U.S.News & WORLD REPORT

ULTIMATE COLLEGE GUIDE
2007

ULTIMATE COLLEGE GUIDE
2007

by the Staff of U.S.News & World Report

Anne McGrath, Editor

Robert Morse, Director of Data Research

Sam Flanigan, Deputy Director of Data Research

Brian Kelly, Series Editor

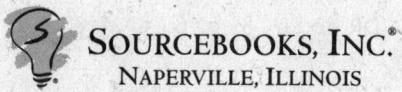

SOURCEBOOKS, INC.
NAPERVILLE, ILLINOIS

Published by Sourcebooks, Inc.

P.O. Box 4410

Naperville, Illinois 60567-4410

(630) 961-3900 FAX: (630) 961-2168

www.sourcebooks.com

ISBN-13: 978-1-4022-0837-9

ISBN-10: 1-4022-0837-5

Fourth Edition

Printed and bound in the United States of America

DR 10 9 8 7 6 5 4 3 2 1

Table of Contents

Now that you have the book, to activate your free 10-day pass to the usnews.com College Premium Online Edition, follow the instructions at www.usnews.com/ultimatecollege

Introduction

In the coming months, you will be tackling the often overwhelming, frequently confusing, always anxiety-producing, and (we hope) ultimately rewarding task of selecting the right college and getting in. We may not be able to completely ease your worries, but we think the 2007 edition of the *Ultimate College Guide* will be a pretty big help on all other counts.

This book will lead you through each step of the process, from figuring out what you want in a college and researching which schools fit the bill to putting together a killer application and negotiating a financial aid package after you make it in. The exclusive Insider's Index, which begins on page 93, contains a rich assortment of data that you can use to compare colleges. The Ultimate College Directory, which begins on page 322, allows you to dig deep into the details.

The first step in the process is to figure out what you want your new life in college to be like. Chapter 1, "How to Choose the Right School for You," will help you frame and find answers to such crucial questions as: What academic programs interest you, and just how tough do you want the coursework to be? Outside of class, how will you create a life that's full and fun? What sort of campus setting will make you feel at home?

The chapter goes on to examine a number of routes you might take, including big universities and small liberal arts colleges, public honors programs, women's colleges, and community colleges. It also offers tips on how to research your potential schools (how to use the Internet wisely as a source of information, for example) and how to make the most of a visit to campus.

In Chapter 2, you'll learn what admissions deans really care about when they start scrutinizing you. You'll find out why your straight As might not be as awesome as you think they are and why being a member of one or two clubs or sports teams might serve you better than having joined 10. You'll hear about the value of "hooks"—the special qualities that make you interesting in a crowded field—and how to sharpen yours. The information in this chapter will be of particular use to the younger brothers and sisters of this year's college applicants because building a truly impressive résumé by senior year takes advance planning—and time. On page 30, Ann Wright, vice president for the southwest region of the College Board, describes how the admissions process works at a selective university.

Chapters 3 and 4 cover the nuts and bolts of getting in: taking the college entrance exams and putting together your application. We help you think through the decision about which test to take—the SAT or ACT—and how to prepare for the big day. If you decide that some test prep might be in order, your options range from expensive private coaching to free online tutorials. In Chapter 4, you'll find detailed instructions on how to write a winning essay, how to ask for and get effective letters of recommendation, and how to stay in touch with the admissions office without driving anyone crazy.

Should you apply using early decision? Maybe, because in many cases an early applicant stands a better chance of getting in. But there are good reasons not to, as well—for one thing, you won't have multiple financial aid offers to consider. On page 59, Joyce Slayton Mitchell, the director of college advising at Nightingale-Bamford School in New York City, discusses common mistakes families make when applying to college.

The final chapter lays out everything you need to know—but probably don't know you need to know—about financial aid and winning scholarships. The fact that three or four colleges can come up with wildly different ideas of how much a family can afford to pay leaves many parents scratching their heads in frustration. This chapter describes how colleges arrive at their figures and all of the tools they have handy to plug the gap between what you're expected to pay and the cost of freshman year. You'll learn about federal sources of aid (Pell grants, Stafford and PLUS loans, and work-study programs), state aid programs, institutional awards based on need or academics or some other talent, and loans from private lenders. And in case you end up with a bottom line you can't live with, we'll teach you how to go back and successfully ask for more.

The Insider's Index will tell you at a glance how your colleges stack up against the competition in areas of special interest to applicants. Take note of which schools have the best record of graduating their students, for example. Note which schools lose the most freshmen before sophomore year—when you're visiting, you might want to ask for an explanation. A look at the table on page 95 ("Schools that are the hardest and easiest to get into") will tell you whether your test scores, grade point average, and class standing put you in the ballpark or not.

Several of the tables should help you deal with money matters. The "Great deals at great schools" table on page 153, for example, features schools that give you the most for your money. The method we use to arrive at the list factors in each school's *U.S. News* rank (which appears in its directory entry in this book) and the cost of attending after aid is taken into account. The higher the quality of the program and the lower the cost, the better the deal. Beginning on page 164, you can see the average size of each school's financial aid package, what proportion of the student body gets aid, and how much of the package comes in the form of grants and loans, on average. You can also see, beginning on page 157, how much debt the average graduate takes on.

The Ultimate College Directory provides detailed profiles of some 1,400 four-year accredited colleges and universities based on an exhaustive survey *U.S. News* sends out annually. The profiles contain the most up-to-date information on everything from programs of study available, to the academic credentials of the most recently admitted class, to housing options and all aspects of extracurricular life. You'll get a sense of the demographic makeup of both student body and faculty; what sorts of services are available to disabled students; and information on tuition, room and board, and the specifics on financial aid.

As you do your research, remember that the choices you make will have a big impact on your quality of life for the next four years. Very likely, they'll influence your career path over the long term, too—and maybe the size of your paycheck. We hope that the leads you find in this guide will point you in the right direction.

Chapter One

How to Choose the Right School for You

You're about to make one of your first grown-up decisions, and it's going to be a tough one. From among the thousands of colleges in the country, you have to choose just a handful to apply to. You could take the easy way out, of course—you know, pick a school according to how well it did in the NCAA Final Four, or the one that has the most luxurious dorms, or just fall in with the driven seniors who will apply indiscriminately to most of the Ivies.

Or you can do the slightly harder work that will pay off for decades to come. You can take a long look in the mirror and ask yourself: Who *is* this person anyway? What does she want out of college? What kind of campus will make him feel at home? If you haven't worried too much about self-awareness before, now's the time—before you make a huge, costly blooper and wind up unhappy.

What kinds of situations have made you feel academically and socially successful in high school? If you haven't been successful, why not? Which kinds of classes have you gotten the most out of? What sorts of people have you enjoyed hanging out with? Which activities have really been fun? How different from high school do you want your college experience to be?

Remember, you're aiming to find the school that best suits *you*—not your friends, not your teachers, and not your parents. This chapter will help you narrow the choices down to a manageable list of five to 10 places where you stand a great chance of being happy for the next four years. Your final list should include "reach" schools (schools that may be a bit too hard to get into), "probables" (schools where your qualifications are apt to get you in), and "safeties" (ones you can count on accepting you).

Don't skimp on the "safeties" category. As the competition to get into college has increased, lots of schools that have been thought of as safeties are suddenly awash in really strong applicants. One persuasive argument for applying to a couple of sure things is that many colleges and universities can get pretty generous with their scholarships when they want to nab candidates whose grades put them near the top of the applicant pool.

Questions to ask yourself

Here's a shocker: As many as one in every three first-year college students decides for some reason not to come back for sophomore year. Many of the students who drop out or transfer are those who didn't do their research and made too hasty a decision the first time around. There's no need for you to find yourself among them. Following are the key questions to ponder as you do your search.

What kinds of academic programs interest me?

First, ask yourself why you want to go to college at all. Are you looking for a chance to dig deep into your studies, think big thoughts, and discuss them late into the night over coffee with your intellectual friends? Or are you mostly after the training that will prepare you for a specific career? Somebody who

thinks of college as a time to burn the midnight oil exploring new lines of inquiry is apt to be happiest with a liberal arts education, which will supply the general knowledge and critical thinking skills needed in any number of jobs. A preprofessional or more practice-oriented education, one with lots of internship opportunities, for example, might suit you better if you already know that you're headed for a career in, say, nursing, nuclear engineering, or graphic design.

But unless you have such a highly specialized career in mind, knowing what type of education you want (liberal arts or practice-oriented) isn't the same thing as knowing exactly what you want to study—nor should it be. College counselors and admissions officers say one of the most common mistakes high school students make when figuring out where to apply is that they worry too much about finding colleges strong in whatever field they think will be their major.

Partly, this is because *not* knowing what they want to study makes them anxious, especially when Aunt Martha, their parents' colleagues, and even the clerks at the local grocery store keep asking them where they're going to go and what they plan to study. Another reason is that with such a long list of colleges to consider, having an intended major to plug into an Internet search engine seems like an obvious and easy way to whittle the list down to size.

However, many students come to regret this overly simple strategy. The fact is, most undergrads change their minds about what they want to study at least once, and a good many switch majors two or three times. "We think that's a healthy thing," says William Hiss, vice president for external affairs at Bates College in Lewiston, Maine. "Some of the jobs young people today will do haven't even been invented yet."

Stay nimble. It's a pretty sure bet that you'll change your mind, too. A better approach when you're not absolutely positive about your career direction is to look for schools that offer you flexibility. Let's say that you're interested in art. If you think it's definitely going to be your life's work, you should consider a specialty school like the San Francisco Art Institute or the Maryland Institute College of Art in

Baltimore. But if you think there's a possibility you'll want to do something else, you might want to pick a liberal arts college or a big university where art is one of a rich menu of choices and where it's easy to get a taste of some other fare. A good rule of thumb, counselors say, is to identify three or four academic fields that excite you and find schools with strong departments in all of them.

Besides giving thought to what you might like to study, it's a good idea to check out how the learning happens. For example, freshmen often feel so lost in the crowd when they come to a big university that many schools now try to help new students connect with other kids and faculty members right from the start. Instead of dumping newcomers all into large introductory lecture courses with 300 or 400 students, they might put each freshman into one small seminar of 15 or 20 that is taught by a professor rather than a graduate assistant.

Many of the larger institutions, including the University of Texas–Austin, the University of Maryland–College Park, and the University of Georgia–Athens, offer honors programs for their most capable undergraduates. These programs typically feature rigorous coursework in smaller-than-normal classes and intensive research with the possibility of a "senior capstone" project, like a thesis. At a small liberal arts college, you're more apt than at a large university to spend much of your time deep in class discussions, working on group projects, or working one-on-one with a professor on some kind of independent study.

Live and learn. On some campuses, students are grouped together in learning communities, sometimes called "living/learning communities." They might take two or more courses together and even live in the same dorm so that discussions can continue long after class ends. You're interested in science? Investigate what the chances are that you'll get to participate in an original research project with a faculty member supervising you. Whether or not you intend to stick with Spanish, you might want to check out how good the study abroad options are. On some campuses, large numbers of students

spend time studying overseas because, in the era of globalization, it is good preparation for working in almost any kind of business. If you've enjoyed community service as a high school student, you might be happy at a college that makes service a class requirement—where architecture students might direct the renovation of a local day-care center, for example, or urban policy students might volunteer at inner-city nonprofit agencies.

Someone who's superfocused on preparing for

> *"Some of the jobs young people today will do haven't even been invented yet."*

the job market might want to think about schools that emphasize internships or that offer cooperative education. In co-op programs, undergrads in fields from marketing to engineering to communications to psychology fit several terms of paid, professional work experience into their schedules. Alternating between full-time work and full-time study means that you get a grasp of the theory in class and then see it in action in the office; then you come back and hash over what worked and what didn't. Employers love to hire graduates of co-op programs because they often show up with already-honed communication skills and have had practice solving problems. They also have lots of experience working in teams, which is how most people work these days. Meanwhile, the paychecks, which can total several thousand dollars a year, go a long way toward covering tuition. The trade-off is that you usually have to put in a fifth year of college and give up your summers from sophomore year until graduation to fit in all the coursework.

How challenging do I want school to be?

Lots of students these days are so determined to impress their friends and families that they automatically limit their list to the most selective colleges they can get into. They don't stop to think about how hard they want to study and how well they handle pressure. These are both important questions to ask

Who am I?

You can't choose the right school unless you know the answer, so get set to take a long look inward. Ask yourself these questions:

- **What do I want to get out of college?** Maybe you're after an intense but broad intellectual experience. Or perhaps you want training for a career in Web design.
- **What's my learning style?** Are you the hide-in-the-back-of-the-lecture-hall type? Or are you someone who thrives on being in the thick of the discussion?
- **How competitive am I?** You may struggle just to stay in the middle of the pack at a college where the whole freshman class consists of former high school stars.
- **What will I want to do with my time outside of class?** Volunteer at a homeless shelter? Hike in the mountains? Go shopping?
- **How important is diversity?** Perhaps you're pretty conservative but don't mind taking the heat from liberals, or maybe you're more relaxed when you're one of the crowd and everyone looks like you.
- **How independent am I?** Remember: A major reason students transfer is that they want to be closer to home.

yourself as you get ready to leave high school for the bigger world. Often, the answer hinges on where you fall now—and where you want to fall—in the academic pecking order. If you loved being at the top of the heap in high school, you might really get bummed out at a college where everybody was a valedictorian, too, and you have to pull all-nighters on a regular basis just to stay in the middle of the pack. Rather than be miserable and stressed out for the next four years, it might be better to pick a somewhat less competitive school where you can get a good education but still stand out.

If, on the other hand, you're jazzed by competition and by people who can match you brilliant thought for brilliant thought, you might be happiest at a really tough school—as long as you come prepared to study and even to fight for resources. The best way to tell if a school has more of a collaborative or cutthroat culture is to ask its current students. Find out, for example, if team learning, in which five or six students work together and all receive the same grade, is common. This kind of learning is becoming more popular as schools look for ways to really engage students in their coursework. Or maybe you have to worry that somebody's going to destroy your science experiment when no one's looking. One New Jersey student ended up choosing the College of William and Mary in Virginia rather than a nearby university after a tour guide at the university let slip that during exam time, students sometimes ripped key pages out of books in the library. "I couldn't deal with a place that competitive," she says.

Will I be happier at a big university or a small liberal arts college?

Howard Payne University in Brownwood, Texas, has an enrollment of slightly under 1,400 students. The population at the University of Texas–Austin, meanwhile, exceeds 36,000 undergrads, plus nearly 13,000 graduate students. Many liberal arts colleges hold the line at a couple thousand students; a mid-sized university might enroll 10,000 or so. It isn't necessarily true that small equals friendly and intimate and big means lost-in-the-shuffle, but a school's size will definitely make a difference to your college experience.

For one thing, size is usually a pretty good indicator of how much a college or university focuses on its undergraduates (at big universities, graduate students often get the attention of the best faculty members and first dibs on things like laboratory space). Smaller schools typically have smaller classes than large universities and fewer students per professor, so faculty members can be available for plenty of give-and-take with undergraduates inside the classroom, during office hours, over coffee in the student center, and sometimes even in their homes. Students in a discussion-oriented class of 20 or 30 can get to know each other a lot more easily than they could in a huge lecture of 300 or 400, are more apt to get to collaborate on projects, and are more likely to be actively engaged in their coursework.

Even though many big schools are making an effort to do a better job of serving undergraduates with freshman seminars and learning communities and other programs, it is still often true that first-year students find themselves lectured to by graduate assistants in one jam-packed auditorium after the next. You'll want to ask both about average class sizes and a school's student-to-faculty ratio, which will give you some indication of how accessible professors will be.

Liberal arts colleges also tend to have many fewer graduate students than universities, if any. That means that students in the sciences, particularly, are likely to get a real crack at doing serious one-on-one research with the school's most accomplished professors. On university campuses, the Ph.D. candidates are going to take precedence, and the faculty stars might never actually work with undergrads.

On the other hand, the typical university offers a much wider variety of majors than most small colleges and many more courses to choose from, although space might be limited to those in the major. Moreover, in fields like science and engineering, where you want cutting-edge research to be reflected in your classwork, it can be a real advantage to be on a campus that is producing Ph.D.s. Many students cherish the freedom that comes along with being anonymous in a large crowd, and they'd rather learn by lecture than be put on the spot in a class discussion. After all, it's not so easy to skip class or let your readings or papers slide when you're one of only a small number of students.

Are you looking for a community where the faces are mostly familiar and there's a sense of common identity? Do you want a place with such a multitude of people—and diverse groups of people—that you're constantly meeting someone new and different from you? A large school is bound to offer

more social and extracurricular options than a small school. A look at Howard Payne's and the University of Texas's websites reveals that the former school has fewer than 40 clubs and organizations, compared to UT's 900-plus.

Small colleges often work hard at making sure new students are all set to succeed on campus and that they're bonding with peers and professors. At a big school, you'll have to take charge of reaching out and forming new relationships, or you will risk being lost among the masses. Richard DiFeliciantonio, vice president of enrollment at Ursinus College, a liberal arts school in Pennsylvania, points to the lower graduation rates at big universities as a sign that such schools can be really rotten choices for even bright students who arrive without a clear direction and focus, because those students are likely to flounder when left completely to their own devices.

It will be up to you to stand up for yourself and be insistent, to go and ask for face time with your professors, and to stop in and see the registrar when it's necessary to get a place in a required course. It will be up to you to find a group of kids with whom you'll feel like you belong. One young woman who chose Pennsylvania State University (undergraduate student body: around 35,000) and loved it recalls that as soon as she arrived for freshman orientation, she began seeking out professors for chats and investigating a list of more than 600 clubs. She discovered student government, and that made her four years great.

What kind of place will make me feel at home?

When you pick a college, you're also committing to where—not to mention how—you'll be spending all your time for the next four years. On the way from your dorm to the library, will you be walking by burned-out buildings on filthy streets or biking past ivy-covered brick buildings and perfect green quads? During your downtime, will you go snowboarding or snorkeling, apple picking or clothes shopping? Is hiking in the country your idea of a good time, or do you really get into the city and the club scene?

Many students, especially those who intend to study hard in college, never give a thought to how much of a boost or a downer weather and geography can be, and how much both can affect their ability to turn out grade-A work. One graduate of a college in Connecticut holds the cloudy days and limited vistas at least partly accountable for her four years of undergraduate misery. Coming from Nevada, she'd known that Connecticut was short on blue skies and mountain views before she decided to attend, but she figured—wrongly—that the scenery wouldn't affect her mood much.

Obviously, the farther you go from home, the tougher (or more expensive) it will be to drop back in for the weekend. How badly do you want to stay in close contact with your family and hometown buddies? Some college counselors advise their clients to page through the calendar and count up the holidays or other events that will be spent at home. How much will all these trips cost in time and fares? Research shows that well over half of all college freshmen attend a school within 100 miles of home.

Weigh the action. Think about how hectic you'd like the pace of life around the campus to be. One rural New Englander was dead set on going to New York University until she spent a summer there and found city life too stressful. She picked a small California college instead. On the other hand, one young man who chose the University of Wisconsin–Madison reports that shortly after classes started, he realized that the quiet setting was going to drive him nuts. Because he wanted to become a financial advisor eventually, he decided to transfer to NYU, where he could take advantage of Wall Street by snagging internships and summer jobs that would prepare him for his career.

Consider where you'll actually be living, too. Some colleges put most of their students in campus housing, and the lounges and rooms are where a whole lot of the fun happens. At other schools, large numbers of students live in off-campus apartments or commute from home. You might like the freedom at a school like that—or you might really miss having the dorm experience.

One final point: local companies tend to recruit on campus, which means that many students end up settling near where they attend college. Do you like your favorite school's location well enough to stick around after graduation? A major move might mean starting out cold in the job search, without any connections.

What will I want to do in my spare time?

Remember, you're moving your whole self to campus, not just your brains. What else really charges your batteries? There aren't too many athletes who get to be stars in college, but if you played lacrosse or field hockey seriously in high school, you might find that there's a big hole in your week if you choose a school without an intramural program. If music or theater has always kept you busy off hours, what will you do if there's no drama club or singing groups? A school's website often includes lists and descriptions of student organizations, sometimes with e-mail links so you can send your questions to current members. Whether you end up at a small college or a university, belonging to an organization of students who share your interests is a great way to make lasting friends.

It's a good idea to talk with students who participate in the clubs or sports that interest you because you'll want to find out how active the club is and how hard it is to get off the sidelines and be involved. There might be a jazz musical ensemble on paper, but maybe there's been no concert in three years. Maybe the drama club or the debate team is so filled with talented people that you'll mostly be sitting in the audience.

Will I fit in?

This question worries even the most confident high schoolers. Yes, you probably want college to be a much bigger and more exciting world than you're used to. And yes, you probably know that living in a diverse community is good preparation for real life. But feeling comfortable is important, too. If you're not, chances are you won't feel able to freely speak up and express your views or be as relaxed and contented socially as you might be.

How much diversity is right for you? Think for a minute about your social life in high school. If you felt you had to blend in with the in crowd no matter what, you probably should stick with schools where many of the students are like you, whether racially, economically, politically, or in their ideas of fun. If you were happy to go your own way, on the other hand, or delight in the idea of being in a diverse community, too much sameness may feel boring and suffocating.

Ease up, Mom and Dad

The following stories are true, but names have been omitted for obvious reasons:

• The day after their son was rejected by a highly selective college, Mom and Dad marched into his guidance counselor's office waving plane tickets. The counselor was instructed to jump on a plane and go straighten out the "mistake."

• One father called his daughter's counselor to read the essay he had written for her Ivy League application. The daughter rejected her father's version and wrote her own, only to learn later that Mom's "typing" was actually heavy editing.

• A parent called her alma mater with a question about the status of her son's application. An admissions officer called the son back with the answer, only to learn that the boy had no idea he'd applied to the school and had no desire to attend. The son withdrew his mother's application.

Are some parents overinvolved in their child's college search? You bet. "Parents, bite your tongues, go to your rooms, back off," advises Wylie Mitchell, dean of admissions at Bates College in

Maine. A kid who spends freshman year at Mom's or Dad's top choice too often spends sophomore year as a transfer student. "A lot of it is a self-fulfilling prophecy," says Karen Levin Coburn, coauthor of *Letting Go: A Parents' Guide to Understanding the College Years.* "If they come in with a chip on their shoulder, they probably won't seek out opportunities that make it a positive experience."

Letting the teenager take the lead leaves parents in an important supporting role. You can help develop a list of schools that all of you are comfortable with by suggestion and by asking questions, rather than by dictating an acceptable five or 10. If your child insists that she wants a diverse, urban environment, don't keep harping on the virtues of a small liberal arts college in the middle of nowhere. In fact, don't harp at all.

You should lay out any financial or geographical constraints up front, however. You need to be serious about the situation for your own sake as well as your child's. It can be devastating to a student who has set his heart on Harvard to hear in April that, despite a $16,000 award, the budget just won't bear it.

College visits require even more restraint. "Top off the tank and stand by," advises Howard Greene, a former admissions officer at Princeton who is now an independent educational consultant in Westport, Connecticut. James Sumner, dean of admissions at Grinnell College in Iowa, recalls attempting to interview one young man whose father first refused to leave the room, then answered all of the questions himself. (The student didn't get in.)

Hands off the application essay as well. Admissions officers can easily distinguish between the writing of a 45-year-old and a 17-year-old, so "editing" is apt to backfire. Instead, plan on reviewing the application folder for mistakes or omissions. Once it has been sent, do not call, write, or e-mail the admissions office. All communication should come from the student.

In the end, if a thin envelope should drop through your mail slot, the best course of action is to receive it philosophically and supportively, and to focus on where the student did get in. If you turn your child's great disappointment into your own, then he's apt to feel that he has failed you, too.

You might be happiest in a great big polyglot population—as long as you can belong to a club or a sports team with others who feel like kindred spirits.

Keep in mind that diversity means much more than the color of the faces you'll encounter. You'll also want to think about students' socioeconomic, political, religious, geographic, and educational backgrounds. How will you feel, as a public school graduate, if many of the kids you're living with graduated from prep school and come from families with tons of money? Or how will you feel as an atheist if a large number share—and actively practice—the same faith? Some students are looking for a chance to be among people with different perspectives; it allows them to test their own worldview and expand or defend it.

Consider what's cool. Whether you'll feel at home on campus will also depend on the dominant culture, if there is one. What's considered cool to do outside of class? Investigate whether everybody heads off to fraternity parties on the weekend or is more apt to be marching at an antiglobalization rally. Or are students 20,000-strong in the football stadium? Maybe there's equal room for all three. Is it perfectly respectable to spend Friday nights at the library, or is it considered kind of nerdy? "We don't have football—we're chess champions," says Freeman Hrabowski, president of the University of Maryland–Baltimore County. "This is a place where it's cool to be smart." To get a fix on these aspects of diversity, it's a good idea to quiz as many current students as possible. The student newspaper and a calendar of events can also help you figure out what matters on campus.

Current students can also tell you how well a highly diverse population actually mixes in practice. Although large, urban schools and big state universities usually score best on diversity measures, sometimes they can also be the most fractured. Students find and hang around with other kids exactly like themselves. If you notice during your campus visit that the African-American students are sitting at one table in the dining hall, Koreans are at another, and female lacrosse players are at a third, it's probably safe to assume that there's not a whole lot of mixing and mingling going on outside the cafeteria, either.

How important is prestige?

When college freshmen are asked to identify what factors made them choose their school, academic reputation usually tops the list. One obvious reason is that it is impressive to get into a name-brand college or university that everybody admires. But there's another reason, too. Many people rely on school reputation because they have so little actual knowledge of the colleges they're considering. A school's prestige is taken as a sign that it's really, really good.

Yes, there's a connection, and not just in the minds of parents. Employers also assume that prestigious schools do a good job of educating their future workers. Some leading companies recruit almost exclusively on elite campuses, and an Ivy League degree definitely can help you get your foot in the door when you're looking for your first job. Being surrounded by crowds of smart, talented students almost certainly means a higher level of discussion and debate than you would find at a less competitive institution, and a list of valuable contacts for later in life, too.

But prestige isn't the only or necessarily the best indicator of quality—particularly when it comes to figuring out which school is right for you. Many other colleges offer top-notch, tough programs with very strong records of sending students on to graduate school. The "top 10" lists of colleges whose graduates go on for Ph.D.s in various disciplines were sprinkled liberally with names like Reed College, Carleton, Oberlin, and Kalamazoo between 1992 and 2001. While national acceptance rates to medical school hover around 50 percent, Knox College in Illinois gets nearly 90 percent of its applicants into med school, while Allegheny College in Pennsylvania placed 94 percent of med school applicants last year.

Ask for the stats. Most colleges keep statistics like these, and you should ask for them, as well as information on the kinds of alumni networking opportunities the schools offer and the kinds of jobs previous graduates have landed.

Will a degree from an Ivy guarantee you a bigger paycheck? Not necessarily. Consider the results of one recent study (headed by a Princeton economist, no less). When the researchers compared the earnings of students who were accepted to elite colleges

It used to be that colleges simply rejected students with learning disabilities—or left them alone to sink or swim. These days, students who learn in nontraditional ways are finding that scores of schools are not only happy to take them, but will take pains to help them succeed. The key to getting help is to be "upfront and know what to ask for," says educational consultant Imy F. Wax, coauthor of the *K&W Guide to Colleges for Students with Learning Disabilities or Attention Deficit Disorder.*

First, you have to find a college whose policies match your needs because approaches to serving learning-disabled students vary considerably from campus to campus. Many schools tend to limit their services to untimed tests in quiet rooms, plus the regular academic counseling that's offered to all students. Others add tutoring and training in time management. Some provide textbooks on tape to students who have a hard time reading; others send a paid note-taker to class with anyone who can't process a lecture. The services are usually free, but not always. Freshmen and sophomores in the University of Arizona's Strategic Alternative Learning Techniques program, for example, get a learning specialist, a writing program, and tutors for $2,100 a semester. Upperclassmen, who use the services less frequently, pay somewhat less.

Ironically, the one college in the country dedicated entirely to students with learning disabilities and AD/HD, two-year Landmark College in southern Vermont, refuses to provide note-takers or books on tape. Landmark, which receives two applications for every $46,560-per-year slot, prides itself instead on arming students with the skills and strategies necessary to pursue a rigorous liberal arts curriculum. Learning communities, a student-to-faculty ratio of 5 to 1, and a "master notebook" system (main ideas of a lecture or text go in one column and supporting details in another) result in 90 percent of graduates transferring to four-year colleges.

To find out how welcoming a college is apt to be, call the admissions office and ask about programs for learning-disabled students. If your call is referred to an academic support office, a learning opportunities program, or another office that handles matters related to the Americans With Disabilities Act, and everyone seems eager to respond, that's a good sign. (You'll want to dig for details about what kinds of supports are available, though, because colleges define LD services in such different ways.) If your questions to admissions are greeted by hemming and hawing, the college may not want to be bothered.

but decided to attend lesser-known schools with the earnings of students who attended the elite schools, they found that the former group earned just as much as the latter. Why? It's the students that matter, not the school, say the economists. Students who are accepted by elite colleges aren't just smart; they are motivated, hardworking, and creative—traits that will help them get ahead regardless of where they actually go to school.

How should you use the *U.S. News* college rankings?

Each year, *U.S. News & World Report* surveys nearly 1,450 four-year colleges and universities in the country to gather information about their academic and extracurricular programs. The results of that survey are published in one form in this book, in the lengthy descriptions of each school that begin on page 326. They are also used to create a yearly ranking of schools that is published each summer in a

St. Mary's College of Maryland and New College of Florida are both innovative small liberal arts schools that do well in the annual *U.S. News* college rankings. Both offer tough academic programs and generally small classes that attract some pretty impressive talent. But because they are public honors colleges within their state university systems, they're downright cheap compared to similar private colleges. A year's tuition, room, and board at St. Mary's runs around $20,000 for in-state students, at New College, about $10,500.

The two schools are unusual in that they have their own separate campuses; the more typical public honors program is a "college within a college" on the grounds of State U, where students live in separate housing, attend accelerated classes, and do research that leads to a publishable paper or a thesis. Often, they collect very generous scholarships. One recent computer science graduate of the University of Delaware who focused his research on natural language processing and artificial intelligence could have gone to the Massachusetts Institute of Technology, Harvard, Columbia, Cornell, or the University of Pennsylvania. But Delaware offered to fully cover the $70,000 cost of his four years there. Some 70 universities now offer honors programs as states fight to keep their best and brightest at home. Among them are the University of South Carolina, California State University–Fresno, Middle Tennessee State University, and Western Washington University.

Not surprisingly, these programs are breeding grounds for future graduate students. A recent survey found that 54 percent of St. Mary's alumni attend graduate school or professional school within three years of graduating. Some 10 percent of New College graduates have gone on to complete their Ph.D.s.

separate guide, "America's Best Colleges," available on newsstands, and on the *U.S. News* website (www.usnews.com). The rankings show how schools stack up against each other based on a number of quality measures, including the proportion of freshmen who return for sophomore year, the proportion of students who graduate within six years, average class size and student-to-faculty ratio, how much a school spends per student on instruction and research, and the capabilities of incoming students as measured by their class standing and test scores. *U.S. News* collects data on up to 15 of these indicators, crunches all the numbers, and ranks schools among their peer institutions.

Many guidance counselors and college admissions deans worry that high schoolers place too much importance on a school's numerical ranking in developing a list of colleges, arguing that it's impossible to reduce all of the intangibles that make a college a good fit to mere numbers. It's true that the ranking alone won't tell you what you need to know to make a decision, but the ranking tables are crammed with hard-to-gather information that allows you to compare schools on key characteristics that contribute to academic excellence. There hasn't been a whole lot of research done on how students pick colleges, but a couple of surveys of current students suggest that most applicants use rankings properly—as one piece of useful information about a school, not as the sole basis for a decision.

Mine the data. The best way to take advantage of the *U.S. News* rankings is to study the data for clues that will help you narrow your search. For instance, you can scan the column of SAT scores to figure out where you could be admitted—or even rise to the top of the applicant pool and possibly qualify for a merit scholarship. You can use the data on class size to get a sense of just how intimate the classroom experience will be—or how good the chances are you can hide in the back of the room. You can check student-to-faculty ratios to see how much attention you're likely to get from professors outside of class, or look at the freshman retention rates to learn how hard schools work to keep students from dropping out. Perhaps you'll find a great candidate or two that you hadn't considered before, or even heard of. The rankings can be used to inform your thinking—they just won't provide an easy answer.

How safe will I be?

Universities have come to understand that they need to do a better job of protecting students from crime. Today, emergency phones and late-night buses or escorts are as common on campus as pizza boxes and laptops. Families can thank the federal government for the increased focus on security. The law now requires all schools receiving federal funding to report their statistics on how many and what kinds of crimes are committed on campus to the Department of Education and to publish the information in an annual report. Often, the information is available in the campus security area of the school's website. If you can't find it there, call and ask for the latest report. By reading the local newspaper and asking the police for crime statistics, you can get a feel for what goes on in the world around the campus, too.

Find out how secure the dorms are and whether outsiders have access to the library, fitness center, or student union. At the University of Maryland–Baltimore County, new dorms have been equipped with a video security system that requires visitors to stand in front of a camera before being buzzed in. The University of Pennsylvania has taken video technology to the campus perimeter, where it has installed a network of closed-circuit television cameras that keep an eye on the surrounding streets. Since the cameras were put in place, the school has seen an impressive drop in robberies and attempted robberies on campus. At the University of Delaware–Newark, students can read about incidents in a crime news box that pops up on the school's customized Web browser the day after they're reported. Depending on where you're looking, you might want to quiz officials about crisis policies and evacuation plans, too.

How much will it cost?

This is one of the first questions most parents are going to want an answer to, and it obviously has to be considered and discussed up front. But don't rule out a wonderful college just because it's expensive! If you're a desirable candidate, a school will usually do its best to meet your need with financial aid or, in some cases, scholarships based on your particular talents. Sometimes, a middle-income family with a highly qualified applicant is offered such a generous package that it's actually less expensive to attend the pricey private school than to go to a $10,000 or $12,000 state university. Desirable students at or under the poverty line probably can count on having all their costs covered with a combination of federal, state, and college grants; student loans; and work-study. That said, Mom and Dad should talk about their financial limits early on. It can be crushing to be accepted by a first-choice school only to find out that it was never a real option. (For more on how to meet the costs of college, see Chapter 5.)

Where might I get the best deal? Universities increasingly use money to attract the most talented applicants possible, so you'll definitely want to investigate schools where your qualifications put you among the cream of the applicant crop. The surest way to stand out is to have a grade point average and board scores that outshine the school's averages. "The institution will treat students at the top of the pecking order more generously," says Barry McCarty, former dean of enrollment services at Lafayette College in Easton, Pennsylvania.

Schools that draw most of their students from a single state or region and are trying to improve diversity on campus may be especially willing to shell out extra cash for students from far-flung places. "We'd like to see more out-of-state students apply," says Julie Rice Mallette, the director of scholarships and financial aid at North Carolina State University–Raleigh. On the other hand, sticking close to home can also save you money. Several states, including Georgia, Kentucky, South Carolina, New Mexico, and West Virginia, offer merit scholarships to state residents if they choose to attend a state school. Eligibility requirements vary by state, but the awards typically go to any student who has a record of achieving good grades. Those who qualify find that these programs generally cover the tuition at State University, and that the grants can be applied toward tuition at in-state private schools, too.

Is community college an option?

Here's a statistic that may surprise you: Forty-four percent of all first-time college freshmen in the country go to a community college. Many of them will stop with a two-year associate's degree and join the workforce, but a growing proportion—now about 30 percent—will continue on and graduate from a four-year college or university. Chances are they'll be well prepared to succeed once they transfer, and students who choose the two-plus-two option will almost certainly save money by starting out closer to home. They might even end up at a better four-year school than they would have as a freshman. "I was absolutely stoked!" says one young man of his transfer to the highly ranked and hard-to-get-into University of California–Berkeley. He had started out at his local community college after high school when every single one of his four-year choices turned him down.

Some high school graduates decide to attend community colleges because they aren't yet academically ready for a four-year program, or are not emotionally prepared to leave family and friends behind. Others want to keep the total cost of a four-year degree as low as possible. It's always been one mission of community colleges to prepare such students to continue successfully at the state public universities. But now that two-year schools have been sprucing up their academic offerings to attract more competitive students, a growing number of students have been using the two-year experience as a stepping stone to more selective private schools as well. Schools like Dickinson College in Carlisle, Pennsylvania; Washington University in St. Louis; New York University; Cornell University in Ithaca, New York; and Johns Hopkins in Baltimore have launched scholarship programs for community college honors students. Some selective universities, including the University of Wisconsin–Madison, feature "dual enrollment" programs with local community colleges. Students admitted to these programs are guaranteed a place at the partnering four-year school their junior year if they complete an associate's degree.

At the same time, community colleges are revamping their course offerings to make them more challenging so that their grads are equipped for the greater rigors of a four-year school. Over the past 10 years, the number of two-year schools with honors programs has jumped by nearly 50 percent to more than 550, says Rod Risley, executive director of Phi Theta Kappa, a community college honors organization. Graduates speak highly of the small classes, dedicated teachers, and opportunities for one-on-one interaction with faculty members.

There's a pretty wide range of quality and mission among two-year colleges, so you'll have to choose carefully if this seems like the route for you. Some schools emphasize job training while others really concentrate on preparing kids to continue a liberal arts education. Ask about schools' transfer rates—and where graduates end up. And ask whether the schools you're considering have any articulation agreements with public universities in your state. Such agreements spell out which community college classes will be accepted by the four-year school, and are one sign that successful transfers are a priority.

Once enrolled, don't specialize too much or choose a major. "We are looking for breadth and balance," says Jennifer Fondiller, dean of admissions at Barnard College in New York City. While four-year universities typically accept credits for most core courses, they often refuse to grant credit for upper-division courses or vocational classes. To avoid haggling later on, you will want to contact the schools you're interested in transferring to as soon as possible freshman year, both to signal your interest and to find out which courses will transfer easily.

The right way to handle the research

Once you've figured out who you are and what type of school you want, it's time to start searching for the college that fits you best. Whittling the possibilities into a short list of the five or eight or 10 that

Low-tech words of wisdom

When your back starts aching from too many hours in front of your computer, try curling up with a more traditional source of information: a book. We reviewed a shelf-load of selections on college admissions and found a number that are well worth your time.

- *Colleges That Change Lives* by Loren Pope (Penguin Books, 2000, $15). An advocate of a liberal arts education, Pope profiles 40 progressive, lesser-known schools that offer a first-class college experience.
- *Don't Miss Out* by Anna and Robert Leider (Octameron, 2003, $11). This is the flagship volume of an inexpensive but quality guidebook series that covers everything from campus visits to how to find scholarships. Available at www.amazon.com or www.octameron.com.
- *Fiske Guide to Colleges 2007* by Edward B. Fiske (Sourcebooks, 2004, $22.95). Check out this guide for detailed, narrative descriptions of universities, including useful dates, such as when applications are due, as well as insider tidbits, like which school's students hold an annual Pumpkin Drop, where they immerse a gourd in liquid nitrogen and drop it from the library's roof (answer: Caltech).
- *Financing College* by Kristin Davis (Kiplinger, 2001, $17.95). This comprehensive book reports on every aspect of paying for higher education, including how to invest college savings and what to do if you haven't put enough away.
- *The Insider's Guide to the Colleges* by the staff of the *Yale Daily News* (St. Martin's Griffin, 2003, $17.99). Editors and writers at Yale's student-run newspaper profile more than 300 top colleges. The style is chatty and informal, though the small type can be difficult to read.
- *Winning the Heart of the College Admissions Dean* by Joyce Slayton Mitchell (Ten Speed Press, 2005, $14.95). Mitchell, director of college advising at the tony Nightingale-Bamford School in New York City, details the process of choosing and getting into your first-choice school.
- *You're Gonna Love This College Guide* by Marty Nemko (Barron's, 1999, $9.95). If you want just one easy-to-read volume skimming the whole college admissions process, this is the book for you.
- *Writing a Successful College Application Essay* by George Ehrenhaft (Barron's, 2000, $10.95). Read this for a step-by-step guide through the process of choosing an essay topic, writing a draft, and revising it.

you'll apply to is going to take some serious digging—at least as much as your parents do when they buy a new house or car. You should plan on spending some time browsing through the college guides in your high school's guidance or college-counseling office, and contact the schools that interest you to get their course catalogs and application materials.

Next, start talking to people. Assuming your guidance counselor isn't too overwhelmed by her workload to give you some quality time, you'll definitely want her input. You might also tell other adults who know you really well—family, friends, and teachers, for example—what it is you're looking for and which schools you've got on your list and take their feedback into account. Later, you might want to ask the admissions office at your favorite schools for the names of a few recent graduates who wouldn't mind giving you their views. And you'll probably want to e-mail or talk to several current students to find out what they like (and don't) about their school.

You may be tempted to bag the college fairs because it's so much easier these days to check out schools on your computer, but it's smart to go anyway. Many colleges interested in ending up with the most enthusiastic freshmen now keep track of how much interest their applicants show, and the fairs are a pretty painless way to make contact. They also offer a quick and easy way to meet admissions representatives from a variety of local and national schools at once and pick up their informational material—and perhaps discover a college or two you hadn't yet thought of. Come armed with a list of fairly specific questions, or you're apt to get nothing more than a sales pitch.

Cultivate your counselor

If your guidance counselor is like most, he's probably too swamped for frequent chatty visits. While it might be a temptation to work without your counselor's input, that's almost always a mistake. Your biggest college resource may be his connections. If he visits campuses regularly and invites lots of admissions officers to your high school, he's probably very familiar with many colleges' strengths, weaknesses, unique qualities, and selectivity. Later in the process, it will be your counselor who writes your letters of recommendation, so introduce yourself, ask questions about colleges, and drop off a résumé that lists your recent accomplishments. Ask for leads on useful guidebooks and websites. Find out whether your school hosts workshops on college admissions. If so, attend them all and sit in the front row.

You won't always want to take your counselor's advice, however. His judgments about your abilities might not be based on the most up-to-date, mature you—or he may not know you well enough to understand how your aspirations and determination might lead you someplace your grades alone won't. One Cincinnati girl remembers having had a really difficult freshman year in high school and being advised to steer clear of the toughest math and science courses from then on. By the time she had to sign up for junior-year courses, she knew she could handle AP biology. She petitioned for the right, won her case, and was accepted senior year at Northwestern University.

Surf the Web

Virtually everybody applying to college nowadays uses the Web for at least part of the research—up from just 4 percent in 1996—and it's easy to see why. College websites are far snazzier and more sophisticated than they were even a few years ago,

and are jammed with information about courses, financial aid, extracurricular opportunities, and campus life. But surf with caution, advises Ken Hartman, executive director of the National Technology Institute for School Counselors in Cherry Hill, New Jersey. Much of what you'll find, he says, is the cyber equivalent of glossy brochure copy.

To arrive at a list of candidate schools, start with a visit to one or two of the college search engines. One of the most extensive sites is www.collegeboard.com, which creates a list of potential schools based on your answers to a number of questions about such factors as cost and geographic location. The search feature at www.usnews.com, the *U.S.News & World Report* site, also generates a customized roster of schools based on your preferences. The site features the annual rankings of colleges and universities produced by *U.S. News*, as well as a tool that permits you to rerank schools according to the criteria that matter most to you, such as student-to-faculty ratio, class size, or acceptance rate. Other search engines include Princeton Review's www.princetonreview.com and CollegeView's www.collegeview.com.

Once you've created a list of possible schools, you typically can click straight through to each college's home page—and to a wealth of good intelligence if you take the time to dig deep. Beyond course descriptions, you can find details about professors' research programs, their e-mail addresses, and possibly even student evaluations of their teaching abilities. A look at the registrar's pages might give you an idea of whether the most interesting classes have long waiting lists. By checking out the home pages of student organizations that intrigue you, and by going through back copies of the student newspaper, you can dig up all kinds of clues about life on campus, from race relations to fraternity and sorority life to how big a problem crime seems to be. And you can take a virtual tour of the campus, from science labs to dining halls.

E-mail offers another way to get the facts you need. If you are an athlete, you might contact coaches at the college you are most eager to attend; one young man checked out crew teams by contacting coaches and ended up rowing for an Ivy League

Why choose a women's college? Views from the top

There are 68 colleges for women in this country, compared to just three for men. What's the appeal? *U.S. News* asked the presidents of Smith College in Northampton, Massachusetts, Barnard College in New York City, and Agnes Scott College just outside Atlanta to describe the benefits of the single-sex experience.

Carol Christ (Smith): Those who have taught in both co-ed and women's colleges know that women participate more actively in discussion in classes composed entirely of women. This difference is particularly important in male-dominated disciplines such as mathematics, science, and engineering. Studies have shown that women's high dropout rates from engineering programs, as well as from majors in math, chemistry, and physics, result from hostility from male peers and instructors. Such hostility obviously doesn't exist at Smith. Engineering students study with a faculty that is more than half female.

Our alumnae consistently tell us that Smith helped them develop intellectual self-confidence and authority, qualities that helped them markedly in their careers. The many leadership roles open to women—in student government, in extracurricular organizations—provide the opportunity for women to develop into leaders accustomed to making a difference. To see this, you need only to look at our graduates. Smith alumnae include Gloria Steinem, founder of *Ms.* magazine; Shelly Lazarus, CEO of Ogilvy & Mather; Laura D'Andrea Tyson, the first woman to head the White House Council of Economic Advisors; Margaret Edson, winner of the 1999 Pulitzer Prize for Drama; and Victoria Murden McClure, the first woman and first American to row solo across the Atlantic Ocean.

Judith Shapiro (Barnard): It is a hard sell to many young women. In fact, most applicants come to Barnard for a host of other reasons: academic quality, the combination of enjoying all the advantages of a liberal arts college plus the opportunities afforded by [partner school] Columbia, a large research university. And then, of course, there is New York. But the overwhelming majority of the students I have known really connect with this aspect of the institution's identity, and come to see it as core to their experience and a highly positive force in their lives.

I often say that [the experience] prepares students exceptionally well for a world that may not be as friendly to women as Barnard, since they will assume that the problem is not with them but with the world—and even as they are savvy enough to adapt to it, they will also be working to change it. I believe that women's college graduates are far less likely to suffer from what one might call "the enemy within," all the things we do to sabotage ourselves through insecurity, because they have developed a strong sense of who they are and what they can do. Our graduates are strongly represented in fields like medicine, among women starting their own businesses, and at the top of various professions where men have dominated. Women's college graduates are hugely overrepresented among women who sit on the boards of Fortune 500 corporations and occupy high positions in the world of finance generally.

Mary Brown Bullock (Agnes Scott): We look at a liberal arts education with a global vantage that is a woman's perspective. Many international issues today—literacy, poverty, old age, children's health, and war and peace—can be seen as women's issues. Women's perspectives are integrated throughout the curriculum. Our NCAA Division III sports program is not an adaptation of a formerly male-dominated program; it has evolved out of more than a century of attention to women's life-long physical and health issues. An athlete at Agnes Scott College can expect to have a grade point average that is higher than the college average.

It is often difficult to articulate the benefits of attending a women's college to girls. For many young women, the media, including movies, have portrayed the idyllic college experience focusing largely on social experi- ences including men, Greek life, and Division I athletics. A student who is more interested in develop- ing a social résumé than an aca- demic record should not consider attending Agnes Scott. A student who is more interested in con- forming to a peer group and less interested in individualizing her academic and leadership experi- ence should not consider attend- ing a women's college. This does not mean that students at women's colleges are nerds. Quite the contrary! After a year of observing, my husband George commented, "I never knew women could have so much fun without men!" At women's col- leges, young women learn that single-sex bonding—sisterhood, if you will—creates uplifting friend- ships that last for life.

---

college. You might not have the nerve to approach a group of students on campus with your queries about how well they like their classes, or how at home minority students feel, but e-mail makes the asking easy. Most schools periodically open chat- room discussions where students who are interested can quiz counselors or other students.

Make the most of your visit

Someone who prefers to go his own way rather than joining the crowd may feel out of place at a school dominated by fraternities; sports fans may feel frus- trated at a college with no school spirit. No matter how much your virtual visit tells you about a college, there's no substitute for a trip to campus if you want to get a real feel for how well you'll fit in. Besides, showing up for an admissions interview and campus visit is an important way to let the decision makers know that you're seriously interested. These days, many colleges are flooded with applications from superqualified students, and your level of interest— measured by visits, number of phone calls or e-mail exchanges, contact with professors and coaches, for example—can influence whether you get a thumbs- up or thumbs-down if it comes to a vote between you and another equally qualified applicant.

The college tour should begin junior year if pos- sible because you definitely want to be nosing around when classes are in session so you can sit in, observe the students in action, and talk to a profes- sor or two. Students themselves should make the interview appointments and sign up for the tours. "It looks bad to have your mother calling," says admissions consultant Katherine Cohen, author of *The Truth About Getting In* and *Rock Hard Apps: How to Write a Killer College Application.*

Overall, you'll probably want to see a number of colleges and universities of different sizes and types in urban, rural, or suburban locations. But cramming five or six schools into a two-day period will only prove to be an exercise in frustration. Not only will you not have time for a thorough check, but your head will be spinning by the time you head home. It is ideal to maintain a one-school-a-day policy.

Once on campus, be aware that your tour guide will present the school in the most favorable light. Ask a few blunt questions. How serious a problem is crime? How big do the classes tend to be? How easy is it to get the classes you need? Does everybody head home on weekends? Then, since it can be tough to form your own impression with opinion- ated parents in tow, spend time wandering around alone. To learn about campus issues, read the col- lege paper. Check out bulletin boards. Flyers—be they for keg parties or Albanian film festivals—give a useful glimpse of the social scene. Athletes might

Your plan of action

Freshman year

Fall

- Buckle down early, since even your ninth-grade As (and Ds) will count in the eyes of college admissions counselors. Consider taking a study skills and time management class or workshop—and then put what you've learned to use.
- Explore clubs and activities in and outside of school that offer you the chance to develop your interests and abilities as well as your leadership skills. Consider volunteering in your community. Too often, students wait until junior or senior year and then hurriedly—and unconvincingly—pad their résumés. Colleges want to see passion and long-term commitment.
- Visit your guidance counselor early in the term to map out a four-year curriculum that will meet college entrance requirements and put you into the most challenging courses you can handle. If you expect to take Advanced Placement courses later, you may need to sign up for prerequisites now.
- Look into National Collegiate Athletic Association requirements if you think you may want to participate in sports in college. And consider whether your sports experience jibes with your college plans. Do schools that interest you need players in your sport?
- Research careers and talk to your parents about your interests and goals. Find opportunities to meet people working in fields that interest you.

Summer

- Those who are old enough to get a summer job may need to work and begin saving money for college. Others who are not old enough might take on volunteer work to gain experience or enroll in an enrichment course or summer camp at a college.
- Read for pleasure—and while you're at it, learn the unfamiliar words. Vocabulary skills come in very handy on the SAT.

Sophomore year

September

- Draw up a list of college majors that intrigue you and review your four-year course load with the majors in mind.
- Register for the PSAT or the practice ACT (the PLAN) if they are offered to sophomores at your school. These tests will prepare you for the SAT and the ACT and can help you identify weaknesses in time to address them.

October and November

- Take the PLAN, which measures your academic development. Or take the PSAT to practice for the SAT.
- College fairs are a great way to "see" many schools at once. Go to www.nacac.com, the website of the National Association for College Admission Counseling, to find the fairs nearest you.

December

- Discuss your test results with your guidance counselor and figure out how to make improvements where needed.
- Explore your reasons for going to college, which may have a huge bearing on where you belong.

April and May

- Talk to your guidance counselor and your parents about whether you should take summer-school classes to improve your grades, to fit in a needed course, or to investigate a subject that appeals to you. Look around, too, for other constructive ways to spend your summer.

June

- Take the ACT or the June SAT Subject Tests, if appropriate. It's best to take the subject tests as soon as you complete biology or geometry, for example—even if that happens to be in ninth grade.
- Spend some time researching colleges.

Junior year

September

- Get serious about your schoolwork if you haven't already; junior-year grades are extremely important in the college admissions process, as is the rigor of your coursework.
- Attend college fairs and gather information. If you are just beginning your college search, click on "Best Colleges" at www.usnews.com for additional information on more than 1,400 schools and to link to the colleges' own websites.
- Talk with your parents about what limitations they plan to set on where you'll attend college. Knowing now how much your parents will contribute or whether they object to a campus far from home may affect your decision about where to apply.
- Start researching scholarships. You may find useful information in your school or public library and at www.finaid.com and www.fastaid.com. The *U.S. News* site features a scholarship search tool, too.
- If you hope to play for a college team, and perhaps qualify for an athletic scholarship, introduce yourself to coaches at colleges you are considering.

October

- Take the PSAT to practice for the SAT and to qualify for scholarships offered by the National Merit Scholarship Corporation.

December

- Review your test results with your counselor, and consider taking an SAT preparation course or using test-prep software.

January and February

- Check with your schools to see if they prefer—or require—the ACT, the SAT, or neither. Most colleges will accept either test, and some counselors recommend taking both, since many students do better on one than on the other.

March

- Identify the characteristics of a college that matter to you—size, location, cost, academic rigor, social environment, and diversity, to name a few. View college brochures in your counselor's office, or go online to search websites such as www.usnews.com or www.collegeview.com, or go to specific colleges' own sites.
- Work up a list of schools to visit during spring break (or in the fall) with your parents or with a counselor who takes groups of students on tour. If you can, it's best to plan to be on campus while schools are in session, so that you can visit classes and talk to students and professors.

April

- Register for June SAT or ACT tests.

May

- Take Advanced Placement tests if you are eligible, and prepare to take June SAT or ACT tests if you plan to apply early.

Summer

- Send for college applications and think about essay topics. Consider whom to ask for recommendations.
- Counselors advise entering senior year with three or four schools in mind that are apt to accept you, as well as one or two "reaches." If you haven't already been to campus, visiting schools now or in the early fall will help you create a list. Map an itinerary and set up admissions interviews.
- Compile a résumé of activities, honors, leadership positions, and job experience. You'll need this information for college applications and scholarship forms.
- Continue to read extensively and work on your writing skills.
- Try to find a job that will give you experience in a field that interests you and that will sharpen your leadership skills—and add to your savings account.
- Talk honestly with your parents about how you will finance your college costs and how much they expect you to supply. Colleges typically expect freshmen to contribute about $1,500 to their own college costs.

Senior year

September

- Check your course list one more time. Are you missing credits required by schools you're applying to? Plan to work really hard this term because your first-quarter or first-semester grades will be included on your transcript.
- Ask colleges to send you their application materials.
- Continue researching scholarships. Begin assembling documents for aid applications.
- Give out recommendation forms and stamped envelopes addressed to the colleges' admissions offices.
- If you plan to apply for early decision, consider what effect that choice could have on financial aid.
- Review your final list of colleges with your counselor.
- As you schedule visits with admissions and financial aid advisors, think about also visiting with faculty and students in the department that interests you.
- Register for the fall ACT and/or SAT.

October

- Request that your transcripts be sent to colleges.
- Mail early-action or early-decision applications.
- Take any tests for which you are registered. Have your test results sent to schools.

November

- Take the SAT Subject Test in Language with Listening (for French, German, Japanese, Spanish, and English proficiency) if required by your colleges.
- Start writing your essays. If you applied early decision, notify the college about honors you have received since you submitted your application and ask your high school to send out a recent transcript.

December

- Mail applications or turn them in at school.
- If you applied early and you were accepted, withdraw applications from other schools.
- Start working with your parents on completing the Free Application for Federal Student Aid form. Apply at www.fafsa.ed.gov, or get forms from your high school or by calling (800) 433-3243.

January

- File all federal financial aid forms and apply for state aid.
- Ask your school to send mid-year grade reports to your colleges.
- Verify that all your application materials have been sent out.

February

- Check with schools to make sure that they have the documentation they require.

March

- Look for your decision letters this month and in April.
- Don't give in to "senioritis." Your college admission is contingent upon your final high school grades.

April

- Evaluate your financial aid offers. You'll have to make a decision about where to go and notify your college by May 1, then let other schools know you won't be coming.

June and summer

- Have your high school send your final transcript to the college you will be attending.
- Know when tuition and room-and-board payments are due.
- Notify the financial aid office if there have been any changes in your family's circumstances that might make you eligible for additional aid. (Perhaps one of your parents was laid off or there was a major illness in the family.)

America's best colleges

Each year, *U.S.News & World Report* ranks more than 1,400 colleges and universities based on such measures of excellence as graduation and freshman retention rates, class size and student-to-faculty ratio, and the expert opinions of college presidents and deans. To see where your schools rank, check out the "America's Best Colleges" guidebook, available on newsstands, or go to www.usnews.com. Here are the schools that top the lists for 2007. Colleges whose ranks are identical are tied.

National Universities

Universities in this category offer a full range of undergraduate, master's, and Ph.D. programs, and emphasize faculty research.

1. Princeton University (NJ)
2. Harvard University (MA)
3. Yale University (CT)
4. California Institute of Technology
4. Massachusetts Inst. of Technology
4. Stanford University (CA)
7. University of Pennsylvania
8. Duke University (NC)
9. Columbia University (NY)
9. Dartmouth College (NH)
9. University of Chicago

Liberal Arts Colleges

Liberal arts colleges focus almost entirely on undergraduate education and award more than half of their degrees in the liberal arts disciplines.

1. Williams College (MA)
2. Amherst College (MA)
3. Swarthmore College (PA)
4. Wellesley College (MA)
5. Middlebury College (VT)
6. Carleton College (MN)
7. Bowdoin College (ME)
7. Pomona College (CA)
9. Haverford College (PA)
10. Davidson College (NC)
10. Wesleyan University (CT)

Universities—Master's

These schools offer a full range of undergraduate degrees and some master's programs but few, if any, doctoral programs.

South
1. Rollins College (FL)
2. James Madison University (VA)
3. Elon University (NC)
4. Samford University (AL)
5. Stetson University (FL)

North
1. Villanova University (PA)
2. Loyola College in Maryland
2. Providence College (RI)
4. Fairfield University (CT)
5. College of New Jersey

West
1. Trinity University (TX)
2. Santa Clara University (CA)
3. Gonzaga University (WA)
4. Loyola Marymount University (CA)
5. University of Portland (OR)
5. Whitworth College (WA)

Midwest
1. Creighton University (NE)
2. Xavier University (OH)
3. Valparaiso University (IN)
4. Drake University (IA)
5. Butler University (IN)
5. John Carroll University (OH)

Comprehensive Colleges—Bachelor's

The comprehensive colleges focus on undergraduate education and offer degree programs in the liberal arts and in such professional fields as business, nursing, and education.

South

1. Berea College (KY)
2. Berry College (GA)
3. Asbury College (KY)
3. Maryville College (TN)
5. Ouachita Baptist University (AR)

North

1. Stonehill College (MA)
2. Simon's Rock College of Bard (MA)
3. Elizabethtown College (PA)
4. Messiah College (PA)
5. Elmira College (NY)
5. Russell Sage College (NY)

West

1. Linfield College (OR)
2. Carroll College (MT)
2. Master's Col. and Seminary (CA)
4. Brigham Young University–Hawaii
5. Oklahoma Baptist University
5. Texas Lutheran University

Midwest

1. Calvin College (MI)
1. St. Mary's College (IN)
3. Taylor University (IN)
4. St. Norbert College (WI)
5. Ohio Northern University

hang out in the sports complex, while performers should see the stages or check out a rehearsal.

Parental prerogatives

Parents should view themselves primarily as chauffeurs whose job it is to get their children to an important meeting unfrazzled and on time. Once on campus, they should take to the background. Many counselors advise parents to skip the tour altogether or go on a separate one.

While formal interviews are no longer required at many schools, a scheduled talk with an admissions officer offers a fine opportunity to both gain information and impress the staff. Even if the talk feels really comfortable and informal, keep in mind that you're being judged the whole time on how enthusiastic you seem to be about the school and its programs, and on your thoughtfulness, intelligence, and humor. Admissions officers don't mind at all if you ask pointed questions (Why do so many freshmen decide not to come back?), but you might want to save your queries about where to find the best weekend parties for your campus tour guide.

The admissions office can arrange for you to spend a night in the dorm—a great way to get insight into what daily life is like. You'll find out pretty quickly whether the hallways are noisy with music and conversation, and with groups of kids congregating to gab or watch TV, or if everybody's quietly cramming behind closed doors. Spending this kind of relaxed time with students will give you a chance to ask questions like: What do you like and hate about this school? What are the classes like—and do professors or graduate students teach the introductory courses? How easy is it to get to know professors and see them outside of class? What do students do for fun on the weekends? How much studying and partying goes on? After you've seen the college, it's a good idea to walk around the city or town to get a sense of what it would feel like to be a part of the larger community.

Every school will make an impression. But count on it: You'll forget a lot of the details by the time you need them. (Which school was it that had the great gym? The unbelievable drama department? The cute tour guide?) It's smart to write down your observations along the way. In April, after all those fat acceptance letters arrive, you're going to be the one weighing the candidates and making the decision.

Chapter Two

What Colleges Will Look for in You

Anybody who's heard the depressing stories of standout students rejected by every school (and of whole classfuls of valedictorians turned away by the Ivy League) might logically wonder how his own not-even-close-to-star-quality credentials will gain him a spot in any college. It's true that getting into highly ranked colleges is harder than ever these days—and that a smaller proportion of applicants is making the cut even at places that used to be considered sure bets, or "safeties." And it's *really* hard, it seems, to make it to the end of the process with your sanity intact. Driven by anxiety and mistaken ideas about what admissions officers expect, too many teenagers treat high school as an endurance test these days, taking on more tough courses and activities than they can handle and leaving little time for friends or sleep. This single-minded focus often means "the battle is lost in terms of a healthy high school education," says Scott White, director of guidance at Montclair High School in New Jersey, who sees more students than ever suffering from anxiety, depression, anorexia, and panic attacks.

But it doesn't have to be that way. *U.S. News* asked several dozen counselors and admissions deans to describe what schools are looking for in applicants and how you can measure up without totally stressing out. The first thing to remember is that most schools still accept more than half of their applicants. And even if you're applying to more competitive colleges, you can greatly improve your chances by preparing early, by pursuing your interests actively (without confusing quality with quantity), and by looking for the right fit. You'll have a much better chance of being accepted by a good school—without going nuts in the process.

First, consider what you're up against

Some students are so anxious about getting into college that they or their families are taking creative—even extreme—measures to gain an edge. For instance, there was the student at a New York City high school who stole Bowdoin College's catalog from the guidance office during the fall of her senior year so that none of her classmates would be tempted to apply there. (She didn't get in.) There was the Miami teenager who surfed the Federal Election Commission website to find out whether any admissions officers she'd be trying to impress had made political donations. Upon discovering that the Colby College interviewer gave money to the Republican Party, "I muted my leftist views," says the future government major. (Also a no-go.) One determined father took a year off from work to run his daughter's get-into-college campaign; a mom used her daughter's e-mail address to contact prestigious colleges with impressively intelligent questions. Meanwhile, Katherine Cohen, a New York college consultant whose firm, IvyWise, collects up to $33,000 for helping students select a college and get in, is booked for a year, with a waiting list. Some of her clients fly 2,000 miles to keep their appointments. Yet even she was surprised when a parent brought in a new charge: a student who had only just finished seventh grade.

Partly, the anxiety that makes applicants and their families take such bizarre steps can be blamed on the fact that so many kids are determined to go to the same small group of prestigious schools. "The quality of the applicant pool is so strong that we could easily have filled a very impressive freshman class just with the students who didn't quite make the grade," says Lee Stetson, dean of admissions at the University of Pennsylvania. Last year, Penn received almost 19,000 applications for about 2,550 spaces.

The simple truth is that there are more students than ever fighting for a limited number of spaces. The Department of Education predicts that the number of high school graduates will increase by 11 percent, to 3.2 million, by the end of the decade. Almost two-thirds of the students graduating from high school today head directly to campus, up from just half only 20 years ago. The University of Wisconsin–Madison, for example, received more than 20 percent more applications for last year's entering class than it received five years earlier. The University of Miami, dismissed not so long ago as "Suntan U," received 18,807 applications for the 2,277 spots in the class of 2008—more than double the number of a decade ago. Colleges are making matters worse by marketing strenuously to the most talented students they can possibly attract. (Thus the pounds and pounds of material you've probably already received in the mail.) The result tends to be that applications go way up—and the schools can be pickier.

Because the students who don't make the cut at the most elite colleges have taken up space in their second and third choices, it's harder to get into schools that have been less selective in the past, too. Muhlenberg College in Pennsylvania is now accepting only about 43 percent of students, down from 74 percent in 1995. Brandeis's acceptance rate has dropped from 60 percent to around 38 percent over that time, and the rate at Adelphi University in New York has dipped from 78 percent to about 68 percent since 1997.

Some students have responded by applying to more schools; instead of five or eight applications, they're spending hundreds of dollars to send off 10 or 15. (Indeed, part of the increase in competition can be blamed on all these multiple applications.) But the real key, say the pros, is to apply to the right

The athlete's edge

Yes, indeed, athletes do have an edge—as do trilingual students and gifted artists. Amherst College, a Division III school that does not offer athletic scholarships, sets aside about 66 places in each freshman class of 425 for athletes who will play 29 varsity sports, from women's field hockey to men's swimming. "There's no question that there's an advantage for a very limited number of 'impact' athletes," says Richard Nesbitt, director of admissions at nearby Williams College, which fills about 66 spots every year with athletes who play 32 varsity sports. But at highly selective schools, grades and recommendations count very heavily, too. "It's hard to justify admitting a mediocre student when you're turning away superior kids," says Monica Inzer, former dean of undergraduate admission and student financial services at Babson College near Boston and now dean of admission and financial aid at Hamilton College.

Athletes who can rise to the level of play at Division I powerhouse universities generally get more leeway when it comes to grades and test scores. While researching their book, *The Game of Life: College Sports and*

Educational Values, William G. Bowen and James L. Shulman analyzed data from 30 colleges and found that the high-profile athletes at Division I schools (which can offer scholarships) have SAT scores 237 points lower than students at large; at liberal arts colleges, there is a 135 point gap. In his book *Intercollegiate Athletics and the American University*, former University of Michigan president James J. Duderstadt says that Division I coaches get "a certain number of 'no questions asked' admits, so that they can confidently go after the very top athletes."

How can the more typical athlete use a sport to his or her advantage? Pay attention to supply and demand. Which sports tend to have a shortage of college players? Which schools are launching teams or graduating players—or just added the only goalie they need? (You can find much of this sort of intelligence by scouring college websites.) Julie Browning, the dean of undergraduate enrollment at Rice University in Houston, recalls that the launch of a women's soccer team a couple years ago created a need to recruit 13 players. When Babson added women's track, the school cre-

ated immediate openings for a range of talent from shot-putters to distance runners. In general, Title IX legislation, meant to ensure gender equity in college sports, has led to a boom in women's athletics and a hearty appetite for players. "There are more programs in some sports than there are quality athletes," says Tracy Coyne, head coach of the women's lacrosse team at the University of Notre Dame.

If you think you've got the talent to make a college team, you should be showcasing your skills at summer camps that draw college scouts; golfers and tennis players should be getting in some tournament play. Ask your high school coach to contact college coaches on your behalf, and follow up with a letter and video highlights of your play. (While NCAA regulations prohibit coaches from approaching you until the summer before senior year, there's nothing stopping you from initiating the contact.) Coaches can't necessarily get you in, but they have enormous pull with admissions. Once you've secured a spot on the "coach's list," Shulman and Bowen found, you've improved your chances for admission by as much as 50 percent.

schools, understand what admissions people are really looking for, and—if you're reading this book before the last minute—start thinking well in advance about how you can become the strongest candidate possible. (Younger brothers and sisters, take note: Eighth-grade algebra is the essential first step toward Advanced Placement calculus.)

"You can't control who else is applying," says Nancy Hargrave Meislahn, dean of admission and financial aid at Wesleyan University in Connecticut. But you can make sure you find activities that allow you to stand out and that you always take the most challenging courses you can handle. Here are a few principles to keep in mind.

Grades don't matter the way you think

Guess what? Perfect As and a standing at the head of the class aren't as impressive as they used to be.

This may be hard to believe, given the scary headlines about how tough the competition is. And, in fact, it's true that your transcript, and what it shows about your four years in high school, is still the most important part of your application. But the numbers by themselves might just mean you've been given a big leg up by grade inflation, or that you've chosen easy courses with an eye toward snagging the top slot. Lots of high school administrators don't even bother calculating class rank for their seniors anymore because they don't believe rank gives a very accurate picture of what a student has actually achieved. So instead of focusing in on your grade point average as a measure of your performance, the people in admissions are going to scour your transcript for signs that you've taken full advantage of all the intellectual opportunities your high school has to offer, that you're determined, and that you're maturing as a student.

How can they tell you've made the most of your school's resources? Your guidance counselor tucks a detailed profile of your school in with your recommendation letter. The profile, which you'll hear more about in Chapter 4, lists all the courses that you've been able to select from, so the people

in admissions can see whether you've challenged yourself by taking honors and Advanced Placement classes or have taken the easiest possible path. If the school's curriculum wasn't all that challenging, it probably won't be held against you—as long as your grades are good. On the other hand, somebody in a competitive high school with 20-plus AP courses might be able to show lower grades without any penalty, but had better also show a courseload that makes the most of the curriculum.

Besides helping admissions staffers gauge what kind of student you are, the profiles allow them to better distinguish among candidates from schools that often differ wildly in resources and rigor. For example, they might decide to reject a class valedictorian from School A in favor of No. 100 at School B if the second school offers far more rigorous courses, and on the assumption that No. 100 is more thoroughly prepared for college work.

This is not to suggest that you ought to be signing up for 10 AP courses. (See pages 27–28 for advice on planning your AP strategy.) But you definitely are going to be judged on whether or not your courses make sense given your previous record. A student who took geometry freshman year and has good grades in math might well be expected to be in AP calculus senior year. On the other hand, admissions officers probably wouldn't hold regular chemistry against a student who's always received only average grades in science.

A mediocre grade in a tough course is going to be looked at closely, so you'd better think carefully about what to do if you're struggling. The questionable grade might not hurt you at all if it's one C among mostly As, say, and you're obviously stretching yourself by taking the course. One high school student considered dropping AP calculus before receiving her first C ever during first semester of senior year. She stuck with the class after an admissions officer told her that he would rather see kids taking accelerated courses than getting straight As. Taken as a whole, her transcript showed a strong student rising to a challenge. If your transcript is not otherwise filled with

As, the grade could instead signal to admissions staffers that you're not quite ready to handle college-level work in the subject. In that case, you might be better off dropping down a level than scraping through an advanced course and finishing unprepared.

Suppose you're someone who floundered freshman year but settled in and succeeded as a junior. You probably won't be penalized for your early erratic performance if the overall direction of your high school record is upward. The people judging your application are looking for evidence of determination and personal growth as well as obvious ability. "We'll be very excited about a student who receives poor advising into the vocational track but who takes college prep courses out of sheer will," says Nancy Cable, former vice president and dean of admissions and financial aid at Davidson College in North Carolina.

On the other hand, your grades might make you a hot prospect

One real benefit of looking for colleges that match your interests and abilities, as opposed to schools with a prestigious name and reputation, is that you're apt to discover that you're in demand. Many fine schools below the top ranks are anxious to attract applicants whose qualifications will help boost the student-body profile. Even better, they're often willing to hand out generous merit awards to induce you to come. Ray Loewe, founder and president of College Money, a Marlton, New Jersey, consulting firm that helps families figure out how to finance college, tells his student clients to search out schools where their grades and test scores will put them in the top quarter of the applicant pool. Not only will these kids become "premium candidates," Loewe says, but "the money comes out on the table. A really sharp kid in the top 25 percent of incoming students has some real negotiating power."

The good news here is that your options beyond the most selective schools have never been stronger. A trickle-down of talent, both of students and pro-

fessors, means that many less selective and less well-known schools just keep getting better and more attractive. Taking advantage of the ultra-tight academic job market, they're scooping up top-notch faculty who haven't managed to get hired at more prestigious places. After aggressively recruiting talented professors, the University of Maryland–Baltimore County regularly sends its students off to graduate schools like the Massachusetts Institute of Technology, Stanford, and Oxford. In a typical year,

---

"A really sharp kid in the top 25 percent of incoming students has some real negotiating power."

---

the top-ranked medical school at Johns Hopkins accepts applicants from many colleges without fancy reputations—places like Oakwood College in Alabama, Frostburg State University in Maryland, and the University of California–Irvine. While Ohio State was luring senior professors away from universities such as Berkeley and Tufts by building state-of-the-art research facilities, it also attracted students with higher ACT scores. The average has gone from 21.9 to 26 since 1987.

Any old AP courses won't do

Colleges send slightly mixed messages about what they want in terms of an AP record. At the same time that admissions officers say they expect applicants to be taking full advantage of challenging courses, they also worry that the academic content of the courses is being diluted. A report by the National Research Council contends that both AP classes and the fast-growing International Baccalaureate (IB) courses (a rigorous two-year curriculum of study that is intended to get kids ready for college anywhere in the world) are often taught by poorly prepared teachers who stress rote memorization rather than problem solving and discussion. About the same time as the report came out, Harvard announced that college credit would only be awarded for perfect AP test scores of 5 because professors were complaining that students with lower scores weren't well-prepared enough to move into advanced classes.

The best approach for college-bound students is to keep on taking AP classes, but to pick them wisely. You're going to be better off if you can show a strong background in core subjects (English, math, the basic sciences, history, and a foreign language), so concentrate your advanced coursework in those areas. Don't expect AP courses such as environmental science or art history, which some critics deride as "AP lite," to impress admissions officers unless you already have a solid grounding in the basics. And plan on taking the AP test. No matter what grade you earn in the class, not showing a score for the test—or showing a low score—may signal to administrators that the course wasn't all that advanced and that you didn't master college-level material.

The number of AP classes your transcript will be expected to show varies widely. One or two will suffice at some schools, while the typical applicant to highly ranked Amherst College applies with four. Most people can't handle a full load of college-level courses in one year, so overdosing on APs may drive you crazy and leave colleges unimpressed. "If AP is truly demanding, it should not be possible to take five classes" over such a short period, says William Shain, dean of undergraduate admissions at Vanderbilt University.

You need to love learning— not just getting As

One way colleges swamped with superqualified applicants differentiate one from the next these days is to look for the spark that says, "I like to learn just for the fun of it." These tend to be students who can be counted on to contribute to a college's intellectual life rather than just passively attend classes.

It may be that all the proof you need exists within your school experience. Perhaps you're a capable mathematician who decides to go to summer school so you can fit in an extra course. Maybe you're a science student passionately interested in the environment who participates in the science fair every year or researches an article for the school paper on the impact of a local highway project. Or maybe you're interested in being a

lawyer someday and you join the debate team to get practice arguing.

But many elite colleges are also noting how much effort goes into intellectual pursuits *outside* of the school day. Sometimes the opportunities are ready-made (a community college course that takes you to the next level in photography; a summer enrichment camp with a focus on astronomy or computer programming; a workshop on local artists and their paintings at your city's museum), and sometimes you have to create the opportunities yourself. Maybe you could volunteer to report on student life for your community newspaper if you love writing. Or start a summer business researching family genealogies if history's your thing.

Fancy internships or exotic field trips that seem to speak more about your family's money and connections than about your love of learning won't dazzle the folks at the most prestigious schools anymore; too many students have friends and relatives who can find them a summer gig at a law firm. The secret is to find experiences that admissions folks can tell are clearly meaningful to you because they make sense in the context of who you show yourself to be.

It's bad to be a joiner, but good to do what you love

That advice—choose meaningful experiences— holds true when it comes to extracurricular activities, too. Why? It used to be that colleges wanted well-rounded students. Now, faced with growing piles of applications padded with indiscriminate club memberships, most selective colleges aim toward a well-rounded freshman class instead. "The embodiment at age 17 of a Renaissance person is difficult to find," says David Gould, a former admissions dean at Brandeis who now runs an independent counseling service in Concord, Massachusetts. "We realized we could accomplish the same thing with lots of different people."

The take-home message is that you should show a commitment to one or two of your burning interests, and not simply join every club in school in a misguided effort to appear really active. What impresses the people who read applications is proof that an interest is a theme of your life, not just during school hours but outside, too. One young TV-sports addict started writing a sports column for his high school paper, coaching basketball in a poor neighborhood, and interning at an all-sports television channel, for example. A Wisconsin girl, a music lover, chose as her essay topic how practicing the piano had helped her develop discipline and confidence. Asked on her applications about community service, she described how she'd raised $1,600 for a missionary effort through her church by putting on two solo recitals. Her extracurricular activities included the school's jazz group, wind ensemble, and the orchestra that accompanied the musicals. Along with her good grades and high SAT scores, the girl's passion for music proved irresistible to Northwestern, Marquette, Tufts—and the University of Chicago, where she enrolled.

It's important to keep in mind that while you don't want to appear to be a person who just racks up memberships, neither do you want to show a complete lack of versatility. Given a choice between a brilliant musician whose whole life is music or a brilliant musician who's also a key member of the diving team, many schools will prefer the multidimensional person.

Leaders tend to have an edge

Many colleges, especially selective ones swamped with desirable candidates, are looking for leadership talent: kids who have the gumption and people skills to influence others and make things happen. Maybe you won't be able to point to a class presidency—after all, few can. But think about what you can point to. Chances are, if you've poured yourself into a couple of activities that really mean something to you, it won't be hard to come up with evidence that you don't just sit back and wait for life to happen. Maybe your years of baseball have included several seasons assisting your brother's Little League coach. Maybe your gift with animals has inspired you to start a pet-sitting business, or to volunteer to help raise funds for the local pound. When colleges compare two applicants whose interests and academic qualifica-

tions are similar, such signs of initiative can make one an obvious pick.

Beach time doesn't count for much

Admissions deans don't look kindly on summers spent lazing at the beach, but otherwise they're surprisingly open-minded. If you need money, take that fast-food restaurant job, then try to make the experience as meaningful as you can. One student who worked in a mailroom ended up changing a computer program to make mail distribution more efficient, which helped lead to an acceptance at Williams College.

If you don't have to spend your whole summer at work, you might really benefit by investing some time in community service. Service is such an integral part of the high school experience for so many students now that many colleges have come to expect it and ask about it; examining an applicant's volunteer efforts can tell an admissions staffer a lot about her leadership abilities, imagination, and capacity to show compassion and concern for others. A superficial one-time effort meant for show won't do you any good—again, colleges are looking for commitment.

The sharper your "hook," the better

What many students don't realize when they start this whole process is that even near *perfection* might not be enough to get them in at selective schools. Although they hate to admit it, many colleges target certain groups of applicants for admission—maybe because they want to increase the diversity of the student body or expand the physics department, say, or add women's ice hockey or a few potential future donors. Most people think of ethnic mix when the importance of diversity is discussed, but colleges want the population to reflect socioeconomic differences, too—and they don't want all their students to come from the same three or four cities. Applications from states with small populations such as Wyoming or Nevada sometimes get a second close read at colleges hoping to boast that their students come from all 50 states. Students in the targeted groups are described as

—by Ann Wright, vice president for the southwest region of the College Board. Wright has also served as dean of enrollment management at Smith College, director of admissions at the University of Rochester, and vice president for enrollment at Rice University.

Several years ago, *Money* magazine's cover featured a poor college applicant in the guise of a martyr—hands tied and body skewered by the arrows of his favored colleges, a victim of the biggest competition of the twentieth century. Well, it might seem that the competition is even bloodier now—and in terms of sheer numbers battling for spots at top schools, it probably is. But there's no excuse for students allowing application panic to ruin their high school years. In reality, colleges are in fierce competition for students who fit *their* profile. The key to making yourself an attractive candidate is to educate yourself about how schools pick their next class, and then figure out which colleges are apt to want you.

Inside the back room

By definition, highly selective colleges receive many more applications than they have spots. If they want a class of 700 and usually enroll 41 percent of the people accepted, they must admit about 1,700 students. Last year, 7,500 people applied to Rice, so only 23 percent could be admitted. And many more than that were qualified! To winnow their lists, colleges create evaluation systems that rank the people in the pool based on whatever qualities the schools value most highly.

At Rice, we rated each applicant on a scale of 1 to 5 in each of five categories: rigor of the high school courseload; overall performance in the college-prep curriculum; recommendations; presentation (the clarity of the student's answers and the quality of the essay, for example); and personal qualities, like leadership, talent, and the potential to add something to college life. A total rating of close to 20 moves you into the next round. Readers also pull out students who may not approach 20 overall, but who are outstanding in one or two areas, and who have "flags"—special achievements such as publications or election to high office. Coursework, grades, and academic recommendations are most important.

Test scores matter, but at Rice they are thought of primarily as verification of a student's record—or sometimes as the sign of a "late bloomer" who might wake up in college. It's not unheard of to see an applicant who dozed through three years of high school, only to find herself in the top 1 percent of all per-formers on the SAT physics exam. Who doesn't want a top-scoring female with a sudden intense interest in nanotechnology research, even if her extracurriculars and grades are on the modest side?

The top half of the Rice applicant pool is read at least three times by members of the admission committee, which includes 43 staffers, professors, alumni, and students. The full-timers in the admissions office might work their way through 200 applications a week during the peak season. Each reader rates the application; then a second, more senior person makes another independent judgment.

Half of the applicants are selected to move on for another review, which narrows the group further. In the third round, where all applicants are academically qualified, a Decision Committee roundtable discusses how each applicant works in terms of "fit." Besides academic achievement, the committee looks for flags, life experiences, subtle warnings, and maturity and enthusiasm. Sometimes, there's heat: "I'd rather have two linguists than five civil engineers!" "This is a bright premed who cares only about getting into med school, not about dealing with people!" "This is my 'one' student; I met him in Knoxville, and I'd sacrifice a week off to admit him!"

Admission by crook or by hook

Some students will go to astonishing lengths to get into a college. We've seen essays obviously written by a third party or plagiarized from the Internet, lists of accomplishments and honors that are clearly contradicted by school records, and outrageously egotistical responses. Don't even think about trying such maneuvers. Application readers are a savvy bunch, and it's the kiss of death to commit one of these sins—an automatic route to Rice's deny pile.

A bit of bragging and name-dropping is fine, however. Rice is obviously interested in great music students and wonderful athletes, and we have a special concern for those who have overcome a difficult situation like illness, family tragedy, or discrimination. And it's OK to talk about family connections, as many colleges that value tradition give special consideration to "legacy" applicants. If you really are related to the governor, colleges may want to know, but don't bother getting recommendations from VIPs who never heard of you but once met your great-uncle at a fundraiser.

Otherwise, the qualities that come through on a successful application, beyond a strong academic record, are enthusiasm, personal pizzazz, and a genuine passion for learning. When I read an essay, I look for answers to these questions: "Can you write? Can you think? Do you care? What do you care about?" You don't have to have experienced a major earthquake to impress us! One of the best essays I've read came from a guy who wrote about how growing a beard changed all his relationships; another came from a girl who wrote wonderfully about the sights and smells of an early-morning bicycle ride. Then there was that disaster titled "dniW eht etouQ swodahS gnivoM," written entirely backward and sent in with a mirror so I could read it.

Remember that attention to details—or lack thereof—can create a big impression. We've heard from too many "candy strippers," members of the "drum and bagel corps," and members of the "honor role." And, a word to people filing multiple e-applications: it won't help your case to (accidentally) tell Rice that "Stanford is my dream school."

When all is said and done, you should feel good about your chances of getting in if you've applied to colleges whose values and standards match your strengths. And you'll be better able to take a rejection philosophically. Students who have chosen well can be pretty sure they were qualified to get in, if only there had been room.

---

having "hooks," attributes so attractive that they're likely to overcome even ho-hum grades.

At superselective schools like Harvard, almost all slots go to kids with some hook, says Joyce Slayton Mitchell, director of college advising at Nightingale-Bamford School in New York and author of *Winning the Heart of the College Admissions Dean*. "To have the freshman community they want," she explains, "colleges need musicians and athletes, leadership in student organizations and government, a certain percentage of alumni children, and minorities and international students. That's almost everybody."

(For Mitchell's views on the biggest goofs applicants and their parents make during the college search process, see page 59.)

An easy way to find out where you might be needed is to call coaches, musical directors, and department chairs, for example, and ask what they're searching for this year. A baseball coach with too many catchers will probably tell you there won't be a place for another one on the team, whereas a conductor desperate for bassoons will demand you FedEx over an audition tape—and more important, will tell the admissions committee if you seem promising.

During the time you spend online and on campus, you'll want to study up on the schools' personalities, too. That's because admissions people are looking for students who will be a good "fit" just as applicants are looking for a college that fits (or should be, anyway). Some universities value initiative and the ability to take risks; Stanford judges all applicants on their "intellectual vitality." Pepperdine routinely turns down top-scoring students in favor of others who share the university's commitment to community service. In the end, success at this whole process hinges on your ability to offer something special that the college needs or wants.

Chapter Three

How to Ace the Big Exam

Have you ever had that nightmare where you're sitting in an empty classroom, No. 2 pencil in hand, feeling nauseated and totally unprepared to take any sort of test, when a faceless teacher places a copy of the SAT in front of you and shouts "go," right before the hands on the clock start speeding around, double-time, and your mind goes absolutely blank? Then you wake up—thankfully— sweaty and screaming?

You're not alone. Students lose sleep about the SATs and ACTs for a reason: They matter. And while some of the hullabaloo regarding the new-and-improved SAT Reasoning Test, which launched in March 2005, has finally died down, there are still lots of questions regarding how to proceed with standardized testing: For example, which of the two college entrance exams should you take in order to maximize your scoring potential? Is it worth shelling out big bucks for professional test prep or are you better off studying on your own? How important are the SAT and ACT writing sections to the admissions office?

It's essential to consider these issues, as standardized test scores are the second most important factor to admissions officers, right behind grades in academic courses, according to a recent survey by the National Association for College Admission Counseling, the professional organization of guidance counselors and admissions deans. And schools—the vast majority of which still require applicants to submit SAT or ACT scores—rely on the results for a range of important decisions.

For example, many large state institutions, including the University of Iowa and the University of Washington, plug scores into a formula along with grade point average to determine a cutoff number below which nobody gets in. Cleveland State University draws the line for entrance to its honors program at a combined SAT score of 1830 (out of a possible 2400) or an ACT of 30 (out of 36), while schools such as Howard University in Washington, D.C., Boston University, and the University of North Carolina–Greensboro, among dozens of others, hand out freshman scholarships based partly on test results.

But don't panic

Even so, there's no need to exaggerate the importance of admissions tests. Many schools, particularly small liberal arts colleges that don't have to screen tens of thousands of applicants, look at SAT or ACT scores in the context of the entire application file; in other words, the scores are just one piece of the puzzle of who you are. Anybody who has been prepping frantically to retake the SAT for a third time in a last-ditch effort to gain a few more points should bear in mind that test scores seldom overshadow the transcript. When there's a mismatch between the two, admissions officers try to figure out why. Often, they give more weight to grades.

This works in favor of diligent and successful students and against underachievers whose test scores suggest brilliance but whose report cards hint at laziness. "If a student with a B in chemistry gets a 750 on the [SAT] subject test, I think, 'This kid knows how to take a test,'" but hasn't shown the sustained effort and mastery needed for a top mark, says William Conley, dean of enrollment and academic services at Johns Hopkins University in Baltimore.

If you find yourself in this boat, about to be tossed overboard with no life preserver, you can use your application essay and interview to explain the discrepancy as best you can, and to point out any achievements in other areas, such as sports or the arts, that make you a good pick anyway. You should also make sure the admissions staff understands that you've matured and plan to work harder in college. If you're particularly excited by a school's new biochemistry department or the stellar eighteenth-century Brit Lit faculty, for instance, ask intelligent questions and make contact with students and professors. Your obvious enthusiasm for academic pursuits, new as it may be, may make admissions officers more willing to take a gamble on your application.

If you lean in the opposite direction, with low scores and a series of stellar report cards, use well-chosen teacher recommendations and the quality of your writing to convince admissions officers that your grades are the more accurate measure of your smarts and not the result of grade inflation at your high school. Ideally, of course, both your standardized exam results and your GPA will be high.

Here's the rest of what you need to know about the testing juggernaut—and how to turn the stuff of nightmares into a big, fat acceptance letter from the school of your dreams.

The SAT versus the ACT

Consider this question: To test best, should Joe take (A) the SAT, (B) the ACT, (C) both of the above? High achievers gunning for top-tier schools often assume they have no choice but to select (A). In the college-crowded state of Massachusetts, for example, 85 percent of 2004's high school graduates took the SAT, while just 12 percent took the ACT Assessment, the college entrance test that dominates at many Midwestern and Southern high schools. Nationally, however, the latter is steadily closing the gap. In the graduating class of 2004, a record-breaking 1.4 million or so students sat for the SAT, and nearly 1.2 million took the ACT—a 15 percent increase since 1999.

Looking past the SAT

If you've taken both the SAT and the ACT and are disappointed with your lackluster results, don't despair. A growing number of the nation's four-year institutions leave standardized test scores out of admissions decisions for many freshman applicants. Among them are schools that give students the option of not submitting test scores, like Bates, Bowdoin (the first school to make the SAT optional, back in 1969), Connecticut College, Dickinson, and Mount Holyoke, and those, like the University of Texas, that admit in-state students near the top of their high school class regardless of SAT performance. The size of this entire cluster of schools has grown nearly 100 percent in recent years, according to the National Center for Fair and Open Testing, to more than 700 institutions. For a list of schools surveyed by *U.S. News* that make the tests optional for some or all students, see page 36.

For additional choices, visit www.fairtest.org/optinit.htm.

Muhlenberg College, in Allentown, Pennsylvania, which made the SAT optional for the class entering in 1997, has a policy that is typical for test-optional schools. Applicants who decide not to submit their scores can now send in a graded paper and come to campus for an interview instead. If you choose this route, one of the best ways to impress admissions committees is to send in a transcript packed with challenging courses, as many administrators say they have found the strength of an applicant's high school curriculum, and how well he or she succeeded at taking advantage of it, to be highly reliable predictors of the applicant's college achievement. Showing Advanced Placement courses, plus high marks on the AP exams, gives you an edge—and, as a bonus, in many cases you will also receive college credit.

Among schools that still require the tests are a number that have de-emphasized their importance. In the past, applicants to the University of California–Berkeley whose grades and SAT scores fell below a numerical cutoff were removed from the pool before deliberations about admissions began. Now there's no cutoff. "When you have so many [qualified] students, you have to go deeper into academics," explains one admissions staffer. Other large schools that get a flood of applications from high achievers, such as the University of North Carolina–Chapel Hill, sort applicants by the numbers and then search for qualities that might override mediocre scores. All of these admissions policies are more equitable, say anti-testing advocates, as they don't penalize those who can't afford expensive prep courses.

Today, virtually all colleges accept both tests, and that means you can present the one that best shows your stuff. Students ahead of the curve on this trend are, well, scoring ahead of the curve. For instance, one young woman from Maryland worried that her combined score of 1100 on the old SAT wouldn't make the grade at her top choice, the University of Michigan–Ann Arbor, and took the ACT as well. She scored a 28 (equal to approximately 1260 on the critical reading and math sections of the SAT) and enrolled at Michigan the next fall.

Why the variation in her scores? Historically, the two exams have assessed different things—the old SAT measured raw aptitude while the ACT measures academic achievement in high school content areas. The overhauled SAT is much more similar to the ACT, but differences remain. To gauge which exam is right for you, it helps to know the basic structure and content of each test.

According to a recent *U.S. News* survey of colleges and universities, these schools have decided not to require SAT or ACT scores from some or all of their applicants. Among them are several that have recently changed their policies in response to the brouhaha over the new writing exam, like the College of the Holy Cross in Worcester, Massachusetts, and Lawrence University in Appleton, Wisconsin. You'll want to check with schools that interest you; some institutions recommend that scores be submitted even though they're not required, and some will consider test results if applicants want them to.

Alabama State University
Albany State University (GA)
Albertus Magnus College (CT)
Albion College (MI)
Allen University (SC)
Antioch College (OH)
Arkansas Baptist College
Art Center College of Design (CA)
Atlantic Union College (MA)
Austin Peay State University (TN)
Baker College of Flint (MI)
Bard College (NY)
Bates College (ME)
Bellevue University (NE)
Benjamin Franklin Institute of Technology (MA)
Bennington College (VT)
Berklee College of Music (MA)
Bethany College (CA)
Black Hills State University (SD)
Boston Architectural College
Boston Conservatory
Bowdoin College (ME)
Brigham Young University–Hawaii
Burlington College (VT)
California College of the Arts
California Institute of the Arts
California State University–East Bay
California State University–Los Angeles
California State University–Sacramento
California State University–San Marcos
California State University–Stanislaus
Calumet College of St. Joseph (IN)
Cazenovia College (NY)
Chadron State College (NE)
City University (WA)
Cleary University (MI)
Cleveland Institute of Music
Cogswell Polytechnical College (CA)
College of New Rochelle (NY)
College of St. Mary (NE)
College of the Atlantic (ME)
College of the Holy Cross (MA)
Colorado Christian University
Columbia College (IL)
Concordia College (AL)
Connecticut College
Cornish College of the Arts (WA)
Culver-Stockton College (MO)
CUNY–College of Staten Island
CUNY–Medgar Evers College
CUNY–New York City College of Technology
CUNY–York College
Curry College (MA)
Curtis Institute of Music (PA)
Daniel Webster College (NH)
Davenport University (MI)
Dickinson College (PA)
Dowling College (NY)
Drew University (NJ)
East-West University (IL)
Edward Waters College (FL)
Excelsior College (NY)
Fashion Institute of Technology (NY)
Florida Memorial College
Franklin and Marshall College (PA)
Franklin University (OH)
Gardner-Webb University (NC)
Goddard College (VT)
Golden Gate University (CA)

Goldey Beacom College (DE)

Graceland University (IA)

Grambling State University (LA)

Granite State College (NH)

Gratz College (PA)

Hamilton College (NY)

Hampshire College (MA)

Hartwick College (NY)

Henry Cogswell College (WA)

Heritage University (WA)

Hilbert College (NY)

Hobart and William Smith Colleges (NY)

Hofstra University (NY)

Humboldt State University (CA)

Humphreys College (CA)

Indiana University East

Indiana University–South Bend

International College (FL)

Jarvis Christian College (TX)

John F. Kennedy University (CA)

Johnson and Wales University (RI)

Judson College (AL)

Juilliard School (NY)

Juniata College (PA)

Knox College (IL)

Laguna College of Art and Design (CA)

Langston University (OK)

Lawrence University (WI)

Lebanon Valley College (PA)

Lewis and Clark College (OR)

Lewis-Clark State College (ID)

Lincoln Memorial University (TN)

Lindsey Wilson College (KY)

Livingstone College (NC)

Long Island University–Brooklyn (NY)

Longy School of Music (MA)

Loras College (IA)

Louisiana State University–Baton Rouge

Lourdes College (OH)

Lyndon State College (VT)

Manhattan School of Music (NY)

Marygrove College (MI)

Marymount Manhattan College (NY)

McDaniel College (MD)

Mercy College (NY)

Messiah College (PA)

Metropolitan State University (MN)

Midway College (KY)

Milwaukee Institute of Art and Design

Minnesota State University–Mankato

Missouri Baptist University

Missouri Western State University

Montana State University–Northern

Montserrat College of Art (MA)

Morris College (SC)

Mountain State University (WV)

Mount Holyoke College (MA)

Muhlenberg College (PA)

National University (CA)

New England College (NH)

New School University (NY)

Nichols College (MA)

North Carolina School of the Arts

North Carolina Wesleyan College

Northern Arizona University

Northern State University (SD)

Northwest Missouri State University

Nyack College (NY)

Oakland University (MI)

Oklahoma Panhandle State University

Ottawa University (KS)

Pacific Northwest College of Art (OR)

Pacific Union College (CA)

Paul Quinn College (TX)

Pennsylvania College of Technology

Peru State College (NE)

Philander Smith College (AR)

Pikeville College (KY)

Pitzer College (CA)

Post University (CT)

Purdue University–Calumet (IN)

Purdue University–North Central (IN)

Regent University (VA)

Ringling School of Art and Design (FL)

Robert Morris College (IL)

San Diego Christian College (CA)

San Francisco Art Institute

San Francisco Conservatory of Music

San Francisco State University

Seton Hill University (PA)

Shawnee State University (OH)

Sheldon Jackson College (AK)

Shimer College (IL)

Siena Heights University (MI)

Sierra Nevada College (NV)

Silver Lake College (WI)

South Carolina State University

Southeastern University (DC)

Southern California Institute of Architecture

Southern Nazarene University (OK)

Southern University–New Orleans

Southern Vermont College

Stephens College (MO)

St. Gregory's University (OK)

St. John's College (NM)

St. Lawrence University (NY)

Sul Ross State University (TX)

SUNY College of A&T–Cobleskill

SUNY–Empire State College

Susquehanna University (PA)

Texas College

Texas Southern University

Texas Wesleyan University

Texas Woman's University

Thiel College (PA)

Thomas College (ME)

Thomas Edison State College (NJ)

Thomas University (GA)

Touro College (NY)

Union Institute and University (OH)

Unity College (ME)

University of Alaska–Southeast

University of Arizona

University of Arkansas–Little Rock

University of Arkansas–Monticello

University of Charleston (WV)

University of Great Falls (MT)

University of Houston–Downtown

University of Maine–Farmington

University of Maine–Fort Kent

University of Maine–Presque Isle

University of Maryland–University College

University of Mississippi

University of Mobile (AL)

University of Nevada–Las Vegas

University of Nevada–Reno

University of New England (ME)

University of Science and Arts of Oklahoma

University of Texas–Brownsville

University of Texas–El Paso

University of the Arts (PA)

University of the District of Columbia

University of Wisconsin–Parkside

University of Wisconsin–Whitewater

Urbana University (OH)

Ursinus College (PA)

Utah Valley State College

Utica College (NY)

Voorhees College (SC)

Walsh College of Accountancy and Bus. Adm. (MI)

Wayne State College (NE)

Weber State University (UT)

West Virginia University–Parkersburg

Wheaton College (MA)

Wichita State University (KS)

Wiley College (TX)

Wilmington College (DE)

Yeshiva University (NY)

The SAT, designed to better measure your academic preparedness (or how much knowledge you have actually mastered) has a maximum score of 2400. The exam takes an endurance-testing three hours and 45 minutes, and costs $41.50. First comes a short handwritten 25-minute essay. Sample query: "Novelty is too often mistaken for progress. Assignment: The statement above suggests that what is new and different is often confused with advancement. To what extent do you agree or disagree with this view?" The essay is scored by two readers and accounts for approximately 30 percent of the writing score. (See page 40 for more on the essay and how it's graded.) The rest of the writing section has 49 multiple-choice grammar and usage questions, which can appear at any time in the test.

The 70-minute "Critical Reading" section consists of 67 multiple-choice questions that include sentence completions and both long and short reading comprehension passages. The 70-minute math section tests your knowledge of geometry, statistics, and Algebra II topics such as exponential growth, absolute value, and functional notation; it includes both multiple-choice and grid-in questions, and calculators are allowed.

The SAT includes an experimental section (used to test new questions) that can be an additional critical reading section, an extra math section, or further multiple-choice writing questions. It does not count toward your score, but you won't know which section it is, so you'll have to take it seriously. SAT questions appear in order of difficulty, from easy to hard, and the style of the test can be tricky. Possible answers include lots of "distractors," or choices that are specifically meant to distract test-takers from the correct response. One SAT question, for example, asked for the antonym of "blue," meaning "sad"; two colors, including "red," appeared as options to throw test-takers off. Students are penalized for wrong answers, which means that guessing isn't a good idea unless you can definitely eliminate one or more incorrect responses.

The ACT, on the other hand, is a roughly three-hour exam that costs $29 and measures academic preparation in four sections: English, which covers usage and mechanics like grammar and punctuation as well as rhetorical skills, takes 45 minutes; Mathematics, which includes questions on pre-algebra, algebra, geometry, and trigonometry, takes 60 minutes; Scientific Reasoning, which measures your ability to design and interpret basic experiments, takes 35 minutes; and Reading Comprehension, in four subject areas, also takes 35 minutes. The 215 multiple-choice questions are presented in random order—simple and killer queries all mixed together from the start—and the style is considered more straightforward than the SAT. There is no penalty for wrong answers, so feel free to take your chances.

Test-takers choosing the ACT also have the option of adding a 30-minute essay that costs an additional $14 and will satisfy colleges that demand a writing score as part of your application. A sample query: "In some high schools, many teachers and parents have encouraged the school to adopt a dress code that sets guidelines for what students can wear in the school building. Some teachers and parents support a dress code because they think it will improve the learning environment in the school. Other teachers and parents do not support a dress code because they think it restricts the individual student's freedom of expression. In your opinion, should high schools adopt dress codes for students? In your essay, take a position on this question. You may write about either one of the two points of view given, or you may present a different point of view on this question. Use specific reasons and examples to support your position."

In 2003–2004, the average score on the SAT was 508 out of a possible 800 for the old verbal section and 518 for the math. Though the content may be slightly different now, these scores are, by design, exactly comparable to results on the new exam. The mean ACT was 20.9 out of a top score of 36. Those who plan to be tested multiple times—or who fear they'll have to be—take note: Although you can choose to submit only your highest ACT score, schools see the results of every SAT you sit for.

To figure out which exam to take, you can buy review books for under $20 apiece and try a practice version of each test. Then compare your scores using a concordance table, which shows how SAT scores and ACT scores equate to each other. (A sample is available at www.collegeboard.com/sat/cbsenior/html/statoof.html.) Until there are national score reports for the writing test, experts suggest simply ignoring that section and comparing the total of your math and critical reading scores on the

senior reader will make the call. This raw score then counts for about 30 percent of the total 200–800 writing score.

According to the College Board's scoring guidelines, a 0 means you completely failed to answer the question; a 6 means you've eloquently and effectively argued your case. "Holistic scoring has far less to do with [what your answer is] and far more to do with whether or not you develop your argument well," says Brian O'Reilly, executive director of SAT information and services for the College Board. "You can take either side of the issue and back up your argument with something you read in a textbook, novel, newspaper article, or even saw in a movie."

> *"Holistic scoring has far less to do with [what your answer is] and far more to do with whether or not you develop your argument well."*

SAT with those portions of the ACT to get a good— if not perfect—idea of how you'll do on one exam versus the other.

If you perform substantially better on the practice SAT, stick with that exam, or go ahead and take both and report the ACT score if it turns out to be a pleasant surprise. Keep in mind that many top-ranking colleges require two or three SAT Subject Tests in addition to the SAT Reasoning Test, but some, like Wesleyan University in Connecticut, will accept the ACT in lieu of all SATs. The upshot: Check with the colleges you think you want to apply to before deciding which tests to take.

How your SAT essay will be graded—and used

What happens to your brilliant ideas and exquisite phrasings once you've put the pencil down? Your essay will be trucked off to two members of an army of readers across the country who've been specially trained in the art of "holistic" scoring—or, in other words, of absorbing and judging your prose in a couple minutes flat.

Each reader will give you a grade of 0 to 6, based on how convincingly you take a stand on an issue and prove your point. Your two scores will be combined for a composite of 0 to 12; if there is a discrepancy of more than one point between the two readers, a more

Believe it or not, as long as your essay is readable, errors in spelling, punctuation, and grammar will not be held against you— the multiple-choice portion of the new writing section will test your knowledge in those areas. And don't spend precious time trying to remember that the French Revolution started in 1789, since you will not be judged on how straight your facts are, either. "We don't want to penalize [students] on a writing assignment because they reference the wrong date historically or the wrong author of a literary work," explains O'Reilly, noting that this would be particularly unfair given that students who use their own personal experiences in an essay could make up stories that fit their argument. "What we're measuring is how well did they develop an argument."

Interestingly enough, a recent analysis of sample SAT essays and grades by a Massachusetts Institute of Technology professor found that the longer a student's answer, the better his or her score. Testing officials insist the correlation was expected. "In the process of developing a full, complete argument— bringing in supporting examples and explaining why they support your side of the argument—length is not unimportant," says O'Reilly. "On average, the longer essays do get higher scores because the student is saying more than his or her fellow student is saying in a short essay." But before you ramble on and on, be forewarned: College Board officials insist that length is not an automatic guarantee of 5 or 6. "There are plenty of examples of longer essays with lower scores," O'Reilly adds.

The readers, many of whom are English teachers experienced in grading the old SAT Subject Test in writing, understand that what you manage to piece together in 25 minutes will be substantially different from a paper handed in at school. "In a testing situation, we are taking a snapshot of a first draft," says Bernard Phelan, an English teacher at Homewood-Flossmoor High School in Flossmoor, Illinois, and a member of the committee that developed the writing section. To be sure that everyone's on the same wavelength, readers are assigned sample essays representing each point level from 0 to 6 and must come up with the right score for each on their own before they can proceed with grading real essays.

In general, says Agnes Yamada, Professor Emerita of English at California State University–Dominguez Hills and an experienced test-reader herself, the people scoring your essay will expect to get a clear sense of your direction—and to see that you actually move forward rather than jump around or get stuck. "At level 3, you often have papers that are so undeveloped that every sentence sounds like the beginning of a new essay," says Yamada. Or the writers just repeat themselves and fail to "advance the paper." Besides direction, she says, readers want "good details, good examples, and specificity." If human rights is the topic, for example, you might start by describing your position and ticking off the several people—Martin Luther King Jr., Elie Wiesel, Nelson Mandela—whose experiences and beliefs you will use to support it, then devote a paragraph to specifics about each that make your case. Suppose you decide that writing about your own life would prove your point. A narrative is completely acceptable—as long as your story is rich in details. "The writer has to remember that we are not familiar with his aunt or grandma," says Yamada.

How much weight will college admissions officers give your written work? Schools are still in the midst of developing their policies, and it remains to be seen whether the result will matter as much as

critical reading and math scores. So far, less than half of the country's colleges and universities have said they will require this year's applicants to submit either SAT or ACT writing scores; nonetheless, this group includes the Ivies, the entire University of California system, and many other highly selective institutions, which, for the most part, were already requiring the old SAT writing exam. "We are using the test because we regard writing as a critically important aspect of college success, and, of course, in measuring the potential for

> *"On average the longer essays do get higher scores because the student is saying more than his or her fellow student is saying in a short essay."*

successful college work," says Ann Wright, vice president for the southwest region of the College Board. Officials at the University of Virginia plan to use test results both for admission and for placement. "We think it will not be greatly different from the SAT Subject Test in writing and its predecessor, the English Composition Achievement Test," says dean of admission Jack Blackburn, who explains that UVA has required one of these earlier tests since the 1960s, and has long felt confident that their scores accurately predict writing ability. "We think that the new test will be quite similar to the old one, and we hope that we can use it in much the same way as in the past."

Because the actual essays will not be included in the SAT score reports, college officials must decide whether to read them online. One tack many will take is to call up the essay when they feel a need to compare it with a polished application essay, which may have been produced as an English assignment, say, and carefully honed over a long period of time—or even written by a parent. Essays of marginal applicants may be download about whom more information is needed, or possibly those by candidates for merit awards. "The short essay will represent the student's ability to think logically, to prepare ideas in draft form, and to demonstrate written communication skills," she says. "We've been trying to find more ways to evaluate students because they are starting to look the same on paper," says Todd

Rinehart, assistant vice chancellor for enrollment at the University of Denver, which has also decided to use the essay in admissions decisions, viewing it as a source of much-needed extra information.

Critics have raised concerns about the usefulness of the brief, timed essay, which clearly doesn't represent the kind of writing most students will do in college. Thus, a number of schools will not be using it in the admissions process at all. "We don't feel that the writing section adds value to the criteria

---

"We've been trying to find more ways to evaluate students because they are starting to look the same on paper."

---

already presented about applicants in their complete package, and we have concerns about implications, in particular, for students who may be socioeconomically disadvantaged—we don't want to potentially disadvantage them even more if they don't have access to a strong writing curriculum," says Julie Green Bataille, spokesperson at Georgetown University, which will ignore writing results. Officials at the University of Chicago, which is known for its unusual and thought-provoking application essay questions, will not look at the SAT essay either, nor do they plan to in the future.

Many who will not be using the essay in admissions decisions right away are taking a wait-and-see approach until sound data about the test's value in predicting ultimate success in college is available, both on a national and institutional level. For example, Kenyon College won't factor in the writing section for now because "we don't quite know how to use it," says Beverly Morse, associate dean of admissions, research, and information management. At the end of every school year, Kenyon conducts a validity study in which the statistics that were used to admit a Kenyon student are correlated with the same student's freshman-year GPA. "I'm going to plug in the writing score as another variable in that study," says Morse. "If there is a high correlation between the writing section and success at Kenyon, we will think about

requiring it." Syracuse University, MIT, and the University of Iowa are taking a similar stance. "While [we] recognize that the development of effective writing skills is essential to success in high school, college and work environments, it does not seem appropriate for us to require a pre-admission writing sample until we know just how it will enhance our ability to serve students through placement decisions or admission processes," says Iowa's director of admissions Michael Barron, who anticipates that as many as half of applicants who take the ACT will elect to include the writing test. "Since the SAT will provide a writing sample and writing sub-scores for each of the students who sit for the exam, we will receive those scores and begin our longitudinal review of their potential impact on placement and admission efforts for our students."

The uncertainty surrounding colleges' use of the new writing exams has exacerbated student confusion and concern, says Alan Crocker, assistant headmaster and college advisor at the New Hampton School in New Hampshire. "It would be nice if there was some consistency in the use" of the new tests, he says. But students shouldn't expend much effort trying to make sense of school policies, advises Joyce Slayton Mitchell, director of college advising at the Nightingale-Bamford School in New York City. "Build the strongest academic record you can build, document the local record with national SATs in as many areas as you can do well. Then see who wants a student just like you. No need to get into who wants what and do they know and what if they change. Do the best you can in as many areas as you can document."

Calculating how much prep you need

Once you decide which test to take, how much time and energy—not to mention money—should you devote to preparing for it? First, you'll need to figure out how important test scores are to the colleges you're interested in attending. Some schools, including Bates College in Maine and Dickinson in Pennsylvania, have dropped the tests entirely as an entrance requirement, reasoning that high school GPA and writing samples are equal or even better predictors of success in college, and that eliminating applicants solely on the basis of test scores penalizes the less affluent who can't afford any sort of fancy test prep. Others have unofficially decided to de-emphasize the importance of test scores in admissions decisions for the same reasons, though you probably won't know this when you apply.

The next step is to calculate how the test results you can expect to get would stack up against scores of the college's entering freshmen. To get a sense of how you'll perform when the big day comes, you'll need to take a look at your success on the PLAN test or the PSAT. PLAN, which schools in the ACT-centric states administer to tenth graders (many of whom also choose to take the PSAT), mirrors the ACT: It is divided into English, math, reading, and scientific-reasoning sections, and is graded on the same 36-point basis. The idea is that if you find you're weak in certain subject areas, you can tailor your course selection or study to get ready for the big test. The PSAT, which students usually take in their sophomore or junior year, closely reflects the SAT exam: The 2 hour and 10 minute test is divided into three sections—50 minutes apiece of math and critical reading and 30 minutes of multiple-choice "writing skills" questions—each of which is scored on a 20-to-80 scale. The PSAT does not include a written essay, mostly because grading it is such a labor-intensive task, but high schools may assign a practice one anyway.

If you add your math, critical reading, and writing PSAT scores together, then tack on a zero, you'll get a number that should roughly approximate the combined score you'll earn on the SAT—although test prep of any sort should give you a boost, and even just having the PSAT under your belt might help your performance on the SAT.

See where you stand

To get an idea of how your PLAN and/or PSAT results measure up against the scores of students who have been accepted at colleges you're interested in, take a look at the math and verbal SAT and ACT score ranges provided in each school's entry in the Ultimate College Directory. Although mean scores on the new 2400-point scale will not be available, experts in counseling, admissions, and testing note that your math and critical reading scores are exactly comparable to the old scores; thus, judging your combined scores in those two sections against the scores reported in a school's directory entry should give you a ballpark idea of where you stand. "Reading and writing are skills that usually overlap," adds the College Board's O'Reilly. "It's not universal—there will be differences—but, in general, most students will see their reading and writing scores be relatively similar, and so they can simply view writing scores in comparison to verbal scores at colleges as well."

If your predicted score is better than the scores of freshmen at schools you're applying to, you probably don't need to do exhaustive studying, except that you will certainly want to take several practice tests to familiarize yourself with the exam's format and pacing. "The new SAT isn't that much harder, it's just longer. You get pretty tired out after the third hour—and there's still more to go," says a student who took the exam, and whose concerns about time have been echoed by countless peers. Think of it this way: You don't want to tackle a marathon without doing some long runs beforehand. In addition, anybody who has been racing down the accelerated math track in high school should also spend some time dusting off long-forgotten algebra and geometry skills.

If your practice test scores are only mediocre, you should absolutely prepare for the real exam more extensively, whether you study by yourself at home or pay for a coaching class. Says Robert Schaeffer, public education director of the National Center for Fair and Open Testing in Cambridge, Massachusetts, an organization that advocates standardized testing reform, "There's no human endeavor, from writing to tennis, that practice doesn't improve. Why should the SAT be any different?"

Studying on your own for the new SAT

Walk into any bookstore and you'll be confronted with shelves upon shelves of the latest-and-greatest SAT and ACT prep materials, from compilations of practice exams to tips on how to beat the system. Still, a good place to start is the source of testing madness. The College Board develops the SAT, and its website, www.collegeboard.com, contains practice questions for all sections as well as a free downloadable practice test that comes with an explanation of correct

---

"The new SAT isn't that much harder, it's just longer. You get pretty tired out after the third hour—and there's still more to go."

---

answers. *The Official SAT Study Guide: For the New SAT*, with eight full-length exams, is another great resource at $19.95. In addition, the ACT student website, www.actstudent.org/testprep/index.html, contains gratis sample questions and exams, test-taking tips, and links to official materials like "The Real ACT Prep Guide," with three full-length exams and a price-tag of $25.

The cast of test-prep characters

If you decide that your SAT or ACT score could use a boost from a professional, you've got plenty of test-prep options to choose from. In fact, teaching nervous teens to ace these tests has turned into a multimillion-dollar industry. A slew of new coaching services, from free online courses to $100-an-hour-and-up private tutors, have joined classroom kings Princeton Review and Kaplan in the business over the past few years. The range of choices means you can probably find a style and method of prep that will work best for you.

Some students need the stimulation and structure of a classroom, while others learn better when cozying up to a computer in their pajamas. One of the big selling points of private tutoring and online courses is that you can learn at your own pace. But the latter route may not be a great idea for unmotivated students, and some parents are understandably wary of encouraging their kids to spend hours online where distractions, like instant messaging, are plentiful.

Both Kaplan and Princeton Review offer 36-hour cram courses that review material likely to appear on the exam and teach key test-taking skills. For example, you'll learn guessing techniques and strategies such as how to gauge when a problem isn't worth the time it will take to answer it. Kaplan's course runs $899, while Princeton Review's is priced between $899 and $1,099, depending on location.

If you can't concentrate in a group and a higher price tag isn't an obstacle, one-on-one help might be the right answer. Private tutoring at Kaplan costs between $2,399 and $4,199, depending on the number of hours and location, while Princeton Review's individualized prep runs from $2,700 for the standard 24-hour package to $7,200 for the same period of time with the most experienced, in-demand tutors.

The online option

If you'd rather do your preparation by computer, possibilities abound—many of them free. SparkNotes, for example, features a free fully searchable version of *The New SAT Book*, which is sold in bookstores for $19.95, at www.sparknotes.com/testprep/books/newsat; you can also download free diagnostic tests and other tools such as a list of a thousand of the most frequently tested vocabulary words. The website Number2.com offers free interactive ACT and SAT courses that teach you how to approach each type of question, let you practice at your own pace, and monitor your progress; these tutorials automatically adjust according to your skill level. Countless other sites provide various forms of help for free; just log on to your favorite search engine to take advantage of these services.

Not to be outdone, Kaplan and Princeton Review also offer a full range of online course options that run anywhere from around $99 to $699 and up, depending on content and duration. (In the latter's new "Live Online Class," students can talk directly to their instructor with a specialized headset, included in the $699 cost.) The College Board's "Official SAT Online course" contains specific lessons like "algebra and functions review" and over 600 practice questions, as well as three official practice tests, which you can take online or on paper—the latter being key to approximating real test-taking conditions—with detailed score and skills reports; a four-month subscription is $69.95.

How much will it help?

Both Kaplan and Princeton Review claim that students who take any of their pricey coaching courses typically see huge gains in their scores. A 2001 study commissioned by the latter firm showed a 136-point jump in the combined verbal and math scores among its students; a former staff member has suggested that pupils in the top 25 percent of their class usually do even better, improving their scores by an average of 250 points. With this sort of information in mind, all Princeton Review students are guaranteed a score increase—between either a PSAT or SAT taken before the class and an SAT taken after the class—or they can retake the course at no cost. In fact, the company is so confident that the new SAT is even more "coachable" than the old—particularly the formulaic writing section—that it is now guaranteeing a 200-point gain. Kaplan charges pupils a nominal fee to take the class over again if their scores don't go up or they aren't satisfied for any reason.

Still, independent reports suggest that the gains are less striking. A study conducted by the College Board found that students who retook the SAT without taking a cram course saw their scores rise an average of 43 points, while the scores of Kaplan and Princeton Review pupils increased only an additional 19 to 42 points, on average. More recently, a study by an education graduate student at the University of California–Berkeley found that preparing for the tests increased overall scores by only an average of 20 to 30 points. Critics point out that the latter study doesn't distinguish between different methods of coaching, and they question both sets of results.

While it's impossible to foretell whether taking a course will boost your scores enough to make the cost worthwhile, you might benefit more if you suffer from test anxiety, say guidance counselors. Indeed, much of what these classes are selling is confidence: There's less chance of going into the testing room and choking if you've been drilling and taking practice tests for weeks or months in advance. Also, students who have had trouble with the math portions of the PSAT may profit quite a bit from

> "There's no human endeavor, from writing to tennis, that practice doesn't improve. Why should the SAT be any different?"

prep programs, because math skills generally are easier to improve through coaching than verbal skills.

Check references

Before shelling out hundreds of dollars for any kind of course or tutor, Judi Robinovitz, a private education consultant who runs several learning centers in Florida and tutoring services in New York City, recommends doing some investigative work. The best referrals are those that come from someone you trust who has had firsthand experience. You'll want to ask about the credentials of an outfit's instructors. Have they been teaching SAT prep for at least five years? Do they take the SAT themselves on a regular basis and continue to score in the top 5 percent of test-takers? Do they teach from real and recent College Board tests? A professional should be able to provide you with several student references, says Robinovitz. She also suggests auditing the first session of any class before you sign up to make sure it's a good fit.

Keeping it all in perspective

It's important not to get carried away with test prepping, especially during the all-important junior year, when your grades matter more than almost anything else. You don't want any obsessing about the SAT to distract you from more worthwhile pursuits, like paying attention to Dickens in AP English or truly grasping the origins of capitalism in history class. And remember that a higher-than-average score will not ensure that your dream schools will be clamoring to admit you, since most look at students holistically, judging the application and the person as a whole. "We consider a student's best test scores," reads Harvard University's admissions website, "but it is generally our experience that taking tests more than twice offers diminishing returns." In addition, while academic preparation is key, don't underestimate the value of simple steps like getting a good night's sleep before the exam, eating a healthy breakfast that morning, and trying to stay calm throughout the entire process. Remember: Even a perfect 2400 or 36 is no magic guarantee of getting in, say admissions officers across the country. At the end of the day, they're just one part of the package.

Chapter Four

Putting Together a Killer Application

You've sweated your way through the challenging courses and put your heart into drama club, student government, four seasons of lacrosse, and hours and hours at the local food bank. You've prepped for the SATs—and taken them twice—and tramped behind tour guides across more than a dozen campuses.

The hard work has only begun.

Now you've got to put all the facts, figures, and that special *je ne sais quoi* together in a package that will blow the minds of the admissions committee and nail you a place in next year's freshman class.

This is no small feat, given the competition. To ace this last, most crucial phase of admissions, you're going to have to give careful thought to each step of the application process. How do you write an essay that will grab a tired staffer who's been plowing through more than 30 a day for weeks? How can you get a recommendation from a teacher who will write as if he knows you, and not just serve up clichés? Is it better to be honest about that trouble you got into—even if it was ages ago in the ninth grade—or not? What do you stand to gain and lose by applying early decision? And how about when your alumni interviewer pressures you to divulge where else you're applying?

What follows are answers to all these questions and more, gleaned from admissions professionals who have judged hundreds of thousands of applicants before you.

Get great guidance

Here's why your high school guidance counselor should be your new best friend: Besides helping you zero in on a sensible list of schools, counselors can get you into any remaining classes you need, suggest which standardized test will best showcase your abilities, and write a recommendation that, come April, will help determine whether you receive fat envelopes or skinny ones.

In fact, your biggest college resource may be your counselor's connections because she's probably well plugged into the college admissions scene. Why does this matter to you? Admissions officers who know and trust her may call for the inside scoop—like who the best candidates from your senior class are. She'll be the one fielding phone calls about everything from a low grade on your transcript to a difficult discipline problem. And if that's not enough to convince you, suppose that—worst-case scenario—you wind up getting rejected everywhere you apply; a sympathetic counselor might plead your case to admissions officials at schools that still have open slots.

These are people you definitely want watching your back, so don't be shy about making the first move. You can be one of the few faces in the hall that your advisor recognizes if you pop into his office often to talk about college, extracurriculars, and the state of the world in general. If your counselor is too swamped for frequent chats, it's a good idea to drop off a résumé that lists your recent accomplishments for her files. "If students are going to brag to anyone, we're the people," says Risa Green, codirector of college counseling at Milken Community High School in Los Angeles. She suggests handing over a portfolio of your best papers and creative projects, too. Be prepared to share any major personal problems. If one of your parents gets seriously ill and your grades slip as a

result, your counselor can explain the situation in her recommendation.

One of your counselor's responsibilities is to send colleges a profile of your high school, which has a big impact on how admissions personnel view your application. The profile clues them in on how thoroughly you've taken advantage of what's been available to you by describing the curriculum that you've chosen from, including all of the Advanced Placement, International Baccalaureate, and honors courses available. It explains the grading system and how class rank is calculated, and supplies a tally of the universities that accepted last year's seniors. Most profiles also describe the demographic makeup of the school and its community.

As a result, admissions officers can interpret your grades in light of what they discover about a school's resources. The less challenging its curriculum, the higher an applicant's grades must be, for example. It's a good idea to take a look at your school's profile to see, for example, whether it reports an average family income that far surpasses your parents' earnings. If so, you might ask your counselor to clarify the situation in the recommendation letter; the added insight will help explain why you're working after school instead of playing sports.

While lots of high schoolers get great counsel, many others have to navigate college admissions with little or no guidance. The numbers tell the story: Although the National Association for College Admission Counseling recommends that the student-to-counselor ratio in a school not exceed 250 to 1 (which already sounds pretty big), at some big public high schools the numbers push as high as 565 to 1. Not only do most counselors have too many students, they also have too many duties, including scheduling classes, finding resources for learning-disabled students, and dealing with troublemakers.

So what do you do if your counselor is permanently missing in action, resists all advances, or doesn't know enough about colleges to be helpful? Experts suggest trying to make an appointment with another counselor at your school—being sure to tell your own advisor that you're gathering information from as many people as possible so he or she doesn't get offended. Eventually you may be able to officially

Does money matter?

It depends. Most colleges claim to keep a wall between admissions and financial aid, so checking the tiny box on an application that says you're going to be applying for assistance shouldn't influence the decision-making process at all. Still, Donald Heller, a Penn State professor of education and coauthor of several studies on financial aid, notes that relatively few schools—mostly the Ivies and a clutch of small, selective institutions like Amherst, Vassar, and Williams—are truly committed to a "need-blind" admissions policy that ignores a student's ability to pay, coupled with a promise to fully meet the need of every student admitted.

Most schools, says Heller, take a "need-aware" approach. In other words, stellar candidates will be admitted regardless of their financial status, but middling students are apt to be judged, in part, by how much they will cost the school. The result is that many applicants who might meet the standards for admission are rejected if the college knows it won't meet their need.

Some schools admit a large percentage of their freshmen without considering whether they will need financial aid; from that point on, the class is filled out with those who can afford full tuition.

In the end, the only way to deal with this situation is to know what you're up against. Ask colleges up front about how their decisions are affected by need. Then use your application and any interviews to make yourself seem so valuable that the committee will want you no matter what.

---

switch counselors, but it isn't easy. A student who argues that she's not getting a fair shake because an older sibling's bad behavior biased the counselor against the whole family may have a shot, but pleas based on personality clashes or alleged incompetence aren't normally approved. However, college admissions committees know that, for a variety of reasons, not everyone gets good advice or a fair recommendation. Says one admissions dean, "We try not to hold [a mediocre letter] against a candidate if the rest of the transcript is strong."

Look into hired help

You may find that you want to investigate outside counseling options as a way to lower your anxiety level a few notches. Counselors-for-hire will coach you on all the basics and more: picking appropriate high school courses and extracurricular activities, researching and selecting colleges to apply to, writing an engaging essay, preparing for your interviews, and applying for financial aid.

Qualified advisors abound these days, but they don't come cheap. At the high end are private educational consultants who sometimes start as early as the eighth or ninth grade, grooming their "clients" as desirable candidates and later helping them develop a list of schools and prepare applications. Their services usually cost from $700 to upwards of $2,200 a year. Kaplan Test Prep and Admissions also offers one-on-one counseling over the phone at $1,399 for 10 hours, with each additional hour costing $139. Less-personalized guidance is available, too, in seminars or online packages. If you are truly needy, you can turn to groups such as the Bottom Line in Boston, which counsels students for free. Many pricey consultants also do pro bono advising, so you may want to call several in your area, explain your situation, and ask if they can help or suggest some other options.

One motive many families who use private counseling share is the desire to keep Mom, Dad, and the kids from strangling each other during these often tense months. "Most parents come to us saying, 'I can't talk to my kids. They won't listen to me. I think it'll be much better coming from you,'" says one California advisor. As for students, they get to spill their guts to a sympathetic ear. In fact, independent counselors often end up acting more as therapists

You can put away the white out

The Internet has put an end to typing and retyping—and erasing and retyping—the same information on dozens of forms. Today, many colleges and universities have their application forms online so that they can be printed and filled out or completed electronically. Among them are state university systems like those in Texas and New York. In addition to college-specific sites, you can log onto one of several that host hundreds of colleges' e-applications, such as www.collegenet.com and www.xap.com. In most cases, their services are free to applicants, although you still have to pay an application fee to the schools. Students can also go to www.commonapp.org for a generic form, called the Common Application, which is accepted by nearly 300 colleges and universities.

Just don't let the relative ease of applying electronically be your downfall, guidance counselors and admissions officers warn. Too often, students who would take care with a paper form hurry through the Internet version. If you decide to apply online, be sure to have a parent or teacher read over your essays before you hit the submit button. Print it out and read it through yourself, too. Keep a copy; Internet delivery is not infallible. Chasing down the mailman to white out that glaring spelling error you just remembered is—sadly or not—no longer an option.

than anything else—a fair, unbiased person who will listen to you stress out about which topic to explore in your essay and offer advice, without screaming.

No matter what kind of program you choose, be sure to check out a prospective counselor's qualifications first. Perhaps the most important question to ask any private consultant is: How much experience have you had? It's smart to expect at least five years as a high school guidance counselor or in college admissions, as well as membership in either the Independent Educational Consultants Association (703-591-4850) or the National Association for College Admission Counseling (800-822-6285). Ask for professional and client references—and call them.

Avoid inexperienced consultants who claim that their Ivy League degrees give them special insight into the admission process, consultants who promise entrance into prestigious schools before viewing your academic record, and independent counselors who have cantankerous relationships with guidance offices. Remember, you can't afford to alienate your high school counselor! He still writes the all-important recommendation, and colleges will still call him if they want to know more about you.

Pull the pieces together

By the time you're sitting down to fill in the blanks, there's not a whole lot you can do about your transcript, which, as the key part of your application, is going to get a thorough going-over. Besides demonstrating how well you've succeeded academically (your grades), the transcript shows whether you've challenged yourself or skated by (your courseload) and, when studied alongside your standardized test scores, often hints at whether you're a consistent and hard worker or an underachiever. (For more on what the admissions office wants to see when it studies your four-year history, see Chapter 2, "What Colleges Will Look for in You.")

Elsewhere in the application, the effort you put out now can greatly improve your odds. Here are some tips.

Hit the mark with your essay

Dante got it wrong. There is another circle of hell: writing the college essay, an exercise that can make or break your chances of being admitted. "Often [test] scores are in the same acceptable range, the kid's done well in the same classes everybody else has taken, and it's the essay we finally refer to," says University of Chicago admissions dean Ted O'Neill.

How to compose the prose that will win you that coveted spot is, of course, what everybody hopes to learn from books like this one. Most start with the premise that essay writing is easy—if you just know the secrets. Well, it's not. Writing about yourself with imagination and the perfect balance of humility and pride is really, really difficult. To succeed, you'll have to start early, be willing to rewrite, and follow a few rules—some of which are even simple.

Let's start with the easiest: Always answer the question. If it's "Why do you want to go to Kalamazoo College?" don't talk about your lifelong ambition to be a trapeze artist; address what's compelling about Kalamazoo. If a university asks, "If you could be a tree, what kind of tree would you be?" try to get into the spirit of things—and don't be snotty, no matter how inane the question might seem.

There's agreement among admissions deans that literary perfection is not necessary; they want an introduction to the real 17-year-old you. "Sometimes the least successful essays are so polished they don't reveal anything about the writer," says O'Neill. Chicago is renowned for its offbeat topics, which have included the significance of given names and the possible extraterrestrial origins of such features of modern life as the tax code. The answers, says O'Neill, can reveal a lot about a student's creativity and thought process.

Many other schools leave the topic open, and settling on a good one is the hardest part of the job for many seniors. If you have no idea where to begin, try taking the advice of Michael Thompson, former dean of admission and financial aid at the University of Southern California in Los Angeles, and tell your readers something they don't already know about you. "When a student writes to us that they work 30 hours a week and the money they make goes into the family income," he says, "then the fact that they weren't president of the chess club makes more

sense." Some favorites that stick in admissions deans' memories:

- A reflection on race by a part-time cashier in a discount clothing store
- A deadpan appreciation of late-night TV game shows
- A young American Indian woman's recounting of moving from a big city in Utah back to the Navajo reservation

---

"Sometimes the least successful essays are so polished they don't reveal anything about the writer."

- A young man's reflection on having his right foot amputated at age two, living with a prosthesis, and growing up to play three varsity sports
- An emotional essay about the torment a young woman went through after severely injuring her father in a skiing accident

Thompson warns that, though tempting, essays about adversity and how you surmounted it can be hard to pull off. The last thing you want to do is sound whiny. He advises focusing on the positive lessons learned. Do not under any circumstances write about breaking up with a boyfriend or girlfriend! A broken heart is one of the few topics admissions officers agree are off limits. If you still have no idea where to begin, try canvassing the people who know you best for their take on your three most compelling qualities, or ask them to help you recall a formative experience.

Once you've chosen a subject, use the KISS principle of writing: Keep It Super Simple. Take a single idea or event, and describe it in loving detail. One mistake college essayists often make is that they write an overview of their lives. A narrow focus is bound to offer your readers more interesting insights about what you think and who you are. Another rule that writers follow: show, don't tell. Telling is making a statement like "I am a very

Tips for homeschoolers

What do you do for teacher recommendations if Dad did the teaching? How do you produce a class rank for the only kid in school? Each year, thousands of homeschooled students must jump through hoops to document their accomplishments for admissions officers.

Use your ingenuity and do some early strategic planning, advises Cafi Cohen, author of *And What about College?: How Homeschooling Can Lead to Admissions to the Best Colleges and Universities.* Selective institutions like the University of Virginia and Stanford insist on a solid curriculum in certain subjects like math and science, and are on the lookout for any extraordinary talent—musical, athletic, or otherwise.

Most schools also want evidence that a student educated alone interacts well with others, such as a history of participation in team sports or a local choir, for example. Some tips:

- *Establish an academic record.* Like many homeschooling parents, Cohen did not grade her homeschooled son, Jeff. When schools wanted a transcript, she awarded As in subjects she felt he had mastered—a tactic she explained up front to admissions officers, and that got him a place at the U.S. Air Force Academy. Another alternative is to present a bibliography of what students have read for each course.
- *Take college classes.* College coursework indicates achievement in much the same way that Advanced Placement courses do for regular applicants.
- *Test your knowledge.* College entrance exams carry extra weight because, as one dean put it, "We can't trust the grades." The University of Virginia, for one, urges homeschoolers to take five or six SAT Subject Tests, if possible.
- *Polish your portfolio.* Essays take on greater importance, too. Articulate why you've been homeschooled and what you've learned from various projects. Supporting evidence of intellectual vitality, like academic papers and samples of artwork, is also welcome.

passionate person." Oh, really? Says who? Show your readers how passionately you feel about, say, scuba diving, with details that put them on the water with you, like how thrilling it is to smell the salty air as the dive boat races toward the reef, how you're filled with anticipation and more than a little fear. Write about how your anxiety dissipates as you sink toward the seafloor, with only the crackle of snapping shrimp and the hiss of your own breathing for company. Caring passionately, it turns out, is one of the personal qualities schools want most in applicants. Admissions officers don't expect every student to be a Renaissance boy or girl—captain of the soccer team, president of the student body, and a member of the French, history, and glee clubs. They want students who are excited about life and scholarship and who can express this—and thus, themselves—in writing.

However, a college essay is no place for the fancy words you memorized for the SATs; your audience wants to hear your thoughts in your own voice. If your expostulation is transmogrified to mephitic pedantry, throw out the thesaurus and try again.

Get a glowing recommendation

The impact of recommendation letters is easy to underestimate, but that would be a big mistake. A recent survey of college admission officers by the National Association for College Admission Counseling showed that nearly 60 percent considered recommendations from teachers and guidance counselors to be of moderate or considerable importance in their efforts to distinguish one qualified student from the next.

Most colleges require letters from your guidance counselor and one or two high school teachers. In a perfect world, the teachers would speak to your fabulous performance in the classroom and the counselor would carry on about your contributions to the school and your community. But overworked guidance counselors often don't know kids well enough to give colleges much more than a school profile and your class rank. So it makes sense to approach teachers who can describe your place in the big picture—preferably somebody who has seen your best work academically over a period of time.

If you've been deeply involved in an organization in or outside of school, consider adding an extra letter from someone who knows you in that context. For example, if ballet is a major part of your life and you spend hours every day after school practicing pirouettes, it's probably a good idea to have the director of your ballet school—who can speak to your dedication, talent, and drive—write a letter on your behalf. Letters from alums (or a CEO or a senator, for that matter) can bolster your chances if they shed light on your abilities or personality, but only if they are written by someone who really knows you well. VIP recommendations that say merely that Jack or Jill mowed the lawn and seemed like a nice kid don't help, no matter who they come from.

Quantity should not be confused with quality. Emory University in Atlanta has a three-recommendation limit; most other schools say they rarely want more than four recommendations total—and definitely not the 14 that filled one recent applicant's folder at Wake Forest University in North Carolina.

Once you've found the right people to ask for letters, there's a lot you can do to make it easier for them to enthuse on your behalf. Obviously, it helps to approach teachers and counselors well before the letters are due; a month in advance of the deadline is a good rule of thumb. For students applying early decision or early action, this can mean asking teachers almost as soon as school starts in the fall. Be sure to come prepared with the appropriate forms along with stamped, preaddressed envelopes, and remember to check the privacy waiver. This reassures admissions officials that the evaluation is an honest one.

If you haven't spent much time recently with the teacher or counselor who will recommend you, make an appointment to talk over your accomplishments during high school and your goals for college. You want to make sure your letter writers have something concrete to say because shallow recommendations do little to further your cause. Ideally, your teachers and counselors will be able to point to specific stories or particular qualities and say this is a great kid "because"—that kind of insight can really make a dif-

---

"Recommendations can highlight things that you can't write about gracefully or talk about without seeming like an arrogant jerk."

---

ference in how admissions staffers view you. Talking yourself up isn't always the easiest job, but if you do your part, your teachers can often get information across that you'd never feel comfortable expressing in your essay or in interviews with admissions officials. "Sometimes it's obnoxious to do a real strong self-presentation," explains Charles Cogan, senior assistant dean of admissions and director of international recruitment at Carleton College in Northfield, Minnesota. "Recommendations can highlight things that you can't write about gracefully or talk about without seeming like an arrogant jerk."

Stick in any relevant extras

So you're a rap-rock guitarist? A successful Internet entrepreneur? A published author? Students who have a special talent or an unusual accomplishment or personal quality that can be captured in a portfolio may want to send the evidence to the admissions office along with their application—particularly if they've received recognition from someone other than Mom. Such "hooks" can help you stand out in a field of outstanding applicants and sway opinion in your favor, even if other aspects of your application aren't top-notch.

Smaller colleges especially welcome extra information, including tapes or CDs, videos, and websites. "We really want to know as much about each candidate as possible," says Paula Mitchell, director

If you can't take the pressure of filling out a slew of applications and then waiting months upon months to learn your fate, there is another answer. Getting accepted into Newbury College in Brookline, Massachusetts, and a number of other schools could take about as long as watching your favorite sitcom. Under these schools' "instant admissions" options, applicants meet with an admissions official who reviews their transcript and test scores and asks them a few questions about their academic interests and extracurricular activities. Applicants then get a thumbs-up or a thumbs-down, usually within half an hour.

Virtually unheard of 20 years ago, "instant" or "on-site" admission has been adopted by a host of state schools over the past decade, including William Paterson University of New Jersey in Wayne and Virginia Tech in Blacksburg. Virginia Tech counselors travel to high schools, where the admissions decisions are made. Now, private colleges like Newbury are jumping on the bandwagon, too. For schools, the advantage of this quickie service is that accepted students are more likely to attend, perhaps because their admittance comes with a smile and a handshake. For their part, high school seniors get a big reduction in stress. While they may be offered admission as early as the fall, they can usually wait until May to give the school an answer. Or they can just say yes on the spot.

Going with an instant-admission interview may or may not affect your chances of getting in. At Western Michigan University, the odds are equal whichever way you apply; Newbury has recently taken about 90 percent of instant-admission applicants and about 80 percent of the regular pool. It's a good idea to call ahead of time to ask what you need to bring to the interview. Newbury still requires a personal essay, for example; Western Michigan does not. Also be sure to practice your interview skills and topics with a guidance counselor or parent before the big day. If you got an F in sophomore English, you should be prepared to explain why and how you've improved. If you can't, you might flunk instant admissions, too.

of the U.S. Office of Higher Education for the Council of International Schools. For example, one Ithaca freshman sent slides of her paintings to emphasize that, although she didn't plan on majoring in art, she devoted lots of time and energy to creating it. Many big state schools don't have the resources to examine your works of genius, however, so find out an institution's policy before dropping them into the mail.

If your talent—as a leader in student politics, for example—can't easily be demonstrated in a portfolio, you might include a résumé instead. This way, you can add detail about what you've accomplished to the bare-bones list of activities on your application.

Don't get caught tweaking the truth

When you're staring down at that blank application form or empty computer screen, it can be tempting to embroider your qualifications or download an essay and call it your own. As the number of qualified students vying for spots at selective colleges grows, the urge to cheat on an application sometimes seizes even the most capable student. For example, one applicant to Pomona College in Claremont, California, seemed like a shoo-in a few years ago. He was valedictorian of his class and scored well into the 1500s on his SAT. But there was something about his essay that seemed familiar to the assistant dean of admissions reading his application file. In fact, it was the third time that afternoon she had read the same work—from applicants scattered around the globe.

The essay, it turned out, was a sample posted on www.essayedge.com, a site that offers editing and writing tips for college essays. Bruce Poch, vice president and dean of admissions at Pomona, returned the papers along with a copy of the EssayEdge sample. The valedictorian confessed to his school's headmaster and soon received a rejection letter in the mail.

Poch figures that the student, "who could have done the essay in his sleep," was simply too overwhelmed to bother—and it seems he's not alone. In fact, a recent survey asked more than 2,100 college students if all of the information on their applications was factually correct. One in 50 answered no. The true number is probably much higher, says Rutgers University professor and study author Donald McCabe, an authority on academic integrity issues, because the line between packaging oneself smartly and stretching the truth can be so blurry nowadays. "You get a lot of students who feel they suffer disadvantages," he explains, so they think they can "make the playing field more level."

Admissions officers warn that they read application folders very carefully and are good at catching this kind of fakery. "That's why we have bags under our eyes," quips Keith White, former associate director of undergraduate admissions at the University of Wisconsin–Madison, who has seen several essays shared among siblings and friends. He says certain topics and word choices often tip him off. Recently, for example, he noticed that two students from the same high school had described their relationships with their parents using words straight from a *Friends* episode. When White compared the essays, he found them to be virtually identical. (In these cases, the UW admissions office asks for an explanation in writing of similarities found; the applicants rarely respond, and that is the end of the matter.)

One desperate father wrote a glowing recommendation for his daughter, signed her guidance counselor's name, and sent it off to Notre Dame. After the school's assistant provost for enrollment smelled a rat—the letter and her transcript just didn't seem to describe the same person—he phoned the guidance counselor, who knew nothing of the missive. Needless to say, the student is not at Notre Dame.

Another red flag is a transcript and an essay that just don't jibe. "You say, 'Gee, this essay seems to have been written by Maya Angelou, but the transcript belongs to Willie Lumplump,'" says William Hiss, former admissions dean at Bates College, who is now vice president of external and alumni affairs there. More often, the transcript belongs to Junior and the essay is written or heavily edited by Mom and Dad.

Getting caught is not the only reason to avoid heavy-handed parental "proofreading." William Shain, dean of admissions at Vanderbilt, says that when he reads an essay that is implausible even for a very literary 17-year-old, "the essay ceases to have any impact, because you lose the natural charm of a high school senior." Remember, admissions people know what high school students sound like.

Most commonly, students embellish the truth, exaggerating a leadership role or their contributions on the soccer field. Spinning a bench-warming career into a star turn is a high-stakes move because admissions folks may contact your high school coach. Pomona's Poch recalls several applicants whose listed number of weekly hours spent on extracurricular activities exceeded what was possible given the number of waking hours in a week. If dance and community service are so much a part of your life, why haven't they been mentioned in your letters of recommendation? In four cases out of five, this sort of fudging backfires, experts warn. You probably won't actually be accused of being dishonest, but you definitely won't get in.

Deal wisely with admissions

This is a relationship you want to manage carefully. Here are a few pointers.

Stay in contact

Colleges want to know just how badly they're wanted, and it can sometimes help your chances to be really clear about your interest. Having a handle on which applicants will enroll if accepted helps schools prevent the expensive error of ending up with too many, or too few, freshmen come fall. As a result, many schools record your every contact with the campus. If you order a video tour of

April may be known as the cruelest month, but that's only because Harvard grad T. S. Eliot never had to sweat out May, June, and even July in today's wait-list wasteland. Many colleges are trimming acceptances and expanding their waiting lists to avoid over-enrolling students, which has meant crowded classes and housing crunches on hundreds of campuses. The result is a growing number of not-quite-yes-but-still-not-quite-no letters and masses of nervous high school grads come spring.

While no magical combination of grades or activities can propel borderline applicants over the top, there's plenty a stranded candidate can do to catch an admissions officer's eye again—starting with an expression of eagerness to attend. "It's e-mail; it's faxes saying, 'I'm still out here and I'm still interested,'" says Michael Steidel, admissions director at Carnegie Mellon University in Pittsburgh. "That's the message we want to hear."

If you're bound and determined to scale the walls of a highly selective school, you'll have a better shot if you give colleges information they don't already have, like updates on grades, new honors, academic awards, lessons learned doing additional community service, or even a letter of recommendation from a senior-year teacher. You should also alert colleges as fast as possible if you no longer need financial aid; funds get doled out early, making those who can pay their way much more attractive late in the game.

Sheer creativity can help, too. Carnegie Mellon's Steidel still keeps a bottle that he received from a wait-listed candidate several years ago in his office. The jug, covered with Life Savers candy, had a scroll inside that read: "SOS SOS SOS. I'm stranded here in South Carolina," and went on to detail how the applicant needed to be rescued by the admissions committee to fulfill her dream of becoming a cosmetic surgeon. "We loved it," recalls Steidel. "It was cute; it was innovative." And it won the girl a seat. Another memorable wait-list winner from Hawaii painted the seascape outside her window on a coconut—a scene she said she'd love to pine for from a dorm room in Pittsburgh. "When you know someone wants it that badly," says Steidel, "it does turn the committee's head."

Emory, an admissions officer will note the request in your application folder; e-mails to Miami University in Oxford, Ohio, will be logged in a database. Most institutions naturally construe a campus visit as a sign of serious interest, so you should be sure to travel to the schools that top your list—and let the admissions office know you've stopped by.

But don't just call for the sake of calling. Every communication should have a point. Maybe you're updating the admissions staff on your latest achievements or searching for information that you really can't find in brochures or on the website. Call to find out which professor you should talk to about research opportunities in biochemistry or study abroad opportunities, for example. Then you might send the appropriate person an e-mail introducing yourself and your interests.

Will admissions officers think you're a pest if you check on your application? That depends on what you mean by "check." Trying to find out whether you've been accepted before decisions are released will almost certainly irritate whoever takes your call, but checking that your application is complete can stave off disaster. One Elon University student didn't realize until March of her senior year of high school that the College Board hadn't sent her SAT scores to any of the schools she'd designated. She had to postpone college for a year and go through the whole process again. The second time around, she says, "I was that annoying person who called every single day." She ended up getting into all of the 12 schools to which she applied.

Schedule an interview

You've heard about the "optional" college interview? Well, it really isn't so optional if you want to show commitment to the school. "All other things being equal, we are more inclined to admit a student if that student has interviewed," says William Caren, associate vice president for enrollment services at the State University of New York–Geneseo. (Most admissions officers will understand if applicants can't visit because the cost is too great or there is some other hardship preventing a trip.) The best way to shine, beyond looking clean and neatly dressed, is to show that you're passionate about your interests and equally passionate about attending the school. Practice speaking about your favorite classes and activities ahead of time, say experts, and avoid one-word answers.

You'll definitely want to research the school thoroughly before the interview because no one will be impressed by a barrage of questions about statistics you could have found on the website. It is better to ask why students transfer, say, or if graduate assistants teach classes. The idea is to gather information that will help you decide whether it's the school for you, while astonishing the interviewer with your curiosity and thoughtful turn of mind. Brandeis, for one, rates students on a 1-to-5 scale on the basis of their intellectual curiosity and personal qualities. At other schools, admissions officers take notes during the session and review them with the admissions committee afterward. Making an incredible impression can push your application over the top.

'Fess up to bad behavior

One important job of the admissions office is to ferret out any bad apples. By probing applicants' disciplinary histories, colleges hope to avoid admitting nasty characters who might harm other students or cause legal headaches down the road. Youthful high jinks don't worry anyone much, but more serious charges like assault, drug dealing, or academic dishonesty will be closely scrutinized.

If you're asked, straight out, whether you've ever been arrested or suspended or expelled from high school, you should absolutely come clean. Getting caught in a lie will kill your chances of being admitted—and you might get kicked out if you've already been accepted. "If a student has falsified [his] answer [to the discipline question], I have no problem pulling the rug out from under them," says

> *"All other things being equal, we are more inclined to admit a student if that student has interviewed."*

Christopher Gruber, vice president and dean of admission and financial aid at Davidson College. The likely leaks? High school counselors who report infractions to colleges and teachers who inadvertently mention in a recommendation letter how much Steve has matured since he burned the gym down sophomore year. Most private schools have policies to notify colleges of suspensions and expulsions. Public school counselors are hampered by state privacy laws, but they can hint at problems with vague phrases like "had difficulty last semester."

The key here is to demonstrate that your brush with authority led to personal growth. Writing a thoughtful explanation of what happened to go along with your application will help, but a special trip to campus to explain yourself in person may be in order if the infraction is serious. One Florida high schooler, who was expelled when marijuana was found in her car, arranged a meeting with officials from the New College of Florida in Sarasota to clarify what had happened. The student had already signed up for drug counseling and taken steps toward earning her GED. Joel Bauman, then dean of admissions and financial aid, was impressed. "She confronted the problem head on and had done things to make up for it," says Bauman, who is now vice president of enrollment management at Westminster College in Utah. "That takes courage, integrity, and character." The student was admitted.

Keep your other colleges to yourself

This is one case where full disclosure may not be in your best interest. In fact, if you do answer the question "Where else are you applying?" you run the risk that the information will actually be used against you.

Sometimes there's an innocent reason for a college's nosiness. The staff may want to figure out what all your schools have in common (strong journalism programs, say), so as to better sell their institution to you. But in many cases, the goal is to guess how likely you are to actually attend if you get in. Colleges that are worried about boosting their "yield," or the fraction of admitted students who ultimately enroll, may reject or wait-list even the most outstanding candidates if they've also applied to more popular or more prestigious schools.

There are two places this issue may come up: on the application or in an interview. What to do? Some counselors suggest supplying the names of a few similarly competitive schools from your list or stating that you are still undecided. You can also leave the question blank on the application, or declare yourself uncomfortable with the question in an interview. For the most part, colleges will let unanswered questions slide. "I respect a student who says they prefer not to answer," says Michael Frantz, vice president of enrollment services at Wilkes University in Pennsylvania.

But don't be surprised if an interviewer pushes for an answer. One recent applicant says a Tufts University alumni interviewer asked four or five times what other schools he was applying to. He tried to evade the question, he says, but the man persisted and he was left with a "sour aftertaste." Although he was admitted to Tufts, he ultimately enrolled at Harvard.

If you're learning disabled, say so

Students who have struggled with learning disabilities will inevitably wonder: to tell or not to tell? Most guidance counselors recommend honesty in this situation—at least if there are any red flags in your history that need explaining. A precipitous drop in English grades or poor test scores are likely to raise questions in an admissions committee. When

there's no clear reason, colleges can be expected to reject a candidate who seemingly doesn't measure up. Plus, so many learning-disabled students today are reaching college age and choosing to apply that many schools are much more open than they used to be to taking kids who learn in nontraditional ways—not to mention helping them succeed.

You can often gauge a college's attitudes before applying by phoning the admissions office and asking who coordinates services for learning-disabled students and what programs and accommodations the school offers. If your questions are met with silence, you may be better off looking elsewhere. (For more on what to seek in a college if you're learning disabled, see page 9.)

Consider early decision—but be careful

While Ivy League presidents and editorial writers continue to debate the pros and cons of early decision, the process is alive and well at some 270 of the nation's four-year colleges and universities. Many admissions offices, in fact, accept a large proportion of each entering class early. The University of Pennsylvania, for instance, took 46 percent of the 2003–2004 freshman class from its early-applicant pool.

So high schoolers intent on getting into one of these schools have to ask themselves, "Should I put myself into that early group?" Three-quarters or more of seniors at some affluent high schools now are doing so, up from around a quarter a decade ago. If you join them, you promise to enroll if you're accepted, and you'll know by mid-December whether you've got a spot. (It used to be that early-decision candidates couldn't apply to more than one school. Revised guidelines from the National Association for College Admission Counseling now allow them to apply elsewhere as regular candidates, as long as they withdraw any pending applications if accepted by their first choice.)

You don't have to be a math major to figure out why so many students apply early. Their odds of getting in go up, sometimes a lot. "The admit rates look so good, it's hard not to be tempted by them," says

—by Joyce Slayton Mitchell, director of college advising at Nightingale-Bamford School in New York City and the author of *Winning the Heart of the College Admissions Dean* (2005, Ten Speed Press, $14.95).

"The handwriting isn't the same throughout the application!" says Johnny's counselor to Johnny's mom. "It looks like you wrote most of it for him."

"But he is so busy with his classes, and soccer, and music, and the school newspaper!" Mom replies. "He has no time to be writing his college applications!"

"Yes, we give interviews. Ask Susie to give us a call before her campus visit."

"Oh, she won't have time to call—she's too busy with classes, and soccer, and music, and the school newspaper to be calling the colleges. I'll make the appointment for her."

"I've got 650's on my SATs, so my parents want me to spend the summer cramming in an SAT-prep program. I've got to get my scores up to get the college I want!"

When I swap stories with my colleagues, I often hear of panicked parents and well-meaning students making these kinds of state-ments. In our experience, here are the most common mistakes families make when applying to college—and how to avoid them.

Parents take the initiative, and that hurts the student

Nowadays, many colleges are so concerned about their image that they are choosing their freshman classes with a very close eye on their "yield" (the proportion of accepted students who actually choose to enroll). What this means for applicants is that enthusiasm about a school counts for a lot to the admis-sions dean, who wants to pick students who won't turn down an offer. But it's the student, not the parent, who has to show the interest.

When parents or a hired con-sultant stand in, even if only to handle clerical chores, the young-ster's image suffers more than you might imagine. The seniors who make it into Selective U are not only very busy, they're also the ones who can manage their academics, sports, music, the-ater, publications, student gov-ernment, friends, and family with sleep deprivation like they will never again have to in their lives until they bring home a new baby—and still have the maturity to take charge of the college selection process and make a case for themselves. They need to be the ones making the phone calls to admissions, contacting professors and coaches with questions, and thinking about and actually doing the writing on their applications. If parents think about it, they'll want their kids to take on this developmen-tal task, which will help them get ready to leave home.

Raising test scores becomes an obsession

Yes, the higher your test scores, the better you'll feel. But test scores usually reflect the kind of curriculum you study and the grades you earn—it doesn't pay to try to eke out a gain at all costs!

Let's think about it. Deans are looking for interesting young people who are eager to learn, kids with great curiosity about the world. Does someone who studied vocab and took practice tests for two months, or every Saturday morning of junior and senior year, sound like an inter-esting kid to you? No, she sounds like an ordinary kid from a fearful family. Harvard, Georgetown, Stanford, Northwestern, Rice, Amherst, and other top schools think noth-ing of turning down the applicant with the perfect SAT scores. As soon as a student is within a cer-tain range of numbers, admis-sions deans want to know, "Who is this kid? What did she do last summer?"

When Fred Hargadon, the former dean of admission at Princeton, was asked by a mother what would be the best thing her son could do the summer before senior year to get into Princeton, his response was, "Pump gas!" He didn't literally mean that pumping gas would open the door, but that it's very important that applicants have had experiences that lead to personal growth—not that they fit some preconceived notion of the ideal applicant. A student might choose a summer of service to others, or sports, or reading, or ceramics, or starting a business, or cutting grass, or working in the supermarket. It matters less what he picks than that he learn something about himself and is able to express that learning in writing.

If the student is interesting enough, 650's on the SAT won't keep him out of any college in the country. And if he's not, no score will get him in.

Application questions aren't taken as seriously as the essay
I try to instill in my students an appreciation for the importance of the application question: Why did you choose to apply to Duke? Admissions staffers want to know whether you understand the match between your personality and the college culture—and they are impressed when they discover that you do. You can imagine my chagrin when Eric Kaplan, director of admissions at Penn, calls to say, "Joyce, I love this kid, but she wants to go to Duke!" I say to my students, "I should be able to take the name of the college out of your response and know what college you are talking about."

When you get to the essay, keep in mind that whatever questions you are asked, all of your colleges are after the same information: an idea of what you've learned about yourself and the world from the opportunities

you've been given. And they want it presented in the authentic voice of a 17-year-old.

If your essay is one of a couple thousand about the war in Iraq, the admissions officer's eyes will glaze over. If it is about one of the three Ds (divorce, depression, or drugs), chances are he will groan. If your essay is about God, love, injustice, or the purpose of life, it had better be funny! Bill Fitzsimmons, the admissions dean at Harvard, once told a group of counselors that a farm boy had chosen not to write about his work on the family farm because he thought, "Those big-time college deans wouldn't want to hear about anything so ordinary." In fact, they do. Think about it: The admissions deans won't know that you're interesting unless they know who you are. It's your job to tell them!

Hector Martinez, director of college guidance at The Webb Schools in Claremont, California. Johns Hopkins University in Baltimore admitted 57 percent of its early-decision applicants in 2004, compared with 29 percent of the regular admission pool. Carleton College in Northfield, Minnesota, which has two early-decision deadlines, took 51 percent of its combined early pools and 27 percent of its regular applicants. Penn took 34 percent in the early round, compared with 17.8 percent of regular applicants. (For a list of schools where applying early boosts your chances most, see page 103.)

Granted, these numbers can be attributed in part to the high grade point averages and board scores of many early applicants; applying early won't help at all if you aren't qualified. But there's no doubt that applying early decision gives many students an edge. Penn admissions dean Lee Stetson openly acknowledges that applicants to his school have a better chance of getting in early than they do during regular admissions. A recent study at Harvard's Kennedy School of Government confirmed that early applicants have a leg up. After analyzing data from 14 top-ranking schools, researchers found that the average advantage of applying early was equivalent to scoring 100 points higher on the SAT.

Still, applying early is by no means a good choice for everyone. For starters, if you're asking for financial aid—and particularly for merit aid that's handed out based on talent rather than need—it's best to apply to several places during the regular admissions cycle. This way, schools get to compete for you, and you can compare offers. Keep in mind that even when colleges do arrive at the same conclusion about how much aid you need, one may be more generous with its outright grants than another. Late bloomers, too, probably should not apply early, in order to leave more time to rack up achievements. A student with a mediocre GPA may be better served by a stellar fall semester than by applying early, which helps, but won't turn old Bs into As.

So who might benefit from taking the plunge? Strong students with a clear sense of what they want out of college—a cutting-edge art department, say—and who are sure that a given college is their first choice. Applicants whose parents are alums ("legacies" in admission office parlance) and wealthy students also have lots of incentive to apply early, particularly if they lack some special quality or talent that would give them a boost during the regular round. Schools often court these applicants, whose families tend to make good donors and who turn into loyal alumni themselves, but they might only give such students preference during the early-admissions cycle.

Applying early just to get the work of filling out forms behind you is dangerous because you risk binding acceptance to a school you wouldn't have picked with a couple of months' more thought. Many students' idea of what's important in a college—an urban location or small size, for example—does a 180-degree turn between November, when early applications are due, and April, when most college-bound kids are weighing their options. Kids who diligently identify their ideal school by the beginning of twelfth grade pay a price, too, in time stolen from academics and extracurriculars during the all-important junior year. Early applicants also take their standardized tests on a shorter timetable and lose the luxury of time to demonstrate their leadership and academic prowess as seniors.

If the binding commitment doesn't appeal to you but shortening that dreadful period of suspense does, consider applying "early action" if it's offered by your top-choice school. These plans generally don't give you the same edge in admissions, but they also don't require a promise to attend. Applicants are notified of their status in December but given until May to accept or reject an offer. Because early action is nonbinding, a student can test his or her chances at one or more early-action schools, see what happens, and still apply to additional colleges in the spring.

Once you're in, don't blow it

When that long-awaited acceptance letter arrives in the mail, you'll obviously want to celebrate—perhaps for the rest of senior year. But forsaking academics for an easy coast into prom week can have serious consequences.

Michele Hernandez, author of *A Is for Admission: The Insider's Guide to Getting into the Ivy League and Other Top Colleges*, points out that an offer of admission is contingent on successful completion of high school. Admissions personnel at most colleges will inspect your final transcript, and you're going to have to explain any big drop in grades in a written statement. The director of admissions reads these accounts and decides what action to take.

She'll probably be sympathetic if there's valid cause for a decline in academic performance—a serious illness in the family, say, or one particularly difficult math class. But genuine slackers do have to answer for their behavior. Summer school may be required, or you might be placed on academic probation for the first semester of freshman year. In the most extreme instances—a straight-A student inexplicably has a straight-D quarter, for example—acceptances can be revoked. In fact, Hernandez estimates that a few students a year are "de-admitted" from each of the more-selective colleges. Less-selective institutions are unlikely to turn errant students away entirely, though they may require corrective action.

Other symptoms of senioritis are of interest to the admissions staff, too, although they generally aren't evident in a transcript. Any criminal violations that come to light, like sexual assault or vandalism, will almost certainly result in a reevaluation of your admittance. So will episodes of cheating or frequent cutting of classes, which are often reported by guidance counselors or teachers.

Aside from fulfilling the "successful completion of senior year" bargain, there are other, more practical reasons to stay engaged in high school until the bittersweet end. Getting superior marks in the final semester is essential for those who have been put on wait lists, for one thing. Those in AP courses can't afford to slack off either, as a high score of 5 or even 4 on an exam often translates into college credit; this can save tuition and may allow you to opt out of an introductory lecture class and get straight into a more advanced seminar. Besides, if you keep working hard until the end of senior year, you'll be far less rusty when you start studying in the fall. Just remember, you'll still have two full months to celebrate after final grades are in hand.

Chapter Five

How to Find the Money to Pay for College

If fall is the season of teenage college dreams, spring is when the grown-ups wake up and face reality. The acceptance letters have come and the first check is due. And it's a big one. Now what?

The sticker shock that families always experience when faced with actually making tuition payments has been exacerbated in recent years by a struggling economy. Even as stock portfolios took a big hit, colleges and universities confronted with depressed endowments, rising energy and health insurance costs, and shrinking state support have been sharply jacking up tuition.

Public schools in states with budget shortfalls have instituted the most staggering increases over the past couple of years. Tuition at Ohio State University in Columbus rose 15 percent last fall for in-state students and again 6 percent this fall to about $8,400 (nonresidents pay around $19,050), for example; in-state students at the

University of Iowa in Iowa City have seen 19 percent, 8 percent, and 4.5 percent jumps. Even the less-arresting percentage increases imposed by private schools translate into big dollars. How can parents possibly satisfy the tuition collectors as well as their starry-eyed children?

OK, take a deep breath. And remember that relatively few families have to come up with the staggering tuitions charged by the Ivy League and many other private institutions. In recent years, four out of five U.S. undergrads have attended public universities, and only 8.4 percent have paid $24,000 or more a year in tuition and fees. The upshot is that almost 70 percent of undergrads have paid less than $8,000 in tuition annually.

Granted, these statistics bring cold comfort to students who have their hearts set on high-priced private schools. But even those colleges don't etch their sticker prices in stone; they offer financial aid to roughly three quarters of their students. The savvier you are about what financial aid is available and how it is doled out, the more likely it is that you'll get a share of the money. In the following pages, you'll learn how aid packages are calculated and put together, how to appeal a school's offer of aid if it seems too low, and how students can boost their chances of winning a merit scholarship (an award that's based on academic performance or some other talent, and not on need). And if it turns out your family doesn't qualify for much—or any—free money, you'll be equipped to better manage the bills with information about low-cost loans, tax breaks available for college expenses, and employment options a student might consider.

How colleges figure out what you "need"

In a nutshell, you fill out a federal or maybe a college-specific form that asks a lot of questions about your income, assets, and expenses. The numbers are crunched, and out pops your "expected family contribution," or EFC in financial aid lingo. The difference between the cost of a year in college and your expected contribution is your "need," or the amount of aid you are eligible for.

Sounds straightforward enough. So why does it turn out that College A says you need so much less than College B? The experience of one upstate New York family is typical. While the federal government estimated that the family should be able to afford to pay $14,450, Arizona State University judged that the family could pay $15,533, and Penn State expected the family to come up with $20,375.

The often-great differences between financial aid awards is one of the aspects of this process that puzzle and frustrate families the most. Colleges argue that it isn't such an easy matter to gauge a family's true need. Thanks to the growth in the value of people's homes, the availability of new financial tools like flexible home-equity credit lines, and the complicated finances of blended families, it's tough to figure out which moms and dads are really hard-pressed for cash and which ones simply don't want to have to sacrifice this year's Caribbean vacation.

What's more, aid officers argue, it's reasonable to expect families to have saved something for college, and to borrow if necessary, because education is an investment that pays off with much higher future earnings. So colleges make their own, and often quite different, judgments about what families have in the way of resources. Finally, aid officials look at their own school's "need" (that is, how badly they want you to attend based on your academic accomplishments or other talents) before deciding how much they'll actually award. Here's a detailed look at how the process works.

You start with the FAFSA...

The first exercise any supplicant must go through is filling out the Department of Education's Free Application for Federal Student Aid, or the FAFSA. (The electronic form, which flags errors and missing data for you before you submit it, can be found at www.fafsa.ed.gov.)

The government applies a formula called the "federal methodology" to the numbers you supply on the FAFSA to determine your eligibility for a slice of the billions of dollars in federal grants and loans awarded each year. States use the results to award their own state aid, too. Most public universities use

Great deals at great schools

To determine which schools offer the best value, we use a formula that relates a school's academic quality, as indicated by its *U.S. News* ranking, to the net cost of attendance for a student who receives the average level of financial aid. The higher the quality of the program and the lower the cost, the better the deal. For more great values, see page 153.

National Universities

Universities in this category offer a full range of undergraduate, master's, and Ph.D. programs, and emphasize faculty research.

1. California Institute of Technology
2. Harvard University (MA)
3. Princeton University (NJ)
4. Yale University (CT)
5. Massachusetts Inst. of Technology
6. Stanford University (CA)
7. Dartmouth College (NH)
8. Rice University (TX)
9. U. of North Carolina–Chapel Hill
10. Duke University (NC)

Liberal Arts Colleges

Liberal arts colleges focus almost entirely on undergraduate education and award more than half of their degrees in the liberal arts disciplines.

1. Williams College (MA)
2. Amherst College (MA)
3. Wellesley College (MA)
4. Skidmore College (NY)
5. Pomona College (CA)
6. Swarthmore College (PA)
7. Middlebury College (VT)
8. Bowdoin College (ME)
9. Macalester College (MN)
10. Grinnell College (IA)

Universities–Master's

These schools offer a full range of undergraduate degrees and some master's programs but few, if any, doctoral programs.

South

1. Rollins College (FL)
2. The Citadel (SC)
3. Converse College (SC)
4. Stetson University (FL)
5. Mercer University (GA)

North

1. Gallaudet University (DC)
2. Alfred University (NY)
3. Hood College (MD)
4. Villanova University (PA)
5. Bentley College (MA)

West

1. Seattle Pacific University
2. University of Redlands (CA)
3. Whitworth College (WA)
4. Trinity University (TX)
5. Pacific University (OR)

Midwest

1. University of Evansville (IN)
2. Valparaiso University (IN)
3. Drury University (MO)
4. Creighton University (NE)
5. Bradley University (IL)

Comprehensive Colleges–Bachelor's

The comprehensive colleges focus on undergraduate education and offer degree programs in the liberal arts and in such professional fields as business, nursing, and education.

South

1. University of the Ozarks (AR)
2. Claflin University (SC)
3. Berry College (GA)
4. Ouachita Baptist University (AR)
5. Maryville College (TN)

North

1. Grove City College (PA)
2. Elizabethtown College (PA)
3. Elmira College (NY)
4. Stonehill College (MA)
5. College of St. Elizabeth (NJ)

West

1. Brigham Young University–Hawaii
2. East Texas Baptist University
3. Univ. of Science and Arts of Okla.
4. Corban College (OR)
5. Carroll College (MT)

Midwest

1. Eureka College (IL)
2. Wartburg College (IA)
3. Manchester College (IN)
4. Simpson College (IA)
5. Clarke College (IA)

the FAFSA to construct your entire aid package, which may include grants or loans from the institution's own budget as well as the government money. How much you'll have to pay depends entirely on your own complex set of financial characteristics. But as a general guideline, a FAFSA form for a family with one student in college and an income of $65,000—in which the older parent is 50, one parent works, and federal taxes total $11,000—would result in an expected family contribution in the neighborhood of $6,600, assuming a state tax rate of 6 percent.

...and maybe the Profile

Applicants to several hundred of the country's most selective (and high-priced) private colleges face an additional and much more detailed aid form, the College Board's CSS/Profile application, which feeds into a far-more-sensitive "institutional methodology." This formula includes home equity as a resource, while the federal formula does not, so a family might wind up with a considerably higher expected contribution. The Profile also takes into account siblings' assets and does not allow any sort of deduction for business or investment losses, which can make a significant difference for some

families. The College Board says that the same $65,000 family would have to contribute about $9,000 when the standard institutional methodology is used.

But colleges may stray from the standard method and fine-tune the formula even further. Each college has its own customized version of the institutional methodology. Many colleges and universities, for example, don't let parents deduct the cost of tuition for private elementary or secondary school from their resources, reasoning that private schooling is a matter of personal choice. Other schools may allow a generous deduction. One institution may expect contributions from both parents whether they're still married or not, while another won't.

You can file the Profile online at http://profileonline.collegeboard.com/index.jsp. The College Board charges applicants $5 to process the form, plus $18 for each college to which you have the profile sent.

Then the college might fiddle...

Once all the formulas have been applied, financial aid officers have the right to use their discretion and adjust the bottom line. Even though the formulas say that your tax-deferred retirement assets won't count against you, for instance, some schools might trim your award if the family nest egg is huge. Or your award might get a boost if an aid officer makes adjustments for expenses that the forms don't ask about, like nursing home care for a family member. (Make sure you bring any such hidden expenses to light.)

Even if all of the colleges in your candidate pool somehow do agree on how much you should be able to afford, their financial aid packages may still vary in significant ways because of "preferential packaging." This means that colleges with a limited amount of aid to dole out are increasingly awarding more money to students they really want. One college might make outright grants a higher proportion of the total package, for instance, while a college less keen on snagging you might offer more of the award in the form of loans and work-study.

Basically, schools handing out money from their own coffers—as opposed to Uncle Sam's—can use the information from the FAFSA and Profile forms in any way they want. And they do, because they're often competing to get the same terrific students. Some colleges even apply the federal methodology to one student and the institutional methodology to another, driving "need" up or down by using whichever formula supports the school's assessment of a student's appeal. Home equity is a favorite tool. For a highly desirable student, information about family assets could come from the FAFSA, which ignores home equity. For a student who is less interesting, assets could be taken from the Profile form, which counts it.

...and you end up happy—or "gapped"

Many colleges pride themselves on "meeting full need," which means they come up with aid packages that fill the entire difference between each family's expected contribution and the cost of freshman year. (Of course, plenty of families don't agree that their need is being met when they realize just how much they're expected to contribute. "The big shocker is that the only place it looks like teachers make a fortune is on the FAFSA," says one dad whose wife is also a teacher. "It says you're good for $16,000 a year. I'm thinking, 'Wow!'") At Princeton University, which has one of the most generous aid policies in the nation and doesn't require students to take out any loans, the $65,000 family could get about $30,000 of the $39,000 cost paid for by grants. With two children in college, even a family with total income of $120,000 and $50,000 in nonretirement savings could receive as much as $29,000 for the Princeton student.

> *"The big shocker is that the only place it looks like teachers make a fortune is on the FAFSA."*

But more and more often when the aid budget is tight, the package doesn't come close to meeting full need, which means that you have to come up with both your family's EFC and whatever the college doesn't cover. "Most schools don't have enough money," says Sandy Baum, a professor of economics at Skidmore College and an expert on financial aid. One school might leave a $3,000 gap, for example, while another might leave a $6,000 gap. (Instead of "gapping," some schools manage their financial aid budgets by practicing "need-conscious" or "need-aware" admissions, which means that the school considers ability to pay when deciding whether to admit some applicants. After 90 or 95 percent of the class is filled, the rest of the hopefuls, even if they're qualified, are likely to be rejected unless they don't need financial aid. Other schools use an "admit-deny" strategy. They admit all students regardless of their need but then decline to offer financial aid to the less qualified.)

Whatever the package, the initial offer is strictly conditional on a double-check of your financial information. The school will at least want corroborating tax information from the previous year. And many private schools and some public universities run all aid applicants through the "verification" mill, an audit-like process in which the college asks for tax returns, bank statements, and other paperwork that can back up your claims about income, assets, and expenses.

Since even schools with generous funds run out, it's smart to file aid applications early. Your FAFSA ought to be in as soon as possible after January 1; due dates for other aid applications vary by school, but waiting until the last moment is a bad idea.

Finally, you weigh your offers

Once all of your aid letters are in hand, you have to make sense of their bottom lines. What will each school really cost you? The price tag includes tuition, fees, room, and board—the charges for which you will receive a bill from the college—plus books, personal expenses, and travel. To figure out how big a burden you'll have to assume, take the total cost and subtract the free money, which includes federal and state grants and institutional grants and scholarships. Then subtract the anticipated earnings from a work-study job, which is usually paid directly to the student and covers personal expenses. The remaining dollar figure is what you will have to pay, either up front or through loans. This should be your real point of comparison between aid packages.

Next, examine which loans each college is offering you (described in detail in the next section of this chapter). Federally subsidized student loans, which are available to families with demonstrated financial need, offer extremely low interest rates and generous grace periods after graduation before interest accrues and repayments begin. Less desirable, but still often a good option, are unsubsidized loans for students and parents, which also carry low rates but begin accruing interest as soon as the loan is in your hands.

Finally, find out whether the aid will be renewed each year, and if it will be renewed in the same form. One young woman whose $20,000 in costs were completely covered by her large state university decided to transfer to another school after she discovered that $8,000 of her grant aid had been converted to loans for sophomore year.

Everything you need to know about the contents of your aid package

What's in an aid package? The first layer usually consists of whatever federal grants or loans you qualify for, plus possibly a work-study job. If you're eligible for aid from your state, that will come next. Then, if you still have remaining need—which you might, because there are caps on how much federal and state aid each person can get—the school will award grants and possibly loans from its own funds.

Government giving

To qualify for any of the following, you must file the Free Application for Federal Student Aid (the FAFSA).

Pell grant. Families with modest household incomes (typically less than $40,000) may be awarded a federal Pell grant of up to $4,050 for each year of undergraduate study. This money, which comes from the federal budget, does not have to be repaid. Because need depends on family size and the number of family members in school as well as income, a large family with a higher income might qualify, for instance. The key is the expected family contribution, which can be no higher than $3,850 for the year.

Federal Supplemental Educational Opportunity Grant. Exceptionally needy students—typically, they can't afford any family contribution at all—may qualify for an FSEOG in additional to a Pell grant. The amount ranges from $100 to $4,000 a year, depending on need and on the funding available at your school. FSEOG grants are an example of "campus-based" federal aid, which means that colleges apply each year to the Department of Education for funding, and the financial aid office determines how much each student receives.

Stafford loan. If you qualify for one of these low-rate loans based on need, your Stafford loan will be subsidized, which means that the federal government pays the interest on the loan while you're in school. You'll qualify if the school's total cost of attendance exceeds your expected family contribution. An unsubsidized Stafford loan, on which interest accrues while you're in school, is available to students regardless of need. You begin repaying your loan six months after you graduate or drop below half-time status, and you can choose from several repayment schedules, including the standard 10-year term, a longer term with lower payments, or payments that are based on your annual income.

If your school participates in the Ford Federal Direct Loan Program, you'll borrow directly from the federal government; otherwise you'll be given a list of banks or other lenders that participate in the Federal Family Education Loan Program. You can borrow up to $2,625 during your freshman year, up to $3,500 during your sophomore year, and up to $5,500 in subsequent years, but no more than $23,000 overall for undergraduate study. Interest rates change annually. Up-front fees total about 4 percent of the loan amount. They vary from bank to bank, though, so it pays to shop around.

Perkins loan. Undergraduates may also qualify for a federal Perkins Loan of up to $4,000, depending on need and on the funds available at their school. The interest rate is a flat 5 percent for the life of the loan, there are no up-front fees, and the loan is repaid directly to the school. (Repayment rates are one of the variables that determine how much a school gets each year from the federal government to fund Perkins loans.)

Federal work-study. After a Stafford loan, a job subsidized by the federal work-study program is one of the most common components of a financial aid package. Some students turn up their noses at this form of "self-help," but a work-study job doesn't necessarily entail washing dishes in the campus cafeteria. Moreover, the pay can be competitive with off-campus employment. You might work 10 hours a week, for example, and earn at least minimum wage; pay usually ranges from $6 to $10 an hour.

Financial aid departments set the standard amount for work-study awards based on their funding each year from the Department of Education, which is determined in part by how much work-study money students at the school have earned in prior years. To some extent, colleges also factor in their philosophy about how many hours full-time students should work. At Amherst College, the standard work-study award is $1,550 a year. At the University of Wisconsin–Madison, the average award is about $2,265 and the maximum is $3,000, which represents 12 to 15 hours of work per week.

Job possibilities run the gamut from checkout at the library to lab research to staffing the office in the psych department. Increasingly, schools also are partnering with organizations in the community to create work-study positions that double as service—tutoring slots with the America Reads program, for example, or lifeguard jobs at the local Y. Once you've earned the full amount of your work-study award, the job officially ends, although sometimes an employer can continue your job and pay you from other funds.

It can be tempting to add hours by taking on a second job, but working too much may interfere with your studies. Two recent surveys by the U.S. Education Department show that students who work more than 15 hours a week during the school year are less likely to complete their degrees than those who work up to 15 hours a week. Undergrads who work up to 15 hours a week also tend to have higher grade

> *"Merit scholarships help to get the attention of exceptional students who might not otherwise look closely at us."*

point averages than those who put in more time.

Accepting a work-study job that is included in your aid package is not mandatory, and many students choose not to work at all or to work for an off-campus employer instead. In a recent year, the University of Wisconsin–Madison offered work-study jobs to 10,544 students. About 3,565 accepted when they signed off on their aid packages, but only 2,053 had earnings. (The rest presumably never took the next step of obtaining a work-study job; you do have to look for the work yourself.) At colleges in urban areas, in particular, you may be able to find better-paying work—or work that's more closely related to your field of study—outside of the work-study program. If you prefer not to work at all, the financial aid office might be able to replace your work-study award with a loan.

Don't be too quick to reject a work-study job in favor of an extra 50 cents an hour somewhere else. What many students don't realize is that what they make from work-study won't be counted next year in the calculation of their expected family contribution. But half of net earnings from other employment must go toward next year's family contribution.

In addition, on-campus bosses are often more willing than other employers to fit your work schedule around classes and exams. "If you're working for your academic department or the library and you ask for time off to work on a paper, generally they'll work with you," says Joe Paul

Case, dean of financial aid at Amherst. That's less likely to happen at McDonald's. Another benefit of on-campus work: the chance to make connections with other students and faculty.

State grants and loans. Many states offer their own grants and loans to residents who attend school in state. Some of the money is awarded to students who show need, and some is given out to any student, regardless of family financial status, who keeps his or her grades up. To find out what your state offers, contact your state's higher education agency. (A listing is available at www.studentaid.ed.gov; click on "funding," then scroll down to "state aid.")

Aid from the college coffers

If a college determines that your financial need is $10,000 and federal and state aid covers $5,000, you're eligible for institutional aid to cover the remaining $5,000 in need.

Need-based grants and loans. In the best-case scenario, you'd get a $5,000 grant from the school to make up the whole difference. Indeed, a student who is especially desirable to a college may get the whole amount covered, while a student who is fortunate to be admitted might receive a far stingier grant. A school's generosity also depends on how much money it has to give away. While Princeton can afford to hand out grants only, less well-financed schools are likely to package a loan or direct you to private lenders.

Merit money. Merit awards are granted by schools recruiting applicants for some special talent or quality—high grades or test scores that will enhance the student body profile, for example, or chess-playing finesse, tromboning skills, or outstanding community service. You don't have to be needy to get one of these scholarships, just really attractive to the people making decisions. "Merit scholarships help to get the attention of exceptional students who might not otherwise look closely at us," says Ben Sandler, special assistant to the chancellor at Washington University in St. Louis.

While there's undeniable appeal in seeing just how prestigious a school you can get into, remember this: If you can earn admission to a top-ranked school, you also have the clout to win a merit scholarship at a very good school with a little less cachet. While it's a mistake to choose a college based entirely on cost, aiming for some merit money with a couple of your applications will give you more flexibility when the time comes to put down a deposit. Schools' goals naturally vary, so the kind of applicant they're willing to lavish aid on varies, too. Still, the quickest way to stand out is to have a grade point average and board scores that outshine the school's averages and put you in the top fifth or top quarter of the student body.

This focus on attracting students with merit aid, and the related trend of granting highly prized applicants more generous need-based financial aid packages, is most pronounced at second- and third-tier colleges. (Many of the most prestigious institutions don't offer merit scholarships.) One caveat is that merit awards don't always add much to your total package. That's because colleges anxious to make their aid money stretch as far as possible often substitute a merit scholarship for need-based aid you would have received otherwise. That's not so bad if the money is used to replace a work-study job or a loan. (Even better if the school uses the money to fill any gap between your official need and the school's aid package.) But if the merit award is large enough, it may also replace all or part of a need-based grant.

How to negotiate for more aid— and win

Financial aid officers often deal with two kinds of disappointed parents: those who reasonably and convincingly make a case that they need more help, and those who rant and rave in frustration. If, in the end, you're bummed out by a puny package, you might find that aid officials have the power to make it grow—assuming you fall into the convincing camp.

These days, most aid administrators will readily hear an appeal. In fact, they pretty much expect to. "Everybody appeals after they get the initial award— I call it 'Let's Make a Deal,'" says Jim Stevenson, director of financial aid at Rensselaer Polytechnic Institute in New York. "We don't increase every pack-

age, but we do make a fair number of adjustments. I have a fund at my disposal for it."

There is a certain etiquette to asking for more money. "I wouldn't say *negotiate*," says Kathy Ruby, the director of financial aid at St. Olaf College in Northfield, Minnesota. Ask her to re-evaluate an aid offer, however, and you'll get another response entirely: "We've certainly been doing a lot more of that."

Walking into an aid office with a better offer in hand and a "match it" attitude won't garner you any sympathy, however. It's a great idea to tell schools that you've received alternative offers (Carnegie Mellon University in Pittsburgh, for example, explicitly encourages admitted students to fax in aid packages from other institutions), but the key to success is giving the college a substantive reason to reconsider.

"If someone says, 'Well, I got this award from Emory, and their award is based on need, and your award is based on need, but it appears that you guys are way off in your assessment of what my need is,'" financial aid officials will be open to a second look, says Rodney Oto, the director of student financial services at Carleton College, also in Northfield, Minnesota.

It may be that some of your family expenses are invisible on federal aid forms. Bates College in Lewiston, Maine, considers costs families incur providing nursing home care for elderly parents, for instance, as well as changes in job status that may have happened after the forms were filed. Some aid officers say they might consider factoring in a younger sibling's upcoming class trip to Europe or, more commonly, the private high school tuition of a younger sibling, if it's clearly creating a hardship. To better the odds of getting the maximum award, follow these few ground rules:

- *Speak up.* Every family's finances are quirky in some way—there's an upcoming bonus that's a one-time event only, a bunch of pending hospital bills because of a sibling's serious illness, a business start-up or serious financial reversal. Let the aid office know about any anomalies; the more the office knows, the better.
- *Beat the application deadlines.* Sure, you don't have to have all of the verification information

in until May 1. But that's what everybody else thinks, too. Dealing with a family's tangled finances during crunch time puts tremendous pressure on overworked aid representatives. That's when mistakes happen.

- *Do your homework.* While aid staffers say they are happy to explain the logic behind an award, they hope you'll be prepared for the discussion. Review the forms that you filed and jot down any changes in your finances or

---

"Everybody appeals after they get the initial award—I call it 'Let's Make a Deal.'"

---

any omissions. Fax any relevant new documentation to the aid office. Finally, calculate how much you can contribute to college costs, and be ready to justify the figures. If you're comparing offers from different schools, consider the example of a Milwaukee mother who prepared a spreadsheet of the offers. It's smart to maintain a call log to verify whom you've been talking with, when, and what about.

- *Go to the top.* If you're not satisfied with what you're hearing from an aid representative, ask politely but firmly to speak with the director of financial aid. Most say their phone lines are open to anyone who makes a specific request.

Not all comers will be warmly received. Students with stellar grades and accomplished athletes, for example, tend to have a bit more bargaining power. Applicants to state schools tend to find less flexibility than at private universities. Families that hire a financial aid consultant to do their bargaining are apt to find the conversation over before it begins. Many schools refuse to barter with consultants on the grounds that doing so would violate the privacy of families.

Finally, it is best not to mistake financial aid officers for pushovers. "I've had people say to me, 'Well, look, we're paying for four cars,'" says Oto, recalling a particularly far-fetched plea. "That isn't going to fly."

Your other borrowing options

You've reviewed a college's aid offer a dozen times, pleaded with the financial aid officer, and even asked your wealthy great-aunt for money, and you still come up short. If you're willing to borrow to go the distance, here are some sources to tap.

The PLUS program

The Department of Education's Parent Loan for Undergraduate Students is available to any creditworthy parent, regardless of need, and can be used to cover all costs of attending an accredited school. That means books and living expenses as well as tuition. The interest rate for loans disbursed on or after July 1, 2006, is fixed at 7.94 percent (for Direct PLUS loans) or 8.5 percent (for FFEL PLUS loans).

The program guarantees that all outstanding debts will be covered if the parent who signs the loan is permanently disabled or dies. And come tax time, families may be able to take a deduction on the paid interest.

Your home equity

Higher-income families may find that borrowing against their home makes more sense than taking out a PLUS loan. Many couples who don't qualify for the interest deduction because they earn too much can take a tax deduction for at least some of the interest on a second mortgage or home-equity line of credit. A line of credit is usually the preferred option, even though rates are variable. Why? Second mortgages disburse the money in a lump sum, which means parents can end up paying interest on the costs of their child's senior year as early as the start of his or her freshman year.

Private lenders

Another borrowing option is a private student loan. These usually cost more than PLUS or home-equity loans because they tend to have higher interest rates. But some families prefer them because the students, rather than the parents, are responsible for paying them off. Moreover, private loans to students tend to

Extra help from Uncle Sam

Mostly, you're going to be writing big checks for the foreseeable future. But come April, parent and student taxpayers can get a little back from the Internal Revenue Service:

Tax credits

Two credits for college expenses are available to parents: the Hope tax credit, which can be used for freshmen and sophomores, and the Lifetime Learning credit, for students in any year of college. The annual credits directly reduce tax, which means a $1,000 credit saves $1,000. The Hope credit is for 100 percent of the first $1,000 of tuition and half of the next $1,000, for a maximum of $1,500. The Lifetime credit allows you to write off 20 percent of the first $10,000 in tuition, so the most you can take is $2,000. Parents putting more than one child through school can claim a Hope credit for each child who qualifies but only up to $2,000 a year total in Lifetime credits. And you can only use one credit per student; you'll have to do the calculations to see which one works best.

Not everyone qualifies, however. Married couples with more than $87,000 in adjusted gross income get a reduced credit, and those making more than $107,000 can't claim a credit at all. The income limits for single taxpayers are $42,000 and $52,000.

Tax deduction for tuition

People whose income barred them from taking a credit for 2004 could possibly claim up to $4,000 of tuition as a tax deduction, though income curbs limited some people to $2,000. Unlike a credit, which reduces your tax, a deduction reduces the income upon which tax is figured. So for someone in the 25 percent tax bracket, a $4,000 deduction saves $1,000. This benefit was available for 2004 to people with incomes up to $130,000 on a married couple's joint return and $65,000 on a single return. Remember: You can't double-dip and take a credit and deduction for the same student.

Tax deduction for student loan interest

Interest on most personal loans isn't deductible, but up to $2,500 a year of interest is deductible on loans used for tuition, room and board, books, transportation, and other expenses. (This doesn't apply to a loan from Grandma, by the way.) The amount of interest that was deductible for 2004 gradually phased out at incomes of $100,000 to $130,000 on a joint return and $50,000 to $65,000 on a single return. And remember, interest on a home equity loan is generally deductible no matter how the funds are used.

---

offer more-flexible repayment terms. For instance, payments on private loans often can be deferred until after graduation, while families must begin repaying each year's PLUS loan soon after the end of the school year.

Your chosen college

Some universities team up with a bank to offer their undergrads private loans with attractive terms. The University of Notre Dame, for instance, offers a loan program in cooperation with Citibank. Still, while the rates on many private loans are ultralow now, they're almost sure to go up. That's one reason many students stick with federal loans, which carry interest rate caps.

Weighing how much debt you can handle

As the cost of tuition keeps going up, so does the weight of the debt. At some institutions, graduates now leave campus with average burdens of $30,000. Most undergraduates misjudge how much they're going to owe—and how debt could affect their post-

Prefer not to borrow? Buy time

If spreading payments out over the academic year will help you avoid borrowing, think about signing up for a tuition payment plan. These programs allow you to pay the room, board, and tuition bills at your child's school in monthly installments instead of sending off big checks at the beginning of each semester. The plans don't charge interest, but do require you to pay an annual enrollment fee of approximately $50.

Some institutions administer the programs themselves; parents send their monthly checks directly to the school. Most colleges partner with outside companies and send enrollment information out with financial aid letters. Parents who sign up start sending their checks to the outside service—almost immediately after their child's high school graduation.

---

college plans—until late senior year, when aid offices provide exit counseling. A recent study by the State Public Interest Research Groups found that more than three in four students underestimate their debt, by an average of nearly $5,000, and that many are unfamiliar with their repayment options.

It's important to think now about how much debt you want to take on over four years and to make sure you stay on track. Financial aid experts advise visiting an aid officer periodically during college, beginning in January of freshman year, both to monitor how fast the loan amounts are piling up and to get some help thinking ahead to how repaying the money will factor into your postcollege plans.

Ask how much the monthly payments are likely to be on your existing and projected levels of debt, and compare that with your expected postgraduation income. Payments on $20,000 in Stafford loans at current rates over 10 years, for instance, would equal about $200 a month, a sizable chunk of an entry-level, $25,000 salary. (You can stretch repayment beyond the standard 10-year repayment schedule to lower the payment, but it will cost you additional interest.)

Credit card debt, too, lies in wait to trap unsuspecting borrowers. According to a study by the student loan agency Nellie Mae, 21 percent of undergraduates with credit cards are carrying balances between $3,000 and $7,000, which represents a 61 percent increase in debt over the span of one year. These balances rack up interest at alarming rates and, unlike subsidized student loans, don't wait until graduation to grow. Keeping up with the monthly payments on an outsize balance will, at best, be a drag on your lifestyle. And not keeping up can really haunt you later on. Late payments and delinquencies on a credit report can make it difficult to borrow for a car, a home, or graduate school. Even worse, some students face financial disaster. According to data collected for Harvard University's Consumer Bankruptcy Project by lead researcher Elizabeth Warren, a professor at the law school, and project director Deborah Thorne, an assistant professor at Ohio University, some 90,000 Americans under age 25 filed for bankruptcy in 2003.

How to find and win an outside scholarship or two

Suppose you don't qualify for any federal or college aid in the first place—or your appeal for more help falls on deaf ears. Thousands of other organizations stand ready to give money away, if only students ask; indeed, over the past several years, new scholarships have popped up like weeds. Some go to brainiacs, some to the best essayists, some to the student who lives in the right place or belongs to the right club. FastWeb, one of the first Internet scholarship search sites, has expanded its database from 180,000 awards in 1996 to more than 600,000 today, worth a total of over $1 billion.

Where to find help on the Web

Looking for authoritative online sources of college aid information? Start here:

- *www.collegeboard.com*. A comprehensive site on college admissions and finances. Under the tab "Pay for college," you'll find a good financial aid calculator, plus debt calculators, a scholarship search, and a worksheet for comparing aid awards.
- *www.fastweb.com*. The leading free scholarship search service features a database of 600,000 scholarships worth more than $1 billion.
- *www.finaid.org*. Devoted solely to college aid, this site covers scholarship, loan, and financial aid basics, with more detail as you drill down through the pages. Includes good tips on maximizing financial aid eligibility.
- *www.studentaid.ed.gov*. If you click on "Publications," you'll find a Department of Education guide entitled "Finding Education Beyond High School: The Guide to Federal Student Aid 2006–2007," which gives all the details on Pell grants and Stafford, Perkins, and PLUS loans.
- *www.usnews.com*. You'll find all the *U.S. News* college rankings and statistics here—plus, under "Find the Money," guidance on scholarships, loans, and other financial aid.
- *www.collegeanswer.com*. You can compare lenders and apply for student loans at this site, created by student-loan giant Sallie Mae. You'll also find loan and financial aid calculators and a scholarship database.

What can you do to collar some of this cash? Apply for it, first and foremost. Online search engines, like those at www.usnews.com and www.fastweb.com, can locate a lot of potential awards fast. You fill out a form about yourself—including every characteristic and hobby you can think of—and all of the relevant scholarships pop up. It's important to be detailed about your interests. One award found on CollegeNET (www.collegenet .com) is for water-skiers, while another is for people who play the recorder.

Don't rely solely on the Internet in your scholarship search, however. Many local scholarships handed out by 4-H clubs, churches, civic groups, and hospitals aren't listed online. Your high school's guidance office probably keeps a list of the possibilities close to home, and it's smart to just call around and ask about awards. Financial aid offices at the colleges you're interested in may also maintain listings of outside scholarships; sometimes they're posted online.

Once you've assembled the necessary application forms, take a deep breath and...slow down. Spending time on an application will mean impressive essays (be sure to get a parent's or teacher's critique). It's OK to file and reuse your essays on other applications, but you'll want to refine them as you go. The process gets easier with practice, says Ben Kaplan, who wrote *How to Go to College Almost for Free* and *The Scholarship Scouting Report: An Insider's Guide to America's Best Scholarships*. Kaplan's first scholarship application took about 16 hours to complete, but by the time his winnings were edging toward $90,000, the Harvard grad could finish some of them in as little as an hour.

Maximizing the money

If you win an award from an outside sponsor, whether it's the prestigious Intel Science Talent Search award or a prize from your local Elks club, you're likely to feel an impact on whatever financial aid you receive from your school. Often, outside awards, like merit awards, are used to replace a portion of your need-based aid. It used to be that colleges simply used the outside scholarship money to replace their own grants, which left students no better off. Now, it's common for colleges to at least use half an outside award to lower your loan burden, while the other half goes to replace school-awarded grants. At the most generous schools, outside scholarships replace your loans first. If you still have scholarship money coming after the school loans are wiped out, the college will sub the remaining funds for its own grant awards. Some schools describe their scholarship policy on their websites, but most do not, which means you'll have to call up your financial aid officer and ask him or her directly.

If you do discover that your school soaks up part of your scholarship by using it to replace grants you would otherwise receive, you can try to negotiate a better deal. Ask your scholarship provider to help you make your plea because providers often have a lot of clout with financial aid officers. If the school upsets a parent or student with its policy, there's just one student and one tuition at stake. But schools risk a wealth of future funding when they displease a scholarship provider.

Picking schools with aid in mind

No, you shouldn't opt for a school just because it's cheap. On the other hand, choosing colleges shrewdly can minimize your costs. One strategy, as we've noted, is to target a couple schools with merit awards to hand out. Here are a couple of additional tips.

Stay in state

Aside from the fact that tuition is cheaper for residents who attend public colleges, several states, including Kentucky, South Carolina, New Mexico, and West Virginia, offer good students (the requirements vary by state) scholarships if they attend a state school. Modeled on Georgia's HOPE scholarship, these programs typically cover tuition at State U, but the grants can be applied toward tuition at in-state private schools as well. So far, Georgia's effort to slow its brain drain is succeeding. Ten years ago, only about a fifth of the stu-

dents who scored 1400 or more on the SAT stayed in state for school. Today, that proportion has nearly doubled.

Apply to colleges in clusters

What do the California Institute of Technology, the Massachusetts Institute of Technology, and Rice University have in common? These schools all compete for the same students—and indeed, most schools have a serious rival or two.

Savvy applicants sometimes can take advantage of these rivalries if they apply to more than one school in a group. While it's a mistake to try to pit one financial aid officer against another, many officers admit that if their school's offer is bested by that of a rival, they're likely to take a second look at their own package. Dan Lundquist, vice president of admissions and financial aid at Union College in Schenectady, New York, says that if a student he has admitted receives a stronger need-based offer from another liberal arts college in New York, "we would want to discuss the differential and reasons behind it." Similarly, Lundquist would want to hear about an offer of merit aid from a rival. "We would give serious consideration to a non-need-based offer to help a student's family feel good about saying yes to Union," he says.

Go north

Canadian colleges continue to be a bargain for Americans. The cost of attending prominent Canadian schools such as McGill University in Montreal and the University of British Columbia in Vancouver ranges from $10,000 to $18,000 (in U.S. dollars) a year. Competition can be fierce. Two years ago, the University of Toronto had more than 75,000 applications for just under 15,000 freshman spots. But think of it this way: As an American bringing some diversity to campus, you might have at least a slight edge.

Glossary

What does it mean if a college is "test-optional" or practices "gapping"? Here, you'll find a key to the large and specialized vocabulary of admissions and financial aid. If a term appears in boldface inside a definition, you can find its own entry elsewhere.

acceptance rate. The proportion of applicants admitted is one measure of how selective a college is. It gives you an idea of how much competition you'll face.

ACT. Most colleges and universities will accept either of two college admissions exams, the ACT Assessment or the **SAT**. The ACT tends to be the more popular of the two among students applying to many Midwestern and Southern institutions. It tests your knowledge in English, reading, mathematics, and science reasoning. The ACT is administered nationally five times a year, in October, December, February, April, and June. Many counselors advise students to take both the ACT and the SAT to see which one better shows off their capabilities.

admissions committee. Your application may be read by several people on this committee, typically made up of faculty and staff members, and sometimes alumni and students, who, along with admissions officers, help evaluate applications. The committee will scrutinize each component of your application, from test scores and transcripts to essays and letters of recommendation.

admissions interview. You probably won't have to sit for an interview with someone on the admissions staff, but it's definitely a good idea. An interview lets you show how interested you are in a school, as well as how intelligent, humorous, and multitalented you are. Many schools use interviews as an opportunity to get to know and assess prospective students in a more personal way than the application allows. Interviews can be done on campus during your visit or by an alumnus in your area.

admit-deny. Schools whose financial aid budgets are stretched sometimes use what's known as an "admit-deny" strategy, admitting students who are academically qualified but offering them little or no aid even though they need it. Because these students often can't enroll, the strategy is typically used for marginal applicants.

Advanced Placement (AP) courses. Admissions staffers like to see some Advanced Placement entries on an applicant's transcript because these more rigorous courses indicate that the student has challenged himself and presumably can handle college-level work. AP tests are given nationwide in the late spring, usually during the first two weeks of May, and are scored on a scale of 1 to 5. If you get a "qualifying" grade on the AP Exam, colleges may give you credit for the course and you can move into an advanced class. A score of 3 may qualify for credit, but some schools demand a 4 or a 5.

aid. See financial aid.

alumna; alumnae. A female graduate or former student of a college or university; more than one female former student.

alumnus; alumni. A male graduate or former student of a college or university; more than one male former student (or a mixed-gender group).

application fee. This fee accompanies your application and typically runs $25 to $60 or more.

articulation agreement. If you're thinking about completing a year or two at a technical or **community college** before transferring to a four-year college or university, you might want to check to see if your community college has an articulation agreement with any colleges or universities. These arrangements make the process of transferring go more smoothly than it otherwise might because they define which community college credits will be honored by the four-year school; the two-year degree would typically satisfy the new college's lower-division general education requirements.

associate's degree. The two-year associate's degree in science awarded by a junior or **community college** might be career-oriented and lead to a job as a veterinary technician, dental hygienist, or legal secretary, for example. The more general associate's degree in arts often is the first part of a four-year bachelor's degree.

board scores. When someone brags about her board scores, she's telling you what she got on the **SAT** entrance exam or the **SAT Subject Tests**, which are administered by the College Board.

campus visit. You can narrow down your choices by studying this book, attending **college fairs**, scouring websites, and collecting school catalogs, but you won't want to actually make a decision until you see and talk to students, sit in on a class or two, spend a night in the dorm, and maybe get a taste of the cafeteria food. Many counselors suggest visiting colleges of varying sizes and types, in urban and more rural locations, to get a feel for how schools differ. They also suggest that the student (not Mom or Dad) call admissions and schedule the visit.

class rank. Your class rank is determined by where your high school **grade point average (GPA)** sits among those of the rest of your class. Many high schools calculate a "weighted rank," which takes into account both your grades and how tough your courses were. Others figure a "straight rank," based strictly on grades. Some have stopped calculating class rank because they don't believe it gives a very accurate idea of achievement.

class size. The number of students in your college classes will determine to a large extent how the teaching and learning happens. An introductory economics course with 500 other students will be taught by lecture, probably supplemented by smaller group discussions led by graduate assistants, who will also grade your tests and papers. By contrast, a seminar on eighteenth-century British literature with only seven other students will center on class discussion and debate and offer students the chance to really get to know the professor. The college profiles in the directory section of this book contain information on class sizes at each school.

college catalog. Unlike a college's **view book**, a heavily illustrated first peek at a school, its catalog is an all-business publication that lists all classes offered, faculty and their credentials, requirements for graduation, and detailed information on costs.

college entrance requirements. The admissions requirements set by a college or university vary from school to school, but typically include a minimum GPA or test scores and a certain number of courses in English, mathematics, social studies, science, and foreign language.

college fair. Here's your chance to meet with admissions representatives from a wide range of colleges and universities in one fell swoop and ask about everything from the types of courses that are offered to admissions and **financial aid** requirements. It may seem easier to stay home and browse the Web, but colleges want to know who's really, truly interested, and showing up is one way to let them know you are. Be sure to complete the student information cards put out by each college you're considering so it's clear that you were there.

college-sponsored loan. A small number of colleges offer their own loans to parents and students. Check each college's aid materials to see if such loans are available, and ask about interest rates.

Common Application. Go to www.common app.org to apply to multiple schools without filling out multiple applications. The Common Application is a generic form accepted by nearly 300 colleges and universities; some require a supplemental essay or other additional information. You can either download the form and submit a hard copy or submit it online to the schools of your choice. Check with the schools you're interested in to see if they accept it.

community college. According to the American Association of Community Colleges (AACC), there are now 1,186 of these two-year postsecondary institutions that offer certificate programs and **associate's degrees**. Some students choose to spend a year or two at a community college and then transfer to a four-year college, which can be a great way to transition to life after high school if you don't feel quite ready to take the plunge and a good way to save some tuition dollars even if you are. Many community colleges have **articulation agreements** with four-year schools that allow credits to transfer smoothly.

cooperative education. Colleges that offer a "co-op" program—particularly popular in business and technical fields—alternate a term in the classroom with time in the workforce. You learn the theory in class, then apply it on the job and, as a bonus, earn money and build connections and a résumé that can come in handy upon graduation. The trade-off: You typically must put in a fifth year of college and several summers.

cost of attendance. The total amount it will cost a student to go to school for a year. The figure includes **tuition** and fees; **room and board** (or a housing and food allowance for off-campus students); and allowances for books, supplies, transportation, and miscellaneous expenses, including the rental or purchase of a personal computer.

counselor-for-hire. See **educational consultant.**

CSS/Profile. Several hundred of the country's most selective private colleges ask financial aid applicants to fill out this detailed form in addition to the federal aid application form, known as the **Free Application for Federal Student Aid (FAFSA).**

curriculum. A set of courses that make up a program. Many schools have a general curriculum, required of all students, that consists of courses in mathematics, English, science, and the humanities. Your major will also have a curriculum of required classes.

diversity. The mix of cultures and ethnic groups, as well as of people from different religious and socioeconomic backgrounds, will have a big impact on the character of a school. Are you comfortable befriending and working with people unlike you, and who hold different views from your own? Or would you rather stick with kids from your home state or your own religion? Statistics on the demographic breakdown of the student body appear in each college's directory profile.

double major. Specialization in two academic fields of study, or majors.

dual enrollment. A majority of states have adopted policies that encourage enrollment partnerships between high schools and colleges. These arrangements allow high school students to take courses that earn credit toward a high school diploma and a college degree at the same time.

early action. Under an early-action plan, you apply to college in the fall and get "action"—which is to say, a decision or deferral—on your application by December or January. You can apply to more than one school and have until May 1 to make your decision. Early action may be a good choice for someone who has narrowed the field to two or three schools and is anxious to be done with the waiting game.

early decision. A growing number of applicants opt for early decision because they want an edge over the competition. Colleges often accept a higher proportion of early-decision applicants than they do of those in the regular pool. But you have to be really sure about a school, because you're obligated to enroll if you're accepted and receive an adequate aid package.

Early-decision applications are usually due in November, and you'll most likely get the decision within a month. The problem, say counselors, is that students may make hasty and poorly researched choices. Plus, they lose the opportunity to compare financial aid offers.

educational consultant. For a fee that usually ranges from several hundred to several thousand dollars, educational consultants guide juniors and seniors and their families through the process of selecting the right schools, getting ready for admissions tests and interviews, and preparing applications. If you choose to hire a consultant and are unable to find one by word of mouth, it's a good idea to interview several from among the membership of the Independent Educational Consultants Association (www.educationalconsulting.org) or the National Association for College Admission Counseling (www.nacac.com).

essay. Colleges typically require a personal statement on the application so the admissions staff can get behind the numbers and see how cogently and creatively you think, as well as how your experiences have contributed to your personal growth. You'll want to do a careful job, because when two candidates are equally qualified, the essay may tip the balance. If the topic is left up to you, counselors and deans alike advise that you write about a familiar subject (as opposed to a theme such as poverty or world peace) and that you spend time drafting and editing. It's a good idea to ask Mom and Dad for feedback and proofreading, but that's all they should do!

expected family contribution (EFC). This number, which appears on financial aid award letters, is the amount your family will be asked to contribute to the cost of your education. It is calculated based on the information you supplied about your income and assets on the Free Application for Federal Student Aid (FAFSA) and on a second form used by many private colleges, the CSS/Profile. Your EFC may vary quite a bit from college to college because schools interpret families' financial situations differently.

extracurricular activities. What life offers outside of class at college will probably have a big impact on your happiness, just as it did in high school. So when you're creating a list of schools, pay attention to whether you'll still be able to play lacrosse, write for the school paper, belong to the drama club (and actually have a shot at some stage time), or work for the local food bank. You'll also want to be able to talk about one or two activities that are particularly important to you when you interview.

FAFSA. See Free Application for Federal Student Aid.

Federal Family Education Loan Program (FFELP). Banks and other lenders that participate in this program are sources of student loan funds. Unless your college is part of a program that allows you to borrow directly from the government, it will give you a list of lenders to contact when it awards financial aid.

federal methodology. In calculating how much financial aid you are eligible for, the federal government takes the information you supply on the federal aid application form and feeds it into this formula to arrive at your expected contribution to the cost of college.

Federal Supplemental Educational Opportunity Grant (FSEOG). This federal grant, which can range from $100 to $4,000 per year, goes to exceptionally needy students whose families typically can't afford to contribute anything at all to college costs. To be considered for this grant, you must complete the **Free Application for Federal Student Aid (FAFSA).**

fifth-year program. Some schools have designed curricula that allow you to complete both a bachelor's degree and a master's degree in five years. This is usually accomplished through some accelerated coursework and an overlap of undergraduate and graduate classes. These programs usually require high levels of academic performance.

financial aid. A financial aid package usually consists of federal **Pell grants** and state grants, which don't have to be repaid; federal **Stafford** and **Perkins** loans for students, which do; and **work-study** programs. Colleges may add in their own grants or **scholarships** as well. Financial aid amounts are based on the information you supply in your **Free Application for Federal Student Aid (FAFSA)** form and other forms, but colleges may use **preferential packaging** as a way to recruit great students, as they offer more in grants and less in loans to someone they really want than to more marginal candidates.

financial aid advisor. If you apply for any type of financial aid from your school, you will be assigned to a financial aid advisor on the staff who puts together your package and is available to help you plan funding throughout your college years.

Ford Federal Direct Loan Program. If your college participates in this program, you'll borrow your student loans directly from the government. If not, you'll be given a list of banks or other lenders to contact.

fraternities/sororities. How strong an influence do these social societies have on campus life? A school where much of the social life revolves around frat parties and where many students choose to live in fraternity and sorority houses may feel inhospitable to someone who prefers not to participate—or just right to someone excited about Greek life.

Free Application for Federal Student Aid (FAFSA). This is the application you'll need to complete if you're applying for federal and state grants, loans, and work-study. The paper version of the FAFSA is available in your guidance office, public library, or the financial aid office of a local college. You can also have a paper copy of the FAFSA mailed to you by calling 800-433-3243. For additional information or to fill the form out online, visit www.fafsa.ed.gov.

freshman retention rate. The proportion of students who return to school for their sophomore year is a number worth looking at. If it's low, you'll want to find out why. Do students feel lost in the shuffle? Do their aid packages tend to shrink after freshman year? We've included each school's rate in its profile.

freshman seminar. Recognizing that a schedule full of large lecture classes makes it difficult for freshmen to connect with professors and peers, many schools make sure each first-year student has at least one enriching small-group class experience. The seminars are typically led by a faculty member, so students can form a bond with a professor earlier than they might otherwise.

full need. In financial aid parlance, colleges that "meet full need" are those that can provide enough in **grants**, **loans**, and **work-study** to fill the whole gap between what a family is expected to pay and the cost of a year in college.

gapping. Many schools' financial aid budgets are too strained to allow them to meet every student's **full need**. Instead, they may "gap" a family, or offer aid that is not sufficient to cover the difference between the **expected family contribution (EFC)** and the cost of college. This gap can be closed through outside scholarships and bigger parent loans. But it will be up to you to find them. Your **financial aid advisor** can offer guidance.

grade point average (GPA). Your grade point average is calculated using a formula that takes into account both your grades and the number of credits earned in each class. An A in a class worth two credits will not influence your GPA as much as an A in a class worth four credits. Some high schools calculate "weighted GPAs" by making grades in AP and honors classes worth extra. Sometimes, the GPA colleges use is figured without grades in nonessential courses such as typing. It's a good idea to know the policies of both your high school and the colleges to which you'll apply. If your high school calculates **class rank**, colleges may consider your rank and your GPA.

graduate assistant. Freshmen at large universities are apt to be taught part of the time by graduate students who work as teaching assistants to university faculty. If you take a large lecture course, you will most likely take part in study sessions facilitated by graduate students, who may also grade your papers.

graduation rate. The proportion of students who have graduated within a certain time period; *U.S. News* uses a six-year graduation rate when calculating its annual rankings of colleges and universities. This number, available in the directory profiles, will give you some perspective on how students fare at a school. If a school's graduation rate seems low, ask the admissions office to explain why. Do students transfer in great numbers? Is it hard to get into courses, so students have to stay longer than expected to get all their credits?

grant. A form of financial aid that never has to be paid back. The federal **Pell grant** is an example.

honors colleges and programs. These programs take different forms, but their purpose is the same: to attract stellar students and to give them the chance to do accelerated work in smaller-than-usual classes with respected faculty members. Some honors programs require a separate application; some offer a spot based on high school performance. Some house honors students separately so that they engage with each other outside of the classroom as well as inside it. Typically, some sort of culminating project or thesis is required.

hook. Many applicants don't realize that admissions decisions are often heavily influenced by what skills or characteristics the school needs in a given year. A school might want to add a women's soccer team, expand the biology department, or be able to boast a student body representing all 50 states. Whatever special qualities or talents you have are apt to put you high on some college's wish list. It's up to you to develop these "hooks" and convey them in your interviews and on your application.

indebtedness. As tuition rises, so does the amount students have to borrow. It's a good idea to talk regularly with the financial aid office during college about how your total indebtedness at graduation might affect your plans afterward. Many students underestimate how much they'll owe and how painful the payback will be on an entry-level salary.

in-state/out-of-state tuition. At private colleges, tuition costs are the same whether you're a resident of the state or not. At colleges and universities funded by taxpayers of a state, the tuition for an out-of-state student is generally far higher than what the in-state student pays.

institutional methodology. Colleges that use the **CSS/Profile** to calculate financial aid feed your family data into a formula that is more sensitive than the federal formula. It counts home equity as a resource, for example, while the federal methodology does not.

intercollegiate sports. Intercollegiate competition pits one college's team against another college's team.

interdisciplinary major. In an increasingly complex world, biologists studying the brain must understand chemistry and physics to make progress, and architects need to understand the environment to design buildings. As a result, college students today sometimes choose a field of study that crosses disciplines. Bioengineering draws from biology, physics, chemistry, and mathematics. Cognitive science combines linguistics, computer science, and psychology. If a school doesn't offer one of those types of majors, it might let you craft your own.

internship. Many colleges encourage or even require short stints in the workplace, on the theory that an internship in a field related to your studies gives you a chance to apply and reinforce what you've learned in class, gain hands-on experience, and build your résumé.

intramural sports. Rather than compete against teams from other colleges, members of an intramural sports program play against other teams from their school.

Ivy League. The term is now used as shorthand for eight of the country's most elite schools: Brown, Columbia, Cornell, Dartmouth, Harvard, the University of Pennsylvania, Princeton, and Yale. Technically, it is the name of the athletic league formed by the eight schools, with shared academic standards and eligibility requirements for athletes.

learning center. The campus learning center provides a wide variety of student services, from academic and career counseling to tutoring services, test preparation, and study skills work-

shops. Check with your school to find out what types of services are available.

learning community, living/learning community. To make sure students are engaged in their studies and bonding with peers and professors, many schools have devised ways to keep the conversations going after class. Typically, students in a learning community take two or more linked courses as a small group and get to know each other especially well. In some cases, they live and eat in the same residence halls, too.

lecture. Courses taught in a lecture format involve little classroom interaction and often have enrollments of a few hundred students. A professor gives the actual lectures, but he or she usually relies on graduate assistants to lead discussion groups and review sessions and to grade papers and exams.

legacy. Someone who is a legacy of a college has a close relative who also attended (usually a parent or grandparent). Some schools may give preferential consideration to these applicants, or perhaps a bit more scholarship aid, while others disregard legacy status entirely in the admissions process.

liberal arts college. These typically small, residential colleges emphasize undergraduate education and a curriculum centered on a broad set of courses as opposed to more specialized technical or professional training. These courses typically include language, literature, philosophy, history, and the natural sciences. Liberal arts colleges award more than half of their degrees in liberal arts disciplines.

loan. Money you receive that must be paid back. See **Perkins loans, PLUS loan, Stafford loan, college-sponsored loans,** and **private loans.**

major. Some students enter college having known since elementary school what their chosen field of study would be; others come to school without a clue as to which path they'll follow. Many students switch majors once or twice as they discover new interests. Usually, you declare your major as you enter junior year and are required to take a certain number of credits in the subject. Many students choose to **double**

major, or major in two subjects. Some colleges offer **interdisciplinary majors**, such as American studies, which combine coursework from several fields.

merit awards or merit scholarships. In order to attract students with outstanding grades and test scores, many colleges award scholarships based not on financial need but on academic achievement. Scholarships are also given out in recognition of other talents or accomplishments the college finds desirable, such as musical ability or community service.

National Association for College Admission Counseling (NACAC). The professional organization of admissions officers and college counselors.

National Association of Intercollegiate Athletics (NAIA). The NAIA is a voluntary association of nearly 300 colleges and universities in 14 regions. The NAIA conducts two dozen national championship events in sports that include basketball, football, swimming, and tennis. Universities that are known as the big intercollegiate sports powerhouses belong to the other athletic governing body, the **National Collegiate Athletic Association (NCAA)**.

National Collegiate Athletic Association (NCAA). The NCAA is a voluntary association of about 1,250 colleges, universities, athletic conferences, and sports organizations responsible for the administration of intercollegiate athletics. Member schools compete in three groups: Division I, Division II, and Division III. The organization administers 88 championships in 22 sports.

National Merit Scholarship Corporation. This group administers two annual scholarship competitions: the National Merit Scholarship Program and the National Achievement Scholarship Program, which recognizes outstanding African-American students. High school students enter this competition by taking the PSAT/National Merit Scholarship Qualifying Test, usually during their junior year. Students whose scores and other academic standards qualify them as finalists are considered for scholarships. Other high scorers are recognized for their achievement.

need-based aid. Need-based financial aid is awarded to students whose family income, assets, and expenses—as indicated on the **Free Application for Federal Student Aid (FAFSA)**—demonstrate that they can't afford to pay the whole cost of college by themselves. Their need is the difference between the amount the family is expected to be able to pay (by each college's calculations) and the cost of a year in college. The aid package usually consists of a combination of **grants**, **loans**, and **work-study**.

need-blind admissions. When a school has a need-blind admissions policy, it judges all applications for admissions without regard to whether or not a student will need financial aid.

need-conscious or need-aware admissions. Schools that can't afford to meet every student's full need sometimes accept most of their students in a need-blind fashion, then make decisions about the final 5 or 10 percent of the incoming class based on ability to pay.

open admission. Under an open-admission policy, a school accepts all applicants who meet or exceed a certain standard. For example, an open-admissions standard may require a high school diploma and a minimum **grade point average**. Anyone who meets those requirements is virtually guaranteed admission. The policy is most often used by community colleges.

orientation. Sometime before class starts, you'll get a chance to spend time on campus forging connections with faculty members and your new classmates. Orientation activities vary widely from school to school. You might go out on a citywide scavenger hunt, take a backpacking or white-water rafting trip, tackle a community service project, or just attend a meeting or two.

Pell grant. These federal grants are awarded to the neediest undergraduate students as part of the financial aid package and do not have to be repaid. To be considered, you must fill out the **Free Application for Federal Student Aid (FAFSA)** form. Your eligibility depends on the size of your **expected family contribution**. It can be no higher than $3,850 for the year. Typically, Pell grants go to families with household incomes of less than $40,000 yearly. The grants are capped at $4,050 per year of undergraduate study.

Perkins loan. Perkins loans, need-based loans of up to $4,000 per year, are awarded by the financial aid office. The interest rate is a flat 5 percent for the life of the loan, and you don't make any loan payments while in school.

PLAN. The PLAN is a "pre-ACT" test typically administered in the fall of sophomore year. It covers the same subject areas as the **ACT** (English, mathematics, reading, and science), making it a predictor of success on the **ACT**. It also includes an "interest inventory" to help students prepare for life after high school.

PLUS loan. The federal Parent Loan for Undergraduate Students is available to any credit-worthy parent of a dependent student, regardless of need, and can be used to cover all costs of attending an accredited school. The PLUS loan lets parents borrow enough to cover any costs not already covered by the student's financial aid package, up to the full cost of attendance. The interest rate for loans disbursed on or after July 1, 2006, is fixed at 7.94 percent (for Direct PLUS loans) or 8.5 percent (for FFEL PLUS loans). Parents interested in this type of loan should submit a completed PLUS application to the school's financial aid office.

preferential packaging. In order to shape their incoming classes and attract the most desirable students, some schools offer more attractive financial aid packages to more appealing students. A very talented applicant might receive almost all grant aid, for example, while a less outstanding contender might be offered a package equally split between grants, loans, and work-study.

private loan. A number of lenders and other financial institutions offer private-education loans for parents and for students. These loans usually carry a higher interest rate than the federal student and **PLUS loans**, and the student loans are not subsidized. The College Board's Signature Loans are an example of a private-loan program for students.

PSAT. The Preliminary SAT is a standardized test that offers practice for the SAT. It also gives you a chance to qualify for the National Merit Scholarship Corporation's scholarship programs. The test measures verbal reasoning skills, critical reading skills, mathematical problem-solving skills, and writing skills. While it is designed to be taken during the junior year of high school, some students choose to take it sophomore year.

reach school. Looking only at your grades and scores, getting into a "reach" school is a long shot. On the other hand, maybe you've got a hook that will compensate. Most students like to include a reach school or two on their list of colleges as well as some that will probably accept them and a couple of safety schools that almost certainly will.

recommendation. Admissions and scholarship committees use letters of recommendation from guidance counselors and teachers to learn about the character and personality of each applicant. You want to ask people to recommend you who know you well enough to say something specific about you or your performance; clichés won't help your case.

rolling admissions. Schools that use rolling admissions evaluate and respond to applicants as the applications come in, rather than waiting to start the process until all applications have been received. They continue accepting students until the class is full.

room and board. Room charges pay for your housing; board charges pay for your food service. These charges can vary from student to student depending on the meal plan and type of campus housing he or she selects.

safety school. You're very likely to make it into your safety schools because you exceed all of the entrance requirements and have grades and test scores that fall above the average. Because most schools are interested in raising the academic profile of their student body, many give out merit scholarships to induce their highly qualified applicants to enroll. Many applicants choose to apply to a couple of safety schools in addition to colleges that will probably accept them and a reach school or two.

SAT Reasoning Test. The SAT college entrance exam takes 3 hours and 45 minutes and measures the critical reading, mathematical, and writing skills students have developed over time. The SAT is scored on a scale of 200-800 and is usually taken by high school juniors and seniors. The test is given several times a year. Because many schools will accept either the SAT or the ACT, students often opt to take both and see which score is strongest. The total score possible on the SAT is 2400.

SAT Subject Test. The SAT Subject Tests are one-hour, mostly multiple choice subject tests designed to measure how much students know about a particular academic subject and how well they can apply that knowledge. Some colleges and universities require applicants to submit SAT Subject Test results; others use them as an additional indicator of academic achievement or as an indicator of where to place you in first-year classes.

scholarship. A scholarship is a form of funding that does not have to be repaid. Usually, scholarships are awarded based on academic, athletic, or other talent.

selectivity. Schools that receive 15 applications for each spot are much more selective than schools that receive only two. They accept a much smaller proportion of their applicant pool and have the luxury of taking only the most highly qualified students.

self-help aid. The part of the aid package that isn't just handed out, but requires some effort on your part—**loans** and **work-study**.

senior capstone. These culminating projects are generally completed over the course of your final year or semester under the guidance of a faculty advisor and might consist of an independent research project (like a thesis), a service-learning project, or an internship experience. You can expect to present a final project, paper, or presentation at the close of the year.

senioritis. Nope, it's not "inflammation of the senior." This affliction plagues some students who have heard that they're accepted at college and are anticipating graduation. Symptoms include the inability or lack of motivation to continue working. Better fight it off, because colleges do look at those final transcripts and may require summer school if grades slip too much.

service learning. Schools that build service learning into the curriculum require volunteer work as a class assignment. Students get practical experience related to what they're studying and work on citizenship, too.

Stafford loan, subsidized. These need-based student loans have an ultralow interest rate, and the federal government pays the yearly interest while you're in school.

Stafford loan, unsubsidized: Students who don't demonstrate significant financial need can still take out a Stafford loan to help pay the family share of costs, but they'll be responsible for the interest on the loan while in school.

student-to-faculty ratio. This measure, which shows how many students are enrolled in a college or university per professor, gives a rough sense of the sort of contact you're apt to have with faculty members. The greater the number of students per professor, the harder it's likely to be to get individual attention. Student-to-faculty ratios can be found in the profiles in this book.

test-optional school. In recent years, a number of schools dissatisfied with standardized tests as a predictor of performance have decided to stop requiring them in admissions decisions. A test-optional school does not require applicants to submit **SAT** or **ACT** scores, although students may choose to.

transcript. This all-important document shows the courses you've taken and the grades received. When studied alongside a profile of your high school that lists all courses available to you, admissions officers can get a sense of whether you've challenged yourself or chosen easier courses.

tuition. Tuition is what you pay to be educated at a college or university, but does not include what you pay for food and housing.

tuition discounting. Schools that give out lots of their own aid (on top of what Uncle Sam hands out) are often said to be discounting their tuition. Students receive different "discounts" depending on how badly the institution wants them.

view book. A college view book is often a prospective applicant's first introduction to a school. It typically contains general information on degree programs, a sense of the student-body profile, and the types of student clubs and organizations.

wait list. If you fit the admissions criteria for a particular school but miss the cut, you may be offered a place on the waiting list. If your heart is set on the school, be sure to keep your grades up, let the admissions office know about any new honors that come your way, and make sure it's clear that you're still interested. Wait-listed candidates are usually encouraged to make a deposit at another school in order to ensure they have a spot in the fall, though they'll forfeit the deposit if their first choice makes an offer.

work-study. Federal work-study money, which may be promised as part of a financial aid package, supports jobs for students with financial need. You can expect to work between eight and 20 hours a week, and earn at least minimum wage (maybe more, depending on the type of work you do and the skills required). Once you've earned the full amount of your work-study award, the job officially ends, although employers often find ways to keep valued workers on the payroll by tapping alternative funds. Your **financial aid advisor** can point you to work-study jobs.

yield. A college's yield is the proportion of admitted students who accept the offer and enroll. It's a number colleges keep a close watch on. For one thing, a high yield indicates that students really want to be at the school. Also, schools are concerned about ending up with too many or too few freshmen.

College Planner

With all the details and dates to remember, applying to college can be a major organizational challenge. This planner can help. You can copy this sheet (or print it out at *www.usnews.com/planner*) and then fill one out for each school you're considering. Your comments will allow you to compare characteristics of different schools—and remind yourself of interesting facts down the line.

SCHOOL: _____

LOCATION	COMMENTS
Region	
Setting (urban, suburban, rural)	
Distance from home	
ACADEMICS	
Rigor of coursework	
Choice of majors	
Class size and student/faculty ratio	
Academic facilities	
Quality of professors	
Access to professors	
CAMPUS LIFE	
Size of student body	
Diversity of student body	
Student attitudes about the school	
Social life	
Extracurricular activities	
Housing options	
Atmosphere	
COSTS	
Affordability	
Access to grants/aid	
CAREER PREPARATION	
Range of internships	
Quality of career services	
OTHER FACTORS	

CAMPUS VISITS: QUESTIONS TO ASK

Once you've decided on a shortlist, it's extremely helpful to visit the campuses, if possible. You'll be overwhelmed with information, but don't forget to ask questions, too. Current students are one of the best candid sources of information. Talk to a few different ones, not just the tour guide. Consider these questions and add a few of your own. (You can print out this sheet at *www.usnews.com/plan-*

SCHOOL: _____

QUESTIONS FOR STUDENTS: What do you like most about this college? What's the worst thing about it? _____

_____

What do you wish you had known when you were making your own decision? _____

_____

What are the students like here? _____

_____

What are the classes like? Lots of small discussion groups? Mostly large lectures? _____

_____

Do graduate students or professors teach introductory classes? _____

_____

How often in the last semester have you participated in class or met with a professor outside of class? ____

_____

Where do students study? Where do students hang out on campus? Off campus? On the weekend? _____

_____

How central are fraternities and sororities to campus social life? What about sports? _____

_____

QUESTIONS FOR ADMINISTRATORS: What percentage of students go on to graduate or professional schools? ____

_____

What percentage of students graduate in four years? What percentage of first-year students return the next year? ____

_____

What was the average tuition increase over the past five years? _____

_____

When must you declare a major? Can you design your own major? _____

_____

(If applicable) Can you take classes at other schools in the area? _____

_____

Who serves as a student's adviser? Do advisers change each year? _____

_____

What are the living options on campus? Off campus? _____

_____

What percentage of students study abroad at some point during their four years? _____

_____

Additional questions: _____

_____

_____

_____

Contact information (names, phone numbers, E-mail addresses) for students and administrators I met: _____

_____

_____

_____

_____

APPLICATION ORGANIZER

With this organizer you can always see at a glance what's done, what needs to be done, and when it has to happen. At the top of each column, write the name of the school you are applying to. Note the deadlines for the application and financial aid forms. Then just check off the squares as you complete each item for each school.

	SCHOOL NAMES									
	1	**2**	**3**	**4**	**5**	**6**	**7**	**8**	**9**	**10**
APPLICATIONS										
Application deadline										
Application form completed	☐	☐	☐	☐	☐	☐	☐	☐	☐	☐
Essays completed	☐	☐	☐	☐	☐	☐	☐	☐	☐	☐
Application mailed or E-mailed	☐	☐	☐	☐	☐	☐	☐	☐	☐	☐
RECOMMENDATIONS										
Gave form to NAME HERE	☐	☐	☐	☐	☐	☐	☐	☐	☐	☐
Writer mailed form or returned it to me	☐	☐	☐	☐	☐	☐	☐	☐	☐	☐
Sent thank-you note	☐	☐	☐	☐	☐	☐	☐	☐	☐	☐
Gave form to NAME HERE	☐	☐	☐	☐	☐	☐	☐	☐	☐	☐
Writer mailed form or returned it to me	☐	☐	☐	☐	☐	☐	☐	☐	☐	☐
Sent thank-you note	☐	☐	☐	☐	☐	☐	☐	☐	☐	☐
Gave form to NAME HERE	☐	☐	☐	☐	☐	☐	☐	☐	☐	☐
Writer mailed form or returned it to me	☐	☐	☐	☐	☐	☐	☐	☐	☐	☐
Sent thank-you note	☐	☐	☐	☐	☐	☐	☐	☐	☐	☐
TRANSCRIPTS										
Gave transcript form to counselor	☐	☐	☐	☐	☐	☐	☐	☐	☐	☐
Form mailed	☐	☐	☐	☐	☐	☐	☐	☐	☐	☐
Gave midyear report form to counselor	☐	☐	☐	☐	☐	☐	☐	☐	☐	☐
Form mailed	☐	☐	☐	☐	☐	☐	☐	☐	☐	☐
TEST SCORES										
Requested that score reports be sent	☐	☐	☐	☐	☐	☐	☐	☐	☐	☐
SAT I	☐	☐	☐	☐	☐	☐	☐	☐	☐	☐
SAT II	☐	☐	☐	☐	☐	☐	☐	☐	☐	☐
ACT	☐	☐	☐	☐	☐	☐	☐	☐	☐	☐
AP exams	☐	☐	☐	☐	☐	☐	☐	☐	☐	☐
FINANCIAL AID FORMS										
Financial aid application deadline										
FAFSA form submitted	☐	☐	☐	☐	☐	☐	☐	☐	☐	☐
Completed Profile registration process	☐	☐	☐	☐	☐	☐	☐	☐	☐	☐
Profile form submitted	☐	☐	☐	☐	☐	☐	☐	☐	☐	☐
If needed, college's form submitted	☐	☐	☐	☐	☐	☐	☐	☐	☐	☐

MY PERSONAL PROFILE

Filling out a personal profile will help you complete the application process more quickly and easily. You can use it as a cheat sheet as you complete your college applications, and give copies to the people who are writing your letters of recommendation. If you haven't thought of that perfect essay topic yet, a thoughtfully completed profile should give you some good ideas.

Name: _____   Phone number: _____

Address: _____   E-mail address: _____

High school counselor's name: _____   Phone number: _____

Colleges I'm applying to: _____

_____

SCORES

SAT: _____   ACT: _____   High school GPA: _____

Verbal: _____   Multiple Choice: _____   AP (subject, score): _____

Math: _____   Writing Test: _____   AP (subject, score): _____

HIGH SCHOOL COURSES (Attach a transcript.) List your favorite courses and a few words about why they interested you.

_____   _____

_____   _____

_____   _____

AWARDS List award, date received, and description.

_____   _____

_____   _____

_____   _____

_____   _____

ACTIVITIES Include jobs, volunteer work, and extracurricular activities. List the dates you participated and/or hours per week, and any leadership positions you held. On a separate sheet, you can summarize what you did and why it was meaningful.

_____   _____

_____   _____

_____   _____

_____   _____

_____   _____

_____   _____

PERSONAL INFO Are you the first member of your family to attend college? Did you have an extraordinary childhood? Do you breed show turtles for fun? Outside of individual awards, activities, and courses, what is most interesting about you? What makes you stand out as a college applicant? Using the space below, write down a few ideas and continue brainstorming on a separate sheet.

_____

_____

_____

_____

_____

How Do Your
Schools Compare?

How to Use the Insider's Index

The Insider's Index will help you see how your schools stack up on key measures, from graduation rate to the size of their financial aid packages to the diversity of the student body. (See page viii in the Introduction for further discussion.) As you search for a particular college or university, you'll notice that the lists are organized by type of institution:

• National Universities, which offer a wide range of undergraduate majors as well as master's and doctoral degrees

• Liberal Arts Colleges, which emphasize undergraduate education and award at least half of their degrees in the liberal arts disciplines

• Universities–Master's, which offer a full range of undergraduate and master's programs but few, if any, doctoral programs

• Comprehensive Colleges–Bachelor's, which offer programs in the liberal arts (accounting for fewer than half of their degrees) and in professional fields such as business, nursing, and education

Schools that did not supply the necessary data do not appear in the tables. "N/A" means "not available."

How much competition are you facing? In this table, colleges and universities are organized by how "selective" they are: that is, how picky they can be in choosing freshmen. Selectivity is determined by the test scores and high school class standing of applicants who enroll, plus the proportion of applicants who are accepted. Within each category, schools are ranked by their acceptance rate. SAT results are the combined math and verbal scores of the last class to take the old test; you can compare your scores on the math and critical reading sections of the new test to get an idea of how well you fit a school's profile. All data are for the fall 2005 entering freshman class.

The hardest to get into

Most Selective Schools	Acceptance rate	SAT I Verbal 25th–75th percentile	SAT I Math 25th–75th percentile	SAT I Composite 25th–75th percentile	ACT Composite 25th–75th percentile	High school class standing Top 10%	Top 25%	Average high school GPA
National Universities								
Harvard University, (MA)	9%	700–790	700–790	1400–1580	30–34	96%	99%	N/A
Yale University, (CT)	10%	700–790	700–790	1400–1580	31–34	95%	99%	N/A
Princeton University, (NJ)	11%	690–770	690–790	1380–1560	N/A	94%	99%	3.8
Stanford University, (CA)	12%	670–770	690–780	1360–1550	29–33	89%	97%	3.9
Columbia University, (NY)	13%	670–760	670–780	1340–1540	28–33	92%	99%	3.9
Massachusetts Institute of Technology	14%	690–770	740–800	1430–1570	31–34	97%	100%	N/A
Brown University, (RI)	15%	660–760	670–780	1330–1540	27–33	90%	99%	N/A
Dartmouth College, (NH)	17%	670–770	680–780	1350–1550	29–34	87%	98%	N/A
Washington University in St. Louis	19%	670–750	690–770	1360–1520	30–33	93%	100%	N/A
California Institute of Technology	20%	700–780	770–800	1470–1580	N/A	94%	98%	N/A
University of Pennsylvania	21%	660–750	680–770	1340–1520	28–33	94%	99%	3.8
Georgetown University, (DC)	22%	640–750	650–740	1290–1490	27–32	86%	97%	3.8
Duke University, (NC)	24%	670–760	690–780	1360–1540	29–33	88%	97%	N/A
Rice University, (TX)	25%	660–760	670–780	1330–1540	30–34	88%	96%	N/A
Cornell University, (NY)	27%	630–720	660–760	1290–1480	28–32	81%	96%	N/A
University of California–Berkeley	27%	590–710	630–740	1220–1450	N/A	99%	100%	3.9
University of California–Los Angeles	27%	570–690	600–720	1170–1410	24–30	97%	100%	4.0
University of Southern California	27%	620–710	650–730	1270–1440	28–32	85%	95%	3.7
Tufts University, (MA)	28%	660–740	670–740	1330–1480	28–32	80%	96%	N/A
Northwestern University, (IL)	30%	650–740	670–760	1320–1500	29–33	82%	96%	N/A
Boston College	31%	610–700	640–720	1250–1420	N/A	75%	95%	N/A
College of William and Mary, (VA)	31%	630–730	630–710	1260–1440	28–31	79%	97%	4.0
University of Notre Dame, (IN)	32%	630–730	660–740	1290–1470	30–33	86%	97%	N/A
Johns Hopkins University, (MD)	35%	630–740	660–760	1290–1500	28–32	81%	97%	3.7
Vanderbilt University, (TN)	35%	630–720	650–740	1280–1460	28–33	77%	93%	N/A
Emory University, (GA)	37%	640–730	660–740	1300–1470	29–33	90%	98%	3.8
New York University	37%	620–710	620–710	1240–1420	27–31	68%	95%	3.6
University of North Carolina–Chapel Hill	37%	600–690	610–700	1210–1390	25–31	74%	95%	4.0
Brandeis University, (MA)	38%	630–720	640–720	1270–1440	28–33	74%	96%	3.9
University of Virginia	38%	600–710	620–720	1220–1430	25–30	86%	97%	4.0
Carnegie Mellon University, (PA)	39%	610–710	680–760	1290–1470	28–32	71%	94%	3.6
Wake Forest University, (NC)	39%	620–700	640–710	1260–1410	N/A	61%	94%	N/A
University of Chicago	40%	680–770	670–760	1350–1530	29–33	79%	95%	N/A
Lehigh University, (PA)	41%	600–680	640–720	1240–1400	N/A	78%	95%	N/A
University of California–San Diego	44%	550–660	600–710	1150–1370	23–29	99%	100%	3.9
Tulane University, (LA)	45%	N/A	N/A	N/A	N/A	65%	86%	N/A
University of Rochester, (NY)	48%	610–710	640–710	1250–1420	26–30	76%	93%	N/A
University of California–Santa Barbara	53%	530–650	560–670	1090–1320	22–28	96%	100%	3.8
University of Florida	57%	570–670	590–690	1160–1360	25–29	85%	90%	4.0
University of Michigan–Ann Arbor	57%	590–690	630–730	1220–1420	26–31	89%	98%	3.7
University of California–Irvine	60%	540–630	570–680	1110–1310	N/A	98%	100%	3.7
Georgia Institute of Technology	68%	600–700	650–740	1250–1440	26–30	66%	96%	3.7
Liberal Arts Colleges								
Amherst College, (MA)	19%	670–780	680–780	1350–1560	29–33	87%	96%	N/A
Pomona College, (CA)	19%	690–770	690–760	1380–1530	29–34	88%	98%	N/A
Williams College, (MA)	19%	670–770	670–760	1340–1530	29–33	88%	98%	N/A
Claremont McKenna College, (CA)	21%	650–750	660–740	1310–1490	29–33	84%	98%	3.9
Swarthmore College, (PA)	22%	680–770	670–760	1350–1530	N/A	88%	95%	N/A
Middlebury College, (VT)	24%	630–745	650–730	1280–1475	27–32	84%	96%	N/A
Bowdoin College, (ME)	25%	660–740	660–730	1320–1470	N/A	78%	96%	N/A
Haverford College, (PA)	26%	640–740	650–730	1290–1470	N/A	91%	96%	N/A
Barnard College, (NY)	27%	650–740	640–710	1290–1450	27–30	83%	99%	3.9

Schools that are the hardest and easiest to get into

Most Selective Schools, continued

	Acceptance rate	SAT I Verbal 25th–75th percentile	SAT I Math 25th–75th percentile	SAT I Composite 25th–75th percentile	ACT Composite 25th–75th percentile	High school class standing Top 10%	High school class standing Top 25%	Average high school GPA
Colgate University, (NY)	27%	630–710	650–720	1280–1430	29–32	68%	90%	3.6
Davidson College, (NC)	27%	640–730	640–710	1280–1440	28–31	77%	97%	3.9
Wesleyan University, (CT)	28%	650–750	650–740	1300–1490	28–32	71%	93%	N/A
Bates College, (ME)	29%	640–710	640–700	1280–1410	N/A	57%	91%	N/A
Carleton College, (MN)	29%	660–760	660–740	1320–1500	27–32	71%	91%	N/A
Vassar College, (NY)	29%	680–730	660–720	1340–1450	28–32	67%	94%	3.7
Washington and Lee University, (VA)	29%	650–730	650–720	1300–1450	28–30	76%	96%	N/A
Bard College, (NY)	32%	650–750	590–690	1240–1440	N/A	63%	85%	3.5
Bucknell University, (PA)	34%	600–680	630–710	1230–1390	27–30	68%	93%	N/A
Oberlin College, (OH)	34%	650–750	620–710	1270–1460	27–32	68%	93%	3.6
Wellesley College, (MA)	34%	660–750	650–730	1310–1480	28–31	77%	95%	N/A
Hamilton College, (NY)	36%	630–720	640–720	1270–1440	N/A	70%	91%	N/A
Harvey Mudd College, (CA)	36%	670–760	710–800	1380–1560	N/A	91%	100%	N/A
Kenyon College, (OH)	36%	630–720	610–700	1240–1420	28–31	59%	89%	3.8
Colby College, (ME)	38%	640–720	640–710	1280–1430	27–31	67%	92%	N/A
Colorado College	38%	610–710	610–690	1220–1400	27–31	66%	90%	N/A
Macalester College, (MN)	44%	630–740	630–710	1260–1450	28–32	65%	94%	N/A
Grinnell College, (IA)	45%	640–750	640–730	1280–1480	29–33	73%	93%	N/A
Scripps College, (CA)	46%	650–740	620–710	1270–1450	26–31	69%	93%	4.0

More Selective Schools

National Universities

	Acceptance rate	SAT I Verbal 25th–75th percentile	SAT I Math 25th–75th percentile	SAT I Composite 25th–75th percentile	ACT Composite 25th–75th percentile	High school class standing Top 10%	High school class standing Top 25%	Average high school GPA
Pepperdine University, (CA)	28%	550–660	570–670	1120–1330	24–35	43%	76%	3.7
George Washington University, (DC)	37%	600–700	600–690	1200–1390	25–29	63%	88%	N/A
Andrews University, (MI)	40%	470–610	460–590	930–1200	20–25	16%	40%	3.4
SUNY–Binghamton	43%	560–660	600–690	1160–1350	25–29	47%	87%	3.7
University of Miami, (FL)	46%	570–670	590–690	1160–1360	26–30	62%	89%	4.0
Northeastern University, (MA)	47%	560–650	580–670	1140–1320	24–28	36%	73%	N/A
Rutgers–Newark, (NJ)	47%	500–590	520–640	1020–1230	N/A	35%	70%	N/A
Stevens Institute of Technology, (NJ)	47%	560–660	620–710	1180–1370	24–28	49%	81%	3.7
University of Delaware	47%	550–640	560–660	1110–1300	24–29	37%	76%	3.6
University of Maryland–College Park	49%	580–670	600–700	1180–1370	N/A	64%	86%	3.9
Fordham University, (NY)	50%	560–660	560–650	1120–1310	24–28	39%	75%	3.7
American University, (DC)	51%	600–690	580–670	1180–1360	26–30	47%	82%	3.5
SUNY–Stony Brook	51%	520–620	560–660	1080–1280	N/A	34%	69%	3.6
University of Connecticut	51%	540–630	550–650	1090–1280	23–27	37%	80%	N/A
University of Texas–Austin	51%	540–670	570–690	1110–1360	23–29	68%	92%	N/A
University of Texas–Dallas	51%	540–670	580–700	1120–1370	24–29	41%	74%	3.6
University of Missouri–St. Louis	52%	460–640	490–610	950–1250	21–26	21%	50%	N/A
University of Pittsburgh	53%	560–660	570–670	1130–1330	24–29	43%	80%	N/A
University of the Pacific, (CA)	56%	530–630	550–670	1080–1300	23–28	43%	73%	3.5
Boston University	57%	580–680	600–690	1180–1370	25–30	58%	87%	3.5
Clemson University, (SC)	57%	550–650	580–670	1130–1320	24–29	45%	79%	3.8
SUNY College of Environmental Science and Forestry	57%	520–610	520–610	1040–1220	22–26	24%	54%	3.6
University at Buffalo–SUNY	57%	510–600	540–640	1050–1240	23–28	24%	59%	3.1
Southern Methodist University, (TX)	58%	560–660	570–670	1130–1330	24–28	35%	64%	3.5
University of Illinois–Chicago	58%	N/A	N/A	N/A	20–26	25%	57%	N/A
University of South Florida	58%	510–600	520–610	1030–1210	21–26	23%	59%	3.5
University of San Diego	60%	530–630	550–650	1080–1280	23–28	41%	79%	3.7
Rutgers–New Brunswick, (NJ)	61%	540–640	570–680	1110–1320	N/A	36%	78%	N/A
University of California–Davis	61%	500–630	560–670	1060–1300	21–27	95%	100%	3.7
Clark University, (MA)	62%	560–660	540–650	1100–1310	24–28	34%	70%	3.4
Florida State University	62%	530–620	540–630	1070–1250	23–27	26%	61%	3.6
Hofstra University, (NY)	62%	520–620	540–620	1060–1240	21–26	24%	47%	3.2
Kansas State University	62%	N/A	N/A	N/A	21–27	32%	60%	N/A
Pennsylvania State University–University Park	62%	530–630	570–670	1100–1300	N/A	40%	78%	3.5
University of Central Florida	62%	520–610	530–620	1050–1230	22–26	35%	75%	3.5
Illinois Institute of Technology	63%	560–660	620–720	1180–1380	25–30	38%	69%	3.9
Syracuse University, (NY)	65%	540–650	570–670	1110–1320	N/A	44%	80%	3.6
University of Georgia	65%	560–660	570–670	1130–1330	24–28	52%	84%	3.7
Baylor University, (TX)	66%	540–650	550–660	1090–1310	22–27	38%	68%	N/A
North Carolina State University–Raleigh	66%	530–620	560–660	1090–1280	23–27	36%	78%	4.0
Texas Christian University	67%	520–630	540–640	1060–1270	23–28	28%	61%	N/A

	Acceptance rate	SAT I Verbal 25th–75th percentile	SAT I Math 25th–75th percentile	SAT I Composite 25th–75th percentile	ACT Composite 25th–75th percentile	High school class standing Top 10%	Top 25%	Average high school GPA
University of Washington	67%	530–650	570–670	1100–1320	23–28	82%	96%	3.7
Case Western Reserve University, (OH)	68%	600–700	640–740	1240–1440	27–31	63%	91%	N/A
University of South Carolina–Columbia	68%	520–630	540–640	1060–1270	22–27	26%	60%	3.8
University of Wisconsin–Madison	68%	560–670	600–700	1160–1370	26–30	56%	91%	3.7
Miami University–Oxford, (OH)	69%	560–650	580–670	1140–1320	25–29	41%	79%	3.8
Mississippi State University	69%	N/A	N/A	N/A	19–27	26%	55%	3.2
Polytechnic University, (NY)	69%	500–610	570–680	1070–1290	N/A	44%	71%	3.2
Marquette University, (WI)	70%	540–650	540–660	1080–1310	24–29	34%	65%	N/A
Texas A&M University–College Station	70%	530–640	560–670	1090–1310	23–28	50%	79%	N/A
University of Maryland–Baltimore County	71%	540–650	570–670	1110–1320	23–27	30%	59%	3.5
University of Minnesota–Twin Cities	71%	540–660	570–690	1110–1350	23–28	34%	74%	N/A
University of Alabama	72%	500–630	500–630	1000–1260	21–27	32%	51%	3.4
Virginia Tech	72%	540–630	570–660	1110–1290	22–27	37%	79%	3.7
Louisiana State University–Baton Rouge	73%	520–630	540–660	1060–1290	22–27	25%	53%	3.5
Ohio State University–Columbus	74%	530–640	550–660	1080–1300	24–28	39%	76%	N/A
University of Kansas	74%	N/A	N/A	N/A	22–27	28%	55%	3.4
University of Tennessee	74%	520–630	530–640	1050–1270	23–28	34%	63%	3.6
Washington State University	74%	490–600	510–610	1000–1210	20–26	37%	57%	3.5
University of California–Santa Cruz	75%	520–630	530–640	1050–1270	21–27	96%	100%	3.5
University of Illinois–Urbana-Champaign	75%	560–670	620–730	1180–1400	26–31	48%	86%	N/A
University of Missouri–Kansas City	75%	N/A	N/A	N/A	21–27	30%	55%	3.3
University of Nebraska–Lincoln	75%	530–660	540–670	1070–1330	22–28	27%	54%	N/A
University of Tulsa, (OK)	75%	540–700	550–710	1090–1410	23–30	63%	81%	3.7
Michigan State University	76%	490–620	520–650	1010–1270	22–27	26%	64%	3.6
University of California–Riverside	76%	460–570	490–630	950–1200	18–23	94%	100%	3.5
University of Cincinnati	76%	500–620	500–640	1000–1260	21–27	19%	48%	3.3
University of Kentucky	77%	510–630	520–640	1030–1270	22–27	28%	57%	3.6
Brigham Young University–Provo, (UT)	78%	550–660	570–670	1120–1330	25–29	49%	84%	3.7
Rensselaer Polytechnic Institute, (NY)	78%	580–690	640–730	1220–1420	24–28	61%	95%	N/A
St. Louis University	78%	550–650	550–670	1100–1320	24–29	36%	66%	3.7
Yeshiva University, (NY)	78%	550–670	560–680	1110–1350	23–29	40%	55%	3.3
University of Louisville, (KY)	79%	500–620	510–640	1010–1260	21–27	22%	51%	3.0
University of Dayton, (OH)	80%	520–620	540–650	1060–1270	23–28	24%	50%	3.5
University of Vermont	80%	530–630	540–630	1070–1260	22–27	21%	55%	N/A
Loyola University Chicago	81%	540–640	530–640	1070–1280	22–27	30%	63%	3.5
New Mexico Institute of Mining and Technology	81%	560–670	570–680	1130–1350	24–29	41%	71%	3.6
Auburn University, (AL)	82%	500–600	520–620	1020–1220	21–27	32%	56%	3.5
Biola University, (CA)	82%	510–630	500–620	1010–1250	21–27	35%	67%	3.5
Drexel University, (PA)	82%	530–630	550–660	1080–1290	N/A	30%	59%	3.5
University of Denver	82%	530–630	530–640	1060–1270	23–28	36%	69%	3.6
Florida Institute of Technology	83%	510–630	550–660	1060–1290	22–29	32%	66%	3.5
University of Iowa	84%	520–650	540–660	1060–1310	22–27	22%	53%	3.6
Michigan Technological University	85%	530–660	580–700	1110–1360	22–28	25%	56%	3.5
Purdue University–West Lafayette, (IN)	85%	500–610	530–650	1030–1260	23–28	27%	58%	3.4
University of Utah	85%	495–630	500–630	995–1260	21–26	27%	51%	3.5
Worcester Polytechnic Institute, (MA)	85%	560–670	620–710	1180–1380	24–29	46%	77%	3.6
Clarkson University, (NY)	86%	520–620	580–670	1100–1290	22–28	33%	69%	3.5
University of Oklahoma	86%	N/A	N/A	N/A	23–28	37%	72%	3.6
University of Alabama–Huntsville	87%	520–630	510–650	1030–1280	22–28	31%	57%	3.4
University of Arkansas	87%	510–640	520–640	1030–1280	22–28	32%	61%	3.6
Oklahoma State University	88%	500–610	510–620	1010–1230	22–27	27%	55%	3.5
University of Arizona	88%	500–620	500–630	1000–1250	21–26	34%	61%	3.4
University of Colorado–Boulder	88%	530–630	550–650	1080–1280	23–28	22%	54%	3.5
University of Missouri–Columbia	89%	540–660	540–650	1080–1310	23–28	27%	57%	N/A
Iowa State University	90%	530–660	550–690	1080–1350	22–27	24%	52%	3.5
University of St. Thomas, (MN)	91%	540–658	530–650	1070–1308	22–27	23%	56%	3.6
University of Missouri–Rolla	92%	550–660	600–690	1150–1350	24–30	38%	69%	3.6
Utah State University	94%	470–620	490–620	960–1240	21–27	25%	51%	3.5

Liberal Arts Colleges

Connecticut College	35%	630–700	620–690	1250–1390	26–29	54%	83%	N/A
Lafayette College, (PA)	37%	580–670	600–700	1180–1370	25–30	62%	88%	3.7
Denison University, (OH)	39%	570–660	580–670	1150–1330	25–29	54%	80%	3.6
Pitzer College, (CA)	39%	570–680	560–660	1130–1340	N/A	45%	76%	3.6
Spelman College, (GA)	39%	510–600	500–580	1010–1180	21–25	33%	71%	3.6
Trinity College, (CT)	39%	610–700	610–700	1220–1400	25–29	53%	89%	N/A
Washington and Jefferson College, (PA)	39%	520–610	530–620	1050–1230	23–27	31%	65%	3.3
Occidental College, (CA)	41%	600–690	610–690	1210–1380	27–31	60%	86%	N/A
Gettysburg College, (PA)	43%	600–680	610–670	1210–1350	27–30	66%	89%	N/A

Schools that are the hardest and easiest to get into

More Selective Schools, continued	Acceptance rate	SAT I Verbal 25th–75th percentile	SAT I Math 25th–75th percentile	SAT I Composite 25th–75th percentile	ACT Composite 25th–75th percentile	High school class standing Top 10%	High school class standing Top 25%	Average high school GPA
Muhlenberg College, (PA)	43%	560–660	570–670	1130–1330	26–29	42%	82%	3.4
Skidmore College, (NY)	44%	580–670	580–660	1160–1330	25–28	46%	78%	3.3
Wheaton College, (MA)	44%	570–670	570–650	1140–1320	26–30	56%	82%	3.5
Franklin and Marshall College, (PA)	45%	580–680	600–690	1180–1370	N/A	54%	83%	N/A
Reed College, (OR)	45%	660–760	620–710	1280–1470	29–32	57%	86%	3.9
Sarah Lawrence College, (NY)	45%	N/A	N/A	N/A	N/A	33%	72%	3.6
Bryn Mawr College, (PA)	46%	620–720	590–680	1210–1400	27–30	62%	87%	N/A
Union College, (NY)	47%	570–660	590–690	1160–1350	25–29	62%	87%	3.5
University of Richmond, (VA)	47%	610–690	630–700	1240–1390	26–30	58%	88%	3.5
College of the Holy Cross, (MA)	48%	620–640	580–680	1200–1320	N/A	66%	93%	N/A
Smith College, (MA)	48%	580–710	570–670	1150–1380	25–31	61%	90%	3.8
Dickinson College, (PA)	49%	600–700	600–680	1200–1380	26–30	52%	81%	N/A
Whitman College, (WA)	49%	620–750	620–700	1240–1450	27–31	60%	91%	3.7
Rhodes College, (TN)	50%	580–680	580–670	1160–1350	25–30	50%	79%	3.6
Wabash College, (IN)	51%	530–650	550–660	1080–1310	23–28	29%	69%	3.6
Wheaton College, (IL)	51%	630–730	620–710	1250–1440	27–31	54%	81%	3.7
Mount Holyoke College, (MA)	52%	620–720	610–690	1230–1410	27–30	51%	80%	3.6
Agnes Scott College, (GA)	53%	570–685	540–650	1110–1335	24–29	48%	75%	3.7
Furman University, (SC)	53%	600–700	600–690	1200–1390	25–30	64%	88%	3.8
Wesleyan College, (GA)	55%	500–630	490–600	990–1230	21–26	34%	66%	3.5
Illinois Wesleyan University	57%	600–690	590–690	1190–1380	26–31	47%	81%	N/A
Marlboro College, (VT)	58%	590–690	510–650	1100–1340	24–32	33%	62%	3.2
Lewis and Clark College, (OR)	59%	610–700	590–680	1200–1380	26–30	42%	78%	3.7
St. Lawrence University, (NY)	59%	520–620	530–630	1050–1250	N/A	38%	71%	3.4
Washington College, (MD)	59%	530–630	520–620	1050–1250	22–27	36%	68%	3.4
New College of Florida	60%	630–720	580–670	1210–1390	25–29	44%	80%	4.0
Allegheny College, (PA)	62%	570–660	570–660	1140–1320	23–28	45%	77%	3.8
Bennington College, (VT)	62%	610–700	540–640	1150–1340	25–28	30%	74%	3.5
Chatham College, (PA)	62%	N/A	N/A	N/A	N/A	23%	54%	N/A
Birmingham-Southern College, (AL)	63%	530–650	530–640	1060–1290	23–29	30%	59%	3.3
Centre College, (KY)	63%	580–690	600–680	1180–1370	25–29	56%	85%	N/A
Lake Forest College, (IL)	63%	540–640	530–650	1070–1290	23–28	32%	54%	3.4
University of North Carolina–Asheville	63%	540–660	540–640	1080–1300	22–27	25%	68%	3.8
Beloit College, (WI)	64%	580–700	560–660	1140–1360	25–29	37%	64%	3.5
Hampshire College, (MA)	64%	600–710	560–660	1160–1370	24–30	28%	63%	3.4
Huntingdon College, (AL)	64%	460–570	430–550	890–1120	20–25	26%	55%	3.3
Stephens College, (MO)	64%	540–610	480–580	1020–1190	21–27	19%	59%	3.5
William Jewell College, (MO)	64%	490–630	480–650	970–1280	23–28	30%	60%	3.7
Hobart and William Smith Colleges, (NY)	65%	540–640	550–640	1090–1280	23–28	33%	67%	3.2
Moravian College, (PA)	65%	520–620	520–630	1040–1250	19–21	31%	64%	N/A
Wells College, (NY)	65%	520–630	480–580	1000–1210	20–26	25%	64%	3.5
College of the Atlantic, (ME)	66%	560–670	530–630	1090–1300	23–28	36%	76%	3.6
Cornell College, (IA)	66%	560–680	550–680	1110–1360	23–29	24%	56%	3.5
DePauw University, (IN)	66%	560–660	570–670	1130–1330	24–29	55%	87%	3.7
Wofford College, (SC)	66%	570–660	580–680	1150–1340	22–27	58%	83%	3.5
Austin College, (TX)	67%	580–680	580–670	1160–1350	23–28	44%	75%	N/A
Goucher College, (MD)	67%	560–670	540–640	1100–1310	23–27	26%	63%	3.2
Sewanee–University of the South, (TN)	67%	588–670	570–660	1158–1330	25–29	42%	78%	3.6
Southwestern University, (TX)	67%	560–670	570–660	1130–1330	24–29	49%	82%	N/A
Juniata College, (PA)	68%	530–630	550–640	1080–1270	N/A	43%	79%	3.8
Kalamazoo College, (MI)	68%	610–710	600–690	1210–1400	26–31	43%	77%	3.6
Lawrence University, (WI)	68%	590–700	600–690	1190–1390	25–30	41%	72%	3.5
St. Mary's College of Maryland	68%	570–690	560–650	1130–1340	N/A	34%	73%	3.4
Westmont College, (CA)	68%	570–670	560–660	1130–1330	24–29	44%	75%	3.7
Earlham College, (IN)	70%	570–700	530–650	1100–1350	23–29	30%	61%	3.5
Erskine College, (SC)	70%	480–620	510–610	990–1230	21–27	31%	58%	3.8
Hanover College, (IN)	70%	540–650	550–650	1090–1300	23–29	44%	80%	N/A
University of Puget Sound, (WA)	71%	580–690	560–660	1140–1350	24–29	37%	68%	3.5
Coe College, (IA)	72%	540–660	540–650	1080–1310	23–28	30%	67%	3.7
Lyon College, (AR)	72%	500–710	530–650	1030–1360	23–28	29%	69%	3.5
St. Olaf College, (MN)	73%	590–700	580–690	1170–1390	25–30	49%	76%	3.6
Willamette University, (OR)	74%	570–670	570–650	1140–1320	25–29	40%	73%	3.7
College of Wooster, (OH)	75%	560–680	550–660	1110–1340	23–28	32%	66%	3.6
Luther College, (IA)	75%	550–670	550–670	1100–1340	22–28	32%	61%	3.6
Ohio Wesleyan University	75%	550–660	570–660	1120–1320	24–29	30%	52%	3.3
Ursinus College, (PA)	75%	550–660	560–665	1110–1325	22–28	44%	73%	3.5
Christendom College, (VA)	76%	600–700	530–630	1130–1330	N/A	15%	75%	3.6
Goshen College, (IN)	76%	510–660	510–650	1020–1310	23–28	30%	63%	3.6

	Acceptance rate	SAT I Verbal 25th–75th percentile	SAT I Math 25th–75th percentile	SAT I Composite 25th–75th percentile	ACT Composite 25th–75th percentile	High school class standing Top 10%	Top 25%	Average high school GPA
Knox College, (IL)	76%	580–700	540–660	1120–1360	25–30	33%	61%	N/A
Drew University, (NJ)	77%	550–660	540–650	1090–1310	24–27	36%	66%	3.3
Hope College, (MI)	77%	550–680	560–680	1110–1360	23–29	34%	61%	3.8
Mills College, (CA)	77%	520–660	490–600	1010–1260	21–28	37%	74%	3.6
West Virginia Wesleyan College	77%	460–580	460–570	920–1150	20–25	22%	53%	3.3
Gustavus Adolphus College, (MN)	79%	570–670	560–680	1130–1350	23–28	41%	71%	3.7
Hillsdale College, (MI)	79%	580–720	540–670	1120–1390	24–29	40%	75%	3.7
Sweet Briar College, (VA)	79%	530–640	500–590	1030–1230	22–27	25%	64%	3.5
Westminster College, (MO)	79%	530–620	490–630	1020–1250	22–27	18%	46%	3.5
Alma College, (MI)	81%	520–670	510–650	1030–1320	21–27	32%	62%	3.5
Ripon College, (WI)	81%	480–650	500–620	980–1270	21–27	23%	50%	3.4
Susquehanna University, (PA)	81%	520–610	530–620	1050–1230	N/A	29%	60%	N/A
Thomas Aquinas College, (CA)	81%	630–740	570–650	1200–1390	24–29	75%	75%	3.7
University of Dallas	81%	580–700	540–650	1120–1350	23–29	34%	66%	3.6
Albion College, (MI)	82%	520–645	540–670	1060–1315	22–27	30%	64%	3.6
Millsaps College, (MS)	82%	538–683	540–650	1078–1333	23–30	38%	63%	3.6
University of Minnesota–Morris	82%	570–680	565–680	1135–1360	22–27	31%	60%	N/A
Concordia College–Moorhead, (MN)	83%	500–620	490–620	990–1240	21–27	30%	59%	N/A
Hendrix College, (AR)	83%	590–700	560–670	1150–1370	25–30	37%	73%	3.6
Albertson College, (ID)	84%	520–643	530–640	1050–1283	23–28	34%	70%	3.6
Augustana College, (IL)	84%	N/A	N/A	N/A	24–29	29%	63%	3.5
Gordon College, (MA)	84%	550–670	540–650	1090–1320	23–29	24%	50%	3.6
Nebraska Wesleyan University	84%	N/A	N/A	N/A	21–26	22%	57%	N/A
Transylvania University, (KY)	84%	500–580	460–590	960–1170	23–28	42%	77%	3.6
Wittenberg University, (OH)	85%	520–630	500–620	1020–1250	21–27	27%	56%	3.5
College of St. Benedict, (MN)	86%	520–630	520–640	1040–1270	23–27	44%	79%	3.7
Randolph-Macon Woman's College, (VA)	87%	540–670	510–630	1050–1300	23–29	36%	70%	3.4
St. John's University, (MN)	87%	530–660	540–650	1070–1310	23–28	22%	51%	3.5
Principia College, (IL)	89%	510–650	500–620	1010–1270	21–30	38%	63%	3.4
Houghton College, (NY)	90%	530–660	520–630	1050–1290	24–28	32%	68%	3.5
Georgetown College, (KY)	95%	480–590	470–590	950–1180	21–26	31%	58%	3.5

Universities—Master's (North)

	Acceptance rate	SAT I Verbal 25th–75th percentile	SAT I Math 25th–75th percentile	SAT I Composite 25th–75th percentile	ACT Composite 25th–75th percentile	High school class standing Top 10%	Top 25%	Average high school GPA
CUNY–Baruch College	33%	460–570	530–630	990–1200	N/A	28%	59%	3.0
Bentley College, (MA)	43%	550–630	600–670	1150–1300	24–27	39%	82%	N/A
College of New Jersey	45%	570–670	600–700	1170–1370	N/A	68%	94%	N/A
Emerson College, (MA)	45%	590–670	560–650	1150–1320	25–29	36%	83%	3.6
St. Joseph's University, (PA)	47%	520–620	530–630	1050–1250	22–24	24%	78%	3.3
SUNY College of Arts and Sciences–Geneseo	49%	600–670	600–670	1200–1340	26–29	51%	89%	3.8
Marist College, (NY)	50%	540–620	550–640	1090–1260	24–28	29%	70%	3.4
Hood College, (MD)	51%	510–600	500–600	1010–1200	20–25	33%	64%	3.3
Quinnipiac University, (CT)	51%	525–605	545–620	1070–1225	24–28	30%	60%	3.5
Villanova University, (PA)	51%	580–660	600–690	1180–1350	27–30	47%	83%	3.7
Rutgers–Camden, (NJ)	53%	510–600	510–610	1020–1210	N/A	27%	64%	N/A
Providence College, (RI)	54%	550–630	560–650	1110–1280	23–27	38%	79%	3.4
Salisbury University, (MD)	57%	520–600	530–610	1050–1210	N/A	18%	56%	3.5
Wagner College, (NY)	61%	530–630	530–640	1060–1270	23–27	17%	64%	3.5
Loyola College in Maryland	64%	560–650	570–660	1130–1310	24–28	35%	74%	3.5
Rochester Institute of Technology, (NY)	69%	540–640	570–670	1110–1310	24–28	28%	59%	3.7
St. Michael's College, (VT)	72%	520–620	520–610	1040–1230	N/A	26%	58%	3.5
Touro College, (NY)	72%	520–640	520–630	1040–1270	22–25	70%	90%	3.2
Fairfield University, (CT)	74%	550–630	560–640	1110–1270	23–27	31%	69%	3.4
Ithaca College, (NY)	76%	540–640	540–640	1080–1280	N/A	29%	64%	N/A
Lebanon Valley College, (PA)	77%	500–610	510–620	1010–1230	N/A	36%	70%	N/A
Arcadia University, (PA)	79%	520–620	500–610	1020–1230	21–26	31%	63%	N/A
Nazareth College of Rochester, (NY)	79%	520–630	530–620	1050–1250	22–28	29%	66%	3.4

Universities—Master's (South)

	Acceptance rate	SAT I Verbal 25th–75th percentile	SAT I Math 25th–75th percentile	SAT I Composite 25th–75th percentile	ACT Composite 25th–75th percentile	High school class standing Top 10%	Top 25%	Average high school GPA
Elon University, (NC)	41%	560–640	570–650	1130–1290	24–28	32%	67%	3.7
Rollins College, (FL)	53%	540–650	540–640	1080–1290	22–27	34%	67%	3.4
University of Central Arkansas	53%	430–575	470–595	900–1170	20–27	21%	44%	3.3
Palm Beach Atlantic University, (FL)	56%	450–540	460–570	910–1110	19–24	21%	47%	3.5
Mississippi College	57%	520–620	500–620	1020–1240	20–26	27%	56%	3.3
Mississippi University for Women	59%	420–500	430–620	850–1120	18–25	34%	61%	3.3
Campbell University, (NC)	61%	510–620	495–630	1005–1250	N/A	37%	78%	3.6
University of North Carolina–Wilmington	61%	520–600	540–610	1060–1210	21–25	21%	60%	3.6
Harding University, (AR)	62%	500–630	490–630	990–1260	20–26	27%	52%	3.5
Centenary College of Louisiana	64%	510–650	500–630	1010–1280	22–27	40%	70%	3.3

Schools that are the hardest and easiest to get into

More Selective Schools, continued	Acceptance rate	SAT I Verbal 25th–75th percentile	SAT I Math 25th–75th percentile	SAT I Composite 25th–75th percentile	ACT Composite 25th–75th percentile	High school class standing Top 10%	High school class standing Top 25%	Average high school GPA
Murray State University, (KY)	64%	N/A	N/A	N/A	21–26	28%	65%	3.6
University of Mary Washington, (VA)	64%	580–670	560–640	1140–1310	25–29	38%	82%	3.7
College of Charleston, (SC)	66%	570–650	570–640	1140–1290	22–25	25%	58%	3.6
James Madison University, (VA)	68%	530–620	540–630	1070–1250	21–26	28%	74%	3.7
Loyola University New Orleans	68%	N/A	N/A	N/A	N/A	28%	60%	N/A
Stetson University, (FL)	69%	520–620	520–615	1040–1235	22–27	27%	57%	3.8
Bellarmine University, (KY)	70%	480–590	490–600	970–1190	21–26	22%	50%	3.5
Belmont University, (TN)	72%	530–640	540–640	1070–1280	23–28	36%	67%	3.5
Christian Brothers University, (TN)	72%	490–630	480–620	970–1250	21–27	35%	60%	3.4
Tennessee Technological University	75%	490–600	500–630	990–1230	20–26	24%	53%	3.2
Lipscomb University, (TN)	76%	510–630	490–630	1000–1260	21–27	25%	51%	3.5
Carson-Newman College, (TN)	78%	N/A	N/A	N/A	19–26	27%	47%	3.3
Mercer University, (GA)	80%	530–640	550–640	1080–1280	22–27	48%	74%	3.6
Spring Hill College, (AL)	80%	480–600	460–610	940–1210	21–26	28%	50%	3.5
Union University, (TN)	86%	550–650	520–620	1070–1270	22–27	37%	66%	3.6
Samford University, (AL)	88%	530–630	530–630	1060–1260	23–28	36%	66%	3.6
Freed-Hardeman University, (TN)	99%	510–600	490–610	1000–1210	20–26	30%	57%	3.5

Universities–Master's (Midwest)

	Acceptance rate	SAT I Verbal 25th–75th percentile	SAT I Math 25th–75th percentile	SAT I Composite 25th–75th percentile	ACT Composite 25th–75th percentile	Top 10%	Top 25%	Average high school GPA
Webster University, (MO)	55%	525–620	495–615	1020–1235	21–27	23%	48%	3.4
Olivet Nazarene University, (IL)	59%	500–620	480–580	980–1200	21–27	25%	53%	3.5
Concordia University–River Forest, (IL)	62%	N/A	N/A	N/A	19–25	25%	50%	3.2
Baker University, (KS)	63%	460–570	443–588	903–1158	21–26	25%	52%	3.5
Xavier University, (OH)	66%	540–640	540–640	1080–1280	23–28	30%	62%	3.6
University of Wisconsin–La Crosse	67%	500–610	520–660	1020–1270	23–27	30%	80%	N/A
Grand Valley State University, (MI)	68%	N/A	N/A	N/A	21–26	22%	55%	N/A
University of Detroit Mercy	69%	N/A	N/A	N/A	20–26	24%	55%	3.3
North Central College, (IL)	70%	510–630	510–650	1020–1280	22–27	20%	50%	3.5
University of Wisconsin–Eau Claire	70%	520–630	540–640	1060–1270	22–26	23%	60%	N/A
University of Michigan–Dearborn	71%	460–598	483–628	943–1226	21–26	27%	58%	3.5
Butler University, (IN)	72%	540–630	540–650	1080–1280	24–29	47%	78%	3.6
Maryville University of St. Louis, (MO)	73%	N/A	N/A	N/A	21–27	24%	54%	3.5
Rockhurst University, (MO)	74%	530–640	530–640	1060–1280	22–28	31%	65%	3.6
Capital University, (OH)	78%	490–600	480–600	970–1200	21–26	29%	55%	N/A
College of St. Catherine, (MN)	78%	518–660	495–650	1013–1310	22–27	34%	75%	3.6
Drury University, (MO)	78%	530–640	523–650	1053–1290	23–28	38%	67%	3.7
Hamline University, (MN)	78%	560–670	530–643	1090–1313	21–27	27%	51%	3.5
Baldwin-Wallace College, (OH)	79%	495–610	500–620	995–1230	21–26	28%	57%	3.5
Dominican University, (IL)	81%	470–580	480–570	950–1150	20–25	24%	52%	3.5
Franciscan University of Steubenville, (OH)	81%	540–660	520–630	1060–1290	22–27	27%	59%	3.6
Drake University, (IA)	82%	520–660	510–650	1030–1310	24–29	37%	73%	3.7
Truman State University, (MO)	82%	570–670	560–660	1130–1330	25–30	48%	80%	3.8
Valparaiso University, (IN)	83%	520–630	520–640	1040–1270	23–28	34%	60%	3.4
John Carroll University, (OH)	85%	530–630	530–630	1060–1260	21–26	28%	58%	3.5
Bethel University, (MN)	87%	520–670	520–630	1040–1300	22–28	32%	63%	N/A
College of St. Scholastica, (MN)	87%	490–600	520–620	1010–1220	21–26	25%	54%	3.5
Creighton University, (NE)	87%	530–660	540–660	1070–1320	23–29	40%	73%	3.7
Bradley University, (IL)	89%	510–650	540–650	1050–1300	23–27	30%	61%	3.6
University of Evansville, (IN)	91%	520–630	520–640	1040–1270	22–28	35%	65%	3.6

Universities–Master's (West)

	Acceptance rate	SAT I Verbal 25th–75th percentile	SAT I Math 25th–75th percentile	SAT I Composite 25th–75th percentile	ACT Composite 25th–75th percentile	Top 10%	Top 25%	Average high school GPA
Cal Poly–San Luis Obispo	45%	540–630	570–670	1110–1300	23–28	37%	76%	3.7
Chapman University, (CA)	53%	543–656	551–662	1094–1318	23–29	51%	92%	3.7
Loyola Marymount University, (CA)	56%	530–630	540–640	1070–1270	24–28	30%	64%	3.6
Santa Clara University, (CA)	61%	550–650	570–670	1120–1320	24–28	40%	72%	3.5
Trinity University, (TX)	63%	600–690	610–690	1210–1380	27–30	47%	81%	3.5
Point Loma Nazarene University, (CA)	65%	520–630	520–640	1040–1270	21–28	38%	75%	3.7
University of Redlands, (CA)	66%	530–620	540–630	1070–1250	21–26	32%	69%	3.6
Whitworth College, (WA)	67%	540–650	540–650	1080–1300	24–29	40%	70%	3.7
Seattle University	68%	520–630	530–620	1050–1250	23–27	32%	60%	3.6
Azusa Pacific University, (CA)	69%	510–610	500–610	1010–1220	21–27	41%	74%	3.7
Gonzaga University, (WA)	73%	540–640	550–650	1090–1290	24–29	40%	71%	3.6
LeTourneau University, (TX)	76%	500–650	520–650	1020–1300	22–28	32%	60%	3.5
Pacific Lutheran University, (WA)	76%	500–620	500–620	1000–1240	21–27	33%	65%	3.6
Oklahoma City University	81%	520–630	500–610	1020–1240	22–27	30%	65%	3.7
Regis University, (CO)	81%	470–600	470–590	940–1190	20–26	24%	55%	3.4
University of Portland, (OR)	81%	540–640	540–640	1080–1280	N/A	44%	76%	3.6
George Fox University, (OR)	83%	490–620	500–620	990–1240	20–26	37%	65%	3.6

	Acceptance rate	SAT I Verbal 25th–75th percentile	SAT I Math 25th–75th percentile	SAT I Composite 25th–75th percentile	ACT Composite 25th–75th percentile	High school class standing Top 10%	High school class standing Top 25%	Average high school GPA
Seattle Pacific University	85%	530–650	520–630	1050–1280	22–28	39%	67%	3.7
Westminster College, (UT)	89%	493–630	470–613	963–1243	21–26	30%	57%	3.5
University of St. Thomas, (TX)	92%	530–640	520–640	1050–1280	22–28	29%	58%	3.0

Comprehensive Colleges–Bachelor's (North)

Ramapo College of New Jersey	41%	540–620	550–640	1090–1260	N/A	31%	80%	3.5
Grove City College, (PA)	45%	579–698	582–698	1161–1396	25–30	54%	83%	3.9
Stonehill College, (MA)	57%	560–640	570–640	1130–1280	23–27	48%	87%	3.6
Elizabethtown College, (PA)	62%	500–610	500–620	1000–1230	19–24	29%	58%	3.6
Elmira College, (NY)	64%	520–630	510–620	1030–1250	23–27	28%	70%	3.5
Messiah College, (PA)	75%	550–660	540–650	1090–1310	23–28	39%	71%	3.8

Comprehensive Colleges–Bachelor's (South)

Flagler College, (FL)	25%	530–620	510–600	1040–1220	22–26	16%	51%	3.4
Berea College, (KY)	27%	510–638	503–618	1013–1256	21–25	30%	66%	3.5
Ouachita Baptist University, (AR)	58%	490–600	470–610	960–1210	20–27	33%	60%	3.5
John Brown University, (AR)	62%	540–660	510–640	1050–1300	22–28	29%	59%	3.6
Lambuth University, (TN)	65%	480–600	500–590	980–1190	21–26	29%	52%	3.4
Asbury College, (KY)	74%	530–660	500–630	1030–1290	21–28	35%	64%	3.6
Maryville College, (TN)	79%	490–620	460–600	950–1220	21–28	33%	63%	N/A
Berry College, (GA)	83%	520–630	520–620	1040–1250	23–28	28%	59%	3.5
Bryan College, (TN)	95%	545–680	505–640	1050–1320	22–27	44%	66%	3.6

Comprehensive Colleges–Bachelor's (Midwest)

Southwestern College, (KS)	34%	440–550	410–590	850–1140	19–26	21%	45%	3.4
McKendree College, (IL)	62%	410–520	470–570	880–1090	21–26	22%	52%	3.3
Illinois College	64%	540–650	560–640	1100–1290	21–27	23%	53%	3.4
Elmhurst College, (IL)	75%	500–640	500–620	1000–1260	20–27	23%	49%	3.4
Northland College, (WI)	75%	510–590	510–620	1020–1210	22–26	26%	50%	3.5
Otterbein College, (OH)	76%	500–620	510–620	1010–1240	21–26	26%	54%	3.4
Augustana College, (SD)	80%	520–700	510–710	1030–1410	22–27	26%	58%	3.6
Ohio Northern University	80%	530–630	530–650	1060–1280	23–28	38%	66%	3.6
St. Mary's College, (IN)	81%	530–630	520–610	1050–1240	23–27	32%	66%	3.7
Taylor University, (IN)	82%	540–660	550–660	1090–1320	23–29	37%	68%	3.8
Wisconsin Lutheran College	82%	N/A	N/A	N/A	22–27	23%	50%	3.5
Cedarville University, (OH)	83%	540–650	520–640	1060–1290	22–28	34%	63%	3.6
Central College, (IA)	84%	460–650	470–610	930–1260	21–26	25%	53%	3.5
St. Norbert College, (WI)	86%	N/A	N/A	N/A	21–27	27%	56%	3.2
Simpson College, (IA)	87%	N/A	N/A	N/A	22–27	30%	61%	N/A
Wartburg College, (IA)	88%	500–600	500–650	1000–1250	21–26	31%	62%	3.6
Northwestern College, (IA)	93%	N/A	N/A	N/A	21–27	26%	58%	3.5
Calvin College, (MI)	98%	540–663	550–670	1090–1333	23–28	26%	54%	3.6
Northwestern College, (MN)	98%	500–660	510–620	1010–1280	21–26	26%	51%	3.5

Comprehensive Colleges–Bachelor's (West)

Brigham Young University–Hawaii	11%	505–630	555–630	1060–1260	20–26	25%	61%	3.3
Master's College and Seminary, (CA)	29%	520–620	490–630	1010–1250	19–27	33%	53%	3.6
Linfield College, (OR)	73%	510–620	520–640	1030–1260	21–27	34%	67%	3.6
Oklahoma Baptist University	99%	520–610	500–600	1020–1210	21–27	36%	60%	3.6
Oklahoma Christian University	100%	580–620	470–620	1050–1240	20–27	23%	46%	3.3

Schools that are the hardest and easiest to get into

The easiest to get into

	Acceptance rate	SAT I Verbal 25th–75th percentile	SAT I Math 25th–75th percentile	SAT I Composite 25th–75th percentile	ACT Composite 25th–75th percentile	High school class standing Top 10%	High school class standing Top 25%	Average high school GPA
Liberal Arts Colleges								
Bennett College, (NC)	57%	360–460	360–430	720–890	13–18	5%	14%	2.5
Virginia Union University	71%	N/A	N/A	N/A	N/A	4%	8%	2.4
Pine Manor College, (MA)	73%	370–490	350–460	720–950	16–18	8%	23%	2.5
Universities–Master's (North)								
Cheyney University of Pennsylvania	56%	N/A	N/A	N/A	N/A	N/A	N/A	N/A
Delaware State University	64%	360–450	360–450	720–900	14–17	5%	12%	2.6
University of Maryland–Eastern Shore	66%	370–460	360–460	730–920	14–18	N/A	N/A	N/A
Gallaudet University, (DC)	76%	320–550	355–520	675–1070	14–18	N/A	N/A	N/A
Trinity University, (DC)	86%	N/A	N/A	N/A	N/A	N/A	N/A	N/A
Universities–Master's (South)								
North Carolina Central University	77%	370–480	380–480	750–960	15–19	5%	16%	2.7
Fayetteville State University, (NC)	80%	370–460	370–470	740–930	15–17	2%	13%	2.7
Virginia State University	83%	380–460	370–460	750–920	16–19	4%	15%	2.7
Universities–Master's (Midwest)								
Lincoln University, (MO)	94%	N/A	N/A	N/A	N/A	5%	17%	2.6
Comprehensive Colleges–Bachelor's (North)								
CUNY–New York City College of Technology	88%	350–450	370–480	720–930	N/A	6%	19%	1.9
CUNY–Medgar Evers College	96%	340–440	340–430	680–870	N/A	N/A	24%	1.7
Comprehensive Colleges–Bachelor's (South)								
Shaw University, (NC)	65%	330–430	320–430	650–860	12–16	1%	8%	2.4
St. Paul's College, (VA)	72%	N/A	N/A	N/A	N/A	1%	1%	N/A
Benedict College, (SC)	73%	N/A	N/A	N/A	N/A	3%	8%	N/A
Bethune-Cookman College, (FL)	74%	360–460	360–460	720–920	14–16	6%	22%	2.8
Elizabeth City State University, (NC)	80%	370–460	380–460	750–920	14–18	6%	20%	2.8
Philander Smith College, (AR)	80%	N/A	N/A	N/A	14–17	10%	24%	2.6
Comprehensive Colleges–Bachelor's (West)								
Wiley College, (TX)	48%	340–470	340–430	680–900	13–17	6%	16%	2.6
Huston-Tillotson University, (TX)	56%	360–440	340–468	700–908	14–17	N/A	N/A	N/A
Jarvis Christian College, (TX)	76%	N/A	N/A	N/A	N/A	7%	14%	2.6

Where applying early may help you most—or not

Applying early can sometimes boost your chances of getting in. One study of 14 elite schools by Harvard researchers found that applying early decision conferred an advantage equivalent to an extra 100 points on the SAT. Acceptance rates and the design of early plans can change from year to year; in this table, colleges are ranked by the size of the difference between their early and non-early acceptance rates for the class that entered in the fall 2005. The difference in acceptance rates is figured using unrounded data.

Most Selective Schools

	Early-decision and/or early-action acceptance rate	Non-early acceptance rate	Difference in acceptance rate	Freshmen enrolled through early plans	Type of plan (early-decision and/or early-action)
National Universities					
Tulane University, (LA)	63%	31%	33%	N/A	EA, ED
Columbia University, (NY)	39%	10%	28%	N/A	ED
Boston College	52%	25%	27%	32%	EA
Princeton University, (NJ)	29%	8%	21%	N/A	ED
Carnegie Mellon University, (PA)	58%	38%	20%	18%	ED
Lehigh University, (PA)	60%	40%	20%	39%	ED
Northwestern University, (IL)	49%	28%	20%	26%	ED
University of North Carolina–Chapel Hill	46%	27%	19%	73%	EA
California Institute of Technology	35%	17%	18%	32%	EA
Emory University, (GA)	52%	35%	17%	N/A	ED
Cornell University, (NY)	42%	25%	16%	N/A	ED
University of Pennsylvania	34%	18%	16%	46%	ED
Wake Forest University, (NC)	53%	37%	16%	32%	ED
Brown University, (RI)	28%	13%	15%	39%	ED
Harvard University, (MA)	21%	7%	15%	50%	EA
Brandeis University, (MA)	52%	37%	14%	22%	ED
Vanderbilt University, (TN)	48%	34%	14%	N/A	ED
New York University	47%	36%	11%	33%	ED
Yale University, (CT)	18%	8%	10%	47%	EA
Duke University, (NC)	32%	23%	9%	27%	ED
Tufts University, (MA)	36%	28%	8%	33%	ED
Rice University, (TX)	29%	22%	7%	57%	EA, ED
University of Virginia	42%	37%	6%	31%	ED
Georgetown University, (DC)	25%	20%	5%	37%	EA
Massachusetts Institute of Technology	14%	15%	-1%	29%	EA
University of Chicago	40%	40%	-1%	35%	EA
University of Rochester, (NY)	47%	48%	-1%	23%	ED
University of Florida	50%	59%	-9%	31%	ED
Liberal Arts Colleges					
Kenyon College, (OH)	64%	34%	30%	38%	ED
Swarthmore College, (PA)	50%	20%	30%	40%	ED
Grinnell College, (IA)	70%	44%	27%	24%	ED
Bucknell University, (PA)	58%	32%	26%	41%	ED
Davidson College, (NC)	49%	24%	25%	46%	ED
Haverford College, (PA)	50%	25%	25%	33%	ED
Carleton College, (MN)	51%	27%	24%	38%	ED
Colgate University, (NY)	49%	25%	24%	42%	ED
Williams College, (MA)	39%	17%	23%	39%	ED
Hamilton College, (NY)	55%	33%	22%	49%	ED
Colorado College	52%	33%	19%	45%	EA
Colby College, (ME)	52%	36%	16%	42%	ED
Barnard College, (NY)	41%	26%	15%	30%	ED
Harvey Mudd College, (CA)	50%	35%	15%	20%	ED
Vassar College, (NY)	42%	27%	15%	38%	ED
Wellesley College, (MA)	47%	33%	15%	19%	ED
Middlebury College, (VT)	35%	22%	13%	47%	ED
Pomona College, (CA)	28%	18%	10%	30%	ED
Washington and Lee University, (VA)	35%	28%	7%	40%	ED
Bowdoin College, (ME)	29%	24%	6%	37%	ED
Claremont McKenna College, (CA)	25%	21%	5%	28%	ED
Scripps College, (CA)	51%	46%	5%	19%	ED
Macalester College, (MN)	47%	44%	3%	22%	ED

Where applying early may help you most—or not

More Selective Schools

	Early-decision and/or early-action acceptance rate	Non-early acceptance rate	Difference in acceptance rate	Freshmen enrolled through early plans	Type of plan (early-decision and/or early-action)
National Universities					
SUNY College of Environmental Science and Forestry	95%	52%	43%	32%	EA
University of Georgia	80%	52%	28%	62%	EA
SUNY–Stony Brook	74%	47%	27%	23%	EA
Stevens Institute of Technology, (NJ)	70%	44%	26%	32%	ED
University of Connecticut	65%	40%	24%	55%	EA
George Washington University, (DC)	58%	36%	22%	38%	ED
Clark University, (MA)	82%	61%	21%	13%	ED
University of Maryland–College Park	53%	32%	21%	91%	EA
Case Western Reserve University, (OH)	82%	64%	18%	39%	EA
SUNY–Binghamton	56%	40%	17%	32%	EA
University of Denver	91%	78%	13%	40%	EA
Worcester Polytechnic Institute, (MA)	94%	82%	12%	36%	EA
Syracuse University, (NY)	76%	64%	11%	16%	ED
Southern Methodist University, (TX)	65%	55%	10%	52%	EA
American University, (DC)	60%	51%	9%	19%	ED
University of Vermont	88%	79%	9%	27%	EA
Rensselaer Polytechnic Institute, (NY)	85%	78%	7%	N/A	ED
University at Buffalo–SUNY	62%	57%	6%	9%	ED
Clarkson University, (NY)	90%	86%	4%	20%	ED
University of the Pacific, (CA)	60%	56%	4%	10%	EA
Boston University	55%	57%	-1%	9%	ED
Fordham University, (NY)	49%	50%	-1%	19%	EA
University of San Diego	58%	60%	-2%	38%	EA
University of Delaware	43%	48%	-4%	N/A	ED
University of Arkansas	83%	91%	-8%	40%	EA
University of Miami, (FL)	39%	47%	-8%	N/A	EA, ED
Hofstra University, (NY)	52%	70%	-18%	27%	EA
Virginia Tech	56%	74%	-18%	21%	ED
University of Maryland–Baltimore County	48%	78%	-30%	14%	EA
North Carolina State University–Raleigh	53%	94%	-41%	77%	EA
Liberal Arts Colleges					
St. Olaf College, (MN)	91%	45%	46%	81%	EA, ED
Denison University, (OH)	82%	37%	45%	25%	ED
Wheaton College, (MA)	83%	42%	41%	39%	ED
Franklin and Marshall College, (PA)	77%	42%	35%	47%	ED
Gettysburg College, (PA)	75%	41%	35%	35%	ED
Beloit College, (WI)	87%	53%	34%	56%	EA
Connecticut College	67%	33%	34%	42%	ED
Knox College, (IL)	94%	63%	31%	54%	EA
Marlboro College, (VT)	81%	52%	30%	49%	EA, ED
Muhlenberg College, (PA)	69%	40%	29%	54%	ED
Smith College, (MA)	76%	47%	29%	N/A	ED
Union College, (NY)	73%	45%	28%	34%	ED
Austin College, (TX)	77%	50%	26%	72%	EA, ED
Trinity College, (CT)	64%	38%	26%	40%	ED
Lake Forest College, (IL)	78%	53%	25%	50%	EA, ED
Ohio Wesleyan University	93%	69%	25%	36%	EA, ED
Centre College, (KY)	79%	54%	24%	55%	EA
Earlham College, (IN)	83%	60%	24%	52%	EA, ED
Skidmore College, (NY)	66%	42%	24%	37%	ED
Whitman College, (WA)	71%	47%	24%	N/A	ED
Wittenberg University, (OH)	97%	73%	24%	63%	EA, ED
College of the Holy Cross, (MA)	69%	46%	23%	N/A	ED
Juniata College, (PA)	90%	67%	23%	16%	EA, ED
Bryn Mawr College, (PA)	67%	45%	22%	26%	ED
St. Lawrence University, (NY)	80%	58%	22%	28%	ED
Ursinus College, (PA)	95%	73%	22%	27%	EA, ED
Wells College, (NY)	83%	61%	22%	38%	EA, ED
Westmont College, (CA)	77%	55%	22%	66%	EA
University of Puget Sound, (WA)	91%	70%	21%	17%	ED
Washington and Jefferson College, (PA)	43%	21%	21%	74%	EA, ED
Willamette University, (OR)	91%	70%	21%	33%	EA
Wofford College, (SC)	82%	61%	21%	47%	ED
Albion College, (MI)	89%	69%	20%	68%	EA
Gordon College, (MA)	93%	73%	20%	66%	EA, ED

	Early-decision and/or early-action acceptance rate	Non-early acceptance rate	Difference in acceptance rate	Freshman enrolled through early plans	Type of plan
College of Wooster, (OH)	93%	74%	19%	12%	ED
Furman University, (SC)	69%	50%	19%	41%	ED
Coe College, (IA)	79%	61%	18%	65%	EA
Wabash College, (IN)	68%	50%	18%	15%	EA, ED
Goucher College, (MD)	78%	61%	17%	38%	EA
Lawrence University, (WI)	81%	65%	17%	28%	EA, ED
Cornell College, (IA)	73%	57%	16%	77%	EA, ED
Lewis and Clark College, (OR)	72%	56%	16%	32%	EA
Sewanee–University of the South, (TN)	82%	66%	16%	N/A	ED
Drew University, (NJ)	92%	77%	15%	18%	ED
Millsaps College, (MS)	90%	75%	15%	50%	EA
Dickinson College, (PA)	58%	45%	14%	62%	EA, ED
Goshen College, (IN)	88%	75%	14%	13%	EA
Hobart and William Smith Colleges, (NY)	78%	64%	14%	29%	ED
Nebraska Wesleyan University	96%	82%	14%	28%	ED
Sweet Briar College, (VA)	92%	78%	14%	34%	ED
Hampshire College, (MA)	77%	64%	13%	13%	EA, ED
Principia College, (IL)	100%	88%	12%	16%	EA
Kalamazoo College, (MI)	79%	68%	11%	N/A	EA, ED
Sarah Lawrence College, (NY)	54%	44%	10%	29%	ED
College of the Atlantic, (ME)	73%	65%	8%	39%	ED
Moravian College, (PA)	72%	64%	8%	37%	ED
University of Richmond, (VA)	55%	47%	7%	19%	ED
DePauw University, (IN)	68%	64%	4%	61%	EA, ED
Mount Holyoke College, (MA)	54%	52%	2%	26%	ED
Allegheny College, (PA)	63%	62%	1%	11%	ED
Occidental College, (CA)	38%	41%	-3%	9%	ED
Randolph-Macon Woman's College, (VA)	84%	87%	-3%	7%	ED
Susquehanna University, (PA)	75%	82%	-7%	23%	ED
Bennington College, (VT)	54%	62%	-8%	16%	ED
Wheaton College, (IL)	44%	58%	-14%	49%	EA
St. Mary's College of Maryland	52%	71%	-19%	25%	ED
Agnes Scott College, (GA)	17%	55%	-39%	5%	ED

Universities–Master's (North)

Marist College, (NY)	69%	41%	27%	42%	EA, ED
St. Michael's College, (VT)	87%	60%	27%	62%	EA
Hood College, (MD)	74%	47%	26%	24%	EA
Bentley College, (MA)	59%	37%	23%	51%	EA, ED
SUNY College of Arts and Sciences–Geneseo	59%	48%	10%	16%	ED
Villanova University, (PA)	55%	50%	6%	26%	EA
Emerson College, (MA)	49%	44%	5%	46%	EA
Rochester Institute of Technology, (NY)	73%	69%	4%	26%	ED
Nazareth College of Rochester, (NY)	81%	78%	3%	43%	EA, ED
Arcadia University, (PA)	79%	79%	0%	1%	ED
Wagner College, (NY)	61%	61%	0%	16%	ED
Ithaca College, (NY)	74%	76%	-2%	6%	ED
CUNY–Baruch College	25%	33%	-8%	0%	ED
College of New Jersey	36%	46%	-10%	16%	ED

Universities–Master's (South)

Mississippi College	97%	53%	44%	46%	ED
Stetson University, (FL)	86%	69%	18%	6%	ED
Elon University, (NC)	49%	34%	15%	66%	EA, ED
Mercer University, (GA)	87%	74%	13%	50%	EA
Rollins College, (FL)	66%	52%	13%	36%	ED
Centenary College of Louisiana	66%	57%	9%	72%	EA, ED
Bellarmine University, (KY)	73%	67%	6%	55%	EA
James Madison University, (VA)	54%	73%	-20%	28%	EA

Universities–Master's (Midwest)

Xavier University, (OH)	79%	50%	30%	68%	EA
Hamline University, (MN)	86%	72%	13%	47%	EA
Valparaiso University, (IN)	90%	77%	12%	57%	EA
Bethel University, (MN)	86%	90%	-4%	N/A	EA

Where applying early may help you most—or not

More Selective Schools, continued

	Early-decision and/or early-action acceptance rate	Non-early acceptance rate	Difference in acceptance rate	Freshman enrolled through early plans	Type of plan
Universities–Master's (West)					
Whitworth College, (WA)	79%	57%	22%	63%	EA
Trinity University, (TX)	72%	51%	21%	68%	EA, ED
Santa Clara University, (CA)	74%	58%	16%	30%	EA
Chapman University, (CA)	61%	48%	13%	54%	EA
Cal Poly–San Luis Obispo	36%	45%	-9%	19%	ED
Comprehensive Colleges–Bachelor's (North)					
Marist College, (NY)	69%	41%	27%	42%	EA, ED
St. Michael's College, (VT)	87%	60%	27%	62%	EA
Hood College, (MD)	74%	47%	26%	24%	EA
Bentley College, (MA)	59%	37%	23%	51%	EA, ED
SUNY College of Arts and Sciences–Geneseo	59%	48%	10%	16%	ED
Villanova University, (PA)	55%	50%	6%	26%	EA
Emerson College, (MA)	49%	44%	5%	46%	EA
Rochester Institute of Technology, (NY)	73%	69%	4%	26%	ED
Nazareth College of Rochester, (NY)	81%	78%	3%	43%	EA, ED
Arcadia University, (PA)	79%	79%	0%	1%	ED
Wagner College, (NY)	61%	61%	0%	16%	ED
Ithaca College, (NY)	74%	76%	-2%	6%	ED
CUNY–Baruch College	25%	33%	-8%	0%	ED
College of New Jersey	36%	46%	-10%	16%	ED
Comprehensive Colleges–Bachelor's (South)					
Flagler College, (FL)	56%	12%	44%	78%	ED
Comprehensive Colleges–Bachelor's (Midwest)					
Taylor University, (IN)	87%	66%	21%	78%	EA
St. Norbert College, (WI)	96%	86%	10%	4%	ED
St. Mary's College, (IN)	85%	80%	5%	19%	ED
Comprehensive Colleges–Bachelor's (West)					
Linfield College, (OR)	97%	68%	29%	31%	EA
Master's College and Seminary, (CA)	29%	29%	0%	20%	EA

Selective Schools

	Early-decision and/or early-action acceptance rate	Non-early acceptance rate	Difference in acceptance rate	Freshman enrolled through early plans	Type of plan
National Universities					
SUNY–Albany	87%	57%	30%	26%	EA
DePaul University, (IL)	84%	63%	22%	51%	EA
George Mason University, (VA)	80%	62%	17%	44%	EA
Pace University, (NY)	76%	72%	4%	8%	EA
Duquesne University, (PA)	66%	84%	-18%	21%	EA, ED
Old Dominion University, (VA)	58%	78%	-20%	45%	EA
University of New Hampshire	58%	77%	-20%	30%	EA
Adelphi University, (NY)	41%	76%	-35%	13%	EA
Liberal Arts Colleges					
Siena College, (NY)	73%	47%	26%	65%	EA, ED
University of Virginia–Wise	87%	63%	24%	62%	EA
Presbyterian College, (SC)	91%	75%	16%	N/A	ED
Whittier College, (CA)	90%	78%	13%	21%	EA
Hollins University, (VA)	97%	85%	11%	N/A	ED
St. Anselm College, (NH)	79%	72%	7%	16%	ED
Hartwick College, (NY)	90%	87%	3%	17%	ED
Hampden-Sydney College, (VA)	69%	67%	2%	0%	EA, ED
Randolph-Macon College, (VA)	79%	79%	0%	9%	EA, ED
Universities–Master's (North)					
SUNY–Purchase College	73%	31%	42%	N/A	ED
Emmanuel College, (MA)	100%	61%	39%	1%	ED
Framingham State College, (MA)	86%	63%	23%	8%	EA
SUNY College–Oneonta	63%	42%	21%	33%	EA
Le Moyne College, (NY)	92%	72%	20%	8%	ED
Bryant University, (RI)	76%	57%	19%	10%	ED
Salve Regina University, (RI)	74%	57%	17%	24%	EA
SUNY College of Arts and Sciences–New Paltz	59%	42%	17%	27%	EA
SUNY–Oswego	66%	56%	11%	N/A	ED
Mount St. Mary's University, (MD)	92%	83%	9%	19%	EA
Monmouth University, (NJ)	72%	65%	7%	60%	EA, ED
Iona College, (NY)	72%	66%	6%	28%	EA
University of Massachusetts–Dartmouth	79%	73%	6%	3%	ED
SUNY–Fredonia	60%	55%	4%	4%	ED
Sacred Heart University, (CT)	64%	64%	0%	19%	ED
Simmons College, (MA)	64%	64%	0%	54%	EA
Manhattanville College, (NY)	54%	60%	-6%	10%	ED
Carlow University, (PA)	58%	65%	-7%	18%	EA
Alfred University, (NY)	69%	77%	-8%	8%	ED
St. John Fisher College, (NY)	51%	66%	-15%	6%	ED
Springfield College, (MA)	43%	71%	-28%	9%	ED
Universities–Master's (South)					
University of North Florida	98%	60%	38%	7%	EA
The Citadel, (SC)	99%	77%	22%	19%	ED
Georgia College and State University	63%	60%	4%	28%	EA
Lynchburg College, (VA)	55%	73%	-17%	8%	ED
Meredith College, (NC)	60%	98%	-38%	12%	ED
University of North Carolina–Charlotte	50%	92%	-42%	21%	EA
Longwood University, (VA)	37%	92%	-55%	19%	EA
Universities–Master's (Midwest)					
Ursuline College, (OH)	89%	58%	31%	37%	EA
Universities–Master's (West)					
Mount St. Mary's College, (CA)	89%	82%	7%	51%	EA
Comprehensive Colleges–Bachelor's (North)					
Daemen College, (NY)	100%	79%	21%	2%	EA
Roger Williams University, (RI)	90%	78%	12%	16%	ED
Russell Sage College, (NY)	89%	81%	8%	14%	ED
Merrimack College, (MA)	69%	72%	-3%	29%	EA

Where applying early may help you most—or not

Selective Schools, continued

	Early-decision and/or early-action acceptance rate	Non-early acceptance rate	Difference in acceptance rate	Freshman enrolled through early plans	Type of plan
Comprehensive Colleges–Bachelor's (South)					
Florida Southern College	98%	73%	25%	9%	ED
Comprehensive Colleges–Bachelor's (South)					
Vanguard University of Southern California	80%	92%	-11%	74%	EA

Less Selective Schools

	Early-decision and/or early-action acceptance rate	Non-early acceptance rate	Difference in acceptance rate	Freshman enrolled through early plans	Type of plan
National Universities					
University of Akron, (OH)	63%	87%	-24%	18%	EA
Universities–Master's (North)					
College of Mount St. Vincent, (NY)	93%	68%	26%	7%	EA
SUNY–Buffalo State College	68%	44%	25%	2%	ED
Wheelock College, (MA)	100%	75%	25%	20%	ED
Bloomsburg University of Pennsylvania	75%	67%	8%	13%	EA, ED
Suffolk University, (MA)	61%	83%	-22%	7%	EA
Comprehensive Colleges–Bachelor's (North)					
Bay Path College, (MA)	74%	62%	13%	76%	EA
Concordia College, (NY)	75%	76%	-1%	5%	EA
Curry College, (MA)	29%	71%	-42%	4%	ED

Schools whose freshmen are least (and most) likely to return

As many as one in three first-year students doesn't make it back for sophomore year. The reasons run the gamut, of course, from family problems to loneliness to academic struggles to a lack of money. If schools you're considering have a low freshman retention rate, you'll want to ask the admissions office why. Some colleges do a great job of taking care of their freshmen; some don't. The retention rates shown below, from lowest to highest, are the average proportion of freshmen entering between 2001 and 2004 who returned the following fall. The freshman enrollment is for the fall 2005 entering class.

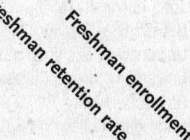

National Universities	Freshman retention rate	Freshman enrollment
National-Louis University (IL)	42%	34
Alliant International University (CA)	52%	29
Texas A&M University–Kingsville	56%	783
Idaho State University	58%	2,490
Cleveland State University	61%	1,079
Portland State University (OR)	65%	1,427
Indiana Univ.-Purdue Univ.–Indianapolis	66%	2,746
University of Akron (OH)	66%	3,082
University of Arkansas–Little Rock	66%	N/A
Nova Southeastern University (FL)	67%	457
University of Bridgeport (CT)	67%	365
University of New Orleans	67%	N/A
East Tennessee State University	68%	1,595
Union Institute and University (OH)	68%	N/A
Alabama Agricultural and Mech. Univ.	69%	1,099
Florida Atlantic University	69%	2,304
Indiana State University	69%	1,642
Northern Arizona University	69%	2,279
Southern Illinois University–Carbondale	69%	2,470
Univ. of Col.–Denver and Health Sci. Center	69%	787
University of South Dakota	69%	1,165
University of Texas–El Paso	69%	2,289
University of Toledo (OH)	69%	3,160
Wichita State University (KS)	69%	1,241
University of Alaska–Fairbanks	70%	1,000
University of Montana	70%	1,864
University of Northern Colorado	70%	2,494
University of South Alabama	70%	1,258
University of Texas–Arlington	70%	2,130
Clark Atlanta University	71%	881
Montana State University–Bozeman	71%	2,236
University of Massachusetts–Boston	71%	781
University of Missouri–St. Louis	71%	532
Wright State University (OH)	71%	2,336
Kent State University (OH)	72%	3,814
Louisiana Tech University	72%	1,797
New Mexico State University	72%	2,019
Oakland University (MI)	72%	2,213
Texas Woman's University	72%	744
University of Louisiana–Lafayette	72%	2,819
University of Nevada–Las Vegas	72%	3,138
University of Wisconsin–Milwaukee	72%	4,300
Utah State University	72%	2,054
Widener University (PA)	72%	650
South Carolina State University	73%	1,013
University of Memphis	73%	2,073
University of Missouri–Kansas City	73%	1,028
University of Southern Mississippi	73%	1,346
Wilmington College (DE)	73%	N/A
New Mexico Inst. of Mining and Tech.	74%	281
Tennessee State University	74%	1,205
University of Massachusetts–Lowell	74%	1,088
Hofstra University (NY)	75%	1,774
Middle Tennessee State University	75%	3,208
South Dakota State University	75%	1,869
University of Alabama–Huntsville	75%	660
University of Hartford (CT)	75%	1,489
University of Nevada–Reno	75%	2,432
Wayne State University (MI)	75%	2,878
Western Michigan University	75%	3,751
Bowling Green State University (OH)	76%	3,603
Indiana University of Pennsylvania	76%	2,509
Jackson State University (MS)	76%	1,159
North Dakota State University	76%	2,021
University of Alabama–Birmingham	76%	1,587
University of Louisville (KY)	76%	2,313
University of New Mexico	76%	3,095
University of North Carolina–Greensboro	76%	2,424
University of North Texas	76%	3,635
University of Wyoming	76%	1,421
Central Michigan University	77%	3,718
East Carolina University (NC)	77%	3,273
Pace University (NY)	77%	1,501
University of Cincinnati	77%	3,138
University of Hawaii–Manoa	77%	2,022
University of Mississippi	77%	2,192
University of North Dakota	77%	1,884
Arizona State University	78%	7,706
Ball State University (IN)	78%	3,692
Florida Institute of Technology	78%	604
Northern Illinois University	78%	3,179
Old Dominion University (VA)	78%	2,094
University of Arizona	78%	5,974
University of Illinois–Chicago	78%	2,776
University of Kentucky	78%	3,835
University of Tennessee	78%	4,265
Andrews University (MI)	79%	305
University of Houston	79%	3,445
University of Maine–Orono	79%	1,800
Virginia Commonwealth University	79%	3,540
West Virginia University	79%	4,574
Adelphi University (NY)	80%	770
Kansas State University	80%	3,309
Oklahoma State University	80%	3,315
St. John's University (NY)	80%	3,159
University of Idaho	80%	1,745
University of Rhode Island	80%	2,461
Michigan Technological University	81%	1,327
Mississippi State University	81%	1,966
New School University (NY)	81%	803
Oregon State University	81%	2,902
Seton Hall University (NJ)	81%	1,120
University of Nebraska–Lincoln	81%	3,560
University of South Florida	81%	4,311
University of Utah	81%	2,821
Colorado State University	82%	3,893
Drexel University (PA)	82%	2,476
George Mason University (VA)	82%	2,529
Georgia State University	82%	2,291
Illinois Institute of Technology	82%	415
New Jersey Institute of Technology	82%	762
Polytechnic University (NY)	82%	304
San Diego State University	82%	4,105
Texas Christian University	82%	1,610
University of Central Florida	82%	6,359
University of Kansas	82%	4,201
University of Maryland–Baltimore County	82%	1,429
University of Texas–Dallas	82%	1,060
University of Tulsa (OK)	82%	631
Baylor University (TX)	83%	3,168
Florida International University	83%	2,506
Illinois State University	83%	3,179
Ohio University	83%	4,163
Temple University (PA)	83%	3,871
Texas Tech University	83%	3,779
University of Arkansas	83%	2,752
University of Colorado–Boulder	83%	5,047
University of Iowa	83%	3,849
Biola University (CA)	84%	781
Catholic University of America (DC)	84%	792
DePaul University (IL)	84%	2,400
Louisiana State University–Baton Rouge	84%	4,970
Loyola University Chicago	84%	2,080
SUNY Col of Environ Science and Forestry	84%	260
SUNY–Albany	84%	2,560
University of Alabama	84%	3,735
University of Massachusetts–Amherst	84%	4,427
University of Missouri–Columbia	84%	4,718
University of Oklahoma	84%	3,245
University of Oregon	84%	3,207
University of South Carolina–Columbia	84%	3,734
Washington State University	84%	2,885
Auburn University (AL)	85%	4,197
Iowa State University	85%	3,769
University of California–Riverside	85%	2,988
University of Missouri–Rolla	85%	884
University of New Hampshire	85%	2,622
University of San Diego	85%	1,136
University of San Francisco	85%	934
University of Vermont	85%	2,394
University of the Pacific (CA)	85%	800
Clark University (MA)	86%	560
Purdue University–West Lafayette (IN)	86%	7,110
Rutgers–Newark (NJ)	86%	704
University at Buffalo–SUNY	86%	3,230
University of Denver	86%	1,092
University of Minnesota–Twin Cities	86%	5,305
Clarkson University (NY)	87%	630
Florida State University	87%	6,067
SUNY–Stony Brook	87%	2,508
Southern Methodist University (TX)	87%	1,402
St. Louis University	87%	1,521

Schools whose freshmen are least (and most) likely to return

National Universities, continued

	Freshman retention rate	Freshman enrollment
Tulane University (LA)	87%	N/A
University of Dayton (OH)	87%	1,981
University of La Verne (CA)	87%	339
University of St. Thomas (MN)	87%	1,326
Virginia Tech	87%	5,049
Yeshiva University (NY)	87%	1,005
American University (DC)	88%	1,223
Duquesne University (PA)	88%	1,328
Indiana University–Bloomington	88%	6,949
Northeastern University (MA)	88%	2,831
Ohio State University–Columbus	88%	5,954
University of California–Santa Cruz	88%	3,000
University of Miami (FL)	88%	2,277
Clemson University (SC)	89%	2,903
Howard University (DC)	89%	1,415
Marquette University (WI)	89%	1,784
Pepperdine University (CA)	89%	765
Rutgers–New Brunswick (NJ)	89%	5,245
Stevens Institute of Technology (NJ)	89%	484
University of Delaware	89%	3,522
University of Pittsburgh	89%	3,249
Boston University	90%	4,212
Fordham University (NY)	90%	1,755
Miami University–Oxford (OH)	90%	3,162
Michigan State University	90%	7,485
North Carolina State University–Raleigh	90%	4,253
Texas A&M University–College Station	90%	7,104
University of Connecticut	90%	3,260

	Freshman retention rate	Freshman enrollment
Georgia Institute of Technology	91%	2,425
SUNY–Binghamton	91%	2,215
University of California–Davis	91%	4,381
University of California–Santa Barbara	91%	3,829
Case Western Reserve University (OH)	92%	1,162
George Washington University (DC)	92%	2,411
New York University	92%	4,676
Pennsylvania State Univ.–Univ. Park	92%	6,496
Rensselaer Polytechnic Institute (NY)	92%	1,240
Syracuse University (NY)	92%	3,248
University of Illinois–Urbana-Champaign	92%	7,582
University of Texas–Austin	92%	6,836
University of Washington	92%	4,924
Worcester Polytechnic Institute (MA)	92%	735
University of Georgia	93%	4,712
University of Maryland–College Park	93%	4,211
University of Wisconsin–Madison	93%	6,141
Brandeis University (MA)	94%	739
Brigham Young University–Provo (UT)	94%	5,335
Carnegie Mellon University (PA)	94%	1,409
Emory University (GA)	94%	1,259
Lehigh University (PA)	94%	1,223
University of California–Irvine	94%	4,338
University of California–San Diego	94%	3,720
University of Florida	94%	7,241
University of Rochester (NY)	94%	997
Wake Forest University (NC)	94%	1,120
Boston College	95%	2,174

	Freshman retention rate	Freshman enrollment
College of William and Mary (VA)	95%	1,344
Johns Hopkins University (MD)	95%	1,154
University of Southern California	95%	2,741
Vanderbilt University (TN)	95%	1,620
California Institute of Technology	96%	234
Cornell University (NY)	96%	3,108
Rice University (TX)	96%	722
Tufts University (MA)	96%	1,365
University of Chicago	96%	1,203
University of Michigan–Ann Arbor	96%	6,113
University of North Carolina–Chapel Hill	96%	3,751
Brown University (RI)	97%	1,439
Dartmouth College (NH)	97%	1,074
Duke University (NC)	97%	1,724
Georgetown University (DC)	97%	1,551
Harvard University (MA)	97%	1,640
Northwestern University (IL)	97%	1,952
University of California–Berkeley	97%	4,101
University of California–Los Angeles	97%	4,422
University of Virginia	97%	3,112
Washington University in St. Louis	97%	1,388
Columbia University (NY)	98%	1,339
Massachusetts Institute of Technology	98%	996
Princeton University (NJ)	98%	1,229
Stanford University (CA)	98%	1,633
University of Notre Dame (IN)	98%	1,966
University of Pennsylvania	98%	2,552
Yale University (CT)	98%	1,321

Liberal Arts Colleges

	Freshman retention rate	Freshman enrollment
Lindsey Wilson College (KY)	52%	414
Talladega College (AL)	54%	182
Virginia Union University	54%	N/A
Fort Lewis College (CO)	57%	910
Shawnee State University (OH)	58%	870
Lees-McRae College (NC)	59%	224
Mesa State College (CO)	59%	1,288
Western State College of Colorado	59%	478
Blackburn College (IL)	61%	211
St. Augustine's College (NC)	61%	262
University of Maine–Presque Isle	61%	211
Schreiner University (TX)	62%	173
Franklin Pierce College (NH)	63%	507
Olivet College (MI)	63%	260
Adrian College (MI)	64%	267
Pine Manor College (MA)	64%	138
University of Pittsburgh–Bradford	64%	239
Antioch College (OH)	65%	53
Paine College (GA)	65%	198
University of Hawaii–Hilo	66%	439
Virginia Wesleyan College	66%	323
Warner Pacific College (OR)	66%	104
Chatham College (PA)	67%	N/A
Greensboro College (NC)	67%	217
Lane College (TN)	67%	504
St. Andrews Presbyterian College (NC)	67%	191
Judson College (AL)	68%	N/A

	Freshman retention rate	Freshman enrollment
Marymount Manhattan College (NY)	69%	448
Wesleyan College (GA)	69%	113
Bennett College (NC)	70%	239
Coastal Carolina University (SC)	70%	1,498
Stephens College (MO)	70%	207
Huntingdon College (AL)	71%	184
Texas A&M University–Galveston	71%	466
Emory and Henry College (VA)	72%	338
Evergreen State College (WA)	72%	605
King College (TN)	72%	209
California State University–Monterey Bay	73%	N/A
Massachusetts College of Liberal Arts	73%	274
Muskingum College (OH)	73%	436
University of Virginia–Wise	73%	366
Christopher Newport University (VA)	74%	1,250
Guilford College (NC)	74%	412
Lyon College (AR)	74%	112
San Diego Christian College (CA)	74%	126
Westminster College (MO)	74%	270
Erskine College (SC)	75%	181
Hastings College (NE)	75%	311
Marlboro College (VT)	75%	75
Randolph-Macon College (VA)	75%	305
University of Pittsburgh–Greensburg	75%	424
Hanover College (IN)	76%	265
Wells College (NY)	76%	130
Albertson College (ID)	77%	196

	Freshman retention rate	Freshman enrollment
Bridgewater College (VA)	77%	394
Hartwick College (NY)	77%	409
Hollins University (VA)	77%	184
Salem College (NC)	77%	131
Seton Hill University (PA)	77%	336
Tougaloo College (MS)	77%	208
Whittier College (CA)	77%	351
Albright College (PA)	78%	451
Eastern Mennonite University (VA)	78%	202
Mills College (CA)	78%	207
Randolph-Macon Woman's College (VA)	78%	184
University of North Carolina–Asheville	78%	472
West Virginia Wesleyan College	78%	371
Bethany College (WV)	79%	219
Georgetown College (KY)	79%	416
Hiram College (OH)	79%	215
Roanoke College (VA)	79%	534
Sweet Briar College (VA)	79%	182
College of the Atlantic (ME)	80%	82
Concordia College–Moorhead (MN)	80%	773
Cornell College (IA)	80%	319
Lake Forest College (IL)	80%	358
Ohio Wesleyan University	80%	595
Wittenberg University (OH)	80%	496
Alma College (MI)	81%	336
Coe College (IA)	81%	316
Goshen College (IN)	81%	197

College	Freshman retention rate	Freshman enrollment
Hampden-Sydney College (VA)	81%	322
Hampshire College (MA)	81%	399
Monmouth College (IL)	81%	N/A
Nebraska Wesleyan University	81%	406
New College of Florida	81%	218
University of Dallas	81%	256
Bennington College (VT)	82%	137
Goucher College (MD)	82%	340
McDaniel College (MD)	82%	448
Millsaps College (MS)	82%	258
Rosemont College (PA)	82%	120
Agnes Scott College (GA)	83%	229
Eckerd College (FL)	83%	505
Richard Stockton College of New Jersey	83%	812
Christendom College (VA)	84%	105
Hendrix College (AR)	84%	281
Houghton College (NY)	84%	323
Lycoming College (PA)	84%	360
Oglethorpe University (GA)	84%	233
Presbyterian College (SC)	84%	313
St. Anselm College (NH)	84%	519
University of Minnesota–Morris	84%	388
Washington and Jefferson College (PA)	84%	388
Albion College (MI)	85%	574
Birmingham-Southern College (AL)	85%	316
Earlham College (IN)	85%	324
Fisk University (TN)	85%	214
Hobart and William Smith Colleges (NY)	85%	545
Lewis and Clark College (OR)	85%	490
Luther College (IA)	85%	631
Morehouse College (GA)	85%	661
Reed College (OR)	85%	354
Ripon College (WI)	85%	262
Transylvania University (KY)	85%	326
University of Judaism (CA)	85%	N/A
Westminster College (PA)	85%	359
Allegheny College (PA)	86%	564
Augustana College (IL)	86%	679
Austin College (TX)	86%	348
Drew University (NJ)	86%	391
Hillsdale College (MI)	86%	368
Juniata College (PA)	86%	388
Moravian College (PA)	86%	382
Pitzer College (CA)	86%	241
Principia College (IL)	86%	139
Rhodes College (TN)	86%	444
Sewanee–University of the South (TN)	86%	421
St. Vincent College (PA)	86%	483
Virginia Military Institute	86%	391
Wabash College (IN)	86%	249
Washington College (MD)	86%	343
Westmont College (CA)	86%	333
William Jewell College (MO)	86%	304
College of Wooster (OH)	87%	537
Gordon College (MA)	87%	414
Hope College (MI)	87%	760
Kalamazoo College (MI)	87%	367
Knox College (IL)	87%	325
Southwestern University (TX)	87%	329
University of Puget Sound (WA)	87%	670
Wheaton College (MA)	87%	467
Bard College (NY)	88%	515
Siena College (NY)	88%	763
St. Lawrence University (NY)	88%	537
Susquehanna University (PA)	88%	512
Thomas Aquinas College (CA)	88%	102
Centre College (KY)	89%	316
College of St. Benedict (MN)	89%	576
Denison University (OH)	89%	622
Gustavus Adolphus College (MN)	89%	705
St. John's University (MN)	89%	447
St. Mary's College of Maryland	89%	488
Willamette University (OR)	89%	444
Dickinson College (PA)	90%	648
Lawrence University (WI)	90%	401
Spelman College (GA)	90%	531
Ursinus College (PA)	90%	426
Wofford College (SC)	90%	321
Colorado College	91%	476
Connecticut College	91%	492
Franklin and Marshall College (PA)	91%	582
Gettysburg College (PA)	91%	697
Oberlin College (OH)	91%	741
Sarah Lawrence College (NY)	91%	376
Scripps College (CA)	91%	234
Smith College (MA)	91%	615
DePauw University (IN)	92%	586
Furman University (SC)	92%	689
Grinnell College (IA)	92%	387
Kenyon College (OH)	92%	440
Occidental College (CA)	92%	436
Skidmore College (NY)	92%	694
Trinity College (CT)	92%	573
Bryn Mawr College (PA)	93%	355
Colby College (ME)	93%	511
Hamilton College (NY)	93%	498
Illinois Wesleyan University	93%	565
Macalester College (MN)	93%	491
Mount Holyoke College (MA)	93%	504
Muhlenberg College (PA)	93%	576
St. Olaf College (MN)	93%	764
Union College (NY)	93%	581
University of Richmond (VA)	93%	772
Barnard College (NY)	94%	571
Bates College (ME)	94%	490
Beloit College (WI)	94%	326
Colgate University (NY)	94%	729
Lafayette College (PA)	94%	603
Wheaton College (IL)	94%	578
Whitman College (WA)	94%	361
Bucknell University (PA)	95%	923
Claremont McKenna College (CA)	95%	271
Vassar College (NY)	95%	650
Washington and Lee University (VA)	95%	465
Wellesley College (MA)	95%	605
College of the Holy Cross (MA)	96%	723
Davidson College (NC)	96%	460
Harvey Mudd College (CA)	96%	193
Haverford College (PA)	96%	316
Middlebury College (VT)	96%	553
Swarthmore College (PA)	96%	389
Wesleyan University (CT)	96%	717
Amherst College (MA)	97%	431
Carleton College (MN)	97%	541
Williams College (MA)	97%	536
Bowdoin College (ME)	98%	478
Pomona College (CA)	99%	383

Schools whose freshmen are least (and most) likely to return

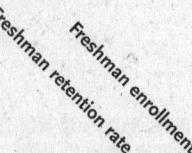

Universities– Master's (North)	Freshman retention rate	Freshman enrollment
Southeastern University (DC)	52%	N/A
Long Island University–Brooklyn (NY)	53%	1,028
University of the District of Columbia	55%	1,137
College of St. Joseph (VT)	57%	44
Mercy College (NY)	59%	605
Cheyney University of Pennsylvania	60%	675
Johnson State College (VT)	61%	N/A
American International College (MA)	62%	331
Lincoln University (PA)	64%	636
Nyack College (NY)	65%	270
Delaware State University	66%	940
Husson College (ME)	66%	327
Anna Maria College (MA)	67%	161
Coppin State University (MD)	67%	690
Dowling College (NY)	67%	465
Mansfield University of Pennsylvania	67%	680
Trinity University (DC)	67%	N/A
University of Maryland–Eastern Shore	68%	1,054
University of Southern Maine	68%	1,010
Castleton State College (VT)	69%	467
Chestnut Hill College (PA)	69%	216
Elms College (MA)	69%	N/A
Gallaudet University (DC)	69%	280
Carlow University (PA)	70%	277
Long Island Univ.–C.W. Post Campus (NY)	70%	1,006
St. Thomas Aquinas College (NY)	70%	328
Edinboro University of Pennsylvania	71%	1,325
New York Institute of Technology	71%	990
Philadelphia University	71%	692
Point Park University (PA)	71%	472
University of New England (ME)	71%	468
Western Connecticut State University	71%	787
Bowie State University (MD)	72%	1,226
Eastern Nazarene College (MA)	72%	213
Framingham State College (MA)	72%	670
Johnson and Wales University (RI)	72%	2,792
La Roche College (PA)	72%	305
Lock Haven University of Pennsylvania	72%	1,247
Morgan State University (MD)	72%	793
Southern Connecticut State University	72%	1,340
St. Peter's College (NJ)	72%	491
CUNY–Lehman College	73%	804
Cabrini College (PA)	73%	539
Frostburg State University (MD)	73%	942
Mount St. Mary College (NY)	73%	360
Rivier College (NH)	73%	305
St. Joseph College (CT)	73%	251
Wheelock College (MA)	73%	181
Clarion University of Pennsylvania	74%	1,241
Fairleigh Dickinson University (NJ)	74%	1,115
Immaculata University (PA)	74%	298
New Jersey City University	74%	690
SUNY–Purchase College	74%	718
Salem State College (MA)	74%	1,226
Suffolk University (MA)	74%	1,136
Waynesburg College (PA)	74%	341
Western New England College (MA)	74%	666
Worcester State College (MA)	74%	648
Fitchburg State College (MA)	75%	607
Monmouth University (NJ)	75%	943
Norwich University (VT)	75%	578
Plymouth State University (NH)	75%	1,003
SUNY College–Potsdam	75%	739
SUNY–Buffalo State College	75%	1,250
University of New Haven (CT)	75%	664
Bridgewater State College (MA)	76%	1,332
California University of Pennsylvania	76%	1,259
East Stroudsburg Univ. of Pennsylvania	76%	1,101
Eastern Connecticut State University	76%	925
Kean University (NJ)	76%	1,432
Robert Morris University (PA)	76%	695
Central Connecticut State University	77%	1,356
Geneva College (PA)	77%	353
Keene State College (NH)	77%	1,008
Kutztown University of Pennsylvania	77%	N/A
Lesley University (MA)	77%	257
Manhattanville College (NY)	77%	515
SUNY College–Oneonta	77%	1,145
SUNY–Oswego	77%	1,354
SUNY–Plattsburgh	77%	1,040
Slippery Rock University of Pennsylvania	77%	1,455
St. Francis University (PA)	77%	366
University of Massachusetts–Dartmouth	77%	1,545
Westfield State College (MA)	77%	1,183
William Paterson University of New Jersey	77%	1,421
College of Mount St. Vincent (NY)	78%	345
Georgian Court University (NJ)	78%	188
Iona College (NY)	78%	779
Rhode Island College	78%	1,098
St. Joseph's College (ME)	78%	360
CUNY–City College	79%	1,326
Eastern University (PA)	79%	404
Niagara University (NY)	79%	735
Rider University (NJ)	79%	948
SUNY College–Cortland	79%	1,110
Shippensburg University of Pennsylvania	79%	1,503
Wilkes University (PA)	79%	572
Alfred University (NY)	80%	429
Arcadia University (PA)	80%	441
CUNY–Hunter College	80%	1,837
Holy Family University (PA)	80%	436
Marywood University (PA)	80%	404
Regis College (MA)	80%	161
SUNY College–Brockport	80%	988
Sacred Heart University (CT)	80%	886
Salve Regina University (RI)	80%	568
Touro College (NY)	80%	913
Bloomsburg University of Pennsylvania	81%	1,697
CUNY–Brooklyn College	81%	1,413
Gannon University (PA)	81%	632
Gwynedd-Mercy College (PA)	81%	345
King's College (PA)	81%	480
Millersville University of Pennsylvania	81%	1,320
Mount St. Mary's University (MD)	81%	439
Roberts Wesleyan College (NY)	81%	228
Salisbury University (MD)	81%	958
St. Bonaventure University (NY)	81%	478
Assumption College (MA)	82%	565
Emmanuel College (MA)	82%	438
Hood College (MD)	82%	237
Molloy College (NY)	82%	294
Springfield College (MA)	82%	574
York College of Pennsylvania	82%	1,098
CUNY–College of Staten Island	83%	2,198
Canisius College (NY)	83%	775
College Misericordia (PA)	83%	335
Manhattan College (NY)	83%	701
Montclair State University (NJ)	83%	1,944
Penn. State–Erie, Behrend College	83%	838
Rutgers–Camden (NJ)	83%	353
Bryant University (RI)	84%	822
College of St. Rose (NY)	84%	598
Nazareth College of Rochester (NY)	84%	453
SUNY Coll. of Arts and Sci.–New Paltz	84%	1,050
Simmons College (MA)	84%	413
St. John Fisher College (NY)	84%	553
West Chester University of Pennsylvania	84%	1,901
DeSales University (PA)	85%	434
Lebanon Valley College (PA)	85%	454
Rowan University (NJ)	85%	1,247
SUNY–Fredonia	85%	1,037
Towson University (MD)	85%	2,327
CUNY–Queens College	86%	1,509
College of Notre Dame of Maryland	86%	147
Emerson College (MA)	86%	721
La Salle University (PA)	86%	822
Le Moyne College (NY)	86%	520
Ithaca College (NY)	87%	1,680
Quinnipiac University (CT)	87%	1,361
CUNY–Baruch College	88%	1,641
University of Scranton (PA)	88%	956
Wagner College (NY)	88%	579
Fairfield University (CT)	89%	940
Marist College (NY)	89%	1,017
Rochester Institute of Technology (NY)	89%	2,217
St. Joseph's University (PA)	89%	1,140
St. Michael's College (VT)	89%	597
Loyola College in Maryland	91%	898
SUNY Coll. of Arts and Sci.–Geneseo	91%	1,029
Providence College (RI)	92%	1,069
Bentley College (MA)	94%	937
Villanova University (PA)	94%	1,628
College of New Jersey	95%	1,236

Universities–Master's (South)

University	Freshman retention rate	Freshman enrollment
Southern University–New Orleans	46%	N/A
Louisiana State University–Shreveport	56%	459
Warren Wilson College (NC)	59%	245
Averett University (VA)	60%	258
Lynn University (FL)	60%	655
University of West Alabama	60%	366
Tusculum College (TN)	61%	259
University of the Cumberlands (KY)	62%	433
Austin Peay State University (TN)	63%	1,408
Campbellsville University (KY)	63%	356
Cumberland University (TN)	63%	262
Henderson State University (AR)	63%	425
Nicholls State University (LA)	63%	1,301
Kentucky State University	64%	825
Lander University (SC)	64%	577
Morehead State University (KY)	64%	1,300
Southern Arkansas University	64%	571
Spalding University (KY)	64%	N/A
Barry University (FL)	65%	563
Mary Baldwin College (VA)	65%	267
Southern Wesleyan University (SC)	65%	138
Armstrong Atlantic State University (GA)	66%	799
Augusta State University (GA)	66%	988
Francis Marion University (SC)	66%	803
St. Thomas University (FL)	66%	206
University of Louisiana–Monroe	66%	N/A
William Carey College (MS)	66%	164
Arkansas Tech University	67%	1,529
Eastern Kentucky University	67%	2,500
McNeese State University (LA)	67%	1,405
Norfolk State University (VA)	67%	1,001
Alabama State University	68%	1,213
Arkansas State University	68%	1,584
Gardner-Webb University (NC)	68%	438
Georgia Southwestern State University	68%	385
Jacksonville State University (AL)	68%	1,151
Jacksonville University (FL)	68%	536
Southeastern Louisiana University	68%	2,578
University of Mobile (AL)	68%	264
University of North Alabama	68%	931
Charleston Southern University (SC)	69%	632
Mississippi University for Women	69%	226
Northern Kentucky University	69%	1,843
Northwestern State University of Louisiana	69%	1,539
Piedmont College (GA)	69%	166
St. Leo University (FL)	69%	454
Trevecca Nazarene University (TN)	69%	250
University of Tennessee–Chattanooga	69%	1,454
Alcorn State University (MS)	70%	497
Delta State University (MS)	70%	398
Pfeiffer University (NC)	70%	200
Shenandoah University (VA)	70%	370
Southern University and A&M College (LA)	70%	1,502
University of North Carolina–Pembroke	70%	984
Columbus State University (GA)	71%	1,184
Florida Gulf Coast University	71%	1,343
Palm Beach Atlantic University (FL)	71%	626
Troy University (AL)	71%	2,250
University of Central Arkansas	71%	2,503
University of Tennessee–Martin	71%	1,250
University of West Georgia	71%	1,983
Western Carolina University (NC)	71%	1,557
Carson-Newman College (TN)	72%	449
Grambling State University (LA)	72%	N/A
Lynchburg College (VA)	72%	554
Savannah State University (GA)	72%	N/A
Tennessee Technological University	72%	1,424
Tuskegee University (AL)	72%	737
Virginia State University	72%	1,107
Brenau University (GA)	73%	176
Marshall University (WV)	73%	1,715
Marymount University (VA)	73%	426
University of West Florida	73%	924
Wheeling Jesuit University (WV)	73%	285
Fayetteville State University (NC)	74%	848
Liberty University (VA)	74%	1,985
Union University (TN)	74%	408
University of Montevallo (AL)	74%	496
University of Tampa (FL)	74%	1,010
Western Kentucky University	74%	3,150
Converse College (SC)	75%	177
Fort Valley State University (GA)	75%	N/A
Kennesaw State University (GA)	75%	2,348
Queens University of Charlotte (NC)	75%	242
Valdosta State University (GA)	75%	1,757
Winthrop University (SC)	75%	1,017
Lipscomb University (TN)	76%	526
Meredith College (NC)	76%	451
Milligan College (TN)	76%	168
Mississippi College	76%	394
North Georgia College and State University	76%	731
Xavier University of Louisiana	76%	N/A
Embry Riddle Aeronautical University (FL)	77%	977
Freed-Hardeman University (TN)	77%	374
Murray State University (KY)	77%	1,030
University of North Carolina–Charlotte	77%	2,890
University of North Florida	77%	2,388
Centenary College of Louisiana	78%	233
Georgia Southern University	78%	3,145
Radford University (VA)	78%	1,896
Stetson University (FL)	78%	550
Belmont University (TN)	79%	797
Campbell University (NC)	79%	730
Georgia College and State University	79%	1,036
Longwood University (VA)	79%	958
Mercer University (GA)	79%	616
North Carolina Central University	79%	1,226
Christian Brothers University (TN)	80%	261
Harding University (AR)	80%	960
Spring Hill College (AL)	80%	275
The Citadel (SC)	80%	585
Albany State University (GA)	81%	N/A
Bellarmine University (KY)	81%	436
Loyola University New Orleans	81%	N/A
Lincoln Memorial University (TN)	82%	N/A
College of Charleston (SC)	83%	1,993
Appalachian State University (NC)	84%	2,543
Florida A&M University	85%	N/A
Hampton University (VA)	85%	1,201
Rollins College (FL)	85%	464
Samford University (AL)	85%	702
University of North Carolina–Wilmington	85%	1,943
Elon University (NC)	87%	1,237
University of Mary Washington (VA)	87%	914
James Madison University (VA)	92%	3,798

Universities–Master's (Midwest)

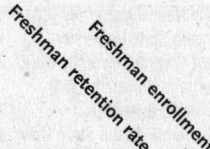
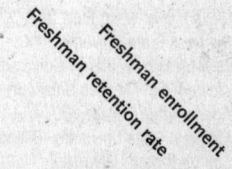

University	Freshman retention rate	Freshman enrollment
Rockford College (IL)	51%	270
Lincoln University (MO)	52%	632
Chicago State University	57%	451
University of St. Mary (KS)	59%	83
Columbia College (IL)	61%	1,829
Minot State University (ND)	61%	471
Peru State College (NE)	61%	213
Indiana University Northwest	62%	604
University of Rio Grande (OH)	62%	473
University of Southern Indiana	62%	2,148
Friends University (KS)	63%	174
Indiana U.-Purdue U.–Fort Wayne	63%	1,895
Marygrove College (MI)	63%	80
Mount Mary College (WI)	63%	160
Oakland City University (IN)	63%	208
Purdue University–Calumet (IN)	63%	1,252
Lake Erie College (OH)	64%	117
University of Wisconsin–Parkside	64%	877
Lake Superior State University (MI)	65%	487
Maharishi University of Management (IA)	65%	N/A
Roosevelt University (IL)	65%	326
Ferris State University (MI)	67%	2,417
Indiana University Southeast	67%	753
Indiana University–South Bend	67%	1,006
Newman University (KS)	67%	N/A
Saginaw Valley State University (MI)	67%	1,267
University of Dubuque (IA)	67%	309
University of Sioux Falls (SD)	67%	224
Emporia State University (KS)	68%	739
Lindenwood University (MO)	68%	821
Minnesota State University–Moorhead	68%	1,135
Quincy University (IL)	68%	202
Ursuline College (OH)	68%	141
Viterbo University (WI)	68%	296
Wayne State College (NE)	68%	593
Chadron State College (NE)	69%	326
Heidelberg College (OH)	69%	328
Northeastern Illinois University	69%	1,058
Park University (MO)	69%	142

Schools whose freshmen are least (and most) likely to return

Universities–Master's (Midwest), continued

	Freshman retention rate	Freshman enrollment
University of Wisconsin–Superior	69%	346
Aurora University (IL)	70%	383
Bemidji State University (MN)	70%	616
Fort Hays State University (KS)	70%	811
Northern State University (SD)	70%	381
Silver Lake College (WI)	70%	33
Central Missouri State University	71%	1,575
Marian College of Fond du Lac (WI)	71%	262
MidAmerica Nazarene University (KS)	71%	216
North Park University (IL)	71%	359
Northwest Missouri State University	71%	N/A
Southeast Missouri State University	71%	1,679
Southwest Baptist University (MO)	71%	393
St. Cloud State University (MN)	71%	2,152
University of Mary (ND)	71%	392
Washburn University (KS)	71%	863
Avila University (MO)	72%	162
Concordia University–River Forest (IL)	72%	210
Cornerstone University (MI)	72%	417
Eastern Michigan University	72%	2,386
Edgewood College (WI)	72%	353
Fontbonne University (MO)	72%	195
University of Findlay (OH)	72%	642
University of St. Francis (IN)	72%	319
William Woods University (MO)	72%	253
Youngstown State University (OH)	72%	2,258
Ashland University (OH)	73%	550
Lawrence Technological University (MI)	73%	332
Missouri State University	73%	2,621
Mount Marty College (SD)	73%	148
Northern Michigan University	73%	1,399
University of Wisconsin–Stout	73%	1,694
Baker University (KS)	74%	239
Carthage College (WI)	74%	598

	Freshman retention rate	Freshman enrollment
Madonna University (MI)	74%	200
Malone College (OH)	74%	361
Southern Illinois University–Edwardsville	74%	1,748
St. Mary's University of Minnesota	74%	311
University of Michigan–Flint	74%	579
University of Nebraska–Omaha	74%	1,758
Walsh University (OH)	74%	618
Anderson University (IN)	75%	580
Cardinal Stritch University (WI)	75%	176
College of Mount St. Joseph (OH)	75%	315
Pittsburg State University (KS)	75%	1,003
University of Minnesota–Duluth	75%	2,164
University of Wisconsin–Oshkosh	75%	1,634
Winona State University (MN)	75%	1,720
Aquinas College (MI)	76%	363
Benedictine University (IL)	76%	311
University of Detroit Mercy	76%	502
University of St. Francis (IL)	76%	190
Capital University (OH)	77%	602
Concordia University Wisconsin	77%	387
Lewis University (IL)	77%	561
Maryville University of St. Louis (MO)	77%	335
North Central College (IL)	77%	425
St. Xavier University (IL)	77%	422
University of Wisconsin–Green Bay	77%	910
University of Wisconsin–Whitewater	77%	1,712
Western Illinois University	77%	1,816
Doane College (NE)	78%	262
Minnesota State University–Mankato	78%	2,257
University of Indianapolis	78%	737
University of Wisconsin–Platteville	78%	1,218
University of Wisconsin–River Falls	78%	1,209
University of Wisconsin–Stevens Point	78%	1,523
Concordia University (NE)	79%	291

	Freshman retention rate	Freshman enrollment
Olivet Nazarene University (IL)	79%	671
Spring Arbor University (MI)	79%	318
St. Ambrose University (IA)	79%	474
Augsburg College (MN)	80%	335
College of St. Catherine (MN)	80%	413
Eastern Illinois University	80%	1,668
Grand Valley State University (MI)	80%	3,412
Indiana Wesleyan University	80%	N/A
University of Evansville (IN)	80%	670
Webster University (MO)	80%	481
Benedictine College (KS)	81%	304
Dominican University (IL)	81%	271
Drury University (MO)	81%	378
University of Northern Iowa	81%	1,737
University of Wisconsin–Eau Claire	81%	2,068
College of St. Scholastica (MN)	82%	490
Rockhurst University (MO)	82%	371
University of Michigan–Dearborn	82%	840
Baldwin-Wallace College (OH)	83%	599
Hamline University (MN)	83%	461
University of Nebraska–Kearney	83%	1,062
Drake University (IA)	84%	809
Franciscan University of Steubenville (OH)	85%	402
Bethel University (MN)	86%	731
John Carroll University (OH)	86%	786
Truman State University (MO)	86%	1,448
Valparaiso University (IN)	86%	673
Butler University (IN)	87%	867
Creighton University (NE)	87%	971
University of Wisconsin–La Crosse	87%	1,764
Bradley University (IL)	88%	1,136
Xavier University (OH)	90%	765

Universities–Master's (West)

	Freshman retention rate	Freshman enrollment
University of Great Falls (MT)	45%	122
Sul Ross State University (TX)	48%	N/A
New Mexico Highlands University	51%	237
Western New Mexico University	54%	309
Adams State College (CO)	56%	N/A
Montana State University–Billings	56%	977
Southern Utah University	57%	1,074
University of Texas–San Antonio	57%	4,452
Cameron University (OK)	58%	943
College of the Southwest (NM)	58%	240
University of Texas–Tyler	58%	549
Eastern New Mexico University	59%	567
Boise State University (ID)	61%	2,501
Marylhurst University (OR)	61%	12
Our Lady of the Lake University (TX)	61%	271
Simpson University (CA)	61%	164
Southeastern Oklahoma State University	61%	619
University of Mary Hardin-Baylor (TX)	61%	502
Colorado Christian University	62%	N/A
Colorado State University–Pueblo	62%	683

	Freshman retention rate	Freshman enrollment
Holy Names University (CA)	62%	90
Angelo State University (TX)	63%	1,304
East Central University (OK)	63%	572
Heritage University (WA)	63%	89
Prescott College (AZ)	63%	54
Stephen F. Austin State University (TX)	63%	1,921
Tarleton State University (TX)	63%	N/A
Texas A&M University–Corpus Christi	63%	1,256
University of Texas of the Permian Basin	63%	307
Midwestern State University (TX)	64%	876
Southwestern Oklahoma State University	64%	792
Texas Wesleyan University	64%	196
California State Univ.–Dominguez Hills	65%	786
Chaminade University of Honolulu	65%	266
La Sierra University (CA)	65%	388
Northwestern Oklahoma State University	66%	291
Sam Houston State University (TX)	66%	2,167
Texas A&M International University	66%	486
University of Alaska–Southeast	66%	190
University of the Incarnate Word (TX)	66%	578

	Freshman retention rate	Freshman enrollment
West Texas A&M University	66%	780
Alaska Pacific University	67%	51
Concordia University (OR)	67%	171
Dallas Baptist University	67%	362
Hardin-Simmons University (TX)	67%	436
Hawaii Pacific University	67%	657
Hope International University (CA)	67%	121
Prairie View A&M University (TX)	67%	1,101
Southern Oregon University	67%	770
University of Alaska–Anchorage	67%	1,561
University of Texas–Brownsville	67%	1,415
University of Texas–Pan American	67%	2,434
Wayland Baptist University (TX)	67%	226
Eastern Oregon University	68%	383
Lamar University (TX)	68%	1,683
University of Colorado–Colorado Springs	68%	1,048
Southern Nazarene University (OK)	69%	284
Walla Walla College (WA)	69%	291
Western Oregon University	69%	834
College of Santa Fe (NM)	70%	129

	Freshman retention rate	Freshman enrollment
Northwest Nazarene University (ID)	70%	264
University of St. Thomas (TX)	71%	295
Weber State University (UT)	71%	2,759
California State University–San Marcos	72%	804
Houston Baptist University	72%	313
LeTourneau University (TX)	72%	352
Northeastern State University (OK)	72%	1,104
Oklahoma City University	72%	370
University of Central Oklahoma	72%	2,169
Westminster College (UT)	72%	350
St. Martin's University (WA)	73%	173
Abilene Christian University (TX)	75%	1,031
California State University–Los Angeles	75%	1,458
Concordia University (CA)	75%	265
Dominican University of California	75%	227
California State University–Northridge	76%	3,720
Eastern Washington University	76%	1,637
Mount St. Mary's College (CA)	76%	372
Notre Dame de Namur University (CA)	76%	145
Texas State University–San Marcos	76%	3,073
California State University–Bakersfield	77%	N/A

	Freshman retention rate	Freshman enrollment
Humboldt State University (CA)	77%	827
Central Washington University	78%	1,435
California State University–Sacramento	79%	2,600
San Francisco State University	79%	N/A
St. Mary's University of San Antonio	79%	494
California State University–Fullerton	80%	3,943
California State Univ.–San Bernardino	80%	1,692
Fresno Pacific University (CA)	80%	212
George Fox University (OR)	80%	588
Oral Roberts University (OK)	80%	465
Pacific University (OR)	80%	326
San Jose State University (CA)	80%	2,551
California Lutheran University	81%	385
St. Edward's University (TX)	81%	650
Woodbury University (CA)	81%	133
California State Polytechnic Univ.–Pomona	82%	2,793
California State University–Chico	82%	2,335
California State University–East Bay	82%	691
California State University–Stanislaus	82%	870
Pacific Lutheran University (WA)	82%	690
Regis University (CO)	82%	402

	Freshman retention rate	Freshman enrollment
Seattle Pacific University	82%	710
Sonoma State University (CA)	82%	1,053
Azusa Pacific University (CA)	83%	881
California State University–Fresno	83%	2,438
Point Loma Nazarene University (CA)	83%	563
Western Washington University	83%	2,382
Seattle University	84%	763
University of Redlands (CA)	84%	615
California State University–Long Beach	85%	4,383
University of Portland (OR)	85%	724
California Baptist University	86%	439
Chapman University (CA)	86%	853
Whitworth College (WA)	86%	451
Loyola Marymount University (CA)	89%	1,346
St. Mary's College of California	89%	675
Trinity University (TX)	89%	651
Cal Poly–San Luis Obispo	90%	3,372
Gonzaga University (WA)	91%	986
Santa Clara University (CA)	92%	1,198

Comprehensive Colleges–Bachelor's (North)

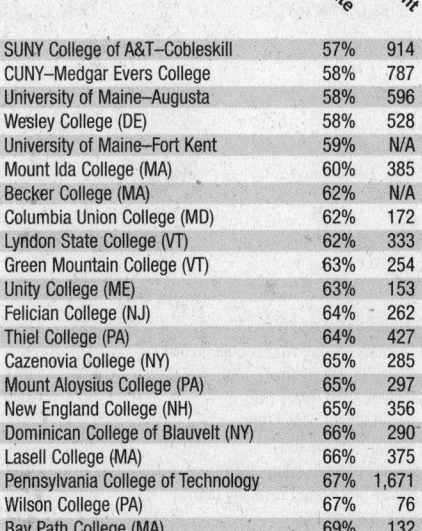

	Freshman retention rate	Freshman enrollment
SUNY College of A&T–Cobleskill	57%	914
CUNY–Medgar Evers College	58%	787
University of Maine–Augusta	58%	596
Wesley College (DE)	58%	528
University of Maine–Fort Kent	59%	N/A
Mount Ida College (MA)	60%	385
Becker College (MA)	62%	N/A
Columbia Union College (MD)	62%	172
Lyndon State College (VT)	62%	333
Green Mountain College (VT)	63%	254
Unity College (ME)	63%	153
Felician College (NJ)	64%	262
Thiel College (PA)	64%	427
Cazenovia College (NY)	65%	285
Mount Aloysius College (PA)	65%	297
New England College (NH)	65%	356
Dominican College of Blauvelt (NY)	66%	290
Lasell College (MA)	66%	375
Pennsylvania College of Technology	67%	1,671
Wilson College (PA)	67%	76
Bay Path College (MA)	69%	132

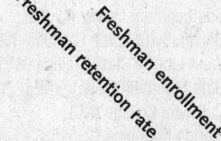

	Freshman retention rate	Freshman enrollment
Bloomfield College (NJ)	69%	413
Curry College (MA)	69%	600
Caldwell College (NJ)	70%	298
Medaille College (NY)	70%	218
SUNY–Farmingdale	70%	1,053
Utica College (NY)	70%	470
Daemen College (NY)	71%	366
University of Maine–Machias	71%	120
Delaware Valley College (PA)	72%	451
Keuka College (NY)	72%	268
Neumann College (PA)	72%	522
University of Maine–Farmington	72%	575
Albertus Magnus College (CT)	73%	484
Centenary College (NJ)	73%	266
Post University (CT)	73%	205
SUNY College–Old Westbury	74%	404
CUNY–New York City Coll. of Technology	75%	2,499
St. Francis College (NY)	75%	505
Concordia College (NY)	76%	175
Hilbert College (NY)	76%	166
Roger Williams University (RI)	76%	1,189

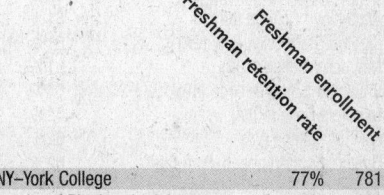

	Freshman retention rate	Freshman enrollment
CUNY–York College	77%	781
University of Pittsburgh–Johnstown	77%	822
Alvernia College (PA)	78%	274
Colby-Sawyer College (NH)	78%	282
Elmira College (NY)	78%	323
Villa Julie College (MD)	79%	543
Champlain College (VT)	80%	466
Endicott College (MA)	81%	502
Merrimack College (MA)	81%	556
Russell Sage College (NY)	81%	117
College of St. Elizabeth (NJ)	83%	130
Mercyhurst College (PA)	83%	696
St. Joseph's College New York–Brooklyn	83%	632
Cedar Crest College (PA)	85%	204
Elizabethtown College (PA)	85%	538
Messiah College (PA)	86%	707
Ramapo College of New Jersey	87%	748
Grove City College (PA)	90%	582
Stonehill College (MA)	90%	619

Schools whose freshmen are least (and most) likely to return

Comprehensive Colleges–Bachelor's (South)

	Freshman retention rate	Freshman enrollment
Allen University (SC)	36%	N/A
International College (FL)	37%	55
Edward Waters College (FL)	43%	N/A
St. Paul's College (VA)	46%	224
Chowan College (NC)	49%	286
Midway College (KY)	51%	161
University of Arkansas–Monticello	51%	668
LeMoyne-Owen College (TN)	54%	112
Brewton-Parker College (GA)	55%	257
Clearwater Christian College (FL)	56%	149
Crichton College (TN)	56%	80
Faulkner University (AL)	56%	204
Morris College (SC)	57%	208
Mountain State University (WV)	57%	365
Rust College (MS)	57%	256
Glenville State College (WV)	58%	270
Martin Methodist College (TN)	58%	221
Mid-Continent University (KY)	58%	94
Pikeville College (KY)	58%	208
Reinhardt College (GA)	58%	222
West Virginia State University	58%	363
West Virginia Univ. Institute of Technology	58%	183
Belmont Abbey College (NC)	60%	227
Brevard College (NC)	60%	148
Lambuth University (TN)	60%	234
North Carolina Wesleyan College	60%	288
Williams Baptist College (AR)	60%	130
Alice Lloyd College (KY)	61%	188
Clayton State University (GA)	61%	1,255
Newberry College (SC)	61%	276
Philander Smith College (AR)	61%	126
Bluefield College (VA)	62%	107
Ferrum College (VA)	62%	347
University of Arkansas–Pine Bluff	62%	719
Johnson C. Smith University (NC)	63%	444
Louisiana College	63%	N/A
Tennessee Wesleyan College	63%	N/A
Thomas More College (KY)	63%	227
Thomas University (GA)	63%	N/A
University of the Ozarks (AR)	63%	170
Barton College (NC)	64%	247
Benedict College (SC)	64%	N/A
Columbia College (SC)	64%	210
Livingstone College (NC)	64%	191
Concord University (WV)	65%	654
Kentucky Wesleyan College	65%	209
Limestone College (SC)	65%	172
University of Charleston (WV)	65%	287
University of South Carolina–Upstate	65%	749
West Virginia University–Parkersburg	65%	659
Anderson University (SC)	66%	371
Bluefield State College (WV)	66%	251
Methodist College (NC)	66%	439
Mississippi Valley State University	66%	407
Ohio Valley University (WV)	66%	89
Peace College (NC)	66%	179
Virginia Intermont College	66%	182
Warner Southern College (FL)	66%	109
Belhaven College (MS)	67%	202
Davis and Elkins College (WV)	67%	104
Emmanuel College (GA)	67%	231
Shaw University (NC)	67%	601
Southeastern University (FL)	67%	521
University of South Carolina–Aiken	67%	610
West Liberty State College (WV)	67%	421
Blue Mountain College (MS)	68%	45
Catawba College (NC)	68%	223
Florida Memorial College	68%	N/A
Mars Hill College (NC)	68%	286
Shepherd University (WV)	68%	675
Coker College (SC)	69%	148
Florida Southern College	70%	464
Maryville College (TN)	70%	333
Toccoa Falls College (GA)	70%	271
Lenoir-Rhyne College (NC)	71%	330
North Greenville University (SC)	71%	439
Oakwood College (AL)	71%	410
Southern Adventist University (TN)	71%	605
Wingate University (NC)	71%	371
Covenant College (GA)	72%	263
Kentucky Christian University	72%	138
Mount Olive College (NC)	72%	314
Stillman College (AL)	72%	275
Bethune-Cookman College (FL)	73%	949
Fairmont State University (WV)	73%	731
Lee University (TN)	73%	761
Shorter College (GA)	73%	291
Bryan College (TN)	74%	184
Flagler College (FL)	74%	458
Elizabeth City State University (NC)	75%	560
Ouachita Baptist University (AR)	75%	368
Our Lady of Holy Cross College (LA)	75%	N/A
LaGrange College (GA)	76%	204
High Point University (NC)	77%	454
Winston-Salem State University (NC)	77%	1,083
Berry College (GA)	78%	514
Dillard University (LA)	78%	N/A
Claflin University (SC)	79%	385
John Brown University (AR)	79%	262
Alderson-Broaddus College (WV)	80%	125
Asbury College (KY)	80%	277
Brescia University (KY)	80%	48
Berea College (KY)	81%	378

Comprehensive Colleges–Bachelor's (Midwest)

	Freshman retention rate	Freshman enrollment
East-West University (IL)	35%	N/A
William Penn University (IA)	45%	168
Missouri Valley College	47%	N/A
Iowa Wesleyan College	51%	135
Central State University (OH)	52%	353
Purdue University–North Central (IN)	53%	683
Black Hills State University (SD)	54%	N/A
Calumet College of St. Joseph (IN)	57%	60
Indiana University East	57%	372
MacMurray College (IL)	57%	320
Mayville State University (ND)	57%	145
Missouri Western State University	57%	N/A
Central Christian College (KS)	58%	97
Kansas Wesleyan University	59%	N/A
Urbana University (OH)	59%	N/A
Indiana University–Kokomo	60%	476
Rochester College (MI)	60%	137
Lourdes College (OH)	61%	129
Ohio Dominican University	61%	381
Central Methodist University (MO)	62%	224
Dakota Wesleyan University (SD)	62%	346
Wilberforce University (OH)	62%	N/A
Columbia College (MO)	63%	192
Dana College (NE)	63%	208
University of Minnesota–Crookston	63%	198
Bethany College (KS)	64%	148
Defiance College (OH)	64%	208
Hannibal-LaGrange College (MO)	64%	119
Missouri Southern State University	64%	897
Sterling College (KS)	64%	127
Waldorf College (IA)	64%	161
Evangel University (MO)	65%	423
Dickinson State University (ND)	66%	376
Eureka College (IL)	66%	138
Grace University (NE)	66%	N/A
Missouri Baptist University	66%	223
Morningside College (IA)	66%	309
Graceland University (IA)	67%	N/A
Tri-State University (IN)	67%	305
Dakota State University (SD)	68%	285
Lakeland College (WI)	68%	243
St. Mary-of-the-Woods College (IN)	68%	N/A
Briar Cliff University (IA)	69%	251
College of St. Mary (NE)	69%	N/A
Grand View College (IA)	69%	221
Marian College (IN)	69%	191
Southwestern College (KS)	69%	136
Valley City State University (ND)	69%	176
York College (NE)	69%	119
Concordia University (MI)	70%	115
Concordia University–St. Paul (MN)	70%	165
Culver-Stockton College (MO)	70%	155
Manchester College (IN)	70%	330
Midland Lutheran College (NE)	70%	249
Southwest Minnesota State University (MN)	70%	590
St. Joseph's College (IN)	70%	233
Crown College (MN)	71%	N/A
Jamestown College (ND)	71%	286
Union College (NE)	71%	180
Bethel College (KS)	72%	96

	Freshman retention rate	Freshman enrollment
Greenville College (IL)	72%	252
Marietta College (OH)	72%	392
Tabor College (KS)	72%	124
Wilmington College (OH)	72%	389
Judson College (IL)	73%	135
Mount Vernon Nazarene University (OH)	73%	380
Alverno College (WI)	74%	280
Bluffton University (OH)	74%	230
Franklin College (IN)	74%	273
Buena Vista University (IA)	75%	287
Grace College and Seminary (IN)	75%	218
Illinois College	75%	256
Mount Mercy College (IA)	75%	181
Carroll College (WI)	76%	610
McKendree College (IL)	76%	273

	Freshman retention rate	Freshman enrollment
Northwestern College (IA)	76%	374
Huntington University (IN)	77%	229
Wisconsin Lutheran College	77%	180
Northwestern College (MN)	78%	469
Trinity Christian College (IL)	78%	229
Wartburg College (IA)	78%	519
Clarke College (IA)	79%	158
Loras College (IA)	79%	366
Millikin University (IL)	79%	573
Mount Union College (OH)	79%	503
Simpson College (IA)	79%	336
Augustana College (SD)	81%	405
Central College (IA)	81%	366
Elmhurst College (IL)	81%	466
Notre Dame College of Ohio	81%	168

	Freshman retention rate	Freshman enrollment
Otterbein College (OH)	81%	627
Cedarville University (OH)	82%	763
Dordt College (IA)	82%	356
McPherson College (KS)	83%	109
Ohio Northern University	83%	809
College of the Ozarks (MO)	84%	242
St. Norbert College (WI)	84%	511
St. Mary's College (IN)	85%	377
Bethel College (IN)	87%	N/A
Calvin College (MI)	87%	1,007
Taylor University (IN)	88%	461
Northland College (WI)	91%	180

Comprehensive Colleges–Bachelor's (West)

	Freshman retention rate	Freshman enrollment
Paul Quinn College (TX)	41%	N/A
Utah Valley State College	49%	3,713
Humphreys College (CA)	50%	117
Texas College	50%	212
Huston-Tillotson University (TX)	52%	168
Jarvis Christian College (TX)	54%	98
Wiley College (TX)	55%	151
Oklahoma Panhandle State University	56%	212
Concordia University–Austin (TX)	57%	195
Lewis-Clark State College (ID)	57%	509
St. Gregory's University (OK)	58%	101
University of Science and Arts of Oklahoma	58%	282
Howard Payne University (TX)	59%	297

	Freshman retention rate	Freshman enrollment
University of Montana–Western	59%	230
East Texas Baptist University	60%	303
Oklahoma Wesleyan University	60%	133
Metropolitan State College of Denver	61%	N/A
University of Houston–Downtown	61%	1,029
McMurry University (TX)	62%	292
Menlo College (CA)	64%	172
Lubbock Christian University (TX)	66%	320
Northwest Christian College (OR)	66%	47
Northwest University (WA)	69%	132
Pacific Union College (CA)	69%	348
Oklahoma Christian University	70%	611
Sierra Nevada College (NV)	70%	69

	Freshman retention rate	Freshman enrollment
Corban College (OR)	71%	205
Oklahoma Baptist University	71%	374
Texas Lutheran University	71%	380
Cogswell Polytechnical College (CA)	72%	24
Brigham Young University–Hawaii	73%	220
Rocky Mountain College (MT)	74%	218
Vanguard University of Southern California	74%	403
Patten University (CA)	75%	59
Carroll College (MT)	79%	304
Master's College and Seminary (CA)	81%	187
Linfield College (OR)	82%	488

Schools whose students are most (and least) likely to graduate

Like retention rates, graduation rates can tell you something about how colleges serve their students: how good a job they do at providing the support and access to courses students need to complete their degrees. A low four-year graduation rate may also indicate a large population of part-time students or a significant cooperative education program, which can require five years or more. Below, we show the average proportion who graduate in six years or less for classes starting in 1996 through 1999, and the proportion who started in 1999 who earned a degree in four years.

National Universities

University	6-year graduation rate	4-year graduation rate
Harvard University (MA)	98%	87%
Princeton University (NJ)	97%	90%
Brown University (RI)	96%	83%
Yale University (CT)	96%	90%
Dartmouth College (NH)	95%	84%
University of Notre Dame (IN)	95%	88%
Duke University (NC)	94%	87%
Stanford University (CA)	94%	76%
Columbia University (NY)	93%	92%
Georgetown University (DC)	93%	88%
Northwestern University (IL)	93%	85%
University of Pennsylvania	93%	87%
Massachusetts Institute of Technology	92%	82%
University of Virginia	92%	84%
College of William and Mary (VA)	91%	81%
Cornell University (NY)	91%	84%
Rice University (TX)	91%	76%
Tufts University (MA)	90%	84%
Washington University in St. Louis	90%	82%
Boston College	89%	88%
Johns Hopkins University (MD)	89%	81%
University of Chicago	89%	85%
California Institute of Technology	88%	83%
Brandeis University (MA)	87%	84%
Emory University (GA)	87%	84%
University of California–Los Angeles	87%	57%
Wake Forest University (NC)	87%	78%
University of California–Berkeley	86%	58%
University of Michigan–Ann Arbor	86%	70%
Lehigh University (PA)	85%	74%
Vanderbilt University (TN)	85%	83%
Carnegie Mellon University (PA)	84%	66%
University of California–San Diego	83%	54%
Penn. State Univ.–University Park	82%	54%
University of North Carolina–Chapel Hill	82%	71%
Yeshiva University (NY)	82%	57%
University of Illinois–Urbana-Champaign	81%	60%
University of Southern California	81%	61%
Miami University–Oxford (OH)	80%	66%
New York University	80%	74%
Rensselaer Polytechnic Institute (NY)	80%	61%
SUNY–Binghamton	80%	67%
University of California–Davis	80%	42%
University of Rochester (NY)	80%	68%
Syracuse University (NY)	79%	68%
University of California–Irvine	79%	42%
Case Western Reserve University (OH)	78%	57%
Pepperdine University (CA)	78%	71%
University of Florida	78%	53%
Fordham University (NY)	77%	72%
Marquette University (WI)	77%	62%
Boston University	76%	65%
George Washington University (DC)	76%	72%
Texas A&M University–College Station	76%	35%
University of Dayton (OH)	76%	60%
University of Wisconsin–Madison	76%	43%
Worcester Polytechnic Institute (MA)	76%	61%
University of California–Santa Barbara	75%	55%
University of Delaware	75%	62%
Virginia Tech	75%	47%
Tulane University (LA)	74%	63%
Clemson University (SC)	73%	44%
St. Louis University	73%	61%
University of New Hampshire	73%	53%
University of Texas–Austin	73%	42%
Baylor University (TX)	72%	45%
Brigham Young University–Provo (UT)	72%	N/A
Rutgers–New Brunswick (NJ)	72%	42%
University of Georgia	72%	41%
University of Maryland–College Park	72%	50%
University of San Diego	72%	62%
University of St. Thomas (MN)	72%	59%
University of Washington	72%	46%
Georgia Institute of Technology	71%	29%
Indiana University–Bloomington	71%	49%
Michigan State University	71%	41%
Southern Methodist University (TX)	71%	55%
University of Connecticut	71%	50%
American University (DC)	70%	63%
Duquesne University (PA)	70%	54%
Ohio University	70%	46%
Stevens Institute of Technology (NJ)	70%	31%
University of Denver	70%	52%
Catholic University of America (DC)	69%	60%
Clark University (MA)	69%	63%
University of Miami (FL)	69%	56%
Loyola University Chicago	68%	51%
University of California–Santa Cruz	68%	49%
University of Vermont	68%	49%
University of the Pacific (CA)	68%	43%
Clarkson University (NY)	67%	62%
SUNY Coll. Environ. Science & Forestry	67%	44%
University of California–Riverside	67%	43%
University of Colorado–Boulder	67%	38%
University of Missouri–Columbia	67%	44%
University of San Francisco	67%	50%
Auburn University (AL)	66%	32%
Iowa State University	66%	31%
North Carolina State University–Raleigh	66%	36%
St. John's University (NY)	66%	40%
Texas Christian University	66%	N/A
University of Pittsburgh	66%	46%
Biola University (CA)	65%	48%
Florida State University	65%	44%
Purdue University–West Lafayette (IN)	65%	32%
University of Iowa	65%	38%
Colorado State University	63%	34%
DePaul University (IL)	63%	40%
Ohio State University–Columbus	63%	35%
SUNY–Albany	63%	50%
University of Massachusetts–Amherst	63%	46%
University of South Carolina–Columbia	63%	41%
Illinois Institute of Technology	62%	64%
Michigan Technological University	62%	23%
University of Alabama	62%	35%
Bowling Green State University (OH)	61%	34%
Oregon State University	61%	31%
University of Missouri–Rolla	61%	16%
University of Oregon	61%	39%
Washington State University	61%	32%
Howard University (DC)	60%	43%
Illinois State University	60%	35%
University of Kentucky	60%	29%
University of Nebraska–Lincoln	60%	22%
University of Tulsa (OK)	60%	43%
Northeastern University (MA)	59%	0%
Widener University (PA)	59%	39%
Drexel University (PA)	58%	14%
Kansas State University	58%	22%
Oklahoma State University	58%	26%
University at Buffalo–SUNY	58%	35%
University of Kansas	58%	31%
University of Tennessee	58%	29%
Louisiana State University–Baton Rouge	57%	26%
Mississippi State University	57%	25%
New School University (NY)	57%	44%
SUNY–Stony Brook	57%	38%
Seton Hall University (NJ)	57%	41%
University of Rhode Island	57%	36%
Pace University (NY)	56%	40%
University of Arizona	56%	32%
University of Maine–Orono	56%	28%
University of Minnesota–Twin Cities	56%	32%
University of Mississippi	56%	34%
University of Wyoming	56%	29%
University of Idaho	55%	23%
University of Maryland–Baltimore County	55%	30%
University of Oklahoma	55%	19%
University of Texas–Dallas	55%	30%
West Virginia University	55%	26%
Western Michigan University	55%	20%
Arizona State University	54%	27%
East Carolina University (NC)	54%	25%
Hofstra University (NY)	54%	36%
South Dakota State University	54%	24%
Texas Tech University	54%	23%
University of Central Florida	54%	30%
University of Hartford (CT)	54%	45%
University of Hawaii–Manoa	54%	12%
Florida Institute of Technology	53%	35%
Rutgers–Newark (NJ)	53%	22%
Temple University (PA)	53%	27%

University	6-year graduation rate	4-year graduation rate
University of North Dakota	53%	23%
Adelphi University (NY)	52%	44%
Central Michigan University	52%	21%
Louisiana Tech University	52%	28%
North Dakota State University	52%	19%
Northern Illinois University	52%	25%
Ball State University (IN)	51%	27%
George Mason University (VA)	51%	26%
New Jersey Institute of Technology	51%	18%
University of Arkansas	51%	30%
University of Utah	51%	20%
Indiana University of Pennsylvania	50%	N/A
University of North Carolina–Greensboro	50%	38%
Northern Arizona University	49%	26%
University of Cincinnati	49%	17%
University of La Verne (CA)	49%	38%
University of Nevada–Reno	49%	16%
University of South Florida	49%	22%
Kent State University (OH)	48%	19%
Polytechnic University (NY)	48%	32%
University of Southern Mississippi	48%	23%
Andrews University (MI)	47%	28%
Florida International University	47%	21%
South Carolina State University	47%	32%
Utah State University	47%	21%
Tennessee State University	46%	N/A
University of Illinois–Chicago	46%	20%
University of Missouri–Kansas City	46%	17%
University of Northern Colorado	46%	26%
University of South Dakota	46%	21%
Montana State University–Bozeman	45%	19%
San Diego State University	45%	14%
University of Massachusetts–Lowell	45%	25%
New Mexico State University	44%	12%
Nova Southeastern University (FL)	44%	N/A
Oakland University (MI)	44%	13%
Old Dominion University (VA)	44%	22%
University of Montana	44%	20%
University of Toledo (OH)	43%	17%
Southern Illinois University–Carbondale	42%	19%
University of Alabama–Huntsville	42%	13%
University of New Mexico	42%	N/A
New Mexico Institute of Mining and Tech	41%	16%
University of Bridgeport (CT)	41%	21%
Univ. of Col.–Denver and Health Science	41%	16%
University of Missouri–St. Louis	41%	23%
Virginia Commonwealth University	41%	21%
Wilmington College (DE)	41%	N/A
Middle Tennessee State University	40%	23%
University of North Texas	40%	15%
University of Wisconsin–Milwaukee	40%	13%
Wright State University (OH)	40%	16%
Indiana State University	39%	18%
University of Houston	39%	10%
University of Nevada–Las Vegas	39%	14%
Texas Woman's University	38%	12%
University of Alabama–Birmingham	38%	14%
University of Texas–Arlington	38%	15%
East Tennessee State University	37%	15%
Florida Atlantic University	37%	14%
Georgia State University	37%	13%
University of Akron (OH)	37%	10%
Alabama Agricultural and Mechanical Univ.	36%	9%
Jackson State University (MS)	36%	N/A
Texas A&M University–Commerce	36%	N/A
Wichita State University (KS)	36%	15%
University of Louisville (KY)	35%	13%
University of Memphis	35%	11%
Alliant International University (CA)	34%	25%
Portland State University (OR)	33%	10%
University of Louisiana–Lafayette	33%	12%
University of Massachusetts–Boston	33%	15%
University of South Alabama	33%	14%
Wayne State University (MI)	33%	7%
Clark Atlanta University	32%	19%
Union Institute and University (OH)	28%	N/A
University of Alaska–Fairbanks	28%	6%
Cleveland State University	27%	11%
University of Texas–El Paso	27%	5%
National-Louis University (IL)	26%	13%
Texas A&M University–Kingsville	26%	7%
Idaho State University	24%	8%
University of New Orleans	24%	N/A
Indiana Univ.-Purdue Univ.–Indianapolis	23%	7%
University of Arkansas–Little Rock	22%	N/A
Texas Southern University	15%	N/A

Liberal Arts Colleges

College	6-year graduation rate	4-year graduation rate
Amherst College (MA)	96%	89%
Williams College (MA)	96%	90%
Swarthmore College (PA)	92%	86%
Wellesley College (MA)	92%	88%
Bowdoin College (ME)	91%	90%
College of the Holy Cross (MA)	91%	89%
Haverford College (PA)	91%	81%
Middlebury College (VT)	91%	85%
Wesleyan University (CT)	91%	83%
Davidson College (NC)	90%	84%
Bucknell University (PA)	89%	85%
Colgate University (NY)	89%	88%
Carleton College (MN)	88%	81%
Colby College (ME)	88%	85%
Pomona College (CA)	88%	87%
Vassar College (NY)	88%	86%
Washington and Lee University (VA)	88%	84%
Barnard College (NY)	87%	82%
Bates College (ME)	87%	84%
Lafayette College (PA)	87%	87%
Connecticut College	86%	84%
Grinnell College (IA)	86%	83%
Hamilton College (NY)	86%	82%
Wheaton College (IL)	86%	77%
Trinity College (CT)	85%	78%
Union College (NY)	85%	80%
Whitman College (WA)	85%	78%
Bryn Mawr College (PA)	84%	80%
Claremont McKenna College (CA)	84%	82%
Furman University (SC)	84%	79%
Harvey Mudd College (CA)	84%	79%
Smith College (MA)	84%	82%
Franklin and Marshall College (PA)	83%	75%
Kenyon College (OH)	83%	80%
Macalester College (MN)	83%	79%
University of Richmond (VA)	83%	78%
Muhlenberg College (PA)	82%	81%
St. Olaf College (MN)	82%	78%
Colorado College	81%	77%
Dickinson College (PA)	81%	81%
Oberlin College (OH)	81%	68%
St. John's University (MN)	81%	71%
Illinois Wesleyan University	80%	77%
Mount Holyoke College (MA)	80%	74%
Sewanee–University of the South (TN)	80%	79%
Skidmore College (NY)	80%	73%
Centre College (KY)	79%	77%
College of St. Benedict (MN)	79%	71%
Occidental College (CA)	79%	78%
Scripps College (CA)	79%	81%
Thomas Aquinas College (CA)	79%	84%
Denison University (OH)	78%	75%
Gustavus Adolphus College (MN)	78%	79%
Principia College (IL)	78%	73%
Rhodes College (TN)	78%	77%
Susquehanna University (PA)	78%	75%
Ursinus College (PA)	78%	72%
Wofford College (SC)	78%	74%
DePauw University (IN)	77%	75%
Kalamazoo College (MI)	77%	73%
Luther College (IA)	77%	65%
Siena College (NY)	77%	73%
Spelman College (GA)	77%	62%
Augustana College (IL)	76%	71%
Gettysburg College (PA)	76%	70%
St. Mary's College of Maryland	76%	63%
Westminster College (PA)	76%	65%
Willamette University (OR)	76%	67%
Austin College (TX)	75%	69%
Juniata College (PA)	75%	67%
Knox College (IL)	75%	67%
St. Anselm College (NH)	75%	71%
University of Puget Sound (WA)	75%	65%
Drew University (NJ)	74%	69%
Hope College (MI)	74%	64%
Southwestern University (TX)	74%	67%
St. Lawrence University (NY)	74%	71%
Birmingham-Southern College (AL)	73%	62%
Hobart and William Smith Colleges (NY)	73%	61%
Presbyterian College (SC)	73%	62%
Sarah Lawrence College (NY)	73%	65%
Wheaton College (MA)	73%	70%
Pitzer College (CA)	72%	61%
Randolph-Macon College (VA)	72%	62%
Alma College (MI)	71%	58%
Earlham College (IN)	71%	54%
Lawrence University (WI)	71%	59%
McDaniel College (MD)	71%	63%
Moravian College (PA)	71%	67%
Reed College (OR)	71%	52%
Wabash College (IN)	71%	66%
Westmont College (CA)	71%	65%
Albion College (MI)	70%	67%

Schools whose students are most (and least) likely to graduate

Liberal Arts Colleges, continued

	6-year graduation rate	4-year graduation rate
Allegheny College (PA)	70%	67%
Bard College (NY)	70%	60%
Beloit College (WI)	70%	62%
Hanover College (IN)	70%	68%
Millsaps College (MS)	70%	63%
New College of Florida	70%	57%
St. Vincent College (PA)	70%	59%
Washington and Jefferson College (PA)	70%	66%
Agnes Scott College (GA)	69%	60%
Coe College (IA)	69%	66%
College of Wooster (OH)	69%	68%
Erskine College (SC)	69%	64%
Houghton College (NY)	69%	56%
Rosemont College (PA)	69%	62%
Gordon College (MA)	68%	54%
Hillsdale College (MI)	68%	64%
Lewis and Clark College (OR)	68%	62%
Wittenberg University (OH)	68%	61%
Fisk University (TN)	67%	44%
Lake Forest College (IL)	67%	63%
Washington College (MD)	67%	62%
Bennington College (VT)	66%	45%
Christendom College (VA)	66%	N/A
Concordia College–Moorhead (MN)	66%	56%
Goucher College (MD)	66%	57%
Lycoming College (PA)	66%	61%
Nebraska Wesleyan University	66%	55%
Ohio Wesleyan University	66%	63%
Ripon College (WI)	66%	60%
St. John's College (MD)	66%	N/A
Sweet Briar College (VA)	66%	65%
Transylvania University (KY)	66%	60%
University of Dallas	66%	61%
Virginia Military Institute	66%	N/A
College of the Atlantic (ME)	65%	45%
Goshen College (IN)	65%	46%
Hampshire College (MA)	65%	52%
Hendrix College (AR)	65%	55%
Cornell College (IA)	64%	60%
Eckerd College (FL)	64%	58%

	6-year graduation rate	4-year graduation rate
Hiram College (OH)	64%	55%
Mills College (CA)	64%	59%
Richard Stockton College of New Jersey	64%	36%
Roanoke College (VA)	64%	57%
Wells College (NY)	64%	54%
Bethany College (WV)	63%	53%
Eastern Mennonite University (VA)	63%	51%
Hastings College (NE)	63%	51%
Hollins University (VA)	63%	55%
Albright College (PA)	62%	52%
Bridgewater College (VA)	62%	65%
Guilford College (NC)	62%	44%
Muskingum College (OH)	62%	49%
Randolph-Macon Woman's College (VA)	62%	63%
Chatham College (PA)	61%	N/A
Hampden-Sydney College (VA)	61%	58%
William Jewell College (MO)	61%	54%
Monmouth College (IL)	60%	N/A
Oglethorpe University (GA)	60%	53%
Georgetown College (KY)	59%	46%
Lyon College (AR)	58%	58%
Hartwick College (NY)	57%	49%
St. John's College (NM)	57%	N/A
University of Judaism (CA)	57%	N/A
Morehouse College (GA)	56%	43%
Salem College (NC)	56%	41%
Emory and Henry College (VA)	55%	43%
King College (TN)	55%	47%
Stephens College (MO)	55%	43%
University of Minnesota–Morris	55%	40%
Seton Hill University (PA)	54%	44%
West Virginia Wesleyan College	54%	45%
Westminster College (MO)	54%	47%
Huntingdon College (AL)	53%	36%
Whittier College (CA)	53%	49%
Albertson College (ID)	52%	48%
Evergreen State College (WA)	52%	42%
University of North Carolina–Asheville	52%	28%
National Hispanic University (CA)	N/A	N/A
Talladega College (AL)	49%	34%

	6-year graduation rate	4-year graduation rate
Antioch College (OH)	48%	32%
San Diego Christian College (CA)	48%	35%
Tougaloo College (MS)	48%	N/A
Adrian College (MI)	47%	30%
Franklin Pierce College (NH)	47%	45%
University of Pittsburgh–Greensburg	47%	N/A
Marlboro College (VT)	46%	45%
Massachusetts College of Liberal Arts	46%	35%
Warner Pacific College (OR)	46%	39%
Judson College (AL)	45%	N/A
Wesleyan College (GA)	45%	40%
Marymount Manhattan College (NY)	44%	28%
University of Pittsburgh–Bradford	44%	17%
Bennett College (NC)	43%	22%
Pine Manor College (MA)	43%	30%
Schreiner University (TX)	42%	27%
University of Virginia–Wise	42%	28%
Greensboro College (NC)	41%	26%
Virginia Wesleyan College	41%	30%
Christopher Newport University (VA)	40%	18%
Coastal Carolina University (SC)	39%	23%
St. Andrews Presbyterian College (NC)	39%	37%
Blackburn College (IL)	38%	N/A
California State University–Monterey Bay	36%	N/A
Lane College (TN)	35%	50%
Olivet College (MI)	35%	34%
University of Maine–Presque Isle	34%	16%
University of Hawaii–Hilo	32%	11%
Western State College of Colorado	32%	N/A
Lees-McRae College (NC)	31%	20%
Texas A&M University–Galveston	31%	11%
Fort Lewis College (CO)	30%	10%
St. Augustine's College (NC)	30%	18%
Mesa State College (CO)	29%	9%
Paine College (GA)	28%	8%
Bethel College (TN)	27%	N/A
Virginia Union University	27%	19%
Shawnee State University (OH)	26%	13%
Arkansas Baptist College	25%	N/A
Lindsey Wilson College (KY)	22%	12%

Universities–Master's (North)

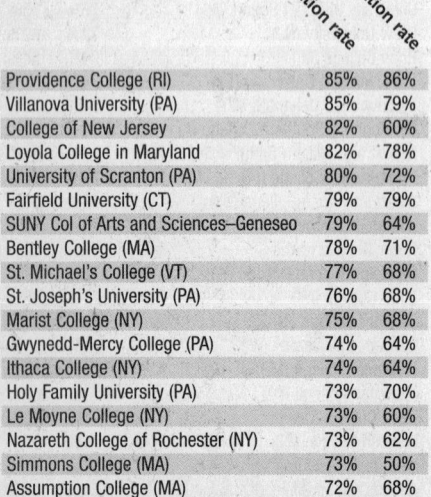

	6-year graduation rate	4-year graduation rate
Providence College (RI)	85%	86%
Villanova University (PA)	85%	79%
College of New Jersey	82%	60%
Loyola College in Maryland	82%	78%
University of Scranton (PA)	80%	72%
Fairfield University (CT)	79%	79%
SUNY Col of Arts and Sciences–Geneseo	79%	64%
Bentley College (MA)	78%	71%
St. Michael's College (VT)	77%	68%
St. Joseph's University (PA)	76%	68%
Marist College (NY)	75%	68%
Gwynedd-Mercy College (PA)	74%	64%
Ithaca College (NY)	74%	64%
Holy Family University (PA)	73%	70%
Le Moyne College (NY)	73%	60%
Nazareth College of Rochester (NY)	73%	62%
Simmons College (MA)	73%	50%
Assumption College (MA)	72%	68%

	6-year graduation rate	4-year graduation rate
La Salle University (PA)	72%	56%
College Misericordia (PA)	71%	66%
King's College (PA)	70%	64%
Lebanon Valley College (PA)	70%	69%
Emerson College (MA)	69%	66%
Hood College (MD)	69%	64%
St. Bonaventure University (NY)	69%	59%
College of Notre Dame of Maryland	68%	57%
Quinnipiac University (CT)	68%	64%
Bryant University (RI)	67%	63%
Canisius College (NY)	67%	51%
Manhattan College (NY)	67%	59%
Salisbury University (MD)	67%	52%
Alfred University (NY)	66%	44%
Marywood University (PA)	66%	42%
Mount St. Mary's University (MD)	66%	64%
Springfield College (MA)	66%	46%
Wagner College (NY)	66%	64%

	6-year graduation rate	4-year graduation rate
Arcadia University (PA)	65%	57%
College of St. Rose (NY)	65%	51%
Gannon University (PA)	65%	50%
Regis College (MA)	65%	64%
DeSales University (PA)	64%	62%
Penn State–Erie, Behrend Col.	64%	39%
York College of Pennsylvania	63%	43%
Millersville University of Pennsylvania	62%	34%
Rowan University (NJ)	62%	36%
SUNY–Fredonia	62%	49%
St. John Fisher College (NY)	62%	53%
Bloomsburg University of Pennsylvania	61%	38%
Eastern University (PA)	61%	50%
Molloy College (NY)	61%	44%
Rider University (NJ)	61%	42%
Shippensburg University of Pennsylvania	61%	42%
Emmanuel College (MA)	60%	45%
Lesley University (MA)	60%	32%

	6-year graduation rate	4-year graduation rate
St. Francis University (PA)	60%	47%
Niagara University (NY)	59%	55%
Rochester Institute of Technology (NY)	59%	N/A
Rutgers–Camden (NJ)	59%	26%
Salve Regina University (RI)	59%	52%
West Chester University of Pennsylvania	59%	26%
Cabrini College (PA)	58%	50%
Roberts Wesleyan College (NY)	58%	51%
Sacred Heart University (CT)	58%	56%
Towson University (MD)	58%	31%
University of New England (ME)	58%	48%
Chestnut Hill College (PA)	57%	42%
College of Mount St. Vincent (NY)	57%	35%
Immaculata University (PA)	57%	60%
Manhattanville College (NY)	57%	51%
Montclair State University (NJ)	57%	23%
SUNY Col. Arts & Sci.–New Paltz	57%	35%
SUNY–Plattsburgh	57%	32%
Western New England College (MA)	57%	46%
Wilkes University (PA)	57%	44%
Anna Maria College (MA)	56%	48%
Geneva College (PA)	56%	42%
Georgian Court University (NJ)	56%	29%
St. Joseph College (CT)	56%	43%
La Roche College (PA)	55%	43%
Mount St. Mary College (NY)	55%	49%
Philadelphia University	55%	35%
Robert Morris University (PA)	55%	30%
SUNY College–Cortland	55%	37%
SUNY–Oswego	55%	33%
Westfield State College (MA)	55%	38%
Wheelock College (MA)	55%	43%
Iona College (NY)	54%	42%
Keene State College (NH)	53%	27%
Monmouth University (NJ)	53%	33%
St. Joseph's College (ME)	53%	48%
Clarion University of Pennsylvania	52%	23%

	6-year graduation rate	4-year graduation rate
SUNY College–Brockport	52%	29%
Waynesburg College (PA)	52%	44%
CUNY–Baruch College	51%	28%
Carlow University (PA)	51%	35%
Rivier College (NH)	51%	42%
St. Thomas Aquinas College (NY)	51%	34%
Suffolk University (MA)	51%	36%
University of Massachusetts–Dartmouth	51%	28%
CUNY–Queens College	50%	23%
East Stroudsburg Univ. of Pennsylvania	50%	19%
Johnson and Wales University (RI)	50%	47%
Lock Haven University of Pennsylvania	50%	25%
Norwich University (VT)	50%	N/A
Slippery Rock University of Pennsylvania	50%	26%
Touro College (NY)	50%	44%
Edinboro University of Pennsylvania	49%	20%
Frostburg State University (MD)	49%	21%
Kutztown University of Pennsylvania	49%	N/A
Mansfield University of Pennsylvania	49%	30%
Bridgewater State College (MA)	48%	19%
Fairleigh Dickinson University (NJ)	48%	30%
Fitchburg State College (MA)	48%	21%
SUNY College–Oneonta	48%	37%
William Paterson University of New Jersey	48%	15%
Husson College (ME)	47%	N/A
Plymouth State University (NH)	46%	28%
St. Peter's College (NJ)	46%	34%
California University of Pennsylvania	45%	17%
Kean University (NJ)	45%	16%
SUNY College–Potsdam	45%	26%
Eastern Nazarene College (MA)	44%	38%
Trinity University (DC)	44%	N/A
American International College (MA)	43%	32%
Castleton State College (VT)	43%	26%
Elms College (MA)	43%	N/A
Rhode Island College	43%	16%
SUNY–Purchase College	43%	32%

	6-year graduation rate	4-year graduation rate
University of New Haven (CT)	43%	23%
CUNY–College of Staten Island	42%	20%
Central Connecticut State University	42%	11%
Eastern Connecticut State University	42%	25%
Framingham State College (MA)	42%	23%
University of Maryland–Eastern Shore	42%	25%
Lincoln University (PA)	41%	27%
New York Institute of Technology	41%	18%
Worcester State College (MA)	41%	30%
CUNY–Brooklyn College	40%	17%
Dowling College (NY)	40%	17%
Morgan State University (MD)	40%	24%
Nyack College (NY)	40%	33%
SUNY–Buffalo State College	40%	15%
Long Island Univ.–C.W. Post Campus	39%	24%
Point Park University (PA)	39%	36%
Salem State College (MA)	38%	15%
CUNY–Hunter College	36%	10%
New Jersey City University	36%	9%
Southern Connecticut State University	36%	12%
College of New Rochelle (NY)	34%	N/A
College of St. Joseph (VT)	34%	N/A
Western Connecticut State University	34%	15%
Bowie State University (MD)	33%	N/A
CUNY–City College	33%	6%
CUNY–Lehman College	33%	7%
Delaware State University	33%	21%
Johnson State College (VT)	33%	N/A
Cheyney University of Pennsylvania	32%	N/A
University of Southern Maine	32%	12%
Gallaudet University (DC)	30%	6%
Goddard College (VT)	28%	N/A
Southeastern University (DC)	25%	N/A
Coppin State University (MD)	24%	9%
Long Island University–Brooklyn (NY)	21%	4%
Mercy College (NY)	20%	9%
University of the District of Columbia	13%	N/A

Universities–Master's (South)

	6-year graduation rate	4-year graduation rate
James Madison University (VA)	80%	62%
University of Mary Washington (VA)	73%	70%
Elon University (NC)	72%	69%
Samford University (AL)	70%	53%
Meredith College (NC)	68%	57%
The Citadel (SC)	67%	55%
Mississippi College	66%	52%
Stetson University (FL)	64%	57%
Spring Hill College (AL)	63%	49%
Appalachian State University (NC)	62%	35%
Christian Brothers University (TN)	62%	49%
Rollins College (FL)	62%	49%
Longwood University (VA)	61%	48%
Loyola University New Orleans	61%	N/A
University of North Carolina–Wilmington	61%	41%
Queens University of Charlotte (NC)	60%	54%
Belmont University (TN)	59%	46%

	6-year graduation rate	4-year graduation rate
Harding University (AR)	59%	33%
Bellarmine University (KY)	58%	56%
Carson-Newman College (TN)	58%	45%
Lynchburg College (VA)	58%	47%
Wheeling Jesuit University (WV)	58%	52%
Murray State University (KY)	57%	38%
Union University (TN)	57%	43%
Winthrop University (SC)	57%	33%
College of Charleston (SC)	56%	41%
Hampton University (VA)	55%	35%
Xavier University of Louisiana	55%	N/A
Centenary College of Louisiana	54%	43%
Converse College (SC)	54%	55%
Embry Riddle Aeronautical University (FL)	54%	33%
Marymount University (VA)	54%	38%
Milligan College (TN)	54%	49%
Radford University (VA)	54%	37%

	6-year graduation rate	4-year graduation rate
Freed-Hardeman University (TN)	53%	39%
Troy University (AL)	53%	33%
Lipscomb University (TN)	52%	29%
University of Tampa (FL)	52%	45%
Mercer University (GA)	51%	35%
Campbell University (NC)	50%	N/A
Mary Baldwin College (VA)	50%	49%
North Carolina Central University	49%	23%
Gardner-Webb University (NC)	48%	35%
Tuskegee University (AL)	48%	17%
University of North Carolina–Charlotte	48%	24%
Delta State University (MS)	47%	23%
Lander University (SC)	47%	22%
North Georgia College and State University	47%	22%
University of North Florida	47%	25%
University of Tennessee–Chattanooga	47%	16%
Western Carolina University (NC)	47%	23%

Schools whose students are most (and least) likely to graduate

Universities–Master's (South), continued

School	6-year graduation rate	4-year graduation rate
Alcorn State University (MS)	46%	24%
Lincoln Memorial University (TN)	46%	N/A
Barry University (FL)	45%	21%
Spalding University (KY)	45%	N/A
Tennessee Technological University	45%	13%
Warren Wilson College (NC)	45%	37%
Averett University (VA)	44%	N/A
Liberty University (VA)	44%	25%
University of Mobile (AL)	44%	31%
Western Kentucky University	44%	27%
Mississippi University for Women	43%	30%
Shenandoah University (VA)	43%	31%
Tusculum College (TN)	43%	33%
University of Montevallo (AL)	43%	22%
Brenau University (GA)	42%	42%
Jacksonville University (FL)	42%	29%
Morehead State University (KY)	42%	16%
Palm Beach Atlantic University (FL)	42%	37%
Southern Wesleyan University (SC)	42%	35%
North Carolina A&T State University	41%	22%
St. Leo University (FL)	41%	25%
University of Central Arkansas	41%	21%
Virginia State University	41%	18%
William Carey College (MS)	41%	26%
University of Tennessee–Martin	40%	19%
University of West Florida	40%	21%

School	6-year graduation rate	4-year graduation rate
Cumberland University (TN)	39%	21%
Francis Marion University (SC)	39%	17%
Marshall University (WV)	39%	17%
Pfeiffer University (NC)	39%	36%
Arkansas Tech University	38%	18%
Fayetteville State University (NC)	38%	24%
Georgia College and State University	38%	21%
Georgia Southern University	38%	12%
Northern Kentucky University	38%	10%
University of North Alabama	38%	16%
Arkansas State University	37%	18%
Campbellsville University (KY)	37%	27%
Florida Gulf Coast University	37%	14%
Jacksonville State University (AL)	37%	18%
Lynn University (FL)	37%	31%
Piedmont College (GA)	37%	26%
Trevecca Nazarene University (TN)	37%	23%
University of North Carolina–Pembroke	37%	20%
University of the Cumberlands (KY)	37%	21%
Albany State University (GA)	36%	N/A
Eastern Kentucky University	36%	13%
Valdosta State University (GA)	36%	18%
Charleston Southern University (SC)	34%	21%
Grambling State University (LA)	34%	N/A
St. Thomas University (FL)	34%	24%
Florida A&M University	33%	N/A

School	6-year graduation rate	4-year graduation rate
Georgia Southwestern State University	32%	16%
Henderson State University (AR)	32%	12%
Kentucky State University	32%	13%
Southern Arkansas University	32%	13%
Austin Peay State University (TN)	31%	10%
University of West Alabama	31%	15%
University of West Georgia	31%	9%
Kennesaw State University (GA)	29%	N/A
McNeese State University (LA)	29%	11%
Northwestern State University of Louisiana	29%	14%
Auburn University–Montgomery (AL)	28%	N/A
Norfolk State University (VA)	28%	12%
University of Louisiana–Monroe	28%	N/A
Nicholls State University (LA)	27%	10%
Columbus State University (GA)	26%	8%
Southern University and A&M College (LA)	26%	7%
Fort Valley State University (GA)	25%	N/A
Savannah State University (GA)	24%	6%
Southeastern Louisiana University	24%	8%
Alabama State University	22%	9%
Southern University–New Orleans	22%	N/A
Armstrong Atlantic State University (GA)	20%	6%
Augusta State University (GA)	20%	5%
Louisiana State University–Shreveport	18%	4%

Universities–Master's (Midwest)

School	6-year graduation rate	4-year graduation rate
Xavier University (OH)	76%	70%
John Carroll University (OH)	75%	65%
Valparaiso University (IN)	73%	59%
Bethel University (MN)	72%	62%
Bradley University (IL)	72%	53%
Creighton University (NE)	72%	63%
Drake University (IA)	70%	55%
Franciscan University of Steubenville (OH)	70%	59%
Butler University (IN)	69%	55%
Hamline University (MN)	69%	63%
Baldwin-Wallace College (OH)	67%	50%
College of Mount St. Joseph (OH)	67%	53%
Truman State University (MO)	66%	41%
Rockhurst University (MO)	65%	50%
University of Northern Iowa	65%	34%
Concordia University Wisconsin	64%	44%
Doane College (NE)	64%	62%
North Central College (IL)	64%	55%
Washburn University (KS)	64%	30%
Dominican University (IL)	63%	54%
Drury University (MO)	63%	48%
Maryville University of St. Louis (MO)	63%	55%
College of St. Scholastica (MN)	62%	50%
Eastern Illinois University	62%	33%
Indiana Wesleyan University	62%	57%
St. Ambrose University (IA)	62%	53%
University of Evansville (IN)	62%	46%

School	6-year graduation rate	4-year graduation rate
St. Mary's University of Minnesota	61%	53%
University of Wisconsin–La Crosse	61%	21%
Baker University (KS)	59%	39%
Capital University (OH)	59%	48%
College of St. Catherine (MN)	59%	40%
Concordia University (NE)	59%	32%
Heidelberg College (OH)	59%	48%
Spring Arbor University (MI)	58%	36%
Anderson University (IN)	57%	42%
University of Wisconsin–Eau Claire	57%	19%
University of Wisconsin–River Falls	57%	26%
University of Wisconsin–Stevens Point	57%	19%
Ashland University (OH)	56%	47%
Silver Lake College (WI)	56%	19%
Webster University (MO)	56%	43%
Carthage College (WI)	55%	44%
Malone College (OH)	55%	39%
Augsburg College (MN)	54%	40%
Fontbonne University (MO)	54%	33%
Mount Mary College (WI)	54%	41%
Olivet Nazarene University (IL)	54%	40%
University of Detroit Mercy	54%	31%
Western Illinois University	54%	32%
Lewis University (IL)	53%	26%
North Park University (IL)	53%	41%
Northwest Missouri State University	53%	N/A
St. Xavier University (IL)	53%	30%

School	6-year graduation rate	4-year graduation rate
University of Findlay (OH)	53%	42%
University of Indianapolis	53%	42%
University of St. Francis (IL)	53%	32%
Concordia University–River Forest (IL)	52%	27%
University of Nebraska–Kearney	52%	20%
University of Wisconsin–Platteville	52%	13%
University of Wisconsin–Whitewater	52%	19%
Winona State University (MN)	52%	23%
Aquinas College (MI)	51%	27%
Benedictine University (IL)	51%	29%
University of Mary (ND)	51%	42%
Grand Valley State University (MI)	50%	20%
Southeast Missouri State University	50%	23%
University of Michigan–Dearborn	50%	12%
William Woods University (MO)	50%	39%
Aurora University (IL)	49%	33%
Benedictine College (KS)	49%	31%
Central Missouri State University	49%	20%
Marian College of Fond du Lac (WI)	49%	32%
MidAmerica Nazarene University (KS)	49%	N/A
Minnesota State University–Mankato	49%	18%
Mount Marty College (SD)	49%	28%
Pittsburg State University (KS)	49%	51%
Quincy University (IL)	49%	N/A
University of Sioux Falls (SD)	49%	27%
Viterbo University (WI)	49%	36%
Fort Hays State University (KS)	48%	24%

University	6-year graduation rate	4-year graduation rate
Madonna University (MI)	48%	17%
Missouri State University	48%	23%
University of Wisconsin–Stout	48%	14%
Ursuline College (OH)	48%	24%
Lake Erie College (OH)	47%	32%
Maharishi University of Management (IA)	47%	N/A
University of St. Francis (IN)	47%	30%
Walsh University (OH)	47%	35%
Lawrence Technological University (MI)	46%	25%
Rockford College (IL)	46%	32%
University of Minnesota–Duluth	46%	21%
University of Wisconsin–Oshkosh	46%	15%
Edgewood College (WI)	45%	25%
Lindenwood University (MO)	45%	27%
Northern Michigan University	45%	14%
Southwest Baptist University (MO)	45%	32%
Wayne State College (NE)	45%	23%
Chadron State College (NE)	44%	26%
Emporia State University (KS)	44%	22%
Newman University (KS)	44%	N/A
University of St. Mary (KS)	44%	28%
University of Wisconsin–Green Bay	44%	18%
Southern Illinois University–Edwardsville	43%	19%
University of Rio Grande (OH)	43%	25%
Cardinal Stritch University (WI)	42%	16%
Friends University (KS)	42%	20%
Minnesota State University–Moorhead	42%	18%
Northern State University (SD)	42%	N/A
Park University (MO)	42%	21%
Siena Heights University (MI)	42%	N/A
St. Cloud State University (MN)	42%	N/A
University of Dubuque (IA)	41%	44%
Bemidji State University (MN)	40%	26%
Cornerstone University (MI)	40%	22%
Lake Superior State University (MI)	40%	21%
Eastern Michigan University	39%	11%
Avila University (MO)	38%	N/A
University of Michigan–Flint	38%	10%
Oakland City University (IN)	37%	51%
Peru State College (NE)	37%	34%
Youngstown State University (OH)	37%	13%
University of Nebraska–Omaha	36%	10%
Ferris State University (MI)	35%	25%
Saginaw Valley State University (MI)	34%	8%
University of Wisconsin–Superior	34%	N/A
Lincoln University (MO)	33%	9%
Minot State University (ND)	32%	10%
Roosevelt University (IL)	32%	20%
University of Southern Indiana	31%	5%
Columbia College (IL)	29%	20%
Indiana University Southeast	29%	8%
University of Wisconsin–Parkside	29%	9%
Bellevue University (NE)	27%	N/A
Metropolitan State University (MN)	26%	N/A
Indiana University Northwest	24%	11%
Indiana University–South Bend	24%	6%
Marygrove College (MI)	23%	5%
Purdue University–Calumet (IN)	21%	4%
Indiana Univ.-Purdue Univ.–Fort Wayne	19%	4%
Chicago State University	16%	2%
Northeastern Illinois University	16%	2%

Universities– Master's (West)

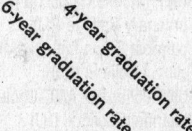

University	6-year graduation rate	4-year graduation rate
Santa Clara University (CA)	84%	77%
Gonzaga University (WA)	76%	58%
Trinity University (TX)	76%	63%
Loyola Marymount University (CA)	73%	63%
Whitworth College (WA)	70%	58%
University of Portland (OR)	69%	57%
St. Mary's College of California	68%	59%
Cal Poly–San Luis Obispo	67%	21%
California Lutheran University	65%	55%
Pacific Lutheran University (WA)	65%	47%
Seattle University	65%	43%
Western Washington University	64%	30%
George Fox University (OR)	62%	54%
Pacific University (OR)	62%	55%
Seattle Pacific University	62%	48%
University of Redlands (CA)	62%	57%
Chapman University (CA)	61%	52%
Mount St. Mary's College (CA)	61%	43%
Azusa Pacific University (CA)	60%	52%
St. Mary's University of San Antonio	60%	34%
Fresno Pacific University (CA)	59%	42%
Regis University (CO)	59%	46%
Point Loma Nazarene University (CA)	57%	54%
Abilene Christian University (TX)	55%	36%
Concordia University (CA)	54%	51%
California Baptist University	53%	8%
New College of California	53%	N/A
St. Edward's University (TX)	53%	28%
Westminster College (UT)	53%	34%
Oklahoma City University	52%	38%
California State University–Chico	51%	15%
Central Washington University	51%	21%
Notre Dame de Namur University (CA)	51%	39%
Houston Baptist University	50%	33%
LeTourneau University (TX)	50%	29%
Woodbury University (CA)	50%	23%
Oral Roberts University (OK)	49%	41%
Sonoma State University (CA)	49%	20%
University of St. Thomas (TX)	49%	24%
California State University–Fullerton	48%	14%
California State University–Stanislaus	48%	21%
Dominican University of California	48%	40%
Hardin-Simmons University (TX)	48%	27%
Texas State University–San Marcos	48%	21%
University of Texas–Tyler	48%	38%
Northwest Nazarene University (ID)	47%	30%
Southern Nazarene University (OK)	47%	26%
Eastern Washington University	46%	18%
Simpson University (CA)	46%	35%
Walla Walla College (WA)	46%	18%
California State University–Fresno	45%	13%
California State University–Long Beach	45%	11%
Dallas Baptist University	45%	33%
California State Polytechnic Univ.–Pomona	43%	9%
Concordia University (OR)	43%	30%
University of Mary Hardin-Baylor (TX)	43%	26%
Weber State University (UT)	43%	15%
California State University–East Bay	42%	N/A
California State Univ.–San Bernardino	42%	9%
Humboldt State University (CA)	42%	12%
Tarleton State University (TX)	41%	N/A
California State University–Bakersfield	40%	N/A
College of Santa Fe (NM)	40%	21%
Alaska Pacific University	39%	19%
California State University–Sacramento	39%	10%
California State University–San Marcos	39%	10%
Chaminade University of Honolulu	39%	20%
Holy Names University (CA)	39%	20%
Prescott College (AZ)	39%	23%
San Francisco State University	39%	N/A
San Jose State University (CA)	39%	7%
University of Colorado–Colorado Springs	39%	16%
Hawaii Pacific University	38%	23%
Heritage University (WA)	38%	N/A
St. Martin's University (WA)	38%	24%
University of the Incarnate Word (TX)	38%	13%
Western Oregon University	38%	18%
Colorado Christian University	37%	N/A
Hope International University (CA)	37%	23%
Prairie View A&M University (TX)	37%	12%
Sam Houston State University (TX)	37%	16%
Texas A&M University–Corpus Christi	37%	19%
Southern Oregon University	36%	19%
Southwestern Oklahoma State University	36%	15%
Stephen F. Austin State University (TX)	36%	15%
Angelo State University (TX)	35%	22%
La Sierra University (CA)	35%	22%
Our Lady of the Lake University (TX)	35%	14%
Texas A&M International University	35%	16%
University of Texas–Brownsville	35%	N/A
West Texas A&M University	35%	13%
California State Univ.–Dominguez Hills	34%	6%
College of the Southwest (NM)	34%	11%
East Central University (OK)	34%	14%
Northeastern State University (OK)	34%	11%
California State University–Los Angeles	33%	N/A
California State University–Northridge	33%	9%
Eastern New Mexico University	32%	10%
Montana State University–Northern	32%	N/A

Schools whose students are most (and least) likely to graduate

Universities–Master's (West), continued

	6-year graduation rate	4-year graduation rate
Southeastern Oklahoma State University	32%	13%
University of Alaska–Anchorage	32%	6%
Wayland Baptist University (TX)	32%	18%
Adams State College (CO)	31%	N/A
Colorado State University–Pueblo	31%	13%
Southern Utah University	31%	18%
University of Central Oklahoma	31%	12%
Midwestern State University (TX)	30%	9%

	6-year graduation rate	4-year graduation rate
Northwestern Oklahoma State University	30%	26%
University of Texas of the Permian Basin	30%	15%
Lamar University (TX)	29%	9%
Eastern Oregon University	28%	N/A
University of Texas–San Antonio	28%	6%
Boise State University (ID)	27%	6%
Montana State University–Billings	27%	12%
University of Texas–Pan American	27%	8%

	6-year graduation rate	4-year graduation rate
Cameron University (OK)	25%	24%
Texas Wesleyan University	24%	14%
University of Great Falls (MT)	23%	N/A
New Mexico Highlands University	21%	N/A
Western New Mexico University	19%	3%
Marylhurst University (OR)	17%	0%
Sul Ross State University (TX)	17%	N/A
University of Alaska–Southeast	13%	3%

Comprehensive Colleges–Bachelor's (North)

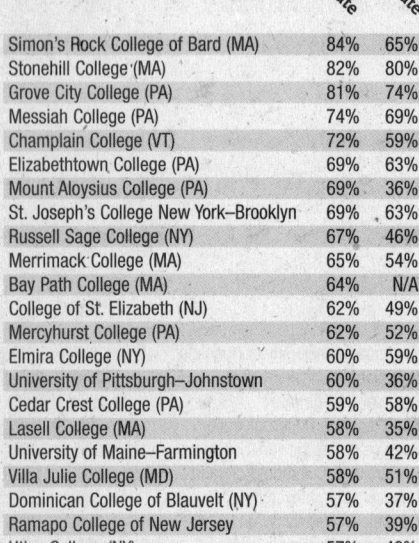

	6-year graduation rate	4-year graduation rate
Simon's Rock College of Bard (MA)	84%	65%
Stonehill College (MA)	82%	80%
Grove City College (PA)	81%	74%
Messiah College (PA)	74%	69%
Champlain College (VT)	72%	59%
Elizabethtown College (PA)	69%	63%
Mount Aloysius College (PA)	69%	36%
St. Joseph's College New York–Brooklyn	69%	63%
Russell Sage College (NY)	67%	46%
Merrimack College (MA)	65%	54%
Bay Path College (MA)	64%	N/A
College of St. Elizabeth (NJ)	62%	49%
Mercyhurst College (PA)	62%	52%
Elmira College (NY)	60%	59%
University of Pittsburgh–Johnstown	60%	36%
Cedar Crest College (PA)	59%	58%
Lasell College (MA)	58%	35%
University of Maine–Farmington	58%	42%
Villa Julie College (MD)	58%	51%
Dominican College of Blauvelt (NY)	57%	37%
Ramapo College of New Jersey	57%	39%
Utica College (NY)	57%	40%
Colby-Sawyer College (NH)	55%	48%

	6-year graduation rate	4-year graduation rate
Albertus Magnus College (CT)	54%	46%
Neumann College (PA)	54%	33%
St. Francis College (NY)	54%	35%
Delaware Valley College (PA)	52%	N/A
Endicott College (MA)	52%	48%
Roger Williams University (RI)	52%	38%
Caldwell College (NJ)	51%	35%
Keuka College (NY)	51%	34%
Wilson College (PA)	51%	42%
Alvernia College (PA)	49%	42%
Mount Ida College (MA)	49%	N/A
New England College (NH)	48%	36%
Unity College (ME)	47%	N/A
Curry College (MA)	46%	36%
Newbury College (MA)	46%	N/A
University of Maine–Machias	46%	21%
Concordia College (NY)	44%	37%
Wesley College (DE)	44%	28%
Becker College (MA)	42%	38%
University of Maine–Fort Kent	41%	21%
Daemen College (NY)	40%	26%
Atlantic Union College (MA)	39%	N/A
Cazenovia College (NY)	39%	42%

	6-year graduation rate	4-year graduation rate
Pennsylvania College of Technology	39%	33%
Hilbert College (NY)	38%	31%
Daniel Webster College (NH)	37%	N/A
Lyndon State College (VT)	37%	24%
Post University (CT)	37%	17%
Thiel College (PA)	37%	31%
Green Mountain College (VT)	36%	N/A
Centenary College (NJ)	35%	N/A
Columbia Union College (MD)	32%	15%
Felician College (NJ)	32%	18%
SUNY College of A&T–Cobleskill	31%	N/A
Bloomfield College (NJ)	29%	9%
CUNY–York College	27%	5%
Southern Vermont College	26%	N/A
University of Maine–Augusta	25%	5%
Medaille College (NY)	24%	28%
SUNY College–Old Westbury	23%	20%
SUNY–Farmingdale	22%	13%
Boricua College (NY)	18%	N/A
CUNY–Medgar Evers College	15%	5%
CUNY–New York City Coll. of Technology	11%	6%

Comprehensive Colleges–Bachelor's (South)

College	6-year graduation rate	4-year graduation rate
Miles College (AL)	72%	N/A
Claflin University (SC)	68%	42%
Asbury College (KY)	65%	61%
Covenant College (GA)	63%	56%
Berry College (GA)	61%	49%
Bryan College (TN)	59%	61%
Florida Southern College	57%	49%
Maryville College (TN)	57%	45%
Ouachita Baptist University (AR)	57%	44%
Berea College (KY)	56%	35%
John Brown University (AR)	56%	43%
Thomas More College (KY)	55%	39%
Flagler College (FL)	54%	44%
Southern Adventist University (TN)	54%	24%
Columbia College (SC)	53%	36%
Winston-Salem State University (NC)	52%	22%
Lenoir-Rhyne College (NC)	51%	41%
Newberry College (SC)	51%	33%
High Point University (NC)	50%	35%
Coker College (SC)	49%	37%
Elizabeth City State University (NC)	49%	27%
University of the Ozarks (AR)	49%	32%
Shorter College (GA)	48%	39%
Wingate University (NC)	48%	34%
Brescia University (KY)	47%	32%
Louisiana College	47%	N/A
Davis and Elkins College (WV)	45%	29%
LaGrange College (GA)	45%	29%
Toccoa Falls College (GA)	45%	32%
Barton College (NC)	44%	29%
Belmont Abbey College (NC)	44%	29%
Dillard University (LA)	44%	N/A
Kentucky Wesleyan College	44%	31%
Lee University (TN)	44%	31%
Tennessee Wesleyan College	44%	N/A
Belhaven College (MS)	43%	32%
Catawba College (NC)	43%	32%
Clearwater Christian College (FL)	43%	36%
Florida Memorial College	43%	N/A
Oakwood College (AL)	43%	16%
Peace College (NC)	43%	39%
University of Charleston (WV)	43%	31%
Alderson-Broaddus College (WV)	42%	N/A
Anderson University (SC)	42%	24%
Blue Mountain College (MS)	42%	33%
North Greenville University (SC)	42%	24%
West Liberty State College (WV)	42%	N/A
Bluefield College (VA)	41%	38%
Lambuth University (TN)	41%	25%
Mars Hill College (NC)	41%	32%
Shepherd University (WV)	41%	16%
University of South Carolina–Aiken	41%	21%
Williams Baptist College (AR)	41%	19%
Fairmont State University (WV)	40%	14%
Johnson C. Smith University (NC)	40%	23%
Southeastern University (FL)	40%	34%
Warner Southern College (FL)	40%	N/A
Kentucky Christian University	39%	20%
Mississippi Valley State University	38%	19%
University of South Carolina–Upstate	38%	16%
West Virginia University Inst. of Tech.	38%	14%
Morris College (SC)	37%	19%
North Carolina Wesleyan College	36%	22%
Virginia Intermont College	36%	19%
Bethune-Cookman College (FL)	35%	20%
Bluefield State College (WV)	35%	33%
Ferrum College (VA)	35%	18%
Concord University (WV)	34%	15%
Limestone College (SC)	34%	38%
Pikeville College (KY)	34%	22%
Emmanuel College (GA)	33%	24%
Methodist College (NC)	32%	22%
International College (FL)	31%	13%
Our Lady of Holy Cross College (LA)	31%	N/A
Voorhees College (SC)	31%	N/A
Alice Lloyd College (KY)	30%	14%
Glenville State College (WV)	30%	12%
Livingstone College (NC)	30%	8%
Rust College (MS)	30%	12%
University of Arkansas–Pine Bluff	30%	12%
Shaw University (NC)	29%	15%
Stillman College (AL)	29%	24%
Mount Olive College (NC)	28%	17%
Ohio Valley University (WV)	28%	27%
Midway College (KY)	27%	24%
Reinhardt College (GA)	27%	16%
University of Arkansas–Monticello	26%	10%
Faulkner University (AL)	25%	N/A
Mid-Continent University (KY)	25%	9%
St. Paul's College (VA)	25%	0%
West Virginia State University	25%	8%
Benedict College (SC)	24%	N/A
Allen University (SC)	23%	N/A
Chowan College (NC)	23%	19%
Brevard College (NC)	22%	21%
Mountain State University (WV)	21%	13%
Clayton State University (GA)	20%	11%
Philander Smith College (AR)	20%	4%
Crichton College (TN)	19%	N/A
Martin Methodist College (TN)	19%	N/A
West Virginia University–Parkersburg	19%	3%
Brewton-Parker College (GA)	18%	N/A
LeMoyne-Owen College (TN)	18%	N/A
Thomas University (GA)	17%	N/A
Edward Waters College (FL)	13%	3%
Concordia College (AL)	8%	N/A

Comprehensive Colleges–Bachelor's (Midwest)

College	6-year graduation rate	4-year graduation rate
Taylor University (IN)	79%	73%
St. Mary's College (IN)	75%	69%
Calvin College (MI)	74%	54%
Elmhurst College (IL)	72%	59%
St. Norbert College (WI)	72%	64%
Cedarville University (OH)	70%	57%
Wartburg College (IA)	69%	62%
Wisconsin Lutheran College	68%	49%
Augustana College (SD)	66%	48%
Central College (IA)	66%	60%
Dordt College (IA)	66%	59%
Loras College (IA)	66%	55%
Mount Union College (OH)	66%	49%
Ohio Northern University	66%	49%
Otterbein College (OH)	66%	50%
Simpson College (IA)	66%	58%
Huntington University (IN)	64%	58%
Mount Mercy College (IA)	63%	50%
Clarke College (IA)	61%	45%
Millikin University (IL)	61%	54%
Bluffton University (OH)	60%	46%
Carroll College (WI)	60%	45%
Grace College and Seminary (IN)	59%	58%
Franklin College (IN)	58%	47%
Illinois College	58%	40%
McKendree College (IL)	58%	41%
Northwestern College (IA)	58%	49%
Buena Vista University (IA)	57%	45%
Northwestern College (MN)	57%	42%
Trinity Christian College (IL)	56%	43%
Wilmington College (OH)	56%	49%
Morningside College (IA)	55%	39%
Southwestern College (KS)	55%	42%
St. Joseph's College (IN)	55%	42%
Eureka College (IL)	54%	47%
Greenville College (IL)	54%	38%
Marietta College (OH)	54%	N/A
St. Mary-of-the-Woods College (IN)	54%	46%
Tri-State University (IN)	54%	39%
Bethel College (IN)	53%	N/A
Jamestown College (ND)	52%	34%
Manchester College (IN)	52%	N/A
Union College (NE)	52%	27%
Briar Cliff University (IA)	51%	40%
Dana College (NE)	51%	35%
Mount Vernon Nazarene University (OH)	51%	37%
Upper Iowa University	51%	N/A
Crown College (MN)	50%	32%
Judson College (IL)	50%	32%
College of the Ozarks (MO)	49%	N/A
Culver-Stockton College (MO)	49%	47%
Defiance College (OH)	49%	36%
Marian College (IN)	49%	35%
Missouri Baptist University	49%	35%
Ohio Dominican University	49%	37%
College of St. Mary (NE)	48%	39%
Graceland University (IA)	48%	N/A

Schools whose students are most (and least) likely to graduate

Comprehensive Colleges–Bachelor's (Midwest), continued

	6-year graduation rate	4-year graduation rate
Bethel College (KS)	47%	43%
Concordia University (MI)	47%	30%
MacMurray College (IL)	47%	N/A
Alverno College (WI)	46%	35%
Dakota State University (SD)	46%	18%
Dakota Wesleyan University (SD)	46%	N/A
Hannibal-LaGrange College (MO)	46%	N/A
Midland Lutheran College (NE)	46%	35%
Sterling College (KS)	46%	55%
Tabor College (KS)	46%	40%
Valley City State University (ND)	46%	21%
Concordia University–St. Paul (MN)	45%	29%
Evangel University (MO)	44%	41%
Bethany College (KS)	43%	32%
Columbia College (MO)	42%	29%
Northland College (WI)	42%	N/A
Southwest Minnesota State University (MN)	42%	18%

	6-year graduation rate	4-year graduation rate
Central Methodist University (MO)	41%	26%
Lakeland College (WI)	41%	25%
Urbana University (OH)	40%	N/A
York College (NE)	40%	18%
Grace University (NE)	38%	N/A
Mayville State University (ND)	38%	31%
Ottawa University (KS)	38%	N/A
University of Minnesota–Crookston	38%	19%
Notre Dame College of Ohio	36%	35%
Grand View College (IA)	35%	25%
Iowa Wesleyan College	35%	22%
McPherson College (KS)	32%	19%
Missouri Southern State University	32%	14%
Missouri Western State University	32%	N/A
Waldorf College (IA)	32%	28%
Wilberforce University (OH)	32%	N/A
William Penn University (IA)	32%	22%

	6-year graduation rate	4-year graduation rate
Kansas Wesleyan University	31%	N/A
Kendall College (IL)	29%	N/A
Lourdes College (OH)	29%	4%
Rochester College (MI)	28%	13%
Baker College of Flint (MI)	25%	N/A
Black Hills State University (SD)	25%	N/A
Dickinson State University (ND)	25%	12%
Central Christian College (KS)	24%	15%
Central State University (OH)	24%	16%
Indiana University East	24%	6%
Indiana University–Kokomo	23%	10%
Missouri Valley College	20%	N/A
Calumet College of St. Joseph (IN)	13%	N/A
Purdue University–North Central (IN)	11%	2%
East-West University (IL)	6%	N/A

Comprehensive Colleges–Bachelor's (West)

	6-year graduation rate	4-year graduation rate
Linfield College (OR)	68%	57%
Carroll College (MT)	61%	42%
Master's College and Seminary (CA)	61%	51%
Oklahoma Baptist University	54%	53%
Vanguard University of Southern California	54%	32%
Humphreys College (CA)	53%	64%
Corban College (OR)	52%	50%
Texas Lutheran University	49%	29%
Cogswell Polytechnical College (CA)	45%	0%
East Texas Baptist University	42%	26%
Rocky Mountain College (MT)	42%	26%
McMurry University (TX)	41%	25%
Oklahoma Christian University	41%	31%
Oklahoma Wesleyan University	41%	19%

	6-year graduation rate	4-year graduation rate
Northwest University (WA)	40%	N/A
Brigham Young University–Hawaii	39%	23%
Howard Payne University (TX)	37%	24%
Langston University (OK)	35%	N/A
Patten University (CA)	35%	N/A
Lubbock Christian University (TX)	34%	22%
Concordia University–Austin (TX)	33%	20%
Northwest Christian College (OR)	33%	30%
Utah Valley State College	33%	2%
Southwestern Adventist University (TX)	32%	N/A
Bethany College (CA)	31%	N/A
University of Science and Arts of Oklahoma	30%	12%
St. Gregory's University (OK)	29%	19%
University of Montana–Western	29%	9%

	6-year graduation rate	4-year graduation rate
Paul Quinn College (TX)	26%	N/A
Texas College	26%	9%
Wiley College (TX)	26%	6%
Lewis-Clark State College (ID)	25%	10%
Oklahoma Panhandle State University	24%	18%
Menlo College (CA)	23%	22%
Pacific Union College (CA)	23%	8%
Sierra Nevada College (NV)	23%	17%
Metropolitan State College of Denver	21%	N/A
Huston-Tillotson University (TX)	17%	5%
Jarvis Christian College (TX)	16%	11%
University of Houston–Downtown	14%	2%

Schools with the most diverse student bodies

If you're looking for a campus culture that features a wealth of different student backgrounds, the *U.S. News* diversity index can point you to institutions with both a healthy proportion of minority students and a mix of different groups. The closer the index number is to 1.0, the more diverse the population and more likely you are to encounter undergraduates from a racial or ethnic group different from your own. All the data are for the 2005–2006 school year; the top 40 percent of each category is shown.

National Universities	Diversity index	Men	Women	American Indian	Asian	Black	Hispanic	White	International	Undergraduates from out of state	Average age of full-time students
Rutgers–Newark (NJ)	0.73	43%	57%	0%	23%	21%	18%	35%	2%	6%	22
University of Houston	0.72	48%	52%	0%	21%	16%	21%	37%	5%	2%	22
Nova Southeastern University (FL)	0.69	27%	73%	0%	5%	27%	25%	37%	6%	20%	26
Polytechnic University (NY)	0.69	82%	18%	0%	32%	12%	11%	37%	8%	5%	20
University of California–Riverside	0.69	47%	53%	0%	42%	7%	24%	25%	2%	1%	21
Stanford University (CA)	0.67	53%	47%	2%	24%	10%	11%	46%	6%	56%	20
St. John's University (NY)	0.66	42%	58%	0%	16%	17%	15%	49%	3%	12%	20
University of Bridgeport (CT)	0.66	36%	64%	0%	4%	33%	14%	35%	13%	40%	23
University of Illinois–Chicago	0.66	47%	53%	0%	25%	9%	17%	49%	1%	2%	21
Alliant International University (CA)	0.65	48%	52%	1%	7%	8%	19%	37%	27%	23%	22
New Jersey Institute of Technology	0.65	81%	19%	0%	21%	11%	13%	49%	6%	4%	22
University of California–Los Angeles	0.65	44%	56%	0%	38%	3%	15%	39%	4%	4%	21
Massachusetts Institute of Technology	0.64	57%	43%	2%	27%	6%	11%	47%	8%	91%	20
Andrews University (MI)	0.63	45%	55%	0%	8%	20%	11%	48%	12%	53%	18
University of San Francisco	0.63	37%	63%	1%	25%	5%	14%	49%	7%	24%	20
University of California–Berkeley	0.62	46%	54%	1%	41%	4%	11%	41%	3%	10%	21
University of California–Davis	0.62	44%	56%	1%	40%	3%	11%	44%	2%	2%	21
University of La Verne (CA)	0.62	35%	65%	1%	5%	9%	38%	47%	1%	5%	20
University of Southern California	0.62	49%	51%	1%	21%	6%	13%	50%	8%	34%	21
University of Texas–Arlington	0.62	47%	53%	1%	11%	14%	15%	54%	5%	2%	22
University of California–Irvine	0.61	49%	51%	0%	49%	2%	12%	34%	2%	1%	21
SUNY–Stony Brook	0.60	50%	50%	0%	22%	10%	9%	54%	5%	4%	21
San Diego State University	0.60	41%	59%	1%	16%	4%	22%	56%	2%	5%	22
Texas Woman's University	0.60	7%	93%	1%	6%	21%	14%	55%	3%	1%	24
University of California–San Diego	0.60	48%	52%	0%	39%	1%	11%	45%	3%	2%	21
University of New Mexico	0.60	42%	58%	6%	3%	3%	35%	52%	1%	11%	22
Florida Atlantic University	0.59	40%	60%	0%	4%	18%	17%	56%	4%	5%	22
Georgia State University	0.59	39%	61%	0%	10%	31%	3%	52%	3%	4%	22
Rutgers–New Brunswick (NJ)	0.58	49%	51%	0%	23%	9%	8%	58%	2%	9%	20
University of Miami (FL)	0.58	43%	57%	0%	5%	9%	23%	56%	6%	46%	20
University of the Pacific (CA)	0.58	44%	56%	1%	29%	3%	10%	54%	2%	13%	20
New Mexico State University	0.57	44%	56%	3%	1%	3%	45%	47%	1%	15%	23
University of Maryland–Baltimore County	0.57	54%	46%	0%	20%	14%	4%	58%	4%	8%	21
University of Texas–Austin	0.57	48%	52%	0%	17%	4%	16%	59%	3%	5%	21
University of Texas–Dallas	0.57	54%	46%	1%	20%	7%	10%	58%	5%	2%	24
California Institute of Technology	0.56	70%	30%	0%	33%	1%	7%	52%	7%	58%	20
Harvard University (MA)	0.56	51%	49%	1%	18%	8%	8%	56%	9%	85%	20
University of California–Santa Cruz	0.56	46%	54%	1%	19%	3%	15%	62%	1%	4%	21
Carnegie Mellon University (PA)	0.55	60%	40%	0%	24%	5%	5%	54%	12%	67%	19
University of Massachusetts–Boston	0.55	43%	57%	1%	12%	15%	7%	62%	4%	4%	25
University of Nevada–Las Vegas	0.55	44%	56%	1%	14%	8%	11%	61%	4%	25%	22
Wayne State University (MI)	0.55	41%	59%	0%	5%	33%	3%	54%	4%	1%	22
Florida International University	0.54	44%	56%	0%	4%	13%	60%	17%	7%	15%	27
Rice University (TX)	0.54	51%	49%	1%	16%	7%	12%	62%	3%	47%	20
University of California–Santa Barbara	0.54	45%	55%	1%	16%	3%	17%	62%	1%	4%	21
DePaul University (IL)	0.53	43%	57%	0%	9%	10%	13%	65%	2%	15%	21
Pace University (NY)	0.53	39%	61%	0%	11%	10%	12%	63%	4%	28%	21
Pepperdine University (CA)	0.53	43%	57%	2%	11%	8%	11%	62%	6%	50%	20
Columbia University (NY)	0.52	52%	48%	0%	16%	7%	8%	61%	7%	74%	20
Duke University (NC)	0.52	52%	48%	0%	14%	11%	7%	63%	5%	85%	20
George Mason University (VA)	0.52	46%	54%	0%	17%	8%	8%	64%	4%	8%	21
National-Louis University (IL)	0.52	26%	74%	0%	2%	26%	8%	64%	0%	2%	34
University of Memphis	0.52	39%	61%	0%	2%	38%	1%	56%	2%	6%	22
University of Washington	0.52	48%	52%	1%	27%	3%	4%	61%	3%	14%	21
Dartmouth College (NH)	0.51	50%	50%	3%	14%	7%	6%	65%	5%	96%	20
University of Alabama–Birmingham	0.51	39%	61%	0%	3%	32%	1%	61%	2%	6%	22
University of Maryland–College Park	0.51	51%	49%	0%	14%	13%	6%	66%	2%	24%	20

Schools with the most diverse student bodies

National Universities, continued

	Diversity index	Men	Women	American Indian	Asian	Black	Hispanic	White	International	Undergraduates from out of state	Average age of full-time students
Virginia Commonwealth University	0.51	40%	60%	1%	9%	20%	3%	64%	2%	5%	22
Johns Hopkins University (MD)	0.50	49%	51%	1%	19%	6%	5%	64%	5%	85%	20
Princeton University (NJ)	0.50	54%	46%	1%	13%	9%	7%	62%	9%	85%	20
Union Institute and University (OH)	0.50	32%	68%	1%	1%	24%	8%	66%	0%	22%	N/A
University of Pennsylvania	0.50	50%	50%	0%	18%	7%	6%	60%	9%	80%	20
Yale University (CT)	0.50	51%	49%	1%	14%	8%	7%	62%	8%	92%	20
Illinois Institute of Technology	0.49	74%	26%	0%	14%	5%	7%	58%	16%	28%	20
New York University	0.49	39%	61%	0%	17%	5%	8%	66%	4%	58%	20
Old Dominion University (VA)	0.49	42%	58%	1%	6%	23%	3%	66%	2%	8%	22
Temple University (PA)	0.49	43%	57%	0%	9%	19%	3%	66%	3%	22%	21
Brown University (RI)	0.48	46%	54%	1%	14%	7%	7%	66%	6%	95%	20
Texas A&M University–Kingsville	0.48	49%	51%	0%	1%	6%	66%	25%	2%	N/A	N/A
University of South Florida	0.48	41%	59%	0%	6%	13%	11%	68%	3%	4%	23
Emory University (GA)	0.47	42%	58%	0%	16%	9%	3%	67%	4%	69%	20
Northwestern University (IL)	0.47	47%	53%	0%	17%	5%	6%	66%	5%	70%	21
Tufts University (MA)	0.47	48%	52%	0%	13%	7%	7%	67%	6%	75%	N/A
University of Florida	0.47	46%	54%	0%	7%	9%	13%	70%	1%	5%	21
University of Hawaii–Manoa	0.47	44%	56%	0%	65%	1%	2%	28%	3%	20%	21
Cornell University (NY)	0.46	50%	50%	0%	16%	5%	5%	66%	8%	61%	20
Loyola University Chicago	0.46	35%	65%	0%	11%	6%	10%	71%	2%	33%	20
University of Chicago	0.46	50%	50%	0%	14%	4%	8%	66%	7%	74%	20
University of North Texas	0.46	44%	56%	1%	5%	12%	11%	69%	3%	26%	N/A
Adelphi University (NY)	0.45	28%	72%	0%	5%	13%	8%	70%	3%	8%	22
New School University (NY)	0.45	30%	70%	0%	11%	5%	6%	56%	22%	N/A	N/A
SUNY–Binghamton	0.45	52%	48%	0%	15%	5%	6%	68%	7%	6%	20
Seton Hall University (NJ)	0.45	46%	54%	0%	7%	11%	9%	71%	1%	26%	20
Stevens Institute of Technology (NJ)	0.45	75%	25%	0%	13%	5%	9%	68%	5%	34%	20
Texas A&M University–Commerce	0.45	39%	61%	1%	2%	19%	7%	70%	1%	N/A	N/A
University of Central Florida	0.45	45%	55%	0%	5%	9%	13%	72%	1%	5%	21
University of Southern Mississippi	0.45	39%	61%	0%	1%	28%	1%	69%	1%	10%	23
Drexel University (PA)	0.44	57%	43%	0%	11%	11%	3%	69%	6%	44%	21
Georgia Institute of Technology	0.44	72%	28%	0%	15%	7%	4%	69%	5%	28%	20
New Mexico Institute of Mining and Technology	0.44	68%	32%	3%	3%	1%	20%	70%	3%	12%	21
University of Alaska–Fairbanks	0.44	41%	59%	18%	4%	3%	3%	70%	2%	13%	22
University of Arizona	0.44	47%	53%	2%	6%	3%	15%	71%	3%	27%	21
University of Colorado–Denver and Health Sciences	0.44	43%	57%	1%	10%	4%	11%	72%	2%	4%	23
University of Illinois–Urbana-Champaign	0.44	53%	47%	0%	13%	7%	6%	70%	4%	11%	20
Cleveland State University	0.43	45%	55%	0%	3%	21%	3%	70%	2%	2%	24
Florida State University	0.43	43%	57%	0%	3%	12%	11%	74%	1%	13%	21
University of Michigan–Ann Arbor	0.43	49%	51%	1%	12%	7%	5%	70%	5%	31%	20
Arizona State University	0.42	48%	52%	2%	5%	4%	13%	73%	3%	24%	21
Baylor University (TX)	0.42	42%	58%	1%	7%	8%	10%	74%	1%	17%	20
University of Missouri–Kansas City	0.42	40%	60%	1%	6%	15%	4%	72%	3%	24%	23

Liberal Arts Colleges

	Diversity index	Men	Women	American Indian	Asian	Black	Hispanic	White	International	Undergraduates from out of state	Average age of full-time students
Pine Manor College (MA)	0.65	0%	100%	1%	5%	42%	12%	31%	9%	25%	20
Rosemont College (PA)	0.59	13%	87%	0%	7%	28%	7%	54%	4%	25%	21
Wellesley College (MA)	0.58	2%	98%	0%	27%	6%	7%	52%	8%	84%	20
Whittier College (CA)	0.57	46%	54%	2%	8%	4%	27%	57%	3%	28%	20
Swarthmore College (PA)	0.54	48%	52%	1%	15%	7%	10%	61%	6%	84%	20
University of Hawaii–Hilo	0.54	41%	59%	1%	39%	1%	3%	48%	8%	30%	23
Occidental College (CA)	0.53	43%	57%	1%	13%	6%	14%	62%	3%	51%	20
Wesleyan College (GA)	0.52	1%	99%	0%	3%	25%	3%	50%	19%	14%	22
Claremont McKenna College (CA)	0.51	54%	46%	0%	15%	4%	12%	64%	4%	50%	20
Pomona College (CA)	0.50	50%	50%	0%	14%	7%	11%	67%	2%	N/A	20
Amherst College (MA)	0.49	52%	48%	0%	13%	9%	6%	64%	7%	87%	19
Pitzer College (CA)	0.49	41%	59%	1%	10%	5%	15%	67%	2%	43%	20
Barnard College (NY)	0.48	0%	100%	0%	17%	5%	7%	67%	3%	66%	20
Williams College (MA)	0.48	49%	51%	0%	9%	9%	9%	66%	6%	82%	20
Marymount Manhattan College (NY)	0.46	23%	77%	0%	5%	12%	11%	69%	2%	66%	21
Mills College (CA)	0.46	0%	100%	1%	8%	8%	9%	68%	6%	23%	25
Agnes Scott College (GA)	0.45	1%	99%	0%	5%	19%	3%	65%	7%	54%	20
Haverford College (PA)	0.45	47%	53%	1%	13%	7%	8%	69%	4%	85%	21

	Diversity index	Men	Women	American Indian	Asian	Black	Hispanic	White	International	Undergraduates from out of state	Average age of full-time students
Bowdoin College (ME)	0.44	49%	51%	1%	12%	6%	7%	71%	3%	87%	20
Guilford College (NC)	0.43	38%	62%	1%	1%	23%	2%	72%	1%	62%	20
Mount Holyoke College (MA)	0.43	0%	100%	1%	12%	4%	5%	63%	14%	75%	20
San Diego Christian College (CA)	0.43	41%	59%	1%	3%	7%	16%	71%	2%	10%	22
Smith College (MA)	0.43	0%	100%	1%	11%	6%	6%	69%	7%	78%	21
Wesleyan University (CT)	0.43	48%	52%	0%	10%	7%	7%	69%	6%	87%	N/A
Harvey Mudd College (CA)	0.42	68%	32%	0%	17%	1%	6%	71%	4%	N/A	20
Oglethorpe University (GA)	0.42	36%	64%	0%	4%	21%	1%	72%	2%	75%	22
Austin College (TX)	0.41	45%	55%	1%	12%	4%	9%	74%	1%	9%	20
Fort Lewis College (CO)	0.41	52%	48%	19%	1%	1%	6%	73%	1%	29%	22
Salem College (NC)	0.41	2%	98%	0%	1%	19%	3%	68%	8%	41%	24
Schreiner University (TX)	0.40	40%	60%	1%	1%	4%	20%	74%	1%	1%	23
Bethel College (TN)	0.38	N/A	N/A	0%	0%	22%	1%	71%	5%	N/A	N/A
Carleton College (MN)	0.38	48%	52%	1%	10%	6%	5%	73%	6%	73%	20
Southwestern University (TX)	0.38	41%	59%	1%	5%	3%	14%	77%	0%	7%	20
University of Dallas	0.38	44%	56%	0%	5%	2%	15%	76%	1%	44%	20
Vassar College (NY)	0.38	41%	59%	0%	9%	5%	6%	75%	5%	74%	20
Scripps College (CA)	0.37	0%	100%	0%	13%	3%	5%	77%	1%	58%	20
Westmont College (CA)	0.36	38%	62%	2%	8%	2%	10%	78%	0%	32%	20
Bryn Mawr College (PA)	0.35	3%	97%	0%	12%	5%	3%	74%	7%	83%	20
Oberlin College (OH)	0.35	44%	56%	1%	8%	5%	5%	75%	6%	93%	N/A
Randolph-Macon Woman's College (VA)	0.33	0%	100%	1%	3%	9%	4%	74%	10%	61%	21
Virginia Wesleyan College	0.33	36%	64%	0%	2%	15%	3%	79%	1%	23%	20
Evergreen State College (WA)	0.32	45%	55%	4%	5%	5%	4%	82%	0%	22%	25
Greensboro College (NC)	0.32	45%	55%	0%	1%	19%	0%	79%	0%	26%	39
Macalester College (MN)	0.32	42%	58%	1%	7%	4%	4%	72%	12%	75%	20
Olivet College (MI)	0.32	56%	44%	1%	1%	14%	2%	79%	3%	11%	N/A
Richard Stockton College of New Jersey	0.32	42%	58%	0%	4%	8%	6%	82%	0%	3%	22
Millsaps College (MS)	0.31	51%	49%	0%	3%	12%	1%	82%	1%	50%	20
Grinnell College (IA)	0.30	45%	55%	0%	6%	4%	4%	75%	11%	78%	20
Whitman College (WA)	0.30	46%	54%	1%	9%	2%	4%	81%	3%	58%	20
Colgate University (NY)	0.29	49%	51%	1%	6%	4%	4%	80%	5%	69%	20
Drew University (NJ)	0.29	43%	57%	0%	6%	3%	6%	84%	1%	44%	20
Lake Forest College (IL)	0.29	42%	58%	0%	3%	5%	6%	77%	8%	54%	20
St. Mary's College of Maryland	0.29	43%	57%	0%	4%	8%	3%	84%	1%	18%	20
Trinity College (CT)	0.29	49%	51%	0%	6%	5%	5%	82%	2%	80%	21
Albright College (PA)	0.28	41%	59%	0%	2%	9%	4%	81%	3%	33%	20
Huntingdon College (AL)	0.28	50%	50%	1%	1%	13%	1%	82%	3%	27%	20
Middlebury College (VT)	0.28	49%	51%	1%	7%	3%	5%	76%	9%	93%	N/A
Texas A&M University–Galveston	0.28	58%	42%	1%	2%	3%	10%	84%	0%	27%	21
University of Minnesota–Morris	0.28	40%	60%	9%	3%	2%	1%	83%	1%	13%	21
University of Puget Sound (WA)	0.28	42%	58%	1%	9%	2%	4%	83%	0%	70%	20
Colorado College	0.27	46%	54%	1%	4%	2%	7%	83%	2%	98%	20
Hamilton College (NY)	0.27	50%	50%	1%	6%	4%	4%	80%	5%	64%	20
Reed College (OR)	0.27	45%	55%	1%	6%	2%	5%	82%	4%	85%	0
Sarah Lawrence College (NY)	0.27	26%	74%	1%	4%	5%	4%	83%	2%	77%	20
Ursinus College (PA)	0.27	47%	53%	0%	4%	7%	3%	84%	1%	39%	20
Wells College (NY)	0.27	9%	91%	0%	3%	7%	4%	83%	2%	30%	20
Coastal Carolina University (SC)	0.26	47%	53%	1%	1%	12%	2%	84%	2%	46%	21
College of the Holy Cross (MA)	0.25	45%	55%	0%	4%	4%	5%	85%	1%	63%	20
Connecticut College	0.25	40%	60%	0%	4%	4%	5%	82%	5%	82%	20
Dickinson College (PA)	0.25	44%	56%	0%	4%	4%	4%	82%	5%	72%	20
Knox College (IL)	0.25	46%	54%	0%	5%	4%	4%	80%	7%	45%	20
Mesa State College (CO)	0.25	41%	59%	2%	2%	2%	8%	86%	1%	8%	23
New College of Florida	0.25	39%	61%	0%	3%	2%	9%	84%	2%	25%	20
St. Andrews Presbyterian College (NC)	0.25	38%	62%	1%	0%	10%	3%	82%	4%	51%	20
Stephens College (MO)	0.25	3%	97%	1%	2%	8%	3%	86%	1%	55%	21
Union College (NY)	0.25	55%	45%	0%	6%	3%	5%	85%	2%	56%	20
Wabash College (IN)	0.25	100%	0%	0%	3%	6%	4%	83%	4%	29%	20
Christopher Newport University (VA)	0.24	46%	54%	1%	2%	8%	2%	87%	0%	3%	20
Davidson College (NC)	0.24	50%	50%	0%	2%	6%	4%	84%	3%	82%	20
Earlham College (IN)	0.24	42%	58%	0%	2%	7%	3%	81%	7%	72%	20
Hampshire College (MA)	0.24	41%	59%	0%	4%	3%	4%	84%	3%	82%	20
Hollins University (VA)	0.24	1%	99%	1%	1%	8%	2%	85%	2%	48%	21
Skidmore College (NY)	0.24	39%	61%	1%	6%	3%	4%	86%	1%	70%	20
Wheaton College (IL)	0.24	49%	51%	0%	7%	2%	3%	87%	1%	72%	20
Willamette University (OR)	0.24	46%	54%	1%	7%	2%	4%	86%	1%	60%	20

Schools with the most diverse student bodies

Universities–Master's (North)

	Diversity index	Men	Women	American Indian	Asian	Black	Hispanic	White	International	Undergraduates from out of state	Average age of full-time students
CUNY–Baruch College	0.72	45%	55%	0%	28%	13%	17%	31%	11%	3%	22
CUNY–City College	0.71	51%	49%	0%	18%	24%	34%	11%	12%	13%	23
CUNY–Hunter College	0.70	32%	68%	0%	17%	14%	20%	42%	7%	4%	22
New Jersey City University	0.70	37%	63%	0%	8%	20%	33%	38%	1%	N/A	N/A
Long Island University–Brooklyn (NY)	0.69	28%	72%	0%	15%	40%	12%	31%	2%	N/A	N/A
Mercy College (NY)	0.69	29%	71%	0%	3%	31%	34%	30%	2%	4%	25
Nyack College (NY)	0.69	39%	61%	0%	6%	35%	20%	34%	5%	N/A	27
St. Peter's College (NJ)	0.68	46%	54%	0%	7%	22%	24%	44%	3%	19%	21
CUNY–Brooklyn College	0.67	40%	60%	0%	11%	28%	12%	41%	7%	2%	22
College of Mount St. Vincent (NY)	0.66	26%	74%	0%	11%	12%	29%	48%	0%	14%	20
CUNY–Queens College	0.65	38%	62%	0%	18%	9%	17%	48%	8%	1%	21
Kean University (NJ)	0.64	36%	64%	0%	6%	21%	20%	50%	2%	2%	22
CUNY–Lehman College	0.62	28%	72%	0%	4%	34%	47%	10%	5%	1%	29
Chestnut Hill College (PA)	0.56	28%	72%	0%	3%	38%	6%	53%	1%	25%	20
William Paterson University of New Jersey	0.54	42%	58%	0%	6%	13%	17%	63%	1%	N/A	22
American International College (MA)	0.53	41%	59%	0%	2%	25%	9%	62%	1%	45%	21
Gallaudet University (DC)	0.52	47%	53%	4%	5%	12%	9%	61%	10%	85%	23
Montclair State University (NJ)	0.52	39%	61%	0%	6%	10%	17%	63%	3%	2%	22
CUNY–College of Staten Island	0.51	40%	60%	0%	8%	11%	12%	63%	5%	1%	21
Fairleigh Dickinson University (NJ)	0.51	45%	55%	0%	5%	14%	12%	64%	5%	N/A	N/A
Molloy College (NY)	0.51	22%	78%	0%	6%	20%	8%	66%	0%	N/A	21
New York Institute of Technology	0.51	61%	39%	0%	10%	11%	10%	64%	6%	28%	21
Touro College (NY)	0.51	38%	62%	0%	4%	18%	11%	67%	0%	N/A	N/A
Regis College (MA)	0.48	3%	97%	0%	7%	14%	10%	69%	1%	11%	20
Rutgers–Camden (NJ)	0.48	42%	58%	0%	8%	15%	6%	69%	1%	8%	21
Springfield College (MA)	0.47	40%	60%	0%	1%	22%	8%	68%	1%	65%	20
College of Notre Dame of Maryland	0.46	6%	94%	0%	2%	25%	3%	68%	1%	13%	21
Manhattanville College (NY)	0.44	31%	69%	1%	3%	6%	15%	68%	8%	37%	20
La Salle University (PA)	0.43	40%	60%	0%	3%	15%	8%	73%	1%	41%	21
St. Joseph College (CT)	0.40	1%	99%	0%	2%	14%	8%	76%	0%	18%	21
SUNY–Purchase College	0.39	45%	55%	0%	4%	8%	10%	76%	1%	18%	21
St. Thomas Aquinas College (NY)	0.39	45%	55%	0%	2%	5%	16%	75%	1%	28%	20
Eastern University (PA)	0.38	35%	65%	0%	2%	15%	5%	76%	2%	46%	N/A
Long Island University–C.W. Post Campus (NY)	0.37	39%	61%	0%	3%	10%	8%	75%	3%	9%	21
Mount St. Mary College (NY)	0.37	27%	73%	0%	3%	11%	9%	78%	0%	12%	21
Dowling College (NY)	0.36	39%	61%	0%	2%	9%	9%	76%	4%	10%	23
Eastern Nazarene College (MA)	0.36	39%	61%	1%	3%	13%	5%	78%	2%	49%	20
Southern Connecticut State University	0.36	38%	62%	0%	2%	12%	6%	78%	1%	6%	21
Iona College (NY)	0.35	46%	54%	0%	2%	7%	11%	77%	2%	19%	20
SUNY College of Arts and Sciences–New Paltz	0.34	33%	67%	0%	3%	6%	10%	78%	3%	3%	20
Carlow University (PA)	0.33	6%	94%	1%	1%	18%	1%	80%	0%	3%	23
Delaware State University	0.33	42%	58%	0%	1%	80%	2%	17%	0%	N/A	N/A
Point Park University (PA)	0.33	41%	59%	0%	1%	18%	2%	79%	1%	17%	23
Rowan University (NJ)	0.33	45%	55%	0%	3%	9%	7%	81%	0%	2%	22
SUNY–Buffalo State College	0.33	41%	59%	0%	2%	13%	4%	81%	0%	1%	22
University of the District of Columbia	0.33	35%	65%	0%	3%	81%	6%	11%	0%	27%	30
College of New Jersey	0.32	42%	58%	0%	5%	6%	7%	82%	0%	5%	20
Frostburg State University (MD)	0.32	51%	49%	0%	2%	15%	2%	80%	1%	11%	21
Gwynedd-Mercy College (PA)	0.32	25%	75%	0%	3%	14%	2%	80%	1%	6%	22
Simmons College (MA)	0.32	1%	99%	0%	8%	7%	3%	80%	2%	39%	20
Hood College (MD)	0.31	25%	75%	0%	2%	12%	3%	80%	3%	19%	21
Central Connecticut State University	0.30	49%	51%	1%	3%	8%	6%	82%	1%	4%	21
Holy Family University (PA)	0.30	24%	76%	0%	4%	8%	3%	82%	2%	N/A	21
Lesley University (MA)	0.30	23%	77%	0%	5%	6%	5%	80%	3%	37%	21
Rider University (NJ)	0.30	41%	59%	0%	3%	9%	5%	81%	2%	24%	22
Towson University (MD)	0.30	39%	61%	0%	4%	11%	2%	81%	2%	18%	21
University of New Haven (CT)	0.30	51%	49%	0%	2%	8%	6%	81%	2%	41%	N/A
Bentley College (MA)	0.29	59%	41%	0%	8%	3%	4%	78%	8%	47%	20
Johnson and Wales University (RI)	0.29	47%	53%	0%	2%	8%	5%	81%	4%	78%	20
Rochester Institute of Technology (NY)	0.29	69%	31%	0%	6%	4%	3%	75%	11%	45%	20
Suffolk University (MA)	0.29	41%	59%	0%	7%	3%	4%	76%	9%	24%	20
University of Maryland–Eastern Shore	0.29	39%	61%	0%	1%	81%	1%	14%	3%	23%	22
Villanova University (PA)	0.29	49%	51%	0%	6%	4%	5%	82%	2%	73%	21
Philadelphia University	0.28	31%	69%	0%	4%	9%	3%	81%	3%	50%	20
Emmanuel College (MA)	0.27	25%	75%	0%	4%	7%	4%	83%	3%	28%	20
Salem State College (MA)	0.27	37%	63%	0%	3%	6%	5%	81%	4%	10%	22

Universities–Master's (South)

	Diversity index	Men	Women	American Indian	Asian	Black	Hispanic	White	International	Undergraduates from out of state	Average age of full-time students
Barry University (FL)	0.67	31%	69%	0%	1%	23%	33%	38%	5%	16%	28
University of North Carolina–Pembroke	0.65	35%	65%	22%	2%	24%	3%	48%	1%	5%	23
St. Thomas University (FL)	0.64	42%	58%	0%	1%	26%	43%	19%	11%	9%	25
Marymount University (VA)	0.56	25%	75%	0%	9%	14%	11%	59%	7%	43%	21
Christian Brothers University (TN)	0.55	45%	55%	0%	5%	36%	2%	55%	2%	24%	22
Troy University (AL)	0.53	46%	54%	1%	1%	36%	4%	57%	2%	60%	27
Francis Marion University (SC)	0.51	35%	65%	0%	1%	42%	1%	55%	1%	4%	21
University of West Alabama	0.51	44%	56%	0%	0%	44%	1%	53%	1%	20%	22
Columbus State University (GA)	0.50	38%	62%	0%	2%	32%	3%	62%	1%	N/A	N/A
Southern Wesleyan University (SC)	0.50	34%	66%	1%	1%	37%	1%	60%	1%	16%	33
Auburn University–Montgomery (AL)	0.49	35%	65%	1%	2%	33%	1%	63%	0%	4%	22
Averett University (VA)	0.49	44%	56%	0%	1%	32%	2%	63%	1%	30%	21
Delta State University (MS)	0.49	40%	60%	0%	1%	39%	1%	60%	0%	8%	22
Georgia Southwestern State University	0.49	35%	65%	1%	1%	34%	1%	62%	2%	2%	22
Northwestern State University of Louisiana	0.49	33%	67%	2%	1%	31%	2%	63%	0%	7%	22
Augusta State University (GA)	0.48	36%	64%	0%	3%	26%	3%	67%	1%	11%	22
Mercer University (GA)	0.48	31%	69%	0%	4%	27%	2%	64%	3%	24%	20
Kentucky State University	0.47	43%	57%	0%	1%	64%	0%	35%	0%	33%	22
Charleston Southern University (SC)	0.46	39%	61%	1%	2%	28%	1%	67%	2%	23%	23
Mississippi University for Women	0.46	16%	84%	0%	1%	32%	1%	65%	1%	10%	24
Southern Arkansas University	0.45	43%	57%	1%	1%	28%	1%	65%	5%	21%	24
Winthrop University (SC)	0.45	31%	69%	0%	1%	28%	1%	67%	2%	11%	N/A
Armstrong Atlantic State University (GA)	0.43	32%	68%	0%	3%	21%	3%	71%	2%	6%	23
Louisiana State University–Shreveport	0.43	37%	63%	1%	2%	23%	2%	72%	0%	N/A	N/A
Mary Baldwin College (VA)	0.43	8%	92%	1%	2%	20%	3%	72%	2%	38%	21
University of Tennessee–Chattanooga	0.43	42%	58%	1%	3%	23%	1%	72%	1%	8%	22
William Carey College (MS)	0.43	29%	71%	1%	1%	26%	1%	70%	1%	13%	24
Palm Beach Atlantic University (FL)	0.42	35%	65%	0%	2%	15%	8%	72%	4%	27%	24
Jacksonville University (FL)	0.41	42%	58%	1%	2%	16%	5%	73%	3%	38%	22
Pfeiffer University (NC)	0.41	41%	59%	1%	1%	22%	2%	71%	3%	11%	23
University of Mobile (AL)	0.41	35%	65%	2%	1%	23%	1%	70%	4%	19%	28
Austin Peay State University (TN)	0.40	37%	63%	1%	2%	18%	4%	74%	0%	8%	25
Jacksonville State University (AL)	0.40	43%	57%	1%	1%	23%	1%	73%	1%	13%	23
Nicholls State University (LA)	0.40	37%	63%	2%	1%	20%	1%	74%	1%	3%	22
University of North Carolina–Charlotte	0.40	47%	53%	0%	5%	15%	3%	75%	1%	9%	22
University of West Georgia	0.40	40%	60%	0%	1%	23%	2%	73%	1%	3%	20
Georgia Southern University	0.39	51%	49%	0%	1%	22%	1%	74%	1%	N/A	N/A
Queens University of Charlotte (NC)	0.39	23%	77%	1%	2%	17%	4%	72%	5%	50%	20
Valdosta State University (GA)	0.39	41%	59%	0%	1%	22%	2%	74%	1%	4%	21
Brenau University (GA)	0.38	0%	100%	1%	2%	16%	3%	74%	4%	12%	22
Fayetteville State University (NC)	0.38	33%	67%	1%	1%	77%	4%	17%	0%	12%	23
Lander University (SC)	0.38	34%	66%	0%	1%	23%	1%	73%	2%	3%	21
Spring Hill College (AL)	0.38	36%	64%	1%	1%	15%	5%	76%	1%	54%	20
Tuskegee University (AL)	0.38	46%	54%	0%	0%	72%	0%	25%	3%	59%	20
University of North Florida	0.38	42%	58%	0%	5%	10%	6%	77%	1%	3%	21
McNeese State University (LA)	0.37	40%	60%	1%	1%	19%	1%	76%	2%	6%	23
Mississippi College	0.36	41%	59%	0%	1%	21%	0%	75%	2%	15%	23
University of Central Arkansas	0.35	41%	59%	1%	2%	17%	1%	77%	2%	5%	21
University of West Florida	0.35	41%	59%	1%	4%	9%	5%	80%	1%	13%	23

Schools with the most diverse student bodies

Universities–Master's (Midwest)	Diversity index	Men	Women	American Indian	Asian	Black	Hispanic	White	International	Undergraduates from out of state	Average age of full-time students
Northeastern Illinois University	0.66	38%	62%	0%	11%	12%	29%	47%	2%	1%	23
Park University (MO)	0.59	52%	48%	1%	3%	21%	16%	57%	2%	N/A	N/A
Roosevelt University (IL)	0.57	33%	67%	0%	5%	24%	11%	58%	2%	8%	24
Indiana University Northwest	0.53	30%	70%	0%	1%	22%	12%	64%	0%	1%	22
Lincoln University (MO)	0.52	42%	58%	0%	0%	48%	1%	45%	5%	15%	21
North Park University (IL)	0.52	36%	64%	1%	10%	12%	9%	63%	5%	35%	21
University of Detroit Mercy	0.52	35%	65%	1%	3%	31%	3%	60%	3%	22%	N/A
Benedictine University (IL)	0.50	40%	60%	0%	14%	10%	7%	67%	1%	4%	21
Purdue University–Calumet (IN)	0.50	43%	57%	0%	1%	16%	14%	67%	1%	8%	22
St. Xavier University (IL)	0.50	28%	72%	0%	2%	18%	13%	67%	0%	4%	22
Fontbonne University (MO)	0.47	25%	75%	0%	1%	32%	1%	65%	0%	10%	25
Dominican University (IL)	0.46	31%	69%	0%	3%	7%	19%	69%	1%	9%	21
Aurora University (IL)	0.45	34%	66%	0%	2%	13%	12%	72%	0%	6%	22
Columbia College (IL)	0.45	49%	51%	1%	3%	14%	9%	71%	2%	22%	22
Mount Mary College (WI)	0.45	3%	97%	1%	5%	18%	5%	70%	1%	3%	24
Avila University (MO)	0.44	34%	66%	2%	2%	17%	6%	68%	5%	N/A	N/A
University of St. Mary (KS)	0.44	42%	58%	0%	3%	13%	11%	72%	1%	35%	22
Ursuline College (OH)	0.44	8%	92%	0%	1%	26%	2%	70%	1%	1%	25
Lewis University (IL)	0.43	39%	61%	0%	4%	12%	9%	72%	3%	6%	22
Cardinal Stritch University (WI)	0.42	30%	70%	1%	1%	21%	3%	72%	2%	19%	34
Eastern Michigan University	0.37	40%	60%	1%	2%	18%	2%	76%	1%	7%	24
Cornerstone University (MI)	0.36	39%	61%	0%	1%	18%	3%	77%	1%	19%	20
University of St. Francis (IL)	0.36	31%	69%	0%	4%	9%	7%	78%	1%	2%	22
University of Wisconsin–Parkside	0.35	43%	57%	1%	3%	9%	6%	79%	1%	7%	22
Bellevue University (NE)	0.34	51%	49%	1%	2%	10%	6%	75%	6%	N/A	N/A
Madonna University (MI)	0.34	25%	75%	0%	2%	14%	3%	77%	3%	1%	26
University of Dubuque (IA)	0.33	62%	38%	2%	1%	11%	4%	80%	1%	40%	20
University of Michigan–Dearborn	0.33	47%	53%	1%	6%	9%	3%	80%	2%	0%	22
College of St. Catherine (MN)	0.32	3%	97%	0%	7%	8%	3%	80%	2%	10%	21
Concordia University Wisconsin	0.31	37%	63%	1%	1%	13%	3%	81%	1%	30%	21
Lawrence Technological University (MI)	0.31	78%	22%	0%	3%	12%	2%	80%	2%	1%	21
Concordia University–River Forest (IL)	0.30	36%	64%	0%	1%	8%	7%	83%	0%	33%	N/A
Webster University (MO)	0.30	41%	59%	0%	1%	10%	2%	71%	15%	28%	22
Creighton University (NE)	0.29	41%	59%	1%	7%	3%	4%	84%	1%	55%	22
Rockhurst University (MO)	0.29	42%	58%	1%	2%	7%	5%	83%	1%	67%	21
Friends University (KS)	0.28	41%	59%	2%	1%	9%	4%	83%	1%	8%	22
Indiana Wesleyan University	0.28	36%	64%	0%	1%	13%	2%	84%	0%	41%	21
Lindenwood University (MO)	0.28	43%	57%	0%	1%	12%	1%	79%	7%	17%	25
University of Michigan–Flint	0.28	37%	63%	1%	2%	11%	3%	83%	1%	1%	24
Xavier University (OH)	0.28	44%	56%	0%	2%	11%	2%	83%	1%	37%	21
Youngstown State University (OH)	0.28	44%	56%	0%	1%	12%	2%	84%	1%	9%	22
Benedictine College (KS)	0.27	48%	52%	0%	2%	4%	9%	82%	3%	55%	21
Capital University (OH)	0.26	36%	64%	0%	2%	12%	1%	84%	1%	4%	23
Baker University (KS)	0.25	42%	58%	1%	1%	8%	4%	86%	0%	27%	20
Lake Superior State University (MI)	0.25	48%	52%	10%	1%	1%	1%	76%	11%	4%	22
Rockford College (IL)	0.25	36%	64%	0%	2%	7%	5%	84%	2%	N/A	N/A
Southern Illinois University–Edwardsville	0.25	45%	55%	0%	2%	10%	2%	85%	1%	N/A	21
University of Indianapolis	0.25	32%	68%	0%	1%	11%	2%	84%	2%	7%	21
Chicago State University	0.24	28%	72%	0%	1%	87%	6%	6%	1%	2%	26
MidAmerica Nazarene University (KS)	0.24	47%	53%	1%	1%	7%	4%	86%	1%	N/A	24
University of Nebraska–Omaha	0.24	47%	53%	0%	3%	6%	3%	85%	2%	7%	21
Oakland City University (IN)	0.23	45%	55%	0%	1%	10%	2%	85%	2%	16%	23
Hamline University (MN)	0.22	39%	61%	1%	6%	3%	2%	85%	3%	15%	20
Indiana University–South Bend	0.22	38%	62%	0%	1%	7%	3%	86%	2%	3%	23
Western Illinois University	0.22	51%	49%	0%	1%	7%	4%	87%	1%	8%	22

Universities–Master's (West)

	Diversity index	Men	Women	American Indian	Asian	Black	Hispanic	White	International	Undergraduates from out of state	Average age of full-time students
La Sierra University (CA)	0.72	41%	59%	1%	22%	9%	28%	29%	10%	13%	21
California State University–Dominguez Hills	0.71	32%	68%	1%	9%	26%	35%	27%	2%	2%	25
California State Polytechnic University–Pomona	0.70	57%	43%	0%	31%	4%	27%	34%	3%	2%	22
California State University–East Bay	0.70	38%	62%	1%	29%	12%	14%	39%	5%	3%	N/A
Holy Names University (CA)	0.70	27%	73%	1%	9%	26%	18%	39%	6%	5%	23
Mount St. Mary's College (CA)	0.69	6%	94%	1%	20%	10%	44%	25%	1%	3%	21
California State University–Long Beach	0.68	40%	60%	1%	22%	6%	25%	42%	5%	1%	22
California State University–Fullerton	0.67	42%	58%	0%	22%	4%	28%	42%	4%	2%	22
California State University–Los Angeles	0.67	39%	61%	0%	21%	8%	46%	20%	4%	1%	24
California State University–San Bernardino	0.67	34%	66%	1%	8%	12%	34%	42%	3%	1%	23
Houston Baptist University	0.67	33%	67%	0%	13%	20%	14%	46%	6%	3%	22
California State University–Northridge	0.66	41%	59%	0%	12%	9%	28%	46%	5%	1%	22
San Francisco State University	0.66	41%	59%	1%	31%	6%	14%	43%	5%	1%	23
San Jose State University (CA)	0.66	49%	51%	0%	38%	5%	16%	37%	3%	0%	22
California State University–Fresno	0.64	42%	58%	1%	14%	5%	30%	48%	2%	1%	22
College of the Southwest (NM)	0.64	39%	61%	8%	4%	4%	37%	42%	6%	36%	24
Hawaii Pacific University	0.64	41%	59%	1%	35%	7%	7%	39%	11%	52%	22
Woodbury University (CA)	0.64	40%	60%	0%	11%	6%	34%	43%	6%	20%	21
Dominican University of California	0.63	23%	77%	1%	20%	8%	15%	53%	3%	6%	22
Notre Dame de Namur University (CA)	0.63	37%	63%	1%	15%	5%	22%	52%	4%	N/A	21
University of St. Thomas (TX)	0.63	38%	62%	1%	12%	6%	30%	49%	3%	4%	21
University of Texas–San Antonio	0.62	47%	53%	1%	5%	7%	46%	39%	2%	4%	21
California State University–Sacramento	0.60	43%	57%	1%	19%	7%	15%	57%	1%	1%	22
California State University–Stanislaus	0.60	34%	66%	1%	12%	4%	28%	54%	1%	1%	23
Loyola Marymount University (CA)	0.60	42%	58%	1%	13%	8%	20%	58%	2%	23%	20
Cameron University (OK)	0.58	40%	60%	8%	3%	19%	9%	59%	3%	18%	22
Heritage University (WA)	0.58	27%	73%	10%	1%	1%	54%	34%	0%	N/A	31
Texas Wesleyan University	0.57	34%	66%	1%	2%	18%	21%	59%	N/A	1%	23
Eastern New Mexico University	0.56	44%	56%	3%	1%	7%	30%	58%	1%	19%	22
New Mexico Highlands University	0.56	38%	62%	8%	1%	5%	60%	25%	0%	7%	25
St. Mary's College of California	0.56	39%	61%	1%	10%	6%	20%	61%	2%	11%	20
Western New Mexico University	0.56	36%	64%	3%	0%	3%	48%	44%	1%	16%	26
University of Texas of the Permian Basin	0.55	39%	61%	1%	1%	4%	37%	56%	0%	5%	N/A
University of the Incarnate Word (TX)	0.55	34%	66%	1%	2%	7%	56%	31%	3%	2%	22
Seattle University	0.54	39%	61%	1%	20%	5%	7%	58%	7%	40%	22
Texas A&M University–Corpus Christi	0.54	40%	60%	1%	2%	3%	38%	55%	1%	3%	23
California State University–San Marcos	0.53	39%	61%	1%	11%	3%	20%	62%	3%	1%	23
Lamar University (TX)	0.53	40%	60%	1%	3%	27%	6%	63%	1%	1%	22
St. Edward's University (TX)	0.53	42%	58%	1%	2%	5%	30%	60%	2%	6%	20
Chaminade University of Honolulu	0.52	31%	69%	1%	64%	4%	7%	23%	2%	50%	22
Fresno Pacific University (CA)	0.52	34%	66%	1%	4%	4%	26%	62%	3%	3%	27
Northeastern State University (OK)	0.52	39%	61%	29%	1%	6%	2%	60%	3%	6%	28
Santa Clara University (CA)	0.52	44%	56%	1%	18%	3%	13%	63%	3%	33%	20
Southeastern Oklahoma State University	0.52	44%	56%	29%	1%	5%	2%	62%	1%	21%	24
Colorado State University–Pueblo	0.51	40%	60%	2%	3%	5%	25%	64%	2%	7%	23
Hope International University (CA)	0.50	38%	62%	1%	4%	8%	18%	66%	3%	32%	26

Comprehensive Colleges–Bachelor's (North)

	Diversity index	Men	Women	American Indian	Asian	Black	Hispanic	White	International	Undergraduates from out of state	Average age of full-time students
CUNY–New York City College of Technology	0.69	50%	50%	0%	12%	39%	25%	12%	11%	0%	22
CUNY–York College	0.67	32%	68%	0%	10%	48%	15%	26%	N/A	28%	24
SUNY College–Old Westbury	0.66	39%	61%	0%	7%	28%	16%	47%	2%	1%	23
Atlantic Union College (MA)	0.62	39%	61%	0%	1%	51%	24%	24%	0%	N/A	N/A
Bloomfield College (NJ)	0.62	31%	69%	0%	4%	53%	18%	23%	2%	3%	24
Columbia Union College (MD)	0.58	36%	64%	0%	6%	56%	8%	27%	4%	44%	22
Dominican College of Blauvelt (NY)	0.58	33%	67%	0%	7%	18%	15%	60%	0%	19%	23
St. Francis College (NY)	0.57	46%	54%	0%	2%	20%	16%	54%	9%	2%	21
College of St. Elizabeth (NJ)	0.56	8%	92%	0%	6%	16%	15%	59%	4%	6%	20
Albertus Magnus College (CT)	0.55	28%	72%	0%	1%	27%	11%	60%	0%	N/A	N/A
Felician College (NJ)	0.55	24%	76%	0%	7%	12%	17%	63%	N/A	N/A	N/A
Post University (CT)	0.53	40%	60%	0%	2%	22%	10%	62%	3%	30%	21

Schools with the most diverse student bodies

Comprehensive Colleges–Bachelor's (North), continued

	Diversity index	Men	Women	American Indian	Asian	Black	Hispanic	White	International	Undergraduates from out of state	Average age of full-time students
Caldwell College (NJ)	0.47	32%	68%	0%	2%	16%	11%	66%	5%	14%	23
SUNY–Farmingdale	0.45	58%	42%	0%	5%	13%	9%	72%	1%	1%	21
Wesley College (DE)	0.44	47%	53%	0%	2%	26%	2%	69%	1%	77%	20
Bay Path College (MA)	0.36	0%	100%	0%	1%	12%	7%	79%	1%	N/A	N/A
Concordia College (NY)	0.36	43%	57%	0%	2%	10%	7%	73%	8%	72%	21
St. Joseph's College New York–Brooklyn	0.36	25%	75%	0%	2%	11%	7%	79%	0%	0%	22
Ramapo College of New Jersey	0.35	40%	60%	0%	4%	7%	8%	78%	3%	7%	21
Alvernia College (PA)	0.34	31%	69%	0%	1%	14%	5%	80%	0%	14%	22
Daemen College (NY)	0.34	23%	77%	1%	1%	15%	2%	79%	1%	4%	21
Mount Ida College (MA)	0.34	31%	69%	0%	2%	10%	6%	75%	6%	N/A	N/A
Villa Julie College (MD)	0.32	29%	71%	0%	3%	15%	1%	81%	0%	4%	21
Simon's Rock College of Bard (MA)	0.30	44%	56%	0%	5%	6%	5%	81%	3%	83%	18
Lasell College (MA)	0.29	31%	69%	0%	3%	6%	6%	82%	3%	44%	20
Medaille College (NY)	0.29	35%	65%	0%	0%	14%	2%	83%	0%	5%	27
Neumann College (PA)	0.29	33%	67%	0%	1%	13%	2%	81%	2%	27%	21

Comprehensive Colleges–Bachelor's (South)

	Diversity index	Men	Women	American Indian	Asian	Black	Hispanic	White	International	Undergraduates from out of state	Average age of full-time students
Clayton State University (GA)	0.57	30%	70%	0%	4%	50%	2%	40%	2%	2%	24
International College (FL)	0.55	31%	69%	1%	1%	18%	18%	62%	0%	N/A	N/A
Columbia College (SC)	0.54	2%	98%	0%	1%	43%	2%	51%	2%	7%	22
North Carolina Wesleyan College	0.54	45%	55%	1%	1%	45%	3%	50%	1%	15%	26
Limestone College (SC)	0.53	37%	63%	0%	1%	46%	2%	51%	1%	41%	20
Belhaven College (MS)	0.52	32%	68%	1%	1%	39%	3%	56%	1%	N/A	N/A
Chowan College (NC)	0.52	55%	45%	1%	1%	37%	3%	57%	1%	51%	19
Crichton College (TN)	0.51	35%	65%	0%	0%	44%	1%	54%	1%	N/A	N/A
Warner Southern College (FL)	0.50	42%	58%	0%	1%	21%	10%	66%	2%	13%	25
Mid-Continent University (KY)	0.49	53%	47%	0%	1%	31%	2%	58%	8%	58%	N/A
Methodist College (NC)	0.47	54%	46%	1%	2%	20%	6%	68%	3%	45%	23
Southern Adventist University (TN)	0.47	46%	54%	0%	5%	11%	12%	67%	5%	70%	20
University of Arkansas–Monticello	0.47	41%	59%	1%	1%	31%	2%	66%	0%	10%	23
University of South Carolina–Upstate	0.46	34%	66%	1%	3%	27%	2%	66%	2%	N/A	23
Faulkner University (AL)	0.45	38%	62%	0%	1%	31%	1%	66%	0%	11%	27
Newberry College (SC)	0.44	60%	40%	0%	1%	26%	2%	68%	3%	N/A	N/A
University of South Carolina–Aiken	0.44	33%	67%	0%	1%	26%	2%	69%	2%	11%	N/A
High Point University (NC)	0.42	37%	63%	0%	1%	23%	2%	70%	3%	51%	21
Barton College (NC)	0.41	27%	73%	0%	1%	23%	2%	72%	2%	20%	22
Brewton-Parker College (GA)	0.40	36%	64%	0%	0%	23%	2%	73%	1%	5%	22
Berea College (KY)	0.38	41%	59%	1%	1%	19%	2%	70%	7%	57%	20
Coker College (SC)	0.38	41%	59%	0%	1%	20%	2%	75%	2%	23%	21
LaGrange College (GA)	0.38	39%	61%	1%	1%	20%	1%	74%	3%	10%	21
Ferrum College (VA)	0.37	58%	42%	1%	1%	20%	2%	76%	1%	15%	21
Lambuth University (TN)	0.37	46%	54%	0%	1%	19%	3%	75%	3%	21%	20
Southeastern University (FL)	0.36	43%	57%	0%	1%	7%	12%	79%	4%	37%	23
Elizabeth City State University (NC)	0.35	38%	62%	0%	1%	78%	0%	21%	0%	14%	22
Peace College (NC)	0.35	0%	100%	0%	2%	15%	3%	78%	1%	9%	20
Bluefield College (VA)	0.33	40%	60%	0%	1%	18%	1%	80%	0%	27%	28
Catawba College (NC)	0.32	48%	52%	1%	1%	16%	1%	80%	2%	30%	22
University of the Ozarks (AR)	0.32	47%	53%	4%	2%	4%	5%	70%	15%	30%	21
Belmont Abbey College (NC)	0.31	44%	56%	0%	1%	12%	4%	77%	6%	35%	24
Emmanuel College (GA)	0.30	43%	57%	0%	1%	15%	1%	82%	1%	21%	20
Martin Methodist College (TN)	0.30	40%	60%	0%	0%	14%	2%	73%	10%	N/A	N/A
Mars Hill College (NC)	0.28	40%	60%	0%	1%	12%	2%	83%	2%	30%	20
Winston-Salem State University (NC)	0.26	30%	70%	0%	1%	85%	1%	13%	0%	9%	23
Florida Southern College	0.25	39%	61%	0%	1%	6%	6%	83%	4%	28%	19
Mountain State University (WV)	0.25	34%	66%	1%	1%	10%	2%	84%	2%	24%	31
Wingate University (NC)	0.25	48%	52%	1%	1%	11%	1%	84%	3%	39%	20

Comprehensive Colleges–Bachelor's (Midwest)

	Diversity index	Men	Women	American Indian	Asian	Black	Hispanic	White	International	Undergraduates from out of state	Average age of full-time students
Calumet College of St. Joseph (IN)	0.63	43%	57%	0%	1%	29%	20%	50%	0%	35%	N/A
Alverno College (WI)	0.55	1%	99%	1%	5%	20%	11%	63%	1%	2%	24
Baker College of Flint (MI)	0.45	30%	70%	0%	1%	28%	2%	69%	0%	N/A	N/A
Notre Dame College of Ohio	0.38	33%	67%	0%	1%	19%	2%	72%	5%	7%	21
Iowa Wesleyan College	0.36	39%	61%	0%	2%	10%	7%	71%	9%	29%	N/A
Ohio Dominican University	0.36	37%	63%	0%	1%	21%	1%	76%	0%	2%	25
Central Christian College (KS)	0.35	47%	53%	2%	0%	9%	7%	78%	3%	56%	21
Rochester College (MI)	0.34	39%	61%	1%	1%	18%	1%	78%	1%	5%	25
Marian College (IN)	0.30	26%	74%	1%	1%	14%	1%	81%	2%	7%	21
Sterling College (KS)	0.30	52%	48%	2%	1%	9%	6%	82%	1%	41%	20
Lourdes College (OH)	0.29	18%	82%	1%	1%	14%	2%	83%	0%	10%	26
McKendree College (IL)	0.28	44%	56%	0%	1%	13%	2%	82%	2%	16%	23
Southwestern College (KS)	0.28	50%	50%	2%	1%	8%	4%	83%	2%	30%	23
Bethany College (KS)	0.27	55%	45%	1%	1%	8%	5%	81%	4%	41%	20
Concordia University (MI)	0.27	44%	56%	1%	1%	10%	2%	84%	1%	17%	24
Dakota Wesleyan University (SD)	0.27	42%	58%	4%	1%	5%	4%	83%	2%	N/A	N/A
Elmhurst College (IL)	0.27	35%	65%	0%	3%	6%	6%	84%	1%	8%	21
Trinity Christian College (IL)	0.27	34%	66%	0%	2%	8%	5%	84%	1%	37%	21
MacMurray College (IL)	0.26	40%	60%	1%	0%	11%	3%	84%	1%	12%	21
Bethel College (KS)	0.25	49%	51%	1%	2%	6%	4%	82%	5%	24%	21
Concordia University–St. Paul (MN)	0.25	39%	61%	0%	5%	7%	2%	85%	0%	23%	25
Grace College and Seminary (IN)	0.25	53%	47%	1%	1%	10%	2%	86%	1%	41%	23
Missouri Baptist University	0.25	41%	59%	0%	0%	11%	2%	82%	4%	N/A	N/A
William Penn University (IA)	0.25	45%	55%	1%	2%	8%	3%	86%	0%	19%	27
McPherson College (KS)	0.24	62%	38%	1%	0%	6%	6%	86%	0%	50%	19
College of St. Mary (NE)	0.22	0%	100%	1%	1%	7%	3%	87%	1%	10%	26
Crown College (MN)	0.22	41%	59%	1%	6%	3%	2%	88%	0%	30%	20
Lakeland College (WI)	0.22	39%	61%	1%	2%	6%	2%	84%	5%	12%	N/A
Millikin University (IL)	0.22	41%	59%	0%	1%	9%	2%	87%	0%	13%	22
Union College (NE)	0.22	45%	55%	1%	2%	2%	6%	79%	10%	79%	22
Central State University (OH)	0.21	51%	49%	0%	0%	87%	1%	11%	1%	30%	21
Columbia College (MO)	0.20	39%	61%	1%	1%	5%	3%	84%	6%	7%	21
Culver-Stockton College (MO)	0.20	42%	58%	0%	0%	7%	3%	88%	1%	34%	19
Greenville College (IL)	0.20	46%	54%	1%	1%	8%	2%	88%	1%	29%	24
Judson College (IL)	0.20	42%	58%	0%	1%	4%	5%	87%	3%	30%	21
Purdue University–North Central (IN)	0.20	41%	59%	1%	1%	4%	4%	89%	0%	1%	24
Tabor College (KS)	0.20	52%	48%	1%	1%	5%	4%	88%	1%	37%	20
Wilmington College (OH)	0.20	46%	54%	1%	0%	9%	1%	88%	1%	4%	21
York College (NE)	0.20	49%	51%	0%	2%	5%	4%	87%	2%	66%	20
Dana College (NE)	0.19	55%	45%	1%	1%	5%	3%	90%	1%	45%	20
Evangel University (MO)	0.19	42%	58%	1%	2%	4%	4%	89%	0%	62%	21

Comprehensive Colleges–Bachelor's (West)

	Diversity index	Men	Women	American Indian	Asian	Black	Hispanic	White	International	Undergraduates from out of state	Average age of full-time students
Patten University (CA)	0.73	61%	39%	0%	21%	25%	17%	37%	0%	23%	23
University of Houston–Downtown	0.72	41%	59%	0%	10%	26%	37%	23%	4%	1%	24
Humphreys College (CA)	0.64	14%	86%	1%	13%	3%	42%	41%	0%	N/A	N/A
Menlo College (CA)	0.59	60%	40%	1%	12%	9%	15%	53%	10%	13%	22
Pacific Union College (CA)	0.58	47%	53%	1%	22%	4%	12%	55%	7%	19%	21
Brigham Young University–Hawaii	0.56	42%	58%	1%	22%	1%	2%	28%	47%	65%	23
St. Gregory's University (OK)	0.47	48%	52%	11%	1%	7%	8%	64%	10%	N/A	N/A
McMurry University (TX)	0.44	50%	50%	1%	1%	11%	14%	72%	1%	4%	21
Concordia University–Austin (TX)	0.42	43%	57%	0%	1%	9%	16%	74%	0%	N/A	N/A
Texas Lutheran University	0.42	46%	54%	0%	2%	8%	16%	73%	1%	3%	20
Vanguard University of Southern California	0.42	34%	66%	1%	4%	4%	17%	74%	1%	17%	21
University of Science and Arts of Oklahoma	0.39	36%	64%	13%	1%	6%	3%	76%	2%	6%	22
Huston-Tillotson University (TX)	0.38	47%	53%	0%	1%	75%	13%	9%	2%	N/A	N/A
Cogswell Polytechnical College (CA)	0.37	88%	12%	0%	11%	2%	9%	78%	N/A	9%	24
Howard Payne University (TX)	0.37	49%	51%	1%	1%	6%	14%	78%	N/A	4%	22
Lubbock Christian University (TX)	0.36	43%	57%	0%	1%	7%	15%	77%	1%	9%	23

Priciest private schools

The sticker price of a year at an elite private school may be a far cry from what most people actually pay, so it's a good idea not to rule out any favorites based just on price. Many high-priced institutions are generous with their financial aid. The schools are listed here by sticker price—the sum of tuition, fees, and room and board—for the 2005–2006 academic year. (Remember, though, some schools don't charge for tuition or room and board.) In addition, the table lists the average need-based financial aid package granted to undergraduates during 2005–2006. The typical aid package has three components: a need based grant, need-based loans, and work study. In order to qualify, students must file an annual aid application that demonstrates financial need. Expenses for 2006–2007 are provided in the directory when available.

National Universities	Tuition, fees, room and board	Average financial aid package
George Washington University (DC)	$44,500	$33,196
New York University	$43,170	$18,652
Georgetown University (DC)	$42,938	$25,600
Columbia University (NY)	$42,584	$28,138
University of Chicago	$42,369	$29,176
Boston College	$42,283	$24,905
Washington University in St. Louis	$42,106	$25,653
Boston University	$42,046	$27,633
Tufts University (MA)	$42,018	$25,749
Vanderbilt University (TN)	$41,986	$31,840
Massachusetts Institute of Technology	$41,800	$29,831
Brown University (RI)	$41,770	$26,477
University of Pennsylvania	$41,766	$28,642
Cornell University (NY)	$41,717	$29,500
Harvard University (MA)	$41,675	$30,715
Northwestern University (IL)	$41,662	$25,831
University of Southern California	$41,618	$29,365
Brandeis University (MA)	$41,551	$23,816
Johns Hopkins University (MD)	$41,544	$26,553
Rensselaer Polytechnic Institute (NY)	$41,363	$26,072
Tulane University (LA)	$41,361	N/A
Dartmouth College (NH)	$41,355	$30,019
Duke University (NC)	$41,240	$29,878
University of Rochester (NY)	$41,135	$24,474
Stanford University (CA)	$41,132	$29,750
Yale University (CT)	$41,000	$30,219
Stevens Institute of Technology (NJ)	$40,895	$21,139
Worcester Polytechnic Institute (MA)	$40,850	$20,849
Carnegie Mellon University (PA)	$40,650	$22,143
Emory University (GA)	$40,546	$27,599
Princeton University (NJ)	$40,213	$28,368
Lehigh University (PA)	$39,980	$25,403
Pepperdine University (CA)	$39,960	$30,991
University of Notre Dame (IN)	$39,552	N/A
Northeastern University (MA)	$39,342	$16,085
Fordham University (NY)	$39,331	$20,104
American University (DC)	$38,719	$26,534
Wake Forest University (NC)	$38,710	$22,581
Syracuse University (NY)	$38,655	$20,716
University of Miami (FL)	$38,410	$23,709
New School University (NY)	$38,200	$14,338
University of San Diego	$37,888	$21,450
Case Western Reserve University (OH)	$37,160	$28,931
University of Denver	$37,159	$20,508
Polytechnic University (NY)	$37,150	$21,955
University of San Francisco	$37,080	$21,153
Southern Methodist University (TX)	$36,187	$23,699
California Institute of Technology	$36,123	$28,508
Catholic University of America (DC)	$35,838	$16,279
Clark University (MA)	$35,165	$21,898
Clarkson University (NY)	$34,930	$18,723
Drexel University (PA)	$34,725	$15,076
University of the Pacific (CA)	$34,566	$23,050
St. John's University (NY)	$34,370	$15,807
Pace University (NY)	$34,324	$15,062
University of Hartford (CT)	$34,044	$16,790
Yeshiva University (NY)	$33,980	$20,434
Seton Hall University (NJ)	$33,622	$15,660
Widener University (PA)	$33,490	$20,192
Loyola University Chicago	$33,296	$20,367
St. Louis University	$33,158	$18,858
Florida Institute of Technology	$31,950	$21,102
University of La Verne (CA)	$31,910	$20,636
Marquette University (WI)	$31,066	$16,770
Hofstra University (NY)	$31,030	$12,750
Illinois Institute of Technology	$30,438	$20,610
Rice University (TX)	$30,100	$20,140
University of St. Thomas (MN)	$30,000	$18,695
DePaul University (IL)	$29,970	$16,309
Biola University (CA)	$29,702	$15,200
University of Bridgeport (CT)	$29,595	N/A
Duquesne University (PA)	$29,534	$15,919
University of Dayton (OH)	$28,826	$7,187
Adelphi University (NY)	$28,820	$14,750
Texas Christian University	$28,300	$14,589
Baylor University (TX)	$27,944	$15,392
Alliant International University (CA)	$26,950	$17,000
University of Tulsa (OK)	$25,348	$21,719
Nova Southeastern University (FL)	$25,048	$13,662
National-Louis University (IL)	$24,390	$9,559
Andrews University (MI)	$21,786	$21,103
Clark Atlanta University	$21,410	N/A
Howard University (DC)	$18,481	$17,077
Brigham Young University-Provo (UT)	$8,980	$4,302

Liberal Arts Colleges

	Tuition, fees, room and board	Average financial aid package
Sarah Lawrence College (NY)	$45,506	$28,671
Trinity College (CT)	$42,220	$27,920
Harvey Mudd College (CA)	$42,150	$25,315
Mount Holyoke College (MA)	$42,148	$27,253
Wesleyan University (CT)	$42,122	$29,341
Middlebury College (VT)	$42,120	$28,295
Bates College (ME)	$42,100	$27,428
Connecticut College	$41,975	$26,014
Bennington College (VT)	$41,890	$25,712
Colby College (ME)	$41,770	$27,177
Vassar College (NY)	$41,700	$27,982
Bowdoin College (ME)	$41,660	$29,090
Hamilton College (NY)	$41,660	$27,035
Pitzer College (CA)	$41,644	$29,002
Bard College (NY)	$41,620	$25,107
Haverford College (PA)	$41,600	$26,990
Union College (NY)	$41,595	$27,359
Barnard College (NY)	$41,592	$28,790
Amherst College (MA)	$41,590	$31,048
Swarthmore College (PA)	$41,280	$28,914
Colgate University (NY)	$41,170	$27,795
Hobart and William Smith Colleges (NY)	$41,123	$24,303
Reed College (OR)	$41,106	N/A
Claremont McKenna College (CA)	$41,070	$25,674
Hampshire College (MA)	$41,038	$27,080
Wellesley College (MA)	$41,030	$27,907
Smith College (MA)	$41,024	$29,776
Scripps College (CA)	$41,000	$27,665
Oberlin College (OH)	$40,904	$23,710
Pomona College (CA)	$40,774	$29,784
College of the Holy Cross (MA)	$40,664	$21,254
Franklin and Marshall College (PA)	$40,590	$24,283
University of Richmond (VA)	$40,510	$23,258
Carleton College (MN)	$40,467	$26,649
Bryn Mawr College (PA)	$40,420	$27,582
Williams College (MA)	$40,310	$30,309
Wheaton College (MA)	$40,180	$23,155
Dickinson College (PA)	$40,170	$27,496
Occidental College (CA)	$39,988	$29,089
Mills College (CA)	$39,870	$29,584
St. Lawrence University (NY)	$39,790	$30,445
Drew University (NJ)	$39,698	$23,012
Bucknell University (PA)	$39,660	$21,000
Gettysburg College (PA)	$39,644	$25,089
Kenyon College (OH)	$39,500	$24,982
Lafayette College (PA)	$39,267	$24,675
Ursinus College (PA)	$38,950	$23,938
Colorado College	$37,668	$27,522
Denison University (OH)	$37,040	$25,367
Davidson College (NC)	$36,825	$18,024
Westmont College (CA)	$36,672	$18,521
Macalester College (MN)	$36,500	$25,238
Goucher College (MD)	$36,400	$19,792
Whitman College (WA)	$36,110	$22,050
Marlboro College (VT)	$35,980	$10,057
Washington and Lee University (VA)	$35,860	$25,158
Ohio Wesleyan University	$35,830	$20,854
University of Puget Sound (WA)	$35,600	$20,466
Willamette University (OR)	$35,416	N/A
Lewis and Clark College (OR)	$35,358	$24,262
College of Wooster (OH)	$35,290	$23,837
Washington College (MD)	$34,990	$16,314
Grinnell College (IA)	$34,814	$23,921
Sewanee–University of the South (TN)	$34,645	$19,574
Wittenberg University (OH)	$34,596	$21,691
Hartwick College (NY)	$34,490	$20,494
Whittier College (CA)	$34,390	$23,742
Illinois Wesleyan University	$34,050	$18,285
DePauw University (IN)	$33,970	$24,873
Lawrence University (WI)	$33,958	$22,900
Lake Forest College (IL)	$33,860	$21,562
St. Anselm College (NH)	$33,730	$18,164
College of the Atlantic (ME)	$33,702	$24,478
Antioch College (OH)	$33,700	$22,853
Albright College (PA)	$33,668	$17,140
Earlham College (IN)	$33,604	$21,500
Allegheny College (PA)	$33,500	$21,250
Washington and Jefferson College (PA)	$33,490	$19,096
Susquehanna University (PA)	$33,465	$18,578
Furman University (SC)	$33,264	$22,162
Eckerd College (FL)	$33,212	$21,718
Juniata College (PA)	$33,130	$18,539
Rhodes College (TN)	$32,860	$24,349
Beloit College (WI)	$32,808	$19,108
St. Olaf College (MN)	$32,800	$21,869
Moravian College (PA)	$32,793	$17,118
Skidmore College (NY)	$32,659	$28,452
Knox College (IL)	$32,385	$21,317
Kalamazoo College (MI)	$32,352	$25,005
Agnes Scott College (GA)	$32,070	$24,314
Franklin Pierce College (NH)	$31,700	$16,346
Randolph-Macon Woman's College (VA)	$31,640	$21,368
McDaniel College (MD)	$31,610	$20,398
Sweet Briar College (VA)	$31,460	$15,293
Hampden-Sydney College (VA)	$31,440	$17,891
Randolph-Macon College (VA)	$31,250	$17,459
Albion College (MI)	$31,224	$20,101
Hollins University (VA)	$31,105	$17,913
Wofford College (SC)	$30,935	$22,401
Centre College (KY)	$30,810	$18,526
Roanoke College (VA)	$30,748	$18,931
Lycoming College (PA)	$30,697	$17,826
Gustavus Adolphus College (MN)	$30,685	$17,200
Chatham College (PA)	$30,520	N/A
Coe College (IA)	$30,190	$20,370
College of St. Benedict (MN)	$30,121	$19,044
Wabash College (IN)	$30,116	$22,192
Cornell College (IA)	$30,110	$18,510
Presbyterian College (SC)	$30,044	$21,609
Augustana College (IL)	$29,862	$17,229
University of Judaism (CA)	$29,860	$19,700
St. John's University (MN)	$29,749	$17,573
Gordon College (MA)	$29,564	$14,540
Southwestern University (TX)	$29,540	$19,315
Oglethorpe University (GA)	$29,400	N/A
Westminster College (PA)	$29,280	$18,665
Seton Hill University (PA)	$29,230	$18,903
Rosemont College (PA)	$29,115	$17,513
Luther College (IA)	$28,800	$19,374
St. Vincent College (PA)	$28,553	$16,963
Alma College (MI)	$28,544	$17,812
Virginia Wesleyan College	$28,433	$14,385
Siena College (NY)	$28,325	$14,486
Millsaps College (MS)	$28,256	$17,774
Birmingham-Southern College (AL)	$28,230	$15,595
Emory and Henry College (VA)	$28,220	$14,362
Hope College (MI)	$28,208	$18,272
Guilford College (NC)	$28,170	$11,661
Hanover College (IN)	$28,150	$17,526
Hendrix College (AR)	$27,946	$15,269
Austin College (TX)	$27,871	$20,989
Bridgewater College (VA)	$27,790	$17,309
Principia College (IL)	$27,765	N/A
Wheaton College (IL)	$27,760	$18,555

Priciest private schools

Liberal Arts Colleges, continued

	Tuition, fees, room and board	Average financial aid package
University of Dallas	$27,432	$17,561
Ripon College (WI)	$27,160	$18,534
Stephens College (MO)	$26,930	$16,894
West Virginia Wesleyan College	$26,800	$21,518
Salem College (NC)	$26,441	$13,980
Transylvania University (KY)	$26,240	$16,537
Houghton College (NY)	$25,980	$14,861
Monmouth College (IL)	$25,950	N/A
Goshen College (IN)	$25,750	$16,555
Erskine College (SC)	$25,468	$18,100
Adrian College (MI)	$25,240	$17,074
Morehouse College (GA)	$25,070	$7,859
Greensboro College (NC)	$25,040	N/A
Pine Manor College (MA)	$25,038	$14,984
Georgetown College (KY)	$24,950	$17,844
Concordia College–Moorhead (MN)	$24,510	$14,468
Warner Pacific College (OR)	$24,510	$14,048
Spelman College (GA)	$24,400	$10,500
Thomas Aquinas College (CA)	$24,400	$16,479
Hillsdale College (MI)	$24,060	$13,000
William Jewell College (MO)	$23,850	$15,288
Nebraska Wesleyan University	$23,425	$12,858
King College (TN)	$23,400	$15,045
Wells College (NY)	$23,070	$17,290
Lees-McRae College (NC)	$23,000	$10,174
Muskingum College (OH)	$22,795	$14,348
St. Andrews Presbyterian College (NC)	$22,730	$12,198
San Diego Christian College (CA)	$22,690	$14,547
Schreiner University (TX)	$22,474	$11,682
Hastings College (NE)	$22,218	N/A
Bethany College (WV)	$22,210	N/A
Olivet College (MI)	$21,944	$14,121
Christendom College (VA)	$21,594	N/A
Huntingdon College (AL)	$21,350	$8,793
Albertson College (ID)	$21,164	$13,993
Westminster College (MO)	$20,040	$16,226
Lyon College (AR)	$19,990	$13,749
Fisk University (TN)	$19,910	N/A
Lindsey Wilson College (KY)	$19,740	$10,491
Wesleyan College (GA)	$19,560	$10,758
Bennett College (NC)	$19,014	$9,036
Blackburn College (IL)	$18,735	$9,808
Marymount Manhattan College (NY)	$18,530	$11,386
Virginia Union University	$18,432	$12,687
St. Augustine's College (NC)	$16,560	$11,688
Bethel College (TN)	$16,066	N/A
Tougaloo College (MS)	$15,025	$4,775
Paine College (GA)	$14,418	$8,964
Lane College (TN)	$11,710	$9,403
Talladega College (AL)	$11,548	N/A
National Hispanic University (CA)	$3,914	N/A

Universities–Master's (North)

	Tuition, fees, room and board	Average financial aid package
Fairfield University (CT)	$39,835	$17,079
Loyola College in Maryland	$38,610	$20,465
Villanova University (PA)	$38,493	$20,503
St. Joseph's University (PA)	$37,395	$13,301
Bentley College (MA)	$36,994	$23,177
Manhattanville College (NY)	$36,610	$21,904
La Salle University (PA)	$35,930	$17,999
Simmons College (MA)	$35,640	$15,085
Ithaca College (NY)	$35,144	$21,810
Emerson College (MA)	$34,995	$13,823
Quinnipiac University (CT)	$34,640	$14,511
Providence College (RI)	$34,580	$17,000
Bryant University (RI)	$34,330	$15,270
University of Scranton (PA)	$33,934	$15,912
Arcadia University (PA)	$33,570	$19,214
Salve Regina University (RI)	$33,450	$16,392
Sacred Heart University (CT)	$33,404	$14,943
Cabrini College (PA)	$33,340	$19,399
St. Michael's College (VT)	$33,330	$19,222
Wagner College (NY)	$33,300	$15,642
Suffolk University (MA)	$33,160	$13,162
Wheelock College (MA)	$33,075	$15,741
Assumption College (MA)	$32,875	$15,462
Fairleigh Dickinson University (NJ)	$32,626	N/A
St. Joseph College (CT)	$32,550	$17,997
University of New Haven (CT)	$32,532	$14,751
Rider University (NJ)	$32,310	$17,454
Canisius College (NY)	$32,257	$18,883
Lesley University (MA)	$32,100	$15,834
Emmanuel College (MA)	$32,000	$16,201
Long Island University–C.W. Post Campus (NY)	$31,930	N/A
Lebanon Valley College (PA)	$31,700	$17,982
Rochester Institute of Technology (NY)	$31,428	N/A
Regis College (MA)	$31,350	$20,003
University of New England (ME)	$31,005	$15,659
Alfred University (NY)	$30,932	$21,663
Mount St. Mary's University (MD)	$30,930	$15,181
Wilkes University (PA)	$30,886	$16,882
Iona College (NY)	$30,878	$13,384
Long Island University–Brooklyn (NY)	$30,720	$12,399
Marywood University (PA)	$30,715	$16,474
Marist College (NY)	$30,546	$13,439
Manhattan College (NY)	$30,245	$13,606
Hood College (MD)	$30,085	$18,020
Philadelphia University	$30,076	$15,474
St. Peter's College (NJ)	$29,962	$17,370
Anna Maria College (MA)	$29,815	$15,242
King's College (PA)	$29,810	$15,220
College of Notre Dame of Maryland	$29,600	$18,061
Le Moyne College (NY)	$29,570	$16,821
Springfield College (MA)	$29,365	$15,637
Chestnut Hill College (PA)	$29,325	$8,500
St. Joseph's College (ME)	$29,185	$16,472
St. Francis University (PA)	$28,978	$18,573
Monmouth University (NJ)	$28,956	$13,765
St. Bonaventure University (NY)	$28,785	$16,944

	Tuition, fees, room and board	Average financial aid package
College of Mount St. Vincent (NY)	$28,750	$17,000
American International College (MA)	$28,710	$20,200
DeSales University (PA)	$28,580	$14,278
Rivier College (NH)	$28,494	$14,176
Norwich University (VT)	$28,448	$16,159
College of New Rochelle (NY)	$28,400	N/A
Nazareth College of Rochester (NY)	$28,376	$15,551
Immaculata University (PA)	$28,350	$13,725
Niagara University (NY)	$28,250	$16,821
College Misericordia (PA)	$27,950	$13,722
St. John Fisher College (NY)	$27,860	$15,727
Johnson and Wales University (RI)	$27,645	$12,009
New York Institute of Technology	$27,266	$13,616
Eastern University (PA)	$26,715	$13,217
Georgian Court University (NJ)	$26,700	$15,700
Roberts Wesleyan College (NY)	$26,108	N/A
Gannon University (PA)	$26,100	$15,226
Gwynedd-Mercy College (PA)	$25,945	$13,189
Holy Family University (PA)	$25,740	$8,500
College of St. Rose (NY)	$25,686	$7,486

	Tuition, fees, room and board	Average financial aid package
St. Thomas Aquinas College (NY)	$25,450	$10,258
Mount St. Mary College (NY)	$25,250	$10,170
Trinity University (DC)	$24,934	$15,347
La Roche College (PA)	$24,524	N/A
Carlow University (PA)	$24,320	$15,815
Geneva College (PA)	$24,250	$13,360
Point Park University (PA)	$24,160	$12,906
Nyack College (NY)	$23,150	$14,124
Western New England College (MA)	$23,064	$13,646
Robert Morris University (PA)	$22,822	$12,784
Waynesburg College (PA)	$21,230	$11,919
College of St. Joseph (VT)	$20,900	$12,874
Gallaudet University (DC)	$18,750	$14,284
Touro College (NY)	$18,647	$11,675
Husson College (ME)	$17,410	$7,835
Molloy College (NY)	$16,560	$10,122
York College of Pennsylvania	$16,550	$7,015
Dowling College (NY)	$13,008	$13,385
Mercy College (NY)	$11,792	N/A
Goddard College (VT)	$10,684	N/A

Universities–Master's (South)

	Tuition, fees, room and board	Average financial aid package
Rollins College (FL)	$38,366	$27,679
Lynn University (FL)	$37,350	$16,051
Stetson University (FL)	$32,640	$21,991
Loyola University New Orleans	$31,462	N/A
Mercer University (GA)	$30,873	$23,102
Embry Riddle Aeronautical University (FL)	$30,436	$13,221
Lynchburg College (VA)	$30,345	N/A
Spring Hill College (AL)	$28,678	$18,907
Wheeling Jesuit University (WV)	$28,150	$17,907
Bellarmine University (KY)	$27,650	$15,600
Converse College (SC)	$27,636	$18,431
Shenandoah University (VA)	$27,600	$14,013
Mary Baldwin College (VA)	$27,550	$19,803
Jacksonville University (FL)	$26,430	$16,571
Marymount University (VA)	$25,934	$12,511
Belmont University (TN)	$25,790	$9,696
University of Tampa (FL)	$25,784	$14,640
Meredith College (NC)	$25,600	$14,059
Elon University (NC)	$25,371	$12,161
Averett University (VA)	$24,920	$11,583
Centenary College of Louisiana	$24,880	$13,618
Christian Brothers University (TN)	$24,650	$14,897
Queens University of Charlotte (NC)	$24,528	$13,121
Warren Wilson College (NC)	$24,382	$11,365
Brenau University (GA)	$23,950	$14,861
Palm Beach Atlantic University (FL)	$23,642	N/A
St. Thomas University (FL)	$23,490	N/A
Barry University (FL)	$22,430	$14,124

	Tuition, fees, room and board	Average financial aid package
Union University (TN)	$22,220	$13,650
Charleston Southern University (SC)	$22,152	$14,086
Milligan College (TN)	$21,990	$14,512
St. Leo University (FL)	$21,940	$15,485
Pfeiffer University (NC)	$21,900	N/A
Gardner-Webb University (NC)	$21,670	$9,305
Tusculum College (TN)	$21,365	$9,092
Campbellsville University (KY)	$21,328	$11,897
Campbell University (NC)	$21,137	$12,204
Lipscomb University (TN)	$20,977	$10,316
Hampton University (VA)	$20,928	$3,220
Southern Wesleyan University (SC)	$20,900	$9,649
Carson-Newman College (TN)	$20,510	$12,839
Piedmont College (GA)	$20,500	$14,989
Samford University (AL)	$20,258	$11,977
Xavier University of Louisiana	$20,200	N/A
Liberty University (VA)	$19,950	$10,001
Trevecca Nazarene University (TN)	$19,594	$8,846
Tuskegee University (AL)	$19,445	$13,824
Cumberland University (TN)	$18,964	$14,455
Freed-Hardeman University (TN)	$18,640	$10,706
Spalding University (KY)	$18,258	N/A
University of the Cumberlands (KY)	$18,184	$13,277
Mississippi College	$17,300	$14,145
Harding University (AR)	$16,512	$8,584
William Carey College (MS)	$11,640	$12,000
University of Mobile (AL)	$10,560	$6,500

Priciest private schools

Universities–Master's (Midwest)

	Tuition, fees, room and board	Average financial aid package
Butler University (IN)	$31,944	$17,500
John Carroll University (OH)	$31,156	$18,007
Maharishi University of Management (IA)	$30,430	$27,088
Capital University (OH)	$29,944	$17,779
Creighton University (NE)	$29,922	$20,201
Xavier University (OH)	$29,890	$14,510
University of Detroit Mercy	$29,798	$23,871
Hamline University (MN)	$29,706	$23,870
Rockford College (IL)	$29,650	$11,679
University of Findlay (OH)	$29,238	$19,308
Carthage College (WI)	$29,000	$15,278
Valparaiso University (IN)	$28,970	$17,707
North Central College (IL)	$28,701	$19,796
University of Evansville (IN)	$28,500	$19,847
College of St. Scholastica (MN)	$28,456	$17,059
Augsburg College (MN)	$28,298	$12,842
Bethel University (MN)	$28,100	$14,918
Lake Erie College (OH)	$27,700	N/A
Drake University (IA)	$27,632	$17,453
College of St. Catherine (MN)	$27,430	$22,474
Baldwin-Wallace College (OH)	$27,256	$13,355
Ashland University (OH)	$27,092	$17,116
Dominican University (IL)	$27,020	$15,046
Concordia University–River Forest (IL)	$26,300	$18,080
Benedictine University (IL)	$25,710	$11,980
St. Xavier University (IL)	$25,598	$15,408
St. Ambrose University (IA)	$25,570	$15,159
Ursuline College (OH)	$25,496	$15,796
Lewis University (IL)	$25,490	$12,416
Lawrence Technological University (MI)	$25,475	$10,157
University of St. Francis (IL)	$25,430	$15,359
Rockhurst University (MO)	$25,240	$19,719
Webster University (MO)	$25,210	$17,299
University of Indianapolis	$25,090	$16,861
Bradley University (IL)	$25,080	$13,098
Anderson University (IN)	$25,050	N/A
Quincy University (IL)	$24,920	$14,835
College of Mount St. Joseph (OH)	$24,860	$15,832
Maryville University of St. Louis (MO)	$24,670	$14,272
Columbia College (IL)	$23,898	N/A
St. Mary's University of Minnesota	$23,857	$14,833
Concordia University Wisconsin	$23,820	$17,213
Roosevelt University (IL)	$23,786	$14,500
Aquinas College (MI)	$23,750	$14,380
University of Dubuque (IA)	$23,440	$17,080
Walsh University (OH)	$23,440	$11,262
Heidelberg College (OH)	$23,242	$14,130
University of St. Francis (IN)	$23,048	$12,457
Malone College (OH)	$23,040	$12,194
Edgewood College (WI)	$22,862	$12,229
Mount Mary College (WI)	$22,805	$11,550
Fontbonne University (MO)	$22,702	$14,500
Olivet Nazarene University (IL)	$22,590	$12,033
Spring Arbor University (MI)	$22,476	$14,116
Doane College (NE)	$22,458	$14,435
Aurora University (IL)	$22,440	$17,348
Concordia University (NE)	$22,434	$15,019
Baker University (KS)	$22,190	$20,977
Avila University (MO)	$22,100	$11,751
Viterbo University (WI)	$22,090	N/A
Cardinal Stritch University (WI)	$22,085	$8,480
Silver Lake College (WI)	$22,050	$12,752
Benedictine College (KS)	$22,038	$13,973
Franciscan University of Steubenville (OH)	$21,950	$10,542
Marian College of Fond du Lac (WI)	$21,775	$16,359
University of St. Mary (KS)	$21,490	$10,420
North Park University (IL)	$21,380	N/A
Newman University (KS)	$21,118	$10,092
William Woods University (MO)	$21,020	$12,617
University of Sioux Falls (SD)	$21,000	N/A
Cornerstone University (MI)	$20,960	$13,320
Mount Marty College (SD)	$20,590	$13,253
MidAmerica Nazarene University (KS)	$20,584	$10,028
Friends University (KS)	$20,190	$9,673
Drury University (MO)	$20,099	$7,737
Marygrove College (MI)	$19,250	N/A
Lindenwood University (MO)	$18,240	N/A
University of Rio Grande (OH)	$17,887	$8,081
Southwest Baptist University (MO)	$17,200	$10,651
Madonna University (MI)	$16,068	$6,381
University of Mary (ND)	$14,927	N/A
Park University (MO)	$12,050	N/A
Bellevue University (NE)	$5,045	$4,424

Universities–Master's (West)

	Tuition, fees, room and board	Average financial aid package
Santa Clara University (CA)	$38,931	$19,706
Chapman University (CA)	$38,339	$21,628
Loyola Marymount University (CA)	$38,127	$22,232
St. Mary's College of California	$37,290	$20,858
University of Redlands (CA)	$36,164	$25,071
Dominican University of California	$35,870	$21,738
Notre Dame de Namur University (CA)	$32,760	$18,378
University of Portland (OR)	$32,300	$21,356
Mount St. Mary's College (CA)	$32,086	N/A
Regis University (CO)	$31,890	$15,599
California Lutheran University	$31,690	$16,600
Trinity University (TX)	$30,307	$17,845
Gonzaga University (WA)	$30,225	$18,255
Woodbury University (CA)	$30,176	$17,132
Seattle University	$30,063	$22,535
Holy Names University (CA)	$29,440	$16,215
Whitworth College (WA)	$29,438	$17,441
Seattle Pacific University	$29,355	$18,525
College of Santa Fe (NM)	$28,978	$18,934
Pacific Lutheran University (WA)	$28,805	$19,269
Azusa Pacific University (CA)	$28,576	N/A
George Fox University (OR)	$28,490	$15,281
Point Loma Nazarene University (CA)	$27,880	$12,525
Pacific University (OR)	$27,520	$17,492
Concordia University (CA)	$26,980	$19,204
St. Martin's University (WA)	$26,170	$17,572

	Tuition, fees, room and board	Average financial aid package
St. Mary's University of San Antonio	$26,162	$19,472
Westminster College (UT)	$25,662	$18,917
Fresno Pacific University (CA)	$25,614	$16,847
Alaska Pacific University	$25,142	$15,748
California Baptist University	$25,100	$11,670
Hope International University (CA)	$25,060	N/A
Concordia University (OR)	$24,800	N/A
La Sierra University (CA)	$24,327	N/A
St. Edward's University (TX)	$23,860	$14,680
University of St. Thomas (TX)	$23,810	$12,487
Walla Walla College (WA)	$23,694	$17,349
Oklahoma City University	$23,458	$15,462
Chaminade University of Honolulu	$23,320	$12,642
University of the Incarnate Word (TX)	$23,306	$13,991
Our Lady of the Lake University (TX)	$22,913	$15,760
Simpson University (CA)	$22,900	N/A
Oral Roberts University (OK)	$22,650	$16,503

	Tuition, fees, room and board	Average financial aid package
Northwest Nazarene University (ID)	$22,590	$13,254
LeTourneau University (TX)	$22,176	$11,288
Abilene Christian University (TX)	$20,830	$11,055
Hawaii Pacific University	$20,580	$10,465
University of Great Falls (MT)	$19,710	$10,989
Texas Wesleyan University	$19,005	N/A
Southern Nazarene University (OK)	$18,904	N/A
Houston Baptist University	$18,660	$10,935
Hardin-Simmons University (TX)	$18,641	$13,530
University of Mary Hardin-Baylor (TX)	$17,700	$12,511
Prescott College (AZ)	$17,365	N/A
Dallas Baptist University	$17,040	$10,262
Marylhurst University (OR)	$14,220	$12,368
Wayland Baptist University (TX)	$13,320	$9,012
College of the Southwest (NM)	$12,465	$8,437
Heritage University (WA)	$7,730	$12,333

Comprehensive Colleges– Bachelor's (North)

	Tuition, fees, room and board	Average financial aid package
Simon's Rock College of Bard (MA)	$42,018	$15,760
Elmira College (NY)	$37,200	$21,435
Roger Williams University (RI)	$34,959	$14,600
Stonehill College (MA)	$34,724	$17,700
Colby-Sawyer College (NH)	$34,190	$16,430
Merrimack College (MA)	$33,180	N/A
Elizabethtown College (PA)	$32,100	$16,420
Curry College (MA)	$31,740	$14,733
New England College (NH)	$31,466	$22,536
Utica College (NY)	$31,396	$18,190
Russell Sage College (NY)	$30,910	$24,647
Cedar Crest College (PA)	$30,615	$15,960
Delaware Valley College (PA)	$29,924	$17,760
Green Mountain College (VT)	$29,874	$19,049
Bay Path College (MA)	$29,362	N/A
Endicott College (MA)	$29,102	N/A
Messiah College (PA)	$28,910	$11,017
Mount Ida College (MA)	$28,750	$11,436
College of St. Elizabeth (NJ)	$28,615	$16,889
Lasell College (MA)	$28,500	$14,900
Centenary College (NJ)	$28,370	$13,647
Concordia College (NY)	$28,000	$20,690
Wilson College (PA)	$27,660	$16,223
Felician College (NJ)	$27,450	$13,161

	Tuition, fees, room and board	Average financial aid package
Cazenovia College (NY)	$26,850	$13,500
Caldwell College (NJ)	$26,680	N/A
Dominican College of Blauvelt (NY)	$26,630	$12,808
Becker College (MA)	$26,420	$9,286
Alvernia College (PA)	$26,388	$12,225
Mercyhurst College (PA)	$26,187	$10,261
Neumann College (PA)	$25,996	$17,000
Keuka College (NY)	$25,850	$16,103
Albertus Magnus College (CT)	$25,768	$6,335
Villa Julie College (MD)	$24,641	$10,438
Champlain College (VT)	$24,605	$9,185
Daemen College (NY)	$24,580	$14,419
Thiel College (PA)	$24,580	$13,265
Unity College (ME)	$23,970	$13,589
Columbia Union College (MD)	$23,532	N/A
Bloomfield College (NJ)	$22,500	$15,061
Medaille College (NY)	$22,460	$18,094
Wesley College (DE)	$22,339	$14,600
Mount Aloysius College (PA)	$20,900	$11,400
Hilbert College (NY)	$20,480	$10,127
Atlantic Union College (MA)	$18,000	$10,995
Grove City College (PA)	$15,784	$5,175
St. Francis College (NY)	$12,970	$4,622
St. Joseph's College New York–Brooklyn	$12,936	$6,560

Priciest private schools

Comprehensive Colleges– Bachelor's (South)

	Tuition, fees, room and board	Average financial aid package
Maryville College (TN)	$29,224	$20,380
University of Charleston (WV)	$27,600	$19,575
Florida Southern College	$25,965	$16,993
Peace College (NC)	$25,824	N/A
Lenoir-Rhyne College (NC)	$25,580	$14,779
Belmont Abbey College (NC)	$25,314	$12,113
Catawba College (NC)	$25,000	$14,174
Columbia College (SC)	$24,982	$20,051
Covenant College (GA)	$24,920	$15,096
Methodist College (NC)	$24,620	$15,822
Thomas More College (KY)	$24,470	$17,432
Berry College (GA)	$24,342	$14,794
Ferrum College (VA)	$24,120	$14,639
Alderson-Broaddus College (WV)	$24,006	$17,211
Asbury College (KY)	$23,762	$13,506
High Point University (NC)	$23,710	$14,750
Wingate University (NC)	$23,300	$12,528
Coker College (SC)	$23,124	$16,829
Davis and Elkins College (WV)	$22,937	$12,846
LaGrange College (GA)	$22,874	$14,651
North Carolina Wesleyan College	$22,670	$17,598
Brevard College (NC)	$22,570	$15,245
Barton College (NC)	$22,550	N/A
Mars Hill College (NC)	$22,483	$13,339
Virginia Intermont College	$22,200	$10,961
Lambuth University (TN)	$21,700	$16,084
Chowan College (NC)	$21,300	$12,504
Anderson University (SC)	$21,250	$15,834
John Brown University (AR)	$20,910	$8,195
Midway College (KY)	$20,150	$12,196
Johnson C. Smith University (NC)	$19,962	$9,725
Limestone College (SC)	$19,840	$10,813
Shorter College (GA)	$19,700	$11,105
Martin Methodist College (TN)	$19,620	N/A
Belhaven College (MS)	$19,530	N/A
University of the Ozarks (AR)	$19,250	$16,375
Reinhardt College (GA)	$19,216	$9,943
Bryan College (TN)	$19,170	$9,832
Ohio Valley University (WV)	$18,972	$10,304
Ouachita Baptist University (AR)	$18,806	$12,992

	Tuition, fees, room and board	Average financial aid package
Tennessee Wesleyan College	$18,650	$10,470
Kentucky Wesleyan College	$18,590	$12,214
Southern Adventist University (TN)	$18,500	$12,500
Brescia University (KY)	$18,100	$13,927
Bethune-Cookman College (FL)	$17,922	$13,981
Livingstone College (NC)	$17,815	$10,531
Warner Southern College (FL)	$17,513	N/A
Southeastern University (FL)	$17,178	$7,005
Bluefield College (VA)	$17,135	$8,308
Toccoa Falls College (GA)	$17,125	$9,653
Stillman College (AL)	$17,105	$16,987
Clearwater Christian College (FL)	$16,930	$8,245
Claflin University (SC)	$16,808	N/A
Mount Olive College (NC)	$16,600	$7,091
Pikeville College (KY)	$16,500	$12,119
Brewton-Parker College (GA)	$16,404	$9,399
Kentucky Christian University	$16,184	$11,728
St. Paul's College (VA)	$16,170	$10,704
Crichton College (TN)	$16,092	$8,381
Mid-Continent University (KY)	$15,800	$7,198
Faulkner University (AL)	$15,725	$7,300
Thomas University (GA)	$15,110	N/A
Louisiana College	$14,990	$8,650
Emmanuel College (GA)	$14,800	$8,650
Lee University (TN)	$14,440	$7,911
LeMoyne-Owen College (TN)	$14,238	$9,421
Flagler College (FL)	$13,790	$10,752
Williams Baptist College (AR)	$13,450	N/A
Mountain State University (WV)	$12,876	$6,280
Philander Smith College (AR)	$12,856	$8,214
Edward Waters College (FL)	$12,300	N/A
Morris College (SC)	$11,999	$12,400
Alice Lloyd College (KY)	$11,260	$8,678
Blue Mountain College (MS)	$11,086	$7,942
International College (FL)	$8,830	N/A
Rust College (MS)	$8,660	N/A
Allen University (SC)	$7,764	N/A
Our Lady of Holy Cross College (LA)	$7,008	$4,259
Berea College (KY)	$5,496	$26,299

Comprehensive Colleges– Bachelor's (Midwest)

	Tuition, fees, room and board	Average financial aid package
Ohio Northern University	$33,765	$22,130
St. Mary's College (IN)	$32,538	$18,964
Marietta College (OH)	$29,102	N/A
Otterbein College (OH)	$28,986	N/A
St. Norbert College (WI)	$28,577	$16,958
Elmhurst College (IL)	$28,216	$15,512
Wilmington College (OH)	$28,062	$16,901
Millikin University (IL)	$27,854	$15,927
Concordia University–St. Paul (MN)	$27,776	$11,847
Buena Vista University (IA)	$27,742	$19,994
Loras College (IA)	$27,193	$18,374

	Tuition, fees, room and board	Average financial aid package
Wartburg College (IA)	$26,895	$17,098
Simpson College (IA)	$26,833	$18,989
Central College (IA)	$26,774	$16,987
St. Joseph's College (IN)	$26,600	$18,976
Taylor University (IN)	$26,376	$14,069
Manchester College (IN)	$26,210	$17,375
Tri-State University (IN)	$26,200	$13,327
Bluffton University (OH)	$26,110	$18,106
Ohio Dominican University	$26,025	N/A
Mount Union College (OH)	$25,840	$16,184
Calvin College (MI)	$25,735	$13,000

	Tuition, fees, room and board	Average financial aid package
Notre Dame College of Ohio	$25,610	$13,941
St. Mary-of-the-Woods College (IN)	$25,480	$12,733
Marian College (IN)	$25,460	$15,345
Clarke College (IA)	$25,390	$16,631
Northland College (WI)	$25,325	$15,302
Northwestern College (MN)	$25,220	$14,453
Judson College (IL)	$25,100	$8,846
Franklin College (IN)	$25,095	$15,508
Concordia University (MI)	$25,053	$14,959
Carroll College (WI)	$24,860	$15,075
Huntington University (IN)	$24,830	$12,751
McKendree College (IL)	$24,800	$15,473
Defiance College (OH)	$24,790	$14,129
Augustana College (SD)	$24,194	$15,183
College of St. Mary (NE)	$24,010	$10,127
Mount Mercy College (IA)	$23,710	$14,744
Morningside College (IA)	$23,704	$16,302
Briar Cliff University (IA)	$23,550	N/A
Trinity Christian College (IL)	$23,386	$7,806
Greenville College (IL)	$23,304	$14,260
Midland Lutheran College (NE)	$23,140	$16,271
Wisconsin Lutheran College	$23,100	$14,493
Dana College (NE)	$22,770	$15,665
Dordt College (IA)	$22,540	$15,719
Northwestern College (IA)	$22,174	$13,700
Grace College and Seminary (IN)	$22,170	$12,941
Iowa Wesleyan College	$22,140	$14,852
Cedarville University (OH)	$22,130	$15,778
Illinois College	$21,900	$13,570
Bethel College (IN)	$21,880	$9,089
Bethel College (KS)	$21,650	$16,297
Tabor College (KS)	$21,614	$15,794

	Tuition, fees, room and board	Average financial aid package
Grand View College (IA)	$21,482	$12,144
Southwestern College (KS)	$21,476	$16,151
Lakeland College (WI)	$21,405	$11,325
Alverno College (WI)	$21,088	N/A
MacMurray College (IL)	$21,064	$13,591
McPherson College (KS)	$21,010	$16,893
Crown College (MN)	$20,878	$11,529
Mount Vernon Nazarene University (OH)	$20,810	$12,008
Bethany College (KS)	$20,660	$16,612
Culver-Stockton College (MO)	$20,625	$11,986
Central Methodist University (MO)	$20,560	N/A
Dakota Wesleyan University (SD)	$20,344	$14,500
Waldorf College (IA)	$20,340	$14,532
William Penn University (IA)	$20,230	N/A
Missouri Valley College	$20,050	$12,891
Sterling College (KS)	$19,892	N/A
Missouri Baptist University	$19,510	$4,602
Eureka College (IL)	$19,280	$15,467
Union College (NE)	$19,130	$8,376
Kendall College (IL)	$19,050	$7,572
Rochester College (MI)	$18,404	$4,635
Central Christian College (KS)	$18,100	$12,372
Evangel University (MO)	$17,420	N/A
Grace University (NE)	$17,380	$7,406
Columbia College (MO)	$16,966	$14,709
Hannibal-LaGrange College (MO)	$16,370	N/A
York College (NE)	$16,330	$5,231
Jamestown College (ND)	$14,130	$8,094
Lourdes College (OH)	$12,270	$8,768
Calumet College of St. Joseph (IN)	$9,900	N/A
Baker College of Flint (MI)	$7,875	N/A
College of the Ozarks (MO)	$4,080	$14,849

Comprehensive Colleges–Bachelor's (West)

	Tuition, fees, room and board	Average financial aid package
Menlo College (CA)	$33,900	$19,510
Linfield College (OR)	$29,632	$17,653
Sierra Nevada College (NV)	$27,100	N/A
Vanguard University of Southern California	$26,996	$13,406
Master's College and Seminary (CA)	$25,850	$15,311
Pacific Union College (CA)	$24,555	$14,150
Corban College (OR)	$24,478	$12,117
Northwest Christian College (OR)	$24,298	$16,195
Concordia University–Austin (TX)	$23,750	$15,222
Carroll College (MT)	$23,324	$15,113
Texas Lutheran University	$23,080	$13,740
Northwest University (WA)	$22,454	$12,446
Rocky Mountain College (MT)	$20,805	$13,378
McMurry University (TX)	$20,213	$15,032
Oklahoma Christian University	$18,992	$12,128

	Tuition, fees, room and board	Average financial aid package
Oklahoma Wesleyan University	$18,950	$7,148
Southwestern Adventist University (TX)	$18,290	N/A
Oklahoma Baptist University	$17,986	$12,278
St. Gregory's University (OK)	$17,956	$9,381
Patten University (CA)	$17,320	$6,692
Humphreys College (CA)	$17,094	$9,850
Howard Payne University (TX)	$17,026	$11,638
Lubbock Christian University (TX)	$16,960	$11,163
East Texas Baptist University	$16,713	$11,930
Huston-Tillotson University (TX)	$14,232	N/A
Cogswell Polytechnical College (CA)	$13,240	N/A
Wiley College (TX)	$12,900	$10,645
Texas College	$12,430	N/A
Jarvis Christian College (TX)	$10,936	$9,800
Brigham Young University–Hawaii	$7,740	$7,900

Cheapest public schools

Four out of five students attend public institutions, where the costs for in-state students run far below the headline-grabbing level. The schools are listed by in-state tuition and fees for the 2005–2006 academic year. Also provided is the 2005–2006 charge for room and board, as well as the tuition and fees for out-of-state students. (Not all schools offer housing, so in some cases no charges appear for room and board–though you'll still have living expenses, of course.) In addition, the table lists the average need-based financial aid package granted to undergraduates during 2005–2006. The typical aid package has three components: a need based grant, need-based loans, and work study. In order to qualify, students must file an annual aid application that demonstrates financial need. Expenses for 2006–2007 are provided in the directory when available.

National Universities

	Tuition, fees (in-state)	Tuition, fees (out-of-state)	Room and board	Average financial aid package
Middle Tennessee State University	$2,258	$7,149	$3,722	N/A
University of Florida	$3,094	$16,579	$6,260	$10,227
San Diego State University	$3,122	$13,292	$9,849	$7,400
Florida State University	$3,175	$16,306	$7,774	$8,752
South Carolina State University	$3,240	$6,604	$2,460	N/A
Florida Atlantic University	$3,259	$16,391	$7,962	$7,012
University of Nevada–Las Vegas	$3,270	$12,740	$9,610	$6,416
University of Louisiana–Lafayette	$3,324	$9,504	$3,566	$5,627
University of Central Florida	$3,339	$16,470	$7,400	$5,448
University of South Florida	$3,384	$16,150	$6,900	$9,237
University of Wyoming	$3,429	$9,819	$6,240	$7,017
East Carolina University (NC)	$3,454	$13,668	N/A	$6,085
University of North Carolina–Greensboro	$3,467	$14,735	$5,400	$7,008
University of South Alabama	$3,510	$6,820	$5,872	$2,951
Utah State University	$3,533	$10,432	$4,330	$5,000
New Mexico Institute of Mining and Technology	$3,644	$10,463	$4,866	$8,040
University of Hawaii–Manoa	$3,697	$10,177	$6,717	$6,039
University of New Orleans	$3,810	$10,854	N/A	N/A
University of Northern Colorado	$3,837	$12,381	$6,412	$9,529
New Mexico State University	$3,918	$13,206	$5,332	$8,728
Louisiana Tech University	$3,921	$9,362	$4,155	$6,406
Jackson State University (MS)	$3,964	$8,872	$4,994	N/A
University of Idaho	$3,968	$12,738	$5,342	$9,287
Idaho State University	$4,000	$7,700	$5,030	$7,494
University of Southern Mississippi	$4,136	$9,306	$4,420	$7,504
Texas A&M University–Commerce	$4,150	$12,430	$6,060	$7,254
University of Alaska–Fairbanks	$4,161	$11,781	$5,580	$8,899
West Virginia University	$4,164	$12,874	$6,144	$7,011
Wichita State University (KS)	$4,232	$11,685	$5,070	$5,924
Tennessee State University	$4,274	$13,356	$4,567	$2,875
University of Utah	$4,298	$13,371	$4,668	$8,086
Mississippi State University	$4,312	$9,772	$5,030	$7,653
Oklahoma State University	$4,365	$12,389	$5,848	$8,867
North Carolina State University–Raleigh	$4,368	$16,566	$6,851	$8,403
Northern Arizona University	$4,393	$13,023	$5,960	$7,919
Arizona State University	$4,406	$14,013	N/A	N/A
University of Oklahoma	$4,408	$12,301	$6,361	$9,782
Louisiana State University–Baton Rouge	$4,419	$12,719	$6,330	$7,070
Alabama Agricultural and Mechanical University	$4,420	$8,320	$4,770	$5,705
University of South Dakota	$4,452	$9,296	$3,741	$5,545
Georgia State University	$4,464	$15,360	$6,980	$8,671
University of Arizona	$4,498	$13,682	$7,460	$7,810
East Tennessee State University	$4,507	$10,141	$5,048	$4,762
Colorado State University	$4,562	$15,524	$6,500	$8,188
Texas A&M University–Kingsville	$4,566	$12,846	$4,672	N/A
University of North Carolina–Chapel Hill	$4,613	$18,411	$6,516	$10,051
University of Georgia	$4,628	$16,848	$6,376	$7,320
Georgia Institute of Technology	$4,648	$18,990	$6,800	$5,461
University of Alabama–Huntsville	$4,688	$9,886	$4,700	$6,064
South Dakota State University	$4,732	$9,719	$4,769	$7,550
University of Alabama–Birmingham	$4,792	$10,732	$8,924	$14,304
Texas Woman's University	$4,830	$11,370	$5,355	$9,718
University of Alabama	$4,864	$13,516	$5,024	$7,980

	Tuition, fees (in-state)	Tuition, fees (out-of-state)	Room and board	Average financial aid package
University of Texas–El Paso	$4,888	$13,168	N/A	$9,294
University of Montana	$4,894	$13,883	$5,658	$7,199
Portland State University (OR)	$4,961	$17,126	$8,445	$7,576
SUNY College of Environmental Science and Forestry	$4,991	$11,251	$10,180	$12,450
University of Colorado–Denver and Health Sciences Center	$5,021	$16,191	N/A	$9,163
University of Memphis	$5,084	$14,898	$5,049	$4,056
Kansas State University	$5,124	$14,454	$6,024	$5,850
Virginia Commonwealth University	$5,124	$17,248	$7,850	$7,932
North Dakota State University	$5,211	$12,524	$4,780	$4,884
Montana State University–Bozeman	$5,221	$14,945	N/A	N/A
Auburn University (AL)	$5,278	$14,878	$7,232	$7,683
University of North Dakota	$5,282	$12,614	$4,727	$8,807
Indiana University–Purdue University–Indianapolis	$5,346	$15,657	N/A	$6,929
University of Colorado–Boulder	$5,372	$22,826	$7,980	$9,973
University of Kansas	$5,413	$13,866	$5,502	$6,401
Oregon State University	$5,442	$17,502	$6,930	$8,696
University of Arkansas	$5,494	$13,222	$6,365	$8,798
University of Louisville (KY)	$5,532	$15,092	$6,036	$8,175
SUNY–Stony Brook	$5,574	$11,834	$8,050	$8,444
University of Washington	$5,610	$19,907	$7,164	$10,900
University of Iowa	$5,612	$16,998	$6,560	$7,445
University of Oregon	$5,613	$17,445	$7,496	$7,656
Old Dominion University (VA)	$5,614	$15,394	$6,292	$6,417
University of Nebraska–Lincoln	$5,620	$14,576	$5,860	$8,258
University of Tennessee	$5,626	$16,696	$5,756	$7,531
Iowa State University	$5,634	$15,724	$6,197	$9,181
University of Kentucky	$5,812	$12,798	$5,129	$7,861
SUNY–Binghamton	$5,838	$12,098	$8,152	$11,516
Indiana State University	$5,864	$12,860	$5,615	$7,321
Central Michigan University	$5,868	$13,632	$6,376	$9,632
George Mason University (VA)	$5,880	$17,160	$6,480	$7,991
SUNY–Albany	$5,887	$12,147	$8,050	$8,258
University of Texas–Arlington	$5,910	$13,843	$5,345	$9,016
Washington State University	$5,980	$14,988	$6,592	$9,141
Indiana University–Bloomington	$6,016	$18,394	$6,240	$6,940
University at Buffalo–SUNY	$6,070	$13,330	$7,226	$6,890
Indiana University of Pennsylvania	$6,085	$13,301	$4,866	$7,498
University of North Texas	$6,100	$14,380	$5,350	$7,830
Texas Tech University	$6,152	$14,432	$6,875	$7,220
Ball State University (IN)	$6,160	$15,336	$6,328	N/A
University of Wisconsin–Milwaukee	$6,246	$18,998	$6,130	$5,966
University of Wisconsin–Madison	$6,284	$20,284	$6,500	$11,288
Virginia Tech	$6,378	$17,717	$6,776	$8,064
Texas A&M University–College Station	$6,399	$14,679	$6,952	$10,747
Southern Illinois University–Carbondale	$6,407	$13,787	$5,560	$10,016
Wayne State University (MI)	$6,439	$13,771	$6,845	$6,958
Purdue University–West Lafayette (IN)	$6,458	$19,824	$6,830	$11,256
Western Michigan University	$6,478	$15,856	$6,651	$8,000
University of California–Los Angeles	$6,485	$24,305	$11,928	$14,036
University of Houston	$6,506	$14,786	$6,058	$7,775
University of California–Riverside	$6,590	$24,410	$10,200	$13,538
University of California–San Diego	$6,681	$24,501	$9,421	$13,342
University of California–Irvine	$6,770	$24,590	$9,176	$12,914
University of Texas–Dallas	$6,832	$15,112	$6,412	$9,016
University of Maine–Orono	$6,910	$17,050	$6,732	$9,460
University of California–Santa Cruz	$6,913	$24,733	$11,571	$14,285
University of California–Santa Barbara	$6,952	$24,772	$10,958	$13,437
University of Texas–Austin	$6,972	$16,310	$7,638	$9,210
Illinois State University	$7,091	$12,971	$5,748	$9,056
University of Virginia	$7,180	$24,100	$6,389	$14,974
Northern Illinois University	$7,229	$12,290	$6,996	$9,489
University of Missouri–Kansas City	$7,250	$17,027	$6,670	$9,859
University of Rhode Island	$7,284	$19,926	$8,114	$11,659
University of South Carolina–Columbia	$7,314	$18,956	$6,083	$9,501
University of Delaware	$7,318	$17,474	$6,824	$11,100
University of Missouri–Columbia	$7,393	$17,170	$6,540	$10,676
Cleveland State University	$7,394	$9,977	$6,809	$7,247
University of California–Berkeley	$7,433	$25,253	$12,554	$15,203
University of Toledo (OH)	$7,494	$16,305	N/A	N/A
University of California–Davis	$7,495	$25,315	$10,791	$11,697
University of Missouri–Rolla	$7,536	$17,313	$5,840	$10,513
University of Missouri–St. Louis	$7,618	$17,395	$6,428	$9,633

Cheapest public schools

National Universities, continued

	Tuition, fees (in-state)	Tuition, fees (out-of-state)	Room and board	Average financial aid package
College of William and Mary (VA)	$7,778	$23,048	$6,369	$10,682
University of Illinois–Chicago	$7,796	$19,044	$7,160	$10,753
University of Maryland–College Park	$7,821	$20,145	$8,075	$12,598
University of Connecticut	$7,912	$20,416	$7,848	$9,070
Kent State University (OH)	$7,954	$15,386	$6,640	$7,040
University of Akron (OH)	$7,958	$16,682	$7,208	$6,798
Ohio State University–Columbus	$7,980	$19,203	$7,275	$9,726
University of Massachusetts–Lowell	$8,166	$15,279	$6,311	$8,733
Michigan Technological University	$8,194	$19,384	$6,375	$8,517
Ohio University	$8,235	$17,199	$7,686	$6,870
University of Massachusetts–Boston	$8,265	$16,309	N/A	N/A
Michigan State University	$8,312	$20,010	$5,788	$8,468
University of Cincinnati	$8,379	$21,351	$7,425	$7,476
University of Maryland–Baltimore County	$8,520	$16,596	$7,936	$9,827
Bowling Green State University (OH)	$8,574	$15,922	$6,434	$8,245
University of Minnesota–Twin Cities	$8,622	$20,252	$6,722	$11,007
University of Illinois–Urbana-Champaign	$8,634	$22,720	$7,176	$9,939
Rutgers–Newark (NJ)	$8,812	$16,410	$8,984	$10,138
Clemson University (SC)	$8,816	$18,440	$5,780	$9,154
Rutgers–New Brunswick (NJ)	$9,221	$16,819	$8,838	$11,569
University of Massachusetts–Amherst	$9,278	$17,501	$6,517	$11,276
Temple University (PA)	$9,640	$17,236	$7,798	$13,365
University of Michigan–Ann Arbor	$9,705	$28,480	$7,374	$10,234
University of New Hampshire	$9,778	$21,498	$7,032	$14,888
New Jersey Institute of Technology	$9,822	$16,026	$8,572	$13,200
University of Vermont	$10,748	$24,934	$7,332	$15,408
University of Pittsburgh	$11,436	$20,784	$7,430	$11,605
Pennsylvania State University–University Park	$11,508	$21,744	$6,530	$7,062
Miami University–Oxford (OH)	$21,487	$21,487	$7,610	$15,665

Liberal Arts Colleges

	Tuition, fees (in-state)	Tuition, fees (out-of-state)	Room and board	Average financial aid package
University of Hawaii–Hilo	$2,610	$8,178	$5,472	N/A
Western State College of Colorado	$3,138	$11,754	$6,806	$8,800
Mesa State College (CO)	$3,217	$11,002	$6,877	$5,206
California State University–Monterey Bay	$3,346	$10,000	$6,700	$6,343
University of North Carolina–Asheville	$3,525	$13,325	$5,712	$8,152
New College of Florida	$3,679	$19,475	$6,330	$11,792
Evergreen State College (WA)	$4,353	$14,715	$6,924	$11,066
Texas A&M University–Galveston	$4,743	$13,023	$4,870	$10,288
University of Maine–Presque Isle	$4,820	$11,210	$5,246	$7,248
University of Virginia–Wise	$5,081	$15,159	$5,965	$7,102
Massachusetts College of Liberal Arts	$5,617	$14,562	$6,282	$7,130
Fort Lewis College (CO)	$5,692	$13,700	$6,160	$7,050
Christopher Newport University (VA)	$5,826	$12,848	$7,500	$6,229
Shawnee State University (OH)	$6,120	$10,008	$6,729	N/A
Coastal Carolina University (SC)	$6,860	$15,100	N/A	$7,427
Richard Stockton College of New Jersey	$7,870	$11,055	$8,109	$11,022
Virginia Military Institute	$8,617	$22,816	$5,715	$14,334
University of Minnesota–Morris	$9,542	$9,542	$5,750	$12,660
University of Pittsburgh–Bradford	$10,538	$20,426	$6,470	$12,000
University of Pittsburgh–Greensburg	$10,562	$20,453	$7,210	$7,063
St. Mary's College of Maryland	$10,896	$19,773	$7,980	$6,250

Universities–Master's (North)

	Tuition, fees (in-state)	Tuition, fees (out-of-state)	Room and board	Average financial aid package
University of the District of Columbia	$2,520	$5,820	N/A	$1,350
Morgan State University (MD)	$3,055	$6,760	$3,365	N/A
CUNY–City College	$4,157	$10,957	N/A	$7,100
CUNY–Lehman College	$4,270	$8,910	N/A	$3,537
CUNY–Baruch College	$4,300	$11,100	$0	$4,800
CUNY–College of Staten Island	$4,328	$8,968	N/A	$6,101
CUNY–Hunter College	$4,329	$8,969	N/A	$5,383
CUNY–Brooklyn College	$4,353	$8,993	N/A	$5,450
CUNY–Queens College	$4,356	$11,156	N/A	$8,400
Rhode Island College	$4,676	$11,988	$6,960	N/A
Westfield State College (MA)	$4,857	$10,937	$5,742	N/A
Coppin State University (MD)	$4,878	$11,369	$6,117	$6,880
Framingham State College (MA)	$4,999	$11,079	$6,157	$6,242
Fitchburg State College (MA)	$5,002	$11,082	$6,104	$6,565
University of Southern Maine	$5,030	$12,440	$6,825	$8,754
Worcester State College (MA)	$5,079	$11,159	$7,420	N/A
SUNY–Buffalo State College	$5,166	$11,426	$6,200	$7,870
SUNY–Oswego	$5,222	$11,482	$8,340	$8,622
SUNY College of Arts and Sciences–New Paltz	$5,260	$11,520	$7,220	$2,367
SUNY College–Brockport	$5,263	$11,213	$7,601	$8,501
SUNY–Plattsburgh	$5,272	$11,532	$7,066	$9,524
SUNY College–Potsdam	$5,289	$11,549	$7,670	$11,771
SUNY College–Oneonta	$5,347	$11,607	$7,230	$9,244
Bridgewater State College (MA)	$5,422	$11,562	$6,614	N/A
SUNY–Fredonia	$5,441	$11,701	$7,330	$7,690
SUNY–Purchase College	$5,463	$11,723	$8,676	$7,804
Bowie State University (MD)	$5,481	$14,786	$6,823	N/A
SUNY College of Arts and Sciences–Geneseo	$5,520	$11,780	$7,390	$9,339
Western Connecticut State University	$5,800	$12,586	$7,158	$3,012
University of Maryland–Eastern Shore	$5,808	$11,964	$6,130	N/A
Eastern Connecticut State University	$5,964	$12,750	$8,600	$11,279
Delaware State University	$5,975	$12,219	$8,298	$6,919
Slippery Rock University of Pennsylvania	$6,096	$8,502	$4,714	$6,938
West Chester University of Pennsylvania	$6,147	$13,507	$6,208	N/A
Shippensburg University of Pennsylvania	$6,175	$13,535	$5,710	$6,256
Bloomsburg University of Pennsylvania	$6,226	$13,586	$5,376	$9,356
Frostburg State University (MD)	$6,230	$14,480	$6,442	$6,906
Millersville University of Pennsylvania	$6,236	$13,596	$5,878	$7,172
Lock Haven University of Pennsylvania	$6,258	$11,618	$5,840	$6,562
Edinboro University of Pennsylvania	$6,290	$11,198	$5,518	$6,402
Salisbury University (MD)	$6,376	$14,054	$6,752	$6,052
East Stroudsburg University of Pennsylvania	$6,399	$13,719	$4,794	$5,224
California University of Pennsylvania	$6,432	$8,886	$7,788	$7,799
Mansfield University of Pennsylvania	$6,434	$13,794	$5,868	$10,934
Clarion University of Pennsylvania	$6,447	$11,355	$5,246	$7,008
Castleton State College (VT)	$6,484	$13,804	$6,674	N/A
Kutztown University of Pennsylvania	$6,527	$14,068	$5,480	$6,189
Lincoln University (PA)	$6,866	$10,542	$6,792	$9,118
Keene State College (NH)	$6,940	$13,380	$5,966	N/A
Southern Connecticut State University	$6,966	$13,752	$7,648	$6,629
Plymouth State University (NH)	$7,028	$13,868	$6,780	N/A
New Jersey City University	$7,040	$12,080	$7,306	$7,628
Towson University (MD)	$7,096	$16,030	$6,828	$7,602
Kean University (NJ)	$7,506	$10,139	$8,374	$7,929
Montclair State University (NJ)	$7,709	$12,156	N/A	$7,826
Central Connecticut State University	$7,916	$14,702	$7,456	$6,820
University of Massachusetts–Dartmouth	$8,036	$14,718	$7,786	$10,805
Rowan University (NJ)	$8,607	$14,901	$8,242	$6,214
William Paterson University of New Jersey	$8,740	$13,856	$9,070	$10,130
Rutgers–Camden (NJ)	$9,028	$16,626	$8,088	$10,112
College of New Jersey	$9,857	$15,120	$8,807	$9,317
Pennsylvania State–Erie, The Behrend College	$10,626	$16,024	$6,530	$7,395

Cheapest public schools

Universities–Master's (South)

	Tuition, fees (in-state)	Tuition, fees (out-of-state)	Room and board	Average financial aid package
Armstrong Atlantic State University (GA)	$2,651	$9,967	$6,192	N/A
Savannah State University (GA)	$2,747	$10,063	$4,716	N/A
University of North Carolina–Pembroke	$2,825	$12,265	$4,890	$6,446
Fayetteville State University (NC)	$2,833	$12,569	$4,120	$8,063
Augusta State University (GA)	$2,920	$10,236	N/A	N/A
Columbus State University (GA)	$2,944	$10,260	$5,880	$3,988
Valdosta State University (GA)	$2,992	$9,960	$5,208	$6,501
Georgia Southwestern State University	$3,016	$10,332	$4,810	$6,219
Kennesaw State University (GA)	$3,044	$10,360	$9,108	$9,524
North Georgia College and State University	$3,044	$10,360	$4,596	N/A
North Carolina Central University	$3,096	$12,840	$4,527	$8,196
North Carolina A&T State University	$3,114	$12,556	$5,979	$5,898
McNeese State University (LA)	$3,159	$9,225	$4,637	N/A
University of West Florida	$3,198	$15,705	$6,600	N/A
Florida Gulf Coast University	$3,260	$15,249	N/A	N/A
University of North Florida	$3,268	$14,910	$6,640	$1,485
University of West Georgia	$3,270	$10,586	$5,568	$6,441
Southeastern Louisiana University	$3,341	$8,669	$5,180	N/A
Nicholls State University (LA)	$3,390	$8,838	N/A	$5,506
Northwestern State University of Louisiana	$3,393	$9,471	$3,626	$5,208
Appalachian State University (NC)	$3,436	$13,178	$4,658	$6,383
Georgia Southern University	$3,462	$10,778	$6,300	$6,625
University of North Carolina–Charlotte	$3,480	$13,900	N/A	$8,730
Mississippi University for Women	$3,495	$8,442	$3,778	$7,084
Southern University and A&M College (LA)	$3,592	$9,384	$4,646	$9,516
Western Carolina University (NC)	$3,624	$13,060	$4,900	$6,574
University of North Carolina–Wilmington	$3,695	$13,630	$6,412	$6,526
Alcorn State University (MS)	$3,919	$8,887	$4,272	$9,500
Marshall University (WV)	$3,932	$10,634	$6,272	$7,230
Jacksonville State University (AL)	$4,040	$8,080	$3,538	$5,200
Georgia College and State University	$4,128	$14,340	$6,878	$5,338
Alabama State University	$4,158	$8,166	$3,400	$7,799
Austin Peay State University (TN)	$4,224	$12,712	$4,296	$6,367
Delta State University (MS)	$4,252	$9,192	$3,947	$8,200
Eastern Kentucky University	$4,252	$10,924	$4,788	$7,185
Southern Arkansas University	$4,310	$6,320	$3,790	$4,158
Troy University (AL)	$4,316	$8,320	$4,812	$3,634
Morehead State University (KY)	$4,320	$11,480	$4,830	$7,826
University of North Alabama	$4,366	$8,014	$4,170	$4,515
Tennessee Technological University	$4,396	$9,312	$6,275	$3,502
Murray State University (KY)	$4,428	$6,100	$4,472	$4,613
Kentucky State University	$4,468	$10,910	$5,620	N/A
University of Tennessee–Martin	$4,476	$13,530	$4,310	$8,443
Auburn University–Montgomery (AL)	$4,640	$13,430	$4,890	$7,516
Henderson State University (AR)	$4,645	$8,695	$4,032	N/A
Arkansas Tech University	$4,700	$8,990	$4,290	$4,381
University of West Alabama	$4,778	$8,616	$3,318	$10,222
Virginia State University	$4,892	$12,243	$6,484	$7,120
Northern Kentucky University	$4,968	$9,696	$5,358	N/A
Radford University (VA)	$5,130	$12,368	$6,120	$6,990
Western Kentucky University	$5,316	$12,732	N/A	N/A
University of Tennessee–Chattanooga	$5,400	$14,424	$6,474	$8,301
Arkansas State University	$5,440	$12,145	$4,190	$6,000
University of Central Arkansas	$5,500	$10,000	$4,180	$7,500
University of Mary Washington (VA)	$5,634	$14,776	$6,002	$4,050
University of Montevallo (AL)	$5,664	$11,124	$3,966	$7,966
James Madison University (VA)	$5,886	$15,322	$6,372	$6,822
Francis Marion University (SC)	$5,984	$11,833	$5,130	N/A
College of Charleston (SC)	$6,668	$15,342	N/A	$8,971
Longwood University (VA)	$7,020	$13,704	$5,586	N/A
The Citadel (SC)	$7,520	$16,916	$4,840	$8,846
Winthrop University (SC)	$8,756	$16,150	$5,352	$8,437

Universities–Master's (Midwest)

	Tuition, fees (in-state)	Tuition, fees (out-of-state)	Room and board	Average financial aid package
Pittsburg State University (KS)	$1,765	$4,944	$4,550	$6,890
Emporia State University (KS)	$3,306	$10,658	$4,787	$5,955
Peru State College (NE)	$3,637	$6,570	$4,676	N/A
Wayne State College (NE)	$3,803	$6,735	$4,300	$3,264
Minot State University (ND)	$4,040	$9,758	$4,460	$6,658
University of Southern Indiana	$4,244	$10,118	$6,368	$5,393
Indiana University Southeast	$4,337	$11,004	N/A	$6,127
Indiana University Northwest	$4,359	$11,026	N/A	$7,363
Indiana University–South Bend	$4,441	$11,851	N/A	$6,050
University of Nebraska–Kearney	$4,492	$8,332	$5,326	$7,227
Lincoln University (MO)	$4,602	$8,249	$3,790	$8,000
Northern State University (SD)	$4,700	$9,687	$3,981	$6,076
University of Nebraska–Omaha	$4,728	$12,775	$5,960	N/A
St. Cloud State University (MN)	$4,760	$10,332	$4,688	$9,634
Southeast Missouri State University	$4,875	$8,460	$5,187	$6,531
University of Wisconsin–Oshkosh	$4,981	$15,027	$4,884	N/A
Washburn University (KS)	$4,982	$11,192	$4,752	$7,426
University of Wisconsin–Parkside	$4,995	$15,043	$4,950	N/A
Northeastern Illinois University	$5,062	$8,842	N/A	$6,870
University of Wisconsin–Stevens Point	$5,063	$15,109	$4,322	$6,885
University of Wisconsin–River Falls	$5,084	$15,130	$4,384	$6,343
University of Wisconsin–Eau Claire	$5,178	$15,224	$4,737	$7,206
University of Wisconsin–Superior	$5,188	$6,302	$4,422	$6,242
Southern Illinois University–Edwardsville	$5,209	$11,734	$5,819	$9,050
University of Wisconsin–La Crosse	$5,229	$15,223	$4,781	$4,885
University of Wisconsin–Whitewater	$5,254	$15,652	$4,170	$6,527
Saginaw Valley State University (MI)	$5,282	$11,891	$6,150	N/A
Minnesota State University–Mankato	$5,402	$10,750	$4,874	$6,939
University of Wisconsin–Green Bay	$5,425	$15,471	$4,810	$7,839
Missouri State University	$5,454	$10,374	$5,294	$6,125
University of Northern Iowa	$5,602	$13,214	$5,537	$6,738
Indiana University-Purdue University–Fort Wayne	$5,630	$12,984	$6,394	$6,546
Winona State University (MN)	$5,700	$9,920	$6,060	N/A
Truman State University (MO)	$5,812	$9,992	$5,380	$6,706
Northern Michigan University	$5,958	$10,232	$6,482	$6,935
Central Missouri State University	$5,970	$11,100	$5,180	$8,450
Bemidji State University (MN)	$6,044	$9,344	$5,166	$7,414
Western Illinois University	$6,182	$10,720	$5,768	$7,891
Grand Valley State University (MI)	$6,220	$12,510	$6,360	$7,049
Lake Superior State University (MI)	$6,306	$12,294	$6,536	$8,157
Youngstown State University (OH)	$6,333	$11,541	$6,280	N/A
Eastern Illinois University	$6,373	$15,631	$6,196	$9,783
University of Michigan–Flint	$6,398	$12,150	N/A	N/A
Eastern Michigan University	$6,541	$17,896	$6,356	$6,472
University of Wisconsin–Stout	$6,592	$16,925	$4,572	$7,467
Chicago State University	$6,625	$11,815	$6,212	$3,912
University of Michigan–Dearborn	$6,784	$14,593	N/A	$4,847
Ferris State University (MI)	$6,882	$13,622	$6,816	$8,000
University of Minnesota–Duluth	$8,944	$20,051	N/A	$8,149

Cheapest public schools

Universities–Master's (West)

	Tuition, fees (in-state)	Tuition, fees (out-of-state)	Room and board	Average financial aid package
New Mexico Highlands University	$2,304	$10,176	$3,456	N/A
Angelo State University (TX)	$2,544	$9,168	$4,763	$6,531
Eastern New Mexico University	$2,784	$8,340	$4,480	$7,598
California State Polytechnic University–Pomona	$2,832	$13,488	$7,506	$9,265
Humboldt State University (CA)	$2,863	$10,999	$7,906	$8,257
California State University–Long Beach	$2,864	$13,034	$6,530	$8,350
California State University–East Bay	$2,916	$8,532	$6,759	$7,973
California State University–Bakersfield	$2,923	$13,093	$5,946	N/A
California State University–Fresno	$2,933	$13,103	$6,584	$5,833
California State University–Fullerton	$2,990	$13,160	N/A	$7,220
California State University–Dominguez Hills	$2,991	$11,127	$7,770	$8,239
California State University–Stanislaus	$3,030	$13,200	$7,094	$7,836
California State University–Los Angeles	$3,035	$11,171	$7,353	$6,894
California State University–Northridge	$3,036	$13,206	$7,616	N/A
East Central University (OK)	$3,042	$7,366	$3,980	$6,325
California State University–San Marcos	$3,062	$13,232	N/A	$6,946
California State University–San Bernardino	$3,090	$11,226	$7,517	$7,773
San Francisco State University	$3,128	$11,264	$10,458	$8,441
Weber State University (UT)	$3,164	$9,599	$6,400	$4,763
University of Texas–Pan American	$3,212	$12,212	$4,233	$7,488
Southwestern Oklahoma State University	$3,240	$7,740	$3,240	$4,368
Northeastern State University (OK)	$3,270	$8,040	$3,080	$3,686
Northwestern Oklahoma State University	$3,270	$8,100	$3,000	$5,598
California State University–Sacramento	$3,348	$13,518	$7,052	$8,753
California State University–Chico	$3,370	$13,459	$7,993	$7,801
Southeastern Oklahoma State University	$3,372	$5,998	$3,190	N/A
Cameron University (OK)	$3,440	$8,060	$3,972	$3,500
University of Alaska–Anchorage	$3,465	$9,561	$7,810	N/A
University of Texas–Brownsville	$3,525	$12,130	$5,015	$3,269
Southern Utah University	$3,565	$10,603	$4,124	N/A
University of Alaska–Southeast	$3,580	$9,676	$3,980	$6,967
Sonoma State University (CA)	$3,606	$11,742	$8,890	$7,498
University of Central Oklahoma	$3,618	$8,628	$4,476	$6,043
West Texas A&M University	$3,756	$12,036	$4,595	N/A
Boise State University (ID)	$3,872	$11,088	$5,545	$8,348
University of Texas of the Permian Basin	$4,149	$12,219	$4,078	$3,302
Texas A&M International University	$4,218	$12,498	$6,390	$3,818
Cal Poly–San Luis Obispo	$4,245	$14,415	$8,145	$7,333
University of Texas–Tyler	$4,252	$12,532	$7,010	$7,270
Texas A&M University–Corpus Christi	$4,279	$12,019	N/A	$6,524
Eastern Washington University	$4,284	$13,557	$5,733	$11,418
Stephen F. Austin State University (TX)	$4,358	$12,638	$5,459	$5,059
Midwestern State University (TX)	$4,461	$12,741	$5,080	$6,459
Western Oregon University	$4,488	$13,719	$6,654	$6,412
Prairie View A&M University (TX)	$4,514	$12,794	$6,204	$6,920
Sam Houston State University (TX)	$4,560	$12,240	$4,400	$6,108
Lamar University (TX)	$4,674	$12,954	$5,410	$1,237
Western Washington University	$4,738	$14,688	$6,524	$8,981
Central Washington University	$4,806	$13,101	$6,924	$7,996
Southern Oregon University	$4,932	$16,362	$7,254	N/A
Texas State University–San Marcos	$5,252	$13,532	$5,610	$7,545
University of Colorado–Colorado Springs	$5,253	$16,575	$7,470	$6,508
University of Texas–San Antonio	$5,520	$13,800	$5,805	$6,381
Eastern Oregon University	$5,905	$5,905	$7,200	N/A
Colorado State University–Pueblo	$6,518	$14,757	$6,088	$7,247

Comprehensive Colleges–Bachelor's (North)

	Tuition, fees (in-state)	Tuition, fees (out-of-state)	Room and board	Average financial aid package
CUNY–York College	$4,242	$8,882	N/A	$3,482
CUNY–Medgar Evers College	$4,252	$8,892	N/A	N/A
CUNY–New York City College of Technology	$4,538	$9,178	N/A	$6,384
University of Maine–Machias	$4,780	$12,130	$5,678	$9,604
University of Maine–Augusta	$5,025	$11,115	$0	$7,929
SUNY College–Old Westbury	$5,041	$10,991	$8,083	$6,283
SUNY–Farmingdale	$5,297	$11,557	$11,168	N/A
SUNY College of A&T–Cobleskill	$5,520	$8,380	$7,570	$6,976
University of Maine–Farmington	$5,541	$12,771	$5,846	$8,156
Lyndon State College (VT)	$6,634	$13,954	$6,674	N/A
Ramapo College of New Jersey	$8,791	$13,708	$9,116	$9,765
Pennsylvania College of Technology	$10,080	$12,660	$5,600	N/A
University of Pittsburgh–Johnstown	$10,540	$20,428	$6,240	$9,214

Comprehensive Colleges–Bachelor's (South)

	Tuition, fees (in-state)	Tuition, fees (out-of-state)	Room and board	Average financial aid package
West Virginia University–Parkersburg	$1,668	$5,892	N/A	$5,700
Winston-Salem State University (NC)	$2,800	$11,439	$5,278	$3,477
Clayton State University (GA)	$2,842	$10,248	N/A	$2,425
Elizabeth City State University (NC)	$3,242	$11,581	$4,710	N/A
Bluefield State College (WV)	$3,410	$7,014	N/A	$5,600
Glenville State College (WV)	$3,628	$8,640	$5,200	$8,736
West Liberty State College (WV)	$3,686	$9,054	$5,006	N/A
Mississippi Valley State University	$3,832	$8,840	$3,506	N/A
University of Arkansas–Monticello	$3,900	$4,650	$3,250	N/A
Shepherd University (WV)	$4,046	$10,618	$6,020	$8,674
Fairmont State University (WV)	$4,218	$7,524	N/A	N/A
University of Arkansas–Pine Bluff	$4,326	$8,511	$5,290	N/A
University of South Carolina–Aiken	$6,080	$12,173	$4,650	N/A
University of South Carolina–Upstate	$6,762	$13,600	$5,195	$7,400

Comprehensive Colleges–Bachelor's (Midwest)

	Tuition, fees (in-state)	Tuition, fees (out-of-state)	Room and board	Average financial aid package
Missouri Southern State University	$3,916	$7,666	$4,480	$6,722
Dickinson State University (ND)	$4,154	$9,713	$3,694	N/A
Indiana University East	$4,263	$10,930	N/A	$5,918
Indiana University–Kokomo	$4,292	$10,959	N/A	$6,081
Purdue University–North Central (IN)	$4,699	$10,890	N/A	$6,808
Black Hills State University (SD)	$4,754	$9,741	$4,310	N/A
Dakota State University (SD)	$4,831	$9,819	$3,726	$6,308
Mayville State University (ND)	$4,943	$10,454	$3,724	$7,420
Valley City State University (ND)	$5,160	$11,265	$4,694	$6,299
Central State University (OH)	$5,294	$11,462	$7,402	N/A
Southwest Minnesota State University (MN)	$5,856	$5,856	$5,120	$6,736
University of Minnesota–Crookston	$7,920	$7,920	$5,039	$10,303

Cheapest public schools

Comprehensive Colleges–Bachelor's (West)	Tuition, fees (in-state)	Tuition, fees (out-of-state)	Room and board	Average financial aid package
Metropolitan State College of Denver	$2,779	$10,007	$0	N/A
Utah Valley State College	$3,022	$9,472	N/A	$7,554
Oklahoma Panhandle State University	$3,309	$5,535	$3,130	N/A
University of Science and Arts of Oklahoma	$3,480	$8,220	$4,310	$6,799
Lewis-Clark State College (ID)	$3,714	$10,484	$4,200	$5,452
University of Houston–Downtown	$4,139	$12,419	$0	N/A
University of Montana–Western	$4,500	$12,360	$4,740	$2,735

Best values: Great deals at great schools

To determine which schools offer the best value, *U.S. News* uses a formula that relates a school's academic quality to the net cost of attendance for a student who receives the average level of financial aid. The higher the quality of the program (as indicated by its *U.S. News* ranking) and the lower the cost, the better the deal. We considered only schools ranked in the top half of their peer groups. The methodology we used is described in detail below.

National Universities

		% receiving grants based on need ('05)	Average cost after receiving grants based on need ('05)	Average discount from total cost ('05)
1	California Institute of Technology	53%	$13,694	67%
2	Harvard University (MA)	49%	$16,346	63%
3	Princeton University (NJ)	51%	$16,917	61%
4	Yale University (CT)	42%	$16,268	63%
5	Massachusetts Institute of Technology	60%	$18,587	58%
6	Stanford University (CA)	43%	$18,767	58%
7	Dartmouth College (NH)	50%	$18,804	58%
8	Rice University (TX)	34%	$15,561	52%
9	University of North Carolina–Chapel Hill	31%	$14,464	47%
10	Duke University (NC)	38%	$20,172	54%
11	University of Pennsylvania	41%	$21,205	53%
12	Columbia University (NY)	45%	$21,690	52%
13	University of Chicago	45%	$21,977	51%
14	Cornell University (NY)	43%	$21,757	50%
15	Vanderbilt University (TN)	38%	$20,154	55%
16	Brown University (RI)	40%	$22,356	50%
17	University of Virginia	24%	$17,906	47%
18	Washington University in St. Louis	42%	$23,645	47%
19	Brigham Young University–Provo (UT)	29%	$11,027	19%
20	Northwestern University (IL)	42%	$23,674	48%
21	Emory University (GA)	35%	$21,710	49%
22	Howard University (DC)	36%	$12,222	44%
23	Case Western Reserve University (OH)	60%	$22,276	45%
24	Rensselaer Polytechnic Institute (NY)	70%	$23,585	45%
25	Texas A&M University–College Station	37%	$15,084	40%
26	Tufts University (MA)	36%	$21,735	51%
27	University of Southern California	42%	$22,709	49%
28	Lehigh University (PA)	42%	$21,749	48%
29	University of Rochester (NY)	56%	$23,478	45%
30	Johns Hopkins University (MD)	41%	$26,118	40%
31	University of Texas–Austin	54%	$19,248	31%
32	North Carolina State University–Raleigh	43%	$15,032	42%
33	Carnegie Mellon University (PA)	48%	$26,234	39%
34	Clark University (MA)	54%	$19,220	48%
35	Brandeis University (MA)	45%	$24,631	43%
36	Pepperdine University (CA)	45%	$21,205	50%
37	Georgetown University (DC)	37%	$26,550	42%
38	University of the Pacific (CA)	64%	$21,040	45%
39	Wake Forest University (NC)	33%	$24,353	41%
40	Yeshiva University (NY)	43%	$22,702	42%
41	Boston College	36%	$24,279	45%
42	Worcester Polytechnic Institute (MA)	68%	$26,678	38%
43	SUNY College of Environmental Science and Forestry	80%	$20,981	11%
44	University of Miami (FL)	51%	$24,507	41%
45	University of Georgia	8%	$15,901	39%
46	Illinois Institute of Technology	57%	$21,254	39%
47	University of California–Berkeley	28%	$27,318	33%
48	St. Louis University	57%	$23,923	35%
49	Syracuse University (NY)	52%	$26,575	36%
50	Marquette University (WI)	52%	$22,071	34%

How we calculated the best values

To be considered, a university or college had to finish in the top half of its category in the U.S. News "America's Best Colleges 2007" rankings. The best values rankings were based on three variables:

1. Ratio of quality to price: A school's ranking—its overall score in the "America's Best Colleges" survey—was divided by the cost to a student receiving an average grant meeting financial need. The higher the ratio, the better the value.

2. Percentage of all undergraduates receiving grants meeting financial need during the 2005–2006 year.

3. Average discount: percentage of a school's 2005–2006 total costs (tuition, room and board, fees, books, and other expenses) covered by the average need-based grant to undergraduates. In the case of public institutions, 2005–2006 out-of-state tuition and percentage of out-of-state students receiving grants meeting need were used.

Overall rank was determined first by standardizing the scores achieved by every school in each of the three variables and weighting those scores. The first variable—the ratio of quality to price—accounted for 60 percent of the overall score; the percentage of all undergraduates receiving grants accounted for 25 percent; and the average discount accounted for 15 percent. The weighted scores for each school were totaled. The school with the highest total weighted points became No. 1 in its category. The scores for the other schools were then ranked in descending order.

Best values: Great deals at great schools

Liberal Arts Colleges

		% receiving grants based on need ('05)	Average cost after receiving grants based on need ('05)	Average discount from total cost ('05)
1	Williams College (MA)	43%	$15,621	64%
2	Amherst College (MA)	46%	$16,177	64%
3	Wellesley College (MA)	58%	$17,547	59%
4	Skidmore College (NY)	41%	$11,952	66%
5	Pomona College (CA)	53%	$17,740	59%
6	Swarthmore College (PA)	48%	$18,692	57%
7	Middlebury College (VT)	44%	$19,216	56%
8	Bowdoin College (ME)	44%	$18,965	57%
9	Macalester College (MN)	69%	$18,774	51%
10	Grinnell College (IA)	54%	$18,395	49%
11	College of the Atlantic (ME)	85%	$13,913	60%
12	Colgate University (NY)	39%	$17,604	59%
13	Colorado College	41%	$16,483	59%
14	Wabash College (IN)	70%	$16,156	49%
15	Carleton College (MN)	58%	$21,525	49%
16	Claremont McKenna College (CA)	50%	$20,097	53%
17	Smith College (MA)	60%	$20,568	53%
18	Centre College (KY)	60%	$16,891	48%
19	Wesleyan University (CT)	45%	$20,502	54%
20	Haverford College (PA)	41%	$20,276	54%
21	Colby College (ME)	36%	$18,318	58%
22	Bryn Mawr College (PA)	52%	$19,882	54%
23	Lyon College (AR)	70%	$12,837	44%
24	Wells College (NY)	74%	$12,802	48%
25	Vassar College (NY)	53%	$21,226	52%
26	Lafayette College (PA)	48%	$18,299	55%
27	Hanover College (IN)	77%	$15,632	49%
28	Agnes Scott College (GA)	63%	$16,754	52%
29	Mount Holyoke College (MA)	60%	$21,148	52%
30	Harvey Mudd College (CA)	51%	$21,788	50%
31	Furman University (SC)	44%	$17,210	52%
32	Occidental College (CA)	54%	$19,784	54%
33	Scripps College (CA)	43%	$19,678	54%
34	Hamilton College (NY)	51%	$22,115	49%
35	Beloit College (WI)	76%	$19,472	43%
36	Thomas Aquinas College (CA)	59%	$15,718	43%
37	Lake Forest College (IL)	78%	$17,529	50%
38	Barnard College (NY)	40%	$19,891	55%
39	Bates College (ME)	39%	$20,150	54%
40	Kenyon College (OH)	41%	$19,583	53%

Universities–Master's (North)

		% receiving grants based on need ('05)	Average cost after receiving grants based on need ('05)	Average discount from total cost ('05)
1	Gallaudet University (DC)	65%	$11,745	51%
2	Alfred University (NY)	83%	$17,184	48%
3	Hood College (MD)	78%	$17,171	46%
4	Villanova University (PA)	39%	$24,741	40%
5	Bentley College (MA)	43%	$21,338	45%
6	Le Moyne College (NY)	79%	$18,555	41%
7	St. Michael's College (VT)	63%	$21,477	39%
8	Lebanon Valley College (PA)	77%	$18,764	44%
9	Ithaca College (NY)	65%	$23,447	37%
10	Gannon University (PA)	83%	$16,981	41%
11	Providence College (RI)	55%	$25,580	30%
12	St. Bonaventure University (NY)	71%	$18,773	39%
13	Nazareth College of Rochester (NY)	78%	$20,027	34%
14	University of Scranton (PA)	63%	$24,891	32%
15	St. Francis University (PA)	83%	$17,601	43%

Universities–Master's (South)

		% receiving grants based on need ('05)	Average cost after receiving grants based on need ('05)	Average discount from total cost ('05)
1	Rollins College (FL)	41%	$18,515	56%
2	The Citadel (SC)	30%	$14,765	43%
3	Converse College (SC)	70%	$15,194	50%
4	Stetson University (FL)	53%	$18,505	48%
5	Mercer University (GA)	64%	$18,617	44%
6	Mississippi College	41%	$12,230	40%
7	Meredith College (NC)	67%	$17,052	39%
8	Centenary College of Louisiana	60%	$17,061	40%
9	Carson-Newman College (TN)	69%	$14,127	39%
10	Brenau University (GA)	73%	$14,389	46%
11	Samford University (AL)	34%	$18,619	26%
12	Spring Hill College (AL)	64%	$18,858	42%
13	Bellarmine University (KY)	65%	$18,302	39%
14	Murray State University (KY)	56%	$15,590	17%
15	Harding University (AR)	47%	$14,340	26%

Universities–Master's (Midwest)

		% receiving grants based on need ('05)	Average cost after receiving grants based on need ('05)	Average discount from total cost ('05)
1	University of Evansville (IN)	69%	$15,822	49%
2	Valparaiso University (IN)	67%	$19,203	39%
3	Drury University (MO)	88%	$16,510	29%
4	Creighton University (NE)	50%	$21,119	36%
5	Bradley University (IL)	69%	$19,445	31%
6	Doane College (NE)	77%	$14,698	41%
7	Drake University (IA)	61%	$20,513	34%
8	University of Detroit Mercy	70%	$16,095	54%
9	Xavier University (OH)	52%	$22,318	31%
10	Dominican University (IL)	80%	$17,583	39%
11	Butler University (IN)	57%	$21,894	37%
12	John Carroll University (OH)	67%	$22,447	33%
13	Baldwin-Wallace College (OH)	77%	$19,600	34%
14	Heidelberg College (OH)	81%	$15,348	39%
15	Capital University (OH)	79%	$19,515	41%

Universities–Master's (West)

		% receiving grants based on need ('05)	Average cost after receiving grants based on need ('05)	Average discount from total cost ('05)
1	Seattle Pacific University	60%	$17,878	45%
2	University of Redlands (CA)	66%	$20,947	47%
3	Whitworth College (WA)	71%	$20,765	37%
4	Trinity University (TX)	38%	$20,995	35%
5	Pacific University (OR)	71%	$18,082	39%
6	Wayland Baptist University (TX)	71%	$9,834	41%
7	Gonzaga University (WA)	57%	$21,626	36%
8	St. Mary's University of San Antonio	61%	$16,809	42%
9	George Fox University (OR)	79%	$19,485	37%
10	University of Portland (OR)	51%	$20,651	41%
11	Houston Baptist University	84%	$14,729	34%
12	Oklahoma City University	47%	$15,937	42%
13	Chapman University (CA)	59%	$23,662	43%
14	Westminster College (UT)	65%	$18,577	35%
15	St. Mary's College of California	56%	$24,208	41%

Comprehensive Colleges–Bachelor's (North)

		% receiving grants based on need ('05)	Average cost after receiving grants based on need ('05)	Average discount from total cost ('05)
1	Grove City College (PA)	33%	$12,563	28%
2	Elizabethtown College (PA)	70%	$19,306	42%
3	Elmira College (NY)	78%	$22,070	42%
4	Stonehill College (MA)	61%	$24,188	35%
5	College of St. Elizabeth (NJ)	69%	$17,842	44%
6	Cedar Crest College (PA)	85%	$19,921	38%
7	Wilson College (PA)	71%	$17,209	42%
8	Neumann College (PA)	82%	$15,596	47%
9	Keuka College (NY)	89%	$18,022	37%
10	Colby-Sawyer College (NH)	69%	$23,946	33%

Comprehensive Colleges–Bachelor's (South)

		% receiving grants based on need ('05)	Average cost after receiving grants based on need ('05)	Average discount from total cost ('05)
1	University of the Ozarks (AR)	52%	$9,536	59%
2	Claflin University (SC)	83%	$10,878	50%
3	Berry College (GA)	57%	$16,214	41%
4	Ouachita Baptist University (AR)	45%	$13,412	39%
5	Maryville College (TN)	74%	$17,704	44%
6	Florida Southern College	68%	$15,587	46%
7	LaGrange College (GA)	73%	$16,183	36%
8	Kentucky Wesleyan College	84%	$14,074	41%
9	Covenant College (GA)	68%	$16,001	41%
10	Pikeville College (KY)	95%	$12,122	45%

Best values: Great deals at great schools

Comprehensive Colleges–Bachelor's (Midwest)

		% receiving grants based on need ('05)	Average cost after receiving grants based on need ('05)	Average discount from total cost ('05)
1	Eureka College (IL)	73%	$9,614	53%
2	Wartburg College (IA)	78%	$16,640	43%
3	Manchester College (IN)	85%	$14,416	49%
4	Simpson College (IA)	85%	$17,100	42%
5	Clarke College (IA)	85%	$14,093	48%
6	Augustana College (SD)	68%	$15,420	41%
7	Mount Union College (OH)	79%	$16,731	40%
8	McKendree College (IL)	77%	$15,256	44%
9	Taylor University (IN)	52%	$18,145	37%
10	Central College (IA)	80%	$18,458	38%

Comprehensive Colleges–Bachelor's (West)

		% receiving grants based on need ('05)	Average cost after receiving grants based on need ('05)	Average discount from total cost ('05)
1	Brigham Young University–Hawaii	67%	$6,840	37%
2	East Texas Baptist University	61%	$11,971	38%
3	University of Science and Arts of Oklahoma	54%	$9,594	43%
4	Corban College (OR)	86%	$18,719	32%
5	Carroll College (MT)	62%	$17,771	34%
6	Northwest Christian College (OR)	90%	$15,608	42%
7	Rocky Mountain College (MT)	73%	$15,180	36%
8	Master's College and Seminary (CA)	67%	$19,178	36%
9	Howard Payne University (TX)	73%	$12,694	37%
10	McMurry University (TX)	78%	$15,894	33%

Schools whose graduates have the most and least debt

How mired in debt will you be when you get your diploma? This table shows the percentage of 2005 graduates who took on debt and the average cumulative amount they borrowed. The data include loans taken out by students from the colleges themselves; from financial institutions; and from federal, state and local governments. Parents' loans are not included.

National Universities

School	% of grads with debt	Average amount of debt
Worcester Polytechnic Institute (MA)	80%	$34,325
Pepperdine University (CA)	62%	$31,848
University of North Dakota	71%	$31,086
New York University	61%	$29,480
Pace University (NY)	67%	$29,060
Biola University (CA)	74%	$28,007
Rensselaer Polytechnic Institute (NY)	75%	$27,235
George Washington University (DC)	50%	$27,041
University of San Francisco	62%	$26,779
Nova Southeastern University (FL)	62%	$26,658
University of St. Thomas (MN)	66%	$26,621
University of San Diego	45%	$26,617
Carnegie Mellon University (PA)	48%	$26,500
Widener University (PA)	79%	$26,348
Marquette University (WI)	52%	$26,345
University of Rochester (NY)	56%	$26,100
Iowa State University	67%	$25,851
Temple University (PA)	71%	$25,493
Drexel University (PA)	85%	$25,347
SUNY Coll. Environ. Sci. & Forestry	92%	$25,000
St. Louis University	67%	$24,552
Florida Institute of Technology	54%	$24,535
Duke University (NC)	46%	$24,391
Loyola University Chicago	68%	$24,299
University of Alaska–Fairbanks	49%	$24,010
University of Tulsa (OK)	59%	$23,824
Georgetown University (DC)	45%	$23,724
Cornell University (NY)	54%	$23,450
Tennessee State University	84%	$23,434
Lehigh University (PA)	52%	$23,418
University of Vermont	62%	$23,328
Andrews University (MI)	66%	$23,195
Indiana U.-Purdue U.-Indianapolis	52%	$23,041
University of Memphis	23%	$22,962
Wake Forest University (NC)	39%	$22,831
University of Denver	43%	$22,663
University of Michigan–Ann Arbor	42%	$22,312
Emory University (GA)	40%	$22,175
Michigan State University	56%	$22,147
Polytechnic University (NY)	78%	$22,125
Adelphi University (NY)	81%	$22,000
Bowling Green State University (OH)	72%	$21,594
Miami University–Oxford (OH)	48%	$21,522
Duquesne University (PA)	78%	$21,493
University of New Hampshire	68%	$21,459
Brandeis University (MA)	61%	$21,437
Tulane University (LA)	49%	$21,379
Auburn University (AL)	65%	$21,339
Indiana University–Bloomington	44%	$21,251
Boston University	57%	$21,196
University of Pennsylvania	41%	$21,133
St. John's University (NY)	69%	$21,122
Kent State University (OH)	69%	$21,066
DePaul University (IL)	65%	$21,061
University of Maine–Orono	75%	$20,930
Case Western Reserve University (OH)	67%	$20,597
North Dakota State University	70%	$20,568
Hofstra University (NY)	61%	$20,500
Indiana State University	65%	$20,494
Washington State University	49%	$20,494
Univ. of Col.–Denver and Health Sci.	51%	$20,444
University of Missouri–Rolla	65%	$20,233
University of Dayton (OH)	67%	$20,151
Virginia Commonwealth University	66%	$20,069
University of Idaho	69%	$20,002
University of South Alabama	71%	$20,000
Clarkson University (NY)	81%	$19,942
Boston College	48%	$19,888
University of Iowa	58%	$19,886
University of Arkansas	51%	$19,862
American University (DC)	50%	$19,766
Massachusetts Institute of Technology	50%	$19,748
East Carolina University (NC)	79%	$19,614
Vanderbilt University (TN)	31%	$19,585
University of South Dakota	80%	$19,535
South Dakota State University	81%	$19,520
Illinois Institute of Technology	54%	$19,483
University of Missouri–St. Louis	56%	$19,435
University of Connecticut	60%	$19,410
Wayne State University (MI)	50%	$19,329
Dartmouth College (NH)	48%	$19,305
Idaho State University	71%	$19,299
Texas Tech University	57%	$19,195
University of Miami (FL)	56%	$19,140
University of Southern California	48%	$19,131
New School University (NY)	61%	$19,071
Univ. of Maryland–Baltimore County	48%	$19,018
Kansas State University	55%	$19,000
Clark University (MA)	88%	$18,990
Purdue University–West Lafayette (IN)	49%	$18,978
University of Illinois–Chicago	46%	$18,800
Univ. of South Carolina–Columbia	50%	$18,699
University of Wisconsin–Madison	45%	$18,630
Yeshiva University (NY)	49%	$18,628
Southern Methodist University (TX)	43%	$18,571
University of Alabama	50%	$18,545
University of Oklahoma	49%	$18,494
University of Tennessee	49%	$18,433
Virginia Tech	54%	$18,385
Northwestern University (IL)	46%	$18,362
Mississippi State University	49%	$18,230
Texas A&M University–Commerce	66%	$18,182
Texas Woman's University	54%	$18,125
Indiana University of Pennsylvania	80%	$18,105
Ohio University	62%	$18,101
Portland State University (OR)	70%	$18,085
Montana State University–Bozeman	66%	$18,081
Wichita State University (KS)	59%	$18,068
University of Oregon	60%	$18,029
East Tennessee State University	58%	$17,988
University of North Texas	42%	$17,950
University of Missouri–Columbia	50%	$17,907
Clemson University (SC)	44%	$17,882
Oklahoma State University	56%	$17,844
University at Buffalo–SUNY	70%	$17,834
Ohio State University–Columbus	58%	$17,821
Northern Illinois University	60%	$17,773
University of Kentucky	68%	$17,692
University of Chicago	51%	$17,651
University of Alabama–Birmingham	53%	$17,650
University of South Florida	53%	$17,546
University of Nevada–Las Vegas	40%	$17,394
University of Kansas	42%	$17,243
Louisiana Tech University	82%	$17,234
University of Colorado–Boulder	44%	$17,225
University of Pittsburgh	63%	$17,051
University of Alabama–Huntsville	53%	$17,043
Fordham University (NY)	61%	$16,976
Oregon State University	62%	$16,952
University of Montana	71%	$16,929
University of Nebraska–Lincoln	61%	$16,909
Colorado State University	52%	$16,887
University of Texas–Austin	39%	$16,850
University of Cincinnati	66%	$16,794
University of Texas–Arlington	42%	$16,780
Old Dominion University (VA)	80%	$16,775
University of Wyoming	46%	$16,742
Florida State University	52%	$16,597
Rutgers–Newark (NJ)	85%	$16,553
Howard University (DC)	80%	$16,546
Columbia University (NY)	47%	$16,541
Central Michigan University	64%	$16,537
University of Wisconsin–Milwaukee	63%	$16,492
Northern Arizona University	60%	$16,473
University of Arizona	47%	$16,422
Georgia Institute of Technology	44%	$16,399
University of Missouri–Kansas City	87%	$16,387
University of Rhode Island	56%	$16,200
Texas A&M University–College Station	32%	$16,027
Alliant International University (CA)	43%	$16,000
New Jersey Institute of Technology	45%	$16,000
Brown University (RI)	46%	$15,940
Univ. of Illinois–Urbana-Champaign	44%	$15,825
University of Washington	50%	$15,700
Illinois State University	59%	$15,616
University of Akron (OH)	62%	$15,500
Rutgers–New Brunswick (NJ)	63%	$15,362
Western Michigan University	47%	$15,300
Univ. of California–Santa Barbara	52%	$15,297
University of Delaware	40%	$15,200
Johns Hopkins University (MD)	51%	$15,177
University of Virginia	30%	$15,176
Stanford University (CA)	45%	$15,172
University of Louisville (KY)	42%	$15,128
University of Houston	55%	$15,004
National-Louis University (IL)	59%	$15,000
University of Massachusetts-Lowell	57%	$14,833
University of Florida	41%	$14,830

Schools whose graduates have the most and least debt

National Universities, continued

	% of grads with debt	Average amount of debt
University of California–Riverside	65%	$14,819
SUNY–Binghamton	60%	$14,734
Southern Illinois Univ.–Carbondale	39%	$14,708
Stevens Institute of Technology (NJ)	68%	$14,700
University of California–San Diego	49%	$14,689
University of Massachusetts–Amherst	61%	$14,672
College of William and Mary (VA)	34%	$14,524
North Carolina State Univ.–Raleigh	52%	$14,505
San Diego State University	49%	$14,500
University of Maryland–College Park	46%	$14,451
University of California–Los Angeles	52%	$14,431
Tufts University (MA)	40%	$14,400
SUNY–Albany	74%	$14,392

	% of grads with debt	Average amount of debt
Yale University (CT)	43%	$14,306
Rice University (TX)	34%	$14,166
Georgia State University	48%	$13,886
Univ. of North Carolina–Chapel Hill	34%	$13,801
West Virginia University	62%	$13,798
Univ. of North Carolina–Greensboro	60%	$13,661
George Mason University (VA)	47%	$13,607
Michigan Technological University	53%	$13,587
University of California–Irvine	55%	$13,587
University of Georgia	43%	$13,422
University of California–Santa Cruz	51%	$13,374
University of California–Berkeley	47%	$13,171
University of Central Florida	44%	$13,095

	% of grads with debt	Average amount of debt
Brigham Young University–Provo (UT)	35%	$12,955
University of Utah	45%	$12,806
University of Southern Mississippi	66%	$12,712
University of California–Davis	50%	$12,701
University of Hawaii–Manoa	33%	$12,579
Utah State University	50%	$12,430
SUNY–Stony Brook	64%	$11,473
Harvard University (MA)	48%	$8,769
N.M. Inst. of Mining and Tech.	58%	$7,292
University of Texas–El Paso	47%	$6,546
California Institute of Technology	45%	$5,395
Princeton University (NJ)	26%	$4,370

Liberal Arts Colleges

	% of grads with debt	Average amount of debt
Marymount Manhattan College (NY)	80%	$29,706
St. Augustine's College (NC)	72%	$28,602
Franklin Pierce College (NH)	80%	$28,036
Whittier College (CA)	78%	$27,335
St. Lawrence University (NY)	74%	$27,222
Seton Hill University (PA)	74%	$26,281
University of Puget Sound (WA)	60%	$25,842
Bridgewater College (VA)	69%	$25,780
Randolph-Macon Woman's Coll. (VA)	70%	$25,500
Albertson College (ID)	94%	$25,343
Smith College (MA)	69%	$25,023
Allegheny College (PA)	78%	$24,825
College of St. Benedict (MN)	72%	$24,764
Albright College (PA)	88%	$24,671
St. John's University (MN)	63%	$24,663
Wesleyan University (CT)	35%	$24,338
Kalamazoo College (MI)	55%	$24,022
Olivet College (MI)	94%	$23,606
Spelman College (GA)	75%	$23,500
Lycoming College (PA)	87%	$23,343
Cornell College (IA)	78%	$23,185
Rosemont College (PA)	78%	$23,091
Albion College (MI)	63%	$23,010
Davidson College (NC)	34%	$22,954
University of Dallas	67%	$22,850
Morehouse College (GA)	90%	$22,625
Ohio Wesleyan University	60%	$22,619
Rhodes College (TN)	46%	$22,575
Connecticut College	44%	$22,542
Wheaton College (MA)	61%	$22,380
Millsaps College (MS)	63%	$22,285
St. Anselm College (NH)	72%	$22,246
Juniata College (PA)	77%	$22,131
Coastal Carolina University (SC)	65%	$22,057
Agnes Scott College (GA)	71%	$22,018
Furman University (SC)	38%	$21,860
Illinois Wesleyan University	67%	$21,846
Gettysburg College (PA)	59%	$21,810
Paine College (GA)	95%	$21,661
Wittenberg University (OH)	69%	$21,615
Concordia College–Moorhead (MN)	72%	$21,532
Ursinus College (PA)	81%	$21,500
Schreiner University (TX)	83%	$21,455
Hobart and William Smith Colleges (NY)	65%	$21,454

	% of grads with debt	Average amount of debt
McDaniel College (MD)	60%	$21,416
Mills College (CA)	73%	$21,228
University of Minnesota–Morris	75%	$21,228
Wesleyan College (GA)	80%	$20,988
Dickinson College (PA)	62%	$20,982
Middlebury College (VT)	42%	$20,957
Pitzer College (CA)	60%	$20,900
Adrian College (MI)	79%	$20,849
Hope College (MI)	62%	$20,812
Washington College (MD)	60%	$20,483
Virginia Wesleyan College	79%	$20,386
Westminster College (PA)	83%	$20,386
Bennington College (VT)	72%	$20,340
Beloit College (WI)	62%	$20,339
Coe College (IA)	76%	$20,237
Guilford College (NC)	61%	$20,150
Lane College (TN)	98%	$20,000
Tougaloo College (MS)	85%	$20,000
Presbyterian College (SC)	64%	$19,998
College of Wooster (OH)	55%	$19,989
Mount Holyoke College (MA)	69%	$19,877
Marlboro College (VT)	85%	$19,758
West Virginia Wesleyan College	63%	$19,750
Knox College (IL)	68%	$19,642
Gustavus Adolphus College (MN)	68%	$19,500
Barnard College (NY)	45%	$19,496
St. Olaf College (MN)	65%	$19,410
Hampshire College (MA)	52%	$19,400
Stephens College (MO)	63%	$19,396
Franklin and Marshall College (PA)	61%	$19,391
College of the Holy Cross (MA)	52%	$19,390
Lafayette College (PA)	51%	$19,373
University of Pittsburgh–Bradford	85%	$19,313
Lawrence University (WI)	66%	$19,294
Kenyon College (OH)	60%	$19,190
Lewis and Clark College (OR)	57%	$19,156
Vassar College (NY)	56%	$19,038
Earlham College (IN)	70%	$19,000
Alma College (MI)	87%	$18,947
Monmouth College (IL)	82%	$18,901
Goshen College (IN)	69%	$18,680
Warner Pacific College (OR)	86%	$18,591
Roanoke College (VA)	72%	$18,543
Luther College (IA)	76%	$18,504

	% of grads with debt	Average amount of debt
University of Richmond (VA)	41%	$18,500
Colby College (ME)	43%	$18,479
Southwestern University (TX)	52%	$18,446
Susquehanna University (PA)	81%	$18,414
Bard College (NY)	71%	$18,345
Lake Forest College (IL)	53%	$18,306
Hanover College (IN)	62%	$18,124
Augustana College (IL)	71%	$18,098
San Diego Christian College (CA)	79%	$18,000
Wheaton College (IL)	55%	$17,936
Carleton College (MN)	60%	$17,842
Sweet Briar College (VA)	56%	$17,808
Mesa State College (CO)	53%	$17,634
Drew University (NJ)	60%	$17,586
Virginia Union University	98%	$17,560
Huntingdon College (AL)	68%	$17,540
Westminster College (MO)	66%	$17,534
Siena College (NY)	73%	$17,415
Bucknell University (PA)	62%	$17,400
Wabash College (IN)	65%	$17,328
Eckerd College (FL)	55%	$17,290
Muskingum College (OH)	72%	$17,277
Reed College (OR)	61%	$17,175
William Jewell College (MO)	71%	$17,133
Antioch College (OH)	97%	$17,125
Salem College (NC)	70%	$17,125
St. Mary's College of Maryland	69%	$17,125
Wells College (NY)	91%	$17,125
Washington and Lee University (VA)	25%	$17,105
Erskine College (SC)	78%	$17,100
Nebraska Wesleyan University	70%	$17,100
Bryn Mawr College (PA)	57%	$17,018
Hillsdale College (MI)	65%	$17,000
Washington and Jefferson College (PA)	75%	$17,000
Westmont College (CA)	74%	$16,999
Fort Lewis College (CO)	60%	$16,966
Oberlin College (OH)	60%	$16,922
Hollins University (VA)	64%	$16,853
Grinnell College (IA)	61%	$16,744
College of the Atlantic (ME)	57%	$16,705
King College (TN)	99%	$16,635
Ripon College (WI)	90%	$16,492
Massachusetts College of Liberal Arts	64%	$16,478
Haverford College (PA)	36%	$16,330

College	% of grads with debt	Average amount of debt
Colorado College	46%	$16,300
Hampden-Sydney College (VA)	54%	$16,244
Whitman College (WA)	45%	$16,200
Harvey Mudd College (CA)	60%	$16,055
Houghton College (NY)	71%	$16,028
Western State College of Colorado	67%	$16,000
Lyon College (AR)	92%	$15,956
Richard Stockton Coll. of New Jersey	64%	$15,875
Skidmore College (NY)	48%	$15,857
Texas A&M University–Galveston	63%	$15,793
Transylvania University (KY)	59%	$15,673
DePauw University (IN)	55%	$15,635
Bennett College (NC)	96%	$15,539
Goucher College (MD)	50%	$15,468
Emory and Henry College (VA)	76%	$15,465
Pine Manor College (MA)	80%	$15,412
University of North Carolina–Asheville	51%	$15,309
Bowdoin College (ME)	54%	$15,300
Union College (NY)	53%	$15,132
Randolph-Macon College (VA)	70%	$15,130
Georgetown College (KY)	69%	$15,018
Sewanee–Univ. of the South (TN)	36%	$14,926
Macalester College (MN)	75%	$14,889
Hendrix College (AR)	77%	$14,885
Denison University (OH)	49%	$14,657
Virginia Military Institute	34%	$14,367
Trinity College (CT)	44%	$14,283
Thomas Aquinas College (CA)	85%	$14,000
Evergreen State College (WA)	59%	$13,818
Christopher Newport University (VA)	53%	$13,772
Centre College (KY)	58%	$13,700
Bates College (ME)	46%	$13,636
Sarah Lawrence College (NY)	63%	$13,607
Colgate University (NY)	38%	$13,452
Scripps College (CA)	49%	$12,907
Birmingham-Southern College (AL)	51%	$12,857
California State Univ.–Monterey Bay	62%	$12,457
Swarthmore College (PA)	36%	$12,413
New College of Florida	38%	$12,252
Blackburn College (IL)	84%	$12,120
Amherst College (MA)	47%	$12,109
Wellesley College (MA)	51%	$11,821
Pomona College (CA)	53%	$11,250
Gordon College (MA)	47%	$11,192
University of Maine–Presque Isle	33%	$11,181
Williams College (MA)	39%	$10,900
Claremont McKenna College (CA)	51%	$10,518
Wofford College (SC)	49%	$10,242
Lees-McRae College (NC)	49%	$9,565
Lindsey Wilson College (KY)	99%	$9,389
St. Andrews Presbyterian College (NC)	55%	$9,329
University of Virginia–Wise	70%	$9,157

Universities—Master's (North)

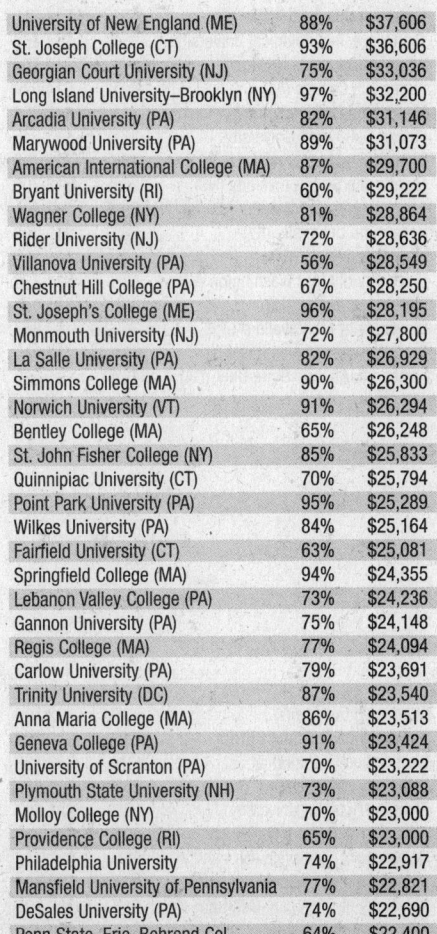

University	% of grads with debt	Average amount of debt
University of New England (ME)	88%	$37,606
St. Joseph College (CT)	93%	$36,606
Georgian Court University (NJ)	75%	$33,036
Long Island University–Brooklyn (NY)	97%	$32,200
Arcadia University (PA)	82%	$31,146
Marywood University (PA)	89%	$31,073
American International College (MA)	87%	$29,700
Bryant University (RI)	60%	$29,222
Wagner College (NY)	81%	$28,864
Rider University (NJ)	72%	$28,636
Villanova University (PA)	56%	$28,549
Chestnut Hill College (PA)	67%	$28,250
St. Joseph's College (ME)	96%	$28,195
Monmouth University (NJ)	72%	$27,800
La Salle University (PA)	82%	$26,929
Simmons College (MA)	90%	$26,300
Norwich University (VT)	91%	$26,294
Bentley College (MA)	65%	$26,248
St. John Fisher College (NY)	85%	$25,833
Quinnipiac University (CT)	70%	$25,794
Point Park University (PA)	95%	$25,289
Wilkes University (PA)	84%	$25,164
Fairfield University (CT)	63%	$25,081
Springfield College (MA)	94%	$24,355
Lebanon Valley College (PA)	73%	$24,236
Gannon University (PA)	75%	$24,148
Regis College (MA)	77%	$24,094
Carlow University (PA)	79%	$23,691
Trinity University (DC)	87%	$23,540
Anna Maria College (MA)	86%	$23,513
Geneva College (PA)	91%	$23,424
University of Scranton (PA)	70%	$23,222
Plymouth State University (NH)	73%	$23,088
Molloy College (NY)	70%	$23,000
Providence College (RI)	65%	$23,000
Philadelphia University	74%	$22,917
Mansfield University of Pennsylvania	77%	$22,821
DeSales University (PA)	74%	$22,690
Penn State–Erie, Behrend Col.	64%	$22,400
California University of Pennsylvania	79%	$21,975
College of St. Joseph (VT)	69%	$21,967
Salve Regina University (RI)	81%	$21,925
East Stroudsburg Univ. of Penn.	69%	$21,900
Canisius College (NY)	72%	$21,801
University of Southern Maine	61%	$21,800
Assumption College (MA)	76%	$21,773
Iona College (NY)	70%	$21,495
Alfred University (NY)	85%	$21,250
Lincoln University (PA)	78%	$21,000
Waynesburg College (PA)	89%	$21,000
New York Institute of Technology	61%	$20,725
St. Michael's College (VT)	72%	$20,706
Eastern University (PA)	71%	$20,541
Marist College (NY)	54%	$20,419
Manhattanville College (NY)	68%	$20,198
Keene State College (NH)	74%	$20,065
Mount St. Mary College (NY)	70%	$20,000
Sacred Heart University (CT)	93%	$19,926
Nazareth College of Rochester (NY)	82%	$19,785
SUNY College–Brockport	80%	$19,556
Lock Haven University of Pennsylvania	75%	$19,500
College of St. Rose (NY)	82%	$19,459
College of Notre Dame of Maryland	71%	$19,211
Le Moyne College (NY)	87%	$19,137
Suffolk University (MA)	61%	$19,012
Dowling College (NY)	81%	$18,920
SUNY Col. Arts & Sci.–New Paltz	75%	$18,900
Gwynedd-Mercy College (PA)	89%	$18,750
University of the District of Columbia	60%	$18,700
College of New Jersey	54%	$18,518
York College of Pennsylvania	68%	$18,198
College Misericordia (PA)	87%	$18,013
Shippensburg Univ. of Pennsylvania	67%	$17,976
Johnson and Wales University (RI)	68%	$17,704
SUNY–Buffalo State College	69%	$17,657
Wheelock College (MA)	95%	$17,525
Millersville University of Pennsylvania	74%	$17,433
SUNY–Plattsburgh	75%	$17,424
Cabrini College (PA)	84%	$17,400
Rutgers–Camden (NJ)	69%	$17,378
King's College (PA)	88%	$17,263
Niagara University (NY)	80%	$17,163
Holy Family University (PA)	68%	$17,125
Immaculata University (PA)	85%	$17,125
Edinboro University of Pennsylvania	67%	$17,034
College of Mount St. Vincent (NY)	80%	$17,000
Husson College (ME)	90%	$16,940
St. Bonaventure University (NY)	72%	$16,900
SUNY College–Oneonta	68%	$16,900
Eastern Connecticut State University	71%	$16,899
CUNY–City College	35%	$16,800
Montclair State University (NJ)	53%	$16,654
Emmanuel College (MA)	69%	$16,475
Bloomsburg University of Pennsylvania	68%	$16,442
Hood College (MD)	74%	$16,295
Emerson College (MA)	55%	$16,222
Univ. of Mass.–Dartmouth	65%	$16,214
St. Joseph's University (PA)	71%	$16,120
SUNY College–Potsdam	82%	$16,117
SUNY Col. Arts & Sci.–Geneseo	75%	$16,000
Mount St. Mary's University (MD)	75%	$15,964
Salisbury University (MD)	63%	$15,831
Loyola College in Maryland	74%	$15,680
Frostburg State University (MD)	61%	$15,678
SUNY–Purchase College	66%	$15,307
Bridgewater State College (MA)	31%	$15,065
Towson University (MD)	53%	$14,808
Clarion University of Pennsylvania	83%	$14,791
St. Francis University (PA)	90%	$14,500
Kutztown University of Pennsylvania	78%	$14,479
Gallaudet University (DC)	59%	$14,071
CUNY–Brooklyn College	30%	$14,000
Coppin State University (MD)	73%	$13,833
Lesley University (MA)	90%	$13,650
Kean University (NJ)	40%	$13,128
Central Connecticut State University	50%	$13,000
Framingham State College (MA)	53%	$12,800

Schools whose graduates have the most and least debt

Universities—Master's (North) continued

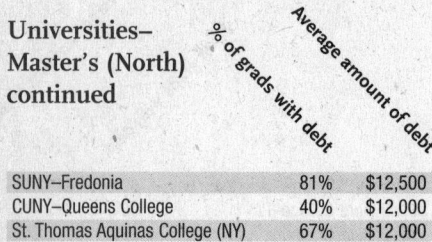
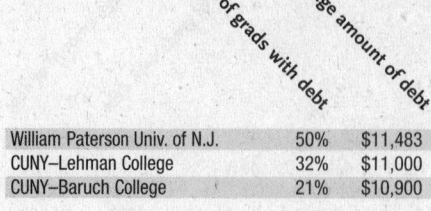

School	% of grads with debt	Average amount of debt
SUNY–Fredonia	81%	$12,500
CUNY–Queens College	40%	$12,000
St. Thomas Aquinas College (NY)	67%	$12,000
William Paterson Univ. of N.J.	50%	$11,483
CUNY–Lehman College	32%	$11,000
CUNY–Baruch College	21%	$10,900
Fitchburg State College (MA)	55%	$10,660
Rowan University (NJ)	97%	$9,575
CUNY–Hunter College	38%	$8,780

Universities—Master's (South)

School	% of grads with debt	Average amount of debt
Embry Riddle Aeronautical Univ. (FL)	68%	$52,276
Lipscomb University (TN)	56%	$33,000
Tuskegee University (AL)	91%	$30,000
Virginia State University	92%	$25,600
Marymount University (VA)	71%	$24,950
Columbus State University (GA)	71%	$24,675
Christian Brothers University (TN)	63%	$24,463
Palm Beach Atlantic University (FL)	80%	$24,393
Charleston Southern University (SC)	90%	$24,251
Barry University (FL)	72%	$24,091
Southern Wesleyan University (SC)	99%	$24,032
Trevecca Nazarene University (TN)	73%	$24,000
University of Tampa (FL)	71%	$23,051
Southern Univ. and A&M College (LA)	90%	$23,000
Elon University (NC)	45%	$21,687
Stetson University (FL)	55%	$21,500
Jacksonville University (FL)	53%	$21,483
Mary Baldwin College (VA)	75%	$21,266
Meredith College (NC)	79%	$21,266
Alabama State University	13%	$21,150
Shenandoah University (VA)	85%	$21,125
Tusculum College (TN)	72%	$20,928
Wheeling Jesuit University (WV)	74%	$20,227
University of Central Arkansas	71%	$20,000
University of Mobile (AL)	92%	$20,000
Union University (TN)	59%	$19,506
Mississippi College	61%	$19,484
Winthrop University (SC)	63%	$18,793
Milligan College (TN)	65%	$18,769
Arkansas State University	68%	$18,500
Cumberland University (TN)	67%	$18,456
Campbellsville University (KY)	80%	$18,437
University of North Carolina–Charlotte	56%	$18,407
University of North Alabama	47%	$18,245
Delta State University (MS)	75%	$18,200
Belmont University (TN)	56%	$18,007
Brenau University (GA)	65%	$17,953
Georgia Southern University	70%	$17,913
Henderson State University (AR)	34%	$17,800
Western Carolina University (NC)	49%	$17,782
Murray State University (KY)	52%	$17,617
Samford University (AL)	46%	$17,532
Northwestern State Univ. of Louisiana	68%	$17,442
Centenary College of Louisiana	53%	$17,300
Radford University (VA)	88%	$17,264
University of West Alabama	57%	$17,255
Arkansas Tech University	53%	$17,064
Marshall University (WV)	60%	$17,053
Alcorn State University (MS)	73%	$17,000
Morehead State University (KY)	59%	$16,995
Eastern Kentucky University	48%	$16,906
University of Tennessee–Martin	57%	$16,749
University of North Florida	46%	$16,707
Converse College (SC)	58%	$16,641
Carson-Newman College (TN)	71%	$16,512
Averett University (VA)	70%	$16,398
Harding University (AR)	66%	$16,310
Queens University of Charlotte (NC)	86%	$16,270
Valdosta State University (GA)	61%	$16,220
Warren Wilson College (NC)	59%	$16,211
College of Charleston (SC)	46%	$16,143
Augusta State University (GA)	64%	$16,092
University of the Cumberlands (KY)	58%	$16,083
William Carey College (MS)	85%	$16,000
Southeastern Louisiana University	61%	$15,793
Univ. of North Carolina–Wilmington	52%	$15,620
Rollins College (FL)	50%	$15,438
Appalachian State University (NC)	50%	$15,433
University of Tennessee–Chattanooga	48%	$15,348
Georgia Southwestern State Univ.	68%	$15,346
Kennesaw State University (GA)	45%	$15,346
St. Leo University (FL)	67%	$15,300
Lynn University (FL)	68%	$15,154
Georgia College and State University	57%	$15,082
Univ. of North Carolina–Pembroke	70%	$14,766
Troy University (AL)	70%	$14,762
University of West Georgia	61%	$14,555
Piedmont College (GA)	66%	$14,408
Campbell University (NC)	65%	$14,200
Tennessee Technological University	35%	$14,164
Southern Arkansas University	58%	$14,162
Spring Hill College (AL)	80%	$14,074
Mississippi University for Women	71%	$13,800
Florida Gulf Coast University	47%	$13,245
Nicholls State University (LA)	48%	$12,738
Fayetteville State University (NC)	85%	$12,700
James Madison University (VA)	53%	$12,591
Bellarmine University (KY)	68%	$12,263
Liberty University (VA)	42%	$11,885
University of Mary Washington (VA)	57%	$11,800
Mercer University (GA)	63%	$11,075
University of Montevallo (AL)	38%	$7,897
Gardner-Webb University (NC)	53%	$7,014
Armstrong Atlantic State Univ. (GA)	40%	$5,500

Universities—Master's (Midwest)

School	% of grads with debt	Average amount of debt
Rockford College (IL)	85%	$30,125
College of St. Scholastica (MN)	84%	$29,942
College of St. Catherine (MN)	77%	$27,528
Augsburg College (MN)	76%	$27,514
St. Mary's University of Minnesota	73%	$26,633
Maryville University of St. Louis (MO)	60%	$26,310
Mount Marty College (SD)	85%	$26,304
Franciscan Univ. of Steubenville (OH)	75%	$26,192
Heidelberg College (OH)	87%	$26,125
Creighton University (NE)	74%	$26,013
Drake University (IA)	70%	$25,800
Bethel University (MN)	75%	$25,325
St. Ambrose University (IA)	79%	$24,728
University of Indianapolis	75%	$24,651
Lawrence Technological University (MI)	50%	$24,250
Capital University (OH)	80%	$24,092
Valparaiso University (IN)	71%	$23,853
Cornerstone University (MI)	79%	$23,710
Hamline University (MN)	81%	$23,311
Ursuline College (OH)	67%	$23,000
Edgewood College (WI)	73%	$22,710
University of St. Francis (IN)	85%	$22,709
Benedictine College (KS)	62%	$22,333
University of Michigan–Flint	66%	$21,888
Eastern Michigan University	58%	$21,397
John Carroll University (OH)	90%	$21,385
University of Evansville (IN)	67%	$21,142
Marian College of Fond du Lac (WI)	90%	$20,800
University of Michigan–Dearborn	51%	$20,509
St. Xavier University (IL)	81%	$20,470

	% of grads with debt	Average amount of debt
St. Cloud State University (MN)	52%	$20,431
University of Northern Iowa	77%	$20,239
University of Minnesota–Duluth	71%	$20,221
Indiana University–South Bend	53%	$20,199
Olivet Nazarene University (IL)	75%	$20,062
Northern State University (SD)	80%	$19,864
Lake Superior State University (MI)	63%	$19,825
Baker University (KS)	86%	$19,602
Maharishi Univ. of Management (IA)	93%	$19,545
Xavier University (OH)	58%	$19,300
Madonna University (MI)	40%	$19,252
MidAmerica Nazarene University (KS)	80%	$19,222
Newman University (KS)	70%	$19,054
Mount Mary College (WI)	75%	$19,040
Silver Lake College (WI)	70%	$18,934
Walsh University (OH)	79%	$18,775
Webster University (MO)	50%	$18,690
Indiana University Southeast	42%	$18,570
University of Wisconsin–Stout	73%	$18,496
Malone College (OH)	72%	$18,482
Indiana University Northwest	45%	$18,394
Aurora University (IL)	74%	$18,374
Ashland University (OH)	75%	$18,250
Bemidji State University (MN)	77%	$18,247
Rockhurst University (MO)	72%	$17,890
Friends University (KS)	100%	$17,750

	% of grads with debt	Average amount of debt
Drury University (MO)	42%	$17,585
Fontbonne University (MO)	85%	$17,500
Concordia University–River Forest (IL)	76%	$17,470
Emporia State University (KS)	72%	$17,435
University of Wisconsin–Whitewater	63%	$17,394
Southern Illinois Univ.–Edwardsville	20%	$17,290
Concordia University Wisconsin	68%	$17,269
University of St. Mary (KS)	72%	$17,125
Univ. of Wisconsin–Stevens Point	69%	$17,065
University of Wisconsin–Eau Claire	65%	$16,953
University of Nebraska–Omaha	48%	$16,900
Indiana Univ.-Purdue Univ.–Ft. Wayne	60%	$16,880
Northern Michigan University	67%	$16,842
University of Wisconsin–La Crosse	67%	$16,793
Grand Valley State University (MI)	73%	$16,606
Winona State University (MN)	66%	$16,588
Truman State University (MO)	43%	$16,546
Minnesota State University–Mankato	75%	$16,500
Lincoln University (MO)	63%	$16,471
Avila University (MO)	100%	$16,398
Baldwin-Wallace College (OH)	95%	$16,250
University of Nebraska–Kearney	74%	$16,175
Quincy University (IL)	80%	$16,134
Southeast Missouri State University	63%	$16,006
University of Wisconsin–Oshkosh	70%	$16,000
Minot State University (ND)	97%	$15,900

	% of grads with debt	Average amount of debt
University of Southern Indiana	60%	$15,724
Purdue University–Calumet (IN)	56%	$15,687
Eastern Illinois University	63%	$15,538
Concordia University (NE)	86%	$15,522
Bradley University (IL)	74%	$15,105
Ferris State University (MI)	85%	$15,000
North Park University (IL)	68%	$14,978
Dominican University (IL)	60%	$14,923
Doane College (NE)	79%	$14,915
Western Illinois University	62%	$14,850
University of Wisconsin–River Falls	68%	$14,756
University of St. Francis (IL)	88%	$14,650
Aquinas College (MI)	65%	$14,645
North Central College (IL)	70%	$14,608
Lewis University (IL)	71%	$14,328
William Woods University (MO)	85%	$13,865
College of Mount St. Joseph (OH)	80%	$13,400
Washburn University (KS)	60%	$13,125
Missouri State University	54%	$12,997
Northeastern Illinois University	34%	$12,284
University of Wisconsin–Green Bay	61%	$12,222
University of Rio Grande (OH)	80%	$12,136
Spring Arbor University (MI)	84%	$11,989
Southwest Baptist University (MO)	73%	$11,268
Pittsburg State University (KS)	93%	$10,742
Central Missouri State University	63%	$9,632

Universities– Master's (West)

	% of grads with debt	Average amount of debt
Oral Roberts University (OK)	83%	$30,471
LeTourneau University (TX)	87%	$28,426
St. Martin's University (WA)	60%	$27,846
Loyola Marymount University (CA)	59%	$27,144
University of Great Falls (MT)	83%	$26,450
Abilene Christian University (TX)	71%	$26,413
Hardin-Simmons University (TX)	72%	$26,144
Our Lady of the Lake University (TX)	83%	$26,058
St. Mary's University of San Antonio	83%	$25,736
Pacific University (OR)	84%	$25,581
Seattle University	68%	$25,311
Prairie View A&M University (TX)	80%	$25,000
Northwest Nazarene University (ID)	94%	$24,405
St. Edward's University (TX)	62%	$24,280
Walla Walla College (WA)	72%	$23,668
University of the Incarnate Word (TX)	80%	$23,383
Gonzaga University (WA)	69%	$23,164
Marylhurst University (OR)	67%	$23,000
Seattle Pacific University	68%	$22,569
Pacific Lutheran University (WA)	69%	$22,372
Chaminade University of Honolulu	56%	$22,263
University of Portland (OR)	64%	$22,253
St. Mary's College of California	62%	$21,892
University of St. Thomas (TX)	63%	$21,626
California Lutheran University	86%	$21,140
Woodbury University (CA)	91%	$20,134
University of Alaska–Southeast	44%	$19,979
California Baptist University	99%	$19,920
East Central University (OK)	60%	$19,882
Azusa Pacific University (CA)	49%	$19,487
Western Oregon University	51%	$19,422

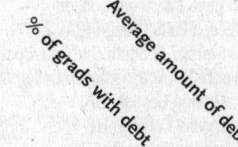

	% of grads with debt	Average amount of debt
Chapman University (CA)	64%	$19,237
Concordia University (CA)	74%	$19,200
Oklahoma City University	47%	$19,178
Heritage University (WA)	98%	$19,120
Dominican University of California	70%	$19,092
Dallas Baptist University	55%	$18,763
Eastern Washington University	65%	$18,600
Point Loma Nazarene University (CA)	79%	$18,415
Whitworth College (WA)	73%	$18,246
Houston Baptist University	75%	$18,238
Prescott College (AZ)	68%	$18,235
University of Texas–San Antonio	63%	$18,000
Notre Dame de Namur University (CA)	79%	$17,844
Northeastern State University (OK)	69%	$17,824
Alaska Pacific University	66%	$17,775
Santa Clara University (CA)	50%	$17,620
Hope International University (CA)	72%	$17,563
College of Santa Fe (NM)	63%	$17,540
College of the Southwest (NM)	66%	$17,420
Texas A&M University–Corpus Christi	60%	$17,367
Hawaii Pacific University	36%	$17,125
Texas State University–San Marcos	59%	$16,863
University of Mary Hardin-Baylor (TX)	80%	$16,725
Holy Names University (CA)	38%	$16,640
Sam Houston State University (TX)	61%	$16,636
Westminster College (UT)	64%	$16,450
Midwestern State University (TX)	46%	$16,041
Central Washington University	65%	$15,824
Western Washington University	58%	$15,784
Montana State University–Billings	68%	$15,719
University of Central Oklahoma	53%	$15,508

	% of grads with debt	Average amount of debt
California State University–Stanislaus	18%	$15,500
San Francisco State University	46%	$15,376
Calif. State Univ.–Dominguez Hills	32%	$15,232
George Fox University (OR)	61%	$15,026
University of Redlands (CA)	78%	$15,024
Univ. of Texas of the Permian Basin	48%	$14,870
Boise State University (ID)	59%	$14,765
Colorado State University–Pueblo	81%	$14,590
University of Texas–Tyler	55%	$14,581
California State University–Fullerton	37%	$14,482
Cal Poly–San Luis Obispo	35%	$14,020
Stephen F. Austin State University (TX)	70%	$14,007
Wayland Baptist University (TX)	78%	$13,972
Fresno Pacific University (CA)	50%	$13,334
Sonoma State University (CA)	47%	$13,328
California State Univ.–San Marcos	40%	$13,112
Lamar University (TX)	54%	$13,000
Humboldt State University (CA)	35%	$12,730
University of Texas–Pan American	84%	$12,453
Univ. of Colorado–Colorado Springs	48%	$12,438
California State University–East Bay	37%	$12,312
Southern Utah University	64%	$11,239
California State University–Fresno	43%	$10,958
California State Univ.–Sacramento	40%	$10,868
California State Univ.–Long Beach	31%	$10,842
Texas A&M International University	57%	$10,627
Northwestern Oklahoma State Univ.	47%	$9,476
Cameron University (OK)	32%	$6,300
Southeastern Oklahoma State Univ.	30%	$6,124

Schools whose graduates have the most and least debt

Comprehensive Colleges–Bachelor's (North)

	% of grads with debt	Average amount of debt
Becker College (MA)	98%	$32,120
Atlantic Union College (MA)	100%	$30,062
New England College (NH)	74%	$29,777
Elizabethtown College (PA)	77%	$29,233
Dominican College of Blauvelt (NY)	73%	$28,601
Roger Williams University (RI)	80%	$28,147
Messiah College (PA)	70%	$27,322
Cazenovia College (NY)	85%	$27,321
Wilson College (PA)	90%	$25,848
Utica College (NY)	89%	$25,565
Elmira College (NY)	69%	$25,347
Curry College (MA)	55%	$25,051
College of St. Elizabeth (NJ)	60%	$24,290
Green Mountain College (VT)	93%	$23,894
Grove City College (PA)	53%	$23,409
Cedar Crest College (PA)	97%	$22,820
University of Pittsburgh–Johnstown	89%	$22,362
Hilbert College (NY)	91%	$21,496
Mercyhurst College (PA)	93%	$21,000
Russell Sage College (NY)	90%	$21,000
Mount Aloysius College (PA)	79%	$20,970
Lasell College (MA)	93%	$20,800
Centenary College (NJ)	98%	$20,383
Neumann College (PA)	80%	$20,000
Thiel College (PA)	87%	$20,000
Stonehill College (MA)	75%	$19,712
Medaille College (NY)	85%	$19,000
Wesley College (DE)	90%	$18,800
Mount Ida College (MA)	77%	$18,328
Concordia College (NY)	75%	$18,265
Colby-Sawyer College (NH)	79%	$18,175
Caldwell College (NJ)	74%	$17,548
Post University (CT)	92%	$17,500
Delaware Valley College (PA)	68%	$17,482
St. Joseph's Coll. New York–Brooklyn	66%	$16,638
University of Maine–Farmington	80%	$16,289
Ramapo College of New Jersey	37%	$15,937
Villa Julie College (MD)	68%	$15,580
Albertus Magnus College (CT)	92%	$15,530
University of Maine–Machias	69%	$15,062
SUNY College–Old Westbury	52%	$14,532
Daemen College (NY)	78%	$13,323
Keuka College (NY)	86%	$13,041
University of Maine–Augusta	62%	$12,861
Simon's Rock College of Bard (MA)	80%	$12,383
Alvernia College (PA)	91%	$6,985
SUNY College of A&T–Cobleskill	77%	$6,300

Comprehensive Colleges–Bachelor's (South)

	% of grads with debt	Average amount of debt
Bethune-Cookman College (FL)	83%	$26,740
Lee University (TN)	71%	$26,482
Philander Smith College (AR)	89%	$26,000
Thomas More College (KY)	70%	$25,779
Kentucky Christian University	84%	$25,731
Johnson C. Smith University (NC)	90%	$25,000
Lenoir-Rhyne College (NC)	92%	$24,951
Alderson-Broaddus College (WV)	80%	$23,579
Mountain State University (WV)	69%	$23,570
Chowan College (NC)	80%	$23,370
University of Charleston (WV)	80%	$22,500
Mars Hill College (NC)	50%	$22,250
Asbury College (KY)	69%	$22,016
Claflin University (SC)	95%	$21,898
Davis and Elkins College (WV)	81%	$20,651
Stillman College (AL)	86%	$20,604
High Point University (NC)	83%	$20,125
Morris College (SC)	99%	$20,000
Methodist College (NC)	75%	$19,989
Brevard College (NC)	63%	$19,293
John Brown University (AR)	60%	$19,262
Brewton-Parker College (GA)	83%	$19,230
Belmont Abbey College (NC)	80%	$18,950
Southeastern University (FL)	93%	$18,933
Faulkner University (AL)	82%	$18,900
Wingate University (NC)	70%	$18,759
Ohio Valley University (WV)	94%	$18,741
Catawba College (NC)	78%	$18,731
Virginia Intermont College	83%	$18,700
Toccoa Falls College (GA)	71%	$17,273
University of South Carolina–Upstate	67%	$17,238
North Carolina Wesleyan College	88%	$17,125
LaGrange College (GA)	79%	$17,074
Maryville College (TN)	90%	$17,026
Lambuth University (TN)	80%	$17,000
Coker College (SC)	87%	$16,859
Bryan College (TN)	60%	$16,521
Clearwater Christian College (FL)	64%	$16,300
Ferrum College (VA)	74%	$16,300
Shorter College (GA)	59%	$16,193
Limestone College (SC)	66%	$16,175
Glenville State College (WV)	71%	$16,079
Florida Southern College	67%	$16,072
LeMoyne-Owen College (TN)	94%	$15,528
Martin Methodist College (TN)	68%	$15,473
Midway College (KY)	80%	$15,407
Pikeville College (KY)	73%	$15,208
Bluefield State College (WV)	45%	$15,200
Tennessee Wesleyan College	82%	$15,154
Anderson University (SC)	76%	$15,125
Flagler College (FL)	55%	$15,037
Covenant College (GA)	58%	$14,980
Shepherd University (WV)	68%	$14,887
Williams Baptist College (AR)	81%	$14,768
Bluefield College (VA)	84%	$14,191
Ouachita Baptist University (AR)	50%	$14,016
University of South Carolina–Aiken	80%	$13,963
Clayton State University (GA)	27%	$13,400
University of the Ozarks (AR)	50%	$12,866
Berry College (GA)	50%	$12,028
St. Paul's College (VA)	86%	$12,011
West Virginia University–Parkersburg	83%	$12,000
Blue Mountain College (MS)	83%	$11,484
Kentucky Wesleyan College	69%	$11,191
Concord University (WV)	79%	$11,178
Southern Adventist University (TN)	67%	$10,935
Livingstone College (NC)	92%	$10,500
Winston-Salem State University (NC)	80%	$10,200
Mount Olive College (NC)	57%	$8,901
Warner Southern College (FL)	42%	$7,869
Berea College (KY)	79%	$7,299
Mid-Continent University (KY)	77%	$7,000
Reinhardt College (GA)	69%	$5,500
Alice Lloyd College (KY)	56%	$3,495

Comprehensive Colleges–Bachelor's (Midwest)

	% of grads with debt	Average amount of debt
Ohio Northern University	78%	$37,017
Alverno College (WI)	88%	$29,542
Buena Vista University (IA)	92%	$29,059
Concordia University (MI)	83%	$28,280
Bluffton University (OH)	77%	$27,441
Morningside College (IA)	91%	$26,816
St. Norbert College (WI)	65%	$24,808
Indiana University East	59%	$24,729
St. Mary's College (IN)	68%	$24,617
Simpson College (IA)	87%	$24,403
Loras College (IA)	94%	$24,320
Central College (IA)	85%	$23,490
St. Joseph's College (IN)	74%	$23,417
Union College (NE)	64%	$23,379
Iowa Wesleyan College	78%	$22,907
Crown College (MN)	87%	$22,672
York College (NE)	89%	$22,581
Mount Mercy College (IA)	72%	$22,530
Northwestern College (IA)	85%	$22,286
Wartburg College (IA)	84%	$22,122
Northwestern College (MN)	62%	$21,778
Franklin College (IN)	90%	$21,263
Jamestown College (ND)	95%	$21,131
Dakota State University (SD)	90%	$20,977
Concordia University–St. Paul (MN)	68%	$20,715
Mount Vernon Nazarene Univ. (OH)	79%	$20,293
Kendall College (IL)	78%	$20,271
Marian College (IN)	75%	$20,197
Tabor College (KS)	82%	$20,180
Dakota Wesleyan University (SD)	93%	$20,068
Central Christian College (KS)	73%	$20,000
Greenville College (IL)	85%	$19,820
Clarke College (IA)	72%	$19,492
Midland Lutheran College (NE)	85%	$19,419
Calvin College (MI)	67%	$19,400
Cedarville University (OH)	67%	$19,258
Judson College (IL)	92%	$19,216
St. Mary-of-the-Woods College (IN)	86%	$19,113
Missouri Baptist University	65%	$19,082
Augustana College (SD)	79%	$18,956
Trinity Christian College (IL)	80%	$18,956
Northland College (WI)	81%	$18,893
Bethel College (KS)	86%	$18,584
Grace University (NE)	98%	$18,502
Grand View College (IA)	94%	$18,463
Culver-Stockton College (MO)	89%	$18,429
Millikin University (IL)	79%	$18,418
Carroll College (WI)	57%	$18,404
Valley City State University (ND)	60%	$18,394
Huntington University (IN)	62%	$18,290
Manchester College (IN)	70%	$18,254
College of St. Mary (NE)	91%	$18,047
McPherson College (KS)	83%	$18,010
Taylor University (IN)	60%	$17,910
Southwestern College (KS)	65%	$17,858
Dana College (NE)	89%	$17,774
Defiance College (OH)	76%	$17,359
Bethany College (KS)	82%	$16,925
Southwest Minnesota State Univ. (MN)	83%	$16,678
Dordt College (IA)	80%	$16,610
McKendree College (IL)	57%	$16,322
Bethel College (IN)	77%	$16,204
Mount Union College (OH)	84%	$16,139
Elmhurst College (IL)	75%	$16,080
Calumet College of St. Joseph (IN)	65%	$16,040
Tri-State University (IN)	61%	$15,400
Eureka College (IL)	89%	$15,352
Indiana University–Kokomo	38%	$15,195
Columbia College (MO)	65%	$14,879
Waldorf College (IA)	63%	$14,782
Wisconsin Lutheran College	71%	$14,638
Missouri Valley College	80%	$14,500
Lakeland College (WI)	85%	$14,210
University of Minnesota–Crookston	60%	$14,194
Purdue University–North Central (IN)	53%	$14,009
MacMurray College (IL)	91%	$12,440
Illinois College	95%	$11,105

Comprehensive Colleges–Bachelor's (West)

	% of grads with debt	Average amount of debt
Humphreys College (CA)	96%	$32,000
Texas Lutheran University	63%	$27,139
Carroll College (MT)	75%	$25,659
McMurry University (TX)	82%	$24,854
Linfield College (OR)	75%	$24,594
Pacific Union College (CA)	72%	$24,200
Corban College (OR)	70%	$23,400
University of Montana–Western	86%	$22,682
Lubbock Christian University (TX)	81%	$22,192
Menlo College (CA)	67%	$21,905
Oklahoma Christian University	74%	$21,096
Oklahoma Wesleyan University	98%	$20,684
Concordia University–Austin (TX)	68%	$20,202
Northwest University (WA)	88%	$19,171
Howard Payne University (TX)	64%	$19,100
Rocky Mountain College (MT)	75%	$18,653
Northwest Christian College (OR)	75%	$17,585
Vanguard Univ. of Southern California	76%	$16,979
East Texas Baptist University	81%	$16,777
Oklahoma Baptist University	51%	$16,614
Master's College and Seminary (CA)	64%	$15,383
Jarvis Christian College (TX)	74%	$14,600
Univ. of Sci. and Arts of Oklahoma	67%	$11,378
St. Gregory's University (OK)	68%	$10,062
Brigham Young University–Hawaii	25%	$9,794
Patten University (CA)	75%	$9,191
Utah Valley State College	54%	$9,046

Where the money is: Schools that award the most need-based aid

The schools at the top of this list handed out the largest need-based financial aid packages, on average, during the 2005–2006 school year. The typical aid package has three components: need based grants, need-based loans, and work study. In order to qualify, students must file an annual aid application that demonstrates financial need. The table also lists the percentage of undergraduates receiving the average need-based aid package, the average need-based grant and loan awarded to undergraduates, and the average percentage of a student's demonstrated need that was met by the school during the 2005–2006 academic year. In addition, some colleges give out merit awards, which are based on academic ability or other talents and not on financial need. The table lists the percentage of undergraduates receiving such awards and the average amount of the award during 2005–2006.

National Universities	Average amount of aid package	% students receiving need-based package	Average need-based grant	Average need-based loan	Average % of need met	Average merit award	% students receiving merit awards
George Washington University (DC)	$33,196	43%	$19,828	$6,806	91%	$19,290	24%
Vanderbilt University (TN)	$31,840	40%	$24,806	$3,870	99%	$17,602	13%
Pepperdine University (CA)	$30,991	49%	$20,855	$9,684	89%	$18,720	15%
Harvard University (MA)	$30,715	50%	$28,004	$3,439	100%	$0	0%
Yale University (CT)	$30,219	42%	$27,932	$1,994	100%	N/A	N/A
Dartmouth College (NH)	$30,019	52%	$25,720	$4,345	100%	$461	0%
Duke University (NC)	$29,878	40%	$23,928	$4,270	100%	$24,016	4%
Massachusetts Institute of Technology	$29,831	62%	$26,013	$4,010	100%	$0	0%
Stanford University (CA)	$29,750	44%	$25,500	$2,390	100%	$3,000	10%
Cornell University (NY)	$29,500	46%	$22,000	$7,400	100%	N/A	N/A
University of Southern California	$29,365	43%	$21,773	$6,538	100%	$12,552	19%
University of Chicago	$29,176	45%	$23,078	$5,494	100%	$11,579	11%
Case Western Reserve University (OH)	$28,931	60%	$18,391	$5,349	92%	$11,852	30%
University of Pennsylvania	$28,642	44%	$23,595	$3,699	100%	N/A	N/A
California Institute of Technology	$28,508	54%	$27,325	$1,491	100%	$29,818	9%
Princeton University (NJ)	$28,368	51%	$26,468	$0	100%	N/A	N/A
Columbia University (NY)	$28,138	48%	$23,874	$4,803	100%	N/A	N/A
Boston University	$27,633	46%	$18,631	$4,835	90%	$16,606	10%
Emory University (GA)	$27,599	38%	$21,236	$5,355	100%	$17,985	6%
Johns Hopkins University (MD)	$26,553	49%	$17,776	$4,087	96%	$12,609	4%
American University (DC)	$26,534	47%	$13,534	$8,191	75%	$15,708	13%
Brown University (RI)	$26,477	42%	$22,224	$4,935	100%	$0	0%
Rensselaer Polytechnic Institute (NY)	$26,072	70%	$19,500	$7,000	81%	$15,800	19%
Northwestern University (IL)	$25,831	43%	$21,489	$4,503	100%	$2,353	2%
Tufts University (MA)	$25,749	38%	$22,465	$4,287	100%	$500	2%
Washington University in St. Louis	$25,653	43%	$21,191	$5,884	100%	$7,090	13%
Georgetown University (DC)	$25,600	42%	$19,300	$3,600	100%	$30,730	0%
Lehigh University (PA)	$25,403	46%	$20,441	$4,325	98%	$9,808	6%
Boston College	$24,905	40%	$19,854	$4,987	100%	$11,233	0%
University of Rochester (NY)	$24,474	56%	$19,585	$5,076	87%	$8,773	33%
Brandeis University (MA)	$23,816	47%	$18,620	$5,744	83%	$12,952	5%
University of Miami (FL)	$23,709	52%	$17,257	$5,104	78%	$14,784	22%
Southern Methodist University (TX)	$23,699	38%	$13,766	$3,924	88%	$5,311	30%
University of the Pacific (CA)	$23,050	67%	$17,486	$5,628	N/A	$8,140	13%
Wake Forest University (NC)	$22,581	35%	$16,797	$6,643	87%	$10,520	29%
Carnegie Mellon University (PA)	$22,143	50%	$16,636	$4,853	81%	$12,318	9%
Polytechnic University (NY)	$21,955	82%	$7,511	$4,928	91%	$16,578	13%
Clark University (MA)	$21,898	54%	$17,645	$3,208	93%	$11,591	26%
University of Tulsa (OK)	$21,719	47%	$4,339	$5,979	88%	$10,881	35%
University of San Diego	$21,450	46%	$15,830	$4,318	71%	$8,556	15%
University of San Francisco	$21,153	57%	$14,973	$4,966	70%	$14,696	3%
Stevens Institute of Technology (NJ)	$21,139	68%	$12,406	$4,158	80%	$10,977	17%
Andrews University (MI)	$21,103	64%	$7,105	$7,477	98%	$5,472	33%
Florida Institute of Technology	$21,102	64%	$14,095	$4,724	84%	$7,526	26%
Worcester Polytechnic Institute (MA)	$20,849	70%	$16,052	$6,245	67%	$18,228	15%
Syracuse University (NY)	$20,716	58%	$15,020	$5,300	80%	$8,840	16%
University of La Verne (CA)	$20,636	83%	$10,620	$4,637	N/A	$7,929	13%
Illinois Institute of Technology	$20,610	58%	$13,484	$4,594	85%	$10,259	39%
University of Denver	$20,508	42%	$16,365	$3,745	71%	$8,313	33%
Yeshiva University (NY)	$20,434	46%	$16,512	$6,002	74%	$9,029	9%
Loyola University Chicago	$20,367	70%	$11,760	$3,971	79%	$7,205	7%

	Average amount of aid package	% students receiving need-based package	Average need-based grant	Average need-based loan	Average % of need met	Average merit award	% students receiving merit awards
Widener University (PA)	$20,192	81%	$10,799	$4,705	77%	$8,201	12%
Rice University (TX)	$20,140	35%	$16,889	$3,044	100%	$6,154	18%
Fordham University (NY)	$20,104	65%	$14,953	$4,386	75%	$7,806	12%
St. Louis University	$18,858	60%	$12,875	$4,192	59%	$9,455	24%
Clarkson University (NY)	$18,723	75%	$11,200	$4,294	87%	$7,873	8%
University of St. Thomas (MN)	$18,695	46%	$9,049	$4,408	99%	$7,920	12%
New York University	$18,652	54%	$12,592	$5,070	64%	$6,925	10%
Howard University (DC)	$17,077	63%	$9,559	$3,636	84%	$10,755	13%
Alliant International University (CA)	$17,000	48%	$6,700	$3,300	70%	$2,000	31%
University of Hartford (CT)	$16,790	62%	$12,322	$4,504	72%	$7,169	30%
Marquette University (WI)	$16,770	58%	$11,445	$4,991	74%	$7,953	7%
DePaul University (IL)	$16,309	59%	$10,461	$4,581	66%	$8,144	7%
Catholic University of America (DC)	$16,279	52%	$12,399	$4,793	83%	$8,962	40%
Northeastern University (MA)	$16,085	60%	$11,629	$4,746	61%	$13,717	20%
Duquesne University (PA)	$15,919	66%	$11,275	$4,257	87%	$8,077	21%
St. John's University (NY)	$15,807	81%	$7,255	$4,268	65%	$8,180	3%
Miami University–Oxford (OH)	$15,665	40%	$4,005	$3,947	75%	$11,606	40%
Seton Hall University (NJ)	$15,660	61%	$4,757	$3,622	66%	$11,959	17%
University of Vermont	$15,408	55%	$10,770	$5,978	78%	$2,157	16%
Baylor University (TX)	$15,392	51%	$10,925	$2,394	67%	$6,981	31%
University of California–Berkeley	$15,203	49%	$10,937	$5,058	89%	$3,402	7%
Biola University (CA)	$15,200	65%	$9,514	$2,969	70%	$11,205	11%
Drexel University (PA)	$15,076	63%	$4,672	$4,299	59%	$9,206	19%
Pace University (NY)	$15,062	70%	$11,094	$4,271	51%	$7,742	5%
University of Virginia	$14,974	24%	$10,916	$4,617	100%	$8,535	14%
University of New Hampshire	$14,888	58%	$2,293	$3,385	78%	$5,827	24%
Adelphi University (NY)	$14,750	66%	$4,850	$4,090	32%	$8,000	18%
Texas Christian University	$14,589	43%	$10,253	$5,957	67%	$8,800	22%
New School University (NY)	$14,338	38%	$10,012	$4,889	81%	$4,157	15%
University of Alabama–Birmingham	$14,304	51%	$3,309	$3,876	40%	$9,814	19%
University of California–Santa Cruz	$14,285	46%	$10,340	$4,656	89%	$6,851	2%
University of California–Los Angeles	$14,036	53%	$10,888	$4,948	83%	$3,412	4%
Nova Southeastern University (FL)	$13,662	94%	$7,125	$4,717	64%	$11,534	6%
University of California–Riverside	$13,538	60%	$9,852	$5,618	84%	$5,606	1%
University of California–Santa Barbara	$13,437	44%	$10,220	$5,807	82%	$5,771	2%
Temple University (PA)	$13,365	71%	$4,904	$3,514	83%	$4,603	24%
University of California–San Diego	$13,342	51%	$9,540	$5,109	84%	$6,824	3%
New Jersey Institute of Technology	$13,200	57%	N/A	N/A	81%	$7,964	13%
University of California–Irvine	$12,914	47%	$10,067	$5,633	85%	$7,381	4%
Hofstra University (NY)	$12,750	59%	$8,475	$4,400	52%	$8,050	14%
University of Maryland–College Park	$12,598	37%	$4,715	$3,794	69%	$6,129	16%
SUNY College of Environmental Science and Forestry	$12,450	75%	$6,500	$6,400	100%	$2,000	2%
University of California–Davis	$11,697	48%	$9,072	$4,515	75%	$4,342	6%
University of Rhode Island	$11,659	51%	$5,883	$6,713	61%	$4,607	4%
University of Pittsburgh	$11,605	52%	$4,486	$4,542	76%	$9,699	7%
Rutgers–New Brunswick (NJ)	$11,569	50%	$8,034	$4,170	72%	$5,311	10%
SUNY–Binghamton	$11,516	46%	$4,788	$4,345	80%	$4,162	3%
University of Wisconsin–Madison	$11,288	39%	$4,928	$3,813	N/A	$2,935	15%
University of Massachusetts–Amherst	$11,276	51%	$7,158	$4,007	87%	$4,796	2%
Purdue University–West Lafayette (IN)	$11,256	41%	$8,293	$4,107	92%	$11,431	14%
University of Delaware	$11,100	38%	$6,300	$4,900	79%	$4,400	22%
University of Minnesota–Twin Cities	$11,007	48%	$6,663	$7,369	83%	$4,363	11%
University of Washington	$10,900	48%	$6,500	$4,500	86%	$4,400	2%
University of Illinois–Chicago	$10,753	54%	$8,389	$3,665	91%	$3,665	7%
Texas A&M University–College Station	$10,747	36%	$6,795	$4,984	87%	$4,406	23%
College of William and Mary (VA)	$10,682	27%	$9,613	$2,648	87%	$5,237	5%
University of Missouri–Columbia	$10,676	42%	$5,404	$4,177	85%	$4,170	23%
University of Missouri–Rolla	$10,513	52%	$6,106	$4,645	78%	$6,220	29%
University of Michigan–Ann Arbor	$10,234	45%	$7,035	$5,695	90%	$5,418	25%
University of Florida	$10,227	38%	$4,604	$3,707	83%	$4,427	54%
Rutgers–Newark (NJ)	$10,138	64%	$7,362	$4,151	72%	$5,087	5%
University of North Carolina–Chapel Hill	$10,051	32%	$7,547	$3,919	100%	$5,425	15%
Southern Illinois University–Carbondale	$10,016	55%	$6,185	$3,884	98%	$3,280	7%
University of Colorado–Boulder	$9,973	32%	$4,411	$5,039	90%	$2,667	37%
University of Illinois–Urbana-Champaign	$9,939	39%	$7,519	$4,487	84%	$3,713	15%
University of Missouri–Kansas City	$9,859	64%	$5,428	$6,311	51%	$4,223	13%
University of Maryland–Baltimore County	$9,827	44%	$4,766	$4,315	73%	$3,667	8%
University of Oklahoma	$9,782	53%	$3,686	$4,612	87%	$3,895	12%
Ohio State University–Columbus	$9,726	52%	$5,713	$4,085	69%	$4,047	17%
Texas Woman's University	$9,718	58%	$4,011	$3,775	95%	$2,705	5%

Where the money is: Schools that award the most need-based aid

	Average amount of aid package	% students receiving need-based package	Average need-based grant	Average need-based loan	Average % of need met	Average merit award	% students receiving merit awards
University of Missouri–St. Louis	$9,633	53%	$4,137	$4,371	65%	$4,701	10%
Central Michigan University	$9,632	51%	$3,929	$5,129	94%	$3,096	10%
National-Louis University (IL)	$9,559	64%	N/A	N/A	49%	$1,863	8%
University of Northern Colorado	$9,529	44%	$3,747	$3,618	100%	$2,632	9%
University of South Carolina–Columbia	$9,501	49%	$3,426	$3,486	71%	$5,950	32%
Northern Illinois University	$9,489	52%	$5,859	$3,968	70%	$1,230	2%
University of Maine–Orono	$9,460	63%	$5,075	$4,228	83%	$5,272	21%
University of Texas–El Paso	$9,294	54%	$4,846	$4,922	78%	$1,482	6%
University of Idaho	$9,287	58%	$3,133	$5,733	76%	$3,562	26%
University of South Florida	$9,237	46%	$4,324	$4,340	25%	$2,503	8%
University of Texas–Austin	$9,210	54%	$5,890	$4,600	90%	$3,120	29%
Iowa State University	$9,181	56%	$4,235	$4,328	81%	$1,880	27%
University of Colorado–Denver and Health Sciences Center	$9,163	48%	$5,138	$4,306	73%	$1,524	3%
Clemson University (SC)	$9,154	38%	$3,337	$4,192	39%	$3,671	18%
Washington State University	$9,141	48%	$5,820	$4,258	80%	$3,026	5%
University of Connecticut	$9,070	47%	$5,958	$5,122	69%	$5,951	7%
Illinois State University	$9,056	44%	$6,844	$4,921	84%	$4,230	2%
University of Texas–Arlington	$9,016	52%	$4,229	$5,798	74%	$2,323	13%
University of Texas–Dallas	$9,016	40%	$4,208	$4,670	72%	$8,114	19%
University of Alaska–Fairbanks	$8,899	40%	$4,354	$6,256	69%	$3,362	16%
Oklahoma State University	$8,867	51%	$3,714	$4,035	73%	$3,396	23%
University of North Dakota	$8,807	54%	$3,129	$4,345	86%	$2,941	4%
University of Arkansas	$8,798	39%	$3,630	$4,276	64%	$5,796	19%
Florida State University	$8,752	32%	$3,003	$3,122	70%	$1,797	4%
University of Massachusetts–Lowell	$8,733	48%	$4,419	$4,270	93%	$3,843	3%
New Mexico State University	$8,728	57%	$5,947	$4,189	65%	$3,066	20%
Oregon State University	$8,696	51%	$2,532	$3,145	67%	$2,327	0%
Georgia State University	$8,671	54%	$4,309	$4,002	76%	$4,270	21%
Michigan Technological University	$8,517	52%	$5,025	$4,394	78%	$3,300	20%
Michigan State University	$8,468	40%	$4,167	$3,861	72%	$3,824	7%
SUNY–Stony Brook	$8,444	55%	$5,375	$4,074	68%	$3,247	5%
North Carolina State University–Raleigh	$8,403	38%	$5,917	$3,066	81%	$7,344	23%
SUNY–Albany	$8,258	54%	$4,673	$4,154	73%	$3,073	7%
University of Nebraska–Lincoln	$8,258	46%	$4,867	$4,011	85%	$4,999	6%
Bowling Green State University (OH)	$8,245	57%	$3,575	$3,757	53%	$5,274	10%
Colorado State University	$8,188	39%	$4,914	$5,355	82%	$2,275	5%
University of Louisville (KY)	$8,175	51%	$5,473	$3,976	55%	$5,184	16%
University of Utah	$8,086	41%	$3,970	$4,622	50%	$3,471	4%
Virginia Tech	$8,064	35%	$4,213	$3,570	77%	$2,122	5%
New Mexico Institute of Mining and Technology	$8,040	39%	$4,186	$4,202	93%	$4,851	35%
Western Michigan University	$8,000	49%	$4,200	$4,000	69%	$3,600	11%
George Mason University (VA)	$7,991	36%	$4,434	$3,830	68%	$4,116	2%
University of Alabama	$7,980	39%	$3,732	$4,895	70%	$5,151	29%
Virginia Commonwealth University	$7,932	49%	$4,008	$3,780	65%	$4,785	4%
Northern Arizona University	$7,919	51%	$4,651	$3,726	64%	$3,416	17%
University of Kentucky	$7,861	38%	$4,854	$3,765	81%	$2,821	3%
University of North Texas	$7,830	45%	$3,960	$3,923	68%	$3,001	7%
University of Arizona	$7,810	39%	$6,167	$4,025	64%	$5,014	20%
University of Houston	$7,775	52%	$4,975	$4,133	52%	$3,884	1%
Auburn University (AL)	$7,683	32%	$4,477	$4,035	48%	$3,230	4%
University of Oregon	$7,656	41%	$4,034	$4,489	64%	$1,701	6%
Mississippi State University	$7,653	51%	$3,767	$3,419	64%	$2,519	16%
Portland State University (OR)	$7,576	53%	$4,420	$4,498	55%	$2,258	1%
South Dakota State University	$7,550	79%	$3,128	$4,486	83%	$1,002	13%
University of Tennessee	$7,531	53%	$5,168	$3,775	65%	$10,145	1%
University of Southern Mississippi	$7,504	69%	$3,601	$4,497	85%	$2,104	7%
Indiana University of Pennsylvania	$7,498	65%	$3,875	$3,698	76%	$2,249	3%
Idaho State University	$7,494	70%	$3,044	$3,560	67%	$2,243	13%
University of Cincinnati	$7,476	54%	$4,449	$3,888	63%	$4,696	15%
University of Iowa	$7,445	51%	$4,459	$3,847	97%	$1,950	14%
San Diego State University	$7,400	48%	$5,700	$4,000	71%	$1,700	2%
Indiana State University	$7,321	56%	$4,844	$3,786	78%	$2,889	8%
University of Georgia	$7,320	25%	$5,731	$3,683	74%	$1,870	6%
Texas A&M University–Commerce	$7,254	65%	$4,697	$3,599	68%	$1,953	13%
Cleveland State University	$7,247	72%	$4,979	$3,901	48%	$8,133	11%
Texas Tech University	$7,220	39%	$4,499	$3,906	66%	$1,847	3%
University of Montana	$7,199	56%	$3,408	$3,386	65%	$4,770	19%
University of Dayton (OH)	$7,187	57%	$2,381	$3,631	93%	$8,793	15%
Louisiana State University–Baton Rouge	$7,070	43%	$4,664	$3,885	57%	$3,603	10%
Pennsylvania State University–University Park	$7,062	49%	$4,509	$4,247	62%	$2,506	11%

	Average amount of aid package	% students receiving need-based package	Average need-based grant	Average need-based loan	Average % of need met	Average merit award	% students receiving merit awards
Kent State University (OH)	$7,040	58%	$4,670	$3,820	56%	$3,761	8%
University of Wyoming	$7,017	43%	$3,272	$4,022	75%	$1,434	17%
Florida Atlantic University	$7,012	46%	$5,796	$3,741	74%	$2,315	4%
West Virginia University	$7,011	50%	$3,225	$4,034	88%	$3,036	37%
University of North Carolina–Greensboro	$7,008	65%	$3,814	$3,654	60%	$3,909	5%
Wayne State University (MI)	$6,958	54%	$3,484	$3,756	64%	$2,030	2%
Indiana University–Bloomington	$6,940	54%	$5,546	$4,161	59%	$4,333	6%
Indiana University-Purdue University–Indianapolis	$6,929	60%	$4,829	$3,704	51%	$3,061	4%
University at Buffalo–SUNY	$6,890	50%	$3,237	$3,246	70%	$2,780	11%
Ohio University	$6,870	48%	N/A	N/A	52%	$3,755	11%
University of Akron (OH)	$6,798	62%	$4,427	$3,415	49%	$3,419	5%
Old Dominion University (VA)	$6,417	56%	$3,610	$3,744	72%	$3,481	4%
University of Nevada–Las Vegas	$6,416	42%	$3,117	$4,104	70%	$2,473	22%
Louisiana Tech University	$6,406	42%	$4,641	$3,037	60%	$2,165	14%
University of Kansas	$6,401	40%	$5,708	$4,284	56%	$4,032	1%
East Carolina University (NC)	$6,085	32%	$3,974	$3,597	65%	$2,593	4%
University of Alabama–Huntsville	$6,064	43%	$3,642	$4,499	60%	$2,475	21%
University of Hawaii–Manoa	$6,039	32%	$3,617	$3,664	66%	$2,393	8%
University of Wisconsin–Milwaukee	$5,966	53%	$4,587	$3,722	57%	$1,970	2%
Wichita State University (KS)	$5,924	62%	$2,754	$2,856	46%	$4,209	14%
Kansas State University	$5,850	49%	$2,442	$3,505	76%	$1,918	6%
Alabama Agricultural and Mechanical University	$5,705	48%	$4,333	$3,006	26%	$8,700	8%
University of Louisiana–Lafayette	$5,627	51%	$3,733	$3,656	56%	$1,763	12%
University of South Dakota	$5,545	60%	$3,061	$3,790	75%	$2,954	17%
Georgia Institute of Technology	$5,461	30%	$4,334	$3,995	42%	$2,964	7%
University of Central Florida	$5,448	48%	$3,118	$4,106	74%	$1,816	12%
Utah State University	$5,000	45%	$3,100	$3,800	59%	$2,900	9%
North Dakota State University	$4,884	59%	$3,130	$4,128	67%	$1,506	8%
East Tennessee State University	$4,762	56%	$3,009	$3,216	82%	$3,054	14%
Brigham Young University–Provo (UT)	$4,302	36%	$2,533	$1,769	43%	$2,914	29%
University of Memphis	$4,056	52%	$2,665	$3,169	80%	$4,193	16%
University of South Alabama	$2,951	44%	$1,734	$1,869	27%	N/A	N/A
Tennessee State University	$2,875	N/A	$108	$777	82%	$8,370	N/A

Liberal Arts Colleges

	Average amount of aid package	% students receiving need-based package	Average need-based grant	Average need-based loan	Average % of need met	Average merit award	% students receiving merit awards
Amherst College (MA)	$31,048	48%	$28,713	$2,935	100%	$0	0%
St. Lawrence University (NY)	$30,445	66%	$16,983	$4,427	92%	$13,726	14%
Williams College (MA)	$30,309	44%	$27,189	$2,976	100%	$0	0%
Pomona College (CA)	$29,784	53%	$25,484	$2,920	100%	$0	0%
Smith College (MA)	$29,776	60%	$23,426	$3,772	100%	$5,709	6%
Mills College (CA)	$29,584	76%	$18,880	$4,952	91%	$15,491	10%
Wesleyan University (CT)	$29,341	48%	$24,335	$4,429	100%	$0	0%
Bowdoin College (ME)	$29,090	45%	$24,785	$3,285	100%	$1,000	3%
Occidental College (CA)	$29,089	55%	$22,840	$5,607	100%	$16,180	27%
Pitzer College (CA)	$29,002	40%	$23,424	$4,171	100%	$8,125	4%
Swarthmore College (PA)	$28,914	48%	$24,980	$3,179	100%	$31,196	1%
Barnard College (NY)	$28,790	42%	$24,611	$3,693	100%	$0	0%
Sarah Lawrence College (NY)	$28,671	50%	$21,981	$3,045	90%	$5,139	6%
Skidmore College (NY)	$28,452	41%	$22,928	$3,818	94%	$10,000	0%
Middlebury College (VT)	$28,295	44%	$24,854	$3,963	100%	$0	0%
Vassar College (NY)	$27,982	54%	$22,754	$3,378	100%	$0	0%
Trinity College (CT)	$27,920	40%	N/A	N/A	100%	$16,807	0%
Wellesley College (MA)	$27,907	60%	$25,283	$3,197	100%	N/A	0%
Colgate University (NY)	$27,795	44%	$25,396	$4,350	100%	$0	0%

Where the money is: Schools that award the most need-based aid

Liberal Arts Colleges, continued

	Average amount of aid package	% students receiving need-based package	Average need-based grant	Average need-based loan	Average % of need met	Average merit award	% students receiving merit awards
Scripps College (CA)	$27,665	43%	$23,122	$3,872	100%	$15,715	11%
Bryn Mawr College (PA)	$27,582	54%	$22,888	$4,479	98%	$11,082	2%
Colorado College	$27,522	45%	$23,717	$4,835	91%	$15,144	11%
Dickinson College (PA)	$27,496	49%	$20,818	$5,224	96%	$12,318	12%
Bates College (ME)	$27,428	40%	$24,000	$3,877	100%	N/A	N/A
Union College (NY)	$27,359	50%	$22,736	$3,856	97%	$11,824	13%
Mount Holyoke College (MA)	$27,253	63%	$22,500	$4,470	100%	$11,981	7%
Colby College (ME)	$27,177	38%	$25,352	$3,306	100%	$0	0%
Hampshire College (MA)	$27,080	55%	$20,600	$4,150	97%	$4,390	10%
Hamilton College (NY)	$27,035	52%	$21,045	$3,996	100%	$9,148	5%
Haverford College (PA)	$26,990	43%	$24,073	$3,884	100%	N/A	N/A
Carleton College (MN)	$26,649	60%	$20,842	$3,691	100%	$4,876	8%
Connecticut College	$26,014	42%	$23,748	$4,076	100%	N/A	N/A
Bennington College (VT)	$25,712	69%	$21,449	$3,798	74%	$7,498	5%
Claremont McKenna College (CA)	$25,674	50%	$22,823	$3,406	100%	$6,116	6%
Denison University (OH)	$25,367	44%	$19,189	$5,013	93%	$12,464	9%
Harvey Mudd College (CA)	$25,315	53%	$22,062	$4,246	100%	$5,157	21%
Macalester College (MN)	$25,238	69%	$19,806	$3,627	100%	$4,686	6%
Washington and Lee University (VA)	$25,158	33%	$19,037	$4,708	99%	$13,824	13%
Bard College (NY)	$25,107	59%	N/A	N/A	89%	$10,750	4%
Gettysburg College (PA)	$25,089	56%	$19,711	$4,495	100%	$9,571	12%
Kalamazoo College (MI)	$25,005	52%	$9,367	N/A	N/A	N/A	N/A
Kenyon College (OH)	$24,982	43%	$21,897	$3,810	98%	$12,072	23%
DePauw University (IN)	$24,873	47%	$14,486	$4,637	98%	$12,245	49%
Lafayette College (PA)	$24,675	54%	$22,543	$4,114	100%	$13,141	7%
College of the Atlantic (ME)	$24,478	93%	$20,849	$3,990	95%	$4,200	6%
Rhodes College (TN)	$24,349	35%	$13,966	$6,015	88%	$9,887	42%
Agnes Scott College (GA)	$24,314	63%	$17,866	$3,923	97%	$12,976	33%
Hobart and William Smith Colleges (NY)	$24,303	61%	$20,480	$3,630	88%	$11,062	16%
Franklin and Marshall College (PA)	$24,283	48%	$19,856	$5,040	100%	$8,826	24%
Lewis and Clark College (OR)	$24,262	61%	$19,851	$5,020	87%	$7,913	14%
Ursinus College (PA)	$23,938	83%	$18,558	$4,607	85%	$9,000	15%
Grinnell College (IA)	$23,921	55%	$17,919	$5,131	100%	$10,564	34%
College of Wooster (OH)	$23,837	58%	$17,286	$6,333	93%	$11,350	27%
Whittier College (CA)	$23,742	69%	$11,316	$7,579	71%	$11,219	17%
Oberlin College (OH)	$23,710	59%	$18,007	$4,248	100%	$11,029	10%
University of Richmond (VA)	$23,258	34%	$20,314	$2,755	100%	$15,469	14%
Wheaton College (MA)	$23,155	49%	$18,303	$4,667	94%	$10,760	12%
Drew University (NJ)	$23,012	48%	$17,577	$4,843	81%	$12,232	28%
Lawrence University (WI)	$22,900	61%	$16,061	$5,660	100%	$9,270	31%
Antioch College (OH)	$22,853	N/A	$13,719	$4,910	100%	$9,571	4%
Wofford College (SC)	$22,401	52%	$16,648	$4,371	89%	$9,884	25%
Wabash College (IN)	$22,192	70%	$15,660	$2,353	100%	$11,150	26%
Furman University (SC)	$22,162	44%	$18,486	$5,083	86%	$10,198	28%
Whitman College (WA)	$22,050	55%	$16,850	$4,250	89%	$8,250	38%
St. Olaf College (MN)	$21,869	62%	$14,973	$5,515	100%	$7,210	17%
Eckerd College (FL)	$21,718	57%	$14,207	$3,237	90%	$9,330	35%
Wittenberg University (OH)	$21,691	75%	$16,720	$3,465	88%	$9,776	18%
Presbyterian College (SC)	$21,609	61%	N/A	N/A	91%	$8,614	32%
Lake Forest College (IL)	$21,562	78%	$17,771	$4,821	100%	$10,967	15%
West Virginia Wesleyan College	$21,518	74%	$16,286	$4,397	88%	$11,945	23%
Earlham College (IN)	$21,500	59%	$13,243	$4,783	85%	$6,916	22%
Randolph-Macon Woman's College (VA)	$21,368	67%	$16,016	$4,379	88%	$14,855	33%
Knox College (IL)	$21,317	67%	$16,117	$5,138	95%	$10,011	29%
College of the Holy Cross (MA)	$21,254	53%	$18,110	$4,198	100%	$15,517	3%
Allegheny College (PA)	$21,250	68%	$14,950	$4,720	92%	$10,635	28%
Bucknell University (PA)	$21,000	48%	$17,300	$5,200	100%	$12,356	1%
Austin College (TX)	$20,989	54%	$13,446	$5,857	99%	$9,199	38%
Ohio Wesleyan University	$20,854	56%	$14,473	$3,525	82%	$11,439	41%
Hartwick College (NY)	$20,494	74%	N/A	N/A	80%	$10,835	22%
University of Puget Sound (WA)	$20,466	59%	$15,106	$5,274	80%	$7,210	27%
McDaniel College (MD)	$20,398	62%	$9,091	$4,505	94%	$10,326	33%
Coe College (IA)	$20,370	77%	$14,228	$6,229	90%	$11,287	20%
Albion College (MI)	$20,101	60%	$15,969	$4,444	94%	$11,250	37%
Goucher College (MD)	$19,792	55%	$16,011	$4,827	82%	$13,652	30%
University of Judaism (CA)	$19,700	83%	$8,573	$4,386	75%	N/A	N/A
Sewanee–University of the South (TN)	$19,574	47%	$16,156	$3,311	97%	$11,581	20%
Luther College (IA)	$19,374	71%	$12,386	$5,150	88%	$6,301	29%
Southwestern University (TX)	$19,315	50%	$13,251	$4,530	97%	$7,935	29%
Beloit College (WI)	$19,108	77%	$14,736	$5,872	100%	$13,410	14%

	Average amount of aid package	% students receiving need-based package	Average need-based grant	Average need-based loan	Average % of need met	Average merit award	% students receiving merit awards
Washington and Jefferson College (PA)	$19,096	73%	$14,301	$3,725	74%	$9,297	20%
College of St. Benedict (MN)	$19,044	66%	$12,290	$6,030	91%	$8,210	29%
Roanoke College (VA)	$18,931	73%	$15,168	$4,267	89%	$10,255	23%
Seton Hill University (PA)	$18,903	75%	$12,100	$3,895	75%	$7,100	4%
Westminster College (PA)	$18,665	78%	$14,511	$4,031	89%	$8,818	20%
Susquehanna University (PA)	$18,578	64%	$14,698	$3,879	81%	$9,655	26%
Wheaton College (IL)	$18,555	49%	$12,710	$5,523	85%	$3,658	19%
Juniata College (PA)	$18,539	76%	$14,789	$3,981	77%	$12,311	23%
Ripon College (WI)	$18,534	75%	$14,326	$4,453	93%	$14,807	18%
Centre College (KY)	$18,526	61%	$15,809	$4,110	88%	$10,381	34%
Westmont College (CA)	$18,521	55%	$13,480	$5,461	67%	$9,990	32%
Cornell College (IA)	$18,510	80%	$15,005	$4,370	91%	$11,705	25%
Illinois Wesleyan University	$18,285	54%	$13,565	$4,935	93%	$8,691	31%
Hope College (MI)	$18,272	59%	$12,828	$4,680	87%	$6,880	29%
St. Anselm College (NH)	$18,164	71%	$12,728	$5,218	83%	$13,306	18%
Erskine College (SC)	$18,100	80%	$10,500	$4,250	88%	$10,360	16%
Davidson College (NC)	$18,024	35%	$15,766	$3,926	100%	$8,824	22%
Hollins University (VA)	$17,913	61%	$14,983	$4,761	75%	$9,830	25%
Hampden-Sydney College (VA)	$17,891	47%	$14,035	$4,134	83%	$16,595	50%
Georgetown College (KY)	$17,844	66%	$13,703	$4,145	92%	$8,581	32%
Lycoming College (PA)	$17,826	83%	$13,513	$4,261	77%	$8,949	13%
Alma College (MI)	$17,812	75%	$13,480	$5,228	84%	$12,840	23%
Millsaps College (MS)	$17,774	57%	$13,773	$4,241	80%	$13,310	38%
St. John's University (MN)	$17,573	58%	N/A	N/A	87%	$7,643	35%
University of Dallas	$17,561	61%	$12,117	$5,041	86%	$9,023	33%
Hanover College (IN)	$17,526	77%	$14,918	$3,371	78%	$14,843	21%
Rosemont College (PA)	$17,513	77%	$14,389	$3,550	76%	$16,134	22%
Randolph-Macon College (VA)	$17,459	60%	$12,821	$4,996	82%	$12,387	36%
Bridgewater College (VA)	$17,309	68%	$13,371	$3,537	84%	$7,895	30%
Wells College (NY)	$17,290	74%	$11,668	$4,737	92%	$4,960	14%
Augustana College (IL)	$17,229	68%	$11,882	$4,541	86%	$8,087	13%
Gustavus Adolphus College (MN)	$17,200	61%	$13,900	$4,350	87%	$5,750	28%
Albright College (PA)	$17,140	74%	$13,532	$4,248	75%	$1,230	16%
Moravian College (PA)	$17,118	74%	$12,278	$4,175	74%	$13,668	22%
Adrian College (MI)	$17,074	78%	$10,282	$4,235	98%	$8,059	20%
St. Vincent College (PA)	$16,963	75%	$12,070	$2,905	85%	$8,933	20%
Stephens College (MO)	$16,894	73%	$6,533	$3,907	83%	$7,714	21%
Goshen College (IN)	$16,555	78%	$11,680	$4,887	86%	$8,031	7%
Transylvania University (KY)	$16,537	60%	$12,598	$3,829	87%	$11,584	38%
Thomas Aquinas College (CA)	$16,479	67%	$11,955	$3,297	100%	$0	0%
Franklin Pierce College (NH)	$16,346	74%	$11,888	$4,486	67%	$11,589	19%
Washington College (MD)	$16,314	44%	$14,939	$4,583	90%	$10,743	40%
Westminster College (MO)	$16,226	58%	$11,001	$2,631	89%	$8,946	41%
Birmingham-Southern College (AL)	$15,595	44%	$12,202	$4,401	79%	$11,106	33%
Sweet Briar College (VA)	$15,293	64%	$13,706	$4,755	39%	$11,213	46%
William Jewell College (MO)	$15,288	57%	$11,260	$4,502	N/A	N/A	N/A
Hendrix College (AR)	$15,269	56%	$10,927	$4,438	82%	$15,672	42%
King College (TN)	$15,045	76%	$12,080	$4,335	77%	$9,793	16%
Pine Manor College (MA)	$14,984	80%	$11,556	$3,470	73%	$6,108	3%
Houghton College (NY)	$14,861	76%	$9,422	$3,691	72%	$10,810	5%
San Diego Christian College (CA)	$14,547	84%	$5,500	$3,850	80%	$4,565	25%
Gordon College (MA)	$14,540	67%	$10,093	$4,473	70%	$12,383	30%
Siena College (NY)	$14,486	68%	$10,784	$4,282	78%	$6,485	13%
Concordia College–Moorhead (MN)	$14,468	70%	$9,349	$4,831	92%	$5,643	27%
Virginia Wesleyan College	$14,385	63%	$3,239	$4,077	66%	$5,992	22%
Emory and Henry College (VA)	$14,362	79%	$10,834	$3,197	72%	$10,072	20%
Muskingum College (OH)	$14,348	77%	$10,498	$3,981	85%	$5,271	18%
Virginia Military Institute	$14,334	40%	$12,636	$3,708	94%	$5,817	15%
Olivet College (MI)	$14,121	83%	$9,990	$3,857	75%	$10,830	12%
Warner Pacific College (OR)	$14,048	89%	$8,146	$3,570	74%	$6,521	4%
Albertson College (ID)	$13,993	64%	$4,060	$4,444	83%	$7,791	32%
Salem College (NC)	$13,980	73%	N/A	N/A	100%	$13,732	7%
Lyon College (AR)	$13,749	70%	$9,953	$4,616	77%	$10,421	27%
Hillsdale College (MI)	$13,000	32%	$8,000	$5,130	80%	$6,750	26%
Nebraska Wesleyan University	$12,858	68%	$8,532	$4,298	69%	$5,881	23%
Virginia Union University	$12,687	82%	$3,681	$3,968	67%	$5,096	1%
University of Minnesota–Morris	$12,660	67%	$5,885	$7,333	82%	$3,052	20%
St. Andrews Presbyterian College (NC)	$12,198	59%	$8,928	$3,401	73%	$8,776	39%
University of Pittsburgh–Bradford	$12,000	83%	$4,000	$4,281	78%	$4,000	12%
New College of Florida	$11,792	36%	$7,549	$3,764	94%	$3,580	49%

Where the money is: Schools that award the most need-based aid

Liberal Arts Colleges, continued

	Average amount of aid package	% students receiving need-based package	Average need-based grant	Average need-based loan	Average % of need met	Average merit award	% students receiving merit awards
St. Augustine's College (NC)	$11,688	73%	$9,164	$1,131	7%	$6,816	32%
Schreiner University (TX)	$11,682	82%	$8,981	$2,795	33%	$12,968	19%
Guilford College (NC)	$11,661	46%	$8,325	$4,145	67%	$7,006	18%
Marymount Manhattan College (NY)	$11,386	63%	$4,222	$3,711	46%	$4,122	12%
Evergreen State College (WA)	$11,066	58%	$5,672	$4,071	81%	$3,793	0%
Richard Stockton College of New Jersey	$11,022	52%	$5,937	$3,980	59%	$2,523	6%
Wesleyan College (GA)	$10,758	62%	$7,913	$3,799	79%	$13,943	38%
Spelman College (GA)	$10,500	75%	N/A	N/A	67%	$24,000	0%
Lindsey Wilson College (KY)	$10,491	91%	N/A	N/A	N/A	N/A	N/A
Texas A&M University–Galveston	$10,288	50%	$4,413	$3,102	22%	$7,103	2%
Lees-McRae College (NC)	$10,174	65%	$4,976	$3,705	90%	$4,800	42%
Marlboro College (VT)	$10,057	75%	$7,621	$3,728	80%	$8,834	91%
Blackburn College (IL)	$9,808	85%	$6,179	$3,030	91%	$6,499	10%
Lane College (TN)	$9,403	82%	$3,852	$3,465	80%	$0	0%
Bennett College (NC)	$9,036	85%	$6,827	$3,183	42%	$14,393	9%
Paine College (GA)	$8,964	93%	$6,054	$2,887	60%	$10,442	5%
Western State College of Colorado	$8,800	37%	$2,500	$5,000	40%	$1,500	25%
Huntingdon College (AL)	$8,793	63%	$3,252	$3,718	59%	$6,561	32%
University of North Carolina–Asheville	$8,152	42%	$3,400	$3,855	78%	$3,389	9%
Morehouse College (GA)	$7,859	99%	$6,125	$4,250	49%	$7,544	68%
Coastal Carolina University (SC)	$7,427	57%	$3,229	$6,524	51%	$8,872	22%
University of Maine–Presque Isle	$7,248	57%	$4,509	$3,323	89%	$4,532	8%
Massachusetts College of Liberal Arts	$7,130	65%	$4,902	$3,241	69%	$4,135	21%
University of Virginia–Wise	$7,102	70%	$3,750	$3,068	94%	$1,581	17%
University of Pittsburgh–Greensburg	$7,063	77%	$3,970	$3,661	54%	$2,676	2%
Fort Lewis College (CO)	$7,050	47%	$4,097	$3,673	72%	$1,916	6%
California State University–Monterey Bay	$6,343	54%	N/A	N/A	63%	$3,000	0%
St. Mary's College of Maryland	$6,250	46%	$4,000	$5,500	62%	$4,000	24%
Christopher Newport University (VA)	$6,229	35%	$4,086	$3,191	76%	$1,661	3%
Mesa State College (CO)	$5,206	58%	$3,546	$3,188	60%	$1,893	4%
Tougaloo College (MS)	$4,775	75%	$2,500	$5,000	50%	$5,000	4%

Universities–Master's (North)

	Average amount of aid package	% students receiving need-based package	Average need-based grant	Average need-based loan	Average % of need met	Average merit award	% students receiving merit awards
Bentley College (MA)	$23,177	52%	$17,666	$5,018	91%	$12,262	10%
Manhattanville College (NY)	$21,904	63%	$10,024	$3,997	79%	$8,496	28%
Ithaca College (NY)	$21,810	70%	$13,967	$6,091	87%	$9,582	10%
Alfred University (NY)	$21,663	84%	$15,798	$5,113	88%	$10,171	7%
Villanova University (PA)	$20,503	44%	$16,202	$4,698	78%	$10,971	5%
Loyola College in Maryland	$20,465	44%	$12,785	$5,730	98%	$11,176	11%
American International College (MA)	$20,200	90%	$10,813	$4,653	82%	$6,741	15%
Regis College (MA)	$20,003	80%	$10,410	$5,166	62%	$7,940	10%
Cabrini College (PA)	$19,399	73%	$5,659	$3,919	84%	$7,154	9%
St. Michael's College (VT)	$19,222	65%	$13,953	$4,744	83%	$7,840	17%
Arcadia University (PA)	$19,214	88%	$12,731	$4,834	78%	$7,652	9%
Canisius College (NY)	$18,883	75%	$13,101	$4,039	79%	$9,761	19%
St. Francis University (PA)	$18,573	84%	$13,427	$5,511	84%	$12,433	15%
College of Notre Dame of Maryland	$18,061	74%	$8,635	$4,221	75%	$9,055	8%
Hood College (MD)	$18,020	79%	$14,814	$4,450	87%	$13,256	20%
La Salle University (PA)	$17,999	73%	$12,804	$4,530	86%	$10,868	20%
St. Joseph College (CT)	$17,997	86%	$11,289	$7,335	70%	$11,492	13%
Lebanon Valley College (PA)	$17,982	78%	$14,836	$4,222	88%	$10,104	18%
Rider University (NJ)	$17,454	67%	$11,825	$3,937	70%	$8,239	16%
St. Peter's College (NJ)	$17,370	64%	$8,033	$3,397	75%	$11,437	14%
Fairfield University (CT)	$17,079	47%	$11,906	$4,111	65%	$10,723	7%
College of Mount St. Vincent (NY)	$17,000	78%	$7,600	$4,100	74%	$0	N/A
Providence College (RI)	$17,000	60%	$11,000	$6,150	86%	$8,500	10%
St. Bonaventure University (NY)	$16,944	71%	$11,762	$4,555	82%	$6,868	16%
Wilkes University (PA)	$16,882	79%	$12,315	$3,787	82%	$8,838	13%
Le Moyne College (NY)	$16,821	80%	$12,945	$4,423	78%	$9,415	10%
Niagara University (NY)	$16,821	75%	$9,334	$4,422	83%	$8,173	19%
Marywood University (PA)	$16,474	82%	$11,226	$4,311	75%	$7,724	15%

	Average amount of aid package	% students receiving need-based package	Average need-based grant	Average need-based loan	Average % of need met	Average merit award	% students receiving merit awards
St. Joseph's College (ME)	$16,472	81%	$10,328	$6,098	83%	$12,702	18%
Salve Regina University (RI)	$16,392	66%	$11,946	$4,688	69%	$6,725	15%
Emmanuel College (MA)	$16,201	78%	$8,209	$4,368	70%	$9,202	14%
Norwich University (VT)	$16,159	78%	$12,289	$4,611	77%	$17,951	24%
University of Scranton (PA)	$15,912	66%	$11,493	$4,572	76%	$7,494	6%
Lesley University (MA)	$15,834	71%	$11,142	$4,183	70%	$6,056	10%
Carlow University (PA)	$15,815	94%	$6,403	$4,382	N/A	N/A	N/A
Wheelock College (MA)	$15,741	91%	$8,248	$4,483	57%	$12,106	6%
St. John Fisher College (NY)	$15,727	81%	$10,103	$6,542	79%	$5,251	16%
Georgian Court University (NJ)	$15,700	92%	$9,651	$8,446	83%	$5,562	8%
University of New England (ME)	$15,659	83%	$10,052	$5,150	67%	$7,770	16%
Wagner College (NY)	$15,642	52%	$11,957	$4,511	73%	$8,286	34%
Springfield College (MA)	$15,637	78%	$11,078	$3,999	77%	$13,898	14%
Nazareth College of Rochester (NY)	$15,551	78%	$10,299	$4,719	76%	$7,811	18%
Philadelphia University	$15,474	68%	$9,974	$4,045	72%	$4,066	26%
Assumption College (MA)	$15,462	70%	$11,400	$4,451	72%	$13,992	23%
Trinity University (DC)	$15,347	84%	$11,345	$4,636	68%	$11,781	7%
Bryant University (RI)	$15,270	65%	$8,615	$4,899	74%	$7,721	15%
Anna Maria College (MA)	$15,242	81%	$10,958	$4,178	75%	$6,913	14%
Gannon University (PA)	$15,226	85%	$11,609	$3,728	72%	$6,260	10%
King's College (PA)	$15,220	81%	$6,373	$4,369	71%	$8,242	17%
Mount St. Mary's University (MD)	$15,181	61%	$11,892	$4,056	77%	$13,552	33%
Simmons College (MA)	$15,085	70%	$10,829	$2,908	58%	$11,898	2%
Sacred Heart University (CT)	$14,943	67%	$9,436	$6,190	70%	$11,498	19%
University of New Haven (CT)	$14,751	74%	$11,257	$4,174	67%	$15,347	13%
Quinnipiac University (CT)	$14,511	57%	$9,613	$4,207	65%	$6,625	10%
Gallaudet University (DC)	$14,284	67%	$12,091	$2,926	75%	$4,323	1%
DeSales University (PA)	$14,278	69%	$11,122	$3,525	75%	$6,118	28%
Rivier College (NH)	$14,176	82%	$8,309	$6,309	77%	$11,230	18%
Nyack College (NY)	$14,124	84%	$8,851	$5,070	65%	$7,089	14%
Emerson College (MA)	$13,823	53%	$11,514	$4,326	67%	$15,260	16%
Monmouth University (NJ)	$13,765	64%	$7,959	$4,413	65%	$4,955	29%
Immaculata University (PA)	$13,725	90%	$7,800	$2,778	50%	$9,463	49%
College Misericordia (PA)	$13,722	81%	$9,527	$6,244	75%	$6,008	10%
Western New England College (MA)	$13,646	71%	$8,462	$3,948	68%	$6,851	9%
New York Institute of Technology	$13,616	74%	$5,089	$3,857	79%	$7,268	13%
Manhattan College (NY)	$13,606	61%	N/A	$3,984	64%	$7,052	16%
Marist College (NY)	$13,439	61%	$9,099	$4,741	68%	$5,837	18%
Dowling College (NY)	$13,385	65%	$2,804	$3,691	87%	$3,690	14%
Iona College (NY)	$13,384	75%	$3,258	$2,794	23%	$9,753	18%
Geneva College (PA)	$13,360	83%	$9,647	$3,634	77%	$8,558	15%
St. Joseph's University (PA)	$13,301	48%	$7,706	$4,890	80%	$7,176	22%
Eastern University (PA)	$13,217	74%	$11,259	$2,678	72%	$7,245	11%
Gwynedd-Mercy College (PA)	$13,189	74%	$10,039	$3,352	73%	$11,737	19%
Suffolk University (MA)	$13,162	54%	$6,828	$4,660	65%	$5,537	9%
Point Park University (PA)	$12,906	80%	$7,234	$5,100	68%	$9,565	18%
College of St. Joseph (VT)	$12,874	91%	$7,430	$5,046	76%	$11,020	9%
Robert Morris University (PA)	$12,784	75%	$6,956	$5,837	70%	$9,451	19%
Long Island University–Brooklyn (NY)	$12,399	84%	$8,744	$4,300	45%	$19,604	4%
Johnson and Wales University (RI)	$12,009	71%	$4,900	$5,788	64%	$4,455	13%
Waynesburg College (PA)	$11,919	84%	$8,890	$3,590	80%	$10,327	12%
SUNY College–Potsdam	$11,771	66%	$4,518	$4,175	78%	$3,637	11%
Touro College (NY)	$11,675	84%	$4,000	$2,625	75%	$2,000	16%
Eastern Connecticut State University	$11,279	66%	$5,742	$6,217	60%	$2,762	5%
Mansfield University of Pennsylvania	$10,934	74%	$3,924	$3,636	56%	$1,830	3%
University of Massachusetts–Dartmouth	$10,805	60%	$5,500	$6,375	95%	$2,500	5%
St. Thomas Aquinas College (NY)	$10,258	61%	$7,947	$3,808	64%	$5,412	14%
Mount St. Mary College (NY)	$10,170	62%	$6,522	$4,461	56%	$10,249	15%
William Paterson University of New Jersey	$10,130	50%	$5,955	$3,800	83%	$4,694	1%
Molloy College (NY)	$10,122	81%	$6,189	$4,797	60%	$10,788	18%
Rutgers–Camden (NJ)	$10,112	62%	$7,063	$4,023	74%	$4,624	6%
SUNY–Plattsburgh	$9,524	59%	$4,262	$6,130	90%	$5,221	27%
SUNY College–Cortland	$9,372	63%	$3,550	$3,784	75%	$6,724	16%
Bloomsburg University of Pennsylvania	$9,356	78%	$4,105	$3,540	65%	$1,642	1%
SUNY College of Arts and Sciences–Geneseo	$9,339	47%	$2,717	$5,424	85%	$1,900	9%
College of New Jersey	$9,317	41%	N/A	N/A	58%	$4,444	22%
SUNY College–Oneonta	$9,244	57%	$3,666	$4,406	64%	$4,893	20%
Lincoln University (PA)	$9,118	83%	$4,889	$3,490	49%	$8,509	6%
University of Southern Maine	$8,754	65%	$3,914	$4,085	76%	$4,409	12%
SUNY–Oswego	$8,622	66%	$3,836	$4,720	84%	$5,746	16%

Where the money is: Schools that award the most need-based aid

Universities–Master's (North), continued

	Average amount of aid package	% students receiving need-based package	Average need-based grant	Average need-based loan	Average % of need met	Average merit award	% students receiving merit awards
SUNY College–Brockport	$8,501	66%	$3,643	$4,571	80%	$3,901	3%
Chestnut Hill College (PA)	$8,500	79%	N/A	N/A	56%	$6,000	11%
Holy Family University (PA)	$8,500	72%	$4,000	$3,875	85%	$6,000	3%
CUNY–Queens College	$8,400	61%	$5,000	$6,000	95%	$1,609	3%
Kean University (NJ)	$7,929	53%	$5,705	$3,848	54%	$2,184	2%
SUNY–Buffalo State College	$7,870	73%	$4,057	$3,889	87%	$3,212	0%
Husson College (ME)	$7,835	65%	$5,363	$3,252	72%	$6,286	15%
Montclair State University (NJ)	$7,826	47%	$2,849	$4,078	54%	$4,789	4%
SUNY–Purchase College	$7,804	53%	$4,757	$4,214	60%	$14,771	17%
California University of Pennsylvania	$7,799	75%	$4,025	$3,571	90%	$3,056	15%
SUNY–Fredonia	$7,690	62%	$2,990	$3,744	79%	$1,605	6%
New Jersey City University	$7,628	73%	$6,049	$3,765	65%	$3,672	1%
Towson University (MD)	$7,602	42%	$5,042	$3,707	64%	$3,906	3%
College of St. Rose (NY)	$7,486	78%	$3,377	$1,987	41%	$2,203	11%
Pennsylvania State–Erie, The Behrend College	$7,395	70%	$4,373	$4,132	63%	$2,593	5%
Millersville University of Pennsylvania	$7,172	50%	$4,002	$3,640	82%	$2,505	3%
CUNY–City College	$7,100	77%	$5,271	$3,200	70%	$2,200	14%
York College of Pennsylvania	$7,015	50%	$4,138	$3,569	71%	$3,090	9%
Clarion University of Pennsylvania	$7,008	69%	$4,535	$3,457	71%	$1,659	5%
Slippery Rock University of Pennsylvania	$6,938	60%	$3,015	$3,162	81%	$5,131	21%
Delaware State University	$6,919	83%	$2,298	$2,950	63%	$8,071	14%
Frostburg State University (MD)	$6,906	48%	$4,075	$3,320	71%	$2,452	10%
Coppin State University (MD)	$6,880	80%	$4,399	$4,034	66%	$2,427	1%
Central Connecticut State University	$6,820	52%	$2,254	$3,294	72%	$2,243	1%
Southern Connecticut State University	$6,629	46%	$4,409	$3,383	79%	$2,935	5%
Fitchburg State College (MA)	$6,565	45%	$3,308	$2,684	93%	$1,767	1%
Lock Haven University of Pennsylvania	$6,562	80%	$4,922	$3,797	77%	$1,575	4%
Edinboro University of Pennsylvania	$6,402	77%	$1,825	$3,227	81%	$1,900	11%
Shippensburg University of Pennsylvania	$6,256	46%	$3,943	$3,446	69%	$615	32%
Framingham State College (MA)	$6,242	56%	$3,393	$2,052	82%	$1,923	2%
Rowan University (NJ)	$6,214	83%	$5,547	$3,476	67%	$2,933	0%
Kutztown University of Pennsylvania	$6,189	60%	$4,133	$3,533	57%	$2,033	3%
CUNY–College of Staten Island	$6,101	52%	$4,991	$3,356	58%	$2,682	5%
Salisbury University (MD)	$6,052	42%	$4,351	$3,356	57%	$3,428	13%
CUNY–Brooklyn College	$5,450	78%	$3,300	$2,850	99%	$4,000	37%
CUNY–Hunter College	$5,383	59%	$4,575	$3,691	80%	$5,805	1%
East Stroudsburg University of Pennsylvania	$5,224	57%	$3,489	$3,780	86%	$7,415	18%
CUNY–Baruch College	$4,800	82%	N/A	N/A	63%	$1,800	7%
CUNY–Lehman College	$3,537	83%	$1,361	$1,559	61%	$1,400	2%
Western Connecticut State University	$3,012	41%	$2,701	$3,503	73%	N/A	1%
SUNY College of Arts and Sciences–New Paltz	$2,367	53%	$2,130	$940	67%	$1,744	3%
University of the District of Columbia	$1,350	N/A	$950	N/A	37%	N/A	N/A

Universities–Master's (South)

	Average amount of aid package	% students receiving need-based package	Average need-based grant	Average need-based loan	Average % of need met	Average merit award	% students receiving merit awards
Rollins College (FL)	$27,679	42%	$23,591	$3,986	90%	$10,122	13%
Mercer University (GA)	$23,102	64%	$14,556	$6,668	91%	$15,854	33%
Stetson University (FL)	$21,991	54%	$16,755	$4,983	86%	$9,975	35%
Mary Baldwin College (VA)	$19,803	71%	$9,693	$3,406	86%	$13,381	24%
Spring Hill College (AL)	$18,907	66%	$13,570	$4,300	80%	$10,316	27%
Converse College (SC)	$18,431	71%	$15,292	$4,426	87%	$16,637	29%
Wheeling Jesuit University (WV)	$17,907	77%	$5,451	$3,758	84%	$8,021	17%
Jacksonville University (FL)	$16,571	71%	$5,331	$3,963	82%	$5,066	16%
Lynn University (FL)	$16,051	36%	$12,320	$4,304	55%	$12,527	29%
Bellarmine University (KY)	$15,600	67%	$11,714	N/A	83%	N/A	N/A
St. Leo University (FL)	$15,485	68%	$10,666	$3,684	86%	$5,845	2%
Piedmont College (GA)	$14,989	71%	$2,312	$4,921	60%	$3,094	11%
Christian Brothers University (TN)	$14,897	68%	$6,028	$4,054	79%	$9,419	25%
Brenau University (GA)	$14,861	73%	$12,411	$3,439	80%	$7,643	18%
University of Tampa (FL)	$14,640	55%	$6,758	$5,036	81%	$6,037	9%
Milligan College (TN)	$14,512	84%	$6,051	$4,098	62%	$5,980	12%

	Average amount of aid package	% students receiving need-based package	Average need-based grant	Average need-based loan	Average % of need met	Average merit award	% students receiving merit awards
Cumberland University (TN)	$14,455	75%	$5,348	$7,143	84%	$4,497	17%
Mississippi College	$14,145	55%	$8,291	$6,706	70%	$8,210	44%
Barry University (FL)	$14,124	74%	$6,639	$4,302	62%	$5,499	7%
Charleston Southern University (SC)	$14,086	84%	$9,858	$4,534	70%	$10,704	14%
Meredith College (NC)	$14,059	68%	$10,948	$3,858	70%	$5,089	12%
Shenandoah University (VA)	$14,013	61%	$7,053	$5,702	85%	$3,950	10%
Tuskegee University (AL)	$13,824	72%	$8,000	$6,006	85%	$6,000	32%
Union University (TN)	$13,650	53%	$4,350	$4,500	N/A	$6,700	22%
Centenary College of Louisiana	$13,618	60%	$11,289	$3,631	75%	$10,270	28%
University of the Cumberlands (KY)	$13,277	83%	$6,032	$3,796	94%	$6,136	4%
Embry Riddle Aeronautical University (FL)	$13,221	60%	$7,070	$4,510	N/A	N/A	N/A
Queens University of Charlotte (NC)	$13,121	58%	$10,304	$3,243	73%	$10,079	39%
Carson-Newman College (TN)	$12,839	72%	$8,983	$3,790	82%	$9,120	26%
Marymount University (VA)	$12,511	56%	$6,834	$3,805	70%	$8,343	17%
Campbell University (NC)	$12,204	57%	$4,083	$4,382	100%	$6,134	14%
Elon University (NC)	$12,161	34%	$6,799	$3,771	67%	$4,119	21%
William Carey College (MS)	$12,000	96%	$6,000	$5,000	85%	$6,000	11%
Samford University (AL)	$11,977	38%	$6,615	$3,487	70%	$4,712	23%
Campbellsville University (KY)	$11,897	77%	$8,953	$3,447	72%	$7,860	16%
Averett University (VA)	$11,583	81%	$8,803	$4,001	68%	$11,412	18%
Warren Wilson College (NC)	$11,365	57%	$8,908	$3,419	75%	$2,203	11%
Freed-Hardeman University (TN)	$10,706	75%	$7,795	$3,875	62%	$12,850	20%
Lipscomb University (TN)	$10,316	52%	$2,916	$4,004	79%	$5,495	46%
University of West Alabama	$10,222	59%	$3,761	$4,239	85%	$3,144	14%
Liberty University (VA)	$10,001	75%	$2,885	$3,737	62%	$5,247	20%
Belmont University (TN)	$9,696	49%	$4,909	$7,215	64%	$5,704	11%
Southern Wesleyan University (SC)	$9,649	27%	$6,873	$3,673	65%	$10,101	5%
Kennesaw State University (GA)	$9,524	38%	$2,690	$3,402	22%	$1,672	30%
Southern University and A&M College (LA)	$9,516	79%	$1,808	$3,997	78%	$2,746	13%
Alcorn State University (MS)	$9,500	85%	N/A	N/A	74%	$5,380	18%
Gardner-Webb University (NC)	$9,305	74%	$2,326	$3,624	67%	$4,291	11%
Tusculum College (TN)	$9,092	68%	$6,313	N/A	61%	$6,043	12%
College of Charleston (SC)	$8,971	37%	$2,897	$3,563	62%	$10,293	10%
The Citadel (SC)	$8,846	49%	N/A	$4,142	58%	$6,578	12%
Trevecca Nazarene University (TN)	$8,846	67%	$6,388	$4,342	52%	$8,622	31%
University of North Carolina–Charlotte	$8,730	45%	$4,215	$3,829	63%	$6,310	16%
Harding University (AR)	$8,584	56%	$4,990	$4,583	68%	$3,370	48%
University of Tennessee–Martin	$8,443	58%	$4,252	$3,613	77%	$4,449	24%
Winthrop University (SC)	$8,437	59%	$6,441	$3,970	64%	$5,409	11%
University of Tennessee–Chattanooga	$8,301	59%	$3,630	$4,671	78%	$3,518	14%
Delta State University (MS)	$8,200	80%	$3,550	$4,280	73%	N/A	N/A
North Carolina Central University	$8,196	80%	$1,818	$3,205	74%	$3,748	1%
Fayetteville State University (NC)	$8,063	77%	$3,460	$4,700	86%	$4,125	7%
University of Montevallo (AL)	$7,966	59%	$6,399	$2,992	63%	$4,985	20%
Morehead State University (KY)	$7,826	67%	$4,263	$3,329	86%	$3,261	18%
Alabama State University	$7,799	84%	$3,592	$3,428	67%	$4,924	2%
Auburn University–Montgomery (AL)	$7,516	52%	$3,275	$3,525	N/A	N/A	N/A
University of Central Arkansas	$7,500	66%	$2,460	$3,500	50%	$3,400	N/A
Marshall University (WV)	$7,230	49%	$3,992	$4,894	58%	$5,115	20%
Eastern Kentucky University	$7,185	56%	$4,823	$3,108	85%	$2,014	24%
Virginia State University	$7,120	88%	$3,255	$4,025	75%	$4,576	10%
Mississippi University for Women	$7,084	67%	$3,822	$4,322	65%	$4,626	18%
Radford University (VA)	$6,990	39%	$4,529	$3,481	74%	$2,787	3%
James Madison University (VA)	$6,822	30%	$5,332	$3,640	50%	$2,049	1%
Georgia Southern University	$6,625	48%	$4,406	$3,849	63%	$1,448	2%
Western Carolina University (NC)	$6,574	47%	$3,416	$3,386	79%	$2,487	12%
University of North Carolina–Wilmington	$6,526	36%	$3,554	$4,006	87%	$1,625	2%
Valdosta State University (GA)	$6,501	57%	$4,631	$3,873	91%	$1,445	25%
University of Mobile (AL)	$6,500	56%	$2,111	$3,765	40%	N/A	4%
University of North Carolina–Pembroke	$6,446	70%	$4,136	$3,357	62%	$1,208	4%
University of West Georgia	$6,441	49%	$4,346	$3,025	78%	$1,635	2%
Appalachian State University (NC)	$6,383	32%	$4,286	$3,399	77%	$2,875	6%
Austin Peay State University (TN)	$6,367	72%	$3,641	N/A	N/A	$4,457	7%
Georgia Southwestern State University	$6,219	62%	$3,018	$3,249	55%	$2,961	8%
Arkansas State University	$6,000	74%	$5,400	$4,100	55%	$5,000	11%
North Carolina A&T State University	$5,898	72%	$4,028	$7,202	50%	$4,466	3%
Nicholls State University (LA)	$5,506	53%	$3,107	$2,973	87%	$2,811	2%
Georgia College and State University	$5,338	37%	$2,859	$2,291	41%	$1,439	2%
Northwestern State University of Louisiana	$5,208	56%	N/A	$4,913	48%	$3,711	23%
Jacksonville State University (AL)	$5,200	78%	$3,500	$5,250	80%	$1,000	14%

Where the money is: Schools that award the most need-based aid

Universities–Master's (South), continued

	Average amount of aid package	% students receiving need-based package	Average need-based grant	Average need-based loan	Average % of need met	Average merit award	% students receiving merit awards
Murray State University (KY)	$4,613	44%	$2,182	$1,955	88%	$2,552	33%
University of North Alabama	$4,515	45%	$2,754	$3,313	68%	$1,590	12%
Arkansas Tech University	$4,381	63%	$2,478	$1,826	41%	$5,643	18%
Southern Arkansas University	$4,158	54%	$2,376	$1,283	100%	$4,557	11%
University of Mary Washington (VA)	$4,050	51%	$2,500	$2,400	56%	$1,200	11%
Columbus State University (GA)	$3,988	47%	$3,214	$3,456	64%	$1,672	27%
Troy University (AL)	$3,634	61%	$3,183	$3,874	70%	$2,610	25%
Tennessee Technological University	$3,502	51%	$2,632	$3,223	80%	$3,481	22%
Hampton University (VA)	$3,220	67%	N/A	N/A	46%	$7,474	6%
University of North Florida	$1,485	15%	$1,052	$1,561	88%	$1,297	9%

Universities–Master's (Midwest)

	Average amount of aid package	% students receiving need-based package	Average need-based grant	Average need-based loan	Average % of need met	Average merit award	% students receiving merit awards
Maharishi University of Management (IA)	$27,088	92%	$19,717	$8,281	87%	$5,900	2%
University of Detroit Mercy	$23,871	78%	$18,567	$4,210	80%	$13,628	6%
Hamline University (MN)	$23,870	75%	$6,841	$3,718	85%	$8,755	16%
College of St. Catherine (MN)	$22,474	69%	$7,248	$4,887	76%	$12,876	16%
Baker University (KS)	$20,977	78%	$5,114	$3,637	85%	$5,809	22%
Creighton University (NE)	$20,201	55%	$12,003	$6,575	86%	$8,627	34%
University of Evansville (IN)	$19,847	71%	$15,028	$4,760	93%	$10,137	23%
North Central College (IL)	$19,796	67%	$11,941	$6,531	86%	$8,669	23%
Rockhurst University (MO)	$19,719	78%	$5,869	$3,314	97%	$8,523	10%
University of Findlay (OH)	$19,308	72%	$8,215	$5,200	75%	$8,100	14%
Concordia University–River Forest (IL)	$18,080	76%	$9,034	$6,573	80%	$8,348	19%
John Carroll University (OH)	$18,007	69%	$11,259	$4,418	83%	$6,829	9%
Capital University (OH)	$17,779	79%	$13,679	$4,379	73%	$9,259	19%
Valparaiso University (IN)	$17,707	68%	$12,137	$4,988	90%	$7,888	25%
Butler University (IN)	$17,500	60%	$12,800	$5,200	78%	$9,400	26%
Drake University (IA)	$17,453	62%	$10,719	$5,472	84%	$9,026	31%
Aurora University (IL)	$17,348	76%	$5,855	$3,811	89%	$8,703	21%
Webster University (MO)	$17,299	68%	$4,900	$4,121	N/A	$9,204	22%
Concordia University Wisconsin	$17,213	77%	$9,147	$5,570	78%	$7,181	15%
Ashland University (OH)	$17,116	78%	$11,409	$4,183	90%	$6,206	16%
University of Dubuque (IA)	$17,080	90%	$8,879	$9,143	85%	$15,378	10%
College of St. Scholastica (MN)	$17,059	77%	$5,618	$4,571	84%	$8,003	17%
University of Indianapolis	$16,861	75%	$8,442	$3,907	85%	$10,014	13%
Marian College of Fond du Lac (WI)	$16,359	79%	$8,986	$5,309	92%	$4,484	14%
College of Mount St. Joseph (OH)	$15,832	68%	$6,998	$4,737	90%	$6,990	12%
Ursuline College (OH)	$15,796	78%	$5,882	$4,231	78%	$3,593	15%
St. Xavier University (IL)	$15,408	80%	$9,018	$3,885	83%	$4,135	18%
University of St. Francis (IL)	$15,359	71%	$6,894	$4,413	73%	$5,793	12%
Carthage College (WI)	$15,278	72%	$10,586	$5,672	73%	$11,549	25%
St. Ambrose University (IA)	$15,159	70%	$8,630	$4,049	16%	$7,603	26%
Dominican University (IL)	$15,046	81%	$11,237	$3,763	80%	$11,282	18%
Concordia University (NE)	$15,019	80%	$4,471	$3,572	91%	$5,896	20%
Bethel University (MN)	$14,918	66%	$8,846	$4,368	78%	$3,545	25%
Quincy University (IL)	$14,835	72%	$9,365	$4,373	85%	$3,867	21%
St. Mary's University of Minnesota	$14,833	79%	$7,900	$5,633	89%	N/A	N/A
Xavier University (OH)	$14,510	54%	$9,872	$4,426	75%	$8,158	29%
Fontbonne University (MO)	$14,500	66%	$5,200	$3,000	46%	$5,000	40%
Roosevelt University (IL)	$14,500	69%	$6,000	N/A	75%	N/A	N/A
Doane College (NE)	$14,435	78%	$10,360	$4,207	95%	$9,358	9%
Aquinas College (MI)	$14,380	72%	$11,245	$3,135	87%	$9,798	28%
Maryville University of St. Louis (MO)	$14,272	72%	$7,795	$3,833	75%	$4,639	18%
Heidelberg College (OH)	$14,130	81%	$9,894	$4,349	86%	$6,518	7%
Spring Arbor University (MI)	$14,116	74%	$7,820	$4,424	83%	$2,785	3%
Benedictine College (KS)	$13,973	77%	$11,150	$6,418	67%	$4,680	17%
Baldwin-Wallace College (OH)	$13,355	77%	$9,956	$3,440	87%	$7,975	23%

	Average amount of aid package	% students receiving need-based package	Average need-based grant	Average need-based loan	Average % of need met	Average merit award	% students receiving merit awards
Cornerstone University (MI)	$13,320	76%	$6,656	$4,077	85%	$3,472	16%
Mount Marty College (SD)	$13,253	88%	$8,552	$4,632	75%	$9,217	10%
Bradley University (IL)	$13,098	73%	$8,755	$5,757	82%	$10,015	23%
Augsburg College (MN)	$12,842	78%	$10,531	$6,122	68%	$7,740	8%
Silver Lake College (WI)	$12,752	79%	$8,555	$3,688	73%	$3,510	8%
William Woods University (MO)	$12,617	63%	$9,235	$3,931	79%	$9,356	34%
University of St. Francis (IN)	$12,457	86%	$8,927	$3,130	74%	$9,793	12%
Lewis University (IL)	$12,416	79%	$5,862	$4,495	76%	$5,388	13%
Edgewood College (WI)	$12,229	76%	$7,391	$4,360	75%	$8,895	18%
Malone College (OH)	$12,194	75%	$8,344	$4,074	71%	$4,524	11%
Olivet Nazarene University (IL)	$12,033	70%	$9,075	$4,056	84%	$6,361	25%
Benedictine University (IL)	$11,980	73%	$6,350	$4,170	85%	$6,720	18%
Avila University (MO)	$11,751	33%	$7,465	$5,221	25%	$8,933	13%
Rockford College (IL)	$11,679	78%	$8,939	$4,060	35%	$6,053	16%
Mount Mary College (WI)	$11,550	67%	$7,158	$4,410	68%	$7,287	19%
Walsh University (OH)	$11,262	74%	$5,827	$4,220	83%	$4,834	13%
Southwest Baptist University (MO)	$10,651	69%	$3,534	$4,372	68%	$5,031	23%
Franciscan University of Steubenville (OH)	$10,542	69%	$6,485	$4,126	57%	$8,207	22%
University of St. Mary (KS)	$10,420	43%	$6,653	$4,124	86%	$4,500	39%
Lawrence Technological University (MI)	$10,157	57%	$6,783	$4,126	80%	$5,816	18%
Newman University (KS)	$10,092	72%	$3,892	$3,919	58%	$2,395	4%
MidAmerica Nazarene University (KS)	$10,028	70%	$6,260	$5,861	60%	$2,921	15%
Eastern Illinois University	$9,783	47%	$2,886	$3,461	19%	$7,140	3%
Friends University (KS)	$9,673	85%	$3,453	$3,480	45%	$1,427	12%
St. Cloud State University (MN)	$9,634	45%	$3,803	$4,187	96%	$1,812	4%
Southern Illinois University–Edwardsville	$9,050	50%	$5,560	$3,700	76%	$3,926	10%
Cardinal Stritch University (WI)	$8,480	89%	$6,069	$3,725	47%	$10,074	11%
Central Missouri State University	$8,450	81%	$3,375	$4,275	88%	$2,065	4%
Lake Superior State University (MI)	$8,157	86%	$3,407	$4,787	75%	$2,774	7%
University of Minnesota–Duluth	$8,149	52%	$5,758	$3,747	66%	$2,240	10%
University of Rio Grande (OH)	$8,081	66%	N/A	N/A	N/A	$0	0%
Ferris State University (MI)	$8,000	66%	$3,500	$3,500	75%	$2,000	4%
Lincoln University (MO)	$8,000	70%	$3,000	$2,000	35%	$3,000	11%
Western Illinois University	$7,891	54%	$5,776	$3,573	67%	$2,306	5%
University of Wisconsin–Green Bay	$7,839	55%	$4,609	$4,030	79%	$2,890	2%
Drury University (MO)	$7,737	89%	$6,889	$5,549	83%	$2,979	14%
University of Wisconsin–Stout	$7,467	50%	$4,177	$3,880	85%	$2,087	7%
Washburn University (KS)	$7,426	58%	$3,264	$3,846	36%	$1,900	20%
Bemidji State University (MN)	$7,414	57%	$4,132	$3,421	78%	$6,656	17%
Indiana University Northwest	$7,363	62%	$4,944	$3,264	64%	$2,983	2%
University of Nebraska–Kearney	$7,227	57%	$3,176	$3,590	79%	$1,994	30%
University of Wisconsin–Eau Claire	$7,206	41%	$4,389	$4,332	94%	$1,670	10%
Grand Valley State University (MI)	$7,049	55%	$3,081	$3,419	85%	$2,078	14%
Minnesota State University–Mankato	$6,939	50%	$3,643	$3,989	79%	$1,801	6%
Northern Michigan University	$6,935	61%	$3,504	$3,602	71%	$2,670	10%
Pittsburg State University (KS)	$6,890	57%	$3,365	$3,657	87%	$1,849	13%
University of Wisconsin–Stevens Point	$6,885	47%	$4,496	$4,234	95%	$1,973	6%
Northeastern Illinois University	$6,870	49%	$5,302	$3,849	64%	$1,377	3%
University of Northern Iowa	$6,738	55%	$2,690	$4,121	66%	$2,900	9%
Truman State University (MO)	$6,706	42%	$2,934	$4,039	78%	$4,002	45%
Minot State University (ND)	$6,658	81%	$1,812	$2,836	97%	$620	10%
Indiana University-Purdue University–Fort Wayne	$6,546	55%	$4,260	$3,112	73%	$1,860	18%
Southeast Missouri State University	$6,531	53%	$4,224	$3,678	65%	$3,795	13%
University of Wisconsin–Whitewater	$6,527	44%	$4,739	$3,822	75%	$2,091	7%
Eastern Michigan University	$6,472	50%	$3,146	$4,044	60%	$2,516	8%
Madonna University (MI)	$6,381	47%	$3,982	$3,348	55%	$6,426	20%
University of Wisconsin–River Falls	$6,343	48%	$2,610	$3,046	82%	$1,510	5%
University of Wisconsin–Superior	$6,242	59%	$4,592	$3,664	N/A	$2,454	3%
Indiana University Southeast	$6,127	58%	$4,560	$3,772	52%	$2,376	3%
Missouri State University	$6,125	60%	$4,308	$3,649	61%	$7,328	33%
Northern State University (SD)	$6,076	59%	$2,540	$3,505	N/A	$1,692	7%
Indiana University–South Bend	$6,050	58%	$4,153	$3,277	58%	$1,966	4%
Emporia State University (KS)	$5,955	58%	$2,192	$2,765	67%	$849	9%
Purdue University–Calumet (IN)	$5,886	42%	N/A	N/A	24%	$1,597	4%
University of Southern Indiana	$5,393	52%	$4,509	$3,260	54%	$2,140	7%
University of Wisconsin–La Crosse	$4,885	66%	N/A	N/A	86%	$3,875	12%
University of Michigan–Dearborn	$4,847	46%	N/A	N/A	43%	$2,921	33%
Bellevue University (NE)	$4,424	94%	$2,127	$4,085	N/A	N/A	N/A
Chicago State University	$3,912	80%	$3,012	$1,993	47%	$2,573	1%
Wayne State College (NE)	$3,264	62%	$1,574	$1,912	37%	N/A	N/A

Where the money is: Schools that award the most need-based aid

Universities–Master's (West)	Average amount of aid package	% students receiving need-based package	Average need-based grant	Average need-based loan	Average % of need met	Average merit award	% students receiving merit awards
University of Redlands (CA)	$25,071	69%	$18,517	$5,377	89%	$9,816	19%
Seattle University	$22,535	67%	N/A	$4,818	84%	$7,847	4%
Loyola Marymount University (CA)	$22,232	60%	$14,941	$4,631	74%	$11,084	3%
Dominican University of California	$21,738	74%	$14,394	$3,416	64%	$7,929	19%
Chapman University (CA)	$21,628	60%	$18,118	$4,596	100%	$16,047	15%
University of Portland (OR)	$21,356	51%	$14,249	$5,511	84%	$16,651	43%
St. Mary's College of California	$20,858	63%	$16,898	$4,535	72%	$7,454	3%
Santa Clara University (CA)	$19,706	42%	$15,990	$4,963	70%	$9,259	15%
St. Mary's University of San Antonio	$19,472	63%	$12,330	$5,559	81%	$6,866	15%
Pacific Lutheran University (WA)	$19,269	67%	$7,987	$7,132	89%	$8,086	20%
Concordia University (CA)	$19,204	66%	$10,480	$4,030	69%	$6,151	20%
College of Santa Fe (NM)	$18,934	67%	$10,083	$4,700	77%	$4,011	15%
Westminster College (UT)	$18,917	66%	$10,210	$6,221	87%	$8,663	29%
Seattle Pacific University	$18,525	61%	$14,723	$5,452	82%	$9,748	28%
Notre Dame de Namur University (CA)	$18,378	69%	$12,643	$4,026	64%	$7,675	14%
Gonzaga University (WA)	$18,255	59%	$12,374	$5,358	89%	$7,205	34%
Trinity University (TX)	$17,845	40%	$11,415	$6,105	89%	$7,869	31%
St. Martin's University (WA)	$17,572	86%	$11,679	$5,197	85%	$9,545	14%
Pacific University (OR)	$17,492	73%	$11,538	$5,429	86%	$8,645	23%
Whitworth College (WA)	$17,441	74%	$12,423	$4,572	79%	$7,382	23%
Walla Walla College (WA)	$17,349	71%	$6,500	$5,751	86%	$3,308	18%
Woodbury University (CA)	$17,132	73%	$13,499	$4,521	60%	$13,031	12%
Fresno Pacific University (CA)	$16,847	73%	$11,617	$4,187	73%	$2,112	13%
California Lutheran University	$16,600	63%	$13,000	$4,300	70%	$8,800	27%
Oral Roberts University (OK)	$16,503	69%	$7,880	$9,813	88%	$7,195	19%
Holy Names University (CA)	$16,215	82%	$9,200	$3,458	84%	$18,286	5%
Our Lady of the Lake University (TX)	$15,760	91%	$6,439	$4,009	80%	$3,768	8%
Alaska Pacific University	$15,748	72%	$2,863	$3,813	81%	$1,736	26%
Regis University (CO)	$15,599	59%	$11,003	$2,417	50%	$7,858	8%
Oklahoma City University	$15,462	50%	$11,621	$3,769	86%	$8,481	14%
George Fox University (OR)	$15,281	83%	$11,305	$4,267	75%	$8,863	15%
St. Edward's University (TX)	$14,680	60%	$10,054	$4,324	76%	$5,826	10%
University of the Incarnate Word (TX)	$13,991	75%	$7,877	$4,229	58%	$6,108	15%
Hardin-Simmons University (TX)	$13,530	69%	$4,812	$3,803	70%	$3,751	13%
Northwest Nazarene University (ID)	$13,254	72%	$2,920	$4,798	74%	$8,446	10%
Chaminade University of Honolulu	$12,642	66%	$8,312	$4,128	65%	$4,840	23%
Point Loma Nazarene University (CA)	$12,525	47%	$9,523	$5,109	46%	$10,485	7%
University of Mary Hardin-Baylor (TX)	$12,511	74%	$5,134	$4,948	73%	$3,314	23%
University of St. Thomas (TX)	$12,487	57%	$8,653	$4,199	64%	$6,613	18%
Marylhurst University (OR)	$12,368	90%	$6,723	$4,732	48%	$0	0%
Heritage University (WA)	$12,333	79%	$8,812	$3,840	69%	$6,641	1%
California Baptist University	$11,670	96%	$8,920	$4,360	67%	$5,900	7%
Eastern Washington University	$11,418	61%	$5,089	$4,052	37%	$3,450	2%
LeTourneau University (TX)	$11,288	63%	$7,757	$3,931	69%	$4,134	17%
Abilene Christian University (TX)	$11,055	60%	$7,814	$3,996	71%	$5,767	28%
University of Great Falls (MT)	$10,989	83%	$3,719	$4,024	41%	$3,933	3%
Houston Baptist University	$10,935	87%	$7,531	$3,434	61%	$14,816	13%
Hawaii Pacific University	$10,465	36%	$3,915	$4,145	71%	$6,543	24%
Dallas Baptist University	$10,262	56%	$2,767	$3,398	79%	$9,093	21%
California State Polytechnic University–Pomona	$9,265	55%	$2,217	$3,894	90%	$1,400	1%
Wayland Baptist University (TX)	$9,012	75%	$6,770	$3,037	76%	$8,514	20%
Western Washington University	$8,981	39%	$5,602	$4,150	87%	$1,586	2%
California State University–Sacramento	$8,753	48%	$2,216	$4,018	67%	$5,960	5%
San Francisco State University	$8,441	46%	$5,911	$2,995	65%	$1,841	1%
College of the Southwest (NM)	$8,437	81%	$4,104	$3,768	62%	$3,402	16%
California State University–Long Beach	$8,350	51%	$4,250	$3,314	82%	$2,068	6%
Boise State University (ID)	$8,348	54%	$3,299	$3,938	65%	$2,207	1%
Humboldt State University (CA)	$8,257	54%	$2,619	$2,851	77%	N/A	N/A
California State University–Dominguez Hills	$8,239	82%	$4,975	$4,258	67%	$2,669	1%
Central Washington University	$7,996	51%	$2,309	$3,387	73%	$731	0%
California State University–East Bay	$7,973	45%	$6,294	$5,849	65%	N/A	0%
California State University–Stanislaus	$7,836	50%	$4,509	$4,004	42%	$1,437	1%
California State University–Chico	$7,801	42%	$5,646	$4,017	26%	$1,517	2%
California State University–San Bernardino	$7,773	63%	$5,710	$3,648	68%	$3,654	0%
Eastern New Mexico University	$7,598	67%	$3,202	$4,215	49%	$3,140	3%
Montana State University–Billings	$7,566	67%	$4,373	$3,250	67%	$9,025	3%
Texas State University–San Marcos	$7,545	51%	$4,059	$3,362	67%	$2,165	2%
Sonoma State University (CA)	$7,498	41%	$4,705	$3,866	63%	$1,567	1%
University of Texas–Pan American	$7,488	83%	N/A	N/A	76%	$4,658	5%
Cal Poly–San Luis Obispo	$7,333	32%	$1,820	$3,879	66%	N/A	N/A

	Average amount of aid package	% students receiving need-based package	Average need-based grant	Average need-based loan	Average % of need met	Average merit award	% students receiving merit awards
University of Texas–Tyler	$7,270	50%	$4,160	$3,512	68%	$2,496	11%
Colorado State University–Pueblo	$7,247	63%	$4,517	$3,252	59%	$7,876	20%
California State University–Fullerton	$7,220	33%	$6,195	$4,179	62%	$4,622	7%
University of Alaska–Southeast	$6,967	45%	$3,413	$4,778	56%	$2,608	4%
California State University–San Marcos	$6,946	40%	$3,831	$4,099	N/A	N/A	N/A
Prairie View A&M University (TX)	$6,920	88%	$3,350	$4,000	73%	$1,300	6%
California State University–Los Angeles	$6,894	64%	$6,413	$5,242	78%	N/A	N/A
Angelo State University (TX)	$6,531	67%	$2,161	$2,566	65%	$2,343	6%
Texas A&M University–Corpus Christi	$6,524	60%	$3,826	$3,753	63%	$4,689	7%
University of Colorado–Colorado Springs	$6,508	51%	$4,960	$3,603	53%	$1,709	8%
Midwestern State University (TX)	$6,459	47%	$4,038	$3,304	70%	$1,472	21%
Western Oregon University	$6,412	73%	$4,261	$3,535	65%	$7,544	22%
University of Texas–San Antonio	$6,381	60%	$3,807	$3,669	52%	$1,539	3%
East Central University (OK)	$6,325	66%	$2,946	$3,511	44%	$1,217	3%
Sam Houston State University (TX)	$6,108	48%	$3,494	$3,517	50%	$1,893	7%
University of Central Oklahoma	$6,043	45%	N/A	$3,787	68%	$2,169	7%
California State University–Fresno	$5,833	59%	$4,660	$3,206	75%	$2,194	2%
Northwestern Oklahoma State University	$5,598	57%	$3,531	$3,053	75%	$1,104	15%
Stephen F. Austin State University (TX)	$5,059	54%	$2,871	$2,166	70%	$2,882	6%
Weber State University (UT)	$4,763	44%	$2,951	$3,523	56%	$1,527	25%
Southwestern Oklahoma State University	$4,368	57%	$1,187	$1,324	91%	$400	25%
Texas A&M International University	$3,818	78%	$2,844	$2,165	29%	$1,603	3%
Northeastern State University (OK)	$3,686	90%	$1,884	$1,758	67%	$1,933	2%
Cameron University (OK)	$3,500	46%	$2,500	$3,930	87%	$750	9%
University of Texas of the Permian Basin	$3,302	67%	$2,327	$1,105	51%	$765	7%
University of Texas–Brownsville	$3,269	78%	$2,404	$1,858	29%	$964	1%
Lamar University (TX)	$1,237	40%	N/A	N/A	30%	$900	17%

Comprehensive Colleges–Bachelor's (North)

	Average amount of aid package	% students receiving need-based package	Average need-based grant	Average need-based loan	Average % of need met	Average merit award	% students receiving merit awards
Russell Sage College (NY)	$24,647	86%	$5,635	$3,371	N/A	$10,701	5%
New England College (NH)	$22,536	74%	$10,140	$8,430	86%	$8,282	5%
Elmira College (NY)	$21,435	78%	$16,130	$5,795	80%	$15,717	18%
Concordia College (NY)	$20,690	68%	$9,700	$3,630	70%	$5,895	12%
Green Mountain College (VT)	$19,049	75%	$12,939	$6,251	78%	$15,767	13%
Utica College (NY)	$18,190	90%	$7,451	$3,956	73%	$6,004	7%
Medaille College (NY)	$18,094	66%	$8,187	$3,437	65%	$10,156	19%
Delaware Valley College (PA)	$17,760	78%	$13,075	$3,709	85%	$8,302	22%
Stonehill College (MA)	$17,700	61%	$12,848	$5,287	80%	$11,571	24%
Neumann College (PA)	$17,000	90%	$14,000	$5,000	65%	N/A	N/A
College of St. Elizabeth (NJ)	$16,889	75%	$14,123	$3,883	75%	$13,073	16%
Colby-Sawyer College (NH)	$16,430	72%	$11,994	$3,926	71%	$4,200	10%
Elizabethtown College (PA)	$16,420	71%	$14,244	$3,914	79%	$15,442	9%
Wilson College (PA)	$16,223	73%	$12,451	$4,407	78%	$14,565	23%
Keuka College (NY)	$16,103	92%	$10,578	$6,004	80%	$16,406	8%
Cedar Crest College (PA)	$15,960	88%	$12,194	$4,110	74%	$13,887	11%
Simon's Rock College of Bard (MA)	$15,760	65%	$10,724	$4,441	55%	$22,250	6%
Post University (CT)	$15,600	78%	$10,000	$4,500	80%	$3,500	7%
Bloomfield College (NJ)	$15,061	86%	$10,205	$4,441	64%	$5,265	3%
Lasell College (MA)	$14,900	84%	$12,200	$2,500	67%	$14,700	13%
Curry College (MA)	$14,733	66%	$9,925	$3,764	68%	$4,379	1%
Roger Williams University (RI)	$14,600	63%	$7,700	$5,100	83%	$6,017	9%
Wesley College (DE)	$14,600	88%	$5,500	$4,700	80%	$2,500	5%
Daemen College (NY)	$14,419	85%	$6,951	$4,054	87%	$5,369	16%
Centenary College (NJ)	$13,647	78%	$10,478	$4,269	65%	$13,205	11%
Unity College (ME)	$13,589	79%	$7,300	$5,751	76%	$8,753	17%
Cazenovia College (NY)	$13,500	81%	$8,000	$3,063	70%	$5,000	7%
Thiel College (PA)	$13,265	87%	$9,236	$3,508	75%	$7,229	13%
Felician College (NJ)	$13,161	76%	$6,000	$4,300	85%	$9,962	8%
Dominican College of Blauvelt (NY)	$12,808	77%	$9,682	$3,788	62%	$10,959	12%

Where the money is: Schools that award the most need-based aid

Comprehensive Colleges–Bachelor's (North), continued

	Average amount of aid package	% students receiving need-based package	Average need-based grant	Average need-based loan	Average % of need met	Average merit award	% students receiving merit awards
Alvernia College (PA)	$12,225	94%	$6,521	$5,482	79%	$6,500	2%
Mount Ida College (MA)	$11,436	79%	$8,240	$3,346	51%	$8,123	20%
Mount Aloysius College (PA)	$11,400	94%	$2,600	$3,530	25%	$2,000	6%
Messiah College (PA)	$11,017	68%	$3,910	$3,010	61%	$7,726	19%
Atlantic Union College (MA)	$10,995	68%	$6,608	$4,295	75%	$7,271	31%
Villa Julie College (MD)	$10,438	56%	$7,876	$3,586	71%	$5,720	24%
Mercyhurst College (PA)	$10,261	76%	$5,433	$3,224	89%	N/A	N/A
Hilbert College (NY)	$10,127	87%	$6,265	$4,303	77%	$9,671	12%
Ramapo College of New Jersey	$9,765	47%	$6,856	$3,860	77%	$7,914	13%
University of Maine–Machias	$9,604	80%	$5,438	$4,172	82%	$6,118	6%
Becker College (MA)	$9,286	86%	$6,642	$2,937	46%	$11,833	13%
University of Pittsburgh–Johnstown	$9,214	75%	$4,175	$3,034	54%	$2,806	3%
Champlain College (VT)	$9,185	57%	$5,134	$5,218	63%	$11,912	16%
University of Maine–Farmington	$8,156	67%	$4,007	$3,671	79%	$1,647	4%
University of Maine–Augusta	$7,929	77%	$4,742	$3,747	72%	$4,416	8%
SUNY College of A&T–Cobleskill	$6,976	64%	$4,467	$3,190	61%	N/A	N/A
St. Joseph's College New York–Brooklyn	$6,560	75%	$4,079	$2,372	43%	$5,410	19%
CUNY–New York City College of Technology	$6,384	80%	$5,708	$5,402	70%	N/A	N/A
Albertus Magnus College (CT)	$6,335	62%	$4,815	$3,638	50%	$4,500	1%
SUNY College–Old Westbury	$6,283	75%	$4,677	$2,341	45%	$0	0%
Grove City College (PA)	$5,175	36%	$4,971	$0	49%	$6,260	34%
St. Francis College (NY)	$4,622	64%	$3,683	$1,825	67%	$3,867	11%
CUNY–York College	$3,482	69%	$2,976	$3,623	30%	N/A	N/A

Comprehensive Colleges–Bachelor's (South)

	Average amount of aid package	% students receiving need-based package	Average need-based grant	Average need-based loan	Average % of need met	Average merit award	% students receiving merit awards
Berea College (KY)	$26,299	100%	$24,062	$1,190	92%	$0	0%
Maryville College (TN)	$20,380	77%	$13,670	$5,086	92%	$1,535	22%
Columbia College (SC)	$20,051	78%	$8,495	$3,810	70%	$7,775	17%
University of Charleston (WV)	$19,575	72%	$3,550	$8,500	68%	$3,850	13%
North Carolina Wesleyan College	$17,598	84%	$12,018	$4,590	88%	$6,983	6%
Thomas More College (KY)	$17,432	73%	$4,608	$2,281	82%	$6,804	13%
Alderson-Broaddus College (WV)	$17,211	95%	$4,961	$3,947	87%	$5,694	6%
Florida Southern College	$16,993	72%	$13,078	$5,199	64%	$13,443	13%
Stillman College (AL)	$16,987	97%	$5,862	$7,500	75%	$2,000	4%
Coker College (SC)	$16,829	81%	$5,674	$3,861	91%	$6,161	18%
University of the Ozarks (AR)	$16,375	52%	$13,862	$3,025	70%	$12,092	44%
Lambuth University (TN)	$16,084	75%	$10,520	$5,022	75%	$6,781	13%
Anderson University (SC)	$15,834	86%	$7,160	$4,596	66%	$5,652	8%
Methodist College (NC)	$15,822	74%	$6,679	$3,505	73%	$5,929	9%
Brevard College (NC)	$15,245	62%	$10,172	$3,829	82%	$6,015	16%
Covenant College (GA)	$15,096	71%	$11,054	$4,218	84%	$6,042	22%
Berry College (GA)	$14,794	57%	$11,398	$2,826	82%	$12,112	42%
Lenoir-Rhyne College (NC)	$14,779	79%	$12,076	$4,237	72%	$6,362	18%
High Point University (NC)	$14,750	68%	$5,500	$5,500	72%	$7,000	13%
LaGrange College (GA)	$14,651	73%	$9,241	$3,889	81%	$5,803	24%
Ferrum College (VA)	$14,639	76%	$10,075	$3,829	85%	$6,487	18%
Catawba College (NC)	$14,174	68%	$4,256	$4,431	81%	$6,628	10%
Bethune-Cookman College (FL)	$13,981	87%	$6,510	$3,412	66%	$7,880	3%
Brescia University (KY)	$13,927	72%	$4,085	$768	75%	$8,293	8%
Asbury College (KY)	$13,506	71%	$8,075	$3,737	78%	$10,356	9%
Mars Hill College (NC)	$13,339	46%	$10,547	$3,567	72%	$12,346	5%
Ouachita Baptist University (AR)	$12,992	48%	$8,419	$3,709	75%	$6,032	33%
Davis and Elkins College (WV)	$12,846	74%	$4,247	$4,388	71%	$5,476	20%
Wingate University (NC)	$12,528	63%	$2,971	$3,966	76%	$4,955	29%
Chowan College (NC)	$12,504	87%	$9,526	$3,560	69%	$11,297	9%
Southern Adventist University (TN)	$12,500	66%	$3,000	$2,600	67%	$3,000	28%
Morris College (SC)	$12,400	99%	$3,500	$3,500	87%	$0	0%
Kentucky Wesleyan College	$12,214	84%	$9,766	$2,902	75%	$10,887	16%
Midway College (KY)	$12,196	81%	$5,792	$3,658	59%	$3,756	1%

	Average amount of aid package	% students receiving need-based package	Average need-based grant	Average need-based loan	Average % of need met	Average merit award	% students receiving merit awards
Pikeville College (KY)	$12,119	96%	$9,978	$3,462	90%	$3,094	1%
Belmont Abbey College (NC)	$12,113	70%	$9,029	$3,398	57%	$11,895	28%
Kentucky Christian University	$11,728	81%	$4,743	$3,656	74%	$2,919	13%
Shorter College (GA)	$11,105	68%	$8,424	$3,525	61%	$8,685	31%
Virginia Intermont College	$10,961	75%	N/A	$3,855	55%	$8,508	16%
Limestone College (SC)	$10,813	88%	$7,807	$3,309	60%	$8,131	18%
Flagler College (FL)	$10,752	46%	$3,060	$3,787	79%	$2,293	3%
St. Paul's College (VA)	$10,704	92%	$2,456	$2,627	85%	$0	0%
Livingstone College (NC)	$10,531	92%	$7,412	$3,479	57%	$7,986	8%
Tennessee Wesleyan College	$10,470	77%	$8,044	$3,462	69%	$7,272	18%
Ohio Valley University (WV)	$10,304	74%	$6,518	$4,230	67%	$8,660	23%
Reinhardt College (GA)	$9,943	80%	$2,000	$4,670	37%	$3,613	71%
Bryan College (TN)	$9,832	86%	$3,721	$4,054	67%	$5,339	12%
Johnson C. Smith University (NC)	$9,725	85%	$3,000	$5,500	60%	$2,717	8%
Toccoa Falls College (GA)	$9,653	78%	$6,486	$3,110	60%	$7,595	20%
LeMoyne-Owen College (TN)	$9,421	91%	$6,750	$3,158	55%	$8,701	6%
Brewton-Parker College (GA)	$9,399	87%	$6,813	$3,187	59%	$6,470	12%
Glenville State College (WV)	$8,736	73%	$4,455	$4,087	82%	$2,387	8%
Alice Lloyd College (KY)	$8,678	54%	$7,087	$501	60%	$4,970	41%
Shepherd University (WV)	$8,674	48%	$3,529	$3,584	74%	$7,458	20%
Emmanuel College (GA)	$8,650	96%	$2,900	$3,502	48%	$3,413	23%
Crichton College (TN)	$8,381	69%	N/A	N/A	61%	$6,173	10%
Bluefield College (VA)	$8,308	72%	$5,283	$4,099	56%	$6,306	21%
Clearwater Christian College (FL)	$8,245	89%	$3,694	$3,923	47%	$0	0%
Philander Smith College (AR)	$8,214	N/A	$5,014	$3,560	N/A	$10,236	N/A
John Brown University (AR)	$8,195	63%	$7,121	$4,496	50%	$4,121	16%
Blue Mountain College (MS)	$7,942	72%	$2,830	$3,592	46%	$4,041	11%
Lee University (TN)	$7,911	56%	$5,752	$4,041	54%	$7,114	24%
University of South Carolina–Upstate	$7,400	64%	$3,340	$3,610	42%	$3,003	2%
Faulkner University (AL)	$7,300	72%	$3,800	$5,300	60%	$2,500	3%
Concord University (WV)	$7,202	65%	$3,688	$3,219	79%	$3,232	13%
Mid-Continent University (KY)	$7,198	73%	$5,309	$2,782	60%	$6,248	5%
Mount Olive College (NC)	$7,091	49%	$4,983	$2,577	67%	$3,919	12%
Southeastern University (FL)	$7,005	69%	$4,839	$575	53%	$10,455	25%
Mountain State University (WV)	$6,280	69%	$3,878	$3,864	47%	$4,044	1%
West Virginia University–Parkersburg	$5,700	85%	$5,000	$3,200	82%	$850	4%
Bluefield State College (WV)	$5,600	N/A	N/A	N/A	68%	$1,400	N/A
Our Lady of Holy Cross College (LA)	$4,259	40%	$3,427	$3,139	15%	$4,943	3%
Winston-Salem State University (NC)	$3,477	86%	$2,666	$3,501	82%	$4,099	2%
Clayton State University (GA)	$2,425	63%	$1,611	$1,856	46%	$730	4%

Comprehensive Colleges–Bachelor's (Midwest)

	Average amount of aid package	% students receiving need-based package	Average need-based grant	Average need-based loan	Average % of need met	Average merit award	% students receiving merit awards
Ohio Northern University	$22,130	81%	$9,754	$5,034	85%	$12,417	16%
Buena Vista University (IA)	$19,994	92%	$9,608	$4,689	91%	$6,550	5%
Simpson College (IA)	$18,989	85%	$12,633	$3,994	87%	$9,198	14%
St. Joseph's College (IN)	$18,976	72%	$12,234	$4,299	84%	$10,042	14%
St. Mary's College (IN)	$18,964	70%	$9,405	$2,961	77%	$7,845	21%
Loras College (IA)	$18,374	76%	$8,170	$4,230	88%	$8,289	32%
Bluffton University (OH)	$18,106	74%	$12,147	$4,759	91%	$8,087	10%
Manchester College (IN)	$17,375	85%	$13,794	$3,202	88%	$8,648	6%
Wartburg College (IA)	$17,098	78%	$12,455	$4,786	85%	$12,721	23%
Central College (IA)	$16,987	81%	$11,542	$4,208	81%	$8,000	19%
St. Norbert College (WI)	$16,958	65%	$11,522	$4,524	88%	$7,054	30%
Wilmington College (OH)	$16,901	87%	$6,489	$5,126	86%	$6,780	10%
McPherson College (KS)	$16,893	84%	$5,077	$5,858	88%	$4,240	13%
Clarke College (IA)	$16,631	86%	$12,897	$4,237	100%	$12,108	11%
Bethany College (KS)	$16,612	82%	$5,404	$4,822	96%	$6,189	5%
Morningside College (IA)	$16,302	87%	$5,702	$3,585	77%	$6,130	12%

Where the money is: Schools that award the most need-based aid

Comprehensive Colleges– Bachelor's (Midwest), continued	Average amount of aid package	% students receiving need-based package	Average need-based grant	Average need-based loan	Average % of need met	Average merit award	% students receiving merit awards
Bethel College (KS)	$16,297	87%	$4,798	$5,242	90%	$8,648	9%
Midland Lutheran College (NE)	$16,271	86%	$9,884	$6,282	91%	$9,192	14%
Mount Union College (OH)	$16,184	79%	$11,209	$4,811	82%	$8,759	20%
Southwestern College (KS)	$16,151	75%	$9,175	$5,899	81%	$6,356	20%
Millikin University (IL)	$15,927	75%	$7,189	$4,230	91%	$7,126	10%
Tabor College (KS)	$15,794	74%	$3,482	$7,072	89%	$5,086	20%
Cedarville University (OH)	$15,778	61%	$1,879	$4,129	38%	$9,457	19%
Dordt College (IA)	$15,719	76%	$8,731	$4,487	86%	$8,179	20%
Dana College (NE)	$15,665	81%	$4,321	$4,133	88%	$5,686	13%
Elmhurst College (IL)	$15,512	70%	$11,156	$3,745	91%	$8,374	20%
Franklin College (IN)	$15,508	81%	$11,681	$4,021	88%	$11,692	18%
McKendree College (IL)	$15,473	78%	$12,144	$3,627	81%	$11,327	21%
Eureka College (IL)	$15,467	78%	$10,666	$3,798	81%	$4,125	2%
Marian College (IN)	$15,345	79%	$5,044	$3,302	72%	$6,901	12%
Northland College (WI)	$15,302	86%	$10,783	$4,397	80%	$10,137	14%
Augustana College (SD)	$15,183	68%	$10,674	$5,007	89%	$7,223	30%
Carroll College (WI)	$15,075	75%	$9,401	$4,013	96%	$7,258	22%
Concordia University (MI)	$14,959	84%	$10,784	$5,194	87%	$6,129	14%
Iowa Wesleyan College	$14,852	92%	$7,833	$5,000	89%	$7,564	5%
College of the Ozarks (MO)	$14,849	90%	$12,519	N/A	86%	$15,220	9%
Mount Mercy College (IA)	$14,744	84%	$9,678	$5,041	81%	$11,522	16%
Columbia College (MO)	$14,709	59%	$7,616	$2,820	83%	$4,379	19%
Waldorf College (IA)	$14,532	83%	$9,868	$4,846	86%	$10,207	16%
Dakota Wesleyan University (SD)	$14,500	90%	$9,500	$3,700	63%	$0	0%
Wisconsin Lutheran College	$14,493	73%	$10,377	$3,580	86%	$10,638	23%
Northwestern College (MN)	$14,453	82%	$10,316	$4,372	75%	$5,089	15%
Greenville College (IL)	$14,260	85%	$9,875	$3,987	76%	$8,163	15%
Defiance College (OH)	$14,129	83%	$1,821	$3,401	83%	$7,863	8%
Taylor University (IN)	$14,069	57%	$10,631	$4,537	78%	$3,898	23%
Notre Dame College of Ohio	$13,941	99%	N/A	N/A	65%	N/A	N/A
Northwestern College (IA)	$13,700	78%	$4,995	$4,155	N/A	$4,908	20%
MacMurray College (IL)	$13,591	90%	$9,942	$4,184	75%	$12,548	9%
Illinois College	$13,570	75%	$6,292	$4,307	85%	$5,587	18%
Tri-State University (IN)	$13,327	73%	$3,552	$3,753	90%	$6,758	31%
Calvin College (MI)	$13,000	61%	$8,300	$6,100	80%	$3,800	29%
Grace College and Seminary (IN)	$12,941	78%	$8,034	$5,568	83%	$12,198	20%
Missouri Valley College	$12,891	76%	$11,300	$3,650	80%	$10,540	24%
Huntington University (IN)	$12,751	73%	$10,409	$4,118	72%	$6,328	13%
St. Mary-of-the-Woods College (IN)	$12,733	99%	$9,720	$3,000	79%	$0	0%
Central Christian College (KS)	$12,372	84%	$3,815	$4,560	61%	$5,460	7%
Grand View College (IA)	$12,144	80%	$8,448	$3,867	74%	$11,108	18%
Mount Vernon Nazarene University (OH)	$12,008	55%	$6,658	$3,876	85%	$2,893	7%
Culver-Stockton College (MO)	$11,986	89%	$8,650	$3,680	75%	$12,103	10%
Concordia University–St. Paul (MN)	$11,847	66%	$9,760	$4,154	65%	$6,202	6%
Crown College (MN)	$11,529	63%	$4,675	$4,075	61%	$2,606	8%
Lakeland College (WI)	$11,325	71%	$8,146	$4,123	75%	$8,232	22%
University of Minnesota–Crookston	$10,303	67%	$5,365	$7,071	82%	$2,667	9%
College of St. Mary (NE)	$10,127	62%	$7,014	$4,213	51%	$8,008	15%
Bethel College (IN)	$9,089	77%	$6,729	$3,783	48%	$10,975	0%
Judson College (IL)	$8,846	75%	$6,691	N/A	33%	$1,523	9%
Lourdes College (OH)	$8,768	80%	$5,048	$3,537	N/A	$0	0%
Union College (NE)	$8,376	61%	$5,334	$4,807	44%	N/A	N/A
Jamestown College (ND)	$8,094	81%	$4,844	$3,848	65%	$7,821	19%
Trinity Christian College (IL)	$7,806	80%	$5,600	$3,966	68%	N/A	N/A
Kendall College (IL)	$7,572	85%	$6,088	$2,560	31%	$18,229	15%
Mayville State University (ND)	$7,420	60%	$3,433	$4,374	86%	N/A	2%
Grace University (NE)	$7,406	80%	$4,495	$3,867	45%	$5,952	17%
Purdue University–North Central (IN)	$6,808	57%	$4,335	$2,854	51%	$1,846	5%
Southwest Minnesota State University (MN)	$6,736	60%	$3,680	$3,432	40%	$1,798	14%
Missouri Southern State University	$6,722	79%	$4,636	$3,249	69%	$2,560	34%
Dakota State University (SD)	$6,308	64%	$3,192	$4,755	85%	$5,840	22%
Valley City State University (ND)	$6,299	63%	$3,028	$3,686	75%	$1,626	13%
Indiana University–Kokomo	$6,081	52%	$4,288	$3,043	73%	$2,022	6%
Indiana University East	$5,918	70%	$4,272	$3,240	59%	$1,737	4%
York College (NE)	$5,231	79%	N/A	N/A	N/A	$0	0%
Rochester College (MI)	$4,635	49%	$2,033	$1,716	N/A	$2,234	14%
Missouri Baptist University	$4,602	72%	$1,663	$5,946	13%	$3,480	24%

Comprehensive Colleges–Bachelor's (West)

	Average amount of aid package	% students receiving need-based package	Average need-based grant	Average need-based loan	Average % of need met	Average merit award	% students receiving merit awards
Menlo College (CA)	$19,510	62%	$15,516	$4,612	74%	$10,820	27%
Linfield College (OR)	$17,653	67%	$6,672	$4,457	85%	$8,946	22%
Northwest Christian College (OR)	$16,195	90%	$11,315	$4,198	76%	$6,880	8%
Master's College and Seminary (CA)	$15,311	72%	$10,632	$4,700	71%	$10,069	20%
Concordia University–Austin (TX)	$15,222	66%	$8,735	$6,411	81%	$6,844	18%
Carroll College (MT)	$15,113	67%	$9,053	$4,831	80%	$6,109	32%
McMurry University (TX)	$15,032	81%	$7,919	$4,128	84%	$4,201	6%
Pacific Union College (CA)	$14,150	62%	$6,589	N/A	67%	N/A	N/A
Texas Lutheran University	$13,740	73%	$6,040	$4,191	72%	$5,881	24%
Vanguard University of Southern California	$13,406	87%	$7,892	$3,190	68%	$5,028	12%
Rocky Mountain College (MT)	$13,378	73%	$8,525	$2,576	71%	$7,335	10%
Northwest University (WA)	$12,446	73%	$8,054	$4,068	68%	$10,199	17%
Oklahoma Baptist University	$12,278	58%	$3,700	$3,871	70%	$5,240	21%
Oklahoma Christian University	$12,128	69%	$1,609	$3,677	46%	$1,827	21%
Corban College (OR)	$12,117	86%	$8,955	$3,846	61%	$7,847	13%
East Texas Baptist University	$11,930	77%	$7,492	$3,743	85%	$5,768	16%
Howard Payne University (TX)	$11,638	75%	$7,582	$3,475	81%	$5,252	19%
Lubbock Christian University (TX)	$11,163	61%	$7,409	$3,655	73%	$10,592	15%
Wiley College (TX)	$10,645	89%	$2,500	$3,229	79%	$2,787	6%
Humphreys College (CA)	$9,850	89%	N/A	N/A	75%	$0	0%
Jarvis Christian College (TX)	$9,800	93%	N/A	$3,700	87%	$11,500	2%
St. Gregory's University (OK)	$9,381	63%	$4,402	$3,981	79%	$2,306	20%
Brigham Young University–Hawaii	$7,900	71%	$4,000	$2,000	80%	$1,400	5%
Utah Valley State College	$7,554	51%	$3,283	$3,391	70%	$2,043	14%
Oklahoma Wesleyan University	$7,148	97%	$3,217	$2,742	58%	$1,958	4%
University of Science and Arts of Oklahoma	$6,799	66%	$4,866	$2,884	68%	$3,857	18%
Patten University (CA)	$6,692	84%	$5,439	$3,074	41%	$9,708	11%
Lewis-Clark State College (ID)	$5,452	70%	$3,125	$3,552	11%	$2,478	7%
University of Montana–Western	$2,735	73%	$2,287	$3,687	18%	$3,037	0%

Getting a late start? All is not lost

Midterms are over and your applications still aren't out. Here's a list of schools whose application deadlines are later in the year or who have "rolling" admissions, meaning they take applications until the freshman class is full. Schools are listed by application deadline for the academic year starting in the fall of 2007.

National Universities

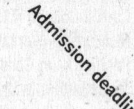

School	Admission deadline
Baylor University (TX)	2/1
Catholic University of America (DC)	2/1
New School University (NY)	2/1
North Carolina State University–Raleigh	2/1
Ohio State University–Columbus	2/1
Ohio University	2/1
Texas A&M University–College Station	2/1
University of Connecticut	2/1
University of Maryland–Baltimore County	2/1
University of Miami (FL)	2/1
University of Michigan–Ann Arbor	2/1
University of Nevada–Las Vegas	2/1
University of New Hampshire	2/1
University of Rhode Island	2/1
University of San Francisco	2/1
University of Texas–Austin	2/1
University of Wisconsin–Madison	2/1
Worcester Polytechnic Institute (MA)	2/1
Brigham Young University–Provo (UT)	2/15
Howard University (DC)	2/15
Stevens Institute of Technology (NJ)	2/15
Texas Christian University	2/15
University of Kentucky	2/15
Yeshiva University (NY)	2/15
Biola University (CA)	3/1
Drexel University (PA)	3/1
Florida State University	3/1
Georgia State University	3/1
Illinois State University	3/1
Pace University (NY)	3/1
SUNY–Albany	3/1
University of Alabama–Birmingham	3/1
University of San Diego	3/5
Clarkson University (NY)	3/15
Old Dominion University (VA)	3/15
Southern Methodist University (TX)	3/15
Temple University (PA)	4/1
University of Arizona	4/1
University of Houston	4/1
University of Iowa	4/1
University of Kansas	4/1
University of Oklahoma	4/1
University of Utah	4/1
Louisiana State University–Baton Rouge	4/15
University of South Florida	4/15
Clemson University (SC)	5/1
Kent State University (OH)	5/1
Texas Tech University	5/1
University of Central Florida	5/1
University of Hawaii–Manoa	5/1
University of Nebraska–Lincoln	5/1
Clark Atlanta University	6/1
Florida Atlantic University	6/1
University of New Mexico	6/15
Colorado State University	7/1
Duquesne University (PA)	7/1
Middle Tennessee State University	7/1
New Jersey Institute of Technology	7/1

School	Admission deadline
South Carolina State University	7/1
University of Memphis	7/1
University of Missouri–Rolla	7/1
University of North Dakota	7/1
University of Texas–Dallas	7/1
Alabama Agricultural and Mechanical University	7/15
Bowling Green State University (OH)	7/15
Cleveland State University	7/15
Texas Woman's University	7/15
University of Mississippi	7/20
Louisiana Tech University	7/31
University of Texas–El Paso	7/31
Auburn University (AL)	8/1
Iowa State University	8/1
Jackson State University (MS)	8/1
New Mexico Institute of Mining and Technology	8/1
Northern Illinois University	8/1
St. Louis University	8/1
Tennessee State University	8/1
Texas A&M University–Commerce	8/1
Texas Southern University	8/1
University of Akron (OH)	8/1
University of Alaska–Fairbanks	8/1
University of Idaho	8/1
University of North Carolina–Greensboro	8/1
University of North Texas	8/1
University of Northern Colorado	8/1
University of Wisconsin–Milwaukee	8/1
Wayne State University (MI)	8/1
West Virginia University	8/1
Western Michigan University	8/1
University of Wyoming	8/10
University of Massachusetts–Boston	8/11
Indiana State University	8/15
North Dakota State University	8/15
University of Alabama–Huntsville	8/15
University of Arkansas	8/15
Southern Illinois University–Carbondale	8/17
University of Louisville (KY)	8/22
University of South Alabama	8/22
University of Southern Mississippi	8/25
New Mexico State University	8/28
University of Missouri–St. Louis	8/28
University of New Orleans	8/30
Adelphi University (NY)	rolling
Alliant International University (CA)	rolling
Andrews University (MI)	rolling
Arizona State University	rolling
Ball State University (IN)	rolling
Central Michigan University	rolling
DePaul University (IL)	rolling
East Tennessee State University	rolling
Florida Institute of Technology	rolling
Hofstra University (NY)	rolling
Idaho State University	rolling
Illinois Institute of Technology	rolling
Indiana University of Pennsylvania	rolling
Indiana University–Bloomington	rolling

School	Admission deadline
Indiana University–Purdue University–Indianapolis	rolling
Kansas State University	rolling
Loyola University Chicago	rolling
Marquette University (WI)	rolling
Michigan State University	rolling
Michigan Technological University	rolling
Mississippi State University	rolling
Montana State University–Bozeman	rolling
National-Louis University (IL)	rolling
Northern Arizona University	rolling
Nova Southeastern University (FL)	rolling
Oakland University (MI)	rolling
Oklahoma State University	rolling
Pennsylvania State University–University Park	rolling
Polytechnic University (NY)	rolling
Portland State University (OR)	rolling
Purdue University–West Lafayette (IN)	rolling
Rutgers–New Brunswick (NJ)	rolling
Rutgers–Newark (NJ)	rolling
SUNY College Environmental Science and Forestry	rolling
SUNY–Binghamton	rolling
SUNY–Stony Brook	rolling
Seton Hall University (NJ)	rolling
South Dakota State University	rolling
St. John's University (NY)	rolling
Texas A&M University–Kingsville	rolling
Union Institute and University (OH)	rolling
University at Buffalo–SUNY	rolling
University of Alabama	rolling
University of Arkansas–Little Rock	rolling
University of Bridgeport (CT)	rolling
Univ. of Colorado–Denver and Health Sciences	rolling
University of Dayton (OH)	rolling
University of Hartford (CT)	rolling
University of La Verne (CA)	rolling
University of Louisiana–Lafayette	rolling
University of Maine–Orono	rolling
University of Massachusetts–Lowell	rolling
University of Minnesota–Twin Cities	rolling
University of Missouri–Columbia	rolling
University of Missouri–Kansas City	rolling
University of Montana	rolling
University of Nevada–Reno	rolling
University of Pittsburgh	rolling
University of South Dakota	rolling
University of St. Thomas (MN)	rolling
University of Tennessee	rolling
University of Texas–Arlington	rolling
University of Toledo (OH)	rolling
University of Tulsa (OK)	rolling
University of the Pacific (CA)	rolling
Utah State University	rolling
Virginia Commonwealth University	rolling
Washington State University	rolling
Wichita State University (KS)	rolling
Widener University (PA)	rolling
Wilmington College (DE)	rolling
Wright State University (OH)	rolling

Liberal Arts Colleges

College	Admission deadline
Centre College (KY)	2/1
DePauw University (IN)	2/1
Dickinson College (PA)	2/1
Franklin and Marshall College (PA)	2/1
Goucher College (MD)	2/1
Guilford College (NC)	2/1
Hobart and William Smith Colleges (NY)	2/1
Knox College (IL)	2/1
Lewis and Clark College (OR)	2/1
McDaniel College (MD)	2/1
Sewanee–University of the South (TN)	2/1
Spelman College (GA)	2/1
Sweet Briar College (VA)	2/1
Transylvania University (KY)	2/1
University of Puget Sound (WA)	2/1
Willamette University (OR)	2/1
Wofford College (SC)	2/1
Allegheny College (PA)	2/15
College of Wooster (OH)	2/15
College of the Atlantic (ME)	2/15
Drew University (NJ)	2/15
Earlham College (IN)	2/15
Gettysburg College (PA)	2/15
Hartwick College (NY)	2/15
Hillsdale College (MI)	2/15
Kalamazoo College (MI)	2/15
Marlboro College (VT)	2/15
Moravian College (PA)	2/15
Morehouse College (GA)	2/15
Muhlenberg College (PA)	2/15
Southwestern University (TX)	2/15
St. Lawrence University (NY)	2/15
Ursinus College (PA)	2/15
Virginia Military Institute	2/15
Westmont College (CA)	2/15
University of North Carolina–Asheville	2/16
Albion College (MI)	3/1
Christopher Newport University (VA)	3/1
Coe College (IA)	3/1
Cornell College (IA)	3/1
Hampden-Sydney College (VA)	3/1
Hanover College (IN)	3/1
Juniata College (PA)	3/1
Ohio Wesleyan University	3/1
Principia College (IL)	3/1
Randolph-Macon College (VA)	3/1
Siena College (NY)	3/1
St. John's College (NM)	3/1
Susquehanna University (PA)	3/1
Washington College (MD)	3/1
Washington and Jefferson College (PA)	3/1
Wells College (NY)	3/1
Roanoke College (VA)	3/15
University of Minnesota–Morris	3/15
Wittenberg University (OH)	3/15
Gustavus Adolphus College (MN)	4/1
Hiram College (OH)	4/15
Agnes Scott College (GA)	5/1
Austin College (TX)	5/1
Lake Forest College (IL)	5/1
New College of Florida	5/1
Richard Stockton College of New Jersey	5/1
St. Vincent College (PA)	5/1
Albertson College (ID)	6/1
Fisk University (TN)	6/1
Lycoming College (PA)	6/1
Millsaps College (MS)	6/1
Lees-McRae College (NC)	7/1
St. Augustine's College (NC)	7/1
University of Hawaii–Hilo	7/1
West Virginia Wesleyan College	7/1
Adrian College (MI)	8/1
Fort Lewis College (CO)	8/1
Georgetown College (KY)	8/1
Hastings College (NE)	8/1
Hendrix College (AR)	8/1
Huntingdon College (AL)	8/1
Lane College (TN)	8/1
Muskingum College (OH)	8/1
Paine College (GA)	8/1
Rosemont College (PA)	8/1
San Diego Christian College (CA)	8/1
Schreiner University (TX)	8/1
University of Dallas	8/1
University of Pittsburgh–Greensburg	8/1
Wesleyan College (GA)	8/1
Western State College of Colorado	8/1
William Jewell College (MO)	8/1
Bethel College (TN)	8/4
Virginia Union University	8/9
Coastal Carolina University (SC)	8/15
Goshen College (IN)	8/15
Mesa State College (CO)	8/15
Nebraska Wesleyan University	8/15
Seton Hill University (PA)	8/15
University of Virginia–Wise	8/15
Olivet College (MI)	8/19
Albright College (PA)	rolling
Alma College (MI)	rolling
Antioch College (OH)	rolling
Arkansas Baptist College	rolling
Augustana College (IL)	rolling
Beloit College (WI)	rolling
Bennett College (NC)	rolling
Bethany College (WV)	rolling
Birmingham-Southern College (AL)	rolling
Blackburn College (IL)	rolling
Bridgewater College (VA)	rolling
California State University–Monterey Bay	rolling
Chatham College (PA)	rolling
Christendom College (VA)	rolling
College of St. Benedict (MN)	rolling
Concordia College–Moorhead (MN)	rolling
Eastern Mennonite University (VA)	rolling
Eckerd College (FL)	rolling
Emory and Henry College (VA)	rolling
Erskine College (SC)	rolling
Evergreen State College (WA)	rolling
Franklin Pierce College (NH)	rolling
Gordon College (MA)	rolling
Greensboro College (NC)	rolling
Hollins University (VA)	rolling
Hope College (MI)	rolling
Houghton College (NY)	rolling
Illinois Wesleyan University	rolling
Judson College (AL)	rolling
King College (TN)	rolling
Lindsey Wilson College (KY)	rolling
Luther College (IA)	rolling
Lyon College (AR)	rolling
Marymount Manhattan College (NY)	rolling
Massachusetts College of Liberal Arts	rolling
Mills College (CA)	rolling
Oglethorpe University (GA)	rolling
Pine Manor College (MA)	rolling
Presbyterian College (SC)	rolling
Randolph-Macon Woman's College (VA)	rolling
Rhodes College (TN)	rolling
Ripon College (WI)	rolling
Salem College (NC)	rolling
Shawnee State University (OH)	rolling
St. Andrews Presbyterian College (NC)	rolling
St. Anselm College (NH)	rolling
St. John's University (MN)	rolling
St. Olaf College (MN)	rolling
Stephens College (MO)	rolling
Talladega College (AL)	rolling
Texas A&M University–Galveston	rolling
Thomas Aquinas College (CA)	rolling
Tougaloo College (MS)	rolling
University of Judaism (CA)	rolling
University of Maine–Presque Isle	rolling
University of Pittsburgh–Bradford	rolling
Virginia Wesleyan College	rolling
Wabash College (IN)	rolling
Westminster College (MO)	rolling
Whittier College (CA)	rolling

Getting a late start? All is not lost

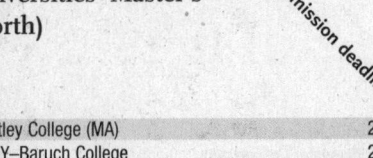

Universities–Master's (North)

	Admission deadline
Bentley College (MA)	2/1
CUNY–Baruch College	2/1
College of St. Rose (NY)	2/1
Ithaca College (NY)	2/1
Quinnipiac University (CT)	2/1
St. Joseph's University (PA)	2/1
St. Michael's College (VT)	2/1
Assumption College (MA)	2/15
Bridgewater State College (MA)	2/15
Bryant University (RI)	2/15
College of New Jersey	2/15
Iona College (NY)	2/15
Marist College (NY)	2/15
Nazareth College of Rochester (NY)	2/15
Towson University (MD)	2/15
Emmanuel College (MA)	3/1
Manhattanville College (NY)	3/1
Monmouth University (NJ)	3/1
Montclair State University (NJ)	3/1
Simmons College (MA)	3/1
Suffolk University (MA)	3/1
Trinity University (DC)	3/1
University of Scranton (PA)	3/1
Wagner College (NY)	3/1
Westfield State College (MA)	3/1
CUNY–Hunter College	3/15
Rowan University (NJ)	3/15
Delaware State University	4/1
East Stroudsburg University of Pennsylvania	4/1
Keene State College (NH)	4/1
New Jersey City University	4/1
Plymouth State University (NH)	4/1
SUNY College of Arts and Sciences–New Paltz	4/1
Springfield College (MA)	4/1
Manhattan College (NY)	4/15
Canisius College (NY)	5/1
Framingham State College (MA)	5/1
Rhode Island College	5/1
Western Connecticut State University	5/1
William Paterson University of New Jersey	5/1
Kean University (NJ)	5/31
Central Connecticut State University	6/1
SUNY–Purchase College	6/1
Worcester State College (MA)	6/1
St. Bonaventure University (NY)	6/15
University of the District of Columbia	6/15
Lincoln University (PA)	7/1
Robert Morris University (PA)	7/1
Southern Connecticut State University	7/1
Mansfield University of Pennsylvania	7/6
Chestnut Hill College (PA)	7/15

	Admission deadline
Coppin State University (MD)	7/15
University of Maryland–Eastern Shore	7/15
Carlow University (PA)	8/1
DeSales University (PA)	8/1
Georgian Court University (NJ)	8/1
Niagara University (NY)	8/1
SUNY–Plattsburgh	8/1
St. Joseph's College (ME)	8/1
CUNY–Lehman College	8/15
Immaculata University (PA)	8/15
St. Peter's College (NJ)	8/15
University of New England (ME)	8/15
Gwynedd-Mercy College (PA)	8/20
Edinboro University of Pennsylvania	8/30
Husson College (ME)	8/30
Rivier College (NH)	8/30
College of New Rochelle (NY)	8/31
Alfred University (NY)	rolling
American International College (MA)	rolling
Anna Maria College (MA)	rolling
Arcadia University (PA)	rolling
Bloomsburg University of Pennsylvania	rolling
CUNY–City College	rolling
CUNY–College of Staten Island	rolling
CUNY–Queens College	rolling
Cabrini College (PA)	rolling
California University of Pennsylvania	rolling
Castleton State College (VT)	rolling
Cheyney University of Pennsylvania	rolling
Clarion University of Pennsylvania	rolling
College Misericordia (PA)	rolling
College of Mount St. Vincent (NY)	rolling
College of Notre Dame of Maryland	rolling
College of St. Joseph (VT)	rolling
Dowling College (NY)	rolling
Eastern Connecticut State University	rolling
Eastern University (PA)	rolling
Elms College (College of Our Lady of the Elms) (MA)	rolling
Fairleigh Dickinson University (NJ)	rolling
Fitchburg State College (MA)	rolling
Frostburg State University (MD)	rolling
Gallaudet University (DC)	rolling
Gannon University (PA)	rolling
Geneva College (PA)	rolling
Goddard College (VT)	rolling
Holy Family University (PA)	rolling
Hood College (MD)	rolling
Johnson State College (VT)	rolling
Johnson and Wales University (RI)	rolling
King's College (PA)	rolling
Kutztown University of Pennsylvania	rolling

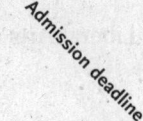

	Admission deadline
La Roche College (PA)	rolling
La Salle University (PA)	rolling
Le Moyne College (NY)	rolling
Lebanon Valley College (PA)	rolling
Lesley University (MA)	rolling
Lock Haven University of Pennsylvania	rolling
Long Island University–C.W. Post Campus (NY)	rolling
Marywood University (PA)	rolling
Mercy College (NY)	rolling
Millersville University of Pennsylvania	rolling
Molloy College (NY)	rolling
Morgan State University (MD)	rolling
Mount St. Mary College (NY)	rolling
Mount St. Mary's University (MD)	rolling
New York Institute of Technology	rolling
Norwich University (VT)	rolling
Nyack College (NY)	rolling
Pennsylvania State–Erie, The Behrend College	rolling
Philadelphia University	rolling
Point Park University (PA)	rolling
Regis College (MA)	rolling
Rider University (NJ)	rolling
Roberts Wesleyan College (NY)	rolling
Rochester Institute of Technology (NY)	rolling
Rutgers–Camden (NJ)	rolling
SUNY College–Brockport	rolling
SUNY College–Cortland	rolling
SUNY College–Potsdam	rolling
SUNY–Buffalo State College	rolling
SUNY–Fredonia	rolling
SUNY–Oswego	rolling
Sacred Heart University (CT)	rolling
Salem State College (MA)	rolling
Salve Regina University (RI)	rolling
Shippensburg University of Pennsylvania	rolling
Slippery Rock University of Pennsylvania	rolling
Southeastern University (DC)	rolling
St. Francis University (PA)	rolling
St. John Fisher College (NY)	rolling
St. Joseph College (CT)	rolling
St. Thomas Aquinas College (NY)	rolling
Touro College (NY)	rolling
University of Massachusetts–Dartmouth	rolling
University of New Haven (CT)	rolling
Waynesburg College (PA)	rolling
West Chester University of Pennsylvania	rolling
Western New England College (MA)	rolling
Wheelock College (MA)	rolling
Wilkes University (PA)	rolling
York College of Pennsylvania	rolling

Universities–Master's (South)

	Admission deadline			Admission deadline			Admission deadline
University of Mary Washington (VA)	2/1	Belmont University (TN)	8/1	Francis Marion University (SC)	rolling
Radford University (VA)	2/1	Campbellsville University (KY)	8/1	Freed-Hardeman University (TN)	rolling
University of Mary Washington (VA)	2/1	Carson-Newman College (TN)	8/1	Gardner-Webb University (NC)	rolling
University of North Carolina–Wilmington	2/1	Centenary College of Louisiana	8/1	Jacksonville State University (AL)	rolling
Rollins College (FL)	2/15	Delta State University (MS)	8/1	Jacksonville University (FL)	rolling
Warren Wilson College (NC)	2/28	Eastern Kentucky University	8/1	Liberty University (VA)	rolling
Hampton University (VA)	3/1	Florida Gulf Coast University	8/1	Lincoln Memorial University (TN)	rolling
Stetson University (FL)	3/15	Louisiana State University–Shreveport	8/1	Lipscomb University (TN)	rolling
Tuskegee University (AL)	3/15	Milligan College (TN)	8/1	Longwood University (VA)	rolling
College of Charleston (SC)	4/1	Murray State University (KY)	8/1	Loyola University New Orleans	rolling
Converse College (SC)	4/1	Northern Kentucky University	8/1	Lynchburg College (VA)	rolling
Georgia College and State University	4/1	Tennessee Technological University	8/1	Lynn University (FL)	rolling
Georgia Southern University	5/1	Union University (TN)	8/1	Marshall University (WV)	rolling
Virginia State University	5/1	University of Montevallo (AL)	8/1	Mary Baldwin College (VA)	rolling
Florida A&M University	5/10	University of Tennessee–Martin	8/1	Marymount University (VA)	rolling
Kennesaw State University (GA)	5/27	Western Carolina University (NC)	8/1	McNeese State University (LA)	rolling
Norfolk State University (VA)	5/31	Western Kentucky University	8/1	Meredith College (NC)	rolling
Armstrong Atlantic State University (GA)	6/30	North Carolina Central University	8/6	Mississippi University for Women	rolling
University of West Florida	6/30	Kentucky State University	8/10	Morehead State University (KY)	rolling
Albany State University (GA)	7/1	University of Mobile (AL)	8/10	Nicholls State University (LA)	rolling
Averett University (VA)	7/1	Southern Wesleyan University (SC)	8/11	North Carolina A&T State University	rolling
Columbus State University (GA)	7/1	Bellarmine University (KY)	8/15	Palm Beach Atlantic University (FL)	rolling
Harding University (AR)	7/1	Lander University (SC)	8/15	Pfeiffer University (NC)	rolling
Mercer University (GA)	7/1	Mississippi College	8/15	Queens University of Charlotte (NC)	rolling
North Georgia College and State University	7/1	Southeastern Louisiana University	8/15	Samford University (AL)	rolling
Piedmont College (GA)	7/1	St. Leo University (FL)	8/15	Shenandoah University (VA)	rolling
Southern University and A&M College (LA)	7/1	University of the Cumberlands (KY)	8/15	Spalding University (KY)	rolling
Southern University–New Orleans	7/1	Arkansas State University	8/21	St. Thomas University (FL)	rolling
University of North Carolina–Charlotte	7/1	Fayetteville State University (NC)	8/25	The Citadel (SC)	rolling
University of West Georgia	7/1	Southern Arkansas University	8/27	Trevecca Nazarene University (TN)	rolling
Xavier University of Louisiana	7/1	Austin Peay State University (TN)	8/28	Troy University (AL)	rolling
University of North Florida	7/2	Charleston Southern University (SC)	8/29	Tusculum College (TN)	rolling
Northwestern State University of Louisiana	7/6	Alcorn State University (MS)	rolling	University of Louisiana–Monroe	rolling
Grambling State University (LA)	7/15	Appalachian State University (NC)	rolling	University of North Alabama	rolling
Henderson State University (AR)	7/15	Arkansas Tech University	rolling	University of North Carolina–Pembroke	rolling
Spring Hill College (AL)	7/15	Augusta State University (GA)	rolling	University of Tampa (FL)	rolling
Valdosta State University (GA)	7/15	Barry University (FL)	rolling	University of Tennessee–Chattanooga	rolling
Georgia Southwestern State University	7/21	Brenau University (GA)	rolling	University of West Alabama	rolling
Fort Valley State University (GA)	7/23	Christian Brothers University (TN)	rolling	Wheeling Jesuit University (WV)	rolling
Auburn University–Montgomery (AL)	7/25	Cumberland University (TN)	rolling	William Carey College (MS)	rolling
Alabama State University	8/1	Embry Riddle Aeronautical University (FL)	rolling	Winthrop University (SC)	rolling

Universities–Master's (Midwest)

	Admission deadline			Admission deadline			Admission deadline
John Carroll University (OH)	2/1	Anderson University (IN)	7/1	Minnesota State University–Moorhead	8/1
University of Evansville (IN)	2/1	Malone College (OH)	7/1	Oakland City University (IN)	8/1
Xavier University (OH)	2/1	Northeastern Illinois University	7/1	Park University (MO)	8/1
Bethel University (MN)	3/1	University of Findlay (OH)	7/1	Rockford College (IL)	8/1
Truman State University (MO)	3/1	Missouri State University	7/20	Spring Arbor University (MI)	8/1
Drury University (MO)	3/15	Cardinal Stritch University (WI)	8/1	University of Minnesota–Duluth	8/1
Grand Valley State University (MI)	5/1	Concordia University (NE)	8/1	University of Nebraska–Omaha	8/1
Southern Illinois University–Edwardsville	5/1	Concordia University Wisconsin	8/1	University of St. Francis (IN)	8/1
St. Mary's University of Minnesota	5/1	Creighton University (NE)	8/1	University of St. Francis (IL)	8/1
Olivet Nazarene University (IL)	5/15	Heidelberg College (OH)	8/1	University of Wisconsin–Parkside	8/1
Western Illinois University	5/15	Indiana University-Purdue University–Fort Wayne	8/1	Washburn University (KS)	8/1
North Park University (IL)	6/1	Indiana Wesleyan University	8/1	Ferris State University (MI)	8/4
St. Cloud State University (MN)	6/1	Lincoln University (MO)	8/1	Augsburg College (MN)	8/15
Webster University (MO)	6/1	Marygrove College (MI)	8/1	College of Mount St. Joseph (OH)	8/15
Rockhurst University (MO)	6/30	MidAmerica Nazarene University (KS)	8/1	Lake Superior State University (MI)	8/15

Getting a late start? All is not lost

Universities–Master's (Midwest), continued

	Admission deadline
Maryville University of St. Louis (MO)	8/15
University of Dubuque (IA)	8/15
University of Northern Iowa	8/15
University of Southern Indiana	8/15
Valparaiso University (IN)	8/15
Walsh University (OH)	8/15
William Woods University (MO)	8/15
Youngstown State University (OH)	8/15
Central Missouri State University	8/19
University of Mary (ND)	8/23
Edgewood College (WI)	8/26
Minnesota State University–Mankato	8/27
Mount Marty College (SD)	8/30
Aquinas College (MI)	rolling
Ashland University (OH)	rolling
Aurora University (IL)	rolling
Avila University (MO)	rolling
Baker University (KS)	rolling
Baldwin-Wallace College (OH)	rolling
Bellevue University (NE)	rolling
Bemidji State University (MN)	rolling
Benedictine College (KS)	rolling
Benedictine University (IL)	rolling
Bradley University (IL)	rolling
Butler University (IN)	rolling
Capital University (OH)	rolling
Carthage College (WI)	rolling
Chadron State College (NE)	rolling
Chicago State University	rolling
College of St. Catherine (MN)	rolling
College of St. Scholastica (MN)	rolling

	Admission deadline
Columbia College (IL)	rolling
Concordia University–River Forest (IL)	rolling
Doane College (NE)	rolling
Dominican University (IL)	rolling
Drake University (IA)	rolling
Eastern Illinois University	rolling
Eastern Michigan University	rolling
Emporia State University (KS)	rolling
Fontbonne University (MO)	rolling
Fort Hays State University (KS)	rolling
Franciscan University of Steubenville (OH)	rolling
Friends University (KS)	rolling
Hamline University (MN)	rolling
Indiana University Northwest	rolling
Indiana University Southeast	rolling
Indiana University–South Bend	rolling
Lake Erie College (OH)	rolling
Lawrence Technological University (MI)	rolling
Lewis University (IL)	rolling
Lindenwood University (MO)	rolling
Madonna University (MI)	rolling
Maharishi University of Management (IA)	rolling
Marian College of Fond du Lac (WI)	rolling
Metropolitan State University (MN)	rolling
Minot State University (ND)	rolling
Mount Mary College (WI)	rolling
Newman University (KS)	rolling
North Central College (IL)	rolling
Northern Michigan University	rolling
Northwest Missouri State University	rolling
Peru State College (NE)	rolling

	Admission deadline
Pittsburg State University (KS)	rolling
Quincy University (IL)	rolling
Saginaw Valley State University (MI)	rolling
Siena Heights University (MI)	rolling
Silver Lake College (WI)	rolling
Southeast Missouri State University	rolling
Southwest Baptist University (MO)	rolling
St. Ambrose University (IA)	rolling
St. Xavier University (IL)	rolling
University of Detroit Mercy	rolling
University of Indianapolis	rolling
University of Michigan–Dearborn	rolling
University of Michigan–Flint	rolling
University of Nebraska–Kearney	rolling
University of Rio Grande (OH)	rolling
University of Sioux Falls (SD)	rolling
University of St. Mary (KS)	rolling
University of Wisconsin–Eau Claire	rolling
University of Wisconsin–Green Bay	rolling
University of Wisconsin–La Crosse	rolling
University of Wisconsin–Oshkosh	rolling
University of Wisconsin–Platteville	rolling
University of Wisconsin–River Falls	rolling
University of Wisconsin–Stevens Point	rolling
University of Wisconsin–Stout	rolling
University of Wisconsin–Superior	rolling
University of Wisconsin–Whitewater	rolling
Ursuline College (OH)	rolling
Viterbo University (WI)	rolling
Wayne State College (NE)	rolling

Universities–Master's (West)

	Admission deadline
California State University–Fresno	2/1
Gonzaga University (WA)	2/1
San Jose State University (CA)	2/1
Trinity University (TX)	2/1
Mount St. Mary's College (CA)	2/15
Point Loma Nazarene University (CA)	3/1
Seattle Pacific University	3/1
Western Washington University	3/1
Whitworth College (WA)	3/1
Central Washington University	4/1
St. Edward's University (TX)	5/1
Tarleton State University (TX)	5/1
Texas State University–San Marcos	5/1
Azusa Pacific University (CA)	6/1
Prairie View A&M University (TX)	6/1
University of Portland (OR)	6/1
University of Redlands (CA)	6/1
California State University–Stanislaus	7/1
Concordia University (OR)	7/1
Montana State University–Billings	7/1
Seattle University	7/1
Texas A&M International University	7/1
Texas A&M University–Corpus Christi	7/1
University of Alaska–Anchorage	7/1
University of Colorado–Colorado Springs	7/1
University of Texas–San Antonio	7/1

	Admission deadline
Boise State University (ID)	7/12
Our Lady of the Lake University (TX)	7/15
California State University–San Bernardino	7/17
California State University–East Bay	7/30
Fresno Pacific University (CA)	7/31
Abilene Christian University (TX)	8/1
Adams State College (CO)	8/1
Alaska Pacific University	8/1
California State University–Sacramento	8/1
Colorado Christian University	8/1
Colorado State University–Pueblo	8/1
Dominican University of California	8/1
Holy Names University (CA)	8/1
Humboldt State University (CA)	8/1
Lamar University (TX)	8/1
LeTourneau University (TX)	8/1
Regis University (CO)	8/1
Sam Houston State University (TX)	8/1
Southern Utah University	8/1
University of Alaska–Southeast	8/1
University of Texas–Brownsville	8/1
Western New Mexico University	8/1
Southern Nazarene University (OK)	8/6
Midwestern State University (TX)	8/7
Northwest Nazarene University (ID)	8/8
University of Texas–Pan American	8/11

	Admission deadline
Angelo State University (TX)	8/15
Eastern Washington University	8/15
Hawaii Pacific University	8/15
Pacific University (OR)	8/15
Prescott College (AZ)	8/15
University of Texas of the Permian Basin	8/15
University of St. Thomas (TX)	8/19
Oklahoma City University	8/21
Weber State University (UT)	8/23
Cameron University (OK)	8/28
University of Great Falls (MT)	8/31
California Baptist University	rolling
California Lutheran University	rolling
California State University–Bakersfield	rolling
California State University–Dominguez Hills	rolling
Chaminade University of Honolulu	rolling
College of Santa Fe (NM)	rolling
College of the Southwest (NM)	rolling
Concordia University (CA)	rolling
Dallas Baptist University	rolling
East Central University (OK)	rolling
Eastern New Mexico University	rolling
George Fox University (OR)	rolling
Hardin-Simmons University (TX)	rolling
Hope International University (CA)	rolling
Houston Baptist University	rolling

	Admission deadline
La Sierra University (CA)	rolling
Loyola Marymount University (CA)	rolling
Marylhurst University (OR)	rolling
Montana State University–Northern	rolling
New Mexico Highlands University	rolling
Northeastern State University (OK)	rolling
Northwestern Oklahoma State University	rolling
Notre Dame de Namur University (CA)	rolling
Oral Roberts University (OK)	rolling
Pacific Lutheran University (WA)	rolling

	Admission deadline
Simpson University (CA)	rolling
Southeastern Oklahoma State University	rolling
Southern Oregon University	rolling
Southwestern Oklahoma State University	rolling
St. Martin's University (WA)	rolling
St. Mary's University of San Antonio	rolling
Stephen F. Austin State University (TX)	rolling
Sul Ross State University (TX)	rolling
Texas Wesleyan University	rolling
University of Central Oklahoma	rolling

	Admission deadline
University of Mary Hardin-Baylor (TX)	rolling
University of Texas–Tyler	rolling
University of the Incarnate Word (TX)	rolling
Walla Walla College (WA)	rolling
Wayland Baptist University (TX)	rolling
West Texas A&M University	rolling
Western Oregon University	rolling
Westminster College (UT)	rolling
Woodbury University (CA)	rolling

Comprehensive Colleges– Bachelor's (North)

	Admission deadline
Grove City College (PA)	2/1
Merrimack College (MA)	2/1
Endicott College (MA)	2/15
Elmira College (NY)	3/1
Ramapo College of New Jersey	3/1
Villa Julie College (MD)	3/1
CUNY–New York City College of Technology	3/14
Colby-Sawyer College (NH)	4/1
Wesley College (DE)	4/30
Simon's Rock College of Bard (MA)	5/31
Thiel College (PA)	6/30
Bloomfield College (NJ)	7/1
Pennsylvania College of Technology	7/1
Atlantic Union College (MA)	8/1
Columbia Union College (MD)	8/1
Neumann College (PA)	8/1
Russell Sage College (NY)	8/1
Unity College (ME)	8/1
Mount Aloysius College (PA)	8/3
Albertus Magnus College (CT)	8/15
Cazenovia College (NY)	8/15

	Admission deadline
Centenary College (NJ)	8/15
College of St. Elizabeth (NJ)	8/15
Concordia College (NY)	8/15
Mount Ida College (MA)	8/15
University of Maine–Machias	8/15
Champlain College (VT)	8/20
CUNY–Medgar Evers College	8/23
University of Maine–Augusta	8/30
St. Joseph's College New York–Brooklyn	8/31
Alvernia College (PA)	rolling
Bay Path College (MA)	rolling
Becker College (MA)	rolling
CUNY–York College	rolling
Caldwell College (NJ)	rolling
Cedar Crest College (PA)	rolling
Curry College (MA)	rolling
Daemen College (NY)	rolling
Daniel Webster College (NH)	rolling
Delaware Valley College (PA)	rolling
Dominican College of Blauvelt (NY)	rolling
Elizabethtown College (PA)	rolling

	Admission deadline
Felician College (NJ)	rolling
Green Mountain College (VT)	rolling
Keuka College (NY)	rolling
Lyndon State College (VT)	rolling
Medaille College (NY)	rolling
Mercyhurst College (PA)	rolling
Messiah College (PA)	rolling
New England College (NH)	rolling
Post University (CT)	rolling
Roger Williams University (RI)	rolling
SUNY College of A&T–Cobleskill	rolling
SUNY College–Old Westbury	rolling
SUNY–Farmingdale	rolling
Southern Vermont College	rolling
St. Francis College (NY)	rolling
University of Maine–Farmington	rolling
University of Maine–Fort Kent	rolling
University of Pittsburgh–Johnstown	rolling
Utica College (NY)	rolling
Wilson College (PA)	rolling

Getting a late start? All is not lost

Comprehensive Colleges– Bachelor's (South)

College	Admission deadline
Allen University (SC)	2/5
Flagler College (FL)	3/1
Maryville College (TN)	3/1
Florida Southern College	4/1
LeMoyne-Owen College (TN)	4/1
Berea College (KY)	4/30
Stillman College (AL)	5/1
Claflin University (SC)	6/30
Voorhees College (SC)	6/30
Alice Lloyd College (KY)	7/1
Anderson University (SC)	7/1
Clayton State University (GA)	7/1
Clearwater Christian College (FL)	7/1
Dillard University (LA)	7/1
Miles College (AL)	7/15
Philander Smith College (AR)	7/15
Winston-Salem State University (NC)	7/15
Our Lady of Holy Cross College (LA)	7/20
Berry College (GA)	7/21
North Carolina Wesleyan College	7/30
Shaw University (NC)	7/30
Bryan College (TN)	7/31
Ohio Valley University (WV)	7/31
Belmont Abbey College (NC)	8/1
Columbia College (SC)	8/1
Elizabeth City State University (NC)	8/1
Emmanuel College (GA)	8/1
Kentucky Christian University	8/1
LaGrange College (GA)	8/1
Martin Methodist College (TN)	8/1
Mississippi Valley State University	8/1
Peace College (NC)	8/1
University of South Carolina–Aiken	8/1
West Virginia State University	8/10

College	Admission deadline
West Virginia University Institute of Technology	8/11
High Point University (NC)	8/15
Lenoir-Rhyne College (NC)	8/15
Louisiana College	8/15
Reinhardt College (GA)	8/15
Thomas More College (KY)	8/15
Pikeville College (KY)	8/16
Shorter College (GA)	8/17
Crichton College (TN)	8/21
Kentucky Wesleyan College	8/21
Alderson-Broaddus College (WV)	8/25
Limestone College (SC)	8/26
North Greenville University (SC)	8/26
Tennessee Wesleyan College	8/31
Asbury College (KY)	rolling
Barton College (NC)	rolling
Belhaven College (MS)	rolling
Benedict College (SC)	rolling
Bethune-Cookman College (FL)	rolling
Bluefield College (VA)	rolling
Bluefield State College (WV)	rolling
Brescia University (KY)	rolling
Brevard College (NC)	rolling
Brewton-Parker College (GA)	rolling
Catawba College (NC)	rolling
Chowan College (NC)	rolling
Coker College (SC)	rolling
Concord University (WV)	rolling
Concordia College (AL)	rolling
Covenant College (GA)	rolling
Davis and Elkins College (WV)	rolling
Edward Waters College (FL)	rolling
Fairmont State University (WV)	rolling
Faulkner University (AL)	rolling

College	Admission deadline
Ferrum College (VA)	rolling
Florida Memorial College	rolling
Glenville State College (WV)	rolling
International College (FL)	rolling
John Brown University (AR)	rolling
Johnson C. Smith University (NC)	rolling
Lambuth University (TN)	rolling
Livingstone College (NC)	rolling
Mars Hill College (NC)	rolling
Methodist College (NC)	rolling
Mid-Continent University (KY)	rolling
Midway College (KY)	rolling
Morris College (SC)	rolling
Mount Olive College (NC)	rolling
Mountain State University (WV)	rolling
Newberry College (SC)	rolling
Oakwood College (AL)	rolling
Ouachita Baptist University (AR)	rolling
Rust College (MS)	rolling
Shepherd University (WV)	rolling
Southeastern University (FL)	rolling
St. Paul's College (VA)	rolling
Thomas University (GA)	rolling
Toccoa Falls College (GA)	rolling
University of Arkansas–Monticello	rolling
University of Arkansas–Pine Bluff	rolling
University of Charleston (WV)	rolling
University of South Carolina–Upstate	rolling
University of the Ozarks (AR)	rolling
Virginia Intermont College	rolling
Warner Southern College (FL)	rolling
West Virginia University–Parkersburg	rolling
Williams Baptist College (AR)	rolling
Wingate University (NC)	rolling

Comprehensive Colleges– Bachelor's (Midwest)

College	Admission deadline
Marietta College (OH)	4/15
Mount Vernon Nazarene University (OH)	5/1
Wilmington College (OH)	5/1
Otterbein College (OH)	6/1
Tri-State University (IN)	6/1
Wilberforce University (OH)	6/1
Black Hills State University (SD)	7/1
Central Christian College (KS)	7/1
Elmhurst College (IL)	7/15
Bethel College (IN)	8/1
Concordia University–St. Paul (MN)	8/1
Dana College (NE)	8/1
Dordt College (IA)	8/1
Eureka College (IL)	8/1
Greenville College (IL)	8/1
Huntington University (IN)	8/1
Illinois College	8/1
Marian College (IN)	8/1
Northwestern College (MN)	8/1
Southwestern College (KS)	8/1
Midland Lutheran College (NE)	8/6
Calvin College (MI)	8/15
Defiance College (OH)	8/15

College	Admission deadline
Evangel University (MO)	8/15
Grace College and Seminary (IN)	8/15
Grand View College (IA)	8/15
Iowa Wesleyan College	8/15
Millikin University (IL)	8/15
Missouri Western State University	8/15
Northland College (WI)	8/15
Northwestern College (IA)	8/15
Ohio Northern University	8/15
Simpson College (IA)	8/15
Bluffton University (OH)	8/20
College of the Ozarks (MO)	8/20
Southwest Minnesota State University (MN)	8/20
Mount Mercy College (IA)	8/25
Hannibal-LaGrange College (MO)	8/26
William Penn University (IA)	8/27
Dakota Wesleyan University (SD)	8/30
Trinity Christian College (IL)	8/31
York College (NE)	8/31
Alverno College (WI)	rolling
Augustana College (SD)	rolling
Bethany College (KS)	rolling
Bethel College (KS)	rolling

College	Admission deadline
Briar Cliff University (IA)	rolling
Buena Vista University (IA)	rolling
Calumet College of St. Joseph (IN)	rolling
Carroll College (WI)	rolling
Cedarville University (OH)	rolling
Central College (IA)	rolling
Central Methodist University (MO)	rolling
Central State University (OH)	rolling
Clarke College (IA)	rolling
College of St. Mary (NE)	rolling
Columbia College (MO)	rolling
Concordia University (MI)	rolling
Crown College (MN)	rolling
Culver-Stockton College (MO)	rolling
Dakota State University (SD)	rolling
Dickinson State University (ND)	rolling
East-West University (IL)	rolling
Franklin College (IN)	rolling
Grace University (NE)	rolling
Graceland University (IA)	rolling
Indiana University East	rolling
Jamestown College (ND)	rolling
Judson College (IL)	rolling

	Admission deadline		Admission deadline		Admission deadline
Kansas Wesleyan University	rolling	Morningside College (IA)	rolling	Sterling College (KS)	rolling
Kendall College (IL)	rolling	Mount Union College (OH)	rolling	Tabor College (KS)	rolling
Loras College (IA)	rolling	Notre Dame College of Ohio	rolling	Union College (NE)	rolling
Lourdes College (OH)	rolling	Ohio Dominican University	rolling	University of Minnesota–Crookston	rolling
MacMurray College (IL)	rolling	Ottawa University (KS)	rolling	Upper Iowa University	rolling
Manchester College (IN)	rolling	Purdue University–North Central (IN)	rolling	Urbana University (OH)	rolling
Mayville State University (ND)	rolling	Rochester College (MI)	rolling	Valley City State University (ND)	rolling
McKendree College (IL)	rolling	St. Joseph's College (IN)	rolling	Waldorf College (IA)	rolling
McPherson College (KS)	rolling	St. Mary's College (IN)	rolling	Wartburg College (IA)	rolling
Missouri Baptist University	rolling	St. Mary-of-the-Woods College (IN)	rolling	Wisconsin Lutheran College	rolling
Missouri Southern State University	rolling	St. Norbert College (WI)	rolling		

Comprehensive Colleges– Bachelor's (West)

	Admission deadline		Admission deadline		Admission deadline
Brigham Young University–Hawaii	2/15	Texas Lutheran University	8/1	Linfield College (OR)	rolling
Carroll College (MT)	6/1	Langston University (OK)	8/10	Master's College and Seminary (CA)	rolling
University of Houston–Downtown	7/1	Howard Payne University (TX)	8/15	Menlo College (CA)	rolling
Bethany College (CA)	7/31	Lubbock Christian University (TX)	8/15	Northwest Christian College (OR)	rolling
Patten University (CA)	7/31	McMurry University (TX)	8/15	Oklahoma Panhandle State University	rolling
Corban College (OR)	8/1	Oklahoma Wesleyan University	8/15	Pacific Union College (CA)	rolling
Huston-Tillotson University (TX)	8/1	Utah Valley State College	8/15	Rocky Mountain College (MT)	rolling
Jarvis Christian College (TX)	8/1	East Texas Baptist University	8/17	Sierra Nevada College (NV)	rolling
Metropolitan State College of Denver	8/1	Cogswell Polytechnical College (CA)	rolling	St. Gregory's University (OK)	rolling
Northwest University (WA)	8/1	Concordia University–Austin (TX)	rolling	Texas College	rolling
Oklahoma Baptist University	8/1	Humphreys College (CA)	rolling	University of Montana–Western	rolling
Paul Quinn College (TX)	8/1	Lewis-Clark State College (ID)	rolling	Vanguard University of Southern California	rolling

Index to Major Fields of Study

You think you'd like to specialize in architectural engineering? Or possibly biblical studies? Use this list to find schools offering majors in subject areas of interest and then learn more about each school by studying its directory entry. For more specifics on programs offered, consult the schools' websites.

Accounting and Computer Science

Houston Baptist Univ.
San Jose State Univ. (CA)
Schreiner Univ. (TX)
Western Washington Univ.

Accounting and Related Services

Abilene Christian Univ. (TX)
Adelphi Univ. (NY)
Adrian College (MI)
Alabama Agricultural and
    Mechanical Univ.
Alabama State Univ.
Alaska Pacific Univ.
Albany State Univ. (GA)
Albertson College (ID)
Albright College (PA)
Alcorn State Univ. (MS)
Alderson-Broaddus College (WV)
Alfred Univ. (NY)
Alma College (MI)
Alvernia College (PA)
American Univ. (DC)
Anderson College (SC)
Anderson Univ. (IN)
Andrews Univ. (MI)
Angelo State Univ. (TX)
Appalachian State Univ. (NC)
Aquinas College (MI)
Arcadia Univ. (PA)
Arizona State Univ.
Arizona State Univ. West
Arkansas State Univ.
Arkansas Tech Univ.
Asbury College (KY)
Ashland Univ. (OH)
Assumption College (MA)
Auburn Univ. (AL)
Auburn Univ.–Montgomery (AL)
Augsburg College (MN)
Augusta State Univ. (GA)
Augustana College (SD)
Augustana College (IL)
Aurora Univ. (IL)
Averett Univ. (VA)
Avila Univ. (MO)
Azusa Pacific Univ. (CA)
Babson College (MA)
Baker College of Flint (MI)
Baker Univ. (KS)
Baldwin-Wallace College (OH)
Ball State Univ. (IN)
Barry Univ. (FL)
Barton College (NC)

Baylor Univ. (TX)
Belhaven College (MS)
Bellarmine Univ. (KY)
Bellevue Univ. (NE)
Belmont Abbey College (NC)
Belmont Univ. (TN)
Bemidji State Univ. (MN)
Benedict College (SC)
Benedictine College (KS)
Benedictine Univ. (IL)
Bennett College (NC)
Bentley College (MA)
Berry College (GA)
Bethany College (WV)
Bethany College (KS)
Bethel College (IN)
Bethel Univ. (MN)
Bethune-Cookman College (FL)
Black Hills State Univ. (SD)
Bloomfield College (NJ)
Bloomsburg Univ. of Pennsylvania
Bluefield College (VA)
Bluefield State College (WV)
Bluffton Univ. (OH)
Boise State Univ. (ID)
Boston Univ.
Bowling Green State Univ. (OH)
Bradley Univ. (IL)
Brenau Univ. (GA)
Brescia Univ. (KY)
Brewton-Parker College (GA)
Briar Cliff Univ. (IA)
Bridgewater State College (MA)
Brigham Young Univ.–Hawaii
Brigham Young Univ.–Provo (UT)
Bryant College (RI)
Bucknell Univ. (PA)
Buena Vista Univ. (IA)
Butler Univ. (IN)
Cabrini College (PA)
Caldwell College (NJ)
California Baptist Univ.
California Lutheran Univ.
California State Polytechnic
    Univ.–Pomona
California State Univ.–Fullerton
California State Univ.–Hayward
California State Univ.–Long Beach
California State Univ.–Sacramento
California State Univ.–San Marcos
California Univ. of Pennsylvania
Calvin College (MI)
Cameron Univ. (OK)
Campbell Univ. (NC)
Campbellsville Univ. (KY)
Canisius College (NY)
Capital Univ. (OH)
Cardinal Stritch Univ. (WI)
Carlow College (PA)
Carroll College (MT)

Carroll College (WI)
Carson-Newman College (TN)
Carthage College (WI)
Case Western Reserve Univ. (OH)
Castleton State College (VT)
Catawba College (NC)
Catholic Univ. of America (DC)
Cazenovia College (NY)
Cedar Crest College (PA)
Cedarville Univ. (OH)
Centenary College (NJ)
Centenary College of Louisiana
Central Connecticut State Univ.
Central Methodist Univ. (MO)
Central Michigan Univ.
Central Missouri State Univ.
Central State Univ. (OH)
Central Washington Univ.
Chaminade Univ. of Honolulu
Champlain College (VT)
Chapman Univ. (CA)
Chatham College (PA)
Chestnut Hill College (PA)
Christopher Newport Univ. (VA)
City Univ. (WA)
Clarion Univ. of Pennsylvania
Clark Atlanta Univ.
Clayton Coll. and State Univ. (GA)
Clearwater Christian College (FL)
Cleary Univ. (MI)
Cleveland State Univ.
Coastal Carolina Univ. (SC)
Coe College (IA)
College Misericordia (PA)
College of Charleston (SC)
College of Mount St. Joseph (OH)
College of New Jersey
College of Santa Fe (NM)
College of St. Benedict (MN)
College of St. Catherine (MN)
College of St. Joseph (VT)
College of St. Rose (NY)
College of St. Scholastica (MN)
College of the Holy Cross (MA)
College of the Ozarks (MO)
Colorado Christian Univ.
Colorado State Univ.
Colorado State Univ.–Pueblo
Columbia College (SC)
Columbia College (MO)
Columbia Union College (MD)
Columbus State Univ. (GA)
Concordia Coll.–Moorhead (MN)
Concordia Univ. (NE)
Concordia Univ. Wisconsin
Concordia Univ.–River Forest (IL)
Concordia Univ.–St. Paul (MN)
Converse College (SC)
Cornerstone Univ. (MI)
Culver-Stockton College (MO)

Cumberland College (KY)
Cumberland Univ. (TN)
CUNY–Baruch College
CUNY–Brooklyn College
CUNY–College of Staten Island
CUNY–Hunter College
CUNY–Lehman College
CUNY–Medgar Evers College
CUNY–York College
Daemen College (NY)
Dakota State Univ. (SD)
Dakota Wesleyan Univ. (SD)
Dallas Baptist Univ.
Davenport Univ. (MI)
David Lipscomb Univ. (TN)
Davis and Elkins College (WV)
Defiance College (OH)
Delaware State Univ.
Delaware Valley College (PA)
Delta State Univ. (MS)
Depaul Univ. (IL)
Desales Univ. (PA)
Dickinson State Univ. (ND)
Dillard Univ. (LA)
Dominican Coll. of Blauvelt (NY)
Dominican Univ. (IL)
Dordt College (IA)
Dowling College (NY)
Drake Univ. (IA)
Drexel Univ. (PA)
Drury Univ. (MO)
Duquesne Univ. (PA)
East Carolina Univ. (NC)
East Central Univ. (OK)
East Tennessee State Univ.
East Texas Baptist Univ.
Eastern Connecticut State Univ.
Eastern Illinois Univ.
Eastern Kentucky Univ.
Eastern Mennonite Univ. (VA)
Eastern Michigan Univ.
Eastern New Mexico Univ.
Eastern Univ. (PA)
Eastern Washington Univ.
Edgewood College (WI)
Edward Waters College (FL)
Elizabeth City State Univ. (NC)
Elizabethtown College (PA)
Elmhurst College (IL)
Elmira College (NY)
Elms College (College of Our Lady
    of the Elms) (MA)
Elon Univ. (NC)
Emory Univ. (GA)
Emporia State Univ. (KS)
Eureka College (IL)
Evangel Univ. (MO)
Excelsior College (NY)
Fairleigh Dickinson Univ. (NJ)
Fairmont State Univ. (WV)

Fayetteville State Univ. (NC)
Ferris State Univ. (MI)
Ferrum College (VA)
Fitchburg State College (MA)
Flagler College (FL)
Florida Atlantic Univ.
Florida Gulf Coast Univ.
Florida Institute of Technology
Florida International Univ.
Florida Southern College
Florida State Univ.
Fordham Univ. (NY)
Fort Hays State Univ. (KS)
Fort Lewis College (CO)
Fort Valley State Univ. (GA)
Francis Marion Univ. (SC)
Franciscan Univ. of Steubenville
    (OH)
Franklin College (IN)
Franklin Pierce College (NH)
Freed-Hardeman Univ. (TN)
Fresno Pacific Univ. (CA)
Friends Univ. (KS)
Frostburg State Univ. (MD)
Furman Univ. (SC)
Gallaudet Univ. (DC)
Gannon Univ. (PA)
Gardner-Webb Univ. (NC)
Geneva College (PA)
George Fox Univ. (OR)
George Mason Univ. (VA)
George Washington Univ. (DC)
Georgetown College (KY)
Georgetown Univ. (DC)
Georgia College and State Univ.
Georgia Southern Univ.
Georgia Southwestern State Univ.
Georgia State Univ.
Georgian Court Univ. (NJ)
Golden Gate Univ. (CA)
Goldey Beacom College (DE)
Gonzaga Univ. (WA)
Gordon College (MA)
Goshen College (IN)
Grace College and Seminary (IN)
Graceland Univ. (IA)
Grambling State Univ. (LA)
Grand Canyon Univ. (AZ)
Grand Valley State Univ. (MI)
Grand View College (IA)
Greensboro College (NC)
Greenville College (IL)
Grove City College (PA)
Guilford College (NC)
Gustavus Adolphus College (MN)
Gwynedd-Mercy College (PA)
Hampton Univ. (VA)
Hardin-Simmons Univ. (TX)
Harding Univ. (AR)
Hartwick College (NY)

Hastings College (NE)
Hawaii Pacific Univ.
Heidelberg College (OH)
Henderson State Univ. (AR)
Hendrix College (AR)
Heritage College (WA)
High Point Univ. (NC)
Hillsdale College (MI)
Hiram College (OH)
Hofstra Univ. (NY)
Holy Family Univ. (PA)
Hope College (MI)
Houghton College (NY)
Houston Baptist Univ.
Howard Payne Univ. (TX)
Howard Univ. (DC)
Humphreys College (CA)
Huntingdon College (AL)
Huntington College (IN)
Husson College (ME)
Idaho State Univ.
Illinois College
Illinois State Univ.
Illinois Wesleyan Univ.
Immaculata Univ. (PA)
Indiana Institute of Technology
Indiana State Univ.
Indiana Univ. of Pennsylvania
Indiana Univ. Southeast
Indiana Univ.–Kokomo
Indiana Univ.–South Bend
Indiana Univ.–Purdue Univ.–Fort
  Wayne
Indiana Wesleyan Univ.
International College (FL)
Iona College (NY)
Ithaca College (NY)
Jacksonville State Univ. (AL)
Jacksonville Univ. (FL)
James Madison Univ. (VA)
Jamestown College (ND)
John Brown Univ. (AR)
John Carroll Univ. (OH)
Johnson and Wales Univ. (RI)
Judson College (IL)
Juniata College (PA)
Kansas State Univ.
Kansas Wesleyan Univ.
Kean Univ. (NJ)
Kennesaw State Univ. (GA)
Kent State Univ. (OH)
Kentucky State Univ.
Kentucky Wesleyan College
Kettering Univ. (MI)
Keuka College (NY)
King's College (PA)
Kutztown Univ. of Pennsylvania
La Roche College (PA)
La Salle Univ. (PA)
La Sierra Univ. (CA)
Lagrange College (GA)
Lake Erie College (OH)
Lake Superior State Univ. (MI)
Lakeland College (WI)
Lamar Univ. (TX)
Lambuth Univ. (TN)
Lasell College (MA)
Le Moyne College (NY)
Lebanon Valley College (PA)
Lehigh Univ. (PA)
Lemoyne-Owen College (TN)

Lenoir-Rhyne College (NC)
Letourneau Univ. (TX)
Lewis Univ. (IL)
Lewis-Clark State College (ID)
Liberty Univ. (VA)
Limestone College (SC)
Lincoln Univ. (PA)
Lincoln Univ. (MO)
Lindenwood Univ. (MO)
Linfield College (OR)
Livingstone College (NC)
Lock Haven Univ. of Pennsylvania
Long Island Univ.–Brooklyn (NY)
Long Island Univ.–C.W. Post
  Campus (NY)
Long Island Univ.–Southampton
  College (NY)
Loras College (IA)
Louisiana College
Louisiana State Univ.–Baton Rouge
Louisiana State Univ.–Shreveport
Louisiana Tech Univ.
Lourdes College (OH)
Loyola College In Maryland
Loyola Marymount Univ. (CA)
Loyola Univ. Chicago
Loyola Univ. New Orleans
Lubbock Christian Univ. (TX)
Luther College (IA)
Lycoming College (PA)
Lynchburg College (VA)
Lyndon State College (VT)
Lyon College (AR)
Macmurray College (IL)
Madonna Univ. (MI)
Malone College (OH)
Manchester College (IN)
Manhattan College (NY)
Mansfield Univ. of Pennsylvania
Marian College (IN)
Marian College of Fond Du Lac
  (WI)
Marietta College (OH)
Marist College (NY)
Marquette Univ. (WI)
Marshall Univ. (WV)
Martin Methodist College (TN)
Martin Univ. (IN)
Marygrove College (MI)
Maryville Univ. of St. Louis (MO)
Marywood Univ. (PA)
Master's Coll. and Seminary (CA)
Mckendree College (IL)
Mcneese State Univ. (LA)
Mcpherson College (KS)
Mercy College (NY)
Mercyhurst College (PA)
Meredith College (NC)
Mesa State College (CO)
Messiah College (PA)
Methodist College (NC)
Metropolitan State College of
  Denver
Miami Univ.–Oxford (OH)
Michigan State Univ.
Middle Tennessee State Univ.
Midland Lutheran College (NE)
Midwestern State Univ. (TX)
Miles College (AL)
Milligan College (TN)
Millikin Univ. (IL)

Millsaps College (MS)
Minnesota State Univ.–Mankato
Minnesota State Univ.–Moorhead
Minot State Univ. (ND)
Mississippi College
Mississippi State Univ.
Mississippi Univ. For Women
Mississippi Valley State Univ.
Missouri Baptist College
Missouri Southern State Univ.
Missouri Valley College
Missouri Western State College
Molloy College (NY)
Monmouth College (IL)
Moravian College (PA)
Morehead State Univ. (KY)
Morgan State Univ. (MD)
Morningside College (IA)
Mount Aloysius College (PA)
Mount Marty College (SD)
Mount Mary College (WI)
Mount Mercy College (IA)
Mount St. Mary College (NY)
Mount St. Mary's Univ. (MD)
Mount Union College (OH)
Mount Vernon Nazarene Univ.
  (OH)
Muhlenberg College (PA)
Murray State Univ. (KY)
Muskingum College (OH)
National Univ. (CA)
National-Louis Univ. (IL)
Nazareth College of Rochester
  (NY)
Nebraska Wesleyan Univ.
Neumann College (PA)
New Mexico Highlands Univ.
New Mexico State Univ.
New York Institute of Technology
New York Univ.
Niagara Univ. (NY)
Nicholls State Univ. (LA)
Nichols College (MA)
Norfolk State Univ. (VA)
North Carolina A&T State Univ.
North Carolina Central Univ.
North Carolina State Univ.–Raleigh
North Central College (IL)
North Dakota State Univ.
North Georgia College and State
  Univ.
North Greenville College (SC)
North Park Univ. (IL)
Northeastern State Univ. (OK)
Northeastern Univ. (MA)
Northern Arizona Univ.
Northern Illinois Univ.
Northern Kentucky Univ.
Northern Michigan Univ.
Northern State Univ. (SD)
Northwest Christian College (OR)
Northwest Missouri State Univ.
Northwest Nazarene Univ. (ID)
Northwestern College (IA)
Northwestern College (MN)
Northwestern Oklahoma State
  Univ.
Northwestern State Univ. of
  Louisiana
Northwood Univ. (MI)
Norwich Univ. (VT)

Notre Dame College of Ohio
Nova Southeastern Univ. (FL)
Nyack College (NY)
Oakland City Univ. (IN)
Oakland Univ. (MI)
Oakwood College (AL)
Oglethorpe Univ. (GA)
Ohio Dominican Univ.
Ohio Northern Univ.
Ohio State Univ.–Columbus
Ohio Univ.
Ohio Valley College (WV)
Ohio Wesleyan Univ.
Oklahoma Baptist Univ.
Oklahoma Christian Univ.
Oklahoma City Univ.
Oklahoma Panhandle State Univ.
Oklahoma State Univ.
Old Dominion Univ. (VA)
Oral Roberts Univ. (OK)
Oregon Institute of Technology
Otterbein College (OH)
Ouachita Baptist Univ. (AR)
Our Lady of Holy Cross Coll. (LA)
Our Lady of the Lake Univ. (TX)
Pace Univ. (NY)
Paine College (GA)
Palm Beach Atlantic Univ. (FL)
Park Univ. (MO)
Paul Quinn College (TX)
Pennsylvania College of Technology
Penn. State Univ.–Univ. Park
Penn. State–Erie, The Behrend
  College
Pepperdine Univ. (CA)
Peru State College (NE)
Pfeiffer Univ. (NC)
Philadelphia Univ.
Plymouth State Univ. (NH)
Point Loma Nazarene Univ. (CA)
Point Park Univ. (PA)
Prairie View A&M Univ. (TX)
Providence College (RI)
Purdue Univ.–Calumet (IN)
Purdue Univ.–West Lafayette (IN)
Quincy Univ. (IL)
Quinnipiac Univ. (CT)
Radford Univ. (VA)
Ramapo College of New Jersey
Randolph-Macon College (VA)
Regis Univ. (CO)
Reinhardt College (GA)
Rhode Island College
Rhodes College (TN)
Rider Univ. (NJ)
Robert Morris Univ. (PA)
Roberts Wesleyan College (NY)
Rochester College (MI)
Rochester Institute of Tech. (NY)
Rockford College (IL)
Rocky Mountain College (MT)
Roger Williams Univ. (RI)
Roosevelt Univ. (IL)
Rosemont College (PA)
Rutgers–Camden (NJ)
Rutgers–New Brunswick (NJ)
Rutgers–Newark (NJ)
Sacred Heart Univ. (CT)
Saginaw Valley State Univ. (MI)
Salem College (NC)
Salisbury Univ. (MD)

Salve Regina Univ. (RI)
Sam Houston State Univ. (TX)
Samford Univ. (AL)
San Diego State Univ.
Santa Clara Univ. (CA)
Savannah State Univ. (GA)
Schreiner Univ. (TX)
Scripps College (CA)
Seattle Univ.
Seton Hall Univ. (NJ)
Seton Hill Univ. (PA)
Shaw Univ. (NC)
Shawnee State Univ. (OH)
Shepherd Univ. (WV)
Shippensburg Univ. of
  Pennsylvania
Shorter College (GA)
Siena College (NY)
Silver Lake College (WI)
Simpson College (IA)
South Carolina State Univ.
Southeast Missouri State Univ.
Southeastern College of the
  Assemblies of God
Southeastern Louisiana Univ.
Southeastern Oklahoma State
  Univ.
Southeastern Univ. (DC)
Southern Adventist Univ. (TN)
Southern Arkansas Univ.
Southern Connecticut State Univ.
Southern Illinois Univ.–Carbondale
Southern Illinois
  Univ.–Edwardsville
Southern Methodist Univ. (TX)
Southern Nazarene Univ. (OK)
Southern New Hampshire Univ.
Southern Univ. and A&M College
  (LA)
Southern Utah Univ.
Southern Wesleyan Univ. (SC)
Southwest Baptist Univ. (MO)
Southwest Minnesota State Univ.
  (MN)
Southwest Missouri State Univ.
Southwestern Adventist Univ. (TX)
Southwestern College (KS)
Southwestern Univ. (TX)
Spalding Univ. (KY)
Spring Arbor Univ. (MI)
St. Ambrose Univ. (IA)
St. Anselm College (NH)
St. Bonaventure Univ. (NY)
St. Cloud State Univ. (MN)
St. Edward's Univ. (TX)
St. Francis College (NY)
St. Francis Univ. (PA)
St. Gregory's Univ. (OK)
St. John Fisher College (NY)
St. John's Univ. (NY)
St. John's Univ. (MN)
St. Joseph's College (ME)
St. Joseph's College (IN)
St. Joseph's College, New York
St. Joseph's Univ. (PA)
St. Leo Univ. (FL)
St. Louis Univ.
St. Martin's College (WA)
St. Mary's College (IN)
St. Mary's College of California
St. Mary's Univ. of Minnesota

St. Mary's Univ. of San Antonio
St. Mary-of-The-Woods Coll. (IN)
St. Michael's College (VT)
St. Norbert College (WI)
St. Paul's College (VA)
St. Peter's College (NJ)
St. Thomas Aquinas College (NY)
St. Thomas Univ. (FL)
St. Vincent College (PA)
St. Xavier Univ. (IL)
State Univ. of West Georgia
Stephen F. Austin State Univ. (TX)
Stephens College (MO)
Stetson Univ. (FL)
Stonehill College (MA)
Suffolk Univ. (MA)
Sul Ross State Univ. (TX)
SUNY College of Arts and
    Sciences–Geneseo
SUNY College–Brockport
SUNY College–Old Westbury
SUNY College–Oneonta
SUNY–Albany
SUNY–Binghamton
SUNY–Fredonia
SUNY–Plattsburgh
Susquehanna Univ. (PA)
Syracuse Univ. (NY)
Tabor College (KS)
Tarleton State Univ. (TX)
Taylor Univ. (IN)
Teikyo Post Univ. (CT)
Temple Univ. (PA)
Tennessee State Univ.
Tennessee Technological Univ.
Tennessee Wesleyan College
Texas A&M International Univ.
Texas A&M Univ.–College Station
Texas A&M Univ.–Commerce
Texas A&M Univ.–Corpus Christi
Texas A&M Univ.–Kingsville
Texas Christian Univ.
Texas Lutheran Univ.
Texas State Univ.–San Marcos
Texas Tech Univ.
Texas Wesleyan Univ.
Texas Woman's Univ.
The Franciscan Univ. (IA)
Thiel College (PA)
Thomas College (ME)
Thomas Edison State College (NJ)
Thomas More College (KY)
Thomas Univ. (GA)
Tiffin Univ. (OH)
Tougaloo College (MS)
Towson Univ. (MD)
Transylvania Univ. (KY)
Trevecca Nazarene Univ. (TN)
Tri-State Univ. (IN)
Trinity Christian College (IL)
Trinity College (DC)
Troy State Univ.–Troy (AL)
Truman State Univ. (MO)
Tulane Univ. (LA)
Tuskegee Univ. (AL)
Union College (NE)
Union Univ. (TN)
Univ. of Akron (OH)
Univ. of Alabama
Univ. of Alabama–Birmingham
Univ. of Alabama–Huntsville

Univ. of Alaska–Anchorage
Univ. of Alaska–Fairbanks
Univ. of Arizona
Univ. of Arkansas
Univ. of Arkansas–Little Rock
Univ. of Arkansas–Pine Bluff
Univ. of Bridgeport (CT)
Univ. of Central Arkansas
Univ. of Central Florida
Univ. of Central Oklahoma
Univ. of Charleston (WV)
Univ. of Connecticut
Univ. of Dayton (OH)
Univ. of Delaware
Univ. of Denver
Univ. of Detroit Mercy
Univ. of Dubuque (IA)
Univ. of Evansville (IN)
Univ. of Findlay (OH)
Univ. of Florida
Univ. of Georgia
Univ. of Great Falls (MT)
Univ. of Hartford (CT)
Univ. of Hawaii–Hilo
Univ. of Hawaii–Manoa
Univ. of Houston
Univ. of Houston–Downtown
Univ. of Illinois–Chicago
Univ. of Illinois–Springfield
Univ. of Ill.–Urbana-Champaign
Univ. of Indianapolis
Univ. of Iowa
Univ. of Kansas
Univ. of Kentucky
Univ. of La Verne (CA)
Univ. of Louisiana–Lafayette
Univ. of Louisiana–Monroe
Univ. of Louisville (KY)
Univ. of Maine–Augusta
Univ. of Maine–Orono
Univ. of Mary (ND)
Univ. of Mary Hardin-Baylor (TX)
Univ. of Maryland–College Park
Univ. of Maryland–Eastern Shore
Univ. of Maryland–Univ. College
Univ. of Massachusetts–Amherst
Univ. of Memphis
Univ. of Miami (FL)
Univ. of Michigan–Dearborn
Univ. of Michigan–Flint
Univ. of Minnesota–Crookston
Univ. of Minnesota–Duluth
Univ. of Minnesota–Twin Cities
Univ. of Mississippi
Univ. of Missouri–Columbia
Univ. of Missouri–Kansas City
Univ. of Missouri–St. Louis
Univ. of Montana
Univ. of Montevallo (AL)
Univ. of Nebraska–Lincoln
Univ. of Nebraska–Omaha
Univ. of Nevada–Las Vegas
Univ. of Nevada–Reno
Univ. of New Hampshire
Univ. of New Haven (CT)
Univ. of New Orleans
Univ. of North Alabama
Univ. of North Carolina–Asheville
Univ. of North Carolina–Charlotte
Univ. of N.C.–Greensboro
Univ. of North Carolina–Pembroke

Univ. of N.C.–Wilmington
Univ. of North Dakota
Univ. of North Florida
Univ. of North Texas
Univ. of Northern Iowa
Univ. of Notre Dame (IN)
Univ. of Oklahoma
Univ. of Oregon
Univ. of Pennsylvania
Univ. of Pittsburgh
Univ. of Pittsburgh–Greensburg
Univ. of Pittsburgh–Johnstown
Univ. of Portland (OR)
Univ. of Redlands (CA)
Univ. of Rhode Island
Univ. of Richmond (VA)
Univ. of Rio Grande (OH)
Univ. of San Diego
Univ. of San Francisco
Univ. of Scranton (PA)
Univ. of Sioux Falls (SD)
Univ. of South Alabama
Univ. of South Carolina–Columbia
Univ. of South Dakota
Univ. of South Florida
Univ. of Southern California
Univ. of Southern Indiana
Univ. of Southern Maine
Univ. of Southern Mississippi
Univ. of St. Francis (IL)
Univ. of St. Francis (IN)
Univ. of St. Mary (KS)
Univ. of St. Thomas (TX)
Univ. of St. Thomas (MN)
Univ. of Tampa (FL)
Univ. of Tennessee
Univ. of Tennessee–Chattanooga
Univ. of Tennessee–Martin
Univ. of Texas of the Permian Basin
Univ. of Texas–Arlington
Univ. of Texas–Austin
Univ. of Texas–Brownsville
Univ. of Texas–Dallas
Univ. of Texas–El Paso
Univ. of Texas–Pan American
Univ. of Texas–San Antonio
Univ. of Texas–Tyler
Univ. of the District of Columbia
Univ. of the Ozarks (AR)
Univ. of Toledo (OH)
Univ. of Tulsa (OK)
Univ. of Utah
Univ. of Virginia–Wise
Univ. of Washington
Univ. of West Alabama
Univ. of West Florida
Univ. of Wisconsin–Eau Claire
Univ. of Wisconsin–Green Bay
Univ. of Wisconsin–La Crosse
Univ. of Wisconsin–Madison
Univ. of Wisconsin–Milwaukee
Univ. of Wisconsin–Oshkosh
Univ. of Wisconsin–Platteville
Univ. of Wisconsin–River Falls
Univ. of Wisconsin–Stevens Point
Univ. of Wisconsin–Superior
Univ. of Wisconsin–Whitewater
Univ. of Wyoming
Upper Iowa Univ.
Urbana Univ. (OH)
Ursuline College (OH)

Utah State Univ.
Utah Valley State College
Utica College (NY)
Valdosta State Univ. (GA)
Valparaiso Univ. (IN)
Vanguard Univ. of Southern
    California
Villanova Univ. (PA)
Virginia Commonwealth Univ.
Virginia State Univ.
Virginia Tech
Viterbo Univ. (WI)
Voorhees College (SC)
Wagner College (NY)
Wake Forest Univ. (NC)
Walsh College of Accountancy and
    Business Adm. (MI)
Walsh Univ. (OH)
Wartburg College (IA)
Washburn Univ. (KS)
Washington and Jefferson College
    (PA)
Washington and Lee Univ. (VA)
Washington State Univ.
Washington Univ. In St. Louis
Wayne State Univ. (MI)
Waynesburg College (PA)
Webber International Univ. (FL)
Weber State Univ. (UT)
Webster Univ. (MO)
Wesley College (DE)
Wesleyan College (GA)
West Chester Univ. of Pennsylvania
West Texas A&M Univ.
West Virginia Univ.
West Virginia Univ. Institute of
    Technology
West Virginia Wesleyan College
Western Baptist College (OR)
Western Carolina Univ. (NC)
Western Connecticut State Univ.
Western Illinois Univ.
Western Kentucky Univ.
Western Michigan Univ.
Western New England College
    (MA)
Western New Mexico Univ.
Western State College of Colorado
Western Washington Univ.
Westminster College (PA)
Westminster College (MO)
Westminster College (UT)
Wheeling Jesuit Univ. (WV)
Whitworth College (WA)
Wichita State Univ. (KS)
Widener Univ. (PA)
Wilberforce Univ. (OH)
Wiley College (TX)
Wilkes Univ. (PA)
William Jewell College (MO)
William Paterson Univ. of New
    Jersey
William Penn Univ. (IA)
William Woods Univ. (MO)
Wilmington College (DE)
Wilmington College (OH)
Wilson College (PA)
Wingate Univ. (NC)
Winston-Salem State Univ. (NC)
Wofford College (SC)
Woodbury Univ. (CA)

Wright State Univ. (OH)
Xavier Univ. (OH)
Yeshiva Univ. (NY)
York College (NE)
York College of Pennsylvania
Youngstown State Univ. (OH)

Aerospace, Aeronautical, and Astronautical Engineering

Arizona State Univ.
Auburn Univ. (AL)
Bethel College (IN)
Boston Univ.
Cal Poly–San Luis Obispo
California Institute of Technology
California State Polytechnic
    Univ.–Pomona
California State Univ.–Long Beach
Capitol College (MD)
Case Western Reserve Univ. (OH)
Clarkson Univ. (NY)
Cornell Univ. (NY)
Dowling College (NY)
Embry Riddle Aeronautical Univ.
    (FL)
Florida Institute of Technology
Georgia Institute of Technology
Illinois Institute of Technology
Iowa State Univ.
Massachusetts Institute of
    Technology
Mississippi State Univ.
North Carolina State Univ.–Raleigh
Ohio State Univ.–Columbus
Oklahoma State Univ.
Penn. State Univ.–Univ. Park
Purdue Univ.–West Lafayette (IN)
Rensselaer Polytechnic Inst. (NY)
Rochester Institute of Tech. (NY)
San Diego State Univ.
San Jose State Univ. (CA)
St. Louis Univ.
Stanford Univ. (CA)
Syracuse Univ. (NY)
Texas A&M Univ.–College Station
Tuskegee Univ. (AL)
United States Air Force Academy
    (CO)
United States Naval Academy
    (MD)
Univ. at Buffalo–SUNY
Univ. of Alabama
Univ. of Arizona
Univ. of California–Davis
Univ. of California–Irvine
Univ. of California–Los Angeles
Univ. of California–San Diego
Univ. of Central Florida
Univ. of Colorado–Boulder
Univ. of Florida
Univ. of Ill.–Urbana-Champaign
Univ. of Kansas
Univ. of Maryland–College Park
Univ. of Miami (FL)
Univ. of Michigan–Ann Arbor
Univ. of Minnesota–Twin Cities
Univ. of Missouri–Rolla
Univ. of Notre Dame (IN)

Univ. of Oklahoma
Univ. of Southern California
Univ. of Tennessee
Univ. of Texas–Arlington
Univ. of Texas–Austin
Univ. of Virginia
Univ. of Washington
Utah State Univ.
Virginia Tech
Washington Univ. In St. Louis
West Virginia Univ.
Western Michigan Univ.
Wichita State Univ. (KS)
Worcester Polytechnic Institute
 (MA)

African Languages, Literatures, and Linguistics

Univ. of California–Los Angeles
Univ. of Wisconsin–Madison

Agricultural and Domestic Animal Services

Averett Univ. (VA)
Bethany College (WV)
Centenary College (NJ)
Colorado State Univ.
Johnson and Wales Univ. (RI)
Lake Erie College (OH)
Midway College (KY)
North Dakota State Univ.
Otterbein College (OH)
Rocky Mountain College (MT)
St. Mary-of-The-Woods Coll. (IN)
Teikyo Post Univ. (CT)
Texas A&M Univ.–College Station
Truman State Univ. (MO)
Univ. of Findlay (OH)
Univ. of Minnesota–Crookston
Univ. of New Hampshire
Virginia Intermont College
West Texas A&M Univ.
William Woods Univ. (MO)
Wilson College (PA)

Agricultural and Food Products Processing

Brewton-Parker College (GA)
Florida A&M Univ.
Kansas State Univ.
Ohio State Univ.–Columbus
Texas A&M Univ.–College Station
Univ. of Florida
Univ. of Missouri–Columbia

Agricultural Business and Management

Abilene Christian Univ. (TX)
Alabama Agricultural and
 Mechanical Univ.
Alcorn State Univ. (MS)
Arkansas State Univ.

Arkansas Tech Univ.
Auburn Univ. (AL)
Austin Peay State Univ. (TN)
Bellarmine Univ. (KY)
Berea College (KY)
Boise State Univ. (ID)
Bradley Univ. (IL)
Cal Poly–San Luis Obispo
California Lutheran Univ.
California State Polytechnic
 Univ.–Pomona
California State Univ.–Chico
California State Univ.–Fresno
Cameron Univ. (OK)
Central Missouri State Univ.
Cleveland State Univ.
College of the Ozarks (MO)
Colorado State Univ.
Cornell Univ. (NY)
Davenport Univ. (MI)
Delaware State Univ.
Delaware Valley College (PA)
Dillard Univ. (LA)
Dordt College (IA)
Eastern Kentucky Univ.
Eastern New Mexico Univ.
Eastern Oregon Univ.
Faulkner Univ. (AL)
Florida A&M Univ.
Florida Southern College
Fort Hays State Univ. (KS)
Fort Lewis College (CO)
Fort Valley State Univ. (GA)
Gettysburg College (PA)
Grace Univ. (NE)
Hannibal-Lagrange College (MO)
Hardin-Simmons Univ. (TX)
Illinois State Univ.
Iowa State Univ.
Johnson and Wales Univ. (RI)
Kansas State Univ.
Lake Erie College (OH)
Lincoln Univ. (MO)
Lindenwood Univ. (MO)
Louisiana State Univ.–Baton Rouge
Louisiana Tech Univ.
Lubbock Christian Univ. (TX)
Marymount Manhattan College
 (NY)
Michigan State Univ.
Middle Tennessee State Univ.
Mississippi State Univ.
Montana State Univ.–Bozeman
Mount Aloysius College (PA)
Neumann College (PA)
New Mexico State Univ.
Nicholls State Univ. (LA)
North Carolina A&T State Univ.
North Carolina State Univ.–Raleigh
North Dakota State Univ.
Northern Michigan Univ.
Northwest Missouri State Univ.
Northwestern College (IA)
Northwestern Oklahoma State
 Univ.
Ohio State Univ.–Columbus
Oklahoma State Univ.
Oregon State Univ.
Penn. State Univ.–Univ. Park
Peru State College (NE)
Purdue Univ.–West Lafayette (IN)

Rocky Mountain College (MT)
Sam Houston State Univ. (TX)
San Diego State Univ.
South Carolina State Univ.
South Dakota State Univ.
Southeast Missouri State Univ.
Southern Arkansas Univ.
Southern Illinois Univ.–Carbondale
Southern Univ. and A&M College
 (LA)
Southwest Minnesota State Univ.
 (MN)
Southwest Missouri State Univ.
Southwestern Univ. (TX)
St. Cloud State Univ. (MN)
Stephen F. Austin State Univ. (TX)
Sul Ross State Univ. (TX)
SUNY College of A&T–Cobleskill
Tarleton State Univ. (TX)
Texas A&M Univ.–College Station
Texas A&M Univ.–Commerce
Texas A&M Univ.–Kingsville
Texas Christian Univ.
Texas State Univ.–San Marcos
Texas Tech Univ.
Truman State Univ. (MO)
Tuskegee Univ. (AL)
Univ. of Arizona
Univ. of Arkansas
Univ. of Arkansas–Pine Bluff
Univ. of California–Davis
Univ. of Connecticut
Univ. of Delaware
Univ. of Florida
Univ. of Georgia
Univ. of Ill.–Urbana-Champaign
Univ. of Kentucky
Univ. of Louisiana–Monroe
Univ. of Maine–Orono
Univ. of Maryland–College Park
Univ. of Maryland–Eastern Shore
Univ. of Minnesota–Crookston
Univ. of Minnesota–Twin Cities
Univ. of Missouri–Columbia
Univ. of Nebraska–Kearney
Univ. of Nebraska–Lincoln
Univ. of Nevada–Reno
Univ. of New Hampshire
Univ. of Tennessee
Univ. of Wisconsin–Madison
Univ. of Wisconsin–Platteville
Univ. of Wisconsin–River Falls
Univ. of Wyoming
Utah State Univ.
Virginia Tech
Washington State Univ.
West Texas A&M Univ.
West Virginia Univ.
York College of Pennsylvania

Agricultural Mechanization

Cal Poly–San Luis Obispo
College of the Ozarks (MO)
Florida A&M Univ.
Kansas State Univ.
Middle Tennessee State Univ.
Montana State Univ.–Bozeman
North Carolina State Univ.–Raleigh

North Dakota State Univ.
Penn. State Univ.–Univ. Park
Purdue Univ.–West Lafayette (IN)
Sam Houston State Univ. (TX)
Stephen F. Austin State Univ. (TX)
SUNY College of A&T–Cobleskill
Tarleton State Univ. (TX)
Texas A&M Univ.–Kingsville
Univ. of Ill.–Urbana-Champaign
Univ. of Nebraska–Lincoln
Univ. of Wisconsin–River Falls
Washington State Univ.

Agricultural Production Operations

Angelo State Univ. (TX)
Auburn Univ. (AL)
Brigham Young Univ.–Provo (UT)
Cornell Univ. (NY)
Delaware Valley College (PA)
Eastern Kentucky Univ.
Florida A&M Univ.
Lake Erie College (OH)
Mesa State College (CO)
Montana State Univ.–Northern
North Dakota State Univ.
Stephen F. Austin State Univ. (TX)
Tarleton State Univ. (TX)
Texas A&M Univ.–College Station
Unity College (ME)
Univ. of Hawaii–Hilo
Univ. of Ill.–Urbana-Champaign
Univ. of Maine–Orono
Univ. of Minnesota–Crookston
Univ. of Missouri–Columbia
Univ. of New England (ME)
Univ. of New Hampshire
Washington State Univ.

Agricultural Public Services

Kansas State Univ.
Michigan State Univ.
North Carolina State Univ.–Raleigh
North Dakota State Univ.
Oklahoma State Univ.
Penn. State Univ.–Univ. Park
Tarleton State Univ. (TX)
Texas Tech Univ.
Univ. of Georgia
Univ. of Ill.–Urbana-Champaign
Univ. of Missouri–Columbia
Univ. of Nebraska–Lincoln
Univ. of Wisconsin–Madison
Univ. of Wyoming
Washington State Univ.

Agricultural/Biological Engineering and Bioengineering

Auburn Univ. (AL)
Cal Poly–San Luis Obispo
Cornell Univ. (NY)
Florida A&M Univ.
Iowa State Univ.

North Dakota State Univ.
Penn. State Univ.–Univ. Park
Purdue Univ.–West Lafayette (IN)
Sam Houston State Univ. (TX)
Stephen F. Austin State Univ. (TX)
SUNY College of A&T–Cobleskill
Tarleton State Univ. (TX)
Texas A&M Univ.–Kingsville
Univ. of Ill.–Urbana-Champaign
Univ. of Nebraska–Lincoln
Univ. of Wisconsin–River Falls
Washington State Univ.

Agriculture, Agriculture Operations, and Related Sciences

Alabama Agricultural and
 Mechanical Univ.
California State Polytechnic
 Univ.–Pomona
California State Univ.–Fresno
California State Univ.–Stanislaus
Michigan State Univ.
North Carolina A&T State Univ.
Ohio State Univ.–Columbus
Prescott College (AZ)
Tennessee State Univ.
Texas A&M Univ.–Commerce
Univ. of Arizona
Univ. of Arkansas–Pine Bluff
Univ. of California–Davis
Univ. of Georgia
Univ. of Massachusetts–Amherst
Univ. of Wyoming

Air Transportation

Averett Univ. (VA)
Baylor Univ. (TX)
Bowling Green State Univ. (OH)
Bridgewater State College (MA)
Central Missouri State Univ.
Central Washington Univ.
Christian Heritage College (CA)
College of the Ozarks (MO)
Delaware State Univ.
Delta State Univ. (MS)

Kansas State Univ.
Michigan State Univ.
North Carolina A&T State Univ.
North Carolina State Univ.–Raleigh
North Dakota State Univ.
Ohio State Univ.–Columbus
Oklahoma State Univ.
Penn. State Univ.–Univ. Park
Purdue Univ.–West Lafayette (IN)
Rutgers–New Brunswick (NJ)
South Dakota State Univ.
SUNY–Binghamton
Texas A&M Univ.–College Station
Univ. of Arizona
Univ. of Arkansas
Univ. of California–Davis
Univ. of California–Los Angeles
Univ. of Florida
Univ. of Georgia
Univ. of Hawaii–Manoa
Univ. of Ill.–Urbana-Champaign
Univ. of Kentucky
Univ. of Maine–Orono
Univ. of Maryland–College Park
Univ. of Minnesota–Twin Cities
Univ. of Missouri–Columbia
Univ. of Nebraska–Lincoln
Univ. of Tennessee
Univ. of the Pacific (CA)
Univ. of Wisconsin–Madison
Utah State Univ.
Virginia Tech
Washington State Univ.

Eastern Kentucky Univ.
Eastern Michigan Univ.
Elizabeth City State Univ. (NC)
Embry Riddle Aeronautical Univ. (FL)
Florida Institute of Technology
Geneva College (PA)
Grace Univ. (NE)
Hampton Univ. (VA)
Henderson State Univ. (AR)
Indiana State Univ.
Jacksonville Univ. (FL)
Kansas State Univ.
Kent State Univ. (OH)
Letourneau Univ. (TX)
Lewis Univ. (IL)
Liberty Univ. (VA)
Louisiana Tech Univ.
Metropolitan State College of Denver
Middle Tennessee State Univ.
Minnesota State Univ.–Mankato
Ohio State Univ.–Columbus
Ohio Univ.
Oklahoma State Univ.
Pacific Union College (CA)
Park Univ. (MO)
Purdue Univ.–West Lafayette (IN)
Quincy Univ. (IL)
Robert Morris Univ. (PA)
Rocky Mountain College (MT)
Salem International Univ. (WV)
San Jose State Univ. (CA)
Southeastern Oklahoma State Univ.
Southern Illinois Univ.–Carbondale
Southern Nazarene Univ. (OK)
St. Cloud State Univ. (MN)
St. Louis Univ.
SUNY–Farmingdale
Tarleton State Univ. (TX)
Thomas Edison State College (NJ)
Univ. of Alaska–Anchorage
Univ. of Dubuque (IA)
Univ. of Ill.–Urbana-Champaign
Univ. of Louisiana–Monroe
Univ. of Maryland–Eastern Shore
Univ. of Minnesota–Crookston
Univ. of Nebraska–Kearney
Univ. of Nebraska–Omaha
Univ. of North Dakota
Univ. of Oklahoma
Univ. of the District of Columbia
Utah State Univ.
Utah Valley State College
Western Michigan Univ.
Westminster College (UT)
Wilmington College (DE)

Allied Health and Medical Assisting Services

Boise State Univ. (ID)
College of St. Mary (NE)
Columbia Union College (MD)
Drury Univ. (MO)
Fairmont State Univ. (WV)
Fort Valley State Univ. (GA)
Medaille College (NY)

Michigan State Univ.
Murray State Univ. (KY)
National-Louis Univ. (IL)
New York Institute of Technology
Newberry College (SC)
North Dakota State Univ.
Purdue Univ.–West Lafayette (IN)
Quinnipiac Univ. (CT)
Shawnee State Univ. (OH)
Southwest Missouri State Univ.
St. John's Univ. (NY)
Tennessee State Univ.
Thomas Edison State College (NJ)
Univ. of Findlay (OH)
Univ. of Louisiana–Monroe
Univ. of Louisville (KY)
Univ. of Maryland–Eastern Shore
Univ. of Nebraska–Lincoln
Wayne State Univ. (MI)
Wilson College (PA)

Allied Health Diagnostic, Intervention, and Treatment Professions

Albion College (MI)
Alderson-Broaddus College (WV)
Alfred Univ. (NY)
Alma College (MI)
Anderson Univ. (IN)
Angelo State Univ. (TX)
Appalachian State Univ. (NC)
Aquinas College (MI)
Arkansas State Univ.
Armstrong Atlantic State Univ. (GA)
Augustana College (SD)
Averett Univ. (VA)
Avila Univ. (MO)
Baldwin-Wallace College (OH)
Ball State Univ. (IN)
Barry Univ. (FL)
Barton College (NC)
Baylor Univ. (TX)
Bellarmine Univ. (KY)
Belmont Univ. (TN)
Benedictine College (KS)
Benedictine Univ. (IL)
Bethel College (KS)
Bethel Univ. (MN)
Bloomfield College (NJ)
Bloomsburg Univ. of Pennsylvania
Boise State Univ. (ID)
Boston Univ.
Bowling Green State Univ. (OH)
Briar Cliff Univ. (IA)
Bridgewater College (VA)
Bridgewater State College (MA)
Brigham Young Univ.–Provo (UT)
Bryan College (TN)
Buena Vista Univ. (IA)
Butler Univ. (IN)
California State Univ.–Long Beach
California State Univ.–Sacramento
California Univ. of Pennsylvania
Campbell Univ. (NC)
Canisius College (NY)
Capital Univ. (OH)
Carlow College (PA)
Carroll College (WI)

Carson-Newman College (TN)
Cedarville Univ. (OH)
Central Connecticut State Univ.
Central Michigan Univ.
Central Washington Univ.
Champlain College (VT)
Chapman Univ. (CA)
Chatham College (PA)
Clarion Univ. of Pennsylvania
Coe College (IA)
Colby-Sawyer College (NH)
College Misericordia (PA)
College of Charleston (SC)
College of Mount St. Joseph (OH)
College of Notre Dame of Maryland
College of St. Catherine (MN)
Colorado State Univ.
Columbia Union College (MD)
Concord College (WV)
Concordia Univ. Wisconsin
Concordia Univ.–River Forest (IL)
Culver-Stockton College (MO)
Cumberland Univ. (TN)
CUNY–City College
CUNY–College of Staten Island
Daemen College (NY)
Dakota State Univ. (SD)
Dakota Wesleyan Univ. (SD)
David Lipscomb Univ. (TN)
Defiance College (OH)
Delta State Univ. (MS)
Depauw Univ. (IN)
Desales Univ. (PA)
Dominican Coll. of Blauvelt (NY)
Drexel Univ. (PA)
Drury Univ. (MO)
Duquesne Univ. (PA)
East Carolina Univ. (NC)
East Stroudsburg Univ. of Pennsylvania
East Texas Baptist Univ.
Eastern Kentucky Univ.
Eastern Michigan Univ.
Eastern Washington Univ.
Elon Univ. (NC)
Emory Univ. (GA)
Emporia State Univ. (KS)
Erskine College (SC)
Fairleigh Dickinson Univ. (NJ)
Florida Southern College
Fort Hays State Univ. (KS)
Fort Lewis College (CO)
Franklin College (IN)
Fresno Pacific Univ. (CA)
Frostburg State Univ. (MD)
Gannon Univ. (PA)
George Washington Univ. (DC)
Georgetown College (KY)
Georgia Southern Univ.
Georgia State Univ.
Georgian Court Univ. (NJ)
Graceland Univ. (IA)
Grand Canyon Univ. (AZ)
Grand Valley State Univ. (MI)
Greensboro College (NC)
Guilford College (NC)
Gustavus Adolphus College (MN)
Gwynedd-Mercy College (PA)
Hardin-Simmons Univ. (TX)
Harding Univ. (AR)

High Point Univ. (NC)
Hofstra Univ. (NY)
Holy Family Univ. (PA)
Hope College (MI)
Howard Payne Univ. (TX)
Howard Univ. (DC)
Huntingdon College (AL)
Idaho State Univ.
Illinois State Univ.
Indiana State Univ.
Indiana Univ. East
Indiana Univ. Northwest
Indiana Univ. of Pennsylvania
Indiana Univ.–Bloomington
Indiana Univ.–Kokomo
Indiana Univ.-Purdue Univ.–Indianapolis
Indiana Wesleyan Univ.
Ithaca College (NY)
James Madison Univ. (VA)
Jamestown College (ND)
John Brown Univ. (AR)
Kansas State Univ.
Keene State College (NH)
King's College (PA)
La Roche College (PA)
Lake Superior State Univ. (MI)
Lambuth Univ. (TN)
Lasell College (MA)
Lees-Mcrae College (NC)
Lenoir-Rhyne College (NC)
Lewis Univ. (IL)
Liberty Univ. (VA)
Limestone College (SC)
Lincoln Memorial Univ. (TN)
Lindenwood Univ. (MO)
Linfield College (OR)
Long Island Univ.–C.W. Post Campus (NY)
Louisiana College
Luther College (IA)
Lynchburg College (VA)
Manchester College (IN)
Mansfield Univ. of Pennsylvania
Marian College of Fond Du Lac (WI)
Marietta College (OH)
Marist College (NY)
Marquette Univ. (WI)
Marshall Univ. (WV)
Marywood Univ. (PA)
Mckendree College (IL)
Mcneese State Univ. (LA)
Merrimack College (MA)
Messiah College (PA)
Methodist College (NC)
Miami Univ.–Oxford (OH)
Midwestern State Univ. (TX)
Millikin Univ. (IL)
Minnesota State Univ.–Mankato
Minnesota State Univ.–Moorhead
Minot State Univ. (ND)
Montana State Univ.–Billings
Montclair State Univ. (NJ)
Morehead State Univ. (KY)
Mount Aloysius College (PA)
Mount Marty College (SD)
Mount Union College (OH)
Mountain State Univ. (WV)
National-Louis Univ. (IL)
Nebraska Wesleyan Univ.

New Mexico State Univ.
Newman Univ. (KS)
North Carolina Central Univ.
North Central College (IL)
North Dakota State Univ.
North Georgia College and State Univ.
Northeastern State Univ. (OK)
Northeastern Univ. (MA)
Northern Arizona Univ.
Northern Kentucky Univ.
Northern Michigan Univ.
Northwestern State Univ. of Louisiana
Norwich Univ. (VT)
Nova Southeastern Univ. (FL)
Ohio Northern Univ.
Ohio State Univ.–Columbus
Ohio Univ.
Oklahoma State Univ.
Old Dominion Univ. (VA)
Olivet Nazarene Univ. (IL)
Oregon Institute of Technology
Otterbein College (OH)
Ouachita Baptist Univ. (AR)
Pace Univ. (NY)
Palm Beach Atlantic Univ. (FL)
Park Univ. (MO)
Philadelphia Univ.
Plymouth State Univ. (NH)
Point Loma Nazarene Univ. (CA)
Quinnipiac Univ. (CT)
Ramapo College of New Jersey
Regis Univ. (CO)
Rhode Island College
Roanoke College (VA)
Rochester Institute of Tech. (NY)
Rocky Mountain College (MT)
Roosevelt Univ. (IL)
Rutgers–Newark (NJ)
Sacred Heart Univ. (CT)
Saginaw Valley State Univ. (MI)
Salem State College (MA)
Salisbury Univ. (MD)
Samford Univ. (AL)
Seattle Univ.
Seton Hill Univ. (PA)
Shaw Univ. (NC)
Shenandoah Univ. (VA)
Slippery Rock Univ. of Pennsylvania
South Dakota State Univ.
Southeastern Louisiana Univ.
Southern Arkansas Univ.
Southern Illinois Univ.–Carbondale
Southern Nazarene Univ. (OK)
Southern Utah Univ.
Southwest Baptist Univ. (MO)
Southwest Missouri State Univ.
Southwestern College (KS)
Springfield College (MA)
St. Cloud State Univ. (MN)
St. Francis College (NY)
St. Francis Univ. (PA)
St. John's Univ. (NY)
St. Louis Univ.
St. Mary's Univ. of Minnesota
St. Vincent College (PA)
Sterling College (KS)
SUNY–Stony Brook
Tabor College (KS)
Tennessee Wesleyan College

Texas Christian Univ.
Texas Lutheran Univ.
Texas State Univ.–San Marcos
Thomas Edison State College (NJ)
Touro College (NY)
Towson Univ. (MD)
Troy State Univ.–Troy (AL)
Tulane Univ. (LA)
Tusculum College (TN)
Union College (NE)
Union Univ. (TN)
Univ. at Buffalo–SUNY
Univ. of Akron (OH)
Univ. of Alabama
Univ. of Alabama–Birmingham
Univ. of Arkansas–Monticello
Univ. of Central Arkansas
Univ. of Central Florida
Univ. of Charleston (WV)
Univ. of Connecticut
Univ. of Delaware
Univ. of Evansville (IN)
Univ. of Findlay (OH)
Univ. of Hartford (CT)
Univ. of Ill.–Urbana-Champaign
Univ. of Indianapolis
Univ. of Iowa
Univ. of Kansas
Univ. of Kentucky
Univ. of La Verne (CA)
Univ. of Louisiana–Lafayette
Univ. of Louisiana–Monroe
Univ. of Louisville (KY)
Univ. of Mary (ND)
Univ. of Mary Hardin-Baylor (TX)
Univ. of Maryland–Baltimore
    County
Univ. of Maryland–Eastern Shore
Univ. of Miami (FL)
Univ. of Michigan–Ann Arbor
Univ. of Michigan–Flint
Univ. of Minnesota–Duluth
Univ. of Minnesota–Twin Cities
Univ. of Missouri–Columbia
Univ. of Nebraska–Kearney
Univ. of Nebraska–Lincoln
Univ. of Nevada–Las Vegas
Univ. of New England (ME)
Univ. of New Hampshire
Univ. of New Mexico
Univ. of N.C.–Chapel Hill
Univ. of North Carolina–Pembroke
Univ. of N.C.–Wilmington
Univ. of North Dakota
Univ. of North Florida
Univ. of Northern Iowa
Univ. of Oklahoma
Univ. of Pittsburgh–Bradford
Univ. of Sioux Falls (SD)
Univ. of South Alabama
Univ. of South Carolina–Columbia
Univ. of South Dakota
Univ. of South Florida
Univ. of Southern Indiana
Univ. of Southern Mississippi
Univ. of St. Francis (IL)
Univ. of St. Francis (IN)
Univ. of Tampa (FL)
Univ. of Texas–Arlington
Univ. of Texas–Austin
Univ. of Texas–Pan American

Univ. of the Incarnate Word (TX)
Univ. of Toledo (OH)
Univ. of Tulsa (OK)
Univ. of Vermont
Univ. of Washington
Univ. of West Alabama
Univ. of Wisconsin–Eau Claire
Univ. of Wisconsin–La Crosse
Univ. of Wisconsin–Madison
Univ. of Wisconsin–Oshkosh
Valdosta State Univ. (GA)
Virginia Commonwealth Univ.
Wagner College (NY)
Washburn Univ. (KS)
Washington State Univ.
Wayne State College (NE)
Wayne State Univ. (MI)
Waynesburg College (PA)
Weber State Univ. (UT)
West Chester Univ. of Pennsylvania
West Texas A&M Univ.
West Virginia Wesleyan College
Western Carolina Univ. (NC)
Western Michigan Univ.
Wheeling Jesuit Univ. (WV)
Whitworth College (WA)
Wichita State Univ. (KS)
William Woods Univ. (MO)
Wilmington College (OH)
Wingate Univ. (NC)
Wright State Univ. (OH)
Xavier Univ. (OH)
York College of Pennsylvania
Youngstown State Univ. (OH)

Alternative and Complementary Medicine and Medical Systems

Maharishi Univ. of Management
    (IA)

American Literature (United States and Canadian)

Ashland Univ. (OH)
Bennington College (VT)
CUNY–Baruch College
Harvard Univ. (MA)
Lawrence Univ. (WI)
Marlboro College (VT)
Middlebury College (VT)
New York Univ.
Tufts Univ. (MA)
Univ. of California–Los Angeles
Univ. of Judaism (CA)
Univ. of Pittsburgh–Johnstown
Univ. of Southern California

American Sign Language (ASL)

Augustana College (SD)
Bethel College (IN)
College of St. Catherine (MN)
Columbia College (IL)
Eastern Kentucky Univ.

Gallaudet Univ. (DC)
Gardner-Webb Univ. (NC)
Goshen College (IN)
Idaho State Univ.
Indiana Univ.–Purdue
    Univ.–Indianapolis
Kent State Univ. (OH)
Madonna Univ. (MI)
Maryville College (TN)
Mount Aloysius College (PA)
Northeastern Univ. (MA)
Quincy Univ. (IL)
Rochester Institute of Tech. (NY)
Univ. of Arkansas–Little Rock
Univ. of Louisville (KY)
Univ. of New Mexico
Univ. of Rochester (NY)
Valdosta State Univ. (GA)

Animal Sciences

Abilene Christian Univ. (TX)
Alabama Agricultural and
    Mechanical Univ.
Alcorn State Univ. (MS)
Andrews Univ. (MI)
Angelo State Univ. (TX)
Arkansas State Univ.
Auburn Univ. (AL)
Berry College (GA)
Cal Poly–San Luis Obispo
California State Polytechnic
    Univ.–Pomona
College of the Ozarks (MO)
Colorado State Univ.
Cornell Univ. (NY)
Delaware State Univ.
Delaware Valley College (PA)
Dordt College (IA)
Fort Valley State Univ. (GA)
Hardin-Simmons Univ. (TX)
Iowa State Univ.
Kansas State Univ.
Louisiana State Univ.–Baton Rouge
Louisiana Tech Univ.
Michigan State Univ.
Mississippi State Univ.
Montana State Univ.–Bozeman
New Mexico State Univ.
North Carolina A&T State Univ.
North Carolina State Univ.–Raleigh
North Dakota State Univ.
Northwest Missouri State Univ.
Ohio State Univ.–Columbus
Oklahoma Panhandle State Univ.
Oklahoma State Univ.
Oregon State Univ.
Penn. State Univ.–Univ. Park
Purdue Univ.–West Lafayette (IN)
Rutgers–New Brunswick (NJ)
South Dakota State Univ.
Southern Illinois Univ.–Carbondale
Southern Univ. and A&M College
    (LA)
Southwest Missouri State Univ.
Stephen F. Austin State Univ. (TX)
Sul Ross State Univ. (TX)
SUNY College of A&T–Cobleskill
Tarleton State Univ. (TX)
Texas A&M Univ.–College Station

Texas A&M Univ.–Commerce
Texas A&M Univ.–Kingsville
Texas State Univ.–San Marcos
Texas Tech Univ.
Truman State Univ. (MO)
Tuskegee Univ. (AL)
Univ. of Arizona
Univ. of Arkansas
Univ. of California–Davis
Univ. of Connecticut
Univ. of Delaware
Univ. of Denver
Univ. of Florida
Univ. of Georgia
Univ. of Hawaii–Hilo
Univ. of Hawaii–Manoa
Univ. of Ill.–Urbana-Champaign
Univ. of Kentucky
Univ. of Maine–Orono
Univ. of Maryland–College Park
Univ. of Maryland–Eastern Shore
Univ. of Massachusetts–Amherst
Univ. of Minnesota–Crookston
Univ. of Minnesota–Twin Cities
Univ. of Missouri–Columbia
Univ. of Nevada–Reno
Univ. of New Hampshire
Univ. of Rhode Island
Univ. of Tennessee
Univ. of Vermont
Univ. of Wisconsin–Madison
Univ. of Wisconsin–Platteville
Univ. of Wisconsin–River Falls
Univ. of Wyoming
Utah State Univ.
Virginia Tech
Washington State Univ.
West Texas A&M Univ.
West Virginia Univ.

Anthropology

Adelphi Univ. (NY)
Albion College (MI)
Alma College (MI)
American Univ. (DC)
Amherst College (MA)
Appalachian State Univ. (NC)
Arizona State Univ.
Auburn Univ. (AL)
Ball State Univ. (IN)
Barnard College (NY)
Bates College (ME)
Baylor Univ. (TX)
Beloit College (WI)
Bennington College (VT)
Bethel Univ. (MN)
Biola Univ. (CA)
Bloomsburg Univ. of Pennsylvania
Boise State Univ. (ID)
Boston Univ.
Bowdoin College (ME)
Brandeis Univ. (MA)
Bridgewater State College (MA)
Brigham Young Univ.–Hawaii
Brigham Young Univ.–Provo (UT)
Brown Univ. (RI)
Bryn Mawr College (PA)
Bucknell Univ. (PA)
Buffalo State College

Butler Univ. (IN)
California State Polytechnic
    Univ.–Pomona
California State Univ.–Bakersfield
California State Univ.–Chico
California State Univ.–Fresno
California State Univ.–Fullerton
California State Univ.–Hayward
California State Univ.–Long Beach
California State Univ.–Los Angeles
California State Univ.–Northridge
California State Univ.–Sacramento
California State Univ.–San
    Bernardino
California State Univ.–Stanislaus
Canisius College (NY)
Carnegie Mellon Univ. (PA)
Case Western Reserve Univ. (OH)
Catholic Univ. of America (DC)
Central College (IA)
Central Connecticut State Univ.
Central Michigan Univ.
Central Missouri State Univ.
Central Washington Univ.
Clarion Univ. of Pennsylvania
Cleveland State Univ.
Colby College (ME)
Colgate Univ. (NY)
College of Charleston (SC)
College of the Holy Cross (MA)
Coll. of William and Mary (VA)
College of Wooster (OH)
Colorado College
Colorado State Univ.
Columbia Univ. (NY)
Connecticut College
Cornell College (IA)
Cornell Univ. (NY)
Creighton Univ. (NE)
CUNY–Brooklyn College
CUNY–City College
CUNY–Hunter College
CUNY–Lehman College
CUNY–Queens College
CUNY–York College
Dartmouth College (NH)
Davidson College (NC)
Denison Univ. (OH)
Depaul Univ. (IL)
Depauw Univ. (IN)
Dickinson College (PA)
Drake Univ. (IA)
Drew Univ. (NJ)
Drexel Univ. (PA)
Duke Univ. (NC)
East Carolina Univ. (NC)
Eastern Kentucky Univ.
Eastern Michigan Univ.
Eastern New Mexico Univ.
Eastern Washington Univ.
Eckerd College (FL)
Edinboro Univ. of Pennsylvania
Elizabethtown College (PA)
Emory and Henry College (VA)
Emory Univ. (GA)
Florida Atlantic Univ.
Florida State Univ.
Fordham Univ. (NY)
Fort Lewis College (CO)
Franciscan Univ. of Steubenville
    (OH)

Franklin and Marshall College (PA)
Franklin Pierce College (NH)
George Mason Univ. (VA)
George Washington Univ. (DC)
Georgetown Univ. (DC)
Georgia Southern Univ.
Georgia State Univ.
Grand Valley State Univ. (MI)
Grinnell College (IA)
Hamilton College (NY)
Hamline Univ. (MN)
Hampshire College (MA)
Hanover College (IN)
Hartwick College (NY)
Harvard Univ. (MA)
Haverford College (PA)
Hawaii Pacific Univ.
Heidelberg College (OH)
Hendrix College (AR)
Hobart and William Smith Colleges (NY)
Hofstra Univ. (NY)
Howard Univ. (DC)
Humboldt State Univ. (CA)
Idaho State Univ.
Illinois State Univ.
Illinois Wesleyan Univ.
Indiana State Univ.
Indiana Univ. of Pennsylvania
Indiana Univ.–Bloomington
Indiana Univ.–Purdue Univ.–Fort Wayne
Indiana Univ.–Purdue Univ.–Indianapolis
Iowa State Univ.
Ithaca College (NY)
James Madison Univ. (VA)
Johns Hopkins Univ. (MD)
Johnson State College (VT)
Juniata College (PA)
Kansas State Univ.
Kent State Univ. (OH)
Kutztown Univ. of Pennsylvania
Lawrence Univ. (WI)
Lehigh Univ. (PA)
Lincoln Univ. (PA)
Linfield College (OR)
Long Island Univ.–Brooklyn (NY)
Longwood Univ. (VA)
Louisiana State Univ.–Baton Rouge
Loyola Univ. Chicago
Loyola Univ. New Orleans
Luther College (IA)
Macalester College (MN)
Marlboro College (VT)
Marquette Univ. (WI)
Marylhurst Univ. (OR)
Massachusetts Institute of Technology
Mercyhurst College (PA)
Metropolitan State Coll. of Denver
Miami Univ.–Oxford (OH)
Michigan State Univ.
Michigan Technological Univ.
Middle Tennessee State Univ.
Millersville Univ. of Pennsylvania
Millsaps College (MS)
Minnesota State Univ.–Mankato
Minnesota State Univ.–Moorhead
Mississippi State Univ.
Monmouth Univ. (NJ)

Montana State Univ.–Bozeman
Montclair State Univ. (NJ)
Mount Holyoke College (MA)
Muhlenberg College (PA)
Nazareth College of Rochester (NY)
New Mexico State Univ.
New York Univ.
North Carolina State Univ.–Raleigh
North Central College (IL)
North Dakota State Univ.
North Park Univ. (IL)
Northeastern Illinois Univ.
Northeastern Univ. (MA)
Northern Arizona Univ.
Northern Illinois Univ.
Northern Kentucky Univ.
Northwestern Univ. (IL)
Oakland Univ. (MI)
Oberlin College (OH)
Occidental College (CA)
Ohio State Univ.–Columbus
Ohio Univ.
Oklahoma Baptist Univ.
Oregon State Univ.
Pacific Lutheran Univ. (WA)
Pacific Univ. (OR)
Penn. State Univ.–Univ. Park
Pitzer College (CA)
Pomona College (CA)
Portland State Univ. (OR)
Princeton Univ. (NJ)
Principia College (IL)
Radford Univ. (VA)
Reed College (OR)
Rhode Island College
Rhodes College (TN)
Rice Univ. (TX)
Ripon College (WI)
Rockford College (IL)
Roger Williams Univ. (RI)
Rollins College (FL)
Rutgers–New Brunswick (NJ)
Rutgers–Newark (NJ)
Salisbury Univ. (MD)
Salve Regina Univ. (RI)
San Diego State Univ.
San Francisco State Univ.
San Jose State Univ. (CA)
Santa Clara Univ. (CA)
Scripps College (CA)
Seton Hall Univ. (NJ)
Sewanee–Univ. of the South (TN)
Skidmore College (NY)
Sonoma State Univ. (CA)
Southeast Missouri State Univ.
Southern Illinois Univ.–Carbondale
Southern Illinois Univ.–Edwardsville
Southern Methodist Univ. (TX)
Southern Oregon Univ.
Southwest Missouri State Univ.
Southwestern Univ. (TX)
St. Cloud State Univ. (MN)
St. John Fisher College (NY)
St. John's Univ. (NY)
St. Lawrence Univ. (NY)
St. Martin's College (WA)
St. Mary's College of California
St. Mary's College of Maryland
St. Michael's College (VT)

St. Vincent College (PA)
Stanford Univ. (CA)
State Univ. of West Georgia
SUNY College of Arts and Sciences–Geneseo
SUNY College–Brockport
SUNY College–Oneonta
SUNY College–Potsdam
SUNY–Albany
SUNY–Binghamton
SUNY–Fredonia
SUNY–Plattsburgh
SUNY–Purchase College
SUNY–Stony Brook
Sweet Briar College (VA)
Syracuse Univ. (NY)
Texas A&M Univ.–College Station
Texas A&M Univ.–Kingsville
Texas Christian Univ.
Texas State Univ.–San Marcos
Texas Tech Univ.
Thomas Edison State College (NJ)
Tougaloo College (MS)
Transylvania Univ. (KY)
Trinity College (CT)
Tufts Univ. (MA)
Tulane Univ. (LA)
Union College (NY)
Univ. at Buffalo–SUNY
Univ. of Alabama
Univ. of Alabama–Birmingham
Univ. of Alaska–Anchorage
Univ. of Alaska–Fairbanks
Univ. of Arizona
Univ. of Arkansas
Univ. of California–Berkeley
Univ. of California–Davis
Univ. of California–Irvine
Univ. of California–Los Angeles
Univ. of California–Riverside
Univ. of California–San Diego
Univ. of California–Santa Barbara
Univ. of California–Santa Cruz
Univ. of Central Florida
Univ. of Chicago
Univ. of Colorado–Boulder
Univ. of Colorado–Colorado Springs
Univ. of Colorado–Denver
Univ. of Connecticut
Univ. of Delaware
Univ. of Denver
Univ. of Florida
Univ. of Georgia
Univ. of Hawaii–Hilo
Univ. of Hawaii–Manoa
Univ. of Houston
Univ. of Illinois–Chicago
Univ. of Ill.–Urbana-Champaign
Univ. of Indianapolis
Univ. of Iowa
Univ. of Kansas
Univ. of Kentucky
Univ. of La Verne (CA)
Univ. of Louisiana–Lafayette
Univ. of Louisville (KY)
Univ. of Maine–Farmington
Univ. of Maine–Orono
Univ. of Mary Washington (VA)
Univ. of Maryland–Baltimore County

Univ. of Maryland–College Park
Univ. of Massachusetts–Amherst
Univ. of Massachusetts–Boston
Univ. of Memphis
Univ. of Miami (FL)
Univ. of Michigan–Ann Arbor
Univ. of Michigan–Dearborn
Univ. of Michigan–Flint
Univ. of Minnesota–Duluth
Univ. of Minnesota–Morris
Univ. of Minnesota–Twin Cities
Univ. of Mississippi
Univ. of Missouri–Columbia
Univ. of Missouri–St. Louis
Univ. of Montana
Univ. of Nebraska–Lincoln
Univ. of Nevada–Las Vegas
Univ. of Nevada–Reno
Univ. of New Hampshire
Univ. of New Mexico
Univ. of New Orleans
Univ. of N.C.–Chapel Hill
Univ. of North Carolina–Charlotte
Univ. of N.C.–Greensboro
Univ. of N.C.–Wilmington
Univ. of North Dakota
Univ. of North Florida
Univ. of North Texas
Univ. of Northern Colorado
Univ. of Northern Iowa
Univ. of Notre Dame (IN)
Univ. of Oklahoma
Univ. of Oregon
Univ. of Pennsylvania
Univ. of Pittsburgh
Univ. of Pittsburgh–Greensburg
Univ. of Redlands (CA)
Univ. of Rhode Island
Univ. of Richmond (VA)
Univ. of Rochester (NY)
Univ. of San Diego
Univ. of South Alabama
Univ. of South Carolina–Columbia
Univ. of South Dakota
Univ. of South Florida
Univ. of Southern California
Univ. of Southern Mississippi
Univ. of Tennessee
Univ. of Texas–Arlington
Univ. of Texas–Austin
Univ. of Texas–El Paso
Univ. of Texas–Pan American
Univ. of Texas–San Antonio
Univ. of Toledo (OH)
Univ. of Tulsa (OK)
Univ. of Utah
Univ. of Vermont
Univ. of Virginia
Univ. of Washington
Univ. of West Florida
Univ. of Wisconsin–Madison
Univ. of Wisconsin–Milwaukee
Univ. of Wisconsin–Oshkosh
Univ. of Wisconsin–Parkside
Univ. of Wyoming
Utah State Univ.
Vanderbilt Univ. (TN)
Vanguard Univ. of Southern California
Vassar College (NY)
Virginia Commonwealth Univ.

Wagner College (NY)
Wake Forest Univ. (NC)
Washburn Univ. (KS)
Washington and Lee Univ. (VA)
Washington College (MD)
Washington State Univ.
Washington Univ. In St. Louis
Wayne State Univ. (MI)
Weber State Univ. (UT)
Webster Univ. (MO)
Wellesley College (MA)
Wesleyan Univ. (CT)
West Chester Univ. of Pennsylvania
Western Carolina Univ. (NC)
Western Kentucky Univ.
Western Michigan Univ.
Western Oregon Univ.
Western State College of Colorado
Western Washington Univ.
Westminster College (MO)
Wheaton College (MA)
Wheaton College (IL)
Whitman College (WA)
Wichita State Univ. (KS)
Widener Univ. (PA)
Willamette Univ. (OR)
William Paterson Univ. of New Jersey
Williams College (MA)
Wright State Univ. (OH)
Yale Univ. (CT)
Youngstown State Univ. (OH)

Apparel and Textiles

Albright College (PA)
Appalachian State Univ. (NC)
Auburn Univ. (AL)
Bluffton Univ. (OH)
California State Polytechnic Univ.–Pomona
California State Univ.–Long Beach
Carson-Newman College (TN)
Central Missouri State Univ.
Cheyney Univ. of Pennsylvania
College of St. Catherine (MN)
College of the Ozarks (MO)
Colorado State Univ.
Concordia Coll.–Moorhead (MN)
David Lipscomb Univ. (TN)
Delaware State Univ.
East Carolina Univ. (NC)
Florida State Univ.
Fontbonne Univ. (MO)
Framingham State College (MA)
Georgia Southern Univ.
Indiana State Univ.
Indiana Univ.–Bloomington
Kansas State Univ.
Kentucky State Univ.
Lambuth Univ. (TN)
Lasell College (MA)
Mars Hill College (NC)
Marygrove College (MI)
Miami Univ.–Oxford (OH)
Middle Tennessee State Univ.
New Mexico State Univ.
North Dakota State Univ.
Northern Illinois Univ.

Northwest Missouri State Univ.
Ohio State Univ.–Columbus
Ohio Univ.
Oregon State Univ.
Purdue Univ.–West Lafayette (IN)
Seattle Pacific Univ.
South Dakota State Univ.
Southern Illinois Univ.–Carbondale
Southwest Missouri State Univ.
Stephens College (MO)
SUNY College–Oneonta
Syracuse Univ. (NY)
Texas Tech Univ.
Univ. of Alabama
Univ. of Arkansas
Univ. of California–Davis
Univ. of Central Oklahoma
Univ. of Delaware
Univ. of Hawaii–Manoa
Univ. of Ill.–Urbana-Champaign
Univ. of Kentucky
Univ. of Minnesota–Twin Cities
Univ. of Missouri–Columbia
Univ. of Nebraska–Lincoln
Univ. of N.C.–Greensboro
Univ. of Northern Iowa
Univ. of Rhode Island
Univ. of Southern Mississippi
Univ. of Texas–Austin
Univ. of Wisconsin–Madison
Univ. of Wisconsin–Stout
Utah State Univ.
Washington State Univ.
Wayne State Univ. (MI)
Western Kentucky Univ.
Western Michigan Univ.

Applied Horticulture/ Horticultural Business Services

Andrews Univ. (MI)
Bethel College (IN)
Brigham Young Univ.–Provo (UT)
Cal Poly–San Luis Obispo
California State Polytechnic
    Univ.–Pomona
Christopher Newport Univ. (VA)
College of the Ozarks (MO)
Colorado State Univ.
Cornell Univ. (NY)
Delaware Valley College (PA)
Eastern Kentucky Univ.
Ferrum College (VA)
Florida Southern College
Heritage College (WA)
Iowa State Univ.
Mississippi State Univ.
North Dakota State Univ.
Ohio State Univ.–Columbus
Oklahoma State Univ.
Oregon State Univ.
Penn. State Univ.–Univ. Park
South Dakota State Univ.
Stephen F. Austin State Univ. (TX)
SUNY–Farmingdale
Tarleton State Univ. (TX)
Temple Univ. (PA)
Texas A&M Univ.–College Station
Texas Tech Univ.

Thomas Edison State College (NJ)
Unity College (ME)
Univ. of Arkansas
Univ. of Delaware
Univ. of Georgia
Univ. of Ill.–Urbana-Champaign
Univ. of Maine–Orono
Univ. of Minnesota–Crookston
Univ. of Nebraska–Lincoln
Univ. of Rhode Island
Univ. of Tennessee

Applied Mathematics

Albertson College (ID)
Alderson-Broaddus College (WV)
American Univ. (DC)
Arizona State Univ.
Asbury College (KY)
Auburn Univ. (AL)
Averett Univ. (VA)
Barnard College (NY)
Baylor Univ. (TX)
Bloomfield College (NJ)
Bowling Green State Univ. (OH)
Brenau Univ. (GA)
Brescia Univ. (KY)
Brown Univ. (RI)
California Institute of Technology
California State Univ.–Fullerton
California State Univ.–Long Beach
Carnegie Mellon Univ. (PA)
Carroll College (WI)
Case Western Reserve Univ. (OH)
Charleston Southern Univ. (SC)
Clarion Univ. of Pennsylvania
Clarkson Univ. (NY)
Coastal Carolina Univ. (SC)
Columbia Univ. (NY)
CUNY–Brooklyn College
CUNY–City College
CUNY–New York City College of
    Technology
Ferris State Univ. (MI)
Florida Institute of Technology
Florida International Univ.
Fresno Pacific Univ. (CA)
Geneva College (PA)
George Washington Univ. (DC)
Georgia Institute of Technology
Gettysburg College (PA)
Grand View College (IA)
Hampden-Sydney College (VA)
Harvard Univ. (MA)
Hawaii Pacific Univ.
Hillsdale College (MI)
Hofstra Univ. (NY)
Humboldt State Univ. (CA)
Illinois Institute of Technology
Indiana Univ. of Pennsylvania
Indiana Univ.–South Bend
Iona College (NY)
Jamestown College (ND)
Johns Hopkins Univ. (MD)
Johnson C. Smith Univ. (NC)
Keene State College (NH)
Kent State Univ. (OH)
Kettering Univ. (MI)
Knox College (IL)
Long Island Univ.–C.W. Post

Campus (NY)
Loyola College In Maryland
Loyola Marymount Univ. (CA)
Lycoming College (PA)
Mansfield Univ. of Pennsylvania
Marist College (NY)
Marquette Univ. (WI)
Mary Baldwin College (VA)
Maryville Univ. of St. Louis (MO)
Michigan State Univ.
Missouri Southern State Univ.
National-Louis Univ. (IL)
New Jersey Institute of Technology
New Mexico Institute of Mining
    and Technology
New York Univ.
North Carolina A&T State Univ.
North Carolina State Univ.–Raleigh
North Central College (IL)
Northwestern Univ. (IL)
Oakland City Univ. (IN)
Oakwood College (AL)
Ohio Univ.
Princeton Univ. (NJ)
Rice Univ. (TX)
Robert Morris Univ. (PA)
Rochester Institute of Tech. (NY)
Rutgers–Newark (NJ)
Saginaw Valley State Univ. (MI)
Salem State College (MA)
San Jose State Univ. (CA)
Seattle Pacific Univ.
Seattle Univ.
Siena College (NY)
St. Louis Univ.
St. Mary's College (IN)
Stanford Univ. (CA)
SUNY–Farmingdale
SUNY–Stony Brook
Texas A&M Univ.–College Station
Texas State Univ.–San Marcos
Tufts Univ. (MA)
Univ. of Akron (OH)
Univ. of Alaska–Fairbanks
Univ. of Arkansas–Pine Bluff
Univ. of California–Berkeley
Univ. of California–Davis
Univ. of California–Los Angeles
Univ. of California–Riverside
Univ. of California–San Diego
Univ. of California–Santa Barbara
Univ. of Colorado–Boulder
Univ. of Connecticut
Univ. of Dayton (OH)
Univ. of Evansville (IN)
Univ. of Houston
Univ. of Houston–Downtown
Univ. of Ill.–Urbana-Champaign
Univ. of Iowa
Univ. of Massachusetts–Lowell
Univ. of Miami (FL)
Univ. of Michigan–Ann Arbor
Univ. of Michigan–Dearborn
Univ. of Missouri–Rolla
Univ. of Nevada–Las Vegas
Univ. of New Hampshire
Univ. of New Haven (CT)
Univ. of N.C.–Chapel Hill
Univ. of Northern Iowa
Univ. of Pittsburgh
Univ. of Pittsburgh–Bradford

Univ. of Pittsburgh–Greensburg
Univ. of Richmond (VA)
Univ. of Rochester (NY)
Univ. of Sioux Falls (SD)
Univ. of South Carolina–Aiken
Univ. of South Carolina–Upstate
Univ. of Texas–Dallas
Univ. of Texas–El Paso
Univ. of the Pacific (CA)
Univ. of Tulsa (OK)
Univ. of Virginia
Univ. of Washington
Univ. of Wisconsin–Madison
Univ. of Wisconsin–Milwaukee
Univ. of Wisconsin–Stout
Univ. of Wyoming
Valdosta State Univ. (GA)
Villa Julie College (MD)
Washington State Univ.
Washington Univ. In St. Louis
Western Michigan Univ.
Western Washington Univ.
Whitworth College (WA)
Yale Univ. (CT)

Archaeology

Baylor Univ. (TX)
Boston Univ.
Bridgewater State College (MA)
Brown Univ. (RI)
College of Wooster (OH)
Columbia Univ. (NY)
Cornell Univ. (NY)
CUNY–Hunter College
Dickinson College (PA)
George Washington Univ. (DC)
Hamilton College (NY)
Haverford College (PA)
Oberlin College (OH)
Penn. State Univ.–Univ. Park
Southern Adventist Univ. (TN)
St. Mary's College of California
Stanford Univ. (CA)
SUNY College–Potsdam
Tufts Univ. (MA)
Univ. of California–San Diego
Univ. of Evansville (IN)
Univ. of Indianapolis
Univ. of Missouri–Columbia
Univ. of Texas–Austin
Univ. of Wisconsin–La Crosse
Washington Univ. In St. Louis
Wesleyan Univ. (CT)
Western Washington Univ.
Wheaton College (IL)
Yale Univ. (CT)

Architectural Engineering

Auburn Univ. (AL)
Cal Poly–San Luis Obispo
California State Univ.–Fresno
Illinois Institute of Technology
Kansas State Univ.
Milwaukee School of Engineering
North Carolina A&T State Univ.
Oklahoma State Univ.

Penn. State Univ.–Univ. Park
Tennessee State Univ.
Tufts Univ. (MA)
Univ. of Colorado–Boulder
Univ. of Kansas
Univ. of Miami (FL)
Univ. of Missouri–Rolla
Univ. of Nebraska–Lincoln
Univ. of Nebraska–Omaha
Univ. of Oklahoma
Univ. of Texas–Austin
Univ. of Wyoming

Architectural Engineering Technologies/Technicians

Bluefield State College (WV)
Central Missouri State Univ.
Eastern Kentucky Univ.
Fairmont State Univ. (WV)
Fitchburg State College (MA)
Indiana State Univ.
Indiana Univ.-Purdue
    Univ.–Indianapolis
Louisiana College
Northern Kentucky Univ.
Purdue Univ.–West Lafayette (IN)
Southern Polytechnic State Univ.
    (GA)
SUNY–Farmingdale
Texas Tech Univ.
Univ. of Hartford (CT)
Univ. of Southern Mississippi
Vermont Technical College
Virginia Tech
Wentworth Institute of Technology
    (MA)

Architectural History and Criticism

Brown Univ. (RI)
Carnegie Mellon Univ. (PA)
Catholic Univ. of America (DC)
Columbia Univ. (NY)
Cornell Univ. (NY)
Roger Williams Univ. (RI)
Univ. of California–Santa Barbara
Univ. of Kansas
Univ. of San Francisco

Architectural Technology/Technician

Carnegie Mellon Univ. (PA)
CUNY–New York City College of
    Technology
Keene State College (NH)
Washington Univ. In St. Louis

Architecture

Andrews Univ. (MI)
Arizona State Univ.
Auburn Univ. (AL)
Ball State Univ. (IN)
Barnard College (NY)

Baylor Univ. (TX)
Bennington College (VT)
Boston Architectural Center
Cal Poly–San Luis Obispo
California College of the Arts
California Institute of Technology
California State Polytechnic
    Univ.–Pomona
Carnegie Mellon Univ. (PA)
Catholic Univ. of America (DC)
Columbia Univ. (NY)
Connecticut College
Cornell Univ. (NY)
CUNY–City College
Drexel Univ. (PA)
Florida A&M Univ.
Florida Atlantic Univ.
Georgia Institute of Technology
Hampton Univ. (VA)
Howard Univ. (DC)
Illinois Institute of Technology
Iowa State Univ.
Jackson State Univ. (MS)
Judson College (IL)
Kansas State Univ.
Kent State Univ. (OH)
Lawrence Technological Univ. (MI)
Lehigh Univ. (PA)
Louisiana State Univ.–Baton Rouge
Massachusetts Institute of
    Technology
Miami Univ.–Oxford (OH)
Mississippi State Univ.
Montana State Univ.–Bozeman
Mount Holyoke College (MA)
New Jersey Institute of Technology
New York Institute of Technology
North Carolina State Univ.–Raleigh
North Dakota State Univ.
Northeastern Univ. (MA)
Norwich Univ. (VT)
Ohio State Univ.–Columbus
Oklahoma State Univ.
Penn. State Univ.–Univ. Park
Philadelphia Univ.
Portland State Univ. (OR)
Prairie View A&M Univ. (TX)
Princeton Univ. (NJ)
Rensselaer Polytechnic Inst. (NY)
Rice Univ. (TX)
Roger Williams Univ. (RI)
Savannah College of Art and
    Design (GA)
School of the Art Institute of
    Chicago
Southern California Institute of
    Architecture
Southern Illinois Univ.–Carbondale
Southern Polytechnic State Univ.
    (GA)
Southern Univ. and A&M College
    (LA)
Syracuse Univ. (NY)
Temple Univ. (PA)
Texas A&M Univ.–College Station
Texas Tech Univ.
Tulane Univ. (LA)
Tuskegee Univ. (AL)
Univ. at Buffalo–SUNY
Univ. of Arizona
Univ. of Arkansas

Univ. of California–Berkeley
Univ. of Detroit Mercy
Univ. of Florida
Univ. of Houston
Univ. of Idaho
Univ. of Ill.–Urbana-Champaign
Univ. of Kansas
Univ. of Kentucky
Univ. of Maryland–College Park
Univ. of Maryland–Eastern Shore
Univ. of Miami (FL)
Univ. of Michigan–Ann Arbor
Univ. of Minnesota–Twin Cities
Univ. of Nebraska–Lincoln
Univ. of Nevada–Las Vegas
Univ. of New Mexico
Univ. of North Carolina–Charlotte
Univ. of Notre Dame (IN)
Univ. of Oklahoma
Univ. of Oregon
Univ. of Pennsylvania
Univ. of Southern California
Univ. of Tennessee
Univ. of Texas–Arlington
Univ. of Texas–Austin
Univ. of Texas–San Antonio
Univ. of the District of Columbia
Univ. of Utah
Univ. of Virginia
Univ. of Washington
Univ. of Wisconsin–Milwaukee
Virginia Tech
Washington State Univ.
Washington Univ. In St. Louis
Wellesley College (MA)
Wentworth Institute of Technology
    (MA)
Woodbury Univ. (CA)
Yale Univ. (CT)

Architecture and Related Services

Carnegie Mellon Univ. (PA)
Catholic Univ. of America (DC)
David Lipscomb Univ. (TN)
Florida International Univ.
Georgia Institute of Technology
Hampshire College (MA)
Hobart and William Smith Colleges
    (NY)
La Roche College (PA)
Louisiana Tech Univ.
Metropolitan State College of
    Denver
New York Institute of Technology
Olivet Nazarene Univ. (IL)
Philadelphia Univ.
Rensselaer Polytechnic Inst. (NY)
Tulane Univ. (LA)
Univ. of Dallas
Univ. of Illinois–Chicago
Univ. of Louisiana–Lafayette
Univ. of Nevada–Las Vegas
Univ. of Utah
Univ. of Virginia

Area Studies

Adelphi Univ. (NY)
Adrian College (MI)
Agnes Scott College (GA)
Albion College (MI)
Albright College (PA)
American International College
    (MA)
American Univ. (DC)
Amherst College (MA)
Arizona State Univ. West
Assumption College (MA)
Augsburg College (MN)
Augustana College (IL)
Austin College (TX)
Barnard College (NY)
Bates College (ME)
Baylor Univ. (TX)
Beloit College (WI)
Bennington College (VT)
Boston Univ.
Bowdoin College (ME)
Bowling Green State Univ. (OH)
Brandeis Univ. (MA)
Bridgewater State College (MA)
Brigham Young Univ.–Hawaii
Brigham Young Univ.–Provo (UT)
Brown Univ. (RI)
Bryn Mawr College (PA)
Bucknell Univ. (PA)
Burlington College (VT)
Cabrini College (PA)
Caldwell College (NJ)
California State Univ.–Chico
California State Univ.–Dominguez
    Hills
California State Univ.–Fullerton
California State Univ.–Hayward
California State Univ.–Long Beach
California State Univ.–Los Angeles
California State Univ.–Sacramento
California State Univ.–San
    Bernardino
Calvin College (MI)
Canisius College (NY)
Carleton College (MN)
Carnegie Mellon Univ. (PA)
Case Western Reserve Univ. (OH)
Cedarville Univ. (OH)
Centenary College of Louisiana
Central Michigan Univ.
Central Washington Univ.
Chatham College (PA)
Claflin Univ. (SC)
Claremont Mckenna College (CA)
Coe College (IA)
Colby College (ME)
Colgate Univ. (NY)
College of Charleston (SC)
College of Santa Fe (NM)
College of St. Elizabeth (NJ)
College of St. Rose (NY)
College of William and Mary (VA)
College of Wooster (OH)
Colorado College
Columbia Univ. (NY)
Concordia College (NY)
Connecticut College
Cornell College (IA)

Cornell Univ. (NY)
Creighton Univ. (NE)
Cumberland Univ. (TN)
CUNY–Brooklyn College
CUNY–College of Staten Island
CUNY–Hunter College
CUNY–Lehman College
CUNY–Queens College
Dartmouth College (NH)
David Lipscomb Univ. (TN)
Denison Univ. (OH)
Depaul Univ. (IL)
Depauw Univ. (IN)
Dickinson College (PA)
Dominican Univ. (IL)
Drew Univ. (NJ)
Drexel Univ. (PA)
Duke Univ. (NC)
Earlham College (IN)
Eastern Michigan Univ.
Eckerd College (FL)
Elmhurst College (IL)
Elmira College (NY)
Emmanuel College (MA)
Emory and Henry College (VA)
Emory Univ. (GA)
Erskine College (SC)
Fairfield Univ. (CT)
Flagler College (FL)
Florida A&M Univ.
Florida International Univ.
Florida State Univ.
Fordham Univ. (NY)
Franklin and Marshall College (PA)
Franklin College (IN)
Franklin Pierce College (NH)
Furman Univ. (SC)
Gannon Univ. (PA)
George Mason Univ. (VA)
George Washington Univ. (DC)
Georgetown College (KY)
Georgetown Univ. (DC)
Gettysburg College (PA)
Gonzaga Univ. (WA)
Goucher College (MD)
Grand Valley State Univ. (MI)
Gustavus Adolphus College (MN)
Hamilton College (NY)
Hamline Univ. (MN)
Hampshire College (MA)
Hanover College (IN)
Harding Univ. (AR)
Harvard Univ. (MA)
Haverford College (PA)
Hendrix College (AR)
Heritage College (WA)
High Point Univ. (NC)
Hillsdale College (MI)
Hobart and William Smith Colleges
    (NY)
Hofstra Univ. (NY)
Hollins Univ. (VA)
Hood College (MD)
Hope College (MI)
Howard Univ. (DC)
Idaho State Univ.
Illinois Wesleyan Univ.
Indiana Univ. Southeast
Indiana Univ.-Purdue
    Univ.–Indianapolis
Iowa State Univ.

Ithaca College (NY)
Johns Hopkins Univ. (MD)
Kalamazoo College (MI)
Keene State College (NH)
Kennesaw State Univ. (GA)
Kent State Univ. (OH)
Knox College (IL)
La Salle Univ. (PA)
Lafayette College (PA)
Lake Forest College (IL)
Lawrence Univ. (WI)
Lebanon Valley College (PA)
Lehigh Univ. (PA)
Lesley Univ. (MA)
Lewis and Clark College (OR)
Lewis Univ. (IL)
Lindenwood Univ. (MO)
Lindsey Wilson College (KY)
Loyola Marymount Univ. (CA)
Lycoming College (PA)
Macalester College (MN)
Madonna Univ. (MI)
Manhattanville College (NY)
Marist College (NY)
Marlboro College (VT)
Mary Baldwin College (VA)
Mercer Univ. (GA)
Meredith College (NC)
Miami Univ.–Oxford (OH)
Michigan State Univ.
Middlebury College (VT)
Millikin Univ. (IL)
Mills College (CA)
Millsaps College (MS)
Minnesota State Univ.–Mankato
Minnesota State Univ.–Moorhead
Montreat College (NC)
Mount Holyoke College (MA)
Mount St. Mary's College (CA)
Mount Union College (OH)
Muhlenberg College (PA)
Nazareth College of Rochester
    (NY)
New York Univ.
North Central College (IL)
North Park Univ. (IL)
Northwestern Univ. (IL)
Oakland Univ. (MI)
Oberlin College (OH)
Occidental College (CA)
Oglethorpe Univ. (GA)
Ohio Univ.
Ohio Wesleyan Univ.
Oklahoma State Univ.
Old Dominion Univ. (VA)
Oregon State Univ.
Penn. State Univ.–Univ. Park
Pepperdine Univ. (CA)
Pfeiffer Univ. (NC)
Pitzer College (CA)
Pomona College (CA)
Princeton Univ. (NJ)
Providence College (RI)
Purdue Univ.–Calumet (IN)
Ramapo College of New Jersey
Randolph-Macon Woman's College
    (VA)
Reed College (OR)
Rhode Island College
Rhodes College (TN)
Rice Univ. (TX)

Rider Univ. (NJ)
Ripon College (WI)
Rollins College (FL)
Roosevelt Univ. (IL)
Rutgers–New Brunswick (NJ)
Rutgers–Newark (NJ)
Salem College (NC)
Salem International Univ. (WV)
Salve Regina Univ. (RI)
Samford Univ. (AL)
San Diego State Univ.
San Francisco State Univ.
Scripps College (CA)
Seattle Univ.
Seton Hall Univ. (NJ)
Sewanee–Univ. of the South (TN)
Shenandoah Univ. (VA)
Siena College (NY)
Simmons College (MA)
Skidmore College (NY)
Southern Methodist Univ. (TX)
Southern Nazarene Univ. (OK)
Southwestern Univ. (TX)
Springfield College (MA)
St. Andrews Presbyterian College (NC)
St. Cloud State Univ. (MN)
St. Edward's Univ. (TX)
St. Francis College (NY)
St. John Fisher College (NY)
St. John's Univ. (NY)
St. Joseph's Univ. (PA)
St. Lawrence Univ. (NY)
St. Louis Univ.
St. Mary's College of California
St. Michael's College (VT)
St. Olaf College (MN)
St. Peter's College (NJ)
St. Xavier Univ. (IL)
Stanford Univ. (CA)
Stetson Univ. (FL)
Stonehill College (MA)
Suffolk Univ. (MA)
SUNY College–Old Westbury
SUNY College–Oneonta
SUNY–Albany
SUNY–Binghamton
SUNY–Plattsburgh
SUNY–Stony Brook
Swarthmore College (PA)
Sweet Briar College (VA)
Syracuse Univ. (NY)
Temple Univ. (PA)
Texas A&M International Univ.
Texas A&M Univ.–College Station
Texas Christian Univ.
Texas State Univ.–San Marcos
Texas Tech Univ.
Towson Univ. (MD)
Trinity College (CT)
Trinity College (DC)
Tufts Univ. (MA)
Tulane Univ. (LA)
Union College (NY)
Univ. at Buffalo–SUNY
Univ. of Alabama
Univ. of Alaska–Fairbanks
Univ. of Arizona
Univ. of Arkansas
Univ. of Bridgeport (CT)
Univ. of California–Berkeley

Univ. of California–Davis
Univ. of California–Irvine
Univ. of California–Los Angeles
Univ. of California–Riverside
Univ. of California–San Diego
Univ. of California–Santa Barbara
Univ. of California–Santa Cruz
Univ. of Chicago
Univ. of Colorado–Boulder
Univ. of Connecticut
Univ. of Dayton (OH)
Univ. of Delaware
Univ. of Florida
Univ. of Hawaii–Hilo
Univ. of Hawaii–Manoa
Univ. of Houston
Univ. of Illinois–Chicago
Univ. of Ill.–Urbana-Champaign
Univ. of Iowa
Univ. of Judaism (CA)
Univ. of Kansas
Univ. of Kentucky
Univ. of Mary Washington (VA)
Univ. of Maryland–Baltimore County
Univ. of Maryland–College Park
Univ. of Maryland–Univ. College
Univ. of Massachusetts–Amherst
Univ. of Massachusetts–Boston
Univ. of Massachusetts–Lowell
Univ. of Miami (FL)
Univ. of Michigan–Ann Arbor
Univ. of Michigan–Dearborn
Univ. of Minnesota–Duluth
Univ. of Minnesota–Morris
Univ. of Minnesota–Twin Cities
Univ. of Mississippi
Univ. of Missouri–Columbia
Univ. of Missouri–Kansas City
Univ. of Nebraska–Lincoln
Univ. of Nebraska–Omaha
Univ. of Nevada–Las Vegas
Univ. of New England (ME)
Univ. of New Hampshire
Univ. of New Mexico
Univ. of N.C.–Chapel Hill
Univ. of North Carolina–Pembroke
Univ. of Northern Iowa
Univ. of Notre Dame (IN)
Univ. of Oregon
Univ. of Pennsylvania
Univ. of Pittsburgh–Johnstown
Univ. of Portland (OR)
Univ. of Puget Sound (WA)
Univ. of Redlands (CA)
Univ. of Rhode Island
Univ. of Richmond (VA)
Univ. of Rio Grande (OH)
Univ. of Rochester (NY)
Univ. of San Francisco
Univ. of South Carolina–Columbia
Univ. of South Florida
Univ. of Southern California
Univ. of Southern Mississippi
Univ. of St. Francis (IN)
Univ. of St. Thomas (MN)
Univ. of Texas–Austin
Univ. of Texas–Dallas
Univ. of Texas–El Paso
Univ. of Texas–Pan American
Univ. of Texas–San Antonio

Univ. of Toledo (OH)
Univ. of Utah
Univ. of Vermont
Univ. of Virginia
Univ. of Washington
Univ. of Wisconsin–Eau Claire
Univ. of Wisconsin–Madison
Univ. of Wyoming
Ursinus College (PA)
Ursuline College (OH)
Utah State Univ.
Valparaiso Univ. (IN)
Vanderbilt Univ. (TN)
Vassar College (NY)
Virginia Commonwealth Univ.
Virginia Wesleyan College
Washington and Lee Univ. (VA)
Washington College (MD)
Washington State Univ.
Washington Univ. In St. Louis
Wayne State Univ. (MI)
Wellesley College (MA)
Wesley College (DE)
Wesleyan College (GA)
Wesleyan Univ. (CT)
West Chester Univ. of Pennsylvania
Western Connecticut State Univ.
Western Michigan Univ.
Western New England College (MA)
Western Washington Univ.
Westmont College (CA)
Wheaton College (MA)
Wheelock College (MA)
Whitman College (WA)
Whittier College (CA)
Whitworth College (WA)
Willamette Univ. (OR)
William Jewell College (MO)
William Paterson Univ. of New Jersey
Williams College (MA)
Wittenberg Univ. (OH)
Wright State Univ. (OH)
Yale Univ. (CT)
Youngstown State Univ. (OH)

Area, Ethnic, Cultural, and Gender Studies

Alfred Univ. (NY)
Azusa Pacific Univ. (CA)
Brown Univ. (RI)
Burlington College (VT)
Carleton College (MN)
Central College (IA)
Chatham College (PA)
Columbia College (IL)
Connecticut College
CUNY–City College
Dartmouth College (NH)
Emmanuel College (MA)
Excelsior College (NY)
Fort Lewis College (CO)
Hawaii Pacific Univ.
Hobart and William Smith Colleges (NY)
Humboldt State Univ. (CA)
Lafayette College (PA)
Madonna Univ. (MI)

Manhattanville College (NY)
Northwest Christian College (OR)
Norwich Univ. (VT)
Pepperdine Univ. (CA)
Point Park Univ. (PA)
Prescott College (AZ)
Savannah State Univ. (GA)
Skidmore College (NY)
Syracuse Univ. (NY)
Texas A&M Univ.–Galveston
Union Univ. (TN)
Univ. of California–Davis
Univ. of California–Riverside
Univ. of California–San Diego
Univ. of Denver
Univ. of Michigan–Ann Arbor
Univ. of N.C.–Chapel Hill
Univ. of North Carolina–Charlotte
Univ. of Oregon
Univ. of Tennessee
Univ. of the Incarnate Word (TX)
Univ. of Wisconsin–Stevens Point
Whitman College (WA)
Williams College (MA)

Astronomy and Astrophysics

Agnes Scott College (GA)
Amherst College (MA)
Barnard College (NY)
Benedictine College (KS)
Bennington College (VT)
Boston Univ.
Brigham Young Univ.–Provo (UT)
Bryn Mawr College (PA)
Buffalo State College
California Institute of Technology
California State Univ.–Los Angeles
California State Univ.–Northridge
Carnegie Mellon Univ. (PA)
Case Western Reserve Univ. (OH)
Central Michigan Univ.
Colgate Univ. (NY)
Colorado State Univ.
Columbia Univ. (NY)
Concordia Univ.–River Forest (IL)
Connecticut College
Cornell Univ. (NY)
Denison Univ. (OH)
Drake Univ. (IA)
Eastern Univ. (PA)
Florida Institute of Technology
Franklin and Marshall College (PA)
George Mason Univ. (VA)
Harvard Univ. (MA)
Haverford College (PA)
Indiana Univ.–Bloomington
Lehigh Univ. (PA)
Lycoming College (PA)
Marlboro College (VT)
Michigan State Univ.
Minnesota State Univ.–Mankato
Mount Holyoke College (MA)
New Mexico Institute of Mining and Technology
Northern Arizona Univ.
Ohio State Univ.–Columbus
Ohio Univ.
Ohio Wesleyan Univ.

Penn. State Univ.–Univ. Park
Princeton Univ. (NJ)
Rice Univ. (TX)
Rutgers–New Brunswick (NJ)
San Diego State Univ.
Savannah State Univ. (GA)
SUNY–Stony Brook
Swarthmore College (PA)
Texas A&M Univ.–Commerce
Texas Christian Univ.
Tufts Univ. (MA)
Union College (NY)
Univ. of Alaska–Fairbanks
Univ. of Arizona
Univ. of California–Berkeley
Univ. of California–Los Angeles
Univ. of California–San Diego
Univ. of Colorado–Boulder
Univ. of Florida
Univ. of Georgia
Univ. of Hawaii–Hilo
Univ. of Ill.–Urbana-Champaign
Univ. of Iowa
Univ. of Kansas
Univ. of Maryland–College Park
Univ. of Massachusetts–Amherst
Univ. of Michigan–Ann Arbor
Univ. of Minnesota–Twin Cities
Univ. of New Mexico
Univ. of Oklahoma
Univ. of Southern California
Univ. of Texas–Austin
Univ. of Texas–El Paso
Univ. of Toledo (OH)
Univ. of Virginia
Univ. of Washington
Univ. of Wisconsin–Madison
Univ. of Wyoming
Valdosta State Univ. (GA)
Vassar College (NY)
Wellesley College (MA)
Wesleyan Univ. (CT)
Western Washington Univ.
Wheaton College (MA)
Whitman College (WA)
Williams College (MA)
Yale Univ. (CT)
Youngstown State Univ. (OH)

Atmospheric Sciences and Meteorology

Central Michigan Univ.
Colorado State Univ.
Cornell Univ. (NY)
Embry Riddle Aeronautical Univ. (FL)
Florida Institute of Technology
Florida State Univ.
Iowa State Univ.
Lyndon State College (VT)
Metropolitan State College of Denver
Millersville Univ. of Pennsylvania
New Mexico Institute of Mining and Technology
North Carolina State Univ.–Raleigh
Northern Illinois Univ.
Northland College (WI)
Ohio Univ.

Penn. State Univ.–Univ. Park
Plymouth State Univ. (NH)
Princeton Univ. (NJ)
Rutgers–New Brunswick (NJ)
San Jose State Univ. (CA)
St. Cloud State Univ. (MN)
St. Louis Univ.
SUNY College–Brockport
SUNY College–Oneonta
SUNY–Albany
United States Air Force Academy
 (CO)
Univ. of Arizona
Univ. of California–Berkeley
Univ. of California–Davis
Univ. of California–Los Angeles
Univ. of Hawaii–Manoa
Univ. of Kansas
Univ. of Louisiana–Monroe
Univ. of Miami (FL)
Univ. of Michigan–Ann Arbor
Univ. of Missouri–Columbia
Univ. of Nebraska–Lincoln
Univ. of North Carolina–Asheville
Univ. of North Dakota
Univ. of Oklahoma
Univ. of South Alabama
Univ. of the Incarnate Word (TX)
Univ. of Utah
Univ. of Washington
Univ. of Wisconsin–Madison
Univ. of Wisconsin–Milwaukee
Valparaiso Univ. (IN)
Western Connecticut State Univ.
Western Illinois Univ.

Audiovisual Communications Technologies/Technicians

American Univ. (DC)
Asbury College (KY)
Ashland Univ. (OH)
California State Univ.–Monterey
 Bay
Columbia College (IL)
CUNY–Brooklyn College
Eastern Michigan Univ.
Ferris State Univ. (MI)
Gannon Univ. (PA)
Gonzaga Univ. (WA)
Greenville College (IL)
Hampshire College (MA)
Ithaca College (NY)
Johns Hopkins Univ. (MD)
Lebanon Valley College (PA)
Liberty Univ. (VA)
Long Island Univ.–C.W. Post
 Campus (NY)
Loyola Marymount Univ. (CA)
Malone College (OH)
Marywood Univ. (PA)
Michigan Technological Univ.
Rowan Univ. (NJ)
San Francisco State Univ.
Savannah College of Art and
 Design (GA)
Southern Oregon Univ.
St. John's Univ. (NY)
Suffolk Univ. (MA)

SUNY–Fredonia
Syracuse Univ. (NY)
Texas State Univ.–San Marcos
Univ. of Arizona
Univ. of Georgia

Behavioral Sciences

Andrews Univ. (MI)
California Baptist Univ.
Carnegie Mellon Univ. (PA)
College For Lifelong Learning (NH)
Concordia Univ. (NE)
Concordia Univ. (CA)
Dakota Wesleyan Univ. (SD)
Drew Univ. (NJ)
George Fox Univ. (OR)
Grand Valley State Univ. (MI)
Hampshire College (MA)
Mercy College (NY)
Mount Mary College (WI)
National Univ. (CA)
Oglethorpe Univ. (GA)
Point Park Univ. (PA)
Rochester College (MI)
San Jose State Univ. (CA)
St. Andrews Presbyterian College
 (NC)
Sterling College (KS)
United States Air Force Academy
 (CO)
Univ. of California–Santa Cruz
Univ. of Kansas
Univ. of La Verne (CA)
Univ. of Maine–Machias
Univ. of Maine–Presque Isle
Univ. of North Texas
Widener Univ. (PA)
Wilmington College (DE)
Wilson College (PA)

Bible/Biblical Studies

Abilene Christian Univ. (TX)
Anderson Univ. (IN)
Asbury College (KY)
Azusa Pacific Univ. (CA)
Bethany College (CA)
Bethel College (IN)
Bethel Univ. (MN)
Biola Univ. (CA)
Blue Mountain College (MS)
Bryan College (TN)
Calvin College (MI)
Cedarville Univ. (OH)
Christian Heritage College (CA)
Clearwater Christian College (FL)
Colorado Christian Univ.
Concordia Univ. Wisconsin
Concordia Univ.–River Forest (IL)
Concordia Univ.–St. Paul (MN)
Cornerstone Univ. (MI)
Covenant College (GA)
Crichton College (TN)
David Lipscomb Univ. (TN)
East Texas Baptist Univ.
Eastern Mennonite Univ. (VA)
Eastern Univ. (PA)
Erskine College (SC)

Faulkner Univ. (AL)
Freed-Hardeman Univ. (TN)
Fresno Pacific Univ. (CA)
Geneva College (PA)
Gordon College (MA)
Grace College and Seminary (IN)
Grace Univ. (NE)
Grand Canyon Univ. (AZ)
Hannibal-Lagrange College (MO)
Hardin-Simmons Univ. (TX)
Harding Univ. (AR)
Hope International Univ. (CA)
Houghton College (NY)
Howard Payne Univ. (TX)
Huntington College (IN)
Judson College (IL)
King College (TN)
Letourneau Univ. (TX)
Liberty Univ. (VA)
Lubbock Christian Univ. (TX)
Malone College (OH)
Master's Coll. and Seminary (CA)
Messiah College (PA)
Mid-Continent College (KY)
Milligan College (TN)
Montreat College (NC)
North Park Univ. (IL)
Northwest Christian College (OR)
Northwest College (WA)
Northwestern College (MN)
Nyack College (NY)
Ohio Valley College (WV)
Oklahoma Baptist Univ.
Oklahoma Christian Univ.
Oklahoma Wesleyan Univ.
Olivet Nazarene Univ. (IL)
Oral Roberts Univ. (OK)
Ouachita Baptist Univ. (AR)
Palm Beach Atlantic Univ. (FL)
Patten College (CA)
Point Loma Nazarene Univ. (CA)
Rochester College (MI)
Simpson Univ. (CA)
Southwest Baptist Univ. (MO)
Taylor Univ. (IN)
Toccoa Falls College (GA)
Union College (NE)
Union Univ. (TN)
Univ. of Judaism (CA)
Univ. of Mary Hardin-Baylor (TX)
Vanguard Univ. of Southern
 California
Warner Southern College (FL)
Western Baptist College (OR)
Wheaton College (IL)
William Carey College (MS)
Williams Baptist College (AR)
York College (NE)

Bilingual, Multilingual, and Multicultural Education

Boise State Univ. (ID)
Boston Univ.
California State Univ.–Fullerton
California State Univ.–Sacramento
Calvin College (MI)
Chicago State Univ.
College of St. Scholastica (MN)

Concordia Univ.–St. Paul (MN)
CUNY–Brooklyn College
CUNY–Lehman College
Heritage College (WA)
Houston Baptist Univ.
Loyola Univ. Chicago
Midwestern State Univ. (TX)
Monmouth College (IL)
Mount Mary College (WI)
SUNY College–Old Westbury
Texas Christian Univ.
Texas Wesleyan Univ.
Univ. of California–Riverside
Univ. of Findlay (OH)
Univ. of Judaism (CA)
Washington State Univ.
Weber State Univ. (UT)
Western Illinois Univ.
Western Oregon Univ.

Biochemistry, Biophysics, and Molecular Biology

Abilene Christian Univ. (TX)
Adelphi Univ. (NY)
Agnes Scott College (GA)
Albright College (PA)
Allegheny College (PA)
Alma College (MI)
Alverno College (WI)
American Univ. (DC)
Anderson Univ. (IN)
Andrews Univ. (MI)
Angelo State Univ. (TX)
Arizona State Univ.
Asbury College (KY)
Ashland Univ. (OH)
Auburn Univ. (AL)
Austin College (TX)
Baker Univ. (KS)
Barnard College (NY)
Barry Univ. (FL)
Bates College (ME)
Baylor Univ. (TX)
Bellarmine Univ. (KY)
Belmont Univ. (TN)
Beloit College (WI)
Benedictine College (KS)
Benedictine Univ. (IL)
Berry College (GA)
Bethany College (WV)
Bethel Univ. (MN)
Biola Univ. (CA)
Blackburn College (IL)
Boston Univ.
Bowdoin College (ME)
Bradley Univ. (IL)
Bridgewater State College (MA)
Brigham Young Univ.–Hawaii
Brigham Young Univ.–Provo (UT)
Brown Univ. (RI)
Cal Poly–San Luis Obispo
California Lutheran Univ.
California State Univ.–Fullerton
California State Univ.–Hayward
California State Univ.–Long Beach
California State Univ.–Los Angeles
California State Univ.–Northridge
California State Univ.–Sacramento
California State Univ.–San Marcos

Calvin College (MI)
Campbell Univ. (NC)
Canisius College (NY)
Capital Univ. (OH)
Carnegie Mellon Univ. (PA)
Carroll College (WI)
Case Western Reserve Univ. (OH)
Catholic Univ. of America (DC)
Cedar Crest College (PA)
Centenary College of Louisiana
Central Connecticut State Univ.
Centre College (KY)
Chapman Univ. (CA)
Charleston Southern Univ. (SC)
Chatham College (PA)
Chestnut Hill College (PA)
Claflin Univ. (SC)
Claremont Mckenna College (CA)
Clarion Univ. of Pennsylvania
Clark Univ. (MA)
Clarke College (IA)
Clarkson Univ. (NY)
Coe College (IA)
Colby College (ME)
Colgate Univ. (NY)
College Misericordia (PA)
College of Mount St. Joseph (OH)
College of Mount St. Vincent (NY)
College of St. Benedict (MN)
College of St. Elizabeth (NJ)
College of St. Rose (NY)
College of St. Scholastica (MN)
College of Wooster (OH)
Colorado College
Colorado State Univ.
Columbia Union College (MD)
Columbia Univ. (NY)
Connecticut College
Converse College (SC)
Cornell College (IA)
Cornell Univ. (NY)
CUNY–College of Staten Island
Daemen College (NY)
Dartmouth College (NH)
David Lipscomb Univ. (TN)
Denison Univ. (OH)
Depauw Univ. (IN)
Dickinson College (PA)
Drake Univ. (IA)
Drew Univ. (NJ)
Duquesne Univ. (PA)
Earlham College (IN)
East Carolina Univ. (NC)
East Stroudsburg Univ. of
 Pennsylvania
Eastern Connecticut State Univ.
Eastern Kentucky Univ.
Eastern Mennonite Univ. (VA)
Eastern Michigan Univ.
Eastern New Mexico Univ.
Eastern Oregon Univ.
Eastern Univ. (PA)
Eckerd College (FL)
Elizabethtown College (PA)
Elmhurst College (IL)
Emmanuel College (MA)
Emporia State Univ. (KS)
Fairleigh Dickinson Univ. (NJ)
Ferris State Univ. (MI)
Florida Institute of Technology
Florida State Univ.

Fort Lewis College (CO)
Franklin and Marshall College (PA)
Freed-Hardeman Univ. (TN)
Georgetown Univ. (DC)
Georgian Court Univ. (NJ)
Gettysburg College (PA)
Goshen College (IN)
Grand Canyon Univ. (AZ)
Grand Valley State Univ. (MI)
Grinnell College (IA)
Grove City College (PA)
Gustavus Adolphus College (MN)
Hamilton College (NY)
Hamline Univ. (MN)
Hardin-Simmons Univ. (TX)
Harding Univ. (AR)
Hartwick College (NY)
Harvard Univ. (MA)
Harvey Mudd College (CA)
Hendrix College (AR)
Hiram College (OH)
Hofstra Univ. (NY)
Holy Family Univ. (PA)
Hood College (MD)
Houston Baptist Univ.
Howard Univ. (DC)
Humboldt State Univ. (CA)
Huntingdon College (AL)
Idaho State Univ.
Illinois Institute of Technology
Illinois State Univ.
Indiana Univ. East
Indiana Univ. of Pennsylvania
Indiana Univ.–Bloomington
Indiana Wesleyan Univ.
Iona College (NY)
Iowa State Univ.
Ithaca College (NY)
Jamestown College (ND)
John Brown Univ. (AR)
Johns Hopkins Univ. (MD)
Juniata College (PA)
Kansas State Univ.
Kennesaw State Univ. (GA)
Keuka College (NY)
King College (TN)
Knox College (IL)
La Salle Univ. (PA)
La Sierra Univ. (CA)
Lafayette College (PA)
Lagrange College (GA)
Lakeland College (WI)
Lawrence Technological Univ. (MI)
Lawrence Univ. (WI)
Le Moyne College (NY)
Lebanon Valley College (PA)
Lehigh Univ. (PA)
Lewis and Clark College (OR)
Lewis Univ. (IL)
Liberty Univ. (VA)
Long Island Univ.–Southampton
    College (NY)
Louisiana State Univ.–Baton Rouge
Loyola Marymount Univ. (CA)
Madonna Univ. (MI)
Manhattan College (NY)
Manhattanville College (NY)
Mansfield Univ. of Pennsylvania
Marietta College (OH)
Marist College (NY)
Marlboro College (VT)

Marquette Univ. (WI)
Mary Baldwin College (VA)
Maryville College (TN)
Mcmurry Univ. (TX)
Mercer Univ. (GA)
Mercyhurst College (PA)
Merrimack College (MA)
Messiah College (PA)
Miami Univ.–Oxford (OH)
Michigan State Univ.
Michigan Technological Univ.
Middlebury College (VT)
Millikin Univ. (IL)
Mills College (CA)
Minnesota State Univ.–Mankato
Mississippi College
Mississippi State Univ.
Missouri Southern State Univ.
Missouri Western State College
Monmouth College (IL)
Montclair State Univ. (NJ)
Moravian College (PA)
Mount Holyoke College (MA)
Mount St. Mary's Univ. (MD)
Mount Union College (OH)
Muhlenberg College (PA)
Muskingum College (OH)
Nazareth College of Rochester
    (NY)
Nebraska Wesleyan Univ.
New Mexico State Univ.
New York Univ.
Newman Univ. (KS)
Niagara Univ. (NY)
North Carolina State Univ.–Raleigh
North Central College (IL)
North Dakota State Univ.
Northeastern Univ. (MA)
Northern Arizona Univ.
Northern Michigan Univ.
Norwich Univ. (VT)
Notre Dame College of Ohio
Notre Dame De Namur Univ. (CA)
Oakland Univ. (MI)
Oakwood College (AL)
Oberlin College (OH)
Occidental College (CA)
Ohio Northern Univ.
Ohio State Univ.–Columbus
Ohio Wesleyan Univ.
Oklahoma Christian Univ.
Oklahoma City Univ.
Oklahoma State Univ.
Oklahoma Wesleyan Univ.
Old Dominion Univ. (VA)
Olivet College (MI)
Oral Roberts Univ. (OK)
Oregon State Univ.
Otterbein College (OH)
Pace Univ. (NY)
Pacific Union College (CA)
Pacific Univ. (OR)
Penn. State Univ.–Univ. Park
Pepperdine Univ. (CA)
Philadelphia Univ.
Pitzer College (CA)
Point Loma Nazarene Univ. (CA)
Pomona College (CA)
Princeton Univ. (NJ)
Providence College (RI)
Purdue Univ.–West Lafayette (IN)

Queens Univ. of Charlotte (NC)
Ramapo College of New Jersey
Reed College (OR)
Regis College (MA)
Regis Univ. (CO)
Rensselaer Polytechnic Inst. (NY)
Rice Univ. (TX)
Richard Stockton College of New
    Jersey
Rider Univ. (NJ)
Roanoke College (VA)
Roberts Wesleyan College (NY)
Rochester Institute of Tech. (NY)
Rockford College (IL)
Rockhurst Univ. (MO)
Rollins College (FL)
Rosemont College (PA)
Rutgers–New Brunswick (NJ)
Sacred Heart Univ. (CT)
Saginaw Valley State Univ. (MI)
Samford Univ. (AL)
San Francisco State Univ.
Schreiner Univ. (TX)
Scripps College (CA)
Seattle Pacific Univ.
Seattle Univ.
Seton Hall Univ. (NJ)
Seton Hill Univ. (PA)
Sewanee–Univ. of the South (TN)
Siena College (NY)
Simmons College (MA)
Skidmore College (NY)
Southern Adventist Univ. (TN)
Southern Illinois Univ.–Carbondale
Southern Methodist Univ. (TX)
Southern Nazarene Univ. (OK)
Southwestern College (KS)
Spelman College (GA)
Spring Arbor Univ. (MI)
Spring Hill College (AL)
St. Anselm College (NH)
St. Bonaventure Univ. (NY)
St. Cloud State Univ. (MN)
St. Edward's Univ. (TX)
St. Francis Univ. (PA)
St. John's Univ. (MN)
St. Joseph College (CT)
St. Joseph's College (IN)
St. Joseph's Univ. (PA)
St. Lawrence Univ. (NY)
St. Louis Univ.
St. Mary's College of California
St. Mary's College of Maryland
St. Mary's Univ. of Minnesota
St. Michael's College (VT)
St. Peter's College (NJ)
St. Vincent College (PA)
Stetson Univ. (FL)
Stevens Institute of Technology
    (NJ)
Stonehill College (MA)
Suffolk Univ. (MA)
SUNY College of Arts and
    Sciences–Geneseo
SUNY College–Potsdam
SUNY–Binghamton
SUNY–Fredonia
SUNY–Plattsburgh
SUNY–Stony Brook
Susquehanna Univ. (PA)
Swarthmore College (PA)

Sweet Briar College (VA)
Syracuse Univ. (NY)
Tabor College (KS)
Temple Univ. (PA)
Texas A&M Univ.–College Station
Texas Christian Univ.
Texas Lutheran Univ.
Texas State Univ.–San Marcos
Texas Tech Univ.
Texas Wesleyan Univ.
Trinity College (DC)
Trinity College (CT)
Tulane Univ. (LA)
Union College (NE)
Union College (NY)
Univ. at Buffalo–SUNY
Univ. of Arizona
Univ. of California–Davis
Univ. of California–Irvine
Univ. of California–Los Angeles
Univ. of California–Riverside
Univ. of California–San Diego
Univ. of California–Santa Barbara
Univ. of California–Santa Cruz
Univ. of Chicago
Univ. of Colorado–Boulder
Univ. of Connecticut
Univ. of Dallas
Univ. of Dayton (OH)
Univ. of Delaware
Univ. of Denver
Univ. of Evansville (IN)
Univ. of Georgia
Univ. of Hartford (CT)
Univ. of Houston
Univ. of Illinois–Chicago
Univ. of Ill.–Urbana-Champaign
Univ. of Iowa
Univ. of Kansas
Univ. of Maine–Orono
Univ. of Maryland–Baltimore
    County
Univ. of Maryland–College Park
Univ. of Massachusetts–Amherst
Univ. of Massachusetts–Boston
Univ. of Miami (FL)
Univ. of Michigan–Ann Arbor
Univ. of Michigan–Dearborn
Univ. of Michigan–Flint
Univ. of Minnesota–Duluth
Univ. of Minnesota–Twin Cities
Univ. of Missouri–Columbia
Univ. of Missouri–St. Louis
Univ. of Nebraska–Lincoln
Univ. of Nevada–Las Vegas
Univ. of Nevada–Reno
Univ. of New England (ME)
Univ. of New Hampshire
Univ. of New Mexico
Univ. of N.C.–Greensboro
Univ. of North Texas
Univ. of Northern Iowa
Univ. of Notre Dame (IN)
Univ. of Oklahoma
Univ. of Oregon
Univ. of Pennsylvania
Univ. of Pittsburgh
Univ. of Puget Sound (WA)
Univ. of Redlands (CA)
Univ. of Richmond (VA)
Univ. of Scranton (PA)

Univ. of Southern California
Univ. of Southern Indiana
Univ. of St. Thomas (MN)
Univ. of Tampa (FL)
Univ. of Tennessee
Univ. of Texas–Arlington
Univ. of Texas–Austin
Univ. of Texas–Dallas
Univ. of the Pacific (CA)
Univ. of Tulsa (OK)
Univ. of Vermont
Univ. of Washington
Univ. of Wisconsin–Eau Claire
Univ. of Wisconsin–La Crosse
Univ. of Wisconsin–Madison
Univ. of Wisconsin–Milwaukee
Univ. of Wisconsin–Parkside
Univ. of Wisconsin–Superior
Univ. of Wyoming
Valparaiso Univ. (IN)
Vanderbilt Univ. (TN)
Vassar College (NY)
Virginia Tech
Viterbo Univ. (WI)
Wartburg College (IA)
Washington and Jefferson College
    (PA)
Washington and Lee Univ. (VA)
Washington State Univ.
Washington Univ. In St. Louis
Wesleyan Univ. (CT)
West Chester Univ. of Pennsylvania
Western Kentucky Univ.
Western Michigan Univ.
Western New England College
    (MA)
Western Washington Univ.
Westminster College (PA)
Wheaton College (MA)
Whitman College (WA)
Whittier College (CA)
Widener Univ. (PA)
Wilkes Univ. (PA)
William Jewell College (MO)
Winston-Salem State Univ. (NC)
Wisconsin Lutheran College
Wittenberg Univ. (OH)
Worcester Polytechnic Institute
    (MA)
Yale Univ. (CT)

Biological and Biomedical Sciences

Alderson-Broaddus College (WV)
Alvernia College (PA)
Arcadia Univ. (PA)
Azusa Pacific Univ. (CA)
Beloit College (WI)
Brown Univ. (RI)
California State Univ.–Sacramento
Capital Univ. (OH)
Carlow College (PA)
Carnegie Mellon Univ. (PA)
Charleston Southern Univ. (SC)
College of Charleston (SC)
Cornell Univ. (NY)
CUNY–City College
CUNY–Hunter College
Dakota State Univ. (SD)

Davis and Elkins College (WV)
Eastern Univ. (PA)
Emory Univ. (GA)
Eureka College (IL)
Fairleigh Dickinson Univ. (NJ)
Florida Southern College
Fresno Pacific Univ. (CA)
Frostburg State Univ. (MD)
Geneva College (PA)
Grand Canyon Univ. (AZ)
Guilford College (NC)
Johns Hopkins Univ. (MD)
Kansas State Univ.
Kent State Univ. (OH)
Letourneau Univ. (TX)
Louisiana State Univ.–Shreveport
Martin Univ. (IN)
Merrimack College (MA)
Midland Lutheran College (NE)
Northwest Missouri State Univ.
Norwich Univ. (VT)
Ohio State Univ.–Columbus
Oral Roberts Univ. (OK)
Our Lady of the Lake Univ. (TX)
Park Univ. (MO)
Penn. State Univ.–Univ. Park
Purdue Univ.–Calumet (IN)
Ramapo College of New Jersey
Regis Univ. (CO)
Rensselaer Polytechnic Inst. (NY)
Rochester Institute of Tech. (NY)
Siena College (NY)
Skidmore College (NY)
Southwestern Univ. (TX)
Springfield College (MA)
St. Mary's College of California
SUNY–Albany
SUNY–Farmingdale
SUNY–Fredonia
Swarthmore College (PA)
Texas A&M Univ.–College Station
Texas A&M Univ.–Galveston
Texas Wesleyan Univ.
Touro College (NY)
Trevecca Nazarene Univ. (TN)
Union College (NY)
Univ. at Buffalo–SUNY
Univ. of California–Riverside
Univ. of Ill.–Urbana-Champaign
Univ. of Kansas
Univ. of Maryland–Univ. College
Univ. of Minnesota–Twin Cities
Univ. of Mississippi
Univ. of North Dakota
Univ. of South Florida
Ursuline College (OH)
Wayland Baptist Univ. (TX)

Biological and Physical Sciences

Adelphi Univ. (NY)
Albertus Magnus College (CT)
Alfred Univ. (NY)
Alma College (MI)
Alvernia College (PA)
Averett Univ. (VA)
Avila Univ. (MO)
Bard College (NY)
Benedictine College (KS)

Benedictine Univ. (IL)
Bluefield State College (WV)
Bowie State Univ. (MD)
Brevard College (NC)
Buena Vista Univ. (IA)
California State Univ.–Fullerton
California State Univ.–Los Angeles
Cameron Univ. (OK)
Charleston Southern Univ. (SC)
Clarion Univ. of Pennsylvania
Clarke College (IA)
College of St. Benedict (MN)
College of the Ozarks (MO)
Colorado Christian Univ.
Columbia Univ. (NY)
Concordia Univ. (MI)
Concordia Univ.–River Forest (IL)
Concordia Univ.–St. Paul (MN)
CUNY–Baruch College
CUNY–Brooklyn College
Dallas Baptist Univ.
Delta State Univ. (MS)
Dominican Univ. (IL)
Dowling College (NY)
Drexel Univ. (PA)
East Stroudsburg Univ. of
    Pennsylvania
Eastern Michigan Univ.
Eastern Nazarene College (MA)
Edinboro Univ. of Pennsylvania
Elmira College (NY)
Evergreen State College (WA)
Fairleigh Dickinson Univ. (NJ)
Florida Institute of Technology
Fordham Univ. (NY)
Fort Hays State Univ. (KS)
Furman Univ. (SC)
George Washington Univ. (DC)
Grand Valley State Univ. (MI)
Heritage College (WA)
Immaculata Univ. (PA)
Indiana Univ. East
Indiana Univ. of Pennsylvania
Indiana Univ.–Kokomo
Indiana Wesleyan Univ.
Johns Hopkins Univ. (MD)
King's College (PA)
Kutztown Univ. of Pennsylvania
Lawrence Univ. (WI)
Le Moyne College (NY)
Lehigh Univ. (PA)
Lock Haven Univ. of Pennsylvania
Louisiana College
Lyndon State College (VT)
Madonna Univ. (MI)
Manchester College (IN)
Maryville Univ. of St. Louis (MO)
Mcmurry Univ. (TX)
Mcpherson College (KS)
Michigan State Univ.
Middle Tennessee State Univ.
Mississippi State Univ.
Mount Mary College (WI)
National-Louis Univ. (IL)
North Central College (IL)
North Park Univ. (IL)
Northwestern Univ. (IL)
Olivet College (MI)
Oral Roberts Univ. (OK)
Oregon State Univ.
Pacific Univ. (OR)

Penn. State Univ.–Univ. Park
Purdue Univ.–West Lafayette (IN)
Ramapo College of New Jersey
San Francisco State Univ.
Shimer College (IL)
Southeastern Oklahoma State
    Univ.
Southern Arkansas Univ.
St. Anselm College (NH)
St. John's Univ. (MN)
St. Mary's College of Maryland
St. Norbert College (WI)
St. Peter's College (NJ)
St. Thomas Aquinas College (NY)
St. Xavier Univ. (IL)
SUNY College–Potsdam
Taylor Univ. (IN)
Texas A&M Univ.–College Station
Texas Tech Univ.
Towson Univ. (MD)
Union College (NY)
Univ. of Alabama
Univ. of Alabama–Birmingham
Univ. of Alaska–Anchorage
Univ. of Alaska–Fairbanks
Univ. of Arkansas–Monticello
Univ. of Central Arkansas
Univ. of Denver
Univ. of Georgia
Univ. of Houston
Univ. of Houston–Downtown
Univ. of Kentucky
Univ. of La Verne (CA)
Univ. of Maine–Orono
Univ. of Massachusetts–Amherst
Univ. of Nevada–Las Vegas
Univ. of New Orleans
Univ. of North Florida
Univ. of Northern Iowa
Univ. of Oregon
Univ. of Pittsburgh
Univ. of Pittsburgh–Greensburg
Univ. of South Florida
Univ. of Southern Indiana
Univ. of St. Francis (IN)
Univ. of Texas of the Permian Basin
Univ. of Texas–El Paso
Univ. of Texas–Pan American
Univ. of Texas–San Antonio
Univ. of the Pacific (CA)
Univ. of West Alabama
Univ. of West Florida
Univ. of Wisconsin–Platteville
Univ. of Wisconsin–River Falls
Univ. of Wisconsin–Stevens Point
Univ. of Wisconsin–Superior
Urbana Univ. (OH)
Ursinus College (PA)
Vanguard Univ. of Southern
    California
Virginia Commonwealth Univ.
Washington State Univ.
Waynesburg College (PA)
Western Washington Univ.
Worcester State College (MA)

Biology

Abilene Christian Univ. (TX)
Adams State College (CO)

Adelphi Univ. (NY)
Adrian College (MI)
Agnes Scott College (GA)
Alabama Agricultural and
    Mechanical Univ.
Alabama State Univ.
Albany State Univ. (GA)
Albertson College (ID)
Albertus Magnus College (CT)
Albion College (MI)
Albright College (PA)
Alcorn State Univ. (MS)
Alderson-Broaddus College (WV)
Alfred Univ. (NY)
Alice Lloyd College (KY)
Allegheny College (PA)
Allen Univ. (SC)
Alma College (MI)
Alvernia College (PA)
Alverno College (WI)
American International College
    (MA)
American Univ. (DC)
Amherst College (MA)
Anderson College (SC)
Anderson Univ. (IN)
Andrews Univ. (MI)
Angelo State Univ. (TX)
Antioch College (OH)
Appalachian State Univ. (NC)
Aquinas College (MI)
Arcadia Univ. (PA)
Arizona State Univ.
Arizona State Univ. West
Arkansas State Univ.
Arkansas Tech Univ.
Armstrong Atlantic State Univ.
    (GA)
Asbury College (KY)
Ashland Univ. (OH)
Assumption College (MA)
Atlantic Union College (MA)
Auburn Univ. (AL)
Auburn Univ.–Montgomery (AL)
Augsburg College (MN)
Augusta State Univ. (GA)
Augustana College (IL)
Augustana College (SD)
Aurora Univ. (IL)
Austin College (TX)
Austin Peay State Univ. (TN)
Averett Univ. (VA)
Avila Univ. (MO)
Azusa Pacific Univ. (CA)
Baker Univ. (KS)
Baldwin-Wallace College (OH)
Ball State Univ. (IN)
Barber Scotia College (NC)
Barnard College (NY)
Barry Univ. (FL)
Barton College (NC)
Bates College (ME)
Bay Path College (MA)
Baylor Univ. (TX)
Belhaven College (MS)
Bellarmine Univ. (KY)
Bellevue Univ. (NE)
Belmont Abbey College (NC)
Belmont Univ. (TN)
Beloit College (WI)
Bemidji State Univ. (MN)

Benedict College (SC)
Benedictine College (KS)
Benedictine Univ. (IL)
Bennett College (NC)
Bennington College (VT)
Berea College (KY)
Berry College (GA)
Bethany College (KS)
Bethany College (WV)
Bethel College (KS)
Bethel College (TN)
Bethel College (IN)
Bethel Univ. (MN)
Bethune-Cookman College (FL)
Biola Univ. (CA)
Birmingham-Southern College (AL)
Black Hills State Univ. (SD)
Blackburn College (IL)
Bloomfield College (NJ)
Bloomsburg Univ. of Pennsylvania
Blue Mountain College (MS)
Bluefield College (VA)
Bluffton Univ. (OH)
Boise State Univ. (ID)
Boston Univ.
Bowdoin College (ME)
Bowie State Univ. (MD)
Bowling Green State Univ. (OH)
Bradley Univ. (IL)
Brandeis Univ. (MA)
Brenau Univ. (GA)
Brescia Univ. (KY)
Brewton-Parker College (GA)
Briar Cliff Univ. (IA)
Bridgewater College (VA)
Bridgewater State College (MA)
Brigham Young Univ.–Hawaii
Brigham Young Univ.–Provo (UT)
Brown Univ. (RI)
Bryn Athyn College (PA)
Bryn Mawr College (PA)
Bucknell Univ. (PA)
Buena Vista Univ. (IA)
Buffalo State College
Butler Univ. (IN)
Cabrini College (PA)
Cal Poly–San Luis Obispo
Caldwell College (NJ)
California Baptist Univ.
California Institute of Technology
California Lutheran Univ.
California State Polytechnic
    Univ.–Pomona
California State Univ.–Bakersfield
California State Univ.–Chico
California State Univ.–Dominguez
    Hills
California State Univ.–Fresno
California State Univ.–Fullerton
California State Univ.–Hayward
California State Univ.–Long Beach
California State Univ.–Los Angeles
California State Univ.–Monterey
    Bay
California State Univ.–Northridge
California State Univ.–Sacramento
California State Univ.–San
    Bernardino
California State Univ.–San Marcos
California State Univ.–Stanislaus
California Univ. of Pennsylvania

Calvin College (MI)
Cameron Univ. (OK)
Campbell Univ. (NC)
Campbellsville Univ. (KY)
Canisius College (NY)
Capital Univ. (OH)
Cardinal Stritch Univ. (WI)
Carleton College (MN)
Carlow College (PA)
Carnegie Mellon Univ. (PA)
Carroll College (MT)
Carroll College (WI)
Carson-Newman College (TN)
Carthage College (WI)
Case Western Reserve Univ. (OH)
Castleton State College (VT)
Catawba College (NC)
Catholic Univ. of America (DC)
Cedar Crest College (PA)
Cedarville Univ. (OH)
Centenary College of Louisiana
Central Christian College (KS)
Central College (IA)
Central Connecticut State Univ.
Central Methodist Univ. (MO)
Central Michigan Univ.
Central Missouri State Univ.
Central State Univ. (OH)
Central Washington Univ.
Centre College (KY)
Chadron State College (NE)
Chaminade Univ. of Honolulu
Chapman Univ. (CA)
Charleston Southern Univ. (SC)
Chatham College (PA)
Chestnut Hill College (PA)
Cheyney Univ. of Pennsylvania
Chicago State Univ.
Chowan College (NC)
Christian Brothers Univ. (TN)
Christian Heritage College (CA)
Christopher Newport Univ. (VA)
Claflin Univ. (SC)
Claremont Mckenna College (CA)
Clarion Univ. of Pennsylvania
Clark Atlanta Univ.
Clark Univ. (MA)
Clarkson Univ. (NY)
Clayton Coll. and State Univ. (GA)
Clearwater Christian College (FL)
Cleveland State Univ.
Coastal Carolina Univ. (SC)
Coe College (IA)
Coker College (SC)
Colby College (ME)
Colby-Sawyer College (NH)
Colgate Univ. (NY)
College Misericordia (PA)
College of Charleston (SC)
College of Mount St. Joseph (OH)
College of Mount St. Vincent (NY)
College of New Jersey
College of Notre Dame of
    Maryland
College of St. Benedict (MN)
College of St. Catherine (MN)
College of St. Elizabeth (NJ)
College of St. Mary (NE)
College of St. Rose (NY)
College of St. Scholastica (MN)
College of the Holy Cross (MA)

College of the Southwest (NM)
College of William and Mary (VA)
College of Wooster (OH)
Colorado Christian Univ.
Colorado College
Colorado State Univ.
Colorado State Univ.–Pueblo
Columbia College (MO)
Columbia College (SC)
Columbia Union College (MD)
Columbus State Univ. (GA)
Concord College (WV)
Concordia College (NY)
Concordia Coll.–Moorhead (MN)
Concordia Univ. (MI)
Concordia Univ. (CA)
Concordia Univ. (NE)
Concordia Univ. (OR)
Concordia Univ. Wisconsin
Concordia Univ.–Austin (TX)
Concordia Univ.–River Forest (IL)
Concordia Univ.–St. Paul (MN)
Connecticut College
Converse College (SC)
Coppin State Univ. (MD)
Cornell College (IA)
Cornell Univ. (NY)
Cornerstone Univ. (MI)
Crichton College (TN)
Crown College (MN)
Culver-Stockton College (MO)
Cumberland College (KY)
Cumberland Univ. (TN)
CUNY–Baruch College
CUNY–Brooklyn College
CUNY–City College
CUNY–College of Staten Island
CUNY–Hunter College
CUNY–Lehman College
CUNY–Medgar Evers College
CUNY–Queens College
CUNY–York College
Curry College (MA)
Daemen College (NY)
Dakota Wesleyan Univ. (SD)
Dallas Baptist Univ.
Dana College (NE)
Dartmouth College (NH)
Davidson College (NC)
Davis and Elkins College (WV)
Defiance College (OH)
Delaware State Univ.
Delaware Valley College (PA)
Delta State Univ. (MS)
Denison Univ. (OH)
Depaul Univ. (IL)
Depauw Univ. (IN)
Desales Univ. (PA)
Dickinson College (PA)
Dickinson State Univ. (ND)
Dillard Univ. (LA)
Dominican Coll. of Blauvelt (NY)
Dominican Univ. (IL)
Dominican Univ. of California (CA)
Dordt College (IA)
Dowling College (NY)
Drake Univ. (IA)
Drew Univ. (NJ)
Drury Univ. (MO)
Duke Univ. (NC)
Duquesne Univ. (PA)

Earlham College (IN)
East Carolina Univ. (NC)
East Central Univ. (OK)
East Stroudsburg Univ. of
    Pennsylvania
East Tennessee State Univ.
East Texas Baptist Univ.
Eastern Connecticut State Univ.
Eastern Illinois Univ.
Eastern Kentucky Univ.
Eastern Mennonite Univ. (VA)
Eastern Michigan Univ.
Eastern Nazarene College (MA)
Eastern New Mexico Univ.
Eastern Oregon Univ.
Eastern Univ. (PA)
Eastern Washington Univ.
Eckerd College (FL)
Edgewood College (WI)
Edinboro Univ. of Pennsylvania
Edward Waters College (FL)
Elizabeth City State Univ. (NC)
Elizabethtown College (PA)
Elmhurst College (IL)
Elmira College (NY)
Elms College (College of Our Lady
    of the Elms) (MA)
Elon Univ. (NC)
Emmanuel College (MA)
Emmanuel College (GA)
Emory and Henry College (VA)
Emory Univ. (GA)
Emporia State Univ. (KS)
Erskine College (SC)
Eureka College (IL)
Evangel Univ. (MO)
Excelsior College (NY)
Fairfield Univ. (CT)
Fairleigh Dickinson Univ. (NJ)
Fairmont State Univ. (WV)
Fayetteville State Univ. (NC)
Felician College (NJ)
Ferris State Univ. (MI)
Ferrum College (VA)
Fisk Univ. (TN)
Fitchburg State College (MA)
Florida Atlantic Univ.
Florida Institute of Technology
Florida International Univ.
Florida Memorial College
Florida Southern College
Florida State Univ.
Fontbonne Univ. (MO)
Fordham Univ. (NY)
Fort Hays State Univ. (KS)
Fort Lewis College (CO)
Fort Valley State Univ. (GA)
Framingham State College (MA)
Francis Marion Univ. (SC)
Franciscan Univ. of Steubenville
    (OH)
Franklin and Marshall College (PA)
Franklin College (IN)
Franklin Pierce College (NH)
Freed-Hardeman Univ. (TN)
Fresno Pacific Univ. (CA)
Friends Univ. (KS)
Frostburg State Univ. (MD)
Furman Univ. (SC)
Gallaudet Univ. (DC)
Gannon Univ. (PA)

Gardner-Webb Univ. (NC)
Geneva College (PA)
George Fox Univ. (OR)
George Mason Univ. (VA)
George Washington Univ. (DC)
Georgetown College (KY)
Georgetown Univ. (DC)
Georgia College and State Univ.
Georgia Institute of Technology
Georgia Southern Univ.
Georgia Southwestern State Univ.
Georgia State Univ.
Georgian Court Univ. (NJ)
Gettysburg College (PA)
Glenville State College (WV)
Gonzaga Univ. (WA)
Gordon College (MA)
Goucher College (MD)
Grace College and Seminary (IN)
Graceland Univ. (IA)
Grambling State Univ. (LA)
Grand Canyon Univ. (AZ)
Grand Valley State Univ. (MI)
Grand View College (IA)
Green Mountain College (VT)
Greensboro College (NC)
Greenville College (IL)
Grinnell College (IA)
Grove City College (PA)
Guilford College (NC)
Gustavus Adolphus College (MN)
Gwynedd-Mercy College (PA)
Hamilton College (NY)
Hamline Univ. (MN)
Hampden-Sydney College (VA)
Hampshire College (MA)
Hampton Univ. (VA)
Hannibal-Lagrange College (MO)
Hanover College (IN)
Hardin-Simmons Univ. (TX)
Harding Univ. (AR)
Hartwick College (NY)
Harvard Univ. (MA)
Harvey Mudd College (CA)
Hastings College (NE)
Haverford College (PA)
Hawaii Pacific Univ.
Heidelberg College (OH)
Henderson State Univ. (AR)
Hendrix College (AR)
Heritage College (WA)
High Point Univ. (NC)
Hillsdale College (MI)
Hiram College (OH)
Hobart and William Smith Colleges
    (NY)
Hofstra Univ. (NY)
Hollins Univ. (VA)
Holy Family Univ. (PA)
Holy Names Univ. (CA)
Hood College (MD)
Hope College (MI)
Houghton College (NY)
Houston Baptist Univ.
Howard Payne Univ. (TX)
Howard Univ. (DC)
Humboldt State Univ. (CA)
Huntingdon College (AL)
Huntington College (IN)
Husson College (ME)
Huston-Tillotson College (TX)

Idaho State Univ.
Illinois College
Illinois Institute of Technology
Illinois State Univ.
Illinois Wesleyan Univ.
Immaculata Univ. (PA)
Indiana State Univ.
Indiana Univ. Northwest
Indiana Univ. of Pennsylvania
Indiana Univ. Southeast
Indiana Univ.–Bloomington
Indiana Univ.–Kokomo
Indiana Univ.–Purdue Univ.–Fort
    Wayne
Indiana Univ.-Purdue
    Univ.–Indianapolis
Indiana Wesleyan Univ.
Iona College (NY)
Iowa State Univ.
Ithaca College (NY)
Jackson State Univ. (MS)
Jacksonville State Univ. (AL)
Jacksonville Univ. (FL)
James Madison Univ. (VA)
Jamestown College (ND)
Jarvis Christian College (TX)
John Brown Univ. (AR)
John Carroll Univ. (OH)
Johns Hopkins Univ. (MD)
Johnson C. Smith Univ. (NC)
Johnson State College (VT)
Judson College (AL)
Judson College (IL)
Juniata College (PA)
Kalamazoo College (MI)
Kansas State Univ.
Kansas Wesleyan Univ.
Kean Univ. (NJ)
Keene State College (NH)
Kennesaw State Univ. (GA)
Kent State Univ. (OH)
Kentucky State Univ.
Kentucky Wesleyan College
Keuka College (NY)
King College (TN)
King's College (PA)
Knox College (IL)
Kutztown Univ. of Pennsylvania
La Roche College (PA)
La Salle Univ. (PA)
La Sierra Univ. (CA)
Lafayette College (PA)
Lagrange College (GA)
Lake Erie College (OH)
Lake Forest College (IL)
Lake Superior State Univ. (MI)
Lakeland College (WI)
Lamar Univ. (TX)
Lambuth Univ. (TN)
Lander Univ. (SC)
Lane College (TN)
Lawrence Univ. (WI)
Le Moyne College (NY)
Lebanon Valley College (PA)
Lees-Mcrae College (NC)
Lehigh Univ. (PA)
Lemoyne-Owen College (TN)
Lenoir-Rhyne College (NC)
Lesley Univ. (MA)
Letourneau Univ. (TX)
Lewis and Clark College (OR)

Lewis Univ. (IL)
Lewis-Clark State College (ID)
Liberty Univ. (VA)
Limestone College (SC)
Lincoln Memorial Univ. (TN)
Lincoln Univ. (PA)
Lincoln Univ. (MO)
Lindenwood Univ. (MO)
Lindsey Wilson College (KY)
Linfield College (OR)
Livingstone College (NC)
Lock Haven Univ. of Pennsylvania
Long Island Univ.–C.W. Post
    Campus (NY)
Long Island Univ.–Southampton
    College (NY)
Longwood Univ. (VA)
Loras College (IA)
Louisiana College
Louisiana State Univ.–Baton Rouge
Louisiana State Univ.–Shreveport
Louisiana Tech Univ.
Lourdes College (OH)
Loyola College In Maryland
Loyola Marymount Univ. (CA)
Loyola Univ. Chicago
Loyola Univ. New Orleans
Lubbock Christian Univ. (TX)
Luther College (IA)
Lycoming College (PA)
Lynchburg College (VA)
Lynn Univ. (FL)
Lyon College (AR)
Macalester College (MN)
Macmurray College (IL)
Madonna Univ. (MI)
Malone College (OH)
Manchester College (IN)
Manhattan College (NY)
Manhattanville College (NY)
Mansfield Univ. of Pennsylvania
Marian College (IN)
Marian College of Fond Du Lac
    (WI)
Marietta College (OH)
Marist College (NY)
Marlboro College (VT)
Marquette Univ. (WI)
Mars Hill College (NC)
Marshall Univ. (WV)
Martin Methodist College (TN)
Martin Univ. (IN)
Mary Baldwin College (VA)
Marygrove College (MI)
Marymount Manhattan College
    (NY)
Marymount Univ. (VA)
Maryville College (TN)
Maryville Univ. of St. Louis (MO)
Marywood Univ. (PA)
Massachusetts Institute of
    Technology
Master's Coll. and Seminary (CA)
Mayville State Univ. (ND)
Mcdaniel College (MD)
Mckendree College (IL)
Mcmurry Univ. (TX)
Mcneese State Univ. (LA)
Mcpherson College (KS)
Medaille College (NY)
Mercer Univ. (GA)

Mercy College (NY)
Mercyhurst College (PA)
Meredith College (NC)
Merrimack College (MA)
Mesa State College (CO)
Messiah College (PA)
Methodist College (NC)
Metropolitan State College of
    Denver
Michigan State Univ.
Michigan Technological Univ.
Middle Tennessee State Univ.
Middlebury College (VT)
Midland Lutheran College (NE)
Midway College (KY)
Midwestern State Univ. (TX)
Millersville Univ. of Pennsylvania
Milligan College (TN)
Millikin Univ. (IL)
Mills College (CA)
Millsaps College (MS)
Minnesota State Univ.–Mankato
Minnesota State Univ.–Moorhead
Minot State Univ. (ND)
Mississippi College
Mississippi State Univ.
Mississippi Univ. For Women
Mississippi Valley State Univ.
Missouri Southern State Univ.
Missouri Valley College
Missouri Western State College
Molloy College (NY)
Monmouth College (IL)
Monmouth Univ. (NJ)
Montana State Univ.–Billings
Montana State Univ.–Bozeman
Montana State Univ.–Northern
Montana Tech of the Univ. of
    Montana
Montclair State Univ. (NJ)
Montreat College (NC)
Moravian College (PA)
Morehead State Univ. (KY)
Morehouse College (GA)
Morgan State Univ. (MD)
Morningside College (IA)
Morris College (SC)
Mount Holyoke College (MA)
Mount Ida College (MA)
Mount Marty College (SD)
Mount Mary College (WI)
Mount Mercy College (IA)
Mount Olive College (NC)
Mount St. Mary College (NY)
Mount St. Mary's College (CA)
Mount St. Mary's Univ. (MD)
Mount Union College (OH)
Muhlenberg College (PA)
Murray State Univ. (KY)
Muskingum College (OH)
National-Louis Univ. (IL)
Nazareth College of Rochester
    (NY)
Nebraska Wesleyan Univ.
Neumann College (PA)
New Jersey City Univ.
New Jersey Institute of Technology
New Mexico Highlands Univ.
New Mexico Institute of Mining
    and Technology
New Mexico State Univ.

New York Institute of Technology
New York Univ.
Newberry College (SC)
Newman Univ. (KS)
Niagara Univ. (NY)
Nicholls State Univ. (LA)
Norfolk State Univ. (VA)
North Carolina A&T State Univ.
North Carolina Central Univ.
North Carolina State Univ.–Raleigh
North Carolina Wesleyan College
North Central College (IL)
North Dakota State Univ.
North Georgia College and State
    Univ.
North Greenville College (SC)
North Park Univ. (IL)
Northeastern Illinois Univ.
Northeastern State Univ. (OK)
Northeastern Univ. (MA)
Northern Arizona Univ.
Northern Illinois Univ.
Northern Kentucky Univ.
Northern Michigan Univ.
Northern State Univ. (SD)
Northland College (WI)
Northwest Nazarene Univ. (ID)
Northwestern College (MN)
Northwestern College (IA)
Northwestern Oklahoma State
    Univ.
Northwestern State Univ. of
    Louisiana
Northwestern Univ. (IL)
Norwich Univ. (VT)
Notre Dame College of Ohio
Notre Dame De Namur Univ. (CA)
Nova Southeastern Univ. (FL)
Oakland City Univ. (IN)
Oakland Univ. (MI)
Oakwood College (AL)
Oberlin College (OH)
Occidental College (CA)
Ohio Dominican Univ.
Ohio Northern Univ.
Ohio State Univ.–Columbus
Ohio Univ.
Ohio Wesleyan Univ.
Oklahoma Baptist Univ.
Oklahoma Christian Univ.
Oklahoma City Univ.
Oklahoma Panhandle State Univ.
Oklahoma State Univ.
Oklahoma Wesleyan Univ.
Old Dominion Univ. (VA)
Olivet College (MI)
Olivet Nazarene Univ. (IL)
Oral Roberts Univ. (OK)
Oregon State Univ.
Otterbein College (OH)
Ouachita Baptist Univ. (AR)
Our Lady of Holy Cross Coll. (LA)
Our Lady of the Lake Univ. (TX)
Pace Univ. (NY)
Pacific Lutheran Univ. (WA)
Pacific Union College (CA)
Pacific Univ. (OR)
Paine College (GA)
Palm Beach Atlantic Univ. (FL)
Park Univ. (MO)
Paul Quinn College (TX)

Peace College (NC)
Penn. State Univ.–Univ. Park
Penn. State–Erie, The Behrend
    College
Pepperdine Univ. (CA)
Peru State College (NE)
Pfeiffer Univ. (NC)
Philadelphia Univ.
Philander Smith College (AR)
Piedmont College (GA)
Pikeville College (KY)
Pine Manor College (MA)
Pittsburg State Univ. (KS)
Pitzer College (CA)
Plymouth State Univ. (NH)
Point Loma Nazarene Univ. (CA)
Point Park Univ. (PA)
Pomona College (CA)
Portland State Univ. (OR)
Prairie View A&M Univ. (TX)
Presbyterian College (SC)
Principia College (IL)
Providence College (RI)
Purdue Univ.–Calumet (IN)
Purdue Univ.–North Central (IN)
Purdue Univ.–West Lafayette (IN)
Queens Univ. of Charlotte (NC)
Quincy Univ. (IL)
Quinnipiac Univ. (CT)
Radford Univ. (VA)
Ramapo College of New Jersey
Randolph-Macon College (VA)
Randolph-Macon Woman's College
    (VA)
Reed College (OR)
Regis College (MA)
Regis Univ. (CO)
Reinhardt College (GA)
Rensselaer Polytechnic Inst. (NY)
Rhode Island College
Rhodes College (TN)
Rice Univ. (TX)
Richard Stockton College of New
    Jersey
Rider Univ. (NJ)
Ripon College (WI)
Rivier College (NH)
Roanoke College (VA)
Roberts Wesleyan College (NY)
Rochester Institute of Tech. (NY)
Rockford College (IL)
Rockhurst Univ. (MO)
Rocky Mountain College (MT)
Roger Williams Univ. (RI)
Rollins College (FL)
Roosevelt Univ. (IL)
Rose-Hulman Institute of
    Technology (IN)
Rosemont College (PA)
Russell Sage College (NY)
Rust College (MS)
Rutgers–Camden (NJ)
Rutgers–New Brunswick (NJ)
Rutgers–Newark (NJ)
Sacred Heart Univ. (CT)
Saginaw Valley State Univ. (MI)
Salem College (NC)
Salem International Univ. (WV)
Salem State College (MA)
Salisbury Univ. (MD)
Salve Regina Univ. (RI)

Sam Houston State Univ. (TX)
Samford Univ. (AL)
San Diego State Univ.
San Francisco State Univ.
San Jose State Univ. (CA)
Santa Clara Univ. (CA)
Savannah State Univ. (GA)
Schreiner Univ. (TX)
Scripps College (CA)
Seattle Pacific Univ.
Seattle Univ.
Seton Hall Univ. (NJ)
Seton Hill Univ. (PA)
Sewanee–Univ. of the South (TN)
Shaw Univ. (NC)
Shawnee State Univ. (OH)
Shenandoah Univ. (VA)
Shepherd Univ. (WV)
Shippensburg Univ. of
    Pennsylvania
Shorter College (GA)
Siena College (NY)
Sierra Nevada College (NV)
Silver Lake College (WI)
Simmons College (MA)
Simon's Rock College of Bard
    (MA)
Simpson College (IA)
Skidmore College (NY)
Slippery Rock Univ. of Pennsylvania
Sonoma State Univ. (CA)
South Carolina State Univ.
South Dakota State Univ.
Southeast Missouri State Univ.
Southeastern College of the
    Assemblies of God
Southeastern Louisiana Univ.
Southeastern Oklahoma State
    Univ.
Southern Adventist Univ. (TN)
Southern Arkansas Univ.
Southern Connecticut State Univ.
Southern Illinois Univ.–Carbondale
Southern Illinois
    Univ.–Edwardsville
Southern Methodist Univ. (TX)
Southern Nazarene Univ. (OK)
Southern Oregon Univ.
Southern Polytechnic State Univ.
    (GA)
Southern Univ. and A&M College
    (LA)
Southern Utah Univ.
Southern Wesleyan Univ. (SC)
Southwest Baptist Univ. (MO)
Southwest Minnesota State Univ.
    (MN)
Southwest Missouri State Univ.
Southwestern Adventist Univ. (TX)
Southwestern College (KS)
Southwestern Oklahoma State
    Univ.
Southwestern Univ. (TX)
Spelman College (GA)
Spring Arbor Univ. (MI)
Spring Hill College (AL)
Springfield College (MA)
St. Ambrose Univ. (IA)
St. Andrews Presbyterian College
    (NC)
St. Anselm College (NH)

St. Augustine's College (NC)
St. Bonaventure Univ. (NY)
St. Cloud State Univ. (MN)
St. Edward's Univ. (TX)
St. Francis College (NY)
St. Francis Univ. (PA)
St. John Fisher College (NY)
St. John's Univ. (NY)
St. John's Univ. (MN)
St. Joseph College (CT)
St. Joseph's College (IN)
St. Joseph's College (ME)
St. Joseph's College, New York
St. Joseph's Univ. (PA)
St. Lawrence Univ. (NY)
St. Leo Univ. (FL)
St. Louis Univ.
St. Martin's College (WA)
St. Mary's College (IN)
St. Mary's College of California
St. Mary's College of Maryland
St. Mary's Univ. of Minnesota
St. Mary's Univ. of San Antonio
St. Michael's College (VT)
St. Norbert College (WI)
St. Olaf College (MN)
St. Peter's College (NJ)
St. Thomas Aquinas College (NY)
St. Thomas Univ. (FL)
St. Vincent College (PA)
St. Xavier Univ. (IL)
Stanford Univ. (CA)
State Univ. of West Georgia
Stephen F. Austin State Univ. (TX)
Stephens College (MO)
Sterling College (KS)
Stetson Univ. (FL)
Stillman College (AL)
Stonehill College (MA)
Suffolk Univ. (MA)
Sul Ross State Univ. (TX)
SUNY College of Arts and
    Sciences–Geneseo
SUNY College–Brockport
SUNY College–Old Westbury
SUNY College–Oneonta
SUNY College–Potsdam
SUNY–Albany
SUNY–Binghamton
SUNY–Fredonia
SUNY–Plattsburgh
SUNY–Purchase College
SUNY–Stony Brook
Susquehanna Univ. (PA)
Swarthmore College (PA)
Sweet Briar College (VA)
Syracuse Univ. (NY)
Tabor College (KS)
Talladega College (AL)
Tarleton State Univ. (TX)
Taylor Univ. (IN)
Teikyo Post Univ. (CT)
Temple Univ. (PA)
Tennessee State Univ.
Tennessee Technological Univ.
Tennessee Wesleyan College
Texas A&M International Univ.
Texas A&M Univ.–College Station
Texas A&M Univ.–Commerce
Texas A&M Univ.–Corpus Christi
Texas A&M Univ.–Kingsville

Texas Christian Univ.
Texas College
Texas Lutheran Univ.
Texas State Univ.–San Marcos
Texas Tech Univ.
Texas Wesleyan Univ.
Texas Woman's Univ.
The Citadel (SC)
The Franciscan Univ. (IA)
Thiel College (PA)
Thomas Edison State College (NJ)
Thomas More College (KY)
Thomas Univ. (GA)
Toccoa Falls College (GA)
Tougaloo College (MS)
Touro College (NY)
Towson Univ. (MD)
Transylvania Univ. (KY)
Trevecca Nazarene Univ. (TN)
Tri-State Univ. (IN)
Trinity Christian College (IL)
Trinity College (DC)
Trinity College (CT)
Troy State Univ.–Troy (AL)
Truman State Univ. (MO)
Tufts Univ. (MA)
Tulane Univ. (LA)
Tusculum College (TN)
Union College (NY)
Union College (NE)
Union Univ. (TN)
United States Air Force Academy
    (CO)
Univ. at Buffalo–SUNY
Univ. of Akron (OH)
Univ. of Alabama
Univ. of Alabama–Birmingham
Univ. of Alabama–Huntsville
Univ. of Alaska–Anchorage
Univ. of Alaska–Fairbanks
Univ. of Alaska–Southeast
Univ. of Arizona
Univ. of Arkansas
Univ. of Arkansas–Pine Bluff
Univ. of Bridgeport (CT)
Univ. of California–Berkeley
Univ. of California–Davis
Univ. of California–Irvine
Univ. of California–Los Angeles
Univ. of California–Riverside
Univ. of California–San Diego
Univ. of California–Santa Barbara
Univ. of California–Santa Cruz
Univ. of Central Arkansas
Univ. of Central Florida
Univ. of Central Oklahoma
Univ. of Charleston (WV)
Univ. of Chicago
Univ. of Colorado–Colorado
    Springs
Univ. of Colorado–Denver
Univ. of Connecticut
Univ. of Dallas
Univ. of Dayton (OH)
Univ. of Delaware
Univ. of Denver
Univ. of Detroit Mercy
Univ. of Dubuque (IA)
Univ. of Evansville (IN)
Univ. of Findlay (OH)
Univ. of Georgia

Univ. of Great Falls (MT)
Univ. of Hartford (CT)
Univ. of Hawaii–Hilo
Univ. of Hawaii–Manoa
Univ. of Houston
Univ. of Houston–Downtown
Univ. of Illinois–Chicago
Univ. of Illinois–Springfield
Univ. of Ill.–Urbana-Champaign
Univ. of Indianapolis
Univ. of Iowa
Univ. of Kansas
Univ. of Kentucky
Univ. of La Verne (CA)
Univ. of Louisiana–Lafayette
Univ. of Louisiana–Monroe
Univ. of Louisville (KY)
Univ. of Maine–Augusta
Univ. of Maine–Farmington
Univ. of Maine–Fort Kent
Univ. of Maine–Machias
Univ. of Maine–Orono
Univ. of Maine–Presque Isle
Univ. of Mary (ND)
Univ. of Mary Hardin-Baylor (TX)
Univ. of Mary Washington (VA)
Univ. of Maryland–Baltimore
    County
Univ. of Maryland–College Park
Univ. of Maryland–Eastern Shore
Univ. of Massachusetts–Amherst
Univ. of Massachusetts–Boston
Univ. of Massachusetts–Lowell
Univ. of Memphis
Univ. of Miami (FL)
Univ. of Michigan–Ann Arbor
Univ. of Michigan–Dearborn
Univ. of Michigan–Flint
Univ. of Minnesota–Duluth
Univ. of Minnesota–Morris
Univ. of Minnesota–Twin Cities
Univ. of Mississippi
Univ. of Missouri–Columbia
Univ. of Missouri–Kansas City
Univ. of Missouri–Rolla
Univ. of Missouri–St. Louis
Univ. of Mobile (AL)
Univ. of Montana
Univ. of Montevallo (AL)
Univ. of Nebraska–Kearney
Univ. of Nebraska–Lincoln
Univ. of Nebraska–Omaha
Univ. of Nevada–Las Vegas
Univ. of Nevada–Reno
Univ. of New England (ME)
Univ. of New Hampshire
Univ. of New Haven (CT)
Univ. of New Mexico
Univ. of New Orleans
Univ. of North Alabama
Univ. of North Carolina–Asheville
Univ. of N.C.–Chapel Hill
Univ. of North Carolina–Charlotte
Univ. of N.C.–Greensboro
Univ. of North Carolina–Pembroke
Univ. of N.C.–Wilmington
Univ. of North Dakota
Univ. of North Florida
Univ. of North Texas
Univ. of Northern Colorado
Univ. of Northern Iowa

Univ. of Notre Dame (IN)
Univ. of Oregon
Univ. of Pennsylvania
Univ. of Pittsburgh
Univ. of Pittsburgh–Bradford
Univ. of Pittsburgh–Greensburg
Univ. of Pittsburgh–Johnstown
Univ. of Portland (OR)
Univ. of Puget Sound (WA)
Univ. of Redlands (CA)
Univ. of Rhode Island
Univ. of Richmond (VA)
Univ. of Rio Grande (OH)
Univ. of Rochester (NY)
Univ. of San Diego
Univ. of San Francisco
Univ. of Science and Arts of
    Oklahoma
Univ. of Scranton (PA)
Univ. of Sioux Falls (SD)
Univ. of South Alabama
Univ. of South Carolina–Aiken
Univ. of South Carolina–Columbia
Univ. of South Carolina–Upstate
Univ. of South Dakota
Univ. of South Florida
Univ. of Southern California
Univ. of Southern Indiana
Univ. of Southern Maine
Univ. of Southern Mississippi
Univ. of St. Francis (IL)
Univ. of St. Francis (IN)
Univ. of St. Mary (KS)
Univ. of St. Thomas (TX)
Univ. of St. Thomas (MN)
Univ. of Tampa (FL)
Univ. of Tennessee
Univ. of Tennessee–Chattanooga
Univ. of Tennessee–Martin
Univ. of Texas of the Permian Basin
Univ. of Texas–Arlington
Univ. of Texas–Austin
Univ. of Texas–Brownsville
Univ. of Texas–Dallas
Univ. of Texas–El Paso
Univ. of Texas–Pan American
Univ. of Texas–San Antonio
Univ. of Texas–Tyler
Univ. of the District of Columbia
Univ. of the Incarnate Word (TX)
Univ. of the Pacific (CA)
Univ. of Toledo (OH)
Univ. of Tulsa (OK)
Univ. of Utah
Univ. of Vermont
Univ. of Virginia
Univ. of Virginia–Wise
Univ. of Washington
Univ. of West Alabama
Univ. of West Florida
Univ. of Wisconsin–Eau Claire
Univ. of Wisconsin–Green Bay
Univ. of Wisconsin–La Crosse
Univ. of Wisconsin–Madison
Univ. of Wisconsin–Milwaukee
Univ. of Wisconsin–Oshkosh
Univ. of Wisconsin–Platteville
Univ. of Wisconsin–River Falls
Univ. of Wisconsin–Stevens Point
Univ. of Wisconsin–Superior
Univ. of Wisconsin–Whitewater

Univ. of Wyoming
Upper Iowa Univ.
Ursinus College (PA)
Ursuline College (OH)
Utah State Univ.
Utah Valley State College
Utica College (NY)
Valdosta State Univ. (GA)
Valley City State Univ. (ND)
Valparaiso Univ. (IN)
Vanderbilt Univ. (TN)
Vassar College (NY)
Villa Julie College (MD)
Villanova Univ. (PA)
Virginia Commonwealth Univ.
Virginia Intermont College
Virginia Military Institute
Virginia State Univ.
Virginia Tech
Virginia Wesleyan College
Viterbo Univ. (WI)
Voorhees College (SC)
Wabash College (IN)
Wagner College (NY)
Wake Forest Univ. (NC)
Walsh Univ. (OH)
Warner Pacific College (OR)
Warner Southern College (FL)
Wartburg College (IA)
Washburn Univ. (KS)
Washington and Jefferson College
    (PA)
Washington and Lee Univ. (VA)
Washington College (MD)
Washington State Univ.
Washington Univ. In St. Louis
Wayland Baptist Univ. (TX)
Wayne State College (NE)
Wayne State Univ. (MI)
Waynesburg College (PA)
Webster Univ. (MO)
Wellesley College (MA)
Wesley College (DE)
Wesleyan College (GA)
Wesleyan Univ. (CT)
West Chester Univ. of Pennsylvania
West Liberty State College (WV)
West Texas A&M Univ.
West Virginia State Univ.
West Virginia Univ.
West Virginia Univ. Institute of
    Technology
West Virginia Wesleyan College
Western Carolina Univ. (NC)
Western Connecticut State Univ.
Western Illinois Univ.
Western Kentucky Univ.
Western Michigan Univ.
Western New England College
    (MA)
Western New Mexico Univ.
Western Oregon Univ.
Western State College of Colorado
Western Washington Univ.
Westfield State College (MA)
Westminster College (UT)
Westminster College (PA)
Westminster College (MO)
Westmont College (CA)
Wheaton College (MA)
Wheaton College (IL)

Wheeling Jesuit Univ. (WV)
Whitman College (WA)
Whittier College (CA)
Whitworth College (WA)
Wichita State Univ. (KS)
Widener Univ. (PA)
Wilberforce Univ. (OH)
Wiley College (TX)
Wilkes Univ. (PA)
Willamette Univ. (OR)
William Carey College (MS)
William Jewell College (MO)
William Paterson Univ. of New
 Jersey
William Penn Univ. (IA)
William Woods Univ. (MO)
Williams Baptist College (AR)
Williams College (MA)
Wilmington College (OH)
Wilson College (PA)
Wingate Univ. (NC)
Winston-Salem State Univ. (NC)
Winthrop Univ. (SC)
Wisconsin Lutheran College
Wittenberg Univ. (OH)
Wofford College (SC)
Worcester Polytechnic Institute
 (MA)
Worcester State College (MA)
Wright State Univ. (OH)
Xavier Univ. (OH)
Xavier Univ. of Louisiana
Yale Univ. (CT)
York College (NE)
York College of Pennsylvania
Youngstown State Univ. (OH)

Biology Technician/ Biotechnology Laboratory Technician

Florida Memorial College
Gannon Univ. (PA)
Mansfield Univ. of Pennsylvania
Penn. State Univ.–Univ. Park
Texas Wesleyan Univ.
Tusculum College (TN)
Univ. of New Haven (CT)

Biomathematics and Bioinformatics

Baylor Univ. (TX)
Brigham Young Univ.–Provo (UT)
Brown Univ. (RI)
Canisius College (NY)
Cedar Crest College (PA)
Chatham College (PA)
Claflin Univ. (SC)
Clark Univ. (MA)
Cornell Univ. (NY)
Emmanuel College (MA)
Gannon Univ. (PA)
Harvey Mudd College (CA)
La Sierra Univ. (CA)
Loyola Univ. Chicago
Michigan Technological Univ.
Pacific Univ. (OR)
Polytechnic Univ. (NY)

Ramapo College of New Jersey
Rochester Institute of Tech. (NY)
Rockhurst Univ. (MO)
St. Edward's Univ. (TX)
St. Vincent College (PA)
Tulane Univ. (LA)
Univ. at Buffalo–SUNY
Univ. of California–San Diego
Univ. of California–Santa Cruz
Univ. of Denver
Univ. of Maryland–Baltimore
 County
Univ. of Michigan–Ann Arbor
Univ. of Nebraska–Omaha
Univ. of N.C.–Chapel Hill
Univ. of Northern Iowa
Univ. of Pennsylvania
Univ. of Scranton (PA)
Univ. of St. Thomas (TX)
Univ. of Wisconsin–Parkside
Virginia Commonwealth Univ.

Biomedical/Medical Engineering

Alfred Univ. (NY)
Arizona State Univ.
Boston Univ.
Brown Univ. (RI)
Bucknell Univ. (PA)
California Lutheran Univ.
Carnegie Mellon Univ. (PA)
Case Western Reserve Univ. (OH)
Catholic Univ. of America (DC)
Cedar Crest College (PA)
College of New Jersey
Columbia Univ. (NY)
Cornell Univ. (NY)
CUNY–City College
Drexel Univ. (PA)
Duke Univ. (NC)
Florida A&M Univ.
Florida International Univ.
George Washington Univ. (DC)
Georgia Institute of Technology
Hofstra Univ. (NY)
Illinois Institute of Technology
Johns Hopkins Univ. (MD)
Kettering Univ. (MI)
Lawrence Technological Univ. (MI)
Lehigh Univ. (PA)
Letourneau Univ. (TX)
Louisiana State Univ.–Baton Rouge
Louisiana Tech Univ.
Marquette Univ. (WI)
Michigan Technological Univ.
Milwaukee School of Engineering
Mississippi State Univ.
New Jersey Institute of Technology
North Carolina State Univ.–Raleigh
Northwestern Univ. (IL)
Oral Roberts Univ. (OK)
Oregon State Univ.
Penn. State Univ.–Univ. Park
Rensselaer Polytechnic Inst. (NY)
Rice Univ. (TX)
Rochester Institute of Tech. (NY)
Rose-Hulman Institute of
 Technology (IN)
Rutgers–New Brunswick (NJ)

St. Louis Univ.
Stanford Univ. (CA)
Stevens Institute of Technology
 (NJ)
SUNY–Stony Brook
Syracuse Univ. (NY)
Texas A&M Univ.–College Station
Trinity College (CT)
Tulane Univ. (LA)
Univ. of Akron (OH)
Univ. of Alabama–Birmingham
Univ. of California–Berkeley
Univ. of California–Davis
Univ. of California–Irvine
Univ. of California–Riverside
Univ. of Central Oklahoma
Univ. of Connecticut
Univ. of Houston
Univ. of Illinois–Chicago
Univ. of Illinois–Urbana-
 Champaign
Univ. of Iowa
Univ. of Louisville (KY)
Univ. of Memphis
Univ. of Miami (FL)
Univ. of Minnesota–Twin Cities
Univ. of Nebraska–Lincoln
Univ. of Pennsylvania
Univ. of Pittsburgh
Univ. of Rhode Island
Univ. of Rochester (NY)
Univ. of South Carolina–Columbia
Univ. of Southern California
Univ. of Texas–Austin
Univ. of the Pacific (CA)
Univ. of Toledo (OH)
Univ. of Utah
Univ. of Virginia
Univ. of Washington
Univ. of Wisconsin–Madison
Vanderbilt Univ. (TN)
Virginia Commonwealth Univ.
Washington State Univ.
Washington Univ. In St. Louis
Western New England College
 (MA)
Worcester Polytechnic Institute
 (MA)
Wright State Univ. (OH)
Yale Univ. (CT)

Biopsychology

Hiram College (OH)
Long Island Univ.–Southampton
 College (NY)
Simmons College (MA)
Tufts Univ. (MA)
Univ. of California–Santa Barbara

Biotechnology

Brigham Young Univ.–Provo (UT)
California State Polytechnic
 Univ.–Pomona
California State Univ.–San Marcos
Calvin College (MI)
Claflin Univ. (SC)
CUNY–York College

East Stroudsburg Univ. of
 Pennsylvania
Elizabethtown College (PA)
Fayetteville State Univ. (NC)
Ferris State Univ. (MI)
Florida Gulf Coast Univ.
Fontbonne Univ. (MO)
James Madison Univ. (VA)
Kennesaw State Univ. (GA)
Kent State Univ. (OH)
Minnesota State Univ.–Mankato
Missouri Southern State Univ.
Montana State Univ.–Bozeman
North Dakota State Univ.
Oregon State Univ.
Penn. State Univ.–Univ. Park
Plymouth State Univ. (NH)
Point Park Univ. (PA)
Purdue Univ.–Calumet (IN)
Rochester Institute of Tech. (NY)
Roosevelt Univ. (IL)
Rutgers–New Brunswick (NJ)
Salem International Univ. (WV)
Southeastern Oklahoma State
 Univ.
SUNY College Environmental
 Science and Forestry
Univ. at Buffalo–SUNY
Univ. of California–Davis
Univ. of California–Los Angeles
Univ. of Georgia
Univ. of Ill.–Urbana-Champaign
Univ. of Nebraska–Omaha
Univ. of Nevada–Reno
Univ. of Northern Iowa
Univ. of Wisconsin–River Falls
Ursuline College (OH)
Villa Julie College (MD)
Washington State Univ.
West Texas A&M Univ.
William Paterson Univ. of New
 Jersey
Winston-Salem State Univ. (NC)
Worcester Polytechnic Institute
 (MA)
Worcester State College (MA)

Botany/Plant Biology

Arizona State Univ.
Bennington College (VT)
Brigham Young Univ.–Provo (UT)
California State Polytechnic
 Univ.–Pomona
California State Univ.–Long Beach
Colorado State Univ.
Connecticut College
Cornell Univ. (NY)
Humboldt State Univ. (CA)
Idaho State Univ.
Iowa State Univ.
Juniata College (PA)
Kent State Univ. (OH)
Lawrence Univ. (WI)
Marlboro College (VT)
Mars Hill College (NC)
Methodist College (NC)
Miami Univ.–Oxford (OH)
Michigan State Univ.
New Mexico State Univ.

North Carolina State Univ.–Raleigh
North Dakota State Univ.
Northern Arizona Univ.
Northern Michigan Univ.
Northwestern Oklahoma State
 Univ.
Ohio State Univ.–Columbus
Ohio Univ.
Ohio Wesleyan Univ.
Oklahoma State Univ.
Oregon State Univ.
Purdue Univ.–West Lafayette (IN)
Rutgers–Newark (NJ)
Southern Illinois Univ.–Carbondale
St. Xavier Univ. (IL)
Texas A&M Univ.–College Station
Texas State Univ.–San Marcos
Univ. of Akron (OH)
Univ. of California–Berkeley
Univ. of California–Davis
Univ. of California–Irvine
Univ. of California–Los Angeles
Univ. of California–Riverside
Univ. of Florida
Univ. of Georgia
Univ. of Hawaii–Manoa
Univ. of Ill.–Urbana-Champaign
Univ. of Maine–Orono
Univ. of Michigan–Ann Arbor
Univ. of Minnesota–Twin Cities
Univ. of Nevada–Las Vegas
Univ. of New Hampshire
Univ. of Oklahoma
Univ. of Rhode Island
Univ. of Texas–Austin
Univ. of Vermont
Univ. of Washington
Univ. of Wisconsin–Madison
Univ. of Wisconsin–Superior
Univ. of Wyoming
Utah State Univ.
Washington State Univ.
Weber State Univ. (UT)
Western New Mexico Univ.
Western Washington Univ.

Building/Construction Finishing, Management, and Inspection

Andrews Univ. (MI)
California State Univ.–Sacramento
Central Connecticut State Univ.
Drexel Univ. (PA)
Roger Williams Univ. (RI)
Southern Utah Univ.
Univ. of Minnesota–Twin Cities
Univ. of the District of Columbia
Weber State Univ. (UT)
Wentworth Institute of Tech. (MA)

Business Administration, Management, and Operations

Abilene Christian Univ. (TX)
Adams State College (CO)
Adelphi Univ. (NY)
Adrian College (MI)

Alabama Agricultural and
  Mechanical Univ.
Alabama State Univ.
Alaska Pacific Univ.
Albany State Univ. (GA)
Albertus Magnus College (CT)
Albion College (MI)
Albright College (PA)
Alcorn State Univ. (MS)
Alderson-Broaddus College (WV)
Alfred Univ. (NY)
Alice Lloyd College (KY)
Allen Univ. (SC)
Alliant International Univ. (CA)
Alma College (MI)
Alverno College (WI)
American Univ. (DC)
Anderson College (SC)
Anderson Univ. (IN)
Andrews Univ. (MI)
Angelo State Univ. (TX)
Anna Maria College (MA)
Appalachian State Univ. (NC)
Aquinas College (MI)
Arcadia Univ. (PA)
Arizona State Univ.
Arkansas State Univ.
Arkansas Tech Univ.
Assumption College (MA)
Atlantic Union College (MA)
Auburn Univ. (AL)
Auburn Univ.–Montgomery (AL)
Augusta State Univ. (GA)
Aurora Univ. (IL)
Austin Peay State Univ. (TN)
Averett Univ. (VA)
Babson College (MA)
Baker College of Flint (MI)
Baker Univ. (KS)
Baldwin-Wallace College (OH)
Ball State Univ. (IN)
Barber Scotia College (NC)
Barry Univ. (FL)
Barton College (NC)
Bay Path College (MA)
Baylor Univ. (TX)
Becker College (MA)
Belhaven College (MS)
Bellevue Univ. (NE)
Belmont Abbey College (NC)
Beloit College (WI)
Bemidji State Univ. (MN)
Benedictine College (KS)
Benedictine Univ. (IL)
Bennett College (NC)
Bentley College (MA)
Berry College (GA)
Bethel College (IN)
Bethune-Cookman College (FL)
Black Hills State Univ. (SD)
Bloomfield College (NJ)
Bloomsburg Univ. of Pennsylvania
Blue Mountain College (MS)
Bluefield College (VA)
Bluefield State College (WV)
Bluffton Univ. (OH)
Boise State Univ. (ID)
Boston Univ.
Bowie State Univ. (MD)
Bowling Green State Univ. (OH)
Brenau Univ. (GA)

Brescia Univ. (KY)
Brevard College (NC)
Brewton-Parker College (GA)
Briar Cliff Univ. (IA)
Bridgewater College (VA)
Bridgewater State College (MA)
Brigham Young Univ.–Hawaii
Bryant College (RI)
Cabrini College (PA)
Cal Poly–San Luis Obispo
Caldwell College (NJ)
California Baptist Univ.
California Lutheran Univ.
California State Polytechnic
  Univ.–Pomona
California State Univ.–Bakersfield
California State Univ.–Chico
California State Univ.–Fresno
California State Univ.–Fullerton
California State Univ.–Hayward
California State Univ.–Los Angeles
California State Univ.–Northridge
California State Univ.–Sacramento
California State Univ.–San
  Bernardino
California State Univ.–San Marcos
California State Univ.–Stanislaus
California Univ. of Pennsylvania
Calumet College of St. Joseph (IN)
Calvin College (MI)
Cameron Univ. (OK)
Campbell Univ. (NC)
Campbellsville Univ. (KY)
Canisius College (NY)
Capital Univ. (OH)
Capitol College (MD)
Cardinal Stritch Univ. (WI)
Carnegie Mellon Univ. (PA)
Carroll College (WI)
Carroll College (MT)
Carson-Newman College (TN)
Carthage College (WI)
Case Western Reserve Univ. (OH)
Castleton State College (VT)
Catawba College (NC)
Catholic Univ. of America (DC)
Cazenovia College (NY)
Cedar Crest College (PA)
Cedarville Univ. (OH)
Centenary College (NJ)
Centenary College of Louisiana
Central Christian College (KS)
Central Connecticut State Univ.
Central Methodist Univ. (MO)
Central Michigan Univ.
Central Missouri State Univ.
Central Washington Univ.
Chadron State College (NE)
Chaminade Univ. of Honolulu
Champlain College (VT)
Chapman Univ. (CA)
Charleston Southern Univ. (SC)
Chatham College (PA)
Chestnut Hill College (PA)
Cheyney Univ. of Pennsylvania
Chicago State Univ.
Chowan College (NC)
Christian Brothers Univ. (TN)
Christian Heritage College (CA)
Christopher Newport Univ. (VA)
City Univ. (WA)

Claflin Univ. (SC)
Clarion Univ. of Pennsylvania
Clark Atlanta Univ.
Clark Univ. (MA)
Clarkson Univ. (NY)
Clayton Coll. and State Univ. (GA)
Clearwater Christian College (FL)
Cleary Univ. (MI)
Coastal Carolina Univ. (SC)
Coe College (IA)
Coker College (SC)
Colby-Sawyer College (NH)
College For Lifelong Learning (NH)
College Misericordia (PA)
College of Charleston (SC)
College of Mount St. Joseph (OH)
College of Mount St. Vincent (NY)
College of New Jersey
College of Notre Dame of
  Maryland
College of Santa Fe (NM)
College of St. Benedict (MN)
College of St. Catherine (MN)
College of St. Elizabeth (NJ)
College of St. Joseph (VT)
College of St. Mary (NE)
College of St. Rose (NY)
College of St. Scholastica (MN)
College of the Ozarks (MO)
College of William and Mary (VA)
Colorado Christian Univ.
Colorado State Univ.
Columbia College (SC)
Columbia College (MO)
Concord College (WV)
Concordia College (AL)
Concordia College (NY)
Concordia Coll.–Moorhead (MN)
Concordia Univ. (NE)
Concordia Univ. (OR)
Concordia Univ. (CA)
Concordia Univ. (MI)
Concordia Univ. Wisconsin
Concordia Univ.–Austin (TX)
Concordia Univ.–River Forest (IL)
Concordia Univ.–St. Paul (MN)
Cornerstone Univ. (MI)
Crichton College (TN)
Culver-Stockton College (MO)
Cumberland College (KY)
CUNY–Baruch College
CUNY–Brooklyn College
CUNY–City College
CUNY–Lehman College
CUNY–Medgar Evers College
CUNY–New York City College of
  Technology
CUNY–York College
Curry College (MA)
Daemen College (NY)
Dakota State Univ. (SD)
Dallas Baptist Univ.
Dana College (NE)
Davenport Univ. (MI)
David Lipscomb Univ. (TN)
Davis and Elkins College (WV)
Defiance College (OH)
Delaware State Univ.
Delaware Valley College (PA)
Delta State Univ. (MS)
Depaul Univ. (IL)

Dickinson State Univ. (ND)
Dillard Univ. (LA)
Dominican Coll. of Blauvelt (NY)
Dominican Univ. (IL)
Dominican Univ. of California (CA)
Dordt College (IA)
Dowling College (NY)
Drexel Univ. (PA)
Drury Univ. (MO)
Duquesne Univ. (PA)
Earlham College (IN)
East Carolina Univ. (NC)
East Central Univ. (OK)
East Stroudsburg Univ. of
  Pennsylvania
East Tennessee State Univ.
Eastern Illinois Univ.
Eastern Kentucky Univ.
Eastern Mennonite Univ. (VA)
Eastern Michigan Univ.
Eastern Nazarene College (MA)
Eastern New Mexico Univ.
Eastern Univ. (PA)
Eastern Washington Univ.
Eckerd College (FL)
Edinboro Univ. of Pennsylvania
Edward Waters College (FL)
Elizabeth City State Univ. (NC)
Elizabethtown College (PA)
Elmhurst College (IL)
Elmira College (NY)
Elon Univ. (NC)
Embry Riddle Aeronautical Univ.
  (FL)
Emmanuel College (GA)
Emmanuel College (MA)
Emory Univ. (GA)
Emporia State Univ. (KS)
Endicott College (MA)
Erskine College (SC)
Eureka College (IL)
Evangel Univ. (MO)
Evergreen State College (WA)
Excelsior College (NY)
Fairfield Univ. (CT)
Fairleigh Dickinson Univ. (NJ)
Fairmont State Univ. (WV)
Faulkner Univ. (AL)
Fayetteville State Univ. (NC)
Felician College (NJ)
Ferris State Univ. (MI)
Ferrum College (VA)
Fitchburg State College (MA)
Flagler College (FL)
Florida Atlantic Univ.
Florida Gulf Coast Univ.
Florida Institute of Technology
Florida International Univ.
Florida Southern College
Florida State Univ.
Fontbonne Univ. (MO)
Fordham Univ. (NY)
Fort Hays State Univ. (KS)
Fort Lewis College (CO)
Fort Valley State Univ. (GA)
Francis Marion Univ. (SC)
Franciscan Univ. of Steubenville
  (OH)
Franklin and Marshall College (PA)
Franklin Pierce College (NH)
Freed-Hardeman Univ. (TN)

Fresno Pacific Univ. (CA)
Friends Univ. (KS)
Frostburg State Univ. (MD)
Furman Univ. (SC)
Gallaudet Univ. (DC)
Gannon Univ. (PA)
Gardner-Webb Univ. (NC)
Geneva College (PA)
George Fox Univ. (OR)
George Mason Univ. (VA)
George Washington Univ. (DC)
Georgetown Univ. (DC)
Georgia College and State Univ.
Georgia Institute of Technology
Georgia Southern Univ.
Georgia Southwestern State Univ.
Georgia State Univ.
Georgian Court Univ. (NJ)
Gettysburg College (PA)
Glenville State College (WV)
Golden Gate Univ. (CA)
Goldey Beacom College (DE)
Gonzaga Univ. (WA)
Gordon College (MA)
Goucher College (MD)
Grace College and Seminary (IN)
Grace Univ. (NE)
Graceland Univ. (IA)
Grambling State Univ. (LA)
Grand Canyon Univ. (AZ)
Grand Valley State Univ. (MI)
Green Mountain College (VT)
Greensboro College (NC)
Greenville College (IL)
Grove City College (PA)
Guilford College (NC)
Gustavus Adolphus College (MN)
Gwynedd-Mercy College (PA)
Hamline Univ. (MN)
Hampton Univ. (VA)
Hanover College (IN)
Hardin-Simmons Univ. (TX)
Harding Univ. (AR)
Hartwick College (NY)
Hastings College (NE)
Hawaii Pacific Univ.
Heidelberg College (OH)
Henry Cogswell College (WA)
Heritage College (WA)
High Point Univ. (NC)
Hofstra Univ. (NY)
Holy Family Univ. (PA)
Holy Names Univ. (CA)
Hood College (MD)
Hope College (MI)
Hope International Univ. (CA)
Houghton College (NY)
Houston Baptist Univ.
Howard Univ. (DC)
Humboldt State Univ. (CA)
Humphreys College (CA)
Huntingdon College (AL)
Huntington College (IN)
Husson College (ME)
Idaho State Univ.
Illinois State Univ.
Immaculata Univ. (PA)
Indiana Institute of Technology
Indiana State Univ.
Indiana Univ. of Pennsylvania
Indiana Univ. Southeast

Indiana Univ.–Kokomo
Indiana Univ.–South Bend
Indiana Univ.-Purdue Univ.–Fort Wayne
Indiana Univ.-Purdue Univ.–Indianapolis
Indiana Wesleyan Univ.
International College (FL)
Iona College (NY)
Iowa State Univ.
Ithaca College (NY)
Jacksonville State Univ. (AL)
Jacksonville Univ. (FL)
James Madison Univ. (VA)
Jamestown College (ND)
Jarvis Christian College (TX)
John Brown Univ. (AR)
John Carroll Univ. (OH)
Johnson C. Smith Univ. (NC)
Judson College (IL)
Judson College (AL)
Juniata College (PA)
Kansas State Univ.
Kansas Wesleyan Univ.
Kean Univ. (NJ)
Keene State College (NH)
Kendall College (IL)
Kennesaw State Univ. (GA)
Kent State Univ. (OH)
Kettering Univ. (MI)
Keuka College (NY)
King College (TN)
King's College (PA)
Kutztown Univ. of Pennsylvania
La Roche College (PA)
La Salle Univ. (PA)
La Sierra Univ. (CA)
Lagrange College (GA)
Lake Superior State Univ. (MI)
Lakeland College (WI)
Lambuth Univ. (TN)
Lander Univ. (SC)
Lane College (TN)
Lasell College (MA)
Lawrence Technological Univ. (MI)
Le Moyne College (NY)
Lebanon Valley College (PA)
Lees-Mcrae College (NC)
Lehigh Univ. (PA)
Lemoyne-Owen College (TN)
Letourneau Univ. (TX)
Lewis Univ. (IL)
Lewis-Clark State College (ID)
Liberty Univ. (VA)
Limestone College (SC)
Lincoln Univ. (PA)
Lincoln Univ. (MO)
Lindenwood Univ. (MO)
Lindsey Wilson College (KY)
Linfield College (OR)
Livingstone College (NC)
Lock Haven Univ. of Pennsylvania
Long Island Univ.–Brooklyn (NY)
Long Island Univ.–C.W. Post Campus (NY)
Long Island Univ.–Southampton College (NY)
Longwood Univ. (VA)
Loras College (IA)
Louisiana College
Louisiana State Univ.–Baton Rouge

Louisiana State Univ.–Shreveport
Louisiana Tech Univ.
Lourdes College (OH)
Loyola Marymount Univ. (CA)
Loyola Univ. Chicago
Loyola Univ. New Orleans
Lubbock Christian Univ. (TX)
Luther College (IA)
Lycoming College (PA)
Lynchburg College (VA)
Lyndon State College (VT)
Lynn Univ. (FL)
Lyon College (AR)
Madonna Univ. (MI)
Maharishi Univ. of Management (IA)
Malone College (OH)
Manchester College (IN)
Manhattan College (NY)
Manhattanville College (NY)
Mansfield Univ. of Pennsylvania
Marian College of Fond Du Lac (WI)
Marietta College (OH)
Marist College (NY)
Marquette Univ. (WI)
Mars Hill College (NC)
Marshall Univ. (WV)
Martin Methodist College (TN)
Martin Univ. (IN)
Mary Baldwin College (VA)
Marygrove College (MI)
Marylhurst Univ. (OR)
Marymount Manhattan College (NY)
Marymount Univ. (VA)
Maryville College (TN)
Maryville Univ. of St. Louis (MO)
Marywood Univ. (PA)
Master's Coll. and Seminary (CA)
Mayville State Univ. (ND)
Mcdaniel College (MD)
Mckendree College (IL)
Mcmurry Univ. (TX)
Mcneese State Univ. (LA)
Mcpherson College (KS)
Mercer Univ. (GA)
Mercy College (NY)
Mercyhurst College (PA)
Meredith College (NC)
Merrimack College (MA)
Mesa State College (CO)
Messiah College (PA)
Methodist College (NC)
Metropolitan State College of Denver
Miami Univ.–Oxford (OH)
Michigan State Univ.
Michigan Technological Univ.
Middle Tennessee State Univ.
Midland Lutheran College (NE)
Midwestern State Univ. (TX)
Miles College (AL)
Millersville Univ. of Pennsylvania
Milligan College (TN)
Millikin Univ. (IL)
Millsaps College (MS)
Milwaukee School of Engineering
Minnesota State Univ.–Mankato
Minnesota State Univ.–Moorhead
Minot State Univ. (ND)

Mississippi College
Mississippi State Univ.
Mississippi Univ. For Women
Mississippi Valley State Univ.
Missouri Baptist College
Missouri Southern State Univ.
Missouri Valley College
Missouri Western State College
Molloy College (NY)
Monmouth College (IL)
Monmouth Univ. (NJ)
Montana State Univ.–Northern
Montclair State Univ. (NJ)
Montreat College (NC)
Moravian College (PA)
Morehead State Univ. (KY)
Morehouse College (GA)
Morgan State Univ. (MD)
Morningside College (IA)
Morris College (SC)
Mount Aloysius College (PA)
Mount Ida College (MA)
Mount Marty College (SD)
Mount Mary College (WI)
Mount Mercy College (IA)
Mount Olive College (NC)
Mount St. Mary College (NY)
Mount St. Mary's College (CA)
Mount Union College (OH)
Mount Vernon Nazarene Univ. (OH)
Mountain State Univ. (WV)
Muhlenberg College (PA)
Murray State Univ. (KY)
National Univ. (CA)
National-Louis Univ. (IL)
Nazareth College of Rochester (NY)
Neumann College (PA)
New Jersey City Univ.
New Jersey Institute of Technology
New Mexico Highlands Univ.
New Mexico Institute of Mining and Technology
New Mexico State Univ.
New York Institute of Technology
New York Univ.
Newberry College (SC)
Nicholls State Univ. (LA)
Nichols College (MA)
North Carolina A&T State Univ.
North Carolina Central Univ.
North Carolina State Univ.–Raleigh
North Central College (IL)
North Dakota State Univ.
North Georgia College and State Univ.
North Greenville College (SC)
North Park Univ. (IL)
Northeastern State Univ. (OK)
Northeastern Univ. (MA)
Northern Arizona Univ.
Northern Illinois Univ.
Northern Kentucky Univ.
Northern Michigan Univ.
Northern State Univ. (SD)
Northwest Christian College (OR)
Northwest Missouri State Univ.
Northwest Nazarene Univ. (ID)
Northwestern College (MN)
Northwestern College (IA)

Northwestern Oklahoma State Univ.
Northwestern State Univ. of Louisiana
Northwood Univ. (MI)
Norwich Univ. (VT)
Notre Dame College of Ohio
Notre Dame De Namur Univ. (CA)
Nova Southeastern Univ. (FL)
Nyack College (NY)
Oakland City Univ. (IN)
Oakwood College (AL)
Oglethorpe Univ. (GA)
Ohio Dominican Univ.
Ohio State Univ.–Columbus
Ohio Univ.
Ohio Valley College (WV)
Oklahoma Christian Univ.
Oklahoma City Univ.
Oklahoma Panhandle State Univ.
Oklahoma State Univ.
Oklahoma Wesleyan Univ.
Old Dominion Univ. (VA)
Olivet College (MI)
Oral Roberts Univ. (OK)
Oregon Institute of Technology
Oregon State Univ.
Otterbein College (OH)
Ouachita Baptist Univ. (AR)
Our Lady of Holy Cross Coll. (LA)
Our Lady of the Lake Univ. (TX)
Pace Univ. (NY)
Pacific Lutheran Univ. (WA)
Pacific Univ. (OR)
Paine College (GA)
Palm Beach Atlantic Univ. (FL)
Park Univ. (MO)
Patten College (CA)
Paul Quinn College (TX)
Peace College (NC)
Pennsylvania College of Technology
Penn. State Univ.–Univ. Park
Penn. State–Erie, The Behrend College
Pepperdine Univ. (CA)
Peru State College (NE)
Pfeiffer Univ. (NC)
Philadelphia Univ.
Philander Smith College (AR)
Piedmont College (GA)
Pikeville College (KY)
Pine Manor College (MA)
Pitzer College (CA)
Plymouth State Univ. (NH)
Point Loma Nazarene Univ. (CA)
Point Park Univ. (PA)
Prairie View A&M Univ. (TX)
Prescott College (AZ)
Principia College (IL)
Providence College (RI)
Purdue Univ.–Calumet (IN)
Purdue Univ.–North Central (IN)
Purdue Univ.–West Lafayette (IN)
Queens Univ. of Charlotte (NC)
Quincy Univ. (IL)
Quinnipiac Univ. (CT)
Radford Univ. (VA)
Ramapo College of New Jersey
Regis Univ. (CO)
Rensselaer Polytechnic Inst. (NY)
Rhode Island College

Rhodes College (TN)
Rice Univ. (TX)
Richard Stockton College of New Jersey
Rider Univ. (NJ)
Ripon College (WI)
Rivier College (NH)
Roanoke College (VA)
Robert Morris College (IL)
Robert Morris Univ. (PA)
Roberts Wesleyan College (NY)
Rochester College (MI)
Rochester Institute of Tech. (NY)
Rockford College (IL)
Rockhurst Univ. (MO)
Rocky Mountain College (MT)
Rust College (MS)
Rutgers–Camden (NJ)
Rutgers–New Brunswick (NJ)
Rutgers–Newark (NJ)
Sacred Heart Univ. (CT)
Saginaw Valley State Univ. (MI)
Salem College (NC)
Salem International Univ. (WV)
Salem State College (MA)
Salisbury Univ. (MD)
Salve Regina Univ. (RI)
Sam Houston State Univ. (TX)
Samford Univ. (AL)
San Diego State Univ.
San Francisco State Univ.
San Jose State Univ. (CA)
Savannah State Univ. (GA)
Schreiner Univ. (TX)
Seattle Univ.
Seton Hall Univ. (NJ)
Seton Hill Univ. (PA)
Shaw Univ. (NC)
Shawnee State Univ. (OH)
Sheldon Jackson College (AK)
Shenandoah Univ. (VA)
Shepherd Univ. (WV)
Shippensburg Univ. of Pennsylvania
Shorter College (GA)
Sierra Nevada College (NV)
Silver Lake College (WI)
Simpson Univ. (CA)
Slippery Rock Univ. of Pennsylvania
Sonoma State Univ. (CA)
South Carolina State Univ.
Southeast Missouri State Univ.
Southeastern College of the Assemblies of God
Southeastern Louisiana Univ.
Southeastern Oklahoma State Univ.
Southeastern Univ. (DC)
Southern Adventist Univ. (TN)
Southern Illinois Univ.–Carbondale
Southern Illinois Univ.–Edwardsville
Southern Methodist Univ. (TX)
Southern Nazarene Univ. (OK)
Southern New Hampshire Univ.
Southern Oregon Univ.
Southern Polytechnic St.Univ. (GA)
Southern Univ. and A&M College (LA)
Southern Utah Univ.
Southern Wesleyan Univ. (SC)

Southwest Baptist Univ. (MO)
Southwest Minnesota State Univ. (MN)
Southwest Missouri State Univ.
Southwestern Adventist Univ. (TX)
Southwestern College (KS)
Southwestern Oklahoma State Univ.
Spring Arbor Univ. (MI)
Spring Hill College (AL)
Springfield College (MA)
St. Ambrose Univ. (IA)
St. Andrews Presbyterian College (NC)
St. Bonaventure Univ. (NY)
St. Cloud State Univ. (MN)
St. Edward's Univ. (TX)
St. Francis Univ. (PA)
St. Gregory's Univ. (OK)
St. John Fisher College (NY)
St. John's Univ. (MN)
St. John's Univ. (NY)
St. Joseph's College (ME)
St. Joseph's College, New York
St. Joseph's Univ. (PA)
St. Leo Univ. (FL)
St. Louis Univ.
St. Martin's College (WA)
St. Mary's College (IN)
St. Mary's Univ. of Minnesota
St. Mary's Univ. of San Antonio
St. Mary-of-The-Woods Coll. (IN)
St. Michael's College (VT)
St. Paul's College (VA)
St. Peter's College (NJ)
St. Thomas Aquinas College (NY)
St. Thomas Univ. (FL)
St. Vincent College (PA)
St. Xavier Univ. (IL)
State Univ. of West Georgia
Stephen F. Austin State Univ. (TX)
Stephens College (MO)
Sterling College (KS)
Stetson Univ. (FL)
Stevens Institute of Technology (NJ)
Stillman College (AL)
Stonehill College (MA)
Suffolk Univ. (MA)
Sul Ross State Univ. (TX)
SUNY College of Arts and Sciences–Geneseo
SUNY College–Brockport
SUNY College–Old Westbury
SUNY College–Potsdam
SUNY–Albany
SUNY–Binghamton
SUNY–Farmingdale
SUNY–Fredonia
SUNY–Oswego
SUNY–Stony Brook
Syracuse Univ. (NY)
Tabor College (KS)
Talladega College (AL)
Tarleton State Univ. (TX)
Taylor Univ. (IN)
Teikyo Post Univ. (CT)
Temple Univ. (PA)
Tennessee State Univ.
Tennessee Technological Univ.
Tennessee Wesleyan College

Texas A&M International Univ.
Texas A&M Univ.–College Station
Texas A&M Univ.–Commerce
Texas A&M Univ.–Corpus Christi
Texas A&M Univ.–Galveston
Texas Christian Univ.
Texas College
Texas Lutheran Univ.
Texas State Univ.–San Marcos
Texas Tech Univ.
Texas Wesleyan Univ.
Texas Woman's Univ.
The Citadel (SC)
The Franciscan Univ. (IA)
Thiel College (PA)
Thomas Edison State College (NJ)
Thomas More College (KY)
Thomas Univ. (GA)
Tiffin Univ. (OH)
Toccoa Falls College (GA)
Tougaloo College (MS)
Touro College (NY)
Towson Univ. (MD)
Trevecca Nazarene Univ. (TN)
Tri-State Univ. (IN)
Trinity College (DC)
Troy State Univ.–Troy (AL)
Truman State Univ. (MO)
Tulane Univ. (LA)
Tusculum College (TN)
Tuskegee Univ. (AL)
Union College (NE)
Union Univ. (TN)
United States Coast Guard Academy (CT)
Univ. at Buffalo–SUNY
Univ. of Akron (OH)
Univ. of Alabama
Univ. of Alabama–Birmingham
Univ. of Alabama–Huntsville
Univ. of Alaska–Anchorage
Univ. of Alaska–Fairbanks
Univ. of Arizona
Univ. of Arkansas
Univ. of Arkansas–Little Rock
Univ. of Arkansas–Pine Bluff
Univ. of California–Berkeley
Univ. of California–Riverside
Univ. of Central Arkansas
Univ. of Central Florida
Univ. of Central Oklahoma
Univ. of Charleston (WV)
Univ. of Colorado–Boulder
Univ. of Colorado–Denver
Univ. of Connecticut
Univ. of Dallas
Univ. of Dayton (OH)
Univ. of Delaware
Univ. of Denver
Univ. of Dubuque (IA)
Univ. of Evansville (IN)
Univ. of Findlay (OH)
Univ. of Florida
Univ. of Georgia
Univ. of Great Falls (MT)
Univ. of Hartford (CT)
Univ. of Hawaii–Hilo
Univ. of Hawaii–Manoa
Univ. of Houston
Univ. of Houston–Downtown
Univ. of Illinois–Springfield

Univ. of Ill.–Urbana-Champaign
Univ. of Indianapolis
Univ. of Iowa
Univ. of Judaism (CA)
Univ. of La Verne (CA)
Univ. of Louisiana–Lafayette
Univ. of Louisiana–Monroe
Univ. of Louisville (KY)
Univ. of Maine–Augusta
Univ. of Maine–Fort Kent
Univ. of Maine–Orono
Univ. of Mary (ND)
Univ. of Mary Hardin-Baylor (TX)
Univ. of Mary Washington (VA)
Univ. of Maryland–College Park
Univ. of Maryland–Eastern Shore
Univ. of Maryland–Univ. College
Univ. of Massachusetts–Amherst
Univ. of Massachusetts–Boston
Univ. of Massachusetts–Lowell
Univ. of Memphis
Univ. of Miami (FL)
Univ. of Michigan–Ann Arbor
Univ. of Michigan–Dearborn
Univ. of Michigan–Flint
Univ. of Minnesota–Crookston
Univ. of Minnesota–Duluth
Univ. of Minnesota–Morris
Univ. of Minnesota–Twin Cities
Univ. of Mississippi
Univ. of Missouri–Rolla
Univ. of Missouri–St. Louis
Univ. of Montana
Univ. of Montevallo (AL)
Univ. of Nebraska–Kearney
Univ. of Nebraska–Lincoln
Univ. of Nebraska–Omaha
Univ. of Nevada–Las Vegas
Univ. of Nevada–Reno
Univ. of New England (ME)
Univ. of New Hampshire
Univ. of New Haven (CT)
Univ. of New Mexico
Univ. of New Orleans
Univ. of North Alabama
Univ. of North Carolina–Asheville
Univ. of N.C.–Chapel Hill
Univ. of North Carolina–Charlotte
Univ. of N.C.–Greensboro
Univ. of North Carolina–Pembroke
Univ. of N.C.–Wilmington
Univ. of North Florida
Univ. of North Texas
Univ. of Northern Colorado
Univ. of Northern Iowa
Univ. of Notre Dame (IN)
Univ. of Oklahoma
Univ. of Pennsylvania
Univ. of Pittsburgh
Univ. of Pittsburgh–Bradford
Univ. of Puget Sound (WA)
Univ. of Redlands (CA)
Univ. of Rhode Island
Univ. of Richmond (VA)
Univ. of Rio Grande (OH)
Univ. of San Diego
Univ. of San Francisco
Univ. of Science and Arts of Oklahoma
Univ. of Scranton (PA)
Univ. of Sioux Falls (SD)

Univ. of South Alabama
Univ. of South Carolina–Aiken
Univ. of South Carolina–Columbia
Univ. of South Carolina–Upstate
Univ. of South Dakota
Univ. of South Florida
Univ. of Southern California
Univ. of Southern Indiana
Univ. of Southern Maine
Univ. of Southern Mississippi
Univ. of St. Francis (IL)
Univ. of St. Francis (IN)
Univ. of St. Mary (KS)
Univ. of St. Thomas (MN)
Univ. of St. Thomas (TX)
Univ. of Tampa (FL)
Univ. of Tennessee
Univ. of Tennessee–Martin
Univ. of Texas of the Permian Basin
Univ. of Texas–Arlington
Univ. of Texas–Austin
Univ. of Texas–Brownsville
Univ. of Texas–Dallas
Univ. of Texas–El Paso
Univ. of Texas–Pan American
Univ. of Texas–San Antonio
Univ. of Texas–Tyler
Univ. of the District of Columbia
Univ. of the Incarnate Word (TX)
Univ. of the Ozarks (AR)
Univ. of the Pacific (CA)
Univ. of Toledo (OH)
Univ. of Tulsa (OK)
Univ. of Utah
Univ. of Vermont
Univ. of Virginia–Wise
Univ. of Washington
Univ. of West Alabama
Univ. of West Florida
Univ. of Wisconsin–Eau Claire
Univ. of Wisconsin–Green Bay
Univ. of Wisconsin–La Crosse
Univ. of Wisconsin–Madison
Univ. of Wisconsin–Milwaukee
Univ. of Wisconsin–Platteville
Univ. of Wisconsin–River Falls
Univ. of Wisconsin–Stevens Point
Univ. of Wisconsin–Stout
Univ. of Wisconsin–Superior
Univ. of Wisconsin–Whitewater
Univ. of Wyoming
Upper Iowa Univ.
Urbana Univ. (OH)
Ursuline College (OH)
Utah State Univ.
Utah Valley State College
Utica College (NY)
Valley City State Univ. (ND)
Valparaiso Univ. (IN)
Vanguard Univ. of Southern California
Villa Julie College (MD)
Villanova Univ. (PA)
Virginia Commonwealth Univ.
Virginia Intermont College
Virginia State Univ.
Virginia Tech
Viterbo Univ. (WI)
Voorhees College (SC)
Wagner College (NY)
Waldorf College (IA)

Walsh College of Accountancy and Business Adm. (MI)
Walsh Univ. (OH)
Warner Pacific College (OR)
Warner Southern College (FL)
Washburn Univ. (KS)
Washington and Lee Univ. (VA)
Washington College (MD)
Washington State Univ.
Washington Univ. In St. Louis
Wayland Baptist Univ. (TX)
Wayne State College (NE)
Wayne State Univ. (MI)
Waynesburg College (PA)
Webber International Univ. (FL)
Weber State Univ. (UT)
Webster Univ. (MO)
Wentworth Institute of Technology (MA)
Wesleyan College (GA)
West Chester Univ. of Pennsylvania
West Liberty State College (WV)
West Texas A&M Univ.
West Virginia State Univ.
West Virginia Univ.
West Virginia Univ. Institute of Technology
West Virginia Univ.–Parkersburg
West Virginia Wesleyan College
Western Baptist College (OR)
Western Carolina Univ. (NC)
Western Connecticut State Univ.
Western Illinois Univ.
Western Kentucky Univ.
Western Michigan Univ.
Western New England College (MA)
Western New Mexico Univ.
Western State College of Colorado
Western Washington Univ.
Westminster College (PA)
Westminster College (UT)
Whittier College (CA)
Whitworth College (WA)
Wichita State Univ. (KS)
Widener Univ. (PA)
Wilberforce Univ. (OH)
Wiley College (TX)
Wilkes Univ. (PA)
William Jewell College (MO)
William Paterson Univ. of New Jersey
William Woods Univ. (MO)
Williams Baptist College (AR)
Wilmington College (OH)
Wilmington College (DE)
Wilson College (PA)
Wingate Univ. (NC)
Winston-Salem State Univ. (NC)
Winthrop Univ. (SC)
Woodbury Univ. (CA)
Worcester Polytechnic Institute (MA)
Worcester State College (MA)
Wright State Univ. (OH)
Xavier Univ. (OH)
Yeshiva Univ. (NY)
York College (NE)
York College of Pennsylvania
Youngstown State Univ. (OH)

Business Operations Support and Assistant Services

Albany State Univ. (GA)
Alcorn State Univ. (MS)
Auburn Univ.–Montgomery (AL)
Ball State Univ. (IN)
Bellevue Univ. (NE)
Central Washington Univ.
Concordia Coll.–Moorhead (MN)
Cumberland College (KY)
Delaware State Univ.
East Carolina Univ. (NC)
East Central Univ. (OK)
Eastern Oregon Univ.
Howard Payne Univ. (TX)
Humphreys College (CA)
Idaho State Univ.
Lewis-Clark State College (ID)
Lincoln Univ. (MO)
Midland Lutheran College (NE)
Minot State Univ. (ND)
New York Institute of Technology
Northern State Univ. (SD)
Northwest Missouri State Univ.
Northwestern Oklahoma State
  Univ.
Roosevelt Univ. (IL)
Suffolk Univ. (MA)
Texas Woman's Univ.
Univ. of Central Oklahoma
Univ. of Rio Grande (OH)
Utah State Univ.
Valdosta State Univ. (GA)
Weber State Univ. (UT)

Business, Management, Marketing, and Related Support Services

Adelphi Univ. (NY)
Arcadia Univ. (PA)
Baylor Univ. (TX)
Bellevue Univ. (NE)
Belmont Abbey College (NC)
Bentley College (MA)
Boise State Univ. (ID)
Bowling Green State Univ. (OH)
Bridgewater State College (MA)
Cabrini College (PA)
California State Univ.–Long Beach
California State Univ.–Stanislaus
Campbellsville Univ. (KY)
Central Michigan Univ.
Central Missouri State Univ.
Claflin Univ. (SC)
Cleary Univ. (MI)
College Misericordia (PA)
College of Mount St. Joseph (OH)
Columbus State Univ. (GA)
Davenport Univ. (MI)
Depaul Univ. (IL)
Desales Univ. (PA)
Dominican Univ. (IL)
Dominican Univ. of California (CA)
Dowling College (NY)
Drake Univ. (IA)
Drexel Univ. (PA)

Duquesne Univ. (PA)
Eastern Univ. (PA)
George Mason Univ. (VA)
Golden Gate Univ. (CA)
Grace Univ. (NE)
Johnson and Wales Univ. (RI)
Johnson State College (VT)
La Sierra Univ. (CA)
Loyola Univ. Chicago
Marquette Univ. (WI)
Mercy College (NY)
Messiah College (PA)
Metropolitan State College of
  Denver
Midland Lutheran College (NE)
Morgan State Univ. (MD)
Nebraska Wesleyan Univ.
New York Institute of Technology
North Carolina A&T State Univ.
Norwich Univ. (VT)
Nyack College (NY)
Ohio Valley College (WV)
Oral Roberts Univ. (OK)
Park Univ. (MO)
Point Park Univ. (PA)
Polytechnic Univ. (NY)
Purdue Univ.–North Central (IN)
Rensselaer Polytechnic Inst. (NY)
Rochester College (MI)
Rochester Institute of Tech. (NY)
Rockford College (IL)
Seton Hill Univ. (PA)
Skidmore College (NY)
Southeastern College of the
  Assemblies of God
Southern New Hampshire Univ.
Southwest Minnesota State Univ.
  (MN)
Southwest Missouri State Univ.
St. Vincent College (PA)
SUNY College of A&T–Cobleskill
SUNY–Fredonia
Sweet Briar College (VA)
Syracuse Univ. (NY)
Texas Wesleyan Univ.
Touro College (NY)
Trevecca Nazarene Univ. (TN)
Troy State Univ.–Troy (AL)
Univ. of Denver
Univ. of Louisiana–Lafayette
Univ. of Missouri–Rolla
Univ. of Toledo (OH)
Univ. of Wisconsin–Stout
Ursuline College (OH)
Wheeling Jesuit Univ. (WV)
Wiley College (TX)
Woodbury Univ. (CA)
Worcester Polytechnic Institute
  (MA)
York College of Pennsylvania

Business/Commerce

Albright College (PA)
Alliant International Univ. (CA)
Alvernia College (PA)
American Univ. (DC)
Asbury College (KY)
Auburn Univ.–Montgomery (AL)
Augustana College (SD)

Augustana College (IL)
Austin College (TX)
Austin Peay State Univ. (TN)
Averett Univ. (VA)
Avila Univ. (MO)
Babson College (MA)
Baker Univ. (KS)
Ball State Univ. (IN)
Baylor Univ. (TX)
Belhaven College (MS)
Bellarmine Univ. (KY)
Bellevue Univ. (NE)
Belmont Univ. (TN)
Bentley College (MA)
Berea College (KY)
Bethel College (TN)
Bethel College (KS)
Biola Univ. (CA)
Black Hills State Univ. (SD)
Bloomsburg Univ. of Pennsylvania
Boise State Univ. (ID)
Bowling Green State Univ. (OH)
Bradley Univ. (IL)
Brenau Univ. (GA)
Brigham Young Univ.–Provo (UT)
Bucknell Univ. (PA)
California Lutheran Univ.
California State Univ.–Hayward
California State Univ.–Monterey
  Bay
Campbellsville Univ. (KY)
Capital Univ. (OH)
Cardinal Stritch Univ. (WI)
Carlow College (PA)
Carson-Newman College (TN)
Catholic Univ. of America (DC)
Central Methodist Univ. (MO)
Central Michigan Univ.
Central State Univ. (OH)
Clayton Coll. and State Univ. (GA)
College of Mount St. Vincent (NY)
College of the Ozarks (MO)
Colorado State Univ.–Pueblo
Concordia Univ. (OR)
Concordia Univ. (NE)
Concordia Univ.–Austin (TX)
Concordia Univ.–River Forest (IL)
Converse College (SC)
Cornerstone Univ. (MI)
Covenant College (GA)
Cumberland Univ. (TN)
CUNY–Baruch College
CUNY–College of Staten Island
Dakota Wesleyan Univ. (SD)
Delta State Univ. (MS)
Depaul Univ. (IL)
Dickinson State Univ. (ND)
Dordt College (IA)
Drexel Univ. (PA)
Duquesne Univ. (PA)
Earlham College (IN)
East Texas Baptist Univ.
East-West Univ. (IL)
Eastern Connecticut State Univ.
Eastern Kentucky Univ.
Eastern Michigan Univ.
Eastern Oregon Univ.
Eckerd College (FL)
Edgewood College (WI)
Elmhurst College (IL)
Excelsior College (NY)

Fisk Univ. (TN)
Florida Southern College
Florida State Univ.
Fort Valley State Univ. (GA)
Framingham State College (MA)
Franklin College (IN)
Gallaudet Univ. (DC)
George Mason Univ. (VA)
George Washington Univ. (DC)
Georgetown College (KY)
Georgia College and State Univ.
Georgia Southwestern State Univ.
Grand View College (IA)
Harding Univ. (AR)
Hastings College (NE)
Hawaii Pacific Univ.
Henderson State Univ. (AR)
Hofstra Univ. (NY)
Hollins Univ. (VA)
Houston Baptist Univ.
Howard Payne Univ. (TX)
Huntington College (IN)
Idaho State Univ.
Illinois Institute of Technology
Illinois Wesleyan Univ.
Indiana Univ. East
Indiana Univ.–Bloomington
Indiana Univ.–Kokomo
Indiana Univ.-Purdue
  Univ.–Indianapolis
Indiana Wesleyan Univ.
Jacksonville Univ. (FL)
Juniata College (PA)
Kansas State Univ.
Kentucky Christian College
Kentucky State Univ.
Kentucky Wesleyan College
La Sierra Univ. (CA)
Lake Forest College (IL)
Lamar Univ. (TX)
Lasell College (MA)
Lenoir-Rhyne College (NC)
Liberty Univ. (VA)
Limestone College (SC)
Lindenwood Univ. (MO)
Linfield College (OR)
Long Island Univ.–Brooklyn (NY)
Louisiana College
Loyola College In Maryland
Loyola Univ. New Orleans
Manhattan College (NY)
Marian College (IN)
Marian College of Fond Du Lac
  (WI)
Marygrove College (MI)
Maryville Univ. of St. Louis (MO)
Marywood Univ. (PA)
Massachusetts Institute of
  Technology
Medaille College (NY)
Mercer Univ. (GA)
Mercy College (NY)
Miami Univ.–Oxford (OH)
Midway College (KY)
Midwestern State Univ. (TX)
Milwaukee School of Engineering
Molloy College (NY)
Montana State Univ.–Billings
Montana State Univ.–Bozeman
Montana Tech of the Univ. of
  Montana

Mount Mercy College (IA)
Mount St. Mary's Univ. (MD)
Murray State Univ. (KY)
Muskingum College (OH)
Nebraska Wesleyan Univ.
New Mexico State Univ.
New York Univ.
Niagara Univ. (NY)
Norfolk State Univ. (VA)
Northern Arizona Univ.
Northern Kentucky Univ.
Northern State Univ. (SD)
Nova Southeastern Univ. (FL)
Oakland Univ. (MI)
Ohio Valley College (WV)
Oklahoma Wesleyan Univ.
Pace Univ. (NY)
Pittsburg State Univ. (KS)
Pitzer College (CA)
Plymouth State Univ. (NH)
Regis College (MA)
Reinhardt College (GA)
Ripon College (WI)
Roger Williams Univ. (RI)
Roosevelt Univ. (IL)
Rosemont College (PA)
Saginaw Valley State Univ. (MI)
Salem International Univ. (WV)
Sam Houston State Univ. (TX)
Schreiner Univ. (TX)
Seattle Univ.
Shorter College (GA)
Simpson College (IA)
Skidmore College (NY)
Southeastern College of the
  Assemblies of God
Southern Arkansas Univ.
Southern Oregon Univ.
Southwest Missouri State Univ.
Southwestern Univ. (TX)
Spalding Univ. (KY)
St. Ambrose Univ. (IA)
St. Anselm College (NH)
St. Cloud State Univ. (MN)
St. Joseph College (CT)
St. Joseph's College (IN)
St. Mary's College of California
St. Mary's Univ. of Minnesota
St. Mary's Univ. of San Antonio
St. Norbert College (WI)
St. Thomas Univ. (FL)
St. Vincent College (PA)
Stephen F. Austin State Univ. (TX)
Stephens College (MO)
Suffolk Univ. (MA)
Sul Ross State Univ. (TX)
SUNY–Empire State College
SUNY–Plattsburgh
Sweet Briar College (VA)
Syracuse Univ. (NY)
Tarleton State Univ. (TX)
Temple Univ. (PA)
Tennessee Wesleyan College
Texas A&M Univ.–Commerce
Texas A&M Univ.–Corpus Christi
Texas A&M Univ.–Kingsville
Texas Lutheran Univ.
Texas Tech Univ.
Thomas More College (KY)
Thomas Univ. (GA)
Transylvania Univ. (KY)

Trinity Christian College (IL)
Troy State Univ.–Troy (AL)
Tulane Univ. (LA)
Union College (NE)
Union Institute and Univ. (OH)
Univ. of Arizona
Univ. of Arkansas
Univ. of Bridgeport (CT)
Univ. of Central Arkansas
Univ. of Central Florida
Univ. of Central Oklahoma
Univ. of Colorado–Colorado
Springs
Univ. of Connecticut
Univ. of Denver
Univ. of Detroit Mercy
Univ. of Evansville (IN)
Univ. of Georgia
Univ. of Hawaii–Manoa
Univ. of Houston–Downtown
Univ. of Illinois–Chicago
Univ. of Illinois–Urbana-
Champaign
Univ. of Judaism (CA)
Univ. of Kansas
Univ. of Kentucky
Univ. of Maine–Orono
Univ. of Mary Hardin-Baylor (TX)
Univ. of Maryland–College Park
Univ. of Maryland–Eastern Shore
Univ. of Michigan–Flint
Univ. of Mississippi
Univ. of Missouri–Columbia
Univ. of Missouri–Kansas City
Univ. of Missouri–Rolla
Univ. of Missouri–St. Louis
Univ. of Montana
Univ. of Nebraska–Omaha
Univ. of Nevada–Las Vegas
Univ. of New Hampshire
Univ. of North Dakota
Univ. of North Texas
Univ. of Notre Dame (IN)
Univ. of Oregon
Univ. of Pittsburgh–Greensburg
Univ. of Pittsburgh–Johnstown
Univ. of Redlands (CA)
Univ. of Rhode Island
Univ. of South Alabama
Univ. of South Florida
Univ. of Southern Indiana
Univ. of Tennessee
Univ. of Tennessee–Chattanooga
Univ. of Texas–Austin
Univ. of Texas–Brownsville
Univ. of Texas–El Paso
Univ. of Texas–San Antonio
Univ. of Toledo (OH)
Univ. of Tulsa (OK)
Univ. of Utah
Univ. of Virginia
Univ. of Washington
Univ. of Wisconsin–Platteville
Univ. of Wisconsin–Superior
Univ. of Wisconsin–Whitewater
Utah State Univ.
Valdosta State Univ. (GA)
Vanguard Univ. of Southern
California
Villanova Univ. (PA)
Virginia Wesleyan College

Wake Forest Univ. (NC)
Walsh Univ. (OH)
Wartburg College (IA)
Washburn Univ. (KS)
Washington and Jefferson College
(PA)
Washington State Univ.
Wayne State Univ. (MI)
Waynesburg College (PA)
Webber International Univ. (FL)
Webster Univ. (MO)
West Chester Univ. of Pennsylvania
West Texas A&M Univ.
West Virginia Univ. Institute of
Technology
Western Michigan Univ.
Western New England College
(MA)
Western State College of Colorado
Western Washington Univ.
Westfield State College (MA)
Westminster College (UT)
Wittenberg Univ. (OH)
Xavier Univ. (OH)
York College of Pennsylvania

Business/Corporate Communications

Aquinas College (MI)
Arcadia Univ. (PA)
Babson College (MA)
Bentley College (MA)
Calvin College (MI)
Chestnut Hill College (PA)
Concordia Univ.–St. Paul (MN)
Creighton Univ. (NE)
CUNY–Baruch College
Duquesne Univ. (PA)
Fort Hays State Univ. (KS)
Harding Univ. (AR)
Hawaii Pacific Univ.
Holy Names Univ. (CA)
Kentucky Wesleyan College
Lindenwood Univ. (MO)
Mercy College (NY)
Morningside College (IA)
North Dakota State Univ.
Ohio Dominican Univ.
Otterbein College (OH)
Pennsylvania College of Technology
Point Loma Nazarene Univ. (CA)
Rochester College (MI)
Rockhurst Univ. (MO)
Rosemont College (PA)
Southwestern College (KS)
St. Leo Univ. (FL)
Susquehanna Univ. (PA)
Trinity Christian College (IL)
Univ. of Houston
Univ. of Mary (ND)
Urbana Univ. (OH)
Villa Julie College (MD)
Walsh Univ. (OH)

Business/Managerial Economics

Albertus Magnus College (CT)

Allegheny College (PA)
Anderson Univ. (IN)
Andrews Univ. (MI)
Arkansas State Univ.
Auburn Univ. (AL)
Auburn Univ.–Montgomery (AL)
Babson College (MA)
Ball State Univ. (IN)
Baylor Univ. (TX)
Benedictine Univ. (IL)
Bentley College (MA)
Bethel College (IN)
Bloomsburg Univ. of Pennsylvania
Bowling Green State Univ. (OH)
Bradley Univ. (IL)
Buena Vista Univ. (IA)
California State Univ.–Fullerton
California State Univ.–Long Beach
Capital Univ. (OH)
Carnegie Mellon Univ. (PA)
Carson-Newman College (TN)
Centenary College of Louisiana
Chapman Univ. (CA)
Christopher Newport Univ. (VA)
Clarion Univ. of Pennsylvania
Cleveland State Univ.
Coastal Carolina Univ. (SC)
College of the Ozarks (MO)
College of Wooster (OH)
Colorado State Univ.–Pueblo
CUNY–Baruch College
David Lipscomb Univ. (TN)
Depaul Univ. (IL)
Drexel Univ. (PA)
Duquesne Univ. (PA)
East Tennessee State Univ.
Eastern Kentucky Univ.
Eastern Michigan Univ.
Eastern Washington Univ.
Emmanuel College (MA)
Fairleigh Dickinson Univ. (NJ)
Fairmont State Univ. (WV)
Fayetteville State Univ. (NC)
Fort Lewis College (CO)
Fort Valley State Univ. (GA)
Francis Marion Univ. (SC)
Georgia College and State Univ.
Georgia Institute of Technology
Georgia Southern Univ.
Georgia State Univ.
Gordon College (MA)
Grambling State Univ. (LA)
Hampden-Sydney College (VA)
Hawaii Pacific Univ.
Hendrix College (AR)
Hofstra Univ. (NY)
Hope College (MI)
Houston Baptist Univ.
Huntington College (IN)
Illinois College
Indiana Univ. Southeast
Indiana Univ.–Purdue Univ.–Fort
Wayne
Jacksonville Univ. (FL)
James Madison Univ. (VA)
John Carroll Univ. (OH)
Kennesaw State Univ. (GA)
Kent State Univ. (OH)
King College (TN)
Kutztown Univ. of Pennsylvania
Lehigh Univ. (PA)

Limestone College (SC)
Lincoln Univ. (MO)
Louisiana College
Louisiana State Univ.–Baton Rouge
Louisiana State Univ.–Shreveport
Louisiana Tech Univ.
Loyola Univ. Chicago
Loyola Univ. New Orleans
Manhattan College (NY)
Marian College of Fond Du Lac
(WI)
Marquette Univ. (WI)
Marshall Univ. (WV)
Messiah College (PA)
Miami Univ.–Oxford (OH)
Middle Tennessee State Univ.
Midland Lutheran College (NE)
Mills College (CA)
Mississippi State Univ.
Missouri Southern State Univ.
Morehead State Univ. (KY)
New York Univ.
Nichols College (MA)
North Carolina State Univ.–Raleigh
North Greenville College (SC)
Northern Arizona Univ.
Northern Kentucky Univ.
Northern State Univ. (SD)
Northland College (WI)
Northwest Missouri State Univ.
Northwood Univ. (MI)
Norwich Univ. (VT)
Oakland Univ. (MI)
Ohio State Univ.–Columbus
Ohio Univ.
Ohio Wesleyan Univ.
Oklahoma City Univ.
Oklahoma State Univ.
Old Dominion Univ. (VA)
Olivet College (MI)
Park Univ. (MO)
Penn. State Univ.–Univ. Park
Penn. State–Erie, The Behrend
College
Purdue Univ.–Calumet (IN)
Randolph-Macon College (VA)
Regis Univ. (CO)
Rhode Island College
Rhodes College (TN)
Rider Univ. (NJ)
Robert Morris Univ. (PA)
Roosevelt Univ. (IL)
Rosemont College (PA)
Sacred Heart Univ. (CT)
Saginaw Valley State Univ. (MI)
Sam Houston State Univ. (TX)
Santa Clara Univ. (CA)
Seattle Univ.
Seton Hall Univ. (NJ)
Shorter College (GA)
South Carolina State Univ.
Southern Illinois Univ.–Carbondale
Southern Illinois
Univ.–Edwardsville
Southern Univ. and A&M College
(LA)
St. Anselm College (NH)
St. Joseph College (CT)
St. Peter's College (NJ)
State Univ. of West Georgia
Stephen F. Austin State Univ. (TX)

Stetson Univ. (FL)
SUNY College–Oneonta
SUNY College–Potsdam
SUNY–Plattsburgh
Susquehanna Univ. (PA)
Taylor Univ. (IN)
Tennessee State Univ.
Texas A&M International Univ.
Texas A&M Univ.–Corpus Christi
Texas State Univ.–San Marcos
Texas Wesleyan Univ.
Tougaloo College (MS)
Tri-State Univ. (IN)
Trinity College (DC)
Tulane Univ. (LA)
Union Univ. (TN)
Univ. of Alabama
Univ. of Alabama–Birmingham
Univ. of Arizona
Univ. of Arkansas
Univ. of Arkansas–Little Rock
Univ. of California–Los Angeles
Univ. of California–Riverside
Univ. of California–Santa Cruz
Univ. of Central Florida
Univ. of Central Oklahoma
Univ. of Dayton (OH)
Univ. of Denver
Univ. of Evansville (IN)
Univ. of Georgia
Univ. of Indianapolis
Univ. of Iowa
Univ. of Kentucky
Univ. of La Verne (CA)
Univ. of Louisiana–Lafayette
Univ. of Louisiana–Monroe
Univ. of Louisville (KY)
Univ. of Maine–Farmington
Univ. of Maine–Orono
Univ. of Memphis
Univ. of Miami (FL)
Univ. of Mississippi
Univ. of Missouri–Rolla
Univ. of Nebraska–Lincoln
Univ. of Nebraska–Omaha
Univ. of Nevada–Reno
Univ. of New Haven (CT)
Univ. of New Orleans
Univ. of North Alabama
Univ. of North Carolina–Charlotte
Univ. of N.C.–Greensboro
Univ. of N.C.–Wilmington
Univ. of North Dakota
Univ. of North Florida
Univ. of North Texas
Univ. of Oklahoma
Univ. of Pittsburgh–Johnstown
Univ. of Redlands (CA)
Univ. of San Diego
Univ. of South Carolina–Columbia
Univ. of South Florida
Univ. of Southern Mississippi
Univ. of Tennessee
Univ. of Tennessee–Martin
Univ. of Texas of the Permian Basin
Univ. of Texas–Arlington
Univ. of Texas–El Paso
Univ. of Texas–San Antonio
Univ. of Texas–Tyler
Univ. of West Florida
Univ. of Wisconsin–Whitewater

Univ. of Wyoming
Utica College (NY)
Valdosta State Univ. (GA)
Villanova Univ. (PA)
Virginia Commonwealth Univ.
Virginia State Univ.
Virginia Tech
Washburn Univ. (KS)
Washington State Univ.
Washington Univ. In St. Louis
Weber State Univ. (UT)
West Chester Univ. of Pennsylvania
West Texas A&M Univ.
West Virginia Univ.
West Virginia Wesleyan College
Western Illinois Univ.
Western Kentucky Univ.
Westminster College (UT)
Wheaton College (IL)
William Jewell College (MO)
Wisconsin Lutheran College
Wofford College (SC)
Wright State Univ. (OH)
Xavier Univ. (OH)
York College of Pennsylvania
Youngstown State Univ. (OH)

Cell/Cellular Biology and Anatomical Sciences

Beloit College (WI)
Bennington College (VT)
Bridgewater State College (MA)
Bucknell Univ. (PA)
California State Univ.–Long Beach
Colby College (ME)
College of St. Rose (NY)
Colorado State Univ.
Dartmouth College (NH)
Fort Lewis College (CO)
Grand Valley State Univ. (MI)
Huntingdon College (AL)
Johns Hopkins Univ. (MD)
Juniata College (PA)
Lawrence Univ. (WI)
Long Island Univ.–C.W. Post
    Campus (NY)
Long Island Univ.–Southampton
    College (NY)
Mansfield Univ. of Pennsylvania
Marymount Univ. (VA)
Master's Coll. and Seminary (CA)
Methodist College (NC)
Montana State Univ.–Bozeman
Northeastern State Univ. (OK)
Northern Arizona Univ.
Ohio Univ.
Oklahoma State Univ.
Rensselaer Polytechnic Inst. (NY)
Rutgers–New Brunswick (NJ)
San Diego State Univ.
Southwest Minnesota State Univ.
    (MN)
Southwest Missouri State Univ.
St. Cloud State Univ. (MN)
SUNY–Albany
SUNY–Plattsburgh
Texas A&M Univ.–College Station
Texas Tech Univ.
Tulane Univ. (LA)

Univ. of Arizona
Univ. of California–Berkeley
Univ. of California–Davis
Univ. of California–Irvine
Univ. of California–Los Angeles
Univ. of California–Riverside
Univ. of California–San Diego
Univ. of California–Santa Barbara
Univ. of California–Santa Cruz
Univ. of Colorado–Boulder
Univ. of Connecticut
Univ. of Georgia
Univ. of Ill.–Urbana-Champaign
Univ. of Kentucky
Univ. of Maine–Orono
Univ. of Michigan–Ann Arbor
Univ. of Minnesota–Duluth
Univ. of Minnesota–Twin Cities
Univ. of Texas–Dallas
Univ. of Utah
Univ. of Wisconsin–Superior
Vanderbilt Univ. (TN)
Washington and Jefferson College
    (PA)
Western Washington Univ.
William Jewell College (MO)

Celtic Languages, Literatures, and Linguistics

Univ. of California–Berkeley

Ceramic Sciences and Engineering

Alfred Univ. (NY)
Rutgers–New Brunswick (NJ)
Univ. of Ill.–Urbana-Champaign
Univ. of Missouri–Rolla

Chemical Engineering

Arizona State Univ.
Auburn Univ. (AL)
Bethel College (IN)
Brigham Young Univ.–Provo (UT)
Bucknell Univ. (PA)
California Institute of Technology
California State Polytechnic
    Univ.–Pomona
California State Univ.–Long Beach
Calvin College (MI)
Carnegie Mellon Univ. (PA)
Case Western Reserve Univ. (OH)
Christian Brothers Univ. (TN)
Clarkson Univ. (NY)
Cleveland State Univ.
Colorado School of Mines
Colorado State Univ.
Columbia Univ. (NY)
Cooper Union (NY)
Cornell Univ. (NY)
CUNY–City College
Drexel Univ. (PA)
Florida A&M Univ.
Florida Institute of Technology
Florida International Univ.

Florida State Univ.
Geneva College (PA)
Georgia Institute of Technology
Hampton Univ. (VA)
Howard Univ. (DC)
Illinois Institute of Technology
Iowa State Univ.
Johns Hopkins Univ. (MD)
Kansas State Univ.
Lafayette College (PA)
Lamar Univ. (TX)
Lehigh Univ. (PA)
Louisiana State Univ.–Baton Rouge
Louisiana Tech Univ.
Manhattan College (NY)
Massachusetts Institute of
    Technology
Miami Univ.–Oxford (OH)
Michigan State Univ.
Michigan Technological Univ.
Mississippi State Univ.
Montana State Univ.–Bozeman
New Jersey Institute of Technology
New Mexico Institute of Mining
    and Technology
New Mexico State Univ.
North Carolina A&T State Univ.
North Carolina State Univ.–Raleigh
Northeastern Univ. (MA)
Northwestern Univ. (IL)
Ohio State Univ.–Columbus
Ohio Univ.
Oklahoma State Univ.
Oregon State Univ.
Penn. State Univ.–Univ. Park
Polytechnic Univ. (NY)
Prairie View A&M Univ. (TX)
Princeton Univ. (NJ)
Purdue Univ.–West Lafayette (IN)
Rensselaer Polytechnic Inst. (NY)
Rice Univ. (TX)
Rose-Hulman Institute of
    Technology (IN)
Rutgers–New Brunswick (NJ)
San Jose State Univ. (CA)
South Dakota School of Mines and
    Technology
Stanford Univ. (CA)
Stevens Institute of Technology
    (NJ)
Syracuse Univ. (NY)
Tennessee Technological Univ.
Texas A&M Univ.–College Station
Texas A&M Univ.–Kingsville
Texas Tech Univ.
Tri-State Univ. (IN)
Tufts Univ. (MA)
Tulane Univ. (LA)
Tuskegee Univ. (AL)
United States Military Academy
    (NY)
Univ. at Buffalo–SUNY
Univ. of Akron (OH)
Univ. of Alabama
Univ. of Alabama–Huntsville
Univ. of Arizona
Univ. of Arkansas
Univ. of California–Berkeley
Univ. of California–Davis
Univ. of California–Irvine
Univ. of California–Los Angeles

Univ. of California–Riverside
Univ. of California–San Diego
Univ. of California–Santa Barbara
Univ. of Colorado–Boulder
Univ. of Connecticut
Univ. of Dayton (OH)
Univ. of Florida
Univ. of Georgia
Univ. of Houston
Univ. of Illinois–Chicago
Univ. of Ill.–Urbana-Champaign
Univ. of Iowa
Univ. of Kansas
Univ. of Kentucky
Univ. of Louisiana–Lafayette
Univ. of Louisville (KY)
Univ. of Maine–Orono
Univ. of Maryland–Baltimore
    County
Univ. of Maryland–College Park
Univ. of Massachusetts–Amherst
Univ. of Massachusetts–Lowell
Univ. of Michigan–Ann Arbor
Univ. of Minnesota–Duluth
Univ. of Minnesota–Twin Cities
Univ. of Mississippi
Univ. of Missouri–Columbia
Univ. of Missouri–Rolla
Univ. of Nebraska–Lincoln
Univ. of Nevada–Reno
Univ. of New Hampshire
Univ. of New Haven (CT)
Univ. of New Mexico
Univ. of North Dakota
Univ. of Notre Dame (IN)
Univ. of Oklahoma
Univ. of Pennsylvania
Univ. of Pittsburgh
Univ. of Rhode Island
Univ. of Rochester (NY)
Univ. of South Alabama
Univ. of South Carolina–Columbia
Univ. of South Florida
Univ. of Southern California
Univ. of Tennessee
Univ. of Texas–Austin
Univ. of Toledo (OH)
Univ. of Tulsa (OK)
Univ. of Utah
Univ. of Virginia
Univ. of Washington
Univ. of Wisconsin–Madison
Univ. of Wyoming
Vanderbilt Univ. (TN)
Villanova Univ. (PA)
Virginia Commonwealth Univ.
Virginia Tech
Washington and Lee Univ. (VA)
Washington State Univ.
Washington Univ. In St. Louis
Wayne State Univ. (MI)
West Virginia Univ.
West Virginia Univ. Institute of
    Technology
Western Michigan Univ.
Widener Univ. (PA)
Worcester Polytechnic Institute
    (MA)
Yale Univ. (CT)
Youngstown State Univ. (OH)

Chemistry

Abilene Christian Univ. (TX)
Adams State College (CO)
Adelphi Univ. (NY)
Adrian College (MI)
Agnes Scott College (GA)
Alabama Agricultural and
    Mechanical Univ.
Alabama State Univ.
Albany State Univ. (GA)
Albertson College (ID)
Albertus Magnus College (CT)
Albion College (MI)
Albright College (PA)
Alcorn State Univ. (MS)
Alderson-Broaddus College (WV)
Allegheny College (PA)
Allen Univ. (SC)
Alma College (MI)
Alvernia College (PA)
Alverno College (WI)
American Univ. (DC)
Amherst College (MA)
Anderson Univ. (IN)
Andrews Univ. (MI)
Angelo State Univ. (TX)
Appalachian State Univ. (NC)
Aquinas College (MI)
Arcadia Univ. (PA)
Arizona State Univ.
Arkansas State Univ.
Arkansas Tech Univ.
Armstrong Atlantic State Univ.
    (GA)
Asbury College (KY)
Ashland Univ. (OH)
Assumption College (MA)
Auburn Univ. (AL)
Augsburg College (MN)
Augusta State Univ. (GA)
Augustana College (IL)
Aurora Univ. (IL)
Austin College (TX)
Austin Peay State Univ. (TN)
Averett Univ. (VA)
Avila Univ. (MO)
Azusa Pacific Univ. (CA)
Baker Univ. (KS)
Baldwin-Wallace College (OH)
Ball State Univ. (IN)
Barnard College (NY)
Barry Univ. (FL)
Barton College (NC)
Bates College (ME)
Baylor Univ. (TX)
Belhaven College (MS)
Bellarmine Univ. (KY)
Belmont Univ. (TN)
Beloit College (WI)
Benedict College (SC)
Benedictine College (KS)
Benedictine Univ. (IL)
Bennington College (VT)
Berea College (KY)
Berry College (GA)
Bethany College (WV)
Bethany College (KS)
Bethel College (IN)
Bethel College (KS)

Bethel Univ. (MN)
Bethune-Cookman College (FL)
Black Hills State Univ. (SD)
Bloomfield College (NJ)
Bloomsburg Univ. of Pennsylvania
Bluefield College (VA)
Bluffton Univ. (OH)
Boise State Univ. (ID)
Boston Univ.
Bowdoin College (ME)
Bowling Green State Univ. (OH)
Bradley Univ. (IL)
Brandeis Univ. (MA)
Brescia Univ. (KY)
Briar Cliff Univ. (IA)
Bridgewater College (VA)
Bridgewater State College (MA)
Brigham Young Univ.–Provo (UT)
Brown Univ. (RI)
Bryn Mawr College (PA)
Bucknell Univ. (PA)
Buena Vista Univ. (IA)
Buffalo State College
Butler Univ. (IN)
Cabrini College (PA)
Cal Poly–San Luis Obispo
Caldwell College (NJ)
California Institute of Technology
California Lutheran Univ.
California State Polytechnic
    Univ.–Pomona
California State Univ.–Bakersfield
California State Univ.–Chico
California State Univ.–Dominguez
    Hills
California State Univ.–Fresno
California State Univ.–Fullerton
California State Univ.–Hayward
California State Univ.–Long Beach
California State Univ.–Los Angeles
California State Univ.–Northridge
California State Univ.–Sacramento
California State Univ.–San
    Bernardino
California State Univ.–San Marcos
California State Univ.–Stanislaus
California Univ. of Pennsylvania
Calvin College (MI)
Cameron Univ. (OK)
Campbellsville Univ. (KY)
Canisius College (NY)
Capital Univ. (OH)
Cardinal Stritch Univ. (WI)
Carleton College (MN)
Carlow College (PA)
Carnegie Mellon Univ. (PA)
Carroll College (MT)
Carroll College (WI)
Carson-Newman College (TN)
Carthage College (WI)
Case Western Reserve Univ. (OH)
Catawba College (NC)
Catholic Univ. of America (DC)
Cedar Crest College (PA)
Cedarville Univ. (OH)
Centenary College of Louisiana
Central Christian College (KS)
Central College (IA)
Central Connecticut State Univ.
Central Methodist Univ. (MO)
Central Michigan Univ.

Central State Univ. (OH)
Central Washington Univ.
Centre College (KY)
Chapman Univ. (CA)
Charleston Southern Univ. (SC)
Chatham College (PA)
Chestnut Hill College (PA)
Cheyney Univ. of Pennsylvania
Chicago State Univ.
Christian Brothers Univ. (TN)
Christopher Newport Univ. (VA)
Claflin Univ. (SC)
Claremont Mckenna College (CA)
Clarion Univ. of Pennsylvania
Clark Atlanta Univ.
Clark Univ. (MA)
Clarke College (IA)
Clarkson Univ. (NY)
Cleveland State Univ.
Coastal Carolina Univ. (SC)
Coe College (IA)
Coker College (SC)
Colby College (ME)
Colgate Univ. (NY)
College Misericordia (PA)
College of Charleston (SC)
College of Mount St. Joseph (OH)
College of Mount St. Vincent (NY)
College of New Jersey
College of Notre Dame of
    Maryland
College of St. Benedict (MN)
College of St. Catherine (MN)
College of St. Elizabeth (NJ)
College of St. Mary (NE)
College of St. Rose (NY)
College of St. Scholastica (MN)
College of the Holy Cross (MA)
College of the Ozarks (MO)
College of William and Mary (VA)
College of Wooster (OH)
Colorado College
Colorado School of Mines
Colorado State Univ.
Colorado State Univ.–Pueblo
Columbia College (MO)
Columbia College (SC)
Columbia Union College (MD)
Columbia Univ. (NY)
Columbus State Univ. (GA)
Concord College (WV)
Concordia Coll.–Moorhead (MN)
Concordia Univ. (MI)
Concordia Univ. (NE)
Concordia Univ. (CA)
Concordia Univ.–River Forest (IL)
Concordia Univ.–St. Paul (MN)
Connecticut College
Converse College (SC)
Coppin State Univ. (MD)
Cornell College (IA)
Cornell Univ. (NY)
Covenant College (GA)
Crichton College (TN)
Cumberland College (KY)
CUNY–Brooklyn College
CUNY–City College
CUNY–College of Staten Island
CUNY–Lehman College
CUNY–Queens College
CUNY–York College

Dana College (NE)
Dartmouth College (NH)
David Lipscomb Univ. (TN)
Davidson College (NC)
Davis and Elkins College (WV)
Defiance College (OH)
Delaware State Univ.
Delaware Valley College (PA)
Delta State Univ. (MS)
Denison Univ. (OH)
Depaul Univ. (IL)
Depauw Univ. (IN)
Desales Univ. (PA)
Dickinson College (PA)
Dickinson State Univ. (ND)
Dillard Univ. (LA)
Dominican Univ. (IL)
Dordt College (IA)
Drake Univ. (IA)
Drew Univ. (NJ)
Drexel Univ. (PA)
Drury Univ. (MO)
Duquesne Univ. (PA)
Earlham College (IN)
East Carolina Univ. (NC)
East Central Univ. (OK)
East Stroudsburg Univ. of
    Pennsylvania
East Tennessee State Univ.
East Texas Baptist Univ.
Eastern Illinois Univ.
Eastern Kentucky Univ.
Eastern Mennonite Univ. (VA)
Eastern Michigan Univ.
Eastern Nazarene College (MA)
Eastern New Mexico Univ.
Eastern Oregon Univ.
Eastern Univ. (PA)
Eastern Washington Univ.
Eckerd College (FL)
Edgewood College (WI)
Edinboro Univ. of Pennsylvania
Elizabeth City State Univ. (NC)
Elizabethtown College (PA)
Elmhurst College (IL)
Elmira College (NY)
Elms College (College of Our Lady
    of the Elms) (MA)
Elon Univ. (NC)
Emmanuel College (MA)
Emory and Henry College (VA)
Emory Univ. (GA)
Emporia State Univ. (KS)
Erskine College (SC)
Eureka College (IL)
Excelsior College (NY)
Fairfield Univ. (CT)
Fairleigh Dickinson Univ. (NJ)
Fairmont State Univ. (WV)
Fayetteville State Univ. (NC)
Ferris State Univ. (MI)
Ferrum College (VA)
Fisk Univ. (TN)
Florida Atlantic Univ.
Florida Institute of Technology
Florida International Univ.
Florida Southern College
Florida State Univ.
Fordham Univ. (NY)
Fort Hays State Univ. (KS)
Fort Lewis College (CO)

Fort Valley State Univ. (GA)
Framingham State College (MA)
Francis Marion Univ. (SC)
Franciscan Univ. of Steubenville
    (OH)
Franklin and Marshall College (PA)
Franklin College (IN)
Freed-Hardeman Univ. (TN)
Fresno Pacific Univ. (CA)
Friends Univ. (KS)
Frostburg State Univ. (MD)
Furman Univ. (SC)
Gallaudet Univ. (DC)
Gannon Univ. (PA)
Gardner-Webb Univ. (NC)
Geneva College (PA)
George Fox Univ. (OR)
George Mason Univ. (VA)
George Washington Univ. (DC)
Georgetown College (KY)
Georgetown Univ. (DC)
Georgia College and State Univ.
Georgia Institute of Technology
Georgia Southern Univ.
Georgia Southwestern State Univ.
Georgia State Univ.
Georgian Court Univ. (NJ)
Gettysburg College (PA)
Glenville State College (WV)
Gonzaga Univ. (WA)
Gordon College (MA)
Goshen College (IN)
Goucher College (MD)
Graceland Univ. (IA)
Grambling State Univ. (LA)
Grand Canyon Univ. (AZ)
Grand Valley State Univ. (MI)
Greensboro College (NC)
Greenville College (IL)
Grinnell College (IA)
Grove City College (PA)
Guilford College (NC)
Gustavus Adolphus College (MN)
Hamilton College (NY)
Hamline Univ. (MN)
Hampden-Sydney College (VA)
Hampshire College (MA)
Hampton Univ. (VA)
Hanover College (IN)
Hardin-Simmons Univ. (TX)
Harding Univ. (AR)
Hartwick College (NY)
Harvard Univ. (MA)
Harvey Mudd College (CA)
Hastings College (NE)
Haverford College (PA)
Heidelberg College (OH)
Henderson State Univ. (AR)
Hendrix College (AR)
Heritage College (WA)
High Point Univ. (NC)
Hillsdale College (MI)
Hiram College (OH)
Hobart and William Smith Colleges
    (NY)
Hofstra Univ. (NY)
Hollins Univ. (VA)
Holy Family Univ. (PA)
Hood College (MD)
Hope College (MI)
Houghton College (NY)

Houston Baptist Univ.
Howard Payne Univ. (TX)
Howard Univ. (DC)
Humboldt State Univ. (CA)
Huntingdon College (AL)
Huntington College (IN)
Huston-Tillotson College (TX)
Idaho State Univ.
Illinois College
Illinois Institute of Technology
Illinois State Univ.
Illinois Wesleyan Univ.
Immaculata Univ. (PA)
Indiana State Univ.
Indiana Univ. Northwest
Indiana Univ. of Pennsylvania
Indiana Univ. Southeast
Indiana Univ.–Bloomington
Indiana Univ.–Kokomo
Indiana Univ.–South Bend
Indiana Univ.-Purdue Univ.–Fort
    Wayne
Indiana Univ.-Purdue
    Univ.–Indianapolis
Indiana Wesleyan Univ.
Iona College (NY)
Iowa State Univ.
Ithaca College (NY)
Jacksonville State Univ. (AL)
Jacksonville Univ. (FL)
James Madison Univ. (VA)
Jamestown College (ND)
Jarvis Christian College (TX)
John Brown Univ. (AR)
John Carroll Univ. (OH)
Johns Hopkins Univ. (MD)
Johnson C. Smith Univ. (NC)
Judson College (IL)
Judson College (AL)
Juniata College (PA)
Kalamazoo College (MI)
Kansas State Univ.
Kansas Wesleyan Univ.
Kean Univ. (NJ)
Keene State College (NH)
Kennesaw State Univ. (GA)
Kent State Univ. (OH)
Kentucky State Univ.
Kentucky Wesleyan College
Kettering Univ. (MI)
King College (TN)
King's College (PA)
Knox College (IL)
Kutztown Univ. of Pennsylvania
La Roche College (PA)
La Salle Univ. (PA)
La Sierra Univ. (CA)
Lafayette College (PA)
Lagrange College (GA)
Lake Forest College (IL)
Lake Superior State Univ. (MI)
Lakeland College (WI)
Lamar Univ. (TX)
Lambuth Univ. (TN)
Lander Univ. (SC)
Lane College (TN)
Lawrence Technological Univ. (MI)
Lawrence Univ. (WI)
Le Moyne College (NY)
Lebanon Valley College (PA)
Lehigh Univ. (PA)

Lemoyne-Owen College (TN)
Lenoir-Rhyne College (NC)
Letourneau Univ. (TX)
Lewis and Clark College (OR)
Lewis Univ. (IL)
Lewis-Clark State College (ID)
Limestone College (SC)
Lincoln Memorial Univ. (TN)
Lincoln Univ. (MO)
Lincoln Univ. (PA)
Lindenwood Univ. (MO)
Linfield College (OR)
Lock Haven Univ. of Pennsylvania
Long Island Univ.–C.W. Post
    Campus (NY)
Longwood Univ. (VA)
Loras College (IA)
Louisiana College
Louisiana State Univ.–Baton Rouge
Louisiana State Univ.–Shreveport
Louisiana Tech Univ.
Loyola College In Maryland
Loyola Marymount Univ. (CA)
Loyola Univ. Chicago
Loyola Univ. New Orleans
Lubbock Christian Univ. (TX)
Luther College (IA)
Lycoming College (PA)
Lynchburg College (VA)
Lyon College (AR)
Macalester College (MN)
Madonna Univ. (MI)
Malone College (OH)
Manchester College (IN)
Manhattan College (NY)
Manhattanville College (NY)
Mansfield Univ. of Pennsylvania
Marian College (IN)
Marian College of Fond Du Lac
    (WI)
Marietta College (OH)
Marist College (NY)
Marquette Univ. (WI)
Mars Hill College (NC)
Marshall Univ. (WV)
Martin Univ. (IN)
Mary Baldwin College (VA)
Marygrove College (MI)
Maryville College (TN)
Maryville Univ. of St. Louis (MO)
Massachusetts Institute of
    Technology
Mayville State Univ. (ND)
Mckendree College (IL)
Mcmurry Univ. (TX)
Mcneese State Univ. (LA)
Mcpherson College (KS)
Mercer Univ. (GA)
Mercyhurst College (PA)
Meredith College (NC)
Merrimack College (MA)
Messiah College (PA)
Methodist College (NC)
Metropolitan State College of
    Denver
Miami Univ.–Oxford (OH)
Michigan State Univ.
Michigan Technological Univ.
Middle Tennessee State Univ.
Middlebury College (VT)
Midway College (KY)

Midwestern State Univ. (TX)
Miles College (AL)
Millersville Univ. of Pennsylvania
Milligan College (TN)
Millikin Univ. (IL)
Mills College (CA)
Millsaps College (MS)
Minnesota State Univ.–Mankato
Minnesota State Univ.–Moorhead
Minot State Univ. (ND)
Mississippi College
Mississippi State Univ.
Mississippi Univ. For Women
Mississippi Valley State Univ.
Missouri Baptist College
Missouri Southern State Univ.
Missouri Western State College
Monmouth College (IL)
Monmouth Univ. (NJ)
Montana State Univ.–Billings
Montana State Univ.–Bozeman
Montana Tech of the Univ. of
    Montana
Montclair State Univ. (NJ)
Moravian College (PA)
Morehead State Univ. (KY)
Morehouse College (GA)
Morgan State Univ. (MD)
Morningside College (IA)
Mount Holyoke College (MA)
Mount Marty College (SD)
Mount Mary College (WI)
Mount St. Mary College (NY)
Mount St. Mary's College (CA)
Mount St. Mary's Univ. (MD)
Mount Union College (OH)
Mount Vernon Nazarene Univ.
    (OH)
Muhlenberg College (PA)
Murray State Univ. (KY)
Muskingum College (OH)
Nazareth College of Rochester
    (NY)
Nebraska Wesleyan Univ.
New Jersey City Univ.
New Jersey Institute of Technology
New Mexico Highlands Univ.
New Mexico Institute of Mining
    and Technology
New Mexico State Univ.
New York Institute of Technology
New York Univ.
Newberry College (SC)
Niagara Univ. (NY)
Nicholls State Univ. (LA)
Norfolk State Univ. (VA)
North Carolina Central Univ.
North Carolina State Univ.–Raleigh
North Carolina Wesleyan College
North Central College (IL)
North Dakota State Univ.
North Georgia College and State
    Univ.
North Park Univ. (IL)
Northeastern Illinois Univ.
Northeastern State Univ. (OK)
Northeastern Univ. (MA)
Northern Arizona Univ.
Northern Illinois Univ.
Northern Kentucky Univ.
Northern Michigan Univ.

Northern State Univ. (SD)
Northland College (WI)
Northwest Missouri State Univ.
Northwest Nazarene Univ. (ID)
Northwestern College (IA)
Northwestern Oklahoma State
    Univ.
Northwestern State Univ. of
    Louisiana
Northwestern Univ. (IL)
Norwich Univ. (VT)
Notre Dame College of Ohio
Oakland Univ. (MI)
Oakwood College (AL)
Oberlin College (OH)
Occidental College (CA)
Oglethorpe Univ. (GA)
Ohio Dominican Univ.
Ohio Northern Univ.
Ohio State Univ.–Columbus
Ohio Univ.
Ohio Wesleyan Univ.
Oklahoma Baptist Univ.
Oklahoma Christian Univ.
Oklahoma City Univ.
Oklahoma Panhandle State Univ.
Oklahoma State Univ.
Oklahoma Wesleyan Univ.
Old Dominion Univ. (VA)
Olivet College (MI)
Olivet Nazarene Univ. (IL)
Oral Roberts Univ. (OK)
Oregon State Univ.
Otterbein College (OH)
Ouachita Baptist Univ. (AR)
Our Lady of the Lake Univ. (TX)
Pace Univ. (NY)
Pacific Lutheran Univ. (WA)
Pacific Union College (CA)
Pacific Univ. (OR)
Paine College (GA)
Park Univ. (MO)
Penn. State Univ.–Univ. Park
Penn. State–Erie, The Behrend
    College
Pepperdine Univ. (CA)
Pfeiffer Univ. (NC)
Philadelphia Univ.
Philander Smith College (AR)
Piedmont College (GA)
Pikeville College (KY)
Pittsburg State Univ. (KS)
Plymouth State Univ. (NH)
Point Loma Nazarene Univ. (CA)
Polytechnic Univ. (NY)
Pomona College (CA)
Portland State Univ. (OR)
Prairie View A&M Univ. (TX)
Presbyterian College (SC)
Princeton Univ. (NJ)
Principia College (IL)
Providence College (RI)
Purdue Univ.–Calumet (IN)
Purdue Univ.–West Lafayette (IN)
Quincy Univ. (IL)
Quinnipiac Univ. (CT)
Radford Univ. (VA)
Ramapo College of New Jersey
Randolph-Macon College (VA)
Randolph-Macon Woman's College
    (VA)

Reed College (OR)
Regis Univ. (CO)
Rensselaer Polytechnic Inst. (NY)
Rhode Island College
Rhodes College (TN)
Rice Univ. (TX)
Richard Stockton College of New
    Jersey
Rider Univ. (NJ)
Ripon College (WI)
Roanoke College (VA)
Roberts Wesleyan College (NY)
Rochester Institute of Tech. (NY)
Rockford College (IL)
Rockhurst Univ. (MO)
Rocky Mountain College (MT)
Roger Williams Univ. (RI)
Rollins College (FL)
Roosevelt Univ. (IL)
Rose-Hulman Institute of
    Technology (IN)
Rosemont College (PA)
Russell Sage College (NY)
Rust College (MS)
Rutgers–Camden (NJ)
Rutgers–New Brunswick (NJ)
Rutgers–Newark (NJ)
Sacred Heart Univ. (CT)
Saginaw Valley State Univ. (MI)
Salem College (NC)
Salem State College (MA)
Salisbury Univ. (MD)
Salve Regina Univ. (RI)
Sam Houston State Univ. (TX)
Samford Univ. (AL)
San Diego State Univ.
San Francisco State Univ.
San Jose State Univ. (CA)
Santa Clara Univ. (CA)
Savannah State Univ. (GA)
Schreiner Univ. (TX)
Scripps College (CA)
Seattle Pacific Univ.
Seattle Univ.
Seton Hall Univ. (NJ)
Seton Hill Univ. (PA)
Shaw Univ. (NC)
Shawnee State Univ. (OH)
Shenandoah Univ. (VA)
Shepherd Univ. (WV)
Shippensburg Univ. of
    Pennsylvania
Shorter College (GA)
Siena College (NY)
Simmons College (MA)
Simpson College (IA)
Skidmore College (NY)
Slippery Rock Univ. of Pennsylvania
Sonoma State Univ. (CA)
South Carolina State Univ.
South Dakota School of Mines and
    Technology
South Dakota State Univ.
Southeast Missouri State Univ.
Southeastern Louisiana Univ.
Southeastern Oklahoma State
    Univ.
Southern Adventist Univ. (TN)
Southern Arkansas Univ.
Southern Connecticut State Univ.
Southern Illinois Univ.–Carbondale

Southern Illinois
    Univ.–Edwardsville
Southern Methodist Univ. (TX)
Southern Nazarene Univ. (OK)
Southern Oregon Univ.
Southern Univ. and A&M College
    (LA)
Southern Utah Univ.
Southern Wesleyan Univ. (SC)
Southwest Baptist Univ. (MO)
Southwest Minnesota State Univ.
    (MN)
Southwestern Adventist Univ. (TX)
Southwestern College (KS)
Southwestern Oklahoma State
    Univ.
Southwestern Univ. (TX)
Spelman College (GA)
Spring Arbor Univ. (MI)
Spring Hill College (AL)
Springfield College (MA)
St. Ambrose Univ. (IA)
St. Andrews Presbyterian College
    (NC)
St. Anselm College (NH)
St. Augustine's College (NC)
St. Bonaventure Univ. (NY)
St. Cloud State Univ. (MN)
St. Edward's Univ. (TX)
St. Francis College (NY)
St. Francis Univ. (PA)
St. Gregory's Univ. (OK)
St. John Fisher College (NY)
St. John's Univ. (NY)
St. John's Univ. (MN)
St. Joseph College (CT)
St. Joseph's College (IN)
St. Joseph's College (ME)
St. Joseph's College, New York
St. Joseph's Univ. (PA)
St. Lawrence Univ. (NY)
St. Louis Univ.
St. Martin's College (WA)
St. Mary's College (IN)
St. Mary's College of California
St. Mary's College of Maryland
St. Mary's Univ. of Minnesota
St. Mary's Univ. of San Antonio
St. Michael's College (VT)
St. Norbert College (WI)
St. Olaf College (MN)
St. Peter's College (NJ)
St. Vincent College (PA)
St. Xavier Univ. (IL)
Stanford Univ. (CA)
State Univ. of West Georgia
Stephen F. Austin State Univ. (TX)
Sterling College (KS)
Stetson Univ. (FL)
Stevens Institute of Tech. (NJ)
Stonehill College (MA)
Suffolk Univ. (MA)
Sul Ross State Univ. (TX)
SUNY College Environmental
    Science and Forestry
SUNY College of Arts and
    Sciences–Geneseo
SUNY College–Brockport
SUNY College–Old Westbury
SUNY College–Oneonta
SUNY College–Potsdam

SUNY–Albany
SUNY–Binghamton
SUNY–Fredonia
SUNY–Oswego
SUNY–Plattsburgh
SUNY–Purchase College
SUNY–Stony Brook
Susquehanna Univ. (PA)
Swarthmore College (PA)
Sweet Briar College (VA)
Syracuse Univ. (NY)
Tabor College (KS)
Talladega College (AL)
Tarleton State Univ. (TX)
Taylor Univ. (IN)
Temple Univ. (PA)
Tennessee State Univ.
Tennessee Technological Univ.
Texas A&M International Univ.
Texas A&M Univ.–College Station
Texas A&M Univ.–Commerce
Texas A&M Univ.–Corpus Christi
Texas A&M Univ.–Kingsville
Texas Christian Univ.
Texas Lutheran Univ.
Texas State Univ.–San Marcos
Texas Tech Univ.
Texas Wesleyan Univ.
Texas Woman's Univ.
The Citadel (SC)
Thiel College (PA)
Thomas More College (KY)
Touro College (NY)
Towson Univ. (MD)
Transylvania Univ. (KY)
Trevecca Nazarene Univ. (TN)
Tri-State Univ. (IN)
Trinity Christian College (IL)
Trinity College (DC)
Trinity College (CT)
Troy State Univ.–Troy (AL)
Truman State Univ. (MO)
Tufts Univ. (MA)
Tulane Univ. (LA)
Union College (NE)
Union College (NY)
Union Univ. (TN)
United States Air Force Academy (CO)
United States Naval Academy (MD)
Univ. at Buffalo–SUNY
Univ. of Akron (OH)
Univ. of Alabama
Univ. of Alabama–Birmingham
Univ. of Alabama–Huntsville
Univ. of Alaska–Anchorage
Univ. of Alaska–Fairbanks
Univ. of Arizona
Univ. of Arkansas
Univ. of Arkansas–Little Rock
Univ. of Arkansas–Monticello
Univ. of Arkansas–Pine Bluff
Univ. of California–Berkeley
Univ. of California–Davis
Univ. of California–Irvine
Univ. of California–Los Angeles
Univ. of California–Riverside
Univ. of California–San Diego
Univ. of California–Santa Barbara
Univ. of California–Santa Cruz

Univ. of Central Arkansas
Univ. of Central Florida
Univ. of Central Oklahoma
Univ. of Charleston (WV)
Univ. of Chicago
Univ. of Colorado–Boulder
Univ. of Colorado–Colorado Springs
Univ. of Colorado–Denver
Univ. of Connecticut
Univ. of Dallas
Univ. of Dayton (OH)
Univ. of Delaware
Univ. of Denver
Univ. of Detroit Mercy
Univ. of Evansville (IN)
Univ. of Florida
Univ. of Georgia
Univ. of Hartford (CT)
Univ. of Hawaii–Hilo
Univ. of Hawaii–Manoa
Univ. of Houston
Univ. of Houston–Downtown
Univ. of Illinois–Chicago
Univ. of Illinois–Springfield
Univ. of Illinois–Urbana-Champaign
Univ. of Indianapolis
Univ. of Iowa
Univ. of Kansas
Univ. of Kentucky
Univ. of La Verne (CA)
Univ. of Louisiana–Lafayette
Univ. of Louisiana–Monroe
Univ. of Louisville (KY)
Univ. of Maine–Orono
Univ. of Mary Hardin-Baylor (TX)
Univ. of Mary Washington (VA)
Univ. of Maryland–Baltimore County
Univ. of Maryland–College Park
Univ. of Maryland–Eastern Shore
Univ. of Massachusetts–Amherst
Univ. of Massachusetts–Boston
Univ. of Mass.–Dartmouth
Univ. of Massachusetts–Lowell
Univ. of Memphis
Univ. of Miami (FL)
Univ. of Michigan–Ann Arbor
Univ. of Michigan–Dearborn
Univ. of Michigan–Flint
Univ. of Minnesota–Duluth
Univ. of Minnesota–Morris
Univ. of Minnesota–Twin Cities
Univ. of Mississippi
Univ. of Missouri–Columbia
Univ. of Missouri–Kansas City
Univ. of Missouri–Rolla
Univ. of Missouri–St. Louis
Univ. of Mobile (AL)
Univ. of Montana
Univ. of Montevallo (AL)
Univ. of Nebraska–Kearney
Univ. of Nebraska–Lincoln
Univ. of Nebraska–Omaha
Univ. of Nevada–Las Vegas
Univ. of Nevada–Reno
Univ. of New England (ME)
Univ. of New Hampshire
Univ. of New Haven (CT)
Univ. of New Mexico

Univ. of New Orleans
Univ. of North Alabama
Univ. of North Carolina–Asheville
Univ. of N.C.–Chapel Hill
Univ. of North Carolina–Charlotte
Univ. of N.C.–Greensboro
Univ. of North Carolina–Pembroke
Univ. of N.C.–Wilmington
Univ. of North Dakota
Univ. of North Florida
Univ. of North Texas
Univ. of Northern Colorado
Univ. of Northern Iowa
Univ. of Notre Dame (IN)
Univ. of Oklahoma
Univ. of Oregon
Univ. of Pennsylvania
Univ. of Pittsburgh
Univ. of Pittsburgh–Bradford
Univ. of Pittsburgh–Johnstown
Univ. of Portland (OR)
Univ. of Puget Sound (WA)
Univ. of Redlands (CA)
Univ. of Rhode Island
Univ. of Richmond (VA)
Univ. of Rochester (NY)
Univ. of San Diego
Univ. of San Francisco
Univ. of Science and Arts of Oklahoma
Univ. of Scranton (PA)
Univ. of Sioux Falls (SD)
Univ. of South Alabama
Univ. of South Carolina–Aiken
Univ. of South Carolina–Columbia
Univ. of South Carolina–Upstate
Univ. of South Dakota
Univ. of South Florida
Univ. of Southern California
Univ. of Southern Indiana
Univ. of Southern Maine
Univ. of Southern Mississippi
Univ. of St. Francis (IN)
Univ. of St. Mary (KS)
Univ. of St. Thomas (MN)
Univ. of St. Thomas (TX)
Univ. of Tampa (FL)
Univ. of Tennessee
Univ. of Tennessee–Chattanooga
Univ. of Tennessee–Martin
Univ. of Texas of the Permian Basin
Univ. of Texas–Arlington
Univ. of Texas–Austin
Univ. of Texas–Brownsville
Univ. of Texas–Dallas
Univ. of Texas–El Paso
Univ. of Texas–Pan American
Univ. of Texas–San Antonio
Univ. of Texas–Tyler
Univ. of the District of Columbia
Univ. of the Incarnate Word (TX)
Univ. of the Ozarks (AR)
Univ. of the Pacific (CA)
Univ. of Toledo (OH)
Univ. of Tulsa (OK)
Univ. of Utah
Univ. of Vermont
Univ. of Virginia
Univ. of Virginia–Wise
Univ. of Washington
Univ. of West Alabama

Univ. of West Florida
Univ. of Wisconsin–Eau Claire
Univ. of Wisconsin–Green Bay
Univ. of Wisconsin–La Crosse
Univ. of Wisconsin–Madison
Univ. of Wisconsin–Milwaukee
Univ. of Wisconsin–Parkside
Univ. of Wisconsin–Platteville
Univ. of Wisconsin–River Falls
Univ. of Wisconsin–Stevens Point
Univ. of Wisconsin–Superior
Univ. of Wisconsin–Whitewater
Univ. of Wyoming
Upper Iowa Univ.
Ursinus College (PA)
Utah State Univ.
Utah Valley State College
Utica College (NY)
Valdosta State Univ. (GA)
Valley City State Univ. (ND)
Valparaiso Univ. (IN)
Vanderbilt Univ. (TN)
Vanguard Univ. of Southern California
Vassar College (NY)
Villa Julie College (MD)
Villanova Univ. (PA)
Virginia Commonwealth Univ.
Virginia Military Institute
Virginia State Univ.
Virginia Tech
Virginia Wesleyan College
Viterbo Univ. (WI)
Wabash College (IN)
Wagner College (NY)
Wake Forest Univ. (NC)
Walsh Univ. (OH)
Wartburg College (IA)
Washburn Univ. (KS)
Washington and Jefferson College (PA)
Washington and Lee Univ. (VA)
Washington College (MD)
Washington State Univ.
Washington Univ. In St. Louis
Wayland Baptist Univ. (TX)
Wayne State College (NE)
Wayne State Univ. (MI)
Waynesburg College (PA)
Weber State Univ. (UT)
Wellesley College (MA)
Wesleyan College (GA)
Wesleyan Univ. (CT)
West Chester Univ. of Pennsylvania
West Liberty State College (WV)
West Texas A&M Univ.
West Virginia State Univ.
West Virginia Univ.
West Virginia Univ. Institute of Technology
West Virginia Wesleyan College
Western Carolina Univ. (NC)
Western Connecticut State Univ.
Western Illinois Univ.
Western Kentucky Univ.
Western Michigan Univ.
Western New England College (MA)
Western New Mexico Univ.
Western State College of Colorado
Western Washington Univ.

Westfield State College (MA)
Westminster College (PA)
Westminster College (UT)
Westminster College (MO)
Westmont College (CA)
Wheaton College (MA)
Wheaton College (IL)
Wheeling Jesuit Univ. (WV)
Whitman College (WA)
Whittier College (CA)
Whitworth College (WA)
Wichita State Univ. (KS)
Wiley College (TX)
Wilkes Univ. (PA)
Willamette Univ. (OR)
William Carey College (MS)
William Jewell College (MO)
William Paterson Univ. of New Jersey
Williams College (MA)
Wilmington College (OH)
Wilson College (PA)
Wingate Univ. (NC)
Winthrop Univ. (SC)
Wisconsin Lutheran College
Wittenberg Univ. (OH)
Wofford College (SC)
Worcester Polytechnic Institute (MA)
Worcester State College (MA)
Wright State Univ. (OH)
Xavier Univ. (OH)
Yale Univ. (CT)
Yeshiva Univ. (NY)
York College of Pennsylvania
Youngstown State Univ. (OH)

Chiropractic (D.C.)

Marywood Univ. (PA)

City/Urban, Community, and Regional Planning

Alabama Agricultural and Mechanical Univ.
Appalachian State Univ. (NC)
Arizona State Univ.
Auburn Univ. (AL)
Ball State Univ. (IN)
Bridgewater State College (MA)
Cal Poly–San Luis Obispo
California State Polytechnic Univ.–Pomona
California State Univ.–San Bernardino
Catholic Univ. of America (DC)
Cornell Univ. (NY)
East Carolina Univ. (NC)
Eastern Michigan Univ.
Eastern Washington Univ.
Florida Atlantic Univ.
Frostburg State Univ. (MD)
Grand Valley State Univ. (MI)
Indiana Univ. of Pennsylvania
Iowa State Univ.
Massachusetts Institute of Technology
Miami Univ.–Oxford (OH)

Michigan State Univ.
New Mexico State Univ.
Northern Michigan Univ.
Plymouth State Univ. (NH)
Savannah College of Art and
    Design (GA).
Southwest Missouri State Univ.
Stanford Univ. (CA)
SUNY–Albany
Temple Univ. (PA)
Texas A&M Univ.–College Station
Texas State Univ.–San Marcos
Univ. of Akron (OH)
Univ. of Arizona
Univ. of California–Davis
Univ. of Ill.–Urbana-Champaign
Univ. of Miami (FL)
Univ. of Missouri–Kansas City
Univ. of Nevada–Las Vegas
Univ. of New Hampshire
Univ. of North Texas
Univ. of San Francisco
Univ. of Virginia
Univ. of Washington
Washington State Univ.
Westfield State College (MA)

Civil Engineering

Alabama Agricultural and
    Mechanical Univ.
Arizona State Univ.
Auburn Univ. (AL)
Bethel College (IN)
Boise State Univ. (ID)
Bradley Univ. (IL)
Brigham Young Univ.–Provo (UT)
Bucknell Univ. (PA)
Cal Poly–San Luis Obispo
California State Polytechnic
    Univ.–Pomona
California State Univ.–Chico
California State Univ.–Fullerton
California State Univ.–Long Beach
California State Univ.–Los Angeles
California State Univ.–Sacramento
Calvin College (MI)
Carnegie Mellon Univ. (PA)
Carroll College (MT)
Case Western Reserve Univ. (OH)
Catholic Univ. of America (DC)
Central Missouri State Univ.
Central Univ. (OH)
Christian Brothers Univ. (TN)
Clarkson Univ. (NY)
Cleveland State Univ.
Colorado State Univ.
Columbia Univ. (NY)
Cooper Union (NY)
Cornell Univ. (NY)
CUNY–City College
Drexel Univ. (PA)
Duke Univ. (NC)
Embry Riddle Aeronautical Univ.
    (FL)
Florida A&M Univ.
Florida Atlantic Univ.
Florida Institute of Technology
Florida International Univ.
Florida State Univ.

George Mason Univ. (VA)
George Washington Univ. (DC)
Georgia Institute of Technology
Gonzaga Univ. (WA)
Hofstra Univ. (NY)
Howard Univ. (DC)
Idaho State Univ.
Illinois Institute of Technology
Iowa State Univ.
Johns Hopkins Univ. (MD)
Johnson and Wales Univ. (RI)
Kansas State Univ.
Lafayette College (PA)
Lamar Univ. (TX)
Lawrence Technological Univ. (MI)
Lehigh Univ. (PA)
Louisiana State Univ.–Baton Rouge
Louisiana Tech Univ.
Loyola Marymount Univ. (CA)
Manhattan College (NY)
Marquette Univ. (WI)
Massachusetts Institute of
    Technology
Merrimack College (MA)
Michigan State Univ.
Michigan Technological Univ.
Mississippi State Univ.
Montana State Univ.–Bozeman
Morgan State Univ. (MD)
New England College (NH)
New Jersey Institute of Technology
New Mexico Institute of Mining
    and Technology
New Mexico State Univ.
North Carolina A&T State Univ.
North Carolina State Univ.–Raleigh
North Dakota State Univ.
Northeastern Univ. (MA)
Northern Arizona Univ.
Northwestern Univ. (IL)
Norwich Univ. (VT)
Ohio Northern Univ.
Ohio State Univ.–Columbus
Ohio Univ.
Oklahoma State Univ.
Old Dominion Univ. (VA)
Oregon Institute of Technology
Oregon State Univ.
Penn. State Univ.–Univ. Park
Polytechnic Univ. (NY)
Portland State Univ. (OR)
Prairie View A&M Univ. (TX)
Princeton Univ. (NJ)
Purdue Univ.–West Lafayette (IN)
Rensselaer Polytechnic Inst. (NY)
Rice Univ. (TX)
Rose-Hulman Institute of
    Technology (IN)
Rutgers–New Brunswick (NJ)
San Diego State Univ.
San Francisco State Univ.
San Jose State Univ. (CA)
Santa Clara Univ. (CA)
Savannah State Univ. (GA)
Seattle Univ.
South Dakota School of Mines and
    Technology
South Dakota State Univ.
Southern Illinois Univ.–Carbondale
Southern Illinois
    Univ.–Edwardsville

Southern Univ. and A&M College
    (LA)
St. Martin's College (WA)
Stanford Univ. (CA)
Stevens Institute of Technology
    (NJ)
Syracuse Univ. (NY)
Temple Univ. (PA)
Tennessee State Univ.
Tennessee Technological Univ.
Texas A&M Univ.–College Station
Texas A&M Univ.–Galveston
Texas A&M Univ.–Kingsville
Texas Tech Univ.
The Citadel (SC)
Tri-State Univ. (IN)
Tufts Univ. (MA)
Tulane Univ. (LA)
United States Air Force Academy
    (CO)
United States Coast Guard
    Academy (CT)
United States Military Academy
    (NY)
Univ. at Buffalo–SUNY
Univ. of Akron (OH)
Univ. of Alabama
Univ. of Alabama–Birmingham
Univ. of Alabama–Huntsville
Univ. of Alaska–Anchorage
Univ. of Alaska–Fairbanks
Univ. of Arizona
Univ. of Arkansas
Univ. of California–Berkeley
Univ. of California–Davis
Univ. of California–Irvine
Univ. of California–Los Angeles
Univ. of California–San Diego
Univ. of Central Florida
Univ. of Colorado–Boulder
Univ. of Colorado–Denver
Univ. of Connecticut
Univ. of Dayton (OH)
Univ. of Detroit Mercy
Univ. of Evansville (IN)
Univ. of Florida
Univ. of Hartford (CT)
Univ. of Hawaii–Manoa
Univ. of Houston
Univ. of Illinois–Chicago
Univ. of Ill.–Urbana-Champaign
Univ. of Iowa
Univ. of Kansas
Univ. of Kentucky
Univ. of Louisiana–Lafayette
Univ. of Louisville (KY)
Univ. of Maine–Orono
Univ. of Maryland–College Park
Univ. of Massachusetts–Amherst
Univ. of Mass.–Dartmouth
Univ. of Massachusetts–Lowell
Univ. of Memphis
Univ. of Miami (FL)
Univ. of Michigan–Ann Arbor
Univ. of Minnesota–Twin Cities
Univ. of Mississippi
Univ. of Missouri–Columbia
Univ. of Missouri–Kansas City
Univ. of Missouri–Rolla
Univ. of Missouri–St. Louis
Univ. of Nebraska–Lincoln

Univ. of Nebraska–Omaha
Univ. of Nevada–Las Vegas
Univ. of Nevada–Reno
Univ. of New Hampshire
Univ. of New Haven (CT)
Univ. of New Mexico
Univ. of New Orleans
Univ. of North Carolina–Charlotte
Univ. of North Dakota
Univ. of North Florida
Univ. of Notre Dame (IN)
Univ. of Oklahoma
Univ. of Pennsylvania
Univ. of Pittsburgh
Univ. of Portland (OR)
Univ. of Rhode Island
Univ. of South Alabama
Univ. of South Carolina–Columbia
Univ. of South Florida
Univ. of Southern California
Univ. of Tennessee
Univ. of Texas–Arlington
Univ. of Texas–Austin
Univ. of Texas–El Paso
Univ. of Texas–San Antonio
Univ. of Texas–Tyler
Univ. of the District of Columbia
Univ. of the Pacific (CA)
Univ. of Toledo (OH)
Univ. of Utah
Univ. of Vermont
Univ. of Virginia
Univ. of Washington
Univ. of Wisconsin–Madison
Univ. of Wisconsin–Milwaukee
Univ. of Wisconsin–Platteville
Univ. of Wyoming
Utah State Univ.
Valparaiso Univ. (IN)
Vanderbilt Univ. (TN)
Villanova Univ. (PA)
Virginia Military Institute
Virginia Tech
Washington State Univ.
Washington Univ. In St. Louis
Wayne State Univ. (MI)
West Virginia Univ.
West Virginia Univ. Institute of
    Technology
Western Kentucky Univ.
Western Michigan Univ.
Widener Univ. (PA)
Worcester Polytechnic Institute
    (MA)
Youngstown State Univ. (OH)

Civil Engineering Technologies/Technicians

Bluefield State College (WV)
Bradley Univ. (IL)
Central Connecticut State Univ.
Colorado State Univ.–Pueblo
Fairleigh Dickinson Univ. (NJ)
Fairmont State Univ. (WV)
Florida A&M Univ.
Georgia Southern Univ.
Lincoln Univ. (MO)
Metropolitan State College of
    Denver

Missouri Western State College
Montana State Univ.–Northern
Murray State Univ. (KY)
Old Dominion Univ. (VA)
Pennsylvania College of Technology
Point Park Univ. (PA)
Rochester Institute of Tech. (NY)
South Carolina State Univ.
Southern Polytechnic State Univ.
    (GA)
Thomas Edison State College (NJ)
Univ. of Houston–Downtown
Univ. of Maine–Orono
Univ. of Maryland–Eastern Shore
Univ. of Massachusetts–Lowell
Univ. of North Carolina–Charlotte
Univ. of Pittsburgh–Johnstown
Univ. of Tennessee–Martin
Univ. of Toledo (OH)
Wentworth Institute of Technology
    (MA)
Western Kentucky Univ.
Youngstown State Univ. (OH)

Classical and Ancient Studies

Agnes Scott College (GA)
Bates College (ME)
Boston Univ.
Bowdoin College (ME)
Brandeis Univ. (MA)
Brown Univ. (RI)
Bryn Mawr College (PA)
Calvin College (MI)
College of Wooster (OH)
Columbia Univ. (NY)
Creighton Univ. (NE)
Furman Univ. (SC)
Hillsdale College (MI)
Lawrence Univ. (WI)
Loyola Marymount Univ. (CA)
Lycoming College (PA)
Michigan State Univ.
Mount Holyoke College (MA)
Mount Union College (OH)
Ohio Wesleyan Univ.
Randolph-Macon Woman's College
    (VA)
Rice Univ. (TX)
Rutgers–Newark (NJ)
Santa Clara Univ. (CA)
St. Olaf College (MN)
SUNY–Albany
Univ. of California–Berkeley
Univ. of California–Davis
Univ. of California–Irvine
Univ. of California–Los Angeles
Univ. of California–Riverside
Univ. of California–Santa Cruz
Univ. of Chicago
Univ. of Illinois–Chicago
Univ. of Iowa
Univ. of Kansas
Univ. of Maryland–Baltimore
    County
Univ. of Minnesota–Twin Cities
Univ. of Nebraska–Lincoln
Univ. of Oregon
Univ. of Texas–Austin

Vassar College (NY)
Washington Univ. In St. Louis
Wellesley College (MA)
Wheaton College (MA)
Yale Univ. (CT)

Classics and Classical Languages, Literatures, and Linguistics

Agnes Scott College (GA)
Amherst College (MA)
Asbury College (KY)
Assumption College (MA)
Augustana College (IL)
Austin College (TX)
Ball State Univ. (IN)
Barnard College (NY)
Baylor Univ. (TX)
Belmont Univ. (TN)
Beloit College (WI)
Berea College (KY)
Boston Univ.
Bowdoin College (ME)
Bowling Green State Univ. (OH)
Brown Univ. (RI)
Bryn Mawr College (PA)
Bucknell Univ. (PA)
Butler Univ. (IN)
California State Univ.–Long Beach
Calvin College (MI)
Carleton College (MN)
Carroll College (MT)
Case Western Reserve Univ. (OH)
Catholic Univ. of America (DC)
Centenary College of Louisiana
Central College (IA)
Centre College (KY)
Christendom College (VA)
Claremont Mckenna College (CA)
Clark Univ. (MA)
Colby College (ME)
Colgate Univ. (NY)
College of Charleston (SC)
College of St. Benedict (MN)
College of the Holy Cross (MA)
College of William and Mary (VA)
Colorado College
Columbia Univ. (NY)
Concordia Coll.–Moorhead (MN)
Concordia Univ. (MI)
Connecticut College
Cornell College (IA)
Cornell Univ. (NY)
Creighton Univ. (NE)
CUNY–Brooklyn College
CUNY–Lehman College
CUNY–Queens College
Dartmouth College (NH)
Davidson College (NC)
Denison Univ. (OH)
Depauw Univ. (IN)
Dickinson College (PA)
Drew Univ. (NJ)
Duke Univ. (NC)
Duquesne Univ. (PA)
Earlham College (IN)
Emory Univ. (GA)
Florida State Univ.
Fordham Univ. (NY)

Franciscan Univ. of Steubenville (OH)
Franklin and Marshall College (PA)
Furman Univ. (SC)
George Washington Univ. (DC)
Georgetown Univ. (DC)
Gettysburg College (PA)
Grace College and Seminary (IN)
Grand Valley State Univ. (MI)
Grinnell College (IA)
Gustavus Adolphus College (MN)
Hampden-Sydney College (VA)
Hanover College (IN)
Harvard Univ. (MA)
Haverford College (PA)
Hillsdale College (MI)
Hiram College (OH)
Hobart and William Smith Colleges (NY)
Hofstra Univ. (NY)
Hollins Univ. (VA)
Hope College (MI)
Howard Univ. (DC)
Illinois Wesleyan Univ.
Indiana Univ.–Bloomington
John Carroll Univ. (OH)
Johns Hopkins Univ. (MD)
Kent State Univ. (OH)
Knox College (IL)
La Salle Univ. (PA)
Lawrence Univ. (WI)
Lehigh Univ. (PA)
Lenoir-Rhyne College (NC)
Louisiana State Univ.–Baton Rouge
Loyola College In Maryland
Loyola Marymount Univ. (CA)
Loyola Univ. Chicago
Loyola Univ. New Orleans
Luther College (IA)
Macalester College (MN)
Manhattanville College (NY)
Marquette Univ. (WI)
Mercer Univ. (GA)
Miami Univ.–Oxford (OH)
Michigan State Univ.
Middlebury College (VT)
Millsaps College (MS)
Monmouth College (IL)
Montclair State Univ. (NJ)
Moravian College (PA)
Mount Holyoke College (MA)
New York Univ.
North Central College (IL)
North Dakota State Univ.
Northwestern Univ. (IL)
Oberlin College (OH)
Ohio State Univ.–Columbus
Ohio Univ.
Ohio Wesleyan Univ.
Pacific Lutheran Univ. (WA)
Penn. State Univ.–Univ. Park
Pitzer College (CA)
Pomona College (CA)
Princeton Univ. (NJ)
Randolph-Macon College (VA)
Randolph-Macon Woman's College (VA)
Reed College (OR)
Rhodes College (TN)
Rice Univ. (TX)
Ripon College (WI)

Rockford College (IL)
Rollins College (FL)
Rutgers–New Brunswick (NJ)
Salisbury Univ. (MD)
Samford Univ. (AL)
San Diego State Univ.
San Francisco State Univ.
Santa Clara Univ. (CA)
Seattle Pacific Univ.
Seton Hall Univ. (NJ)
Sewanee–Univ. of the South (TN)
Siena College (NY)
Skidmore College (NY)
Southern Illinois Univ.–Carbondale
Southwest Missouri State Univ.
Southwestern Univ. (TX)
St. Anselm College (NH)
St. John's Univ. (MN)
St. Joseph College (CT)
St. Joseph's College (ME)
St. Joseph's Univ. (PA)
St. Louis Univ.
St. Mary's College of California
St. Michael's College (VT)
St. Olaf College (MN)
St. Peter's College (NJ)
Stanford Univ. (CA)
SUNY–Albany
SUNY–Binghamton
Swarthmore College (PA)
Sweet Briar College (VA)
Syracuse Univ. (NY)
Temple Univ. (PA)
Texas Tech Univ.
Transylvania Univ. (KY)
Trinity College (CT)
Truman State Univ. (MO)
Tufts Univ. (MA)
Tulane Univ. (LA)
Union College (NY)
Univ. at Buffalo–SUNY
Univ. of Akron (OH)
Univ. of Alabama
Univ. of Arizona
Univ. of Arkansas
Univ. of California–Berkeley
Univ. of California–Davis
Univ. of California–Irvine
Univ. of California–Los Angeles
Univ. of California–Riverside
Univ. of California–Santa Barbara
Univ. of Chicago
Univ. of Colorado–Boulder
Univ. of Connecticut
Univ. of Dallas
Univ. of Evansville (IN)
Univ. of Florida
Univ. of Georgia
Univ. of Hawaii–Manoa
Univ. of Houston
Univ. of Illinois–Chicago
Univ. of Ill.–Urbana-Champaign
Univ. of Iowa
Univ. of Kansas
Univ. of Kentucky
Univ. of Maine–Orono
Univ. of Mary Washington (VA)
Univ. of Maryland–College Park
Univ. of Massachusetts–Amherst
Univ. of Massachusetts–Boston
Univ. of Michigan–Ann Arbor

Univ. of Minnesota–Twin Cities
Univ. of Mississippi
Univ. of Missouri–Columbia
Univ. of Montana
Univ. of Nebraska–Lincoln
Univ. of New Hampshire
Univ. of New Mexico
Univ. of North Carolina–Asheville
Univ. of N.C.–Chapel Hill
Univ. of N.C.–Greensboro
Univ. of North Texas
Univ. of Notre Dame (IN)
Univ. of Oklahoma
Univ. of Oregon
Univ. of Pennsylvania
Univ. of Pittsburgh
Univ. of Puget Sound (WA)
Univ. of Rhode Island
Univ. of Richmond (VA)
Univ. of Rochester (NY)
Univ. of Scranton (PA)
Univ. of South Carolina–Columbia
Univ. of South Florida
Univ. of Southern California
Univ. of St. Thomas (MN)
Univ. of Tennessee
Univ. of Texas–Arlington
Univ. of Texas–Austin
Univ. of Texas–San Antonio
Univ. of Utah
Univ. of Vermont
Univ. of Virginia
Univ. of Washington
Univ. of Wisconsin–Madison
Univ. of Wisconsin–Milwaukee
Ursinus College (PA)
Valparaiso Univ. (IN)
Vanderbilt Univ. (TN)
Vassar College (NY)
Villanova Univ. (PA)
Virginia Wesleyan College
Wabash College (IN)
Wake Forest Univ. (NC)
Washington and Lee Univ. (VA)
Washington Univ. In St. Louis
Wayne State Univ. (MI)
Wellesley College (MA)
West Chester Univ. of Pennsylvania
Western Michigan Univ.
Wheaton College (IL)
Wheaton College (MA)
Whitman College (WA)
Willamette Univ. (OR)
Williams College (MA)
Wright State Univ. (OH)
Xavier Univ. (OH)
Yale Univ. (CT)
Yeshiva Univ. (NY)

Clinical Psychology

Auburn Univ. (AL)
Averett Univ. (VA)
California State Univ.–Dominguez Hills
Columbia Union College (MD)
Gallaudet Univ. (DC)
Husson College (ME)
Indiana Univ. of Pennsylvania
Keene State College (NH)

Liberty Univ. (VA)
Pacific Univ. (OR)
Seattle Pacific Univ.
St. Xavier Univ. (IL)
Tufts Univ. (MA)

Clinical/Medical Laboratory Science and Allied Professions

Gwynedd-Mercy College (PA)
Lake Superior State Univ. (MI)
Marywood Univ. (PA)
Union College (NE)
Univ. of Washington
Univ. of Wisconsin–Oshkosh

Cognitive Psychology and Psycholinguistics

Averett Univ. (VA)
California State Univ.–Stanislaus
Massachusetts Institute of Technology
Northwestern Univ. (IL)
Occidental College (CA)
Pomona College (CA)
Rice Univ. (TX)
Univ. of California–Los Angeles
Univ. of California–San Diego
Univ. of Connecticut
Univ. of Georgia
Univ. of Kansas
Univ. of Michigan–Ann Arbor
Vanderbilt Univ. (TN)
Wellesley College (MA)

Cognitive Science

Brown Univ. (RI)
Carnegie Mellon Univ. (PA)
Case Western Reserve Univ. (OH)
Dartmouth College (NH)
George Fox Univ. (OR)
Hampshire College (MA)
Lawrence Univ. (WI)
Lehigh Univ. (PA)
Rice Univ. (TX)
Univ. of California–Berkeley
Univ. of California–Los Angeles
Univ. of Pennsylvania
Univ. of Richmond (VA)
Univ. of Texas–Dallas
Vassar College (NY)
Wellesley College (MA)
Yale Univ. (CT)

Communication and Media Studies

Adelphi Univ. (NY)
Adrian College (MI)
Alabama State Univ.
Albion College (MI)
Albright College (PA)
Alcorn State Univ. (MS)
Alderson-Broaddus College (WV)

Alfred Univ. (NY)
Allegheny College (PA)
Alma College (MI)
Alvernia College (PA)
Alverno College (WI)
American International Coll. (MA)
American Univ. (DC)
Anderson College (SC)
Anderson Univ. (IN)
Andrews Univ. (MI)
Angelo State Univ. (TX)
Antioch College (OH)
Aquinas College (MI)
Arcadia Univ. (PA)
Arizona State Univ.
Arizona State Univ. West
Ashland Univ. (OH)
Auburn Univ.–Montgomery (AL)
Augsburg College (MN)
Augusta State Univ. (GA)
Augustana College (SD)
Aurora Univ. (IL)
Austin College (TX)
Austin Peay State Univ. (TN)
Avila Univ. (MO)
Azusa Pacific Univ. (CA)
Baker Univ. (KS)
Baldwin-Wallace College (OH)
Barber Scotia College (NC)
Barry Univ. (FL)
Barton College (NC)
Baylor Univ. (TX)
Belhaven College (MS)
Bellarmine Univ. (KY)
Bellevue Univ. (NE)
Belmont Univ. (TN)
Bemidji State Univ. (MN)
Benedict College (SC)
Benedictine College (KS)
Benedictine Univ. (IL)
Bennett College (NC)
Berea College (KY)
Bethany College (WV)
Bethel College (IN)
Bethel College (KS)
Bethel Univ. (MN)
Biola Univ. (CA)
Black Hills State Univ. (SD)
Blackburn College (IL)
Bloomsburg Univ. of Pennsylvania
Bluefield College (VA)
Bluffton Univ. (OH)
Boston Univ.
Bradley Univ. (IL)
Brenau Univ. (GA)
Brewton-Parker College (GA)
Bridgewater College (VA)
Brigham Young Univ.–Provo (UT)
Bryan College (TN)
Bryant College (RI)
Buena Vista Univ. (IA)
Buffalo State College
Butler Univ. (IN)
Cabrini College (PA)
Caldwell College (NJ)
California Baptist Univ.
California Lutheran Univ.
California State Univ.–Bakersfield
California State Univ.–Chico
California State Univ.–Dominguez Hills

California State Univ.–Fullerton
California State Univ.–Hayward
California State Univ.–Long Beach
California State Univ.–Los Angeles
California State Univ.–Sacramento
California State Univ.–San Bernardino
California State Univ.–Stanislaus
California Univ. of Pennsylvania
Calvin College (MI)
Campbell Univ. (NC)
Canisius College (NY)
Capital Univ. (OH)
Cardinal Stritch Univ. (WI)
Carlow College (PA)
Carnegie Mellon Univ. (PA)
Carroll College (WI)
Carson-Newman College (TN)
Carthage College (WI)
Catawba College (NC)
Catholic Univ. of America (DC)
Cazenovia College (NY)
Cedar Crest College (PA)
Centenary College (NJ)
Centenary College of Louisiana
Central Christian College (KS)
Central College (IA)
Central Connecticut State Univ.
Central Methodist Univ. (MO)
Central Missouri State Univ.
Central Washington Univ.
Chaminade Univ. of Honolulu
Champlain College (VT)
Chapman Univ. (CA)
Chatham College (PA)
Christopher Newport Univ. (VA)
Claflin Univ. (SC)
Clarion Univ. of Pennsylvania
Clark Atlanta Univ.
Clark Univ. (MA)
Clarke College (IA)
Clayton Coll. and State Univ. (GA)
Clearwater Christian College (FL)
Cleveland State Univ.
Coastal Carolina Univ. (SC)
Coe College (IA)
Coker College (SC)
Colby-Sawyer College (NH)
College Misericordia (PA)
College of Charleston (SC)
College of Mount St. Joseph (OH)
College of Mount St. Vincent (NY)
College of Notre Dame of Maryland
College of St. Catherine (MN)
College of St. Elizabeth (NJ)
College of St. Joseph (VT)
College of St. Scholastica (MN)
College of the Ozarks (MO)
College of Wooster (OH)
Colorado Christian Univ.
Colorado State Univ.–Pueblo
Columbia College (SC)
Columbia Union College (MD)
Concordia Coll.–Moorhead (MN)
Concordia Univ. (MI)
Concordia Univ. (CA)
Concordia Univ. (NE)
Concordia Univ.–Austin (TX)
Concordia Univ.–St. Paul (MN)
Cornell Univ. (NY)

Cornerstone Univ. (MI)
Cumberland College (KY)
CUNY–City College
CUNY–College of Staten Island
CUNY–Hunter College
CUNY–Lehman College
CUNY–Queens College
Curry College (MA)
Dakota Wesleyan Univ. (SD)
Dallas Baptist Univ.
David Lipscomb Univ. (TN)
Davis and Elkins College (WV)
Defiance College (OH)
Denison Univ. (OH)
Depaul Univ. (IL)
Depauw Univ. (IN)
Dickinson State Univ. (ND)
Dillard Univ. (LA)
Dominican Univ. (IL)
Dordt College (IA)
Dowling College (NY)
Drury Univ. (MO)
Duquesne Univ. (PA)
East Carolina Univ. (NC)
East Central Univ. (OK)
East Stroudsburg Univ. of Pennsylvania
East Tennessee State Univ.
East Texas Baptist Univ.
Eastern Connecticut State Univ.
Eastern Kentucky Univ.
Eastern Mennonite Univ. (VA)
Eastern Michigan Univ.
Eastern New Mexico Univ.
Eastern Univ. (PA)
Eastern Washington Univ.
Eckerd College (FL)
Edgewood College (WI)
Edinboro Univ. of Pennsylvania
Edward Waters College (FL)
Elizabeth City State Univ. (NC)
Elms College (College of Our Lady of the Elms) (MA)
Elon Univ. (NC)
Embry Riddle Aeronautical Univ. (FL)
Emmanuel College (GA)
Emmanuel College (MA)
Emory and Henry College (VA)
Emporia State Univ. (KS)
Endicott College (MA)
Evangel Univ. (MO)
Evergreen State College (WA)
Excelsior College (NY)
Fairfield Univ. (CT)
Fairleigh Dickinson Univ. (NJ)
Fairmont State Univ. (WV)
Ferris State Univ. (MI)
Fitchburg State College (MA)
Florida A&M Univ.
Florida Institute of Technology
Florida International Univ.
Florida State Univ.
Fontbonne Univ. (MO)
Fordham Univ. (NY)
Fort Hays State Univ. (KS)
Fort Lewis College (CO)
Francis Marion Univ. (SC)
Franciscan Univ. of Steubenville (OH)
Franklin Pierce College (NH)

Freed-Hardeman Univ. (TN)
Fresno Pacific Univ. (CA)
Frostburg State Univ. (MD)
Furman Univ. (SC)
Gallaudet Univ. (DC)
Gardner-Webb Univ. (NC)
Geneva College (PA)
George Fox Univ. (OR)
George Mason Univ. (VA)
George Washington Univ. (DC)
Georgetown College (KY)
Georgia Southern Univ.
Gordon College (MA)
Goucher College (MD)
Grace College and Seminary (IN)
Graceland Univ. (IA)
Grambling State Univ. (LA)
Grand Valley State Univ. (MI)
Grand View College (IA)
Green Mountain College (VT)
Greenville College (IL)
Gustavus Adolphus College (MN)
Hamilton College (NY)
Hamline Univ. (MN)
Hampshire College (MA)
Hannibal-Lagrange College (MO)
Hardin-Simmons Univ. (TX)
Harding Univ. (AR)
Hastings College (NE)
Hawaii Pacific Univ.
Heidelberg College (OH)
High Point Univ. (NC)
Hilbert College (NY)
Hiram College (OH)
Hobart and William Smith Colleges (NY)
Hofstra Univ. (NY)
Hollins Univ. (VA)
Hood College (MD)
Hope College (MI)
Houghton College (NY)
Houston Baptist Univ.
Howard Payne Univ. (TX)
Howard Univ. (DC)
Huntington College (IN)
Idaho State Univ.
Illinois State Univ.
Indiana State Univ.
Indiana Univ. East
Indiana Univ. Northwest
Indiana Univ. of Pennsylvania
Indiana Univ.–Kokomo
Indiana Univ.–South Bend
Indiana Univ.-Purdue Univ.–Fort Wayne
Indiana Univ.-Purdue Univ.–Indianapolis
Indiana Wesleyan Univ.
Iona College (NY)
Ithaca College (NY)
Jacksonville Univ. (FL)
James Madison Univ. (VA)
Jamestown College (ND)
John Carroll Univ. (OH)
Johnson C. Smith Univ. (NC)
Judson College (IL)
Juniata College (PA)
Kansas Wesleyan Univ.
Kean Univ. (NJ)
Keene State College (NH)
Kennesaw State Univ. (GA)

Kent State Univ. (OH)
Kentucky Wesleyan College
Keuka College (NY)
King's College (PA)
La Roche College (PA)
La Salle Univ. (PA)
La Sierra Univ. (CA)
Lake Erie College (OH)
Lake Forest College (IL)
Lamar Univ. (TX)
Lambuth Univ. (TN)
Lane College (TN)
Le Moyne College (NY)
Lees-Mcrae College (NC)
Lenoir-Rhyne College (NC)
Lewis and Clark College (OR)
Lewis Univ. (IL)
Lewis-Clark State College (ID)
Liberty Univ. (VA)
Lincoln Univ. (PA)
Lindenwood Univ. (MO)
Lindsey Wilson College (KY)
Linfield College (OR)
Long Island Univ.–Southampton College (NY)
Longwood Univ. (VA)
Loras College (IA)
Louisiana College
Louisiana State Univ.–Baton Rouge
Louisiana State Univ.–Shreveport
Loyola College In Maryland
Loyola Univ. Chicago
Loyola Univ. New Orleans
Lubbock Christian Univ. (TX)
Luther College (IA)
Lycoming College (PA)
Lynchburg College (VA)
Lyndon State College (VT)
Lynn Univ. (FL)
Madonna Univ. (MI)
Manchester College (IN)
Manhattan College (NY)
Mansfield Univ. of Pennsylvania
Marian College (IN)
Marian College of Fond Du Lac (WI)
Marietta College (OH)
Marist College (NY)
Marquette Univ. (WI)
Martin Univ. (IN)
Mary Baldwin College (VA)
Marylhurst Univ. (OR)
Marymount Manhattan College (NY)
Marymount Univ. (VA)
Maryville Univ. of St. Louis (MO)
Massachusetts Institute of Technology
Mcdaniel College (MD)
Mckendree College (IL)
Mcneese State Univ. (LA)
Medaille College (NY)
Mercer Univ. (GA)
Mercyhurst College (PA)
Meredith College (NC)
Merrimack College (MA)
Mesa State College (CO)
Messiah College (PA)
Methodist College (NC)
Miami Univ.–Oxford (OH)

Michigan State Univ.
Michigan Technological Univ.
Midamerica Nazarene Univ. (KS)
Middle Tennessee State Univ.
Midwestern State Univ. (TX)
Millersville Univ. of Pennsylvania
Milligan College (TN)
Millikin Univ. (IL)
Mills College (CA)
Minnesota State Univ.–Mankato
Minnesota State Univ.–Moorhead
Minot State Univ. (ND)
Mississippi College
Mississippi State Univ.
Mississippi Univ. For Women
Missouri Baptist College
Missouri Southern State Univ.
Missouri Valley College
Molloy College (NY)
Monmouth Univ. (NJ)
Montana State Univ.–Billings
Montana State Univ.–Northern
Montclair State Univ. (NJ)
Morehead State Univ. (KY)
Morehouse College (GA)
Morgan State Univ. (MD)
Morningside College (IA)
Mount Mary College (WI)
Mount St. Mary College (NY)
Mount St. Mary's Univ. (MD)
Mount Union College (OH)
Muhlenberg College (PA)
Muskingum College (OH)
National Univ. (CA)
Nazareth Coll. of Rochester (NY)
Nebraska Wesleyan Univ.
Neumann College (PA)
New Jersey City Univ.
New Mexico Highlands Univ.
New York Institute of Technology
New York Univ.
Newberry College (SC)
Niagara Univ. (NY)
Nicholls State Univ. (LA)
North Carolina A&T State Univ.
North Carolina Central Univ.
North Carolina State Univ.–Raleigh
North Central College (IL)
North Greenville College (SC)
North Park Univ. (IL)
Northeastern Univ. (MA)
Northern Arizona Univ.
Northern Illinois Univ.
Northern Michigan Univ.
Northwest Christian College (OR)
Northwest Nazarene Univ. (ID)
Northwestern College (MN)
Northwestern College (IA)
Northwestern Oklahoma State
    Univ.
Northwestern Univ. (IL)
Notre Dame College of Ohio
Notre Dame De Namur Univ. (CA)
Nova Southeastern Univ. (FL)
Nyack College (NY)
Oakland Univ. (MI)
Oakwood College (AL)
Ohio Dominican Univ.
Ohio Northern Univ.
Ohio State Univ.–Columbus
Ohio Univ.

Oklahoma Baptist Univ.
Oklahoma City Univ.
Oklahoma Wesleyan Univ.
Old Dominion Univ. (VA)
Olivet College (MI)
Oral Roberts Univ. (OK)
Oregon Institute of Technology
Oregon State Univ.
Otterbein College (OH)
Ouachita Baptist Univ. (AR)
Pace Univ. (NY)
Pacific Lutheran Univ. (WA)
Palm Beach Atlantic Univ. (FL)
Park Univ. (MO)
Paul Quinn College (TX)
Peace College (NC)
Penn. State Univ.–Univ. Park
Penn. State–Erie, The Behrend
    College
Pepperdine Univ. (CA)
Pfeiffer Univ. (NC)
Piedmont College (GA)
Pikeville College (KY)
Pine Manor College (MA)
Pittsburg State Univ. (KS)
Plymouth State Univ. (NH)
Point Loma Nazarene Univ. (CA)
Point Park Univ. (PA)
Pomona College (CA)
Portland State Univ. (OR)
Prairie View A&M Univ. (TX)
Prescott College (AZ)
Principia College (IL)
Purdue Univ.–Calumet (IN)
Purdue Univ.–North Central (IN)
Purdue Univ.–West Lafayette (IN)
Queens Univ. of Charlotte (NC)
Radford Univ. (VA)
Ramapo College of New Jersey
Randolph-Macon Woman's College
    (VA)
Regent Univ. (VA)
Regis College (MA)
Regis Univ. (CO)
Reinhardt College (GA)
Rensselaer Polytechnic Inst. (NY)
Rhode Island College
Richard Stockton College of New
    Jersey
Ripon College (WI)
Robert Morris Univ. (PA)
Roberts Wesleyan College (NY)
Rochester College (MI)
Rochester Institute of Tech. (NY)
Rockhurst Univ. (MO)
Rocky Mountain College (MT)
Roger Williams Univ. (RI)
Roosevelt Univ. (IL)
Rosemont College (PA)
Russell Sage College (NY)
Rutgers–New Brunswick (NJ)
Sacred Heart Univ. (CT)
Saginaw Valley State Univ. (MI)
Salem College (NC)
Salisbury Univ. (MD)
Salve Regina Univ. (RI)
Samford Univ. (AL)
San Diego State Univ.
San Jose State Univ. (CA)
Santa Clara Univ. (CA)
Scripps College (CA)

Seattle Pacific Univ.
Seattle Univ.
Seton Hall Univ. (NJ)
Seton Hill Univ. (PA)
Shaw Univ. (NC)
Shenandoah Univ. (VA)
Shepherd Univ. (WV)
Shorter College (GA)
Simmons College (MA)
Simpson College (IA)
Simpson Univ. (CA)
Slippery Rock Univ. of Pennsylvania
Sonoma State Univ. (CA)
Southeast Missouri State Univ.
Southeastern College of the
    Assemblies of God
Southeastern Louisiana Univ.
Southeastern Oklahoma State
    Univ.
Southern Connecticut State Univ.
Southern Illinois Univ.–Carbondale
Southern Illinois
    Univ.–Edwardsville
Southern New Hampshire Univ.
Southern Polytechnic State Univ.
    (GA)
Southern Univ. and A&M College
    (LA)
Southern Utah Univ.
Southern Wesleyan Univ. (SC)
Southwest Baptist Univ. (MO)
Southwest Minnesota State Univ.
    (MN)
Southwest Missouri State Univ.
Southwestern College (KS)
Southwestern Univ. (TX)
Spalding Univ. (KY)
Spring Arbor Univ. (MI)
Spring Hill College (AL)
Springfield College (MA)
St. Ambrose Univ. (IA)
St. Andrews Presbyterian College
    (NC)
St. Augustine's College (NC)
St. Edward's Univ. (TX)
St. Francis College (NY)
St. Francis Univ. (PA)
St. Gregory's Univ. (OK)
St. John Fisher College (NY)
St. John's Univ. (NY)
St. Joseph's College (IN)
St. Joseph's Univ. (PA)
St. Leo Univ. (FL)
St. Louis Univ.
St. Mary's College (IN)
St. Mary's College of California
St. Mary's Univ. of San Antonio
St. Norbert College (WI)
St. Peter's College (NJ)
St. Thomas Aquinas College (NY)
St. Thomas Univ. (FL)
St. Vincent College (PA)
St. Xavier Univ. (IL)
Stanford Univ. (CA)
Stephen F. Austin State Univ. (TX)
Stephens College (MO)
Sterling College (KS)
Stetson Univ. (FL)
Stonehill College (MA)
Suffolk Univ. (MA)
SUNY College–Brockport

SUNY College–Old Westbury
SUNY College–Oneonta
SUNY–Albany
SUNY–Fredonia
SUNY–Plattsburgh
SUNY–Purchase College
Susquehanna Univ. (PA)
Syracuse Univ. (NY)
Tabor College (KS)
Talladega College (AL)
Tarleton State Univ. (TX)
Taylor Univ. (IN)
Temple Univ. (PA)
Texas A&M International Univ.
Texas A&M Univ.–Corpus Christi
Texas A&M Univ.–Kingsville
Texas Christian Univ.
Texas Lutheran Univ.
Texas State Univ.–San Marcos
Texas Wesleyan Univ.
Thiel College (PA)
Thomas Edison State College (NJ)
Thomas More College (KY)
Tiffin Univ. (OH)
Toccoa Falls College (GA)
Towson Univ. (MD)
Trevecca Nazarene Univ. (TN)
Tri-State Univ. (IN)
Trinity Christian College (IL)
Trinity College (DC)
Truman State Univ. (MO)
Tulane Univ. (LA)
Tusculum College (TN)
Union College (NE)
Union Institute and Univ. (OH)
Univ. at Buffalo–SUNY
Univ. of Akron (OH)
Univ. of Alabama
Univ. of Alabama–Birmingham
Univ. of Alaska–Fairbanks
Univ. of Arkansas
Univ. of Arkansas–Little Rock
Univ. of Bridgeport (CT)
Univ. of California–Berkeley
Univ. of California–Santa Barbara
Univ. of Central Florida
Univ. of Central Oklahoma
Univ. of Colorado–Boulder
Univ. of Colorado–Colorado
    Springs
Univ. of Colorado–Denver
Univ. of Connecticut
Univ. of Dayton (OH)
Univ. of Denver
Univ. of Detroit Mercy
Univ. of Evansville (IN)
Univ. of Hartford (CT)
Univ. of Hawaii–Hilo
Univ. of Hawaii–Manoa
Univ. of Houston
Univ. of Illinois–Chicago
Univ. of Illinois–Springfield
Univ. of Illinois–Urbana-
    Champaign
Univ. of Indianapolis
Univ. of Iowa
Univ. of Kentucky
Univ. of La Verne (CA)
Univ. of Louisiana–Lafayette
Univ. of Louisiana–Monroe
Univ. of Louisville (KY)

Univ. of Maine–Orono
Univ. of Mary (ND)
Univ. of Mary Hardin-Baylor (TX)
Univ. of Maryland–College Park
Univ. of Maryland–Univ. College
Univ. of Massachusetts–Amherst
Univ. of Memphis
Univ. of Miami (FL)
Univ. of Michigan–Ann Arbor
Univ. of Michigan–Dearborn
Univ. of Michigan–Flint
Univ. of Minnesota–Crookston
Univ. of Minnesota–Duluth
Univ. of Missouri–Columbia
Univ. of Missouri–St. Louis
Univ. of Montana
Univ. of Nebraska–Lincoln
Univ. of Nebraska–Omaha
Univ. of Nevada–Las Vegas
Univ. of Nevada–Reno
Univ. of New Hampshire
Univ. of New Haven (CT)
Univ. of New Orleans
Univ. of North Carolina–Asheville
Univ. of N.C.–Chapel Hill
Univ. of North Carolina–Charlotte
Univ. of N.C.–Greensboro
Univ. of North Carolina–Pembroke
Univ. of North Dakota
Univ. of North Florida
Univ. of Northern Colorado
Univ. of Northern Iowa
Univ. of Oklahoma
Univ. of Oregon
Univ. of Pennsylvania
Univ. of Pittsburgh
Univ. of Pittsburgh–Johnstown
Univ. of Portland (OR)
Univ. of Puget Sound (WA)
Univ. of Rhode Island
Univ. of Rio Grande (OH)
Univ. of San Diego
Univ. of San Francisco
Univ. of Science and Arts of
    Oklahoma
Univ. of Scranton (PA)
Univ. of Sioux Falls (SD)
Univ. of South Alabama
Univ. of South Carolina–Aiken
Univ. of South Carolina–Upstate
Univ. of South Dakota
Univ. of South Florida
Univ. of Southern California
Univ. of Southern Indiana
Univ. of Southern Maine
Univ. of Southern Mississippi
Univ. of St. Francis (IN)
Univ. of St. Francis (IL)
Univ. of St. Mary (KS)
Univ. of St. Thomas (MN)
Univ. of St. Thomas (TX)
Univ. of Tampa (FL)
Univ. of Tennessee–Chattanooga
Univ. of Tennessee–Martin
Univ. of Texas of the Permian Basin
Univ. of Texas–Austin
Univ. of Texas–Brownsville
Univ. of Texas–El Paso
Univ. of Texas–Pan American
Univ. of Texas–San Antonio
Univ. of the Arts (PA)

Univ. of the Incarnate Word (TX)
Univ. of the Ozarks (AR)
Univ. of the Pacific (CA)
Univ. of Toledo (OH)
Univ. of Tulsa (OK)
Univ. of Utah
Univ. of Virginia–Wise
Univ. of Washington
Univ. of West Florida
Univ. of Wisconsin–Eau Claire
Univ. of Wisconsin–La Crosse
Univ. of Wisconsin–Madison
Univ. of Wisconsin–Milwaukee
Univ. of Wisconsin–Oshkosh
Univ. of Wisconsin–Platteville
Univ. of Wisconsin–River Falls
Univ. of Wisconsin–Stevens Point
Univ. of Wisconsin–Superior
Univ. of Wyoming
Upper Iowa Univ.
Urbana Univ. (OH)
Ursinus College (PA)
Utica College (NY)
Valdosta State Univ. (GA)
Valley City State Univ. (ND)
Valparaiso Univ. (IN)
Vanderbilt Univ. (TN)
Villanova Univ. (PA)
Virginia Commonwealth Univ.
Virginia State Univ.
Virginia Tech
Wake Forest Univ. (NC)
Waldorf College (IA)
Walsh Univ. (OH)
Warner Southern College (FL)
Wartburg College (IA)
Washburn Univ. (KS)
Washington State Univ.
Wayland Baptist Univ. (TX)
Wayne State College (NE)
Wayne State Univ. (MI)
Waynesburg College (PA)
Weber State Univ. (UT)
Webster Univ. (MO)
Wesley College (DE)
West Chester Univ. of Pennsylvania
West Liberty State College (WV)
West Virginia Wesleyan College
Western Baptist College (OR)
Western Carolina Univ. (NC)
Western Connecticut State Univ.
Western Illinois Univ.
Western Kentucky Univ.
Western Michigan Univ.
Western New England College (MA)
Western State College of Colorado
Western Washington Univ.
Westfield State College (MA)
Westminster College (PA)
Westminster College (UT)
Westmont College (CA)
Wheaton College (IL)
Whitman College (WA)
Whitworth College (WA)
Wichita State Univ. (KS)
Widener Univ. (PA)
Wilberforce Univ. (OH)
Wiley College (TX)
Wilkes Univ. (PA)
William Carey College (MS)

William Jewell College (MO)
William Paterson Univ. of New Jersey
Wilson College (PA)
Wingate Univ. (NC)
Winston-Salem State Univ. (NC)
Winthrop Univ. (SC)
Wisconsin Lutheran College
Wittenberg Univ. (OH)
Woodbury Univ. (CA)
Worcester State College (MA)
Wright State Univ. (OH)
Yeshiva Univ. (NY)
York College of Pennsylvania
Youngstown State Univ. (OH)

Communication Disorders Sciences and Services

Abilene Christian Univ. (TX)
Adelphi Univ. (NY)
Andrews Univ. (MI)
Appalachian State Univ. (NC)
Arizona State Univ.
Arkansas State Univ.
Armstrong Atlantic State Univ. (GA)
Auburn Univ. (AL)
Augustana College (SD)
Augustana College (IL)
Baldwin-Wallace College (OH)
Ball State Univ. (IN)
Baylor Univ. (TX)
Biola Univ. (CA)
Bloomsburg Univ. of Pennsylvania
Boston Univ.
Bowling Green State Univ. (OH)
Brescia Univ. (KY)
Bridgewater State College (MA)
Brigham Young Univ.–Provo (UT)
Butler Univ. (IN)
California State Univ.–Chico
California State Univ.–Fresno
California State Univ.–Fullerton
California State Univ.–Hayward
California State Univ.–Long Beach
California State Univ.–Los Angeles
California State Univ.–Sacramento
California Univ. of Pennsylvania
Calvin College (MI)
Case Western Reserve Univ. (OH)
Central Michigan Univ.
Central Missouri State Univ.
Clarion Univ. of Pennsylvania
Cleveland State Univ.
College Misericordia (PA)
College of St. Rose (NY)
College of Wooster (OH)
Columbia College (SC)
CUNY–Brooklyn College
CUNY–Hunter College
CUNY–Lehman College
CUNY–Queens College
Delta State Univ. (MS)
Duquesne Univ. (PA)
East Carolina Univ. (NC)
East Stroudsburg Univ. of Pennsylvania
Eastern Illinois Univ.
Eastern Kentucky Univ.

Eastern Michigan Univ.
Eastern New Mexico Univ.
Eastern Washington Univ.
Edinboro Univ. of Pennsylvania
Elmhurst College (IL)
Elmira College (NY)
Elms College (College of Our Lady of the Elms) (MA)
Emerson College (MA)
Florida State Univ.
Fontbonne Univ. (MO)
Fort Hays State Univ. (KS)
Geneva College (PA)
George Washington Univ. (DC)
Grambling State Univ. (LA)
Hampton Univ. (VA)
Hardin-Simmons Univ. (TX)
Harding Univ. (AR)
Hofstra Univ. (NY)
Howard Univ. (DC)
Idaho State Univ.
Illinois State Univ.
Indiana State Univ.
Indiana Univ. of Pennsylvania
Indiana Univ.–Bloomington
Indiana Univ.-Purdue Univ.–Fort Wayne
Iona College (NY)
Ithaca College (NY)
James Madison Univ. (VA)
Kansas State Univ.
Kent State Univ. (OH)
La Salle Univ. (PA)
Lamar Univ. (TX)
Lambuth Univ. (TN)
Long Island Univ.–Brooklyn (NY)
Long Island Univ.–C.W. Post Campus (NY)
Longwood Univ. (VA)
Louisiana State Univ.–Baton Rouge
Louisiana State Univ.–Shreveport
Louisiana Tech Univ.
Loyola College In Maryland
Marquette Univ. (WI)
Marshall Univ. (WV)
Marymount Manhattan College (NY)
Maryville College (TN)
Marywood Univ. (PA)
Miami Univ.–Oxford (OH)
Michigan State Univ.
Minnesota State Univ.–Mankato
Minnesota State Univ.–Moorhead
Minot State Univ. (ND)
Mississippi Univ. For Women
Molloy College (NY)
Murray State Univ. (KY)
Nazareth College of Rochester (NY)
Nicholls State Univ. (LA)
Northeastern State Univ. (OK)
Northeastern Univ. (MA)
Northern Illinois Univ.
Northern Michigan Univ.
Northwestern Univ. (IL)
Ohio State Univ.–Columbus
Ohio Univ.
Oklahoma State Univ.
Old Dominion Univ. (VA)
Ouachita Baptist Univ. (AR)
Our Lady of the Lake Univ. (TX)

Pace Univ. (NY)
Penn. State Univ.–Univ. Park
Portland State Univ. (OR)
Purdue Univ.–West Lafayette (IN)
Radford Univ. (VA)
Richard Stockton College of New Jersey
Rockhurst Univ. (MO)
San Diego State Univ.
San Francisco State Univ.
San Jose State Univ. (CA)
Shaw Univ. (NC)
South Carolina State Univ.
Southeast Missouri State Univ.
Southern Illinois Univ.–Carbondale
Southern Illinois Univ.–Edwardsville
Southern Univ. and A&M College (LA)
Southwest Missouri State Univ.
St. Cloud State Univ. (MN)
St. John's Univ. (NY)
St. Louis Univ.
St. Xavier Univ. (IL)
State Univ. of West Georgia
Stephen F. Austin State Univ. (TX)
SUNY College of Arts and Sciences–Geneseo
SUNY–Fredonia
SUNY–Plattsburgh
Syracuse Univ. (NY)
Temple Univ. (PA)
Tennessee State Univ.
Texas A&M Univ.–Kingsville
Texas Christian Univ.
Texas State Univ.–San Marcos
Texas Woman's Univ.
Thiel College (PA)
Towson Univ. (MD)
Truman State Univ. (MO)
Univ. at Buffalo–SUNY
Univ. of Akron (OH)
Univ. of Alabama
Univ. of Arizona
Univ. of Arkansas
Univ. of Central Arkansas
Univ. of Central Florida
Univ. of Central Oklahoma
Univ. of Colorado–Boulder
Univ. of Florida
Univ. of Georgia
Univ. of Hawaii–Manoa
Univ. of Houston
Univ. of Ill.–Urbana-Champaign
Univ. of Iowa
Univ. of Kansas
Univ. of Kentucky
Univ. of Louisiana–Lafayette
Univ. of Louisiana–Monroe
Univ. of Maine–Orono
Univ. of Maryland–College Park
Univ. of Massachusetts–Amherst
Univ. of Michigan–Ann Arbor
Univ. of Minnesota–Duluth
Univ. of Minnesota–Twin Cities
Univ. of Mississippi
Univ. of Missouri–Columbia
Univ. of Montevallo (AL)
Univ. of Nebraska–Kearney
Univ. of Nebraska–Lincoln
Univ. of Nevada–Reno

Univ. of New Hampshire
Univ. of New Mexico
Univ. of N.C.–Greensboro
Univ. of North Dakota
Univ. of North Texas
Univ. of Northern Colorado
Univ. of Northern Iowa
Univ. of Oklahoma
Univ. of Oregon
Univ. of Pittsburgh
Univ. of Redlands (CA)
Univ. of Rhode Island
Univ. of Science and Arts of Oklahoma
Univ. of South Alabama
Univ. of South Dakota
Univ. of South Florida
Univ. of Southern Mississippi
Univ. of Tennessee
Univ. of Texas–Austin
Univ. of Texas–Dallas
Univ. of Texas–El Paso
Univ. of Texas–Pan American
Univ. of the District of Columbia
Univ. of the Pacific (CA)
Univ. of Toledo (OH)
Univ. of Tulsa (OK)
Univ. of Utah
Univ. of Vermont
Univ. of Virginia
Univ. of Washington
Univ. of Wisconsin–Eau Claire
Univ. of Wisconsin–Madison
Univ. of Wisconsin–Milwaukee
Univ. of Wisconsin–River Falls
Univ. of Wisconsin–Stevens Point
Univ. of Wisconsin–Whitewater
Univ. of Wyoming
Utah State Univ.
Valdosta State Univ. (GA)
Washington State Univ.
Wayne State Univ. (MI)
West Chester Univ. of Pennsylvania
West Texas A&M Univ.
West Virginia Univ.
Western Carolina Univ. (NC)
Western Illinois Univ.
Western Michigan Univ.
Western Washington Univ.
Wichita State Univ. (KS)
Winthrop Univ. (SC)
Worcester State College (MA)
Yeshiva Univ. (NY)

Communication, Journalism, and Related Programs

Abilene Christian Univ. (TX)
Albertus Magnus College (CT)
Aquinas College (MI)
Arkansas State Univ.
Austin College (TX)
Berry College (GA)
Bethel College (IN)
Bowling Green State Univ. (OH)
Bridgewater State College (MA)
Buena Vista Univ. (IA)
Carlow College (PA)
Central Methodist Univ. (MO)

Central Missouri State Univ.
Champlain College (VT)
Chestnut Hill College (PA)
College of Santa Fe (NM)
Columbia College (SC)
Concordia Univ. (NE)
Culver-Stockton College (MO)
CUNY–Brooklyn College
Dana College (NE)
Dominican Univ. of California (CA)
Elmhurst College (IL)
Flagler College (FL)
Fort Hays State Univ. (KS)
Friends Univ. (KS)
Hope College (MI)
Humboldt State Univ. (CA)
Illinois Institute of Technology
Immaculata Univ. (PA)
Indiana Univ. Northwest
Ithaca College (NY)
Judson College (IL)
King College (TN)
Lehigh Univ. (PA)
Malone College (OH)
Marquette Univ. (WI)
Mary Baldwin College (VA)
Mercer Univ. (GA)
Michigan Technological Univ.
Milwaukee School of Engineering
Mount St. Mary College (NY)
Norfolk State Univ. (VA)
Northern Arizona Univ.
Northwest Christian College (OR)
Northwest Missouri State Univ.
Norwich Univ. (VT)
Ohio State Univ.–Columbus
Ohio Univ.
Oral Roberts Univ. (OK)
Our Lady of the Lake Univ. (TX)
Pace Univ. (NY)
Pacific Univ. (OR)
Patten College (CA)
Penn. State Univ.–Univ. Park
Pepperdine Univ. (CA)
Quincy Univ. (IL)
Rivier College (NH)
Rochester Institute of Tech. (NY)
San Diego State Univ.
St. Mary's College of California
St. Mary's Univ. of San Antonio
SUNY College of Arts and
　Sciences–Geneseo
SUNY–Fredonia
Syracuse Univ. (NY)
Trevecca Nazarene Univ. (TN)
Tulane Univ. (LA)
Univ. of Akron (OH)
Univ. of Findlay (OH)
Univ. of Miami (FL)
Univ. of Minnesota–Twin Cities
Univ. of Mississippi
Univ. of Missouri–Kansas City
Univ. of the Arts (PA)
Univ. of Wisconsin–Green Bay
Virginia Intermont College
Virginia Wesleyan College
Waldorf College (IA)
Washington Univ. In St. Louis
Webster Univ. (MO)
Wesleyan College (GA)
West Virginia Univ.

Western Michigan Univ.
Wingate Univ. (NC)
Wisconsin Lutheran College

Communications Technologies/Technicians and Support Services

Alverno College (WI)
California State Univ.–Monterey
　Bay
Chestnut Hill College (PA)
Fort Hays State Univ. (KS)
Framingham State College (MA)
Hampton Univ. (VA)
Indiana Univ.–Bloomington
Touro College (NY)
Univ. of Wisconsin–Platteville

Communications Technology/Technician

California State Univ.–Monterey
　Bay
Cedarville Univ. (OH)
College of St. Rose (NY)
East Stroudsburg Univ. of
　Pennsylvania
Eastern Michigan Univ.
Hastings College (NE)
Jackson State Univ. (MS)
Kent State Univ. (OH)
Lawrence Technological Univ. (MI)
Lesley Univ. (MA)
Lyndon State College (VT)
Marywood Univ. (PA)
Minot State Univ. (ND)
New York Univ.
San Diego State Univ.
Southern Adventist Univ. (TN)
Suffolk Univ. (MA)
Texas A&M Univ.–College Station

Community Organization and Advocacy

Albertus Magnus College (CT)
Alverno College (WI)
Aquinas College (MI)
Black Hills State Univ. (SD)
Cornell Univ. (NY)
CUNY–Brooklyn College
Delta State Univ. (MS)
Elmira College (NY)
Lynn Univ. (FL)
Mercer Univ. (GA)
New Mexico State Univ.
Northern State Univ. (SD)
Northwestern Univ. (IL)
Pace Univ. (NY)
Portland State Univ. (OR)
Prescott College (AZ)
Providence College (RI)
Southern Arkansas Univ.
Springfield College (MA)
St. Leo Univ. (FL)
St. Martin's College (WA)
St. Thomas Univ. (FL)

SUNY–Empire State College
Thomas Edison State College (NJ)
Univ. of Alaska–Fairbanks
Univ. of Bridgeport (CT)
Univ. of Massachusetts–Boston
Univ. of New Mexico
Univ. of Tennessee
West Virginia Univ. Institute of
　Technology
Western Illinois Univ.

Community Psychology

Clayton Coll. and State Univ. (GA)
Montana State Univ.–Billings
National-Louis Univ. (IL)
New York Institute of Technology
North Georgia College and State
　Univ.
Northern Michigan Univ.
Northwestern Univ. (IL)
Pikeville College (KY)
Seton Hill Univ. (PA)
Southern Nazarene Univ. (OK)
Univ. of St. Mary (KS)
Walsh Univ. (OH)

Comparative Linguistics and Related Language Studies and Services

Albright College (PA)
Antioch College (OH)
Arkansas Tech Univ.
Assumption College (MA)
Auburn Univ.–Montgomery (AL)
Austin Peay State Univ. (TN)
Barnard College (NY)
Baylor Univ. (TX)
Beloit College (WI)
Benedict College (SC)
Benedictine Univ. (IL)
Bennington College (VT)
Boise State Univ. (ID)
Boston Univ.
Brandeis Univ. (MA)
Brigham Young Univ.–Provo (UT)
Brown Univ. (RI)
Bryn Mawr College (PA)
Cal Poly–San Luis Obispo
California State Univ.–Fresno
California State Univ.–Fullerton
California State Univ.–Long Beach
California State Univ.–Northridge
Cameron Univ. (OK)
Carnegie Mellon Univ. (PA)
Case Western Reserve Univ. (OH)
Centenary College of Louisiana
Central Washington Univ.
Clark Univ. (MA)
Cleveland State Univ.
College of Mount St. Vincent (NY)
College of Notre Dame of
　Maryland
College of the Holy Cross (MA)
College of William and Mary (VA)
College of Wooster (OH)
Colorado College
Colorado State Univ.

Colorado State Univ.–Pueblo
Columbia Univ. (NY)
Converse College (SC)
Cornell Univ. (NY)
CUNY–Baruch College
CUNY–Brooklyn College
CUNY–City College
CUNY–Hunter College
CUNY–Lehman College
CUNY–Queens College
Dartmouth College (NH)
Delta State Univ. (MS)
Dowling College (NY)
Duke Univ. (NC)
Duquesne Univ. (PA)
Earlham College (IN)
East Tennessee State Univ.
Eastern Illinois Univ.
Eastern Michigan Univ.
Eckerd College (FL)
Elmira College (NY)
Emporia State Univ. (KS)
Florida Atlantic Univ.
Fordham Univ. (NY)
Fort Hays State Univ. (KS)
Framingham State College (MA)
Francis Marion Univ. (SC)
Frostburg State Univ. (MD)
Gallaudet Univ. (DC)
Gannon Univ. (PA)
George Mason Univ. (VA)
Georgetown Univ. (DC)
Gordon College (MA)
Grace College and Seminary (IN)
Graceland Univ. (IA)
Hamilton College (NY)
Hampshire College (MA)
Hartwick College (NY)
Harvard Univ. (MA)
Hastings College (NE)
Haverford College (PA)
Heidelberg College (OH)
High Point Univ. (NC)
Hobart and William Smith Colleges
　(NY)
Hofstra Univ. (NY)
Indiana Univ. Northwest
Indiana Univ.–Bloomington
Iowa State Univ.
Jacksonville State Univ. (AL)
James Madison Univ. (VA)
Johns Hopkins Univ. (MD)
Judson College (AL)
Juniata College (PA)
Kansas State Univ.
King College (TN)
Knox College (IL)
Lambuth Univ. (TN)
Lawrence Univ. (WI)
Lewis and Clark College (OR)
Long Island Univ.–C.W. Post
　Campus (NY)
Longwood Univ. (VA)
Loras College (IA)
Louisiana College
Lycoming College (PA)
Macalester College (MN)
Manhattan College (NY)
Marian College (IN)
Marian College of Fond Du Lac
　(WI)

Marquette Univ. (WI)
Marshall Univ. (WV)
Massachusetts Institute of
　Technology
Mercyhurst College (PA)
Metropolitan State College of
　Denver
Miami Univ.–Oxford (OH)
Michigan State Univ.
Middle Tennessee State Univ.
Mills College (CA)
Minnesota State Univ.–Moorhead
Minot State Univ. (ND)
Mississippi College
Mississippi State Univ.
Monmouth Univ. (NJ)
Montana State Univ.–Bozeman
Montclair State Univ. (NJ)
Nazareth College of Rochester
　(NY)
New Mexico State Univ.
New York Univ.
Newberry College (SC)
Northeastern Univ. (MA)
Northern Arizona Univ.
Northwestern Univ. (IL)
Oakland Univ. (MI)
Ohio State Univ.–Columbus
Ohio Univ.
Old Dominion Univ. (VA)
Pace Univ. (NY)
Pacific Univ. (OR)
Penn. State Univ.–Univ. Park
Pittsburg State Univ. (KS)
Pitzer College (CA)
Portland State Univ. (OR)
Presbyterian College (SC)
Princeton Univ. (NJ)
Purdue Univ.–West Lafayette (IN)
Radford Univ. (VA)
Ramapo College of New Jersey
Reed College (OR)
Rice Univ. (TX)
Richard Stockton College of New
　Jersey
Ripon College (WI)
Roosevelt Univ. (IL)
Rosemont College (PA)
Rutgers–New Brunswick (NJ)
Salisbury Univ. (MD)
Samford Univ. (AL)
San Diego State Univ.
San Francisco State Univ.
San Jose State Univ. (CA)
Seattle Univ.
Seton Hall Univ. (NJ)
Southern Adventist Univ. (TN)
Southern Illinois Univ.–Carbondale
Southern Illinois
　Univ.–Edwardsville
Spelman College (GA)
St. Ambrose Univ. (IA)
St. Louis Univ.
St. Mary's College of Maryland
St. Peter's College (NJ)
Stanford Univ. (CA)
Stonehill College (MA)
Suffolk Univ. (MA)
SUNY College of Arts and
　Sciences–Geneseo
SUNY–Albany

SUNY–Binghamton
SUNY–Purchase College
SUNY–Stony Brook
Swarthmore College (PA)
Sweet Briar College (VA)
Syracuse Univ. (NY)
Temple Univ. (PA)
Tennessee State Univ.
Thomas Edison State College (NJ)
Tufts Univ. (MA)
Tulane Univ. (LA)
Union College (NY)
Univ. at Buffalo–SUNY
Univ. of Alabama–Birmingham
Univ. of Alabama–Huntsville
Univ. of Alaska–Anchorage
Univ. of Alaska–Fairbanks
Univ. of Arizona
Univ. of California–Berkeley
Univ. of California–Davis
Univ. of California–Irvine
Univ. of California–Los Angeles
Univ. of California–Riverside
Univ. of California–San Diego
Univ. of California–Santa Barbara
Univ. of California–Santa Cruz
Univ. of Central Florida
Univ. of Central Oklahoma
Univ. of Chicago
Univ. of Colorado–Boulder
Univ. of Connecticut
Univ. of Dayton (OH)
Univ. of Delaware
Univ. of Florida
Univ. of Georgia
Univ. of Hartford (CT)
Univ. of Hawaii–Hilo
Univ. of Ill.–Urbana-Champaign
Univ. of Iowa
Univ. of Kansas
Univ. of Kentucky
Univ. of La Verne (CA)
Univ. of Louisiana–Lafayette
Univ. of Maine–Fort Kent
Univ. of Maine–Orono
Univ. of Mary Washington (VA)
Univ. of Maryland–Baltimore County
Univ. of Maryland–College Park
Univ. of Massachusetts–Amherst
Univ. of Massachusetts–Lowell
Univ. of Memphis
Univ. of Michigan–Ann Arbor
Univ. of Minnesota–Twin Cities
Univ. of Mississippi
Univ. of Missouri–Columbia
Univ. of Montana
Univ. of Montevallo (AL)
Univ. of Nevada–Las Vegas
Univ. of New Hampshire
Univ. of New Mexico
Univ. of North Alabama
Univ. of N.C.–Chapel Hill
Univ. of North Dakota
Univ. of Northern Colorado
Univ. of Northern Iowa
Univ. of Oklahoma
Univ. of Oregon
Univ. of Pennsylvania
Univ. of Pittsburgh
Univ. of Rhode Island

Univ. of Rochester (NY)
Univ. of San Francisco
Univ. of South Alabama
Univ. of South Carolina–Columbia
Univ. of Southern California
Univ. of Southern Maine
Univ. of Southern Mississippi
Univ. of Tennessee–Chattanooga
Univ. of Texas–Arlington
Univ. of Texas–Austin
Univ. of Texas–El Paso
Univ. of Texas–Tyler
Univ. of Toledo (OH)
Univ. of Utah
Univ. of Virginia
Univ. of Virginia–Wise
Univ. of Washington
Univ. of Wisconsin–Madison
Univ. of Wisconsin–Milwaukee
Univ. of Wisconsin–Platteville
Univ. of Wisconsin–River Falls
Virginia Commonwealth Univ.
Virginia Military Institute
Virginia Tech
Virginia Wesleyan College
Washington and Lee Univ. (VA)
Washington College (MD)
Washington State Univ.
Washington Univ. In St. Louis
Wayne State College (NE)
Wayne State Univ. (MI)
Weber State Univ. (UT)
West Chester Univ. of Pennsylvania
West Virginia Univ.
Western Washington Univ.
Westmont College (CA)
Whitman College (WA)
Wichita State Univ. (KS)
Willamette Univ. (OR)
William Woods Univ. (MO)
Williams College (MA)
Winthrop Univ. (SC)
Yale Univ. (CT)
York College of Pennsylvania
Youngstown State Univ. (OH)

Computer and Information Sciences

Adelphi Univ. (NY)
Alabama Agricultural and Mechanical Univ.
Albany State Univ. (GA)
Albright College (PA)
Alcorn State Univ. (MS)
Alvernia College (PA)
Alverno College (WI)
American International College (MA)
Andrews Univ. (MI)
Angelo State Univ. (TX)
Aquinas College (MI)
Arcadia Univ. (PA)
Arkansas State Univ.
Arkansas Tech Univ.
Armstrong Atlantic State Univ. (GA)
Atlantic Union College (MA)
Auburn Univ. (AL)
Augusta State Univ. (GA)

Augustana College (SD)
Austin Peay State Univ. (TN)
Avila Univ. (MO)
Azusa Pacific Univ. (CA)
Babson College (MA)
Ball State Univ. (IN)
Barton College (NC)
Belhaven College (MS)
Bellarmine Univ. (KY)
Bellevue Univ. (NE)
Belmont Abbey College (NC)
Belmont Univ. (TN)
Benedict College (SC)
Benedictine Univ. (IL)
Bennett College (NC)
Bentley College (MA)
Bethel College (IN)
Bethel Univ. (MN)
Biola Univ. (CA)
Bloomfield College (NJ)
Bloomsburg Univ. of Pennsylvania
Bluefield State College (WV)
Bluffton Univ. (OH)
Boise State Univ. (ID)
Bowie State Univ. (MD)
Bowling Green State Univ. (OH)
Bradley Univ. (IL)
Brigham Young Univ.–Hawaii
Brigham Young Univ.–Provo (UT)
Brown Univ. (RI)
Bryan College (TN)
Bryant College (RI)
Butler Univ. (IN)
Cabrini College (PA)
Caldwell College (NJ)
California Lutheran Univ.
California State Polytechnic Univ.–Pomona
California State Univ.–Chico
California State Univ.–Dominguez Hills
California State Univ.–Fresno
California State Univ.–Los Angeles
California State Univ.–Monterey Bay
California State Univ.–Northridge
California State Univ.–Sacramento
California State Univ.–San Bernardino
California State Univ.–Stanislaus
California Univ. of Pennsylvania
Calvin College (MI)
Campbellsville Univ. (KY)
Capitol College (MD)
Carroll College (WI)
Carson-Newman College (TN)
Catawba College (NC)
Cedar Crest College (PA)
Cedarville Univ. (OH)
Central College (IA)
Central Connecticut State Univ.
Central Michigan Univ.
Central Missouri State Univ.
Central Washington Univ.
Chaminade Univ. of Honolulu
Chapman Univ. (CA)
Chestnut Hill College (PA)
Cheyney Univ. of Pennsylvania
Christian Brothers Univ. (TN)
Christopher Newport Univ. (VA)
Clarion Univ. of Pennsylvania

Clark Atlanta Univ.
Clarke College (IA)
Clayton Coll. and State Univ. (GA)
Cleveland State Univ.
Coastal Carolina Univ. (SC)
College Misericordia (PA)
College of Charleston (SC)
College of Mount St. Joseph (OH)
College of Mount St. Vincent (NY)
College of New Jersey
College of Notre Dame of Maryland
College of Santa Fe (NM)
College of St. Joseph (VT)
College of St. Rose (NY)
College of St. Scholastica (MN)
College of the Holy Cross (MA)
College of the Ozarks (MO)
College of William and Mary (VA)
Colorado Christian Univ.
Colorado State Univ.
Columbia College (SC)
Columbia College (MO)
Columbia Univ. (NY)
Concordia Coll.–Moorhead (MN)
Concordia Univ. (CA)
Concordia Univ.–River Forest (IL)
Converse College (SC)
Coppin State Univ. (MD)
Cornell Univ. (NY)
Covenant College (GA)
Cumberland College (KY)
Cumberland Univ. (TN)
CUNY–Baruch College
CUNY–Brooklyn College
CUNY–City College
CUNY–Hunter College
CUNY–Lehman College
CUNY–Queens College
Curry College (MA)
Dakota State Univ. (SD)
Dallas Baptist Univ.
Davenport Univ. (MI)
David Lipscomb Univ. (TN)
Defiance College (OH)
Delaware State Univ.
Denison Univ. (OH)
Depaul Univ. (IL)
Depauw Univ. (IN)
Dickinson College (PA)
Dickinson State Univ. (ND)
Dominican Coll. of Blauvelt (NY)
Dordt College (IA)
Dowling College (NY)
Drury Univ. (MO)
Duke Univ. (NC)
East Stroudsburg Univ. of Pennsylvania
East Tennessee State Univ.
East-West Univ. (IL)
Eastern Connecticut State Univ.
Eastern Illinois Univ.
Eastern Kentucky Univ.
Eastern Michigan Univ.
Eastern Nazarene College (MA)
Eastern New Mexico Univ.
Eastern Oregon Univ.
Eastern Washington Univ.
Edgewood College (WI)
Edinboro Univ. of Pennsylvania
Edward Waters College (FL)

Elizabeth City State Univ. (NC)
Elmhurst College (IL)
Elms College (College of Our Lady of the Elms) (MA)
Elon Univ. (NC)
Emmanuel College (GA)
Emory and Henry College (VA)
Emory Univ. (GA)
Emporia State Univ. (KS)
Eureka College (IL)
Evangel Univ. (MO)
Evergreen State College (WA)
Excelsior College (NY)
Fairfield Univ. (CT)
Fairleigh Dickinson Univ. (NJ)
Fairmont State Univ. (WV)
Faulkner Univ. (AL)
Felician College (NJ)
Ferris State Univ. (MI)
Ferrum College (VA)
Fitchburg State College (MA)
Florida A&M Univ.
Florida Atlantic Univ.
Florida Gulf Coast Univ.
Florida International Univ.
Florida Memorial College
Florida State Univ.
Fontbonne Univ. (MO)
Fordham Univ. (NY)
Fort Hays State Univ. (KS)
Fort Lewis College (CO)
Fort Valley State Univ. (GA)
Framingham State College (MA)
Francis Marion Univ. (SC)
Franciscan Univ. of Steubenville (OH)
Franklin College (IN)
Freed-Hardeman Univ. (TN)
Friends Univ. (KS)
Frostburg State Univ. (MD)
Furman Univ. (SC)
Gallaudet Univ. (DC)
Gannon Univ. (PA)
Geneva College (PA)
George Fox Univ. (OR)
George Mason Univ. (VA)
George Washington Univ. (DC)
Georgetown College (KY)
Georgia College and State Univ.
Georgia Institute of Technology
Georgia Southern Univ.
Georgia Southwestern State Univ.
Georgia State Univ.
Goldey Beacom College (DE)
Gonzaga Univ. (WA)
Grace Univ. (NE)
Grand Valley State Univ. (MI)
Grand View College (IA)
Grove City College (PA)
Guilford College (NC)
Gwynedd-Mercy College (PA)
Hamilton College (NY)
Hampden-Sydney College (VA)
Hannibal-Lagrange College (MO)
Hanover College (IN)
Harding Univ. (AR)
Hartwick College (NY)
Harvey Mudd College (CA)
Hastings College (NE)
Haverford College (PA)
Heidelberg College (OH)

Henderson State Univ. (AR)
Hendrix College (AR)
High Point Univ. (NC)
Hobart and William Smith Colleges (NY)
Holy Family Univ. (PA)
Hope College (MI)
Houghton College (NY)
Humboldt State Univ. (CA)
Huntington College (IN)
Huston-Tillotson College (TX)
Idaho State Univ.
Illinois Institute of Technology
Illinois State Univ.
Indiana Institute of Technology
Indiana State Univ.
Indiana Univ. Northwest
Indiana Univ. of Pennsylvania
Indiana Univ.–Bloomington
Indiana Univ.–Kokomo
Indiana Univ.-Purdue Univ.–Fort Wayne
Indiana Univ.-Purdue Univ.–Indianapolis
Indiana Wesleyan Univ.
International College (FL)
Iowa State Univ.
Ithaca College (NY)
Jacksonville State Univ. (AL)
Jacksonville Univ. (FL)
James Madison Univ. (VA)
Jamestown College (ND)
Jarvis Christian College (TX)
Johns Hopkins Univ. (MD)
Johnson C. Smith Univ. (NC)
Juniata College (PA)
Kalamazoo College (MI)
Kansas State Univ.
Kansas Wesleyan Univ.
Kean Univ. (NJ)
Keene State College (NH)
Kennesaw State Univ. (GA)
Kentucky State Univ.
Kentucky Wesleyan College
Kettering Univ. (MI)
King College (TN)
King's College (PA)
Kutztown Univ. of Pennsylvania
La Roche College (PA)
La Salle Univ. (PA)
La Sierra Univ. (CA)
Lafayette College (PA)
Lagrange College (GA)
Lake Superior State Univ. (MI)
Lamar Univ. (TX)
Lander Univ. (SC)
Lane College (TN)
Lawrence Technological Univ. (MI)
Lenoir-Rhyne College (NC)
Lewis-Clark State College (ID)
Liberty Univ. (VA)
Limestone College (SC)
Lincoln Memorial Univ. (TN)
Lincoln Univ. (PA)
Lindenwood Univ. (MO)
Livingstone College (NC)
Lock Haven Univ. of Pennsylvania
Loyola Marymount Univ. (CA)
Loyola Univ. Chicago
Loyola Univ. New Orleans
Lubbock Christian Univ. (TX)

Lycoming College (PA)
Lynchburg College (VA)
Lyndon State College (VT)
Macalester College (MN)
Macmurray College (IL)
Madonna Univ. (MI)
Manchester College (IN)
Manhattan College (NY)
Manhattanville College (NY)
Marian College of Fond Du Lac (WI)
Marist College (NY)
Marquette Univ. (WI)
Mars Hill College (NC)
Mary Baldwin College (VA)
Marygrove College (MI)
Marymount Univ. (VA)
Maryville College (TN)
Maryville Univ. of St. Louis (MO)
Marywood Univ. (PA)
Mayville State Univ. (ND)
Mcdaniel College (MD)
Mcmurry Univ. (TX)
Mcpherson College (KS)
Medaille College (NY)
Mercyhurst College (PA)
Meredith College (NC)
Merrimack College (MA)
Methodist College (NC)
Miami Univ.–Oxford (OH)
Michigan State Univ.
Michigan Technological Univ.
Midland Lutheran College (NE)
Midwestern State Univ. (TX)
Miles College (AL)
Millersville Univ. of Pennsylvania
Milligan College (TN)
Mills College (CA)
Millsaps College (MS)
Minnesota State Univ.–Mankato
Minnesota State Univ.–Moorhead
Minot State Univ. (ND)
Mississippi College
Mississippi State Univ.
Mississippi Valley State Univ.
Missouri Baptist College
Missouri Southern State Univ.
Missouri Valley College
Missouri Western State College
Molloy College (NY)
Monmouth College (IL)
Monmouth Univ. (NJ)
Montana State Univ.–Northern
Montclair State Univ. (NJ)
Montreat College (NC)
Morehead State Univ. (KY)
Morehouse College (GA)
Morgan State Univ. (MD)
Mount Marty College (SD)
Mount Mercy College (IA)
Mount Olive College (NC)
Mount St. Mary College (NY)
Mount St. Mary's Univ. (MD)
Mountain State Univ. (WV)
Muhlenberg College (PA)
Murray State Univ. (KY)
Myers Univ. (OH)
National Univ. (CA)
National-Louis Univ. (IL)
Neumann College (PA)
New Jersey City Univ.

New Jersey Institute of Technology
New Mexico Highlands Univ.
New Mexico Institute of Mining and Technology
New Mexico State Univ.
New York Institute of Technology
New York Univ.
Niagara Univ. (NY)
Norfolk State Univ. (VA)
North Carolina Wesleyan College
North Georgia College and State Univ.
Northeastern Univ. (MA)
Northern Arizona Univ.
Northern Kentucky Univ.
Northern Michigan Univ.
Northern State Univ. (SD)
Northland College (WI)
Northwest Christian College (OR)
Northwest Missouri State Univ.
Northwestern College (IA)
Northwestern Oklahoma State Univ.
Northwestern Univ. (IL)
Northwood Univ. (MI)
Norwich Univ. (VT)
Notre Dame De Namur Univ. (CA)
Nova Southeastern Univ. (FL)
Nyack College (NY)
Oakland City Univ. (IN)
Oakland Univ. (MI)
Oberlin College (OH)
Ohio State Univ.–Columbus
Ohio Univ.
Oklahoma Baptist Univ.
Oklahoma Christian Univ.
Oklahoma City Univ.
Oklahoma Panhandle State Univ.
Oklahoma State Univ.
Old Dominion Univ. (VA)
Olivet College (MI)
Olivet Nazarene Univ. (IL)
Oral Roberts Univ. (OK)
Oregon Institute of Technology
Oregon State Univ.
Otterbein College (OH)
Our Lady of the Lake Univ. (TX)
Pace Univ. (NY)
Pacific Lutheran Univ. (WA)
Palm Beach Atlantic Univ. (FL)
Park Univ. (MO)
Paul Quinn College (TX)
Penn. State Univ.–Univ. Park
Peru State College (NE)
Pfeiffer Univ. (NC)
Pikeville College (KY)
Pittsburg State Univ. (KS)
Plymouth State Univ. (NH)
Point Park Univ. (PA)
Prairie View A&M Univ. (TX)
Prescott College (AZ)
Principia College (IL)
Purdue Univ.–West Lafayette (IN)
Quinnipiac Univ. (CT)
Ramapo College of New Jersey
Randolph-Macon College (VA)
Regis College (MA)
Regis Univ. (CO)
Rensselaer Polytechnic Inst. (NY)
Rhode Island College
Rice Univ. (TX)

Rider Univ. (NJ)
Ripon College (WI)
Rivier College (NH)
Robert Morris College (IL)
Rochester Institute of Tech. (NY)
Rockford College (IL)
Rocky Mountain College (MT)
Roger Williams Univ. (RI)
Rutgers–Camden (NJ)
Rutgers–New Brunswick (NJ)
Rutgers–Newark (NJ)
Saginaw Valley State Univ. (MI)
Salem International Univ. (WV)
Salem State College (MA)
Salisbury Univ. (MD)
San Diego State Univ.
San Francisco State Univ.
Scripps College (CA)
Seattle Pacific Univ.
Seton Hall Univ. (NJ)
Sewanee–Univ. of the South (TN)
Shaw Univ. (NC)
Shepherd Univ. (WV)
Shippensburg Univ. of Pennsylvania
Shorter College (GA)
Siena College (NY)
Silver Lake College (WI)
Simmons College (MA)
Simpson College (IA)
Skidmore College (NY)
Slippery Rock Univ. of Pennsylvania
Sonoma State Univ. (CA)
South Carolina State Univ.
South Dakota School of Mines and Technology
South Dakota State Univ.
Southeast Missouri State Univ.
Southeastern Oklahoma State Univ.
Southeastern Univ. (DC)
Southern Adventist Univ. (TN)
Southern Arkansas Univ.
Southern Nazarene Univ. (OK)
Southern New Hampshire Univ.
Southern Oregon Univ.
Southern Polytechnic State Univ. (GA)
Southern Utah Univ.
Southern Wesleyan Univ. (SC)
Southwest Baptist Univ. (MO)
Southwest Minnesota State Univ. (MN)
Southwest Missouri State Univ.
Southwestern College (KS)
Southwestern Oklahoma State Univ.
Southwestern Univ. (TX)
Spelman College (GA)
Springfield College (MA)
St. Augustine's College (NC)
St. Cloud State Univ. (MN)
St. Edward's Univ. (TX)
St. Francis College (NY)
St. John Fisher College (NY)
St. John's Univ. (NY)
St. Joseph's College (ME)
St. Joseph's College (IN)
St. Joseph's Univ. (PA)
St. Lawrence Univ. (NY)
St. Louis Univ.

St. Mary's College of Maryland
St. Mary's Univ. of San Antonio
St. Mary-of-The-Woods Coll. (IN)
St. Norbert College (WI)
St. Peter's College (NJ)
St. Thomas Aquinas College (NY)
St. Thomas Univ. (FL)
St. Vincent College (PA)
Stanford Univ. (CA)
State Univ. of West Georgia
Stephen F. Austin State Univ. (TX)
Sterling College (KS)
Stetson Univ. (FL)
Suffolk Univ. (MA)
Sul Ross State Univ. (TX)
SUNY College–Brockport
SUNY College–Old Westbury
SUNY College–Potsdam
SUNY–Albany
SUNY–Binghamton
SUNY–Fredonia
SUNY–Plattsburgh
Susquehanna Univ. (PA)
Swarthmore College (PA)
Syracuse Univ. (NY)
Taylor Univ. (IN)
Teikyo Post Univ. (CT)
Temple Univ. (PA)
Tennessee Wesleyan College
Texas A&M International Univ.
Texas A&M Univ.–College Station
Texas A&M Univ.–Commerce
Texas A&M Univ.–Corpus Christi
Texas A&M Univ.–Kingsville
Texas Christian Univ.
Texas Lutheran Univ.
Texas State Univ.–San Marcos
Texas Tech Univ.
Texas Wesleyan Univ.
Texas Woman's Univ.
The Citadel (SC)
The Franciscan Univ. (IA)
Thiel College (PA)
Thomas College (ME)
Thomas More College (KY)
Tiffin Univ. (OH)
Touro College (NY)
Transylvania Univ. (KY)
Trevecca Nazarene Univ. (TN)
Tri-State Univ. (IN)
Trinity College (DC)
Troy State Univ.–Troy (AL)
Truman State Univ. (MO)
Tufts Univ. (MA)
Tulane Univ. (LA)
Tuskegee Univ. (AL)
Union College (NY)
Union College (NE)
United States Naval Academy (MD)
Univ. of Alabama
Univ. of Alabama–Birmingham
Univ. of Alabama–Huntsville
Univ. of Alaska–Anchorage
Univ. of Arizona
Univ. of Arkansas
Univ. of Arkansas–Little Rock
Univ. of Arkansas–Pine Bluff
Univ. of Bridgeport (CT)
Univ. of California–Davis
Univ. of California–Irvine

Univ. of California–Los Angeles
Univ. of Central Arkansas
Univ. of Central Florida
Univ. of Central Oklahoma
Univ. of Charleston (WV)
Univ. of Chicago
Univ. of Colorado–Denver
Univ. of Delaware
Univ. of Detroit Mercy
Univ. of Dubuque (IA)
Univ. of Evansville (IN)
Univ. of Florida
Univ. of Great Falls (MT)
Univ. of Hartford (CT)
Univ. of Hawaii–Manoa
Univ. of Houston
Univ. of Houston–Downtown
Univ. of Ill.–Urbana-Champaign
Univ. of Iowa
Univ. of Kansas
Univ. of Kentucky
Univ. of La Verne (CA)
Univ. of Maine–Augusta
Univ. of Maine–Farmington
Univ. of Maine–Fort Kent
Univ. of Maine–Orono
Univ. of Mary Hardin-Baylor (TX)
Univ. of Mary Washington (VA)
Univ. of Maryland–College Park
Univ. of Maryland–Eastern Shore
Univ. of Maryland–Univ. College
Univ. of Michigan–Ann Arbor
Univ. of Michigan–Dearborn
Univ. of Mississippi
Univ. of Missouri–Columbia
Univ. of Missouri–Kansas City
Univ. of Missouri–Rolla
Univ. of Missouri–St. Louis
Univ. of Mobile (AL)
Univ. of Nebraska–Kearney
Univ. of Nebraska–Lincoln
Univ. of Nevada–Reno
Univ. of New Hampshire
Univ. of New Haven (CT)
Univ. of New Mexico
Univ. of North Alabama
Univ. of North Dakota
Univ. of North Florida
Univ. of North Texas
Univ. of Northern Iowa
Univ. of Notre Dame (IN)
Univ. of Oregon
Univ. of Pittsburgh–Johnstown
Univ. of Portland (OR)
Univ. of Redlands (CA)
Univ. of Rhode Island
Univ. of Richmond (VA)
Univ. of San Francisco
Univ. of Sioux Falls (SD)
Univ. of South Alabama
Univ. of South Carolina–Columbia
Univ. of South Carolina–Upstate
Univ. of South Dakota
Univ. of South Florida
Univ. of Southern California
Univ. of Southern Indiana
Univ. of Southern Mississippi
Univ. of St. Francis (IL)
Univ. of St. Mary (KS)
Univ. of St. Thomas (MN)
Univ. of Tampa (FL)

Univ. of Tennessee–Chattanooga
Univ. of Texas of the Permian Basin
Univ. of Texas–Austin
Univ. of Texas–Brownsville
Univ. of Texas–Dallas
Univ. of Texas–El Paso
Univ. of Texas–Pan American
Univ. of Texas–San Antonio
Univ. of Texas–Tyler
Univ. of the District of Columbia
Univ. of the Incarnate Word (TX)
Univ. of Tulsa (OK)
Univ. of Virginia
Univ. of Virginia–Wise
Univ. of Washington
Univ. of West Florida
Univ. of Wisconsin–Eau Claire
Univ. of Wisconsin–Green Bay
Univ. of Wisconsin–La Crosse
Univ. of Wisconsin–Madison
Univ. of Wisconsin–Milwaukee
Univ. of Wisconsin–Oshkosh
Univ. of Wisconsin–Platteville
Univ. of Wisconsin–River Falls
Univ. of Wisconsin–Stevens Point
Univ. of Wisconsin–Whitewater
Upper Iowa Univ.
Utah State Univ.
Utica College (NY)
Valdosta State Univ. (GA)
Valley City State Univ. (ND)
Vanderbilt Univ. (TN)
Vassar College (NY)
Villanova Univ. (PA)
Virginia Commonwealth Univ.
Virginia State Univ.
Virginia Tech
Virginia Union Univ.
Viterbo Univ. (WI)
Voorhees College (SC)
Wake Forest Univ. (NC)
Waldorf College (IA)
Wartburg College (IA)
Washburn Univ. (KS)
Washington and Jefferson College (PA)
Washington and Lee Univ. (VA)
Washington College (MD)
Washington State Univ.
Wayne State College (NE)
Wayne State Univ. (MI)
Waynesburg College (PA)
Webber International Univ. (FL)
Weber State Univ. (UT)
Webster Univ. (MO)
Wesleyan College (GA)
West Chester Univ. of Pennsylvania
West Texas A&M Univ.
West Virginia Univ.
West Virginia Univ. Institute of Technology
West Virginia Wesleyan College
Western Connecticut State Univ.
Western Illinois Univ.
Western Kentucky Univ.
Western Michigan Univ.
Western New Mexico Univ.
Western State College of Colorado
Western Washington Univ.
Westfield State College (MA)
Westminster College (MO)

Westmont College (CA)
Wheeling Jesuit Univ. (WV)
Whitworth College (WA)
Wichita State Univ. (KS)
Wilberforce Univ. (OH)
Wiley College (TX)
Wilkes Univ. (PA)
Willamette Univ. (OR)
William Paterson Univ. of New Jersey
William Woods Univ. (MO)
Williams Baptist College (AR)
Wilmington College (DE)
Winston-Salem State Univ. (NC)
Winthrop Univ. (SC)
Worcester Polytechnic Institute (MA)
Yeshiva Univ. (NY)
York College of Pennsylvania
Youngstown State Univ. (OH)

Computer and Information Sciences and Support Services

Arizona State Univ. West
Cabrini College (PA)
Capitol College (MD)
Carlow College (PA)
Central Michigan Univ.
Champlain College (VT)
CUNY–Brooklyn College
CUNY–College of Staten Island
Delaware Valley College (PA)
Depaul Univ. (IL)
Dowling College (NY)
Elmhurst College (IL)
Ferris State Univ. (MI)
Georgian Court Univ. (NJ)
Humboldt State Univ. (CA)
Indiana Univ. East
Indiana Univ. Southeast
Indiana Univ.-Purdue Univ.–Indianapolis
Johnson and Wales Univ. (RI)
Johnson State College (VT)
Lehigh Univ. (PA)
Long Island Univ.–C.W. Post Campus (NY)
Loyola Univ. New Orleans
Mayville State Univ. (ND)
Mount Marty College (SD)
Mount St. Mary College (NY)
Norwich Univ. (VT)
Park Univ. (MO)
Pepperdine Univ. (CA)
Purdue Univ.–North Central (IN)
Purdue Univ.–West Lafayette (IN)
Regis College (MA)
Seattle Pacific Univ.
Southern Adventist Univ. (TN)
Southern Nazarene Univ. (OK)
Southwestern College (KS)
St. Louis Univ.
SUNY College of A&T–Cobleskill
SUNY College–Brockport
Syracuse Univ. (NY)
Towson Univ. (MD)
Univ. of Findlay (OH)
Univ. of Michigan–Ann Arbor

Univ. of Missouri–Rolla
Univ. of Notre Dame (IN)
Univ. of Pittsburgh
Univ. of Wisconsin–Milwaukee
Utah State Univ.
Valley City State Univ. (ND)
William Woods Univ. (MO)
Wilmington College (DE)
Woodbury Univ. (CA)
Worcester Polytechnic Institute (MA)

Computer Engineering

Abilene Christian Univ. (TX)
Allegheny College (PA)
Arizona State Univ.
Auburn Univ. (AL)
Bellarmine Univ. (KY)
Benedict College (SC)
Bethel College (IN)
Bethune-Cookman College (FL)
Brigham Young Univ.–Provo (UT)
Bucknell Univ. (PA)
Cal Poly–San Luis Obispo
California State Polytechnic Univ.–Pomona
California State Univ.–Chico
California State Univ.–Fresno
California State Univ.–Fullerton
California State Univ.–Long Beach
California State Univ.–Sacramento
Capital Univ. (OH)
Capitol College (MD)
Carnegie Mellon Univ. (PA)
Carroll College (WI)
Case Western Reserve Univ. (OH)
Cedarville Univ. (OH)
Champlain College (VT)
Christopher Newport Univ. (VA)
Claflin Univ. (SC)
Clarkson Univ. (NY)
Cleveland State Univ.
College of New Jersey
Columbia Univ. (NY)
CUNY–City College
David Lipscomb Univ. (TN)
Drexel Univ. (PA)
Eastern Nazarene College (MA)
Elizabethtown College (PA)
Embry Riddle Aeronautical Univ. (FL)
Florida A&M Univ.
Florida Atlantic Univ.
Florida Institute of Technology
Florida International Univ.
Florida State Univ.
George Mason Univ. (VA)
George Washington Univ. (DC)
Georgia Institute of Technology
Grand Valley State Univ. (MI)
Harding Univ. (AR)
Hofstra Univ. (NY)
Howard Univ. (DC)
Illinois Institute of Technology
Indiana Institute of Technology
Indiana Univ.-Purdue Univ.–Fort Wayne
Indiana Univ.-Purdue Univ.–Indianapolis

Iowa State Univ.
Johns Hopkins Univ. (MD)
Johnson C. Smith Univ. (NC)
Kansas State Univ.
Kettering Univ. (MI)
Lake Superior State Univ. (MI)
Lawrence Technological Univ. (MI)
Lehigh Univ. (PA)
Letourneau Univ. (TX)
Louisiana State Univ.–Baton Rouge
Manhattan College (NY)
Marquette Univ. (WI)
Merrimack College (MA)
Miami Univ.–Oxford (OH)
Michigan State Univ.
Michigan Technological Univ.
Milwaukee School of Engineering
Minnesota State Univ.–Mankato
Mississippi State Univ.
Monmouth Univ. (NJ)
Montana State Univ.–Bozeman
Montana Tech of the Univ. of Montana
National Univ. (CA)
New Jersey Institute of Technology
North Carolina State Univ.–Raleigh
North Dakota State Univ.
Northeastern Univ. (MA)
Northwestern Univ. (IL)
Norwich Univ. (VT)
Oakland Univ. (MI)
Ohio Northern Univ.
Oklahoma Christian Univ.
Old Dominion Univ. (VA)
Oral Roberts Univ. (OK)
Oregon State Univ.
Pacific Lutheran Univ. (WA)
Penn. State Univ.–Univ. Park
Penn. State–Erie, The Behrend College
Polytechnic Univ. (NY)
Portland State Univ. (OR)
Princeton Univ. (NJ)
Purdue Univ.–Calumet (IN)
Purdue Univ.–West Lafayette (IN)
Rensselaer Polytechnic Inst. (NY)
Rice Univ. (TX)
Robert Morris Univ. (PA)
Rochester Institute of Tech. (NY)
Roger Williams Univ. (RI)
Rose-Hulman Institute of Technology (IN)
San Diego State Univ.
San Jose State Univ. (CA)
Santa Clara Univ. (CA)
Seattle Pacific Univ.
Seattle Univ.
South Dakota School of Mines and Technology
South Dakota State Univ.
Southern Illinois Univ.–Carbondale
Southern Illinois Univ.–Edwardsville
Southern Methodist Univ. (TX)
Southern Polytechnic State Univ. (GA)
St. Cloud State Univ. (MN)
St. Mary's Univ. of Minnesota
St. Mary's Univ. of San Antonio
Stevens Institute of Technology (NJ)

Stonehill College (MA)
Suffolk Univ. (MA)
SUNY–Binghamton
SUNY–Stony Brook
Syracuse Univ. (NY)
Taylor Univ. (IN)
Tennessee Technological Univ.
Texas A&M Univ.–College Station
Texas A&M Univ.–Kingsville
Texas Tech Univ.
Tri-State Univ. (IN)
Trinity College (CT)
Tufts Univ. (MA)
Tulane Univ. (LA)
United States Air Force Academy
   (CO)
Univ. at Buffalo–SUNY
Univ. of Akron (OH)
Univ. of Alabama–Huntsville
Univ. of Arizona
Univ. of Arkansas
Univ. of Bridgeport (CT)
Univ. of California–Davis
Univ. of California–Irvine
Univ. of California–Los Angeles
Univ. of California–Riverside
Univ. of California–San Diego
Univ. of California–Santa Barbara
Univ. of California–Santa Cruz
Univ. of Central Florida
Univ. of Colorado–Boulder
Univ. of Colorado–Colorado
   Springs
Univ. of Connecticut
Univ. of Dayton (OH)
Univ. of Denver
Univ. of Evansville (IN)
Univ. of Florida
Univ. of Georgia
Univ. of Hartford (CT)
Univ. of Houston
Univ. of Illinois–Chicago
Univ. of Illinois–Urbana-
   Champaign
Univ. of Indianapolis
Univ. of Kansas
Univ. of Louisiana–Lafayette
Univ. of Louisville (KY)
Univ. of Maine–Orono
Univ. of Maryland–Baltimore
   County
Univ. of Maryland–College Park
Univ. of Massachusetts–Amherst
Univ. of Mass.–Dartmouth
Univ. of Massachusetts–Lowell
Univ. of Memphis
Univ. of Miami (FL)
Univ. of Michigan–Ann Arbor
Univ. of Michigan–Dearborn
Univ. of Minnesota–Duluth
Univ. of Minnesota–Twin Cities
Univ. of Missouri–Columbia
Univ. of Missouri–Kansas City
Univ. of Missouri–Rolla
Univ. of Nebraska–Lincoln
Univ. of Nebraska–Omaha
Univ. of Nevada–Las Vegas
Univ. of Nevada–Reno
Univ. of New Hampshire
Univ. of New Haven (CT)
Univ. of New Mexico

Univ. of North Carolina–Charlotte
Univ. of North Texas
Univ. of Notre Dame (IN)
Univ. of Oklahoma
Univ. of Pennsylvania
Univ. of Pittsburgh
Univ. of Rhode Island
Univ. of Scranton (PA)
Univ. of South Alabama
Univ. of South Carolina–Columbia
Univ. of South Florida
Univ. of Southern California
Univ. of Tennessee
Univ. of Texas–Arlington
Univ. of Texas–Dallas
Univ. of the Pacific (CA)
Univ. of Toledo (OH)
Univ. of Utah
Univ. of Virginia
Univ. of Washington
Univ. of West Florida
Univ. of Wisconsin–Madison
Univ. of Wisconsin–Platteville
Univ. of Wyoming
Utah State Univ.
Valparaiso Univ. (IN)
Vanderbilt Univ. (TN)
Vermont Technical College
Villanova Univ. (PA)
Virginia Commonwealth Univ.
Virginia Military Institute
Virginia State Univ.
Virginia Tech
Washington State Univ.
Washington Univ. In St. Louis
West Virginia Univ.
Western Michigan Univ.
Wichita State Univ. (KS)
Wilberforce Univ. (OH)
Wright State Univ. (OH)
York College of Pennsylvania

Computer Engineering Technologies/Technicians

Andrews Univ. (MI)
California State Polytechnic
   Univ.–Pomona
California State Univ.–Long Beach
California Univ. of Pennsylvania
Capitol College (MD)
Central Michigan Univ.
Cogswell Polytechnical College
   (CA)
CUNY–New York City College of
   Technology
Eastern Kentucky Univ.
Eastern Michigan Univ.
Eastern Washington Univ.
Georgia Southwestern State Univ.
Indiana State Univ.
Indiana Univ.-Purdue Univ.–Fort
   Wayne
Indiana Univ.-Purdue
   Univ.–Indianapolis
Letourneau Univ. (TX)
Martin Univ. (IN)
Minnesota State Univ.–Mankato
Missouri Western State College
Montana State Univ.–Northern

Norfolk State Univ. (VA)
Northeastern Univ. (MA)
Oregon Institute of Technology
Prairie View A&M Univ. (TX)
Rochester Institute of Tech. (NY)
Shawnee State Univ. (OH)
Southern Polytechnic State Univ.
   (GA)
SUNY–Farmingdale
Thomas Edison State College (NJ)
Univ. of Central Florida
Univ. of Dayton (OH)
Univ. of Hartford (CT)
Univ. of Houston
Univ. of Houston–Downtown
Univ. of Memphis
Univ. of Minnesota–Crookston
Univ. of Southern Mississippi
Utah State Univ.
Vermont Technical College
Wayne State Univ. (MI)
Weber State Univ. (UT)
Wentworth Institute of Tech. (MA)

Computer Programming

Bellevue Univ. (NE)
California Lutheran Univ.
Calvin College (MI)
Capitol College (MD)
Champlain College (VT)
Charleston Southern Univ. (SC)
City Univ. (WA)
Clayton Coll. and State Univ. (GA)
Cleary Univ. (MI)
College For Lifelong Learning (NH)
Friends Univ. (KS)
Gannon Univ. (PA)
Grand Valley State Univ. (MI)
Grand View College (IA)
Hardin-Simmons Univ. (TX)
Indiana Univ.–South Bend
Johnson and Wales Univ. (RI)
Kent State Univ. (OH)
Limestone College (SC)
Minot State Univ. (ND)
Missouri Southern State Univ.
Morningside College (IA)
Mount Marty College (SD)
National Univ. (CA)
New Jersey City Univ.
New Mexico Institute of Mining
   and Technology
Northern Michigan Univ.
Northwest Christian College (OR)
Pepperdine Univ. (CA)
Purdue Univ.–Calumet (IN)
Southeast Missouri State Univ.
Southern Adventist Univ. (TN)
SUNY–Farmingdale
Temple Univ. (PA)
Tufts Univ. (MA)
Univ. of Evansville (IN)
Univ. of Ill.–Urbana-Champaign
Univ. of Michigan–Dearborn
Univ. of Missouri–Rolla
Western Michigan Univ.
Youngstown State Univ. (OH)

Computer Science

Abilene Christian Univ. (TX)
Alabama State Univ.
Albion College (MI)
Alderson-Broaddus College (WV)
Allegheny College (PA)
Alma College (MI)
American International College
   (MA)
American Univ. (DC)
Amherst College (MA)
Anderson Univ. (IN)
Appalachian State Univ. (NC)
Arizona State Univ.
Assumption College (MA)
Atlantic Union College (MA)
Augustana College (IL)
Augustana College (SD)
Aurora Univ. (IL)
Austin College (TX)
Baker Univ. (KS)
Baldwin-Wallace College (OH)
Barnard College (NY)
Barry Univ. (FL)
Baylor Univ. (TX)
Bellevue Univ. (NE)
Beloit College (WI)
Bemidji State Univ. (MN)
Benedict College (SC)
Benedictine College (KS)
Bennington College (VT)
Berry College (GA)
Bethany College (WV)
Bethel College (KS)
Bethel College (IN)
Bethune-Cookman College (FL)
Blackburn College (IL)
Bloomsburg Univ. of Pennsylvania
Bluffton Univ. (OH)
Boston Univ.
Bowdoin College (ME)
Bradley Univ. (IL)
Brandeis Univ. (MA)
Briar Cliff Univ. (IA)
Bridgewater College (VA)
Bridgewater State College (MA)
Brigham Young Univ.–Hawaii
Brigham Young Univ.–Provo (UT)
Brown Univ. (RI)
Bryn Mawr College (PA)
Buena Vista Univ. (IA)
Cal Poly–San Luis Obispo
Caldwell College (NJ)
California Institute of Technology
California Lutheran Univ.
California State Univ.–Bakersfield
California State Univ.–Chico
California State Univ.–Fullerton
California State Univ.–Hayward
California State Univ.–Long Beach
California State Univ.–Los Angeles
California State Univ.–Sacramento
California State Univ.–San
   Bernardino
California State Univ.–San Marcos
California State Univ.–Stanislaus
Calvin College (MI)
Cameron Univ. (OK)
Campbell Univ. (NC)

Canisius College (NY)
Capital Univ. (OH)
Cardinal Stritch Univ. (WI)
Carleton College (MN)
Carlow College (PA)
Carnegie Mellon Univ. (PA)
Carson-Newman College (TN)
Carthage College (WI)
Case Western Reserve Univ. (OH)
Catholic Univ. of America (DC)
Central Methodist Univ. (MO)
Central State Univ. (OH)
Centre College (KY)
Chapman Univ. (CA)
Charleston Southern Univ. (SC)
Chicago State Univ.
Christopher Newport Univ. (VA)
Claflin Univ. (SC)
Clark Atlanta Univ.
Clarke College (IA)
Clarkson Univ. (NY)
Coe College (IA)
Coker College (SC)
Colby College (ME)
Colgate Univ. (NY)
College of Santa Fe (NM)
College of St. Benedict (MN)
College of St. Elizabeth (NJ)
College of the Ozarks (MO)
College of the Southwest (NM)
College of Wooster (OH)
Columbia College (MO)
Columbia Union College (MD)
Columbia Univ. (NY)
Concordia Coll.–Moorhead (MN)
Concordia Univ. (NE)
Concordia Univ.–Austin (TX)
Connecticut College
Cornell College (IA)
Cornerstone Univ. (MI)
CUNY–Baruch College
CUNY–College of Staten Island
CUNY–Lehman College
Dana College (NE)
Dartmouth College (NH)
David Lipscomb Univ. (TN)
Delaware State Univ.
Dominican Univ. (IL)
Drew Univ. (NJ)
Drexel Univ. (PA)
Drury Univ. (MO)
Duquesne Univ. (PA)
Earlham College (IN)
East Carolina Univ. (NC)
Eastern Kentucky Univ.
Eastern Mennonite Univ. (VA)
Eastern Michigan Univ.
Eastern Nazarene College (MA)
Eckerd College (FL)
Elizabethtown College (PA)
Elmhurst College (IL)
Elon Univ. (NC)
Fairleigh Dickinson Univ. (NJ)
Fayetteville State Univ. (NC)
Ferrum College (VA)
Fisk Univ. (TN)
Fitchburg State College (MA)
Florida Institute of Technology
Florida Southern College
Franciscan Univ. of Steubenville
   (OH)

Franklin College (IN)
Franklin Pierce College (NH)
Furman Univ. (SC)
Gallaudet Univ. (DC)
Gardner-Webb Univ. (NC)
Georgetown Univ. (DC)
Georgia Southwestern State Univ.
Georgia State Univ.
Georgian Court Univ. (NJ)
Gettysburg College (PA)
Gordon College (MA)
Goshen College (IN)
Goucher College (MD)
Graceland Univ. (IA)
Grambling State Univ. (LA)
Greenville College (IL)
Grinnell College (IA)
Gustavus Adolphus College (MN)
Hampshire College (MA)
Hampton Univ. (VA)
Hannibal-Lagrange College (MO)
Harding Univ. (AR)
Harvard Univ. (MA)
Hastings College (NE)
Hawaii Pacific Univ.
Heidelberg College (OH)
Henry Cogswell College (WA)
Heritage College (WA)
High Point Univ. (NC)
Hofstra Univ. (NY)
Hood College (MD)
Houghton College (NY)
Illinois College
Illinois Institute of Technology
Illinois State Univ.
Illinois Wesleyan Univ.
Indiana Univ. Southeast
Indiana Univ.–South Bend
Indiana Univ.-Purdue Univ.–Fort
    Wayne
Iona College (NY)
Jamestown College (ND)
John Brown Univ. (AR)
John Carroll Univ. (OH)
Kettering Univ. (MI)
King's College (PA)
Knox College (IL)
La Roche College (PA)
La Salle Univ. (PA)
La Sierra Univ. (CA)
Lake Forest College (IL)
Lakeland College (WI)
Lamar Univ. (TX)
Lawrence Technological Univ. (MI)
Lawrence Univ. (WI)
Lebanon Valley College (PA)
Lehigh Univ. (PA)
Lemoyne-Owen College (TN)
Letourneau Univ. (TX)
Lewis and Clark College (OR)
Lewis Univ. (IL)
Lewis-Clark State College (ID)
Limestone College (SC)
Lindenwood Univ. (MO)
Linfield College (OR)
Lock Haven Univ. of Pennsylvania
Longwood Univ. (VA)
Loras College (IA)
Louisiana State Univ.–Baton Rouge
Louisiana State Univ.–Shreveport
Louisiana Tech Univ.

Loyola College In Maryland
Luther College (IA)
Lyon College (AR)
Madonna Univ. (MI)
Maharishi Univ. of Management
    (IA)
Malone College (OH)
Mansfield Univ. of Pennsylvania
Marietta College (OH)
Marist College (NY)
Marymount Univ. (VA)
Marywood Univ. (PA)
Massachusetts Institute of
    Technology
Master's Coll. and Seminary (CA)
Mckendree College (IL)
Mcmurry Univ. (TX)
Mcneese State Univ. (LA)
Mercer Univ. (GA)
Meredith College (NC)
Messiah College (PA)
Metropolitan State College of
    Denver
Middle Tennessee State Univ.
Middlebury College (VT)
Millikin Univ. (IL)
Minnesota State Univ.–Mankato
Minnesota State Univ.–Moorhead
Mississippi College
Monmouth College (IL)
Montana State Univ.–Bozeman
Montana Tech of the Univ. of
    Montana
Moravian College (PA)
Mount Holyoke College (MA)
Mount Marty College (SD)
Mount Mary College (WI)
Mount Union College (OH)
Mountain State Univ. (WV)
Muskingum College (OH)
National Univ. (CA)
Nebraska Wesleyan Univ.
New Mexico Institute of Mining
    and Technology
New York Univ.
Niagara Univ. (NY)
Nicholls State Univ. (LA)
North Carolina A&T State Univ.
North Carolina Central Univ.
North Carolina State Univ.–Raleigh
North Central College (IL)
North Dakota State Univ.
Northeastern Illinois Univ.
Northeastern State Univ. (OK)
Northern Arizona Univ.
Northern Illinois Univ.
Northwest Nazarene Univ. (ID)
Northwestern College (IA)
Northwestern Univ. (IL)
Norwich Univ. (VT)
Notre Dame De Namur Univ. (CA)
Nova Southeastern Univ. (FL)
Ohio Northern Univ.
Ohio Univ.
Ohio Wesleyan Univ.
Oklahoma Christian Univ.
Ouachita Baptist Univ. (AR)
Pace Univ. (NY)
Pacific Union College (CA)
Pacific Univ. (OR)
Park Univ. (MO)

Penn. State–Erie, The Behrend
    College
Philander Smith College (AR)
Plymouth State Univ. (NH)
Point Loma Nazarene Univ. (CA)
Polytechnic Univ. (NY)
Pomona College (CA)
Portland State Univ. (OR)
Presbyterian College (SC)
Providence College (RI)
Purdue Univ.–Calumet (IN)
Quincy Univ. (IL)
Radford Univ. (VA)
Regis College (MA)
Regis Univ. (CO)
Rhodes College (TN)
Roanoke College (VA)
Roberts Wesleyan College (NY)
Rochester Institute of Tech. (NY)
Rockford College (IL)
Rockhurst Univ. (MO)
Rocky Mountain College (MT)
Rollins College (FL)
Roosevelt Univ. (IL)
Rose-Hulman Institute of
    Technology (IN)
Rust College (MS)
Sacred Heart Univ. (CT)
Samford Univ. (AL)
Seattle Pacific Univ.
Seattle Univ.
Seton Hill Univ. (PA)
Shaw Univ. (NC)
Sierra Nevada College (NV)
Simmons College (MA)
Simpson College (IA)
Sonoma State Univ. (CA)
Southeastern Louisiana Univ.
Southeastern Oklahoma State
    Univ.
Southeastern Univ. (DC)
Southern Adventist Univ. (TN)
Southern Connecticut State Univ.
Southern Illinois Univ.–Carbondale
Southern Illinois
    Univ.–Edwardsville
Southern Methodist Univ. (TX)
Southern Polytechnic State Univ.
    (GA)
Southern Univ. and A&M College
    (LA)
Southern Utah Univ.
Southwest Baptist Univ. (MO)
Spring Arbor Univ. (MI)
St. Ambrose Univ. (IA)
St. Anselm College (NH)
St. Bonaventure Univ. (NY)
St. Edward's Univ. (TX)
St. Francis Univ. (PA)
St. John's Univ. (MN)
St. Martin's College (WA)
St. Mary's Univ. of Minnesota
St. Michael's College (VT)
St. Olaf College (MN)
St. Thomas Univ. (FL)
St. Xavier Univ. (IL)
Stetson Univ. (FL)
Stevens Institute of Technology
    (NJ)
Stillman College (AL)
Stonehill College (MA)

Suffolk Univ. (MA)
SUNY College of Arts and
    Sciences–Geneseo
SUNY College–Oneonta
SUNY–Stony Brook
Sweet Briar College (VA)
Tabor College (KS)
Talladega College (AL)
Tennessee State Univ.
Tennessee Technological Univ.
Texas A&M Univ.–Kingsville
Texas College
Thomas Edison State College (NJ)
Trinity Christian College (IL)
Trinity College (CT)
Tufts Univ. (MA)
Tulane Univ. (LA)
Tuskegee Univ. (AL)
Union College (NE)
Union Univ. (TN)
United States Air Force Academy
    (CO)
United States Military Academy
    (NY)
Univ. at Buffalo–SUNY
Univ. of Akron (OH)
Univ. of Alaska–Anchorage
Univ. of Alaska–Fairbanks
Univ. of California–Berkeley
Univ. of California–Irvine
Univ. of California–Riverside
Univ. of California–San Diego
Univ. of California–Santa Barbara
Univ. of California–Santa Cruz
Univ. of Colorado–Boulder
Univ. of Colorado–Colorado
    Springs
Univ. of Connecticut
Univ. of Dayton (OH)
Univ. of Denver
Univ. of Detroit Mercy
Univ. of Findlay (OH)
Univ. of Georgia
Univ. of Great Falls (MT)
Univ. of Hawaii–Hilo
Univ. of Hawaii–Manoa
Univ. of Illinois–Chicago
Univ. of Illinois–Springfield
Univ. of Ill.–Urbana-Champaign
Univ. of Indianapolis
Univ. of Iowa
Univ. of Louisiana–Lafayette
Univ. of Louisiana–Monroe
Univ. of Mary Hardin-Baylor (TX)
Univ. of Maryland–Baltimore
    County
Univ. of Maryland–College Park
Univ. of Massachusetts–Amherst
Univ. of Massachusetts–Boston
Univ. of Massachusetts–Lowell
Univ. of Memphis
Univ. of Miami (FL)
Univ. of Michigan–Ann Arbor
Univ. of Michigan–Flint
Univ. of Minnesota–Duluth
Univ. of Minnesota–Morris
Univ. of Minnesota–Twin Cities
Univ. of Missouri–Rolla
Univ. of Montana
Univ. of Nebraska–Omaha
Univ. of Nevada–Las Vegas

Univ. of Nevada–Reno
Univ. of New Hampshire
Univ. of New Orleans
Univ. of North Carolina–Asheville
Univ. of N.C.–Chapel Hill
Univ. of North Carolina–Charlotte
Univ. of N.C.–Greensboro
Univ. of North Carolina–Pembroke
Univ. of N.C.–Wilmington
Univ. of Northern Iowa
Univ. of Oklahoma
Univ. of Pittsburgh
Univ. of Pittsburgh–Bradford
Univ. of Puget Sound (WA)
Univ. of Rio Grande (OH)
Univ. of Rochester (NY)
Univ. of San Diego
Univ. of Science and Arts of
    Oklahoma
Univ. of Scranton (PA)
Univ. of Sioux Falls (SD)
Univ. of Southern Maine
Univ. of St. Francis (IL)
Univ. of St. Thomas (MN)
Univ. of Tennessee
Univ. of Tennessee–Martin
Univ. of Texas–Arlington
Univ. of Texas–Pan American
Univ. of the District of Columbia
Univ. of the Pacific (CA)
Univ. of Tulsa (OK)
Univ. of Utah
Univ. of Vermont
Univ. of Washington
Univ. of Wisconsin–Superior
Univ. of Wyoming
Ursinus College (PA)
Utah Valley State College
Valparaiso Univ. (IN)
Virginia Military Institute
Virginia State Univ.
Virginia Wesleyan College
Wagner College (NY)
Walsh Univ. (OH)
Washington State Univ.
Washington Univ. In St. Louis
Weber State Univ. (UT)
Wellesley College (MA)
Wentworth Institute of Technology
    (MA)
Wesleyan Univ. (CT)
West Virginia Univ.
West Virginia Wesleyan College
Western Baptist College (OR)
Western Carolina Univ. (NC)
Western Michigan Univ.
Western New England College
    (MA)
Westfield State College (MA)
Westminster College (UT)
Westminster College (PA)
Wheaton College (IL)
Wheaton College (MA)
Widener Univ. (PA)
Wilberforce Univ. (OH)
Wiley College (TX)
William Jewell College (MO)
Williams College (MA)
Wilmington College (OH)
Wingate Univ. (NC)
Winston-Salem State Univ. (NC)

Wittenberg Univ. (OH)
Worcester Polytechnic Institute (MA)
Worcester State College (MA)
Wright State Univ. (OH)
Xavier Univ. (OH)
Yale Univ. (CT)
Youngstown State Univ. (OH)

Computer Software and Media Applications

Baker Univ. (KS)
Baldwin-Wallace College (OH)
Bellevue Univ. (NE)
California State Univ.–Chico
Cameron Univ. (OK)
Champlain College (VT)
City Univ. (WA)
Clarkson Univ. (NY)
Columbia College (IL)
CUNY–Lehman College
Dakota State Univ. (SD)
Dakota Wesleyan Univ. (SD)
Dana College (NE)
Dominican Univ. (IL)
Drexel Univ. (PA)
Duquesne Univ. (PA)
Elmhurst College (IL)
Hampshire College (MA)
Holy Names Univ. (CA)
Husson College (ME)
Indiana Univ.–South Bend
Iona College (NY)
Jacksonville Univ. (FL)
La Salle Univ. (PA)
Lasell College (MA)
Lewis Univ. (IL)
Limestone College (SC)
Louisiana College
Minot State Univ. (ND)
Montana Tech of the Univ. of Montana
Mount Mary College (WI)
National Univ. (CA)
Purdue Univ.–Calumet (IN)
Rochester Institute of Tech. (NY)
Savannah College of Art and Design (GA)
Stetson Univ. (FL)
SUNY College–Oneonta
Trevecca Nazarene Univ. (TN)
Union Univ. (TN)
Univ. of Denver
Univ. of Dubuque (IA)
Univ. of Mary Hardin-Baylor (TX)
Univ. of Miami (FL)
Univ. of North Carolina–Asheville
Univ. of Pennsylvania
Univ. of Tampa (FL)
Univ. of the Incarnate Word (TX)
Univ. of Wisconsin–Stevens Point

Computer Systems Analysis

Arkansas Tech Univ.
Baldwin-Wallace College (OH)
Bellevue Univ. (NE)

California State Polytechnic Univ.–Pomona
Clayton Coll. and State Univ. (GA)
College For Lifelong Learning (NH)
Eastern Mennonite Univ. (VA)
Husson College (ME)
Kent State Univ. (OH)
Marshall Univ. (WV)
Miami Univ.–Oxford (OH)
New Jersey City Univ.
Northern Michigan Univ.
Pace Univ. (NY)
Pittsburg State Univ. (KS)
Purdue Univ.–Calumet (IN)
Saginaw Valley State Univ. (MI)
Seattle Pacific Univ.
Shippensburg Univ. of Pennsylvania
Tabor College (KS)
Tulane Univ. (LA)
Univ. of Denver
Univ. of Great Falls (MT)
Univ. of Houston
Univ. of Missouri–Rolla
Univ. of North Dakota
Univ. of Vermont
Univ. of Wisconsin–Whitewater
Washburn Univ. (KS)

Computer Systems Networking and Telecommunications

Baldwin-Wallace College (OH)
Bellevue Univ. (NE)
Bloomfield College (NJ)
Boston Univ.
California State Univ.–Hayward
Champlain College (VT)
City Univ. (WA)
Illinois State Univ.
Iona College (NY)
Kansas State Univ.
Kean Univ. (NJ)
Lake Superior State Univ. (MI)
Michigan Technological Univ.
Northeastern State Univ. (OK)
Northern Michigan Univ.
Our Lady of the Lake Univ. (TX)
Rochester Institute of Tech. (NY)
Roosevelt Univ. (IL)
St. Ambrose Univ. (IA)
Syracuse Univ. (NY)
Univ. of Akron (OH)
Univ. of Minnesota–Duluth
Univ. of Minnesota–Twin Cities
Univ. of N.C.–Greensboro
Univ. of Northern Iowa
Univ. of Oklahoma
Univ. of Pennsylvania
Univ. of Wisconsin–Stout
Weber State Univ. (UT)
Widener Univ. (PA)

Computer/Information Techn. Administration and Management

Albertus Magnus College (CT)

Bellevue Univ. (NE)
Husson College (ME)
Master's Coll. and Seminary (CA)
Oklahoma Baptist Univ.
Purdue Univ.–Calumet (IN)
Univ. of Great Falls (MT)
Univ. of Missouri–Rolla
Widener Univ. (PA)

Construction Engineering

Bradley Univ. (IL)
Iowa State Univ.
National Univ. (CA)
North Carolina State Univ.–Raleigh
North Dakota State Univ.
Oregon State Univ.
Purdue Univ.–West Lafayette (IN)
Univ. of Alabama
Univ. of Ill.–Urbana-Champaign

Construction Engineering Technologies

California State Univ.–Long Beach
SUNY–Farmingdale

Construction Management

California State Univ.–Sacramento
Univ. of Washington

Construction Trades

Boise State Univ. (ID)
Mesa State College (CO)
Tuskegee Univ. (AL)
Univ. of Maryland–Eastern Shore

Counseling Psychology

Auburn Univ. (AL)
Bellevue Univ. (NE)
Chestnut Hill College (PA)
Christian Heritage College (CA)
Coker College (SC)
College of Santa Fe (NM)
Coppin State Univ. (MD)
Emmanuel College (MA)
Grace College and Seminary (IN)
Grace Univ. (NE)
Jamestown College (ND)
Kentucky Christian College
Lesley Univ. (MA)
Liberty Univ. (VA)
Martin Univ. (IN)
Methodist College (NC)
Mid-Continent College (KY)
Midwestern State Univ. (TX)
Morningside College (IA)
Our Lady of Holy Cross Coll. (LA)
Pacific Univ. (OR)
Paine College (GA)
Rochester College (MI)

Slippery Rock Univ. of Pennsylvania
South Dakota State Univ.
St. Joseph College (CT)
Texas A&M Univ.–Commerce
Texas Wesleyan Univ.
Toccoa Falls College (GA)
Univ. of North Alabama
Univ. of North Texas
Wayne State College (NE)
West Virginia Wesleyan College
Western Washington Univ.
William Carey College (MS)

Crafts/Craft Design, Folk Art, and Artisanry

Bowling Green State Univ. (OH)
Bridgewater State College (MA)
Brigham Young Univ.–Provo (UT)
Indiana Univ.-Purdue Univ.–Fort Wayne
Kent State Univ. (OH)
Kutztown Univ. of Pennsylvania
Massachusetts College of Art
Rochester Institute of Tech. (NY)
Univ. of Ill.–Urbana-Champaign
Univ. of the Arts (PA)
Virginia Commonwealth Univ.

Creative Writing

Agnes Scott College (GA)
Alderson-Broaddus College (WV)
Allegheny College (PA)
Antioch College (OH)
Arkansas Tech Univ.
Ashland Univ. (OH)
Beloit College (WI)
Benedictine Univ. (IL)
Bennington College (VT)
Bluffton Univ. (OH)
Bowling Green State Univ. (OH)
Bridgewater State College (MA)
Brown Univ. (RI)
Butler Univ. (IN)
California College of the Arts
California State Univ.–Long Beach
California State Univ.–Sacramento
Capital Univ. (OH)
Cardinal Stritch Univ. (WI)
Carlow College (PA)
Carnegie Mellon Univ. (PA)
Carroll College (WI)
Central Michigan Univ.
Chapman Univ. (CA)
Colby College (ME)
College of Santa Fe (NM)
Colorado College
Colorado State Univ.
Columbia College (IL)
Columbia Univ. (NY)
Concordia College–Moorhead (MN)
Converse College (SC)
Cornerstone Univ. (MI)
CUNY–Baruch College
CUNY–Brooklyn College
Dartmouth College (NH)
Denison Univ. (OH)

Depauw Univ. (IN)
Dickinson State Univ. (ND)
Drake Univ. (IA)
Drury Univ. (MO)
Eastern Michigan Univ.
Eastern Washington Univ.
Eckerd College (FL)
Elon Univ. (NC)
Emerson College (MA)
Emory and Henry College (VA)
Emory Univ. (GA)
Fairleigh Dickinson Univ. (NJ)
Franklin and Marshall College (PA)
Gallaudet Univ. (DC)
George Washington Univ. (DC)
Grand Valley State Univ. (MI)
Green Mountain College (VT)
Hamilton College (NY)
Hampshire College (MA)
Hastings College (NE)
Hofstra Univ. (NY)
Hollins Univ. (VA)
Houghton College (NY)
Huntingdon College (AL)
Indiana Wesleyan Univ.
Ithaca College (NY)
Johns Hopkins Univ. (MD)
Johnson State College (VT)
Knox College (IL)
Lewis-Clark State College (ID)
Linfield College (OR)
Loras College (IA)
Loyola College In Maryland
Loyola Univ. New Orleans
Marlboro College (VT)
Massachusetts Institute of Technology
Mcmurry Univ. (TX)
Medaille College (NY)
Methodist College (NC)
Miami Univ.–Oxford (OH)
Millikin Univ. (IL)
Minnesota State Univ.–Mankato
Moravian College (PA)
Mount Union College (OH)
North Central College (IL)
Northern Michigan Univ.
Northwestern Univ. (IL)
Oberlin College (OH)
Ohio Northern Univ.
Ohio Univ.
Ohio Wesleyan Univ.
Oklahoma Christian Univ.
Pacific Univ. (OR)
Penn. State–Erie, The Behrend College
Prescott College (AZ)
Queens Univ. of Charlotte (NC)
Randolph-Macon Woman's College (VA)
Roger Williams Univ. (RI)
Savannah College of Art and Design (GA)
School of the Art Institute of Chicago
Seattle Univ.
Seton Hill Univ. (PA)
Southeastern Oklahoma State Univ.
Southern Illinois Univ.–Carbondale
Southern Methodist Univ. (TX)

Southern New Hampshire Univ.
Southwest Minnesota State Univ. (MN)
St. Andrews Presbyterian College (NC)
St. Joseph's College (IN)
St. Leo Univ. (FL)
St. Mary's College (IN)
St. Mary's College of California
Stephens College (MO)
Suffolk Univ. (MA)
SUNY–Purchase College
Susquehanna Univ. (PA)
Sweet Briar College (VA)
Syracuse Univ. (NY)
Union College (NE)
Univ. of Arizona
Univ. of California–Riverside
Univ. of Charleston (WV)
Univ. of Evansville (IN)
Univ. of Findlay (OH)
Univ. of Houston
Univ. of Maine–Farmington
Univ. of Miami (FL)
Univ. of Michigan–Ann Arbor
Univ. of Michigan–Flint
Univ. of Nebraska–Omaha
Univ. of N.C.–Wilmington
Univ. of Pittsburgh
Univ. of Pittsburgh–Bradford
Univ. of Pittsburgh–Greensburg
Univ. of Pittsburgh–Johnstown
Univ. of Redlands (CA)
Univ. of San Francisco
Univ. of Southern California
Univ. of St. Thomas (MN)
Univ. of Tampa (FL)
Univ. of Texas–El Paso
Valparaiso Univ. (IN)
Weber State Univ. (UT)
West Virginia Wesleyan College
Western Michigan Univ.
Western New England Coll. (MA)
Western Washington Univ.
Wheeling Jesuit Univ. (WV)
Widener Univ. (PA)

Criminal Justice and Corrections

Adelphi Univ. (NY)
Adrian College (MI)
Alabama State Univ.
Albany State Univ. (GA)
Albertus Magnus College (CT)
Alcorn State Univ. (MS)
Alfred Univ. (NY)
Alvernia College (PA)
American Univ. (DC)
Anderson College (SC)
Anderson Univ. (IN)
Angelo State Univ. (TX)
Anna Maria College (MA)
Appalachian State Univ. (NC)
Arizona State Univ.
Arizona State Univ. West
Arkansas State Univ.
Armstrong Atlantic State Univ. (GA)
Ashland Univ. (OH)

Auburn Univ.–Montgomery (AL)
Augusta State Univ. (GA)
Aurora Univ. (IL)
Austin Peay State Univ. (TN)
Averett Univ. (VA)
Baldwin-Wallace College (OH)
Ball State Univ. (IN)
Barry Univ. (FL)
Barton College (NC)
Bay Path College (MA)
Baylor Univ. (TX)
Becker College (MA)
Bellarmine Univ. (KY)
Bellevue Univ. (NE)
Bemidji State Univ. (MN)
Benedict College (SC)
Bethany College (KS)
Bethel College (IN)
Bethune-Cookman College (FL)
Bloomsburg Univ. of Pennsylvania
Bluefield College (VA)
Bluefield State College (WV)
Bluffton Univ. (OH)
Boise State Univ. (ID)
Bowling Green State Univ. (OH)
Bradley Univ. (IL)
Briar Cliff Univ. (IA)
Bridgewater State College (MA)
Buena Vista Univ. (IA)
Buffalo State College
Butler Univ. (IN)
Caldwell College (NJ)
California Baptist Univ.
California Lutheran Univ.
California State Univ.–Bakersfield
California State Univ.–Chico
California State Univ.–Fullerton
California State Univ.–Hayward
California State Univ.–Long Beach
California State Univ.–Los Angeles
California State Univ.–Sacramento
California State Univ.–San Bernardino
California State Univ.–Stanislaus
California Univ. of Pennsylvania
Calumet College of St. Joseph (IN)
Campbell Univ. (NC)
Canisius College (NY)
Carroll College (WI)
Carthage College (WI)
Castleton State College (VT)
Cedar Crest College (PA)
Cedarville Univ. (OH)
Centenary College (NJ)
Central Christian College (KS)
Central Methodist Univ. (MO)
Central Missouri State Univ.
Central Washington Univ.
Chadron State College (NE)
Chaminade Univ. of Honolulu
Champlain College (VT)
Charleston Southern Univ. (SC)
Chatham College (PA)
Chestnut Hill College (PA)
Chicago State Univ.
Chowan College (NC)
Claflin Univ. (SC)
Clark Atlanta Univ.
Clayton Coll. and State Univ. (GA)
Coker College (SC)
College For Lifelong Learning (NH)

College of New Jersey
College of Santa Fe (NM)
College of St. Catherine (MN)
College of St. Rose (NY)
College of the Ozarks (MO)
College of the Southwest (NM)
Columbia College (MO)
Concordia Univ. (MI)
Concordia Univ.–Austin (TX)
Coppin State Univ. (MD)
Culver-Stockton College (MO)
Cumberland Univ. (TN)
Curry College (MA)
Dakota Wesleyan Univ. (SD)
Dallas Baptist Univ.
Dana College (NE)
Defiance College (OH)
Delaware Valley College (PA)
Delta State Univ. (MS)
Desales Univ. (PA)
Dillard Univ. (LA)
Drexel Univ. (PA)
Drury Univ. (MO)
East Carolina Univ. (NC)
East Central Univ. (OK)
East Tennessee State Univ.
Eastern Kentucky Univ.
Eastern Nazarene College (MA)
Eastern New Mexico Univ.
Edgewood College (WI)
Edinboro Univ. of Pennsylvania
Edward Waters College (FL)
Elizabeth City State Univ. (NC)
Elmira College (NY)
Endicott College (MA)
Eureka College (IL)
Excelsior College (NY)
Fairleigh Dickinson Univ. (NJ)
Fairmont State Univ. (WV)
Faulkner Univ. (AL)
Fayetteville State Univ. (NC)
Ferris State Univ. (MI)
Ferrum College (VA)
Fitchburg State College (MA)
Florida Atlantic Univ.
Florida Gulf Coast Univ.
Florida International Univ.
Florida Southern College
Florida State Univ.
Fort Hays State Univ. (KS)
Fort Valley State Univ. (GA)
Franklin Pierce College (NH)
Friends Univ. (KS)
Frostburg State Univ. (MD)
Gannon Univ. (PA)
George Mason Univ. (VA)
George Washington Univ. (DC)
Georgia College and State Univ.
Georgia Southern Univ.
Georgia State Univ.
Georgian Court Univ. (NJ)
Gonzaga Univ. (WA)
Grace College and Seminary (IN)
Graceland Univ. (IA)
Grambling State Univ. (LA)
Grand Canyon Univ. (AZ)
Grand Valley State Univ. (MI)
Grand View College (IA)
Greenville College (IL)
Guilford College (NC)
Gustavus Adolphus College (MN)

Gwynedd-Mercy College (PA)
Hamline Univ. (MN)
Hannibal-Lagrange College (MO)
Hardin-Simmons Univ. (TX)
Harding Univ. (AR)
Hastings College (NE)
Hawaii Pacific Univ.
High Point Univ. (NC)
Hilbert College (NY)
Holy Family Univ. (PA)
Howard Univ. (DC)
Husson College (ME)
Huston-Tillotson College (TX)
Illinois State Univ.
Immaculata Univ. (PA)
Indiana Univ. East
Indiana Univ. Northwest
Indiana Univ. Southeast
Indiana Univ.–Bloomington
Indiana Univ.–Kokomo
Indiana Univ.-Purdue Univ.–Fort Wayne
Indiana Univ.-Purdue Univ.–Indianapolis
Indiana Wesleyan Univ.
International College (FL)
Iona College (NY)
Jacksonville State Univ. (AL)
Jamestown College (ND)
Johnson and Wales Univ. (RI)
Judson College (AL)
Judson College (IL)
Kansas Wesleyan Univ.
Kean Univ. (NJ)
Kennesaw State Univ. (GA)
Kent State Univ. (OH)
Kentucky State Univ.
Kentucky Wesleyan College
Keuka College (NY)
King College (TN)
King's College (PA)
Kutztown Univ. of Pennsylvania
La Roche College (PA)
La Salle Univ. (PA)
Lake Superior State Univ. (MI)
Lakeland College (WI)
Lamar Univ. (TX)
Lambuth Univ. (TN)
Lane College (TN)
Lasell College (MA)
Lewis Univ. (IL)
Lewis-Clark State College (ID)
Liberty Univ. (VA)
Limestone College (SC)
Lincoln Univ. (PA)
Lincoln Univ. (MO)
Lindenwood Univ. (MO)
Lindsey Wilson College (KY)
Livingstone College (NC)
Lock Haven Univ. of Pennsylvania
Long Island Univ.–C.W. Post Campus (NY)
Longwood Univ. (VA)
Louisiana College
Louisiana State Univ.–Shreveport
Lourdes College (OH)
Loyola Univ. Chicago
Loyola Univ. New Orleans
Lubbock Christian Univ. (TX)
Lycoming College (PA)
Lynn Univ. (FL)

Macmurray College (IL)
Madonna Univ. (MI)
Mansfield Univ. of Pennsylvania
Marian College of Fond Du Lac (WI)
Marist College (NY)
Marshall Univ. (WV)
Martin Univ. (IN)
Marymount Univ. (VA)
Marywood Univ. (PA)
Mcneese State Univ. (LA)
Medaille College (NY)
Mercer Univ. (GA)
Mercy College (NY)
Mercyhurst College (PA)
Mesa State College (CO)
Messiah College (PA)
Methodist College (NC)
Metropolitan State College of Denver
Michigan State Univ.
Middle Tennessee State Univ.
Midwestern State Univ. (TX)
Minnesota State Univ.–Mankato
Minnesota State Univ.–Moorhead
Minot State Univ. (ND)
Mississippi College
Mississippi Valley State Univ.
Missouri Baptist College
Missouri Valley College
Missouri Western State College
Molloy College (NY)
Monmouth Univ. (NJ)
Morris College (SC)
Mount Marty College (SD)
Mount Mary College (WI)
Mount Olive College (NC)
Mount St. Mary's Univ. (MD)
Mount Vernon Nazarene Univ. (OH)
Mountain State Univ. (WV)
Murray State Univ. (KY)
Muskingum College (OH)
National Univ. (CA)
Neumann College (PA)
New Jersey City Univ.
New Mexico Highlands Univ.
New Mexico State Univ.
New York Institute of Technology
Niagara Univ. (NY)
Nichols College (MA)
North Carolina Central Univ.
North Carolina Wesleyan College
North Dakota State Univ.
North Georgia College and State Univ.
Northeastern Illinois Univ.
Northeastern State Univ. (OK)
Northeastern Univ. (MA)
Northern Arizona Univ.
Northern Kentucky Univ.
Northern Michigan Univ.
Northwestern College (MN)
Northwestern Oklahoma State Univ.
Northwestern State Univ. of Louisiana
Nova Southeastern Univ. (FL)
Oakland City Univ. (IN)
Ohio Dominican Univ.
Ohio Northern Univ.

Olivet College (MI)
Olivet Nazarene Univ. (IL)
Pace Univ. (NY)
Park Univ. (MO)
Penn. State Univ.–Univ. Park
Pepperdine Univ. (CA)
Peru State College (NE)
Pfeiffer Univ. (NC)
Piedmont College (GA)
Pikeville College (KY)
Pittsburg State Univ. (KS)
Plymouth State Univ. (NH)
Point Park Univ. (PA)
Prairie View A&M Univ. (TX)
Purdue Univ.–Calumet (IN)
Quincy Univ. (IL)
Quinnipiac Univ. (CT)
Radford Univ. (VA)
Regis Univ. (CO)
Rhode Island College
Rivier College (NH)
Roanoke College (VA)
Roberts Wesleyan College (NY)
Rochester Institute of Tech. (NY)
Roger Williams Univ. (RI)
Roosevelt Univ. (IL)
Rutgers–Camden (NJ)
Rutgers–New Brunswick (NJ)
Rutgers–Newark (NJ)
Sacred Heart Univ. (CT)
Saginaw Valley State Univ. (MI)
Salem International Univ. (WV)
Salem State College (MA)
Salve Regina Univ. (RI)
Sam Houston State Univ. (TX)
San Diego State Univ.
San Francisco State Univ.
San Jose State Univ. (CA)
Savannah State Univ. (GA)
Seattle Univ.
Seton Hall Univ. (NJ)
Seton Hill Univ. (PA)
Shaw Univ. (NC)
Shenandoah Univ. (VA)
Shippensburg Univ. of
   Pennsylvania
Simpson College (IA)
Sonoma State Univ. (CA)
South Carolina State Univ.
Southeast Missouri State Univ.
Southeastern Louisiana Univ.
Southeastern Oklahoma State
   Univ.
Southern Arkansas Univ.
Southern Illinois Univ.–Carbondale
Southern Illinois
   Univ.–Edwardsville
Southern Oregon Univ.
Southern Univ. and A&M College
   (LA)
Southern Utah Univ.
Southern Wesleyan Univ. (SC)
Southwest Baptist Univ. (MO)
Southwest Minnesota State Univ.
   (MN)
Southwest Missouri State Univ.
Southwestern Adventist Univ. (TX)
Southwestern Oklahoma State
   Univ.
Springfield College (MA)
St. Ambrose Univ. (IA)

St. Andrews Presbyterian College
   (NC)
St. Augustine's College (NC)
St. Cloud State Univ. (MN)
St. Edward's Univ. (TX)
St. Francis College (NY)
St. Francis Univ. (PA)
St. Gregory's Univ. (OK)
St. John's Univ. (NY)
St. Joseph's College (ME)
St. Joseph's College (IN)
St. Leo Univ. (FL)
St. Louis Univ.
St. Mary's Univ. of Minnesota
St. Paul's College (VA)
St. Peter's College (NJ)
St. Thomas Aquinas College (NY)
St. Thomas Univ. (FL)
St. Xavier Univ. (IL)
Stephen F. Austin State Univ. (TX)
Stonehill College (MA)
Suffolk Univ. (MA)
Sul Ross State Univ. (TX)
SUNY College–Brockport
SUNY College–Oneonta
SUNY College–Potsdam
SUNY–Albany
SUNY–Farmingdale
SUNY–Plattsburgh
Syracuse Univ. (NY)
Tarleton State Univ. (TX)
Teikyo Post Univ. (CT)
Temple Univ. (PA)
Tennessee State Univ.
Texas A&M International Univ.
Texas A&M Univ.–Commerce
Texas A&M Univ.–Corpus Christi
Texas A&M Univ.–Kingsville
Texas Christian Univ.
Texas State Univ.–San Marcos
Texas Wesleyan Univ.
Texas Woman's Univ.
The Citadel (SC)
Thomas College (ME)
Thomas Edison State College (NJ)
Thomas More College (KY)
Thomas Univ. (GA)
Tiffin Univ. (OH)
Tri-State Univ. (IN)
Trinity College (DC)
Troy State Univ.–Troy (AL)
Truman State Univ. (MO)
Tulane Univ. (LA)
Union Institute and Univ. (OH)
Univ. of Akron (OH)
Univ. of Alabama
Univ. of Alabama–Birmingham
Univ. of Alaska–Anchorage
Univ. of Alaska–Fairbanks
Univ. of Arizona
Univ. of Arkansas
Univ. of Arkansas–Little Rock
Univ. of Arkansas–Monticello
Univ. of Arkansas–Pine Bluff
Univ. of Central Florida
Univ. of Central Oklahoma
Univ. of Dayton (OH)
Univ. of Detroit Mercy
Univ. of Dubuque (IA)
Univ. of Findlay (OH)
Univ. of Georgia

Univ. of Great Falls (MT)
Univ. of Hartford (CT)
Univ. of Houston–Downtown
Univ. of Illinois–Chicago
Univ. of Illinois–Springfield
Univ. of Indianapolis
Univ. of Louisiana–Lafayette
Univ. of Louisiana–Monroe
Univ. of Louisville (KY)
Univ. of Maine–Augusta
Univ. of Maine–Presque Isle
Univ. of Mary (ND)
Univ. of Mary Hardin-Baylor (TX)
Univ. of Maryland–Eastern Shore
Univ. of Maryland–Univ. College
Univ. of Massachusetts–Boston
Univ. of Massachusetts–Lowell
Univ. of Memphis
Univ. of Michigan–Dearborn
Univ. of Michigan–Flint
Univ. of Mississippi
Univ. of Missouri–Kansas City
Univ. of Nebraska–Kearney
Univ. of Nebraska–Omaha
Univ. of Nevada–Las Vegas
Univ. of New Haven (CT)
Univ. of New Mexico
Univ. of North Alabama
Univ. of North Carolina–Charlotte
Univ. of North Carolina–Pembroke
Univ. of N.C.–Wilmington
Univ. of North Dakota
Univ. of North Florida
Univ. of North Texas
Univ. of Northern Colorado
Univ. of Pittsburgh
Univ. of Pittsburgh–Bradford
Univ. of Pittsburgh–Greensburg
Univ. of Richmond (VA)
Univ. of Scranton (PA)
Univ. of Sioux Falls (SD)
Univ. of South Alabama
Univ. of South Carolina–Columbia
Univ. of South Carolina–Upstate
Univ. of South Dakota
Univ. of Southern Mississippi
Univ. of Tennessee–Chattanooga
Univ. of Tennessee–Martin
Univ. of Texas of the Permian Basin
Univ. of Texas–Arlington
Univ. of Texas–Brownsville
Univ. of Texas–El Paso
Univ. of Texas–Pan American
Univ. of Texas–San Antonio
Univ. of Texas–Tyler
Univ. of the District of Columbia
Univ. of Toledo (OH)
Univ. of Washington
Univ. of West Florida
Univ. of Wisconsin–Eau Claire
Univ. of Wisconsin–Milwaukee
Univ. of Wisconsin–Parkside
Univ. of Wisconsin–Platteville
Univ. of Wisconsin–Superior
Univ. of Wyoming
Urbana Univ. (OH)
Utah Valley State College
Utica College (NY)
Valdosta State Univ. (GA)
Virginia Commonwealth Univ.
Virginia Intermont College

Virginia State Univ.
Viterbo Univ. (WI)
Voorhees College (SC)
Washburn Univ. (KS)
Washington State Univ.
Wayland Baptist Univ. (TX)
Wayne State College (NE)
Wayne State Univ. (MI)
Waynesburg College (PA)
Weber State Univ. (UT)
West Chester Univ. of Pennsylvania
West Liberty State College (WV)
West Texas A&M Univ.
West Virginia State Univ.
West Virginia Univ.
West Virginia Wesleyan College
Western Carolina Univ. (NC)
Western Connecticut State Univ.
Western Illinois Univ.
Western Michigan Univ.
Western New England College
   (MA)
Western New Mexico Univ.
Western Oregon Univ.
Westfield State College (MA)
Wheeling Jesuit Univ. (WV)
Wichita State Univ. (KS)
Widener Univ. (PA)
Wiley College (TX)
Wilkes Univ. (PA)
William Woods Univ. (MO)
Wilmington College (OH)
Wilmington College (DE)
Winona State Univ. (MN)
Winston-Salem State Univ. (NC)
Worcester State College (MA)
Xavier Univ. (OH)
York College of Pennsylvania
Youngstown State Univ. (OH)

Criminology

Albright College (PA)
Arcadia Univ. (PA)
Arkansas State Univ.
Auburn Univ. (AL)
Ball State Univ. (IN)
Barber Scotia College (NC)
Buffalo State College
Butler Univ. (IN)
Cabrini College (PA)
California State Univ.–Fresno
Cameron Univ. (OK)
Capital Univ. (OH)
Central Connecticut State Univ.
Coker College (SC)
College of Mount St. Joseph (OH)
College of Notre Dame of
   Maryland
College of the Ozarks (MO)
Columbus State Univ. (GA)
Concordia Univ.–River Forest (IL)
Concordia Univ.–St. Paul (MN)
Delaware State Univ.
Dominican Univ. (IL)
Drury Univ. (MO)
Eastern Michigan Univ.
Eastern Washington Univ.
Elizabethtown College (PA)
Evangel Univ. (MO)

Florida Memorial College
Gallaudet Univ. (DC)
Indiana State Univ.
Indiana Univ. of Pennsylvania
Johnson C. Smith Univ. (NC)
Juniata College (PA)
Le Moyne College (NY)
Lees-Mcrae College (NC)
Lemoyne-Owen College (TN)
Longwood Univ. (VA)
Loras College (IA)
Lycoming College (PA)
Mansfield Univ. of Pennsylvania
Marquette Univ. (WI)
Marymount Univ. (VA)
Maryville Univ. of St. Louis (MO)
Midland Lutheran College (NE)
Mount Mercy College (IA)
New England College (NH)
Niagara Univ. (NY)
North Carolina State Univ.–Raleigh
North Carolina Wesleyan College
Ohio State Univ.–Columbus
Ohio Univ.
Old Dominion Univ. (VA)
Our Lady of Holy Cross Coll. (LA)
Paine College (GA)
Purdue Univ.–Calumet (IN)
Richard Stockton College of New
   Jersey
Russell Sage College (NY)
San Diego State Univ.
St. Anselm College (NH)
St. Edward's Univ. (TX)
St. Joseph's Univ. (PA)
St. Martin's College (WA)
State Univ. of West Georgia
Stonehill College (MA)
Suffolk Univ. (MA)
SUNY College–Old Westbury
Texas A&M Univ.–Commerce
Texas A&M Univ.–Kingsville
Thiel College (PA)
Univ. of Akron (OH)
Univ. of California–Irvine
Univ. of Delaware
Univ. of Denver
Univ. of Florida
Univ. of Great Falls (MT)
Univ. of Hawaii–Hilo
Univ. of La Verne (CA)
Univ. of Maryland–College Park
Univ. of Miami (FL)
Univ. of Minnesota–Duluth
Univ. of Minnesota–Twin Cities
Univ. of Missouri–St. Louis
Univ. of Nevada–Reno
Univ. of New Hampshire
Univ. of Northern Iowa
Univ. of South Florida
Univ. of Southern Maine
Univ. of St. Thomas (MN)
Univ. of Tampa (FL)
Univ. of Texas of the Permian Basin
Univ. of Texas–Dallas
Univ. of Virginia–Wise
Upper Iowa Univ.
Valparaiso Univ. (IN)
Virginia Wesleyan College
Western Michigan Univ.
William Penn Univ. (IA)

Culinary Arts and Related Services

Drexel Univ. (PA)
Johnson and Wales Univ. (RI)
Kendall College (IL)
Mississippi Univ. For Women
Mountain State Univ. (WV)
Nicholls State Univ. (LA)
Pennsylvania College of Technology
Southern New Hampshire Univ.
Texas A&M Univ.–Kingsville
Thiel College (PA)
Univ. of Alaska–Anchorage
Univ. of Nevada–Las Vegas
Univ. of New Hampshire
Virginia Intermont College

Curriculum and Instruction

California State Univ.–Sacramento
Campbellsville Univ. (KY)
College of the Southwest (NM)
Colorado Christian Univ.
Coppin State Univ. (MD)
Keene State College (NH)
Lake Erie College (OH)
Lincoln Memorial Univ. (TN)
Long Island Univ.–Brooklyn (NY)
Midwestern State Univ. (TX)
Northern State Univ. (SD)
Seattle Pacific Univ.
South Dakota State Univ.
Southern Illinois Univ.–Carbondale
Texas A&M Univ.–College Station
Texas Wesleyan Univ.
Univ. of California–Riverside
Univ. of Judaism (CA)
Univ. of Nevada–Las Vegas
Univ. of Redlands (CA)
Univ. of Wisconsin–Oshkosh
Utah State Univ.
Washington State Univ.

Dance

Adelphi Univ. (NY)
Alma College (MI)
Antioch College (OH)
Arizona State Univ.
Ball State Univ. (IN)
Barnard College (NY)
Belhaven College (MS)
Beloit College (WI)
Bennington College (VT)
Boston Conservatory
Brenau Univ. (GA)
Brigham Young Univ.–Provo (UT)
Butler Univ. (IN)
California Institute of the Arts
California State Univ.–Fullerton
California State Univ.–Long Beach
California State Univ.–Sacramento
Cedar Crest College (PA)
Centenary College of Louisiana
Chapman Univ. (CA)
Coker College (SC)

Colorado College
Colorado State Univ.
Columbia College (IL)
Columbia College (SC)
Columbia Univ. (NY)
Connecticut College
Cornell Univ. (NY)
Cornish College of the Arts (WA)
CUNY–Hunter College
CUNY–Lehman College
CUNY–Queens College
Denison Univ. (OH)
Desales Univ. (PA)
East Carolina Univ. (NC)
Eastern Michigan Univ.
Eastern Univ. (PA)
Elon Univ. (NC)
Emory Univ. (GA)
Florida International Univ.
Florida State Univ.
Fordham Univ. (NY)
Franklin and Marshall College (PA)
Friends Univ. (KS)
Frostburg State Univ. (MD)
George Mason Univ. (VA)
George Washington Univ. (DC)
Goucher College (MD)
Gustavus Adolphus College (MN)
Hamilton College (NY)
Hampshire College (MA)
Hobart and William Smith Colleges (NY)
Hofstra Univ. (NY)
Hollins Univ. (VA)
Hope College (MI)
Howard Univ. (DC)
Indiana Univ.–Bloomington
Jacksonville Univ. (FL)
Juilliard School (NY)
Keene State College (NH)
Kent State Univ. (OH)
La Roche College (PA)
Lamar Univ. (TX)
Lees-Mcrae College (NC)
Lindenwood Univ. (MO)
Long Island Univ.–Brooklyn (NY)
Long Island Univ.–C.W. Post Campus (NY)
Loyola Marymount Univ. (CA)
Manhattanville College (NY)
Marygrove College (MI)
Marymount Manhattan College (NY)
Marywood Univ. (PA)
Mercyhurst College (PA)
Meredith College (NC)
Middlebury College (VT)
Mills College (CA)
Montclair State Univ. (NJ)
Mount Holyoke College (MA)
Muhlenberg College (PA)
New Jersey City Univ.
New Mexico State Univ.
New School Univ. (NY)
New York Univ.
North Carolina School of the Arts
Northwestern Univ. (IL)
Oberlin College (OH)
Ohio State Univ.–Columbus
Ohio Univ.
Ohio Wesleyan Univ.

Oklahoma City Univ.
Palm Beach Atlantic Univ. (FL)
Pitzer College (CA)
Point Park Univ. (PA)
Pomona College (CA)
Prescott College (AZ)
Radford Univ. (VA)
Randolph-Macon Woman's College (VA)
Rhode Island College
Rockford College (IL)
Roger Williams Univ. (RI)
Rutgers–New Brunswick (NJ)
Salisbury Univ. (MD)
Sam Houston State Univ. (TX)
San Diego State Univ.
San Francisco State Univ.
San Jose State Univ. (CA)
Scripps College (CA)
Shenandoah Univ. (VA)
Skidmore College (NY)
Slippery Rock Univ. of Pennsylvania
Southern Methodist Univ. (TX)
Southern Utah Univ.
Southwest Missouri State Univ.
Springfield College (MA)
St. Gregory's Univ. (OK)
St. Mary's College of California
St. Olaf College (MN)
Stephen F. Austin State Univ. (TX)
Stephens College (MO)
SUNY College–Brockport
SUNY College–Potsdam
SUNY–Purchase College
Swarthmore College (PA)
Sweet Briar College (VA)
Temple Univ. (PA)
Texas Christian Univ.
Texas State Univ.–San Marcos
Texas Tech Univ.
Texas Woman's Univ.
Towson Univ. (MD)
Trinity College (CT)
Tulane Univ. (LA)
Univ. at Buffalo–SUNY
Univ. of Akron (OH)
Univ. of Alabama
Univ. of Arizona
Univ. of California–Berkeley
Univ. of California–Irvine
Univ. of California–Riverside
Univ. of California–Santa Barbara
Univ. of Central Oklahoma
Univ. of Colorado–Boulder
Univ. of Florida
Univ. of Georgia
Univ. of Hartford (CT)
Univ. of Hawaii–Hilo
Univ. of Hawaii–Manoa
Univ. of Houston
Univ. of Ill.–Urbana-Champaign
Univ. of Iowa
Univ. of Kansas
Univ. of Maryland–Baltimore County
Univ. of Maryland–College Park
Univ. of Massachusetts–Amherst
Univ. of Michigan–Ann Arbor
Univ. of Michigan–Flint
Univ. of Minnesota–Twin Cities
Univ. of Missouri–Kansas City

Univ. of Montana
Univ. of Nebraska–Lincoln
Univ. of Nevada–Las Vegas
Univ. of New Mexico
Univ. of North Carolina–Charlotte
Univ. of N.C.–Greensboro
Univ. of North Texas
Univ. of Oklahoma
Univ. of Oregon
Univ. of South Florida
Univ. of Southern Mississippi
Univ. of St. Francis (IN)
Univ. of Texas–Austin
Univ. of Texas–El Paso
Univ. of Texas–Pan American
Univ. of the Arts (PA)
Univ. of Utah
Univ. of Washington
Univ. of Wisconsin–Madison
Univ. of Wisconsin–Milwaukee
Ursinus College (PA)
Utah State Univ.
Utah Valley State College
Virginia Commonwealth Univ.
Virginia Intermont College
Washington Univ. In St. Louis
Wayne State Univ. (MI)
Weber State Univ. (UT)
Webster Univ. (MO)
Wesleyan Univ. (CT)
West Texas A&M Univ.
Western Michigan Univ.
Western Oregon Univ.
Winthrop Univ. (SC)
Wright State Univ. (OH)

Data Processing

Arkansas State Univ.
Clayton Coll. and State Univ. (GA)
Indiana Univ.–Kokomo
Mcmurry Univ. (TX)
Pace Univ. (NY)
Roosevelt Univ. (IL)
Stephen F. Austin State Univ. (TX)
Texas State Univ.–San Marcos
Univ. of Arkansas
Univ. of Southern Indiana
Univ. of Southern Mississippi
Utah Valley State College

Demography and Population Studies

Alfred Univ. (NY)
Bennett College (NC)
Campbell Univ. (NC)
Central Missouri State Univ.
Chadron State College (NE)
Concordia Coll.–Moorhead (MN)
CUNY–Hunter College
Duke Univ. (NC)
Grace Univ. (NE)
Hampshire College (MA)
North Carolina A&T State Univ.
Northern Arizona Univ.
Princeton Univ. (NJ)
Southwest Missouri State Univ.
Univ. of North Carolina–Pembroke

Western New Mexico Univ.

Dental Support Services and Allied Professions

Armstrong Atlantic State Univ. (GA)
Clayton Coll. and State Univ. (GA)
East Tennessee State Univ.
Eastern Washington Univ.
Idaho State Univ.
Indiana Univ.-Purdue Univ.–Indianapolis
Louisiana College
Midwestern State Univ. (TX)
Minnesota State Univ.–Mankato
Mount Ida College (MA)
Northern Arizona Univ.
Ohio State Univ.–Columbus
Old Dominion Univ. (VA)
Oregon Institute of Technology
Pennsylvania College of Technology
SUNY–Farmingdale
Tennessee State Univ.
Texas Woman's Univ.
Thomas Edison State College (NJ)
Univ. of Bridgeport (CT)
Univ. of Colorado–Denver
Univ. of Detroit Mercy
Univ. of Hawaii–Manoa
Univ. of Louisiana–Lafayette
Univ. of Louisiana–Monroe
Univ. of Louisville (KY)
Univ. of Maine–Augusta
Univ. of Maryland–Eastern Shore
Univ. of Michigan–Ann Arbor
Univ. of Minnesota–Twin Cities
Univ. of Missouri–Kansas City
Univ. of New England (ME)
Univ. of New Haven (CT)
Univ. of New Mexico
Univ. of N.C.–Chapel Hill
Univ. of Oklahoma
Univ. of Pittsburgh
Univ. of Rhode Island
Univ. of Southern California
Univ. of Southern Indiana
Univ. of Tennessee
Univ. of the Pacific (CA)
Univ. of Washington
Univ. of Wyoming
Virginia Commonwealth Univ.
Weber State Univ. (UT)
West Liberty State College (WV)
West Virginia Univ.
Western Kentucky Univ.
Wichita State Univ. (KS)

Design and Applied Arts

Abilene Christian Univ. (TX)
Adrian College (MI)
Albertus Magnus College (CT)
Albright College (PA)
Alma College (MI)
American Univ. (DC)
Anderson College (SC)
Anderson Univ. (IN)

Andrews Univ. (MI)
Anna Maria College (MA)
Appalachian State Univ. (NC)
Arcadia Univ. (PA)
Arizona State Univ.
Arkansas State Univ.
Art Academy of Cincinnati
Art Center College of Design (CA)
Ashland Univ. (OH)
Atlanta College of Art
Atlantic Union College (MA)
Auburn Univ. (AL)
Augusta State Univ. (GA)
Baker College of Flint (MI)
Baylor Univ. (TX)
Becker College (MA)
Bellevue Univ. (NE)
Belmont Univ. (TN)
Bemidji State Univ. (MN)
Bennington College (VT)
Bethel College (IN)
Black Hills State Univ. (SD)
Boise State Univ. (ID)
Boston Univ.
Bowling Green State Univ. (OH)
Brenau Univ. (GA)
Brescia Univ. (KY)
Briar Cliff Univ. (IA)
Bridgewater State College (MA)
Brigham Young Univ.–Provo (UT)
Buena Vista Univ. (IA)
Buffalo State College
Cabrini College (PA)
Cal Poly–San Luis Obispo
California Baptist Univ.
California College of the Arts
California Institute of the Arts
California State Polytechnic
    Univ.–Pomona
California State Univ.–Chico
California State Univ.–Long Beach
California State Univ.–Sacramento
California Univ. of Pennsylvania
Campbell Univ. (NC)
Cardinal Stritch Univ. (WI)
Carlow College (PA)
Carnegie Mellon Univ. (PA)
Carroll College (WI)
Carson-Newman College (TN)
Carthage College (WI)
Cazenovia College (NY)
Cedarville Univ. (OH)
Centenary College (NJ)
Central Connecticut State Univ.
Central Michigan Univ.
Central Missouri State Univ.
Central Washington Univ.
Chaminade Univ. of Honolulu
Chapman Univ. (CA)
Chatham College (PA)
Chowan College (NC)
Cleveland Institute of Art
Cogswell Polytechnical College
    (CA)
Coker College (SC)
Colby-Sawyer College (NH)
College For Creative Studies (MI)
College of Mount St. Joseph (OH)
College of New Jersey
College of Santa Fe (NM)
College of St. Catherine (MN)

College of St. Rose (NY)
College of the Ozarks (MO)
College of Visual Arts (MN)
Colorado State Univ.
Columbia College (MO)
Columbia College (IL)
Columbus College of Art and
    Design (OH)
Concord College (WV)
Concordia Univ. (NE)
Concordia Univ. Wisconsin
Converse College (SC)
Corcoran College of Art and Design
    (DC)
Cornell Univ. (NY)
Cornish College of the Arts (WA)
Creighton Univ. (NE)
CUNY–Baruch College
CUNY–Lehman College
CUNY–New York City College of
    Technology
CUNY–Queens College
Daemen College (NY)
David Lipscomb Univ. (TN)
Defiance College (OH)
Depaul Univ. (IL)
Dominican Univ. (IL)
Dordt College (IA)
Dowling College (NY)
Drake Univ. (IA)
Drexel Univ. (PA)
Drury Univ. (MO)
Duke Univ. (NC)
East Carolina Univ. (NC)
East Stroudsburg Univ. of
    Pennsylvania
Eastern Kentucky Univ.
Eastern Michigan Univ.
Eastern Washington Univ.
Edgewood College (WI)
Elizabeth City State Univ. (NC)
Elmhurst College (IL)
Emmanuel College (MA)
Emory and Henry College (VA)
Endicott College (MA)
Ferris State Univ. (MI)
Fitchburg State College (MA)
Flagler College (FL)
Florida A&M Univ.
Florida International Univ.
Florida Southern College
Florida State Univ.
Fort Valley State Univ. (GA)
Franklin Pierce College (NH)
Freed-Hardeman Univ. (TN)
Gallaudet Univ. (DC)
George Washington Univ. (DC)
Georgia Institute of Technology
Georgia Southern Univ.
Grace College and Seminary (IN)
Graceland Univ. (IA)
Grand Canyon Univ. (AZ)
Grand Valley State Univ. (MI)
Grand View College (IA)
Hampshire College (MA)
Hardin-Simmons Univ. (TX)
Harding Univ. (AR)
Henry Cogswell College (WA)
High Point Univ. (NC)
Hofstra Univ. (NY)
Howard Univ. (DC)

Huntingdon College (AL)
Huntington College (IN)
Indiana Univ. of Pennsylvania
Indiana Univ.–Bloomington
Indiana Univ.-Purdue Univ.–Fort
    Wayne
Indiana Wesleyan Univ.
Iowa State Univ.
Jacksonville Univ. (FL)
John Brown Univ. (AR)
Judson College (IL)
Kansas City Art Institute (MO)
Kansas State Univ.
Kean Univ. (NJ)
Keene State College (NH)
Kent State Univ. (OH)
Kutztown Univ. of Pennsylvania
La Roche College (PA)
La Sierra Univ. (CA)
Lambuth Univ. (TN)
Lawrence Technological Univ. (MI)
Lehigh Univ. (PA)
Liberty Univ. (VA)
Limestone College (SC)
Lindenwood Univ. (MO)
Long Island Univ.–C.W. Post
    Campus (NY)
Long Island Univ.–Southampton
    College (NY)
Louisiana College
Louisiana Tech Univ.
Loyola Univ. New Orleans
Lyndon State College (VT)
Lynn Univ. (FL)
Madonna Univ. (MI)
Maine College of Art
Marian College (IN)
Marian College of Fond Du Lac
    (WI)
Marietta College (OH)
Marist College (NY)
Maryland Institute College of Art
Marylhurst Univ. (OR)
Marymount Univ. (VA)
Maryville Univ. of St. Louis (MO)
Marywood Univ. (PA)
Massachusetts College of Art
Mcmurry Univ. (TX)
Mcpherson College (KS)
Meredith College (NC)
Metropolitan State College of
    Denver
Michigan State Univ.
Middle Tennessee State Univ.
Midland Lutheran College (NE)
Millikin Univ. (IL)
Milwaukee Institute of Art and
    Design
Minneapolis College of Art and
    Design
Minnesota State Univ.–Mankato
Minnesota State Univ.–Moorhead
Mississippi College
Missouri Western State College
Monmouth College (IL)
Montana State Univ.–Northern
Montclair State Univ. (NJ)
Montserrat College of Art (MA)
Moore College of Art and Design
    (PA)
Morningside College (IA)

Mount Mary College (WI)
Mount Mercy College (IA)
Mount Vernon Nazarene Univ.
    (OH)
New England College (NH)
New Mexico Highlands Univ.
New School Univ. (NY)
New York Institute of Technology
North Carolina A&T State Univ.
North Carolina State Univ.–Raleigh
North Central College (IL)
North Dakota State Univ.
North Georgia College and State
    Univ.
Northeastern State Univ. (OK)
Northeastern Univ.·(MA)
Northern Arizona Univ.
Northern Kentucky Univ.
Northern Michigan Univ.
Northwestern College (MN)
Notre Dame De Namur Univ. (CA)
Oakland City Univ. (IN)
Ohio Dominican Univ.
Ohio State Univ.–Columbus
Ohio Univ.
Oklahoma Christian Univ.
Oklahoma City Univ.
Oregon State Univ.
Otis College of Art and Design
    (CA)
Ouachita Baptist Univ. (AR)
Palm Beach Atlantic Univ. (FL)
Park Univ. (MO)
Peace College (NC)
Pennsylvania College of Technology
Penn. State Univ.–Univ. Park
Philadelphia Univ.
Pittsburg State Univ. (KS)
Point Loma Nazarene Univ. (CA)
Point Park Univ. (PA)
Prairie View A&M Univ. (TX)
Purdue Univ.–West Lafayette (IN)
Quincy Univ. (IL)
Quinnipiac Univ. (CT)
Radford Univ. (VA)
Regis College (MA)
Rhode Island School of Design
Ringling School of Art and Design
    (FL)
River College (NH)
Robert Morris College (IL)
Robert Morris Univ. (PA)
Rochester Institute of Tech. (NY)
Roger Williams Univ. (RI)
Sacred Heart Univ. (CT)
Saginaw Valley State Univ. (MI)
Salem College (NC)
Sam Houston State Univ. (TX)
Samford Univ. (AL)
San Diego State Univ.
San Jose State Univ. (CA)
Savannah College of Art and
    Design (GA)
School of the Art Institute of
    Chicago
Schreiner Univ. (TX)
Seton Hall Univ. (NJ)
Seton Hill Univ. (PA)
Shawnee State Univ. (OH)
South Dakota State Univ.
Southeastern Oklahoma St. Univ.

Southern Adventist Univ. (TN)
Southern Illinois Univ.–Carbondale
Southern New Hampshire Univ.
Southern Utah Univ.
Southwest Baptist Univ. (MO)
Southwest Missouri State Univ.
Southwestern Oklahoma State
    Univ.
Spring Arbor Univ. (MI)
Spring Hill College (AL)
Springfield College (MA)
St. Ambrose Univ. (IA)
St. Edward's Univ. (TX)
St. John's Univ. (NY)
St. Mary's Univ. of Minnesota
St. Norbert College (WI)
St. Thomas Aquinas College
    (NY)
St. Vincent College (PA)
Stephens College (MO)
Suffolk Univ. (MA)
SUNY–Farmingdale
SUNY–Fredonia
SUNY–Purchase College
Susquehanna Univ. (PA)
Syracuse Univ. (NY)
Tabor College (KS)
Temple Univ. (PA)
Texas A&M Univ.–Commerce
Texas Christian Univ.
Texas State Univ.–San Marcos
Texas Tech Univ.
Texas Woman's Univ.
Truman State Univ. (MO)
Union College (NE)
Univ. of Akron (OH)
Univ. of Alabama
Univ. of Bridgeport (CT)
Univ. of California–Davis
Univ. of California–Los Angeles
Univ. of Central Oklahoma
Univ. of Charleston (WV)
Univ. of Dayton (OH)
Univ. of Delaware
Univ. of Denver
Univ. of Florida
Univ. of Georgia
Univ. of Hartford (CT)
Univ. of Houston
Univ. of Illinois–Chicago
Univ. of Ill.–Urbana-Champaign
Univ. of Indianapolis
Univ. of Kansas
Univ. of Kentucky
Univ. of Louisiana–Lafayette
Univ. of Louisville (KY)
Univ. of Maryland–Eastern Shore
Univ. of Massachusetts–Amherst
Univ. of Mass.–Dartmouth
Univ. of Miami (FL)
Univ. of Michigan–Ann Arbor
Univ. of Michigan–Flint
Univ. of Minnesota–Duluth
Univ. of Minnesota–Twin Cities
Univ. of Missouri–St. Louis
Univ. of Montana
Univ. of New Haven (CT)
Univ. of N.C.–Greensboro
Univ. of North Texas
Univ. of Northern Iowa
Univ. of Notre Dame (IN)

Univ. of Oklahoma
Univ. of Oregon
Univ. of San Francisco
Univ. of South Carolina–Upstate
Univ. of St. Francis (IN)
Univ. of Tampa (FL)
Univ. of Tennessee
Univ. of Texas–Austin
Univ. of Texas–El Paso
Univ. of Texas–Pan American
Univ. of the Arts (PA)
Univ. of the Incarnate Word (TX)
Univ. of the Pacific (CA)
Univ. of Wisconsin–Madison
Univ. of Wisconsin–Stevens Point
Univ. of Wisconsin–Stout
Upper Iowa Univ.
Ursuline College (OH)
Utah State Univ.
Utah Valley State College
Valdosta State Univ. (GA)
Villa Julie College (MD)
Virginia Commonwealth Univ.
Virginia Tech
Viterbo Univ. (WI)
Wartburg College (IA)
Washington Univ. In St. Louis
Wayne State College (NE)
Waynesburg College (PA)
Weber State Univ. (UT)
Wentworth Institute of Technology (MA)
West Liberty State College (WV)
West Texas A&M Univ.
West Virginia Wesleyan College
Western Carolina Univ. (NC)
Western Michigan Univ.
Western Washington Univ.
Wichita State Univ. (KS)
William Woods Univ. (MO)
Wilmington College (DE)
Woodbury Univ. (CA)
York College of Pennsylvania
Youngstown State Univ. (OH)

Developmental and Child Psychology

Bridgewater State College (MA)
Cal Poly–San Luis Obispo
Colby-Sawyer College (NH)
Eastern Washington Univ.
Emmanuel College (MA)
Fitchburg State College (MA)
Gallaudet Univ. (DC)
Keene State College (NH)
Letourneau Univ. (TX)
Liberty Univ. (VA)
Long Island Univ.–Southampton College (NY)
Maryville College (TN)
National-Louis Univ. (IL)
Peace College (NC)
Prescott College (AZ)
Rivier College (NH)
Sonoma State Univ. (CA)
St. Mary's College of California
Suffolk Univ. (MA)
Tufts Univ. (MA)
Univ. of Detroit Mercy

Univ. of Judaism (CA)
Univ. of Kansas
Univ. of Minnesota–Twin Cities
Univ. of Wisconsin–Green Bay
Utica College (NY)
Vanderbilt Univ. (TN)
Warner Pacific College (OR)
Western Washington Univ.
Whittier College (CA)

Dietetics and Clinical Nutrition Services

Abilene Christian Univ. (TX)
Andrews Univ. (MI)
Ball State Univ. (IN)
Bowling Green State Univ. (OH)
Brigham Young Univ.–Provo (UT)
Buffalo State College
Cal Poly–San Luis Obispo
California State Univ.–Chico
California State Univ.–San Bernardino
Case Western Reserve Univ. (OH)
Central Missouri State Univ.
Cheyney Univ. of Pennsylvania
College of St. Benedict (MN)
College of St. Catherine (MN)
College of St. Elizabeth (NJ)
College of the Ozarks (MO)
David Lipscomb Univ. (TN)
Dominican Univ. (IL)
East Carolina Univ. (NC)
Eastern Kentucky Univ.
Eastern Michigan Univ.
Florida International Univ.
Florida State Univ.
Fontbonne Univ. (MO)
Gannon Univ. (PA)
Harding Univ. (AR)
Idaho State Univ.
Immaculata Univ. (PA)
Indiana Univ. of Pennsylvania
Iowa State Univ.
Kansas State Univ.
Keene State College (NH)
La Salle Univ. (PA)
Louisiana State Univ.–Baton Rouge
Louisiana Tech Univ.
Loyola Univ. Chicago
Madonna Univ. (MI)
Mansfield Univ. of Pennsylvania
Marshall Univ. (WV)
Meredith College (NC)
Messiah College (PA)
Miami Univ.–Oxford (OH)
Michigan State Univ.
Mount Mary College (WI)
Nicholls State Univ. (LA)
North Dakota State Univ.
Northern Illinois Univ.
Northern Michigan Univ.
Ohio State Univ.–Columbus
Ohio Univ.
Olivet Nazarene Univ. (IL)
Ouachita Baptist Univ. (AR)
Point Loma Nazarene Univ. (CA)
Rochester Institute of Tech. (NY)
Seton Hill Univ. (PA)
Southwest Missouri State Univ.

St. John's Univ. (MN)
SUNY College–Oneonta
Tarleton State Univ. (TX)
Texas Christian Univ.
Texas Tech Univ.
Texas Woman's Univ.
Univ. of Akron (OH)
Univ. of Alabama
Univ. of Connecticut
Univ. of Dayton (OH)
Univ. of Delaware
Univ. of Georgia
Univ. of Illinois–Chicago
Univ. of Ill.–Urbana-Champaign
Univ. of Louisiana–Lafayette
Univ. of Maryland–College Park
Univ. of New Hampshire
Univ. of New Haven (CT)
Univ. of North Dakota
Univ. of Northern Colorado
Univ. of Pittsburgh
Univ. of Rhode Island
Univ. of Southern Mississippi
Univ. of Texas–Pan American
Univ. of Vermont
Univ. of Wisconsin–Stout
Virginia Intermont College
Viterbo Univ. (WI)
Wayne State Univ. (MI)
West Chester Univ. of Pennsylvania
Western Carolina Univ. (NC)
Western Michigan Univ.
Youngstown State Univ. (OH)

Drafting/Design Engineering Technologies/Technicians

Eastern Michigan Univ.
Grambling State Univ. (LA)
Indiana Univ.-Purdue Univ.–Indianapolis
Lewis-Clark State College (ID)
Montana State Univ.–Northern
Prairie View A&M Univ. (TX)
Purdue Univ.–West Lafayette (IN)
Southern Utah Univ.
Southwest Missouri State Univ.
Thomas Edison State College (NJ)
Tri-State Univ. (IN)
Weber State Univ. (UT)

Drama/Theater Arts and Stagecraft

Abilene Christian Univ. (TX)
Adams State College (CO)
Adelphi Univ. (NY)
Adrian College (MI)
Agnes Scott College (GA)
Alabama State Univ.
Albertson College (ID)
Albertus Magnus College (CT)
Albion College (MI)
Albright College (PA)
Alfred Univ. (NY)
Allegheny College (PA)
Alma College (MI)
American Univ. (DC)

Amherst College (MA)
Anderson College (SC)
Anderson Univ. (IN)
Angelo State Univ. (TX)
Appalachian State Univ. (NC)
Aquinas College (MI)
Arcadia Univ. (PA)
Arizona State Univ.
Arkansas State Univ.
Armstrong Atlantic St. Univ. (GA)
Ashland Univ. (OH)
Auburn Univ. (AL)
Augsburg College (MN)
Augustana College (SD)
Augustana College (IL)
Averett Univ. (VA)
Avila Univ. (MO)
Azusa Pacific Univ. (CA)
Baker Univ. (KS)
Baldwin-Wallace College (OH)
Ball State Univ. (IN)
Barnard College (NY)
Barry Univ. (FL)
Barton College (NC)
Bates College (ME)
Baylor Univ. (TX)
Belhaven College (MS)
Bellevue Univ. (NE)
Belmont Univ. (TN)
Beloit College (WI)
Bemidji State Univ. (MN)
Benedictine College (KS)
Bennington College (VT)
Berea College (KY)
Berklee College of Music (MA)
Berry College (GA)
Bethany College (WV)
Bethany College (CA)
Bethel College (IN)
Bethel Univ. (MN)
Bloomsburg Univ. of Pennsylvania
Bluefield College (VA)
Boise State Univ. (ID)
Boston Univ.
Bowdoin College (ME)
Bowling Green State Univ. (OH)
Bradley Univ. (IL)
Brandeis Univ. (MA)
Brenau Univ. (GA)
Brevard College (NC)
Briar Cliff Univ. (IA)
Bridgewater State College (MA)
Brigham Young Univ.–Provo (UT)
Brown Univ. (RI)
Bucknell Univ. (PA)
Buena Vista Univ. (IA)
Buffalo State College
Butler Univ. (IN)
Cal Poly–San Luis Obispo
Caldwell College (NJ)
California Baptist Univ.
California Institute of the Arts
California Lutheran Univ.
California State Polytechnic Univ.–Pomona
California State Univ.–Bakersfield
California State Univ.–Chico
California State Univ.–Dominguez Hills
California State Univ.–Fresno
California State Univ.–Fullerton

California State Univ.–Hayward
California State Univ.–Long Beach
California State Univ.–Los Angeles
California State Univ.–Northridge
California State Univ.–Sacramento
California State Univ.–San Bernardino
California State Univ.–San Marcos
California State Univ.–Stanislaus
California Univ. of Pennsylvania
Calvin College (MI)
Cameron Univ. (OK)
Campbell Univ. (NC)
Campbellsville Univ. (KY)
Capital Univ. (OH)
Cardinal Stritch Univ. (WI)
Carnegie Mellon Univ. (PA)
Carroll College (MT)
Carroll College (WI)
Carthage College (WI)
Case Western Reserve Univ. (OH)
Castleton State College (VT)
Catawba College (NC)
Catholic Univ. of America (DC)
Cedar Crest College (PA)
Cedarville Univ. (OH)
Centenary College of Louisiana
Central Christian College (KS)
Central College (IA)
Central Connecticut State Univ.
Central Methodist Univ. (MO)
Central Michigan Univ.
Central Missouri State Univ.
Central Washington Univ.
Centre College (KY)
Chadron State College (NE)
Chapman Univ. (CA)
Charleston Southern Univ. (SC)
Chatham College (PA)
Cheyney Univ. of Pennsylvania
Christopher Newport Univ. (VA)
Claremont Mckenna College (CA)
Clarion Univ. of Pennsylvania
Clark Univ. (MA)
Cleveland State Univ.
Coastal Carolina Univ. (SC)
Coe College (IA)
Coker College (SC)
Colby College (ME)
Colgate Univ. (NY)
College of Charleston (SC)
College of Santa Fe (NM)
College of St. Benedict (MN)
College of St. Catherine (MN)
College of the Holy Cross (MA)
College of the Ozarks (MO)
College of the Southwest (NM)
College of William and Mary (VA)
Colorado Christian Univ.
Colorado College
Colorado State Univ.
Columbia College (IL)
Columbia Univ. (NY)
Columbus State Univ. (GA)
Concordia Coll.–Moorhead (MN)
Concordia Univ. (NE)
Concordia Univ. (CA)
Concordia Univ. (MI)
Concordia Univ.–St. Paul (MN)
Connecticut College
Converse College (SC)

Cornell College (IA)
Cornell Univ. (NY)
Cornish College of the Arts (WA)
Creighton Univ. (NE)
Culver-Stockton College (MO)
Cumberland College (KY)
Cumberland Univ. (TN)
CUNY–Brooklyn College
CUNY–City College
CUNY–College of Staten Island
CUNY–Hunter College
CUNY–Lehman College
CUNY–New York City College of
    Technology
CUNY–Queens College
CUNY–York College
Dartmouth College (NH)
David Lipscomb Univ. (TN)
Davidson College (NC)
Davis and Elkins College (WV)
Denison Univ. (OH)
Depaul Univ. (IL)
Depauw Univ. (IN)
Desales Univ. (PA)
Dickinson College (PA)
Dickinson State Univ. (ND)
Dillard Univ. (LA)
Dominican Univ. (IL)
Dordt College (IA)
Drake Univ. (IA)
Drew Univ. (NJ)
Drexel Univ. (PA)
Drury Univ. (MO)
Duke Univ. (NC)
Duquesne Univ. (PA)
Earlham College (IN)
East Carolina Univ. (NC)
East Stroudsburg Univ. of
    Pennsylvania
East Texas Baptist Univ.
Eastern Illinois Univ.
Eastern Kentucky Univ.
Eastern Mennonite Univ. (VA)
Eastern Michigan Univ.
Eastern New Mexico Univ.
Eastern Oregon Univ.
Eastern Washington Univ.
Eckerd College (FL)
Edinboro Univ. of Pennsylvania
Elizabethtown College (PA)
Elmhurst College (IL)
Elmira College (NY)
Elon Univ. (NC)
Emerson College (MA)
Emory and Henry College (VA)
Emory Univ. (GA)
Emporia State Univ. (KS)
Eureka College (IL)
Evangel Univ. (MO)
Evergreen State College (WA)
Fairleigh Dickinson Univ. (NJ)
Fairmont State Univ. (WV)
Ferrum College (VA)
Fisk Univ. (TN)
Fitchburg State College (MA)
Flagler College (FL)
Florida A&M Univ.
Florida Atlantic Univ.
Florida International Univ.
Florida Southern College
Florida State Univ.

Fontbonne Univ. (MO)
Fordham Univ. (NY)
Fort Lewis College (CO)
Francis Marion Univ. (SC)
Franklin and Marshall College (PA)
Franklin College (IN)
Franklin Pierce College (NH)
Freed-Hardeman Univ. (TN)
Fresno Pacific Univ. (CA)
Friends Univ. (KS)
Frostburg State Univ. (MD)
Furman Univ. (SC)
Gallaudet Univ. (DC)
Gannon Univ. (PA)
Gardner-Webb Univ. (NC)
George Fox Univ. (OR)
George Mason Univ. (VA)
George Washington Univ. (DC)
Georgetown College (KY)
Georgia College and State Univ.
Georgia Southern Univ.
Georgia Southwestern State Univ.
Gettysburg College (PA)
Gonzaga Univ. (WA)
Gordon College (MA)
Goshen College (IN)
Goucher College (MD)
Graceland Univ. (IA)
Grand Valley State Univ. (MI)
Grand View College (IA)
Greensboro College (NC)
Greenville College (IL)
Grinnell College (IA)
Guilford College (NC)
Gustavus Adolphus College (MN)
Hamilton College (NY)
Hamline Univ. (MN)
Hampshire College (MA)
Hampton Univ. (VA)
Hannibal-Lagrange College (MO)
Hanover College (IN)
Hardin-Simmons Univ. (TX)
Hartwick College (NY)
Hastings College (NE)
Heidelberg College (OH)
Henderson State Univ. (AR)
Hendrix College (AR)
High Point Univ. (NC)
Hillsdale College (MI)
Hiram College (OH)
Hofstra Univ. (NY)
Hollins Univ. (VA)
Hope College (MI)
Howard Univ. (DC)
Humboldt State Univ. (CA)
Huntington College (IN)
Idaho State Univ.
Illinois State Univ.
Illinois Wesleyan Univ.
Indiana State Univ.
Indiana Univ. Northwest
Indiana Univ. of Pennsylvania
Indiana Univ. Southeast
Indiana Univ.–Bloomington
Indiana Univ.–South Bend
Indiana Univ.-Purdue Univ.–Fort
    Wayne
Iona College (NY)
Ithaca College (NY)
Jacksonville State Univ. (AL)
Jacksonville Univ. (FL)

James Madison Univ. (VA)
Jamestown College (ND)
Johnson State College (VT)
Juilliard School (NY)
Juniata College (PA)
Kalamazoo College (MI)
Kansas State Univ.
Kansas Wesleyan Univ.
Kean Univ. (NJ)
Keene State College (NH)
Kennesaw State Univ. (GA)
Kent State Univ. (OH)
King's College (PA)
Knox College (IL)
Kutztown Univ. of Pennsylvania
Lagrange College (GA)
Lake Erie College (OH)
Lamar Univ. (TX)
Lambuth Univ. (TN)
Lawrence Univ. (WI)
Le Moyne College (NY)
Lees-Mcrae College (NC)
Lehigh Univ. (PA)
Lenoir-Rhyne College (NC)
Lewis and Clark College (OR)
Liberty Univ. (VA)
Limestone College (SC)
Lindenwood Univ. (MO)
Linfield College (OR)
Lock Haven Univ. of Pennsylvania
Long Island Univ.–Brooklyn (NY)
Long Island Univ.–C.W. Post
    Campus (NY)
Louisiana College
Louisiana State Univ.–Baton Rouge
Loyola Marymount Univ. (CA)
Loyola Univ. Chicago
Loyola Univ. New Orleans
Luther College (IA)
Lycoming College (PA)
Lynchburg College (VA)
Lyon College (AR)
Macalester College (MN)
Macmurray College (IL)
Manhattanville College (NY)
Marietta College (OH)
Marquette Univ. (WI)
Mars Hill College (NC)
Mary Baldwin College (VA)
Marymount Manhattan College
    (NY)
Maryville College (TN)
Marywood Univ. (PA)
Mcdaniel College (MD)
Mckendree College (IL)
Mcmurry Univ. (TX)
Mcneese State Univ. (LA)
Mcpherson College (KS)
Mercer Univ. (GA)
Meredith College (NC)
Mesa State College (CO)
Messiah College (PA)
Methodist College (NC)
Miami Univ.–Oxford (OH)
Michigan State Univ.
Michigan Technological Univ.
Middle Tennessee State Univ.
Middlebury College (VT)
Midland Lutheran College (NE)
Midwestern State Univ. (TX)
Millikin Univ. (IL)

Millsaps College (MS)
Minnesota State Univ.–Mankato
Minnesota State Univ.–Moorhead
Minot State Univ. (ND)
Missouri Southern State Univ.
Missouri Valley College
Montana State Univ.–Billings
Montclair State Univ. (NJ)
Morehead State Univ. (KY)
Morehouse College (GA)
Morgan State Univ. (MD)
Morningside College (IA)
Mount Holyoke College (MA)
Mount Mercy College (IA)
Mount Union College (OH)
Mount Vernon Nazarene Univ.
    (OH)
Muhlenberg College (PA)
Murray State Univ. (KY)
National-Louis Univ. (IL)
Nazareth College of Rochester
    (NY)
Nebraska Wesleyan Univ.
New England College (NH)
New Jersey City Univ.
New Mexico State Univ.
New School Univ. (NY)
New York Univ.
Newberry College (SC)
North Carolina A&T State Univ.
North Carolina Central Univ.
North Carolina School of the Arts
North Carolina Wesleyan College
North Central College (IL)
North Dakota State Univ.
North Greenville College (SC)
Northeastern State Univ. (OK)
Northeastern Univ. (MA)
Northern Arizona Univ.
Northern Illinois Univ.
Northern Kentucky Univ.
Northern Michigan Univ.
Northwest Missouri State Univ.
Northwestern College (IA)
Northwestern State Univ. of
    Louisiana
Northwestern Univ. (IL)
Notre Dame De Namur Univ. (CA)
Oakland Univ. (MI)
Oberlin College (OH)
Occidental College (CA)
Oglethorpe Univ. (GA)
Ohio State Univ.–Columbus
Ohio Univ.
Ohio Wesleyan Univ.
Oklahoma Baptist Univ.
Oklahoma Christian Univ.
Oklahoma City Univ.
Oklahoma State Univ.
Old Dominion Univ. (VA)
Olivet College (MI)
Ouachita Baptist Univ. (AR)
Our Lady of the Lake Univ. (TX)
Pace Univ. (NY)
Pacific Lutheran Univ. (WA)
Pacific Univ. (OR)
Paine College (GA)
Palm Beach Atlantic Univ. (FL)
Penn. State Univ.–Univ. Park
Pepperdine Univ. (CA)
Piedmont College (GA)

Pitzer College (CA)
Plymouth State Univ. (NH)
Point Loma Nazarene Univ. (CA)
Point Park Univ. (PA)
Pomona College (CA)
Portland State Univ. (OR)
Prairie View A&M Univ. (TX)
Principia College (IL)
Purdue Univ.–West Lafayette (IN)
Radford Univ. (VA)
Ramapo College of New Jersey
Randolph-Macon College (VA)
Randolph-Macon Woman's College
    (VA)
Reed College (OR)
Regis College (MA)
Rhode Island College
Rhodes College (TN)
Ripon College (WI)
Roanoke College (VA)
Rockford College (IL)
Rocky Mountain College (MT)
Roger Williams Univ. (RI)
Rollins College (FL)
Roosevelt Univ. (IL)
Rutgers–Camden (NJ)
Rutgers–New Brunswick (NJ)
Rutgers–Newark (NJ)
Saginaw Valley State Univ. (MI)
Salem State College (MA)
Salisbury Univ. (MD)
Salve Regina Univ. (RI)
Sam Houston State Univ. (TX)
Samford Univ. (AL)
San Diego State Univ.
San Francisco State Univ.
San Jose State Univ. (CA)
Santa Clara Univ. (CA)
Savannah College of Art and
    Design (GA)
Schreiner Univ. (TX)
Scripps College (CA)
Seattle Pacific Univ.
Seattle Univ.
Seton Hill Univ. (PA)
Sewanee–Univ. of the South (TN)
Shaw Univ. (NC)
Shenandoah Univ. (VA)
Shorter College (GA)
Simpson College (IA)
Skidmore College (NY)
Slippery Rock Univ. of Pennsylvania
Sonoma State Univ. (CA)
South Carolina State Univ.
Southeast Missouri State Univ.
Southeastern College of the
    Assemblies of God
Southeastern Oklahoma State
    Univ.
Southern Arkansas Univ.
Southern Connecticut State Univ.
Southern Illinois Univ.–Carbondale
Southern Illinois
    Univ.–Edwardsville
Southern Methodist Univ. (TX)
Southern Oregon Univ.
Southern Univ. and A&M Coll. (LA)
Southern Utah Univ.
Southwest Baptist Univ. (MO)
Southwest Minnesota State Univ.
    (MN)

Southwest Missouri State Univ.
Southwestern College (KS)
Southwestern Univ. (TX)
Spelman College (GA)
Spring Hill College (AL)
St. Ambrose Univ. (IA)
St. Cloud State Univ. (MN)
St. Edward's Univ. (TX)
St. John's Univ. (MN)
St. Joseph's College (IN)
St. Lawrence Univ. (NY)
St. Louis Univ.
St. Martin's College (WA)
St. Mary's College (IN)
St. Mary's College of California
St. Mary's College of Maryland
St. Mary's Univ. of Minnesota
St. Michael's College (VT)
St. Olaf College (MN)
St. Vincent College (PA)
Stanford Univ. (CA)
State Univ. of West Georgia
Stephen F. Austin State Univ. (TX)
Stephens College (MO)
Sterling College (KS)
Stetson Univ. (FL)
Suffolk Univ. (MA)
Sul Ross State Univ. (TX)
SUNY College of Arts and
    Sciences–Geneseo
SUNY College–Brockport
SUNY College–Oneonta
SUNY College–Potsdam
SUNY–Albany
SUNY–Binghamton
SUNY–Fredonia
SUNY–Plattsburgh
SUNY–Purchase College
SUNY–Stony Brook
Susquehanna Univ. (PA)
Swarthmore College (PA)
Sweet Briar College (VA)
Syracuse Univ. (NY)
Tarleton State Univ. (TX)
Taylor Univ. (IN)
Temple Univ. (PA)
Tennessee State Univ.
Texas A&M Univ.–College Station
Texas A&M Univ.–Commerce
Texas A&M Univ.–Corpus Christi
Texas A&M Univ.–Kingsville
Texas Christian Univ.
Texas Lutheran Univ.
Texas State Univ.–San Marcos
Texas Tech Univ.
Texas Wesleyan Univ.
Texas Woman's Univ.
Thomas Edison State College (NJ)
Thomas More College (KY)
Towson Univ. (MD)
Transylvania Univ. (KY)
Trevecca Nazarene Univ. (TN)
Trinity College (CT)
Truman State Univ. (MO)
Tufts Univ. (MA)
Tulane Univ. (LA)
Univ. at Buffalo–SUNY
Univ. of Akron (OH)
Univ. of Alabama
Univ. of Alaska–Anchorage
Univ. of Alaska–Fairbanks

Univ. of Arizona
Univ. of Arkansas
Univ. of Arkansas–Little Rock
Univ. of California–Berkeley
Univ. of California–Davis
Univ. of California–Irvine
Univ. of California–Los Angeles
Univ. of California–Riverside
Univ. of California–Santa Barbara
Univ. of California–Santa Cruz
Univ. of Central Arkansas
Univ. of Central Florida
Univ. of Central Oklahoma
Univ. of Colorado–Boulder
Univ. of Colorado–Denver
Univ. of Connecticut
Univ. of Dallas
Univ. of Dayton (OH)
Univ. of Delaware
Univ. of Denver
Univ. of Detroit Mercy
Univ. of Evansville (IN)
Univ. of Findlay (OH)
Univ. of Florida
Univ. of Georgia
Univ. of Hartford (CT)
Univ. of Hawaii–Hilo
Univ. of Hawaii–Manoa
Univ. of Houston
Univ. of Illinois–Chicago
Univ. of Illinois–Urbana-
    Champaign
Univ. of Indianapolis
Univ. of Iowa
Univ. of Kansas
Univ. of Kentucky
Univ. of La Verne (CA)
Univ. of Louisville (KY)
Univ. of Maine–Farmington
Univ. of Maine–Orono
Univ. of Mary Hardin-Baylor (TX)
Univ. of Maryland–Baltimore
    County
Univ. of Maryland–College Park
Univ. of Massachusetts–Amherst
Univ. of Massachusetts–Boston
Univ. of Memphis
Univ. of Miami (FL)
Univ. of Michigan–Ann Arbor
Univ. of Michigan–Flint
Univ. of Minnesota–Duluth
Univ. of Minnesota–Morris
Univ. of Minnesota–Twin Cities
Univ. of Mississippi
Univ. of Missouri–Columbia
Univ. of Missouri–Kansas City
Univ. of Montana
Univ. of Montevallo (AL)
Univ. of Nebraska–Kearney
Univ. of Nebraska–Lincoln
Univ. of Nebraska–Omaha
Univ. of Nevada–Las Vegas
Univ. of Nevada–Reno
Univ. of New Mexico
Univ. of North Carolina–Asheville
Univ. of N.C.–Chapel Hill
Univ. of North Carolina–Charlotte
Univ. of N.C.–Greensboro
Univ. of North Carolina–Pembroke
Univ. of N.C.–Wilmington
Univ. of North Dakota

Univ. of North Texas
Univ. of Northern Colorado
Univ. of Northern Iowa
Univ. of Notre Dame (IN)
Univ. of Oklahoma
Univ. of Oregon
Univ. of Pennsylvania
Univ. of Pittsburgh
Univ. of Pittsburgh–Johnstown
Univ. of Portland (OR)
Univ. of Puget Sound (WA)
Univ. of Redlands (CA)
Univ. of Rhode Island
Univ. of Richmond (VA)
Univ. of San Diego
Univ. of Science and Arts of
    Oklahoma
Univ. of Scranton (PA)
Univ. of South Alabama
Univ. of South Carolina–Columbia
Univ. of South Dakota
Univ. of South Florida
Univ. of Southern California
Univ. of Southern Indiana
Univ. of Southern Mississippi
Univ. of St. Mary (KS)
Univ. of St. Thomas (MN)
Univ. of St. Thomas (TX)
Univ. of Tennessee
Univ. of Tennessee–Chattanooga
Univ. of Texas–Arlington
Univ. of Texas–Austin
Univ. of Texas–El Paso
Univ. of Texas–Pan American
Univ. of Texas–Tyler
Univ. of the Arts (PA)
Univ. of the District of Columbia
Univ. of the Incarnate Word (TX)
Univ. of the Ozarks (AR)
Univ. of the Pacific (CA)
Univ. of Toledo (OH)
Univ. of Tulsa (OK)
Univ. of Utah
Univ. of Vermont
Univ. of Virginia
Univ. of Virginia–Wise
Univ. of Washington
Univ. of West Florida
Univ. of Wisconsin–Eau Claire
Univ. of Wisconsin–Green Bay
Univ. of Wisconsin–La Crosse
Univ. of Wisconsin–Madison
Univ. of Wisconsin–Milwaukee
Univ. of Wisconsin–River Falls
Univ. of Wisconsin–Stevens Point
Univ. of Wisconsin–Superior
Univ. of Wisconsin–Whitewater
Univ. of Wyoming
Ursinus College (PA)
Utah State Univ.
Valparaiso Univ. (IN)
Vanderbilt Univ. (TN)
Vanguard Univ. of Southern
    California
Vassar College (NY)
Virginia Commonwealth Univ.
Virginia Intermont College
Virginia Tech
Virginia Wesleyan College
Viterbo Univ. (WI)
Wabash College (IN)

Wagner College (NY)
Wake Forest Univ. (NC)
Waldorf College (IA)
Wartburg College (IA)
Washburn Univ. (KS)
Washington and Jefferson College
    (PA)
Washington and Lee Univ. (VA)
Washington College (MD)
Washington State Univ.
Washington Univ. In St. Louis
Wayland Baptist Univ. (TX)
Wayne State College (NE)
Wayne State Univ. (MI)
Weber State Univ. (UT)
Webster Univ. (MO)
Wellesley College (MA)
Wesleyan College (GA)
Wesleyan Univ. (CT)
West Chester Univ. of Pennsylvania
West Texas A&M Univ.
West Virginia Univ.
West Virginia Wesleyan College
Western Carolina Univ. (NC)
Western Connecticut State Univ.
Western Illinois Univ.
Western Kentucky Univ.
Western Michigan Univ.
Western Oregon Univ.
Western State College of Colorado
Western Washington Univ.
Westfield State College (MA)
Westminster College (PA)
Westmont College (CA)
Wheaton College (MA)
Whitman College (WA)
Whittier College (CA)
Whitworth College (WA)
Wichita State Univ. (KS)
Wilkes Univ. (PA)
Willamette Univ. (OR)
William Carey College (MS)
William Jewell College (MO)
William Woods Univ. (MO)
Williams College (MA)
Wilmington College (OH)
Winona State Univ. (MN)
Winthrop Univ. (SC)
Wisconsin Lutheran College
Wofford College (SC)
Wright State Univ. (OH)
Yale Univ. (CT)
York College of Pennsylvania
Youngstown State Univ. (OH)

**East Asian Languages,
Literatures, and
Linguistics**

Antioch College (OH)
Arizona State Univ.
Ball State Univ. (IN)
Bates College (ME)
Beloit College (WI)
Bennington College (VT)
Brigham Young Univ.–Provo (UT)
California State Univ.–Fullerton
California State Univ.–Los Angeles
Carnegie Mellon Univ. (PA)
Central College (IA)

Colgate Univ. (NY)
Columbia Univ. (NY)
Connecticut College
CUNY–Hunter College
Dartmouth College (NH)
Eastern Michigan Univ.
Elizabethtown College (PA)
Emory Univ. (GA)
George Washington Univ. (DC)
Georgetown Univ. (DC)
Gettysburg College (PA)
Grinnell College (IA)
Gustavus Adolphus College (MN)
Hamilton College (NY)
Hollins Univ. (VA)
Indiana Univ.–Bloomington
La Salle Univ. (PA)
Lawrence Univ. (WI)
Lincoln Univ. (PA)
Linfield College (OR)
Macalester College (MN)
Michigan State Univ.
Middlebury College (VT)
Mount Union College (OH)
North Central College (IL)
Northwestern Univ. (IL)
Ohio State Univ.–Columbus
Pacific Lutheran Univ. (WA)
Pacific Univ. (OR)
Penn. State Univ.–Univ. Park
Pomona College (CA)
Reed College (OR)
Rutgers–New Brunswick (NJ)
San Diego State Univ.
San Francisco State Univ.
San Jose State Univ. (CA)
Scripps College (CA)
Stanford Univ. (CA)
Swarthmore College (PA)
Trinity College (CT)
Tufts Univ. (MA)
Univ. of Alaska–Fairbanks
Univ. of California–Berkeley
Univ. of California–Davis
Univ. of California–Irvine
Univ. of California–Los Angeles
Univ. of California–Riverside
Univ. of California–Santa Barbara
Univ. of Colorado–Boulder
Univ. of Findlay (OH)
Univ. of Florida
Univ. of Georgia
Univ. of Hawaii–Hilo
Univ. of Hawaii–Manoa
Univ. of Ill.–Urbana-Champaign
Univ. of Iowa
Univ. of Kansas
Univ. of Maryland–College Park
Univ. of Massachusetts–Amherst
Univ. of Minnesota–Twin Cities
Univ. of Montana
Univ. of Notre Dame (IN)
Univ. of Oklahoma
Univ. of Oregon
Univ. of Pennsylvania
Univ. of Pittsburgh
Univ. of Rochester (NY)
Univ. of Southern California
Univ. of St. Thomas (MN)
Univ. of Texas–Austin
Univ. of the Pacific (CA)

Univ. of Utah
Univ. of Washington
Univ. of Wisconsin–Madison
Vassar College (NY)
Washington and Lee Univ. (VA)
Washington Univ. In St. Louis
Wellesley College (MA)
Williams College (MA)
Yale Univ. (CT)

Ecology, Evolution, Systematics, and Population Biology

Alaska Pacific Univ.
Appalachian State Univ. (NC)
Arizona State Univ.
Arkansas Tech Univ.
Auburn Univ. (AL)
Averett Univ. (VA)
Bemidji State Univ. (MN)
Bennington College (VT)
Bethel College (IN)
Blackburn College (IL)
Bradley Univ. (IL)
Brevard College (NC)
Bridgewater State College (MA)
Brigham Young Univ.–Provo (UT)
Brown Univ. (RI)
Cal Poly–San Luis Obispo
California State Polytechnic
    Univ.–Pomona
California State Univ.–Hayward
California State Univ.–Long Beach
California State Univ.–Sacramento
California State Univ.–San Marcos
Carlow College (PA)
Case Western Reserve Univ. (OH)
Cedar Crest College (PA)
Clarkson Univ. (NY)
Coastal Carolina Univ. (SC)
Coe College (IA)
Colby College (ME)
College of Santa Fe (NM)
Colorado State Univ.
Columbia Univ. (NY)
Concordia College (NY)
Connecticut College
Cornell Univ. (NY)
Cornerstone Univ. (MI)
CUNY–Queens College
Dartmouth College (NH)
Desales Univ. (PA)
Dowling College (NY)
East Stroudsburg Univ. of
    Pennsylvania
Eastern Kentucky Univ.
Eckerd College (FL)
Elizabethtown College (PA)
Fairleigh Dickinson Univ. (NJ)
Ferris State Univ. (MI)
Fitchburg State College (MA)
Florida Institute of Technology
Florida International Univ.
Fort Lewis College (CO)
Friends Univ. (KS)
Georgetown College (KY)
Greenville College (IL)
Hamline Univ. (MN)
Hawaii Pacific Univ.

Humboldt State Univ. (CA)
Idaho State Univ.
Illinois College
Iona College (NY)
Iowa State Univ.
Jacksonville Univ. (FL)
Johns Hopkins Univ. (MD)
Juniata College (PA)
Lawrence Univ. (WI)
Lehigh Univ. (PA)
Lindenwood Univ. (MO)
Long Island Univ.–Southampton
    College (NY)
Mansfield Univ. of Pennsylvania
Marywood Univ. (PA)
Master's Coll. and Seminary (CA)
Michigan State Univ.
Missouri Southern State Univ.
Molloy College (NY)
Monmouth College (IL)
Monmouth Univ. (NJ)
Moravian College (PA)
Morehead State Univ. (KY)
Mount Union College (OH)
Nazareth College of Rochester
    (NY)
New Mexico State Univ.
Northeastern State Univ. (OK)
Northern Arizona Univ.
Northern Michigan Univ.
Northwest Missouri State Univ.
Northwestern Univ. (IL)
Nova Southeastern Univ. (FL)
Ohio State Univ.–Columbus
Oklahoma State Univ.
Olivet Nazarene Univ. (IL)
Oral Roberts Univ. (OK)
Philadelphia Univ.
Plymouth State Univ. (NH)
Prescott College (AZ)
Princeton Univ. (NJ)
Queens Univ. of Charlotte (NC)
Rice Univ. (TX)
Richard Stockton College of New
    Jersey
Rutgers–New Brunswick (NJ)
Salisbury Univ. (MD)
Samford Univ. (AL)
San Diego State Univ.
Savannah State Univ. (GA)
Siena College (NY)
Slippery Rock Univ. of Pennsylvania
Southern Nazarene Univ. (OK)
Southwestern College (KS)
St. Francis Univ. (PA)
St. Gregory's Univ. (OK)
St. Joseph's College (ME)
St. Mary's Univ. of Minnesota
Stetson Univ. (FL)
Suffolk Univ. (MA)
SUNY College Environmental
    Science and Forestry
SUNY College–Oneonta
Susquehanna Univ. (PA)
Taylor Univ. (IN)
Tennessee Technological Univ.
Texas A&M Univ.–Galveston
Texas State Univ.–San Marcos
Troy State Univ.–Troy (AL)
Tufts Univ. (MA)
Tulane Univ. (LA)

Unity College (ME)
Univ. of Akron (OH)
Univ. of Alabama
Univ. of Arizona
Univ. of California–Davis
Univ. of California–Irvine
Univ. of California–Los Angeles
Univ. of California–San Diego
Univ. of California–Santa Barbara
Univ. of California–Santa Cruz
Univ. of Charleston (WV)
Univ. of Colorado–Boulder
Univ. of Connecticut
Univ. of Dayton (OH)
Univ. of Denver
Univ. of Georgia
Univ. of Hawaii–Hilo
Univ. of Hawaii–Manoa
Univ. of Louisiana–Lafayette
Univ. of Maine–Machias
Univ. of Maine–Orono
Univ. of Maryland–College Park
Univ. of Maryland–Eastern Shore
Univ. of Miami (FL)
Univ. of Michigan–Ann Arbor
Univ. of Michigan–Flint
Univ. of Minnesota–Twin Cities
Univ. of Missouri–Rolla
Univ. of Nevada–Reno
Univ. of New England (ME)
Univ. of New Haven (CT)
Univ. of North Alabama
Univ. of N.C.–Wilmington
Univ. of Northern Iowa
Univ. of Oregon
Univ. of Pittsburgh
Univ. of Rhode Island
Univ. of San Diego
Univ. of South Carolina–Columbia
Univ. of Southern Mississippi
Univ. of Tampa (FL)
Univ. of Tennessee
Univ. of Texas–Austin
Univ. of Virginia–Wise
Univ. of West Alabama
Univ. of Wisconsin–Madison
Univ. of Wisconsin–Superior
Ursuline College (OH)
Washington College (MD)
Waynesburg College (PA)
Western Washington Univ.
William Jewell College (MO)
Wingate Univ. (NC)

Economics

Adelphi Univ. (NY)
Adrian College (MI)
Agnes Scott College (GA)
Alabama Agricultural and
    Mechanical Univ.
Albion College (MI)
Albright College (PA)
Alcorn State Univ. (MS)
Alfred Univ. (NY)
Allegheny College (PA)
Alma College (MI)
American Univ. (DC)
Amherst College (MA)
Antioch College (OH)

Appalachian State Univ. (NC)
Aquinas College (MI)
Arizona State Univ.
Arkansas State Univ.
Arkansas Tech Univ.
Armstrong Atlantic State Univ.
    (GA)
Ashland Univ. (OH)
Assumption College (MA)
Auburn Univ. (AL)
Augsburg College (MN)
Augustana College (SD)
Augustana College (IL)
Aurora Univ. (IL)
Austin College (TX)
Babson College (MA)
Baker Univ. (KS)
Baldwin-Wallace College (OH)
Ball State Univ. (IN)
Barnard College (NY)
Barry Univ. (FL)
Barton College (NC)
Bates College (ME)
Bellarmine Univ. (KY)
Belmont Abbey College (NC)
Belmont Univ. (TN)
Beloit College (WI)
Bemidji State Univ. (MN)
Benedict College (SC)
Benedictine College (KS)
Benedictine Univ. (IL)
Berea College (KY)
Berry College (GA)
Bethany College (WV)
Bethel Univ. (MN)
Bloomfield College (NJ)
Bloomsburg Univ. of Pennsylvania
Bluffton Univ. (OH)
Boise State Univ. (ID)
Boston Univ.
Bowdoin College (ME)
Bowling Green State Univ. (OH)
Bradley Univ. (IL)
Brandeis Univ. (MA)
Bridgewater College (VA)
Bridgewater State College (MA)
Brigham Young Univ.–Provo (UT)
Brown Univ. (RI)
Bryant College (RI)
Bryn Mawr College (PA)
Bucknell Univ. (PA)
Buffalo State College
Butler Univ. (IN)
Cal Poly–San Luis Obispo
California Institute of Technology
California Lutheran Univ.
California State Polytechnic
    Univ.–Pomona
California State Univ.–Bakersfield
California State Univ.–Chico
California State Univ.–Fresno
California State Univ.–Fullerton
California State Univ.–Hayward
California State Univ.–Long Beach
California State Univ.–Los Angeles
California State Univ.–Northridge
California State Univ.–Sacramento
California State Univ.–San
    Bernardino
California State Univ.–San Marcos
California State Univ.–Stanislaus

Calvin College (MI)
Campbell Univ. (NC)
Canisius College (NY)
Capital Univ. (OH)
Carleton College (MN)
Carnegie Mellon Univ. (PA)
Carson-Newman College (TN)
Carthage College (WI)
Case Western Reserve Univ. (OH)
Catholic Univ. of America (DC)
Centenary College of Louisiana
Central College (IA)
Central Connecticut State Univ.
Central Methodist Univ. (MO)
Central Michigan Univ.
Central Missouri State Univ.
Central State Univ. (OH)
Central Washington Univ.
Centre College (KY)
Charleston Southern Univ. (SC)
Chatham College (PA)
Cheyney Univ. of Pennsylvania
Chicago State Univ.
Claremont Mckenna College (CA)
Clarion Univ. of Pennsylvania
Clark Atlanta Univ.
Clark Univ. (MA)
Cleveland State Univ.
Coe College (IA)
Colby College (ME)
Colgate Univ. (NY)
College of Charleston (SC)
College of Mount St. Vincent (NY)
College of New Jersey
College of Notre Dame of
    Maryland
College of St. Benedict (MN)
College of St. Catherine (MN)
College of St. Elizabeth (NJ)
College of St. Scholastica (MN)
College of the Holy Cross (MA)
College of William and Mary (VA)
College of Wooster (OH)
Colorado College
Colorado School of Mines
Colorado State Univ.
Columbia Univ. (NY)
Concordia Coll.–Moorhead (MN)
Concordia Univ. Wisconsin
Connecticut College
Converse College (SC)
Cornell College (IA)
Cornell Univ. (NY)
Covenant College (GA)
Creighton Univ. (NE)
CUNY–Baruch College
CUNY–Brooklyn College
CUNY–City College
CUNY–College of Staten Island
CUNY–Hunter College
CUNY–Lehman College
CUNY–Queens College
CUNY–York College
Dartmouth College (NH)
Davidson College (NC)
Davis and Elkins College (WV)
Denison Univ. (OH)
Depaul Univ. (IL)
Depauw Univ. (IN)
Dickinson College (PA)
Dillard Univ. (LA)

Dominican Coll. of Blauvelt (NY)
Dominican Univ. (IL)
Dowling College (NY)
Drake Univ. (IA)
Drew Univ. (NJ)
Drexel Univ. (PA)
Drury Univ. (MO)
Duke Univ. (NC)
Duquesne Univ. (PA)
Earlham College (IN)
East Carolina Univ. (NC)
East Stroudsburg Univ. of
   Pennsylvania
East Tennessee State Univ.
Eastern Connecticut State Univ.
Eastern Illinois Univ.
Eastern Kentucky Univ.
Eastern Mennonite Univ. (VA)
Eastern Michigan Univ.
Eastern Univ. (PA)
Eastern Washington Univ.
Eckerd College (FL)
Edgewood College (WI)
Edinboro Univ. of Pennsylvania
Elizabethtown College (PA)
Elmhurst College (IL)
Elmira College (NY)
Elon Univ. (NC)
Emory and Henry College (VA)
Emory Univ. (GA)
Emporia State Univ. (KS)
Excelsior College (NY)
Fairfield Univ. (CT)
Fairleigh Dickinson Univ. (NJ)
Fayetteville State Univ. (NC)
Fitchburg State College (MA)
Florida Atlantic Univ.
Florida International Univ.
Florida Southern College
Florida State Univ.
Fordham Univ. (NY)
Fort Hays State Univ. (KS)
Fort Lewis College (CO)
Framingham State College (MA)
Francis Marion Univ. (SC)
Franciscan Univ. of Steubenville
   (OH)
Franklin and Marshall College (PA)
Franklin College (IN)
Frostburg State Univ. (MD)
Furman Univ. (SC)
Gallaudet Univ. (DC)
George Fox Univ. (OR)
George Mason Univ. (VA)
George Washington Univ. (DC)
Georgetown College (KY)
Georgetown Univ. (DC)
Georgia Southern Univ.
Georgia State Univ.
Gettysburg College (PA)
Golden Gate Univ. (CA)
Gonzaga Univ. (WA)
Gordon College (MA)
Goucher College (MD)
Graceland Univ. (IA)
Grand Valley State Univ. (MI)
Grinnell College (IA)
Grove City College (PA)
Guilford College (NC)
Gustavus Adolphus College (MN)
Hamilton College (NY)

Hamline Univ. (MN)
Hampden-Sydney College (VA)
Hampshire College (MA)
Hampton Univ. (VA)
Hanover College (IN)
Hardin-Simmons Univ. (TX)
Harding Univ. (AR)
Hartwick College (NY)
Harvard Univ. (MA)
Hastings College (NE)
Haverford College (PA)
Hawaii Pacific Univ.
Heidelberg College (OH)
Hendrix College (AR)
Hillsdale College (MI)
Hiram College (OH)
Hobart and William Smith Colleges
   (NY)
Hofstra Univ. (NY)
Hollins Univ. (VA)
Holy Family Univ. (PA)
Hood College (MD)
Hope College (MI)
Howard Univ. (DC)
Humboldt State Univ. (CA)
Idaho State Univ.
Illinois College
Illinois State Univ.
Illinois Wesleyan Univ.
Immaculata Univ. (PA)
Indiana State Univ.
Indiana Univ. Northwest
Indiana Univ. of Pennsylvania
Indiana Univ.–Bloomington
Indiana Univ.–Kokomo
Indiana Univ.–South Bend
Indiana Univ.-Purdue Univ.–Fort
   Wayne
Indiana Univ.-Purdue
   Univ.–Indianapolis
Indiana Wesleyan Univ.
Iona College (NY)
Iowa State Univ.
Ithaca College (NY)
Jackson State Univ. (MS)
Jacksonville State Univ. (AL)
Jacksonville Univ. (FL)
James Madison Univ. (VA)
Jamestown College (ND)
John Carroll Univ. (OH)
Johns Hopkins Univ. (MD)
Johnson C. Smith Univ. (NC)
Juniata College (PA)
Kalamazoo College (MI)
Kansas State Univ.
Kean Univ. (NJ)
Keene State College (NH)
King's College (PA)
Knox College (IL)
Kutztown Univ. of Pennsylvania
La Salle Univ. (PA)
Lafayette College (PA)
Lake Forest College (IL)
Lamar Univ. (TX)
Lawrence Univ. (WI)
Le Moyne College (NY)
Lebanon Valley College (PA)
Lenoir-Rhyne College (NC)
Lewis and Clark College (OR)
Lewis Univ. (IL)
Limestone College (SC)

Lincoln Univ. (PA)
Linfield College (OR)
Lock Haven Univ. of Pennsylvania
Long Island Univ.–Brooklyn (NY)
Long Island Univ.–C.W. Post
   Campus (NY)
Longwood Univ. (VA)
Loras College (IA)
Louisiana College
Louisiana State Univ.–Baton Rouge
Loyola College In Maryland
Loyola Marymount Univ. (CA)
Loyola Univ. New Orleans
Luther College (IA)
Lycoming College (PA)
Lynchburg College (VA)
Lyon College (AR)
Macalester College (MN)
Manchester College (IN)
Manhattan College (NY)
Manhattanville College (NY)
Mansfield Univ. of Pennsylvania
Marian College (IN)
Marietta College (OH)
Marist College (NY)
Marlboro College (VT)
Marquette Univ. (WI)
Marshall Univ. (WV)
Mary Baldwin College (VA)
Marymount Univ. (VA)
Maryville College (TN)
Massachusetts Institute of
   Technology
Mcdaniel College (MD)
Mckendree College (IL)
Mercer Univ. (GA)
Meredith College (NC)
Merrimack College (MA)
Messiah College (PA)
Metropolitan State College of
   Denver
Miami Univ.–Oxford (OH)
Michigan State Univ.
Michigan Technological Univ.
Middle Tennessee State Univ.
Middlebury College (VT)
Midwestern State Univ. (TX)
Millersville Univ. of Pennsylvania
Mills College (CA)
Millsaps College (MS)
Minnesota State Univ.–Mankato
Minnesota State Univ.–Moorhead
Minot State Univ. (ND)
Mississippi State Univ.
Missouri Valley College
Missouri Western State College
Montana State Univ.–Bozeman
Montclair State Univ. (NJ)
Moravian College (PA)
Morehouse College (GA)
Mount Holyoke College (MA)
Mount St. Mary's Univ. (MD)
Mount Union College (OH)
Muhlenberg College (PA)
Murray State Univ. (KY)
Muskingum College (OH)
Nazareth College of Rochester
   (NY)
Nebraska Wesleyan Univ.
New Jersey City Univ.
New Mexico State Univ.

New York Institute of Technology
New York Univ.
North Carolina A&T State Univ.
North Central College (IL)
North Dakota State Univ.
North Park Univ. (IL)
Northeastern Illinois Univ.
Northeastern Univ. (MA)
Northern Arizona Univ.
Northern Illinois Univ.
Northern Michigan Univ.
Northern State Univ. (SD)
Northland College (WI)
Northwest Missouri State Univ.
Northwestern College (IA)
Northwestern Univ. (IL)
Norwich Univ. (VT)
Oakland Univ. (MI)
Oberlin College (OH)
Occidental College (CA)
Oglethorpe Univ. (GA)
Ohio Dominican Univ.
Ohio State Univ.–Columbus
Ohio Univ.
Ohio Wesleyan Univ.
Oklahoma State Univ.
Old Dominion Univ. (VA)
Olivet Nazarene Univ. (IL)
Oregon State Univ.
Otterbein College (OH)
Pace Univ. (NY)
Pacific Lutheran Univ. (WA)
Pacific Univ. (OR)
Park Univ. (MO)
Penn. State Univ.–Univ. Park
Pepperdine Univ. (CA)
Pfeiffer Univ. (NC)
Pittsburg State Univ. (KS)
Pitzer College (CA)
Point Loma Nazarene Univ. (CA)
Pomona College (CA)
Portland State Univ. (OR)
Prairie View A&M Univ. (TX)
Presbyterian College (SC)
Princeton Univ. (NJ)
Principia College (IL)
Providence College (RI)
Purdue Univ.–West Lafayette (IN)
Quinnipiac Univ. (CT)
Radford Univ. (VA)
Ramapo College of New Jersey
Randolph-Macon College (VA)
Randolph-Macon Woman's College
   (VA)
Reed College (OR)
Regis Univ. (CO)
Rensselaer Polytechnic Inst. (NY)
Rhode Island College
Rhodes College (TN)
Rice Univ. (TX)
Richard Stockton College of New
   Jersey
Rider Univ. (NJ)
Ripon College (WI)
Roanoke College (VA)
Robert Morris Univ. (PA)
Rochester Institute of Tech. (NY)
Rockford College (IL)
Rockhurst Univ. (MO)
Rocky Mountain College (MT)
Rollins College (FL)

Roosevelt Univ. (IL)
Rose-Hulman Institute of
   Technology (IN)
Rosemont College (PA)
Rutgers–Camden (NJ)
Rutgers–New Brunswick (NJ)
Rutgers–Newark (NJ)
Sacred Heart Univ. (CT)
Saginaw Valley State Univ. (MI)
Salem College (NC)
Salem State College (MA)
Salisbury Univ. (MD)
Salve Regina Univ. (RI)
Sam Houston State Univ. (TX)
San Diego State Univ.
San Francisco State Univ.
San Jose State Univ. (CA)
Santa Clara Univ. (CA)
Scripps College (CA)
Seattle Univ.
Seton Hall Univ. (NJ)
Seton Hill Univ. (PA)
Sewanee–Univ. of the South (TN)
Shepherd Univ. (WV)
Shippensburg Univ. of
   Pennsylvania
Siena College (NY)
Simmons College (MA)
Simpson College (IA)
Skidmore College (NY)
Slippery Rock Univ. of Pennsylvania
Sonoma State Univ. (CA)
South Dakota State Univ.
Southeast Missouri State Univ.
Southern Illinois Univ.–Carbondale
Southern Illinois
   Univ.–Edwardsville
Southern Methodist Univ. (TX)
Southern New Hampshire Univ.
Southern Oregon Univ.
Southern Utah Univ.
Southwest Missouri State Univ.
Southwestern College (KS)
Southwestern Univ. (TX)
Spelman College (GA)
St. Ambrose Univ. (IA)
St. Cloud State Univ. (MN)
St. Edward's Univ. (TX)
St. Francis College (NY)
St. Francis Univ. (PA)
St. John Fisher College (NY)
St. John's Univ. (NY)
St. John's Univ. (MN)
St. Joseph College (CT)
St. Joseph's College (IN)
St. Joseph's Univ. (PA)
St. Lawrence Univ. (NY)
St. Louis Univ.
St. Mary's College (IN)
St. Mary's College of California
St. Mary's College of Maryland
St. Mary's Univ. of San Antonio
St. Michael's College (VT)
St. Norbert College (WI)
St. Olaf College (MN)
St. Peter's College (NJ)
St. Vincent College (PA)
Stanford Univ. (CA)
State Univ. of West Georgia
Stephen F. Austin State Univ. (TX)
Stetson Univ. (FL)

Stonehill College (MA)
Suffolk Univ. (MA)
SUNY College of Arts and Sciences–Geneseo
SUNY College–Oneonta
SUNY College–Potsdam
SUNY–Albany
SUNY–Binghamton
SUNY–Farmingdale
SUNY–Fredonia
SUNY–Plattsburgh
SUNY–Purchase College
SUNY–Stony Brook
Susquehanna Univ. (PA)
Swarthmore College (PA)
Sweet Briar College (VA)
Syracuse Univ. (NY)
Tarleton State Univ. (TX)
Temple Univ. (PA)
Tennessee Technological Univ.
Texas A&M Univ.–College Station
Texas A&M Univ.–Commerce
Texas A&M Univ.–Corpus Christi
Texas Christian Univ.
Texas Lutheran Univ.
Texas State Univ.–San Marcos
Texas Tech Univ.
Thomas Edison State College (NJ)
Thomas More College (KY)
Tougaloo College (MS)
Touro College (NY)
Towson Univ. (MD)
Transylvania Univ. (KY)
Trinity College (DC)
Trinity College (CT)
Truman State Univ. (MO)
Tufts Univ. (MA)
Tulane Univ. (LA)
Tuskegee Univ. (AL)
Union College (NY)
Union Univ. (TN)
United States Air Force Academy (CO)
United States Naval Academy (MD)
Univ. at Buffalo–SUNY
Univ. of Akron (OH)
Univ. of Alaska–Anchorage
Univ. of Alaska–Fairbanks
Univ. of Arizona
Univ. of Arkansas
Univ. of California–Berkeley
Univ. of California–Davis
Univ. of California–Irvine
Univ. of California–Los Angeles
Univ. of California–Riverside
Univ. of California–San Diego
Univ. of California–Santa Barbara
Univ. of California–Santa Cruz
Univ. of Central Arkansas
Univ. of Central Florida
Univ. of Central Oklahoma
Univ. of Chicago
Univ. of Colorado–Boulder
Univ. of Colorado–Colorado Springs
Univ. of Colorado–Denver
Univ. of Connecticut
Univ. of Dallas
Univ. of Dayton (OH)
Univ. of Delaware

Univ. of Denver
Univ. of Detroit Mercy
Univ. of Evansville (IN)
Univ. of Findlay (OH)
Univ. of Florida
Univ. of Georgia
Univ. of Hartford (CT)
Univ. of Hawaii–Hilo
Univ. of Hawaii–Manoa
Univ. of Houston
Univ. of Illinois–Chicago
Univ. of Illinois–Springfield
Univ. of Ill.–Urbana-Champaign
Univ. of Iowa
Univ. of Judaism (CA)
Univ. of Kansas
Univ. of Kentucky
Univ. of La Verne (CA)
Univ. of Louisville (KY)
Univ. of Maine–Orono
Univ. of Mary Washington (VA)
Univ. of Maryland–Baltimore County
Univ. of Maryland–College Park
Univ. of Massachusetts–Amherst
Univ. of Massachusetts–Boston
Univ. of Mass.–Dartmouth
Univ. of Massachusetts–Lowell
Univ. of Memphis
Univ. of Miami (FL)
Univ. of Michigan–Ann Arbor
Univ. of Michigan–Dearborn
Univ. of Michigan–Flint
Univ. of Minnesota–Duluth
Univ. of Minnesota–Morris
Univ. of Minnesota–Twin Cities
Univ. of Mississippi
Univ. of Missouri–Columbia
Univ. of Missouri–Kansas City
Univ. of Missouri–Rolla
Univ. of Missouri–St. Louis
Univ. of Montana
Univ. of Nebraska–Kearney
Univ. of Nebraska–Lincoln
Univ. of Nevada–Las Vegas
Univ. of Nevada–Reno
Univ. of New Hampshire
Univ. of New Mexico
Univ. of New Orleans
Univ. of North Carolina–Asheville
Univ. of N.C.–Chapel Hill
Univ. of North Carolina–Charlotte
Univ. of N.C.–Greensboro
Univ. of N.C.–Wilmington
Univ. of North Dakota
Univ. of North Florida
Univ. of North Texas
Univ. of Northern Colorado
Univ. of Northern Iowa
Univ. of Notre Dame (IN)
Univ. of Oklahoma
Univ. of Oregon
Univ. of Pennsylvania
Univ. of Pittsburgh
Univ. of Pittsburgh–Bradford
Univ. of Pittsburgh–Johnstown
Univ. of Puget Sound (WA)
Univ. of Redlands (CA)
Univ. of Rhode Island
Univ. of Richmond (VA)
Univ. of Rochester (NY)

Univ. of San Diego
Univ. of San Francisco
Univ. of Science and Arts of Oklahoma
Univ. of Scranton (PA)
Univ. of South Carolina–Columbia
Univ. of South Dakota
Univ. of South Florida
Univ. of Southern California
Univ. of Southern Indiana
Univ. of Southern Maine
Univ. of St. Thomas (TX)
Univ. of St. Thomas (MN)
Univ. of Tampa (FL)
Univ. of Tennessee
Univ. of Tennessee–Martin
Univ. of Texas–Arlington
Univ. of Texas–Austin
Univ. of Texas–Dallas
Univ. of Texas–Pan American
Univ. of the District of Columbia
Univ. of the Ozarks (AR)
Univ. of the Pacific (CA)
Univ. of Toledo (OH)
Univ. of Tulsa (OK)
Univ. of Utah
Univ. of Vermont
Univ. of Virginia
Univ. of Virginia–Wise
Univ. of Washington
Univ. of West Florida
Univ. of Wisconsin–Eau Claire
Univ. of Wisconsin–Green Bay
Univ. of Wisconsin–La Crosse
Univ. of Wisconsin–Madison
Univ. of Wisconsin–Milwaukee
Univ. of Wisconsin–Oshkosh
Univ. of Wisconsin–Parkside
Univ. of Wisconsin–Platteville
Univ. of Wisconsin–River Falls
Univ. of Wisconsin–Stevens Point
Univ. of Wisconsin–Superior
Univ. of Wisconsin–Whitewater
Ursinus College (PA)
Utah State Univ.
Utica College (NY)
Valparaiso Univ. (IN)
Vanderbilt Univ. (TN)
Vassar College (NY)
Virginia Military Institute
Virginia Tech
Wabash College (IN)
Wagner College (NY)
Wake Forest Univ. (NC)
Wartburg College (IA)
Washburn Univ. (KS)
Washington and Jefferson College (PA)
Washington and Lee Univ. (VA)
Washington College (MD)
Washington State Univ.
Washington Univ. In St. Louis
Wayne State Univ. (MI)
Webster Univ. (MO)
Wellesley College (MA)
Wesleyan College (GA)
Wesleyan Univ. (CT)
West Texas A&M Univ.
West Virginia State Univ.
West Virginia Univ.
West Virginia Wesleyan College

Western Connecticut State Univ.
Western Illinois Univ.
Western Kentucky Univ.
Western Michigan Univ.
Western New England College (MA)
Western Oregon Univ.
Western State College of Colorado
Western Washington Univ.
Westfield State College (MA)
Westminster College (PA)
Westminster College (MO)
Westmont College (CA)
Wheaton College (MA)
Wheaton College (IL)
Whitman College (WA)
Whittier College (CA)
Whitworth College (WA)
Wichita State Univ. (KS)
Widener Univ. (PA)
Willamette Univ. (OR)
Williams College (MA)
Winston-Salem State Univ. (NC)
Winthrop Univ. (SC)
Wittenberg Univ. (OH)
Wofford College (SC)
Worcester Polytechnic Institute (MA)
Worcester State College (MA)
Wright State Univ. (OH)
Xavier Univ. (OH)
Yale Univ. (CT)
Yeshiva Univ. (NY)
York College of Pennsylvania
Youngstown State Univ. (OH)

Education

Adrian College (MI)
Albany State Univ. (GA)
Albertus Magnus College (CT)
Alice Lloyd College (KY)
Allegheny College (PA)
Allen Univ. (SC)
Alma College (MI)
Alverno College (WI)
Anderson Univ. (IN)
Antioch College (OH)
Arcadia Univ. (PA)
Ashland Univ. (OH)
Auburn Univ. (AL)
Augsburg College (MN)
Augustana College (SD)
Baldwin-Wallace College (OH)
Bay Path College (MA)
Belhaven College (MS)
Belmont Abbey College (NC)
Belmont Univ. (TN)
Beloit College (WI)
Benedict College (SC)
Bennington College (VT)
Berea College (KY)
Bethany College (KS)
Bethany College (WV)
Bethel College (IN)
Bethel College (TN)
Bethune-Cookman College (FL)
Bloomfield College (NJ)
Bluefield College (VA)
Bluffton Univ. (OH)

Bowling Green State Univ. (OH)
Brevard College (NC)
Brewton-Parker College (GA)
Brown Univ. (RI)
Bryn Athyn College (PA)
Bucknell Univ. (PA)
Cabrini College (PA)
California State Polytechnic Univ.–Pomona
California State Univ.–Fullerton
California State Univ.–Monterey Bay
California State Univ.–San Bernardino
California Univ. of Pennsylvania
Calumet College of St. Joseph (IN)
Calvin College (MI)
Capital Univ. (OH)
Cardinal Stritch Univ. (WI)
Carroll College (WI)
Carson-Newman College (TN)
Carthage College (WI)
Case Western Reserve Univ. (OH)
Castleton State College (VT)
Catawba College (NC)
Catholic Univ. of America (DC)
Cedarville Univ. (OH)
Centenary College of Louisiana
Central College (IA)
Central Missouri State Univ.
Charleston Southern Univ. (SC)
Clarion Univ. of Pennsylvania
Clarke College (IA)
Cleveland State Univ.
Coker College (SC)
Colgate Univ. (NY)
College of New Jersey
College of Wooster (OH)
Columbia College (MO)
Columbia Univ. (NY)
Concordia College (NY)
Concordia Univ.–River Forest (IL)
Concordia Univ.–St. Paul (MN)
Converse College (SC)
Cornell Univ. (NY)
Cornerstone Univ. (MI)
Crichton College (TN)
Culver-Stockton College (MO)
Cumberland Univ. (TN)
CUNY–Brooklyn College
CUNY–City College
CUNY–Lehman College
Curry College (MA)
Dakota Wesleyan Univ. (SD)
Dallas Baptist Univ.
Dana College (NE)
David Lipscomb Univ. (TN)
Defiance College (OH)
Denison Univ. (OH)
Dowling College (NY)
Drury Univ. (MO)
Duquesne Univ. (PA)
East Texas Baptist Univ.
Eastern Nazarene College (MA)
Edgewood College (WI)
Elmhurst College (IL)
Elmira College (NY)
Emory Univ. (GA)
Endicott College (MA)
Eureka College (IL)
Ferris State Univ. (MI)

Ferrum College (VA)
Fitchburg State College (MA)
Florida Memorial College
Florida Southern College
Fordham Univ. (NY)
Furman Univ. (SC)
Gallaudet Univ. (DC)
George Washington Univ. (DC)
Goddard College (VT)
Goucher College (MD)
Graceland Univ. (IA)
Grand Canyon Univ. (AZ)
Hampshire College (MA)
Hardin-Simmons Univ. (TX)
Harding Univ. (AR)
Hastings College (NE)
Heidelberg College (OH)
Heritage College (WA)
Hiram College (OH)
Houston Baptist Univ.
Howard Payne Univ. (TX)
Humboldt State Univ. (CA)
Huntington College (IN)
Huston-Tillotson College (TX)
Illinois Wesleyan Univ.
Jacksonville Univ. (FL)
Jarvis Christian College (TX)
Johnson and Wales Univ. (RI)
Juniata College (PA)
Kent State Univ. (OH)
Kentucky Christian College
King College (TN)
Knox College (IL)
Lake Forest College (IL)
Lakeland College (WI)
Lamar Univ. (TX)
Lasell College (MA)
Lees-Mcrae College (NC)
Limestone College (SC)
Lincoln Memorial Univ. (TN)
Lindenwood Univ. (MO)
Long Island Univ.–Brooklyn (NY)
Loras College (IA)
Louisiana College
Louisiana Tech Univ.
Lourdes College (OH)
Madonna Univ. (MI)
Manchester College (IN)
Manhattanville College (NY)
Mansfield Univ. of Pennsylvania
Marietta College (OH)
Martin Univ. (IN)
Maryville College (TN)
Marywood Univ. (PA)
Mercer Univ. (GA)
Michigan State Univ.
Midwestern State Univ. (TX)
Miles College (AL)
Millikin Univ. (IL)
Millsaps College (MS)
Mississippi Valley State Univ.
Missouri Baptist College
Monmouth College (IL)
Monmouth Univ. (NJ)
Morehouse College (GA)
Morningside College (IA)
Mount Holyoke College (MA)
Mount Mercy College (IA)
Mount St. Mary's College (CA)
Newberry College (SC)
Niagara Univ. (NY)

Nichols College (MA)
North Carolina State Univ.–Raleigh
Northeastern State Univ. (OK)
Northern Arizona Univ.
Northern State Univ. (SD)
Northland College (WI)
Northwestern College (IA)
Northwestern Oklahoma State
   Univ.
Northwestern Univ. (IL)
Nova Southeastern Univ. (FL)
Ohio Northern Univ.
Oklahoma Baptist Univ.
Oklahoma Christian Univ.
Oklahoma City Univ.
Oklahoma State Univ.
Oregon State Univ.
Our Lady of Holy Cross Coll. (LA)
Pace Univ. (NY)
Pacific Lutheran Univ. (WA)
Palm Beach Atlantic Univ. (FL)
Park Univ. (MO)
Paul Quinn College (TX)
Peru State College (NE)
Point Loma Nazarene Univ. (CA)
Prescott College (AZ)
Principia College (IL)
Purdue Univ.–West Lafayette
   (IN)
Randolph-Macon Woman's College
   (VA)
Regis Univ. (CO)
Ripon College (WI)
Rockford College (IL)
Roger Williams Univ. (RI)
Rollins College (FL)
Roosevelt Univ. (IL)
Salem State College (MA)
Salisbury Univ. (MD)
San Jose State Univ. (CA)
Schreiner Univ. (TX)
Seattle Pacific Univ.
Shaw Univ. (NC)
Shawnee State Univ. (OH)
Shepherd Univ. (WV)
Simmons College (MA)
Southeastern College of the
   Assemblies of God
Southern Nazarene Univ. (OK)
Southwest Minnesota State Univ.
   (MN)
Southwestern Univ. (TX)
Spalding Univ. (KY)
Spelman College (GA)
Spring Arbor Univ. (MI)
Springfield College (MA)
St. Andrews Presbyterian College
   (NC)
St. John Fisher College (NY)
St. Joseph College (CT)
St. Joseph's Univ. (PA)
St. Louis Univ.
Suffolk Univ. (MA)
SUNY College–Potsdam
SUNY–Empire State College
Swarthmore College (PA)
Syracuse Univ. (NY)
Tabor College (KS)
Tarleton State Univ. (TX)
Texas College
Texas Wesleyan Univ.

Thomas More College (KY)
Thomas Univ. (GA)
Trinity Christian College (IL)
Trinity College (CT)
Tusculum College (TN)
Tuskegee Univ. (AL)
Union Institute and Univ. (OH)
Unity College (ME)
Univ. of Alaska–Fairbanks
Univ. of Alaska–Southeast
Univ. of California–Riverside
Univ. of Charleston (WV)
Univ. of Dayton (OH)
Univ. of Evansville (IN)
Univ. of Findlay (OH)
Univ. of Great Falls (MT)
Univ. of Judaism (CA)
Univ. of La Verne (CA)
Univ. of Maine–Orono
Univ. of Maryland–Eastern Shore
Univ. of Massachusetts–Amherst
Univ. of Michigan–Ann Arbor
Univ. of Michigan–Dearborn
Univ. of Michigan–Flint
Univ. of Minnesota–Morris
Univ. of Minnesota–Twin Cities
Univ. of Mississippi
Univ. of Missouri–Columbia
Univ. of Missouri–Kansas City
Univ. of Missouri–Rolla
Univ. of Missouri–St. Louis
Univ. of Montana
Univ. of Montevallo (AL)
Univ. of Nevada–Las Vegas
Univ. of New England (ME)
Univ. of Oregon
Univ. of Pennsylvania
Univ. of Redlands (CA)
Univ. of Southern California
Univ. of St. Mary (KS)
Univ. of Tennessee–Chattanooga
Univ. of Tennessee–Martin
Univ. of the District of Columbia
Univ. of the Pacific (CA)
Univ. of Toledo (OH)
Univ. of Tulsa (OK)
Univ. of Utah
Univ. of Vermont
Univ. of Wisconsin–Green Bay
Univ. of Wisconsin–Milwaukee
Upper Iowa Univ.
Vanderbilt Univ. (TN)
Vassar College (NY)
Virginia Intermont College
Wake Forest Univ. (NC)
Waldorf College (IA)
Walsh Univ. (OH)
Washburn Univ. (KS)
Washington and Jefferson College
   (PA)
Washington State Univ.
Washington Univ. In St. Louis
Wayland Baptist Univ. (TX)
Webster Univ. (MO)
Wellesley College (MA)
Wesley College (DE)
West Virginia Wesleyan College
Western Michigan Univ.
Western State College of Colorado
Wheaton College (IL)
Widener Univ. (PA)

William Paterson Univ. of New
   Jersey
William Woods Univ. (MO)
Wilmington College (DE)
Wilmington College (OH)
Xavier Univ. (OH)
Yeshiva Univ. (NY)
York College of Pennsylvania
Youngstown State Univ. (OH)

Educational Administration and Supervision

Albany State Univ. (GA)
Auburn Univ. (AL)
California State Univ.–Fullerton
California State Univ.–Sacramento
California State Univ.–San
   Bernardino
Cazenovia College (NY)
Centenary College of Louisiana
Charleston Southern Univ. (SC)
College of the Southwest (NM)
Colorado State Univ.
Fayetteville State Univ. (NC)
Gallaudet Univ. (DC)
Grace Univ. (NE)
Grand Canyon Univ. (AZ)
Harding Univ. (AR)
Indiana Univ.–South Bend
Jacksonville State Univ. (AL)
Keene State College (NH)
Lincoln Memorial Univ. (TN)
Lynn Univ. (FL)
Marshall Univ. (WV)
North Georgia College and State
   Univ.
Pacific Lutheran Univ. (WA)
Penn. State Univ.–Univ. Park
Philander Smith College (AR)
Pittsburg State Univ. (KS)
Point Loma Nazarene Univ. (CA)
Regis Univ. (CO)
Salisbury Univ. (MD)
Seattle Pacific Univ.
Slippery Rock Univ. of Pennsylvania
South Dakota State Univ.
Southern Illinois Univ.–Carbondale
Springfield College (MA)
St. Mary's Univ. of San Antonio
SUNY–Oswego
Texas A&M Univ.–College Station
Union College (NE)
Univ. of Arkansas–Monticello
Univ. of California–Riverside
Univ. of Judaism (CA)
Univ. of Michigan–Flint
Univ. of Nevada–Las Vegas
Univ. of North Alabama
Univ. of Redlands (CA)
Univ. of Wisconsin–Milwaukee
Univ. of Wisconsin–Oshkosh
Univ. of Wisconsin–River Falls
Washington State Univ.
Western Washington Univ.

Educational Assessment, Evaluation, and Research

College of the Southwest (NM)
Midwestern State Univ. (TX)
Washington State Univ.

Educational Psychology

Alcorn State Univ. (MS)
Marymount Univ. (VA)
Mississippi State Univ.
Shenandoah Univ. (VA)
Southern Illinois Univ.–Carbondale
Univ. of California–Riverside
Univ. of Georgia
Univ. of Pittsburgh
Utah State Univ.

Educational/Instructional Media Design

Auburn Univ. (AL)
Bellevue Univ. (NE)
California State Univ.–Chico
California State Univ.–Fullerton
California State Univ.–Sacramento
Clarke College (IA)
Jacksonville State Univ. (AL)
Pittsburg State Univ. (KS)
St. Cloud State Univ. (MN)
SUNY–Oswego
Western Illinois Univ.

Electrical Engineering Technologies/Technicians

Alabama Agricultural and
   Mechanical Univ.
Andrews Univ. (MI)
Bluefield State College (WV)
Boston Univ.
Bowling Green State Univ. (OH)
Buffalo State College
California State Univ.–Long Beach
California Univ. of Pennsylvania
Capitol College (MD)
Central Michigan Univ.
Central Washington Univ.
Cleveland State Univ.
Cogswell Polytechnical Coll. (CA)
Colorado State Univ.–Pueblo
CUNY–New York City College of
   Technology
East-West Univ. (IL)
Eastern Michigan Univ.
Embry Riddle Aeronautical Univ.
   (FL)
Fairleigh Dickinson Univ. (NJ)
Fairmont State Univ. (WV)
Ferris State Univ. (MI)
Fitchburg State College (MA)
Florida A&M Univ.
Fort Valley State Univ. (GA)
Georgia Southern Univ.
Grambling State Univ. (LA)
Indiana State Univ.

Indiana Univ.–South Bend
Indiana Univ.-Purdue Univ.–Fort
Wayne
Indiana Univ.-Purdue
Univ.–Indianapolis
Jacksonville State Univ. (AL)
Johnson and Wales Univ. (RI)
Kean Univ. (NJ)
Letourneau Univ. (TX)
Louisiana Tech Univ.
Michigan Technological Univ.
Milwaukee School of Engineering
Minnesota State Univ.–Mankato
Missouri Western State College
Montana State Univ.–Bozeman
New York Institute of Technology
Norfolk State Univ. (VA)
North Carolina A&T State Univ.
Northeastern Univ. (MA)
Northern Kentucky Univ.
Northwestern State Univ. of
Louisiana
Oklahoma State Univ.
Old Dominion Univ. (VA)
Oregon Institute of Technology
Penn. State–Erie, The Behrend
College
Pittsburg State Univ. (KS)
Point Park Univ. (PA)
Portland State Univ. (OR)
Prairie View A&M Univ. (TX)
Purdue Univ.–Calumet (IN)
Purdue Univ.–West Lafayette (IN)
Rochester Institute of Tech. (NY)
Roosevelt Univ. (IL)
Savannah State Univ. (GA)
South Carolina State Univ.
South Dakota State Univ.
Southern Illinois Univ.–Carbondale
Southern Polytechnic State Univ.
(GA)
Southern Univ. and A&M College
(LA)
St. John's Univ. (NY)
SUNY–Farmingdale
Texas A&M Univ.–College Station
Texas Tech Univ.
Thomas Edison State College (NJ)
Troy State Univ.–Troy (AL)
Univ. of Akron (OH)
Univ. of Arkansas–Little Rock
Univ. of Central Florida
Univ. of Dayton (OH)
Univ. of Hartford (CT)
Univ. of Houston
Univ. of Maine–Orono
Univ. of Massachusetts–Lowell
Univ. of Memphis
Univ. of Nebraska–Lincoln
Univ. of North Carolina–Charlotte
Univ. of North Texas
Univ. of Pittsburgh–Johnstown
Univ. of Southern Mississippi
Univ. of Tennessee–Martin
Univ. of Texas–Brownsville
Univ. of the District of Columbia
Virginia State Univ.
Wayne State Univ. (MI)
Wentworth Institute of Technology
(MA)
Western Carolina Univ. (NC)

Western Kentucky Univ.
Western Washington Univ.
Wichita State Univ. (KS)
Youngstown State Univ. (OH)

Electrical, Electronics, and Communications Engineering

California State Univ.–Sacramento
Christian Brothers Univ. (TN)
Clarkson Univ. (NY)
CUNY–City College
Grove City College (PA)
Hampton Univ. (VA)
Howard Univ. (DC)
Indiana Institute of Technology
Kettering Univ. (MI)
Lafayette College (PA)
Lake Superior State Univ. (MI)
Loras College (IA)
Miami Univ.–Oxford (OH)
Morgan State Univ. (MD)
Oklahoma Christian Univ.
Purdue Univ.–Calumet (IN)
Rice Univ. (TX)
Seattle Pacific Univ.
South Dakota School of Mines and
Technology
Tennessee State Univ.
Texas A&M Univ.–Kingsville
Tri-State Univ. (IN)
Tufts Univ. (MA)
Tuskegee Univ. (AL)
United States Military Academy
(NY)
Univ. of California–San Diego
Univ. of California–Santa Barbara
Univ. of California–Santa Cruz
Univ. of Kentucky
Univ. of Missouri–Rolla
Univ. of Portland (OR)
Univ. of Tennessee
Univ. of Texas–Dallas
Univ. of Texas–El Paso
Univ. of Washington
Vanderbilt Univ. (TN)
Widener Univ. (PA)
York College of Pennsylvania

Electrical/Electronics Maintenance and Repair Technology

Lewis-Clark State College (ID)

Electromechanical Instr. and Maint. Technologies/Technicians

Buffalo State College
Excelsior College (NY)
Hampshire College (MA)
Indiana State Univ.
Indiana Univ.-Purdue
Univ.–Indianapolis
Keene State College (NH)
Murray State Univ. (KY)

New York Institute of Technology
Purdue Univ.–West Lafayette (IN)
Suffolk Univ. (MA)
Texas A&M Univ.–Corpus Christi
Thomas Edison State College (NJ)
Univ. of Northern Iowa
Univ. of Toledo (OH)
Vermont Technical College
Wayne State Univ. (MI)
Wentworth Institute of Technology
(MA)

Engineering

Abilene Christian Univ. (TX)
Albertson College (ID)
Alfred Univ. (NY)
Andrews Univ. (MI)
Arcadia Univ. (PA)
Arizona State Univ.
Arkansas State Univ.
Auburn Univ. (AL)
Augustana College (IL)
Ball State Univ. (IN)
Baylor Univ. (TX)
Beloit College (WI)
Bethel College (IN)
Brown Univ. (RI)
Cal Poly–San Luis Obispo
California Institute of Technology
California State Univ.–Chico
California State Univ.–Fresno
California State Univ.–Fullerton
California State Univ.–Long Beach
California State Univ.–Los Angeles
Calvin College (MI)
Carnegie Mellon Univ. (PA)
Case Western Reserve Univ. (OH)
Catholic Univ. of America (DC)
Charleston Southern Univ. (SC)
Chatham College (PA)
Claremont Mckenna College (CA)
Clark Atlanta Univ.
Clarkson Univ. (NY)
College of Notre Dame of
Maryland
Colorado School of Mines
Colorado State Univ.–Pueblo
Cornell Univ. (NY)
CUNY–City College
CUNY–College of Staten Island
Dartmouth College (NH)
David Lipscomb Univ. (TN)
Dickinson College (PA)
Dordt College (IA)
Dowling College (NY)
Drexel Univ. (PA)
East Carolina Univ. (NC)
Eastern Illinois Univ.
Eastern Nazarene College (MA)
Elizabethtown College (PA)
Elon Univ. (NC)
Embry Riddle Aeronautical Univ.
(FL)
Florida Institute of Technology
Fort Lewis College (CO)
Geneva College (PA)
George Fox Univ. (OR)
George Mason Univ. (VA)

George Washington Univ. (DC)
Gonzaga Univ. (WA)
Harvey Mudd College (CA)
Hope College (MI)
Idaho State Univ.
Illinois College
Indiana Univ.-Purdue
Univ.–Indianapolis
Iowa State Univ.
John Brown Univ. (AR)
Johns Hopkins Univ. (MD)
Johnson and Wales Univ. (RI)
Juniata College (PA)
Kent State Univ. (OH)
Kentucky State Univ.
Lafayette College (PA)
Lehigh Univ. (PA)
Letourneau Univ. (TX)
Lincoln Univ. (PA)
Livingstone College (NC)
Louisiana College
Louisiana Tech Univ.
Loyola College In Maryland
Loyola Marymount Univ. (CA)
Lubbock Christian Univ. (TX)
Manchester College (IN)
Marquette Univ. (WI)
Maryville College (TN)
Maryville Univ. of St. Louis (MO)
Mcneese State Univ. (LA)
Mercer Univ. (GA)
Messiah College (PA)
Miami Univ.–Oxford (OH)
Michigan State Univ.
Michigan Technological Univ.
Midwestern State Univ. (TX)
Mills College (CA)
Milwaukee School of Engineering
Mississippi State Univ.
Montana State Univ.–Bozeman
Montana Tech of the Univ. of
Montana
Moravian College (PA)
Morehouse College (GA)
National Univ. (CA)
New Mexico Highlands Univ.
New York Institute of Technology
Norfolk State Univ. (VA)
North Carolina State Univ.–Raleigh
Northeastern Univ. (MA)
Northern Arizona Univ.
Northwestern Univ. (IL)
Oakland Univ. (MI)
Oberlin College (OH)
Ohio State Univ.–Columbus
Oral Roberts Univ. (OK)
Park Univ. (MO)
Penn. State Univ.–Univ. Park
Pfeiffer Univ. (NC)
Philadelphia Univ.
Purdue Univ.–Calumet (IN)
Purdue Univ.–West Lafayette (IN)
Rensselaer Polytechnic Inst. (NY)
Robert Morris Univ. (PA)
Rochester Institute of Tech. (NY)
Rockford College (IL)
Roger Williams Univ. (RI)
Rose-Hulman Institute of
Technology (IN)
Salisbury Univ. (MD)

San Jose State Univ. (CA)
Santa Clara Univ. (CA)
Schreiner Univ. (TX)
South Dakota State Univ.
Southern Illinois Univ.–Carbondale
Southwestern Oklahoma State
Univ.
Spelman College (GA)
Spring Hill College (AL)
St. Anselm College (NH)
St. Cloud State Univ. (MN)
St. Francis Univ. (PA)
St. Mary's Univ. of San Antonio
St. Michael's College (VT)
St. Vincent College (PA)
Stanford Univ. (CA)
Stevens Institute of Technology
(NJ)
SUNY College Environmental
Science and Forestry
SUNY–Stony Brook
Swarthmore College (PA)
Syracuse Univ. (NY)
Tarleton State Univ. (TX)
Temple Univ. (PA)
Texas Christian Univ.
Texas Tech Univ.
Thiel College (PA)
Transylvania Univ. (KY)
Trinity College (CT)
Trinity College (DC)
Tufts Univ. (MA)
Tulane Univ. (LA)
United States Air Force Academy
(CO)
United States Military Academy
(NY)
United States Naval Academy
(MD)
Univ. at Buffalo–SUNY
Univ. of Akron (OH)
Univ. of Alabama–Huntsville
Univ. of Arizona
Univ. of California–Irvine
Univ. of California–Riverside
Univ. of Dallas
Univ. of Denver
Univ. of Hartford (CT)
Univ. of Ill.–Urbana-Champaign
Univ. of Iowa
Univ. of Louisville (KY)
Univ. of Maine–Orono
Univ. of Maryland–Baltimore
County
Univ. of Maryland–College Park
Univ. of Maryland–Eastern Shore
Univ. of Massachusetts–Amherst
Univ. of Michigan–Ann Arbor
Univ. of Michigan–Dearborn
Univ. of Mississippi
Univ. of Missouri–Columbia
Univ. of Missouri–Rolla
Univ. of Nebraska–Lincoln
Univ. of Nevada–Las Vegas
Univ. of New Hampshire
Univ. of New Haven (CT)
Univ. of North Carolina–Asheville
Univ. of Oklahoma
Univ. of Pennsylvania
Univ. of Pittsburgh
Univ. of Pittsburgh–Bradford

Univ. of Portland (OR)
Univ. of Rhode Island
Univ. of Rochester (NY)
Univ. of South Florida
Univ. of Southern California
Univ. of Southern Indiana
Univ. of Tennessee–Chattanooga
Univ. of Tennessee–Martin
Univ. of the Incarnate Word (TX)
Univ. of the Pacific (CA)
Univ. of Toledo (OH)
Univ. of Tulsa (OK)
Univ. of Utah
Univ. of Washington
Ursinus College (PA)
Vanderbilt Univ. (TN)
Villanova Univ. (PA)
Wake Forest Univ. (NC)
Washington State Univ.
Washington Univ. In St. Louis
Wesleyan College (GA)
West Virginia Univ. Institute of
    Technology
Western Michigan Univ.
Wheaton College (IL)
Widener Univ. (PA)
Yeshiva Univ. (NY)
York College of Pennsylvania
Youngstown State Univ. (OH)

Engineering Mechanics

Columbia Univ. (NY)
David Lipscomb Univ. (TN)
Johns Hopkins Univ. (MD)
Lehigh Univ. (PA)
Michigan State Univ.
New Mexico Institute of Mining
    and Technology
United States Air Force Academy
    (CO)
Univ. of California–San Diego
Univ. of Ill.–Urbana-Champaign
Univ. of Missouri–Rolla
Univ. of Wisconsin–Madison
Virginia Tech

Engineering Physics

Abilene Christian Univ. (TX)
Arkansas Tech Univ.
Aurora Univ. (IL)
Barnard College (NY)
Belmont Univ. (TN)
Bradley Univ. (IL)
Brown Univ. (RI)
Case Western Reserve Univ. (OH)
Christian Brothers Univ. (TN)
Colorado School of Mines
Connecticut College
Cornell Univ. (NY)
Dartmouth College (NH)
Eastern Michigan Univ.
Eastern Nazarene College (MA)
Elizabethtown College (PA)
Elon Univ. (NC)
Embry Riddle Aeronautical Univ.
    (FL)
Fordham Univ. (NY)

Fort Lewis College (CO)
Hope College (MI)
Humboldt State Univ. (CA)
John Carroll Univ. (OH)
Juniata College (PA)
Lehigh Univ. (PA)
Loyola Marymount Univ. (CA)
Miami Univ.–Oxford (OH)
Morgan State Univ. (MD)
Morningside College (IA)
Murray State Univ. (KY)
New Mexico State Univ.
North Carolina A&T State Univ.
Northeastern State Univ. (OK)
Northern Arizona Univ.
Northwest Nazarene Univ. (ID)
Oakland Univ. (MI)
Ohio State Univ.–Columbus
Oklahoma Christian Univ.
Oral Roberts Univ. (OK)
Oregon State Univ.
Ouachita Baptist Univ. (AR)
Point Loma Nazarene Univ. (CA)
Providence College (RI)
Purdue Univ.–Calumet (IN)
Randolph-Macon Woman's College
    (VA)
Rensselaer Polytechnic Inst. (NY)
Rose-Hulman Institute of
    Technology (IN)
Samford Univ. (AL)
Santa Clara Univ. (CA)
South Dakota State Univ.
Southeast Missouri State Univ.
Southwestern College (KS)
Southwestern Oklahoma State
    Univ.
Spring Arbor Univ. (MI)
St. Ambrose Univ. (IA)
St. Mary's Univ. of Minnesota
Stevens Institute of Technology
    (NJ)
Syracuse Univ. (NY)
Tarleton State Univ. (TX)
Taylor Univ. (IN)
Texas Tech Univ.
Tufts Univ. (MA)
Union Univ. (TN)
Univ. at Buffalo–SUNY
Univ. of Arizona
Univ. of California–Berkeley
Univ. of California–San Diego
Univ. of Colorado–Boulder
Univ. of Connecticut
Univ. of Illinois–Chicago
Univ. of Ill.–Urbana-Champaign
Univ. of Kansas
Univ. of Maine–Orono
Univ. of Massachusetts–Boston
Univ. of Michigan–Ann Arbor
Univ. of Nebraska–Omaha
Univ. of Nevada–Reno
Univ. of Northern Iowa
Univ. of Oklahoma
Univ. of Pittsburgh
Univ. of Tennessee
Univ. of Texas–Brownsville
Univ. of the Pacific (CA)
Univ. of Tulsa (OK)
Univ. of Wisconsin–Madison
Univ. of Wisconsin–Platteville

Washington and Lee Univ. (VA)
Washington Univ. In St. Louis
West Virginia Univ. Institute of
    Technology
Westmont College (CA)
Worcester Polytechnic Inst. (MA)
Wright State Univ. (OH)
Yale Univ. (CT)

Engineering Science

Abilene Christian Univ. (TX)
Bethel Univ. (MN)
California State Univ.–Fullerton
Case Western Reserve Univ. (OH)
College of New Jersey
Colorado State Univ.
David Lipscomb Univ. (TN)
Dordt College (IA)
Franciscan Univ. of Steubenville
    (OH)
Harvard Univ. (MA)
Hofstra Univ. (NY)
Iowa State Univ.
King College (TN)
Merrimack College (MA)
New Jersey Institute of Technology
Northwestern Univ. (IL)
Penn. State Univ.–Univ. Park
Principia College (IL)
Rutgers–New Brunswick (NJ)
Seattle Pacific Univ.
Southern Utah Univ.
St. Mary's Univ. of San Antonio
Sweet Briar College (VA)
Tufts Univ. (MA)
Tulane Univ. (LA)
Univ. of California–Berkeley
Univ. of California–San Diego
Univ. of Florida
Univ. of Miami (FL)
Univ. of Michigan–Ann Arbor
Univ. of Michigan–Flint
Univ. of New Mexico
Univ. of New Orleans
Univ. of Rochester (NY)
Univ. of Tennessee
Univ. of Virginia
Wartburg College (IA)
Washington State Univ.
West Virginia Univ. Institute of
    Technology
Yale Univ. (CT)

Engineering Technologies/Technicians

Andrews Univ. (MI)
Appalachian State Univ. (NC)
Arkansas State Univ.
Ball State Univ. (IN)
Bowling Green State Univ. (OH)
Capitol College (MD)
Central Missouri State Univ.
East Carolina Univ. (NC)
Eastern Washington Univ.
Excelsior College (NY)
Jacksonville State Univ. (AL)
Letourneau Univ. (TX)

New York Institute of Technology
North Carolina A&T State Univ.
Old Dominion Univ. (VA)
Pittsburg State Univ. (KS)
Rochester Institute of Tech. (NY)
Southwest Missouri State Univ.
St. Cloud State Univ. (MN)
Thomas Edison State College (NJ)
Univ. of Alaska–Fairbanks
Univ. of Hartford (CT)
Univ. of Maryland–Eastern Shore
Univ. of Northern Iowa
Univ. of Southern Indiana
Univ. of West Alabama
Virginia State Univ.
Western Michigan Univ.

Engineering Technology

Austin Peay State Univ. (TN)
Berry College (GA)
California State Univ.–Long Beach
California Univ. of Pennsylvania
Cameron Univ. (OK)
Columbia Univ. (NY)
East Tennessee State Univ.
Eastern New Mexico Univ.
Jackson State Univ. (MS)
Kansas State Univ.
Lawrence Technological Univ. (MI)
Mcneese State Univ. (LA)
New Jersey Institute of Technology
New Mexico State Univ.
Northern Illinois Univ.
Paul Quinn College (TX)
Southern Illinois Univ.–Carbondale
Southern Polytechnic State Univ.
    (GA)
Texas A&M Univ.–College Station
Texas A&M Univ.–Galveston
Texas State Univ.–San Marcos
Univ. of North Texas
Univ. of Wisconsin–Stout
Wentworth Institute of Tech. (MA)
Western Carolina Univ. (NC)
Youngstown State Univ. (OH)

Engineering-Related Fields

Eastern Michigan Univ.
Illinois Institute of Technology
Kansas State Univ.
Lake Superior State Univ. (MI)
Lawrence Technological Univ. (MI)
Marquette Univ. (WI)
Miami Univ.–Oxford (OH)
Montana State Univ.–Bozeman
Pittsburg State Univ. (KS)
South Dakota State Univ.
St. Louis Univ.
Stanford Univ. (CA)
Stevens Institute of Tech. (NJ)
SUNY–Farmingdale
Sweet Briar College (VA)
Univ. of Evansville (IN)
Univ. of Illinois–Chicago
Univ. of Scranton (PA)
Univ. of the Pacific (CA)

Washpolton State Univ.
West Virginia Univ.–Parkersburg
Western Michigan Univ.
Worcester Polytechnic Institute
    (MA)
York College of Pennsylvania

Engineering-Related Technologies

Boise State Univ. (ID)
East Tennessee State Univ.
Fairfield Univ. (CT)
Ferris State Univ. (MI)
Idaho State Univ.
Metropolitan State College of
    Denver
Miami Univ.–Oxford (OH)
Middle Tennessee State Univ.
New Mexico State Univ.
Nicholls State Univ. (LA)
Ohio State Univ.–Columbus
Oregon Institute of Technology
Pennsylvania College of Technology
Purdue Univ.–West Lafayette (IN)
Savannah State Univ. (GA)
Southern Polytechnic State Univ.
    (GA)
St. Cloud State Univ. (MN)
Tarleton State Univ. (TX)
Texas A&M Univ.–Corpus Christi
Thomas Edison State College (NJ)
Troy State Univ.–Troy (AL)
Univ. of Akron (OH)
Univ. of Arizona
Univ. of Delaware
Univ. of Florida
Univ. of Houston
Univ. of Maine–Orono
Univ. of Texas–Tyler

English Composition

Baylor Univ. (TX)
Benedict College (SC)
Bennington College (VT)
Bethel Univ. (MN)
Boise State Univ. (ID)
Briar Cliff Univ. (IA)
California State Univ.–Long Beach
California State Univ.–San
    Bernardino
Carroll College (MT)
Delaware State Univ.
Drury Univ. (MO)
Eastern Michigan Univ.
Eureka College (IL)
Ferris State Univ. (MI)
Florida Southern College
Geneva College (PA)
Georgia Southern Univ.
Graceland Univ. (IA)
Huntington College (IN)
Indiana Univ. Southeast
Jamestown College (ND)
La Roche College (PA)
Lakeland College (WI)
Marian College of Fond Du Lac
    (WI)

Marquette Univ. (WI)
Morgan State Univ. (MD)
Purdue Univ.–Calumet (IN)
St. Edward's Univ. (TX)
Tulane Univ. (LA)
Univ. of Central Arkansas
Univ. of Colorado–Denver
Univ. of Great Falls (MT)
Univ. of Ill.–Urbana-Champaign
Univ. of Judaism (CA)
Univ. of Michigan–Flint
Upper Iowa Univ.
Wartburg College (IA)
Western Connecticut State Univ.
Western Michigan Univ.

English Language and Literature

Abilene Christian Univ. (TX)
Adams State College (CO)
Adelphi Univ. (NY)
Adrian College (MI)
Agnes Scott College (GA)
Alabama Agricultural and
    Mechanical Univ.
Alabama State Univ.
Albany State Univ. (GA)
Albertson College (ID)
Albertus Magnus College (CT)
Albion College (MI)
Albright College (PA)
Alcorn State Univ. (MS)
Alfred Univ. (NY)
Alice Lloyd College (KY)
Allegheny College (PA)
Allen Univ. (SC)
Alma College (MI)
Alvernia College (PA)
Alverno College (WI)
American International College
    (MA)
American Univ. (DC)
Amherst College (MA)
Anderson College (SC)
Anderson Univ. (IN)
Andrews Univ. (MI)
Angelo State Univ. (TX)
Anna Maria College (MA)
Antioch College (OH)
Appalachian State Univ. (NC)
Aquinas College (MI)
Arcadia Univ. (PA)
Arizona State Univ.
Arizona State Univ. West
Arkansas State Univ.
Arkansas Tech Univ.
Armstrong Atlantic State Univ.
    (GA)
Asbury College (KY)
Assumption College (MA)
Atlantic Union College (MA)
Auburn Univ. (AL)
Auburn Univ.–Montgomery (AL)
Augusta State Univ. (GA)
Augustana College (IL)
Augustana College (SD)
Aurora Univ. (IL)
Austin College (TX)
Austin Peay State Univ. (TN)

Averett Univ. (VA)
Avila Univ. (MO)
Azusa Pacific Univ. (CA)
Baker Univ. (KS)
Baldwin-Wallace College (OH)
Ball State Univ. (IN)
Barber Scotia College (NC)
Barry Univ. (FL)
Barton College (NC)
Bates College (ME)
Baylor Univ. (TX)
Belhaven College (MS)
Bellarmine Univ. (KY)
Belmont Abbey College (NC)
Belmont Univ. (TN)
Beloit College (WI)
Bemidji State Univ. (MN)
Benedictine College (KS)
Benedictine Univ. (IL)
Bennett College (NC)
Bennington College (VT)
Bentley College (MA)
Berea College (KY)
Berry College (GA)
Bethany College (WV)
Bethel College (KS)
Bethel College (IN)
Bethel College (TN)
Bethel Univ. (MN)
Bethune-Cookman College (FL)
Biola Univ. (CA)
Black Hills State Univ. (SD)
Blackburn College (IL)
Bloomfield College (NJ)
Bloomsburg Univ. of Pennsylvania
Blue Mountain College (MS)
Bluefield College (VA)
Bluffton Univ. (OH)
Boise State Univ. (ID)
Boston Univ.
Bowdoin College (ME)
Bowie State Univ. (MD)
Bowling Green State Univ. (OH)
Bradley Univ. (IL)
Brandeis Univ. (MA)
Brenau Univ. (GA)
Brescia Univ. (KY)
Brevard College (NC)
Brewton-Parker College (GA)
Briar Cliff Univ. (IA)
Bridgewater College (VA)
Bridgewater State College (MA)
Brigham Young Univ.–Hawaii
Brown Univ. (RI)
Bryan College (TN)
Bryant College (RI)
Bryn Athyn College (PA)
Bryn Mawr College (PA)
Bucknell Univ. (PA)
Buena Vista Univ. (IA)
Buffalo State College
Butler Univ. (IN)
Cabrini College (PA)
Caldwell College (NJ)
California Baptist Univ.
California Lutheran Univ.
California State Polytechnic
    Univ.–Pomona
California State Univ.–Bakersfield
California State Univ.–Chico

California State Univ.–Fresno
California State Univ.–Fullerton
California State Univ.–Hayward
California State Univ.–Long Beach
California State Univ.–Los Angeles
California State Univ.–Monterey
    Bay
California State Univ.–Northridge
California State Univ.–Sacramento
California State Univ.–San
    Bernardino
California State Univ.–Stanislaus
California Univ. of Pennsylvania
Calumet College of St. Joseph (IN)
Calvin College (MI)
Cameron Univ. (OK)
Campbell Univ. (NC)
Campbellsville Univ. (KY)
Canisius College (NY)
Capital Univ. (OH)
Cardinal Stritch Univ. (WI)
Carleton College (MN)
Carlow College (PA)
Carnegie Mellon Univ. (PA)
Carroll College (MT)
Carthage College (WI)
Case Western Reserve Univ. (OH)
Castleton State College (VT)
Catawba College (NC)
Catholic Univ. of America (DC)
Cazenovia College (NY)
Cedarville Univ. (OH)
Centenary College (NJ)
Centenary College of Louisiana
Central College (IA)
Central Connecticut State Univ.
Central Methodist Univ. (MO)
Central Michigan Univ.
Central Missouri State Univ.
Central State Univ. (OH)
Central Washington Univ.
Centre College (KY)
Chadron State College (NE)
Chaminade Univ. of Honolulu
Chapman Univ. (CA)
Charleston Southern Univ. (SC)
Chatham College (PA)
Chestnut Hill College (PA)
Cheyney Univ. of Pennsylvania
Chicago State Univ.
Chowan College (NC)
Christendom College (VA)
Christian Heritage College (CA)
Christopher Newport Univ. (VA)
Claflin Univ. (SC)
Claremont Mckenna College (CA)
Clarion Univ. of Pennsylvania
Clark Atlanta Univ.
Clark Univ. (MA)
Clearwater Christian College (FL)
Cleveland State Univ.
Coastal Carolina Univ. (SC)
Coe College (IA)
Coker College (SC)
Colby College (ME)
Colby-Sawyer College (NH)
Colgate Univ. (NY)
College Misericordia (PA)
College of Charleston (SC)
College of Mount St. Joseph (OH)
College of Mount St. Vincent (NY)

College of New Jersey
College of Notre Dame of
    Maryland
College of Santa Fe (NM)
College of St. Benedict (MN)
College of St. Catherine (MN)
College of St. Elizabeth (NJ)
College of St. Joseph (VT)
College of St. Mary (NE)
College of St. Rose (NY)
College of St. Scholastica (MN)
College of the Holy Cross (MA)
College of the Ozarks (MO)
College of the Southwest (NM)
College of William and Mary (VA)
College of Wooster (OH)
Colorado Christian Univ.
Colorado College
Colorado State Univ.
Colorado State Univ.–Pueblo
Columbia College (MO)
Columbia College (SC)
Columbia Union College (MD)
Columbia Univ. (NY)
Columbus State Univ. (GA)
Concord College (WV)
Concordia College (NY)
Concordia Coll.–Moorhead (MN)
Concordia Univ. (OR)
Concordia Univ. (NE)
Concordia Univ. (MI)
Concordia Univ. (CA)
Concordia Univ.–Austin (TX)
Concordia Univ.–River Forest (IL)
Concordia Univ.–St. Paul (MN)
Connecticut College
Converse College (SC)
Coppin State Univ. (MD)
Cornell College (IA)
Cornell Univ. (NY)
Cornerstone Univ. (MI)
Covenant College (GA)
Creighton Univ. (NE)
Crichton College (TN)
Culver-Stockton College (MO)
Cumberland Univ. (TN)
CUNY–Brooklyn College
CUNY–City College
CUNY–College of Staten Island
CUNY–Hunter College
CUNY–Lehman College
CUNY–Medgar Evers College
CUNY–Queens College
CUNY–York College
Curry College (MA)
Daemen College (NY)
Dakota Wesleyan Univ. (SD)
Dallas Baptist Univ.
Dartmouth College (NH)
David Lipscomb Univ. (TN)
Davidson College (NC)
Davis and Elkins College (WV)
Delaware Valley College (PA)
Delta State Univ. (MS)
Denison Univ. (OH)
Depaul Univ. (IL)
Depauw Univ. (IN)
Desales Univ. (PA)
Dickinson College (PA)
Dickinson State Univ. (ND)
Dominican Coll. of Blauvelt (NY)

Dominican Univ. (IL)
Dominican Univ. of California (CA)
Dordt College (IA)
Dowling College (NY)
Drake Univ. (IA)
Drew Univ. (NJ)
Drury Univ. (MO)
Duke Univ. (NC)
Duquesne Univ. (PA)
Earlham College (IN)
East Carolina Univ. (NC)
East Stroudsburg Univ. of
    Pennsylvania
East Tennessee State Univ.
East Texas Baptist Univ.
Eastern Connecticut State Univ.
Eastern Illinois Univ.
Eastern Kentucky Univ.
Eastern Mennonite Univ. (VA)
Eastern Michigan Univ.
Eastern Nazarene College (MA)
Eastern New Mexico Univ.
Eastern Oregon Univ.
Eastern Washington Univ.
Eckerd College (FL)
Edgewood College (WI)
Edinboro Univ. of Pennsylvania
Elizabeth City State Univ. (NC)
Elizabethtown College (PA)
Elmhurst College (IL)
Elmira College (NY)
Elms College (College of Our Lady
    of the Elms) (MA)
Elon Univ. (NC)
Emmanuel College (GA)
Emmanuel College (MA)
Emory and Henry College (VA)
Emory Univ. (GA)
Emporia State Univ. (KS)
Endicott College (MA)
Erskine College (SC)
Eureka College (IL)
Evangel Univ. (MO)
Fairfield Univ. (CT)
Fairleigh Dickinson Univ. (NJ)
Fairmont State Univ. (WV)
Faulkner Univ. (AL)
Fayetteville State Univ. (NC)
Ferrum College (VA)
Fisk Univ. (TN)
Fitchburg State College (MA)
Flagler College (FL)
Florida Atlantic Univ.
Florida International Univ.
Florida Southern College
Florida State Univ.
Fontbonne Univ. (MO)
Fordham Univ. (NY)
Fort Hays State Univ. (KS)
Fort Lewis College (CO)
Fort Valley State Univ. (GA)
Framingham State College (MA)
Francis Marion Univ. (SC)
Franciscan Univ. of Steubenville
    (OH)
Franklin and Marshall College (PA)
Franklin College (IN)
Franklin Pierce College (NH)
Freed-Hardeman Univ. (TN)
Fresno Pacific Univ. (CA)
Friends Univ. (KS)

Frostburg State Univ. (MD)
Gallaudet Univ. (DC)
Gardner-Webb Univ. (NC)
Geneva College (PA)
George Mason Univ. (VA)
George Washington Univ. (DC)
Georgetown College (KY)
Georgetown Univ. (DC)
Georgia College and State Univ.
Georgia Southern Univ.
Georgia State Univ.
Georgian Court Univ. (NJ)
Gettysburg College (PA)
Glenville State College (WV)
Gonzaga Univ. (WA)
Gordon College (MA)
Goshen College (IN)
Goucher College (MD)
Grace College and Seminary (IN)
Graceland Univ. (IA)
Grambling State Univ. (LA)
Grand Canyon Univ. (AZ)
Grand Valley State Univ. (MI)
Grand View College (IA)
Green Mountain College (VT)
Greensboro College (NC)
Greenville College (IL)
Grinnell College (IA)
Grove City College (PA)
Guilford College (NC)
Gustavus Adolphus College (MN)
Hamline Univ. (MN)
Hampden-Sydney College (VA)
Hampshire College (MA)
Hampton Univ. (VA)
Hannibal-Lagrange College (MO)
Hanover College (IN)
Hardin-Simmons Univ. (TX)
Harding Univ. (AR)
Hartwick College (NY)
Harvard Univ. (MA)
Hastings College (NE)
Haverford College (PA)
Hawaii Pacific Univ.
Henderson State Univ. (AR)
Hendrix College (AR)
Heritage College (WA)
High Point Univ. (NC)
Hilbert College (NY)
Hiram College (OH)
Hobart and William Smith Colleges (NY)
Hofstra Univ. (NY)
Hollins Univ. (VA)
Holy Family Univ. (PA)
Holy Names Univ. (CA)
Hood College (MD)
Hope College (MI)
Houghton College (NY)
Houston Baptist Univ.
Howard Payne Univ. (TX)
Howard Univ. (DC)
Humboldt State Univ. (CA)
Huntingdon College (AL)
Huntington College (IN)
Huston-Tillotson College (TX)
Idaho State Univ.
Illinois College
Illinois State Univ.
Illinois Wesleyan Univ.
Immaculata Univ. (PA)

Indiana State Univ.
Indiana Univ. East
Indiana Univ. Northwest
Indiana Univ. of Pennsylvania
Indiana Univ. Southeast
Indiana Univ.–Bloomington
Indiana Univ.–Kokomo
Indiana Univ.–South Bend
Indiana Univ.-Purdue Univ.–Fort Wayne
Indiana Univ.-Purdue Univ.–Indianapolis
Indiana Wesleyan Univ.
Iona College (NY)
Iowa State Univ.
Ithaca College (NY)
Jackson State Univ. (MS)
Jacksonville State Univ. (AL)
James Madison Univ. (VA)
Jamestown College (ND)
Jarvis Christian College (TX)
John Brown Univ. (AR)
John Carroll Univ. (OH)
Johns Hopkins Univ. (MD)
Johnson C. Smith Univ. (NC)
Johnson State College (VT)
Judson College (IL)
Judson College (AL)
Juniata College (PA)
Kalamazoo College (MI)
Kansas State Univ.
Kansas Wesleyan Univ.
Kean Univ. (NJ)
Keene State College (NH)
Kennesaw State Univ. (GA)
Kent State Univ. (OH)
Kentucky State Univ.
Kentucky Wesleyan College
Keuka College (NY)
King College (TN)
King's College (PA)
Knox College (IL)
Kutztown Univ. of Pennsylvania
La Roche College (PA)
La Salle Univ. (PA)
La Sierra Univ. (CA)
Lafayette College (PA)
Lagrange College (GA)
Lake Superior State Univ. (MI)
Lakeland College (WI)
Lamar Univ. (TX)
Lambuth Univ. (TN)
Lander Univ. (SC)
Lane College (TN)
Lawrence Univ. (WI)
Le Moyne College (NY)
Lebanon Valley College (PA)
Lees-Mcrae College (NC)
Lehigh Univ. (PA)
Lemoyne-Owen College (TN)
Lenoir-Rhyne College (NC)
Letourneau Univ. (TX)
Lewis and Clark College (OR)
Lewis-Clark State College (ID)
Liberty Univ. (VA)
Limestone College (SC)
Lincoln Memorial Univ. (TN)
Lincoln Univ. (MO)
Lincoln Univ. (PA)
Lindenwood Univ. (MO)
Lindsey Wilson College (KY)

Linfield College (OR)
Livingstone College (NC)
Lock Haven Univ. of Pennsylvania
Long Island Univ.–C.W. Post Campus (NY)
Long Island Univ.–Southampton College (NY)
Loras College (IA)
Louisiana College
Louisiana State Univ.–Baton Rouge
Louisiana State Univ.–Shreveport
Louisiana Tech Univ.
Lourdes College (OH)
Loyola College In Maryland
Loyola Marymount Univ. (CA)
Loyola Univ. Chicago
Loyola Univ. New Orleans
Luther College (IA)
Lycoming College (PA)
Lynchburg College (VA)
Lyon College (AR)
Macalester College (MN)
Macmurray College (IL)
Madonna Univ. (MI)
Maharishi Univ. of Management (IA)
Malone College (OH)
Manchester College (IN)
Manhattan College (NY)
Manhattanville College (NY)
Mansfield Univ. of Pennsylvania
Marian College (IN)
Marian College of Fond Du Lac (WI)
Marietta College (OH)
Marist College (NY)
Marquette Univ. (WI)
Mars Hill College (NC)
Marshall Univ. (WV)
Martin Methodist College (TN)
Martin Univ. (IN)
Mary Baldwin College (VA)
Marygrove College (MI)
Marylhurst Univ. (OR)
Marymount Manhattan College (NY)
Marymount Univ. (VA)
Maryville College (TN)
Maryville Univ. of St. Louis (MO)
Massachusetts Institute of Technology
Master's Coll. and Seminary (CA)
Mayville State Univ. (ND)
Mcdaniel College (MD)
Mckendree College (IL)
Mcmurry Univ. (TX)
Mcpherson College (KS)
Medaille College (NY)
Mercer Univ. (GA)
Mercyhurst College (PA)
Meredith College (NC)
Merrimack College (MA)
Mesa State College (CO)
Messiah College (PA)
Methodist College (NC)
Metropolitan State College of Denver
Miami Univ.–Oxford (OH)
Michigan State Univ.
Middle Tennessee State Univ.
Middlebury College (VT)

Midland Lutheran College (NE)
Midway College (KY)
Midwestern State Univ. (TX)
Miles College (AL)
Millersville Univ. of Pennsylvania
Milligan College (TN)
Millikin Univ. (IL)
Mills College (CA)
Millsaps College (MS)
Minnesota State Univ.–Mankato
Minnesota State Univ.–Moorhead
Minot State Univ. (ND)
Mississippi College
Mississippi State Univ.
Mississippi Univ. For Women
Mississippi Valley State Univ.
Missouri Baptist College
Missouri Southern State Univ.
Missouri Valley College
Missouri Western State College
Molloy College (NY)
Monmouth Univ. (NJ)
Montana State Univ.–Billings
Montana State Univ.–Bozeman
Montana State Univ.–Northern
Montclair State Univ. (NJ)
Montreat College (NC)
Moravian College (PA)
Morehead State Univ. (KY)
Morehouse College (GA)
Morningside College (IA)
Morris College (SC)
Mount Marty College (SD)
Mount Mary College (WI)
Mount Mercy College (IA)
Mount Olive College (NC)
Mount St. Mary College (NY)
Mount St. Mary's College (CA)
Mount St. Mary's Univ. (MD)
Mount Union College (OH)
Muhlenberg College (PA)
Murray State Univ. (KY)
Muskingum College (OH)
National Univ. (CA)
National-Louis Univ. (IL)
Nazareth College of Rochester (NY)
Nebraska Wesleyan Univ.
Neumann College (PA)
New Jersey City Univ.
New Mexico Highlands Univ.
New Mexico State Univ.
New York Institute of Technology
Newberry College (SC)
Nicholls State Univ. (LA)
Nichols College (MA)
Norfolk State Univ. (VA)
North Carolina A&T State Univ.
North Carolina Central Univ.
North Carolina State Univ.–Raleigh
North Carolina Wesleyan College
North Central College (IL)
North Dakota State Univ.
North Georgia College and State Univ.
North Greenville College (SC)
North Park Univ. (IL)
Northeastern Illinois Univ.
Northeastern Univ. (MA)
Northern Arizona Univ.
Northern Illinois Univ.

Northern Kentucky Univ.
Northern Michigan Univ.
Northern State Univ. (SD)
Northwest College (WA)
Northwest Missouri State Univ.
Northwest Nazarene Univ. (ID)
Northwestern College (MN)
Northwestern College (IA)
Northwestern Oklahoma State Univ.
Northwestern State Univ. of Louisiana
Northwestern Univ. (IL)
Norwich Univ. (VT)
Notre Dame College of Ohio
Notre Dame De Namur Univ. (CA)
Nova Southeastern Univ. (FL)
Nyack College (NY)
Oakland City Univ. (IN)
Oakland Univ. (MI)
Oakwood College (AL)
Oberlin College (OH)
Ohio Dominican Univ.
Ohio State Univ.–Columbus
Ohio Univ.
Ohio Wesleyan Univ.
Oklahoma Baptist Univ.
Oklahoma Christian Univ.
Oklahoma City Univ.
Oklahoma Panhandle State Univ.
Oklahoma State Univ.
Oklahoma Wesleyan Univ.
Old Dominion Univ. (VA)
Olivet College (MI)
Olivet Nazarene Univ. (IL)
Oregon State Univ.
Otterbein College (OH)
Ouachita Baptist Univ. (AR)
Our Lady of Holy Cross Coll. (LA)
Our Lady of the Lake Univ. (TX)
Pace Univ. (NY)
Pacific Lutheran Univ. (WA)
Pacific Union College (CA)
Pacific Univ. (OR)
Paine College (GA)
Palm Beach Atlantic Univ. (FL)
Park Univ. (MO)
Paul Quinn College (TX)
Peace College (NC)
Penn. State Univ.–Univ. Park
Penn. State–Erie, The Behrend College
Pepperdine Univ. (CA)
Peru State College (NE)
Pfeiffer Univ. (NC)
Philander Smith College (AR)
Piedmont College (GA)
Pikeville College (KY)
Pine Manor College (MA)
Pittsburg State Univ. (KS)
Pitzer College (CA)
Plymouth State Univ. (NH)
Point Loma Nazarene Univ. (CA)
Point Park Univ. (PA)
Pomona College (CA)
Prairie View A&M Univ. (TX)
Presbyterian College (SC)
Prescott College (AZ)
Princeton Univ. (NJ)
Principia College (IL)
Providence College (RI)

Purdue Univ.–Calumet (IN)
Purdue Univ.–North Central (IN)
Purdue Univ.–West Lafayette (IN)
Queens Univ. of Charlotte (NC)
Quincy Univ. (IL)
Quinnipiac Univ. (CT)
Radford Univ. (VA)
Randolph-Macon College (VA)
Randolph-Macon Woman's College (VA)
Reed College (OR)
Regis College (MA)
Regis Univ. (CO)
Reinhardt College (GA)
Rhode Island College
Rhodes College (TN)
Richard Stockton College of New Jersey
Rider Univ. (NJ)
Ripon College (WI)
Rivier College (NH)
Roanoke College (VA)
Robert Morris Univ. (PA)
Roberts Wesleyan College (NY)
Rochester College (MI)
Rockford College (IL)
Rockhurst Univ. (MO)
Rocky Mountain College (MT)
Roger Williams Univ. (RI)
Rollins College (FL)
Roosevelt Univ. (IL)
Rosemont College (PA)
Russell Sage College (NY)
Rutgers–Camden (NJ)
Rutgers–New Brunswick (NJ)
Rutgers–Newark (NJ)
Saginaw Valley State Univ. (MI)
Salem College (NC)
Salem State College (MA)
Salisbury Univ. (MD)
Salve Regina Univ. (RI)
Sam Houston State Univ. (TX)
Samford Univ. (AL)
San Diego State Univ.
San Francisco State Univ.
San Jose State Univ. (CA)
Santa Clara Univ. (CA)
Savannah State Univ. (GA)
Schreiner Univ. (TX)
Seattle Univ.
Seton Hall Univ. (NJ)
Seton Hill Univ. (PA)
Sewanee–Univ. of the South (TN)
Shaw Univ. (NC)
Shawnee State Univ. (OH)
Shenandoah Univ. (VA)
Shepherd Univ. (WV)
Shippensburg Univ. of Pennsylvania
Shorter College (GA)
Siena College (NY)
Sierra Nevada College (NV)
Silver Lake College (WI)
Simmons College (MA)
Simon's Rock College of Bard (MA)
Simpson College (IA)
Simpson Univ. (CA)
Skidmore College (NY)
Slippery Rock Univ. of Pennsylvania
Sonoma State Univ. (CA)

South Carolina State Univ.
South Dakota State Univ.
Southeast Missouri State Univ.
Southeastern College of the Assemblies of God
Southeastern Louisiana Univ.
Southeastern Oklahoma State Univ.
Southern Adventist Univ. (TN)
Southern Arkansas Univ.
Southern Illinois Univ.–Carbondale
Southern Illinois Univ.–Edwardsville
Southern Methodist Univ. (TX)
Southern Nazarene Univ. (OK)
Southern New Hampshire Univ.
Southern Oregon Univ.
Southern Univ. and A&M College (LA)
Southern Utah Univ.
Southern Wesleyan Univ. (SC)
Southwest Baptist Univ. (MO)
Southwest Minnesota State Univ. (MN)
Southwest Missouri State Univ.
Southwestern Adventist Univ. (TX)
Southwestern College (KS)
Southwestern Oklahoma State Univ.
Southwestern Univ. (TX)
Spelman College (GA)
Spring Arbor Univ. (MI)
Spring Hill College (AL)
Springfield College (MA)
St. Ambrose Univ. (IA)
St. Andrews Presbyterian College (NC)
St. Anselm College (NH)
St. Augustine's College (NC)
St. Cloud State Univ. (MN)
St. Edward's Univ. (TX)
St. Francis College (NY)
St. Francis Univ. (PA)
St. Gregory's Univ. (OK)
St. John Fisher College (NY)
St. John's Univ. (NY)
St. John's Univ. (MN)
St. Joseph College (CT)
St. Joseph's College (IN)
St. Joseph's College (ME)
St. Joseph's College, New York
St. Joseph's Univ. (PA)
St. Lawrence Univ. (NY)
St. Leo Univ. (FL)
St. Louis Univ.
St. Martin's College (WA)
St. Mary's College of California
St. Mary's College of Maryland
St. Mary's Univ. of Minnesota
St. Mary's Univ. of San Antonio
St. Mary-of-The-Woods Coll. (IN)
St. Norbert College (WI)
St. Olaf College (MN)
St. Peter's College (NJ)
St. Thomas Aquinas College (NY)
St. Thomas Univ. (FL)
St. Vincent College (PA)
St. Xavier Univ. (IL)
Stanford Univ. (CA)
State Univ. of West Georgia
Stephen F. Austin State Univ. (TX)

Stephens College (MO)
Sterling College (KS)
Stetson Univ. (FL)
Stillman College (AL)
Stonehill College (MA)
Suffolk Univ. (MA)
Sul Ross State Univ. (TX)
SUNY College of Arts and Sciences–Geneseo
SUNY College–Brockport
SUNY College–Oneonta
SUNY College–Potsdam
SUNY–Albany
SUNY–Binghamton
SUNY–Empire State College
SUNY–Oswego
SUNY–Plattsburgh
SUNY–Purchase College
SUNY–Stony Brook
Susquehanna Univ. (PA)
Swarthmore College (PA)
Sweet Briar College (VA)
Syracuse Univ. (NY)
Tabor College (KS)
Talladega College (AL)
Tarleton State Univ. (TX)
Taylor Univ. (IN)
Teikyo Post Univ. (CT)
Temple Univ. (PA)
Tennessee State Univ.
Tennessee Technological Univ.
Texas A&M International Univ.
Texas A&M Univ.–College Station
Texas A&M Univ.–Commerce
Texas A&M Univ.–Corpus Christi
Texas Christian Univ.
Texas College
Texas Lutheran Univ.
Texas State Univ.–San Marcos
Texas Tech Univ.
Texas Wesleyan Univ.
Texas Woman's Univ.
The Citadel (SC)
Thiel College (PA)
Thomas Edison State College (NJ)
Thomas More College (KY)
Tiffin Univ. (OH)
Toccoa Falls College (GA)
Tougaloo College (MS)
Touro College (NY)
Towson Univ. (MD)
Transylvania Univ. (KY)
Trevecca Nazarene Univ. (TN)
Tri-State Univ. (IN)
Trinity Christian College (IL)
Trinity College (CT)
Trinity College (DC)
Troy State Univ.–Troy (AL)
Truman State Univ. (MO)
Tulane Univ. (LA)
Tusculum College (TN)
Tuskegee Univ. (AL)
Union College (NY)
Union College (NE)
Union Univ. (TN)
United States Air Force Academy (CO)
United States Naval Academy (MD)
Univ. at Buffalo–SUNY
Univ. of Akron (OH)

Univ. of Alabama
Univ. of Alabama–Birmingham
Univ. of Alabama–Huntsville
Univ. of Alaska–Anchorage
Univ. of Alaska–Fairbanks
Univ. of Arizona
Univ. of Arkansas
Univ. of Arkansas–Little Rock
Univ. of Arkansas–Pine Bluff
Univ. of California–Berkeley
Univ. of California–Davis
Univ. of California–Irvine
Univ. of California–Los Angeles
Univ. of California–Riverside
Univ. of California–San Diego
Univ. of Central Arkansas
Univ. of Central Florida
Univ. of Central Oklahoma
Univ. of Charleston (WV)
Univ. of Chicago
Univ. of Colorado–Boulder
Univ. of Colorado–Colorado Springs
Univ. of Colorado–Denver
Univ. of Connecticut
Univ. of Dallas
Univ. of Dayton (OH)
Univ. of Delaware
Univ. of Denver
Univ. of Dubuque (IA)
Univ. of Evansville (IN)
Univ. of Findlay (OH)
Univ. of Florida
Univ. of Georgia
Univ. of Great Falls (MT)
Univ. of Hartford (CT)
Univ. of Hawaii–Hilo
Univ. of Hawaii–Manoa
Univ. of Houston
Univ. of Houston–Downtown
Univ. of Illinois–Chicago
Univ. of Illinois–Springfield
Univ. of Ill.–Urbana-Champaign
Univ. of Indianapolis
Univ. of Iowa
Univ. of Judaism (CA)
Univ. of Kansas
Univ. of Kentucky
Univ. of La Verne (CA)
Univ. of Louisiana–Lafayette
Univ. of Louisville (KY)
Univ. of Maine–Farmington
Univ. of Maine–Fort Kent
Univ. of Maine–Machias
Univ. of Maine–Orono
Univ. of Mary (ND)
Univ. of Mary Hardin-Baylor (TX)
Univ. of Mary Washington (VA)
Univ. of Maryland–Baltimore County
Univ. of Maryland–College Park
Univ. of Maryland–Eastern Shore
Univ. of Maryland–Univ. College
Univ. of Massachusetts–Amherst
Univ. of Massachusetts–Boston
Univ. of Massachusetts–Lowell
Univ. of Memphis
Univ. of Miami (FL)
Univ. of Michigan–Ann Arbor
Univ. of Michigan–Dearborn
Univ. of Michigan–Flint

Univ. of Minnesota–Duluth
Univ. of Minnesota–Twin Cities
Univ. of Mississippi
Univ. of Missouri–Columbia
Univ. of Missouri–Kansas City
Univ. of Missouri–Rolla
Univ. of Missouri–St. Louis
Univ. of Mobile (AL)
Univ. of Montana
Univ. of Montevallo (AL)
Univ. of Nebraska–Kearney
Univ. of Nebraska–Lincoln
Univ. of Nebraska–Omaha
Univ. of Nevada–Las Vegas
Univ. of Nevada–Reno
Univ. of New England (ME)
Univ. of New Hampshire
Univ. of New Haven (CT)
Univ. of New Mexico
Univ. of New Orleans
Univ. of North Alabama
Univ. of North Carolina–Asheville
Univ. of N.C.–Chapel Hill
Univ. of North Carolina–Charlotte
Univ. of N.C.–Greensboro
Univ. of North Carolina–Pembroke
Univ. of N.C.–Wilmington
Univ. of North Dakota
Univ. of North Florida
Univ. of North Texas
Univ. of Northern Colorado
Univ. of Northern Iowa
Univ. of Notre Dame (IN)
Univ. of Oklahoma
Univ. of Oregon
Univ. of Pennsylvania
Univ. of Pittsburgh–Bradford
Univ. of Portland (OR)
Univ. of Puget Sound (WA)
Univ. of Redlands (CA)
Univ. of Rhode Island
Univ. of Richmond (VA)
Univ. of Rio Grande (OH)
Univ. of Rochester (NY)
Univ. of San Diego
Univ. of Science and Arts of Oklahoma
Univ. of Sioux Falls (SD)
Univ. of South Alabama
Univ. of South Carolina–Aiken
Univ. of South Carolina–Columbia
Univ. of South Dakota
Univ. of South Florida
Univ. of Southern California
Univ. of Southern Indiana
Univ. of Southern Maine
Univ. of Southern Mississippi
Univ. of St. Francis (IN)
Univ. of St. Francis (IL)
Univ. of St. Mary (KS)
Univ. of St. Thomas (TX)
Univ. of St. Thomas (MN)
Univ. of Tampa (FL)
Univ. of Tennessee
Univ. of Tennessee–Chattanooga
Univ. of Tennessee–Martin
Univ. of Texas of the Permian Basin
Univ. of Texas–Arlington
Univ. of Texas–Austin
Univ. of Texas–Brownsville
Univ. of Texas–Pan American

Univ. of Texas–San Antonio
Univ. of Texas–Tyler
Univ. of the District of Columbia
Univ. of the Incarnate Word (TX)
Univ. of the Ozarks (AR)
Univ. of the Pacific (CA)
Univ. of Toledo (OH)
Univ. of Tulsa (OK)
Univ. of Utah
Univ. of Vermont
Univ. of Virginia
Univ. of Virginia–Wise
Univ. of Washington
Univ. of West Alabama
Univ. of West Florida
Univ. of Wisconsin–Eau Claire
Univ. of Wisconsin–Green Bay
Univ. of Wisconsin–La Crosse
Univ. of Wisconsin–Madison
Univ. of Wisconsin–Milwaukee
Univ. of Wisconsin–Platteville
Univ. of Wisconsin–River Falls
Univ. of Wisconsin–Stevens Point
Univ. of Wisconsin–Whitewater
Univ. of Wyoming
Urbana Univ. (OH)
Ursinus College (PA)
Ursuline College (OH)
Utah State Univ.
Utah Valley State College
Utica College (NY)
Valdosta State Univ. (GA)
Valley City State Univ. (ND)
Valparaiso Univ. (IN)
Vanderbilt Univ. (TN)
Vanguard Univ. of Southern
    California
Vassar College (NY)
Villa Julie College (MD)
Villanova Univ. (PA)
Virginia Commonwealth Univ.
Virginia Intermont College
Virginia Military Institute
Virginia State Univ.
Virginia Tech
Virginia Wesleyan College
Viterbo Univ. (WI)
Wabash College (IN)
Wagner College (NY)
Wake Forest Univ. (NC)
Waldorf College (IA)
Walsh Univ. (OH)
Warner Pacific College (OR)
Warner Southern College (FL)
Wartburg College (IA)
Washington and Jefferson College
    (PA)
Washington and Lee Univ. (VA)
Washington College (MD)
Washington State Univ.
Washington Univ. In St. Louis
Wayland Baptist Univ. (TX)
Wayne State College (NE)
Wayne State Univ. (MI)
Waynesburg College (PA)
Weber State Univ. (UT)
Webster Univ. (MO)
Wesley College (DE)
Wesleyan College (GA)
West Chester Univ. of Pennsylvania
West Liberty State College (WV)

West Texas A&M Univ.
West Virginia Univ.
West Virginia Wesleyan College
Western Baptist College (OR)
Western Carolina Univ. (NC)
Western Connecticut State Univ.
Western Illinois Univ.
Western Kentucky Univ.
Western Michigan Univ.
Western New England College
    (MA)
Western New Mexico Univ.
Western Oregon Univ.
Western State College of Colorado
Western Washington Univ.
Westfield State College (MA)
Westminster College (MO)
Westminster College (PA)
Westminster College (UT)
Westmont College (CA)
Wheaton College (MA)
Wheaton College (IL)
Wheeling Jesuit Univ. (WV)
Whitman College (WA)
Whittier College (CA)
Whitworth College (WA)
Wichita State Univ. (KS)
Wiley College (TX)
Wilkes Univ. (PA)
Willamette Univ. (OR)
William Carey College (MS)
William Jewell College (MO)
William Paterson Univ. of New
    Jersey
William Woods Univ. (MO)
Williams College (MA)
Wilmington College (OH)
Wilson College (PA)
Wingate Univ. (NC)
Winston-Salem State Univ. (NC)
Winthrop Univ. (SC)
Wisconsin Lutheran College
Wittenberg Univ. (OH)
Wofford College (SC)
Worcester State College (MA)
Wright State Univ. (OH)
Xavier Univ. (OH)
Yale Univ. (CT)
York College (NE)
York College of Pennsylvania
Youngstown State Univ. (OH)

English Language and Literature/Letters

Bard College (NY)
Beloit College (WI)
Boise State Univ. (ID)
Burlington College (VT)
California State Univ.–Hayward
California State Univ.–Long Beach
Columbia College (SC)
CUNY–College of Staten Island
Dakota State Univ. (SD)
Drexel Univ. (PA)
Duke Univ. (NC)
Duquesne Univ. (PA)
Eastern Univ. (PA)
Edward Waters College (FL)
Emmanuel College (MA)

Eureka College (IL)
Ferris State Univ. (MI)
Florida Southern College
Hannibal-Lagrange College (MO)
Harvard Univ. (MA)
Hillsdale College (MI)
Hofstra Univ. (NY)
Houghton College (NY)
Houston Baptist Univ.
Johns Hopkins Univ. (MD)
Lindenwood Univ. (MO)
Milligan College (TN)
Mills College (CA)
Minnesota State Univ.–Moorhead
Monmouth College (IL)
Northern Arizona Univ.
Ohio Wesleyan Univ.
Rust College (MS)
Skidmore College (NY)
Southeastern College of the
    Assemblies of God
Spring Hill College (AL)
St. Gregory's Univ. (OK)
St. Leo Univ. (FL)
St. Mary's College of California
SUNY College–Old Westbury
Tulane Univ. (LA)
Unity College (ME)
Univ. of California–Los Angeles
Univ. of California–San Diego
Univ. of Findlay (OH)
Univ. of Iowa
Univ. of La Verne (CA)
Univ. of Maine–Augusta
Univ. of Pennsylvania
Univ. of Southern California
Viterbo Univ. (WI)
Washington Univ. In St. Louis
Western Kentucky Univ.
Whitman College (WA)
Wilberforce Univ. (OH)
Williams College (MA)
Yale Univ. (CT)

English Literature (British and Commonwealth)

Bennington College (VT)
CUNY–Baruch College
CUNY–Hunter College
Elmira College (NY)
Emory Univ. (GA)
Excelsior College (NY)
Gannon Univ. (PA)
Hofstra Univ. (NY)
Lawrence Univ. (WI)
Marian College of Fond Du Lac
    (WI)
Marlboro College (VT)
Mills College (CA)
New York Univ.
Ohio Northern Univ.
Oral Roberts Univ. (OK)
St. Mary's College (IN)
Syracuse Univ. (NY)
Tufts Univ. (MA)
Univ. of California–San Diego
Univ. of Miami (FL)
Univ. of New Hampshire

Univ. of Pittsburgh
Univ. of Pittsburgh–Greensburg
Univ. of Redlands (CA)

Entrepreneurial and Small Business Operations

Babson College (MA)
Baylor Univ. (TX)
Belmont Univ. (TN)
Black Hills State Univ. (SD)
Boston Univ.
Bradley Univ. (IL)
Buena Vista Univ. (IA)
California State Univ.–Fullerton
Canisius College (NY)
Central Michigan Univ.
Cleary Univ. (MI)
Columbia Union College (MD)
Davenport Univ. (MI)
Dickinson State Univ. (ND)
Drake Univ. (IA)
Duquesne Univ. (PA)
Eastern Michigan Univ.
Fairleigh Dickinson Univ. (NJ)
Ferris State Univ. (MI)
Gallaudet Univ. (DC)
Grove City College (PA)
Hampton Univ. (VA)
Hawaii Pacific Univ.
Hofstra Univ. (NY)
Houston Baptist Univ.
Huntington College (IN)
Husson College (ME)
Juniata College (PA)
Lewis-Clark State College (ID)
Lyndon State College (VT)
Messiah College (PA)
Middle Tennessee State Univ.
Mountain State Univ. (WV)
North Central College (IL)
Northeastern State Univ. (OK)
Northeastern Univ. (MA)
Northern Michigan Univ.
Northwood Univ. (MI)
Oregon Institute of Technology
Pace Univ. (NY)
Palm Beach Atlantic Univ. (FL)
Pepperdine Univ. (CA)
Purdue Univ.–Calumet (IN)
Reinhardt College (GA)
Rhode Island College
Seton Hill Univ. (PA)
Shaw Univ. (NC)
Sierra Nevada College (NV)
Southern Adventist Univ. (TN)
Southern Polytechnic State Univ.
    (GA)
Southwestern College (KS)
St. Cloud State Univ. (MN)
St. Edward's Univ. (TX)
St. Mary's Univ. of San Antonio
Stetson Univ. (FL)
Susquehanna Univ. (PA)
Syracuse Univ. (NY)
Temple Univ. (PA)
Thomas Edison State College (NJ)
Union College (NE)
Univ. of Arizona

Univ. of Dayton (OH)
Univ. of Hartford (CT)
Univ. of Illinois–Chicago
Univ. of Ill.–Urbana-Champaign
Univ. of Indianapolis
Univ. of Iowa
Univ. of Louisiana–Monroe
Univ. of Massachusetts–Lowell
Univ. of Miami (FL)
Univ. of New Hampshire
Univ. of Pittsburgh–Bradford
Univ. of Rio Grande (OH)
Univ. of St. Thomas (MN)
Univ. of Toledo (OH)
Univ. of Utah
Univ. of Washington
Washington State Univ.
Washington Univ. In St. Louis
Waynesburg College (PA)
Wichita State Univ. (KS)
Wilkes Univ. (PA)
Xavier Univ. (OH)

Environmental Control Technologies/Technicians

California State Univ.–Long Beach
Central Missouri State Univ.
Davis and Elkins College (WV)
Eastern Kentucky Univ.
Fairmont State Univ. (WV)
Ferris State Univ. (MI)
Fitchburg State College (MA)
Florida International Univ.
Mesa State College (CO)
Middle Tennessee State Univ.
Montana State Univ.–Northern
Murray State Univ. (KY)
New York Institute of Technology
North Carolina State Univ.–Raleigh
Oregon Institute of Technology
Pennsylvania College of Technology
Rochester Institute of Tech. (NY)
Shawnee State Univ. (OH)
Univ. of Findlay (OH)
West Liberty State College (WV)
Western Kentucky Univ.

Environmental Design

Auburn Univ. (AL)
Ball State Univ. (IN)
Boston Architectural Center
Bowling Green State Univ. (OH)
Cornell Univ. (NY)
Lawrence Technological Univ. (MI)
Miami Univ.–Oxford (OH)
Montana State Univ.–Bozeman
Morgan State Univ. (MD)
New School Univ. (NY)
North Carolina State Univ.–Raleigh
North Dakota State Univ.
Otis College of Art and Design
    (CA)
Rutgers–New Brunswick (NJ)
Texas A&M Univ.–College Station
Univ. at Buffalo–SUNY
Univ. of California–Davis
Univ. of California–Irvine

Univ. of Colorado–Boulder
Univ. of Houston
Univ. of Massachusetts–Amherst
Univ. of Memphis
Univ. of Michigan–Ann Arbor
Univ. of Minnesota–Twin Cities
Univ. of New Mexico
Univ. of Oklahoma
Univ. of Pennsylvania
Univ. of Texas–Arlington

Environmental Psychology

Embry Riddle Aeronautical Univ. (FL)

Environmental/ Environmental Health Engineering

Cal Poly–San Luis Obispo
Clarkson Univ. (NY)
Columbia Univ. (NY)
Cornell Univ. (NY)
Drexel Univ. (PA)
Gannon Univ. (PA)
Hofstra Univ. (NY)
Humboldt State Univ. (CA)
Johns Hopkins Univ. (MD)
Lehigh Univ. (PA)
Louisiana State Univ.–Baton Rouge
Manhattan College (NY)
Marquette Univ. (WI)
Massachusetts Institute of Technology
Michigan Technological Univ.
Montana Tech of the Univ. of Montana
New Jersey Institute of Technology
New Mexico Institute of Mining and Technology
North Carolina State Univ.–Raleigh
Northeastern State Univ. (OK)
Northern Arizona Univ.
Northwestern Univ. (IL)
Old Dominion Univ. (VA)
Oregon State Univ.
Penn. State Univ.–Univ. Park
Rensselaer Polytechnic Inst. (NY)
Rice Univ. (TX)
Roger Williams Univ. (RI)
San Diego State Univ.
Southern Methodist Univ. (TX)
Stanford Univ. (CA)
Stevens Institute of Technology (NJ)
Suffolk Univ. (MA)
Syracuse Univ. (NY)
Taylor Univ. (IN)
Temple Univ. (PA)
Texas A&M Univ.–Kingsville
Texas Tech Univ.
Tufts Univ. (MA)
Tulane Univ. (LA)
United States Air Force Academy (CO)
United States Military Academy (NY)

Univ. at Buffalo–SUNY
Univ. of California–Berkeley
Univ. of California–Irvine
Univ. of California–Riverside
Univ. of California–San Diego
Univ. of Central Florida
Univ. of Colorado–Boulder
Univ. of Connecticut
Univ. of Florida
Univ. of Georgia
Univ. of Ill.–Urbana-Champaign
Univ. of Miami (FL)
Univ. of Michigan–Ann Arbor
Univ. of Missouri–Rolla
Univ. of Nevada–Reno
Univ. of New Hampshire
Univ. of North Dakota
Univ. of Notre Dame (IN)
Univ. of Oklahoma
Univ. of Pennsylvania
Univ. of Southern California
Univ. of Vermont
Univ. of Wisconsin–Platteville
Utah State Univ.
Washington State Univ.
Wentworth Institute of Tech. (MA)
Wilkes Univ. (PA)
Worcester Polytechnic Institute (MA)
Yale Univ. (CT)

Ethnic, Cultural Minority, and Gender Studies

Agnes Scott College (GA)
Albion College (MI)
Albright College (PA)
Allegheny College (PA)
American Univ. (DC)
Amherst College (MA)
Antioch College (OH)
Arizona State Univ.
Arizona State Univ. West
Augsburg College (MN)
Ball State Univ. (IN)
Barnard College (NY)
Bates College (ME)
Beloit College (WI)
Bennington College (VT)
Berea College (KY)
Black Hills State Univ. (SD)
Boise State Univ. (ID)
Bowdoin College (ME)
Bowling Green State Univ. (OH)
Brandeis Univ. (MA)
Brenau Univ. (GA)
Brown Univ. (RI)
Bucknell Univ. (PA)
California State Polytechnic Univ.–Pomona
California State Univ.–Chico
California State Univ.–Dominguez Hills
California State Univ.–Fresno
California State Univ.–Fullerton
California State Univ.–Hayward
California State Univ.–Long Beach
California State Univ.–Los Angeles
California State Univ.–Monterey Bay

California State Univ.–Northridge
California State Univ.–Sacramento
California State Univ.–San Marcos
Carleton College (MN)
Carnegie Mellon Univ. (PA)
Case Western Reserve Univ. (OH)
Central Michigan Univ.
Central Missouri State Univ.
Chatham College (PA)
Chicago State Univ.
Claflin Univ. (SC)
Claremont Mckenna College (CA)
Clark Univ. (MA)
Cleveland State Univ.
Coe College (IA)
Colby College (ME)
Colgate Univ. (NY)
College of New Jersey
College of St. Catherine (MN)
College of St. Rose (NY)
College of William and Mary (VA)
College of Wooster (OH)
Colorado College
Columbia Univ. (NY)
Connecticut College
Cornell College (IA)
Cornell Univ. (NY)
Creighton Univ. (NE)
CUNY–Brooklyn College
CUNY–College of Staten Island
CUNY–Hunter College
CUNY–Lehman College
CUNY–Queens College
CUNY–York College
Dartmouth College (NH)
Denison Univ. (OH)
Depaul Univ. (IL)
Depauw Univ. (IN)
Dickinson College (PA)
Dominican Univ. (IL)
Dominican Univ. of California (CA)
Drew Univ. (NJ)
Duke Univ. (NC)
Earlham College (IN)
East Carolina Univ. (NC)
Eastern Illinois Univ.
Eastern Michigan Univ.
Eckerd College (FL)
Emory Univ. (GA)
Evergreen State College (WA)
Florida A&M Univ.
Florida International Univ.
Fordham Univ. (NY)
Fort Lewis College (CO)
Fresno Pacific Univ. (CA)
Furman Univ. (SC)
Gallaudet Univ. (DC)
George Washington Univ. (DC)
Georgetown Univ. (DC)
Georgia State Univ.
Goshen College (IN)
Goucher College (MD)
Guilford College (NC)
Gustavus Adolphus College (MN)
Hamilton College (NY)
Hamline Univ. (MN)
Hampshire College (MA)
Harvard Univ. (MA)
Hobart and William Smith Colleges (NY)
Hofstra Univ. (NY)

Hollins Univ. (VA)
Hope College (MI)
Houghton College (NY)
Howard Univ. (DC)
Humboldt State Univ. (CA)
Illinois Wesleyan Univ.
Indiana State Univ.
Indiana Univ. Northwest
Indiana Univ.–South Bend
Indiana Univ.-Purdue Univ.–Fort Wayne
Indiana Univ.-Purdue Univ.–Indianapolis
Indiana Wesleyan Univ.
Iowa State Univ.
Johns Hopkins Univ. (MD)
Kansas State Univ.
Kent State Univ. (OH)
Knox College (IL)
Lawrence Univ. (WI)
Lehigh Univ. (PA)
Lincoln Univ. (PA)
Louisiana State Univ.–Baton Rouge
Loyola Marymount Univ. (CA)
Luther College (IA)
Macalester College (MN)
Martin Univ. (IN)
Mercer Univ. (GA)
Meredith College (NC)
Metropolitan State College of Denver
Miami Univ.–Oxford (OH)
Michigan State Univ.
Middlebury College (VT)
Mills College (CA)
Minnesota State Univ.–Mankato
Minnesota State Univ.–Moorhead
Montclair State Univ. (NJ)
Morehouse College (GA)
Morgan State Univ. (MD)
Mount Holyoke College (MA)
Nebraska Wesleyan Univ.
New York Univ.
North Dakota State Univ.
North Park Univ. (IL)
Northeastern Illinois Univ.
Northeastern State Univ. (OK)
Northeastern Univ. (MA)
Northern Arizona Univ.
Northwestern Univ. (IL)
Oakland Univ. (MI)
Oberlin College (OH)
Occidental College (CA)
Ohio State Univ.–Columbus
Ohio Univ.
Ohio Wesleyan Univ.
Old Dominion Univ. (VA)
Oregon State Univ.
Pace Univ. (NY)
Penn. State Univ.–Univ. Park
Pitzer College (CA)
Pomona College (CA)
Portland State Univ. (OR)
Prescott College (AZ)
Purdue Univ.–West Lafayette (IN)
Randolph-Macon College (VA)
Regis Univ. (CO)
Rhode Island College
Rice Univ. (TX)
Roosevelt Univ. (IL)
Rosemont College (PA)

Russell Sage College (NY)
Rutgers–Camden (NJ)
Rutgers–New Brunswick (NJ)
Rutgers–Newark (NJ)
San Diego State Univ.
San Francisco State Univ.
San Jose State Univ. (CA)
Scripps College (CA)
Seton Hall Univ. (NJ)
Simmons College (MA)
Skidmore College (NY)
Sonoma State Univ. (CA)
Southern Adventist Univ. (TN)
Southern Methodist Univ. (TX)
Southwestern Univ. (TX)
Spelman College (GA)
St. Bonaventure Univ. (NY)
St. Cloud State Univ. (MN)
St. Francis College (NY)
St. Louis Univ.
St. Mary's College of California
St. Olaf College (MN)
Stanford Univ. (CA)
Stonehill College (MA)
Suffolk Univ. (MA)
Sul Ross State Univ. (TX)
SUNY College of Arts and Sciences–Geneseo
SUNY College–Brockport
SUNY–Albany
SUNY–Binghamton
SUNY–Plattsburgh
SUNY–Purchase College
SUNY–Stony Brook
Syracuse Univ. (NY)
Talladega College (AL)
Temple Univ. (PA)
Tennessee State Univ.
Towson Univ. (MD)
Trinity College (CT)
Tufts Univ. (MA)
Tulane Univ. (LA)
Univ. at Buffalo–SUNY
Univ. of Alabama–Birmingham
Univ. of Alaska–Fairbanks
Univ. of Arizona
Univ. of California–Berkeley
Univ. of California–Davis
Univ. of California–Irvine
Univ. of California–Los Angeles
Univ. of California–Riverside
Univ. of California–San Diego
Univ. of California–Santa Barbara
Univ. of California–Santa Cruz
Univ. of Central Arkansas
Univ. of Chicago
Univ. of Colorado–Boulder
Univ. of Connecticut
Univ. of Dayton (OH)
Univ. of Delaware
Univ. of Denver
Univ. of Florida
Univ. of Georgia
Univ. of Hartford (CT)
Univ. of Hawaii–Manoa
Univ. of Illinois–Chicago
Univ. of Illinois–Urbana-Champaign
Univ. of Iowa
Univ. of Kansas
Univ. of Louisville (KY)

Univ. of Maine–Farmington
Univ. of Maine–Orono
Univ. of Maryland–Baltimore
County
Univ. of Maryland–College Park
Univ. of Maryland–Eastern Shore
Univ. of Massachusetts–Amherst
Univ. of Massachusetts–Boston
Univ. of Memphis
Univ. of Miami (FL)
Univ. of Michigan–Ann Arbor
Univ. of Michigan–Dearborn
Univ. of Michigan–Flint
Univ. of Minnesota–Duluth
Univ. of Minnesota–Morris
Univ. of Minnesota–Twin Cities
Univ. of Mississippi
Univ. of Montana
Univ. of Nebraska–Lincoln
Univ. of Nebraska–Omaha
Univ. of Nevada–Las Vegas
Univ. of Nevada–Reno
Univ. of New Hampshire
Univ. of New Mexico
Univ. of New Orleans
Univ. of North Carolina–Asheville
Univ. of N.C.–Chapel Hill
Univ. of North Carolina–Charlotte
Univ. of N.C.–Greensboro
Univ. of North Carolina–Pembroke
Univ. of North Dakota
Univ. of Northern Colorado
Univ. of Oklahoma
Univ. of Oregon
Univ. of Pennsylvania
Univ. of Pittsburgh
Univ. of Rhode Island
Univ. of Richmond (VA)
Univ. of Rochester (NY)
Univ. of Science and Arts of
Oklahoma
Univ. of South Carolina–Columbia
Univ. of South Dakota
Univ. of South Florida
Univ. of Southern California
Univ. of Southern Maine
Univ. of St. Thomas (MN)
Univ. of Texas–Austin
Univ. of Texas–Dallas
Univ. of Texas–El Paso
Univ. of Texas–Pan American
Univ. of Texas–San Antonio
Univ. of the Incarnate Word (TX)
Univ. of Toledo (OH)
Univ. of Utah
Univ. of Vermont
Univ. of Virginia
Univ. of Washington
Univ. of Wisconsin–Eau Claire
Univ. of Wisconsin–Madison
Univ. of Wisconsin–Milwaukee
Univ. of Wisconsin–Whitewater
Univ. of Wyoming
Vanderbilt Univ. (TN)
Vassar College (NY)
Virginia Commonwealth Univ.
Virginia Wesleyan College
Washington State Univ.
Washington Univ. In St. Louis
Wayne State Univ. (MI)
Wellesley College (MA)

Wesleyan Univ. (CT)
West Chester Univ. of Pennsylvania
Western Illinois Univ.
Western Michigan Univ.
Westfield State College (MA)
Wheaton College (MA)
Whitman College (WA)
Wichita State Univ. (KS)
Willamette Univ. (OR)
William Paterson Univ. of New
Jersey
Williams College (MA)
Wright State Univ. (OH)
Yale Univ. (CT)
Youngstown State Univ. (OH)

Experimental Psychology

Keene State College (NH)
Millikin Univ. (IL)
Moravian College (PA)
Northern Michigan Univ.
Paine College (GA)
Tufts Univ. (MA)
Univ. of Judaism (CA)
Univ. of Rochester (NY)
Univ. of South Carolina–Columbia

Family and Consumer Economics and Related Studies

Arizona State Univ.
Bradley Univ. (IL)
Brigham Young Univ.–Provo (UT)
Buffalo State College
California State Polytechnic
Univ.–Pomona
Concordia Coll.–Moorhead (MN)
Cornell Univ. (NY)
Indiana Univ. of Pennsylvania
Iowa State Univ.
Kent State Univ. (OH)
Louisiana Tech Univ.
Middle Tennessee State Univ.
New Mexico State Univ.
Oakwood College (AL)
Ohio State Univ.–Columbus
South Dakota State Univ.
St. Joseph College (CT)
Syracuse Univ. (NY)
Tennessee State Univ.
Univ. of Alabama
Univ. of Arizona
Univ. of Delaware
Univ. of Georgia
Univ. of Hawaii–Manoa
Univ. of Ill.–Urbana-Champaign
Univ. of Kentucky
Univ. of Minnesota–Twin Cities
Univ. of Missouri–Columbia
Univ. of Nebraska–Kearney
Univ. of Nebraska–Lincoln
Univ. of Tennessee
Univ. of Utah
Univ. of Wisconsin–Madison
Utah State Univ.
Virginia State Univ.

Weber State Univ. (UT)

Family and Consumer Sciences/Human Sciences

Alabama Agricultural and
Mechanical Univ.
Alcorn State Univ. (MS)
Ashland Univ. (OH)
Ball State Univ. (IN)
Baylor Univ. (TX)
Berea College (KY)
Bluffton Univ. (OH)
Boise State Univ. (ID)
Bridgewater College (VA)
Brigham Young Univ.–Provo (UT)
Cal Poly–San Luis Obispo
California State Univ.–Fresno
California State Univ.–Long Beach
California State Univ.–Los Angeles
California State Univ.–Northridge
California State Univ.–Sacramento
Cameron Univ. (OK)
Campbell Univ. (NC)
Central Missouri State Univ.
Central Washington Univ.
Chadron State College (NE)
Cheyney Univ. of Pennsylvania
College of the Ozarks (MO)
Colorado State Univ.
Concordia Coll.–Moorhead (MN)
Cornell Univ. (NY)
CUNY–Queens College
David Lipscomb Univ. (TN)
Delta State Univ. (MS)
East Tennessee State Univ.
Eastern Illinois Univ.
Eastern Kentucky Univ.
Eastern New Mexico Univ.
Fairmont State Univ. (WV)
Florida State Univ.
Framingham State College (MA)
Gallaudet Univ. (DC)
Grambling State Univ. (LA)
Harding Univ. (AR)
Henderson State Univ. (AR)
Idaho State Univ.
Illinois State Univ.
Indiana State Univ.
Indiana Univ. of Pennsylvania
Jacksonville State Univ. (AL)
Kansas State Univ.
Kent State Univ. (OH)
Lambuth Univ. (TN)
Liberty Univ. (VA)
Louisiana State Univ.–Baton Rouge
Madonna Univ. (MI)
Marshall Univ. (WV)
Master's Coll. and Seminary (CA)
Mcneese State Univ. (LA)
Mercyhurst College (PA)
Meredith College (NC)
Michigan State Univ.
Minnesota State Univ.–Mankato
Mississippi State Univ.
Montana State Univ.–Bozeman
Montclair State Univ. (NJ)
Morehead State Univ. (KY)
New Jersey City Univ.

New Mexico Highlands Univ.
Nicholls State Univ. (LA)
Norfolk State Univ. (VA)
North Carolina A&T State Univ.
North Carolina Central Univ.
Northeastern State Univ. (OK)
Northwestern Oklahoma State
Univ.
Northwestern State Univ. of
Louisiana
Ohio State Univ.–Columbus
Oklahoma Baptist Univ.
Oklahoma Christian Univ.
Oklahoma State Univ.
Oregon State Univ.
Pittsburg State Univ. (KS)
Point Loma Nazarene Univ. (CA)
Prairie View A&M Univ. (TX)
Purdue Univ.–Calumet (IN)
Purdue Univ.–West Lafayette (IN)
Sam Houston State Univ. (TX)
San Francisco State Univ.
Seattle Pacific Univ.
Seton Hill Univ. (PA)
South Carolina State Univ.
Southeast Missouri State Univ.
Southeastern Louisiana Univ.
Southern Utah Univ.
Stephen F. Austin State Univ. (TX)
SUNY College–Oneonta
Syracuse Univ. (NY)
Tarleton State Univ. (TX)
Texas State Univ.–San Marcos
Texas Tech Univ.
Texas Woman's Univ.
Univ. of Akron (OH)
Univ. of Alabama
Univ. of Arkansas
Univ. of Arkansas–Pine Bluff
Univ. of Central Arkansas
Univ. of Central Oklahoma
Univ. of Delaware
Univ. of Houston
Univ. of Louisiana–Monroe
Univ. of Maryland–Eastern Shore
Univ. of Mississippi
Univ. of Missouri–Columbia
Univ. of Montevallo (AL)
Univ. of New Mexico
Univ. of North Alabama
Univ. of Southern Mississippi
Univ. of Tennessee
Univ. of Tennessee–Chattanooga
Univ. of Tennessee–Martin
Univ. of Texas–Austin
Univ. of Wisconsin–Madison
Univ. of Wyoming
Utah State Univ.
Washington State Univ.
Wayne State College (NE)
West Virginia Univ.
Western Illinois Univ.
Youngstown State Univ. (OH)

Family and Consumer Sci./Human Sciences Business Services

Ashland Univ. (OH)
California State Univ.–Long Beach

Eastern Kentucky Univ.
Lasell College (MA)
Madonna Univ. (MI)
Northwestern Oklahoma State
Univ.
Our Lady of the Lake Univ. (TX)
San Jose State Univ. (CA)
Univ. of Georgia
Univ. of Houston
Univ. of Wisconsin–Madison
Virginia Tech

Family Psychology

Seattle Pacific Univ.
Walsh Univ. (OH)
Western Baptist College (OR)

Film/Video and Photographic Arts

American Univ. (DC)
Arcadia Univ. (PA)
Arizona State Univ.
Art Academy of Cincinnati
Art Center College of Design (CA)
Atlanta College of Art
Baldwin-Wallace College (OH)
Barnard College (NY)
Barry Univ. (FL)
Bellevue Univ. (NE)
Bennington College (VT)
Berklee College of Music (MA)
Bethel College (IN)
Boston Univ.
Bowling Green State Univ. (OH)
Briar Cliff Univ. (IA)
Bridgewater State College (MA)
Brigham Young Univ.–Provo (UT)
Buffalo State College
Burlington College (VT)
California College of the Arts
California Institute of the Arts
California State Univ.–Long Beach
California State Univ.–Sacramento
Calvin College (MI)
Cardinal Stritch Univ. (WI)
Carlow College (PA)
Carroll College (WI)
Carson-Newman College (TN)
Cazenovia College (NY)
Central Missouri State Univ.
Chapman Univ. (CA)
Chatham College (PA)
Claremont Mckenna College (CA)
Clark Univ. (MA)
Cleveland Institute of Art
Coker College (SC)
College For Creative Studies (MI)
College of Santa Fe (NM)
College of Visual Arts (MN)
Colorado College
Colorado State Univ.
Columbia College (MO)
Columbia College (IL)
Columbia Univ. (NY)
Columbus College of Art and
Design (OH)
Connecticut College

Corcoran College of Art and Design (DC)
Cornell Univ. (NY)
CUNY–Brooklyn College
CUNY–College of Staten Island
CUNY–Hunter College
CUNY–Queens College
Dartmouth College (NH)
Denison Univ. (OH)
Desales Univ. (PA)
Dominican Univ. (IL)
Drexel Univ. (PA)
Eastern Michigan Univ.
Eastern Washington Univ.
Emerson College (MA)
Emory Univ. (GA)
Evergreen State College (WA)
Fairleigh Dickinson Univ. (NJ)
Ferris State Univ. (MI)
Fitchburg State College (MA)
Florida State Univ.
George Fox Univ. (OR)
Georgia State Univ.
Grand Valley State Univ. (MI)
Hampshire College (MA)
Hofstra Univ. (NY)
Hollins Univ. (VA)
Howard Univ. (DC)
Huntington College (IN)
Indiana Univ.–South Bend
Indiana Univ.–Purdue Univ.–Fort Wayne
Indiana Wesleyan Univ.
Ithaca College (NY)
Kansas City Art Institute (MO)
Keene State College (NH)
Kent State Univ. (OH)
La Roche College (PA)
Long Island Univ.–Brooklyn (NY)
Long Island Univ.–C.W. Post Campus (NY)
Long Island Univ.–Southampton College (NY)
Louisiana Tech Univ.
Loyola Marymount Univ. (CA)
Macmurray College (IL)
Maine College of Art
Maryland Institute College of Art
Marywood Univ. (PA)
Massachusetts College of Art
Middlebury College (VT)
Milwaukee Institute of Art and Design
Minneapolis College of Art and Design
Minnesota State Univ.–Moorhead
Montana State Univ.–Bozeman
Montserrat College of Art (MA)
Moore College of Art and Design (PA)
Morningside College (IA)
Mount Holyoke College (MA)
Mountain State Univ. (WV)
Muhlenberg College (PA)
National Univ. (CA)
New Jersey City Univ.
New Mexico Highlands Univ.
New School Univ. (NY)
New York Univ.
North Carolina School of the Arts
Northern Arizona Univ.

Ohio State Univ.–Columbus
Ohio Univ.
Oklahoma City Univ.
Otis College of Art and Design (CA)
Pacific Union College (CA)
Penn. State Univ.–Univ. Park
Pitzer College (CA)
Point Park Univ. (PA)
Prescott College (AZ)
Providence College (RI)
Rhode Island College
Rhode Island School of Design
Ringling School of Art and Design (FL)
Rochester Institute of Tech. (NY)
Sam Houston State Univ. (TX)
San Francisco Art Institute
San Francisco State Univ.
San Jose State Univ. (CA)
Savannah College of Art and Design (GA)
School of the Art Institute of Chicago
Seattle Univ.
Shawnee State Univ. (OH)
Southern Adventist Univ. (TN)
Southern Illinois Univ.–Carbondale
Southern Methodist Univ. (TX)
Southwest Missouri State Univ.
Spring Arbor Univ. (MI)
St. Augustine's College (NC)
St. Cloud State Univ. (MN)
St. Edward's Univ. (TX)
St. John's Univ. (NY)
Stanford Univ. (CA)
Suffolk Univ. (MA)
SUNY–Binghamton
SUNY–Fredonia
SUNY–Purchase College
Swarthmore College (PA)
Syracuse Univ. (NY)
Temple Univ. (PA)
Texas A&M Univ.–Commerce
Texas Christian Univ.
Thomas Edison State College (NJ)
Tulane Univ. (LA)
Univ. at Buffalo–SUNY
Univ. of Akron (OH)
Univ. of California–Berkeley
Univ. of California–Davis
Univ. of California–Irvine
Univ. of California–Los Angeles
Univ. of California–Riverside
Univ. of California–Santa Barbara
Univ. of California–Santa Cruz
Univ. of Central Florida
Univ. of Chicago
Univ. of Colorado–Boulder
Univ. of Dayton (OH)
Univ. of Georgia
Univ. of Hartford (CT)
Univ. of Houston
Univ. of Illinois–Chicago
Univ. of Ill.–Urbana-Champaign
Univ. of Iowa
Univ. of Mass.–Dartmouth
Univ. of Miami (FL)
Univ. of Michigan–Ann Arbor
Univ. of Michigan–Flint
Univ. of Minnesota–Twin Cities

Univ. of Missouri–St. Louis
Univ. of Montana
Univ. of Nebraska–Lincoln
Univ. of Nevada–Las Vegas
Univ. of New Mexico
Univ. of N.C.–Wilmington
Univ. of North Texas
Univ. of Oklahoma
Univ. of Oregon
Univ. of Pennsylvania
Univ. of Pittsburgh
Univ. of Rochester (NY)
Univ. of South Carolina–Columbia
Univ. of Southern California
Univ. of the Arts (PA)
Univ. of Toledo (OH)
Univ. of Tulsa (OK)
Univ. of Utah
Univ. of Vermont
Univ. of Wisconsin–Milwaukee
Vanguard Univ. of Southern California
Vassar College (NY)
Virginia Commonwealth Univ.
Virginia Intermont College
Washington Univ. In St. Louis
Wayne State Univ. (MI)
Weber State Univ. (UT)
Webster Univ. (MO)
Wellesley College (MA)
Wesleyan Univ. (CT)
Western Michigan Univ.
Western Washington Univ.
Wilmington College (DE)
Woodbury Univ. (CA)
Wright State Univ. (OH)
Yale Univ. (CT)
Youngstown State Univ. (OH)

Finance and Financial Management Services

Abilene Christian Univ. (TX)
Adelphi Univ. (NY)
Alabama Agricultural and Mechanical Univ.
Alabama State Univ.
Alfred Univ. (NY)
Alma College (MI)
American Univ. (DC)
Anderson College (SC)
Anderson Univ. (IN)
Andrews Univ. (MI)
Angelo State Univ. (TX)
Appalachian State Univ. (NC)
Arcadia Univ. (PA)
Arizona State Univ.
Arkansas State Univ.
Ashland Univ. (OH)
Auburn Univ. (AL)
Auburn Univ.–Montgomery (AL)
Augsburg College (MN)
Augusta State Univ. (GA)
Aurora Univ. (IL)
Averett Univ. (VA)
Avila Univ. (MO)
Azusa Pacific Univ. (CA)
Babson College (MA)
Baldwin-Wallace College (OH)
Ball State Univ. (IN)

Baylor Univ. (TX)
Belmont Univ. (TN)
Benedictine Univ. (IL)
Bentley College (MA)
Berry College (GA)
Bethel College (IN)
Bethel Univ. (MN)
Boise State Univ. (ID)
Boston Univ.
Bowling Green State Univ. (OH)
Bradley Univ. (IL)
Bridgewater State College (MA)
Bryant College (RI)
Buena Vista Univ. (IA)
Butler Univ. (IN)
Cabrini College (PA)
California State Polytechnic Univ.–Pomona
California State Univ.–Fullerton
California State Univ.–Long Beach
California State Univ.–Sacramento
Canisius College (NY)
Capital Univ. (OH)
Carroll College (WI)
Catholic Univ. of America (DC)
Cedarville Univ. (OH)
Centenary College of Louisiana
Central Connecticut State Univ.
Central Michigan Univ.
Central Missouri State Univ.
Chestnut Hill College (PA)
Christopher Newport Univ. (VA)
Clarion Univ. of Pennsylvania
Clarkson Univ. (NY)
Cleary Univ. (MI)
Cleveland State Univ.
Coastal Carolina Univ. (SC)
College of New Jersey
College of William and Mary (VA)
Colorado State Univ.
Columbia College (MO)
Columbia Union College (MD)
Columbus State Univ. (GA)
Concordia Coll.–Moorhead (MN)
Concordia Univ. Wisconsin
Concordia Univ.–St. Paul (MN)
Culver-Stockton College (MO)
CUNY–Baruch College
CUNY–Queens College
Dakota State Univ. (SD)
Dallas Baptist Univ.
Davenport Univ. (MI)
David Lipscomb Univ. (TN)
Defiance College (OH)
Delaware State Univ.
Delta State Univ. (MS)
Depaul Univ. (IL)
Desales Univ. (PA)
Dominican Coll. of Blauvelt (NY)
Dowling College (NY)
Drake Univ. (IA)
Drexel Univ. (PA)
Duquesne Univ. (PA)
East Carolina Univ. (NC)
East Tennessee State Univ.
Eastern Illinois Univ.
Eastern Kentucky Univ.
Eastern Michigan Univ.
Eastern New Mexico Univ.
Eastern Washington Univ.
Elmhurst College (IL)

Evangel Univ. (MO)
Excelsior College (NY)
Fairmont State Univ. (WV)
Fayetteville State Univ. (NC)
Ferris State Univ. (MI)
Fitchburg State College (MA)
Florida Atlantic Univ.
Florida Gulf Coast Univ.
Florida International Univ.
Florida Southern College
Florida State Univ.
Fort Hays State Univ. (KS)
Fort Lewis College (CO)
Francis Marion Univ. (SC)
Franklin Pierce College (NH)
Freed-Hardeman Univ. (TN)
Gannon Univ. (PA)
Gardner-Webb Univ. (NC)
George Mason Univ. (VA)
George Washington Univ. (DC)
Georgetown Univ. (DC)
Georgia Southern Univ.
Georgia Southwestern State Univ.
Georgia State Univ.
Golden Gate Univ. (CA)
Goldey Beacom College (DE)
Gordon College (MA)
Grand Valley State Univ. (MI)
Grove City College (PA)
Gwynedd-Mercy College (PA)
Hampton Univ. (VA)
Hardin-Simmons Univ. (TX)
Hawaii Pacific Univ.
Hillsdale College (MI)
Hofstra Univ. (NY)
Holy Family Univ. (PA)
Houston Baptist Univ.
Howard Univ. (DC)
Huntington College (IN)
Husson College (ME)
Idaho State Univ.
Illinois College
Illinois State Univ.
Immaculata Univ. (PA)
Indiana State Univ.
Indiana Univ. of Pennsylvania
Indiana Univ. Southeast
Indiana Univ.–Kokomo
Indiana Univ.–South Bend
Indiana Univ.–Purdue Univ.–Fort Wayne
Indiana Wesleyan Univ.
Iona College (NY)
Iowa State Univ.
Jacksonville State Univ. (AL)
Jacksonville Univ. (FL)
James Madison Univ. (VA)
Jamestown College (ND)
John Carroll Univ. (OH)
Johnson and Wales Univ. (RI)
Juniata College (PA)
Kansas State Univ.
Kean Univ. (NJ)
Kennesaw State Univ. (GA)
Kent State Univ. (OH)
King's College (PA)
Kutztown Univ. of Pennsylvania
La Roche College (PA)
La Salle Univ. (PA)
La Sierra Univ. (CA)
Lake Superior State Univ. (MI)

Lamar Univ. (TX)
Lasell College (MA)
Le Moyne College (NY)
Lehigh Univ. (PA)
Lenoir-Rhyne College (NC)
Letourneau Univ. (TX)
Lincoln Univ. (PA)
Lindenwood Univ. (MO)
Linfield College (OR)
Loras College (IA)
Louisiana College
Louisiana State Univ.–Baton Rouge
Louisiana State Univ.–Shreveport
Louisiana Tech Univ.
Loyola Univ. Chicago
Loyola Univ. New Orleans
Macmurray College (IL)
Manchester College (IN)
Manhattan College (NY)
Manhattanville College (NY)
Marian College (IN)
Marquette Univ. (WI)
Marshall Univ. (WV)
Marywood Univ. (PA)
Master's Coll. and Seminary (CA)
Mcneese State Univ. (LA)
Medaille College (NY)
Mercy College (NY)
Methodist College (NC)
Metropolitan State College of Denver
Miami Univ.–Oxford (OH)
Michigan State Univ.
Middle Tennessee State Univ.
Midwestern State Univ. (TX)
Millikin Univ. (IL)
Minnesota State Univ.–Mankato
Minnesota State Univ.–Moorhead
Minot State Univ. (ND)
Mississippi State Univ.
Missouri Southern State Univ.
Missouri Western State College
Morehead State Univ. (KY)
Morgan State Univ. (MD)
Morningside College (IA)
Mount Vernon Nazarene Univ. (OH)
Mountain State Univ. (WV)
Murray State Univ. (KY)
National Univ. (CA)
New Mexico Highlands Univ.
New Mexico State Univ.
New York Institute of Technology
New York Univ.
Nicholls State Univ. (LA)
Nichols College (MA)
North Carolina A&T State Univ.
North Central College (IL)
North Georgia Coll. and State Univ.
North Park Univ. (IL)
Northeastern State Univ. (OK)
Northeastern Univ. (MA)
Northern Arizona Univ.
Northern Illinois Univ.
Northern Kentucky Univ.
Northern Michigan Univ.
Northern State Univ. (SD)
Northwest Missouri State Univ.
Northwestern College (MN)
Northwestern Oklahoma State Univ.

Northwood Univ. (MI)
Nova Southeastern Univ. (FL)
Oakland Univ. (MI)
Oakwood College (AL)
Ohio Dominican Univ.
Ohio State Univ.–Columbus
Ohio Univ.
Oklahoma Baptist Univ.
Oklahoma City Univ.
Oklahoma State Univ.
Old Dominion Univ. (VA)
Olivet College (MI)
Oral Roberts Univ. (OK)
Pace Univ. (NY)
Park Univ. (MO)
Penn. State Univ.–Univ. Park
Penn. State–Erie, The Behrend College
Pepperdine Univ. (CA)
Philadelphia Univ.
Pittsburg State Univ. (KS)
Polytechnic Univ. (NY)
Prairie View A&M Univ. (TX)
Princeton Univ. (NJ)
Providence College (RI)
Quincy Univ. (IL)
Quinnipiac Univ. (CT)
Radford Univ. (VA)
Regis Univ. (CO)
Rhode Island College
Rider Univ. (NJ)
Robert Morris Univ. (PA)
Rochester Institute of Tech. (NY)
Roger Williams Univ. (RI)
Roosevelt Univ. (IL)
Rutgers–Camden (NJ)
Rutgers–New Brunswick (NJ)
Rutgers–Newark (NJ)
Sacred Heart Univ. (CT)
Saginaw Valley State Univ. (MI)
Salisbury Univ. (MD)
Salve Regina Univ. (RI)
Sam Houston State Univ. (TX)
San Diego State Univ.
Santa Clara Univ. (CA)
Schreiner Univ. (TX)
Seattle Univ.
Seton Hall Univ. (NJ)
Seton Hill Univ. (PA)
Shippensburg Univ. of Pennsylvania
Siena College (NY)
Southeast Missouri State Univ.
Southeastern College of the Assemblies of God
Southeastern Louisiana Univ.
Southeastern Oklahoma State Univ.
Southeastern Univ. (DC)
Southern Adventist Univ. (TN)
Southern Connecticut State Univ.
Southern Illinois Univ.–Carbondale
Southern Methodist Univ. (TX)
Southern Nazarene Univ. (OK)
Southern Univ. and A&M College (LA)
Southern Utah Univ.
Southwest Missouri State Univ.
Southwestern College (KS)
St. Ambrose Univ. (IA)
St. Anselm College (NH)

St. Bonaventure Univ. (NY)
St. Cloud State Univ. (MN)
St. Edward's Univ. (TX)
St. Francis Univ. (PA)
St. John Fisher College (NY)
St. John's Univ. (NY)
St. Joseph's College (ME)
St. Joseph's Univ. (PA)
St. Louis Univ.
St. Mary's College of California
St. Mary's Univ. of San Antonio
St. Thomas Aquinas College (NY)
St. Thomas Univ. (FL)
St. Vincent College (PA)
St. Xavier Univ. (IL)
State Univ. of West Georgia
Stephen F. Austin State Univ. (TX)
Stetson Univ. (FL)
Stonehill College (MA)
Suffolk Univ. (MA)
Sul Ross State Univ. (TX)
SUNY College of Arts and Sciences–New Paltz
SUNY College–Old Westbury
Susquehanna Univ. (PA)
Syracuse Univ. (NY)
Talladega College (AL)
Tarleton State Univ. (TX)
Taylor Univ. (IN)
Teikyo Post Univ. (CT)
Temple Univ. (PA)
Tennessee Technological Univ.
Tennessee Wesleyan College
Texas A&M International Univ.
Texas A&M Univ.–College Station
Texas A&M Univ.–Commerce
Texas A&M Univ.–Corpus Christi
Texas A&M Univ.–Kingsville
Texas Christian Univ.
Texas State Univ.–San Marcos
Texas Tech Univ.
Thomas College (ME)
Thomas Edison State College (NJ)
Tiffin Univ. (OH)
Troy State Univ.–Troy (AL)
Tulane Univ. (LA)
Tuskegee Univ. (AL)
Union College (NE)
Univ. of Akron (OH)
Univ. of Alabama
Univ. of Alabama–Birmingham
Univ. of Alabama–Huntsville
Univ. of Alaska–Anchorage
Univ. of Arizona
Univ. of Arkansas
Univ. of Arkansas–Little Rock
Univ. of Bridgeport (CT)
Univ. of Central Arkansas
Univ. of Central Florida
Univ. of Central Oklahoma
Univ. of Charleston (WV)
Univ. of Connecticut
Univ. of Dayton (OH)
Univ. of Delaware
Univ. of Denver
Univ. of Evansville (IN)
Univ. of Findlay (OH)
Univ. of Florida
Univ. of Georgia
Univ. of Hartford (CT)
Univ. of Hawaii–Hilo

Univ. of Hawaii–Manoa
Univ. of Houston
Univ. of Houston–Downtown
Univ. of Illinois–Chicago
Univ. of Illinois–Urbana-Champaign
Univ. of Indianapolis
Univ. of Iowa
Univ. of Kansas
Univ. of Kentucky
Univ. of Louisiana–Lafayette
Univ. of Louisiana–Monroe
Univ. of Louisville (KY)
Univ. of Maine–Augusta
Univ. of Maine–Orono
Univ. of Mary Hardin-Baylor (TX)
Univ. of Maryland–College Park
Univ. of Maryland–Univ. College
Univ. of Massachusetts–Amherst
Univ. of Memphis
Univ. of Miami (FL)
Univ. of Michigan–Dearborn
Univ. of Michigan–Flint
Univ. of Minnesota–Duluth
Univ. of Minnesota–Twin Cities
Univ. of Mississippi
Univ. of Missouri–Rolla
Univ. of Montana
Univ. of Montevallo (AL)
Univ. of Nebraska–Lincoln
Univ. of Nebraska–Omaha
Univ. of Nevada–Las Vegas
Univ. of Nevada–Reno
Univ. of New Hampshire
Univ. of New Haven (CT)
Univ. of New Orleans
Univ. of North Alabama
Univ. of North Carolina–Charlotte
Univ. of N.C.–Greensboro
Univ. of N.C.–Wilmington
Univ. of North Dakota
Univ. of North Florida
Univ. of North Texas
Univ. of Northern Iowa
Univ. of Notre Dame (IN)
Univ. of Oklahoma
Univ. of Pennsylvania
Univ. of Pittsburgh
Univ. of Pittsburgh–Johnstown
Univ. of Portland (OR)
Univ. of Rhode Island
Univ. of Rio Grande (OH)
Univ. of San Francisco
Univ. of Scranton (PA)
Univ. of South Alabama
Univ. of South Carolina–Columbia
Univ. of South Dakota
Univ. of South Florida
Univ. of Southern Indiana
Univ. of Southern Mississippi
Univ. of St. Francis (IL)
Univ. of St. Thomas (MN)
Univ. of St. Thomas (TX)
Univ. of Tampa (FL)
Univ. of Tennessee
Univ. of Texas of the Permian Basin
Univ. of Texas–Arlington
Univ. of Texas–Austin
Univ. of Texas–Brownsville
Univ. of Texas–Dallas
Univ. of Texas–El Paso

Univ. of Texas–Pan American
Univ. of Texas–San Antonio
Univ. of Texas–Tyler
Univ. of the District of Columbia
Univ. of Toledo (OH)
Univ. of Tulsa (OK)
Univ. of Utah
Univ. of Washington
Univ. of West Florida
Univ. of Wisconsin–Eau Claire
Univ. of Wisconsin–La Crosse
Univ. of Wisconsin–Madison
Univ. of Wisconsin–Milwaukee
Univ. of Wisconsin–Oshkosh
Univ. of Wisconsin–Superior
Univ. of Wisconsin–Whitewater
Univ. of Wyoming
Utah State Univ.
Valdosta State Univ. (GA)
Valparaiso Univ. (IN)
Vanguard Univ. of Southern California
Villanova Univ. (PA)
Virginia Commonwealth Univ.
Virginia Tech
Wagner College (NY)
Wake Forest Univ. (NC)
Waldorf College (IA)
Walsh College of Accountancy and Business Adm. (MI)
Walsh Univ. (OH)
Washburn Univ. (KS)
Washington State Univ.
Washington Univ. In St. Louis
Wayne State Univ. (MI)
Waynesburg College (PA)
Webber International Univ. (FL)
Weber State Univ. (UT)
West Chester Univ. of Pennsylvania
West Texas A&M Univ.
West Virginia Univ.
West Virginia Wesleyan College
Western Carolina Univ. (NC)
Western Connecticut State Univ.
Western Illinois Univ.
Western Kentucky Univ.
Western Michigan Univ.
Western New England College (MA)
Western Washington Univ.
Westminster College (UT)
Wichita State Univ. (KS)
Widener Univ. (PA)
Williams Baptist College (AR)
Wingate Univ. (NC)
Wofford College (SC)
Wright State Univ. (OH)
Xavier Univ. (OH)
York College of Pennsylvania
Youngstown State Univ. (OH)

Fine and Studio Art

Abilene Christian Univ. (TX)
Adams State College (CO)
Adelphi Univ. (NY)
Adrian College (MI)
Agnes Scott College (GA)
Alabama Agricultural and Mechanical Univ.

Alabama State Univ.
Albany State Univ. (GA)
Albertson College (ID)
Albertus Magnus College (CT)
Albion College (MI)
Albright College (PA)
Alfred Univ. (NY)
Allegheny College (PA)
Alma College (MI)
Alverno College (WI)
American Univ. (DC)
Amherst College (MA)
Anderson College (SC)
Anderson Univ. (IN)
Andrews Univ. (MI)
Angelo State Univ. (TX)
Anna Maria College (MA)
Antioch College (OH)
Appalachian State Univ. (NC)
Aquinas College (MI)
Arcadia Univ. (PA)
Arizona State Univ.
Arkansas State Univ.
Arkansas Tech Univ.
Armstrong Atlantic State Univ.
 (GA)
Art Academy of Cincinnati
Art Center College of Design (CA)
Asbury College (KY)
Atlanta College of Art
Atlantic Union College (MA)
Auburn Univ. (AL)
Auburn Univ.–Montgomery (AL)
Augsburg College (MN)
Augustana College (SD)
Augustana College (IL)
Austin College (TX)
Austin Peay State Univ. (TN)
Averett Univ. (VA)
Avila Univ. (MO)
Azusa Pacific Univ. (CA)
Baker College of Flint (MI)
Baker Univ. (KS)
Baldwin-Wallace College (OH)
Ball State Univ. (IN)
Bard College (NY)
Barnard College (NY)
Barry Univ. (FL)
Barton College (NC)
Bates College (ME)
Baylor Univ. (TX)
Belhaven College (MS)
Bellarmine Univ. (KY)
Bellevue Univ. (NE)
Belmont Univ. (TN)
Beloit College (WI)
Bemidji State Univ. (MN)
Benedict College (SC)
Benedictine College (KS)
Benedictine Univ. (IL)
Bennington College (VT)
Berea College (KY)
Berry College (GA)
Bethany College (KS)
Bethany College (WV)
Bethel College (IN)
Bethel College (KS)
Bethel Univ. (MN)
Biola Univ. (CA)
Black Hills State Univ. (SD)
Bloomsburg Univ. of Pennsylvania

Bluefield College (VA)
Bluffton Univ. (OH)
Boise State Univ. (ID)
Boston Univ.
Bowdoin College (ME)
Bowie State Univ. (MD)
Bowling Green State Univ. (OH)
Bradley Univ. (IL)
Brandeis Univ. (MA)
Brenau Univ. (GA)
Brescia Univ. (KY)
Brevard College (NC)
Briar Cliff Univ. (IA)
Bridgewater College (VA)
Bridgewater State College (MA)
Brigham Young Univ.–Hawaii
Brigham Young Univ.–Provo (UT)
Brown Univ. (RI)
Bryn Mawr College (PA)
Bucknell Univ. (PA)
Buena Vista Univ. (IA)
Buffalo State College
Burlington College (VT)
Butler Univ. (IN)
Cabrini College (PA)
Cal Poly–San Luis Obispo
Caldwell College (NJ)
California Baptist Univ.
California College of the Arts
California Institute of the Arts
California Lutheran Univ.
California State Polytechnic
 Univ.–Pomona
California State Univ.–Bakersfield
California State Univ.–Chico
California State Univ.–Dominguez
 Hills
California State Univ.–Fresno
California State Univ.–Fullerton
California State Univ.–Hayward
California State Univ.–Long Beach
California State Univ.–Los Angeles
California State Univ.–Northridge
California State Univ.–Sacramento
California State Univ.–San
 Bernardino
California State Univ.–Stanislaus
California Univ. of Pennsylvania
Calvin College (MI)
Cameron Univ. (OK)
Campbell Univ. (NC)
Campbellsville Univ. (KY)
Canisius College (NY)
Capital Univ. (OH)
Cardinal Stritch Univ. (WI)
Carleton College (MN)
Carlow College (PA)
Carnegie Mellon Univ. (PA)
Carroll College (WI)
Carson-Newman College (TN)
Carthage College (WI)
Case Western Reserve Univ. (OH)
Castleton State College (VT)
Catholic Univ. of America (DC)
Cazenovia College (NY)
Cedar Crest College (PA)
Centenary College of Louisiana
Central College (IA)
Central Connecticut State Univ.
Central Michigan Univ.
Central Missouri State Univ.

Central State Univ. (OH)
Central Washington Univ.
Centre College (KY)
Chadron State College (NE)
Champlain College (VT)
Chapman Univ. (CA)
Chatham College (PA)
Cheyney Univ. of Pennsylvania
Chicago State Univ.
Chowan College (NC)
Christopher Newport Univ. (VA)
Claflin Univ. (SC)
Clarion Univ. of Pennsylvania
Clark Atlanta Univ.
Clark Univ. (MA)
Cleveland Institute of Art
Cleveland State Univ.
Coastal Carolina Univ. (SC)
Coe College (IA)
Coker College (SC)
Colby College (ME)
Colby-Sawyer College (NH)
Colgate Univ. (NY)
College For Creative Studies (MI)
College of Charleston (SC)
College of Mount St. Joseph (OH)
College of New Jersey
College of Notre Dame of
 Maryland
College of Santa Fe (NM)
College of St. Benedict (MN)
College of St. Catherine (MN)
College of St. Elizabeth (NJ)
College of St. Mary (NE)
College of St. Rose (NY)
College of the Holy Cross (MA)
College of the Ozarks (MO)
College of Visual Arts (MN)
College of William and Mary (VA)
College of Wooster (OH)
Colorado Christian Univ.
Colorado College
Colorado State Univ.
Colorado State Univ.–Pueblo
Columbia College (IL)
Columbia College (SC)
Columbia College (MO)
Columbia Univ. (NY)
Columbus College of Art and
 Design (OH)
Columbus State Univ. (GA)
Concord College (WV)
Concordia College (NY)
Concordia Coll.–Moorhead (MN)
Concordia Univ. (NE)
Concordia Univ. (CA)
Concordia Univ. (MI)
Concordia Univ. Wisconsin
Concordia Univ.–St. Paul (MN)
Connecticut College
Converse College (SC)
Cooper Union (NY)
Corcoran College of Art and Design
 (DC)
Cornell College (IA)
Cornell Univ. (NY)
Cornish College of the Arts (WA)
Creighton Univ. (NE)
Culver-Stockton College (MO)
Cumberland College (KY)
Cumberland Univ. (TN)

CUNY–Baruch College
CUNY–Brooklyn College
CUNY–City College
CUNY–College of Staten Island
CUNY–Hunter College
CUNY–Lehman College
CUNY–Queens College
CUNY–York College
Curry College (MA)
Daemen College (NY)
Dakota Wesleyan Univ. (SD)
Dallas Baptist Univ.
Dana College (NE)
Dartmouth College (NH)
David Lipscomb Univ. (TN)
Davidson College (NC)
Davis and Elkins College (WV)
Defiance College (OH)
Delaware State Univ.
Denison Univ. (OH)
Depaul Univ. (IL)
Depauw Univ. (IN)
Dickinson College (PA)
Dickinson State Univ. (ND)
Dillard Univ. (LA)
Dominican Univ. (IL)
Dominican Univ. of California (CA)
Dordt College (IA)
Dowling College (NY)
Drake Univ. (IA)
Drew Univ. (NJ)
Drury Univ. (MO)
Duke Univ. (NC)
Duquesne Univ. (PA)
Earlham College (IN)
East Carolina Univ. (NC)
East Central Univ. (OK)
East Tennessee State Univ.
Eastern Connecticut State Univ.
Eastern Illinois Univ.
Eastern Kentucky Univ.
Eastern Mennonite Univ. (VA)
Eastern Michigan Univ.
Eastern New Mexico Univ.
Eastern Oregon Univ.
Eastern Univ. (PA)
Eastern Washington Univ.
Eckerd College (FL)
Edgewood College (WI)
Edinboro Univ. of Pennsylvania
Elizabeth City State Univ. (NC)
Elizabethtown College (PA)
Elmhurst College (IL)
Elmira College (NY)
Elms College (College of Our Lady
 of the Elms) (MA)
Elon Univ. (NC)
Emmanuel College (MA)
Emory and Henry College (VA)
Emory Univ. (GA)
Emporia State Univ. (KS)
Endicott College (MA)
Erskine College (SC)
Eureka College (IL)
Evangel Univ. (MO)
Evergreen State College (WA)
Fairfield Univ. (CT)
Felician College (NJ)
Ferris State Univ. (MI)
Ferrum College (VA)
Flagler College (FL)

Florida A&M Univ.
Florida Atlantic Univ.
Florida International Univ.
Florida Southern College
Florida State Univ.
Fontbonne Univ. (MO)
Fordham Univ. (NY)
Fort Hays State Univ. (KS)
Fort Lewis College (CO)
Framingham State College (MA)
Francis Marion Univ. (SC)
Franklin and Marshall College (PA)
Franklin Pierce College (NH)
Freed-Hardeman Univ. (TN)
Fresno Pacific Univ. (CA)
Friends Univ. (KS)
Furman Univ. (SC)
Gallaudet Univ. (DC)
George Fox Univ. (OR)
George Mason Univ. (VA)
George Washington Univ. (DC)
Georgetown College (KY)
Georgetown Univ. (DC)
Georgia College and State Univ.
Georgia Southern Univ.
Georgia Southwestern State Univ.
Georgia State Univ.
Georgian Court Univ. (NJ)
Gettysburg College (PA)
Gonzaga Univ. (WA)
Gordon College (MA)
Goshen College (IN)
Goucher College (MD)
Grace College and Seminary (IN)
Graceland Univ. (IA)
Grambling State Univ. (LA)
Grand Valley State Univ. (MI)
Grand View College (IA)
Green Mountain College (VT)
Greensboro College (NC)
Greenville College (IL)
Grinnell College (IA)
Guilford College (NC)
Gustavus Adolphus College (MN)
Hamilton College (NY)
Hamline Univ. (MN)
Hampshire College (MA)
Hampton Univ. (VA)
Hannibal-Lagrange College (MO)
Hanover College (IN)
Hardin-Simmons Univ. (TX)
Harding Univ. (AR)
Hartwick College (NY)
Harvard Univ. (MA)
Hastings College (NE)
Haverford College (PA)
Henderson State Univ. (AR)
Hendrix College (AR)
High Point Univ. (NC)
Hillsdale College (MI)
Hiram College (OH)
Hobart and William Smith Colleges
 (NY)
Hofstra Univ. (NY)
Hollins Univ. (VA)
Holy Family Univ. (PA)
Hood College (MD)
Hope College (MI)
Houghton College (NY)
Houston Baptist Univ.
Howard Payne Univ. (TX)

Howard Univ. (DC)
Humboldt State Univ. (CA)
Huntingdon College (AL)
Huntington College (IN)
Idaho State Univ.
Illinois College
Illinois State Univ.
Illinois Wesleyan Univ.
Indiana State Univ.
Indiana Univ. East
Indiana Univ. Northwest
Indiana Univ. of Pennsylvania
Indiana Univ. Southeast
Indiana Univ.–Bloomington
Indiana Univ.–South Bend
Indiana Univ.-Purdue Univ.–Fort Wayne
Indiana Univ.-Purdue Univ.–Indianapolis
Indiana Wesleyan Univ.
Ithaca College (NY)
Jacksonville State Univ. (AL)
Jacksonville Univ. (FL)
James Madison Univ. (VA)
Jamestown College (ND)
John Carroll Univ. (OH)
Johns Hopkins Univ. (MD)
Johnson State College (VT)
Judson College (IL)
Juniata College (PA)
Kalamazoo College (MI)
Kansas City Art Institute (MO)
Kansas State Univ.
Kean Univ. (NJ)
Keene State College (NH)
Kennesaw State Univ. (GA)
Kent State Univ. (OH)
Kentucky State Univ.
Kentucky Wesleyan College
Knox College (IL)
Kutztown Univ. of Pennsylvania
La Salle Univ. (PA)
La Sierra Univ. (CA)
Lafayette College (PA)
Lake Erie College (OH)
Lake Forest College (IL)
Lake Superior State Univ. (MI)
Lambuth Univ. (TN)
Lander Univ. (SC)
Lawrence Univ. (WI)
Lebanon Valley College (PA)
Lehigh Univ. (PA)
Lemoyne-Owen College (TN)
Lesley Univ. (MA)
Lewis and Clark College (OR)
Lewis Univ. (IL)
Limestone College (SC)
Lincoln Univ. (PA)
Lincoln Univ. (MO)
Lindenwood Univ. (MO)
Lindsey Wilson College (KY)
Linfield College (OR)
Lock Haven Univ. of Pennsylvania
Long Island Univ.–Brooklyn (NY)
Long Island Univ.–C.W. Post Campus (NY)
Long Island Univ.–Southampton College (NY)
Loras College (IA)
Louisiana College
Louisiana State Univ.–Baton Rouge

Louisiana Tech Univ.
Lourdes College (OH)
Loyola College In Maryland
Loyola Marymount Univ. (CA)
Loyola Univ. Chicago
Loyola Univ. New Orleans
Luther College (IA)
Lycoming College (PA)
Lynchburg College (VA)
Lyon College (AR)
Macalester College (MN)
Macmurray College (IL)
Madonna Univ. (MI)
Maine College of Art
Malone College (OH)
Manchester College (IN)
Manhattanville College (NY)
Mansfield Univ. of Pennsylvania
Marian College (IN)
Marian College of Fond Du Lac (WI)
Marietta College (OH)
Marist College (NY)
Mars Hill College (NC)
Marshall Univ. (WV)
Mary Baldwin College (VA)
Marygrove College (MI)
Maryland Institute College of Art
Marylhurst Univ. (OR)
Marymount Manhattan College (NY)
Marymount Univ. (VA)
Maryville College (TN)
Maryville Univ. of St. Louis (MO)
Marywood Univ. (PA)
Massachusetts College of Art
Mcdaniel College (MD)
Mckendree College (IL)
Mcmurry Univ. (TX)
Mcneese State Univ. (LA)
Mcpherson College (KS)
Memphis College of Art
Mercer Univ. (GA)
Mercyhurst College (PA)
Meredith College (NC)
Merrimack College (MA)
Mesa State College (CO)
Messiah College (PA)
Methodist College (NC)
Metropolitan State College of Denver
Miami Univ.–Oxford (OH)
Michigan State Univ.
Middle Tennessee State Univ.
Middlebury College (VT)
Midland Lutheran College (NE)
Midwestern State Univ. (TX)
Millersville Univ. of Pennsylvania
Millikin Univ. (IL)
Mills College (CA)
Millsaps College (MS)
Milwaukee Institute of Art and Design
Minneapolis College of Art and Design
Minnesota State Univ.–Mankato
Minnesota State Univ.–Moorhead
Minot State Univ. (ND)
Mississippi College
Missouri Southern State Univ.
Missouri Valley College

Missouri Western State College
Molloy College (NY)
Monmouth Univ. (NJ)
Montana State Univ.–Billings
Montana State Univ.–Bozeman
Montclair State Univ. (NJ)
Montserrat College of Art (MA)
Moore College of Art and Design (PA)
Moravian College (PA)
Morehead State Univ. (KY)
Morehouse College (GA)
Morgan State Univ. (MD)
Morningside College (IA)
Mount Holyoke College (MA)
Mount Mary College (WI)
Mount Mercy College (IA)
Mount St. Mary's College (CA)
Mount Union College (OH)
Mount Vernon Nazarene Univ. (OH)
Muhlenberg College (PA)
Murray State Univ. (KY)
Muskingum College (OH)
National-Louis Univ. (IL)
Nazareth College of Rochester (NY)
Nebraska Wesleyan Univ.
New England College (NH)
New Jersey City Univ.
New Mexico Highlands Univ.
New Mexico State Univ.
New School Univ. (NY)
New York Institute of Technology
New York Univ.
Newberry College (SC)
Newman Univ. (KS)
Nicholls State Univ. (LA)
Norfolk State Univ. (VA)
North Carolina A&T State Univ.
North Carolina Central Univ.
North Carolina State Univ.–Raleigh
North Central College (IL)
North Dakota State Univ.
North Georgia College and State Univ.
North Park Univ. (IL)
Northeastern Illinois Univ.
Northeastern State Univ. (OK)
Northeastern Univ. (MA)
Northern Arizona Univ.
Northern Illinois Univ.
Northern Kentucky Univ.
Northern Michigan Univ.
Northern State Univ. (SD)
Northland College (WI)
Northwest Missouri State Univ.
Northwest Nazarene Univ. (ID)
Northwestern College (MN)
Northwestern College (IA)
Northwestern Oklahoma State Univ.
Northwestern State Univ. of Louisiana
Northwestern Univ. (IL)
Notre Dame College of Ohio
Notre Dame De Namur Univ. (CA)
Oakland City Univ. (IN)
Oakland Univ. (MI)
Oberlin College (OH)
Occidental College (CA)

Oglethorpe Univ. (GA)
Ohio Dominican Univ.
Ohio Northern Univ.
Ohio State Univ.–Columbus
Ohio Univ.
Ohio Wesleyan Univ.
Oklahoma Baptist Univ.
Oklahoma State Univ.
Old Dominion Univ. (VA)
Olivet College (MI)
Olivet Nazarene Univ. (IL)
Oregon State Univ.
Otis College of Art and Design (CA)
Ouachita Baptist Univ. (AR)
Our Lady of the Lake Univ. (TX)
Pace Univ. (NY)
Pacific Lutheran Univ. (WA)
Pacific Union College (CA)
Pacific Univ. (OR)
Palm Beach Atlantic Univ. (FL)
Park Univ. (MO)
Penn. State Univ.–Univ. Park
Pepperdine Univ. (CA)
Pfeiffer Univ. (NC)
Philadelphia Univ.
Piedmont College (GA)
Pikeville College (KY)
Pine Manor College (MA)
Pittsburg State Univ. (KS)
Pitzer College (CA)
Plymouth State Univ. (NH)
Point Loma Nazarene Univ. (CA)
Pomona College (CA)
Portland State Univ. (OR)
Presbyterian College (SC)
Prescott College (AZ)
Princeton Univ. (NJ)
Principia College (IL)
Providence College (RI)
Purdue Univ.–West Lafayette (IN)
Queens Univ. of Charlotte (NC)
Radford Univ. (VA)
Ramapo College of New Jersey
Randolph-Macon College (VA)
Reed College (OR)
Regis College (MA)
Reinhardt College (GA)
Rhode Island College
Rhode Island School of Design
Rhodes College (TN)
Rice Univ. (TX)
Rider Univ. (NJ)
Ringling School of Art and Design (FL)
Ripon College (WI)
Rivier College (NH)
Roanoke College (VA)
Roberts Wesleyan College (NY)
Rochester Institute of Tech. (NY)
Rockford College (IL)
Rocky Mountain College (MT)
Roger Williams Univ. (RI)
Rollins College (FL)
Roosevelt Univ. (IL)
Rosemont College (PA)
Rutgers–Camden (NJ)
Rutgers–New Brunswick (NJ)
Rutgers–Newark (NJ)
Sacred Heart Univ. (CT)
Saginaw Valley State Univ. (MI)

Salem College (NC)
Salisbury Univ. (MD)
Salve Regina Univ. (RI)
Sam Houston State Univ. (TX)
Samford Univ. (AL)
San Diego State Univ.
San Francisco Art Institute
San Francisco State Univ.
San Jose State Univ. (CA)
Santa Clara Univ. (CA)
Savannah College of Art and Design (GA)
School of the Art Institute of Chicago
Scripps College (CA)
Seattle Pacific Univ.
Seattle Univ.
Seton Hall Univ. (NJ)
Seton Hill Univ. (PA)
Sewanee–Univ. of the South (TN)
Shawnee State Univ. (OH)
Shenandoah Univ. (VA)
Shepherd Univ. (WV)
Shippensburg Univ. of Pennsylvania
Shorter College (GA)
Sierra Nevada College (NV)
Silver Lake College (WI)
Simmons College (MA)
Simpson College (IA)
Skidmore College (NY)
Slippery Rock Univ. of Pennsylvania
Sonoma State Univ. (CA)
South Carolina State Univ.
Southeast Missouri State Univ.
Southeastern Louisiana Univ.
Southeastern Oklahoma St. Univ.
Southern Adventist Univ. (TN)
Southern Arkansas Univ.
Southern Connecticut State Univ.
Southern Illinois Univ.–Carbondale
Southern Illinois Univ.–Edwardsville
Southern Methodist Univ. (TX)
Southern Oregon Univ.
Southern Univ. and A&M College (LA)
Southern Utah Univ.
Southwest Baptist Univ. (MO)
Southwest Minnesota State Univ. (MN)
Southwest Missouri State Univ.
Southwestern Adventist Univ. (TX)
Southwestern Univ. (TX)
Spelman College (GA)
Spring Arbor Univ. (MI)
Spring Hill College (AL)
Springfield College (MA)
St. Ambrose Univ. (IA)
St. Andrews Presbyterian College (NC)
St. Anselm College (NH)
St. Cloud State Univ. (MN)
St. Edward's Univ. (TX)
St. Gregory's Univ. (OK)
St. John's Univ. (NY)
St. John's Univ. (MN)
St. Joseph College (CT)
St. Joseph's College (IN)
St. Lawrence Univ. (NY)
St. Louis Univ.

St. Mary's College (IN)
St. Mary's College of California
St. Mary's College of Maryland
St. Mary's Univ. of Minnesota
St. Mary-of-The-Woods Coll. (IN)
St. Michael's College (VT)
St. Norbert College (WI)
St. Olaf College (MN)
St. Peter's College (NJ)
St. Thomas Aquinas College (NY)
St. Vincent College (PA)
St. Xavier Univ. (IL)
Stanford Univ. (CA)
State Univ. of West Georgia
Stephen F. Austin State Univ. (TX)
Sterling College (KS)
Stetson Univ. (FL)
Stevens Institute of Technology (NJ)
Stillman College (AL)
Stonehill College (MA)
Suffolk Univ. (MA)
Sul Ross State Univ. (TX)
SUNY College–Brockport
SUNY College–Old Westbury
SUNY College–Oneonta
SUNY College–Potsdam
SUNY–Albany
SUNY–Binghamton
SUNY–Empire State College
SUNY–Fredonia
SUNY–Oswego
SUNY–Plattsburgh
SUNY–Purchase College
SUNY–Stony Brook
Susquehanna Univ. (PA)
Swarthmore College (PA)
Sweet Briar College (VA)
Syracuse Univ. (NY)
Tarleton State Univ. (TX)
Taylor Univ. (IN)
Temple Univ. (PA)
Tennessee State Univ.
Tennessee Technological Univ.
Texas A&M Univ.–Commerce
Texas A&M Univ.–Corpus Christi
Texas A&M Univ.–Kingsville
Texas Christian Univ.
Texas College
Texas Lutheran Univ.
Texas State Univ.–San Marcos
Texas Tech Univ.
Texas Wesleyan Univ.
Texas Woman's Univ.
Thomas Edison State College (NJ)
Thomas More College (KY)
Tiffin Univ. (OH)
Towson Univ. (MD)
Transylvania Univ. (KY)
Trinity Christian College (IL)
Trinity College (DC)
Trinity College (CT)
Troy State Univ.–Troy (AL)
Truman State Univ. (MO)
Tufts Univ. (MA)
Tulane Univ. (LA)
Union College (NY)
Union College (NE)
Union Univ. (TN)
Univ. at Buffalo–SUNY
Univ. of Akron (OH)

Univ. of Alabama
Univ. of Alabama–Birmingham
Univ. of Alabama–Huntsville
Univ. of Alaska–Anchorage
Univ. of Alaska–Fairbanks
Univ. of Arizona
Univ. of Arkansas
Univ. of Arkansas–Little Rock
Univ. of Arkansas–Pine Bluff
Univ. of California–Berkeley
Univ. of California–Davis
Univ. of California–Irvine
Univ. of California–Los Angeles
Univ. of California–Riverside
Univ. of California–Santa Barbara
Univ. of California–Santa Cruz
Univ. of Central Arkansas
Univ. of Central Florida
Univ. of Central Oklahoma
Univ. of Charleston (WV)
Univ. of Chicago
Univ. of Colorado–Boulder
Univ. of Colorado–Colorado Springs
Univ. of Colorado–Denver
Univ. of Connecticut
Univ. of Dallas
Univ. of Dayton (OH)
Univ. of Delaware
Univ. of Denver
Univ. of Evansville (IN)
Univ. of Findlay (OH)
Univ. of Florida
Univ. of Georgia
Univ. of Great Falls (MT)
Univ. of Hartford (CT)
Univ. of Hawaii–Hilo
Univ. of Hawaii–Manoa
Univ. of Houston
Univ. of Illinois–Chicago
Univ. of Illinois–Springfield
Univ. of Illinois–Urbana-Champaign
Univ. of Indianapolis
Univ. of Iowa
Univ. of Kansas
Univ. of Kentucky
Univ. of La Verne (CA)
Univ. of Louisiana–Lafayette
Univ. of Louisiana–Monroe
Univ. of Louisville (KY)
Univ. of Maine–Augusta
Univ. of Maine–Farmington
Univ. of Maine–Orono
Univ. of Maine–Presque Isle
Univ. of Mary Hardin-Baylor (TX)
Univ. of Mary Washington (VA)
Univ. of Maryland–Baltimore County
Univ. of Maryland–College Park
Univ. of Massachusetts–Amherst
Univ. of Massachusetts–Boston
Univ. of Mass.–Dartmouth
Univ. of Massachusetts–Lowell
Univ. of Memphis
Univ. of Miami (FL)
Univ. of Michigan–Ann Arbor
Univ. of Michigan–Dearborn
Univ. of Michigan–Flint
Univ. of Minnesota–Duluth
Univ. of Minnesota–Morris

Univ. of Minnesota–Twin Cities
Univ. of Mississippi
Univ. of Missouri–Columbia
Univ. of Missouri–Kansas City
Univ. of Missouri–St. Louis
Univ. of Montana
Univ. of Montevallo (AL)
Univ. of Nebraska–Kearney
Univ. of Nebraska–Lincoln
Univ. of Nebraska–Omaha
Univ. of Nevada–Las Vegas
Univ. of Nevada–Reno
Univ. of New Hampshire
Univ. of New Haven (CT)
Univ. of New Mexico
Univ. of New Orleans
Univ. of North Alabama
Univ. of North Carolina–Asheville
Univ. of N.C.–Chapel Hill
Univ. of North Carolina–Charlotte
Univ. of N.C.–Greensboro
Univ. of North Carolina–Pembroke
Univ. of N.C.–Wilmington
Univ. of North Dakota
Univ. of North Florida
Univ. of North Texas
Univ. of Northern Colorado
Univ. of Northern Iowa
Univ. of Notre Dame (IN)
Univ. of Oklahoma
Univ. of Oregon
Univ. of Pennsylvania
Univ. of Pittsburgh
Univ. of Puget Sound (WA)
Univ. of Redlands (CA)
Univ. of Rhode Island
Univ. of Richmond (VA)
Univ. of Rio Grande (OH)
Univ. of Rochester (NY)
Univ. of San Diego
Univ. of San Francisco
Univ. of Science and Arts of Oklahoma
Univ. of Sioux Falls (SD)
Univ. of South Alabama
Univ. of South Carolina–Aiken
Univ. of South Carolina–Columbia
Univ. of South Dakota
Univ. of South Florida
Univ. of Southern California
Univ. of Southern Indiana
Univ. of Southern Maine
Univ. of St. Francis (IN)
Univ. of St. Mary (KS)
Univ. of St. Thomas (MN)
Univ. of St. Thomas (TX)
Univ. of Tampa (FL)
Univ. of Tennessee
Univ. of Tennessee–Chattanooga
Univ. of Texas of the Permian Basin
Univ. of Texas–Arlington
Univ. of Texas–Austin
Univ. of Texas–Brownsville
Univ. of Texas–Dallas
Univ. of Texas–El Paso
Univ. of Texas–Pan American
Univ. of Texas–San Antonio
Univ. of Texas–Tyler
Univ. of the Arts (PA)
Univ. of the District of Columbia
Univ. of the Incarnate Word (TX)

Univ. of the Pacific (CA)
Univ. of Toledo (OH)
Univ. of Tulsa (OK)
Univ. of Utah
Univ. of Vermont
Univ. of Virginia
Univ. of Virginia–Wise
Univ. of Washington
Univ. of West Florida
Univ. of Wisconsin–Eau Claire
Univ. of Wisconsin–Green Bay
Univ. of Wisconsin–La Crosse
Univ. of Wisconsin–Madison
Univ. of Wisconsin–Milwaukee
Univ. of Wisconsin–Platteville
Univ. of Wisconsin–River Falls
Univ. of Wisconsin–Stevens Point
Univ. of Wisconsin–Superior
Univ. of Wisconsin–Whitewater
Univ. of Wyoming
Ursinus College (PA)
Ursuline College (OH)
Utah State Univ.
Valdosta State Univ. (GA)
Valley City State Univ. (ND)
Valparaiso Univ. (IN)
Vanderbilt Univ. (TN)
Vassar College (NY)
Villanova Univ. (PA)
Virginia Commonwealth Univ.
Virginia Intermont College
Virginia Tech
Virginia Wesleyan College
Viterbo Univ. (WI)
Wabash College (IN)
Wagner College (NY)
Wake Forest Univ. (NC)
Wartburg College (IA)
Washburn Univ. (KS)
Washington and Jefferson College (PA)
Washington and Lee Univ. (VA)
Washington College (MD)
Washington State Univ.
Washington Univ. In St. Louis
Wayland Baptist Univ. (TX)
Wayne State College (NE)
Wayne State Univ. (MI)
Waynesburg College (PA)
Weber State Univ. (UT)
Webster Univ. (MO)
Wellesley College (MA)
Wesleyan College (GA)
Wesleyan Univ. (CT)
West Chester Univ. of Pennsylvania
West Texas A&M Univ.
West Virginia Univ.
West Virginia Wesleyan College
Western Carolina Univ. (NC)
Western Connecticut State Univ.
Western Illinois Univ.
Western Kentucky Univ.
Western Michigan Univ.
Western New Mexico Univ.
Western Oregon Univ.
Western State College of Colorado
Western Washington Univ.
Westfield State College (MA)
Westminster College (UT)
Westminster College (PA)
Westmont College (CA)

Wheaton College (IL)
Wheaton College (MA)
Whitman College (WA)
Whittier College (CA)
Whitworth College (WA)
Wichita State Univ. (KS)
Willamette Univ. (OR)
William Carey College (MS)
William Jewell College (MO)
William Paterson Univ. of New Jersey
William Woods Univ. (MO)
Williams Baptist College (AR)
Williams College (MA)
Wilmington College (OH)
Wilson College (PA)
Wingate Univ. (NC)
Winston-Salem State Univ. (NC)
Winthrop Univ. (SC)
Wisconsin Lutheran College
Wittenberg Univ. (OH)
Wofford College (SC)
Wright State Univ. (OH)
Xavier Univ. (OH)
Yale Univ. (CT)
York College of Pennsylvania
Youngstown State Univ. (OH)

Fire Protection

Anna Maria College (MA)
California State Univ.–Los Angeles
Cogswell Polytechnical College (CA)
Concordia Univ. (MI)
Eastern Kentucky Univ.
Eastern Oregon Univ.
Holy Family Univ. (PA)
Lake Superior State Univ. (MI)
Lewis-Clark State College (ID)
Lindenwood Univ. (MO)
Madonna Univ. (MI)
Oklahoma State Univ.
Park Univ. (MO)
Providence College (RI)
Salem State College (MA)
Southern Illinois Univ.–Carbondale
Southwest Minnesota State Univ. (MN)
Thomas Edison State College (NJ)
Univ. of Akron (OH)
Univ. of Florida
Univ. of Maryland–Univ. College
Univ. of Nebraska–Lincoln
Univ. of New Haven (CT)
Univ. of North Carolina–Charlotte
Univ. of the District of Columbia
Utah Valley State College
Western Oregon Univ.

Fishing and Fisheries Sciences and Management

Colorado State Univ.
Humboldt State Univ. (CA)
Northland College (WI)
Ohio State Univ.–Columbus
Oregon State Univ.

Texas A&M Univ.–College Station
Texas A&M Univ.–Galveston
Texas Tech Univ.
Univ. of Alaska–Fairbanks
Univ. of California–Davis
Univ. of Georgia
Univ. of Michigan–Ann Arbor
Univ. of Minnesota–Twin Cities
Univ. of Missouri–Columbia
Univ. of Rhode Island
Univ. of Washington
Valley City State Univ. (ND)

Food Science and Technology

California State Polytechnic
    Univ.–Pomona
Penn. State Univ.–Univ. Park
Tarleton State Univ. (TX)
Univ. of Kentucky
Univ. of Tennessee

Foods, Nutrition, and Related Services

Alcorn State Univ. (MS)
Andrews Univ. (MI)
Appalachian State Univ. (NC)
Ashland Univ. (OH)
Ball State Univ. (IN)
Baylor Univ. (TX)
Benedictine Univ. (IL)
Bluffton Univ. (OH)
Bowling Green State Univ. (OH)
Bridgewater College (VA)
California State Polytechnic
    Univ.–Pomona
California State Univ.–Los Angeles
Campbell Univ. (NC)
Carson-Newman College (TN)
Case Western Reserve Univ. (OH)
Cedar Crest College (PA)
Central Michigan Univ.
Central Washington Univ.
College of St. Catherine (MN)
College of the Ozarks (MO)
Colorado State Univ.
Concordia Coll.–Moorhead (MN)
Cornell Univ. (NY)
CUNY–Hunter College
CUNY–Lehman College
David Lipscomb Univ. (TN)
Delaware State Univ.
Dominican Univ. (IL)
Eastern Kentucky Univ.
Fort Valley State Univ. (GA)
Framingham State College (MA)
Georgia Southern Univ.
Georgia State Univ.
Indiana State Univ.
Indiana Univ. of Pennsylvania
Iowa State Univ.
James Madison Univ. (VA)
Johnson and Wales Univ. (RI)
Kansas State Univ.
Kent State Univ. (OH)
Lambuth Univ. (TN)
Madonna Univ. (MI)

Mansfield Univ. of Pennsylvania
Marygrove College (MI)
Marywood Univ. (PA)
Middle Tennessee State Univ.
Montclair State Univ. (NJ)
Morgan State Univ. (MD)
Murray State Univ. (KY)
New Mexico State Univ.
New York Univ.
North Carolina A&T State Univ.
North Dakota State Univ.
Northeastern State Univ. (OK)
Northern Michigan Univ.
Northwest Missouri State Univ.
Ohio State Univ.–Columbus
Ohio Univ.
Oklahoma State Univ.
Oregon State Univ.
Penn. State Univ.–Univ. Park
Pepperdine Univ. (CA)
Point Loma Nazarene Univ. (CA)
Prairie View A&M Univ. (TX)
Purdue Univ.–West Lafayette (IN)
Radford Univ. (VA)
Rochester Institute of Tech. (NY)
Sam Houston State Univ. (TX)
Samford Univ. (AL)
San Diego State Univ.
San Francisco State Univ.
Seattle Pacific Univ.
South Carolina State Univ.
South Dakota State Univ.
Southern Illinois Univ.–Carbondale
St. Louis Univ.
Stephen F. Austin State Univ. (TX)
SUNY College–Oneonta
SUNY–Plattsburgh
Syracuse Univ. (NY)
Tarleton State Univ. (TX)
Texas A&M Univ.–College Station
Texas State Univ.–San Marcos
Texas Tech Univ.
Texas Woman's Univ.
Univ. of Arkansas
Univ. of California–Davis
Univ. of Dayton (OH)
Univ. of Georgia
Univ. of Houston
Univ. of Ill.–Urbana-Champaign
Univ. of Kentucky
Univ. of Maine–Orono
Univ. of Maryland–College Park
Univ. of Massachusetts–Amherst
Univ. of Missouri–Columbia
Univ. of Nevada–Reno
Univ. of New Hampshire
Univ. of New Mexico
Univ. of N.C.–Chapel Hill
Univ. of N.C.–Greensboro
Univ. of Rhode Island
Univ. of Tennessee
Univ. of Texas–Austin
Univ. of the District of Columbia
Univ. of Wisconsin–Stout
Utah State Univ.
Virginia Tech
Washington State Univ.
Wayne State Univ. (MI)
Weber State Univ. (UT)
Western Michigan Univ.
Winthrop Univ. (SC)

Youngstown State Univ. (OH)

Foreign Languages, Literatures, and Linguistics

Andrews Univ. (MI)
Clark Atlanta Univ.
Edinboro Univ. of Pennsylvania
Excelsior College (NY)
Harvard Univ. (MA)
Hobart and William Smith Colleges
    (NY)
Indiana State Univ.
Indiana Univ. of Pennsylvania
Kennesaw State Univ. (GA)
Keuka College (NY)
Mississippi College
Purdue Univ.–Calumet (IN)
Scripps College (CA)
Southern Illinois Univ.–Carbondale
Southern Oregon Univ.
St. Lawrence Univ. (NY)
St. Mary's College of California
St. Thomas Aquinas College (NY)
Univ. of Alaska–Fairbanks
Univ. of California–Berkeley
Univ. of California–Riverside
Univ. of California–San Diego
Univ. of Findlay (OH)
Univ. of Scranton (PA)

Forensic Psychology

Bay Path College (MA)
Florida Institute of Technology
Lake Erie College (OH)
St. Ambrose Univ. (IA)
St. Andrews Presbyterian Coll. (NC)
Tiffin Univ. (OH)

Forest Engineering

Oregon State Univ.
Univ. of Maine–Orono
Univ. of Washington

Forestry

Alabama Agr. and Mechanical Univ.
Albright College (PA)
Auburn Univ. (AL)
Baylor Univ. (TX)
Cal Poly–San Luis Obispo
Colorado State Univ.
Davis and Elkins College (WV)
Elizabethtown College (PA)
High Point Univ. (NC)
Humboldt State Univ. (CA)
Iowa State Univ.
Louisiana State Univ.–Baton Rouge
Louisiana Tech Univ.
Miami Univ.–Oxford (OH)
Michigan State Univ.
Michigan Technological Univ.
Mississippi State Univ.
New Mexico Highlands Univ.

North Carolina State Univ.–Raleigh
Northern Arizona Univ.
Northland College (WI)
Ohio State Univ.–Columbus
Oklahoma State Univ.
Oregon State Univ.
Penn. State Univ.–Univ. Park
Purdue Univ.–West Lafayette (IN)
Sewanee–Univ. of the South (TN)
Southern Illinois Univ.–Carbondale
Southern Univ. and A&M Coll. (LA)
St. Francis Univ. (PA)
Stephen F. Austin State Univ. (TX)
SUNY College Environmental
    Science and Forestry
Texas A&M Univ.–College Station
Thomas Edison State College (NJ)
Unity College (ME)
Univ. of Alaska–Fairbanks
Univ. of Arkansas–Monticello
Univ. of California–Berkeley
Univ. of California–Davis
Univ. of Florida
Univ. of Georgia
Univ. of Ill.–Urbana-Champaign
Univ. of Kentucky
Univ. of Maine–Orono
Univ. of Maryland–Eastern Shore
Univ. of Massachusetts–Amherst
Univ. of Minnesota–Twin Cities
Univ. of Missouri–Columbia
Univ. of Montana
Univ. of Nevada–Reno
Univ. of New Hampshire
Univ. of Tennessee
Univ. of Vermont
Univ. of Washington
Univ. of Wisconsin–Madison
Univ. of Wisconsin–Stevens Point
Utah State Univ.
Virginia Tech
Wake Forest Univ. (NC)
Washington State Univ.
West Virginia Univ.

Funeral Service and Mortuary Science

Gannon Univ. (PA)
Lindenwood Univ. (MO)
Point Park Univ. (PA)
St. John's Univ. (NY)
Thiel College (PA)
Univ. of Central Oklahoma
Univ. of Minnesota–Twin Cities
Wayne State Univ. (MI)

General Sales, Merch., and Related Marketing Operations

Babson College (MA)
Baylor Univ. (TX)
College of St. Catherine (MN)
CUNY–Baruch College
Dowling College (NY)
Eastern Michigan Univ.
Fordham Univ. (NY)
Franklin Pierce College (NH)

Harding Univ. (AR)
Johnson and Wales Univ. (RI)
Keuka College (NY)
Lindenwood Univ. (MO)
Marywood Univ. (PA)
Michigan State Univ.
Oral Roberts Univ. (OK)
Our Lady of Holy Cross Coll. (LA)
Purdue Univ.–Calumet (IN)
Rochester Institute of Tech. (NY)
Seton Hill Univ. (PA)
Simmons College (MA)
Simpson College (IA)
Southern Adventist Univ. (TN)
Southern New Hampshire Univ.
St. Joseph's Univ. (PA)
St. Mary's Univ. of Minnesota
Stephens College (MO)
Syracuse Univ. (NY)
Texas A&M Univ.–College Station
Tuskegee Univ. (AL)
Univ. of Akron (OH)
Univ. of Georgia
Univ. of Houston
Univ. of Ill.–Urbana-Champaign
Univ. of Memphis
Univ. of Minnesota–Twin Cities
Univ. of North Dakota
Univ. of North Texas
Univ. of Pennsylvania
Univ. of South Carolina–Columbia
Univ. of Texas–San Antonio
Univ. of Texas–Tyler
Univ. of Wisconsin–Stout
Weber State Univ. (UT)
West Chester Univ. of Pennsylvania
William Paterson Univ. of New
    Jersey
Youngstown State Univ. (OH)

Genetics

Cedar Crest College (PA)
Cornell Univ. (NY)
Iowa State Univ.
Lawrence Univ. (WI)
Marlboro College (VT)
Missouri Southern State Univ.
Ohio State Univ.–Columbus
Ohio Wesleyan Univ.
Rutgers–New Brunswick (NJ)
SUNY College–Oneonta
Tulane Univ. (LA)
Univ. of California–Davis
Univ. of California–Irvine
Univ. of California–Riverside
Univ. of Georgia
Univ. of Michigan–Ann Arbor
Univ. of Wisconsin–Madison
Washington State Univ.
Western Kentucky Univ.

Geography and Cartography

Appalachian State Univ. (NC)
Aquinas College (MI)
Arizona State Univ.
Arkansas State Univ.

Auburn Univ. (AL)
Augustana College (IL)
Austin Peay State Univ. (TN)
Ball State Univ. (IN)
Bemidji State Univ. (MN)
Bloomsburg Univ. of Pennsylvania
Boston Univ.
Bowling Green State Univ. (OH)
Bridgewater State College (MA)
Brigham Young Univ.–Provo (UT)
Bucknell Univ. (PA)
California State Polytechnic
    Univ.–Pomona
California State Univ.–Chico
California State Univ.–Fresno
California State Univ.–Fullerton
California State Univ.–Hayward
California State Univ.–Long Beach
California State Univ.–Los Angeles
California State Univ.–Northridge
California State Univ.–Sacramento
California State Univ.–San
    Bernardino
California State Univ.–Stanislaus
California Univ. of Pennsylvania
Calvin College (MI)
Carthage College (WI)
Central Connecticut State Univ.
Central Michigan Univ.
Central Missouri State Univ.
Central Washington Univ.
Cheyney Univ. of Pennsylvania
Chicago State Univ.
Clarion Univ. of Pennsylvania
Clark Univ. (MA)
Colgate Univ. (NY)
Concord College (WV)
Concordia Univ. (NE)
Concordia Univ.–River Forest (IL)
CUNY–Hunter College
CUNY–Lehman College
Dartmouth College (NH)
Denison Univ. (OH)
Depaul Univ. (IL)
East Carolina Univ. (NC)
East Central Univ. (OK)
East Stroudsburg Univ. of
    Pennsylvania
East Tennessee State Univ.
Eastern Illinois Univ.
Eastern Kentucky Univ.
Eastern Michigan Univ.
Eastern Washington Univ.
Edinboro Univ. of Pennsylvania
Elmhurst College (IL)
Elon Univ. (NC)
Emory and Henry College (VA)
Excelsior College (NY)
Fayetteville State Univ. (NC)
Fitchburg State College (MA)
Florida Atlantic Univ.
Florida International Univ.
Florida State Univ.
Fort Hays State Univ. (KS)
Framingham State College (MA)
Frostburg State Univ. (MD)
George Mason Univ. (VA)
George Washington Univ. (DC)
Georgia Southern Univ.
Georgia State Univ.
Grand Valley State Univ. (MI)

Gustavus Adolphus College (MN)
Hofstra Univ. (NY)
Humboldt State Univ. (CA)
Illinois State Univ.
Indiana State Univ.
Indiana Univ. of Pennsylvania
Indiana Univ. Southeast
Indiana Univ.–Bloomington
Indiana Univ.-Purdue
    Univ.–Indianapolis
Jacksonville State Univ. (AL)
Jacksonville Univ. (FL)
James Madison Univ. (VA)
Johns Hopkins Univ. (MD)
Kansas State Univ.
Keene State College (NH)
Kennesaw State Univ. (GA)
Kent State Univ. (OH)
Kutztown Univ. of Pennsylvania
Lock Haven Univ. of Pennsylvania
Long Island Univ.–C.W. Post
    Campus (NY)
Louisiana State Univ.–Baton Rouge
Louisiana State Univ.–Shreveport
Louisiana Tech Univ.
Macalester College (MN)
Mansfield Univ. of Pennsylvania
Marshall Univ. (WV)
Miami Univ.–Oxford (OH)
Michigan State Univ.
Middlebury College (VT)
Millersville Univ. of Pennsylvania
Minnesota State Univ.–Mankato
Montclair State Univ. (NJ)
Morehead State Univ. (KY)
Mount Holyoke College (MA)
New Mexico State Univ.
North Carolina Central Univ.
Northeastern Illinois Univ.
Northeastern State Univ. (OK)
Northern Arizona Univ.
Northern Illinois Univ.
Northern Kentucky Univ.
Northern Michigan Univ.
Northwest Missouri State Univ.
Northwestern Univ. (IL)
Ohio State Univ.–Columbus
Ohio Univ.
Ohio Wesleyan Univ.
Oklahoma State Univ.
Old Dominion Univ. (VA)
Oregon State Univ.
Penn. State Univ.–Univ. Park
Pittsburg State Univ. (KS)
Plymouth State Univ. (NH)
Portland State Univ. (OR)
Prairie View A&M Univ. (TX)
Radford Univ. (VA)
Rhode Island College
Roosevelt Univ. (IL)
Rutgers–New Brunswick (NJ)
Salem State College (MA)
Salisbury Univ. (MD)
Sam Houston State Univ. (TX)
Samford Univ. (AL)
San Diego State Univ.
San Francisco State Univ.
San Jose State Univ. (CA)
Shippensburg Univ. of
    Pennsylvania
Slippery Rock Univ. of Pennsylvania

Sonoma State Univ. (CA)
South Dakota State Univ.
Southeast Missouri State Univ.
Southern Illinois Univ.–Carbondale
Southern Illinois
    Univ.–Edwardsville
Southern Oregon Univ.
Southwest Missouri State Univ.
St. Cloud State Univ. (MN)
State Univ. of West Georgia
Stephen F. Austin State Univ. (TX)
Stetson Univ. (FL)
SUNY College of Arts and
    Sciences–Geneseo
SUNY College–Oneonta
SUNY–Albany
SUNY–Binghamton
SUNY–Plattsburgh
Syracuse Univ. (NY)
Taylor Univ. (IN)
Texas A&M Univ.–College Station
Texas A&M Univ.–Commerce
Texas A&M Univ.–Corpus Christi
Texas A&M Univ.–Kingsville
Texas Christian Univ.
Texas State Univ.–San Marcos
Texas Tech Univ.
Towson Univ. (MD)
United States Air Force Academy
    (CO)
Univ. at Buffalo–SUNY
Univ. of Akron (OH)
Univ. of Alabama
Univ. of Alaska–Fairbanks
Univ. of Arizona
Univ. of Arkansas
Univ. of California–Berkeley
Univ. of California–Los Angeles
Univ. of California–Riverside
Univ. of California–Santa Barbara
Univ. of Central Arkansas
Univ. of Central Oklahoma
Univ. of Chicago
Univ. of Colorado–Boulder
Univ. of Colorado–Colorado
    Springs
Univ. of Colorado–Denver
Univ. of Connecticut
Univ. of Delaware
Univ. of Denver
Univ. of Florida
Univ. of Georgia
Univ. of Hawaii–Hilo
Univ. of Hawaii–Manoa
Univ. of Ill.–Urbana-Champaign
Univ. of Iowa
Univ. of Kansas
Univ. of Kentucky
Univ. of Louisville (KY)
Univ. of Maine–Farmington
Univ. of Mary Washington (VA)
Univ. of Maryland–Baltimore
    County
Univ. of Maryland–College Park
Univ. of Massachusetts–Amherst
Univ. of Massachusetts–Boston
Univ. of Memphis
Univ. of Miami (FL)
Univ. of Michigan–Ann Arbor
Univ. of Minnesota–Duluth
Univ. of Minnesota–Twin Cities

Univ. of Missouri–Columbia
Univ. of Missouri–Kansas City
Univ. of Montana
Univ. of Nebraska–Kearney
Univ. of Nebraska–Lincoln
Univ. of Nebraska–Omaha
Univ. of Nevada–Reno
Univ. of New Hampshire
Univ. of New Mexico
Univ. of New Orleans
Univ. of North Alabama
Univ. of N.C.–Chapel Hill
Univ. of North Carolina–Charlotte
Univ. of N.C.–Greensboro
Univ. of N.C.–Wilmington
Univ. of North Dakota
Univ. of North Texas
Univ. of Northern Colorado
Univ. of Northern Iowa
Univ. of Oklahoma
Univ. of Oregon
Univ. of Pittsburgh–Johnstown
Univ. of South Alabama
Univ. of South Carolina–Columbia
Univ. of South Florida
Univ. of Southern California
Univ. of Southern Mississippi
Univ. of St. Thomas (MN)
Univ. of Tennessee
Univ. of Texas–Austin
Univ. of Texas–Dallas
Univ. of Texas–San Antonio
Univ. of Toledo (OH)
Univ. of Utah
Univ. of Vermont
Univ. of Washington
Univ. of Wisconsin–Eau Claire
Univ. of Wisconsin–La Crosse
Univ. of Wisconsin–Madison
Univ. of Wisconsin–Milwaukee
Univ. of Wisconsin–Oshkosh
Univ. of Wisconsin–Parkside
Univ. of Wisconsin–Platteville
Univ. of Wisconsin–River Falls
Univ. of Wisconsin–Stevens Point
Univ. of Wisconsin–Whitewater
Univ. of Wyoming
Utah State Univ.
Valparaiso Univ. (IN)
Vassar College (NY)
Virginia Tech
Wayne State College (NE)
Wayne State Univ. (MI)
Weber State Univ. (UT)
West Chester Univ. of Pennsylvania
West Texas A&M Univ.
West Virginia Univ.
Western Carolina Univ. (NC)
Western Illinois Univ.
Western Kentucky Univ.
Western Michigan Univ.
Western Oregon Univ.
Western State College of Colorado
Western Washington Univ.
Westfield State College (MA)
William Paterson Univ. of New
    Jersey
Wittenberg Univ. (OH)
Worcester State College (MA)
Wright State Univ. (OH)
Youngstown State Univ. (OH)

Geological and Earth Sciences/Geosciences

Adams State College (CO)
Adrian College (MI)
Albion College (MI)
Alfred Univ. (NY)
Allegheny College (PA)
Amherst College (MA)
Antioch College (OH)
Appalachian State Univ. (NC)
Arizona State Univ.
Arkansas Tech Univ.
Ashland Univ. (OH)
Auburn Univ. (AL)
Augustana College (IL)
Austin Peay State Univ. (TN)
Ball State Univ. (IN)
Bates College (ME)
Baylor Univ. (TX)
Beloit College (WI)
Bloomsburg Univ. of Pennsylvania
Boise State Univ. (ID)
Boston Univ.
Bowdoin College (ME)
Bowling Green State Univ. (OH)
Bradley Univ. (IL)
Bridgewater State College (MA)
Brigham Young Univ.–Provo (UT)
Brown Univ. (RI)
Bryn Mawr College (PA)
Bucknell Univ. (PA)
Cal Poly–San Luis Obispo
California Institute of Technology
California Lutheran Univ.
California State Polytechnic
    Univ.–Pomona
California State Univ.–Bakersfield
California State Univ.–Chico
California State Univ.–Fresno
California State Univ.–Fullerton
California State Univ.–Hayward
California State Univ.–Long Beach
California State Univ.–Los Angeles
California State Univ.–Northridge
California State Univ.–Sacramento
California State Univ.–San
    Bernardino
California State Univ.–Stanislaus
California Univ. of Pennsylvania
Calvin College (MI)
Carleton College (MN)
Case Western Reserve Univ. (OH)
Castleton State College (VT)
Centenary College of Louisiana
Central Connecticut State Univ.
Central Michigan Univ.
Central State Univ. (OH)
Central Washington Univ.
Clarion Univ. of Pennsylvania
Cleveland State Univ.
Colby College (ME).
Colgate Univ. (NY)
College of Charleston (SC)
College of William and Mary (VA)
College of Wooster (OH)
Colorado College
Colorado School of Mines
Colorado State Univ.
Columbia Univ. (NY)

Columbus State Univ. (GA)
Cornell College (IA)
Cornell Univ. (NY)
CUNY–Brooklyn College
CUNY–City College
CUNY–Lehman College
CUNY–Queens College
CUNY–York College
Dartmouth College (NH)
Denison Univ. (OH)
Depauw Univ. (IN)
Dickinson College (PA)
Duke Univ. (NC)
Earlham College (IN)
East Carolina Univ. (NC)
East Stroudsburg Univ. of
    Pennsylvania
Eastern Connecticut State Univ.
Eastern Illinois Univ.
Eastern Kentucky Univ.
Eastern Michigan Univ.
Eastern New Mexico Univ.
Eastern Washington Univ.
Edinboro Univ. of Pennsylvania
Elizabeth City State Univ. (NC)
Elmira College (NY)
Emporia State Univ. (KS)
Excelsior College (NY)
Florida Atlantic Univ.
Florida Institute of Technology
Florida International Univ.
Florida State Univ.
Fort Hays State Univ. (KS)
Fort Lewis College (CO)
Franklin and Marshall College (PA)
Furman Univ. (SC)
George Mason Univ. (VA)
Georgia Institute of Technology
Georgia Southern Univ.
Georgia Southwestern State Univ.
Georgia State Univ.
Grand Valley State Univ. (MI)
Guilford College (NC)
Gustavus Adolphus College (MN)
Hamilton College (NY)
Hampshire College (MA)
Hanover College (IN)
Hardin-Simmons Univ. (TX)
Hartwick College (NY)
Harvard Univ. (MA)
Haverford College (PA)
Hawaii Pacific Univ.
Heidelberg College (OH)
Hofstra Univ. (NY)
Hope College (MI)
Humboldt State Univ. (CA)
Idaho State Univ.
Illinois State Univ.
Indiana State Univ.
Indiana Univ. Northwest
Indiana Univ. of Pennsylvania
Indiana Univ.–Bloomington
Indiana Univ.–Purdue Univ.–Fort
    Wayne
Indiana Univ.–Purdue
    Univ.–Indianapolis
Iowa State Univ.
James Madison Univ. (VA)
Johns Hopkins Univ. (MD)
Juniata College (PA)
Kansas State Univ.

Kean Univ. (NJ)
Keene State College (NH)
Kent State Univ. (OH)
Kutztown Univ. of Pennsylvania
La Salle Univ. (PA)
Lafayette College (PA)
Lake Superior State Univ. (MI)
Lamar Univ. (TX)
Lawrence Univ. (WI)
Lehigh Univ. (PA)
Lock Haven Univ. of Pennsylvania
Long Island Univ.–C.W. Post
    Campus (NY)
Louisiana State Univ.–Baton Rouge
Macalester College (MN)
Marietta College (OH)
Marshall Univ. (WV)
Massachusetts Institute of
    Technology
Mercyhurst College (PA)
Miami Univ.–Oxford (OH)
Michigan State Univ.
Michigan Technological Univ.
Middle Tennessee State Univ.
Middlebury College (VT)
Midwestern State Univ. (TX)
Millersville Univ. of Pennsylvania
Millsaps College (MS)
Minnesota State Univ.–Mankato
Minnesota State Univ.–Moorhead
Minot State Univ. (ND)
Mississippi State Univ.
Montana State Univ.–Bozeman
Montclair State Univ. (NJ)
Moravian College (PA)
Morehead State Univ. (KY)
Mount Holyoke College (MA)
Mount Union College (OH)
Murray State Univ. (KY)
Muskingum College (OH)
National Univ. (CA)
New Jersey City Univ.
New Mexico Highlands Univ.
New Mexico Institute of Mining
    and Technology
New Mexico State Univ.
North Carolina State Univ.–Raleigh
North Dakota State Univ.
Northeastern Univ. (MA)
Northern Arizona Univ.
Northern Illinois Univ.
Northern Kentucky Univ.
Northern Michigan Univ.
Northwest Missouri State Univ.
Norwich Univ. (VT)
Oberlin College (OH)
Occidental College (CA)
Ohio State Univ.–Columbus
Ohio Univ.
Ohio Wesleyan Univ.
Oklahoma State Univ.
Old Dominion Univ. (VA)
Olivet Nazarene Univ. (IL)
Oregon State Univ.
Pace Univ. (NY)
Pacific Lutheran Univ. (WA)
Penn. State Univ.–Univ. Park
Pomona College (CA)
Portland State Univ. (OR)
Princeton Univ. (NJ)

Purdue Univ.–West Lafayette (IN)
Radford Univ. (VA)
Rensselaer Polytechnic Inst. (NY)
Rice Univ. (TX)
Richard Stockton College of New
    Jersey
Rider Univ. (NJ)
Rocky Mountain College (MT)
Rutgers–New Brunswick (NJ)
Rutgers–Newark (NJ)
Salem State College (MA)
Salisbury Univ. (MD)
San Diego State Univ.
San Francisco State Univ.
San Jose State Univ. (CA)
Scripps College (CA)
Sewanee–Univ. of the South (TN)
Shippensburg Univ. of
    Pennsylvania
Skidmore College (NY)
Slippery Rock Univ. of Pennsylvania
Sonoma State Univ. (CA)
South Dakota School of Mines and
    Technology
Southern Connecticut State Univ.
Southern Illinois Univ.–Carbondale
Southern Methodist Univ. (TX)
Southern Oregon Univ.
Southern Utah Univ.
Southwest Missouri State Univ.
Southwestern Adventist Univ. (TX)
St. Cloud State Univ. (MN)
St. Lawrence Univ. (NY)
St. Louis Univ.
St. Mary's Univ. of San Antonio
St. Norbert College (WI)
Stanford Univ. (CA)
State Univ. of West Georgia
Stephen F. Austin State Univ. (TX)
Sul Ross State Univ. (TX)
SUNY College of Arts and
    Sciences–Geneseo
SUNY College–Brockport
SUNY College–Oneonta
SUNY College–Potsdam
SUNY–Albany
SUNY–Binghamton
SUNY–Fredonia
SUNY–Plattsburgh
SUNY–Stony Brook
Susquehanna Univ. (PA)
Syracuse Univ. (NY)
Tarleton State Univ. (TX)
Taylor Univ. (IN)
Temple Univ. (PA)
Tennessee Technological Univ.
Texas A&M Univ.–College Station
Texas A&M Univ.–Corpus Christi
Texas A&M Univ.–Galveston
Texas A&M Univ.–Kingsville
Texas Christian Univ.
Texas Tech Univ.
Towson Univ. (MD)
Tufts Univ. (MA)
Tulane Univ. (LA)
Union College (NY)
United States Coast Guard
    Academy (CT)
United States Naval Academy
    (MD)
Univ. at Buffalo–SUNY

Univ. of Akron (OH)
Univ. of Alabama
Univ. of Alaska–Fairbanks
Univ. of Arizona
Univ. of Arkansas
Univ. of California–Berkeley
Univ. of California–Davis
Univ. of California–Irvine
Univ. of California–Los Angeles
Univ. of California–Riverside
Univ. of California–San Diego
Univ. of California–Santa Barbara
Univ. of California–Santa Cruz
Univ. of Chicago
Univ. of Colorado–Boulder
Univ. of Connecticut
Univ. of Dayton (OH)
Univ. of Delaware
Univ. of Florida
Univ. of Georgia
Univ. of Hawaii–Hilo
Univ. of Hawaii–Manoa
Univ. of Houston
Univ. of Illinois–Chicago
Univ. of Ill.–Urbana-Champaign
Univ. of Indianapolis
Univ. of Iowa
Univ. of Kansas
Univ. of Kentucky
Univ. of Louisiana–Lafayette
Univ. of Maine–Farmington
Univ. of Maine–Orono
Univ. of Maine–Presque Isle
Univ. of Maryland–College Park
Univ. of Massachusetts–Amherst
Univ. of Memphis
Univ. of Miami (FL)
Univ. of Michigan–Ann Arbor
Univ. of Michigan–Dearborn
Univ. of Minnesota–Duluth
Univ. of Minnesota–Morris
Univ. of Minnesota–Twin Cities
Univ. of Mississippi
Univ. of Missouri–Columbia
Univ. of Missouri–Kansas City
Univ. of Missouri–Rolla
Univ. of Montana
Univ. of Nebraska–Lincoln
Univ. of Nebraska–Omaha
Univ. of Nevada–Las Vegas
Univ. of Nevada–Reno
Univ. of New Hampshire
Univ. of New Mexico
Univ. of New Orleans
Univ. of North Alabama
Univ. of N.C.–Chapel Hill
Univ. of North Carolina–Charlotte
Univ. of N.C.–Wilmington
Univ. of North Dakota
Univ. of North Texas
Univ. of Northern Colorado
Univ. of Northern Iowa
Univ. of Oklahoma
Univ. of Oregon
Univ. of Pennsylvania
Univ. of Pittsburgh
Univ. of Pittsburgh–Bradford
Univ. of Pittsburgh–Johnstown
Univ. of Puget Sound (WA)
Univ. of Rhode Island
Univ. of Rochester (NY)

Univ. of South Alabama
Univ. of South Carolina–Columbia
Univ. of South Dakota
Univ. of South Florida
Univ. of Southern California
Univ. of Southern Indiana
Univ. of Southern Maine
Univ. of Southern Mississippi
Univ. of St. Thomas (MN)
Univ. of Tennessee
Univ. of Tennessee–Chattanooga
Univ. of Tennessee–Martin
Univ. of Texas of the Permian Basin
Univ. of Texas–Arlington
Univ. of Texas–Austin
Univ. of Texas–Dallas
Univ. of Texas–El Paso
Univ. of Texas–San Antonio
Univ. of the Pacific (CA)
Univ. of Toledo (OH)
Univ. of Tulsa (OK)
Univ. of Utah
Univ. of Vermont
Univ. of Washington
Univ. of West Florida
Univ. of Wisconsin–Eau Claire
Univ. of Wisconsin–Green Bay
Univ. of Wisconsin–Madison
Univ. of Wisconsin–Milwaukee
Univ. of Wisconsin–Parkside
Univ. of Wisconsin–River Falls
Univ. of Wyoming
Utah State Univ.
Utah Valley State College
Valparaiso Univ. (IN)
Vanderbilt Univ. (TN)
Vassar College (NY)
Virginia Tech
Washington and Lee Univ. (VA)
Washington State Univ.
Washington Univ. In St. Louis
Wayne State Univ. (MI)
Weber State Univ. (UT)
Wellesley College (MA)
West Chester Univ. of Pennsylvania
West Texas A&M Univ.
West Virginia Univ.
Western Carolina Univ. (NC)
Western Connecticut State Univ.
Western Illinois Univ.
Western Kentucky Univ.
Western Michigan Univ.
Western State College of Colorado
Western Washington Univ.
Wheaton College (IL)
Whitman College (WA)
Wichita State Univ. (KS)
Wilkes Univ. (PA)
Williams College (MA)
Wittenberg Univ. (OH)
Wright State Univ. (OH)
Yale Univ. (CT)
Youngstown State Univ. (OH)

Geological/Geophysical Engineering

Michigan Technological Univ.
Montana Tech of the Univ. of
    Montana

New Jersey Institute of Technology
Rutgers–Newark (NJ)
South Dakota School of Mines and Technology
Univ. of Alaska–Fairbanks
Univ. of Arizona
Univ. of California–Berkeley
Univ. of California–Los Angeles
Univ. of Michigan–Ann Arbor
Univ. of Minnesota–Twin Cities
Univ. of Mississippi
Univ. of Missouri–Rolla
Univ. of Nevada–Reno
Univ. of North Dakota
Univ. of Rochester (NY)
Univ. of Utah
Univ. of Wisconsin–Madison

Germanic Languages, Literatures, and Linguistics

Adrian College (MI)
Albion College (MI)
Alfred Univ. (NY)
Allegheny College (PA)
Alma College (MI)
American Univ. (DC)
Amherst College (MA)
Angelo State Univ. (TX)
Aquinas College (MI)
Arizona State Univ.
Auburn Univ. (AL)
Augsburg College (MN)
Augustana College (SD)
Augustana College (IL)
Austin College (TX)
Baker Univ. (KS)
Baldwin-Wallace College (OH)
Ball State Univ. (IN)
Barnard College (NY)
Bates College (ME)
Baylor Univ. (TX)
Belmont Univ. (TN)
Beloit College (WI)
Bemidji State Univ. (MN)
Berea College (KY)
Berry College (GA)
Bethany College (WV)
Bethel College (KS)
Bloomsburg Univ. of Pennsylvania
Boise State Univ. (ID)
Boston Univ.
Bowdoin College (ME)
Bowling Green State Univ. (OH)
Bradley Univ. (IL)
Brandeis Univ. (MA)
Brigham Young Univ.–Provo (UT)
Bryn Mawr College (PA)
Bucknell Univ. (PA)
Butler Univ. (IN)
California Lutheran Univ.
California State Univ.–Chico
California State Univ.–Fullerton
California State Univ.–Long Beach
California State Univ.–Northridge
California State Univ.–Sacramento
Calvin College (MI)
Canisius College (NY)
Carleton College (MN)

Carnegie Mellon Univ. (PA)
Carson-Newman College (TN)
Carthage College (WI)
Case Western Reserve Univ. (OH)
Catholic Univ. of America (DC)
Centenary College of Louisiana
Central College (IA)
Central Connecticut State Univ.
Central Michigan Univ.
Central Missouri State Univ.
Centre College (KY)
Christopher Newport Univ. (VA)
Claremont Mckenna College (CA)
Cleveland State Univ.
Coe College (IA)
Colby College (ME)
Colgate Univ. (NY)
College of Charleston (SC)
College of St. Benedict (MN)
College of the Holy Cross (MA)
College of the Ozarks (MO)
College of William and Mary (VA)
College of Wooster (OH)
Colorado College
Columbia Univ. (NY)
Concordia Coll.–Moorhead (MN)
Concordia Univ. Wisconsin
Connecticut College
Converse College (SC)
Cornell College (IA)
Cornell Univ. (NY)
Creighton Univ. (NE)
CUNY–Hunter College
CUNY–Queens College
Dana College (NE)
Dartmouth College (NH)
David Lipscomb Univ. (TN)
Davidson College (NC)
Denison Univ. (OH)
Depaul Univ. (IL)
Depauw Univ. (IN)
Dickinson College (PA)
Dordt College (IA)
Drew Univ. (NJ)
Drury Univ. (MO)
Duke Univ. (NC)
Earlham College (IN)
East Carolina Univ. (NC)
Eastern Michigan Univ.
Eckerd College (FL)
Edinboro Univ. of Pennsylvania
Elizabethtown College (PA)
Elmhurst College (IL)
Emory Univ. (GA)
Fairfield Univ. (CT)
Florida Atlantic Univ.
Florida International Univ.
Florida State Univ.
Fordham Univ. (NY)
Franciscan Univ. of Steubenville (OH)
Franklin and Marshall College (PA)
Furman Univ. (SC)
Georgetown College (KY)
Georgetown Univ. (DC)
Georgia Southern Univ.
Georgia State Univ.
Gettysburg College (PA)
Gordon College (MA)
Grace College and Seminary (IN)
Graceland Univ. (IA)

Grand Valley State Univ. (MI)
Grinnell College (IA)
Guilford College (NC)
Gustavus Adolphus College (MN)
Hamilton College (NY)
Hamline Univ. (MN)
Hampden-Sydney College (VA)
Hanover College (IN)
Harvard Univ. (MA)
Hastings College (NE)
Haverford College (PA)
Heidelberg College (OH)
Hendrix College (AR)
Hillsdale College (MI)
Hofstra Univ. (NY)
Hood College (MD)
Hope College (MI)
Howard Univ. (DC)
Humboldt State Univ. (CA)
Idaho State Univ.
Illinois College
Illinois State Univ.
Illinois Wesleyan Univ.
Immaculata Univ. (PA)
Indiana State Univ.
Indiana Univ. of Pennsylvania
Indiana Univ.–Bloomington
Indiana Univ.–South Bend
Indiana Univ.–Purdue Univ.–Fort Wayne
Indiana Univ.–Purdue Univ.–Indianapolis
Iowa State Univ.
Ithaca College (NY)
Jamestown College (ND)
John Carroll Univ. (OH)
Johns Hopkins Univ. (MD)
Juniata College (PA)
Kalamazoo College (MI)
Kent State Univ. (OH)
Knox College (IL)
Kutztown Univ. of Pennsylvania
La Salle Univ. (PA)
Lafayette College (PA)
Lakeland College (WI)
Lambuth Univ. (TN)
Lawrence Univ. (WI)
Lebanon Valley College (PA)
Lehigh Univ. (PA)
Lenoir-Rhyne College (NC)
Lewis and Clark College (OR)
Linfield College (OR)
Lock Haven Univ. of Pennsylvania
Louisiana State Univ.–Baton Rouge
Loyola College In Maryland
Loyola Univ. Chicago
Loyola Univ. New Orleans
Luther College (IA)
Lycoming College (PA)
Macalester College (MN)
Mansfield Univ. of Pennsylvania
Marquette Univ. (WI)
Mcdaniel College (MD)
Mcmurry Univ. (TX)
Mcpherson College (KS)
Mercer Univ. (GA)
Messiah College (PA)
Miami Univ.–Oxford (OH)
Michigan State Univ.
Middlebury College (VT)
Millersville Univ. of Pennsylvania

Millsaps College (MS)
Minnesota State Univ.–Mankato
Minot State Univ. (ND)
Missouri Southern State Univ.
Moravian College (PA)
Mount St. Mary's Univ. (MD)
Mount Union College (OH)
Muhlenberg College (PA)
Murray State Univ. (KY)
Muskingum College (OH)
Nazareth College of Rochester (NY)
Nebraska Wesleyan Univ.
New York Univ.
Newberry College (SC)
North Central College (IL)
North Park Univ. (IL)
Northeastern Univ. (MA)
Northern Arizona Univ.
Northern Illinois Univ.
Northern State Univ. (SD)
Northwestern Univ. (IL)
Oakland Univ. (MI)
Oberlin College (OH)
Ohio Northern Univ.
Ohio State Univ.–Columbus
Ohio Univ.
Ohio Wesleyan Univ.
Oklahoma Baptist Univ.
Oklahoma City Univ.
Oklahoma State Univ.
Oral Roberts Univ. (OK)
Oregon State Univ.
Pacific Lutheran Univ. (WA)
Pacific Univ. (OR)
Penn. State Univ.–Univ. Park
Pepperdine Univ. (CA)
Pomona College (CA)
Presbyterian College (SC)
Princeton Univ. (NJ)
Purdue Univ.–Calumet (IN)
Randolph-Macon College (VA)
Reed College (OR)
Rhodes College (TN)
Rice Univ. (TX)
Rider Univ. (NJ)
Ripon College (WI)
Rockford College (IL)
Rosemont College (PA)
Rutgers–Camden (NJ)
Rutgers–New Brunswick (NJ)
Rutgers–Newark (NJ)
Salem College (NC)
Salisbury Univ. (MD)
Sam Houston State Univ. (TX)
Samford Univ. (AL)
San Diego State Univ.
San Francisco State Univ.
San Jose State Univ. (CA)
Santa Clara Univ. (CA)
Scripps College (CA)
Seattle Pacific Univ.
Seattle Univ.
Sewanee–Univ. of the South (TN)
Simpson College (IA)
Skidmore College (NY)
South Dakota State Univ.
Southeast Missouri State Univ.
Southern Connecticut State Univ.
Southern Illinois Univ.–Carbondale
Southern Methodist Univ. (TX)

Southern Utah Univ.
Southwestern Univ. (TX)
St. Ambrose Univ. (IA)
St. Cloud State Univ. (MN)
St. John Fisher College (NY)
St. John's Univ. (MN)
St. Joseph's Univ. (PA)
St. Lawrence Univ. (NY)
St. Louis Univ.
St. Norbert College (WI)
St. Olaf College (MN)
St. Peter's College (NJ)
Stanford Univ. (CA)
State Univ. of West Georgia
Stetson Univ. (FL)
Suffolk Univ. (MA)
SUNY–Binghamton
SUNY–Fredonia
SUNY–Stony Brook
Susquehanna Univ. (PA)
Swarthmore College (PA)
Sweet Briar College (VA)
Syracuse Univ. (NY)
Temple Univ. (PA)
Texas A&M Univ.–College Station
Texas State Univ.–San Marcos
Texas Tech Univ.
The Citadel (SC)
Towson Univ. (MD)
Trinity College (CT)
Truman State Univ. (MO)
Tufts Univ. (MA)
Tulane Univ. (LA)
Union College (NE)
Univ. at Buffalo–SUNY
Univ. of Alabama
Univ. of Arizona
Univ. of Arkansas
Univ. of Arkansas–Little Rock
Univ. of California–Berkeley
Univ. of California–Davis
Univ. of California–Irvine
Univ. of California–Los Angeles
Univ. of California–Riverside
Univ. of California–San Diego
Univ. of California–Santa Barbara
Univ. of Chicago
Univ. of Colorado–Boulder
Univ. of Connecticut
Univ. of Dallas
Univ. of Dayton (OH)
Univ. of Denver
Univ. of Evansville (IN)
Univ. of Florida
Univ. of Georgia
Univ. of Hawaii–Manoa
Univ. of Houston
Univ. of Illinois–Chicago
Univ. of Ill.–Urbana-Champaign
Univ. of Indianapolis
Univ. of Iowa
Univ. of Kansas
Univ. of Kentucky
Univ. of La Verne (CA)
Univ. of Louisville (KY)
Univ. of Maine–Orono
Univ. of Maryland–College Park
Univ. of Massachusetts–Amherst
Univ. of Massachusetts–Boston
Univ. of Miami (FL)
Univ. of Michigan–Ann Arbor

Univ. of Minnesota–Morris
Univ. of Minnesota–Twin Cities
Univ. of Mississippi
Univ. of Missouri–Columbia
Univ. of Missouri–Kansas City
Univ. of Missouri–St. Louis
Univ. of Montana
Univ. of Nebraska–Kearney
Univ. of Nebraska–Lincoln
Univ. of Nebraska–Omaha
Univ. of Nevada–Las Vegas
Univ. of Nevada–Reno
Univ. of New Hampshire
Univ. of New Mexico
Univ. of North Carolina–Asheville
Univ. of N.C.–Chapel Hill
Univ. of North Carolina–Charlotte
Univ. of N.C.–Greensboro
Univ. of N.C.–Wilmington
Univ. of North Dakota
Univ. of North Texas
Univ. of Northern Iowa
Univ. of Notre Dame (IN)
Univ. of Oklahoma
Univ. of Oregon
Univ. of Pennsylvania
Univ. of Pittsburgh
Univ. of Portland (OR)
Univ. of Puget Sound (WA)
Univ. of Redlands (CA)
Univ. of Rhode Island
Univ. of Richmond (VA)
Univ. of Rochester (NY)
Univ. of Scranton (PA)
Univ. of South Carolina–Columbia
Univ. of South Dakota
Univ. of South Florida
Univ. of Southern California
Univ. of Southern Indiana
Univ. of St. Thomas (MN)
Univ. of Tennessee
Univ. of Texas–Arlington
Univ. of Texas–Austin
Univ. of Texas–San Antonio
Univ. of the Pacific (CA)
Univ. of Toledo (OH)
Univ. of Tulsa (OK)
Univ. of Utah
Univ. of Vermont
Univ. of Virginia
Univ. of Washington
Univ. of Wisconsin–Eau Claire
Univ. of Wisconsin–Green Bay
Univ. of Wisconsin–La Crosse
Univ. of Wisconsin–Madison
Univ. of Wisconsin–Milwaukee
Univ. of Wisconsin–Parkside
Univ. of Wisconsin–Stevens Point
Univ. of Wisconsin–Whitewater
Univ. of Wyoming
Ursinus College (PA)
Utah State Univ.
Valparaiso Univ. (IN)
Vanderbilt Univ. (TN)
Vassar College (NY)
Villanova Univ. (PA)
Virginia Wesleyan College
Wabash College (IN)
Wake Forest Univ. (NC)
Wartburg College (IA)
Washburn Univ. (KS)

Washington and Jefferson College (PA)
Washington and Lee Univ. (VA)
Washington College (MD)
Washington State Univ.
Washington Univ. In St. Louis
Wayne State Univ. (MI)
Weber State Univ. (UT)
Webster Univ. (MO)
Wellesley College (MA)
West Chester Univ. of Pennsylvania
Western Carolina Univ. (NC)
Western Kentucky Univ.
Western Michigan Univ.
Western Oregon Univ.
Western Washington Univ.
Westminster College (PA)
Wheaton College (MA)
Wheaton College (IL)
Whitman College (WA)
Willamette Univ. (OR)
Williams College (MA)
Wittenberg Univ. (OH)
Wofford College (SC)
Wright State Univ. (OH)
Xavier Univ. (OH)
Yale Univ. (CT)
Youngstown State Univ. (OH)

Gerontology

Alfred Univ. (NY)
Alma College (MI)
Barton College (NC)
Bethune-Cookman College (FL)
Bowling Green State Univ. (OH)
California State Univ.–Fullerton
California State Univ.–Sacramento
California Univ. of Pennsylvania
Case Western Reserve Univ. (OH)
Central Washington Univ.
CUNY–York College
Dominican Univ. (IL)
Edward Waters College (FL)
Ithaca College (NY)
Kansas State Univ.
Lander Univ. (SC)
Lindenwood Univ. (MO)
Miami Univ.–Oxford (OH)
Minnesota State Univ.–Moorhead
Molloy College (NY)
Roosevelt Univ. (IL)
San Diego State Univ.
Southwest Missouri State Univ.
Springfield College (MA)
St. Ambrose Univ. (IA)
Stephen F. Austin State Univ. (TX)
Thomas Edison State College (NJ)
Univ. of Massachusetts–Boston
Univ. of Nebraska–Omaha
Univ. of North Texas
Univ. of Northern Iowa
Univ. of South Alabama
Univ. of South Florida
Univ. of Southern California
Washburn Univ. (KS)
Wichita State Univ. (KS)
Winston-Salem State Univ. (NC)

Graphic Communications

American Univ. (DC)
Arkansas State Univ.
Atlanta College of Art
Bellevue Univ. (NE)
Bennington College (VT)
Bradley Univ. (IL)
Brigham Young Univ.–Provo (UT)
California State Univ.–Long Beach
Carroll College (WI)
Central Missouri State Univ.
Chatham College (PA)
Chowan College (NC)
College of the Ozarks (MO)
Dakota Wesleyan Univ. (SD)
East Tennessee State Univ.
Eastern Kentucky Univ.
Fairmont State Univ. (WV)
Ferris State Univ. (MI)
Georgia Southern Univ.
Grand View College (IA)
Kean Univ. (NJ)
Lewis-Clark State College (ID)
Louisiana College
Loyola Marymount Univ. (CA)
Marywood Univ. (PA)
Minneapolis College of Art and Design
Mount Marty College (SD)
Murray State Univ. (KY)
North Central College (IL)
Otis College of Art and Design (CA)
Pennsylvania College of Technology
Philadelphia Univ.
Pittsburg State Univ. (KS)
Point Loma Nazarene Univ. (CA)
Purdue Univ.–Calumet (IN)
Rochester Institute of Tech. (NY)
Savannah College of Art and Design (GA)
Southern Adventist Univ. (TN)
Southern Nazarene Univ. (OK)
Texas A&M Univ.–Commerce
Texas State Univ.–San Marcos
The Franciscan Univ. (IA)
Touro College (NY)
Univ. of Northern Iowa
Univ. of Wisconsin–Stout
West Virginia Univ. Institute of Technology
Western Illinois Univ.

Health and Medical Administrative Services

Alabama State Univ.
Alaska Pacific Univ.
Alfred Univ. (NY)
Alvernia College (PA)
Anderson College (SC)
Andrews Univ. (MI)
Appalachian State Univ. (NC)
Arcadia Univ. (PA)
Arkansas Tech Univ.
Auburn Univ. (AL)
Barry Univ. (FL)

Bellevue Univ. (NE)
Bemidji State Univ. (MN)
Benedictine Univ. (IL)
Black Hills State Univ. (SD)
Boise State Univ. (ID)
Bowling Green State Univ. (OH)
Brescia Univ. (KY)
California State Univ.–Long Beach
California State Univ.–Los Angeles
California State Univ.–San Bernardino
Carson-Newman College (TN)
Catawba College (NC)
Central Michigan Univ.
Chestnut Hill College (PA)
Cheyney Univ. of Pennsylvania
Chicago State Univ.
Clark Atlanta Univ.
Clayton Coll. and State Univ. (GA)
College Misericordia (PA)
College of St. Catherine (MN)
College of St. Mary (NE)
College of St. Scholastica (MN)
Columbia Union College (MD)
Concordia Coll.–Moorhead (MN)
Cornell Univ. (NY)
CUNY–Lehman College
CUNY–New York City College of Technology
Dakota State Univ. (SD)
Dallas Baptist Univ.
Drexel Univ. (PA)
Duquesne Univ. (PA)
East Carolina Univ. (NC)
East Central Univ. (OK)
Eastern Kentucky Univ.
Eastern Michigan Univ.
Eastern Washington Univ.
Elmhurst College (IL)
Elon Univ. (NC)
Ferris State Univ. (MI)
Florida Atlantic Univ.
Florida International Univ.
Freed-Hardeman Univ. (TN)
George Washington Univ. (DC)
Graceland Univ. (IA)
Gwynedd-Mercy College (PA)
Harding Univ. (AR)
Hastings College (NE)
Howard Payne Univ. (TX)
Howard Univ. (DC)
Idaho State Univ.
Illinois State Univ.
Immaculata Univ. (PA)
Indiana Univ. East
Indiana Univ.–Bloomington
Indiana Univ.-Purdue Univ.–Indianapolis
Indiana Wesleyan Univ.
International College (FL)
Iona College (NY)
Ithaca College (NY)
James Madison Univ. (VA)
Johnson and Wales Univ. (RI)
Kean Univ. (NJ)
Lamar Univ. (TX)
Lebanon Valley College (PA)
Lewis-Clark State College (ID)
Lindenwood Univ. (MO)
Long Island Univ.–C.W. Post Campus (NY)

Louisiana Tech Univ.
Lynn Univ. (FL)
Madonna Univ. (MI)
Manchester College (IN)
Mary Baldwin College (VA)
Marywood Univ. (PA)
Methodist College (NC)
Midway College (KY)
Minnesota State Univ.–Moorhead
Missouri Southern State Univ.
Molloy College (NY)
Montana State Univ.–Billings
Mount Mercy College (IA)
National-Louis Univ. (IL)
New York Univ.
Norfolk State Univ. (VA)
North Greenville College (SC)
Northeastern State Univ. (OK)
Northwestern Oklahoma State Univ.
Ohio State Univ.–Columbus
Ohio Univ.
Oklahoma Panhandle State Univ.
Olivet Nazarene Univ. (IL)
Oregon State Univ.
Pennsylvania College of Technology
Penn. State Univ.–Univ. Park
Pepperdine Univ. (CA)
Pfeiffer Univ. (NC)
Providence College (RI)
Regis Univ. (CO)
Rhode Island College
Robert Morris Univ. (PA)
Roosevelt Univ. (IL)
San Francisco State Univ.
Shawnee State Univ. (OH)
Shippensburg Univ. of Pennsylvania
Southeastern Univ. (DC)
Southern Adventist Univ. (TN)
Southern Illinois Univ.–Carbondale
Southwestern Oklahoma State Univ.
Spring Arbor Univ. (MI)
Springfield College (MA)
St. John's Univ. (NY)
St. Joseph's College, New York
St. Joseph's Univ. (PA)
St. Leo Univ. (FL)
St. Louis Univ.
St. Mary's College of California
St. Peter's College (NJ)
St. Thomas Univ. (FL)
St. Xavier Univ. (IL)
Stephens College (MO)
Stonehill College (MA)
SUNY–Fredonia
Temple Univ. (PA)
Tennessee State Univ.
Texas State Univ.–San Marcos
Thomas Edison State College (NJ)
Touro College (NY)
Tulane Univ. (LA)
Univ. of Alabama
Univ. of Alabama–Birmingham
Univ. of Central Florida
Univ. of Central Oklahoma
Univ. of Connecticut
Univ. of Illinois–Chicago
Univ. of Kansas
Univ. of Kentucky

Univ. of Louisiana–Lafayette
Univ. of Louisville (KY)
Univ. of Maryland–Baltimore County
Univ. of Michigan–Dearborn
Univ. of Michigan–Flint
Univ. of Minnesota–Crookston
Univ. of Minnesota–Twin Cities
Univ. of Nebraska–Omaha
Univ. of Nevada–Las Vegas
Univ. of New England (ME)
Univ. of New Hampshire
Univ. of N.C.–Chapel Hill
Univ. of Northern Colorado
Univ. of Pennsylvania
Univ. of Pittsburgh
Univ. of Rhode Island
Univ. of South Dakota
Univ. of St. Francis (IL)
Univ. of St. Francis (IN)
Univ. of Tennessee
Univ. of Texas–El Paso
Univ. of Toledo (OH)
Univ. of Washington
Univ. of Wisconsin–Eau Claire
Univ. of Wisconsin–Milwaukee
Ursuline College (OH)
Utica College (NY)
Washington State Univ.
Weber State Univ. (UT)
West Chester Univ. of Pennsylvania
West Liberty State College (WV)
Western Carolina Univ. (NC)
Western Illinois Univ.
Western Kentucky Univ.
Western Michigan Univ.
Wheeling Jesuit Univ. (WV)
Wichita State Univ. (KS)
Wilberforce Univ. (OH)
York College of Pennsylvania
Youngstown State Univ. (OH)

Health and Physical Education/Fitness

Abilene Christian Univ. (TX)
Adams State College (CO)
Adrian College (MI)
Albertson College (ID)
Albion College (MI)
Alderson-Broaddus College (WV)
Alice Lloyd College (KY)
Alma College (MI)
Alvernia College (PA)
American Univ. (DC)
Anderson College (SC)
Anderson Univ. (IN)
Angelo State Univ. (TX)
Appalachian State Univ. (NC)
Aquinas College (MI)
Arizona State Univ.
Arkansas State Univ.
Asbury College (KY)
Augustana College (SD)
Austin Peay State Univ. (TN)
Averett Univ. (VA)
Avila Univ. (MO)
Baker Univ. (KS)
Baldwin-Wallace College (OH)
Ball State Univ. (IN)

Barry Univ. (FL)
Barton College (NC)
Baylor Univ. (TX)
Belhaven College (MS)
Belmont Univ. (TN)
Bemidji State Univ. (MN)
Bethel College (KS)
Bethel College (IN)
Bethel Univ. (MN)
Black Hills State Univ. (SD)
Bloomsburg Univ. of Pennsylvania
Blue Mountain College (MS)
Bluefield College (VA)
Bluffton Univ. (OH)
Boise State Univ. (ID)
Bowling Green State Univ. (OH)
Brenau Univ. (GA)
Brevard College (NC)
Brewton-Parker College (GA)
Briar Cliff Univ. (IA)
Bridgewater College (VA)
Bridgewater State College (MA)
Brigham Young Univ.–Hawaii
Brigham Young Univ.–Provo (UT)
Bryan College (TN)
Buena Vista Univ. (IA)
Cabrini College (PA)
Cal Poly–San Luis Obispo
California Baptist Univ.
California Lutheran Univ.
California State Polytechnic Univ.–Pomona
California State Univ.–Chico
California State Univ.–Fullerton
California State Univ.–Long Beach
California State Univ.–Sacramento
California State Univ.–San Bernardino
California State Univ.–Stanislaus
California Univ. of Pennsylvania
Calvin College (MI)
Campbell Univ. (NC)
Campbellsville Univ. (KY)
Capital Univ. (OH)
Carroll College (WI)
Carroll College (MT)
Carson-Newman College (TN)
Carthage College (WI)
Castleton State College (VT)
Catawba College (NC)
Cedarville Univ. (OH)
Centenary College of Louisiana
Central Christian College (KS)
Central Connecticut State Univ.
Central Michigan Univ.
Central Washington Univ.
Charleston Southern Univ. (SC)
Chatham College (PA)
Chowan College (NC)
Christian Heritage College (CA)
Claflin Univ. (SC)
Clearwater Christian College (FL)
Cleveland State Univ.
Coastal Carolina Univ. (SC)
Coker College (SC)
Colby-Sawyer College (NH)
College Misericordia (PA)
College of St. Catherine (MN)
College of the Ozarks (MO)
College of William and Mary (VA)
Colorado Christian Univ.

Colorado State Univ.
Colorado State Univ.–Pueblo
Columbia Union College (MD)
Concordia Coll.–Moorhead (MN)
Concordia Univ. (OR)
Concordia Univ. (MI)
Concordia Univ. (NE)
Concordia Univ. (CA)
Concordia Univ. Wisconsin
Concordia Univ.–Austin (TX)
Concordia Univ.–St. Paul (MN)
Coppin State Univ. (MD)
Cornell College (IA)
Cornerstone Univ. (MI)
Cumberland Univ. (TN)
CUNY–Brooklyn College
CUNY–Queens College
CUNY–York College
Dakota State Univ. (SD)
Dakota Wesleyan Univ. (SD)
Dana College (NE)
David Lipscomb Univ. (TN)
Davis and Elkins College (WV)
Defiance College (OH)
Delaware State Univ.
Depauw Univ. (IN)
Desales Univ. (PA)
Doane College (NE)
Dordt College (IA)
Drexel Univ. (PA)
Drury Univ. (MO)
East Carolina Univ. (NC)
East Stroudsburg Univ. of Pennsylvania
East Tennessee State Univ.
East Texas Baptist Univ.
Eastern Connecticut State Univ.
Eastern Mennonite Univ. (VA)
Eastern Michigan Univ.
Eastern Nazarene College (MA)
Eastern New Mexico Univ.
Eastern Univ. (PA)
Eastern Washington Univ.
Edinboro Univ. of Pennsylvania
Elmhurst College (IL)
Elon Univ. (NC)
Emmanuel College (GA)
Emory and Henry College (VA)
Endicott College (MA)
Erskine College (SC)
Evangel Univ. (MO)
Faulkner Univ. (AL)
Ferrum College (VA)
Fitchburg State College (MA)
Flagler College (FL)
Florida Atlantic Univ.
Florida Gulf Coast Univ.
Florida International Univ.
Florida Southern College
Fontbonne Univ. (MO)
Fort Lewis College (CO)
Franklin Pierce College (NH)
Freed-Hardeman Univ. (TN)
Fresno Pacific Univ. (CA)
Friends Univ. (KS)
Frostburg State Univ. (MD)
Furman Univ. (SC)
Gardner-Webb Univ. (NC)
George Fox Univ. (OR)
George Mason Univ. (VA)
Georgetown College (KY)

Georgia Southern Univ.
Georgia State Univ.
Gordon College (MA)
Grace College and Seminary (IN)
Graceland Univ. (IA)
Grand Canyon Univ. (AZ)
Grand Valley State Univ. (MI)
Greensboro College (NC)
Greenville College (IL)
Guilford College (NC)
Gustavus Adolphus College (MN)
Hamline Univ. (MN)
Hampton Univ. (VA)
Hanover College (IN)
Hardin-Simmons Univ. (TX)
Harding Univ. (AR)
Hastings College (NE)
Heidelberg College (OH)
Hendrix College (AR)
High Point Univ. (NC)
Holy Family Univ. (PA)
Hope College (MI)
Houghton College (NY)
Houston Baptist Univ.
Howard Payne Univ. (TX)
Huntingdon College (AL)
Huntington College (IN)
Illinois College
Illinois State Univ.
Immaculata Univ. (PA)
Indiana Univ. of Pennsylvania
Indiana Wesleyan Univ.
Iowa State Univ.
Ithaca College (NY)
Jacksonville Univ. (FL)
James Madison Univ. (VA)
John Brown Univ. (AR)
Johnson C. Smith Univ. (NC)
Judson College (IL)
Kansas State Univ.
Kansas Wesleyan Univ.
Keene State College (NH)
Kennesaw State Univ. (GA)
Kentucky Wesleyan College
La Sierra Univ. (CA)
Lake Superior State Univ. (MI)
Lambuth Univ. (TN)
Lander Univ. (SC)
Lasell College (MA)
Lenoir-Rhyne College (NC)
Letourneau Univ. (TX)
Lewis Univ. (IL)
Lewis-Clark State College (ID)
Liberty Univ. (VA)
Limestone College (SC)
Lincoln Memorial Univ. (TN)
Lincoln Univ. (PA)
Lincoln Univ. (MO)
Lindenwood Univ. (MO)
Linfield College (OR)
Livingstone College (NC)
Lock Haven Univ. of Pennsylvania
Longwood Univ. (VA)
Louisiana College
Louisiana Tech Univ.
Lubbock Christian Univ. (TX)
Luther College (IA)
Lynchburg College (VA)
Macmurray College (IL)
Malone College (OH)
Marian College (IN)

Marian College of Fond Du Lac (WI)
Martin Methodist College (TN)
Marymount Univ. (VA)
Maryville College (TN)
Master's Coll. and Seminary (CA)
Mayville State Univ. (ND)
Mcpherson College (KS)
Medaille College (NY)
Meredith College (NC)
Mesa State College (CO)
Messiah College (PA)
Methodist College (NC)
Miami Univ.–Oxford (OH)
Michigan State Univ.
Michigan Technological Univ.
Middle Tennessee State Univ.
Midland Lutheran College (NE)
Midwestern State Univ. (TX)
Milligan College (TN)
Millikin Univ. (IL)
Minnesota State Univ.–Mankato
Minnesota State Univ.–Moorhead
Minot State Univ. (ND)
Mississippi College
Mississippi Univ. For Women
Missouri Baptist College
Missouri Southern State Univ.
Missouri Western State College
Montana State Univ.–Billings
Montana State Univ.–Bozeman
Montana State Univ.–Northern
Morehead State Univ. (KY)
Morehouse College (GA)
Mount Marty College (SD)
Mount St. Mary's Univ. (MD)
Mount Union College (OH)
Mount Vernon Nazarene Univ. (OH)
Murray State Univ. (KY)
Nebraska Wesleyan Univ.
Neumann College (PA)
New York Univ.
Newberry College (SC)
Nichols College (MA)
Norfolk State Univ. (VA)
North Carolina A&T State Univ.
North Carolina Central Univ.
North Carolina State Univ.–Raleigh
North Carolina Wesleyan College
North Central College (IL)
North Dakota State Univ.
North Greenville College (SC)
Northeastern State Univ. (OK)
Northern Arizona Univ.
Northern Kentucky Univ.
Northern Michigan Univ.
Northern State Univ. (SD)
Northwest Nazarene Univ. (ID)
Northwestern College (IA)
Northwestern College (MN)
Northwood Univ. (MI)
Notre Dame De Namur Univ. (CA)
Nova Southeastern Univ. (FL)
Occidental College (CA)
Ohio Dominican Univ.
Ohio Northern Univ.
Ohio State Univ.–Columbus
Ohio Univ.
Ohio Wesleyan Univ.
Oklahoma Baptist Univ.

Oklahoma Christian Univ.
Oklahoma Panhandle State Univ.
Oklahoma Wesleyan Univ.
Olivet College (MI)
Olivet Nazarene Univ. (IL)
Oregon State Univ.
Otterbein College (OH)
Ouachita Baptist Univ. (AR)
Pacific Lutheran Univ. (WA)
Pacific Union College (CA)
Pacific Univ. (OR)
Penn. State Univ.–Univ. Park
Pepperdine Univ. (CA)
Pfeiffer Univ. (NC)
Plymouth State Univ. (NH)
Point Loma Nazarene Univ. (CA)
Portland State Univ. (OR)
Prairie View A&M Univ. (TX)
Principia College (IL)
Purdue Univ.–Calumet (IN)
Quincy Univ. (IL)
Rice Univ. (TX)
Ripon College (WI)
Roanoke College (VA)
Robert Morris Univ. (PA)
Rockford College (IL)
Rocky Mountain College (MT)
Sacred Heart Univ. (CT)
Saginaw Valley State Univ. (MI)
Salem International Univ. (WV)
Salisbury Univ. (MD)
Sam Houston State Univ. (TX)
Samford Univ. (AL)
San Jose State Univ. (CA)
Schreiner Univ. (TX)
Seton Hall Univ. (NJ)
Shaw Univ. (NC)
Shawnee State Univ. (OH)
Shippensburg Univ. of Penn.
Simpson College (IA)
Skidmore College (NY)
Slippery Rock Univ. of Pennsylvania
Sonoma State Univ. (CA)
South Carolina State Univ.
South Dakota State Univ.
Southeast Missouri State Univ.
Southeastern College of the
    Assemblies of God
Southeastern Oklahoma State
    Univ.
Southern Adventist Univ. (TN)
Southern Arkansas Univ.
Southern Connecticut State Univ.
Southern Illinois
    Univ.–Edwardsville
Southern Nazarene Univ. (OK)
Southern New Hampshire Univ.
Southern Wesleyan Univ. (SC)
Southwest Baptist Univ. (MO)
Southwest Minnesota State Univ.
    (MN)
Southwestern College (KS)
Southwestern Oklahoma State
    Univ.
Spring Arbor Univ. (MI)
Springfield College (MA)
St. Augustine's College (NC)
St. Cloud State Univ. (MN)
St. Edward's Univ. (TX)
St. John Fisher College (NY)
St. John's Univ. (NY)

St. Joseph's College (ME)
St. Leo Univ. (FL)
St. Louis Univ.
St. Mary's College of California
St. Mary's Univ. of San Antonio
St. Olaf College (MN)
St. Thomas Univ. (FL)
Stephen F. Austin State Univ. (TX)
Sterling College (KS)
Stetson Univ. (FL)
Stillman College (AL)
Sul Ross State Univ. (TX)
Syracuse Univ. (NY)
Tabor College (KS)
Tarleton State Univ. (TX)
Taylor Univ. (IN)
Tennessee State Univ.
Tennessee Technological Univ.
Tennessee Wesleyan College
Texas A&M International Univ.
Texas A&M Univ.–College Station
Texas A&M Univ.–Commerce
Texas A&M Univ.–Corpus Christi
Texas A&M Univ.–Kingsville
Texas Christian Univ.
Texas College
Texas Lutheran Univ.
Texas State Univ.–San Marcos
Texas Tech Univ.
Texas Wesleyan Univ.
Texas Woman's Univ.
Thomas College (ME)
Thomas More College (KY)
Tiffin Univ. (OH)
Towson Univ. (MD)
Transylvania Univ. (KY)
Trevecca Nazarene Univ. (TN)
Tri-State Univ. (IN)
Trinity Christian College (IL)
Troy State Univ.–Troy (AL)
Truman State Univ. (MO)
Tulane Univ. (LA)
Tusculum College (TN)
Union College (NE)
Union Univ. (TN)
Univ. at Buffalo–SUNY
Univ. of Akron (OH)
Univ. of Alaska–Fairbanks
Univ. of Arkansas
Univ. of Arkansas–Monticello
Univ. of Central Arkansas
Univ. of Charleston (WV)
Univ. of Dayton (OH)
Univ. of Delaware
Univ. of Dubuque (IA)
Univ. of Evansville (IN)
Univ. of Findlay (OH)
Univ. of Florida
Univ. of Georgia
Univ. of Great Falls (MT)
Univ. of Hawaii–Hilo
Univ. of Hawaii–Manoa
Univ. of Houston
Univ. of Illinois–Chicago
Univ. of Illinois–Urbana-
    Champaign
Univ. of Indianapolis
Univ. of Iowa
Univ. of Kansas
Univ. of Louisville (KY)
Univ. of Maine–Presque Isle

Univ. of Mary (ND)
Univ. of Mary Hardin-Baylor (TX)
Univ. of Maryland–College Park
Univ. of Maryland–Eastern Shore
Univ. of Massachusetts–Amherst
Univ. of Memphis
Univ. of Miami (FL)
Univ. of Michigan–Ann Arbor
Univ. of Minnesota–Crookston
Univ. of Minnesota–Duluth
Univ. of Minnesota–Twin Cities
Univ. of Mississippi
Univ. of Montevallo (AL)
Univ. of Nebraska–Kearney
Univ. of Nebraska–Lincoln
Univ. of Nevada–Las Vegas
Univ. of New England (ME)
Univ. of New Hampshire
Univ. of N.C.–Chapel Hill
Univ. of North Carolina–Charlotte
Univ. of N.C.–Greensboro
Univ. of North Carolina–Pembroke
Univ. of N.C.–Wilmington
Univ. of North Texas
Univ. of Northern Colorado
Univ. of Northern Iowa
Univ. of Oklahoma
Univ. of Pittsburgh–Bradford
Univ. of Puget Sound (WA)
Univ. of Rio Grande (OH)
Univ. of San Francisco
Univ. of Science and Arts of
    Oklahoma
Univ. of Scranton (PA)
Univ. of Sioux Falls (SD)
Univ. of South Carolina–Aiken
Univ. of South Carolina–Columbia
Univ. of Southern California
Univ. of Southern Indiana
Univ. of Southern Maine
Univ. of Southern Mississippi
Univ. of St. Mary (KS)
Univ. of St. Thomas (MN)
Univ. of Tennessee
Univ. of Tennessee–Chattanooga
Univ. of Tennessee–Martin
Univ. of Texas of the Permian Basin
Univ. of Texas–Arlington
Univ. of Texas–Austin
Univ. of Texas–Brownsville
Univ. of Texas–El Paso
Univ. of Texas–Pan American
Univ. of Texas–San Antonio
Univ. of Texas–Tyler
Univ. of the District of Columbia
Univ. of the Incarnate Word (TX)
Univ. of the Pacific (CA)
Univ. of Toledo (OH)
Univ. of Tulsa (OK)
Univ. of Utah
Univ. of West Florida
Univ. of Wisconsin–Eau Claire
Univ. of Wisconsin–La Crosse
Univ. of Wisconsin–Madison
Univ. of Wisconsin–Milwaukee
Univ. of Wisconsin–Parkside
Univ. of Wisconsin–Stevens Point
Univ. of Wyoming
Upper Iowa Univ.
Urbana Univ. (OH)
Ursinus College (PA)

Utah Valley State College
Valdosta State Univ. (GA)
Valley City State Univ. (ND)
Valparaiso Univ. (IN)
Vanguard Univ. of Southern
    California
Virginia Intermont College
Voorhees College (SC)
Wake Forest Univ. (NC)
Walla Walla College (WA)
Walsh Univ. (OH)
Warner Pacific College (OR)
Warner Southern College (FL)
Wartburg College (IA)
Washburn Univ. (KS)
Washington State Univ.
Wayne State College (NE)
Wesley College (DE)
West Chester Univ. of Pennsylvania
West Texas A&M Univ.
West Virginia Univ.
West Virginia Wesleyan College
Western Baptist College (OR)
Western Carolina Univ. (NC)
Western Illinois Univ.
Western Michigan Univ.
Western New England College
    (MA)
Western New Mexico Univ.
Western Washington Univ.
Westfield State College (MA)
Westmont College (CA)
Wheaton College (IL)
Wichita State Univ. (KS)
Willamette Univ. (OR)
William Carey College (MS)
William Penn Univ. (IA)
William Woods Univ. (MO)
Wilmington College (DE)
Wilmington College (OH)
Wilson College (PA)
Wingate Univ. (NC)
Winston-Salem State Univ. (NC)
Winthrop Univ. (SC)
Xavier Univ. (OH)
York College of Pennsylvania
Youngstown State Univ. (OH)

Health Professions and Related Clinical Sciences

Albany State Univ. (GA)
Albertus Magnus College (CT)
Alcorn State Univ. (MS)
Alvernia College (PA)
Armstrong Atlantic State Univ.
    (GA)
Baldwin-Wallace College (OH)
Boise State Univ. (ID)
Boston Univ.
Bowling Green State Univ. (OH)
California State Univ.–Fresno
California State Univ.–Fullerton
California State Univ.–Los Angeles
California State Univ.–Northridge
Campbell Univ. (NC)
Carlow College (PA)
Clark Atlanta Univ.
College Misericordia (PA)

CUNY–Brooklyn College
CUNY–Hunter College
Curry College (MA)
Dominican Univ. of California (CA)
Dowling College (NY)
Drexel Univ. (PA)
East Tennessee State Univ.
Eastern Nazarene College (MA)
Edward Waters College (FL)
Emmanuel College (GA)
Excelsior College (NY)
Gannon Univ. (PA)
George Mason Univ. (VA)
Georgetown Univ. (DC)
Goddard College (VT)
Grand Canyon Univ. (AZ)
Gwynedd-Mercy College (PA)
Howard Univ. (DC)
Kalamazoo College (MI)
Keuka College (NY)
King's College (PA)
Lock Haven Univ. of Pennsylvania
Long Island Univ.–C.W. Post
    Campus (NY)
Marquette Univ. (WI)
Mars Hill College (NC)
Maryville College (TN)
Molloy College (NY)
Montana State Univ.–Northern
Nazareth College of Rochester
    (NY)
New Jersey City Univ.
New York Institute of Technology
Northern Arizona Univ.
Nova Southeastern Univ. (FL)
Oakland Univ. (MI)
Ohio State Univ.–Columbus
Old Dominion Univ. (VA)
Oral Roberts Univ. (OK)
Pennsylvania College of Technology
Point Park Univ. (PA)
Purdue Univ.–West Lafayette (IN)
Quinnipiac Univ. (CT)
Rochester Institute of Tech. (NY)
Salisbury Univ. (MD)
San Diego State Univ.
San Francisco State Univ.
Southeastern Louisiana Univ.
Southwestern Oklahoma State
    Univ.
Southwestern Univ. (TX)
Springfield College (MA)
St. Francis College (NY)
St. Joseph's College, New York
St. Joseph's Univ. (PA)
St. Mary's College of California
SUNY College–Brockport
SUNY College–Potsdam
SUNY–Stony Brook
Syracuse Univ. (NY)
Towson Univ. (MD)
Tulane Univ. (LA)
Union College (NE)
Union Institute and Univ. (OH)
Univ. of Alabama
Univ. of Alabama–Birmingham
Univ. of Alaska–Anchorage
Univ. of Arkansas
Univ. of Central Arkansas
Univ. of Dallas
Univ. of Findlay (OH)

Univ. of Maryland–Baltimore
County
Univ. of Miami (FL)
Univ. of Nevada–Las Vegas
Univ. of N.C.–Wilmington
Univ. of Northern Iowa
Univ. of Pittsburgh
Univ. of Scranton (PA)
Univ. of Southern Indiana
Univ. of Southern Maine
Univ. of St. Francis (IN)
Univ. of Tennessee–Martin
Univ. of Texas–El Paso
Waldorf College (IA)
Wayne State Univ. (MI)
Worcester State College (MA)
Youngstown State Univ. (OH)

Health Psychology

Bridgewater State College (MA)

Health Services/Allied Health/Health Sciences

Albertson College (ID)
Alderson-Broaddus College (WV)
Anna Maria College (MA)
California State Univ.–Chico
California State Univ.–Hayward
California State Univ.–Monterey
Bay
California State Univ.–San
Bernardino
Centenary College of Louisiana
Central Christian College (KS)
Chatham College (PA)
Chicago State Univ.
College of St. Scholastica (MN)
Covenant College (GA)
Daemen College (NY)
Emmanuel College (MA)
Evergreen State College (WA)
Felician College (NJ)
Ferrum College (VA)
Florida Atlantic Univ.
Florida Gulf Coast Univ.
Florida International Univ.
Gardner-Webb Univ. (NC)
Geneva College (PA)
Graceland Univ. (IA)
Grand Valley State Univ. (MI)
Greensboro College (NC)
Idaho State Univ.
Ithaca College (NY)
Lebanon Valley College (PA)
Liberty Univ. (VA)
Macmurray College (IL)
Marietta College (OH)
Mercyhurst College (PA)
Merrimack College (MA)
Metropolitan State College of
Denver
Montclair State Univ. (NJ)
Nicholls State Univ. (LA)
Pacific Univ. (OR)
Quinnipiac Univ. (CT)
Sam Houston State Univ. (TX)
San Jose State Univ. (CA)

Southwestern Oklahoma State
Univ.
St. Joseph's Univ. (PA)
Stephen F. Austin State Univ. (TX)
Stetson Univ. (FL)
Texas State Univ.–San Marcos
Texas Tech Univ.
Texas Woman's Univ.
Thomas Edison State College (NJ)
Trevecca Nazarene Univ. (TN)
Union College (NE)
Univ. of Arizona
Univ. of Central Florida
Univ. of Colorado–Colorado
Springs
Univ. of Florida
Univ. of Hartford (CT)
Univ. of Houston
Univ. of Michigan–Flint
Univ. of Minnesota–Crookston
Univ. of Mobile (AL)
Univ. of New England (ME)
Univ. of North Florida
Univ. of North Texas
Univ. of Northern Colorado
Univ. of Southern Mississippi
Univ. of Texas–Austin
Univ. of Texas–Brownsville
Univ. of Texas–Pan American
Univ. of Texas–San Antonio
Univ. of Utah
Univ. of West Florida
Univ. of Wyoming
Ursuline College (OH)
Utica College (NY)
Viterbo Univ. (WI)
Washburn Univ. (KS)
Western Baptist College (OR)
Widener Univ. (PA)
William Carey College (MS)
York College of Pennsylvania

Health/Medical Preparatory Programs

Abilene Christian Univ. (TX)
Adrian College (MI)
Albertson College (ID)
Allegheny College (PA)
Alma College (MI)
American International College
(MA)
Andrews Univ. (MI)
Arcadia Univ. (PA)
Asbury College (KY)
Augustana College (SD)
Augustana College (IL)
Aurora Univ. (IL)
Austin Peay State Univ. (TN)
Averett Univ. (VA)
Avila Univ. (MO)
Azusa Pacific Univ. (CA)
Ball State Univ. (IN)
Baylor Univ. (TX)
Becker College (MA)
Benedictine Univ. (IL)
Bennington College (VT)
Bethel College (IN)
Bluffton Univ. (OH)
Boise State Univ. (ID)

Brevard College (NC)
California Baptist Univ.
Calvin College (MI)
Carroll College (WI)
Carroll College (MT)
Chadron State College (NE)
Chapman Univ. (CA)
Charleston Southern Univ. (SC)
Chatham College (PA)
Clearwater Christian College (FL)
College of Charleston (SC)
College of the Ozarks (MO)
Concordia Coll.–Moorhead (MN)
Concordia Univ. (MI)
Cornerstone Univ. (MI)
Crichton College (TN)
Cumberland College (KY)
Dakota Wesleyan Univ. (SD)
Dana College (NE)
David Lipscomb Univ. (TN)
Defiance College (OH)
Delaware State Univ.
Desales Univ. (PA)
Dordt College (IA)
Drexel Univ. (PA)
Duquesne Univ. (PA)
Eastern Mennonite Univ. (VA)
Eastern Nazarene College (MA)
Elmhurst College (IL)
Ferrum College (VA)
Furman Univ. (SC)
Gannon Univ. (PA)
Geneva College (PA)
Graceland Univ. (IA)
Grand Valley State Univ. (MI)
Guilford College (NC)
Hardin-Simmons Univ. (TX)
Harding Univ. (AR)
Hartwick College (NY)
Hastings College (NE)
Hawaii Pacific Univ.
High Point Univ. (NC)
Hofstra Univ. (NY)
Howard Payne Univ. (TX)
Humboldt State Univ. (CA)
Huntington College (IN)
Immaculata Univ. (PA)
Indiana Wesleyan Univ.
International College (FL)
Jarvis Christian College (TX)
Juniata College (PA)
Kansas State Univ.
Kent State Univ. (OH)
Lambuth Univ. (TN)
Lehigh Univ. (PA)
Lenoir-Rhyne College (NC)
Lewis Univ. (IL)
Limestone College (SC)
Lincoln Memorial Univ. (TN)
Lindenwood Univ. (MO)
Lock Haven Univ. of Pennsylvania
Louisiana College
Macmurray College (IL)
Manchester College (IN)
Mansfield Univ. of Pennsylvania
Marian College (IN)
Marywood Univ. (PA)
Mercer Univ. (GA)
Michigan State Univ.
Midwestern State Univ. (TX)
Millikin Univ. (IL)

Minnesota State Univ.–Moorhead
Mississippi College
Missouri Southern State Univ.
Monmouth College (IL)
Montana State Univ.–Bozeman
Mount Mary College (WI)
New York Institute of Technology
New York Univ.
North Park Univ. (IL)
Northeastern State Univ. (OK)
Northern Arizona Univ.
Northern Illinois Univ.
Northwest Missouri State Univ.
Northwestern Univ. (IL)
Notre Dame College of Ohio
Notre Dame De Namur Univ. (CA)
Ohio Wesleyan Univ.
Oklahoma Baptist Univ.
Oklahoma State Univ.
Olivet Nazarene Univ. (IL)
Oral Roberts Univ. (OK)
Oregon Institute of Technology
Ouachita Baptist Univ. (AR)
Penn. State Univ.–Univ. Park
Pfeiffer Univ. (NC)
Philadelphia Univ.
Rensselaer Polytechnic Inst. (NY)
Rochester Institute of Tech. (NY)
Roosevelt Univ. (IL)
Sacred Heart Univ. (CT)
Salisbury Univ. (MD)
Samford Univ. (AL)
Shawnee State Univ. (OH)
Slippery Rock Univ. of Pennsylvania
Southern Wesleyan Univ. (SC)
St. Francis College (NY)
St. Gregory's Univ. (OK)
St. Thomas Univ. (FL)
St. Xavier Univ. (IL)
SUNY College–Oneonta
Tarleton State Univ. (TX)
Texas A&M Univ.–College Station
Texas Wesleyan Univ.
Tri-State Univ. (IN)
Truman State Univ. (MO)
Tusculum College (TN)
Union Univ. (TN)
Univ. of Akron (OH)
Univ. of Arizona
Univ. of Arkansas
Univ. of California–Riverside
Univ. of Connecticut
Univ. of Dayton (OH)
Univ. of Evansville (IN)
Univ. of Findlay (OH)
Univ. of Hawaii–Hilo
Univ. of Ill.–Urbana-Champaign
Univ. of Iowa
Univ. of Louisville (KY)
Univ. of Maryland–College Park
Univ. of Maryland–Eastern Shore
Univ. of Massachusetts–Amherst
Univ. of Miami (FL)
Univ. of Missouri–Rolla
Univ. of Nebraska–Lincoln
Univ. of Nevada–Las Vegas
Univ. of Nevada–Reno
Univ. of New Mexico
Univ. of New Orleans
Univ. of Notre Dame (IN)
Univ. of Pittsburgh–Johnstown

Univ. of South Alabama
Univ. of St. Francis (IN)
Univ. of St. Thomas (MN)
Univ. of the Ozarks (AR)
Univ. of Tulsa (OK)
Univ. of Utah
Univ. of Wisconsin–Madison
Univ. of Wisconsin–Milwaukee
Utah State Univ.
Utica College (NY)
Valley City State Univ. (ND)
Virginia Intermont College
Walsh Univ. (OH)
Washburn Univ. (KS)
Washington State Univ.
West Chester Univ. of Pennsylvania
West Virginia Wesleyan College
Wheaton College (IL)
Widener Univ. (PA)
Winona State Univ. (MN)
York College of Pennsylvania
Youngstown State Univ. (OH)

Heating, Air Cond., Vent., and Refrig. Maint. Technology/ Technician

Lewis-Clark State College (ID)

Heavy/Industrial Equipment Maintenance Technologies

Ferris State Univ. (MI)
San Francisco State Univ.

Historic Preservation and Conservation

College of Charleston (SC)
Goucher College (MD)
Northwestern State Univ. of
Louisiana
Roger Williams Univ. (RI)
Salve Regina Univ. (RI)
Savannah College of Art and
Design (GA)
Univ. of Delaware
Univ. of Mary Washington (VA)
Ursuline College (OH)

History

Abilene Christian Univ. (TX)
Adelphi Univ. (NY)
Adrian College (MI)
Alabama Agricultural and
Mechanical Univ.
Alabama State Univ.
Albertson College (ID)
Albertus Magnus College (CT)
Albion College (MI)
Albright College (PA)
Alcorn State Univ. (MS)
Alderson-Broaddus College (WV)
Alfred Univ. (NY)
Allegheny College (PA)

Alma College (MI)
Alverno College (WI)
American Univ. (DC)
Amherst College (MA)
Anderson College (SC)
Anderson Univ. (IN)
Angelo State Univ. (TX)
Anna Maria College (MA)
Appalachian State Univ. (NC)
Aquinas College (MI)
Arcadia Univ. (PA)
Arizona State Univ.
Arizona State Univ. West
Arkansas State Univ.
Arkansas Tech Univ.
Armstrong Atlantic State Univ.
    (GA)
Asbury College (KY)
Ashland Univ. (OH)
Assumption College (MA)
Atlantic Union College (MA)
Auburn Univ. (AL)
Auburn Univ.–Montgomery (AL)
Augusta State Univ. (GA)
Augustana College (IL)
Augustana College (SD)
Aurora Univ. (IL)
Austin College (TX)
Austin Peay State Univ. (TN)
Averett Univ. (VA)
Avila Univ. (MO)
Azusa Pacific Univ. (CA)
Babson College (MA)
Baker Univ. (KS)
Baldwin-Wallace College (OH)
Ball State Univ. (IN)
Barnard College (NY)
Barry Univ. (FL)
Barton College (NC)
Bates College (ME)
Baylor Univ. (TX)
Belhaven College (MS)
Bellarmine Univ. (KY)
Bellevue Univ. (NE)
Belmont Abbey College (NC)
Belmont Univ. (TN)
Beloit College (WI)
Bemidji State Univ. (MN)
Benedict College (SC)
Benedictine College (KS)
Bennington College (VT)
Bentley College (MA)
Berry College (GA)
Bethany College (KS)
Bethany College (WV)
Bethel College (KS)
Bethel College (TN)
Bethel Univ. (MN)
Bethune-Cookman College (FL)
Biola Univ. (CA)
Black Hills State Univ. (SD)
Bloomfield College (NJ)
Bloomsburg Univ. of Pennsylvania
Blue Mountain College (MS)
Bluefield College (VA)
Bluffton Univ. (OH)
Boise State Univ. (ID)
Bowie State Univ. (MD)
Bowling Green State Univ. (OH)
Bradley Univ. (IL)
Brenau Univ. (GA)

Brescia Univ. (KY)
Brevard College (NC)
Brewton-Parker College (GA)
Bridgewater College (VA)
Bridgewater State College (MA)
Brigham Young Univ.–Hawaii
Brigham Young Univ.–Provo (UT)
Brown Univ. (RI)
Bryan College (TN)
Bryant College (RI)
Bryn Athyn College (PA)
Bryn Mawr College (PA)
Bucknell Univ. (PA)
Buena Vista Univ. (IA)
Buffalo State College
Butler Univ. (IN)
Cabrini College (PA)
Cal Poly–San Luis Obispo
California Baptist Univ.
California Institute of Technology
California Lutheran Univ.
California State Polytechnic
    Univ.–Pomona
California State Univ.–Chico
California State Univ.–Dominguez
    Hills
California State Univ.–Fresno
California State Univ.–Fullerton
California State Univ.–Hayward
California State Univ.–Long Beach
California State Univ.–Los Angeles
California State Univ.–Monterey
    Bay
California State Univ.–Northridge
California State Univ.–Sacramento
California State Univ.–San
    Bernardino
California State Univ.–Stanislaus
California Univ. of Pennsylvania
Calvin College (MI)
Cameron Univ. (OK)
Canisius College (NY)
Capital Univ. (OH)
Carleton College (MN)
Carlow College (PA)
Carnegie Mellon Univ. (PA)
Carroll College (WI)
Carson-Newman College (TN)
Carthage College (WI)
Case Western Reserve Univ. (OH)
Castleton State College (VT)
Catawba College (NC)
Catholic Univ. of America (DC)
Cedar Crest College (PA)
Cedarville Univ. (OH)
Centenary College (NJ)
Centenary College of Louisiana
Central College (IA)
Central Connecticut State Univ.
Central Methodist Univ. (MO)
Central Michigan Univ.
Central Missouri State Univ.
Central State Univ. (OH)
Central Washington Univ.
Centre College (KY)
Chadron State College (NE)
Chaminade Univ. of Honolulu
Chapman Univ. (CA)
Chatham College (PA)
Chestnut Hill College (PA)
Chicago State Univ.

Chowan College (NC)
Christendom College (VA)
Christian Heritage College (CA)
Christopher Newport Univ. (VA)
Claflin Univ. (SC)
Claremont Mckenna College (CA)
Clarion Univ. of Pennsylvania
Clark Atlanta Univ.
Clark Univ. (MA)
Clarkson Univ. (NY)
Clayton Coll. and State Univ. (GA)
Clearwater Christian College (FL)
Cleveland State Univ.
Coastal Carolina Univ. (SC)
Coe College (IA)
Coker College (SC)
Colby College (ME)
Colgate Univ. (NY)
College Misericordia (PA)
College of Charleston (SC)
College of Mount St. Joseph (OH)
College of Mount St. Vincent (NY)
College of New Jersey
College of Notre Dame of
    Maryland
College of St. Benedict (MN)
College of St. Catherine (MN)
College of St. Elizabeth (NJ)
College of St. Rose (NY)
College of St. Scholastica (MN)
College of the Holy Cross (MA)
College of the Ozarks (MO)
College of the Southwest (NM)
College of William and Mary (VA)
Colorado Christian Univ.
Colorado College
Colorado State Univ.
Colorado State Univ.–Pueblo
Columbia College (MO)
Columbia College (SC)
Columbia Union College (MD)
Columbia Univ. (NY)
Concord College (WV)
Concordia College (NY)
Concordia Coll.–Moorhead (MN)
Concordia Univ. (CA)
Concordia Univ. (OR)
Concordia Univ. (MI)
Concordia Univ. (NE)
Concordia Univ.–Austin (TX)
Concordia Univ.–River Forest (IL)
Concordia Univ.–St. Paul (MN)
Connecticut College
Converse College (SC)
Cornell College (IA)
Cornell Univ. (NY)
Cornerstone Univ. (MI)
Covenant College (GA)
Creighton Univ. (NE)
Crichton College (TN)
Culver-Stockton College (MO)
Cumberland College (KY)
Cumberland Univ. (TN)
CUNY–Baruch College
CUNY–Brooklyn College
CUNY–City College
CUNY–College of Staten Island
CUNY–Hunter College
CUNY–Lehman College
CUNY–Queens College
CUNY–York College

Daemen College (NY)
Dakota Wesleyan Univ. (SD)
Dana College (NE)
Dartmouth College (NH)
David Lipscomb Univ. (TN)
Davidson College (NC)
Davis and Elkins College (WV)
Defiance College (OH)
Delta State Univ. (MS)
Denison Univ. (OH)
Depauw Univ. (IN)
Desales Univ. (PA)
Dickinson College (PA)
Dickinson State Univ. (ND)
Dillard Univ. (LA)
Dominican Coll. of Blauvelt (NY)
Dominican Univ. (IL)
Dominican Univ. of California (CA)
Dordt College (IA)
Dowling College (NY)
Drake Univ. (IA)
Drew Univ. (NJ)
Drexel Univ. (PA)
Duke Univ. (NC)
Duquesne Univ. (PA)
Earlham College (IN)
East Carolina Univ. (NC)
East Central Univ. (OK)
East Stroudsburg Univ. of
    Pennsylvania
East Tennessee State Univ.
East Texas Baptist Univ.
Eastern Connecticut State Univ.
Eastern Illinois Univ.
Eastern Kentucky Univ.
Eastern Mennonite Univ. (VA)
Eastern Michigan Univ.
Eastern Nazarene College (MA)
Eastern New Mexico Univ.
Eastern Oregon Univ.
Eastern Univ. (PA)
Eastern Washington Univ.
Eckerd College (FL)
Edgewood College (WI)
Edinboro Univ. of Pennsylvania
Elizabeth City State Univ. (NC)
Elmhurst College (IL)
Elmira College (NY)
Elms College (College of Our Lady
    of the Elms) (MA)
Elon Univ. (NC)
Emmanuel College (GA)
Emmanuel College (MA)
Emory and Henry College (VA)
Emory Univ. (GA)
Emporia State Univ. (KS)
Erskine College (SC)
Eureka College (IL)
Evangel Univ. (MO)
Excelsior College (NY)
Fairfield Univ. (CT)
Fairleigh Dickinson Univ. (NJ)
Fairmont State Univ. (WV)
Fayetteville State Univ. (NC)
Felician College (NJ)
Ferris State Univ. (MI)
Ferrum College (VA)
Fisk Univ. (TN)
Fitchburg State College (MA)
Flagler College (FL)
Florida Atlantic Univ.

Florida International Univ.
Florida Southern College
Florida State Univ.
Fontbonne Univ. (MO)
Fordham Univ. (NY)
Fort Hays State Univ. (KS)
Fort Lewis College (CO)
Fort Valley State Univ. (GA)
Framingham State College (MA)
Francis Marion Univ. (SC)
Franciscan Univ. of Steubenville
    (OH)
Franklin and Marshall College (PA)
Franklin College (IN)
Franklin Pierce College (NH)
Freed-Hardeman Univ. (TN)
Fresno Pacific Univ. (CA)
Friends Univ. (KS)
Frostburg State Univ. (MD)
Furman Univ. (SC)
Gallaudet Univ. (DC)
Gannon Univ. (PA)
Gardner-Webb Univ. (NC)
Geneva College (PA)
George Fox Univ. (OR)
George Mason Univ. (VA)
George Washington Univ. (DC)
Georgetown College (KY)
Georgetown Univ. (DC)
Georgia College and State Univ.
Georgia Institute of Technology
Georgia Southern Univ.
Georgia Southwestern State Univ.
Georgia State Univ.
Georgian Court Univ. (NJ)
Gettysburg College (PA)
Glenville State College (WV)
Gonzaga Univ. (WA)
Gordon College (MA)
Goshen College (IN)
Goucher College (MD)
Graceland Univ. (IA)
Grambling State Univ. (LA)
Grand Valley State Univ. (MI)
Green Mountain College (VT)
Greensboro College (NC)
Greenville College (IL)
Grinnell College (IA)
Grove City College (PA)
Guilford College (NC)
Gustavus Adolphus College (MN)
Gwynedd-Mercy College (PA)
Hamilton College (NY)
Hamline Univ. (MN)
Hampden-Sydney College (VA)
Hampshire College (MA)
Hampton Univ. (VA)
Hardin-Simmons Univ. (TX)
Harding Univ. (AR)
Hartwick College (NY)
Harvard Univ. (MA)
Hastings College (NE)
Haverford College (PA)
Henderson State Univ. (AR)
Hendrix College (AR)
High Point Univ. (NC)
Hobart and William Smith Colleges
    (NY)
Hofstra Univ. (NY)
Hollins Univ. (VA)
Hood College (MD)

Hope College (MI)
Houghton College (NY)
Houston Baptist Univ.
Howard Payne Univ. (TX)
Humboldt State Univ. (CA)
Huntingdon College (AL)
Huntington College (IN)
Huston-Tillotson College (TX)
Idaho State Univ.
Illinois College
Illinois State Univ.
Illinois Wesleyan Univ.
Immaculata Univ. (PA)
Indiana State Univ.
Indiana Univ. East
Indiana Univ. Northwest
Indiana Univ. of Pennsylvania
Indiana Univ. Southeast
Indiana Univ.–Bloomington
Indiana Univ.–South Bend
Indiana Univ.–Purdue Univ.–Fort
   Wayne
Indiana Univ.–Purdue
   Univ.–Indianapolis
Indiana Wesleyan Univ.
Iona College (NY)
Iowa State Univ.
Ithaca College (NY)
Jacksonville State Univ. (AL)
Jacksonville Univ. (FL)
James Madison Univ. (VA)
Jamestown College (ND)
Jarvis Christian College (TX)
John Brown Univ. (AR)
John Carroll Univ. (OH)
Johns Hopkins Univ. (MD)
Johnson C. Smith Univ. (NC)
Johnson State College (VT)
Judson College (IL)
Judson College (AL)
Juniata College (PA)
Kalamazoo College (MI)
Kansas State Univ.
Kansas Wesleyan Univ.
Kean Univ. (NJ)
Keene State College (NH)
Kennesaw State Univ. (GA)
Kent State Univ. (OH)
Kentucky Christian College
Kentucky State Univ.
Kentucky Wesleyan College
King College (TN)
King's College (PA)
Knox College (IL)
Kutztown Univ. of Pennsylvania
La Roche College (PA)
La Salle Univ. (PA)
La Sierra Univ. (CA)
Lafayette College (PA)
Lagrange College (GA)
Lake Erie College (OH)
Lake Forest College (IL)
Lake Superior State Univ. (MI)
Lakeland College (WI)
Lamar Univ. (TX)
Lambuth Univ. (TN)
Lander Univ. (SC)
Lane College (TN)
Lasell College (MA)
Le Moyne College (NY)
Lebanon Valley College (PA)

Lees-Mcrae College (NC)
Lehigh Univ. (PA)
Lenoir-Rhyne College (NC)
Letourneau Univ. (TX)
Lewis and Clark College (OR)
Liberty Univ. (VA)
Limestone College (SC)
Lincoln Memorial Univ. (TN)
Lincoln Univ. (PA)
Lindenwood Univ. (MO)
Lindsey Wilson College (KY)
Linfield College (OR)
Livingstone College (NC)
Lock Haven Univ. of Pennsylvania
Long Island Univ.–Brooklyn (NY)
Long Island Univ.–C.W. Post
   Campus (NY)
Long Island Univ.–Southampton
   College (NY)
Loras College (IA)
Louisiana College
Louisiana State Univ.–Baton Rouge
Louisiana Tech Univ.
Lourdes College (OH)
Loyola College In Maryland
Loyola Marymount Univ. (CA)
Loyola Univ. Chicago
Loyola Univ. New Orleans
Luther College (IA)
Lycoming College (PA)
Lynchburg College (VA)
Lyon College (AR)
Macalester College (MN)
Macmurray College (IL)
Madonna Univ. (MI)
Malone College (OH)
Manchester College (IN)
Manhattan College (NY)
Manhattanville College (NY)
Mansfield Univ. of Pennsylvania
Marian College (IN)
Marian College of Fond Du Lac
   (WI)
Marietta College (OH)
Marist College (NY)
Marlboro College (VT)
Marquette Univ. (WI)
Mars Hill College (NC)
Marshall Univ. (WV)
Martin Univ. (IN)
Mary Baldwin College (VA)
Marygrove College (MI)
Marymount Manhattan College
   (NY)
Marymount Univ. (VA)
Maryville College (TN)
Maryville Univ. of St. Louis (MO)
Massachusetts Institute of
   Technology
Master's Coll. and Seminary (CA)
Mcdaniel College (MD)
Mckendree College (IL)
Mcmurry Univ. (TX)
Mcneese State Univ. (LA)
Mcpherson College (KS)
Mercer Univ. (GA)
Mercy College (NY)
Mercyhurst College (PA)
Meredith College (NC)
Merrimack College (MA)
Mesa State College (CO)

Messiah College (PA)
Methodist College (NC)
Metropolitan State College of
   Denver
Miami Univ.–Oxford (OH)
Michigan State Univ.
Michigan Technological Univ.
Middle Tennessee State Univ.
Middlebury College (VT)
Midland Lutheran College (NE)
Midwestern State Univ. (TX)
Milligan College (TN)
Millikin Univ. (IL)
Mills College (CA)
Millsaps College (MS)
Minnesota State Univ.–Mankato
Minnesota State Univ.–Moorhead
Minot State Univ. (ND)
Mississippi College
Mississippi State Univ.
Mississippi Univ. For Women
Missouri Baptist College
Missouri Southern State Univ.
Missouri Valley College
Missouri Western State College
Molloy College (NY)
Monmouth College (IL)
Monmouth Univ. (NJ)
Montana State Univ.–Billings
Montana State Univ.–Bozeman
Montclair State Univ. (NJ)
Montreat College (NC)
Moravian College (PA)
Morehead State Univ. (KY)
Morehouse College (GA)
Morningside College (IA)
Morris College (SC)
Mount Holyoke College (MA)
Mount Marty College (SD)
Mount Mary College (WI)
Mount Mercy College (IA)
Mount Olive College (NC)
Mount St. Mary College (NY)
Mount St. Mary's College (CA)
Mount St. Mary's Univ. (MD)
Mount Union College (OH)
Mount Vernon Nazarene Univ.
   (OH)
Muhlenberg College (PA)
Murray State Univ. (KY)
Muskingum College (OH)
Nazareth College of Rochester
   (NY)
Nebraska Wesleyan Univ.
New England College (NH)
New Jersey City Univ.
New Jersey Institute of Technology
New Mexico Highlands Univ.
New Mexico State Univ.
New York Univ.
Newberry College (SC)
Newman Univ. (KS)
Niagara Univ. (NY)
Nicholls State Univ. (LA)
Nichols College (MA)
Norfolk State Univ. (VA)
North Carolina A&T State Univ.
North Carolina Central Univ.
North Carolina State Univ.–Raleigh
North Carolina Wesleyan College
North Central College (IL)

North Dakota State Univ.
North Georgia College and State
   Univ.
North Greenville College (SC)
Northeastern State Univ. (OK)
Northeastern Univ. (MA)
Northern Arizona Univ.
Northern Illinois Univ.
Northern Kentucky Univ.
Northern Michigan Univ.
Northern State Univ. (SD)
Northland College (WI)
Northwest College (WA)
Northwest Missouri State Univ.
Northwest Nazarene Univ. (ID)
Northwestern College (MN)
Northwestern College (IA)
Northwestern State Univ. of
   Louisiana
Northwestern Univ. (IL)
Norwich Univ. (VT)
Notre Dame College of Ohio
Notre Dame De Namur Univ. (CA)
Nova Southeastern Univ. (FL)
Nyack College (NY)
Oakland Univ. (MI)
Oberlin College (OH)
Oglethorpe Univ. (GA)
Ohio Dominican Univ.
Ohio Northern Univ.
Ohio State Univ.–Columbus
Ohio Univ.
Ohio Wesleyan Univ.
Oklahoma Baptist Univ.
Oklahoma Christian Univ.
Oklahoma City Univ.
Oklahoma Panhandle State Univ.
Oklahoma State Univ.
Oklahoma Wesleyan Univ.
Old Dominion Univ. (VA)
Olivet College (MI)
Oral Roberts Univ. (OK)
Oregon State Univ.
Otterbein College (OH)
Ouachita Baptist Univ. (AR)
Our Lady of Holy Cross Coll. (LA)
Our Lady of the Lake Univ. (TX)
Pace Univ. (NY)
Pacific Lutheran Univ. (WA)
Paine College (GA)
Palm Beach Atlantic Univ. (FL)
Park Univ. (MO)
Paul Quinn College (TX)
Penn. State Univ.–Univ. Park
Penn. State–Erie, The Behrend
   College
Pepperdine Univ. (CA)
Pfeiffer Univ. (NC)
Piedmont College (GA)
Pikeville College (KY)
Pine Manor College (MA)
Pittsburg State Univ. (KS)
Pitzer College (CA)
Plymouth State Univ. (NH)
Point Loma Nazarene Univ. (CA)
Point Park Univ. (PA)
Polytechnic Univ. (NY)
Pomona College (CA)
Prairie View A&M Univ. (TX)
Princeton Univ. (NJ)
Principia College (IL)

Providence College (RI)
Purdue Univ.–Calumet (IN)
Purdue Univ.–West Lafayette (IN)
Quincy Univ. (IL)
Quinnipiac Univ. (CT)
Ramapo College of New Jersey
Randolph-Macon College (VA)
Randolph-Macon Woman's College
   (VA)
Reed College (OR)
Regis College (MA)
Reinhardt College (GA)
Rhode Island College
Rhodes College (TN)
Rice Univ. (TX)
Richard Stockton College of New
   Jersey
Rider Univ. (NJ)
Ripon College (WI)
Rivier College (NH)
Roanoke College (VA)
Rochester College (MI)
Rockford College (IL)
Rockhurst Univ. (MO)
Rocky Mountain College (MT)
Roger Williams Univ. (RI)
Rollins College (FL)
Rosemont College (PA)
Rutgers–Camden (NJ)
Rutgers–New Brunswick (NJ)
Rutgers–Newark (NJ)
Sacred Heart Univ. (CT)
Saginaw Valley State Univ. (MI)
Salem College (NC)
Salem State College (MA)
Salisbury Univ. (MD)
Salve Regina Univ. (RI)
Samford Univ. (AL)
San Diego State Univ.
San Francisco State Univ.
San Jose State Univ. (CA)
Santa Clara Univ. (CA)
Savannah State Univ. (GA)
Schreiner Univ. (TX)
Scripps College (CA)
Seton Hall Univ. (NJ)
Seton Hill Univ. (PA)
Sewanee–Univ. of the South (TN)
Shawnee State Univ. (OH)
Shenandoah Univ. (VA)
Shippensburg Univ. of
   Pennsylvania
Shorter College (GA)
Siena College (NY)
Silver Lake College (WI)
Simmons College (MA)
Simon's Rock College of Bard
   (MA)
Simpson College (IA)
Simpson Univ. (CA)
Skidmore College (NY)
Slippery Rock Univ. of Pennsylvania
Sonoma State Univ. (CA)
South Carolina State Univ.
South Dakota State Univ.
Southeast Missouri State Univ.
Southeastern Louisiana Univ.
Southeastern Oklahoma State
   Univ.
Southern Arkansas Univ.
Southern Illinois Univ.–Carbondale

Southern Illinois Univ.–Edwardsville
Southern Methodist Univ. (TX)
Southern Nazarene Univ. (OK)
Southern New Hampshire Univ.
Southern Oregon Univ.
Southern Univ. and A&M College (LA)
Southern Utah Univ.
Southern Wesleyan Univ. (SC)
Southwest Baptist Univ. (MO)
Southwest Minnesota State Univ. (MN)
Southwest Missouri State Univ.
Southwestern Adventist Univ. (TX)
Southwestern College (KS)
Southwestern Oklahoma State Univ.
Southwestern Univ. (TX)
Spring Arbor Univ. (MI)
Spring Hill College (AL)
St. Ambrose Univ. (IA)
St. Andrews Presbyterian College (NC)
St. Anselm College (NH)
St. Bonaventure Univ. (NY)
St. Edward's Univ. (TX)
St. Francis College (NY)
St. Gregory's Univ. (OK)
St. John Fisher College (NY)
St. John's Univ. (NY)
St. John's Univ. (MN)
St. Joseph's College (ME)
St. Joseph's College (IN)
St. Joseph's College, New York
St. Joseph's Univ. (PA)
St. Lawrence Univ. (NY)
St. Leo Univ. (FL)
St. Louis Univ.
St. Martin's College (WA)
St. Mary's College (IN)
St. Mary's College of California
St. Mary's College of Maryland
St. Mary's Univ. of Minnesota
St. Mary's Univ. of San Antonio
St. Michael's College (VT)
St. Norbert College (WI)
St. Olaf College (MN)
St. Peter's College (NJ)
St. Thomas Aquinas College (NY)
St. Thomas Univ. (FL)
St. Vincent College (PA)
St. Xavier Univ. (IL)
Stanford Univ. (CA)
State Univ. of West Georgia
Stephen F. Austin State Univ. (TX)
Sterling College (KS)
Stetson Univ. (FL)
Stillman College (AL)
Stonehill College (MA)
Suffolk Univ. (MA)
SUNY College of Arts and Sciences–Geneseo
SUNY College–Brockport
SUNY–Albany
SUNY–Binghamton
SUNY–Empire State College
SUNY–Oswego
SUNY–Plattsburgh
SUNY–Purchase College
SUNY–Stony Brook

Susquehanna Univ. (PA)
Swarthmore College (PA)
Sweet Briar College (VA)
Syracuse Univ. (NY)
Tabor College (KS)
Tarleton State Univ. (TX)
Taylor Univ. (IN)
Teikyo Post Univ. (CT)
Temple Univ. (PA)
Tennessee State Univ.
Tennessee Wesleyan College
Texas A&M International Univ.
Texas A&M Univ.–College Station
Texas A&M Univ.–Commerce
Texas A&M Univ.–Corpus Christi
Texas A&M Univ.–Kingsville
Texas Christian Univ.
Texas College
Texas Lutheran Univ.
Texas State Univ.–San Marcos
Texas Tech Univ.
Texas Woman's Univ.
The Citadel (SC)
Thiel College (PA)
Thomas Edison State College (NJ)
Thomas More College (KY)
Tougaloo College (MS)
Touro College (NY)
Towson Univ. (MD)
Transylvania Univ. (KY)
Trevecca Nazarene Univ. (TN)
Tri-State Univ. (IN)
Trinity Christian College (IL)
Trinity College (CT)
Trinity College (DC)
Troy State Univ.–Troy (AL)
Truman State Univ. (MO)
Tufts Univ. (MA)
Tulane Univ. (LA)
Tusculum College (TN)
Tuskegee Univ. (AL)
Union College (NY)
Union College (NE)
Union Univ. (TN)
United States Air Force Academy (CO)
United States Naval Academy (MD)
Univ. at Buffalo–SUNY
Univ. of Akron (OH)
Univ. of Alabama
Univ. of Alabama–Birmingham
Univ. of Alabama–Huntsville
Univ. of Alaska–Anchorage
Univ. of Alaska–Fairbanks
Univ. of Arizona
Univ. of Arkansas
Univ. of Arkansas–Little Rock
Univ. of Arkansas–Pine Bluff
Univ. of California–Berkeley
Univ. of California–Davis
Univ. of California–Irvine
Univ. of California–Los Angeles
Univ. of California–Riverside
Univ. of California–San Diego
Univ. of Central Arkansas
Univ. of Central Florida
Univ. of Central Oklahoma
Univ. of Charleston (WV)
Univ. of Chicago
Univ. of Colorado–Boulder

Univ. of Colorado–Colorado Springs
Univ. of Colorado–Denver
Univ. of Connecticut
Univ. of Dallas
Univ. of Dayton (OH)
Univ. of Delaware
Univ. of Denver
Univ. of Evansville (IN)
Univ. of Findlay (OH)
Univ. of Florida
Univ. of Georgia
Univ. of Great Falls (MT)
Univ. of Hawaii–Hilo
Univ. of Hawaii–Manoa
Univ. of Houston
Univ. of Houston–Downtown
Univ. of Illinois–Chicago
Univ. of Illinois–Springfield
Univ. of Illinois–Urbana-Champaign
Univ. of Indianapolis
Univ. of Iowa
Univ. of Judaism (CA)
Univ. of Kansas
Univ. of Kentucky
Univ. of La Verne (CA)
Univ. of Louisiana–Lafayette
Univ. of Louisiana–Monroe
Univ. of Louisville (KY)
Univ. of Maine–Farmington
Univ. of Maine–Fort Kent
Univ. of Maine–Machias
Univ. of Maine–Orono
Univ. of Mary (ND)
Univ. of Mary Hardin-Baylor (TX)
Univ. of Maryland–Baltimore County
Univ. of Maryland–College Park
Univ. of Maryland–Eastern Shore
Univ. of Maryland–Univ. College
Univ. of Massachusetts–Amherst
Univ. of Massachusetts–Boston
Univ. of Massachusetts–Lowell
Univ. of Memphis
Univ. of Miami (FL)
Univ. of Michigan–Ann Arbor
Univ. of Michigan–Dearborn
Univ. of Michigan–Flint
Univ. of Minnesota–Duluth
Univ. of Minnesota–Morris
Univ. of Minnesota–Twin Cities
Univ. of Mississippi
Univ. of Missouri–Columbia
Univ. of Missouri–Kansas City
Univ. of Missouri–Rolla
Univ. of Missouri–St. Louis
Univ. of Mobile (AL)
Univ. of Montana
Univ. of Montevallo (AL)
Univ. of Nebraska–Kearney
Univ. of Nebraska–Lincoln
Univ. of Nebraska–Omaha
Univ. of Nevada–Las Vegas
Univ. of Nevada–Reno
Univ. of New England (ME)
Univ. of New Hampshire
Univ. of New Haven (CT)
Univ. of New Mexico
Univ. of New Orleans
Univ. of North Alabama

Univ. of North Carolina–Asheville
Univ. of N.C.–Chapel Hill
Univ. of North Carolina–Charlotte
Univ. of N.C.–Greensboro
Univ. of North Carolina–Pembroke
Univ. of N.C.–Wilmington
Univ. of North Dakota
Univ. of North Florida
Univ. of North Texas
Univ. of Northern Colorado
Univ. of Northern Iowa
Univ. of Notre Dame (IN)
Univ. of Oklahoma
Univ. of Oregon
Univ. of Pennsylvania
Univ. of Pittsburgh
Univ. of Pittsburgh–Greensburg
Univ. of Pittsburgh–Johnstown
Univ. of Portland (OR)
Univ. of Puget Sound (WA)
Univ. of Redlands (CA)
Univ. of Rhode Island
Univ. of Richmond (VA)
Univ. of Rochester (NY)
Univ. of San Diego
Univ. of San Francisco
Univ. of Science and Arts of Oklahoma
Univ. of Scranton (PA)
Univ. of Sioux Falls (SD)
Univ. of South Alabama
Univ. of South Carolina–Aiken
Univ. of South Carolina–Columbia
Univ. of South Dakota
Univ. of South Florida
Univ. of Southern California
Univ. of Southern Indiana
Univ. of Southern Mississippi
Univ. of St. Francis (IN)
Univ. of St. Francis (IL)
Univ. of St. Mary (KS)
Univ. of St. Thomas (MN)
Univ. of St. Thomas (TX)
Univ. of Tampa (FL)
Univ. of Tennessee
Univ. of Tennessee–Chattanooga
Univ. of Tennessee–Martin
Univ. of Texas of the Permian Basin
Univ. of Texas–Arlington
Univ. of Texas–Austin
Univ. of Texas–Brownsville
Univ. of Texas–El Paso
Univ. of Texas–Pan American
Univ. of Texas–San Antonio
Univ. of Texas–Tyler
Univ. of the District of Columbia
Univ. of the Incarnate Word (TX)
Univ. of the Ozarks (AR)
Univ. of the Pacific (CA)
Univ. of Toledo (OH)
Univ. of Tulsa (OK)
Univ. of Utah
Univ. of Vermont
Univ. of Virginia
Univ. of Virginia–Wise
Univ. of Washington
Univ. of West Alabama
Univ. of West Florida
Univ. of Wisconsin–Eau Claire
Univ. of Wisconsin–Green Bay
Univ. of Wisconsin–La Crosse

Univ. of Wisconsin–Madison
Univ. of Wisconsin–Milwaukee
Univ. of Wisconsin–Oshkosh
Univ. of Wisconsin–Platteville
Univ. of Wisconsin–River Falls
Univ. of Wisconsin–Stevens Point
Univ. of Wisconsin–Superior
Univ. of Wisconsin–Whitewater
Univ. of Wyoming
Urbana Univ. (OH)
Ursinus College (PA)
Ursuline College (OH)
Utah Valley State College
Utica College (NY)
Valdosta State Univ. (GA)
Valley City State Univ. (ND)
Valparaiso Univ. (IN)
Vanderbilt Univ. (TN)
Vanguard Univ. of Southern California
Vassar College (NY)
Villa Julie College (MD)
Villanova Univ. (PA)
Virginia Commonwealth Univ.
Virginia Intermont College
Virginia Military Institute
Virginia State Univ.
Virginia Tech
Virginia Wesleyan College
Wagner College (NY)
Wake Forest Univ. (NC)
Waldorf College (IA)
Walsh Univ. (OH)
Warner Pacific College (OR)
Warner Southern College (FL)
Wartburg College (IA)
Washburn Univ. (KS)
Washington and Jefferson College (PA)
Washington and Lee Univ. (VA)
Washington College (MD)
Washington State Univ.
Washington Univ. In St. Louis
Wayland Baptist Univ. (TX)
Wayne State College (NE)
Wayne State Univ. (MI)
Waynesburg College (PA)
Webster Univ. (MO)
Wellesley College (MA)
Wesley College (DE)
Wesleyan College (GA)
Wesleyan Univ. (CT)
West Chester Univ. of Pennsylvania
West Liberty State College (WV)
West Virginia State Univ.
West Virginia Univ.
West Virginia Wesleyan College
Western Carolina Univ. (NC)
Western Connecticut State Univ.
Western Illinois Univ.
Western Kentucky Univ.
Western Michigan Univ.
Western New England Coll. (MA)
Western New Mexico Univ.
Western State College of Colorado
Western Washington Univ.
Westfield State College (MA)
Westminster College (MO)
Westminster College (PA)
Westminster College (UT)
Westmont College (CA)

Wheaton College (MA)
Wheaton College (IL)
Wheeling Jesuit Univ. (WV)
Whitman College (WA)
Whittier College (CA)
Whitworth College (WA)
Wichita State Univ. (KS)
Wiley College (TX)
Wilkes Univ. (PA)
Willamette Univ. (OR)
William Carey College (MS)
William Jewell College (MO)
William Paterson Univ. of New
    Jersey
William Penn Univ. (IA)
William Woods Univ. (MO)
Williams College (MA)
Wilmington College (OH)
Winston-Salem State Univ. (NC)
Winthrop Univ. (SC)
Wisconsin Lutheran College
Wittenberg Univ. (OH)
Wofford College (SC)
Worcester State College (MA)
Wright State Univ. (OH)
Xavier Univ. (OH)
Yale Univ. (CT)
Yeshiva Univ. (NY)
York College of Pennsylvania
Youngstown State Univ. (OH)

Hospitality Administration/ Management

Alliant International Univ. (CA)
Appalachian State Univ. (NC)
Arkansas State Univ.
Arkansas Tech Univ.
Ashland Univ. (OH)
Auburn Univ. (AL)
Barber Scotia College (NC)
Bethune-Cookman College (FL)
Black Hills State Univ. (SD)
Boston Univ.
Bowling Green State Univ. (OH)
Brigham Young Univ.–Hawaii
Buffalo State College
California State Polytechnic
    Univ.–Pomona
Campbell Univ. (NC)
Central Michigan Univ.
Central Missouri State Univ.
Champlain College (VT)
Cheyney Univ. of Pennsylvania
Clark Atlanta Univ.
Coastal Carolina Univ. (SC)
College of Charleston (SC)
College of St. Joseph (VT)
College of the Ozarks (MO)
Concordia Univ. (MI)
Cornell Univ. (NY)
CUNY–New York City College of
    Technology
Davis and Elkins College (WV)
Delaware State Univ.
Delta State Univ. (MS)
Dowling College (NY)
Drexel Univ. (PA)
East Carolina Univ. (NC)

East Stroudsburg Univ. of
    Pennsylvania
Eastern Kentucky Univ.
Eastern Michigan Univ.
Edward Waters College (FL)
Endicott College (MA)
Excelsior College (NY)
Fairleigh Dickinson Univ. (NJ)
Fairmont State Univ. (WV)
Ferris State Univ. (MI)
Florida Atlantic Univ.
Florida Gulf Coast Univ.
Florida International Univ.
Florida State Univ.
George Washington Univ. (DC)
Georgia Southern Univ.
Georgia State Univ.
Golden Gate Univ. (CA)
Grand Valley State Univ. (MI)
Green Mountain College (VT)
Hawaii Pacific Univ.
Howard Univ. (DC)
Husson College (ME)
Indiana Univ. of Pennsylvania
Indiana Univ.–Purdue Univ.–Fort
    Wayne
Indiana Univ.–Purdue
    Univ.–Indianapolis
Iowa State Univ.
James Madison Univ. (VA)
Johnson and Wales Univ. (RI)
Johnson State College (VT)
Kansas State Univ.
Kendall College (IL)
Keuka College (NY)
Lakeland College (WI)
Lasell College (MA)
Lewis-Clark State College (ID)
Lindenwood Univ. (MO)
Lynn Univ. (FL)
Madonna Univ. (MI)
Mansfield Univ. of Pennsylvania
Marywood Univ. (PA)
Mercyhurst College (PA)
Methodist College (NC)
Metropolitan State College of
    Denver
Michigan State Univ.
Morgan State Univ. (MD)
Mount Ida College (MA)
Mountain State Univ. (WV)
New Mexico State Univ.
New York Institute of Technology
New York Univ.
Niagara Univ. (NY)
North Carolina Central Univ.
North Dakota State Univ.
Northeastern State Univ. (OK)
Northern Arizona Univ.
Northwestern State Univ. of
    Louisiana
Northwood Univ. (MI)
Ohio State Univ.–Columbus
Oklahoma State Univ.
Pace Univ. (NY)
Purdue Univ.–West Lafayette (IN)
Robert Morris Univ. (PA)
Rochester Institute of Tech. (NY)
Roosevelt Univ. (IL)
Rutgers–Camden (NJ)
San Diego State Univ.

San Francisco State Univ.
Seton Hill Univ. (PA)
Sierra Nevada College (NV)
South Dakota State Univ.
Southern New Hampshire Univ.
Southern Utah Univ.
Southwest Minnesota State Univ.
    (MN)
Southwest Missouri State Univ.
St. John's Univ. (NY)
St. Leo Univ. (FL)
St. Thomas Univ. (FL)
Stephen F. Austin State Univ. (TX)
SUNY College–Brockport
SUNY–Plattsburgh
Tennessee State Univ.
Texas A&M International Univ.
Texas A&M Univ.–College Station
Texas Tech Univ.
Thomas Edison State College (NJ)
Tiffin Univ. (OH)
Tougaloo College (MS)
Tuskegee Univ. (AL)
Univ. of Akron (OH)
Univ. of Alabama
Univ. of Central Florida
Univ. of Central Oklahoma
Univ. of Delaware
Univ. of Denver
Univ. of Findlay (OH)
Univ. of Hawaii–Manoa
Univ. of Houston
Univ. of Ill.–Urbana-Champaign
Univ. of Kentucky
Univ. of Louisiana–Lafayette
Univ. of Maryland–Eastern Shore
Univ. of Massachusetts–Amherst
Univ. of Memphis
Univ. of Minnesota–Crookston
Univ. of Missouri–Columbia
Univ. of Nebraska–Kearney
Univ. of Nevada–Las Vegas
Univ. of New Hampshire
Univ. of New Haven (CT)
Univ. of New Orleans
Univ. of N.C.–Greensboro
Univ. of North Texas
Univ. of San Francisco
Univ. of South Carolina–Columbia
Univ. of South Florida
Univ. of Southern Mississippi
Univ. of Tennessee
Univ. of Texas–San Antonio
Univ. of West Florida
Univ. of Wisconsin–Stout
Utah Valley State College
Virginia State Univ.
Virginia Tech
Viterbo Univ. (WI)
Washington State Univ.
Webber International Univ. (FL)
Western Carolina Univ. (NC)
Western Kentucky Univ.
Widener Univ. (PA)
Wiley College (TX)
Youngstown State Univ. (OH)

Housing and Human Environments

CUNY–New York City College of
    Technology
Eastern Kentucky Univ.
Eastern Michigan Univ.
Iowa State Univ.
Miami Univ.–Oxford (OH)
North Dakota State Univ.
Ohio Univ.
Oklahoma State Univ.
Oregon State Univ.
Southwest Missouri State Univ.
Univ. of Arkansas
Univ. of Georgia
Univ. of Minnesota–Twin Cities
Univ. of Missouri–Columbia
Univ. of Nevada–Reno
Utah State Univ.

Human Development, Family Studies, and Related Services

Abilene Christian Univ. (TX)
Adrian College (MI)
Alcorn State Univ. (MS)
Alderson-Broaddus College (WV)
Anderson Univ. (IN)
Andrews Univ. (MI)
Appalachian State Univ. (NC)
Auburn Univ. (AL)
Baker College of Flint (MI)
Ball State Univ. (IN)
Baylor Univ. (TX)
Boston College
Bowling Green State Univ. (OH)
California State Univ.–Bakersfield
California State Univ.–Hayward
California State Univ.–Long Beach
California State Univ.–San
    Bernardino
California State Univ.–San Marcos
Carson-Newman College (TN)
Central Michigan Univ.
Chestnut Hill College (PA)
Christian Heritage College (CA)
College of the Ozarks (MO)
Colorado State Univ.
Columbia College (SC)
Concordia Univ. (MI)
Concordia Univ.–St. Paul (MN)
Connecticut College
Cornell Univ. (NY)
Cornerstone Univ. (MI)
David Lipscomb Univ. (TN)
Desales Univ. (PA)
East Carolina Univ. (NC)
East Tennessee State Univ.
Eastern Kentucky Univ.
Eastern Washington Univ.
Eckerd College (FL)
Ferris State Univ. (MI)
Florida State Univ.
Freed-Hardeman Univ. (TN)
Gallaudet Univ. (DC)
Georgia Southern Univ.
Harding Univ. (AR)

Hope International Univ. (CA)
Houston Baptist Univ.
Howard Univ. (DC)
Indiana State Univ.
Indiana Univ. of Pennsylvania
Iowa State Univ.
John Brown Univ. (AR)
Kansas State Univ.
Kent State Univ. (OH)
Kentucky State Univ.
Lesley Univ. (MA)
Lewis-Clark State College (ID)
Liberty Univ. (VA)
Louisiana Tech Univ.
Lubbock Christian Univ. (TX)
Lynchburg College (VA)
Madonna Univ. (MI)
Mayville State Univ. (ND)
Meredith College (NC)
Messiah College (PA)
Miami Univ.–Oxford (OH)
Michigan State Univ.
Mills College (CA)
Mississippi Univ. For Women
Missouri Baptist College
Murray State Univ. (KY)
New Mexico State Univ.
North Carolina A&T State Univ.
North Dakota State Univ.
Northern Illinois Univ.
Northern Michigan Univ.
Northwest Missouri State Univ.
Oakwood College (AL)
Ohio State Univ.–Columbus
Ohio Univ.
Oklahoma Baptist Univ.
Oklahoma Christian Univ.
Oklahoma State Univ.
Oregon State Univ.
Penn. State Univ.–Univ. Park
Point Loma Nazarene Univ. (CA)
Purdue Univ.–Calumet (IN)
Purdue Univ.–West Lafayette (IN)
Quinnipiac Univ. (CT)
Samford Univ. (AL)
San Diego State Univ.
Seton Hill Univ. (PA)
South Dakota State Univ.
Southern Adventist Univ. (TN)
Southern Nazarene Univ. (OK)
Southern New Hampshire Univ.
Southwest Missouri State Univ.
Spring Arbor Univ. (MI)
St. Joseph College (CT)
St. Joseph's College, New York
St. Olaf College (MN)
Stephen F. Austin State Univ. (TX)
SUNY College of A&T–Cobleskill
SUNY College–Oneonta
SUNY–Plattsburgh
Syracuse Univ. (NY)
Texas State Univ.–San Marcos
Texas Tech Univ.
Texas Woman's Univ.
Thomas Edison State College (NJ)
Univ. of Akron (OH)
Univ. of Alabama
Univ. of Alaska–Anchorage
Univ. of Arizona
Univ. of Arkansas
Univ. of Arkansas–Pine Bluff

Univ. of California–Davis
Univ. of California–San Diego
Univ. of Central Oklahoma
Univ. of Connecticut
Univ. of Delaware
Univ. of Florida
Univ. of Georgia
Univ. of Houston
Univ. of Ill.–Urbana-Champaign
Univ. of La Verne (CA)
Univ. of Louisiana–Lafayette
Univ. of Maine–Orono
Univ. of Maryland–College Park
Univ. of Missouri–Columbia
Univ. of Nevada–Reno
Univ. of New Hampshire
Univ. of New Mexico
Univ. of North Carolina–Charlotte
Univ. of N.C.–Greensboro
Univ. of North Texas
Univ. of Northern Colorado
Univ. of Northern Iowa
Univ. of Rhode Island
Univ. of Scranton (PA)
Univ. of Southern Mississippi
Univ. of St. Mary (KS)
Univ. of Tennessee
Univ. of Texas of the Permian Basin
Univ. of Texas–Arlington
Univ. of Texas–Austin
Univ. of the Incarnate Word (TX)
Univ. of Utah
Univ. of Vermont
Univ. of Wisconsin–Madison
Univ. of Wisconsin–Stout
Utah State Univ.
Villa Julie College (MD)
Virginia Tech
Warner Pacific College (OR)
Washington State Univ.
Wayne State College (NE)
Wayne State Univ. (MI)
Weber State Univ. (UT)
Western Michigan Univ.
Western Washington Univ.
Wheelock College (MA)
York College of Pennsylvania
Youngstown State Univ. (OH)

Human Resources Management and Services

Arcadia Univ. (PA)
Bellevue Univ. (NE)
California State Polytechnic
    Univ.–Pomona
Converse College (SC)
Defiance College (OH)
Gwynedd-Mercy College (PA)
Lewis Univ. (IL)
North Park Univ. (IL)
Oakland City Univ. (IN)
Otterbein College (OH)
St. Mary-of-The-Woods Coll. (IN)
Tennessee Wesleyan College
Texas A&M Univ.–Commerce
Thomas College (ME)
Univ. of Central Oklahoma
Wright State Univ. (OH)

York College (NE)

Human Services

Alaska Pacific Univ.
Anna Maria College (MA)
Bellevue Univ. (NE)
Bethel College (TN)
Burlington College (VT)
California State Univ.–Fullerton
California State Univ.–Monterey
    Bay
California State Univ.–Sacramento
California State Univ.–San
    Bernardino
Calumet College of St. Joseph (IN)
Cazenovia College (NY)
Central Washington Univ.
Chestnut Hill College (PA)
College of Notre Dame of
    Maryland
College of St. Joseph (VT)
College of St. Mary (NE)
College of the Southwest (NM)
Concordia Univ.–St. Paul (MN)
Coppin State Univ. (MD)
CUNY–New York City College of
    Technology
Dakota Wesleyan Univ. (SD)
East Central Univ. (OK)
Elmhurst College (IL)
Elon Univ. (NC)
Florida Gulf Coast Univ.
Fontbonne Univ. (MO)
Geneva College (PA)
Grand View College (IA)
Hannibal-Lagrange College (MO)
Hawaii Pacific Univ.
High Point Univ. (NC)
Holy Names Univ. (CA)
Indiana Univ.-Purdue Univ.–Fort
    Wayne
Judson College (IL)
Kennesaw State Univ. (GA)
Kentucky Wesleyan College
La Roche College (PA)
Lake Superior State Univ. (MI)
Lasell College (MA)
Lenoir-Rhyne College (NC)
Lesley Univ. (MA)
Lewis Univ. (IL)
Lincoln Univ. (PA)
Lindenwood Univ. (MO)
Lindsey Wilson College (KY)
Loyola Univ. Chicago
Martin Methodist College (TN)
Mcmurry Univ. (TX)
Medaille College (NY)
Mercer Univ. (GA)
Missouri Baptist College
Montreat College (NC)
Mount Ida College (MA)
Mount St. Mary College (NY)
New York Univ.
Northeastern Univ. (MA)
Northwest Christian College (OR)
Notre Dame De Namur Univ. (CA)
Pfeiffer Univ. (NC)
Seton Hill Univ. (PA)
Sheldon Jackson College (AK)

Southwest Baptist Univ. (MO)
Spelman College (GA)
St. John's Univ. (NY)
St. Mary's Univ. of Minnesota
Teikyo Post Univ. (CT)
Thomas Edison State College (NJ)
Tiffin Univ. (OH)
Touro College (NY)
Univ. of Detroit Mercy
Univ. of Maine–Presque Isle
Univ. of Massachusetts–Boston
Univ. of Minnesota–Morris
Univ. of Northern Colorado
Univ. of Oregon
Univ. of Tennessee–Chattanooga
Univ. of Wisconsin–Oshkosh
Villanova Univ. (PA)
Waynesburg College (PA)
William Penn Univ. (IA)
William Woods Univ. (MO)
Wingate Univ. (NC)

Industrial and Organizational Psychology

Abilene Christian Univ. (TX)
Albright College (PA)
Averett Univ. (VA)
Bridgewater State College (MA)
College of Santa Fe (NM)
CUNY–Baruch College
East Texas Baptist Univ.
Fitchburg State College (MA)
Georgia Institute of Technology
High Point Univ. (NC)
Holy Family Univ. (PA)
Ithaca College (NY)
Lincoln Univ. (PA)
Maryville Univ. of St. Louis (MO)
Middle Tennessee State Univ.
Morningside College (IA)
Nebraska Wesleyan Univ.
Northwest Missouri State Univ.
Pepperdine Univ. (CA)
Point Loma Nazarene Univ. (CA)
St. Joseph's Univ. (PA)
St. Mary's College of California
St. Xavier Univ. (IL)
Texas Wesleyan Univ.
Tiffin Univ. (OH)
Univ. of Missouri–Rolla
Washington Univ. In St. Louis
Western Baptist College (OR)
William Carey College (MS)

Industrial Engineering

Andrews Univ. (MI)
Arizona State Univ.
Auburn Univ. (AL)
Bethel College (IN)
Bradley Univ. (IL)
Cal Poly–San Luis Obispo
California State Polytechnic
    Univ.–Pomona
California State Univ.–Fresno
California State Univ.–Long Beach
Cleveland State Univ.

Colorado State Univ.–Pueblo
Columbia Univ. (NY)
Elizabethtown College (PA)
Florida A&M Univ.
Florida State Univ.
Gannon Univ. (PA)
George Washington Univ. (DC)
Georgia Institute of Technology
Hofstra Univ. (NY)
Indiana Institute of Technology
Iowa State Univ.
Kansas State Univ.
Kent State Univ. (OH)
Kettering Univ. (MI)
Lamar Univ. (TX)
Lehigh Univ. (PA)
Louisiana State Univ.–Baton Rouge
Louisiana Tech Univ.
Milwaukee School of Engineering
Mississippi State Univ.
Montana State Univ.–Bozeman
Morgan State Univ. (MD)
New Jersey Institute of Technology
New Mexico State Univ.
North Carolina A&T State Univ.
North Carolina State Univ.–Raleigh
North Dakota State Univ.
Northeastern State Univ. (OK)
Northeastern Univ. (MA)
Northern Illinois Univ.
Northwestern Univ. (IL)
Ohio State Univ.–Columbus
Ohio Univ.
Oklahoma State Univ.
Oregon State Univ.
Penn. State Univ.–Univ. Park
Philadelphia Univ.
Purdue Univ.–West Lafayette (IN)
Rensselaer Polytechnic Inst. (NY)
Rochester Institute of Tech. (NY)
Roosevelt Univ. (IL)
Rutgers–New Brunswick (NJ)
San Jose State Univ. (CA)
South Dakota School of Mines and
    Technology
Southern Illinois
    Univ.–Edwardsville
St. Ambrose Univ. (IA)
St. Mary's Univ. of San Antonio
Stanford Univ. (CA)
SUNY–Binghamton
Syracuse Univ. (NY)
Tennessee Technological Univ.
Texas A&M Univ.–College Station
Texas State Univ.–San Marcos
Texas Tech Univ.
Tri-State Univ. (IN)
Univ. at Buffalo–SUNY
Univ. of Alabama
Univ. of Alabama–Huntsville
Univ. of Arizona
Univ. of Arkansas
Univ. of Central Florida
Univ. of Connecticut
Univ. of Houston
Univ. of Illinois–Chicago
Univ. of Ill.–Urbana-Champaign
Univ. of Iowa
Univ. of Louisville (KY)
Univ. of Massachusetts–Amherst
Univ. of Miami (FL)

Univ. of Michigan–Ann Arbor
Univ. of Michigan–Dearborn
Univ. of Minnesota–Crookston
Univ. of Minnesota–Duluth
Univ. of Minnesota–Twin Cities
Univ. of Missouri–Rolla
Univ. of Nebraska–Lincoln
Univ. of Oklahoma
Univ. of Pittsburgh
Univ. of Rhode Island
Univ. of San Diego
Univ. of South Florida
Univ. of Southern California
Univ. of Southern Maine
Univ. of Tennessee
Univ. of Texas–Arlington
Univ. of Texas–El Paso
Univ. of Texas–Pan American
Univ. of Toledo (OH)
Univ. of Vermont
Univ. of Washington
Univ. of Wisconsin–Madison
Univ. of Wisconsin–Platteville
Utah State Univ.
Virginia Tech
Washington State Univ.
Wayne State Univ. (MI)
West Virginia Univ.
Western Michigan Univ.
Western New England College
    (MA)
Wichita State Univ. (KS)
Worcester Polytechnic Institute
    (MA)
Youngstown State Univ. (OH)

Industrial Production Technologies/Technicians

Alabama Agricultural and
    Mechanical Univ.
Alcorn State Univ. (MS)
Andrews Univ. (MI)
Appalachian State Univ. (NC)
Baker College of Flint (MI)
Ball State Univ. (IN)
Bemidji State Univ. (MN)
Berea College (KY)
Black Hills State Univ. (SD)
Bowling Green State Univ. (OH)
Buffalo State College
California State Univ.–Long Beach
California Univ. of Pennsylvania
Central Connecticut State Univ.
Central Michigan Univ.
Central Missouri State Univ.
Central State Univ. (OH)
Central Washington Univ.
Chadron State College (NE)
Colorado State Univ.–Pueblo
East Carolina Univ. (NC)
Eastern Illinois Univ.
Eastern Kentucky Univ.
Eastern Michigan Univ.
Elizabeth City State Univ. (NC)
Ferris State Univ. (MI)
Fitchburg State College (MA)
Florida A&M Univ.
Georgia Southern Univ.
Humboldt State Univ. (CA)

Illinois Institute of Technology
Illinois State Univ.
Indiana State Univ.
Indiana Univ.–South Bend
Indiana Univ.-Purdue Univ.–Fort Wayne
Jacksonville State Univ. (AL)
Kean Univ. (NJ)
Lamar Univ. (TX)
Lawrence Technological Univ. (MI)
Letourneau Univ. (TX)
Lewis-Clark State College (ID)
Mcpherson College (KS)
Metropolitan State College of Denver
Michigan Technological Univ.
Middle Tennessee State Univ.
Midwestern State Univ. (TX)
Millersville Univ. of Pennsylvania
Minnesota State Univ.–Mankato
Minnesota State Univ.–Moorhead
Mississippi State Univ.
Mississippi Valley State Univ.
Montana State Univ.–Northern
Morehead State Univ. (KY)
Murray State Univ. (KY)
North Carolina A&T State Univ.
Northern Illinois Univ.
Northern Kentucky Univ.
Northwest Missouri State Univ.
Northwestern State Univ. of Louisiana
Ohio Northern Univ.
Ohio Univ.
Oklahoma Panhandle State Univ.
Oregon Institute of Technology
Pennsylvania College of Technology
Penn. State–Erie, The Behrend College
Pittsburg State Univ. (KS)
Prairie View A&M Univ. (TX)
Purdue Univ.–Calumet (IN)
Purdue Univ.–North Central (IN)
Rhode Island College
Rochester Institute of Tech. (NY)
Saginaw Valley State Univ. (MI)
Sam Houston State Univ. (TX)
Shawnee State Univ. (OH)
South Carolina State Univ.
South Dakota State Univ.
Southeast Missouri State Univ.
Southeastern Louisiana Univ.
Southern Arkansas Univ.
Southern Illinois Univ.–Carbondale
Southern Polytechnic State Univ. (GA)
Southern Utah Univ.
Southwest Missouri State Univ.
Southwestern Oklahoma State Univ.
St. Mary's Univ. of Minnesota
Sul Ross State Univ. (TX)
SUNY–Farmingdale
Tarleton State Univ. (TX)
Tennessee Technological Univ.
Texas A&M Univ.–College Station
Texas A&M Univ.–Commerce
Texas A&M Univ.–Kingsville
Texas State Univ.–San Marcos
Thomas Edison State College (NJ)
Univ. of Akron (OH)

Univ. of Arkansas–Pine Bluff
Univ. of Dayton (OH)
Univ. of Houston
Univ. of Louisiana–Lafayette
Univ. of Massachusetts–Lowell
Univ. of Memphis
Univ. of Minnesota–Crookston
Univ. of Nebraska–Lincoln
Univ. of North Carolina–Charlotte
Univ. of North Dakota
Univ. of North Texas
Univ. of Northern Iowa
Univ. of Rio Grande (OH)
Univ. of Southern Mississippi
Univ. of Texas of the Permian Basin
Univ. of Texas–Brownsville
Univ. of Texas–Tyler
Univ. of West Alabama
Univ. of Wisconsin–Platteville
Univ. of Wisconsin–Stout
Utah State Univ.
Valdosta State Univ. (GA)
Wayne State College (NE)
Wayne State Univ. (MI)
Weber State Univ. (UT)
Wentworth Institute of Tech. (MA)
West Texas A&M Univ.
Western Carolina Univ. (NC)
Western Illinois Univ.
Western Kentucky Univ.
Western Michigan Univ.
Western Washington Univ.

Information Science/ Studies

Adelphi Univ. (NY)
Alabama State Univ.
Albright College (PA)
American Univ. (DC)
Anderson Univ. (IN)
Armstrong Atlantic State Univ. (GA)
Averett Univ. (VA)
Babson College (MA)
Baker Univ. (KS)
Barry Univ. (FL)
Bemidji State Univ. (MN)
Benedictine Univ. (IL)
Bethune-Cookman College (FL)
Bluffton Univ. (OH)
Boise State Univ. (ID)
Bradley Univ. (IL)
Brewton-Parker College (GA)
Brigham Young Univ.–Hawaii
Buffalo State College
Butler Univ. (IN)
California State Univ.–Fullerton
California State Univ.–Sacramento
Carlow College (PA)
Carnegie Mellon Univ. (PA)
Carroll College (WI)
Cedar Crest College (PA)
Central Michigan Univ.
Chadron State College (NE)
Clarion Univ. of Pennsylvania
Clayton Coll. and State Univ. (GA)
College of Charleston (SC)
College of Notre Dame of Maryland

College of St. Catherine (MN)
Colorado State Univ.–Pueblo
Columbia Union College (MD)
Concord College (WV)
CUNY–Baruch College
CUNY–College of Staten Island
CUNY–Lehman College
CUNY–New York City College of Technology
Dakota State Univ. (SD)
Davis and Elkins College (WV)
Delaware State Univ.
Depaul Univ. (IL)
Desales Univ. (PA)
Dominican Univ. (IL)
Dordt College (IA)
Drexel Univ. (PA)
Eastern Connecticut State Univ.
Eastern Kentucky Univ.
Elizabethtown College (PA)
Elmhurst College (IL)
Elmira College (NY)
Emporia State Univ. (KS)
Eureka College (IL)
Excelsior College (NY)
Florida Institute of Technology
Florida State Univ.
Fordham Univ. (NY)
Fort Valley State Univ. (GA)
Franklin Pierce College (NH)
Frostburg State Univ. (MD)
Gallaudet Univ. (DC)
George Washington Univ. (DC)
Georgia Southern Univ.
Golden Gate Univ. (CA)
Grambling State Univ. (LA)
Grand Valley State Univ. (MI)
Guilford College (NC)
Howard Payne Univ. (TX)
Idaho State Univ.
Immaculata Univ. (PA)
Jacksonville Univ. (FL)
James Madison Univ. (VA)
John Carroll Univ. (OH)
Johns Hopkins Univ. (MD)
Johnson and Wales Univ. (RI)
Kansas State Univ.
Kennesaw State Univ. (GA)
Lehigh Univ. (PA)
Lenoir-Rhyne College (NC)
Letourneau Univ. (TX)
Lincoln Univ. (MO)
Long Island Univ.–C.W. Post Campus (NY)
Loyola Univ. New Orleans
Mansfield Univ. of Pennsylvania
Marist College (NY)
Marymount Univ. (VA)
Marywood Univ. (PA)
Mckendree College (IL)
Mercer Univ. (GA)
Messiah College (PA)
Minnesota State Univ.–Mankato
Minot State Univ. (ND)
Missouri Western State College
Molloy College (NY)
Mount Union College (OH)
Murray State Univ. (KY)
Nazareth College of Rochester (NY)
Nebraska Wesleyan Univ.

New Jersey Institute of Technology
New Mexico Highlands Univ.
New Mexico State Univ.
New York Univ.
Niagara Univ. (NY)
North Carolina Central Univ.
North Georgia College and State Univ.
Northeastern Univ. (MA)
Northwestern College (IA)
Northwestern State Univ. of Louisiana
Northwestern Univ. (IL)
Norwich Univ. (VT)
Oakwood College (AL)
Ohio Dominican Univ.
Oklahoma Baptist Univ.
Oklahoma Christian Univ.
Olivet Nazarene Univ. (IL)
Pace Univ. (NY)
Penn. State Univ.–Univ. Park
Philadelphia Univ.
Prairie View A&M Univ. (TX)
Queens Univ. of Charlotte (NC)
Quincy Univ. (IL)
Quinnipiac Univ. (CT)
Radford Univ. (VA)
Ramapo College of New Jersey
Regis College (MA)
Regis Univ. (CO)
Richard Stockton College of New Jersey
Roanoke College (VA)
Robert Morris Univ. (PA)
Rochester Institute of Tech. (NY)
Rutgers–New Brunswick (NJ)
Rutgers–Newark (NJ)
Salisbury Univ. (MD)
Salve Regina Univ. (RI)
San Diego State Univ.
Savannah State Univ. (GA)
Southeastern College of the Assemblies of God
Southern Illinois Univ.–Carbondale
Southern Methodist Univ. (TX)
Southern Nazarene Univ. (OK)
Southern Utah Univ.
St. Ambrose Univ. (IA)
St. Francis Univ. (PA)
St. Joseph's College, New York
St. Joseph's Univ. (PA)
St. Mary's Univ. of Minnesota
St. Michael's College (VT)
St. Peter's College (NJ)
Suffolk Univ. (MA)
SUNY College–Old Westbury
SUNY–Albany
SUNY–Stony Brook
Susquehanna Univ. (PA)
Syracuse Univ. (NY)
Texas A&M Univ.–Commerce
Texas Christian Univ.
Texas Lutheran Univ.
Tiffin Univ. (OH)
Towson Univ. (MD)
Trinity Christian College (IL)
Univ. of Arkansas–Little Rock
Univ. of California–Irvine
Univ. of California–Riverside
Univ. of Dayton (OH)
Univ. of Hartford (CT)

Univ. of Houston
Univ. of Illinois–Chicago
Univ. of Maine–Orono
Univ. of Mary (ND)
Univ. of Mary Hardin-Baylor (TX)
Univ. of Maryland–Baltimore County
Univ. of Maryland–College Park
Univ. of Maryland–Univ. College
Univ. of Massachusetts–Lowell
Univ. of Miami (FL)
Univ. of Michigan–Flint
Univ. of Missouri–Rolla
Univ. of New Haven (CT)
Univ. of N.C.–Chapel Hill
Univ. of North Texas
Univ. of Oklahoma
Univ. of Pittsburgh
Univ. of Redlands (CA)
Univ. of San Francisco
Univ. of Scranton (PA)
Univ. of South Florida
Univ. of Texas of the Permian Basin
Univ. of Texas–Brownsville
Univ. of the District of Columbia
Univ. of the Pacific (CA)
Univ. of Toledo (OH)
Univ. of Tulsa (OK)
Urbana Univ. (OH)
Utah State Univ.
Valdosta State Univ. (GA)
Vermont Technical College
Villa Julie College (MD)
Villanova Univ. (PA)
Virginia Commonwealth Univ.
Wayne State College (NE)
Wayne State Univ. (MI)
Weber State Univ. (UT)
West Virginia Wesleyan College
Westminster College (PA)
Widener Univ. (PA)
Wilkes Univ. (PA)
William Jewell College (MO)
York College of Pennsylvania

Insurance

Appalachian State Univ. (NC)
Baylor Univ. (TX)
Bradley Univ. (IL)
California State Univ.–Sacramento
Delta State Univ. (MS)
Eastern Kentucky Univ.
Excelsior College (NY)
Florida International Univ.
Florida State Univ.
Gannon Univ. (PA)
Georgia State Univ.
Howard Univ. (DC)
Illinois State Univ.
Illinois Wesleyan Univ.
Indiana State Univ.
Martin Univ. (IN)
Mississippi State Univ.
Ohio State Univ.–Columbus
Olivet College (MI)
Roosevelt Univ. (IL)
Southwest Missouri State Univ.
St. John's Univ. (NY)

Temple Univ. (PA)
Thomas Edison State College (NJ)
Univ. of Central Arkansas
Univ. of Connecticut
Univ. of Florida
Univ. of Georgia
Univ. of Hartford (CT)
Univ. of Illinois–Urbana-
    Champaign
Univ. of Louisiana–Lafayette
Univ. of Minnesota–Twin Cities
Univ. of Mississippi
Univ. of North Texas
Univ. of Pennsylvania
Univ. of South Carolina–Columbia
Univ. of Wisconsin–Madison
Washington State Univ.

Intercultural/ Multicultural and Diversity Studies

Blackburn College (IL)
Brigham Young Univ.–Hawaii
College of St. Catherine (MN)
Covenant College (GA)
Elmhurst College (IL)
Evergreen State College (WA)
Hampshire College (MA)
Ithaca College (NY)
Lawrence Univ. (WI)
Nyack College (NY)
St. Andrews Presbyterian Coll. (NC)
Univ. of San Diego
Westfield State College (MA)
Wofford College (SC)

Interior Architecture

Arizona State Univ.
Auburn Univ. (AL)
Boston Architectural Center
Bowling Green State Univ. (OH)
California State Univ.–Sacramento
Central Michigan Univ.
Central Missouri State Univ.
Cooper Union (NY)
Indiana State Univ.
Kansas State Univ.
La Roche College (PA)
Lawrence Technological Univ. (MI)
Louisiana State Univ.–Baton Rouge
Louisiana Tech Univ.
Miami Univ.–Oxford (OH)
Philadelphia Univ.
Sam Houston State Univ. (TX)
School of the Art Institute of
    Chicago
Stephen F. Austin State Univ. (TX)
Syracuse Univ. (NY)
Texas Tech Univ.
Univ. of Bridgeport (CT)
Univ. of Houston
Univ. of Louisiana–Lafayette
Univ. of Mississippi
Univ. of Nebraska–Lincoln
Univ. of Nevada–Las Vegas
Univ. of New Haven (CT)
Univ. of North Texas

Univ. of Oregon
Univ. of Southern Mississippi
Univ. of Texas–San Antonio
Woodbury Univ. (CA)

International Agriculture

California State Polytechnic
    Univ.–Pomona
Cornell College (IA)
Cornell Univ. (NY)
Eastern Mennonite Univ. (VA)
Iowa State Univ.
Lewis Univ. (IL)
Southern Connecticut State Univ.
Tarleton State Univ. (TX)
Univ. of California–Davis
Univ. of Minnesota–Morris
Univ. of Pittsburgh–Bradford
Utah State Univ.
Wesleyan Univ. (CT)

International Business

Adrian College (MI)
Alliant International Univ. (CA)
Alma College (MI)
Alverno College (WI)
American Univ. (DC)
Angelo State Univ. (TX)
Appalachian State Univ. (NC)
Aquinas College (MI)
Arizona State Univ. West
Arkansas State Univ.
Assumption College (MA)
Auburn Univ. (AL)
Avila Univ. (MO)
Azusa Pacific Univ. (CA)
Babson College (MA)
Baker Univ. (KS)
Barry Univ. (FL)
Baylor Univ. (TX)
Bellarmine Univ. (KY)
Bellevue Univ. (NE)
Belmont Abbey College (NC)
Benedictine Univ. (IL)
Bethel College (IN)
Bethel Univ. (MN)
Bethune-Cookman College (FL)
Boise State Univ. (ID)
Bowling Green State Univ. (OH)
Bradley Univ. (IL)
Bridgewater State College (MA)
Brigham Young Univ.–Hawaii
Bryant College (RI)
Buena Vista Univ. (IA)
Butler Univ. (IN)
Caldwell College (NJ)
California State Polytechnic
    Univ.–Pomona
California State Univ.–Fullerton
California State Univ.–Long Beach
California State Univ.–Sacramento
Campbell Univ. (NC)
Canisius College (NY)
Cardinal Stritch Univ. (WI)
Carlow College (PA)
Carson-Newman College (TN)

Catholic Univ. of America (DC)
Cedarville Univ. (OH)
Central Connecticut State Univ.
Central Michigan Univ.
Champlain College (VT)
Chatham College (PA)
Chestnut Hill College (PA)
College of Charleston (SC)
College of New Jersey
College of Santa Fe (NM)
College of the Ozarks (MO)
Columbia College (MO)
Columbia Union College (MD)
Converse College (SC)
Cornell College (IA)
CUNY–Queens College
Davenport Univ. (MI)
Davis and Elkins College (WV)
Dickinson College (PA)
Dominican Coll. of Blauvelt (NY)
Dominican Univ. (IL)
Dowling College (NY)
Drake Univ. (IA)
Drexel Univ. (PA)
Drury Univ. (MO)
Duquesne Univ. (PA)
Eastern Mennonite Univ. (VA)
Eastern Michigan Univ.
Eckerd College (FL)
Elizabethtown College (PA)
Elmhurst College (IL)
Emory and Henry College (VA)
Excelsior College (NY)
Ferris State Univ. (MI)
Fitchburg State College (MA)
Florida Atlantic Univ.
Florida International Univ.
Florida Southern College
Florida State Univ.
Fort Lewis College (CO)
Fresno Pacific Univ. (CA)
Gannon Univ. (PA)
George Washington Univ. (DC)
Georgetown Univ. (DC)
Georgia College and State Univ.
Golden Gate Univ. (CA)
Goldey Beacom College (DE)
Grace College and Seminary (IN)
Graceland Univ. (IA)
Grand Canyon Univ. (AZ)
Grand Valley State Univ. (MI)
Gustavus Adolphus College (MN)
Gwynedd-Mercy College (PA)
Hamline Univ. (MN)
Hardin-Simmons Univ. (TX)
Harding Univ. (AR)
Hawaii Pacific Univ.
High Point Univ. (NC)
Hillsdale College (MI)
Hofstra Univ. (NY)
Holy Family Univ. (PA)
Howard Univ. (DC)
Husson College (ME)
Illinois State Univ.
Illinois Wesleyan Univ.
Indiana Univ. of Pennsylvania
Iona College (NY)
Iowa State Univ.
Jacksonville Univ. (FL)
James Madison Univ. (VA)
Jamestown College (ND)

John Brown Univ. (AR)
Johnson and Wales Univ. (RI)
Juniata College (PA)
King's College (PA)
Kutztown Univ. of Pennsylvania
La Roche College (PA)
Lake Superior State Univ. (MI)
Lakeland College (WI)
Lambuth Univ. (TN)
Lasell College (MA)
Lenoir-Rhyne College (NC)
Letourneau Univ. (TX)
Lindenwood Univ. (MO)
Linfield College (OR)
Louisiana State Univ.–Baton Rouge
Loyola Univ. Chicago
Loyola Univ. New Orleans
Madonna Univ. (MI)
Manchester College (IN)
Manhattan College (NY)
Mansfield Univ. of Pennsylvania
Marietta College (OH)
Marquette Univ. (WI)
Marygrove College (MI)
Maryville College (TN)
Marywood Univ. (PA)
Mercyhurst College (PA)
Messiah College (PA)
Midwestern State Univ. (TX)
Millikin Univ. (IL)
Milwaukee School of Engineering
Minnesota State Univ.–Mankato
Minnesota State Univ.–Moorhead
Minot State Univ. (ND)
Missouri Southern State Univ.
Monmouth College (IL)
Monmouth Univ. (NJ)
Moravian College (PA)
Morningside College (IA)
Mount Union College (OH)
Mount Vernon Nazarene Univ.
    (OH)
Murray State Univ. (KY)
Muskingum College (OH)
Nebraska Wesleyan Univ.
Neumann College (PA)
New Mexico State Univ.
New York Institute of Technology
New York Univ.
North Central College (IL)
North Greenville College (SC)
North Park Univ. (IL)
Northeastern State Univ. (OK)
Northeastern Univ. (MA)
Northern State Univ. (SD)
Northwest Missouri State Univ.
Northwestern College (MN)
Northwood Univ. (MI)
Ohio Dominican Univ.
Ohio Northern Univ.
Ohio State Univ.–Columbus
Ohio Univ.
Ohio Wesleyan Univ.
Oklahoma Baptist Univ.
Oklahoma State Univ.
Old Dominion Univ. (VA)
Oral Roberts Univ. (OK)
Pace Univ. (NY)
Paine College (GA)
Palm Beach Atlantic Univ. (FL)
Penn. State Univ.–Univ. Park

Penn. State–Erie, The Behrend
    College
Pepperdine Univ. (CA)
Pfeiffer Univ. (NC)
Philadelphia Univ.
Quinnipiac Univ. (CT)
Ramapo College of New Jersey
Rhode Island College
Rider Univ. (NJ)
Rochester Institute of Tech. (NY)
Roger Williams Univ. (RI)
Rollins College (FL)
Sacred Heart Univ. (CT)
Saginaw Valley State Univ. (MI)
Salem College (NC)
Sam Houston State Univ. (TX)
Samford Univ. (AL)
San Diego State Univ.
Savannah State Univ. (GA)
Schreiner Univ. (TX)
Seattle Univ.
Seton Hill Univ. (PA)
Shaw Univ. (NC)
Simpson College (IA)
Southeastern College of the
    Assemblies of God
Southern Adventist Univ. (TN)
Southern New Hampshire Univ.
St. Ambrose Univ. (IA)
St. Anselm College (NH)
St. Cloud State Univ. (MN)
St. Edward's Univ. (TX)
St. Francis Univ. (PA)
St. Joseph's College (ME)
St. Joseph's Univ. (PA)
St. Leo Univ. (FL)
St. Louis Univ.
St. Mary's College of California
St. Mary's Univ. of Minnesota
St. Mary's Univ. of San Antonio
St. Norbert College (WI)
St. Peter's College (NJ)
St. Thomas Univ. (FL)
St. Vincent College (PA)
St. Xavier Univ. (IL)
Stephen F. Austin State Univ. (TX)
Stetson Univ. (FL)
Stonehill College (MA)
Suffolk Univ. (MA)
SUNY College–Brockport
Susquehanna Univ. (PA)
Taylor Univ. (IN)
Teikyo Post Univ. (CT)
Temple Univ. (PA)
Texas A&M Univ.–Galveston
Texas A&M Univ.–Kingsville
Texas Christian Univ.
Texas Tech Univ.
Texas Wesleyan Univ.
Thomas College (ME)
Thomas Edison State College (NJ)
Tiffin Univ. (OH)
Tulane Univ. (LA)
Union College (NE)
Union Univ. (TN)
Univ. of Akron (OH)
Univ. of Arkansas
Univ. of Arkansas–Little Rock
Univ. of Bridgeport (CT)
Univ. of Dayton (OH)
Univ. of Denver

Univ. of Evansville (IN)
Univ. of Findlay (OH)
Univ. of Georgia
Univ. of Hawaii–Manoa
Univ. of Houston–Downtown
Univ. of Indianapolis
Univ. of Iowa
Univ. of La Verne (CA)
Univ. of Maryland–College Park
Univ. of Maryland–Univ. College
Univ. of Memphis
Univ. of Miami (FL)
Univ. of Minnesota–Twin Cities
Univ. of Mississippi
Univ. of Montana
Univ. of Nebraska–Lincoln
Univ. of Nevada–Las Vegas
Univ. of Nevada–Reno
Univ. of New Haven (CT)
Univ. of North Carolina–Charlotte
Univ. of N.C.–Greensboro
Univ. of North Florida
Univ. of Pennsylvania
Univ. of Portland (OR)
Univ. of Rhode Island
Univ. of Rio Grande (OH)
Univ. of San Francisco
Univ. of Scranton (PA)
Univ. of South Carolina–Columbia
Univ. of South Florida
Univ. of Southern Mississippi
Univ. of St. Mary (KS)
Univ. of St. Thomas (MN)
Univ. of Tampa (FL)
Univ. of Texas–Arlington
Univ. of Texas–Pan American
Univ. of Texas–San Antonio
Univ. of Toledo (OH)
Univ. of Tulsa (OK)
Univ. of Wisconsin–La Crosse
Univ. of Wisconsin–Madison
Univ. of Wisconsin–Superior
Valparaiso Univ. (IN)
Vanguard Univ. of Southern
   California
Villanova Univ. (PA)
Virginia Intermont College
Wagner College (NY)
Washington and Jefferson College
   (PA)
Washington State Univ.
Washington Univ. In St. Louis
Webber International Univ. (FL)
Wesley College (DE)
Wesleyan College (GA)
West Virginia Wesleyan College
Western Carolina Univ. (NC)
Western Washington Univ.
Westminster College (UT)
Westminster College (PA)
Wheeling Jesuit Univ. (WV)
Whitworth College (WA)
Wichita State Univ. (KS)
Widener Univ. (PA)
William Jewell College (MO)
Wofford College (SC)
Wright State Univ. (OH)
Xavier Univ. (OH)

International Relations and Affairs

Adrian College (MI)
Agnes Scott College (GA)
Albertson College (ID)
Allegheny College (PA)
Alliant International Univ. (CA)
Alverno College (WI)
American Univ. (DC)
Antioch College (OH)
Aquinas College (MI)
Arcadia Univ. (PA)
Ashland Univ. (OH)
Augustana College (SD)
Austin College (TX)
Baylor Univ. (TX)
Beloit College (WI)
Benedictine Univ. (IL)
Bennington College (VT)
Berry College (GA)
Bethany College (WV)
Bethel Univ. (MN)
Bethune-Cookman College (FL)
Boston Univ.
Bowling Green State Univ. (OH)
Bradley Univ. (IL)
Brenau Univ. (GA)
Bridgewater College (VA)
Bridgewater State College (MA)
Brigham Young Univ.–Provo (UT)
Brown Univ. (RI)
Bryant College (RI)
Bucknell Univ. (PA)
Butler Univ. (IN)
California State Univ.–Chico
California State Univ.–Hayward
California State Univ.–Sacramento
California State Univ.–San
   Bernardino
Calvin College (MI)
Canisius College (NY)
Capital Univ. (OH)
Carleton College (MN)
Carnegie Mellon Univ. (PA)
Carroll College (WI)
Carroll College (MT)
Case Western Reserve Univ. (OH)
Centenary College (NJ)
Central Michigan Univ.
Chaminade Univ. of Honolulu
Chapman Univ. (CA)
Chatham College (PA)
Claremont Mckenna College (CA)
Clark Univ. (MA)
Cleveland State Univ.
Colgate Univ. (NY)
College of New Jersey
College of Notre Dame of
   Maryland
College of St. Catherine (MN)
College of William and Mary (VA)
College of Wooster (OH)
Connecticut College
Cornell College (IA)
Creighton Univ. (NE)
CUNY–City College
CUNY–College of Staten Island
CUNY–Hunter College
Denison Univ. (OH)

Depaul Univ. (IL)
Dickinson College (PA)
Dominican Univ. (IL)
Drake Univ. (IA)
Drury Univ. (MO)
Duquesne Univ. (PA)
Eastern Washington Univ.
Eckerd College (FL)
Edgewood College (WI)
Elmira College (NY)
Endicott College (MA)
Fairfield Univ. (CT)
Fairleigh Dickinson Univ. (NJ)
Ferrum College (VA)
Florida International Univ.
Florida State Univ.
Fordham Univ. (NY)
Francis Marion Univ. (SC)
Frostburg State Univ. (MD)
George Washington Univ. (DC)
Georgetown Univ. (DC)
Georgia Institute of Technology
Georgia Southern Univ.
Gonzaga Univ. (WA)
Gordon College (MA)
Goucher College (MD)
Graceland Univ. (IA)
Grand Canyon Univ. (AZ)
Grand Valley State Univ. (MI)
Guilford College (NC)
Hastings College (NE)
Hawaii Pacific Univ.
Hendrix College (AR)
Hobart and William Smith Colleges
   (NY)
Holy Names Univ. (CA)
Houghton College (NY)
Idaho State Univ.
Immaculata Univ. (PA)
Indiana Univ. of Pennsylvania
Indiana Univ. Southeast
Indiana Wesleyan Univ.
Jacksonville Univ. (FL)
James Madison Univ. (VA)
Johns Hopkins Univ. (MD)
Juniata College (PA)
Kennesaw State Univ. (GA)
Kent State Univ. (OH)
Knox College (IL)
La Roche College (PA)
Lafayette College (PA)
Lake Forest College (IL)
Lambuth Univ. (TN)
Le Moyne College (NY)
Lees-Mcrae College (NC)
Lehigh Univ. (PA)
Lewis and Clark College (OR)
Lincoln Univ. (PA)
Lindenwood Univ. (MO)
Lock Haven Univ. of Pennsylvania
Long Island Univ.–C.W. Post
   Campus (NY)
Loyola Univ. Chicago
Lynchburg College (VA)
Lynn Univ. (FL)
Macalester College (MN)
Manhattan College (NY)
Mars Hill College (NC)
Marshall Univ. (WV)
Mary Baldwin College (VA)
Marymount Manhattan Coll. (NY)

Maryville College (TN)
Mckendree College (IL)
Mercer Univ. (GA)
Methodist College (NC)
Miami Univ.–Oxford (OH)
Michigan State Univ.
Middle Tennessee State Univ.
Middlebury College (VT)
Millikin Univ. (IL)
Mills College (CA)
Minnesota State Univ.–Mankato
Missouri Southern State Univ.
Morehouse College (GA)
Morningside College (IA)
Mount Holyoke College (MA)
Mount Mary College (WI)
Mount St. Mary's Univ. (MD)
Mount Union College (OH)
Muhlenberg College (PA)
Murray State Univ. (KY)
Muskingum College (OH)
Nazareth College of Rochester
   (NY)
New York Univ.
Newberry College (SC)
North Central College (IL)
North Park Univ. (IL)
Northeastern Univ. (MA)
Northern Arizona Univ.
Northern Kentucky Univ.
Northern Michigan Univ.
Northwest Nazarene Univ. (ID)
Northwestern Univ. (IL)
Norwich Univ. (VT)
Nova Southeastern Univ. (FL)
Occidental College (CA)
Oglethorpe Univ. (GA)
Ohio Northern Univ.
Ohio State Univ.–Columbus
Ohio Univ.
Ohio Wesleyan Univ.
Old Dominion Univ. (VA)
Oral Roberts Univ. (OK)
Otterbein College (OH)
Pacific Univ. (OR)
Penn. State Univ.–Univ. Park
Point Park Univ. (PA)
Pomona College (CA)
Portland State Univ. (OR)
Queens Univ. of Charlotte (NC)
Reed College (OR)
Regis College (MA)
Rhodes College (TN)
Rider Univ. (NJ)
Roanoke College (VA)
Rochester Institute of Tech.
   (NY)
Rockford College (IL)
Rollins College (FL)
Roosevelt Univ. (IL)
Salem College (NC)
Samford Univ. (AL)
San Diego State Univ.
San Francisco State Univ.
Scripps College (CA)
Seattle Univ.
Seton Hall Univ. (NJ)
Seton Hill Univ. (PA)
Shaw Univ. (NC)
Shawnee State Univ. (OH)
Simmons College (MA)

Simpson College (IA)
Sonoma State Univ. (CA)
Southern Methodist Univ. (TX)
Southern Nazarene Univ. (OK)
Southern Oregon Univ.
Southern Polytechnic State Univ.
   (GA)
Southwestern Univ. (TX)
Spring Hill College (AL)
St. Anselm College (NH)
St. Cloud State Univ. (MN)
St. Edward's Univ. (TX)
St. John Fisher College (NY)
St. Joseph College (CT)
St. Joseph's College (IN)
St. Joseph's Univ. (PA)
St. Leo Univ. (FL)
St. Louis Univ.
St. Mary's Univ. of San Antonio
St. Norbert College (WI)
Stanford Univ. (CA)
State Univ. of West Georgia
Stetson Univ. (FL)
Stonehill College (MA)
SUNY College of Arts and
   Sciences–Geneseo
SUNY College–Brockport
Susquehanna Univ. (PA)
Sweet Briar College (VA)
Syracuse Univ. (NY)
Taylor Univ. (IN)
Texas A&M Univ.–Commerce
Texas Christian Univ.
Texas State Univ.–San Marcos
Texas Wesleyan Univ.
Thomas More College (KY)
Tiffin Univ. (OH)
Towson Univ. (MD)
Trinity College (DC)
Tufts Univ. (MA)
Tulane Univ. (LA)
Union College (NE)
Univ. of Akron (OH)
Univ. of Alabama
Univ. of Arkansas
Univ. of Bridgeport (CT)
Univ. of California–Davis
Univ. of California–Riverside
Univ. of Chicago
Univ. of Delaware
Univ. of Denver
Univ. of Evansville (IN)
Univ. of Georgia
Univ. of Indianapolis
Univ. of Judaism (CA)
Univ. of Kansas
Univ. of La Verne (CA)
Univ. of Maine–Farmington
Univ. of Maine–Orono
Univ. of Mary Washington (VA)
Univ. of Massachusetts–Boston
Univ. of Memphis
Univ. of Miami (FL)
Univ. of Minnesota–Duluth
Univ. of Minnesota–Twin Cities
Univ. of Mississippi
Univ. of Nebraska–Kearney
Univ. of Nebraska–Lincoln
Univ. of Nevada–Reno
Univ. of New Hampshire
Univ. of Pennsylvania

Univ. of Redlands (CA)
Univ. of Richmond (VA)
Univ. of San Diego
Univ. of Scranton (PA)
Univ. of South Carolina–Columbia
Univ. of South Florida
Univ. of Southern California
Univ. of Southern Indiana
Univ. of St. Mary (KS)
Univ. of St. Thomas (MN)
Univ. of Tennessee–Martin
Univ. of the Pacific (CA)
Univ. of Toledo (OH)
Univ. of Virginia
Univ. of West Florida
Univ. of Wisconsin–Parkside
Univ. of Wisconsin–Whitewater
Univ. of Wyoming
Ursinus College (PA)
Utica College (NY)
Valparaiso Univ. (IN)
Vassar College (NY)
Virginia Military Institute
Virginia Tech
Wagner College (NY)
Wartburg College (IA)
Washington College (MD)
Washington Univ. In St. Louis
Webster Univ. (MO)
Wellesley College (MA)
Wesleyan College (GA)
West Virginia Wesleyan College
Westminster College (PA)
Westminster College (MO)
Wheaton College (MA)
Wheaton College (IL)
Wheeling Jesuit Univ. (WV)
Widener Univ. (PA)
Wilkes Univ. (PA)
William Jewell College (MO)
William Woods Univ. (MO)
Wilson College (PA)
Xavier Univ. (OH)
York College of Pennsylvania

International/Global Studies

Assumption College (MA)
Bethel College (IN)
Brandeis Univ. (MA)
Clark Univ. (MA)
Elon Univ. (NC)
Hampshire College (MA)
Hanover College (IN)
High Point Univ. (NC)
Lawrence Univ. (WI)
National Univ. (CA)
Oglethorpe Univ. (GA)
Russell Sage College (NY)
Shorter College (GA)
SUNY College–Oneonta
Univ. of California–San Diego
Univ. of California–Santa Barbara
Wright State Univ. (OH)

Iranian/Persian Languages, Literatures, and Linguistics

Univ. of Texas–Austin

Journalism

Abilene Christian Univ. (TX)
Adrian College (MI)
Allegheny College (PA)
American Univ. (DC)
Anderson College (SC)
Andrews Univ. (MI)
Angelo State Univ. (TX)
Appalachian State Univ. (NC)
Arcadia Univ. (PA)
Arizona State Univ.
Arkansas State Univ.
Arkansas Tech Univ.
Asbury College (KY)
Ashland Univ. (OH)
Auburn Univ. (AL)
Augustana College (SD)
Averett Univ. (VA)
Ball State Univ. (IN)
Barry Univ. (FL)
Baylor Univ. (TX)
Belmont Univ. (TN)
Bennington College (VT)
Bethel Univ. (MN)
Bethune-Cookman College (FL)
Biola Univ. (CA)
Boston Univ.
Bowie State Univ. (MD)
Bowling Green State Univ. (OH)
Bradley Univ. (IL)
Briar Cliff Univ. (IA)
Brigham Young Univ.–Provo (UT)
Butler Univ. (IN)
Cal Poly–San Luis Obispo
California Baptist Univ.
California Lutheran Univ.
California State Univ.–Chico
California State Univ.–Fullerton
California State Univ.–Long Beach
California State Univ.–Monterey
   Bay
California State Univ.–Northridge
California State Univ.–Sacramento
Campbell Univ. (NC)
Campbellsville Univ. (KY)
Carroll College (WI)
Carson-Newman College (TN)
Central Michigan Univ.
Central Missouri State Univ.
Central State Univ. (OH)
Central Washington Univ.
Champlain College (VT)
Chapman Univ. (CA)
Chatham College (PA)
Clarke College (IA)
College of St. Joseph (VT)
College of the Ozarks (MO)
Colorado State Univ.
Columbia College (IL)
Columbia College (SC)
Columbia Union College (MD)
Concord College (WV)

Concordia Coll.–Moorhead (MN)
Concordia Univ. (MI)
Concordia Univ. (NE)
Corcoran College of Art and Design
   (DC)
Creighton Univ. (NE)
CUNY–Baruch College
CUNY–Brooklyn College
CUNY–Lehman College
Dana College (NE)
David Lipscomb Univ. (TN)
Delaware State Univ.
Delta State Univ. (MS)
Dominican Univ. (IL)
Dordt College (IA)
Drake Univ. (IA)
Drury Univ. (MO)
Duquesne Univ. (PA)
East Carolina Univ. (NC)
Eastern Illinois Univ.
Eastern Kentucky Univ.
Eastern Michigan Univ.
Eastern Washington Univ.
Edinboro Univ. of Pennsylvania
Edward Waters College (FL)
Elon Univ. (NC)
Emerson College (MA)
Evangel Univ. (MO)
Florida A&M Univ.
Fort Valley State Univ. (GA)
Franklin College (IN)
Gardner-Webb Univ. (NC)
George Washington Univ. (DC)
Georgia College and State Univ.
Georgia Southern Univ.
Georgia State Univ.
Gonzaga Univ. (WA)
Grand Canyon Univ. (AZ)
Grand Valley State Univ. (MI)
Grand View College (IA)
Hampton Univ. (VA)
Hardin-Simmons Univ. (TX)
Harding Univ. (AR)
Hastings College (NE)
Hawaii Pacific Univ.
Heidelberg College (OH)
Henderson State Univ. (AR)
Hillsdale College (MI)
Hofstra Univ. (NY)
Howard Univ. (DC)
Humboldt State Univ. (CA)
Huntington College (IN)
Illinois State Univ.
Indiana State Univ.
Indiana Univ. Northwest
Indiana Univ. of Pennsylvania
Indiana Univ. Southeast
Indiana Univ.–South Bend
Indiana Univ.-Purdue
   Univ.–Indianapolis
Iona College (NY)
Iowa State Univ.
Ithaca College (NY)
John Brown Univ. (AR)
Johnson State College (VT)
Kansas State Univ.
Keene State College (NH)
Kent State Univ. (OH)
Lake Erie College (OH)
Lehigh Univ. (PA)
Liberty Univ. (VA)

Lincoln Univ. (MO)
Lincoln Univ. (PA)
Lock Haven Univ. of Pennsylvania
Long Island Univ.–Brooklyn (NY)
Long Island Univ.–C.W. Post
   Campus (NY)
Louisiana College
Louisiana Tech Univ.
Loyola Univ. Chicago
Lyndon State College (VT)
Macmurray College (IL)
Madonna Univ. (MI)
Mansfield Univ. of Pennsylvania
Marian College of Fond Du Lac
   (WI)
Marietta College (OH)
Marist College (NY)
Marquette Univ. (WI)
Marshall Univ. (WV)
Marywood Univ. (PA)
Master's Coll. and Seminary (CA)
Mercer Univ. (GA)
Messiah College (PA)
Metropolitan State College of
   Denver
Miami Univ.–Oxford (OH)
Michigan State Univ.
Midland Lutheran College (NE)
Mississippi Univ. For Women
Morningside College (IA)
Morris College (SC)
Murray State Univ. (KY)
Muskingum College (OH)
New Mexico State Univ.
New York Univ.
Norfolk State Univ. (VA)
North Carolina A&T State Univ.
North Central College (IL)
North Greenville College (SC)
Northeastern State Univ. (OK)
Northeastern Univ. (MA)
Northern Arizona Univ.
Northern Illinois Univ.
Northern Kentucky Univ.
Northwestern State Univ. of
   Louisiana
Northwestern Univ. (IL)
Oakland Univ. (MI)
Ohio Northern Univ.
Ohio State Univ.–Columbus
Ohio Univ.
Ohio Wesleyan Univ.
Oklahoma Baptist Univ.
Oklahoma Christian Univ.
Oklahoma State Univ.
Olivet Nazarene Univ. (IL)
Oral Roberts Univ. (OK)
Otterbein College (OH)
Paine College (GA)
Palm Beach Atlantic Univ. (FL)
Penn. State Univ.–Univ. Park
Pepperdine Univ. (CA)
Point Loma Nazarene Univ. (CA)
Point Park Univ. (PA)
Polytechnic Univ. (NY)
Prescott College (AZ)
Queens Univ. of Charlotte (NC)
Radford Univ. (VA)
Rider Univ. (NJ)
Rivier College (NH)
Rochester Institute of Tech. (NY)

Roosevelt Univ. (IL)
Rust College (MS)
Rutgers–New Brunswick (NJ)
Rutgers–Newark (NJ)
Sam Houston State Univ. (TX)
Samford Univ. (AL)
San Diego State Univ.
San Francisco State Univ.
San Jose State Univ. (CA)
Savannah State Univ. (GA)
Seattle Univ.
Seton Hill Univ. (PA)
Shippensburg Univ. of
   Pennsylvania
Simpson College (IA)
South Dakota State Univ.
Southeastern College of the
   Assemblies of God
Southern Adventist Univ. (TN)
Southern Arkansas Univ.
Southern Connecticut State Univ.
Southern Illinois Univ.–Carbondale
Southern Nazarene Univ. (OK)
Southern Oregon Univ.
Southwest Missouri State Univ.
Southwestern Adventist Univ. (TX)
St. Ambrose Univ. (IA)
St. Bonaventure Univ. (NY)
St. Gregory's Univ. (OK)
St. John's Univ. (NY)
St. Joseph's College (ME)
St. Mary-of-The-Woods Coll. (IN)
St. Michael's College (VT)
State Univ. of West Georgia
Stephen F. Austin State Univ. (TX)
Stephens College (MO)
Suffolk Univ. (MA)
SUNY College–Brockport
SUNY–Plattsburgh
SUNY–Purchase College
Susquehanna Univ. (PA)
Syracuse Univ. (NY)
Temple Univ. (PA)
Tennessee Technological Univ.
Texas A&M Univ.–College Station
Texas A&M Univ.–Commerce
Texas Christian Univ.
Texas State Univ.–San Marcos
Texas Tech Univ.
Texas Wesleyan Univ.
Texas Woman's Univ.
Thomas Edison State College (NJ)
Tougaloo College (MS)
Troy State Univ.–Troy (AL)
Truman State Univ. (MO)
Tulane Univ. (LA)
Union College (NE)
Union Univ. (TN)
Univ. of Akron (OH)
Univ. of Alabama
Univ. of Alaska–Anchorage
Univ. of Alaska–Fairbanks
Univ. of Arizona
Univ. of Arkansas
Univ. of Arkansas–Little Rock
Univ. of Arkansas–Pine Bluff
Univ. of California–Irvine
Univ. of Central Arkansas
Univ. of Central Florida
Univ. of Central Oklahoma
Univ. of Colorado–Boulder

Univ. of Connecticut
Univ. of Dayton (OH)
Univ. of Denver
Univ. of Findlay (OH)
Univ. of Florida
Univ. of Georgia
Univ. of Hawaii–Manoa
Univ. of Houston
Univ. of Ill.–Urbana-Champaign
Univ. of Iowa
Univ. of Judaism (CA)
Univ. of Kansas
Univ. of Kentucky
Univ. of La Verne (CA)
Univ. of Maine–Orono
Univ. of Maryland–College Park
Univ. of Massachusetts–Amherst
Univ. of Memphis
Univ. of Miami (FL)
Univ. of Michigan–Ann Arbor
Univ. of Minnesota–Twin Cities
Univ. of Mississippi
Univ. of Missouri–Columbia
Univ. of Montana
Univ. of Nebraska–Kearney
Univ. of Nebraska–Lincoln
Univ. of Nebraska–Omaha
Univ. of Nevada–Reno
Univ. of New Hampshire
Univ. of New Mexico
Univ. of North Texas
Univ. of Northern Colorado
Univ. of Oklahoma
Univ. of Oregon
Univ. of Pittsburgh–Johnstown
Univ. of Rhode Island
Univ. of Richmond (VA)
Univ. of Rio Grande (OH)
Univ. of South Carolina–Columbia
Univ. of Southern California
Univ. of Southern Indiana
Univ. of Southern Mississippi
Univ. of St. Thomas (MN)
Univ. of Tennessee
Univ. of Texas–Arlington
Univ. of Texas–Austin
Univ. of Texas–Pan American
Univ. of Texas–Tyler
Univ. of Washington
Univ. of Wisconsin–Eau Claire
Univ. of Wisconsin–Madison
Univ. of Wisconsin–Oshkosh
Univ. of Wisconsin–River Falls
Univ. of Wisconsin–Superior
Univ. of Wisconsin–Whitewater
Univ. of Wyoming
Utah State Univ.
Utica College (NY)
Valparaiso Univ. (IN)
Waldorf College (IA)
Washington and Lee Univ. (VA)
Wayne State Univ. (MI)
Weber State Univ. (UT)
Webster Univ. (MO)
West Texas A&M Univ.
West Virginia Univ.
Western Baptist College (OR)
Western Illinois Univ.
Western Kentucky Univ.
Western Michigan Univ.
Western Washington Univ.

Whitworth College (WA)
Widener Univ. (PA)
William Carey College (MS)
William Woods Univ. (MO)
Youngstown State Univ. (OH)

Landscape Architecture

Arizona State Univ.
Auburn Univ. (AL)
Ball State Univ. (IN)
Boston Architectural Center
Cal Poly–San Luis Obispo
California State Polytechnic
    Univ.–Pomona
Colorado State Univ.
Cornell Univ. (NY)
CUNY–City College
Iowa State Univ.
Kansas State Univ.
Louisiana State Univ.–Baton Rouge
Michigan State Univ.
Mississippi State Univ.
North Carolina A&T State Univ.
North Carolina State Univ.–Raleigh
North Dakota State Univ.
Ohio State Univ.–Columbus
Oklahoma State Univ.
Penn. State Univ.–Univ. Park
Philadelphia Univ.
Purdue Univ.–West Lafayette (IN)
SUNY College Environmental
    Science and Forestry
Temple Univ. (PA)
Texas A&M Univ.–College Station
Texas Tech Univ.
Univ. of Arkansas
Univ. of California–Berkeley
Univ. of California–Davis
Univ. of Connecticut
Univ. of Florida
Univ. of Georgia
Univ. of Ill.–Urbana-Champaign
Univ. of Kentucky
Univ. of Maine–Orono
Univ. of Maryland–College Park
Univ. of Massachusetts–Amherst
Univ. of Michigan–Ann Arbor
Univ. of Nebraska–Lincoln
Univ. of Nevada–Las Vegas
Univ. of Oregon
Univ. of Rhode Island
Univ. of Southern California
Univ. of Washington
Univ. of Wisconsin–Madison
Utah State Univ.
Virginia Tech
Washington State Univ.
West Virginia Univ.

Law (LL.B., J.D.)

North Carolina Central Univ.
Ohio Northern Univ.
Quinnipiac Univ. (CT)
Roger Williams Univ. (RI)
Southern Illinois Univ.–Carbondale
Texas Wesleyan Univ.
Tulane Univ. (LA)

Legal Professions and Studies

Ball State Univ. (IN)
Becker College (MA)
Brenau Univ. (GA)
Burlington College (VT)
Drake Univ. (IA)
Elms College (College of Our Lady
    of the Elms) (MA)
International College (FL)
Johnson and Wales Univ. (RI)
Pennsylvania College of Technology
Quinnipiac Univ. (CT)
Ramapo College of New Jersey
Regis College (MA)
St. Augustine's College (NC)
St. Joseph's Univ. (PA)
Syracuse Univ. (NY)
Teikyo Post Univ. (CT)
Tulane Univ. (LA)
United States Military Academy
    (NY)
Univ. of Dallas
Univ. of Findlay (OH)
Univ. of Illinois–Springfield
Univ. of Nebraska–Lincoln
Univ. of Pennsylvania
Univ. of Tulsa (OK)
William Woods Univ. (MO)

Legal Research and Advanced Professional Studies (Post-LL.B./J.D.)

Grambling State Univ. (LA)
James Madison Univ. (VA)

Legal Support Services

Anna Maria College (MA)
Avila Univ. (MO)
Bay Path College (MA)
Bentley College (MA)
Champlain College (VT)
College of Mount St. Joseph (OH)
CUNY–New York City College of
    Technology
Davenport Univ. (MI)
Drury Univ. (MO)
East Central Univ. (OK)
Eastern Kentucky Univ.
Eastern Michigan Univ.
Elms College (College of Our Lady
    of the Elms) (MA)
Florida Gulf Coast Univ.
Gannon Univ. (PA)
Grambling State Univ. (LA)
Hilbert College (NY)
Husson College (ME)
Indiana Wesleyan Univ.
Johnson and Wales Univ. (RI)
Kent State Univ. (OH)
Lake Superior State Univ. (MI)
Lewis-Clark State College (ID)
Lock Haven Univ. of Pennsylvania
Madonna Univ. (MI)
Marymount Univ. (VA)

Maryville Univ. of St. Louis (MO)
Marywood Univ. (PA)
Minnesota State Univ.–Moorhead
Mississippi College
Mississippi Univ. For Women
Morehead State Univ. (KY)
Mountain State Univ. (WV)
Myers Univ. (OH)
Northeastern State Univ. (OK)
Nova Southeastern Univ. (FL)
Roger Williams Univ. (RI)
Roosevelt Univ. (IL)
Shawnee State Univ. (OH)
Southern Illinois Univ.–Carbondale
Stephen F. Austin State Univ. (TX)
Suffolk Univ. (MA)
Texas A&M Univ.–Commerce
Texas Woman's Univ.
Thomas Edison State College (NJ)
Tulane Univ. (LA)
Univ. of Central Florida
Univ. of Detroit Mercy
Univ. of Great Falls (MT)
Univ. of Mississippi
Univ. of Southern Mississippi
Univ. of Tennessee–Chattanooga
Univ. of Toledo (OH)
Univ. of West Florida
Ursuline College (OH)
Utah Valley State College
Valdosta State Univ. (GA)
Villa Julie College (MD)
Virginia Intermont College
Washburn Univ. (KS)
Wesley College (DE)
William Jewell College (MO)
William Woods Univ. (MO)

Liberal Arts and Sciences Studies, and Humanities

Abilene Christian Univ. (TX)
Adams State College (CO)
Adelphi Univ. (NY)
Alaska Pacific Univ.
Albertson College (ID)
Albertus Magnus College (CT)
Albion College (MI)
Alcorn State Univ. (MS)
Alderson-Broaddus College (WV)
Alfred Univ. (NY)
Allen Univ. (SC)
Alma College (MI)
Alvernia College (PA)
Alverno College (WI)
American Univ. (DC)
Anderson Univ. (IN)
Andrews Univ. (MI)
Angelo State Univ. (TX)
Anna Maria College (MA)
Antioch College (OH)
Appalachian State Univ. (NC)
Aquinas College (MI)
Arcadia Univ. (PA)
Arizona State Univ.
Arkansas State Univ.
Arkansas Tech Univ.
Armstrong Atlantic State Univ.
    (GA)

Atlantic Union College (MA)
Auburn Univ.–Montgomery (AL)
Augustana College (SD)
Aurora Univ. (IL)
Austin Peay State Univ. (TN)
Averett Univ. (VA)
Avila Univ. (MO)
Azusa Pacific Univ. (CA)
Ball State Univ. (IN)
Barry Univ. (FL)
Barton College (NC)
Bay Path College (MA)
Baylor Univ. (TX)
Becker College (MA)
Belhaven College (MS)
Bellarmine Univ. (KY)
Bellevue Univ. (NE)
Belmont Abbey College (NC)
Belmont Univ. (TN)
Bemidji State Univ. (MN)
Benedictine Univ. (IL)
Bennington College (VT)
Bentley College (MA)
Bethel College (IN)
Bethel College (TN)
Bethune-Cookman College (FL)
Biola Univ. (CA)
Bluefield State College (WV)
Bowling Green State Univ. (OH)
Brenau Univ. (GA)
Brescia Univ. (KY)
Brewton-Parker College (GA)
Bridgewater College (VA)
Brigham Young Univ.–Hawaii
Brigham Young Univ.–Provo (UT)
Brown Univ. (RI)
Bryan College (TN)
Bucknell Univ. (PA)
Buffalo State College
Burlington College (VT)
Butler Univ. (IN)
Cabrini College (PA)
Cal Poly–San Luis Obispo
California Baptist Univ.
California Institute of Technology
California Lutheran Univ.
California State Univ.–Bakersfield
California State Univ.–Chico
California State Univ.–Dominguez
    Hills
California State Univ.–Fresno
California State Univ.–Fullerton
California State Univ.–Hayward
California State Univ.–Long Beach
California State Univ.–Los Angeles
California State Univ.–Monterey
    Bay
California State Univ.–Northridge
California State Univ.–Sacramento
California State Univ.–San
    Bernardino
California State Univ.–San Marcos
California State Univ.–Stanislaus
California Univ. of Pennsylvania
Calumet College of St. Joseph (IN)
Calvin College (MI)
Canisius College (NY)
Carlow College (PA)
Carnegie Mellon Univ. (PA)
Carson-Newman College (TN)
Carthage College (WI)

Catholic Univ. of America (DC)
Cazenovia College (NY)
Cedar Crest College (PA)
Centenary College (NJ)
Centenary College of Louisiana
Central Christian College (KS)
Central College (IA)
Central Michigan Univ.
Central Missouri State Univ.
Central Washington Univ.
Chadron State College (NE)
Champlain College (VT)
Chapman Univ. (CA)
Charleston Southern Univ. (SC)
Chestnut Hill College (PA)
Chicago State Univ.
Chowan College (NC)
Christian Brothers Univ. (TN)
Christian Heritage College (CA)
Clarion Univ. of Pennsylvania
Clark Atlanta Univ.
Clarkson Univ. (NY)
Clayton Coll. and State Univ. (GA)
Clearwater Christian College (FL)
Cleveland State Univ.
Coastal Carolina Univ. (SC)
Colgate Univ. (NY)
College For Lifelong Learning (NH)
College Misericordia (PA)
College of Mount St. Joseph (OH)
College of Mount St. Vincent (NY)
College of Notre Dame of
    Maryland
College of Santa Fe (NM)
College of St. Benedict (MN)
College of St. Joseph (VT)
College of St. Mary (NE)
College of St. Rose (NY)
College of St. Scholastica (MN)
College of the Southwest (NM)
Colorado Christian Univ.
Colorado College
Colorado State Univ.
Colorado State Univ.–Pueblo
Columbia College (MO)
Columbia College (IL)
Columbia College (SC)
Columbia Union College (MD)
Concord College (WV)
Concordia College (NY)
Concordia Univ. (CA)
Concordia Univ. (OR)
Concordia Univ. Wisconsin
Concordia Univ.–Austin (TX)
Concordia Univ.–River Forest (IL)
Cornell College (IA)
Cornell Univ. (NY)
Crichton College (TN)
Cumberland Univ. (TN)
CUNY–Baruch College
CUNY–Brooklyn College
CUNY–City College
CUNY–College of Staten Island
CUNY–Hunter College
Curry College (MA)
Dakota Wesleyan Univ. (SD)
Dallas Baptist Univ.
Dartmouth College (NH)
David Lipscomb Univ. (TN)
Delta State Univ. (MS)
Depaul Univ. (IL)

Desales Univ. (PA)
Dickinson State Univ. (ND)
Dominican Coll. of Blauvelt (NY)
Dominican Univ. (IL)
Dominican Univ. of California (CA)
Dordt College (IA)
Dowling College (NY)
Drexel Univ. (PA)
Drury Univ. (MO)
Duquesne Univ. (PA)
East Carolina Univ. (NC)
East Central Univ. (OK)
East Stroudsburg Univ. of
    Pennsylvania
East Tennessee State Univ.
East Texas Baptist Univ.
East-West Univ. (IL)
Eastern Connecticut State Univ.
Eastern Illinois Univ.
Eastern Kentucky Univ.
Eastern Mennonite Univ. (VA)
Eastern Nazarene College (MA)
Eastern New Mexico Univ.
Eastern Oregon Univ.
Eastern Washington Univ.
Eckerd College (FL)
Edinboro Univ. of Pennsylvania
Elmhurst College (IL)
Elmira College (NY)
Elms College (College of Our Lady
    of the Elms) (MA)
Emporia State Univ. (KS)
Endicott College (MA)
Evergreen State College (WA)
Excelsior College (NY)
Fairfield Univ. (CT)
Fairleigh Dickinson Univ. (NJ)
Faulkner Univ. (AL)
Felician College (NJ)
Ferrum College (VA)
Fitchburg State College (MA)
Flagler College (FL)
Florida Atlantic Univ.
Florida Gulf Coast Univ.
Florida Institute of Technology
Florida International Univ.
Florida Southern College
Florida State Univ.
Fontbonne Univ. (MO)
Fordham Univ. (NY)
Fort Hays State Univ. (KS)
Fort Lewis College (CO)
Framingham State College (MA)
Francis Marion Univ. (SC)
Franciscan Univ. of Steubenville
    (OH)
Franklin Pierce College (NH)
Fresno Pacific Univ. (CA)
Friends Univ. (KS)
Frostburg State Univ. (MD)
Gannon Univ. (PA)
George Mason Univ. (VA)
George Washington Univ. (DC)
Georgetown College (KY)
Georgetown Univ. (DC)
Georgia College and State Univ.
Georgia Southern Univ.
Georgian Court Univ. (NJ)
Glenville State College (WV)
Goddard College (VT)
Golden Gate Univ. (CA)

Gonzaga Univ. (WA)
Grace Univ. (NE)
Graceland Univ. (IA)
Grand Canyon Univ. (AZ)
Grand Valley State Univ. (MI)
Grand View College (IA)
Green Mountain College (VT)
Greenville College (IL)
Hampden-Sydney College (VA)
Hannibal-Lagrange College (MO)
Harding Univ. (AR)
Harvard Univ. (MA)
Hastings College (NE)
Haverford College (PA)
Hawaii Pacific Univ.
Heritage College (WA)
Hilbert College (NY)
Hobart and William Smith Colleges
    (NY)
Hofstra Univ. (NY)
Holy Family Univ. (PA)
Holy Names Univ. (CA)
Hope College (MI)
Houghton College (NY)
Houston Baptist Univ.
Howard Payne Univ. (TX)
Humboldt State Univ. (CA)
Huntingdon College (AL)
Idaho State Univ.
Illinois State Univ.
Indiana State Univ.
Indiana Univ. East
Indiana Univ. Northwest
Indiana Univ. of Pennsylvania
Indiana Univ. Southeast
Indiana Univ.–Bloomington
Indiana Univ.–Kokomo
Indiana Univ.–South Bend
Indiana Univ.–Purdue Univ.–Fort
    Wayne
Indiana Univ.-Purdue
    Univ.–Indianapolis
Indiana Wesleyan Univ.
Iona College (NY)
Iowa State Univ.
Ithaca College (NY)
Jacksonville State Univ. (AL)
Jacksonville Univ. (FL)
James Madison Univ. (VA)
John Carroll Univ. (OH)
Johns Hopkins Univ. (MD)
Johnson C. Smith Univ. (NC)
Johnson State College (VT)
Juniata College (PA)
Kalamazoo College (MI)
Kansas State Univ.
Kean Univ. (NJ)
Keene State College (NH)
Kent State Univ. (OH)
Kentucky Christian College
Kentucky State Univ.
Keuka College (NY)
Knox College (IL)
Kutztown Univ. of Pennsylvania
La Roche College (PA)
La Sierra Univ. (CA)
Lake Forest College (IL)
Lake Superior State Univ. (MI)
Lambuth Univ. (TN)
Lander Univ. (SC)
Lasell College (MA)

Lawrence Technological Univ. (MI)
Lemoyne-Owen College (TN)
Lenoir-Rhyne College (NC)
Lesley Univ. (MA)
Lewis and Clark College (OR)
Liberty Univ. (VA)
Limestone College (SC)
Lincoln Memorial Univ. (TN)
Lincoln Univ. (MO)
Lindenwood Univ. (MO)
Lindsey Wilson College (KY)
Lock Haven Univ. of Pennsylvania
Long Island Univ.–C.W. Post
    Campus (NY)
Longwood Univ. (VA)
Louisiana College
Louisiana State Univ.–Baton Rouge
Louisiana State Univ.–Shreveport
Louisiana Tech Univ.
Loyola Marymount Univ. (CA)
Loyola Univ. Chicago
Loyola Univ. New Orleans
Lubbock Christian Univ. (TX)
Lynn Univ. (FL)
Macalester College (MN)
Macmurray College (IL)
Madonna Univ. (MI)
Malone College (OH)
Manhattan College (NY)
Manhattanville College (NY)
Mansfield Univ. of Pennsylvania
Marian College of Fond Du Lac
    (WI)
Marist College (NY)
Marlboro College (VT)
Marshall Univ. (WV)
Martin Univ. (IN)
Marylhurst Univ. (OR)
Marymount Manhattan College
    (NY)
Marymount Univ. (VA)
Maryville Univ. of St. Louis (MO)
Massachusetts Institute of
    Technology
Master's Coll. and Seminary (CA)
Mayville State Univ. (ND)
Mckendree College (IL)
Mcneese State Univ. (LA)
Medaille College (NY)
Mercer Univ. (GA)
Mercyhurst College (PA)
Merrimack College (MA)
Mesa State College (CO)
Messiah College (PA)
Michigan State Univ.
Michigan Technological Univ.
Middle Tennessee State Univ.
Middlebury College (VT)
Midwestern State Univ. (TX)
Milligan College (TN)
Mills College (CA)
Minnesota State Univ.–Mankato
Minot State Univ. (ND)
Mississippi State Univ.
Missouri Valley College
Molloy College (NY)
Montana State Univ.–Billings
Montana State Univ.–Bozeman
Montana State Univ.–Northern
Montana Tech of the Univ. of
    Montana

Montclair State Univ. (NJ)
Morehead State Univ. (KY)
Morris College (SC)
Mount Ida College (MA)
Mount Marty College (SD)
Mount St. Mary's College (CA)
Murray State Univ. (KY)
Muskingum College (OH)
National Univ. (CA)
Neumann College (PA)
New Mexico Institute of Mining
    and Technology
New Mexico State Univ.
New School Univ. (NY)
New York Univ.
Nicholls State Univ. (LA)
North Carolina State Univ.–Raleigh
North Central College (IL)
North Dakota State Univ.
Northeastern State Univ. (OK)
Northeastern Univ. (MA)
Northern Arizona Univ.
Northern Illinois Univ.
Northern Kentucky Univ.
Northern Michigan Univ.
Northern State Univ. (SD)
Northland College (WI)
Northwest Christian College (OR)
Northwest Missouri State Univ.
Northwest Nazarene Univ. (ID)
Northwestern College (IA)
Northwestern Oklahoma State
    Univ.
Northwestern State Univ. of
    Louisiana
Northwestern Univ. (IL)
Notre Dame De Namur Univ. (CA)
Nova Southeastern Univ. (FL)
Nyack College (NY)
Oakland City Univ. (IN)
Oakland Univ. (MI)
Oakwood College (AL)
Ohio Dominican Univ.
Ohio State Univ.–Columbus
Ohio Univ.
Ohio Valley College (WV)
Ohio Wesleyan Univ.
Oklahoma Baptist Univ.
Oklahoma Christian Univ.
Oklahoma City Univ.
Oklahoma Panhandle State Univ.
Oklahoma State Univ.
Olivet College (MI)
Olivet Nazarene Univ. (IL)
Oral Roberts Univ. (OK)
Oregon State Univ.
Otterbein College (OH)
Our Lady of Holy Cross Coll. (LA)
Our Lady of the Lake Univ. (TX)
Pace Univ. (NY)
Pacific Univ. (OR)
Palm Beach Atlantic Univ. (FL)
Park Univ. (MO)
Patten College (CA)
Peace College (NC)
Penn. State Univ.–Univ. Park
Penn. State–Erie, The Behrend
    College
Pepperdine Univ. (CA)
Peru State College (NE)
Pfeiffer Univ. (NC)

Pine Manor College (MA)
Pittsburg State Univ. (KS)
Plymouth State Univ. (NH)
Point Loma Nazarene Univ. (CA)
Point Park Univ. (PA)
Polytechnic Univ. (NY)
Providence College (RI)
Purdue Univ.–North Central (IN)
Purdue Univ.–West Lafayette (IN)
Quincy Univ. (IL)
Quinnipiac Univ. (CT)
Radford Univ. (VA)
Ramapo College of New Jersey
Regis College (MA)
Regis Univ. (CO)
Reinhardt College (GA)
Rhode Island College
Richard Stockton College of New Jersey
Rider Univ. (NJ)
Rivier College (NH)
Roberts Wesleyan College (NY)
Roger Williams Univ. (RI)
Roosevelt Univ. (IL)
Rosemont College (PA)
Rutgers–Camden (NJ)
Sacred Heart Univ. (CT)
Salem International Univ. (WV)
Salem State College (MA)
Salisbury Univ. (MD)
Salve Regina Univ. (RI)
Samford Univ. (AL)
San Diego State Univ.
San Francisco State Univ.
San Jose State Univ. (CA)
Santa Clara Univ. (CA)
Sarah Lawrence College (NY)
Schreiner Univ. (TX)
Seattle Univ.
Seton Hall Univ. (NJ)
Seton Hill Univ. (PA)
Shaw Univ. (NC)
Shawnee State Univ. (OH)
Sheldon Jackson College (AK)
Shenandoah Univ. (VA)
Shimer College (IL)
Shorter College (GA)
Sierra Nevada College (NV)
Simpson College (IA)
Simpson Univ. (CA)
Skidmore College (NY)
Sonoma State Univ. (CA)
South Dakota State Univ.
Southeast Missouri State Univ.
Southeastern Louisiana Univ.
Southeastern Oklahoma State Univ.
Southeastern Univ. (DC)
Southern Arkansas Univ.
Southern Connecticut State Univ.
Southern Illinois Univ.–Carbondale
Southern Illinois Univ.–Edwardsville
Southern Methodist Univ. (TX)
Southern New Hampshire Univ.
Southwest Missouri State Univ.
Southwestern Adventist Univ. (TX)
Southwestern College (KS)
Southwestern Univ. (TX)
Spalding Univ. (KY)
Spring Hill College (AL)

Springfield College (MA)
St. Andrews Presbyterian College (NC)
St. Anselm College (NH)
St. Cloud State Univ. (MN)
St. Edward's Univ. (TX)
St. Francis College (NY)
St. Gregory's Univ. (OK)
St. John Fisher College (NY)
St. John's Univ. (MN)
St. John's Univ. (NY)
St. Joseph College (CT)
St. Joseph's College, New York
St. Joseph's Univ. (PA)
St. Lawrence Univ. (NY)
St. Louis Univ.
St. Martin's College (WA)
St. Mary's College (IN)
St. Mary's College of California
St. Mary-of-The-Woods Coll. (IN)
St. Norbert College (WI)
St. Olaf College (MN)
St. Peter's College (NJ)
St. Thomas Aquinas College (NY)
St. Thomas Univ. (FL)
St. Vincent College (PA)
St. Xavier Univ. (IL)
Stephen F. Austin State Univ. (TX)
Stetson Univ. (FL)
Stevens Institute of Technology (NJ)
Suffolk Univ. (MA)
SUNY College–Old Westbury
SUNY College–Potsdam
SUNY–Fredonia
SUNY–Plattsburgh
SUNY–Stony Brook
Sweet Briar College (VA)
Syracuse Univ. (NY)
Tabor College (KS)
Tarleton State Univ. (TX)
Teikyo Post Univ. (CT)
Temple Univ. (PA)
Tennessee State Univ.
Texas A&M Univ.–Galveston
Texas Christian Univ.
Texas College
Texas Tech Univ.
Texas Woman's Univ.
The Franciscan Univ. (IA)
Thomas Aquinas College (CA)
Thomas Edison State College (NJ)
Thomas More College (KY)
Thomas Univ. (GA)
Tiffin Univ. (OH)
Tougaloo College (MS)
Touro College (NY)
Transylvania Univ. (KY)
Tri-State Univ. (IN)
Trinity College (DC)
Troy State Univ.–Troy (AL)
Tulane Univ. (LA)
Union College (NY)
Union College (NE)
Union Institute and Univ. (OH)
United States Air Force Academy (CO)
Unity College (ME)
Univ. at Buffalo–SUNY
Univ. of Akron (OH)
Univ. of Alaska–Anchorage

Univ. of Alaska–Fairbanks
Univ. of Alaska–Southeast
Univ. of Arizona
Univ. of Arkansas–Little Rock
Univ. of Arkansas–Pine Bluff
Univ. of Bridgeport (CT)
Univ. of California–Irvine
Univ. of California–Los Angeles
Univ. of California–Riverside
Univ. of Central Florida
Univ. of Central Oklahoma
Univ. of Charleston (WV)
Univ. of Chicago
Univ. of Colorado–Boulder
Univ. of Colorado–Colorado Springs
Univ. of Connecticut
Univ. of Dayton (OH)
Univ. of Delaware
Univ. of Detroit Mercy
Univ. of Evansville (IN)
Univ. of Georgia
Univ. of Hartford (CT)
Univ. of Hawaii–Manoa
Univ. of Houston–Downtown
Univ. of Illinois–Chicago
Univ. of Illinois–Springfield
Univ. of Ill.–Urbana-Champaign
Univ. of Indianapolis
Univ. of Iowa
Univ. of Judaism (CA)
Univ. of Kansas
Univ. of Kentucky
Univ. of La Verne (CA)
Univ. of Louisiana–Lafayette
Univ. of Louisiana–Monroe
Univ. of Louisville (KY)
Univ. of Maine–Farmington
Univ. of Maine–Fort Kent
Univ. of Maine–Machias
Univ. of Maine–Orono
Univ. of Maine–Presque Isle
Univ. of Mary (ND)
Univ. of Mary Hardin-Baylor (TX)
Univ. of Mary Washington (VA)
Univ. of Maryland–Eastern Shore
Univ. of Maryland–Univ. College
Univ. of Massachusetts–Amherst
Univ. of Massachusetts–Lowell
Univ. of Memphis
Univ. of Miami (FL)
Univ. of Michigan–Ann Arbor
Univ. of Michigan–Dearborn
Univ. of Michigan–Flint
Univ. of Minnesota–Morris
Univ. of Mississippi
Univ. of Missouri–Columbia
Univ. of Missouri–Kansas City
Univ. of Missouri–St. Louis
Univ. of Montana
Univ. of Montana–Western
Univ. of Nebraska–Kearney
Univ. of Nebraska–Lincoln
Univ. of Nebraska–Omaha
Univ. of Nevada–Las Vegas
Univ. of Nevada–Reno
Univ. of New England (ME)
Univ. of New Hampshire
Univ. of New Haven (CT)
Univ. of New Mexico
Univ. of New Orleans

Univ. of North Alabama
Univ. of North Carolina–Asheville
Univ. of N.C.–Chapel Hill
Univ. of N.C.–Greensboro
Univ. of North Dakota
Univ. of North Florida
Univ. of North Texas
Univ. of Northern Iowa
Univ. of Notre Dame (IN)
Univ. of Oklahoma
Univ. of Oregon
Univ. of Pennsylvania
Univ. of Pittsburgh
Univ. of Pittsburgh–Greensburg
Univ. of Pittsburgh–Johnstown
Univ. of Redlands (CA)
Univ. of Rhode Island
Univ. of Richmond (VA)
Univ. of Rochester (NY)
Univ. of San Diego
Univ. of San Francisco
Univ. of Scranton (PA)
Univ. of Sioux Falls (SD)
Univ. of South Alabama
Univ. of South Carolina–Columbia
Univ. of South Carolina–Upstate
Univ. of South Dakota
Univ. of South Florida
Univ. of Southern California
Univ. of Southern Indiana
Univ. of Southern Maine
Univ. of St. Francis (IN)
Univ. of St. Francis (IL)
Univ. of St. Mary (KS)
Univ. of St. Thomas (MN)
Univ. of St. Thomas (TX)
Univ. of Tampa (FL)
Univ. of Tennessee–Chattanooga
Univ. of Texas of the Permian Basin
Univ. of Texas–Austin
Univ. of Texas–Dallas
Univ. of Texas–Pan American
Univ. of Texas–San Antonio
Univ. of Texas–Tyler
Univ. of the Ozarks (AR)
Univ. of the Pacific (CA)
Univ. of Toledo (OH)
Univ. of Tulsa (OK)
Univ. of Utah
Univ. of Vermont
Univ. of Virginia
Univ. of Virginia–Wise
Univ. of Washington
Univ. of West Florida
Univ. of Wisconsin–Green Bay
Univ. of Wisconsin–Milwaukee
Univ. of Wisconsin–Parkside
Univ. of Wisconsin–River Falls
Univ. of Wisconsin–Stevens Point
Univ. of Wisconsin–Superior
Univ. of Wisconsin–Whitewater
Univ. of Wyoming
Urbana Univ. (OH)
Ursuline College (OH)
Utah State Univ.
Utica College (NY)
Valdosta State Univ. (GA)
Vanguard Univ. of Southern California
Vassar College (NY)
Villanova Univ. (PA)

Virginia Commonwealth Univ.
Virginia Intermont College
Virginia State Univ.
Virginia Tech
Virginia Wesleyan College
Viterbo Univ. (WI)
Waldorf College (IA)
Warner Pacific College (OR)
Washburn Univ. (KS)
Washington and Jefferson College (PA)
Washington College (MD)
Washington State Univ.
Washington Univ. In St. Louis
Wesley College (DE)
Wesleyan College (GA)
West Chester Univ. of Pennsylvania
West Liberty State College (WV)
West Texas A&M Univ.
West Virginia Univ.
West Virginia Univ. Institute of Technology
Western Baptist College (OR)
Western Carolina Univ. (NC)
Western Connecticut State Univ.
Western Illinois Univ.
Western Kentucky Univ.
Western Michigan Univ.
Western New England College (MA)
Western New Mexico Univ.
Western Washington Univ.
Westfield State College (MA)
Westmont College (CA)
Wheeling Jesuit Univ. (WV)
Wheelock College (MA)
Whittier College (CA)
Whitworth College (WA)
Wichita State Univ. (KS)
Wilkes Univ. (PA)
Willamette Univ. (OR)
William Carey College (MS)
Williams Baptist College (AR)
Wilmington College (DE)
Wilmington College (OH)
Wingate Univ. (NC)
Winston-Salem State Univ. (NC)
Wittenberg Univ. (OH)
Wofford College (SC)
Woodbury Univ. (CA)
Worcester Polytechnic Institute (MA)
Wright State Univ. (OH)
Xavier Univ. (OH)
Yale Univ. (CT)
York College (NE)
York College of Pennsylvania
Youngstown State Univ. (OH)

Library Science

Univ. of Washington

Library Science/ Librarianship

Ball State Univ. (IN)
Chadron State College (NE)
Clarion Univ. of Pennsylvania

Kutztown Univ. of Pennsylvania
Miami Univ.–Oxford (OH)
Northwestern Oklahoma State Univ.
Univ. of Maine–Augusta
Univ. of Nebraska–Omaha
Univ. of Southern Mississippi

Management Information Systems and Services

Albertus Magnus College (CT)
Alliant International Univ. (CA)
American Univ. (DC)
Anderson College (SC)
Andrews Univ. (MI)
Angelo State Univ. (TX)
Anna Maria College (MA)
Appalachian State Univ. (NC)
Arcadia Univ. (PA)
Arizona State Univ.
Ashland Univ. (OH)
Auburn Univ. (AL)
Auburn Univ.–Montgomery (AL)
Augsburg College (MN)
Augusta State Univ. (GA)
Aurora Univ. (IL)
Avila Univ. (MO)
Azusa Pacific Univ. (CA)
Babson College (MA)
Baker College of Flint (MI)
Baker Univ. (KS)
Barry Univ. (FL)
Baylor Univ. (TX)
Bellevue Univ. (NE)
Belmont Univ. (TN)
Boston Univ.
Bowling Green State Univ. (OH)
Bradley Univ. (IL)
Bridgewater College (VA)
Bridgewater State College (MA)
Brigham Young Univ.–Provo (UT)
Buena Vista Univ. (IA)
Cabrini College (PA)
California State Univ.–Long Beach
California State Univ.–Sacramento
Calvin College (MI)
Campbell Univ. (NC)
Canisius College (NY)
Cardinal Stritch Univ. (WI)
Carroll College (WI)
Carthage College (WI)
Catholic Univ. of America (DC)
Cedarville Univ. (OH)
Central Connecticut State Univ.
Central Michigan Univ.
Chatham College (PA)
City Univ. (WA)
Claflin Univ. (SC)
Clarkson Univ. (NY)
Cleary Univ. (MI)
Cleveland State Univ.
College Misericordia (PA)
College of Santa Fe (NM)
College of St. Catherine (MN)
Colorado Christian Univ.
Colorado State Univ.
Columbus State Univ. (GA)
Concordia Coll.–Moorhead (MN)

Concordia Univ. (NE)
Concordia Univ.–St. Paul (MN)
Cornerstone Univ. (MI)
Culver-Stockton College (MO)
CUNY–Baruch College
CUNY–York College
Dallas Baptist Univ.
Davis and Elkins College (WV)
Delaware Valley College (PA)
Delta State Univ. (MS)
Desales Univ. (PA)
Dominican Coll. of Blauvelt (NY)
Drake Univ. (IA)
Drexel Univ. (PA)
Duquesne Univ. (PA)
East Carolina Univ. (NC)
East Texas Baptist Univ.
Eastern Kentucky Univ.
Eastern New Mexico Univ.
Eastern Univ. (PA)
Eastern Washington Univ.
Edgewood College (WI)
Excelsior College (NY)
Fairmont State Univ. (WV)
Fayetteville State Univ. (NC)
Florida Atlantic Univ.
Florida Gulf Coast Univ.
Florida Institute of Technology
Florida International Univ.
Florida Southern College
Florida State Univ.
Fort Lewis College (CO)
Framingham State College (MA)
Francis Marion Univ. (SC)
Freed-Hardeman Univ. (TN)
Fresno Pacific Univ. (CA)
Friends Univ. (KS)
Gallaudet Univ. (DC)
Gannon Univ. (PA)
Gardner-Webb Univ. (NC)
George Fox Univ. (OR)
Georgetown Univ. (DC)
Georgia Southern Univ.
Georgia Southwestern State Univ.
Grace College and Seminary (IN)
Graceland Univ. (IA)
Greenville College (IL)
Hawaii Pacific Univ.
Henderson State Univ. (AR)
High Point Univ. (NC)
Hofstra Univ. (NY)
Holy Family Univ. (PA)
Houston Baptist Univ.
Howard Univ. (DC)
Humphreys College (CA)
Illinois College
Indiana State Univ.
Indiana Univ. of Pennsylvania
Indiana Univ. Southeast
Indiana Wesleyan Univ.
Iona College (NY)
Iowa State Univ.
Jamestown College (ND)
John Carroll Univ. (OH)
Judson College (IL)
Juniata College (PA)
Kent State Univ. (OH)
Kettering Univ. (MI)
La Salle Univ. (PA)
La Sierra Univ. (CA)
Lake Erie College (OH)

Lamar Univ. (TX)
Lasell College (MA)
Le Moyne College (NY)
Lenoir-Rhyne College (NC)
Letourneau Univ. (TX)
Lewis Univ. (IL)
Liberty Univ. (VA)
Lindenwood Univ. (MO)
Loras College (IA)
Louisiana Tech Univ.
Loyola Univ. Chicago
Luther College (IA)
Macmurray College (IL)
Madonna Univ. (MI)
Marian College (IN)
Maryville Univ. of St. Louis (MO)
Marywood Univ. (PA)
Master's Coll. and Seminary (CA)
Mesa State College (CO)
Metropolitan State College of Denver
Miami Univ.–Oxford (OH)
Middle Tennessee State Univ.
Midland Lutheran College (NE)
Midwestern State Univ. (TX)
Millikin Univ. (IL)
Milwaukee School of Engineering
Minot State Univ. (ND)
Mississippi State Univ.
Missouri Southern State Univ.
Monmouth College (IL)
Montana Tech of the Univ. of Montana
Morehead State Univ. (KY)
Mount St. Mary's Univ. (MD)
Muhlenberg College (PA)
Murray State Univ. (KY)
National-Louis Univ. (IL)
New Mexico Highlands Univ.
New York Institute of Technology
Nicholls State Univ. (LA)
Nichols College (MA)
North Central College (IL)
North Dakota State Univ.
North Park Univ. (IL)
Northeastern State Univ. (OK)
Northeastern Univ. (MA)
Northern Arizona Univ.
Northern Kentucky Univ.
Northern Michigan Univ.
Northern State Univ. (SD)
Northwest Christian College (OR)
Northwest Missouri State Univ.
Northwestern College (MN)
Northwood Univ. (MI)
Notre Dame College of Ohio
Oakland City Univ. (IN)
Oakland Univ. (MI)
Ohio State Univ.–Columbus
Ohio Univ.
Oklahoma State Univ.
Oklahoma Wesleyan Univ.
Old Dominion Univ. (VA)
Oral Roberts Univ. (OK)
Oregon Institute of Technology
Paine College (GA)
Park Univ. (MO)
Penn. State Univ.–Univ. Park
Penn. State–Erie, The Behrend College
Pfeiffer Univ. (NC)

Point Loma Nazarene Univ. (CA)
Polytechnic Univ. (NY)
Prairie View A&M Univ. (TX)
Purdue Univ.–Calumet (IN)
Reinhardt College (GA)
Rhode Island College
Rivier College (NH)
Robert Morris Univ. (PA)
Rochester Institute of Tech. (NY)
Rocky Mountain College (MT)
Roger Williams Univ. (RI)
Rutgers–Newark (NJ)
Sam Houston State Univ. (TX)
Santa Clara Univ. (CA)
Schreiner Univ. (TX)
Seton Hall Univ. (NJ)
Seton Hill Univ. (PA)
Shawnee State Univ. (OH)
Simmons College (MA)
Simpson Univ. (CA)
Southeastern College of the Assemblies of God
Southern Adventist Univ. (TN)
Southern Connecticut State Univ.
Southern Illinois Univ.–Edwardsville
Southern New Hampshire Univ.
Southwest Missouri State Univ.
Southwestern College (KS)
Spring Arbor Univ. (MI)
St. Bonaventure Univ. (NY)
St. Cloud State Univ. (MN)
St. Gregory's Univ. (OK)
St. John's Univ. (NY)
St. Joseph's College (IN)
St. Joseph's Univ. (PA)
St. Leo Univ. (FL)
St. Louis Univ.
St. Mary's College (IN)
St. Mary's Univ. of San Antonio
St. Paul's College (VA)
St. Xavier Univ. (IL)
State Univ. of West Georgia
Stetson Univ. (FL)
Stevens Institute of Technology (NJ)
Suffolk Univ. (MA)
Tarleton State Univ. (TX)
Temple Univ. (PA)
Texas A&M International Univ.
Texas A&M Univ.–Commerce
Texas A&M Univ.–Corpus Christi
Texas State Univ.–San Marcos
Texas Tech Univ.
Texas Wesleyan Univ.
Thiel College (PA)
Thomas Edison State College (NJ)
Touro College (NY)
Trevecca Nazarene Univ. (TN)
Tri-State Univ. (IN)
Tulane Univ. (LA)
Univ. of Akron (OH)
Univ. of Alabama
Univ. of Alabama–Birmingham
Univ. of Alabama–Huntsville
Univ. of Alaska–Anchorage
Univ. of Arizona
Univ. of Arkansas–Little Rock
Univ. of Bridgeport (CT)
Univ. of Central Arkansas
Univ. of Central Florida

Univ. of Connecticut
Univ. of Dayton (OH)
Univ. of Denver
Univ. of Georgia
Univ. of Hartford (CT)
Univ. of Hawaii–Manoa
Univ. of Houston
Univ. of Houston–Downtown
Univ. of Illinois–Chicago
Univ. of Ill.–Urbana-Champaign
Univ. of Indianapolis
Univ. of Kansas
Univ. of Louisiana–Lafayette
Univ. of Louisiana–Monroe
Univ. of Louisville (KY)
Univ. of Maine–Orono
Univ. of Mary Hardin-Baylor (TX)
Univ. of Memphis
Univ. of Michigan–Dearborn
Univ. of Minnesota–Crookston
Univ. of Minnesota–Duluth
Univ. of Minnesota–Twin Cities
Univ. of Mississippi
Univ. of Missouri–Rolla
Univ. of Missouri–St. Louis
Univ. of Montana
Univ. of Montevallo (AL)
Univ. of Nebraska–Omaha
Univ. of Nevada–Las Vegas
Univ. of Nevada–Reno
Univ. of New Orleans
Univ. of North Alabama
Univ. of North Carolina–Charlotte
Univ. of N.C.–Wilmington
Univ. of North Texas
Univ. of Northern Iowa
Univ. of Notre Dame (IN)
Univ. of Oklahoma
Univ. of Pennsylvania
Univ. of Puget Sound (WA)
Univ. of Redlands (CA)
Univ. of Rhode Island
Univ. of Rio Grande (OH)
Univ. of South Florida
Univ. of Southern Mississippi
Univ. of St. Thomas (TX)
Univ. of Tennessee–Martin
Univ. of Texas–Arlington
Univ. of Texas–Austin
Univ. of Texas–El Paso
Univ. of Texas–Pan American
Univ. of Texas–San Antonio
Univ. of Toledo (OH)
Univ. of Tulsa (OK)
Univ. of Utah
Univ. of Washington
Univ. of West Alabama
Univ. of West Florida
Univ. of Wisconsin–Eau Claire
Univ. of Wisconsin–Green Bay
Univ. of Wisconsin–La Crosse
Univ. of Wisconsin–Madison
Univ. of Wisconsin–Milwaukee
Univ. of Wisconsin–Oshkosh
Univ. of Wisconsin–Parkside
Univ. of Wisconsin–Superior
Univ. of Wyoming
Upper Iowa Univ.
Ursuline College (OH)
Villa Julie College (MD)
Villanova Univ. (PA)

Viterbo Univ. (WI)
Wake Forest Univ. (NC)
Walsh Univ. (OH)
Washington State Univ.
Wayne State Univ. (MI)
Weber State Univ. (UT)
West Texas A&M Univ.
West Virginia Univ.
West Virginia Univ. Institute of
 Technology
Western Baptist College (OR)
Western Carolina Univ. (NC)
Western Connecticut State Univ.
Western Illinois Univ.
Western Kentucky Univ.
Western Michigan Univ.
Western New England College
 (MA)
Western New Mexico Univ.
Western State College of Colorado
Western Washington Univ.
Westminster College (UT)
Westminster College (MO)
Wichita State Univ. (KS)
Widener Univ. (PA)
William Penn Univ. (IA)
Wilmington College (DE)
Worcester Polytechnic Institute
 (MA)
Wright State Univ. (OH)
Xavier Univ. (OH)
York College of Pennsylvania
Youngstown State Univ. (OH)

Management Sciences and Quantitative Methods

Antioch College (OH)
Arcadia Univ. (PA)
Aurora Univ. (IL)
Averett Univ. (VA)
Babson College (MA)
Ball State Univ. (IN)
Bellarmine Univ. (KY)
Bellevue Univ. (NE)
Belmont Univ. (TN)
Boston Univ.
Bradley Univ. (IL)
Brigham Young Univ.–Provo (UT)
Bryant College (RI)
Butler Univ. (IN)
Caldwell College (NJ)
Carroll College (WI)
Central Michigan Univ.
Central Missouri State Univ.
Christopher Newport Univ. (VA)
Cleveland State Univ.
Colorado Christian Univ.
Colorado State Univ.
Columbus State Univ. (GA)
Cumberland Univ. (TN)
CUNY–Baruch College
CUNY–Queens College
Delaware State Univ.
Drake Univ. (IA)
Duquesne Univ. (PA)
Eastern Illinois Univ.
Eastern Michigan Univ.
Elizabethtown College (PA)

Elmhurst College (IL)
Fitchburg State College (MA)
Florida State Univ.
Georgia College and State Univ.
Georgia State Univ.
Grand Valley State Univ. (MI)
Gwynedd-Mercy College (PA)
Hampton Univ. (VA)
Hardin-Simmons Univ. (TX)
Hofstra Univ. (NY)
Illinois State Univ.
Indiana State Univ.
Indiana Univ. Northwest
Indiana Univ. Southeast
Iowa State Univ.
John Brown Univ. (AR)
Kent State Univ. (OH)
La Roche College (PA)
Lamar Univ. (TX)
Lasell College (MA)
Lebanon Valley College (PA)
Lehigh Univ. (PA)
Lincoln Univ. (PA)
Lindenwood Univ. (MO)
Louisiana State Univ.–Baton Rouge
Lourdes College (OH)
Manhattan College (NY)
Maryville Univ. of St. Louis (MO)
Mckendree College (IL)
Miami Univ.–Oxford (OH)
Mount Ida College (MA)
Mount Mercy College (IA)
Mount Vernon Nazarene Univ.
 (OH)
National Univ. (CA)
National-Louis Univ. (IL)
New York Univ.
North Central College (IL)
North Greenville College (SC)
Northeastern State Univ. (OK)
Northern Illinois Univ.
Northwestern College (IA)
Ohio Northern Univ.
Ohio State Univ.–Columbus
Ohio Univ.
Oklahoma Baptist Univ.
Oklahoma Christian Univ.
Oklahoma State Univ.
Oral Roberts Univ. (OK)
Pace Univ. (NY)
Penn. State Univ.–Univ. Park
Quincy Univ. (IL)
Regis Univ. (CO)
Rider Univ. (NJ)
Robert Morris Univ. (PA)
Rocky Mountain College (MT)
Roosevelt Univ. (IL)
Rutgers–New Brunswick (NJ)
Salve Regina Univ. (RI)
Shippensburg Univ. of
 Pennsylvania
Simmons College (MA)
Southern Adventist Univ. (TN)
Southern Connecticut State Univ.
Southern Illinois Univ.–Carbondale
Southern Methodist Univ. (TX)
St. Ambrose Univ. (IA)
St. Bonaventure Univ. (NY)
St. Francis Univ. (PA)
St. Gregory's Univ. (OK)
St. John's Univ. (NY)

St. Joseph's Univ. (PA)
St. Louis Univ.
Stetson Univ. (FL)
SUNY–Albany
Temple Univ. (PA)
Texas A&M Univ.–Kingsville
Texas Christian Univ.
Troy State Univ.–Troy (AL)
Tulane Univ. (LA)
Tuskegee Univ. (AL)
United States Air Force Academy
 (CO)
Univ. of Alabama
Univ. of Central Florida
Univ. of Central Oklahoma
Univ. of Connecticut
Univ. of Denver
Univ. of Florida
Univ. of Illinois–Chicago
Univ. of Ill.–Urbana-Champaign
Univ. of Iowa
Univ. of Kentucky
Univ. of Mary (ND)
Univ. of Maryland–College Park
Univ. of Michigan–Flint
Univ. of Nebraska–Lincoln
Univ. of Nevada–Las Vegas
Univ. of Nevada–Reno
Univ. of Northern Iowa
Univ. of Oklahoma
Univ. of Pennsylvania
Univ. of South Carolina–Columbia
Univ. of Texas–San Antonio
Univ. of the Ozarks (AR)
Univ. of Toledo (OH)
Univ. of Wisconsin–Madison
Univ. of Wyoming
Valparaiso Univ. (IN)
Virginia Tech
Wake Forest Univ. (NC)
Washington State Univ.
Western Michigan Univ.
Western New Mexico Univ.
Worcester Polytechnic Institute
 (MA)
Wright State Univ. (OH)
Xavier Univ. (OH)

Manufacturing Engineering

Boston Univ.
Bradley Univ. (IL)
Brigham Young Univ.–Provo (UT)
Cal Poly–San Luis Obispo
California State Polytechnic
 Univ.–Pomona
Central Michigan Univ.
Central State Univ. (OH)
Cleveland State Univ.
Grand Valley State Univ. (MI)
Hofstra Univ. (NY)
Kettering Univ. (MI)
Marquette Univ. (WI)
Miami Univ.–Oxford (OH)
New Jersey Institute of Technology
North Carolina A&T State Univ.
North Dakota State Univ.
Northwestern Univ. (IL)
Oregon State Univ.

Robert Morris Univ. (PA)
Rochester Institute of Tech. (NY)
Southern Illinois
 Univ.–Edwardsville
Stanford Univ. (CA)
Texas State Univ.–San Marcos
Univ. of California–Berkeley
Univ. of California–Los Angeles
Univ. of Detroit Mercy
Univ. of Hartford (CT)
Univ. of Ill.–Urbana-Champaign
Univ. of Louisville (KY)
Univ. of Miami (FL)
Univ. of Michigan–Dearborn
Univ. of Missouri–Rolla
Univ. of Southern Maine
Univ. of Wisconsin–Milwaukee
Univ. of Wisconsin–Stout
Utah State Univ.
Virginia State Univ.
Washington State Univ.
Western Michigan Univ.
Wichita State Univ. (KS)
Worcester Polytechnic Institute
 (MA)

Marine Transportation

Humboldt State Univ. (CA)
Texas A&M Univ.–Galveston
United States Merchant Marine
 Academy (NY)

Marketing

Abilene Christian Univ. (TX)
Adrian College (MI)
Alabama Agricultural and
 Mechanical Univ.
Alabama State Univ.
Albany State Univ. (GA)
Alderson-Broaddus College (WV)
Alfred Univ. (NY)
Alma College (MI)
American Univ. (DC)
Anderson Univ. (IN)
Andrews Univ. (MI)
Angelo State Univ. (TX)
Appalachian State Univ. (NC)
Arcadia Univ. (PA)
Arizona State Univ.
Arkansas State Univ.
Assumption College (MA)
Auburn Univ. (AL)
Augsburg College (MN)
Augusta State Univ. (GA)
Aurora Univ. (IL)
Averett Univ. (VA)
Avila Univ. (MO)
Azusa Pacific Univ. (CA)
Babson College (MA)
Baker College of Flint (MI)
Baldwin-Wallace College (OH)
Ball State Univ. (IN)
Barry Univ. (FL)
Baylor Univ. (TX)
Bellevue Univ. (NE)
Belmont Univ. (TN)
Benedict College (SC)

Benedictine Univ. (IL)
Bentley College (MA)
Berry College (GA)
Bethel Univ. (MN)
Black Hills State Univ. (SD)
Bloomfield College (NJ)
Boise State Univ. (ID)
Boston Univ.
Bowling Green State Univ. (OH)
Bradley Univ. (IL)
Brenau Univ. (GA)
Bridgewater State College (MA)
Bryant College (RI)
Buena Vista Univ. (IA)
Butler Univ. (IN)
Cabrini College (PA)
Caldwell College (NJ)
California State Polytechnic
 Univ.–Pomona
California State Univ.–Fullerton
California State Univ.–Long Beach
California State Univ.–Sacramento
Canisius College (NY)
Capital Univ. (OH)
Cardinal Stritch Univ. (WI)
Carlow College (PA)
Carroll College (WI)
Carthage College (WI)
Catholic Univ. of America (DC)
Cedarville Univ. (OH)
Central Connecticut State Univ.
Central Michigan Univ.
Champlain College (VT)
Chatham College (PA)
Chestnut Hill College (PA)
Christopher Newport Univ. (VA)
City Univ. (WA)
Claflin Univ. (SC)
Clarion Univ. of Pennsylvania
Clark Atlanta Univ.
Clarkson Univ. (NY)
Clayton Coll. and State Univ. (GA)
Cleary Univ. (MI)
Cleveland State Univ.
Coastal Carolina Univ. (SC)
College Misericordia (PA)
College of New Jersey
College of St. Scholastica (MN)
College of the Ozarks (MO)
College of the Southwest (NM)
Columbia College (IL)
Columbia College (MO)
Columbia Union College (MD)
Columbus State Univ. (GA)
Concordia Univ.–St. Paul (MN)
Cornerstone Univ. (MI)
Cumberland Univ. (TN)
CUNY–York College
Dakota State Univ. (SD)
Dallas Baptist Univ.
Davenport Univ. (MI)
David Lipscomb Univ. (TN)
Davis and Elkins College (WV)
Defiance College (OH)
Delaware State Univ.
Delaware Valley College (PA)
Delta State Univ. (MS)
Depaul Univ. (IL)
Desales Univ. (PA)
Dominican Coll. of Blauvelt (NY)
Drake Univ. (IA)

Drexel Univ. (PA)
Duquesne Univ. (PA)
East Carolina Univ. (NC)
East Tennessee State Univ.
Eastern Illinois Univ.
Eastern Kentucky Univ.
Eastern Michigan Univ.
Eastern New Mexico Univ.
Eastern Univ. (PA)
Eastern Washington Univ.
Elmhurst College (IL)
Emerson College (MA)
Emporia State Univ. (KS)
Evangel Univ. (MO)
Excelsior College (NY)
Fairfield Univ. (CT)
Fairleigh Dickinson Univ. (NJ)
Fairmont State Univ. (WV)
Felician College (NJ)
Ferris State Univ. (MI)
Fitchburg State College (MA)
Florida Atlantic Univ.
Florida Gulf Coast Univ.
Florida International Univ.
Florida Southern College
Florida State Univ.
Fort Hays State Univ. (KS)
Fort Lewis College (CO)
Fort Valley State Univ. (GA)
Francis Marion Univ. (SC)
Freed-Hardeman Univ. (TN)
Fresno Pacific Univ. (CA)
Friends Univ. (KS)
Gannon Univ. (PA)
Gardner-Webb Univ. (NC)
George Mason Univ. (VA)
George Washington Univ. (DC)
Georgetown Univ. (DC)
Georgia College and State Univ.
Georgia Southern Univ.
Georgia Southwestern State Univ.
Georgia State Univ.
Goldey Beacom College (DE)
Grambling State Univ. (LA)
Grand Canyon Univ. (AZ)
Grand Valley State Univ. (MI)
Greenville College (IL)
Grove City College (PA)
Gwynedd-Mercy College (PA)
Hampton Univ. (VA)
Hardin-Simmons Univ. (TX)
Harding Univ. (AR)
Hastings College (NE)
Hawaii Pacific Univ.
High Point Univ. (NC)
Hillsdale College (MI)
Hofstra Univ. (NY)
Holy Family Univ. (PA)
Holy Names Univ. (CA)
Houston Baptist Univ.
Howard Univ. (DC)
Husson College (ME)
Idaho State Univ.
Illinois State Univ.
Indiana State Univ.
Indiana Univ. of Pennsylvania
Indiana Univ. Southeast
Indiana Univ.–Kokomo
Indiana Univ.–South Bend
Indiana Univ.-Purdue Univ.–Fort
    Wayne

Indiana Wesleyan Univ.
Iona College (NY)
Iowa State Univ.
Jacksonville State Univ. (AL)
Jacksonville Univ. (FL)
James Madison Univ. (VA)
Jamestown College (ND)
John Brown Univ. (AR)
John Carroll Univ. (OH)
Johnson and Wales Univ. (RI)
Juniata College (PA)
Kansas State Univ.
Kean Univ. (NJ)
Kennesaw State Univ. (GA)
Kent State Univ. (OH)
Kentucky State Univ.
Kettering Univ. (MI)
King's College (PA)
Kutztown Univ. of Pennsylvania
La Roche College (PA)
La Salle Univ. (PA)
Lake Superior State Univ. (MI)
Lakeland College (WI)
Lamar Univ. (TX)
Lambuth Univ. (TN)
Lasell College (MA)
Le Moyne College (NY)
Lehigh Univ. (PA)
Lenoir-Rhyne College (NC)
Letourneau Univ. (TX)
Lewis Univ. (IL)
Limestone College (SC)
Lindenwood Univ. (MO)
Loras College (IA)
Louisiana College
Louisiana State Univ.–Baton Rouge
Louisiana State Univ.–Shreveport
Louisiana Tech Univ.
Lourdes College (OH)
Loyola Univ. Chicago
Loyola Univ. New Orleans
Lynchburg College (VA)
Macmurray College (IL)
Madonna Univ. (MI)
Manhattan College (NY)
Mansfield Univ. of Pennsylvania
Marian College (IN)
Marian College of Fond Du Lac
    (WI)
Marietta College (OH)
Marquette Univ. (WI)
Marshall Univ. (WV)
Martin Univ. (IN)
Maryville Univ. of St. Louis (MO)
Marywood Univ. (PA)
Mckendree College (IL)
Mcneese State Univ. (LA)
Messiah College (PA)
Methodist College (NC)
Miami Univ.–Oxford (OH)
Michigan State Univ.
Middle Tennessee State Univ.
Midwestern State Univ. (TX)
Millikin Univ. (IL)
Minnesota State Univ.–Mankato
Minnesota State Univ.–Moorhead
Minot State Univ. (ND)
Mississippi College
Mississippi State Univ.
Missouri Baptist College
Missouri Southern State Univ.

Missouri Western State College
Morehead State Univ. (KY)
Morgan State Univ. (MD)
Morningside College (IA)
Mount Mary College (WI)
Mount Mercy College (IA)
Mount Vernon Nazarene Univ.
    (OH)
Murray State Univ. (KY)
Neumann College (PA)
New Mexico Highlands Univ.
New Mexico State Univ.
New York Institute of Technology
Nicholls State Univ. (LA)
Nichols College (MA)
North Central College (IL)
North Georgia College and State
    Univ.
North Greenville College (SC)
North Park Univ. (IL)
Northeastern State Univ. (OK)
Northeastern Univ. (MA)
Northern Arizona Univ.
Northern Illinois Univ.
Northern Kentucky Univ.
Northern Michigan Univ.
Northern State Univ. (SD)
Northwest Missouri State Univ.
Northwestern College (MN)
Northwood Univ. (MI)
Notre Dame College of Ohio
Nova Southeastern Univ. (FL)
Oakland Univ. (MI)
Ohio State Univ.–Columbus
Ohio Univ.
Ohio Valley College (WV)
Oklahoma Baptist Univ.
Oklahoma Christian Univ.
Oklahoma City Univ.
Oklahoma State Univ.
Old Dominion Univ. (VA)
Olivet College (MI)
Oregon Institute of Technology
Our Lady of the Lake Univ. (TX)
Pace Univ. (NY)
Paine College (GA)
Palm Beach Atlantic Univ. (FL)
Park Univ. (MO)
Penn. State Univ.–Univ. Park
Penn. State–Erie, The Behrend
    College
Pepperdine Univ. (CA)
Philadelphia Univ.
Pittsburg State Univ. (KS)
Plymouth State Univ. (NH)
Point Park Univ. (PA)
Prairie View A&M Univ. (TX)
Providence College (RI)
Purdue Univ.–Calumet (IN)
Quincy Univ. (IL)
Radford Univ. (VA)
Regis Univ. (CO)
Rider Univ. (NJ)
Robert Morris Univ. (PA)
Rochester College (MI)
Rochester Institute of Tech. (NY)
Roger Williams Univ. (RI)
Rutgers–Camden (NJ)
Rutgers–New Brunswick (NJ)
Rutgers–Newark (NJ)
Saginaw Valley State Univ. (MI)

Salisbury Univ. (MD)
Salve Regina Univ. (RI)
Sam Houston State Univ. (TX)
Santa Clara Univ. (CA)
Schreiner Univ. (TX)
Seattle Univ.
Seton Hall Univ. (NJ)
Seton Hill Univ. (PA)
Shippensburg Univ. of
    Pennsylvania
Siena College (NY)
South Carolina State Univ.
Southeast Missouri State Univ.
Southeastern College of the
    Assemblies of God
Southeastern Louisiana Univ.
Southeastern Oklahoma State
    Univ.
Southeastern Univ. (DC)
Southern Adventist Univ. (TN)
Southern Connecticut State Univ.
Southern Illinois Univ.–Carbondale
Southern Methodist Univ. (TX)
Southern Nazarene Univ. (OK)
Southern New Hampshire Univ.
Southern Univ. and A&M College
    (LA)
Southern Utah Univ.
Southwest Minnesota State Univ.
    (MN)
Southwestern Adventist Univ. (TX)
Southwestern College (KS)
St. Ambrose Univ. (IA)
St. Bonaventure Univ. (NY)
St. Cloud State Univ. (MN)
St. Edward's Univ. (TX)
St. Francis Univ. (PA)
St. Gregory's Univ. (OK)
St. John's Univ. (NY)
St. Joseph's College (ME)
St. Joseph's Univ. (PA)
St. Leo Univ. (FL)
St. Mary's Univ. of Minnesota
St. Mary's Univ. of San Antonio
St. Mary-of-The-Woods Coll. (IN)
St. Paul's College (VA)
St. Peter's College (NJ)
St. Thomas Aquinas College (NY)
St. Vincent College (PA)
St. Xavier Univ. (IL)
State Univ. of West Georgia
Stephen F. Austin State Univ. (TX)
Stephens College (MO)
Stetson Univ. (FL)
Stonehill College (MA)
Suffolk Univ. (MA)
SUNY College–Old Westbury
Susquehanna Univ. (PA)
Syracuse Univ. (NY)
Talladega College (AL)
Tarleton State Univ. (TX)
Taylor Univ. (IN)
Teikyo Post Univ. (CT)
Temple Univ. (PA)
Tennessee Technological Univ.
Texas A&M Univ.–College Station
Texas A&M Univ.–Commerce
Texas A&M Univ.–Corpus Christi
Texas A&M Univ.–Kingsville
Texas Christian Univ.
Texas State Univ.–San Marcos

Texas Tech Univ.
Texas Wesleyan Univ.
Texas Woman's Univ.
Thomas College (ME)
Thomas Edison State College (NJ)
Tiffin Univ. (OH)
Trevecca Nazarene Univ. (TN)
Tri-State Univ. (IN)
Troy State Univ.–Troy (AL)
Tulane Univ. (LA)
Union College (NE)
Union Univ. (TN)
Univ. of Akron (OH)
Univ. of Alabama
Univ. of Alabama–Birmingham
Univ. of Alabama–Huntsville
Univ. of Alaska–Anchorage
Univ. of Arkansas
Univ. of Arkansas–Little Rock
Univ. of Bridgeport (CT)
Univ. of Central Arkansas
Univ. of Central Florida
Univ. of Central Oklahoma
Univ. of Connecticut
Univ. of Dayton (OH)
Univ. of Delaware
Univ. of Denver
Univ. of Evansville (IN)
Univ. of Findlay (OH)
Univ. of Florida
Univ. of Georgia
Univ. of Hartford (CT)
Univ. of Hawaii–Hilo
Univ. of Hawaii–Manoa
Univ. of Houston
Univ. of Houston–Downtown
Univ. of Illinois–Chicago
Univ. of Ill.–Urbana-Champaign
Univ. of Indianapolis
Univ. of Iowa
Univ. of Kansas
Univ. of Kentucky
Univ. of La Verne (CA)
Univ. of Louisiana–Lafayette
Univ. of Louisiana–Monroe
Univ. of Louisville (KY)
Univ. of Mary Hardin-Baylor (TX)
Univ. of Maryland–College Park
Univ. of Maryland–Univ. College
Univ. of Massachusetts–Amherst
Univ. of Memphis
Univ. of Miami (FL)
Univ. of Michigan–Dearborn
Univ. of Michigan–Flint
Univ. of Minnesota–Crookston
Univ. of Minnesota–Duluth
Univ. of Minnesota–Twin Cities
Univ. of Mississippi
Univ. of Montana
Univ. of Montevallo (AL)
Univ. of Nebraska–Lincoln
Univ. of Nebraska–Omaha
Univ. of Nevada–Las Vegas
Univ. of Nevada–Reno
Univ. of New Haven (CT)
Univ. of New Orleans
Univ. of North Alabama
Univ. of North Carolina–Charlotte
Univ. of N.C.–Wilmington
Univ. of North Dakota
Univ. of North Florida

Univ. of North Texas
Univ. of Northern Iowa
Univ. of Notre Dame (IN)
Univ. of Oklahoma
Univ. of Pennsylvania
Univ. of Pittsburgh
Univ. of Portland (OR)
Univ. of Rhode Island
Univ. of Rio Grande (OH)
Univ. of San Francisco
Univ. of Scranton (PA)
Univ. of South Alabama
Univ. of South Carolina–Columbia
Univ. of South Florida
Univ. of Southern Indiana
Univ. of St. Francis (IL)
Univ. of St. Thomas (TX)
Univ. of St. Thomas (MN)
Univ. of Tampa (FL)
Univ. of Tennessee
Univ. of Tennessee–Chattanooga
Univ. of Tennessee–Martin
Univ. of Texas of the Permian Basin
Univ. of Texas–Arlington
Univ. of Texas–Austin
Univ. of Texas–Brownsville
Univ. of Texas–El Paso
Univ. of Texas–Pan American
Univ. of Texas–San Antonio
Univ. of Texas–Tyler
Univ. of the District of Columbia
Univ. of the Ozarks (AR)
Univ. of Toledo (OH)
Univ. of Tulsa (OK)
Univ. of Utah
Univ. of Washington
Univ. of West Florida
Univ. of Wisconsin–Eau Claire
Univ. of Wisconsin–La Crosse
Univ. of Wisconsin–Madison
Univ. of Wisconsin–Milwaukee
Univ. of Wisconsin–Oshkosh
Univ. of Wisconsin–Superior
Univ. of Wisconsin–Whitewater
Univ. of Wyoming
Upper Iowa Univ.
Urbana Univ. (OH)
Ursuline College (OH)
Utah State Univ.
Valdosta State Univ. (GA)
Valparaiso Univ. (IN)
Vanguard Univ. of Southern
    California
Villanova Univ. (PA)
Virginia Commonwealth Univ.
Virginia Intermont College
Virginia State Univ.
Viterbo Univ. (WI)
Wagner College (NY)
Walsh College of Accountancy and
    Business Adm. (MI)
Walsh Univ. (OH)
Washburn Univ. (KS)
Washington State Univ.
Washington Univ. In St. Louis
Wayne State Univ. (MI)
Waynesburg College (PA)
Webber International Univ. (FL)
Weber State Univ. (UT)
Wesley College (DE)
West Texas A&M Univ.

West Virginia Univ.
West Virginia Wesleyan College
Western Carolina Univ. (NC)
Western Connecticut State Univ.
Western Illinois Univ.
Western Kentucky Univ.
Western Michigan Univ.
Western New England College
    (MA)
Western New Mexico Univ.
Western Washington Univ.
Westminster College (UT)
Wheeling Jesuit Univ. (WV)
Whitworth College (WA)
Wichita State Univ. (KS)
Widener Univ. (PA)
Wilberforce Univ. (OH)
William Penn Univ. (IA)
Wilmington College (DE)
Wingate Univ. (NC)
Woodbury Univ. (CA)
Wright State Univ. (OH)
Xavier Univ. (OH)
York College of Pennsylvania
Youngstown State Univ. (OH)

Mason/Masonry

Northwestern Oklahoma State
    Univ.

Materials Engineering

Alfred Univ. (NY)
Arizona State Univ.
Auburn Univ. (AL)
Cal Poly–San Luis Obispo
California State Polytechnic
    Univ.–Pomona
California State Univ.–Long Beach
Colorado School of Mines
Columbia Univ. (NY)
Cornell Univ. (NY)
Drexel Univ. (PA)
Georgia Institute of Technology
Iowa State Univ.
Johns Hopkins Univ. (MD)
Lehigh Univ. (PA)
Massachusetts Institute of
    Technology
Michigan Technological Univ.
New Mexico Institute of Mining
    and Technology
North Carolina State Univ.–Raleigh
Northwestern Univ. (IL)
Ohio State Univ.–Columbus
Purdue Univ.–West Lafayette (IN)
Rensselaer Polytechnic Inst. (NY)
Rice Univ. (TX)
Stevens Institute of Technology
    (NJ)
Univ. of Alabama–Birmingham
Univ. of California–Davis
Univ. of California–Irvine
Univ. of California–Los Angeles
Univ. of Connecticut
Univ. of Florida
Univ. of Ill.–Urbana-Champaign
Univ. of Kentucky

Univ. of Maryland–College Park
Univ. of Minnesota–Twin Cities
Univ. of Missouri–Rolla
Univ. of Nevada–Reno
Univ. of New Hampshire
Univ. of Pennsylvania
Univ. of Pittsburgh
Univ. of Tennessee
Univ. of Utah
Univ. of Washington
Univ. of Wisconsin–Madison
Univ. of Wisconsin–Milwaukee
Virginia Tech
Washington State Univ.
Western Michigan Univ.
Winona State Univ. (MN)
Wright State Univ. (OH)
Youngstown State Univ. (OH)

Materials Science

Alfred Univ. (NY)
Carnegie Mellon Univ. (PA)
Case Western Reserve Univ. (OH)
Columbia Univ. (NY)
Michigan State Univ.
Northwestern Univ. (IL)
Stevens Institute of Technology
    (NJ)
Temple Univ. (PA)
Univ. of Arizona
Univ. of California–Berkeley
Univ. of California–Los Angeles
Univ. of Connecticut
Univ. of Ill.–Urbana-Champaign
Univ. of Michigan–Ann Arbor
Univ. of New Hampshire
Washington State Univ.
Wright State Univ. (OH)

Mathematics

Abilene Christian Univ. (TX)
Adams State College (CO)
Adelphi Univ. (NY)
Adrian College (MI)
Agnes Scott College (GA)
Alabama Agricultural and
    Mechanical Univ.
Alabama State Univ.
Albany State Univ. (GA)
Albertson College (ID)
Albertus Magnus College (CT)
Albion College (MI)
Albright College (PA)
Alcorn State Univ. (MS)
Alfred Univ. (NY)
Allegheny College (PA)
Allen Univ. (SC)
Alma College (MI)
Alvernia College (PA)
Alverno College (WI)
American International College
    (MA)
American Univ. (DC)
Amherst College (MA)
Anderson College (SC)
Anderson Univ. (IN)
Andrews Univ. (MI)

Angelo State Univ. (TX)
Appalachian State Univ. (NC)
Aquinas College (MI)
Arcadia Univ. (PA)
Arizona State Univ.
Arkansas State Univ.
Arkansas Tech Univ.
Armstrong Atlantic State Univ.
    (GA)
Asbury College (KY)
Ashland Univ. (OH)
Assumption College (MA)
Atlantic Union College (MA)
Auburn Univ. (AL)
Auburn Univ.–Montgomery (AL)
Augsburg College (MN)
Augusta State Univ. (GA)
Augustana College (SD)
Augustana College (IL)
Aurora Univ. (IL)
Austin College (TX)
Austin Peay State Univ. (TN)
Averett Univ. (VA)
Avila Univ. (MO)
Azusa Pacific Univ. (CA)
Baker Univ. (KS)
Baldwin-Wallace College (OH)
Ball State Univ. (IN)
Barber Scotia College (NC)
Barnard College (NY)
Barry Univ. (FL)
Barton College (NC)
Bates College (ME)
Baylor Univ. (TX)
Belhaven College (MS)
Bellarmine Univ. (KY)
Belmont Univ. (TN)
Beloit College (WI)
Bemidji State Univ. (MN)
Benedict College (SC)
Benedictine College (KS)
Benedictine Univ. (IL)
Bennett College (NC)
Bennington College (VT)
Bentley College (MA)
Berea College (KY)
Berry College (GA)
Bethany College (KS)
Bethany College (WV)
Bethel College (IN)
Bethel College (TN)
Bethel College (KS)
Bethel Univ. (MN)
Bethune-Cookman College (FL)
Biola Univ. (CA)
Black Hills State Univ. (SD)
Blackburn College (IL)
Bloomfield College (NJ)
Bloomsburg Univ. of Pennsylvania
Blue Mountain College (MS)
Bluefield College (VA)
Bluffton Univ. (OH)
Boise State Univ. (ID)
Boston Univ.
Bowdoin College (ME)
Bowie State Univ. (MD)
Bowling Green State Univ. (OH)
Bradley Univ. (IL)
Brandeis Univ. (MA)
Brevard College (NC)
Brewton-Parker College (GA)

Briar Cliff Univ. (IA)
Bridgewater College (VA)
Bridgewater State College (MA)
Brigham Young Univ.–Hawaii
Brigham Young Univ.–Provo (UT)
Brown Univ. (RI)
Bryn Mawr College (PA)
Bucknell Univ. (PA)
Buena Vista Univ. (IA)
Buffalo State College
Butler Univ. (IN)
Cabrini College (PA)
Cal Poly–San Luis Obispo
Caldwell College (NJ)
California Baptist Univ.
California Institute of Technology
California Lutheran Univ.
California State Polytechnic
    Univ.–Pomona
California State Univ.–Bakersfield
California State Univ.–Chico
California State Univ.–Dominguez
    Hills
California State Univ.–Fresno
California State Univ.–Fullerton
California State Univ.–Hayward
California State Univ.–Long Beach
California State Univ.–Los Angeles
California State Univ.–Northridge
California State Univ.–Sacramento
California State Univ.–San
    Bernardino
California State Univ.–San Marcos
California State Univ.–Stanislaus
California Univ. of Pennsylvania
Calvin College (MI)
Cameron Univ. (OK)
Campbell Univ. (NC)
Campbellsville Univ. (KY)
Capital Univ. (OH)
Cardinal Stritch Univ. (WI)
Carleton College (MN)
Carlow College (PA)
Carroll College (MT)
Carroll College (WI)
Carson-Newman College (TN)
Carthage College (WI)
Case Western Reserve Univ. (OH)
Catawba College (NC)
Catholic Univ. of America (DC)
Cedar Crest College (PA)
Cedarville Univ. (OH)
Centenary College (NJ)
Centenary College of Louisiana
Central Christian College (KS)
Central College (IA)
Central Connecticut State Univ.
Central Methodist Univ. (MO)
Central Michigan Univ.
Central Missouri State Univ.
Central State Univ. (OH)
Central Washington Univ.
Centre College (KY)
Chadron State College (NE)
Chapman Univ. (CA)
Charleston Southern Univ. (SC)
Chatham College (PA)
Cheyney Univ. of Pennsylvania
Chicago State Univ.
Chowan College (NC)
Christian Brothers Univ. (TN)

Christian Heritage College (CA)
Christopher Newport Univ. (VA)
Claflin Univ. (SC)
Claremont Mckenna College (CA)
Clarion Univ. of Pennsylvania
Clark Atlanta Univ.
Clark Univ. (MA)
Clarke College (IA)
Clarkson Univ. (NY)
Clearwater Christian College (FL)
Cleveland State Univ.
Coe College (IA)
Coker College (SC)
Colby College (ME)
Colgate Univ. (NY)
College Misericordia (PA)
College of Charleston (SC)
College of Mount St. Joseph (OH)
College of Mount St. Vincent (NY)
College of New Jersey
College of Notre Dame of
    Maryland
College of St. Benedict (MN)
College of St. Catherine (MN)
College of St. Elizabeth (NJ)
College of St. Mary (NE)
College of St. Rose (NY)
College of St. Scholastica (MN)
College of the Holy Cross (MA)
College of the Ozarks (MO)
College of the Southwest (NM)
College of William and Mary (VA)
College of Wooster (OH)
Colorado Christian Univ.
Colorado College
Colorado School of Mines
Colorado State Univ.
Colorado State Univ.–Pueblo
Columbia College (SC)
Columbia College (MO)
Columbia Union College (MD)
Columbia Univ. (NY)
Columbus State Univ. (GA)
Concord College (WV)
Concordia College (NY)
Concordia Coll.–Moorhead (MN)
Concordia Univ. (MI)
Concordia Univ. (CA)
Concordia Univ. (NE)
Concordia Univ. Wisconsin
Concordia Univ.–Austin (TX)
Concordia Univ.–River Forest (IL)
Concordia Univ.–St. Paul (MN)
Connecticut College
Converse College (SC)
Coppin State Univ. (MD)
Cornell College (IA)
Cornell Univ. (NY)
Covenant College (GA)
Culver-Stockton College (MO)
Cumberland College (KY)
Cumberland Univ. (TN)
CUNY–Baruch College
CUNY–Brooklyn College
CUNY–City College
CUNY–College of Staten Island
CUNY–Hunter College
CUNY–Lehman College
CUNY–Medgar Evers College
CUNY–Queens College
CUNY–York College

Daemen College (NY)
Dakota Wesleyan Univ. (SD)
Dallas Baptist Univ.
Dana College (NE)
Dartmouth College (NH)
David Lipscomb Univ. (TN)
Davidson College (NC)
Davis and Elkins College (WV)
Defiance College (OH)
Delaware State Univ.
Delaware Valley College (PA)
Delta State Univ. (MS)
Denison Univ. (OH)
Depaul Univ. (IL)
Depauw Univ. (IN)
Desales Univ. (PA)
Dickinson College (PA)
Dickinson State Univ. (ND)
Dillard Univ. (LA)
Dominican Coll. of Blauvelt (NY)
Dominican Univ. (IL)
Dordt College (IA)
Dowling College (NY)
Drake Univ. (IA)
Drew Univ. (NJ)
Drexel Univ. (PA)
Drury Univ. (MO)
Duke Univ. (NC)
Duquesne Univ. (PA)
Earlham College (IN)
East Carolina Univ. (NC)
East Central Univ. (OK)
East Stroudsburg Univ. of
    Pennsylvania
East Tennessee State Univ.
East Texas Baptist Univ.
East-West Univ. (IL)
Eastern Connecticut State Univ.
Eastern Illinois Univ.
Eastern Kentucky Univ.
Eastern Mennonite Univ. (VA)
Eastern Michigan Univ.
Eastern Nazarene College (MA)
Eastern New Mexico Univ.
Eastern Oregon Univ.
Eastern Univ. (PA)
Eastern Washington Univ.
Eckerd College (FL)
Edgewood College (WI)
Edinboro Univ. of Pennsylvania
Edward Waters College (FL)
Elizabeth City State Univ. (NC)
Elizabethtown College (PA)
Elmhurst College (IL)
Elmira College (NY)
Elms College (College of Our Lady
    of the Elms) (MA)
Elon Univ. (NC)
Emmanuel College (MA)
Emmanuel College (GA)
Emory and Henry College (VA)
Emory Univ. (GA)
Emporia State Univ. (KS)
Erskine College (SC)
Eureka College (IL)
Evangel Univ. (MO)
Excelsior College (NY)
Fairfield Univ. (CT)
Fairleigh Dickinson Univ. (NJ)
Fairmont State Univ. (WV)
Faulkner Univ. (AL)

Fayetteville State Univ. (NC)
Felician College (NJ)
Ferris State Univ. (MI)
Ferrum College (VA)
Fitchburg State College (MA)
Florida Atlantic Univ.
Florida Institute of Technology
Florida International Univ.
Florida Memorial College
Florida Southern College
Florida State Univ.
Fontbonne Univ. (MO)
Fordham Univ. (NY)
Fort Hays State Univ. (KS)
Fort Lewis College (CO)
Fort Valley State Univ. (GA)
Framingham State College (MA)
Francis Marion Univ. (SC)
Franciscan Univ. of Steubenville
    (OH)
Franklin and Marshall College (PA)
Franklin College (IN)
Franklin Pierce College (NH)
Freed-Hardeman Univ. (TN)
Fresno Pacific Univ. (CA)
Friends Univ. (KS)
Frostburg State Univ. (MD)
Furman Univ. (SC)
Gallaudet Univ. (DC)
Gannon Univ. (PA)
Gardner-Webb Univ. (NC)
George Fox Univ. (OR)
George Mason Univ. (VA)
George Washington Univ. (DC)
Georgetown College (KY)
Georgetown Univ. (DC)
Georgia College and State Univ.
Georgia Southern Univ.
Georgia Southwestern State Univ.
Georgia State Univ.
Georgian Court Univ. (NJ)
Gettysburg College (PA)
Gonzaga Univ. (WA)
Gordon College (MA)
Goshen College (IN)
Goucher College (MD)
Grace College and Seminary (IN)
Graceland Univ. (IA)
Grambling State Univ. (LA)
Grand Canyon Univ. (AZ)
Grand Valley State Univ. (MI)
Greensboro College (NC)
Greenville College (IL)
Grinnell College (IA)
Grove City College (PA)
Guilford College (NC)
Gustavus Adolphus College (MN)
Gwynedd-Mercy College (PA)
Hamilton College (NY)
Hamline Univ. (MN)
Hampden-Sydney College (VA)
Hampshire College (MA)
Hampton Univ. (VA)
Hannibal-Lagrange College (MO)
Hanover College (IN)
Hardin-Simmons Univ. (TX)
Harding Univ. (AR)
Hartwick College (NY)
Harvard Univ. (MA)
Harvey Mudd College (CA)
Hastings College (NE)

Haverford College (PA)
Heidelberg College (OH)
Henderson State Univ. (AR)
Hendrix College (AR)
Heritage College (WA)
High Point Univ. (NC)
Hillsdale College (MI)
Hiram College (OH)
Hobart and William Smith Colleges
    (NY)
Hofstra Univ. (NY)
Holy Family Univ. (PA)
Hood College (MD)
Hope College (MI)
Houghton College (NY)
Houston Baptist Univ.
Howard Payne Univ. (TX)
Howard Univ. (DC)
Humboldt State Univ. (CA)
Huntingdon College (AL)
Huntington College (IN)
Huston-Tillotson College (TX)
Idaho State Univ.
Illinois College
Illinois State Univ.
Illinois Wesleyan Univ.
Immaculata Univ. (PA)
Indiana State Univ.
Indiana Univ. East
Indiana Univ. Northwest
Indiana Univ. of Pennsylvania
Indiana Univ. Southeast
Indiana Univ.–Bloomington
Indiana Univ.–Kokomo
Indiana Univ.–South Bend
Indiana Univ.-Purdue Univ.–Fort
    Wayne
Indiana Univ.-Purdue
    Univ.–Indianapolis
Indiana Wesleyan Univ.
Iona College (NY)
Iowa State Univ.
Ithaca College (NY)
Jackson State Univ. (MS)
Jacksonville State Univ. (AL)
Jacksonville Univ. (FL)
James Madison Univ. (VA)
Jamestown College (ND)
Jarvis Christian College (TX)
John Brown Univ. (AR)
John Carroll Univ. (OH)
Johns Hopkins Univ. (MD)
Johnson C. Smith Univ. (NC)
Judson College (AL)
Judson College (IL)
Juniata College (PA)
Kalamazoo College (MI)
Kansas State Univ.
Kansas Wesleyan Univ.
Kean Univ. (NJ)
Keene State College (NH)
Kennesaw State Univ. (GA)
Kent State Univ. (OH)
Kentucky State Univ.
Kentucky Wesleyan College
Keuka College (NY)
King College (TN)
King's College (PA)
Knox College (IL)
Kutztown Univ. of Pennsylvania
La Roche College (PA)

La Salle Univ. (PA)
La Sierra Univ. (CA)
Lafayette College (PA)
Lagrange College (GA)
Lake Erie College (OH)
Lake Forest College (IL)
Lakeland College (WI)
Lamar Univ. (TX)
Lambuth Univ. (TN)
Lander Univ. (SC)
Lane College (TN)
Lawrence Technological Univ. (MI)
Lawrence Univ. (WI)
Le Moyne College (NY)
Lebanon Valley College (PA)
Lehigh Univ. (PA)
Lemoyne-Owen College (TN)
Lenoir-Rhyne College (NC)
Lesley Univ. (MA)
Letourneau Univ. (TX)
Lewis and Clark College (OR)
Lewis Univ. (IL)
Lewis-Clark State College (ID)
Liberty Univ. (VA)
Limestone College (SC)
Lincoln Memorial Univ. (TN)
Lincoln Univ. (MO)
Lincoln Univ. (PA)
Lindenwood Univ. (MO)
Lindsey Wilson College (KY)
Linfield College (OR)
Livingstone College (NC)
Lock Haven Univ. of Pennsylvania
Long Island Univ.–C.W. Post
    Campus (NY)
Longwood Univ. (VA)
Louisiana College
Louisiana State Univ.–Baton Rouge
Louisiana State Univ.–Shreveport
Louisiana Tech Univ.
Loyola Marymount Univ. (CA)
Loyola Univ. Chicago
Loyola Univ. New Orleans
Lubbock Christian Univ. (TX)
Luther College (IA)
Lycoming College (PA)
Lynchburg College (VA)
Lyon College (AR)
Macalester College (MN)
Macmurray College (IL)
Madonna Univ. (MI)
Maharishi Univ. of Management
    (IA)
Malone College (OH)
Manchester College (IN)
Manhattan College (NY)
Manhattanville College (NY)
Mansfield Univ. of Pennsylvania
Marian College (IN)
Marian College of Fond Du Lac
    (WI)
Marietta College (OH)
Marist College (NY)
Marquette Univ. (WI)
Mars Hill College (NC)
Marshall Univ. (WV)
Martin Univ. (IN)
Mary Baldwin College (VA)
Marygrove College (MI)
Marymount Univ. (VA)
Maryville College (TN)

Maryville Univ. of St. Louis (MO)
Marywood Univ. (PA)
Massachusetts Institute of Technology
Master's Coll. and Seminary (CA)
Mayville State Univ. (ND)
Mcdaniel College (MD)
Mckendree College (IL)
Mcmurry Univ. (TX)
Mercer Univ. (GA)
Mercy College (NY)
Mercyhurst College (PA)
Meredith College (NC)
Merrimack College (MA)
Mesa State College (CO)
Messiah College (PA)
Methodist College (NC)
Metropolitan State College of Denver
Miami Univ.–Oxford (OH)
Michigan State Univ.
Michigan Technological Univ.
Middle Tennessee State Univ.
Middlebury College (VT)
Midland Lutheran College (NE)
Midway College (KY)
Midwestern State Univ. (TX)
Millersville Univ. of Pennsylvania
Milligan College (TN)
Millikin Univ. (IL)
Mills College (CA)
Millsaps College (MS)
Minnesota State Univ.–Mankato
Minnesota State Univ.–Moorhead
Mississippi College
Mississippi State Univ.
Mississippi Univ. For Women
Mississippi Valley State Univ.
Missouri Baptist College
Missouri Southern State Univ.
Missouri Valley College
Missouri Western State College
Molloy College (NY)
Monmouth College (IL)
Monmouth Univ. (NJ)
Montana State Univ.–Billings
Montana State Univ.–Bozeman
Montana Tech of the Univ. of Montana
Montclair State Univ. (NJ)
Moravian College (PA)
Morehead State Univ. (KY)
Morehouse College (GA)
Morgan State Univ. (MD)
Morningside College (IA)
Morris College (SC)
Mount Holyoke College (MA)
Mount Marty College (SD)
Mount Mary College (WI)
Mount Mercy College (IA)
Mount Olive College (NC)
Mount St. Mary College (NY)
Mount St. Mary's College (CA)
Mount St. Mary's Univ. (MD)
Mount Union College (OH)
Mount Vernon Nazarene Univ. (OH)
Muhlenberg College (PA)
Murray State Univ. (KY)
Muskingum College (OH)
National Univ. (CA)

Nazareth College of Rochester (NY)
Nebraska Wesleyan Univ.
New England College (NH)
New Jersey City Univ.
New Mexico Highlands Univ.
New Mexico Institute of Mining and Technology
New Mexico State Univ.
New York Univ.
Newberry College (SC)
Newman Univ. (KS)
Niagara Univ. (NY)
Nicholls State Univ. (LA)
Nichols College (MA)
Norfolk State Univ. (VA)
North Carolina A&T State Univ.
North Carolina Central Univ.
North Carolina State Univ.–Raleigh
North Carolina Wesleyan College
North Central College (IL)
North Dakota State Univ.
North Georgia College and State Univ.
North Greenville College (SC)
North Park Univ. (IL)
Northeastern Illinois Univ.
Northeastern State Univ. (OK)
Northeastern Univ. (MA)
Northern Arizona Univ.
Northern Illinois Univ.
Northern Kentucky Univ.
Northern Michigan Univ.
Northern State Univ. (SD)
Northland College (WI)
Northwest Missouri State Univ.
Northwestern College (MN)
Northwestern College (IA)
Northwestern Oklahoma State Univ.
Northwestern State Univ. of Louisiana
Northwestern Univ. (IL)
Norwich Univ. (VT)
Notre Dame College of Ohio
Nyack College (NY)
Oakland Univ. (MI)
Oakwood College (AL)
Oberlin College (OH)
Occidental College (CA)
Oglethorpe Univ. (GA)
Ohio Dominican Univ.
Ohio Northern Univ.
Ohio State Univ.–Columbus
Ohio Univ.
Ohio Wesleyan Univ.
Oklahoma Baptist Univ.
Oklahoma Christian Univ.
Oklahoma City Univ.
Oklahoma Panhandle State Univ.
Oklahoma State Univ.
Oklahoma Wesleyan Univ.
Old Dominion Univ. (VA)
Olivet College (MI)
Olivet Nazarene Univ. (IL)
Oral Roberts Univ. (OK)
Oregon State Univ.
Otterbein College (OH)
Ouachita Baptist Univ. (AR)
Our Lady of the Lake Univ. (TX)
Pace Univ. (NY)

Pacific Lutheran Univ. (WA)
Pacific Union College (CA)
Pacific Univ. (OR)
Paine College (GA)
Palm Beach Atlantic Univ. (FL)
Penn. State Univ.–Univ. Park
Penn. State–Erie, The Behrend College
Pepperdine Univ. (CA)
Peru State College (NE)
Pfeiffer Univ. (NC)
Philander Smith College (AR)
Pikeville College (KY)
Pittsburg State Univ. (KS)
Pitzer College (CA)
Plymouth State Univ. (NH)
Point Loma Nazarene Univ. (CA)
Polytechnic Univ. (NY)
Pomona College (CA)
Prairie View A&M Univ. (TX)
Presbyterian College (SC)
Prescott College (AZ)
Princeton Univ. (NJ)
Principia College (IL)
Providence College (RI)
Purdue Univ.–Calumet (IN)
Purdue Univ.–West Lafayette (IN)
Queens Univ. of Charlotte (NC)
Quincy Univ. (IL)
Quinnipiac Univ. (CT)
Radford Univ. (VA)
Ramapo College of New Jersey
Randolph-Macon College (VA)
Randolph-Macon Woman's College (VA)
Reed College (OR)
Regis Univ. (CO)
Rensselaer Polytechnic Inst. (NY)
Rhode Island College
Rhodes College (TN)
Rice Univ. (TX)
Richard Stockton College of New Jersey
Rider Univ. (NJ)
Ripon College (WI)
Rivier College (NH)
Roanoke College (VA)
Roberts Wesleyan College (NY)
Rockford College (IL)
Rockhurst Univ. (MO)
Rocky Mountain College (MT)
Roger Williams Univ. (RI)
Rollins College (FL)
Roosevelt Univ. (IL)
Rose-Hulman Institute of Technology (IN)
Rosemont College (PA)
Russell Sage College (NY)
Rust College (MS)
Rutgers–Camden (NJ)
Rutgers–New Brunswick (NJ)
Rutgers–Newark (NJ)
Sacred Heart Univ. (CT)
Saginaw Valley State Univ. (MI)
Salem College (NC)
Salem State College (MA)
Salisbury Univ. (MD)
Salve Regina Univ. (RI)
Sam Houston State Univ. (TX)
Samford Univ. (AL)
San Diego State Univ.

San Francisco State Univ.
San Jose State Univ. (CA)
Santa Clara Univ. (CA)
Savannah State Univ. (GA)
Schreiner Univ. (TX)
Scripps College (CA)
Seattle Pacific Univ.
Seattle Univ.
Seton Hall Univ. (NJ)
Seton Hill Univ. (PA)
Sewanee–Univ. of the South (TN)
Shaw Univ. (NC)
Shawnee State Univ. (OH)
Shenandoah Univ. (VA)
Shepherd Univ. (WV)
Shippensburg Univ. of Pennsylvania
Shorter College (GA)
Siena College (NY)
Silver Lake College (WI)
Simmons College (MA)
Simpson College (IA)
Simpson Univ. (CA)
Skidmore College (NY)
Slippery Rock Univ. of Pennsylvania
Sonoma State Univ. (CA)
South Carolina State Univ.
South Dakota School of Mines and Technology
South Dakota State Univ.
Southeast Missouri State Univ.
Southeastern College of the Assemblies of God
Southeastern Louisiana Univ.
Southeastern Oklahoma State Univ.
Southern Adventist Univ. (TN)
Southern Arkansas Univ.
Southern Connecticut State Univ.
Southern Illinois Univ.–Carbondale
Southern Illinois Univ.–Edwardsville
Southern Methodist Univ. (TX)
Southern Nazarene Univ. (OK)
Southern Polytechnic State Univ. (GA)
Southern Univ. and A&M College (LA)
Southern Utah Univ.
Southern Wesleyan Univ. (SC)
Southwest Baptist Univ. (MO)
Southwest Minnesota State Univ. (MN)
Southwest Missouri State Univ.
Southwestern Adventist Univ. (TX)
Southwestern College (KS)
Southwestern Oklahoma State Univ.
Southwestern Univ. (TX)
Spelman College (GA)
Spring Arbor Univ. (MI)
Spring Hill College (AL)
Springfield College (MA)
St. Ambrose Univ. (IA)
St. Andrews Presbyterian College (NC)
St. Anselm College (NH)
St. Augustine's College (NC)
St. Bonaventure Univ. (NY)
St. Cloud State Univ. (MN)
St. Edward's Univ. (TX)

St. Francis College (NY)
St. Francis Univ. (PA)
St. Gregory's Univ. (OK)
St. John Fisher College (NY)
St. John's Univ. (MN)
St. John's Univ. (NY)
St. Joseph College (CT)
St. Joseph's College (ME)
St. Joseph's College (IN)
St. Joseph's College, New York
St. Joseph's Univ. (PA)
St. Lawrence Univ. (NY)
St. Leo Univ. (FL)
St. Louis Univ.
St. Martin's College (WA)
St. Mary's College (IN)
St. Mary's College of California
St. Mary's College of Maryland
St. Mary's Univ. of Minnesota
St. Mary's Univ. of San Antonio
St. Michael's College (VT)
St. Norbert College (WI)
St. Olaf College (MN)
St. Peter's College (NJ)
St. Vincent College (PA)
St. Xavier Univ. (IL)
Stanford Univ. (CA)
State Univ. of West Georgia
Stephen F. Austin State Univ. (TX)
Sterling College (KS)
Stetson Univ. (FL)
Stevens Institute of Technology (NJ)
Stillman College (AL)
Stonehill College (MA)
Suffolk Univ. (MA)
Sul Ross State Univ. (TX)
SUNY College of Arts and Sciences–Geneseo
SUNY College–Brockport
SUNY College–Old Westbury
SUNY College–Oneonta
SUNY College–Potsdam
SUNY–Albany
SUNY–Binghamton
SUNY–Fredonia
SUNY–Oswego
SUNY–Plattsburgh
SUNY–Purchase College
SUNY–Stony Brook
Susquehanna Univ. (PA)
Swarthmore College (PA)
Sweet Briar College (VA)
Syracuse Univ. (NY)
Tabor College (KS)
Talladega College (AL)
Tarleton State Univ. (TX)
Taylor Univ. (IN)
Temple Univ. (PA)
Tennessee State Univ.
Tennessee Technological Univ.
Tennessee Wesleyan College
Texas A&M International Univ.
Texas A&M Univ.–College Station
Texas A&M Univ.–Commerce
Texas A&M Univ.–Corpus Christi
Texas A&M Univ.–Kingsville
Texas Christian Univ.
Texas College
Texas Lutheran Univ.
Texas State Univ.–San Marcos

Texas Tech Univ.
Texas Wesleyan Univ.
Texas Woman's Univ.
The Citadel (SC)
Thiel College (PA)
Thomas Edison State College (NJ)
Thomas More College (KY)
Touro College (NY)
Towson Univ. (MD)
Transylvania Univ. (KY)
Trevecca Nazarene Univ. (TN)
Tri-State Univ. (IN)
Trinity Christian College (IL)
Trinity College (CT)
Trinity College (DC)
Troy State Univ.–Troy (AL)
Truman State Univ. (MO)
Tufts Univ. (MA)
Tulane Univ. (LA)
Tusculum College (TN)
Tuskegee Univ. (AL)
Union College (NE)
Union College (NY)
Union Univ. (TN)
United States Military Academy (NY)
United States Naval Academy (MD)
Univ. at Buffalo–SUNY
Univ. of Akron (OH)
Univ. of Alabama
Univ. of Alabama–Birmingham
Univ. of Alabama–Huntsville
Univ. of Alaska–Anchorage
Univ. of Alaska–Fairbanks
Univ. of Arizona
Univ. of Arkansas
Univ. of Arkansas–Little Rock
Univ. of Arkansas–Pine Bluff
Univ. of Bridgeport (CT)
Univ. of California–Berkeley
Univ. of California–Davis
Univ. of California–Irvine
Univ. of California–Los Angeles
Univ. of California–Riverside
Univ. of California–San Diego
Univ. of California–Santa Barbara
Univ. of California–Santa Cruz
Univ. of Central Florida
Univ. of Central Oklahoma
Univ. of Chicago
Univ. of Cincinnati
Univ. of Colorado–Boulder
Univ. of Colorado–Colorado Springs
Univ. of Colorado–Denver
Univ. of Connecticut
Univ. of Dallas
Univ. of Dayton (OH)
Univ. of Delaware
Univ. of Denver
Univ. of Detroit Mercy
Univ. of Evansville (IN)
Univ. of Findlay (OH)
Univ. of Florida
Univ. of Georgia
Univ. of Great Falls (MT)
Univ. of Hartford (CT)
Univ. of Hawaii–Hilo
Univ. of Hawaii–Manoa
Univ. of Houston

Univ. of Idaho
Univ. of Illinois–Chicago
Univ. of Illinois–Springfield
Univ. of Ill.–Urbana-Champaign
Univ. of Indianapolis
Univ. of Iowa
Univ. of Kansas
Univ. of Kentucky
Univ. of La Verne (CA)
Univ. of Louisiana–Lafayette
Univ. of Louisiana–Monroe
Univ. of Louisville (KY)
Univ. of Maine–Farmington
Univ. of Maine–Orono
Univ. of Mary (ND)
Univ. of Mary Hardin-Baylor (TX)
Univ. of Mary Washington (VA)
Univ. of Maryland–Baltimore County
Univ. of Maryland–College Park
Univ. of Maryland–Eastern Shore
Univ. of Massachusetts–Amherst
Univ. of Massachusetts–Boston
Univ. of Massachusetts–Lowell
Univ. of Memphis
Univ. of Miami (FL)
Univ. of Michigan–Ann Arbor
Univ. of Michigan–Dearborn
Univ. of Michigan–Flint
Univ. of Minnesota–Duluth
Univ. of Minnesota–Morris
Univ. of Minnesota–Twin Cities
Univ. of Mississippi
Univ. of Missouri–Columbia
Univ. of Missouri–Kansas City
Univ. of Missouri–Rolla
Univ. of Missouri–St. Louis
Univ. of Mobile (AL)
Univ. of Montana
Univ. of Montevallo (AL)
Univ. of Nebraska–Kearney
Univ. of Nebraska–Lincoln
Univ. of Nebraska–Omaha
Univ. of Nevada–Las Vegas
Univ. of Nevada–Reno
Univ. of New England (ME)
Univ. of New Hampshire
Univ. of New Haven (CT)
Univ. of New Mexico
Univ. of New Orleans
Univ. of North Alabama
Univ. of North Carolina–Asheville
Univ. of N.C.–Chapel Hill
Univ. of North Carolina–Charlotte
Univ. of N.C.–Greensboro
Univ. of North Carolina–Pembroke
Univ. of N.C.–Wilmington
Univ. of North Dakota
Univ. of North Florida
Univ. of North Texas
Univ. of Northern Colorado
Univ. of Northern Iowa
Univ. of Notre Dame (IN)
Univ. of Oklahoma
Univ. of Oregon
Univ. of Pennsylvania
Univ. of Pittsburgh
Univ. of Pittsburgh–Johnstown
Univ. of Portland (OR)
Univ. of Puget Sound (WA)
Univ. of Redlands (CA)

Univ. of Rhode Island
Univ. of Richmond (VA)
Univ. of Rio Grande (OH)
Univ. of Rochester (NY)
Univ. of San Diego
Univ. of San Francisco
Univ. of Science and Arts of Oklahoma
Univ. of Scranton (PA)
Univ. of Sioux Falls (SD)
Univ. of South Carolina–Columbia
Univ. of South Carolina–Upstate
Univ. of South Dakota
Univ. of South Florida
Univ. of Southern California
Univ. of Southern Indiana
Univ. of Southern Maine
Univ. of Southern Mississippi
Univ. of St. Francis (IN)
Univ. of St. Francis (IL)
Univ. of St. Mary (KS)
Univ. of St. Thomas (TX)
Univ. of St. Thomas (MN)
Univ. of Tampa (FL)
Univ. of Tennessee
Univ. of Tennessee–Chattanooga
Univ. of Tennessee–Martin
Univ. of Texas of the Permian Basin
Univ. of Texas–Arlington
Univ. of Texas–Austin
Univ. of Texas–Brownsville
Univ. of Texas–Dallas
Univ. of Texas–El Paso
Univ. of Texas–Pan American
Univ. of Texas–San Antonio
Univ. of Texas–Tyler
Univ. of the District of Columbia
Univ. of the Incarnate Word (TX)
Univ. of the Ozarks (AR)
Univ. of the Pacific (CA)
Univ. of Toledo (OH)
Univ. of Tulsa (OK)
Univ. of Utah
Univ. of Vermont
Univ. of Virginia
Univ. of Virginia–Wise
Univ. of Washington
Univ. of West Alabama
Univ. of West Florida
Univ. of Wisconsin–Eau Claire
Univ. of Wisconsin–Green Bay
Univ. of Wisconsin–La Crosse
Univ. of Wisconsin–Madison
Univ. of Wisconsin–Milwaukee
Univ. of Wisconsin–Oshkosh
Univ. of Wisconsin–Parkside
Univ. of Wisconsin–Platteville
Univ. of Wisconsin–River Falls
Univ. of Wisconsin–Stevens Point
Univ. of Wisconsin–Superior
Univ. of Wisconsin–Whitewater
Univ. of Wyoming
Upper Iowa Univ.
Urbana Univ. (OH)
Ursinus College (PA)
Ursuline College (OH)
Utah State Univ.
Utah Valley State College
Utica College (NY)
Valdosta State Univ. (GA)
Valley City State Univ. (ND)

Valparaiso Univ. (IN)
Vanderbilt Univ. (TN)
Vassar College (NY)
Villanova Univ. (PA)
Virginia Commonwealth Univ.
Virginia Military Institute
Virginia State Univ.
Virginia Tech
Virginia Wesleyan College
Viterbo Univ. (WI)
Voorhees College (SC)
Wabash College (IN)
Wagner College (NY)
Wake Forest Univ. (NC)
Walsh Univ. (OH)
Wartburg College (IA)
Washburn Univ. (KS)
Washington and Jefferson College (PA)
Washington and Lee Univ. (VA)
Washington College (MD)
Washington State Univ.
Washington Univ. In St. Louis
Wayland Baptist Univ. (TX)
Wayne State College (NE)
Wayne State Univ. (MI)
Waynesburg College (PA)
Weber State Univ. (UT)
Webster Univ. (MO)
Wellesley College (MA)
Wesleyan College (GA)
Wesleyan Univ. (CT)
West Chester Univ. of Pennsylvania
West Liberty State College (WV)
West Texas A&M Univ.
West Virginia State Univ.
West Virginia Univ.
West Virginia Univ. Institute of Technology
Western Baptist College (OR)
Western Carolina Univ. (NC)
Western Connecticut State Univ.
Western Illinois Univ.
Western Kentucky Univ.
Western Michigan Univ.
Western New England College (MA)
Western New Mexico Univ.
Western Oregon Univ.
Western State College of Colorado
Western Washington Univ.
Westfield State College (MA)
Westminster College (MO)
Westminster College (PA)
Westminster College (UT)
Westmont College (CA)
Wheaton College (MA)
Wheaton College (IL)
Wheeling Jesuit Univ. (WV)
Whitman College (WA)
Whittier College (CA)
Whitworth College (WA)
Wichita State Univ. (KS)
Widener Univ. (PA)
Wiley College (TX)
Wilkes Univ. (PA)
Willamette Univ. (OR)
William Carey College (MS)
William Jewell College (MO)
William Paterson Univ. of New Jersey

William Penn Univ. (IA)
William Woods Univ. (MO)
Williams College (MA)
Wilmington College (OH)
Wilson College (PA)
Wingate Univ. (NC)
Winston-Salem State Univ. (NC)
Winthrop Univ. (SC)
Wisconsin Lutheran College
Wittenberg Univ. (OH)
Wofford College (SC)
Worcester Polytechnic Institute (MA)
Worcester State College (MA)
Wright State Univ. (OH)
Xavier Univ. (OH)
Yale Univ. (CT)
Yeshiva Univ. (NY)
York College of Pennsylvania
Youngstown State Univ. (OH)

Mathematics and Computer Science

Alfred Univ. (NY)
Anderson Univ. (IN)
Augustana College (IL)
Belhaven College (MS)
Bennington College (VT)
Bethel College (IN)
Boston Univ.
Bowdoin College (ME)
Brescia Univ. (KY)
Brown Univ. (RI)
Chestnut Hill College (PA)
Colby College (ME)
Colgate Univ. (NY)
College of St. Benedict (MN)
Colorado College
Concordia Univ.–River Forest (IL)
CUNY–Brooklyn College
Delaware State Univ.
Dominican Univ. (IL)
Drew Univ. (NJ)
Eastern Illinois Univ.
Friends Univ. (KS)
Furman Univ. (SC)
Gonzaga Univ. (WA)
Goshen College (IN)
Hampden-Sydney College (VA)
Harvey Mudd College (CA)
Hofstra Univ. (NY)
Immaculata Univ. (PA)
Ithaca College (NY)
Keene State College (NH)
Lake Superior State Univ. (MI)
Lawrence Technological Univ. (MI)
Lawrence Univ. (WI)
Letourneau Univ. (TX)
Loyola Univ. Chicago
Mary Baldwin College (VA)
Maryville College (TN)
Massachusetts Institute of Technology
Mount Aloysius College (PA)
Newberry College (SC)
Oakwood College (AL)
Oglethorpe Univ. (GA)
Paine College (GA)
Pepperdine Univ. (CA)

Pfeiffer Univ. (NC)
Salem International Univ. (WV)
San Diego State Univ.
Santa Clara Univ. (CA)
Springfield College (MA)
St. Gregory's Univ. (OK)
St. John's Univ. (MN)
St. Lawrence Univ. (NY)
St. Mary's College (IN)
St. Mary's College of California
St. Mary's Univ. of Minnesota
Stanford Univ. (CA)
Stevens Institute of Technology
    (NJ)
SUNY–Albany
Swarthmore College (PA)
Touro College (NY)
Tusculum College (TN)
United States Air Force Academy
    (CO)
Univ. of Akron (OH)
Univ. of Illinois–Chicago
Univ. of Ill.–Urbana-Champaign
Univ. of Kentucky
Univ. of Michigan–Dearborn
Univ. of Oregon
Univ. of South Carolina–Aiken
Univ. of St. Francis (IL)
Univ. of Tampa (FL)
Western Connecticut State Univ.
Wheaton College (MA)
Wingate Univ. (NC)
Yale Univ. (CT)

Mathematics and Statistics

Anderson Univ. (IN)
Asbury College (KY)
Canisius College (NY)
Carnegie Mellon Univ. (PA)
College of Mount St. Joseph (OH)
Dakota State Univ. (SD)
Fresno Pacific Univ. (CA)
Grand Canyon Univ. (AZ)
Hofstra Univ. (NY)
Indiana Univ. of Pennsylvania
Ithaca College (NY)
Long Island Univ.–C.W. Post
    Campus (NY)
Lycoming College (PA)
Northwestern Univ. (IL)
Ohio State Univ.–Columbus
Ohio Univ.
Oregon State Univ.
Siena College (NY)
St. Joseph's College, New York
St. Mary's College of California
SUNY–Fredonia
Taylor Univ. (IN)
Tulane Univ. (LA)
United States Coast Guard
    Academy (CT)
Univ. of Miami (FL)
Univ. of Missouri–Kansas City
Univ. of Missouri–Rolla
Univ. of Pittsburgh
Univ. of Rochester (NY)
Univ. of South Alabama
William Jewell College (MO)

Worcester Polytechnic Institute
    (MA)

Mechanic and Repair Technologies/Technicians

Mesa State College (CO)

Mechanical Engineering

Alabama Agricultural and
    Mechanical Univ.
Alfred Univ. (NY)
Arizona State Univ.
Arkansas Tech Univ.
Auburn Univ. (AL)
Baker College of Flint (MI)
Baylor Univ. (TX)
Bethel College (IN)
Boise State Univ. (ID)
Boston Univ.
Bradley Univ. (IL)
Brigham Young Univ.–Provo (UT)
Bucknell Univ. (PA)
Cal Poly–San Luis Obispo
California Institute of Technology
California State Polytechnic
    Univ.–Pomona
California State Univ.–Chico
California State Univ.–Fresno
California State Univ.–Fullerton
California State Univ.–Long Beach
California State Univ.–Los Angeles
California State Univ.–Sacramento
Calvin College (MI)
Carnegie Mellon Univ. (PA)
Case Western Reserve Univ. (OH)
Catholic Univ. of America (DC)
Cedarville Univ. (OH)
Central Michigan Univ.
Christian Brothers Univ. (TN)
Clarkson Univ. (NY)
Cleveland State Univ.
College of New Jersey
Colorado State Univ.
Columbia Univ. (NY)
Cooper Union (NY)
Cornell Univ. (NY)
CUNY–City College
Dordt College (IA)
Drexel Univ. (PA)
Duke Univ. (NC)
Fairfield Univ. (CT)
Florida A&M Univ.
Florida Atlantic Univ.
Florida Institute of Technology
Florida International Univ.
Florida State Univ.
Gannon Univ. (PA)
George Washington Univ. (DC)
Georgia Institute of Technology
Gonzaga Univ. (WA)
Grand Valley State Univ. (MI)
Grove City College (PA)
Hofstra Univ. (NY)
Howard Univ. (DC)
Idaho State Univ.
Illinois Institute of Technology
Indiana Institute of Technology

Indiana Univ.-Purdue Univ.–Fort
    Wayne
Indiana Univ.-Purdue
    Univ.–Indianapolis
Iowa State Univ.
Johns Hopkins Univ. (MD)
Kansas State Univ.
Kettering Univ. (MI)
Lafayette College (PA)
Lake Superior State Univ. (MI)
Lamar Univ. (TX)
Lawrence Technological Univ. (MI)
Lehigh Univ. (PA)
Letourneau Univ. (TX)
Louisiana State Univ.–Baton Rouge
Louisiana Tech Univ.
Loyola Marymount Univ. (CA)
Manhattan College (NY)
Marquette Univ. (WI)
Massachusetts Institute of
    Technology
Miami Univ.–Oxford (OH)
Michigan State Univ.
Michigan Technological Univ.
Midwestern State Univ. (TX)
Milwaukee School of Engineering
Minnesota State Univ.–Mankato
Mississippi State Univ.
Montana State Univ.–Bozeman
New Jersey Institute of Technology
New Mexico Institute of Mining
    and Technology
New Mexico State Univ.
New York Institute of Technology
North Carolina A&T State Univ.
North Carolina State Univ.–Raleigh
North Dakota State Univ.
Northeastern Univ. (MA)
Northern Arizona Univ.
Northern Illinois Univ.
Northwestern Univ. (IL)
Norwich Univ. (VT)
Oakland Univ. (MI)
Ohio Northern Univ.
Ohio State Univ.–Columbus
Ohio Univ.
Oklahoma Christian Univ.
Oklahoma State Univ.
Old Dominion Univ. (VA)
Oral Roberts Univ. (OK)
Oregon State Univ.
Penn. State Univ.–Univ. Park
Penn. State–Erie, The Behrend
    College
Polytechnic Univ. (NY)
Portland State Univ. (OR)
Prairie View A&M Univ. (TX)
Princeton Univ. (NJ)
Purdue Univ.–Calumet (IN)
Purdue Univ.–West Lafayette (IN)
Rensselaer Polytechnic Inst. (NY)
Rice Univ. (TX)
Rochester Institute of Tech. (NY)
Rose-Hulman Institute of
    Technology (IN)
Rutgers–New Brunswick (NJ)
Saginaw Valley State Univ. (MI)
San Diego State Univ.
San Francisco State Univ.
San Jose State Univ. (CA)
Santa Clara Univ. (CA)

Seattle Univ.
South Dakota School of Mines and
    Technology
South Dakota State Univ.
Southern Illinois Univ.–Carbondale
Southern Illinois
    Univ.–Edwardsville
Southern Univ. and A&M College
    (LA)
St. Cloud State Univ. (MN)
St. Louis Univ.
St. Martin's College (WA)
Stanford Univ. (CA)
Stevens Institute of Technology
    (NJ)
SUNY–Binghamton
SUNY–Stony Brook
Syracuse Univ. (NY)
Temple Univ. (PA)
Tennessee State Univ.
Tennessee Technological Univ.
Texas A&M Univ.–Kingsville
Texas Tech Univ.
Tri-State Univ. (IN)
Trinity College (CT)
Tufts Univ. (MA)
Tulane Univ. (LA)
Tuskegee Univ. (AL)
Union College (NY)
Union Univ. (TN)
United States Air Force Academy
    (CO)
United States Coast Guard
    Academy (CT)
United States Military Academy
    (NY)
United States Naval Academy
    (MD)
Univ. at Buffalo–SUNY
Univ. of Akron (OH)
Univ. of Alabama
Univ. of Alabama–Birmingham
Univ. of Alabama–Huntsville
Univ. of Alaska–Fairbanks
Univ. of Arizona
Univ. of Arkansas
Univ. of California–Berkeley
Univ. of California–Davis
Univ. of California–Irvine
Univ. of California–Los Angeles
Univ. of California–Riverside
Univ. of California–San Diego
Univ. of California–Santa Barbara
Univ. of Central Florida
Univ. of Colorado–Boulder
Univ. of Colorado–Colorado
    Springs
Univ. of Colorado–Denver
Univ. of Connecticut
Univ. of Dayton (OH)
Univ. of Denver
Univ. of Detroit Mercy
Univ. of Evansville (IN)
Univ. of Florida
Univ. of Hartford (CT)
Univ. of Hawaii–Manoa
Univ. of Houston
Univ. of Illinois–Chicago
Univ. of Ill.–Urbana-Champaign
Univ. of Indianapolis
Univ. of Iowa

Univ. of Kansas
Univ. of Kentucky
Univ. of Louisiana–Lafayette
Univ. of Louisville (KY)
Univ. of Maine–Orono
Univ. of Maryland–Baltimore
    County
Univ. of Maryland–College Park
Univ. of Massachusetts–Amherst
Univ. of Mass.–Dartmouth
Univ. of Massachusetts–Lowell
Univ. of Memphis
Univ. of Miami (FL)
Univ. of Michigan–Ann Arbor
Univ. of Michigan–Dearborn
Univ. of Minnesota–Duluth
Univ. of Minnesota–Twin Cities
Univ. of Mississippi
Univ. of Missouri–Columbia
Univ. of Missouri–Kansas City
Univ. of Missouri–Rolla
Univ. of Missouri–St. Louis
Univ. of Nebraska–Lincoln
Univ. of Nevada–Las Vegas
Univ. of Nevada–Reno
Univ. of New Hampshire
Univ. of New Haven (CT)
Univ. of New Mexico
Univ. of New Orleans
Univ. of North Carolina–Charlotte
Univ. of North Dakota
Univ. of North Florida
Univ. of Notre Dame (IN)
Univ. of Oklahoma
Univ. of Pennsylvania
Univ. of Pittsburgh
Univ. of Portland (OR)
Univ. of Rhode Island
Univ. of Rochester (NY)
Univ. of San Diego
Univ. of South Alabama
Univ. of South Carolina–Columbia
Univ. of South Florida
Univ. of Southern California
Univ. of St. Thomas (MN)
Univ. of Tennessee
Univ. of Texas–Arlington
Univ. of Texas–Austin
Univ. of Texas–El Paso
Univ. of Texas–Pan American
Univ. of Texas–San Antonio
Univ. of Texas–Tyler
Univ. of the District of Columbia
Univ. of the Pacific (CA)
Univ. of Toledo (OH)
Univ. of Tulsa (OK)
Univ. of Utah
Univ. of Vermont
Univ. of Virginia
Univ. of Washington
Univ. of Wisconsin–Madison
Univ. of Wisconsin–Milwaukee
Univ. of Wisconsin–Platteville
Univ. of Wyoming
Utah State Univ.
Valparaiso Univ. (IN)
Vanderbilt Univ. (TN)
Villanova Univ. (PA)
Virginia Commonwealth Univ.
Virginia Military Institute
Virginia Tech

Washington State Univ.
Washington Univ. In St. Louis
Wayne State Univ. (MI)
Weber State Univ. (UT)
West Texas A&M Univ.
West Virginia Univ.
West Virginia Univ. Institute of
  Technology
Western Kentucky Univ.
Western Michigan Univ.
Western New England College
  (MA)
Wichita State Univ. (KS)
Widener Univ. (PA)
Wilkes Univ. (PA)
William Penn Univ. (IA)
Worcester Polytechnic Institute
  (MA)
Wright State Univ. (OH)
Yale Univ. (CT)
York College of Pennsylvania
Youngstown State Univ. (OH)

Mechanical Engineering Related Technologies/ Technicians

Alabama Agricultural and
  Mechanical Univ.
Andrews Univ. (MI)
Benjamin Franklin Institute of
  Technology (MA)
Bluefield State College (WV)
Bowling Green State Univ. (OH)
Buffalo State College
California State Univ.–Sacramento
Central Connecticut State Univ.
Central Michigan Univ.
Central Missouri State Univ.
Central Washington Univ.
Cleveland State Univ.
Colorado State Univ.–Pueblo
Eastern Michigan Univ.
Eastern Washington Univ.
Embry Riddle Aeronautical Univ.
  (FL)
Fairleigh Dickinson Univ. (NJ)
Fairmont State Univ. (WV)
Ferris State Univ. (MI)
Georgia Southern Univ.
Henry Cogswell College (WA)
Indiana State Univ.
Indiana Univ.–South Bend
Indiana Univ.-Purdue Univ.–Fort
  Wayne
Indiana Univ.-Purdue
  Univ.–Indianapolis
Johnson and Wales Univ. (RI)
Letourneau Univ. (TX)
Lincoln Univ. (MO)
Metropolitan State College of
  Denver
Michigan Technological Univ.
Milwaukee School of Engineering
Minnesota State Univ.–Mankato
Montana State Univ.–Bozeman
New York Institute of Technology
Nicholls State Univ. (LA)
Norfolk State Univ. (VA)
Northeastern Univ. (MA)

Oklahoma State Univ.
Old Dominion Univ. (VA)
Oregon Institute of Technology
Pennsylvania College of Technology
Penn. State–Erie, The Behrend
  College
Pittsburg State Univ. (KS)
Point Park Univ. (PA)
Prairie View A&M Univ. (TX)
Purdue Univ.–Calumet (IN)
Purdue Univ.–North Central (IN)
Purdue Univ.–West Lafayette (IN)
Rochester Institute of Tech. (NY)
Savannah State Univ. (GA)
South Carolina State Univ.
Southern Illinois Univ.–Carbondale
Southern Polytechnic State Univ.
  (GA)
Southern Univ. and A&M College
  (LA)
Southwest Missouri State Univ.
SUNY–Farmingdale
Tennessee State Univ.
Texas A&M Univ.–College Station
Texas A&M Univ.–Corpus Christi
Texas Tech Univ.
Thomas Edison State College (NJ)
Univ. of Akron (OH)
Univ. of Arkansas–Little Rock
Univ. of Central Florida
Univ. of Dayton (OH)
Univ. of Hartford (CT)
Univ. of Houston
Univ. of Houston–Downtown
Univ. of Maine–Orono
Univ. of Massachusetts–Lowell
Univ. of North Carolina–Charlotte
Univ. of North Texas
Univ. of Pittsburgh–Johnstown
Univ. of Tennessee–Martin
Univ. of Texas–Brownsville
Univ. of Toledo (OH)
Utah State Univ.
Virginia State Univ.
Wayne State Univ. (MI)
Weber State Univ. (UT)
Wentworth Institute of Technology
  (MA)
Youngstown State Univ. (OH)

Mechanics and Repairers

Boise State Univ. (ID)
Lewis-Clark State College (ID)

Medical Illustration and Informatics

Alma College (MI)
Cleveland Institute of Art
Iowa State Univ.
Montana Tech of the Univ. of
  Montana
Rochester Institute of Tech. (NY)

Medicine (M.D.)

Southern Illinois Univ.–Carbondale

Tulane Univ. (LA)
Univ. of Washington

Medieval and Renaissance Studies

Barnard College (NY)
Brown Univ. (RI)
Catholic Univ. of America (DC)
College of William and Mary (VA)
Connecticut College
Dickinson College (PA)
Duke Univ. (NC)
Hanover College (IN)
Mount Holyoke College (MA)
New York Univ.
Ohio State Univ.–Columbus
Ohio Wesleyan Univ.
Penn. State Univ.–Univ. Park
Rhode Island College
Rice Univ. (TX)
Rutgers–New Brunswick (NJ)
Southern Methodist Univ. (TX)
SUNY–Albany
SUNY–Binghamton
Swarthmore College (PA)
Tulane Univ. (LA)
Univ. of California–Davis
Univ. of California–Santa Barbara
Univ. of Chicago
Univ. of Iowa
Univ. of Michigan–Ann Arbor
Univ. of Nebraska–Lincoln
Univ. of Notre Dame (IN)
Univ. of Oregon
Univ. of Toledo (OH)
Vassar College (NY)
Washington and Lee Univ. (VA)
Wesleyan Univ. (CT)
Yale Univ. (CT)

Mental and Social Health Services and Allied Professions

Alvernia College (PA)
Bemidji State Univ. (MN)
Bethany College (CA)
California State Univ.–Sacramento
Central Washington Univ.
Clarion Univ. of Pennsylvania
Clark Atlanta Univ.
Dominican Univ. (IL)
Drexel Univ. (PA)
Eastern Kentucky Univ.
Eastern Washington Univ.
Edgewood College (WI)
Franciscan Univ. of Steubenville
  (OH)
Graceland Univ. (IA)
Harding Univ. (AR)
Hilbert College (NY)
Indiana State Univ.
James Madison Univ. (VA)
John Brown Univ. (AR)
Keene State College (NH)
Minnesota State Univ.–Mankato
Minnesota State Univ.–Moorhead
Minot State Univ. (ND)

Missouri Valley College
Montana State Univ.–Northern
Morris College (SC)
Mount Olive College (NC)
New Mexico Highlands Univ.
Northern Illinois Univ.
Northern Kentucky Univ.
Northwestern State Univ. of
  Louisiana
Ohio State Univ.–Columbus
Ohio Univ.
Old Dominion Univ. (VA)
Pennsylvania College of Technology
Roger Williams Univ. (RI)
Seton Hill Univ. (PA)
Slippery Rock Univ. of Pennsylvania
St. Cloud State Univ. (MN)
St. John Fisher College (NY)
Texas A&M Univ.–College Station
Texas A&M Univ.–Commerce
Texas State Univ.–San Marcos
Thomas Edison State College (NJ)
Univ. of Central Arkansas
Univ. of Florida
Univ. of Kansas
Univ. of Maine–Augusta
Univ. of Maine–Farmington
Univ. of Mary (ND)
Univ. of Nebraska–Lincoln
Univ. of Nebraska–Omaha
Univ. of Pennsylvania
Univ. of South Dakota
Univ. of St. Thomas (MN)
Univ. of Texas–Pan American
Univ. of Texas–Tyler
Univ. of Toledo (OH)
Univ. of West Florida
Washburn Univ. (KS)
Western Connecticut State Univ.
Western Kentucky Univ.
Western Michigan Univ.
Western New Mexico Univ.
Western Washington Univ.
Youngstown State Univ. (OH)

Metallurgical Engineering

South Dakota School of Mines and
  Technology
Univ. of Missouri–Rolla
Univ. of Texas–El Paso
Univ. of Washington

Microbiological Sciences and Immunology

Arizona State Univ.
Auburn Univ. (AL)
Bowling Green State Univ. (OH)
Brigham Young Univ.–Provo (UT)
Cal Poly–San Luis Obispo
California State Polytechnic
  Univ.–Pomona
California State Univ.–Chico
California State Univ.–Fresno
California State Univ.–Long Beach
California State Univ.–Los Angeles
California State Univ.–Sacramento
Central Michigan Univ.

Colorado State Univ.
Cornell Univ. (NY)
Humboldt State Univ. (CA)
Idaho State Univ.
Indiana Univ.–Bloomington
Iowa State Univ.
Juniata College (PA)
Kansas State Univ.
Lawrence Univ. (WI)
Louisiana State Univ.–Baton Rouge
Miami Univ.–Oxford (OH)
Michigan State Univ.
Mississippi State Univ.
Mississippi Univ. For Women
Montana State Univ.–Bozeman
New Mexico State Univ.
North Carolina State Univ.–Raleigh
North Dakota State Univ.
Northern Arizona Univ.
Northern Michigan Univ.
Ohio State Univ.–Columbus
Ohio Univ.
Ohio Wesleyan Univ.
Oklahoma State Univ.
Oregon State Univ.
Penn. State Univ.–Univ. Park
Quinnipiac Univ. (CT)
Rutgers–New Brunswick (NJ)
San Diego State Univ.
South Dakota State Univ.
Southern Illinois Univ.–Carbondale
Syracuse Univ. (NY)
Texas A&M Univ.–College Station
Texas State Univ.–San Marcos
Texas Tech Univ.
Tulane Univ. (LA)
Univ. of Akron (OH)
Univ. of Alabama
Univ. of Arizona
Univ. of California–Berkeley
Univ. of California–Davis
Univ. of California–Los Angeles
Univ. of California–Riverside
Univ. of California–San Diego
Univ. of California–Santa Barbara
Univ. of Central Florida
Univ. of Florida
Univ. of Georgia
Univ. of Hawaii–Manoa
Univ. of Houston–Downtown
Univ. of Ill.–Urbana-Champaign
Univ. of Iowa
Univ. of Kansas
Univ. of Louisiana–Lafayette
Univ. of Maine–Orono
Univ. of Maryland–College Park
Univ. of Massachusetts–Amherst
Univ. of Miami (FL)
Univ. of Michigan–Ann Arbor
Univ. of Michigan–Dearborn
Univ. of Minnesota–Twin Cities
Univ. of Missouri–Columbia
Univ. of Montana
Univ. of New Hampshire
Univ. of Northern Iowa
Univ. of Oklahoma
Univ. of Pittsburgh
Univ. of Rhode Island
Univ. of South Florida
Univ. of Tennessee
Univ. of Texas–Arlington

Univ. of Texas–Austin
Univ. of Texas–El Paso
Univ. of Vermont
Univ. of Washington
Univ. of Wisconsin–La Crosse
Univ. of Wisconsin–Madison
Univ. of Wisconsin–Oshkosh
Univ. of Wyoming
Utah State Univ.
Wagner College (NY)
Washington State Univ.
Weber State Univ. (UT)

Middle/Near Eastern and Semitic Lang., Lit., and Linguistics

Asbury College (KY)
Baylor Univ. (TX)
Brandeis Univ. (MA)
Brigham Young Univ.–Provo (UT)
Calvin College (MI)
Central College (IA)
Columbia Univ. (NY)
Concordia Univ. (MI)
Cornerstone Univ. (MI)
CUNY–Hunter College
CUNY–Queens College
Dartmouth College (NH)
Georgetown Univ. (DC)
Hofstra Univ. (NY)
Indiana Univ.–Bloomington
Lawrence Univ. (WI)
Loyola Marymount Univ. (CA)
Lubbock Christian Univ. (TX)
Luther College (IA)
Master's Coll. and Seminary (CA)
Mid-Continent College (KY)
New York Univ.
Ohio State Univ.–Columbus
SUNY–Binghamton
Temple Univ. (PA)
Touro College (NY)
Union Univ. (TN)
Univ. of California–Los Angeles
Univ. of Chicago
Univ. of Ill.–Urbana-Champaign
Univ. of Michigan–Ann Arbor
Univ. of Minnesota–Twin Cities
Univ. of Notre Dame (IN)
Univ. of Pennsylvania
Univ. of Texas–Austin
Univ. of Washington
Univ. of Wisconsin–Madison
Univ. of Wisconsin–Milwaukee
Washington Univ. In St. Louis
Wayne State Univ. (MI)
Yale Univ. (CT)
Yeshiva Univ. (NY)

Military Technologies

Eastern Washington Univ.

Mining and Mineral Engineering

Colorado School of Mines

Montana Tech of the Univ. of Montana
New Mexico Institute of Mining and Technology
Penn. State Univ.–Univ. Park
South Dakota School of Mines and Technology
Southern Illinois Univ.–Carbondale
Univ. of Alaska–Fairbanks
Univ. of Arizona
Univ. of Kentucky
Univ. of Missouri–Rolla
Univ. of Nevada–Reno
Univ. of Utah
Virginia Tech
West Virginia Univ.

Mining and Petroleum Technologies/Technicians

Bluefield State College (WV)
Nicholls State Univ. (LA)

Missions/Missionary Studies and Missiology

Abilene Christian Univ. (TX)
Asbury College (KY)
Bethany College (CA)
Bethel College (IN)
Bethel Univ. (MN)
Biola Univ. (CA)
Cedarville Univ. (OH)
Christian Heritage College (CA)
Concordia Univ. Wisconsin
Concordia Univ.–St. Paul (MN)
Cornerstone Univ. (MI)
Covenant College (GA)
Crown College (MN)
David Lipscomb Univ. (TN)
East Texas Baptist Univ.
Eastern Univ. (PA)
Grace College and Seminary (IN)
Grace Univ. (NE)
Hardin-Simmons Univ. (TX)
Harding Univ. (AR)
Hope International Univ. (CA)
Huntington College (IN)
John Brown Univ. (AR)
King College (TN)
Liberty Univ. (VA)
Lubbock Christian Univ. (TX)
Master's Coll. and Seminary (CA)
Mid-Continent College (KY)
North Greenville College (SC)
Northwest College (WA)
Northwestern College (MN)
Nyack College (NY)
Oklahoma Baptist Univ.
Oklahoma Christian Univ.
Oklahoma Wesleyan Univ.
Oral Roberts Univ. (OK)
Ouachita Baptist Univ. (AR)
Patten College (CA)
Pfeiffer Univ. (NC)
Rochester College (MI)
Simpson Univ. (CA)
Southern Nazarene Univ. (OK)
Southwest Baptist Univ. (MO)

Toccoa Falls College (GA)
Vanguard Univ. of Southern California
Western Baptist College (OR)
Williams Baptist College (AR)

Modern Greek Language and Literature

Boston Univ.
Butler Univ. (IN)
Columbia Univ. (NY)
CUNY–Queens College
Lawrence Univ. (WI)
New York Univ.
Ohio State Univ.–Columbus
St. Louis Univ.
Univ. of New Hampshire
Wellesley College (MA)
Wright State Univ. (OH)
Yale Univ. (CT)

Movement and Mind-Body Therapies and Education

Texas Christian Univ.
Univ. of Vermont

Multi/Interdisciplinary Studies

Abilene Christian Univ. (TX)
Adelphi Univ. (NY)
Albertson College (ID)
Albright College (PA)
Alfred Univ. (NY)
Allegheny College (PA)
Alverno College (WI)
Amherst College (MA)
Angelo State Univ. (TX)
Antioch College (OH)
Arizona State Univ.
Arizona State Univ. West
Arkansas Tech Univ.
Austin College (TX)
Austin Peay State Univ. (TN)
Baldwin-Wallace College (OH)
Bard College (NY)
Bates College (ME)
Baylor Univ. (TX)
Bellarmine Univ. (KY)
Beloit College (WI)
Bennett College (NC)
Bentley College (MA)
Berea College (KY)
Berry College (GA)
Bethany College (WV)
Bethel Univ. (MN)
Blackburn College (IL)
Bluffton Univ. (OH)
Boise State Univ. (ID)
Bowdoin College (ME)
Bowling Green State Univ. (OH)
Brescia Univ. (KY)
Brevard College (NC)
Brown Univ. (RI)
Bryn Athyn College (PA)

Bucknell Univ. (PA)
Buena Vista Univ. (IA)
Buffalo State College
Caldwell College (NJ)
California State Univ.–Chico
California State Univ.–Fresno
California State Univ.–Long Beach
California State Univ.–Los Angeles
California State Univ.–Northridge
California State Univ.–Sacramento
California State Univ.–San Bernardino
California State Univ.–Stanislaus
Cameron Univ. (OK)
Capital Univ. (OH)
Carlow College (PA)
Cedarville Univ. (OH)
Central College (IA)
Central Connecticut State Univ.
Central Methodist Univ. (MO)
Central Washington Univ.
Chaminade Univ. of Honolulu
Chestnut Hill College (PA)
Chowan College (NC)
Christopher Newport Univ. (VA)
Claremont Mckenna College (CA)
Clark Univ. (MA)
Clearwater Christian College (FL)
Cleveland State Univ.
College Misericordia (PA)
College of Notre Dame of Maryland
College of Santa Fe (NM)
College of St. Benedict (MN)
College of St. Elizabeth (NJ)
College of the Atlantic (ME)
College of William and Mary (VA)
Colorado College
Columbia College (SC)
Columbia College (MO)
Columbia College (IL)
Concord College (WV)
Connecticut College
Cornell Univ. (NY)
Cornerstone Univ. (MI)
CUNY–Hunter College
Curry College (MA)
Dartmouth College (NH)
Davidson College (NC)
Delta State Univ. (MS)
Dickinson College (PA)
Dickinson State Univ. (ND)
Duke Univ. (NC)
Earlham College (IN)
East Tennessee State Univ.
East-West Univ. (IL)
Eastern Connecticut State Univ.
Eastern Illinois Univ.
Eastern Mennonite Univ. (VA)
Eastern Michigan Univ.
Eastern New Mexico Univ.
Eastern Oregon Univ.
Eastern Washington Univ.
Edgewood College (WI)
Edward Waters College (FL)
Elmhurst College (IL)
Elms College (College of Our Lady of the Elms) (MA)
Emmanuel College (MA)
Emporia State Univ. (KS)
Evergreen State College (WA)

Fairfield Univ. (CT)
Fairleigh Dickinson Univ. (NJ)
Florida Institute of Technology
Fordham Univ. (NY)
Fort Lewis College (CO)
Franklin and Marshall College (PA)
Freed-Hardeman Univ. (TN)
Frostburg State Univ. (MD)
Gannon Univ. (PA)
George Mason Univ. (VA)
George Washington Univ. (DC)
Georgetown College (KY)
Georgia Institute of Technology
Georgia State Univ.
Georgian Court Univ. (NJ)
Gettysburg College (PA)
Glenville State College (WV)
Goddard College (VT)
Gonzaga Univ. (WA)
Goucher College (MD)
Green Mountain College (VT)
Greenville College (IL)
Grinnell College (IA)
Gustavus Adolphus College (MN)
Hampshire College (MA)
Hartwick College (NY)
Hastings College (NE)
Haverford College (PA)
Hawaii Pacific Univ.
Hendrix College (AR)
Heritage College (WA)
Hofstra Univ. (NY)
Hood College (MD)
Hope College (MI)
Humboldt State Univ. (CA)
Huntingdon College (AL)
Idaho State Univ.
Illinois College
Illinois Institute of Technology
Illinois Wesleyan Univ.
Immaculata Univ. (PA)
Indiana Univ. Northwest
Indiana Univ.–Bloomington
Indiana Univ.-Purdue Univ.–Indianapolis
International College (FL)
Iowa State Univ.
Ithaca College (NY)
John Brown Univ. (AR)
Johns Hopkins Univ. (MD)
Judson College (IL)
Juniata College (PA)
Kalamazoo College (MI)
Keene State College (NH)
Kent State Univ. (OH)
Kentucky Christian College
Kentucky Wesleyan College
King College (TN)
Lafayette College (PA)
Lambuth Univ. (TN)
Lane College (TN)
Lawrence Univ. (WI)
Lebanon Valley College (PA)
Lees-Mcrae College (NC)
Lemoyne-Owen College (TN)
Letourneau Univ. (TX)
Lewis-Clark State College (ID)
Liberty Univ. (VA)
Long Island Univ.–Brooklyn (NY)
Long Island Univ.–Southampton College (NY)

Louisiana College
Lourdes College (OH)
Loyola College In Maryland
Loyola Marymount Univ. (CA)
Luther College (IA)
Lycoming College (PA)
Madonna Univ. (MI)
Maharishi Univ. of Management (IA)
Marian College of Fond Du Lac (WI)
Marquette Univ. (WI)
Marshall Univ. (WV)
Mary Baldwin College (VA)
Marylhurst Univ. (OR)
Maryville College (TN)
Marywood Univ. (PA)
Mercer Univ. (GA)
Mercyhurst College (PA)
Meredith College (NC)
Messiah College (PA)
Metropolitan State College of Denver
Miami Univ.–Oxford (OH)
Middle Tennessee State Univ.
Middlebury College (VT)
Midwestern State Univ. (TX)
Millikin Univ. (IL)
Mills College (CA)
Millsaps College (MS)
Minnesota State Univ.–Moorhead
Mississippi State Univ.
Missouri Baptist College
Missouri Western State College
Montana State Univ.–Billings
Montana State Univ.–Bozeman
Montclair State Univ. (NJ)
Moravian College (PA)
Mount Holyoke College (MA)
Mount St. Mary College (NY)
Mount St. Mary's Univ. (MD)
Mountain State Univ. (WV)
Muskingum College (OH)
New York Institute of Technology
Norfolk State Univ. (VA)
North Carolina Wesleyan College
North Central College (IL)
North Dakota State Univ.
North Greenville College (SC)
Northern Arizona Univ.
Northwest Christian College (OR)
Northwestern College (MN)
Northwestern Univ. (IL)
Oberlin College (OH)
Ohio State Univ.–Columbus
Ohio Wesleyan Univ.
Old Dominion Univ. (VA)
Olivet College (MI)
Oral Roberts Univ. (OK)
Oregon State Univ.
Pace Univ. (NY)
Pacific Lutheran Univ. (WA)
Park Univ. (MO)
Penn. State Univ.–Univ. Park
Pfeiffer Univ. (NC)
Piedmont College (GA)
Plymouth State Univ. (NH)
Pomona College (CA)
Prairie View A&M Univ. (TX)
Princeton Univ. (NJ)
Providence College (RI)

Purdue Univ.–West Lafayette (IN)
Quinnipiac Univ. (CT)
Radford Univ. (VA)
Reed College (OR)
Regis College (MA)
Regis Univ. (CO)
Rhode Island College
Rhodes College (TN)
Rivier College (NH)
Robert Morris Univ. (PA)
Rochester College (MI)
Rochester Institute of Tech. (NY)
Rocky Mountain College (MT)
Rollins College (FL)
Rutgers–Camden (NJ)
Rutgers–New Brunswick (NJ)
Rutgers–Newark (NJ)
Saginaw Valley State Univ. (MI)
Sam Houston State Univ. (TX)
San Diego State Univ.
San Francisco State Univ.
Santa Clara Univ. (CA)
Sheldon Jackson College (AK)
Shippensburg Univ. of Pennsylvania
Simmons College (MA)
Sonoma State Univ. (CA)
South Dakota School of Mines and Technology
Southeast Missouri State Univ.
Southern Adventist Univ. (TN)
Southern Arkansas Univ.
Southern Illinois Univ.–Carbondale
Southern Methodist Univ. (TX)
Southern Oregon Univ.
Southern Utah Univ.
Southwest Baptist Univ. (MO)
Southwestern Oklahoma State Univ.
Southwestern Univ. (TX)
Spring Hill College (AL)
St. Ambrose Univ. (IA)
St. Edward's Univ. (TX)
St. John's Univ. (MN)
St. Louis Univ.
St. Mary's College (IN)
St. Mary's College of Maryland
St. Mary's Univ. of San Antonio
St. Olaf College (MN)
St. Peter's College (NJ)
Stephen F. Austin State Univ. (TX)
Sterling College (KS)
Stillman College (AL)
Stonehill College (MA)
Sul Ross State Univ. (TX)
SUNY–Albany
SUNY–Binghamton
SUNY–Empire State College
SUNY–Farmingdale
SUNY–Oswego
SUNY–Purchase College
SUNY–Stony Brook
Sweet Briar College (VA)
Syracuse Univ. (NY)
Tarleton State Univ. (TX)
Taylor Univ. (IN)
Tennessee Wesleyan College
Texas A&M International Univ.
Texas A&M Univ.–College Station
Texas A&M Univ.–Commerce
Texas A&M Univ.–Corpus Christi

Texas State Univ.–San Marcos
Texas Tech Univ.
Texas Wesleyan Univ.
Texas Woman's Univ.
Tiffin Univ. (OH)
Tulane Univ. (LA)
Tusculum College (TN)
Univ. at Buffalo–SUNY
Univ. of Akron (OH)
Univ. of Alabama
Univ. of Alaska–Anchorage
Univ. of Alaska–Fairbanks
Univ. of Arizona
Univ. of Bridgeport (CT)
Univ. of California–Berkeley
Univ. of California–Davis
Univ. of California–Irvine
Univ. of California–Los Angeles
Univ. of Colorado–Boulder
Univ. of Colorado–Denver
Univ. of Connecticut
Univ. of Dallas
Univ. of Delaware
Univ. of Denver
Univ. of Florida
Univ. of Hartford (CT)
Univ. of Houston
Univ. of Houston–Downtown
Univ. of Maine–Farmington
Univ. of Mary Washington (VA)
Univ. of Maryland–Baltimore County
Univ. of Maryland–College Park
Univ. of Maryland–Eastern Shore
Univ. of Maryland–Univ. College
Univ. of Massachusetts–Amherst
Univ. of Memphis
Univ. of Michigan–Dearborn
Univ. of Minnesota–Crookston
Univ. of Minnesota–Duluth
Univ. of Minnesota–Twin Cities
Univ. of Missouri–Columbia
Univ. of Missouri–Kansas City
Univ. of Missouri–St. Louis
Univ. of Montana
Univ. of Montana–Western
Univ. of Nebraska–Omaha
Univ. of Nevada–Las Vegas
Univ. of North Dakota
Univ. of North Texas
Univ. of Northern Colorado
Univ. of Pittsburgh–Greensburg
Univ. of Puget Sound (WA)
Univ. of Redlands (CA)
Univ. of Rhode Island
Univ. of Richmond (VA)
Univ. of South Florida
Univ. of Southern California
Univ. of St. Francis (IL)
Univ. of St. Mary (KS)
Univ. of St. Thomas (MN)
Univ. of Tennessee–Martin
Univ. of Texas of the Permian Basin
Univ. of Texas–Arlington
Univ. of Texas–Austin
Univ. of Texas–Brownsville
Univ. of Texas–Dallas
Univ. of Texas–El Paso
Univ. of Texas–San Antonio
Univ. of Texas–Tyler
Univ. of the Arts (PA)

Univ. of Toledo (OH)
Univ. of Virginia
Univ. of Virginia–Wise
Univ. of Washington
Univ. of Wisconsin–Green Bay
Univ. of Wisconsin–Madison
Univ. of Wisconsin–Milwaukee
Univ. of Wisconsin–Platteville
Univ. of Wisconsin–Stevens Point
Univ. of Wisconsin–Superior
Univ. of Wisconsin–Whitewater
Univ. of Wyoming
Ursinus College (PA)
Ursuline College (OH)
Utah State Univ.
Utah Valley State College
Valley City State Univ. (ND)
Valparaiso Univ. (IN)
Vanderbilt Univ. (TN)
Vassar College (NY)
Villa Julie College (MD)
Virginia State Univ.
Viterbo Univ. (WI)
Washington and Lee Univ. (VA)
Washington College (MD)
Washington State Univ.
Washington Univ. In St. Louis
Wayne State College (NE)
Wayne State Univ. (MI)
Waynesburg College (PA)
Wesleyan College (GA)
West Liberty State College (WV)
West Texas A&M Univ.
West Virginia Univ.
West Virginia Univ. Institute of Technology
Western Kentucky Univ.
Western Michigan Univ.
Western Oregon Univ.
Western Washington Univ.
Wheaton College (IL)
Wheaton College (MA)
Wheeling Jesuit Univ. (WV)
Widener Univ. (PA)
Wilkes Univ. (PA)
William Jewell College (MO)
William Woods Univ. (MO)
Wisconsin Lutheran College
Worcester Polytechnic Institute (MA)
Yale Univ. (CT)
York College of Pennsylvania

Museology/Museum Studies

Baylor Univ. (TX)
Juniata College (PA)
Regis College (MA)
Texas A&M Univ.–College Station
Tusculum College (TN)
Univ. of Iowa

Music

Abilene Christian Univ. (TX)
Adams State College (CO)
Adelphi Univ. (NY)
Adrian College (MI)

Agnes Scott College (GA)
Alabama State Univ.
Albany State Univ. (GA)
Albertson College (ID)
Albion College (MI)
Albright College (PA)
Alcorn State Univ. (MS)
Alderson-Broaddus College (WV)
Allegheny College (PA)
Allen Univ. (SC)
Alma College (MI)
Alverno College (WI)
American Univ. (DC)
Amherst College (MA)
Anderson College (SC)
Anderson Univ. (IN)
Andrews Univ. (MI)
Angelo State Univ. (TX)
Anna Maria College (MA)
Appalachian State Univ. (NC)
Aquinas College (MI)
Arizona State Univ.
Arkansas State Univ.
Arkansas Tech Univ.
Armstrong Atlantic State Univ. (GA)
Asbury College (KY)
Auburn Univ. (AL)
Augusta State Univ. (GA)
Augustana College (IL)
Austin College (TX)
Austin Peay State Univ. (TN)
Averett Univ. (VA)
Avila Univ. (MO)
Azusa Pacific Univ. (CA)
Baker College of Flint (MI)
Baker Univ. (KS)
Baldwin-Wallace College (OH)
Ball State Univ. (IN)
Barnard College (NY)
Barry Univ. (FL)
Bates College (ME)
Baylor Univ. (TX)
Bellarmine Univ. (KY)
Belmont Univ. (TN)
Beloit College (WI)
Bemidji State Univ. (MN)
Benedictine College (KS)
Benedictine Univ. (IL)
Bennington College (VT)
Berea College (KY)
Berklee College of Music (MA)
Berry College (GA)
Bethany College (KS)
Bethany College (WV)
Bethany College (CA)
Bethel College (KS)
Bethel College (IN)
Bethel Univ. (MN)
Bethune-Cookman College (FL)
Biola Univ. (CA)
Black Hills State Univ. (SD)
Bloomsburg Univ. of Pennsylvania
Blue Mountain College (MS)
Bluefield College (VA)
Bluffton Univ. (OH)
Boise State Univ. (ID)
Boston Conservatory
Boston Univ.
Bowdoin College (ME)
Bowling Green State Univ. (OH)

Bradley Univ. (IL)
Brandeis Univ. (MA)
Brenau Univ. (GA)
Brevard College (NC)
Brewton-Parker College (GA)
Briar Cliff Univ. (IA)
Bridgewater College (VA)
Bridgewater State College (MA)
Brigham Young Univ.–Hawaii
Brigham Young Univ.–Provo (UT)
Brown Univ. (RI)
Bryan College (TN)
Bryn Mawr College (PA)
Bucknell Univ. (PA)
Buena Vista Univ. (IA)
Buffalo State College
Butler Univ. (IN)
Cal Poly–San Luis Obispo
Caldwell College (NJ)
California Baptist Univ.
California Institute of the Arts
California Lutheran Univ.
California State Polytechnic
　Univ.–Pomona
California State Univ.–Bakersfield
California State Univ.–Chico
California State Univ.–Fresno
California State Univ.–Fullerton
California State Univ.–Hayward
California State Univ.–Long Beach
California State Univ.–Los Angeles
California State Univ.–Northridge
California State Univ.–Sacramento
California State Univ.–San
　Bernardino
California State Univ.–San Marcos
California State Univ.–Stanislaus
Calvin College (MI)
Cameron Univ. (OK)
Campbell Univ. (NC)
Campbellsville Univ. (KY)
Canisius College (NY)
Capital Univ. (OH)
Cardinal Stritch Univ. (WI)
Carleton College (MN)
Carnegie Mellon Univ. (PA)
Carroll College (WI)
Carson-Newman College (TN)
Carthage College (WI)
Case Western Reserve Univ. (OH)
Castleton State College (VT)
Catholic Univ. of America (DC)
Cedar Crest College (PA)
Cedarville Univ. (OH)
Centenary College of Louisiana
Central Christian College (KS)
Central College (IA)
Central Connecticut State Univ.
Central Methodist Univ. (MO)
Central Michigan Univ.
Central Missouri State Univ.
Central State Univ. (OH)
Central Washington Univ.
Centre College (KY)
Chadron State College (NE)
Chapman Univ. (CA)
Charleston Southern Univ. (SC)
Chatham College (PA)
Chestnut Hill College (PA)
Cheyney Univ. of Pennsylvania
Chicago State Univ.

Chowan College (NC)
Christian Heritage College (CA)
Christopher Newport Univ. (VA)
Claflin Univ. (SC)
Clarion Univ. of Pennsylvania
Clark Atlanta Univ.
Clark Univ. (MA)
Clayton Coll. and State Univ. (GA)
Clearwater Christian College (FL)
Cleveland Institute of Music
Cleveland State Univ.
Coastal Carolina Univ. (SC)
Coe College (IA)
Coker College (SC)
Colby College (ME)
Colgate Univ. (NY)
College of Charleston (SC)
College of Mount St. Joseph (OH)
College of New Jersey
College of Santa Fe (NM)
College of St. Benedict (MN)
College of St. Catherine (MN)
College of St. Elizabeth (NJ)
College of St. Rose (NY)
College of St. Scholastica (MN)
College of the Holy Cross (MA)
College of the Ozarks (MO)
College of William and Mary (VA)
College of Wooster (OH)
Colorado Christian Univ.
Colorado College
Colorado State Univ.
Columbia College (SC)
Columbia College (IL)
Columbia Union College (MD)
Columbia Univ. (NY)
Columbus State Univ. (GA)
Concordia College (NY)
Concordia Coll.–Moorhead (MN)
Concordia Univ. (NE)
Concordia Univ. (CA)
Concordia Univ. (MI)
Concordia Univ. Wisconsin
Concordia Univ.–St. Paul (MN)
Connecticut College
Converse College (SC)
Cornell College (IA)
Cornell Univ. (NY)
Cornerstone Univ. (MI)
Cornish College of the Arts (WA)
Covenant College (GA)
Creighton Univ. (NE)
Culver-Stockton College (MO)
Cumberland College (KY)
Cumberland Univ. (TN)
CUNY–Baruch College
CUNY–Brooklyn College
CUNY–City College
CUNY–College of Staten Island
CUNY–Hunter College
CUNY–Lehman College
CUNY–Queens College
CUNY–York College
Dakota Wesleyan Univ. (SD)
Dallas Baptist Univ.
Dana College (NE)
Dartmouth College (NH)
David Lipscomb Univ. (TN)
Davidson College (NC)
Davis and Elkins College (WV)
Delaware State Univ.

Delta State Univ. (MS)
Denison Univ. (OH)
Depaul Univ. (IL)
Depauw Univ. (IN)
Dickinson College (PA)
Dickinson State Univ. (ND)
Dillard Univ. (LA)
Dominican Univ. of California (CA)
Dordt College (IA)
Dowling College (NY)
Drew Univ. (NJ)
Drexel Univ. (PA)
Drury Univ. (MO)
Duke Univ. (NC)
Duquesne Univ. (PA)
Earlham College (IN)
East Carolina Univ. (NC)
East Central Univ. (OK)
East Tennessee State Univ.
East Texas Baptist Univ.
Eastern Illinois Univ.
Eastern Kentucky Univ.
Eastern Mennonite Univ. (VA)
Eastern Michigan Univ.
Eastern Nazarene College (MA)
Eastern New Mexico Univ.
Eastern Oregon Univ.
Eastern Univ. (PA)
Eastern Washington Univ.
Eckerd College (FL)
Edgewood College (WI)
Edinboro Univ. of Pennsylvania
Edward Waters College (FL)
Elizabeth City State Univ. (NC)
Elizabethtown College (PA)
Elmhurst College (IL)
Elmira College (NY)
Elon Univ. (NC)
Emmanuel College (GA)
Emory and Henry College (VA)
Emory Univ. (GA)
Emporia State Univ. (KS)
Erskine College (SC)
Eureka College (IL)
Evangel Univ. (MO)
Excelsior College (NY)
Faulkner Univ. (AL)
Fayetteville State Univ. (NC)
Ferris State Univ. (MI)
Florida A&M Univ.
Florida Atlantic Univ.
Florida International Univ.
Florida Southern College
Florida State Univ.
Fordham Univ. (NY)
Fort Hays State Univ. (KS)
Fort Lewis College (CO)
Franklin and Marshall College (PA)
Franklin Pierce College (NH)
Freed-Hardeman Univ. (TN)
Fresno Pacific Univ. (CA)
Friends Univ. (KS)
Frostburg State Univ. (MD)
Furman Univ. (SC)
Geneva College (PA)
George Fox Univ. (OR)
George Mason Univ. (VA)
George Washington Univ. (DC)
Georgetown College (KY)
Georgia College and State Univ.
Georgia Southern Univ.

Georgia Southwestern State Univ.
Georgia State Univ.
Georgian Court Univ. (NJ)
Gettysburg College (PA)
Gonzaga Univ. (WA)
Gordon College (MA)
Goshen College (IN)
Goucher College (MD)
Grace College and Seminary (IN)
Grace Univ. (NE)
Graceland Univ. (IA)
Grambling State Univ. (LA)
Grand Valley State Univ. (MI)
Greensboro College (NC)
Greenville College (IL)
Grinnell College (IA)
Grove City College (PA)
Guilford College (NC)
Gustavus Adolphus College (MN)
Hamilton College (NY)
Hamline Univ. (MN)
Hampshire College (MA)
Hampton Univ. (VA)
Hannibal-Lagrange College (MO)
Hanover College (IN)
Hardin-Simmons Univ. (TX)
Harding Univ. (AR)
Hartwick College (NY)
Harvard Univ. (MA)
Hastings College (NE)
Haverford College (PA)
Heidelberg College (OH)
Henderson State Univ. (AR)
Hendrix College (AR)
Hillsdale College (MI)
Hiram College (OH)
Hobart and William Smith Colleges
　(NY)
Hofstra Univ. (NY)
Hollins Univ. (VA)
Holy Names Univ. (CA)
Hood College (MD)
Hope College (MI)
Houghton College (NY)
Howard Payne Univ. (TX)
Howard Univ. (DC)
Humboldt State Univ. (CA)
Huntingdon College (AL)
Huntington College (IN)
Huston-Tillotson College (TX)
Idaho State Univ.
Illinois College
Illinois State Univ.
Illinois Wesleyan Univ.
Immaculata Univ. (PA)
Indiana State Univ.
Indiana Univ. of Pennsylvania
Indiana Univ. Southeast
Indiana Univ.–Bloomington
Indiana Univ.–South Bend
Indiana Univ.–Purdue Univ.–Fort
　Wayne
Indiana Wesleyan Univ.
Ithaca College (NY)
Jacksonville State Univ. (AL)
Jacksonville Univ. (FL)
James Madison Univ. (VA)
Jamestown College (ND)
John Brown Univ. (AR)
Johns Hopkins Univ. (MD)
Johnson C. Smith Univ. (NC)

Johnson State College (VT)
Judson College (IL)
Juilliard School (NY)
Kalamazoo College (MI)
Kansas State Univ.
Kean Univ. (NJ)
Keene State College (NH)
Kennesaw State Univ. (GA)
Kent State Univ. (OH)
Kentucky State Univ.
Kentucky Wesleyan College
Knox College (IL)
Kutztown Univ. of Pennsylvania
La Salle Univ. (PA)
La Sierra Univ. (CA)
Lafayette College (PA)
Lagrange College (GA)
Lake Forest College (IL)
Lakeland College (WI)
Lamar Univ. (TX)
Lambuth Univ. (TN)
Lander Univ. (SC)
Lane College (TN)
Lawrence Univ. (WI)
Lebanon Valley College (PA)
Lehigh Univ. (PA)
Lemoyne-Owen College (TN)
Lenoir-Rhyne College (NC)
Lewis and Clark College (OR)
Lewis Univ. (IL)
Liberty Univ. (VA)
Limestone College (SC)
Lincoln Univ. (PA)
Lindenwood Univ. (MO)
Linfield College (OR)
Livingstone College (NC)
Lock Haven Univ. of Pennsylvania
Long Island Univ.–Brooklyn (NY)
Long Island Univ.–C.W. Post
　Campus (NY)
Longy School of Music (MA)
Loras College (IA)
Louisiana College
Louisiana State Univ.–Baton Rouge
Louisiana Tech Univ.
Loyola Marymount Univ. (CA)
Loyola Univ. Chicago
Loyola Univ. New Orleans
Lubbock Christian Univ. (TX)
Luther College (IA)
Lycoming College (PA)
Lynchburg College (VA)
Lynn Univ. (FL)
Lyon College (AR)
Macalester College (MN)
Macmurray College (IL)
Madonna Univ. (MI)
Malone College (OH)
Manchester College (IN)
Manhattanville College (NY)
Mansfield Univ. of Pennsylvania
Marian College (IN)
Marian College of Fond Du Lac
　(WI)
Marietta College (OH)
Mars Hill College (NC)
Martin Univ. (IN)
Mary Baldwin College (VA)
Marygrove College (MI)
Marylhurst Univ. (OR)
Maryville College (TN)

Marywood Univ. (PA)
Massachusetts Institute of Technology
Master's Coll. and Seminary (CA)
Mcdaniel College (MD)
Mckendree College (IL)
Mcmurry Univ. (TX)
Mcneese State Univ. (LA)
Mcpherson College (KS)
Mercer Univ. (GA)
Mercyhurst College (PA)
Meredith College (NC)
Mesa State College (CO)
Messiah College (PA)
Methodist College (NC)
Metropolitan State College of Denver
Miami Univ.–Oxford (OH)
Michigan State Univ.
Middle Tennessee State Univ.
Middlebury College (VT)
Midland Lutheran College (NE)
Midwestern State Univ. (TX)
Millersville Univ. of Pennsylvania
Milligan College (TN)
Millikin Univ. (IL)
Mills College (CA)
Millsaps College (MS)
Minnesota State Univ.–Mankato
Minnesota State Univ.–Moorhead
Minot State Univ. (ND)
Mississippi College
Mississippi Univ. For Women
Mississippi Valley State Univ.
Missouri Baptist College
Missouri Southern State Univ.
Molloy College (NY)
Monmouth College (IL)
Monmouth Univ. (NJ)
Montana State Univ.–Billings
Montana State Univ.–Bozeman
Montclair State Univ. (NJ)
Montreat College (NC)
Moravian College (PA)
Morehead State Univ. (KY)
Morehouse College (GA)
Morgan State Univ. (MD)
Morningside College (IA)
Mount Holyoke College (MA)
Mount Marty College (SD)
Mount Mercy College (IA)
Mount St. Mary's College (CA)
Mount Union College (OH)
Mount Vernon Nazarene Univ. (OH)
Muhlenberg College (PA)
Murray State Univ. (KY)
Muskingum College (OH)
Nazareth College of Rochester (NY)
Nebraska Wesleyan Univ.
New England Conservatory of Music (MA)
New Jersey City Univ.
New Mexico Highlands Univ.
New Mexico State Univ.
New School Univ. (NY)
New York Univ.
Newberry College (SC)
Nicholls State Univ. (LA)
Norfolk State Univ. (VA)

North Carolina A&T State Univ.
North Carolina Central Univ.
North Carolina School of the Arts
North Central College (IL)
North Dakota State Univ.
North Georgia College and State Univ.
North Greenville College (SC)
North Park Univ. (IL)
Northeastern Illinois Univ.
Northeastern State Univ. (OK)
Northeastern Univ. (MA)
Northern Arizona Univ.
Northern Illinois Univ.
Northern Kentucky Univ.
Northern State Univ. (SD)
Northland College (WI)
Northwest Christian College (OR)
Northwest Missouri State Univ.
Northwest Nazarene Univ. (ID)
Northwestern College (IA)
Northwestern College (MN)
Northwestern Oklahoma State Univ.
Northwestern State Univ. of Louisiana
Northwestern Univ. (IL)
Notre Dame De Namur Univ. (CA)
Nyack College (NY)
Oakland Univ. (MI)
Oakwood College (AL)
Oberlin College (OH)
Occidental College (CA)
Ohio Northern Univ.
Ohio State Univ.–Columbus
Ohio Univ.
Ohio Wesleyan Univ.
Oklahoma Baptist Univ.
Oklahoma Christian Univ.
Oklahoma City Univ.
Oklahoma State Univ.
Oklahoma Wesleyan Univ.
Old Dominion Univ. (VA)
Olivet College (MI)
Olivet Nazarene Univ. (IL)
Oregon State Univ.
Ouachita Baptist Univ. (AR)
Our Lady of the Lake Univ. (TX)
Pacific Lutheran Univ. (WA)
Pacific Union College (CA)
Pacific Univ. (OR)
Paine College (GA)
Palm Beach Atlantic Univ. (FL)
Patten College (CA)
Peace College (NC)
Penn. State Univ.–Univ. Park
Pepperdine Univ. (CA)
Pfeiffer Univ. (NC)
Philander Smith College (AR)
Piedmont College (GA)
Pittsburg State Univ. (KS)
Plymouth State Univ. (NH)
Point Loma Nazarene Univ. (CA)
Pomona College (CA)
Portland State Univ. (OR)
Prairie View A&M Univ. (TX)
Presbyterian College (SC)
Princeton Univ. (NJ)
Principia College (IL)
Providence College (RI)
Queens Univ. of Charlotte (NC)

Quincy Univ. (IL)
Radford Univ. (VA)
Ramapo College of New Jersey
Randolph-Macon College (VA)
Randolph-Macon Woman's College (VA)
Reed College (OR)
Reinhardt College (GA)
Rhode Island College
Rhodes College (TN)
Rice Univ. (TX)
Rider Univ. (NJ)
Ripon College (WI)
Roanoke College (VA)
Roberts Wesleyan College (NY)
Rochester College (MI)
Rockford College (IL)
Rocky Mountain College (MT)
Rollins College (FL)
Roosevelt Univ. (IL)
Rust College (MS)
Rutgers–Camden (NJ)
Rutgers–New Brunswick (NJ)
Rutgers–Newark (NJ)
Saginaw Valley State Univ. (MI)
Salem College (NC)
Salisbury Univ. (MD)
Salve Regina Univ. (RI)
Sam Houston State Univ. (TX)
Samford Univ. (AL)
San Diego State Univ.
San Francisco Conservatory of Music
San Francisco State Univ.
San Jose State Univ. (CA)
Santa Clara Univ. (CA)
Savannah State Univ. (GA)
Schreiner Univ. (TX)
Scripps College (CA)
Seattle Pacific Univ.
Seattle Univ.
Seton Hall Univ. (NJ)
Seton Hill Univ. (PA)
Sewanee–Univ. of the South (TN)
Shaw Univ. (NC)
Shenandoah Univ. (VA)
Shepherd Univ. (WV)
Shorter College (GA)
Silver Lake College (WI)
Simmons College (MA)
Simpson College (IA)
Simpson Univ. (CA)
Skidmore College (NY)
Slippery Rock Univ. of Pennsylvania
Sonoma State Univ. (CA)
South Carolina State Univ.
South Dakota State Univ.
Southeast Missouri State Univ.
Southeastern College of the Assemblies of God
Southeastern Louisiana Univ.
Southeastern Oklahoma State Univ.
Southern Adventist Univ. (TN)
Southern Arkansas Univ.
Southern Connecticut State Univ.
Southern Illinois Univ.–Carbondale
Southern Illinois Univ.–Edwardsville
Southern Methodist Univ. (TX)
Southern Nazarene Univ. (OK)

Southern Oregon Univ.
Southern Univ. and A&M College (LA)
Southern Utah Univ.
Southern Wesleyan Univ. (SC)
Southwest Baptist Univ. (MO)
Southwest Minnesota State Univ. (MN)
Southwest Missouri State Univ.
Southwestern Adventist Univ. (TX)
Southwestern College (KS)
Southwestern Oklahoma State Univ.
Southwestern Univ. (TX)
Spelman College (GA)
Spring Arbor Univ. (MI)
St. Ambrose Univ. (IA)
St. Augustine's College (NC)
St. Cloud State Univ. (MN)
St. John's Univ. (MN)
St. Joseph's College (IN)
St. Lawrence Univ. (NY)
St. Louis Univ.
St. Martin's College (WA)
St. Mary's College (IN)
St. Mary's College of California
St. Mary's College of Maryland
St. Mary's Univ. of Minnesota
St. Mary's Univ. of San Antonio
St. Mary-of-The-Woods Coll. (IN)
St. Michael's College (VT)
St. Norbert College (WI)
St. Olaf College (MN)
St. Vincent College (PA)
St. Xavier Univ. (IL)
Stanford Univ. (CA)
State Univ. of West Georgia
Stephen F. Austin State Univ. (TX)
Sterling College (KS)
Stetson Univ. (FL)
Stevens Institute of Technology (NJ)
Stillman College (AL)
Sul Ross State Univ. (TX)
SUNY College of Arts and Sciences–Geneseo
SUNY College–Oneonta
SUNY College–Potsdam
SUNY–Albany
SUNY–Binghamton
SUNY–Fredonia
SUNY–Plattsburgh
SUNY–Purchase College
SUNY–Stony Brook
Susquehanna Univ. (PA)
Swarthmore College (PA)
Sweet Briar College (VA)
Syracuse Univ. (NY)
Tabor College (KS)
Talladega College (AL)
Tarleton State Univ. (TX)
Taylor Univ. (IN)
Temple Univ. (PA)
Tennessee State Univ.
Tennessee Technological Univ.
Texas A&M International Univ.
Texas A&M Univ.–College Station
Texas A&M Univ.–Commerce
Texas A&M Univ.–Corpus Christi
Texas A&M Univ.–Kingsville
Texas Christian Univ.

Texas College
Texas Lutheran Univ.
Texas State Univ.–San Marcos
Texas Tech Univ.
Texas Wesleyan Univ.
Texas Woman's Univ.
Thomas Edison State College (NJ)
Toccoa Falls College (GA)
Towson Univ. (MD)
Transylvania Univ. (KY)
Trevecca Nazarene Univ. (TN)
Trinity Christian College (IL)
Trinity College (CT)
Troy State Univ.–Troy (AL)
Truman State Univ. (MO)
Tufts Univ. (MA)
Tulane Univ. (LA)
Union College (NE)
Union Univ. (TN)
Univ. at Buffalo–SUNY
Univ. of Akron (OH)
Univ. of Alabama
Univ. of Alabama–Birmingham
Univ. of Alabama–Huntsville
Univ. of Alaska–Anchorage
Univ. of Alaska–Fairbanks
Univ. of Arizona
Univ. of Arkansas
Univ. of Arkansas–Little Rock
Univ. of Arkansas–Monticello
Univ. of Arkansas–Pine Bluff
Univ. of Bridgeport (CT)
Univ. of California–Berkeley
Univ. of California–Irvine
Univ. of California–Los Angeles
Univ. of California–Riverside
Univ. of California–Santa Barbara
Univ. of California–Santa Cruz
Univ. of Central Arkansas
Univ. of Central Florida
Univ. of Central Oklahoma
Univ. of Charleston (WV)
Univ. of Chicago
Univ. of Colorado–Boulder
Univ. of Colorado–Denver
Univ. of Connecticut
Univ. of Dayton (OH)
Univ. of Delaware
Univ. of Denver
Univ. of Evansville (IN)
Univ. of Florida
Univ. of Georgia
Univ. of Hartford (CT)
Univ. of Hawaii–Hilo
Univ. of Hawaii–Manoa
Univ. of Houston
Univ. of Illinois–Chicago
Univ. of Ill.–Urbana-Champaign
Univ. of Indianapolis
Univ. of Iowa
Univ. of Kansas
Univ. of Kentucky
Univ. of La Verne (CA)
Univ. of Louisiana–Lafayette
Univ. of Louisiana–Monroe
Univ. of Louisville (KY)
Univ. of Maine–Augusta
Univ. of Maine–Farmington
Univ. of Maine–Orono
Univ. of Mary (ND)
Univ. of Mary Hardin-Baylor (TX)

Univ. of Mary Washington (VA)
Univ. of Maryland–Baltimore County
Univ. of Maryland–College Park
Univ. of Massachusetts–Amherst
Univ. of Massachusetts–Boston
Univ. of Mass.–Dartmouth
Univ. of Massachusetts–Lowell
Univ. of Memphis
Univ. of Miami (FL)
Univ. of Michigan–Ann Arbor
Univ. of Michigan–Flint
Univ. of Minnesota–Duluth
Univ. of Minnesota–Morris
Univ. of Minnesota–Twin Cities
Univ. of Mississippi
Univ. of Missouri–Columbia
Univ. of Missouri–Kansas City
Univ. of Missouri–St. Louis
Univ. of Montana
Univ. of Montevallo (AL)
Univ. of Nebraska–Kearney
Univ. of Nebraska–Lincoln
Univ. of Nebraska–Omaha
Univ. of Nevada–Las Vegas
Univ. of Nevada–Reno
Univ. of New Hampshire
Univ. of New Haven (CT)
Univ. of New Mexico
Univ. of New Orleans
Univ. of North Alabama
Univ. of North Carolina–Asheville
Univ. of N.C.–Chapel Hill
Univ. of North Carolina–Charlotte
Univ. of N.C.–Greensboro
Univ. of North Carolina–Pembroke
Univ. of N.C.–Wilmington
Univ. of North Dakota
Univ. of North Florida
Univ. of North Texas
Univ. of Northern Colorado
Univ. of Northern Iowa
Univ. of Notre Dame (IN)
Univ. of Oklahoma
Univ. of Oregon
Univ. of Pennsylvania
Univ. of Pittsburgh
Univ. of Portland (OR)
Univ. of Puget Sound (WA)
Univ. of Redlands (CA)
Univ. of Rhode Island
Univ. of Richmond (VA)
Univ. of Rochester (NY)
Univ. of San Diego
Univ. of Science and Arts of Oklahoma
Univ. of Sioux Falls (SD)
Univ. of South Alabama
Univ. of South Carolina–Columbia
Univ. of South Dakota
Univ. of South Florida
Univ. of Southern California
Univ. of Southern Maine
Univ. of Southern Mississippi
Univ. of St. Francis (IL)
Univ. of St. Thomas (MN)
Univ. of St. Thomas (TX)
Univ. of Tampa (FL)
Univ. of Tennessee
Univ. of Tennessee–Chattanooga
Univ. of Tennessee–Martin

Univ. of Texas–Arlington
Univ. of Texas–Austin
Univ. of Texas–Brownsville
Univ. of Texas–El Paso
Univ. of Texas–Pan American
Univ. of Texas–San Antonio
Univ. of Texas–Tyler
Univ. of the Arts (PA)
Univ. of the District of Columbia
Univ. of the Incarnate Word (TX)
Univ. of the Ozarks (AR)
Univ. of the Pacific (CA)
Univ. of Toledo (OH)
Univ. of Tulsa (OK)
Univ. of Utah
Univ. of Vermont
Univ. of Virginia
Univ. of Washington
Univ. of West Florida
Univ. of Wisconsin–Eau Claire
Univ. of Wisconsin–Green Bay
Univ. of Wisconsin–La Crosse
Univ. of Wisconsin–Madison
Univ. of Wisconsin–Milwaukee
Univ. of Wisconsin–Platteville
Univ. of Wisconsin–River Falls
Univ. of Wisconsin–Stevens Point
Univ. of Wisconsin–Superior
Univ. of Wisconsin–Whitewater
Univ. of Wyoming
Utah State Univ.
Valdosta State Univ. (GA)
Valley City State Univ. (ND)
Valparaiso Univ. (IN)
Vanderbilt Univ. (TN)
Vanguard Univ. of Southern California
Vassar College (NY)
Virginia Commonwealth Univ.
Virginia State Univ.
Virginia Tech
Virginia Wesleyan College
Viterbo Univ. (WI)
Wabash College (IN)
Wagner College (NY)
Wake Forest Univ. (NC)
Waldorf College (IA)
Warner Pacific College (OR)
Wartburg College (IA)
Washburn Univ. (KS)
Washington and Jefferson College (PA)
Washington and Lee Univ. (VA)
Washington College (MD)
Washington State Univ.
Washington Univ. In St. Louis
Wayland Baptist Univ. (TX)
Wayne State College (NE)
Wayne State Univ. (MI)
Weber State Univ. (UT)
Webster Univ. (MO)
Wellesley College (MA)
Wesleyan College (GA)
Wesleyan Univ. (CT)
West Chester Univ. of Pennsylvania
West Texas A&M Univ.
West Virginia Univ.
West Virginia Wesleyan College
Western Baptist College (OR)
Western Carolina Univ. (NC)
Western Connecticut State Univ.

Western Illinois Univ.
Western Kentucky Univ.
Western Michigan Univ.
Western New Mexico Univ.
Western Oregon Univ.
Western State College of Colorado
Western Washington Univ.
Westfield State College (MA)
Westminster College (PA)
Westmont College (CA)
Wheaton College (MA)
Wheaton College (IL)
Whitman College (WA)
Whittier College (CA)
Whitworth College (WA)
Wichita State Univ. (KS)
Wilberforce Univ. (OH)
Wiley College (TX)
Wilkes Univ. (PA)
Willamette Univ. (OR)
William Carey College (MS)
William Jewell College (MO)
William Paterson Univ. of New Jersey
Williams College (MA)
Wingate Univ. (NC)
Winston-Salem State Univ. (NC)
Winthrop Univ. (SC)
Wisconsin Lutheran College
Wittenberg Univ. (OH)
Wright State Univ. (OH)
Yale Univ. (CT)
Yeshiva Univ. (NY)
York College (NE)
York College of Pennsylvania
Youngstown State Univ. (OH)

Natural Resources and Conservation

Cal Poly–San Luis Obispo
California State Univ.–Sacramento
Depaul Univ. (IL)
Humboldt State Univ. (CA)
Penn. State Univ.–Univ. Park
Prescott College (AZ)
Springfield College (MA)
Stephen F. Austin State Univ. (TX)
Sul Ross State Univ. (TX)
Univ. of Alaska–Fairbanks
Univ. of California–Davis
Univ. of Louisiana–Lafayette
Univ. of Washington
Univ. of Wisconsin–Platteville
Univ. of Wisconsin–Stevens Point
Utah State Univ.

Natural Resources Conservation and Research

Abilene Christian Univ. (TX)
Adelphi Univ. (NY)
Adrian College (MI)
Alaska Pacific Univ.
Albertson College (ID)
Albright College (PA)
Alderson-Broaddus College (WV)
Alfred Univ. (NY)

Allegheny College (PA)
Alverno College (WI)
American Univ. (DC)
Andrews Univ. (MI)
Anna Maria College (MA)
Antioch College (OH)
Aquinas College (MI)
Assumption College (MA)
Auburn Univ. (AL)
Augustana College (IL)
Aurora Univ. (IL)
Averett Univ. (VA)
Ball State Univ. (IN)
Barnard College (NY)
Barry Univ. (FL)
Barton College (NC)
Bates College (ME)
Baylor Univ. (TX)
Bemidji State Univ. (MN)
Benedictine Univ. (IL)
Bennington College (VT)
Berry College (GA)
Bethany College (WV)
Bethel Univ. (MN)
Boston Univ.
Bowdoin College (ME)
Bradley Univ. (IL)
Brandeis Univ. (MA)
Brenau Univ. (GA)
Brevard College (NC)
Briar Cliff Univ. (IA)
Bridgewater College (VA)
Brown Univ. (RI)
Bucknell Univ. (PA)
California Lutheran Univ.
California State Univ.–Chico
California State Univ.–Hayward
California State Univ.–Long Beach
California State Univ.–Monterey Bay
California State Univ.–Sacramento
California State Univ.–San Bernardino
California Univ. of Pennsylvania
Calvin College (MI)
Canisius College (NY)
Capital Univ. (OH)
Carlow College (PA)
Carroll College (MT)
Carroll College (WI)
Carthage College (WI)
Case Western Reserve Univ. (OH)
Catawba College (NC)
Cazenovia College (NY)
Central College (IA)
Central Methodist Univ. (MO)
Central Michigan Univ.
Chatham College (PA)
Chestnut Hill College (PA)
Christopher Newport Univ. (VA)
Claflin Univ. (SC)
Claremont Mckenna College (CA)
Clarion Univ. of Pennsylvania
Clark Univ. (MA)
Cleveland State Univ.
Colby College (ME)
Colby-Sawyer College (NH)
Colgate Univ. (NY)
College of Santa Fe (NM)
College of St. Benedict (MN)
College of St. Rose (NY)

Colorado College
Colorado State Univ.
Columbia College (MO)
Columbia Univ. (NY)
Concordia Univ. (OR)
Concordia Univ.–Austin (TX)
Concordia Univ.–St. Paul (MN)
Cornell College (IA)
Cornell Univ. (NY)
CUNY–Brooklyn College
CUNY–Medgar Evers College
CUNY–Queens College
Curry College (MA)
Dana College (NE)
Dartmouth College (NH)
David Lipscomb Univ. (TN)
Delaware State Univ.
Denison Univ. (OH)
Depauw Univ. (IN)
Dickinson College (PA)
Dominican Univ. (IL)
Dordt College (IA)
Drake Univ. (IA)
Drexel Univ. (PA)
Drury Univ. (MO)
Duke Univ. (NC)
Duquesne Univ. (PA)
Earlham College (IN)
Eastern Kentucky Univ.
Eastern Mennonite Univ. (VA)
Eastern Univ. (PA)
Eastern Washington Univ.
Eckerd College (FL)
Edinboro Univ. of Pennsylvania
Elon Univ. (NC)
Emmanuel College (MA)
Emory and Henry College (VA)
Emory Univ. (GA)
Endicott College (MA)
Evergreen State College (WA)
Fairleigh Dickinson Univ. (NJ)
Ferrum College (VA)
Florida A&M Univ.
Florida Institute of Technology
Florida International Univ.
Franklin and Marshall College (PA)
Franklin Pierce College (NH)
Fresno Pacific Univ. (CA)
Frostburg State Univ. (MD)
Gannon Univ. (PA)
Georgia College and State Univ.
Gettysburg College (PA)
Goshen College (IN)
Grand Canyon Univ. (AZ)
Grand Valley State Univ. (MI)
Green Mountain College (VT)
Guilford College (NC)
Gustavus Adolphus College (MN)
Hamline Univ. (MN)
Hampshire College (MA)
Hampton Univ. (VA)
Hardin-Simmons Univ. (TX)
Harvard Univ. (MA)
Hawaii Pacific Univ.
Hendrix College (AR)
Heritage College (WA)
Hiram College (OH)
Hobart and William Smith Colleges (NY)
Hofstra Univ. (NY)
Hollins Univ. (VA)

Hood College (MD)
Hope College (MI)
Humboldt State Univ. (CA)
Huntington College (IN)
Illinois Wesleyan Univ.
Immaculata Univ. (PA)
Indiana Univ. East
Indiana Univ.–South Bend
Indiana Univ.-Purdue
  Univ.–Indianapolis
Iowa State Univ.
Ithaca College (NY)
John Brown Univ. (AR)
Johnson State College (VT)
Juniata College (PA)
Keene State College (NH)
Kent State Univ. (OH)
Kentucky Christian College
King's College (PA)
Knox College (IL)
Kutztown Univ. of Pennsylvania
La Salle Univ. (PA)
Lake Forest College (IL)
Lake Superior State Univ. (MI)
Lamar Univ. (TX)
Lambuth Univ. (TN)
Lander Univ. (SC)
Lawrence Univ. (WI)
Lees-Mcrae College (NC)
Lehigh Univ. (PA)
Lenoir-Rhyne College (NC)
Lesley Univ. (MA)
Lewis and Clark College (OR)
Lewis Univ. (IL)
Lincoln Memorial Univ. (TN)
Linfield College (OR)
Louisiana State Univ.–Baton Rouge
Louisiana State Univ.–Shreveport
Louisiana Tech Univ.
Loyola Univ. Chicago
Lynchburg College (VA)
Lyon College (AR)
Macalester College (MN)
Madonna Univ. (MI)
Maharishi Univ. of Management
  (IA)
Manchester College (IN)
Marietta College (OH)
Marist College (NY)
Marshall Univ. (WV)
Marylhurst Univ. (OR)
Marymount Univ. (VA)
Maryville College (TN)
Maryville Univ. of St. Louis (MO)
Mcdaniel College (MD)
Mcmurry Univ. (TX)
Mercer Univ. (GA)
Meredith College (NC)
Merrimack College (MA)
Mesa State College (CO)
Messiah College (PA)
Miami Univ.–Oxford (OH)
Michigan State Univ.
Michigan Technological Univ.
Middlebury College (VT)
Midwestern State Univ. (TX)
Mills College (CA)
Minnesota State Univ.–Mankato
Montana State Univ.–Billings
Montana State Univ.–Bozeman
Montreat College (NC)

Moravian College (PA)
Mount Holyoke College (MA)
Muhlenberg College (PA)
Neumann College (PA)
New England College (NH)
New Jersey Institute of Technology
New Mexico Highlands Univ.
New Mexico State Univ.
North Carolina Central Univ.
North Carolina State Univ.–Raleigh
North Carolina Wesleyan College
North Dakota State Univ.
Northeastern Illinois Univ.
Northeastern State Univ. (OK)
Northeastern Univ. (MA)
Northern Arizona Univ.
Northern Kentucky Univ.
Northern Michigan Univ.
Northland College (WI)
Northwest College (WA)
Northwestern Univ. (IL)
Nova Southeastern Univ. (FL)
Oberlin College (OH)
Occidental College (CA)
Ohio Northern Univ.
Ohio State Univ.–Columbus
Ohio Wesleyan Univ.
Oklahoma State Univ.
Olivet College (MI)
Oregon Institute of Technology
Oregon State Univ.
Otterbein College (OH)
Pace Univ. (NY)
Pacific Univ. (OR)
Paine College (GA)
Penn. State Univ.–Univ. Park
Pfeiffer Univ. (NC)
Pitzer College (CA)
Point Park Univ. (PA)
Pomona College (CA)
Portland State Univ. (OR)
Prescott College (AZ)
Principia College (IL)
Purdue Univ.–West Lafayette (IN)
Ramapo College of New Jersey
Randolph-Macon College (VA)
Richard Stockton College of New
  Jersey
Rider Univ. (NJ)
Ripon College (WI)
Roanoke College (VA)
Robert Morris Univ. (PA)
Rochester Institute of Tech. (NY)
Rocky Mountain College (MT)
Roosevelt Univ. (IL)
Rosemont College (PA)
Russell Sage College (NY)
Rutgers–Camden (NJ)
Rutgers–New Brunswick (NJ)
Rutgers–Newark (NJ)
Sacred Heart Univ. (CT)
Salisbury Univ. (MD)
Sam Houston State Univ. (TX)
Samford Univ. (AL)
San Diego State Univ.
San Francisco State Univ.
San Jose State Univ. (CA)
Santa Clara Univ. (CA)
Scripps College (CA)
Seattle Univ.
Sewanee–Univ. of the South (TN)

Shaw Univ. (NC)
Sheldon Jackson College (AK)
Shenandoah Univ. (VA)
Shepherd Univ. (WV)
Shippensburg Univ. of
  Pennsylvania
Shorter College (GA)
Simmons College (MA)
Simpson College (IA)
Skidmore College (NY)
Slippery Rock Univ. of Pennsylvania
Sonoma State Univ. (CA)
Southeast Missouri State Univ.
Southeastern Oklahoma State
  Univ.
Southern Methodist Univ. (TX)
Southern New Hampshire Univ.
Southern Oregon Univ.
Southwest Minnesota State Univ.
  (MN)
Spelman College (GA)
St. Anselm College (NH)
St. Bonaventure Univ. (NY)
St. Cloud State Univ. (MN)
St. Edward's Univ. (TX)
St. Francis Univ. (PA)
St. John's Univ. (NY)
St. John's Univ. (MN)
St. Joseph's College (ME)
St. Joseph's Univ. (PA)
St. Lawrence Univ. (NY)
St. Leo Univ. (FL)
St. Louis Univ.
St. Michael's College (VT)
St. Norbert College (WI)
St. Olaf College (MN)
St. Vincent College (PA)
Stanford Univ. (CA)
State Univ. of West Georgia
Stephen F. Austin State Univ. (TX)
Stetson Univ. (FL)
Suffolk Univ. (MA)
SUNY College Environmental
  Science and Forestry
SUNY College–Brockport
SUNY College–Oneonta
SUNY–Albany
SUNY–Binghamton
SUNY–Plattsburgh
SUNY–Stony Brook
Sweet Briar College (VA)
Taylor Univ. (IN)
Teikyo Post Univ. (CT)
Temple Univ. (PA)
Texas A&M International Univ.
Texas A&M Univ.–College Station
Texas A&M Univ.–Corpus Christi
Texas Christian Univ.
Texas State Univ.–San Marcos
Texas Tech Univ.
Thiel College (PA)
Thomas Edison State College (NJ)
Thomas Univ. (GA)
Tri-State Univ. (IN)
Trinity College (DC)
Trinity College (CT)
Troy State Univ.–Troy (AL)
Tulane Univ. (LA)
Tusculum College (TN)
Unity College (ME)
Univ. of Alabama

Univ. of Alaska–Fairbanks
Univ. of Alaska–Southeast
Univ. of Arizona
Univ. of Arkansas
Univ. of Arkansas–Pine Bluff
Univ. of California–Berkeley
Univ. of California–Davis
Univ. of California–Riverside
Univ. of California–Santa Barbara
Univ. of California–Santa Cruz
Univ. of Central Arkansas
Univ. of Charleston (WV)
Univ. of Chicago
Univ. of Colorado–Boulder
Univ. of Colorado–Colorado
  Springs
Univ. of Connecticut
Univ. of Delaware
Univ. of Denver
Univ. of Dubuque (IA)
Univ. of Evansville (IN)
Univ. of Florida
Univ. of Georgia
Univ. of Hawaii–Manoa
Univ. of Houston
Univ. of Ill.–Urbana-Champaign
Univ. of Indianapolis
Univ. of Iowa
Univ. of Kansas
Univ. of Kentucky
Univ. of La Verne (CA)
Univ. of Maine–Farmington
Univ. of Maine–Fort Kent
Univ. of Maine–Machias
Univ. of Maine–Orono
Univ. of Maine–Presque Isle
Univ. of Maryland–Baltimore
  County
Univ. of Maryland–College Park
Univ. of Maryland–Univ. College
Univ. of Massachusetts–Amherst
Univ. of Michigan–Ann Arbor
Univ. of Michigan–Dearborn
Univ. of Michigan–Flint
Univ. of Minnesota–Crookston
Univ. of Minnesota–Duluth
Univ. of Minnesota–Twin Cities
Univ. of Missouri–Columbia
Univ. of Missouri–Kansas City
Univ. of Montana
Univ. of Nebraska–Lincoln
Univ. of Nebraska–Omaha
Univ. of Nevada–Las Vegas
Univ. of Nevada–Reno
Univ. of New England (ME)
Univ. of New Hampshire
Univ. of New Mexico
Univ. of New Orleans
Univ. of North Carolina–Asheville
Univ. of N.C.–Chapel Hill
Univ. of North Carolina–Pembroke
Univ. of N.C.–Wilmington
Univ. of Northern Iowa
Univ. of Notre Dame (IN)
Univ. of Oklahoma
Univ. of Oregon
Univ. of Pennsylvania
Univ. of Pittsburgh–Johnstown
Univ. of Portland (OR)
Univ. of Redlands (CA)
Univ. of Rhode Island

Univ. of Richmond (VA)
Univ. of Rio Grande (OH)
Univ. of Rochester (NY)
Univ. of San Diego
Univ. of San Francisco
Univ. of South Florida
Univ. of Southern California
Univ. of Southern Maine
Univ. of St. Francis (IL)
Univ. of St. Francis (IN)
Univ. of St. Thomas (TX)
Univ. of St. Thomas (MN)
Univ. of Tampa (FL)
Univ. of Tennessee–Chattanooga
Univ. of Texas of the Permian Basin
Univ. of Texas–Brownsville
Univ. of Texas–El Paso
Univ. of Texas–San Antonio
Univ. of the District of Columbia
Univ. of the Incarnate Word (TX)
Univ. of the Pacific (CA)
Univ. of Toledo (OH)
Univ. of Tulsa (OK)
Univ. of Utah
Univ. of Vermont
Univ. of Virginia
Univ. of Washington
Univ. of West Florida
Univ. of Wisconsin–Green Bay
Univ. of Wisconsin–Milwaukee
Univ. of Wisconsin–River Falls
Univ. of Wisconsin–Stevens Point
Univ. of Wyoming
Upper Iowa Univ.
Ursinus College (PA)
Valdosta State Univ. (GA)
Valparaiso Univ. (IN)
Vassar College (NY)
Virginia Commonwealth Univ.
Virginia Intermont College
Virginia Tech
Virginia Wesleyan College
Washington College (MD)
Washington State Univ.
Washington Univ. In St. Louis
Wayne State Univ. (MI)
Webster Univ. (MO)
Wellesley College (MA)
Wesleyan Univ. (CT)
West Texas A&M Univ.
West Virginia Wesleyan College
Western Carolina Univ. (NC)
Western Michigan Univ.
Western State College of Colorado
Western Washington Univ.
Westfield State College (MA)
Westminster College (MO)
Westminster College (PA)
Wheaton College (IL)
Wheaton College (MA)
Whittier College (CA)
Willamette Univ. (OR)
William Paterson Univ. of New
  Jersey
Wilson College (PA)
Winthrop Univ. (SC)
Yale Univ. (CT)
Youngstown State Univ. (OH)

Natural Resources Management and Policy

Alaska Pacific Univ.
Angelo State Univ. (TX)
Bowling Green State Univ. (OH)
California State Univ.–Bakersfield
Carnegie Mellon Univ. (PA)
Charleston Southern Univ. (SC)
Colorado State Univ.
Drury Univ. (MO)
Elmhurst College (IL)
Glenville State College (WV)
Heidelberg College (OH)
Humboldt State Univ. (CA)
Louisiana State Univ.–Baton Rouge
Marywood Univ. (PA)
Michigan State Univ.
Montana State Univ.–Bozeman
New Mexico Highlands Univ.
North Carolina State Univ.–Raleigh
Northland College (WI)
Nova Southeastern Univ. (FL)
Ohio State Univ.–Columbus
Oregon State Univ.
Prescott College (AZ)
Roanoke College (VA)
Rochester Institute of Tech. (NY)
Rutgers–New Brunswick (NJ)
Sewanee–Univ. of the South (TN)
South Dakota State Univ.
Southern Illinois Univ.–Carbondale
St. Vincent College (PA)
SUNY College Environmental
    Science and Forestry
Texas A&M Univ.–Galveston
Texas State Univ.–San Marcos
Tuskegee Univ. (AL)
Unity College (ME)
Univ. of Alaska–Fairbanks
Univ. of Arizona
Univ. of California–Berkeley
Univ. of California–Davis
Univ. of Delaware
Univ. of Georgia
Univ. of Hawaii–Manoa
Univ. of Illinois–Urbana-
    Champaign
Univ. of Maine–Farmington
Univ. of Maine–Orono
Univ. of Massachusetts–Amherst
Univ. of Michigan–Ann Arbor
Univ. of Minnesota–Twin Cities
Univ. of Nebraska–Lincoln
Univ. of Nevada–Reno
Univ. of New Hampshire
Univ. of Rhode Island
Univ. of Tennessee–Martin
Univ. of Vermont
Univ. of Wisconsin–River Falls
Washington State Univ.
Western Carolina Univ. (NC)
Western Oregon Univ.
Xavier Univ. (OH)

Natural Sciences

Bethel College (KS)
Blue Mountain College (MS)

California State Univ.–San
    Bernardino
Calvin College (MI)
Case Western Reserve Univ. (OH)
Central Washington Univ.
Christian Brothers Univ. (TN)
Colgate Univ. (NY)
College of Mount St. Joseph (OH)
Concordia Univ. (NE)
Covenant College (GA)
Daemen College (NY)
Dominican Univ. (IL)
Edgewood College (WI)
Evergreen State College (WA)
Hofstra Univ. (NY)
Houghton College (NY)
Johns Hopkins Univ. (MD)
Johnson C. Smith Univ. (NC)
Juniata College (PA)
Lawrence Univ. (WI)
Lewis-Clark State College (ID)
Loyola Marymount Univ. (CA)
Madonna Univ. (MI)
Marygrove College (MI)
Mount St. Mary College (NY)
Muhlenberg College (PA)
National Univ. (CA)
Oklahoma Baptist Univ.
Park Univ. (MO)
Pepperdine Univ. (CA)
Spelman College (GA)
St. Gregory's Univ. (OK)
SUNY College of Arts and
    Sciences–Geneseo
Tabor College (KS)
Thomas Edison State College (NJ)
Univ. of La Verne (CA)
Univ. of Maine–Orono
Univ. of Nebraska–Omaha
Univ. of New Hampshire
Univ. of Pennsylvania
Univ. of Puget Sound (WA)
Univ. of Science and Arts of
    Oklahoma
Virginia Wesleyan College
Xavier Univ. (OH)

Naval Architecture and Marine Engineering

Texas A&M Univ.–Galveston
United States Coast Guard
    Academy (CT)
United States Merchant Marine
    Academy (NY)
United States Naval Academy
    (MD)
Univ. of Michigan–Ann Arbor
Univ. of New Orleans
Univ. of Wisconsin–Madison
Webb Institute (NY)

Neuroscience

Allegheny College (PA)
Amherst College (MA)
Baldwin-Wallace College (OH)
Barnard College (NY)
Bates College (ME)

Baylor Univ. (TX)
Bowdoin College (ME)
Bowling Green State Univ. (OH)
Brandeis Univ. (MA)
Brigham Young Univ.–Provo (UT)
Brown Univ. (RI)
Carthage College (WI)
Centenary College of Louisiana
Central Michigan Univ.
Claremont Mckenna College (CA)
Colby College (ME)
Colgate Univ. (NY)
College of William and Mary (VA)
Colorado College
Columbia Univ. (NY)
Connecticut College
Cornell Univ. (NY)
CUNY–Queens College
Dickinson College (PA)
Drake Univ. (IA)
Drew Univ. (NJ)
Fairfield Univ. (CT)
Franklin and Marshall College (PA)
Furman Univ. (SC)
Hampshire College (MA)
Johns Hopkins Univ. (MD)
King College (TN)
King's College (PA)
Knox College (IL)
Lafayette College (PA)
Lawrence Univ. (WI)
Macalester College (MN)
Mount Holyoke College (MA)
Mount Union College (OH)
Muskingum College (OH)
New York Univ.
Northeastern Univ. (MA)
Northwestern Univ. (IL)
Oberlin College (OH)
Ohio Wesleyan Univ.
Pomona College (CA)
St. Andrews Presbyterian College
    (NC)
St. Lawrence Univ. (NY)
Texas Christian Univ.
Tulane Univ. (LA)
Union College (NY)
Univ. of California–Irvine
Univ. of California–Los Angeles
Univ. of California–Riverside
Univ. of California–San Diego
Univ. of California–Santa Cruz
Univ. of Miami (FL)
Univ. of Michigan–Ann Arbor
Univ. of Minnesota–Twin Cities
Univ. of Pennsylvania
Univ. of Pittsburgh
Univ. of Scranton (PA)
Univ. of Southern California
Univ. of Texas–Dallas
Ursinus College (PA)
Vanderbilt Univ. (TN)
Washington and Lee Univ. (VA)
Washington State Univ.
Wellesley College (MA)
Westminster College (PA)
Westmont College (CA)

Nonprofessional General Legal Studies (Undergraduate)

Abilene Christian Univ. (TX)
Allegheny College (PA)
Alma College (MI)
Amherst College (MA)
Anna Maria College (MA)
Arizona State Univ.
Babson College (MA)
Ball State Univ. (IN)
Barry Univ. (FL)
Bay Path College (MA)
Benedictine Univ. (IL)
Bennington College (VT)
Bethel College (IN)
Bowling Green State Univ. (OH)
Brevard College (NC)
Bridgewater State College (MA)
California Lutheran Univ.
Calumet College of St. Joseph (IN)
Calvin College (MI)
Campbell Univ. (NC)
Carroll College (MT)
Catawba College (NC)
Cedarville Univ. (OH)
Central Christian College (KS)
Chapman Univ. (CA)
Charleston Southern Univ. (SC)
Chatham College (PA)
Claremont Mckenna College (CA)
Clearwater Christian College (FL)
College of St. Mary (NE)
College of the Ozarks (MO)
College of William and Mary (VA)
Concordia Univ. (MI)
Cornerstone Univ. (MI)
Crichton College (TN)
Dakota Wesleyan Univ. (SD)
Dana College (NE)
David Lipscomb Univ. (TN)
Defiance College (OH)
Desales Univ. (PA)
Dickinson College (PA)
Dillard Univ. (LA)
Dominican Coll. of Blauvelt (NY)
Drury Univ. (MO)
Elizabethtown College (PA)
Emmanuel College (GA)
Fontbonne Univ. (MO)
Franciscan Univ. of Steubenville
    (OH)
Geneva College (PA)
Golden Gate Univ. (CA)
Grand Valley State Univ. (MI)
Hamline Univ. (MN)
Hampshire College (MA)
Hardin-Simmons Univ. (TX)
Harding Univ. (AR)
Hastings College (NE)
Hofstra Univ. (NY)
Hood College (MD)
Howard Payne Univ. (TX)
Huntington College (IN)
Indiana Univ.-Purdue Univ.–Fort
    Wayne
Ithaca College (NY)
Juniata College (PA)
Lake Erie College (OH)

Lambuth Univ. (TN)
Lasell College (MA)
Lawrence Univ. (WI)
Liberty Univ. (VA)
Limestone College (SC)
Lindenwood Univ. (MO)
Louisiana College
Macmurray College (IL)
Mansfield Univ. of Pennsylvania
Marlboro College (VT)
Maryville Univ. of St. Louis (MO)
Marywood Univ. (PA)
Master's Coll. and Seminary (CA)
Mercy College (NY)
Michigan State Univ.
Midwestern State Univ. (TX)
Minnesota State Univ.–Moorhead
Monmouth College (IL)
Mount Mary College (WI)
Mount Mercy College (IA)
National Univ. (CA)
New England College (NH)
New York Univ.
Northern Arizona Univ.
Northwestern Univ. (IL)
Notre Dame College of Ohio
Nova Southeastern Univ. (FL)
Oberlin College (OH)
Ohio Wesleyan Univ.
Oklahoma Baptist Univ.
Oklahoma Christian Univ.
Oral Roberts Univ. (OK)
Ouachita Baptist Univ. (AR)
Pacific Lutheran Univ. (WA)
Palm Beach Atlantic Univ. (FL)
Park Univ. (MO)
Pfeiffer Univ. (NC)
Point Park Univ. (PA)
Regis Univ. (CO)
Rensselaer Polytechnic Inst. (NY)
Rochester Institute of Tech. (NY)
Roger Williams Univ. (RI)
Sacred Heart Univ. (CT)
Schreiner Univ. (TX)
Southeastern College of the
    Assemblies of God
Southeastern Univ. (DC)
Southwestern Adventist Univ. (TX)
Spelman College (GA)
St. Ambrose Univ. (IA)
St. Augustine's College (NC)
St. Bonaventure Univ. (NY)
St. Francis Univ. (PA)
St. Gregory's Univ. (OK)
St. John's Univ. (NY)
St. Joseph's Univ. (PA)
Stephens College (MO)
Suffolk Univ. (MA)
SUNY College–Oneonta
Temple Univ. (PA)
Texas Wesleyan Univ.
Thiel College (PA)
Toccoa Falls College (GA)
Tougaloo College (MS)
Truman State Univ. (MO)
United States Air Force Academy
    (CO)
Univ. of California–Berkeley
Univ. of California–Riverside
Univ. of California–Santa Barbara
Univ. of California–Santa Cruz

Univ. of Dayton (OH)
Univ. of Evansville (IN)
Univ. of Iowa
Univ. of La Verne (CA)
Univ. of Maryland–College Park
Univ. of Maryland–Eastern Shore
Univ. of Maryland–Univ. College
Univ. of Massachusetts–Amherst
Univ. of Massachusetts–Boston
Univ. of Miami (FL)
Univ. of Missouri–Rolla
Univ. of Nevada–Las Vegas
Univ. of New Haven (CT)
Univ. of Pittsburgh
Univ. of Pittsburgh–Johnstown
Univ. of St. Francis (IN)
Univ. of St. Thomas (MN)
Univ. of Toledo (OH)
Univ. of Utah
Univ. of Wisconsin–Madison
Univ. of Wisconsin–Superior
Utah State Univ.
Vanguard Univ. of Southern
    California
Virginia Intermont College
Washburn Univ. (KS)
Webber International Univ. (FL)
Webster Univ. (MO)
West Texas A&M Univ.
West Virginia Wesleyan College
Western Baptist College (OR)
Widener Univ. (PA)
William Woods Univ. (MO)
Wilmington College (DE)
Winona State Univ. (MN)
Youngstown State Univ. (OH)

Nuclear and Industrial Radiologic Technologies/Technicians

Univ. of North Texas

Nuclear Engineering

Georgia Institute of Technology
Idaho State Univ.
Massachusetts Institute of
    Technology
North Carolina State Univ.–Raleigh
Oregon State Univ.
Penn. State Univ.–Univ. Park
Purdue Univ.–West Lafayette (IN)
Rensselaer Polytechnic Inst. (NY)
South Carolina State Univ.
Texas A&M Univ.–College Station
United States Military Academy
    (NY)
Univ. of California–Berkeley
Univ. of Florida
Univ. of Ill.–Urbana-Champaign
Univ. of Michigan–Ann Arbor
Univ. of Missouri–Rolla
Univ. of New Mexico
Univ. of Tennessee
Univ. of Wisconsin–Madison

Nuclear Engineering Technologies/Technicians

Excelsior College (NY)
Thomas Edison State College (NJ)

Nursing

Abilene Christian Univ. (TX)
Adelphi Univ. (NY)
Albany State Univ. (GA)
Alcorn State Univ. (MS)
Alderson-Broaddus College (WV)
Alvernia College (PA)
Alverno College (WI)
American International College
    (MA)
Anderson Univ. (IN)
Andrews Univ. (MI)
Angelo State Univ. (TX)
Anna Maria College (MA)
Arizona State Univ.
Arkansas State Univ.
Arkansas Tech Univ.
Armstrong Atlantic State Univ.
    (GA)
Atlantic Union College (MA)
Auburn Univ. (AL)
Auburn Univ.–Montgomery (AL)
Augsburg College (MN)
Augustana College (SD)
Aurora Univ. (IL)
Austin Peay State Univ. (TN)
Avila Univ. (MO)
Azusa Pacific Univ. (CA)
Baker Univ. (KS)
Ball State Univ. (IN)
Barry Univ. (FL)
Barton College (NC)
Baylor Univ. (TX)
Bellarmine Univ. (KY)
Belmont Univ. (TN)
Bemidji State Univ. (MN)
Benedictine Univ. (IL)
Berea College (KY)
Berry College (GA)
Bethel College (KS)
Bethel College (IN)
Bethel Univ. (MN)
Bethune-Cookman College (FL)
Biola Univ. (CA)
Bloomfield College (NJ)
Bloomsburg Univ. of Pennsylvania
Bluefield State College (WV)
Boise State Univ. (ID)
Boston College
Bowie State Univ. (MD)
Bowling Green State Univ. (OH)
Bradley Univ. (IL)
Brenau Univ. (GA)
Briar Cliff Univ. (IA)
Brigham Young Univ.–Provo (UT)
California Baptist Univ.
California State Univ.–Bakersfield
California State Univ.–Chico
California State Univ.–Fresno
California State Univ.–Fullerton
California State Univ.–Hayward
California State Univ.–Long Beach

California State Univ.–Los Angeles
California State Univ.–Northridge
California State Univ.–Sacramento
California State Univ.–San
    Bernardino
California State Univ.–Stanislaus
California Univ. of Pennsylvania
Calvin College (MI)
Capital Univ. (OH)
Carlow College (PA)
Carroll College (MT)
Carroll College (WI)
Carson-Newman College (TN)
Case Western Reserve Univ. (OH)
Catholic Univ. of America (DC)
Cedar Crest College (PA)
Cedarville Univ. (OH)
Central Connecticut State Univ.
Central Methodist Univ. (MO)
Central Missouri State Univ.
Charleston Southern Univ. (SC)
Chicago State Univ.
Clarion Univ. of Pennsylvania
Clayton Coll. and State Univ. (GA)
Cleveland State Univ.
Colby-Sawyer College (NH)
College Misericordia (PA)
College of Mount St. Joseph (OH)
College of Mount St. Vincent (NY)
College of New Jersey
College of Notre Dame of
    Maryland
College of St. Benedict (MN)
College of St. Catherine (MN)
College of St. Elizabeth (NJ)
College of St. Mary (NE)
College of St. Scholastica (MN)
College of the Ozarks (MO)
Colorado State Univ.–Pueblo
Columbia Union College (MD)
Columbus State Univ. (GA)
Concordia Coll.–Moorhead (MN)
Concordia Univ. Wisconsin
Concordia Univ.–River Forest (IL)
Coppin State Univ. (MD)
Culver-Stockton College (MO)
Cumberland Univ. (TN)
CUNY–City College
CUNY–College of Staten Island
CUNY–Hunter College
CUNY–Lehman College
CUNY–Medgar Evers College
CUNY–York College
Curry College (MA)
Daemen College (NY)
Dakota Wesleyan Univ. (SD)
Davenport Univ. (MI)
David Lipscomb Univ. (TN)
Delaware State Univ.
Delta State Univ. (MS)
Depaul Univ. (IL)
Desales Univ. (PA)
Dickinson State Univ. (ND)
Dominican Coll. of Blauvelt (NY)
Dominican Univ. (IL)
Drexel Univ. (PA)
Duquesne Univ. (PA)
East Carolina Univ. (NC)
East Central Univ. (OK)
East Stroudsburg Univ. of
    Pennsylvania

East Tennessee State Univ.
East Texas Baptist Univ.
Eastern Kentucky Univ.
Eastern Mennonite Univ. (VA)
Eastern Michigan Univ.
Eastern New Mexico Univ.
Eastern Oregon Univ.
Eastern Univ. (PA)
Eastern Washington Univ.
Edgewood College (WI)
Edinboro Univ. of Pennsylvania
Elmhurst College (IL)
Elmira College (NY)
Elms College (College of Our Lady
    of the Elms) (MA)
Emmanuel College (MA)
Emory Univ. (GA)
Emporia State Univ. (KS)
Endicott College (MA)
Evangel Univ. (MO)
Excelsior College (NY)
Fairfield Univ. (CT)
Fairleigh Dickinson Univ. (NJ)
Fairmont State Univ. (WV)
Felician College (NJ)
Ferris State Univ. (MI)
Fitchburg State College (MA)
Florida Atlantic Univ.
Florida Gulf Coast Univ.
Florida International Univ.
Florida Southern College
Florida State Univ.
Fort Hays State Univ. (KS)
Framingham State College (MA)
Francis Marion Univ. (SC)
Franciscan Univ. of Steubenville
    (OH)
Gannon Univ. (PA)
Gardner-Webb Univ. (NC)
George Fox Univ. (OR)
George Mason Univ. (VA)
Georgetown Univ. (DC)
Georgia College and State Univ.
Georgia Southern Univ.
Georgia Southwestern State Univ.
Georgia State Univ.
Glenville State College (WV)
Gonzaga Univ. (WA)
Goshen College (IN)
Grace Univ. (NE)
Graceland Univ. (IA)
Grambling State Univ. (LA)
Grand Valley State Univ. (MI)
Grand View College (IA)
Gustavus Adolphus College (MN)
Gwynedd-Mercy College (PA)
Hampton Univ. (VA)
Hannibal-Lagrange College (MO)
Hardin-Simmons Univ. (TX)
Harding Univ. (AR)
Hartwick College (NY)
Hawaii Pacific Univ.
Henderson State Univ. (AR)
Holy Family Univ. (PA)
Holy Names Univ. (CA)
Hope College (MI)
Houston Baptist Univ.
Howard Univ. (DC)
Humboldt State Univ. (CA)
Husson College (ME)
Idaho State Univ.

Illinois State Univ.
Illinois Wesleyan Univ.
Immaculata Univ. (PA)
Indiana State Univ.
Indiana Univ. East
Indiana Univ. Northwest
Indiana Univ. of Pennsylvania
Indiana Univ. Southeast
Indiana Univ.–Bloomington
Indiana Univ.–Kokomo
Indiana Univ.–Purdue Univ.–Fort
    Wayne
Indiana Univ.–Purdue
    Univ.–Indianapolis
Indiana Wesleyan Univ.
Jacksonville State Univ. (AL)
Jacksonville Univ. (FL)
James Madison Univ. (VA)
Jamestown College (ND)
Kansas Wesleyan Univ.
Kean Univ. (NJ)
Kennesaw State Univ. (GA)
Kent State Univ. (OH)
Kentucky Christian College
Kentucky State Univ.
Keuka College (NY)
King College (TN)
Kutztown Univ. of Pennsylvania
La Roche College (PA)
La Salle Univ. (PA)
Lagrange College (GA)
Lake Superior State Univ. (MI)
Lamar Univ. (TX)
Lander Univ. (SC)
Le Moyne College (NY)
Lees-Mcrae College (NC)
Lenoir-Rhyne College (NC)
Lewis Univ. (IL)
Lewis-Clark State College (ID)
Liberty Univ. (VA)
Lincoln Memorial Univ. (TN)
Lincoln Univ. (MO)
Long Island Univ.–C.W. Post
    Campus (NY)
Louisiana College
Lourdes College (OH)
Loyola Univ. Chicago
Loyola Univ. New Orleans
Lubbock Christian Univ. (TX)
Luther College (IA)
Lynchburg College (VA)
Macmurray College (IL)
Madonna Univ. (MI)
Malone College (OH)
Mansfield Univ. of Pennsylvania
Marian College (IN)
Marian College of Fond Du Lac
    (WI)
Marquette Univ. (WI)
Marshall Univ. (WV)
Marymount Univ. (VA)
Maryville Univ. of St. Louis (MO)
Marywood Univ. (PA)
Mckendree College (IL)
Mcmurry Univ. (TX)
Mcneese State Univ. (LA)
Mercer Univ. (GA)
Mesa State College (CO)
Messiah College (PA)
Metropolitan State College of
    Denver

Miami Univ.–Oxford (OH)
Michigan State Univ.
Middle Tennessee State Univ.
Midland Lutheran College (NE)
Midway College (KY)
Midwestern State Univ. (TX)
Milligan College (TN)
Millikin Univ. (IL)
Milwaukee School of Engineering
Minnesota State Univ.–Mankato
Minnesota State Univ.–Moorhead
Minot State Univ. (ND)
Mississippi Univ. For Women
Missouri Southern State Univ.
Missouri Western State College
Molloy College (NY)
Monmouth Univ. (NJ)
Montana State Univ.–Bozeman
Montana State Univ.–Northern
Montana Tech of the Univ. of
　Montana
Moravian College (PA)
Morehead State Univ. (KY)
Morningside College (IA)
Mount Aloysius College (PA)
Mount Marty College (SD)
Mount Mary College (WI)
Mount Mercy College (IA)
Mount St. Mary College (NY)
Mount St. Mary's College (CA)
Mountain State Univ. (WV)
Murray State Univ. (KY)
National Univ. (CA)
Nazareth College of Rochester
　(NY)
Nebraska Wesleyan Univ.
Neumann College (PA)
New Jersey City Univ.
New Mexico State Univ.
New York Institute of Technology
New York Univ.
Newman Univ. (KS)
Nicholls State Univ. (LA)
Norfolk State Univ. (VA)
North Carolina A&T State Univ.
North Carolina Central Univ.
North Dakota State Univ.
North Georgia College and State
　Univ.
Northeastern State Univ. (OK)
Northeastern Univ. (MA)
Northern Arizona Univ.
Northern Illinois Univ.
Northern Kentucky Univ.
Northern Michigan Univ.
Northwest College (WA)
Northwest Nazarene Univ. (ID)
Northwestern College (IA)
Northwestern Oklahoma State
　Univ.
Northwestern State Univ. of
　Louisiana
Norwich Univ. (VT)
Nova Southeastern Univ. (FL)
Oakland Univ. (MI)
Oakwood College (AL)
Ohio Northern Univ.
Ohio State Univ.–Columbus
Oklahoma Baptist Univ.
Oklahoma City Univ.
Oklahoma Panhandle State Univ.

Oklahoma Wesleyan Univ.
Old Dominion Univ. (VA)
Oral Roberts Univ. (OK)
Oregon Institute of Technology
Otterbein College (OH)
Pace Univ. (NY)
Pacific Lutheran Univ. (WA)
Pacific Union College (CA)
Palm Beach Atlantic Univ. (FL)
Pennsylvania College of Technology
Penn. State Univ.–Univ. Park
Pittsburg State Univ. (KS)
Point Loma Nazarene Univ. (CA)
Prairie View A&M Univ. (TX)
Purdue Univ.–Calumet (IN)
Purdue Univ.–North Central (IN)
Purdue Univ.–West Lafayette (IN)
Queens Univ. of Charlotte (NC)
Quincy Univ. (IL)
Quinnipiac Univ. (CT)
Radford Univ. (VA)
Ramapo College of New Jersey
Regis College (MA)
Regis Univ. (CO)
Rhode Island College
Richard Stockton College of New
　Jersey
Rivier College (NH)
Robert Morris Univ. (PA)
Roberts Wesleyan College (NY)
Rockford College (IL)
Rockhurst Univ. (MO)
Russell Sage College (NY)
Rutgers–Camden (NJ)
Rutgers–Newark (NJ)
Sacred Heart Univ. (CT)
Saginaw Valley State Univ. (MI)
Salem State College (MA)
Salisbury Univ. (MD)
Salve Regina Univ. (RI)
Samford Univ. (AL)
San Diego State Univ.
San Francisco State Univ.
San Jose State Univ. (CA)
Seattle Pacific Univ.
Seattle Univ.
Seton Hall Univ. (NJ)
Shawnee State Univ. (OH)
Shenandoah Univ. (VA)
Shepherd Univ. (WV)
Simmons College (MA)
Slippery Rock Univ. of Pennsylvania
Sonoma State Univ. (CA)
South Carolina State Univ.
South Dakota State Univ.
Southeast Missouri State Univ.
Southeastern Louisiana Univ.
Southern Adventist Univ. (TN)
Southern Arkansas Univ.
Southern Connecticut State Univ.
Southern Illinois
　Univ.–Edwardsville
Southern Nazarene Univ. (OK)
Southern Univ. and A&M College
　(LA)
Southern Utah Univ.
Southwest Baptist Univ. (MO)
Southwest Missouri State Univ.
Southwestern College (KS)
Southwestern Oklahoma State
　Univ.

Spalding Univ. (KY)
Spring Arbor Univ. (MI)
Spring Hill College (AL)
St. Ambrose Univ. (IA)
St. Anselm College (NH)
St. Cloud State Univ. (MN)
St. Francis College (NY)
St. Francis Univ. (PA)
St. John Fisher College (NY)
St. John's Univ. (MN)
St. Joseph College (CT)
St. Joseph's College (ME)
St. Joseph's College (IN)
St. Joseph's College, New York
St. Louis Univ.
St. Mary's College (IN)
St. Olaf College (MN)
St. Peter's College (NJ)
St. Xavier Univ. (IL)
State Univ. of West Georgia
Stephen F. Austin State Univ. (TX)
SUNY College–Brockport
SUNY–Binghamton
SUNY–Farmingdale
SUNY–Plattsburgh
SUNY–Stony Brook
Tabor College (KS)
Tarleton State Univ. (TX)
Temple Univ. (PA)
Tennessee State Univ.
Tennessee Technological Univ.
Tennessee Wesleyan College
Texas A&M International Univ.
Texas A&M Univ.–Corpus Christi
Texas Christian Univ.
Texas Wesleyan Univ.
Texas Woman's Univ.
Thomas Edison State College (NJ)
Thomas More College (KY)
Thomas Univ. (GA)
Towson Univ. (MD)
Trevecca Nazarene Univ. (TN)
Trinity Christian College (IL)
Troy State Univ.–Troy (AL)
Truman State Univ. (MO)
Tuskegee Univ. (AL)
Union College (NE)
Union Univ. (TN)
Univ. at Buffalo–SUNY
Univ. of Akron (OH)
Univ. of Alabama
Univ. of Alabama–Birmingham
Univ. of Alabama–Huntsville
Univ. of Alaska–Anchorage
Univ. of Arizona
Univ. of Arkansas
Univ. of Arkansas–Monticello
Univ. of Arkansas–Pine Bluff
Univ. of California–Los Angeles
Univ. of Central Arkansas
Univ. of Central Florida
Univ. of Central Oklahoma
Univ. of Charleston (WV)
Univ. of Colorado–Colorado
　Springs
Univ. of Colorado–Denver
Univ. of Connecticut
Univ. of Delaware
Univ. of Detroit Mercy
Univ. of Dubuque (IA)
Univ. of Evansville (IN)

Univ. of Findlay (OH)
Univ. of Florida
Univ. of Hartford (CT)
Univ. of Hawaii–Hilo
Univ. of Hawaii–Manoa
Univ. of Illinois–Chicago
Univ. of Indianapolis
Univ. of Iowa
Univ. of Kansas
Univ. of Kentucky
Univ. of Louisiana–Lafayette
Univ. of Louisiana–Monroe
Univ. of Louisville (KY)
Univ. of Maine–Fort Kent
Univ. of Maine–Orono
Univ. of Mary (ND)
Univ. of Mary Hardin-Baylor (TX)
Univ. of Maryland–Eastern Shore
Univ. of Massachusetts–Amherst
Univ. of Massachusetts–Boston
Univ. of Massachusetts–Lowell
Univ. of Memphis
Univ. of Miami (FL)
Univ. of Michigan–Ann Arbor
Univ. of Michigan–Flint
Univ. of Minnesota–Twin Cities
Univ. of Missouri–Columbia
Univ. of Missouri–Kansas City
Univ. of Missouri–St. Louis
Univ. of Nevada–Las Vegas
Univ. of Nevada–Reno
Univ. of New England (ME)
Univ. of New Hampshire
Univ. of New Mexico
Univ. of North Alabama
Univ. of N.C.–Chapel Hill
Univ. of North Carolina–Charlotte
Univ. of N.C.–Greensboro
Univ. of North Carolina–Pembroke
Univ. of N.C.–Wilmington
Univ. of North Dakota
Univ. of North Florida
Univ. of Northern Colorado
Univ. of Oklahoma
Univ. of Pennsylvania
Univ. of Pittsburgh
Univ. of Pittsburgh–Bradford
Univ. of Portland (OR)
Univ. of Rhode Island
Univ. of Rio Grande (OH)
Univ. of Rochester (NY)
Univ. of San Diego
Univ. of San Francisco
Univ. of Scranton (PA)
Univ. of South Alabama
Univ. of South Carolina–Aiken
Univ. of South Carolina–Columbia
Univ. of South Carolina–Upstate
Univ. of South Florida
Univ. of Southern Indiana
Univ. of Southern Maine
Univ. of Southern Mississippi
Univ. of St. Francis (IL)
Univ. of St. Francis (IN)
Univ. of Tampa (FL)
Univ. of Tennessee
Univ. of Tennessee–Chattanooga
Univ. of Tennessee–Martin
Univ. of Texas–Arlington
Univ. of Texas–Austin
Univ. of Texas–Brownsville

Univ. of Texas–El Paso
Univ. of Texas–Pan American
Univ. of Texas–Tyler
Univ. of the District of Columbia
Univ. of the Incarnate Word (TX)
Univ. of Toledo (OH)
Univ. of Tulsa (OK)
Univ. of Utah
Univ. of Vermont
Univ. of Virginia
Univ. of Washington
Univ. of West Florida
Univ. of Wisconsin–Eau Claire
Univ. of Wisconsin–Green Bay
Univ. of Wisconsin–Madison
Univ. of Wisconsin–Milwaukee
Univ. of Wisconsin–Oshkosh
Univ. of Wisconsin–Parkside
Univ. of Wyoming
Urbana Univ. (OH)
Ursuline College (OH)
Utah Valley State College
Utica College (NY)
Valdosta State Univ. (GA)
Valparaiso Univ. (IN)
Villa Julie College (MD)
Villanova Univ. (PA)
Virginia Commonwealth Univ.
Virginia State Univ.
Viterbo Univ. (WI)
Wagner College (NY)
Walla Walla College (WA)
Walsh Univ. (OH)
Washburn Univ. (KS)
Washington State Univ.
Wayne State Univ. (MI)
Waynesburg College (PA)
Weber State Univ. (UT)
Webster Univ. (MO)
Wesley College (DE)
West Chester Univ. of Pennsylvania
West Liberty State College (WV)
West Texas A&M Univ.
West Virginia Univ.
West Virginia Univ. Institute of
　Technology
Western Carolina Univ. (NC)
Western Connecticut State Univ.
Western Kentucky Univ.
Western Michigan Univ.
Western New Mexico Univ.
Westminster College (UT)
Wheaton College (IL)
Wheeling Jesuit Univ. (WV)
Whitworth College (WA)
Wichita State Univ. (KS)
Widener Univ. (PA)
Wilkes Univ. (PA)
William Carey College (MS)
William Jewell College (MO)
William Paterson Univ. of New
　Jersey
Wilmington College (DE)
Winona State Univ. (MN)
Winston-Salem State Univ. (NC)
Worcester State College (MA)
Wright State Univ. (OH)
Xavier Univ. (OH)
York College of Pennsylvania
Youngstown State Univ. (OH)

Nutrition Sciences

Auburn Univ. (AL)
Boston Univ.
Brigham Young Univ.–Provo (UT)
Case Western Reserve Univ. (OH)
Chapman Univ. (CA)
College of St. Benedict (MN)
Cornell Univ. (NY)
Drexel Univ. (PA)
Howard Univ. (DC)
Michigan State Univ.
Ohio State Univ.–Columbus
Russell Sage College (NY)
Rutgers–New Brunswick (NJ)
San Jose State Univ. (CA)
Simmons College (MA)
St. John's Univ. (MN)
Texas Woman's Univ.
Tulane Univ. (LA)
Univ. of Arizona
Univ. of California–Berkeley
Univ. of California–Davis
Univ. of Connecticut
Univ. of Delaware
Univ. of Hawaii–Manoa
Univ. of Maine–Orono
Univ. of Michigan–Ann Arbor
Univ. of Minnesota–Twin Cities
Univ. of N.C.–Greensboro
Univ. of Oklahoma
Univ. of the Incarnate Word (TX)
Univ. of Vermont
Univ. of Wisconsin–Green Bay
Univ. of Wisconsin–Madison
Washington State Univ.

Ocean Engineering

Florida Atlantic Univ.
Florida Institute of Technology
Massachusetts Institute of Technology
Texas A&M Univ.–College Station
Texas A&M Univ.–Galveston
United States Naval Academy (MD)
Univ. of New Hampshire
Univ. of Rhode Island

Operations Research

Carnegie Mellon Univ. (PA)
Columbia Univ. (NY)
Cornell Univ. (NY)
CUNY–Baruch College
Princeton Univ. (NJ)
Syracuse Univ. (NY)
United States Air Force Academy (CO)
United States Military Academy (NY)
Univ. of California–Berkeley
Univ. of Ill.–Urbana-Champaign

Ophthalmic and Optometric Support Services and Allied Prof.

Excelsior College (NY)
Lindenwood Univ. (MO)

Optometry (O.D.)

Gannon Univ. (PA)
Indiana Univ.–Bloomington
Marywood Univ. (PA)
Univ. of California–Berkeley

Parks, Recreation, and Leisure Facilities Management

Alabama State Univ.
Alderson-Broaddus College (WV)
American International College (MA)
Appalachian State Univ. (NC)
Arkansas Tech Univ.
Asbury College (KY)
Bluffton Univ. (OH)
California Univ. of Pennsylvania
Carroll College (WI)
Central Methodist Univ. (MO)
Central Michigan Univ.
Central Washington Univ.
Cheyney Univ. of Pennsylvania
Chicago State Univ.
College of the Ozarks (MO)
Colorado State Univ.
Colorado State Univ.–Pueblo
Cumberland Univ. (TN)
East Carolina Univ. (NC)
East Stroudsburg Univ. of Pennsylvania
Eastern Illinois Univ.
Eastern Kentucky Univ.
Eastern Michigan Univ.
Eastern Washington Univ.
Elmhurst College (IL)
Ferris State Univ. (MI)
Florida International Univ.
Florida State Univ.
Gallaudet Univ. (DC)
Green Mountain College (VT)
Hannibal-Lagrange College (MO)
Hastings College (NE)
Henderson State Univ. (AR)
High Point Univ. (NC)
Huntington College (IN)
Illinois State Univ.
Indiana State Univ.
Indiana Wesleyan Univ.
Johnson and Wales Univ. (RI)
Johnson State College (VT)
Kansas State Univ.
Kean Univ. (NJ)
Kent State Univ. (OH)
Lock Haven Univ. of Pennsylvania
Lyndon State College (VT)
Lynn Univ. (FL)
Marshall Univ. (WV)
Michigan State Univ.

Middle Tennessee State Univ.
Midland Lutheran College (NE)
Minnesota State Univ.–Mankato
Missouri Valley College
Missouri Western State College
Morris College (SC)
Mount Marty College (SD)
Murray State Univ. (KY)
New Mexico Highlands Univ.
New Mexico State Univ.
North Carolina A&T State Univ.
North Carolina Central Univ.
North Carolina State Univ.–Raleigh
Northwest Missouri State Univ.
Ohio State Univ.–Columbus
Oklahoma Baptist Univ.
Old Dominion Univ. (VA)
Penn. State Univ.–Univ. Park
Prairie View A&M Univ. (TX)
San Jose State Univ. (CA)
Savannah State Univ. (GA)
Slippery Rock Univ. of Pennsylvania
South Dakota State Univ.
Southwestern Oklahoma State Univ.
Springfield College (MA)
St. Joseph's College, New York
St. Thomas Aquinas College (NY)
State Univ. of West Georgia
Stephen F. Austin State Univ. (TX)
Texas A&M Univ.–College Station
Texas State Univ.–San Marcos
Tri-State Univ. (IN)
Unity College (ME)
Univ. of Connecticut
Univ. of Delaware
Univ. of Florida
Univ. of Hawaii–Hilo
Univ. of Maine–Machias
Univ. of Maine–Orono
Univ. of Maine–Presque Isle
Univ. of Minnesota–Duluth
Univ. of Minnesota–Twin Cities
Univ. of Mississippi
Univ. of Montana
Univ. of N.C.–Chapel Hill
Univ. of North Carolina–Pembroke
Univ. of N.C.–Wilmington
Univ. of North Dakota
Univ. of North Texas
Univ. of Northern Colorado
Univ. of St. Francis (IL)
Univ. of Tennessee
Univ. of Vermont
Univ. of Wisconsin–La Crosse
Univ. of Wisconsin–Madison
Univ. of Wyoming
Webber International Univ. (FL)
West Virginia Univ.
Western Carolina Univ. (NC)
Western Illinois Univ.
Western Kentucky Univ.
York College of Pennsylvania

Parks, Recreation, and Leisure Studies

Alaska Pacific Univ.
Alcorn State Univ. (MS)
Aquinas College (MI)

Arizona State Univ.
Arizona State Univ. West
Atlantic Union College (MA)
Aurora Univ. (IL)
Barber Scotia College (NC)
Benedict College (SC)
Black Hills State Univ. (SD)
Bowling Green State Univ. (OH)
Brevard College (NC)
Bridgewater State College (MA)
Brigham Young Univ.–Provo (UT)
Cal Poly–San Luis Obispo
California State Univ.–Chico
California State Univ.–Fresno
California State Univ.–Hayward
California State Univ.–Long Beach
California State Univ.–Northridge
California State Univ.–Sacramento
Calvin College (MI)
Carson-Newman College (TN)
Catawba College (NC)
Central Michigan Univ.
Central Missouri State Univ.
Central State Univ. (OH)
College of St. Joseph (VT)
Eastern Washington Univ.
Emporia State Univ. (KS)
Ferrum College (VA)
Frostburg State Univ. (MD)
Gallaudet Univ. (DC)
Georgia College and State Univ.
Georgia Southern Univ.
Gordon College (MA)
Graceland Univ. (IA)
Grambling State Univ. (LA)
Grand Valley State Univ. (MI)
Green Mountain College (VT)
Greenville College (IL)
Houghton College (NY)
Howard Payne Univ. (TX)
Huntingdon College (AL)
Huntington College (IN)
Huston-Tillotson College (TX)
Indiana Univ. Northwest
Indiana Univ.–Bloomington
Ithaca College (NY)
Jacksonville State Univ. (AL)
Lake Superior State Univ. (MI)
Mars Hill College (NC)
Maryville College (TN)
Messiah College (PA)
Metropolitan State College of Denver
Montreat College (NC)
Mount Olive College (NC)
Mountain State Univ. (WV)
New Mexico Highlands Univ.
Newberry College (SC)
North Dakota State Univ.
Northern Arizona Univ.
Northern Michigan Univ.
Ohio Univ.
Oklahoma Baptist Univ.
Oklahoma State Univ.
Oregon State Univ.
Radford Univ. (VA)
San Diego State Univ.
San Francisco State Univ.
Shaw Univ. (NC)
Sheldon Jackson College (AK)
Shepherd Univ. (WV)

Shorter College (GA)
South Dakota State Univ.
Southeast Missouri State Univ.
Southern Connecticut State Univ.
Southern Illinois Univ.–Carbondale
Southern Univ. and A&M College (LA)
Southwest Baptist Univ. (MO)
Southwest Missouri State Univ.
Spring Arbor Univ. (MI)
Springfield College (MA)
St. Cloud State Univ. (MN)
Temple Univ. (PA)
Texas A&M Univ.–College Station
Thomas Edison State College (NJ)
Towson Univ. (MD)
Unity College (ME)
Univ. of Arkansas
Univ. of Arkansas–Pine Bluff
Univ. of Ill.–Urbana-Champaign
Univ. of Iowa
Univ. of Maine–Presque Isle
Univ. of Mary Hardin-Baylor (TX)
Univ. of Michigan–Ann Arbor
Univ. of Minnesota–Twin Cities
Univ. of Mississippi
Univ. of Missouri–Columbia
Univ. of Nebraska–Kearney
Univ. of Nebraska–Omaha
Univ. of Nevada–Las Vegas
Univ. of New Hampshire
Univ. of N.C.–Greensboro
Univ. of Northern Iowa
Univ. of South Alabama
Univ. of South Dakota
Univ. of Southern Mississippi
Univ. of Toledo (OH)
Univ. of Utah
Utah State Univ.
Virginia Commonwealth Univ.
Virginia Wesleyan College
Washington State Univ.
West Virginia State Univ.
Western Michigan Univ.
Western State College of Colorado
Western Washington Univ.
William Jewell College (MO)
Wingate Univ. (NC)
York College of Pennsylvania

Parks, Recreation, Leisure, and Fitness Studies

Becker College (MA)
Brigham Young Univ.–Provo (UT)
Central Methodist Univ. (MO)
Central Michigan Univ.
Central Missouri State Univ.
Chadron State College (NE)
Coker College (SC)
Culver-Stockton College (MO)
Elon Univ. (NC)
Ferrum College (VA)
Franklin College (IN)
Howard Univ. (DC)
Huntington College (IN)
Lambuth Univ. (TN)
Malone College (OH)
North Greenville College (SC)

Pittsburg State Univ. (KS)
Plymouth State Univ. (NH)
Prescott College (AZ)
Southern Wesleyan Univ. (SC)
Springfield College (MA)
St. Edward's Univ. (TX)
SUNY College–Brockport
The Franciscan Univ. (IA)
Univ. of Maryland–Eastern Shore
Univ. of North Alabama
Urbana Univ. (OH)
Utah State Univ.

Pastoral Counseling and Specialized Ministries

Abilene Christian Univ. (TX)
Anna Maria College (MA)
Asbury College (KY)
Augsburg College (MN)
Bethany College (CA)
Bethel College (IN)
Bethel Univ. (MN)
Bluffton Univ. (OH)
Brescia Univ. (KY)
Cedarville Univ. (OH)
Charleston Southern Univ. (SC)
Christian Heritage College (CA)
Clearwater Christian College (FL)
College of Mount St. Joseph (OH)
Colorado Christian Univ.
Concordia Univ.–St. Paul (MN)
Cornerstone Univ. (MI)
Crichton College (TN)
Crown College (MN)
Dallas Baptist Univ.
David Lipscomb Univ. (TN)
Dominican Univ. (IL)
Dordt College (IA)
East Texas Baptist Univ.
Eastern Nazarene College (MA)
Eastern Univ. (PA)
Gordon College (MA)
Grace College and Seminary (IN)
Grace Univ. (NE)
Greenville College (IL)
Hardin-Simmons Univ. (TX)
Harding Univ. (AR)
Hope International Univ. (CA)
Howard Payne Univ. (TX)
Huntington College (IN)
Indiana Wesleyan Univ.
John Brown Univ. (AR)
Judson College (IL)
Liberty Univ. (VA)
Lindenwood Univ. (MO)
Lubbock Christian Univ. (TX)
Macmurray College (IL)
Madonna Univ. (MI)
Malone College (OH)
Master's Coll. and Seminary (CA)
Midland Lutheran College (NE)
Northwest College (WA)
Northwestern College (IA)
Northwestern College (MN)
Notre Dame College of Ohio
Ohio Northern Univ.
Oklahoma Baptist Univ.
Oklahoma Christian Univ.
Oklahoma City Univ.

Olivet Nazarene Univ. (IL)
Oral Roberts Univ. (OK)
Ouachita Baptist Univ. (AR)
Patten College (CA)
Pfeiffer Univ. (NC)
Rochester College (MI)
Simpson Univ. (CA)
Southern Nazarene Univ. (OK)
Southwest Baptist Univ. (MO)
Spring Arbor Univ. (MI)
St. Gregory's Univ. (OK)
St. Joseph's College (IN)
St. Mary's Univ. of Minnesota
Tabor College (KS)
Texas Lutheran Univ.
Toccoa Falls College (GA)
Union College (NE)
Union Univ. (TN)
Univ. of Mary Hardin-Baylor (TX)
Univ. of Sioux Falls (SD)
Univ. of St. Mary (KS)
Univ. of St. Thomas (TX)
Ursuline College (OH)
Valparaiso Univ. (IN)
Vanguard Univ. of Southern
    California
Warner Pacific College (OR)
Western Baptist College (OR)
York College (NE)

Peace Studies and Conflict Resolution

Antioch College (OH)
Bennington College (VT)
Bethel Univ. (MN)
Bluffton Univ. (OH)
California State Univ.–Long Beach
Chapman Univ. (CA)
Clarke College (IA)
Colgate Univ. (NY)
College of St. Benedict (MN)
Creighton Univ. (NE)
Depauw Univ. (IN)
Earlham College (IN)
Eastern Mennonite Univ. (VA)
George Mason Univ. (VA)
Goshen College (IN)
Goucher College (MD)
Guilford College (NC)
Gustavus Adolphus College (MN)
Hamline Univ. (MN)
Hampshire College (MA)
Juniata College (PA)
Kent State Univ. (OH)
Le Moyne College (NY)
Long Island Univ.–Southampton
    College (NY)
Manchester College (IN)
Manhattan College (NY)
Nazareth College of Rochester
    (NY)
Salisbury Univ. (MD)
St. John's Univ. (MN)
Tufts Univ. (MA)
Univ. of California–Berkeley
Univ. of N.C.–Chapel Hill
Univ. of St. Thomas (MN)
Wellesley College (MA)

Personal and Culinary Services

Kendall College (IL)

Petroleum Engineering

Colorado School of Mines
Louisiana State Univ.–Baton Rouge
Marietta College (OH)
Montana Tech of the Univ. of
    Montana
New Mexico Institute of Mining
    and Technology
Penn. State Univ.–Univ. Park
Stanford Univ. (CA)
Texas A&M Univ.–College Station
Texas A&M Univ.–Kingsville
Texas Tech Univ.
Univ. of Alaska–Fairbanks
Univ. of Kansas
Univ. of Louisiana–Lafayette
Univ. of Missouri–Rolla
Univ. of Oklahoma
Univ. of Texas–Austin
Univ. of Tulsa (OK)
West Virginia Univ.

Pharmacy, Pharmaceutical Sciences, and Administration

Gannon Univ. (PA)
Univ. of Missouri–Kansas City

Philosophy

Adelphi Univ. (NY)
Adrian College (MI)
Agnes Scott College (GA)
Albertson College (ID)
Albion College (MI)
Albright College (PA)
Alfred Univ. (NY)
Allegheny College (PA)
Alma College (MI)
Alvernia College (PA)
Alverno College (WI)
American International College
    (MA)
American Univ. (DC)
Amherst College (MA)
Anderson Univ. (IN)
Antioch College (OH)
Aquinas College (MI)
Arizona State Univ.
Arkansas State Univ.
Asbury College (KY)
Ashland Univ. (OH)
Assumption College (MA)
Auburn Univ. (AL)
Augsburg College (MN)
Augustana College (IL)
Augustana College (SD)
Austin College (TX)
Austin Peay State Univ. (TN)
Azusa Pacific Univ. (CA)

Babson College (MA)
Baker Univ. (KS)
Baldwin-Wallace College (OH)
Ball State Univ. (IN)
Barnard College (NY)
Barry Univ. (FL)
Bates College (ME)
Baylor Univ. (TX)
Belhaven College (MS)
Bellarmine Univ. (KY)
Belmont Abbey College (NC)
Belmont Univ. (TN)
Beloit College (WI)
Bemidji State Univ. (MN)
Benedictine College (KS)
Benedictine Univ. (IL)
Bennington College (VT)
Bentley College (MA)
Berea College (KY)
Bethel College (IN)
Bethel Univ. (MN)
Biola Univ. (CA)
Bloomfield College (NJ)
Bloomsburg Univ. of Pennsylvania
Boise State Univ. (ID)
Boston Univ.
Bowdoin College (ME)
Bowling Green State Univ. (OH)
Bradley Univ. (IL)
Brandeis Univ. (MA)
Bridgewater State College (MA)
Brigham Young Univ.–Provo (UT)
Brown Univ. (RI)
Bryn Mawr College (PA)
Bucknell Univ. (PA)
Buffalo State College
Butler Univ. (IN)
Cabrini College (PA)
Cal Poly–San Luis Obispo
California Baptist Univ.
California Lutheran Univ.
California State Polytechnic
    Univ.–Pomona
California State Univ.–Bakersfield
California State Univ.–Chico
California State Univ.–Fresno
California State Univ.–Fullerton
California State Univ.–Hayward
California State Univ.–Long Beach
California State Univ.–Los Angeles
California State Univ.–Monterey
    Bay
California State Univ.–Northridge
California State Univ.–Sacramento
California State Univ.–San
    Bernardino
California State Univ.–Stanislaus
California Univ. of Pennsylvania
Calvin College (MI)
Canisius College (NY)
Capital Univ. (OH)
Carleton College (MN)
Carlow Univ. (PA)
Carnegie Mellon Univ. (PA)
Carroll College (MT)
Carson-Newman College (TN)
Carthage College (WI)
Case Western Reserve Univ. (OH)
Catholic Univ. of America (DC)
Cedarville Univ. (OH)
Centenary College of Louisiana

Central College (IA)
Central Connecticut State Univ.
Central Methodist Univ. (MO)
Central Michigan Univ.
Central Washington Univ.
Centre College (KY)
Chaminade Univ. of Honolulu
Chapman Univ. (CA)
Christendom College (VA)
Christopher Newport Univ. (VA)
Claremont Mckenna College (CA)
Clarion Univ. of Pennsylvania
Clark Atlanta Univ.
Clark Univ. (MA)
Clarke College (IA)
Cleveland State Univ.
Coastal Carolina Univ. (SC)
Coe College (IA)
Colby College (ME)
Colgate Univ. (NY)
College Misericordia (PA)
College of Charleston (SC)
College of Mount St. Vincent (NY)
College of New Jersey
College of Notre Dame of
    Maryland
College of St. Benedict (MN)
College of St. Catherine (MN)
College of St. Elizabeth (NJ)
College of the Holy Cross (MA)
College of William and Mary (VA)
College of Wooster (OH)
Colorado College
Colorado State Univ.
Columbia Univ. (NY)
Concordia Coll.–Moorhead (MN)
Concordia Univ. (MI)
Connecticut College
Cornell College (IA)
Cornell Univ. (NY)
Cornerstone Univ. (MI)
Covenant College (GA)
Creighton Univ. (NE)
CUNY–Baruch College
CUNY–Brooklyn College
CUNY–City College
CUNY–College of Staten Island
CUNY–Hunter College
CUNY–Lehman College
CUNY–Queens College
CUNY–York College
Curry College (MA)
Dallas Baptist Univ.
Dartmouth College (NH)
David Lipscomb Univ. (TN)
Davidson College (NC)
Denison Univ. (OH)
Depaul Univ. (IL)
Depauw Univ. (IN)
Desales Univ. (PA)
Dickinson College (PA)
Dominican Univ. (IL)
Dordt College (IA)
Dowling College (NY)
Drake Univ. (IA)
Drew Univ. (NJ)
Drury Univ. (MO)
Duke Univ. (NC)
Duquesne Univ. (PA)
Earlham College (IN)
East Carolina Univ. (NC)

East Stroudsburg Univ. of Pennsylvania
East Tennessee State Univ.
Eastern Illinois Univ.
Eastern Kentucky Univ.
Eastern Michigan Univ.
Eckerd College (FL)
Edinboro Univ. of Pennsylvania
Elizabethtown College (PA)
Elmhurst College (IL)
Elon Univ. (NC)
Emory and Henry College (VA)
Emory Univ. (GA)
Erskine College (SC)
Evangel Univ. (MO)
Excelsior College (NY)
Fairfield Univ. (CT)
Fairleigh Dickinson Univ. (NJ)
Ferrum College (VA)
Florida Atlantic Univ.
Florida International Univ.
Florida Southern College
Florida State Univ.
Fordham Univ. (NY)
Fort Hays State Univ. (KS)
Fort Lewis College (CO)
Franciscan Univ. of Steubenville (OH)
Franklin and Marshall College (PA)
Franklin College (IN)
Freed-Hardeman Univ. (TN)
Fresno Pacific Univ. (CA)
Frostburg State Univ. (MD)
Furman Univ. (SC)
Gallaudet Univ. (DC)
Gannon Univ. (PA)
Geneva College (PA)
George Fox Univ. (OR)
George Mason Univ. (VA)
George Washington Univ. (DC)
Georgetown College (KY)
Georgetown Univ. (DC)
Georgia College and State Univ.
Georgia Southern Univ.
Georgia State Univ.
Gettysburg College (PA)
Gonzaga Univ. (WA)
Gordon College (MA)
Goucher College (MD)
Grand Valley State Univ. (MI)
Green Mountain College (VT)
Greenville College (IL)
Grinnell College (IA)
Grove City College (PA)
Guilford College (NC)
Gustavus Adolphus College (MN)
Hamilton College (NY)
Hamline Univ. (MN)
Hampden-Sydney College (VA)
Hampshire College (MA)
Hanover College (IN)
Hardin-Simmons Univ. (TX)
Hartwick College (NY)
Harvard Univ. (MA)
Hastings College (NE)
Haverford College (PA)
Heidelberg College (OH)
Hendrix College (AR)
High Point Univ. (NC)
Hillsdale College (MI)
Hiram College (OH)

Hobart and William Smith Colleges (NY)
Hofstra Univ. (NY)
Hollins Univ. (VA)
Holy Names Univ. (CA)
Hood College (MD)
Hope College (MI)
Houghton College (NY)
Howard Payne Univ. (TX)
Howard Univ. (DC)
Humboldt State Univ. (CA)
Huntington College (IN)
Idaho State Univ.
Illinois College
Illinois State Univ.
Illinois Wesleyan Univ.
Indiana State Univ.
Indiana Univ. Northwest
Indiana Univ. of Pennsylvania
Indiana Univ.–Bloomington
Indiana Univ.–South Bend
Indiana Univ.-Purdue Univ.–Fort Wayne
Indiana Univ.-Purdue Univ.–Indianapolis
Iona College (NY)
Iowa State Univ.
Ithaca College (NY)
Jacksonville Univ. (FL)
John Carroll Univ. (OH)
Johns Hopkins Univ. (MD)
Juniata College (PA)
Kalamazoo College (MI)
Kansas State Univ.
Kent State Univ. (OH)
King's College (PA)
Knox College (IL)
Kutztown Univ. of Pennsylvania
La Salle Univ. (PA)
Lafayette College (PA)
Lake Forest College (IL)
Lawrence Univ. (WI)
Le Moyne College (NY)
Lebanon Valley College (PA)
Lehigh Univ. (PA)
Lenoir-Rhyne College (NC)
Lewis and Clark College (OR)
Lewis Univ. (IL)
Liberty Univ. (VA)
Lincoln Univ. (PA)
Lindenwood Univ. (MO)
Linfield College (OR)
Lock Haven Univ. of Pennsylvania
Long Island Univ.–Brooklyn (NY)
Long Island Univ.-C.W. Post Campus (NY)
Loras College (IA)
Louisiana State Univ.–Baton Rouge
Loyola College In Maryland
Loyola Marymount Univ. (CA)
Loyola Univ. Chicago
Loyola Univ. New Orleans
Luther College (IA)
Lycoming College (PA)
Lynchburg College (VA)
Macalester College (MN)
Macmurray College (IL)
Madonna Univ. (MI)
Malone College (OH)
Manchester College (IN)
Manhattan College (NY)

Manhattanville College (NY)
Mansfield Univ. of Pennsylvania
Marian College (IN)
Marist College (NY)
Mary Baldwin College (VA)
Marymount Univ. (VA)
Marywood Univ. (PA)
Massachusetts Institute of Technology
Mcdaniel College (MD)
Mckendree College (IL)
Mcpherson College (KS)
Mercer Univ. (GA)
Mercy College (NY)
Mercyhurst College (PA)
Merrimack College (MA)
Messiah College (PA)
Metropolitan State College of Denver
Miami Univ.–Oxford (OH)
Michigan State Univ.
Middle Tennessee State Univ.
Middlebury College (VT)
Millersville Univ. of Pennsylvania
Millikin Univ. (IL)
Mills College (CA)
Millsaps College (MS)
Minnesota State Univ.–Mankato
Minnesota State Univ.–Moorhead
Mississippi State Univ.
Molloy College (NY)
Monmouth College (IL)
Montana State Univ.–Bozeman
Montclair State Univ. (NJ)
Moravian College (PA)
Morehead State Univ. (KY)
Morehouse College (GA)
Morningside College (IA)
Mount Holyoke College (MA)
Mount Mary College (WI)
Mount Mercy College (IA)
Mount St. Mary's College (CA)
Mount St. Mary's Univ. (MD)
Mount Union College (OH)
Muhlenberg College (PA)
Murray State Univ. (KY)
Nazareth College of Rochester (NY)
Nebraska Wesleyan Univ.
New England College (NH)
New Jersey City Univ.
New Mexico State Univ.
New York Univ.
Niagara Univ. (NY)
North Carolina State Univ.–Raleigh
North Central College (IL)
North Dakota State Univ.
North Park Univ. (IL)
Northeastern Illinois Univ.
Northeastern Univ. (MA)
Northern Arizona Univ.
Northern Illinois Univ.
Northern Kentucky Univ.
Northern Michigan Univ.
Northland College (WI)
Northwest Missouri State Univ.
Northwest Nazarene Univ. (ID)
Northwestern College (IA)
Northwestern Univ. (IL)
Notre Dame De Namur Univ. (CA)
Nyack College (NY)

Oakland Univ. (MI)
Oberlin College (OH)
Occidental College (CA)
Oglethorpe Univ. (GA)
Ohio Dominican Univ.
Ohio Northern Univ.
Ohio State Univ.–Columbus
Ohio Univ.
Ohio Wesleyan Univ.
Oklahoma Baptist Univ.
Oklahoma City Univ.
Oklahoma State Univ.
Old Dominion Univ. (VA)
Oregon State Univ.
Otterbein College (OH)
Ouachita Baptist Univ. (AR)
Our Lady of the Lake Univ. (TX)
Pacific Lutheran Univ. (WA)
Pacific Univ. (OR)
Paine College (GA)
Penn. State Univ.–Univ. Park
Pepperdine Univ. (CA)
Plymouth State Univ. (NH)
Point Loma Nazarene Univ. (CA)
Pomona College (CA)
Portland State Univ. (OR)
Presbyterian College (SC)
Princeton Univ. (NJ)
Principia College (IL)
Providence College (RI)
Purdue Univ.–Calumet (IN)
Purdue Univ.–West Lafayette (IN)
Randolph-Macon College (VA)
Randolph-Macon Woman's College (VA)
Reed College (OR)
Regis Univ. (CO)
Rensselaer Polytechnic Inst. (NY)
Rhode Island College
Rhodes College (TN)
Rice Univ. (TX)
Rider Univ. (NJ)
Ripon College (WI)
Roanoke College (VA)
Rockford College (IL)
Rockhurst Univ. (MO)
Roger Williams Univ. (RI)
Rollins College (FL)
Roosevelt Univ. (IL)
Rosemont College (PA)
Rutgers–Camden (NJ)
Rutgers–New Brunswick (NJ)
Rutgers–Newark (NJ)
Sacred Heart Univ. (CT)
Salem College (NC)
Salisbury Univ. (MD)
Salve Regina Univ. (RI)
Sam Houston State Univ. (TX)
Samford Univ. (AL)
San Diego State Univ.
San Francisco State Univ.
San Jose State Univ. (CA)
Santa Clara Univ. (CA)
Scripps College (CA)
Seattle Pacific Univ.
Seattle Univ.
Seton Hall Univ. (NJ)
Sewanee–Univ. of the South (TN)
Siena College (NY)
Simmons College (MA)
Simpson College (IA)

Skidmore College (NY)
Slippery Rock Univ. of Pennsylvania
Sonoma State Univ. (CA)
Southeast Missouri State Univ.
Southern Connecticut State Univ.
Southern Illinois Univ.–Carbondale
Southern Illinois Univ.–Edwardsville
Southern Methodist Univ. (TX)
Southern Nazarene Univ. (OK)
Southwest Minnesota State Univ. (MN)
Southwest Missouri State Univ.
Southwestern Univ. (TX)
Spelman College (GA)
Spring Arbor Univ. (MI)
Spring Hill College (AL)
St. Ambrose Univ. (IA)
St. Andrews Presbyterian College (NC)
St. Anselm College (NH)
St. Bonaventure Univ. (NY)
St. Cloud State Univ. (MN)
St. Edward's Univ. (TX)
St. Francis College (NY)
St. Francis Univ. (PA)
St. Gregory's Univ. (OK)
St. John Fisher College (NY)
St. John's Univ. (MN)
St. John's Univ. (NY)
St. Joseph College (CT)
St. Joseph's College (IN)
St. Joseph's College (ME)
St. Joseph's Univ. (PA)
St. Lawrence Univ. (NY)
St. Louis Univ.
St. Mary's College (IN)
St. Mary's College of California
St. Mary's College of Maryland
St. Mary's Univ. of Minnesota
St. Mary's Univ. of San Antonio
St. Norbert College (WI)
St. Olaf College (MN)
St. Peter's College (NJ)
St. Vincent College (PA)
St. Xavier Univ. (IL)
Stanford Univ. (CA)
State Univ. of West Georgia
Stetson Univ. (FL)
Stonehill College (MA)
SUNY College of Arts and Sciences–Geneseo
SUNY College–Brockport
SUNY College–Oneonta
SUNY College–Potsdam
SUNY–Albany
SUNY–Binghamton
SUNY–Fredonia
SUNY–Plattsburgh
SUNY–Purchase College
SUNY–Stony Brook
Susquehanna Univ. (PA)
Swarthmore College (PA)
Sweet Briar College (VA)
Syracuse Univ. (NY)
Tabor College (KS)
Taylor Univ. (IN)
Temple Univ. (PA)
Texas A&M Univ.–College Station
Texas Christian Univ.
Texas Lutheran Univ.

Texas State Univ.–San Marcos
Texas Tech Univ.
Thiel College (PA)
Thomas Edison State College (NJ)
Thomas More College (KY)
Touro College (NY)
Towson Univ. (MD)
Transylvania Univ. (KY)
Trinity Christian College (IL)
Trinity College (CT)
Tufts Univ. (MA)
Tulane Univ. (LA)
Union College (NY)
Union Univ. (TN)
Univ. at Buffalo–SUNY
Univ. of Akron (OH)
Univ. of Alabama
Univ. of Alabama–Birmingham
Univ. of Alabama–Huntsville
Univ. of Alaska–Anchorage
Univ. of Alaska–Fairbanks
Univ. of Arizona
Univ. of Arkansas
Univ. of Arkansas–Little Rock
Univ. of California–Berkeley
Univ. of California–Davis
Univ. of California–Irvine
Univ. of California–Los Angeles
Univ. of California–Riverside
Univ. of California–San Diego
Univ. of California–Santa Barbara
Univ. of California–Santa Cruz
Univ. of Central Arkansas
Univ. of Central Florida
Univ. of Central Oklahoma
Univ. of Chicago
Univ. of Colorado–Boulder
Univ. of Colorado–Colorado
    Springs
Univ. of Colorado–Denver
Univ. of Connecticut
Univ. of Dallas
Univ. of Dayton (OH)
Univ. of Delaware
Univ. of Denver
Univ. of Detroit Mercy
Univ. of Dubuque (IA)
Univ. of Evansville (IN)
Univ. of Findlay (OH)
Univ. of Florida
Univ. of Georgia
Univ. of Hartford (CT)
Univ. of Hawaii–Hilo
Univ. of Hawaii–Manoa
Univ. of Houston
Univ. of Houston–Downtown
Univ. of Illinois–Chicago
Univ. of Illinois–Springfield
Univ. of Illinois–Urbana-
    Champaign
Univ. of Indianapolis
Univ. of Iowa
Univ. of Kansas
Univ. of Kentucky
Univ. of La Verne (CA)
Univ. of Louisiana–Lafayette
Univ. of Louisville (KY)
Univ. of Maine–Orono
Univ. of Maryland–Baltimore
    County
Univ. of Maryland–College Park

Univ. of Massachusetts–Amherst
Univ. of Massachusetts–Boston
Univ. of Massachusetts–Lowell
Univ. of Memphis
Univ. of Miami (FL)
Univ. of Michigan–Ann Arbor
Univ. of Michigan–Dearborn
Univ. of Michigan–Flint
Univ. of Minnesota–Duluth
Univ. of Minnesota–Morris
Univ. of Minnesota–Twin Cities
Univ. of Mississippi
Univ. of Missouri–Columbia
Univ. of Missouri–Kansas City
Univ. of Missouri–Rolla
Univ. of Missouri–St. Louis
Univ. of Montana
Univ. of Nebraska–Kearney
Univ. of Nebraska–Lincoln
Univ. of Nebraska–Omaha
Univ. of Nevada–Las Vegas
Univ. of Nevada–Reno
Univ. of New Hampshire
Univ. of New Mexico
Univ. of New Orleans
Univ. of North Carolina–Asheville
Univ. of N.C.–Chapel Hill
Univ. of North Carolina–Charlotte
Univ. of N.C.–Greensboro
Univ. of North Dakota
Univ. of North Florida
Univ. of North Texas
Univ. of Northern Colorado
Univ. of Northern Iowa
Univ. of Notre Dame (IN)
Univ. of Oklahoma
Univ. of Oregon
Univ. of Pennsylvania
Univ. of Pittsburgh
Univ. of Portland (OR)
Univ. of Puget Sound (WA)
Univ. of Redlands (CA)
Univ. of Rhode Island
Univ. of Richmond (VA)
Univ. of Rochester (NY)
Univ. of San Diego
Univ. of San Francisco
Univ. of Scranton (PA)
Univ. of South Alabama
Univ. of South Carolina–Columbia
Univ. of South Dakota
Univ. of South Florida
Univ. of Southern California
Univ. of Southern Indiana
Univ. of Southern Maine
Univ. of Southern Mississippi
Univ. of St. Francis (IN)
Univ. of St. Thomas (MN)
Univ. of St. Thomas (TX)
Univ. of Tennessee
Univ. of Tennessee–Martin
Univ. of Texas–Arlington
Univ. of Texas–Austin
Univ. of Texas–El Paso
Univ. of Texas–Pan American
Univ. of Texas–San Antonio
Univ. of the Incarnate Word (TX)
Univ. of the Pacific (CA)
Univ. of Toledo (OH)
Univ. of Tulsa (OK)
Univ. of Utah

Univ. of Vermont
Univ. of Virginia
Univ. of Washington
Univ. of West Florida
Univ. of Wisconsin–Eau Claire
Univ. of Wisconsin–Green Bay
Univ. of Wisconsin–La Crosse
Univ. of Wisconsin–Madison
Univ. of Wisconsin–Milwaukee
Univ. of Wisconsin–Oshkosh
Univ. of Wisconsin–Parkside
Univ. of Wisconsin–Platteville
Univ. of Wisconsin–Stevens Point
Univ. of Wyoming
Ursinus College (PA)
Ursuline College (OH)
Utah State Univ.
Utah Valley State College
Utica College (NY)
Valdosta State Univ. (GA)
Valparaiso Univ. (IN)
Vanderbilt Univ. (TN)
Vassar College (NY)
Villanova Univ. (PA)
Virginia Commonwealth Univ.
Virginia Tech
Virginia Wesleyan College
Wabash College (IN)
Wagner College (NY)
Wake Forest Univ. (NC)
Walsh Univ. (OH)
Wartburg College (IA)
Washburn Univ. (KS)
Washington and Jefferson College
    (PA)
Washington and Lee Univ. (VA)
Washington College (MD)
Washington State Univ.
Washington Univ. In St. Louis
Wayne State Univ. (MI)
Webster Univ. (MO)
Wellesley College (MA)
Wesleyan College (GA)
Wesleyan Univ. (CT)
West Chester Univ. of Pennsylvania
West Virginia Univ.
West Virginia Wesleyan College
Western Carolina Univ. (NC)
Western Illinois Univ.
Western Kentucky Univ.
Western Michigan Univ.
Western New England College
    (MA)
Western Oregon Univ.
Western State College of Colorado
Western Washington Univ.
Westfield State College (MA)
Westminster College (PA)
Westminster College (MO)
Westminster College (UT)
Westmont College (CA)
Wheaton College (IL)
Wheaton College (MA)
Wheeling Jesuit Univ. (WV)
Whitman College (WA)
Whittier College (CA)
Whitworth College (WA)
Wichita State Univ. (KS)
Wilkes Univ. (PA)
Willamette Univ. (OR)
William Jewell College (MO)

William Paterson Univ. of New
    Jersey
Williams College (MA)
Wingate Univ. (NC)
Wisconsin Lutheran College
Wittenberg Univ. (OH)
Wofford College (SC)
Wright State Univ. (OH)
Xavier Univ. (OH)
Yale Univ. (CT)
Yeshiva Univ. (NY)
York College of Pennsylvania
Youngstown State Univ. (OH)

Philosophy and Religious Studies

Alderson-Broaddus College (WV)
Appalachian State Univ. (NC)
Barton College (NC)
Benedictine College (KS)
Berry College (GA)
Bethel College (IN)
Bethune-Cookman College (FL)
Bridgewater College (VA)
Buena Vista Univ. (IA)
Butler Univ. (IN)
Campbell Univ. (NC)
Claflin Univ. (SC)
Colgate Univ. (NY)
College of the Ozarks (MO)
Covenant College (GA)
Eastern Mennonite Univ. (VA)
Elmira College (NY)
Eureka College (IL)
Fisk Univ. (TN)
Flagler College (FL)
Graceland Univ. (IA)
Greenville College (IL)
Holy Names Univ. (CA)
Indiana Univ. Southeast
Ithaca College (NY)
James Madison Univ. (VA)
Jamestown College (ND)
Juniata College (PA)
Kean Univ. (NJ)
Lambuth Univ. (TN)
Louisiana College
Lyon College (AR)
Marquette Univ. (WI)
Mary Baldwin College (VA)
Marywood Univ. (PA)
Midland Lutheran College (NE)
Muskingum College (OH)
Newman Univ. (KS)
Northwest Nazarene Univ. (ID)
Ohio Northern Univ.
Ohio State Univ.–Columbus
Pace Univ. (NY)
Pepperdine Univ. (CA)
Philander Smith College (AR)
Point Loma Nazarene Univ. (CA)
Queens Univ. of Charlotte (NC)
Quincy Univ. (IL)
Radford Univ. (VA)
Richard Stockton College of New
    Jersey
Roberts Wesleyan College (NY)
Rocky Mountain College (MT)
Samford Univ. (AL)

Shaw Univ. (NC)
Southwestern College (KS)
St. Joseph's College (IN)
St. Thomas Aquinas College (NY)
Sterling College (KS)
SUNY College–Old Westbury
Syracuse Univ. (NY)
Toccoa Falls College (GA)
Union Univ. (TN)
Univ. of La Verne (CA)
Univ. of Maine–Farmington
Univ. of Mary Washington (VA)
Univ. of North Carolina–Pembroke
Univ. of N.C.–Wilmington
Univ. of Notre Dame (IN)
Univ. of Sioux Falls (SD)
Univ. of Tennessee–Chattanooga
Urbana Univ. (OH)
Ursinus College (PA)
Vanderbilt Univ. (TN)
Wheaton College (MA)
William Jewell College (MO)
Wilson College (PA)
Winthrop Univ. (SC)

Physical Science Technologies/Technicians

Dakota State Univ. (SD)
Marian College (IN)
Southwest Missouri State Univ.
Univ. of Alaska–Anchorage

Physical Sciences

Alfred Univ. (NY)
Arkansas Tech Univ.
Asbury College (KY)
Auburn Univ.–Montgomery (AL)
Azusa Pacific Univ. (CA)
Baldwin-Wallace College (OH)
Bennington College (VT)
Biola Univ. (CA)
Black Hills State Univ. (SD)
Cal Poly–San Luis Obispo
California Institute of Technology
California State Univ.–Fresno
California State Univ.–Sacramento
California State Univ.–Stanislaus
California Univ. of Pennsylvania
Carthage College (WI)
Central College (IA)
Central Connecticut State Univ.
Central Michigan Univ.
Charleston Southern Univ. (SC)
Colgate Univ. (NY)
Columbia Univ. (NY)
Concordia Univ. (NE)
Concordia Univ.–River Forest (IL)
Cornell College (IA)
Dakota State Univ. (SD)
Defiance College (OH)
East Stroudsburg Univ. of Penn.
Eastern Michigan Univ.
Eastern Washington Univ.
Emporia State Univ. (KS)
Eureka College (IL)
Evangel Univ. (MO)
Florida Institute of Technology

Fort Hays State Univ. (KS)
Freed-Hardeman Univ. (TN)
Frostburg State Univ. (MD)
Grace College and Seminary (IN)
Grace Univ. (NE)
Graceland Univ. (IA)
Grand View College (IA)
Hampshire College (MA)
Hobart and William Smith Colleges (NY)
Humboldt State Univ. (CA)
Indiana Univ.–Kokomo
Johns Hopkins Univ. (MD)
Juniata College (PA)
Kansas State Univ.
Kent State Univ. (OH)
Keuka College (NY)
La Sierra Univ. (CA)
Lawrence Univ. (WI)
Lincoln Univ. (PA)
Linfield College (OR)
Long Island Univ.–C.W. Post Campus (NY)
Marian College (IN)
Marlboro College (VT)
Mayville State Univ. (ND)
Mcdaniel College (MD)
Michigan State Univ.
Minot State Univ. (ND)
Mississippi Univ. For Women
Montana Tech of the Univ. of Montana
Muhlenberg College (PA)
Northern Arizona Univ.
Northland College (WI)
Northwest Nazarene Univ. (ID)
Olivet Nazarene Univ. (IL)
Oral Roberts Univ. (OK)
Otterbein College (OH)
Pacific Univ. (OR)
Penn. State–Erie, The Behrend College
Pitzer College (CA)
Radford Univ. (VA)
Ripon College (WI)
Roberts Wesleyan College (NY)
Rochester Institute of Tech. (NY)
San Diego State Univ.
Seattle Univ.
Southern Nazarene Univ. (OK)
Southwestern Univ. (TX)
St. Ambrose Univ. (IA)
St. Francis Univ. (PA)
St. John's Univ. (NY)
St. Joseph College (CT)
St. Michael's College (VT)
Suffolk Univ. (MA)
SUNY–Empire State College
SUNY–Stony Brook
Texas A&M International Univ.
Texas A&M Univ.–College Station
Tri-State Univ. (IN)
Trinity College (DC)
Troy State Univ.–Troy (AL)
Tusculum College (TN)
United States Naval Academy (MD)
Univ. of Alaska–Anchorage
Univ. of California–Berkeley
Univ. of California–Davis
Univ. of California–Riverside

Univ. of Dayton (OH)
Univ. of Hartford (CT)
Univ. of Mary Washington (VA)
Univ. of Maryland–College Park
Univ. of Massachusetts–Lowell
Univ. of Missouri–Rolla
Univ. of North Alabama
Univ. of N.C.–Chapel Hill
Univ. of Pittsburgh
Univ. of Pittsburgh–Bradford
Univ. of Rio Grande (OH)
Univ. of Southern California
Univ. of Southern Maine
Univ. of St. Francis (IN)
Univ. of Texas–El Paso
Univ. of Utah
Utah State Univ.
Villanova Univ. (PA)
Washburn Univ. (KS)
Washington State Univ.
Wayland Baptist Univ. (TX)
Western New Mexico Univ.
Westfield State College (MA)
Wheeling Jesuit Univ. (WV)
Williams College (MA)
Xavier Univ. (OH)
York College of Pennsylvania

Physics

Abilene Christian Univ. (TX)
Adelphi Univ. (NY)
Adrian College (MI)
Agnes Scott College (GA)
Alabama Agricultural and Mechanical Univ.
Alabama State Univ.
Albion College (MI)
Albright College (PA)
Alfred Univ. (NY)
Allegheny College (PA)
Alma College (MI)
American Univ. (DC)
Amherst College (MA)
Anderson Univ. (IN)
Andrews Univ. (MI)
Angelo State Univ. (TX)
Appalachian State Univ. (NC)
Arizona State Univ.
Arkansas State Univ.
Armstrong Atlantic State Univ. (GA)
Ashland Univ. (OH)
Auburn Univ. (AL)
Augsburg College (MN)
Augusta State Univ. (GA)
Augustana College (IL)
Austin College (TX)
Austin Peay State Univ. (TN)
Baker Univ. (KS)
Baldwin-Wallace College (OH)
Ball State Univ. (IN)
Barnard College (NY)
Bates College (ME)
Baylor Univ. (TX)
Belmont Univ. (TN)
Beloit College (WI)
Benedict College (SC)
Benedictine College (KS)
Benedictine Univ. (IL)

Bennington College (VT)
Berea College (KY)
Berry College (GA)
Bethany College (WV)
Bethel College (KS)
Bethel College (IN)
Bethel Univ. (MN)
Bethune-Cookman College (FL)
Bloomsburg Univ. of Pennsylvania
Bluffton Univ. (OH)
Boise State Univ. (ID)
Boston Univ.
Bowdoin College (ME)
Bowling Green State Univ. (OH)
Bradley Univ. (IL)
Brandeis Univ. (MA)
Bridgewater College (VA)
Bridgewater State College (MA)
Brigham Young Univ.–Provo (UT)
Brown Univ. (RI)
Bryn Mawr College (PA)
Bucknell Univ. (PA)
Buena Vista Univ. (IA)
Buffalo State College
Butler Univ. (IN)
Cal Poly–San Luis Obispo
California Institute of Technology
California Lutheran Univ.
California State Polytechnic Univ.–Pomona
California State Univ.–Bakersfield
California State Univ.–Chico
California State Univ.–Fresno
California State Univ.–Fullerton
California State Univ.–Hayward
California State Univ.–Long Beach
California State Univ.–Los Angeles
California State Univ.–Northridge
California State Univ.–Sacramento
California State Univ.–San Bernardino
California State Univ.–Stanislaus
California Univ. of Pennsylvania
Calvin College (MI)
Cameron Univ. (OK)
Campbellsville Univ. (KY)
Canisius College (NY)
Carleton College (MN)
Carnegie Mellon Univ. (PA)
Carthage College (WI)
Case Western Reserve Univ. (OH)
Catholic Univ. of America (DC)
Cedarville Univ. (OH)
Centenary College of Louisiana
Central College (IA)
Central Connecticut State Univ.
Central Methodist Univ. (MO)
Central Michigan Univ.
Central Washington Univ.
Centre College (KY)
Chadron State College (NE)
Chatham College (PA)
Chicago State Univ.
Christian Brothers Univ. (TN)
Christopher Newport Univ. (VA)
Claremont Mckenna College (CA)
Clarion Univ. of Pennsylvania
Clark Atlanta Univ.
Clark Univ. (MA)
Clarke College (IA)
Clarkson Univ. (NY)

Cleveland State Univ.
Coastal Carolina Univ. (SC)
Coe College (IA)
Colby College (ME)
Colgate Univ. (NY)
College of Charleston (SC)
College of Mount St. Vincent (NY)
College of New Jersey
College of Notre Dame of Maryland
College of St. Benedict (MN)
College of St. Catherine (MN)
College of the Holy Cross (MA)
College of William and Mary (VA)
College of Wooster (OH)
Colorado College
Colorado State Univ.
Colorado State Univ.–Pueblo
Columbia Univ. (NY)
Concordia Coll.–Moorhead (MN)
Concordia Univ. (MI)
Connecticut College
Cornell Univ. (NY)
Covenant College (GA)
Cumberland College (KY)
CUNY–Brooklyn College
CUNY–College of Staten Island
CUNY–Hunter College
CUNY–Lehman College
CUNY–Queens College
CUNY–York College
Dartmouth College (NH)
David Lipscomb Univ. (TN)
Davidson College (NC)
Delaware State Univ.
Denison Univ. (OH)
Depaul Univ. (IL)
Depauw Univ. (IN)
Dickinson College (PA)
Dillard Univ. (LA)
Dordt College (IA)
Drake Univ. (IA)
Drew Univ. (NJ)
Drexel Univ. (PA)
Drury Univ. (MO)
Duke Univ. (NC)
Duquesne Univ. (PA)
Earlham College (IN)
East Carolina Univ. (NC)
East Central Univ. (OK)
East Stroudsburg Univ. of Pennsylvania
East Tennessee State Univ.
Eastern Illinois Univ.
Eastern Kentucky Univ.
Eastern Michigan Univ.
Eastern Nazarene College (MA)
Eastern New Mexico Univ.
Eastern Oregon Univ.
Eastern Washington Univ.
Eckerd College (FL)
Edinboro Univ. of Pennsylvania
Elizabeth City State Univ. (NC)
Elizabethtown College (PA)
Elmhurst College (IL)
Elon Univ. (NC)
Emory and Henry College (VA)
Emory Univ. (GA)
Emporia State Univ. (KS)
Erskine College (SC)
Excelsior College (NY)

Fairfield Univ. (CT)
Fisk Univ. (TN)
Florida Atlantic Univ.
Florida Institute of Technology
Florida International Univ.
Florida State Univ.
Fordham Univ. (NY)
Fort Hays State Univ. (KS)
Fort Lewis College (CO)
Francis Marion Univ. (SC)
Franklin and Marshall College (PA)
Frostburg State Univ. (MD)
Furman Univ. (SC)
Gallaudet Univ. (DC)
Geneva College (PA)
George Mason Univ. (VA)
George Washington Univ. (DC)
Georgetown College (KY)
Georgetown Univ. (DC)
Georgia Institute of Technology
Georgia Southern Univ.
Georgia State Univ.
Georgian Court Univ. (NJ)
Gettysburg College (PA)
Gonzaga Univ. (WA)
Gordon College (MA)
Goshen College (IN)
Goucher College (MD)
Grambling State Univ. (LA)
Grand Valley State Univ. (MI)
Greenville College (IL)
Grinnell College (IA)
Grove City College (PA)
Guilford College (NC)
Gustavus Adolphus College (MN)
Hamilton College (NY)
Hamline Univ. (MN)
Hampden-Sydney College (VA)
Hampshire College (MA)
Hampton Univ. (VA)
Hanover College (IN)
Hardin-Simmons Univ. (TX)
Harding Univ. (AR)
Hartwick College (NY)
Harvard Univ. (MA)
Harvey Mudd College (CA)
Hastings College (NE)
Haverford College (PA)
Heidelberg College (OH)
Henderson State Univ. (AR)
Hendrix College (AR)
Hillsdale College (MI)
Hiram College (OH)
Hobart and William Smith Colleges (NY)
Hofstra Univ. (NY)
Hollins Univ. (VA)
Hope College (MI)
Houghton College (NY)
Houston Baptist Univ.
Howard Univ. (DC)
Humboldt State Univ. (CA)
Huntington College (IN)
Idaho State Univ.
Illinois College
Illinois Institute of Technology
Illinois State Univ.
Illinois Wesleyan Univ.
Indiana State Univ.
Indiana Univ. of Pennsylvania
Indiana Univ.–Bloomington

Indiana Univ.-Purdue Univ.–Fort Wayne
Indiana Univ.-Purdue Univ.–Indianapolis
Iona College (NY)
Iowa State Univ.
Ithaca College (NY)
Jacksonville Univ. (FL)
James Madison Univ. (VA)
John Carroll Univ. (OH)
Johns Hopkins Univ. (MD)
Juniata College (PA)
Kalamazoo College (MI)
Kansas State Univ.
Kent State Univ. (OH)
Kentucky Wesleyan College
Kettering Univ. (MI)
King College (TN)
Knox College (IL)
Kutztown Univ. of Pennsylvania
La Salle Univ. (PA)
Lafayette College (PA)
Lake Forest College (IL)
Lamar Univ. (TX)
Lane College (TN)
Lawrence Technological Univ. (MI)
Lawrence Univ. (WI)
Le Moyne College (NY)
Lebanon Valley College (PA)
Lehigh Univ. (PA)
Lenoir-Rhyne College (NC)
Lewis and Clark College (OR)
Lewis Univ. (IL)
Lincoln Univ. (PA)
Lincoln Univ. (MO)
Linfield College (OR)
Lock Haven Univ. of Pennsylvania
Long Island Univ.–C.W. Post Campus (NY)
Longwood Univ. (VA)
Loras College (IA)
Louisiana State Univ.–Baton Rouge
Louisiana State Univ.–Shreveport
Louisiana Tech Univ.
Loyola College In Maryland
Loyola Marymount Univ. (CA)
Loyola Univ. Chicago
Loyola Univ. New Orleans
Luther College (IA)
Lycoming College (PA)
Lynchburg College (VA)
Macalester College (MN)
Madonna Univ. (MI)
Manchester College (IN)
Manhattan College (NY)
Manhattanville College (NY)
Mansfield Univ. of Pennsylvania
Marian College (IN)
Marietta College (OH)
Marquette Univ. (WI)
Marshall Univ. (WV)
Mary Baldwin College (VA)
Maryville College (TN)
Massachusetts Institute of Technology
Mcmurry Univ. (TX)
Mcneese State Univ. (LA)
Mercer Univ. (GA)
Merrimack College (MA)
Messiah College (PA)
Metropolitan State Coll. of Denver

Miami Univ.–Oxford (OH)
Michigan State Univ.
Michigan Technological Univ.
Middle Tennessee State Univ.
Middlebury College (VT)
Midwestern State Univ. (TX)
Millersville Univ. of Pennsylvania
Millikin Univ. (IL)
Millsaps College (MS)
Minnesota State Univ.–Mankato
Minnesota State Univ.–Moorhead
Minot State Univ. (ND)
Mississippi College
Mississippi State Univ.
Missouri Southern State Univ.
Monmouth College (IL)
Montana State Univ.–Bozeman
Montclair State Univ. (NJ)
Moravian College (PA)
Morehead State Univ. (KY)
Morehouse College (GA)
Morgan State Univ. (MD)
Morningside College (IA)
Mount Holyoke College (MA)
Mount Union College (OH)
Muhlenberg College (PA)
Murray State Univ. (KY)
Muskingum College (OH)
Nebraska Wesleyan Univ.
New Jersey City Univ.
New Jersey Institute of Technology
New Mexico Highlands Univ.
New Mexico Institute of Mining and Technology
New Mexico State Univ.
New York Institute of Technology
New York Univ.
Norfolk State Univ. (VA)
North Carolina A&T State Univ.
North Carolina Central Univ.
North Carolina State Univ.–Raleigh
North Central College (IL)
North Dakota State Univ.
North Georgia College and State Univ.
North Park Univ. (IL)
Northeastern Illinois Univ.
Northeastern Univ. (MA)
Northern Arizona Univ.
Northern Illinois Univ.
Northern Kentucky Univ.
Northern Michigan Univ.
Northland College (WI)
Northwest Missouri State Univ.
Northwest Nazarene Univ. (ID)
Northwestern Oklahoma State Univ.
Northwestern State Univ. of Louisiana
Northwestern Univ. (IL)
Norwich Univ. (VT)
Oakland Univ. (MI)
Oberlin College (OH)
Occidental College (CA)
Oglethorpe Univ. (GA)
Ohio Northern Univ.
Ohio State Univ.–Columbus
Ohio Univ.
Ohio Wesleyan Univ.
Oklahoma Baptist Univ.
Oklahoma City Univ.

Oklahoma State Univ.
Old Dominion Univ. (VA)
Oral Roberts Univ. (OK)
Oregon State Univ.
Otterbein College (OH)
Ouachita Baptist Univ. (AR)
Pace Univ. (NY)
Pacific Lutheran Univ. (WA)
Pacific Union College (CA)
Pacific Univ. (OR)
Penn. State Univ.–Univ. Park
Penn. State–Erie, The Behrend College
Pepperdine Univ. (CA)
Pittsburg State Univ. (KS)
Point Loma Nazarene Univ. (CA)
Polytechnic Univ. (NY)
Pomona College (CA)
Portland State Univ. (OR)
Prairie View A&M Univ. (TX)
Presbyterian College (SC)
Princeton Univ. (NJ)
Principia College (IL)
Purdue Univ.–Calumet (IN)
Purdue Univ.–West Lafayette (IN)
Ramapo College of New Jersey
Randolph-Macon College (VA)
Randolph-Macon Woman's College (VA)
Reed College (OR)
Rensselaer Polytechnic Inst. (NY)
Rhode Island College
Rhodes College (TN)
Rice Univ. (TX)
Richard Stockton College of New Jersey
Rider Univ. (NJ)
Ripon College (WI)
Roanoke College (VA)
Rochester Institute of Tech. (NY)
Rockhurst Univ. (MO)
Rollins College (FL)
Roosevelt Univ. (IL)
Rose-Hulman Institute of Technology (IN)
Rutgers–Camden (NJ)
Rutgers–New Brunswick (NJ)
Rutgers–Newark (NJ)
Saginaw Valley State Univ. (MI)
Salisbury Univ. (MD)
Sam Houston State Univ. (TX)
Samford Univ. (AL)
San Diego State Univ.
San Francisco State Univ.
San Jose State Univ. (CA)
Santa Clara Univ. (CA)
Scripps College (CA)
Seattle Pacific Univ.
Seattle Univ.
Seton Hall Univ. (NJ)
Seton Hill Univ. (PA)
Sewanee–Univ. of the South (TN)
Shaw Univ. (NC)
Shippensburg Univ. of Pennsylvania
Siena College (NY)
Simmons College (MA)
Skidmore College (NY)
Slippery Rock Univ. of Pennsylvania
Sonoma State Univ. (CA)
South Carolina State Univ.

South Dakota School of Mines and Technology
South Dakota State Univ.
Southeast Missouri State Univ.
Southeastern Louisiana Univ.
Southern Adventist Univ. (TN)
Southern Arkansas Univ.
Southern Connecticut State Univ.
Southern Illinois Univ.–Carbondale
Southern Illinois Univ.–Edwardsville
Southern Methodist Univ. (TX)
Southern Nazarene Univ. (OK)
Southern Oregon Univ.
Southern Polytechnic State Univ. (GA)
Southern Univ. and A&M College (LA)
Southwest Missouri State Univ.
Southwestern Adventist Univ. (TX)
Southwestern College (KS)
Southwestern Oklahoma State Univ.
Southwestern Univ. (TX)
Spelman College (GA)
Spring Arbor Univ. (MI)
St. Ambrose Univ. (IA)
St. Anselm College (NH)
St. Bonaventure Univ. (NY)
St. Cloud State Univ. (MN)
St. John Fisher College (NY)
St. John's Univ. (NY)
St. John's Univ. (MN)
St. Joseph's Univ. (PA)
St. Lawrence Univ. (NY)
St. Louis Univ.
St. Mary's College of California
St. Mary's College of Maryland
St. Mary's Univ. of San Antonio
St. Michael's College (VT)
St. Norbert College (WI)
St. Olaf College (MN)
St. Peter's College (NJ)
St. Vincent College (PA)
Stanford Univ. (CA)
State Univ. of West Georgia
Stephen F. Austin State Univ. (TX)
Stetson Univ. (FL)
Stevens Institute of Technology (NJ)
Suffolk Univ. (MA)
SUNY College of Arts and Sciences–Geneseo
SUNY College–Brockport
SUNY College–Oneonta
SUNY College–Potsdam
SUNY–Albany
SUNY–Binghamton
SUNY–Fredonia
SUNY–Plattsburgh
SUNY–Stony Brook
Susquehanna Univ. (PA)
Swarthmore College (PA)
Sweet Briar College (VA)
Syracuse Univ. (NY)
Talladega College (AL)
Tarleton State Univ. (TX)
Taylor Univ. (IN)
Temple Univ. (PA)
Tennessee State Univ.
Tennessee Technological Univ.

Texas A&M Univ.–College Station
Texas A&M Univ.–Commerce
Texas A&M Univ.–Kingsville
Texas Christian Univ.
Texas Lutheran Univ.
Texas State Univ.–San Marcos
Texas Tech Univ.
The Citadel (SC)
Thiel College (PA)
Thomas More College (KY)
Towson Univ. (MD)
Transylvania Univ. (KY)
Trevecca Nazarene Univ. (TN)
Trinity College (CT)
Truman State Univ. (MO)
Tufts Univ. (MA)
Tulane Univ. (LA)
Tuskegee Univ. (AL)
Union College (NE)
Union College (NY)
Union Univ. (TN)
United States Air Force Academy (CO)
United States Naval Academy (MD)
Univ. at Buffalo–SUNY
Univ. of Akron (OH)
Univ. of Alabama
Univ. of Alabama–Birmingham
Univ. of Alabama–Huntsville
Univ. of Alaska–Fairbanks
Univ. of Arizona
Univ. of Arkansas
Univ. of Arkansas–Little Rock
Univ. of Arkansas–Pine Bluff
Univ. of California–Berkeley
Univ. of California–Davis
Univ. of California–Irvine
Univ. of California–Los Angeles
Univ. of California–Riverside
Univ. of California–San Diego
Univ. of California–Santa Barbara
Univ. of California–Santa Cruz
Univ. of Central Arkansas
Univ. of Central Florida
Univ. of Central Oklahoma
Univ. of Chicago
Univ. of Colorado–Boulder
Univ. of Colorado–Colorado Springs
Univ. of Colorado–Denver
Univ. of Connecticut
Univ. of Dallas
Univ. of Dayton (OH)
Univ. of Delaware
Univ. of Denver
Univ. of Evansville (IN)
Univ. of Florida
Univ. of Georgia
Univ. of Hartford (CT)
Univ. of Hawaii–Hilo
Univ. of Hawaii–Manoa
Univ. of Houston
Univ. of Houston–Downtown
Univ. of Illinois–Chicago
Univ. of Illinois–Urbana-Champaign
Univ. of Indianapolis
Univ. of Iowa
Univ. of Kansas
Univ. of Kentucky

Univ. of La Verne (CA)
Univ. of Louisiana–Lafayette
Univ. of Louisville (KY)
Univ. of Maine–Orono
Univ. of Mary Washington (VA)
Univ. of Maryland–Baltimore
County
Univ. of Maryland–College Park
Univ. of Massachusetts–Amherst
Univ. of Massachusetts–Boston
Univ. of Mass.–Dartmouth
Univ. of Massachusetts–Lowell
Univ. of Memphis
Univ. of Miami (FL)
Univ. of Michigan–Ann Arbor
Univ. of Michigan–Dearborn
Univ. of Michigan–Flint
Univ. of Minnesota–Duluth
Univ. of Minnesota–Morris
Univ. of Minnesota–Twin Cities
Univ. of Mississippi
Univ. of Missouri–Columbia
Univ. of Missouri–Kansas City
Univ. of Missouri–Rolla
Univ. of Missouri–St. Louis
Univ. of Montana
Univ. of Nebraska–Kearney
Univ. of Nebraska–Lincoln
Univ. of Nebraska–Omaha
Univ. of Nevada–Las Vegas
Univ. of Nevada–Reno
Univ. of New Hampshire
Univ. of New Mexico
Univ. of New Orleans
Univ. of North Alabama
Univ. of North Carolina–Asheville
Univ. of N.C.–Chapel Hill
Univ. of North Carolina–Charlotte
Univ. of N.C.–Greensboro
Univ. of North Carolina–Pembroke
Univ. of N.C.–Wilmington
Univ. of North Dakota
Univ. of North Florida
Univ. of North Texas
Univ. of Northern Colorado
Univ. of Northern Iowa
Univ. of Notre Dame (IN)
Univ. of Oklahoma
Univ. of Oregon
Univ. of Pennsylvania
Univ. of Pittsburgh
Univ. of Portland (OR)
Univ. of Puget Sound (WA)
Univ. of Redlands (CA)
Univ. of Rhode Island
Univ. of Richmond (VA)
Univ. of Rochester (NY)
Univ. of San Diego
Univ. of San Francisco
Univ. of Science and Arts of
Oklahoma
Univ. of Scranton (PA)
Univ. of South Alabama
Univ. of South Carolina–Columbia
Univ. of South Dakota
Univ. of South Florida
Univ. of Southern California
Univ. of Southern Mississippi
Univ. of St. Thomas (MN)
Univ. of Tennessee
Univ. of Tennessee–Chattanooga

Univ. of Texas–Arlington
Univ. of Texas–Austin
Univ. of Texas–Brownsville
Univ. of Texas–Dallas
Univ. of Texas–El Paso
Univ. of Texas–Pan American
Univ. of Texas–San Antonio
Univ. of the District of Columbia
Univ. of the Pacific (CA)
Univ. of Toledo (OH)
Univ. of Tulsa (OK)
Univ. of Utah
Univ. of Vermont
Univ. of Virginia
Univ. of Washington
Univ. of West Florida
Univ. of Wisconsin–Eau Claire
Univ. of Wisconsin–La Crosse
Univ. of Wisconsin–Madison
Univ. of Wisconsin–Milwaukee
Univ. of Wisconsin–Parkside
Univ. of Wisconsin–River Falls
Univ. of Wisconsin–Stevens Point
Univ. of Wisconsin–Whitewater
Univ. of Wyoming
Ursinus College (PA)
Utah State Univ.
Utah Valley State College
Utica College (NY)
Valdosta State Univ. (GA)
Valparaiso Univ. (IN)
Vanderbilt Univ. (TN)
Vassar College (NY)
Villanova Univ. (PA)
Virginia Commonwealth Univ.
Virginia Military Institute
Virginia State Univ.
Virginia Tech
Wabash College (IN)
Wagner College (NY)
Wake Forest Univ. (NC)
Wartburg College (IA)
Washburn Univ. (KS)
Washington and Jefferson College
(PA)
Washington and Lee Univ. (VA)
Washington College (MD)
Washington State Univ.
Washington Univ. In St. Louis
Wayne State Univ. (MI)
Weber State Univ. (UT)
Wellesley College (MA)
Wesleyan College (GA)
Wesleyan Univ. (CT)
West Chester Univ. of Pennsylvania
West Texas A&M Univ.
West Virginia Univ.
West Virginia Wesleyan College
Western Illinois Univ.
Western Kentucky Univ.
Western Michigan Univ.
Western Washington Univ.
Westminster College (UT)
Westminster College (MO)
Westmont College (CA)
Wheaton College (IL)
Wheaton College (MA)
Wheeling Jesuit Univ. (WV)
Whitman College (WA)
Whittier College (CA)
Whitworth College (WA)

Wichita State Univ. (KS)
Willamette Univ. (OR)
William Jewell College (MO)
Williams College (MA)
Wittenberg Univ. (OH)
Wofford College (SC)
Worcester Polytechnic Institute
(MA)
Wright State Univ. (OH)
Xavier Univ. (OH)
Yale Univ. (CT)
Yeshiva Univ. (NY)
York College of Pennsylvania
Youngstown State Univ. (OH)

Physiological Psychology/Psychobiology

Albright College (PA)
Averett Univ. (VA)
Centre College (KY)
College of William and Mary (VA)
Florida Atlantic Univ.
Holy Names Univ. (CA)
Lebanon Valley College (PA)
Lincoln Univ. (PA)
Medaille College (NY)
Mills College (CA)
Northwest Missouri State Univ.
Occidental College (CA)
Pepperdine Univ. (CA)
Quinnipiac Univ. (CT)
St. Mary's College of California
SUNY–Binghamton
Swarthmore College (PA)
Univ. of California–Los Angeles
Univ. of California–Santa Cruz
Univ. of Colorado–Denver
Univ. of Miami (FL)
Univ. of New England (ME)
Wheaton College (MA)
Wilson College (PA)
York College (NE)

Physiology, Pathology, and Related Sciences

Augustana College (SD)
Baldwin-Wallace College (OH)
Baylor Univ. (TX)
Black Hills State Univ. (SD)
Boise State Univ. (ID)
Boston Univ.
Brigham Young Univ.–Provo (UT)
California State Univ.–Dominguez
Hills
California State Univ.–Long Beach
Chapman Univ. (CA)
Colby College (ME)
College of St. Scholastica (MN)
Colorado State Univ.
Concordia Univ.–River Forest (IL)
Denison Univ. (OH)
East Carolina Univ. (NC)
Fitchburg State College (MA)
Gettysburg College (PA)
Gonzaga Univ. (WA)
Hamilton College (NY)
High Point Univ. (NC)

Hiram College (OH)
Huntington College (IN)
Lafayette College (PA)
Lasell College (MA)
Lynchburg College (VA)
Manchester College (IN)
Marquette Univ. (WI)
Metropolitan State College of
Denver
Miami Univ.–Oxford (OH)
Michigan State Univ.
North Park Univ. (IL)
Northern Arizona Univ.
Northern Michigan Univ.
Northwest Christian College (OR)
Ohio Northern Univ.
Oklahoma State Univ.
Olivet Nazarene Univ. (IL)
Oral Roberts Univ. (OK)
Regis Univ. (CO)
Sacred Heart Univ. (CT)
San Diego State Univ.
Southern Illinois Univ.–Carbondale
Tennessee Wesleyan College
Tulane Univ. (LA)
Univ. of Arizona
Univ. of California–Davis
Univ. of California–Los Angeles
Univ. of California–Santa Barbara
Univ. of Colorado–Boulder
Univ. of Connecticut
Univ. of Delaware
Univ. of Ill.–Urbana-Champaign
Univ. of Maine–Orono
Univ. of Miami (FL)
Univ. of Minnesota–Twin Cities
Univ. of N.C.–Chapel Hill
Univ. of Oregon
Univ. of Tennessee
Univ. of Washington
Utah State Univ.
West Liberty State College (WV)
West Virginia Univ.

Plant Sciences

Alabama Agricultural and
Mechanical Univ.
Alcorn State Univ. (MS)
Arkansas State Univ.
Auburn Univ. (AL)
Cal Poly–San Luis Obispo
California State Polytechnic
Univ.–Pomona
Chadron State College (NE)
College of the Ozarks (MO)
Colorado State Univ.
Cornell Univ. (NY)
Delaware State Univ.
Delaware Valley College (PA)
Dordt College (IA)
Eastern Kentucky Univ.
Eastern Oregon Univ.
Florida Southern College
Hardin-Simmons Univ. (TX)
Humboldt State Univ. (CA)
Iowa State Univ.
Kansas State Univ.
Louisiana State Univ.–Baton Rouge
Michigan State Univ.

Mississippi State Univ.
Montana State Univ.–Bozeman
New Mexico State Univ.
North Carolina State Univ.–Raleigh
North Dakota State Univ.
Northwest Missouri State Univ.
Ohio State Univ.–Columbus
Oklahoma Panhandle State Univ.
Oklahoma State Univ.
Oregon State Univ.
Penn. State Univ.–Univ. Park
Purdue Univ.–West Lafayette (IN)
Rutgers–New Brunswick (NJ)
South Dakota State Univ.
Southeastern Louisiana Univ.
Southern Illinois Univ.–Carbondale
Southwest Missouri State Univ.
Stephen F. Austin State Univ. (TX)
SUNY College of A&T–Cobleskill
Tarleton State Univ. (TX)
Texas A&M Univ.–College Station
Texas A&M Univ.–Commerce
Texas A&M Univ.–Kingsville
Texas Tech Univ.
Truman State Univ. (MO)
Tuskegee Univ. (AL)
Univ. of Arizona
Univ. of Arkansas
Univ. of California–Davis
Univ. of California–Riverside
Univ. of Connecticut
Univ. of Delaware
Univ. of Florida
Univ. of Hawaii–Hilo
Univ. of Hawaii–Manoa
Univ. of Ill.–Urbana-Champaign
Univ. of Kentucky
Univ. of Maine–Orono
Univ. of Massachusetts–Amherst
Univ. of Minnesota–Crookston
Univ. of Minnesota–Twin Cities
Univ. of Missouri–Columbia
Univ. of Nebraska–Lincoln
Univ. of Nevada–Reno
Univ. of New Hampshire
Univ. of Tennessee
Univ. of Vermont
Univ. of Wisconsin–Madison
Univ. of Wisconsin–Platteville
Univ. of Wisconsin–River Falls
Univ. of Wyoming
Utah State Univ.
Virginia Tech
Washington State Univ.
West Virginia Univ.

Podiatric Medicine/Podiatry (D.P.M.)

Gannon Univ. (PA)

Political Science and Government

Agnes Scott College (GA)
Arcadia Univ. (PA)
Assumption College (MA)
Augsburg College (MN)
Belhaven College (MS)

Bemidji State Univ. (MN)
Benedict College (SC)
Benedictine College (KS)
Benedictine Univ. (IL)
Bowdoin College (ME)
Bowie State Univ. (MD)
Brandeis Univ. (MA)
Bryan College (TN)
California Lutheran Univ.
California State Polytechnic
 Univ.–Pomona
California State Univ.–Sacramento
California State Univ.–San Marcos
Carthage College (WI)
Clark Univ. (MA)
Clarkson Univ. (NY)
Coe College (IA)
Columbus State Univ. (GA)
Concordia Univ. (CA)
CUNY–York College
Denison Univ. (OH)
Dillard Univ. (LA)
Earlham College (IN)
East Central Univ. (OK)
Elizabethtown College (PA)
Emory and Henry College (VA)
Eureka College (IL)
Evergreen State College (WA)
Furman Univ. (SC)
Greensboro College (NC)
Grinnell College (IA)
Grove City College (PA)
Hamilton College (NY)
Hampshire College (MA)
Hanover College (IN)
High Point Univ. (NC)
Hillsdale College (MI)
Hiram College (OH)
Hollins Univ. (VA)
Huston-Tillotson College (TX)
Indiana Univ.–South Bend
Indiana Wesleyan Univ.
Johnson State College (VT)
La Salle Univ. (PA)
Lake Forest College (IL)
Lawrence Univ. (WI)
Lemoyne-Owen College (TN)
Lewis Univ. (IL)
Long Island Univ.–Brooklyn (NY)
Long Island Univ.–Southampton
 College (NY)
Loras College (IA)
Macmurray College (IL)
Manchester College (IN)
Manhattan College (NY)
Manhattanville College (NY)
Marlboro College (VT)
Marymount Manhattan College
 (NY)
Mcdaniel College (MD)
Methodist College (NC)
Mount Mercy College (IA)
Mount St. Mary's Univ. (MD)
North Carolina Wesleyan College
North Park Univ. (IL)
Northeastern Illinois Univ.
Northland College (WI)
Northwest College (WA)
Norwich Univ. (VT)
Occidental College (CA)
Oglethorpe Univ. (GA)

Oklahoma City Univ.
Olivet Nazarene Univ. (IL)
Otterbein College (OH)
Pitzer College (CA)
Principia College (IL)
Randolph-Macon Woman's College
 (VA)
Rice Univ. (TX)
Ripon College (WI)
Russell Sage College (NY)
Scripps College (CA)
Seattle Pacific Univ.
Sewanee–Univ. of the South (TN)
Shepherd Univ. (WV)
Simmons College (MA)
Southern New Hampshire Univ.
Spelman College (GA)
St. Bonaventure Univ. (NY)
St. Martin's College (WA)
St. Mary's Univ. of Minnesota
St. Mary-of-The-Woods Coll. (IN)
Stephens College (MO)
SUNY College–Oneonta
SUNY–Albany
SUNY–Purchase College
Texas A&M Univ.–Kingsville
Thiel College (PA)
Thomas College (ME)
Towson Univ. (MD)
Univ. of California–Santa Barbara
Univ. of Chicago
Univ. of Colorado–Colorado
 Springs
Univ. of Judaism (CA)
Univ. of Kentucky
Univ. of Louisville (KY)
Univ. of Mass.–Dartmouth
Univ. of Portland (OR)
Univ. of South Carolina–Upstate
Univ. of St. Thomas (MN)
Univ. of Tennessee–Martin
Univ. of Washington
Univ. of Wisconsin–Whitewater
Wabash College (IN)
Wellesley College (MA)
Western State College of Colorado
Westminster College (MO)
Yeshiva Univ. (NY)

Polymer/Plastics Engineering

Case Western Reserve Univ. (OH)
Kettering Univ. (MI)
Stevens Institute of Technology
 (NJ)
Univ. of Akron (OH)
Univ. of Ill.–Urbana-Champaign
Univ. of Massachusetts–Lowell

Precision Metalworking

Lewis-Clark State College (ID)
Utah State Univ.

Precision Production Trades

Boise State Univ. (ID)
Mesa State College (CO)

Psychology

Abilene Christian Univ. (TX)
Adams State College (CO)
Adelphi Univ. (NY)
Adrian College (MI)
Alabama Agricultural and
 Mechanical Univ.
Alabama State Univ.
Alaska Pacific Univ.
Albany State Univ. (GA)
Albertson College (ID)
Albertus Magnus College (CT)
Albion College (MI)
Albright College (PA)
Alcorn State Univ. (MS)
Alderson-Broaddus College (WV)
Alfred Univ. (NY)
Allegheny College (PA)
Alma College (MI)
Alvernia College (PA)
Alverno College (WI)
American Univ. (DC)
Amherst College (MA)
Anderson College (SC)
Anderson Univ. (IN)
Andrews Univ. (MI)
Angelo State Univ. (TX)
Anna Maria College (MA)
Appalachian State Univ. (NC)
Aquinas College (MI)
Arcadia Univ. (PA)
Arizona State Univ.
Arizona State Univ. West
Arkansas State Univ.
Arkansas Tech Univ.
Armstrong Atlantic State Univ.
 (GA)
Asbury College (KY)
Ashland Univ. (OH)
Assumption College (MA)
Atlantic Union College (MA)
Auburn Univ. (AL)
Auburn Univ.–Montgomery (AL)
Augusta State Univ. (GA)
Augustana College (IL)
Augustana College (SD)
Aurora Univ. (IL)
Austin College (TX)
Austin Peay State Univ. (TN)
Avila Univ. (MO)
Azusa Pacific Univ. (CA)
Baker Univ. (KS)
Baldwin-Wallace College (OH)
Ball State Univ. (IN)
Barnard College (NY)
Barry Univ. (FL)
Barton College (NC)
Bates College (ME)
Bay Path College (MA)
Baylor Univ. (TX)
Becker College (MA)
Belhaven College (MS)

Bellarmine Univ. (KY)
Bellevue Univ. (NE)
Belmont Abbey College (NC)
Belmont Univ. (TN)
Beloit College (WI)
Bemidji State Univ. (MN)
Benedictine College (KS)
Benedictine Univ. (IL)
Bennett College (NC)
Bennington College (VT)
Berea College (KY)
Berry College (GA)
Bethany College (KS)
Bethany College (WV)
Bethel College (TN)
Bethel College (KS)
Bethel Univ. (MN)
Bethune-Cookman College (FL)
Biola Univ. (CA)
Black Hills State Univ. (SD)
Bloomfield College (NJ)
Bloomsburg Univ. of Pennsylvania
Blue Mountain College (MS)
Bluefield College (VA)
Bluffton Univ. (OH)
Boise State Univ. (ID)
Bowie State Univ. (MD)
Bowling Green State Univ. (OH)
Bradley Univ. (IL)
Brenau Univ. (GA)
Brescia Univ. (KY)
Brevard College (NC)
Brewton-Parker College (GA)
Briar Cliff Univ. (IA)
Bridgewater College (VA)
Bridgewater State College (MA)
Brigham Young Univ.–Hawaii
Brigham Young Univ.–Provo (UT)
Brown Univ. (RI)
Bryan College (TN)
Bryant College (RI)
Bryn Mawr College (PA)
Bucknell Univ. (PA)
Buena Vista Univ. (IA)
Buffalo State College
Burlington College (VT)
Butler Univ. (IN)
Cabrini College (PA)
Cal Poly–San Luis Obispo
California Baptist Univ.
California Lutheran Univ.
California State Polytechnic
 Univ.–Pomona
California State Univ.–Chico
California State Univ.–Dominguez
 Hills
California State Univ.–Fresno
California State Univ.–Fullerton
California State Univ.–Hayward
California State Univ.–Long Beach
California State Univ.–Los Angeles
California State Univ.–Northridge
California State Univ.–Sacramento
California State Univ.–San
 Bernardino
California State Univ.–Stanislaus
California Univ. of Pennsylvania
Calumet College of St. Joseph (IN)
Calvin College (MI)
Cameron Univ. (OK)
Campbell Univ. (NC)

Campbellsville Univ. (KY)
Canisius College (NY)
Capital Univ. (OH)
Cardinal Stritch Univ. (WI)
Carleton College (MN)
Carlow College (PA)
Carnegie Mellon Univ. (PA)
Carroll College (WI)
Carson-Newman College (TN)
Carthage College (WI)
Case Western Reserve Univ. (OH)
Castleton State College (VT)
Catawba College (NC)
Catholic Univ. of America (DC)
Cazenovia College (NY)
Cedar Crest College (PA)
Cedarville Univ. (OH)
Centenary College (NJ)
Centenary College of Louisiana
Central Christian College (KS)
Central College (IA)
Central Connecticut State Univ.
Central Methodist Univ. (MO)
Central Michigan Univ.
Central Missouri State Univ.
Central State Univ. (OH)
Central Washington Univ.
Centre College (KY)
Chadron State College (NE)
Chaminade Univ. of Honolulu
Champlain College (VT)
Chapman Univ. (CA)
Charleston Southern Univ. (SC)
Chatham College (PA)
Chestnut Hill College (PA)
Cheyney Univ. of Pennsylvania
Chicago State Univ.
Chowan College (NC)
Christian Brothers Univ. (TN)
Christian Heritage College (CA)
Christopher Newport Univ. (VA)
City Univ. (WA)
Claremont Mckenna College (CA)
Clarion Univ. of Pennsylvania
Clark Atlanta Univ.
Clark Univ. (MA)
Clarke College (IA)
Clarkson Univ. (NY)
Clearwater Christian College (FL)
Cleveland State Univ.
Coastal Carolina Univ. (SC)
Coker College (SC)
Colby College (ME)
Colby-Sawyer College (NH)
Colgate Univ. (NY)
College Misericordia (PA)
College of Charleston (SC)
College of Mount St. Joseph (OH)
College of Mount St. Vincent (NY)
College of New Jersey
College of Notre Dame of
 Maryland
College of Santa Fe (NM)
College of St. Benedict (MN)
College of St. Catherine (MN)
College of St. Elizabeth (NJ)
College of St. Joseph (VT)
College of St. Mary (NE)
College of St. Rose (NY)
College of St. Scholastica (MN)
College of the Holy Cross (MA)

College of the Ozarks (MO)
College of the Southwest (NM)
College of William and Mary (VA)
Colorado Christian Univ.
Colorado College
Colorado State Univ.
Colorado State Univ.–Pueblo
Columbia College (MO)
Columbia College (SC)
Columbia Union College (MD)
Columbia Univ. (NY)
Concord College (WV)
Concordia Coll.–Moorhead (MN)
Concordia Univ. (NE)
Concordia Univ. (MI)
Concordia Univ. (OR)
Concordia Univ.–River Forest (IL)
Concordia Univ.–St. Paul (MN)
Connecticut College
Converse College (SC)
Cornell College (IA)
Cornell Univ. (NY)
Cornerstone Univ. (MI)
Covenant College (GA)
Creighton Univ. (NE)
Crichton College (TN)
Culver-Stockton College (MO)
Cumberland College (KY)
Cumberland Univ. (TN)
CUNY–Baruch College
CUNY–Brooklyn College
CUNY–City College
CUNY–College of Staten Island
CUNY–Hunter College
CUNY–Lehman College
CUNY–Medgar Evers College
CUNY–Queens College
Curry College (MA)
Daemen College (NY)
Dakota Wesleyan Univ. (SD)
Dallas Baptist Univ.
Dana College (NE)
Dartmouth College (NH)
David Lipscomb Univ. (TN)
Davidson College (NC)
Davis and Elkins College (WV)
Defiance College (OH)
Delaware State Univ.
Delta State Univ. (MS)
Denison Univ. (OH)
Depaul Univ. (IL)
Depauw Univ. (IN)
Desales Univ. (PA)
Dickinson College (PA)
Dickinson State Univ. (ND)
Dillard Univ. (LA)
Dominican Coll. of Blauvelt (NY)
Dominican Univ. (IL)
Dominican Univ. of California (CA)
Dordt College (IA)
Dowling College (NY)
Drake Univ. (IA)
Drew Univ. (NJ)
Drexel Univ. (PA)
Drury Univ. (MO)
Duke Univ. (NC)
Duquesne Univ. (PA)
East Carolina Univ. (NC)
East Stroudsburg Univ. of
    Pennsylvania
East Tennessee State Univ.

East Texas Baptist Univ.
Eastern Connecticut State Univ.
Eastern Illinois Univ.
Eastern Kentucky Univ.
Eastern Mennonite Univ. (VA)
Eastern Michigan Univ.
Eastern New Mexico Univ.
Eastern Oregon Univ.
Eastern Univ. (PA)
Eastern Washington Univ.
Eckerd College (FL)
Edgewood College (WI)
Edinboro Univ. of Pennsylvania
Edward Waters College (FL)
Elizabeth City State Univ. (NC)
Elmhurst College (IL)
Elmira College (NY)
Elon Univ. (NC)
Emmanuel College (MA)
Emmanuel College (GA)
Emory and Henry College (VA)
Emory Univ. (GA)
Emporia State Univ. (KS)
Endicott College (MA)
Erskine College (SC)
Eureka College (IL)
Evangel Univ. (MO)
Evergreen State College (WA)
Excelsior College (NY)
Fairfield Univ. (CT)
Fairleigh Dickinson Univ. (NJ)
Fairmont State Univ. (WV)
Faulkner Univ. (AL)
Fayetteville State Univ. (NC)
Ferris State Univ. (MI)
Ferrum College (VA)
Fisk Univ. (TN)
Fitchburg State College (MA)
Flagler College (FL)
Florida Atlantic Univ.
Florida Institute of Technology
Florida International Univ.
Florida Southern College
Florida State Univ.
Fontbonne Univ. (MO)
Fordham Univ. (NY)
Fort Hays State Univ. (KS)
Fort Lewis College (CO)
Fort Valley State Univ. (GA)
Framingham State College (MA)
Francis Marion Univ. (SC)
Franciscan Univ. of Steubenville
    (OH)
Franklin and Marshall College (PA)
Franklin College (IN)
Franklin Pierce College (NH)
Freed-Hardeman Univ. (TN)
Fresno Pacific Univ. (CA)
Friends Univ. (KS)
Frostburg State Univ. (MD)
Gallaudet Univ. (DC)
Gannon Univ. (PA)
Gardner-Webb Univ. (NC)
George Fox Univ. (OR)
George Mason Univ. (VA)
George Washington Univ. (DC)
Georgetown College (KY)
Georgetown Univ. (DC)
Georgia College and State Univ.
Georgia Southern Univ.
Georgia Southwestern State Univ.

Georgia State Univ.
Georgian Court Univ. (NJ)
Gettysburg College (PA)
Goddard College (VT)
Golden Gate Univ. (CA)
Gonzaga Univ. (WA)
Gordon College (MA)
Goucher College (MD)
Grace College and Seminary (IN)
Graceland Univ. (IA)
Grambling State Univ. (LA)
Grand Valley State Univ. (MI)
Grand View College (IA)
Green Mountain College (VT)
Greensboro College (NC)
Greenville College (IL)
Grinnell College (IA)
Guilford College (NC)
Gustavus Adolphus College
    (MN)
Gwynedd-Mercy College (PA)
Hamline Univ. (MN)
Hampden-Sydney College (VA)
Hampshire College (MA)
Hannibal-Lagrange College (MO)
Hardin-Simmons Univ. (TX)
Harding Univ. (AR)
Hartwick College (NY)
Harvard Univ. (MA)
Hastings College (NE)
Haverford College (PA)
Hawaii Pacific Univ.
Heidelberg College (OH)
Henderson State Univ. (AR)
Hendrix College (AR)
Heritage College (WA)
High Point Univ. (NC)
Hilbert College (NY)
Hobart and William Smith Colleges
    (NY)
Hofstra Univ. (NY)
Hollins Univ. (VA)
Holy Family Univ. (PA)
Holy Names Univ. (CA)
Hood College (MD)
Hope College (MI)
Hope International Univ. (CA)
Houghton College (NY)
Houston Baptist Univ.
Howard Payne Univ. (TX)
Howard Univ. (DC)
Humboldt State Univ. (CA)
Huntingdon College (AL)
Huntington College (IN)
Huston-Tillotson College (TX)
Idaho State Univ.
Illinois College
Illinois Institute of Technology
Illinois State Univ.
Illinois Wesleyan Univ.
Immaculata Univ. (PA)
Indiana State Univ.
Indiana Univ. East
Indiana Univ. Northwest
Indiana Univ. of Pennsylvania
Indiana Univ. Southeast
Indiana Univ.–Bloomington
Indiana Univ.–Kokomo
Indiana Univ.–South Bend
Indiana Univ.–Purdue Univ.–Fort
    Wayne

Indiana Univ.–Purdue
    Univ.–Indianapolis
Indiana Wesleyan Univ.
International College (FL)
Iona College (NY)
Iowa State Univ.
Ithaca College (NY)
Jacksonville State Univ. (AL)
Jacksonville Univ. (FL)
James Madison Univ. (VA)
John Carroll Univ. (OH)
Johns Hopkins Univ. (MD)
Johnson C. Smith Univ. (NC)
Johnson State College (VT)
Judson College (AL)
Judson College (IL)
Juniata College (PA)
Kalamazoo College (MI)
Kansas State Univ.
Kansas Wesleyan Univ.
Kean Univ. (NJ)
Kennesaw State Univ. (GA)
Kent State Univ. (OH)
Kentucky Christian College
Kentucky State Univ.
Kentucky Wesleyan College
Keuka College (NY)
King College (TN)
King's College (PA)
Knox College (IL)
Kutztown Univ. of Pennsylvania
La Roche College (PA)
La Salle Univ. (PA)
La Sierra Univ. (CA)
Lafayette College (PA)
Lagrange College (GA)
Lake Erie College (OH)
Lake Forest College (IL)
Lake Superior State Univ. (MI)
Lakeland College (WI)
Lambuth Univ. (TN)
Lasell College (MA)
Lawrence Technological Univ. (MI)
Le Moyne College (NY)
Lebanon Valley College (PA)
Lees-Mcrae College (NC)
Lehigh Univ. (PA)
Lenoir-Rhyne College (NC)
Letourneau Univ. (TX)
Lewis and Clark College (OR)
Lewis-Clark State College (ID)
Liberty Univ. (VA)
Limestone College (SC)
Lincoln Memorial Univ. (TN)
Lincoln Univ. (PA)
Lincoln Univ. (MO)
Lindenwood Univ. (MO)
Lindsey Wilson College (KY)
Linfield College (OR)
Livingstone College (NC)
Lock Haven Univ. of Pennsylvania
Long Island Univ.–C.W. Post
    Campus (NY)
Long Island Univ.–Southampton
    College (NY)
Louisiana College
Louisiana State Univ.–Baton Rouge
Louisiana State Univ.–Shreveport
Louisiana Tech Univ.
Lourdes College (OH)
Loyola College In Maryland

Loyola Marymount Univ. (CA)
Loyola Univ. Chicago
Loyola Univ. New Orleans
Lubbock Christian Univ. (TX)
Luther College (IA)
Lycoming College (PA)
Lynchburg College (VA)
Lynn Univ. (FL)
Lyon College (AR)
Macalester College (MN)
Macmurray College (IL)
Madonna Univ. (MI)
Malone College (OH)
Manchester College (IN)
Manhattan College (NY)
Manhattanville College (NY)
Mansfield Univ. of Pennsylvania
Marian College (IN)
Marian Coll. of Fond Du Lac (WI)
Marietta College (OH)
Marist College (NY)
Marquette Univ. (WI)
Mars Hill College (NC)
Marshall Univ. (WV)
Martin Methodist College (TN)
Martin Univ. (IN)
Mary Baldwin College (VA)
Marygrove College (MI)
Marylhurst Univ. (OR)
Marymount Manhattan College
    (NY)
Marymount Univ. (VA)
Maryville College (TN)
Maryville Univ. of St. Louis (MO)
Marywood Univ. (PA)
Mayville State Univ. (ND)
Mcdaniel College (MD)
Mckendree College (IL)
Mcmurry Univ. (TX)
Mcneese State Univ. (LA)
Mcpherson College (KS)
Medaille College (NY)
Mercer Univ. (GA)
Mercy College (NY)
Mercyhurst College (PA)
Meredith College (NC)
Merrimack College (MA)
Mesa State College (CO)
Messiah College (PA)
Methodist College (NC)
Metropolitan State College of
    Denver
Miami Univ.–Oxford (OH)
Michigan State Univ.
Michigan Technological Univ.
Middle Tennessee State Univ.
Middlebury College (VT)
Midland Lutheran College (NE)
Midway College (KY)
Midwestern State Univ. (TX)
Millersville Univ. of Pennsylvania
Milligan College (TN)
Millikin Univ. (IL)
Mills College (CA)
Millsaps College (MS)
Minnesota State Univ.–Mankato
Minnesota State Univ.–Moorhead
Minot State Univ. (ND)
Mississippi College
Mississippi State Univ.
Mississippi Univ. For Women

Missouri Baptist College
Missouri Southern State Univ.
Missouri Valley College
Missouri Western State College
Molloy College (NY)
Monmouth College (IL)
Monmouth Univ. (NJ)
Montana State Univ.–Billings
Montana State Univ.–Bozeman
Montclair State Univ. (NJ)
Moravian College (PA)
Morehead State Univ. (KY)
Morehouse College (GA)
Morningside College (IA)
Mount Aloysius College (PA)
Mount Holyoke College (MA)
Mount Marty College (SD)
Mount Mary College (WI)
Mount Mercy College (IA)
Mount Olive College (NC)
Mount St. Mary College (NY)
Mount St. Mary's College (CA)
Mount St. Mary's Univ. (MD)
Mount Union College (OH)
Muhlenberg College (PA)
Murray State Univ. (KY)
Muskingum College (OH)
National Univ. (CA)
National-Louis Univ. (IL)
Nazareth College of Rochester
   (NY)
Nebraska Wesleyan Univ.
Neumann College (PA)
New England College (NH)
New Jersey City Univ.
New Mexico Highlands Univ.
New Mexico Institute of Mining
   and Technology
New Mexico State Univ.
New York Institute of Technology
New York Univ.
Newberry College (SC)
Newman Univ. (KS)
Niagara Univ. (NY)
Nicholls State Univ. (LA)
Nichols College (MA)
Norfolk State Univ. (VA)
North Carolina A&T State Univ.
North Carolina Central Univ.
North Carolina State Univ.–Raleigh
North Carolina Wesleyan College
North Central College (IL)
North Dakota State Univ.
North Georgia College and State
   Univ.
North Greenville College (SC)
North Park Univ. (IL)
Northeastern Illinois Univ.
Northeastern State Univ. (OK)
Northeastern Univ. (MA)
Northern Arizona Univ.
Northern Illinois Univ.
Northern Kentucky Univ.
Northern Michigan Univ.
Northern State Univ. (SD)
Northland College (WI)
Northwest Christian College (OR)
Northwest Missouri State Univ.
Northwest Nazarene Univ. (ID)
Northwestern College (IA)
Northwestern College (MN)

Northwestern Oklahoma State
   Univ.
Northwestern State Univ. of
   Louisiana
Northwestern Univ. (IL)
Norwich Univ. (VT)
Notre Dame College of Ohio
Notre Dame De Namur Univ. (CA)
Nova Southeastern Univ. (FL)
Nyack College (NY)
Oakland Univ. (MI)
Oakwood College (AL)
Oberlin College (OH)
Occidental College (CA)
Ohio Dominican Univ.
Ohio Northern Univ.
Ohio State Univ.–Columbus
Ohio Univ.
Ohio Valley College (WV)
Ohio Wesleyan Univ.
Oklahoma Baptist Univ.
Oklahoma Christian Univ.
Oklahoma Panhandle State Univ.
Oklahoma State Univ.
Oklahoma Wesleyan Univ.
Old Dominion Univ. (VA)
Olivet College (MI)
Olivet Nazarene Univ. (IL)
Oral Roberts Univ. (OK)
Oregon Institute of Technology
Oregon State Univ.
Otterbein College (OH)
Ouachita Baptist Univ. (AR)
Our Lady of the Lake Univ. (TX)
Pace Univ. (NY)
Pacific Lutheran Univ. (WA)
Pacific Univ. (OR)
Paine College (GA)
Palm Beach Atlantic Univ. (FL)
Park Univ. (MO)
Patten College (CA)
Peace College (NC)
Penn. State Univ.–Univ. Park
Penn. State–Erie, The Behrend
   College
Pepperdine Univ. (CA)
Peru State College (NE)
Pfeiffer Univ. (NC)
Philadelphia Univ.
Philander Smith College (AR)
Piedmont College (GA)
Pikeville College (KY)
Pine Manor College (MA)
Pittsburg State Univ. (KS)
Pitzer College (CA)
Plymouth State Univ. (NH)
Point Loma Nazarene Univ. (CA)
Point Park Univ. (PA)
Pomona College (CA)
Prairie View A&M Univ. (TX)
Presbyterian College (SC)
Prescott College (AZ)
Princeton Univ. (NJ)
Providence College (RI)
Purdue Univ.–Calumet (IN)
Purdue Univ.–West Lafayette (IN)
Queens Univ. of Charlotte (NC)
Quincy Univ. (IL)
Quinnipiac Univ. (CT)
Radford Univ. (VA)
Ramapo College of New Jersey

Randolph-Macon College (VA)
Randolph-Macon Woman's College
   (VA)
Reed College (OR)
Regis College (MA)
Regis Univ. (CO)
Reinhardt College (GA)
Rensselaer Polytechnic Inst. (NY)
Rhode Island College
Rhodes College (TN)
Rice Univ. (TX)
Richard Stockton College of New
   Jersey
Rider Univ. (NJ)
Ripon College (WI)
Rivier College (NH)
Roanoke College (VA)
Robert Morris Univ. (PA)
Roberts Wesleyan College (NY)
Rochester College (MI)
Rochester Institute of Tech. (NY)
Rockford College (IL)
Rockhurst Univ. (MO)
Rocky Mountain College (MT)
Roger Williams Univ. (RI)
Rollins College (FL)
Roosevelt Univ. (IL)
Rosemont College (PA)
Russell Sage College (NY)
Rutgers–Camden (NJ)
Rutgers–New Brunswick (NJ)
Rutgers–Newark (NJ)
Sacred Heart Univ. (CT)
Saginaw Valley State Univ. (MI)
Salem College (NC)
Salem State College (MA)
Salisbury Univ. (MD)
Salve Regina Univ. (RI)
Sam Houston State Univ. (TX)
Samford Univ. (AL)
San Diego State Univ.
San Francisco State Univ.
San Jose State Univ. (CA)
Santa Clara Univ. (CA)
Schreiner Univ. (TX)
Seattle Univ.
Seton Hall Univ. (NJ)
Seton Hill Univ. (PA)
Shaw Univ. (NC)
Shawnee State Univ. (OH)
Shenandoah Univ. (VA)
Shippensburg Univ. of
   Pennsylvania
Shorter College (GA)
Siena College (NY)
Sierra Nevada College (NV)
Silver Lake College (WI)
Simmons College (MA)
Simon's Rock College of Bard
   (MA)
Simpson College (IA)
Simpson Univ. (CA)
Skidmore College (NY)
Slippery Rock Univ. of Pennsylvania
Sonoma State Univ. (CA)
South Carolina State Univ.
South Dakota State Univ.
Southeast Missouri State Univ.
Southeastern College of the
   Assemblies of God
Southeastern Louisiana Univ.

Southeastern Oklahoma State
   Univ.
Southern Adventist Univ. (TN)
Southern Arkansas Univ.
Southern Illinois Univ.–Carbondale
Southern Illinois
   Univ.–Edwardsville
Southern Methodist Univ. (TX)
Southern Nazarene Univ. (OK)
Southern New Hampshire Univ.
Southern Oregon Univ.
Southern Univ. and A&M College
   (LA)
Southern Utah Univ.
Southern Wesleyan Univ. (SC)
Southwest Baptist Univ. (MO)
Southwest Minnesota State Univ.
   (MN)
Southwest Missouri State Univ.
Southwestern College (KS)
Southwestern Oklahoma State
   Univ.
Southwestern Univ. (TX)
Spalding Univ. (KY)
Spring Arbor Univ. (MI)
Spring Hill College (AL)
Springfield College (MA)
St. Ambrose Univ. (IA)
St. Andrews Presbyterian College
   (NC)
St. Anselm College (NH)
St. Augustine's College (NC)
St. Cloud State Univ. (MN)
St. Edward's Univ. (TX)
St. Francis College (NY)
St. Gregory's Univ. (OK)
St. John Fisher College (NY)
St. John's Univ. (MN)
St. John's Univ. (NY)
St. Joseph College (CT)
St. Joseph's College (IN)
St. Joseph's College (ME)
St. Joseph's College, New York
St. Joseph's Univ. (PA)
St. Lawrence Univ. (NY)
St. Leo Univ. (FL)
St. Louis Univ.
St. Martin's College (WA)
St. Mary's College (IN)
St. Mary's College of California
St. Mary's College of Maryland
St. Mary's Univ. of Minnesota
St. Mary's Univ. of San Antonio
St. Mary-of-The-Woods Coll. (IN)
St. Michael's College (VT)
St. Norbert College (WI)
St. Olaf College (MN)
St. Peter's College (NJ)
St. Thomas Aquinas College (NY)
St. Thomas Univ. (FL)
St. Vincent College (PA)
Stanford Univ. (CA)
State Univ. of West Georgia
Stephen F. Austin State Univ. (TX)
Stetson Univ. (FL)
Stonehill College (MA)
Suffolk Univ. (MA)
Sul Ross State Univ. (TX)
SUNY College of Arts and
   Sciences–Geneseo
SUNY College–Brockport

SUNY College–Old Westbury
SUNY College–Potsdam
SUNY–Albany
SUNY–Binghamton
SUNY–Empire State College
SUNY–Farmingdale
SUNY–Fredonia
SUNY–Oswego
SUNY–Plattsburgh
SUNY–Purchase College
SUNY–Stony Brook
Susquehanna Univ. (PA)
Swarthmore College (PA)
Sweet Briar College (VA)
Syracuse Univ. (NY)
Tabor College (KS)
Tarleton State Univ. (TX)
Taylor Univ. (IN)
Teikyo Post Univ. (CT)
Temple Univ. (PA)
Tennessee State Univ.
Tennessee Technological Univ.
Tennessee Wesleyan College
Texas A&M International Univ.
Texas A&M Univ.–College Station
Texas A&M Univ.–Commerce
Texas A&M Univ.–Corpus Christi
Texas A&M Univ.–Kingsville
Texas Christian Univ.
Texas Lutheran Univ.
Texas State Univ.–San Marcos
Texas Tech Univ.
Texas Wesleyan Univ.
Texas Woman's Univ.
The Citadel (SC)
Thiel College (PA)
Thomas College (ME)
Thomas Edison State College (NJ)
Thomas More College (KY)
Tiffin Univ. (OH)
Tougaloo College (MS)
Touro College (NY)
Towson Univ. (MD)
Transylvania Univ. (KY)
Trevecca Nazarene Univ. (TN)
Tri-State Univ. (IN)
Trinity Christian College (IL)
Trinity College (DC)
Trinity College (CT)
Troy State Univ.–Troy (AL)
Truman State Univ. (MO)
Tufts Univ. (MA)
Tulane Univ. (LA)
Tusculum College (TN)
Union College (NY)
Union College (NE)
Union Institute and Univ. (OH)
Union Univ. (TN)
Univ. at Buffalo–SUNY
Univ. of Akron (OH)
Univ. of Alabama
Univ. of Alabama–Birmingham
Univ. of Alabama–Huntsville
Univ. of Alaska–Anchorage
Univ. of Alaska–Fairbanks
Univ. of Arizona
Univ. of Arkansas
Univ. of Arkansas–Little Rock
Univ. of Arkansas–Pine Bluff
Univ. of Bridgeport (CT)
Univ. of California–Berkeley

Univ. of California–Davis
Univ. of California–Irvine
Univ. of California–Los Angeles
Univ. of California–Riverside
Univ. of California–San Diego
Univ. of Central Arkansas
Univ. of Central Florida
Univ. of Central Oklahoma
Univ. of Charleston (WV)
Univ. of Chicago
Univ. of Colorado–Boulder
Univ. of Colorado–Colorado
   Springs
Univ. of Colorado–Denver
Univ. of Connecticut
Univ. of Dallas
Univ. of Dayton (OH)
Univ. of Denver
Univ. of Detroit Mercy
Univ. of Evansville (IN)
Univ. of Findlay (OH)
Univ. of Florida
Univ. of Georgia
Univ. of Hartford (CT)
Univ. of Hawaii–Hilo
Univ. of Hawaii–Manoa
Univ. of Houston
Univ. of Houston–Downtown
Univ. of Illinois–Chicago
Univ. of Illinois–Springfield
Univ. of Ill.–Urbana-Champaign
Univ. of Indianapolis
Univ. of Iowa
Univ. of Judaism (CA)
Univ. of Kansas
Univ. of Kentucky
Univ. of La Verne (CA)
Univ. of Louisiana–Lafayette
Univ. of Louisiana–Monroe
Univ. of Louisville (KY)
Univ. of Maine–Farmington
Univ. of Maine–Orono
Univ. of Maine–Presque Isle
Univ. of Mary (ND)
Univ. of Mary Hardin-Baylor (TX)
Univ. of Mary Washington (VA)
Univ. of Maryland–Baltimore
   County
Univ. of Maryland–College Park
Univ. of Maryland–Univ. College
Univ. of Massachusetts–Amherst
Univ. of Massachusetts–Boston
Univ. of Massachusetts–Lowell
Univ. of Memphis
Univ. of Miami (FL)
Univ. of Michigan–Ann Arbor
Univ. of Michigan–Dearborn
Univ. of Michigan–Flint
Univ. of Minnesota–Duluth
Univ. of Minnesota–Morris
Univ. of Minnesota–Twin Cities
Univ. of Mississippi
Univ. of Missouri–Columbia
Univ. of Missouri–Kansas City
Univ. of Missouri–Rolla
Univ. of Missouri–St. Louis
Univ. of Mobile (AL)
Univ. of Montevallo (AL)
Univ. of Nebraska–Kearney
Univ. of Nebraska–Lincoln
Univ. of Nebraska–Omaha

Univ. of Nevada–Las Vegas
Univ. of Nevada–Reno
Univ. of New England (ME)
Univ. of New Hampshire
Univ. of New Haven (CT)
Univ. of New Mexico
Univ. of New Orleans
Univ. of North Alabama
Univ. of North Carolina–Asheville
Univ. of N.C.–Chapel Hill
Univ. of North Carolina–Charlotte
Univ. of N.C.–Greensboro
Univ. of North Carolina–Pembroke
Univ. of N.C.–Wilmington
Univ. of North Dakota
Univ. of North Florida
Univ. of North Texas
Univ. of Northern Colorado
Univ. of Northern Iowa
Univ. of Notre Dame (IN)
Univ. of Oklahoma
Univ. of Oregon
Univ. of Pennsylvania
Univ. of Pittsburgh
Univ. of Pittsburgh–Bradford
Univ. of Pittsburgh–Johnstown
Univ. of Portland (OR)
Univ. of Puget Sound (WA)
Univ. of Redlands (CA)
Univ. of Rhode Island
Univ. of Richmond (VA)
Univ. of Rio Grande (OH)
Univ. of Rochester (NY)
Univ. of San Diego
Univ. of San Francisco
Univ. of Science and Arts of
   Oklahoma
Univ. of Scranton (PA)
Univ. of Sioux Falls (SD)
Univ. of South Alabama
Univ. of South Carolina–Aiken
Univ. of South Carolina–Upstate
Univ. of South Dakota
Univ. of South Florida
Univ. of Southern California
Univ. of Southern Indiana
Univ. of Southern Maine
Univ. of Southern Mississippi
Univ. of St. Francis (IL)
Univ. of St. Francis (IN)
Univ. of St. Mary (KS)
Univ. of St. Thomas (TX)
Univ. of Tampa (FL)
Univ. of Tennessee
Univ. of Tennessee–Chattanooga
Univ. of Tennessee–Martin
Univ. of Texas of the Permian Basin
Univ. of Texas–Arlington
Univ. of Texas–Austin
Univ. of Texas–Brownsville
Univ. of Texas–Dallas
Univ. of Texas–El Paso
Univ. of Texas–Pan American
Univ. of Texas–San Antonio
Univ. of Texas–Tyler
Univ. of the District of Columbia
Univ. of the Incarnate Word (TX)
Univ. of the Pacific (CA)
Univ. of Toledo (OH)
Univ. of Tulsa (OK)
Univ. of Utah

Univ. of Vermont
Univ. of Virginia
Univ. of Virginia–Wise
Univ. of Washington
Univ. of West Alabama
Univ. of West Florida
Univ. of Wisconsin–Eau Claire
Univ. of Wisconsin–Green Bay
Univ. of Wisconsin–La Crosse
Univ. of Wisconsin–Madison
Univ. of Wisconsin–Milwaukee
Univ. of Wisconsin–Oshkosh
Univ. of Wisconsin–Platteville
Univ. of Wisconsin–River Falls
Univ. of Wisconsin–Stevens Point
Univ. of Wisconsin–Stout
Univ. of Wisconsin–Superior
Univ. of Wisconsin–Whitewater
Univ. of Wyoming
Upper Iowa Univ.
Urbana Univ. (OH)
Ursinus College (PA)
Ursuline College (OH)
Utah State Univ.
Utah Valley State College
Utica College (NY)
Valdosta State Univ. (GA)
Valley City State Univ. (ND)
Valparaiso Univ. (IN)
Vanderbilt Univ. (TN)
Vanguard Univ. of Southern
   California
Vassar College (NY)
Villa Julie College (MD)
Villanova Univ. (PA)
Virginia Commonwealth Univ.
Virginia Intermont College
Virginia Military Institute
Virginia State Univ.
Virginia Tech
Virginia Wesleyan College
Viterbo Univ. (WI)
Wabash College (IN)
Wagner College (NY)
Wake Forest Univ. (NC)
Walsh Univ. (OH)
Warner Southern College (FL)
Wartburg College (IA)
Washburn Univ. (KS)
Washington and Jefferson College
   (PA)
Washington and Lee Univ. (VA)
Washington College (MD)
Washington State Univ.
Washington Univ. In St. Louis
Wayland Baptist Univ. (TX)
Wayne State College (NE)
Wayne State Univ. (MI)
Waynesburg College (PA)
Weber State Univ. (UT)
Webster Univ. (MO)
Wesley College (DE)
Wesleyan College (GA)
West Chester Univ. of Pennsylvania
West Liberty State College (WV)
West Texas A&M Univ.
West Virginia State Univ.
West Virginia Univ.
West Virginia Wesleyan College
Western Baptist College (OR)
Western Carolina Univ. (NC)

Western Connecticut State Univ.
Western Illinois Univ.
Western Kentucky Univ.
Western Michigan Univ.
Western New England College
   (MA)
Western New Mexico Univ.
Western Oregon Univ.
Western State College of Colorado
Western Washington Univ.
Westfield State College (MA)
Westminster College (UT)
Westminster College (PA)
Westminster College (MO)
Westmont College (CA)
Wheaton College (MA)
Wheaton College (IL)
Wheeling Jesuit Univ. (WV)
Whitman College (WA)
Whittier College (CA)
Whitworth College (WA)
Wichita State Univ. (KS)
Wilberforce Univ. (OH)
Wilkes Univ. (PA)
Willamette Univ. (OR)
William Carey College (MS)
William Jewell College (MO)
William Paterson Univ. of New
   Jersey
William Penn Univ. (IA)
William Woods Univ. (MO)
Williams College (MA)
Wilmington College (DE)
Wilmington College (OH)
Wingate Univ. (NC)
Winthrop Univ. (SC)
Wisconsin Lutheran College
Wittenberg Univ. (OH)
Wofford College (SC)
Woodbury Univ. (CA)
Worcester State College (MA)
Wright State Univ. (OH)
Xavier Univ. (OH)
Yale Univ. (CT)
Yeshiva Univ. (NY)
York College of Pennsylvania
Youngstown State Univ. (OH)

Psychometrics and Quantitative Psychology

North Dakota State Univ.

Public Administration

Albany State Univ. (GA)
Alfred Univ. (NY)
Auburn Univ. (AL)
Augustana College (IL)
Barry Univ. (FL)
Baylor Univ. (TX)
Bowling Green State Univ. (OH)
Brenau Univ. (GA)
Buena Vista Univ. (IA)
California State Univ.–Bakersfield
California State Univ.–Chico
California State Univ.–Fresno
California State Univ.–Fullerton
California State Univ.–Sacramento

California State Univ.–San
   Bernardino
Calvin College (MI)
Campbell Univ. (NC)
Capital Univ. (OH)
Carroll College (MT)
Cedarville Univ. (OH)
Central Methodist Univ. (MO)
Cleveland State Univ.
College of Santa Fe (NM)
Cornell Univ. (NY)
CUNY–Baruch College
CUNY–Medgar Evers College
Dallas Baptist Univ.
David Lipscomb Univ. (TN)
Eastern Michigan Univ.
Elon Univ. (NC)
Ferris State Univ. (MI)
Florida Atlantic Univ.
Florida International Univ.
Florida Memorial College
George Mason Univ. (VA)
Golden Gate Univ. (CA)
Grambling State Univ. (LA)
Grand Valley State Univ. (MI)
Hampton Univ. (VA)
Harding Univ. (AR)
Hawaii Pacific Univ.
Henderson State Univ. (AR)
Indiana Univ. East
Indiana Univ. Northwest
Indiana Univ.–Bloomington
Indiana Univ.–Kokomo
Indiana Univ.–South Bend
Indiana Univ.-Purdue Univ.–Fort
   Wayne
Indiana Univ.-Purdue
   Univ.–Indianapolis
Iowa State Univ.
Jacksonville State Univ. (AL)
James Madison Univ. (VA)
Juniata College (PA)
Kean Univ. (NJ)
Kentucky State Univ.
Kentucky Wesleyan College
Kutztown Univ. of Pennsylvania
La Salle Univ. (PA)
Lewis Univ. (IL)
Lewis-Clark State College (ID)
Lincoln Univ. (MO)
Lincoln Univ. (PA)
Lindenwood Univ. (MO)
Long Island Univ.–C.W. Post
   Campus (NY)
Louisiana College
Miami Univ.–Oxford (OH)
Michigan State Univ.
Mississippi Valley State Univ.
Murray State Univ. (KY)
Myers Univ. (OH)
New York Univ.
North Georgia College and State
   Univ.
Northeastern State Univ. (OK)
Northern Michigan Univ.
Northwest Missouri State Univ.
Oakland Univ. (MI)
Park Univ. (MO)
Plymouth State Univ. (NH)
Point Park Univ. (PA)
Princeton Univ. (NJ)

Rhode Island College
Roosevelt Univ. (IL)
Saginaw Valley State Univ. (MI)
Samford Univ. (AL)
San Diego State Univ.
Seattle Univ.
Shaw Univ. (NC)
Shenandoah Univ. (VA)
Shippensburg Univ. of
    Pennsylvania
Silver Lake College (WI)
Southeastern Univ. (DC)
Southern Illinois Univ.–Carbondale
Southern New Hampshire Univ.
Southwest Minnesota State Univ.
    (MN)
Southwest Missouri State Univ.
St. Ambrose Univ. (IA)
St. Cloud State Univ. (MN)
St. Francis Univ. (PA)
St. John's Univ. (NY)
St. Joseph's Univ. (PA)
St. Mary's Univ. of San Antonio
Stephen F. Austin State Univ. (TX)
Stonehill College (MA)
Suffolk Univ. (MA)
Syracuse Univ. (NY)
Talladega College (AL)
Texas State Univ.–San Marcos
Thomas Edison State College (NJ)
Union Institute and Univ. (OH)
Univ. of Arizona
Univ. of Arkansas
Univ. of California–Riverside
Univ. of Central Arkansas
Univ. of Central Florida
Univ. of Evansville (IN)
Univ. of Kansas
Univ. of La Verne (CA)
Univ. of Maine–Augusta
Univ. of Maine–Orono
Univ. of Massachusetts–Boston
Univ. of Michigan–Flint
Univ. of Missouri–St. Louis
Univ. of Nevada–Las Vegas
Univ. of New Haven (CT)
Univ. of North Carolina–Pembroke
Univ. of North Dakota
Univ. of North Texas
Univ. of Northern Iowa
Univ. of Oklahoma
Univ. of Oregon
Univ. of Pittsburgh
Univ. of San Francisco
Univ. of Southern California
Univ. of St. Thomas (MN)
Univ. of Tennessee
Univ. of Texas–Dallas
Univ. of Wisconsin–La Crosse
Univ. of Wisconsin–Stevens Point
Univ. of Wisconsin–Superior
Univ. of Wisconsin–Whitewater
Virginia Intermont College
Virginia State Univ.
Washburn Univ. (KS)
Wayne State Univ. (MI)
Waynesburg College (PA)
West Texas A&M Univ.
Western Carolina Univ. (NC)
Western Michigan Univ.
Western New Mexico Univ.

Western Oregon Univ.
York College of Pennsylvania
Youngstown State Univ. (OH)

Public Administration and Social Service Professions

Cleveland State Univ.
Columbia College (SC)
Eastern Oregon Univ.
Elmira College (NY)
Jacksonville State Univ. (AL)
Merrimack College (MA)
Milligan College (TN)
Mountain State Univ. (WV)
Ohio Wesleyan Univ.
Pfeiffer Univ. (NC)
Quincy Univ. (IL)
Roosevelt Univ. (IL)
Samford Univ. (AL)
Syracuse Univ. (NY)
Troy State Univ.–Troy (AL)
Virginia Wesleyan College

Public Health

Appalachian State Univ. (NC)
Baker College of Flint (MI)
Bethel Univ. (MN)
Bloomsburg Univ. of Pennsylvania
Boise State Univ. (ID)
Bowling Green State Univ. (OH)
Brandeis Univ. (MA)
Brown Univ. (RI)
California State Univ.–Long Beach
California State Univ.–Northridge
California State Univ.–Sacramento
Case Western Reserve Univ. (OH)
Central Michigan Univ.
Central Washington Univ.
Coastal Carolina Univ. (SC)
Colorado State Univ.
Concordia Univ. (OR)
Cumberland College (KY)
CUNY–York College
Davenport Univ. (MI)
Delaware State Univ.
Dickinson State Univ. (ND)
East Carolina Univ. (NC)
East Central Univ. (OK)
East Stroudsburg Univ. of
    Pennsylvania
East Tennessee State Univ.
Eastern Kentucky Univ.
Eastern Washington Univ.
Elizabethtown College (PA)
Emporia State Univ. (KS)
Georgia Southern Univ.
Grand Valley State Univ. (MI)
Hofstra Univ. (NY)
Illinois State Univ.
Indiana State Univ.
Indiana Univ. of Pennsylvania
Indiana Univ.–Bloomington
Indiana Univ.-Purdue Univ.–Fort
    Wayne
Indiana Univ.-Purdue
    Univ.–Indianapolis

Ithaca College (NY)
Johns Hopkins Univ. (MD)
Liberty Univ. (VA)
Malone College (OH)
Mississippi Valley State Univ.
Missouri Southern State Univ.
Montana State Univ.–Northern
Montana Tech of the Univ. of
    Montana
Mountain State Univ. (WV)
New Mexico State Univ.
North Carolina A&T State Univ.
North Carolina Central Univ.
Northern Arizona Univ.
Northwest Christian College (OR)
Oakland Univ. (MI)
Ohio Univ.
Oklahoma State Univ.
Old Dominion Univ. (VA)
Oregon State Univ.
Plymouth State Univ. (NH)
Quinnipiac Univ. (CT)
Richard Stockton College of New
    Jersey
Robert Morris Univ. (PA)
Rutgers–New Brunswick (NJ)
Slippery Rock Univ. of Pennsylvania
Southeastern Louisiana Univ.
Southern Connecticut State Univ.
St. Cloud State Univ. (MN)
Temple Univ. (PA)
Tennessee State Univ.
Thomas Edison State College (NJ)
Tulane Univ. (LA)
Univ. of Arkansas–Little Rock
Univ. of California–Berkeley
Univ. of Evansville (IN)
Univ. of Georgia
Univ. of Ill.–Urbana-Champaign
Univ. of Kentucky
Univ. of Maryland–College Park
Univ. of Michigan–Flint
Univ. of Nevada–Las Vegas
Univ. of New Hampshire
Univ. of North Carolina–Asheville
Univ. of N.C.–Chapel Hill
Univ. of N.C.–Greensboro
Univ. of North Carolina–Pembroke
Univ. of Northern Colorado
Univ. of Southern California
Univ. of Southern Maine
Univ. of Southern Mississippi
Univ. of St. Thomas (MN)
Univ. of Toledo (OH)
Univ. of Utah
Univ. of Washington
Univ. of Wisconsin–Eau Claire
Univ. of Wisconsin–La Crosse
Utah State Univ.
Utah Valley State College
West Chester Univ. of Pennsylvania
West Virginia Univ. Institute of
    Technology
Western Carolina Univ. (NC)
Winona State Univ. (MN)

Public Policy Analysis

Albion College (MI)
Anna Maria College (MA)

Bentley College (MA)
Brown Univ. (RI)
California State Univ.–Sacramento
Carlow College (PA)
Carnegie Mellon Univ. (PA)
Central Washington Univ.
Chatham College (PA)
College of William and Mary (VA)
Cornell Univ. (NY)
Depaul Univ. (IL)
Dickinson College (PA)
Duke Univ. (NC)
Emory and Henry College (VA)
Franklin and Marshall College (PA)
Georgia Institute of Technology
Hobart and William Smith Colleges
    (NY)
Immaculata Univ. (PA)
Mills College (CA)
Northern Arizona Univ.
Northwestern Univ. (IL)
Olivet Nazarene Univ. (IL)
Pomona College (CA)
Rice Univ. (TX)
Rochester Institute of Tech. (NY)
Southern Methodist Univ. (TX)
St. Mary's College of Maryland
St. Peter's College (NJ)
St. Vincent College (PA)
Stanford Univ. (CA)
Suffolk Univ. (MA)
SUNY–Albany
Trinity College (DC)
Trinity College (CT)
Univ. of Chicago
Univ. of Denver
Univ. of Massachusetts–Boston
Univ. of Mississippi
Univ. of Nevada–Las Vegas
Univ. of N.C.–Chapel Hill
Univ. of Pennsylvania
Univ. of Rhode Island
Univ. of Southern California
Univ. of Wisconsin–Superior
Univ. of Wisconsin–Whitewater
Virginia Tech
Wagner College (NY)
Washington and Lee Univ. (VA)
Washington State Univ.

Public Relations, Advertising, and Applied Communication

American Univ. (DC)
Anderson College (SC)
Andrews Univ. (MI)
Appalachian State Univ. (NC)
Assumption College (MA)
Auburn Univ. (AL)
Augustana College (SD)
Babson College (MA)
Baldwin-Wallace College (OH)
Barry Univ. (FL)
Bellevue Univ. (NE)
Belmont Univ. (TN)
Boston Univ.
Bowling Green State Univ. (OH)
Bradley Univ. (IL)
Brigham Young Univ.–Provo (UT)

Buena Vista Univ. (IA)
California Lutheran Univ.
California State Univ.–Fullerton
California State Univ.–Long Beach
California State Univ.–Sacramento
Campbell Univ. (NC)
Capital Univ. (OH)
Carroll College (MT)
Carroll College (WI)
Central Michigan Univ.
Central Missouri State Univ.
Central Washington Univ.
Champlain College (VT)
Chapman Univ. (CA)
Chatham College (PA)
Christian Brothers Univ. (TN)
Clarke College (IA)
Coe College (IA)
College of St. Scholastica (MN)
College of the Ozarks (MO)
Colorado State Univ.
Concordia Coll.–Moorhead (MN)
Concordia Univ. (MI)
Creighton Univ. (NE)
CUNY–Baruch College
Dana College (NE)
David Lipscomb Univ. (TN)
Delaware State Univ.
Dominican Univ. (IL)
Dordt College (IA)
Drake Univ. (IA)
Drury Univ. (MO)
Duquesne Univ. (PA)
Eastern Kentucky Univ.
Eastern Michigan Univ.
Emerson College (MA)
Ferris State Univ. (MI)
Fitchburg State College (MA)
Florida A&M Univ.
Florida Southern College
Fontbonne Univ. (MO)
Franklin Pierce College (NH)
Freed-Hardeman Univ. (TN)
Gannon Univ. (PA)
Georgia Southern Univ.
Gonzaga Univ. (WA)
Grand Valley State Univ. (MI)
Greenville College (IL)
Gwynedd-Mercy College (PA)
Hampton Univ. (VA)
Hannibal-Lagrange College (MO)
Hardin-Simmons Univ. (TX)
Harding Univ. (AR)
Hastings College (NE)
Hawaii Pacific Univ.
Heidelberg College (OH)
Hofstra Univ. (NY)
Howard Payne Univ. (TX)
Humboldt State Univ. (CA)
Huntington College (IN)
Illinois State Univ.
Indiana State Univ.
Indiana Univ. Southeast
Indiana Univ.–South Bend
Indiana Univ.-Purdue Univ.–Fort
    Wayne
Iona College (NY)
Iowa State Univ.
Ithaca College (NY)
John Brown Univ. (AR)
Johnson and Wales Univ. (RI)

Juniata College (PA)
Kent State Univ. (OH)
Lake Erie College (OH)
Lambuth Univ. (TN)
Liberty Univ. (VA)
Long Island Univ.–C.W. Post
    Campus (NY)
Long Island Univ.–Southampton
    College (NY)
Loras College (IA)
Louisiana College
Loyola Univ. Chicago
Mansfield Univ. of Pennsylvania
Marian College of Fond Du Lac
    (WI)
Marietta College (OH)
Marist College (NY)
Marquette Univ. (WI)
Marylhurst Univ. (OR)
Marywood Univ. (PA)
Master's Coll. and Seminary (CA)
Methodist College (NC)
Metropolitan State College of
    Denver
Michigan State Univ.
Midland Lutheran College (NE)
Montana State Univ.–Billings
Morningside College (IA)
Mount Mary College (WI)
Murray State Univ. (KY)
Nebraska Wesleyan Univ.
North Carolina A&T State Univ.
North Central College (IL)
North Dakota State Univ.
North Park Univ. (IL)
Northern Arizona Univ.
Northern Kentucky Univ.
Northern Michigan Univ.
Northwest Missouri State Univ.
Northwood Univ. (MI)
Notre Dame De Namur Univ. (CA)
Ohio Dominican Univ.
Ohio Northern Univ.
Ohio Univ.
Oklahoma Baptist Univ.
Oklahoma Christian Univ.
Oral Roberts Univ. (OK)
Otis College of Art and Design
    (CA)
Otterbein College (OH)
Pace Univ. (NY)
Paine College (GA)
Palm Beach Atlantic Univ. (FL)
Penn. State Univ.–Univ. Park
Pepperdine Univ. (CA)
Pfeiffer Univ. (NC)
Point Park Univ. (PA)
Purdue Univ.–Calumet (IN)
Quinnipiac Univ. (CT)
Regis College (MA)
Rider Univ. (NJ)
Rivier College (NH)
Rochester Institute of Tech. (NY)
Rockhurst Univ. (MO)
Roosevelt Univ. (IL)
San Diego State Univ.
San Jose State Univ. (CA)
Shorter College (GA)
Southern Adventist Univ. (TN)
Southern Methodist Univ. (TX)
Southern New Hampshire Univ.

Southwest Minnesota State Univ.
    (MN)
Southwestern Adventist Univ. (TX)
St. Ambrose Univ. (IA)
St. John's Univ. (NY)
St. Joseph's College (ME)
St. Mary's Univ. of Minnesota
Stephens College (MO)
Suffolk Univ. (MA)
SUNY–Fredonia
Susquehanna Univ. (PA)
Syracuse Univ. (NY)
Tabor College (KS)
Texas A&M Univ.–Commerce
Texas Christian Univ.
Texas State Univ.–San Marcos
Texas Tech Univ.
Texas Wesleyan Univ.
Thomas Edison State College (NJ)
Tiffin Univ. (OH)
Toccoa Falls College (GA)
Tougaloo College (MS)
Trevecca Nazarene Univ. (TN)
Trinity Christian College (IL)
Tulane Univ. (LA)
Union College (NE)
Union Univ. (TN)
Univ. of Akron (OH)
Univ. of Alabama
Univ. of Arkansas–Little Rock
Univ. of Central Florida
Univ. of Dayton (OH)
Univ. of Findlay (OH)
Univ. of Florida
Univ. of Georgia
Univ. of Houston
Univ. of Illinois–Urbana-
    Champaign
Univ. of Kentucky
Univ. of Louisiana–Lafayette
Univ. of Miami (FL)
Univ. of Michigan–Flint
Univ. of Nebraska–Lincoln
Univ. of North Texas
Univ. of Northern Iowa
Univ. of Oklahoma
Univ. of Oregon
Univ. of Pittsburgh–Bradford
Univ. of Rhode Island
Univ. of South Carolina–Columbia
Univ. of Southern California
Univ. of Southern Indiana
Univ. of St. Thomas (MN)
Univ. of Tennessee
Univ. of Texas–Arlington
Univ. of Texas–Austin
Univ. of Texas–El Paso
Univ. of Texas–San Antonio
Univ. of Vermont
Univ. of Wisconsin–River Falls
Ursuline College (OH)
Utica College (NY)
Valparaiso Univ. (IN)
Wayne State Univ. (MI)
Waynesburg College (PA)
Webster Univ. (MO)
Wesleyan College (GA)
West Texas A&M Univ.
West Virginia Wesleyan College
Western Kentucky Univ.
Western Michigan Univ.

Western New England Coll. (MA)
Westminster College (PA)
Westminster College (MO)
Widener Univ. (PA)
William Jewell College (MO)
Winthrop Univ. (SC)
Wright State Univ. (OH)
Xavier Univ. (OH)
York College of Pennsylvania
Youngstown State Univ. (OH)

Quality Control and Safety Technologies/Technicians

Bowling Green State Univ. (OH)
California State Univ.–Long Beach
California State Univ.–Los Angeles
Central Missouri State Univ.
Central Washington Univ.
Embry Riddle Aeronautical Univ.
    (FL)
Ferris State Univ. (MI)
Indiana State Univ.
Indiana Univ. of Pennsylvania
Jacksonville State Univ. (AL)
Keene State College (NH)
Madonna Univ. (MI)
Marshall Univ. (WV)
Millersville Univ. of Pennsylvania
Murray State Univ. (KY)
Northeastern State Univ. (OK)
Rochester Institute of Tech. (NY)
Slippery Rock Univ. of Pennsylvania
South Dakota State Univ.
Southeastern Louisiana Univ.
Southeastern Oklahoma State
    Univ.
Southwest Baptist Univ. (MO)
Univ. of Houston–Downtown
Univ. of New Haven (CT)
Univ. of North Dakota
Univ. of Texas–Tyler
Univ. of Wisconsin–Whitewater
Utah State Univ.

Radio, Television, and Digital Communication

Abilene Christian Univ. (TX)
Alabama Agricultural and
    Mechanical Univ.
American Univ. (DC)
Appalachian State Univ. (NC)
Arkansas State Univ.
Ashland Univ. (OH)
Atlanta College of Art
Auburn Univ. (AL)
Barry Univ. (FL)
Baylor Univ. (TX)
Belmont Univ. (TN)
Biola Univ. (CA)
Bowie State Univ. (MD)
Bradley Univ. (IL)
Butler Univ. (IN)
California State Univ.–Fullerton
California State Univ.–Los Angeles
California State Univ.–Northridge
California State Univ.–Sacramento
Calvin College (MI)

Campbell Univ. (NC)
Campbellsville Univ. (KY)
Canisius College (NY)
Capital Univ. (OH)
Central Michigan Univ.
Central Missouri State Univ.
Central State Univ. (OH)
Chicago State Univ.
College of Notre Dame of
    Maryland
College of the Ozarks (MO)
Columbia College (IL)
Corcoran College of Art and Design
    (DC)
Cornerstone Univ. (MI)
CUNY–Brooklyn College
CUNY–City College
Delaware State Univ.
Dordt College (IA)
Drake Univ. (IA)
Eastern Kentucky Univ.
Emerson College (MA)
Fitchburg State College (MA)
Florida A&M Univ.
Florida Atlantic Univ.
Freed-Hardeman Univ. (TN)
George Washington Univ. (DC)
Georgia Institute of Technology
Georgia Southern Univ.
Grace Univ. (NE)
Grand Valley State Univ. (MI)
Grand View College (IA)
Hampshire College (MA)
Hardin-Simmons Univ. (TX)
Harding Univ. (AR)
Hastings College (NE)
Hawaii Pacific Univ.
Heidelberg College (OH)
Hofstra Univ. (NY)
Howard Payne Univ. (TX)
Howard Univ. (DC)
Humboldt State Univ. (CA)
Huntington College (IN)
Indiana State Univ.
Indiana Univ.–Purdue
    Univ.–Indianapolis
Iona College (NY)
Ithaca College (NY)
Jacksonville State Univ. (AL)
John Brown Univ. (AR)
Juniata College (PA)
Kent State Univ. (OH)
Kutztown Univ. of Pennsylvania
Lebanon Valley College (PA)
Long Island Univ.–Southampton
    College (NY)
Lyndon State College (VT)
Madonna Univ. (MI)
Mansfield Univ. of Pennsylvania
Marietta College (OH)
Marist College (NY)
Marywood Univ. (PA)
Master's Coll. and Seminary (CA)
Messiah College (PA)
Michigan State Univ.
Minot State Univ. (ND)
Montclair State Univ. (NJ)
Morningside College (IA)
Mount Vernon Nazarene Univ.
    (OH)
Murray State Univ. (KY)

New York Institute of Technology
New York Univ.
North Carolina A&T State Univ.
North Central College (IL)
North Dakota State Univ.
Northern Arizona Univ.
Northern Kentucky Univ.
Northern Michigan Univ.
Northwest Missouri State Univ.
Northwestern College (MN)
Northwestern Univ. (IL)
Ohio Univ.
Oklahoma Christian Univ.
Oral Roberts Univ. (OK)
Otterbein College (OH)
Palm Beach Atlantic Univ. (FL)
Pepperdine Univ. (CA)
Philadelphia Univ.
Purdue Univ.–Calumet (IN)
Roosevelt Univ. (IL)
Sam Houston State Univ. (TX)
San Diego State Univ.
San Jose State Univ. (CA)
Savannah College of Art and
    Design (GA)
Southeastern College of the
    Assemblies of God
Southern Illinois Univ.–Carbondale
Southern Methodist Univ. (TX)
Southern New Hampshire Univ.
Southern Oregon Univ.
Southwest Minnesota State Univ.
    (MN)
Southwest Missouri State Univ.
St. Ambrose Univ. (IA)
St. Edward's Univ. (TX)
St. Joseph's College (ME)
Stephen F. Austin State Univ. (TX)
Stephens College (MO)
SUNY–Fredonia
Susquehanna Univ. (PA)
Syracuse Univ. (NY)
Temple Univ. (PA)
Texas A&M Univ.–Commerce
Texas Christian Univ.
Texas State Univ.–San Marcos
Texas Tech Univ.
Texas Wesleyan Univ.
Towson Univ. (MD)
Trevecca Nazarene Univ. (TN)
Troy State Univ.–Troy (AL)
Univ. of Alabama
Univ. of Arkansas–Little Rock
Univ. of Central Florida
Univ. of Dayton (OH)
Univ. of Denver
Univ. of Florida
Univ. of Houston
Univ. of Kentucky
Univ. of La Verne (CA)
Univ. of Miami (FL)
Univ. of Michigan–Ann Arbor
Univ. of Montana
Univ. of Montevallo (AL)
Univ. of New Hampshire
Univ. of North Texas
Univ. of Northern Iowa
Univ. of Oregon
Univ. of Scranton (PA)
Univ. of South Carolina–Columbia
Univ. of Southern Indiana

Univ. of Southern Mississippi
Univ. of Tennessee
Univ. of Texas–Arlington
Univ. of Texas–Austin
Univ. of Wisconsin–Oshkosh
Utah Valley State College
Valparaiso Univ. (IN)
Waldorf College (IA)
Washington State Univ.
Wayne State Univ. (MI)
Weber State Univ. (UT)
Western Illinois Univ.
Western Kentucky Univ.
Western Michigan Univ.
Westminster College (PA)
Wilkes Univ. (PA)
William Jewell College (MO)
William Woods Univ. (MO)
Xavier Univ. (OH)
York College of Pennsylvania
Youngstown State Univ. (OH)

Real Estate

Angelo State Univ. (TX)
Baylor Univ. (TX)
California State Univ.–Sacramento
Clarion Univ. of Pennsylvania
Colorado State Univ.
CUNY–Baruch College
Eastern Kentucky Univ.
Florida Atlantic Univ.
Florida International Univ.
Florida State Univ.
Georgia State Univ.
Kent State Univ. (OH)
La Roche College (PA)
Marquette Univ. (WI)
Marylhurst Univ. (OR)
Mississippi State Univ.
Morehead State Univ. (KY)
New York Univ.
Ohio State Univ.–Columbus
St. Cloud State Univ. (MN)
State Univ. of West Georgia
Temple Univ. (PA)
Texas Christian Univ.
Thomas Edison State College (NJ)
Univ. of Central Oklahoma
Univ. of Connecticut
Univ. of Denver
Univ. of Florida
Univ. of Georgia
Univ. of Ill.–Urbana-Champaign
Univ. of Mississippi
Univ. of Nebraska–Omaha
Univ. of Nevada–Las Vegas
Univ. of North Texas
Univ. of Northern Iowa
Univ. of Pennsylvania
Univ. of South Carolina–Columbia
Univ. of St. Thomas (MN)
Univ. of Texas–Arlington
Univ. of Wisconsin–Madison
Washington State Univ.
Weber State Univ. (UT)

Rehabilitation and Therapeutic Professions

Alabama State Univ.
Alcorn State Univ. (MS)
Alderson-Broaddus College (WV)
Alvernia College (PA)
Alverno College (WI)
Anna Maria College (MA)
Appalachian State Univ. (NC)
Arizona State Univ.
Arkansas Tech Univ.
Assumption College (MA)
Baker College of Flint (MI)
Baldwin-Wallace College (OH)
Barry Univ. (FL)
Bay Path College (MA)
Bellarmine Univ. (KY)
Boston Univ.
Bowling Green State Univ. (OH)
Brenau Univ. (GA)
Bridgewater State College (MA)
California State Univ.–Long Beach
California State Univ.–Los Angeles
California State Univ.–Sacramento
California State Univ.–San Bernardino
Calvin College (MI)
Capital Univ. (OH)
Carlow College (PA)
Cedar Crest College (PA)
Central Michigan Univ.
Central Missouri State Univ.
Chapman Univ. (CA)
Charleston Southern Univ. (SC)
Cleveland State Univ.
College Misericordia (PA)
College of Santa Fe (NM)
College of St. Catherine (MN)
College of Wooster (OH)
Colorado State Univ.
CUNY–College of Staten Island
CUNY–Lehman College
CUNY–York College
Dominican Coll. of Blauvelt (NY)
Dominican Univ. (IL)
Duquesne Univ. (PA)
East Carolina Univ. (NC)
East Stroudsburg Univ. of Pennsylvania
Eastern Kentucky Univ.
Eastern Michigan Univ.
Eastern Washington Univ.
Edgewood College (WI)
Elizabethtown College (PA)
Emmanuel College (MA)
Emporia State Univ. (KS)
Endicott College (MA)
Florida Gulf Coast Univ.
Florida International Univ.
Florida State Univ.
Fresno Pacific Univ. (CA)
Gallaudet Univ. (DC)
Gannon Univ. (PA)
Georgia College and State Univ.
Green Mountain College (VT)
Harding Univ. (AR)
Hilbert College (NY)
Howard Univ. (DC)
Huntington College (IN)

Illinois College
Immaculata Univ. (PA)
Indiana Univ. East
Indiana Univ. Northwest
Indiana Univ.–Bloomington
Indiana Univ.–Kokomo
Indiana Univ.-Purdue Univ.–Fort Wayne
Indiana Wesleyan Univ.
Ithaca College (NY)
Kean Univ. (NJ)
Keuka College (NY)
Lenoir-Rhyne College (NC)
Lesley Univ. (MA)
Lincoln Univ. (PA)
Longwood Univ. (VA)
Louisiana College
Loyola Marymount Univ. (CA)
Loyola Univ. New Orleans
Marian College of Fond Du Lac (WI)
Marygrove College (MI)
Marylhurst Univ. (OR)
Maryville Univ. of St. Louis (MO)
Marywood Univ. (PA)
Master's Coll. and Seminary (CA)
Mckendree College (IL)
Mercyhurst College (PA)
Messiah College (PA)
Michigan State Univ.
Midwestern State Univ. (TX)
Millikin Univ. (IL)
Mississippi Univ. For Women
Montana State Univ.–Billings
Montclair State Univ. (NJ)
Moravian College (PA)
Mount Aloysius College (PA)
Mount Mary College (WI)
Mount St. Mary College (NY)
Nazareth College of Rochester (NY)
New York Institute of Technology
Newman Univ. (KS)
North Georgia College and State Univ.
Northeastern Univ. (MA)
Northern Illinois Univ.
Northwest Nazarene Univ. (ID)
Oakland Univ. (MI)
Oral Roberts Univ. (OK)
Penn. State Univ.–Univ. Park
Queens Univ. of Charlotte (NC)
Quinnipiac Univ. (CT)
Regis Univ. (CO)
Russell Sage College (NY)
Saginaw Valley State Univ. (MI)
Salem State College (MA)
Sam Houston State Univ. (TX)
San Jose State Univ. (CA)
Seton Hill Univ. (PA)
Shaw Univ. (NC)
Shenandoah Univ. (VA)
Slippery Rock Univ. of Pennsylvania
Southern Adventist Univ. (TN)
Southern Illinois Univ.–Carbondale
Southern Methodist Univ. (TX)
Southern Univ. and A&M College (LA)
Spalding Univ. (KY)
Spring Hill College (AL)
Springfield College (MA)

St. Ambrose Univ. (IA)
St. Andrews Presbyterian College (NC)
St. Francis Univ. (PA)
St. Louis Univ.
St. Mary's Univ. of Minnesota
St. Vincent College (PA)
Stephen F. Austin State Univ. (TX)
Temple Univ. (PA)
Tennessee State Univ.
Texas Woman's Univ.
Thomas Univ. (GA)
Touro College (NY)
Towson Univ. (MD)
Troy State Univ.–Troy (AL)
Truman State Univ. (MO)
Tuskegee Univ. (AL)
Unity College (ME)
Univ. at Buffalo–SUNY
Univ. of Akron (OH)
Univ. of Arkansas–Little Rock
Univ. of Arkansas–Pine Bluff
Univ. of Connecticut
Univ. of Dayton (OH)
Univ. of Evansville (IN)
Univ. of Findlay (OH)
Univ. of Georgia
Univ. of Hartford (CT)
Univ. of Ill.–Urbana-Champaign
Univ. of Indianapolis
Univ. of Iowa
Univ. of Kansas
Univ. of Kentucky
Univ. of Louisville (KY)
Univ. of Maine–Farmington
Univ. of Maryland–Eastern Shore
Univ. of Massachusetts–Lowell
Univ. of Miami (FL)
Univ. of Michigan–Flint
Univ. of Minnesota–Twin Cities
Univ. of Missouri–Columbia
Univ. of Nevada–Las Vegas
Univ. of New Hampshire
Univ. of N.C.–Wilmington
Univ. of North Dakota
Univ. of North Texas
Univ. of Northern Colorado
Univ. of Pittsburgh
Univ. of Pittsburgh–Bradford
Univ. of Scranton (PA)
Univ. of Southern California
Univ. of Southern Indiana
Univ. of Southern Maine
Univ. of Tennessee
Univ. of Texas–El Paso
Univ. of Texas–Pan American
Univ. of the Incarnate Word (TX)
Univ. of the Pacific (CA)
Univ. of Toledo (OH)
Univ. of Utah
Univ. of Washington
Univ. of Wisconsin–Eau Claire
Univ. of Wisconsin–La Crosse
Univ. of Wisconsin–Madison
Univ. of Wisconsin–Milwaukee
Univ. of Wisconsin–Stout
Univ. of Wisconsin–Superior
Utah State Univ.
Utica College (NY)
Wartburg College (IA)
Wayne State Univ. (MI)

West Texas A&M Univ.
Western Carolina Univ. (NC)
Western Michigan Univ.
Western New Mexico Univ.
Western Washington Univ.
Wilberforce Univ. (OH)
William Carey College (MS)
Wilson College (PA)
Winston-Salem State Univ. (NC)
Worcester State College (MA)
Wright State Univ. (OH)
York College of Pennsylvania

Religion/Religious Studies

Adrian College (MI)
Agnes Scott College (GA)
Albertson College (ID)
Albion College (MI)
Albright College (PA)
Allegheny College (PA)
Allen Univ. (SC)
Alma College (MI)
Alvernia College (PA)
Alverno College (WI)
American Univ. (DC)
Amherst College (MA)
Anderson College (SC)
Anderson Univ. (IN)
Andrews Univ. (MI)
Aquinas College (MI)
Arizona State Univ.
Ashland Univ. (OH)
Atlantic Union College (MA)
Augsburg College (MN)
Augustana College (IL)
Augustana College (SD)
Austin College (TX)
Averett Univ. (VA)
Avila Univ. (MO)
Baker Univ. (KS)
Baldwin-Wallace College (OH)
Ball State Univ. (IN)
Barnard College (NY)
Bates College (ME)
Baylor Univ. (TX)
Belhaven College (MS)
Belmont Univ. (TN)
Beloit College (WI)
Benedictine College (KS)
Berea College (KY)
Bethany College (WV)
Bethel College (IN)
Bethel College (KS)
Bloomfield College (NJ)
Bluefield College (VA)
Bluffton Univ. (OH)
Boston Univ.
Bowdoin College (ME)
Bradley Univ. (IL)
Brevard College (NC)
Brewton-Parker College (GA)
Brown Univ. (RI)
Bryan College (TN)
Bryn Athyn College (PA)
Bryn Mawr College (PA)
Bucknell Univ. (PA)
Butler Univ. (IN)
Cabrini College (PA)
California Baptist Univ.

California Lutheran Univ.
California State Univ.–Bakersfield
California State Univ.–Chico
California State Univ.–Fullerton
California State Univ.–Long Beach
California State Univ.–Northridge
California State Univ.–Sacramento
Calumet College of St. Joseph (IN)
Calvin College (MI)
Canisius College (NY)
Capital Univ. (OH)
Cardinal Stritch Univ. (WI)
Carleton College (MN)
Carroll College (WI)
Carson-Newman College (TN)
Carthage College (WI)
Case Western Reserve Univ. (OH)
Catawba College (NC)
Catholic Univ. of America (DC)
Centenary College of Louisiana
Central College (IA)
Central Methodist Univ. (MO)
Central Michigan Univ.
Centre College (KY)
Chaminade Univ. of Honolulu
Chapman Univ. (CA)
Charleston Southern Univ. (SC)
Chowan College (NC)
Claremont Mckenna College (CA)
Clarke College (IA)
Cleveland State Univ.
Coe College (IA)
Colby College (ME)
Colgate Univ. (NY)
College of Charleston (SC)
College of Mount St. Joseph (OH)
College of Mount St. Vincent (NY)
College of Notre Dame of
    Maryland
College of Santa Fe (NM)
College of St. Rose (NY)
College of St. Scholastica (MN)
College of William and Mary (VA)
College of Wooster (OH)
Colorado College
Columbia College (SC)
Columbia Univ. (NY)
Concordia College (NY)
Concordia Coll.–Moorhead (MN)
Concordia Univ. (MI)
Connecticut College
Converse College (SC)
Cornell College (IA)
Cornell Univ. (NY)
Cornerstone Univ. (MI)
Culver-Stockton College (MO)
CUNY–Brooklyn College
CUNY–Hunter College
CUNY–Queens College
Daemen College (NY)
Dakota Wesleyan Univ. (SD)
Dana College (NE)
Dartmouth College (NH)
Davidson College (NC)
Davis and Elkins College (WV)
Defiance College (OH)
Denison Univ. (OH)
Depaul Univ. (IL)
Depauw Univ. (IN)
Dickinson College (PA)
Dominican Univ. (IL)

Dominican Univ. of California (CA)
Drake Univ. (IA)
Drew Univ. (NJ)
Drury Univ. (MO)
Duke Univ. (NC)
Earlham College (IN)
East Texas Baptist Univ.
Eastern Nazarene College (MA)
Eastern New Mexico Univ.
Eckerd College (FL)
Edgewood College (WI)
Elizabethtown College (PA)
Elmhurst College (IL)
Elon Univ. (NC)
Emmanuel College (MA)
Emory and Henry College (VA)
Emory Univ. (GA)
Erskine College (SC)
Evangel Univ. (MO)
Fairfield Univ. (CT)
Ferrum College (VA)
Florida Atlantic Univ.
Florida International Univ.
Florida Southern College
Florida State Univ.
Fordham Univ. (NY)
Franklin and Marshall College (PA)
Franklin College (IN)
Friends Univ. (KS)
Furman Univ. (SC)
Gallaudet Univ. (DC)
Gardner-Webb Univ. (NC)
George Fox Univ. (OR)
George Mason Univ. (VA)
George Washington Univ. (DC)
Georgetown College (KY)
Georgetown Univ. (DC)
Georgia State Univ.
Georgian Court Univ. (NJ)
Gettysburg College (PA)
Gonzaga Univ. (WA)
Goshen College (IN)
Goucher College (MD)
Graceland Univ. (IA)
Grand Canyon Univ. (AZ)
Grand View College (IA)
Greensboro College (NC)
Greenville College (IL)
Grinnell College (IA)
Grove City College (PA)
Guilford College (NC)
Gustavus Adolphus College (MN)
Hamilton College (NY)
Hamline Univ. (MN)
Hampden-Sydney College (VA)
Hampshire College (MA)
Harding Univ. (AR)
Hartwick College (NY)
Harvard Univ. (MA)
Hastings College (NE)
Haverford College (PA)
Heidelberg College (OH)
Hendrix College (AR)
High Point Univ. (NC)
Hillsdale College (MI)
Hiram College (OH)
Hobart and William Smith Colleges
    (NY)
Hofstra Univ. (NY)
Hollins Univ. (VA)
Holy Family Univ. (PA)

Holy Names Univ. (CA)
Hood College (MD)
Hope College (MI)
Houghton College (NY)
Houston Baptist Univ.
Howard Payne Univ. (TX)
Humboldt State Univ. (CA)
Huntingdon College (AL)
Huntington College (IN)
Illinois College
Illinois Wesleyan Univ.
Indiana Univ. of Pennsylvania
Indiana Univ.–Bloomington
Indiana Univ.–South Bend
Indiana Univ.–Purdue
    Univ.–Indianapolis
Indiana Wesleyan Univ.
Iona College (NY)
Iowa State Univ.
Jarvis Christian College (TX)
John Carroll Univ. (OH)
Judson College (AL)
Juniata College (PA)
Kalamazoo College (MI)
Kansas Wesleyan Univ.
Kentucky Christian College
Kentucky Wesleyan College
La Roche College (PA)
La Salle Univ. (PA)
La Sierra Univ. (CA)
Lafayette College (PA)
Lagrange College (GA)
Lakeland College (WI)
Lambuth Univ. (TN)
Lane College (TN)
Lawrence Univ. (WI)
Le Moyne College (NY)
Lebanon Valley College (PA)
Lees-Mcrae College (NC)
Lehigh Univ. (PA)
Lenoir-Rhyne College (NC)
Lewis and Clark College (OR)
Liberty Univ. (VA)
Lincoln Univ. (PA)
Lindenwood Univ. (MO)
Lindsey Wilson College (KY)
Linfield College (OR)
Loras College (IA)
Lourdes College (OH)
Loyola College In Maryland
Loyola Univ. New Orleans
Luther College (IA)
Lycoming College (PA)
Lynchburg College (VA)
Macalester College (MN)
Macmurray College (IL)
Manchester College (IN)
Manhattan College (NY)
Manhattanville College (NY)
Marian College (IN)
Mars Hill College (NC)
Martin Univ. (IN)
Marygrove College (MI)
Marylhurst Univ. (OR)
Marymount Univ. (VA)
Maryville College (TN)
Marywood Univ. (PA)
Mcdaniel College (MD)
Mckendree College (IL)
Mcmurry Univ. (TX)
Mercer Univ. (GA)

Mercyhurst College (PA)
Meredith College (NC)
Merrimack College (MA)
Messiah College (PA)
Methodist College (NC)
Miami Univ.–Oxford (OH)
Michigan State Univ.
Middlebury College (VT)
Millsaps College (MS)
Mississippi College
Missouri Baptist College
Molloy College (NY)
Monmouth College (IL)
Montclair State Univ. (NJ)
Moravian College (PA)
Morehouse College (GA)
Morningside College (IA)
Mount Holyoke College (MA)
Mount Marty College (SD)
Mount Mary College (WI)
Mount Mercy College (IA)
Mount Olive College (NC)
Mount St. Mary's College (CA)
Mount Union College (OH)
Muhlenberg College (PA)
Muskingum College (OH)
Nazareth College of Rochester
    (NY)
Nebraska Wesleyan Univ.
New York Univ.
Niagara Univ. (NY)
North Carolina State Univ.–Raleigh
North Carolina Wesleyan College
North Central College (IL)
North Greenville College (SC)
Northern Arizona Univ.
Northland College (WI)
Northwestern College (IA)
Northwestern Univ. (IL)
Notre Dame De Namur Univ. (CA)
Nyack College (NY)
Oakland City Univ. (IN)
Oakwood College (AL)
Oberlin College (OH)
Occidental College (CA)
Ohio Northern Univ.
Ohio State Univ.–Columbus
Ohio Univ.
Ohio Wesleyan Univ.
Oklahoma Baptist Univ.
Oklahoma City Univ.
Oklahoma Wesleyan Univ.
Olivet Nazarene Univ. (IL)
Otterbein College (OH)
Our Lady of the Lake Univ. (TX)
Pacific Lutheran Univ. (WA)
Paine College (GA)
Palm Beach Atlantic Univ. (FL)
Paul Quinn College (TX)
Penn. State Univ.–Univ. Park
Pepperdine Univ. (CA)
Pfeiffer Univ. (NC)
Pikeville College (KY)
Point Loma Nazarene Univ. (CA)
Pomona College (CA)
Presbyterian College (SC)
Princeton Univ. (NJ)
Principia College (IL)
Randolph-Macon College (VA)
Randolph-Macon Woman's College
    (VA)

Reed College (OR)
Reinhardt College (GA)
Rhodes College (TN)
Rice Univ. (TX)
Ripon College (WI)
Roanoke College (VA)
Rockhurst Univ. (MO)
Rollins College (FL)
Rosemont College (PA)
Rutgers–New Brunswick (NJ)
Sacred Heart Univ. (CT)
Salem College (NC)
Salve Regina Univ. (RI)
Samford Univ. (AL)
San Diego State Univ.
San Jose State Univ. (CA)
Santa Clara Univ. (CA)
Schreiner Univ. (TX)
Scripps College (CA)
Seattle Pacific Univ.
Seattle Univ.
Seton Hall Univ. (NJ)
Seton Hill Univ. (PA)
Sewanee–Univ. of the South (TN)
Shenandoah Univ. (VA)
Shorter College (GA)
Siena College (NY)
Simpson College (IA)
Simpson Univ. (CA)
Skidmore College (NY)
Southern Adventist Univ. (TN)
Southern Methodist Univ. (TX)
Southern Wesleyan Univ. (SC)
Southwest Missouri State Univ.
Southwestern Adventist Univ. (TX)
Southwestern Univ. (TX)
Spelman College (GA)
Spring Arbor Univ. (MI)
St. Andrews Presbyterian College
    (NC)
St. Francis College (NY)
St. Francis Univ. (PA)
St. Gregory's Univ. (OK)
St. John Fisher College (NY)
St. Joseph College (CT)
St. Joseph's Univ. (PA)
St. Lawrence Univ. (NY)
St. Martin's College (WA)
St. Mary's College (IN)
St. Mary's College of California
St. Mary's College of Maryland
St. Norbert College (WI)
St. Olaf College (MN)
St. Paul's College (VA)
St. Peter's College (NJ)
St. Thomas Univ. (FL)
St. Xavier Univ. (IL)
Stanford Univ. (CA)
Stetson Univ. (FL)
Stillman College (AL)
Stonehill College (MA)
SUNY–Albany
SUNY–Binghamton
SUNY–Stony Brook
Susquehanna Univ. (PA)
Swarthmore College (PA)
Sweet Briar College (VA)
Syracuse Univ. (NY)
Tabor College (KS)
Temple Univ. (PA)
Texas Christian Univ.

Texas Wesleyan Univ.
Thiel College (PA)
Thomas Edison State College (NJ)
Thomas More College (KY)
Touro College (NY)
Transylvania Univ. (KY)
Trevecca Nazarene Univ. (TN)
Trinity College (CT)
Tufts Univ. (MA)
Tulane Univ. (LA)
Union College (NE)
Union Univ. (TN)
Univ. of Alabama
Univ. of Arizona
Univ. of Bridgeport (CT)
Univ. of California–Berkeley
Univ. of California–Davis
Univ. of California–Los Angeles
Univ. of California–Riverside
Univ. of California–Santa Barbara
Univ. of Central Arkansas
Univ. of Colorado–Boulder
Univ. of Dayton (OH)
Univ. of Denver
Univ. of Detroit Mercy
Univ. of Dubuque (IA)
Univ. of Evansville (IN)
Univ. of Findlay (OH)
Univ. of Florida
Univ. of Georgia
Univ. of Hartford (CT)
Univ. of Hawaii–Hilo
Univ. of Hawaii–Manoa
Univ. of Ill.–Urbana-Champaign
Univ. of Indianapolis
Univ. of Iowa
Univ. of Judaism (CA)
Univ. of Kansas
Univ. of La Verne (CA)
Univ. of Mary (ND)
Univ. of Mary Hardin-Baylor (TX)
Univ. of Maryland–College Park
Univ. of Massachusetts–Amherst
Univ. of Miami (FL)
Univ. of Michigan–Ann Arbor
Univ. of Minnesota–Twin Cities
Univ. of Missouri–Columbia
Univ. of Mobile (AL)
Univ. of Nebraska–Omaha
Univ. of New Mexico
Univ. of N.C.–Chapel Hill
Univ. of North Carolina–Charlotte
Univ. of N.C.–Greensboro
Univ. of North Dakota
Univ. of Northern Iowa
Univ. of Oklahoma
Univ. of Oregon
Univ. of Pennsylvania
Univ. of Pittsburgh
Univ. of Puget Sound (WA)
Univ. of Redlands (CA)
Univ. of Richmond (VA)
Univ. of Rochester (NY)
Univ. of San Diego
Univ. of San Francisco
Univ. of Scranton (PA)
Univ. of South Carolina–Columbia
Univ. of South Florida
Univ. of Southern California
Univ. of Southern Mississippi
Univ. of St. Francis (IN)

Univ. of St. Thomas (MN)
Univ. of Tennessee
Univ. of Texas–Austin
Univ. of the Incarnate Word (TX)
Univ. of the Pacific (CA)
Univ. of Toledo (OH)
Univ. of Tulsa (OK)
Univ. of Vermont
Univ. of Virginia
Univ. of Washington
Univ. of West Florida
Univ. of Wisconsin–Eau Claire
Univ. of Wisconsin–Madison
Univ. of Wisconsin–Milwaukee
Univ. of Wisconsin–Oshkosh
Ursuline College (OH)
Vanguard Univ. of Southern
   California
Vassar College (NY)
Villanova Univ. (PA)
Virginia Commonwealth Univ.
Virginia Intermont College
Virginia Wesleyan College
Viterbo Univ. (WI)
Wabash College (IN)
Wake Forest Univ. (NC)
Warner Pacific College (OR)
Wartburg College (IA)
Washburn Univ. (KS)
Washington and Lee Univ. (VA)
Washington State Univ.
Washington Univ. In St. Louis
Wayland Baptist Univ. (TX)
Webster Univ. (MO)
Wellesley College (MA)
Wesleyan College (GA)
Wesleyan Univ. (CT)
West Chester Univ. of Pennsylvania
West Virginia Wesleyan College
Western Kentucky Univ.
Western Michigan Univ.
Westminster College (MO)
Westminster College (PA)
Westmont College (CA)
Wheaton College (MA)
Whitman College (WA)
Whittier College (CA)
Whitworth College (WA)
Willamette Univ. (OR)
William Jewell College (MO)
Williams College (MA)
Wingate Univ. (NC)
Wittenberg Univ. (OH)
Wofford College (SC)
Wright State Univ. (OH)
Yale Univ. (CT)
Yeshiva Univ. (NY)
Youngstown State Univ. (OH)

Religious Education

Asbury College (KY)
Azusa Pacific Univ. (CA)
Bethel College (IN)
Biola Univ. (CA)
Bryan College (TN)
Campbellsville Univ. (KY)
Cedarville Univ. (OH)
College of Mount St. Joseph (OH)
Columbia College (SC)

Columbia Union College (MD)
Concordia Univ. (OR)
Concordia Univ. (MI)
Concordia Univ.–Austin (TX)
Concordia Univ.–St. Paul (MN)
Cornerstone Univ. (MI)
Cumberland College (KY)
Dallas Baptist Univ.
Davis and Elkins College (WV)
East Texas Baptist Univ.
Eastern Nazarene College (MA)
Erskine College (SC)
Florida Southern College
Franciscan Univ. of Steubenville
   (OH)
Grace College and Seminary (IN)
Grace Univ. (NE)
Grand Canyon Univ. (AZ)
Harding Univ. (AR)
Holy Family Univ. (PA)
Houghton College (NY)
Howard Payne Univ. (TX)
Huntington College (IN)
Indiana Wesleyan Univ.
La Roche College (PA)
Liberty Univ. (VA)
Louisiana College
Loyola Univ. Chicago
Malone College (OH)
Marian College (IN)
Master's Coll. and Seminary (CA)
Mercyhurst College (PA)
Messiah College (PA)
Mid-Continent College (KY)
Missouri Baptist College
Morris College (SC)
Mount Mary College (WI)
North Park Univ. (IL)
Northwest College (WA)
Northwestern College (MN)
Northwestern College (IA)
Nyack College (NY)
Oklahoma Christian Univ.
Olivet Nazarene Univ. (IL)
Oral Roberts Univ. (OK)
Patten College (CA)
Pfeiffer Univ. (NC)
Presbyterian College (SC)
Regis Univ. (CO)
Seattle Pacific Univ.
Seton Hall Univ. (NJ)
Simpson Univ. (CA)
Southern Adventist Univ. (TN)
Southern Nazarene Univ. (OK)
Southwest Baptist Univ. (MO)
St. Edward's Univ. (TX)
St. Mary's Univ. of Minnesota
St. Vincent College (PA)
Sterling College (KS)
Taylor Univ. (IN)
Texas Wesleyan Univ.
Toccoa Falls College (GA)
Union College (NE)
Univ. of California–San Diego
Univ. of Judaism (CA)
Vanguard Univ. of Southern
   California
Viterbo Univ. (WI)
Wayland Baptist Univ. (TX)
West Virginia Wesleyan College
Western Baptist College (OR)

Westminster College (PA)
Wheaton College (IL)
Williams Baptist College (AR)

Religious/Sacred Music

Anderson College (SC)
Anderson Univ. (IN)
Aquinas College (MI)
Baylor Univ. (TX)
Bethel College (IN)
Bethel Univ. (MN)
Biola Univ. (CA)
Bluefield College (VA)
Calvin College (MI)
Campbellsville Univ. (KY)
Carson-Newman College (TN)
Cedarville Univ. (OH)
Charleston Southern Univ. (SC)
Clearwater Christian College (FL)
College of the Ozarks (MO)
Concordia College (NY)
Concordia Univ. (MI)
Concordia Univ. (NE)
Concordia Univ.–Austin (TX)
Concordia Univ.–St. Paul (MN)
Cumberland College (KY)
Dakota Wesleyan Univ. (SD)
Dordt College (IA)
East Texas Baptist Univ.
Eastern Nazarene College (MA)
Emmanuel College (GA)
Furman Univ. (SC)
Grace Univ. (NE)
Grand Canyon Univ. (AZ)
Greenville College (IL)
Hannibal-Lagrange College (MO)
Hardin-Simmons Univ. (TX)
Hope International Univ. (CA)
Howard Payne Univ. (TX)
Huntington College (IN)
Indiana Wesleyan Univ.
Jacksonville Univ. (FL)
John Brown Univ. (AR)
Judson College (IL)
Kent State Univ. (OH)
Lambuth Univ. (TN)
Lenoir-Rhyne College (NC)
Liberty Univ. (VA)
Lincoln Univ. (MO)
Louisiana College
Malone College (OH)
Marian College (IN)
Mississippi College
Missouri Baptist College
Newberry College (SC)
North Greenville College (SC)
Northwest College (WA)
Nyack College (NY)
Oklahoma City Univ.
Oklahoma Wesleyan Univ.
Oral Roberts Univ. (OK)
Ouachita Baptist Univ. (AR)
Palm Beach Atlantic Univ. (FL)
Pfeiffer Univ. (NC)
Point Loma Nazarene Univ. (CA)
Presbyterian College (SC)
Rider Univ. (NJ)
Samford Univ. (AL)
Seton Hill Univ. (PA)

Shorter College (GA)
Southeastern College of the
   Assemblies of God
Southern Nazarene Univ. (OK)
Southwest Baptist Univ. (MO)
Susquehanna Univ. (PA)
Texas Christian Univ.
Toccoa Falls College (GA)
Trevecca Nazarene Univ. (TN)
Union Univ. (TN)
Univ. of Mary Hardin-Baylor (TX)
Warner Southern College (FL)
Wartburg College (IA)
Wayland Baptist Univ. (TX)
Western Baptist College (OR)
William Carey College (MS)
William Jewell College (MO)

Romance Languages, Literatures, and Linguistics

Abilene Christian Univ. (TX)
Adams State College (CO)
Adelphi Univ. (NY)
Adrian College (MI)
Agnes Scott College (GA)
Albany State Univ. (GA)
Albertson College (ID)
Albertus Magnus College (CT)
Albion College (MI)
Albright College (PA)
Alfred Univ. (NY)
Allegheny College (PA)
Alma College (MI)
American International College
   (MA)
American Univ. (DC)
Amherst College (MA)
Anderson College (SC)
Anderson Univ. (IN)
Andrews Univ. (MI)
Angelo State Univ. (TX)
Anna Maria College (MA)
Antioch College (OH)
Appalachian State Univ. (NC)
Aquinas College (MI)
Arcadia Univ. (PA)
Arizona State Univ.
Arizona State Univ. West
Arkansas State Univ.
Armstrong Atlantic State Univ.
   (GA)
Asbury College (KY)
Assumption College (MA)
Auburn Univ. (AL)
Augsburg College (MN)
Augusta State Univ. (GA)
Augustana College (SD)
Augustana College (IL)
Austin College (TX)
Austin Peay State Univ. (TN)
Azusa Pacific Univ. (CA)
Baker Univ. (KS)
Baldwin-Wallace College (OH)
Ball State Univ. (IN)
Barnard College (NY)
Barry Univ. (FL)
Barton College (NC)
Bates College (ME)

Baylor Univ. (TX)
Belmont Univ. (TN)
Beloit College (WI)
Bemidji State Univ. (MN)
Benedictine College (KS)
Benedictine Univ. (IL)
Bennington College (VT)
Berea College (KY)
Berry College (GA)
Bethany College (WV)
Bethel College (KS)
Bethel Univ. (MN)
Biola Univ. (CA)
Black Hills State Univ. (SD)
Bloomsburg Univ. of Pennsylvania
Blue Mountain College (MS)
Bluffton Univ. (OH)
Boise State Univ. (ID)
Boston Univ.
Bowdoin College (ME)
Bowling Green State Univ. (OH)
Bradley Univ. (IL)
Brandeis Univ. (MA)
Brescia Univ. (KY)
Briar Cliff Univ. (IA)
Bridgewater College (VA)
Bridgewater State College (MA)
Brigham Young Univ.–Provo (UT)
Brown Univ. (RI)
Bryan College (TN)
Bryn Mawr College (PA)
Bucknell Univ. (PA)
Buena Vista Univ. (IA)
Buffalo State College
Butler Univ. (IN)
Cabrini College (PA)
Caldwell College (NJ)
California Baptist Univ.
California Lutheran Univ.
California State Polytechnic
    Univ.–Pomona
California State Univ.–Bakersfield
California State Univ.–Chico
California State Univ.–Dominguez
    Hills
California State Univ.–Fresno
California State Univ.–Fullerton
California State Univ.–Hayward
California State Univ.–Long Beach
California State Univ.–Los Angeles
California State Univ.–Northridge
California State Univ.–Sacramento
California State Univ.–San
    Bernardino
California State Univ.–San Marcos
California State Univ.–Stanislaus
California Univ. of Pennsylvania
Calvin College (MI)
Campbell Univ. (NC)
Canisius College (NY)
Capital Univ. (OH)
Cardinal Stritch Univ. (WI)
Carleton College (MN)
Carlow College (PA)
Carnegie Mellon Univ. (PA)
Carroll College (MT)
Carroll College (WI)
Carson-Newman College (TN)
Carthage College (WI)
Case Western Reserve Univ. (OH)
Catawba College (NC)

Catholic Univ. of America (DC)
Cedar Crest College (PA)
Cedarville Univ. (OH)
Centenary College of Louisiana
Central College (IA)
Central Connecticut State Univ.
Central Methodist Univ. (MO)
Central Michigan Univ.
Central Missouri State Univ.
Centre College (KY)
Chadron State College (NE)
Chapman Univ. (CA)
Charleston Southern Univ. (SC)
Chatham College (PA)
Chestnut Hill College (PA)
Cheyney Univ. of Pennsylvania
Chicago State Univ.
Christendom College (VA)
Christopher Newport Univ. (VA)
Claremont Mckenna College (CA)
Clarion Univ. of Pennsylvania
Clark Univ. (MA)
Clarke College (IA)
Cleveland State Univ.
Coastal Carolina Univ. (SC)
Coe College (IA)
Coker College (SC)
Colby College (ME)
Colgate Univ. (NY)
College of Charleston (SC)
College of Mount St. Vincent (NY)
College of New Jersey
College of Notre Dame of
    Maryland
College of St. Benedict (MN)
College of St. Catherine (MN)
College of St. Elizabeth (NJ)
College of St. Rose (NY)
College of the Holy Cross (MA)
College of the Ozarks (MO)
College of William and Mary (VA)
College of Wooster (OH)
Colorado College
Columbia College (SC)
Columbia Univ. (NY)
Columbus State Univ. (GA)
Concordia Coll.–Moorhead (MN)
Concordia Univ. (MI)
Concordia Univ. Wisconsin
Connecticut College
Converse College (SC)
Cornell College (IA)
Cornell Univ. (NY)
Creighton Univ. (NE)
CUNY–Baruch College
CUNY–Brooklyn College
CUNY–College of Staten Island
CUNY–Hunter College
CUNY–Lehman College
CUNY–Queens College
CUNY–York College
Daemen College (NY)
Dana College (NE)
Dartmouth College (NH)
David Lipscomb Univ. (TN)
Davidson College (NC)
Davis and Elkins College (WV)
Denison Univ. (OH)
Depaul Univ. (IL)
Depauw Univ. (IN)
Desales Univ. (PA)

Dickinson College (PA)
Dickinson State Univ. (ND)
Dominican Coll. of Blauvelt (NY)
Dominican Univ. (IL)
Dordt College (IA)
Drew Univ. (NJ)
Drury Univ. (MO)
Duke Univ. (NC)
Duquesne Univ. (PA)
Earlham College (IN)
East Carolina Univ. (NC)
East Stroudsburg Univ. of
    Pennsylvania
East Texas Baptist Univ.
Eastern Connecticut State Univ.
Eastern Kentucky Univ.
Eastern Mennonite Univ. (VA)
Eastern Michigan Univ.
Eastern New Mexico Univ.
Eastern Univ. (PA)
Eastern Washington Univ.
Eckerd College (FL)
Edgewood College (WI)
Edinboro Univ. of Pennsylvania
Elizabethtown College (PA)
Elmhurst College (IL)
Elms College (College of Our Lady
    of the Elms) (MA)
Elon Univ. (NC)
Emmanuel College (MA)
Emory and Henry College (VA)
Emory Univ. (GA)
Erskine College (SC)
Evangel Univ. (MO)
Fairfield Univ. (CT)
Fairleigh Dickinson Univ. (NJ)
Fayetteville State Univ. (NC)
Ferrum College (VA)
Fisk Univ. (TN)
Flagler College (FL)
Florida Atlantic Univ.
Florida International Univ.
Florida Southern College
Florida State Univ.
Fordham Univ. (NY)
Fort Lewis College (CO)
Franciscan Univ. of Steubenville
    (OH)
Franklin and Marshall College (PA)
Franklin College (IN)
Fresno Pacific Univ. (CA)
Friends Univ. (KS)
Furman Univ. (SC)
Gallaudet Univ. (DC)
Gardner-Webb Univ. (NC)
George Fox Univ. (OR)
George Washington Univ. (DC)
Georgetown College (KY)
Georgetown Univ. (DC)
Georgia College and State Univ.
Georgia Southern Univ.
Georgia State Univ.
Georgian Court Univ. (NJ)
Gettysburg College (PA)
Gonzaga Univ. (WA)
Gordon College (MA)
Goshen College (IN)
Goucher College (MD)
Grace College and Seminary (IN)
Graceland Univ. (IA)
Grambling State Univ. (LA)

Grand Valley State Univ. (MI)
Greensboro College (NC)
Greenville College (IL)
Grinnell College (IA)
Guilford College (NC)
Gustavus Adolphus College (MN)
Hamilton College (NY)
Hamline Univ. (MN)
Hampden-Sydney College (VA)
Hampshire College (MA)
Hampton Univ. (VA)
Hanover College (IN)
Hardin-Simmons Univ. (TX)
Harding Univ. (AR)
Harvard Univ. (MA)
Hastings College (NE)
Haverford College (PA)
Heidelberg College (OH)
Henderson State Univ. (AR)
Hendrix College (AR)
High Point Univ. (NC)
Hillsdale College (MI)
Hiram College (OH)
Hofstra Univ. (NY)
Hollins Univ. (VA)
Holy Family Univ. (PA)
Holy Names Univ. (CA)
Hood College (MD)
Hope College (MI)
Houghton College (NY)
Houston Baptist Univ.
Howard Payne Univ. (TX)
Howard Univ. (DC)
Humboldt State Univ. (CA)
Idaho State Univ.
Illinois College
Illinois State Univ.
Illinois Wesleyan Univ.
Immaculata Univ. (PA)
Indiana State Univ.
Indiana Univ. Northwest
Indiana Univ. of Pennsylvania
Indiana Univ. Southeast
Indiana Univ.–Bloomington
Indiana Univ.–South Bend
Indiana Univ.–Purdue Univ.–Fort
    Wayne
Indiana Univ.–Purdue
    Univ.–Indianapolis
Indiana Wesleyan Univ.
Iona College (NY)
Iowa State Univ.
Ithaca College (NY)
Jacksonville Univ. (FL)
Jamestown College (ND)
John Brown Univ. (AR)
John Carroll Univ. (OH)
Johns Hopkins Univ. (MD)
Johnson C. Smith Univ. (NC)
Juniata College (PA)
Kalamazoo College (MI)
Kean Univ. (NJ)
Keene State College (NH)
Kent State Univ. (OH)
Kentucky Wesleyan College
King College (TN)
King's College (PA)
Knox College (IL)
Kutztown Univ. of Pennsylvania
La Salle Univ. (PA)
La Sierra Univ. (CA)

Lafayette College (PA)
Lagrange College (GA)
Lake Forest College (IL)
Lake Superior State Univ. (MI)
Lakeland College (WI)
Lamar Univ. (TX)
Lambuth Univ. (TN)
Lander Univ. (SC)
Lane College (TN)
Lawrence Univ. (WI)
Le Moyne College (NY)
Lebanon Valley College (PA)
Lehigh Univ. (PA)
Lenoir-Rhyne College (NC)
Lewis and Clark College (OR)
Liberty Univ. (VA)
Lincoln Univ. (PA)
Lincoln Univ. (MO)
Lindenwood Univ. (MO)
Linfield College (OR)
Lock Haven Univ. of Pennsylvania
Long Island Univ.–Brooklyn (NY)
Long Island Univ.–C.W. Post
    Campus (NY)
Loras College (IA)
Louisiana College
Louisiana State Univ.–Baton Rouge
Louisiana State Univ.–Shreveport
Louisiana Tech Univ.
Loyola College In Maryland
Loyola Marymount Univ. (CA)
Loyola Univ. Chicago
Loyola Univ. New Orleans
Luther College (IA)
Lycoming College (PA)
Lynchburg College (VA)
Lyon College (AR)
Macalester College (MN)
Macmurray College (IL)
Madonna Univ. (MI)
Malone College (OH)
Manchester College (IN)
Manhattan College (NY)
Manhattanville College (NY)
Mansfield Univ. of Pennsylvania
Marian College of Fond Du Lac
    (WI)
Marietta College (OH)
Marist College (NY)
Marquette Univ. (WI)
Mars Hill College (NC)
Martin Univ. (IN)
Mary Baldwin College (VA)
Maryville College (TN)
Mcdaniel College (MD)
Mcmurry Univ. (TX)
Mcneese State Univ. (LA)
Mcpherson College (KS)
Mercer Univ. (GA)
Mercy College (NY)
Meredith College (NC)
Merrimack College (MA)
Messiah College (PA)
Methodist College (NC)
Metropolitan State College of
    Denver
Miami Univ.–Oxford (OH)
Michigan State Univ.
Middlebury College (VT)
Midland Lutheran College (NE)
Midwestern State Univ. (TX)

Millersville Univ. of Pennsylvania
Millikin Univ. (IL)
Mills College (CA)
Millsaps College (MS)
Minnesota State Univ.–Mankato
Minnesota State Univ.–Moorhead
Minot State Univ. (ND)
Mississippi College
Mississippi Univ. For Women
Missouri Southern State Univ.
Missouri Western State College
Molloy College (NY)
Monmouth College (IL)
Montana State Univ.–Billings
Montclair State Univ. (NJ)
Moravian College (PA)
Morehead State Univ. (KY)
Morehouse College (GA)
Morningside College (IA)
Mount Holyoke College (MA)
Mount Mary College (WI)
Mount St. Mary College (NY)
Mount St. Mary's College (CA)
Mount St. Mary's Univ. (MD)
Mount Union College (OH)
Mount Vernon Nazarene Univ.
   (OH)
Muhlenberg College (PA)
Murray State Univ. (KY)
Muskingum College (OH)
Nazareth College of Rochester
   (NY)
Nebraska Wesleyan Univ.
New Jersey City Univ.
New Mexico Highlands Univ.
New York Univ.
Newberry College (SC)
Niagara Univ. (NY)
Nicholls State Univ. (LA)
North Carolina A&T State Univ.
North Carolina Central Univ.
North Carolina State Univ.–Raleigh
North Central College (IL)
North Dakota State Univ.
North Georgia College and State
   Univ.
North Park Univ. (IL)
Northeastern Illinois Univ.
Northeastern State Univ. (OK)
Northeastern Univ. (MA)
Northern Arizona Univ.
Northern Illinois Univ.
Northern Kentucky Univ.
Northern Michigan Univ.
Northern State Univ. (SD)
Northwest Missouri State Univ.
Northwest Nazarene Univ. (ID)
Northwestern College (IA)
Northwestern Oklahoma State
   Univ.
Northwestern Univ. (IL)
Oakland Univ. (MI)
Oakwood College (AL)
Oberlin College (OH)
Occidental College (CA)
Ohio Northern Univ.
Ohio State Univ.–Columbus
Ohio Univ.
Ohio Wesleyan Univ.
Oklahoma Baptist Univ.
Oklahoma Christian Univ.

Oklahoma City Univ.
Oklahoma State Univ.
Olivet Nazarene Univ. (IL)
Oral Roberts Univ. (OK)
Oregon State Univ.
Otterbein College (OH)
Ouachita Baptist Univ. (AR)
Our Lady of the Lake Univ. (TX)
Pace Univ. (NY)
Pacific Lutheran Univ. (WA)
Pacific Union College (CA)
Pacific Univ. (OR)
Park Univ. (MO)
Peace College (NC)
Penn. State Univ.–Univ. Park
Pepperdine Univ. (CA)
Piedmont College (GA)
Pitzer College (CA)
Plymouth State Univ. (NH)
Point Loma Nazarene Univ. (CA)
Pomona College (CA)
Prairie View A&M Univ. (TX)
Presbyterian College (SC)
Princeton Univ. (NJ)
Providence College (RI)
Purdue Univ.–Calumet (IN)
Queens Univ. of Charlotte (NC)
Quinnipiac Univ. (CT)
Ramapo College of New Jersey
Randolph-Macon College (VA)
Randolph-Macon Woman's College
   (VA)
Reed College (OR)
Regis College (MA)
Regis Univ. (CO)
Rhode Island College
Rhodes College (TN)
Rice Univ. (TX)
Rider Univ. (NJ)
Ripon College (WI)
Rivier College (NH)
Roanoke College (VA)
Rockford College (IL)
Rockhurst Univ. (MO)
Rollins College (FL)
Roosevelt Univ. (IL)
Rosemont College (PA)
Russell Sage College (NY)
Rutgers–Camden (NJ)
Rutgers–New Brunswick (NJ)
Rutgers–Newark (NJ)
Sacred Heart Univ. (CT)
Saginaw Valley State Univ. (MI)
Salem College (NC)
Salem State College (MA)
Salisbury Univ. (MD)
Salve Regina Univ. (RI)
Sam Houston State Univ. (TX)
Samford Univ. (AL)
San Diego State Univ.
San Francisco State Univ.
San Jose State Univ. (CA)
Santa Clara Univ. (CA)
Scripps College (CA)
Seattle Pacific Univ.
Seattle Univ.
Seton Hall Univ. (NJ)
Seton Hill Univ. (PA)
Sewanee–Univ. of the South (TN)
Shaw Univ. (NC)
Shenandoah Univ. (VA)

Shippensburg Univ. of
   Pennsylvania
Shorter College (GA)
Siena College (NY)
Simmons College (MA)
Simpson College (IA)
Skidmore College (NY)
Slippery Rock Univ. of Pennsylvania
Sonoma State Univ. (CA)
South Carolina State Univ.
South Dakota State Univ.
Southeast Missouri State Univ.
Southeastern Louisiana Univ.
Southeastern Oklahoma State
   Univ.
Southern Adventist Univ. (TN)
Southern Arkansas Univ.
Southern Connecticut State Univ.
Southern Illinois Univ.–Carbondale
Southern Methodist Univ. (TX)
Southern Nazarene Univ. (OK)
Southern Oregon Univ.
Southern Univ. and A&M College
   (LA)
Southern Utah Univ.
Southwest Baptist Univ. (MO)
Southwest Minnesota State Univ.
   (MN)
Southwest Missouri State Univ.
Southwestern Adventist Univ. (TX)
Southwestern Univ. (TX)
Spring Arbor Univ. (MI)
Spring Hill College (AL)
St. Ambrose Univ. (IA)
St. Anselm College (NH)
St. Bonaventure Univ. (NY)
St. Cloud State Univ. (MN)
St. Edward's Univ. (TX)
St. Francis College (NY)
St. Francis Univ. (PA)
St. John Fisher College (NY)
St. John's Univ. (NY)
St. John's Univ. (MN)
St. Joseph College (CT)
St. Joseph's College, New York
St. Joseph's Univ. (PA)
St. Lawrence Univ. (NY)
St. Louis Univ.
St. Mary's College (IN)
St. Mary's College of California
St. Mary's Univ. of Minnesota
St. Mary's Univ. of San Antonio
St. Michael's College (VT)
St. Norbert College (WI)
St. Olaf College (MN)
St. Peter's College (NJ)
St. Thomas Aquinas College (NY)
St. Vincent College (PA)
St. Xavier Univ. (IL)
Stanford Univ. (CA)
State Univ. of West Georgia
Stephen F. Austin State Univ. (TX)
Stetson Univ. (FL)
Suffolk Univ. (MA)
Sul Ross State Univ. (TX)
SUNY College of Arts and
   Sciences–Geneseo
SUNY College–Brockport
SUNY College–Old Westbury
SUNY College–Oneonta
SUNY College–Potsdam

SUNY–Albany
SUNY–Binghamton
SUNY–Fredonia
SUNY–Plattsburgh
SUNY–Stony Brook
Susquehanna Univ. (PA)
Swarthmore College (PA)
Sweet Briar College (VA)
Syracuse Univ. (NY)
Talladega College (AL)
Tarleton State Univ. (TX)
Taylor Univ. (IN)
Temple Univ. (PA)
Texas A&M International Univ.
Texas A&M Univ.–College Station
Texas A&M Univ.–Corpus Christi
Texas A&M Univ.–Kingsville
Texas Christian Univ.
Texas Lutheran Univ.
Texas State Univ.–San Marcos
Texas Tech Univ.
Texas Wesleyan Univ.
The Citadel (SC)
Towson Univ. (MD)
Transylvania Univ. (KY)
Trinity Christian College (IL)
Trinity College (CT)
Truman State Univ. (MO)
Tufts Univ. (MA)
Tulane Univ. (LA)
Union College (NE)
Union Univ. (TN)
Univ. at Buffalo–SUNY
Univ. of Akron (OH)
Univ. of Alabama
Univ. of Arizona
Univ. of Arkansas
Univ. of Arkansas–Little Rock
Univ. of California–Berkeley
Univ. of California–Davis
Univ. of California–Irvine
Univ. of California–Los Angeles
Univ. of California–Riverside
Univ. of California–San Diego
Univ. of California–Santa Barbara
Univ. of Central Arkansas
Univ. of Central Florida
Univ. of Chicago
Univ. of Colorado–Boulder
Univ. of Colorado–Colorado
   Springs
Univ. of Colorado–Denver
Univ. of Connecticut
Univ. of Dallas
Univ. of Dayton (OH)
Univ. of Denver
Univ. of Evansville (IN)
Univ. of Findlay (OH)
Univ. of Florida
Univ. of Georgia
Univ. of Hawaii–Manoa
Univ. of Houston
Univ. of Houston–Downtown
Univ. of Illinois–Chicago
Univ. of Ill.–Urbana-Champaign
Univ. of Indianapolis
Univ. of Iowa
Univ. of Kansas
Univ. of Kentucky
Univ. of La Verne (CA)
Univ. of Louisiana–Monroe

Univ. of Louisville (KY)
Univ. of Maine–Orono
Univ. of Maine–Presque Isle
Univ. of Mary Hardin-Baylor (TX)
Univ. of Maryland–College Park
Univ. of Massachusetts–Amherst
Univ. of Massachusetts–Boston
Univ. of Mass.–Dartmouth
Univ. of Miami (FL)
Univ. of Michigan–Ann Arbor
Univ. of Michigan–Dearborn
Univ. of Michigan–Flint
Univ. of Minnesota–Duluth
Univ. of Minnesota–Morris
Univ. of Minnesota–Twin Cities
Univ. of Mississippi
Univ. of Missouri–Columbia
Univ. of Missouri–Kansas City
Univ. of Missouri–St. Louis
Univ. of Montana
Univ. of Nebraska–Kearney
Univ. of Nebraska–Lincoln
Univ. of Nebraska–Omaha
Univ. of Nevada–Las Vegas
Univ. of Nevada–Reno
Univ. of New Hampshire
Univ. of New Mexico
Univ. of New Orleans
Univ. of North Carolina–Asheville
Univ. of N.C.–Chapel Hill
Univ. of North Carolina–Charlotte
Univ. of N.C.–Greensboro
Univ. of North Carolina–Pembroke
Univ. of N.C.–Wilmington
Univ. of North Dakota
Univ. of North Florida
Univ. of North Texas
Univ. of Northern Colorado
Univ. of Northern Iowa
Univ. of Notre Dame (IN)
Univ. of Oklahoma
Univ. of Oregon
Univ. of Pennsylvania
Univ. of Pittsburgh
Univ. of Portland (OR)
Univ. of Puget Sound (WA)
Univ. of Redlands (CA)
Univ. of Rhode Island
Univ. of Richmond (VA)
Univ. of Rochester (NY)
Univ. of San Diego
Univ. of San Francisco
Univ. of Scranton (PA)
Univ. of South Carolina–Columbia
Univ. of South Carolina–Upstate
Univ. of South Dakota
Univ. of South Florida
Univ. of Southern California
Univ. of Southern Indiana
Univ. of Southern Maine
Univ. of St. Thomas (TX)
Univ. of St. Thomas (MN)
Univ. of Tampa (FL)
Univ. of Tennessee
Univ. of Tennessee–Martin
Univ. of Texas of the Permian Basin
Univ. of Texas–Arlington
Univ. of Texas–Austin
Univ. of Texas–Brownsville
Univ. of Texas–El Paso
Univ. of Texas–Pan American

Univ. of Texas–San Antonio
Univ. of Texas–Tyler
Univ. of the District of Columbia
Univ. of the Incarnate Word (TX)
Univ. of the Pacific (CA)
Univ. of Toledo (OH)
Univ. of Tulsa (OK)
Univ. of Utah
Univ. of Vermont
Univ. of Virginia
Univ. of Virginia–Wise
Univ. of Washington
Univ. of Wisconsin–Eau Claire
Univ. of Wisconsin–Green Bay
Univ. of Wisconsin–La Crosse
Univ. of Wisconsin–Madison
Univ. of Wisconsin–Milwaukee
Univ. of Wisconsin–Parkside
Univ. of Wisconsin–Stevens Point
Univ. of Wisconsin–Whitewater
Univ. of Wyoming
Ursinus College (PA)
Utah State Univ.
Utah Valley State College
Valdosta State Univ. (GA)
Valley City State Univ. (ND)
Valparaiso Univ. (IN)
Vanderbilt Univ. (TN)
Vanguard Univ. of Southern
   California
Vassar College (NY)
Villanova Univ. (PA)
Virginia Wesleyan College
Viterbo Univ. (WI)
Wabash College (IN)
Wagner College (NY)
Wake Forest Univ. (NC)
Walsh Univ. (OH)
Wartburg College (IA)
Washburn Univ. (KS)
Washington and Jefferson College
   (PA)
Washington and Lee Univ. (VA)
Washington College (MD)
Washington State Univ.
Washington Univ. In St. Louis
Wayland Baptist Univ. (TX)
Wayne State College (NE)
Wayne State Univ. (MI)
Weber State Univ. (UT)
Webster Univ. (MO)
Wellesley College (MA)
Wesleyan College (GA)
Wesleyan Univ. (CT)
West Chester Univ. of Pennsylvania
West Texas A&M Univ.
Western Carolina Univ. (NC)
Western Connecticut State Univ.
Western Illinois Univ.
Western Kentucky Univ.
Western Michigan Univ.
Western New Mexico Univ.
Western State College of Colorado
Western Washington Univ.
Westfield State College (MA)
Westminster College (PA)
Westminster College (MO)
Westmont College (CA)
Wheaton College (IL)
Wheeling Jesuit Univ. (WV)
Whitman College (WA)

Whittier College (CA)
Whitworth College (WA)
Widener Univ. (PA)
Wilkes Univ. (PA)
Willamette Univ. (OR)
William Jewell College (MO)
William Paterson Univ. of New
   Jersey
Williams College (MA)
Wilmington College (OH)
Wilson College (PA)
Wingate Univ. (NC)
Winston-Salem State Univ. (NC)
Wisconsin Lutheran College
Wittenberg Univ. (OH)
Wofford College (SC)
Worcester State College (MA)
Wright State Univ. (OH)
Xavier Univ. (OH)
Yale Univ. (CT)
Yeshiva Univ. (NY)
York College of Pennsylvania
Youngstown State Univ. (OH)

School Psychology

Gallaudet Univ. (DC)
Pittsburg State Univ. (KS)
SUNY–Oswego
Texas Wesleyan Univ.
Univ. of California–Riverside
Univ. of Wisconsin–River Falls
Western Illinois Univ.

Science Technologies/ Technicians

Bridgewater State College (MA)
Carlow College (PA)
Charleston Southern Univ. (SC)
Edward Waters College (FL)
Humboldt State Univ. (CA)
Kean Univ. (NJ)
Madonna Univ. (MI)
Northern Arizona Univ.
Univ. of Alaska–Anchorage
Univ. of Virginia–Wise
Univ. of Wisconsin–Stout

Science, Technology, and Society

Brown Univ. (RI)
Butler Univ. (IN)
Carnegie Mellon Univ. (PA)
Clark Univ. (MA)
Colby College (ME)
Cornell Univ. (NY)
Georgetown Univ. (DC)
Georgia Institute of Technology
Hampshire College (MA)
James Madison Univ. (VA)
La Salle Univ. (PA)
Lehigh Univ. (PA)
Massachusetts Institute of
   Technology
Michigan State Univ.
New Jersey Institute of Technology

North Carolina State Univ.–Raleigh
Northwestern Univ. (IL)
Pomona College (CA)
Prescott College (AZ)
Rutgers–Newark (NJ)
Scripps College (CA)
Slippery Rock Univ. of Pennsylvania
St. Cloud State Univ. (MN)
Stanford Univ. (CA)
Univ. of California–Davis
Univ. of Puget Sound (WA)
Vassar College (NY)
Wesleyan Univ. (CT)
Willamette Univ. (OR)
Worcester Polytechnic Institute
   (MA)

Security and Protective Services

Anna Maria College (MA)
Arkansas Tech Univ.
Eastern Michigan Univ.
La Roche College (PA)
North Dakota State Univ.
Point Park Univ. (PA)
Thomas Edison State College (NJ)
Tiffin Univ. (OH)
Virginia Commonwealth Univ.
York College of Pennsylvania

Slavic, Baltic and Albanian Languages, Literatures, and Linguistics

American Univ. (DC)
Amherst College (MA)
Arizona State Univ.
Barnard College (NY)
Bates College (ME)
Baylor Univ. (TX)
Beloit College (WI)
Boston Univ.
Bowdoin College (ME)
Bowling Green State Univ. (OH)
Brandeis Univ. (MA)
Brigham Young Univ.–Provo (UT)
Bryn Mawr College (PA)
Bucknell Univ. (PA)
Carleton College (MN)
Colby College (ME)
Colgate Univ. (NY)
College of the Holy Cross (MA)
Colorado College
Columbia Univ. (NY)
Concordia Coll.–Moorhead (MN)
Connecticut College
Cornell College (IA)
Cornell Univ. (NY)
CUNY–Brooklyn College
CUNY–Hunter College
CUNY–Lehman College
CUNY–Queens College
Dartmouth College (NH)
Dickinson College (PA)
Duke Univ. (NC)
Emory Univ. (GA)
Ferrum College (VA)
Florida State Univ.

Fordham Univ. (NY)
George Washington Univ. (DC)
Georgetown Univ. (DC)
Goucher College (MD)
Grinnell College (IA)
Harvard Univ. (MA)
Haverford College (PA)
Hofstra Univ. (NY)
Howard Univ. (DC)
Indiana Univ.–Bloomington
Juniata College (PA)
Kent State Univ. (OH)
Kutztown Univ. of Pennsylvania
La Salle Univ. (PA)
Lawrence Univ. (WI)
Lincoln Univ. (PA)
Long Island Univ.–Brooklyn (NY)
Loyola Univ. New Orleans
Madonna Univ. (MI)
Miami Univ.–Oxford (OH)
Michigan State Univ.
Middlebury College (VT)
New York Univ.
Northern Illinois Univ.
Northwestern Univ. (IL)
Oberlin College (OH)
Ohio State Univ.–Columbus
Ohio Univ.
Oklahoma State Univ.
Oral Roberts Univ. (OK)
Ouachita Baptist Univ. (AR)
Penn. State Univ.–Univ. Park
Pomona College (CA)
Princeton Univ. (NJ)
Reed College (OR)
Rice Univ. (TX)
Rider Univ. (NJ)
Rutgers–New Brunswick (NJ)
Salisbury Univ. (MD)
San Diego State Univ.
San Francisco State Univ.
Scripps College (CA)
Seattle Pacific Univ.
Sewanee–Univ. of the South (TN)
St. Louis Univ.
St. Olaf College (MN)
Stanford Univ. (CA)
SUNY–Albany
SUNY–Stony Brook
Swarthmore College (PA)
Syracuse Univ. (NY)
Temple Univ. (PA)
Trinity College (CT)
Truman State Univ. (MO)
Tufts Univ. (MA)
Tulane Univ. (LA)
Univ. of Alaska–Fairbanks
Univ. of Arizona
Univ. of California–Berkeley
Univ. of California–Davis
Univ. of California–Irvine
Univ. of California–Los Angeles
Univ. of California–Riverside
Univ. of California–San Diego
Univ. of California–Santa Barbara
Univ. of Chicago
Univ. of Denver
Univ. of Florida
Univ. of Georgia
Univ. of Hawaii–Manoa
Univ. of Illinois–Chicago

Univ. of Ill.–Urbana-Champaign
Univ. of Iowa
Univ. of Kansas
Univ. of Kentucky
Univ. of Maryland–College Park
Univ. of Massachusetts–Boston
Univ. of Michigan–Ann Arbor
Univ. of Minnesota–Twin Cities
Univ. of Missouri–Columbia
Univ. of Montana
Univ. of Nebraska–Lincoln
Univ. of New Hampshire
Univ. of New Mexico
Univ. of N.C.–Chapel Hill
Univ. of Northern Iowa
Univ. of Notre Dame (IN)
Univ. of Oklahoma
Univ. of Oregon
Univ. of Pennsylvania
Univ. of Pittsburgh
Univ. of Rochester (NY)
Univ. of South Carolina–Columbia
Univ. of South Florida
Univ. of Southern California
Univ. of Tennessee
Univ. of Texas–Arlington
Univ. of Texas–Austin
Univ. of Utah
Univ. of Vermont
Univ. of Virginia
Univ. of Washington
Univ. of Wisconsin–Madison
Univ. of Wisconsin–Milwaukee
Univ. of Wyoming
Vanderbilt Univ. (TN)
Vassar College (NY)
Wake Forest Univ. (NC)
Washington State Univ.
Wayne State Univ. (MI)
Wellesley College (MA)
Wesleyan Univ. (CT)
West Chester Univ. of Pennsylvania
Wheaton College (MA)
Williams College (MA)
Yale Univ. (CT)

Social and Philosophical Foundations of Education

Goddard College (VT)
Northwestern Univ. (IL)

Social Psychology

Atlantic Union College (MA)
Bellevue Univ. (NE)
Bennington College (VT)
Clarion Univ. of Pennsylvania
Florida Atlantic Univ.
Hannibal-Lagrange College (MO)
Maryville Univ. of St. Louis (MO)
Northwest Missouri State Univ.
Notre Dame De Namur Univ. (CA)
Our Lady of the Lake Univ. (TX)
Paine College (GA)
Park Univ. (MO)
Suffolk Univ. (MA)
SUNY–Oswego
Trinity College (DC)

Tufts Univ. (MA)
Univ. of California–Irvine
Walsh Univ. (OH)
Western Michigan Univ.

Social Sciences

Abilene Christian Univ. (TX)
Adams State College (CO)
Adelphi Univ. (NY)
Adrian College (MI)
Agnes Scott College (GA)
Albany State Univ. (GA)
Albertson College (ID)
Albertus Magnus College (CT)
Albright College (PA)
Alice Lloyd College (KY)
Allen Univ. (SC)
Alma College (MI)
Alvernia College (PA)
Alverno College (WI)
Anna Maria College (MA)
Aquinas College (MI)
Arizona State Univ. West
Asbury College (KY)
Atlantic Union College (MA)
Azusa Pacific Univ. (CA)
Bard College (NY)
Belhaven College (MS)
Bemidji State Univ. (MN)
Benedictine College (KS)
Benedictine Univ. (IL)
Bennington College (VT)
Berry College (GA)
Biola Univ. (CA)
Black Hills State Univ. (SD)
Bloomsburg Univ. of Pennsylvania
Blue Mountain College (MS)
Bluefield College (VA)
Bluefield State College (WV)
Bluffton Univ. (OH)
Boise State Univ. (ID)
Bowie State Univ. (MD)
Brescia Univ. (KY)
Brewton-Parker College (GA)
Briar Cliff Univ. (IA)
Brown Univ. (RI)
Buena Vista Univ. (IA)
Buffalo State College
Butler Univ. (IN)
Cal Poly–San Luis Obispo
California Lutheran Univ.
California State Polytechnic
    Univ.–Pomona
California State Univ.–Chico
California State Univ.–Fresno
California State Univ.–Los Angeles
California State Univ.–Monterey
    Bay
California State Univ.–Northridge
California State Univ.–Sacramento
California State Univ.–San
    Bernardino
California State Univ.–Stanislaus
California Univ. of Pennsylvania
Calvin College (MI)
Campbell Univ. (NC)
Campbellsville Univ. (KY)
Canisius College (NY)
Carleton College (MN)

Carnegie Mellon Univ. (PA)
Carthage College (WI)
Castleton State College (VT)
Central Christian College (KS)
Central College (IA)
Central Connecticut State Univ.
Central Methodist Univ. (MO)
Central Michigan Univ.
Central Washington Univ.
Centre College (KY)
Chaminade Univ. of Honolulu
Charleston Southern Univ. (SC)
Cheyney Univ. of Pennsylvania
Clarion Univ. of Pennsylvania
Clark Univ. (MA)
Cleveland State Univ.
Colby-Sawyer College (NH)
Colgate Univ. (NY)
College of St. Benedict (MN)
College of St. Catherine (MN)
College of St. Scholastica (MN)
College of the Southwest (NM)
Colorado Christian Univ.
Colorado State Univ.–Pueblo
Columbia College (SC)
Concordia College (NY)
Concordia Univ. (MI)
Concordia Univ.–Austin (TX)
Connecticut College
Cornell Univ. (NY)
CUNY–City College
CUNY–College of Staten Island
CUNY–Queens College
Curry College (MA)
Dakota Wesleyan Univ. (SD)
Delta State Univ. (MS)
Depaul Univ. (IL)
Dickinson State Univ. (ND)
Dominican Coll. of Blauvelt (NY)
Dominican Univ. (IL)
Dordt College (IA)
Dowling College (NY)
Duke Univ. (NC)
East Stroudsburg Univ. of
    Pennsylvania
East Texas Baptist Univ.
Eastern Mennonite Univ. (VA)
Eastern Michigan Univ.
Eastern New Mexico Univ.
Eastern Oregon Univ.
Edgewood College (WI)
Edinboro Univ. of Pennsylvania
Elmira College (NY)
Emporia State Univ. (KS)
Eureka College (IL)
Evangel Univ. (MO)
Ferrum College (VA)
Florida Atlantic Univ.
Florida Southern College
Florida State Univ.
Fordham Univ. (NY)
Fresno Pacific Univ. (CA)
Friends Univ. (KS)
Frostburg State Univ. (MD)
Gannon Univ. (PA)
Gardner-Webb Univ. (NC)
Georgetown Univ. (DC)
Georgia Southwestern State Univ.
Gettysburg College (PA)
Glenville State College (WV)
Graceland Univ. (IA)

Grand Valley State Univ. (MI)
Green Mountain College (VT)
Greensboro College (NC)
Hamline Univ. (MN)
Hampshire College (MA)
Harding Univ. (AR)
Harvard Univ. (MA)
Hawaii Pacific Univ.
Hobart and William Smith Colleges
    (NY)
Hofstra Univ. (NY)
Hope College (MI)
Hope International Univ. (CA)
Howard Payne Univ. (TX)
Humboldt State Univ. (CA)
Indiana Univ. of Pennsylvania
Indiana Univ.–Bloomington
Indiana Univ.–Kokomo
Indiana Wesleyan Univ.
Ithaca College (NY)
James Madison Univ. (VA)
Jamestown College (ND)
John Brown Univ. (AR)
Johns Hopkins Univ. (MD)
Johnson C. Smith Univ. (NC)
Juniata College (PA)
Kalamazoo College (MI)
Kansas State Univ.
Keene State College (NH)
Kentucky State Univ.
Keuka College (NY)
King College (TN)
Knox College (IL)
Kutztown Univ. of Pennsylvania
La Sierra Univ. (CA)
Lafayette College (PA)
Lake Forest College (IL)
Lake Superior State Univ. (MI)
Lasell College (MA)
Lehigh Univ. (PA)
Lemoyne-Owen College (TN)
Lenoir-Rhyne College (NC)
Letourneau Univ. (TX)
Lewis-Clark State College (ID)
Liberty Univ. (VA)
Lindsey Wilson College (KY)
Livingstone College (NC)
Lock Haven Univ. of Pennsylvania
Long Island Univ.–Brooklyn (NY)
Louisiana College
Loyola Univ. New Orleans
Macmurray College (IL)
Manhattan College (NY)
Marygrove College (MI)
Marylhurst Univ. (OR)
Mayville State Univ. (ND)
Mckendree College (IL)
Medaille College (NY)
Mesa State College (CO)
Metropolitan State College of
    Denver
Michigan State Univ.
Michigan Technological Univ.
Mid-Continent College (KY)
Midland Lutheran College (NE)
Millersville Univ. of Pennsylvania
Mills College (CA)
Minnesota State Univ.–Mankato
Minot State Univ. (ND)
Mississippi Univ. For Women
Mississippi Valley State Univ.

Missouri Baptist College
Monmouth Univ. (NJ)
Morehead State Univ. (KY)
Mount Aloysius College (PA)
Mount Holyoke College (MA)
Mount Marty College (SD)
Mount Mary College (WI)
Mount St. Mary College (NY)
Mount St. Mary's College (CA)
Mount St. Mary's Univ. (MD)
Muhlenberg College (PA)
National-Louis Univ. (IL)
Nazareth College of Rochester
    (NY)
New Jersey City Univ.
New Mexico Highlands Univ.
New York Institute of Technology
New York Univ.
North Central College (IL)
North Dakota State Univ.
North Georgia College and State
    Univ.
North Park Univ. (IL)
Northern Arizona Univ.
Northern Illinois Univ.
Northern Kentucky Univ.
Northern Michigan Univ.
Northwest Christian College (OR)
Northwestern College (MN)
Northwestern Univ. (IL)
Notre Dame De Namur Univ. (CA)
Nyack College (NY)
Oakland City Univ. (IN)
Oakland Univ. (MI)
Oglethorpe Univ. (GA)
Oklahoma Panhandle State Univ.
Oklahoma Wesleyan Univ.
Olivet College (MI)
Olivet Nazarene Univ. (IL)
Oral Roberts Univ. (OK)
Ouachita Baptist Univ. (AR)
Our Lady of Holy Cross Coll. (LA)
Our Lady of the Lake Univ. (TX)
Pace Univ. (NY)
Pikeville College (KY)
Pittsburg State Univ. (KS)
Plymouth State Univ. (NH)
Point Loma Nazarene Univ. (CA)
Point Park Univ. (PA)
Portland State Univ. (OR)
Prescott College (AZ)
Providence College (RI)
Purdue Univ.–North Central (IN)
Purdue Univ.–West Lafayette (IN)
Quinnipiac Univ. (CT)
Radford Univ. (VA)
Regis Univ. (CO)
Rensselaer Polytechnic Inst. (NY)
Rhode Island College
Robert Morris Univ. (PA)
Roberts Wesleyan College (NY)
Rockford College (IL)
Roger Williams Univ. (RI)
Roosevelt Univ. (IL)
Rosemont College (PA)
Rust College (MS)
Rutgers–New Brunswick (NJ)
Sam Houston State Univ. (TX)
Samford Univ. (AL)
San Diego State Univ.
San Francisco State Univ.

San Jose State Univ. (CA)
Shawnee State Univ. (OH)
Shimer College (IL)
Simon's Rock College of Bard
    (MA)
Simpson College (IA)
Simpson Univ. (CA)
Skidmore College (NY)
Sonoma State Univ. (CA)
South Carolina State Univ.
Southern Arkansas Univ.
Southern Illinois Univ.–Carbondale
Southern Methodist Univ. (TX)
Southern New Hampshire Univ.
Southern Oregon Univ.
Southern Wesleyan Univ. (SC)
Spalding Univ. (KY)
Spring Arbor Univ. (MI)
Spring Hill College (AL)
Springfield College (MA)
St. Andrews Presbyterian College
    (NC)
St. Augustine's College (NC)
St. Cloud State Univ. (MN)
St. Gregory's Univ. (OK)
St. John's Univ. (MN)
St. John's Univ. (NY)
St. Joseph College (CT)
St. Joseph's College, New York
St. Lawrence Univ. (NY)
St. Louis Univ.
St. Martin's College (WA)
St. Mary's Univ. of Minnesota
St. Mary-of-The-Woods Coll. (IN)
St. Peter's College (NJ)
St. Thomas Aquinas College (NY)
St. Xavier Univ. (IL)
Stephen F. Austin State Univ. (TX)
Stetson Univ. (FL)
Stevens Institute of Technology
    (NJ)
Suffolk Univ. (MA)
Sul Ross State Univ. (TX)
SUNY College–Old Westbury
SUNY–Binghamton
SUNY–Empire State College
SUNY–Purchase College
SUNY–Stony Brook
Swarthmore College (PA)
Syracuse Univ. (NY)
Tabor College (KS)
Talladega College (AL)
Texas A&M International Univ.
Texas A&M Univ.–College Station
Texas A&M Univ.–Commerce
Texas Wesleyan Univ.
The Franciscan Univ. (IA)
Thomas Edison State College
    (NJ)
Touro College (NY)
Towson Univ. (MD)
Transylvania Univ. (KY)
Trevecca Nazarene Univ. (TN)
Tri-State Univ. (IN)
Trinity College (DC)
Troy State Univ.–Troy (AL)
Tulane Univ. (LA)
Union College (NY)
Union College (NE)
Union Institute and Univ. (OH)
Union Univ. (TN)

United States Air Force Academy (CO)
Univ. of Akron (OH)
Univ. of Alabama–Birmingham
Univ. of Bridgeport (CT)
Univ. of California–Berkeley
Univ. of California–Irvine
Univ. of California–Riverside
Univ. of California–San Diego
Univ. of Central Florida
Univ. of Chicago
Univ. of Denver
Univ. of Findlay (OH)
Univ. of Hartford (CT)
Univ. of Houston–Downtown
Univ. of Illinois–Springfield
Univ. of Judaism (CA)
Univ. of Kentucky
Univ. of La Verne (CA)
Univ. of Maine–Augusta
Univ. of Maine–Farmington
Univ. of Maine–Fort Kent
Univ. of Maine–Presque Isle
Univ. of Mary (ND)
Univ. of Maryland–Univ. College
Univ. of Massachusetts–Amherst
Univ. of Massachusetts–Boston
Univ. of Michigan–Ann Arbor
Univ. of Michigan–Dearborn
Univ. of Michigan–Flint
Univ. of Minnesota–Morris
Univ. of Mobile (AL)
Univ. of Montevallo (AL)
Univ. of Nevada–Las Vegas
Univ. of North Dakota
Univ. of North Texas
Univ. of Northern Colorado
Univ. of Pennsylvania
Univ. of Pittsburgh
Univ. of Pittsburgh–Bradford
Univ. of Pittsburgh–Greensburg
Univ. of Pittsburgh–Johnstown
Univ. of Rhode Island
Univ. of Rio Grande (OH)
Univ. of Rochester (NY)
Univ. of Sioux Falls (SD)
Univ. of South Florida
Univ. of Southern Indiana
Univ. of Southern Maine
Univ. of St. Thomas (MN)
Univ. of Tampa (FL)
Univ. of Tennessee–Chattanooga
Univ. of Texas–Pan American
Univ. of Texas–San Antonio
Univ. of the Pacific (CA)
Univ. of Utah
Univ. of Washington
Univ. of West Florida
Univ. of Wisconsin–Green Bay
Univ. of Wisconsin–Platteville
Univ. of Wisconsin–River Falls
Univ. of Wisconsin–Stevens Point
Univ. of Wisconsin–Superior
Univ. of Wisconsin–Whitewater
Univ. of Wyoming
Upper Iowa Univ.
Utah State Univ.
Valley City State Univ. (ND)
Vanderbilt Univ. (TN)
Vanguard Univ. of Southern California

Vassar College (NY)
Villanova Univ. (PA)
Virginia Wesleyan College
Viterbo Univ. (WI)
Walsh Univ. (OH)
Warner Southern College (FL)
Washington State Univ.
Washington Univ. In St. Louis
Wayland Baptist Univ. (TX)
Wayne State College (NE)
Wayne State Univ. (MI)
Waynesburg College (PA)
Webster Univ. (MO)
West Liberty State College (WV)
West Texas A&M Univ.
Western Baptist College (OR)
Western Carolina Univ. (NC)
Western Connecticut State Univ.
Western Kentucky Univ.
Western Michigan Univ.
Western New Mexico Univ.
Western Oregon Univ.
Western State College of Colorado
Western Washington Univ.
Westminster College (UT)
Westmont College (CA)
William Carey College (MS)
Williams College (MA)
Wilson College (PA)
Wisconsin Lutheran College
Worcester Polytechnic Inst. (MA)
Wright State Univ. (OH)
York College of Pennsylvania
Youngstown State Univ. (OH)

Social Work

Abilene Christian Univ. (TX)
Adelphi Univ. (NY)
Adrian College (MI)
Alabama Agricultural and Mechanical Univ.
Alabama State Univ.
Albany State Univ. (GA)
Alvernia College (PA)
Anderson Univ. (IN)
Andrews Univ. (MI)
Anna Maria College (MA)
Appalachian State Univ. (NC)
Arizona State Univ.
Arizona State Univ. West
Arkansas State Univ.
Asbury College (KY)
Ashland Univ. (OH)
Atlantic Union College (MA)
Auburn Univ. (AL)
Augsburg College (MN)
Augusta State Univ. (GA)
Aurora Univ. (IL)
Austin Peay State Univ. (TN)
Avila Univ. (MO)
Azusa Pacific Univ. (CA)
Ball State Univ. (IN)
Barry Univ. (FL)
Barton College (NC)
Baylor Univ. (TX)
Bellevue Univ. (NE)
Belmont Univ. (TN)
Bemidji State Univ. (MN)
Benedict College (SC)

Bennett College (NC)
Bethany College (WV)
Bethany College (KS)
Bethel College (KS)
Bethel Univ. (MN)
Bloomsburg Univ. of Pennsylvania
Bluffton Univ. (OH)
Boise State Univ. (ID)
Bowie State Univ. (MD)
Bowling Green State Univ. (OH)
Bradley Univ. (IL)
Brescia Univ. (KY)
Briar Cliff Univ. (IA)
Bridgewater State College (MA)
Brigham Young Univ.–Hawaii
Brigham Young Univ.–Provo (UT)
Buena Vista Univ. (IA)
Buffalo State College
Cabrini College (PA)
California State Univ.–Chico
California State Univ.–Fresno
California State Univ.–Long Beach
California State Univ.–Los Angeles
California State Univ.–Sacramento
California State Univ.–San Bernardino
California Univ. of Pennsylvania
Calvin College (MI)
Campbell Univ. (NC)
Capital Univ. (OH)
Carlow College (PA)
Carthage College (WI)
Castleton State College (VT)
Catholic Univ. of America (DC)
Cazenovia College (NY)
Cedar Crest College (PA)
Cedarville Univ. (OH)
Central Connecticut State Univ.
Central Michigan Univ.
Central Missouri State Univ.
Central State Univ. (OH)
Chadron State College (NE)
Champlain College (VT)
Chapman Univ. (CA)
Chatham College (PA)
Christopher Newport Univ. (VA)
Clark Atlanta Univ.
Clarke College (IA)
Cleveland State Univ.
Coker College (SC)
College Misericordia (PA)
College of Mount St. Joseph (OH)
College of St. Benedict (MN)
College of St. Catherine (MN)
College of St. Rose (NY)
College of St. Scholastica (MN)
College of the Ozarks (MO)
Colorado State Univ.
Colorado State Univ.–Pueblo
Columbia College (MO)
Columbia College (SC)
Concord College (WV)
Concordia College (NY)
Concordia Coll.–Moorhead (MN)
Concordia Univ. (OR)
Concordia Univ. Wisconsin
Concordia Univ.–River Forest (IL)
Concordia Univ.–St. Paul (MN)
Coppin State Univ. (MD)
Cornerstone Univ. (MI)
Cumberland College (KY)

CUNY–College of Staten Island
CUNY–Lehman College
CUNY–York College
Daemen College (NY)
Dana College (NE)
David Lipscomb Univ. (TN)
Defiance College (OH)
Delaware State Univ.
Delta State Univ. (MS)
Dillard Univ. (LA)
Dominican Coll. of Blauvelt (NY)
Dordt College (IA)
East Carolina Univ. (NC)
East Central Univ. (OK)
East Tennessee State Univ.
Eastern Connecticut State Univ.
Eastern Kentucky Univ.
Eastern Mennonite Univ. (VA)
Eastern Michigan Univ.
Eastern Nazarene College (MA)
Eastern New Mexico Univ.
Eastern Univ. (PA)
Eastern Washington Univ.
Edinboro Univ. of Pennsylvania
Elizabeth City State Univ. (NC)
Elizabethtown College (PA)
Elms College (College of Our Lady of the Elms) (MA)
Ferris State Univ. (MI)
Ferrum College (VA)
Fitchburg State College (MA)
Florida Atlantic Univ.
Florida International Univ.
Florida State Univ.
Fordham Univ. (NY)
Fort Hays State Univ. (KS)
Fort Valley State Univ. (GA)
Franciscan Univ. of Steubenville (OH)
Franklin Pierce College (NH)
Freed-Hardeman Univ. (TN)
Fresno Pacific Univ. (CA)
Frostburg State Univ. (MD)
Gallaudet Univ. (DC)
Gannon Univ. (PA)
George Fox Univ. (OR)
George Mason Univ. (VA)
Georgia State Univ.
Georgian Court Univ. (NJ)
Gordon College (MA)
Goshen College (IN)
Grace College and Seminary (IN)
Grace Univ. (NE)
Graceland Univ. (IA)
Grambling State Univ. (LA)
Grand Valley State Univ. (MI)
Greenville College (IL)
Gwynedd-Mercy College (PA)
Hannibal-Lagrange College (MO)
Hardin-Simmons Univ. (TX)
Harding Univ. (AR)
Hawaii Pacific Univ.
Henderson State Univ. (AR)
Heritage College (WA)
Holy Family Univ. (PA)
Hood College (MD)
Hope College (MI)
Humboldt State Univ. (CA)
Huntington College (IN)
Idaho State Univ.
Illinois State Univ.

Indiana State Univ.
Indiana Univ. East
Indiana Univ.–Kokomo
Indiana Univ.–South Bend
Indiana Univ.-Purdue Univ.–Indianapolis
Indiana Wesleyan Univ.
Iona College (NY)
Jacksonville State Univ. (AL)
James Madison Univ. (VA)
Johnson C. Smith Univ. (NC)
Juniata College (PA)
Kansas State Univ.
Kean Univ. (NJ)
Kent State Univ. (OH)
Kentucky Christian College
Kentucky State Univ.
Keuka College (NY)
Kutztown Univ. of Pennsylvania
La Salle Univ. (PA)
La Sierra Univ. (CA)
Lewis Univ. (IL)
Limestone College (SC)
Lincoln Memorial Univ. (TN)
Lindenwood Univ. (MO)
Livingstone College (NC)
Lock Haven Univ. of Pennsylvania
Long Island Univ.–Brooklyn (NY)
Long Island Univ.–C.W. Post Campus (NY)
Longwood Univ. (VA)
Loras College (IA)
Louisiana College
Lourdes College (OH)
Loyola Univ. Chicago
Lubbock Christian Univ. (TX)
Luther College (IA)
Macmurray College (IL)
Madonna Univ. (MI)
Malone College (OH)
Manchester College (IN)
Mansfield Univ. of Pennsylvania
Marian College of Fond Du Lac (WI)
Marist College (NY)
Marquette Univ. (WI)
Mars Hill College (NC)
Marshall Univ. (WV)
Mary Baldwin College (VA)
Marygrove College (MI)
Marywood Univ. (PA)
Mcdaniel College (MD)
Medaille College (NY)
Mercy College (NY)
Mercyhurst College (PA)
Meredith College (NC)
Messiah College (PA)
Methodist College (NC)
Metropolitan State College of Denver
Miami Univ.–Oxford (OH)
Michigan State Univ.
Middle Tennessee State Univ.
Midwestern State Univ. (TX)
Miles College (AL)
Millersville Univ. of Pennsylvania
Millikin Univ. (IL)
Minnesota State Univ.–Mankato
Minnesota State Univ.–Moorhead
Minot State Univ. (ND)
Mississippi College

Mississippi State Univ.
Mississippi Valley State Univ.
Missouri Western State College
Molloy College (NY)
Monmouth Univ. (NJ)
Morehead State Univ. (KY)
Mount Mary College (WI)
Mount Mercy College (IA)
Mount St. Mary's College (CA)
Mountain State Univ. (WV)
Murray State Univ. (KY)
National-Louis Univ. (IL)
Nazareth College of Rochester (NY)
Nebraska Wesleyan Univ.
New Mexico State Univ.
New York Univ.
Norfolk State Univ. (VA)
North Carolina A&T State Univ.
North Carolina Central Univ.
North Carolina State Univ.–Raleigh
Northeastern Illinois Univ.
Northeastern State Univ. (OK)
Northern Arizona Univ.
Northern Kentucky Univ.
Northern Michigan Univ.
Northern State Univ. (SD)
Northwest Nazarene Univ. (ID)
Northwestern College (IA)
Northwestern Oklahoma State Univ.
Northwestern State Univ. of Louisiana
Nyack College (NY)
Oakwood College (AL)
Oglethorpe Univ. (GA)
Ohio Dominican Univ.
Ohio State Univ.–Columbus
Ohio Univ.
Olivet Nazarene Univ. (IL)
Oral Roberts Univ. (OK)
Our Lady of the Lake Univ. (TX)
Pacific Lutheran Univ. (WA)
Pacific Union College (CA)
Pacific Univ. (OR)
Philander Smith College (AR)
Pittsburg State Univ. (KS)
Plymouth State Univ. (NH)
Point Loma Nazarene Univ. (CA)
Prairie View A&M Univ. (TX)
Providence College (RI)
Quincy Univ. (IL)
Radford Univ. (VA)
Ramapo College of New Jersey
Regis College (MA)
Rhode Island College
Richard Stockton College of New Jersey
Roberts Wesleyan College (NY)
Rockford College (IL)
Rust College (MS)
Rutgers–Camden (NJ)
Rutgers–New Brunswick (NJ)
Rutgers–Newark (NJ)
Sacred Heart Univ. (CT)
Saginaw Valley State Univ. (MI)
Salem State College (MA)
Salisbury Univ. (MD)
Salve Regina Univ. (RI)
San Diego State Univ.
San Francisco State Univ.

San Jose State Univ. (CA)
Savannah State Univ. (GA)
Seattle Univ.
Seton Hall Univ. (NJ)
Seton Hill Univ. (PA)
Shaw Univ. (NC)
Shepherd Univ. (WV)
Shippensburg Univ. of Pennsylvania
Siena College (NY)
Skidmore College (NY)
Slippery Rock Univ. of Pennsylvania
South Carolina State Univ.
Southeast Missouri State Univ.
Southeastern College of the Assemblies of God
Southeastern Louisiana Univ.
Southern Adventist Univ. (TN)
Southern Arkansas Univ.
Southern Connecticut State Univ.
Southern Illinois Univ.–Carbondale
Southern Illinois Univ.–Edwardsville
Southern Univ. and A&M College (LA)
Southwest Minnesota State Univ. (MN)
Southwest Missouri State Univ.
Southwestern Adventist Univ. (TX)
Southwestern Oklahoma State Univ.
Spalding Univ. (KY)
Spring Arbor Univ. (MI)
Springfield College (MA)
St. Cloud State Univ. (MN)
St. Edward's Univ. (TX)
St. Francis Univ. (PA)
St. John's Univ. (MN)
St. Joseph College (CT)
St. Joseph's College (IN)
St. Leo Univ. (FL)
St. Louis Univ.
St. Mary's College (IN)
St. Olaf College (MN)
Stephen F. Austin State Univ. (TX)
SUNY College–Brockport
SUNY–Albany
SUNY–Fredonia
SUNY–Oswego
SUNY–Plattsburgh
SUNY–Stony Brook
Syracuse Univ. (NY)
Tarleton State Univ. (TX)
Taylor Univ. (IN)
Temple Univ. (PA)
Tennessee State Univ.
Tennessee Wesleyan College
Texas A&M International Univ.
Texas A&M Univ.–Commerce
Texas A&M Univ.–Kingsville
Texas Christian Univ.
Texas College
Texas State Univ.–San Marcos
Texas Tech Univ.
Texas Woman's Univ.
Thomas Univ. (GA)
Trevecca Nazarene Univ. (TN)
Trinity Christian College (IL)
Troy State Univ.–Troy (AL)
Tulane Univ. (LA)
Tuskegee Univ. (AL)

Union College (NE)
Union Institute and Univ. (OH)
Union Univ. (TN)
Univ. of Akron (OH)
Univ. of Alabama
Univ. of Alabama–Birmingham
Univ. of Alaska–Anchorage
Univ. of Alaska–Fairbanks
Univ. of Arkansas
Univ. of Arkansas–Little Rock
Univ. of Arkansas–Monticello
Univ. of Arkansas–Pine Bluff
Univ. of California–Berkeley
Univ. of Central Florida
Univ. of Detroit Mercy
Univ. of Findlay (OH)
Univ. of Georgia
Univ. of Hawaii–Manoa
Univ. of Illinois–Chicago
Univ. of Illinois–Springfield
Univ. of Indianapolis
Univ. of Iowa
Univ. of Kansas
Univ. of Kentucky
Univ. of Louisiana–Monroe
Univ. of Maine–Orono
Univ. of Maine–Presque Isle
Univ. of Mary (ND)
Univ. of Mary Hardin-Baylor (TX)
Univ. of Maryland–Baltimore County
Univ. of Memphis
Univ. of Michigan–Flint
Univ. of Mississippi
Univ. of Missouri–Columbia
Univ. of Missouri–St. Louis
Univ. of Montana
Univ. of Montevallo (AL)
Univ. of Nebraska–Kearney
Univ. of Nebraska–Omaha
Univ. of Nevada–Las Vegas
Univ. of Nevada–Reno
Univ. of New Hampshire
Univ. of North Alabama
Univ. of North Carolina–Charlotte
Univ. of N.C.–Greensboro
Univ. of North Carolina–Pembroke
Univ. of N.C.–Wilmington
Univ. of North Dakota
Univ. of North Texas
Univ. of Northern Iowa
Univ. of Oklahoma
Univ. of Pittsburgh
Univ. of Portland (OR)
Univ. of Rio Grande (OH)
Univ. of Sioux Falls (SD)
Univ. of South Alabama
Univ. of South Florida
Univ. of Southern Indiana
Univ. of Southern Maine
Univ. of Southern Mississippi
Univ. of St. Francis (IL)
Univ. of St. Francis (IN)
Univ. of St. Thomas (MN)
Univ. of Tennessee
Univ. of Tennessee–Martin
Univ. of Texas of the Permian Basin
Univ. of Texas–Arlington
Univ. of Texas–Austin
Univ. of Texas–El Paso
Univ. of Texas–Pan American

Univ. of the District of Columbia
Univ. of Toledo (OH)
Univ. of Utah
Univ. of Vermont
Univ. of Washington
Univ. of West Florida
Univ. of Wisconsin–Eau Claire
Univ. of Wisconsin–Madison
Univ. of Wisconsin–Milwaukee
Univ. of Wisconsin–Oshkosh
Univ. of Wisconsin–River Falls
Univ. of Wisconsin–Superior
Univ. of Wisconsin–Whitewater
Univ. of Wyoming
Ursuline College (OH)
Utah State Univ.
Valparaiso Univ. (IN)
Virginia Commonwealth Univ.
Virginia Intermont College
Virginia State Univ.
Viterbo Univ. (WI)
Warner Pacific College (OR)
Warner Southern College (FL)
Wartburg College (IA)
Washburn Univ. (KS)
Wayne State Univ. (MI)
Weber State Univ. (UT)
West Chester Univ. of Pennsylvania
West Texas A&M Univ.
West Virginia State Univ.
West Virginia Univ.
Western Carolina Univ. (NC)
Western Connecticut State Univ.
Western Illinois Univ.
Western Kentucky Univ.
Western Michigan Univ.
Western New England College (MA)
Western New Mexico Univ.
Westfield State College (MA)
Wheelock College (MA)
Whittier College (CA)
Wichita State Univ. (KS)
Widener Univ. (PA)
Wilberforce Univ. (OH)
William Woods Univ. (MO)
Wilmington College (OH)
Winston-Salem State Univ. (NC)
Winthrop Univ. (SC)
Wright State Univ. (OH)
Xavier Univ. (OH)
Youngstown State Univ. (OH)

Sociology

Abilene Christian Univ. (TX)
Adams State College (CO)
Adelphi Univ. (NY)
Adrian College (MI)
Alabama Agricultural and Mechanical Univ.
Alabama State Univ.
Albany State Univ. (GA)
Albertus Magnus College (CT)
Albion College (MI)
Albright College (PA)
Alcorn State Univ. (MS)
Alfred Univ. (NY)
Alma College (MI)
Alverno College (WI)

American Univ. (DC)
Amherst College (MA)
Anderson Univ. (IN)
Andrews Univ. (MI)
Angelo State Univ. (TX)
Appalachian State Univ. (NC)
Aquinas College (MI)
Arcadia Univ. (PA)
Arizona State Univ.
Arizona State Univ. West
Arkansas State Univ.
Arkansas Tech Univ.
Asbury College (KY)
Ashland Univ. (OH)
Assumption College (MA)
Auburn Univ. (AL)
Auburn Univ.–Montgomery (AL)
Augsburg College (MN)
Augusta State Univ. (GA)
Augustana College (SD)
Augustana College (IL)
Aurora Univ. (IL)
Austin College (TX)
Austin Peay State Univ. (TN)
Averett Univ. (VA)
Avila Univ. (MO)
Azusa Pacific Univ. (CA)
Baker Univ. (KS)
Baldwin-Wallace College (OH)
Ball State Univ. (IN)
Barber Scotia College (NC)
Barnard College (NY)
Barry Univ. (FL)
Bates College (ME)
Baylor Univ. (TX)
Bellarmine Univ. (KY)
Bellevue Univ. (NE)
Belmont Abbey College (NC)
Belmont Univ. (TN)
Beloit College (WI)
Bemidji State Univ. (MN)
Benedict College (SC)
Benedictine College (KS)
Benedictine Univ. (IL)
Bennett College (NC)
Bennington College (VT)
Berea College (KY)
Bethel College (IN)
Bethel Univ. (MN)
Bethune-Cookman College (FL)
Biola Univ. (CA)
Black Hills State Univ. (SD)
Bloomfield College (NJ)
Bloomsburg Univ. of Pennsylvania
Bluffton Univ. (OH)
Boise State Univ. (ID)
Boston Univ.
Bowdoin College (ME)
Bowie State Univ. (MD)
Bowling Green State Univ. (OH)
Bradley Univ. (IL)
Brandeis Univ. (MA)
Brewton-Parker College (GA)
Briar Cliff Univ. (IA)
Bridgewater College (VA)
Bridgewater State College (MA)
Brigham Young Univ.–Provo (UT)
Brown Univ. (RI)
Bryn Mawr College (PA)
Bucknell Univ. (PA)
Buena Vista Univ. (IA)

Butler Univ. (IN)
Cabrini College (PA)
Caldwell College (NJ)
California Baptist Univ.
California Lutheran Univ.
California State Polytechnic
    Univ.–Pomona
California State Univ.–Bakersfield
California State Univ.–Chico
California State Univ.–Fresno
California State Univ.–Fullerton
California State Univ.–Hayward
California State Univ.–Long Beach
California State Univ.–Los Angeles
California State Univ.–Northridge
California State Univ.–Sacramento
California State Univ.–San
    Bernardino
California State Univ.–San Marcos
California State Univ.–Stanislaus
Calvin College (MI)
Cameron Univ. (OK)
Campbellsville Univ. (KY)
Canisius College (NY)
Capital Univ. (OH)
Carlow College (PA)
Carroll College (WI)
Carroll College (MT)
Carson-Newman College (TN)
Carthage College (WI)
Case Western Reserve Univ. (OH)
Castleton State College (VT)
Catawba College (NC)
Catholic Univ. of America (DC)
Cedarville Univ. (OH)
Centenary College (NJ)
Centenary College of Louisiana
Central College (IA)
Central Connecticut State Univ.
Central Methodist Univ. (MO)
Central Michigan Univ.
Central Missouri State Univ.
Central State Univ. (OH)
Central Washington Univ.
Chadron State College (NE)
Chapman Univ. (CA)
Charleston Southern Univ. (SC)
Chestnut Hill College (PA)
Chicago State Univ.
Christopher Newport Univ. (VA)
Claflin Univ. (SC)
Clarion Univ. of Pennsylvania
Clark Atlanta Univ.
Clark Univ. (MA)
Clarke College (IA)
Clarkson Univ. (NY)
Cleveland State Univ.
Coastal Carolina Univ. (SC)
Coe College (IA)
Coker College (SC)
Colby College (ME)
Colgate Univ. (NY)
College of Charleston (SC)
College of Mount St. Joseph (OH)
College of Mount St. Vincent (NY)
College of New Jersey
College of St. Benedict (MN)
College of St. Catherine (MN)
College of St. Elizabeth (NJ)
College of St. Rose (NY)
College of the Holy Cross (MA)

College of the Ozarks (MO)
College of William and Mary (VA)
College of Wooster (OH)
Colorado College
Colorado State Univ.
Colorado State Univ.–Pueblo
Columbia College (MO)
Columbia Univ. (NY)
Columbus State Univ. (GA)
Concord College (WV)
Concordia Coll.–Moorhead (MN)
Concordia Univ. (MI)
Concordia Univ.–River Forest (IL)
Concordia Univ.–St. Paul (MN)
Connecticut College
Cornell College (IA)
Cornell Univ. (NY)
Cornerstone Univ. (MI)
Covenant College (GA)
Creighton Univ. (NE)
Cumberland Univ. (TN)
CUNY–Baruch College
CUNY–Brooklyn College
CUNY–City College
CUNY–Hunter College
CUNY–Lehman College
CUNY–Queens College
CUNY–York College
Curry College (MA)
Dakota Wesleyan Univ. (SD)
Dallas Baptist Univ.
Dartmouth College (NH)
Davidson College (NC)
Davis and Elkins College (WV)
Delaware State Univ.
Denison Univ. (OH)
Depaul Univ. (IL)
Depauw Univ. (IN)
Dickinson College (PA)
Dillard Univ. (LA)
Dominican Univ. (IL)
Dowling College (NY)
Drake Univ. (IA)
Drew Univ. (NJ)
Drexel Univ. (PA)
Drury Univ. (MO)
Duke Univ. (NC)
Duquesne Univ. (PA)
East Carolina Univ. (NC)
East Central Univ. (OK)
East Stroudsburg Univ. of
    Pennsylvania
East Tennessee State Univ.
Eastern Connecticut State Univ.
Eastern Illinois Univ.
Eastern Kentucky Univ.
Eastern Mennonite Univ. (VA)
Eastern Michigan Univ.
Eastern Nazarene College (MA)
Eastern New Mexico Univ.
Eastern Univ. (PA)
Eckerd College (FL)
Edgewood College (WI)
Edinboro Univ. of Pennsylvania
Edward Waters College (FL)
Elizabeth City State Univ. (NC)
Elizabethtown College (PA)
Elmhurst College (IL)
Elms College (College of Our Lady
    of the Elms) (MA)
Elon Univ. (NC)

Emmanuel College (MA)
Emory and Henry College (VA)
Emory Univ. (GA)
Emporia State Univ. (KS)
Evangel Univ. (MO)
Evergreen State College (WA)
Excelsior College (NY)
Fairfield Univ. (CT)
Fairleigh Dickinson Univ. (NJ)
Fairmont State Univ. (WV)
Fayetteville State Univ. (NC)
Ferris State Univ. (MI)
Fisk Univ. (TN)
Fitchburg State College (MA)
Flagler College (FL)
Florida Atlantic Univ.
Florida International Univ.
Florida Memorial College
Florida Southern College
Florida State Univ.
Fordham Univ. (NY)
Fort Hays State Univ. (KS)
Fort Lewis College (CO)
Framingham State College (MA)
Francis Marion Univ. (SC)
Franciscan Univ. of Steubenville
    (OH)
Franklin and Marshall College (PA)
Franklin College (IN)
Franklin Pierce College (NH)
Fresno Pacific Univ. (CA)
Friends Univ. (KS)
Furman Univ. (SC)
Gallaudet Univ. (DC)
Gardner-Webb Univ. (NC)
Geneva College (PA)
George Fox Univ. (OR)
George Mason Univ. (VA)
George Washington Univ. (DC)
Georgetown College (KY)
Georgetown Univ. (DC)
Georgia College and State Univ.
Georgia Southern Univ.
Georgia State Univ.
Georgian Court Univ. (NJ)
Gettysburg College (PA)
Gonzaga Univ. (WA)
Gordon College (MA)
Goshen College (IN)
Goucher College (MD)
Grace College and Seminary (IN)
Graceland Univ. (IA)
Grambling State Univ. (LA)
Grand Canyon Univ. (AZ)
Greensboro College (NC)
Greenville College (IL)
Grinnell College (IA)
Grove City College (PA)
Guilford College (NC)
Gustavus Adolphus College (MN)
Gwynedd-Mercy College (PA)
Hamilton College (NY)
Hamline Univ. (MN)
Hampshire College (MA)
Hampton Univ. (VA)
Hanover College (IN)
Hardin-Simmons Univ. (TX)
Hartwick College (NY)
Harvard Univ. (MA)
Hastings College (NE)
Haverford College (PA)

Hawaii Pacific Univ.
Henderson State Univ. (AR)
Hendrix College (AR)
High Point Univ. (NC)
Hillsdale College (MI)
Hiram College (OH)
Hobart and William Smith Colleges
    (NY)
Hofstra Univ. (NY)
Hollins Univ. (VA)
Holy Family Univ. (PA)
Holy Names Univ. (CA)
Hood College (MD)
Hope College (MI)
Houghton College (NY)
Houston Baptist Univ.
Howard Payne Univ. (TX)
Howard Univ. (DC)
Humboldt State Univ. (CA)
Huntington College (IN)
Huston-Tillotson College (TX)
Idaho State Univ.
Illinois College
Illinois State Univ.
Illinois Wesleyan Univ.
Immaculata Univ. (PA)
Indiana State Univ.
Indiana Univ. East
Indiana Univ. Northwest
Indiana Univ. of Pennsylvania
Indiana Univ. Southeast
Indiana Univ.–Bloomington
Indiana Univ.–Kokomo
Indiana Univ.–South Bend
Indiana Univ.-Purdue Univ.–Fort
    Wayne
Indiana Univ.-Purdue
    Univ.–Indianapolis
Indiana Wesleyan Univ.
Iona College (NY)
Iowa State Univ.
Ithaca College (NY)
Jacksonville State Univ. (AL)
Jacksonville Univ. (FL)
James Madison Univ. (VA)
Jarvis Christian College (TX)
John Carroll Univ. (OH)
Johns Hopkins Univ. (MD)
Johnson C. Smith Univ. (NC)
Judson College (IL)
Juniata College (PA)
Kalamazoo College (MI)
Kansas State Univ.
Kansas Wesleyan Univ.
Kean Univ. (NJ)
Keene State College (NH)
Kennesaw State Univ. (GA)
Kent State Univ. (OH)
Kentucky State Univ.
Kentucky Wesleyan College
Keuka College (NY)
King's College (PA)
Kutztown Univ. of Pennsylvania
La Roche College (PA)
La Salle Univ. (PA)
Lagrange College (GA)
Lake Forest College (IL)
Lake Superior State Univ. (MI)
Lakeland College (WI)
Lamar Univ. (TX)
Lambuth Univ. (TN)

Lander Univ. (SC)
Lane College (TN)
Lasell College (MA)
Le Moyne College (NY)
Lebanon Valley College (PA)
Lees-Mcrae College (NC)
Lehigh Univ. (PA)
Lemoyne-Owen College (TN)
Lenoir-Rhyne College (NC)
Lewis and Clark College (OR)
Lincoln Univ. (PA)
Lincoln Univ. (MO)
Lindenwood Univ. (MO)
Linfield College (OR)
Livingstone College (NC)
Lock Haven Univ. of Pennsylvania
Long Island Univ.–Brooklyn (NY)
Long Island Univ.–C.W. Post
    Campus (NY)
Long Island Univ.–Southampton
    College (NY)
Longwood Univ. (VA)
Loras College (IA)
Louisiana College
Louisiana State Univ.–Baton Rouge
Louisiana State Univ.–Shreveport
Louisiana Tech Univ.
Lourdes College (OH)
Loyola College In Maryland
Loyola Marymount Univ. (CA)
Loyola Univ. Chicago
Loyola Univ. New Orleans
Luther College (IA)
Lycoming College (PA)
Lynchburg College (VA)
Macalester College (MN)
Madonna Univ. (MI)
Manchester College (IN)
Manhattan College (NY)
Manhattanville College (NY)
Mansfield Univ. of Pennsylvania
Marian College (IN)
Marlboro College (VT)
Marquette Univ. (WI)
Mars Hill College (NC)
Marshall Univ. (WV)
Martin Univ. (IN)
Mary Baldwin College (VA)
Marylhurst Univ. (OR)
Marymount Manhattan College
    (NY)
Marymount Univ. (VA)
Maryville College (TN)
Maryville Univ. of St. Louis (MO)
Marywood Univ. (PA)
Mcdaniel College (MD)
Mckendree College (IL)
Mcmurry Univ. (TX)
Mcneese State Univ. (LA)
Mcpherson College (KS)
Mercer Univ. (GA)
Mercyhurst College (PA)
Meredith College (NC)
Merrimack College (MA)
Mesa State College (CO)
Messiah College (PA)
Methodist College (NC)
Metropolitan State College of
    Denver
Miami Univ.–Oxford (OH)
Michigan State Univ.

Middle Tennessee State Univ.
Middlebury College (VT)
Midland Lutheran College (NE)
Midwestern State Univ. (TX)
Millersville Univ. of Pennsylvania
Milligan College (TN)
Millikin Univ. (IL)
Mills College (CA)
Millsaps College (MS)
Minnesota State Univ.–Mankato
Minnesota State Univ.–Moorhead
Minot State Univ. (ND)
Mississippi College
Mississippi State Univ.
Mississippi Valley State Univ.
Missouri Southern State Univ.
Missouri Valley College
Molloy College (NY)
Monmouth College (IL)
Monmouth Univ. (NJ)
Montana State Univ.–Billings
Montana State Univ.–Bozeman
Montclair State Univ. (NJ)
Moravian College (PA)
Morehead State Univ. (KY)
Morehouse College (GA)
Morgan State Univ. (MD)
Morris College (SC)
Mount Holyoke College (MA)
Mount Mercy College (IA)
Mount St. Mary College (NY)
Mount St. Mary's College (CA)
Mount St. Mary's Univ. (MD)
Mount Union College (OH)
Mount Vernon Nazarene Univ.
    (OH)
Muhlenberg College (PA)
Murray State Univ. (KY)
Muskingum College (OH)
Nazareth College of Rochester
    (NY)
Nebraska Wesleyan Univ.
New England College (NH)
New Jersey City Univ.
New Mexico State Univ.
New York Institute of Technology
New York Univ.
Newberry College (SC)
Newman Univ. (KS)
Niagara Univ. (NY)
Nicholls State Univ. (LA)
Norfolk State Univ. (VA)
North Carolina A&T State Univ.
North Carolina Central Univ.
North Carolina State Univ.–Raleigh
North Carolina Wesleyan College
North Central College (IL)
North Dakota State Univ.
North Georgia College and State
    Univ.
North Park Univ. (IL)
Northeastern Illinois Univ.
Northeastern State Univ. (OK)
Northeastern Univ. (MA)
Northern Arizona Univ.
Northern Illinois Univ.
Northern Kentucky Univ.
Northern Michigan Univ.
Northern State Univ. (SD)
Northland College (WI)
Northwest Missouri State Univ.

Northwestern College (IA)
Northwestern State Univ. of
    Louisiana
Northwestern Univ. (IL)
Notre Dame De Namur Univ. (CA)
Oakland City Univ. (IN)
Oakland Univ. (MI)
Oberlin College (OH)
Occidental College (CA)
Oglethorpe Univ. (GA)
Ohio Dominican Univ.
Ohio Northern Univ.
Ohio State Univ.–Columbus
Ohio Univ.
Ohio Wesleyan Univ.
Oklahoma Baptist Univ.
Oklahoma City Univ.
Oklahoma State Univ.
Old Dominion Univ. (VA)
Olivet College (MI)
Olivet Nazarene Univ. (IL)
Oral Roberts Univ. (OK)
Oregon State Univ.
Otterbein College (OH)
Ouachita Baptist Univ. (AR)
Our Lady of the Lake Univ. (TX)
Pacific Lutheran Univ. (WA)
Pacific Union College (CA)
Pacific Univ. (OR)
Paine College (GA)
Park Univ. (MO)
Paul Quinn College (TX)
Penn. State Univ.–Univ. Park
Pepperdine Univ. (CA)
Pfeiffer Univ. (NC)
Philander Smith College (AR)
Piedmont College (GA)
Pikeville College (KY)
Pittsburg State Univ. (KS)
Pitzer College (CA)
Point Loma Nazarene Univ. (CA)
Pomona College (CA)
Portland State Univ. (OR)
Prairie View A&M Univ. (TX)
Presbyterian College (SC)
Princeton Univ. (NJ)
Principia College (IL)
Providence College (RI)
Purdue Univ.–Calumet (IN)
Purdue Univ.–West Lafayette (IN)
Quinnipiac Univ. (CT)
Radford Univ. (VA)
Ramapo College of New Jersey
Randolph-Macon College (VA)
Randolph-Macon Woman's College
    (VA)
Reed College (OR)
Regis College (MA)
Regis Univ. (CO)
Reinhardt College (GA)
Rhode Island College
Rhodes College (TN)
Rice Univ. (TX)
Richard Stockton College of New
    Jersey
Rider Univ. (NJ)
Ripon College (WI)
Rivier College (NH)
Roanoke College (VA)
Roberts Wesleyan College (NY)
Rockhurst Univ. (MO)

Rocky Mountain College (MT)
Roger Williams Univ. (RI)
Rollins College (FL)
Roosevelt Univ. (IL)
Rosemont College (PA)
Russell Sage College (NY)
Rust College (MS)
Rutgers–Camden (NJ)
Rutgers–New Brunswick (NJ)
Rutgers–Newark (NJ)
Sacred Heart Univ. (CT)
Saginaw Valley State Univ. (MI)
Salem College (NC)
Salem State College (MA)
Salisbury Univ. (MD)
Salve Regina Univ. (RI)
Sam Houston State Univ. (TX)
Samford Univ. (AL)
San Diego State Univ.
San Francisco State Univ.
Santa Clara Univ. (CA)
Savannah State Univ. (GA)
Scripps College (CA)
Seattle Pacific Univ.
Seattle Univ.
Seton Hall Univ. (NJ)
Seton Hill Univ. (PA)
Shaw Univ. (NC)
Shawnee State Univ. (OH)
Shenandoah Univ. (VA)
Shepherd Univ. (WV)
Shippensburg Univ. of
    Pennsylvania
Shorter College (GA)
Siena College (NY)
Simmons College (MA)
Simpson College (IA)
Skidmore College (NY)
Slippery Rock Univ. of Pennsylvania
Sonoma State Univ. (CA)
South Carolina State Univ.
South Dakota State Univ.
Southeast Missouri State Univ.
Southeastern Louisiana Univ.
Southeastern Oklahoma State
    Univ.
Southern Arkansas Univ.
Southern Illinois Univ.–Carbondale
Southern Illinois
    Univ.–Edwardsville
Southern Methodist Univ. (TX)
Southern Nazarene Univ. (OK)
Southern Oregon Univ.
Southern Univ. and A&M College
    (LA)
Southern Utah Univ.
Southwest Baptist Univ. (MO)
Southwest Minnesota State Univ.
    (MN)
Southwest Missouri State Univ.
Southwestern Univ. (TX)
Spelman College (GA)
Spring Arbor Univ. (MI)
Spring Hill College (AL)
Springfield College (MA)
St. Ambrose Univ. (IA)
St. Anselm College (NH)
St. Bonaventure Univ. (NY)
St. Cloud State Univ. (MN)
St. Edward's Univ. (TX)
St. Francis College (NY)

St. Francis Univ. (PA)
St. Gregory's Univ. (OK)
St. John Fisher College (NY)
St. John's Univ. (NY)
St. John's Univ. (MN)
St. Joseph College (CT)
St. Joseph's College (IN)
St. Joseph's College (ME)
St. Joseph's Univ. (PA)
St. Lawrence Univ. (NY)
St. Leo Univ. (FL)
St. Louis Univ.
St. Mary's College (IN)
St. Mary's College of California
St. Mary's College of Maryland
St. Mary's Univ. of Minnesota
St. Mary's Univ. of San Antonio
St. Michael's College (VT)
St. Norbert College (WI)
St. Olaf College (MN)
St. Peter's College (NJ)
St. Vincent College (PA)
St. Xavier Univ. (IL)
Stanford Univ. (CA)
State Univ. of West Georgia
Stephen F. Austin State Univ. (TX)
Stetson Univ. (FL)
Stonehill College (MA)
Suffolk Univ. (MA)
SUNY College of Arts and
    Sciences–Geneseo
SUNY College–Brockport
SUNY College–Old Westbury
SUNY College–Oneonta
SUNY College–Potsdam
SUNY–Albany
SUNY–Binghamton
SUNY–Fredonia
SUNY–Plattsburgh
SUNY–Stony Brook
Susquehanna Univ. (PA)
Sweet Briar College (VA)
Syracuse Univ. (NY)
Tabor College (KS)
Talladega College (AL)
Tarleton State Univ. (TX)
Taylor Univ. (IN)
Teikyo Post Univ. (CT)
Temple Univ. (PA)
Tennessee State Univ.
Tennessee Technological Univ.
Texas A&M International Univ.
Texas A&M Univ.–College Station
Texas A&M Univ.–Commerce
Texas A&M Univ.–Corpus Christi
Texas A&M Univ.–Kingsville
Texas Christian Univ.
Texas College
Texas Lutheran Univ.
Texas State Univ.–San Marcos
Texas Tech Univ.
Texas Wesleyan Univ.
Texas Woman's Univ.
Thiel College (PA)
Thomas Edison State College (NJ)
Thomas More College (KY)
Tougaloo College (MS)
Touro College (NY)
Transylvania Univ. (KY)
Trinity Christian College (IL)
Trinity College (CT)

Trinity College (DC)
Troy State Univ.–Troy (AL)
Truman State Univ. (MO)
Tufts Univ. (MA)
Tulane Univ. (LA)
Tuskegee Univ. (AL)
Union College (NY)
Union Univ. (TN)
Univ. at Buffalo–SUNY
Univ. of Akron (OH)
Univ. of Alabama
Univ. of Alabama–Birmingham
Univ. of Alabama–Huntsville
Univ. of Alaska–Anchorage
Univ. of Alaska–Fairbanks
Univ. of Arizona
Univ. of Arkansas
Univ. of Arkansas–Little Rock
Univ. of Arkansas–Pine Bluff
Univ. of California–Berkeley
Univ. of California–Davis
Univ. of California–Irvine
Univ. of California–Los Angeles
Univ. of California–Riverside
Univ. of California–San Diego
Univ. of California–Santa Barbara
Univ. of California–Santa Cruz
Univ. of Central Florida
Univ. of Central Oklahoma
Univ. of Chicago
Univ. of Colorado–Boulder
Univ. of Colorado–Colorado
    Springs
Univ. of Colorado–Denver
Univ. of Connecticut
Univ. of Dayton (OH)
Univ. of Delaware
Univ. of Denver
Univ. of Detroit Mercy
Univ. of Dubuque (IA)
Univ. of Evansville (IN)
Univ. of Findlay (OH)
Univ. of Florida
Univ. of Georgia
Univ. of Great Falls (MT)
Univ. of Hartford (CT)
Univ. of Hawaii–Hilo
Univ. of Hawaii–Manoa
Univ. of Houston
Univ. of Houston–Downtown
Univ. of Illinois–Chicago
Univ. of Ill.–Urbana-Champaign
Univ. of Indianapolis
Univ. of Iowa
Univ. of Kansas
Univ. of Kentucky
Univ. of La Verne (CA)
Univ. of Louisiana–Lafayette
Univ. of Louisiana–Monroe
Univ. of Louisville (KY)
Univ. of Maine–Orono
Univ. of Maine–Presque Isle
Univ. of Mary Hardin-Baylor (TX)
Univ. of Mary Washington (VA)
Univ. of Maryland–Baltimore
    County
Univ. of Maryland–College Park
Univ. of Maryland–Eastern Shore
Univ. of Massachusetts–Amherst
Univ. of Massachusetts–Boston
Univ. of Mass.–Dartmouth

Univ. of Massachusetts–Lowell
Univ. of Memphis
Univ. of Miami (FL)
Univ. of Michigan–Ann Arbor
Univ. of Michigan–Dearborn
Univ. of Michigan–Flint
Univ. of Minnesota–Duluth
Univ. of Minnesota–Morris
Univ. of Minnesota–Twin Cities
Univ. of Mississippi
Univ. of Missouri–Columbia
Univ. of Missouri–Kansas City
Univ. of Missouri–St. Louis
Univ. of Montana
Univ. of Montevallo (AL)
Univ. of Nebraska–Kearney
Univ. of Nebraska–Lincoln
Univ. of Nebraska–Omaha
Univ. of Nevada–Reno
Univ. of New England (ME)
Univ. of New Hampshire
Univ. of New Mexico
Univ. of New Orleans
Univ. of North Alabama
Univ. of North Carolina–Asheville
Univ. of N.C.–Chapel Hill
Univ. of North Carolina–Charlotte
Univ. of N.C.–Greensboro
Univ. of North Carolina–Pembroke
Univ. of N.C.–Wilmington
Univ. of North Dakota
Univ. of North Florida
Univ. of North Texas
Univ. of Northern Colorado
Univ. of Northern Iowa
Univ. of Notre Dame (IN)
Univ. of Oklahoma
Univ. of Oregon
Univ. of Pennsylvania
Univ. of Pittsburgh
Univ. of Pittsburgh–Bradford
Univ. of Pittsburgh–Johnstown
Univ. of Portland (OR)
Univ. of Puget Sound (WA)
Univ. of Redlands (CA)
Univ. of Rhode Island
Univ. of Richmond (VA)
Univ. of San Diego
Univ. of San Francisco
Univ. of Science and Arts of
    Oklahoma
Univ. of Scranton (PA)
Univ. of Sioux Falls (SD)
Univ. of South Alabama
Univ. of South Carolina–Aiken
Univ. of South Carolina–Columbia
Univ. of South Carolina–Upstate
Univ. of South Dakota
Univ. of South Florida
Univ. of Southern California
Univ. of Southern Indiana
Univ. of Southern Maine
Univ. of Southern Mississippi
Univ. of St. Francis (IN)
Univ. of St. Mary (KS)
Univ. of St. Thomas (MN)
Univ. of Tampa (FL)
Univ. of Tennessee
Univ. of Tennessee–Martin
Univ. of Texas of the Permian Basin
Univ. of Texas–Arlington

Univ. of Texas–Austin
Univ. of Texas–Brownsville
Univ. of Texas–Dallas
Univ. of Texas–El Paso
Univ. of Texas–Pan American
Univ. of Texas–San Antonio
Univ. of Texas–Tyler
Univ. of the District of Columbia
Univ. of the Incarnate Word (TX)
Univ. of the Ozarks (AR)
Univ. of the Pacific (CA)
Univ. of Toledo (OH)
Univ. of Tulsa (OK)
Univ. of Utah
Univ. of Vermont
Univ. of Virginia
Univ. of Virginia–Wise
Univ. of Washington
Univ. of West Alabama
Univ. of West Florida
Univ. of Wisconsin–Eau Claire
Univ. of Wisconsin–La Crosse
Univ. of Wisconsin–Madison
Univ. of Wisconsin–Milwaukee
Univ. of Wisconsin–Parkside
Univ. of Wisconsin–River Falls
Univ. of Wisconsin–Stevens Point
Univ. of Wisconsin–Superior
Univ. of Wisconsin–Whitewater
Univ. of Wyoming
Urbana Univ. (OH)
Ursuline College (OH)
Utah State Univ.
Utica College (NY)
Valdosta State Univ. (GA)
Valparaiso Univ. (IN)
Vanderbilt Univ. (TN)
Vanguard Univ. of Southern
    California
Vassar College (NY)
Villanova Univ. (PA)
Virginia Commonwealth Univ.
Virginia State Univ.
Virginia Tech
Virginia Wesleyan College
Viterbo Univ. (WI)
Voorhees College (SC)
Wagner College (NY)
Wake Forest Univ. (NC)
Walsh Univ. (OH)
Wartburg College (IA)
Washburn Univ. (KS)
Washington and Jefferson College
    (PA)
Washington and Lee Univ. (VA)
Washington College (MD)
Washington State Univ.
Wayne State College (NE)
Wayne State Univ. (MI)
Weber State Univ. (UT)
Webster Univ. (MO)
Wellesley College (MA)
Wesleyan Univ. (CT)
West Chester Univ. of Pennsylvania
West Liberty State College (WV)
West Texas A&M Univ.
West Virginia State Univ.
West Virginia Univ.
West Virginia Wesleyan College
Western Carolina Univ. (NC)
Western Connecticut State Univ.

Western Illinois Univ.
Western Kentucky Univ.
Western Michigan Univ.
Western New England College
    (MA)
Western New Mexico Univ.
Western Oregon Univ.
Western State College of Colorado
Western Washington Univ.
Westfield State College (MA)
Westminster College (UT)
Westminster College (MO)
Westminster College (PA)
Westmont College (CA)
Wheaton College (IL)
Wheaton College (MA)
Whitman College (WA)
Whittier College (CA)
Whitworth College (WA)
Wichita State Univ. (KS)
Widener Univ. (PA)
Wilberforce Univ. (OH)
Wiley College (TX)
Wilkes Univ. (PA)
Willamette Univ. (OR)
William Paterson Univ. of New
    Jersey
William Penn Univ. (IA)
Williams College (MA)
Wingate Univ. (NC)
Winston-Salem State Univ. (NC)
Winthrop Univ. (SC)
Wittenberg Univ. (OH)
Wofford College (SC)
Worcester State College (MA)
Wright State Univ. (OH)
Xavier Univ. (OH)
Yale Univ. (CT)
Yeshiva Univ. (NY)
York College of Pennsylvania
Youngstown State Univ. (OH)

Soil Sciences

Brigham Young Univ.–Provo (UT)
Cal Poly–San Luis Obispo
California State Polytechnic
    Univ.–Pomona
Humboldt State Univ. (CA)
Michigan State Univ.
New Mexico State Univ.
North Dakota State Univ.
Oklahoma State Univ.
Penn. State Univ.–Univ. Park
Texas A&M Univ.–College Station
Tuskegee Univ. (AL)
Univ. of Arizona
Univ. of California–Davis
Univ. of California–Riverside
Univ. of Delaware
Univ. of Florida
Univ. of Georgia
Univ. of Hawaii–Manoa
Univ. of Maine–Orono
Univ. of Nebraska–Lincoln
Univ. of Rhode Island
Univ. of Wisconsin–Madison
Utah State Univ.
Washington State Univ.

South Asian Languages, Literatures, and Linguistics

Brown Univ. (RI)
Univ. of Chicago

Southeast Asian and Australasian/Pacific Lang., Lit., and Ling.

Univ. of Chicago
Univ. of Hawaii–Manoa

Special Education and Teaching

Benedictine Univ. (IL)
Boston Univ.
Carthage College (WI)
Cazenovia College (NY)
Cheyney Univ. of Pennsylvania
College of St. Joseph (VT)
Columbus State Univ. (GA)
Coppin State Univ. (MD)
CUNY–Lehman College
East Central Univ. (OK)
Felician College (NJ)
Fisk Univ. (TN)
Greensboro College (NC)
Gwynedd-Mercy College (PA)
Indiana Wesleyan Univ.
Long Island Univ.–Brooklyn (NY)
Longwood Univ. (VA)
Marygrove College (MI)
Mount Vernon Nazarene Univ.
    (OH)
Oklahoma Christian Univ.
Prescott College (AZ)
Seattle Pacific Univ.
Simmons College (MA)
Southern Connecticut State Univ.
St. Bonaventure Univ. (NY)
St. Martin's College (WA)
St. Mary-of-The-Woods Coll. (IN)
SUNY–Oswego
Touro College (NY)
Tusculum College (TN)
Univ. of Great Falls (MT)
Univ. of Kentucky
Univ. of Wisconsin–Oshkosh
Wheelock College (MA)
Widener Univ. (PA)

Specialized Sales, Merchandising, and Marketing Operations

Ashland Univ. (OH)
Baylor Univ. (TX)
Bowling Green State Univ. (OH)
Brenau Univ. (GA)
California State Polytechnic
    Univ.–Pomona
Cazenovia College (NY)
Centenary College (NJ)
Central Connecticut State Univ.

Central Missouri State Univ.
Central Washington Univ.
Clark Atlanta Univ.
College of St. Catherine (MN)
Concord College (WV)
David Lipscomb Univ. (TN)
Dominican Univ. (IL)
Eastern Kentucky Univ.
Eastern Michigan Univ.
Ferris State Univ. (MI)
Gannon Univ. (PA)
Grand Valley State Univ. (MI)
Harding Univ. (AR)
Howard Univ. (DC)
Immaculata Univ. (PA)
Indiana Univ. of Pennsylvania
Johnson and Wales Univ. (RI)
Kent State Univ. (OH)
Lasell College (MA)
Liberty Univ. (VA)
Louisiana State Univ.–Baton Rouge
Marist College (NY)
Marymount Univ. (VA)
Meredith College (NC)
Mount Ida College (MA)
Mount Mary College (WI)
New Mexico State Univ.
Niagara Univ. (NY)
Northern Arizona Univ.
Northwood Univ. (MI)
Ohio State Univ.–Columbus
Olivet Nazarene Univ. (IL)
Philadelphia Univ.
Purdue Univ.–Calumet (IN)
Rhode Island College
St. Joseph's Univ. (PA)
Stephen F. Austin State Univ. (TX)
Stephens College (MO)
Texas Christian Univ.
Texas State Univ.–San Marcos
Texas Tech Univ.
Texas Woman's Univ.
Univ. of Akron (OH)
Univ. of Arizona
Univ. of Central Oklahoma
Univ. of Georgia
Univ. of Louisiana–Lafayette
Univ. of Massachusetts–Amherst
Univ. of North Texas
Univ. of Rhode Island
Ursuline College (OH)
Utah State Univ.
Western Carolina Univ. (NC)
Western Michigan Univ.
Woodbury Univ. (CA)
Youngstown State Univ. (OH)

Speech and Rhetorical Studies

Ashland Univ. (OH)
CUNY–York College
Dillard Univ. (LA)
Hillsdale College (MI)
Huntington College (IN)
Missouri Valley College
Northeastern Illinois Univ.
Northwestern Oklahoma State
    Univ.
Oglethorpe Univ. (GA)

Olivet Nazarene Univ. (IL)
Texas A&M Univ.–Commerce
Univ. of Judaism (CA)
Univ. of Minnesota–Morris
Univ. of Pittsburgh–Greensburg
Univ. of Tennessee
Univ. of Washington

Statistics

American Univ. (DC)
Appalachian State Univ. (NC)
Auburn Univ. (AL)
Babson College (MA)
Barnard College (NY)
Bowling Green State Univ. (OH)
Brown Univ. (RI)
Cal Poly–San Luis Obispo
California State Univ.–Fullerton
California State Univ.–Hayward
Carnegie Mellon Univ. (PA)
Case Western Reserve Univ. (OH)
Central Michigan Univ.
Colorado State Univ.
Columbia Univ. (NY)
CUNY–Baruch College
CUNY–Hunter College
Eastern Kentucky Univ.
Eastern Michigan Univ.
Eastern Washington Univ.
Florida International Univ.
Florida State Univ.
George Washington Univ. (DC)
Grand Valley State Univ. (MI)
Harvard Univ. (MA)
Howard Univ. (DC)
Iowa State Univ.
Kansas State Univ.
Lehigh Univ. (PA)
Loyola Univ. Chicago
Luther College (IA)
Master's Coll. and Seminary (CA)
Miami Univ.–Oxford (OH)
Michigan State Univ.
Mount Holyoke College (MA)
New Mexico Institute of Mining
    and Technology
New York Univ.
North Carolina State Univ.–Raleigh
North Dakota State Univ.
Northwest Missouri State Univ.
Northwestern Univ. (IL)
Oakland Univ. (MI)
Ohio Northern Univ.
Oklahoma State Univ.
Penn. State Univ.–Univ. Park
Purdue Univ.–West Lafayette (IN)
Rice Univ. (TX)
Rochester Institute of Tech. (NY)
Roosevelt Univ. (IL)
Rutgers–New Brunswick (NJ)
San Diego State Univ.
Southern Methodist Univ. (TX)
St. Cloud State Univ. (MN)
SUNY College–Oneonta
Texas A&M Univ.–College Station
Tulane Univ. (LA)
Univ. of Akron (OH)
Univ. of Alaska–Fairbanks
Univ. of California–Berkeley

Univ. of California–Davis
Univ. of California–Los Angeles
Univ. of California–Riverside
Univ. of California–Santa Barbara
Univ. of Central Florida
Univ. of Connecticut
Univ. of Florida
Univ. of Georgia
Univ. of Illinois–Chicago
Univ. of Ill.–Urbana-Champaign
Univ. of Iowa
Univ. of Maryland–Baltimore
    County
Univ. of Miami (FL)
Univ. of Michigan–Ann Arbor
Univ. of Minnesota–Morris
Univ. of Minnesota–Twin Cities
Univ. of Missouri–Columbia
Univ. of Nevada–Las Vegas
Univ. of New Mexico
Univ. of N.C.–Wilmington
Univ. of North Florida
Univ. of Pennsylvania
Univ. of Pittsburgh
Univ. of Rochester (NY)
Univ. of South Carolina–Columbia
Univ. of Tennessee
Univ. of Texas–Dallas
Univ. of Texas–El Paso
Univ. of Texas–San Antonio
Univ. of Vermont
Univ. of Washington
Univ. of Wisconsin–Madison
Univ. of Wyoming
Utah State Univ.
Virginia Tech
Western Michigan Univ.

Student Counseling and Personnel Services

Albany State Univ. (GA)
Auburn Univ. (AL)
Bellevue Univ. (NE)
Buena Vista Univ. (IA)
California State Univ.–Fullerton
California State Univ.–Sacramento
California State Univ.–San
    Bernardino
College of the Southwest (NM)
CUNY–Lehman College
Gallaudet Univ. (DC)
Goddard College (VT)
Harding Univ. (AR)
Indiana Univ.–Bloomington
Keene State College (NH)
Lincoln Memorial Univ. (TN)
Long Island Univ.–Brooklyn (NY)
Marshall Univ. (WV)
Northern State Univ. (SD)
Pittsburg State Univ. (KS)
Samford Univ. (AL)
Springfield College (MA)
Stephens College (MO)
SUNY–Oswego
Univ. of Nevada–Las Vegas
Univ. of North Alabama
Univ. of North Carolina–Pembroke
Univ. of Redlands (CA)
Univ. of St. Francis (IN)

Univ. of Wisconsin–Oshkosh
Univ. of Wisconsin–River Falls
Washington State Univ.
Western Washington Univ.

Surveying Engineering

California State Univ.–Fresno
Michigan Technological Univ.
Univ. of Arkansas–Monticello
Univ. of Maine–Orono

Systems Engineering

California State Univ.–Fullerton
Case Western Reserve Univ. (OH)
Fairfield Univ. (CT)
Florida International Univ.
George Mason Univ. (VA)
Howard Univ. (DC)
Oakland Univ. (MI)
Providence College (RI)
Stanford Univ. (CA)
Stevens Institute of Technology
    (NJ)
United States Merchant Marine
    Academy (NY)
United States Military Academy
    (NY)
United States Naval Academy
    (MD)
Univ. of Arizona
Univ. of Arkansas–Little Rock
Univ. of Florida
Univ. of Maine–Orono
Univ. of Missouri–Rolla
Univ. of Pennsylvania
Univ. of Virginia
Washington Univ. In St. Louis

Systems Science and Theory

Carnegie Mellon Univ. (PA)
Indiana Univ.–Bloomington
Marshall Univ. (WV)
Stanford Univ. (CA)
Wheeling Jesuit Univ. (WV)

Taxation

California State Univ.–Fullerton
Grand Valley State Univ. (MI)

Teacher Education and Professional Development

Abilene Christian Univ. (TX)
Adelphi Univ. (NY)
Adrian College (MI)
Alabama Agricultural and
    Mechanical Univ.
Alabama State Univ.
Alaska Pacific Univ.
Albany State Univ. (GA)
Albertson College (ID)

Albion College (MI)
Albright College (PA)
Alcorn State Univ. (MS)
Alderson-Broaddus College (WV)
Alfred Univ. (NY)
Allen Univ. (SC)
Alma College (MI)
Alvernia College (PA)
Alverno College (WI)
American Univ. (DC)
Anderson College (SC)
Anderson Univ. (IN)
Andrews Univ. (MI)
Anna Maria College (MA)
Appalachian State Univ. (NC)
Aquinas College (MI)
Arcadia Univ. (PA)
Arizona State Univ.
Arizona State Univ. West
Arkansas State Univ.
Arkansas Tech Univ.
Armstrong Atlantic State Univ.
    (GA)
Asbury College (KY)
Ashland Univ. (OH)
Atlantic Union College (MA)
Auburn Univ. (AL)
Auburn Univ.–Montgomery (AL)
Augsburg College (MN)
Augusta State Univ. (GA)
Augustana College (IL)
Augustana College (SD)
Aurora Univ. (IL)
Austin College (TX)
Austin Peay State Univ. (TN)
Averett Univ. (VA)
Avila Univ. (MO)
Azusa Pacific Univ. (CA)
Baker Univ. (KS)
Baldwin-Wallace College (OH)
Ball State Univ. (IN)
Barber Scotia College (NC)
Barry Univ. (FL)
Barton College (NC)
Baylor Univ. (TX)
Bellarmine Univ. (KY)
Bellevue Univ. (NE)
Belmont Abbey College (NC)
Belmont Univ. (TN)
Bemidji State Univ. (MN)
Benedict College (SC)
Benedictine College (KS)
Benedictine Univ. (IL)
Bennett College (NC)
Bennington College (VT)
Berea College (KY)
Berry College (GA)
Bethany College (CA)
Bethany College (WV)
Bethany College (KS)
Bethel College (IN)
Bethel College (KS)
Bethel Univ. (MN)
Bethune-Cookman College (FL)
Biola Univ. (CA)
Black Hills State Univ. (SD)
Blackburn College (IL)
Bloomsburg Univ. of Pennsylvania
Blue Mountain College (MS)
Bluefield College (VA)
Bluefield State College (WV)

Bluffton Univ. (OH)
Boise State Univ. (ID)
Boston Univ.
Bowie State Univ. (MD)
Bowling Green State Univ. (OH)
Bradley Univ. (IL)
Brenau Univ. (GA)
Brescia Univ. (KY)
Brevard College (NC)
Brewton-Parker College (GA)
Briar Cliff Univ. (IA)
Bridgewater College (VA)
Bridgewater State College (MA)
Brigham Young Univ.–Hawaii
Brigham Young Univ.–Provo (UT)
Bryan College (TN)
Bucknell Univ. (PA)
Buena Vista Univ. (IA)
Buffalo State College
Butler Univ. (IN)
Cabrini College (PA)
Cal Poly–San Luis Obispo
California State Polytechnic
    Univ.–Pomona
California State Univ.–Bakersfield
California State Univ.–Chico
California State Univ.–Fresno
California State Univ.–Fullerton
California State Univ.–Long Beach
California State Univ.–Los Angeles
California State Univ.–Monterey
    Bay
California State Univ.–Northridge
California State Univ.–Sacramento
California State Univ.–San
    Bernardino
California State Univ.–Stanislaus
California Univ. of Pennsylvania
Calumet College of St. Joseph (IN)
Calvin College (MI)
Cameron Univ. (OK)
Campbell Univ. (NC)
Canisius College (NY)
Capital Univ. (OH)
Cardinal Stritch Univ. (WI)
Carlow College (PA)
Carroll College (MT)
Carroll College (WI)
Carson-Newman College (TN)
Carthage College (WI)
Case Western Reserve Univ. (OH)
Catholic Univ. of America (DC)
Cazenovia College (NY)
Cedar Crest College (PA)
Cedarville Univ. (OH)
Centenary College of Louisiana
Central College (IA)
Central Connecticut State Univ.
Central Methodist Univ. (MO)
Central Michigan Univ.
Central Missouri State Univ.
Central State Univ. (OH)
Central Washington Univ.
Centre College (KY)
Chadron State College (NE)
Chaminade Univ. of Honolulu
Champlain College (VT)
Chapman Univ. (CA)
Charleston Southern Univ. (SC)
Chatham College (PA)
Chestnut Hill College (PA)

Cheyney Univ. of Pennsylvania
Chicago State Univ.
Chowan College (NC)
City Univ. (WA)
Claflin Univ. (SC)
Clarion Univ. of Pennsylvania
Clark Atlanta Univ.
Clarke College (IA)
Clayton Coll. and State Univ. (GA)
Clearwater Christian College (FL)
Cleveland State Univ.
Coastal Carolina Univ. (SC)
Coe College (IA)
Coker College (SC)
Colby-Sawyer College (NH)
College For Lifelong Learning (NH)
College Misericordia (PA)
College of Charleston (SC)
College of Mount St. Joseph (OH)
College of Mount St. Vincent (NY)
College of New Jersey
College of Notre Dame of Maryland
College of Santa Fe (NM)
College of St. Benedict (MN)
College of St. Catherine (MN)
College of St. Elizabeth (NJ)
College of St. Joseph (VT)
College of St. Mary (NE)
College of St. Rose (NY)
College of St. Scholastica (MN)
College of the Ozarks (MO)
College of the Southwest (NM)
College of Wooster (OH)
Colorado Christian Univ.
Colorado State Univ.
Columbia College (IL)
Columbia College (SC)
Columbia Union College (MD)
Columbus State Univ. (GA)
Concord College (WV)
Concordia College (AL)
Concordia College (NY)
Concordia Coll.-Moorhead (MN)
Concordia Univ. (NE)
Concordia Univ. (MI)
Concordia Univ. (OR)
Concordia Univ.-Austin (TX)
Concordia Univ.-River Forest (IL)
Concordia Univ.-St. Paul (MN)
Connecticut College
Converse College (SC)
Coppin State Univ. (MD)
Corcoran College of Art and Design (DC)
Cornell College (IA)
Cornell Univ. (NY)
Cornerstone Univ. (MI)
Covenant College (GA)
Creighton Univ. (NE)
Crichton College (TN)
Culver-Stockton College (MO)
Cumberland College (KY)
Cumberland Univ. (TN)
CUNY-Brooklyn College
CUNY-City College
CUNY-College of Staten Island
CUNY-Hunter College
CUNY-Lehman College
CUNY-Medgar Evers College

CUNY-New York City College of Technology
CUNY-Queens College
CUNY-York College
Curry College (MA)
Daemen College (NY)
Dakota State Univ. (SD)
Dakota Wesleyan Univ. (SD)
Dallas Baptist Univ.
Dana College (NE)
David Lipscomb Univ. (TN)
Davis and Elkins College (WV)
Defiance College (OH)
Delaware State Univ.
Delaware Valley College (PA)
Delta State Univ. (MS)
Denison Univ. (OH)
Depaul Univ. (IL)
Depauw Univ. (IN)
Desales Univ. (PA)
Dickinson State Univ. (ND)
Dominican Coll. of Blauvelt (NY)
Dominican Univ. of California (CA)
Dordt College (IA)
Dowling College (NY)
Drake Univ. (IA)
Drexel Univ. (PA)
Drury Univ. (MO)
Duquesne Univ. (PA)
East Carolina Univ. (NC)
East Central Univ. (OK)
East Stroudsburg Univ. of Penn.
East Texas Baptist Univ.
Eastern Connecticut State Univ.
Eastern Illinois Univ.
Eastern Kentucky Univ.
Eastern Mennonite Univ. (VA)
Eastern Michigan Univ.
Eastern Nazarene College (MA)
Eastern New Mexico Univ.
Eastern Oregon Univ.
Eastern Univ. (PA)
Eastern Washington Univ.
Edgewood College (WI)
Edinboro Univ. of Pennsylvania
Edward Waters College (FL)
Elizabeth City State Univ. (NC)
Elizabethtown College (PA)
Elmhurst College (IL)
Elmira College (NY)
Elms College (College of Our Lady of the Elms) (MA)
Elon Univ. (NC)
Emmanuel College (MA)
Emmanuel College (GA)
Emory and Henry College (VA)
Emporia State Univ. (KS)
Endicott College (MA)
Erskine College (SC)
Eureka College (IL)
Evangel Univ. (MO)
Fairmont State Univ. (WV)
Faulkner Univ. (AL)
Fayetteville State Univ. (NC)
Felician College (NJ)
Ferris State Univ. (MI)
Fitchburg State College (MA)
Flagler College (FL)
Florida A&M Univ.
Florida Atlantic Univ.
Florida Gulf Coast Univ.

Florida Institute of Technology
Florida International Univ.
Florida Southern College
Florida State Univ.
Fontbonne Univ. (MO)
Fordham Univ. (NY)
Fort Hays State Univ. (KS)
Fort Lewis College (CO)
Fort Valley State Univ. (GA)
Framingham State College (MA)
Francis Marion Univ. (SC)
Franciscan Univ. of Steubenville (OH)
Franklin College (IN)
Fresno Pacific Univ. (CA)
Friends Univ. (KS)
Frostburg State Univ. (MD)
Furman Univ. (SC)
Gallaudet Univ. (DC)
Gannon Univ. (PA)
Gardner-Webb Univ. (NC)
Geneva College (PA)
George Fox Univ. (OR)
George Mason Univ. (VA)
George Washington Univ. (DC)
Georgetown College (KY)
Georgia College and State Univ.
Georgia Southern Univ.
Georgia Southwestern State Univ.
Georgia State Univ.
Georgian Court Univ. (NJ)
Gettysburg College (PA)
Glenville State College (WV)
Goddard College (VT)
Gonzaga Univ. (WA)
Gordon College (MA)
Goshen College (IN)
Goucher College (MD)
Grace College and Seminary (IN)
Grace Univ. (NE)
Graceland Univ. (IA)
Grambling State Univ. (LA)
Grand Canyon Univ. (AZ)
Grand Valley State Univ. (MI)
Grand View College (IA)
Green Mountain College (VT)
Greensboro College (NC)
Greenville College (IL)
Grove City College (PA)
Guilford College (NC)
Gustavus Adolphus College (MN)
Gwynedd-Mercy College (PA)
Hannibal-Lagrange College (MO)
Hardin-Simmons Univ. (TX)
Harding Univ. (AR)
Hartwick College (NY)
Hastings College (NE)
Heidelberg College (OH)
Henderson State Univ. (AR)
Hendrix College (AR)
Heritage College (WA)
High Point Univ. (NC)
Hillsdale College (MI)
Hiram College (OH)
Hofstra Univ. (NY)
Holy Family Univ. (PA)
Hood College (MD)
Hope College (MI)
Hope International Univ. (CA)
Houghton College (NY)
Houston Baptist Univ.

Howard Payne Univ. (TX)
Howard Univ. (DC)
Humboldt State Univ. (CA)
Huntingdon College (AL)
Huntington College (IN)
Husson College (ME)
Idaho State Univ.
Illinois College
Illinois State Univ.
Illinois Wesleyan Univ.
Immaculata Univ. (PA)
Indiana State Univ.
Indiana Univ. East
Indiana Univ. Northwest
Indiana Univ. of Pennsylvania
Indiana Univ. Southeast
Indiana Univ.-Bloomington
Indiana Univ.-Kokomo
Indiana Univ.-South Bend
Indiana Univ.-Purdue Univ.-Fort Wayne
Indiana Univ.-Purdue Univ.-Indianapolis
Indiana Wesleyan Univ.
Iona College (NY)
Iowa State Univ.
Ithaca College (NY)
Jacksonville State Univ. (AL)
Jacksonville Univ. (FL)
James Madison Univ. (VA)
Jamestown College (ND)
John Brown Univ. (AR)
John Carroll Univ. (OH)
Johns Hopkins Univ. (MD)
Johnson and Wales Univ. (RI)
Johnson C. Smith Univ. (NC)
Johnson State College (VT)
Judson College (AL)
Judson College (IL)
Juniata College (PA)
Kansas State Univ.
Kansas Wesleyan Univ.
Kean Univ. (NJ)
Keene State College (NH)
Kendall College (IL)
Kennesaw State Univ. (GA)
Kent State Univ. (OH)
Kentucky State Univ.
Kentucky Wesleyan College
Keuka College (NY)
King College (TN)
King's College (PA)
Kutztown Univ. of Pennsylvania
La Roche College (PA)
La Salle Univ. (PA)
La Sierra Univ. (CA)
Lagrange College (GA)
Lake Erie College (OH)
Lake Superior State Univ. (MI)
Lakeland College (WI)
Lamar Univ. (TX)
Lambuth Univ. (TN)
Lander Univ. (SC)
Lane College (TN)
Lasell College (MA)
Lawrence Univ. (WI)
Lebanon Valley College (PA)
Lees-Mcrae College (NC)
Lenoir-Rhyne College (NC)
Lesley Univ. (MA)
Letourneau Univ. (TX)

Lewis Univ. (IL)
Lewis-Clark State College (ID)
Liberty Univ. (VA)
Limestone College (SC)
Lincoln Memorial Univ. (TN)
Lincoln Univ. (MO)
Lincoln Univ. (PA)
Lindenwood Univ. (MO)
Lindsey Wilson College (KY)
Linfield College (OR)
Livingstone College (NC)
Lock Haven Univ. of Pennsylvania
Long Island Univ.-Brooklyn (NY)
Long Island Univ.-C.W. Post Campus (NY)
Long Island Univ.-Southampton College (NY)
Longwood Univ. (VA)
Louisiana College
Louisiana State Univ.-Baton Rouge
Louisiana State Univ.-Shreveport
Louisiana Tech Univ.
Lourdes College (OH)
Loyola College In Maryland
Loyola Univ. Chicago
Loyola Univ. New Orleans
Lubbock Christian Univ. (TX)
Luther College (IA)
Lynchburg College (VA)
Lyndon State College (VT)
Lynn Univ. (FL)
Lyon College (AR)
Macmurray College (IL)
Madonna Univ. (MI)
Maharishi Univ. of Management (IA)
Malone College (OH)
Manchester College (IN)
Manhattan College (NY)
Mansfield Univ. of Pennsylvania
Marian College (IN)
Marian Coll. of Fond Du Lac (WI)
Marietta College (OH)
Marist College (NY)
Marquette Univ. (WI)
Mars Hill College (NC)
Marshall Univ. (WV)
Martin Methodist College (TN)
Martin Univ. (IN)
Marygrove College (MI)
Maryland Institute College of Art
Maryville College (TN)
Maryville Univ. of St. Louis (MO)
Marywood Univ. (PA)
Massachusetts College of Art
Master's Coll. and Seminary (CA)
Mayville State Univ. (ND)
Mcdaniel College (MD)
Mckendree College (IL)
Mcmurry Univ. (TX)
Mcneese State Univ. (LA)
Mcpherson College (KS)
Medaille College (NY)
Mercer Univ. (GA)
Mercyhurst College (PA)
Meredith College (NC)
Mesa State College (CO)
Messiah College (PA)
Methodist College (NC)
Metropolitan State College of Denver

Miami Univ.–Oxford (OH)
Michigan State Univ.
Mid-Continent College (KY)
Midamerica Nazarene Univ. (KS)
Middle Tennessee State Univ.
Midland Lutheran College (NE)
Midway College (KY)
Midwestern State Univ. (TX)
Miles College (AL)
Millersville Univ. of Pennsylvania
Milligan College (TN)
Millikin Univ. (IL)
Minnesota State Univ.–Mankato
Minnesota State Univ.–Moorhead
Minot State Univ. (ND)
Mississippi College
Mississippi State Univ.
Mississippi Univ. For Women
Mississippi Valley State Univ.
Missouri Baptist College
Missouri Southern State Univ.
Missouri Valley College
Missouri Western State College
Molloy College (NY)
Monmouth College (IL)
Montana State Univ.–Billings
Montana State Univ.–Bozeman
Montana State Univ.–Northern
Montclair State Univ. (NJ)
Montreat College (NC)
Moravian College (PA)
Morehead State Univ. (KY)
Morgan State Univ. (MD)
Morningside College (IA)
Morris College (SC)
Mount Aloysius College (PA)
Mount Ida College (MA)
Mount Marty College (SD)
Mount Mary College (WI)
Mount Mercy College (IA)
Mount Olive College (NC)
Mount St. Mary College (NY)
Mount St. Mary's Univ. (MD)
Mount Union College (OH)
Mount Vernon Nazarene Univ.
　(OH)
Murray State Univ. (KY)
Muskingum College (OH)
National Univ. (CA)
National-Louis Univ. (IL)
Nazareth College of Rochester
　(NY)
Nebraska Wesleyan Univ.
Neumann College (PA)
New England College (NH)
New Jersey City Univ.
New Mexico Highlands Univ.
New Mexico State Univ.
New York Institute of Technology
New York Univ.
Newberry College (SC)
Newman Univ. (KS)
Niagara Univ. (NY)
Nicholls State Univ. (LA)
Norfolk State Univ. (VA)
North Carolina A&T State Univ.
North Carolina Central Univ.
North Carolina State Univ.–Raleigh
North Carolina Wesleyan College
North Central College (IL)
North Dakota State Univ.

North Georgia College and State
　Univ.
North Greenville College (SC)
North Park Univ. (IL)
Northeastern State Univ. (OK)
Northeastern Univ. (MA)
Northern Arizona Univ.
Northern Illinois Univ.
Northern Kentucky Univ.
Northern Michigan Univ.
Northern State Univ. (SD)
Northland College (WI)
Northwest Christian College (OR)
Northwest College (WA)
Northwest Missouri State Univ.
Northwest Nazarene Univ. (ID)
Northwestern College (MN)
Northwestern College (IA)
Northwestern Oklahoma State
　Univ.
Northwestern State Univ. of
　Louisiana
Northwestern Univ. (IL)
Notre Dame College of Ohio
Nova Southeastern Univ. (FL)
Nyack College (NY)
Oakland City Univ. (IN)
Oakland Univ. (MI)
Oakwood College (AL)
Oberlin College (OH)
Ohio Dominican Univ.
Ohio Northern Univ.
Ohio State Univ.–Columbus
Ohio Univ.
Ohio Valley College (WV)
Ohio Wesleyan Univ.
Oklahoma Baptist Univ.
Oklahoma Christian Univ.
Oklahoma City Univ.
Oklahoma Panhandle State Univ.
Oklahoma State Univ.
Oklahoma Wesleyan Univ.
Old Dominion Univ. (VA)
Olivet College (MI)
Olivet Nazarene Univ. (IL)
Oral Roberts Univ. (OK)
Ouachita Baptist Univ. (AR)
Our Lady of the Lake Univ. (TX)
Pace Univ. (NY)
Pacific Lutheran Univ. (WA)
Pacific Union College (CA)
Paine College (GA)
Palm Beach Atlantic Univ. (FL)
Park Univ. (MO)
Patten College (CA)
Penn. State Univ.–Univ. Park
Pepperdine Univ. (CA)
Peru State College (NE)
Pfeiffer Univ. (NC)
Philander Smith College (AR)
Piedmont College (GA)
Pikeville College (KY)
Pittsburg State Univ. (KS)
Plymouth State Univ. (NH)
Point Loma Nazarene Univ. (CA)
Point Park Univ. (PA)
Presbyterian College (SC)
Prescott College (AZ)
Providence College (RI)
Purdue Univ.–Calumet (IN)
Purdue Univ.–North Central (IN)

Purdue Univ.–West Lafayette (IN)
Queens Univ. of Charlotte (NC)
Quincy Univ. (IL)
Radford Univ. (VA)
Regent Univ. (VA)
Regis College (MA)
Regis Univ. (CO)
Reinhardt College (GA)
Rhode Island College
Richard Stockton College of New
　Jersey
Rider Univ. (NJ)
Rivier College (NH)
Robert Morris Univ. (PA)
Roberts Wesleyan College (NY)
Rochester College (MI)
Rockford College (IL)
Rockhurst Univ. (MO)
Rocky Mountain College (MT)
Roger Williams Univ. (RI)
Roosevelt Univ. (IL)
Russell Sage College (NY)
Rust College (MS)
Rutgers–New Brunswick (NJ)
Saginaw Valley State Univ. (MI)
Salem International Univ. (WV)
Salem State College (MA)
Salisbury Univ. (MD)
Salve Regina Univ. (RI)
Sam Houston State Univ. (TX)
Samford Univ. (AL)
San Diego State Univ.
San Francisco State Univ.
San Jose State Univ. (CA)
School of the Art Institute of
　Chicago
Schreiner Univ. (TX)
Seattle Pacific Univ.
Seton Hall Univ. (NJ)
Seton Hill Univ. (PA)
Shaw Univ. (NC)
Shawnee State Univ. (OH)
Sheldon Jackson College (AK)
Shenandoah Univ. (VA)
Shippensburg Univ. of
　Pennsylvania
Shorter College (GA)
Silver Lake College (WI)
Simpson College (IA)
Simpson Univ. (CA)
Skidmore College (NY)
Slippery Rock Univ. of Pennsylvania
Sonoma State Univ. (CA)
South Carolina State Univ.
South Dakota State Univ.
Southeast Missouri State Univ.
Southeastern College of the
　Assemblies of God
Southeastern Louisiana Univ.
Southeastern Oklahoma State
　Univ.
Southern Adventist Univ. (TN)
Southern Arkansas Univ.
Southern Connecticut State Univ.
Southern Illinois Univ.–Carbondale
Southern Illinois
　Univ.–Edwardsville
Southern Methodist Univ. (TX)
Southern Nazarene Univ. (OK)
Southern New Hampshire Univ.
Southern Oregon Univ.

Southern Univ. and A&M College
　(LA)
Southern Utah Univ.
Southern Wesleyan Univ. (SC)
Southwest Baptist Univ. (MO)
Southwest Minnesota State Univ.
　(MN)
Southwest Missouri State Univ.
Southwestern College (KS)
Southwestern Oklahoma State
　Univ.
Southwestern Univ. (TX)
Spalding Univ. (KY)
Spring Arbor Univ. (MI)
Spring Hill College (AL)
Springfield College (MA)
St. Ambrose Univ. (IA)
St. Andrews Presbyterian College
　(NC)
St. Augustine's College (NC)
St. Bonaventure Univ. (NY)
St. Cloud State Univ. (MN)
St. Edward's Univ. (TX)
St. Francis College (NY)
St. Francis Univ. (PA)
St. Gregory's Univ. (OK)
St. John Fisher College (NY)
St. John's Univ. (MN)
St. John's Univ. (NY)
St. Joseph's College (IN)
St. Joseph's College (ME)
St. Joseph's College, New York
St. Joseph's Univ. (PA)
St. Leo Univ. (FL)
St. Louis Univ.
St. Martin's College (WA)
St. Mary's College (IN)
St. Mary's Univ. of Minnesota
St. Mary's Univ. of San Antonio
St. Mary-of-The-Woods Coll. (IN)
St. Michael's College (VT)
St. Norbert College (WI)
St. Olaf College (MN)
St. Peter's College (NJ)
St. Thomas Aquinas College (NY)
St. Thomas Univ. (FL)
St. Vincent College (PA)
St. Xavier Univ. (IL)
State Univ. of West Georgia
Stephens College (MO)
Sterling College (KS)
Stetson Univ. (FL)
Stillman College (AL)
Stonehill College (MA)
SUNY College of Arts and
　Sciences–Geneseo
SUNY College–Brockport
SUNY College–Old Westbury
SUNY College–Oneonta
SUNY College–Potsdam
SUNY–Albany
SUNY–Fredonia
SUNY–Oswego
SUNY–Plattsburgh
Susquehanna Univ. (PA)
Syracuse Univ. (NY)
Tabor College (KS)
Talladega College (AL)
Taylor Univ. (IN)
Temple Univ. (PA)
Tennessee State Univ.

Tennessee Technological Univ.
Texas A&M Univ.–Kingsville
Texas Christian Univ.
Texas Lutheran Univ.
Texas Wesleyan Univ.
The Citadel (SC)
The Franciscan Univ. (IA)
Thiel College (PA)
Thomas College (ME)
Thomas More College (KY)
Thomas Univ. (GA)
Toccoa Falls College (GA)
Tougaloo College (MS)
Towson Univ. (MD)
Transylvania Univ. (KY)
Trevecca Nazarene Univ. (TN)
Tri-State Univ. (IN)
Trinity Christian College (IL)
Trinity College (DC)
Troy State Univ.–Troy (AL)
Tufts Univ. (MA)
Tusculum College (TN)
Tuskegee Univ. (AL)
Union College (NE)
Union Institute and Univ. (OH)
Union Univ. (TN)
Univ. of Akron (OH)
Univ. of Alabama
Univ. of Alabama–Birmingham
Univ. of Alabama–Huntsville
Univ. of Alaska–Anchorage
Univ. of Alaska–Fairbanks
Univ. of Alaska–Southeast
Univ. of Arizona
Univ. of Arkansas
Univ. of Arkansas–Little Rock
Univ. of Arkansas–Monticello
Univ. of Arkansas–Pine Bluff
Univ. of California–Riverside
Univ. of Central Arkansas
Univ. of Central Florida
Univ. of Central Oklahoma
Univ. of Charleston (WV)
Univ. of Colorado–Boulder
Univ. of Connecticut
Univ. of Dallas
Univ. of Dayton (OH)
Univ. of Delaware
Univ. of Denver
Univ. of Detroit Mercy
Univ. of Dubuque (IA)
Univ. of Evansville (IN)
Univ. of Findlay (OH)
Univ. of Florida
Univ. of Georgia
Univ. of Great Falls (MT)
Univ. of Hartford (CT)
Univ. of Hawaii–Hilo
Univ. of Hawaii–Manoa
Univ. of Illinois–Chicago
Univ. of Illinois–Urbana-
　Champaign
Univ. of Indianapolis
Univ. of Iowa
Univ. of Kansas
Univ. of Kentucky
Univ. of La Verne (CA)
Univ. of Louisiana–Lafayette
Univ. of Louisiana–Monroe
Univ. of Louisville (KY)
Univ. of Maine–Farmington

Univ. of Maine–Fort Kent
Univ. of Maine–Machias
Univ. of Maine–Orono
Univ. of Maine–Presque Isle
Univ. of Mary (ND)
Univ. of Mary Hardin-Baylor (TX)
Univ. of Maryland–College Park
Univ. of Maryland–Eastern Shore
Univ. of Massachusetts–Boston
Univ. of Mass.–Dartmouth
Univ. of Massachusetts–Lowell
Univ. of Memphis
Univ. of Miami (FL)
Univ. of Michigan–Ann Arbor
Univ. of Michigan–Dearborn
Univ. of Michigan–Flint
Univ. of Minnesota–Crookston
Univ. of Minnesota–Duluth
Univ. of Minnesota–Morris
Univ. of Minnesota–Twin Cities
Univ. of Mississippi
Univ. of Missouri–Columbia
Univ. of Missouri–Kansas City
Univ. of Missouri–Rolla
Univ. of Missouri–St. Louis
Univ. of Mobile (AL)
Univ. of Montana
Univ. of Montana–Western
Univ. of Montevallo (AL)
Univ. of Nebraska–Kearney
Univ. of Nebraska–Lincoln
Univ. of Nebraska–Omaha
Univ. of Nevada–Las Vegas
Univ. of Nevada–Reno
Univ. of New England (ME)
Univ. of New Hampshire
Univ. of New Mexico
Univ. of New Orleans
Univ. of North Alabama
Univ. of N.C.–Chapel Hill
Univ. of North Carolina–Charlotte
Univ. of N.C.–Greensboro
Univ. of North Carolina–Pembroke
Univ. of N.C.–Wilmington
Univ. of North Dakota
Univ. of North Florida
Univ. of Northern Colorado
Univ. of Northern Iowa
Univ. of Notre Dame (IN)
Univ. of Oklahoma
Univ. of Oregon
Univ. of Pennsylvania
Univ. of Pittsburgh
Univ. of Pittsburgh–Bradford
Univ. of Pittsburgh–Johnstown
Univ. of Portland (OR)
Univ. of Puget Sound (WA)
Univ. of Redlands (CA)
Univ. of Rhode Island
Univ. of Rio Grande (OH)
Univ. of Rochester (NY)
Univ. of Science and Arts of
    Oklahoma
Univ. of Scranton (PA)
Univ. of Sioux Falls (SD)
Univ. of South Alabama
Univ. of South Carolina–Aiken
Univ. of South Carolina–Columbia
Univ. of South Carolina–Upstate
Univ. of South Dakota
Univ. of South Florida

Univ. of Southern California
Univ. of Southern Indiana
Univ. of Southern Maine
Univ. of Southern Mississippi
Univ. of St. Francis (IL)
Univ. of St. Francis (IN)
Univ. of St. Mary (KS)
Univ. of St. Thomas (TX)
Univ. of St. Thomas (MN)
Univ. of Tampa (FL)
Univ. of Tennessee
Univ. of Tennessee–Martin
Univ. of the Arts (PA)
Univ. of the District of Columbia
Univ. of the Incarnate Word (TX)
Univ. of the Pacific (CA)
Univ. of Toledo (OH)
Univ. of Tulsa (OK)
Univ. of Utah
Univ. of Vermont
Univ. of Virginia
Univ. of West Alabama
Univ. of West Florida
Univ. of Wisconsin–Eau Claire
Univ. of Wisconsin–La Crosse
Univ. of Wisconsin–Madison
Univ. of Wisconsin–Milwaukee
Univ. of Wisconsin–Oshkosh
Univ. of Wisconsin–Platteville
Univ. of Wisconsin–River Falls
Univ. of Wisconsin–Stevens Point
Univ. of Wisconsin–Stout
Univ. of Wisconsin–Superior
Univ. of Wisconsin–Whitewater
Univ. of Wyoming
Upper Iowa Univ.
Urbana Univ. (OH)
Ursuline College (OH)
Utah State Univ.
Utah Valley State College
Valdosta State Univ. (GA)
Valley City State Univ. (ND)
Valparaiso Univ. (IN)
Vanderbilt Univ. (TN)
Vandercook College of Music (IL)
Villa Julie College (MD)
Villanova Univ. (PA)
Virginia Commonwealth Univ.
Virginia Intermont College
Virginia State Univ.
Virginia Tech
Virginia Wesleyan College
Viterbo Univ. (WI)
Wagner College (NY)
Waldorf College (IA)
Walsh Univ. (OH)
Warner Pacific College (OR)
Warner Southern College (FL)
Wartburg College (IA)
Washburn Univ. (KS)
Washington and Jefferson College
    (PA)
Washington State Univ.
Washington Univ. In St. Louis
Wayland Baptist Univ. (TX)
Wayne State College (NE)
Wayne State Univ. (MI)
Waynesburg College (PA)
Weber State Univ. (UT)
Webster Univ. (MO)
Wesleyan College (GA)

West Chester Univ. of Pennsylvania
West Liberty State College (WV)
West Virginia State Univ.
West Virginia Univ.
West Virginia Univ. Institute of
    Technology
West Virginia Univ.–Parkersburg
West Virginia Wesleyan College
Western Baptist College (OR)
Western Carolina Univ. (NC)
Western Connecticut State Univ.
Western Illinois Univ.
Western Kentucky Univ.
Western Michigan Univ.
Western New England Coll. (MA)
Western New Mexico Univ.
Western Oregon Univ.
Western Washington Univ.
Westfield State College (MA)
Westminster College (UT)
Westminster College (PA)
Westminster College (MO)
Wheaton College (IL)
Wheelock College (MA)
Whittier College (CA)
Whitworth College (WA)
Wichita State Univ. (KS)
Widener Univ. (PA)
Wiley College (TX)
Wilkes Univ. (PA)
William Carey College (MS)
William Jewell College (MO)
William Paterson Univ. of New
    Jersey
William Woods Univ. (MO)
Williams Baptist College (AR)
Wilmington College (DE)
Wilson College (PA)
Wingate Univ. (NC)
Winston-Salem State Univ. (NC)
Winthrop Univ. (SC)
Wisconsin Lutheran College
Wittenberg Univ. (OH)
Worcester State College (MA)
Wright State Univ. (OH)
Xavier Univ. (OH)
York College (NE)
York College of Pennsylvania
Youngstown State Univ. (OH)

Teaching Assistants/Aides

Tougaloo College (MS)
Univ. of Central Oklahoma

Teaching English or French as a Second or Foreign Language

Bethel Univ. (MN)
Brigham Young Univ.–Hawaii
California State Univ.–Sacramento
Carnegie Mellon Univ. (PA)
Carroll College (MT)
Concordia Univ.–St. Paul (MN)
Cornerstone Univ. (MI)
CUNY–Queens College
Elms College (College of Our Lady
    of the Elms) (MA)

Grace Univ. (NE)
Grand Canyon Univ. (AZ)
Hawaii Pacific Univ.
Heritage College (WA)
Howard Payne Univ. (TX)
Liberty Univ. (VA)
Master's Coll. and Seminary (CA)
Northern State Univ. (SD)
Northwest College (WA)
Northwestern College (MN)
Nyack College (NY)
Oklahoma Christian Univ.
Salisbury Univ. (MD)
Seattle Pacific Univ.
Southern Illinois Univ.–Carbondale
Texas Wesleyan Univ.
Union Univ. (TN)
Univ. of Evansville (IN)
Univ. of Findlay (OH)
Univ. of Nebraska–Lincoln
Univ. of Northern Iowa
Univ. of Wisconsin–Oshkosh
Univ. of Wisconsin–River Falls
Washington State Univ.

Technical and Business Writing

Allegheny College (PA)
Auburn Univ. (AL)
Bowling Green State Univ. (OH)
Carlow College (PA)
Carnegie Mellon Univ. (PA)
Cedarville Univ. (OH)
Chatham College (PA)
Coker College (SC)
College of Santa Fe (NM)
Colorado State Univ.
Dominican Univ. (IL)
Drexel Univ. (PA)
Eastern Michigan Univ.
Eastern Washington Univ.
Ferris State Univ. (MI)
Fitchburg State College (MA)
Grand Valley State Univ. (MI)
Illinois Institute of Technology
James Madison Univ. (VA)
Kutztown Univ. of Pennsylvania
Madonna Univ. (MI)
Maryville College (TN)
Medaille College (NY)
Miami Univ.–Oxford (OH)
Michigan State Univ.
Montana Tech of the Univ. of
    Montana
Mount Mary College (WI)
New Jersey Institute of Technology
New Mexico Institute of Mining
    and Technology
Northern Michigan Univ.
Ohio Northern Univ.
Southwest Missouri State Univ.
SUNY–Farmingdale
Univ. of Findlay (OH)
Univ. of Hartford (CT)
Univ. of Houston–Downtown
Univ. of Texas–San Antonio
Univ. of Washington
Univ. of Wisconsin–Stout
Valparaiso Univ. (IN)

Weber State Univ. (UT)
Winthrop Univ. (SC)
Worcester Polytechnic Inst. (MA)
York College of Pennsylvania
Youngstown State Univ. (OH)

Textile Sciences and Engineering

Auburn Univ. (AL)
Georgia Institute of Technology
North Carolina State Univ.–Raleigh
Philadelphia Univ.
Univ. of Mass.–Dartmouth

Theological and Ministerial Studies

Alma College (MI)
Anderson Univ. (IN)
Andrews Univ. (MI)
Anna Maria College (MA)
Assumption College (MA)
Atlantic Union College (MA)
Azusa Pacific Univ. (CA)
Barry Univ. (FL)
Bellarmine Univ. (KY)
Belmont Abbey College (NC)
Bethany College (KS)
Bethany College (CA)
Bethel College (IN)
Bethel Univ. (MN)
Bluefield College (VA)
Boston Univ.
Brescia Univ. (KY)
Brewton-Parker College (GA)
Briar Cliff Univ. (IA)
Calvin College (MI)
Campbell Univ. (NC)
Carlow College (PA)
Carroll College (MT)
Carson-Newman College (TN)
Cedarville Univ. (OH)
Central Christian College (KS)
Christendom College (VA)
Clearwater Christian College
    (FL)
College of St. Benedict (MN)
College of St. Catherine (MN)
College of St. Elizabeth (NJ)
College of the Holy Cross (MA)
Columbia Union College (MD)
Concordia Univ. (NE)
Concordia Univ. (CA)
Concordia Univ. (OR)
Concordia Univ. (MI)
Concordia Univ. Wisconsin
Concordia Univ.–River Forest (IL)
Concordia Univ.–St. Paul (MN)
Creighton Univ. (NE)
Crown College (MN)
Defiance College (OH)
Desales Univ. (PA)
Dominican Univ. (IL)
Dordt College (IA)
Duquesne Univ. (PA)
East Texas Baptist Univ.
Eastern Mennonite Univ. (VA)
Eastern Univ. (PA)

Elmhurst College (IL)
Elms College (College of Our Lady
of the Elms) (MA)
Emmanuel College (GA)
Franciscan Univ. of Steubenville
(OH)
Gannon Univ. (PA)
Grace Univ. (NE)
Grove City College (PA)
Hanover College (IN)
Hardin-Simmons Univ. (TX)
Harding Univ. (AR)
Hope International Univ. (CA)
Howard Payne Univ. (TX)
Huntington College (IN)
Immaculata Univ. (PA)
Indiana Wesleyan Univ.
John Brown Univ. (AR)
Juniata College (PA)
King's College (PA)
Lambuth Univ. (TN)
Livingstone College (NC)
Louisiana College
Loyola Marymount Univ. (CA)
Loyola Univ. Chicago
Madonna Univ. (MI)
Marian College (IN)
Marquette Univ. (WI)
Master's Coll. and Seminary (CA)
Morris College (SC)
Mount Olive College (NC)
Mount St. Mary's Univ. (MD)
Newman Univ. (KS)
Northwest Christian College (OR)
Northwest Nazarene Univ. (ID)
Northwestern College (MN)
Notre Dame College of Ohio
Nyack College (NY)
Oakwood College (AL)
Ohio Dominican Univ.
Ohio Wesleyan Univ.
Olivet Nazarene Univ. (IL)
Oral Roberts Univ. (OK)
Ouachita Baptist Univ. (AR)
Palm Beach Atlantic Univ. (FL)
Point Loma Nazarene Univ. (CA)
Providence College (RI)
Regent Univ. (VA)
Regis Univ. (CO)
Roanoke College (VA)
Roberts Wesleyan College (NY)
Seattle Pacific Univ.
Shorter College (GA)
Silver Lake College (WI)
Southern Adventist Univ. (TN)
Southern Nazarene Univ. (OK)
Southwest Baptist Univ. (MO)
Southwestern Adventist Univ. (TX)
Spring Hill College (AL)
St. Ambrose Univ. (IA)
St. Anselm College (NH)
St. Bonaventure Univ. (NY)
St. Gregory's Univ. (OK)
St. John's Univ. (NY)
St. John's Univ. (MN)
St. Joseph's College (ME)
St. Leo Univ. (FL)
St. Louis Univ.
St. Mary's Univ. of Minnesota
St. Mary's Univ. of San Antonio
St. Mary-of-The-Woods Coll. (IN)

St. Vincent College (PA)
Tabor College (KS)
Tennessee Wesleyan College
Texas Lutheran Univ.
Toccoa Falls College (GA)
Trinity Christian College (IL)
Union College (NE)
Union Univ. (TN)
Univ. of Chicago
Univ. of Dallas
Univ. of Great Falls (MT)
Univ. of Judaism (CA)
Univ. of Mary (ND)
Univ. of Mary Hardin-Baylor (TX)
Univ. of Notre Dame (IN)
Univ. of Portland (OR)
Univ. of San Francisco
Univ. of Sioux Falls (SD)
Univ. of St. Francis (IL)
Univ. of St. Francis (IN)
Univ. of St. Mary (KS)
Univ. of St. Thomas (TX)
Univ. of St. Thomas (MN)
Valparaiso Univ. (IN)
Vanguard Univ. of Southern
California
Viterbo Univ. (WI)
Walsh Univ. (OH)
Warner Southern College (FL)
Western Baptist College (OR)
Wheeling Jesuit Univ. (WV)
Williams Baptist College (AR)
Wisconsin Lutheran College
Xavier Univ. (OH)

Theology and Religious Vocations

Abilene Christian Univ. (TX)
Campbellsville Univ. (KY)
King College (TN)
Letourneau Univ. (TX)
Lubbock Christian Univ. (TX)
Martin Methodist College (TN)
Missouri Valley College
Nyack College (NY)
Oklahoma Wesleyan Univ.
Oral Roberts Univ. (OK)
Patten College (CA)
Simpson Univ. (CA)
Southeastern College of the
Assemblies of God
Southern Nazarene Univ. (OK)
St. Edward's Univ. (TX)
Trinity Christian College (IL)
Union Univ. (TN)
Univ. of St. Thomas (TX)
Univ. of Washington
Wayland Baptist Univ. (TX)

Transportation and Materials Moving

Dowling College (NY)
Syracuse Univ. (NY)

Turkic, Ural-Altaic, Caucasian, and Central Asian Lang., Lit., and Ling.

Univ. of Texas–Austin

Urban Studies/Affairs

Aquinas College (MI)
Ball State Univ. (IN)
Barnard College (NY)
Bethel Univ. (MN)
Boston Univ.
Brown Univ. (RI)
Bryn Mawr College (PA)
Buffalo State College
Butler Univ. (IN)
Canisius College (NY)
Cleveland State Univ.
College of Charleston (SC)
College of Mount St. Vincent (NY)
College of Wooster (OH)
Columbia Univ. (NY)
Connecticut College
CUNY–Hunter College
CUNY–Queens College
David Lipscomb Univ. (TN)
Depaul Univ. (IL)
Dillard Univ. (LA)
Eastern Univ. (PA)
Elmhurst College (IL)
Evergreen State College (WA)
Fordham Univ. (NY)
Furman Univ. (SC)
Georgia State Univ.
Hamline Univ. (MN)
Hampshire College (MA)
Hobart and William Smith Colleges
(NY)
Indiana Univ.–South Bend
Lehigh Univ. (PA)
Long Island Univ.–Brooklyn (NY)
Loyola Marymount Univ. (CA)
Manhattan College (NY)
Minnesota State Univ.–Mankato
Morehouse College (GA)
Mount Mercy College (IA)
New York Univ.
Northeastern Univ. (MA)
Northwestern Univ. (IL)
Occidental College (CA)
Ohio Univ.
Ohio Wesleyan Univ.
Rhodes College (TN)
Roosevelt Univ. (IL)
Rutgers–Camden (NJ)
Rutgers–New Brunswick (NJ)
San Diego State Univ.
San Francisco State Univ.
St. Cloud State Univ. (MN)
St. Louis Univ.
St. Peter's College (NJ)
Stanford Univ. (CA)
SUNY–Albany
Syracuse Univ. (NY)
Temple Univ. (PA)
Texas A&M International Univ.
Trinity College (CT)
Univ. of California–Berkeley

Univ. of California–San Diego
Univ. of Connecticut
Univ. of Minnesota–Duluth
Univ. of Minnesota–Twin Cities
Univ. of Missouri–Kansas City
Univ. of Nebraska–Omaha
Univ. of New Orleans
Univ. of Pennsylvania
Univ. of Pittsburgh
Univ. of Richmond (VA)
Univ. of Texas–Austin
Univ. of the District of Columbia
Univ. of Utah
Univ. of Washington
Univ. of Wisconsin–Green Bay
Vassar College (NY)
Virginia Commonwealth Univ.
Worcester State College (MA)
Wright State Univ. (OH)
York College of Pennsylvania

Vehicle Maintenance and Repair Technologies

Andrews Univ. (MI)
College of the Ozarks (MO)
Hampton Univ. (VA)
Kansas State Univ.
Lewis-Clark State College (ID)
Montana State Univ.–Northern
Pennsylvania College of
Technology
Southern Illinois Univ.–Carbondale
Thomas Edison State College (NJ)
Univ. of Alaska–Anchorage
Utah State Univ.
Western Michigan Univ.

Veterinary Biomedical and Clinical Sciences (Cert., M.S., Ph.D.)

Auburn Univ. (AL)
Washington State Univ.

Veterinary Medicine (D.V.M.)

Auburn Univ. (AL)
Cornell Univ. (NY)
Univ. of Minnesota–Twin Cities
Washington State Univ.

Visual and Performing Arts

Adrian College (MI)
Alma College (MI)
Arizona State Univ. West
Assumption College (MA)
Baldwin-Wallace College (OH)
Ball State Univ. (IN)
Bennington College (VT)
Berklee College of Music (MA)
Bethany College (WV)
Bloomfield College (NJ)
Bluefield College (VA)

Boston Conservatory
Brigham Young Univ.–Hawaii
California Baptist Univ.
California College of the Arts
California Institute of the Arts
California State Polytechnic
Univ.–Pomona
California State Univ.–Monterey
Bay
California State Univ.–Sacramento
Cazenovia College (NY)
Cedar Crest College (PA)
Centenary College of Louisiana
Chatham College (PA)
Cogswell Polytechnical Coll. (CA)
College For Creative Studies (MI)
Coppin State Univ. (MD)
Covenant College (GA)
Delta State Univ. (MS)
Dominican Univ. (IL)
East Stroudsburg Univ. of
Pennsylvania
Edgewood College (WI)
Elmira College (NY)
Fairleigh Dickinson Univ. (NJ)
Fayetteville State Univ. (NC)
Fisk Univ. (TN)
Franklin College (IN)
Friends Univ. (KS)
Frostburg State Univ. (MD)
Gallaudet Univ. (DC)
Gannon Univ. (PA)
George Mason Univ. (VA)
George Washington Univ. (DC)
Grace College and Seminary (IN)
Green Mountain College (VT)
Hampden-Sydney College (VA)
Hampshire College (MA)
Harvard Univ. (MA)
Haverford College (PA)
Heritage College (WA)
Howard Univ. (DC)
Huntington College (IN)
Illinois College
Illinois State Univ.
Illinois Wesleyan Univ.
Indiana Univ. of Pennsylvania
Iowa State Univ.
Ithaca College (NY)
Judson College (AL)
Kansas Wesleyan Univ.
Kent State Univ. (OH)
King College (TN)
Kutztown Univ. of Pennsylvania
Lagrange College (GA)
Lamar Univ. (TX)
Lambuth Univ. (TN)
Lawrence Univ. (WI)
Lincoln Memorial Univ. (TN)
Lindenwood Univ. (MO)
Long Island Univ.–C.W. Post
Campus (NY)
Longwood Univ. (VA)
Loyola Univ. New Orleans
Maharishi Univ. of Management
(IA)
Mary Baldwin College (VA)
Marywood Univ. (PA)
Medaille College (NY)
Milligan College (TN)
Millikin Univ. (IL)

Mississippi State Univ.
Mississippi Univ. For Women
Mississippi Valley State Univ.
Molloy College (NY)
Montana State Univ.–Billings
Mount Olive College (NC)
Mount St. Mary's Univ. (MD)
Nebraska Wesleyan Univ.
New Mexico Highlands Univ.
New Mexico State Univ.
New York Univ.
Niagara Univ. (NY)
Northwestern Univ. (IL)
Oakland Univ. (MI)
Oberlin College (OH)
Oklahoma Baptist Univ.
Oregon State Univ.
Pacific Lutheran Univ. (WA)
Penn. State Univ.–Univ. Park
Pepperdine Univ. (CA)
Pitzer College (CA)
Prescott College (AZ)
Providence College (RI)
Ramapo College of New Jersey
Regis Univ. (CO)
Rensselaer Polytechnic Inst. (NY)
Rhode Island School of Design
Rice Univ. (TX)
Richard Stockton College of New
    Jersey
Rockford College (IL)
Roger Williams Univ. (RI)
Salem State College (MA)
Samford Univ. (AL)
School of the Art Institute of
    Chicago
Seattle Univ.
Seton Hall Univ. (NJ)
Shenandoah Univ. (VA)
Siena College (NY)
Simon's Rock College of Bard
    (MA)
Sonoma State Univ. (CA)
South Dakota State Univ.
Southeast Missouri State Univ.
Southwest Missouri State Univ.
Southwestern Oklahoma State
    Univ.
Southwestern Univ. (TX)
St. Andrews Presbyterian College
    (NC)
St. Augustine's College (NC)
St. Gregory's Univ. (OK)
St. Joseph College (CT)
St. Joseph's Univ. (PA)
St. Mary's College of California

St. Peter's College (NJ)
Suffolk Univ. (MA)
SUNY College–Old Westbury
SUNY College–Potsdam
SUNY–Fredonia
SUNY–Purchase College
Swarthmore College (PA)
Texas Lutheran Univ.
Texas Wesleyan Univ.
Thomas More College (KY)
Truman State Univ. (MO)
Tulane Univ. (LA)
Tusculum College (TN)
Univ. of Alabama–Birmingham
Univ. of Arkansas–Monticello
Univ. of California–Los Angeles
Univ. of California–Riverside
Univ. of Hartford (CT)
Univ. of Louisiana–Lafayette
Univ. of Maine–Machias
Univ. of Mary Washington (VA)
Univ. of Maryland–Baltimore
    County
Univ. of Miami (FL)
Univ. of Minnesota–Duluth
Univ. of Mississippi
Univ. of Missouri–St. Louis
Univ. of Montana
Univ. of New Hampshire
Univ. of Oklahoma
Univ. of Pennsylvania
Univ. of Pittsburgh–Bradford
Univ. of San Francisco
Univ. of South Florida
Univ. of Southern Maine
Univ. of Southern Mississippi
Univ. of St. Francis (IL)
Univ. of Tampa (FL)
Univ. of Tennessee–Martin
Univ. of Texas–Austin
Univ. of Texas–Dallas
Univ. of the Arts (PA)
Univ. of Utah
Univ. of Wisconsin–Green Bay
Univ. of Wisconsin–Superior
Valdosta State Univ. (GA)
Villa Julie College (MD)
Virginia State Univ.
Viterbo Univ. (WI)
Washburn Univ. (KS)
Waynesburg College (PA)
West Virginia Univ.
Western Kentucky Univ.
Western Oregon Univ.
Western Washington Univ.
Wheaton College (IL)

Wheelock College (MA)
Wichita State Univ. (KS)
Wittenberg Univ. (OH)
York College of Pennsylvania
Youngstown State Univ. (OH)

Wildlife and Wildlands Science and Management

Arkansas State Univ.
Auburn Univ. (AL)
Brigham Young Univ.–Provo (UT)
Colorado State Univ.
Delaware Valley College (PA)
Eastern Kentucky Univ.
Eastern New Mexico Univ.
Frostburg State Univ. (MD)
Humboldt State Univ. (CA)
Lake Superior State Univ. (MI)
Lincoln Memorial Univ. (TN)
Mcneese State Univ. (LA)
Michigan State Univ.
Michigan Technological Univ.
Mississippi State Univ.
Murray State Univ. (KY)
New Mexico State Univ.
Northland College (WI)
Northwest Missouri State Univ.
Ohio State Univ.–Columbus
Purdue Univ.–West Lafayette (IN)
South Dakota State Univ.
Southwest Missouri State Univ.
Stephen F. Austin State Univ. (TX)
Tarleton State Univ. (TX)
Tennessee Technological Univ.
Texas A&M Univ.–College Station
Texas A&M Univ.–Kingsville
Texas Tech Univ.
Unity College (ME)
Univ. of Alaska–Fairbanks
Univ. of Arizona
Univ. of Arkansas–Monticello
Univ. of California–Davis
Univ. of Delaware
Univ. of Georgia
Univ. of Ill.–Urbana-Champaign
Univ. of Maine–Orono
Univ. of Massachusetts–Amherst
Univ. of Michigan–Ann Arbor
Univ. of Missouri–Columbia
Univ. of Montana
Univ. of Nevada–Reno
Univ. of New Hampshire
Univ. of Rhode Island
Univ. of Tennessee

Univ. of Washington
Univ. of Wisconsin–Madison
Univ. of Wisconsin–Stevens Point
Utah State Univ.
Washington State Univ.
West Texas A&M Univ.
West Virginia Univ.
Western New Mexico Univ.

Woodworking

Ferris State Univ. (MI)
Rochester Institute of Tech. (NY)

Work and Family Studies

Ashland Univ. (OH)
Indiana Univ.–South Bend
Portland State Univ. (OR)
Rockford College (IL)
Texas Tech Univ.
Union Univ. (TN)
Ursuline College (OH)

Zoology/Animal Biology

Auburn Univ. (AL)
Baker Univ. (KS)
Bennington College (VT)
California State Polytechnic
    Univ.–Pomona
California State Univ.–Long Beach
Carroll College (WI)
Colorado State Univ.
Cornell Univ. (NY)
Delaware Valley College (PA)
Friends Univ. (KS)
Humboldt State Univ. (CA)
Idaho State Univ.
Iowa State Univ.
Juniata College (PA)
Kansas State Univ.
Kent State Univ. (OH)
Kentucky Wesleyan College
Lawrence Univ. (WI)
Malone College (OH)
Mars Hill College (NC)
Methodist College (NC)
Miami Univ.–Oxford (OH)
Michigan State Univ.
North Carolina State Univ.–Raleigh
North Dakota State Univ.
Northern Arizona Univ.

Northern Michigan Univ.
Northland College (WI)
Northwestern Oklahoma State
    Univ.
Ohio State Univ.–Columbus
Ohio Univ.
Ohio Wesleyan Univ.
Oklahoma State Univ.
Olivet Nazarene Univ. (IL)
Oregon State Univ.
Prescott College (AZ)
Purdue Univ.–West Lafayette (IN)
Rutgers–Newark (NJ)
San Diego State Univ.
Southern Illinois Univ.–Carbondale
Tarleton State Univ. (TX)
Texas A&M Univ.–College Station
Texas State Univ.–San Marcos
Texas Tech Univ.
Texas Woman's Univ.
Tulane Univ. (LA)
Unity College (ME)
Univ. of Akron (OH)
Univ. of California–Davis
Univ. of California–Riverside
Univ. of California–San Diego
Univ. of California–Santa Barbara
Univ. of Connecticut
Univ. of Delaware
Univ. of Florida
Univ. of Georgia
Univ. of Hawaii–Manoa
Univ. of Ill.–Urbana-Champaign
Univ. of Maine–Orono
Univ. of Michigan–Ann Arbor
Univ. of Michigan–Flint
Univ. of Minnesota–Twin Cities
Univ. of Nebraska–Lincoln
Univ. of New Hampshire
Univ. of Oklahoma
Univ. of Rhode Island
Univ. of Tennessee
Univ. of Texas–Austin
Univ. of Vermont
Univ. of Washington
Univ. of Wisconsin–Madison
Univ. of Wyoming
Utah State Univ.
Washington State Univ.
Weber State Univ. (UT)
Western New Mexico Univ.
Western Washington Univ.

U.S.News & World Report

Ultimate College Directory

How to Use the Directory

In the following pages, you'll find exhaustive profiles of the more than 1,400 colleges and universities *U.S. News* surveys each year. The directory is organized by state, and schools are presented alphabetically within each state. The online version of the directory at www.usnews.com allows you to do a customized search of our database. Want to know which liberal arts colleges with no more than 2,000 students offer anthropology and are located within 100 miles of your home? Enter those criteria and pull up a list.

The vital statistics shown in each directory entry are explained below. The data were collected from the schools themselves during 2006. If a college did not supply the data requested, the information either does not appear or is marked as "N/A" for "not available." If a school did not return the full *U.S. News* questionnaire, only limited information appears in its write-up. In some cases, data reported in previous years were used if current-year data were unavailable.

Addresses and essential stats

This section supplies the basics: college name and address, whether the institution is public or private, year founded, religious affiliation, and contact information. Use the admissions office phone number or email address to request information or an application. Visit the school's website to research its programs, take a virtual tour, or submit an application.

- **Selectivity:** How competitive is the admissions process at the schools you are considering? Schools are designated "Most selective," "More selective," "Selective," "Less selective," or "Least selective" based on a formula that accounts for enrollees' test scores and class standing, and the school's acceptance rate (the percentage of applicants who are accepted). Since all of these factors are considered, a school that enrolls a high percentage of its applicants may still be considered selective if the students are of a high academic caliber.

- **Expenses:** Figures cited for tuition (including any required fees) are for the 2006–2007 academic year. For public schools, we list both in-state and out-of-state tuition. If data for the 2006–2007 academic year are not available, we provide figures for 2005–2006 or, in some cases, the school's estimate for 2006–2007.

- **SAT verbal/math or ACT score (25th/75th percentile):** The SAT or ACT composite scores shown represent the range within which half the students scored; 25 percent of students scored at or below the lower end of the range, and 25 percent scored at or above the upper end of the range. If no range was available, an average score was provided.

- **Rank in the 2007 edition of *U.S News*'s "America's Best Colleges":** The school's rank indicates where it sits among its peers in the 2007 ranking of colleges and universities published by *U.S. News* at www.usnews.com and in its annual guide "America's Best Colleges." You'll see the school's rank, followed by the category of institution it falls into. The categories are National University, Liberal Arts College, University–Master's, and Comprehensive College–Bachelor's. The master's and comprehensive schools further subdivide by location: North, South, West, and Midwest. Colleges and universities in the top half of their categories are ranked numerically. Others are placed in third and fourth tiers. You cannot compare the ranks of institutions in different categories because schools are assessed only against their peers. Schools that specialize in business, engineering, and art are labeled as such, but are not ranked; nor are the service academies, schools with fewer than 200 students, or schools with a high percentage of older or part-time students.

- **Acceptance rate:** The percentage of applicants accepted, a measure of how hard the school is to get into, is provided for the class entering in fall 2005.

Student body stats

What will your classmates be like? This section supplies the breakdown of full-time and part-time undergraduate students, the male and female enrollments, the ethnic makeup of the student body, and the percentage of students from countries other than the United States. In addition, a breakdown is given where reported of the percentage of students with various religious preferences. All figures are for the 2005–2006 academic year. Note that students who did not identify themselves as members of any demographic group are classified by schools as "White" and that numbers may not add up to 100 percent because of rounding.

Admissions facts and figures

Along with contact information for the admissions office, all of the application deadlines for fall 2007 admission—regular decision, early decision, and early action—are provided. You'll find out whether there is a date by which you must accept or turn down an offer, what the application fee is, and whether admission can be deferred. A school with rolling admissions makes decisions as applications are received, accepting students until the class has been filled. If the "common application" is accepted, the school is one of about 800 that recognize the standard application form distributed by the National Association of Secondary School Principals. For schools that allow you to apply online, the URL is provided.

Admissions requirements/recommendations: The high school academic courses required or recommended of applicants are noted. The number of required units stands alone, and the number of recommended units is enclosed in parentheses—e.g., English: 3 (4). If the information was unavailable, it does not appear. The section also tells you whether the school does or doesn't require SAT or ACT scores or uses them in admissions decisions. Be aware that a school may consider SAT or ACT scores if they are available even if they do not require them for admission. Finally, information is provided on whether campus visits, admissions interviews, and off-campus interviews are available or recommended.

Factors that count in admissions decisions: Various academic and nonacademic factors that are—or might be—considered in admission decisions are rated on their relative importance: "Very important,"

"Important," "Considered," and "Not considered."

Overlap schools: Up to five schools are provided whose applicant pools have the greatest overlap with the school's own applicant pool.

Admissions statistics for the fall 2005 entering class: A look at the admissions statistics for the fall 2005 entering class will tell you the proportion of all applicants who were accepted, as well as the proportion of early-decision and early-action applicants who got in compared to the acceptance rate of non-early applicants. You'll find how many of the freshmen enrolled were men, how many were women, and how many were from out of state. You will see statistics on how many students were put on the waiting list and how many of those students eventually enrolled.

Credentials of fall 2005 freshman: Of those who submitted their high school class standing when they applied, you will see how many ranked among the top 10 percent of their high school class, in the top quarter, and in the top half. We supply the average high school grade point average of the 2005 freshmen, the percentage submitting SAT and ACT scores, and, for both tests, the range within which half the students scored. The 25th/75th percentiles shown tell you that 25 percent of students scored at or below the lower end of the range and 25 percent scored at or above the upper end.

Academics

Academic calendar: This tells you whether the school year operates on a traditional semester schedule or a different type of schedule, such as trimesters or 4-1-4.

Degrees offered: A list of what types of degrees the school offers is provided.

Most popular majors: Here you will find a list of the five most popular majors among 2005 graduates with a bachelor's degree (and the percentage of students who majored in each).

Majors offered: Undergraduate majors offered are listed here by main field of study. For a more specific idea of majors offered, consult the index of majors that begins on page 190. When a school did not submit information about its majors, *U.S. News* obtained the data from the U.S. Department of Education.

Course requirements: For graduation, does the school require a general education or core curriculum, a minor, physical education, or religion/theology courses? Areas of required coursework are listed.

Pre-professional programs: A list of pre-professional programs offered. If the information was not available, this section does not appear.

Special academic programs (% participating): A list of special academic programs offered. If the information was not available, this section does not appear.

Teacher certification is offered in: Information on teacher certification offered by the school. If the information was not available, this section does not appear.

Cooperative education programs: A list of cooperative education programs offered. If the information was not available, this section does not appear.

Reserve Officers Training Corps (ROTC): This section indicates whether the school offers Army, Navy, or Air Force ROTC programs on campus or at a cooperating institution. If the information was not available, this section does not appear.

Faculty and instruction: Information on faculty includes the number of full-time and part-time professors and the breakdown of men, women, and minorities. You can also see what percentage has earned a Ph.D. or other terminal degree in their field. The student-to-faculty ratio is provided. Class-size figures tell you the percentage of classes during the fall 2005 term that had fewer than 20 students, the percentage with 20 to 49 students, and the percentage with 50 or more. (Labs and discussion sections are excluded.)

Advanced Placement and International Baccalaureate credit: If Advanced Placement (AP) and International Baccalaureate (IB) courses can be used for college credit or placement, that information is listed, along with the accepted AP scores.

Graduation and freshman retention rate: Two key numbers that applicants should consider are a school's freshman retention rate and its graduation rate. The freshman retention rate tells you the average proportion of the freshmen who started in 2001 through 2004 and returned the following fall. The graduation rates show the proportion starting college in 1999 who earned a degree in four years and in five years. We also show the average proportion of graduates who earned a degree in six years or less for classes starting in 1996

through 1999. Because these data were collected in different years, the percentage of students who graduate in six years may be lower than the percentage who graduate in four or five years.

Graduate study: You can see the proportion of students who pursue further study immediately upon graduation, within one year, and within five years. Additionally, we provide a breakdown of the proportion of graduates who pursue further study in business, law, medicine, dentistry, engineering, theology (or the seminary), education, arts and sciences, and veterinary medicine, if those subject areas apply and the information was available.

Costs and financial aid

Expenses: One statistic you will surely want to know is the sticker price: tuition, room, board, and required fees. We provide figures for the 2006–2007 academic year. For public schools, we list both in-state and out-of-state tuition. If data for the 2006–2007 academic year are not available, we provide figures for 2005–2006 or, in some cases, the school's estimate for 2006–2007. We also provide estimates of the cost of books and supplies, transportation, and personal expenses.

Financial aid information: Anyone planning on applying for financial aid for the fall of 2007 will find the necessary deadlines as well as any priority filing dates. The data on financial aid packages are for those awarded to undergraduates during the 2005–2006 school year and include the percentage of undergraduates who applied for aid; the percentage determined by the school to have financial need; and the percentage whose need was fully met by an aid package that excluded parent or other private loans. In addition, we give the average financial aid package (including grants, loans, and jobs) and the proportion of students awarded a package; the average amount of gift aid (scholarships or grants) and the proportion awarded such aid; the average amount of self-help aid (work study or loans) and the proportion awarded such aid; and the average need-based student loan. Among students who received need-based aid, what percentage of their need was met, on average? Among students who were awarded aid based only on merit, what was the average amount and the proportion awarded such merit aid? What was the average athletic scholarship awarded and the proportion receiving such an award?

Debt burden: This section informs you what the average debt was for the students in the Class of 2005 who borrowed money to finance their education and the proportion of students who borrowed.

Campus life and extracurricular activities

Housing: What types of college-owned, operated, or affiliated housing are available for undergraduates on campus, and what percentage of students live there? Is housing available for married students? What percentage live in college-owned or operated housing? These questions are answered in this section.

Student employment: Find out what proportion of undergraduates worked on campus during the 2005–2006 academic year and how much undergraduates can expect to earn per year from part-time, on-campus work.

Clubs and organizations: A sense of the extracurricular opportunities on campus can be gleaned from a list of major clubs and organizations, the numbers of fraternities and sororities and proportion of undergraduates who are members, and what percentage of students spend their weekends on campus.

2005–2006 sports program: This section includes information about the school's intercollegiate varsity sports program. Is the school a member of either the National Collegiate Athletic Association (NCAA) or the National Association of Intercollegiate Athletics (NAIA)? During the 2005–2006 year, how many intercollegiate varsity sports—and which ones—were played by men and women? When a school did not submit its sports data, *U.S. News* attempted to compile the information from the websites of the National Collegiate Athletic Association (NCAA), the National

Association of Intercollegiate Athletics (NAIA), or from the school's own website; in some cases, the information we supply may not be complete.

Services and facilities

Basic services: In this section, you'll find out what student services are offered, such as counseling services, remedial assistance, and career placement services.

Services for learning-disabled students: Find out if the school offers a separate structured program for learning-disabled students with separate admissions and additional fees as well as how many undergraduates are either enrolled in a learning-disabled program or are otherwise receiving services. Services offered to learning-disabled students are listed.

Library: This section gives an idea of the size of the library's collection.

Information and technology resources: Are students required to lease or own a computer? How many computers does the school have for students to use? Does the school have a wireless network and if so, approximately how many users can be accommodated on the network? What proportion of college housing is wired for high-speed Internet access?

Campus security: A list of security services offered.

Transfer and international students

Transfer students: Students thinking of transferring can quickly find out when to apply and whether applicants need a minimum number of credits. We provide the number of transfer applications received for fall 2005, the number of transfer applicants offered admission, and the number who enrolled.

International students: We note how many undergraduates come from other countries and how many countries are represented. Minimum and average TOEFL scores are also listed, if they are available.

Alabama

Alabama Agricultural and Mechanical Univ.

- **Address:** PO Box 1357, Normal, AL 35762
- **Website:** http://www.aamu.edu
- **Public**
- **Enrollment:** 4,631 full-time; 416 part-time

KEY STATS
- ✔ **U.S News College Ranking:** fourth tier, National Universities
- ✔ **ACT Score (25th/75th percentile):** 16-20
- ✔ **Tuition:** 2006-2007: $4,420 in state, $8,320 out of state

Selectivity: Less selective	**Room/board:** $4,770
Acceptance rate: 43%	**Average debt:** N/A
Student/faculty ratio: 16/1	**Proportion who borrowed:** N/A

UNDERGRADUATE STUDENT BODY STATS
2005-2006 enrollment: 4,631 full-time; 416 part-time. Men: 47%; women: 53%. **Ethnic makeup:** African American: 94%; White: 2%; International: 3%.

ADMISSIONS FACTS AND FIGURES
Phone: (256) 372-5245. **Email:** aboyle@aamu.edu. **Website:** http://www.aamu.edu. **Application deadlines for fall 2007:** Regular decision: July 15. Early decision: Not offered. Early action: Not offered. Admission can be deferred. **Application fee:** $10. Common application is not accepted. **To apply online, go to:** http://www.aamu.edu/Admission/admissionsapp.htm. **Admissions requirements/recommendations:** High school units required (recommended): English: 4; Mathematics: 4; Science: 2. Tests: The college uses SAT or ACT scores in admissions decisions. ACT required. Admissions interview: Neither required nor recommended. **Factors that count in admissions decisions:** *Academic:* Secondary school record: Important. Class rank: Considered. Letters of recommendation: Important. Standardized test scores: Very important. Essay: Considered. *Nonacademic:* Interview: Not considered. Extracurricular activities: Considered. Talent/ability: Not considered. Character/personal qualities: Considered. Alumni/ae relationship: Not considered. Geographical residence: Not considered. State residency: Important. Religious affiliation/commitment: Not considered. Minority status: Considered. Volunteer work: Not considered. Work experience: Not considered. **Admissions statistics for the fall 2005 entering class:** Total applicants: 6,784. Total accepted: 2,934. Freshmen enrolled: 1,099; 9% were from out of state. Overall acceptance rate: 43%. **First-year students submitting ACT scores:** 97%. Scores (25/75 percentile): English: 15-20, Math: 15-18, Composite: 16-20.

ACADEMICS
Year founded: 1875. **Academic calendar:** Semester. **Degrees offered:** associate, bachelor's, master's, doctorate. **Most popular majors:** 21% business, management, marketing, and related support services, 20% education, 13% engineering technologies/technicians, 7% biological and biomedical sciences, 7% computer and information sciences and support services. **Major fields of study:** agriculture, agriculture operations, and related sciences; architecture and related services; biological and biomedical sciences; business, management, marketing, and related support services; communication, journalism, and related programs; computer and information sciences and support services; education; engineering; engineering technologies/technicians; English language and literature/letters; family and consumer sciences/human sciences; history; mathematics and statistics; natural resources and conservation; physical sciences; psychology; public administration and social service professions; social sciences; visual and performing arts. **Areas of required coursework:** arts/fine arts, humanities, computer literacy, mathematics, English (including composition), philosophy, sciences (biological or physical), history, social science. **Special academic programs:** accelerated program, cooperative (work-study plan) program, distance learning, double major, dual enrollment, exchange student program (domestic), honors program, independent study, internships, study abroad, teacher certificate program, weekend college. **Cooperative education programs:** computer science. **Reserve Officers Training Corps (ROTC):** Army ROTC: Offered on campus. **Faculty and instruction (2005-2006):** Total instructional faculty: 321 full-time, 78 part-time (59% men; 41% women). Full-time faculty with Ph.D. or other terminal degree: 47%. Student/faculty ratio: 16/1. Classes of fewer than 20 students: 43%; of 20 to 49 students: 49%; of 50 or more students: 9%. **Freshmen returning for sophomore year:** 69%. **Graduation rates:** Four-year: 9%; five-year: 25%; six-year: 33%.

COSTS AND FINANCIAL AID
Financial aid office: (256) 372-5400. **Expenses (2006-2007):** Tuition and fees 2006-2007: $4,420 in state, $8,320 out of state; room/board: $4,770. Estimated books and supplies: $1,800; transportation: $2,400; personal expenses: $2,600. **Financial aid:** Priority filing date for institution's financial aid form: February 1; deadline: July 15. In 2005-2006, 92% of undergraduates applied for financial aid. Of those, 82% were determined to have financial need; 5% had their need fully met. Average financial aid package (proportion receiving): $5,705 (48%). Average amount of gift aid, such as scholarships or grants (proportion receiving): $4,333 (42%). Average amount of self-help aid, such as work study or loans (proportion receiving): $3,117 (30%). Average need-based loan (excluding PLUS or other private loans): $3,006. Among students who received need-based aid, the average percentage of need met: 26%. Among students who received aid based on merit, the average award (and the proportion receiving): $8,700 (8%). The average athletic scholarship (and the proportion receiving): $0 (0%).

CAMPUS LIFE AND EXTRACURRICULAR ACTIVITIES
Campus housing available: women's dorms, men's dorms. Students who live in college-owned, operated, or affiliated housing: 44%. Activities include: choral groups, concert band, dance, drama/theater, jazz band, marching band, music ensembles, pep band, radio station, student government, student newspaper, television station, yearbook. **Sports program (2005-2006):** Member of NCAA I. *Men's intercollegiate varsity sports:* baseball, basketball, cross-country, football, golf, soccer, tennis, track and field (indoor), track and field (outdoor). *Women's intercollegiate varsity sports:* basketball, bowling, cross-country, golf, soccer, softball, tennis, track and field (indoor), track and field (outdoor), volleyball.

SERVICES AND FACILITIES
Basic services: placement service, day care, health service, health insurance. **Remedial assistance:** math, writing. **Counseling services:** career, military. **Information technology resources:** Students are not required to lease or own a computer. School does not have a wireless network. **Campus safety:** Security services offered: 24-hour emergency telephones.

TRANSFER AND INTERNATIONAL STUDENTS
Transfer students: May apply for admission for the following academic terms: Fall, Spring, Summer. Applicants need a minimum number of credits to apply. For fall 2005: Transfer applications received: 1,039. Transfer applicants offered admission: 335. Transfer applicants enrolled: 201. **International students:** Number of foreign undergraduates: 134 (3% of student body). Minimum TOEFL score required: 500 (paper); 213 (computer).

Alabama State University

- **Address:** 915 S. Jackson Street, Montgomery, AL 36101
- **Website:** http://www.alasu.edu
- **Public**
- **Enrollment:** 3,958 full-time; 527 part-time

KEY STATS
- ✔ **U.S News College Ranking:** fourth tier, Universities–Master's (South)
- ✔ **ACT Score (25th/75th percentile):** 13-17
- ✔ **Tuition:** 2005-2006: $4,158 in state, $8,166 out of state

Selectivity: Less selective	**Room/board:** $3,400
Acceptance rate: 67%	**Average debt:** $21,150
Student/faculty ratio: 13/1	**Proportion who borrowed:** 13%

UNDERGRADUATE STUDENT BODY STATS

2005-2006 enrollment: 3,958 full-time; 527 part-time. Men: 40%; women: 60%. **Ethnic makeup:** African American: 96%; White: 3%.

ADMISSIONS FACTS AND FIGURES

Phone: (334) 229-4291. **Email:** dlamar@asunet.alasu.edu. **Website:** http://www.alasu.edu. **Application deadlines for fall 2007:** Regular decision: August 1. Early decision: Not offered. Early action: Not offered. Admission can be deferred. Common application is not accepted. **Admissions requirements/recommendations:** High school units required (recommended): English: (3); Mathematics: (2); Science: (2); Foreign language: (2); Social studies: (2); Total units: (11). Tests: The college does not use SAT or ACT scores in admissions decisions. Neither SAT nor ACT required. For admission to the fall 2007 entering class, the school will accept: ACT with writing, ACT without writing. Campus visit: Recommended. Admissions interview: Recommended. Off-campus interview: May not be arranged. **Factors that count in admissions decisions:** *Academic:* Secondary school record: Very important. Class rank: Important. Letters of recommendation: Considered. Standardized test scores: Important. Essay: Not considered. *Nonacademic:* Interview: Not considered. Extracurricular activities: Not considered. Talent/ability: Not considered. Character/personal qualities: Not considered. Alumni/ae relationship: Not considered. Geographical residence: Not considered. State residency: Not considered. Religious affiliation/commitment: Not considered. Minority status: Not considered. Volunteer work: Not considered. Work experience: Not considered. **Admissions statistics for the fall 2005 entering class:** Total applicants: 6,202. Total accepted: 4,154. Freshmen enrolled: 1,213; 40% were from out of state. Overall acceptance rate: 67%. **Average high school grade point average:** 2.8. **First-year students who submitted SAT scores:** 16%. Scores (25/75 percentile): Verbal: 330-430, Math: 330-430, Combined: 660-860. **First-year students submitting ACT scores:** 72%. Scores (25/75 percentile): English: N/A, Math: N/A, Composite: 13-17.

ACADEMICS

Year founded: 1867. **Academic calendar:** Semester. **Degrees offered:** certificate, bachelor's, post-bachelor's certificate, master's, post-master's certificate, doctorate. **Most popular majors:** 12% information science/studies, 10% elementary education and teaching, 9% criminal justice/safety studies, 8% secondary education and teaching, 7% communication studies/speech communication and rhetoric. **Major fields of study:** biological and biomedical sciences; business, management, marketing, and related support services; communication, journalism, and related programs; computer and information sciences and support services; education; English language and literature/letters; health professions and related clinical sciences; history; mathematics and statistics; parks, recreation, leisure, and fitness studies; physical sciences; psychology; public administration and social service professions; security and protective services; social sciences; visual and performing arts. **Areas of required coursework:** arts/fine arts, humanities, computer literacy, mathematics, English (including composition), sciences (biological or physical), history, social science. **Special academic programs:** cooperative (work-study plan) program, cross-registration, double major, honors program, internships, liberal arts/career combination, teacher certificate program. **Teacher certification offered in:** early childhood, special education, elementary, secondary. **Cooperative education programs:** art, business, computer science, education, humanities, natural science, social/behavioral science, vocational arts. **Reserve Officers Training Corps (ROTC):** Army ROTC: Offered at cooperating institution; Air Force ROTC: Offered on campus. **Faculty and instruction (2005-2006):** Total instructional faculty: 228 full-time, 180 part-time (43% men; 57% women; 74% minorities). Full-time faculty with Ph.D. or other terminal degree: 60%. Student/faculty ratio: 13/1. **Advanced Placement and International Baccalaureate credit:** AP tests may be used for: Placement only. Scores accepted: 4, 5. **Freshmen returning for sophomore year:** 68%. **Graduation rates:** Four-year: 9%; five-year: 18%; six-year: 22%.

COSTS AND FINANCIAL AID

Financial aid office: (334) 229-4323. **Expenses (2005-2006):** Tuition and fees 2005-2006: $4,158 in state, $8,166 out of state; room/board: $3,400. Estimated books and supplies: $1,000; transportation: $930; personal expenses: $930. **Financial aid:** Priority filing date for institution's financial aid form: May 1. In 2005-2006, 97% of undergraduates applied for financial aid. Of those, 90% were determined to have financial need; 15% had their need fully met. Average financial aid package (proportion receiving): $7,799 (84%). Average amount of gift aid, such as scholarships or grants (proportion receiving): $3,592 (70%). Average amount of self-help aid, such as work study or loans (proportion receiving): $3,871 (75%). Average need-based loan (excluding PLUS or other private loans): $3,428. Among students who received need-based aid, the average percentage of need met: 67%. Among students who received aid based on merit, the average award (and the proportion receiving): $4,924 (2%). The average athletic scholarship (and the proportion receiving): $8,356 (5%). Average amount of debt of borrowers graduating in 2005: $21,150. Proportion who borrowed: 13%.

CAMPUS LIFE AND EXTRACURRICULAR ACTIVITIES

Campus housing available (% using): women's dorms (58%), men's dorms (38%), other housing options (4%). Students who live in college-owned, operated, or affiliated housing: 45%. **Student employment:** During the 2005-2006 academic year, 10% of undergraduates worked on campus. Average per-year earnings: $4,017. **Clubs and organizations:** Number of student organizations: 64. Activities include: choral groups, concert band, dance, drama/theater, jazz band, marching band, music ensembles, musical theater, pep band, radio station, student government, student newspaper, symphony orchestra, yearbook. Number of fraternities: 5; sororities: 4. **Sports program (2005-2006):** Member of NCAA I. *Men's intercollegiate varsity sports:* baseball, basketball, cross-country, football, golf, tennis, track and field (indoor), track and field (outdoor). *Women's intercollegiate varsity sports:* basketball, bowling, cross-country, golf, soccer, softball, tennis, track and field (indoor), track and field (outdoor), volleyball.

SERVICES AND FACILITIES

Basic services: nonremedial tutoring, placement service, health service, health insurance. **Remedial assistance:** reading, math, writing, study skills. **Counseling services:** minority student, career, military, personal, veteran student, academic, older student, psychological, birth control. **For learning-disabled students:** School does not offer a structured program with separate admission and additional fees. Services include: remedial math, remedial English, remedial reading, tape recorders, untimed tests, note-taking services, oral tests, learning center, extended time for tests, tutors. **Library:** Number of titles: 286,270; number of current serial subscriptions: 126,616. **Information technology resources:** Students are not required to lease or own a computer. Number of campus computers available to all students: 550. School has a wireless network. Proportion of college-owned housing units wired for high-speed internet access: 10%. **Campus safety:** Security services offered: 24-hour foot-and-vehicle patrols, late-night transport/escort service, 24-hour emergency telephones, controlled dormitory access (key, security card, etc).

TRANSFER AND INTERNATIONAL STUDENTS

Transfer students: May apply for admission for the following academic terms: Fall, Spring, Summer. Applicants need a minimum number of credits to apply. For fall 2005: Transfer applicants enrolled: 166. **International students:** Number of foreign undergraduates: 16. Minimum TOEFL score required: 500 (paper).

Auburn University

- **Address:** 202 Martin Hall, Auburn University, AL 36849
- **Website:** http://www.auburn.edu
- **Public**
- **Enrollment:** 17,778 full-time; 1,476 part-time

KEY STATS

- ✔ **U.S News College Ranking:** 88, National Universities
- ✔ **ACT Score (25th/75th percentile):** 21-27
- ✔ **Tuition:** 2006-2007: $5,496 in state, $15,496 out of state

Selectivity: More selective	**Room/board:** $7,564
Acceptance rate: 82%	**Average debt:** $21,339
Student/faculty ratio: 17/1	**Proportion who borrowed:** 65%

UNDERGRADUATE STUDENT BODY STATS

2005-2006 enrollment: 17,778 full-time; 1,476 part-time. Men: 52%; women: 48%. **Ethnic makeup:** African American: 8%; American-Indian: 1%; Asian American: 2%; Hispanic: 2%; White: 88%; International: 1%.

ADMISSIONS FACTS AND FIGURES

Phone: (334) 844-4080. **Email:** admissions@auburn.edu. **Website:** http://www.auburn.edu. **Application deadlines for fall 2007:** Regular decision: August 1. Early decision: Not offered. Early action: Send application by:

November 1; Decision sent by: N/A. Admission can be deferred. **Application fee:** $25. Common application is not accepted. **To apply online, go to:** http://www.auburn.edu/admissions. **Admissions requirements/recommendations:** High school units required (recommended): English: 4 (4); Mathematics: 3 (3); Science: 2 (3); Foreign language: 0 (1); Social studies: 3 (4); History: 0 (0); Academic electives: 0 (0); Total units: 12 (15). Tests: The college uses SAT or ACT scores in admissions decisions. Either SAT or ACT required. For admission to the fall 2007 entering class, the school will accept: ACT with writing, ACT without writing. Campus visit: Recommended. Admissions interview: Neither required nor recommended. Off-campus interview: May be arranged. **Factors that count in admissions decisions:** *Academic:* Secondary school record: Very important. Class rank: Considered. Letters of recommendation: Considered. Standardized test scores: Very important. Essay: Considered. *Nonacademic:* Interview: Not considered. Extracurricular activities: Considered. Talent/ability: Considered. Character/personal qualities: Not considered. Alumni/ae relationship: Considered. Geographical residence: Considered. State residency: Important. Religious affiliation/commitment: Not considered. Minority status: Considered. Volunteer work: Considered. Work experience: Not considered. **Other schools with the greatest overlap in applicants:** Clemson University; Georgia Institute of Technology; University of Alabama; University of Florida; University of Georgia. **Admissions statistics for the fall 2005 entering class:** Total applicants: 14,249. Total accepted: 11,616. Freshmen enrolled: 4,197; 41% were from out of state. Overall acceptance rate: 82%. Non-early acceptance rate: 82%. **Size of waiting list:** 879 applicants; enrolled from waiting list: N/A. **Credentials of fall 2005 freshmen:** 32% ranked in the top 10 percent of their high school class; 56% were in the top 25 percent, and 85% were in the top half. (Proportion submitting class standing: 61%.) **Average high school grade point average:** 3.5. **First-year students who submitted SAT scores:** 31%. Scores (25/75 percentile): Verbal: 500-600, Math: 520-620, Combined: 1020-1220. **First-year students submitting ACT scores:** 69%. Scores (25/75 percentile): English: 21-28, Math: 20-26, Composite: 21-27.

ACADEMICS

Year founded: 1856. **Academic calendar:** Semester. **Degrees offered:** bachelor's, master's, post-master's certificate, first professional, doctorate. **Most popular majors:** 26% business, management, marketing, and related support services, 15% engineering, 9% education, 4% health professions and related clinical sciences, 4% psychology. **Major fields of study:** agriculture, agriculture operations, and related sciences; architecture and related services; biological and biomedical sciences; business, management, and related support services; communication, journalism, and related programs; computer and information sciences and support services; education; engineering; English language and literature/letters; family and consumer sciences/human sciences; foreign languages, literatures, and linguistics; health professions and related clinical sciences; history; mathematics and statistics; multi/interdisciplinary studies; natural resources and conservation; philosophy and religious studies; physical sciences; psychology; public administration and social service professions; social sciences; visual and performing arts. **Areas of required coursework:** arts/fine arts, humanities, computer literacy, mathematics, English (including composition), philosophy, sciences (biological or physical), history, social science. **Pre-professional programs:** pre-law, pre-dentistry, pre-medicine, pre-veterinary science, pre-optometry, pre-pharmacy. **Special academic programs (% participation):** accelerated program, cooperative (work-study plan) program (4.92%), distance learning (5.46%), double major (1.89%), dual enrollment, English as a Second Language (ESL) (10%), honors program (5.33%), independent study (17.57%), internships (30.66%), liberal arts/career combination, study abroad (6.31%), teacher certificate program (6.64%). **Teacher certification offered in:** early childhood, special education, elementary, vo-tech, adult education, secondary. **Cooperative education programs:** agriculture, art, business, computer science, engineering, humanities, natural science, social/behavioral science, technologies, other. **Reserve Officers Training Corps (ROTC):** Army ROTC: Offered on campus; Navy ROTC: Offered on campus; Air Force ROTC: Offered on campus. **Faculty and instruction (2005-2006):** Total instructional faculty: 1,176 full-time, 155 part-time (69% men; 31% women; 15% minorities). Full-time faculty with Ph.D. or other terminal degree: 93%. Student/faculty ratio: 17/1. Classes of fewer than 20 students: 27%; of 20 to 49 students: 59%; of 50 or more students: 13%. **Advanced Placement and International Baccalaureate credit:** AP tests may be used for: Credit and/or placement. Scores accepted: 3, 4, 5. International Baccalaureate exams may be used for: Credit and/or placement. **Freshmen returning for sophomore year:** 85%. **Graduation rates:** Four-year: 32%; five-year: 56%; six-year: 62%. **Graduate study:** Fields in which graduates pursue

further study: Master of Business Administration (MBA), 16%; law, 8%; medicine, 18%; engineering, 9%; education, 20%.

COSTS AND FINANCIAL AID

Financial aid office: (334) 844-4634. **Expenses (2006-2007):** Tuition and fees 2006-2007: $5,496 in state, $15,496 out of state; room/board: $7,564. Estimated books and supplies: $1,000; transportation: $1,804; personal expenses: $2,484. **Financial aid:** Priority filing date for institution's financial aid form: March 1. In 2005-2006, 44% of undergraduates applied for financial aid. Of those, 33% were determined to have financial need; 12% had their need fully met. Average financial aid package (proportion receiving): $7,683 (32%). Average amount of gift aid, such as scholarships or grants (proportion receiving): $4,477 (20%). Average amount of self-help aid, such as work study or loans (proportion receiving): $4,240 (28%). Average need-based loan (excluding PLUS or other private loans): $4,035. Among students who received need-based aid, the average percentage of need met: 48%. Among students who received aid based on merit, the average award (and the proportion receiving): $3,230 (4%). The average athletic scholarship (and the proportion receiving): $14,720 (2%). Average amount of debt of borrowers graduating in 2005: $21,339. Proportion who borrowed: 65%.

CAMPUS LIFE AND EXTRACURRICULAR ACTIVITIES

Campus housing available (% using): coed dorms (30%), women's dorms (20%), fraternity housing, apartment for single students (21%), special housing for disabled students (1%), other housing options (28%). Students who live in college-owned, operated, or affiliated housing: 16%. **Student employment:** During the 2005-2006 academic year, 13% of undergraduates worked on campus. Average per-year earnings: $4,500. **Clubs and organizations:** Number of student organizations: 250. Activities include: choral groups, concert band, dance, drama/theater, jazz band, literary magazine, marching band, music ensembles, musical theater, opera, pep band, radio station, student government, student newspaper, student film society, symphony orchestra, television station, yearbook. Number of fraternities: 26; sororities: 16. Proportion of men in fraternities: 20%; of women in sororities: 32%. Average proportion of students who stay on campus on weekends: 70%. **Sports program (2005-2006):** Member of NCAA I. *Men's intercollegiate varsity sports:* baseball, basketball, cross-country, football, golf, swimming and diving, tennis, track and field (indoor), track and field (outdoor). *Women's intercollegiate varsity sports:* basketball, cross-country, equestrian sports, golf, gymnastics, soccer, softball, swimming and diving, tennis, track and field (indoor), track and field (outdoor), volleyball.

SERVICES AND FACILITIES

Basic services: nonremedial tutoring, placement service, health service, health insurance. **Counseling services:** minority student, career, military, personal, veteran student, academic, older student, psychological, birth control, religious, other. **For learning-disabled students:** School does not offer a structured program with separate admission and additional fees. Total undergraduates in learning-disabled program or receiving services: 200. Services include: reading machines, diagnostic testing service, note-taking services, oral tests, learning center, readers, extended time for tests, tutors, priority registration, priority seating, exams on tape or computer, other testing accomodations, other. **Library:** Number of titles: 2,768,765; number of current serial subscriptions: 39,318. **Information technology resources:** Students are not required to lease or own a computer. Number of campus computers available to all students: 1,722. School has a wireless network. Approximate number of users that can be accommodated: 1,500. Proportion of college-owned housing units wired for high-speed internet access: 100%. **Campus safety:** Security services offered: 24-hour foot-and-vehicle patrols, late-night transport/escort service, 24-hour emergency telephones, lighted pathways/sidewalks, controlled dormitory access (key, security card, etc).

TRANSFER AND INTERNATIONAL STUDENTS

Transfer students: May apply for admission for the following academic terms: Fall, Spring, Summer. Applicants need a minimum number of credits to apply. For fall 2005: Transfer applications received: 2,474. Transfer applicants offered admission: 1,496. Transfer applicants enrolled: 1,057. **International students:** Number of foreign undergraduates: 140 (1% of student body). Number of countries represented: 55. Minimum TOEFL score required: 550 (paper); 213 (computer). Average TOEFL score: 580 (paper).

Auburn University–Montgomery

- **Address:** PO Box 244023, Montgomery, AL 36124
- **Website:** http://www.aum.edu
- **Public**
- **Enrollment:** 2,702 full-time; 1,598 part-time

KEY STATS

✔ **U.S News College Ranking:** third tier, Universities–Master's (South)
✔ **ACT Score (25th/75th percentile):** 18-23
✔ **Tuition:** 2006-2007: $4,640 in state, $13,430 out of state

Selectivity: Less selective	**Room/board:** $4,890
Acceptance rate: 98%	**Average debt:** N/A
Student/faculty ratio: 16/1	**Proportion who borrowed:** N/A

UNDERGRADUATE STUDENT BODY STATS

2005-2006 enrollment: 2,702 full-time; 1,598 part-time. Men: 35%; women: 65%. **Ethnic makeup:** African American: 33%; American-Indian: 1%; Asian American: 2%; Hispanic: 1%; White: 63%.

ADMISSIONS FACTS AND FIGURES

Phone: (334) 244-3611. **Email:** AdmitMe@mail.aum.edu. **Website:** http://www.aum.edu. **Application deadlines for fall 2007:** Regular decision: July 25. Early decision: Not offered. Early action: Not offered. Admission can be deferred. **Application fee:** $25. Common application is accepted. **Admissions requirements/recommendations:** High school units required (recommended): English: 4 (4); Mathematics: 4 (3); Science: 3 (2); Foreign language: 2 (2); Social studies: 2 (2); History: 2 (2); Academic electives: 2 (2). Tests: The college uses SAT or ACT scores in admissions decisions. Either SAT or ACT required. For admission to the fall 2007 entering class, the school will accept: ACT with writing, ACT without writing. Campus visit: Required. Admissions interview: Recommended. **Factors that count in admissions decisions:** *Academic:* Secondary school record: Very important. Class rank: Very important. Letters of recommendation: Considered. Standardized test scores: Very important. Essay: Not considered. *Nonacademic:* Interview: Not considered. Extracurricular activities: Not considered. Talent/ability: Not considered. Character/personal qualities: Not considered. Alumni/ae relationship: Not considered. Geographical residence: Not considered. State residency: Not considered. Religious affiliation/commitment: Not considered. Minority status: Not considered. Volunteer work: Not considered. Work experience: Not considered. **Admissions statistics for the fall 2005 entering class:** Total applicants: 814. Total accepted: 798. Freshmen enrolled: 758; Overall acceptance rate: 98%. **First-year students submitting ACT scores:** 95%. Scores (25/75 percentile): English: 18-24, Math: 16-21, Composite: 18-23.

ACADEMICS

Year founded: 1967. **Academic calendar:** Semester. **Degrees offered:** bachelor's, post-bachelor's certificate, master's, doctorate. **Most popular majors:** 36% business, management, marketing, and related support services, 17% education, 11% health professions and related clinical sciences, 6% psychology, 6% security and protective services. **Major fields of study:** biological and biomedical sciences; business, management, marketing, and related support services; communication, journalism, and related programs; education; English language and literature/letters; foreign languages, literatures, and linguistics; health professions and related clinical sciences; history; liberal arts and sciences studies, and humanities; mathematics and statistics; physical sciences; psychology; security and protective services; social sciences; visual and performing arts. **Areas of required coursework:** arts/fine arts, computer literacy, mathematics, English (including composition), history. **Special academic programs:** accelerated program, cooperative (work-study) plan) program, cross-registration, distance learning, double major, dual enrollment, English as a Second Language (ESL), exchange student program (domestic), honors program, independent study, internships, liberal arts/career combination, student-designed major, study abroad, teacher certificate program, weekend college. **Teacher certification offered in:** early childhood, special education, elementary, secondary. **Cooperative education programs:** art, business, computer science, education, engineering, health professions, natural science, social/behavioral science. **Reserve Officers Training Corps (ROTC):** Army ROTC: Offered on campus; Air Force ROTC: Offered at cooperating institution (Alabama State University). **Faculty and instruction (2005-2006):** Total instructional faculty: 186 full-time, 119 part-time (53% men; 47% women; 11% minorities). Full-time faculty with Ph.D.

or other terminal degree: 80%. Student/faculty ratio: 16/1. Classes of fewer than 20 students: 50%; of 20 to 49 students: 49%; of 50 or more students: 1%. **Advanced Placement and International Baccalaureate credit:** AP tests may be used for: Credit and/or placement. International Baccalaureate exams may be used for: Credit and/or placement. **Graduation rates:** Six-year: 28%.

COSTS AND FINANCIAL AID

Financial aid office: (334) 244-3570. **Expenses (2006-2007):** Tuition and fees 2006-2007: $4,640 in state, $13,430 out of state; room/board: $4,890. Estimated books and supplies: $600; transportation: $850; personal expenses: $1,060. **Financial aid:** In 2005-2006, 72% of undergraduates applied for financial aid. Of those, 67% were determined to have financial need; 16% had their need fully met. Average financial aid package (proportion receiving): $7,516 (52%). Average amount of gift aid, such as scholarships or grants (proportion receiving): $3,275 (39%). Average amount of self-help aid, such as work study or loans (proportion receiving): N/A (47%). Average need-based loan (excluding PLUS or other private loans): $3,525.

CAMPUS LIFE AND EXTRACURRICULAR ACTIVITIES

Campus housing available: coed dorms, special housing for disabled students. Students who live in college-owned, operated, or affiliated housing: 12%. **Clubs and organizations:** Number of student organizations: 65. Activities include: choral groups, drama/theater, student government, student newspaper. Number of fraternities: 6; sororities: 6. Proportion of men in fraternities: 6%; of women in sororities: 4%. Average proportion of students who stay on campus on weekends: 10%. **Sports program (2005-2006):** Member of NAIA. *Men's intercollegiate varsity sports:* baseball, basketball, soccer, tennis. *Women's intercollegiate varsity sports:* basketball, soccer, tennis.

SERVICES AND FACILITIES

Basic services: placement service. **Remedial assistance:** math. **For learning-disabled students:** School does not offer a structured program with separate admission and additional fees. Services include: remedial math, remedial English, reading machines, remedial reading, tape recorders, videotaped classes, untimed tests, note-taking services, oral tests, learning center, readers, extended time for tests, tutors, other. **Library:** Number of titles: 328,134; number of current serial subscriptions: 2,245. **Information technology resources:** Students are not required to lease or own a computer. Number of campus computers available to all students: 200. **Campus safety:** Security services offered: 24-hour foot-and-vehicle patrols, 24-hour emergency telephones, lighted pathways/sidewalks, student patrols.

TRANSFER AND INTERNATIONAL STUDENTS

Transfer students: May apply for admission for the following academic terms: Fall, Spring, Summer. Applicants need a minimum number of credits to apply. **International students:** Number of foreign undergraduates: 20. Minimum TOEFL score required: 500 (paper); 173 (computer).

Birmingham-Southern College

- **Address:** 900 Arkadelphia Road, Birmingham, AL 35254
- **Website:** http://www.bsc.edu
- **Private; Religious affiliation:** United Methodist
- **Enrollment:** 1,294 full-time; 30 part-time

KEY STATS

✔ **U.S News College Ranking:** 74, Liberal Arts Colleges
✔ **ACT Score (25th/75th percentile):** 23-29
✔ **Tuition:** 2006-2007: $22,940

Selectivity: More selective	**Room/board:** $7,200
Acceptance rate: 63%	**Average debt:** $12,857
Student/faculty ratio: 12/1	**Proportion who borrowed:** 51%

UNDERGRADUATE STUDENT BODY STATS

2005-2006 enrollment: 1,294 full-time; 30 part-time. Men: 44%; women: 56%. **Ethnic makeup:** African American: 7%; Asian American: 3%; Hispanic: 1%; White: 89%. **Religious preference:** Roman Catholic: 12%; Protestant: 28%; Jewish: 1%; Hindu: 1%; No preference: 15%; United Methodist: 30%; Episcopal: 8%; Other: 5%.

ADMISSIONS FACTS AND FIGURES

Phone: (205) 226-4696. **Email:** admission@bsc.edu. **Website:** http://www.bsc.edu. **Application deadlines for fall 2007:** Regular decision: Rolling. Early decision: Not offered. Early action: Send application by: December 1; Decision sent by: December 15. Admission can be deferred. **Application fee:** $25. Common application is accepted. **To apply online, go to:** http://www.bsc.edu/admission/online.htm. **Admissions requirements/recommendations:** High school units required (recommended): English: 4; Mathematics: (4); Science: (4); Foreign language: (2); Social studies: (2); History: (2); Academic electives: (10); Total units: 16. Tests: The college uses SAT or ACT scores in admissions decisions. Either SAT or ACT required. For admission to the fall 2007 entering class, the school will accept; ACT with writing, ACT without writing. Campus visit: Recommended. Admissions interview: Recommended. Off-campus interview: Not available. **Factors that count in admissions decisions:** *Academic:* Secondary school record: Very important. Class rank: Not considered. Letters of recommendation: Very important. Standardized test scores: Very important. Essay: Very important. *Nonacademic:* Interview: Considered. Extracurricular activities: Considered. Talent/ability: Considered. Character/personal qualities: Important. Alumni/ae relationship: Not considered. Geographical residence: Not considered. State residency: Not considered. Religious affiliation/commitment: Not considered. Minority status: Not considered. Volunteer work: Considered. Work experience: Considered. **Other schools with the greatest overlap in applicants:** Auburn University; Millsaps College; Rhodes College; Sewanee–University of the South; University of Alabama. **Admissions statistics for the fall 2005 entering class:** Total applicants: 2,217. Total accepted: 1,395. Freshmen enrolled: 316; 29% were from out of state. Overall acceptance rate: 63%. Non-early acceptance rate: 63%. **Credentials of fall 2005 freshmen:** 30% ranked in the top 10 percent of their high school class; 59% were in the top 25 percent, and 84% were in the top half. (Proportion submitting class standing: 72%.) **Average high school grade point average:** 3.3. **First-year students who submitted SAT scores:** 49%. Scores (25/75 percentile): Verbal: 530-650, Math: 530-640, Combined: 1060-1290. **First-year students submitting ACT scores:** 84%. Scores (25/75 percentile): English: 23-30, Math: 22-27, Composite: 23-29.

ACADEMICS

Year founded: 1856. **Academic calendar:** 4-1-4. **Degrees offered:** bachelor's, master's. **Most popular majors:** 22% business, management, marketing, and related support services, 11% multi/interdisciplinary studies, 10% biological and biomedical sciences, 9% visual and performing arts, 8% English language and literature/letters. **Major fields of study:** biological and biomedical sciences; computer and information sciences and support services; education; engineering; engineering technologies/technicians; English language and literature/letters; foreign languages, literatures, and linguistics; health professions and related clinical sciences; mathematics and statistics; multi/interdisciplinary studies; philosophy and religious studies; physical sciences; psychology; science technologies/technicians; social sciences; theology and religious vocations; visual and performing arts. **Areas of required coursework:** arts/fine arts, humanities, computer literacy, mathematics, English (including composition), philosophy, foreign languages, sciences (biological or physical), history, social science. **Pre-professional programs:** pre-law, pre-dentistry, pre-medicine, pre-theology, pre-veterinary science, pre-optometry, pre-pharmacy, other. **Special academic programs (% participation):** cooperative (work-study plan) program (19%), cross-registration (3%), double major (1%), dual enrollment, exchange student program (domestic), honors program (5%), independent study (16%), internships (15%), student-designed major (1%), study abroad (1%), teacher certificate program (4%). **Teacher certification offered in:** special education, elementary, secondary. **Reserve Officers Training Corps (ROTC):** Army ROTC: Offered at cooperating institution (University of Alabama at Birmingham); Air Force ROTC: Offered at cooperating institution (Samford University). **Faculty and instruction (2005-2006):** Total instructional faculty: 100 full-time, 37 part-time (58% men; 42% women; 2% minorities). Full-time faculty with Ph.D. or other terminal degree: 96%. Student/faculty ratio: 12/1. Classes of fewer than 20 students: 62%; of 20 to 49 students: 37%; of 50 or more students: 1%. **Advanced Placement and International Baccalaureate credit:** AP tests may be used for: Credit and/or placement. Scores accepted: 4, 5. International Baccalaureate exams may be used for: Credit and/or placement. **Freshmen returning for sophomore year:** 85%. **Graduation rates:** Four-year: 62%; five-year: 67%; six-year: 70%. **Graduate study:** 44% of students pursue further study immediately upon graduation; 5% within one year. Fields in which graduates pursue further study: Master of Business Administration (MBA), 5%; law, 28%; medicine, 15%; dentistry, 4%; engineering, 5%; theology (or the seminary), 10%; education, 4%; arts and sciences, 4%.

COSTS AND FINANCIAL AID

Financial aid office: (205) 226-4688. **Expenses (2006-2007):** Tuition and fees 2006-2007: $22,940; room/board: $7,200. Estimated books and supplies: $1,100; transportation: $1,200; personal expenses: $2,330. **Financial aid:** Priority filing date for institution's financial aid form: March 1; deadline: August 1. In 2005-2006, 59% of undergraduates applied for financial aid. Of those, 44% were determined to have financial need; 35% had their need fully met. Average financial aid package (proportion receiving): $15,595 (44%). Average amount of gift aid, such as scholarships or grants (proportion receiving): $12,202 (31%). Average amount of self-help aid, such as work study or loans (proportion receiving): $4,926 (41%). Average need-based loan (excluding PLUS or other private loans): $4,401. Among students who received need-based aid, the average percentage of need met: 79%. Among students who received aid based on merit, the average award (and the proportion receiving): $11,106 (33%). The average athletic scholarship (and the proportion receiving): $20,598 (5%). Average amount of debt of borrowers graduating in 2005: $12,857. Proportion who borrowed: 51%.

CAMPUS LIFE AND EXTRACURRICULAR ACTIVITIES

Campus housing available (% using): women's dorms (47%), men's dorms (33%), sorority housing (4%), fraternity housing (11%), apartments for married students, apartment for single students (5%), special housing for disabled students. Students who live in college-owned, operated, or affiliated housing: 79%. **Student employment:** During the 2005-2006 academic year, 0% of undergraduates worked on campus. **Clubs and organizations:** Number of student organizations: 84. Activities include: choral groups, dance, drama/theater, jazz band, literary magazine, music ensembles, musical theater, opera, pep band, student government, student newspaper, yearbook. Number of fraternities: 6; sororities: 8. Proportion of men in fraternities: 44%; of women in sororities: 51%. Average proportion of students who stay on campus on weekends: 75%. **Sports program (2005-2006):** Member of NCAA I. *Men's intercollegiate varsity sports:* baseball, basketball, cross-country, golf, soccer, tennis. *Women's intercollegiate varsity sports:* basketball, cross-country, golf, riflery, soccer, softball, tennis, volleyball.

SERVICES AND FACILITIES

Basic services: nonremedial tutoring, health service, health insurance, other. **Counseling services:** minority student, career, personal, academic, psychological, religious. **For learning-disabled students:** School does not offer a structured program with separate admission and additional fees. Total undergraduates in learning-disabled program or receiving services: 80. Services include: tape recorders, untimed tests, oral tests, extended time for tests, tutors, priority seating, other testing accomodations. **Library:** Number of titles: 282,934; number of current serial subscriptions: 1,215. **Information technology resources:** Students are not required to lease or own a computer. Number of campus computers available to all students: 510. School has a wireless network. Approximate number of users that can be accommodated: 400. Proportion of college-owned housing units wired for high-speed internet access: 100%. **Campus safety:** Security services offered: 24-hour foot-and-vehicle patrols, late-night transport/escort service, 24-hour emergency telephones, lighted pathways/sidewalks, controlled dormitory access (key, security card, etc).

TRANSFER AND INTERNATIONAL STUDENTS

Transfer students: May apply for admission for the following academic terms: Fall, Winter, Spring, Summer. Applicants need a minimum number of credits to apply. For fall 2005: Transfer applications received: 74. Transfer applicants offered admission: 42. Transfer applicants enrolled: 33. **International students:** Number of foreign undergraduates: 4. Number of countries represented: 14. Minimum TOEFL score required: 500 (paper); 173 (computer).

Concordia College

- **Address:** 1804 Green Street, Selma, AL 36703-3323
- **Website:** http://www.concordiaselma.edu/
- **Private; Religious affiliation:** Lutheran
- **Enrollment:** N/A

KEY STATS
✔ **U.S News College Ranking:** fourth tier, Comp. Coll.–Bachelor's (South)
✔ **SAT or ACT Score (25th/75th percentile):** N/A
✔ **Tuition:** N/A

Selectivity: Less selective	**Room/board:** N/A
Acceptance rate: N/A	**Average debt:** N/A
Student/faculty ratio: N/A	**Proportion who borrowed:** N/A

Faulkner University

- **Address:** 5345 Atlanta Highway, Montgomery, AL 36109
- **Website:** http://www.faulkner.edu
- **Private; Religious affiliation:** Church of Christ
- **Enrollment:** 1,510 full-time; 603 part-time

KEY STATS
✔ **U.S News College Ranking:** third tier, Comp. Colleges–Bachelor's (South)
✔ **ACT Score (25th/75th percentile):** 18-23
✔ **Tuition:** 2006-2007: $11,425

Selectivity: Selective	**Room/board:** $5,400
Acceptance rate: 49%	**Average debt:** $18,900
Student/faculty ratio: 19/1	**Proportion who borrowed:** 82%

UNDERGRADUATE STUDENT BODY STATS
2005-2006 enrollment: 1,510 full-time; 603 part-time. Men: 38%; women: 62%. **Ethnic makeup:** African American: 31%; Asian American: 1%; Hispanic: 1%; White: 66%. **Religious preference:** Roman Catholic: 2%; Protestant: 41%; Unknown: 4%; Church of Christ: 53%.

ADMISSIONS FACTS AND FIGURES
Phone: (334) 386-7200. **Email:** kmock@faulkner.edu. **Website:** http://www.faulkner.edu. **Application deadlines for fall 2007:** Regular decision: Rolling. Early decision: Not offered. Early action: Not offered. Admission cannot be deferred. **Application fee:** $10. Common application is accepted. **Admissions requirements/recommendations:** High school units required (recommended): English: 3; Mathematics: 3; Science: 3; Foreign language: 0; Social studies: 0; History: 3; Academic electives: 0; Total units: 15. Tests: The college uses SAT or ACT scores in admissions decisions. Either SAT or ACT required. For admission to the fall 2007 entering class, the school will accept: ACT with writing, ACT without writing. Campus visit: Recommended. Admissions interview: Recommended. Off-campus interview: May be arranged. **Factors that count in admissions decisions:** *Academic:* Secondary school record: Very important. Class rank: Important. Letters of recommendation: Very important. Standardized test scores: Very important. Essay: Important. *Nonacademic:* Interview: Very important. Extracurricular activities: Very important. Talent/ability: Important. Character/personal qualities: Very important. Alumni/ae relationship: Very important. Geographical residence: Not considered. State residency: Not considered. Religious affiliation/commitment: Important. Minority status: Not considered. Volunteer work: Important. Work experience: Important. **Other schools with the greatest overlap in applicants:** Auburn University; Auburn University–Montgomery; Freed-Hardeman University; Harding University; Lipscomb University. **Admissions statistics for the fall 2005 entering class:** Total applicants: 630. Total accepted: 311. Freshmen enrolled: 204; 27% were from out of state. Overall acceptance rate: 49%. **Credentials of fall 2005 freshmen:** 19% ranked in the top 10 percent of their high school class; 53% were in the top 25 percent, and 86% were in the top half. (Proportion submitting class standing: 62%.) **Average high school grade point average:** 3.2. **First-year students who submitted SAT scores:** 12%. Scores (25/75 percentile): Verbal: 430-570, Math: 450-570, Combined: 880-1140. **First-year students submitting ACT scores:** 87%. Scores (25/75 percentile): English: 18-24, Math: 17-23, Composite: 18-23.

ACADEMICS
Year founded: 1942. **Academic calendar:** Semester. **Degrees offered:** certificate, associate, bachelor's, master's, doctorate. **Most popular majors:** 47% business administration and management, 8% criminal justice/police science, 2% psychology, 1% computer science, 1% education. **Major fields of study:** agriculture, agriculture operations, and related sciences; business, management, marketing, and related support services; computer and information sciences and support services; education; English language and literature/letters; liberal arts and sciences studies, and humanities; mathematics and statistics; parks, recreation, leisure, and fitness studies; psychology; security and protective services; theology and religious vocations; visual and performing arts. **Areas of required coursework:** arts/fine arts, humanities, computer literacy, mathematics, English (including composition), foreign languages, sciences (biological or physical), history, social science, other. **Pre-professional programs:** pre-law, pre-dentistry, pre-medicine, pre-veterinary science, pre-optometry, pre-pharmacy. **Special academic programs:** cross-registration, distance learning, double major, dual enrollment, honors program, independent study, internships, study abroad, weekend college. **Teacher certification offered in:** elementary, secondary. **Cooperative education programs:** computer science, education, natural science. **Reserve Officers Training Corps (ROTC):** Army ROTC: Offered at cooperating institution (Auburn University at Montgomery); Air Force ROTC: Offered at cooperating institution (Alabama State University). **Faculty and instruction (2005-2006):** Total instructional faculty: 89 full-time, 50 part-time (69% men; 31% women; 23% minorities). Full-time faculty with Ph.D. or other terminal degree: 63%. Student/faculty ratio: 19/1. Classes of fewer than 20 students: 81%; of 20 to 49 students: 19%; of 50 or more students: 1%. **Advanced Placement and International Baccalaureate credit:** AP tests may be used for: Credit only. Scores accepted: 2. International Baccalaureate exams may be used for: Credit only. **Freshmen returning for sophomore year:** 56%. **Graduation rates:** Five-year: 14%; six-year: 25%. **Graduate study:** 22% of students pursue further study immediately upon graduation. Fields in which graduates pursue further study: Master of Business Administration (MBA), 30%; law, 24%; medicine, 1%; engineering, 3%; theology (or the seminary), 6%; education, 10%.

COSTS AND FINANCIAL AID
Financial aid office: (334) 386-7195. **Expenses (2006-2007):** Tuition and fees 2006-2007: $11,425; room/board: $5,400. Estimated books and supplies: $1,200; transportation: $1,500; personal expenses: $1,200. **Financial aid:** Priority filing date for institution's financial aid form: May 1. In 2005-2006, 90% of undergraduates applied for financial aid. Of those, 72% were determined to have financial need; 10% had their need fully met. Average financial aid package (proportion receiving): $7,300 (72%). Average amount of gift aid, such as scholarships or grants (proportion receiving): $3,800 (50%). Average amount of self-help aid, such as work study or loans (proportion receiving): $4,600 (65%). Average need-based loan (excluding PLUS or other private loans): $5,300. Among students who received need-based aid, the average percentage of need met: 60%. Among students who received aid based on merit, the average award (and the proportion receiving): $2,500 (3%). The average athletic scholarship (and the proportion receiving): $6,400 (19%). Average amount of debt of borrowers graduating in 2005: $18,900. Proportion who borrowed: 82%.

CAMPUS LIFE AND EXTRACURRICULAR ACTIVITIES
Campus housing available (% using): women's dorms (32%), men's dorms (31%), apartment for single students (37%), special housing for disabled students. Students who live in college-owned, operated, or affiliated housing: 15%. **Student employment:** During the 2005-2006 academic year, 45% of undergraduates worked on campus. Average per-year earnings: $1,600. **Clubs and organizations:** Number of student organizations: 11. Activities include: choral groups, drama/theater, jazz band, literary magazine, music ensembles, musical theater, pep band, student government, student newspaper, student film society, yearbook. Number of fraternities: 0; sororities: 0. Average proportion of students who stay on campus on weekends: 60%. **Sports program (2005-2006):** Member of NAIA. *Men's intercollegiate varsity sports:* baseball, basketball, cross-country, golf, soccer. *Women's intercollegiate varsity sports:* cross-country, soccer, softball, volleyball.

SERVICES AND FACILITIES
Basic services: health service, health insurance. **Remedial assistance:** reading, math, writing. **Counseling services:** career, personal, academic, psychological, religious. **For learning-disabled students:** School does not offer a structured program with separate admission and additional fees. Total undergraduates in learning-disabled program or receiving services: 30. Services include: remedial math, remedial English, reading machines,

remedial reading, tape recorders, untimed tests, note-taking services, oral tests, learning center, readers, extended time for tests, tutors, priority registration, priority seating, texts on tape, typist/scribe, exams on tape or computer, other testing accomodations, other. **Library:** Number of titles: 122,056; number of current serial subscriptions: 3,233. **Information technology resources:** Students are not required to lease or own a computer. Number of campus computers available to all students: 668. School has a wireless network. Approximate number of users that can be accommodated: 968. Proportion of college-owned housing units wired for high-speed internet access: 50%. **Campus safety:** Security services offered: 24-hour foot-and-vehicle patrols, late-night transport/escort service, lighted pathways/sidewalks, student patrols, controlled dormitory access (key, security card, etc).

TRANSFER AND INTERNATIONAL STUDENTS

Transfer students: May apply for admission for the following academic terms: Fall, Winter, Spring, Summer. Applicants need a minimum number of credits to apply. For fall 2005: Transfer applications received: 154. Transfer applicants offered admission: 101. Transfer applicants enrolled: 69. **International students:** Number of foreign undergraduates: 6. Number of countries represented: 4. Minimum TOEFL score required: 450 (paper); 133 (computer).

Huntingdon College

- **Address:** 1500 E. Fairview Avenue, Montgomery, AL 36106-2148
- **Website:** http://www.huntingdon.edu
- **Private; Religious affiliation:** Methodist
- **Enrollment:** 733 full-time; 57 part-time

KEY STATS

✔ **U.S News College Ranking:** fourth tier, Liberal Arts Colleges
✔ **ACT Score (25th/75th percentile):** 20-25
✔ **Tuition:** 2006-2007: $16,690

Selectivity: More selective	**Room/board:** $6,400
Acceptance rate: 64%	**Average debt:** $17,540
Student/faculty ratio: 18/1	**Proportion who borrowed:** 68%

UNDERGRADUATE STUDENT BODY STATS

2005-2006 enrollment: 733 full-time; 57 part-time. Men: 50%; women: 50%. **Ethnic makeup:** African American: 13%; American-Indian: 1%; Asian American: 1%; Hispanic: 1%; White: 82%; International: 3%. **Religious preference:** Roman Catholic: 3%; Protestant: 40%; Unknown: 25%; Methodist: 32%.

ADMISSIONS FACTS AND FIGURES

Phone: (334) 833-4497. **Email:** admis@huntingdon.edu. **Website:** http://www.huntingdon.edu. **Application deadlines for fall 2007:** Regular decision: August 1. Early decision: Not offered. Early action: Not offered. Admission can be deferred. **Application fee:** $20. Common application is accepted. **Admissions requirements/recommendations:** High school units required (recommended): English: 4; Mathematics: 3; Science: 2; Foreign language: 2; History: 2; Total units: 15. Tests: The college uses SAT or ACT scores in admissions decisions. Either SAT or ACT required. For admission to the fall 2007 entering class, the school will accept: ACT with writing, ACT without writing. Campus visit: Recommended. Admissions interview: Recommended. Off-campus interview: May be arranged. **Factors that count in admissions decisions:** *Academic:* Secondary school record: Very important. Class rank: Considered. Letters of recommendation: Considered. Standardized test scores: Very important. Essay: Considered. *Nonacademic:* Interview: Considered. Extracurricular activities: Considered. Talent/ability: Considered. Character/personal qualities: Very important. Alumni/ae relationship: Considered. Geographical residence: Not considered. State residency: Not considered. Religious affiliation/commitment: Not considered. Minority status: Not considered. Volunteer work: Considered. Work experience: Considered. **Other schools with the greatest overlap in applicants:** Auburn University; Auburn University–Montgomery; Birmingham-Southern College; Troy University; University of Alabama. **Admissions statistics for the fall 2005 entering class:** Total applicants: 774. Total accepted: 495. Freshmen enrolled: 184; 19% were from out of state. Overall acceptance rate: 64%. **Credentials of fall 2005 freshmen:** 26% ranked in the top 10 percent of their high school class; 55% were in the top 25 percent, and 86% were in the top half. (Proportion submitting class standing: 76%.) **Average high school grade point average:** 3.3. **First-year students who submitted SAT scores:** 15%. Scores (25/75 percentile): Verbal: 460-570, Math: 430-550;

Combined: 890-1120. **First-year students submitting ACT scores:** 92%. Scores (25/75 percentile): English: 20-27, Math: 18-26, Composite: 20-25.

ACADEMICS

Year founded: 1854. **Academic calendar:** Semester. **Degrees offered:** associate, bachelor's. **Most popular majors:** 18% biology/biological sciences, 15% kinesiology and exercise science, 11% business administration and management, 9% speech and rhetorical studies, 7% English language and literature. **Major fields of study:** biological and biomedical sciences; business, management, marketing, and related support services; education; English language and literature/letters; health professions and related clinical sciences; history; liberal arts and sciences studies, and humanities; mathematics and statistics; multi/interdisciplinary studies; parks, recreation, leisure, and fitness studies; philosophy and religious studies; physical sciences; psychology; social sciences; visual and performing arts. **Areas of required coursework:** arts/fine arts, humanities, computer literacy, mathematics, English (including composition), philosophy, foreign languages, sciences (biological or physical), history, social science. **Pre-professional programs:** pre-law, pre-dentistry, pre-medicine, pre-theology, pre-veterinary science, pre-optometry, pre-pharmacy, other. **Special academic programs (% participation):** accelerated program (3%), cross-registration (2%), double major (8%), honors program (10%), independent study (15%), internships (20%), student-designed major (1%), study abroad (91%), teacher certificate program (5%). **Teacher certification offered in:** elementary, middle/junior high, secondary. **Reserve Officers Training Corps (ROTC):** Army ROTC: Offered at cooperating institution (Auburn University at Montgomery); Air Force ROTC: Offered at cooperating institution (Alabama State University). **Faculty and instruction (2005-2006):** Total instructional faculty: 35 full-time, 19 part-time (59% men; 41% women; 6% minorities). Full-time faculty with Ph.D. or other terminal degree: 89%. Student/faculty ratio: 18/1. Classes of fewer than 20 students: 68%; of 20 to 49 students: 32%; of 50 or more students: 0%. **Advanced Placement and International Baccalaureate credit:** AP tests may be used for: Credit only. Scores accepted: 3, 4, 5. International Baccalaureate exams may be used for: Credit only. **Freshmen returning for sophomore year:** 71%. **Graduation rates:** Four-year: 36%; five-year: 43%; six-year: 45%. **Graduate study:** 22% of students pursue further study immediately upon graduation; 25% within one year; 50% within five years. Fields in which graduates pursue further study: Master of Business Administration (MBA), 4%; law, 8%; medicine, 3%; dentistry, 2%; engineering, 1%; theology (or the seminary), 7%; education, 6%; arts and sciences, 67%; veterinary medicine, 2%.

COSTS AND FINANCIAL AID

Financial aid office: (334) 833-4519. **Expenses (2006-2007):** Tuition and fees 2006-2007: $16,690; room/board: $6,400. Estimated books and supplies: $900; transportation: $600; personal expenses: $900. **Financial aid:** Priority filing date for institution's financial aid form: April 15. In 2005-2006, 74% of undergraduates applied for financial aid. Of those, 64% were determined to have financial need; 25% had their need fully met. Average financial aid package (proportion receiving): $8,793 (63%). Average amount of gift aid, such as scholarships or grants (proportion receiving): $3,252 (40%). Average amount of self-help aid, such as work study or loans (proportion receiving): $4,006 (49%). Average need-based loan (excluding PLUS or other private loans): $3,718. Among students who received need-based aid, the average percentage of need met: 59%. Among students who received aid based on merit, the average award (and the proportion receiving): $6,561 (32%). The average athletic scholarship (and the proportion receiving): $0 (0%). Average amount of debt of borrowers graduating in 2005: $17,540. Proportion who borrowed: 68%.

CAMPUS LIFE AND EXTRACURRICULAR ACTIVITIES

Campus housing available (% using): coed dorms (18%), women's dorms (40%), men's dorms (40%), special housing for disabled students (2%). Students who live in college-owned, operated, or affiliated housing: 76%. **Student employment:** During the 2005-2006 academic year, 5% of undergraduates worked on campus. Average per-year earnings: $2,500. **Clubs and organizations:** Number of student organizations: 40. Activities include: choral groups, drama/theater, jazz band, literary magazine, marching band, music ensembles, pep band, student government, student newspaper, student film society, yearbook. Number of fraternities: 2; sororities: 3. Proportion of men in fraternities: 22%; of women in sororities: 26%. Average proportion of students who stay on campus on weekends: 60%. **Sports program (2005-2006):** Member of NCAA III. *Men's intercollegiate varsity sports:* baseball, basketball, cross-country, golf, soccer, tennis. *Women's intercollegiate varsity sports:* basketball, soccer, softball, tennis, volleyball.

SERVICES AND FACILITIES

Basic services: nonremedial tutoring, placement service, health service, health insurance. **Remedial assistance:** reading, math, writing, study skills. **Counseling services:** career, personal, psychological, birth control, religious. **For learning-disabled students:** School does not offer a structured program with separate admission and additional fees. Total undergraduates in learning-disabled program or receiving services: 25. Services include: remedial reading, untimed tests, note-taking services, oral tests, readers, extended time for tests, tutors, other testing accomodations. **Library:** Number of titles: 105,769; number of current serial subscriptions: 239. **Information technology resources:** Students are required to lease or own a computer. Number of campus computers available to all students: 175. School has a wireless network. Approximate number of users that can be accommodated: 600. Proportion of college-owned housing units wired for high-speed internet access: 100%. **Campus safety:** Security services offered: 24-hour foot-and-vehicle patrols, late-night transport/escort service, 24-hour emergency telephones, lighted pathways/sidewalks, student patrols, controlled dormitory access (key, security card, etc).

TRANSFER AND INTERNATIONAL STUDENTS

Transfer students: May apply for admission for the following academic terms: Fall, Spring, Summer. Applicants do not need a minimum number of credits to apply. For fall 2005: Transfer applications received: 220. Transfer applicants offered admission: 103. Transfer applicants enrolled: 74. **International students:** Number of foreign undergraduates: 21 (3% of student body). Number of countries represented: 12. Minimum TOEFL score required: 500 (paper); 173 (computer). Average TOEFL score: 570 (paper).

Jacksonville State University

- **Address:** 700 Pelham Road N, Jacksonville, AL 36265-1602
- **Website:** http://www.jsu.edu
- **Public**
- **Enrollment:** 5,813 full-time; 1,472 part-time

KEY STATS

✔ **U.S News College Ranking:** third tier, Universities–Master's (South)
✔ **ACT Score (25th/75th percentile):** 17-22
✔ **Tuition:** 2006-2007: $4,056 in state, $8,112 out of state

Selectivity: Less selective	**Room/board:** $3,820
Acceptance rate: 88%	**Average debt:** N/A
Student/faculty ratio: 21/1	**Proportion who borrowed:** N/A

UNDERGRADUATE STUDENT BODY STATS

2005-2006 enrollment: 5,813 full-time; 1,472 part-time. Men: 43%; women: 57%. **Ethnic makeup:** African American: 23%; American-Indian: 1%; Asian American: 1%; Hispanic: 1%; White: 73%; International: 1%.

ADMISSIONS FACTS AND FIGURES

Phone: (256) 782-5268. **Email:** info@jsu.edu. **Website:** http://www.jsu.edu. **Application deadlines for fall 2007:** Regular decision: Rolling. Early decision: Not offered. Early action: Not offered. Admission can be deferred. **Application fee:** $20. Common application is not accepted. **To apply online, go to:** http://www.jsu.edu/depart/undergraduate/. **Admissions requirements/recommendations:** Tests: The college uses SAT or ACT scores in admissions decisions. Either SAT or ACT required. For admission to the fall 2007 entering class, the school will accept: ACT with writing, ACT without writing. Campus visit: Recommended. Admissions interview: Neither required nor recommended. Off-campus interview: Not available. **Factors that count in admissions decisions:** *Academic:* Secondary school record: Very important. Class rank: Not considered. Letters of recommendation: Not considered. Standardized test scores: Very important. Essay: Not considered. *Nonacademic:* Interview: Not considered. Extracurricular activities: Not considered. Talent/ability: Not considered. Character/personal qualities: Not considered. Alumni/ae relationship: Not considered. Geographical residence: Not considered. State residency: Not considered. Religious affiliation/commitment: Not considered. Minority status: Not considered. Volunteer work: Not considered. Work experience: Not considered. **Other schools with the greatest overlap in applicants:** Auburn University; Auburn University–Montgomery; Troy University; University of Alabama–Birmingham; University of Alabama–Huntsville. **Admissions statistics for the fall 2005 entering class:** Total applicants: 2,839. Total accepted:

2,499. Freshmen enrolled: 1,151; 23% were from out of state. Overall acceptance rate: 88%. **Credentials of fall 2005 freshmen:** 3% ranked in the top 10 percent of their high school class; 13% were in the top 25 percent, and 35% were in the top half. (Proportion submitting class standing: 70%.) **Average high school grade point average:** 3.0. **First-year students who submitted SAT scores:** 23%. Scores (25/75 percentile): Verbal: 420-530, Math: 410-520, Combined: 830-1050. **First-year students submitting ACT scores:** 81%. Scores (25/75 percentile): English: 16-23, Math: 16-21, Composite: 17-22.

ACADEMICS

Year founded: 1883. **Academic calendar:** Semester. **Degrees offered:** bachelor's, master's, post-master's certificate. **Most popular majors:** 13% elementary education and teaching, 9% criminal justice/safety studies, 8% nursing/registered nurse training (R.N., A.S.N., B.S.N., M.S.N.), 6% social work, 4% business administration and management. **Major fields of study:** biological and biomedical sciences; business, management, marketing, and related support services; communication, journalism, and related programs; computer and information sciences and support services; education; engineering technologies/technicians; English language and literature/letters; family and consumer sciences/human sciences; foreign languages, literatures, and linguistics; health professions and related clinical sciences; history; liberal arts and sciences studies, and humanities; mathematics and statistics; parks, recreation, leisure, and fitness studies; physical sciences; psychology; public administration and social service professions; security and protective services; social sciences; visual and performing arts. **Areas of required coursework:** arts/fine arts, humanities, computer literacy, mathematics, English (including composition), sciences (biological or physical), history, social science. **Pre-professional programs:** pre-law, pre-medicine. **Special academic programs:** accelerated program, cooperative (work-study plan) program, cross-registration, distance learning, double major, dual enrollment, English as a Second Language (ESL), honors program, independent study, internships, liberal arts/career combination, study abroad, teacher certificate program, weekend college. **Teacher certification offered in:** early childhood, special education, elementary, secondary. **Cooperative education programs:** art, business, computer science, engineering, technologies, vocational arts. **Reserve Officers Training Corps (ROTC):** Army ROTC: Offered on campus. **Faculty and instruction (2005-2006):** Total instructional faculty: 305 full-time, 129 part-time (51% men; 49% women; 10% minorities). Full-time faculty with Ph.D. or other terminal degree: 63%. Student/faculty ratio: 21/1. Classes of fewer than 20 students: 45%; of 20 to 49 students: 47%; of 50 or more students: 7%. **Freshmen returning for sophomore year:** 68%. **Graduation rates:** Four-year: 18%; five-year: 29%; six-year: 37%.

COSTS AND FINANCIAL AID

Financial aid office: (256) 782-5006. **Expenses (2006-2007):** Tuition and fees 2006-2007: $4,056 in state, $8,112 out of state; room/board: $3,820. **Financial aid:** Priority filing date for institution's financial aid form: March 15. In 2005-2006, 82% of undergraduates applied for financial aid. Of those, 78% were determined to have financial need; 50% had their need fully met. Average financial aid package (proportion receiving): $5,200 (78%). Average amount of gift aid, such as scholarships or grants (proportion receiving): $3,500 (6%). Average amount of self-help aid, such as work study or loans (proportion receiving): $5,000 (61%). Average need-based loan (excluding PLUS or other private loans): $5,250. Among students who received need-based aid, the average percentage of need met: 80%. Among students who received aid based on merit, the average award (and the proportion receiving): $1,000 (14%).

CAMPUS LIFE AND EXTRACURRICULAR ACTIVITIES

Campus housing available (% using): coed dorms (46%), women's dorms (21%), men's dorms (11%), fraternity housing (1%), apartments for married students (2%), apartment for single students (15%), special housing for disabled students (1%), special housing for international students (3%). Students who live in college-owned, operated, or affiliated housing: 20%. Average per-year earnings: $3,476. **Clubs and organizations:** Number of student organizations: 90. Activities include: choral groups, concert band, dance, drama/theater, jazz band, literary magazine, marching band, music ensembles, musical theater, opera, pep band, radio station, student government, student newspaper, symphony orchestra, television station, yearbook. Number of fraternities: 11; sororities: 8. Proportion of men in fraternities: 10%; of women in sororities: 10%. Average proportion of students who stay on campus on weekends: 25%. **Sports program (2005-2006):** Member of NCAA I. *Men's intercollegiate varsity sports:* baseball, basketball, cross-country, football, golf, riflery, tennis. *Women's intercollegiate varsity sports:* basketball, cross-country, golf, soccer, softball, tennis, track and field (indoor), track and field (outdoor), volleyball.

SERVICES AND FACILITIES
Basic services: nonremedial tutoring, placement service, day care, health service. **Remedial assistance:** reading, math, writing, study skills. **Counseling services:** minority student, career, military, personal, veteran student, academic, psychological, birth control. **For learning-disabled students:** School does not offer a structured program with separate admission and additional fees. Services include: remedial math, remedial English, reading machines, remedial reading, tape recorders, other special classes, untimed tests, note-taking services, oral tests, learning center, readers, extended time for tests, tutors, priority registration, priority seating, other testing accomodations. **Library:** Number of titles: 684,342; number of current serial subscriptions: 20,791. **Information technology resources:** Students are not required to lease or own a computer. Number of campus computers available to all students: 636. School has a wireless network. Approximate number of users that can be accommodated: 100. Proportion of college-owned housing units wired for high-speed internet access: 75%. **Campus safety:** Security services offered: 24-hour foot-and-vehicle patrols, late-night transport/escort service, 24-hour emergency telephones, lighted pathways/sidewalks, controlled dormitory access (key, security card, etc).

TRANSFER AND INTERNATIONAL STUDENTS
Transfer students: May apply for admission for the following academic terms: Fall, Spring, Summer. Applicants need a minimum number of credits to apply. For fall 2005: Transfer applications received: 1,162. Transfer applicants offered admission: 1,151. Transfer applicants enrolled: 726. **International students:** Number of foreign undergraduates: 57 (1% of student body). Number of countries represented: 73. Minimum TOEFL score required: 500 (paper); 173 (computer).

Judson College

- **Address:** PO Box 120, Marion, AL 36756
- **Website:** http://home.judson.edu
- **Private; Religious affiliation:** Baptist
- **Enrollment:** N/A

KEY STATS
✔ **U.S News College Ranking:** fourth tier, Liberal Arts Colleges
✔ **SAT or ACT Score (25th/75th percentile):** N/A
✔ **Tuition:** N/A

Selectivity: Selective	**Room/board:** N/A
Acceptance rate: N/A	**Average debt:** N/A
Student/faculty ratio: N/A	**Proportion who borrowed:** N/A

Miles College

- **Address:** PO Box 3800, Birmingham, AL 35208
- **Website:** http://www.miles.edu
- **Private; Religious affiliation:** Christian Methodist Episcopal
- **Enrollment:** 1,623 full-time; 135 part-time

KEY STATS
✔ **U.S News College Ranking:** 44, Comp. Colleges–Bachelor's (South)
✔ **ACT Score (25th/75th percentile):** 17
✔ **Tuition:** N/A

Selectivity: Less selective	**Room/board:** N/A
Acceptance rate: 28%	**Average debt:** N/A
Student/faculty ratio: 16/1	**Proportion who borrowed:** N/A

UNDERGRADUATE STUDENT BODY STATS
2005-2006 enrollment: 1,623 full-time; 135 part-time. Men: 44%; women: 56%. **Ethnic makeup:** African American: 97%; White: 3%.

ADMISSIONS FACTS AND FIGURES
Phone: (800) 445-0708. **Email:** admissions@mail.miles.edu. **Website:** http://www.miles.edu. **Application deadlines for fall 2007:** Regular decision:

July 15. Early decision: Not offered. Early action: Not offered. Admission can be deferred. Common application is accepted. **Admissions requirements/recommendations:** High school units required (recommended): English: 20 (20); Mathematics: 20 (20); Science: 20 (20); Social studies: 20 (20); History: 20 (20); Total units: 100 (100). Tests: The college does not use SAT or ACT scores in admissions decisions. Neither SAT nor ACT required. Campus visit: Neither required nor recommended. Admissions interview: Neither required nor recommended. Off-campus interview: Not available. **Factors that count in admissions decisions:** *Academic:* Secondary school record: Considered. Class rank: Considered. Letters of recommendation: Not considered. Standardized test scores: Considered. Essay: Not considered. *Nonacademic:* Interview: Not considered. Extracurricular activities: Not considered. Talent/ability: Not considered. Character/personal qualities: Not considered. Alumni/ae relationship: Considered. Geographical residence: Considered. State residency: Not considered. Religious affiliation/commitment: Considered. Minority status: Not considered. Volunteer work: Not considered. Work experience: Not considered. **Other schools with the greatest overlap in applicants:** Alabama Agricultural and Mechanical University; Alabama State University; Oakwood College; Stillman College; Talladega College. **Admissions statistics for the fall 2005 entering class:** Freshmen enrolled: 400; 33% were from out of state. Overall acceptance rate: 28%.

ACADEMICS
Year founded: 1905. **Academic calendar:** Semester. **Degrees offered:** certificate, bachelor's. **Most popular majors:** 17% business administration and management, 17% management science, 11% social work, 9% English/language arts teacher education, 6% computer systems networking and telecommunications. **Major fields of study:** business, management, marketing, and related support services; communication, journalism, and related programs; computer and information sciences and support services; education; English language and literature/letters; physical sciences; public administration and social service professions; social sciences. **Areas of required coursework:** arts/fine arts, humanities, computer literacy, mathematics, English (including composition), sciences (biological or physical), history, social science. **Special academic programs (% participation):** double major (1%), honors program, internships, teacher certificate program, weekend college. **Teacher certification offered in:** early childhood, elementary, secondary. **Faculty and instruction (2005-2006):** Total instructional faculty: 92 full-time, 40 part-time (50% men; 50% women; 85% minorities). Full-time faculty with Ph.D. or other terminal degree: 38%. Student/faculty ratio: 16/1. **Advanced Placement and International Baccalaureate credit:** International Baccalaureate exams may be used for: Placement only. **Graduation rates:** Six-year: 72%.

COSTS AND FINANCIAL AID
Financial aid office: (205) 929-1665.

CAMPUS LIFE AND EXTRACURRICULAR ACTIVITIES
Campus housing available (% using): coed dorms (15%), women's dorms (26%), men's dorms (29%), apartment for single students (27%), other housing options (3%). Students who live in college-owned, operated, or affiliated housing: 40%. **Clubs and organizations:** Number of student organizations: 40. Activities include: choral groups, concert band, drama/theater, jazz band, marching band, music ensembles, musical theater, student government, student newspaper, student film society, television station. Number of fraternities: 4; sororities: 4. Average proportion of students who stay on campus on weekends: 34%. **Sports program (2005-2006):** Member of NCAA II. *Men's intercollegiate varsity sports:* baseball, basketball, cross-country, football, track and field (outdoor). *Women's intercollegiate varsity sports:* basketball, cross-country, softball, track and field (outdoor), volleyball.

SERVICES AND FACILITIES
Basic services: placement service, health service, health insurance. **Remedial assistance:** reading, math, writing, study skills. **Counseling services:** career, personal, academic, religious. **For learning-disabled students:** School does not offer a structured program with separate admission and additional fees. Services include: remedial math, remedial English, remedial reading, diagnostic testing service, tutors, other testing accomodations. **Library:** Number of titles: 102,230; number of current serial subscriptions: 400. **Information technology resources:** Students are not required to lease or own a computer. School has a wireless network. Proportion of college-owned housing units wired for high-speed internet access: 100%. **Campus safety:** Security services offered: 24-hour foot-and-vehicle patrols, lighted pathways/sidewalks.

TRANSFER AND INTERNATIONAL STUDENTS

Transfer students: May apply for admission for the following academic terms: Fall, Winter, Spring, Summer. Applicants need a minimum number of credits to apply. For fall 2005: Transfer applicants enrolled: 111. **International students:** Number of foreign undergraduates: 1.

Oakwood College

- ■ **Address:** 7000 Adventist Boulevard, Huntsville, AL 35896
- ■ **Website:** http://www.oakwood.edu
- ■ **Private; Religious affiliation:** Seventh-day Adventist
- ■ **Enrollment:** 1,559 full-time; 192 part-time

KEY STATS

✔ **U.S News College Ranking:** 53, Comp. Colleges–Bachelor's (South)
✔ **ACT Score (25th/75th percentile):** 16-21
✔ **Tuition:** N/A

Selectivity: Less selective	**Room/board:** N/A
Acceptance rate: 60%	**Average debt:** N/A
Student/faculty ratio: 13/1	**Proportion who borrowed:** N/A

UNDERGRADUATE STUDENT BODY STATS

2005-2006 enrollment: 1,559 full-time; 192 part-time. Men: 43%; women: 57%. **Ethnic makeup:** African American: 90%; White: 3%; International: 7%.

ADMISSIONS FACTS AND FIGURES

Phone: (256) 726-7356. **Email:** admission@oakwood.edu. **Website:** http://www.oakwood.edu. **Application deadlines for fall 2007:** Regular decision: Rolling. Early decision: Not offered. Early action: Send application by: N/A; Decision sent by: N/A. Admission can be deferred. **Application fee:** $20. Common application is accepted. **To apply online, go to:** http://www.oakwood.edu/admissions. **Admissions requirements/recommendations:** High school units required (recommended): English: (4); Mathematics: (2); Science: (2); Foreign language: (2); Social studies: (1); History: (1); Total units: (18). Tests: The college uses SAT or ACT scores in admissions decisions. Either SAT or ACT required. Campus visit: Recommended. Admissions interview: Neither required nor recommended. **Factors that count in admissions decisions:** *Academic:* Secondary school record: Very important. Class rank: Considered. Letters of recommendation: Very important. Standardized test scores: Very important. Essay: Considered. *Nonacademic:* Interview: Not considered. Extracurricular activities: Not considered. Talent/ability: Not considered. Character/personal qualities: Not considered. Alumni/ae relationship: Not considered. Geographical residence: Not considered. State residency: Not considered. Religious affiliation/commitment: Not considered. Minority status: Not considered. Volunteer work: Not considered. Work experience: Not considered. **Admissions statistics for the fall 2005 entering class:** Total applicants: 1,155. Total accepted: 691. Freshmen enrolled: 410; 88% were from out of state. Overall acceptance rate: 60%. Non-early acceptance rate: 60%. **Credentials of fall 2005 freshmen:** 6% ranked in the top 10 percent of their high school class; 21% were in the top 25 percent, and 48% were in the top half. (Proportion submitting class standing: 47%.) **Average high school grade point average:** 2.9. **First-year students who submitted SAT scores:** 55%. Scores (25/75 percentile): Verbal: 410-520, Math: 370-480, Combined: 780-1000. **First-year students submitting ACT scores:** 59%. Scores (25/75 percentile): English: 15-22, Math: 15-19, Composite: 16-21.

ACADEMICS

Year founded: 1896. **Academic calendar:** Semester. **Degrees offered:** associate, bachelor's. **Most popular majors:** 20% business, management, marketing, and related support services, 12% biological and biomedical sciences, 11% psychology, 9% education, 9% theology and religious vocations. **Major fields of study:** biological and biomedical sciences; business, management, marketing, and related support services; communication, journalism, and related programs; computer and information sciences and support services; education; English language and literature/letters; family and consumer sciences/human sciences; foreign languages, literatures, and linguistics; health professions and related clinical sciences; liberal arts and sciences studies, and humanities; mathematics and statistics; multi/interdisciplinary studies; philosophy and religious studies; physical sciences; psychology; public administration and social service professions; theology and religious

vocations; visual and performing arts. **Areas of required coursework:** humanities, computer literacy, mathematics, English (including composition), foreign languages, sciences (biological or physical), history, social science, other. **Special academic programs:** double major, honors program, internships, study abroad, teacher certificate program. **Teacher certification offered in:** elementary, secondary. **Faculty and instruction (2005-2006):** Total instructional faculty: 103 full-time, 67 part-time (49% men; 51% women; 77% minorities). Full-time faculty with Ph.D. or other terminal degree: 58%. Student/faculty ratio: 13/1. Classes of fewer than 20 students: 58%; of 20 to 49 students: 38%; of 50 or more students: 4%. **Freshmen returning for sophomore year:** 71%. **Graduation rates:** Four-year: 16%; five-year: 36%; six-year: 43%.

COSTS AND FINANCIAL AID

Financial aid office: (256) 726-7210. **Financial aid:** Priority filing date for institution's financial aid form: March 31.

CAMPUS LIFE AND EXTRACURRICULAR ACTIVITIES

Campus housing available (% using): women's dorms (54%), men's dorms (36%), apartments for married students, apartment for single students (10%). Students who live in college-owned, operated, or affiliated housing: 66%. Activities include: music ensembles, radio station, student government, student newspaper, yearbook. Number of fraternities: 0; sororities: 0. **Sports program (2005-2006):** *Men's intercollegiate varsity sports:* basketball. *Women's intercollegiate varsity sports:* basketball.

SERVICES AND FACILITIES

Basic services: health service, health insurance. **Remedial assistance:** reading, math, writing, study skills. **Counseling services:** career, personal, academic. **Library:** Number of titles: 123,571; number of current serial subscriptions: 516. **Information technology resources:** Students are not required to lease or own a computer. Number of campus computers available to all students: 350. School has a wireless network. **Campus safety:** Security services offered: 24-hour foot-and-vehicle patrols, 24-hour emergency telephones, student patrols.

TRANSFER AND INTERNATIONAL STUDENTS

Transfer students: May apply for admission for the following academic terms: Fall, Spring. Applicants need a minimum number of credits to apply. For fall 2005: Transfer applications received: 222. Transfer applicants offered admission: 151. Transfer applicants enrolled: 107. **International students:** Number of foreign undergraduates: 116 (7% of student body). Number of countries represented: 19. Minimum TOEFL score required: 500 (paper); 173 (computer).

Samford University

- ■ **Address:** 800 Lakeshore Drive, Birmingham, AL 35229
- ■ **Website:** http://www.samford.edu
- ■ **Private; Religious affiliation:** Baptist
- ■ **Enrollment:** 2,742 full-time; 199 part-time

KEY STATS

✔ **U.S News College Ranking:** 4, Universities–Master's (South)
✔ **ACT Score (25th/75th percentile):** 23-28
✔ **Tuition:** 2006-2007: $16,000

Selectivity: More selective	**Room/board:** $5,750
Acceptance rate: 88%	**Average debt:** $17,532
Student/faculty ratio: 12/1	**Proportion who borrowed:** 46%

UNDERGRADUATE STUDENT BODY STATS

2005-2006 enrollment: 2,742 full-time; 199 part-time. Men: 35%; women: 65%. **Ethnic makeup:** African American: 6%; Asian American: 1%; Hispanic: 1%; White: 91%; International: 1%. **Religious preference:** Roman Catholic: 4%; Protestant: 26%; Unknown: 20%; Baptist: 50%.

ADMISSIONS FACTS AND FIGURES

Phone: (800) 888-7218. **Email:** admiss@samford.edu. **Website:** http://www.samford.edu. **Application deadlines for fall 2007:** Regular decision: Rolling. Early decision: Not offered. Early action: Not offered. Admission can be deferred. **Application fee:** $35. Common application is accepted. **To apply online, go to:** https://www.samford.edu/groups/

admiss/applyonline.html. **Admissions requirements/recommendations:** High school units required (recommended): English: 4; Mathematics: 3; Science: 3; Foreign language: (2); Social studies: 2; History: 2. Tests: The college uses SAT or ACT scores in admissions decisions. Either SAT or ACT required. For admission to the fall 2007 entering class, the school will accept: ACT with writing, ACT without writing. Campus visit: Recommended. Admissions interview: Recommended. Off-campus interview: May be arranged. **Factors that count in admissions decisions:** *Academic:* Secondary school record: Very important. Class rank: Important. Letters of recommendation: Very important. Standardized test scores: Very important. Essay: Very important. *Nonacademic:* Interview: Important. Extracurricular activities: Important. Talent/ability: Considered. Character/personal qualities: Very important. Alumni/ae relationship: Important. Geographical residence: Considered. State residency: Considered. Religious affiliation/commitment: Very important. Minority status: Considered. Volunteer work: Considered. Work experience: Considered. **Other schools with the greatest overlap in applicants:** Auburn University; Birmingham-Southern College; Furman University; University of Alabama; University of Georgia. **Admissions statistics for the fall 2005 entering class:** Total applicants: 2,025. Total accepted: 1,792. Freshmen enrolled: 702; 64% were from out of state. Overall acceptance rate: 88%. **Credentials of fall 2005 freshmen:** 36% ranked in the top 10 percent of their high school class; 66% were in the top 25 percent, and 86% were in the top half. (Proportion submitting class standing: 62%.) **Average high school grade point average:** 3.6. **First-year students who submitted SAT scores:** 49%. Scores (25/75 percentile): Verbal: 530-630, Math: 530-630, Combined: 1060-1260. **First-year students submitting ACT scores:** 72%. Scores (25/75 percentile): English: 22-29, Math: 21-27, Composite: 23-28.

ACADEMICS

Year founded: 1841. **Academic calendar:** 4-1-4. **Degrees offered:** certificate, associate, terminal-associate, bachelor's, master's, post-master's certificate, first professional, doctorate. **Most popular majors:** 11% business administration and management, 8% teacher education, 7% nursing/registered nurse training (R.N., A.S.N., B.S.N., M.S.N.), 6% biology/biological sciences, 6% journalism. **Major fields of study:** area, ethnic, cultural, and gender studies; biological and biomedical sciences; business, management, marketing, and related support services; communication, journalism, and related programs; computer and information sciences and support services; education; engineering; English language and literature/letters; family and consumer sciences/human sciences; foreign languages, literatures, and linguistics; health professions and related clinical sciences; history; liberal arts and sciences studies, and humanities; mathematics and statistics; natural resources and conservation; parks, recreation, leisure, and fitness studies; philosophy and religious studies; physical sciences; psychology; public administration and social service professions; social sciences; theology and religious vocations; visual and performing arts. **Areas of required coursework:** arts/fine arts, humanities, mathematics, English (including composition), foreign languages, sciences (biological or physical), history, social science, other. **Pre-professional programs:** pre-law, pre-dentistry, pre-medicine, pre-veterinary science, pre-optometry, pre-pharmacy. **Special academic programs:** accelerated program, cooperative (work-study plan) program, distance learning, double major, dual enrollment, exchange student program (domestic), honors program, independent study, internships, study abroad, teacher certificate program. **Teacher certification offered in:** early childhood, special education, elementary, secondary. **Cooperative education programs:** art, business, computer science, health professions, humanities, natural science. **Reserve Officers Training Corps (ROTC):** Army ROTC: Offered at cooperating institution (University of Alabama at Birmingham); Air Force ROTC: Offered on campus. **Faculty and instruction (2005-2006):** Total instructional faculty: 278 full-time, 147 part-time (52% men; 48% women; 8% minorities). Full-time faculty with Ph.D. or other terminal degree: 79%. Student/faculty ratio: 12/1. Classes of fewer than 20 students: 56%; of 20 to 49 students: 41%; of 50 or more students: 2%. **Advanced Placement and International Baccalaureate credit:** AP tests may be used for: Credit and/or placement. Scores accepted: 3, 4, 5. International Baccalaureate exams may be used for: Credit and/or placement. **Freshmen returning for sophomore year:** 85%. **Graduation rates:** Four-year: 53%; five-year: 63%; six-year: 70%.

COSTS AND FINANCIAL AID

Financial aid office: (205) 726-2905. **Expenses (2006-2007):** Tuition and fees 2006-2007: $16,000; room/board: $5,750. Estimated books and supplies: $1,050; transportation: $1,050; personal expenses: $3,140. **Financial aid:** Priority filing date for institution's financial aid form: March 1. In 2005-2006, 55% of undergraduates applied for financial aid. Of those, 38% were determined to have financial need; 27% had their need fully met. Average

financial aid package (proportion receiving): $11,977 (38%). Average amount of gift aid, such as scholarships or grants (proportion receiving): $6,615 (34%). Average amount of self-help aid, such as work study or loans (proportion receiving): $4,727 (34%). Average need-based loan (excluding PLUS or other private loans): $3,487. Among students who received need-based aid, the average percentage of need met: 70%. Among students who received aid based on merit, the average award (and the proportion receiving): $4,712 (23%). The average athletic scholarship (and the proportion receiving): $12,885 (7%). Average amount of debt of borrowers graduating in 2005: $17,532. Proportion who borrowed: 46%.

CAMPUS LIFE AND EXTRACURRICULAR ACTIVITIES

Campus housing available: women's dorms, men's dorms, special housing for disabled students, cooperative housing. Students who live in college-owned, operated, or affiliated housing: 66%. **Student employment:** During the 2005-2006 academic year, 30% of undergraduates worked on campus. Average per-year earnings: $2,000. **Clubs and organizations:** Number of student organizations: 106. Activities include: choral groups, concert band, dance, drama/theater, jazz band, literary magazine, marching band, music ensembles, musical theater, pep band, radio station, student government, student newspaper, symphony orchestra, yearbook. Number of fraternities: 7; sororities: 7. Proportion of men in fraternities: 24%; of women in sororities: 37%. Average proportion of students who stay on campus on weekends: 50%. **Sports program (2005-2006):** Member of NCAA I. *Men's intercollegiate varsity sports:* baseball, basketball, cross-country, football, golf, tennis, track and field (indoor), track and field (outdoor). *Women's intercollegiate varsity sports:* basketball, cross-country, golf, soccer, softball, tennis, track and field (indoor), track and field (outdoor), volleyball.

SERVICES AND FACILITIES

Basic services: nonremedial tutoring, placement service, health service, health insurance, other. **Counseling services:** minority student, career, personal, academic, older student, psychological, birth control, religious. **For learning-disabled students:** School does not offer a structured program with separate admission and additional fees. Total undergraduates in learning-disabled program or receiving services: 51. Services include: reading machines, tape recorders, videotaped classes, untimed tests, note-taking services, oral tests, learning center, readers, extended time for tests, tutors, priority registration, priority seating, texts on tape, other testing accommodations, other. **Library:** Number of titles: 644,024; number of current serial subscriptions: 3,293. **Information technology resources:** Students are not required to lease or own a computer. Number of campus computers available to all students: 630. School has a wireless network. Approximate number of users that can be accommodated: 1,700. Proportion of college-owned housing units wired for high-speed internet access: 100%. **Campus safety:** Security services offered: 24-hour foot-and-vehicle patrols, late-night transport/escort service, 24-hour emergency telephones, lighted pathways/sidewalks, controlled dormitory access (key, security card, etc).

TRANSFER AND INTERNATIONAL STUDENTS

Transfer students: May apply for admission for the following academic terms: Fall, Spring, Summer. Applicants need a minimum number of credits to apply. For fall 2005: Transfer applications received: 331. Transfer applicants offered admission: 220. Transfer applicants enrolled: 99. **International students:** Number of foreign undergraduates: 15 (1% of student body). Number of countries represented: 15. Minimum TOEFL score required: 550 (paper); 213 (computer).

Spring Hill College

- **Address:** 4000 Dauphin Street, Mobile, AL 36608
- **Website:** http://www.shc.edu
- **Private; Religious affiliation:** Catholic
- **Enrollment:** 1,174 full-time; 125 part-time

KEY STATS

✔ **U.S News College Ranking:** 15, Universities–Master's (South)
✔ **ACT Score (25th/75th percentile):** 21-26
✔ **Tuition:** 2006-2007: $22,000

Selectivity: More selective	Room/board: $8,120
Acceptance rate: 80%	Average debt: $14,074
Student/faculty ratio: 14/1	Proportion who borrowed: 80%

UNDERGRADUATE STUDENT BODY STATS

2005-2006 enrollment: 1,174 full-time; 125 part-time. Men: 36%; women: 64%. **Ethnic makeup:** African American: 15%; American-Indian: 1%; Asian American: 1%; Hispanic: 5%; White: 76%; International: 1%. **Religious preference:** Protestant: 22%; Unknown: 25%; Catholic: 52%; Other: 1%.

ADMISSIONS FACTS AND FIGURES

Phone: (251) 380-3030. **Email:** admit@shc.edu. **Website:** http://www.shc.edu. **Application deadlines for fall 2007:** Regular decision: July 15. Early decision: Not offered. Early action: Not offered. Admission can be deferred. **Application fee:** $25. Common application is accepted. **To apply online, go to:** http://www.shc.edu/admission/apply. **Admissions requirements/recommendations:** High school units required (recommended): English: (4); Mathematics: (3); Science: (3); Foreign language: (2); Social studies: (2); History: (1); Academic electives: (1); Total units: (16). Tests: The college uses SAT or ACT scores in admissions decisions. Either SAT or ACT required. For admission to the fall 2007 entering class, the school will accept: ACT without writing. Campus visit: Recommended. Admissions interview: Recommended. Off-campus interview: May be arranged. **Factors that count in admissions decisions:** *Academic:* Secondary school record: Very important. Class rank: Important. Letters of recommendation: Important. Standardized test scores: Very important. Essay: Considered. *Nonacademic:* Interview: Important. Extracurricular activities: Considered. Talent/ability: Considered. Character/personal qualities: Considered. Alumni/ae relationship: Considered. Geographical residence: Not considered. State residency: Not considered. Religious affiliation/commitment: Not considered. Minority status: Not considered. Volunteer work: Considered. Work experience: Not considered. **Other schools with the greatest overlap in applicants:** Louisiana State University–Baton Rouge; Loyola University New Orleans; Millsaps College; University of South Alabama. **Admissions statistics for the fall 2005 entering class:** Total applicants: 1,190. Total accepted: 953. Freshmen enrolled: 275; 67% were from out of state. Overall acceptance rate: 80%. **Credentials of fall 2005 freshmen:** 28% ranked in the top 10 percent of their high school class; 50% were in the top 25 percent, and 82% were in the top half. (Proportion submitting class standing: 71%.) **Average high school grade point average:** 3.5. **First-year students who submitted SAT scores:** 36%. Scores (25/75 percentile): Verbal: 480-600, Math: 460-610, Combined: 940-1210. **First-year students submitting ACT scores:** 87%. Scores (25/75 percentile): English: 21-28, Math: 19-25, Composite: 21-26.

ACADEMICS

Year founded: 1830. **Academic calendar:** Semester. **Degrees offered:** certificate, associate, transfer-associate, terminal-associate, bachelor's, post-bachelor's certificate, master's. **Most popular majors:** 19% business, management, marketing, and related support services, 12% biological and biomedical sciences, 11% communication, journalism, and related programs, 10% psychology, 8% health professions and related clinical sciences. **Major fields of study:** biological and biomedical sciences; business, management, marketing, and related support services; communication, journalism, and related programs; education; engineering; English language and literature/letters; foreign languages, literatures, and linguistics; health professions and related clinical sciences; history; liberal arts and sciences studies, and humanities; mathematics and statistics; multi/interdisciplinary studies; philosophy and religious studies; physical sciences; psychology; social sciences; theology and religious vocations; visual and performing arts. **Areas of required coursework:** arts/fine arts, mathematics, English (including composition), philosophy, foreign languages, sciences (biological or physical), history, social science, other. **Pre-professional programs:** pre-law, pre-dentistry, pre-medicine, pre-veterinary science, pre-optometry. **Special academic programs (% participation):** accelerated program (3%), distance learning, double major (9%), dual enrollment, honors program (14%), independent study (26%), internships (49%), student-designed major (2%), study abroad, teacher certificate program (6%). **Teacher certification offered in:** early childhood, elementary, secondary. **Reserve Officers Training Corps (ROTC):** Army ROTC: Offered at cooperating institution (University of South Alabama); Air Force ROTC: Offered at cooperating institution (University of South Alabama). **Faculty and instruction (2005-2006):** Total instructional faculty: 72 full-time, 66 part-time (53% men; 47% women; 8% minorities). Full-time faculty with Ph.D. or other terminal degree: 86%. Student/faculty ratio: 14/1. Classes of fewer than 20 students: 47%; of 20 to 49 students: 52%; of 50 or more students: 0%. **Advanced Placement and International Baccalaureate credit:** AP tests may be used for: Credit and/or placement. Scores accepted: 3, 4, 5. International Baccalaureate exams may be used for: Credit and/or placement. **Freshmen returning for sophomore year:** 80%. **Graduation rates:** Four-year: 49%; five-year: 60%; six-year: 63%. **Graduate study:** 34% of students pursue further study immediately upon graduation;

34% within one year. Fields in which graduates pursue further study: Master of Business Administration (MBA), 9%; law, 16%; medicine, 14%; education, 7%; arts and sciences, 54%.

COSTS AND FINANCIAL AID

Financial aid office: (251) 380-3460. **Expenses (2006-2007):** Tuition and fees 2006-2007: $22,000; room/board: $8,120. Estimated books and supplies: $1,250; transportation: $1,100; personal expenses: $1,250. **Financial aid:** Priority filing date for institution's financial aid form: March 1. In 2005-2006, 79% of undergraduates applied for financial aid. Of those, 66% were determined to have financial need; 25% had their need fully met. Average financial aid package (proportion receiving): $18,907 (66%). Average amount of gift aid, such as scholarships or grants (proportion receiving): $13,570 (64%). Average amount of self-help aid, such as work study or loans (proportion receiving): $4,778 (50%). Average need-based loan (excluding PLUS or other private loans): $4,300. Among students who received need-based aid, the average percentage of need met: 80%. Among students who received aid based on merit, the average award (and the proportion receiving): $10,316 (27%). The average athletic scholarship (and the proportion receiving): $5,763 (10%). Average amount of debt of borrowers graduating in 2005: $14,074. Proportion who borrowed: 80%.

CAMPUS LIFE AND EXTRACURRICULAR ACTIVITIES

Campus housing available (% using): coed dorms (56%), women's dorms (16%), men's dorms (12%), apartment for single students (16%). Students who live in college-owned, operated, or affiliated housing: 73%. **Student employment:** During the 2005-2006 academic year, 10% of undergraduates worked on campus. Average per-year earnings: $878. **Clubs and organizations:** Number of student organizations: 38. Activities include: choral groups, dance, drama/theater, literary magazine, student government, student newspaper, yearbook. Number of fraternities: 2; sororities: 3. Proportion of men in fraternities: 14%; of women in sororities: 23%. Average proportion of students who stay on campus on weekends: 55%. **Sports program (2005-2006):** Member of NAIA. *Men's intercollegiate varsity sports:* baseball, basketball, cross-country, golf, soccer, swimming and diving, tennis. *Women's intercollegiate varsity sports:* basketball, cross-country, golf, soccer, softball, swimming and diving, tennis, volleyball.

SERVICES AND FACILITIES

Basic services: nonremedial tutoring, placement service, health service. **Remedial assistance:** study skills. **Counseling services:** minority student, career, personal, academic, older student, psychological, religious. **For learning-disabled students:** School does not offer a structured program with separate admission and additional fees. Total undergraduates in learning-disabled program or receiving services: 40. Services include: tape recorders, readers, extended time for tests, tutors, priority seating, other testing accomodations. **Library:** Number of titles: 180,835; number of current serial subscriptions: 1,023. **Information technology resources:** Students are not required to lease or own a computer. Number of campus computers available to all students: 194. School has a wireless network. Approximate number of users that can be accommodated: 500. Proportion of college-owned housing units wired for high-speed internet access: 100%. **Campus safety:** Security services offered: 24-hour foot-and-vehicle patrols, late-night transport/escort service, 24-hour emergency telephones, lighted pathways/sidewalks, controlled dormitory access (key, security card, etc).

TRANSFER AND INTERNATIONAL STUDENTS

Transfer students: May apply for admission for the following academic terms: Fall, Spring, Summer. Applicants do not need a minimum number of credits to apply. For fall 2005: Transfer applications received: 146. Transfer applicants offered admission: 65. Transfer applicants enrolled: 43. **International students:** Number of foreign undergraduates: 10 (1% of student body). Number of countries represented: 8. Minimum TOEFL score required: 550 (paper); 213 (computer).

Stillman College

- **Address:** PO Box 1430, 3600 Stillman Boulevard, Tuscaloosa, AL 35403
- **Website:** http://www.stillman.edu
- **Private; Religious affiliation:** Presbyterian (U.S.A.)
- **Enrollment:** 772 full-time; 32 part-time

KEY STATS
- ✔ **U.S News College Ranking:** 35, Comp. Colleges–Bachelor's (South)
- ✔ **ACT Score (25th/75th percentile):** 15-19
- ✔ **Tuition:** 2006-2007: $11,605
  - **Selectivity:** Less selective **Room/board:** $5,500
  - **Acceptance rate:** 23% **Average debt:** $20,604
  - **Student/faculty ratio:** 14/1 **Proportion who borrowed:** 86%

UNDERGRADUATE STUDENT BODY STATS
2005-2006 enrollment: 772 full-time; 32 part-time. Men: 51%; women: 49%. **Ethnic makeup:** African American: 92%; White: 7%. **Religious preference:** Protestant: 98%; Other: 2%.

ADMISSIONS FACTS AND FIGURES
Phone: (205) 366-8837. **Email:** admissions@stillman.edu. **Website:** http://www.stillman.edu. **Application deadlines for fall 2007:** Regular decision: May 1. Early decision: Send application by: July 1; Decision sent by: July 15. Early action: Not offered. Admission can be deferred. **Application fee:** $50. Common application is accepted. **To apply online, go to:** http://www.stillman.edu/applyonline/apply.asp. **Admissions requirements/recommendations:** High school units required (recommended): English: 4 (4); Mathematics: 1 (1); Science: 1 (1); Foreign language: 0 (0); Social studies: 0 (0); History: 1 (1); Academic electives: 16 (16); Total units: 24 (24). Tests: The college uses SAT or ACT scores in admissions decisions. Either SAT or ACT required. For admission to the fall 2007 entering class, the school will accept: ACT with writing. Campus visit: Recommended. Admissions interview: Recommended. Off-campus interview: May be arranged. **Factors that count in admissions decisions:** *Academic:* Secondary school record: Very important. Class rank: Very important. Letters of recommendation: Very important. Standardized test scores: Very important. Essay: Very important. *Nonacademic:* Interview: Important. Extracurricular activities: Important. Talent/ability: Considered. Character/personal qualities: Very important. Alumni/ae relationship: Not considered. Geographical residence: Not considered. State residency: Not considered. Religious affiliation/commitment: Not considered. Minority status: Not considered. Volunteer work: Considered. Work experience: Not considered. **Other schools with the greatest overlap in applicants:** Alabama Agricultural and Mechanical University; Alabama State University; Spelman College; Tuskegee University; University of Alabama–Birmingham. **Admissions statistics for the fall 2005 entering class:** Total applicants: 1,622. Total accepted: 370. Freshmen enrolled: 275; 47% were from out of state. Overall acceptance rate: 23%. Non-early acceptance rate: 23%. **Size of waiting list:** 0 applicants; enrolled from waiting list: 0. **First-year students who submitted SAT scores:** 8%. Scores (25/75 percentile): Verbal: 440-490, Math: 320-420, Combined: 760-910. **First-year students submitting ACT scores:** 58%. Scores (25/75 percentile): English: 14-19, Math: 17-19, Composite: 15-19.

ACADEMICS
Year founded: 1876. **Academic calendar:** Semester. **Degrees offered:** bachelor's. **Most popular majors:** 32% business administration, management, and operations, 14% biology/biological sciences, 13% elementary education and teaching, 11% English language and literature, 11% history. **Major fields of study:** biological and biomedical sciences; business, management, marketing, and related support services; computer and information sciences and support services; education; English language and literature/letters; history; mathematics and statistics; multi/interdisciplinary studies; parks, recreation, leisure, and fitness studies; philosophy and religious studies; visual and performing arts. **Areas of required coursework:** humanities, computer literacy, mathematics, English (including composition), philosophy, sciences (biological or physical), history, social science. **Pre-professional programs:** pre-law, pre-medicine. **Special academic programs (% participation):** cooperative (work-study plan) program (12%), cross-registration (2%), double major (1%), honors program, independent study (3%), internships (5%), teacher certificate program (20%). **Teacher certification offered in:** elementary, secondary. **Cooperative education programs:** business, health professions, social/behavioral science. **Reserve Officers Training Corps (ROTC):** Army ROTC: Offered at cooperating institution (University of Alabama); Air Force ROTC: Offered at cooperating institution (University of Alabama). **Faculty and instruction (2005-2006):** Total instructional faculty: 57 full-time, 1 part-time (59% men; 41% women; 57% minorities). Full-time faculty with Ph.D. or other terminal degree: 81%. Student/faculty ratio: 14/1. Classes of fewer than 20 students: 67%; of 20 to 49 students: 28%; of 50 or more students: 5%. **Advanced Placement and International Baccalaureate credit:** AP tests may be used for: Credit and/or placement. **Freshmen returning for sophomore year:** 72%. **Graduation rates:** Four-year: 24%; five-year: 24%; six-year: 29%. **Graduate study:** 20% of students pursue further study immediately upon graduation; 20% within one year; 27% within five years. Fields in which graduates pursue further study: Master of Business Administration (MBA), 85%; law, 5%; medicine, 1%; theology (or the seminary), 1%; education, 5%; arts and sciences, 3%.

COSTS AND FINANCIAL AID
Financial aid office: (205) 366-8817. **Expenses (2006-2007):** Tuition and fees 2006-2007: $11,605; room/board: $5,500. Estimated books and supplies: $1,000; transportation: $1,000; personal expenses: $1,200. **Financial aid:** Priority filing date for institution's financial aid form: April 15; deadline: July 1. In 2005-2006, 94% of undergraduates applied for financial aid. Of those, 94% were determined to have financial need; 59% had their need fully met. Average financial aid package (proportion receiving): $16,987 (97%). Average amount of gift aid, such as scholarships or grants (proportion receiving): $5,862 (38%). Average amount of self-help aid, such as work study or loans (proportion receiving): $1,292 (57%). Average need-based loan (excluding PLUS or other private loans): $7,500. Among students who received need-based aid, the average percentage of need met: 75%. Among students who received aid based on merit, the average award (and the proportion receiving): $2,000 (4%). The average athletic scholarship (and the proportion receiving): $4,829 (5%). Average amount of debt of borrowers graduating in 2005: $20,604. Proportion who borrowed: 86%.

CAMPUS LIFE AND EXTRACURRICULAR ACTIVITIES
Campus housing available (% using): women's dorms (47%), men's dorms (39%), apartment for single students (14%). Students who live in college-owned, operated, or affiliated housing: 50%. **Clubs and organizations:** Number of student organizations: 21. Activities include: choral groups, concert band, dance, drama/theater, jazz band, literary magazine, marching band, music ensembles, pep band, student government, student newspaper, symphony orchestra, yearbook. Number of fraternities: 4; sororities: 4. Proportion of men in fraternities: 5%; of women in sororities: 12%. Average proportion of students who stay on campus on weekends: 60%. **Sports program (2005-2006):** Member of NCAA II. *Men's intercollegiate varsity sports:* baseball, basketball, cross-country, football, tennis, track and field (outdoor). *Women's intercollegiate varsity sports:* basketball, cross-country, softball, tennis, track and field (outdoor), volleyball.

SERVICES AND FACILITIES
Basic services: nonremedial tutoring, placement service, health service, health insurance. **Remedial assistance:** reading, math, writing, study skills. **Counseling services:** minority student, career, personal, academic, older student, psychological, religious. **For learning-disabled students:** School does not offer a structured program with separate admission and additional fees. Total undergraduates in learning-disabled program or receiving services: 0. Services include: remedial math, remedial English, reading machines, tape recorders, untimed tests, oral tests, readers, extended time for tests, tutors, priority seating. **Library:** Number of titles: 116,924; number of current serial subscriptions: 242. **Information technology resources:** Students are required to lease or own a computer. Number of campus computers available to all students: 1,224. School has a wireless network. Approximate number of users that can be accommodated: 1,500. Proportion of college-owned housing units wired for high-speed internet access: 95%. **Campus safety:** Security services offered: 24-hour foot-and-vehicle patrols, lighted pathways/sidewalks, controlled dormitory access (key, security card, etc).

TRANSFER AND INTERNATIONAL STUDENTS
Transfer students: May apply for admission for the following academic terms: Fall, Spring, Summer. Applicants do not need a minimum number of credits to apply. **International students:** Number of foreign undergraduates: 4 (1% of student body). Number of countries represented: 6. Minimum TOEFL score required: 550 (paper).

Talladega College

- **Address:** 627 W. Battle Street, Talladega, AL 35160
- **Website:** http://www.talladega.edu
- **Private; Religious affiliation:** United Church of Christ
- **Enrollment:** 339 full-time; 29 part-time

KEY STATS

✔ **U.S News College Ranking:** third tier, Liberal Arts Colleges
✔ **SAT or ACT Score (25th/75th percentile):** N/A
✔ **Tuition:** 2006-2007: $7,128

Selectivity: Selective	**Room/board:** N/A
Acceptance rate: 38%	**Average debt:** N/A
Student/faculty ratio: 10/1	**Proportion who borrowed:** N/A

UNDERGRADUATE STUDENT BODY STATS

2005-2006 enrollment: 339 full-time; 29 part-time. Men: 39%; women: 61%. **Ethnic makeup:** African American: 94%; White: 6%.

ADMISSIONS FACTS AND FIGURES

Phone: (256) 761-6235. **Email:** admissions@talladega.edu. **Website:** http://www.talladega.edu. **Application deadlines for fall 2007:** Regular decision: Rolling. Early decision: Not offered. Early action: Not offered. Admission can be deferred. **Application fee:** $25. Common application is not accepted. **Admissions requirements/recommendations:** High school units required (recommended): English: 4 (4); Mathematics: 2 (2); Science: 2 (2); Social studies: 3 (3); Academic electives: 2 (2); Total units: 15 (15). Tests: The college uses SAT or ACT scores in admissions decisions. Either SAT or ACT required. For admission to the fall 2007 entering class, the school will accept: ACT with writing, ACT without writing. Campus visit: Recommended. Admissions interview: Recommended. Off-campus interview: May be arranged. **Factors that count in admissions decisions:** *Academic:* Secondary school record: Very important. Class rank: Important. Letters of recommendation: Very important. Standardized test scores: Very important. Essay: Very important. *Nonacademic:* Interview: Not considered. Extracurricular activities: Considered. Talent/ability: Very important. Character/personal qualities: Important. Alumni/ae relationship: Not considered. Geographical residence: Not considered. State residency: Not considered. Religious affiliation/commitment: Not considered. Minority status: Not considered. Volunteer work: Not considered. Work experience: Not considered. **Admissions statistics for the fall 2005 entering class:** Total applicants: 1,947. Total accepted: 743. Freshmen enrolled: 182; 48% were from out of state. Overall acceptance rate: 38%. **Average high school grade point average:** 2.5.

ACADEMICS

Year founded: 1867. **Academic calendar:** Semester. **Degrees offered:** bachelor's. **Most popular majors:** 23% biology, 13% business administration and management, 10% psychology, 8% sociology, 7% English language and literature. **Major fields of study:** area, ethnic, cultural, and gender studies; biological and biomedical sciences; business, management, marketing, and related support services; communication, journalism, and related programs; computer and information sciences and support services; education; English language and literature/letters; foreign languages, literatures, and linguistics; history; mathematics and statistics; physical sciences; psychology; public administration and social service professions; social sciences; visual and performing arts. **Areas of required coursework:** humanities, mathematics, foreign languages, sciences (biological or physical), social science, other. **Pre-professional programs:** pre-law, pre-dentistry, pre-medicine, pre-veterinary science, other. **Special academic programs (% participation):** cooperative (work-study plan) program (36%), double major (1%), dual enrollment (1%), independent study (1%), internships (2%), teacher certificate program (2%). **Teacher certification offered in:** secondary. **Cooperative education programs:** engineering, health professions, natural science. **Reserve Officers Training Corps (ROTC):** Army ROTC: Offered at cooperating institution (Jacksonville State University). **Faculty and instruction (2005-2006):** Total instructional faculty: 36 full-time, 15 part-time (47% men; 53% women; 76% minorities). Full-time faculty with Ph.D. or other terminal degree: 50%. Student/faculty ratio: 10/1. **Advanced Placement and International Baccalaureate credit:** International Baccalaureate exams may be used for: Credit only. **Freshmen returning for sophomore year:** 54%. **Graduation rates:** Four-year: 34%; five-year: 74%; six-year: 77%. **Graduate study:** 45% of students pursue further study immediately upon graduation;

54% within one year; 56% within five years. Fields in which graduates pursue further study: Master of Business Administration (MBA), 5%; law, 10%; medicine, 45%; dentistry, 20%; education, 5%; arts and sciences, 15%.

COSTS AND FINANCIAL AID

Financial aid office: (256) 761-6341. **Expenses (2006-2007):** Tuition and fees 2006-2007: $7,128; room/board: N/A. Estimated books and supplies: $1,000. **Financial aid:** Priority filing date for institution's financial aid form: April 15; deadline: June 30. In 2005-2006, 100% of undergraduates applied for financial aid. Of those, 100% were determined to have financial need; Average financial aid package (proportion receiving): N/A (100%). Average amount of gift aid, such as scholarships or grants (proportion receiving): N/A (100%). Among students who received need-based aid, the average percentage of need met: 100%.

CAMPUS LIFE AND EXTRACURRICULAR ACTIVITIES

Campus housing available (% using): women's dorms (62%), men's dorms (38%). **Clubs and organizations:** Number of student organizations: 41. Activities include: choral groups, dance, drama/theater, literary magazine, music ensembles, student government, student film society, yearbook. Number of fraternities: 4; sororities: 4. Proportion of men in fraternities: 8%; of women in sororities: 9%. Average proportion of students who stay on campus on weekends: 30%.

SERVICES AND FACILITIES

Basic services: nonremedial tutoring, placement service, health service, health insurance. **Remedial assistance:** reading, math, writing, study skills. **Counseling services:** career, academic, psychological, birth control, religious. **For learning-disabled students:** School does not offer a structured program with separate admission and additional fees. Services include: remedial math, remedial English, remedial reading, tape recorders, diagnostic testing service, untimed tests, note-taking services, oral tests, learning center, readers, extended time for tests, tutors, early syllabus, texts on tape, typist/scribe, exams on tape or computer, take home exams. **Library:** Number of titles: 127,158; number of current serial subscriptions: 100. **Information technology resources:** Students are not required to lease or own a computer. Number of campus computers available to all students: 219. School has a wireless network. Approximate number of users that can be accommodated: 35. Proportion of college-owned housing units wired for high-speed internet access: 50%. **Campus safety:** Security services offered: 24-hour foot-and-vehicle patrols, late-night transport/escort service.

TRANSFER AND INTERNATIONAL STUDENTS

Transfer students: May apply for admission for the following academic terms: Fall, Spring. Applicants do not need a minimum number of credits to apply. For fall 2005: Transfer applications received: 0. **International students:** Number of foreign undergraduates: 0. Number of countries represented: 2.

Troy University

- **Address:** University Avenue, Troy, AL 36082
- **Website:** http://www.troy.edu/
- **Public**
- **Enrollment:** 8,395 full-time; 10,383 part-time

KEY STATS

✔ **U.S News College Ranking:** 63, Universities–Master's (South)
✔ **ACT Score (25th/75th percentile):** 21
✔ **Tuition:** 2006-2007: $4,316 in state, $8,320 out of state

Selectivity: Selective	**Room/board:** $4,920
Acceptance rate: 81%	**Average debt:** $14,762
Student/faculty ratio: 21/1	**Proportion who borrowed:** 70%

UNDERGRADUATE STUDENT BODY STATS

2005-2006 enrollment: 8,395 full-time; 10,383 part-time. Men: 46%; women: 54%. **Ethnic makeup:** African American: 36%; American-Indian: 1%; Asian American: 1%; Hispanic: 4%; White: 57%; International: 2%.

ADMISSIONS FACTS AND FIGURES

Phone: (334) 670-3179. **Email:** admit@troy.edu. **Website:** http://www.troy.edu/. **Application deadlines for fall 2007:** Regular decision: Rolling. Early decision: Not offered. Early action: Not offered. Admission can be deferred. **Application fee:** $30. Common application is not accepted. **Admissions requirements/recommendations:** High school units required (recommended): English: 4; Mathematics: 4; Science: 4; Foreign language: (2); Social studies: 4; Total units: 18. Tests: The college uses SAT or ACT scores in admissions decisions. Either SAT or ACT required. For admission to the fall 2007 entering class, the school will accept: ACT with writing, ACT without writing. Campus visit: Recommended. Admissions interview: Recommended. Off-campus interview: Not available. **Factors that count in admissions decisions:** *Academic:* Secondary school record: Very important. Class rank: Not considered. Letters of recommendation: Considered. Standardized test scores: Very important. Essay: Considered. *Nonacademic:* Interview: Considered. Extracurricular activities: Considered. Talent/ability: Considered. Character/personal qualities: Considered. Alumni/ae relationship: Considered. Geographical residence: Not considered. State residency: Not considered. Religious affiliation/commitment: Not considered. Minority status: Not considered. Volunteer work: Not considered. Work experience: Not considered. **Admissions statistics for the fall 2005 entering class:** Total applicants: 4,758. Total accepted: 3,866. Freshmen enrolled: 2,250; 7% were from out of state. Overall acceptance rate: 81%. **Credentials of fall 2005 freshmen:** 48% were in the top 25 percent, and 86% were in the top half. (Proportion submitting class standing: 80%.) **First-year students submitting ACT scores:** 54%. Scores (25/75 percentile): English: N/A, Math: N/A, Composite: N/A.

ACADEMICS

Year founded: 1887. **Academic calendar:** Semester. **Degrees offered:** associate, bachelor's, master's, post-master's certificate. **Most popular majors:** 43% business, management, marketing, and related support services, 11% security and protective services, 9% education, 9% psychology, 9% social sciences. **Major fields of study:** biological and biomedical sciences; business, management, marketing, and related support services; communication, journalism, and related programs; computer and information sciences and support services; education; engineering technologies/technicians; English language and literature/letters; health professions and related clinical sciences; history; liberal arts and sciences studies, and humanities; mathematics and statistics; natural resources and conservation; parks, recreation, leisure, and fitness studies; physical sciences; psychology; public administration and social service professions; security and protective services; social sciences; visual and performing arts. **Areas of required coursework:** arts/fine arts, humanities, computer literacy, mathematics, English (including composition), sciences (biological or physical), history. **Pre-professional programs:** pre-law, pre-dentistry, pre-medicine, pre-theology, pre-veterinary science, pre-optometry, pre-pharmacy, other. **Special academic programs:** accelerated program, cross-registration, distance learning, double major, dual enrollment, English as a Second Language (ESL), honors program, independent study, internships, study abroad, teacher certificate program, weekend college. **Teacher certification offered in:** early childhood, special education, elementary, middle/junior high, adult education, secondary. **Reserve Officers Training Corps (ROTC):** Army ROTC: Offered on campus; Air Force ROTC: Offered on campus. **Faculty and instruction (2005-2006):** Total instructional faculty: 456 full-time, 949 part-time (56% men; 44% women; 16% minorities). Full-time faculty with Ph.D. or other terminal degree: 56%. Student/faculty ratio: 21/1. Classes of fewer than 20 students: 62%; of 20 to 49 students: 36%; of 50 or more students: 2%. **Advanced Placement and International Baccalaureate credit:** AP tests may be used for: Credit and/or placement. Scores accepted: 3. **Freshmen returning for sophomore year:** 71%. **Graduation rates:** Four-year: 33%; five-year: 46%; six-year: 53%.

COSTS AND FINANCIAL AID

Financial aid office: (334) 670-3186. **Expenses (2006-2007):** Tuition and fees 2006-2007: $4,316 in state, $8,320 out of state; room/board: $4,920. **Financial aid:** Priority filing date for institution's financial aid form: May 1. In 2005-2006, 67% of undergraduates applied for financial aid. Of those, 61% were determined to have financial need; Average financial aid package (proportion receiving): $3,634 (61%). Average amount of gift aid, such as scholarships or grants (proportion receiving): $3,183 (44%). Average amount of self-help aid, such as work study or loans (proportion receiving): $2,075 (60%). Average need-based loan (excluding PLUS or other private loans): $3,874. Among students who received need-based aid, the average percentage of need met: 70%. Among students who received aid based on merit, the average award (and the proportion receiving): $2,610 (25%). The average athletic scholarship (and the proportion receiving): $4,587 (2%). Average amount of debt of borrowers graduating in 2005: $14,762. Proportion who borrowed: 70%.

CAMPUS LIFE AND EXTRACURRICULAR ACTIVITIES

Campus housing available (% using): coed dorms (16%), women's dorms (24%), men's dorms (29%), sorority housing (5%), fraternity housing (5%), apartments for married students (3%), apartment for single students (9%), special housing for international students (8%), other housing options (1%). Students who live in college-owned, operated, or affiliated housing: 29%. **Student employment:** During the 2005-2006 academic year, 3% of undergraduates worked on campus. Average per-year earnings: $2,300. **Clubs and organizations:** Number of student organizations: 135. Activities include: choral groups, concert band, dance, drama/theater, jazz band, marching band, music ensembles, musical theater, opera, pep band, radio station, student government, student newspaper, symphony orchestra, television station, yearbook. Number of fraternities: 11; sororities: 9. Proportion of men in fraternities: 16%; of women in sororities: 17%. Average proportion of students who stay on campus on weekends: 55%. **Sports program (2005-2006):** Member of NCAA I. *Men's intercollegiate varsity sports:* baseball, basketball, cross-country, football, golf, tennis, track and field (outdoor). *Women's intercollegiate varsity sports:* basketball, cross-country, golf, soccer, softball, tennis, track and field (indoor), track and field (outdoor), volleyball.

SERVICES AND FACILITIES

Basic services: nonremedial tutoring, placement service, day care, health service, health insurance. **Remedial assistance:** math, writing, study skills. **Counseling services:** minority student, career, military, personal, veteran student, academic, older student, psychological, birth control, religious. **For learning-disabled students:** School does not offer a structured program with separate admission and additional fees. Total undergraduates in learning-disabled program or receiving services: 86. Services include: remedial math, remedial English, tape recorders, note-taking services, oral tests, readers, extended time for tests, tutors, priority seating, proofreading services, texts on tape, typist/scribe, other. **Library:** Number of titles: 579,558; number of current serial subscriptions: 2,249. **Information technology resources:** Students are not required to lease or own a computer. Number of campus computers available to all students: 557. School has a wireless network. Approximate number of users that can be accommodated: 1,206. Proportion of college-owned housing units wired for high-speed internet access: 95%. **Campus safety:** Security services offered: 24-hour foot-and-vehicle patrols, late-night transport/escort service, 24-hour emergency telephones, lighted pathways/sidewalks, student patrols, controlled dormitory access (key, security card, etc).

TRANSFER AND INTERNATIONAL STUDENTS

Transfer students: May apply for admission for the following academic terms: Fall, Spring, Summer. Applicants need a minimum number of credits to apply. For fall 2005: Transfer applications received: 5,399. Transfer applicants offered admission: 3,760. Transfer applicants enrolled: 2,746. **International students:** Number of foreign undergraduates: 410 (2% of student body). Minimum TOEFL score required: 500 (paper); 175 (computer).

Tuskegee University

- **Address:** PO Box 1239, Tuskegee, AL 36088
- **Website:** http://www.tuskegee.edu
- **Private**
- **Enrollment:** 2,391 full-time; 119 part-time

KEY STATS

✔ **U.S News College Ranking:** 37, Universities–Master's (South)
✔ **ACT Score (25th/75th percentile):** 17-21
✔ **Tuition:** 2006-2007: $12,985

Selectivity: Less selective	**Room/board:** $6,460
Acceptance rate: 81%	**Average debt:** $30,000
Student/faculty ratio: 12/1	**Proportion who borrowed:** 91%

UNDERGRADUATE STUDENT BODY STATS

2005-2006 enrollment: 2,391 full-time; 119 part-time. Men: 46%; women: 54%. **Ethnic makeup:** African American: 72%; White: 25%; International: 3%. **Religious preference:** Roman Catholic: 2%; Protestant: 96%; Unknown: 2%.

ADMISSIONS FACTS AND FIGURES

Phone: (334) 727-8500. **Email:** admiweb@tusk.edu. **Website:** http://www.tuskegee.edu. **Application deadlines for fall 2007:** Regular decision: March 15. Early decision: Not offered. Early action: Not offered. Admission can be deferred. **Application fee:** $25. Common application is not accepted. **Admissions requirements/recommendations:** High school units required (recommended): English: 4 (4); Mathematics: 3 (3); Science: 2 (2); Foreign language: 0 (0); Social studies: 3 (3); Academic electives: 4 (4); Total units: 16 (16). Tests: The college uses SAT or ACT scores in admissions decisions. Either SAT or ACT required. Campus visit: Recommended. Admissions interview: Neither required nor recommended. Off-campus interview: May be arranged. **Factors that count in admissions decisions:** *Academic:* Secondary school record: Very important. Class rank: Considered. Letters of recommendation: Considered. Standardized test scores: Important. Essay: Considered. *Nonacademic:* Interview: Not considered. Extracurricular activities: Considered. Talent/ability: Considered. Character/personal qualities: Important. Alumni/ae relationship: Considered. State residency: Considered. Religious affiliation/commitment: Not considered. Minority status: Considered. Volunteer work: Important. Work experience: Considered. **Other schools with the greatest overlap in applicants:** Alabama State University; Alcorn State University; Benedict College; Bennett College; Clark Atlanta University. **Admissions statistics for the fall 2005 entering class:** Total applicants: 2,037. Total accepted: 1,640. Freshmen enrolled: 737; 52% were from out of state. Overall acceptance rate: 81%. Size of waiting list: 0 applicants; enrolled from waiting list: 0. **Credentials of fall 2005 freshmen:** 20% ranked in the top 10 percent of their high school class; 59% were in the top 25 percent, and 100% were in the top half. (Proportion submitting class standing: 95%.) **Average high school grade point average:** 3.0. **First-year students who submitted SAT scores:** 55%. Scores (25/75 percentile): Verbal: 390-500, Math: 390-500, Combined: 780-1000. **First-year students submitting ACT scores:** 60%. Scores (25/75 percentile): English: N/A, Math: N/A, Composite: 17-21.

ACADEMICS

Year founded: 1881. **Academic calendar:** Semester. **Degrees offered:** bachelor's, master's, first professional, doctorate. **Most popular majors:** 40% business, management, marketing, and related support services, 21% psychology, 19% human resources management and services, 12% engineering, 8% biology/biological sciences. **Major fields of study:** agriculture, agriculture operations, and related sciences; architecture and related services; business, management, marketing, and related support services; computer and information sciences and support services; construction trades; education; engineering; English language and literature/letters; health professions and related clinical sciences; history; mathematics and statistics; natural resources and conservation; physical sciences; psychology; public administration and social service professions; social sciences. **Areas of required coursework:** arts/fine arts, mathematics, English (including composition), foreign languages, sciences (biological or physical), history, social science. **Pre-professional programs:** pre-dentistry, pre-medicine, pre-veterinary science. **Special academic programs (% participation):** cooperative (work-study plan) program (40%), double major (10%), honors program, independent study, internships, liberal arts/career combination, teacher certificate program. **Teacher certification offered in:** early childhood, special education, elementary. **Cooperative education programs:** agriculture, business, computer science, education, engineering, health professions. **Reserve Officers Training Corps (ROTC):** Army ROTC: Offered on campus; Air Force ROTC: Offered on campus. **Faculty and instruction (2005-2006):** Total instructional faculty: 223 full-time, 42 part-time (64% men; 36% women; 62% minorities). Full-time faculty with Ph.D. or other terminal degree: 78%. Student/faculty ratio: 12/1. Classes of fewer than 20 students: 55%; of 20 to 49 students: 35%; of 50 or more students: 11%. **Advanced Placement and International Baccalaureate credit:** AP tests may be used for: Credit and/or placement. Scores accepted: 3. **Freshmen returning for sophomore year:** 72%. **Graduation rates:** Four-year: 17%; five-year: 31%; six-year: 48%. **Graduate study:** 21% of students pursue further study immediately upon graduation; 45% within one year; 50% within five years. Fields in which graduates pursue further study: Master of Business Administration (MBA), 6%; law, 4%; medicine, 11%; dentistry, 2%; engineering, 16%; theology (or the seminary), 2%; education, 4%; arts and sciences, 2%; veterinary medicine, 13%.

COSTS AND FINANCIAL AID

Financial aid office: (334) 727-8201. **Expenses (2006-2007):** Tuition and fees 2006-2007: $12,985; room/board: $6,460. Estimated books and supplies: $949; transportation: $1,464; personal expenses: $1,537. **Financial aid:** Priority filing date for institution's financial aid form: March 31; deadline:

March 31. In 2005-2006, 92% of undergraduates applied for financial aid. Of those, 78% were determined to have financial need; 64% had their need fully met. Average financial aid package (proportion receiving): $13,824 (72%). Average amount of gift aid, such as scholarships or grants (proportion receiving): $8,000 (61%). Average amount of self-help aid, such as work study or loans (proportion receiving): $5,666 (56%). Average need-based loan (excluding PLUS or other private loans): $6,006. Among students who received need-based aid, the average percentage of need met: 85%. Among students who received aid based on merit, the average award (and the proportion receiving): $6,000 (32%). The average athletic scholarship (and the proportion receiving): $11,690 (1%). Average amount of debt of borrowers graduating in 2005: $30,000. Proportion who borrowed: 91%.

CAMPUS LIFE AND EXTRACURRICULAR ACTIVITIES

Campus housing available (% using): women's dorms (14%), men's dorms (12%), apartments for married students (10%), apartment for single students (15%). Students who live in college-owned, operated, or affiliated housing: 55%. Average per-year earnings: $1,540. Activities include: choral groups, marching band, music ensembles, student government, student newspaper, student film society, yearbook. Number of fraternities: 8; sororities: 4. Proportion of men in fraternities: 6%; of women in sororities: 5%. **Sports program (2005-2006):** Member of NCAA II. *Men's intercollegiate varsity sports:* baseball, basketball, cross-country, football, tennis, track and field (outdoor). *Women's intercollegiate varsity sports:* basketball, cross-country, softball, tennis, track and field (outdoor), volleyball.

SERVICES AND FACILITIES

Basic services: placement service, day care, health service, health insurance. **Remedial assistance:** reading, math, writing, study skills. **Counseling services:** minority student, career, personal, veteran student, academic, birth control, religious. **For learning-disabled students:** School does not offer a structured program with separate admission and additional fees. Services include: remedial math, remedial English, remedial reading, diagnostic testing service, learning center. **Library:** Number of titles: 310,000; number of current serial subscriptions: 53,000. **Information technology resources:** Students are not required to lease or own a computer. Number of campus computers available to all students: 1,200. School has a wireless network. Proportion of college-owned housing units wired for high-speed internet access: 100%. **Campus safety:** Security services offered: 24-hour foot-and-vehicle patrols, late-night transport/escort service, 24-hour emergency telephones, lighted pathways/sidewalks, controlled dormitory access (key, security card, etc).

TRANSFER AND INTERNATIONAL STUDENTS

Transfer students: May apply for admission for the following academic terms: Fall, Spring, Summer. Applicants do not need a minimum number of credits to apply. For fall 2005: Transfer applications received: 352. Transfer applicants offered admission: 190. Transfer applicants enrolled: 80. **International students:** Number of foreign undergraduates: 72 (3% of student body). Minimum TOEFL score required: 500 (paper); 173 (computer).

University of Alabama

- **Address:** Box 870100, Tuscaloosa, AL 35487-0100
- **Website:** http://www.ua.edu
- **Public**
- **Enrollment:** 15,832 full-time; 1,718 part-time

KEY STATS

✔ **U.S News College Ranking:** 88, National Universities
✔ **ACT Score (25th/75th percentile):** 21-27
✔ **Tuition:** 2006-2007: $5,278 in state, $15,294 out of state

Selectivity: More selective	**Room/board:** $5,380
Acceptance rate: 72%	**Average debt:** $18,545
Student/faculty ratio: 19/1	**Proportion who borrowed:** 50%

UNDERGRADUATE STUDENT BODY STATS

2005-2006 enrollment: 15,832 full-time; 1,718 part-time. Men: 47%; women: 53%. **Ethnic makeup:** African American: 12%; American-Indian: 1%; Asian American: 1%; Hispanic: 2%; White: 84%; International: 1%. **Religious pref-**

erence: Roman Catholic: 10%; Protestant: 64%; Jewish: 1%; No preference: 12%; Unknown: 12%; Other: 1%.

ADMISSIONS FACTS AND FIGURES

Phone: (205) 348-5666. **Email:** admissions@ua.edu. **Website:** http://www.ua.edu. **Application deadlines for fall 2007:** Regular decision: Rolling. Early decision: Not offered. Early action: Not offered. Admission cannot be deferred. **Application fee:** $35. Common application is accepted. **To apply online, go to:** https://www.ssc.ua.edu/application/. **Admissions requirements/recommendations:** High school units required (recommended); English: 4 (4); Mathematics: 3 (3); Science: 3 (3); Foreign language: 1 (1); Social studies: 3 (3); History: 1 (1); Academic electives: 5 (5); Total units: 15 (15). Tests: The college uses SAT or ACT scores in admissions decisions. Either SAT or ACT required. For admission to the fall 2007 entering class, the school will accept: ACT with writing, ACT without writing. Campus visit: Recommended. Admissions interview: Neither required nor recommended. Off-campus interview: May be arranged. **Factors that count in admissions decisions:** *Academic:* Secondary school record: Very important. Class rank: Important. Letters of recommendation: Considered. Standardized test scores: Very important. Essay: Considered. *Nonacademic:* Interview: Considered. Extracurricular activities: Considered. Talent/ability: Considered. Character/personal qualities: Considered. Alumni/ae relationship: Considered. Geographical residence: Not considered. State residency: Not considered. Religious affiliation/commitment: Not considered. Minority status: Not considered. Volunteer work: Considered. Work experience: Considered. **Other schools with the greatest overlap in applicants:** Auburn University; University of Alabama–Birmingham; University of Georgia; University of Mississippi; University of Tennessee. **Admissions statistics for the fall 2005 entering class:** Total applicants: 10,707. Total accepted: 7,755. Freshmen enrolled: 3,735; 27% were from out of state. Overall acceptance rate: 72%. **Credentials of fall 2005 freshmen:** 32% ranked in the top 10 percent of their high school class; 51% were in the top 25 percent, and 77% were in the top half. (Proportion submitting class standing: 50%.) **Average high school grade point average:** 3.4. **First-year students who submitted SAT scores:** 35%. Scores (25/75 percentile): Verbal: 500-630, Math: 500-630, Combined: 1000-1260. **First-year students submitting ACT scores:** 86%. Scores (25/75 percentile): English: 21-28, Math: 19-26, Composite: 21-27.

ACADEMICS

Year founded: 1831. **Academic calendar:** Semester. **Degrees offered:** bachelor's, master's, post-master's certificate, first professional, doctorate. **Most popular majors:** 29% business, management, marketing, and related support services, 11% communication, journalism, and related programs, 8% family and consumer sciences/human sciences, 7% education, 7% health professions and related clinical sciences. **Major fields of study:** area, ethnic, cultural, and gender studies; biological and biomedical sciences; business, management, marketing, and related support services; communication, journalism, and related programs; computer and information sciences and support services; education; engineering; English language and literature/letters; family and consumer sciences/human sciences; foreign languages, literatures, and linguistics; health professions and related clinical sciences; history; mathematics and statistics; multi/interdisciplinary studies; natural resources and conservation; philosophy and religious studies; physical sciences; psychology; public administration and social service professions; security and protective services; social sciences; visual and performing arts. **Areas of required coursework:** arts/fine arts, humanities, computer literacy, mathematics, English (including composition), philosophy, foreign languages, sciences (biological or physical), history, social science. **Pre-professional programs:** pre-law, pre-dentistry, pre-medicine, pre-veterinary science, pre-optometry, pre-pharmacy, other. **Special academic programs (% participation):** accelerated program (.1%), cooperative (work-study plan) program (3.6%), cross-registration (.1%), distance learning (22.6%), double major (3.5%), dual enrollment (.2%), English as a Second Language (ESL) (.7%), exchange student program (domestic) (.1%), external degree program (2%), honors program (13.1%), independent study (33.8%), internships (34.2%), liberal arts/career combination (.1%), student-designed major (.9%), study abroad (3.8%), teacher certificate program (6.3%), weekend college (4.8%). **Teacher certification offered in:** special education, elementary, middle/junior high, secondary, bilingual/bicultural. **Cooperative education programs:** art, business, computer science, engineering, health professions, home economics, humanities, natural science, social/behavioral science, technologies. **Reserve Officers Training Corps (ROTC):** Army ROTC: Offered on campus; Air Force ROTC: Offered on campus. **Faculty and instruction (2005-2006):** Total instructional faculty: 893 full-time, 217 part-time (60% men; 40% women; 12% minorities). Full-time faculty with Ph.D. or other terminal degree: 92%. Student/faculty ratio: 19/1. Classes of

fewer than 20 students: 45%; of 20 to 49 students: 41%; of 50 or more students: 14%. **Advanced Placement and International Baccalaureate credit:** AP tests may be used for: Credit and/or placement. Scores accepted: 3, 4. International Baccalaureate exams may be used for: Credit and/or placement. **Freshmen returning for sophomore year:** 84%. **Graduation rates:** Four-year: 35%; five-year: 57%; six-year: 63%. **Graduate study:** 27% of students pursue further study within one year.

COSTS AND FINANCIAL AID

Financial aid office: (205) 348-2976. **Expenses (2006-2007):** Tuition and fees 2006-2007: $5,278 in state, $15,294 out of state; room/board: $5,380. **Financial aid:** Priority filing date for institution's financial aid form: March 1. In 2005-2006, 74% of undergraduates applied for financial aid. Of those, 39% were determined to have financial need; 31% had their need fully met. Average financial aid package (proportion receiving): $7,980 (39%). Average amount of gift aid, such as scholarships or grants (proportion receiving): $3,732 (23%). Average amount of self-help aid, such as work study or loans (proportion receiving): $4,237 (32%). Average need-based loan (excluding PLUS or other private loans): $4,895. Among students who received need-based aid, the average percentage of need met: 70%. Among students who received aid based on merit, the average award (and the proportion receiving): $5,151 (29%). The average athletic scholarship (and the proportion receiving): $18,899 (1%). Average amount of debt of borrowers graduating in 2005: $18,545. Proportion who borrowed: 50%.

CAMPUS LIFE AND EXTRACURRICULAR ACTIVITIES

Campus housing available (% using): coed dorms (45%), women's dorms (22%), men's dorms (13%), sorority housing (10%), fraternity housing (6%), apartments for married students (2%), apartment for single students (1%), special housing for disabled students (0%), other housing options (1%). Students who live in college-owned, operated, or affiliated housing: 26%. **Student employment:** During the 2005-2006 academic year, 11% of undergraduates worked on campus. Average per-year earnings: $2,592. **Clubs and organizations:** Number of student organizations: 263. Activities include: choral groups, concert band, dance, drama/theater, jazz band, literary magazine, marching band, music ensembles, musical theater, opera, pep band, radio station, student government, student newspaper, student film society, symphony orchestra, television station, yearbook. Number of fraternities: 28; sororities: 21. Proportion of men in fraternities: 21%; of women in sororities: 27%. Average proportion of students who stay on campus on weekends: 60%. **Sports program (2005-2006):** Member of NCAA I. *Men's intercollegiate varsity sports:* baseball, basketball, cross-country, football, golf, swimming and diving, tennis, track and field (indoor), track and field (outdoor). *Women's intercollegiate varsity sports:* basketball, cross-country, golf, gymnastics, soccer, softball, swimming and diving, tennis, track and field (indoor), track and field (outdoor), volleyball.

SERVICES AND FACILITIES

Basic services: nonremedial tutoring, women's center, placement service, day care, health service, health insurance. **Remedial assistance:** math, study skills. **Counseling services:** minority student, career, military, personal, veteran student, academic, older student, psychological, birth control, religious. **For learning-disabled students:** School does not offer a structured program with separate admission and additional fees. Total undergraduates in learning-disabled program or receiving services: 642. Services include: remedial math, reading machines, note-taking services, oral tests, learning center, extended time for tests, tutors, priority registration, priority seating, texts on tape, exams on tape or computer, other testing accomodations, other. **Library:** Number of titles: 2,518,290; number of current serial subscriptions: 33,355. **Information technology resources:** Students are not required to lease or own a computer. Number of campus computers available to all students: 2,500. School has a wireless network. Approximate number of users that can be accommodated: 6,000. Proportion of college-owned housing units wired for high-speed internet access: 100%. **Campus safety:** Security services offered: 24-hour foot-and-vehicle patrols, late-night transport/escort service, 24-hour emergency telephones, lighted pathways/sidewalks, student patrols, controlled dormitory access (key, security card, etc).

TRANSFER AND INTERNATIONAL STUDENTS

Transfer students: May apply for admission for the following academic terms: Fall, Spring, Summer. Applicants need a minimum number of credits to apply. For fall 2005: Transfer applications received: 2,665. Transfer applicants offered admission: 1,720. Transfer applicants enrolled: 1,445. **International students:** Number of foreign undergraduates: 187 (1% of student body). Number of countries represented: 900. Minimum TOEFL score required: 500 (paper); 173 (computer).

University of Alabama–Birmingham

- **Address:** 1530 Third Avenue S, Birmingham, AL 35294
- **Website:** http://www.uab.edu
- **Public**
- **Enrollment:** 8,059 full-time; 3,411 part-time

KEY STATS

✔ **U.S News College Ranking:** third tier, National Universities
✔ **ACT Score (25th/75th percentile):** 20-26
✔ **Tuition:** 2005-2006: $4,792 in state, $10,732 out of state

Selectivity: Selective	**Room/board:** $8,924
Acceptance rate: 88%	**Average debt:** $17,650
Student/faculty ratio: 18/1	**Proportion who borrowed:** 53%

UNDERGRADUATE STUDENT BODY STATS
2005-2006 enrollment: 8,059 full-time; 3,411 part-time. Men: 39%; women: 61%. **Ethnic makeup:** African American: 32%; Asian American: 3%; Hispanic: 1%; White: 61%; International: 2%.

ADMISSIONS FACTS AND FIGURES
Phone: (205) 934-8221. **Email:** undergradadmit@uab.edu. **Website:** http://www.uab.edu. **Application deadlines for fall 2007:** Regular decision: March 1. Early decision: Not offered. Early action: Not offered. Admission can be deferred. **Application fee:** $30. Common application is accepted. **To apply online, go to:** https://studentaffairs.sass.uab.edu/admissions/application/. **Admissions requirements/recommendations:** High school units required (recommended): English: 4 (4); Mathematics: 4 (4); Science: 4 (4); Foreign language: 1 (1); Social studies: 4 (4); Total units: 12 (12). Tests: The college uses SAT or ACT scores in admissions decisions. Either SAT or ACT required. For admission to the fall 2007 entering class, the school will accept: ACT with writing, ACT without writing. Campus visit: Neither required nor recommended. Admissions interview: Neither required nor recommended. Off-campus interview: May be arranged. **Factors that count in admissions decisions:** *Academic:* Secondary school record: Important. Class rank: Not considered. Letters of recommendation: Not considered. Standardized test scores: Very important. Essay: Not considered. *Nonacademic:* Interview: Not considered. Extracurricular activities: Not considered. Talent/ability: Not considered. Character/personal qualities: Not considered. Alumni/ae relationship: Not considered. Geographical residence: Not considered. State residency: Not considered. Religious affiliation/commitment: Not considered. Minority status: Not considered. Volunteer work: Not considered. Work experience: Not considered. **Other schools with the greatest overlap in applicants:** Auburn University; University of Alabama; University of Alabama–Huntsville. **Admissions statistics for the fall 2005 entering class:** Total applicants: 4,255. Total accepted: 3,731. Freshmen enrolled: 1,587; 8% were from out of state. Overall acceptance rate: 88%. **Credentials of fall 2005 freshmen:** 23% ranked in the top 10 percent of their high school class; 49% were in the top 25 percent, and 77% were in the top half. (Proportion submitting class standing: 55%.) **Average high school grade point average:** 3.3. **First-year students who submitted SAT scores:** 10%. Scores (25/75 percentile): Verbal: N/A, Math: N/A, Combined: N/A. **First-year students submitting ACT scores:** 87%. Scores (25/75 percentile): English: 20-27, Math: 18-24, Composite: 20-26.

ACADEMICS
Year founded: 1969. **Academic calendar:** Semester. **Degrees offered:** certificate, bachelor's, post-bachelor's certificate, master's, post-master's certificate, first professional, doctorate. **Most popular majors:** 24% business, management, marketing, and related support services, 18% health professions and related clinical sciences, 8% psychology, 7% education, 5% communication, journalism, and related programs. **Major fields of study:** area, ethnic, cultural, and gender studies; biological and biomedical sciences; business, management, marketing, and related support services; communication, journalism, and related programs; computer and information sciences and support services; education; engineering; English language and literature/letters; foreign languages, literatures, and linguistics; health professions and related clinical sciences; history; mathematics and statistics; multi/interdisciplinary studies; philosophy and religious studies; physical

sciences; psychology; public administration and social service professions; security and protective services; social sciences; visual and performing arts. **Areas of required coursework:** arts/fine arts, computer literacy, mathematics, English (including composition), philosophy, foreign languages, sciences (biological or physical), history, social science, other. **Pre-professional programs:** pre-law, pre-dentistry, pre-medicine, pre-optometry, other. **Special academic programs:** cooperative (work-study plan) program, cross-registration, distance learning, double major, dual enrollment, honors program, independent study, internships, student-designed major, study abroad, teacher certificate program, weekend college. **Teacher certification offered in:** early childhood, special education, elementary, secondary. **Cooperative education programs:** art, business, computer science, engineering, health professions, humanities, natural science, social/behavioral science. **Reserve Officers Training Corps (ROTC):** Army ROTC: Offered on campus; Air Force ROTC: Offered at cooperating institution (Samford University). **Faculty and instruction (2005-2006):** Total instructional faculty: 793 full-time, 122 part-time (63% men; 37% women; 16% minorities). Full-time faculty with Ph.D. or other terminal degree: 90%. Student/faculty ratio: 18/1. Classes of fewer than 20 students: 35%; of 20 to 49 students: 50%; of 50 or more students: 15%. **Advanced Placement and International Baccalaureate credit:** AP tests may be used for: Credit only. Scores accepted: 3, 4, 5. International Baccalaureate exams may be used for: Credit only. **Freshmen returning for sophomore year:** 76%. **Graduation rates:** Four-year: 14%; five-year: 30%; six-year: 36%.

COSTS AND FINANCIAL AID
Financial aid office: (205) 934-8223. **Expenses (2005-2006):** Tuition and fees 2005-2006: $4,792 in state, $10,732 out of state; room/board: $8,924. Estimated books and supplies: $900; transportation: $938; personal expenses: $1,500. **Financial aid:** Priority filing date for institution's financial aid form: April 1. In 2005-2006, 63% of undergraduates applied for financial aid. Of those, 51% were determined to have financial need; 13% had their need fully met. Average financial aid package (proportion receiving): $14,304 (51%). Average amount of gift aid, such as scholarships or grants (proportion receiving): $3,309 (31%). Average amount of self-help aid, such as work study or loans (proportion receiving): $3,702 (50%). Average need-based loan (excluding PLUS or other private loans): $3,876. Among students who received need-based aid, the average percentage of need met: 40%. Among students who received aid based on merit, the average award (and the proportion receiving): $9,814 (19%). The average athletic scholarship (and the proportion receiving): $12,026 (3%). Average amount of debt of borrowers graduating in 2005: $17,650. Proportion who borrowed: 53%.

CAMPUS LIFE AND EXTRACURRICULAR ACTIVITIES
Campus housing available (% using): coed dorms, apartments for married students (3%), apartment for single students (97%), special housing for disabled students. Students who live in college-owned, operated, or affiliated housing: 14%. **Clubs and organizations:** Number of student organizations: 200. Activities include: choral groups, concert band, dance, drama/theater, jazz band, literary magazine, marching band, music ensembles, musical theater, opera, pep band, radio station, student government, student newspaper. Number of fraternities: 9; sororities: 7. Proportion of men in fraternities: 6%; of women in sororities: 6%. Average proportion of students who stay on campus on weekends: 80%. **Sports program (2005-2006):** Member of NCAA I. *Men's intercollegiate varsity sports:* baseball, basketball, football, golf, soccer, tennis. *Women's intercollegiate varsity sports:* basketball, cross-country, golf, riflery, soccer, softball, synchronized swimming, tennis, track and field (indoor), track and field (outdoor), volleyball.

SERVICES AND FACILITIES
Basic services: nonremedial tutoring, women's center, placement service, day care, health service, health insurance. **Remedial assistance:** reading, math, writing, study skills. **Counseling services:** career, personal, veteran student, academic. **For learning-disabled students:** School does not offer a structured program with separate admission and additional fees. Total undergraduates in learning-disabled program or receiving services: 72. Services include: remedial math, remedial English, reading machines, tape recorders, note-taking services, oral tests, readers, extended time for tests, priority registration, priority seating, texts on tape, other testing accomodations. **Library:** Number of titles: 1,257,166; number of current serial subscriptions: 3,934. **Information technology resources:** Students are not required to lease or own a computer. Number of campus computers available to all students: 466. School has a wireless network. Proportion of college-owned housing units wired for high-speed internet access: 100%. **Campus safety:** Security services offered: 24-hour foot-and-vehicle patrols,

late-night transport/escort service, 24-hour emergency telephones, lighted pathways/sidewalks, controlled dormitory access (key, security card, etc).

TRANSFER AND INTERNATIONAL STUDENTS

Transfer students: May apply for admission for the following academic terms: Fall, Spring, Summer. Applicants need a minimum number of credits to apply. For fall 2005: Transfer applications received: 2,523. Transfer applicants offered admission: 2,289. Transfer applicants enrolled: 975. **International students:** Number of foreign undergraduates: 264 (2% of student body). Number of countries represented: 74. Minimum TOEFL score required: 500 (paper); 173 (computer).

University of Alabama–Huntsville

- **Address:** 301 Sparkman Drive, Huntsville, AL 35899
- **Website:** http://www.uah.edu
- **Public**
- **Enrollment:** 4,101 full-time; 1,589 part-time

KEY STATS

✔ **U.S News College Ranking:** third tier, National Universities
✔ **ACT Score (25th/75th percentile):** 22-28
✔ **Tuition:** 2006-2007: $4,848 in state, $10,224 out of state

Selectivity: More selective	**Room/board:** $5,690
Acceptance rate: 87%	**Average debt:** $17,043
Student/faculty ratio: 16/1	**Proportion who borrowed:** 53%

UNDERGRADUATE STUDENT BODY STATS

2005-2006 enrollment: 4,101 full-time; 1,589 part-time. Men: 51%; women: 49%. **Ethnic makeup:** African American: 14%; American-Indian: 1%; Asian American: 3%; Hispanic: 2%; White: 75%; International: 4%.

ADMISSIONS FACTS AND FIGURES

Phone: (256) 824-6070. **Email:** admitme@email.uah.edu. **Website:** http://www.uah.edu. **Application deadlines for fall 2007:** Regular decision: August 15. Early decision: Not offered. Early action: Not offered. Admission can be deferred. **Application fee:** $30. Common application is accepted. **Admissions requirements/recommendations:** High school units required (recommended): English: 4; Mathematics: 3; Science: 3; Social studies: 4; Academic electives: 6; Total units: 20. Tests: The college uses SAT or ACT scores in admissions decisions. Either SAT or ACT required. For admission to the fall 2007 entering class, the school will accept: ACT with writing, ACT without writing. Campus visit: Recommended. Admissions interview: Recommended. Off-campus interview: Not available. **Factors that count in admissions decisions:** *Academic:* Secondary school record: Very important. Class rank: Not considered. Letters of recommendation: Not considered. Standardized test scores: Very important. Essay: Not considered. *Nonacademic:* Interview: Not considered. Extracurricular activities: Not considered. Talent/ability: Not considered. Character/personal qualities: Not considered. Alumni/ae relationship: Not considered. Geographical residence: Not considered. State residency: Not considered. Religious affiliation/commitment: Not considered. Minority status: Not considered. Volunteer work: Not considered. Work experience: Not considered. **Other schools with the greatest overlap in applicants:** Alabama Agricultural and Mechanical University; Auburn University; University of Alabama; University of Alabama–Birmingham. **Admissions statistics for the fall 2005 entering class:** Total applicants: 1,698. Total accepted: 1,480. Freshmen enrolled: 660; 17% were from out of state. Overall acceptance rate: 87%. **Credentials of fall 2005 freshmen:** 31% ranked in the top 10 percent of their high school class; 57% were in the top 25 percent, and 83% were in the top half. (Proportion submitting class standing: 37%.) **Average high school grade point average:** 3.4. **First-year students who submitted SAT scores:** 27%. Scores (25/75 percentile): Verbal: 520-630, Math: 510-650, Combined: 1030-1280. **First-year students submitting ACT scores:** 88%. Scores (25/75 percentile): English: 22-29, Math: 20-27, Composite: 22-28.

ACADEMICS

Year founded: 1950. **Academic calendar:** Semester. **Degrees offered:** certificate, bachelor's, post-bachelor's certificate, master's, post-master's certificate, doctorate. **Most popular majors:** 27% business, management, marketing, and related support services, 24% engineering, 17% health professions and related clinical sciences, 6% biological and biomedical sci-

ences, 5% computer and information sciences and support services. **Major fields of study:** biological and biomedical sciences; business, management, marketing, and related support services; computer and information sciences and support services; education; engineering; English language and literature/letters; foreign languages, literatures, and linguistics; health professions and related clinical sciences; history; mathematics and statistics; philosophy and religious studies; physical sciences; psychology; social sciences; visual and performing arts. **Areas of required coursework:** arts/fine arts, humanities, computer literacy, mathematics, English (including composition), sciences (biological or physical), history, social science. **Pre-professional programs:** pre-law, pre-dentistry, pre-medicine, pre-veterinary science, pre-optometry, pre-pharmacy, other. **Special academic programs (% participation):** accelerated program, cooperative (work-study plan) program (6%), cross-registration, distance learning, double major (4%), dual enrollment (3%), English as a Second Language (ESL) (2%), honors program (3%), independent study, internships (2%), liberal arts/career combination (2%), teacher certificate program (3%), other. **Teacher certification offered in:** elementary, middle/junior high, secondary. **Cooperative education programs:** art, business, computer science, education, engineering, health professions, humanities, natural science, social/behavioral science, technologies. **Reserve Officers Training Corps (ROTC):** Army ROTC: Offered at cooperating institution (Alabama A&M University). **Faculty and instruction (2005-2006):** Total instructional faculty: 280 full-time, 188 part-time (60% men; 40% women; 14% minorities). Full-time faculty with Ph.D. or other terminal degree: 91%. Student/faculty ratio: 16/1. Classes of fewer than 20 students: 37%; of 20 to 49 students: 53%; of 50 or more students: 10%. **Advanced Placement and International Baccalaureate credit:** AP tests may be used for: Credit and/or placement. Scores accepted: 3, 4, 5. International Baccalaureate exams may be used for: Credit and/or placement. **Freshmen returning for sophomore year:** 75%. **Graduation rates:** Four-year: 13%; five-year: 36%; six-year: 44%. **Graduate study:** 9% of students pursue further study immediately upon graduation. Fields in which graduates pursue further study: Master of Business Administration (MBA), 2%; law, 7%; medicine, 2%; dentistry, 2%; engineering, 7%; theology (or the seminary), 2%; education, 2%; arts and sciences, 30%.

COSTS AND FINANCIAL AID

Financial aid office: (256) 824-6241. **Expenses (2006-2007):** Tuition and fees 2006-2007: $4,848 in state, $10,224 out of state; room/board: $5,690. **Financial aid:** Priority filing date for institution's financial aid form: April 1; deadline: July 31. In 2005-2006, 83% of undergraduates applied for financial aid. Of those, 43% were determined to have financial need; 14% had their need fully met. Average financial aid package (proportion receiving): $6,064 (43%). Average amount of gift aid, such as scholarships or grants (proportion receiving): $3,642 (33%). Average amount of self-help aid, such as work study or loans (proportion receiving): $4,616 (36%). Average need-based loan (excluding PLUS or other private loans): $4,499. Among students who received need-based aid, the average percentage of need met: 60%. Among students who received aid based on merit, the average award (and the proportion receiving): $2,475 (21%). The average athletic scholarship (and the proportion receiving): $5,049 (5%). Average amount of debt of borrowers graduating in 2005: $17,043. Proportion who borrowed: 53%.

CAMPUS LIFE AND EXTRACURRICULAR ACTIVITIES

Campus housing available (% using): coed dorms (90%), sorority housing (1%), fraternity housing (1%), apartments for married students (2%), apartment for single students (4%), special housing for disabled students (1%), other housing options (4%). Students who live in college-owned, operated, or affiliated housing: 16%. **Student employment:** During the 2005-2006 academic year, 20% of undergraduates worked on campus. Average per-year earnings: $5,924. **Clubs and organizations:** Number of student organizations: 78. Activities include: choral groups, concert band, dance, drama/theater, jazz band, literary magazine, music ensembles, musical theater, opera, pep band, student government, student newspaper, symphony orchestra. Number of fraternities: 7; sororities: 4. Proportion of men in fraternities: 5%; of women in sororities: 4%. Average proportion of students who stay on campus on weekends: 55%. **Sports program (2005-2006):** Member of NCAA II. **Men's intercollegiate varsity sports:** baseball, basketball, cross-country, ice hockey, soccer, tennis, track and field (indoor), track and field (outdoor). **Women's intercollegiate varsity sports:** basketball, cross-country, soccer, softball, tennis, track and field (indoor), track and field (outdoor), volleyball.

SERVICES AND FACILITIES

Basic services: nonremedial tutoring, women's center, placement service, day care, health service, health insurance. **Remedial assistance:** math, writing, study skills. **Counseling services:** minority student, career, military, personal, veteran student, academic, older student, psychological, birth control, religious. **For learning-disabled students:** School does not offer a structured program with separate admission and additional fees. Total undergraduates in learning-disabled program or receiving services: 32. Services include: remedial math, remedial English, reading machines, remedial reading, tape recorders, videotaped classes, untimed tests, note-taking services, oral tests, readers, extended time for tests, tutors, priority seating, texts on tape, exams on tape or computer, other testing accomodations. **Library:** Number of titles: 329,686; number of current serial subscriptions: 1,044. **Information technology resources:** Students are not required to lease or own a computer. Number of campus computers available to all students: 1,091. School has a wireless network. Approximate number of users that can be accommodated: 832. Proportion of college-owned housing units wired for high-speed internet access: 100%. **Campus safety:** Security services offered: 24-hour foot-and-vehicle patrols, late-night transport/escort service, lighted pathways/sidewalks, controlled dormitory access (key, security card, etc).

TRANSFER AND INTERNATIONAL STUDENTS

Transfer students: May apply for admission for the following academic terms: Fall, Spring, Summer. Applicants need a minimum number of credits to apply. For fall 2005: Transfer applications received: 989. Transfer applicants offered admission: 925. Transfer applicants enrolled: 616. **International students:** Number of foreign undergraduates: 189 (4% of student body). Minimum TOEFL score required: 500 (paper); 173 (computer). Average TOEFL score: 588 (paper).

University of Mobile

- **Address:** 5735 College Parkway, Mobile, AL 36613-2842
- **Website:** http://www.umobile.edu
- **Private; Religious affiliation:** Baptist
- **Enrollment:** 1,273 full-time; 276 part-time

KEY STATS

✔ **U.S News College Ranking:** third tier, Universities–Master's (South)
✔ **ACT Score (25th/75th percentile):** 20-30
✔ **Tuition:** 2006-2007: $12,260

Selectivity: Selective	**Room/board:** N/A
Acceptance rate: 53%	**Average debt:** $20,000
Student/faculty ratio: 13/1	**Proportion who borrowed:** 92%

UNDERGRADUATE STUDENT BODY STATS

2005-2006 enrollment: 1,273 full-time; 276 part-time. Men: 35%; women: 65%. **Ethnic makeup:** African American: 23%; American-Indian: 2%; Asian American: 1%; Hispanic: 1%; White: 70%; International: 4%. **Religious preference:** Baptist: 49%; Other: 51%.

ADMISSIONS FACTS AND FIGURES

Phone: (251) 442-2273. **Email:** adminfo@umobile.edu. **Website:** http://www.umobile.edu. **Application deadlines for fall 2007:** Regular decision: August 10. Early decision: Not offered. Early action: Send application by: N/A; Decision sent by: N/A. Admission cannot be deferred. **Application fee:** $30. Common application is accepted. **Admissions requirements/recommendations:** High school units required (recommended): English: (4); Mathematics: (3); Social studies: (2); History: (3); Total units: (22). Tests: The college uses SAT or ACT scores in admissions decisions. Neither SAT nor ACT required. Campus visit: Recommended. Admissions interview: Required. Off-campus interview: May be arranged. **Factors that count in admissions decisions:** *Academic:* Secondary school record: Very important. Class rank: Considered. Letters of recommendation: Considered. Standardized test scores: Very important. Essay: Not considered. *Nonacademic:* Interview: Considered. Extracurricular activities: Not considered. Talent/ability: Not considered. Character/personal qualities: Not considered. Alumni/ae relationship: Not considered. Geographical residence: Not considered. State residency: Not considered. Religious affiliation/commitment: Not considered. Minority status: Not considered. Volunteer work: Not considered. Work experience: Not considered. **Other schools with the greatest overlap in applicants:** Faulkner University; Spring Hill College; University of South Alabama. **Admissions statistics for the fall 2005 entering class:** Total applicants: 504. Total accepted: 266. Freshmen enrolled: 264; 25% were from out of state. Overall acceptance rate: 53%. Non-early accept-

ance rate: 53%. **Credentials of fall 2005 freshmen:** 21% ranked in the top 10 percent of their high school class; 40% were in the top 25 percent, and 71% were in the top half. (Proportion submitting class standing: 25%.) **First-year students who submitted SAT scores:** 2%. Scores (25/75 percentile): Verbal: N/A; Math: N/A, Combined: N/A. **First-year students submitting ACT scores:** 98%. Scores (25/75 percentile): English: N/A, Math: N/A, Composite: 20-30.

ACADEMICS

Year founded: 1961. **Academic calendar:** Semester. **Degrees offered:** associate, bachelor's, master's. **Most popular majors:** 16% education, 10% business, management, marketing, and related support services, 10% health professions and related clinical sciences. **Major fields of study:** biological and biomedical sciences; business, management, marketing, and related support services; communication, journalism, and related programs; computer and information sciences and support services; education; English language and literature/letters; health professions and related clinical sciences; history; mathematics and statistics; multi/interdisciplinary studies; philosophy and religious studies; physical sciences; psychology; social sciences; visual and performing arts. **Areas of required coursework:** arts/fine arts, humanities, computer literacy, mathematics, English (including composition), sciences (biological or physical), history, social science, other. **Pre-professional programs:** pre-law, pre-dentistry, pre-medicine, pre-veterinary science, pre-pharmacy. **Special academic programs (% participation):** accelerated program (10%), double major, dual enrollment (1%), independent study (1%), internships, teacher certificate program (16%). **Teacher certification offered in:** early childhood, elementary, middle/junior high, secondary. **Cooperative education programs:** art, business, computer science, education, health professions, humanities, natural science, social/behavioral science. **Reserve Officers Training Corps (ROTC):** Army ROTC: Offered at cooperating institution (University of South Alabama); Air Force ROTC: Offered at cooperating institution (University of South Alabama). **Faculty and instruction (2005-2006):** Total instructional faculty: 91 full-time, 65 part-time (45% men; 55% women; 5% minorities). Full-time faculty with Ph.D. or other terminal degree: 60%. Student/faculty ratio: 13/1. Classes of fewer than 20 students: 53%; of 20 to 49 students: 46%; of 50 or more students: 1%. **Advanced Placement and International Baccalaureate credit:** AP tests may be used for: Credit only. Scores accepted: 3, 4, 5. International Baccalaureate exams may be used for: Credit only. **Freshmen returning for sophomore year:** 68%. **Graduation rates:** Four-year: 31%; five-year: 46%; six-year: 44%.

COSTS AND FINANCIAL AID

Financial aid office: (251) 442-2385. **Expenses (2006-2007):** Tuition and fees 2006-2007: $12,260; room/board: N/A. Estimated books and supplies: $750; transportation: $500; personal expenses: $500. **Financial aid:** Priority filing date for institution's financial aid form: March 31. In 2005-2006, 64% of undergraduates applied for financial aid. Of those, 56% were determined to have financial need; Average financial aid package (proportion receiving): $6,500 (56%). Average amount of gift aid, such as scholarships or grants (proportion receiving): $2,111 (56%). Average amount of self-help aid, such as work study or loans (proportion receiving): $1,545 (51%). Average need-based loan (excluding PLUS or other private loans): $3,765. Among students who received need-based aid, the average percentage of need met: 40%. Among students who received aid based on merit, the average award (and the proportion receiving): N/A (4%). The average athletic scholarship (and the proportion receiving): $0 (0%). Average amount of debt of borrowers graduating in 2005: $20,000. Proportion who borrowed: 92%.

CAMPUS LIFE AND EXTRACURRICULAR ACTIVITIES

Campus housing available (% using): women's dorms (20%), men's dorms (5%). Students who live in college-owned, operated, or affiliated housing: 15%. Average per-year earnings: $1,500. **Clubs and organizations:** Number of student organizations: 33. Activities include: choral groups, concert band, drama/theater, jazz band, music ensembles, musical theater, opera, pep band, student government. Number of fraternities: 0; sororities: 0. Average proportion of students who stay on campus on weekends: 10%. **Sports program (2005-2006):** Member of NAIA. *Men's intercollegiate varsity sports:* baseball, basketball, cheerleading, golf, soccer. *Women's intercollegiate varsity sports:* basketball, cheerleading, golf, soccer, softball, tennis.

SERVICES AND FACILITIES

Basic services: health service, health insurance. **Remedial assistance:** reading, math, writing, study skills. **Counseling services:** career, military, personal, veteran student, academic, older student, religious. **For learning-disabled students:** School does not offer a structured program with separate admission and additional fees. Total undergraduates in learning-disabled program or receiving services: 10. Services include: remedial math, remedial English, remedial reading, tape recorders, untimed tests, learning center, extended time for tests. **Library:** Number of titles: 69,544; number of current serial subscriptions: 587. **Information technology resources:** Students are not required to lease or own a computer. Number of campus computers available to all students: 120. School does not have a wireless network. **Campus safety:** Security services offered: 24-hour foot-and-vehicle patrols, lighted pathways/sidewalks.

TRANSFER AND INTERNATIONAL STUDENTS

Transfer students: May apply for admission for the following academic terms: Fall, Spring, Summer. Applicants do not need a minimum number of credits to apply. **International students:** Number of foreign undergraduates: 59 (4% of student body). Minimum TOEFL score required: 550 (paper). Average TOEFL score: 550 (paper).

University of Montevallo

- **Address:** Station 6030, Montevallo, AL 35115
- **Website:** http://www.montevallo.edu
- **Public**
- **Enrollment:** 2,357 full-time; 259 part-time

KEY STATS

✔ **U.S News College Ranking:** 59, Universities–Master's (South)
✔ **ACT Score (25th/75th percentile):** 19-24
✔ **Tuition:** 2005-2006: $5,664 in state, $11,124 out of state

Selectivity: Selective	**Room/board:** $3,966
Acceptance rate: 74%	**Average debt:** $7,897
Student/faculty ratio: 17/1	**Proportion who borrowed:** 38%

UNDERGRADUATE STUDENT BODY STATS

2005-2006 enrollment: 2,357 full-time; 259 part-time. Men: 32%; women: 68%. **Ethnic makeup:** African American: 13%; American-Indian: 1%; Asian American: 1%; Hispanic: 1%; White: 82%; International: 2%. **Religious preference:** Roman Catholic: 5%; Protestant: 48%; No preference: 37%; Unknown: 4%; Other: 6%.

ADMISSIONS FACTS AND FIGURES

Phone: (205) 665-6030. **Email:** admissions@um.montevallo.edu. **Website:** http://www.montevallo.edu. **Application deadlines for fall 2007:** Regular decision: August 1. Early decision: Not offered. Early action: Not offered. Admission can be deferred. **Application fee:** $25. Common application is accepted. **Admissions requirements/recommendations:** High school units required (recommended): English: 4; Mathematics: 2 (3); Science: 2 (3); Foreign language: (2); Social studies: 2; History: 2; Academic electives: 4; Total units: 16. Tests: The college uses SAT or ACT scores in admissions decisions. Either SAT or ACT required. For admission to the fall 2007 entering class, the school will accept: ACT with writing, ACT without writing. Campus visit: Recommended. Admissions interview: Recommended. Off-campus interview: May be arranged. **Factors that count in admissions decisions:** *Academic:* Secondary school record: Very important. Class rank: Considered. Letters of recommendation: Considered. Standardized test scores: Very important. *Nonacademic:* Interview: Considered. Extracurricular activities: Considered. Talent/ability: Considered. Character/personal qualities: Considered. Alumni/ae relationship: Considered. Geographical residence: Not considered. State residency: Not considered. Religious affiliation/commitment: Not considered. Minority status: Not considered. Volunteer work: Not considered. Work experience: Considered. **Other schools with the greatest overlap in applicants:** Auburn University; University of Alabama; University of Alabama–Birmingham. **Admissions statistics for the fall 2005 entering class:** Total applicants: 1,426. Total accepted: 1,054. Freshmen enrolled: 496; 3% were from out of state. Overall acceptance rate: 74%. **Average high school grade point average:** 3.3. **First-year students submitting ACT scores:** 96%. Scores (25/75 percentile): English: 19-25, Math: 17-23, Composite: 19-24.

ACADEMICS

Year founded: 1896. **Academic calendar:** Semester. **Degrees offered:** bachelor's, master's, post-master's certificate. **Most popular majors:** 16% business, management, marketing, and related support services, 13% visual and performing arts, 12% education, 7% family and consumer sciences/human sciences, 6% health professions and related clinical sciences. **Major fields of study:** biological and biomedical sciences; business, management, marketing, and related support services; communication, journalism, and related programs; education; English language and literature/letters; family and consumer sciences/human sciences; foreign languages, literatures, and linguistics; health professions and related clinical sciences; history; mathematics and statistics; parks, recreation, leisure, and fitness studies; physical sciences; psychology; public administration and social service professions; social sciences; visual and performing arts. **Areas of required coursework:** arts/fine arts, humanities, computer literacy, mathematics, English (including composition), philosophy, foreign languages, sciences (biological or physical), history, social science, other. **Pre-professional programs:** pre-law, pre-dentistry, pre-medicine, pre-veterinary science, pre-optometry, pre-pharmacy, other. **Special academic programs (% participation):** accelerated program (40%), cross-registration (0%), double major (5%), honors program (1%), independent study (12%), internships (5%), study abroad (1%), teacher certificate program (21%). **Teacher certification offered in:** early childhood, elementary, middle/junior high, secondary. **Cooperative education programs:** business. **Reserve Officers Training Corps (ROTC):** Army ROTC: Offered at cooperating institution (University of Alabama, Birmingham); Air Force ROTC: Offered at cooperating institution (Samford University). **Faculty and instruction (2005-2006):** Total instructional faculty: 140 full-time, 60 part-time (49% men; 51% women; 7% minorities). Full-time faculty with Ph.D. or other terminal degree: 84%. Student/faculty ratio: 17/1. Classes of fewer than 20 students: 41%; of 20 to 49 students: 57%; of 50 or more students: 2%. **Advanced Placement and International Baccalaureate credit:** AP tests may be used for: Credit only. Scores accepted: 3, 4, 5. International Baccalaureate exams may be used for: Credit only. **Freshmen returning for sophomore year:** 74%. **Graduation rates:** Four-year: 22%; five-year: 41%; six-year: 43%.

COSTS AND FINANCIAL AID

Financial aid office: (205) 665-6050. **Expenses (2005-2006):** Tuition and fees 2005-2006: $5,664 in state, $11,124 out of state; room/board: $3,966. Estimated books and supplies: $600; transportation: $1,024; personal expenses: $1,690. **Financial aid:** Priority filing date for institution's financial aid form: April 15. In 2005-2006, 82% of undergraduates applied for financial aid. Of those, 60% were determined to have financial need; 25% had their need fully met. Average financial aid package (proportion receiving): $7,966 (59%). Average amount of gift aid, such as scholarships or grants (proportion receiving): $6,399 (36%). Average amount of self-help aid, such as work study or loans (proportion receiving): $3,197 (41%). Average need-based loan (excluding PLUS or other private loans): $2,992. Among students who received need-based aid, the average percentage of need met: 63%. Among students who received aid based on merit, the average award (and the proportion receiving): $4,985 (20%). The average athletic scholarship (and the proportion receiving): $7,134 (3%). Average amount of debt of borrowers graduating in 2005: $7,897. Proportion who borrowed: 38%.

CAMPUS LIFE AND EXTRACURRICULAR ACTIVITIES

Campus housing available (% using): coed dorms, women's dorms (70%), men's dorms (30%), sorority housing, fraternity housing, apartments for married students, apartment for single students, special housing for disabled students. Students who live in college-owned, operated, or affiliated housing: 36%. **Student employment:** During the 2005-2006 academic year, 18% of undergraduates worked on campus. Average per-year earnings: $2,500. **Clubs and organizations:** Number of student organizations: 772. Activities include: choral groups, concert band, dance, drama/theater, jazz band, literary magazine, music ensembles, musical theater, pep band, student government, student newspaper, television station, yearbook. Number of fraternities: 6; sororities: 5. Proportion of men in fraternities: 20%; of women in sororities: 16%. Average proportion of students who stay on campus on weekends: 30%. **Sports program (2005-2006):** Member of NCAA II. *Men's intercollegiate varsity sports:* baseball, basketball, golf, soccer. *Women's intercollegiate varsity sports:* basketball, cross-country, golf, soccer, tennis, volleyball.

SERVICES AND FACILITIES

Basic services: nonremedial tutoring, placement service, health service. **Remedial assistance:** reading, math, writing, study skills. **Counseling services:** minority student, career, personal, academic. **For learning-disabled students:** School does not offer a structured program with separate admission and additional fees. Total undergraduates in learning-disabled program or receiving services: 75. Services include: tape recorders, note-taking services, readers, extended time for tests, tutors, priority registration, priority seating, texts on tape, exams on tape or computer, other. **Library:** Number of titles: 258,169; number of current serial subscriptions: 813. **Information technol-**

ogy resources: Students are not required to lease or own a computer. Number of campus computers available to all students: 340. School has a wireless network. Approximate number of users that can be accommodated: 2,000. Proportion of college-owned housing units wired for high-speed internet access: 100%. **Campus safety:** Security services offered: 24-hour foot-and-vehicle patrols, late-night transport/escort service, lighted pathways/sidewalks, controlled dormitory access (key, security card, etc.).

TRANSFER AND INTERNATIONAL STUDENTS

Transfer students: May apply for admission for the following academic terms: Fall, Spring, Summer. Applicants need a minimum number of credits to apply. For fall 2005: Transfer applications received: 563. Transfer applicants offered admission: 411. Transfer applicants enrolled: 279. **International students:** Number of foreign undergraduates: 49 (2% of student body). Number of countries represented: 23. Minimum TOEFL score required: 525 (paper); 195 (computer). Average TOEFL score: 525 (paper).

University of North Alabama

- **Address:** UNA–Box 5121, Florence, AL 35632
- **Website:** http://www.una.edu
- **Public**
- **Enrollment:** 4,444 full-time; 973 part-time

KEY STATS

✔ **U.S News College Ranking:** third tier, Universities–Master's (South)
✔ **ACT Score (25th/75th percentile):** 18-23
✔ **Tuition:** 2006-2007: $4,646 in state, $8,414 out of state

Selectivity: Selective	**Room/board:** $4,372
Acceptance rate: 80%	**Average debt:** $18,245
Student/faculty ratio: 21/1	**Proportion who borrowed:** 47%

UNDERGRADUATE STUDENT BODY STATS

2005-2006 enrollment: 4,444 full-time; 973 part-time. Men: 42%; women: 58%. **Ethnic makeup:** African American: 10%; American-Indian: 1%; Asian American: 1%; Hispanic: 1%; White: 81%; International: 7%.

ADMISSIONS FACTS AND FIGURES

Phone: (256) 765-4608. **Email:** admissions@una.edu. **Website:** http://www.una.edu. **Application deadlines for fall 2007:** Regular decision: Rolling. Early decision: Not offered. Early action: Not offered. Admission can be deferred. **Application fee:** $25. Common application is not accepted. **Admissions requirements/recommendations:** High school units required (recommended): English: 4; Mathematics: 2; Science: 2; Foreign language: 2; Social studies: 3; Total units: 13. Tests: The college uses SAT or ACT scores in admissions decisions. Either SAT or ACT required. For admission to the fall 2007 entering class, the school will accept: ACT without writing. Campus visit: Recommended. Admissions interview: Recommended. Off-campus interview: May be arranged. **Factors that count in admissions decisions:** *Academic:* Secondary school record: Important. Class rank: Very important. Letters of recommendation: Not considered. Standardized test scores: Very important. Essay: Not considered. *Nonacademic:* Interview: Not considered. Extracurricular activities: Not considered. Talent/ability: Not considered. Character/personal qualities: Important. Alumni/ae relationship: Not considered. Geographical residence: Not considered. State residency: Not considered. Religious affiliation/commitment: Not considered. Minority status: Not considered. Volunteer work: Not considered. Work experience: Not considered. **Other schools with the greatest overlap in applicants:** Auburn University; University of Alabama; University of Alabama–Huntsville; University of Montevallo. **Admissions statistics for the fall 2005 entering class:** Total applicants: 2,125. Total accepted: 1,704. Freshmen enrolled: 931; 14% were from out of state. Overall acceptance rate: 80%. **Credentials of fall 2005 freshmen:** 30% ranked in the top 10 percent of their high school class; 44% were in the top 25 percent, and 76% were in the top half. (Proportion submitting class standing: 89%.) **Average high school grade point average:** 2.9. **First-year students who submitted SAT scores:** 4%. Scores (25/75 percentile): Verbal: 400-530, Math: 460-600, Combined: 860-1130. **First-year students submitting ACT scores:** 91%. Scores (25/75 percentile): English: 18-25, Math: 17-24, Composite: 18-23.

ACADEMICS

Year founded: 1830. **Academic calendar:** Semester. **Degrees offered:** bachelor's, master's, post-master's certificate. **Most popular majors:** 30% business, management, marketing, and related support services, 15% education, 14% health professions and related clinical sciences, 8% English language and literature/letters, 7% social sciences. **Major fields of study:** biological and biomedical sciences; business, management, marketing, and related support services; computer and information sciences and support services; education; English language and literature/letters; family and consumer sciences/human sciences; foreign languages, literatures, and linguistics; health professions and related clinical sciences; history; liberal arts and sciences studies, and humanities; mathematics and statistics; parks, recreation, leisure, and fitness studies; physical sciences; psychology; public administration and social service professions; security and protective services; social sciences; visual and performing arts. **Areas of required coursework:** arts/fine arts, humanities, computer literacy, mathematics, English (including composition), foreign languages, sciences (biological or physical), history, social science. **Pre-professional programs:** pre-law, pre-dentistry, pre-medicine, pre-theology, pre-veterinary science, pre-optometry, pre-pharmacy, other. **Special academic programs:** accelerated program, cooperative (work-study plan) program, distance learning, double major, dual enrollment, English as a Second Language (ESL), honors program, independent study, internships, student-designed major, teacher certificate program, weekend college. **Teacher certification offered in:** special education, elementary, secondary. **Cooperative education programs:** business, technologies. **Reserve Officers Training Corps (ROTC):** Army ROTC: Offered on campus. **Faculty and instruction (2005-2006):** Total instructional faculty: 209 full-time, 104 part-time (55% men; 45% women; 10% minorities). Full-time faculty with Ph.D. or other terminal degree: 79%. Student/faculty ratio: 21/1. Classes of fewer than 20 students: 44%; of 20 to 49 students: 53%; of 50 or more students: 3%. **Advanced Placement and International Baccalaureate credit:** AP tests may be used for: Credit only. Scores accepted: 3, 4, 5. **Freshmen returning for sophomore year:** 68%. **Graduation rates:** Four-year: 16%; five-year: 33%; six-year: 38%.

COSTS AND FINANCIAL AID

Financial aid office: (256) 765-4278. **Expenses (2006-2007):** Tuition and fees 2006-2007: $4,646 in state, $8,414 out of state; room/board: $4,372. **Financial aid:** Priority filing date for institution's financial aid form: April 4. In 2005-2006, 60% of undergraduates applied for financial aid. Of those, 47% were determined to have financial need; 43% had their need fully met. Average financial aid package (proportion receiving): $4,515 (45%). Average amount of gift aid, such as scholarships or grants (proportion receiving): $2,754 (29%). Average amount of self-help aid, such as work study or loans (proportion receiving): $3,099 (34%). Average need-based loan (excluding PLUS or other private loans): $3,313. Among students who received need-based aid, the average percentage of need met: 68%. Among students who received aid based on merit, the average award (and the proportion receiving): $1,590 (12%). The average athletic scholarship (and the proportion receiving): $4,592 (5%). Average amount of debt of borrowers graduating in 2005: $18,245. Proportion who borrowed: 47%.

CAMPUS LIFE AND EXTRACURRICULAR ACTIVITIES

Campus housing available (% using): coed dorms (31%), women's dorms (28%), men's dorms (25%), apartments for married students (9%), apartment for single students (7%). Students who live in college-owned, operated, or affiliated housing: 21%. **Clubs and organizations:** Number of student organizations: 226. Activities include: choral groups, concert band, drama/theater, jazz band, literary magazine, marching band, music ensembles, musical theater, pep band, radio station, student government, student newspaper, student film society, symphony orchestra, yearbook. Number of fraternities: 9; sororities: 6. Proportion of men in fraternities: 9%; of women in sororities: 8%. Average proportion of students who stay on campus on weekends: 30%. **Sports program (2005-2006):** Member of NCAA II. *Men's intercollegiate varsity sports:* baseball, basketball, cross-country, football, golf, tennis. *Women's intercollegiate varsity sports:* basketball, cross-country, soccer, softball, tennis, volleyball.

SERVICES AND FACILITIES

Basic services: nonremedial tutoring, women's center, placement service, day care, health service. **Remedial assistance:** reading, math, writing, study skills, other. **Counseling services:** minority student, career, academic, older student, other. **For learning-disabled students:** School does not offer a structured program with separate admission and additional fees. Services include: remedial math, remedial English, remedial reading, tape recorders, untimed tests, note-taking services, oral tests, learning center, readers, extended time for tests, tutors, other. **Library:** Number of titles: 371,123; number of current serial subscriptions: 3,540. **Information technology resources:** Students are not required to lease or own a computer. Number of campus computers available to all students: 800. School does not have a wireless network. Approximate number of users that can be accommodated: 1,000. Proportion of college-owned housing units wired for high-speed internet access: 90%. **Campus safety:** Security services offered: 24-hour foot-and-vehicle patrols, late-night transport/escort service, 24-hour emergency telephones, lighted pathways/sidewalks, student patrols, controlled dormitory access (key, security card, etc).

TRANSFER AND INTERNATIONAL STUDENTS

Transfer students: May apply for admission for the following academic terms: Fall, Spring, Summer. Applicants need a minimum number of credits to apply. For fall 2005: Transfer applications received: 896. Transfer applicants offered admission: 781. Transfer applicants enrolled: 561. **International students:** Number of foreign undergraduates: 356 (7% of student body). Number of countries represented: 42. Minimum TOEFL score required: 500 (paper); 173 (computer). Average TOEFL score: 530 (paper).

University of South Alabama

- **Address:** 307 University Boulevard, Mobile, AL 36688-0002
- **Website:** http://www.southalabama.edu
- **Public**
- **Enrollment:** 7,495 full-time; 2,649 part-time

KEY STATS

✔ **U.S News College Ranking:** fourth tier, National Universities
✔ **ACT Score (25th/75th percentile):** 19-25
✔ **Tuition:** 2006-2007: $3,510 in state, $6,820 out of state

Selectivity: Selective	**Room/board:** $5,872
Acceptance rate: 87%	**Average debt:** $20,000
Student/faculty ratio: N/A	**Proportion who borrowed:** 71%

UNDERGRADUATE STUDENT BODY STATS

2005-2006 enrollment: 7,495 full-time; 2,649 part-time. Men: 40%; women: 60%. **Ethnic makeup:** African American: 20%; American-Indian: 1%; Asian American: 2%; Hispanic: 1%; White: 72%; International: 4%. **Religious preference:** Roman Catholic: 12%; Protestant: 40%; No preference: 2%; Unknown: 42%; Other: 4%.

ADMISSIONS FACTS AND FIGURES

Phone: (251) 460-6141. **Email:** admiss@usouthal.edu. **Website:** http://www.southalabama.edu. **Application deadlines for fall 2007:** Regular decision: August 22. Early decision: Not offered. Early action: Not offered. Admission can be deferred. **Application fee:** $25. Common application is not accepted. **To apply online, go to:** http://admissions.usouthal.edu/appls.html. **Admissions requirements/recommendations:** High school units required (recommended): English: (4); Mathematics: (3); Science: (2); Social studies: (2); Academic electives: (2); Total units: (16). Tests: The college uses SAT or ACT scores in admissions decisions. Either SAT or ACT required. Campus visit: Neither required nor recommended. Admissions interview: Neither required nor recommended. Off-campus interview: May be arranged. **Factors that count in admissions decisions:** *Academic:* Secondary school record: Very important. Standardized test scores: Very important. **Admissions statistics for the fall 2005 entering class:** Total applicants: 2,681. Total accepted: 2,321. Freshmen enrolled: 1,258; Overall acceptance rate: 87%. **Credentials of fall 2005 freshmen:** 46% were in the top 25 percent.

ACADEMICS

Year founded: 1963. **Academic calendar:** Semester. **Degrees offered:** certificate, bachelor's, post-bachelor's certificate, master's, post-master's certificate, first professional, doctorate. **Most popular majors:** 16% nursing/registered nurse training (R.N., A.S.N., B.S.N., M.S.N.), 10% elementary education and teaching, 5% communication studies/speech communication and rhetoric, 5% marketing/marketing management, 3% computer and information sciences. **Major fields of study:** biological and biomedical sciences; business, management, marketing, and related support services; communication, journalism, and related programs; computer and information sciences and support services; education; engineering; English language and literature/letters; foreign languages, literatures, and

linguistics; health professions and related clinical sciences; history; liberal arts and sciences studies, and humanities; mathematics and statistics; multi/interdisciplinary studies; parks, recreation, leisure, and fitness studies; philosophy and religious studies; physical sciences; psychology; public administration and social service professions; security and protective services; social sciences; visual and performing arts. **Areas of required coursework:** arts/fine arts, humanities, computer literacy, mathematics, English (including composition), sciences (biological or physical), history, social science. **Pre-professional programs:** pre-law, pre-dentistry, pre-medicine, pre-veterinary science, pre-optometry, pre-pharmacy. **Special academic programs:** cooperative (work-study plan) program, distance learning, double major, English as a Second Language (ESL), honors program, independent study, internships, student-designed major, study abroad, teacher certificate program, weekend college. **Teacher certification offered in:** early childhood, special education, elementary, middle/junior high, secondary. **Cooperative education programs:** art, business, computer science, education, engineering, humanities, natural science, social/behavioral science. **Reserve Officers Training Corps (ROTC):** Army ROTC: Offered on campus; Air Force ROTC: Offered on campus. **Faculty and instruction (2005-2006):** Total instructional faculty: 700 full-time, 273 part-time. Full-time faculty with Ph.D. or other terminal degree: 78%. **Advanced Placement and International Baccalaureate credit:** AP tests may be used for: Credit and/or placement. Scores accepted: 3. **Freshmen returning for sophomore year:** 70%. **Graduation rates:** Four-year: 14%; five-year: 26%; six-year: 33%.

COSTS AND FINANCIAL AID

Financial aid office: (251) 460-6231. **Expenses (2006-2007):** Tuition and fees 2006-2007: $3,510 in state, $6,820 out of state; room/board: $5,872. Estimated books and supplies: $1,200; transportation: $504; personal expenses: $1,950. **Financial aid:** Priority filing date for institution's financial aid form: May 1. In 2005-2006, 44% of undergraduates applied for financial aid. Of those, 44% were determined to have financial need; 86% had their need fully met. Average financial aid package (proportion receiving): $2,951 (44%). Average amount of gift aid, such as scholarships or grants (proportion receiving): $1,734 (31%). Average amount of self-help aid, such as work study or loans (proportion receiving): $1,869 (37%). Average need-based loan (excluding PLUS or other private loans): $1,869. Among students who received need-based aid, the average percentage of need met: 27%. Average amount of debt of borrowers graduating in 2005: $20,000. Proportion who borrowed: 71%.

CAMPUS LIFE AND EXTRACURRICULAR ACTIVITIES

Campus housing available: coed dorms, sorority housing, fraternity housing, apartments for married students, apartment for single students, special housing for disabled students. Students who live in college-owned, operated, or affiliated housing: 12%. **Clubs and organizations:** Number of student organizations: 180. Activities include: choral groups, concert band, dance, drama/theater, jazz band, literary magazine, music ensembles, musical theater, opera, pep band, student government, student newspaper, student film society, symphony orchestra, television station. Number of fraternities: 9; sororities: 8. **Sports program (2005-2006):** Member of NCAA I. *Men's intercollegiate varsity sports:* baseball, bowling, cheerleading, cross-country, golf, tennis, track and field (indoor), track and field (outdoor). *Women's intercollegiate varsity sports:* basketball, cross-country, golf, soccer, tennis, track and field (indoor), track and field (outdoor), volleyball.

SERVICES AND FACILITIES

Basic services: nonremedial tutoring, placement service, health service, health insurance. **Remedial assistance:** reading, math, writing, study skills. **Counseling services:** minority student, career, military, personal, veteran student, academic, older student, psychological. **For learning-disabled students:** School does not offer a structured program with separate admission and additional fees. Services include: remedial math, remedial English, reading machines, remedial reading, tape recorders, diagnostic testing service, untimed tests, note-taking services, oral tests, learning center, readers, extended time for tests, tutors. **Library:** Number of titles: 1,068,209; number of current serial subscriptions: 1,847. **Information technology resources:** Students are not required to lease or own a computer. Proportion of college-owned housing units wired for high-speed internet access: 100%. **Campus safety:** Security services offered: 24-hour foot-and-vehicle patrols, late-night transport/escort service, 24-hour emergency telephones, lighted pathways/sidewalks, controlled dormitory access (key, security card, etc).

TRANSFER AND INTERNATIONAL STUDENTS

Transfer students: May apply for admission for the following academic terms: Fall, Spring, Summer. Applicants do not need a minimum number of credits to apply. For fall 2005: Transfer applications received: 1,770. Transfer applicants offered admission: 1,501. Transfer applicants enrolled: 1,077. **International students:** Number of foreign undergraduates: 31 (4% of student body). Minimum TOEFL score required: 500 (paper); 173 (computer). Average TOEFL score: 580 (paper).

University of West Alabama

- **Address:** Station 4, Livingston, AL 35470
- **Website:** http://www.uwa.edu
- **Public**
- **Enrollment:** 1,522 full-time; 219 part-time

KEY STATS
✔ **U.S News College Ranking:** fourth tier, Universities–Master's (South)
✔ **ACT Score (25th/75th percentile):** 15-22
✔ **Tuition:** 2006-2007: $4,778 in state, $8,616 out of state

Selectivity: Less selective	**Room/board:** $3,318
Acceptance rate: 78%	**Average debt:** $17,255
Student/faculty ratio: 25/1	**Proportion who borrowed:** 57%

UNDERGRADUATE STUDENT BODY STATS
2005-2006 enrollment: 1,522 full-time; 219 part-time. Men: 44%; women: 56%. **Ethnic makeup:** African American: 44%; Hispanic: 1%; White: 53%; International: 1%.

ADMISSIONS FACTS AND FIGURES
Phone: (205) 652-3578. **Email:** admissions@uwa.edu. **Website:** http://www.uwa.edu. **Application deadlines for fall 2007:** Regular decision: Rolling. Early decision: Not offered. Early action: Not offered. Admission can be deferred. **Application fee:** $20. Common application is not accepted. **To apply online, go to:** http://admissions.uwa.edu/applications.htm. **Admissions requirements/recommendations:** High school units required (recommended): English: 3; Mathematics: 3; Science: 3; Foreign language: 0; Social studies: 3; History: 0; Academic electives: 3; Total units: 15. Tests: The college uses SAT or ACT scores in admissions decisions. ACT required. For admission to the fall 2007 entering class, the school will accept: ACT with writing, ACT without writing. Campus visit: Recommended. Admissions interview: Neither required nor recommended. Off-campus interview: Not available. **Factors that count in admissions decisions:** *Academic:* Secondary school record: Very important. Class rank: Considered. Letters of recommendation: Considered. Standardized test scores: Very important. Essay: Considered. *Nonacademic:* Interview: Considered. Extracurricular activities: Considered. Talent/ability: Considered. Character/personal qualities: Considered. Alumni/ae relationship: Considered. Geographical residence: Considered. State residency: Considered. Religious affiliation/commitment: Considered. Minority status: Considered. Volunteer work: Considered. Work experience: Considered. **Other schools with the greatest overlap in applicants:** Auburn University; University of Alabama; University of South Alabama. **Admissions statistics for the fall 2005 entering class:** Total applicants: 832. Total accepted: 646. Freshmen enrolled: 366; 12% were from out of state. Overall acceptance rate: 78%. **First-year students who submitted SAT scores:** 1%. Scores (25/75 percentile): Verbal: N/A, Math: N/A, Combined: N/A. **First-year students submitting ACT scores:** 99%. Scores (25/75 percentile): English: N/A, Math: N/A, Composite: 15-22.

ACADEMICS
Year founded: 1835. **Academic calendar:** Semester. **Degrees offered:** associate, bachelor's, master's. **Most popular majors:** 18% elementary education and teaching, 11% business administration and management, 10% sociology, 9% English language and literature, 9% physical education teaching and coaching. **Major fields of study:** biological and biomedical sciences; business, management, marketing, and related support services; education; engineering technologies/technicians; English language and literature/letters; health professions and related clinical sciences; history; mathematics and statistics; multi/interdisciplinary studies; physical sciences; psychology; social sciences. **Areas of required coursework:** arts/fine arts, humanities, mathematics, English (including composition), sciences (biological or physical), history, social science. **Special academic programs:** accelerated program, cooperative (work-study plan) program, distance learning, double major, dual enrollment, honors program, internships, teacher certificate program. **Teacher certification offered in:** early childhood, special education,

elementary, middle/junior high, secondary. **Reserve Officers Training Corps (ROTC):** Air Force ROTC: Offered at cooperating institution (University of Alabama). **Faculty and instruction (2005-2006):** Total instructional faculty: 93 full-time, 7 part-time (58% men; 42% women; 10% minorities). Full-time faculty with Ph.D. or other terminal degree: 68%. Student/faculty ratio: 25/1. **Advanced Placement and International Baccalaureate credit:** AP tests may be used for: Credit and/or placement. Scores accepted: 3, 4, 5. **Freshmen returning for sophomore year:** 60%. **Graduation rates:** Four-year: 15%; five-year: 24%; six-year: 31%.

COSTS AND FINANCIAL AID
Financial aid office: (205) 652-3576. **Expenses (2006-2007):** Tuition and fees 2006-2007: $4,778 in state, $8,616 out of state; room/board: $3,318. Estimated books and supplies: $900; transportation: $900; personal expenses: $1,200. **Financial aid:** Priority filing date for institution's financial aid form: April 1. In 2005-2006, 83% of undergraduates applied for financial aid. Of those, 70% were determined to have financial need; 41% had their need fully met. Average financial aid package (proportion receiving): $10,222 (59%). Average amount of gift aid, such as scholarships or grants (proportion receiving): $3,761 (47%). Average amount of self-help aid, such as work study or loans (proportion receiving): $4,896 (47%). Average need-based loan (excluding PLUS or other private loans): $4,239. Among students who received need-based aid, the average percentage of need met: 85%. Among students who received aid based on merit, the average award (and the proportion receiving): $3,144 (14%). The average athletic scholarship (and the proportion receiving): $3,983 (12%). Average amount of debt of borrowers graduating in 2005: $17,255. Proportion who borrowed: 57%.

CAMPUS LIFE AND EXTRACURRICULAR ACTIVITIES
Campus housing available (% using): coed dorms (30%), women's dorms (22%), men's dorms (32%), apartments for married students (5%), apartment for single students (11%). **Student employment:** During the 2005-2006 academic year, 10% of undergraduates worked on campus. Average per-year earnings: $1,200. **Clubs and organizations:** Number of student organizations: 85. Activities include: choral groups, concert band, drama/theater, jazz band, marching band, student government, student newspaper, yearbook. Number of fraternities: 13; sororities: 5. Average proportion of students who stay on campus on weekends: 45%. **Sports program (2005-2006):** Member of NCAA II. *Men's intercollegiate varsity sports:* baseball, basketball, cross-country, football, rodeo. *Women's intercollegiate varsity sports:* basketball, cross-country, rodeo, softball, volleyball.

SERVICES AND FACILITIES
Basic services: nonremedial tutoring, placement service, health service. **Remedial assistance:** reading, math, writing, study skills. **Counseling services:** career, personal, academic, psychological. **For learning-disabled students:** School does not offer a structured program with separate admission and additional fees. Services include: remedial math, remedial English, remedial reading, tape recorders, diagnostic testing service, untimed tests, note-taking services, oral tests, learning center, readers, extended time for tests, tutors. **Library:** Number of titles: 151,991; number of current serial subscriptions: 257. **Information technology resources:** Students are not required to lease or own a computer. Number of campus computers available to all students: 350. School has a wireless network. Proportion of college-owned housing units wired for high-speed internet access: 100%. **Campus safety:** Security services offered: 24-hour foot-and-vehicle patrols, lighted pathways/sidewalks, controlled dormitory access (key, security card, etc).

TRANSFER AND INTERNATIONAL STUDENTS
Transfer students: May apply for admission for the following academic terms: Fall, Winter, Spring, Summer. Applicants do not need a minimum number of credits to apply. For fall 2005: Transfer applications received: 309. Transfer applicants offered admission: 229. Transfer applicants enrolled: 197. **International students:** Number of foreign undergraduates: 22 (1% of student body). Number of countries represented: 15. Minimum TOEFL score required: 500 (paper); 175 (computer). Average TOEFL score: 550 (paper).

Alaska

Alaska Pacific University

- **Address:** 4101 University Drive, Anchorage, AK 99508-3051
- **Website:** http://www.alaskapacific.edu
- **Private**
- **Enrollment:** 336 full-time; 244 part-time

KEY STATS
✔ **U.S News College Ranking:** 47, Universities–Master's (West)
✔ **SAT Score (25th/75th percentile):** 890-1130
✔ **Tuition:** 2006-2007: $19,610

Selectivity: Selective	**Room/board:** $7,100
Acceptance rate: 98%	**Average debt:** $17,775
Student/faculty ratio: 10/1	**Proportion who borrowed:** 66%

UNDERGRADUATE STUDENT BODY STATS
2005-2006 enrollment: 336 full-time; 244 part-time. Men: 30%; women: 70%. **Ethnic makeup:** African American: 6%; American-Indian: 16%; Asian American: 4%; Hispanic: 4%; White: 70%.

ADMISSIONS FACTS AND FIGURES
Phone: (800) 252-7528. **Email:** admissions@alaskapacific.edu. **Website:** http://www.alaskapacific.edu. **Application deadlines for fall 2007:** Regular decision: August 1. Early decision: Not offered. Early action: Not offered. Admission can be deferred. **Application fee:** $25. Common application is accepted. **Admissions requirements/recommendations:** High school units required (recommended): English: (4); Mathematics: (3); Science: (2); Foreign language: (2); Social studies: (1); History: (1); Academic electives: (0); Total units: (10). Tests: The college uses SAT or ACT scores in admissions decisions. Either SAT or ACT required. For admission to the fall 2007 entering class, the school will accept: ACT with writing, ACT without writing. Campus visit: Neither required nor recommended. Admissions interview: Recommended. Off-campus interview: May be arranged. **Factors that count in admissions decisions:** *Academic:* Secondary school record: Very important. Class rank: Considered. Letters of recommendation: Important. Standardized test scores: Important. Essay: Very important. *Nonacademic:* Interview: Important. Extracurricular activities: Considered. Talent/ability: Considered. Character/personal qualities: Considered. Alumni/ae relationship: Not considered. Geographical residence: Not considered. State residency: Not considered. Religious affiliation/commitment: Not considered. Minority status: Not considered. Volunteer work: Considered. Work experience: Considered. **Admissions statistics for the fall 2005 entering class:** Total applicants: 140. Total accepted: 137. Freshmen enrolled: 51; 71% were from out of state. Overall acceptance rate: 98%. **Credentials of fall 2005 freshmen:** 11% ranked in the top 10 percent of their high school class; 50% were in the top 25 percent, and 68% were in the top half. (Proportion submitting class standing: 67%.) **Average high school grade point average:** 3.3. **First-year students who submitted SAT scores:** 50%. Scores (25/75 percentile): Verbal: 450-570, Math: 440-560, Combined: 890-1130. **First-year students submitting ACT scores:** 36%. Scores (25/75 percentile): English: 15-29, Math: 17-22, Composite: 19-24.

ACADEMICS
Year founded: 1957. **Academic calendar:** Semester. **Degrees offered:** certificate, associate, bachelor's, master's. **Most popular majors:** 23% parks, recreation, and leisure facilities management, 21% elementary education and teaching, 16% environmental science, 14% psychology, 12% liberal arts and sciences/liberal studies. **Major fields of study:** biological and biomedical sciences; business, management, marketing, and related support services; education; health professions and related clinical sciences; liberal arts and sciences studies, and humanities; natural resources and conservation; parks, recreation, leisure, and fitness studies; psychology; public administration and social service professions. **Areas of required coursework:** humanities, mathematics, English (including composition), foreign languages, sciences (biological or physical), social science, other. **Pre-professional programs:** pre-law. **Special academic programs (% participation):** double major

(2%), independent study (52%), internships (4%), teacher certificate program (21%). **Teacher certification offered in:** elementary, middle/junior high. **Faculty and instruction (2005-2006):** Total instructional faculty: 40 full-time, 48 part-time (48% men; 52% women; 7% minorities). Full-time faculty with Ph.D. or other terminal degree: 63%. Student/faculty ratio: 10/1. Classes of fewer than 20 students: 95%; of 20 to 49 students: 5%; of 50 or more students: 0%. **Advanced Placement and International Baccalaureate credit:** AP tests may be used for: Credit only. Scores accepted: 3, 4, 5. International Baccalaureate exams may be used for: Credit only. **Freshmen returning for sophomore year:** 67%. **Graduation rates:** Four-year: 19%; five-year: 34%; six-year: 39%.

COSTS AND FINANCIAL AID
Financial aid office: (907) 564-8341. **Expenses (2006-2007):** Tuition and fees 2006-2007: $19,610; room/board: $7,100. Estimated books and supplies: $840; transportation: $350; personal expenses: $1,111. **Financial aid:** Priority filing date for institution's financial aid form: April 15. In 2005-2006, 80% of undergraduates applied for financial aid. Of those, 72% were determined to have financial need; 35% had their need fully met. Average financial aid package (proportion receiving): $15,748 (72%). Average amount of gift aid, such as scholarships or grants (proportion receiving): $2,863 (63%). Average amount of self-help aid, such as work study or loans (proportion receiving): $3,813 (59%). Average need-based loan (excluding PLUS or other private loans): $3,813. Among students who received need-based aid, the average percentage of need met: 81%. Among students who received aid based on merit, the average award (and the proportion receiving): $1,736 (26%). The average athletic scholarship (and the proportion receiving): $0 (0%). Average amount of debt of borrowers graduating in 2005: $17,775. Proportion who borrowed: 66%.

CAMPUS LIFE AND EXTRACURRICULAR ACTIVITIES
Campus housing available (% using): coed dorms (94%), special housing for disabled students, cooperative housing (6%). Students who live in college-owned, operated, or affiliated housing: 22%. **Student employment:** During the 2005-2006 academic year, 23% of undergraduates worked on campus. Average per-year earnings: $1,690. **Clubs and organizations:** Number of student organizations: 15. Activities include: drama/theater, literary magazine, music ensembles, student government, student newspaper, yearbook. Number of fraternities: 0; sororities: 0. Average proportion of students who stay on campus on weekends: 98%.

SERVICES AND FACILITIES
Basic services: health insurance. **Remedial assistance:** reading, math, writing. **Counseling services:** minority student, career, personal, academic, psychological, religious. **For learning-disabled students:** School does not offer a structured program with separate admission and additional fees. Total undergraduates in learning-disabled program or receiving services: 8. Services include: remedial math, remedial English, remedial reading, tape recorders, untimed tests, note-taking services, tutors, other. **Library:** Number of titles: 788,000; number of current serial subscriptions: 3,434. **Information technology resources:** Students are not required to lease or own a computer. Number of campus computers available to all students: 50. School does not have a wireless network. Approximate number of users that can be accommodated: 100. **Campus safety:** Security services offered: late-night transport/escort service, 24-hour emergency telephones, lighted pathways/sidewalks, controlled dormitory access (key, security card, etc).

TRANSFER AND INTERNATIONAL STUDENTS
Transfer students: May apply for admission for the following academic terms: Fall, Spring, Summer. Applicants need a minimum number of credits to apply. For fall 2005: Transfer applications received: 125. Transfer applicants offered admission: 122. Transfer applicants enrolled: 89. **International students:** Number of foreign undergraduates: 2. Number of countries represented: 2. Minimum TOEFL score required: 550 (paper); 213 (computer).

Sheldon Jackson College

- **Address:** 801 Lincoln Street, Sitka, AK 99835
- **Website:** http://www.sj-alaska.edu
- **Private; Religious affiliation:** Presbyterian
- **Enrollment:** N/A

KEY STATS

✔ **U.S News College Ranking:** Unranked, Comp. Coll.–Bachelor's (West)
✔ **SAT or ACT Score (25th/75th percentile):** N/A
✔ **Tuition:** 2006-2007: $11,536

Selectivity: N/A	**Room/board:** $7,700
Acceptance rate: N/A	**Average debt:** N/A
Student/faculty ratio: N/A	**Proportion who borrowed:** N/A

University of Alaska–Anchorage

- **Address:** 3211 Providence Drive, Anchorage, AK 99508
- **Website:** http://www.uaa.alaska.edu
- **Public**
- **Enrollment:** 6,908 full-time; 8,703 part-time

KEY STATS

✔ **U.S News College Ranking:** 57, Universities–Master's (West)
✔ **SAT Score (25th/75th percentile):** 890-1150
✔ **Tuition:** 2005-2006: $3,465 in state, $9,561 out of state

Selectivity: Less selective	**Room/board:** $7,810
Acceptance rate: 74%	**Average debt:** N/A
Student/faculty ratio: 18/1	**Proportion who borrowed:** N/A

UNDERGRADUATE STUDENT BODY STATS

2005-2006 enrollment: 6,908 full-time; 8,703 part-time. Men: 39%; women: 61%. **Ethnic makeup:** African American: 4%; American-Indian: 9%; Asian American: 6%; Hispanic: 5%; White: 74%; International: 2%.

ADMISSIONS FACTS AND FIGURES

Phone: (907) 786-1480. **Email:** enroll@uaa.alaska.edu. **Website:** http://www.uaa.alaska.edu. **Application deadlines for fall 2007:** Regular decision: July 1. Early decision: Not offered. Early action: Not offered. Admission can be deferred. **Application fee:** $40. Common application is not accepted. **To apply online, go to:** http://www.uaa.alaska.edu/prostudents. **Admissions requirements/recommendations:** High school units required (recommended): English: (4); Mathematics: (2); Science: (3); Foreign language: (1); Social studies: (3); History: (1). Tests: The college uses SAT or ACT scores in admissions decisions. Either SAT or ACT required. For admission to the fall 2007 entering class, the school will accept: ACT with writing, ACT without writing. Campus visit: Recommended. Admissions interview: Neither required nor recommended. Off-campus interview: Not available. **Factors that count in admissions decisions: Academic:** Secondary school record: Very important. Class rank: Considered. Letters of recommendation: Not considered. Standardized test scores: Considered. Essay: Not considered. *Nonacademic:* Interview: Not considered. Extracurricular activities: Not considered. Talent/ability: Considered. Character/personal qualities: Not considered. Alumni/ae relationship: Not considered. Geographical residence: Not considered. State residency: Not considered. Religious affiliation/commitment: Not considered. Minority status: Not considered. Volunteer work: Not considered. Work experience: Not considered. **Other schools with the greatest overlap in applicants:** Arizona State University; Boise State University; Montana State University–Bozeman; University of Idaho; University of Maryland–University College. **Admissions statistics for the fall 2005 entering class:** Total applicants: 2,760. Total accepted: 2,056. Freshmen enrolled: 1,561; 5% were from out of state. Overall acceptance rate: 74%. **Credentials of fall 2005 freshmen:** 9% ranked in the top 10 percent of their high school class; 28% were in the top 25 percent, and 59% were in the top half. (Proportion submitting class standing: 76%.) **Average high school grade point average:** 3.1. **First-year students who submitted SAT scores:** 52%. Scores (25/75 percentile): Verbal: 440-580, Math: 450-570, Combined: 890-1150. **First-year students submitting ACT scores:** 22%. Scores (25/75 percentile): English: 16-24, Math: 17-24, Composite: 18-24.

ACADEMICS

Year founded: 1954. **Academic calendar:** Semester. **Degrees offered:** certificate, associate, bachelor's, post-bachelor's certificate, master's, post-master's certificate. **Most popular majors:** 21% business administration and management, 18% dental assisting/assistant, 9% psychology, 7% English language and literature, 5% history. **Major fields of study:** biological and biomedical sciences; business, management, marketing, and related support services; communication, journalism, and related programs; computer and information sciences and support services; education; engineering; English language and literature/letters; family and consumer sciences/human sciences; foreign languages, literatures, and linguistics; health professions and related clinical sciences; history; liberal arts and sciences studies, and humanities; mathematics and statistics; mechanic and repair technologies/technicians; multi/interdisciplinary studies; personal and culinary services; philosophy and religious studies; physical sciences; psychology; public administration and social service professions; science technologies/technicians; security and protective services; social sciences; transportation and materials moving; visual and performing arts. **Areas of required coursework:** arts/fine arts, humanities, computer literacy, mathematics, English (including composition), sciences (biological or physical), history, social science, other. **Special academic programs:** accelerated program, cooperative (work-study plan) program, cross-registration, distance learning, double major, dual enrollment, English as a Second Language (ESL), exchange student program (domestic), honors program, independent study, internships, liberal arts/career combination, student-designed major, study abroad, teacher certificate program, other. **Teacher certification offered in:** early childhood, special education, elementary, vo-tech, middle/junior high, secondary, bilingual/bicultural. **Cooperative education programs:** art, business, computer science, education, engineering, health professions, humanities, natural science, social/behavioral science, technologies, vocational arts. **Reserve Officers Training Corps (ROTC):** Air Force ROTC: Offered on campus. **Faculty and instruction (2005-2006):** Total instructional faculty: 551 full-time, 657 part-time (46% men; 54% women; 11% minorities). Full-time faculty with Ph.D. or other terminal degree: 61%. Student/faculty ratio: 18/1. Classes of fewer than 20 students: 56%; of 20 to 49 students: 40%; of 50 or more students: 4%. **Advanced Placement and International Baccalaureate credit:** AP tests may be used for: Credit and/or placement. Scores accepted: 3, 4, 5. **Freshmen returning for sophomore year:** 67%. **Graduation rates:** Four-year: 6%; five-year: 24%; six-year: 32%.

COSTS AND FINANCIAL AID

Financial aid office: (907) 786-1586. **Expenses (2005-2006):** Tuition and fees 2005-2006: $3,465 in state, $9,561 out of state; room/board: $7,810. Estimated books and supplies: $1,036; transportation: $1,721; personal expenses: $1,997. **Financial aid:** Priority filing date for institution's financial aid form: April 1.

CAMPUS LIFE AND EXTRACURRICULAR ACTIVITIES

Campus housing available (% using): coed dorms (32%), apartment for single students (36%), special housing for disabled students (2%), other housing options (30%). Students who live in college-owned, operated, or affiliated housing: 5%. **Clubs and organizations:** Number of student organizations: 70. Activities include: choral groups, dance, drama/theater, jazz band, literary magazine, music ensembles, radio station, student government, student newspaper. Number of fraternities: 3; sororities: 3. Average proportion of students who stay on campus on weekends: 75%. **Sports program (2005-2006):** Member of NCAA II. *Men's intercollegiate varsity sports:* basketball, cross-country, ice hockey, skiing, track and field (outdoor). *Women's intercollegiate varsity sports:* basketball, cross-country, gymnastics, skiing, track and field (outdoor), volleyball.

SERVICES AND FACILITIES

Basic services: placement service, day care, health service. **Remedial assistance:** reading, math, writing, study skills. **Counseling services:** minority student, career, military, veteran student, academic, psychological, birth control. **For learning-disabled students:** School does not offer a structured program with separate admission and additional fees. Total undergraduates in learning-disabled program or receiving services: 450. Services include: remedial math, remedial English, reading machines, remedial reading, tape recorders, note-taking services, oral tests, learning center, readers, extended time for tests, tutors, priority registration, priority seating, texts on tape, exams on tape or computer, other testing accomodations, other. **Library:** Number of titles: 935,756; number of current serial subscriptions: 3,580. **Information technology resources:** Students are not required to lease or own a computer. Number of campus computers available to all students: 680. School has a wireless network. Approximate number of users that can be accommodated: 6,000. Proportion of college-owned housing units wired for high-speed internet access: 100%. **Campus safety:** Security services offered: 24-hour foot-and-vehicle patrols, late-night transport/escort service, 24-hour emergency telephones, lighted pathways/sidewalks, controlled dormitory access (key, security card, etc).

TRANSFER AND INTERNATIONAL STUDENTS

Transfer students: May apply for admission for the following academic terms: Fall, Spring, Summer. Applicants need a minimum number of credits to apply. For fall 2005: Transfer applications received: 1,425. Transfer applicants offered admission: 983. Transfer applicants enrolled: 644. **International students:** Number of foreign undergraduates: 207 (2% of student body). Number of countries represented: 12. Minimum TOEFL score required: 450 (paper); 133 (computer).

University of Alaska–Fairbanks

■ **Address:** PO Box 757500, Fairbanks, AK 99775-7500
■ **Website:** http://www.uaf.edu
■ **Public**
■ **Enrollment:** 3,462 full-time; 3,674 part-time

KEY STATS

✔ **U.S News College Ranking:** fourth tier, National Universities
✔ **SAT Score (25th/75th percentile):** 900-1180
✔ **Tuition:** 2006-2007: $4,521 in state, $12,888 out of state
  Selectivity: Less selective   **Room/board:** $5,580
  Acceptance rate: 78%   **Average debt:** $24,010
  Student/faculty ratio: 16/1   **Proportion who borrowed:** 49%

UNDERGRADUATE STUDENT BODY STATS

2005-2006 enrollment: 3,462 full-time; 3,674 part-time. Men: 41%; women: 59%. **Ethnic makeup:** African American: 3%; American-Indian: 18%; Asian American: 4%; Hispanic: 3%; White: 70%; International: 2%.

ADMISSIONS FACTS AND FIGURES

Phone: (800) 478-1823. **Email:** fyapply@uaf.edu. **Website:** http://www.uaf.edu. **Application deadlines for fall 2007:** Regular decision: August 1. Early decision: Not offered. Early action: Not offered. Admission can be deferred. **Application fee:** $40. Common application is not accepted. **To apply online, go to:** http://www.uaf.edu/admissions/apply/index.html. **Admissions requirements/recommendations:** High school units required (recommended): English: 4; Mathematics: 3; Science: 3; Foreign language: (2); Social studies: 3; Academic electives: 3; Total units: 16. Tests: The college uses SAT or ACT scores in admissions decisions. Either SAT or ACT required. For admission to the fall 2007 entering class, the school will accept: ACT with writing, ACT without writing. Campus visit: Neither required nor recommended. Admissions interview: Neither required nor recommended. Off-campus interview: Not available. **Factors that count in admissions decisions:** *Academic:* Secondary school record: Not considered. Class rank: Not considered. Letters of recommendation: Not considered. Standardized test scores: Very important. Essay: Not considered. *Nonacademic:* Interview: Not considered. Extracurricular activities: Not considered. Talent/ability: Not considered. Character/personal qualities: Not considered. Alumni/ae relationship: Not considered. Geographical residence: Not considered. State residency: Not considered. Religious affiliation/commitment: Not considered. Minority status: Not considered. Volunteer work: Not considered. Work experience: Not considered. **Other schools with the greatest overlap in applicants:** Montana State University–Bozeman; Oregon State University; University of Montana; University of Nevada–Reno; Western Washington University. **Admissions statistics for the fall 2005 entering class:** Total applicants: 1,777. Total accepted: 1,383. Freshmen enrolled: 1,000; 8% were from out of state. Overall acceptance rate: 78%. **Credentials of fall 2005 freshmen:** 15% ranked in the top 10 percent of their high school class; 34% were in the top 25 percent, and 61% were in the top half. (Proportion submitting class standing: 55%.) **Average high school grade point average:** 3.0. **First-year students who submitted SAT scores:** 48%. Scores (25/75 percentile): Verbal: 450-600, Math: 450-580, Combined: 900-1180. **First-year students submitting ACT scores:** 32%. Scores (25/75 percentile): English: 15-23, Math: 16-23, Composite: 17-24.

ACADEMICS

Year founded: 1917. **Academic calendar:** Semester. **Degrees offered:** certificate, associate, terminal-associate, bachelor's, master's, doctorate. **Most pop-**

ular majors: 12% engineering, 9% business, management, marketing, and related support services, 7% biological and biomedical sciences, 7% communication, journalism, and related programs, 5% psychology. **Major fields of study:** area, ethnic, cultural, and gender studies; biological and biomedical sciences; business, management, marketing, and related support services; communication, journalism, and related programs; computer and information sciences and support services; education; engineering; engineering technologies/technicians; English language and literature/letters; foreign languages, literatures, and linguistics; history; liberal arts and sciences studies, and humanities; mathematics and statistics; multi/interdisciplinary studies; natural resources and conservation; parks, recreation, leisure, and fitness studies; philosophy and religious studies; physical sciences; psychology; public administration and social service professions; security and protective services; social sciences; visual and performing arts. **Areas of required coursework:** arts/fine arts, humanities, computer literacy, mathematics, English (including composition), philosophy, sciences (biological or physical), history, social science, other. **Pre-professional programs:** pre-law, pre-dentistry, pre-medicine, pre-veterinary science, other. **Special academic programs:** accelerated program, cooperative (work-study plan) program, distance learning, double major, dual enrollment, English as a Second Language (ESL), exchange student program (domestic), honors program, independent study, internships, student-designed major, study abroad, teacher certificate program. **Teacher certification offered in:** elementary, secondary. **Cooperative education programs:** agriculture, art, business, computer science, education, engineering, health professions, humanities, natural science, social/behavioral science, technologies, vocational arts, other. **Reserve Officers Training Corps (ROTC):** Army ROTC: Offered on campus. **Faculty and instruction (2005-2006):** Total instructional faculty: 288 full-time, 7 part-time (61% men; 39% women; 15% minorities). Student/faculty ratio: 16/1. Classes of fewer than 20 students: 67%; of 20 to 49 students: 30%; of 50 or more students: 3%. **Advanced Placement and International Baccalaureate credit:** AP tests may be used for: Credit and/or placement. Scores accepted: 3, 4, 5. International Baccalaureate exams may be used for: Credit and/or placement. **Freshmen returning for sophomore year:** 70%. **Graduation rates:** Four-year: 6%; five-year: 17%; six-year: 23%. **Graduate study:** 54% of students pursue further study immediately upon graduation. Fields in which graduates pursue further study: Master of Business Administration (MBA), 10%; law, 8%; engineering, 5%; education, 17%; arts and sciences, 47%.

COSTS AND FINANCIAL AID

Financial aid office: (907) 474-7256. **Expenses (2006-2007):** Tuition and fees 2006-2007: $4,521 in state, $12,888 out of state; room/board: $5,580. Estimated books and supplies: $1,100; transportation: $324; personal expenses: $2,250. **Financial aid:** Priority filing date for institution's financial aid form: July 1. In 2005-2006, 100% of undergraduates applied for financial aid. Of those, 42% were determined to have financial need; 27% had their need fully met. Average financial aid package (proportion receiving): $8,899 (40%). Average amount of gift aid, such as scholarships or grants (proportion receiving): $4,354 (26%). Average amount of self-help aid, such as work study or loans (proportion receiving): $8,294 (31%). Average need-based loan (excluding PLUS or other private loans): $6,256. Among students who received need-based aid, the average percentage of need met: 69%. Among students who received aid based on merit, the average award (and the proportion receiving): $3,362 (16%). The average athletic scholarship (and the proportion receiving): $8,082 (2%). Average amount of debt of borrowers graduating in 2005: $24,010. Proportion who borrowed: 49%.

CAMPUS LIFE AND EXTRACURRICULAR ACTIVITIES

Campus housing available: coed dorms, apartments for married students, apartment for single students, special housing for disabled students, other housing options. Students who live in college-owned, operated, or affiliated housing: 29%. **Student employment:** During the 2005-2006 academic year, 15% of undergraduates worked on campus. Average per-year earnings: $10,880. **Clubs and organizations:** Number of student organizations: 53. Activities include: choral groups, concert band, dance, drama/theater, jazz band, literary magazine, music ensembles, musical theater, opera, pep band, radio station, student government, student newspaper, student film society, symphony orchestra, television station. Number of fraternities: 1; sororities: 1. Average proportion of students who stay on campus on weekends: 30%. **Sports program (2005-2006):** Member of NCAA II. *Men's intercollegiate varsity sports:* alpine skiing, basketball, cross-country, ice hockey, riflery. *Women's intercollegiate varsity sports:* alpine skiing, basketball, cross-country, riflery, swimming and diving, volleyball.

SERVICES AND FACILITIES

Basic services: nonremedial tutoring, women's center, placement service, day care, health service, health insurance, other. **Remedial assistance:** math, writing, study skills. **Counseling services:** minority student, military, personal, veteran student, academic, psychological, birth control. **For learning-disabled students:** School does not offer a structured program with separate admission and additional fees. Services include: remedial math, remedial English, reading machines, tape recorders, diagnostic testing service, untimed tests, note-taking services, oral tests, readers, extended time for tests, tutors, other. **Library:** Number of titles: 1,059,001; number of current serial subscriptions: 3,000. **Information technology resources:** Students are not required to lease or own a computer. Number of campus computers available to all students: 718. School has a wireless network. Proportion of college-owned housing units wired for high-speed internet access: 100%. **Campus safety:** Security services offered: 24-hour foot-and-vehicle patrols, late-night transport/escort service, 24-hour emergency telephones, lighted pathways/sidewalks, controlled dormitory access (key, security card, etc).

TRANSFER AND INTERNATIONAL STUDENTS

Transfer students: May apply for admission for the following academic terms: Fall, Spring, Summer. Applicants need a minimum number of credits to apply. For fall 2005: Transfer applications received: 872. Transfer applicants offered admission: 657. Transfer applicants enrolled: 430. **International students:** Number of foreign undergraduates: 96 (2% of student body). Number of countries represented: 20. Minimum TOEFL score required: 550 (paper); 213 (computer). Average TOEFL score: 582 (paper).

University of Alaska–Southeast

- **Address:** 11120 Glacier Highway, Juneau, AK 99801
- **Website:** http://www.uas.alaska.edu
- **Public**
- **Enrollment:** 866 full-time; 2,048 part-time

KEY STATS

✔ **U.S News College Ranking:** fourth tier, Universities–Master's (West)
✔ **SAT Score (25th/75th percentile):** 777-1287
✔ **Tuition:** 2006-2007: $3,856 in state, $10,552 out of state

Selectivity: Less selective	**Room/board:** $3,980
Acceptance rate: 63%	**Average debt:** $19,979
Student/faculty ratio: N/A	**Proportion who borrowed:** 44%

UNDERGRADUATE STUDENT BODY STATS

2005-2006 enrollment: 866 full-time; 2,048 part-time. Men: 36%; women: 64%. **Ethnic makeup:** African American: 1%; American-Indian: 18%; Asian American: 5%; Hispanic: 3%; White: 73%; International: 1%.

ADMISSIONS FACTS AND FIGURES

Phone: (907) 465-6350. **Email:** admissions@uas.alaska.edu. **Website:** http://www.uas.alaska.edu. **Application deadlines for fall 2007:** Regular decision: August 1. Early decision: Not offered. Early action: Not offered. Admission can be deferred. **Application fee:** $40. Common application is accepted. **To apply online, go to:** http://www.uas.alaska.edu/apply/. **Admissions requirements/recommendations:** Tests: The college uses SAT or ACT scores in admissions decisions. Neither SAT nor ACT required. For admission to the fall 2007 entering class, the school will accept: ACT with writing, ACT without writing. Campus visit: Recommended. Admissions interview: Neither required nor recommended. Off-campus interview: Not available. **Factors that count in admissions decisions:** *Academic:* Secondary school record: Important. Class rank: Not considered. Letters of recommendation: Not considered. Standardized test scores: Not considered. Essay: Not considered. *Nonacademic:* Interview: Not considered. Extracurricular activities: Not considered. Talent/ability: Not considered. Character/personal qualities: Not considered. Alumni/ae relationship: Not considered. Geographical residence: Not considered. State residency: Not considered. Religious affiliation/commitment: Not considered. Minority status: Not considered. Volunteer work: Not considered. Work experience: Not considered. **Admissions statistics for the fall 2005 entering class:** Total applicants: 383. Total accepted: 242. Freshmen enrolled: 190; 18% were from out of state. Overall acceptance rate: 63%. **Credentials of fall 2005 freshmen:** 7% ranked in the top 10 percent of their high school class; 24% were in the top 25 percent, and 51% were in the top half. (Proportion submitting class standing: 62%.)

Average high school grade point average: 2.9. **First-year students who submitted SAT scores:** 44%. Scores (25/75 percentile): Verbal: 396-652, Math: 381-635, Combined: 777-1287. **First-year students submitting ACT scores:** 18%. Scores (25/75 percentile): English: 16-27, Math: 16-27, Composite: 17-27.

ACADEMICS

Year founded: 1986. **Academic calendar:** Semester. **Degrees offered:** certificate, associate, bachelor's, master's. **Most popular majors:** 49% business, management, marketing, and related support services, 32% liberal arts and sciences studies, and humanities, 7% biological and biomedical sciences, 5% natural resources and conservation, 4% social sciences. **Major fields of study:** biological and biomedical sciences; education; liberal arts and sciences studies, and humanities; natural resources and conservation. **Areas of required coursework:** arts/fine arts, humanities, mathematics, English (including composition), sciences (biological or physical), social science. **Special academic programs:** cooperative (work-study plan) program, distance learning, dual enrollment, exchange student program (domestic), external degree program, independent study, internships, study abroad, teacher certificate program. **Teacher certification offered in:** early childhood, special education, elementary, secondary. **Cooperative education programs:** education. **Faculty and instruction (2005-2006):** Total instructional faculty: N/A. Classes of fewer than 20 students: 71%; of 20 to 49 students: 28%; of 50 or more students: 1%. **Advanced Placement and International Baccalaureate credit:** AP tests may be used for: Credit and/or placement. Scores accepted: 3, 4, 5. International Baccalaureate exams may be used for: Credit and/or placement. **Freshmen returning for sophomore year:** 66%. **Graduation rates:** Four-year: 3%; five-year: 10%; six-year: 13%.

COSTS AND FINANCIAL AID

Financial aid office: (907) 796-6255. **Expenses (2006-2007):** Tuition and fees 2006-2007: $3,856 in state, $10,552 out of state; room/board: $3,980. Estimated books and supplies: $550; transportation: $782; personal expenses: $1,643. **Financial aid:** Priority filing date for institution's financial aid form: June 1. In 2005-2006, 77% of undergraduates applied for financial aid. Of those, 49% were determined to have financial need; 18% had their need fully met. Average financial aid package (proportion receiving): $6,967 (45%). Average amount of gift aid, such as scholarships or grants (proportion receiving): $3,413 (28%). Average amount of self-help aid, such as work study or loans (proportion receiving): $7,565 (37%). Average need-based loan (excluding PLUS or other private loans): $4,778. Among students who received need-based aid, the average percentage of need met: 56%. Among students who received aid based on merit, the average award (and the proportion receiving): $2,608 (4%). The average athletic scholarship (and the proportion receiving): $0 (0%). Average amount of debt of borrowers graduating in 2005: $19,979. Proportion who borrowed: 44%.

CAMPUS LIFE AND EXTRACURRICULAR ACTIVITIES

Campus housing available: coed dorms, apartments for married students, apartment for single students, special housing for disabled students. Students who live in college-owned, operated, or affiliated housing: 0%. Activities include: dance, literary magazine, student government, student newspaper. Number of fraternities: 0; sororities: 0.

SERVICES AND FACILITIES

Basic services: nonremedial tutoring, placement service, health service, health insurance. **Remedial assistance:** reading, math, writing, study skills. **Counseling services:** minority student, career, personal, academic, psychological, birth control. **For learning-disabled students:** School does not offer a structured program with separate admission and additional fees. Services include: remedial math, remedial English, remedial reading, tape recorders, untimed tests, note-taking services, oral tests, learning center, readers, extended time for tests, tutors, proofreading services, texts on tape, typist/scribe, other testing accomodations. **Information technology resources:** Students are not required to lease or own a computer. Number of campus computers available to all students: 60. School has a wireless network. Proportion of college-owned housing units wired for high-speed internet access: 100%. **Campus safety:** Security services offered: 24-hour emergency telephones, lighted pathways/sidewalks, controlled dormitory access (key, security card, etc).

TRANSFER AND INTERNATIONAL STUDENTS

Transfer students: May apply for admission for the following academic terms: Fall, Spring, Summer. Applicants need a minimum number of credits to apply. For fall 2005: Transfer applications received: 292. Transfer applicants offered admission: 208. Transfer applicants enrolled: 142. **International students:** Number of foreign undergraduates: 12 (1% of student body). Minimum TOEFL score required: 550 (paper); 219 (computer).

Arizona

Arizona State University

- **Address:** Tempe, AZ 85287
- **Website:** http://www.asu.edu
- **Public**
- **Enrollment:** 32,865 full-time; 8,391 part-time

KEY STATS
✔ **U.S News College Ranking:** third tier, National Universities
✔ **SAT Score (25th/75th percentile):** 990-1230
✔ **Tuition:** 2006-2007: $4,688 in state, $15,847 out of state
  Selectivity: Selective   **Room/board:** N/A
  Acceptance rate: 91%   **Average debt:** N/A
  Student/faculty ratio: 22/1   **Proportion who borrowed:** N/A

UNDERGRADUATE STUDENT BODY STATS
2005-2006 enrollment: 32,865 full-time; 8,391 part-time. Men: 48%; women: 52%. **Ethnic makeup:** African American: 4%; American-Indian: 2%; Asian American: 5%; Hispanic: 13%; White: 73%; International: 3%.

ADMISSIONS FACTS AND FIGURES
Phone: (480) 965-7788. **Email:** information@asu.edu. **Website:** http://www.asu.edu. **Application deadlines for fall 2007:** Regular decision: Rolling. Early decision: Not offered. Early action: Not offered. Admission cannot be deferred. **Application fee:** $50. Common application is not accepted. **To apply online, go to:** http://www.asu.edu/admissions. **Admissions requirements/recommendations:** High school units required (recommended): English: 4; Mathematics: 4; Science: 3; Foreign language: 2; Social studies: 1; History: 1; Total units: 16. Tests: The college uses SAT or ACT scores in admissions decisions. Either SAT or ACT required. For admission to the fall 2007 entering class, the school will accept: ACT without writing. Campus visit: Recommended. Admissions interview: Neither required nor recommended. Off-campus interview: Not available. **Factors that count in admissions decisions:** *Academic:* Secondary school record: Not considered. Class rank: Very important. Letters of recommendation: Not considered. Standardized test scores: Very important. Essay: Not considered. *Nonacademic:* Interview: Not considered. Extracurricular activities: Not considered. Talent/ability: Not considered. Character/personal qualities: Not considered. Alumni/ae relationship: Not considered. Geographical residence: Not considered. State residency: Important. Religious affiliation/commitment: Not considered. Minority status: Not considered. Volunteer work: Not considered. Work experience: Not considered. **Other schools with the greatest overlap in applicants:** Northern Arizona University; San Diego State University; University of Arizona; University of California–Los Angeles; University of Southern California. **Admissions statistics for the fall 2005 entering class:** Total applicants: 19,914. Total accepted: 18,126. Freshmen enrolled: 7,706; 35% were from out of state. Overall acceptance rate: 91%. **Credentials of fall 2005 freshmen:** 27% ranked in the top 10 percent of their high school class; 53% were in the top 25 percent, and 83% were in the top half. (Proportion submitting class standing: 74%.) **Average high school grade point average:** 3.3. **First-year students who submitted SAT scores:** 77%. Scores (25/75 percentile): Verbal: 490-610, Math: 500-620, Combined: 990-1230. **First-year students submitting ACT scores:** 43%. Scores (25/75 percentile): English: 19-26, Math: 20-27, Composite: 20-26.

ACADEMICS
Year founded: 1885. **Academic calendar:** Semester. **Degrees offered:** bachelor's, post-bachelor's certificate, master's, post-master's certificate, first professional, doctorate. **Most popular majors:** 18% business, management, marketing, and related support services, 10% communication, journalism, and related programs, 10% multi/interdisciplinary studies, 9% education, 7% social sciences. **Major fields of study:** architecture and related services; area, ethnic, cultural, and gender studies; biological and biomedical sciences; business, management, marketing, and related support services; communication, journalism, and related programs; computer and informa-

tion sciences and support services; education; engineering; English language and literature/letters; family and consumer sciences/human sciences; foreign languages, literatures, and linguistics; health professions and related clinical sciences; history; legal professions and studies; liberal arts and sciences studies, and humanities; mathematics and statistics; multi/interdisciplinary studies; parks, recreation, leisure, and fitness studies; philosophy and religious studies; physical sciences; psychology; public administration and social service professions; security and protective services; social sciences; visual and performing arts. **Areas of required coursework:** arts/fine arts, humanities, computer literacy, mathematics, English (including composition), foreign languages, sciences (biological or physical), history, social science. **Pre-professional programs:** pre-law, pre-dentistry, pre-medicine, pre-optometry, pre-pharmacy. **Special academic programs:** accelerated program, cooperative (work-study plan) program, distance learning, double major, dual enrollment, exchange student program (domestic), honors program, independent study, internships, study abroad, teacher certificate program, weekend college. **Teacher certification offered in:** early childhood, special education, elementary, secondary, bilingual/bicultural. **Cooperative education programs:** business, engineering. **Reserve Officers Training Corps (ROTC):** Army ROTC: Offered on campus; Air Force ROTC: Offered on campus. **Faculty and instruction (2005-2006):** Total instructional faculty: 1,878 full-time, 404 part-time (59% men; 41% women; 20% minorities). Full-time faculty with Ph.D. or other terminal degree: 84%. Student/faculty ratio: 22/1. Classes of fewer than 20 students: 41%; of 20 to 49 students: 44%; of 50 or more students: 15%. **Advanced Placement and International Baccalaureate credit:** AP tests may be used for: Credit only. Scores accepted: 3, 4, 5. International Baccalaureate exams may be used for: Credit only. **Freshmen returning for sophomore year:** 78%. **Graduation rates:** Four-year: 27%; five-year: 49%; six-year: 55%.

COSTS AND FINANCIAL AID
Financial aid office: (480) 965-3355. **Expenses (2006-2007):** Tuition and fees 2006-2007: $4,688 in state, $15,847 out of state; room/board: N/A. Estimated books and supplies: $950; transportation: $1,300; personal expenses: $2,500. **Financial aid:** Priority filing date for institution's financial aid form: March 1.

CAMPUS LIFE AND EXTRACURRICULAR ACTIVITIES
Campus housing available: coed dorms, sorority housing, fraternity housing, apartment for single students, special housing for disabled students, other housing options. Students who live in college-owned, operated, or affiliated housing: 14%. **Clubs and organizations:** Number of student organizations: 563. Activities include: choral groups, concert band, dance, drama/theater, jazz band, literary magazine, marching band, music ensembles, musical theater, opera, pep band, radio station, student government, student newspaper, symphony orchestra, television station. Number of fraternities: 25; sororities: 21. Proportion of men in fraternities: 6%; of women in sororities: 6%. **Sports program (2005-2006):** Member of NCAA I. *Men's intercollegiate varsity sports:* baseball, basketball, cross-country, football, golf, swimming and diving, tennis, track and field (indoor), track and field (outdoor), wrestling. *Women's intercollegiate varsity sports:* basketball, cross-country, golf, gymnastics, soccer, softball, swimming and diving, tennis, track and field (indoor), track and field (outdoor), volleyball, water polo.

SERVICES AND FACILITIES
Basic services: nonremedial tutoring, women's center, placement service, day care, health service, health insurance. **Counseling services:** minority student, career, military, personal, veteran student, academic, older student, psychological, birth control, religious. **For learning-disabled students:** School does not offer a structured program with separate admission and additional fees. **Library:** Number of titles: 3,593,677; number of current serial subscriptions: 32,001. **Information technology resources:** Students are not required to lease or own a computer. Number of campus computers available to all students: 8,000. School has a wireless network. Proportion of college-owned housing units wired for high-speed internet access: 100%. **Campus safety:** Security services offered: 24-hour foot-and-vehicle patrols, late-night transport/escort service, 24-hour emergency telephones, lighted pathways/sidewalks, controlled dormitory access (key, security card, etc).

TRANSFER AND INTERNATIONAL STUDENTS

Transfer students: May apply for admission for the following academic terms: Fall, Winter, Spring, Summer. Applicants need a minimum number of credits to apply. For fall 2005: Transfer applications received: 6,816. Transfer applicants offered admission: 6,189. Transfer applicants enrolled: 3,744. **International students:** Number of foreign undergraduates: 1081 (3% of student body). Number of countries represented: 104. Minimum TOEFL score required: 500 (paper); 173 (computer).

Arizona State University West

- **Address:** PO Box 37100, Phoenix, AZ 85069-7100
- **Website:** http://www.west.asu.edu/
- **Public**
- **Enrollment:** 4,843 full-time; 1,777 part-time

KEY STATS

✔ **U.S News College Ranking:** Unranked, Universities–Master's (West)

✔ **SAT Score (25th/75th percentile):** 930-1150

✔ **Tuition:** 2006-2007: $4,498 in state, $15,848 out of state

Selectivity: N/A	Room/board: $6,900
Acceptance rate: 63%	Average debt: $16,438
Student/faculty ratio: 19/1	Proportion who borrowed: 56%

UNDERGRADUATE STUDENT BODY STATS

2005-2006 enrollment: 4,843 full-time; 1,777 part-time. Men: 35%; women: 65%. **Ethnic makeup:** African American: 5%; American-Indian: 2%; Asian American: 4%; Hispanic: 19%; White: 69%; International: 1%.

ADMISSIONS FACTS AND FIGURES

Phone: (602) 543-8203. **Email:** west-admissions@asu.edu. **Website:** http://www.west.asu.edu/. **Application deadlines for fall 2007:** Regular decision: Rolling. Early decision: Not offered. Early action: Send application by: November 1; Decision sent by: December 1. Admission cannot be deferred. **Application fee:** $50. Common application is not accepted. **To apply online, go to:** http://www.west.asu.edu/gowest. **Admissions requirements/recommendations:** High school units required (recommended): English: 4; Mathematics: 4; Science: 3; Foreign language: 2; Social studies: 1; History: 1; Academic electives: 0; Total units: 16. Tests: The college uses SAT or ACT scores in admissions decisions. Either SAT or ACT required. For admission to the fall 2007 entering class, the school will accept: ACT without writing. Campus visit: Neither required nor recommended. Admissions interview: Neither required nor recommended. Off-campus interview: Not available. **Factors that count in admissions decisions:** *Academic:* Secondary school record: Very important. Class rank: Very important. Letters of recommendation: Considered. Standardized test scores: Very important. Essay: Considered. *Nonacademic:* Interview: Considered. Extracurricular activities: Considered. Talent/ability: Considered. Character/personal qualities: Not considered. Alumni/ae relationship: Not considered. Geographical residence: Not considered. State residency: Important. Religious affiliation/commitment: Not considered. Minority status: Not considered. Volunteer work: Not considered. Work experience: Not considered. **Admissions statistics for the fall 2005 entering class:** Total applicants: 1,403. Total accepted: 882. Freshmen enrolled: 487; 14% were from out of state. Overall acceptance rate: 63%. Non-early acceptance rate: 63%. **Credentials of fall 2005 freshmen:** 31% ranked in the top 10 percent of their high school class; 60% were in the top 25 percent, and 88% were in the top half. (Proportion submitting class standing: 82%.) **Average high school grade point average:** 3.4. **First-year students who submitted SAT scores:** 69%. Scores (25/75 percentile): Verbal: 460-580, Math: 470-570, Combined: 930-1150. **First-year students submitting ACT scores:** 36%. Scores (25/75 percentile): English: 18-24, Math: 18-25, Composite: 19-24.

ACADEMICS

Year founded: 1984. **Academic calendar:** Semester. **Degrees offered:** certificate, bachelor's, master's. **Most popular majors:** 29% business, management, marketing, and related support services, 25% education, 7% psychology, 7% security and protective services, 6% communication, journalism, and related programs. **Major fields of study:** area, ethnic, cultural, and gender studies; biological and biomedical sciences; business, management, marketing, and related support services; communication, journalism, and related programs; computer and information sciences and support serv-

ices; education; English language and literature/letters; foreign languages, literatures, and linguistics; history; multi/interdisciplinary studies; parks, recreation, leisure, and fitness studies; psychology; public administration and social service professions; security and protective services; social sciences; visual and performing arts. **Areas of required coursework:** humanities, computer literacy, mathematics, English (including composition), sciences (biological or physical), history, social science. **Special academic programs (% participation):** double major (2%), honors program (3%), independent study (11%), internships (19%), teacher certificate program (25%). **Teacher certification offered in:** special education, elementary, secondary. **Faculty and instruction (2005-2006):** Total instructional faculty: 233 full-time, 155 part-time (45% men; 55% women; 19% minorities). Full-time faculty with Ph.D. or other terminal degree: 88%. Student/faculty ratio: 19/1. Classes of fewer than 20 students: 21%; of 20 to 49 students: 72%; of 50 or more students: 7%. **Advanced Placement and International Baccalaureate credit:** International Baccalaureate exams may be used for: Credit and/or placement. **Freshmen returning for sophomore year:** 74%.

COSTS AND FINANCIAL AID

Financial aid office: (602) 543-8178. **Expenses (2006-2007):** Tuition and fees 2006-2007: $4,498 in state, $15,848 out of state; room/board: $6,900. **Financial aid:** Priority filing date for institution's financial aid form: March 1. Average amount of debt of borrowers graduating in 2005: $16,438. Proportion who borrowed: 56%.

CAMPUS LIFE AND EXTRACURRICULAR ACTIVITIES

Campus housing available (% using): apartment for single students (100%). Students who live in college-owned, operated, or affiliated housing: 3%. **Student employment:** During the 2005-2006 academic year, 7% of undergraduates worked on campus. Average per-year earnings: $2,500. **Clubs and organizations:** Number of student organizations: 27. Activities include: drama/theater, literary magazine, student government, student newspaper. Number of fraternities: 0; sororities: 0.

SERVICES AND FACILITIES

Basic services: nonremedial tutoring, women's center, placement service, day care, health service, health insurance. **Counseling services:** minority student, career, personal, veteran student, academic, birth control. **For learning-disabled students:** School does not offer a structured program with separate admission and additional fees. Total undergraduates in learning-disabled program or receiving services: 64. Services include: reading machines, tape recorders, note-taking services, oral tests, learning center, readers, extended time for tests, tutors, priority registration, priority seating, texts on tape, other testing accomodations, other. **Library:** Number of titles: 335,000; number of current serial subscriptions: 2,453. **Information technology resources:** Students are not required to lease or own a computer. Number of campus computers available to all students: 674. School has a wireless network. Approximate number of users that can be accommodated: 2,300. Proportion of college-owned housing units wired for high-speed internet access: 100%. **Campus safety:** Security services offered: 24-hour foot-and-vehicle patrols, late-night transport/escort service, 24-hour emergency telephones, lighted pathways/sidewalks, controlled dormitory access (key, security card, etc).

TRANSFER AND INTERNATIONAL STUDENTS

Transfer students: May apply for admission for the following academic terms: Fall, Spring, Summer. Applicants need a minimum number of credits to apply. For fall 2005: Transfer applications received: 2,029. Transfer applicants offered admission: 1,556. Transfer applicants enrolled: 1,125. **International students:** Number of foreign undergraduates: 29 (1% of student body). Number of countries represented: 21. Minimum TOEFL score required: 500 (paper); 173 (computer). Average TOEFL score: 453 (paper).

Northern Arizona University

- **Address:** PO Box 4084, Flagstaff, AZ 86011-4084
- **Website:** http://www.nau.edu
- **Public**
- **Enrollment:** 11,261 full-time; 1,991 part-time

KEY STATS
✔ **U.S News College Ranking:** fourth tier, National Universities
✔ **SAT Score (25th/75th percentile):** 960-1180
✔ **Tuition:** 2006-2007: $4,545 in state, $13,656 out of state
  Selectivity: Selective   **Room/board:** $6,260
  Acceptance rate: 86%   **Average debt:** $16,473
  Student/faculty ratio: 16/1   **Proportion who borrowed:** 60%

UNDERGRADUATE STUDENT BODY STATS
2005-2006 enrollment: 11,261 full-time; 1,991 part-time. Men: 40%; women: 60%. **Ethnic makeup:** African American: 2%; American-Indian: 7%; Asian American: 2%; Hispanic: 12%; White: 75%; International: 2%.

ADMISSIONS FACTS AND FIGURES
Phone: (928) 523-5511. **Email:** undergraduate.admissions@nau.edu. **Website:** http://www.nau.edu. **Application deadlines for fall 2007:** Regular decision: Rolling. Early decision: Not offered. Early action: Not offered. Admission can be deferred. **Application fee:** $25. Common application is not accepted. **To apply online, go to:** http://www4.nau.edu/uadmissions. **Admissions requirements/recommendations:** High school units required (recommended): English: 4 (4); Mathematics: 4 (4); Science: 3 (3); Foreign language: 2 (2); Social studies: 1 (1); History: 1 (1). Tests: The college uses SAT or ACT scores in admissions decisions. Neither SAT nor ACT required. Campus visit: Recommended. Admissions interview: Neither required nor recommended. Off-campus interview: May be arranged. **Factors that count in admissions decisions:** *Academic:* Secondary school record: Very important. Class rank: Very important. Letters of recommendation: Not considered. Standardized test scores: Very important. Essay: Not considered. *Nonacademic:* Interview: Not considered. Extracurricular activities: Not considered. Talent/ability: Not considered. Character/personal qualities: Not considered. Alumni/ae relationship: Not considered. Geographical residence: Not considered. State residency: Not considered. Religious affiliation/commitment: Not considered. Minority status: Not considered. Volunteer work: Not considered. Work experience: Not considered. **Admissions statistics for the fall 2005 entering class:** Total applicants: 7,304. Total accepted: 6,312. Freshmen enrolled: 2,279; 27% were from out of state. Overall acceptance rate: 86%. **Credentials of fall 2005 freshmen:** 17% ranked in the top 10 percent of their high school class; 47% were in the top 25 percent. **Average high school grade point average:** 3.4. **First-year students who submitted SAT scores:** 69%. Scores (25/75 percentile): Verbal: 480-590, Math: 480-590, Combined: 960-1180. **First-year students submitting ACT scores:** 47%. Scores (25/75 percentile): English: 19-23, Math: 18-24, Composite: 19-25.

ACADEMICS
Year founded: 1899. **Academic calendar:** Semester. **Degrees offered:** certificate, bachelor's, post-bachelor's certificate, master's, post-master's certificate, first professional, doctorate. **Most popular majors:** 24% education, 19% business, management, marketing, and related support services, 6% communication, journalism, and related programs, 6% liberal arts and sciences studies, and humanities, 6% visual and performing arts. **Major fields of study:** area, ethnic, cultural, and gender studies; biological and biomedical sciences; business, management, marketing, and related support services; communication, journalism, and related programs; computer and information sciences and support services; education; engineering; English language and literature/letters; foreign languages, literatures, and linguistics; health professions and related clinical sciences; history; legal professions and studies; liberal arts and sciences studies, and humanities; mathematics and statistics; multi/interdisciplinary studies; natural resources and conservation; parks, recreation, leisure, and fitness studies; philosophy and religious studies; physical sciences; psychology; public administration and social service professions; science technologies/technicians; security and protective services; social sciences; visual and performing arts. **Areas of required coursework:** arts/fine arts, humanities, computer literacy, mathematics, English (including composition), philosophy, foreign languages, sciences (biological or physical), history, social science. **Pre-professional**

programs: pre-law, pre-medicine, pre-veterinary science, pre-pharmacy. **Special academic programs (% participation):** accelerated program (1%), cooperative (work-study plan) program (1%), distance learning (27%), double major (3%), dual enrollment, English as a Second Language (ESL) (.5%), exchange student program (domestic) (.5%), honors program (4%), independent study (16%), internships (5%), study abroad (6%), teacher certificate program (6%). **Teacher certification offered in:** special education, elementary, secondary. **Cooperative education programs:** business, education, other. **Reserve Officers Training Corps (ROTC):** Army ROTC: Offered on campus; Air Force ROTC: Offered on campus. **Faculty and instruction (2005-2006):** Total instructional faculty: 723 full-time, 651 part-time (49% men; 51% women; 12% minorities). Full-time faculty with Ph.D. or other terminal degree: 78%. Student/faculty ratio: 16/1. Classes of fewer than 20 students: 39%; of 20 to 49 students: 52%; of 50 or more students: 9%. **Freshmen returning for sophomore year:** 69%. **Graduation rates:** Four-year: 26%; five-year: 42%; six-year: 48%. **Graduate study:** 50% of students pursue further study immediately upon graduation.

COSTS AND FINANCIAL AID
Financial aid office: (928) 523-4951. **Expenses (2006-2007):** Tuition and fees 2006-2007: $4,545 in state, $13,656 out of state; room/board: $6,260. Estimated books and supplies: $828; transportation: $1,358; personal expenses: $2,220. **Financial aid:** Priority filing date for institution's financial aid form: February 14. In 2005-2006, 69% of undergraduates applied for financial aid. Of those, 52% were determined to have financial need; 17% had their need fully met. Average financial aid package (proportion receiving): $7,919 (51%). Average amount of gift aid, such as scholarships or grants (proportion receiving): $4,651 (34%). Average amount of self-help aid, such as work study or loans (proportion receiving): $4,055 (40%). Average need-based loan (excluding PLUS or other private loans): $3,726. Among students who received need-based aid, the average percentage of need met: 64%. Among students who received aid based on merit, the average award (and the proportion receiving): $3,416 (17%). The average athletic scholarship (and the proportion receiving): $11,923 (1%). Average amount of debt of borrowers graduating in 2005: $16,473. Proportion who borrowed: 60%.

CAMPUS LIFE AND EXTRACURRICULAR ACTIVITIES
Campus housing available (% using): coed dorms (68%), women's dorms (2%), men's dorms (2%), sorority housing (5%), fraternity housing (4%), apartments for married students (4%), apartment for single students (14%), special housing for disabled students (1%). Students who live in college-owned, operated, or affiliated housing: 37%. **Student employment:** During the 2005-2006 academic year, 26% of undergraduates worked on campus. Average per-year earnings: $2,054. **Clubs and organizations:** Number of student organizations: 182. Activities include: concert band, dance, drama/theater, jazz band, marching band, music ensembles, musical theater, opera, pep band, radio station, student government, student newspaper, symphony orchestra, television station. Number of fraternities: 13; sororities: 7. Proportion of men in fraternities: 8%; of women in sororities: 6%. **Sports program (2005-2006):** Member of NCAA I. *Men's intercollegiate varsity sports:* basketball, cross-country, football, tennis, track and field (indoor), track and field (outdoor). *Women's intercollegiate varsity sports:* basketball, cross-country, golf, soccer, swimming and diving, tennis, track and field (indoor), track and field (outdoor), volleyball.

SERVICES AND FACILITIES
Basic services: placement service, health service, health insurance. **Counseling services:** minority student, career, military, personal, veteran student, academic, older student, psychological. **For learning-disabled students:** School does not offer a structured program with separate admission and additional fees. Total undergraduates in learning-disabled program or receiving services: 141. Services include: remedial math, reading machines, tape recorders, note-taking services, oral tests, extended time for tests, tutors, priority registration, priority seating, texts on tape, exams on tape or computer, other testing accomodations. **Library:** Number of titles: 1,102,728; number of current serial subscriptions: 26,628. **Information technology resources:** Students are not required to lease or own a computer. Number of campus computers available to all students: 1,000. School has a wireless network. Approximate number of users that can be accommodated: 1,900. Proportion of college-owned housing units wired for high-speed internet access: 100%. **Campus safety:** Security services offered: 24-hour foot-and-vehicle patrols, late-night transport/escort service, 24-hour emergency telephones, lighted pathways/sidewalks, controlled dormitory access (key, security card, etc.).

TRANSFER AND INTERNATIONAL STUDENTS

Transfer students: May apply for admission for the following academic terms: Fall, Winter, Spring, Summer. Applicants do not need a minimum number of credits to apply. For fall 2005: Transfer applications received: 3,553. Transfer applicants offered admission: 2,895. Transfer applicants enrolled: 1,603. **International students:** Number of foreign undergraduates: 265 (2% of student body). Number of countries represented: 34. Minimum TOEFL score required: 500 (paper); 173 (computer). Average TOEFL score: 549 (paper).

Prescott College

- **Address:** 220 Grove Avenue, Prescott, AZ 86301
- **Website:** http://www.prescott.edu/
- **Private**
- **Enrollment:** 723 full-time; 70 part-time

KEY STATS

✔ **U.S News College Ranking:** third tier, Universities–Master's (West)
✔ **SAT Score (25th/75th percentile):** 1030-1290
✔ **Tuition:** 2006-2007: $18,661

Selectivity: Selective	**Room/board:** N/A
Acceptance rate: 88%	**Average debt:** $18,235
Student/faculty ratio: 7/1	**Proportion who borrowed:** 68%

UNDERGRADUATE STUDENT BODY STATS

2005-2006 enrollment: 723 full-time; 70 part-time. Men: 37%; women: 63%. **Ethnic makeup:** African American: 1%; American-Indian: 3%; Asian American: 1%; Hispanic: 6%; White: 90%.

ADMISSIONS FACTS AND FIGURES

Phone: (800) 628-6364. **Email:** admissions@prescott.edu. **Website:** http://www.prescott.edu/. **Application deadlines for fall 2007:** Regular decision: August 15. Early decision: Send application by: December 1; Decision sent by: December 15. Early action: Not offered. Admission can be deferred. **Application fee:** $25. Common application is accepted. **To apply online, go to:** http://www.prescott.edu/apply/index.html. **Admissions requirements/recommendations:** High school units required (recommended): English: (4); Mathematics: (3); Science: (2); Foreign language: (3); Social studies: (1); History: (2); Academic electives: (0); Total units: (16). Tests: The college uses SAT or ACT scores in admissions decisions. Either SAT or ACT required. For admission to the fall 2007 entering class, the school will accept: ACT with writing, ACT without writing. Campus visit: Recommended. Admissions interview: Recommended. Off-campus interview: May be arranged. **Factors that count in admissions decisions:** *Academic:* Secondary school record: Very important. Class rank: Not considered. Letters of recommendation: Very important. Standardized test scores: Important. Essay: Very important. *Nonacademic:* Interview: Important. Extracurricular activities: Important. Talent/ability: Important. Character/personal qualities: Important. Alumni/ae relationship: Not considered. Geographical residence: Not considered. State residency: Not considered. Religious affiliation/commitment: Not considered. Minority status: Not considered. Volunteer work: Considered. Work experience: Considered. **Other schools with the greatest overlap in applicants:** Antioch College; College of the Atlantic; Hampshire College; Sterling College; Warren Wilson College. **Admissions statistics for the fall 2005 entering class:** Total applicants: 147. Total accepted: 129. Freshmen enrolled: 54; Overall acceptance rate: 88%. Non-early acceptance rate: 88%. **Size of waiting list:** 0 applicants; enrolled from waiting list: 0. **Credentials of fall 2005 freshmen:** 12% ranked in the top 10 percent of their high school class; 19% were in the top 25 percent, and 50% were in the top half. (Proportion submitting class standing: 38%.) **Average high school grade point average:** 3.0. **First-year students who submitted SAT scores:** 69%. Scores (25/75 percentile): Verbal: 540-680, Math: 490-610, Combined: 1030-1290. **First-year students submitting ACT scores:** 31%. Scores (25/75 percentile): English: N/A, Math: N/A, Composite: 20-28.

ACADEMICS

Year founded: 1966. **Academic calendar:** Semester. **Degrees offered:** bachelor's, post-bachelor's certificate, master's, doctorate. **Most popular majors:** 26% natural resources and conservation, 15% education, 14% psychology, 8% English language and literature/letters, 7% biological and biomedical sciences. **Major fields of study:** agriculture, agriculture operations, and related sciences; area, ethnic, cultural, and gender studies; biological and biomedical sciences; business, management, marketing, and related support services; communication, journalism, and related programs; computer and information sciences and support services; education; English language and literature/letters; foreign languages, literatures, and linguistics; history; liberal arts and sciences studies, and humanities; library science; mathematics and statistics; multi/interdisciplinary studies; natural resources and conservation; parks, recreation, leisure, and fitness studies; philosophy and religious studies; psychology; public administration and social service professions; social sciences; visual and performing arts. **Areas of required coursework:** mathematics, English (including composition). **Special academic programs:** cross-registration, double major, dual enrollment, exchange student program (domestic), external degree program, independent study, internships, liberal arts/career combination, student-designed major, teacher certificate program. **Teacher certification offered in:** early childhood, special education, elementary, secondary, bilingual/bicultural. **Cooperative education programs:** other. **Faculty and instruction (2005-2006):** Total instructional faculty: 50 full-time, 37 part-time (61% men; 39% women; 6% minorities). Full-time faculty with Ph.D. or other terminal degree: 58%. Student/faculty ratio: 7/1. **Advanced Placement and International Baccalaureate credit:** AP tests may be used for: Credit and/or placement. Scores accepted: 4, 5. International Baccalaureate exams may be used for: Credit and/or placement. **Freshmen returning for sophomore year:** 63%. **Graduation rates:** Four-year: 23%; five-year: 41%; six-year: 39%.

COSTS AND FINANCIAL AID

Financial aid office: (928) 350-1111. **Expenses (2006-2007):** Tuition and fees 2006-2007: $18,661; room/board: N/A. **Financial aid:** Average amount of debt of borrowers graduating in 2005: $18,235. Proportion who borrowed: 68%.

CAMPUS LIFE AND EXTRACURRICULAR ACTIVITIES

Clubs and organizations: Number of student organizations: 10. Activities include: dance, drama/theater, literary magazine, music ensembles, student government, student newspaper. Number of fraternities: 0; sororities: 0.

SERVICES AND FACILITIES

Basic services: nonremedial tutoring, health insurance. **Remedial assistance:** reading, math, writing, study skills. **Counseling services:** career, personal, academic, psychological. **For learning-disabled students:** School does not offer a structured program with separate admission and additional fees. Total undergraduates in learning-disabled program or receiving services: 50. Services include: tape recorders, untimed tests, note-taking services, readers, extended time for tests, tutors, typist/scribe, other testing accomodations, other. **Library:** Number of titles: 23,468; number of current serial subscriptions: 254. **Information technology resources:** Students are not required to lease or own a computer. Number of campus computers available to all students: 50. School has a wireless network. **Campus safety:** Security services offered: lighted pathways/sidewalks.

TRANSFER AND INTERNATIONAL STUDENTS

Transfer students: May apply for admission for the following academic terms: Fall, Spring. Applicants do not need a minimum number of credits to apply. For fall 2005: Transfer applications received: 156. Transfer applicants offered admission: 133. Transfer applicants enrolled: 76. **International students:** Number of foreign undergraduates: 1. Minimum TOEFL score required: 500 (paper); 173 (computer). Average TOEFL score: 600 (paper).

University of Arizona

- **Address:** PO Box 210066, Tucson, AZ 85721-0066
- **Website:** http://www.arizona.edu
- **Public**
- **Enrollment:** 24,725 full-time; 3,737 part-time

KEY STATS

✔ **U.S News College Ranking:** 98, National Universities
✔ **SAT Score (25th/75th percentile):** 1000-1250
✔ **Tuition:** 2006-2007: $4,666 in state, $15,128 out of state

Selectivity: More selective	**Room/board:** $7,850
Acceptance rate: 88%	**Average debt:** $16,422
Student/faculty ratio: 19/1	**Proportion who borrowed:** 47%

UNDERGRADUATE STUDENT BODY STATS

2005-2006 enrollment: 24,725 full-time; 3,737 part-time. Men: 47%; women: 53%. **Ethnic makeup:** African American: 3%; American-Indian: 2%; Asian American: 6%; Hispanic: 15%; White: 71%; International: 3%.

ADMISSIONS FACTS AND FIGURES

Phone: (520) 621-3237. **Email:** appinfo@arizona.edu. **Website:** http://www.arizona.edu. **Application deadlines for fall 2007:** Regular decision: April 1. Early decision: Not offered. Early action: Not offered. Admission cannot be deferred. **Application fee:** $50. Common application is not accepted. **To apply online, go to:** http://www.admissions.arizona.edu. **Admissions requirements/recommendations:** High school units required (recommended): English: 4 (4); Mathematics: 4 (4); Science: 3 (3); Foreign language: 2 (2); Social studies: 1 (1); History: 1 (1); Total units: 16 (16). Tests: The college uses SAT or ACT scores in admissions decisions. Neither SAT nor ACT required. For admission to the fall 2007 entering class, the school will accept: ACT with writing, ACT without writing. Campus visit: Neither required nor recommended. Admissions interview: Neither required nor recommended. Off-campus interview: May be arranged. **Factors that count in admissions decisions:** *Academic:* Secondary school record: Very important. Class rank: Considered. Letters of recommendation: Considered. Standardized test scores: Considered. Essay: Considered. *Nonacademic:* Interview: Considered. Extracurricular activities: Considered. Talent/ability: Considered. Character/personal qualities: Considered. Alumni/ae relationship: Not considered. Geographical residence: Considered. State residency: Considered. Religious affiliation/commitment: Not considered. Minority status: Considered. Volunteer work: Considered. Work experience: Considered. **Other schools with the greatest overlap in applicants:** Arizona State University; Northern Arizona University; San Diego State University; University of California–Irvine; University of California–San Diego. **Admissions statistics for the fall 2005 entering class:** Total applicants: 17,904. Total accepted: 15,701. Freshmen enrolled: 5,974; 35% were from out of state. Overall acceptance rate: 88%. **Credentials of fall 2005 freshmen:** 34% ranked in the top 10 percent of their high school class; 61% were in the top 25 percent, and 88% were in the top half. (Proportion submitting class standing: 66%.) **Average high school grade point average:** 3.4. **First-year students who submitted SAT scores:** 83%. Scores (25/75 percentile): Verbal: 500-620, Math: 500-630, Combined: 1000-1250. **First-year students submitting ACT scores:** 41%. Scores (25/75 percentile): English: 20-27, Math: 20-27, Composite: 21-26.

ACADEMICS

Year founded: 1885. **Academic calendar:** Semester. **Degrees offered:** bachelor's, post-bachelor's certificate, master's, first professional, doctorate. **Most popular majors:** 17% business, management, marketing, and related support services, 9% communication, journalism, and related programs, 9% social sciences, 8% biological and biomedical sciences, 8% education. **Major fields of study:** agriculture, agriculture operations, and related sciences; architecture and related services; area, ethnic, cultural, and gender studies; biological and biomedical sciences; business, management, marketing, and related support services; communication, journalism, and related programs; communications technologies/technicians and support services; computer and information sciences and support services; education; engineering; engineering technologies/technicians; English language and literature/letters; family and consumer sciences/human sciences; foreign languages, literatures, and linguistics; health professions and related clinical sciences; history; liberal arts and sciences studies, and humanities; mathematics and statistics; multi/interdisciplinary studies; natural resources and conservation; philosophy and religious studies; physical sciences; psychology; public administration and social service professions; security and protective services; social sciences; visual and performing arts. **Areas of required coursework:** arts/fine arts, humanities, mathematics, English (including composition), foreign languages, sciences (biological or physical), social science. **Pre-professional programs:** pre-law, pre-medicine, pre-veterinary science, pre-pharmacy. **Special academic programs:** cooperative (work-study plan) program, cross-registration, distance learning, double major, dual enrollment, English as a Second Language (ESL), exchange student program (domestic), honors program, independent study, internships, student-designed major, study abroad, teacher certificate program, weekend college. **Teacher certification offered in:** special education, elementary, secondary, bilingual/bicultural. **Reserve Officers Training Corps (ROTC):** Army ROTC: Offered on campus; Navy ROTC: Offered on campus; Air Force ROTC: Offered on campus. **Faculty and instruction (2005-2006):** Total instructional faculty: 1,378 full-time, 46 part-time (69% men; 31% women; 13% minorities). Full-time faculty with Ph.D. or other terminal degree: 99%. Student/faculty ratio: 19/1. Classes of fewer than 20 students: 30%; of 20 to 49 students: 55%; of 50 or more students: 15%. **Advanced Placement and International Baccalaureate credit:** AP tests may be used for: Credit and/or placement. Scores accepted: 4, 5. International Baccalaureate exams may be used for: Credit and/or placement. **Freshmen returning for sophomore year:** 78%. **Graduation rates:** Four-year: 32%; five-year: 53%; six-year: 58%.

COSTS AND FINANCIAL AID

Financial aid office: (520) 621-5200. **Expenses (2006-2007):** Tuition and fees 2006-2007: $4,666 in state, $15,128 out of state; room/board: $7,850. Estimated books and supplies: $816; transportation: $600; personal expenses: $2,520. **Financial aid:** Priority filing date for institution's financial aid form: March 1. In 2005-2006, 54% of undergraduates applied for financial aid. Of those, 40% were determined to have financial need; 10% had their need fully met. Average financial aid package (proportion receiving): $7,810 (39%). Average amount of gift aid, such as scholarships or grants (proportion receiving): $6,167 (34%). Average amount of self-help aid, such as work study or loans (proportion receiving): $4,145 (26%). Average need-based loan (excluding PLUS or other private loans): $4,025. Among students who received need-based aid, the average percentage of need met: 64%. Among students who received aid based on merit, the average award (and the proportion receiving): $5,014 (20%). The average athletic scholarship (and the proportion receiving): $10,796 (1%). Average amount of debt of borrowers graduating in 2005: $16,422. Proportion who borrowed: 47%.

CAMPUS LIFE AND EXTRACURRICULAR ACTIVITIES

Campus housing available: coed dorms, women's dorms, sorority housing, fraternity housing, apartment for single students, special housing for disabled students, special housing for international students. Students who live in college-owned, operated, or affiliated housing: 20%. **Clubs and organizations:** Number of student organizations: 445. Activities include: choral groups, concert band, dance, drama/theater, jazz band, literary magazine, marching band, music ensembles, musical theater, opera, pep band, radio station, student government, student newspaper, symphony orchestra, television station, yearbook. Number of fraternities: 25; sororities: 20. Proportion of men in fraternities: 10%; of women in sororities: 11%. **Sports program (2005-2006):** Member of NCAA I. *Men's intercollegiate varsity sports:* baseball, basketball, cross-country, football, golf, swimming and diving, tennis, track and field (indoor), track and field (outdoor). *Women's intercollegiate varsity sports:* basketball, cross-country, golf, gymnastics, soccer, softball, swimming and diving, tennis, track and field (indoor), track and field (outdoor), volleyball.

SERVICES AND FACILITIES

Basic services: nonremedial tutoring, women's center, placement service, health service, health insurance. **Counseling services:** minority student, career, military, personal, veteran student, academic, psychological, birth control. **For learning-disabled students:** School does not offer a structured program with separate admission and additional fees. Total undergraduates in learning-disabled program or receiving services: 750. Services include: remedial math, remedial English, reading machines, tape recorders, note-taking services, learning center, readers, extended time for tests, tutors, substitution of courses, texts on tape, typist/scribe, exams on tape or computer, other testing accomodations. **Information technology resources:** Students are not required to lease or own a computer. Number of campus computers available to all students: 2,600. School has a wireless network. Proportion of college-owned housing units wired for high-speed internet access: 100%. **Campus safety:** Security services offered: 24-hour foot-and-vehicle patrols, late-night transport/escort service, 24-hour emergency telephones, lighted pathways/sidewalks, controlled dormitory access (key, security card, etc).

TRANSFER AND INTERNATIONAL STUDENTS

Transfer students: May apply for admission for the following academic terms: Fall, Spring, Summer. Applicants need a minimum number of credits to apply. For fall 2005: Transfer applications received: 3,495. Transfer applicants offered admission: 2,713. Transfer applicants enrolled: 2,007. **International students:** Number of foreign undergraduates: 770 (3% of student body). Number of countries represented: 124. Minimum TOEFL score required: 500 (paper); 173 (computer). Average TOEFL score: 590 (paper).

Arkansas

Arkansas Baptist College

- **Address:** 1600 Bishop Street, Little Rock, AR 72202
- **Website:** http://www.arbaptcol.edu
- **Private; Religious affiliation:** Baptist
- **Enrollment:** N/A

KEY STATS
- ✔ **U.S News College Ranking:** fourth tier, Liberal Arts Colleges
- ✔ **SAT or ACT Score (25th/75th percentile):** N/A
- ✔ **Tuition:** N/A

Selectivity: Selective	**Room/board:** N/A
Acceptance rate: N/A	**Average debt:** N/A
Student/faculty ratio: N/A	**Proportion who borrowed:** N/A

Arkansas State University

- **Address:** PO Box 10, State University, AR 72467
- **Website:** http://www.astate.edu
- **Public**
- **Enrollment:** 7,194 full-time; 1,944 part-time

KEY STATS
- ✔ **U.S News College Ranking:** third tier, Universities–Master's (South)
- ✔ **ACT Score (25th/75th percentile):** 18-24
- ✔ **Tuition:** 2005-2006: $5,440 in state, $12,145 out of state

Selectivity: Selective	**Room/board:** $4,190
Acceptance rate: 65%	**Average debt:** $18,500
Student/faculty ratio: 17/1	**Proportion who borrowed:** 68%

UNDERGRADUATE STUDENT BODY STATS
2005-2006 enrollment: 7,194 full-time; 1,944 part-time. Men: 41%; women: 59%. **Ethnic makeup:** African American: 17%; Asian American: 1%; Hispanic: 1%; White: 80%; International: 1%.

ADMISSIONS FACTS AND FIGURES
Phone: (870) 972-3024. **Email:** admissions@astate.edu. **Website:** http://www.astate.edu. **Application deadlines for fall 2007:** Regular decision: August 21. Early decision: Not offered. Early action: Not offered. Admission can be deferred. **Application fee:** $15. Common application is not accepted. **To apply online, go to:** https://asu.astate.edu. **Admissions requirements/recommendations:** High school units required (recommended): English: 4 (4); Mathematics: 4 (4); Science: 3 (3); Foreign language: 2 (2); Social studies: 1 (1); History: 2 (2); Total units: 16 (15). Tests: The college uses SAT or ACT scores in admissions decisions. Either SAT or ACT required. For admission to the fall 2007 entering class, the school will accept: ACT with writing, ACT without writing. Campus visit: Recommended. Admissions interview: Neither required nor recommended. Off-campus interview: Not available. **Factors that count in admissions decisions: *Academic:*** Secondary school record: Very important. Class rank: Considered. Letters of recommendation: Considered. Standardized test scores: Very important. Essay: Not considered. ***Nonacademic:*** Interview: Not considered. Extracurricular activities: Not considered. Talent/ability: Considered. Character/personal qualities: Not considered. Alumni/ae relationship: Not considered. Geographical residence: Not considered. State residency: Not considered. Religious affiliation/commitment: Not considered. Minority status: Not considered. Volunteer work: Not considered. Work experience: Not considered. **Other schools with the greatest overlap in applicants:** Arkansas Tech University; University of Arkansas; University of Arkansas–Little Rock; University of Central Arkansas; University of Memphis. **Admissions statistics for the fall 2005 entering class:** Total applicants: 3,488. Total accepted: 2,259. Freshmen enrolled: 1,584; 12% were from out of state. Overall acceptance rate: 65%. **Average high school grade point average:** 3.2. **First-year students who sub-**mitted SAT scores: 1%. Scores (25/75 percentile): Verbal: N/A, Math: N/A, Combined: N/A. **First-year students submitting ACT scores:** 92%. Scores (25/75 percentile): English: 18-26, Math: 17-24, Composite: 18-24.

ACADEMICS
Year founded: 1909. **Academic calendar:** Semester. **Degrees offered:** certificate, associate, bachelor's, post-bachelor's certificate, master's, post-master's certificate, doctorate. **Most popular majors:** 19% business, management, marketing, and related support services, 18% education, 11% health professions and related clinical sciences, 6% social sciences, 5% agriculture, agriculture operations, and related sciences. **Major fields of study:** agriculture, agriculture operations, and related sciences; biological and biomedical sciences; business, management, marketing, and related support services; communication, journalism, and related programs; communications technologies/technicians and support services; computer and information sciences and support services; education; engineering; engineering technologies/technicians; English language and literature/letters; foreign languages, literatures, and linguistics; health professions and related clinical sciences; history; liberal arts and sciences studies, and humanities; mathematics and statistics; natural resources and conservation; parks, recreation, leisure, and fitness studies; philosophy and religious studies; physical sciences; psychology; public administration and social service professions; security and protective services; social sciences; visual and performing arts. **Areas of required coursework:** arts/fine arts, humanities, mathematics, English (including composition), philosophy, sciences (biological or physical), history, social science, other. **Special academic programs:** accelerated program, distance learning, double major, dual enrollment, exchange student program (domestic), honors program, independent study, internships, study abroad, teacher certificate program. **Teacher certification offered in:** early childhood, special education, elementary, vo-tech, middle/junior high, adult education, secondary, bilingual/bicultural. **Reserve Officers Training Corps (ROTC):** Army ROTC: Offered on campus. **Faculty and instruction (2005-2006):** Total instructional faculty: 447 full-time, 159 part-time (51% men; 49% women; 11% minorities). Full-time faculty with Ph.D. or other terminal degree: 66%. Student/faculty ratio: 17/1. Classes of fewer than 20 students: 43%; of 20 to 49 students: 51%; of 50 or more students: 6%. **Advanced Placement and International Baccalaureate credit:** AP tests may be used for: Credit only. Scores accepted: 3. **Freshmen returning for sophomore year:** 68%. **Graduation rates:** Four-year: 18%; five-year: 34%; six-year: 37%.

COSTS AND FINANCIAL AID
Financial aid office: (870) 972-2310. **Expenses (2005-2006):** Tuition and fees 2005-2006: $5,440 in state, $12,145 out of state; room/board: $4,190. Estimated books and supplies: $1,000 personal expenses: $2,996. **Financial aid:** Priority filing date for institution's financial aid form: February 15; deadline: July 1. In 2005-2006, 89% of undergraduates applied for financial aid. Of those, 78% were determined to have financial need; 27% had their need fully met. Average financial aid package (proportion receiving): $6,000 (74%). Average amount of gift aid, such as scholarships or grants (proportion receiving): $5,400 (66%). Average amount of self-help aid, such as work study or loans (proportion receiving): $3,300 (50%). Average need-based loan (excluding PLUS or other private loans): $4,100. Among students who received need-based aid, the average percentage of need met: 55%. Among students who received aid based on merit, the average award (and the proportion receiving): $5,000 (11%). The average athletic scholarship (and the proportion receiving): $7,400 (4%). Average amount of debt of borrowers graduating in 2005: $18,500. Proportion who borrowed: 68%.

CAMPUS LIFE AND EXTRACURRICULAR ACTIVITIES
Campus housing available (% using): coed dorms (12%), women's dorms (34%), men's dorms (24%), fraternity housing (5%), apartments for married students (7%), apartment for single students (16%), other housing options (2%). Students who live in college-owned, operated, or affiliated housing: 21%. **Student employment:** During the 2005-2006 academic year, 10% of undergraduates worked on campus. Average per-year earnings: $3,500. **Clubs and organizations:** Number of student organizations: 148. Activities include: choral groups, concert band, dance, drama/theater, jazz band, marching band, music ensembles, musical theater, opera, pep band, radio station, stu-

dent government, student newspaper, symphony orchestra, television station, yearbook. Number of fraternities: 13; sororities: 9. Proportion of men in fraternities: 15%; of women in sororities: 7%. Average proportion of students who stay on campus on weekends: 6%. **Sports program (2005-2006):** Member of NCAA I. *Men's intercollegiate varsity sports:* baseball, basketball, cross-country, football, golf, track and field (indoor), track and field (outdoor). *Women's intercollegiate varsity sports:* basketball, bowling, cross-country, golf, soccer, tennis, track and field (indoor), track and field (outdoor), volleyball.

SERVICES AND FACILITIES

Basic services: nonremedial tutoring, placement service, health service, other. **Remedial assistance:** reading, math, writing, study skills, other. **Counseling services:** career, personal, academic, psychological. **For learning-disabled students:** School does not offer a structured program with separate admission and additional fees. Total undergraduates in learning-disabled program or receiving services: 116. Services include: remedial math, remedial English, remedial reading, tape recorders, note-taking services, readers, extended time for tests, other testing accomodations, other. **Library:** Number of titles: 595,791; number of current serial subscriptions: 1,691. **Information technology resources:** Students are not required to lease or own a computer. Number of campus computers available to all students: 510. School has a wireless network. Approximate number of users that can be accommodated: 6,500. Proportion of college-owned housing units wired for high-speed internet access: 100%. **Campus safety:** Security services offered: 24-hour foot-and-vehicle patrols, late-night transport/escort service, 24-hour emergency telephones, lighted pathways/sidewalks, student patrols, controlled dormitory access (key, security card, etc).

TRANSFER AND INTERNATIONAL STUDENTS

Transfer students: May apply for admission for the following academic terms: Fall, Spring, Summer. Applicants need a minimum number of credits to apply. For fall 2005: Transfer applications received: 1,446. Transfer applicants offered admission: 1,110. Transfer applicants enrolled: 842. **International students:** Number of foreign undergraduates: 83 (1% of student body). Number of countries represented: 38. Minimum TOEFL score required: 500 (paper); 173 (computer). Average TOEFL score: 500 (paper).

Arkansas Tech University

- **Address:** 1509 N. Boulder Avenue, Russellville, AR 72801-2222
- **Website:** http://www.atu.edu
- **Public**
- **Enrollment:** 5,365 full-time; 963 part-time

KEY STATS
- ✔ **U.S News College Ranking:** third tier, Universities–Master's (South)
- ✔ **ACT Score (25th/75th percentile):** 19-25
- ✔ **Tuition:** 2006-2007: $4,880 in state, $9,350 out of state

Selectivity: Selective	Room/board: $4,422
Acceptance rate: 48%	Average debt: $17,064
Student/faculty ratio: 19/1	Proportion who borrowed: 53%

UNDERGRADUATE STUDENT BODY STATS

2005-2006 enrollment: 5,365 full-time; 963 part-time. Men: 47%; women: 53%. **Ethnic makeup:** African American: 5%; American-Indian: 1%; Asian American: 1%; Hispanic: 2%; White: 89%; International: 2%.

ADMISSIONS FACTS AND FIGURES

Phone: (479) 968-0343. **Email:** tech.enroll@atu.edu. **Website:** http://www.atu.edu. **Application deadlines for fall 2007:** Regular decision: Rolling. Early decision: Not offered. Early action: Not offered. Admission can be deferred. Common application is not accepted. **To apply online, go to:** http://admissions.atu.edu. **Admissions requirements/recommendations:** High school units required (recommended): English: 4; Mathematics: 4; Science: 3; Foreign language: 0 (2); Social studies: 1; History: 2; Academic electives: 4; Total units: 21. Tests: The college uses SAT or ACT scores in admissions decisions. Either SAT or ACT required. For admission to the fall 2007 entering class, the school will accept: ACT with writing, ACT without writing. Campus visit: Recommended. Admissions interview: Neither required nor recommended. Off-campus interview: May be arranged. **Factors that count in admissions decisions:** *Academic:* Secondary school record: Very important. Class rank: Considered. Letters of recommendation:

Not considered. Standardized test scores: Very important. Essay: Not considered. *Nonacademic:* Interview: Not considered. Extracurricular activities: Not considered. Talent/ability: Not considered. Character/personal qualities: Not considered. Alumni/ae relationship: Not considered. Geographical residence: Not considered. State residency: Not considered. Religious affiliation/commitment: Not considered. Minority status: Not considered. Volunteer work: Not considered. Work experience: Not considered. **Other schools with the greatest overlap in applicants:** University of Arkansas, University of Central Arkansas. **Admissions statistics for the fall 2005 entering class:** Total applicants: 3,459. Total accepted: 1,673. Freshmen enrolled: 1,529; 4% were from out of state. Overall acceptance rate: 48%. **Credentials of fall 2005 freshmen:** 17% ranked in the top 10 percent of their high school class; 43% were in the top 25 percent, and 70% were in the top half. (Proportion submitting class standing: 87%.) **Average high school grade point average:** 3.2. **First-year students who submitted SAT scores:** 1%. Scores (25/75 percentile): Verbal: 410-510, Math: 480-550, Combined: 890-1060. **First-year students submitting ACT scores:** 82%. Scores (25/75 percentile): English: 19-27, Math: 18-25, Composite: 19-25.

ACADEMICS

Year founded: 1909. **Academic calendar:** Semester. **Degrees offered:** certificate, associate, terminal-associate, bachelor's, master's. **Most popular majors:** 11% business administration and management, 7% early childhood education and teaching, 7% nursing/registered nurse training (R.N., A.S.N., B.S.N., M.S.N.), 5% history, 5% physical education teaching and coaching. **Major fields of study:** agriculture, agriculture operations, and related sciences; biological and biomedical sciences; business, management, marketing, and related support services; communication, journalism, and related programs; computer and information sciences and support services; education; engineering; English language and literature/letters; foreign languages, literatures, and linguistics; health professions and related clinical sciences; history; liberal arts and sciences studies, and humanities; mathematics and statistics; multi/interdisciplinary studies; parks, recreation, leisure, and fitness studies; physical sciences; psychology; security and protective services; social sciences; visual and performing arts. **Areas of required coursework:** arts/fine arts, humanities, computer literacy, mathematics, English (including composition), sciences (biological or physical), history, social science, other. **Special academic programs:** accelerated program, cooperative (work-study plan) program, distance learning, double major, dual enrollment, English as a Second Language (ESL), external degree program, honors program, independent study, internships, student-designed major, teacher certificate program, weekend college. **Teacher certification offered in:** early childhood, elementary, middle/junior high, secondary, bilingual/bicultural. **Reserve Officers Training Corps (ROTC):** Army ROTC: Offered at cooperating institution (University of Central Arkansas). **Faculty and instruction (2005-2006):** Total instructional faculty: 252 full-time, 146 part-time (45% men; 55% women; 6% minorities). Full-time faculty with Ph.D. or other terminal degree: 62%. Student/faculty ratio: 19/1. Classes of fewer than 20 students: 37%; of 20 to 49 students: 54%; of 50 or more students: 9%. **Advanced Placement and International Baccalaureate credit:** International Baccalaureate exams may be used for: Placement only. **Freshmen returning for sophomore year:** 67%. **Graduation rates:** Four-year: 18%; five-year: 31%; six-year: 38%.

COSTS AND FINANCIAL AID

Financial aid office: (479) 968-0399. **Expenses (2006-2007):** Tuition and fees 2006-2007: $4,880 in state, $9,350 out of state; room/board: $4,422. Estimated books and supplies: $1,090 personal expenses: $2,280. **Financial aid:** Priority filing date for institution's financial aid form: April 15. In 2005-2006, 72% of undergraduates applied for financial aid. Of those, 63% were determined to have financial need; 25% had their need fully met. Average financial aid package (proportion receiving): $4,381 (63%). Average amount of gift aid, such as scholarships or grants (proportion receiving): $2,478 (47%). Average amount of self-help aid, such as work study or loans (proportion receiving): $1,903 (38%). Average need-based loan (excluding PLUS or other private loans): $1,826. Among students who received need-based aid, the average percentage of need met: 41%. Among students who received aid based on merit, the average award (and the proportion receiving): $5,643 (18%). The average athletic scholarship (and the proportion receiving): $3,717 (4%). Average amount of debt of borrowers graduating in 2005: $17,064. Proportion who borrowed: 53%.

CAMPUS LIFE AND EXTRACURRICULAR ACTIVITIES

Campus housing available: coed dorms, women's dorms, men's dorms, apartment for single students, special housing for disabled students. Students who live in college-owned, operated, or affiliated housing: 31%. **Clubs and organizations:** Number of student organizations: 111. Activities include: choral groups, concert band, dance, drama/theater, jazz band, literary magazine, marching band, music ensembles, musical theater, opera, pep band, radio station, student government, student newspaper, symphony orchestra, television station, yearbook. Number of fraternities: 5; sororities: 2. Proportion of men in fraternities: 5%; of women in sororities: 4%. **Sports program (2005-2006):** Member of NCAA II. *Men's intercollegiate varsity sports:* baseball, basketball, football, golf. *Women's intercollegiate varsity sports:* basketball, cross-country, golf, softball, tennis, volleyball.

SERVICES AND FACILITIES

Basic services: nonremedial tutoring, placement service, health service, health insurance. **Remedial assistance:** reading, math, writing, other. **Counseling services:** minority student, career, personal, academic, older student, psychological. **For learning-disabled students:** School does not offer a structured program with separate admission and additional fees. Total undergraduates in learning-disabled program or receiving services: 69. Services include: remedial math, remedial English, reading machines, remedial reading, tape recorders, untimed tests, note-taking services, oral tests, readers, extended time for tests, tutors, exams on tape or computer, other testing accomodations. **Library:** Number of titles: 281,445; number of current serial subscriptions: 1,038. **Information technology resources:** Students are not required to lease or own a computer. Number of campus computers available to all students: 628. School has a wireless network. Approximate number of users that can be accommodated: 600. Proportion of college-owned housing units wired for high-speed internet access: 99%. **Campus safety:** Security services offered: 24-hour foot-and-vehicle patrols, late-night transport/escort service, 24-hour emergency telephones, lighted pathways/sidewalks, student patrols, controlled dormitory access (key, security card, etc).

TRANSFER AND INTERNATIONAL STUDENTS

Transfer students: May apply for admission for the following academic terms: Fall, Spring, Summer. Applicants do not need a minimum number of credits to apply. For fall 2005: Transfer applications received: 785. Transfer applicants offered admission: 392. Transfer applicants enrolled: 326. **International students:** Number of foreign undergraduates: 124 (2% of student body). Number of countries represented: 32. Minimum TOEFL score required: 500 (paper); 173 (computer).

Harding University

- **Address:** 900 E. Market Avenue, Searcy, AR 72149
- **Website:** http://www.harding.edu
- **Private; Religious affiliation:** Church of Christ
- **Enrollment:** 3,879 full-time; 213 part-time

KEY STATS

✔ **U.S News College Ranking:** 24, Universities–Master's (South)
✔ **ACT Score (25th/75th percentile):** 20-26
✔ **Tuition:** 2006-2007: $11,650

Selectivity: More selective	**Room/board:** $5,442
Acceptance rate: 62%	**Average debt:** $16,310
Student/faculty ratio: 18/1	**Proportion who borrowed:** 66%

UNDERGRADUATE STUDENT BODY STATS

2005-2006 enrollment: 3,879 full-time; 213 part-time. Men: 46%; women: 54%. **Ethnic makeup:** African American: 4%; American-Indian: 1%; Asian American: 1%; Hispanic: 1%; White: 89%; International: 4%.

ADMISSIONS FACTS AND FIGURES

Phone: (800) 477-4407. **Email:** admissions@harding.edu. **Website:** http://www.harding.edu. **Application deadlines for fall 2007:** Regular decision: July 1. Early decision: Not offered. Early action: Not offered. Admission can be deferred. **Application fee:** $35. Common application is not accepted. **Admissions requirements/recommendations:** High school units required (recommended): English: 4 (4); Mathematics: 3 (4); Science: 2 (4); Foreign language: (2); Social studies: 3 (4); Academic electives: 3 (2); Total units: 15 (20). Tests: The college uses SAT or ACT scores in admissions decisions. Either SAT or ACT required. For admission to the fall 2007 entering class, the school will accept: ACT with writing, ACT without writing. Campus visit: Required. Admissions interview: Required. Off-campus interview: May be arranged. **Factors that count in admissions decisions:** *Academic:* Secondary school record: Very important. Class rank: Important. Letters of recommenda-

tion: Very important. Standardized test scores: Very important. Essay: Considered. *Nonacademic:* Interview: Very important. Extracurricular activities: Considered. Talent/ability: Important. Character/personal qualities: Very important. Alumni/ae relationship: Considered. Geographical residence: Considered. State residency: Considered. Religious affiliation/commitment: Not considered. Minority status: Not considered. Volunteer work: Considered. Work experience: Considered. **Other schools with the greatest overlap in applicants:** Abilene Christian University; Arkansas State University; University of Arkansas; University of Tennessee; University of Texas–Austin. **Admissions statistics for the fall 2005 entering class:** Total applicants: 1,658. Total accepted: 1,020. Freshmen enrolled: 960; 77% were from out of state. Overall acceptance rate: 62%. Size of waiting list: 0 applicants; enrolled from waiting list: 0. **Credentials of fall 2005 freshmen:** 27% ranked in the top 10 percent of their high school class; 52% were in the top 25 percent, and 76% were in the top half. (Proportion submitting class standing: 75%.) **Average high school grade point average:** 3.5. **First-year students who submitted SAT scores:** 41%. Scores (25/75 percentile): Verbal: 500-630, Math: 490-630, Combined: 990-1260. **First-year students submitting ACT scores:** 75%. Scores (25/75 percentile): English: 20-28, Math: 19-26, Composite: 20-26.

ACADEMICS

Year founded: 1924. **Academic calendar:** Semester. **Degrees offered:** bachelor's, master's, doctorate. **Most popular majors:** 20% business, management, marketing, and related support services, 15% education, 9% health professions and related clinical sciences, 6% computer and information sciences and support services, 6% theology and religious vocations. **Major fields of study:** area, ethnic, cultural, and gender studies; biological and biomedical sciences; business, management, marketing, and related support services; communication, journalism, and related programs; computer and information sciences and support services; education; engineering; English language and literature/letters; family and consumer sciences/human sciences; foreign languages, literatures, and linguistics; health professions and related clinical sciences; history; legal professions and studies; liberal arts and sciences studies, and humanities; mathematics and statistics; multi/interdisciplinary studies; parks, recreation, leisure, and fitness studies; philosophy and religious studies; physical sciences; psychology; public administration and social service professions; security and protective services; social sciences; theology and religious vocations; visual and performing arts. **Areas of required coursework:** arts/fine arts, humanities, mathematics, English (including composition), philosophy, sciences (biological or physical), history, social science, other. **Pre-professional programs:** pre-law, pre-dentistry, pre-medicine, pre-theology, pre-veterinary science, pre-optometry, pre-pharmacy. **Special academic programs (% participation):** accelerated program (1%), cooperative (work-study plan) program (5%), distance learning, double major (9%), dual enrollment (2%), English as a Second Language (ESL) (1%), exchange student program (domestic) (1%), honors program (18%), independent study (3%), internships (35%), liberal arts/career combination (1%), study abroad (28%), teacher certificate program (13%). **Teacher certification offered in:** early childhood, special education, elementary, middle/junior high, adult education, secondary, bilingual/bicultural. **Cooperative education programs:** art, business, computer science, education, engineering, health professions, home economics, humanities, natural science, social/behavioral science. **Reserve Officers Training Corps (ROTC):** Army ROTC: Offered at cooperating institution (University of Central Arkansas). **Faculty and instruction (2005-2006):** Total instructional faculty: 226 full-time, 106 part-time (60% men; 40% women; 2% minorities). Full-time faculty with Ph.D. or other terminal degree: 60%. Student/faculty ratio: 18/1. Classes of fewer than 20 students: 51%; of 20 to 49 students: 38%; of 50 or more students: 10%. **Advanced Placement and International Baccalaureate credit:** AP tests may be used for: Credit and/or placement. Scores accepted: 3, 4, 5. International Baccalaureate exams may be used for: Credit and/or placement. **Freshmen returning for sophomore year:** 80%. **Graduation rates:** Four-year: 33%; five-year: 54%; six-year: 59%. **Graduate study:** 20% of students pursue further study immediately upon graduation; 25% within one year; 35% within five years. Fields in which graduates pursue further study: Master of Business Administration (MBA), 20%; law, 5%; medicine, 10%; dentistry, 3%; engineering, 2%; theology (or the seminary), 15%; education, 30%; arts and sciences, 15%.

COSTS AND FINANCIAL AID

Financial aid office: (501) 279-5278. **Expenses (2006-2007):** Tuition and fees 2006-2007: $11,650; room/board: $5,442. Estimated books and supplies: $850; transportation: $1,000; personal expenses: $1,000. **Financial aid:** Priority filing date for institution's financial aid form: April 15. In 2005-2006, 76% of undergraduates applied for financial aid. Of those, 56% were determined to have financial need; 22% had their need fully met. Average financial aid package (proportion receiving): $8,584 (56%). Average amount of gift aid, such as scholarships or grants (proportion receiving): $4,990

(47%). Average amount of self-help aid, such as work study or loans (proportion receiving): $4,703 (48%). Average need-based loan (excluding PLUS or other private loans): $4,583. Among students who received need-based aid, the average percentage of need met: 68%. Among students who received aid based on merit, the average award (and the proportion receiving): $3,370 (48%). The average athletic scholarship (and the proportion receiving): $6,145 (2%). Average amount of debt of borrowers graduating in 2005: $16,310. Proportion who borrowed: 66%.

CAMPUS LIFE AND EXTRACURRICULAR ACTIVITIES

Campus housing available (% using): women's dorms (53%), men's dorms (38%), apartments for married students (4%), apartment for single students (5%), special housing for disabled students. Students who live in college-owned, operated, or affiliated housing: 72%. **Student employment:** During the 2005-2006 academic year, 30% of undergraduates worked on campus. Average per-year earnings: $1,500. **Clubs and organizations:** Number of student organizations: 80. Activities include: choral groups, concert band, drama/theater, jazz band, marching band, music ensembles, musical theater, pep band, radio station, student government, student newspaper, symphony orchestra, television station, yearbook. Number of fraternities: 15; sororities: 15. Proportion of men in fraternities: 41%; of women in sororities: 43%. Average proportion of students who stay on campus on weekends: 90%. **Sports program (2005-2006):** Member of NCAA II. *Men's intercollegiate varsity sports:* baseball, basketball, cross-country, football, golf, soccer, tennis, track and field (indoor), track and field (outdoor). *Women's intercollegiate varsity sports:* basketball, cross-country, golf, soccer, tennis, track and field (indoor), track and field (outdoor), volleyball.

SERVICES AND FACILITIES

Basic services: nonremedial tutoring, placement service, day care, health service, health insurance. **Remedial assistance:** reading, math, writing, study skills. **Counseling services:** minority student, career, personal, academic, psychological, religious. **For learning-disabled students:** School does not offer a structured program with separate admission and additional fees. Total undergraduates in learning-disabled program or receiving services: 144. Services include: remedial math, remedial English, reading machines, remedial reading, tape recorders, other special classes, note-taking services, oral tests, readers, extended time for tests, tutors, priority registration, priority seating, texts on tape, other. **Library:** Number of titles: 236,733; number of current serial subscriptions: 15,232. **Information technology resources:** Students are not required to lease or own a computer. Number of campus computers available to all students: 500. School has a wireless network. Approximate number of users that can be accommodated: 250. Proportion of college-owned housing units wired for high-speed internet access: 100%. **Campus safety:** Security services offered: 24-hour foot-and-vehicle patrols, late-night transport/escort service, 24-hour emergency telephones, lighted pathways/sidewalks, student patrols, controlled dormitory access (key, security card, etc).

TRANSFER AND INTERNATIONAL STUDENTS

Transfer students: May apply for admission for the following academic terms: Fall, Spring, Summer. Applicants need a minimum number of credits to apply. For fall 2005: Transfer applications received: 291. Transfer applicants offered admission: 208. Transfer applicants enrolled: 185. **International students:** Number of foreign undergraduates: 148 (4% of student body). Number of countries represented: 45. Minimum TOEFL score required: 500 (paper); 173 (computer). Average TOEFL score: 550 (paper).

Henderson State University

- ■ **Address:** 1100 Henderson Street, Arkadelphia, AR 71999-0001
- ■ **Website:** http://www.getreddie.com
- ■ **Public**
- ■ **Enrollment:** 2,713 full-time; 376 part-time

KEY STATS

✔ **U.S News College Ranking:** third tier, Universities–Master's (South)
✔ **ACT Score (25th/75th percentile):** 19-25
✔ **Tuition:** 2006-2007: $5,210 in state, $9,620 out of state

Selectivity: Selective	**Room/board:** $4,176
Acceptance rate: 60%	**Average debt:** $17,800
Student/faculty ratio: 14/1	**Proportion who borrowed:** 34%

UNDERGRADUATE STUDENT BODY STATS

2005-2006 enrollment: 2,713 full-time; 376 part-time. Men: 43%; women: 57%. **Ethnic makeup:** African American: 18%; American-Indian: 1%; Hispanic: 2%; White: 77%; International: 2%.

ADMISSIONS FACTS AND FIGURES

Phone: (870) 230-5028. **Email:** admissions@hsu.edu. **Website:** http://www.getreddie.com. **Application deadlines for fall 2007:** Regular decision: July 15. Early decision: Not offered. Early action: Not offered. Admission can be deferred. Common application is not accepted. **To apply online, go to:** http://www.hsu.edu/dept/ura/application.html. **Admissions requirements/recommendations:** High school units required (recommended): English: 4 (4); Mathematics: 4 (4); Science: 3 (3); Foreign language: 0 (2); Social studies: 2 (2); History: 1 (2); Academic electives: 0 (3); Total units: 14 (22). Tests: The college uses SAT or ACT scores in admissions decisions. Either SAT or ACT required. For admission to the fall 2007 entering class, the school will accept: ACT with writing, ACT without writing. Campus visit: Recommended. Admissions interview: Neither required nor recommended. Off-campus interview: Not available. **Factors that count in admissions decisions:** *Academic:* Secondary school record: Very important. Class rank: Considered. Letters of recommendation: Considered. Standardized test scores: Very important. Essay: Considered. *Nonacademic:* Interview: Considered. Extracurricular activities: Not considered. Talent/ability: Not considered. Character/personal qualities: Considered. Alumni/ae relationship: Not considered. Geographical residence: Not considered. State residency: Not considered. Religious affiliation/commitment: Not considered. Minority status: Not considered. Volunteer work: Not considered. Work experience: Not considered. **Admissions statistics for the fall 2005 entering class:** Total applicants: 2,020. Total accepted: 1,206. Freshmen enrolled: 425; 16% were from out of state. Overall acceptance rate: 60%. **Credentials of fall 2005 freshmen:** 18% ranked in the top 10 percent of their high school class; 43% were in the top 25 percent, and 75% were in the top half. (Proportion submitting class standing: 87%.) **Average high school grade point average:** 3.3. **First-year students who submitted SAT scores:** 5%. Scores (25/75 percentile): Verbal: 420-540, Math: 460-600, Combined: 880-1140. **First-year students submitting ACT scores:** 95%. Scores (25/75 percentile): English: N/A, Math: N/A, Composite: 19-25.

ACADEMICS

Year founded: 1890. **Academic calendar:** Semester. **Degrees offered:** associate, bachelor's, master's. **Most popular majors:** 26% education, 25% business, management, marketing, and related support services, 9% social sciences, 6% health professions and related clinical sciences, 6% visual and performing arts. **Major fields of study:** biological and biomedical sciences; business, management, marketing, and related support services; communication, journalism, and related programs; computer and information sciences and support services; education; English language and literature/letters; family and consumer sciences/human sciences; foreign languages, literatures, and linguistics; health professions and related clinical sciences; history; mathematics and statistics; parks, recreation, leisure, and fitness studies; physical sciences; psychology; public administration and social service professions; social sciences; transportation and materials moving; visual and performing arts. **Areas of required coursework:** arts/fine arts, humanities, mathematics, English (including composition), sciences (biological or physical), history, social science, other. **Pre-professional programs:** pre-law, pre-dentistry, pre-medicine, pre-optometry, pre-pharmacy. **Special academic programs:** cross-registration, honors program, internships, liberal arts/career combination, teacher certificate program. **Teacher certification offered in:** early childhood, special education, elementary, middle/junior high, secondary. **Reserve Officers Training Corps (ROTC):** Army ROTC: Offered on campus. **Faculty and instruction (2005-2006):** Total instructional faculty: 162 full-time, 67 part-time (53% men; 47% women; 7% minorities). Full-time faculty with Ph.D. or other terminal degree: 95%. Student/faculty ratio: 14/1. **Freshmen returning for sophomore year:** 63%. **Graduation rates:** Four-year: 12%; five-year: 30%; six-year: 32%.

COSTS AND FINANCIAL AID

Financial aid office: (870) 230-5148. **Expenses (2006-2007):** Tuition and fees 2006-2007: $5,210 in state, $9,620 out of state; room/board: $4,176. **Financial aid:** Priority filing date for institution's financial aid form: June 1; deadline: June 1. Average amount of debt of borrowers graduating in 2005: $17,800. Proportion who borrowed: 34%.

CAMPUS LIFE AND EXTRACURRICULAR ACTIVITIES

Campus housing available: women's dorms, men's dorms, special housing for international students, cooperative housing, other housing options.

Students who live in college-owned, operated, or affiliated housing: 28%. **Clubs and organizations:** Number of student organizations: 80. Activities include: choral groups, concert band, dance, drama/theater, jazz band, literary magazine, marching band, music ensembles, radio station, student government, student newspaper, symphony orchestra, television station, yearbook. Number of fraternities: 8; sororities: 7. Average proportion of students who stay on campus on weekends: 12%. **Sports program (2005-2006):** Member of NCAA II. *Men's intercollegiate varsity sports:* baseball, basketball, football, golf, swimming and diving. *Women's intercollegiate varsity sports:* basketball, cross-country, golf, softball, swimming and diving, tennis, volleyball.

SERVICES AND FACILITIES

Basic services: nonremedial tutoring, health service. **Remedial assistance:** reading, math, writing. **Counseling services:** minority student, career, veteran student, academic, psychological. **For learning-disabled students:** School does not offer a structured program with separate admission and additional fees. Services include: tape recorders, untimed tests, note-taking services, tutors, texts on tape. **Library:** Number of titles: 260,443; number of current serial subscriptions: 1,496. **Information technology resources:** Students are not required to lease or own a computer. Number of campus computers available to all students: 350. School has a wireless network. Approximate number of users that can be accommodated: 500. Proportion of college-owned housing units wired for high-speed internet access: 100%. **Campus safety:** Security services offered: 24-hour foot-and-vehicle patrols, 24-hour emergency telephones, lighted pathways/sidewalks, controlled dormitory access (key, security card, etc).

TRANSFER AND INTERNATIONAL STUDENTS

Transfer students: May apply for admission for the following academic terms: Fall, Spring, Summer. Applicants need a minimum number of credits to apply. For fall 2005: Transfer applications received: 732. Transfer applicants offered admission: 421. Transfer applicants enrolled: 345. **International students:** Number of foreign undergraduates: 63 (2% of student body). Number of countries represented: 27. Minimum TOEFL score required: 500 (paper); 173 (computer).

Hendrix College

- **Address:** 1600 Washington Avenue, Conway, AR 72032
- **Website:** http://www.hendrix.edu
- **Private; Religious affiliation:** United Methodist
- **Enrollment:** 1,001 full-time; 21 part-time

KEY STATS

✔ **U.S News College Ranking:** 69, Liberal Arts Colleges
✔ **ACT Score (25th/75th percentile):** 25-30
✔ **Tuition:** 2006-2007: $22,916

Selectivity: More selective	**Room/board:** $6,358
Acceptance rate: 83%	**Average debt:** $14,885
Student/faculty ratio: 11/1	**Proportion who borrowed:** 77%

UNDERGRADUATE STUDENT BODY STATS

2005-2006 enrollment: 1,001 full-time; 21 part-time. Men: 44%; women: 56%. **Ethnic makeup:** African American: 4%; American-Indian: 1%; Asian American: 3%; Hispanic: 3%; White: 89%. **Religious preference:** Roman Catholic: 10%; Protestant: 24%; Jewish: 2%; No preference: 3%; Unknown: 39%; United Methodist: 19%; Other: 3%.

ADMISSIONS FACTS AND FIGURES

Phone: (800) 277-9017. **Email:** adm@hendrix.edu. **Website:** http://www.hendrix.edu. **Application deadlines for fall 2007:** Regular decision: August 1. Early decision: Not offered. Early action: Not offered. Admission can be deferred. **Application fee:** $40. Common application is accepted. **To apply online, go to:** http://www.hendrix.edu/admission/applicationprcs.htm. **Admissions requirements/recommendations:** High school units required (recommended): English: 4 (4); Mathematics: 3 (3); Science: 2 (2); Foreign language: 2 (2); Social studies: 3 (3); History: 0 (0); Academic electives: 0 (0); Total units: 14 (14). Tests: The college uses SAT or ACT scores in admissions decisions. Either SAT or ACT required. For admission to the fall 2007 entering class, the school will accept: ACT with writing, ACT without writing. Campus visit: Recommended. Admissions interview: Recommended.

Off-campus interview: May be arranged. **Factors that count in admissions decisions:** *Academic:* Secondary school record: Very important. Class rank: Important. Letters of recommendation: Important. Standardized test scores: Very important. Essay: Very important. *Nonacademic:* Interview: Important. Extracurricular activities: Important. Talent/ability: Considered. Character/personal qualities: Important. Alumni/ae relationship: Not considered. Geographical residence: Not considered. State residency: Not considered. Religious affiliation/commitment: Not considered. Minority status: Considered. Volunteer work: Considered. Work experience: Not considered. **Other schools with the greatest overlap in applicants:** Louisiana State University–Baton Rouge; Millsaps College; Rhodes College; University of Arkansas; University of Central Arkansas. **Admissions statistics for the fall 2005 entering class:** Total applicants: 1,086. Total accepted: 896. Freshmen enrolled: 281; 47% were from out of state. Overall acceptance rate: 83%. **Size of waiting list:** 10 applicants; enrolled from waiting list: 0. **Credentials of fall 2005 freshmen:** 37% ranked in the top 10 percent of their high school class; 73% were in the top 25 percent, and 91% were in the top half. (Proportion submitting class standing: 69%.) **Average high school grade point average:** 3.6. **First-year students who submitted SAT scores:** 63%. Scores (25/75 percentile): Verbal: 590-700, Math: 560-670, Combined: 1150-1370. **First-year students submitting ACT scores:** 84%. Scores (25/75 percentile): English: 26-32, Math: 23-28, Composite: 25-30.

ACADEMICS

Year founded: 1876. **Academic calendar:** Semester. **Degrees offered:** bachelor's, master's. **Most popular majors:** 22% social sciences, 16% psychology, 14% biological and biomedical sciences, 11% history, 7% visual and performing arts. **Major fields of study:** area, ethnic, cultural, and gender studies; biological and biomedical sciences; business, management, marketing, and related support services; computer and information sciences and support services; education; English language and literature/letters; foreign languages, literatures, and linguistics; history; mathematics and statistics; multi/interdisciplinary studies; natural resources and conservation; parks, recreation, leisure, and fitness studies; philosophy and religious studies; physical sciences; psychology; social sciences; visual and performing arts. **Areas of required coursework:** arts/fine arts, humanities, mathematics, English (including composition), philosophy, foreign languages, sciences (biological or physical), history, social science, other. **Pre-professional programs:** pre-law, pre-dentistry, pre-medicine, pre-theology, pre-veterinary science, pre-pharmacy, other. **Special academic programs (% participation):** double major (10%), independent study (40%), internships (15%), student-designed major (4%), study abroad (16%), teacher certificate program (4%). **Teacher certification offered in:** early childhood, elementary, secondary. **Reserve Officers Training Corps (ROTC):** Army ROTC: Offered at cooperating institution (University of Central Arkansas). **Faculty and instruction (2005-2006):** Total instructional faculty: 85 full-time, 22 part-time (60% men; 40% women; 8% minorities). Full-time faculty with Ph.D. or other terminal degree: 100%. Student/faculty ratio: 11/1. Classes of fewer than 20 students: 67%; of 20 to 49 students: 33%; of 50 or more students: 0%. **Advanced Placement and International Baccalaureate credit:** AP tests may be used for: Credit and/or placement. Scores accepted: 4, 5. International Baccalaureate exams may be used for: Credit and/or placement. **Freshmen returning for sophomore year:** 84%. **Graduation rates:** Four-year: 55%; five-year: 58%; six-year: 61%. **Graduate study:** 56% of students pursue further study immediately upon graduation; 58% within one year. Fields in which graduates pursue further study: Master of Business Administration (MBA), 10%; law, 5%; medicine, 10%; dentistry, 1%; education, 9%; arts and sciences, 10%; veterinary medicine, 1%.

COSTS AND FINANCIAL AID

Financial aid office: (501) 450-1368. **Expenses (2006-2007):** Tuition and fees 2006-2007: $22,916; room/board: $6,358. Estimated books and supplies: $900; transportation: $900; personal expenses: $1,928. **Financial aid:** Priority filing date for institution's financial aid form: February 15. In 2005-2006, 72% of undergraduates applied for financial aid. Of those, 56% were determined to have financial need; 34% had their need fully met. Average financial aid package (proportion receiving): $15,269 (56%). Average amount of gift aid, such as scholarships or grants (proportion receiving): $10,927 (55%). Average amount of self-help aid, such as work study or loans (proportion receiving): $5,438 (46%). Average need-based loan (excluding PLUS or other private loans): $4,438. Among students who received need-based aid, the average percentage of need met: 82%. Among students who received aid based on merit, the average award (and the proportion receiving): $15,672 (42%). The average athletic scholarship (and the proportion receiving): $0 (0%). Average amount of debt of borrowers graduating in 2005: $14,885. Proportion who borrowed: 77%.

CAMPUS LIFE AND EXTRACURRICULAR ACTIVITIES

Campus housing available (% using): coed dorms (27%), women's dorms (34%), men's dorms (30%), apartment for single students (8%), other housing options (1%). Students who live in college-owned, operated, or affiliated housing: 85%. **Student employment:** During the 2005-2006 academic year, 19% of undergraduates worked on campus. Average per-year earnings: $1,165. **Clubs and organizations:** Number of student organizations: 78. Activities include: choral groups, concert band, dance, drama/theater, jazz band, literary magazine, music ensembles, musical theater, pep band, radio station, student government, student newspaper, symphony orchestra, yearbook. Number of fraternities: 0; sororities: 0. Average proportion of students who stay on campus on weekends: 75%. **Sports program (2005-2006):** Member of NCAA III. *Men's intercollegiate varsity sports:* baseball, basketball, cross-country, golf, soccer, swimming and diving, tennis, track and field (outdoor). *Women's intercollegiate varsity sports:* basketball, cross-country, golf, soccer, softball, swimming and diving, tennis, track and field (outdoor), volleyball.

SERVICES AND FACILITIES

Basic services: nonremedial tutoring, placement service, health service, health insurance. **Counseling services:** minority student, career, military, personal, veteran student, academic, older student, psychological, birth control, religious, other. **For learning-disabled students:** School does not offer a structured program with separate admission and additional fees. Total undergraduates in learning-disabled program or receiving services: 16. Services include: tape recorders, extended time for tests, tutors, priority registration, texts on tape, other testing accomodations. **Library:** Number of titles: 218,390; number of current serial subscriptions: 617. **Information technology resources:** Students are not required to lease or own a computer. Number of campus computers available to all students: 75. School has a wireless network. Approximate number of users that can be accommodated: 300. Proportion of college-owned housing units wired for high-speed internet access: 100%. **Campus safety:** Security services offered: 24-hour foot-and-vehicle patrols, late-night transport/escort service, 24-hour emergency telephones, lighted pathways/sidewalks, controlled dormitory access (key, security card, etc).

TRANSFER AND INTERNATIONAL STUDENTS

Transfer students: May apply for admission for the following academic terms: Fall, Spring. Applicants need a minimum number of credits to apply. For fall 2005: Transfer applications received: 43. Transfer applicants offered admission: 26. Transfer applicants enrolled: 14. **International students:** Number of foreign undergraduates: 5 (1% of student body). Number of countries represented: 5. Minimum TOEFL score required: 550 (paper); 215 (computer). Average TOEFL score: 601 (paper).

John Brown University

- **Address:** 2000 W. University Street, Siloam Springs, AR 72761
- **Website:** http://www.jbu.edu
- **Private; Religious affiliation:** Protestant interdenominational
- **Enrollment:** 1,581 full-time; 78 part-time

KEY STATS

✔ **U.S News College Ranking:** 6, Comp. Colleges–Bachelor's (South)
✔ **ACT Score (25th/75th percentile):** 22-28
✔ **Tuition:** 2006-2007: $16,158

Selectivity: More selective	**Room/board:** $5,956
Acceptance rate: 62%	**Average debt:** $19,262
Student/faculty ratio: 12/1	**Proportion who borrowed:** 60%

UNDERGRADUATE STUDENT BODY STATS

2005-2006 enrollment: 1,581 full-time; 78 part-time. Men: 49%; women: 51%. **Ethnic makeup:** African American: 3%; American-Indian: 2%; Asian American: 1%; Hispanic: 3%; White: 85%; International: 6%.

ADMISSIONS FACTS AND FIGURES

Phone: (877) 528-4636. **Email:** jbuinfo@jbu.edu. **Website:** http://www.jbu.edu. **Application deadlines for fall 2007:** Regular decision: Rolling. Early decision: Not offered. Early action: Not offered. Admission can be deferred. **Application fee:** $25. Common application is not accepted. **To apply online, go to:** http://www.jbu.edu/apply_online. **Admissions requirements/recommendations:** High school units required (recommended): English: (4); Mathematics: (3); Science: (2); Foreign language: (2);

Social studies: (2); History: (1); Total units: (14). Tests: The college uses SAT or ACT scores in admissions decisions. Either SAT or ACT required. For admission to the fall 2007 entering class, the school will accept: ACT with writing, ACT without writing. Campus visit: Recommended. Admissions interview: Recommended. Off-campus interview: May be arranged. **Factors that count in admissions decisions:** *Academic:* Secondary school record: Very important. Class rank: Considered. Letters of recommendation: Very important. Standardized test scores: Very important. Essay: Important. *Nonacademic:* Interview: Important. Extracurricular activities: Considered. Talent/ability: Considered. Character/personal qualities: Important. Alumni/ae relationship: Considered. Geographical residence: Not considered. State residency: Not considered. Religious affiliation/commitment: Important. Minority status: Not considered. Volunteer work: Not considered. Work experience: Not considered. **Other schools with the greatest overlap in applicants:** Azusa Pacific University; Oklahoma Baptist University; Oklahoma State University; Texas A&M University–College Station; University of Arkansas. **Admissions statistics for the fall 2005 entering class:** Total applicants: 874. Total accepted: 545. Freshmen enrolled: 262; 72% were from out of state. Overall acceptance rate: 62%. **Credentials of fall 2005 freshmen:** 29% ranked in the top 10 percent of their high school class; 59% were in the top 25 percent, and 87% were in the top half. (Proportion submitting class standing: 51%.) **Average high school grade point average:** 3.6. **First-year students who submitted SAT scores:** 40%. Scores (25/75 percentile): Verbal: 540-660, Math: 510-640, Combined: 1050-1300. **First-year students submitting ACT scores:** 77%. Scores (25/75 percentile): English: 22-29, Math: 21-26, Composite: 22-28.

ACADEMICS

Year founded: 1919. **Academic calendar:** Semester. **Degrees offered:** associate, bachelor's, master's. **Most popular majors:** 58% business, management, marketing, and related support services, 9% communication, journalism, and related programs, 6% visual and performing arts, 5% education, 4% theology and religious vocations. **Major fields of study:** biological and biomedical sciences; business, management, marketing, and related support services; communication, journalism, and related programs; computer and information sciences and support services; education; engineering; English language and literature/letters; family and consumer sciences/human sciences; foreign languages, literatures, and linguistics; health professions and related clinical sciences; history; mathematics and statistics; multi/interdisciplinary studies; natural resources and conservation; parks, recreation, leisure, and fitness studies; physical sciences; social sciences; theology and religious vocations; visual and performing arts. **Areas of required coursework:** arts/fine arts, humanities, mathematics, English (including composition), philosophy, foreign languages, sciences (biological or physical), history, social science, other. **Pre-professional programs:** pre-law, pre-dentistry, pre-medicine, pre-theology, pre-veterinary science, pre-optometry, pre-pharmacy. **Special academic programs (% participation):** cooperative (work-study plan) program (40%), distance learning (5%), double major (5%), English as a Second Language (ESL) (2%), exchange student program (domestic) (2%), honors program (12%), independent study (2%), internships (60%), study abroad (10%). **Teacher certification offered in:** early childhood, special education, elementary, middle/junior high, secondary. **Reserve Officers Training Corps (ROTC):** Army ROTC: Offered at cooperating institution (University of Arkansas); Air Force ROTC: Offered on campus. **Faculty and instruction (2005-2006):** Total instructional faculty: 83 full-time, 65 part-time (73% men; 27% women; 3% minorities). Full-time faculty with Ph.D. or other terminal degree: 73%. Student/faculty ratio: 12/1. Classes of fewer than 20 students: 53%; of 20 to 49 students: 46%; of 50 or more students: 0%. **Advanced Placement and International Baccalaureate credit:** AP tests may be used for: Credit only. Scores accepted: 3, 4, 5. International Baccalaureate exams may be used for: Credit only. **Freshmen returning for sophomore year:** 79%. **Graduation rates:** Four-year: 43%; five-year: 57%; six-year: 56%. **Graduate study:** 26% of students pursue further study immediately upon graduation; 26% within one year. Fields in which graduates pursue further study: Master of Business Administration (MBA), 15%; law, 4%; medicine, 18%; engineering, 4%; arts and sciences, 59%.

COSTS AND FINANCIAL AID

Financial aid office: (479) 524-7115. **Expenses (2006-2007):** Tuition and fees 2006-2007: $16,158; room/board: $5,956. Estimated books and supplies: $800; transportation: $1,500; personal expenses: $1,350. **Financial aid:** Priority filing date for institution's financial aid form: March 1. In 2005-2006, 74% of undergraduates applied for financial aid. Of those, 63% were determined to have financial need; 6% had their need fully met. Average financial aid package (proportion receiving): $8,195 (63%). Average amount of gift aid, such as scholarships or grants (proportion receiving): $7,121

(48%). Average amount of self-help aid, such as work study or loans (proportion receiving): $4,763 (57%). Average need-based loan (excluding PLUS or other private loans): $4,496. Among students who received need-based aid, the average percentage of need met: 50%. Among students who received aid based on merit, the average award (and the proportion receiving): $4,121 (16%). The average athletic scholarship (and the proportion receiving): $11,168 (3%). Average amount of debt of borrowers graduating in 2005: $19,262. Proportion who borrowed: 60%.

CAMPUS LIFE AND EXTRACURRICULAR ACTIVITIES
Campus housing available (% using): coed dorms (30%), women's dorms (27%), men's dorms (26%), other housing options (17%). Students who live in college-owned, operated, or affiliated housing: 70%. **Student employment:** During the 2005-2006 academic year, 8% of undergraduates worked on campus. Average per-year earnings: $1,500. **Clubs and organizations:** Number of student organizations: 45. Activities include: choral groups, drama/theater, literary magazine, music ensembles, musical theater, opera, pep band, radio station, student government, student newspaper, television station, yearbook. Number of fraternities: 0; sororities: 0. Average proportion of students who stay on campus on weekends: 75%. **Sports program (2005-2006):** Member of NAIA. *Men's intercollegiate varsity sports:* basketball, soccer, swimming and diving, tennis. *Women's intercollegiate varsity sports:* basketball, soccer, swimming and diving, tennis, volleyball.

SERVICES AND FACILITIES
Basic services: nonremedial tutoring, health service. **Remedial assistance:** reading, math, writing, study skills. **Counseling services:** minority student, career, personal, academic, older student, psychological, birth control, religious. **For learning-disabled students:** School does not offer a structured program with separate admission and additional fees. Total undergraduates in learning-disabled program or receiving services: 22. Services include: remedial math, tape recorders, note-taking services, oral tests, learning center, readers, extended time for tests, tutors, priority seating, texts on tape, typist/scribe, exams on tape or computer, other testing accomodations, other. **Library:** Number of titles: 102,031; number of current serial subscriptions: 751. **Information technology resources:** Students are not required to lease or own a computer. Number of campus computers available to all students: 225. School has a wireless network. Approximate number of users that can be accommodated: 600. Proportion of college-owned housing units wired for high-speed internet access: 95%. **Campus safety:** Security services offered; 24-hour foot-and-vehicle patrols, late-night transport/escort service, lighted pathways/sidewalks, student patrols, controlled dormitory access (key, security card, etc).

TRANSFER AND INTERNATIONAL STUDENTS
Transfer students: May apply for admission for the following academic terms: Fall, Spring. Applicants need a minimum number of credits to apply. For fall 2005: Transfer applications received: 184. Transfer applicants offered admission: 94. Transfer applicants enrolled: 53. **International students:** Number of foreign undergraduates: 101 (6% of student body). Number of countries represented: 39. Minimum TOEFL score required: 500 (paper); 173 (computer).

Lyon College

- **Address:** PO Box 2317, Batesville, AR 72503-2317
- **Website:** http://www.lyon.edu
- **Private; Religious affiliation:** Presbyterian
- **Enrollment:** 458 full-time; 30 part-time

KEY STATS
✔ **U.S News College Ranking:** third tier, Liberal Arts Colleges
✔ **ACT Score (25th/75th percentile):** 23-28
✔ **Tuition:** 2006-2007: $14,860

Selectivity: More selective	**Room/board:** $6,270
Acceptance rate: 72%	**Average debt:** $15,956
Student/faculty ratio: 10/1	**Proportion who borrowed:** 92%

UNDERGRADUATE STUDENT BODY STATS
2005-2006 enrollment: 458 full-time; 30 part-time. Men: 49%; women: 51%. **Ethnic makeup:** African American: 5%; American-Indian: 1%; Asian American: 1%; Hispanic: 2%; White: 88%; International: 3%. **Religious pref-**

erence: Roman Catholic: 8%; Protestant: 62%; No preference: 21%; Presbyterian: 4%; Other: 5%.

ADMISSIONS FACTS AND FIGURES
Phone: (800) 423-2542. **Email:** admissions@lyon.edu. **Website:** http://www.lyon.edu. **Application deadlines for fall 2007:** Regular decision: Rolling. Early decision: Not offered. Early action: Not offered. Admission can be deferred. **Application fee:** $25. Common application is accepted. **To apply online, go to:** http://www.lyon.edu/apply/applyonline.html. **Admissions requirements/recommendations:** High school units required (recommended): English: 4 (4); Mathematics: 3 (4); Science: 3 (4); Foreign language: 2 (2); Social studies: 1 (1); History: 2 (2); Academic electives: 1 (1); Total units: 16 (18). Tests: The college uses SAT or ACT scores in admissions decisions. Either SAT or ACT required. For admission to the fall 2007 entering class, the school will accept: ACT with writing, ACT without writing. Campus visit: Recommended. Admissions interview: Neither required nor recommended. Off-campus interview: Not available. **Factors that count in admissions decisions:** *Academic:* Secondary school record: Important. Class rank: Considered. Letters of recommendation: Considered. Standardized test scores: Very important. Essay: Considered. *Nonacademic:* Interview: Considered. Extracurricular activities: Considered. Talent/ability: Considered. Character/personal qualities: Considered. Alumni/ae relationship: Not considered. Geographical residence: Not considered. State residency: Not considered. Religious affiliation/commitment: Not considered. Minority status: Not considered. Volunteer work: Considered. Work experience: Considered. **Other schools with the greatest overlap in applicants:** Arkansas State University; Hendrix College; Rhodes College; University of Arkansas; University of Central Arkansas. **Admissions statistics for the fall 2005 entering class:** Total applicants: 470. Total accepted: 337. Freshmen enrolled: 112; 22% were from out of state. Overall acceptance rate: 72%. **Credentials of fall 2005 freshmen:** 29% ranked in the top 10 percent of their high school class; 69% were in the top 25 percent, and 93% were in the top half. (Proportion submitting class standing: 78%.) **Average high school grade point average:** 3.5. **First-year students who submitted SAT scores:** 18%. Scores (25/75 percentile): Verbal: 500-710, Math: 530-650, Combined: 1030-1360. **First-year students submitting ACT scores:** 96%. Scores (25/75 percentile): English: 23-30, Math: 22-27, Composite: 23-28.

ACADEMICS
Year founded: 1872. **Academic calendar:** Semester. **Degrees offered:** bachelor's. **Most popular majors:** 20% business administration and management, 18% biology/biological sciences, 13% psychology, 10% English language and literature, 9% history. **Major fields of study:** biological and biomedical sciences; business, management, marketing, and related support services; computer and information sciences and support services; education; English language and literature/letters; foreign languages, literatures, and linguistics; history; mathematics and statistics; natural resources and conservation; philosophy and religious studies; physical sciences; psychology; social sciences; visual and performing arts. **Areas of required coursework:** arts/fine arts, humanities, mathematics, English (including composition), foreign languages, sciences (biological or physical), history, social science, other. **Pre-professional programs:** pre-law, pre-dentistry, pre-medicine, pre-theology, pre-veterinary science, pre-optometry, pre-pharmacy, other. **Special academic programs (% participation):** accelerated program (2%), cross-registration (10%), double major (16%), dual enrollment (0%), independent study (14%), internships (53%), student-designed major (2%), study abroad (46%), teacher certificate program (14%). **Teacher certification offered in:** early childhood, elementary, middle/junior high, secondary. **Faculty and instruction (2005-2006):** Total instructional faculty: 44 full-time, 15 part-time (69% men; 31% women; 10% minorities). Full-time faculty with Ph.D. or other terminal degree: 91%. Student/faculty ratio: 10/1. Classes of fewer than 20 students: 74%; of 20 to 49 students: 25%; of 50 or more students: 1%. **Advanced Placement and International Baccalaureate credit:** AP tests may be used for: Credit only. Scores accepted: 4, 5. International Baccalaureate exams may be used for: Credit only. **Freshmen returning for sophomore year:** 74%. **Graduation rates:** Four-year: 58%; five-year: 67%; six-year: 68%. **Graduate study:** 27% of students pursue further study immediately upon graduation; 44% within one year; 48% within five years. Fields in which graduates pursue further study: Master of Business Administration (MBA), 7%; law, 1%; medicine, 2%; dentistry, 4%; arts and sciences, 12%.

COSTS AND FINANCIAL AID
Financial aid office: (870) 698-4257. **Expenses (2006-2007):** Tuition and fees 2006-2007: $14,860; room/board: $6,270. Estimated books and supplies: $1,000; transportation: $900; personal expenses: $900. **Financial aid:**

Priority filing date for institution's financial aid form: March 15. In 2005-2006, 81% of undergraduates applied for financial aid. Of those, 70% were determined to have financial need; 29% had their need fully met. Average financial aid package (proportion receiving): $13,749 (70%). Average amount of gift aid, such as scholarships or grants (proportion receiving): $9,953 (70%). Average amount of self-help aid, such as work study or loans (proportion receiving): $5,211 (51%). Average need-based loan (excluding PLUS or other private loans): $4,616. Among students who received need-based aid, the average percentage of need met: 77%. Among students who received aid based on merit, the average award (and the proportion receiving): $10,421 (27%). The average athletic scholarship (and the proportion receiving): $6,241 (17%). Average amount of debt of borrowers graduating in 2005: $15,956. Proportion who borrowed: 92%.

CAMPUS LIFE AND EXTRACURRICULAR ACTIVITIES

Campus housing available (% using): coed dorms (22%), women's dorms (21%), men's dorms (34%), apartment for single students (23%), other housing options (0%). Students who live in college-owned, operated, or affiliated housing: 76%. **Student employment:** During the 2005-2006 academic year, 14% of undergraduates worked on campus. Average per-year earnings: $1,400. **Clubs and organizations:** Number of student organizations: 44. Activities include: choral groups, dance, drama/theater, literary magazine, music ensembles, student government, student newspaper, yearbook. Number of fraternities: 3; sororities: 2. Proportion of men in fraternities: 10%; of women in sororities: 13%. Average proportion of students who stay on campus on weekends: 60%. **Sports program (2005-2006):** Member of NAIA. *Men's intercollegiate varsity sports:* baseball, basketball, cross-country, golf, soccer, tennis. *Women's intercollegiate varsity sports:* basketball, cross-country, golf, soccer, tennis, volleyball.

SERVICES AND FACILITIES

Basic services: nonremedial tutoring, placement service, health service, health insurance. **Counseling services:** minority student, career, personal, academic, psychological, other. **For learning-disabled students:** School does not offer a structured program with separate admission and additional fees. Total undergraduates in learning-disabled program or receiving services: 12. Services include: tape recorders, untimed tests, oral tests, readers, extended time for tests, other testing accomodations, other. **Library:** Number of titles: 146,280; number of current serial subscriptions: 625. **Information technology resources:** Students are not required to lease or own a computer. Number of campus computers available to all students: 110. School has a wireless network. Approximate number of users that can be accommodated: 150. Proportion of college-owned housing units wired for high-speed internet access: 100%. **Campus safety:** Security services offered: 24-hour foot-and-vehicle patrols, lighted pathways/sidewalks, controlled dormitory access (key, security card, etc).

TRANSFER AND INTERNATIONAL STUDENTS

Transfer students: May apply for admission for the following academic terms: Fall, Spring. Applicants do not need a minimum number of credits to apply. For fall 2005: Transfer applications received: 92. Transfer applicants offered admission: 68. Transfer applicants enrolled: 47. **International students:** Number of foreign undergraduates: 13 (3% of student body). Number of countries represented: 14. Minimum TOEFL score required: 550 (paper); 213 (computer).

Ouachita Baptist University

- **Address:** 410 Ouachita, Arkadelphia, AR 71998
- **Website:** http://www.obu.edu
- **Private; Religious affiliation:** Southern Baptist
- **Enrollment:** 1,399 full-time; 100 part-time

KEY STATS

✔ **U.S News College Ranking:** 5, Comp. Colleges—Bachelor's (South)
✔ **ACT Score (25th/75th percentile):** 20-27
✔ **Tuition:** 2006-2007: $15,560

Selectivity: More selective	**Room/board:** $4,900
Acceptance rate: 58%	**Average debt:** $14,016
Student/faculty ratio: 11/1	**Proportion who borrowed:** 50%

UNDERGRADUATE STUDENT BODY STATS

2005-2006 enrollment: 1,399 full-time; 100 part-time. Men: 45%; women: 55%. **Ethnic makeup:** African American: 6%; Asian American: 1%; Hispanic: 2%; White: 88%; International: 4%. **Religious preference:** Roman Catholic: 2%; Protestant: 8%; Unknown: 13%; Southern Baptist: 77%.

ADMISSIONS FACTS AND FIGURES

Phone: (870) 245-5110. **Email:** admissions@obu.edu. **Website:** http://www.obu.edu. **Application deadlines for fall 2007:** Regular decision: Rolling. Early decision: Not offered. Early action: Send application by: December 1; Decision sent by: December 8. Admission can be deferred. **Application fee:** $50. Common application is not accepted. **Admissions requirements/recommendations:** High school units required (recommended): English: 4 (4); Mathematics: 2 (3); Science: 2 (3); Foreign language: (2); Social studies: 1 (1); History: 2 (2); Total units: 15 (19). Tests: The college uses SAT or ACT scores in admissions decisions. Either SAT or ACT required. For admission to the fall 2007 entering class, the school will accept: ACT with writing, ACT without writing. Campus visit: Recommended. Admissions interview: Recommended. Off-campus interview: May be arranged. **Factors that count in admissions decisions:** *Academic:* Secondary school record: Very important. Class rank: Very important. Letters of recommendation: Considered. Standardized test scores: Very important. Essay: Not considered. *Nonacademic:* Interview: Important. Extracurricular activities: Considered. Talent/ability: Considered. Character/personal qualities: Considered. Alumni/ae relationship: Not considered. Geographical residence: Not considered. State residency: Not considered. Religious affiliation/commitment: Not considered. Minority status: Not considered. Volunteer work: Considered. Work experience: Considered. **Other schools with the greatest overlap in applicants:** Baylor University; Henderson State University; Southern Arkansas University; University of Arkansas; University of Central Arkansas. **Admissions statistics for the fall 2005 entering class:** Total applicants: 1,058. Total accepted: 613. Freshmen enrolled: 368; 48% were from out of state. Overall acceptance rate: 58%. Non-early acceptance rate: 58%. **Credentials of fall 2005 freshmen:** 33% ranked in the top 10 percent of their high school class; 60% were in the top 25 percent, and 82% were in the top half. (Proportion submitting class standing: 72%.) **Average high school grade point average:** 3.5. **First-year students who submitted SAT scores:** 39%. Scores (25/75 percentile): Verbal: 490-600, Math: 470-610, Combined: 960-1210. **First-year students submitting ACT scores:** 77%. Scores (25/75 percentile): English: 21-29, Math: 19-26, Composite: 20-27.

ACADEMICS

Year founded: 1886. **Academic calendar:** Semester. **Degrees offered:** associate, bachelor's. **Most popular majors:** 16% business, management, marketing, and related support services, 9% theology and religious vocations, 9% communication, journalism, and related programs, 8% health professions and related clinical sciences, 8% visual and performing arts. **Major fields of study:** biological and biomedical sciences; business, management, marketing, and related support services; communication, journalism, and related programs; computer and information sciences and support services; education; engineering; English language and literature/letters; foreign languages, literatures, and linguistics; health professions and related clinical sciences; history; legal professions and studies; mathematics and statistics; parks, recreation, leisure, and fitness studies; philosophy and religious studies; physical sciences; psychology; social sciences; theology and religious vocations; visual and performing arts. **Areas of required coursework:** arts/fine arts, humanities, mathematics, English (including composition), philosophy, foreign languages, sciences (biological or physical), history, social science, other. **Pre-professional programs:** pre-law, pre-dentistry, pre-medicine, pre-veterinary science, pre-optometry, pre-pharmacy, other. **Special academic programs (% participation):** cross-registration (11%), double major (14%), English as a Second Language (ESL) (1%), honors program (6%), internships (2%), study abroad (4%), teacher certificate program (15%). **Teacher certification offered in:** early childhood, middle/junior high, secondary. **Reserve Officers Training Corps (ROTC):** Army ROTC: Offered on campus. **Faculty and instruction (2005-2006):** Total instructional faculty: 114 full-time, 33 part-time (60% men; 40% women; 1% minorities). Full-time faculty with Ph.D. or other terminal degree: 79%. Student/faculty ratio: 11/1. Classes of fewer than 20 students: 70%; of 20 to 49 students: 30%; of 50 or more students: 0%. **Advanced Placement and International Baccalaureate credit:** AP tests may be used for: Credit and/or placement. Scores accepted: 4. International Baccalaureate exams may be used for: Credit and/or placement. **Freshmen returning for sophomore year:** 75%. **Graduation rates:** Four-year: 44%; five-year: 58%; six-year: 57%. **Graduate study:** 20% of students pursue further study immediately upon graduation; 25% within one year;

30% within five years. Fields in which graduates pursue further study: Master of Business Administration (MBA), 3%; law, 5%; medicine, 5%; dentistry, 2%; engineering, 1%; theology (or the seminary), 5%; education, 4%; arts and sciences, 4%; veterinary medicine, 1%.

COSTS AND FINANCIAL AID

Financial aid office: (870) 245-5570. **Expenses (2006-2007):** Tuition and fees 2006-2007: $15,560; room/board: $4,900. Estimated books and supplies: $775; transportation: $850; personal expenses: $1,400. **Financial aid:** Priority filing date for institution's financial aid form: February 15; deadline: June 1. In 2005-2006, 63% of undergraduates applied for financial aid. Of those, 49% were determined to have financial need; 30% had their need fully met. Average financial aid package (proportion receiving): $12,992 (48%). Average amount of gift aid, such as scholarships or grants (proportion receiving): $8,419 (45%). Average amount of self-help aid, such as work study or loans (proportion receiving): $4,001 (32%). Average need-based loan (excluding PLUS or other private loans): $3,709. Among students who received need-based aid, the average percentage of need met: 75%. Among students who received aid based on merit, the average award (and the proportion receiving): $6,032 (33%). The average athletic scholarship (and the proportion receiving): $11,175 (6%). Average amount of debt of borrowers graduating in 2005: $14,016. Proportion who borrowed: 50%.

CAMPUS LIFE AND EXTRACURRICULAR ACTIVITIES

Campus housing available (% using): women's dorms (48%), men's dorms (37%), apartments for married students (1%), apartment for single students (14%). Students who live in college-owned, operated, or affiliated housing: 84%. **Clubs and organizations:** Number of student organizations: 32. Activities include: choral groups, concert band, drama/theater, jazz band, marching band, music ensembles, musical theater, opera, pep band, student government, student newspaper, yearbook. Number of fraternities: 5; sororities: 5. Proportion of men in fraternities: 20%; of women in sororities: 30%. Average proportion of students who stay on campus on weekends: 50%. **Sports program (2005-2006):** Member of NCAA II. *Men's intercollegiate varsity sports:* baseball, basketball, football, golf, soccer, swimming and diving, tennis. *Women's intercollegiate varsity sports:* basketball, cross-country, soccer, softball, swimming and diving, tennis, volleyball.

SERVICES AND FACILITIES

Basic services: nonremedial tutoring, placement service, health service, health insurance. **Remedial assistance:** reading, math, study skills. **Counseling services:** minority student, career, military, personal, veteran student, academic, religious. **For learning-disabled students:** School does not offer a structured program with separate admission and additional fees. Total undergraduates in learning-disabled program or receiving services: 26. Services include: remedial math, remedial English, reading machines, remedial reading, tape recorders, other special classes, videotaped classes, note-taking services, oral tests, readers, extended time for tests, tutors. **Library:** Number of titles: 723,962; number of current serial subscriptions: 885. **Information technology resources:** Students are not required to lease or own a computer. Number of campus computers available to all students: 240. School has a wireless network. Approximate number of users that can be accommodated: 750. Proportion of college-owned housing units wired for high-speed internet access: 100%. **Campus safety:** Security services offered: 24-hour foot-and-vehicle patrols, 24-hour emergency telephones, lighted pathways/sidewalks, controlled dormitory access (key, security card, etc).

TRANSFER AND INTERNATIONAL STUDENTS

Transfer students: May apply for admission for the following academic terms: Fall, Spring, Summer. Applicants need a minimum number of credits to apply. For fall 2005: Transfer applications received: 165. Transfer applicants offered admission: 96. Transfer applicants enrolled: 77. **International students:** Number of foreign undergraduates: 54 (4% of student body). Number of countries represented: 33. Minimum TOEFL score required: 550 (paper); 213 (computer). Average TOEFL score: 700 (paper).

Philander Smith College

■ **Address:** 1 Trudie Kibbe Reed Drive, Little Rock, AR 72202-3718
■ **Website:** http://www.philander.edu
■ **Private; Religious affiliation:** United Methodist
■ **Enrollment:** 670 full-time; 115 part-time

KEY STATS

✔ **U.S News College Ranking:** fourth tier, Comp. Coll.–Bachelor's (South)
✔ **ACT Score (25th/75th percentile):** 14-17
✔ **Tuition:** 2005-2006: $7,766
  Selectivity: Least selective   **Room/board:** $5,090
  Acceptance rate: 80%   **Average debt:** $26,000
  Student/faculty ratio: 12/1   **Proportion who borrowed:** 89%

UNDERGRADUATE STUDENT BODY STATS

2005-2006 enrollment: 670 full-time; 115 part-time. Men: 34%; women: 66%. **Ethnic makeup:** African American: 97%; Hispanic: 1%; White: 1%; International: 1%.

ADMISSIONS FACTS AND FIGURES

Phone: (501) 370-5221. **Email:** admissions@philander.edu. **Website:** http://www.philander.edu. **Application deadlines for fall 2007:** Regular decision: July 15. Early decision: Not offered. Early action: Not offered. Admission can be deferred. **Application fee:** $25. Common application is accepted. **Admissions requirements/recommendations:** Tests: The college does not use SAT or ACT scores in admissions decisions. Neither SAT nor ACT required. Campus visit: Recommended. Admissions interview: Neither required nor recommended. Off-campus interview: May be arranged. **Factors that count in admissions decisions:** *Academic:* Standardized test scores: Considered. **Other schools with the greatest overlap in applicants:** Arkansas State University; University of Arkansas–Little Rock; University of Arkansas–Pine Bluff; University of Central Arkansas. **Admissions statistics for the fall 2005 entering class:** Total applicants: 344. Total accepted: 274. Freshmen enrolled: 126; 37% were from out of state. Overall acceptance rate: 80%. **Credentials of fall 2005 freshmen:** 10% ranked in the top 10 percent of their high school class; 24% were in the top 25 percent, and 63% were in the top half. (Proportion submitting class standing: 75%.) **Average high school grade point average:** 2.6. **First-year students submitting ACT scores:** 86%. Scores (25/75 percentile): English: 12-16, Math: 14-17, Composite: 14-17.

ACADEMICS

Year founded: 1877. **Academic calendar:** Semester. **Degrees offered:** bachelor's. **Most popular majors:** 29% business administration, management, and operations, 25% business administration and management, 9% social work, 5% early childhood education and teaching, 5% sociology. **Major fields of study:** biological and biomedical sciences; business, management, marketing, and related support services; computer and information sciences and support services; education; English language and literature/letters; mathematics and statistics; philosophy and religious studies; physical sciences; psychology; public administration and social service professions; social sciences; visual and performing arts. **Areas of required coursework:** arts/fine arts, humanities, mathematics, English (including composition), philosophy, sciences (biological or physical), history, social science. **Pre-professional programs:** pre-medicine. **Special academic programs:** double major, honors program, independent study, internships, study abroad, teacher certificate program, weekend college. **Teacher certification offered in:** early childhood, vo-tech, middle/junior high. **Reserve Officers Training Corps (ROTC):** Army ROTC: Offered at cooperating institution (Univ. Of Arkansas at Little Rock). **Faculty and instruction (2005-2006):** Total instructional faculty: 44 full-time, 45 part-time (45% men; 55% women; 81% minorities). Full-time faculty with Ph.D. or other terminal degree: 48%. Student/faculty ratio: 12/1. Classes of fewer than 20 students: 82%; of 20 to 49 students: 18%. **Freshmen returning for sophomore year:** 61%. **Graduation rates:** Four-year: 4%; five-year: 14%; six-year: 20%. **Graduate study:** 28% of students pursue further study immediately upon graduation.

COSTS AND FINANCIAL AID

Financial aid office: (501) 370-5350. **Expenses (2005-2006):** Tuition and fees 2005-2006: $7,766; room/board: $5,090. Estimated books and supplies: $900; estimated transportation: $2,344; personal expenses: $1,446. **Financial aid:** Priority filing date for institution's financial aid form: March 1. Average financial aid package (proportion receiving): $8,214 (N/A). Average amount of gift aid, such as scholarships or grants (proportion receiving): $5,014 (N/A). Average amount of self-help aid, such as work study or loans (proportion receiving): $3,860 (N/A). Average need-based loan (excluding PLUS or other private loans): $3,560. Among students who received aid based on merit, the average award (and the proportion receiving): $10,236 (N/A). The average athletic scholarship (and the proportion receiving): $0 (N/A). Average amount of debt of borrowers graduating in 2005: $26,000. Proportion who borrowed: 89%.

CAMPUS LIFE AND EXTRACURRICULAR ACTIVITIES

Campus housing available (% using): coed dorms (100%). Students who live in college-owned, operated, or affiliated housing: 26%. **Student employment:** During the 2005-2006 academic year, 7% of undergraduates worked on campus. Average per-year earnings: $3,000. **Clubs and organizations:** Number of student organizations: 10. Activities include: choral groups, drama/theater, music ensembles, musical theater, opera, pep band, student government, student newspaper, yearbook. Number of fraternities: 3; sororities: 3. Proportion of men in fraternities: 4%; of women in sororities: 2%. **Sports program (2005-2006):** Member of NAIA. *Men's intercollegiate varsity sports:* basketball. *Women's intercollegiate varsity sports:* basketball, volleyball.

SERVICES AND FACILITIES

Basic services: nonremedial tutoring, placement service, health service, health insurance. **Remedial assistance:** reading, math, writing, study skills. **Counseling services:** career, personal, veteran student, academic, psychological, religious. **For learning-disabled students:** School does not offer a structured program with separate admission and additional fees. Total undergraduates in learning-disabled program or receiving services: 0. **Library:** Number of titles: 67,756; number of current serial subscriptions: 283. **Information technology resources:** Students are not required to lease or own a computer. School does not have a wireless network. Proportion of college-owned housing units wired for high-speed internet access: 100%. **Campus safety:** Security services offered: 24-hour foot-and-vehicle patrols, controlled dormitory access (key, security card, etc).

TRANSFER AND INTERNATIONAL STUDENTS

Transfer students: May apply for admission for the following academic terms: Fall, Spring, Summer. Applicants need a minimum number of credits to apply. For fall 2005: Transfer applications received: 93. Transfer applicants offered admission: 61. Transfer applicants enrolled: 40. **International students:** Number of foreign undergraduates: 10 (1% of student body). Number of countries represented: 9. Minimum TOEFL score required: 500 (paper); 173 (computer).

Southern Arkansas University

- **Address:** Box 9392, Magnolia, AR 71754-9392
- **Website:** http://www.saumag.edu
- **Public**
- **Enrollment:** 2,408 full-time; 468 part-time

KEY STATS

✔ **U.S News College Ranking:** fourth tier, Universities–Master's (South)
✔ **ACT Score (25th/75th percentile):** 17-24
✔ **Tuition:** 2006-2007: $4,890 in state, $7,080 out of state

Selectivity: Selective	**Room/board:** $3,930
Acceptance rate: 82%	**Average debt:** $14,162
Student/faculty ratio 19/1	**Proportion who borrowed:** 58%

UNDERGRADUATE STUDENT BODY STATS

2005-2006 enrollment: 2,408 full-time; 468 part-time. Men: 43%; women: 57%. **Ethnic makeup:** African American: 28%; American-Indian: 1%; Asian American: 1%; Hispanic: 1%; White: 65%; International: 5%. **Religious preference:** Roman Catholic: 3%; Protestant: 80%; No preference: 4%; Unknown: 3%; Other: 10%.

ADMISSIONS FACTS AND FIGURES

Phone: (870) 235-4040. **Email:** muleriders@saumag.edu. **Website:** http://www.saumag.edu. **Application deadlines for fall 2007:** Regular decision: August 27. Early decision: Not offered. Early action: Not offered. Admission can be deferred. **Application fee:** None. Common application is accepted. **Admissions requirements/recommendations:** High school units

required (recommended): English: (4); Mathematics: (4); Science: (3); Foreign language: (2); Social studies: (3). Tests: The college uses SAT or ACT scores in admissions decisions. Either SAT or ACT required. For admission to the fall 2007 entering class, the school will accept: ACT with writing, ACT without writing. Campus visit: Recommended. Admissions interview: Neither required nor recommended. Off-campus interview: May be arranged. **Factors that count in admissions decisions:** *Academic:* Secondary school record: Very important. Class rank: Very important. Letters of recommendation: Considered. Standardized test scores: Very important. Essay: Considered. *Nonacademic:* Interview: Not considered. Extracurricular activities: Not considered. Talent/ability: Not considered. Character/personal qualities: Not considered. Alumni/ae relationship: Not considered. Geographical residence: Not considered. State residency: Not considered. Religious affiliation/commitment: Not considered. Minority status: Not considered. Volunteer work: Not considered. Work experience: Not considered. **Admissions statistics for the fall 2005 entering class:** Total applicants: 1,356. Total accepted: 1,107. Freshmen enrolled: 571; 20% were from out of state. Overall acceptance rate: 82%. **Credentials of fall 2005 freshmen:** 35% were in the top 25 percent, and 70% were in the top half. (Proportion submitting class standing: 97%.) **Average high school grade point average:** 3.1. **First-year students who submitted SAT scores:** 8%. Scores (25/75 percentile): Verbal: N/A, Math: N/A, Combined: N/A. **First-year students submitting ACT scores:** 98%. Scores (25/75 percentile): English: 17-25, Math: 17-23, Composite: 17-24.

ACADEMICS

Year founded: 1909. **Academic calendar:** Semester. **Degrees offered:** associate, bachelor's, master's. **Most popular majors:** 32% business, management, marketing, and related support services, 16% education, 9% security and protective services, 8% agriculture, agriculture operations, and related sciences, 6% biological and biomedical sciences. **Major fields of study:** agriculture, agriculture operations, and related sciences; biological and biomedical sciences; business, management, marketing, and related support services; communication, journalism, and related programs; computer and information sciences and support services; education; engineering technologies/technicians; English language and literature/letters; foreign languages, literatures, and linguistics; health professions and related clinical sciences; history; liberal arts and sciences studies, and humanities; mathematics and statistics; multi/interdisciplinary studies; parks, recreation, leisure, and fitness studies; physical sciences; psychology; public administration and social service professions; security and protective services; social sciences; visual and performing arts. **Areas of required coursework:** arts/fine arts, humanities, computer literacy, mathematics, English (including composition), sciences (biological or physical), history, social science. **Pre-professional programs:** pre-law, pre-dentistry, pre-medicine, pre-veterinary science, pre-optometry, pre-pharmacy, other. **Special academic programs:** distance learning, double major, dual enrollment, honors program, independent study, internships, teacher certificate program. **Teacher certification offered in:** early childhood, special education, elementary, middle/junior high, secondary. **Cooperative education programs:** health professions. **Faculty and instruction (2005-2006):** Total instructional faculty: 120 full-time, 62 part-time (54% men; 46% women; 13% minorities). Full-time faculty with Ph.D. or other terminal degree: 67%. Student/faculty ratio: 19/1. Classes of fewer than 20 students: 50%; of 20 to 49 students: 44%; of 50 or more students: 6%. **Advanced Placement and International Baccalaureate credit:** International Baccalaureate exams may be used for: Credit and/or placement. **Freshmen returning for sophomore year:** 64%. **Graduation rates:** Four-year: 13%; five-year: 27%; six-year: 32%.

COSTS AND FINANCIAL AID

Financial aid office: (870) 235-4023. **Expenses (2006-2007):** Tuition and fees 2006-2007: $4,890 in state, $7,080 out of state; room/board: $3,930. Estimated books and supplies: $1,000; transportation: $1,200; personal expenses: $2,000. **Financial aid:** Priority filing date for institution's financial aid form: July 1. In 2005-2006, 63% of undergraduates applied for financial aid. Of those, 55% were determined to have financial need; 80% had their need fully met. Average financial aid package (proportion receiving): $4,158 (54%). Average amount of gift aid, such as scholarships or grants (proportion receiving): $2,376 (52%). Average amount of self-help aid, such as work study or loans (proportion receiving): $2,210 (45%). Average need-based loan (excluding PLUS or other private loans): $1,283. Among students who received need-based aid, the average percentage of need met: 100%. Among students who received aid based on merit, the average award (and the proportion receiving): $4,557 (11%). The average athletic scholarship (and the proportion receiving): $4,119 (5%). Average amount of debt of borrowers graduating in 2005: $14,162. Proportion who borrowed: 58%.

CAMPUS LIFE AND EXTRACURRICULAR ACTIVITIES

Campus housing available: coed dorms, women's dorms, men's dorms, apartments for married students, apartment for single students. Students who live in college-owned, operated, or affiliated housing: 38%. **Student employment:** During the 2005-2006 academic year, 28% of undergraduates worked on campus. Average per-year earnings: $2,700. **Clubs and organizations:** Number of student organizations: 80. Activities include: choral groups, concert band, drama/theater, jazz band, marching band, music ensembles, pep band, radio station, student government, student newspaper, yearbook. Number of fraternities: 7; sororities: 7. Proportion of men in fraternities: 10%; of women in sororities: 10%. Average proportion of students who stay on campus on weekends: 25%. **Sports program (2005-2006):** Member of NCAA II. *Men's intercollegiate varsity sports:* baseball, basketball, cross-country, football, golf, track and field (outdoor). *Women's intercollegiate varsity sports:* basketball, cross-country, golf, softball, tennis, track and field (outdoor), volleyball.

SERVICES AND FACILITIES

Basic services: nonremedial tutoring, placement service, health service, health insurance, other. **Remedial assistance:** reading, math, writing. **Counseling services:** minority student, career, personal, veteran student, academic, older student, psychological. **For learning-disabled students:** Services include: remedial math, remedial English, remedial reading, tape recorders, note-taking services, learning center, readers, extended time for tests, tutors. **Library:** Number of titles: 167,762; number of current serial subscriptions: 1,018. **Information technology resources:** Students are not required to lease or own a computer. Number of campus computers available to all students: 220. School has a wireless network. **Campus safety:** Security services offered: 24-hour foot-and-vehicle patrols, late-night transport/escort service, 24-hour emergency telephones, lighted pathways/sidewalks, student patrols, controlled dormitory access (key, security card, etc.).

TRANSFER AND INTERNATIONAL STUDENTS

Transfer students: May apply for admission for the following academic terms: Fall, Spring, Summer. Applicants need a minimum number of credits to apply. For fall 2005: Transfer applicants enrolled: 173. **International students:** Number of foreign undergraduates: 146 (5% of student body). Minimum TOEFL score required: 500 (paper); 173 (computer). Average TOEFL score: 560 (paper).

University of Arkansas

- **Address:** 232 Silas Hunt Hall, Fayetteville, AR 72701
- **Website:** http://www.uark.edu
- **Public**
- **Enrollment:** 11,743 full-time; 2,538 part-time

KEY STATS

✔ **U.S News College Ranking:** third tier, National Universities
✔ **ACT Score (25th/75th percentile):** 22-28
✔ **Tuition:** 2006-2007: $5,808 in state, $13,942 out of state

Selectivity: More selective	**Room/board:** $6,522
Acceptance rate: 87%	**Average debt:** $19,862
Student/faculty ratio: 18/1	**Proportion who borrowed:** 51%

UNDERGRADUATE STUDENT BODY STATS

2005-2006 enrollment: 11,743 full-time; 2,538 part-time. Men: 51%; women: 49%. **Ethnic makeup:** African American: 5%; American-Indian: 2%; Asian American: 3%; Hispanic: 2%; White: 86%; International: 2%.

ADMISSIONS FACTS AND FIGURES

Phone: (800) 377-8632. **Email:** uofa@uark.edu. **Website:** http://www.uark.edu. **Application deadlines for fall 2007:** Regular decision: August 15. Early decision: Not offered. Early action: Send application by: November 15; Decision sent by: December 15. Admission can be deferred. **Application fee:** $40. Common application is accepted. **To apply online, go to:** http://apply.uark.edu. **Admissions requirements/recommendations:** High school units required (recommended): English: 4; Mathematics: 4; Science: 3; Foreign language: (2); Social studies: 3; Academic electives: 2; Total units: 16. Tests: The college uses SAT or ACT scores in admissions decisions. Either SAT or ACT required. For admission to the fall 2007 entering class, the school will accept: ACT with writing, ACT without writing. Campus visit: Recommended. Admissions interview: Recommended. Off-campus interview: May be arranged. **Factors that count in admissions decisions:** *Academic:* Secondary school record: Very important. Class rank: Very important. Letters of recommendation: Considered. Standardized test scores: Very important. Essay: Considered. *Nonacademic:* Interview: Not considered. Extracurricular activities: Considered. Talent/ability: Considered. Character/personal qualities: Considered. Alumni/ae relationship: Considered. Geographical residence: Considered. State residency: Considered. Religious affiliation/commitment: Not considered. Minority status: Considered. Volunteer work: Considered. Work experience: Considered. **Other schools with the greatest overlap in applicants:** Oklahoma State University; University of Mississippi; University of Missouri–Columbia; University of Oklahoma; University of Texas–Austin. **Admissions statistics for the fall 2005 entering class:** Total applicants: 6,041. Total accepted: 5,283. Freshmen enrolled: 2,752; 30% were from out of state. Accepted through early-decision or early-action plans: 40%. Overall acceptance rate: 87%. Non-early acceptance rate: 91%. **Credentials of fall 2005 freshmen:** 32% ranked in the top 10 percent of their high school class; 61% were in the top 25 percent, and 86% were in the top half. (Proportion submitting class standing: 82%.) **Average high school grade point average:** 3.6. **First-year students who submitted SAT scores:** 27%. Scores (25/75 percentile): Verbal: 510-640, Math: 520-640, Combined: 1030-1280. **First-year students submitting ACT scores:** 93%. Scores (25/75 percentile): English: 22-29, Math: 21-27, Composite: 22-28.

ACADEMICS

Year founded: 1871. **Academic calendar:** Semester. **Degrees offered:** bachelor's, post-bachelor's certificate, master's, post-master's certificate, first professional, doctorate. **Most popular majors:** 7% marketing/marketing management, 6% finance, 5% journalism, 4% accounting, 4% business administration and management. **Major fields of study:** agriculture, agriculture operations, and related sciences; architecture and related services; area, ethnic, cultural, and gender studies; biological and biomedical sciences; business, management, marketing, and related support services; communication, journalism, and related programs; computer and information sciences and support services; education; engineering; English language and literature/letters; family and consumer sciences/human sciences; foreign languages, literatures, and linguistics; health professions and related clinical sciences; history; mathematics and statistics; natural resources and conservation; parks, recreation, leisure, and fitness studies; philosophy and religious studies; physical sciences; psychology; public administration and social service professions; security and protective services; social sciences; visual and performing arts. **Areas of required coursework:** arts/fine arts, humanities, mathematics, English (including composition), philosophy, foreign languages, sciences (biological or physical), history, social science. **Preprofessional programs:** pre-law, pre-dentistry, pre-medicine, pre-veterinary science, pre-optometry, pre-pharmacy, other. **Special academic programs (% participation):** accelerated program, cooperative (work-study plan) program, distance learning, double major, dual enrollment, English as a Second Language (ESL), honors program (16.2%), independent study, internships, liberal arts/career combination, study abroad, teacher certificate program. **Teacher certification offered in:** early childhood, special education, elementary, middle/junior high, adult education, secondary, bilingual/bicultural. **Cooperative education programs:** art, business, computer science, engineering, humanities, natural science, social/behavioral science, technologies, other. **Reserve Officers Training Corps (ROTC):** Army ROTC: Offered on campus; Air Force ROTC: Offered on campus. **Faculty and instruction (2005-2006):** Total instructional faculty: 787 full-time, 37 part-time (68% men; 32% women; 12% minorities). Full-time faculty with Ph.D. or other terminal degree: 90%. Student/faculty ratio: 18/1. Classes of fewer than 20 students: 36%; of 20 to 49 students: 49%; of 50 or more students: 15%. **Advanced Placement and International Baccalaureate credit:** AP tests may be used for: Credit and/or placement. Scores accepted: 3, 4, 5. International Baccalaureate exams may be used for: Credit and/or placement. **Freshmen returning for sophomore year:** 83%. **Graduation rates:** Four-year: 30%; five-year: 52%; six-year: 56%.

COSTS AND FINANCIAL AID

Financial aid office: (479) 575-3806. **Expenses (2006-2007):** Tuition and fees 2006-2007: $5,808 in state, $13,942 out of state; room/board: $6,522. Estimated books and supplies: $956; transportation: $1,178; personal expenses: $1,934. **Financial aid:** Priority filing date for institution's financial aid form: March 15. In 2005-2006, 52% of undergraduates applied for financial aid. Of those, 40% were determined to have financial need; 18% had their need fully met. Average financial aid package (proportion receiving): $8,798 (39%). Average amount of gift aid, such as scholarships or grants (proportion receiving): $3,630 (24%). Average amount of self-help aid, such as work study or loans (proportion receiving): $4,666 (31%). Average need-based loan (excluding PLUS or other private loans): $4,276. Among students who received need-based aid, the average percentage of need met: 64%. Among students who received aid based on merit, the average award (and the proportion receiving): $5,796 (19%). The average athletic scholarship (and the proportion receiving): $8,365 (4%). Average amount of debt of borrowers graduating in 2005: $19,862. Proportion who borrowed: 51%.

CAMPUS LIFE AND EXTRACURRICULAR ACTIVITIES

Campus housing available (% using): coed dorms (39%), women's dorms (11%), men's dorms (2%), sorority housing (12%), fraternity housing (10%), apartments for married students (1%), apartment for single students (3%), special housing for disabled students (1%), other housing options (21%). Students who live in college-owned, operated, or affiliated housing: 28%. **Student employment:** During the 2005-2006 academic year, 13% of undergraduates worked on campus. Average per-year earnings: $4,986. **Clubs and organizations:** Number of student organizations: 238. Activities include: choral groups, concert band, dance, drama/theater, jazz band, literary magazine, marching band, music ensembles, musical theater, opera, pep band, radio station, student government, student newspaper, student film society, symphony orchestra, television station, yearbook. Number of fraternities: 15; sororities: 10. Proportion of men in fraternities: 11%; of women in sororities: 19%. Average proportion of students who stay on campus on weekends: 76%. **Sports program (2005-2006):** Member of NCAA I. *Men's intercollegiate varsity sports:* baseball, basketball, cross-country, football, golf, tennis, track and field (indoor), track and field (outdoor). *Women's intercollegiate varsity sports:* basketball, cross-country, golf, gymnastics, soccer, softball, swimming and diving, tennis, track and field (indoor), track and field (outdoor), volleyball.

SERVICES AND FACILITIES

Basic services: nonremedial tutoring, placement service, day care, health service, health insurance, other. **Remedial assistance:** reading, math, writing, study skills. **Counseling services:** minority student, career, military, personal, veteran student, academic, older student, psychological, birth control, religious. **For learning-disabled students:** School does not offer a structured program with separate admission and additional fees. Total undergraduates in learning-disabled program or receiving services: 130. Services include: remedial math, remedial English, reading machines, remedial reading, tape recorders, other special classes, note-taking services, oral tests, learning center, readers, extended time for tests, tutors, priority registration, priority seating, substitution of courses, texts on tape, typist/scribe, exams on tape or computer, other. **Library:** Number of titles: 1,727,892; number of current serial subscriptions: 18,131. **Information technology resources:** Students are not required to lease or own a computer. Number of campus computers available to all students: 2,002. School has a wireless network. Approximate number of users that can be accommodated: 8,850. Proportion of college-owned housing units wired for high-speed internet access: 99%. **Campus safety:** Security services offered: 24-hour foot-and-vehicle patrols, late-night transport/escort service, 24-hour emergency telephones, lighted pathways/sidewalks, student patrols, controlled dormitory access (key, security card, etc).

TRANSFER AND INTERNATIONAL STUDENTS

Transfer students: May apply for admission for the following academic terms: Fall, Spring, Summer. Applicants need a minimum number of credits to apply. For fall 2005: Transfer applications received: 2,333. Transfer applicants offered admission: 1,780. Transfer applicants enrolled: 1,240. **International students:** Number of foreign undergraduates: 262 (2% of student body). Number of countries represented: 63. Minimum TOEFL score required: 550 (paper); 213 (computer). Average TOEFL score: 587 (paper).

University of Arkansas—Little Rock

- **Address:** 2801 S. University Avenue, Little Rock, AR 72204-1099
- **Website:** http://www.ualr.edu
- **Public**
- **Enrollment:** N/A

KEY STATS

✔ **U.S News College Ranking:** fourth tier, National Universities
✔ **SAT or ACT Score (25th/75th percentile):** N/A
✔ **Tuition:** 2006-2007: $5,510 in state, $12,726 out of state

Selectivity: Selective	**Room/board:** N/A
Acceptance rate: N/A	**Average debt:** N/A
Student/faculty ratio: N/A	**Proportion who borrowed:** N/A

University of Arkansas—Monticello

- **Address:** UAM Box 3478, Monticello, AR 71656
- **Website:** http://www.uamont.edu
- **Public**
- **Enrollment:** 2,218 full-time; 342 part-time

KEY STATS

✔ **U.S News College Ranking:** fourth tier, Comp. Coll.–Bachelor's (South)
✔ **SAT or ACT Score (25th/75th percentile):** N/A
✔ **Tuition:** 2006-2007: $4,150 in state, $4,930 out of state

Selectivity: Less selective	**Room/board:** $3,366
Acceptance rate: 60%	**Average debt:** $13,599
Student/faculty ratio: 16/1	**Proportion who borrowed:** N/A

UNDERGRADUATE STUDENT BODY STATS

2005-2006 enrollment: 2,218 full-time; 342 part-time. Men: 41%; women: 59%. **Ethnic makeup:** African American: 31%; American-Indian: 1%; Asian American: 1%; Hispanic: 2%; White: 66%.

ADMISSIONS FACTS AND FIGURES

Phone: (870) 460-1026. **Email:** admissions@uamont.edu. **Website:** http://www.uamont.edu. **Application deadlines for fall 2007:** Regular decision: Rolling. Early decision: Not offered. Early action: Not offered. Admission cannot be deferred. Common application is not accepted. **To apply online, go to:** http://www.uamont.edu/admissions/AdmissionsFormdraft.htm. **Admissions requirements/recommendations:** High school units required (recommended): English: (4); Mathematics: (4); Science: (3); Social studies: (3); Total units: (14). Tests: The college does not use SAT or ACT scores in admissions decisions. Neither SAT nor ACT required. Campus visit: Recommended. Admissions interview: Neither required nor recommended. **Other schools with the greatest overlap in applicants:** Southern Arkansas University; University of Arkansas–Little Rock; University of Arkansas–Pine Bluff. **Admissions statistics for the fall 2005 entering class:** Total applicants: 1,564. Total accepted: 943. Freshmen enrolled: 668; 11% were from out of state. Overall acceptance rate: 60%. **Average high school grade point average:** 2.9.

ACADEMICS

Year founded: 1910. **Academic calendar:** Semester. **Degrees offered:** certificate, associate, bachelor's, post-bachelor's certificate, master's. **Most popular majors:** 19% business administration and management, 11% management information systems, 7% accounting, 7% health and physical education, 7% kindergarten/preschool education and teaching. **Major fields of study:** agriculture, agriculture operations, and related sciences; biological and biomedical sciences; business, management, marketing, and related support services; education; engineering; English language and literature/letters; health professions and related clinical sciences; history; mathematics and statistics; multi/interdisciplinary studies; natural resources and conservation; parks, recreation, leisure, and fitness studies; physical sciences; psychology; public administration and social service professions; security and protective services; social sciences; visual and performing arts. **Areas of required coursework:** arts/fine arts, humanities, mathematics, English (including composition), sciences (biological or physical), history, social science. **Pre-professional programs:** pre-law, pre-medicine, pre-veterinary science, pre-pharmacy. **Special academic programs:** cooperative (work-study plan) program, cross-registration, distance learning, double major, independent study, internships, teacher certificate program. **Teacher certification offered in:** early childhood, middle/junior high, secondary. **Reserve Officers Training Corps (ROTC):** Army ROTC: Offered on campus. **Faculty and instruction (2005-2006):** Total instructional faculty: 157 full-time, 31 part-time (51% men; 49% women; 8% minorities). Full-time faculty with Ph.D. or other terminal degree: 52%. Student/faculty ratio: 16/1. Classes of fewer than 20 students: 58%; of 20 to 49 students: 39%; of 50 or more students: 3%. **Advanced Placement and International Baccalaureate credit:** AP tests may be used for: Credit only. Scores accepted: 3, 4, 5. International Baccalaureate exams may be used for: Credit and/or placement. **Freshmen returning for sophomore year:** 51%. **Graduation rates:** Four-year: 10%; five-year: 25%; six-year: 26%.

COSTS AND FINANCIAL AID
Financial aid office: (870) 460-1050. **Expenses (2006-2007):** Tuition and fees 2006-2007: $4,150 in state, $4,930 out of state; room/board: $3,366. Estimated books and supplies: $800; transportation: $1,350; personal expenses: $1,980. Average amount of debt of borrowers graduating in 2005: $13,599.

CAMPUS LIFE AND EXTRACURRICULAR ACTIVITIES
Campus housing available (% using): coed dorms (17%), women's dorms (26%), men's dorms (30%), apartments for married students (5%), apartment for single students (21%). Students who live in college-owned, operated, or affiliated housing: 18%. **Clubs and organizations:** Number of student organizations: 72. Activities include: choral groups, concert band, jazz band, literary magazine, marching band, music ensembles, musical theater, student government, student newspaper, yearbook. Number of fraternities: 8; sororities: 5. Proportion of men in fraternities: 5%; of women in sororities: 3%. **Sports program (2005-2006):** Member of NCAA II. *Men's intercollegiate varsity sports:* baseball, basketball, cross-country, football, golf. *Women's intercollegiate varsity sports:* basketball, cross-country, softball, volleyball.

SERVICES AND FACILITIES
Basic services: nonremedial tutoring, placement service, health service. **Remedial assistance:** reading, math, writing. **Counseling services:** career, academic. **For learning-disabled students:** School does not offer a structured program with separate admission and additional fees. Total undergraduates in learning-disabled program or receiving services: 36. Services include: remedial math, remedial English, remedial reading, tape recorders, videotaped classes, untimed tests, note-taking services, oral tests, readers, extended time for tests, tutors, early syllabus, priority registration, priority seating, texts on tape, typist/scribe, other testing accomodations. **Library:** Number of titles: 241,040; number of current serial subscriptions: 969. **Information technology resources:** Students are not required to lease or own a computer. School does not have a wireless network. Proportion of college-owned housing units wired for high-speed internet access: 95%. **Campus safety:** Security services offered: 24-hour foot-and-vehicle patrols, 24-hour emergency telephones, lighted pathways/sidewalks, controlled dormitory access (key, security card, etc).

TRANSFER AND INTERNATIONAL STUDENTS
Transfer students: May apply for admission for the following academic terms: Fall, Spring, Summer. Applicants do not need a minimum number of credits to apply. For fall 2005: Transfer applications received: 542. Transfer applicants offered admission: 312. Transfer applicants enrolled: 224. **International students:** Number of foreign undergraduates: 0. Minimum TOEFL score required: 500 (paper); 173 (computer).

University of Arkansas–Pine Bluff

- **Address:** 1200 N. University Drive, Pine Bluff, AR 71601
- **Website:** http://www.uapb.edu/
- **Public**
- **Enrollment:** 2,831 full-time; 301 part-time

KEY STATS
✔ **U.S News College Ranking:** fourth tier, Comp. Coll.–Bachelor's (South)
✔ **ACT Score (25th/75th percentile):** 14-19
✔ **Tuition:** 2005-2006: $4,326 in state, $8,511 out of state
Selectivity: Less selective **Room/board:** $5,290
Acceptance rate: 51% **Average debt:** N/A
Student/faculty ratio: N/A **Proportion who borrowed:** N/A

UNDERGRADUATE STUDENT BODY STATS
2005-2006 enrollment: 2,831 full-time; 301 part-time. Men: 44%; women: 56%. **Ethnic makeup:** African American: 96%; White: 3%; International: 1%.

ADMISSIONS FACTS AND FIGURES
Phone: (870) 575-8492. **Email:** fulton_e@uapb.edu. **Website:** http://www.uapb.edu/. **Application deadlines for fall 2007:** Regular decision: Rolling. Early decision: Not offered. Early action: Not offered. Admission can be deferred. Common application is accepted. **Admissions requirements/recommendations:** High school units required (recommended): English: 4; Mathematics: 3; Science: 3; Foreign language: 2; Social studies: 3; Academic electives: 4; Total units: 21. Tests: The college uses SAT or ACT scores in admissions decisions. Either SAT or ACT required. For admission to the fall 2007 entering class, the school will accept: ACT with writing, ACT without writing. **Factors that count in admissions decisions:** *Academic:* Secondary school record: Important. Class rank: Considered. Letters of recommendation: Considered. Standardized test scores: Very important. Essay: Considered. *Nonacademic:* Interview: Considered. Extracurricular activities: Considered. Talent/ability: Considered. Character/personal qualities: Considered. Alumni/ae relationship: Considered. Geographical residence: Considered. State residency: Considered. Religious affiliation/commitment: Considered. Minority status: Considered. Volunteer work: Considered. Work experience: Considered. **Admissions statistics for the fall 2005 entering class:** Total applicants: 2,256. Total accepted: 1,157. Freshmen enrolled: 719; Overall acceptance rate: 51%. **First-year students who submitted SAT scores:** 5%. Scores (25/75 percentile): Verbal: 370-483, Math: 363-488, Combined: 733-971. **First-year students submitting ACT scores:** 95%. Scores (25/75 percentile): English: 13-19, Math: 14-17, Composite: 14-19.

ACADEMICS
Year founded: 1873. **Academic calendar:** Semester. **Degrees offered:** certificate, associate, transfer-associate, terminal-associate, bachelor's, master's. **Most popular majors:** 20% business administration and management, 10% criminal justice/safety studies, 8% psychology, 7% biology/biological sciences, 5% family and consumer sciences/human sciences. **Major fields of study:** agriculture, agriculture operations, and related sciences; biological and biomedical sciences; business, management, marketing, and related support services; communication, journalism, and related programs; computer and information sciences and support services; education; engineering technologies/technicians; English language and literature/letters; family and consumer sciences/human sciences; health professions and related clinical sciences; history; liberal arts and sciences studies, and humanities; mathematics and statistics; natural resources and conservation; parks, recreation, leisure, and fitness studies; physical sciences; psychology; public administration and social service professions; security and protective services; social sciences; visual and performing arts. **Areas of required coursework:** arts/fine arts, humanities, mathematics, English (including composition), philosophy, foreign languages, sciences (biological or physical), history, social science. **Special academic programs:** cooperative (work-study plan) program, cross-registration, distance learning, double major, dual enrollment, honors program, independent study, internships, teacher certificate program. **Teacher certification offered in:** early childhood, special education, middle/junior high, secondary. **Reserve Officers Training Corps (ROTC):** Army ROTC: Offered on campus. **Faculty and instruction (2005-2006):** Total instructional faculty: N/A. Classes of fewer than 20 students: 44%; of 20 to 49 students: 50%; of 50 or more students: 6%. **Freshmen returning for sophomore year:** 62%. **Graduation rates:** Four-year: 12%; five-year: 23%; six-year: 30%.

COSTS AND FINANCIAL AID

Financial aid office: (870) 575-8302. **Expenses (2005-2006):** Tuition and fees 2005-2006: $4,326 in state, $8,511 out of state; room/board: $5,290. Estimated books and supplies: $1,200; transportation: $1,900; personal expenses: $2,428. **Financial aid:** Priority filing date for institution's financial aid form: April 1.

CAMPUS LIFE AND EXTRACURRICULAR ACTIVITIES

Campus housing available (% using): women's dorms (52%), men's dorms (48%). Activities include: choral groups, concert band, drama/theater, jazz band, marching band, music ensembles, pep band, radio station, student government, student newspaper, symphony orchestra, television station, yearbook. **Sports program (2005-2006):** Member of NCAA I. *Men's intercollegiate varsity sports:* baseball, basketball, cross-country, football, golf, tennis, track and field (indoor), track and field (outdoor). *Women's intercollegiate varsity sports:* basketball, bowling, cross-country, golf, soccer, softball, tennis, track and field (indoor), track and field (outdoor), volleyball.

SERVICES AND FACILITIES

Basic services: placement service, health service. **Remedial assistance:** reading, math. **Counseling services:** career, academic.

TRANSFER AND INTERNATIONAL STUDENTS

Transfer students: May apply for admission for the following academic terms: Fall, Spring, Summer. Applicants need a minimum number of credits to apply. For fall 2005: Transfer applications received: 295. Transfer applicants offered admission: 207. Transfer applicants enrolled: 165. **International students:** Number of foreign undergraduates: 21 (1% of student body). Minimum TOEFL score required: 500 (paper); 173 (computer). Average TOEFL score: 520 (paper).

University of Central Arkansas

- **Address:** 201 Donaghey Avenue, Conway, AR 72035
- **Website:** http://www.uca.edu
- **Public**
- **Enrollment:** 9,127 full-time; 842 part-time

KEY STATS

✔ **U.S News College Ranking:** 61, Universities–Master's (South)
✔ **ACT Score (25th/75th percentile):** 20-27
✔ **Tuition:** 2006-2007: $6,010 in state, $10,706 out of state
  Selectivity: More selective   **Room/board:** $4,320
  Acceptance rate: 53%   **Average debt:** $20,000
  Student/faculty ratio: 20/1   **Proportion who borrowed:** 71%

UNDERGRADUATE STUDENT BODY STATS

2005-2006 enrollment: 9,127 full-time; 842 part-time. Men: 41%; women: 59%. **Ethnic makeup:** African American: 17%; American-Indian: 1%; Asian American: 2%; Hispanic: 1%; White: 77%; International: 2%.

ADMISSIONS FACTS AND FIGURES

Phone: (501) 450-3128. **Email:** admissions@uca.edu. **Website:** http://www.uca.edu. **Application deadlines for fall 2007:** Regular decision: September 1. Early decision: Not offered. Early action: Not offered. Admission can be deferred. Common application is not accepted. **To apply online, go to:** https://www.uca.edu/admissions/reg/register.php. **Admissions requirements/recommendations:** High school units required (recommended): English: 4 (4); Mathematics: 4 (4); Science: 3 (3); Social studies: 3 (3); Academic electives: 6 (6); Total units: 21 (21). Tests: The college uses SAT or ACT scores in admissions decisions. Either SAT or ACT required. For admission to the fall 2007 entering class, the school will accept: ACT with writing, ACT without writing. Campus visit: Recommended. Admissions interview: Neither required nor recommended. Off-campus interview: May be arranged. **Factors that count in admissions decisions:** *Academic:* Secondary school record: Very important. Class rank: Very important. Letters of recommendation: Considered. Standardized test scores: Very important. Essay: Not considered. *Nonacademic:* Interview: Considered. Extracurricular activities: Considered. Talent/ability: Considered. Character/personal qualities: Considered. Alumni/ae relationship: Considered. Geographical residence: Not considered. State residency: Not considered. Religious affiliation/commitment: Not considered. Minority sta-

tus: Not considered. Volunteer work: Considered. Work experience: Considered. **Other schools with the greatest overlap in applicants:** Arkansas State University; Arkansas Tech University; Hendrix College; University of Arkansas; University of Arkansas–Little Rock. **Admissions statistics for the fall 2005 entering class:** Total applicants: 5,899. Total accepted: 3,154. Freshmen enrolled: 2,503; 5% were from out of state. Overall acceptance rate: 53%. **Credentials of fall 2005 freshmen:** 21% ranked in the top 10 percent of their high school class; 44% were in the top 25 percent, and 74% were in the top half. (Proportion submitting class standing: 66%.) **Average high school grade point average:** 3.3. **First-year students who submitted SAT scores:** 1%. Scores (25/75 percentile): Verbal: 430-575, Math: 470-595, Combined: 900-1170. **First-year students submitting ACT scores:** 93%. Scores (25/75 percentile): English: 20-28, Math: 18-25, Composite: 20-27.

ACADEMICS

Year founded: 1907. **Academic calendar:** Semester. **Degrees offered:** associate, bachelor's, master's, post-master's certificate, doctorate. **Most popular majors:** 8% family and consumer sciences/human sciences, 6% health professions and related clinical sciences, 5% biology/biological sciences, 5% management information systems, 5% psychology. **Major fields of study:** area, ethnic, cultural, and gender studies; biological and biomedical sciences; business, management, marketing, and related support services; communication, journalism, and related programs; computer and information sciences and support services; education; English language and literature/letters; family and consumer sciences/human sciences; foreign languages, literatures, and linguistics; health professions and related clinical sciences; history; multi/interdisciplinary studies; natural resources and conservation; parks, recreation, leisure, and fitness studies; philosophy and religious studies; physical sciences; psychology; public administration and social service professions; social sciences; visual and performing arts. **Areas of required coursework:** arts/fine arts, humanities, mathematics, English (including composition), sciences (biological or physical), history, social science. **Pre-professional programs:** pre-law, pre-dentistry, pre-medicine, pre-veterinary science, pre-optometry, pre-pharmacy. **Special academic programs:** cooperative (work-study plan) program, distance learning, double major, dual enrollment, English as a Second Language (ESL), exchange student program (domestic), honors program, independent study, internships, liberal arts/career combination, study abroad, teacher certificate program. **Teacher certification offered in:** early childhood, special education, elementary, middle/junior high, secondary. **Reserve Officers Training Corps (ROTC):** Army ROTC: Offered on campus. **Faculty and instruction (2005-2006):** Total instructional faculty: 478 full-time, 129 part-time (50% men; 50% women; 9% minorities). Full-time faculty with Ph.D. or other terminal degree: 64%. Student/faculty ratio: 20/1. Classes of fewer than 20 students: 43%; of 20 to 49 students: 54%; of 50 or more students: 3%. **Freshmen returning for sophomore year:** 71%. **Graduation rates:** Four-year: 21%; five-year: 43%; six-year: 41%.

COSTS AND FINANCIAL AID

Financial aid office: (501) 450-3140. **Expenses (2006-2007):** Tuition and fees 2006-2007: $6,010 in state, $10,706 out of state; room/board: $4,320. **Financial aid:** Priority filing date for institution's financial aid form: February 15; deadline: September 1. In 2005-2006, 85% of undergraduates applied for financial aid. Of those, 66% were determined to have financial need; 5% had their need fully met. Average financial aid package (proportion receiving): $7,500 (66%). Average amount of gift aid, such as scholarships or grants (proportion receiving): $2,460 (66%). Average amount of self-help aid, such as work study or loans (proportion receiving): $3,750 (47%). Average need-based loan (excluding PLUS or other private loans): $3,500. Among students who received need-based aid, the average percentage of need met: 50%. Among students who received aid based on merit, the average award (and the proportion receiving): $3,400 (N/A). The average athletic scholarship (and the proportion receiving): $3,306 (N/A). Average amount of debt of borrowers graduating in 2005: $20,000. Proportion who borrowed: 71%.

CAMPUS LIFE AND EXTRACURRICULAR ACTIVITIES

Campus housing available: coed dorms, women's dorms, men's dorms, fraternity housing, apartments for married students, apartment for single students, special housing for disabled students. Students who live in college-owned, operated, or affiliated housing: 38%. Activities include: choral groups, concert band, dance, drama/theater, jazz band, literary magazine, marching band, music ensembles, musical theater, pep band, radio station, student government, student newspaper, symphony orchestra, television station, yearbook. Number of fraternities: 11; sororities: 8. Proportion of men in fraternities: 10%; of women in sororities: 10%. **Sports program (2005-2006):** Member of NCAA II. *Men's intercollegiate varsity sports:* baseball, basketball, cross-country, football, golf, soccer. **Women's intercollegiate varsity sports:** basketball, cross-country, golf, soccer, softball, tennis, track and field (outdoor), volleyball.

SERVICES AND FACILITIES
Basic services: nonremedial tutoring, placement service, health service. **Remedial assistance:** reading, math, writing, study skills. **Counseling services:** minority student, career, personal, veteran student, academic, older student, psychological, birth control. **For learning-disabled students:** School does not offer a structured program with separate admission and additional fees. Total undergraduates in learning-disabled program or receiving services: 30. Services include: tape recorders, note-taking services, readers, extended time for tests, priority registration, priority seating, texts on tape. **Library:** Number of titles: 1,300,592; number of current serial subscriptions: 1,696. **Information technology resources:** Students are not required to lease or own a computer. Number of campus computers available to all students: 1,500. School has a wireless network. Approximate number of users that can be accommodated: 10,000. Proportion of college-owned housing units wired for high-speed internet access: 100%. **Campus safety:** Security services offered: 24-hour foot-and-vehicle patrols, late-night transport/escort service, 24-hour emergency telephones, lighted pathways/sidewalks.

TRANSFER AND INTERNATIONAL STUDENTS
Transfer students: May apply for admission for the following academic terms: Fall, Spring, Summer. Applicants need a minimum number of credits to apply. For fall 2005: Transfer applications received: 1,561. Transfer applicants offered admission: 852. Transfer applicants enrolled: 720. **International students:** Number of foreign undergraduates: 217 (2% of student body). Number of countries represented: 54. Minimum TOEFL score required: 500 (paper); 173 (computer).

University of the Ozarks

- **Address:** 415 N. College Avenue, Clarksville, AR 72830
- **Website:** http://www.ozarks.edu
- **Private; Religious affiliation:** Presbyterian
- **Enrollment:** 588 full-time; 40 part-time

KEY STATS
✔ **U.S News College Ranking:** 10, Comp. Colleges–Bachelor's (South)
✔ **ACT Score (25th/75th percentile):** 17-27
✔ **Tuition:** 2006-2007: $14,950

Selectivity: Selective	**Room/board:** $5,260
Acceptance rate: 84%	**Average debt:** $12,866
Student/faculty ratio: 13/1	**Proportion who borrowed:** 50%

UNDERGRADUATE STUDENT BODY STATS
2005-2006 enrollment: 588 full-time; 40 part-time. Men: 47%; women: 53%. **Ethnic makeup:** African American: 4%; American-Indian: 4%; Asian American: 2%; Hispanic: 5%; White: 70%; International: 15%. **Religious preference:** Roman Catholic: 15%; Protestant: 55%; No preference: 24%; Presbyterian: 5%; Other: 1%.

ADMISSIONS FACTS AND FIGURES
Phone: (479) 979-1227. **Email:** admiss@ozarks.edu. **Website:** http://www.ozarks.edu. **Application deadlines for fall 2007:** Regular decision: Rolling. Early decision: Not offered. Early action: Not offered. Admission can be deferred. **Application fee:** None. Common application is accepted. **Admissions requirements/recommendations:** High school units required (recommended): English: 4 (4); Mathematics: 4 (4); Science: 3 (3); Foreign language: 2 (2); Social studies: 1 (1); History: 2 (2); Total units: (18). Tests: The college uses SAT or ACT scores in admissions decisions. Either SAT or ACT required. For admission to the fall 2007 entering class, the school will accept: ACT with writing, ACT without writing. Campus visit: Recommended. Admissions interview: Recommended. Off-campus interview: Not available. **Factors that count in admissions decisions:** *Academic:* Secondary school record: Very important. Class rank: Important. Letters of recommendation: Considered. Standardized test scores: Very important. Essay: Considered. *Nonacademic:* Interview: Important. Extracurricular activities: Considered. Talent/ability: Considered. Character/personal qualities: Considered. Alumni/ae relationship: Considered. Geographical residence: Considered. State residency: Not considered. Religious affiliation/commit-

ment: Not considered. Minority status: Not considered. Volunteer work: Considered. Work experience: Considered. **Other schools with the greatest overlap in applicants:** Arkansas Tech University. **Admissions statistics for the fall 2005 entering class:** Total applicants: 632. Total accepted: 530. Freshmen enrolled: 170; 31% were from out of state. Overall acceptance rate: 84%. **Credentials of fall 2005 freshmen:** 20% ranked in the top 10 percent of their high school class; 40% were in the top 25 percent, and 78% were in the top half. (Proportion submitting class standing: 92%.) **Average high school grade point average:** 3.3. **First-year students who submitted SAT scores:** 23%. Scores (25/75 percentile): Verbal: 450-640, Math: 440-620, Combined: 890-1260. **First-year students submitting ACT scores:** 75%. Scores (25/75 percentile): English: 19-28, Math: 16-26, Composite: 17-27.

ACADEMICS
Year founded: 1834. **Academic calendar:** Semester. **Degrees offered:** bachelor's. **Most popular majors:** 38% business administration and management, 22% marketing/marketing management, 13% political science and government, 9% general studies, 8% accounting. **Major fields of study:** business, management, marketing, and related support services; communication, journalism, and related programs; English language and literature/letters; health professions and related clinical sciences; history; liberal arts and sciences studies, and humanities; mathematics and statistics; natural resources and conservation; philosophy and religious studies; physical sciences; psychology; social sciences; visual and performing arts. **Areas of required coursework:** arts/fine arts, humanities, mathematics, English (including composition), sciences (biological or physical), history, social science, other. **Pre-professional programs:** pre-law, pre-dentistry, pre-medicine, pre-veterinary science, pre-pharmacy, other. **Special academic programs (% participation):** double major (19%), English as a Second Language (ESL) (2%), independent study (2%), internships (10%), student-designed major (10%), study abroad (3%), teacher certificate program (18%). **Teacher certification offered in:** early childhood, special education, middle/junior high, secondary. **Faculty and instruction (2005-2006):** Total instructional faculty: 44 full-time, 13 part-time (67% men; 33% women; 5% minorities). Full-time faculty with Ph.D. or other terminal degree: 82%. Student/faculty ratio: 13/1. Classes of fewer than 20 students: 82%; of 20 to 49 students: 18%. **Advanced Placement and International Baccalaureate credit:** AP tests may be used for: Credit only. Scores accepted: 4. International Baccalaureate exams may be used for: Credit only. **Freshmen returning for sophomore year:** 63%. **Graduation rates:** Four-year: 32%; five-year: 49%; six-year: 49%. **Graduate study:** 21% of students pursue further study immediately upon graduation. Fields in which graduates pursue further study: Master of Business Administration (MBA), 25%; law, 11%; medicine, 7%; engineering, 4%; education, 11%; arts and sciences, 43%.

COSTS AND FINANCIAL AID
Financial aid office: (479) 979-1221. **Expenses (2006-2007):** Tuition and fees 2006-2007: $14,950; room/board: $5,260. Estimated books and supplies: $700; transportation: $954; personal expenses: $2,610. **Financial aid:** Priority filing date for institution's financial aid form: February 15. In 2005-2006, 57% of undergraduates applied for financial aid. Of those, 52% were determined to have financial need; 15% had their need fully met. Average financial aid package (proportion receiving): $16,375 (52%). Average amount of gift aid, such as scholarships or grants (proportion receiving): $13,862 (52%). Average amount of self-help aid, such as work study or loans (proportion receiving): $3,521 (43%). Average need-based loan (excluding PLUS or other private loans): $3,025. Among students who received need-based aid, the average percentage of need met: 70%. Among students who received aid based on merit, the average award (and the proportion receiving): $12,092 (44%). Average amount of debt of borrowers graduating in 2005: $12,866. Proportion who borrowed: 50%.

CAMPUS LIFE AND EXTRACURRICULAR ACTIVITIES
Campus housing available (% using): coed dorms (80%), women's dorms (8%), apartment for single students (10%), special housing for disabled students, other housing options (2%). Students who live in college-owned, operated, or affiliated housing: 36%. **Student employment:** During the 2005-2006 academic year, 33% of undergraduates worked on campus. Average per-year earnings: $1,494. **Clubs and organizations:** Number of student organizations: 40. Activities include: choral groups, dance, drama/theater, literary magazine, radio station, student government, television station, yearbook. Number of fraternities: 0; sororities: 0. Average proportion of students who stay on campus on weekends: 50%. **Sports program (2005-2006):** Member of NCAA III. **Men's intercollegiate varsity sports:** baseball, basketball, cross-country, soccer, tennis. **Women's intercollegiate varsity sports:** basketball, cross-country, soccer, softball, tennis.

SERVICES AND FACILITIES

Basic services: nonremedial tutoring, placement service, health service. **Remedial assistance:** reading, math, writing, study skills. **Counseling services:** minority student, career, personal, academic, psychological, religious. **For learning-disabled students:** School does not offer a structured program with separate admission and additional fees. Total undergraduates in learning-disabled program or receiving services: 80. Services include: remedial math, remedial English, reading machines, remedial reading, tape recorders, other special classes, diagnostic testing service, note-taking services, oral tests, learning center, readers, extended time for tests, tutors, priority registration, proof-reading services, texts on tape, typist/scribe, other. **Library:** Number of titles: 106,620; number of current serial subscriptions: 502. **Information technology resources:** Students are not required to lease or own a computer. Number of campus computers available to all students: 150. School does not have a wireless network. Proportion of college-owned housing units wired for high-speed internet access: 100%. **Campus safety:** Security services offered: 24-hour foot-and-vehicle patrols, 24-hour emergency telephones, lighted pathways/sidewalks, controlled dormitory access (key, security card, etc).

TRANSFER AND INTERNATIONAL STUDENTS

Transfer students: May apply for admission for the following academic terms: Fall, Spring, Summer. Applicants do not need a minimum number of credits to apply. For fall 2005: Transfer applications received: 60. Transfer applicants offered admission: 48. Transfer applicants enrolled: 34. **International students:** Number of foreign undergraduates: 92 (15% of student body). Number of countries represented: 22. Minimum TOEFL score required: 500 (paper); 173 (computer).

Williams Baptist College

- **Address:** PO Box 3665, Walnut Ridge, AR 72476
- **Website:** http://www.wbcoll.edu
- **Private; Religious affiliation:** Southern Baptist Convention
- **Enrollment:** 492 full-time; 123 part-time

KEY STATS

✔ **U.S News College Ranking:** third tier, Comp. Colleges–Bachelor's (South)
✔ **ACT Score (25th/75th percentile):** 22
✔ **Tuition:** 2006-2007: $9,850

Selectivity: Selective	**Room/board:** N/A
Acceptance rate: 65%	**Average debt:** $14,768
Student/faculty ratio: 16/1	**Proportion who borrowed:** 81%

UNDERGRADUATE STUDENT BODY STATS

2005-2006 enrollment: 492 full-time; 123 part-time. Men: 42%; women: 58%. **Ethnic makeup:** African American: 2%; Hispanic: 1%; White: 95%; International: 1%. **Religious preference:** Roman Catholic: 2%; Protestant: 45%; Southern Baptist Convention: 47%; Other: 6%.

ADMISSIONS FACTS AND FIGURES

Phone: (800) 722-4434. **Email:** admissions@wbcoll.edu. **Website:** http://www.wbcoll.edu. **Application deadlines for fall 2007:** Regular decision: Rolling. Early decision: Not offered. Early action: Not offered. Admission can be deferred. **Application fee:** $20. Common application is not accepted. **Admissions requirements/recommendations:** High school units required (recommended): English: (4); Mathematics: (4); Science: (3); Foreign language: (2); Social studies: (3). Tests: The college uses SAT or ACT scores in admissions decisions. Either SAT or ACT required. For admission to the fall 2007 entering class, the school will accept: ACT with writing, ACT without writing. Campus visit: Recommended. Admissions interview: Recommended. Off-campus interview: May be arranged. **Factors that count in admissions decisions:** *Academic:* Secondary school record: Very important. Class rank: Important. Letters of recommendation: Considered. Standardized test scores: Very important. Essay: Considered. *Nonacademic:* Interview: Important. Extracurricular activities: Considered. Talent/ability: Important. Character/personal qualities: Important. Alumni/ae relationship: Not considered. Geographical residence: Not considered. State residency: Not considered. Religious affiliation/commitment: Not considered. Minority status: Not considered. Volunteer work: Considered. Work experience: Not considered. **Admissions statistics for the fall 2005 entering class:** Total applicants: 479. Total accepted: 310. Freshmen enrolled: 130; Overall acceptance rate: 65%. **Credentials of fall 2005 freshmen:** 21% ranked in the top 10 percent of their high school class; 50% were in the top 25 percent, and 82% were in the top half. (Proportion submitting class standing: 63%.) **Average high school grade point average:** 3.3. **First-year students who submitted SAT scores:** 2%. Scores (25/75 percentile): Verbal: N/A, Math: N/A, Combined: N/A. **First-year students submitting ACT scores:** 95%. Scores (25/75 percentile): English: N/A, Math: N/A, Composite: N/A.

ACADEMICS

Year founded: 1941. **Academic calendar:** Semester. **Degrees offered:** associate, bachelor's. **Most popular majors:** 40% education, 19% psychology, 15% business, management, marketing, and related support services, 11% theology and religious vocations, 6% liberal arts and sciences studies, and humanities. **Major fields of study:** agriculture, agriculture operations, and related sciences; biological and biomedical sciences; business, management, marketing, and related support services; computer and information sciences and support services; education; history; liberal arts and sciences studies, and humanities; psychology; theology and religious vocations; visual and performing arts. **Areas of required coursework:** arts/fine arts, humanities, computer literacy, mathematics, English (including composition), philosophy, foreign languages, sciences (biological or physical), history, social science, other. **Special academic programs:** double major, internships, study abroad. **Teacher certification offered in:** early childhood, elementary, middle/junior high, secondary. **Reserve Officers Training Corps (ROTC):** Army ROTC: Offered at cooperating institution (Arkansas State University). **Faculty and instruction (2005-2006):** Total instructional faculty: 28 full-time, 13 part-time (49% men; 51% women; 2% minorities). Full-time faculty with Ph.D. or other terminal degree: 57%. Student/faculty ratio: 16/1. Classes of fewer than 20 students: 66%; of 20 to 49 students: 34%; of 50 or more students: 0%. **Advanced Placement and International Baccalaureate credit:** International Baccalaureate exams may be used for: Credit and/or placement. **Freshmen returning for sophomore year:** 60%. **Graduation rates:** Four-year: 19%; five-year: 32%; six-year: 41%. **Graduate study:** 20% of students pursue further study immediately upon graduation; 5% within one year; 5% within five years.

COSTS AND FINANCIAL AID

Financial aid office: (870) 759-4112. **Expenses (2006-2007):** Tuition and fees 2006-2007: $9,850; room/board: N/A. Estimated books and supplies: $900; transportation: $1,000; personal expenses: $1,125. **Financial aid:** Priority filing date for institution's financial aid form: May 3. Average amount of debt of borrowers graduating in 2005: $14,768. Proportion who borrowed: 81%.

CAMPUS LIFE AND EXTRACURRICULAR ACTIVITIES

Campus housing available (% using): women's dorms (44%), men's dorms (39%), apartments for married students (8%), apartment for single students (9%). **Student employment:** During the 2005-2006 academic year, 45% of undergraduates worked on campus. Average per-year earnings: $1,200. **Clubs and organizations:** Number of student organizations: 30. Activities include: choral groups, drama/theater, literary magazine, student government. Number of fraternities: 0; sororities: 0. Average proportion of students who stay on campus on weekends: 25%. **Sports program (2005-2006):** Member of NAIA. *Men's intercollegiate varsity sports:* baseball, basketball, soccer. *Women's intercollegiate varsity sports:* basketball, softball, volleyball.

SERVICES AND FACILITIES

Basic services: placement service, health service. **Remedial assistance:** reading, math, writing, study skills. **Counseling services:** career, personal, academic, psychological, religious. **For learning-disabled students:** School does not offer a structured program with separate admission and additional fees. Total undergraduates in learning-disabled program or receiving services: 10. Services include: remedial math, remedial English, reading machines, remedial reading, tape recorders, other special classes, untimed tests, note-taking services, oral tests, learning center, readers, extended time for tests, tutors, priority seating, texts on tape. **Library:** Number of titles: 68,347; number of current serial subscriptions: 191. **Information technology resources:** Students are not required to lease or own a computer. Number of campus computers available to all students: 70. School does not have a wireless network. Proportion of college-owned housing units wired for high-speed internet access: 85%. **Campus safety:** Security services offered: 24-hour foot-and-vehicle patrols, lighted pathways/sidewalks, student patrols, controlled dormitory access (key, security card, etc).

TRANSFER AND INTERNATIONAL STUDENTS

Transfer students: May apply for admission for the following academic terms: Fall, Spring, Summer. Applicants do not need a minimum number of credits to apply. **International students:** Number of foreign undergraduates: 4 (1% of student body). Minimum TOEFL score required: 500 (paper).

California

Alliant International University

- **Address:** 10455 Pomerado Road, San Diego, CA 92131-1799
- **Website:** http://www.alliant.edu
- **Private**
- **Enrollment:** 227 full-time; 28 part-time

KEY STATS

✔ **U.S News College Ranking:** fourth tier, National Universities
✔ **SAT Score (25th/75th percentile):** 933
✔ **Tuition:** 2006-2007: $14,360

Selectivity: Less selective	**Room/board:** $7,980
Acceptance rate: 77%	**Average debt:** $16,000
Student/faculty ratio: 15/1	**Proportion who borrowed:** 43%

UNDERGRADUATE STUDENT BODY STATS

2005-2006 enrollment: 227 full-time; 28 part-time. Men: 48%; women: 52%. **Ethnic makeup:** African American: 8%; American-Indian: 1%; Asian American: 7%; Hispanic: 19%; White: 37%; International: 27%.

ADMISSIONS FACTS AND FIGURES

Phone: (858) 635-4772. **Email:** admissions@alliant.edu. **Website:** http://www.alliant.edu. **Application deadlines for fall 2007:** Regular decision: Rolling. Early decision: Not offered. Early action: Not offered. Admission can be deferred. **Application fee:** $40. Common application is accepted. **To apply online, go to:** http://www.alliant.edu/applyonline/. **Admissions requirements/recommendations:** High school units required (recommended): English: (4); Mathematics: (2); Science: (2); Foreign language: (2). Tests: The college uses SAT or ACT scores in admissions decisions. Either SAT or ACT required. Campus visit: Recommended. Admissions interview: Neither required nor recommended. Off-campus interview: Not available. **Factors that count in admissions decisions:** *Academic:* Secondary school record: Very important. Class rank: Considered. Letters of recommendation: Not considered. Standardized test scores: Considered. Essay: Not considered. *Nonacademic:* Interview: Not considered. Extracurricular activities: Considered. Talent/ability: Not considered. Character/personal qualities: Important. Alumni/ae relationship: Considered. Geographical residence: Not considered. State residency: Not considered. Religious affiliation/commitment: Not considered. Minority status: Not considered. Volunteer work: Not considered. Work experience: Not considered. **Admissions statistics for the fall 2005 entering class:** Total applicants: 163. Total accepted: 125. Freshmen enrolled: 29; 38% were from out of state. Overall acceptance rate: 77%. **Average high school grade point average:** 2.9. **First-year students who submitted SAT scores:** 59%. Scores (25/75 percentile): Verbal: N/A, Math: N/A, Combined: N/A. **First-year students submitting ACT scores:** 14%. Scores (25/75 percentile): English: N/A, Math: N/A, Composite: N/A.

ACADEMICS

Year founded: 1969. **Academic calendar:** Semester. **Degrees offered:** certificate, bachelor's, post-bachelor's certificate, master's, doctorate. **Most popular majors:** 40% international business/trade/commerce, 16% business administration and management, 14% psychology, 5% management information systems, 4% international relations and affairs. **Major fields of study:** business, management, marketing, and related support services; psychology; social sciences. **Areas of required coursework:** humanities, computer literacy, mathematics, English (including composition), foreign languages, sciences (biological or physical), social science, other. **Special academic programs (% participation):** cooperative (work-study plan) program, English as a Second Language (ESL) (5%), honors program (14%), independent study, internships, study abroad (7%), teacher certificate program (3%). **Faculty and instruction (2005-2006):** Total instructional faculty: 132 full-time, 379 part-time (56% men; 44% women; 19% minorities). Full-time faculty with Ph.D. or other terminal degree: 98%. Student/faculty ratio: 15/1. Classes of fewer than 20 students: 86%; of 20 to 49 students: 14%. **Advanced Placement and International Baccalaureate credit:** AP tests may be used for: Credit and/or placement. Scores accepted: 3. **Freshmen returning for sophomore year:** 52%.

Graduation rates: Four-year: 25%; five-year: 29%; six-year: 33%. **Graduate study:** 65% of students pursue further study immediately upon graduation; 30% within one year; 5% within five years. Fields in which graduates pursue further study: Master of Business Administration (MBA), 64%; education, 9%; arts and sciences, 27%.

COSTS AND FINANCIAL AID

Financial aid office: (858) 635-4700. **Expenses (2006-2007):** Tuition and fees 2006-2007: $14,360; room/board: $7,980. Estimated books and supplies: $1,242; transportation: $738; personal expenses: $1,980. **Financial aid:** Priority filing date for institution's financial aid form: March 2. In 2005-2006, 52% of undergraduates applied for financial aid. Of those, 48% were determined to have financial need; 19% had their need fully met. Average financial aid package (proportion receiving): $17,000 (48%). Average amount of gift aid, such as scholarships or grants (proportion receiving): $6,700 (48%). Average amount of self-help aid, such as work study or loans (proportion receiving): $6,000 (37%). Average need-based loan (excluding PLUS or other private loans): $3,300. Among students who received need-based aid, the average percentage of need met: 70%. Among students who received aid based on merit, the average award (and the proportion receiving): $2,000 (31%). The average athletic scholarship (and the proportion receiving): $5,000 (13%). Average amount of debt of borrowers graduating in 2005: $16,000. Proportion who borrowed: 43%.

CAMPUS LIFE AND EXTRACURRICULAR ACTIVITIES

Campus housing available (% using): coed dorms (100%), other housing options. Students who live in college-owned, operated, or affiliated housing: 36%. **Student employment:** During the 2005-2006 academic year, 7% of undergraduates worked on campus. Average per-year earnings: $1,200. **Clubs and organizations:** Number of student organizations: 15. Activities include: student government, student newspaper, yearbook. Number of fraternities: 0; sororities: 0. Average proportion of students who stay on campus on weekends: 35%. **Sports program (2005-2006):** Member of NAIA. **Men's intercollegiate varsity sports:** cross-country, soccer, tennis, track and field (indoor), track and field (outdoor). **Women's intercollegiate varsity sports:** cross-country, soccer, tennis, track and field (indoor), track and field (outdoor), volleyball.

SERVICES AND FACILITIES

Basic services: nonremedial tutoring, placement service, health service, health insurance, other. **Remedial assistance:** reading, math, writing, study skills, other. **Counseling services:** minority student, career, personal, veteran student, academic, older student, psychological, other. **For learning-disabled students:** School does not offer a structured program with separate admission and additional fees. Total undergraduates in learning-disabled program or receiving services: 10. Services include: remedial math, remedial English, reading machines, remedial reading, tape recorders, videotaped classes, untimed tests, note-taking services, oral tests, readers, extended time for tests, tutors, priority registration, priority seating, texts on tape, other testing accomodations, other. **Information technology resources:** Students are not required to lease or own a computer. Number of campus computers available to all students: 100. School has a wireless network. Proportion of college-owned housing units wired for high-speed internet access: 100%. **Campus safety:** Security services offered: 24-hour foot-and-vehicle patrols, late-night transport/escort service, 24-hour emergency telephones, lighted pathways/sidewalks, controlled dormitory access (key, security card, etc).

TRANSFER AND INTERNATIONAL STUDENTS

Transfer students: May apply for admission for the following academic terms: Fall, Spring, Summer. Applicants need a minimum number of credits to apply. For fall 2005: Transfer applications received: 128. Transfer applicants offered admission: 118. Transfer applicants enrolled: 32. **International students:** Number of foreign undergraduates: 70 (27% of student body). Number of countries represented: 58. Minimum TOEFL score required: 550 (paper); 213 (computer).

Art Center College of Design

■ **Address:** 1700 Lida Street, Pasadena, CA 91103
■ **Website:** http://www.artcenter.edu
■ **Private**
■ **Enrollment:** 1,304 full-time; 208 part-time

KEY STATS

✔ **U.S News College Ranking:** Unranked Specialty School–Fine Arts
✔ **SAT Score (25th/75th percentile):** 1109
✔ **Tuition:** 2006-2007: $26,712

Selectivity: Selective	**Room/board:** N/A
Acceptance rate: 74%	**Average debt:** N/A
Student/faculty ratio: 9/1	**Proportion who borrowed:** 70%

UNDERGRADUATE STUDENT BODY STATS

2005-2006 enrollment: 1,304 full-time; 208 part-time. Men: 60%; women: 40%. **Ethnic makeup:** African American: 2%; Asian American: 37%; Hispanic: 11%; White: 33%; International: 17%.

ADMISSIONS FACTS AND FIGURES

Phone: (626) 396-2373. **Email:** admissions@artcenter.edu. **Website:** http://www.artcenter.edu. **Application deadlines for fall 2007:** Regular decision: Rolling. Early decision: Not offered. Early action: Not offered. Admission can be deferred. **Application fee:** $45. Common application is not accepted. **Admissions requirements/recommendations:** Tests: The college uses SAT or ACT scores in admissions decisions. Neither SAT nor ACT required. Campus visit: Recommended. Admissions interview: Recommended. Off-campus interview: Not available. **Factors that count in admissions decisions:** *Academic:* Secondary school record: Very important. Class rank: Very important. Letters of recommendation: Considered. Standardized test scores: Considered. Essay: Very important. *Nonacademic:* Interview: Considered. Extracurricular activities: Considered. Talent/ability: Very important. Character/personal qualities: Considered. Alumni/ae relationship: Not considered. Geographical residence: Not considered. State residency: Not considered. Religious affiliation/commitment: Not considered. Minority status: Considered. Volunteer work: Considered. Work experience: Considered. **Other schools with the greatest overlap in applicants:** California Institute of the Arts; Otis College of Art and Design; Pratt Institute; Rhode Island School of Design; University of California–Los Angeles. **Admissions statistics for the fall 2005 entering class:** Total applicants: 1,079. Total accepted: 796. Freshmen enrolled: 588; 23% were from out of state. Overall acceptance rate: 74%. **Size of waiting list:** 0 applicants; enrolled from waiting list: 0. **Credentials of fall 2005 freshmen:** 19% ranked in the top 10 percent of their high school class; 19% were in the top 25 percent. **Average high school grade point average:** 3.3. **First-year students who submitted SAT scores:** 21%. Scores (25/75 percentile): Verbal: N/A, Math: N/A, Combined: N/A.

ACADEMICS

Year founded: 1930. **Academic calendar:** Trimester. **Degrees offered:** bachelor's, master's. **Most popular majors:** 100% visual and performing arts. **Major fields of study:** visual and performing arts. **Areas of required coursework:** arts/fine arts, humanities, computer literacy, mathematics, English (including composition), philosophy, sciences (biological or physical), social science. **Special academic programs (% participation):** cross-registration (3%), independent study (20%), internships (15%). **Faculty and instruction (2005-2006):** Total instructional faculty: 66 full-time, 341 part-time (74% men; 26% women; 14% minorities). Student/faculty ratio: 9/1. Classes of fewer than 20 students: 90%; of 20 to 49 students: 10%; of 50 or more students: 0%. **Advanced Placement and International Baccalaureate credit:** AP tests may be used for: Credit only. Scores accepted: 4, 5. International Baccalaureate exams may be used for: Credit only. **Freshmen returning for sophomore year:** 91%. **Graduation rates:** Four-year: 62%; five-year: 62%; six-year: 72%.

COSTS AND FINANCIAL AID

Financial aid office: (626) 396-2215. **Expenses (2006-2007):** Tuition and fees 2006-2007: $26,712; room/board: N/A. **Financial aid:** Priority filing date for institution's financial aid form: March 1. In 2005-2006, 85% of undergraduates applied for financial aid. Of those, 81% were determined to have financial need; Average financial aid package (proportion receiving): $13,708 (78%). Average amount of gift aid, such as scholarships or grants (proportion receiving): $8,227 (65%). Average amount of self-help aid, such as

work study or loans (proportion receiving): $5,481 (77%). Average need-based loan (excluding PLUS or other private loans): $5,283. Among students who received need-based aid, the average percentage of need met: 60%. Among students who received aid based on merit, the average award (and the proportion receiving): $0 (0%). The average athletic scholarship (and the proportion receiving): $0 (0%). Proportion who borrowed: 70%.

CAMPUS LIFE AND EXTRACURRICULAR ACTIVITIES

Students who live in college-owned, operated, or affiliated housing: 0%. **Student employment:** During the 2005-2006 academic year, 22% of undergraduates worked on campus. Average per-year earnings: $2,200. **Clubs and organizations:** Number of student organizations: 14. Activities include: student government. Number of fraternities: 0; sororities: 0.

SERVICES AND FACILITIES

Basic services: placement service, health insurance. **Remedial assistance:** writing. **Counseling services:** career, personal, academic, psychological. **For learning-disabled students:** School does not offer a structured program with separate admission and additional fees. Total undergraduates in learning-disabled program or receiving services: 0. Services include: remedial English, extended time for tests. **Library:** Number of titles: 85,000; number of current serial subscriptions: 400. **Information technology resources:** Students are not required to lease or own a computer. Number of campus computers available to all students: 280. School has a wireless network. **Campus safety:** Security services offered: 24-hour foot-and-vehicle patrols, 24-hour emergency telephones.

TRANSFER AND INTERNATIONAL STUDENTS

Transfer students: May apply for admission for the following academic terms: Fall, Spring, Summer. Applicants need a minimum number of credits to apply. For fall 2005: Transfer applications received: 35. Transfer applicants offered admission: 29. Transfer applicants enrolled: 27. **International students:** Number of foreign undergraduates: 244 (17% of student body). Minimum TOEFL score required: 550 (paper); 213 (computer). Average TOEFL score: 565 (paper).

Azusa Pacific University

■ **Address:** 901 E. Alosta Avenue, Azusa, CA 91702
■ **Website:** http://www.apu.edu
■ **Private; Religious affiliation:** Christian interdenominatial
■ **Enrollment:** 3,947 full-time; 655 part-time

KEY STATS

✔ **U.S News College Ranking:** 15, Universities–Master's (West)
✔ **SAT Score (25th/75th percentile):** 1010-1220
✔ **Tuition:** 2006-2007: $23,750

Selectivity: More selective	**Room/board:** $7,328
Acceptance rate: 69%	**Average debt:** $19,487
Student/faculty ratio: 11/1	**Proportion who borrowed:** 49%

UNDERGRADUATE STUDENT BODY STATS

2005-2006 enrollment: 3,947 full-time; 655 part-time. Men: 36%; women: 64%. **Ethnic makeup:** African American: 3%; Asian American: 6%; Hispanic: 12%; White: 77%; International: 2%. **Religious preference:** Roman Catholic: 7%; Protestant: 1%; No preference: 1%; Unknown: 2%; Christian interdenominatial: 87%; Other: 1%.

ADMISSIONS FACTS AND FIGURES

Phone: (800) 825-5278. **Email:** admissions@apu.edu. **Website:** http://www.apu.edu. **Application deadlines for fall 2007:** Regular decision: June 1. Early decision: Not offered. Early action: Send application by: December 1; Decision sent by: January 15. Admission can be deferred. **Application fee:** $45. Common application is not accepted. **Admissions requirements/recommendations:** High school units required (recommended): English: (4); Mathematics: (3); Science: (2); Foreign language: (3); Social studies: (1); History: (2). Tests: The college uses SAT or ACT scores in admissions decisions. Either SAT or ACT required. Campus visit: Neither required nor recommended. Admissions interview: Neither required nor recommended. Off-campus interview: Not available. **Factors that count in admissions decisions:** *Academic:* Secondary school record: Very important. Class rank: Very important. Letters of recommendation: Very important.

Standardized test scores: Very important. Essay: Very important. **Nonacademic:** Interview: Considered. Extracurricular activities: Considered. Talent/ability: Considered. Character/personal qualities: Important. Alumni/ae relationship: Considered. Geographical residence: Not considered. State residency: Important. Religious affiliation/commitment: Not considered. Minority status: Considered. Volunteer work: Considered. Work experience: Considered. **Other schools with the greatest overlap in applicants:** Biola University; California State University–Long Beach; Point Loma Nazarene University; University of California–Los Angeles; Westmont College. **Admissions statistics for the fall 2005 entering class:** Total applicants: 3,127. Total accepted: 2,151. Freshmen enrolled: 881; 28% were from out of state. Overall acceptance rate: 69%. Non-early acceptance rate: 69%. **Size of waiting list:** 383 applicants; enrolled from waiting list: 56. **Credentials of fall 2005 freshmen:** 41% ranked in the top 10 percent of their high school class; 74% were in the top 25 percent, and 89% were in the top half. (Proportion submitting class standing: 66%.) **Average high school grade point average:** 3.7. **First-year students who submitted SAT scores:** 90%. Scores (25/75 percentile): Verbal: 510-610, Math: 500-610, Combined: 1010-1220. **First-year students submitting ACT scores:** 37%. Scores (25/75 percentile): English: N/A, Math: N/A, Composite: 21-27.

ACADEMICS

Year founded: 1899. **Academic calendar:** Semester. **Degrees offered:** bachelor's, master's, first professional, doctorate. **Most popular majors:** 27% liberal arts and sciences studies, and humanities, 22% business, management, marketing, and related support services, 9% communication, journalism, and related programs, 6% health professions and related clinical sciences, 5% theology and religious vocations. **Major fields of study:** area, ethnic, cultural, and gender studies; biological and biomedical sciences; business, management, marketing, and related support services; communication, journalism, and related programs; computer and information sciences and support services; education; English language and literature/letters; foreign languages, literatures, and linguistics; health professions and related clinical sciences; history; liberal arts and sciences studies, and humanities; mathematics and statistics; philosophy and religious studies; physical sciences; psychology; public administration and social service professions; social sciences; theology and religious vocations; visual and performing arts. **Areas of required coursework:** arts/fine arts, humanities, mathematics, English (including composition), philosophy, foreign languages, sciences (biological or physical), history, social science. **Pre-professional programs:** pre-law, other. **Special academic programs:** accelerated program, cooperative (work-study plan) program, distance learning, double major, English as a Second Language (ESL), exchange student program (domestic), honors program, independent study, internships, study abroad, teacher certificate program. **Reserve Officers Training Corps (ROTC):** Army ROTC: Offered at cooperating institution (Reserve Officers' Training Corps). **Faculty and instruction (2005-2006):** Total instructional faculty: 333 full-time, 36 part-time (55% men; 45% women; 19% minorities). Full-time faculty with Ph.D. or other terminal degree: 70%. Student/faculty ratio: 11/1. Classes of fewer than 20 students: 64%; of 20 to 49 students: 35%; of 50 or more students: 2%. **Advanced Placement and International Baccalaureate credit:** AP tests may be used for: Credit only. Scores accepted: 3, 4, 5. International Baccalaureate exams may be used for: Credit only. **Freshmen returning for sophomore year:** 83%. **Graduation rates:** Four-year: 52%; five-year: 63%; six-year: 60%.

COSTS AND FINANCIAL AID

Financial aid office: (626) 815-6000. **Expenses (2006-2007):** Tuition and fees 2006-2007: $23,750; room/board: $7,328. **Financial aid:** Priority filing date for institution's financial aid form: March 2; deadline: July 1. Average amount of debt of borrowers graduating in 2005: $19,487. Proportion who borrowed: 49%.

CAMPUS LIFE AND EXTRACURRICULAR ACTIVITIES

Campus housing available (% using): coed dorms (29%), women's dorms (9%), men's dorms (6%), apartment for single students (56%). Students who live in college-owned, operated, or affiliated housing: 47%. **Student employment:** During the 2005-2006 academic year, 25% of undergraduates worked on campus. Average per-year earnings: $3,800. **Clubs and organizations:** Number of student organizations: 32. Activities include: choral groups, concert band, drama/theater, jazz band, marching band, music ensembles, musical theater, opera, pep band, radio station, student government, student newspaper, symphony orchestra, television station, yearbook. Number of fraternities: 0; sororities: 0. **Sports program (2005-2006):** Member of NAIA. **Men's intercollegiate varsity sports:** baseball, basketball, cross-country, football, soccer, tennis, track and field (indoor), track and field (outdoor), ultimate frisbee, volleyball, water polo, water skiing, wrestling.

Women's intercollegiate varsity sports: basketball, cross-country, soccer, softball, tennis, track and field (indoor), track and field (outdoor), volleyball.

SERVICES AND FACILITIES

Basic services: nonremedial tutoring, women's center, health service, health insurance. **Remedial assistance:** reading, math, writing. **Counseling services:** minority student, career, personal, academic, psychological, religious, other. **For learning-disabled students:** School does not offer a structured program with separate admission and additional fees. Services include: remedial math, remedial reading, note-taking services, learning center, extended time for tests, tutors, other. **Library:** Number of titles: 185,708; number of current serial subscriptions: 14,031. **Information technology resources:** Students are not required to lease or own a computer. Number of campus computers available to all students: 456. School has a wireless network. Approximate number of users that can be accommodated: 8,000. Proportion of college-owned housing units wired for high-speed internet access: 100%. **Campus safety:** Security services offered: 24-hour foot-and-vehicle patrols, late-night transport/escort service, 24-hour emergency telephones, lighted pathways/sidewalks, controlled dormitory access (key, security card, etc).

TRANSFER AND INTERNATIONAL STUDENTS

Transfer students: May apply for admission for the following academic terms: Fall, Spring. Applicants need a minimum number of credits to apply. For fall 2005: Transfer applications received: 1,025. Transfer applicants offered admission: 500. Transfer applicants enrolled: 372. **International students:** Number of foreign undergraduates: 80 (2% of student body). Number of countries represented: 29. Minimum TOEFL score required: 500 (paper); 173 (computer). Average TOEFL score: 500 (paper).

Bethany College

- **Address:** 800 Bethany Drive, Scotts Valley, CA 95066
- **Website:** http://www.bethany.edu
- **Private; Religious affiliation:** Assemblies of God
- **Enrollment:** N/A

KEY STATS
- ✔ **U.S News College Ranking:** third tier, Comp. Colleges–Bachelor's (West)
- ✔ **SAT or ACT Score (25th/75th percentile):** N/A
- ✔ **Tuition:** N/A
  - **Selectivity:** Less selective   **Room/board:** N/A
  - **Acceptance rate:** N/A   **Average debt:** N/A
  - **Student/faculty ratio:** N/A   **Proportion who borrowed:** N/A

Biola University

- **Address:** 13800 Biola Avenue, La Mirada, CA 90639-0001
- **Website:** http://www.biola.edu
- **Private; Religious affiliation:** Christian interdenominational
- **Enrollment:** 3,310 full-time; 484 part-time

KEY STATS
- ✔ **U.S News College Ranking:** fourth tier, National Universities
- ✔ **SAT Score (25th/75th percentile):** 1010-1250
- ✔ **Tuition:** 2006-2007: $23,782
  - **Selectivity:** More selective   **Room/board:** $7,440
  - **Acceptance rate:** 82%   **Average debt:** $28,007
  - **Student/faculty ratio:** 16/1   **Proportion who borrowed:** 74%

UNDERGRADUATE STUDENT BODY STATS

2005-2006 enrollment: 3,310 full-time; 484 part-time. Men: 40%; women: 60%. **Ethnic makeup:** African American: 4%; Asian American: 8%; Hispanic: 11%; White: 74%; International: 2%.

ADMISSIONS FACTS AND FIGURES

Phone: (562) 903-4752. **Email:** admissions@biola.edu. **Website:** http://www.biola.edu. **Application deadlines for fall 2007:** Regular decision: March 1; decision sent by April 1. Early decision: Not offered. Early action: Send application by: December 1; Decision sent by: January 15. Admission can be deferred. **Application fee:** $45. Common application is not accepted. **To apply online, go to:** http://www.biola.edu/applynow. **Admissions requirements/recommendations:** High school units required (recommended): English: (4); Mathematics: (3); Science: (2); Foreign language: (4); Social studies: (2); Total units: (15). Tests: The college uses SAT or ACT scores in admissions decisions. Either SAT or ACT required. For admission to the fall 2007 entering class, the school will accept: ACT with writing, ACT without writing. Campus visit: Recommended. Admissions interview: Recommended. Off-campus interview: May be arranged. **Factors that count in admissions decisions:** *Academic:* Secondary school record: Very important. Class rank: Considered. Letters of recommendation: Very important. Standardized test scores: Very important. Essay: Very important. *Nonacademic:* Interview: Considered. Extracurricular activities: Considered. Talent/ability: Not considered. Character/personal qualities: Important. Alumni/ae relationship: Considered. Geographical residence: Not considered. State residency: Not considered. Religious affiliation/commitment: Very important. Minority status: Considered. Volunteer work: Considered. Work experience: Considered. **Admissions statistics for the fall 2005 entering class:** Total applicants: 2,077. Total accepted: 1,709. Freshmen enrolled: 781; 26% were from out of state. Overall acceptance rate: 82%. **Credentials of fall 2005 freshmen:** 35% ranked in the top 10 percent of their high school class; 67% were in the top 25 percent, and 90% were in the top half. (Proportion submitting class standing: 59%.) **Average high school grade point average:** 3.5. **First-year students who submitted SAT scores:** 92%. Scores (25/75 percentile): Verbal: 510-630, Math: 500-620, Combined: 1010-1250. **First-year students submitting ACT scores:** 28%. Scores (25/75 percentile): English: 21-28, Math: N/A, Composite: 21-27.

ACADEMICS

Year founded: 1908. **Academic calendar:** 4-1-4. **Degrees offered:** bachelor's, master's, post-master's certificate, first professional, doctorate. **Most popular majors:** 24% business, management, marketing, and related support services, 15% theology and religious vocations, 13% communication, journalism, and related programs, 8% education, 7% psychology. **Major fields of study:** biological and biomedical sciences; business, management, marketing, and related support services; communication, journalism, and related programs; computer and information sciences and support services; education; English language and literature/letters; foreign languages, literatures, and linguistics; health professions and related clinical sciences; history; liberal arts and sciences studies, and humanities; mathematics and statistics; philosophy and religious studies; physical sciences; psychology; social sciences; theology and religious vocations; visual and performing arts. **Areas of required coursework:** arts/fine arts, mathematics, English (including composition), philosophy, foreign languages, sciences (biological or physical), history, social science, other. **Pre-professional programs:** pre-law, pre-dentistry, pre-medicine, pre-theology, pre-veterinary science, pre-optometry, pre-pharmacy. **Special academic programs (% participation):** double major (1%), English as a Second Language (ESL) (1%), exchange student program (domestic) (2%), honors program (8%), independent study, internships (60%), student-designed major, study abroad (10%), teacher certificate program (4%). **Teacher certification offered in:** elementary, secondary. **Reserve Officers Training Corps (ROTC):** Army ROTC: Offered at cooperating institution (California State University, Fullerton); Air Force ROTC: Offered at cooperating institution (Loyola Marymount University). **Faculty and instruction (2005-2006):** Total instructional faculty: 190 full-time, 250 part-time (; 10% minorities). Full-time faculty with Ph.D. or other terminal degree: 78%. Student/faculty ratio: 16/1. **Advanced Placement and International Baccalaureate credit:** AP tests may be used for: Credit and/or placement. Scores accepted: 3, 4, 5. International Baccalaureate exams may be used for: Credit and/or placement. **Freshmen returning for sophomore year:** 84%. **Graduation rates:** Four-year: 48%; five-year: 66%; six-year: 70%.

COSTS AND FINANCIAL AID

Financial aid office: (562) 903-4742. **Expenses (2006-2007):** Tuition and fees 2006-2007: $23,782; room/board: $7,440. Estimated books and supplies: $1,314; transportation: $774; personal expenses: $2,088. **Financial aid:** Priority filing date for institution's financial aid form: March 2. In 2005-2006, 75% of undergraduates applied for financial aid. Of those, 65% were determined to have financial need; 13% had their need fully met. Average financial aid package (proportion receiving): $15,200 (65%). Average amount of gift aid, such as scholarships or grants (proportion receiving): $9,514 (52%). Average amount of self-help aid, such as work study or loans (proportion receiving): $4,486 (64%). Average need-based loan (excluding PLUS or other private loans): $2,969. Among students who received need-based aid, the average percentage of need met: 70%. Among students who received aid based on merit, the average award (and the proportion receiv-

ing): $11,205 (11%). The average athletic scholarship (and the proportion receiving): $1,449 (3%). Average amount of debt of borrowers graduating in 2005: $28,007. Proportion who borrowed: 74%.

CAMPUS LIFE AND EXTRACURRICULAR ACTIVITIES

Campus housing available (% using): women's dorms (15%), apartment for single students (15%), other housing options (70%). **Student employment:** During the 2005-2006 academic year, 37% of undergraduates worked on campus. Average per-year earnings: $3,000. **Clubs and organizations:** Number of student organizations: 37. Activities include: choral groups, concert band, dance, drama/theater, jazz band, music ensembles, musical theater, radio station, student government, student newspaper, student film society, symphony orchestra, television station, yearbook. Number of fraternities: 0; sororities: 0. **Sports program (2005-2006):** Member of NAIA. *Men's intercollegiate varsity sports:* baseball, basketball, cross-country, soccer, swimming and diving, track and field (indoor), track and field (outdoor). *Women's intercollegiate varsity sports:* basketball, cross-country, soccer, softball, swimming and diving, tennis, track and field (indoor), track and field (outdoor), volleyball.

SERVICES AND FACILITIES

Basic services: nonremedial tutoring, health service, health insurance. **Remedial assistance:** reading, math, writing, study skills. **Counseling services:** minority student, career, military, personal, veteran student, academic, older student, psychological, birth control, religious, other. **For learning-disabled students:** School does not offer a structured program with separate admission and additional fees. Total undergraduates in learning-disabled program or receiving services: 60. Services include: reading machines, tape recorders, diagnostic testing service, note-taking services, readers, extended time for tests, tutors, priority registration, priority seating, texts on tape, other testing accomodations. **Library:** Number of titles: 279,560; number of current serial subscriptions: 13,123. **Information technology resources:** Students are not required to lease or own a computer. Number of campus computers available to all students: 165. School has a wireless network. Approximate number of users that can be accommodated: 100. Proportion of college-owned housing units wired for high-speed internet access: 100%. **Campus safety:** Security services offered: 24-hour foot-and-vehicle patrols, late-night transport/escort service, 24-hour emergency telephones, lighted pathways/sidewalks, student patrols, controlled dormitory access (key, security card, etc).

TRANSFER AND INTERNATIONAL STUDENTS

Transfer students: May apply for admission for the following academic terms: Fall, Spring. Applicants need a minimum number of credits to apply. For fall 2005: Transfer applications received: 657. Transfer applicants offered admission: 505. Transfer applicants enrolled: 280. **International students:** Number of foreign undergraduates: 86 (2% of student body). Minimum TOEFL score required: 500 (paper); 173 (computer).

California Baptist University

- **Address:** 8432 Magnolia Avenue, Riverside, CA 92504
- **Website:** http://www.calbaptist.edu
- **Private; Religious affiliation:** California Southern Baptist Convention
- **Enrollment:** 1,976 full-time; 439 part-time

KEY STATS

✔ U.S News College Ranking: 51, Universities–Master's (West)
✔ SAT Score (25th/75th percentile): 900-1110
✔ Tuition: 2006-2007: $19,030

Selectivity: Selective	Room/board: $8,222
Acceptance rate: 71%	Average debt: $19,920
Student/faculty ratio: 17/1	Proportion who borrowed: 99%

UNDERGRADUATE STUDENT BODY STATS

2005-2006 enrollment: 1,976 full-time; 439 part-time. Men: 35%; women: 65%. **Ethnic makeup:** African American: 9%; American-Indian: 1%; Asian American: 2%; Hispanic: 17%; White: 70%; International: 1%. **Religious preference:** Roman Catholic: 6%; Protestant: 47%; Unknown: 6%; California Southern Baptist Convention: 27%; Other: 14%.

ADMISSIONS FACTS AND FIGURES

Phone: (877) 228-8866. **Email:** admissions@calbaptist.edu. **Website:** http://www.calbaptist.edu. **Application deadlines for fall 2007:** Regular decision: Rolling. Early decision: Not offered. Early action: Send application by: November 19; Decision sent by: December 20. Admission can be deferred. **Application fee:** $45. Common application is accepted. **Admissions requirements/recommendations:** High school units required (recommended): English: 4 (4); Mathematics: 3 (4); Science: 2 (3); Foreign language: 2 (3); Social studies: 2 (2); History: 2 (2); Academic electives: (3); Total units: 15 (19). Tests: The college uses SAT or ACT scores in admissions decisions. Either SAT or ACT required. For admission to the fall 2007 entering class, the school will accept: ACT with writing, ACT without writing. Campus visit: Recommended. Admissions interview: Recommended. Off-campus interview: May be arranged. **Factors that count in admissions decisions:** *Academic:* Secondary school record: Important. Class rank: Considered. Letters of recommendation: Important. Standardized test scores: Important. Essay: Important. *Nonacademic:* Interview: Considered. Extracurricular activities: Considered. Talent/ability: Considered. Character/personal qualities: Important. Alumni/ae relationship: Not considered. Geographical residence: Not considered. State residency: Not considered. Religious affiliation/commitment: Not considered. Minority status: Not considered. Volunteer work: Not considered. Work experience: Not considered. **Other schools with the greatest overlap in applicants:** Azusa Pacific University; Biola University; California State University–San Bernardino; Point Loma Nazarene University; Vanguard University of Southern California. **Admissions statistics for the fall 2005 entering class:** Total applicants: 1,072. Total accepted: 764. Freshmen enrolled: 439; 9% were from out of state. Overall acceptance rate: 71%. Non-early acceptance rate: 71%. **Credentials of fall 2005 freshmen:** 12% ranked in the top 10 percent of their high school class; 42% were in the top 25 percent, and 44% were in the top half. (Proportion submitting class standing: 72%.) **Average high school grade point average:** 3.1. **First-year students who submitted SAT scores:** 73%. Scores (25/75 percentile): Verbal: 450-560, Math: 450-550, Combined: 900-1110. **First-year students submitting ACT scores:** 27%. Scores (25/75 percentile): English: 19-23, Math: 18-20, Composite: 18-23.

ACADEMICS

Year founded: 1950. **Academic calendar:** Semester. **Degrees offered:** certificate, bachelor's, master's. **Most popular majors:** 31% liberal arts and sciences/liberal studies, 16% psychology, 15% business/commerce, 6% kinesiology and exercise science, 5% theology/theological studies. **Major fields of study:** biological and biomedical sciences; business, management, marketing, and related support services; communication, journalism, and related programs; English language and literature/letters; foreign languages, literatures, and linguistics; health professions and related clinical sciences; history; liberal arts and sciences studies, and humanities; mathematics and statistics; multi/interdisciplinary studies; parks, recreation, leisure, and fitness studies; philosophy and religious studies; psychology; security and protective services; social sciences; theology and religious vocations; visual and performing arts. **Areas of required coursework:** arts/fine arts, humanities, computer literacy, mathematics, English (including composition), philosophy, sciences (biological or physical), history, social science. **Pre-professional programs:** pre-law, pre-dentistry, pre-medicine, pre-theology, other. **Special academic programs (% participation):** accelerated program (35%), distance learning, double major, English as a Second Language (ESL), exchange student program (domestic), honors program, internships, liberal arts/career combination, study abroad, teacher certificate program, weekend college. **Teacher certification offered in:** special education, elementary, middle/junior high, secondary, bilingual/bicultural. **Reserve Officers Training Corps (ROTC):** Army ROTC: Offered at cooperating institution (Claremont-McKenna); Air Force ROTC: Offered at cooperating institution (California State University-San Bernardino). **Faculty and instruction (2005-2006):** Total instructional faculty: 96 full-time, 130 part-time (54% men; 46% women; 21% minorities). Full-time faculty with Ph.D. or other terminal degree: 64%. Student/faculty ratio: 17/1. Classes of fewer than 20 students: 50%; of 20 to 49 students: 46%; of 50 or more students: 5%. **Advanced Placement and International Baccalaureate credit:** AP tests may be used for: Credit and/or placement. Scores accepted: 3. International Baccalaureate exams may be used for: Credit and/or placement. **Freshmen returning for sophomore year:** 86%. **Graduation rates:** Four-year: 8%; five-year: 66%; six-year: 53%.

COSTS AND FINANCIAL AID

Financial aid office: (951) 343-4236. **Expenses (2006-2007):** Tuition and fees 2006-2007: $19,030; room/board: $8,222. Estimated books and supplies: $1,314; transportation: $774; personal expenses: $2,088. **Financial aid:**

Priority filing date for institution's financial aid form: March 2. In 2005-2006, 99% of undergraduates applied for financial aid. Of those, 96% were determined to have financial need; 20% had their need fully met. Average financial aid package (proportion receiving): $11,670 (96%). Average amount of gift aid, such as scholarships or grants (proportion receiving): $8,920 (95%). Average amount of self-help aid, such as work study or loans (proportion receiving): $4,970 (95%). Average need-based loan (excluding PLUS or other private loans): $4,360. Among students who received need-based aid, the average percentage of need met: 67%. Among students who received aid based on merit, the average award (and the proportion receiving): $5,900 (7%). The average athletic scholarship (and the proportion receiving): $9,780 (12%). Average amount of debt of borrowers graduating in 2005: $19,920. Proportion who borrowed: 99%.

CAMPUS LIFE AND EXTRACURRICULAR ACTIVITIES

Campus housing available (% using): women's dorms (21%), men's dorms (12%), apartments for married students (7%), apartment for single students (60%), other housing options (0%). Students who live in college-owned, operated, or affiliated housing: 37%. **Student employment:** During the 2005-2006 academic year, 23% of undergraduates worked on campus. Average per-year earnings: $4,050. **Clubs and organizations:** Number of student organizations: 31. Activities include: choral groups, concert band, drama/theater, jazz band, music ensembles, musical theater, pep band, student government, student newspaper, symphony orchestra, yearbook. Number of fraternities: 0; sororities: 0. Average proportion of students who stay on campus on weekends: 50%. **Sports program (2005-2006):** Member of NAIA. **Men's intercollegiate varsity sports:** baseball, basketball, cross-country, soccer, swimming and diving. **Women's intercollegiate varsity sports:** basketball, cross-country, soccer, softball, swimming and diving, tennis, volleyball.

SERVICES AND FACILITIES

Basic services: nonremedial tutoring, placement service. **Remedial assistance:** reading, math, writing, study skills. **Counseling services:** career, personal, veteran student, academic, psychological, religious. **For learning-disabled students:** School does not offer a structured program with separate admission and additional fees. Total undergraduates in learning-disabled program or receiving services: 11. Services include: remedial English, tape recorders, note-taking services, oral tests, learning center, readers, extended time for tests, tutors, priority registration, priority seating, texts on tape, other testing accomodations. **Library:** Number of titles: 104,415; number of current serial subscriptions: 360. **Information technology resources:** Students are not required to lease or own a computer. Number of campus computers available to all students: 179. School has a wireless network. Approximate number of users that can be accommodated: 150. Proportion of college-owned housing units wired for high-speed internet access: 100%. **Campus safety:** Security services offered: 24-hour foot-and-vehicle patrols, late-night transport/escort service, 24-hour emergency telephones, lighted pathways/sidewalks, controlled dormitory access (key, security card, etc).

TRANSFER AND INTERNATIONAL STUDENTS

Transfer students: May apply for admission for the following academic terms: Fall, Spring, Summer. Applicants need a minimum number of credits to apply. For fall 2005: Transfer applications received: 461. Transfer applicants offered admission: 322. Transfer applicants enrolled: 247. **International students:** Number of foreign undergraduates: 29 (1% of student body). Number of countries represented: 15. Minimum TOEFL score required: 500 (paper); 153 (computer).

California College of the Arts

- **Address:** 1111 Eighth Street, San Francisco, CA 94107
- **Website:** http://www.cca.edu
- **Private**
- **Enrollment:** 1,227 full-time; 85 part-time

KEY STATS
- ✔ **U.S News College Ranking:** Unranked Specialty School–Fine Arts
- ✔ **SAT Score (25th/75th percentile):** 970-1220
- ✔ **Tuition:** 2006-2007: $27,914

Selectivity: Selective	**Room/board:** $5,880
Acceptance rate: 78%	**Average debt:** $28,549
Student/faculty ratio: N/A	**Proportion who borrowed:** 62%

UNDERGRADUATE STUDENT BODY STATS
2005-2006 enrollment: 1,227 full-time; 85 part-time. Men: 41%; women: 59%. **Ethnic makeup:** African American: 2%; American-Indian: 1%; Asian American: 12%; Hispanic: 9%; White: 70%; International: 7%.

ADMISSIONS FACTS AND FIGURES
Phone: (800) 447-1278. **Email:** enroll@cca.edu. **Website:** http://www.cca.edu. **Application deadlines for fall 2007:** Regular decision: Rolling. Early decision: Not offered. Early action: Not offered. Admission can be deferred. **Application fee:** $50. Common application is accepted. **Admissions requirements/recommendations:** Tests: The college uses SAT or ACT scores in admissions decisions. Neither SAT nor ACT required. For admission to the fall 2007 entering class, the school will accept: ACT with writing, ACT without writing. Campus visit: Recommended. Admissions interview: Recommended. Off-campus interview: Not available. **Factors that count in admissions decisions:** *Academic:* Secondary school record: Considered. Class rank: Not considered. Letters of recommendation: Important. Standardized test scores: Considered. Essay: Very important. *Nonacademic:* Interview: Important. Extracurricular activities: Considered. Talent/ability: Very important. Character/personal qualities: Considered. Alumni/ae relationship: Not considered. Geographical residence: Not considered. State residency: Not considered. Religious affiliation/commitment: Not considered. Minority status: Not considered. Volunteer work: Considered. Work experience: Considered. **Other schools with the greatest overlap in applicants:** California Institute of the Arts; Maryland Institute College of Art; Pratt Institute; Rhode Island School of Design; San Francisco Art Institute. **Admissions statistics for the fall 2005 entering class:** Total applicants: 785. Total accepted: 616. Freshmen enrolled: 181; 40% were from out of state. Overall acceptance rate: 78%. **Credentials of fall 2005 freshmen:** 9% ranked in the top 10 percent of their high school class; 36% were in the top 25 percent, and 86% were in the top half. (Proportion submitting class standing: 36%.) **Average high school grade point average:** 3.1. **First-year students who submitted SAT scores:** 60%. Scores (25/75 percentile): Verbal: 480-620, Math: 490-600, Combined: 970-1220. **First-year students submitting ACT scores:** 20%. Scores (25/75 percentile): English: 20-28, Math: 17-24, Composite: 18-24.

ACADEMICS
Year founded: 1907. **Academic calendar:** Semester. **Degrees offered:** bachelor's, master's. **Most popular majors:** 14% graphic design, 12% architecture (B.Arch., B.A./B.S., M.Arch., M.A./M.S., Ph.D.), 12% painting, 9% illustration, 7% photography. **Major fields of study:** architecture and related services; English language and literature/letters; visual and performing arts. **Areas of required coursework:** arts/fine arts, humanities. **Special academic programs:** independent study, internships, study abroad. **Faculty and instruction (2005-2006):** Total instructional faculty: 42 full-time, 328 part-time (54% men; 46% women; 16% minorities). Full-time faculty with Ph.D. or other terminal degree: 81%. **Advanced Placement and International Baccalaureate credit:** AP tests may be used for: Credit and/or placement. International Baccalaureate exams may be used for: Credit and/or placement. **Freshmen returning for sophomore year:** 78%. **Graduation rates:** Six-year: 43%.

COSTS AND FINANCIAL AID
Financial aid office: (415) 703-9573. **Expenses (2006-2007):** Tuition and fees 2006-2007: $27,914; room/board: $5,880. Estimated books and supplies: $1,300; transportation: $1,050; personal expenses: $1,880. **Financial aid:** Priority filing date for institution's financial aid form: March 1. In 2005-

2006, 76% of undergraduates applied for financial aid. Of those, 71% were determined to have financial need; 4% had their need fully met. Average financial aid package (proportion receiving): $17,807 (71%). Average amount of gift aid, such as scholarships or grants (proportion receiving): $11,553 (71%). Average amount of self-help aid, such as work study or loans (proportion receiving): $6,594 (68%). Average need-based loan (excluding PLUS or other private loans): $4,982. Among students who received need-based aid, the average percentage of need met: 57%. Among students who received aid based on merit, the average award (and the proportion receiving): $5,404 (11%). The average athletic scholarship (and the proportion receiving): $0 (0%). Average amount of debt of borrowers graduating in 2005: $28,549. Proportion who borrowed: 62%.

CAMPUS LIFE AND EXTRACURRICULAR ACTIVITIES
Campus housing available: coed dorms, apartment for single students, special housing for international students, cooperative housing, other housing options. Students who live in college-owned, operated, or affiliated housing: 17%. **Clubs and organizations:** Number of student organizations: 18. Activities include: literary magazine, student government, student film society, yearbook. Number of fraternities: 0; sororities: 0.

SERVICES AND FACILITIES
Basic services: health insurance. **Remedial assistance:** reading. **Counseling services:** career, personal, academic. **For learning-disabled students:** School does not offer a structured program with separate admission and additional fees. Services include: remedial English, tape recorders, untimed tests, note-taking services, extended time for tests, tutors. **Information technology resources:** Students are not required to lease or own a computer. Number of campus computers available to all students: 238. School has a wireless network. **Campus safety:** Security services offered: late-night transport/escort service, lighted pathways/sidewalks, controlled dormitory access (key, security card, etc).

TRANSFER AND INTERNATIONAL STUDENTS
Transfer students: May apply for admission for the following academic terms: Fall, Spring. Applicants do not need a minimum number of credits to apply. For fall 2005: Transfer applications received: 559. Transfer applicants offered admission: 417. Transfer applicants enrolled: 195. **International students:** Number of foreign undergraduates: 91 (7% of student body). Minimum TOEFL score required: 550 (paper); 213 (computer).

California Institute of Technology

- **Address:** 1200 E. California Boulevard, Pasadena, CA 91125
- **Website:** http://www.caltech.edu
- **Private**
- **Enrollment:** 913 full-time

KEY STATS
- ✔ **U.S News College Ranking:** 4, National Universities
- ✔ **SAT Score (25th/75th percentile):** 1470-1580
- ✔ **Tuition:** 2006-2007: $29,595

Selectivity: Most selective	**Room/board:** $9,102
Acceptance rate: 20%	**Average debt:** $5,395
Student/faculty ratio: 3/1	**Proportion who borrowed:** 45%

UNDERGRADUATE STUDENT BODY STATS
2005-2006 enrollment: 913 full-time. Men: 70%; women: 30%. **Ethnic makeup:** African American: 1%; Asian American: 33%; Hispanic: 7%; White: 52%; International: 7%.

ADMISSIONS FACTS AND FIGURES
Phone: (626) 395-6341. **Email:** ugadmissions@caltech.edu. **Website:** http://www.caltech.edu. **Application deadlines for fall 2007:** Regular decision: January 1; decision sent by April 1. Early decision: Not offered. Early action: Send application by: November 1; Decision sent by: December 31. Admission can be deferred. **Application fee:** $60. Common application is accepted. **To apply online, go to:** http://admissions.caltech.edu/admissions/applying. **Admissions requirements/recommendations:** High school units required (recommended): English: 3 (4); Mathematics: 4; Science: 2 (4); Social studies: 1; History: 1. Tests: The college uses SAT or ACT scores in admissions decisions. Either

SAT or ACT required. For admission to the fall 2007 entering class, the school will accept: ACT with writing, ACT without writing. Campus visit: Neither required nor recommended. Admissions interview: Neither required nor recommended. Off-campus interview: Not available. **Factors that count in admissions decisions:** *Academic:* Secondary school record: Very important. Class rank: Important. Letters of recommendation: Important. Standardized test scores: Important. Essay: Important. *Nonacademic:* Interview: Not considered. Extracurricular activities: Important. Talent/ability: Considered. Character/personal qualities: Important. Alumni/ae relationship: Considered. Geographical residence: Not considered. State residency: Not considered. Religious affiliation/commitment: Not considered. Minority status: Considered. Volunteer work: Considered. Work experience: Considered. **Other schools with the greatest overlap in applicants:** Harvard University; Massachusetts Institute of Technology; Princeton University; Stanford University; University of California–Berkeley. **Admissions statistics for the fall 2005 entering class:** Total applicants: 2,760. Total accepted: 551. Freshmen enrolled: 234; 62% were from out of state. Accepted through early-decision or early-action plans: 32%. Overall acceptance rate: 20%. Non-early acceptance rate: 17%. **Size of waiting list:** 379 applicants; enrolled from waiting list: 0. **Credentials of fall 2005 freshmen:** 94% ranked in the top 10 percent of their high school class; 98% were in the top 25 percent, and 100% were in the top half. (Proportion submitting class standing: 53%.) **First-year students who submitted SAT scores:** 99%. Scores (25/75 percentile): Verbal: 700-780, Math: 770-800, Combined: 1470-1580. **First-year students submitting ACT scores:** 16%. Scores (25/75 percentile): English: N/A, Math: N/A, Composite: N/A.

ACADEMICS

Year founded: 1891. **Academic calendar:** Quarter. **Degrees offered:** bachelor's, master's, post-master's certificate, doctorate. **Most popular majors:** 35% engineering, 35% physical sciences, 13% biological and biomedical sciences, 6% computer and information sciences and support services, 6% social sciences. **Major fields of study:** architecture and related services; biological and biomedical sciences; computer and information sciences and support services; engineering; history; liberal arts and sciences studies, and humanities; mathematics and statistics; physical sciences; social sciences. **Areas of required coursework:** humanities, mathematics, sciences (biological or physical), social science. **Special academic programs (% participation):** cross-registration, double major (10%), English as a Second Language (ESL), exchange student program (domestic), independent study, liberal arts/career combination, student-designed major, study abroad. **Reserve Officers Training Corps (ROTC):** Army ROTC: Offered at cooperating institution (University of Southern California); Air Force ROTC: Offered at cooperating institution (University of Southern California, California State University–San Bernardino, Harvey Mudd College). **Faculty and instruction (2005-2006):** Total instructional faculty: 284 full-time, 16 part-time (84% men; 16% women; 12% minorities). Full-time faculty with Ph.D. or other terminal degree: 97%. Student/faculty ratio: 3/1. Classes of fewer than 20 students: 67%; of 20 to 49 students: 25%; of 50 or more students: 8%. **Freshmen returning for sophomore year:** 96%. **Graduation rates:** Four-year: 83%; five-year: 89%; six-year: 90%. **Graduate study:** 53% of students pursue further study immediately upon graduation. Fields in which graduates pursue further study: law, 1%; medicine, 5%; engineering, 29%; arts and sciences, 65%.

COSTS AND FINANCIAL AID

Financial aid office: (626) 395-6280. **Expenses (2006-2007):** Tuition and fees 2006-2007: $29,595; room/board: $9,102. Estimated books and supplies: $1,077 personal expenses: $2,907. **Financial aid:** Priority filing date for institution's financial aid form: January 15. In 2005-2006, 70% of undergraduates applied for financial aid. Of those, 54% were determined to have financial need; 100% had their need fully met. Average financial aid package (proportion receiving): $28,508 (54%). Average amount of gift aid, such as scholarships or grants (proportion receiving): $27,325 (53%). Average amount of self-help aid, such as work study or loans (proportion receiving): $2,283 (38%). Average need-based loan (excluding PLUS or other private loans): $1,491. Among students who received need-based aid, the average percentage of need met: 100%. Among students who received aid based on merit, the average award (and the proportion receiving): $29,818 (9%). The average athletic scholarship (and the proportion receiving): $0 (0%). Average amount of debt of borrowers graduating in 2005: $5,395. Proportion who borrowed: 45%.

CAMPUS LIFE AND EXTRACURRICULAR ACTIVITIES

Campus housing available (% using): coed dorms (89%), apartments for married students (1%), special housing for disabled students (1%), other

housing options (9%). Students who live in college-owned, operated, or affiliated housing: 90%. **Student employment:** During the 2005-2006 academic year, 34% of undergraduates worked on campus. Average per-year earnings: $3,713. **Clubs and organizations:** Number of student organizations: 80. Activities include: choral groups, concert band, dance, drama/theater, jazz band, literary magazine, music ensembles, musical theater, pep band, student government, student newspaper, student film society, symphony orchestra, yearbook. Number of fraternities: 0; sororities: 0. Average proportion of students who stay on campus on weekends: 90%. **Sports program (2005-2006):** Member of NCAA III. *Men's intercollegiate varsity sports:* baseball, basketball, cross-country, fencing, golf, soccer, swimming and diving, tennis, track and field (outdoor), water polo. *Women's intercollegiate varsity sports:* basketball, cross-country, fencing, swimming and diving, tennis, track and field (outdoor), volleyball, water polo.

SERVICES AND FACILITIES

Basic services: nonremedial tutoring, women's center, health service, health insurance. **Counseling services:** minority student, career, personal, academic, older student, psychological, birth control, religious. **For learning-disabled students:** School does not offer a structured program with separate admission and additional fees. Total undergraduates in learning-disabled program or receiving services: 15. Services include: tape recorders, untimed tests, note-taking services, oral tests, readers, extended time for tests, tutors. **Library:** Number of titles: 344,020; number of current serial subscriptions: 2,620. **Information technology resources:** Students are not required to lease or own a computer. Number of campus computers available to all students: 50. School has a wireless network. Approximate number of users that can be accommodated: 10,000. Proportion of college-owned housing units wired for high-speed internet access: 100%. **Campus safety:** Security services offered: 24-hour foot-and-vehicle patrols, late-night transport/escort service, 24-hour emergency telephones, lighted pathways/sidewalks, controlled dormitory access (key, security card, etc).

TRANSFER AND INTERNATIONAL STUDENTS

Transfer students: May apply for admission for the following academic terms: Fall. Applicants do not need a minimum number of credits to apply. For fall 2005: Transfer applications received: 134. Transfer applicants offered admission: 3. Transfer applicants enrolled: 3. **International students:** Number of foreign undergraduates: 64 (7% of student body). Number of countries represented: 23.

California Institute of the Arts

- **Address:** 24700 McBean Parkway, Valencia, CA 91355
- **Website:** http://www.calarts.edu
- **Private**
- **Enrollment:** 794 full-time; 9 part-time

KEY STATS

✔ **U.S News College Ranking:** Unranked Specialty School–Fine Arts
✔ **SAT or ACT Score (25th/75th percentile):** N/A
✔ **Tuition:** 2006-2007: $29,815

Selectivity: Least selective	Room/board: $8,130
Acceptance rate: 31%	Average debt: $34,602
Student/faculty ratio: 7/1	Proportion who borrowed: 76%

UNDERGRADUATE STUDENT BODY STATS

2005-2006 enrollment: 794 full-time; 9 part-time. Men: 55%; women: 45%. **Ethnic makeup:** African American: 7%; American-Indian: 1%; Asian American: 10%; Hispanic: 12%; White: 61%; International: 8%.

ADMISSIONS FACTS AND FIGURES

Phone: (661) 255-1050. **Email:** admiss@calarts.edu. **Website:** http://www.calarts.edu. **Application deadlines for fall 2007:** Regular decision: January 5. Early decision: Not offered. Early action: Not offered. Admission cannot be deferred. **Application fee:** $65. Common application is not accepted. **Admissions requirements/recommendations:** Tests: The college does not use SAT or ACT scores in admissions decisions. Neither SAT nor ACT required. Campus visit: Recommended. Admissions interview: Recommended. Off-campus interview: Not available. **Factors that count in admissions decisions:** *Academic:* Secondary school record: Considered. Class rank: Not considered. Letters of recommendation: Considered.

Standardized test scores: Not considered. Essay: Very important. *Nonacademic:* Interview: Very important. Extracurricular activities: Considered. Talent/ability: Very important. Character/personal qualities: Important. Alumni/ae relationship: Not considered. Geographical residence: Not considered. State residency: Not considered. Religious affiliation/commitment: Not considered. Minority status: Not considered. Volunteer work: Not considered. Work experience: Not considered. **Other schools with the greatest overlap in applicants:** Juilliard School; New York University; Rhode Island School of Design; School of the Art Institute of Chicago; University of Southern California. **Admissions statistics for the fall 2005 entering class:** Total applicants: 2,975. Total accepted: 923. Freshmen enrolled: 228; Overall acceptance rate: 31%. **Size of waiting list:** 63 applicants; enrolled from waiting list: 3. **Credentials of fall 2005 freshmen:** 25% ranked in the top 10 percent of their high school class.

ACADEMICS
Year founded: 1961. **Academic calendar:** Semester. **Degrees offered:** bachelor's, master's. **Most popular majors:** 100% visual and performing arts. **Major fields of study:** visual and performing arts. **Areas of required coursework:** arts/fine arts, humanities, computer literacy, mathematics, English (including composition), history, social science. **Faculty and instruction (2005-2006):** Total instructional faculty: 147 full-time, 140 part-time (62% men; 38% women; 15% minorities). Student/faculty ratio: 7/1. **Advanced Placement and International Baccalaureate credit:** AP tests may be used for: Credit only. Scores accepted: 3, 4, 5. International Baccalaureate exams may be used for: Credit only. **Freshmen returning for sophomore year:** 84%. **Graduation rates:** Four-year: 39%; five-year: 46%; six-year: 56%.

COSTS AND FINANCIAL AID
Financial aid office: (661) 253-7869. **Expenses (2006-2007):** Tuition and fees 2006-2007: $29,815; room/board: $8,130. Estimated books and supplies: $1,730; transportation: $825; personal expenses: $1,585. **Financial aid:** Priority filing date for institution's financial aid form: March 2. In 2005-2006, 82% of undergraduates applied for financial aid. Of those, 67% were determined to have financial need; 9% had their need fully met. Average financial aid package (proportion receiving): $26,206 (66%). Average amount of gift aid, such as scholarships or grants (proportion receiving): $11,781 (66%). Average amount of self-help aid, such as work study or loans (proportion receiving): $6,198 (62%). Average need-based loan (excluding PLUS or other private loans): $5,431. Among students who received need-based aid, the average percentage of need met: 85%. Among students who received aid based on merit, the average award (and the proportion receiving): $5,032 (11%). Average amount of debt of borrowers graduating in 2005: $34,602. Proportion who borrowed: 76%.

CAMPUS LIFE AND EXTRACURRICULAR ACTIVITIES
Campus housing available (% using): coed dorms (40%), other housing options (60%). Students who live in college-owned, operated, or affiliated housing: 40%. Average per-year earnings: $2,500. Activities include: dance, drama/theater, jazz band, literary magazine, music ensembles, radio station, student government, student newspaper, student film society, television station. Number of fraternities: 0; sororities: 0. Average proportion of students who stay on campus on weekends: 90%.

SERVICES AND FACILITIES
Basic services: health service, health insurance. **Counseling services:** career, personal, psychological, birth control. **For learning-disabled students:** School does not offer a structured program with separate admission and additional fees. **Library:** Number of titles: 94,839; number of current serial subscriptions: 309. **Information technology resources:** Students are not required to lease or own a computer. Number of campus computers available to all students: 250. School has a wireless network. Proportion of college-owned housing units wired for high-speed internet access: 100%. **Campus safety:** Security services offered: 24-hour foot-and-vehicle patrols, lighted pathways/sidewalks, controlled dormitory access (key, security card, etc).

TRANSFER AND INTERNATIONAL STUDENTS
Transfer students: May apply for admission for the following academic terms: Fall, Spring. Applicants do not need a minimum number of credits to apply. For fall 2005: Transfer applications received: 218. Transfer applicants offered admission: 63. Transfer applicants enrolled: 42. **International students:** Number of foreign undergraduates: 64 (8% of student body). Number of countries represented: 37. Minimum TOEFL score required: 550 (paper); 213 (computer).

California Lutheran University

- **Address:** 60 W. Olsen Road, Thousand Oaks, CA 91360
- **Website:** http://www.clunet.edu
- **Private; Religious affiliation:** Lutheran
- **Enrollment:** 1,884 full-time; 211 part-time

KEY STATS
✔ **U.S News College Ranking:** 17, Universities–Master's (West)
✔ **SAT Score (25th/75th percentile):** 990-1180
✔ **Tuition:** 2006-2007: $24,530
   Selectivity: Selective   **Room/board:** $8,740
   Acceptance rate: 69%   **Average debt:** $21,140
   Student/faculty ratio: 15/1   **Proportion who borrowed:** 86%

UNDERGRADUATE STUDENT BODY STATS
2005-2006 enrollment: 1,884 full-time; 211 part-time. Men: 44%; women: 56%. **Ethnic makeup:** African American: 3%; American-Indian: 2%; Asian American: 5%; Hispanic: 17%; White: 71%; International: 2%. **Religious preference:** Roman Catholic: 23%; Protestant: 25%; Jewish: 2%; No preference: 1%; Unknown: 24%; Lutheran: 23%; Other: 2%.

ADMISSIONS FACTS AND FIGURES
Phone: (877) 258-3678. **Email:** CLUADM@clunet.edu. **Website:** http://www.clunet.edu. **Application deadlines for fall 2007:** Regular decision: Rolling. Early decision: Not offered. Early action: Not offered. Admission can be deferred. **Application fee:** $45. Common application is accepted. **Admissions requirements/recommendations:** High school units required (recommended): English: 4; Mathematics: 3; Science: 2; Foreign language: 2; Social studies: 2. Tests: The college uses SAT or ACT scores in admissions decisions. Either SAT or ACT required. For admission to the fall 2007 entering class, the school will accept: ACT with writing, ACT without writing. Campus visit: Recommended. Admissions interview: Recommended. Off-campus interview: May be arranged. **Factors that count in admissions decisions: Academic:** Secondary school record: Very important. Class rank: Considered. Letters of recommendation: Very important. Standardized test scores: Very important. Essay: Important. *Nonacademic:* Interview: Considered. Extracurricular activities: Important. Talent/ability: Important. Character/personal qualities: Considered. Alumni/ae relationship: Considered. Geographical residence: Considered. State residency: Considered. Religious affiliation/commitment: Considered. Minority status: Considered. Volunteer work: Considered. Work experience: Considered. **Other schools with the greatest overlap in applicants:** Cal Poly–San Luis Obispo; Chapman University; Pepperdine University; University of California–Santa Barbara; University of San Diego. **Admissions statistics for the fall 2005 entering class:** Total applicants: 1,977. Total accepted: 1,362. Freshmen enrolled: 385; 28% were from out of state. Overall acceptance rate: 69%. **Credentials of fall 2005 freshmen:** 23% ranked in the top 10 percent of their high school class; 58% were in the top 25 percent, and 88% were in the top half. (Proportion submitting class standing: 50%.) **Average high school grade point average:** 3.5. **First-year students who submitted SAT scores:** 91%. Scores (25/75 percentile): Verbal: 490-580, Math: 500-600, Combined: 990-1180. **First-year students submitting ACT scores:** 36%. Scores (25/75 percentile): English: 20-25, Math: 20-25, Composite: 20-25.

ACADEMICS
Year founded: 1959. **Academic calendar:** Semester. **Degrees offered:** certificate, bachelor's, post-bachelor's certificate, master's, post-master's certificate, doctorate. **Most popular majors:** 28% business, management, marketing, and related support services; 11% communication, journalism, and related programs; 11% social sciences; 9% psychology; 6% liberal arts and sciences studies, and humanities. **Major fields of study:** agriculture, agriculture operations, and related sciences; biological and biomedical sciences; business, management, marketing, and related support services; communication, journalism, and related programs; computer and information sciences and support services; engineering; English language and literature/letters; foreign languages, literatures, and linguistics; history; legal professions and studies; liberal arts and sciences studies, and humanities; mathematics and statistics; natural resources and conservation; parks, recreation, leisure, and fitness studies; philosophy and religious studies; physical sciences; psychology; security and protective services; social sciences; visual and performing arts. **Areas of required coursework:** arts/fine arts, humanities, computer literacy, mathematics, English (including composition), phi-

losophy, foreign languages, sciences (biological or physical), history, social science, other. **Pre-professional programs:** pre-law, pre-dentistry, pre-medicine, pre-theology, pre-veterinary science, pre-pharmacy. **Special academic programs (% participation):** accelerated program (15.9%), cooperative (work-study plan) program (40%), double major (5.3%), exchange student program (domestic) (3.4%), honors program (5.3%), independent study (23%), internships (32.1%), liberal arts/career combination (6.6%), student-designed major (.63%), study abroad (3.4%). **Teacher certification offered in:** special education, elementary, secondary, bilingual/bicultural. **Cooperative education programs:** art, business, computer science, engineering, humanities, natural science, social/behavioral science, other. **Reserve Officers Training Corps (ROTC):** Army ROTC: Offered at cooperating institution (UCSB); Air Force ROTC: Offered at cooperating institution (UCLA). **Faculty and instruction (2005-2006):** Total instructional faculty: 130 full-time, 130 part-time (54% men; 46% women; 15% minorities). Full-time faculty with Ph.D. or other terminal degree: 85%. Student/faculty ratio: 15/1. Classes of fewer than 20 students: 64%; of 20 to 49 students: 34%; of 50 or more students: 1%. **Advanced Placement and International Baccalaureate credit:** AP tests may be used for: Credit and/or placement. Scores accepted: 4, 5. International Baccalaureate exams may be used for: Credit and/or placement. **Freshmen returning for sophomore year:** 81%. **Graduation rates:** Four-year: 55%; five-year: 65%; six-year: 65%. **Graduate study:** 33% of students pursue further study immediately upon graduation; 48% within one year. Fields in which graduates pursue further study: Master of Business Administration (MBA), 5%; law, 5%; medicine, 4%; dentistry, 5%; theology (or the seminary), 1%; education, 35%; arts and sciences, 38%; veterinary medicine, 11%.

COSTS AND FINANCIAL AID

Financial aid office: (805) 493-3115. **Expenses (2006-2007):** Tuition and fees 2006-2007: $24,530; room/board: $8,740. Estimated books and supplies: $1,310; transportation: $649; personal expenses: $2,046. **Financial aid:** Priority filing date for institution's financial aid form: March 2. In 2005-2006, 92% of undergraduates applied for financial aid. Of those, 63% were determined to have financial need; 15% had their need fully met. Average financial aid package (proportion receiving): $16,600 (63%). Average amount of gift aid, such as scholarships or grants (proportion receiving): $13,000 (61%). Average amount of self-help aid, such as work study or loans (proportion receiving): $7,500 (54%). Average need-based loan (excluding PLUS or other private loans): $4,300. Among students who received need-based aid, the average percentage of need met: 70%. Among students who received aid based on merit, the average award (and the proportion receiving): $8,800 (27%). The average athletic scholarship (and the proportion receiving): $0 (0%). Average amount of debt of borrowers graduating in 2005: $21,140. Proportion who borrowed: 86%.

CAMPUS LIFE AND EXTRACURRICULAR ACTIVITIES

Campus housing available (% using): coed dorms (89%), apartment for single students (10%), special housing for disabled students (1%). Students who live in college-owned, operated, or affiliated housing: 65%. **Student employment:** During the 2005-2006 academic year, 40% of undergraduates worked on campus. Average per-year earnings: $1,950. **Clubs and organizations:** Number of student organizations: 69. Activities include: choral groups, concert band, dance, drama/theater, jazz band, literary magazine, music ensembles, musical theater, opera, pep band, radio station, student government, student newspaper, student film society, symphony orchestra, television station, yearbook. Number of fraternities: 0; sororities: 0. Average proportion of students who stay on campus on weekends: 60%. **Sports program (2005-2006):** Member of NCAA III. **Men's intercollegiate varsity sports:** baseball, basketball, cross-country, football, golf, soccer, swimming and diving, tennis, track and field (indoor), track and field (outdoor), water polo. **Women's intercollegiate varsity sports:** basketball, cross-country, soccer, softball, swimming and diving, tennis, track and field (indoor), track and field (outdoor), volleyball, water polo.

SERVICES AND FACILITIES

Basic services: nonremedial tutoring, women's center, placement service, health service, health insurance. **Remedial assistance:** reading, math, writing, study skills. **Counseling services:** minority student, career, military, personal, veteran student, academic, older student, psychological, birth control, religious. **For learning-disabled students:** School does not offer a structured program with separate admission and additional fees. Total undergraduates in learning-disabled program or receiving services: 158. Services include: remedial math, remedial English, reading machines, remedial reading, tape recorders, untimed tests, note-taking services, oral tests, learning center, readers, extended time for tests, tutors, priority registration, priority seating,

texts on tape, other testing accomodations, other. **Library:** Number of titles: 127,244; number of current serial subscriptions: 597. **Information technology resources:** Students are not required to lease or own a computer. Number of campus computers available to all students: 283. School has a wireless network. Approximate number of users that can be accommodated: 3,000. Proportion of college-owned housing units wired for high-speed internet access: 100%. **Campus safety:** Security services offered: 24-hour foot-and-vehicle patrols, late-night transport/escort service, 24-hour emergency telephones, lighted pathways/sidewalks, student patrols, controlled dormitory access (key, security card, etc).

TRANSFER AND INTERNATIONAL STUDENTS

Transfer students: May apply for admission for the following academic terms: Fall, Spring. Applicants need a minimum number of credits to apply. For fall 2005: Transfer applications received: 408. Transfer applicants offered admission: 268. Transfer applicants enrolled: 161. **International students:** Number of foreign undergraduates: 52 (2% of student body). Number of countries represented: 20. Minimum TOEFL score required: 550 (paper); 213 (computer). Average TOEFL score: 550 (paper).

California State Polytechnic Univ.–Pomona

- **Address:** 3801 W. Temple Avenue, Pomona, CA 91768-2557
- **Website:** http://www.csupomona.edu
- **Public**
- **Enrollment:** 14,982 full-time; 2,992 part-time

KEY STATS

✔ **U.S News College Ranking:** 32, Universities–Master's (West)
✔ **SAT Score (25th/75th percentile):** 900-1150
✔ **Tuition:** 2006-2007: $3,015 in state, $13,185 out of state

Selectivity: Selective	**Room/board:** $7,908
Acceptance rate: 24%	**Average debt:** N/A
Student/faculty ratio: 23/1	**Proportion who borrowed:** N/A

UNDERGRADUATE STUDENT BODY STATS

2005-2006 enrollment: 14,982 full-time; 2,992 part-time. Men: 57%; women: 43%. **Ethnic makeup:** African American: 4%; Asian American: 31%; Hispanic: 27%; White: 34%; International: 3%.

ADMISSIONS FACTS AND FIGURES

Phone: (909) 869-3210. **Email:** generalinfo@csupomona.edu. **Website:** http://www.csupomona.edu. **Application deadlines for fall 2007:** Regular decision: November 30. Early decision: Not offered. Early action: Not offered. Admission cannot be deferred. **Application fee:** $55. Common application is not accepted. **To apply online, go to:** http://www.csumentor.edu/. **Admissions requirements/recommendations:** High school units required (recommended): English: 4; Mathematics: 3 (4); Science: 2; Foreign language: 2; Social studies: 1; History: 1; Academic electives: 1; Total units: 15. Tests: The college uses SAT or ACT scores in admissions decisions. Either SAT or ACT required. For admission to the fall 2007 entering class, the school will accept: ACT with writing, ACT without writing. Campus visit: Recommended. Admissions interview: Neither required nor recommended. Off-campus interview: May be arranged. **Factors that count in admissions decisions:** *Academic:* Secondary school record: Very important. Class rank: Not considered. Letters of recommendation: Not considered. Standardized test scores: Very important. Essay: Not considered. *Nonacademic:* Interview: Not considered. Extracurricular activities: Not considered. Talent/ability: Not considered. Character/personal qualities: Not considered. Alumni/ae relationship: Not considered. Geographical residence: Not considered. State residency: Not considered. Religious affiliation/commitment: Not considered. Minority status: Not considered. Volunteer work: Not considered. Work experience: Not considered. **Other schools with the greatest overlap in applicants:** Cal Poly–San Luis Obispo; California State University–Fullerton; California State University–Long Beach; University of California–Irvine; University of California–Los Angeles. **Admissions statistics for the fall 2005 entering class:** Total applicants: 17,252. Total accepted: 4,121. Freshmen enrolled: 2,793; 2% were from out of state. Overall acceptance rate: 24%. **Average high school grade point average:** 3.2. **First-year students who submitted SAT scores:** 96%. Scores (25/75 percentile): Verbal: 440-550, Math: 460-600, Combined: 900-1150. **First-year students submitting ACT scores:** 17%. Scores (25/75 percentile): English: 16-23, Math: 18-25, Composite: 17-23.

ACADEMICS

Year founded: 1938. **Academic calendar:** Quarter. **Degrees offered:** bachelor's, master's. **Most popular majors:** 38% business, management, marketing, and related support services, 14% engineering, 6% liberal arts and sciences studies, and humanities, 5% visual and performing arts, 4% social sciences. **Major fields of study:** agriculture, agriculture operations, and related sciences; architecture and related services; area, ethnic, cultural, and gender studies; biological and biomedical sciences; business, management, marketing, and related support services; communication, journalism, and related programs; computer and information sciences and support services; education; engineering; engineering technologies/technicians; English language and literature/letters; family and consumer sciences/human sciences; foreign languages, literatures, and linguistics; history; liberal arts and sciences studies, and humanities; mathematics and statistics; parks, recreation, leisure, and fitness studies; philosophy and religious studies; physical sciences; psychology; public administration and social service professions; social sciences; visual and performing arts. **Areas of required coursework:** arts/fine arts, humanities, computer literacy, mathematics, English (including composition), philosophy, foreign languages, sciences (biological or physical), history, social science. **Pre-professional programs:** pre-dentistry, pre-medicine, pre-veterinary science. **Special academic programs:** cooperative (work-study plan) program, cross-registration, double major, dual enrollment, English as a Second Language (ESL), exchange student program (domestic), external degree program, honors program, internships, study abroad, teacher certificate program, other. **Teacher certification offered in:** special education, elementary, middle/junior high, secondary, bilingual/bicultural. **Cooperative education programs:** agriculture, art, business, computer science, education, engineering, natural science, social/behavioral science. **Reserve Officers Training Corps (ROTC):** Army ROTC: Offered on campus; Air Force ROTC: Offered at cooperating institution (University of Southern California, California State University-San Bernardino, Harvey Mudd). **Faculty and instruction (2005-2006):** Total instructional faculty: 659 full-time, 622 part-time (61% men; 39% women; 29% minorities). Full-time faculty with Ph.D. or other terminal degree: 74%. Student/faculty ratio: 23/1. Classes of fewer than 20 students: 36%; of 20 to 49 students: 56%; of 50 or more students: 8%. **Advanced Placement and International Baccalaureate credit:** AP tests may be used for: Credit only. Scores accepted: 3, 4, 5. International Baccalaureate exams may be used for: Credit only. **Freshmen returning for sophomore year:** 82%. **Graduation rates:** Four-year: 9%; five-year: 31%; six-year: 43%.

COSTS AND FINANCIAL AID

Financial aid office: (909) 869-3700. **Expenses (2006-2007):** Tuition and fees 2006-2007: $3,015 in state, $13,185 out of state; room/board: $7,908. Estimated books and supplies: $1,242; transportation: $612; personal expenses: $1,740. **Financial aid:** Priority filing date for institution's financial aid form: March 2. In 2005-2006, 67% of undergraduates applied for financial aid. Of those, 57% were determined to have financial need; 92% had their need fully met. Average financial aid package (proportion receiving): $9,265 (55%). Average amount of gift aid, such as scholarships or grants (proportion receiving): $2,217 (52%). Average amount of self-help aid, such as work study or loans (proportion receiving): $2,887 (47%). Average need-based loan (excluding PLUS or other private loans): $3,894. Among students who received need-based aid, the average percentage of need met: 90%. Among students who received aid based on merit, the average award (and the proportion receiving): $1,400 (1%). The average athletic scholarship (and the proportion receiving): $1,900 (0%).

CAMPUS LIFE AND EXTRACURRICULAR ACTIVITIES

Campus housing available (% using): coed dorms (56%), apartment for single students (44%), special housing for disabled students (0%). Students who live in college-owned, operated, or affiliated housing: 10%. **Student employment:** During the 2005-2006 academic year, 10% of undergraduates worked on campus. Average per-year earnings: $1,800. **Clubs and organizations:** Number of student organizations: 250. Activities include: choral groups, concert band, dance, drama/theater, jazz band, literary magazine, music ensembles, musical theater, opera, pep band, student government, student newspaper, symphony orchestra, television station, yearbook. Number of fraternities: 14; sororities: 9. Proportion of men in fraternities: 3%; of women in sororities: 3%. Average proportion of students who stay on campus on weekends: 60%. **Sports program (2005-2006):** Member of NCAA II. *Men's intercollegiate varsity sports:* baseball, basketball, cross-country, soccer, tennis, track and field (outdoor). *Women's intercollegiate varsity sports:* basketball, cross-country, soccer, tennis, track and field (outdoor), volleyball.

SERVICES AND FACILITIES

Basic services: nonremedial tutoring, women's center, day care, health service, health insurance. **Remedial assistance:** reading, math, writing, study skills. **Counseling services:** career, academic, older student, psychological. **For learning-disabled students:** School does not offer a structured program with separate admission and additional fees. Total undergraduates in learning-disabled program or receiving services: 445. Services include: reading machines, tape recorders, note-taking services, oral tests, learning center, extended time for tests, priority registration, other. **Library:** Number of titles: 755,671; number of current serial subscriptions: 5,153. **Information technology resources:** Students are not required to lease or own a computer. Number of campus computers available to all students: 1,225. School has a wireless network. Approximate number of users that can be accommodated: 600. Proportion of college-owned housing units wired for high-speed internet access: 100%. **Campus safety:** Security services offered: 24-hour foot-and-vehicle patrols, late-night transport/escort service, 24-hour emergency telephones, lighted pathways/sidewalks, student patrols, controlled dormitory access (key, security card, etc).

TRANSFER AND INTERNATIONAL STUDENTS

Transfer students: May apply for admission for the following academic terms: Fall, Winter, Spring, Summer. Applicants need a minimum number of credits to apply. For fall 2005: Transfer applications received: 4,792. Transfer applicants offered admission: 3,517. Transfer applicants enrolled: 1,496. **International students:** Number of foreign undergraduates: 575 (3% of student body). Number of countries represented: 65. Minimum TOEFL score required: 525 (paper); 195 (computer).

California State University–Bakersfield

- ■ **Address:** 9001 Stockdale Highway, Bakersfield, CA 93311
- ■ **Website:** http://www.csub.edu
- ■ **Public**
- ■ **Enrollment:** N/A

KEY STATS

- ✔ **U.S News College Ranking:** third tier, Universities–Master's (West)
- ✔ **ACT Score (25th/75th percentile):** 16-22
- ✔ **Tuition:** 2006-2007: $3,591 in state, $13,761 out of state

Selectivity: Less selective	**Room/board:** $6,043
Acceptance rate: 49%	**Average debt:** N/A
Student/faculty ratio: N/A	**Proportion who borrowed:** N/A

California State University–Chico

- ■ **Address:** 400 W. First Street, Chico, CA 95929-0722
- ■ **Website:** http://www.csuchico.edu
- ■ **Public**
- ■ **Enrollment:** 13,079 full-time; 1,447 part-time

KEY STATS

- ✔ **U.S News College Ranking:** 31, Universities–Master's (West)
- ✔ **SAT Score (25th/75th percentile):** 930-1150
- ✔ **Tuition:** 2006-2007: $3,402 in state, $13,491 out of state

Selectivity: Selective	**Room/board:** $8,314
Acceptance rate: 87%	**Average debt:** N/A
Student/faculty ratio: 21/1	**Proportion who borrowed:** N/A

UNDERGRADUATE STUDENT BODY STATS

2005-2006 enrollment: 13,079 full-time; 1,447 part-time. Men: 47%; women: 53%. **Ethnic makeup:** African American: 2%; American-Indian: 1%; Asian American: 5%; Hispanic: 11%; White: 79%; International: 2%.

ADMISSIONS FACTS AND FIGURES

Phone: (800) 542-4426. **Email:** info@csuchico.edu. **Website:** http://www.csuchico.edu. **Application deadlines for fall 2007:** Regular decision: November 30; decision sent by March 1. Early decision: Not offered. Early action: Not offered. Admission can be deferred. **Application fee:** $55. Common application is not accepted. **To apply online, go to:** http://www.csumentor.edu. **Admissions requirements/recommendations:** High school units required (recommended): English: 4; Mathematics: 3; Science: 2; Foreign language: 2; Social studies: 2; History: 0; Academic electives: 1; Total units: 15. Tests: The college uses SAT or ACT scores in admissions decisions. Either SAT or ACT required. For admission to the fall 2007 entering class, the school will accept: ACT with writing, ACT without writing. Campus visit: Recommended. Admissions interview: Neither required nor recommended. Off-campus interview: Not available. **Factors that count in admissions decisions:** *Academic:* Secondary school record: Not considered. Class rank: Not considered. Letters of recommendation: Not considered. Standardized test scores: Very important. Essay: Not considered. *Nonacademic:* Interview: Not considered. Extracurricular activities: Not considered. Talent/ability: Not considered. Character/personal qualities: Not considered. Alumni/ae relationship: Not considered. Geographical residence: Important. State residency: Important. Religious affiliation/commitment: Not considered. Minority status: Not considered. Volunteer work: Not considered. Work experience: Not considered. **Other schools with the greatest overlap in applicants:** Cal Poly–San Luis Obispo; California State University–Long Beach; San Diego State University; University of California–Davis; University of California–Santa Barbara. **Admissions statistics for the fall 2005 entering class:** Total applicants: 12,457. Total accepted: 10,881. Freshmen enrolled: 2,335; 1% were from out of state. Overall acceptance rate: 87%. **Credentials of fall 2005 freshmen:** 35% ranked in the top 10 percent of their high school class; 76% were in the top 25 percent, and 100% were in the top half. (Proportion submitting class standing: 50%.) **Average high school grade point average:** 3.2. **First-year students who submitted SAT scores:** 92%. Scores (25/75 percentile): Verbal: 460-570, Math: 470-580, Combined: 930-1150. **First-year students submitting ACT scores:** 27%. Scores (25/75 percentile): English: 18-23, Math: 18-24, Composite: 19-23.

ACADEMICS

Year founded: 1887. **Academic calendar:** Semester. **Degrees offered:** certificate, bachelor's, post-bachelor's certificate, master's, post-master's certificate. **Most popular majors:** 16% business, management, marketing, and related support services, 12% liberal arts and sciences studies, and humanities, 9% social sciences, 9% visual and performing arts, 6% health professions and related clinical sciences. **Major fields of study:** agriculture, agriculture operations, and related sciences; area, ethnic, cultural, and gender studies; biological and biomedical sciences; business, management, marketing, and related support services; communication, journalism, and related programs; computer and information sciences and support services; education; engineering; engineering technologies/technicians; English language and literature/letters; foreign languages, literatures, and linguistics; health professions and related clinical sciences; history; liberal arts and sciences studies, and humanities; mathematics and statistics; multi/interdisciplinary studies; natural resources and conservation; parks, recreation, leisure, and fitness studies; philosophy and religious studies; physical sciences; psychology; public administration and social service professions; security and protective services; social sciences; visual and performing arts. **Areas of required coursework:** arts/fine arts, humanities, computer literacy, mathematics, English (including composition), philosophy, sciences (biological or physical), history, social science. **Pre-professional programs:** pre-law, pre-dentistry, pre-medicine, pre-theology, pre-veterinary science, pre-optometry, pre-pharmacy, other. **Special academic programs:** cooperative (work-study plan) program, cross-registration, distance learning, double major, dual enrollment, English as a Second Language (ESL), exchange student program (domestic), external degree program, honors program, independent study, internships, student-designed major, study abroad, teacher certificate program. **Teacher certification offered in:** early childhood, special education, elementary, middle/junior high, secondary, bilingual/bicultural. **Cooperative education programs:** agriculture, art, business, computer science, education, engineering, health professions, humanities, natural science, social/behavioral science, technologies. **Faculty and instruction (2005-2006):** Total instructional faculty: 499 full-time, 414 part-time (57% men; 43% women; 12% minorities). Full-time faculty with Ph.D. or other terminal degree: 88%. Student/faculty ratio: 21/1. Classes of fewer than 20 students: 36%; of 20 to 49 students: 56%; of 50 or more students: 9%. **Advanced Placement and International Baccalaureate credit:** AP tests may be used for: Credit and/or placement. Scores accepted: 3, 4, 5. International Baccalaureate exams may be used for: Credit and/or placement. **Freshmen returning for sophomore year:** 82%. **Graduation rates:** Four-year: 15%; five-year: 42%; six-year: 51%. **Graduate study:** 21% of students pursue further study immediately upon graduation.

COSTS AND FINANCIAL AID

Financial aid office: (530) 898-6451. **Expenses (2006-2007):** Tuition and fees 2006-2007: $3,402 in state, $13,491 out of state; room/board: $8,314. Estimated books and supplies: $1,219; transportation: $899; personal expenses: $2,132. **Financial aid:** Priority filing date for institution's financial aid form: March 2. In 2005-2006, 56% of undergraduates applied for financial aid. Of those, 44% were determined to have financial need; 24% had their need fully met. Average financial aid package (proportion receiving): $7,801 (42%). Average amount of gift aid, such as scholarships or grants (proportion receiving): $5,646 (33%). Average amount of self-help aid, such as work study or loans (proportion receiving): $4,464 (34%). Average need-based loan (excluding PLUS or other private loans): $4,017. Among students who received need-based aid, the average percentage of need met: 26%. Among students who received aid based on merit, the average award (and the proportion receiving): $1,517 (2%). The average athletic scholarship (and the proportion receiving): $2,287 (1%).

CAMPUS LIFE AND EXTRACURRICULAR ACTIVITIES

Campus housing available: coed dorms, apartment for single students, special housing for disabled students, special housing for international students, other housing options. Students who live in college-owned, operated, or affiliated housing: 13%. **Student employment:** During the 2005-2006 academic year, 9% of undergraduates worked on campus. Average per-year earnings: $2,500. **Clubs and organizations:** Number of student organizations: 187. Activities include: choral groups, concert band, dance, drama/theater, jazz band, literary magazine, music ensembles, musical theater, opera, pep band, radio station, student government, student newspaper, student film society, symphony orchestra, yearbook. Number of fraternities: 16; sororities: 11. Proportion of men in fraternities: 4%; of women in sororities: 4%. **Sports program (2005-2006):** Member of NCAA II. *Men's intercollegiate varsity sports:* baseball, basketball, cross-country, golf, soccer, track and field (outdoor). *Women's intercollegiate varsity sports:* basketball, cross-country, golf, soccer, softball, track and field (outdoor), volleyball.

SERVICES AND FACILITIES

Basic services: nonremedial tutoring, women's center, placement service, day care, health service, health insurance. **Remedial assistance:** math, writing, study skills. **Counseling services:** minority student, career, personal, veteran student, academic, older student, psychological, birth control. **For learning-disabled students:** School does not offer a structured program with separate admission and additional fees. Total undergraduates in learning-disabled program or receiving services: 247. Services include: remedial math, remedial English, reading machines, tape recorders, diagnostic testing service, note-taking services, oral tests, learning center, readers, extended time for tests, tutors, priority registration, priority seating, texts on tape, other testing accomodations, other. **Library:** Number of titles: 967,024; number of current serial subscriptions: 24,244. **Information technology resources:** Students are not required to lease or own a computer. Number of campus computers available to all students: 1,160. School has a wireless network. Approximate number of users that can be accommodated: 625. Proportion of college-owned housing units wired for high-speed internet access: 80%. **Campus safety:** Security services offered: 24-hour foot-and-vehicle patrols, late-night transport/escort service, 24-hour emergency telephones, lighted pathways/sidewalks, student patrols, controlled dormitory access (key, security card, etc).

TRANSFER AND INTERNATIONAL STUDENTS

Transfer students: May apply for admission for the following academic terms: Fall, Spring. Applicants do not need a minimum number of credits to apply. For fall 2005: Transfer applications received: 2,757. Transfer applicants offered admission: 2,647. Transfer applicants enrolled: 1,386. **International students:** Number of foreign undergraduates: 228 (2% of student body). Number of countries represented: 25. Minimum TOEFL score required: 500 (paper); 173 (computer). Average TOEFL score: 569 (paper).

California State Univ.–Dominguez Hills

- **Address:** 1000 E. Victoria Street, Carson, CA 90747
- **Website:** http://www.csudh.edu
- **Public**
- **Enrollment:** 5,322 full-time; 3,621 part-time

KEY STATS

✔ **U.S News College Ranking:** fourth tier, Universities–Master's (West)
✔ **SAT Score (25th/75th percentile):** 730-950
✔ **Tuition:** 2006-2007: $3,011 in state, $11,147 out of state

Selectivity: Less selective	**Room/board:** $7,548
Acceptance rate: 45%	**Average debt:** $15,232
Student/faculty ratio: N/A	**Proportion who borrowed:** 32%

UNDERGRADUATE STUDENT BODY STATS

2005-2006 enrollment: 5,322 full-time; 3,621 part-time. Men: 32%; women: 68%. **Ethnic makeup:** African American: 26%; American-Indian: 1%; Asian American: 9%; Hispanic: 35%; White: 27%; International: 2%.

ADMISSIONS FACTS AND FIGURES

Phone: (310) 243-3300. **Email:** info@csudh.edu. **Website:** http://www.csudh.edu. **Application deadlines for fall 2007:** Regular decision: Rolling. Early decision: Not offered. Early action: Not offered. Admission cannot be deferred. **Application fee:** $55. Common application is not accepted. **Admissions requirements/recommendations:** High school units required (recommended): English: 4; Mathematics: 3; Science: 2; Foreign language: 2; Social studies: 2; History: 1; Academic electives: 1; Total units: 15. Tests: The college uses SAT or ACT scores in admissions decisions. Either SAT or ACT required. For admission to the fall 2007 entering class, the school will accept: ACT with writing. Campus visit: Recommended. Admissions interview: Recommended. Off-campus interview: Not available. **Factors that count in admissions decisions:** *Academic:* Secondary school record: Not considered. Class rank: Not considered. Letters of recommendation: Not considered. Standardized test scores: Not considered. Essay: Not considered. *Nonacademic:* Interview: Not considered. Extracurricular activities: Not considered. Talent/ability: Not considered. Character/personal qualities: Not considered. Alumni/ae relationship: Not considered. Geographical residence: Not considered. State residency: Not considered. Religious affiliation/commitment: Not considered. Minority status: Not considered. Volunteer work: Not considered. Work experience: Not considered. **Admissions statistics for the fall 2005 entering class:** Total applicants: 2,323. Total accepted: 1,045. Freshmen enrolled: 786; Overall acceptance rate: 45%. **First-year students who submitted SAT scores:** 76%. Scores (25/75 percentile): Verbal: N/A, Math: N/A, Combined: N/A. **First-year students submitting ACT scores:** 24%. Scores (25/75 percentile): English: N/A, Math: N/A, Composite: N/A.

ACADEMICS

Year founded: 1960. **Academic calendar:** Semester. **Degrees offered:** certificate, bachelor's, master's, post-master's certificate. **Most popular majors:** 22% liberal arts and sciences studies, and humanities, 19% business, management, marketing, and related support services, 13% health professions and related clinical sciences, 10% social sciences, 9% public administration and social service professions. **Major fields of study:** area, ethnic, cultural, and gender studies; biological and biomedical sciences; communication, journalism, and related programs; computer and information sciences and support services; English language and literature/letters; foreign languages, literatures, and linguistics; history; liberal arts and sciences studies, and humanities; mathematics and statistics; multi/interdisciplinary studies; physical sciences; psychology; visual and performing arts. **Areas of required coursework:** arts/fine arts, humanities, mathematics, English (including composition), philosophy, foreign languages, sciences (biological or physical), history, social science. **Special academic programs:** distance learning, double major, dual enrollment, external degree program, honors program, independent study, internships, liberal arts/career combination, student-designed major, study abroad, teacher certificate program, weekend college. **Reserve Officers Training Corps (ROTC):** Army ROTC: Offered on campus; Air Force ROTC: Offered at cooperating institution (Loyola Marymount University). **Freshmen returning for sophomore year:** 65%. **Graduation rates:** Four-year: 6%; five-year: 25%; six-year: 34%.

COSTS AND FINANCIAL AID

Financial aid office: (310) 243-3691. **Expenses (2006-2007):** Tuition and fees 2006-2007: $3,011 in state, $11,147 out of state; room/board: $7,548. Estimated books and supplies: $1,200; transportation: $774; personal expenses: $2,000. **Financial aid:** Priority filing date for institution's financial aid form: March 2; deadline: April 15. In 2005-2006, 89% of undergraduates applied for financial aid. Of those, 84% were determined to have financial need; 5% had their need fully met. Average financial aid package (proportion receiving): $8,239 (82%). Average amount of gift aid, such as scholarships or grants (proportion receiving): $4,975 (82%). Average amount of self-help aid, such as work study or loans (proportion receiving): $3,700 (42%). Average need-based loan (excluding PLUS or other private loans): $4,258. Among students who received need-based aid, the average percentage of need met: 67%. Among students who received aid based on merit, the average award (and the proportion receiving): $2,669 (1%). The average athletic scholarship (and the proportion receiving): $4,360 (0%). Average amount of debt of borrowers graduating in 2005: $15,232. Proportion who borrowed: 32%.

CAMPUS LIFE AND EXTRACURRICULAR ACTIVITIES

Campus housing available: apartments for married students, apartment for single students, special housing for disabled students. Students who live in college-owned, operated, or affiliated housing: 4%. Activities include: choral groups, dance, drama/theater, jazz band, music ensembles, radio station, student government, student newspaper, television station. Number of fraternities: 5; sororities: 6. Average proportion of students who stay on campus on weekends: 5%. **Sports program (2005-2006):** Member of NCAA II. **Men's intercollegiate varsity sports:** baseball, basketball, golf, soccer. **Women's intercollegiate varsity sports:** basketball, cross-country, soccer, softball, track and field (indoor), track and field (outdoor), volleyball.

SERVICES AND FACILITIES

Basic services: women's center, day care, health service. **Remedial assistance:** math, writing. **Counseling services:** career, personal, veteran student, older student, psychological. **Information technology resources:** Students are not required to lease or own a computer. **Campus safety:** Security services offered: 24-hour foot-and-vehicle patrols, late-night transport/escort service, 24-hour emergency telephones, lighted pathways/sidewalks, student patrols.

TRANSFER AND INTERNATIONAL STUDENTS

Transfer students: May apply for admission for the following academic terms: Fall, Spring, Summer. Applicants do not need a minimum number of credits to apply. For fall 2005: Transfer applications received: 2,328. Transfer applicants offered admission: 1,991. Transfer applicants enrolled: 1,374. **International students:** Number of foreign undergraduates: 166 (2% of student body).

California State University–East Bay

- **Address:** 25800 Carlos Bee Boulevard, Hayward, CA 94542
- **Website:** http://www.csueastbay.edu
- **Public**
- **Enrollment:** 7,262 full-time; 1,867 part-time

KEY STATS

✔ **U.S News College Ranking:** fourth tier, Universities–Master's (West)
✔ **SAT Score (25th/75th percentile):** 620-1120
✔ **Tuition:** 2006-2007: $2,928 in state, $8,544 out of state

Selectivity: Less selective	**Room/board:** $7,263
Acceptance rate: 28%	**Average debt:** $12,312
Student/faculty ratio: 17/1	**Proportion who borrowed:** 37%

UNDERGRADUATE STUDENT BODY STATS

2005-2006 enrollment: 7,262 full-time; 1,867 part-time. Men: 38%; women: 62%. **Ethnic makeup:** African American: 12%; American-Indian: 1%; Asian American: 29%; Hispanic: 14%; White: 39%; International: 5%.

ADMISSIONS FACTS AND FIGURES

Phone: (510) 885-2784. **Email:** askes@csuhayward.edu. **Website:** http://www.csueastbay.edu. **Application deadlines for fall 2007:** Regular decision: July 30. Early decision: Not offered. Early action: Not offered. Admission can be deferred. **Application fee:** $55. Common application is not accepted. **To apply online, go to:** http://www.csumentor.edu. **Admissions requirements/recommendations:** High school units required (recommended): English: 4 (4); Mathematics: 3 (4); Science: 2 (2); Foreign language: 2 (2); Social studies: 0 (0); History: 2 (2); Academic electives: 1 (0); Total units: 15 (15). Tests: The college uses SAT or ACT scores in admissions decisions. Neither SAT nor ACT required. For admission to the fall 2007 entering class, the school will accept: ACT with writing, ACT without writing. Campus visit: Recommended. Admissions interview: Neither required nor recommended. Off-campus interview: Not available. **Factors that count in admissions decisions:** *Academic:* Secondary school record: Very important. Class rank: Not considered. Letters of recommendation: Considered. Standardized test scores: Very important. Essay: Not considered. *Nonacademic:* Interview: Not considered. Extracurricular activities: Not considered. Talent/ability: Not considered. Character/personal qualities: Not considered. Alumni/ae relationship: Not considered. Geographical residence: Not considered. State residency: Considered. Religious affiliation/commitment: Not considered. Minority status: Not considered. Volunteer work: Not considered. Work experience: Not considered. **Other schools with the greatest overlap in applicants:** California State University–Sacramento; San Francisco State University; San Jose State University. **Admissions statistics for the fall 2005 entering class:** Total applicants: 7,110. Total accepted: 1,991. Freshmen enrolled: 691; Overall acceptance rate: 28%. **Average high school grade point average:** 3.1. **First-year students who submitted SAT scores:** 76%. Scores (25/75 percentile): Verbal: 200-520, Math: 420-600, Combined: 620-1120. **First-year students submitting ACT scores:** 15%. Scores (25/75 percentile): English: 15-33, Math: 16-23, Composite: 16-23.

ACADEMICS

Year founded: 1957. **Academic calendar:** Quarter. **Degrees offered:** certificate, bachelor's, master's. **Most popular majors:** Information not available. **Major fields of study:** area, ethnic, cultural, and gender studies; biological and biomedical sciences; business, management, marketing, and related support services; communication, journalism, and related programs; computer and information sciences and support services; English language and literature/letters; family and consumer sciences/human sciences; foreign languages, literatures, and linguistics; health professions and related clinical sciences; history; liberal arts and sciences studies, and humanities; mathematics and statistics; natural resources and conservation; parks, recreation, leisure, and fitness studies; philosophy and religious studies; physical sciences; psychology; security and protective services; social sciences; visual and performing arts. **Areas of required coursework:** arts/fine arts, humanities, mathematics, English (including composition), sciences (biological or physical), history, social science. **Pre-professional programs:** pre-law, predentistry, pre-medicine, pre-veterinary science, pre-optometry, pre-pharmacy. **Special academic programs (% participation):** cooperative (work-study plan) program (3%), cross-registration, distance learning, double major (2%), exchange student program (domestic), independent study (9%), internships (4%), student-designed major (1%), study abroad. **Teacher certification offered in:** special education, elementary, middle/junior high, secondary, bilingual/bicultural. **Cooperative education programs:** art, business, computer science, health professions, humanities, natural science, social/behavioral science. **Faculty and instruction (2005-2006):** Total instructional faculty: 324 full-time, 417 part-time (49% men; 51% women). Student/faculty ratio: 17/1. **Advanced Placement and International Baccalaureate credit:** AP tests may be used for: Credit and/or placement. Scores accepted: 3, 4, 5. International Baccalaureate exams may be used for: Credit and/or placement. **Freshmen returning for sophomore year:** 82%. **Graduation rates:** Six-year: 42%.

COSTS AND FINANCIAL AID

Financial aid office: (510) 885-2784. **Expenses (2006-2007):** Tuition and fees 2006-2007: $2,928 in state, $8,544 out of state; room/board: $7,263. Estimated books and supplies: $1,314; transportation: $774; personal expenses: $2,646. **Financial aid:** Priority filing date for institution's financial aid form: March 2. In 2005-2006, 46% of undergraduates applied for financial aid. Of those, 45% were determined to have financial need; 9% had their need fully met. Average financial aid package (proportion receiving): $7,973 (45%). Average amount of gift aid, such as scholarships or grants (proportion receiving): $6,294 (37%). Average amount of self-help aid, such as work study or loans (proportion receiving): $5,628 (27%). Average need-based loan (excluding PLUS or other private loans): $5,849. Among students who received need-based aid, the average percentage of need met: 65%. Average amount of debt of borrowers graduating in 2005: $12,312. Proportion who borrowed: 37%.

CAMPUS LIFE AND EXTRACURRICULAR ACTIVITIES

Campus housing available: coed dorms, apartment for single students, special housing for international students. Students who live in college-owned, operated, or affiliated housing: 3%. **Clubs and organizations:** Number of student organizations: 89. Activities include: choral groups, concert band, dance, drama/theater, jazz band, literary magazine, music ensembles, musical theater, opera, pep band, radio station, student government, student newspaper, symphony orchestra, television station. Number of fraternities: 9; sororities: 8. Average proportion of students who stay on campus on weekends: 2%. **Sports program (2005-2006):** Member of NCAA III. *Men's intercollegiate varsity sports:* baseball, basketball, cross-country, golf, soccer, track and field (outdoor). *Women's intercollegiate varsity sports:* basketball, cross-country, golf, soccer, softball, swimming and diving, track and field (outdoor), volleyball, water polo.

SERVICES AND FACILITIES

Basic services: nonremedial tutoring, placement service, day care, health service, health insurance. **Remedial assistance:** reading, math, writing, study skills. **Counseling services:** career, personal, veteran student, academic, psychological. **For learning-disabled students:** School does not offer a structured program with separate admission and additional fees. Services include: remedial math, remedial English, tape recorders, untimed tests, note-taking services, learning center, readers, extended time for tests, tutors. **Information technology resources:** Students are not required to lease or own a computer. Number of campus computers available to all students: 90. School has a wireless network. Proportion of college-owned housing units wired for high-speed internet access: 100%. **Campus safety:** Security services offered: 24-hour foot-and-vehicle patrols, late-night transport/escort service, 24-hour emergency telephones, lighted pathways/sidewalks, controlled dormitory access (key, security card, etc).

TRANSFER AND INTERNATIONAL STUDENTS

Transfer students: May apply for admission for the following academic terms: Fall, Winter, Spring, Summer. Applicants do not need a minimum number of credits to apply. **International students:** Number of foreign undergraduates: 475 (5% of student body). Minimum TOEFL score required: 525 (paper); 197 (computer).

California State University–Fresno

- **Address:** 5150 N. Maple, Fresno, CA 93740
- **Website:** http://www.csufresno.edu
- **Public**
- **Enrollment:** 14,786 full-time; 2,642 part-time

KEY STATS

✔ **U.S News College Ranking:** 47, Universities–Master's (West)
✔ **SAT Score (25th/75th percentile):** 820-1080
✔ **Tuition:** 2006-2007: $3,037 in state, $13,207 out of state

Selectivity: Less selective	**Room/board:** $6,880
Acceptance rate: 65%	**Average debt:** $10,958
Student/faculty ratio: 20/1	**Proportion who borrowed:** 43%

UNDERGRADUATE STUDENT BODY STATS

2005-2006 enrollment: 14,786 full-time; 2,642 part-time. Men: 42%; women: 58%. **Ethnic makeup:** African American: 5%; American-Indian: 1%; Asian American: 14%; Hispanic: 30%; White: 48%; International: 2%.

ADMISSIONS FACTS AND FIGURES

Phone: (559) 278-2261. **Email:** vivian_franco@csufresno.edu. **Website:** http://www.csufresno.edu. **Application deadlines for fall 2007:** Regular decision: February 1. Early decision: Not offered. Early action: Not offered. Admission cannot be deferred. **Application fee:** $55. Common application is not accepted. **Admissions requirements/recommendations:** High school units required (recommended): English: 4 (4); Mathematics: 3 (3); Science: 2 (1); Foreign language: 2 (2); Social studies: 0 (1); History: 2 (1); Academic electives: 1 (3); Total units: 15 (0). Tests: The college uses SAT or ACT scores in admissions decisions. Either SAT or ACT required. Campus visit: Neither required nor recommended. Admissions interview: Recommended. Off-campus interview: Not available. **Factors that count in admissions decisions:** *Academic:* Secondary school record: Very important. Class rank: Not considered. Letters of recommendation: Very important. Standardized test scores:

Not considered. Essay: Not considered. **Nonacademic:** Interview: Not considered. Extracurricular activities: Not considered. Talent/ability: Not considered. Character/personal qualities: Not considered. Alumni/ae relationship: Not considered. Geographical residence: Not considered. State residency: Not considered. Religious affiliation/commitment: Not considered. Minority status: Not considered. Volunteer work: Not considered. Work experience: Not considered. **Admissions statistics for the fall 2005 entering class:** Total applicants: 13,252. Total accepted: 8,656. Freshmen enrolled: 2,438; 1% were from out of state. Overall acceptance rate: 65%. **Average high school grade point average:** 3.3. **First-year students who submitted SAT scores:** 88%. Scores (25/75 percentile): Verbal: 400-530, Math: 420-550, Combined: 820-1080. **First-year students submitting ACT scores:** 31%. Scores (25/75 percentile): English: 14-21, Math: 21-24, Composite: 16-22.

ACADEMICS

Year founded: 1911. **Academic calendar:** Semester. **Degrees offered:** certificate, bachelor's, master's, doctorate. **Most popular majors:** 18% liberal arts and sciences studies, and humanities, 5% criminology, 5% psychology, 4% communication, journalism, and related programs, 4% nursing. **Major fields of study:** agriculture, agriculture operations, and related sciences; area, ethnic, cultural, and gender studies; biological and biomedical sciences; business, management, marketing, and related support services; computer and information sciences and support services; education; engineering; English language and literature/letters; family and consumer sciences/human sciences; foreign languages, literatures, and linguistics; health professions and related clinical sciences; history; liberal arts and sciences studies, and humanities; mathematics and statistics; multi/interdisciplinary studies; parks, recreation, leisure, and fitness studies; philosophy and religious studies; physical sciences; psychology; public administration and social service professions; social sciences; visual and performing arts. **Areas of required coursework:** arts/fine arts, humanities, computer literacy, mathematics, English (including composition), philosophy, foreign languages, sciences (biological or physical), history, social science, other. **Special academic programs:** accelerated program, cooperative (work-study plan) program, cross-registration, distance learning, double major, dual enrollment, English as a Second Language (ESL), exchange student program (domestic), honors program, independent study, internships, student-designed major, study abroad, teacher certificate program, other. **Reserve Officers Training Corps (ROTC):** Army ROTC: Offered on campus; Air Force ROTC: Offered on campus. **Faculty and instruction (2005-2006):** Total instructional faculty: 754 full-time, 513 part-time (57% men; 43% women; 22% minorities). Student/faculty ratio: 20/1. Classes of fewer than 20 students: 32%; of 20 to 49 students: 59%; of 50 or more students: 9%. **Freshmen returning for sophomore year:** 83%. **Graduation rates:** Four-year: 13%; five-year: 32%; six-year: 45%.

COSTS AND FINANCIAL AID

Financial aid office: (559) 278-2182. **Expenses (2006-2007):** Tuition and fees 2006-2007: $3,037 in state, $13,207 out of state; room/board: $6,880. Estimated books and supplies: $1,008; transportation: $740; personal expenses: $1,612. **Financial aid:** Priority filing date for institution's financial aid form: March 1. In 2005-2006, 72% of undergraduates applied for financial aid. Of those, 66% were determined to have financial need; 39% had their need fully met. Average financial aid package (proportion receiving): $5,833 (59%). Average amount of gift aid, such as scholarships or grants (proportion receiving): $4,660 (48%). Average amount of self-help aid, such as work study or loans (proportion receiving): $3,045 (28%). Average need-based loan (excluding PLUS or other private loans): $3,206. Among students who received need-based aid, the average percentage of need met: 75%. Among students who received aid based on merit, the average award (and the proportion receiving): $2,194 (2%). The average athletic scholarship (and the proportion receiving): $7,645 (3%). Average amount of debt of borrowers graduating in 2005: $10,958. Proportion who borrowed: 43%.

CAMPUS LIFE AND EXTRACURRICULAR ACTIVITIES

Campus housing available: coed dorms, women's dorms, men's dorms, sorority housing, fraternity housing, apartments for married students, apartment for single students. Students who live in college-owned, operated, or affiliated housing: 6%. **Clubs and organizations:** Number of student organizations: 250. Activities include: choral groups, concert band, dance, drama/theater, jazz band, literary magazine, marching band, music ensembles, musical theater, pep band, radio station, student government, student newspaper, symphony orchestra, television station, yearbook. Number of fraternities: 13; sororities: 13. Proportion of men in fraternities: 3%; of women in sororities: 3%. **Sports program (2005-2006):** Member of NCAA I. **Men's intercollegiate varsity sports:** baseball, basketball, cross-country, football, golf, tennis, track and field (indoor), track and field (outdoor), wrestling. **Women's intercollegiate varsity sports:** basketball, cross-country, equestrian sports, golf, soccer, softball, tennis, track and field (indoor), track and field (outdoor), volleyball.

SERVICES AND FACILITIES

Basic services: nonremedial tutoring, women's center, placement service, day care, health service, health insurance. **Remedial assistance:** reading, math, writing, study skills. **Counseling services:** minority student, career, personal, academic, psychological, birth control. **For learning-disabled students:** School does not offer a structured program with separate admission and additional fees. **Library:** Number of titles: 1,025,691; number of current serial subscriptions: 2,617. **Information technology resources:** Students are not required to lease or own a computer. School has a wireless network. **Campus safety:** Security services offered: 24-hour foot-and-vehicle patrols, 24-hour emergency telephones, lighted pathways/sidewalks, student patrols, controlled dormitory access (key, security card, etc).

TRANSFER AND INTERNATIONAL STUDENTS

Transfer students: May apply for admission for the following academic terms: Fall, Spring. Applicants need a minimum number of credits to apply. For fall 2005: Transfer applications received: 4,019. Transfer applicants offered admission: 3,288. Transfer applicants enrolled: 1,637. **International students:** Number of foreign undergraduates: 397 (2% of student body). Number of countries represented: 55. Minimum TOEFL score required: 550 (paper); 213 (computer).

California State University—Fullerton

- **Address:** 800 N. State College Boulevard, Fullerton, CA 92834
- **Website:** http://www.fullerton.edu
- **Public**
- **Enrollment:** 21,187 full-time; 8,275 part-time

KEY STATS

✔ **U.S News College Ranking:** 37, Universities–Master's (West)
✔ **SAT Score (25th/75th percentile):** 880-1100
✔ **Tuition:** 2006-2007: $3,010 in state, $14,156 out of state

Selectivity: Selective	**Room/board:** N/A
Acceptance rate: 64%	**Average debt:** $14,482
Student/faculty ratio: 23/1	**Proportion who borrowed:** 37%

UNDERGRADUATE STUDENT BODY STATS

2005-2006 enrollment: 21,187 full-time; 8,275 part-time. Men: 42%; women: 58%. **Ethnic makeup:** African American: 4%; Asian American: 22%; Hispanic: 28%; White: 42%; International: 4%.

ADMISSIONS FACTS AND FIGURES

Phone: (714) 278-2370. **Email:** admissions@fullerton.edu. **Website:** http://www.fullerton.edu. **Application deadlines for fall 2007:** Regular decision: November 30. Early decision: Not offered. Early action: Not offered. Admission cannot be deferred. **Application fee:** $55. Common application is not accepted. **To apply online, go to:** http://www.calstate.edu. **Admissions requirements/recommendations:** High school units required (recommended): English: 4 (4); Mathematics: 3 (3); Science: 2 (2); Foreign language: 2 (3); Social studies: 1 (1); History: 1 (1); Academic electives: 1 (1); Total units: 15 (16). Tests: The college uses SAT or ACT scores in admissions decisions. SAT required. For admission to the fall 2007 entering class, the school will accept: ACT without writing. Campus visit: Required. Admissions interview: Neither required nor recommended. Off-campus interview: Not available. **Factors that count in admissions decisions:** **Academic:** Secondary school record: Considered. Class rank: Not considered. Letters of recommendation: Not considered. Standardized test scores: Very important. Essay: Not considered. **Nonacademic:** Interview: Not considered. Extracurricular activities: Not considered. Talent/ability: Not considered. Character/personal qualities: Not considered. Alumni/ae relationship: Not considered. Geographical residence: Important. State residency: Very important. Religious affiliation/commitment: Not considered. Minority status: Not considered. Volunteer work: Not considered. Work experience: Not considered. **Other schools with the greatest overlap in applicants:** California State Polytechnic University–Pomona; California State University–Long Beach; University of California–Irvine; University of California–Los Angeles;

University of Southern California. **Admissions statistics for the fall 2005 entering class:** Total applicants: 25,525. Total accepted: 16,304. Freshmen enrolled: 3,943; 2% were from out of state. Overall acceptance rate: 64%. **Credentials of fall 2005 freshmen:** 14% ranked in the top 10 percent of their high school class; 48% were in the top 25 percent, and 62% were in the top half. (Proportion submitting class standing: 63%.) **Average high school grade point average:** 3.2. **First-year students who submitted SAT scores:** 97%. Scores (25/75 percentile): Verbal: 430-540, Math: 450-560, Combined: 880-1100. **First-year students submitting ACT scores:** 20%. Scores (25/75 percentile): English: 16-22, Math: 17-23, Composite: 17-22.

ACADEMICS

Year founded: 1957. **Academic calendar:** Semester. **Degrees offered:** bachelor's, master's. **Most popular majors:** 10% mass communication/media studies, 8% liberal arts and sciences/liberal studies, 8% teacher education, 7% finance, 5% psychology. **Major fields of study:** area, ethnic, cultural, and gender studies; biological and biomedical sciences; business, management, marketing, and related support services; communication, journalism, and related programs; computer and information sciences and support services; education; engineering; English language and literature/letters; foreign languages, literatures, and linguistics; health professions and related clinical sciences; history; liberal arts and sciences studies, and humanities; mathematics and statistics; multi/interdisciplinary studies; parks, recreation, leisure, and fitness studies; philosophy and religious studies; physical sciences; psychology; public administration and social service professions; security and protective services; social sciences; visual and performing arts. **Areas of required coursework:** arts/fine arts, humanities, mathematics, English (including composition), philosophy, foreign languages, sciences (biological or physical), history, social science. **Special academic programs:** cooperative (work-study plan) program, distance learning, double major, honors program, independent study, internships, student-designed major, study abroad, teacher certificate program, other. **Teacher certification offered in:** special education, elementary, vo-tech, middle/junior high, secondary, bilingual/bicultural. **Reserve Officers Training Corps (ROTC):** Army ROTC: Offered on campus. **Faculty and instruction (2005-2006):** Total instructional faculty: 744 full-time, 1,287 part-time. Full-time faculty with Ph.D. or other terminal degree: 85%. Student/faculty ratio: 23/1. Classes of fewer than 20 students: 26%; of 20 to 49 students: 66%; of 50 or more students: 8%. **Advanced Placement and International Baccalaureate credit:** AP tests may be used for: Credit and/or placement. Scores accepted: 3, 4, 5. International Baccalaureate exams may be used for: Credit and/or placement. **Freshmen returning for sophomore year:** 80%. **Graduation rates:** Four-year: 14%; five-year: 37%; six-year: 48%.

COSTS AND FINANCIAL AID

Financial aid office: (714) 278-3128. **Expenses (2006-2007):** Tuition and fees 2006-2007: $3,010 in state, $14,156 out of state; room/board: N/A. **Financial aid:** Priority filing date for institution's financial aid form: March 2; deadline: May 30. In 2005-2006, 57% of undergraduates applied for financial aid. Of those, 45% were determined to have financial need; 2% had their need fully met. Average financial aid package (proportion receiving): $7,220 (33%). Average amount of gift aid, such as scholarships or grants (proportion receiving): $6,195 (26%). Average amount of self-help aid, such as work study or loans (proportion receiving): $4,247 (18%). Average need-based loan (excluding PLUS or other private loans): $4,179. Among students who received need-based aid, the average percentage of need met: 62%. Among students who received aid based on merit, the average award (and the proportion receiving): $4,622 (7%). The average athletic scholarship (and the proportion receiving): $5,520 (1%). Average amount of debt of borrowers graduating in 2005: $14,482. Proportion who borrowed: 37%.

CAMPUS LIFE AND EXTRACURRICULAR ACTIVITIES

Campus housing available: sorority housing, fraternity housing, apartment for single students. Students who live in college-owned, operated, or affiliated housing: 2%. Average per-year earnings: $6,000. **Clubs and organizations:** Number of student organizations: 250. Activities include: choral groups, concert band, dance, drama/theater, jazz band, music ensembles, musical theater, radio station, student government, student newspaper, symphony orchestra, television station. Number of fraternities: 17; sororities: 10. Proportion of men in fraternities: 3%; of women in sororities: 3%. Average proportion of students who stay on campus on weekends: 2%. **Sports program (2005-2006):** Member of NCAA I. *Men's intercollegiate varsity sports:* baseball, basketball, cross-country, fencing, soccer, track and field (outdoor), wrestling. *Women's intercollegiate varsity sports:* basketball, cross-country, fencing, gymnastics, soccer, softball, tennis, track and field (indoor), track and field (outdoor), volleyball.

SERVICES AND FACILITIES

Basic services: nonremedial tutoring, women's center, placement service, day care, health service, health insurance. **Remedial assistance:** reading, math, writing, study skills. **Counseling services:** minority student, career, military, personal, veteran student, academic, older student, psychological, birth control. **For learning-disabled students:** School does not offer a structured program with separate admission and additional fees. Services include: remedial math, remedial English, tape recorders, diagnostic testing service, note-taking services, learning center, readers, extended time for tests, tutors, other testing accomodations. **Library:** Number of titles: 1,189,727; number of current serial subscriptions: 3,690. **Information technology resources:** Students are not required to lease or own a computer. Number of campus computers available to all students: 2,000. School has a wireless network. Proportion of college-owned housing units wired for high-speed internet access: 100%. **Campus safety:** Security services offered: 24-hour foot-and-vehicle patrols, late-night transport/escort service, 24-hour emergency telephones, lighted pathways/sidewalks, student patrols, controlled dormitory access (key, security card, etc).

TRANSFER AND INTERNATIONAL STUDENTS

Transfer students: May apply for admission for the following academic terms: Fall, Spring. Applicants need a minimum number of credits to apply. For fall 2005: Transfer applications received: 12,138. Transfer applicants offered admission: 6,356. Transfer applicants enrolled: 3,676. **International students:** Number of foreign undergraduates: 1071 (4% of student body). Minimum TOEFL score required: 500 (paper); 173 (computer). Average TOEFL score: 555 (paper).

California State University—Long Beach

- **Address:** 1250 Bellflower Boulevard, Long Beach, CA 90840
- **Website:** http://www.csulb.edu
- **Public**
- **Enrollment:** 22,525 full-time; 5,989 part-time

KEY STATS

✔ **U.S News College Ranking:** 27, Universities–Master's (West)
✔ **SAT Score (25th/75th percentile):** 920-1140
✔ **Tuition:** 2006-2007: $2,864 in state, $13,034 out of state

Selectivity: Selective	**Room/board:** $6,648
Acceptance rate: 55%	**Average debt:** $10,842
Student/faculty ratio: 20/1	**Proportion who borrowed:** 31%

UNDERGRADUATE STUDENT BODY STATS

2005-2006 enrollment: 22,525 full-time; 5,989 part-time. Men: 40%; women: 60%. **Ethnic makeup:** African American: 6%; American-Indian: 1%; Asian American: 22%; Hispanic: 25%; White: 42%; International: 5%.

ADMISSIONS FACTS AND FIGURES

Phone: (562) 985-5471. **Website:** http://www.csulb.edu. **Application deadlines for fall 2007:** Regular decision: November 30. Early decision: Not offered. Early action: Not offered. Admission cannot be deferred. **Application fee:** $55. Common application is not accepted. **To apply online, go to:** http://www.csumentor.edu. **Admissions requirements/recommendations:** High school units required (recommended): English: 4 (4); Mathematics: 3 (3); Science: 2 (2); Foreign language: 2 (2); Social studies: 1 (1); History: 1 (1); Academic electives: 1 (1); Total units: 15 (15). Tests: The college uses SAT or ACT scores in admissions decisions. Either SAT or ACT required. For admission to the fall 2007 entering class, the school will accept: ACT with writing, ACT without writing. Campus visit: Neither required nor recommended. Admissions interview: Neither required nor recommended. Off-campus interview: Not available. **Factors that count in admissions decisions:** *Academic:* Secondary school record: Very important. Class rank: Not considered. Letters of recommendation: Considered. Standardized test scores: Very important. Essay: Considered. *Nonacademic:* Interview: Not considered. Extracurricular activities: Considered. Talent/ability: Important. Character/personal qualities: Considered. Alumni/ae relationship: Not considered. Geographical residence: Very important. State residency: Very important. Religious affiliation/commitment: Not considered. Minority status: Not considered. Volunteer work: Considered. Work experience: Considered. **Other schools with the greatest overlap in applicants:** California State University–Fullerton; San Diego State University; University of California–Irvine; University of California–Riverside; University of California–Santa Barbara. **Admissions statistics for the fall 2005 entering class:** Total applicants: 38,579. Total accepted: 21,037. Freshmen enrolled: 4,383; 2% were from out of state. Overall acceptance rate: 55%. **Credentials of fall 2005 freshmen:** 84% were in the top 25 percent, and 100% were in the top half. (Proportion submitting class standing: 69%.) **Average high school grade point average:** 3.3. **First-year students who submitted SAT scores:** 97%. Scores (25/75 percentile): Verbal: 450-560, Math: 470-580, Combined: 920-1140. **First-year students submitting ACT scores:** 27%. Scores (25/75 percentile): English: 16-23, Math: 17-24, Composite: 17-23.

ACADEMICS

Year founded: 1949. **Academic calendar:** Semester. **Degrees offered:** bachelor's, post-bachelor's certificate, master's. **Most popular majors:** 22% business, management, marketing, and related support services, 10% liberal arts and sciences studies, and humanities, 9% visual and performing arts, 8% English language and literature/letters, 6% social sciences. **Major fields of study:** area, ethnic, cultural, and gender studies; biological and biomedical sciences; business, management, marketing, and related support services; communication, journalism, and related programs; communications technologies/technicians and support services; computer and information sciences and support services; education; engineering; engineering technologies/technicians; English language and literature/letters; family and consumer sciences/human sciences; foreign languages, literatures, and linguistics; health professions and related clinical sciences; history; liberal arts and sciences studies, and humanities; mathematics and statistics; multi/interdisciplinary studies; natural resources and conservation; parks, recreation, leisure, and fitness studies; philosophy and religious studies; physical sciences; psychology; public administration and social service professions; security and protective services; social sciences; visual and performing arts. **Areas of required coursework:** arts/fine arts, humanities, mathematics, English (including composition), sciences (biological or physical), history, social science. **Pre-professional programs:** pre-law, pre-dentistry, pre-medicine, pre-veterinary science, pre-optometry, pre-pharmacy. **Special academic programs:** accelerated program, cross-registration, distance learning, double major, dual enrollment, English as a Second Language (ESL), honors program, independent study, internships, student-designed major, study abroad, teacher certificate program. **Teacher certification offered in:** early childhood, special education, elementary, vo-tech, middle/junior high, adult education, secondary, bilingual/bicultural. **Cooperative education programs:** art, business, computer science, education, engineering, health professions, humanities, natural science, social/behavioral science, technologies, other. **Reserve Officers Training Corps (ROTC):** Army ROTC: Offered on campus. **Faculty and instruction (2005-2006):** Total instructional faculty: 966 full-time, 1,108 part-time (52% men; 48% women; 25% minorities). Full-time faculty with Ph.D. or other terminal degree: 88%. Student/faculty ratio: 20/1. Classes of fewer than 20 students: 29%; of 20 to 49 students: 61%; of 50 or more students: 10%. **Advanced Placement and International Baccalaureate credit:** AP tests may be used for: Placement only. Scores accepted: 3, 4, 5. International Baccalaureate exams may be used for: Placement only. **Freshmen returning for sophomore year:** 85%. **Graduation rates:** Four-year: 11%; five-year: 11%; six-year: 45%.

COSTS AND FINANCIAL AID

Financial aid office: (562) 985-8403. **Expenses (2006-2007):** Tuition and fees 2006-2007: $2,864 in state, $13,034 out of state; room/board: $6,648. Estimated books and supplies: $1,314; transportation: $1,116; personal expenses: $1,868. **Financial aid:** Priority filing date for institution's financial aid form: March 2. In 2005-2006, 68% of undergraduates applied for financial aid. Of those, 57% were determined to have financial need; 45% had their need fully met. Average financial aid package (proportion receiving): $8,350 (51%). Average amount of gift aid, such as scholarships or grants (proportion receiving): $4,250 (42%). Average amount of self-help aid, such as work study or loans (proportion receiving): $3,217 (39%). Average need-based loan (excluding PLUS or other private loans): $3,314. Among students who received need-based aid, the average percentage of need met: 82%. Among students who received aid based on merit, the average award (and the proportion receiving): $2,068 (6%). The average athletic scholarship (and the proportion receiving): $4,219 (1%). Average amount of debt of borrowers graduating in 2005: $10,842. Proportion who borrowed: 31%.

CAMPUS LIFE AND EXTRACURRICULAR ACTIVITIES

Campus housing available: coed dorms, special housing for international students. Students who live in college-owned, operated, or affiliated housing: 7%. Average per-year earnings: $5,440. **Clubs and organizations:** Number of student organizations: 235. Activities include: choral groups, concert band, dance, drama/theater, jazz band, literary magazine, music ensembles, musical theater, opera, radio station, student government, student newspaper, student film society, symphony orchestra, television station, yearbook. Number of fraternities: 17; sororities: 14. Proportion of men in fraternities: 4%; of women in sororities: 4%. Average proportion of students who stay on campus on weekends: 50%. **Sports program (2005-2006):** Member of NCAA I. *Men's intercollegiate varsity sports:* baseball, basketball, cross-country, golf, track and field (indoor), track and field (outdoor), volleyball, water polo. *Women's intercollegiate varsity sports:* basketball, cross-country, golf, soccer, softball, tennis, track and field (indoor), track and field (outdoor), volleyball, water polo.

SERVICES AND FACILITIES

Basic services: nonremedial tutoring, women's center, placement service, day care, health service, health insurance. **Remedial assistance:** reading, math, writing, study skills. **Counseling services:** career, personal, veteran student, academic, older student, psychological, birth control, religious. **For learning-disabled students:** School does not offer a structured program with separate admission and additional fees. Total undergraduates in learning-disabled program or receiving services: 500. Services include: remedial math, remedial English, reading machines, tape recorders, diagnostic testing service, untimed tests, note-taking services, oral tests, learning center, readers, extended time for tests, tutors, early syllabus, priority registration, priority seating, proofreading services, substitution of courses, texts on tape, typist/scribe, exams on tape or computer, other testing accomodations, waiver of foreign language degree requirement, waiver of math degree requirement, other. **Library:** Number of titles: 1,445,244; number of current serial subscriptions: 26,478. **Information technology resources:** Students are not required to lease or own a computer. Number of campus computers available to all students: 2,026. School does not have a wireless network. **Campus safety:** Security services offered: 24-hour foot-and-vehicle patrols, late-night transport/escort service, 24-hour emergency telephones, lighted pathways/sidewalks, controlled dormitory access (key, security card, etc).

TRANSFER AND INTERNATIONAL STUDENTS

Transfer students: May apply for admission for the following academic terms: Fall. Applicants need a minimum number of credits to apply. For fall 2005: Transfer applications received: 11,282. Transfer applicants offered admission: 6,053. Transfer applicants enrolled: 2,886. **International students:** Number of foreign undergraduates: 1344 (5% of student body). Minimum TOEFL score required: 500 (paper); 173 (computer).

California State University–Los Angeles

- **Address:** 5151 State University Drive, Los Angeles, CA 90032
- **Website:** http://www.calstatela.edu
- **Public**
- **Enrollment:** 10,872 full-time; 4,083 part-time

KEY STATS

✔ **U.S News College Ranking:** third tier, Universities–Master's (West)
✔ **SAT Score (25th/75th percentile):** 780-1020
✔ **Tuition:** 2006-2007: $3,035 in state, $11,171 out of state
  Selectivity: Less selective   **Room/board:** $7,866
  Acceptance rate: 62%   **Average debt:** N/A
  Student/faculty ratio: 16/1   **Proportion who borrowed:** N/A

UNDERGRADUATE STUDENT BODY STATS

2005-2006 enrollment: 10,872 full-time; 4,083 part-time. Men: 39%; women: 61%. **Ethnic makeup:** African American: 8%; Asian American: 21%; Hispanic: 46%; White: 20%; International: 4%.

ADMISSIONS FACTS AND FIGURES

Phone: (323) 343-3901. **Email:** admission@calstatela.edu. **Website:** http://www.calstatela.edu. **Application deadlines for fall 2007:** Regular decision: November 30. Early decision: Not offered. Early action: Not offered. Admission cannot be deferred. **Application fee:** $55. Common application is not accepted. **To apply online, go to:** http://www.csumentor.edu. **Admissions requirements/recommendations:** High school units required (recommended): English: 4 (4); Mathematics: 3 (3); Science: 2 (2); Foreign language: 2 (2); Social studies: 1 (1); History: 1 (1); Academic electives: 1 (1); Total units: 15 (15). Tests: The college uses SAT or ACT scores in admissions decisions. Neither SAT nor ACT required. For admission to the fall 2007 entering class, the school will accept: ACT with writing, ACT without writing. Campus visit: Neither required nor recommended. Admissions interview: Neither required nor recommended. Off-campus interview: Not available. **Factors that count in admissions decisions:** *Academic:* Secondary school record: Very important. Class rank: Not considered. Letters of recommendation: Not considered. Standardized test scores: Very important. Essay: Not considered. *Nonacademic:* Interview: Not considered. Extracurricular activities: Not considered. Talent/ability: Not considered. Character/personal qualities: Not considered. Alumni/ae relationship: Not considered. Geographical residence: Not considered. State residency: Important. Religious affiliation/commitment: Not considered. Minority status: Not considered. Volunteer work: Not considered. Work experience: Not considered. **Admissions statistics for the fall 2005 entering class:** Total applicants: 17,150. Total accepted: 10,617. Freshmen enrolled: 1,458; 1% were from out of state. Overall acceptance rate: 62%. **Average high school grade point average:** 3.1. **First-year students who submitted SAT scores:** 86%. Scores (25/75 percentile): Verbal: 380-500, Math: 400-520, Combined: 780-1020. **First-year students submitting ACT scores:** 15%. Scores (25/75 percentile): English: 14-20, Math: 15-20, Composite: 15-20.

ACADEMICS

Year founded: 1947. **Academic calendar:** Quarter. **Degrees offered:** certificate, bachelor's, post-bachelor's certificate, master's, doctorate. **Most popular majors:** 21% business, management, marketing, and related support services, 12% public administration and social service professions, 11% education, 10% liberal arts and sciences studies, and humanities, 8% social sciences. **Major fields of study:** area, ethnic, cultural, and gender studies; biological and biomedical sciences; business, management, marketing, and related support services; communication, journalism, and related programs; computer and information sciences and support services; education; engineering; engineering technologies/technicians; English language and literature/letters; family and consumer sciences/human sciences; foreign languages, literatures, and linguistics; health professions and related clinical sciences; history; liberal arts and sciences studies, and humanities; mathematics and statistics; multi/interdisciplinary studies; philosophy and religious studies; physical sciences; psychology; public administration and social service professions; security and protective services; social sciences; visual and performing arts. **Areas of required coursework:** arts/fine arts, humanities, computer literacy, mathematics, English (including composition), philosophy, sciences (biological or physical), history, social science. **Pre-professional programs:** other. **Special academic programs:** accelerated program, cooperative (work-study plan) program, cross-registration, distance learning, double major, dual enrollment, English as a Second Language (ESL), exchange student program (domestic), honors program, independent study, internships, student-designed major, study abroad, teacher certificate program. **Teacher certification offered in:** early childhood, special education, elementary, secondary, bilingual/bicultural. **Cooperative education programs:** art, business, computer science, engineering, health professions, natural science, social/behavioral science, technologies. **Reserve Officers Training Corps (ROTC):** Army ROTC: Offered at cooperating institution (University of California, Los Angeles (UCLA)); Air Force ROTC: Offered at cooperating institution (University of Southern California, California State University–San Bernardino, Harvey Mudd College). **Faculty and instruction (2005-2006):** Total instructional faculty: 581 full-time, 560 part-time (55% men; 45% women; 51% minorities). Full-time faculty with Ph.D. or other terminal degree: 89%. Student/faculty ratio: 16/1. Classes of fewer than 20 students: 36%; of 20 to 49 students: 56%; of 50 or more students: 8%. **Advanced Placement and International Baccalaureate credit:** AP tests may be used for: Credit only. Scores accepted: 3, 4, 5. International Baccalaureate exams may be used for: Credit only. **Freshmen returning for sophomore year:** 75%. **Graduation rates:** Six-year: 33%.

COSTS AND FINANCIAL AID

Financial aid office: (323) 343-1784. **Expenses (2006-2007):** Tuition and fees 2006-2007: $3,035 in state, $11,171 out of state; room/board: $7,866. Estimated books and supplies: $1,314; transportation: $1,032; personal expenses: $2,466. **Financial aid:** Priority filing date for institution's financial aid form: March 2. In 2005-2006, 70% of undergraduates applied for financial aid. Of those, 67% were determined to have financial need; 33% had their need fully met. Average financial aid package (proportion receiving):

$6,894 (64%). Average amount of gift aid, such as scholarships or grants (proportion receiving): $6,413 (54%). Average amount of self-help aid, such as work study or loans (proportion receiving): $5,172 (23%). Average need-based loan (excluding PLUS or other private loans): $5,242. Among students who received need-based aid, the average percentage of need met: 78%.

CAMPUS LIFE AND EXTRACURRICULAR ACTIVITIES

Campus housing available: coed dorms, sorority housing, fraternity housing, apartment for single students. Students who live in college-owned, operated, or affiliated housing: 4%. **Student employment:** During the 2005-2006 academic year, 3% of undergraduates worked on campus. Average per-year earnings: $7,200. **Clubs and organizations:** Number of student organizations: 96. Activities include: choral groups, dance, drama/theater, jazz band, literary magazine, music ensembles, musical theater, opera, student government, student newspaper, student film society, symphony orchestra, yearbook. Number of fraternities: 8; sororities: 7. Average proportion of students who stay on campus on weekends: 20%. **Sports program (2005-2006):** Member of NCAA II. *Men's intercollegiate varsity sports:* baseball, basketball, soccer, track and field (outdoor). *Women's intercollegiate varsity sports:* basketball, cross-country, soccer, tennis, track and field (indoor), track and field (outdoor), volleyball.

SERVICES AND FACILITIES

Basic services: nonremedial tutoring, women's center, placement service, day care, health service. **Remedial assistance:** reading, math, writing, study skills. **Counseling services:** minority student, career, personal, veteran student, academic, psychological, birth control. **For learning-disabled students:** School does not offer a structured program with separate admission and additional fees. Services include: remedial math, remedial English, reading machines, remedial reading, tape recorders, diagnostic testing service, note-taking services, oral tests, learning center, readers, extended time for tests, tutors, priority registration, priority seating, texts on tape, exams on tape or computer, other testing accomodations. **Library:** Number of titles: 1,185,989; number of current serial subscriptions: 78,000. **Information technology resources:** Students are not required to lease or own a computer. Number of campus computers available to all students: 1,500. School has a wireless network. Approximate number of users that can be accommodated: 0. Proportion of college-owned housing units wired for high-speed internet access: 100%. **Campus safety:** Security services offered: 24-hour foot-and-vehicle patrols, late-night transport/escort service, 24-hour emergency telephones, lighted pathways/sidewalks, student patrols.

TRANSFER AND INTERNATIONAL STUDENTS

Transfer students: May apply for admission for the following academic terms: Fall, Winter, Spring, Summer. Applicants need a minimum number of credits to apply. For fall 2005: Transfer applications received: 8,382. Transfer applicants offered admission: 6,294. Transfer applicants enrolled: 2,027. **International students:** Number of foreign undergraduates: 618 (4% of student body). Number of countries represented: 73. Minimum TOEFL score required: 500 (paper); 173 (computer).

California State University–Monterey Bay

- **Address:** 100 Campus Center, Seaside, CA 93955-8001
- **Website:** http://www.csumb.edu
- **Public**
- **Enrollment:** N/A

KEY STATS

✔ **U.S News College Ranking:** fourth tier, Liberal Arts Colleges
✔ **ACT Score (25th/75th percentile):** 17-23
✔ **Tuition:** 2006-2007: $3,502 in state, $10,300 out of state

Selectivity: Selective	**Room/board:** $7,100
Acceptance rate: 62%	**Average debt:** $12,457
Student/faculty ratio: N/A	**Proportion who borrowed:** 62%

California State University–Northridge

- **Address:** 18111 Nordhoff Street, Northridge, CA 91330
- **Website:** http://www.csun.edu
- **Public**
- **Enrollment:** 20,638 full-time; 6,216 part-time

KEY STATS
✔ **U.S News College Ranking:** third tier, Universities–Master's (West)
✔ **SAT Score (25th/75th percentile):** 810-1080
✔ **Tuition:** 2006-2007: $3,042 in state, $13,212 out of state
   Selectivity: Less selective   Room/board: $8,880
   Acceptance rate: 75%   Average debt: N/A
   Student/faculty ratio: 23/1   Proportion who borrowed: N/A

UNDERGRADUATE STUDENT BODY STATS
2005-2006 enrollment: 20,638 full-time; 6,216 part-time. Men: 41%; women: 59%. **Ethnic makeup:** African American: 9%; Asian American: 12%; Hispanic: 28%; White: 46%; International: 5%.

ADMISSIONS FACTS AND FIGURES
Phone: (818) 677-3700. **Email:** admissions.records@csun.edu. **Website:** http://www.csun.edu. **Application deadlines for fall 2007:** Regular decision: November 30. Early decision: Not offered. Early action: Not offered. Admission cannot be deferred. **Application fee:** $55. Common application is accepted. **Admissions requirements/recommendations:** High school units required (recommended): English: 4; Mathematics: 3; Science: 2; Foreign language: 2; Social studies: 1; History: 1; Academic electives: 1; Total units: 15. Tests: The college uses SAT or ACT scores in admissions decisions. Either SAT or ACT required. Campus visit: Recommended. Admissions interview: Neither required nor recommended. Off-campus interview: Not available. **Factors that count in admissions decisions:** *Academic:* Secondary school record: Not considered. Class rank: Not considered. Letters of recommendation: Not considered. Standardized test scores: Very important. Essay: Not considered. *Nonacademic:* Interview: Not considered. Extracurricular activities: Not considered. Talent/ability: Not considered. Character/personal qualities: Not considered. Alumni/ae relationship: Not considered. Geographical residence: Considered. State residency: Considered. Religious affiliation/commitment: Not considered. Minority status: Not considered. Volunteer work: Not considered. Work experience: Not considered. **Admissions statistics for the fall 2005 entering class:** Total applicants: 18,178. Total accepted: 13,575. Freshmen enrolled: 3,720; 1% were from out of state. Overall acceptance rate: 75%. **Average high school grade point average:** 3.1. **First-year students who submitted SAT scores:** 81%. Scores (25/75 percentile): Verbal: 400-530, Math: 410-550, Combined: 810-1080. **First-year students submitting ACT scores:** 18%. Scores (25/75 percentile): English: 14-21, Math: 16-20, Composite: 15-20.

ACADEMICS
Year founded: 1958. **Academic calendar:** Semester. **Degrees offered:** bachelor's, master's. **Most popular majors:** 22% business, management, marketing, and related support services, 12% social sciences, 9% liberal arts and sciences studies, and humanities, 9% psychology, 7% English language and literature/letters. **Major fields of study:** area, ethnic, cultural, and gender studies; biological and biomedical sciences; business, management, marketing, and related support services; communication, journalism, and related programs; computer and information sciences and support services; education; English language and literature/letters; family and consumer sciences/human sciences; foreign languages, literatures, and linguistics; health professions and related clinical sciences; history; liberal arts and sciences studies, and humanities; mathematics and statistics; multi/interdisciplinary studies; parks, recreation, leisure, and fitness studies; philosophy and religious studies; physical sciences; psychology; social sciences; visual and performing arts. **Special academic programs (% participation):** double major (4%), exchange student program (domestic) (1%), liberal arts/career combination (9%), student-designed major (1%), teacher certificate program (1%). **Teacher certification offered in:** special education, elementary, secondary, bilingual/bicultural. **Faculty and instruction (2005-2006):** Total instructional faculty: 803 full-time, 1,019 part-time (51% men; 49% women; 26% minorities). Student/faculty ratio: 23/1. Classes of fewer than 20 students: 16%; of 20 to 49 students: 71%; of 50 or more students: 13%. **Freshmen returning for sophomore year:** 76%. **Graduation rates:** Four-year: 9%; five-year: 25%; six-year: 33%.

COSTS AND FINANCIAL AID
Financial aid office: (818) 677-4085. **Expenses (2006-2007):** Tuition and fees 2006-2007: $3,042 in state, $13,212 out of state; room/board: $8,880. Estimated books and supplies: $1,242; transportation: $1,134; personal expenses: $2,500. **Financial aid:** Priority filing date for institution's financial aid form: March 2.

CAMPUS LIFE AND EXTRACURRICULAR ACTIVITIES
Sports program (2005-2006): Member of NCAA I. *Men's intercollegiate varsity sports:* baseball, basketball, cross-country, golf, soccer, swimming and diving, track and field (indoor), track and field (outdoor), volleyball. *Women's intercollegiate varsity sports:* basketball, cross-country, golf, soccer, softball, swimming and diving, tennis, track and field (indoor), track and field (outdoor), volleyball, water polo.

SERVICES AND FACILITIES
Library: Number of titles: 2,854,723; number of current serial subscriptions: 3,292.

TRANSFER AND INTERNATIONAL STUDENTS
Transfer students: May apply for admission for the following academic terms: Fall, Spring. Applicants do not need a minimum number of credits to apply. For fall 2005: Transfer applications received: 10,680. Transfer applicants offered admission: 7,021. Transfer applicants enrolled: 3,771. **International students:** Number of foreign undergraduates: 1373 (5% of student body). Minimum TOEFL score required: 500 (paper); 173 (computer).

California State University–Sacramento

- **Address:** 6000 J Street, Sacramento, CA 95819
- **Website:** http://www.csus.edu
- **Public**
- **Enrollment:** 17,864 full-time; 5,164 part-time

KEY STATS
✔ **U.S News College Ranking:** 57, Universities–Master's (West)
✔ **SAT Score (25th/75th percentile):** 860-1090
✔ **Tuition:** 2006-2007: $3,660 in state, $13,830 out of state
   Selectivity: Less selective   Room/board: $7,052
   Acceptance rate: 47%   Average debt: $10,868
   Student/faculty ratio: 22/1   Proportion who borrowed: 40%

UNDERGRADUATE STUDENT BODY STATS
2005-2006 enrollment: 17,864 full-time; 5,164 part-time. Men: 43%; women: 57%. **Ethnic makeup:** African American: 7%; American-Indian: 1%; Asian American: 19%; Hispanic: 15%; White: 57%; International: 1%.

ADMISSIONS FACTS AND FIGURES
Phone: (916) 278-3901. **Email:** admissions@csus.edu. **Website:** http://www.csus.edu. **Application deadlines for fall 2007:** Regular decision: August 1. Early decision: Not offered. Early action: Send application by: November 30; Decision sent by: November 1. Admission can be deferred. **Application fee:** $55. Common application is not accepted. **To apply online, go to:** http://www.csumentor.edu. **Admissions requirements/recommendations:** High school units required (recommended): English: 4; Mathematics: 3; Science: 2; Foreign language: 2; Social studies: 1; History: 1; Academic electives: 1; Total units: 15. Tests: The college uses SAT or ACT scores in admissions decisions. Neither SAT nor ACT required. For admission to the fall 2007 entering class, the school will accept: ACT with writing, ACT without writing. Campus visit: Recommended. Admissions interview: Neither required nor recommended. **Factors that count in admissions decisions:** *Academic:* Secondary school record: Very important. Class rank: Not considered. Letters of recommendation: Considered. Standardized test scores: Very important. Essay: Not considered. *Nonacademic:* Interview: Considered. Extracurricular activities: Considered. Talent/ability: Considered. Character/personal qualities: Not considered. Alumni/ae relationship: Not considered. Geographical residence: Considered. State residency: Important. Religious affiliation/commitment: Not considered. Minority status: Not considered. Volunteer work: Not considered. Work experience: Not considered. **Admissions statistics for the fall 2005 entering class:** Total applicants: 15,980. Total accepted: 7,584. Freshmen enrolled: 2,600; 1% were from out of state. Overall acceptance rate: 47%. Non-early

acceptance rate: 47%. **Credentials of fall 2005 freshmen:** 100% were in the top half of their high school class. **Average high school grade point average:** 3.2. **First-year students who submitted SAT scores:** 80%. Scores (25/75 percentile): Verbal: 420-540, Math: 440-550, Combined: 860-1090. **First-year students submitting ACT scores:** 20%. Scores (25/75 percentile): English: 15-21, Math: 17-23, Composite: 17-22.

ACADEMICS

Year founded: 1947. **Academic calendar:** Semester. **Degrees offered:** bachelor's, master's, doctorate. **Most popular majors:** 11% counseling psychology, 9% public administration, 9% social work, 6% English language and literature, 6% special education and teaching. **Major fields of study:** architecture and related services; area, ethnic, cultural, and gender studies; biological and biomedical sciences; business, management, marketing, and related support services; communication, journalism, and related programs; computer and information sciences and support services; construction trades; education; engineering; engineering technologies/technicians; English language and literature/letters; family and consumer sciences/human sciences; foreign languages, literatures, and linguistics; health professions and related clinical sciences; history; liberal arts and sciences studies, and humanities; mathematics and statistics; multi/interdisciplinary studies; natural resources and conservation; parks, recreation, leisure, and fitness studies; philosophy and religious studies; physical sciences; psychology; public administration and social service professions; security and protective services; social sciences; visual and performing arts. **Areas of required coursework:** arts/fine arts, humanities, mathematics, English (including composition), foreign languages, sciences (biological or physical), history, social science, other. **Special academic programs:** accelerated program, cooperative (work-study plan) program, cross-registration, distance learning, double major, dual enrollment, English as a Second Language (ESL), honors program, independent study, internships, student-designed major, study abroad, teacher certificate program, weekend college. **Teacher certification offered in:** early childhood, special education, elementary, middle/junior high, secondary, bilingual/bicultural. **Cooperative education programs:** art, business, computer science, education, engineering, health professions, humanities, natural science, social/behavioral science, technologies. **Reserve Officers Training Corps (ROTC):** Army ROTC: Offered at cooperating institution (UC Davis); Air Force ROTC: Offered on campus. **Faculty and instruction (2005-2006):** Total instructional faculty: 812 full-time, 718 part-time (52% men; 48% women; 21% minorities). Full-time faculty with Ph.D. or other terminal degree: 78%. Student/faculty ratio: 22/1. Classes of fewer than 20 students: 23%; of 20 to 49 students: 65%; of 50 or more students: 11%. **Advanced Placement and International Baccalaureate credit:** AP tests may be used for: Credit and/or placement. Scores accepted: 3, 4, 5. International Baccalaureate exams may be used for: Credit and/or placement. **Freshmen returning for sophomore year:** 79%. **Graduation rates:** Four-year: 10%; five-year: 29%; six-year: 39%.

COSTS AND FINANCIAL AID

Financial aid office: (916) 278-6554. **Expenses (2006-2007):** Tuition and fees 2006-2007: $3,660 in state, $13,830 out of state; room/board: $7,052. Estimated books and supplies: $1,314; transportation: $894; personal expenses: $2,018. **Financial aid:** Priority filing date for institution's financial aid form: March 2. In 2005-2006, 61% of undergraduates applied for financial aid. Of those, 52% were determined to have financial need; 8% had their need fully met. Average financial aid package (proportion receiving): $8,753 (48%). Average amount of gift aid, such as scholarships or grants (proportion receiving): $2,216 (38%). Average amount of self-help aid, such as work study or loans (proportion receiving): $3,892 (29%). Average need-based loan (excluding PLUS or other private loans): $4,018. Among students who received need-based aid, the average percentage of need met: 67%. Among students who received aid based on merit, the average award (and the proportion receiving): $5,960 (5%). The average athletic scholarship (and the proportion receiving): $7,003 (0%). Average amount of debt of borrowers graduating in 2005: $10,868. Proportion who borrowed: 40%.

CAMPUS LIFE AND EXTRACURRICULAR ACTIVITIES

Campus housing available: coed dorms, special housing for disabled students. Students who live in college-owned, operated, or affiliated housing: 5%. **Clubs and organizations:** Number of student organizations: 230. Activities include: choral groups, concert band, dance, drama/theater, jazz band, marching band, music ensembles, musical theater, opera, pep band, radio station, student government, student newspaper, symphony orchestra. Number of fraternities: 19; sororities: 19. Proportion of men in fraternities: 7%; of women in sororities: 5%. Average proportion of students who stay on campus on weekends: 40%. **Sports program (2005-2006):** Member of

NCAA I. **Men's intercollegiate varsity sports:** baseball, basketball, cross-country, football, golf, soccer, tennis, track and field (indoor), track and field (outdoor). **Women's intercollegiate varsity sports:** basketball, cross-country, golf, gymnastics, rowing, soccer, softball, tennis, track and field (indoor), track and field (outdoor), volleyball.

SERVICES AND FACILITIES

Basic services: nonremedial tutoring, women's center, placement service, day care, health service, health insurance. **Remedial assistance:** reading, math, writing, study skills. **Counseling services:** career, personal, veteran student, academic, older student, psychological, birth control, other. **For learning-disabled students:** School does not offer a structured program with separate admission and additional fees. Services include: remedial math, remedial English, tape recorders, diagnostic testing service, note-taking services, learning center, readers, tutors, other testing accomodations, other. **Library:** Number of titles: 1,327,983; number of current serial subscriptions: 3,143. **Information technology resources:** Students are not required to lease or own a computer. Number of campus computers available to all students: 800. School has a wireless network. Proportion of college-owned housing units wired for high-speed internet access: 100%. **Campus safety:** Security services offered: 24-hour foot-and-vehicle patrols, late-night transport/escort service, 24-hour emergency telephones, lighted pathways/sidewalks, student patrols, controlled dormitory access (key, security card, etc).

TRANSFER AND INTERNATIONAL STUDENTS

Transfer students: May apply for admission for the following academic terms: Fall, Spring. Applicants need a minimum number of credits to apply. For fall 2005: Transfer applications received: 8,195. Transfer applicants offered admission: 4,264. Transfer applicants enrolled: 2,970. **International students:** Number of foreign undergraduates: 307 (1% of student body). Number of countries represented: 122. Minimum TOEFL score required: 510 (paper); 180 (computer). Average TOEFL score: 520 (paper).

California State University–San Bernardino

- **Address:** 5500 University Parkway, San Bernardino, CA 92407
- **Website:** http://www.csusb.edu
- **Public**
- **Enrollment:** 10,375 full-time; 2,089 part-time

KEY STATS
✔ **U.S News College Ranking:** 61, Universities–Master's (West)
✔ **SAT Score (25th/75th percentile):** 810-1030
✔ **Tuition:** 2006-2007: $3,092 in state, $11,228 out of state

Selectivity: Selective	**Room/board:** $7,517
Acceptance rate: 19%	**Average debt:** N/A
Student/faculty ratio: 22/1	**Proportion who borrowed:** N/A

UNDERGRADUATE STUDENT BODY STATS

2005-2006 enrollment: 10,375 full-time; 2,089 part-time. Men: 34%; women: 66%. **Ethnic makeup:** African American: 12%; American-Indian: 1%; Asian American: 8%; Hispanic: 34%; White: 42%; International: 3%.

ADMISSIONS FACTS AND FIGURES

Phone: (909) 537-5188. **Email:** moreinfo@csusb.edu. **Website:** http://www.csusb.edu. **Application deadlines for fall 2007:** Regular decision: July 17. Early decision: Not offered. Early action: Not offered. Admission cannot be deferred. **Application fee:** $55. Common application is not accepted. **To apply online, go to:** http://www.csumentor.edu. **Admissions requirements/recommendations:** High school units required (recommended): English: 4 (4); Mathematics: 3 (3); Science: 2 (2); Foreign language: 2 (2); Social studies: 1 (1); History: 1 (1); Academic electives: 1 (1); Total units: 15 (15). Tests: The college uses SAT or ACT scores in admissions decisions. Either SAT or ACT required. For admission to the fall 2007 entering class, the school will accept: ACT with writing, ACT without writing. Campus visit: Recommended. Admissions interview: Neither required nor recommended. Off-campus interview: Not available. **Factors that count in admissions decisions:** *Academic:* Secondary school record: Very important. Class rank: Not considered. Letters of recommendation: Not considered. Standardized test scores: Very important. Essay: Not considered. *Nonacademic:* Interview: Not considered. Extracurricular activities: Not considered. Talent/ability: Not considered. Character/personal qualities: Not considered. Alumni/ae relationship: Not considered. Geographical residence: Not considered. State residency: Important. Religious affiliation/commitment: Not considered. Minority status: Not considered. Volunteer work: Not considered. Work experience: Not considered. **Other schools with the greatest overlap in applicants:** California State University–Fullerton; California State University–Los Angeles; University of California–Riverside. **Admissions statistics for the fall 2005 entering class:** Total applicants: 9,547. Total accepted: 1,841. Freshmen enrolled: 1,692; 2% were from out of state. Overall acceptance rate: 19%. **Credentials of fall 2005 freshmen:** 20% ranked in the top 10 percent of their high school class; 36% were in the top 25 percent, and 92% were in the top half. (Proportion submitting class standing: 100%.) **Average high school grade point average:** 3.1. **First-year students who submitted SAT scores:** 88%. Scores (25/75 percentile): Verbal: 400-510, Math: 410-520, Combined: 810-1030. **First-year students submitting ACT scores:** 16%. Scores (25/75 percentile): English: 14-21, Math: 16-21, Composite: 16-21.

ACADEMICS

Year founded: 1962. **Academic calendar:** Quarter. **Degrees offered:** bachelor's, master's. **Most popular majors:** 22% business, management, marketing, and related support services, 21% liberal arts and sciences studies, and humanities, 10% social sciences, 7% psychology, 6% security and protective services. **Major fields of study:** architecture and related services; area, ethnic, cultural, and gender studies; biological and biomedical sciences; business, management, marketing, and related support services; communication, journalism, and related programs; computer and information sciences and support services; education; English language and literature/letters; family and consumer sciences/human sciences; foreign languages, literatures, and linguistics; health professions and related clinical sciences; history; liberal arts and sciences studies, and humanities; mathematics and statistics; multi/interdisciplinary studies; natural resources and conservation; parks, recreation, leisure, and fitness studies; philosophy and religious studies; physical sciences; psychology; public administration and social service professions; security and protective services; social sciences; visual and performing arts. **Areas of required coursework:** arts/fine arts, humanities, computer literacy, mathematics, English (including composition), philosophy, foreign languages, sciences (biological or physical), history, social science, other. **Pre-professional programs:** pre-law, pre-dentistry, pre-medicine, pre-veterinary science, pre-pharmacy, other. **Special academic programs:** cooperative (work-study plan) program, cross-registration, distance learning, double major, dual enrollment, exchange student program (domestic), honors program, independent study, internships, study abroad, teacher certificate program. **Teacher certification offered in:** early childhood, special education, elementary, vo-tech, middle/junior high, secondary, bilingual/bicultural. **Reserve Officers Training Corps (ROTC):** Army ROTC: Offered on campus; Air Force ROTC: Offered on campus. **Faculty and instruction (2005-2006):** Total instructional faculty: 447 full-time, 158 part-time (55% men; 45% women; 24% minorities). Student/faculty ratio: 22/1. Classes of fewer than 20 students: 26%; of 20 to 49 students: 59%; of 50 or more students: 15%. **Freshmen returning for sophomore year:** 80%. **Graduation rates:** Four-year: 9%; five-year: 31%; six-year: 42%.

COSTS AND FINANCIAL AID

Financial aid office: (909) 537-7800. **Expenses (2006-2007):** Tuition and fees 2006-2007: $3,092 in state, $11,228 out of state; room/board: $7,517. Estimated books and supplies: $1,314; transportation: $774; personal expenses: $2,088. **Financial aid:** Priority filing date for institution's financial aid form: March 2. In 2005-2006, 74% of undergraduates applied for financial aid. Of those, 66% were determined to have financial need; 12% had their need fully met. Average financial aid package (proportion receiving): $7,773 (63%). Average amount of gift aid, such as scholarships or grants (proportion receiving): $5,710 (52%). Average amount of self-help aid, such as work study or loans (proportion receiving): $3,911 (49%). Average need-based loan (excluding PLUS or other private loans): $3,648. Among students who received need-based aid, the average percentage of need met: 68%. Among students who received aid based on merit, the average award (and the proportion receiving): $3,654 (0%). The average athletic scholarship (and the proportion receiving): $3,240 (1%).

CAMPUS LIFE AND EXTRACURRICULAR ACTIVITIES

Campus housing available (% using): coed dorms (27%), women's dorms (1%), apartment for single students (72%). Students who live in college-owned, operated, or affiliated housing: 10%. **Clubs and organizations:** Number of student organizations: 100. Activities include: choral groups, dance, drama/theater, jazz band, music ensembles, musical theater, radio station, student government, student newspaper. Number of fraternities: 9;

sororities: 7. Proportion of men in fraternities: 3%; of women in sororities: 6%. Average proportion of students who stay on campus on weekends: 40%. **Sports program (2005-2006):** Member of NCAA II. *Men's intercollegiate varsity sports:* baseball, basketball, golf, soccer. *Women's intercollegiate varsity sports:* basketball, cross-country, soccer, softball, tennis, volleyball, water polo.

SERVICES AND FACILITIES

Basic services: nonremedial tutoring, women's center, day care, health service, health insurance. **Remedial assistance:** math, writing. **Counseling services:** minority student, career, personal, veteran student, academic, older student, psychological, birth control. **For learning-disabled students:** School does not offer a structured program with separate admission and additional fees. Total undergraduates in learning-disabled program or receiving services: 102. Services include: remedial math, remedial English, reading machines, remedial reading, tape recorders, other special classes, diagnostic testing service, note-taking services, oral tests, learning center, readers, extended time for tests, tutors, priority registration, priority seating, texts on tape, other testing accomodations. **Library:** Number of titles: 775,594; number of current serial subscriptions: 1,407. **Information technology resources:** Students are not required to lease or own a computer. Number of campus computers available to all students: 1,500. School does not have a wireless network. **Campus safety:** Security services offered: 24-hour foot-and-vehicle patrols, late-night transport/escort service, 24-hour emergency telephones, lighted pathways/sidewalks, controlled dormitory access (key, security card, etc).

TRANSFER AND INTERNATIONAL STUDENTS

Transfer students: May apply for admission for the following academic terms: Fall, Winter, Spring, Summer. Applicants do not need a minimum number of credits to apply. For fall 2005: Transfer applications received: 4,871. Transfer applicants offered admission: 2,165. Transfer applicants enrolled: 1,610. **International students:** Number of foreign undergraduates: 370 (3% of student body). Number of countries represented: 55. Minimum TOEFL score required: 500 (paper).

California State University–San Marcos

- ■ **Address:** 333 S. Twin Oaks Valley Road, San Marcos, CA 92096-0001
- ■ **Website:** http://www.csusm.edu
- ■ **Public**
- ■ **Enrollment:** 4,658 full-time; 1,669 part-time

KEY STATS

✔ **U.S News College Ranking:** third tier, Universities–Master's (West)
✔ **SAT Score (25th/75th percentile):** 880-1080
✔ **Tuition:** 2006-2007: $3,092 in state, $13,262 out of state

Selectivity: Less selective	Room/board: N/A
Acceptance rate: 44%	Average debt: $13,112
Student/faculty ratio: 22/1	Proportion who borrowed: 40%

UNDERGRADUATE STUDENT BODY STATS

2005-2006 enrollment: 4,658 full-time; 1,669 part-time. Men: 39%; women: 61%. **Ethnic makeup:** African American: 3%; American-Indian: 1%; Asian American: 11%; Hispanic: 20%; White: 62%; International: 3%.

ADMISSIONS FACTS AND FIGURES

Phone: (760) 750-4848. **Email:** apply@csusm.edu. **Website:** http://www.csusm.edu. **Application deadlines for fall 2007:** Regular decision: November 30. Early decision: Not offered. Early action: Not offered. Admission cannot be deferred. **Application fee:** $55. Common application is not accepted. **To apply online, go to:** http://www.csumentor.edu/AdmissionApp/. **Admissions requirements/recommendations:** High school units required (recommended): English: 4 (4); Mathematics: 3 (4); Science: 2 (2); Foreign language: 2 (2); Social studies: 2 (2); History: 0 (0); Academic electives: 1 (1); Total units: 15 (16). **Tests:** The college uses SAT or ACT scores in admissions decisions. Neither SAT nor ACT required. Campus visit: Recommended. Admissions interview: Neither required nor recommended. Off-campus interview: Not available. **Factors that count in admissions decisions:** *Academic:* Secondary school record: Very important. Class rank: Not considered. Letters of recommendation: Not considered. Standardized test scores: Considered. Essay: Not considered.

Nonacademic: Interview: Not considered. Extracurricular activities: Not considered. Talent/ability: Not considered. Character/personal qualities: Not considered. Alumni/ae relationship: Not considered. Geographical residence: Not considered. State residency: Not considered. Religious affiliation/commitment: Not considered. Minority status: Not considered. Volunteer work: Not considered. Work experience: Not considered. **Admissions statistics for the fall 2005 entering class:** Total applicants: 6,586. Total accepted: 2,877. Freshmen enrolled: 804; 2% were from out of state. Overall acceptance rate: 44%. **Average high school grade point average:** 3.2. **First-year students who submitted SAT scores:** 97%. Scores (25/75 percentile): Verbal: 430-530, Math: 450-550, Combined: 880-1080. **First-year students submitting ACT scores:** 21%. Scores (25/75 percentile): English: N/A, Math: N/A, Composite: N/A.

ACADEMICS

Year founded: 1989. **Academic calendar:** Semester. **Degrees offered:** bachelor's, master's. **Most popular majors:** Information not available. **Major fields of study:** area, ethnic, cultural, and gender studies; biological and biomedical sciences; business, management, marketing, and related support services; communication, journalism, and related programs; computer and information sciences and support services; English language and literature/letters; family and consumer sciences/human sciences; foreign languages, literatures, and linguistics; history; liberal arts and sciences studies, and humanities; mathematics and statistics; multi/interdisciplinary studies; physical sciences; psychology; social sciences; visual and performing arts. **Areas of required coursework:** humanities, computer literacy, mathematics, English (including composition), foreign languages, sciences (biological or physical), history, social science, other. **Special academic programs:** cross-registration, distance learning, double major, dual enrollment, English as a Second Language (ESL), independent study, internships, student-designed major, study abroad, teacher certificate program, weekend college, other. **Reserve Officers Training Corps (ROTC):** Army ROTC: Offered at cooperating institution (San Diego State University); Navy ROTC: Offered at cooperating institution (San Diego State University); Air Force ROTC: Offered at cooperating institution (San Diego State University). **Faculty and instruction (2005-2006):** Total instructional faculty: 203 full-time, 220 part-time (45% men; 55% women; 28% minorities). Full-time faculty with Ph.D. or other terminal degree: 99%. Student/faculty ratio: 22/1. Classes of fewer than 20 students: 21%; of 20 to 49 students: 71%; of 50 or more students: 8%. **Freshmen returning for sophomore year:** 72%. **Graduation rates:** Four-year: 10%; five-year: 32%; six-year: 39%.

COSTS AND FINANCIAL AID

Financial aid office: (760) 750-4850. **Expenses (2006-2007):** Tuition and fees 2006-2007: $3,092 in state, $13,262 out of state; room/board: N/A. Estimated books and supplies: $1,260; transportation: $990; personal expenses: $2,304. **Financial aid:** Priority filing date for institution's financial aid form: March 2. In 2005-2006, 52% of undergraduates applied for financial aid. Of those, 43% were determined to have financial need; Average financial aid package (proportion receiving): $6,946 (40%). Average amount of gift aid, such as scholarships or grants (proportion receiving): $3,831 (40%). Average amount of self-help aid, such as work study or loans (proportion receiving): $4,103 (26%). Average need-based loan (excluding PLUS or other private loans): $4,099. The average athletic scholarship (and the proportion receiving): $3,424 (1%). Average amount of debt of borrowers graduating in 2005: $13,112. Proportion who borrowed: 40%.

CAMPUS LIFE AND EXTRACURRICULAR ACTIVITIES

Campus housing available: apartment for single students, special housing for disabled students, special housing for international students, other housing options. Students who live in college-owned, operated, or affiliated housing: 6%. Activities include: choral groups, dance, drama/theater, music ensembles, student newspaper. **Sports program (2005-2006):** Member of NAIA. **Men's intercollegiate varsity sports:** cross-country, golf, track and field (outdoor). **Women's intercollegiate varsity sports:** cross-country, golf, track and field (outdoor).

SERVICES AND FACILITIES

Basic services: women's center, placement service, day care, health service. **Remedial assistance:** reading, math, writing, study skills. **Counseling services:** minority student, career, veteran student, birth control. **Library:** Number of titles: 241,706; number of current serial subscriptions: 2,181. **Information technology resources:** Students are not required to lease or own a computer. Number of campus computers available to all students: 1,100. **Campus safety:** Security services offered: 24-hour emergency telephones,

lighted pathways/sidewalks, controlled dormitory access (key, security card, etc).

TRANSFER AND INTERNATIONAL STUDENTS

Transfer students: May apply for admission for the following academic terms: Fall, Spring. Applicants need a minimum number of credits to apply. For fall 2005: Transfer applications received: 2,859. Transfer applicants offered admission: 1,595. **International students:** Number of foreign undergraduates: 163 (3% of student body).

California State University—Stanislaus

- ■ **Address:** 801 W. Monte Vista Avenue, Turlock, CA 95382
- ■ **Website:** http://www.csustan.edu
- ■ **Public**
- ■ **Enrollment:** 4,499 full-time; 1,980 part-time

KEY STATS

✔ **U.S News College Ranking:** 51, Universities–Master's (West)
✔ **SAT Score (25th/75th percentile):** 830-1080
✔ **Tuition:** 2006-2007: $3,043 in state, $13,213 out of state
  Selectivity: Less selective   **Room/board:** $7,178
  Acceptance rate: 92%   **Average debt:** $15,500
  Student/faculty ratio: 18/1   **Proportion who borrowed:** 18%

UNDERGRADUATE STUDENT BODY STATS

2005-2006 enrollment: 4,499 full-time; 1,980 part-time. Men: 34%; women: 66%. **Ethnic makeup:** African American: 4%; American-Indian: 1%; Asian American: 12%; Hispanic: 28%; White: 54%; International: 1%.

ADMISSIONS FACTS AND FIGURES

Phone: (209) 667-3152. **Email:** Outreach_Help_Desk@csustan.edu. **Website:** http://www.csustan.edu. **Application deadlines for fall 2007:** Regular decision: July 1. Early decision: Not offered. Early action: Send application by: November 30; Decision sent by: March 1. Admission cannot be deferred. **Application fee:** $55. Common application is not accepted. **To apply online, go to:** http://www.csumentor.edu/admissionApp. **Admissions requirements/recommendations:** High school units required (recommended): English: 4; Mathematics: 3; Science: 2; Foreign language: 2; Social studies: 1; History: 1; Academic electives: 1; Total units: 15. Tests: The college uses SAT or ACT scores in admissions decisions. Neither SAT nor ACT required. For admission to the fall 2007 entering class, the school will accept: ACT with writing, ACT without writing. Campus visit: Recommended. Admissions interview: Neither required nor recommended. Off-campus interview: May be arranged. **Factors that count in admissions decisions:** *Academic:* Secondary school record: Very important. Class rank: Important. Letters of recommendation: Not considered. Standardized test scores: Very important. Essay: Not considered. *Nonacademic:* Interview: Not considered. Extracurricular activities: Not considered. Talent/ability: Not considered. Character/personal qualities: Not considered. Alumni/ae relationship: Not considered. Geographical residence: Not considered. State residency: Not considered. Religious affiliation/commitment: Not considered. Minority status: Not considered. Volunteer work: Not considered. Work experience: Not considered. **Admissions statistics for the fall 2005 entering class:** Total applicants: 3,016. Total accepted: 2,778. Freshmen enrolled: 870; 1% were from out of state. Accepted through early-decision or early-action plans: 17%. Overall acceptance rate: 92%. **Average high school grade point average:** 3.2. **First-year students who submitted SAT scores:** 88%. Scores (25/75 percentile): Verbal: 410-540, Math: 420-540, Combined: 830-1080. **First-year students submitting ACT scores:** 25%. Scores (25/75 percentile): English: 15-22, Math: 17-24, Composite: 17-22.

ACADEMICS

Year founded: 1957. **Academic calendar:** 4-1-4. **Degrees offered:** bachelor's, master's. **Most popular majors:** 24% liberal arts and sciences/liberal studies, 16% business administration and management, 8% psychology, 7% criminal justice/safety studies, 5% sociology. **Major fields of study:** agriculture, agriculture operations, and related sciences; biological and biomedical sciences; business, management, marketing, and related support services; communication, journalism, and related programs; computer and information sciences and support services; education; English language and literature/letters; foreign languages, literatures, and linguistics; health.

professions and related clinical sciences; history; liberal arts and sciences studies, and humanities; mathematics and statistics; multi/interdisciplinary studies; parks, recreation, leisure, and fitness studies; philosophy and religious studies; physical sciences; psychology; security and protective services; social sciences; visual and performing arts. **Areas of required coursework:** arts/fine arts, humanities, computer literacy, mathematics, English (including composition), philosophy, foreign languages, sciences (biological or physical), history, social science, other. **Pre-professional programs:** pre-law, other. **Special academic programs:** accelerated program, cooperative (work-study plan) program, cross-registration, distance learning, double major, dual enrollment, English as a Second Language (ESL), exchange student program (domestic), external degree program, honors program, independent study, internships, liberal arts/career combination, student-designed major, study abroad, teacher certificate program. **Teacher certification offered in:** special education, elementary, secondary, bilingual/bicultural. **Cooperative education programs:** art, business, computer science, education, engineering, social/behavioral science. **Faculty and instruction (2005-2006):** Total instructional faculty: 285 full-time, 210 part-time (53% men; 47% women; 18% minorities). Full-time faculty with Ph.D. or other terminal degree: 88%. Student/faculty ratio: 18/1. Classes of fewer than 20 students: 40%; of 20 to 49 students: 57%; of 50 or more students: 3%. **Advanced Placement and International Baccalaureate credit:** AP tests may be used for: Credit only. Scores accepted: 3. International Baccalaureate exams may be used for: Credit only. **Freshmen returning for sophomore year:** 82%. **Graduation rates:** Four-year: 21%; five-year: 42%; six-year: 48%.

COSTS AND FINANCIAL AID

Financial aid office: (209) 667-3336. **Expenses (2006-2007):** Tuition and fees 2006-2007: $3,043 in state, $13,213 out of state; room/board: $7,178. Estimated books and supplies: $1,314; transportation: $774; personal expenses: $1,935. **Financial aid:** Priority filing date for institution's financial aid form: March 2. In 2005-2006, 76% of undergraduates applied for financial aid. Of those, 51% were determined to have financial need; 4% had their need fully met. Average financial aid package (proportion receiving): $7,836 (50%). Average amount of gift aid, such as scholarships or grants (proportion receiving): $4,509 (44%). Average amount of self-help aid, such as work study or loans (proportion receiving): $3,956 (33%). Average need-based loan (excluding PLUS or other private loans): $4,004. Among students who received need-based aid, the average percentage of need met: 42%. Among students who received aid based on merit, the average award (and the proportion receiving): $1,437 (1%). The average athletic scholarship (and the proportion receiving): $2,302 (3%). Average amount of debt of borrowers graduating in 2005: $15,500. Proportion who borrowed: 18%.

CAMPUS LIFE AND EXTRACURRICULAR ACTIVITIES

Campus housing available: coed dorms, apartment for single students. Students who live in college-owned, operated, or affiliated housing: 10%. **Student employment:** During the 2005-2006 academic year, 11% of undergraduates worked on campus. Average per-year earnings: $6,720. **Clubs and organizations:** Number of student organizations: 82. Activities include: choral groups, concert band, dance, drama/theater, jazz band, music ensembles, musical theater, opera, radio station, student government, student newspaper, symphony orchestra. Number of fraternities: 5; sororities: 7. Proportion of men in fraternities: 3%; of women in sororities: 3%. Average proportion of students who stay on campus on weekends: 30%. **Sports program (2005-2006):** Member of NCAA II. *Men's intercollegiate varsity sports:* baseball, basketball, cross-country, golf, soccer, track and field (indoor), track and field (outdoor). *Women's intercollegiate varsity sports:* basketball, cross-country, soccer, softball, track and field (indoor), track and field (outdoor), volleyball.

SERVICES AND FACILITIES

Basic services: nonremedial tutoring, women's center, placement service, day care, health service, health insurance. **Remedial assistance:** reading, math, writing, study skills. **Counseling services:** minority student, career, military, personal, veteran student, academic, older student, psychological, birth control. **For learning-disabled students:** School does not offer a structured program with separate admission and additional fees. Total undergraduates in learning-disabled program or receiving services: 87. Services include: remedial math, remedial English, reading machines, tape recorders, note-taking services, readers, extended time for tests, tutors, priority registration, priority seating, substitution of courses, texts on tape, exams on tape or computer, other testing accomodations, waiver of foreign language degree requirement, waiver of math degree requirement. **Library:** Number of titles: 363,479; number of current serial subscriptions: 1,398. **Information technology resources:** Students are not required to lease or own

a computer. Number of campus computers available to all students: 150. School has a wireless network. Approximate number of users that can be accommodated: 100. Proportion of college-owned housing units wired for high-speed internet access: 100%. **Campus safety:** Security services offered: 24-hour foot-and-vehicle patrols, late-night transport/escort service, 24-hour emergency telephones, lighted pathways/sidewalks, student patrols, controlled dormitory access (key, security card, etc).

TRANSFER AND INTERNATIONAL STUDENTS

Transfer students: May apply for admission for the following academic terms: Fall, Winter, Spring, Summer. Applicants need a minimum number of credits to apply. For fall 2005: Transfer applications received: 2,210. Transfer applicants offered admission: 1,369. Transfer applicants enrolled: 878. **International students:** Number of foreign undergraduates: 86 (1% of student body). Number of countries represented: 27. Minimum TOEFL score required: 500 (paper); 173 (computer). Average TOEFL score: 505 (paper).

Cal Poly–San Luis Obispo

- **Address:** 1 Grand Avenue, San Luis Obispo, CA 93407
- **Website:** http://www.calpoly.edu
- **Public**
- **Enrollment:** 16,591 full-time; 897 part-time

KEY STATS

✔ **U.S News College Ranking:** 7, Universities–Master's (West)
✔ **SAT Score (25th/75th percentile):** 1110-1300
✔ **Tuition:** 2006-2007: $4,350 in state, $11,130 out of state

Selectivity: More selective	**Room/board:** $8,453
Acceptance rate: 45%	**Average debt:** $14,020
Student/faculty ratio: 20/1	**Proportion who borrowed:** 35%

UNDERGRADUATE STUDENT BODY STATS

2005-2006 enrollment: 16,591 full-time; 897 part-time. Men: 57%; women: 43%. **Ethnic makeup:** African American: 1%; American-Indian: 1%; Asian American: 11%; Hispanic: 10%; White: 76%.

ADMISSIONS FACTS AND FIGURES

Phone: (805) 756-2311. **Email:** admissions@calpoly.edu. **Website:** http://www.calpoly.edu. **Application deadlines for fall 2007:** Regular decision: November 30. Early decision: Send application by: October 31; Decision sent by: December 15. Early action: Not offered. Admission cannot be deferred. **Application fee:** $55. Common application is not accepted. **To apply online, go to:** http://www.ess.calpoly.edu/_admiss/. **Admissions requirements/recommendations:** High school units required (recommended): English: 4; Mathematics: 3; Science: 3; Foreign language: 2; Social studies: 2; History: 1; Academic electives: 1; Total units: 15. Tests: The college uses SAT or ACT scores in admissions decisions. Either SAT or ACT required. For admission to the fall 2007 entering class, the school will accept: ACT with writing, ACT without writing. Campus visit: Neither required nor recommended. Admissions interview: Neither required nor recommended. Off-campus interview: Not available. **Factors that count in admissions decisions:** *Academic:* Secondary school record: Very important. Class rank: Not considered. Letters of recommendation: Not considered. Standardized test scores: Very important. Essay: Not considered. *Nonacademic:* Interview: Not considered. Extracurricular activities: Considered. Talent/ability: Considered. Character/personal qualities: Not considered. Alumni/ae relationship: Not considered. Geographical residence: Not considered. State residency: Not considered. Religious affiliation/commitment: Not considered. Minority status: Not considered. Volunteer work: Considered. Work experience: Considered. **Admissions statistics for the fall 2005 entering class:** Total applicants: 23,691. Total accepted: 10,551. Freshmen enrolled: 3,372; Accepted through early-decision or early-action plans: 19%. Overall acceptance rate: 45%. Early-decision acceptance rate: 36%. Non-early acceptance rate: 45%. **Credentials of fall 2005 freshmen:** 37% ranked in the top 10 percent of their high school class; 76% were in the top 25 percent, and 96% were in the top half. (Proportion submitting class standing: 68%.) **Average high school grade point average:** 3.7. **First-year students who submitted SAT scores:** 99%. Scores (25/75 percentile): Verbal: 540-630, Math: 570-670, Combined: 1110-1300. **First-year**

students submitting ACT scores: 43%. Scores (25/75 percentile): English: 22-28, Math: 24-29, Composite: 23-28.

ACADEMICS
Year founded: 1901. **Academic calendar:** Quarter. **Degrees offered:** bachelor's, master's. **Most popular majors:** 15% business administration and management, 7% agricultural business and management, 5% mechanical engineering, 4% architecture (B.Arch., B.A./B.S., M.Arch., M.A./M.S., Ph.D.), 3% electrical, electronics, and communications engineering. **Major fields of study:** agriculture, agriculture operations, and related sciences; architecture and related services; biological and biomedical sciences; business, management, marketing, and related support services; communication, journalism, and related programs; computer and information sciences and support services; education; engineering; English language and literature/letters; family and consumer sciences/human sciences; foreign languages, literatures, and linguistics; health professions and related clinical sciences; history; liberal arts and sciences studies, and humanities; mathematics and statistics; natural resources and conservation; parks, recreation, leisure, and fitness studies; philosophy and religious studies; physical sciences; psychology; social sciences; visual and performing arts. **Areas of required coursework:** arts/fine arts, humanities, mathematics, English (including composition), philosophy, sciences (biological or physical), history, social science, other. **Special academic programs:** cooperative (work-study plan) program, cross-registration, distance learning, double major, dual enrollment, English as a Second Language (ESL), exchange student program (domestic), external degree program, honors program, independent study, internships, study abroad, teacher certificate program. **Teacher certification offered in:** bilingual/bicultural. **Reserve Officers Training Corps (ROTC):** Army ROTC: Offered on campus. **Faculty and instruction (2005-2006):** Total instructional faculty: 726 full-time, 520 part-time (67% men; 33% women; 15% minorities). Full-time faculty with Ph.D. or other terminal degree: 72%. Student/faculty ratio: 20/1. Classes of fewer than 20 students: 19%; of 20 to 49 students: 72%; of 50 or more students: 10%. **Advanced Placement and International Baccalaureate credit:** AP tests may be used for: Credit only. Scores accepted: 3, 4, 5. **Freshmen returning for sophomore year:** 90%. **Graduation rates:** Four-year: 21%; five-year: 56%; six-year: 67%.

COSTS AND FINANCIAL AID
Financial aid office: (805) 756-2927. **Expenses (2006-2007):** Tuition and fees 2006-2007: $4,350 in state, $11,130 out of state; room/board: $8,453. **Financial aid:** Priority filing date for institution's financial aid form: March 2; deadline: June 30. In 2005-2006, 51% of undergraduates applied for financial aid. Of those, 34% were determined to have financial need; 7% had their need fully met. Average financial aid package (proportion receiving): $7,333 (32%). Average amount of gift aid, such as scholarships or grants (proportion receiving): $1,820 (23%). Average amount of self-help aid, such as work study or loans (proportion receiving): $4,047 (25%). Average need-based loan (excluding PLUS or other private loans): $3,879. Among students who received need-based aid, the average percentage of need met: 66%. Average amount of debt of borrowers graduating in 2005: $14,020. Proportion who borrowed: 35%.

CAMPUS LIFE AND EXTRACURRICULAR ACTIVITIES
Campus housing available: coed dorms, women's dorms, men's dorms, other housing options. Students who live in college-owned, operated, or affiliated housing: 19%. **Student employment:** During the 2005-2006 academic year, 15% of undergraduates worked on campus. Average per-year earnings: $3,100. **Clubs and organizations:** Number of student organizations: 350. Activities include: choral groups, concert band, dance, drama/theater, jazz band, literary magazine, marching band, music ensembles, musical theater, pep band, radio station, student government, student newspaper, television station. Number of fraternities: 23; sororities: 10. Proportion of men in fraternities: 10%; of women in sororities: 11%. **Sports program (2005-2006):** Member of NCAA I. *Men's intercollegiate varsity sports:* baseball, basketball, cross-country, football, golf, soccer, swimming and diving, tennis, track and field (outdoor), wrestling. *Women's intercollegiate varsity sports:* basketball, cross-country, golf, soccer, softball, swimming and diving, tennis, track and field (indoor), track and field (outdoor), volleyball.

SERVICES AND FACILITIES
Basic services: nonremedial tutoring, women's center, placement service, day care, health service, health insurance. **Remedial assistance:** reading, math, writing, study skills. **Counseling services:** personal, academic, psychological, birth control. **For learning-disabled students:** School does not offer a structured program with separate admission and additional fees. Total

undergraduates in learning-disabled program or receiving services: 275. Services include: tape recorders, note-taking services, special bookstore section, extended time for tests, texts on tape, other testing accomodations. **Library:** Number of titles: 1,151,800; number of current serial subscriptions: 2,617. **Information technology resources:** Students are not required to lease or own a computer. Number of campus computers available to all students: 300. School has a wireless network. Approximate number of users that can be accommodated: 1,500. Proportion of college-owned housing units wired for high-speed internet access: 100%. **Campus safety:** Security services offered: 24-hour foot-and-vehicle patrols, late-night transport/escort service, 24-hour emergency telephones, lighted pathways/sidewalks, student patrols, controlled dormitory access (key, security card, etc).

TRANSFER AND INTERNATIONAL STUDENTS
Transfer students: May apply for admission for the following academic terms: Fall, Winter, Spring, Summer. Applicants do not need a minimum number of credits to apply. For fall 2005: Transfer applications received: 3,993. Transfer applicants offered admission: 1,744. Transfer applicants enrolled: 868. **International students:** Number of foreign undergraduates: 61. Minimum TOEFL score required: 550 (paper); 213 (computer).

Chapman University

- **Address:** 1 University Drive, Orange, CA 92866
- **Website:** http://www.chapman.edu
- **Private; Religious affiliation:** Disciples of Christ
- **Enrollment:** 3,661 full-time; 203 part-time

KEY STATS
✔ **U.S News College Ranking:** 11, Universities–Master's (West)
✔ **SAT Score (25th/75th percentile):** 1094-1318
✔ **Tuition:** 2006-2007: $29,712

Selectivity: More selective	**Room/board:** $11,314
Acceptance rate: 53%	**Average debt:** $19,237
Student/faculty ratio: 15/1	**Proportion who borrowed:** 64%

UNDERGRADUATE STUDENT BODY STATS
2005-2006 enrollment: 3,661 full-time; 203 part-time. Men: 41%; women: 59%. **Ethnic makeup:** African American: 2%; American-Indian: 1%; Asian American: 8%; Hispanic: 11%; White: 76%; International: 2%. **Religious preference:** Roman Catholic: 23%; Protestant: 29%; Jewish: 4%; Muslim: 1%; Buddhist: 1%; No preference: 6%; Unknown: 31%; Disciples of Christ: 3%; Greek Orthodox: 1%; Other: 1%.

ADMISSIONS FACTS AND FIGURES
Phone: (888) 282-7759. **Email:** admit@chapman.edu. **Website:** http://www.chapman.edu. **Application deadlines for fall 2007:** Regular decision: January 31. Early decision: Not offered. Early action: Send application by: November 30; Decision sent by: January 15. Admission cannot be deferred. **Application fee:** $55. Common application is accepted. **Admissions requirements/recommendations:** High school units required (recommended): English: 2; Mathematics: 2; Science: 2; Foreign language: 2; Social studies: 3; Total units: 11. Tests: The college uses SAT or ACT scores in admissions decisions. Either SAT or ACT required. For admission to the fall 2007 entering class, the school will accept: ACT with writing. Campus visit: Recommended. Admissions interview: Recommended. Off-campus interview: May be arranged. **Factors that count in admissions decisions:** *Academic:* Secondary school record: Very important. Class rank: Very important. Letters of recommendation: Considered. Standardized test scores: Very important. Essay: Very important. *Nonacademic:* Interview: Important. Extracurricular activities: Important. Talent/ability: Important. Character/personal qualities: Very important. Alumni/ae relationship: Considered. Geographical residence: Not considered. State residency: Not considered. Religious affiliation/commitment: Not considered. Minority status: Considered. Volunteer work: Important. Work experience: Considered. **Other schools with the greatest overlap in applicants:** Loyola Marymount University; University of California–Irvine; University of Redlands; University of San Diego; University of Southern California. **Admissions statistics for the fall 2005 entering class:** Total applicants: 3,862. Total accepted: 2,044. Freshmen enrolled: 853; 31% were from out of state. Accepted through early-decision or early-action plans: 54%. Overall acceptance rate: 53%. Non-early acceptance rate: 48%. **Size of waiting list:** 264 applicants;

enrolled from waiting list: 27. **Credentials of fall 2005 freshmen:** 51% ranked in the top 10 percent of their high school class; 92% were in the top 25 percent, and 99% were in the top half. (Proportion submitting class standing: 44%.) **Average high school grade point average:** 3.7. **First-year students who submitted SAT scores:** 88%. Scores (25/75 percentile): Verbal: 543-656, Math: 551-662, Combined: 1094-1318. **First-year students submitting ACT scores:** 39%. Scores (25/75 percentile): English: 22-29, Math: 22-29, Composite: 23-29.

ACADEMICS

Year founded: 1861. **Academic calendar:** 4-1-4. **Degrees offered:** bachelor's, post-bachelor's certificate, master's, first professional, doctorate. **Most popular majors:** 16% business/commerce, 15% cinematography and film/video production, 6% liberal arts and sciences/liberal studies, 5% psychology, 4% advertising. **Major fields of study:** biological and biomedical sciences; business, management, marketing, and related support services; communication, journalism, and related programs; computer and information sciences and support services; education; English language and literature/letters; foreign languages, literatures, and linguistics; health professions and related clinical sciences; history; legal professions and studies; liberal arts and sciences studies, and humanities; mathematics and statistics; multi/interdisciplinary studies; philosophy and religious studies; physical sciences; psychology; public administration and social service professions; social sciences; visual and performing arts. **Areas of required coursework:** arts/fine arts, humanities, mathematics, English (including composition), philosophy, foreign languages, sciences (biological or physical), history, social science, other. **Pre-professional programs:** pre-law, pre-dentistry, pre-medicine, pre-veterinary science. **Special academic programs (% participation):** cooperative (work-study plan) program, distance learning (21%), double major (4%), English as a Second Language (ESL) (2%), exchange student program (domestic) (1%), honors program (4%), independent study (27%), internships (35%), student-designed major (0%), study abroad (12%). **Teacher certification offered in:** special education, elementary, secondary. **Cooperative education programs:** business. **Reserve Officers Training Corps (ROTC):** Army ROTC: Offered at cooperating institution (CSU Pomona, Claremont Colleges, CSU Fullerton); Air Force ROTC: Offered at cooperating institution (Loyola Marymount University). **Faculty and instruction (2005-2006):** Total instructional faculty: 264 full-time, 231 part-time. Full-time faculty with Ph.D. or other terminal degree: 89%. Student/faculty ratio: 15/1. Classes of fewer than 20 students: 39%; of 20 to 49 students: 60%; of 50 or more students: 1%. **Advanced Placement and International Baccalaureate credit:** AP tests may be used for: Credit and/or placement. Scores accepted: 3, 4, 5. International Baccalaureate exams may be used for: Credit and/or placement. **Freshmen returning for sophomore year:** 86%. **Graduation rates:** Four-year: 52%; five-year: 62%; six-year: 61%. **Graduate study:** 34% of students pursue further study within one year. Fields in which graduates pursue further study: Master of Business Administration (MBA), 12%; law, 3%; medicine, 3%.

COSTS AND FINANCIAL AID

Financial aid office: (714) 997-6741. **Expenses (2006-2007):** Tuition and fees 2006-2007: $29,712; room/board: $11,314. Estimated books and supplies: $1,100; transportation: $741; personal expenses: $1,450. **Financial aid:** Priority filing date for institution's financial aid form: March 2. In 2005-2006, 96% of undergraduates applied for financial aid. Of those, 60% were determined to have financial need; 100% had their need fully met. Average financial aid package (proportion receiving): $21,628 (60%). Average amount of gift aid, such as scholarships or grants (proportion receiving): $18,118 (59%). Average amount of self-help aid, such as work study or loans (proportion receiving): $6,628 (50%). Average need-based loan (excluding PLUS or other private loans): $4,596. Among students who received need-based aid, the average percentage of need met: 100%. Among students who received aid based on merit, the average award (and the proportion receiving): $16,047 (15%). The average athletic scholarship (and the proportion receiving): $0 (0%). Average amount of debt of borrowers graduating in 2005: $19,237. Proportion who borrowed: 64%.

CAMPUS LIFE AND EXTRACURRICULAR ACTIVITIES

Campus housing available (% using): coed dorms (86%), apartment for single students (12%), special housing for disabled students, other housing options (2%). Students who live in college-owned, operated, or affiliated housing: 37%. **Student employment:** During the 2005-2006 academic year, 25% of undergraduates worked on campus. Average per-year earnings: $2,800. **Clubs and organizations:** Number of student organizations: 56. Activities include: choral groups, concert band, dance, drama/theater, jazz band, literary magazine, music ensembles, musical theater, opera, pep

band, radio station, student government, student newspaper, student film society, symphony orchestra, yearbook. Number of fraternities: 5; sororities: 5. Proportion of men in fraternities: 15%; of women in sororities: 17%. **Sports program (2005-2006):** Member of NCAA III. **Men's intercollegiate varsity sports:** baseball, basketball, cross-country, football, golf, soccer, tennis, water polo. **Women's intercollegiate varsity sports:** basketball, crew, cross-country, rowing, soccer, softball, swimming and diving, tennis, track and field (outdoor), volleyball, water polo.

SERVICES AND FACILITIES

Basic services: nonremedial tutoring, day care, health service, health insurance. **Remedial assistance:** reading, math, writing, study skills. **Counseling services:** minority student, career, personal, veteran student, academic, older student, psychological, birth control, religious. **For learning-disabled students:** School does not offer a structured program with separate admission and additional fees. Total undergraduates in learning-disabled program or receiving services: 265. Services include: remedial math, remedial English, remedial reading, tape recorders, note-taking services, oral tests, learning center, readers, extended time for tests, tutors, priority registration. **Library:** Number of titles: 183,336; number of current serial subscriptions: 1,825. **Information technology resources:** Students are not required to lease or own a computer. Number of campus computers available to all students: 543. School has a wireless network. Approximate number of users that can be accommodated: 2,400. Proportion of college-owned housing units wired for high-speed internet access: 100%. **Campus safety:** Security services offered: 24-hour foot-and-vehicle patrols, late-night transport/escort service, 24-hour emergency telephones, lighted pathways/sidewalks, student patrols, controlled dormitory access (key, security card, etc).

TRANSFER AND INTERNATIONAL STUDENTS

Transfer students: May apply for admission for the following academic terms: Fall, Spring. Applicants need a minimum number of credits to apply. For fall 2005: Transfer applications received: 936. Transfer applicants offered admission: 530. Transfer applicants enrolled: 301. **International students:** Number of foreign undergraduates: 75 (2% of student body). Number of countries represented: 53. Minimum TOEFL score required: 500 (paper); 173 (computer). Average TOEFL score: 601 (paper).

Claremont McKenna College

- **Address:** 890 Columbia Avenue, Claremont, CA 91711
- **Website:** http://www.claremontmckenna.edu
- **Private**
- **Enrollment:** 1,139 full-time

KEY STATS

✔ **U.S News College Ranking:** 12, Liberal Arts Colleges
✔ **SAT Score (25th/75th percentile):** 1310-1490
✔ **Tuition:** 2006-2007: $33,210

Selectivity: Most selective	**Room/board:** $10,740
Acceptance rate: 21%	**Average debt:** $10,518
Student/faculty ratio: 9/1	**Proportion who borrowed:** 51%

UNDERGRADUATE STUDENT BODY STATS

2005-2006 enrollment: 1,139 full-time. Men: 54%; women: 46%. **Ethnic makeup:** African American: 4%; Asian American: 15%; Hispanic: 12%; White: 64%; International: 4%. **Religious preference:** Roman Catholic: 19%; Protestant: 34%; Jewish: 9%; Muslim: 2%; Hindu: 2%; Buddhist: 2%; No preference: 32%.

ADMISSIONS FACTS AND FIGURES

Phone: (909) 621-8088. **Email:** admission@claremontmckenna.edu. **Website:** http://www.claremontmckenna.edu. **Application deadlines for fall 2007:** Regular decision: January 2; decision sent by April 1. Early decision: Send application by: November 15; Decision sent by: December 15. Early action: Not offered. Admission can be deferred. **Application fee:** $60. Common application is accepted. **To apply online, go to:** http://www.commonapp.org. **Admissions requirements/recommendations:** High school units required (recommended): English: 4 (4); Mathematics: 3 (4); Science: 2 (3); Foreign language: 3 (3); Social studies: 1 (2); History: 1 (1); Academic electives: 0 (0); Total units: 16 (20). Tests: The college uses SAT or ACT scores in admissions decisions. Either SAT or ACT required. For admission to the fall 2007 entering class, the school will accept: ACT with writing. Campus visit: Recommended. Admissions interview: Recommended. Off-campus interview: May be arranged. **Factors that count in admissions decisions: Academic:** Secondary school record: Very important. Class rank: Very important. Letters of recommendation: Very important. Standardized test scores: Very important. Essay: Very important. **Nonacademic:** Interview: Important. Extracurricular activities: Very important. Talent/ability: Very important. Character/personal qualities: Very important. Alumni/ae relationship: Important. Geographical residence: Important. State residency: Not considered. Religious affiliation/commitment: Not considered. Minority status: Considered. Volunteer work: Important. Work experience: Important. **Other schools with the greatest overlap in applicants:** Georgetown University; Pomona College; Stanford University; University of California–Berkeley; University of California–Los Angeles. **Admissions statistics for the fall 2005 entering class:** Total applicants: 3,734. Total accepted: 786. Freshmen enrolled: 271; 62% were from out of state. Accepted through early-decision or early-action plans: 28%. Overall acceptance rate: 21%. Early-decision acceptance rate: 25%. Non-early acceptance rate: 21%. **Size of waiting list:** 562 applicants; enrolled from waiting list: 24. **Credentials of fall 2005 freshmen:** 84% ranked in the top 10 percent of their high school class; 98% were in the top 25 percent, and 100% were in the top half. (Proportion submitting class standing: 53%.) **Average high school grade point average:** 3.9. **First-year students who submitted SAT scores:** 88%. Scores (25/75 percentile): Verbal: 650-750, Math: 660-740, Combined: 1310-1490. **First-year students submitting ACT scores:** 35%. Scores (25/75 percentile): English: 29-33, Math: 28-32, Composite: 29-33.

ACADEMICS

Year founded: 1946. **Academic calendar:** Semester. **Degrees offered:** bachelor's. **Most popular majors:** 22% economics, 22% political science and government, 15% psychology, 12% international relations and affairs, 11% history. **Major fields of study:** area, ethnic, cultural, and gender studies; biological and biomedical sciences; engineering; English language and literature/letters; foreign languages, literatures, and linguistics; history; legal professions and studies; mathematics and statistics; multi/interdisciplinary studies; natural resources and conservation; philosophy and religious studies; physical sciences; psychology; social sciences; visual and performing arts. **Areas of required coursework:** humanities, mathematics, English (including composition), philosophy, foreign languages, sciences (biological or physical), history, social science, other. **Special academic programs (% participation):** cross-registration (99%), double major (8.1%), exchange student program (domestic) (0%), independent study (12.6%), internships (21%), student-designed major (0%), study abroad (49%). **Reserve Officers Training Corps (ROTC):** Army ROTC: Offered on campus; Air Force ROTC: Offered at cooperating institution (University of Southern California). **Faculty and instruction (2005-2006):** Total instructional faculty: 116 full-time, 18 part-time (63% men; 37% women; 17% minorities). Full-time faculty with Ph.D. or other terminal degree: 96%. Student/faculty ratio: 9/1. Classes of fewer than 20 students: 82%; of 20 to 49 students: 17%; of 50 or more students: 1%. **Advanced Placement and International Baccalaureate credit:** AP tests may be used for: Credit and/or placement. Scores accepted: 3, 4, 5. International Baccalaureate exams may be used for: Credit and/or placement. **Freshmen returning for sophomore year:** 95%. **Graduation rates:** Four-year: 82%; five-year: 87%; six-year: 88%. **Graduate study:** 21% of students pursue further study immediately upon graduation. Fields in which graduates pursue further study: Master of Business Administration (MBA), 13%; law, 25%; medicine, 9%; dentistry, 5%; education, 4%; arts and sciences, 42%; veterinary medicine, 2%.

COSTS AND FINANCIAL AID

Financial aid office: (909) 621-8356. **Expenses (2006-2007):** Tuition and fees 2006-2007: $33,210; room/board: $10,740. Estimated books and supplies: $850; transportation: $1,000. **Financial aid:** Priority filing date for institution's financial aid form: February 1; deadline: February 1. In 2005-2006, 58% of undergraduates applied for financial aid. Of those, 50% were determined to have financial need; 42% had their need fully met. Average financial aid package (proportion receiving): $25,674 (50%). Average amount of gift aid, such as scholarships or grants (proportion receiving): $22,823 (50%). Average amount of self-help aid, such as work study or loans (proportion receiving): $3,642 (40%). Average need-based loan (excluding PLUS or other private loans): $3,406. Among students who received need-based aid, the average percentage of need met: 100%. Among students who received aid based on merit, the average award (and the proportion receiving): $6,116 (6%). The average athletic scholarship (and the proportion receiving): $0 (0%). Average amount of debt of borrowers graduating in 2005: $10,518. Proportion who borrowed: 51%.

CAMPUS LIFE AND EXTRACURRICULAR ACTIVITIES

Campus housing available (% using): coed dorms (87%), apartment for single students (13%), special housing for disabled students (0%). Students who live in college-owned, operated, or affiliated housing: 94%. **Student employment:** During the 2005-2006 academic year, 40% of undergraduates worked on campus. Average per-year earnings: $1,600. **Clubs and organizations:** Number of student organizations: 110. Activities include: choral groups, dance, drama/theater, literary magazine, music ensembles, musical theater, radio station, student government, student newspaper, yearbook. Number of fraternities: 0; sororities: 0. Average proportion of students who stay on campus on weekends: 90%. **Sports program (2005-2006):** Member of NCAA III. **Men's intercollegiate varsity sports:** baseball, basketball, cross-country, football, golf, soccer, swimming and diving, tennis, track and field (outdoor), water polo. **Women's intercollegiate varsity sports:** basketball, cross-country, lacrosse, soccer, softball, swimming and diving, tennis, track and field (outdoor), volleyball, water polo.

SERVICES AND FACILITIES

Basic services: nonremedial tutoring, women's center, placement service, health service, health insurance. **Remedial assistance:** writing. **Counseling services:** minority student, career, military, personal, academic, older student, psychological, birth control, religious, other. **For learning-disabled students:** School does not offer a structured program with separate admission and additional fees. Total undergraduates in learning-disabled program or receiving services: 40. Services include: tape recorders, untimed tests, note-taking services, extended time for tests, tutors, other testing accomodations, other. **Library:** Number of titles: 2,476,503; number of current serial subscriptions: 17,052. **Information technology resources:** Students are not required to lease or own a computer. Number of campus computers available to all students: 220. School has a wireless network. Approximate number of users that can be accommodated: 502. Proportion of college-owned housing units wired for high-speed internet access: 100%. **Campus safety:** Security services offered: 24-hour foot-and-vehicle patrols, late-night transport/escort service, 24-hour emergency telephones, lighted pathways/sidewalks, controlled dormitory access (key, security card, etc).

TRANSFER AND INTERNATIONAL STUDENTS

Transfer students: May apply for admission for the following academic terms: Fall, Spring. Applicants do not need a minimum number of credits to apply. For fall 2005: Transfer applications received: 194. Transfer applicants offered admission: 60. Transfer applicants enrolled: 38. **International students:** Number of foreign undergraduates: 47 (4% of student body). Number of countries represented: 15. Minimum TOEFL score required: 600 (paper); 250 (computer). Average TOEFL score: 643 (paper).

Cogswell Polytechnical College

- **Address:** 1175 Bordeaux Drive, Sunnyvale, CA 94089-9772
- **Website:** http://www.cogswell.edu
- **Private**
- **Enrollment:** 135 full-time; 147 part-time

KEY STATS

✔ **U.S News College Ranking:** 16, Comp. Colleges–Bachelor's (West)
✔ **SAT or ACT Score (25th/75th percentile):** N/A
✔ **Tuition:** 2006-2007: $13,760

Selectivity: Less selective	**Room/board:** N/A
Acceptance rate: 77%	**Average debt:** N/A
Student/faculty ratio: 9/1	**Proportion who borrowed:** N/A

UNDERGRADUATE STUDENT BODY STATS

2005-2006 enrollment: 135 full-time; 147 part-time. Men: 88%; women: 12%. **Ethnic makeup:** African American: 2%; Asian American: 11%; Hispanic: 9%; White: 78%.

ADMISSIONS FACTS AND FIGURES

Phone: (408) 541-0100. **Email:** info@cogswell.edu. **Website:** http://www.cogswell.edu. **Application deadlines for fall 2007:** Regular decision: Rolling. Early decision: Not offered. Early action: Not offered. Admission can be deferred. **Application fee:** $55. Common application is not accepted. **Admissions requirements/recommendations:** High school units required (recommended): English: 3; Mathematics: 3; Science: 1. Tests: The college does not use SAT or ACT scores in admissions decisions. Neither SAT nor ACT required. Campus visit: Recommended. Admissions interview: Neither required nor recommended. Off-campus interview: May be arranged. **Factors that count in admissions decisions:** *Academic:* Secondary school record: Very important. Class rank: Important. Letters of recommendation: Important. Standardized test scores: Not considered. Essay: Very important. *Nonacademic:* Interview: Considered. Extracurricular activities: Not considered. Talent/ability: Very important. Character/personal qualities: Not considered. Alumni/ae relationship: Not considered. Geographical residence: Not considered. State residency: Not considered. Religious affiliation/commitment: Not considered. Minority status: Not considered. Volunteer work: Not considered. Work experience: Not considered. **Admissions statistics for the fall 2005 entering class:** Total applicants: 74. Total accepted: 57. Freshmen enrolled: 24; 1% were from out of state. Overall acceptance rate: 77%. **Average high school grade point average:** 3.0.

ACADEMICS

Year founded: 1887. **Academic calendar:** Semester. **Degrees offered:** bachelor's. **Most popular majors:** 66% visual and performing arts, 22% security and protective services, 12% engineering technologies/technicians. **Major fields of study:** engineering technologies/technicians; security and protective services; visual and performing arts. **Areas of required coursework:** arts/fine arts, humanities, computer literacy, mathematics, English (including composition), sciences (biological or physical), history, social science. **Special academic programs (% participation):** distance learning (31%), internships (.7%). **Faculty and instruction (2005-2006):** Total instructional faculty: 15 full-time, 27 part-time (64% men; 36% women). Full-time faculty with Ph.D. or other terminal degree: 13%. Student/faculty ratio: 9/1. Classes of fewer than 20 students: 98%; of 20 to 49 students: 2%; of 50 or more students: 0%. **Advanced Placement and International Baccalaureate credit:** International Baccalaureate exams may be used for: Credit only. **Freshmen returning for sophomore year:** 72%. **Graduation rates:** Four-year: 0%; five-year: 50%; six-year: 45%.

COSTS AND FINANCIAL AID

Financial aid office: (408) 541-0100. **Expenses (2006-2007):** Tuition and fees 2006-2007: $13,760; room/board: N/A. Estimated books and supplies: $1,260; transportation: $688; personal expenses: $2,192. **Financial aid:** Priority filing date for institution's financial aid form: March 2. In 2005-2006, 61% of undergraduates applied for financial aid. Of those, 60% were determined to have financial need; Average financial aid package (proportion receiving): N/A (60%). Average amount of gift aid, such as scholarships or grants (proportion receiving): $3,078 (35%). Average amount of self-help aid, such as work study or loans (proportion receiving): $2,140 (N/A). Average need-based loan (excluding PLUS or other private loans): $2,968. Among students who received aid based on merit, the average award (and the proportion receiving): $1,025 (16%). The average athletic scholarship (and the proportion receiving): $0 (0%).

CAMPUS LIFE AND EXTRACURRICULAR ACTIVITIES

Campus housing available (% using): apartment for single students (100%). Students who live in college-owned, operated, or affiliated housing: 4%. **Student employment:** During the 2005-2006 academic year, 5% of undergraduates worked on campus. Average per-year earnings: $5,120. Activities include: student government. Number of fraternities: 0; sororities: 0. Average proportion of students who stay on campus on weekends: 1%.

SERVICES AND FACILITIES

Counseling services: academic. **Library:** Number of titles: 1,511; number of current serial subscriptions: 5. **Information technology resources:** Students are not required to lease or own a computer. Number of campus computers available to all students: 140. School has a wireless network. Approximate number of users that can be accommodated: 50. **Campus safety:** Security services offered: 24-hour emergency telephones, lighted pathways/sidewalks, controlled dormitory access (key, security card, etc).

TRANSFER AND INTERNATIONAL STUDENTS

Transfer students: May apply for admission for the following academic terms: Fall, Spring, Summer. Applicants need a minimum number of credits to apply. For fall 2005: Transfer applications received: 74. Transfer applicants offered admission: 57. Transfer applicants enrolled: 40. **International students:** Number of countries represented: 0. Minimum TOEFL score required: 525 (paper); 213 (computer).

Concordia University

- **Address:** 1530 Concordia W, Irvine, CA 92612-3299
- **Website:** http://www.cui.edu
- **Private; Religious affiliation:** Lutheran Church-Missouri Synod
- **Enrollment:** 1,370 full-time; 75 part-time

KEY STATS
- ✔ **U.S News College Ranking:** 49, Universities–Master's (West)
- ✔ **SAT Score (25th/75th percentile):** 940-1150
- ✔ **Tuition:** 2006-2007: $21,130

Selectivity: Selective	Room/board: $7,270
Acceptance rate: 68%	Average debt: $19,200
Student/faculty ratio: 15/1	Proportion who borrowed: 74%

UNDERGRADUATE STUDENT BODY STATS

2005-2006 enrollment: 1,370 full-time; 75 part-time. Men: 37%; women: 63%. **Ethnic makeup:** African American: 4%; American-Indian: 1%; Asian American: 4%; Hispanic: 13%; White: 76%; International: 2%. **Religious preference:** Roman Catholic: 14%; Protestant: 10%; No preference: 7%; Lutheran Church-Missouri Synod: 37%; Non-Denominational: 11%; Other: 21%.

ADMISSIONS FACTS AND FIGURES

Phone: (949) 854-8002. **Email:** admission@cui.edu. **Website:** http://www.cui.edu. **Application deadlines for fall 2007:** Regular decision: Rolling. Early decision: Not offered. Early action: Not offered. Admission can be deferred. **Application fee:** $50. Common application is accepted. **To apply online, go to:** http://www.aiccumentor.org/applications/Concordia_University/apply.html. **Admissions requirements/recommendations:** High school units required (recommended): English: 4; Mathematics: 3; Science: 3; Foreign language: 2; Social studies: 2 (4); Total units: 16. Tests: The college uses SAT or ACT scores in admissions decisions. Either SAT or ACT required. Campus visit: Recommended. Admissions interview: Neither required nor recommended. Off-campus interview: May be arranged. **Factors that count in admissions decisions:** *Academic:* Secondary school record: Very important. Class rank: Very important. Letters of recommendation: Important. Standardized test scores: Very important. Essay: Considered. *Nonacademic:* Interview: Considered. Extracurricular activities: Considered. Talent/ability: Considered. Character/personal qualities: Important. Alumni/ae relationship: Considered. Geographical residence: Not considered. State residency: Not considered. Religious affiliation/commitment: Important. Minority status: Considered. Volunteer work: Considered. Work experience: Considered. **Admissions statistics for the fall 2005 entering class:** Total applicants: 998. Total accepted: 680. Freshmen enrolled: 265; 22% were from out of state. Overall acceptance rate: 68%. **Size of waiting list:** 0 applicants; enrolled from waiting list: N/A. **Credentials of fall 2005 freshmen:** 15% ranked in the top 10 percent of their high school class; 53% were in the top 25 percent, and 93% were in the top half. (Proportion submitting class standing: 51%.) **Average high school grade point average:** 3.5. **First-year students who submitted SAT scores:** 66%. Scores (25/75 percentile): Verbal: 470-570, Math: 470-580, Combined: 940-1150. **First-year students submitting ACT scores:** 23%. Scores (25/75 percentile): English: N/A, Math: N/A, Composite: 20-25.

ACADEMICS

Year founded: 1972. **Academic calendar:** Semester. **Degrees offered:** associate, bachelor's, post-bachelor's certificate, master's. **Most popular majors:** 18% business administration and management, 17% education, 17% liberal arts and sciences/liberal studies, 11% social sciences, 7% philosophy and religious studies. **Major fields of study:** biological and biomedical sciences; business, management, marketing, and related support services; communication, journalism, and related programs; computer and information sciences and support services; English language and literature/letters; history; liberal arts and sciences studies, and humanities; mathematics and statistics; multi/interdisciplinary studies; parks, recreation, leisure, and fitness studies; physical sciences; psychology; social sciences; theology and religious vocations; visual and performing arts. **Areas of required coursework:** arts/fine arts, humanities, computer literacy, mathematics, English (including composition), philosophy, foreign languages, sciences (biological or physical), history, social science, other. **Pre-professional programs:** pre-law, pre-medicine, pre-theology, other. **Special academic programs:** accelerated program, cross-registration, distance learning, double major, dual enrollment, English as a Second Language (ESL), exchange student program (domestic), honors program, independent study, internships, student-designed major, study abroad, teacher certificate program. **Teacher certification offered in:** elementary, secondary. **Faculty and instruction (2005-2006):** Total instructional faculty: 77 full-time, 131 part-time (60% men; 40% women). Full-time faculty with Ph.D. or other terminal degree: 62%. Student/faculty ratio: 15/1. Classes of fewer than 20 students: 51%; of 20 to 49 students: 46%; of 50 or more students: 2%. **Advanced Placement and International Baccalaureate credit:** Scores accepted: 3, 4, 5. International Baccalaureate exams may be used for: Credit only. **Freshmen returning for sophomore year:** 75%. **Graduation rates:** Four-year: 51%; five-year: 55%; six-year: 54%.

COSTS AND FINANCIAL AID

Financial aid office: (949) 854-8002. **Expenses (2006-2007):** Tuition and fees 2006-2007: $21,130; room/board: $7,270. Estimated books and supplies: $1,200; transportation: $900; personal expenses: $2,000. **Financial aid:** Priority filing date for institution's financial aid form: March 2; deadline: April 1. In 2005-2006, 93% of undergraduates applied for financial aid. Of those, 66% were determined to have financial need; 25% had their need fully met. Average financial aid package (proportion receiving): $19,204 (66%). Average amount of gift aid, such as scholarships or grants (proportion receiving): $10,480 (60%). Average amount of self-help aid, such as work study or loans (proportion receiving): $4,342 (50%). Average need-based loan (excluding PLUS or other private loans): $4,030. Among students who received need-based aid, the average percentage of need met: 69%. Among students who received aid based on merit, the average award (and the proportion receiving): $6,151 (20%). The average athletic scholarship (and the proportion receiving): $10,610 (4%). Average amount of debt of borrowers graduating in 2005: $19,200. Proportion who borrowed: 74%.

CAMPUS LIFE AND EXTRACURRICULAR ACTIVITIES

Campus housing available: coed dorms, special housing for disabled students. Students who live in college-owned, operated, or affiliated housing: 64%. **Student employment:** During the 2005-2006 academic year, 30% of undergraduates worked on campus. Average per-year earnings: $2,000. **Clubs and organizations:** Number of student organizations: 5. Activities include: choral groups, dance, drama/theater, literary magazine, music ensembles, musical theater, pep band, radio station, student government, student newspaper, student film society, yearbook. Number of fraternities: 0; sororities: 0. Average proportion of students who stay on campus on weekends: 70%. **Sports program (2005-2006):** Member of NAIA. **Men's intercollegiate varsity sports:** baseball, basketball, cross-country, soccer, track and field (indoor), track and field (outdoor). **Women's intercollegiate varsity sports:** basketball, cross-country, soccer, softball, track and field (indoor), track and field (outdoor), volleyball.

SERVICES AND FACILITIES

Basic services: health service, health insurance, other. **Remedial assistance:** math, study skills, other. **Counseling services:** minority student, career, personal, academic, religious. **For learning-disabled students:** School does not offer a structured program with separate admission and additional fees. Services include: remedial math, untimed tests, oral tests, learning center, extended time for tests. **Library:** Number of titles: 85,432; number of current serial subscriptions: 414. **Information technology resources:** Students are not required to lease or own a computer. Number of campus computers available to all students: 38. School has a wireless network. Approximate number of users that can be accommodated: 275. Proportion of college-owned housing units wired for high-speed internet access: 100%. **Campus safety:** Security services offered: 24-hour foot-and-vehicle patrols, late-night transport/escort service, lighted pathways/sidewalks, controlled dormitory access (key, security card, etc).

TRANSFER AND INTERNATIONAL STUDENTS

Transfer students: May apply for admission for the following academic terms: Fall, Spring. Applicants need a minimum number of credits to apply. For fall 2005: Transfer applications received: 370. Transfer applicants offered admission: 251. Transfer applicants enrolled: 174. **International students:** Number of foreign undergraduates: 22 (2% of student body). Number of countries represented: 6. Minimum TOEFL score required: 550 (paper); 213 (computer). Average TOEFL score: 530 (paper).

Dominican University of California

- **Address:** 50 Acacia Avenue, San Rafael, CA 94901-2298
- **Website:** http://www.dominican.edu
- **Private; Religious affiliation:** Roman Catholic
- **Enrollment:** 1,058 full-time; 119 part-time

KEY STATS

✔ **U.S News College Ranking:** 38, Universities–Master's (West)
✔ **SAT Score (25th/75th percentile):** 910-1140
✔ **Tuition:** 2006-2007: $28,172

Selectivity: Selective	**Room/board:** $11,300
Acceptance rate: 53%	**Average debt:** $19,092
Student/faculty ratio: 10/1	**Proportion who borrowed:** 70%

UNDERGRADUATE STUDENT BODY STATS

2005-2006 enrollment: 1,058 full-time; 119 part-time. Men: 23%; women: 77%. **Ethnic makeup:** African American: 8%; American-Indian: 1%; Asian American: 20%; Hispanic: 15%; White: 53%; International: 3%. **Religious preference:** Roman Catholic: 1%; Protestant: 12%; Jewish: 1%; Buddhist: 1%; No preference: 6%; Unknown: 32%; Roman Catholic: 42%; Baptist: 2%; Other: 3%.

ADMISSIONS FACTS AND FIGURES

Phone: (415) 485-3204. **Email:** enroll@dominican.edu. **Website:** http://www.dominican.edu. **Application deadlines for fall 2007:** Regular decision: August 1; decision sent by September 1. Early decision: Not offered. Early action: Not offered. Admission can be deferred. **Application fee:** $40. Common application is accepted. **Admissions requirements/recommendations:** High school units required (recommended): English: (4); Mathematics: (2); Science: (1); Foreign language: (2); History: (1); Total units: (10). Tests: The college uses SAT or ACT scores in admissions decisions. Either SAT or ACT required. For admission to the fall 2007 entering class, the school will accept: ACT with writing, ACT without writing. Campus visit: Recommended. Admissions interview: Recommended. Off-campus interview: May be arranged. **Factors that count in admissions decisions:** *Academic:* Secondary school record: Very important. Class rank: Considered. Letters of recommendation: Very important. Standardized test scores: Very important. Essay: Very important. *Nonacademic:* Interview: Considered. Extracurricular activities: Important. Talent/ability: Considered. Character/personal qualities: Important. Alumni/ae relationship: Considered. Geographical residence: Not considered. State residency: Not considered. Religious affiliation/commitment: Not considered. Minority status: Not considered. Volunteer work: Considered. Work experience: Considered. **Other schools with the greatest overlap in applicants:** San Francisco State University; Sonoma State University; St. Mary's College of California; University of California–Davis; University of San Francisco. **Admissions statistics for the fall 2005 entering class:** Total applicants: 2,564. Total accepted: 1,354. Freshmen enrolled: 227; 10% were from out of state. Overall acceptance rate: 53%. **Credentials of fall 2005 freshmen:** 25% ranked in the top 10 percent of their high school class; 47% were in the top 25 percent, and 79% were in the top half. (Proportion submitting class standing: 48%.) **Average high school grade point average:** 3.2. **First-year students who submitted SAT scores:** 93%. Scores (25/75 percentile): Verbal: 450-580, Math: 460-560, Combined: 910-1140. **First-year students submitting ACT scores:** 29%. Scores (25/75 percentile): English: N/A, Math: N/A, Composite: 19-24.

ACADEMICS

Year founded: 1890. **Academic calendar:** Semester. **Degrees offered:** certificate, bachelor's, master's. **Most popular majors:** 27% nursing, 15% psychology, 10% international business, 8% biology, 8% legal professions and studies. **Major fields of study:** area, ethnic, cultural, and gender studies; biological and biomedical sciences; business, management, marketing, and related support services; communication, journalism, and related programs; education; English language and literature/letters; health professions and related clinical sciences; history; liberal arts and sciences studies, and humanities; multi/interdisciplinary studies; philosophy and religious studies; psychology; social sciences; visual and performing arts. **Areas of required coursework:** arts/fine arts, humanities, computer literacy, mathematics, English (including composition), philosophy, sciences (biological or physical), social science. **Pre-professional programs:** pre-law, other. **Special academic programs:** accelerated program, cross-registration, distance learning, double major, dual enrollment, English as a Second Language (ESL), exchange student program (domestic), honors program, independent study, internships, student-designed major, study abroad, teacher certificate program, other. **Teacher certification offered in:** special education, elementary, middle/junior high, secondary. **Faculty and instruction (2005-2006):** Total instructional faculty: 71 full-time, 216 part-time (36% men; 64% women; 13% minorities). Full-time faculty with Ph.D. or other terminal degree: 83%. Student/faculty ratio: 10/1. Classes of fewer than 20 students: 72%; of 20 to 49 students: 28%. **Advanced Placement and International Baccalaureate credit:** AP tests may be used for: Credit and/or placement. Scores accepted: 3, 4, 5. International Baccalaureate exams may be used for: Credit only. **Freshmen returning for sophomore year:** 75%. **Graduation rates:** Four-year: 40%; five-year: 41%; six-year: 48%.

COSTS AND FINANCIAL AID

Financial aid office: (415) 257-1321. **Expenses (2006-2007):** Tuition and fees 2006-2007: $28,172; room/board: $11,300. Estimated books and supplies: $1,314; transportation: $774; personal expenses: $2,088. **Financial aid:** Priority filing date for institution's financial aid form: March 2. In 2005-2006, 94% of undergraduates applied for financial aid. Of those, 74% were determined to have financial need; 15% had their need fully met. Average financial aid package (proportion receiving): $21,738 (74%). Average amount of gift aid, such as scholarships or grants (proportion receiving): $14,394 (73%). Average amount of self-help aid, such as work study or loans (proportion receiving): $4,524 (72%). Average need-based loan (excluding PLUS or other private loans): $3,416. Among students who received need-based aid, the average percentage of need met: 64%. Among students who received aid based on merit, the average award (and the proportion receiving): $7,929 (19%). The average athletic scholarship (and the proportion receiving): $4,279 (5%). Average amount of debt of borrowers graduating in 2005: $19,092. Proportion who borrowed: 70%.

CAMPUS LIFE AND EXTRACURRICULAR ACTIVITIES

Campus housing available (% using): coed dorms (100%). Students who live in college-owned, operated, or affiliated housing: 30%. **Student employment:** During the 2005-2006 academic year, 30% of undergraduates worked on campus. Average per-year earnings: $2,923. **Clubs and organizations:** Number of student organizations: 19. Activities include: choral groups, concert band, drama/theater, jazz band, literary magazine, radio station, student government, student newspaper. Number of fraternities: 0; sororities: 0. Average proportion of students who stay on campus on weekends: 35%. **Sports program (2005-2006):** Member of NAIA. *Men's intercollegiate varsity sports:* basketball, golf, soccer, tennis. *Women's intercollegiate varsity sports:* basketball, golf, soccer, softball, tennis, volleyball.

SERVICES AND FACILITIES

Basic services: nonremedial tutoring, placement service, health service. **Remedial assistance:** math, writing, study skills. **Counseling services:** minority student, career, personal, academic, older student, psychological, birth control, religious. **For learning-disabled students:** School does not offer a structured program with separate admission and additional fees. Total undergraduates in learning-disabled program or receiving services: 63. Services include: remedial math, remedial English, tape recorders, note-taking services, readers, extended time for tests, tutors, priority registration, priority seating, texts on tape, other testing accomodations. **Library:** Number of titles: 92,536; number of current serial subscriptions: 597. **Information technology resources:** Students are not required to lease or own a computer. Number of campus computers available to all students: 140. School has a wireless network. Approximate number of users that can be accommodated: 500. Proportion of college-owned housing units wired for high-speed internet access: 100%. **Campus safety:** Security services offered: 24-hour foot-and-vehicle patrols, late-night transport/escort service, 24-hour emergency telephones, lighted pathways/sidewalks.

TRANSFER AND INTERNATIONAL STUDENTS

Transfer students: May apply for admission for the following academic terms: Fall, Spring. Applicants need a minimum number of credits to apply. For fall 2005: Transfer applications received: 477. Transfer applicants offered admission: 366. Transfer applicants enrolled: 200. **International students:** Number of foreign undergraduates: 34 (3% of student body). Number of countries represented: 17. Minimum TOEFL score required: 550 (paper); 213 (computer).

Fresno Pacific University

- **Address:** 1717 S. Chestnut Avenue, Fresno, CA 93702
- **Website:** http://www.fresno.edu
- **Private; Religious affiliation:** Mennonite Brethren
- **Enrollment:** 1,319 full-time; 173 part-time

KEY STATS

✔ **U.S News College Ranking:** 34, Universities–Master's (West)
✔ **SAT Score (25th/75th percentile):** 910-1130
✔ **Tuition:** 2006-2007: $20,790

Selectivity: Selective	**Room/board:** $5,990
Acceptance rate: 68%	**Average debt:** $13,334
Student/faculty ratio: 16/1	**Proportion who borrowed:** 50%

UNDERGRADUATE STUDENT BODY STATS

2005-2006 enrollment: 1,319 full-time; 173 part-time. Men: 34%; women: 66%. **Ethnic makeup:** African American: 4%; American-Indian: 1%; Asian American: 4%; Hispanic: 26%; White: 62%; International: 3%. **Religious preference:** Roman Catholic: 12%; Protestant: 63%; No preference: 4%; Unknown: 2%; Mennonite Brethren: 18%; Other: 1%.

ADMISSIONS FACTS AND FIGURES

Phone: (559) 453-2039. **Email:** ugadmis@fresno.edu. **Website:** http://www.fresno.edu. **Application deadlines for fall 2007:** Regular decision: July 31. Early decision: Not offered. Early action: Not offered. Admission can be deferred. **Application fee:** $40. Common application is not accepted. **To apply online, go to:** http://fresno.edu/apply. **Admissions requirements/recommendations:** High school units required (recommended): English: 4; Mathematics: 3; Science: 1; Foreign language: 2; Social studies: 2; Total units: 13. Tests: The college uses SAT or ACT scores in admissions decisions. Either SAT or ACT required. For admission to the fall 2007 entering class, the school will accept: ACT with writing, ACT without writing. Campus visit: Recommended. Admissions interview: Neither required nor recommended. Off-campus interview: May be arranged. **Factors that count in admissions decisions:** *Academic:* Secondary school record: Very important. Class rank: Important. Letters of recommendation: Important. Standardized test scores: Very important. Essay: Important. *Nonacademic:* Interview: Not considered. Extracurricular activities: Not considered. Talent/ability: Not considered. Character/personal qualities: Considered. Alumni/ae relationship: Not considered. Geographical residence: Not considered. State residency: Not considered. Religious affiliation/commitment: Important. Minority status: Not considered. Volunteer work: Not considered. Work experience: Not considered. **Other schools with the greatest overlap in applicants:** Azusa Pacific University; Biola University; California State University–Fresno; Point Loma Nazarene University; University of California–Davis. **Admissions statistics for the fall 2005 entering class:** Total applicants: 608. Total accepted: 413. Freshmen enrolled: 212; 3% were from out of state. Overall acceptance rate: 68%. **Credentials of fall 2005 freshmen:** 35% ranked in the top 10 percent of their high school class; 64% were in the top 25 percent, and 88% were in the top half. (Proportion submitting class standing: 60%.) **Average high school grade point average:** 3.6. **First-year students who submitted SAT scores:** 85%. Scores (25/75 percentile): Verbal: 450-560, Math: 460-570, Combined: 910-1130. **First-year students submitting ACT scores:** 25%. Scores (25/75 percentile): English: 16-24, Math: 17-24, Composite: 17-23.

ACADEMICS

Year founded: 1944. **Academic calendar:** Semester. **Degrees offered:** associate, bachelor's, master's. **Most popular majors:** 35% education, 34% business, management, marketing, and related support services, 8% theology and religious vocations, 5% psychology, 3% public administration and social service professions. **Major fields of study:** area, ethnic, cultural, and gender studies; biological and biomedical sciences; business, management, marketing, and related support services; communication, journalism, and related programs; education; English language and literature/letters; foreign languages, literatures, and linguistics; health professions and related clinical sciences; history; liberal arts and sciences studies, and humanities; mathematics and statistics; natural resources and conservation; parks, recreation, leisure, and fitness studies; philosophy and religious studies; physical sciences; psychology; public administration and social service professions; social sciences; theology and religious vocations; visual and performing arts. **Areas of required coursework:** arts/fine arts, humanities, mathematics,

English (including composition), foreign languages, sciences (biological or physical), history, social science, other. **Pre-professional programs:** pre-law, pre-dentistry, pre-medicine, pre-theology, pre-veterinary science, other. **Special academic programs (% participation):** cooperative (work-study plan) program (54%), double major (8%), English as a Second Language (ESL) (1%), exchange student program (domestic) (5%), independent study (11%), internships (18%), student-designed major (2%), study abroad (1%). **Teacher certification offered in:** special education, elementary, middle/junior high, secondary, bilingual/bicultural. **Cooperative education programs:** health professions. **Faculty and instruction (2005-2006):** Total instructional faculty: 81 full-time, 117 part-time (58% men; 42% women; 9% minorities). Full-time faculty with Ph.D. or other terminal degree: 64%. Student/faculty ratio: 16/1. Classes of fewer than 20 students: 64%; of 20 to 49 students: 34%; of 50 or more students: 3%. **Advanced Placement and International Baccalaureate credit:** International Baccalaureate exams may be used for: Credit only. **Freshmen returning for sophomore year:** 80%. **Graduation rates:** Four-year: 42%; five-year: 52%; six-year: 59%. **Graduate study:** 31% of students pursue further study within one year; 60% within five years.

COSTS AND FINANCIAL AID

Financial aid office: (559) 453-2027. **Expenses (2006-2007):** Tuition and fees 2006-2007: $20,790; room/board: $5,990. Estimated books and supplies: $1,314; transportation: $774; personal expenses: $2,088. **Financial aid:** Priority filing date for institution's financial aid form: March 2. In 2005-2006, 88% of undergraduates applied for financial aid. Of those, 73% were determined to have financial need; 20% had their need fully met. Average financial aid package (proportion receiving): $16,847 (73%). Average amount of gift aid, such as scholarships or grants (proportion receiving): $11,617 (68%). Average amount of self-help aid, such as work study or loans (proportion receiving): $5,391 (65%). Average need-based loan (excluding PLUS or other private loans): $4,187. Among students who received need-based aid, the average percentage of need met: 73%. Among students who received aid based on merit, the average award (and the proportion receiving): $2,112 (13%). The average athletic scholarship (and the proportion receiving): $8,980 (12%). Average amount of debt of borrowers graduating in 2005: $13,334. Proportion who borrowed: 50%.

CAMPUS LIFE AND EXTRACURRICULAR ACTIVITIES

Campus housing available (% using): women's dorms (40%), men's dorms (23%), apartment for single students (19%), other housing options (18%). Students who live in college-owned, operated, or affiliated housing: 53%. **Student employment:** During the 2005-2006 academic year, 23% of undergraduates worked on campus. Average per-year earnings: $2,000. **Clubs and organizations:** Number of student organizations: 20. Activities include: choral groups, concert band, drama/theater, jazz band, literary magazine, music ensembles, pep band, student government, student newspaper, yearbook. Number of fraternities: 0; sororities: 0. Average proportion of students who stay on campus on weekends: 50%. **Sports program (2005-2006):** Member of NAIA. *Men's intercollegiate varsity sports:* basketball, cross-country, soccer, track and field (indoor), track and field (outdoor). *Women's intercollegiate varsity sports:* basketball, cross-country, soccer, track and field (indoor), track and field (outdoor), volleyball.

SERVICES AND FACILITIES

Basic services: nonremedial tutoring, health service, health insurance, other. **Remedial assistance:** study skills. **Counseling services:** career, personal, academic, psychological, religious, other. **For learning-disabled students:** School does not offer a structured program with separate admission and additional fees. Total undergraduates in learning-disabled program or receiving services: 16. Services include: tape recorders, untimed tests, note-taking services, oral tests, learning center, readers, extended time for tests, tutors, texts on tape, typist/scribe, other testing accomodations. **Library:** Number of titles: 197,032; number of current serial subscriptions: 1,600. **Information technology resources:** Students are not required to lease or own a computer. Number of campus computers available to all students: 75. School has a wireless network. Approximate number of users that can be accommodated: 768. Proportion of college-owned housing units wired for high-speed internet access: 100%. **Campus safety:** Security services offered: 24-hour foot-and-vehicle patrols, late-night transport/escort service, 24-hour emergency telephones, lighted pathways/sidewalks, controlled dormitory access (key, security card, etc).

TRANSFER AND INTERNATIONAL STUDENTS

Transfer students: May apply for admission for the following academic terms: Fall, Spring, Summer. Applicants need a minimum number of credits to apply. For fall 2005: Transfer applications received: 403. Transfer applicants offered admission: 273. Transfer applicants enrolled: 190.

International students: Number of foreign undergraduates: 48 (3% of student body). Number of countries represented: 41. Minimum TOEFL score required: 500 (paper); 173 (computer).

Golden Gate University

- **Address:** 536 Mission Street, San Francisco, CA 94105
- **Website:** http://www.ggu.edu
- **Private**
- **Enrollment:** 135 full-time; 432 part-time

KEY STATS

✔ **U.S News College Ranking:** Unranked Specialty School–Business
✔ **SAT or ACT Score (25th/75th percentile):** N/A
✔ **Tuition:** 2005-2006: $10,800
  Selectivity: Least selective   **Room/board:** N/A
  Acceptance rate: N/A   **Average debt:** N/A
  Student/faculty ratio: N/A   **Proportion who borrowed:** N/A

UNDERGRADUATE STUDENT BODY STATS

2005-2006 enrollment: 135 full-time; 432 part-time. Men: 47%; women: 53%. **Ethnic makeup:** African American: 9%; American-Indian: 1%; Asian American: 17%; Hispanic: 11%; White: 54%; International: 8%.

ADMISSIONS FACTS AND FIGURES

Phone: (415) 442-7800. **Email:** info@ggu.edu. **Website:** http://www.ggu.edu. **Application deadlines for fall 2007:** Regular decision: Rolling. Early decision: Not offered. Early action: Not offered. Admission can be deferred. **Application fee:** $55. Common application is accepted. **Admissions requirements/recommendations:** High school units required (recommended): English: (4); Mathematics: (3); Science: (2); Foreign language: (2); Social studies: (1); History: (1); Total units: (14). Tests: The college uses SAT or ACT scores in admissions decisions. Neither SAT nor ACT required. Campus visit: Neither required nor recommended. Admissions interview: Recommended. Off-campus interview: Not available. **Factors that count in admissions decisions:** *Academic:* Secondary school record: Very important. Class rank: Considered. Letters of recommendation: Considered. Standardized test scores: Considered. Essay: Considered. *Nonacademic:* Interview: Not considered. Extracurricular activities: Not considered. Talent/ability: Not considered. Character/personal qualities: Not considered. Alumni/ae relationship: Not considered. Geographical residence: Not considered. State residency: Not considered. Religious affiliation/commitment: Not considered. Minority status: Considered. Volunteer work: Considered. Work experience: Considered.

ACADEMICS

Year founded: 1901. **Academic calendar:** Trimester. **Degrees offered:** certificate, bachelor's, master's, first professional, doctorate. **Most popular majors:** Information not available. **Major fields of study:** business, management, marketing, and related support services; computer and information sciences and support services; legal professions and studies; liberal arts and sciences studies, and humanities; psychology; public administration and social service professions; social sciences. **Areas of required coursework:** humanities, mathematics, English (including composition), philosophy, history, social science. **Special academic programs:** accelerated program, cooperative (work-study plan) program, distance learning, double major, dual enrollment, English as a Second Language (ESL), independent study, internships, weekend college. **Faculty and instruction (2005-2006):** Total instructional faculty: 70 full-time, 757 part-time (70% men; 30% women). **Graduation rates:** Six-year: 32%.

COSTS AND FINANCIAL AID

Financial aid office: (415) 442-7270. **Expenses (2005-2006):** Tuition and fees 2005-2006: $10,800; room/board: N/A.

SERVICES AND FACILITIES

Counseling services: minority student, career, personal, academic, older student. **Information technology resources:** Students are not required to lease or own a computer. **Campus safety:** Security services offered: 24-hour emergency telephones, lighted pathways/sidewalks.

TRANSFER AND INTERNATIONAL STUDENTS
Transfer students: May apply for admission for the following academic terms: Fall, Spring, Summer. Applicants need a minimum number of credits to apply. For fall 2005: Transfer applications received: 353. Transfer applicants offered admission: 224. Transfer applicants enrolled: 123. **International students:** Number of foreign undergraduates: 46 (8% of student body). Minimum TOEFL score required: 525 (paper); 197 (computer).

Harvey Mudd College

- **Address:** 301 Platt Boulevard, Claremont, CA 91711
- **Website:** http://www.hmc.edu
- **Private**
- **Enrollment:** 746 full-time

KEY STATS
✔ **U.S News College Ranking:** 14, Liberal Arts Colleges
✔ **SAT Score (25th/75th percentile):** 1380-1560
✔ **Tuition:** 2006-2007: $33,325

Selectivity: Most selective	**Room/board:** $10,933
Acceptance rate: 36%	**Average debt:** $16,055
Student/faculty ratio: 9/1	**Proportion who borrowed:** 60%

UNDERGRADUATE STUDENT BODY STATS
2005-2006 enrollment: 746 full-time. Men: 68%; women: 32%. **Ethnic makeup:** African American: 1%; Asian American: 17%; Hispanic: 6%; White: 71%; International: 4%.

ADMISSIONS FACTS AND FIGURES
Phone: (909) 621-8011. **Email:** admission@hmc.edu. **Website:** http://www.hmc.edu. **Application deadlines for fall 2007:** Regular decision: January 15; decision sent by April 1. Early decision: Send application by: November 15; Decision sent by: December 15. Early action: Not offered. Admission can be deferred. **Application fee:** $50. Common application is accepted. **To apply online, go to:** http://www.hmc.edu/admin/admission/. **Admissions requirements/recommendations:** High school units required (recommended): English: 4; Mathematics: 4; Science: 4; Foreign language: (2); Social studies: 2; History: (1); Total units: 17 (3). Tests: The college uses SAT or ACT scores in admissions decisions. Either SAT or ACT required. Campus visit: Recommended. Admissions interview: Recommended. Off-campus interview: May be arranged. **Factors that count in admissions decisions:** *Academic:* Secondary school record: Very important. Class rank: Very important. Letters of recommendation: Very important. Standardized test scores: Very important. Essay: Very important. *Nonacademic:* Interview: Important. Extracurricular activities: Important. Talent/ability: Important. Character/personal qualities: Very important. Alumni/ae relationship: Important. Geographical residence: Considered. State residency: Considered. Religious affiliation/commitment: Not considered. Minority status: Important. Volunteer work: Considered. Work experience: Considered. **Other schools with the greatest overlap in applicants:** California Institute of Technology; Cornell University; Massachusetts Institute of Technology; Rice University; Stanford University. **Admissions statistics for the fall 2005 entering class:** Total applicants: 1,898. Total accepted: 683. Freshmen enrolled: 193; 52% were from out of state. Accepted through early-decision or early-action plans: 20%. Overall acceptance rate: 36%. Early-decision acceptance rate: 50%. Non-early acceptance rate: 35%. **Size of waiting list:** 259 applicants; enrolled from waiting list: 0. **Credentials of fall 2005 freshmen:** 91% ranked in the top 10 percent of their high school class; 100% were in the top 25 percent, and 100% were in the top half. (Proportion submitting class standing: 65%.) **First-year students who submitted SAT scores:** 100%. Scores (25/75 percentile): Verbal: 670-760, Math: 710-800, Combined: 1380-1560.

ACADEMICS
Year founded: 1955. **Academic calendar:** Semester. **Degrees offered:** bachelor's. **Most popular majors:** 37% engineering, 19% physical sciences, 14% mathematics and statistics, 11% computer and information sciences and support services, 7% biological and biomedical sciences. **Major fields of study:** biological and biomedical sciences; computer and information sci-

ences and support services; engineering; mathematics and statistics; multi/interdisciplinary studies; physical sciences. **Areas of required coursework:** arts/fine arts, humanities, computer literacy, mathematics, English (including composition), sciences (biological or physical), social science, other. **Special academic programs (% participation):** cross-registration (100%), double major (7%), dual enrollment (1%), exchange student program (domestic) (0%), liberal arts/career combination (100%), student-designed major (1%), study abroad (14%), other (1%). **Reserve Officers Training Corps (ROTC):** Army ROTC: Offered at cooperating institution (Claremont McKenna College); Air Force ROTC: Offered on campus. **Faculty and instruction (2005-2006):** Total instructional faculty: 84 full-time, 9 part-time (65% men; 35% women; 15% minorities). Full-time faculty with Ph.D. or other terminal degree: 100%. Student/faculty ratio: 9/1. Classes of fewer than 20 students: 64%; of 20 to 49 students: 32%; of 50 or more students: 4%. **Advanced Placement and International Baccalaureate credit:** International Baccalaureate exams may be used for: Credit and/or placement. **Freshmen returning for sophomore year:** 96%. **Graduation rates:** Four-year: 79%; five-year: 87%; six-year: 88%. **Graduate study:** 42% of students pursue further study immediately upon graduation.

COSTS AND FINANCIAL AID
Financial aid office: (909) 621-8055. **Expenses (2006-2007):** Tuition and fees 2006-2007: $33,325; room/board: $10,933. Estimated books and supplies: $800; transportation: $0; personal expenses: $900. **Financial aid:** Priority filing date for institution's financial aid form: February 1; deadline: February 1. In 2005-2006, 63% of undergraduates applied for financial aid. Of those, 53% were determined to have financial need; 100% had their need fully met. Average financial aid package (proportion receiving): $25,315 (53%). Average amount of gift aid, such as scholarships or grants (proportion receiving): $22,062 (51%). Average amount of self-help aid, such as work study or loans (proportion receiving): $5,262 (39%). Average need-based loan (excluding PLUS or other private loans): $4,246. Among students who received need-based aid, the average percentage of need met: 100%. Among students who received aid based on merit, the average award (and the proportion receiving): $5,157 (21%). The average athletic scholarship (and the proportion receiving): $0 (0%). Average amount of debt of borrowers graduating in 2005: $16,055. Proportion who borrowed: 60%.

CAMPUS LIFE AND EXTRACURRICULAR ACTIVITIES
Campus housing available (% using): coed dorms (99%), apartments for married students (1%), apartment for single students (0%), special housing for disabled students (0%), other housing options (0%). Students who live in college-owned, operated, or affiliated housing: 99%. **Student employment:** During the 2005-2006 academic year, 35% of undergraduates worked on campus. Average per-year earnings: $1,080. **Clubs and organizations:** Number of student organizations: 90. Activities include: choral groups, concert band, dance, drama/theater, jazz band, literary magazine, music ensembles, musical theater, pep band, radio station, student government, student newspaper, student film society, symphony orchestra, television station, yearbook. Number of fraternities: 0; sororities: 0. Average proportion of students who stay on campus on weekends: 85%. **Sports program (2005-2006):** Member of NCAA III. *Men's intercollegiate varsity sports:* baseball, basketball, cross-country, football, golf, soccer, swimming and diving, tennis, track and field (outdoor), water polo. *Women's intercollegiate varsity sports:* basketball, cross-country, lacrosse, soccer, softball, swimming and diving, tennis, track and field (outdoor), volleyball, water polo.

SERVICES AND FACILITIES
Basic services: nonremedial tutoring, placement service, health service, health insurance. **Counseling services:** minority student, career, personal, academic, psychological, birth control, religious. **For learning-disabled students:** School does not offer a structured program with separate admission and additional fees. Services include: tape recorders, untimed tests, extended time for tests, tutors. **Library:** Number of titles: 2,476,503; number of current serial subscriptions: 17,052. **Information technology resources:** Students are not required to lease or own a computer. Number of campus computers available to all students: 360. School has a wireless network. Proportion of college-owned housing units wired for high-speed internet access: 100%. **Campus safety:** Security services offered: 24-hour foot-and-vehicle patrols, late-night transport/escort service, 24-hour emergency telephones, lighted pathways/sidewalks, controlled dormitory access (key, security card, etc).

TRANSFER AND INTERNATIONAL STUDENTS
Transfer students: May apply for admission for the following academic terms: Fall. Applicants need a minimum number of credits to apply. For fall

2005: Transfer applications received: 60. Transfer applicants offered admission: 5. Transfer applicants enrolled: 4. **International students:** Number of foreign undergraduates: 24 (4% of student body). Minimum TOEFL score required: 600 (paper).

Holy Names University

- **Address:** 3500 Mountain Boulevard, Oakland, CA 94619
- **Website:** http://www.hnu.edu
- **Private; Religious affiliation:** Roman Catholic
- **Enrollment:** 465 full-time; 221 part-time

KEY STATS

✔ **U.S News College Ranking:** third tier, Universities–Master's (West)
✔ **SAT Score (25th/75th percentile):** 950-1030
✔ **Tuition:** 2006-2007: $22,710

Selectivity: Less selective	**Room/board:** $8,000
Acceptance rate: 76%	**Average debt:** $16,640
Student/faculty ratio: 13/1	**Proportion who borrowed:** 38%

UNDERGRADUATE STUDENT BODY STATS

2005-2006 enrollment: 465 full-time; 221 part-time. Men: 27%; women: 73%. **Ethnic makeup:** African American: 26%; American-Indian: 1%; Asian American: 9%; Hispanic: 18%; White: 39%; International: 6%.

ADMISSIONS FACTS AND FIGURES

Phone: (510) 436-1351. **Email:** admissions@hnu.edu. **Website:** http://www.hnu.edu. **Application deadlines for fall 2007:** Regular decision: August 1. Early decision: Not offered. Early action: Not offered. Admission can be deferred. **Application fee:** $50. Common application is accepted. **To apply online, go to:** http://www.hnu.edu/apply/. **Admissions requirements/recommendations:** High school units required (recommended): English: 4; Mathematics: 3; Science: 1; Foreign language: 2 (3); History: 1; Academic electives: 3 (1); Total units: 15. Tests: The college uses SAT or ACT scores in admissions decisions. Either SAT or ACT required. For admission to the fall 2007 entering class, the school will accept: ACT with writing, ACT without writing. Campus visit: Recommended. Admissions interview: Recommended. Off-campus interview: May be arranged. **Factors that count in admissions decisions:** *Academic:* Secondary school record: Considered. Class rank: Considered. Letters of recommendation: Important. Standardized test scores: Considered. Essay: Important. *Nonacademic:* Interview: Considered. Extracurricular activities: Considered. Talent/ability: Considered. Character/personal qualities: Considered. Alumni/ae relationship: Considered. Geographical residence: Not considered. State residency: Not considered. Religious affiliation/commitment: Not considered. Minority status: Not considered. Volunteer work: Considered. Work experience: Considered. **Other schools with the greatest overlap in applicants:** California State University–East Bay; Dominican University of California; Menlo College; Notre Dame de Namur University; St. Mary's College of California. **Admissions statistics for the fall 2005 entering class:** Total applicants: 308. Total accepted: 235. Freshmen enrolled: 90; 18% were from out of state. Overall acceptance rate: 76%. **Credentials of fall 2005 freshmen:** 21% ranked in the top 10 percent of their high school class; 41% were in the top 25 percent, and 74% were in the top half. (Proportion submitting class standing: 59%.) **Average high school grade point average:** 3.3. **First-year students who submitted SAT scores:** 76%. Scores (25/75 percentile): Verbal: 480-520, Math: 470-510, Combined: 950-1030. **First-year students submitting ACT scores:** 13%. Scores (25/75 percentile): English: N/A, Math: N/A, Composite: 16-20.

ACADEMICS

Year founded: 1868. **Academic calendar:** Semester. **Degrees offered:** bachelor's, post-bachelor's certificate, master's, post-master's certificate. **Most popular majors:** 30% nursing/registered nurse training (R.N., A.S.N., B.S.N., M.S.N.), 20% business administration and management, 9% psychology, 8% liberal arts and sciences/liberal studies, 8% sociology. **Major fields of study:** biological and biomedical sciences; business, management, marketing, and related support services; computer and information sciences and support services; English language and literature/letters; foreign languages, literatures, and linguistics; health professions and related clinical sciences; liberal arts and sciences studies, and humanities; multi/interdisciplinary studies; philosophy and religious studies; psychology; public administration and social service professions; social sciences; visual and performing arts. **Areas of required coursework:** arts/fine arts, computer literacy, mathematics, English (including composition), philosophy, foreign languages, sciences (biological or physical), social science, other. **Pre-professional programs:** pre-law, pre-dentistry, pre-medicine, pre-veterinary science, pre-optometry, pre-pharmacy. **Special academic programs (% participation):** accelerated program (10%), cross-registration (4%), distance learning (36%), double major (7%), English as a Second Language (ESL) (1%), exchange student program (domestic) (0%), independent study (12%), internships (14%), liberal arts/career combination (0%), student-designed major (1%), study abroad (0%), weekend college (23%). **Reserve Officers Training Corps (ROTC):** Army ROTC: Offered at cooperating institution (University of California–Berkeley); Air Force ROTC: Offered at cooperating institution (University of California–Berkeley). **Faculty and instruction (2005-2006):** Total instructional faculty: 34 full-time, 106 part-time (39% men; 61% women; 20% minorities). Full-time faculty with Ph.D. or other terminal degree: 85%. Student/faculty ratio: 13/1. Classes of fewer than 20 students: 64%; of 20 to 49 students: 36%; of 50 or more students: 0%. **Advanced Placement and International Baccalaureate credit:** AP tests may be used for: Credit only. Scores accepted: 3, 4, 5. International Baccalaureate exams may be used for: Credit only. **Freshmen returning for sophomore year:** 62%. **Graduation rates:** Four-year: 20%; five-year: 30%; six-year: 39%.

COSTS AND FINANCIAL AID

Financial aid office: (510) 436-1327. **Expenses (2006-2007):** Tuition and fees 2006-2007: $22,710; room/board: $8,000. Estimated books and supplies: $1,025; transportation: $954; personal expenses: $2,088. **Financial aid:** Priority filing date for institution's financial aid form: March 2. In 2005-2006, 91% of undergraduates applied for financial aid. Of those, 85% were determined to have financial need; 8% had their need fully met. Average financial aid package (proportion receiving): $16,215 (82%). Average amount of gift aid, such as scholarships or grants (proportion receiving): $9,200 (58%). Average amount of self-help aid, such as work study or loans (proportion receiving): $3,610 (70%). Average need-based loan (excluding PLUS or other private loans): $3,458. Among students who received need-based aid, the average percentage of need met: 84%. Among students who received aid based on merit, the average award (and the proportion receiving): $18,286 (5%). The average athletic scholarship (and the proportion receiving): $10,550 (54%). Average amount of debt of borrowers graduating in 2005: $16,640. Proportion who borrowed: 38%.

CAMPUS LIFE AND EXTRACURRICULAR ACTIVITIES

Campus housing available (% using): coed dorms (100%). Students who live in college-owned, operated, or affiliated housing: 35%. **Student employment:** During the 2005-2006 academic year, 0% of undergraduates worked on campus. Average per-year earnings: $0. **Clubs and organizations:** Number of student organizations: 10. Activities include: choral groups, drama/theater, music ensembles, student government, symphony orchestra. Number of fraternities: 0; sororities: 0. Average proportion of students who stay on campus on weekends: 65%. **Sports program (2005-2006):** Member of NAIA. *Men's intercollegiate varsity sports:* basketball, cross-country, golf, soccer. *Women's intercollegiate varsity sports:* basketball, cross-country, soccer, volleyball.

SERVICES AND FACILITIES

Basic services: nonremedial tutoring, health insurance, other. **Remedial assistance:** math, writing, study skills, other. **Counseling services:** career, personal, academic, psychological, religious. **For learning-disabled students:** School does not offer a structured program with separate admission and additional fees. Total undergraduates in learning-disabled program or receiving services: 40. Services include: remedial math, remedial English, reading machines, tape recorders, videotaped classes, note-taking services, oral tests, learning center, readers, extended time for tests, tutors, texts on tape, other testing accomodations. **Library:** Number of titles: 111,643; number of current serial subscriptions: 187. **Information technology resources:** Students are not required to lease or own a computer. Number of campus computers available to all students: 86. School has a wireless network. Approximate number of users that can be accommodated: 100. Proportion of college-owned housing units wired for high-speed internet access: 100%. **Campus safety:** Security services offered: late-night transport/escort service, 24-hour emergency telephones, lighted pathways/sidewalks, controlled dormitory access (key, security card, etc).

TRANSFER AND INTERNATIONAL STUDENTS

Transfer students: May apply for admission for the following academic terms: Fall, Winter, Spring. Applicants do not need a minimum number of credits to apply. For fall 2005: Transfer applications received: 278. Transfer applicants offered admission: 178. Transfer applicants enrolled: 117. **International students:** Number of foreign undergraduates: 42 (6% of student body). Number of countries represented: 16. Minimum TOEFL score required: 490 (paper); 163 (computer).

Hope International University

- **Address:** 2500 E. Nutwood Avenue, Fullerton, CA 92831
- **Website:** http://www.hiu.edu
- **Private; Religious affiliation:** Christian Church/Church of Christ
- **Enrollment:** 660 full-time; 205 part-time

KEY STATS
✔ **U.S News College Ranking:** fourth tier, Universities–Master's (West)
✔ **SAT Score (25th/75th percentile):** 880-1100
✔ **Tuition:** 2006-2007: $18,700

Selectivity: Less selective	**Room/board:** $7,250
Acceptance rate: 67%	**Average debt:** $17,563
Student/faculty ratio: 26/1	**Proportion who borrowed:** 72%

UNDERGRADUATE STUDENT BODY STATS
2005-2006 enrollment: 660 full-time; 205 part-time. Men: 38%; women: 62%. **Ethnic makeup:** African American: 8%; American-Indian: 1%; Asian American: 4%; Hispanic: 18%; White: 66%; International: 3%.

ADMISSIONS FACTS AND FIGURES
Phone: (714) 879-3901. **Email:** ug-admissions@hiu.edu. **Website:** http://www.hiu.edu. **Application deadlines for fall 2007:** Regular decision: Rolling. Early decision: Not offered. Early action: Not offered. Admission can be deferred. **Application fee:** $40. Common application is not accepted. **To apply online, go to:** http://www.hiu.edu/prospective_students/apply/index.htm. **Admissions requirements/recommendations:** High school units required (recommended): English: (4); Mathematics: (2); Science: (1); Foreign language: (1); Social studies: (1); History: (1); Academic electives: (3); Total units: (15). Tests: The college uses SAT or ACT scores in admissions decisions. Either SAT or ACT required. For admission to the fall 2007 entering class, the school will accept: ACT with writing, ACT without writing. Campus visit: Recommended. Admissions interview: Recommended. Off-campus interview: May be arranged. **Factors that count in admissions decisions:** *Academic:* Secondary school record: Very important. Class rank: Important. Letters of recommendation: Important. Standardized test scores: Very important. Essay: Very important. *Nonacademic:* Interview: Considered. Extracurricular activities: Considered. Talent/ability: Considered. Character/personal qualities: Important. Alumni/ae relationship: Not considered. Geographical residence: Not considered. State residency: Not considered. Religious affiliation/commitment: Considered. Minority status: Not considered. Volunteer work: Considered. Work experience: Not considered. **Other schools with the greatest overlap in applicants:** Azusa Pacific University; Biola University; California Baptist University; Concordia University; Vanguard University of Southern California. **Admissions statistics for the fall 2005 entering class:** Total applicants: 260. Total accepted: 174. Freshmen enrolled: 121; 26% were from out of state. Overall acceptance rate: 67%. **Credentials of fall 2005 freshmen:** (Proportion submitting class standing: 66%.) **Average high school grade point average:** 3.3. **First-year students who submitted SAT scores:** 72%. Scores (25/75 percentile): Verbal: 440-550, Math: 440-550, Combined: 880-1100. **First-year students submitting ACT scores:** 34%. Scores (25/75 percentile): English: 16-22, Math: 16-22, Composite: 17-21.

ACADEMICS
Year founded: 1928. **Academic calendar:** 4-1-4. **Degrees offered:** associate, bachelor's, master's. **Most popular majors:** 48% family and consumer sciences/human sciences, 25% theology and religious vocations, 15% business, management, marketing, and related support services, 4% education, 4% social sciences. **Major fields of study:** business, management, marketing, and related support services; education; family and consumer sciences/human sciences; psychology; social sciences; theology and religious vocations. **Areas of required coursework:** arts/fine arts, humanities, mathematics, English (including composition), sciences (biological or physical), history, social science. **Pre-professional programs:** pre-medicine. **Special

academic programs: accelerated program, cooperative (work-study plan) program, distance learning, double major, dual enrollment, English as a Second Language (ESL), independent study, internships, liberal arts/career combination, student-designed major, study abroad, teacher certificate program, other. **Teacher certification offered in:** early childhood, elementary. **Cooperative education programs:** business, education, humanities, social/behavioral science. **Faculty and instruction (2005-2006):** Total instructional faculty: 27 full-time, 184 part-time (68% men; 32% women; 14% minorities). Full-time faculty with Ph.D. or other terminal degree: 70%. Student/faculty ratio: 26/1. Classes of fewer than 20 students: 77%; of 20 to 49 students: 21%; of 50 or more students: 1%. **Advanced Placement and International Baccalaureate credit:** AP tests may be used for: Credit only. **Freshmen returning for sophomore year:** 67%. **Graduation rates:** Four-year: 23%; five-year: 36%; six-year: 37%.

COSTS AND FINANCIAL AID
Financial aid office: (714) 879-3901. **Expenses (2006-2007):** Tuition and fees 2006-2007: $18,700; room/board: $7,250. Estimated books and supplies: $400. **Financial aid:** Priority filing date for institution's financial aid form: February 28. In 2005-2006, 90% of undergraduates applied for financial aid. Of those, 86% were determined to have financial need; Average financial aid package (proportion receiving): N/A (86%). Average amount of gift aid, such as scholarships or grants (proportion receiving): N/A (86%). Average amount of self-help aid, such as work study or loans (proportion receiving): N/A (86%). Among students who received need-based aid, the average percentage of need met: 70%. Among students who received aid based on merit, the average award (and the proportion receiving): $3,000 (6%). The average athletic scholarship (and the proportion receiving): $4,500 (6%). Average amount of debt of borrowers graduating in 2005: $17,563. Proportion who borrowed: 72%.

CAMPUS LIFE AND EXTRACURRICULAR ACTIVITIES
Campus housing available (% using): women's dorms (61%), men's dorms (39%). **Student employment:** During the 2005-2006 academic year, 22% of undergraduates worked on campus. Average per-year earnings: $1,598. **Clubs and organizations:** Number of student organizations: 2. Activities include: choral groups, drama/theater, music ensembles, musical theater, student government, student newspaper, yearbook. Number of fraternities: 0; sororities: 0. **Sports program (2005-2006):** Member of NAIA. *Men's intercollegiate varsity sports:* basketball, soccer, tennis. *Women's intercollegiate varsity sports:* basketball, soccer, softball, tennis, volleyball.

SERVICES AND FACILITIES
Basic services: health insurance. **Remedial assistance:** reading, math, writing, study skills. **Counseling services:** minority student, career, academic, psychological, religious. **Library:** Number of titles: 91,000; number of current serial subscriptions: 400. **Information technology resources:** Students are not required to lease or own a computer. Number of campus computers available to all students: 57. School has a wireless network. **Campus safety:** Security services offered: 24-hour foot-and-vehicle patrols, late-night transport/escort service, 24-hour emergency telephones, lighted pathways/sidewalks, student patrols, controlled dormitory access (key, security card, etc).

TRANSFER AND INTERNATIONAL STUDENTS
Transfer students: May apply for admission for the following academic terms: Fall, Winter, Spring, Summer. Applicants do not need a minimum number of credits to apply. For fall 2005: Transfer applications received: 101. Transfer applicants offered admission: 75. Transfer applicants enrolled: 57. **International students:** Number of foreign undergraduates: 24 (3% of student body). Number of countries represented: 24. Minimum TOEFL score required: 500 (paper); 173 (computer). Average TOEFL score: 590 (paper).

Humboldt State University

- **Address:** 1 Harpst Street, Arcata, CA 95521-8299
- **Website:** http://www.humboldt.edu
- **Public**
- **Enrollment:** 5,753 full-time; 642 part-time

KEY STATS

✔ **U.S News College Ranking:** 40, Universities–Master's (West)

✔ **SAT Score (25th/75th percentile):** 920-1160

✔ **Tuition:** 2006-2007: $3,172 in state, $10,822 out of state

Selectivity: Selective	**Room/board:** $8,522
Acceptance rate: 69%	**Average debt:** $12,730
Student/faculty ratio: 19/1	**Proportion who borrowed:** 35%

UNDERGRADUATE STUDENT BODY STATS

2005-2006 enrollment: 5,753 full-time; 642 part-time. Men: 46%; women: 54%. **Ethnic makeup:** African American: 3%; American-Indian: 2%; Asian American: 4%; Hispanic: 10%; White: 80%; International: 1%.

ADMISSIONS FACTS AND FIGURES

Phone: (707) 826-4402. **Email:** hsuinfo@humboldt.edu. **Website:** http://www.humboldt.edu. **Application deadlines for fall 2007:** Regular decision: August 1. Early decision: Not offered. Early action: Not offered. Admission cannot be deferred. **Application fee:** $55. Common application is not accepted. **To apply online, go to:** http://www.csumentor.edu/AdmissionApp/. **Admissions requirements/recommendations:** High school units required (recommended): English: 4; Mathematics: 3; Science: 2; Foreign language: 2; Social studies: 1; History: 1; Academic electives: 1; Total units: 15. Tests: The college uses SAT or ACT scores in admissions decisions. Neither SAT nor ACT required. For admission to the fall 2007 entering class, the school will accept: ACT with writing, ACT without writing. Campus visit: Neither required nor recommended. Admissions interview: Neither required nor recommended. Off-campus interview: Not available. **Factors that count in admissions decisions:** *Academic:* Secondary school record: Very important. Class rank: Not considered. Letters of recommendation: Not considered. Standardized test scores: Very important. Essay: Not considered. *Nonacademic:* Interview: Not considered. Extracurricular activities: Not considered. Talent/ability: Not considered. Character/personal qualities: Not considered. Alumni/ae relationship: Not considered. Geographical residence: Not considered. State residency: Considered. Religious affiliation/commitment: Not considered. Minority status: Not considered. Volunteer work: Not considered. Work experience: Not considered. **Admissions statistics for the fall 2005 entering class:** Total applicants: 7,206. Total accepted: 4,988. Freshmen enrolled: 827; 6% were from out of state. Overall acceptance rate: 69%. **Credentials of fall 2005 freshmen:** 10% ranked in the top 10 percent of their high school class; 36% were in the top 25 percent, and 75% were in the top half. (Proportion submitting class standing: 92%.) **Average high school grade point average:** 3.2. **First-year students who submitted SAT scores:** 90%. Scores (25/75 percentile): Verbal: 460-590, Math: 460-570, Combined: 920-1160. **First-year students submitting ACT scores:** 36%. Scores (25/75 percentile): English: 19-25, Math: 19-25, Composite: 19-25.

ACADEMICS

Year founded: 1913. **Academic calendar:** Semester. **Degrees offered:** certificate, diploma, bachelor's, master's. **Most popular majors:** 14% natural resources and conservation, 12% social sciences, 11% liberal arts and sciences studies, and humanities, 10% visual and performing arts, 7% biological and biomedical sciences. **Major fields of study:** agriculture, agriculture operations, and related sciences; area, ethnic, cultural, and gender studies; biological and biomedical sciences; business, management, marketing, and related support services; communication, journalism, and related programs; computer and information sciences and support services; education; engineering; engineering technologies/technicians; English language and literature/letters; foreign languages, literatures, and linguistics; health professions and related clinical sciences; history; liberal arts and sciences studies, and humanities; mathematics and statistics; multi/interdisciplinary studies; natural resources and conservation; philosophy and religious studies; physical sciences; psychology; public administration and social service professions; science technologies/technicians; social sciences; transportation and materials moving; visual and performing arts. **Areas of required coursework:** humanities, mathematics, English (including composition),

history. **Pre-professional programs:** pre-dentistry, pre-medicine, pre-veterinary science. **Special academic programs:** cooperative (work-study plan) program, cross-registration, distance learning, double major, dual enrollment, English as a Second Language (ESL), exchange student program (domestic), honors program, independent study, internships, student-designed major, study abroad, teacher certificate program. **Teacher certification offered in:** early childhood, special education, elementary, middle/junior high, secondary, bilingual/bicultural. **Faculty and instruction (2005-2006):** Total instructional faculty: 276 full-time, 257 part-time (62% men; 38% women; 16% minorities). Full-time faculty with Ph.D. or other terminal degree: 80%. Student/faculty ratio: 19/1. Classes of fewer than 20 students: 40%; of 20 to 49 students: 54%; of 50 or more students: 6%. **Advanced Placement and International Baccalaureate credit:** AP tests may be used for: Credit and/or placement. Scores accepted: 3, 4, 5. **Freshmen returning for sophomore year:** 77%. **Graduation rates:** Four-year: 12%; five-year: 33%; six-year: 42%.

COSTS AND FINANCIAL AID

Financial aid office: (707) 826-4321. **Expenses (2006-2007):** Tuition and fees 2006-2007: $3,172 in state, $10,822 out of state; room/board: $8,522. Estimated books and supplies: $1,142; transportation: $1,116; personal expenses: $1,745. **Financial aid:** Priority filing date for institution's financial aid form: March 2. In 2005-2006, 66% of undergraduates applied for financial aid. Of those, 56% were determined to have financial need; 10% had their need fully met. Average financial aid package (proportion receiving): $8,257 (54%). Average amount of gift aid, such as scholarships or grants (proportion receiving): $2,619 (46%). Average amount of self-help aid, such as work study or loans (proportion receiving): $2,793 (44%). Average need-based loan (excluding PLUS or other private loans): $2,851. Among students who received need-based aid, the average percentage of need met: 77%. Average amount of debt of borrowers graduating in 2005: $12,730. Proportion who borrowed: 35%.

CAMPUS LIFE AND EXTRACURRICULAR ACTIVITIES

Campus housing available (% using): coed dorms (80%), apartment for single students (3%), other housing options (17%). Students who live in college-owned, operated, or affiliated housing: 20%. **Clubs and organizations:** Number of student organizations: 168. Activities include: choral groups, concert band, dance, drama/theater, jazz band, literary magazine, marching band, music ensembles, musical theater, radio station, student government, student newspaper, student film society. Number of fraternities: 2; sororities: 2. Average proportion of students who stay on campus on weekends: 100%. **Sports program (2005-2006):** Member of NCAA II. *Men's intercollegiate varsity sports:* basketball, cross-country, football, soccer, track and field (outdoor). *Women's intercollegiate varsity sports:* basketball, cross-country, soccer, softball, track and field (outdoor), volleyball, rowing.

SERVICES AND FACILITIES

Basic services: nonremedial tutoring, women's center, day care, health service, health insurance. **Remedial assistance:** reading, math, writing, study skills. **Counseling services:** career, personal, veteran student, academic, psychological, birth control. **For learning-disabled students:** School does not offer a structured program with separate admission and additional fees. Services include: remedial math, remedial English, reading machines, remedial reading, tape recorders, note-taking services, learning center, readers, extended time for tests, tutors, other. **Information technology resources:** Students are not required to lease or own a computer. Number of campus computers available to all students: 336. School has a wireless network. Proportion of college-owned housing units wired for high-speed internet access: 100%. **Campus safety:** Security services offered: 24-hour foot-and-vehicle patrols, late-night transport/escort service, 24-hour emergency telephones, lighted pathways/sidewalks, controlled dormitory access (key, security card, etc).

TRANSFER AND INTERNATIONAL STUDENTS

Transfer students: May apply for admission for the following academic terms: Fall, Spring, Summer. Applicants do not need a minimum number of credits to apply. For fall 2005: Transfer applications received: 2,463. Transfer applicants offered admission: 1,402. Transfer applicants enrolled: 792. **International students:** Number of foreign undergraduates: 45 (1% of student body). Minimum TOEFL score required: 550 (paper); 213 (computer).

Humphreys College

- **Address:** 6650 Inglewood Avenue, Stockton, CA 95207
- **Website:** http://www.humphreys.edu
- **Private**
- **Enrollment:** 554 full-time; 339 part-time

KEY STATS
- ✔ **U.S News College Ranking:** fourth tier, Comp. Colleges–Bachelor's (West)
- ✔ **SAT or ACT Score (25th/75th percentile):** N/A
- ✔ **Tuition:** 2006-2007: $11,088

Selectivity: Less selective	**Room/board:** $6,696
Acceptance rate: 100%	**Average debt:** $32,000
Student/faculty ratio: N/A	**Proportion who borrowed:** 96%

UNDERGRADUATE STUDENT BODY STATS
2005-2006 enrollment: 554 full-time; 339 part-time. Men: 14%; women: 86%. **Ethnic makeup:** African American: 3%; American-Indian: 1%; Asian American: 13%; Hispanic: 42%; White: 41%.

ADMISSIONS FACTS AND FIGURES
Phone: (209) 478-0800. **Email:** ugadmission@humphreys.edu. **Website:** http://www.humphreys.edu. **Application deadlines for fall 2007:** Regular decision: Rolling. Early decision: Not offered. Early action: Not offered. Admission can be deferred. **Application fee:** $35. Common application is not accepted. **Admissions requirements/recommendations:** Tests: The college does not use SAT or ACT scores in admissions decisions. Neither SAT nor ACT required. Campus visit: Neither required nor recommended. Admissions interview: Required. Off-campus interview: May be arranged. **Factors that count in admissions decisions:** *Academic:* Secondary school record: Important. Class rank: Not considered. Letters of recommendation: Considered. Standardized test scores: Not considered. Essay: Important. *Nonacademic:* Interview: Important. Extracurricular activities: Not considered. Talent/ability: Important. Character/personal qualities: Important. Alumni/ae relationship: Not considered. Geographical residence: Not considered. State residency: Not considered. Religious affiliation/commitment: Not considered. Minority status: Not considered. Volunteer work: Not considered. Work experience: Not considered. **Other schools with the greatest overlap in applicants:** California State University–Chico; California State University–Los Angeles; California State University–Sacramento; California State University–Stanislaus; University of St. Mary. **Admissions statistics for the fall 2005 entering class:** Total applicants: 117. Total accepted: 117. Freshmen enrolled: 117; Overall acceptance rate: 100%. **Size of waiting list:** 0 applicants; enrolled from waiting list: 0.

ACADEMICS
Year founded: 1896. **Academic calendar:** Quarter. **Degrees offered:** certificate, associate, bachelor's, first professional. **Most popular majors:** Information not available. **Major fields of study:** business, management, marketing, and related support services. **Areas of required coursework:** arts/fine arts, humanities, computer literacy, mathematics, English (including composition), philosophy, foreign languages, sciences (biological or physical), history, social science. **Special academic programs (% participation):** double major (5%), internships (1%), weekend college (6%). **Teacher certification offered in:** early childhood. **Cooperative education programs:** computer science, social/behavioral science, vocational arts. **Advanced Placement and International Baccalaureate credit:** AP tests may be used for: Credit only. Scores accepted: 2. International Baccalaureate exams may be used for: Credit and/or placement. **Freshmen returning for sophomore year:** 50%. **Graduation rates:** Four-year: 64%; five-year: 66%; six-year: 53%. **Graduate study:** 30% of students pursue further study immediately upon graduation; 40% within one year; 30% within five years. Fields in which graduates pursue further study: Master of Business Administration (MBA), 40%; law, 30%; education, 30%.

COSTS AND FINANCIAL AID
Financial aid office: (209) 478-0800. **Expenses (2006-2007):** Tuition and fees 2006-2007: $11,088; room/board: $6,696. Estimated books and supplies: $1,314; transportation: $774; personal expenses: $1,980. **Financial aid:** Priority filing date for institution's financial aid form: March 2; deadline: June 1. In 2005-2006, 91% of undergraduates applied for financial aid. Of those, 89% were determined to have financial need; 100% had their need fully met. Average financial aid package (proportion receiving): $9,850

(89%). Average amount of gift aid, such as scholarships or grants (proportion receiving): N/A (1%). Among students who received need-based aid, the average percentage of need met: 75%. Among students who received aid based on merit, the average award (and the proportion receiving): $0 (0%). The average athletic scholarship (and the proportion receiving): $0 (0%). Average amount of debt of borrowers graduating in 2005: $32,000. Proportion who borrowed: 96%.

CAMPUS LIFE AND EXTRACURRICULAR ACTIVITIES
Campus housing available (% using): women's dorms (60%), men's dorms (40%). **Clubs and organizations:** Number of student organizations: 0. Number of fraternities: 0; sororities: 0. Average proportion of students who stay on campus on weekends: 10%.

SERVICES AND FACILITIES
Basic services: placement service, day care. **Remedial assistance:** reading, math, writing, study skills. **Counseling services:** career, academic. **For learning-disabled students:** School does not offer a structured program with separate admission and additional fees. Services include: remedial math, remedial English, remedial reading, learning center, extended time for tests, tutors, priority seating. **Library:** Number of titles: 30,905; number of current serial subscriptions: 98. **Information technology resources:** Students are not required to lease or own a computer. Number of campus computers available to all students: 88. School has a wireless network. Approximate number of users that can be accommodated: 254. Proportion of college-owned housing units wired for high-speed internet access: 0%. **Campus safety:** Security services offered: 24-hour foot-and-vehicle patrols, late-night transport/escort service, lighted pathways/sidewalks, controlled dormitory access (key, security card, etc).

TRANSFER AND INTERNATIONAL STUDENTS
Transfer students: May apply for admission for the following academic terms: Fall, Winter, Spring, Summer. Applicants do not need a minimum number of credits to apply. **International students:** Number of foreign undergraduates: 0. Number of countries represented: 1. Minimum TOEFL score required: 450 (paper); 135 (computer).

John F. Kennedy University

- **Address:** 100 Ellinwood Way, Pleasant Hill, CA 94523
- **Website:** http://www.jfku.edu
- **Private**
- **Enrollment:** N/A

KEY STATS
- ✔ **U.S News College Ranking:** Unranked, Universities–Master's (West)
- ✔ **SAT or ACT Score (25th/75th percentile):** N/A
- ✔ **Tuition:** N/A

Selectivity: N/A	**Room/board:** N/A
Acceptance rate: N/A	**Average debt:** N/A
Student/faculty ratio: N/A	**Proportion who borrowed:** N/A

Laguna College of Art and Design

- **Address:** 2222 Laguna Canyon Road, Laguna Beach, CA 92651
- **Website:** http://www.lagunacollege.edu
- **Private**
- **Enrollment:** N/A

KEY STATS
- ✔ **U.S News College Ranking:** Unranked Specialty School–Fine Arts
- ✔ **SAT or ACT Score (25th/75th percentile):** N/A
- ✔ **Tuition:** N/A

Selectivity: Least selective	**Room/board:** N/A
Acceptance rate: N/A	**Average debt:** N/A
Student/faculty ratio: N/A	**Proportion who borrowed:** N/A

La Sierra University

- **Address:** 4500 Riverwalk Parkway, Riverside, CA 92515
- **Website:** http://www.lasierra.edu
- **Private; Religious affiliation:** Seventh-day Adventist
- **Enrollment:** 1,454 full-time; 184 part-time

KEY STATS

✔ **U.S News College Ranking:** third tier, Universities–Master's (West)
✔ **SAT Score (25th/75th percentile):** 840-1100
✔ **Tuition:** 2005-2006: $19,083

Selectivity: Selective	**Room/board:** $5,244
Acceptance rate: 38%	**Average debt:** N/A
Student/faculty ratio: 15/1	**Proportion who borrowed:** N/A

UNDERGRADUATE STUDENT BODY STATS

2005-2006 enrollment: 1,454 full-time; 184 part-time. Men: 41%; women: 59%. **Ethnic makeup:** African American: 9%; American-Indian: 1%; Asian American: 22%; Hispanic: 28%; White: 29%; International: 10%. **Religious preference:** Roman Catholic: 8%; Protestant: 11%; Buddhist: 1%; No preference: 8%; Seventh-day Adventist: 71%; Other: 1%.

ADMISSIONS FACTS AND FIGURES

Phone: (951) 785-2176. **Email:** admissions@lasierra.edu. **Website:** http://www.lasierra.edu. **Application deadlines for fall 2007:** Regular decision: Rolling. Early decision: Not offered. Early action: Not offered. Admission can be deferred. **Application fee:** $30. Common application is not accepted. **Admissions requirements/recommendations:** High school units required (recommended): English: 4; Mathematics: 3; Science: 3; Foreign language: 2; Social studies: 2; Total units: 18. Tests: The college uses SAT or ACT scores in admissions decisions. Either SAT or ACT required. For admission to the fall 2007 entering class, the school will accept: ACT with writing, ACT without writing. Campus visit: Recommended. Admissions interview: Recommended. Off-campus interview: May be arranged. **Factors that count in admissions decisions:** *Academic:* Secondary school record: Very important. Class rank: Not considered. Letters of recommendation: Important. Standardized test scores: Very important. Essay: Important. *Nonacademic:* Interview: Considered. Extracurricular activities: Not considered. Talent/ability: Not considered. Character/personal qualities: Important. Alumni/ae relationship: Not considered. Geographical residence: Not considered. State residency: Not considered. Religious affiliation/commitment: Important. Minority status: Not considered. Volunteer work: Not considered. Work experience: Not considered. **Admissions statistics for the fall 2005 entering class:** Total applicants: 1,389. Total accepted: 533. Freshmen enrolled: 388; 12% were from out of state. Overall acceptance rate: 38%. **Credentials of fall 2005 freshmen:** 14% ranked in the top 10 percent of their high school class; 38% were in the top 25 percent, and 72% were in the top half. (Proportion submitting class standing: 60%.) **Average high school grade point average:** 3.3. **First-year students who submitted SAT scores:** 79%. Scores (25/75 percentile): Verbal: 420-540, Math: 420-560, Combined: 840-1100. **First-year students submitting ACT scores:** 32%. Scores (25/75 percentile): English: 15-22, Math: 16-22, Composite: 17-22.

ACADEMICS

Year founded: 1922. **Academic calendar:** Quarter. **Degrees offered:** certificate, bachelor's, master's, post-master's certificate, first professional, doctorate. **Most popular majors:** 28% business administration and management, 15% biology/biological sciences, 13% liberal arts and sciences/liberal studies, 11% psychology, 7% social work. **Major fields of study:** biological and biomedical sciences; business, management, marketing, and related support services; communication, journalism, and related programs; computer and information sciences and support services; education; English language and literature/letters; foreign languages, literatures, and linguistics; history; liberal arts and sciences studies, and humanities; mathematics and statistics; parks, recreation, leisure, and fitness studies; philosophy and religious studies; physical sciences; psychology; public administration and social service professions; social sciences; visual and performing arts. **Areas of required coursework:** arts/fine arts, humanities, computer literacy, mathematics, English (including composition), foreign languages, sciences (biological or physical), history, social science. **Pre-professional programs:** pre-law, pre-dentistry, pre-medicine, pre-theology, pre-veterinary science, pre-optometry, pre-pharmacy. **Special academic programs:** accelerated program, cross-registration, distance learning, double major, dual enrollment, English as a

Second Language (ESL), honors program, independent study, internships, student-designed major, study abroad, teacher certificate program. **Teacher certification offered in:** elementary, middle/junior high, secondary. **Faculty and instruction (2005-2006):** Total instructional faculty: 88 full-time, 76 part-time (57% men; 43% women; 30% minorities). Full-time faculty with Ph.D. or other terminal degree: 84%. Student/faculty ratio: 15/1. Classes of fewer than 20 students: 56%; of 20 to 49 students: 37%; of 50 or more students: 7%. **Advanced Placement and International Baccalaureate credit:** AP tests may be used for: Credit only. Scores accepted: 3, 4, 5. **Freshmen returning for sophomore year:** 65%. **Graduation rates:** Four-year: 22%; five-year: 35%; six-year: 35%.

COSTS AND FINANCIAL AID

Financial aid office: (909) 785-2175. **Expenses (2005-2006):** Tuition and fees 2005-2006: $19,083; room/board: $5,244. Estimated books and supplies: $1,242; transportation: $738; personal expenses: $1,980. **Financial aid:** Priority filing date for institution's financial aid form: March 2.

CAMPUS LIFE AND EXTRACURRICULAR ACTIVITIES

Campus housing available: women's dorms, men's dorms, apartments for married students, apartment for single students. Students who live in college-owned, operated, or affiliated housing: 44%. Activities include: choral groups, concert band, drama/theater, jazz band, literary magazine, music ensembles, student government, student newspaper, symphony orchestra, yearbook. Number of fraternities: 0; sororities: 0. **Sports program (2005-2006):** Member of NCAA III.

SERVICES AND FACILITIES

Basic services: nonremedial tutoring, women's center, placement service, health service, health insurance. **Remedial assistance:** reading, math, writing, study skills. **Counseling services:** career, personal, academic, psychological, religious. **For learning-disabled students:** School does not offer a structured program with separate admission and additional fees. **Library:** Number of titles: 258,612; number of current serial subscriptions: 1,081. **Information technology resources:** Students are not required to lease or own a computer. School has a wireless network. **Campus safety:** Security services offered: 24-hour foot-and-vehicle patrols, 24-hour emergency telephones, lighted pathways/sidewalks.

TRANSFER AND INTERNATIONAL STUDENTS

Transfer students: May apply for admission for the following academic terms: Fall, Winter, Spring, Summer. Applicants need a minimum number of credits to apply. For fall 2005: Transfer applications received: 470. Transfer applicants offered admission: 235. Transfer applicants enrolled: 228. **International students:** Number of foreign undergraduates: 161 (10% of student body). Number of countries represented: 38. Minimum TOEFL score required: 550 (paper).

Loyola Marymount University

- **Address:** 1 LMU Drive, Los Angeles, CA 90045-2659
- **Website:** http://www.lmu.edu
- **Private; Religious affiliation:** Roman Catholic
- **Enrollment:** 5,381 full-time; 343 part-time

KEY STATS

✔ **U.S News College Ranking:** 4, Universities–Master's (West)
✔ **SAT Score (25th/75th percentile):** 1070-1270
✔ **Tuition:** 2006-2007: $29,897

Selectivity: More selective	**Room/board:** $11,290
Acceptance rate: 56%	**Average debt:** $27,144
Student/faculty ratio: 11/1	**Proportion who borrowed:** 59%

UNDERGRADUATE STUDENT BODY STATS

2005-2006 enrollment: 5,381 full-time; 343 part-time. Men: 42%; women: 58%. **Ethnic makeup:** African American: 8%; American-Indian: 1%; Asian American: 13%; Hispanic: 20%; White: 58%; International: 2%. **Religious preference:** Protestant: 1%; Jewish: 2%; Muslim: 1%; Buddhist: 1%; No preference: 17%; Roman Catholic: 51%; Other: 27%.

ADMISSIONS FACTS AND FIGURES

Phone: (310) 338-2750. **Email:** admissions@lmu.edu. **Website:** http://www.lmu.edu. **Application deadlines for fall 2007:** Regular decision: Rolling. Early decision: Not offered. Early action: Not offered. Admission can be deferred. **Application fee:** $50. Common application is accepted. **To apply online, go to:** http://www.lmu.edu/admissions. **Admissions requirements/recommendations:** High school units required (recommended): English: 4 (4); Mathematics: 3 (3); Science: 2 (2); Foreign language: 3 (3); Social studies: 3 (3); Academic electives: 1 (1); Total units: 16 (18). Tests: The college uses SAT or ACT scores in admissions decisions. Either SAT or ACT required. For admission to the fall 2007 entering class, the school will accept: ACT without writing. Campus visit: Recommended. Admissions interview: Recommended. Off-campus interview: Not available. **Factors that count in admissions decisions:** *Academic:* Secondary school record: Important. Class rank: Considered. Letters of recommendation: Considered. Standardized test scores: Important. Essay: Important. *Nonacademic:* Interview: Not considered. Extracurricular activities: Considered. Talent/ability: Important. Character/personal qualities: Important. Alumni/ae relationship: Considered. Geographical residence: Not considered. State residency: Not considered. Religious affiliation/commitment: Not considered. Minority status: Not considered. Volunteer work: Considered. Work experience: Considered. **Other schools with the greatest overlap in applicants:** Santa Clara University; University of California–Los Angeles; University of California–Santa Barbara; University of San Diego; University of Southern California. **Admissions statistics for the fall 2005 entering class:** Total applicants: 7,733. Total accepted: 4,367. Freshmen enrolled: 1,346; 26% were from out of state. Overall acceptance rate: 56%. **Size of waiting list:** 864 applicants; enrolled from waiting list: 206. **Credentials of fall 2005 freshmen:** 30% ranked in the top 10 percent of their high school class; 64% were in the top 25 percent, and 95% were in the top half. (Proportion submitting class standing: 54%.) **Average high school grade point average:** 3.6. **First-year students who submitted SAT scores:** 95%. Scores (25/75 percentile): Verbal: 530-630, Math: 540-640, Combined: 1070-1270. **First-year students submitting ACT scores:** 43%. Scores (25/75 percentile): English: N/A, Math: N/A, Composite: 24-28.

ACADEMICS

Year founded: 1911. **Academic calendar:** Semester. **Degrees offered:** bachelor's, post-bachelor's certificate, master's, first professional, doctorate. **Most popular majors:** 25% business/commerce, 7% communication studies/speech communication and rhetoric, 6% English language and literature, 6% psychology, 5% political science and government. **Major fields of study:** area, ethnic, cultural, and gender studies; biological and biomedical sciences; business, management, marketing, and related support services; communications technologies/technicians and support services; computer and information sciences and support services; engineering; English language and literature/letters; foreign languages, literatures, and linguistics; health professions and related clinical sciences; history; liberal arts and sciences studies, and humanities; mathematics and statistics; multi/interdisciplinary studies; philosophy and religious studies; physical sciences; psychology; social sciences; theology and religious vocations; visual and performing arts. **Areas of required coursework:** arts/fine arts, humanities, mathematics, English (including composition), philosophy, sciences (biological or physical), history, social science, other. **Pre-professional programs:** pre-law, pre-dentistry, pre-medicine, pre-theology, pre-veterinary science, pre-optometry, pre-pharmacy, other. **Special academic programs (% participation):** cross-registration, distance learning, double major (11.73%), dual enrollment, honors program (2.67%), independent study (37.42%), internships, liberal arts/career combination, study abroad (21.43%), teacher certificate program, other. **Teacher certification offered in:** special education, elementary, middle/junior high, secondary, bilingual/bicultural. **Reserve Officers Training Corps (ROTC):** Army ROTC: Offered at cooperating institution (UCLA); Navy ROTC: Offered at cooperating institution (UCLA); Air Force ROTC: Offered on campus. **Faculty and instruction (2005-2006):** Total instructional faculty: 460 full-time, 396 part-time (58% men; 42% women; 23% minorities). Full-time faculty with Ph.D. or other terminal degree: 98%. Student/faculty ratio: 11/1. Classes of fewer than 20 students: 46%; of 20 to 49 students: 53%; of 50 or more students: 1%. **Advanced Placement and International Baccalaureate credit:** AP tests may be used for: Credit only. Scores accepted: 4, 5. International Baccalaureate exams may be used for: Credit only. **Freshmen returning for sophomore year:** 89%. **Graduation rates:** Four-year: 63%; five-year: 73%; six-year: 73%. **Graduate study:** 36% of students pursue further study immediately upon graduation; 51% within one year. Fields in which graduates pursue further study: Master of Business Administration (MBA), 11%; law, 43%; engineering, 4%; theology (or the seminary), 3%; education, 32%; arts and sciences, 7%.

COSTS AND FINANCIAL AID

Financial aid office: (310) 338-2753. **Expenses (2006-2007):** Tuition and fees 2006-2007: $29,897; room/board: $11,290. Estimated books and supplies: $1,314; transportation: $500; personal expenses: $1,530. **Financial aid:** Priority filing date for institution's financial aid form: February 15; deadline: July 30. In 2005-2006, 74% of undergraduates applied for financial aid. Of those, 58% were determined to have financial need; 15% had their need fully met. Average financial aid package (proportion receiving): $22,232 (60%). Average amount of gift aid, such as scholarships or grants (proportion receiving): $14,941 (43%). Average amount of self-help aid, such as work study or loans (proportion receiving): $7,004 (47%). Average need-based loan (excluding PLUS or other private loans): $4,631. Among students who received need-based aid, the average percentage of need met: 74%. Among students who received aid based on merit, the average award (and the proportion receiving): $11,084 (3%). The average athletic scholarship (and the proportion receiving): $19,686 (3%). Average amount of debt of borrowers graduating in 2005: $27,144. Proportion who borrowed: 59%.

CAMPUS LIFE AND EXTRACURRICULAR ACTIVITIES

Campus housing available (% using): coed dorms (48%), women's dorms (12%), men's dorms (4%), apartment for single students (35%), other housing options (1%). Students who live in college-owned, operated, or affiliated housing: 49%. **Student employment:** During the 2005-2006 academic year, 46% of undergraduates worked on campus. Average per-year earnings: $3,200. **Clubs and organizations:** Number of student organizations: 122. Activities include: choral groups, dance, drama/theater, literary magazine, music ensembles, musical theater, opera, pep band, radio station, student government, student newspaper, student film society, television station, yearbook. Number of fraternities: 6; sororities: 8. Proportion of men in fraternities: 15%; of women in sororities: 22%. Average proportion of students who stay on campus on weekends: 50%. **Sports program (2005-2006):** Member of NCAA I. *Men's intercollegiate varsity sports:* baseball, basketball, crew, cross-country, golf, soccer, tennis, water polo. *Women's intercollegiate varsity sports:* basketball, crew, cross-country, lightweight crew, soccer, softball, swimming and diving, tennis, track and field (outdoor), volleyball, water polo.

SERVICES AND FACILITIES

Basic services: nonremedial tutoring, placement service, day care, health service, health insurance, other. **Remedial assistance:** reading, math, writing, study skills, other. **Counseling services:** minority student, career, military, personal, academic, older student, psychological, religious. **For learning-disabled students:** School does not offer a structured program with separate admission and additional fees. Total undergraduates in learning-disabled program or receiving services: 135. Services include: remedial math, remedial English, reading machines, remedial reading, tape recorders, other special classes, note-taking services, oral tests, learning center, readers, extended time for tests, tutors, priority registration, priority seating, texts on tape, other testing accomodations. **Library:** Number of titles: 469,585; number of current serial subscriptions: 18,459. **Information technology resources:** Students are not required to lease or own a computer. Number of campus computers available to all students: 725. School has a wireless network. Approximate number of users that can be accommodated: 300. Proportion of college-owned housing units wired for high-speed internet access: 100%. **Campus safety:** Security services offered: 24-hour foot-and-vehicle patrols, late-night transport/escort service, 24-hour emergency telephones, lighted pathways/sidewalks, controlled dormitory access (key, security card, etc).

TRANSFER AND INTERNATIONAL STUDENTS

Transfer students: May apply for admission for the following academic terms: Fall, Spring. Applicants need a minimum number of credits to apply. For fall 2005: Transfer applications received: 965. Transfer applicants offered admission: 276. Transfer applicants enrolled: 176. **International students:** Number of foreign undergraduates: 82 (2% of student body). Number of countries represented: 58. Minimum TOEFL score required: 550 (paper); 213 (computer).

Master's College and Seminary

- **Address:** 21726 Placerita Canyon Road, Santa Clarita, CA 91321-1200
- **Website:** http://www.masters.edu
- **Private; Religious affiliation:** Evangelical nondenominational
- **Enrollment:** 957 full-time; 182 part-time

KEY STATS

✔ **U.S News College Ranking:** 2, Comp. Colleges–Bachelor's (West)
✔ **SAT Score (25th/75th percentile):** 1010-1250
✔ **Tuition:** 2006-2007: $20,770

Selectivity: More selective	**Room/board:** $6,900
Acceptance rate: 29%	**Average debt:** $15,383
Student/faculty ratio: 16/1	**Proportion who borrowed:** 64%

UNDERGRADUATE STUDENT BODY STATS

2005-2006 enrollment: 957 full-time; 182 part-time. Men: 49%; women: 51%. **Ethnic makeup:** African American: 3%; American-Indian: 1%; Asian American: 4%; Hispanic: 7%; White: 83%; International: 3%.

ADMISSIONS FACTS AND FIGURES

Phone: (800) 568-6248. **Email:** admissions@masters.edu. **Website:** http://www.masters.edu. **Application deadlines for fall 2007:** Regular decision: Rolling. Early decision: Not offered. Early action: Send application by: November 1; Decision sent by: December 22. Admission can be deferred. **Application fee:** $55. Common application is not accepted. **Admissions requirements/recommendations:** High school units required (recommended): English: 4; Mathematics: 3; Science: 2; History: 2; Academic electives: (3). Tests: The college uses SAT or ACT scores in admissions decisions. Either SAT or ACT required. For admission to the fall 2007 entering class, the school will accept: ACT with writing. Campus visit: Recommended. Admissions interview: Required. Off-campus interview: May be arranged. **Factors that count in admissions decisions:** *Academic:* Secondary school record: Very important. Class rank: Considered. Letters of recommendation: Very important. Standardized test scores: Very important. Essay: Very important. *Nonacademic:* Interview: Very important. Extracurricular activities: Considered. Talent/ability: Considered. Character/personal qualities: Very important. Alumni/ae relationship: Considered. Geographical residence: Not considered. State residency: Not considered. Religious affiliation/commitment: Very important. Minority status: Not considered. Volunteer work: Not considered. Work experience: Not considered. **Other schools with the greatest overlap in applicants:** Azusa Pacific University; Biola University; Point Loma Nazarene University; Westmont College. **Admissions statistics for the fall 2005 entering class:** Total applicants: 654. Total accepted: 187. Freshmen enrolled: 187; 35% were from out of state. Accepted through early-decision or early-action plans: 20%. Overall acceptance rate: 29%. Non-early acceptance rate: 29%. **Credentials of fall 2005 freshmen:** 33% ranked in the top 10 percent of their high school class; 53% were in the top 25 percent, and 78% were in the top half. (Proportion submitting class standing: 41%.) **Average high school grade point average:** 3.6. **First-year students who submitted SAT scores:** 81%. Scores (25/75 percentile): Verbal: 520-620, Math: 490-630, Combined: 1010-1250. **First-year students submitting ACT scores:** 34%. Scores (25/75 percentile): English: 19-29, Math: 18-26, Composite: 19-27.

ACADEMICS

Year founded: 1927. **Academic calendar:** Semester. **Degrees offered:** certificate, bachelor's, master's, first professional, first professional certificate, doctorate. **Most popular majors:** 33% religion/religious studies, 18% business, management, marketing, and related support services, 16% liberal arts and sciences studies, and humanities, 8% history, 6% communication, journalism, and related programs. **Major fields of study:** biological and biomedical sciences; business, management, marketing, and related support services; communication, journalism, and related programs; computer and information sciences and support services; education; English language and literature/letters; family and consumer sciences/human sciences; foreign languages, literatures, and linguistics; health professions and related clinical sciences; history; legal professions and studies; liberal arts and sciences studies, and humanities; mathematics and statistics; parks, recreation, leisure, and fitness studies; social sciences; theology and religious vocations; visual and performing arts. **Areas of required coursework:** arts/fine arts, humanities, computer literacy, mathematics, English (including composition), philosophy, sciences (biological or physical), history, social science,

other. **Pre-professional programs:** pre-law, pre-dentistry, pre-medicine, pre-theology. **Special academic programs (% participation):** accelerated program, cooperative (work-study plan) program, double major (8%), independent study (35%), internships (5%), study abroad (25%), teacher certificate program (9%). **Teacher certification offered in;** elementary, secondary. **Cooperative education programs:** education, home economics. **Faculty and instruction (2005-2006):** Total instructional faculty: 72 full-time, 116 part-time (82% men; 18% women; 8% minorities). Full-time faculty with Ph.D. or other terminal degree: 88%. Student/faculty ratio: 16/1. Classes of fewer than 20 students: 72%; of 20 to 49 students: 20%; of 50 or more students: 8%. **Advanced Placement and International Baccalaureate credit:** AP tests may be used for: Credit and/or placement. Scores accepted: 3, 4, 5. International Baccalaureate exams may be used for: Credit and/or placement. **Freshmen returning for sophomore year:** 81%. **Graduation rates:** Four-year: 51%; five-year: 60%; six-year: 61%. **Graduate study:** 20% of students pursue further study immediately upon graduation; 35% within five years. Fields in which graduates pursue further study: law, 8%; theology (or the seminary), 14%; education, 8%; arts and sciences, 14%.

COSTS AND FINANCIAL AID

Financial aid office: (661) 259-3540. **Expenses (2006-2007):** Tuition and fees 2006-2007: $20,770; room/board: $6,900. Estimated books and supplies: $1,314; transportation: $774; personal expenses: $2,088. **Financial aid:** Priority filing date for institution's financial aid form: March 2; deadline: March 2. In 2005-2006, 82% of undergraduates applied for financial aid. Of those, 72% were determined to have financial need; 14% had their need fully met. Average financial aid package (proportion receiving): $15,311 (72%). Average amount of gift aid, such as scholarships or grants (proportion receiving): $10,632 (67%). Average amount of self-help aid, such as work study or loans (proportion receiving): $6,018 (64%). Average need-based loan (excluding PLUS or other private loans): $4,700. Among students who received need-based aid, the average percentage of need met: 71%. Among students who received aid based on merit, the average award (and the proportion receiving): $10,069 (20%). The average athletic scholarship (and the proportion receiving): $8,102 (5%). Average amount of debt of borrowers graduating in 2005: $15,383. Proportion who borrowed: 64%.

CAMPUS LIFE AND EXTRACURRICULAR ACTIVITIES

Campus housing available (% using): women's dorms (47%), men's dorms (40%), apartment for single students (11%), special housing for international students (2%). Students who live in college-owned, operated, or affiliated housing: 75%. **Student employment:** During the 2005-2006 academic year, 52% of undergraduates worked on campus. Average per-year earnings: $1,200. **Clubs and organizations:** Number of student organizations: 0. Activities include: choral groups, concert band, jazz band, music ensembles, opera, pep band, student government, symphony orchestra. Number of fraternities: 0; sororities: 0. Average proportion of students who stay on campus on weekends: 50%. **Sports program (2005-2006):** Member of NAIA. *Men's intercollegiate varsity sports:* baseball, basketball, cross-country, golf, soccer. *Women's intercollegiate varsity sports:* basketball, cross-country, soccer, tennis, volleyball.

SERVICES AND FACILITIES

Basic services: placement service, health service, other. **Remedial assistance:** math. **Counseling services:** career, personal, veteran student, older student, religious, other. **For learning-disabled students:** School does not offer a structured program with separate admission and additional fees. Total undergraduates in learning-disabled program or receiving services: 2. Services include: remedial math, extended time for tests, tutors, other. **Library:** Number of titles: 215,650; number of current serial subscriptions: 446. **Information technology resources:** Students are required to lease or own a computer. Number of campus computers available to all students: 60. School has a wireless network. Approximate number of users that can be accommodated: 800. Proportion of college-owned housing units wired for high-speed internet access: 100%. **Campus safety:** Security services offered: 24-hour foot-and-vehicle patrols, late-night transport/escort service, 24-hour emergency telephones, lighted pathways/sidewalks, student patrols, controlled dormitory access (key, security card, etc).

TRANSFER AND INTERNATIONAL STUDENTS

Transfer students: May apply for admission for the following academic terms: Fall, Spring. Applicants need a minimum number of credits to apply. For fall 2005: Transfer applications received: 270. Transfer applicants offered admission: 227. Transfer applicants enrolled: 137. **International students:** Number of foreign undergraduates: 34 (3% of student body). Number of countries represented: 19. Minimum TOEFL score required: 525 (paper); 197 (computer). Average TOEFL score: 530 (paper).

Menlo College

- **Address:** 1000 El Camino Real, Atherton, CA 94027
- **Website:** http://www.menlo.edu
- **Private**
- **Enrollment:** 669 full-time; 100 part-time

KEY STATS

- ✔ **U.S News College Ranking:** third tier, Comp. Colleges–Bachelor's (West)
- ✔ **SAT Score (25th/75th percentile):** 830-1050
- ✔ **Tuition:** 2006-2007: $26,220

Selectivity: Less selective	**Room/board:** $9,800
Acceptance rate: 69%	**Average debt:** $21,905
Student/faculty ratio: 19/1	**Proportion who borrowed:** 67%

UNDERGRADUATE STUDENT BODY STATS

2005-2006 enrollment: 669 full-time; 100 part-time. Men: 60%; women: 40%. **Ethnic makeup:** African American: 9%; American-Indian: 1%; Asian American: 12%; Hispanic: 15%; White: 53%; International: 10%.

ADMISSIONS FACTS AND FIGURES

Phone: (800) 556-3656. **Email:** admissions@menlo.edu. **Website:** http://www.menlo.edu. **Application deadlines for fall 2007:** Regular decision: Rolling. Early decision: Not offered. Early action: Send application by: December 1; Decision sent by: January 30. Admission can be deferred. **Application fee:** $40. Common application is accepted. **Admissions requirements/recommendations:** High school units required (recommended): English: 0 (4); Mathematics: 0 (3); Science: 0 (3); Foreign language: 0 (2); Social studies: 0 (3); History: 0 (3); Academic electives: 0 (0); Total units: 0 (24). Tests: The college uses SAT or ACT scores in admissions decisions. Either SAT or ACT required. For admission to the fall 2007 entering class, the school will accept: ACT with writing, ACT without writing. Campus visit: Recommended. Admissions interview: Recommended. Off-campus interview: May be arranged. **Factors that count in admissions decisions:** *Academic:* Secondary school record: Very important. Class rank: Very important. Letters of recommendation: Very important. Standardized test scores: Very important. Essay: Very important. *Nonacademic:* Interview: Considered. Extracurricular activities: Important. Talent/ability: Considered. Character/personal qualities: Important. Alumni/ae relationship: Considered. Geographical residence: Considered. State residency: Considered. Religious affiliation/commitment: Not considered. Minority status: Not considered. Volunteer work: Considered. Work experience: Considered. **Admissions statistics for the fall 2005 entering class:** Total applicants: 753. Total accepted: 522. Freshmen enrolled: 172; 24% were from out of state. Overall acceptance rate: 69%. Non-early acceptance rate: 69%. **Credentials of fall 2005 freshmen:** 6% ranked in the top 10 percent of their high school class; 26% were in the top 25 percent, and 67% were in the top half. (Proportion submitting class standing: 47%.) **Average high school grade point average:** 3.1. **First-year students who submitted SAT scores:** 80%. Scores (25/75 percentile): Verbal: 410-520, Math: 420-530, Combined: 830-1050. **First-year students submitting ACT scores:** 20%. Scores (25/75 percentile): English: 15-20, Math: 17-21, Composite: 14-21.

ACADEMICS

Year founded: 1927. **Academic calendar:** Semester. **Degrees offered:** bachelor's. **Most popular majors:** 83% business, management, marketing, and related support services, 9% mass communication/media studies, 8% liberal arts and sciences studies, and humanities. **Areas of required coursework:** humanities, computer literacy, mathematics, English (including composition), foreign languages, sciences (biological or physical), history, social science, other. **Special academic programs:** accelerated program, double major, honors program, independent study, internships, student-designed major, study abroad. **Reserve Officers Training Corps (ROTC):** Army ROTC: Offered at cooperating institution (San Jose State University); Navy ROTC: Offered at cooperating institution (San Jose State University); Air Force ROTC: Offered at cooperating institution (San Jose State University). **Faculty and instruction (2005-2006):** Total instructional faculty: 23 full-time, 48 part-time (61% men; 39% women; 11% minorities). Full-time faculty with Ph.D. or other terminal degree: 65%. Student/faculty

ratio: 19/1. Classes of fewer than 20 students: 53%; of 20 to 49 students: 46%; of 50 or more students: 1%. **Advanced Placement and International Baccalaureate credit:** AP tests may be used for: Credit and/or placement. Scores accepted: 3, 4, 5. International Baccalaureate exams may be used for: Credit and/or placement. **Freshmen returning for sophomore year:** 64%. **Graduation rates:** Four-year: 22%; five-year: 28%; six-year: 23%.

COSTS AND FINANCIAL AID

Financial aid office: (650) 543-3880. **Expenses (2006-2007):** Tuition and fees 2006-2007: $26,220; room/board: $9,800. Estimated books and supplies: $1,212; transportation: $774; personal expenses: $1,990. **Financial aid:** Priority filing date for institution's financial aid form: March 2. In 2005-2006, 68% of undergraduates applied for financial aid. Of those, 62% were determined to have financial need; 12% had their need fully met. Average financial aid package (proportion receiving): $19,510 (62%). Average amount of gift aid, such as scholarships or grants (proportion receiving): $15,516 (60%). Average amount of self-help aid, such as work study or loans (proportion receiving): $5,127 (54%). Average need-based loan (excluding PLUS or other private loans): $4,612. Among students who received need-based aid, the average percentage of need met: 74%. Among students who received aid based on merit, the average award (and the proportion receiving): $10,820 (27%). The average athletic scholarship (and the proportion receiving): $0 (0%). Average amount of debt of borrowers graduating in 2005: $21,905. Proportion who borrowed: 67%.

CAMPUS LIFE AND EXTRACURRICULAR ACTIVITIES

Campus housing available (% using): coed dorms (76%), women's dorms, men's dorms (24%). Students who live in college-owned, operated, or affiliated housing: 66%. **Student employment:** During the 2005-2006 academic year, 7% of undergraduates worked on campus. Average per-year earnings: $4,800. **Clubs and organizations:** Number of student organizations: 29. Activities include: radio station, student government, student newspaper, television station. Number of fraternities: 0; sororities: 0. Average proportion of students who stay on campus on weekends: 50%. **Sports program (2005-2006):** Member of NCAA III. *Men's intercollegiate varsity sports:* baseball, basketball, cross-country, football, golf, soccer, wrestling. *Women's intercollegiate varsity sports:* basketball, cross-country, golf, soccer, softball, volleyball.

SERVICES AND FACILITIES

Basic services: nonremedial tutoring, health insurance. **Remedial assistance:** math, writing, study skills. **Counseling services:** career, academic, psychological. **For learning-disabled students:** School does not offer a structured program with separate admission and additional fees. Services include: remedial math, remedial English, tape recorders, other special classes, note-taking services, learning center, extended time for tests, tutors, other testing accomodations, other. **Library:** Number of titles: 64,700; number of current serial subscriptions: 175. **Information technology resources:** Students are not required to lease or own a computer. Number of campus computers available to all students: 150. School has a wireless network. Approximate number of users that can be accommodated: 35. Proportion of college-owned housing units wired for high-speed internet access: 100%. **Campus safety:** Security services offered: 24-hour foot-and-vehicle patrols, late-night transport/escort service, 24-hour emergency telephones, lighted pathways/sidewalks, controlled dormitory access (key, security card, etc).

TRANSFER AND INTERNATIONAL STUDENTS

Transfer students: May apply for admission for the following academic terms: Fall, Spring. Applicants do not need a minimum number of credits to apply. For fall 2005: Transfer applications received: 279. Transfer applicants offered admission: 157. Transfer applicants enrolled: 88. **International students:** Number of foreign undergraduates: 74 (10% of student body). Number of countries represented: 34. Minimum TOEFL score required: 500 (paper); 173 (computer). Average TOEFL score: 520 (paper).

Mills College

- **Address:** 5000 MacArthur Boulevard, Oakland, CA 94613
- **Website:** http://www.mills.edu
- **Private**
- **Enrollment:** 842 full-time; 39 part-time

KEY STATS

✔ **U.S News College Ranking:** 82, Liberal Arts Colleges
✔ **SAT Score (25th/75th percentile):** 1010-1260
✔ **Tuition:** 2006-2007: $33,024

Selectivity: More selective	**Room/board:** $10,290
Acceptance rate: 77%	**Average debt:** $21,228
Student/faculty ratio: 11/1	**Proportion who borrowed:** 73%

UNDERGRADUATE STUDENT BODY STATS

2005-2006 enrollment: 842 full-time; 39 part-time. Men: 0%; women: 100%. **Ethnic makeup:** African American: 8%; American-Indian: 1%; Asian American: 8%; Hispanic: 9%; White: 68%; International: 6%.

ADMISSIONS FACTS AND FIGURES

Phone: (510) 430-2135. **Email:** admission@mills.edu. **Website:** http://www.mills.edu. **Application deadlines for fall 2007:** Regular decision: Rolling. Early decision: Not offered. Early action: Send application by: November 15; Decision sent by: December 15. Admission can be deferred. **Application fee:** $40. Common application is accepted. **To apply online, go to:** http://www.applyweb.com/apply/millsug/menu.html. **Admissions requirements/recommendations:** High school units required (recommended): English: (4); Mathematics: (3); Science: (3); Foreign language: (3); Social studies: (3); History: (3). Tests: The college uses SAT or ACT scores in admissions decisions. Either SAT or ACT required. For admission to the fall 2007 entering class, the school will accept: ACT without writing. Campus visit: Recommended. Admissions interview: Recommended. Off-campus interview: May be arranged. **Factors that count in admissions decisions:** *Academic:* Secondary school record: Very important. Class rank: Important. Letters of recommendation: Important. Standardized test scores: Important. Essay: Important. *Nonacademic:* Interview: Considered. Extracurricular activities: Considered. Talent/ability: Considered. Character/personal qualities: Important. Alumni/ae relationship: Not considered. Geographical residence: Not considered. State residency: Considered. Religious affiliation/commitment: Not considered. Minority status: Considered. Volunteer work: Considered. Work experience: Considered. **Other schools with the greatest overlap in applicants:** Occidental College; Scripps College; Smith College; University of California–Berkeley; University of California–Santa Cruz. **Admissions statistics for the fall 2005 entering class:** Total applicants: 783. Total accepted: 604. Freshmen enrolled: 207; 26% were from out of state. Overall acceptance rate: 77%. Non-early acceptance rate: 77%. **Credentials of fall 2005 freshmen:** 37% ranked in the top 10 percent of their high school class; 74% were in the top 25 percent, and 95% were in the top half. (Proportion submitting class standing: 69%.) **Average high school grade point average:** 3.6. **First-year students who submitted SAT scores:** 92%. Scores (25/75 percentile): Verbal: 520-660, Math: 490-600, Combined: 1010-1260. **First-year students submitting ACT scores:** 25%. Scores (25/75 percentile): English: N/A, Math: N/A, Composite: 21-28.

ACADEMICS

Year founded: 1852. **Academic calendar:** Semester. **Degrees offered:** certificate, bachelor's, post-bachelor's certificate, master's, doctorate. **Most popular majors:** 13% English language and literature, 9% political science and government, 8% art/art studies, 8% psychology, 8% social sciences. **Major fields of study:** area, ethnic, cultural, and gender studies; biological and biomedical sciences; business, management, marketing, and related support services; communication, journalism, and related programs; computer and information sciences and support services; engineering; English language and literature/letters; family and consumer sciences/human sciences; foreign languages, literatures, and linguistics; history; liberal arts and sciences studies, and humanities; mathematics and statistics; multi/interdisciplinary studies; natural resources and conservation; philosophy and religious studies; physical sciences; psychology; public administration and social service professions; social sciences; visual and performing arts. **Areas of required coursework:** arts/fine arts, humanities, computer literacy, mathematics, English (including composition), philosophy, sciences (biological or physical), history, social science. **Pre-professional programs:** pre-law, pre-medi-

cine. **Special academic programs (% participation):** cross-registration (1%), double major (6%), exchange student program (domestic) (1%), independent study (10%), internships (1%), student-designed major (1%), study abroad (30%). **Faculty and instruction (2005-2006):** Total instructional faculty: 89 full-time, 94 part-time (33% men; 67% women; 23% minorities). Full-time faculty with Ph.D. or other terminal degree: 91%. Student/faculty ratio: 11/1. Classes of fewer than 20 students: 75%; of 20 to 49 students: 24%; of 50 or more students: 1%. **Advanced Placement and International Baccalaureate credit:** AP tests may be used for: Placement only. Scores accepted: 4, 5. International Baccalaureate exams may be used for: Credit only. **Freshmen returning for sophomore year:** 78%. **Graduation rates:** Four-year: 59%; five-year: 66%; six-year: 69%. **Graduate study:** 40% of students pursue further study immediately upon graduation; 40% within one year; 60% within five years. Fields in which graduates pursue further study: Master of Business Administration (MBA), 15%; law, 10%; medicine, 5%; dentistry, 3%; engineering, 1%; theology (or the seminary), 1%; education, 15%; arts and sciences, 45%; veterinary medicine, 5%.

COSTS AND FINANCIAL AID

Financial aid office: (510) 430-2000. **Expenses (2006-2007):** Tuition and fees 2006-2007: $33,024; room/board: $10,290. Estimated books and supplies: $1,100; transportation: $0; personal expenses: $2,000. **Financial aid:** Priority filing date for institution's financial aid form: February 15. In 2005-2006, 82% of undergraduates applied for financial aid. Of those, 76% were determined to have financial need; 19% had their need fully met. Average financial aid package (proportion receiving): $29,584 (76%). Average amount of gift aid, such as scholarships or grants (proportion receiving): $18,880 (75%). Average amount of self-help aid, such as work study or loans (proportion receiving): $7,032 (71%). Average need-based loan (excluding PLUS or other private loans): $4,952. Among students who received need-based aid, the average percentage of need met: 91%. Among students who received aid based on merit, the average award (and the proportion receiving): $15,491 (10%). The average athletic scholarship (and the proportion receiving): $0 (0%). Average amount of debt of borrowers graduating in 2005: $21,228. Proportion who borrowed: 73%.

CAMPUS LIFE AND EXTRACURRICULAR ACTIVITIES

Campus housing available (% using): coed dorms (1%), women's dorms (90%), apartments for married students (2%), apartment for single students (4%), special housing for disabled students (1%), cooperative housing (1%), other housing options (1%). Students who live in college-owned, operated, or affiliated housing: 52%. **Student employment:** During the 2005-2006 academic year, 25% of undergraduates worked on campus. Average per-year earnings: $1,884. **Clubs and organizations:** Number of student organizations: 45. Activities include: dance, drama/theater, literary magazine, music ensembles, student government, student newspaper, student film society, yearbook. Number of fraternities: 0; sororities: 0. Average proportion of students who stay on campus on weekends: 50%. **Sports program (2005-2006):** Member of NCAA III. *Women's intercollegiate varsity sports:* crew, cross-country, soccer, swimming and diving, tennis, volleyball.

SERVICES AND FACILITIES

Basic services: nonremedial tutoring, women's center, placement service, day care, health service, health insurance. **Counseling services:** minority student, career, personal, academic, older student, psychological, religious. **For learning-disabled students:** School does not offer a structured program with separate admission and additional fees. Services include: reading machines, tape recorders, note-taking services, readers, extended time for tests, tutors. **Library:** Number of titles: 227,903; number of current serial subscriptions: 873. **Information technology resources:** Students are not required to lease or own a computer. Number of campus computers available to all students: 292. School has a wireless network. Approximate number of users that can be accommodated: 1,000. Proportion of college-owned housing units wired for high-speed internet access: 100%. **Campus safety:** Security services offered: 24-hour foot-and-vehicle patrols, late-night transport/escort service, 24-hour emergency telephones, lighted pathways/sidewalks, controlled dormitory access (key, security card, etc).

TRANSFER AND INTERNATIONAL STUDENTS

Transfer students: May apply for admission for the following academic terms: Fall, Spring. Applicants do not need a minimum number of credits to apply. For fall 2005: Transfer applications received: 251. Transfer applicants offered admission: 193. Transfer applicants enrolled: 128. **International students:** Number of foreign undergraduates: 49 (6% of student body). Number of countries represented: 10. Minimum TOEFL score required: 550 (paper); 213 (computer).

Mount St. Mary's College

- **Address:** 12001 Chalon Road, Los Angeles, CA 90049
- **Website:** http://www.msmc.la.edu
- **Private; Religious affiliation:** Roman Catholic
- **Enrollment:** 1,470 full-time; 510 part-time

KEY STATS

✔ **U.S News College Ranking:** 22, Universities–Master's (West)
✔ **SAT Score (25th/75th percentile):** 930-1108
✔ **Tuition:** 2006-2007: $24,150

Selectivity: Selective	**Room/board:** $8,747
Acceptance rate: 85%	**Average debt:** N/A
Student/faculty ratio: 20/1	**Proportion who borrowed:** N/A

UNDERGRADUATE STUDENT BODY STATS

2005-2006 enrollment: 1,470 full-time; 510 part-time. Men: 6%; women: 94%. **Ethnic makeup:** African American: 10%; American-Indian: 1%; Asian American: 20%; Hispanic: 44%; White: 25%; International: 1%. **Religious preference:** Roman Catholic: 48%; Protestant: 10%; Jewish: 1%; No preference: 1%; Unknown: 39%; Other: 1%.

ADMISSIONS FACTS AND FIGURES

Phone: (310) 954-4250. **Email:** admissions@msmc.la.edu. **Website:** http://www.msmc.la.edu. **Application deadlines for fall 2007:** Regular decision: February 15. Early decision: Not offered. Early action: Send application by: December 1; Decision sent by: January 1. Admission can be deferred. **Application fee:** $40. Common application is accepted. **To apply online, go to:** http://www.msmc.la.edu/admissions/applyingtoMSMC/apply_online.htm. **Admissions requirements/recommendations:** High school units required (recommended): English: 4 (4); Mathematics: 3 (4); Science: 2 (3); Foreign language: 2 (3); Social studies: 2 (3); History: 2 (3); Academic electives: 2 (3); Total units: 25 (30). Tests: The college uses SAT or ACT scores in admissions decisions. Either SAT or ACT required. For admission to the fall 2007 entering class, the school will accept: ACT with writing, ACT without writing. Campus visit: Recommended. Admissions interview: Recommended. Off-campus interview: May be arranged. **Factors that count in admissions decisions:** *Academic:* Secondary school record: Very important. Class rank: Considered. Letters of recommendation: Important. Standardized test scores: Very important. Essay: Very important. *Nonacademic:* Interview: Considered. Extracurricular activities: Considered. Talent/ability: Considered. Character/personal qualities: Considered. Alumni/ae relationship: Considered. Geographical residence: Considered. State residency: Not considered. Religious affiliation/commitment: Not considered. Minority status: Not considered. Volunteer work: Considered. Work experience: Considered. **Other schools with the greatest overlap in applicants:** California State University–Long Beach; California State University–Los Angeles; California State University–Northridge; Loyola Marymount University; University of California–Los Angeles. **Admissions statistics for the fall 2005 entering class:** Total applicants: 1,035. Total accepted: 881. Freshmen enrolled: 372; 7% were from out of state. Accepted through early-decision or early-action plans: 51%. Overall acceptance rate: 85%. Non-early acceptance rate: 82%. **Credentials of fall 2005 freshmen:** 31% ranked in the top 10 percent of their high school class; 64% were in the top 25 percent, and 93% were in the top half. (Proportion submitting class standing: 50%.) **Average high school grade point average:** 3.5. **First-year students who submitted SAT scores:** 94%. Scores (25/75 percentile): Verbal: 470-560, Math: 460-548, Combined: 930-1108. **First-year students submitting ACT scores:** 6%. Scores (25/75 percentile): English: N/A, Math: N/A, Composite: N/A.

ACADEMICS

Year founded: 1925. **Academic calendar:** Semester. **Degrees offered:** associate, bachelor's, master's, doctorate. **Most popular majors:** 28% nursing, 20% sociology, 13% business/commerce, 8% liberal arts and sciences studies, and humanities, 8% psychology. **Major fields of study:** area, ethnic, cultural, and gender studies; biological and biomedical sciences; business, management, marketing, and related support services; education; English language and literature/letters; foreign languages, literatures, and linguistics; health professions and related clinical sciences; history; liberal arts and sciences studies, and humanities; mathematics and statistics; philosophy and religious studies; physical sciences; psychology; public administration and social service professions; social sciences; visual and performing arts. **Areas**

of required coursework: arts/fine arts, mathematics, English (including composition), philosophy, foreign languages, sciences (biological or physical), history, social science. **Special academic programs:** cooperative (work-study plan) program, cross-registration, double major, honors program, independent study, internships, student-designed major, study abroad, teacher certificate program, weekend college. **Faculty and instruction (2005-2006):** Total instructional faculty: 72 full-time, 225 part-time (24% men; 76% women; 22% minorities). Full-time faculty with Ph.D. or other terminal degree: 69%. Student/faculty ratio: 20/1. Classes of fewer than 20 students: 61%; of 20 to 49 students: 38%; of 50 or more students: 1%. **Advanced Placement and International Baccalaureate credit:** AP tests may be used for: Credit and/or placement. Scores accepted: 3, 4, 5. **Freshmen returning for sophomore year:** 76%. **Graduation rates:** Four-year: 43%; five-year: 54%; six-year: 61%.

COSTS AND FINANCIAL AID

Financial aid office: (310) 954-4191. **Expenses (2006-2007):** Tuition and fees 2006-2007: $24,150; room/board: $8,747. Estimated books and supplies: $1,046; transportation: $722; personal expenses: $1,794. **Financial aid:** Priority filing date for institution's financial aid form: March 1; deadline: May 15.

CAMPUS LIFE AND EXTRACURRICULAR ACTIVITIES

Campus housing available: women's dorms. Students who live in college-owned, operated, or affiliated housing: 49%. Activities include: choral groups, dance, drama/theater, literary magazine, music ensembles, student government, student newspaper, yearbook. Number of fraternities: 0; sororities: 1. Average proportion of students who stay on campus on weekends: 10%. **Sports program (2005-2006):** Member of NCAA I. *Men's intercollegiate varsity sports:* baseball, basketball, cross-country, golf, lacrosse, soccer, tennis, track and field (indoor), track and field (outdoor). *Women's intercollegiate varsity sports:* basketball, cross-country, golf, lacrosse, soccer, tennis, track and field (indoor), track and field (outdoor).

SERVICES AND FACILITIES

Basic services: health service, health insurance. **Remedial assistance:** reading, math, writing, study skills. **Counseling services:** career, academic, psychological. **For learning-disabled students:** School does not offer a structured program with separate admission and additional fees. Services include: remedial math, remedial English, remedial reading, learning center, extended time for tests, tutors, other testing accomodations. **Library:** Number of titles: 130,000; number of current serial subscriptions: 15,700. **Information technology resources:** Students are not required to lease or own a computer. School has a wireless network. Approximate number of users that can be accommodated: 600. Proportion of college-owned housing units wired for high-speed internet access: 100%. **Campus safety:** Security services offered: controlled dormitory access (key, security card, etc).

TRANSFER AND INTERNATIONAL STUDENTS

Transfer students: May apply for admission for the following academic terms: Fall, Spring. Applicants need a minimum number of credits to apply. For fall 2005: Transfer applications received: 370. Transfer applicants offered admission: 135. Transfer applicants enrolled: 63. **International students:** Number of foreign undergraduates: 16 (1% of student body). Minimum TOEFL score required: 550 (paper); 213 (computer).

National Hispanic University

- **Address:** 14271 Story Road, San Jose, CA 95127-3823
- **Website:** http://www.nhu.edu
- **Private**
- **Enrollment:** N/A

KEY STATS

✔ **U.S News College Ranking:** fourth tier, Liberal Arts Colleges
✔ **SAT or ACT Score (25th/75th percentile):** N/A
✔ **Tuition:** 2005-2006: $3,914

Selectivity: Selective	**Room/board:** N/A
Acceptance rate: N/A	**Average debt:** N/A
Student/faculty ratio: N/A	**Proportion who borrowed:** N/A

National University

■ **Address:** 11255 N. Torrey Pines Road, La Jolla, CA 92037
■ **Website:** http://www.nu.edu
■ **Private**
■ **Enrollment:** 1,631 full-time; 4,890 part-time

KEY STATS

✔ **U.S News College Ranking:** Unranked, Universities–Master's (West)
✔ **SAT or ACT Score (25th/75th percentile):** N/A
✔ **Tuition:** 2005-2006: $8,412

Selectivity: N/A	Room/board: N/A
Acceptance rate: N/A	Average debt: $23,432
Student/faculty ratio: 13/1	Proportion who borrowed: 79%

UNDERGRADUATE STUDENT BODY STATS

2005-2006 enrollment: 1,631 full-time; 4,890 part-time. Men: 44%; women: 56%. **Ethnic makeup:** African American: 12%; American-Indian: 1%; Asian American: 9%; Hispanic: 18%; White: 58%; International: 1%.

ADMISSIONS FACTS AND FIGURES

Phone: (800) 628-8648. **Email:** advisor@nu.edu. **Website:** http://www.nu.edu. **Application deadlines for fall 2007:** Regular decision: Rolling. Early decision: Not offered. Early action: Not offered. Admission can be deferred. **Application fee:** $60. Common application is not accepted. **To apply online, go to:** http://www.nu.edu/Admissions/ApplyOnline.html. **Admissions requirements/recommendations:** High school units required (recommended): English: 0 (0); Mathematics: 0 (0); Science: 0 (0); Foreign language: 0 (0); Social studies: 0 (0); History: 0 (0); Academic electives: 0 (0); Total units: 0 (0). Tests: The college does not use SAT or ACT scores in admissions decisions. Neither SAT nor ACT required. Campus visit: Recommended. Admissions interview: Required. Off-campus interview: May be arranged. **Factors that count in admissions decisions:** *Academic:* Secondary school record: Important. Class rank: Considered. Letters of recommendation: Considered. Standardized test scores: Considered. Essay: Not considered. *Nonacademic:* Interview: Very important. Extracurricular activities: Not considered. Talent/ability: Not considered. Character/personal qualities: Considered. Alumni/ae relationship: Not considered. Geographical residence: Not considered. State residency: Not considered. Religious affiliation/commitment: Not considered. Minority status: Not considered. Volunteer work: Not considered. Work experience: Considered. **Other schools with the greatest overlap in applicants:** California State University–Los Angeles; Chapman University; University of California–San Diego; University of San Diego. **Admissions statistics for the fall 2005 entering class:** Total applicants: 1,767. Freshmen enrolled: 685; 8% were from out of state.

ACADEMICS

Year founded: 1971. **Academic calendar:** Other. **Degrees offered:** certificate, associate, bachelor's, post-bachelor's certificate, master's. **Most popular majors:** 32% business, management, marketing, and related support services, 16% multi/interdisciplinary studies, 14% psychology, 13% computer and information sciences and support services, 9% security and protective services. **Major fields of study:** area, ethnic, cultural, and gender studies; business, management, marketing, and related support services; communication, journalism, and related programs; computer and information sciences and support services; education; engineering; English language and literature/letters; health professions and related clinical sciences; legal professions and studies; liberal arts and sciences studies, and humanities; mathematics and statistics; multi/interdisciplinary studies; physical sciences; psychology; security and protective services; visual and performing arts. **Areas of required coursework:** arts/fine arts, humanities, computer literacy, mathematics, English (including composition), foreign languages, sciences (biological or physical), history, social science. **Pre-professional programs:** pre-law, other. **Special academic programs (% participation):** accelerated program (100%), distance learning, double major, dual enrollment, English as a Second Language (ESL), independent study, internships, liberal arts/career combination, teacher certificate program. **Teacher certification offered in:** early childhood, special education, elementary, middle/junior high, secondary, bilingual/bicultural. **Reserve Officers Training Corps (ROTC):** Navy ROTC: Offered at cooperating institution (SDSU); Air Force ROTC: Offered at cooperating institution (SDSU). **Faculty and instruction (2005-2006):** Total instructional faculty: 209 full-time, 2,676 part-time (53% men; 47% women; 24% minorities). Full-time faculty with Ph.D. or other terminal degree: 82%. Student/faculty ratio: 13/1. Classes of fewer than 20 students: 84%; of 20 to 49 students: 16%. **Advanced Placement and International Baccalaureate credit:** International Baccalaureate exams may be used for: Credit only. **Freshmen returning for sophomore year:** 94%. **Graduation rates:** Four-year: 50%; five-year: 50%; six-year: 62%.

COSTS AND FINANCIAL AID

Financial aid office: (858) 642-8500. **Expenses (2005-2006):** Tuition and fees 2005-2006: $8,412; room/board: N/A. Estimated books and supplies: $1,104; transportation: $1,120; personal expenses: $2,600. **Financial aid:** In 2005-2006, 85% of undergraduates applied for financial aid. Of those, 68% were determined to have financial need; Average financial aid package (proportion receiving): $5,785 (63%). Average amount of gift aid, such as scholarships or grants (proportion receiving): $1,325 (13%). Average amount of self-help aid, such as work study or loans (proportion receiving): $4,506 (59%). Average need-based loan (excluding PLUS or other private loans): $3,574. Among students who received need-based aid, the average percentage of need met: 82%. Among students who received aid based on merit, the average award (and the proportion receiving): $0 (0%). The average athletic scholarship (and the proportion receiving): $0 (0%). Average amount of debt of borrowers graduating in 2005: $23,432. Proportion who borrowed: 79%.

CAMPUS LIFE AND EXTRACURRICULAR ACTIVITIES

Clubs and organizations: Number of student organizations: 0. Activities include: literary magazine, television station. Number of fraternities: 0; sororities: 0.

SERVICES AND FACILITIES

Basic services: nonremedial tutoring. **Remedial assistance:** reading, math, writing, study skills. **Counseling services:** career, military, veteran student, academic. **For learning-disabled students:** School does not offer a structured program with separate admission and additional fees. Total undergraduates in learning-disabled program or receiving services: 30. Services include: remedial math, remedial English, reading machines, tape recorders, videotaped classes, diagnostic testing service, untimed tests, note-taking services, readers, extended time for tests, tutors. **Library:** Number of titles: 247,528; number of current serial subscriptions: 19,348. **Information technology resources:** Students are not required to lease or own a computer. Number of campus computers available to all students: 2,152. School has a wireless network. Approximate number of users that can be accommodated: 30. **Campus safety:** Security services offered: 24-hour foot-and-vehicle patrols, late-night transport/escort service, 24-hour emergency telephones, lighted pathways/sidewalks.

TRANSFER AND INTERNATIONAL STUDENTS

Transfer students: May apply for admission for the following academic terms: Fall, Winter, Spring, Summer. Applicants do not need a minimum number of credits to apply. For fall 2005: Transfer applications received: 1,333. Transfer applicants enrolled: 1,077. **International students:** Number of foreign undergraduates: 61 (1% of student body). Number of countries represented: 76. Minimum TOEFL score required: 550 (paper); 213 (computer). Average TOEFL score: 550 (paper).

New College of California

■ **Address:** 50 Fell Street, San Francisco, CA 94102
■ **Website:** http://www.newcollege.edu
■ **Private**
■ **Enrollment:** N/A

KEY STATS

✔ **U.S News College Ranking:** fourth tier, Universities–Master's (West)
✔ **SAT or ACT Score (25th/75th percentile):** N/A
✔ **Tuition:** N/A

Selectivity: Less selective	Room/board: N/A
Acceptance rate: N/A	Average debt: N/A
Student/faculty ratio: N/A	Proportion who borrowed: N/A

Notre Dame de Namur University

- **Address:** 1500 Ralston Avenue, Belmont, CA 94002-1908
- **Website:** http://www.ndnu.edu
- **Private; Religious affiliation:** Catholic
- **Enrollment:** 631 full-time; 259 part-time

KEY STATS

✔ **U.S News College Ranking:** 41, Universities–Master's (West)
✔ **SAT Score (25th/75th percentile):** 880-1080
✔ **Tuition:** 2006-2007: $23,850

Selectivity: Less selective	**Room/board:** $10,380
Acceptance rate: 96%	**Average debt:** $17,844
Student/faculty ratio: 13/1	**Proportion who borrowed:** 79%

UNDERGRADUATE STUDENT BODY STATS

2005-2006 enrollment: 631 full-time; 259 part-time. Men: 37%; women: 63%. **Ethnic makeup:** African American: 5%; American-Indian: 1%; Asian American: 15%; Hispanic: 22%; White: 52%; International: 4%. **Religious preference:** Protestant: 15%; Jewish: 1%; Muslim: 1%; Hindu: 1%; Buddhist: 1%; No preference: 31%; Catholic: 47%; Other: 3%.

ADMISSIONS FACTS AND FIGURES

Phone: (650) 508-3600. **Email:** admissions@ndnu.edu. **Website:** http://www.ndnu.edu. **Application deadlines for fall 2007:** Regular decision: Rolling. Early decision: Not offered. Early action: Send application by: December 1; Decision sent by: December 15. Admission can be deferred. **Application fee:** $40. Common application is accepted. **To apply online, go to:** https://www.applyweb.com/aw?cnd. **Admissions requirements/recommendations:** High school units required (recommended): English: 4; Mathematics: 2 (3); Science: 1 (2); Foreign language: 2 (3); Social studies: 2; History: 1; Academic electives: 3; Total units: 15 (10). Tests: The college uses SAT or ACT scores in admissions decisions. Either SAT or ACT required. For admission to the fall 2007 entering class, the school will accept: ACT with writing. Campus visit: Recommended. Admissions interview: Recommended. Off-campus interview: May be arranged. **Factors that count in admissions decisions:** *Academic:* Secondary school record: Very important. Class rank: Important. Letters of recommendation: Important. Standardized test scores: Important. Essay: Important. *Nonacademic:* Interview: Considered. Extracurricular activities: Important. Talent/ability: Important. Character/personal qualities: Very important. Alumni/ae relationship: Not considered. Geographical residence: Not considered. State residency: Not considered. Religious affiliation/commitment: Not considered. Minority status: Not considered. Volunteer work: Important. Work experience: Considered. **Other schools with the greatest overlap in applicants:** Dominican University of California; San Francisco State University; San Jose State University; St. Mary's College of California; University of California–Berkeley. **Admissions statistics for the fall 2005 entering class:** Total applicants: 642. Total accepted: 619. Freshmen enrolled: 145; 30% were from out of state. Accepted through early-decision or early-action plans: 10%. Overall acceptance rate: 96%. **Size of waiting list:** 0 applicants; enrolled from waiting list: 0. **Credentials of fall 2005 freshmen:** 17% ranked in the top 10 percent of their high school class; 40% were in the top 25 percent, and 66% were in the top half. (Proportion submitting class standing: 50%.) **Average high school grade point average:** 3.0. **First-year students who submitted SAT scores:** 88%. Scores (25/75 percentile): Verbal: 440-530, Math: 440-550, Combined: 880-1080. **First-year students submitting ACT scores:** 21%. Scores (25/75 percentile): English: N/A, Math: N/A, Composite: 16-24.

ACADEMICS

Year founded: 1851. **Academic calendar:** Semester. **Degrees offered:** certificate, bachelor's, post-bachelor's certificate, master's. **Most popular majors:** 28% business administration and management, 14% human services, 12% liberal arts and sciences/liberal studies, 12% psychology, 10% biology/biological sciences. **Major fields of study:** biological and biomedical sciences; business, management, marketing, and related support services; communication, journalism, and related programs; computer and information sciences and support services; English language and literature/letters; health professions and related clinical sciences; history; liberal arts and sciences studies, and humanities; parks, recreation, leisure, and fitness studies; philosophy and religious studies; psychology; public administration and social service professions; social sciences; visual and performing arts. **Areas of required coursework:** arts/fine arts, humanities, computer literacy, mathe-

matics, English (including composition), philosophy, foreign languages, sciences (biological or physical), history, social science, other. **Pre-professional programs:** pre-law, pre-dentistry, pre-medicine, pre-veterinary science, pre-pharmacy, other. **Special academic programs:** accelerated program, double major, English as a Second Language (ESL), exchange student program (domestic), independent study, internships, liberal arts/career combination, student-designed major, study abroad, teacher certificate program. **Teacher certification offered in:** special education, elementary, middle/junior high, secondary, bilingual/bicultural. **Faculty and instruction (2005-2006):** Total instructional faculty: 50 full-time, 93 part-time (42% men; 58% women; 17% minorities). Full-time faculty with Ph.D. or other terminal degree: 98%. Student/faculty ratio: 13/1. Classes of fewer than 20 students: 68%; of 20 to 49 students: 32%; of 50 or more students: 0%. **Advanced Placement and International Baccalaureate credit:** AP tests may be used for: Credit and/or placement. Scores accepted: 3, 4, 5. International Baccalaureate exams may be used for: Credit and/or placement. **Freshmen returning for sophomore year:** 76%. **Graduation rates:** Four-year: 39%; five-year: 49%; six-year: 51%.

COSTS AND FINANCIAL AID

Financial aid office: (650) 508-3600. **Expenses (2006-2007):** Tuition and fees 2006-2007: $23,850; room/board: $10,380. Estimated books and supplies: $1,330; transportation: $646; personal expenses: $2,454. **Financial aid:** Priority filing date for institution's financial aid form: March 2. In 2005-2006, 87% of undergraduates applied for financial aid. Of those, 69% were determined to have financial need; 9% had their need fully met. Average financial aid package (proportion receiving): $18,378 (69%). Average amount of gift aid, such as scholarships or grants (proportion receiving): $12,643 (67%). Average amount of self-help aid, such as work study or loans (proportion receiving): $4,896 (58%). Average need-based loan (excluding PLUS or other private loans): $4,026. Among students who received need-based aid, the average percentage of need met: 64%. Among students who received aid based on merit, the average award (and the proportion receiving): $7,675 (14%). The average athletic scholarship (and the proportion receiving): $8,613 (7%). Average amount of debt of borrowers graduating in 2005: $17,844. Proportion who borrowed: 79%.

CAMPUS LIFE AND EXTRACURRICULAR ACTIVITIES

Campus housing available (% using): coed dorms (75%), apartment for single students (25%). Students who live in college-owned, operated, or affiliated housing: 47%. **Student employment:** During the 2005-2006 academic year, 10% of undergraduates worked on campus. Average per-year earnings: $2,000. **Clubs and organizations:** Number of student organizations: 12. Activities include: choral groups, dance, drama/theater, literary magazine, music ensembles, musical theater, opera, student government, student newspaper, symphony orchestra, television station. Number of fraternities: 0; sororities: 0. Average proportion of students who stay on campus on weekends: 90%. **Sports program (2005-2006):** Member of NAIA. *Men's intercollegiate varsity sports:* basketball, cross-country, golf, lacrosse, soccer, track and field (outdoor). *Women's intercollegiate varsity sports:* basketball, cross-country, golf, soccer, softball, track and field (outdoor), volleyball.

SERVICES AND FACILITIES

Basic services: nonremedial tutoring, placement service, health service, health insurance. **Remedial assistance:** reading, math, writing, study skills. **Counseling services:** minority student, career, personal, academic, older student, psychological, religious. **For learning-disabled students:** School does not offer a structured program with separate admission and additional fees. Total undergraduates in learning-disabled program or receiving services: 53. Services include: remedial math, remedial reading, tape recorders, diagnostic testing service, untimed tests, note-taking services, oral tests, learning center, readers, extended time for tests, tutors, priority seating, texts on tape, other testing accomodations. **Library:** Number of titles: 89,963; number of current serial subscriptions: 13,500. **Information technology resources:** Students are not required to lease or own a computer. Number of campus computers available to all students: 150. School has a wireless network. Approximate number of users that can be accommodated: 300. Proportion of college-owned housing units wired for high-speed internet access: 100%. **Campus safety:** Security services offered: 24-hour foot-and-vehicle patrols, late-night transport/escort service, 24-hour emergency telephones, lighted pathways/sidewalks, controlled dormitory access (key, security card, etc).

TRANSFER AND INTERNATIONAL STUDENTS

Transfer students: May apply for admission for the following academic terms: Fall, Spring, Summer. Applicants need a minimum number of credits to apply. For fall 2005: Transfer applications received: 210. Transfer applicants offered admission: 209. Transfer applicants enrolled: 100. **International students:** Number of foreign undergraduates: 33 (4% of student body). Number of countries represented: 29. Minimum TOEFL score required: 500 (paper); 173 (computer). Average TOEFL score: 533 (paper).

Occidental College

- **Address:** 1600 Campus Road, Los Angeles, CA 90041-3314
- **Website:** http://www.oxy.edu
- **Private**
- **Enrollment:** 1,794 full-time; 25 part-time

KEY STATS

✔ **U.S News College Ranking:** 36, Liberal Arts Colleges
✔ **SAT Score (25th/75th percentile):** 1210-1380
✔ **Tuition:** 2006-2007: $33,644
   Selectivity: More selective   Room/board: $9,042
   Acceptance rate: 41%   Average debt: N/A
   Student/faculty ratio: 10/1   Proportion who borrowed: 52%

UNDERGRADUATE STUDENT BODY STATS

2005-2006 enrollment: 1,794 full-time; 25 part-time. Men: 43%; women: 57%. **Ethnic makeup:** African American: 6%; American-Indian: 1%; Asian American: 13%; Hispanic: 14%; White: 62%; International: 3%. **Religious preference:** Roman Catholic: 19%; Protestant: 35%; Jewish: 11%; Muslim: 1%; Buddhist: 2%; No preference: 1%; Other: 27%.

ADMISSIONS FACTS AND FIGURES

Phone: (800) 825-5262. **Email:** admission@oxy.edu. **Website:** http://www.oxy.edu. **Application deadlines for fall 2007:** Regular decision: January 10; decision sent by April 1. Early decision: Send application by: November 15; Decision sent by: December 15. Early action: Not offered. Admission can be deferred. **Application fee:** $50. Common application is accepted. **To apply online, go to:** http://www.oxy.edu/Apply.xml. **Admissions requirements/recommendations:** High school units required (recommended): English: (4); Mathematics: (4); Science: (3); Foreign language: (3); Social studies: (2); History: (2); Academic electives: (2); Total units: (20). Tests: The college uses SAT or ACT scores in admissions decisions. Either SAT or ACT required. For admission to the fall 2007 entering class, the school will accept: ACT with writing. Campus visit: Recommended. Admissions interview: Recommended. Off-campus interview: May be arranged. **Factors that count in admissions decisions:** *Academic:* Secondary school record: Very important. Class rank: Important. Letters of recommendation: Important. Standardized test scores: Important. Essay: Important. *Nonacademic:* Interview: Considered. Extracurricular activities: Very important. Talent/ability: Considered. Character/personal qualities: Important. Alumni/ae relationship: Considered. Geographical residence: Considered. State residency: Not considered. Religious affiliation/commitment: Not considered. Minority status: Considered. Volunteer work: Very important. Work experience: Very important. **Other schools with the greatest overlap in applicants:** Claremont McKenna College; Pomona College; University of California–Berkeley; University of California–Los Angeles; University of Southern California. **Admissions statistics for the fall 2005 entering class:** Total applicants: 5,114. Total accepted: 2,086. Freshmen enrolled: 436; 56% were from out of state. Accepted through early-decision or early-action plans: 9%. Overall acceptance rate: 41%. Early-decision acceptance rate: 38%. Non-early acceptance rate: 41%. **Size of waiting list:** 727 applicants; enrolled from waiting list: 24. **Credentials of fall 2005 freshmen:** 60% ranked in the top 10 percent of their high school class; 86% were in the top 25 percent, and 100% were in the top half. **First-year students who submitted SAT scores:** 86%. Scores (25/75 percentile): Verbal: 600-690, Math: 610-690, Combined: 1210-1380. **First-year students submitting ACT scores:** 14%. Scores (25/75 percentile): English: N/A, Math: N/A, Composite: 27-31.

ACADEMICS

Year founded: 1887. **Academic calendar:** Semester. **Degrees offered:** bachelor's, master's. **Most popular majors:** 11% economics, 11% psychology, 8% English language and literature/letters, 8% international relations and affairs, 8% visual and performing arts. **Major fields of study:** area, ethnic, cultural, and gender studies; biological and biomedical sciences; English language and literature/letters; foreign languages, literatures, and linguis-

tics; history; mathematics and statistics; natural resources and conservation; parks, recreation, leisure, and fitness studies; philosophy and religious studies; physical sciences; psychology; social sciences; visual and performing arts. **Areas of required coursework:** arts/fine arts, humanities, mathematics, English (including composition), foreign languages, sciences (biological or physical), history, social science. **Pre-professional programs:** pre-law, pre-dentistry, pre-medicine, pre-veterinary science, other. **Special academic programs (% participation):** cross-registration (3.2%), double major (8.2%), exchange student program (domestic) (5.9%), honors program (18%), independent study (58.8%), internships (16.5%), student-designed major (.7%), study abroad (26.5%). **Teacher certification offered in:** elementary, secondary. **Reserve Officers Training Corps (ROTC):** Army ROTC: Offered at cooperating institution (University of Southern California, University of California–Los Angeles); Air Force ROTC: Offered at cooperating institution (University of Southern California, University of California–Los Angeles). **Faculty and instruction (2005-2006):** Total instructional faculty: 148 full-time, 72 part-time (54% men; 46% women; 29% minorities). Full-time faculty with Ph.D. or other terminal degree: 94%. Student/faculty ratio: 10/1. Classes of fewer than 20 students: 64%; of 20 to 49 students: 35%; of 50 or more students: 1%. **Advanced Placement and International Baccalaureate credit:** AP tests may be used for: Credit and/or placement. Scores accepted: 4, 5. International Baccalaureate exams may be used for: Credit and/or placement. **Freshmen returning for sophomore year:** 92%. **Graduation rates:** Four-year: 78%; five-year: 81%; six-year: 84%. **Graduate study:** 25% of students pursue further study immediately upon graduation; 30% within one year. Fields in which graduates pursue further study: Master of Business Administration (MBA), 13%; law, 13%; medicine, 7%; dentistry, 1%; theology (or the seminary), 1%; education, 18%; arts and sciences, 47%; veterinary medicine, 1%.

COSTS AND FINANCIAL AID

Financial aid office: (323) 259-2548. **Expenses (2006-2007):** Tuition and fees 2006-2007: $33,644; room/board: $9,042. Estimated books and supplies: $914; transportation: $422; personal expenses: $1,300. **Financial aid:** Priority filing date for institution's financial aid form: February 1; deadline: February 1. In 2005-2006, 63% of undergraduates applied for financial aid. Of those, 55% were determined to have financial need; 99% had their need fully met. Average financial aid package (proportion receiving): $29,089 (55%). Average amount of gift aid, such as scholarships or grants (proportion receiving): $22,840 (54%). Average amount of self-help aid, such as work study or loans (proportion receiving): $7,315 (50%). Average need-based loan (excluding PLUS or other private loans): $5,607. Among students who received need-based aid, the average percentage of need met: 100%. Among students who received aid based on merit, the average award (and the proportion receiving): $16,180 (27%). The average athletic scholarship (and the proportion receiving): $0 (0%). Proportion who borrowed: 52%.

CAMPUS LIFE AND EXTRACURRICULAR ACTIVITIES

Campus housing available (% using): coed dorms (96%), women's dorms (3%), fraternity housing (1%). Students who live in college-owned, operated, or affiliated housing: 70%. **Student employment:** During the 2005-2006 academic year, 10% of undergraduates worked on campus. **Clubs and organizations:** Number of student organizations: 109. Activities include: choral groups, concert band, dance, drama/theater, jazz band, literary magazine, music ensembles, musical theater, radio station, student government, student newspaper, student film society, symphony orchestra, yearbook. Number of fraternities: 3; sororities: 4. Proportion of men in fraternities: 6%; of women in sororities: 13%. Average proportion of students who stay on campus on weekends: 60%. **Sports program (2005-2006):** Member of NCAA III. *Men's intercollegiate varsity sports:* baseball, basketball, cross-country, football, soccer, swimming and diving, tennis, track and field (indoor), track and field (outdoor), water polo, mixed golf. *Women's intercollegiate varsity sports:* basketball, cross-country, soccer, softball, swimming and diving, tennis, track and field (indoor), track and field (outdoor), volleyball, water polo, mixed golf.

SERVICES AND FACILITIES

Basic services: nonremedial tutoring, women's center, health service, health insurance. **Counseling services:** minority student, career, personal, academic, psychological, birth control, religious. **For learning-disabled students:** School does not offer a structured program with separate admission and additional fees. Total undergraduates in learning-disabled program or receiving services: 65. Services include: tape recorders, learning center, extended time for tests, other testing accomodations, other. **Library:** Number of titles: 482,386; number of current serial subscriptions: 1,230. **Information**

technology resources: Students are not required to lease or own a computer. Number of campus computers available to all students: 300. School has a wireless network. Approximate number of users that can be accommodated: 1,800. Proportion of college-owned housing units wired for high-speed internet access: 100%. **Campus safety:** Security services offered: 24-hour foot-and-vehicle patrols, late-night transport/escort service, 24-hour emergency telephones, lighted pathways/sidewalks, controlled dormitory access (key, security card, etc).

TRANSFER AND INTERNATIONAL STUDENTS

Transfer students: May apply for admission for the following academic terms: Fall, Spring. Applicants need a minimum number of credits to apply. For fall 2005: Transfer applications received: 283. Transfer applicants offered admission: 66. Transfer applicants enrolled: 35. **International students:** Number of foreign undergraduates: 64 (3% of student body). Number of countries represented: 22. Minimum TOEFL score required: 600 (paper); 250 (computer).

Otis College of Art and Design

- ■ **Address:** 9045 Lincoln Boulevard, Los Angeles, CA 90045
- ■ **Website:** http://www.otis.edu
- ■ **Private**
- ■ **Enrollment:** 1,020 full-time; 20 part-time

KEY STATS

✔ **U.S News College Ranking:** Unranked Specialty School–Fine Arts
✔ **SAT Score (25th/75th percentile):** 860-1130
✔ **Tuition:** 2006-2007: $27,546

Selectivity: Less selective	**Room/board:** $9,000
Acceptance rate: 58%	**Average debt:** $29,717
Student/faculty ratio: 9/1	**Proportion who borrowed:** 78%

UNDERGRADUATE STUDENT BODY STATS

2005-2006 enrollment: 1,020 full-time; 20 part-time. Men: 35%; women: 65%. **Ethnic makeup:** African American: 3%; American-Indian: 1%; Asian American: 28%; Hispanic: 13%; White: 45%; International: 11%.

ADMISSIONS FACTS AND FIGURES

Phone: (310) 665-6820. **Email:** admissions@otis.edu. **Website:** http://www.otis.edu. **Application deadlines for fall 2007:** Regular decision: Rolling. Early decision: Not offered. Early action: Not offered. Admission cannot be deferred. **Application fee:** $50. Common application is not accepted. **Admissions requirements/recommendations:** High school units required (recommended): English: 4 (4); Mathematics: 3 (4); Science: 2 (4); Foreign language: (2); Social studies: 1 (2); History: 2 (3); Total units: 13 (23). Tests: The college uses SAT or ACT scores in admissions decisions. Either SAT or ACT required. For admission to the fall 2007 entering class, the school will accept: ACT with writing, ACT without writing. Campus visit: Neither required nor recommended. Admissions interview: Neither required nor recommended. Off-campus interview: Not available. **Factors that count in admissions decisions: *Academic:*** Secondary school record: Very important. Class rank: Not considered. Letters of recommendation: Considered. Standardized test scores: Important. Essay: Important. *Nonacademic:* Interview: Considered. Extracurricular activities: Considered. Talent/ability: Very important. Character/personal qualities: Considered. Alumni/ae relationship: Considered. Geographical residence: Not considered. State residency: Not considered. Religious affiliation/commitment: Not considered. Minority status: Not considered. Volunteer work: Considered. Work experience: Considered. **Admissions statistics for the fall 2005 entering class:** Overall acceptance rate: 58%. **Average high school grade point average:** 3.2. **First-year students who submitted SAT scores:** 79%. Scores (25/75 percentile): Verbal: 420-550, Math: 440-580, Combined: 860-1130. **First-year students submitting ACT scores:** 8%. Scores (25/75 percentile): English: N/A, Math: N/A, Composite: 17-22.

ACADEMICS

Year founded: 1918. **Academic calendar:** Semester. **Degrees offered:** bachelor's, master's. **Most popular majors:** 100% visual and performing arts. **Major fields of study:** architecture and related services; communication, journalism, and related programs; communications technologies/technicians and support services; visual and performing arts. **Areas of required**

coursework: arts/fine arts, computer literacy, mathematics, English (including composition), sciences (biological or physical), social science. **Special academic programs:** English as a Second Language (ESL), exchange student program (domestic), honors program, independent study, internships, study abroad. **Faculty and instruction (2005-2006):** Total instructional faculty: 51 full-time, 226 part-time (54% men; 46% women; 19% minorities). Full-time faculty with Ph.D. or other terminal degree: 41%. Student/faculty ratio: 9/1. Classes of fewer than 20 students: 78%; of 20 to 49 students: 20%; of 50 or more students: 2%. **Freshmen returning for sophomore year:** 72%. **Graduation rates:** Six-year: 39%.

COSTS AND FINANCIAL AID

Financial aid office: (310) 665-6880. **Expenses (2006-2007):** Tuition and fees 2006-2007: $27,546; room/board: $9,000. Estimated books and supplies: $2,400; transportation: $2,600; personal expenses: $300. **Financial aid:** Priority filing date for institution's financial aid form: February 15. In 2005-2006, 78% of undergraduates applied for financial aid. Of those, 75% were determined to have financial need; 2% had their need fully met. Average financial aid package (proportion receiving): $14,663 (75%). Average amount of gift aid, such as scholarships or grants (proportion receiving): $8,926 (75%). Average amount of self-help aid, such as work study or loans (proportion receiving): $4,337 (47%). Average need-based loan (excluding PLUS or other private loans): $3,323. Among students who received need-based aid, the average percentage of need met: 56%. Among students who received aid based on merit, the average award (and the proportion receiving): $2,734 (9%). Average amount of debt of borrowers graduating in 2005: $29,717. Proportion who borrowed: 78%.

CAMPUS LIFE AND EXTRACURRICULAR ACTIVITIES

Campus housing available: apartment for single students. Activities include: literary magazine, student government, student newspaper. Number of fraternities: 0; sororities: 0.

SERVICES AND FACILITIES

Basic services: health insurance. **Remedial assistance:** reading, writing, study skills. **Counseling services:** personal, veteran student, psychological. **Information technology resources:** Students are not required to lease or own a computer. School has a wireless network. **Campus safety:** Security services offered: 24-hour foot-and-vehicle patrols, 24-hour emergency telephones, lighted pathways/sidewalks.

TRANSFER AND INTERNATIONAL STUDENTS

Transfer students: May apply for admission for the following academic terms: Fall, Spring. Applicants need a minimum number of credits to apply. **International students:** Number of foreign undergraduates: 116 (11% of student body). Minimum TOEFL score required: 550 (paper); 213 (computer).

Pacific Union College

- ■ **Address:** One Angwin Avenue, Angwin, CA 94508
- ■ **Website:** http://www.puc.edu
- ■ **Private; Religious affiliation:** Seventh-day Adventist
- ■ **Enrollment:** 1,370 full-time; 146 part-time

KEY STATS

✔ **U.S News College Ranking:** 14, Comp. Colleges–Bachelor's (West)
✔ **SAT Score (25th/75th percentile):** 890-1170
✔ **Tuition:** 2006-2007: $20,265

Selectivity: Selective	**Room/board:** $5,652
Acceptance rate: 29%	**Average debt:** $24,200
Student/faculty ratio: 16/1	**Proportion who borrowed:** 72%

UNDERGRADUATE STUDENT BODY STATS

2005-2006 enrollment: 1,370 full-time; 146 part-time. Men: 47%; women: 53%. **Ethnic makeup:** African American: 4%; American-Indian: 1%; Asian American: 22%; Hispanic: 12%; White: 55%; International: 7%.

ADMISSIONS FACTS AND FIGURES

Phone: (707) 965-6336. **Email:** enroll@puc.edu. **Website:** http://www.puc.edu. **Application deadlines for fall 2007:** Regular decision: Rolling. Early decision: Not offered. Early action: Not offered. Admission can be deferred. **Application fee:** $30. Common application is not accepted.

To apply online, go to:
http://www.puc.edu/PUC/enrollment/application.shtml. **Admissions requirements/recommendations:** High school units required (recommended): English: 4; Mathematics: 2 (3); Science: 1 (3); Foreign language: (2); History: 1 (2); Total units: 8. Tests: The college does not use SAT or ACT scores in admissions decisions. Neither SAT nor ACT required. For admission to the fall 2007 entering class, the school will accept: ACT with writing, ACT without writing. Campus visit: Recommended. Admissions interview: Neither required nor recommended. Off-campus interview: May be arranged. **Factors that count in admissions decisions:** *Academic:* Secondary school record: Very important. Class rank: Not considered. Letters of recommendation: Very important. Standardized test scores: Considered. Essay: Not considered. *Nonacademic:* Interview: Considered. Extracurricular activities: Considered. Talent/ability: Not considered. Character/personal qualities: Important. Alumni/ae relationship: Not considered. Geographical residence: Not considered. State residency: Not considered. Religious affiliation/commitment: Considered. Minority status: Not considered. Volunteer work: Not considered. Work experience: Not considered. **Other schools with the greatest overlap in applicants:** La Sierra University; Walla Walla College. **Admissions statistics for the fall 2005 entering class:** Total applicants: 2,174. Total accepted: 640. Freshmen enrolled: 348; 17% were from out of state. Overall acceptance rate: 29%. **Average high school grade point average:** 3.3. **First-year students who submitted SAT scores:** 52%. Scores (25/75 percentile): Verbal: 450-590, Math: 440-580, Combined: 890-1170. **First-year students submitting ACT scores:** 30%. Scores (25/75 percentile): English: 16-24, Math: 17-24, Composite: 18-24.

ACADEMICS
Year founded: 1882. **Academic calendar:** Quarter. **Degrees offered:** associate, bachelor's, master's. **Most popular majors:** 15% business, management, marketing, and related support services, 14% education, 14% health professions and related clinical sciences, 10% biological and biomedical sciences, 9% visual and performing arts. **Major fields of study:** biological and biomedical sciences; business, management, marketing, and related support services; communication, journalism, and related programs; computer and information sciences and support services; education; English language and literature/letters; foreign languages, literatures, and linguistics; health professions and related clinical sciences; history; mathematics and statistics; parks, recreation, leisure, and fitness studies; physical sciences; psychology; public administration and social service professions; social sciences; theology and religious vocations; transportation and materials moving; visual and performing arts. **Areas of required coursework:** arts/fine arts, computer literacy, mathematics, English (including composition), philosophy, sciences (biological or physical), history, social science. **Pre-professional programs:** pre-law, pre-dentistry, pre-medicine, pre-theology, pre-veterinary science, pre-optometry, pre-pharmacy. **Special academic programs (% participation):** cooperative (work-study plan) program, double major, external degree program, honors program (5%), independent study (6%), internships (14%), study abroad (5%), teacher certificate program (3%). **Teacher certification offered in:** early childhood, elementary, middle/junior high, secondary. **Cooperative education programs:** education, social/behavioral science. **Faculty and instruction (2005-2006):** Total instructional faculty: 80 full-time, 19 part-time (60% men; 40% women; 6% minorities). Full-time faculty with Ph.D. or other terminal degree: 61%. Student/faculty ratio: 16/1. Classes of fewer than 20 students: 64%; of 20 to 49 students: 32%; of 50 or more students: 4%. **Advanced Placement and International Baccalaureate credit:** AP tests may be used for: Credit only. Scores accepted: 3. **Freshmen returning for sophomore year:** 69%. **Graduation rates:** Four-year: 8%; five-year: 20%; six-year: 23%.

COSTS AND FINANCIAL AID
Financial aid office: (707) 965-7200. **Expenses (2006-2007):** Tuition and fees 2006-2007: $20,265; room/board: $5,652. Estimated books and supplies: $1,314; transportation: $744; personal expenses: $2,088. **Financial aid:** Priority filing date for institution's financial aid form: March 2. In 2005-2006, 94% of undergraduates applied for financial aid. Of those, 62% were determined to have financial need; 43% had their need fully met. Average financial aid package (proportion receiving): $14,150 (62%). Average amount of gift aid, such as scholarships or grants (proportion receiving): $6,589 (62%). Average amount of self-help aid, such as work study or loans (proportion receiving): $1,200 (52%). Among students who received need-based aid, the average percentage of need met: 67%. Average amount of debt of borrowers graduating in 2005: $24,200. Proportion who borrowed: 72%.

CAMPUS LIFE AND EXTRACURRICULAR ACTIVITIES
Campus housing available (% using): women's dorms (38%), men's dorms (35%), apartments for married students. Students who live in college-owned, operated, or affiliated housing: 83%. **Student employment:** During the 2005-2006 academic year, 52% of undergraduates worked on campus. Average per-year earnings: $2,000. **Clubs and organizations:** Number of student organizations: 37. Activities include: choral groups, concert band, drama/theater, jazz band, literary magazine, music ensembles, musical theater, radio station, student government, student newspaper, symphony orchestra, yearbook. Number of fraternities: 0; sororities: 0. Average proportion of students who stay on campus on weekends: 45%. **Sports program (2005-2006):** Member of NAIA. *Men's intercollegiate varsity sports:* basketball, cross-country, golf. *Women's intercollegiate varsity sports:* basketball, cross-country, volleyball.

SERVICES AND FACILITIES
Basic services: nonremedial tutoring, day care, health service. **Remedial assistance:** reading, math, writing, study skills. **Counseling services:** minority student, career, personal, academic, psychological, birth control, religious. **For learning-disabled students:** School does not offer a structured program with separate admission and additional fees. Total undergraduates in learning-disabled program or receiving services: 119. Services include: remedial math, remedial English, reading machines, tape recorders, diagnostic testing service, note-taking services, oral tests, learning center, readers, extended time for tests, tutors, priority seating, texts on tape, other testing accomodations, other. **Library:** Number of titles: 176,008; number of current serial subscriptions: 805. **Information technology resources:** Students are not required to lease or own a computer. Number of campus computers available to all students: 195. School has a wireless network. Approximate number of users that can be accommodated: 1,000. Proportion of college-owned housing units wired for high-speed internet access: 100%. **Campus safety:** Security services offered: 24-hour foot-and-vehicle patrols, late-night transport/escort service, lighted pathways/sidewalks.

TRANSFER AND INTERNATIONAL STUDENTS
Transfer students: May apply for admission for the following academic terms: Fall, Winter, Spring, Summer. Applicants need a minimum number of credits to apply. For fall 2005: Transfer applications received: 221. Transfer applicants offered admission: 170. Transfer applicants enrolled: 148. **International students:** Number of foreign undergraduates: 93 (7% of student body). Number of countries represented: 18. Minimum TOEFL score required: 525 (paper); 195 (computer).

Patten University

- **Address:** 2433 Coolidge Avenue, Oakland, CA 94601
- **Website:** http://www.patten.edu/
- **Private; Religious affiliation:** Independent Christian
- **Enrollment:** 272 full-time; 379 part-time

KEY STATS
✔ **U.S News College Ranking:** third tier, Comp. Colleges–Bachelor's (West)
✔ **SAT Score (25th/75th percentile):** 1000-1200
✔ **Tuition:** 2006-2007: $11,880

Selectivity: Selective	**Room/board:** $6,160
Acceptance rate: 86%	**Average debt:** $9,191
Student/faculty ratio: 14/1	**Proportion who borrowed:** 75%

UNDERGRADUATE STUDENT BODY STATS
2005-2006 enrollment: 272 full-time; 379 part-time. Men: 61%; women: 39%. **Ethnic makeup:** African American: 25%; Asian American: 21%; Hispanic: 17%; White: 37%. **Religious preference:** Roman Catholic: 3%; Protestant: 94%; No preference: 2%; Unknown: 1%.

ADMISSIONS FACTS AND FIGURES
Phone: (877) 472-8836. **Email:** Admissions@patten.edu. **Website:** http://www.patten.edu/. **Application deadlines for fall 2007:** Regular decision: July 31. Early decision: Not offered. Early action: Not offered. Admission can be deferred. **Application fee:** $30. Common application is accepted. **Admissions requirements/recommendations:** High school units required (recommended): English: 4 (4); Mathematics: 3 (3); Science: 3 (2);

Foreign language: 2 (2); Social studies: 3 (4); History: 3 (4); Academic electives: 4 (4); Total units: 23 (26). Tests: The college uses SAT or ACT scores in admissions decisions. Either SAT or ACT required. For admission to the fall 2007 entering class, the school will accept: ACT with writing. Campus visit: Recommended. Admissions interview: Recommended. Off-campus interview: May be arranged. **Factors that count in admissions decisions:** *Academic:* Secondary school record: Very important. Class rank: Important. Letters of recommendation: Very important. Standardized test scores: Important. Essay: Very important. *Nonacademic:* Interview: Considered. Extracurricular activities: Important. Talent/ability: Considered. Character/personal qualities: Very important. Alumni/ae relationship: Not considered. Geographical residence: Not considered. State residency: Not considered. Religious affiliation/commitment: Very important. Minority status: Not considered. Volunteer work: Important. Work experience: Important. **Other schools with the greatest overlap in applicants:** Bethany College; California State University–East Bay; San Francisco State University; Simpson University; Vanguard University of Southern California. **Admissions statistics for the fall 2005 entering class:** Total applicants: 85. Total accepted: 73. Freshmen enrolled: 59; 12% were from out of state. Overall acceptance rate: 86%. **Credentials of fall 2005 freshmen:** 21% ranked in the top 10 percent of their high school class; 33% were in the top 25 percent, and 77% were in the top half. (Proportion submitting class standing: 90%.) **Average high school grade point average:** 3.5. **First-year students who submitted SAT scores:** 89%. Scores (25/75 percentile): Verbal: 525-600, Math: 475-600, Combined: 1000-1200. **First-year students submitting ACT scores:** 6%. Scores (25/75 percentile): English: N/A-25, Math: N/A-25, Composite: 18-25.

ACADEMICS

Year founded: 1944. **Academic calendar:** Semester. **Degrees offered:** certificate, associate, bachelor's, post-bachelor's certificate, master's. **Most popular majors:** 37% business administration and management, 32% theology and religious vocations, 31% liberal arts and sciences/liberal studies. **Major fields of study:** business, management, marketing, and related support services; communication, journalism, and related programs; education; liberal arts and sciences studies, and humanities; psychology; theology and religious vocations; visual and performing arts. **Areas of required coursework:** arts/fine arts, humanities, computer literacy, mathematics, English (including composition), philosophy, sciences (biological or physical), history, social science, other. **Pre-professional programs:** pre-theology, other. **Special academic programs (% participation):** accelerated program (5%), independent study (3%), internships (100%), teacher certificate program (22%). **Teacher certification offered in:** early childhood, elementary, middle/junior high, secondary, bilingual/bicultural. **Cooperative education programs:** business, health professions, other. **Faculty and instruction (2005-2006):** Total instructional faculty: 22 full-time, 84 part-time (64% men; 36% women; 19% minorities). Full-time faculty with Ph.D. or other terminal degree: 68%. Student/faculty ratio: 14/1. Classes of fewer than 20 students: 76%; of 20 to 49 students: 24%. **Advanced Placement and International Baccalaureate credit:** AP tests may be used for: Credit and/or placement. Scores accepted: 3, 4, 5. International Baccalaureate exams may be used for: Credit and/or placement. **Freshmen returning for sophomore year:** 75%. **Graduation rates:** Six-year: 35%. **Graduate study:** 35% of students pursue further study immediately upon graduation; 53% within one year; 55% within five years. Fields in which graduates pursue further study: Master of Business Administration (MBA), 12%; law, 2%; theology (or the seminary), 37%; education, 37%; arts and sciences, 13%.

COSTS AND FINANCIAL AID

Financial aid office: (510) 261-8500. **Expenses (2006-2007):** Tuition and fees 2006-2007: $11,880; room/board: $6,160. Estimated books and supplies: $1,260; transportation: $738; personal expenses: $1,980. **Financial aid:** Priority filing date for institution's financial aid form: March 2. In 2005-2006, 95% of undergraduates applied for financial aid. Of those, 89% were determined to have financial need; 7% had their need fully met. Average financial aid package (proportion receiving): $6,692 (84%). Average amount of gift aid, such as scholarships or grants (proportion receiving): $5,439 (79%). Average amount of self-help aid, such as work study or loans (proportion receiving): $3,243 (41%). Average need-based loan (excluding PLUS or other private loans): $3,074. Among students who received need-based aid, the average percentage of need met: 41%. Among students who received aid based on merit, the average award (and the proportion receiving): $9,708 (11%). The average athletic scholarship (and the proportion receiving): $0 (0%). Average amount of debt of borrowers graduating in 2005: $9,191. Proportion who borrowed: 75%.

CAMPUS LIFE AND EXTRACURRICULAR ACTIVITIES

Campus housing available (% using): women's dorms (33%), men's dorms (21%), apartments for married students (29%), apartment for single students (0%), special housing for disabled students (2%). Students who live in college-owned, operated, or affiliated housing: 30%. **Student employment:** During the 2005-2006 academic year, 69% of undergraduates worked on campus. Average per-year earnings: $4,480. Activities include: choral groups, jazz band, literary magazine, music ensembles, student government, student newspaper, symphony orchestra, yearbook. Number of fraternities: 0; sororities: 0. Average proportion of students who stay on campus on weekends: 75%. **Sports program (2005-2006):** Member of NAIA. *Women's intercollegiate varsity sports:* softball.

SERVICES AND FACILITIES

Basic services: nonremedial tutoring, placement service, health insurance, other. **Remedial assistance:** math, writing, study skills. **Counseling services:** personal, academic, older student, psychological, religious. **For learning-disabled students:** School does not offer a structured program with separate admission and additional fees. Total undergraduates in learning-disabled program or receiving services: 1. Services include: remedial math, remedial English, remedial reading, tape recorders, videotaped classes, untimed tests, note-taking services, oral tests, learning center, readers, extended time for tests, tutors. **Library:** Number of titles: 36,160; number of current serial subscriptions: 110. **Information technology resources:** Students are not required to lease or own a computer. Number of campus computers available to all students: 35. School has a wireless network. Approximate number of users that can be accommodated: 44. Proportion of college-owned housing units wired for high-speed internet access: 100%. **Campus safety:** Security services offered: late-night transport/escort service, lighted pathways/sidewalks, student patrols, controlled dormitory access (key, security card, etc).

TRANSFER AND INTERNATIONAL STUDENTS

Transfer students: May apply for admission for the following academic terms: Fall, Spring, Summer. Applicants do not need a minimum number of credits to apply. For fall 2005: Transfer applications received: 92. Transfer applicants offered admission: 70. Transfer applicants enrolled: 41. **International students:** Number of foreign undergraduates: 0. Number of countries represented: 12. Minimum TOEFL score required: 550 (paper); 219 (computer). Average TOEFL score: 600 (paper).

Pepperdine University

- **Address:** 24255 Pacific Coast Highway, Malibu, CA 90263
- **Website:** http://www.pepperdine.edu
- **Private; Religious affiliation:** Church of Christ
- **Enrollment:** 2,740 full-time; 458 part-time

KEY STATS

✔ **U.S News College Ranking:** 54, National Universities
✔ **SAT Score (25th/75th percentile):** 1120-1330
✔ **Tuition:** 2006-2007: $32,740

Selectivity: More selective	**Room/board:** $9,500
Acceptance rate: 28%	**Average debt:** $31,848
Student/faculty ratio: 12/1	**Proportion who borrowed:** 62%

UNDERGRADUATE STUDENT BODY STATS

2005-2006 enrollment: 2,740 full-time; 458 part-time. Men: 43%; women: 57%. **Ethnic makeup:** African American: 8%; American-Indian: 2%; Asian American: 11%; Hispanic: 11%; White: 62%; International: 6%. **Religious preference:** Roman Catholic: 16%; Protestant: 5%; Jewish: 1%; Buddhist: 1%; No preference: 2%; Church of Christ: 21%; Other: 54%.

ADMISSIONS FACTS AND FIGURES

Phone: (310) 506-4392. **Email:** admission-seaver@pepperdine.edu. **Website:** http://www.pepperdine.edu. **Application deadlines for fall 2007:** Regular decision: January 15; decision sent by April 1. Early decision: Not offered. Early action: Not offered. Admission cannot be deferred. **Application fee:** $65. Common application is not accepted. **To apply online, go to:** http://www.seaver.pepperdine.edu/admission/information/apply.htm. **Admissions requirements/recommendations:** High school units required (recommended): English: (4); Mathematics: (4); Science: (4); Foreign language: (3); Social studies: (3); History: (3); Academic electives: (3); Total units: (28). Tests: The college uses SAT or ACT scores in admissions decisions. Either SAT or ACT required. For admission to the fall 2007 entering class, the school will accept: ACT with writing. Campus visit: Neither required nor recommended. Admissions interview: Neither required nor recommended. Off-campus interview: Not available. **Factors that count in admissions decisions:** *Academic:* Secondary school record: Very important. Class rank: Not considered. Letters of recommendation: Very important. Standardized test scores: Very important. Essay: Very important. *Nonacademic:* Interview: Not considered. Extracurricular activities: Very important. Talent/ability: Very important. Character/personal qualities: Very important. Alumni/ae relationship: Considered. Geographical residence: Not considered. State residency: Not considered. Religious affiliation/commitment: Important. Minority status: Considered. Volunteer work: Important. Work experience: Considered. **Other schools with the greatest overlap in applicants:** Stanford University; University of California–Berkeley; University of California–Los Angeles; University of Southern California; Vanderbilt University. **Admissions statistics for the fall 2005 entering class:** Total applicants: 7,307. Total accepted: 2,077. Freshmen enrolled: 765; 48% were from out of state. Overall acceptance rate: 28%. **Size of waiting list:** 834 applicants; enrolled from waiting list: 31. **Credentials of fall 2005 freshmen:** 43% ranked in the top 10 percent of their high school class; 76% were in the top 25 percent, and 96% were in the top half. (Proportion submitting class standing: 51%.) **Average high school grade point average:** 3.7. **First-year students who submitted SAT scores:** 91%. Scores (25/75 percentile): Verbal: 550-660, Math: 570-670, Combined: 1120-1330. **First-year students submitting ACT scores:** 39%. Scores (25/75 percentile): English: N/A, Math: N/A, Composite: 24-35.

ACADEMICS

Year founded: 1937. **Academic calendar:** Semester. **Degrees offered:** bachelor's, master's, first professional, doctorate. **Most popular majors:** 40% business, management, marketing, and related support services, 16% communication, journalism, and related programs, 9% social sciences, 7% psychology, 6% multi/interdisciplinary studies. **Major fields of study:** area, ethnic, cultural, and gender studies; biological and biomedical sciences; business, management, marketing, and related support services; communication, journalism, and related programs; computer and information sciences and support services; education; English language and literature/letters; family and consumer sciences/human sciences; foreign languages, literatures, and linguistics; health professions and related clinical sciences; history; liberal arts and sciences studies, and humanities; mathematics and statistics; multi/interdisciplinary studies; parks, recreation, leisure, and fitness studies; philosophy and religious studies; physical sciences; psychology; security and protective services; social sciences; visual and performing arts. **Areas of required coursework:** arts/fine arts, humanities, mathematics, English (including composition), foreign languages, sciences (biological or physical), history, social science, other. **Pre-professional programs:** pre-law, pre-dentistry, pre-medicine, pre-theology, pre-veterinary science. **Special academic programs:** double major, honors program, independent study, internships, student-designed major, study abroad, teacher certificate program, weekend college, other. **Teacher certification offered in:** elementary, secondary. **Reserve Officers Training Corps (ROTC):** Army ROTC: Offered at cooperating institution (UCLA); Air Force ROTC: Offered at cooperating institution (USC, Loyola Marymount Univ.). **Faculty and instruction (2005-2006):** Total instructional faculty: 400 full-time, 326 part-time (55% men; 45% women; 12% minorities). Full-time faculty with Ph.D. or other terminal degree: 97%. Student/faculty ratio: 12/1. Classes of fewer than 20 students: 64%; of 20 to 49 students: 33%; of 50 or more students: 3%. **Advanced Placement and International Baccalaureate credit:** Scores accepted: 3, 4, 5. International Baccalaureate exams may be used for: Credit and/or placement. **Freshmen returning for sophomore year:** 89%. **Graduation rates:** Four-year: 71%; five-year: 79%; six-year: 80%. **Graduate study:** 20% of students pursue further study immediately upon graduation; 50% within one year; 60% within five years.

COSTS AND FINANCIAL AID

Financial aid office: (310) 506-4301. **Expenses (2006-2007):** Tuition and fees 2006-2007: $32,740; room/board: $9,500. Estimated books and supplies: $800; transportation: $600; personal expenses: $900. **Financial aid:** Priority filing date for institution's financial aid form: February 15; deadline: February 15. In 2005-2006, 69% of undergraduates applied for financial aid. Of those, 49% were determined to have financial need; 41% had their need fully met. Average financial aid package (proportion receiving): $30,991 (49%). Average amount of gift aid, such as scholarships or grants (proportion receiving): $20,855 (45%). Average amount of self-help aid, such as work study or loans (proportion receiving): $10,618 (47%). Average

need-based loan (excluding PLUS or other private loans): $9,684. Among students who received need-based aid, the average percentage of need met: 89%. Among students who received aid based on merit, the average award (and the proportion receiving): $18,720 (15%). The average athletic scholarship (and the proportion receiving): $25,822 (5%). Average amount of debt of borrowers graduating in 2005: $31,848. Proportion who borrowed: 62%.

CAMPUS LIFE AND EXTRACURRICULAR ACTIVITIES

Campus housing available (% using): women's dorms (37%), men's dorms (28%), apartments for married students (1%), apartment for single students (33%), special housing for disabled students (0%), other housing options (1%). Students who live in college-owned, operated, or affiliated housing: 62%. **Student employment:** During the 2005-2006 academic year, 10% of undergraduates worked on campus. Average per-year earnings: $3,000. **Clubs and organizations:** Number of student organizations: 64. Activities include: choral groups, concert band, dance, drama/theater, jazz band, literary magazine, music ensembles, musical theater, opera, pep band, radio station, student government, student newspaper, student film society, symphony orchestra, television station, yearbook. Number of fraternities: 5; sororities: 7. Proportion of men in fraternities: 25%; of women in sororities: 25%. Average proportion of students who stay on campus on weekends: 50%. **Sports program (2005-2006):** Member of NCAA I. *Men's intercollegiate varsity sports:* baseball, basketball, cross-country, golf, tennis, volleyball, water polo. *Women's intercollegiate varsity sports:* basketball, cross-country, golf, soccer, swimming and diving, tennis, track and field (outdoor), volleyball.

SERVICES AND FACILITIES

Basic services: health service, health insurance. **Remedial assistance:** writing. **Counseling services:** career, personal, academic, psychological, religious. **For learning-disabled students:** School does not offer a structured program with separate admission and additional fees. Total undergraduates in learning-disabled program or receiving services: 55. Services include: reading machines, tape recorders, note-taking services, oral tests, readers, extended time for tests, priority registration, priority seating, substitution of courses, texts on tape, other testing accomodations. **Library:** Number of titles: 339,753; number of current serial subscriptions: 3,510. **Information technology resources:** Students are not required to lease or own a computer. Number of campus computers available to all students: 500. School has a wireless network. Approximate number of users that can be accommodated: 4,000. Proportion of college-owned housing units wired for high-speed internet access: 100%. **Campus safety:** Security services offered: 24-hour foot-and-vehicle patrols, late-night transport/escort service, 24-hour emergency telephones, lighted pathways/sidewalks, student patrols, controlled dormitory access (key, security card, etc).

TRANSFER AND INTERNATIONAL STUDENTS

Transfer students: May apply for admission for the following academic terms: Fall, Spring. Applicants need a minimum number of credits to apply. For fall 2005: Transfer applications received: 519. Transfer applicants offered admission: 104. Transfer applicants enrolled: 59. **International students:** Number of foreign undergraduates: 189 (6% of student body). Number of countries represented: 60. Minimum TOEFL score required: 550 (paper); 220 (computer). Average TOEFL score: 603 (paper).

Pitzer College

- **Address:** 1050 N. Mills Avenue, Claremont, CA 91711-6101
- **Website:** http://www.pitzer.edu
- **Private**
- **Enrollment:** 911 full-time; 52 part-time

KEY STATS

✔ **U.S News College Ranking:** 51, Liberal Arts Colleges
✔ **SAT Score (25th/75th percentile):** 1130-1340
✔ **Tuition:** 2006-2007: $34,038
  Selectivity: More selective   **Room/board:** $9,670
  Acceptance rate: 39%   **Average debt:** $20,900
  Student/faculty ratio: 12/1   **Proportion who borrowed:** 60%

UNDERGRADUATE STUDENT BODY STATS

2005-2006 enrollment: 911 full-time; 52 part-time. Men: 41%; women: 59%. **Ethnic makeup:** African American: 5%; American-Indian: 1%; Asian American: 10%; Hispanic: 15%; White: 67%; International: 2%.

ADMISSIONS FACTS AND FIGURES

Phone: (909) 621-8129. **Email:** admission@pitzer.edu. **Website:** http://www.pitzer.edu. **Application deadlines for fall 2007:** Regular decision: January 1; decision sent by April 1. Early decision: Send application by: November 15; Decision sent by: December 15. Early action: Not offered. Admission can be deferred. **Application fee:** $50. Common application is accepted. **To apply online, go to:** http://www.pitzer.edu/admissionfinancialaid/admission/onlineapp.html. **Admissions requirements/recommendations:** High school units required (recommended): English: 4 (4); Mathematics: 3 (3); Science: 3 (3); Foreign language: 3 (3); Social studies: 3 (2); History: (1). Tests: The college uses SAT or ACT scores in admissions decisions. Neither SAT nor ACT required. For admission to the fall 2007 entering class, the school will accept: ACT without writing. Campus visit: Recommended. Admissions interview: Recommended. Off-campus interview: May be arranged. **Factors that count in admissions decisions:** *Academic:* Secondary school record: Very important. Class rank: Very important. Letters of recommendation: Very important. Standardized test scores: Considered. Essay: Very important. *Nonacademic:* Interview: Important. Extracurricular activities: Very important. Talent/ability: Important. Character/personal qualities: Important. Alumni/ae relationship: Considered. Geographical residence: Important. State residency: Important. Religious affiliation/commitment: Not considered. Minority status: Important. Volunteer work: Important. Work experience: Important. **Other schools with the greatest overlap in applicants:** Claremont McKenna College; Occidental College; Pomona College; Scripps College; University of Southern California. **Admissions statistics for the fall 2005 entering class:** Total applicants: 3,251. Total accepted: 1,276. Freshmen enrolled: 241; 51% were from out of state. Overall acceptance rate: 39%. Non-early acceptance rate: 39%. **Size of waiting list:** 704 applicants; enrolled from waiting list: 0. **Credentials of fall 2005 freshmen:** 45% ranked in the top 10 percent of their high school class; 76% were in the top 25 percent, and 92% were in the top half. (Proportion submitting class standing: 39%.) **Average high school grade point average:** 3.6. **First-year students who submitted SAT scores:** 59%. Scores (25/75 percentile): Verbal: 570-680, Math: 560-660, Combined: 1130-1340.

ACADEMICS

Year founded: 1963. **Academic calendar:** Semester. **Degrees offered:** bachelor's. **Most popular majors:** 29% social sciences, 13% psychology, 9% English language and literature, 9% visual and performing arts, 5% biology. **Major fields of study:** area, ethnic, cultural, and gender studies; biological and biomedical sciences; business, management, marketing, and related support services; English language and literature/letters; foreign languages, literatures, and linguistics; history; mathematics and statistics; multi/interdisciplinary studies; natural resources and conservation; philosophy and religious studies; physical sciences; psychology; social sciences; visual and performing arts. **Areas of required coursework:** humanities, mathematics, English (including composition), sciences (biological or physical), social science, other. **Pre-professional programs:** pre-medicine. **Special academic programs (% participation):** cross-registration (99%), double major (19.5%), English as a Second Language (ESL) (1.4%), exchange student program (domestic) (0%), honors program (14.5%), independent study (45.2%), internships, student-designed major (12.2%), study abroad (54.8%). **Cooperative education programs:** computer science, health professions, social/behavioral science. **Reserve Officers Training Corps (ROTC):** Army ROTC: Offered at cooperating institution (Claremont McKenna College); Air Force ROTC: Offered at cooperating institution (Harvey Mudd College). **Faculty and instruction (2005-2006):** Total instructional faculty: 65 full-time, 25 part-time (52% men; 48% women; 30% minorities). Full-time faculty with Ph.D. or other terminal degree: 95%. Student/faculty ratio: 12/1. Classes of fewer than 20 students: 65%; of 20 to 49 students: 35%; of 50 or more students: 1%. **Advanced Placement and International Baccalaureate credit:** International Baccalaureate exams may be used for: Credit only. **Freshmen returning for sophomore year:** 86%. **Graduation rates:** Four-year: 61%; five-year: 68%; six-year: 70%. **Graduate study:** 17% of students pursue further study immediately upon graduation; 28% within one year. Fields in which graduates pursue further study: Master of Business Administration (MBA), 6%; law, 16%; medicine, 9%; dentistry, 9%; engineering, 3%; education, 25%.

COSTS AND FINANCIAL AID

Financial aid office: (909) 621-8208. **Expenses (2006-2007):** Tuition and fees 2006-2007: $34,038; room/board: $9,670. Estimated books and supplies: $1,000; transportation: $300; personal expenses: $1,000. **Financial aid:** Priority filing date for institution's financial aid form: February 1; deadline: February 1. In 2005-2006, 46% of undergraduates applied for financial aid. Of those, 41% were determined to have financial need; 98% had their need fully met. Average financial aid package (proportion receiving): $29,002 (40%). Average amount of gift aid, such as scholarships or grants (proportion receiving): $23,424 (40%). Average amount of self-help aid, such as work study or loans (proportion receiving): $6,426 (37%). Average need-based loan (excluding PLUS or other private loans): $4,171. Among students who received need-based aid, the average percentage of need met: 100%. Among students who received aid based on merit, the average award (and the proportion receiving): $8,125 (4%). The average athletic scholarship (and the proportion receiving): $0 (0%). Average amount of debt of borrowers graduating in 2005: $20,900. Proportion who borrowed: 60%.

CAMPUS LIFE AND EXTRACURRICULAR ACTIVITIES

Campus housing available (% using): coed dorms (94%), apartment for single students (5%), special housing for disabled students (1%). Students who live in college-owned, operated, or affiliated housing: 73%. **Clubs and organizations:** Number of student organizations: 68. Activities include: choral groups, dance, drama/theater, literary magazine, music ensembles, musical theater, radio station, student government, student newspaper, student film society, symphony orchestra. Number of fraternities: 0; sororities: 0. Average proportion of students who stay on campus on weekends: 75%. **Sports program (2005-2006):** Member of NCAA III. *Men's intercollegiate varsity sports:* baseball, basketball, cross-country, football, golf, soccer, swimming and diving, tennis, track and field (outdoor), water polo. *Women's intercollegiate varsity sports:* basketball, cross-country, soccer, softball, swimming and diving, tennis, track and field (outdoor), volleyball, water polo.

SERVICES AND FACILITIES

Basic services: nonremedial tutoring, women's center, placement service, health service, health insurance. **Remedial assistance:** writing. **Counseling services:** minority student, career, personal, academic, older student, psychological, birth control, religious. **For learning-disabled students:** School does not offer a structured program with separate admission and additional fees. Total undergraduates in learning-disabled program or receiving services: 105. Services include: reading machines, tape recorders, note-taking services, readers, extended time for tests, tutors. **Library:** Number of titles: 2,476,503; number of current serial subscriptions: 17,052. **Information technology resources:** Students are not required to lease or own a computer. Number of campus computers available to all students: 100. School has a wireless network. Approximate number of users that can be accommodated: 500. Proportion of college-owned housing units wired for high-speed internet access: 100%. **Campus safety:** Security services offered: 24-hour foot-and-vehicle patrols, late-night transport/escort service, 24-hour emergency telephones, lighted pathways/sidewalks, controlled dormitory access (key, security card, etc).

TRANSFER AND INTERNATIONAL STUDENTS

Transfer students: May apply for admission for the following academic terms: Fall, Spring. Applicants need a minimum number of credits to apply. For fall 2005: Transfer applications received: 144. Transfer applicants offered admission: 59. Transfer applicants enrolled: 25. **International students:** Number of foreign undergraduates: 20 (2% of student body). Number of countries represented: 14. Minimum TOEFL score required: 590 (paper); 240 (computer). Average TOEFL score: 600 (paper).

Point Loma Nazarene University

- **Address:** 3900 Lomaland Drive, San Diego, CA 92106
- **Website:** http://www.ptloma.edu
- **Private; Religious affiliation:** Nazarene
- **Enrollment:** 2,282 full-time; 78 part-time

KEY STATS
✔ **U.S News College Ranking:** 22, Universities–Master's (West)
✔ **SAT Score (25th/75th percentile):** 1040-1270
✔ **Tuition:** 2006-2007: $22,150
  Selectivity: More selective   **Room/board:** $7,160
  Acceptance rate: 65%   **Average debt:** $18,415
  Student/faculty ratio: 16/1   **Proportion who borrowed:** 79%

UNDERGRADUATE STUDENT BODY STATS
2005-2006 enrollment: 2,282 full-time; 78 part-time. Men: 40%; women: 60%. **Ethnic makeup:** African American: 2%; American-Indian: 1%; Asian American: 5%; Hispanic: 10%; White: 82%; International: 1%. **Religious preference:** Roman Catholic: 4%; No preference: 1%; Nazarene: 30%; Non-denominational: 24%; Other: 41%.

ADMISSIONS FACTS AND FIGURES
Phone: (619) 849-2273. **Email:** admissions@ptloma.edu. **Website:** http://www.ptloma.edu. **Application deadlines for fall 2007:** Regular decision: March 1. Early decision: Not offered. Early action: Send application by: December 1; Decision sent by: January 15. Admission can be deferred. **Application fee:** $50. Common application is not accepted. **To apply online, go to:** http://www.ptloma.edu/Admissions/Apply/menu.htm. **Admissions requirements/recommendations:** High school units required (recommended): English: 4; Mathematics: 2; Science: 1; Foreign language: 2; History: 1; Total units: 10. Tests: The college uses SAT or ACT scores in admissions decisions. Either SAT or ACT required. For admission to the fall 2007 entering class, the school will accept: ACT with writing, ACT without writing. Campus visit: Recommended. Admissions interview: Required. Off-campus interview: May be arranged. **Factors that count in admissions decisions:** *Academic:* Secondary school record: Very important. Class rank: Considered. Letters of recommendation: Important. Standardized test scores: Very important. Essay: Important. *Nonacademic:* Interview: Important. Extracurricular activities: Considered. Talent/ability: Considered. Character/personal qualities: Very important. Alumni/ae relationship: Considered. Geographical residence: Not considered. State residency: Not considered. Religious affiliation/commitment: Considered. Minority status: Not considered. Volunteer work: Not considered. Work experience: Not considered. **Admissions statistics for the fall 2005 entering class:** Total applicants: 1,857. Total accepted: 1,216. Freshmen enrolled: 563; 21% were from out of state. Overall acceptance rate: 65%. Non-early acceptance rate: 65%. **Credentials of fall 2005 freshmen:** 38% ranked in the top 10 percent of their high school class; 75% were in the top 25 percent, and 90% were in the top half. (Proportion submitting class standing: 74%.) **Average high school grade point average:** 3.7. **First-year students who submitted SAT scores:** 94%. Scores (25/75 percentile): Verbal: 520-630, Math: 520-640, Combined: 1040-1270. **First-year students submitting ACT scores:** 36%. Scores (25/75 percentile): English: N/A, Math: N/A, Composite: 21-28.

ACADEMICS
Year founded: 1902. **Academic calendar:** Semester. **Degrees offered:** bachelor's, master's. **Most popular majors:** 17% business, management, marketing, and related support services, 10% liberal arts and sciences studies, and humanities, 10% psychology, 8% health professions and related clinical sciences, 8% visual and performing arts. **Major fields of study:** biological and biomedical sciences; business, management, marketing, and related support services; communication, journalism, and related programs; communications technologies/technicians and support services; computer and information sciences and support services; education; engineering; English language and literature/letters; family and consumer sciences/human sciences; foreign languages, literatures, and linguistics; health professions and related clinical sciences; history; liberal arts and sciences studies, and humanities; mathematics and statistics; multi/interdisciplinary studies; parks, recreation, leisure, and fitness studies; philosophy and religious studies; physical sciences; psychology; public administration and social service professions; social sciences; theology and religious vocations; visual and performing arts. **Areas of required coursework:** arts/fine arts, mathematics,

English (including composition), philosophy, foreign languages, sciences (biological or physical), history, social science, other. **Pre-professional programs:** pre-law, pre-dentistry, pre-medicine, pre-theology, other. **Special academic programs:** double major, honors program, independent study, internships, study abroad, teacher certificate program. **Teacher certification offered in:** special education, elementary, middle/junior high, secondary. **Cooperative education programs:** art, business, computer science, education, health professions, home economics, humanities, natural science, social/behavioral science. **Reserve Officers Training Corps (ROTC):** Army ROTC: Offered at cooperating institution (San Diego State University); Navy ROTC: Offered at cooperating institution (University of San Diego); Air Force ROTC: Offered at cooperating institution (San Diego State University). **Faculty and instruction (2005-2006):** Total instructional faculty: 139 full-time, 199 part-time (50% men; 50% women; 12% minorities). Full-time faculty with Ph.D. or other terminal degree: 79%. Student/faculty ratio: 16/1. Classes of fewer than 20 students: 44%; of 20 to 49 students: 52%; of 50 or more students: 3%. **Advanced Placement and International Baccalaureate credit:** AP tests may be used for: Credit only. Scores accepted: 3, 4, 5. International Baccalaureate exams may be used for: Credit only. **Freshmen returning for sophomore year:** 83%. **Graduation rates:** Four-year: 54%; five-year: 67%; six-year: 57%.

COSTS AND FINANCIAL AID
Financial aid office: (619) 849-2538. **Expenses (2006-2007):** Tuition and fees 2006-2007: $22,150; room/board: $7,160. Estimated books and supplies: $1,260; transportation: $776; personal expenses: $2,096. **Financial aid:** Priority filing date for institution's financial aid form: March 2. In 2005-2006, 94% of undergraduates applied for financial aid. Of those, 59% were determined to have financial need; 14% had their need fully met. Average financial aid package (proportion receiving): $12,525 (47%). Average amount of gift aid, such as scholarships or grants (proportion receiving): $9,523 (43%). Average amount of self-help aid, such as work study or loans (proportion receiving): $5,551 (31%). Average need-based loan (excluding PLUS or other private loans): $5,109. Among students who received need-based aid, the average percentage of need met: 46%. Among students who received aid based on merit, the average award (and the proportion receiving): $10,485 (7%). The average athletic scholarship (and the proportion receiving): $0 (0%). Average amount of debt of borrowers graduating in 2005: $18,415. Proportion who borrowed: 79%.

CAMPUS LIFE AND EXTRACURRICULAR ACTIVITIES
Campus housing available: women's dorms, men's dorms, apartments for married students, apartment for single students. Students who live in college-owned, operated, or affiliated housing: 70%. **Clubs and organizations:** Number of student organizations: 31. Activities include: choral groups, concert band, drama/theater, jazz band, literary magazine, music ensembles, musical theater, opera, pep band, radio station, student government, student newspaper, yearbook. Number of fraternities: 2; sororities: 3. **Sports program (2005-2006):** Member of NAIA. *Men's intercollegiate varsity sports:* baseball, basketball, cross-country, golf, soccer, tennis, track and field (outdoor). *Women's intercollegiate varsity sports:* basketball, cross-country, soccer, softball, tennis, track and field (outdoor), volleyball.

SERVICES AND FACILITIES
Basic services: nonremedial tutoring, women's center, health service, health insurance. **Remedial assistance:** math, writing, study skills. **Counseling services:** career, personal, academic, psychological, religious, other. **For learning-disabled students:** School does not offer a structured program with separate admission and additional fees. Total undergraduates in learning-disabled program or receiving services: 69. Services include: tape recorders, untimed tests, note-taking services, oral tests, extended time for tests, tutors, texts on tape. **Library:** Number of titles: 152,377; number of current serial subscriptions: 25,505. **Information technology resources:** Students are not required to lease or own a computer. Number of campus computers available to all students: 196. School has a wireless network. Proportion of college-owned housing units wired for high-speed internet access: 89%. **Campus safety:** Security services offered: 24-hour foot-and-vehicle patrols, late-night transport/escort service, lighted pathways/sidewalks, controlled dormitory access (key, security card, etc).

TRANSFER AND INTERNATIONAL STUDENTS
Transfer students: May apply for admission for the following academic terms: Fall, Spring. Applicants do not need a minimum number of credits to apply. **International students:** Number of foreign undergraduates: 16 (1% of student body). Number of countries represented: 11. Minimum TOEFL score required: 550 (paper); 216 (computer).

Pomona College

- **Address:** 550 N. College Avenue, Claremont, CA 91711
- **Website:** http://www.pomona.edu
- **Private**
- **Enrollment:** 1,533 full-time

KEY STATS

✔ **U.S News College Ranking:** 7, Liberal Arts Colleges
✔ **SAT Score (25th/75th percentile):** 1380-1530
✔ **Tuition:** 2006-2007: $31,865

Selectivity: Most selective	**Room/board:** $11,291
Acceptance rate: 19%	**Average debt:** $11,250
Student/faculty ratio: 8/1	**Proportion who borrowed:** 53%

UNDERGRADUATE STUDENT BODY STATS

2005-2006 enrollment: 1,533 full-time. Men: 50%; women: 50%. **Ethnic makeup:** African American: 7%; Asian American: 14%; Hispanic: 11%; White: 67%; International: 2%.

ADMISSIONS FACTS AND FIGURES

Phone: (909) 621-8134. **Email:** admissions@pomona.edu. **Website:** http://www.pomona.edu. **Application deadlines for fall 2007:** Regular decision: January 2; decision sent by April 10. Early decision: Send application by: November 15; Decision sent by: December 15. Early action: Not offered. Admission can be deferred. **Application fee:** $65. Common application is accepted. **To apply online, go to:** http://www.pomona.edu/adwr/admissions/Applying/Information.shtml. **Admissions requirements/recommendations:** High school units required (recommended): English: 4 (4); Mathematics: 3 (4); Science: 3 (3); Foreign language: 3 (3); Social studies: 2 (2). Tests: The college uses SAT or ACT scores in admissions decisions. Either SAT or ACT required. For admission to the fall 2007 entering class, the school will accept ACT without writing. Campus visit: Recommended. Admissions interview: Recommended. Off-campus interview: May be arranged. **Factors that count in admissions decisions:** *Academic:* Secondary school record: Very important. Class rank: Very important. Letters of recommendation: Very important. Standardized test scores: Very important. Essay: Very important. *Nonacademic:* Interview: Important. Extracurricular activities: Very important. Talent/ability: Very important. Character/personal qualities: Very important. Alumni/ae relationship: Considered. Geographical residence: Considered. State residency: Not considered. Religious affiliation/commitment: Not considered. Minority status: Considered. Volunteer work: Considered. Work experience: Considered. **Other schools with the greatest overlap in applicants:** Amherst College; Harvard University; Stanford University; University of California–Berkeley; Yale University. **Admissions statistics for the fall 2005 entering class:** Total applicants: 5,050. Total accepted: 951. Freshmen enrolled: 383; 66% were from out of state. Accepted through early-decision or early-action plans: 30%. Overall acceptance rate: 19%. Early-decision acceptance rate: 28%. Non-early acceptance rate: 18%. **Size of waiting list:** N/A applicants; enrolled from waiting list: 13. **Credentials of fall 2005 freshmen:** 88% ranked in the top 10 percent of their high school class; 98% were in the top 25 percent, and 100% were in the top half. (Proportion submitting class standing: 61%.) **First-year students who submitted SAT scores:** 93%. Scores (25/75 percentile): Verbal: 690-770, Math: 690-760, Combined: 1380-1530. **First-year students submitting ACT scores:** 26%. Scores (25/75 percentile): English: 29-34, Math: 29-34, Composite: 29-34.

ACADEMICS

Year founded: 1887. **Academic calendar:** Semester. **Degrees offered:** bachelor's. **Most popular majors:** 11% economics, 9% English language and literature, 6% biology/biological sciences, 6% political science and government, 5% history. **Major fields of study:** area, ethnic, cultural, and gender studies; biological and biomedical sciences; communication, journalism, and related programs; computer and information sciences and support services; English language and literature/letters; foreign languages, literatures, and linguistics; history; mathematics and statistics; multi/interdisciplinary studies; natural resources and conservation; philosophy and religious studies; physical sciences; psychology; public administration and social service professions; social sciences; visual and performing arts. **Areas of required coursework:** arts/fine arts, humanities, mathematics, English (including composition), foreign languages, sciences (biological or physical), history, social science, other. **Pre-professional programs:** pre-law, pre-medicine.

Special academic programs (% participation): cross-registration (96%), double major (8%), exchange student program (domestic) (1%), independent study (30%), student-designed major (1%), study abroad (48%). **Cooperative education programs:** engineering. **Faculty and instruction (2005-2006):** Total instructional faculty: 172 full-time, 34 part-time (57% men; 43% women; 28% minorities). Full-time faculty with Ph.D. or other terminal degree: 95%. Student/faculty ratio: 8/1. Classes of fewer than 20 students: 67%; of 20 to 49 students: 32%; of 50 or more students: 1%. **Advanced Placement and International Baccalaureate credit:** AP tests may be used for: Credit only. Scores accepted: 4, 5. International Baccalaureate exams may be used for: Credit and/or placement. **Freshmen returning for sophomore year:** 99%. **Graduation rates:** Four-year: 87%; five-year: 93%; six-year: 95%. **Graduate study:** 23% of students pursue further study immediately upon graduation; 85% within five years. Fields in which graduates pursue further study: Master of Business Administration (MBA), 12%; law, 12%; medicine, 12%; dentistry, 1%; engineering, 1%; arts and sciences, 48%.

COSTS AND FINANCIAL AID

Financial aid office: (909) 621-8205. **Expenses (2006-2007):** Tuition and fees 2006-2007: $31,865; room/board: $11,291. Estimated books and supplies: $850; transportation: $600; personal expenses: $1,000. **Financial aid:** Priority filing date for institution's financial aid form: February 1; deadline: February 1. In 2005-2006, 65% of undergraduates applied for financial aid. Of those, 53% were determined to have financial need; 100% had their need fully met. Average financial aid package (proportion receiving): $29,784 (53%). Average amount of gift aid, such as scholarships or grants (proportion receiving): $25,484 (53%). Average amount of self-help aid, such as work study or loans (proportion receiving): $4,300 (53%). Average need-based loan (excluding PLUS or other private loans): $2,920. Among students who received need-based aid, the average percentage of need met: 100%. Among students who received aid based on merit, the average award (and the proportion receiving): $0 (0%). The average athletic scholarship (and the proportion receiving): $0 (0%). Average amount of debt of borrowers graduating in 2005: $11,250. Proportion who borrowed: 53%.

CAMPUS LIFE AND EXTRACURRICULAR ACTIVITIES

Campus housing available (% using): coed dorms (97%), other housing options (3%). Students who live in college-owned, operated, or affiliated housing: 97%. **Clubs and organizations:** Number of student organizations: 150. Activities include: choral groups, dance, drama/theater, jazz band, literary magazine, music ensembles, musical theater, pep band, radio station, student government, student newspaper, student film society, symphony orchestra, television station, yearbook. Number of fraternities: 3; sororities: 0. Proportion of men in fraternities: 5%; Average proportion of students who stay on campus on weekends: 90%. **Sports program (2005-2006):** Member of NCAA II. *Men's intercollegiate varsity sports:* baseball, basketball, cross-country, football, golf, soccer, swimming and diving, tennis, track and field (outdoor), water polo. *Women's intercollegiate varsity sports:* basketball, cross-country, golf, soccer, softball, swimming and diving, tennis, track and field (outdoor), volleyball, water polo.

SERVICES AND FACILITIES

Basic services: nonremedial tutoring, women's center, placement service, health service, health insurance. **Counseling services:** minority student, career, personal, academic, psychological, birth control, religious. **For learning-disabled students:** School does not offer a structured program with separate admission and additional fees. Services include: tape recorders, note-taking services, oral tests, readers, extended time for tests, tutors. **Library:** Number of titles: 2,476,503; number of current serial subscriptions: 17,052. **Information technology resources:** Students are not required to lease or own a computer. Number of campus computers available to all students: 225. School has a wireless network. Approximate number of users that can be accommodated: 7,600. Proportion of college-owned housing units wired for high-speed internet access: 100%. **Campus safety:** Security services offered: 24-hour foot-and-vehicle patrols, late-night transport/escort service, 24-hour emergency telephones, lighted pathways/sidewalks, student patrols, controlled dormitory access (key, security card, etc).

TRANSFER AND INTERNATIONAL STUDENTS

Transfer students: May apply for admission for the following academic terms: Fall. Applicants need a minimum number of credits to apply. For fall 2005: Transfer applications received: 193. Transfer applicants offered admission: 15. Transfer applicants enrolled: 6. **International students:** Number of foreign undergraduates: 32 (2% of student body). Number of countries represented: 10. Minimum TOEFL score required: 600 (paper); 250 (computer).

San Diego Christian College

- **Address:** 2100 Greenfield Drive, El Cajon, CA 92019
- **Website:** http://www.sdcc.edu/
- **Private; Religious affiliation:** Christian, nondenominational
- **Enrollment:** 457 full-time; 54 part-time

KEY STATS

✔ **U.S News College Ranking:** fourth tier, Liberal Arts Colleges
✔ **SAT Score (25th/75th percentile):** 860-1100
✔ **Tuition:** 2006-2007: $17,142

Selectivity: Less selective	**Room/board:** $7,180
Acceptance rate: 72%	**Average debt:** $18,000
Student/faculty ratio: 9/1	**Proportion who borrowed:** 79%

UNDERGRADUATE STUDENT BODY STATS

2005-2006 enrollment: 457 full-time; 54 part-time. Men: 41%; women: 59%. **Ethnic makeup:** African American: 7%; American-Indian: 1%; Asian American: 3%; Hispanic: 16%; White: 71%; International: 2%.

ADMISSIONS FACTS AND FIGURES

Phone: (619) 588-7747. **Email:** admissions@sdcc.edu. **Website:** http://www.sdcc.edu/. **Application deadlines for fall 2007:** Regular decision: August 1. Early decision: Not offered. Early action: Not offered. Admission can be deferred. **Application fee:** $25. Common application is not accepted. **Admissions requirements/recommendations:** High school units required (recommended): English: (4); Mathematics: (3); Science: (3); Foreign language: (2); Social studies: (3); Total units: (15). Tests: The college uses SAT or ACT scores in admissions decisions. Neither SAT nor ACT required. For admission to the fall 2007 entering class, the school will accept: ACT with writing, ACT without writing. Campus visit: Recommended. Admissions interview: Recommended. Off-campus interview: May be arranged. **Factors that count in admissions decisions:** *Academic:* Secondary school record: Important. Class rank: Important. Letters of recommendation: Very important. Standardized test scores: Very important. Essay: Important. *Nonacademic:* Interview: Considered. Extracurricular activities: Considered. Talent/ability: Not considered. Character/personal qualities: Very important. Alumni/ae relationship: Not considered. Geographical residence: Not considered. State residency: Not considered. Religious affiliation/commitment: Very important. Minority status: Not considered. Volunteer work: Considered. Work experience: Not considered. **Other schools with the greatest overlap in applicants:** Azusa Pacific University; Biola University; California Baptist University; Master's College and Seminary; Point Loma Nazarene University. **Admissions statistics for the fall 2005 entering class:** Total applicants: 493. Total accepted: 353. Freshmen enrolled: 126; 18% were from out of state. Overall acceptance rate: 72%. **Average high school grade point average:** 3.3. First-year students who submitted SAT scores: 77%. Scores (25/75 percentile): Verbal: 450-560, Math: 410-540, Combined: 860-1100. **First-year students submitting ACT scores:** 24%. Scores (25/75 percentile): English: 16-23, Math: 16-23, Composite: 18-25.

ACADEMICS

Year founded: 1970. **Academic calendar:** Semester. **Degrees offered:** certificate, bachelor's, post-bachelor's certificate. **Most popular majors:** 27% multi/interdisciplinary studies, 18% human development and family studies, 12% counseling psychology, 11% Bible/biblical studies, 7% liberal arts and sciences/liberal studies. **Major fields of study:** biological and biomedical sciences; business, management, marketing, and related support services; English language and literature/letters; family and consumer sciences/human sciences; history; liberal arts and sciences studies, and humanities; mathematics and statistics; multi/interdisciplinary studies; parks, recreation, leisure, and fitness studies; psychology; theology and religious vocations; transportation and materials moving; visual and performing arts. **Areas of required coursework:** arts/fine arts, humanities, computer literacy, mathematics, English (including composition), philosophy, sciences (biological or physical), history, social science, other. **Special academic programs (% participation):** double major (0%), honors program (.01%), internships (12%), student-designed major (27%), study abroad (.01%). **Teacher certification offered in:** elementary, secondary. **Reserve Officers Training Corps (ROTC):** Navy ROTC: Offered at cooperating institution (San Diego State University); Air Force ROTC: Offered at cooperating institution (San Diego State University). **Faculty and instruction (2005-2006):** Total instructional faculty: 29 full-time, 36 part-time. Student/faculty ratio: 9/1. Classes

of fewer than 20 students: 71%; of 20 to 49 students: 28%; of 50 or more students: 1%. **Advanced Placement and International Baccalaureate credit:** AP tests may be used for: Credit only. Scores accepted: 3, 4, 5. **Freshmen returning for sophomore year:** 74%. **Graduation rates:** Four-year: 35%; five-year: 48%; six-year: 51%. **Graduate study:** 30% of students pursue further study within five years. Fields in which graduates pursue further study: law, 2%; medicine, 1%; theology (or the seminary), 5%; education, 16%.

COSTS AND FINANCIAL AID

Financial aid office: (619) 590-1786. **Expenses (2006-2007):** Tuition and fees 2006-2007: $17,142; room/board: $7,180. Estimated books and supplies: $1,314; transportation: $774; personal expenses: $2,088. **Financial aid:** Priority filing date for institution's financial aid form: March 2; deadline: August 1. In 2005-2006, 99% of undergraduates applied for financial aid. Of those, 84% were determined to have financial need; 70% had their need fully met. Average financial aid package (proportion receiving): $14,547 (84%). Average amount of gift aid, such as scholarships or grants (proportion receiving): $5,500 (56%). Average amount of self-help aid, such as work study or loans (proportion receiving): $4,500 (84%). Average need-based loan (excluding PLUS or other private loans): $3,850. Among students who received need-based aid, the average percentage of need met: 80%. Among students who received aid based on merit, the average award (and the proportion receiving): $4,565 (25%). The average athletic scholarship (and the proportion receiving): $9,277 (5%). Average amount of debt of borrowers graduating in 2005: $18,000. Proportion who borrowed: 79%.

CAMPUS LIFE AND EXTRACURRICULAR ACTIVITIES

Campus housing available (% using): women's dorms (58%), men's dorms (42%). Students who live in college-owned, operated, or affiliated housing: 48%. **Student employment:** During the 2005-2006 academic year, 3% of undergraduates worked on campus. Average per-year earnings: $8. **Clubs and organizations:** Number of student organizations: 8. Activities include: choral groups, music ensembles, musical theater, student government, student newspaper, yearbook. Number of fraternities: 0; sororities: 0. Average proportion of students who stay on campus on weekends: 30%. **Sports program (2005-2006):** Member of NAIA. *Men's intercollegiate varsity sports:* basketball, cross-country, soccer. *Women's intercollegiate varsity sports:* basketball, cross-country, soccer, volleyball.

SERVICES AND FACILITIES

Basic services: nonremedial tutoring, placement service, health service, health insurance. **Remedial assistance:** reading, math, writing, study skills. **Counseling services:** career, personal, academic, psychological, religious. **For learning-disabled students:** School does not offer a structured program with separate admission and additional fees. Total undergraduates in learning-disabled program or receiving services: 5. Services include: remedial math, remedial English, remedial reading, diagnostic testing service, note-taking services, extended time for tests, tutors, early syllabus, other testing accomodations. **Library:** Number of titles: 63,050; number of current serial subscriptions: 246. **Information technology resources:** Students are not required to lease or own a computer. School has a wireless network. Approximate number of users that can be accommodated: 100. Proportion of college-owned housing units wired for high-speed internet access: 100%. **Campus safety:** Security services offered: 24-hour foot-and-vehicle patrols, late-night transport/escort service, 24-hour emergency telephones, lighted pathways/sidewalks, student patrols.

TRANSFER AND INTERNATIONAL STUDENTS

Transfer students: May apply for admission for the following academic terms: Fall, Spring, Summer. Applicants need a minimum number of credits to apply. **International students:** Number of foreign undergraduates: 12 (2% of student body). Number of countries represented: 5. Minimum TOEFL score required: 500 (paper).

San Diego State University

- **Address:** 5500 Campanile Drive, San Diego, CA 92182-7455
- **Website:** http://www.sdsu.edu
- **Public**
- **Enrollment:** 21,912 full-time; 4,938 part-time

KEY STATS

✔ **U.S News College Ranking:** fourth tier, National Universities
✔ **SAT Score (25th/75th percentile):** 980-1180
✔ **Tuition:** 2006-2007: $3,122 in state, $13,292 out of state

Selectivity: Selective	**Room/board:** $10,093
Acceptance rate: 44%	**Average debt:** $14,500
Student/faculty ratio: 19/1	**Proportion who borrowed:** 49%

UNDERGRADUATE STUDENT BODY STATS

2005-2006 enrollment: 21,912 full-time; 4,938 part-time. Men: 41%; women: 59%. **Ethnic makeup:** African American: 4%; American-Indian: 1%; Asian American: 16%; Hispanic: 22%; White: 56%; International: 2%.

ADMISSIONS FACTS AND FIGURES

Phone: (619) 594-6336. **Email:** admissions@sdsu.edu. **Website:** http://www.sdsu.edu. **Application deadlines for fall 2007:** Regular decision: November 30; decision sent by March 1. Early decision: Not offered. Early action: Not offered. Admission cannot be deferred. **Application fee:** $55. Common application is not accepted. **To apply online, go to:** http://www.sdsu.edu/apply. **Admissions requirements/recommendations:** High school units required (recommended): English: 4; Mathematics: 3 (4); Science: 2; Foreign language: 2; Social studies: 1; History: 1; Academic electives: 1; Total units: 15. Tests: The college uses SAT or ACT scores in admissions decisions. Either SAT or ACT required. For admission to the fall 2007 entering class, the school will accept: ACT with writing, ACT without writing. Campus visit: Neither required nor recommended. Admissions interview: Neither required nor recommended. Off-campus interview: Not available. **Factors that count in admissions decisions:** *Academic:* Secondary school record: Very important; Class rank: Not considered. Letters of recommendation: Not considered. Standardized test scores: Very important. Essay: Not considered. *Nonacademic:* Interview: Not considered. Extracurricular activities: Not considered. Talent/ability: Not considered. Character/personal qualities: Not considered. Alumni/ae relationship: Not considered. Geographical residence: Important. State residency: Important. Religious affiliation/commitment: Not considered. Minority status: Not considered. Volunteer work: Not considered. Work experience: Not considered. **Admissions statistics for the fall 2005 entering class:** Total applicants: 36,718. Total accepted: 16,266. Freshmen enrolled: 4,105; 5% were from out of state. Overall acceptance rate: 44%. **Average high school grade point average:** 3.5. **First-year students who submitted SAT scores:** 97%. Scores (25/75 percentile): Verbal: 480-580, Math: 500-600, Combined: 980-1180. **First-year students submitting ACT scores:** 37%. Scores (25/75 percentile): English: 19-25, Math: 20-26, Composite: 20-25.

ACADEMICS

Year founded: 1897. **Academic calendar:** Semester. **Degrees offered:** bachelor's, post-bachelor's certificate, master's, post-master's certificate, doctorate. **Most popular majors:** 18% business, management, marketing, and related support services, 11% social sciences, 10% liberal arts and sciences studies, and humanities, 7% English language and literature/letters, 7% psychology. **Major fields of study:** agriculture, agriculture operations, and related sciences; area, ethnic, cultural, and gender studies; biological and biomedical sciences; business, management, marketing, and related support services; communication, journalism, and related programs; communications technologies/technicians and support services; computer and information sciences and support services; education; engineering; English language and literature/letters; family and consumer sciences/human sciences; foreign languages, literatures, and linguistics; health professions and related clinical sciences; history; liberal arts and sciences studies, and humanities; mathematics and statistics; multi/interdisciplinary studies; natural resources and conservation; parks, recreation, leisure, and fitness studies; philosophy and religious studies; physical sciences; psychology; public administration and social service professions; security and protective services; social sciences; visual and performing arts. **Areas of required coursework:** arts/fine arts, humanities, mathematics, English (including composition), philosophy, foreign languages, sciences (biological or physical), history, social science. Pre-

professional programs: pre-law, pre-dentistry, pre-medicine, pre-veterinary science. **Special academic programs:** cross-registration, distance learning, double major, dual enrollment, English as a Second Language (ESL), exchange student program (domestic), honors program, independent study, internships, student-designed major, study abroad, teacher certificate program. **Teacher certification offered in:** early childhood, special education, elementary, vo-tech, middle/junior high, adult education, secondary, bilingual/bicultural. **Reserve Officers Training Corps (ROTC):** Army ROTC: Offered on campus; Navy ROTC: Offered on campus; Air Force ROTC: Offered on campus. **Faculty and instruction (2005-2006):** Total instructional faculty: 969 full-time, 783 part-time (53% men; 47% women; 22% minorities). Student/faculty ratio: 19/1. Classes of fewer than 20 students: 23%; of 20 to 49 students: 59%; of 50 or more students: 18%. **Advanced Placement and International Baccalaureate credit:** AP tests may be used for: Credit only. Scores accepted: 3, 4, 5. International Baccalaureate exams may be used for: Credit only. **Freshmen returning for sophomore year:** 82%. **Graduation rates:** Four-year: 14%; five-year: 42%; six-year: 53%.

COSTS AND FINANCIAL AID

Financial aid office: (619) 594-6323. **Expenses (2006-2007):** Tuition and fees 2006-2007: $3,122 in state, $13,292 out of state; room/board: $10,093. Estimated books and supplies: $1,283; transportation: $816; personal expenses: $2,392. **Financial aid:** In 2005-2006, 64% of undergraduates applied for financial aid. Of those, 51% were determined to have financial need; 11% had their need fully met. Average financial aid package (proportion receiving): $7,400 (48%). Average amount of gift aid, such as scholarships or grants (proportion receiving): $5,700 (37%). Average amount of self-help aid, such as work study or loans (proportion receiving): $4,000 (43%). Average need-based loan (excluding PLUS or other private loans): $4,000. Among students who received need-based aid, the average percentage of need met: 71%. Among students who received aid based on merit, the average award (and the proportion receiving): $1,700 (2%). The average athletic scholarship (and the proportion receiving): $8,100 (1%). Average amount of debt of borrowers graduating in 2005: $14,500. Proportion who borrowed: 49%.

CAMPUS LIFE AND EXTRACURRICULAR ACTIVITIES

Campus housing available: coed dorms, sorority housing, fraternity housing, apartment for single students, special housing for disabled students, special housing for international students, other housing options. Students who live in college-owned, operated, or affiliated housing: 13%. Average per-year earnings: $3,000. **Clubs and organizations:** Number of student organizations: 225. Activities include: choral groups, concert band, dance, drama/theater, jazz band, literary magazine, marching band, music ensembles, musical theater, opera, pep band, radio station, student government, student newspaper, student film society, symphony orchestra, television station. Number of fraternities: 24; sororities: 24. Proportion of men in fraternities: 10%; of women in sororities: 8%. **Sports program (2005-2006):** Member of NCAA I. *Men's intercollegiate varsity sports:* baseball, basketball, football, golf, soccer, tennis. *Women's intercollegiate varsity sports:* basketball, crew, cross-country, golf, soccer, softball, swimming and diving, tennis, track and field (indoor), track and field (outdoor), volleyball, water polo.

SERVICES AND FACILITIES

Basic services: nonremedial tutoring, placement service, day care, health service, health insurance. **Remedial assistance:** reading, math. **Counseling services:** career, military, academic, psychological, birth control. **For learning-disabled students:** School does not offer a structured program with separate admission and additional fees. Total undergraduates in learning-disabled program or receiving services: 217. Services include: remedial math, remedial English, other special classes, learning center, extended time for tests, tutors. **Information technology resources:** Students are not required to lease or own a computer. Number of campus computers available to all students: 400. School does not have a wireless network. Proportion of college-owned housing units wired for high-speed internet access: 100%. **Campus safety:** Security services offered: 24-hour foot-and-vehicle patrols, late-night transport/escort service, 24-hour emergency telephones, lighted pathways/sidewalks, student patrols.

TRANSFER AND INTERNATIONAL STUDENTS

Transfer students: May apply for admission for the following academic terms: Fall, Spring. Applicants need a minimum number of credits to apply. For fall 2005: Transfer applications received: 11,381. Transfer applicants offered admission: 7,333. Transfer applicants enrolled: 3,813. **International students:** Number of foreign undergraduates: 525 (2% of student body). Minimum TOEFL score required: 550 (paper); 213 (computer). Average TOEFL score: 588 (paper).

San Francisco Art Institute

- **Address:** 800 Chestnut Street, San Francisco, CA 94133
- **Website:** http://www.sfai.edu
- **Private**
- **Enrollment:** N/A

KEY STATS

✔ **U.S News College Ranking:** Unranked Specialty School–Fine Arts
✔ **SAT or ACT Score (25th/75th percentile):** N/A
✔ **Tuition:** 2005-2006: $25,670

Selectivity: Least selective	**Room/board:** $8,100
Acceptance rate: N/A	**Average debt:** N/A
Student/faculty ratio: N/A	**Proportion who borrowed:** N/A

San Francisco Conservatory of Music

- **Address:** 1201 Ortega Street, San Francisco, CA 94122
- **Website:** http://www.sfcm.edu
- **Private**
- **Enrollment:** 169 full-time; 6 part-time

KEY STATS

✔ **U.S News College Ranking:** Unranked Specialty School–Fine Arts
✔ **SAT or ACT Score (25th/75th percentile):** N/A
✔ **Tuition:** 2006-2007: $28,280

Selectivity: Least selective	**Room/board:** N/A
Acceptance rate: 51%	**Average debt:** $28,125
Student/faculty ratio: 7/1	**Proportion who borrowed:** 82%

UNDERGRADUATE STUDENT BODY STATS

2005-2006 enrollment: 169 full-time; 6 part-time. Men: 49%; women: 51%. **Ethnic makeup:** African American: 3%; Asian American: 20%; Hispanic: 3%; White: 63%; International: 11%.

ADMISSIONS FACTS AND FIGURES

Phone: (800) 899-7326. **Email:** admit@sfcm.edu. **Website:** http://www.sfcm.edu. **Application deadlines for fall 2007:** Regular decision: December 15; decision sent by April 1. Early decision: Not offered. Early action: Not offered. Admission cannot be deferred. **Application fee:** $100. Common application is not accepted. **To apply online, go to:** http://www.unifiedapps.org. **Admissions requirements/recommendations:** Tests: The college does not use SAT or ACT scores in admissions decisions. Neither SAT nor ACT required. Campus visit: Recommended. Admissions interview: Neither required nor recommended. Off-campus interview: Not available. **Factors that count in admissions decisions:** *Academic:* Secondary school record: Considered. Class rank: Considered. Letters of recommendation: Important. Standardized test scores: Considered. Essay: Considered. *Nonacademic:* Interview: Not considered. Extracurricular activities: Very important. Talent/ability: Very important. Character/personal qualities: Important. Alumni/ae relationship: Not considered. Geographical residence: Not considered. State residency: Not considered. Religious affiliation/commitment: Not considered. Minority status: Not considered. Volunteer work: Not considered. Work experience: Not considered. **Other schools with the greatest overlap in applicants:** Boston Conservatory; Cleveland Institute of Music; Juilliard School; Manhattan School of Music; New England Conservatory of Music. **Admissions statistics for the fall 2005 entering class:** Total applicants: 214. Total accepted: 110. Freshmen enrolled: 47; Overall acceptance rate: 51%. **Size of waiting list:** 18 applicants; enrolled from waiting list: 4.

ACADEMICS

Year founded: 1917. **Academic calendar:** Semester. **Degrees offered:** certificate, diploma, bachelor's, master's. **Most popular majors:** 100% visual and performing arts. **Major fields of study:** visual and performing arts. **Areas of required coursework:** arts/fine arts, humanities, other. **Special academic programs (% participation):** double major (1%), independent study (3%). **Faculty and instruction (2005-2006):** Total instructional faculty: 24 full-time, 73 part-time (67% men; 33% women). Student/faculty ratio: 7/1. Classes of fewer than 20 students: 76%; of 20 to 49 students: 19%; of 50 or more students: 5%. **Advanced Placement and International Baccalaureate credit:** AP tests may be used for:

Credit and/or placement. Scores accepted: 3. **Freshmen returning for sophomore year:** 76%. **Graduation rates:** Four-year: 62%; five-year: 67%; six-year: 66%. **Graduate study:** 15% of students pursue further study immediately upon graduation; 20% within one year; 25% within five years. Fields in which graduates pursue further study: education, 10%; arts and sciences, 90%.

COSTS AND FINANCIAL AID

Financial aid office: (415) 759-3414. **Expenses (2006-2007):** Tuition and fees 2006-2007: $28,280; room/board: N/A. **Financial aid:** Priority filing date for institution's financial aid form: March 1; deadline: March 1. In 2005-2006, 82% of undergraduates applied for financial aid. Of those, 82% were determined to have financial need; 5% had their need fully met. Average financial aid package (proportion receiving): $17,350 (79%). Average amount of gift aid, such as scholarships or grants (proportion receiving): $12,800 (76%). Average amount of self-help aid, such as work study or loans (proportion receiving): $4,281 (69%). Average need-based loan (excluding PLUS or other private loans): $4,281. Among students who received need-based aid, the average percentage of need met: 62%. Among students who received aid based on merit, the average award (and the proportion receiving): $8,000 (6%). The average athletic scholarship (and the proportion receiving): $0 (0%). Average amount of debt of borrowers graduating in 2005: $28,125. Proportion who borrowed: 82%.

CAMPUS LIFE AND EXTRACURRICULAR ACTIVITIES

Student employment: During the 2005-2006 academic year, 17% of undergraduates worked on campus. Average per-year earnings: $3,000. Activities include: choral groups, music ensembles, musical theater, opera, symphony orchestra. Number of fraternities: 0; sororities: 0.

SERVICES AND FACILITIES

Basic services: health insurance. **Counseling services:** psychological. **For learning-disabled students:** School does not offer a structured program with separate admission and additional fees. Total undergraduates in learning-disabled program or receiving services: 3. Services include: tutors. **Library:** Number of titles: 32,640; number of current serial subscriptions: 77. **Information technology resources:** Students are not required to lease or own a computer. Number of campus computers available to all students: 12. School has a wireless network. Approximate number of users that can be accommodated: 315.

TRANSFER AND INTERNATIONAL STUDENTS

Transfer students: May apply for admission for the following academic terms: Fall, Spring. Applicants do not need a minimum number of credits to apply. For fall 2005: Transfer applications received: 70. Transfer applicants offered admission: 31. Transfer applicants enrolled: 16. **International students:** Number of foreign undergraduates: 13 (11% of student body). Number of countries represented: 11. Minimum TOEFL score required: 500 (paper); 173 (computer). Average TOEFL score: 513 (paper).

San Francisco State University

- **Address:** 1600 Holloway Avenue, San Francisco, CA 94132
- **Website:** http://www.sfsu.edu
- **Public**
- **Enrollment:** 17,917 full-time; 5,157 part-time

KEY STATS

✔ **U.S News College Ranking:** 51, Universities–Master's (West)
✔ **SAT Score (25th/75th percentile):** 890-1130
✔ **Tuition:** 2006-2007: $3,370 in state, $13,540 out of state

Selectivity: Less selective	**Room/board:** $9,124
Acceptance rate: 67%	**Average debt:** $15,376
Student/faculty ratio: 21/1	**Proportion who borrowed:** 46%

UNDERGRADUATE STUDENT BODY STATS

2005-2006 enrollment: 17,917 full-time; 5,157 part-time. Men: 41%; women: 59%. **Ethnic makeup:** African American: 6%; American-Indian: 1%; Asian American: 31%; Hispanic: 14%; White: 43%; International: 5%.

ADMISSIONS FACTS AND FIGURES

Phone: (415) 338-1113. **Email:** ugadmit@sfsu.edu. **Website:** http://www.sfsu.edu. **Application deadlines for fall 2007:** Early decision: Not offered. Early action: Not offered. Admission cannot be deferred. **Application fee:** $55. Common application is not accepted. **To apply online, go to:** http://www.sfsu.edu/apply.htm. **Admissions requirements/recommendations:** High school units required (recommended): English: 4; Mathematics: 3; Science: 2; Foreign language: 2; Social studies: 1; History: 1; Academic electives: (1). Tests: The college uses SAT or ACT scores in admissions decisions. Neither SAT nor ACT required. For admission to the fall 2007 entering class, the school will accept: ACT with writing, ACT without writing. Campus visit: Neither required nor recommended. Admissions interview: Neither required nor recommended. Off-campus interview: Not available. **Factors that count in admissions decisions:** *Academic:* Secondary school record: Very important. Class rank: Not considered. Letters of recommendation: Considered. Standardized test scores: Very important. Essay: Not considered. *Nonacademic:* Interview: Not considered. Extracurricular activities: Not considered. Talent/ability: Considered. Character/personal qualities: Not considered. Alumni/ae relationship: Considered. Geographical residence: Not considered. State residency: Not considered. Religious affiliation/commitment: Not considered. Minority status: Not considered. Volunteer work: Not considered. Work experience: Not considered. **Admissions statistics for the fall 2005 entering class:** 3% were from out of state. Overall acceptance rate: 67%. **First-year students who submitted SAT scores:** 77%. Scores (25/75 percentile): Verbal: 440-560, Math: 450-570, Combined: 890-1130. **First-year students submitting ACT scores:** 18%. Scores (25/75 percentile): English: 16-24, Math: 17-23, Composite: 17-23.

ACADEMICS

Year founded: 1899. **Academic calendar:** Semester. **Degrees offered:** certificate, bachelor's, post-bachelor's certificate, master's, doctorate. **Most popular majors:** Information not available. **Major fields of study:** area, ethnic, cultural, and gender studies; biological and biomedical sciences; business, management, marketing, and related support services; communication, journalism, and related programs; communications technologies/technicians and support services; computer and information sciences and support services; education; engineering; English language and literature/letters; family and consumer sciences/human sciences; foreign languages, literatures, and linguistics; health professions and related clinical sciences; history; liberal arts and sciences studies, and humanities; mathematics and statistics; mechanic and repair technologies/technicians; multi/interdisciplinary studies; natural resources and conservation; parks, recreation, leisure, and fitness studies; philosophy and religious studies; physical sciences; psychology; public administration and social service professions; security and protective services; social sciences; visual and performing arts. **Areas of required coursework:** arts/fine arts, humanities, mathematics, English (including composition), foreign languages, sciences (biological or physical), history, social science. **Pre-professional programs:** pre-law, pre-medicine, other. **Special academic programs:** cooperative (work-study plan) program, cross-registration, distance learning, double major, dual enrollment, English as a Second Language (ESL), exchange student program (domestic), honors program, independent study, internships, liberal arts/career combination, student-designed major, study abroad, teacher certificate program. **Teacher certification offered in:** early childhood, special education, elementary, vo-tech, middle/junior high, adult education, secondary, bilingual/bicultural. **Reserve Officers Training Corps (ROTC):** Army ROTC: Offered at cooperating institution (University of San Francisco); Navy ROTC: Offered at cooperating institution (University of California, Berkeley); Air Force ROTC: Offered at cooperating institution (University of California, Berkeley). **Faculty and instruction (2005-2006):** Total instructional faculty: 865 full-time, 860 part-time (49% men; 51% women; 33% minorities). Full-time faculty with Ph.D. or other terminal degree: 77%. Student/faculty ratio: 21/1. Classes of fewer than 20 students: 25%; of 20 to 49 students: 54%; of 50 or more students: 21%. **Freshmen returning for sophomore year:** 79%. **Graduation rates:** Six-year: 39%.

COSTS AND FINANCIAL AID

Financial aid office: (415) 338-7000. **Expenses (2006-2007):** Tuition and fees 2006-2007: $3,370 in state, $13,540 out of state; room/board: $9,124. Estimated books and supplies: $1,400; transportation: $1,200; personal expenses: $2,400. **Financial aid:** Priority filing date for institution's financial aid form: March 2. In 2005-2006, 56% of undergraduates applied for financial aid. Of those, 48% were determined to have financial need; 8% had their need fully met. Average financial aid package (proportion receiving): $8,441 (46%). Average amount of gift aid, such as scholarships or grants (proportion receiving): $5,911 (34%). Average amount of self-help aid, such as work study or loans (proportion receiving): $4,140 (45%). Average need-based loan (excluding PLUS or other private loans): $2,995. Among students who received need-based aid, the average percentage of need met:

65%. Among students who received aid based on merit, the average award (and the proportion receiving): $1,841 (1%). The average athletic scholarship (and the proportion receiving): $2,088 (0%). Average amount of debt of borrowers graduating in 2005: $15,376. Proportion who borrowed: 46%.

CAMPUS LIFE AND EXTRACURRICULAR ACTIVITIES

Campus housing available: coed dorms, apartments for married students, apartment for single students, special housing for disabled students, special housing for international students. Students who live in college-owned, operated, or affiliated housing: 10%. Activities include: choral groups, concert band, dance, drama/theater, jazz band, literary magazine, marching band, music ensembles, musical theater, opera, pep band, radio station, student government, student newspaper, student film society, symphony orchestra, television station. Proportion of men in fraternities: 1%; of women in sororities: 1%. **Sports program (2005-2006):** Member of NCAA II. **Men's intercollegiate varsity sports:** baseball, basketball, cross-country, soccer, swimming and diving, track and field (outdoor), wrestling. **Women's intercollegiate varsity sports:** basketball, cross-country, soccer, softball, swimming and diving, tennis, track and field (indoor), track and field (outdoor), volleyball.

SERVICES AND FACILITIES

Basic services: nonremedial tutoring, women's center, placement service, day care, health service, health insurance. **Remedial assistance:** reading, math, writing, study skills. **Counseling services:** minority student, career, personal, veteran student, academic, older student, psychological, birth control, other. **For learning-disabled students:** Services include: other special classes, note-taking services. **Campus safety:** Security services offered: 24-hour foot-and-vehicle patrols, late-night transport/escort service, 24-hour emergency telephones, lighted pathways/sidewalks, student patrols, controlled dormitory access (key, security card, etc).

TRANSFER AND INTERNATIONAL STUDENTS

Transfer students: May apply for admission for the following academic terms: Fall, Spring. Applicants need a minimum number of credits to apply. For fall 2005: Transfer applications received: 10,254. Transfer applicants offered admission: 7,944. Transfer applicants enrolled: 3,029. **International students:** Number of foreign undergraduates: 1234 (5% of student body).

San Jose State University

- **Address:** 1 Washington Square, San Jose, CA 95192
- **Website:** http://www.sjsu.edu
- **Public**
- **Enrollment:** 16,968 full-time; 5,783 part-time

KEY STATS
✔ **U.S News College Ranking:** 41, Universities–Master's (West)
✔ **SAT Score (25th/75th percentile):** 850-1100
✔ **Tuition:** N/A

Selectivity: Less selective **Room/board:** N/A
Acceptance rate: 65% **Average debt:** N/A
Student/faculty ratio: 20/1 **Proportion who borrowed:** N/A

UNDERGRADUATE STUDENT BODY STATS

2005-2006 enrollment: 16,968 full-time; 5,783 part-time. Men: 49%; women: 51%. **Ethnic makeup:** African American: 5%; Asian American: 38%; Hispanic: 16%; White: 37%; International: 3%.

ADMISSIONS FACTS AND FIGURES

Phone: (408) 924-2013. **Email:** contact@sjsu.edu. **Website:** http://www.sjsu.edu. **Application deadlines for fall 2007:** Regular decision: February 1; decision sent by February 1. Early decision: Not offered. Early action: Not offered. Admission cannot be deferred. **Application fee:** $55. Common application is not accepted. **To apply online, go to:** http://www.csu-mentor.edu/AdmissionApp/. **Admissions requirements/recommendations:** High school units required (recommended): English: 4; Mathematics: 3; Science: 2; Foreign language: 2; Social studies: 1; History: 1; Academic electives: 1; Total units: 15. Tests: The college uses SAT or ACT scores in admissions decisions. Either SAT or ACT required. For admission to the fall 2007 entering class, the school will accept: ACT with writing, ACT without writing. Campus visit: Required. Admissions interview: Neither required nor recommended. Off-campus interview: Not available. **Factors that count in admissions decisions:** *Academic:* Secondary school record: Very important. Class rank: Not considered. Letters of recommendation: Not considered. Standardized test scores: Very important. Essay: Not considered. *Nonacademic:* Interview: Not considered. Extracurricular activities: Not considered. Talent/ability: Not considered. Character/personal qualities: Not considered. Alumni/ae relationship: Not considered. Geographical residence: Not considered. State residency: Not considered. Religious affiliation/commitment: Not considered. Minority status: Not considered. Volunteer work: Not considered. Work experience: Not considered. **Other schools with the greatest overlap in applicants:** Cal Poly–San Luis Obispo; California State University–Long Beach; San Diego State University; San Francisco State University; University of California–Davis. **Admissions statistics for the fall 2005 entering class:** Total applicants: 16,893. Total accepted: 11,040. Freshmen enrolled: 2,551; 1% were from out of state. Overall acceptance rate: 65%. **Average high school grade point average:** 3.0. **First-year students who submitted SAT scores:** 91%. Scores (25/75 percentile): Verbal: 410-530; Math: 440-570; Combined: 850-1100. **First-year students submitting ACT scores:** 16%. Scores (25/75 percentile): English: 14-22, Math: 16-24, Composite: 16-23.

ACADEMICS

Year founded: 1857. **Academic calendar:** Semester. **Degrees offered:** certificate, bachelor's, post-bachelor's certificate, master's, post-master's certificate. **Most popular majors:** 33% business, management, marketing, and related support services, 11% engineering, 8% visual and performing arts, 6% communication, journalism, and related programs, 6% health professions and related clinical sciences. **Major fields of study:** area, ethnic, cultural, and gender studies; biological and biomedical sciences; business, management, marketing, and related support services; communication, journalism, and related programs; education; engineering; English language and literature/letters; family and consumer sciences/human sciences; foreign languages, literatures, and linguistics; health professions and related clinical sciences; history; liberal arts and sciences studies, and humanities; mathematics and statistics; multi/interdisciplinary studies; natural resources and conservation; parks, recreation, leisure, and fitness studies; philosophy and religious studies; physical sciences; psychology; public administration and social service professions; security and protective services; social sciences; transportation and materials moving; visual and performing arts. **Areas of required coursework:** arts/fine arts, humanities, mathematics, English (including composition), sciences (biological or physical), history, social science. **Pre-professional programs:** pre-law. **Special academic programs (% participation):** distance learning (15%), double major (1%), honors program, independent study, internships, student-designed major, study abroad (1%), teacher certificate program (8%). **Teacher certification offered in:** early childhood, special education, elementary, middle/junior high, secondary, bilingual/bicultural. **Cooperative education programs:** engineering, technologies. **Reserve Officers Training Corps (ROTC):** Army ROTC: Offered on campus; Air Force ROTC: Offered on campus. **Faculty and instruction (2005-2006):** Total instructional faculty: 781 full-time, 1,090 part-time (51% men; 49% women; 27% minorities). Full-time faculty with Ph.D. or other terminal degree: 80%. Student/faculty ratio: 20/1. Classes of fewer than 20 students: 26%; of 20 to 49 students: 61%; of 50 or more students: 13%. **Advanced Placement and International Baccalaureate credit:** AP tests may be used for: Credit only. Scores accepted: 3, 4, 5. International Baccalaureate exams may be used for: Credit only. **Freshmen returning for sophomore year:** 80%. **Graduation rates:** Four-year: 7%; five-year: 26%; six-year: 39%. **Graduate study:** 10% of students pursue further study immediately upon graduation.

COSTS AND FINANCIAL AID

Financial aid office: (408) 283-7500.

CAMPUS LIFE AND EXTRACURRICULAR ACTIVITIES

Campus housing available (% using): coed dorms (65%), apartment for single students (34%), special housing for disabled students (1%), special housing for international students. Students who live in college-owned, operated, or affiliated housing: 30%. **Student employment:** During the 2005-2006 academic year, 5% of undergraduates worked on campus. Average per-year earnings: $6,000. **Clubs and organizations:** Number of student organizations: 245. Activities include: choral groups, concert band, dance, drama/theater, jazz band, literary magazine, marching band, music ensembles, musical theater, opera, pep band, radio station, student government, student newspaper, student film society, television station. Number of fraternities: 20; sororities: 15. Proportion of men in fraternities: 5%; of women in sororities: 3%. Average proportion of students who stay on campus on

weekends: 60%. **Sports program (2005-2006):** Member of NCAA I. **Men's intercollegiate varsity sports:** baseball, basketball, cross-country, football, golf, soccer. **Women's intercollegiate varsity sports:** basketball, cross-country, golf, gymnastics, soccer, softball, swimming and diving, tennis, volleyball, water polo.

SERVICES AND FACILITIES

Basic services: nonremedial tutoring, women's center, placement service, day care, health service, health insurance. **Remedial assistance:** reading, math, writing, study skills. **Counseling services:** minority student, career, military, personal, veteran student, academic, older student, psychological, birth control, religious. **For learning-disabled students:** School does not offer a structured program with separate admission and additional fees. Total undergraduates in learning-disabled program or receiving services: 483. Services include: remedial math, remedial English, reading machines, diagnostic testing service, note-taking services, oral tests, learning center, readers, extended time for tests, tutors, typist/scribe, exams on tape or computer, other testing accomodations, other. **Library:** Number of titles: 1,282,750; number of current serial subscriptions: 1,031. **Information technology resources:** Students are not required to lease or own a computer. Number of campus computers available to all students: 1,321. School has a wireless network. Approximate number of users that can be accommodated: 32,000. Proportion of college-owned housing units wired for high-speed internet access: 100%. **Campus safety:** Security services offered: 24-hour foot-and-vehicle patrols, late-night transport/escort service, 24-hour emergency telephones, lighted pathways/sidewalks, student patrols, controlled dormitory access (key, security card, etc).

TRANSFER AND INTERNATIONAL STUDENTS

Transfer students: May apply for admission for the following academic terms: Fall, Spring. Applicants need a minimum number of credits to apply. For fall 2005: Transfer applications received: 9,329. Transfer applicants offered admission: 6,318. Transfer applicants enrolled: 2,838. **International students:** Number of foreign undergraduates: 783 (3% of student body). Number of countries represented: 104. Minimum TOEFL score required: 500 (paper); 173 (computer). Average TOEFL score: 515 (paper).

Santa Clara University

- **Address:** 500 El Camino Real, Santa Clara, CA 95053
- **Website:** http://www.scu.edu
- **Private; Religious affiliation:** Roman Catholic
- **Enrollment:** 4,525 full-time; 113 part-time

KEY STATS

✔ **U.S News College Ranking:** 2, Universities–Master's (West)
✔ **SAT Score (25th/75th percentile):** 1120-1320
✔ **Tuition:** 2006-2007: $30,900

Selectivity: More selective	**Room/board:** $10,380
Acceptance rate: 61%	**Average debt:** $17,620
Student/faculty ratio: 12/1	**Proportion who borrowed:** 50%

UNDERGRADUATE STUDENT BODY STATS

2005-2006 enrollment: 4,525 full-time; 113 part-time. Men: 44%; women: 56%. **Ethnic makeup:** African American: 3%; American-Indian: 1%; Asian American: 18%; Hispanic: 13%; White: 63%; International: 3%. **Religious preference:** Protestant: 14%; Jewish: 1%; Muslim: 1%; Hindu: 1%; Buddhist: 2%; No preference: 18%; Unknown: 2%; Roman Catholic: 51%; Other Christian: 10%.

ADMISSIONS FACTS AND FIGURES

Phone: (408) 554-4700. **Website:** http://www.scu.edu. **Application deadlines for fall 2007:** Regular decision: January 15; decision sent by April 1. Early decision: Not offered. Early action: Send application by: November 1; Decision sent by: December 23. Admission can be deferred. **Application fee:** $55. Common application is accepted. **To apply online, go to:** https://www.scu.edu/apply/undergraduate/. **Admissions requirements/recommendations:** High school units required (recommended): English: 4 (4); Mathematics: 4 (4); Science: 3 (4); Foreign language: 3 (4); Social studies: 1 (2); History: 1 (1); Academic electives: 2 (2); Total units: 18 (20). Tests: The college uses SAT or ACT scores in admissions decisions. Either SAT or ACT required. For admission to the fall 2007 entering class, the school will accept: ACT without writing. **Campus visit:** Recommended. **Admissions interview:** Neither required nor recommended. **Off-campus interview:** Not available. **Factors that count in admissions decisions:** *Academic:* Secondary school record: Very important. Class rank: Considered. Letters of recommendation: Important. Standardized test scores: Important. Essay: Important. *Nonacademic:* Interview: Not considered. Extracurricular activities: Considered. Talent/ability: Important. Character/personal qualities: Important. Alumni/ae relationship: Considered. Geographical residence: Considered. State residency: Not considered. Religious affiliation/commitment: Not considered. Minority status: Considered. Volunteer work: Important. Work experience: Considered. **Other schools with the greatest overlap in applicants:** University of California–Berkeley; University of California–Davis; University of California–Los Angeles; University of California–San Diego; University of California–Santa Barbara. **Admissions statistics for the fall 2005 entering class:** Total applicants: 8,904. Total accepted: 5,419. Freshmen enrolled: 1,198; 41% were from out of state. Accepted through early-decision or early-action plans: 30%. Overall acceptance rate: 61%. Non-early acceptance rate: 58%. **Size of waiting list:** 1856 applicants; enrolled from waiting list: 351. **Credentials of fall 2005 freshmen:** 40% ranked in the top 10 percent of their high school class; 72% were in the top 25 percent, and 95% were in the top half. (Proportion submitting class standing: 39%.) **Average high school grade point average:** 3.5. **First-year students who submitted SAT scores:** 93%. Scores (25/75 percentile): Verbal: 550-650, Math: 570-670, Combined: 1120-1320. **First-year students submitting ACT scores:** 35%. Scores (25/75 percentile): English: N/A, Math: N/A, Composite: 24-28.

ACADEMICS

Year founded: 1851. **Academic calendar:** Quarter. **Degrees offered:** bachelor's, post-bachelor's certificate, master's, post-master's certificate, first professional, first professional certificate, doctorate. **Most popular majors:** 31% business, management, marketing, and related support services, 12% social sciences, 11% engineering, 8% psychology, 7% communication, journalism, and related programs. **Major fields of study:** biological and biomedical sciences; business, management, marketing, and related support services; communication, journalism, and related programs; engineering; English language and literature/letters; foreign languages, literatures, and linguistics; history; liberal arts and sciences studies, and humanities; mathematics and statistics; multi/interdisciplinary studies; natural resources and conservation; philosophy and religious studies; physical sciences; psychology; social sciences; visual and performing arts. **Areas of required coursework:** arts/fine arts, humanities, computer literacy, mathematics, English (including composition), philosophy, foreign languages, sciences (biological or physical), history, social science, other. **Pre-professional programs:** pre-law, pre-dentistry, pre-medicine, pre-veterinary science, pre-optometry, pre-pharmacy, other. **Special academic programs:** cooperative (work-study plan) program, double major, exchange student program (domestic), honors program, independent study, internships, student-designed major, study abroad, teacher certificate program. **Teacher certification offered in:** special education, elementary, middle/junior high, secondary. **Cooperative education programs:** engineering. **Reserve Officers Training Corps (ROTC):** Army ROTC: Offered on campus; Air Force ROTC: Offered at cooperating institution (San Jose State University). **Faculty and instruction (2005-2006):** Total instructional faculty: 447 full-time, 299 part-time (61% men; 39% women; 15% minorities). Full-time faculty with Ph.D. or other terminal degree: 91%. Student/faculty ratio: 12/1. Classes of fewer than 20 students: 33%; of 20 to 49 students: 64%; of 50 or more students: 3%. **Advanced Placement and International Baccalaureate credit:** AP tests may be used for: Credit and/or placement. Scores accepted: 4, 5. International Baccalaureate exams may be used for: Credit and/or placement. **Freshmen returning for sophomore year:** 92%. **Graduation rates:** Four-year: 77%; five-year: 83%; six-year: 84%. **Graduate study:** 18% of students pursue further study immediately upon graduation; 31% within one year; 81% within five years. Fields in which graduates pursue further study: Master of Business Administration (MBA), 25%; law, 12%; medicine, 5%; dentistry, 1%; engineering, 9%; theology (or the seminary), 1%; education, 10%; arts and sciences, 36%; veterinary medicine, 1%.

COSTS AND FINANCIAL AID

Financial aid office: (408) 554-4505. **Expenses (2006-2007):** Tuition and fees 2006-2007: $30,900; room/board: $10,380. Estimated books and supplies: $1,314; transportation: $774; personal expenses: $2,088. **Financial aid:** Priority filing date for institution's financial aid form: February 1. In 2005-2006, 62% of undergraduates applied for financial aid. Of those, 50% were determined to have financial need; 48% had their need fully met. Average financial aid package (proportion receiving): $19,706 (42%). Average

amount of gift aid, such as scholarships or grants (proportion receiving): $15,990 (38%). Average amount of self-help aid, such as work study or loans (proportion receiving): $5,605 (29%). Average need-based loan (excluding PLUS or other private loans): $4,963. Among students who received need-based aid, the average percentage of need met: 70%. Among students who received aid based on merit, the average award (and the proportion receiving): $9,259 (15%). The average athletic scholarship (and the proportion receiving): $15,787 (4%). Average amount of debt of borrowers graduating in 2005: $17,620. Proportion who borrowed: 50%.

CAMPUS LIFE AND EXTRACURRICULAR ACTIVITIES

Campus housing available (% using): coed dorms (89%), apartment for single students (11%). Students who live in college-owned, operated, or affiliated housing: 46%. **Student employment:** During the 2005-2006 academic year, 32% of undergraduates worked on campus. Average per-year earnings: $4,653. **Clubs and organizations:** Number of student organizations: 90. Activities include: choral groups, dance, drama/theater, jazz band, literary magazine, music ensembles, musical theater, opera, pep band, radio station, student government, student newspaper, symphony orchestra, yearbook. Number of fraternities: 0; sororities: 0. Average proportion of students who stay on campus on weekends: 50%. **Sports program (2005-2006):** Member of NCAA I. *Men's intercollegiate varsity sports:* baseball, basketball, crew, cross-country, golf, soccer, tennis, track and field (outdoor), water polo. *Women's intercollegiate varsity sports:* basketball, crew, cross-country, golf, soccer, softball, tennis, track and field (outdoor), volleyball, water polo.

SERVICES AND FACILITIES

Basic services: nonremedial tutoring, day care, health service, health insurance. **Counseling services:** minority student, career, military, personal, veteran student, academic, older student, psychological, birth control, religious. **For learning-disabled students:** School does not offer a structured program with separate admission and additional fees. Total undergraduates in learning-disabled program or receiving services: 80. Services include: reading machines, tape recorders, note-taking services, readers, extended time for tests, tutors, priority registration, priority seating, texts on tape, other testing accomodations. **Library:** Number of titles: 1,175,020; number of current serial subscriptions: 8,727. **Information technology resources:** Students are not required to lease or own a computer. Number of campus computers available to all students: 802. School has a wireless network. Approximate number of users that can be accommodated: 5,700. Proportion of college-owned housing units wired for high-speed internet access: 100%. **Campus safety:** Security services offered: 24-hour foot-and-vehicle patrols, late-night transport/escort service, 24-hour emergency telephones, lighted pathways/sidewalks, controlled dormitory access (key, security card, etc).

TRANSFER AND INTERNATIONAL STUDENTS

Transfer students: May apply for admission for the following academic terms: Fall, Winter. Applicants need a minimum number of credits to apply. For fall 2005: Transfer applications received: 663. Transfer applicants offered admission: 442. Transfer applicants enrolled: 224. **International students:** Number of foreign undergraduates: 123 (3% of student body). Number of countries represented: 10. Minimum TOEFL score required: 550 (paper); 213 (computer).

Scripps College

- **Address:** 1030 Columbia Avenue, Claremont, CA 91711
- **Website:** http://www.scrippscol.edu
- **Private**
- **Enrollment:** 879 full-time; 8 part-time

KEY STATS

✔ **U.S News College Ranking:** 26, Liberal Arts Colleges
✔ **SAT Score (25th/75th percentile):** 1270-1450
✔ **Tuition:** 2006-2007 $33,700

Selectivity: Most selective	**Room/board:** $10,100
Acceptance rate: 46%	**Average debt:** $12,907
Student/faculty ratio: 11/1	**Proportion who borrowed:** 49%

UNDERGRADUATE STUDENT BODY STATS

2005-2006 enrollment: 879 full-time; 8 part-time. Men: 0%; women: 100%. **Ethnic makeup:** African American: 3%; Asian American: 13%; Hispanic: 5%; White: 77%; International: 1%.

ADMISSIONS FACTS AND FIGURES

Phone: (800) 770-1333. **Email:** admission@scrippscollege.edu. **Website:** http://www.scrippscol.edu. **Application deadlines for fall 2007:** Regular decision: January 1; decision sent by April 1. Early decision: Send application by: November 1; Decision sent by: December 15. Early action: Not offered. Admission can be deferred. **Application fee:** $50. Common application is accepted. **Admissions requirements/recommendations:** High school units required (recommended): English: 4; Mathematics: 3; Science: 3; Foreign language: 3; Social studies: 3; Total units: 16. Tests: The college uses SAT or ACT scores in admissions decisions. Either SAT or ACT required. For admission to the fall 2007 entering class, the school will accept: ACT with writing, ACT without writing. Campus visit: Recommended. Admissions interview: Recommended. Off-campus interview: May be arranged. **Factors that count in admissions decisions:** *Academic:* Secondary school record: Very important. Class rank: Very important. Letters of recommendation: Very important. Standardized test scores: Very important. Essay: Very important. *Nonacademic:* Interview: Very important. Extracurricular activities: Very important. Talent/ability: Very important. Character/personal qualities: Very important. Alumni/ae relationship: Very important. Geographical residence: Important. State residency: Not considered. Religious affiliation/commitment: Not considered. Minority status: Very important. Volunteer work: Very important. Work experience: Very important. **Other schools with the greatest overlap in applicants:** Pomona College; University of California–Berkeley; University of California–Los Angeles; University of Southern California; Wellesley College. **Admissions statistics for the fall 2005 entering class:** Total applicants: 1,836. Total accepted: 847. Freshmen enrolled: 234; 60% were from out of state. Accepted through early-decision or early-action plans: 19%. Overall acceptance rate: 46%. Early-decision acceptance rate: 51%. Non-early acceptance rate: 46%. **Size of waiting list:** 428 applicants; enrolled from waiting list: 1. **Credentials of fall 2005 freshmen:** 69% ranked in the top 10 percent of their high school class; 93% were in the top 25 percent, and 98% were in the top half. (Proportion submitting class standing: 48%.) **Average high school grade point average:** 4.0. **First-year students who submitted SAT scores:** 93%. Scores (25/75 percentile): Verbal: 650-740, Math: 620-710, Combined: 1270-1450. **First-year students submitting ACT scores:** 30%. Scores (25/75 percentile): English: N/A, Math: N/A, Composite: 26-31.

ACADEMICS

Year founded: 1926. **Academic calendar:** Semester. **Degrees offered:** certificate, bachelor's. **Most popular majors:** 12% psychology, 9% English language and literature/letters, 9% visual and performing arts, 8% political science and government, 6% biological and biomedical sciences. **Major fields of study:** area, ethnic, cultural, and gender studies; biological and biomedical sciences; business, management, marketing, and related support services; communication, journalism, and related programs; computer and information sciences and support services; engineering; English language and literature/letters; foreign languages, literatures, and linguistics; history; mathematics and statistics; multi/interdisciplinary studies; natural resources and conservation; philosophy and religious studies; physical sciences; psychology; social sciences; visual and performing arts. **Areas of required coursework:** arts/fine arts, humanities, mathematics, English (including composition), foreign languages, sciences (biological or physical), social science, other. **Pre-professional programs:** pre-medicine. **Special academic programs (% participation):** accelerated program (3%), cross-registration (100%), double major (19%), dual enrollment, exchange student program (domestic) (2%), honors program, independent study (15%), internships, student-designed major, study abroad (58%). **Reserve Officers Training Corps (ROTC):** Army ROTC: Offered at cooperating institution (Claremont McKenna College); Air Force ROTC: Offered at cooperating institution (Harvey Mudd College). **Faculty and instruction (2005-2006):** Total instructional faculty: 66 full-time, 34 part-time (39% men; 61% women; 17% minorities). Full-time faculty with Ph.D. or other terminal degree: 100%. Student/faculty ratio: 11/1. Classes of fewer than 20 students: 67%; of 20 to 49 students: 31%; of 50 or more students: 2%. **Advanced Placement and International Baccalaureate credit:** AP tests may be used for: Credit only. Scores accepted: 4, 5. International Baccalaureate exams may be used for: Credit only. **Freshmen returning for sophomore year:** 91%. **Graduation rates:** Four-year: 81%; five-year: 83%; six-year: 84%. **Graduate study:** 31% of students pursue further study immediately upon graduation; 31% within one year; 39% within five years. Fields in which graduates pur-

sue further study: law, 12%; medicine, 23%; education, 6%; arts and sciences, 41%.

COSTS AND FINANCIAL AID

Financial aid office: (909) 621-8275. **Expenses (2006-2007):** Tuition and fees 2006-2007: $33,700; room/board: $10,100. Estimated books and supplies: $800; transportation: $0; personal expenses: $1,000. **Financial aid:** Priority filing date for institution's financial aid form: February 1. In 2005-2006, 53% of undergraduates applied for financial aid. Of those, 43% were determined to have financial need; 100% had their need fully met. Average financial aid package (proportion receiving): $27,665 (43%). Average amount of gift aid, such as scholarships or grants (proportion receiving): $23,122 (43%). Average amount of self-help aid, such as work study or loans (proportion receiving): $4,871 (40%). Average need-based loan (excluding PLUS or other private loans): $3,872. Among students who received need-based aid, the average percentage of need met: 100%. Among students who received aid based on merit, the average award (and the proportion receiving): $15,715 (11%). The average athletic scholarship (and the proportion receiving): $0 (0%). Average amount of debt of borrowers graduating in 2005: $12,907. Proportion who borrowed: 49%.

CAMPUS LIFE AND EXTRACURRICULAR ACTIVITIES

Campus housing available: women's dorms, apartment for single students, special housing for disabled students, other housing options. Students who live in college-owned, operated, or affiliated housing: 96%. **Student employment:** During the 2005-2006 academic year, 5% of undergraduates worked on campus. Average per-year earnings: $3,600. **Clubs and organizations:** Number of student organizations: 30. Activities include: choral groups, dance, drama/theater, literary magazine, music ensembles, radio station, student government, student newspaper, symphony orchestra, yearbook. Number of fraternities: 0; sororities: 0. Average proportion of students who stay on campus on weekends: 80%. **Sports program (2005-2006):** Member of NCAA III. *Men's intercollegiate varsity sports:* baseball, basketball, cross-country, football, golf, soccer, swimming and diving, tennis, track and field (outdoor), water polo. *Women's intercollegiate varsity sports:* basketball, cross-country, lacrosse, soccer, softball, swimming and diving, tennis, track and field (outdoor), volleyball, water polo.

SERVICES AND FACILITIES

Basic services: nonremedial tutoring, women's center, placement service, health service, health insurance. **Counseling services:** minority student, career, military, personal, academic, older student, psychological, birth control, religious. **For learning-disabled students:** School does not offer a structured program with separate admission and additional fees. Services include: remedial math, remedial reading, tape recorders, untimed tests, readers, extended time for tests, tutors, priority registration, priority seating, other. **Library:** Number of titles: 2,476,503; number of current serial subscriptions: 17,502. **Information technology resources:** Students are not required to lease or own a computer. Number of campus computers available to all students: 85. School has a wireless network. Approximate number of users that can be accommodated: 350. Proportion of college-owned housing units wired for high-speed internet access: 100%. **Campus safety:** Security services offered: late-night transport/escort service, 24-hour emergency telephones, lighted pathways/sidewalks, controlled dormitory access (key, security card, etc).

TRANSFER AND INTERNATIONAL STUDENTS

Transfer students: May apply for admission for the following academic terms: Fall, Spring. Applicants need a minimum number of credits to apply. For fall 2005: Transfer applications received: 79. Transfer applicants offered admission: 36. Transfer applicants enrolled: 18. **International students:** Number of foreign undergraduates: 11 (1% of student body). Number of countries represented: 6. Minimum TOEFL score required: 600 (paper); 250 (computer).

Simpson University

- **Address:** 2211 College View Drive, Redding, CA 96003-8606
- **Website:** http://www.simpsonuniversity.edu
- **Private; Religious affiliation:** Christian and Missionary Alliance
- **Enrollment:** 896 full-time; 28 part-time

KEY STATS

✔ **U.S News College Ranking:** third tier, Universities–Master's (West)
✔ **SAT Score (25th/75th percentile):** 890-1120
✔ **Tuition:** 2005-2006: $17,000

Selectivity: Selective	**Room/board:** $5,900
Acceptance rate: 54%	**Average debt:** N/A
Student/faculty ratio: 17/1	**Proportion who borrowed:** N/A

UNDERGRADUATE STUDENT BODY STATS

2005-2006 enrollment: 896 full-time; 28 part-time. Men: 35%; women: 65%. **Ethnic makeup:** African American: 1%; American-Indian: 1%; Asian American: 5%; Hispanic: 5%; White: 87%; International: 1%. **Religious preference:** Protestant: 74%; No preference: 3%; Unknown: 1%; Christian and Missionary Alliance: 22%.

ADMISSIONS FACTS AND FIGURES

Phone: (530) 226-4606. **Email:** admissions@simpsonuniversity.edu. **Website:** http://www.simpsonuniversity.edu. **Application deadlines for fall 2007:** Regular decision: Rolling. Early decision: Not offered. Early action: Not offered. Admission can be deferred. **Application fee:** $40. Common application is not accepted. **To apply online, go to:** https://www.applyweb.com/apply/simpson/menu.html. **Admissions requirements/recommendations:** High school units required (recommended): English: (4); Mathematics: (3); Science: (2); Foreign language: (2); Social studies: (3); History: (0); Academic electives: (0). Tests: The college uses SAT or ACT scores in admissions decisions. Either SAT or ACT required. For admission to the fall 2007 entering class, the school will accept: ACT with writing. Campus visit: Recommended. Admissions interview: Neither required nor recommended. Off-campus interview: Not available. **Factors that count in admissions decisions: Academic:** Secondary school record: Very important. Class rank: Considered. Letters of recommendation: Very important. Standardized test scores: Very important. Essay: Considered. **Nonacademic:** Interview: Considered. Extracurricular activities: Considered. Talent/ability: Important. Character/personal qualities: Very important. Alumni/ae relationship: Not considered. Geographical residence: Not considered. State residency: Not considered. Religious affiliation/commitment: Very important. Minority status: Not considered. Volunteer work: Considered. Work experience: Considered. **Other schools with the greatest overlap in applicants:** Azusa Pacific University; Fresno Pacific University; George Fox University; Seattle Pacific University; Vanguard University of Southern California. **Admissions statistics for the fall 2005 entering class:** Total applicants: 1,251. Total accepted: 675. Freshmen enrolled: 164; 27% were from out of state. Overall acceptance rate: 54%. **Size of waiting list:** 0 applicants; enrolled from waiting list: 0. **Credentials of fall 2005 freshmen:** 19% ranked in the top 10 percent of their high school class; 40% were in the top 25 percent, and 67% were in the top half. (Proportion submitting class standing: 77%.) **Average high school grade point average:** 3.3. **First-year students who submitted SAT scores:** 94%. Scores (25/75 percentile): Verbal: 460-570, Math: 430-550, Combined: 890-1120. **First-year students submitting ACT scores:** 32%. Scores (25/75 percentile): English: 17-26, Math: 16-22, Composite: 17-25.

ACADEMICS

Year founded: 1921. **Academic calendar:** Semester. **Degrees offered:** certificate, associate, bachelor's, master's. **Most popular majors:** 25% liberal arts and sciences/liberal studies, 19% psychology, 17% human resources management/personnel administration, 6% missions/missionary studies and missiology, 5% business administration and management. **Major fields of study:** business, management, marketing, and related support services; communication, journalism, and related programs; education; English language and literature/letters; history; liberal arts and sciences studies, and humanities; mathematics and statistics; philosophy and religious studies; psychology; social sciences; theology and religious vocations; visual and performing arts. **Areas of required coursework:** arts/fine arts, humanities, mathematics, English (including composition), philosophy, sciences (biological or physical), history. **Special academic programs:** accelerated program, double major, honors program, independent study, internships, student-

designed major, study abroad, teacher certificate program, weekend college. **Teacher certification offered in:** elementary, middle/junior high, secondary. **Faculty and instruction (2005-2006):** Total instructional faculty: 40 full-time, 59 part-time (73% men; 27% women; 2% minorities). Full-time faculty with Ph.D. or other terminal degree: 63%. Student/faculty ratio: 17/1. Classes of fewer than 20 students: 66%; of 20 to 49 students: 30%; of 50 or more students: 4%. **Advanced Placement and International Baccalaureate credit:** AP tests may be used for: Credit and/or placement. Scores accepted: 3, 4, 5. **Freshmen returning for sophomore year:** 61%. **Graduation rates:** Four-year: 35%; five-year: 48%; six-year: 46%.

COSTS AND FINANCIAL AID

Financial aid office: (530) 226-4111. **Expenses (2005-2006):** Tuition and fees 2005-2006: $17,000; room/board: $5,900. Estimated books and supplies: $1,200; transportation: $700; personal expenses: $1,780. **Financial aid:** Priority filing date for institution's financial aid form: March 2.

CAMPUS LIFE AND EXTRACURRICULAR ACTIVITIES

Campus housing available (% using): women's dorms (56%), men's dorms (37%), apartments for married students (2%), apartment for single students (2%), special housing for disabled students (1%), special housing for international students (2%). Students who live in college-owned, operated, or affiliated housing: 68%. **Student employment:** During the 2005-2006 academic year, 34% of undergraduates worked on campus. Average per-year earnings: $2,616. **Clubs and organizations:** Number of student organizations: 11. Activities include: choral groups, drama/theater, jazz band, music ensembles, pep band, student government, student newspaper, yearbook. Number of fraternities: 0; sororities: 0. Average proportion of students who stay on campus on weekends: 85%. **Sports program (2005-2006):** Member of NAIA. **Men's intercollegiate varsity sports:** baseball, basketball, soccer. **Women's intercollegiate varsity sports:** basketball, soccer, volleyball.

SERVICES AND FACILITIES

Basic services: nonremedial tutoring, other. **Remedial assistance:** math, writing. **Counseling services:** career, personal, psychological, religious. **For learning-disabled students:** School does not offer a structured program with separate admission and additional fees. Total undergraduates in learning-disabled program or receiving services: 50. Services include: untimed tests, note-taking services, oral tests, readers, extended time for tests, tutors, priority registration, priority seating, other testing accomodations. **Library:** Number of titles: 89,080; number of current serial subscriptions: 316. **Information technology resources:** Students are not required to lease or own a computer. Number of campus computers available to all students: 50. School has a wireless network. Approximate number of users that can be accommodated: 50. Proportion of college-owned housing units wired for high-speed internet access: 100%. **Campus safety:** Security services offered: 24-hour foot-and-vehicle patrols, late-night transport/escort service, 24-hour emergency telephones, lighted pathways/sidewalks, student patrols, controlled dormitory access (key, security card, etc).

TRANSFER AND INTERNATIONAL STUDENTS

Transfer students: May apply for admission for the following academic terms: Fall, Spring, Summer. Applicants need a minimum number of credits to apply. For fall 2005: Transfer applications received: 254. Transfer applicants offered admission: 208. Transfer applicants enrolled: 79. **International students:** Number of foreign undergraduates: 6 (1% of student body). Minimum TOEFL score required: 500 (paper); 180 (computer).

Sonoma State University

- **Address:** 1801 E. Cotati Avenue, Rohnert Park, CA 94928
- **Website:** http://www.sonoma.edu
- **Public**
- **Enrollment:** 5,653 full-time; 946 part-time

KEY STATS

✔ **U.S News College Ranking:** 32, Universities–Master's (West)
✔ **SAT Score (25th/75th percentile):** 930-1140
✔ **Tuition:** 2006-2007: $3,648 in state, $11,784 out of state

Selectivity: Selective	**Room/board:** $9,130
Acceptance rate: 66%	**Average debt:** $13,328
Student/faculty ratio: 23/1	**Proportion who borrowed:** 47%

UNDERGRADUATE STUDENT BODY STATS

2005-2006 enrollment: 5,653 full-time; 946 part-time. Men: 37%; women: 63%. **Ethnic makeup:** African American: 2%; American-Indian: 1%; Asian American: 5%; Hispanic: 11%; White: 80%; International: 1%.

ADMISSIONS FACTS AND FIGURES

Phone: (707) 664-2778. **Email:** student.outreach@sonoma.edu. **Website:** http://www.sonoma.edu. **Application deadlines for fall 2007:** Regular decision: December 31. Early decision: Not offered. Early action: Not offered. Admission cannot be deferred. **Application fee:** $55. Common application is not accepted. **To apply online, go to:** http://www.csumentor.edu. **Admissions requirements/recommendations:** High school units required (recommended): English: 4; Mathematics: 3; Science: 2; Foreign language: 2; History: 2; Academic electives: 1; Total units: 15. Tests: The college uses SAT or ACT scores in admissions decisions. Either SAT or ACT required. For admission to the fall 2007 entering class, the school will accept: ACT with writing, ACT without writing. Campus visit: Recommended. Admissions interview: Neither required nor recommended. Off-campus interview: Not available. **Factors that count in admissions decisions:** *Academic:* Secondary school record: Very important. Class rank: Not considered. Letters of recommendation: Not considered. Standardized test scores: Very important. Essay: Not considered. *Nonacademic:* Interview: Not considered. Extracurricular activities: Not considered. Talent/ability: Not considered. Character/personal qualities: Not considered. Alumni/ae relationship: Not considered. Geographical residence: Important. State residency: Important. Religious affiliation/commitment: Not considered. Minority status: Important. Volunteer work: Not considered. Work experience: Not considered. **Other schools with the greatest overlap in applicants:** San Francisco State University; University of California–Berkeley; University of California–Davis; University of California–Santa Cruz. **Admissions statistics for the fall 2005 entering class:** Total applicants: 9,787. Total accepted: 6,444. Freshmen enrolled: 1,053; 2% were from out of state. Overall acceptance rate: 66%. **Average high school grade point average:** 3.1. **First-year students who submitted SAT scores:** 96%. Scores (25/75 percentile): Verbal: 470-570, Math: 460-570, Combined: 930-1140. **First-year students submitting ACT scores:** 26%. Scores (25/75 percentile): English: N/A, Math: N/A, Composite: 19-24.

ACADEMICS

Year founded: 1960. **Academic calendar:** Semester. **Degrees offered:** bachelor's, master's. **Most popular majors:** 17% business administration and management, 10% liberal arts and sciences/liberal studies, 10% psychology, 7% sociology, 6% English language and literature. **Major fields of study:** area, ethnic, cultural, and gender studies; biological and biomedical sciences; business, management, marketing, and related support services; communication, journalism, and related programs; computer and information sciences and support services; education; English language and literature/letters; foreign languages, literatures, and linguistics; health professions and related clinical sciences; history; liberal arts and sciences studies, and humanities; mathematics and statistics; multi/interdisciplinary studies; natural resources and conservation; parks, recreation, leisure, and fitness studies; philosophy and religious studies; physical sciences; psychology; security and protective services; social sciences; visual and performing arts. **Areas of required coursework:** arts/fine arts, humanities, computer literacy, mathematics, English (including composition), philosophy, sciences (biological or physical), history, social science. **Pre-professional programs:** pre-law, pre-dentistry, pre-medicine, pre-veterinary science, pre-optometry, pre-pharmacy. **Special academic programs:** accelerated program, cooperative (work-study plan) program, cross-registration, distance learning, double major, dual enrollment, English as a Second Language (ESL), exchange student program (domestic), external degree program, honors program, independent study, internships, liberal arts/career combination, student-designed major, study abroad, teacher certificate program. **Teacher certification offered in:** early childhood, special education, elementary, middle/junior high, secondary, bilingual/bicultural. **Cooperative education programs:** natural science, social/behavioral science. **Reserve Officers Training Corps (ROTC):** Army ROTC: Offered at cooperating institution (UC San Francisco); Navy ROTC: Offered at cooperating institution (UC San Francisco); Air Force ROTC: Offered at cooperating institution (UC San Francisco). **Faculty and instruction (2005-2006):** Total instructional faculty: 277 full-time, 300 part-time (49% men; 51% women; 14% minorities). Full-time faculty with Ph.D. or other terminal degree: 100%. Student/faculty ratio: 23/1. Classes of fewer than 20 students: 32%; of 20 to 49 students: 59%; of 50 or more students: 8%. **Advanced Placement and International Baccalaureate credit:** AP tests may be used for: Credit only. Scores accepted: 3, 4. International Baccalaureate exams may be used for: Credit and/or

placement. **Freshmen returning for sophomore year:** 82%. **Graduation rates:** Four-year: 20%; five-year: 43%; six-year: 49%.

COSTS AND FINANCIAL AID

Financial aid office: (707) 664-2287. **Expenses (2006-2007):** Tuition and fees 2006-2007: $3,648 in state, $11,784 out of state; room/board: $9,130. Estimated books and supplies: $1,314; transportation: $1,116; personal expenses: $2,466. **Financial aid:** Priority filing date for institution's financial aid form: January 31. In 2005-2006, 53% of undergraduates applied for financial aid. Of those, 42% were determined to have financial need; 18% had their need fully met. Average financial aid package (proportion receiving): $7,498 (41%). Average amount of gift aid, such as scholarships or grants (proportion receiving): $4,705 (32%). Average amount of self-help aid, such as work study or loans (proportion receiving): $4,151 (35%). Average need-based loan (excluding PLUS or other private loans): $3,866. Among students who received need-based aid, the average percentage of need met: 63%. Among students who received aid based on merit, the average award (and the proportion receiving): $1,567 (1%). The average athletic scholarship (and the proportion receiving): $1,292 (0%). Average amount of debt of borrowers graduating in 2005: $13,328. Proportion who borrowed: 47%.

CAMPUS LIFE AND EXTRACURRICULAR ACTIVITIES

Campus housing available: coed dorms, apartment for single students, special housing for international students, other housing options. Students who live in college-owned, operated, or affiliated housing: 33%. **Student employment:** During the 2005-2006 academic year, 10% of undergraduates worked on campus. Average per-year earnings: $1,950. **Clubs and organizations:** Number of student organizations: 109. Activities include: choral groups, dance, drama/theater, jazz band, literary magazine, music ensembles, musical theater, opera, pep band, radio station, student government, student newspaper, symphony orchestra. Number of fraternities: 5; sororities: 7. Proportion of men in fraternities: 5%; of women in sororities: 5%. Average proportion of students who stay on campus on weekends: 60%. **Sports program (2005-2006):** Member of NCAA II. *Men's intercollegiate varsity sports:* baseball, basketball, golf, soccer, tennis. *Women's intercollegiate varsity sports:* basketball, cross-country, soccer, softball, tennis, track and field (outdoor), volleyball, water polo.

SERVICES AND FACILITIES

Basic services: nonremedial tutoring, women's center, placement service, day care, health service. **Remedial assistance:** reading, math, writing, study skills. **Counseling services:** minority student, career, military, personal, veteran student, academic, older student, psychological, birth control. **For learning-disabled students:** School does not offer a structured program with separate admission and additional fees. Total undergraduates in learning-disabled program or receiving services: 200. Services include: remedial math, remedial English, reading machines, remedial reading, tape recorders, other special classes, note-taking services, learning center, readers, extended time for tests, priority registration, texts on tape, other testing accomodations. **Library:** Number of titles: 636,613; number of current serial subscriptions: 21,115. **Information technology resources:** Students are required to lease or own a computer. Number of campus computers available to all students: 430. School has a wireless network. Approximate number of users that can be accommodated: 13,400. Proportion of college-owned housing units wired for high-speed internet access: 100%. **Campus safety:** Security services offered: 24-hour foot-and-vehicle patrols, late-night transport/escort service, 24-hour emergency telephones, lighted pathways/sidewalks, controlled dormitory access (key, security card, etc).

TRANSFER AND INTERNATIONAL STUDENTS

Transfer students: May apply for admission for the following academic terms: Fall, Spring. Applicants need a minimum number of credits to apply. For fall 2005: Transfer applications received: 1,271. Transfer applicants offered admission: 1,060. Transfer applicants enrolled: 649. **International students:** Number of foreign undergraduates: 73 (1% of student body). Minimum TOEFL score required: 500 (paper); 173 (computer). Average TOEFL score: 550 (paper).

Southern Calif. Institute of Architecture

■ **Address:** 960 E. Third Street, Los Angeles, CA 90013
■ **Website:** http://www.sciarc.edu
■ **Private**
■ **Enrollment:** 209 full-time

KEY STATS
✔ **U.S News College Ranking:** Unranked Specialty School–Fine Arts
✔ **SAT or ACT Score (25th/75th percentile):** N/A
✔ **Tuition:** 2006-2007: $9,708

Selectivity: Least selective	**Room/board:** N/A
Acceptance rate: 72%	**Average debt:** N/A
Student/faculty ratio: 15/1	**Proportion who borrowed:** N/A

UNDERGRADUATE STUDENT BODY STATS
2005-2006 enrollment: 209 full-time. Men: 75%; women: 25%. **Ethnic makeup:** African American: 1%; Asian American: 14%; Hispanic: 20%; White: 37%; International: 27%.

ADMISSIONS FACTS AND FIGURES
Phone: (800) 774-7242. **Email:** admissions@sciarc.edu. **Website:** http://www.sciarc.edu. **Application deadlines for fall 2007:** Regular decision: July 1; decision sent by August 1. Early decision: Not offered. Early action: Send application by: N/A; Decision sent by: N/A. Admission can be deferred. **Application fee:** $60. Common application is not accepted. **Admissions requirements/recommendations:** High school units required (recommended): English: 4; Mathematics: 3; Science: 2; Foreign language: 2; Social studies: 1; History: 2; Academic electives: 2; Total units: 17. Tests: The college uses SAT or ACT scores in admissions decisions. Neither SAT nor ACT required. Campus visit: Recommended. Admissions interview: Recommended. Off-campus interview: Not available. **Factors that count in admissions decisions:** *Academic:* Secondary school record: Very important. Class rank: Considered. Letters of recommendation: Very important. Standardized test scores: Important. Essay: Very important. *Nonacademic:* Interview: Important. Extracurricular activities: Considered. Talent/ability: Very important. Character/personal qualities: Important. Alumni/ae relationship: Not considered. Geographical residence: Not considered. State residency: Not considered. Religious affiliation/commitment: Not considered. Minority status: Considered. Volunteer work: Considered. Work experience: Considered. **Other schools with the greatest overlap in applicants:** Otis College of Art and Design; Pratt Institute; Savannah College of Art and Design; University of Southern California; Woodbury University. **Admissions statistics for the fall 2005 entering class:** Total applicants: 29. Total accepted: 21. Freshmen enrolled: 6; Overall acceptance rate: 72%. Non-early acceptance rate: 72%. **Size of waiting list:** 0 applicants; enrolled from waiting list: N/A.

ACADEMICS
Year founded: 1972. **Academic calendar:** Trimester. **Degrees offered:** bachelor's, master's. **Most popular majors:** Information not available. **Major fields of study:** architecture and related services. **Faculty and instruction (2005-2006):** Total instructional faculty: 33 full-time, 89 part-time (68% men; 32% women). Student/faculty ratio: 15/1. Classes of fewer than 20 students: 53%; of 20 to 49 students: 47%; of 50 or more students: 0%. **Freshmen returning for sophomore year:** 68%. **Graduation rates:** Six-year: 47%.

COSTS AND FINANCIAL AID
Financial aid office: (213) 613-2200. **Expenses (2006-2007):** Tuition and fees 2006-2007: $9,708; room/board: N/A.

CAMPUS LIFE AND EXTRACURRICULAR ACTIVITIES
Activities include: student government. Number of fraternities: 0; sororities: 0.

SERVICES AND FACILITIES
Remedial assistance: writing, study skills. **Counseling services:** personal, veteran student, academic, psychological. **Campus safety:** Security services offered: 24-hour foot-and-vehicle patrols, late-night transport/escort service.

TRANSFER AND INTERNATIONAL STUDENTS
Transfer students: May apply for admission for the following academic terms: Fall, Spring. Applicants need a minimum number of credits to apply.

International students: Number of foreign undergraduates: 57 (27% of student body). Minimum TOEFL score required: 560 (paper); 220 (computer).

Stanford University

■ **Address:** Stanford, CA 94305
■ **Website:** http://www.stanford.edu
■ **Private**
■ **Enrollment:** 6,515 full-time; 61 part-time

KEY STATS
✔ **U.S News College Ranking:** 4, National Universities
✔ **SAT Score (25th/75th percentile):** 1360-1550
✔ **Tuition:** 2006-2007: $32,994

Selectivity: Most selective	**Room/board:** $10,367
Acceptance rate: 12%	**Average debt:** $15,172
Student/faculty ratio: 6/1	**Proportion who borrowed:** 45%

UNDERGRADUATE STUDENT BODY STATS
2005-2006 enrollment: 6,515 full-time; 61 part-time. Men: 53%; women: 47%. **Ethnic makeup:** African American: 10%; American-Indian: 2%; Asian American: 24%; Hispanic: 11%; White: 46%; International: 6%.

ADMISSIONS FACTS AND FIGURES
Phone: (650) 723-2091. **Email:** admission@stanford.edu. **Website:** http://www.stanford.edu. **Application deadlines for fall 2007:** Regular decision: December 15; decision sent by April 1. Early decision: Not offered. Early action: Send application by: November 1; Decision sent by: December 15. Admission can be deferred. **Application fee:** $75. Common application is not accepted. **To apply online, go to:** http://www.stanford.edu/dept/uga/applying/index.html. **Admissions requirements/recommendations:** High school units required (recommended): English: (4); Mathematics: (4); Science: (3); Foreign language: (3); Social studies: (2); History: (1); Total units: (20). Tests: The college uses SAT or ACT scores in admissions decisions. Either SAT or ACT required. For admission to the fall 2007 entering class, the school will accept: ACT with writing. Campus visit: Neither required nor recommended. Admissions interview: Neither required nor recommended. Off-campus interview: Not available. **Factors that count in admissions decisions:** *Academic:* Secondary school record: Very important. Class rank: Very important. Letters of recommendation: Very important. Standardized test scores: Very important. Essay: Very important. *Nonacademic:* Interview: Not considered. Extracurricular activities: Important. Talent/ability: Important. Character/personal qualities: Very important. Alumni/ae relationship: Considered. Geographical residence: Considered. State residency: Not considered. Religious affiliation/commitment: Not considered. Minority status: Considered. Volunteer work: Considered. Work experience: Considered. **Other schools with the greatest overlap in applicants:** Harvard University; Massachusetts Institute of Technology; Princeton University; University of California–Berkeley; Yale University. **Admissions statistics for the fall 2005 entering class:** Total applicants: 20,195. Total accepted: 2,426. Freshmen enrolled: 1,633; 60% were from out of state. Overall acceptance rate: 12%. Non-early acceptance rate: 12%. **Size of waiting list:** N/A applicants; enrolled from waiting list: 13. **Credentials of fall 2005 freshmen:** 89% ranked in the top 10 percent of their high school class; 97% were in the top 25 percent, and 100% were in the top half. (Proportion submitting class standing: 80%.) **Average high school grade point average:** 3.9. **First-year students who submitted SAT scores:** 97%. Scores (25/75 percentile): Verbal: 670-770, Math: 690-780, Combined: 1360-1550. **First-year students submitting ACT scores:** 23%. Scores (25/75 percentile): English: 29-34, Math: 29-34, Composite: 29-33.

ACADEMICS
Year founded: 1885. **Academic calendar:** Quarter. **Degrees offered:** bachelor's, master's, first professional, doctorate. **Most popular majors:** 25% social sciences, 13% multi/interdisciplinary studies, 11% engineering, 7% biology/biological sciences, 6% psychology. **Major fields of study:** architecture and related services; area, ethnic, cultural, and gender studies; biological and biomedical sciences; communication, journalism, and related programs; computer and information sciences and support services; engineering; engineering technologies/technicians; English language and literature/letters; foreign languages, literatures, and linguistics; history;

mathematics and statistics; multi/interdisciplinary studies; natural resources and conservation; philosophy and religious studies; physical sciences; psychology; public administration and social service professions; social sciences; visual and performing arts. **Areas of required coursework:** humanities, mathematics, English (including composition), foreign languages, sciences (biological or physical), social science. **Special academic programs (% participation):** accelerated program (2%), double major (78%), dual enrollment (13%), exchange student program (domestic) (1%), honors program (21%), independent study (75%), internships, student-designed major (1%), study abroad (25%), other (5%). **Reserve Officers Training Corps (ROTC):** Army ROTC: Offered at cooperating institution (Santa Clara University); Navy ROTC: Offered at cooperating institution (University of California–Berkeley); Air Force ROTC: Offered at cooperating institution (San Jose University). **Faculty and instruction (2005-2006):** Total instructional faculty: 956 full-time, 19 part-time (77% men; 23% women; 16% minorities). Full-time faculty with Ph.D. or other terminal degree: 98%. Student/faculty ratio: 6/1. Classes of fewer than 20 students: 70%; of 20 to 49 students: 19%; of 50 or more students: 11%. **Advanced Placement and International Baccalaureate credit:** AP tests may be used for: Credit and/or placement. Scores accepted: 3, 4, 5. International Baccalaureate exams may be used for: Credit and/or placement. **Freshmen returning for sophomore year:** 98%. **Graduation rates:** Four-year: 76%; five-year: 90%; six-year: 94%. **Graduate study:** 33% of students pursue further study immediately upon graduation. Fields in which graduates pursue further study: Master of Business Administration (MBA), 1%; law, 12%; medicine, 22%; arts and sciences, 56%.

COSTS AND FINANCIAL AID

Financial aid office: (650) 723-3058. **Expenses (2006-2007):** Tuition and fees 2006-2007: $32,994; room/board: $10,367. Estimated books and supplies: $1,290 personal expenses: $1,935. **Financial aid:** Priority filing date for institution's financial aid form: February 1. In 2005-2006, 52% of undergraduates applied for financial aid. Of those, 45% were determined to have financial need; 86% had their need fully met. Average financial aid package (proportion receiving): $29,750 (44%). Average amount of gift aid, such as scholarships or grants (proportion receiving): $25,500 (43%). Average amount of self-help aid, such as work study or loans (proportion receiving): $3,800 (32%). Average need-based loan (excluding PLUS or other private loans): $2,390. Among students who received need-based aid, the average percentage of need met: 100%. Among students who received aid based on merit, the average award (and the proportion receiving): $3,000 (10%). The average athletic scholarship (and the proportion receiving): $30,500 (6%). Average amount of debt of borrowers graduating in 2005: $15,172. Proportion who borrowed: 45%.

CAMPUS LIFE AND EXTRACURRICULAR ACTIVITIES

Campus housing available (% using): coed dorms (64%), women's dorms (1%), sorority housing (3%), fraternity housing (5%), apartments for married students (1%), apartment for single students (10%), special housing for disabled students (2%), cooperative housing (5%), other housing options (9%). Students who live in college-owned, operated, or affiliated housing: 91%. **Clubs and organizations:** Number of student organizations: 640. Activities include: choral groups, concert band, dance, drama/theater, jazz band, literary magazine, marching band, music ensembles, musical theater, opera, pep band, radio station, student government, student newspaper, student film society, symphony orchestra, television station, yearbook. Number of fraternities: 15; sororities: 11. Average proportion of students who stay on campus on weekends: 94%. **Sports program (2005-2006):** Member of NCAA I. *Men's intercollegiate varsity sports:* baseball, basketball, crew, cross-country, fencing, football, golf, gymnastics, sailing, soccer, swimming and diving, tennis, track and field (indoor), track and field (outdoor), volleyball, water polo, wrestling. *Women's intercollegiate varsity sports:* basketball, crew, cross-country, fencing, field hockey, golf, gymnastics, lacrosse, lightweight crew, sailing, soccer, softball, swimming and diving, syncronized swimming, tennis, track and field (indoor), track and field (outdoor), volleyball, water polo.

SERVICES AND FACILITIES

Basic services: nonremedial tutoring, women's center, placement service, day care, health service, health insurance, other. **Counseling services:** career, personal, academic, psychological, birth control, religious. **For learning-disabled students:** School does not offer a structured program with separate admission and additional fees. Total undergraduates in learning-disabled program or receiving services: 125. Services include: reading machines, tape recorders, diagnostic testing service, note-taking services, oral tests, learning center, readers, extended time for tests, tutors, texts on tape, typist/scribe,

other testing accomodations, other. **Library:** Number of titles: 8,267,412; number of current serial subscriptions: 52,000. **Information technology resources:** Students are not required to lease or own a computer. Number of campus computers available to all students: 1,500. School has a wireless network. Approximate number of users that can be accommodated: 5,000. Proportion of college-owned housing units wired for high-speed internet access: 100%. **Campus safety:** Security services offered: 24-hour foot-and-vehicle patrols, late-night transport/escort service, 24-hour emergency telephones, lighted pathways/sidewalks, controlled dormitory access (key, security card, etc).

TRANSFER AND INTERNATIONAL STUDENTS

Transfer students: May apply for admission for the following academic terms: Fall. Applicants need a minimum number of credits to apply. For fall 2005: Transfer applications received: 1,281. Transfer applicants offered admission: 62. Transfer applicants enrolled: 50. **International students:** Number of foreign undergraduates: 401 (6% of student body). Number of countries represented: 68.

St. Mary's College of California

- **Address:** 1928 St. Mary's Road, Moraga, CA 94556
- **Website:** http://www.stmarys-ca.edu
- **Private; Religious affiliation:** Roman Catholic
- **Enrollment:** 2,442 full-time; 83 part-time

KEY STATS
✔ **U.S News College Ranking:** 10, Universities–Master's (West)
✔ **SAT Score (25th/75th percentile):** 980-1200
✔ **Tuition:** 2006-2007: $29,050

Selectivity: Selective	**Room/board:** $10,566
Acceptance rate: 85%	**Average debt:** $21,892
Student/faculty ratio: 12/1	**Proportion who borrowed:** 62%

UNDERGRADUATE STUDENT BODY STATS

2005-2006 enrollment: 2,442 full-time; 83 part-time. Men: 39%; women: 61%. **Ethnic makeup:** African American: 6%; American-Indian: 1%; Asian American: 10%; Hispanic: 20%; White: 61%; International: 2%. **Religious preference:** Jewish: 1%; Hindu: 1%; Buddhist: 1%; No preference: 17%; Roman Catholic: 55%; Christian: 7%; Other: 18%.

ADMISSIONS FACTS AND FIGURES

Phone: (925) 631-4224. **Email:** smcadmit@stmarys-ca.edu. **Website:** http://www.stmarys-ca.edu. **Application deadlines for fall 2007:** Regular decision: January 15. Early decision: Not offered. Early action: Send application by: November 30; Decision sent by: December 30. Admission can be deferred. **Application fee:** $55. Common application is accepted. **To apply online, go to:** http://www.stmarys-ca.edu/prospective/undergraduate_admissions/first_year_students/application.html. **Admissions requirements/recommendations:** High school units required (recommended): English: 4 (4); Mathematics: 3 (4); Science: 2 (3); Foreign language: 2 (3); Social studies: 1 (1); History: 1 (1); Academic electives: 2 (2); Total units: 16 (19). Tests: The college uses SAT or ACT scores in admissions decisions. Either SAT or ACT required. For admission to the fall 2007 entering class, the school will accept: ACT with writing, ACT without writing. Campus visit: Recommended. Admissions interview: Neither required nor recommended. Off-campus interview: May be arranged. **Factors that count in admissions decisions:** *Academic:* Secondary school record: Very important. Class rank: Considered. Letters of recommendation: Important. Standardized test scores: Very important. Essay: Important. *Nonacademic:* Interview: Considered. Extracurricular activities: Considered. Talent/ability: Considered. Character/personal qualities: Considered. Alumni/ae relationship: Considered. Geographical residence: Considered. State residency: Not considered. Religious affiliation/commitment: Considered. Minority status: Considered. Volunteer work: Considered. Work experience: Considered. **Other schools with the greatest overlap in applicants:** Loyola Marymount University; Santa Clara University; University of California–Davis; University of California–Santa Barbara; University of San Diego. **Admissions statistics for the fall 2005 entering class:** Total applicants: 3,381. Total accepted: 2,861. Freshmen enrolled: 675; 16% were from out of state. Accepted through early-decision or early-action plans: 25%. Overall acceptance rate: 85%. **Size of waiting list:** 115 applicants; enrolled from waiting list:

40. Credentials of fall 2005 freshmen: 30% ranked in the top 10 percent of their high school class; 73% were in the top 25 percent, and 90% were in the top half. (Proportion submitting class standing: 32%.) **Average high school grade point average:** 3.3. **First-year students who submitted SAT scores:** 90%. Scores (25/75 percentile): Verbal: 490-600, Math: 490-600, Combined: 980-1200. **First-year students submitting ACT scores:** 10%. Scores (25/75 percentile): English: N/A, Math: N/A, Composite: 22-27.

ACADEMICS

Year founded: 1863. **Academic calendar:** 4-1-4. **Degrees offered:** bachelor's, master's, doctorate. **Most popular majors:** 27% business/commerce, 12% communication studies/speech communication and rhetoric, 11% social sciences, 10% liberal arts and sciences/liberal studies, 9% psychology. **Major fields of study:** area, ethnic, cultural, and gender studies; biological and biomedical sciences; business, management, marketing, and related support services; communication, journalism, and related programs; English language and literature/letters; foreign languages, literatures, and linguistics; health professions and related clinical sciences; history; liberal arts and sciences studies, and humanities; mathematics and statistics; multi/interdisciplinary studies; parks, recreation, leisure, and fitness studies; philosophy and religious studies; physical sciences; psychology; social sciences; visual and performing arts. **Areas of required coursework:** arts/fine arts, humanities, mathematics, English (including composition), philosophy, foreign languages, sciences (biological or physical), history, social science, other. **Pre-professional programs:** pre-law, pre-dentistry, pre-medicine, pre-veterinary science, pre-optometry, pre-pharmacy. **Special academic programs (% participation):** cross-registration (4%), double major (23%), English as a Second Language (ESL) (1%), exchange student program (domestic) (5%), honors program (7%), independent study (11%), internships (27%), liberal arts/career combination (4%), student-designed major (4%), study abroad (29%). **Teacher certification offered in:** early childhood, special education, elementary, secondary. **Reserve Officers Training Corps (ROTC):** Army ROTC: Offered at cooperating institution (University of California–Berkeley); Air Force ROTC: Offered at cooperating institution (University of California–Berkeley). **Faculty and instruction (2005-2006):** Total instructional faculty: 197 full-time, 396 part-time (46% men; 54% women; 12% minorities). Full-time faculty with Ph.D. or other terminal degree: 90%. Student/faculty ratio: 12/1. Classes of fewer than 20 students: 46%; of 20 to 49 students: 54%; of 50 or more students: 0%. **Advanced Placement and International Baccalaureate credit:** AP tests may be used for: Credit only. International Baccalaureate exams may be used for: Credit and/or placement. **Freshmen returning for sophomore year:** 89%. **Graduation rates:** Four-year: 59%; five-year: 65%; six-year: 68%. **Graduate study:** 18% of students pursue further study immediately upon graduation; 35% within one year; 51% within five years. Fields in which graduates pursue further study: Master of Business Administration (MBA), 10%; law, 4%; medicine, 9%; dentistry, 1%; theology (or the seminary), 2%; education, 32%; arts and sciences, 41%.

COSTS AND FINANCIAL AID

Financial aid office: (925) 631-4370. **Expenses (2006-2007):** Tuition and fees 2006-2007: $29,050; room/board: $10,566. Estimated books and supplies: $1,152; transportation: $774; personal expenses: $2,088. **Financial aid:** Priority filing date for institution's financial aid form: March 2; deadline: March 2. In 2005-2006, 70% of undergraduates applied for financial aid. Of those, 64% were determined to have financial need; 8% had their need fully met. Average financial aid package (proportion receiving): $20,858 (63%). Average amount of gift aid, such as scholarships or grants (proportion receiving): $16,898 (56%). Average amount of self-help aid, such as work study or loans (proportion receiving): $5,894 (58%). Average need-based loan (excluding PLUS or other private loans): $4,535. Among students who received need-based aid, the average percentage of need met: 72%. Among students who received aid based on merit, the average award (and the proportion receiving): $7,454 (3%). The average athletic scholarship (and the proportion receiving): $16,870 (10%). Average amount of debt of borrowers graduating in 2005: $21,892. Proportion who borrowed: 62%.

CAMPUS LIFE AND EXTRACURRICULAR ACTIVITIES

Campus housing available (% using): coed dorms (96%), special housing for disabled students (4%). Students who live in college-owned, operated, or affiliated housing: 63%. **Student employment:** During the 2005-2006 academic year, 4% of undergraduates worked on campus. Average per-year earnings: $3,500. **Clubs and organizations:** Number of student organizations: 43. Activities include: choral groups, dance, drama/theater, jazz band, literary magazine, music ensembles, musical theater, pep band, radio station, student government, student newspaper, television station, yearbook.

Number of fraternities: 0; sororities: 0. Average proportion of students who stay on campus on weekends: 50%. **Sports program (2005-2006):** Member of NCAA I. **Men's intercollegiate varsity sports:** baseball, basketball, cross-country, football, golf, soccer, tennis. **Women's intercollegiate varsity sports:** basketball, crew, cross-country, lacrosse, soccer, softball, tennis, volleyball.

SERVICES AND FACILITIES

Basic services: nonremedial tutoring, women's center, health service. **Remedial assistance:** writing. **Counseling services:** minority student, career, personal, academic, psychological, birth control, religious. **For learning-disabled students:** School does not offer a structured program with separate admission and additional fees. Services include: remedial English, reading machines, tape recorders, untimed tests, note-taking services, oral tests, readers, extended time for tests, tutors, priority registration, substitution of courses, typist/scribe, exams on tape or computer, other testing accomodations, other. **Library:** Number of titles: 216,733; number of current serial subscriptions: 14,089. **Information technology resources:** Students are not required to lease or own a computer. Number of campus computers available to all students: 400. School has a wireless network. Approximate number of users that can be accommodated: 1,000. Proportion of college-owned housing units wired for high-speed internet access: 100%. **Campus safety:** Security services offered: 24-hour foot-and-vehicle patrols, late-night transport/escort service, 24-hour emergency telephones, lighted pathways/sidewalks, controlled dormitory access (key, security card, etc).

TRANSFER AND INTERNATIONAL STUDENTS

Transfer students: May apply for admission for the following academic terms: Fall, Winter, Spring. Applicants need a minimum number of credits to apply. For fall 2005: Transfer applications received: 446. Transfer applicants offered admission: 285. Transfer applicants enrolled: 118. **International students:** Number of foreign undergraduates: 60 (2% of student body). Number of countries represented: 33. Minimum TOEFL score required: 525 (paper); 197 (computer). Average TOEFL score: 550 (paper).

Thomas Aquinas College

- **Address:** 10000 N. Ojai Road, Santa Paula, CA 93060-9621
- **Website:** http://www.thomasaquinas.edu
- **Private; Religious affiliation:** Roman Catholic
- **Enrollment:** 359 full-time

KEY STATS

- ✔ **U.S News College Ranking:** 73, Liberal Arts Colleges
- ✔ **SAT Score (25th/75th percentile):** 1200-1390
- ✔ **Tuition:** 2006-2007: $19,300

Selectivity: More selective	**Room/board:** $6,000
Acceptance rate: 81%	**Average debt:** $14,000
Student/faculty ratio: 12/1	**Proportion who borrowed:** 85%

UNDERGRADUATE STUDENT BODY STATS

2005-2006 enrollment: 359 full-time. Men: 49%; women: 51%. **Ethnic makeup:** American-Indian: 1%; Asian American: 3%; Hispanic: 7%; White: 82%; International: 7%. **Religious preference:** Protestant: 5%; No preference: 1%; Unknown: 1%; Roman Catholic: 93%.

ADMISSIONS FACTS AND FIGURES

Phone: (800) 634-9797. **Email:** admissions@thomasaquinas.edu. **Website:** http://www.thomasaquinas.edu. **Application deadlines for fall 2007:** Regular decision: Rolling. Early decision: Not offered. Early action: Not offered. Admission can be deferred. Common application is not accepted. **Admissions requirements/recommendations:** High school units required (recommended): English: 4 (4); Mathematics: 3 (4); Science: (3); Foreign language: 2 (2); History: 2 (2); Academic electives: (3); Total units: 11 (18). Tests: The college uses SAT or ACT scores in admissions decisions. Either SAT or ACT required. For admission to the fall 2007 entering class, the school will accept: ACT with writing, ACT without writing. Campus visit: Recommended. Admissions interview: Neither required nor recommended. Off-campus interview: May be arranged. **Factors that count in admissions decisions:** *Academic:* Secondary school record: Very important. Class rank: Considered. Letters of recommendation: Very important. Standardized test scores: Very important. Essay: Very important. *Nonacademic:* Interview: Considered. Extracurricular activities: Considered. Talent/ability:

Considered. **Character/personal qualities:** Very important. **Alumni/ae relationship:** Not considered. **Geographical residence:** Not considered. **State residency:** Not considered. **Religious affiliation/commitment:** Important. **Minority status:** Not considered. **Volunteer work:** Considered. **Work experience:** Considered. **Other schools with the greatest overlap in applicants:** Catholic University of America; Christendom College; Franciscan University of Steubenville; University of Dallas; University of Notre Dame. **Admissions statistics for the fall 2005 entering class:** Total applicants: 196. Total accepted: 159. Freshmen enrolled: 102; 60% were from out of state. Overall acceptance rate: 81%. **Size of waiting list:** 57 applicants; enrolled from waiting list: 37. **Credentials of fall 2005 freshmen:** 75% ranked in the top 10 percent of their high school class; 75% were in the top 25 percent, and 100% were in the top half. (Proportion submitting class standing: 8%.) **Average high school grade point average:** 3.7. **First-year students who submitted SAT scores:** 94%. Scores (25/75 percentile): Verbal: 630-740, Math: 570-650, Combined: 1200-1390. **First-year students submitting ACT scores:** 8%. Scores (25/75 percentile): English: 25-31, Math: 24-31, Composite: 24-29.

ACADEMICS

Year founded: 1971. **Academic calendar:** Semester. **Degrees offered:** bachelor's. **Most popular majors:** Information not available. **Major fields of study:** liberal arts and sciences studies, and humanities. **Areas of required coursework:** humanities, mathematics, English (including composition), philosophy, foreign languages, sciences (biological or physical), history, social science, other. **Faculty and instruction (2005-2006):** Total instructional faculty: 29 full-time, 5 part-time (91% men; 9% women). Full-time faculty with Ph.D. or other terminal degree: 62%. Student/faculty ratio: 12/1. Classes of fewer than 20 students: 98%; of 20 to 49 students: 3%. **Freshmen returning for sophomore year:** 88%. **Graduation rates:** Four-year: 84%; five-year: 84%; six-year: 85%. **Graduate study:** 21% of students pursue further study immediately upon graduation; 24% within one year; 32% within five years. Fields in which graduates pursue further study: Master of Business Administration (MBA), 1%; law, 10%; medicine, 1%; dentistry, 1%; engineering, 1%; theology (or the seminary), 11%; education, 5%; arts and sciences, 55%.

COSTS AND FINANCIAL AID

Financial aid office: (805) 525-4417. **Expenses (2006-2007):** Tuition and fees 2006-2007: $19,300; room/board: $6,000. Estimated books and supplies: $450; transportation: $774; personal expenses: $400. **Financial aid:** In 2005-2006, 71% of undergraduates applied for financial aid. Of those, 67% were determined to have financial need; 100% had their need fully met. Average financial aid package (proportion receiving): $16,479 (67%). Average amount of gift aid, such as scholarships or grants (proportion receiving): $11,955 (59%). Average amount of self-help aid, such as work study or loans (proportion receiving): $5,805 (65%). Average need-based loan (excluding PLUS or other private loans): $3,297. Among students who received need-based aid, the average percentage of need met: 100%. Among students who received aid based on merit, the average award (and the proportion receiving): $0 (0%). The average athletic scholarship (and the proportion receiving): $0 (0%). Average amount of debt of borrowers graduating in 2005: $14,000. Proportion who borrowed: 85%.

CAMPUS LIFE AND EXTRACURRICULAR ACTIVITIES

Campus housing available (% using): women's dorms (51%), men's dorms (48%), other housing options (1%). Students who live in college-owned, operated, or affiliated housing: 99%. **Clubs and organizations:** Number of student organizations: 7. Activities include: choral groups, dance, drama/theater, literary magazine, music ensembles, musical theater. Number of fraternities: 0; sororities: 0. Average proportion of students who stay on campus on weekends: 95%.

SERVICES AND FACILITIES

Basic services: health service. **Remedial assistance:** math, writing. **Counseling services:** career, personal, academic, psychological, religious. **For learning-disabled students:** School does not offer a structured program with separate admission and additional fees. **Library:** Number of titles: 61,700; number of current serial subscriptions: 70. **Information technology resources:** Students are not required to lease or own a computer. Number of campus computers available to all students: 11. School does not have a wireless network. Proportion of college-owned housing units wired for high-speed internet access: 0%. **Campus safety:** Security services offered: lighted pathways/sidewalks, student patrols, controlled dormitory access (key, security card, etc).

TRANSFER AND INTERNATIONAL STUDENTS

International students: Number of foreign undergraduates: 25 (7% of student body). Number of countries represented: 9. Minimum TOEFL score required: 570 (paper); 230 (computer). Average TOEFL score: 597 (paper).

University of California–Berkeley

- **Address:** 110 Sproul Hall, Berkeley, CA 94720-5800
- **Website:** http://www.berkeley.edu
- **Public**
- **Enrollment:** 22,295 full-time; 1,187 part-time

KEY STATS

✔ **U.S News College Ranking:** 21, National Universities
✔ **SAT Score (25th/75th percentile):** 1220-1450
✔ **Tuition:** 2006-2007: $7,703 in state, $26,387 out of state
Selectivity: Most selective   **Room/board:** $13,074
Acceptance rate: 27%   **Average debt:** $13,171
Student/faculty ratio: 15/1   **Proportion who borrowed:** 47%

UNDERGRADUATE STUDENT BODY STATS

2005-2006 enrollment: 22,295 full-time; 1,187 part-time. Men: 46%; women: 54%. **Ethnic makeup:** African American: 4%; American-Indian: 1%; Asian American: 41%; Hispanic: 11%; White: 41%; International: 3%.

ADMISSIONS FACTS AND FIGURES

Phone: (510) 642-3175. **Website:** http://www.berkeley.edu. **Application deadlines for fall 2007:** Regular decision: November 30. Early decision: Not offered. Early action: Not offered. Admission cannot be deferred. **Application fee:** $60. Common application is not accepted. **To apply online, go to:** http://www.ucop.edu/pathways/. **Admissions requirements/recommendations:** High school units required (recommended): English: 4 (4); Mathematics: 3 (4); Science: 2 (3); Foreign language: 2 (3); Social studies: 2 (2); History: 2 (2); Academic electives: 1 (1); Total units: 15 (19). Tests: The college uses SAT or ACT scores in admissions decisions. Either SAT or ACT required. For admission to the fall 2007 entering class, the school will accept: ACT with writing. **Factors that count in admissions decisions:** *Academic:* Secondary school record: Very important. Class rank: Not considered. Letters of recommendation: Not considered. Standardized test scores: Important. Essay: Very important. *Nonacademic:* Interview: Not considered. Extracurricular activities: Important. Talent/ability: Important. Character/personal qualities: Important. Alumni/ae relationship: Not considered. Geographical residence: Considered. State residency: Very important. Religious affiliation/commitment: Not considered. Minority status: Not considered. Volunteer work: Important. Work experience: Important. **Admissions statistics for the fall 2005 entering class:** Total applicants: 36,989. Total accepted: 9,809. Freshmen enrolled: 4,101; 7% were from out of state. Overall acceptance rate: 27%. **Credentials of fall 2005 freshmen:** 99% ranked in the top 10 percent of their high school class; 100% were in the top 25 percent, and 100% were in the top half. (Proportion submitting class standing: 100%.) **Average high school grade point average:** 3.9. **First-year students who submitted SAT scores:** 99%. Scores (25/75 percentile): Verbal: 590-710, Math: 630-740, Combined: 1220-1450.

ACADEMICS

Year founded: 1868. **Academic calendar:** Semester. **Degrees offered:** certificate, bachelor's, master's, first professional, doctorate. **Most popular majors:** 9% biochemistry, biophysics, and molecular biology, 7% political science and government, 6% business administration, management, and operations, 6% economics, 4% psychology. **Major fields of study:** architecture and related services; area, ethnic, cultural, and gender studies; biological and biomedical sciences; business, management, marketing, and related support services; communication, journalism, and related programs; computer and information sciences and support services; engineering; English language and literature/letters; foreign languages, literatures, and linguistics; health professions and related clinical sciences; history; legal professions and studies; mathematics and statistics; multi/interdisciplinary studies; natural resources and conservation; philosophy and religious studies; physical sciences; psychology; public administration and social service professions; social sciences; visual and performing arts. **Areas of required coursework:** arts/fine arts, English (including composition), philosophy, sciences (biological or physical), history, social science, other. **Special academic programs:**

accelerated program, cross-registration, distance learning, double major, dual enrollment, English as a Second Language (ESL), exchange student program (domestic), honors program, independent study, internships, student-designed major, study abroad, teacher certificate program, other. **Reserve Officers Training Corps (ROTC):** Army ROTC: Offered on campus; Navy ROTC: Offered on campus; Air Force ROTC: Offered on campus. **Faculty and instruction (2005-2006):** Total instructional faculty: 1,543 full-time, 483 part-time (66% men; 34% women; 18% minorities). Full-time faculty with Ph.D. or other terminal degree: 99%. Student/faculty ratio: 15/1. Classes of fewer than 20 students: 59%; of 20 to 49 students: 26%; of 50 or more students: 15%. **Freshmen returning for sophomore year:** 97%. **Graduation rates:** Four-year: 58%; five-year: 84%; six-year: 87%.

COSTS AND FINANCIAL AID

Financial aid office: (510) 642-6442. **Expenses (2006-2007):** Tuition and fees 2006-2007: $7,703 in state, $26,387 out of state; room/board: $13,074. Estimated books and supplies: $1,326; transportation: $684; personal expenses: $1,388. **Financial aid:** Priority filing date for institution's financial aid form: March 2; deadline: March 2. In 2005-2006, 62% of undergraduates applied for financial aid. Of those, 50% were determined to have financial need; 55% had their need fully met. Average financial aid package (proportion receiving): $15,203 (49%). Average amount of gift aid, such as scholarships or grants (proportion receiving): $10,937 (45%). Average amount of self-help aid, such as work study or loans (proportion receiving): $6,146 (39%). Average need-based loan (excluding PLUS or other private loans): $5,058. Among students who received need-based aid, the average percentage of need met: 89%. Among students who received aid based on merit, the average award (and the proportion receiving): $3,402 (7%). The average athletic scholarship (and the proportion receiving): $14,504 (2%). Average amount of debt of borrowers graduating in 2005: $13,171. Proportion who borrowed: 47%.

CAMPUS LIFE AND EXTRACURRICULAR ACTIVITIES

Campus housing available: coed dorms, women's dorms, men's dorms, sorority housing, fraternity housing, apartments for married students, apartment for single students, special housing for disabled students, special housing for international students, cooperative housing, other housing options. Students who live in college-owned, operated, or affiliated housing: 35%. Activities include: choral groups, concert band, dance, drama/theater, jazz band, literary magazine, marching band, music ensembles, musical theater, pep band, radio station, student government, student newspaper, student film society, symphony orchestra, television station, yearbook. Proportion of men in fraternities: 10%; of women in sororities: 10%. **Sports program (2005-2006):** Member of NCAA I. *Men's intercollegiate varsity sports:* baseball, basketball, crew, cross-country, football, golf, gymnastics, rugby, soccer, swimming and diving, tennis, track and field (indoor), track and field (outdoor), water polo. *Women's intercollegiate varsity sports:* basketball, crew, cross-country, field hockey, golf, gymnastics, lacrosse, soccer, softball, swimming and diving, tennis, track and field (indoor), track and field (outdoor), volleyball, water polo.

TRANSFER AND INTERNATIONAL STUDENTS

Transfer students: May apply for admission for the following academic terms: Fall. Applicants need a minimum number of credits to apply. For fall 2005: Transfer applications received: 10,439. Transfer applicants offered admission: 3,020. Transfer applicants enrolled: 1,994. **International students:** Number of foreign undergraduates: 774 (3% of student body). Minimum TOEFL score required: 550 (paper); 220 (computer).

University of California–Davis

- **Address:** 1 Shields Avenue, Davis, CA 95616
- **Website:** http://www.ucdavis.edu
- **Public**
- **Enrollment:** 22,445 full-time; 290 part-time

KEY STATS

✔ **U.S News College Ranking:** 47, National Universities
✔ **SAT Score (25th/75th percentile):** 1060-1300
✔ **Tuition:** 2006-2007: $7,593 in state, $25,761 out of state
   Selectivity: More selective   Room/board: $11,239
   Acceptance rate: 61%   Average debt: $12,701
   Student/faculty ratio: 19/1   Proportion who borrowed: 50%

UNDERGRADUATE STUDENT BODY STATS

2005-2006 enrollment: 22,445 full-time; 290 part-time. Men: 44%; women: 56%. **Ethnic makeup:** African American: 3%; American-Indian: 1%; Asian American: 40%; Hispanic: 11%; White: 44%; International: 2%.

ADMISSIONS FACTS AND FIGURES

Phone: (530) 752-2971. **Email:** undergraduateadmissions@ucdavis.edu. **Website:** http://www.ucdavis.edu. **Application deadlines for fall 2007:** Regular decision: November 30; decision sent by March 15. Early decision: Not offered. Early action: Not offered. Admission can be deferred. **Application fee:** $60. Common application is not accepted. **To apply online, go to:** http://www.universityofcalifornia.edu/apply. **Admissions requirements/recommendations:** High school units required (recommended): English: 4 (4); Mathematics: 3 (4); Science: 2 (3); Foreign language: 2 (3); Social studies: 2 (2); Academic electives: 1 (1); Total units: 15 (18). Tests: The college uses SAT or ACT scores in admissions decisions. Either SAT or ACT required. For admission to the fall 2007 entering class, the school will accept: ACT with writing. Campus visit: Neither required nor recommended. Admissions interview: Neither required nor recommended. Off-campus interview: Not available. **Factors that count in admissions decisions:** *Academic:* Secondary school record: Very important. Class rank: Not considered. Letters of recommendation: Not considered. Standardized test scores: Very important. Essay: Important. *Nonacademic:* Interview: Not considered. Extracurricular activities: Important. Talent/ability: Important. Character/personal qualities: Important. Alumni/ae relationship: Not considered. Geographical residence: Not considered. State residency: Considered. Religious affiliation/commitment: Not considered. Minority status: Not considered. Volunteer work: Considered. Work experience: Considered. **Admissions statistics for the fall 2005 entering class:** Total applicants: 30,079. Total accepted: 18,264. Freshmen enrolled: 4,381; 3% were from out of state. Overall acceptance rate: 61%. **Credentials of fall 2005 freshmen:** 95% ranked in the top 10 percent of their high school class; 100% were in the top 25 percent, and 100% were in the top half. (Proportion submitting class standing: 100%.) **Average high school grade point average:** 3.7. **First-year students who submitted SAT scores:** 98%. Scores (25/75 percentile): Verbal: 500-630, Math: 560-670, Combined: 1060-1300. **First-year students submitting ACT scores:** 34%. Scores (25/75 percentile): English: 20-27, Math: 23-28, Composite: 21-27.

ACADEMICS

Year founded: 1905. **Academic calendar:** Quarter. **Degrees offered:** bachelor's, post-bachelor's certificate, master's, post-master's certificate, first professional, doctorate. **Most popular majors:** 8% psychology, 6% communication studies/speech communication and rhetoric, 6% economics, 5% biology/biological sciences, 5% political science and government. **Major fields of study:** agriculture, agriculture operations, and related sciences; architecture and related services; area, ethnic, cultural, and gender studies; biological and biomedical sciences; computer and information sciences and support services; engineering; English language and literature/letters; family and consumer sciences/human sciences; foreign languages, literatures, and linguistics; history; mathematics and statistics; multi/interdisciplinary studies; natural resources and conservation; philosophy and religious studies; physical sciences; psychology; social sciences; visual and performing arts. **Areas of required coursework:** English (including composition), other. **Special academic programs:** accelerated program, cross-registration, double major, dual enrollment, English as a Second Language (ESL), honors program, independent study, internships, student-designed major, study abroad, teacher certificate program, other. **Teacher certification offered in:**

elementary, middle/junior high, secondary, bilingual/bicultural. **Cooperative education programs:** education, health professions. **Reserve Officers Training Corps (ROTC):** Army ROTC: Offered on campus; Navy ROTC: Offered at cooperating institution (University of California–Berkeley); Air Force ROTC: Offered at cooperating institution (CSU-Sacramento). **Faculty and instruction (2005-2006):** Total instructional faculty: 1,610 full-time, 273 part-time (68% men; 32% women; 19% minorities). Full-time faculty with Ph.D. or other terminal degree: 98%. Student/faculty ratio: 19/1. Classes of fewer than 20 students: 35%; of 20 to 49 students: 37%; of 50 or more students: 28%. **Advanced Placement and International Baccalaureate credit:** AP tests may be used for: Credit only. Scores accepted: 3, 4, 5. **Freshmen returning for sophomore year:** 91%. **Graduation rates:** Four-year: 42%; five-year: 75%; six-year: 80%. **Graduate study:** 38% of students pursue further study within one year. Fields in which graduates pursue further study: Master of Business Administration (MBA), 10%; law, 9%; medicine, 10%; dentistry, 2%; engineering, 6%; theology (or the seminary), 1%; education, 20%; arts and sciences, 50%; veterinary medicine, 3%.

COSTS AND FINANCIAL AID
Financial aid office: (530) 752-2390. **Expenses (2006-2007):** Tuition and fees 2006-2007: $7,593 in state, $25,761 out of state; room/board: $11,239. Estimated books and supplies: $1,513; transportation: $748; personal expenses: $2,125. **Financial aid:** Priority filing date for institution's financial aid form: March 2. In 2005-2006, 61% of undergraduates applied for financial aid. Of those, 51% were determined to have financial need; 17% had their need fully met. Average financial aid package (proportion receiving): $11,697 (48%). Average amount of gift aid, such as scholarships or grants (proportion receiving): $9,072 (44%). Average amount of self-help aid, such as work study or loans (proportion receiving): $4,681 (35%). Average need-based loan (excluding PLUS or other private loans): $4,515. Among students who received need-based aid, the average percentage of need met: 75%. Among students who received aid based on merit, the average award (and the proportion receiving): $4,342 (6%). The average athletic scholarship (and the proportion receiving): $0 (0%). Average amount of debt of borrowers graduating in 2005: $12,701. Proportion who borrowed: 50%.

CAMPUS LIFE AND EXTRACURRICULAR ACTIVITIES
Campus housing available (% using): coed dorms (77%), women's dorms (8%), men's dorms (1%), sorority housing (1%), fraternity housing (2%), apartments for married students (5%), apartment for single students (4%), special housing for disabled students (0%), special housing for international students (1%), cooperative housing (1%), other housing options. Students who live in college-owned, operated, or affiliated housing: 19%. **Student employment:** During the 2005-2006 academic year, 12% of undergraduates worked on campus. Average per-year earnings: $2,745. **Clubs and organizations:** Number of student organizations: 452. Activities include: choral groups, concert band, dance, drama/theater, jazz band, literary magazine, marching band, music ensembles, musical theater, pep band, radio station, student government, student newspaper, student film society, symphony orchestra, television station, yearbook. Number of fraternities: 28; sororities: 25. Proportion of men in fraternities: 9%; of women in sororities: 8%. **Sports program (2005-2006):** Member of NCAA II. **Men's intercollegiate varsity sports:** baseball, basketball, cross-country, football, golf, soccer, swimming and diving, tennis, track and field (indoor), track and field (outdoor), water polo, wrestling. **Women's intercollegiate varsity sports:** basketball, crew, cross-country, gymnastics, lacrosse, rowing, soccer, softball, swimming and diving, tennis, track and field (indoor), track and field (outdoor), volleyball, water polo.

SERVICES AND FACILITIES
Basic services: nonremedial tutoring, women's center, placement service, day care, health service, health insurance. **Remedial assistance:** reading, math, writing, study skills. **Counseling services:** minority student, career, military, personal, veteran student, academic, older student, psychological, birth control. **For learning-disabled students:** School does not offer a structured program with separate admission and additional fees. Total undergraduates in learning-disabled program or receiving services: 191. Services include: reading machines, tape recorders, note-taking services, learning center, readers, extended time for tests, priority registration, texts on tape. **Information technology resources:** Students are required to lease or own a computer. Number of campus computers available to all students: 1,500. School has a wireless network. Approximate number of users that can be accommodated: 1,500. Proportion of college-owned housing units wired for high-speed internet access: 100%. **Campus safety:** Security services offered: 24-hour foot-and-vehicle patrols, late-night transport/escort service, 24-hour emergency telephones, lighted pathways/sidewalks, student patrols, controlled dormitory access (key, security card, etc).

TRANSFER AND INTERNATIONAL STUDENTS
Transfer students: May apply for admission for the following academic terms: Fall, Winter, Spring. Applicants need a minimum number of credits to apply. For fall 2005: Transfer applications received: 7,856. Transfer applicants offered admission: 4,578. Transfer applicants enrolled: 1,730. **International students:** Number of foreign undergraduates: 354 (2% of student body). Number of countries represented: 31. Minimum TOEFL score required: 500 (paper); 213 (computer).

University of California–Irvine

- **Address:** Irvine, CA 92697
- **Website:** http://www.uci.edu
- **Public**
- **Enrollment:** 19,333 full-time; 597 part-time

KEY STATS
- ✔ **U.S News College Ranking:** 44, National Universities
- ✔ **SAT Score (25th/75th percentile):** 1110-1310
- ✔ **Tuition:** 2006-2007: $6,770 in state, $25,454 out of state

Selectivity: Most selective	**Room/board:** $9,815
Acceptance rate: 60%	**Average debt:** $13,587
Student/faculty ratio: 17/1	**Proportion who borrowed:** 55%

UNDERGRADUATE STUDENT BODY STATS
2005-2006 enrollment: 19,333 full-time; 597 part-time. Men: 49%; women: 51%. **Ethnic makeup:** African American: 2%; Asian American: 49%; Hispanic: 12%; White: 34%; International: 2%.

ADMISSIONS FACTS AND FIGURES
Phone: (949) 824-6703. **Email:** admissions@uci.edu. **Website:** http://www.uci.edu. **Application deadlines for fall 2007:** Regular decision: November 30; decision sent by March 31. Early decision: Not offered. Early action: Not offered. Admission cannot be deferred. **Application fee:** $60. Common application is not accepted. **To apply online, go to:** http://www.universityofcalifornia.edu/admissions/. **Admissions requirements/recommendations:** High school units required (recommended): English: 4 (4); Mathematics: 3 (4); Science: 2 (3); Foreign language: 2 (3); Social studies: 0 (0); History: 2 (2); Academic electives: 1 (1); Total units: 15 (18). Tests: The college uses SAT or ACT scores in admissions decisions. Either SAT or ACT required. For admission to the fall 2007 entering class, the school will accept: ACT with writing. Campus visit: Neither required nor recommended. Admissions interview: Neither required nor recommended. Off-campus interview: Not available. **Factors that count in admissions decisions:** *Academic:* Secondary school record: Very important. Class rank: Considered. Letters of recommendation: Not considered. Standardized test scores: Very important. Essay: Very important. *Nonacademic:* Interview: Not considered. Extracurricular activities: Very important. Talent/ability: Very important. Character/personal qualities: Important. Alumni/ae relationship: Not considered. Geographical residence: Not considered. State residency: Considered. Religious affiliation/commitment: Not considered. Minority status: Not considered. Volunteer work: Very important. Work experience: Very important. **Admissions statistics for the fall 2005 entering class:** Total applicants: 34,531. Total accepted: 20,825. Freshmen enrolled: 4,338; 1% were from out of state. Overall acceptance rate: 60%. **Credentials of fall 2005 freshmen:** 98% ranked in the top 10 percent of their high school class; 100% were in the top 25 percent, and 100% were in the top half. (Proportion submitting class standing: 86%.) **Average high school grade point average:** 3.7. **First-year students who submitted SAT scores:** 100%. Scores (25/75 percentile): Verbal: 540-630, Math: 570-680, Combined: 1110-1310.

ACADEMICS
Year founded: 1965. **Academic calendar:** Quarter. **Degrees offered:** bachelor's, post-bachelor's certificate, master's, first professional, doctorate. **Most popular majors:** 12% biology/biological sciences, 9% computer and information sciences, 8% economics, 6% social psychology, 5% psychology. **Major fields of study:** architecture and related services; area, ethnic, cultural, and gender studies; biological and biomedical sciences; communication, journalism, and related programs; computer and information sciences and support services; engineering; English language and literature/letters; foreign languages, literatures, and linguistics; history; liberal arts and sciences studies,

and humanities; mathematics and statistics; multi/interdisciplinary studies; philosophy and religious studies; physical sciences; psychology; social sciences; visual and performing arts. **Areas of required coursework:** humanities, computer literacy, mathematics, English (including composition), foreign languages, sciences (biological or physical), social science, other. **Pre-professional programs:** pre-medicine. **Special academic programs (% participation):** distance learning, double major (12%), English as a Second Language (ESL) (2%), honors program (8%), independent study (63%), internships (18%), study abroad (13%), teacher certificate program. **Teacher certification offered in:** elementary, middle/junior high, secondary, bilingual/bicultural. **Reserve Officers Training Corps (ROTC):** Army ROTC: Offered at cooperating institution (Univ. of Southern California, Claremont Colleges, Extension Office at Cal State University Fullerton); Air Force ROTC: Offered at cooperating institution (Loyola Marymount University, UC Los Angeles, University of Southern California). **Faculty and instruction (2005-2006):** Total instructional faculty: 1,038 full-time, 324 part-time (66% men; 34% women; 24% minorities). Full-time faculty with Ph.D. or other terminal degree: 98%. Student/faculty ratio: 17/1. Classes of fewer than 20 students: 45%; of 20 to 49 students: 31%; of 50 or more students: 24%. **Advanced Placement and International Baccalaureate credit:** AP tests may be used for: Credit and/or placement. Scores accepted: 3, 4, 5. International Baccalaureate exams may be used for: Credit and/or placement. **Freshmen returning for sophomore year:** 94%. **Graduation rates:** Four-year: 42%; five-year: 74%; six-year: 80%. **Graduate study:** 31% of students pursue further study immediately upon graduation; 21% within five years. Fields in which graduates pursue further study: Master of Business Administration (MBA), 6%; law, 13%; medicine, 12%; dentistry, 4%; engineering, 7%; education, 15%; arts and sciences, 43%.

COSTS AND FINANCIAL AID
Financial aid office: (949) 824-5337. **Expenses (2006-2007):** Tuition and fees 2006-2007: $6,770 in state, $25,454 out of state; room/board: $9,815. Estimated books and supplies: $1,631; transportation: $1,276; personal expenses: $1,622. **Financial aid:** Priority filing date for institution's financial aid form: March 2; deadline: May 2. In 2005-2006, 62% of undergraduates applied for financial aid. Of those, 50% were determined to have financial need; 43% had their need fully met. Average financial aid package (proportion receiving): $12,914 (47%). Average amount of gift aid, such as scholarships or grants (proportion receiving): $10,067 (41%). Average amount of self-help aid, such as work study or loans (proportion receiving): $5,661 (35%). Average need-based loan (excluding PLUS or other private loans): $5,633. Among students who received need-based aid, the average percentage of need met: 85%. Among students who received aid based on merit, the average award (and the proportion receiving): $7,381 (4%). The average athletic scholarship (and the proportion receiving): $9,544 (1%). Average amount of debt of borrowers graduating in 2005: $13,587. Proportion who borrowed: 55%.

CAMPUS LIFE AND EXTRACURRICULAR ACTIVITIES
Campus housing available (% using): coed dorms (51%), women's dorms (1%), sorority housing (3%), fraternity housing (1%), apartments for married students (2%), apartment for single students (31%), special housing for disabled students (0%), cooperative housing (0%), other housing options (11%). Students who live in college-owned, operated, or affiliated housing: 34%. **Student employment:** During the 2005-2006 academic year, 21% of undergraduates worked on campus. Average per-year earnings: $8,550. **Clubs and organizations:** Number of student organizations: 401. Activities include: choral groups, concert band, dance, drama/theater, jazz band, literary magazine, music ensembles, musical theater, opera, pep band, radio station, student government, student newspaper, student film society, symphony orchestra, yearbook. Number of fraternities: 20; sororities: 20. Proportion of men in fraternities: 8%; of women in sororities: 9%. Average proportion of students who stay on campus on weekends: 50%. **Sports program (2005-2006):** Member of NCAA I. *Men's intercollegiate varsity sports:* baseball, basketball, crew, golf, sailing, soccer, swimming and diving, tennis, track and field (outdoor), volleyball, water polo. *Women's intercollegiate varsity sports:* basketball, crew, cross-country, golf, sailing, soccer, swimming and diving, tennis, track and field (indoor), track and field (outdoor), volleyball, water polo.

SERVICES AND FACILITIES
Basic services: nonremedial tutoring, women's center, placement service, day care, health service, health insurance. **Remedial assistance:** reading, math, writing, study skills. **Counseling services:** minority student, career, personal, veteran student, academic, psychological, birth control, other. **For learning-disabled students:** School does not offer a structured program with

separate admission and additional fees. Total undergraduates in learning-disabled program or receiving services: 119. Services include: reading machines, tape recorders, note-taking services, readers, extended time for tests, priority registration, texts on tape, other. **Library:** Number of titles: 2,610,255; number of current serial subscriptions: 26,493. **Information technology resources:** Students are not required to lease or own a computer. Number of campus computers available to all students: 2,156. School has a wireless network. Approximate number of users that can be accommodated: 20,400. Proportion of college-owned housing units wired for high-speed internet access: 100%. **Campus safety:** Security services offered: late-night transport/escort service, 24-hour emergency telephones, lighted pathways/sidewalks, student patrols, controlled dormitory access (key, security card, etc).

TRANSFER AND INTERNATIONAL STUDENTS
Transfer students: May apply for admission for the following academic terms: Fall, Winter. Applicants need a minimum number of credits to apply. For fall 2005: Transfer applications received: 8,598. Transfer applicants offered admission: 5,519. Transfer applicants enrolled: 1,425. **International students:** Number of foreign undergraduates: 475 (2% of student body). Number of countries represented: 52. Minimum TOEFL score required: 550 (paper); 213 (computer).

University of California—Los Angeles

- **Address:** 405 Hilgard Avenue, Los Angeles, CA 90095
- **Website:** http://www.ucla.edu/
- **Public**
- **Enrollment:** 23,852 full-time; 959 part-time

KEY STATS
- ✔ **U.S News College Ranking:** 26, National Universities
- ✔ **SAT Score (25th/75th percentile):** 1170-1410
- ✔ **Tuition:** 2006-2007: $6,504 in state, $24,672 out of state
  Selectivity: Most selective **Room/board:** $12,312
  Acceptance rate: 27% **Average debt:** $14,431
  Student/faculty ratio: 18/1 **Proportion who borrowed:** 52%

UNDERGRADUATE STUDENT BODY STATS
2005-2006 enrollment: 23,852 full-time; 959 part-time. Men: 44%; women: 56%. **Ethnic makeup:** African American: 3%; Asian American: 38%; Hispanic: 15%; White: 39%; International: 4%.

ADMISSIONS FACTS AND FIGURES
Phone: (310) 825-3101. **Email:** ugadm@saonet.ucla.edu. **Website:** http://www.ucla.edu/. **Application deadlines for fall 2007:** Regular decision: November 30. Early decision: Not offered. Early action: Not offered. Admission cannot be deferred. **Application fee:** $60. Common application is not accepted. **To apply online, go to:** http://www.universityofcalifornia.edu/admissions/undergrad_adm/apply_to_uc.html. **Admissions requirements/recommendations:** High school units required (recommended): English: 4 (4); Mathematics: 3 (4); Science: 2 (3); Foreign language: 2 (3); History: 2 (2); Academic electives: 1 (1); Total units: 15 (18). Tests: The college uses SAT or ACT scores in admissions decisions. Either SAT or ACT required. For admission to the fall 2007 entering class, the school will accept: ACT with writing. Campus visit: Recommended. Admissions interview: Neither required nor recommended. Off-campus interview: Not available. **Factors that count in admissions decisions:** *Academic:* Secondary school record: Very important. Class rank: Not considered. Letters of recommendation: Not considered. Standardized test scores: Very important. Essay: Very important. *Nonacademic:* Interview: Not considered. Extracurricular activities: Important. Talent/ability: Very important. Character/personal qualities: Not considered. Alumni/ae relationship: Not considered. Geographical residence: Not considered. State residency: Not considered. Religious affiliation/commitment: Not considered. Minority status: Not considered. Volunteer work: Important. Work experience: Important. **Admissions statistics for the fall 2005 entering class:** Total applicants: 42,227. Total accepted: 11,361. Freshmen enrolled: 4,422; 4% were from out of state. Overall acceptance rate: 27%. **Credentials of fall 2005 freshmen:** 97% ranked in the top 10 percent of their high school class; 100% were in the top 25 percent, and 100% were in the top half. (Proportion submitting class standing: 100%.) **Average high school grade**

point average: 4.0. **First-year students who submitted SAT scores:** 99%. Scores (25/75 percentile): Verbal: 570-690, Math: 600-720, Combined: 1170-1410. **First-year students submitting ACT scores:** 33%. Scores (25/75 percentile): English: 23-30, Math: 24-31, Composite: 24-30.

ACADEMICS

Year founded: 1919. **Academic calendar:** Quarter. **Degrees offered:** bachelor's, master's, first professional, doctorate. **Most popular majors:** 9% political science and government, 9% psychology, 8% history, 8% sociology, 7% economics. **Major fields of study:** area, ethnic, cultural, and gender studies; biological and biomedical sciences; business, management, marketing, and related support services; computer and information sciences and support services; engineering; English language and literature/letters; foreign languages, literatures, and linguistics; health professions and related clinical sciences; history; liberal arts and sciences studies, and humanities; mathematics and statistics; multi/interdisciplinary studies; philosophy and religious studies; physical sciences; psychology; social sciences; visual and performing arts. **Areas of required coursework:** arts/fine arts, humanities, mathematics, English (including composition), philosophy, foreign languages, sciences (biological or physical), history, social science. **Pre-professional programs:** pre-law, pre-optometry, pre-pharmacy, other. **Special academic programs:** cross-registration, distance learning, double major, dual enrollment, English as a Second Language (ESL), exchange student program (domestic), honors program, independent study, internships, liberal arts/career combination, student-designed major, study abroad, teacher certificate program. **Cooperative education programs:** engineering. **Reserve Officers Training Corps (ROTC):** Army ROTC: Offered on campus; Navy ROTC: Offered on campus; Air Force ROTC: Offered on campus. **Faculty and instruction (2005-2006):** Total instructional faculty: 1,890 full-time, 615 part-time (68% men; 32% women; 24% minorities). Full-time faculty with Ph.D. or other terminal degree: 98%. Student/faculty ratio: 18/1. Classes of fewer than 20 students: 51%; of 20 to 49 students: 28%; of 50 or more students: 21%. **Advanced Placement and International Baccalaureate credit:** AP tests may be used for: Credit and/or placement. Scores accepted: 3, 4, 5. International Baccalaureate exams may be used for: Credit and/or placement. **Freshmen returning for sophomore year:** 97%. **Graduation rates:** Four-year: 57%; five-year: 85%; six-year: 87%.

COSTS AND FINANCIAL AID

Financial aid office: (310) 206-0400. **Expenses (2006-2007):** Tuition and fees 2006-2007: $6,504 in state, $24,672 out of state; room/board: $12,312. Estimated books and supplies: $1,554; transportation: $764; personal expenses: $2,137. **Financial aid:** In 2005-2006, 59% of undergraduates applied for financial aid. Of those, 53% were determined to have financial need; 40% had their need fully met. Average financial aid package (proportion receiving): $14,036 (53%). Average amount of gift aid, such as scholarships or grants (proportion receiving): $10,888 (51%). Average amount of self-help aid, such as work study or loans (proportion receiving): $4,859 (39%). Average need-based loan (excluding PLUS or other private loans): $4,948. Among students who received need-based aid, the average percentage of need met: 83%. Among students who received aid based on merit, the average award (and the proportion receiving): $3,412 (4%). The average athletic scholarship (and the proportion receiving): $12,744 (2%). Average amount of debt of borrowers graduating in 2005: $14,431. Proportion who borrowed: 52%.

CAMPUS LIFE AND EXTRACURRICULAR ACTIVITIES

Campus housing available (% using): coed dorms (62%), sorority housing (4%), fraternity housing (4%), apartments for married students (8%), apartment for single students (21%), special housing for disabled students, cooperative housing (1%). Students who live in college-owned, operated, or affiliated housing: 38%. **Clubs and organizations:** Number of student organizations: 700. Activities include: choral groups, concert band, dance, drama/theater, jazz band, literary magazine, marching band, music ensembles, musical theater, opera, pep band, radio station, student government, student newspaper, student film society, symphony orchestra, television station, yearbook. Number of fraternities: 27; sororities: 18. Proportion of men in fraternities: 15%; of women in sororities: 11%. Average proportion of students who stay on campus on weekends: 50%. **Sports program (2005-2006):** Member of NCAA I. **Men's intercollegiate varsity sports:** baseball, basketball, cross-country, football, golf, soccer, tennis, track and field (indoor), track and field (outdoor), volleyball, water polo. **Women's intercollegiate varsity sports:** basketball, crew, cross-country, golf, gymnastics, soccer, softball, swimming and diving, tennis, track and field (indoor), track and field (outdoor), volleyball, water polo.

SERVICES AND FACILITIES

Basic services: nonremedial tutoring, women's center, placement service, health service, health insurance. **Counseling services:** minority student, career, military, personal, veteran student, academic, older student, psychological, birth control. **For learning-disabled students:** School does not offer a structured program with separate admission and additional fees. Services include: reading machines, tape recorders, diagnostic testing service, note-taking services, readers, extended time for tests, priority registration, texts on tape, other testing accomodations, other. **Library:** Number of titles: 8,064,896; number of current serial subscriptions: 65,953. **Information technology resources:** Students are not required to lease or own a computer. Number of campus computers available to all students: 155. School has a wireless network. Approximate number of users that can be accommodated: 3,000. Proportion of college-owned housing units wired for high-speed internet access: 100%. **Campus safety:** Security services offered: 24-hour foot-and-vehicle patrols, late-night transport/escort service, 24-hour emergency telephones, lighted pathways/sidewalks, student patrols, controlled dormitory access (key, security card, etc).

TRANSFER AND INTERNATIONAL STUDENTS

Transfer students: May apply for admission for the following academic terms: Fall. Applicants need a minimum number of credits to apply. For fall 2005: Transfer applications received: 13,189. Transfer applicants offered admission: 4,076. Transfer applicants enrolled: 3,150. **International students:** Number of foreign undergraduates: 893 (4% of student body). Minimum TOEFL score required: 550 (paper); 230 (computer).

University of California–Riverside

- **Address:** 900 University Avenue, Riverside, CA 92521
- **Website:** http://www.ucr.edu
- **Public**
- **Enrollment:** 13,769 full-time; 802 part-time

KEY STATS

✔ **U.S News College Ranking:** 88, National Universities
✔ **SAT Score (25th/75th percentile):** 950-1200
✔ **Tuition:** 2006-2007: $6,680 in state, $25,365 out of state

Selectivity: More selective	**Room/board:** $10,200
Acceptance rate: 76%	**Average debt:** $14,819
Student/faculty ratio: 18/1	**Proportion who borrowed:** 65%

UNDERGRADUATE STUDENT BODY STATS

2005-2006 enrollment: 13,769 full-time; 802 part-time. Men: 47%; women: 53%. **Ethnic makeup:** African American: 7%; Asian American: 42%; Hispanic: 24%; White: 25%; International: 2%.

ADMISSIONS FACTS AND FIGURES

Phone: (951) 827-4531. **Email:** discover@ucr.edu. **Website:** http://www.ucr.edu. **Application deadlines for fall 2007:** Regular decision: November 30. Early decision: Not offered. Early action: Not offered. Admission cannot be deferred. **Application fee:** $60. Common application is not accepted. **To apply online, go to:** http://www.ucop.edu/pathways. **Admissions requirements/recommendations:** High school units required (recommended): English: 4; Mathematics: 3 (4); Science: 2 (3); Foreign language: 2 (3); History: 2; Academic electives: 1; Total units: 15 (18). Tests: The college uses SAT or ACT scores in admissions decisions. Either SAT or ACT required. For admission to the fall 2007 entering class, the school will accept: ACT with writing. Campus visit: Recommended. Admissions interview: Neither required nor recommended. Off-campus interview: Not available. **Factors that count in admissions decisions: *Academic:*** Secondary school record: Very important. Class rank: Very important. Letters of recommendation: Not considered. Standardized test scores: Very important. Essay: Very important. ***Nonacademic:*** Interview: Not considered. Extracurricular activities: Not considered. Talent/ability: Not considered. Character/personal qualities: Important. Alumni/ae relationship: Not considered. Geographical residence: Not considered. State residency: Not considered. Religious affiliation/commitment: Not considered. Minority status: Not considered. Volunteer work: Not considered. Work experience: Not considered. **Other schools with the greatest overlap in applicants:** University of California–Davis; University of California–Irvine; University of California–Los Angeles; University of California–San Diego; University of

California–Santa Barbara. **Admissions statistics for the fall 2005 entering class:** Total applicants: 19,060. Total accepted: 14,474. Freshmen enrolled: 2,988; 0% were from out of state. Overall acceptance rate: 76%. **Credentials of fall 2005 freshmen:** 94% ranked in the top 10 percent of their high school class; 100% were in the top 25 percent, and 100% were in the top half. (Proportion submitting class standing: 100%.) **Average high school grade point average:** 3.5. **First-year students who submitted SAT scores:** 99%. Scores (25/75 percentile): Verbal: 460-570, Math: 490-630, Combined: 950-1200. **First-year students submitting ACT scores:** 28%. Scores (25/75 percentile): English: N/A, Math: N/A, Composite: 18-23.

ACADEMICS

Year founded: 1954. **Academic calendar:** Quarter. **Degrees offered:** bachelor's, post-bachelor's certificate, master's, doctorate. **Most popular majors:** 26% business, management, marketing, and related support services, 18% social sciences, 12% biological and biomedical sciences, 9% psychology, 8% liberal arts and sciences studies, and humanities. **Major fields of study:** agriculture, agriculture operations, and related sciences; area, ethnic, cultural, and gender studies; biological and biomedical sciences; business, management, marketing, and related support services; computer and information sciences and support services; education; engineering; English language and literature/letters; foreign languages, literatures, and linguistics; health professions and related clinical sciences; history; legal professions and studies; liberal arts and sciences studies, and humanities; mathematics and statistics; multi/interdisciplinary studies; natural resources and conservation; philosophy and religious studies; physical sciences; psychology; public administration and social service professions; social sciences; visual and performing arts. **Areas of required coursework:** arts/fine arts, humanities, mathematics, English (including composition), foreign languages, sciences (biological or physical), history, social science, other. **Special academic programs:** accelerated program, cooperative (work-study plan) program, cross-registration, double major, dual enrollment, English as a Second Language (ESL), honors program, independent study, internships, liberal arts/career combination, student-designed major, study abroad, teacher certificate program. **Teacher certification offered in:** special education, elementary. **Reserve Officers Training Corps (ROTC):** Army ROTC: Offered at cooperating institution (California State University, San Bernardino); Air Force ROTC: Offered at cooperating institution (California State University, San Bernardino, Claremont McKenna College). **Faculty and instruction (2005-2006):** Total instructional faculty: 709 full-time, 140 part-time (67% men; 33% women; 26% minorities). Full-time faculty with Ph.D. or other terminal degree: 98%. Student/faculty ratio: 18/1. Classes of fewer than 20 students: 33%; of 20 to 49 students: 45%; of 50 or more students: 22%. **Advanced Placement and International Baccalaureate credit:** International Baccalaureate exams may be used for: Credit and/or placement. **Freshmen returning for sophomore year:** 85%. **Graduation rates:** Four-year: 43%; five-year: 68%; six-year: 72%. **Graduate study:** 33% of students pursue further study immediately upon graduation. Fields in which graduates pursue further study: Master of Business Administration (MBA), 7%; law, 6%; medicine, 16%; engineering, 4%; education, 31%; arts and sciences, 36%.

COSTS AND FINANCIAL AID

Financial aid office: (951) 827-3878. **Expenses (2006-2007):** Tuition and fees 2006-2007: $6,680 in state, $25,365 out of state; room/board: $10,200. Estimated books and supplies: $1,700; transportation: $1,300; personal expenses: $1,700. **Financial aid:** Priority filing date for institution's financial aid form: March 2; deadline: March 2. In 2005-2006, 73% of undergraduates applied for financial aid. Of those, 62% were determined to have financial need; 43% had their need fully met. Average financial aid package (proportion receiving): $13,538 (60%). Average amount of gift aid, such as scholarships or grants (proportion receiving): $9,852 (53%). Average amount of self-help aid, such as work study or loans (proportion receiving): $5,979 (47%). Average need-based loan (excluding PLUS or other private loans): $5,618. Among students who received need-based aid, the average percentage of need met: 84%. Among students who received aid based on merit, the average award (and the proportion receiving): $5,606 (1%). The average athletic scholarship (and the proportion receiving): $10,597 (1%). Average amount of debt of borrowers graduating in 2005: $14,819. Proportion who borrowed: 65%.

CAMPUS LIFE AND EXTRACURRICULAR ACTIVITIES

Campus housing available (% using): coed dorms (69%), apartments for married students (3%), apartment for single students (28%). Students who live in college-owned, operated, or affiliated housing: 27%. **Student employment:** During the 2005-2006 academic year, 14% of undergraduates worked on campus. Average per-year earnings: $2,380. **Clubs and organizations:**

Number of student organizations: 279. Activities include: choral groups, concert band, dance, drama/theater, jazz band, literary magazine, music ensembles, musical theater, pep band, radio station, student government, student newspaper, student film society. Number of fraternities: 21; sororities: 21. Proportion of men in fraternities: 8%; of women in sororities: 7%. Average proportion of students who stay on campus on weekends: 30%. **Sports program (2005-2006):** Member of NCAA I. *Men's intercollegiate varsity sports:* baseball, basketball, golf, soccer, tennis, track and field (indoor), track and field (outdoor). *Women's intercollegiate varsity sports:* basketball, golf, soccer, softball, tennis, track and field (indoor), track and field (outdoor), volleyball.

SERVICES AND FACILITIES

Basic services: nonremedial tutoring, women's center, placement service, day care, health service, health insurance. **Remedial assistance:** reading, math, writing, study skills. **Counseling services:** minority student, career, military, personal, veteran student, academic, older student, psychological, birth control, religious. **For learning-disabled students:** School does not offer a structured program with separate admission and additional fees. Total undergraduates in learning-disabled program or receiving services: 49. **Library:** Number of titles: 2,305,526; number of current serial subscriptions: 28,151. **Information technology resources:** Students are not required to lease or own a computer. Number of campus computers available to all students: 408. School has a wireless network. Approximate number of users that can be accommodated: 22,500. Proportion of college-owned housing units wired for high-speed internet access: 100%. **Campus safety:** Security services offered: 24-hour foot-and-vehicle patrols, late-night transport/escort service, 24-hour emergency telephones, lighted pathways/sidewalks, student patrols, controlled dormitory access (key, security card, etc).

TRANSFER AND INTERNATIONAL STUDENTS

Transfer students: May apply for admission for the following academic terms: Fall. Applicants do not need a minimum number of credits to apply. For fall 2005: Transfer applications received: 4,682. Transfer applicants offered admission: 3,350. Transfer applicants enrolled: 877. **International students:** Number of foreign undergraduates: 297 (2% of student body). Number of countries represented: 33. Minimum TOEFL score required: 550 (paper); 213 (computer).

University of California–San Diego

- **Address:** 9500 Gilman Drive, La Jolla, CA 92093
- **Website:** http://www.ucsd.edu/
- **Public**
- **Enrollment:** 20,321 full-time; 358 part-time

KEY STATS

✔ **U.S News College Ranking:** 38, National Universities
✔ **SAT Score (25th/75th percentile):** 1150-1370
✔ **Tuition:** 2006-2007: $7,318 in state, $25,485 out of state
  Selectivity: Most selective   **Room/board:** $9,657
  Acceptance rate: 44%   **Average debt:** $14,689
  Student/faculty ratio: 19/1   **Proportion who borrowed:** 49%

UNDERGRADUATE STUDENT BODY STATS

2005-2006 enrollment: 20,321 full-time; 358 part-time. Men: 48%; women: 52%. **Ethnic makeup:** African American: 1%; Asian American: 39%; Hispanic: 11%; White: 45%; International: 3%. **Religious preference:** Roman Catholic: 21%; Protestant: 10%; Jewish: 4%; Muslim: 2%; Hindu: 2%; Buddhist: 7%; No preference: 33%; Unknown: 4%; Christian: 11%; Other: 6%.

ADMISSIONS FACTS AND FIGURES

Phone: (858) 534-4831. **Email:** admissionsinfo@ucsd.edu. **Website:** http://www.ucsd.edu/. **Application deadlines for fall 2007:** Regular decision: November 30; decision sent by March 31. Early decision: Not offered. Early action: Not offered. Admission cannot be deferred. **Application fee:** $40. Common application is not accepted. **To apply online, go to:** http://www.ucop.edu/pathways. **Admissions requirements/recommendations:** High school units required (recommended): English: 4; Mathematics: 3 (4); Science: 2 (3); Foreign language: 2 (3); History: 2; Academic electives: 1; Total units: 17 (13). Tests: The college uses SAT or ACT scores in admissions decisions. Either SAT or ACT required. For admission to the fall 2007 entering class, the school will accept: ACT with writing. Campus visit: Recommended. Admissions interview: Neither required nor recommended. Off-campus interview: Not available. **Factors that count in admissions decisions:** *Academic:* Secondary school record: Very important. Class rank: Not considered. Letters of recommendation: Not considered. Standardized test scores: Very important. Essay: Very important. *Nonacademic:* Interview: Not considered. Extracurricular activities: Important. Talent/ability: Very important. Character/personal qualities: Considered. Alumni/ae relationship: Not considered. Geographical residence: Not considered. State residency: Important. Religious affiliation/commitment: Not considered. Minority status: Not considered. Volunteer work: Important. Work experience: Important. **Other schools with the greatest overlap in applicants:** Harvard University; Stanford University; University of California–Berkeley; University of California–Los Angeles; University of Southern California. **Admissions statistics for the fall 2007 entering class:** Total applicants: 40,518. Total accepted: 17,891. Freshmen enrolled: 3,720; 2% were from out of state. Overall acceptance rate: 44%. **Credentials of fall 2005 freshmen:** 99% ranked in the top 10 percent of their high school class; 100% were in the top 25 percent, and 100% were in the top half. (Proportion submitting class standing: 100%.) **Average high school grade point average:** 3.9. **First-year students who submitted SAT scores:** 99%. Scores (25/75 percentile): Verbal: 550-660, Math: 600-710, Combined: 1150-1370. **First-year students submitting ACT scores:** 25%. Scores (25/75 percentile): English: N/A, Math: N/A, Composite: 23-29.

ACADEMICS

Year founded: 1960. **Academic calendar:** Quarter. **Degrees offered:** bachelor's, master's, doctorate. **Most popular majors:** 15% biology, 12% economics, 9% political science and government, 8% electrical engineering technologies/technicians, 8% psychology. **Major fields of study:** area, ethnic, cultural, and gender studies; biological and biomedical sciences; communication, journalism, and related programs; computer and information sciences and support services; engineering; English language and literature/letters; family and consumer sciences/human sciences; foreign languages, literatures, and linguistics; history; mathematics and statistics; multi/interdisciplinary studies; philosophy and religious studies; physical sciences; psychology; social sciences; theology and religious vocations. **Areas of required coursework:** arts/fine arts, humanities, mathematics, English (including composition), philosophy, foreign languages, sciences (biological or physical), history, social science. **Pre-professional programs:** pre-law, pre-medicine, pre-pharmacy, other. **Special academic programs:** cross-registration, double major, dual enrollment, English as a Second Language (ESL), exchange student program (domestic), honors program, independent study, internships, liberal arts/career combination, student-designed major, study abroad, teacher certificate program. **Teacher certification offered in:** special education, elementary, middle/junior high, secondary, bilingual/bicultural. **Faculty and instruction (2005-2006):** Total instructional faculty: 941 full-time, 183 part-time (72% men; 28% women; 20% minorities). Full-time faculty with Ph.D. or other terminal degree: 98%. Student/faculty ratio: 19/1. Classes of fewer than 20 students: 46%; of 20 to 49 students: 24%; of 50 or more students: 30%. **Advanced Placement and International Baccalaureate credit:** AP tests may be used for: Credit and/or placement. Scores accepted: 3, 4, 5. International Baccalaureate exams may be used for: Credit and/or placement. **Freshmen returning for sophomore year:** 94%. **Graduation rates:** Four-year: 54%; five-year: 80%; six-year: 85%. **Graduate study:** 33% of students pursue further study immediately upon graduation; 45% within one year; 57% within five years. Fields in which graduates pursue further study: Master of Business Administration (MBA), 8%; law, 15%; medicine, 16%; dentistry, 4%; engineering, 8%; education, 19%; arts and sciences, 37%; veterinary medicine, 1%.

COSTS AND FINANCIAL AID

Financial aid office: (858) 534-4480. **Expenses (2006-2007):** Tuition and fees 2006-2007: $7,318 in state, $25,485 out of state; room/board: $9,657. Estimated books and supplies: $1,504; transportation: $1,097; personal expenses: $2,336. **Financial aid:** Priority filing date for institution's financial aid form: March 2. In 2005-2006, 64% of undergraduates applied for financial aid. Of those, 53% were determined to have financial need; 27% had their need fully met. Average financial aid package (proportion receiving): $13,342 (51%). Average amount of gift aid, such as scholarships or grants (proportion receiving): $9,540 (47%). Average amount of self-help aid, such as work study or loans (proportion receiving): $5,473 (41%). Average need-based loan (excluding PLUS or other private loans): $5,109. Among students who received need-based aid, the average percentage of need met: 84%. Among students who received aid based on merit, the aver-

age award (and the proportion receiving): $6,824 (3%). The average athletic scholarship (and the proportion receiving): $0 (0%). Average amount of debt of borrowers graduating in 2005: $14,689. Proportion who borrowed: 49%.

CAMPUS LIFE AND EXTRACURRICULAR ACTIVITIES

Campus housing available (% using): coed dorms (74%), apartments for married students (5%), apartment for single students (16%), special housing for disabled students (1%), special housing for international students (3%), other housing options (1%). Students who live in college-owned, operated, or affiliated housing: 33%. **Student employment:** During the 2005-2006 academic year, 25% of undergraduates worked on campus. Average per-year earnings: $3,500. **Clubs and organizations:** Number of student organizations: 405. Activities include: choral groups, dance, drama/theater, jazz band, literary magazine, music ensembles, musical theater, opera, pep band, radio station, student government, student newspaper, student film society, symphony orchestra, television station, yearbook. Number of fraternities: 19; sororities: 14. Proportion of men in fraternities: 10%; of women in sororities: 10%. Average proportion of students who stay on campus on weekends: 35%. **Sports program (2005-2006):** Member of NCAA II. *Men's intercollegiate varsity sports:* baseball, basketball, cross-country, fencing, golf, soccer, swimming and diving, tennis, track and field (outdoor), volleyball, water polo. *Women's intercollegiate varsity sports:* basketball, cross-country, fencing, soccer, softball, swimming and diving, tennis, track and field (outdoor), volleyball, water polo, rowing.

SERVICES AND FACILITIES

Basic services: nonremedial tutoring, women's center, placement service, day care, health service, health insurance, other. **Counseling services:** minority student, career, military, personal, veteran student, academic, older student, psychological, birth control, religious. **For learning-disabled students:** School does not offer a structured program with separate admission and additional fees. Services include: reading machines, tape recorders, diagnostic testing service, untimed tests, note-taking services, special bookstore section, oral tests, learning center, readers, extended time for tests, tutors, priority registration, priority seating, texts on tape, other testing accomodations. **Library:** Number of titles: 3,071,461; number of current serial subscriptions: 25,559. **Information technology resources:** Students are not required to lease or own a computer. Number of campus computers available to all students: 2,300. School has a wireless network. Approximate number of users that can be accommodated: 7,000. Proportion of college-owned housing units wired for high-speed internet access: 100%. **Campus safety:** Security services offered: 24-hour foot-and-vehicle patrols, late-night transport/escort service, 24-hour emergency telephones, lighted pathways/sidewalks, student patrols, controlled dormitory access (key, security card, etc).

TRANSFER AND INTERNATIONAL STUDENTS

Transfer students: May apply for admission for the following academic terms: Fall. Applicants need a minimum number of credits to apply. For fall 2005: Transfer applications received: 9,291. Transfer applicants offered admission: 5,939. Transfer applicants enrolled: 1,680. **International students:** Number of foreign undergraduates: 594 (3% of student body). Minimum TOEFL score required: 550 (paper); 220 (computer).

University of California–Santa Barbara

- **Address:** Santa Barbara, CA 93106
- **Website:** http://www.ucsb.edu
- **Public**
- **Enrollment:** 17,432 full-time; 645 part-time

KEY STATS

✔ **U.S News College Ranking:** 47, National Universities
✔ **SAT Score (25th/75th percentile):** 1090-1320
✔ **Tuition:** 2006-2007: $6,993 in state, $25,161 out of state
  Selectivity: Most selective   **Room/board:** $11,493
  Acceptance rate: 53%   **Average debt:** $15,297
  Student/faculty ratio: 17/1   **Proportion who borrowed:** 52%

UNDERGRADUATE STUDENT BODY STATS

2005-2006 enrollment: 17,432 full-time; 645 part-time. Men: 45%; women: 55%. **Ethnic makeup:** African American: 3%; American-Indian: 1%; Asian American: 16%; Hispanic: 17%; White: 62%; International: 1%.

ADMISSIONS FACTS AND FIGURES

Phone: (805) 893-2485. **Email:** appinfo@sa.ucsb.edu. **Website:** http://www.ucsb.edu. **Application deadlines for fall 2007:** Regular decision: November 30; decision sent by March 15. Early decision: Not offered. Early action: Not offered. Admission cannot be deferred. **Application fee:** $40. Common application is not accepted. **To apply online, go to:** http://www.ucop.edu/pathways/appctr.html. **Admissions requirements/recommendations:** High school units required (recommended): English: 4 (4); Mathematics: 3 (4); Science: 2 (3); Foreign language: 2 (3); Social studies: 0 (0); History: 2 (2); Academic electives: 0 (0); Total units: 15 (18). Tests: The college uses SAT or ACT scores in admissions decisions. Either SAT or ACT required. For admission to the fall 2007 entering class, the school will accept ACT with writing. Campus visit: Recommended. Admissions interview: Neither required nor recommended. Off-campus interview: Not available. **Factors that count in admissions decisions:** *Academic:* Secondary school record: Very important. Class rank: Important. Letters of recommendation: Not considered. Standardized test scores: Important. Essay: Important. *Nonacademic:* Interview: Not considered. Extracurricular activities: Important. Talent/ability: Important. Character/personal qualities: Considered. Alumni/ae relationship: Not considered. Geographical residence: Not considered. State residency: Not considered. Religious affiliation/commitment: Not considered. Minority status: Not considered. Volunteer work: Considered. Work experience: Considered. **Other schools with the greatest overlap in applicants:** University of California–Berkeley; University of California–Davis; University of California–Irvine; University of California–Los Angeles; University of California–San Diego. **Admissions statistics for the fall 2005 entering class:** Total applicants: 37,522. Total accepted: 19,821. Freshmen enrolled: 3,829; 4% were from out of state. Overall acceptance rate: 53%. **Credentials of fall 2005 freshmen:** 96% ranked in the top 10 percent of their high school class; 100% were in the top 25 percent, and 100% were in the top half. (Proportion submitting class standing: 95%.) **Average high school grade point average:** 3.8. **First-year students who submitted SAT scores:** 86%. Scores (25/75 percentile): Verbal: 530-650, Math: 560-670, Combined: 1090-1320. **First-year students submitting ACT scores:** 37%. Scores (25/75 percentile): English: N/A, Math: N/A, Composite: 22-28.

ACADEMICS

Year founded: 1909. **Academic calendar:** Quarter. **Degrees offered:** certificate, bachelor's, master's, doctorate. **Most popular majors:** 11% business, management, marketing, and related support services, 9% sociology, 7% psychology, 6% international/global studies, 5% communication and media studies. **Major fields of study:** architecture and related services; area, ethnic, cultural, and gender studies; biological and biomedical sciences; business, management, marketing, and related support services; communication, journalism, and related programs; computer and information sciences and support services; engineering; English language and literature/letters; foreign languages, literatures, and linguistics; history; legal professions and studies; mathematics and statistics; multi/interdisciplinary studies; natural resources and conservation; philosophy and religious studies; physical sciences; psychology; social sciences; visual and performing arts. **Areas of required coursework:** arts/fine arts, humanities, mathematics, English (including composition), foreign languages, sciences (biological or physical), history, social science, other. **Special academic programs:** accelerated program, cooperative (work-study plan) program, cross-registration, double major, English as a Second Language (ESL), exchange student program (domestic), honors program, independent study, internships, student-designed major, study abroad, teacher certificate program. **Teacher certification offered in:** elementary, secondary, bilingual/bicultural. **Reserve Officers Training Corps (ROTC):** Army ROTC: Offered on campus; Air Force ROTC: Offered at cooperating institution (University of California Los Angeles). **Faculty and instruction (2005-2006):** Total instructional faculty: 917 full-time, 150 part-time (68% men; 32% women; 16% minorities). Full-time faculty with Ph.D. or other terminal degree: 100%. Student/faculty ratio: 17/1. Classes of fewer than 20 students: 51%; of 20 to 49 students: 32%; of 50 or more students: 17%. **Advanced Placement and International Baccalaureate credit:** AP tests may be used for: Credit and/or placement. Scores accepted: 3, 4, 5. International Baccalaureate exams may be used for: Credit only. **Freshmen returning for sophomore year:** 91%. **Graduation rates:** Four-year: 55%; five-year: 75%; six-year: 79%.

COSTS AND FINANCIAL AID

Financial aid office: (805) 893-2432. **Expenses (2006-2007):** Tuition and fees 2006-2007: $6,993 in state, $25,161 out of state; room/board: $11,493. Estimated books and supplies: $1,504; transportation: $1,042; personal expenses: $2,233. **Financial aid:** Priority filing date for institution's financial aid form: March 2; deadline: May 31. In 2005-2006, 60% of undergraduates applied for financial aid. Of those, 47% were determined to have financial need; 37% had their need fully met. Average financial aid package (proportion receiving): $13,437 (44%). Average amount of gift aid, such as scholarships or grants (proportion receiving): $10,220 (38%). Average amount of self-help aid, such as work study or loans (proportion receiving): $5,916 (35%). Average need-based loan (excluding PLUS or other private loans): $5,807. Among students who received need-based aid, the average percentage of need met: 82%. Among students who received aid based on merit, the average award (and the proportion receiving): $5,771 (2%). The average athletic scholarship (and the proportion receiving): $8,807 (1%). Average amount of debt of borrowers graduating in 2005: $15,297. Proportion who borrowed: 52%.

CAMPUS LIFE AND EXTRACURRICULAR ACTIVITIES

Campus housing available: coed dorms, sorority housing, fraternity housing, apartments for married students, apartment for single students, special housing for disabled students. Students who live in college-owned, operated, or affiliated housing: 29%. **Student employment:** During the 2005-2006 academic year, 17% of undergraduates worked on campus. **Clubs and organizations:** Number of student organizations: 535. Activities include: choral groups, concert band, dance, drama/theater, jazz band, literary magazine, music ensembles, musical theater, opera, pep band, radio station, student government, student newspaper, student film society, symphony orchestra, yearbook. Number of fraternities: 15; sororities: 15. Proportion of men in fraternities: 4%; of women in sororities: 7%. **Sports program (2005-2006):** Member of NCAA I. *Men's intercollegiate varsity sports:* baseball, basketball, cross-country, golf, soccer, swimming and diving, tennis, track and field (outdoor), volleyball, water polo. *Women's intercollegiate varsity sports:* basketball, cross-country, soccer, softball, swimming and diving, tennis, track and field (outdoor), volleyball, water polo.

SERVICES AND FACILITIES

Basic services: nonremedial tutoring, women's center, day care, health service. **Remedial assistance:** reading, math, writing, study skills. **Counseling services:** minority student, career, military, personal, academic, psychological, birth control. **For learning-disabled students:** School does not offer a structured program with separate admission and additional fees. **Library:** Number of titles: 3,249,784; number of current serial subscriptions: 26,566. **Information technology resources:** Students are not required to lease or own a computer. Number of campus computers available to all students: 250. School has a wireless network. Proportion of college-owned housing units wired for high-speed internet access: 100%. **Campus safety:** Security services offered: 24-hour foot-and-vehicle patrols, late-night transport/escort service, 24-hour emergency telephones, lighted pathways/sidewalks, student patrols, controlled dormitory access (key, security card, etc).

TRANSFER AND INTERNATIONAL STUDENTS

Transfer students: May apply for admission for the following academic terms: Fall, Winter. Applicants do not need a minimum number of credits to apply. For fall 2005: Transfer applications received: 8,630. Transfer applicants offered admission: 5,460. Transfer applicants enrolled: 1,343. **International students:** Number of foreign undergraduates: 212 (1% of student body). Number of countries represented: 69. Minimum TOEFL score required: 500 (paper); 173 (computer).

University of California–Santa Cruz

- **Address:** 1156 High Street, Santa Cruz, CA 95064
- **Website:** http://www.ucsc.edu
- **Public**
- **Enrollment:** 13,139 full-time; 486 part-time

KEY STATS

- ✔ **U.S News College Ranking:** 76, National Universities
- ✔ **SAT Score (25th/75th percentile):** 1050-1270
- ✔ **Tuition:** 2006-2007: $6,949 in state, $25,633 out of state
- **Selectivity:** More selective **Room/board:** $11,805
- **Acceptance rate:** 75% **Average debt:** $13,374
- **Student/faculty ratio:** 19/1 **Proportion who borrowed:** 51%

UNDERGRADUATE STUDENT BODY STATS

2005-2006 enrollment: 13,139 full-time; 486 part-time. Men: 46%; women: 54%. **Ethnic makeup:** African American: 3%; American-Indian: 1%; Asian American: 19%; Hispanic: 15%; White: 62%; International: 1%.

ADMISSIONS FACTS AND FIGURES

Phone: (831) 459-4008. **Email:** admissions@cats.ucsc.edu. **Website:** http://www.ucsc.edu. **Application deadlines for fall 2007:** Regular decision: November 30; decision sent by March 31. Early decision: Not offered. Early action: Not offered. Admission cannot be deferred. **Application fee:** $60. Common application is not accepted. **To apply online, go to:** http://www.ucop.edu/pathways. **Admissions requirements/recommendations:** High school units required (recommended): English: 4 (4); Mathematics: 3 (4); Science: 2 (3); Foreign language: 2 (3); Social studies: 1 (1); History: 1 (1); Academic electives: 1 (1); Total units: 15 (18). Tests: The college uses SAT or ACT scores in admissions decisions. Either SAT or ACT required. For admission to the fall 2007 entering class, the school will accept: ACT with writing. Campus visit: Recommended. Admissions interview: Neither required nor recommended. Off-campus interview: Not available. **Factors that count in admissions decisions:** *Academic:* Secondary school record: Very important. Class rank: Very important. Letters of recommendation: Not considered. Standardized test scores: Very important. Essay: Very important. *Nonacademic:* Interview: Not considered. Extracurricular activities: Important. Talent/ability: Important. Character/personal qualities: Important. Alumni/ae relationship: Not considered. Geographical residence: Important. State residency: Very important. Religious affiliation/commitment: Not considered. Minority status: Not considered. Volunteer work: Considered. Work experience: Considered. **Other schools with the greatest overlap in applicants:** University of California–Berkeley; University of California–Davis; University of California–Los Angeles; University of California–San Diego; University of California–Santa Barbara. **Admissions statistics for the fall 2005 entering class:** Total applicants: 23,003. Total accepted: 17,342. Freshmen enrolled: 3,000; 4% were from out of state. Overall acceptance rate: 75%. **Credentials of fall 2005 freshmen:** 96% ranked in the top 10 percent of their high school class; 100% were in the top 25 percent, and 100% were in the top half. (Proportion submitting class standing: 75%.) **Average high school grade point average:** 3.5. **First-year students who submitted SAT scores:** 98%. Scores (25/75 percentile): Verbal: 520-630, Math: 530-640, Combined: 1050-1270. **First-year students submitting ACT scores:** 27%. Scores (25/75 percentile): English: N/A, Math: N/A, Composite: 21-27.

ACADEMICS

Year founded: 1965. **Academic calendar:** Quarter. **Degrees offered:** bachelor's, post-bachelor's certificate, master's, doctorate. **Most popular majors:** 10% psychology, 8% business/managerial economics, 7% English language and literature/letters, 7% sociology, 5% political science and government. **Major fields of study:** area, ethnic, cultural, and gender studies; biological and biomedical sciences; business, management, marketing, and related support services; computer and information sciences and support services; engineering; foreign languages, literatures, and linguistics; health professions and related clinical sciences; history; legal professions and studies; mathematics and statistics; multi/interdisciplinary studies; natural resources and conservation; philosophy and religious studies; physical sciences; psychology; social sciences; visual and performing arts. **Areas of required coursework:** arts/fine arts, humanities, English (including composition), sciences (biological or physical), social science, other. **Pre-professional programs:** pre-law, pre-medicine. **Special academic programs:** cooperative (work-study

plan) program, double major, dual enrollment, English as a Second Language (ESL), exchange student program (domestic), independent study, internships, student-designed major, study abroad, teacher certificate program. **Teacher certification offered in:** elementary, middle/junior high, secondary, bilingual/bicultural. **Reserve Officers Training Corps (ROTC):** Army ROTC: Offered at cooperating institution (Santa Clara University); Air Force ROTC: Offered at cooperating institution (UC Berkeley). **Faculty and instruction (2005-2006):** Total instructional faculty: 548 full-time, 211 part-time (59% men; 41% women; 19% minorities). Full-time faculty with Ph.D. or other terminal degree: 98%. Student/faculty ratio: 19/1. Classes of fewer than 20 students: 39%; of 20 to 49 students: 41%; of 50 or more students: 20%. **Advanced Placement and International Baccalaureate credit:** AP tests may be used for: Credit and/or placement. Scores accepted: 3, 4, 5. International Baccalaureate exams may be used for: Placement only. **Freshmen returning for sophomore year:** 88%. **Graduation rates:** Four-year: 49%; five-year: 66%; six-year: 70%.

COSTS AND FINANCIAL AID

Financial aid office: (831) 459-2963. **Expenses (2006-2007):** Tuition and fees 2006-2007: $6,949 in state, $25,633 out of state; room/board: $11,805. Estimated books and supplies: $1,395; transportation: $870; personal expenses: $2,192. **Financial aid:** Priority filing date for institution's financial aid form: March 17; deadline: June 1. In 2005-2006, 62% of undergraduates applied for financial aid. Of those, 48% were determined to have financial need; 48% had their need fully met. Average financial aid package (proportion receiving): $14,285 (46%). Average amount of gift aid, such as scholarships or grants (proportion receiving): $10,340 (41%). Average amount of self-help aid, such as work study or loans (proportion receiving): $5,696 (40%). Average need-based loan (excluding PLUS or other private loans): $4,656. Among students who received need-based aid, the average percentage of need met: 89%. Among students who received aid based on merit, the average award (and the proportion receiving): $6,851 (2%). The average athletic scholarship (and the proportion receiving): $0 (0%). Average amount of debt of borrowers graduating in 2005: $13,374. Proportion who borrowed: 51%.

CAMPUS LIFE AND EXTRACURRICULAR ACTIVITIES

Campus housing available: coed dorms, women's dorms, apartments for married students, apartment for single students, special housing for disabled students, special housing for international students, other housing options. Students who live in college-owned, operated, or affiliated housing: 45%. **Student employment:** During the 2005-2006 academic year, 37% of undergraduates worked on campus. Average per-year earnings: $2,010. **Clubs and organizations:** Number of student organizations: 129. Activities include: choral groups, dance, drama/theater, literary magazine, music ensembles, radio station, student government, student newspaper, student film society, symphony orchestra. Number of fraternities: 5; sororities: 6. Proportion of men in fraternities: 1%; of women in sororities: 1%. **Sports program (2005-2006):** Member of NCAA III. *Men's intercollegiate varsity sports:* basketball, soccer, swimming and diving, tennis, volleyball, water polo. *Women's intercollegiate varsity sports:* basketball, cross-country, golf, soccer, swimming and diving, tennis, volleyball, water polo.

SERVICES AND FACILITIES

Basic services: nonremedial tutoring, women's center, placement service, day care, health service. **Counseling services:** minority student, career, personal, academic, psychological, birth control. **For learning-disabled students:** School does not offer a structured program with separate admission and additional fees. Total undergraduates in learning-disabled program or receiving services: 163. Services include: reading machines, tape recorders, videotaped classes, note-taking services, oral tests, learning center, readers, extended time for tests, tutors, priority registration, proofreading services, texts on tape, typist/scribe, other. **Library:** Number of titles: 1,540,634; number of current serial subscriptions: 22,646. **Information technology resources:** Students are not required to lease or own a computer. Number of campus computers available to all students: 593. School has a wireless network. Approximate number of users that can be accommodated: 5,280. Proportion of college-owned housing units wired for high-speed internet access: 100%. **Campus safety:** Security services offered: 24-hour foot-and-vehicle patrols, late-night transport/escort service, 24-hour emergency telephones, lighted pathways/sidewalks, controlled dormitory access (key, security card, etc).

TRANSFER AND INTERNATIONAL STUDENTS

Transfer students: May apply for admission for the following academic terms: Fall, Winter. Applicants need a minimum number of credits to apply.

For fall 2005: Transfer applications received: 5,112. Transfer applicants offered admission: 3,548. Transfer applicants enrolled: 894. **International students:** Number of foreign undergraduates: 115 (1% of student body). Number of countries represented: 89. Minimum TOEFL score required: 550 (paper); 220 (computer). Average TOEFL score: 580 (paper).

University of Judaism

- ■ **Address:** 15600 Mulholland Drive, Bel Air, CA 90077
- ■ **Website:** http://www.uj.edu
- ■ **Private; Religious affiliation:** Jewish
- ■ **Enrollment:** 115 full-time

KEY STATS
✔ **U.S News College Ranking:** fourth tier, Liberal Arts Colleges
✔ **SAT or ACT Score (25th/75th percentile):** N/A
✔ **Tuition:** 2006-2007: $20,300

Selectivity: Selective	**Room/board:** $10,778
Acceptance rate: N/A	**Average debt:** N/A
Student/faculty ratio: N/A	**Proportion who borrowed:** 90%

UNDERGRADUATE STUDENT BODY STATS
2005-2006 enrollment: 115 full-time. Men: 45%; women: 55%.

ADMISSIONS FACTS AND FIGURES
Phone: (888) 853-6763. **Email:** admissions@uj.edu. **Website:** http://www.uj.edu. **Application deadlines for fall 2007:** Regular decision: Rolling. Early decision: Send application by: N/A; Decision sent by: N/A. Early action: Not offered. Admission can be deferred. **Application fee:** $35. Common application is not accepted. **Admissions requirements/recommendations:** Tests: The college uses SAT or ACT scores in admissions decisions. Either SAT or ACT required. Campus visit: Recommended. Admissions interview: Recommended. Off-campus interview: May be arranged. **Factors that count in admissions decisions:** *Academic:* Secondary school record: Important. Class rank: Not considered. Letters of recommendation: Very important. Standardized test scores: Considered. Essay: Very important. *Nonacademic:* Interview: Very important. Extracurricular activities: Very important. Talent/ability: Important. Character/personal qualities: Very important. Alumni/ae relationship: Not considered. Geographical residence: Not considered. State residency: Not considered. Religious affiliation/commitment: Not considered. Minority status: Not considered. Volunteer work: Very important. Work experience: Considered.

ACADEMICS
Year founded: 1947. **Academic calendar:** Semester. **Degrees offered:** bachelor's, master's. **Most popular majors:** Information not available. **Major fields of study:** area, ethnic, cultural, and gender studies; biological and biomedical sciences; business, management, marketing, and related support services; communication, journalism, and related programs; education; English language and literature/letters; history; liberal arts and sciences studies, and humanities; philosophy and religious studies; psychology; social sciences; theology and religious vocations. **Areas of required coursework:** humanities, computer literacy, English (including composition), sciences (biological or physical), history, social science. **Pre-professional programs:** pre-law, pre-dentistry, pre-medicine, pre-veterinary science, pre-pharmacy. **Special academic programs (% participation):** double major (15%), exchange student program (domestic) (5%), independent study (17%), internships (78%), student-designed major (9%), study abroad (87%). **Advanced Placement and International Baccalaureate credit:** AP tests may be used for: Credit only. Scores accepted: 3. International Baccalaureate exams may be used for: Credit and/or placement. **Freshmen returning for sophomore year:** 85%. **Graduation rates:** Six-year: 57%.

COSTS AND FINANCIAL AID
Financial aid office: (310) 476-9777. **Expenses (2006-2007):** Tuition and fees 2006-2007: $20,300; room/board: $10,778. Estimated books and supplies: $1,260; transportation: $745; personal expenses: $1,980. **Financial aid:** Priority filing date for institution's financial aid form: March 2. In 2005-2006, 83% of undergraduates applied for financial aid. Of those, 83% were determined to have financial need; 65% had their need fully met. Average financial aid package (proportion receiving): $19,700 (83%). Average amount of gift aid, such as scholarships or grants (proportion receiving):

$8,573 (53%). Average amount of self-help aid, such as work study or loans (proportion receiving): N/A (20%). Average need-based loan (excluding PLUS or other private loans): $4,386. Among students who received need-based aid, the average percentage of need met: 75%. Proportion who borrowed: 90%.

CAMPUS LIFE AND EXTRACURRICULAR ACTIVITIES
Campus housing available: coed dorms, apartments for married students, apartment for single students, special housing for disabled students. **Student employment:** During the 2005-2006 academic year, 45% of undergraduates worked on campus. Average per-year earnings: $2,500. Activities include: concert band, dance, drama/theater, literary magazine, radio station, student government, student newspaper, yearbook. Number of fraternities: 0; sororities: 0.

SERVICES AND FACILITIES
Basic services: nonremedial tutoring, placement service, health service. **Remedial assistance:** writing, study skills. **Counseling services:** career, personal, academic, psychological, religious. **For learning-disabled students:** Services include: tape recorders, untimed tests, note-taking services, oral tests, readers, extended time for tests, tutors. **Information technology resources:** Students are not required to lease or own a computer. Number of campus computers available to all students: 50. School has a wireless network. **Campus safety:** Security services offered: 24-hour foot-and-vehicle patrols, 24-hour emergency telephones, lighted pathways/sidewalks, controlled dormitory access (key, security card, etc).

TRANSFER AND INTERNATIONAL STUDENTS
Transfer students: May apply for admission for the following academic terms: Fall, Spring. Applicants need a minimum number of credits to apply. **International students:** Minimum TOEFL score required: 600 (paper).

University of La Verne

- ■ **Address:** 1950 Third Street, La Verne, CA 91750
- ■ **Website:** http://www.ulv.edu
- ■ **Private; Religious affiliation:** Church of the Brethren
- ■ **Enrollment:** 1,583 full-time; 102 part-time

KEY STATS
✔ **U.S News College Ranking:** third tier, National Universities
✔ **SAT Score (25th/75th percentile):** 930-1130
✔ **Tuition:** 2006-2007: $24,260

Selectivity: Selective	**Room/board:** $9,210
Acceptance rate: 62%	**Average debt:** N/A
Student/faculty ratio: 12/1	**Proportion who borrowed:** N/A

UNDERGRADUATE STUDENT BODY STATS
2005-2006 enrollment: 1,583 full-time; 102 part-time. Men: 35%; women: 65%. **Ethnic makeup:** African American: 9%; American-Indian: 1%; Asian American: 5%; Hispanic: 38%; White: 47%; International: 1%.

ADMISSIONS FACTS AND FIGURES
Phone: (800) 876-4858. **Email:** admissions@ulv.edu. **Website:** http://www.ulv.edu. **Application deadlines for fall 2007:** Regular decision: Rolling. Early decision: Not offered. Early action: Not offered. Admission can be deferred. **Application fee:** $50. Common application is accepted. **To apply online, go to:** http://www.ulv.edu/admissions/app_online.shtml. **Admissions requirements/recommendations:** High school units required (recommended): English: 4 (4); Mathematics: 3 (4); Science: 2 (2); Foreign language: 0 (2); Social studies: 2 (2); History: 3 (3); Academic electives: 0 (2); Total units: 14 (19). Tests: The college uses SAT or ACT scores in admissions decisions. Either SAT or ACT required. For admission to the fall 2007 entering class, the school will accept: ACT with writing. Campus visit: Recommended. Admissions interview: Recommended. Off-campus interview: May be arranged. **Factors that count in admissions decisions:** *Academic:* Secondary school record: Very important. Class rank: Important. Letters of recommendation: Very important. Standardized test scores: Very important. Essay: Very important. *Nonacademic:* Interview: Considered. Extracurricular activities: Important. Talent/ability: Considered. Character/personal qualities: Very important. Alumni/ae relationship: Considered. Geographical residence: Not considered. State residency: Not

considered. Religious affiliation/commitment: Not considered. Minority status: Considered. Volunteer work: Considered. Work experience: Considered. **Other schools with the greatest overlap in applicants:** California State Polytechnic University–Pomona; California State University–Fullerton; Chapman University; University of Redlands; Whittier College. **Admissions statistics for the fall 2005 entering class:** Total applicants: 1,638. Total accepted: 1,008. Freshmen enrolled: 339; 6% were from out of state. Overall acceptance rate: 62%. **Credentials of fall 2005 freshmen:** 33% ranked in the top 10 percent of their high school class; 68% were in the top 25 percent, and 93% were in the top half. (Proportion submitting class standing: 63%.) **Average high school grade point average:** 3.5. **First-year students who submitted SAT scores:** 96%. Scores (25/75 percentile): Verbal: 460-560, Math: 470-570, Combined: 930-1130. **First-year students submitting ACT scores:** 24%. Scores (25/75 percentile): English: 17-23, Math: 17-23, Composite: 18-23.

ACADEMICS

Year founded: 1891. **Academic calendar:** 4-1-4. **Degrees offered:** certificate, bachelor's, post-bachelor's certificate, master's, post-master's certificate, first professional, doctorate. **Most popular majors:** 19% business administration and management, 13% liberal arts and sciences/liberal studies, 12% psychology, 7% physical education teaching and coaching, 5% criminology. **Major fields of study:** biological and biomedical sciences; business, management, marketing, and related support services; communication, journalism, and related programs; computer and information sciences and support services; education; English language and literature/letters; family and consumer sciences/human sciences; foreign languages, literatures, and linguistics; health professions and related clinical sciences; history; legal professions and studies; liberal arts and sciences studies, and humanities; mathematics and statistics; multi/interdisciplinary studies; natural resources and conservation; philosophy and religious studies; physical sciences; psychology; public administration and social service professions; social sciences; visual and performing arts. **Areas of required coursework:** arts/fine arts, humanities, mathematics, English (including composition), philosophy, foreign languages, sciences (biological or physical), history, social science, other. **Pre-professional programs:** pre-law, pre-dentistry, pre-medicine, other. **Special academic programs:** accelerated program, distance learning, double major, English as a Second Language (ESL), exchange student program (domestic), honors program, independent study, internships, liberal arts/career combination, student-designed major, study abroad, teacher certificate program, weekend college. **Teacher certification offered in:** early childhood, special education, elementary, middle/junior high, secondary, bilingual/bicultural. **Reserve Officers Training Corps (ROTC):** Army ROTC: Offered at cooperating institution (Claremont Colleges/Claremont McKenna College/Pomona College). **Faculty and instruction (2005-2006):** Total instructional faculty: 187 full-time, 211 part-time (53% men; 47% women; 17% minorities). Full-time faculty with Ph.D. or other terminal degree: 96%. Student/faculty ratio: 12/1. Classes of fewer than 20 students: 71%; of 20 to 49 students: 29%; of 50 or more students: 0%. **Advanced Placement and International Baccalaureate credit:** AP tests may be used for: Credit and/or placement. Scores accepted: 3, 4, 5. International Baccalaureate exams may be used for: Credit and/or placement. **Freshmen returning for sophomore year:** 87%. **Graduation rates:** Four-year: 38%; five-year: 44%; six-year: 52%.

COSTS AND FINANCIAL AID

Financial aid office: (800) 649-0160. **Expenses (2006-2007):** Tuition and fees 2006-2007: $24,260; room/board: $9,210. Estimated books and supplies: $1,314; transportation: $774; personal expenses: $3,033. **Financial aid:** Priority filing date for institution's financial aid form: March 2. In 2005-2006, 88% of undergraduates applied for financial aid. Of those, 83% were determined to have financial need; 2% had their need fully met. Average financial aid package (proportion receiving): $20,636 (83%). Average amount of gift aid, such as scholarships or grants (proportion receiving): $10,620 (75%). Average amount of self-help aid, such as work study or loans (proportion receiving): $2,163 (23%). Average need-based loan (excluding PLUS or other private loans): $4,637. Among students who received aid based on merit, the average award (and the proportion receiving): $7,929 (13%). The average athletic scholarship (and the proportion receiving): $7,881 (84%).

CAMPUS LIFE AND EXTRACURRICULAR ACTIVITIES

Campus housing available: coed dorms, women's dorms, special housing for disabled students, other housing options. Students who live in college-owned, operated, or affiliated housing: 32%. **Student employment:** During the 2005-2006 academic year, 21% of undergraduates worked on campus.

Average per-year earnings: $1,800. **Clubs and organizations:** Number of student organizations: 34. Activities include: choral groups, dance, drama/theater, jazz band, literary magazine, music ensembles, musical theater, radio station, student government, student newspaper, television station, yearbook. Number of fraternities: 3; sororities: 5. Proportion of men in fraternities: 9%; of women in sororities: 16%. Average proportion of students who stay on campus on weekends: 25%. **Sports program (2005-2006):** Member of NCAA III. *Men's intercollegiate varsity sports:* baseball, basketball, cross-country, football, golf, soccer, swimming and diving, tennis, track and field (indoor), track and field (outdoor), volleyball, water polo. *Women's intercollegiate varsity sports:* basketball, cross-country, soccer, softball, swimming and diving, tennis, track and field (indoor), track and field (outdoor), volleyball, water polo.

SERVICES AND FACILITIES

Basic services: nonremedial tutoring, placement service, health service, health insurance. **Remedial assistance:** math, writing, study skills. **Counseling services:** minority student, career, military, personal, veteran student, academic, older student, psychological, birth control, religious. **For learning-disabled students:** School does not offer a structured program with separate admission and additional fees. Services include: remedial math, remedial English, reading machines, tape recorders, untimed tests, note-taking services, oral tests, learning center, readers, extended time for tests, tutors, priority registration, priority seating, texts on tape, other testing accomodations, other. **Library:** Number of titles: 148,790; number of current serial subscriptions: 11,585. **Information technology resources:** Students are not required to lease or own a computer. School has a wireless network. Approximate number of users that can be accommodated: 750. Proportion of college-owned housing units wired for high-speed internet access: 100%. **Campus safety:** Security services offered: 24-hour foot-and-vehicle patrols, late-night transport/escort service, 24-hour emergency telephones, lighted pathways/sidewalks, controlled dormitory access (key, security card, etc).

TRANSFER AND INTERNATIONAL STUDENTS

Transfer students: May apply for admission for the following academic terms: Fall, Spring. Applicants need a minimum number of credits to apply. For fall 2005: Transfer applications received: 395. Transfer applicants offered admission: 235. Transfer applicants enrolled: 136. **International students:** Number of foreign undergraduates: 14 (1% of student body). Number of countries represented: 6. Minimum TOEFL score required: 500 (paper); 213 (computer). Average TOEFL score: 583 (paper).

University of Redlands

- **Address:** PO Box 3080, Redlands, CA 92373
- **Website:** http://www.redlands.edu
- **Private**
- **Enrollment:** 2,429 full-time; 664 part-time

KEY STATS
✔ **U.S News College Ranking:** 9, Universities–Master's (West)
✔ **SAT Score (25th/75th percentile):** 1070-1250
✔ **Tuition:** 2006-2007: $28,776

Selectivity: More selective	**Room/board:** $9,360
Acceptance rate: 66%	**Average debt:** $15,024
Student/faculty ratio: 11/1	**Proportion who borrowed:** 78%

UNDERGRADUATE STUDENT BODY STATS

2005-2006 enrollment: 2,429 full-time; 664 part-time. Men: 42%; women: 58%. **Ethnic makeup:** African American: 4%; American-Indian: 1%; Asian American: 6%; Hispanic: 14%; White: 74%; International: 1%.

ADMISSIONS FACTS AND FIGURES

Phone: (800) 455-5064. **Email:** admissions@redlands.edu. **Website:** http://www.redlands.edu. **Application deadlines for fall 2007:** Regular decision: June 1. Early decision: Not offered. Early action: Not offered. Admission can be deferred. **Application fee:** $45. Common application is accepted. **Admissions requirements/recommendations:** High school units required (recommended): English: 4 (4); Mathematics: 3 (3); Science: 2 (3); Foreign language: 2 (3); Social studies: 2 (3); Total units: 13 (16). Tests: The college uses SAT or ACT scores in admissions decisions. Either SAT or ACT required. For admission to the fall 2007 entering class, the school will accept: ACT with writing, ACT without writing. **Campus visit:** Recommended. Admissions interview: Recommended. Off-campus interview: May be arranged. **Factors that count in admissions decisions:** *Academic:* Secondary school record: Very important. Class rank: Not considered. Letters of recommendation: Very important. Standardized test scores: Important. Essay: Important. *Nonacademic:* Interview: Considered. Extracurricular activities: Considered. Talent/ability: Very important. Character/personal qualities: Very important. Alumni/ae relationship: Considered. Geographical residence: Considered. State residency: Not considered. Religious affiliation/commitment: Not considered. Minority status: Considered. Volunteer work: Considered. Work experience: Considered. **Other schools with the greatest overlap in applicants:** Chapman University; Loyola Marymount University; Occidental College; University of San Diego; University of Southern California. **Admissions statistics for the fall 2005 entering class:** Total applicants: 3,395. Total accepted: 2,226. Freshmen enrolled: 615; 37% were from out of state. Overall acceptance rate: 66%. **Size of waiting list:** 25 applicants; enrolled from waiting list: 3. **Credentials of fall 2005 freshmen:** 32% ranked in the top 10 percent of their high school class; 69% were in the top 25 percent, and 93% were in the top half. (Proportion submitting class standing: 68%.) **Average high school grade point average:** 3.6. **First-year students who submitted SAT scores:** 79%. Scores (25/75 percentile): Verbal: 530-620, Math: 540-630, Combined: 1070-1250. **First-year students submitting ACT scores:** 33%. Scores (25/75 percentile): English: N/A, Math: N/A, Composite: 21-26.

ACADEMICS

Year founded: 1907. **Academic calendar:** Other. **Degrees offered:** bachelor's, post-bachelor's certificate, master's, post-master's certificate. **Most popular majors:** 48% business, management, marketing, and related support services, 15% liberal arts and sciences studies, and humanities, 9% social sciences, 4% psychology, 4% visual and performing arts. **Major fields of study:** area, ethnic, cultural, and gender studies; biological and biomedical sciences; business, management, marketing, and related support services; computer and information sciences and support services; education; English language and literature/letters; foreign languages, literatures, and linguistics; health professions and related clinical sciences; history; liberal arts and sciences studies, and humanities; mathematics and statistics; multi/interdisciplinary studies; natural resources and conservation; philosophy and religious studies; physical sciences; psychology; social sciences; visual and performing arts. **Areas of required coursework:** arts/fine arts, humanities, computer literacy, mathematics, English (including composition), philosophy, foreign languages, sciences (biological or physical), history, social science. **Pre-professional programs:** pre-law, pre-medicine. **Special academic programs:** cross-registration, double major, exchange student program (domestic), honors program, independent study, internships, liberal arts/career combination, student-designed major, study abroad, teacher certification program. **Teacher certification offered in:** elementary, middle/junior high, secondary. **Reserve Officers Training Corps (ROTC):** Army ROTC: Offered at cooperating institution (CSUSB); Navy ROTC: Offered at cooperating institution (CSUSB); Air Force ROTC: Offered at cooperating institution (CSUSB). **Faculty and instruction (2005-2006):** Total instructional faculty: 202 full-time, 247 part-time (58% men; 42% women; 15% minorities). Full-time faculty with Ph.D. or other terminal degree: 88%. Student/faculty ratio: 11/1. Classes of fewer than 20 students: 72%; of 20 to 49 students: 28%; of 50 or more students: 0%. **Advanced Placement and International Baccalaureate credit:** AP tests may be used for: Credit and/or placement. Scores accepted: 3, 4, 5. International Baccalaureate exams may be used for: Credit only. **Freshmen returning for sophomore year:** 84%. **Graduation rates:** Four-year: 57%; five-year: 64%; six-year: 62%. **Graduate study:** 20% of students pursue further study immediately upon graduation; 12% within one year; 20% within five years. Fields in which graduates pursue further study: Master of Business Administration (MBA), 6%; law, 6%; medicine, 2%; dentistry, 2%; education, 22%; veterinary medicine, 1%.

COSTS AND FINANCIAL AID

Financial aid office: (909) 335-4047. **Expenses (2006-2007):** Tuition and fees 2006-2007: $28,776; room/board: $9,360. Estimated books and supplies: $1,300 personal expenses: $2,862. **Financial aid:** Priority filing date for institution's financial aid form: February 15. In 2005-2006, 83% of undergraduates applied for financial aid. Of those, 69% were determined to have financial need; 43% had their need fully met. Average financial aid package (proportion receiving): $25,071 (69%). Average amount of gift aid, such as scholarships or grants (proportion receiving): $18,517 (66%). Average amount of self-help aid, such as work study or loans (proportion receiving): $6,483 (60%). Average need-based loan (excluding PLUS or other private loans): $5,377. Among students who received need-based aid, the average

percentage of need met: 89%. Among students who received aid based on merit, the average award (and the proportion receiving): $9,816 (19%). The average athletic scholarship (and the proportion receiving): $0 (0%). Average amount of debt of borrowers graduating in 2005: $15,024. Proportion who borrowed: 78%.

CAMPUS LIFE AND EXTRACURRICULAR ACTIVITIES

Campus housing available (% using): coed dorms (63%), women's dorms (13%), men's dorms (5%), sorority housing (1%), fraternity housing (1%), apartment for single students (14%), special housing for disabled students (1%), other housing options (2%). Students who live in college-owned, operated, or affiliated housing: 67%. **Student employment:** During the 2005-2006 academic year, 48% of undergraduates worked on campus. Average per-year earnings: $1,200. **Clubs and organizations:** Number of student organizations: 102. Activities include: choral groups, concert band, dance, drama/theater, jazz band, literary magazine, music ensembles, musical theater, opera, student government, student newspaper, symphony orchestra. Number of fraternities: 7; sororities: 5. **Sports program (2005-2006):** Member of NCAA III. *Men's intercollegiate varsity sports:* baseball, basketball, cross-country, football, golf, soccer, swimming and diving, tennis, track and field (outdoor), water polo. *Women's intercollegiate varsity sports:* basketball, cross-country, lacrosse, soccer, softball, swimming and diving, tennis, track and field (outdoor), volleyball, water polo.

SERVICES AND FACILITIES

Basic services: nonremedial tutoring, women's center, health service. **Counseling services:** career, personal, academic, psychological, religious. **For learning-disabled students:** School does not offer a structured program with separate admission and additional fees. Total undergraduates in learning-disabled program or receiving services: 281. Services include: tape recorders, untimed tests, note-taking services, oral tests, readers, extended time for tests, tutors, texts on tape, other testing accomodations, other. **Library:** Number of titles: 381,219; number of current serial subscriptions: 12,800. **Information technology resources:** Students are not required to lease or own a computer. Number of campus computers available to all students: 712. School has a wireless network. Approximate number of users that can be accommodated: 750. Proportion of college-owned housing units wired for high-speed internet access: 100%. **Campus safety:** Security services offered: 24-hour foot-and-vehicle patrols, late-night transport/escort service, 24-hour emergency telephones, lighted pathways/sidewalks, controlled dormitory access (key, security card, etc).

TRANSFER AND INTERNATIONAL STUDENTS

Transfer students: May apply for admission for the following academic terms: Fall, Spring. Applicants need a minimum number of credits to apply. For fall 2005: Transfer applications received: 357. Transfer applicants offered admission: 195. Transfer applicants enrolled: 104. **International students:** Number of foreign undergraduates: 35 (1% of student body). Number of countries represented: 14. Minimum TOEFL score required: 550 (paper); 213 (computer).

University of San Diego

- **Address:** 5998 Alcala Park, San Diego, CA 92110-2492
- **Website:** http://www.SanDiego.edu
- **Private; Religious affiliation:** Roman Catholic
- **Enrollment:** 4,801 full-time; 169 part-time

KEY STATS

✔ **U.S News College Ranking:** 105, National Universities
✔ **SAT Score (25th/75th percentile):** 1080-1280
✔ **Tuition:** 2006-2007: $30,716

Selectivity: More selective	**Room/board:** $10,960
Acceptance rate: 60%	**Average debt:** $26,617
Student/faculty ratio: 15/1	**Proportion who borrowed:** 45%

UNDERGRADUATE STUDENT BODY STATS

2005-2006 enrollment: 4,801 full-time; 169 part-time. Men: 40%; women: 60%. **Ethnic makeup:** African American: 2%; American-Indian: 1%; Asian American: 7%; Hispanic: 13%; White: 75%; International: 2%. **Religious preference:** Roman Catholic: 55%; Protestant: 30%; Jewish: 2%; Muslim: 1%; Buddhist: 1%; No preference: 5%; Unknown: 3%; Other: 3%.

ADMISSIONS FACTS AND FIGURES

Phone: (619) 260-4506. **Email:** admissions@SanDiego.edu. **Website:** http://www.SanDiego.edu. **Application deadlines for fall 2007:** Regular decision: March 5; decision sent by April 15. Early decision: Not offered. Early action: Send application by: November 15; Decision sent by: January 31. Admission can be deferred. **Application fee:** $55. Common application is accepted. **Admissions requirements/recommendations:** High school units required (recommended): English: 4 (4); Mathematics: 3 (4); Science: 3 (4); Foreign language: 2 (3); Social studies: 3 (4); Total units: 17 (22). Tests: The college uses SAT or ACT scores in admissions decisions. Either SAT or ACT required. For admission to the fall 2007 entering class, the school will accept: ACT with writing. Campus visit: Recommended. Admissions interview: Neither required nor recommended. Off-campus interview: Not available. **Factors that count in admissions decisions:** *Academic:* Secondary school record: Very important. Class rank: Important. Letters of recommendation: Considered. Standardized test scores: Very important. Essay: Important. *Nonacademic:* Interview: Not considered. Extracurricular activities: Important. Talent/ability: Important. Character/personal qualities: Important. Alumni/ae relationship: Considered. Geographical residence: Not considered. State residency: Not considered. Religious affiliation/commitment: Considered. Minority status: Considered. Volunteer work: Important. Work experience: Considered. **Other schools with the greatest overlap in applicants:** Pepperdine University; Santa Clara University; University of California–San Diego; University of California–Santa Barbara; University of Southern California. **Admissions statistics for the fall 2005 entering class:** Total applicants: 7,862. Total accepted: 4,687. Freshmen enrolled: 1,136; 43% were from out of state. Accepted through early-decision or early-action plans: 38%. Overall acceptance rate: 60%. Non-early acceptance rate: 60%. **Size of waiting list:** 548 applicants; enrolled from waiting list: 4. **Credentials of fall 2005 freshmen:** 41% ranked in the top 10 percent of their high school class; 79% were in the top 25 percent, and 96% were in the top half. (Proportion submitting class standing: 57%.) **Average high school grade point average:** 3.7. **First-year students who submitted SAT scores:** 93%. Scores (25/75 percentile): Verbal: 530-630, Math: 550-650, Combined: 1080-1280. **First-year students submitting ACT scores:** 42%. Scores (25/75 percentile): English: 23-28, Math: 23-28, Composite: 23-28.

ACADEMICS

Year founded: 1949. **Academic calendar:** 4-1-4. **Degrees offered:** bachelor's, post-bachelor's certificate, master's, post-master's certificate, first professional, first professional certificate, doctorate. **Most popular majors:** 36% business, management, marketing, and related support services, 17% social sciences, 9% communication, journalism, and related programs, 7% liberal arts and sciences studies, and humanities, 6% psychology. **Major fields of study:** biological and biomedical sciences; business, management, marketing, and related support services; communication, journalism, and related programs; computer and information sciences and support services; engineering; English language and literature/letters; foreign languages, literatures, and linguistics; health professions and related clinical sciences; history; liberal arts and sciences studies, and humanities; mathematics and statistics; multi/interdisciplinary studies; natural resources and conservation; philosophy and religious studies; physical sciences; psychology; social sciences; visual and performing arts. **Areas of required coursework:** arts/fine arts, humanities, mathematics, English (including composition), philosophy, foreign languages, sciences (biological or physical), history, social science, other. **Pre-professional programs:** pre-law, pre-dentistry, pre-medicine, pre-theology, pre-veterinary science, pre-optometry, pre-pharmacy. **Special academic programs:** double major, English as a Second Language (ESL), honors program, independent study, internships, liberal arts/career combination, study abroad, teacher certificate program. **Teacher certification offered in:** early childhood, special education, elementary, middle/junior high, secondary. **Reserve Officers Training Corps (ROTC):** Army ROTC: Offered at cooperating institution (San Diego State University); Navy ROTC: Offered on campus; Air Force ROTC: Offered at cooperating institution (San Diego State University). **Faculty and instruction (2005-2006):** Total instructional faculty: 359 full-time, 363 part-time (53% men; 47% women; 15% minorities). Full-time faculty with Ph.D. or other terminal degree: 96%. Student/faculty ratio: 15/1. Classes of fewer than 20 students: 40%; of 20 to 49 students: 60%; of 50 or more students: 0%. **Advanced Placement and International Baccalaureate credit:** AP tests may be used for: Credit and/or placement. Scores accepted: 3, 4, 5. International Baccalaureate exams may be used for: Credit and/or placement. **Freshmen returning for sophomore year:** 85%. **Graduation rates:** Four-year: 62%; five-year: 72%; six-year: 73%. **Graduate study:** 15% of students pursue further study within one year.

COSTS AND FINANCIAL AID

Financial aid office: (619) 260-4514. **Expenses (2006-2007):** Tuition and fees 2006-2007: $30,716; room/board: $10,960. Estimated books and supplies: $1,300; transportation: $774; personal expenses: $2,088. **Financial aid:** Priority filing date for institution's financial aid form: February 20. In 2005-2006, 53% of undergraduates applied for financial aid. Of those, 46% were determined to have financial need; 19% had their need fully met. Average financial aid package (proportion receiving): $21,450 (46%). Average amount of gift aid, such as scholarships or grants (proportion receiving): $15,830 (45%). Average amount of self-help aid, such as work study or loans (proportion receiving): $5,919 (44%). Average need-based loan (excluding PLUS or other private loans): $4,318. Among students who received need-based aid, the average percentage of need met: 71%. Among students who received aid based on merit, the average award (and the proportion receiving): $8,556 (15%). The average athletic scholarship (and the proportion receiving): $18,581 (6%). Average amount of debt of borrowers graduating in 2005: $26,617. Proportion who borrowed: 45%.

CAMPUS LIFE AND EXTRACURRICULAR ACTIVITIES

Campus housing available (% using): coed dorms (88%), women's dorms (7%), men's dorms (5%), apartments for married students, apartment for single students, special housing for disabled students. Students who live in college-owned, operated, or affiliated housing: 50%. **Student employment:** During the 2005-2006 academic year, 33% of undergraduates worked on campus. Average per-year earnings: $1,800. **Clubs and organizations:** Number of student organizations: 60. Activities include: choral groups, dance, drama/theater, jazz band, literary magazine, music ensembles, musical theater, pep band, student government, student newspaper, symphony orchestra, television station, yearbook. Number of fraternities: 4; sororities: 6. Proportion of men in fraternities: 12%; of women in sororities: 19%. Average proportion of students who stay on campus on weekends: 50%. **Sports program (2005-2006):** Member of NCAA I. *Men's intercollegiate varsity sports:* baseball, basketball, cross-country, football, golf, soccer, tennis. *Women's intercollegiate varsity sports:* basketball, cross-country, soccer, softball, swimming and diving, tennis, volleyball, rowing.

SERVICES AND FACILITIES

Basic services: nonremedial tutoring, women's center, placement service, day care, health service, health insurance. **Counseling services:** minority student, career, military, personal, veteran student, academic, psychological, religious. **For learning-disabled students:** School does not offer a structured program with separate admission and additional fees. Services include: tape recorders, other. **Library:** Number of titles: 538,034; number of current serial subscriptions: 6,367. **Information technology resources:** Students are not required to lease or own a computer. Number of campus computers available to all students: 275. School has a wireless network. Approximate number of users that can be accommodated: 2,220. Proportion of college-owned housing units wired for high-speed internet access: 100%. **Campus safety:** Security services offered: 24-hour foot-and-vehicle patrols, late-night transport/escort service, 24-hour emergency telephones, lighted pathways/sidewalks, controlled dormitory access (key, security card, etc).

TRANSFER AND INTERNATIONAL STUDENTS

Transfer students: May apply for admission for the following academic terms: Fall, Spring. Applicants need a minimum number of credits to apply. For fall 2005: Transfer applications received: 1,039. Transfer applicants offered admission: 610. Transfer applicants enrolled: 305. **International students:** Number of foreign undergraduates: 99 (2% of student body). Number of countries represented: 37. Minimum TOEFL score required: 550 (paper); 213 (computer).

University of San Francisco

- **Address:** Ignatian Heights, San Francisco, CA 94117-1080
- **Website:** http://www.usfca.edu
- **Private; Religious affiliation:** Roman Catholic
- **Enrollment:** 4,981 full-time; 231 part-time

KEY STATS

✔ **U.S News College Ranking:** 112, National Universities
✔ **SAT Score (25th/75th percentile):** 1010-1240
✔ **Tuition:** 2006-2007: $28,580

Selectivity: Selective   **Room/board:** $10,580
Acceptance rate: 72%   **Average debt:** $26,779
Student/faculty ratio: 14/1   **Proportion who borrowed:** 62%

UNDERGRADUATE STUDENT BODY STATS

2005-2006 enrollment: 4,981 full-time; 231 part-time. Men: 37%; women: 63%. **Ethnic makeup:** African American: 5%; American-Indian: 1%; Asian American: 25%; Hispanic: 14%; White: 49%; International: 7%. **Religious preference:** Roman Catholic: 44%; Protestant: 6%; Jewish: 2%; Muslim: 1%; Hindu: 1%; Buddhist: 2%; No preference: 4%; Other: 37%.

ADMISSIONS FACTS AND FIGURES

Phone: (415) 422-6563. **Email:** admission@usfca.edu. **Website:** http://www.usfca.edu. **Application deadlines for fall 2007:** Regular decision: February 1. Early decision: Not offered. Early action: Send application by: November 15; Decision sent by: January 16. Admission can be deferred. **Application fee:** $55. Common application is accepted. **Admissions requirements/recommendations:** High school units required (recommended): English: 4; Mathematics: 3; Science: 2; Foreign language: 2; Social studies: 3; Academic electives: 6; Total units: 20. Tests: The college uses SAT or ACT scores in admissions decisions. Either SAT or ACT required. For admission to the fall 2007 entering class, the school will accept: ACT with writing. Campus visit: Recommended. Admissions interview: Recommended. Off-campus interview: May be arranged. **Factors that count in admissions decisions: Academic:** Secondary school record: Very important. Class rank: Important. Letters of recommendation: Very important. Standardized test scores: Very important. Essay: Important. **Nonacademic:** Interview: Considered. Extracurricular activities: Considered. Talent/ability: Considered. Character/personal qualities: Considered. Alumni/ae relationship: Considered. Geographical residence: Not considered. State residency: Not considered. Religious affiliation/commitment: Not considered. Minority status: Considered. Volunteer work: Considered. Work experience: Not considered. **Other schools with the greatest overlap in applicants:** San Francisco State University; Santa Clara University; St. Mary's College; Stanford University; University of California–Berkeley. **Admissions statistics for the fall 2005 entering class:** Total applicants: 6,090. Total accepted: 4,376. Freshmen enrolled: 934; 29% were from out of state. Overall acceptance rate: 72%. Non-early acceptance rate: 72%. **Size of waiting list:** 334 applicants; enrolled from waiting list: N/A. **Credentials of fall 2005 freshmen:** 17% ranked in the top 10 percent of their high school class; 54% were in the top 25 percent, and 90% were in the top half. (Proportion submitting class standing: 37%.) **Average high school grade point average:** 3.5. **First-year students who submitted SAT scores:** 99%. Scores (25/75 percentile): Verbal: 510-620, Math: 500-620, Combined: 1010-1240. **First-year students submitting ACT scores:** 33%. Scores (25/75 percentile): English: 21-27, Math: 20-26, Composite: 21-26.

ACADEMICS

Year founded: 1855. **Academic calendar:** 4-1-4. **Degrees offered:** bachelor's, master's, post-master's certificate, first professional, doctorate. **Most popular majors:** 30% business, management, marketing, and related support services, 12% social sciences, 10% communication and media studies, 9% psychology, 8% nursing/registered nurse training (R.N., A.S.N., B.S.N., M.S.N.). **Major fields of study:** architecture and related services; area, ethnic, cultural, and gender studies; biological and biomedical sciences; business, management, marketing, and related support services; communication, journalism, and related programs; computer and information sciences and support services; English language and literature/letters; foreign languages, literatures, and linguistics; health professions and related clinical sciences; history; liberal arts and sciences studies, and humanities; mathematics and statistics; natural resources and conservation; parks, recreation, leisure, and fitness studies; philosophy and religious studies; physical sciences; psychol-

ogy; public administration and social service professions; social sciences; theology and religious vocations; visual and performing arts. **Areas of required coursework:** arts/fine arts, humanities, mathematics, English (including composition), philosophy, sciences (biological or physical), history, social science, other. **Pre-professional programs:** pre-law, pre-dentistry, pre-medicine, pre-veterinary science, pre-optometry, pre-pharmacy. **Special academic programs:** accelerated program, cross-registration, distance learning, double major, English as a Second Language (ESL), exchange student program (domestic), external degree program, honors program, independent study, internships, liberal arts/career combination, student-designed major, study abroad, teacher certificate program. **Teacher certification offered in:** early childhood, special education, elementary, middle/junior high, secondary, bilingual/bicultural. **Reserve Officers Training Corps (ROTC):** Army ROTC: Offered on campus; Air Force ROTC: Offered at cooperating institution (University of California–Berkeley). **Faculty and instruction (2005-2006):** Total instructional faculty: 348 full-time, 171 part-time (54% men; 46% women; 17% minorities). Full-time faculty with Ph.D. or other terminal degree: 93%. Student/faculty ratio: 14/1. Classes of fewer than 20 students: 51%; of 20 to 49 students: 45%; of 50 or more students: 3%. **Advanced Placement and International Baccalaureate credit:** AP tests may be used for: Credit only. Scores accepted: 3. International Baccalaureate exams may be used for: Credit and/or placement. **Freshmen returning for sophomore year:** 85%. **Graduation rates:** Four-year: 50%; five-year: 64%; six-year: 67%.

COSTS AND FINANCIAL AID

Financial aid office: (415) 422-2620. **Expenses (2006-2007):** Tuition and fees 2006-2007: $28,580; room/board: $10,580. Estimated books and supplies: $900; transportation: $800; personal expenses: $2,400. **Financial aid:** Priority filing date for institution's financial aid form: February 15. In 2005-2006, 65% of undergraduates applied for financial aid. Of those, 58% were determined to have financial need; 11% had their need fully met. Average financial aid package (proportion receiving): $21,153 (57%). Average amount of gift aid, such as scholarships or grants (proportion receiving): $14,973 (49%). Average amount of self-help aid, such as work study or loans (proportion receiving): $6,675 (51%). Average need-based loan (excluding PLUS or other private loans): $4,966. Among students who received need-based aid, the average percentage of need met: 70%. Among students who received aid based on merit, the average award (and the proportion receiving): $14,696 (3%). The average athletic scholarship (and the proportion receiving): $23,315 (4%). Average amount of debt of borrowers graduating in 2005: $26,779. Proportion who borrowed: 62%.

CAMPUS LIFE AND EXTRACURRICULAR ACTIVITIES

Campus housing available (% using): coed dorms (71%), women's dorms (8%), apartment for single students (20%), other housing options (1%). Students who live in college-owned, operated, or affiliated housing: 46%. **Student employment:** During the 2005-2006 academic year, 20% of undergraduates worked on campus. Average per-year earnings: $3,425. **Clubs and organizations:** Number of student organizations: 81. Activities include: choral groups, dance, drama/theater, literary magazine, music ensembles, musical theater, pep band, radio station, student government, student newspaper, yearbook. Number of fraternities: 1; sororities: 1. Proportion of men in fraternities: 1%; of women in sororities: 1%. Average proportion of students who stay on campus on weekends: 35%. **Sports program (2005-2006):** Member of NCAA I. **Men's intercollegiate varsity sports:** baseball, basketball, cross-country, golf, riflery, soccer, tennis, track and field (outdoor). **Women's intercollegiate varsity sports:** basketball, cross-country, golf, riflery, soccer, tennis, track and field (outdoor), volleyball.

SERVICES AND FACILITIES

Basic services: nonremedial tutoring, placement service, health service, health insurance. **Counseling services:** minority student, career, personal, academic, psychological, religious, other. **For learning-disabled students:** School does not offer a structured program with separate admission and additional fees. Total undergraduates in learning-disabled program or receiving services: 215. Services include: reading machines, tape recorders, other special classes, videotaped classes, diagnostic testing service, untimed tests, note-taking services, learning center, readers, extended time for tests, tutors, other. **Library:** Number of titles: 1,026,387; number of current serial subscriptions: 4,500. **Information technology resources:** Students are not required to lease or own a computer. Number of campus computers available to all students: 250. School has a wireless network. Proportion of college-owned housing units wired for high-speed internet access: 100%. **Campus safety:** Security services offered: 24-hour foot-and-vehicle patrols, late-night transport/escort service, 24-hour emergency telephones, lighted pathways/sidewalks, controlled dormitory access (key, security card, etc).

TRANSFER AND INTERNATIONAL STUDENTS

Transfer students: May apply for admission for the following academic terms: Fall, Spring. Applicants need a minimum number of credits to apply. **International students:** Number of foreign undergraduates: 286 (7% of student body). Minimum TOEFL score required: 550 (paper); 213 (computer). Average TOEFL score: 545 (paper).

University of Southern California

- **Address:** University Park, Los Angeles, CA 90089
- **Website:** http://www.usc.edu/
- **Private**
- **Enrollment:** 16,072 full-time; 825 part-time

KEY STATS

✔ **U.S News College Ranking:** 27, National Universities
✔ **SAT Score (25th/75th percentile):** 1270-1440
✔ **Tuition:** 2006-2007: $33,892

Selectivity: Most selective	**Room/board:** $10,144
Acceptance rate: 27%	**Average debt:** $19,131
Student/faculty ratio: 10/1	**Proportion who borrowed:** 48%

UNDERGRADUATE STUDENT BODY STATS

2005-2006 enrollment: 16,072 full-time; 825 part-time. Men: 49%; women: 51%. **Ethnic makeup:** African American: 6%; American-Indian: 1%; Asian American: 21%; Hispanic: 13%; White: 50%; International: 8%.

ADMISSIONS FACTS AND FIGURES

Phone: (213) 740-1111. **Email:** admitusc@usc.edu. **Website:** http://www.usc.edu/. **Application deadlines for fall 2007:** Regular decision: January 10; decision sent by April 1. Early decision: Not offered. Early action: Not offered. Admission cannot be deferred. **Application fee:** $65. Common application is not accepted. **To apply online, go to:** http://www.usc.edu/admission/undergraduate/apply/. **Admissions requirements/recommendations:** High school units required (recommended): English: 4 (4); Mathematics: 3 (4); Science: 2 (3); Foreign language: 2 (3); Social studies: 2 (3); History: 0 (0); Academic electives: 3 (3); Total units: 16 (20). Tests: The college uses SAT or ACT scores in admissions decisions. Either SAT or ACT required. For admission to the fall 2007 entering class, the school will accept: ACT with writing. Campus visit: Recommended. Admissions interview: Neither required nor recommended. Off-campus interview: May be arranged. **Factors that count in admissions decisions:** *Academic:* Secondary school record: Very important. Class rank: Considered. Letters of recommendation: Very important. Standardized test scores: Very important. Essay: Very important. *Nonacademic:* Interview: Considered. Extracurricular activities: Important. Talent/ability: Important. Character/personal qualities: Considered. Alumni/ae relationship: Considered. Geographical residence: Not considered. State residency: Not considered. Religious affiliation/commitment: Not considered. Minority status: Considered. Volunteer work: Considered. Work experience: Considered. **Other schools with the greatest overlap in applicants:** New York University; Stanford University; University of California–Berkeley; University of California–Los Angeles; University of California–San Diego. **Admissions statistics for the fall 2005 entering class:** Total applicants: 31,634. Total accepted: 8,418. Freshmen enrolled: 2,741; 45% were from out of state. Overall acceptance rate: 27%. **Credentials of fall 2005 freshmen:** 85% ranked in the top 10 percent of their high school class; 95% were in the top 25 percent, and 100% were in the top half. (Proportion submitting class standing: 50%.) **Average high school grade point average:** 3.7. **First-year students who submitted SAT scores:** 86%. Scores (25/75 percentile): Verbal: 620-710, Math: 650-730, Combined: 1270-1440. **First-year students submitting ACT scores:** 28%. Scores (25/75 percentile): English: 27-33, Math: 27-33, Composite: 28-32.

ACADEMICS

Year founded: 1880. **Academic calendar:** Semester. **Degrees offered:** bachelor's, post-bachelor's certificate, master's, post-master's certificate, first professional, first professional certificate, doctorate. **Most popular majors:** 25% business, management, marketing, and related support services, 15% social sciences, 15% visual and performing arts, 9% communication, journalism, and related programs, 7% engineering. **Major fields of study:** architecture and related services; area, ethnic, cultural, and gender studies; biological

and biomedical sciences; business, management, marketing, and related support services; communication, journalism, and related programs; computer and information sciences and support services; education; engineering; English language and literature/letters; foreign languages, literatures, and linguistics; health professions and related clinical sciences; history; liberal arts and sciences studies, and humanities; mathematics and statistics; multi/interdisciplinary studies; natural resources and conservation; parks, recreation, leisure, and fitness studies; philosophy and religious studies; physical sciences; psychology; public administration and social service professions; social sciences; visual and performing arts. **Areas of required coursework:** humanities, English (including composition), foreign languages, sciences (biological or physical), history, social science, other. **Preprofessional programs:** pre-law, pre-dentistry, pre-medicine, pre-pharmacy, other. **Special academic programs (% participation):** cooperative (work-study plan) program, cross-registration, distance learning, double major, English as a Second Language (ESL), exchange student program (domestic), honors program, independent study (59%), internships (57%), liberal arts/career combination, student-designed major, study abroad, teacher certificate program, other. **Teacher certification offered in:** elementary, middle/junior high, secondary, bilingual/bicultural. **Cooperative education programs:** engineering. **Reserve Officers Training Corps (ROTC):** Army ROTC: Offered on campus; Navy ROTC: Offered on campus; Air Force ROTC: Offered on campus. **Faculty and instruction (2005-2006):** Total instructional faculty: 1,495 full-time, 984 part-time (67% men; 33% women; 22% minorities). Full-time faculty with Ph.D. or other terminal degree: 89%. Student/faculty ratio: 10/1. Classes of fewer than 20 students: 63%; of 20 to 49 students: 27%; of 50 or more students: 10%. **Advanced Placement and International Baccalaureate credit:** AP tests may be used for: Credit and/or placement. Scores accepted: 3, 4, 5. International Baccalaureate exams may be used for: Credit and/or placement. **Freshmen returning for sophomore year:** 95%. **Graduation rates:** Four-year: 61%; five-year: 79%; six-year: 83%. **Graduate study:** 24% of students pursue further study immediately upon graduation.

COSTS AND FINANCIAL AID

Financial aid office: (213) 740-1111. **Expenses (2006-2007):** Tuition and fees 2006-2007: $33,892; room/board: $10,144. Estimated books and supplies: $750; transportation: $580; personal expenses: $1,634. **Financial aid:** Priority filing date for institution's financial aid form: January 20. In 2005-2006, 55% of undergraduates applied for financial aid. Of those, 43% were determined to have financial need; 96% had their need fully met. Average financial aid package (proportion receiving): $29,365 (43%). Average amount of gift aid, such as scholarships or grants (proportion receiving): $21,773 (42%). Average amount of self-help aid, such as work study or loans (proportion receiving): $8,423 (43%). Average need-based loan (excluding PLUS or other private loans): $6,538. Among students who received need-based aid, the average percentage of need met: 100%. Among students who received aid based on merit, the average award (and the proportion receiving): $12,552 (19%). The average athletic scholarship (and the proportion receiving): $32,341 (2%). Average amount of debt of borrowers graduating in 2005: $19,131. Proportion who borrowed: 48%.

CAMPUS LIFE AND EXTRACURRICULAR ACTIVITIES

Campus housing available (% using): coed dorms (42%), fraternity housing (4%), apartments for married students (1%), apartment for single students (52%), special housing for disabled students (1%). Students who live in college-owned, operated, or affiliated housing: 35%. **Clubs and organizations:** Number of student organizations: 600. Activities include: choral groups, concert band, dance, drama/theater, jazz band, literary magazine, marching band, music ensembles, musical theater, opera, pep band, radio station, student government, student newspaper, student film society, symphony orchestra, television station, yearbook. Number of fraternities: 29; sororities: 24. Proportion of men in fraternities: 17%; of women in sororities: 21%. Average proportion of students who stay on campus on weekends: 75%. **Sports program (2005-2006):** Member of NCAA I. *Men's intercollegiate varsity sports:* baseball, basketball, football, golf, swimming and diving, tennis, track and field (outdoor), volleyball, water polo. *Women's intercollegiate varsity sports:* basketball, crew, cross-country, golf, soccer, swimming and diving, tennis, track and field (outdoor), volleyball, water polo.

SERVICES AND FACILITIES

Basic services: nonremedial tutoring, women's center, placement service, day care, health service, health insurance. **Counseling services:** minority student, career, personal, veteran student, academic, psychological, birth control, religious. **For learning-disabled students:** School does not offer a structured program with separate admission and additional fees. Total undergraduates in learning-disabled program or receiving services: 512.

Services include: reading machines, tape recorders, videotaped classes, note-taking services, oral tests, learning center, readers, extended time for tests, tutors, texts on tape, typist/scribe, other testing accomodations, other. **Library:** Number of titles: 3,921,704; number of current serial subscriptions: 37,809. **Information technology resources:** Students are not required to lease or own a computer. Number of campus computers available to all students: 2,500. School has a wireless network. Approximate number of users that can be accommodated: 8,655. Proportion of college-owned housing units wired for high-speed internet access: 100%. **Campus safety:** Security services offered: 24-hour foot-and-vehicle patrols, late-night transport/escort service, 24-hour emergency telephones, lighted pathways/sidewalks, student patrols, controlled dormitory access (key, security card, etc).

TRANSFER AND INTERNATIONAL STUDENTS

Transfer students: May apply for admission for the following academic terms: Fall, Spring. Applicants do not need a minimum number of credits to apply. For fall 2005: Transfer applications received: 8,131. Transfer applicants offered admission: 2,245. Transfer applicants enrolled: 1,423. **International students:** Number of foreign undergraduates: 1393 (8% of student body). Number of countries represented: 89.

University of the Pacific

- **Address:** 3601 Pacific Avenue, Stockton, CA 95211
- **Website:** http://www.pacific.edu
- **Private**
- **Enrollment:** 3,357 full-time; 100 part-time

KEY STATS

✔ **U.S News College Ranking:** 98, National Universities
✔ **SAT Score (25th/75th percentile):** 1080-1300
✔ **Tuition:** 2006-2007: $27,350

Selectivity: More selective	**Room/board:** $8,700
Acceptance rate: 56%	**Average debt:** N/A
Student/faculty ratio: 14/1	**Proportion who borrowed:** N/A

UNDERGRADUATE STUDENT BODY STATS

2005-2006 enrollment: 3,357 full-time; 100 part-time. Men: 44%; women: 56%. **Ethnic makeup:** African American: 3%; American-Indian: 1%; Asian American: 29%; Hispanic: 10%; White: 54%; International: 2%.

ADMISSIONS FACTS AND FIGURES

Phone: (800) 959-2867. **Email:** admissions@pacific.edu. **Website:** http://www.pacific.edu. **Application deadlines for fall 2007:** Regular decision: Rolling. Early decision: Not offered. Early action: Send application by: November 15; Decision sent by: January 15. Admission can be deferred. **Application fee:** $60. Common application is accepted. **Admissions requirements/recommendations:** High school units required (recommended): English: 4 (4); Mathematics: 3 (3); Science: 2 (2); Foreign language: 2 (2); Social studies: 0; History: 1 (1); Academic electives: 3 (3); Total units: 16. Tests: The college uses SAT or ACT scores in admissions decisions. Either SAT or ACT required. For admission to the fall 2007 entering class, the school will accept: ACT with writing, ACT without writing. Campus visit: Neither required nor recommended. Admissions interview: Neither required nor recommended. Off-campus interview: May be arranged. **Factors that count in admissions decisions:** *Academic:* Secondary school record: Very important. Class rank: Considered. Letters of recommendation: Important. Standardized test scores: Important. Essay: Important. *Nonacademic:* Interview: Not considered. Extracurricular activities: Important. Talent/ability: Considered. Character/personal qualities: Considered. Alumni/ae relationship: Considered. Geographical residence: Considered. State residency: Not considered. Religious affiliation/commitment: Not considered. Minority status: Considered. Volunteer work: Considered. Work experience: Considered. **Other schools with the greatest overlap in applicants:** Pepperdine University; Santa Clara University; University of California–Davis. **Admissions statistics for the fall 2005 entering class:** Total applicants: 5,869. Total accepted: 3,304. Freshmen enrolled: 800; 20% were from out of state. Accepted through early-decision or early-action plans: 10%. Overall acceptance rate: 56%. Non-early acceptance rate: 56%. **Size of waiting list:** 130 applicants; enrolled from waiting list: 60. **Credentials of fall 2005 freshmen:** 43% ranked in the top 10 percent of their high school class; 73% were in the top 25 percent, and 92% were in the top

half. (Proportion submitting class standing: 55%.) **Average high school grade point average:** 3.5. **First-year students who submitted SAT scores:** 95%. Scores (25/75 percentile): Verbal: 530-630, Math: 550-670, Combined: 1080-1300. **First-year students submitting ACT scores:** 38%. Scores (25/75 percentile): English: N/A, Math: N/A, Composite: 23-28.

ACADEMICS

Year founded: 1851. **Academic calendar:** Semester. **Degrees offered:** bachelor's, master's, first professional, first professional certificate, doctorate. **Most popular majors:** 20% business administration and management, 13% biology/biological sciences, 13% engineering, 6% education, 6% psychology. **Major fields of study:** biological and biomedical sciences; business, management, marketing, and related support services; communication, journalism, and related programs; computer and information sciences and support services; education; engineering; engineering technologies/technicians; English language and literature/letters; foreign languages, literatures, and linguistics; health professions and related clinical sciences; history; liberal arts and sciences studies, and humanities; mathematics and statistics; multi/inter-disciplinary studies; natural resources and conservation; parks, recreation, leisure, and fitness studies; philosophy and religious studies; physical sciences; psychology; social sciences; visual and performing arts. **Areas of required coursework:** arts/fine arts, humanities, computer literacy, mathematics, English (including composition), philosophy, foreign languages, sciences (biological or physical), history, social science, other. **Pre-professional programs:** pre-dentistry, pre-pharmacy. **Special academic programs (% participation):** accelerated program (7%), cooperative (work-study plan) program (33%), double major (3%), dual enrollment, English as a Second Language (ESL) (3%), exchange student program (domestic), honors program (15%), independent study (39%), internships (49%), liberal arts/career combination (8%), student-designed major (1%), study abroad (11%), teacher certificate program. **Teacher certification offered in:** special education, elementary, middle/junior high, secondary. **Cooperative education programs:** business, education, engineering, health professions. **Faculty and instruction (2005-2006):** Total instructional faculty: 392 full-time, 260 part-time (61% men; 39% women; 19% minorities). Full-time faculty with Ph.D. or other terminal degree: 92%. Student/faculty ratio: 14/1. Classes of fewer than 20 students: 61%; of 20 to 49 students: 34%; of 50 or more students: 5%. **Advanced Placement and International Baccalaureate credit:** AP tests may be used for: Credit only. Scores accepted: 3, 4, 5. International Baccalaureate exams may be used for: Credit only. **Freshmen returning for sophomore year:** 85%. **Graduation rates:** Four-year: 43%; five-year: 59%; six-year: 65%. **Graduate study:** 21% of students pursue further study immediately upon graduation.

COSTS AND FINANCIAL AID

Financial aid office: (209) 946-2421. **Expenses (2006-2007):** Tuition and fees 2006-2007: $27,350; room/board: $8,700. Estimated books and supplies: $1,314; transportation: $714; personal expenses: $2,088. **Financial aid:** Priority filing date for institution's financial aid form: February 15. In 2005-2006, 76% of undergraduates applied for financial aid. Of those, 67% were determined to have financial need; 25% had their need fully met. Average financial aid package (proportion receiving): $23,050 (67%). Average amount of gift aid, such as scholarships or grants (proportion receiving): $17,486 (64%). Average amount of self-help aid, such as work study or loans (proportion receiving): $6,516 (62%). Average need-based loan (excluding PLUS or other private loans): $5,628. Among students who received aid based on merit, the average award (and the proportion receiving): $8,140 (13%). The average athletic scholarship (and the proportion receiving): $21,345 (3%).

CAMPUS LIFE AND EXTRACURRICULAR ACTIVITIES

Campus housing available (% using): coed dorms (59%), sorority housing (4%), fraternity housing (4%), apartments for married students (1%), apartment for single students (31%), special housing for disabled students (1%). Students who live in college-owned, operated, or affiliated housing: 58%. **Student employment:** During the 2005-2006 academic year, 21% of undergraduates worked on campus. Average per-year earnings: $1,242. **Clubs and organizations:** Number of student organizations: 100. Activities include: choral groups, concert band, dance, drama/theater, jazz band, literary magazine, music ensembles, musical theater, opera, pep band, radio station, student government, student newspaper, student film society, symphony orchestra, yearbook. Number of fraternities: 8; sororities: 7. Proportion of men in fraternities: 19%; of women in sororities: 18%. Average proportion of students who stay on campus on weekends: 75%. **Sports program (2005-2006):** Member of NCAA I. *Men's intercollegiate varsity sports:* baseball, basketball, golf, swimming and diving, tennis, volleyball, water polo.

Women's intercollegiate varsity sports: basketball, cross-country, field hockey, soccer, softball, swimming and diving, tennis, volleyball, water polo.

SERVICES AND FACILITIES

Basic services: nonremedial tutoring, placement service, health service, health insurance. **Remedial assistance:** reading, math, writing. **Counseling services:** career, personal, veteran student, academic, psychological. **For learning-disabled students:** School does not offer a structured program with separate admission and additional fees. Total undergraduates in learning-disabled program or receiving services: 180. Services include: remedial math, remedial English, reading machines, remedial reading, learning center, extended time for tests, tutors. **Library:** Number of titles: 364,030; number of current serial subscriptions: 1,285. **Information technology resources:** Students are not required to lease or own a computer. Number of campus computers available to all students: 750. School has a wireless network. Approximate number of users that can be accommodated: 2,000. Proportion of college-owned housing units wired for high-speed internet access: 100%. **Campus safety:** Security services offered: 24-hour foot-and-vehicle patrols, late-night transport/escort service, 24-hour emergency telephones, lighted pathways/sidewalks, student patrols, controlled dormitory access (key, security card, etc).

TRANSFER AND INTERNATIONAL STUDENTS

Transfer students: May apply for admission for the following academic terms: Fall, Spring, Summer. Applicants need a minimum number of credits to apply. For fall 2005: Transfer applications received: 774. Transfer applicants offered admission: 410. Transfer applicants enrolled: 229. **International students:** Number of foreign undergraduates: 78 (2% of student body). Number of countries represented: 55. Minimum TOEFL score required: 475 (paper); 150 (computer). Average TOEFL score: 530 (paper).

Vanguard University of Southern California

- **Address:** 55 Fair Drive, Costa Mesa, CA 92626
- **Website:** http://www.vanguard.edu
- **Private; Religious affiliation:** Assemblies of God
- **Enrollment:** 1,496 full-time; 407 part-time

KEY STATS

✔ **U.S News College Ranking:** 7, Comp. Coll.–Bachelor's (West)
✔ **SAT Score (25th/75th percentile):** 880-1130
✔ **Tuition:** 2006-2007: $21,564

Selectivity: Selective	**Room/board:** $7,058
Acceptance rate: 86%	**Average debt:** $16,979
Student/faculty ratio: 14/1	**Proportion who borrowed:** 76%

UNDERGRADUATE STUDENT BODY STATS

2005-2006 enrollment: 1,496 full-time; 407 part-time. Men: 34%; women: 66%. **Ethnic makeup:** African American: 4%; American-Indian: 1%; Asian American: 4%; Hispanic: 17%; White: 74%; International: 1%. **Religious preference:** Roman Catholic: 2%; Protestant: 57%; No preference: 3%; Assemblies of God: 27%.

ADMISSIONS FACTS AND FIGURES

Phone: (800) 722-6279. **Email:** admissions@vanguard.edu. **Website:** http://www.vanguard.edu. **Application deadlines for fall 2007:** Regular decision: Rolling; decision sent by January 15. Early decision: Not offered. Early action: Send application by: December 1; Decision sent by: January 15. Admission can be deferred. **Application fee:** $45. Common application is not accepted. **To apply online, go to:** http://www.vanguard.edu/admissions/index.cfm?doc_id=1409. **Admissions requirements/recommendations:** High school units required (recommended): English: (4); Mathematics: (2); Science: (2); Social studies: (3). Tests: The college uses SAT or ACT scores in admissions decisions. Either SAT or ACT required. For admission to the fall 2007 entering class, the school will accept: ACT without writing. Campus visit: Recommended. Admissions interview: Recommended. Off-campus interview: Not available. **Factors that count in admissions decisions:** *Academic:* Secondary school record: Very important. Class rank: Not considered. Letters of recommendation: Very important. Standardized test scores: Important. Essay: Very important. *Nonacademic:* Interview: Considered. Extracurricular activities: Considered. Talent/ability: Considered. Character/personal qualities: Very important. Alumni/ae relationship: Not considered. Geographical residence: Not considered. State residency: Not considered. Religious affiliation/commitment: Very important. Minority status: Not considered. Volunteer work: Considered. Work experience: Considered. **Other schools with the greatest overlap in applicants:** Azusa Pacific University; Biola University; Point Loma Nazarene University. **Admissions statistics for the fall 2005 entering class:** Total applicants: 903. Total accepted: 775. Freshmen enrolled: 403; 20% were from out of state. Accepted through early-decision or early-action plans: 74%. Overall acceptance rate: 86%. Non-early acceptance rate: 92%. **Credentials of fall 2005 freshmen:** 24% ranked in the top 10 percent of their high school class; 47% were in the top 25 percent, and 79% were in the top half. (Proportion submitting class standing: 60%.) **Average high school grade point average:** 3.4. **First-year students who submitted SAT scores:** 84%. Scores (25/75 percentile): Verbal: 450-570, Math: 430-560, Combined: 880-1130. **First-year students submitting ACT scores:** 25%. Scores (25/75 percentile): English: 18-24, Math: 17-24, Composite: 19-24.

ACADEMICS

Year founded: 1920. **Academic calendar:** Semester. **Degrees offered:** certificate, bachelor's, master's. **Most popular majors:** 30% business, management, marketing, and related support services, 16% psychology, 11% education, 10% theology and religious vocations, 8% social sciences. **Major fields of study:** business, management, marketing, and related support services; education; English language and literature/letters; foreign languages, literatures, and linguistics; history; legal professions and studies; liberal arts and sciences studies, and humanities; multi/interdisciplinary studies; parks, recreation, leisure, and fitness studies; philosophy and religious studies; physical sciences; psychology; social sciences; theology and religious vocations; visual and performing arts. **Areas of required coursework:** arts/fine arts, humanities, computer literacy, mathematics, English (including composition), sciences (biological or physical), history, social science, other. **Pre-professional programs:** pre-law, pre-dentistry, pre-medicine, pre-theology, pre-veterinary science, pre-optometry, pre-pharmacy. **Special academic programs (% participation):** accelerated program (35%), cooperative (work-study plan) program, cross-registration, double major, dual enrollment, external degree program, independent study, internships, study abroad, teacher certificate program, weekend college. **Teacher certification offered in:** early childhood, elementary, middle/junior high, secondary. **Reserve Officers Training Corps (ROTC):** Air Force ROTC: Offered at cooperating institution (Loyola Marymount). **Faculty and instruction (2005-2006):** Total instructional faculty: 66 full-time, 131 part-time (59% men; 41% women; 14% minorities). Full-time faculty with Ph.D. or other terminal degree: 76%. Student/faculty ratio: 14/1. Classes of fewer than 20 students: 62%; of 20 to 49 students: 32%; of 50 or more students: 6%. **Advanced Placement and International Baccalaureate credit:** AP tests may be used for: Credit and/or placement. Scores accepted: 3. International Baccalaureate exams may be used for: Credit and/or placement. **Freshmen returning for sophomore year:** 74%. **Graduation rates:** Four-year: 32%; five-year: 43%; six-year: 54%.

COSTS AND FINANCIAL AID

Financial aid office: (714) 556-3610. **Expenses (2006-2007):** Tuition and fees 2006-2007: $21,564; room/board: $7,058. Estimated books and supplies: $1,242; transportation: $738; personal expenses: $1,980. **Financial aid:** Priority filing date for institution's financial aid form: March 2; deadline: March 2. In 2005-2006, 99% of undergraduates applied for financial aid. Of those, 87% were determined to have financial need; 15% had their need fully met. Average financial aid package (proportion receiving): $13,406 (87%). Average amount of gift aid, such as scholarships or grants (proportion receiving): $7,892 (58%). Average amount of self-help aid, such as work study or loans (proportion receiving): $3,419 (79%). Average need-based loan (excluding PLUS or other private loans): $3,190. Among students who received need-based aid, the average percentage of need met: 68%. Among students who received aid based on merit, the average award (and the proportion receiving): $5,028 (12%). The average athletic scholarship (and the proportion receiving): $5,453 (2%). Average amount of debt of borrowers graduating in 2005: $16,979. Proportion who borrowed: 76%.

CAMPUS LIFE AND EXTRACURRICULAR ACTIVITIES

Campus housing available (% using): coed dorms (10%), women's dorms (50%), men's dorms (30%), apartments for married students (2%), apartment for single students (8%), special housing for disabled students (0%). Students who live in college-owned, operated, or affiliated housing: 73%. **Student employment:** During the 2005-2006 academic year, 16% of undergraduates worked on campus. Average per-year earnings: $1,522. Activities include: choral groups, concert band, dance, drama/theater, jazz band, music ensembles, musical theater, student government, student newspaper, yearbook. Number of fraternities: 0; sororities: 0. Average proportion of students who stay on campus on weekends: 65%. **Sports program (2005-2006):** Member of NAIA. **_Men's intercollegiate varsity sports:_** baseball, basketball, cross-country, soccer, tennis, track and field (indoor), track and field (outdoor). **_Women's intercollegiate varsity sports:_** basketball, cross-country, soccer, softball, tennis, track and field (indoor), track and field (outdoor), volleyball.

SERVICES AND FACILITIES
Basic services: placement service, other. **Remedial assistance:** other. **Counseling services:** career, personal, academic, psychological, religious. **For learning-disabled students:** School does not offer a structured program with separate admission and additional fees. Total undergraduates in learning-disabled program or receiving services: 31. Services include: untimed tests, note-taking services, oral tests, extended time for tests, tutors, other. **Library:** Number of titles: 139,889; number of current serial subscriptions: 10,482. **Information technology resources:** Students are not required to lease or own a computer. Number of campus computers available to all students: 145. School has a wireless network. Approximate number of users that can be accommodated: 600. Proportion of college-owned housing units wired for high-speed internet access: 100%. **Campus safety:** Security services offered: 24-hour foot-and-vehicle patrols, late-night transport/escort service, 24-hour emergency telephones, lighted pathways/sidewalks, controlled dormitory access (key, security card, etc).

TRANSFER AND INTERNATIONAL STUDENTS
Transfer students: May apply for admission for the following academic terms: Fall, Spring. Applicants need a minimum number of credits to apply. For fall 2005: Transfer applications received: 304. Transfer applicants offered admission: 215. Transfer applicants enrolled: 131. **International students:** Number of foreign undergraduates: 16 (1% of student body). Number of countries represented: 16. Minimum TOEFL score required: 550 (paper); 213 (computer).

Westmont College

- **Address:** 955 La Paz Road, Santa Barbara, CA 93108
- **Website:** http://www.westmont.edu
- **Private; Religious affiliation:** Christian nondenominational
- **Enrollment:** 1,360 full-time; 13 part-time

KEY STATS
✔ **U.S News College Ranking:** 104, Liberal Arts Colleges
✔ **SAT Score (25th/75th percentile):** 1130-1330
✔ **Tuition:** 2006-2007: $29,470

Selectivity: More selective	**Room/board:** $9,232
Acceptance rate: 68%	**Average debt:** $16,999
Student/faculty ratio: 13/1	**Proportion who borrowed:** 74%

UNDERGRADUATE STUDENT BODY STATS
2005-2006 enrollment: 1,360 full-time; 13 part-time. Men: 38%; women: 62%. **Ethnic makeup:** African American: 2%; American-Indian: 2%; Asian American: 8%; Hispanic: 10%; White: 78%. **Religious preference:** Roman Catholic: 3%; Protestant: 90%; Unknown: 7%.

ADMISSIONS FACTS AND FIGURES
Phone: (800) 777-9011. **Email:** admissions@westmont.edu. **Website:** http://www.westmont.edu. **Application deadlines for fall 2007:** Regular decision: February 15; decision sent by April 1. Early decision: Not offered. Early action: Send application by: November 1; Decision sent by: December 20. Admission cannot be deferred. **Application fee:** $50. Common application is accepted. **Admissions requirements/recommendations:** High school units required (recommended): English: 4; Mathematics: 3; Science: 3; Foreign language: 2 (3); Social studies: 1; History: 1; Total units: 16. Tests: The college uses SAT or ACT scores in admissions decisions. Either SAT or ACT required. For admission to the fall 2007 entering class, the school will accept: ACT with writing. Campus visit: Recommended. Admissions interview: Recommended. Off-campus interview: May be arranged. **Factors that count in admissions decisions:** *Academic:* Secondary school record: Very important. Class rank: Considered. Letters of recommendation: Important. Standardized test scores: Very important. Essay: Important. *Nonacademic:* Interview: Important. Extracurricular activities: Important. Talent/ability:

Considered. Character/personal qualities: Very important. Alumni/ae relationship: Considered. Geographical residence: Considered. State residency: Not considered. Religious affiliation/commitment: Very important. Minority status: Considered. Volunteer work: Considered. Work experience: Considered. **Other schools with the greatest overlap in applicants:** Azusa Pacific University; Biola University; Pepperdine University; Point Loma Nazarene University; University of California–Santa Barbara. **Admissions statistics for the fall 2005 entering class:** Total applicants: 1,813. Total accepted: 1,231. Freshmen enrolled: 333; 37% were from out of state. Accepted through early-decision or early-action plans: 66%. Overall acceptance rate: 68%. Non-early acceptance rate: 55%. **Size of waiting list:** 249 applicants; enrolled from waiting list: 69. **Credentials of fall 2005 freshmen:** 44% ranked in the top 10 percent of their high school class; 75% were in the top 25 percent, and 96% were in the top half. (Proportion submitting class standing: 62%.) **Average high school grade point average:** 3.7. **First-year students who submitted SAT scores:** 93%. Scores (25/75 percentile): Verbal: 570-670, Math: 560-660, Combined: 1130-1330. **First-year students submitting ACT scores:** 36%. Scores (25/75 percentile): English: 24-31, Math: 24-29, Composite: 24-29.

ACADEMICS
Year founded: 1937. **Academic calendar:** Semester. **Degrees offered:** bachelor's, post-bachelor's certificate. **Most popular majors:** 15% English language and literature, 13% communication studies/speech communication and rhetoric, 11% biology/biological sciences, 8% economics, 6% liberal arts and sciences/liberal studies. **Major fields of study:** area, ethnic, cultural, and gender studies; biological and biomedical sciences; communication, journalism, and related programs; computer and information sciences and support services; engineering; English language and literature/letters; foreign languages, literatures, and linguistics; history; liberal arts and sciences studies, and humanities; mathematics and statistics; multi/interdisciplinary studies; parks, recreation, leisure, and fitness studies; philosophy and religious studies; physical sciences; psychology; social sciences; visual and performing arts. **Areas of required coursework:** arts/fine arts, humanities, mathematics, English (including composition), philosophy, foreign languages, sciences (biological or physical), history, social science, other. **Pre-professional programs:** pre-law, pre-dentistry, pre-medicine, pre-theology, pre-veterinary science. **Special academic programs (% participation):** accelerated program (5%), cooperative (work-study plan) program (15%), cross-registration (1%), double major (10%), exchange student program (domestic) (35%), honors program (30%), independent study (60%), internships (65%), liberal arts/career combination (1%), student-designed major (1%), study abroad (50%), teacher certificate program (5%). **Teacher certification offered in:** elementary, secondary, bilingual/bicultural. **Reserve Officers Training Corps (ROTC):** Army ROTC: Offered at cooperating institution (U.C. Santa Barbara); Air Force ROTC: Offered at cooperating institution (Loyola Marymount University). **Faculty and instruction (2005-2006):** Total instructional faculty: 91 full-time, 51 part-time (58% men; 42% women; 14% minorities). Full-time faculty with Ph.D. or other terminal degree: 86%. Student/faculty ratio: 13/1. Classes of fewer than 20 students: 60%; of 20 to 49 students: 37%; of 50 or more students: 2%. **Advanced Placement and International Baccalaureate credit:** AP tests may be used for: Credit and/or placement. Scores accepted: 4, 5. International Baccalaureate exams may be used for: Credit and/or placement. **Freshmen returning for sophomore year:** 86%. **Graduation rates:** Four-year: 65%; five-year: 70%; six-year: 72%. **Graduate study:** 30% of students pursue further study immediately upon graduation; 60% within five years. Fields in which graduates pursue further study: Master of Business Administration (MBA), 10%; law, 3%; medicine, 5%; dentistry, 1%; engineering, 2%; theology (or the seminary), 10%; education, 25%; arts and sciences, 40%; veterinary medicine, 1%.

COSTS AND FINANCIAL AID
Financial aid office: (805) 565-6063. **Expenses (2006-2007):** Tuition and fees 2006-2007: $29,470; room/board: $9,232. Estimated books and supplies: $1,314; transportation: $774; personal expenses: $2,088. **Financial aid:** Priority filing date for institution's financial aid form: March 1. In 2005-2006, 65% of undergraduates applied for financial aid. Of those, 55% were determined to have financial need; 10% had their need fully met. Average financial aid package (proportion receiving): $18,521 (55%). Average amount of gift aid, such as scholarships or grants (proportion receiving): $13,480 (54%). Average amount of self-help aid, such as work study or loans (proportion receiving): $6,119 (47%). Average need-based loan (excluding PLUS or other private loans): $5,461. Among students who received need-based aid, the average percentage of need met: 67%. Among students who received aid based on merit, the average award (and the proportion receiving): $9,990 (32%). The average athletic scholarship (and the proportion

receiving): $7,042 (4%). Average amount of debt of borrowers graduating in 2005: $16,999. Proportion who borrowed: 74%.

CAMPUS LIFE AND EXTRACURRICULAR ACTIVITIES

Campus housing available (% using): coed dorms (93%), apartments for married students (1%), apartment for single students (5%), special housing for disabled students (1%). Students who live in college-owned, operated, or affiliated housing: 85%. **Student employment:** During the 2005-2006 academic year, 35% of undergraduates worked on campus. Average per-year earnings: $1,500. **Clubs and organizations:** Number of student organizations: 0. Activities include: choral groups, concert band, dance, drama/theater, jazz band, literary magazine, music ensembles, musical theater, pep band, radio station, student government, student newspaper, symphony orchestra, yearbook. Number of fraternities: 0; sororities: 0. Average proportion of students who stay on campus on weekends: 50%. **Sports program (2005-2006):** Member of NAIA. *Men's intercollegiate varsity sports:* baseball, basketball, cross-country, soccer, tennis, track and field (indoor), track and field (outdoor). *Women's intercollegiate varsity sports:* basketball, cross-country, soccer, tennis, track and field (indoor), track and field (outdoor), volleyball.

SERVICES AND FACILITIES

Basic services: nonremedial tutoring, placement service, health service, health insurance. **Remedial assistance:** math, writing, study skills. **Counseling services:** minority student, career, personal, academic, psychological, birth control, religious. **For learning-disabled students:** School does not offer a structured program with separate admission and additional fees. Total undergraduates in learning-disabled program or receiving services: 33. Services include: tape recorders, untimed tests, note-taking services, oral tests, readers, extended time for tests, tutors, priority registration, texts on tape, other testing accomodations, other. **Library:** Number of titles: 150,385; number of current serial subscriptions: 465. **Information technology resources:** Students are not required to lease or own a computer. Number of campus computers available to all students: 90. School has a wireless network. Approximate number of users that can be accommodated: 477. Proportion of college-owned housing units wired for high-speed internet access: 100%. **Campus safety:** Security services offered: 24-hour foot-and-vehicle patrols, late-night transport/escort service, 24-hour emergency telephones, lighted pathways/sidewalks, controlled dormitory access (key, security card, etc).

TRANSFER AND INTERNATIONAL STUDENTS

Transfer students: May apply for admission for the following academic terms: Fall, Spring. Applicants do not need a minimum number of credits to apply. For fall 2005: Transfer applications received: 239. Transfer applicants offered admission: 139. Transfer applicants enrolled: 90. **International students:** Number of foreign undergraduates: 3. Number of countries represented: 8. Minimum TOEFL score required: 560 (paper); 220 (computer). Average TOEFL score: 600 (paper).

Whittier College

- **Address:** 13406 Philadelphia Street, PO Box 634, Whittier, CA 90608
- **Website:** http://www.whittier.edu
- **Private**
- **Enrollment:** 1,295 full-time; 32 part-time

KEY STATS

✔ **U.S News College Ranking:** third tier, Liberal Arts Colleges
✔ **SAT Score (25th/75th percentile):** 950-1193
✔ **Tuition:** 2006-2007: $28,206

Selectivity: Selective	**Room/board:** $8,542
Acceptance rate: 80%	**Average debt:** $27,335
Student/faculty ratio: 13/1	**Proportion who borrowed:** 78%

UNDERGRADUATE STUDENT BODY STATS

2005-2006 enrollment: 1,295 full-time; 32 part-time. Men: 46%; women: 54%. **Ethnic makeup:** African American: 4%; American-Indian: 2%; Asian American: 8%; Hispanic: 27%; White: 57%; International: 3%. **Religious preference:** Roman Catholic: 27%; Protestant: 28%; Jewish: 3%; Muslim: 1%; Hindu: 2%; Buddhist: 2%; No preference: 32%.

ADMISSIONS FACTS AND FIGURES

Phone: (562) 907-4238. **Email:** admission@whittier.edu. **Website:** http://www.whittier.edu. **Application deadlines for fall 2007:** Regular decision: Rolling. Early decision: Not offered. Early action: Send application by: December 1; Decision sent by: December 30. Admission can be deferred. **Application fee:** $50. Common application is accepted. **To apply online, go to:** http://www.aiccumentor.org/applications/whittier_college/apply.html. **Admissions requirements/recommendations:** High school units required (recommended): English: 3 (4); Mathematics: 2 (4); Science: 1 (3); Foreign language: 2 (3); Social studies: 1 (3); History: 1 (0); Total units: 11 (17). Tests: The college uses SAT or ACT scores in admissions decisions. Either SAT or ACT required. For admission to the fall 2007 entering class, the school will accept: ACT with writing. Campus visit: Recommended. Admissions interview: Recommended. Off-campus interview: May be arranged. **Factors that count in admissions decisions:** *Academic:* Secondary school record: Very important. Class rank: Considered. Letters of recommendation: Important. Standardized test scores: Important. Essay: Very important. *Nonacademic:* Interview: Important. Extracurricular activities: Important. Talent/ability: Important. Character/personal qualities: Important. Alumni/ae relationship: Considered. Geographical residence: Considered. State residency: Considered. Religious affiliation/commitment: Not considered. Minority status: Considered. Volunteer work: Important. Work experience: Considered. **Other schools with the greatest overlap in applicants:** California State University–Fullerton; Chapman University; Loyola Marymount University; Occidental College; University of Redlands. **Admissions statistics for the fall 2005 entering class:** Total applicants: 1,823. Total accepted: 1,458. Freshmen enrolled: 351; 29% were from out of state. Accepted through early-decision or early-action plans: 21%. Overall acceptance rate: 80%. Non-early acceptance rate: 78%. **Credentials of fall 2005 freshmen:** 25% ranked in the top 10 percent of their high school class; 52% were in the top 25 percent, and 79% were in the top half. (Proportion submitting class standing: 58%.) **Average high school grade point average:** 3.4. **First-year students who submitted SAT scores:** 96%. Scores (25/75 percentile): Verbal: 480-593, Math: 470-600, Combined: 950-1193. **First-year students submitting ACT scores:** 26%. Scores (25/75 percentile): English: N/A, Math: N/A, Composite: 19-25.

ACADEMICS

Year founded: 1887. **Academic calendar:** 4-1-4. **Degrees offered:** bachelor's, master's, first professional. **Most popular majors:** 17% social sciences, 16% business, management, marketing, and related support services; 10% English language and literature/letters, 9% biological and biomedical sciences, 9% family and consumer sciences/human sciences. **Major fields of study:** area, ethnic, cultural, and gender studies; biological and biomedical sciences; business, management, marketing, and related support services; education; English language and literature/letters; foreign languages, literatures, and linguistics; history; liberal arts and sciences studies, and humanities; mathematics and statistics; natural resources and conservation; philosophy and religious studies; physical sciences; psychology; public administration and social service professions; social sciences; visual and performing arts. **Areas of required coursework:** arts/fine arts, humanities, mathematics, English (including composition), sciences (biological or physical), history, social science. **Pre-professional programs:** pre-law, pre-dentistry, pre-medicine, pre-veterinary science, pre-pharmacy. **Special academic programs (% participation):** double major (7.7%), independent study (20%), internships (30%), liberal arts/career combination (50%), student-designed major (10%), study abroad (20%), teacher certificate program (15%). **Teacher certification offered in:** elementary, middle/junior high, secondary. **Reserve Officers Training Corps (ROTC):** Army ROTC: Offered at cooperating institution (USC, Cal State Fullerton, Loyola Marymount); Navy ROTC: Offered at cooperating institution (USC, Cal State Fullerton, Loyola Marymount); Air Force ROTC: Offered at cooperating institution (USC, Cal State Fullerton, Loyola Marymount). **Faculty and instruction (2005-2006):** Total instructional faculty: 86 full-time, 55 part-time (47% men; 53% women; 26% minorities). Full-time faculty with Ph.D. or other terminal degree: 100%. Student/faculty ratio: 13/1. Classes of fewer than 20 students: 53%; of 20 to 49 students: 44%; of 50 or more students: 2%. **Advanced Placement and International Baccalaureate credit:** AP tests may be used for: Credit and/or placement. Scores accepted: 4, 5. International Baccalaureate exams may be used for: Credit and/or placement. **Freshmen returning for sophomore year:** 77%. **Graduation rates:** Four-year: 49%; five-year: 55%; six-year: 56%. **Graduate study:** 30% of students pursue further study immediately upon graduation; 28% within five years. Fields in which graduates pursue further study: law, 3%; medicine, 8%; dentistry, 1%; education, 11%; arts and sciences, 17%.

COSTS AND FINANCIAL AID

Financial aid office: (562) 907-4285. **Expenses (2006-2007):** Tuition and fees 2006-2007: $28,206; room/board: $8,542. Estimated books and supplies: $800; transportation: $402; personal expenses: $1,700. **Financial aid:** Priority filing date for institution's financial aid form: February 1; deadline: March 2. In 2005-2006, 100% of undergraduates applied for financial aid. Of those, 69% were determined to have financial need; 35% had their need fully met. Average financial aid package (proportion receiving): $23,742 (69%). Average amount of gift aid, such as scholarships or grants (proportion receiving): $11,316 (58%). Average amount of self-help aid, such as work study or loans (proportion receiving): $8,917 (66%). Average need-based loan (excluding PLUS or other private loans): $7,579. Among students who received need-based aid, the average percentage of need met: 71%. Among students who received aid based on merit, the average award (and the proportion receiving): $11,219 (17%). Average amount of debt of borrowers graduating in 2005: $27,335. Proportion who borrowed: 78%.

CAMPUS LIFE AND EXTRACURRICULAR ACTIVITIES

Campus housing available (% using): coed dorms (75%). Students who live in college-owned, operated, or affiliated housing: 59%. **Student employment:** During the 2005-2006 academic year, 55% of undergraduates worked on campus. Average per-year earnings: $1,296. **Clubs and organizations:** Number of student organizations: 68. Activities include: choral groups, dance, drama/theater, jazz band, literary magazine, music ensembles, musical theater, radio station, student government, student newspaper, yearbook. Number of fraternities: 4; sororities: 5. Proportion of men in fraternities: 5%; of women in sororities: 11%. Average proportion of students who stay on campus on weekends: 75%. **Sports program (2005-2006):** Member of NCAA III. *Men's intercollegiate varsity sports:* baseball, basketball, cross-country, football, golf, lacrosse, soccer, swimming and diving, tennis, track and field (outdoor), water polo. *Women's intercollegiate varsity sports:* basketball, cross-country, lacrosse, soccer, softball, swimming and diving, tennis, track and field (outdoor), volleyball, water polo.

SERVICES AND FACILITIES

Basic services: nonremedial tutoring, health service, health insurance. **Counseling services:** minority student, career, personal, academic, psychological, birth control. **For learning-disabled students:** School does not offer a structured program with separate admission and additional fees. Total undergraduates in learning-disabled program or receiving services: 174. Services include: reading machines, tape recorders, note-taking services, oral tests, learning center, readers, extended time for tests, tutors, texts on tape, typist/scribe, other testing accomodations. **Library:** Number of titles: 297,613; number of current serial subscriptions: 3,388. **Information technology resources:** Students are not required to lease or own a computer. Number of campus computers available to all students: 312. School has a wireless network. Approximate number of users that can be accommodated: 1,000. Proportion of college-owned housing units wired for high-speed internet access: 100%. **Campus safety:** Security services offered: 24-hour foot-and-vehicle patrols, late-night transport/escort service, 24-hour emergency telephones, lighted pathways/sidewalks, student patrols, controlled dormitory access (key, security card, etc).

TRANSFER AND INTERNATIONAL STUDENTS

Transfer students: May apply for admission for the following academic terms: Fall, Spring. Applicants need a minimum number of credits to apply. For fall 2005: Transfer applications received: 217. Transfer applicants offered admission: 113. Transfer applicants enrolled: 56. **International students:** Number of foreign undergraduates: 45 (3% of student body). Number of countries represented: 18. Minimum TOEFL score required: 550 (paper); 213 (computer).

Woodbury University

- **Address:** 7500 Glenoaks Boulevard, Burbank, CA 91510
- **Website:** http://www.woodbury.edu
- **Private**
- **Enrollment:** 1,027 full-time; 240 part-time

KEY STATS

- ✔ **U.S News College Ranking:** third tier, Universities–Master's (West)
- ✔ **SAT Score (25th/75th percentile):** 800-1040
- ✔ **Tuition:** 2006-2007: $23,474
- **Selectivity:** Less selective   **Room/board:** $8,198
- **Acceptance rate:** 80%   **Average debt:** $20,134
- **Student/faculty ratio:** 12/1   **Proportion who borrowed:** 91%

UNDERGRADUATE STUDENT BODY STATS

2005-2006 enrollment: 1,027 full-time; 240 part-time. Men: 40%; women: 60%. **Ethnic makeup:** African American: 6%; Asian American: 11%; Hispanic: 34%; White: 43%; International: 6%. **Religious preference:** Roman Catholic: 28%; Protestant: 23%; Buddhist: 2%; No preference: 25%.

ADMISSIONS FACTS AND FIGURES

Phone: (818) 767-0888. **Email:** info@woodbury.edu. **Website:** http://www.woodbury.edu. **Application deadlines for fall 2007:** Regular decision: Rolling. Early decision: Not offered. Early action: Not offered. Admission can be deferred. **Application fee:** $35. Common application is accepted. **Admissions requirements/recommendations:** High school units required (recommended): English: (4); Mathematics: (3); Science: (3); Foreign language: (2); Social studies: (3); History: (2); Academic electives: (0); Total units: (17). Tests: The college uses SAT or ACT scores in admissions decisions. Either SAT or ACT required. For admission to the fall 2007 entering class, the school will accept: ACT with writing, ACT without writing. Campus visit: Recommended. Admissions interview: Recommended. Off-campus interview: May be arranged. **Factors that count in admissions decisions:** *Academic:* Secondary school record: Very important. Class rank: Not considered. Letters of recommendation: Important. Standardized test scores: Very important. Essay: Considered. *Nonacademic:* Interview: Not considered. Extracurricular activities: Considered. Talent/ability: Not considered. Character/personal qualities: Not considered. Alumni/ae relationship: Considered. Geographical residence: Not considered. State residency: Not considered. Religious affiliation/commitment: Not considered. Minority status: Not considered. Volunteer work: Considered. Work experience: Considered. **Other schools with the greatest overlap in applicants:** California State Polytechnic University–Pomona; California State University–Northridge; Pepperdine University; University of California–Los Angeles; University of Southern California. **Admissions statistics for the fall 2005 entering class:** Total applicants: 390. Total accepted: 311. Freshmen enrolled: 133; 20% were from out of state. Overall acceptance rate: 80%. **Size of waiting list:** 20 applicants; enrolled from waiting list: 20. **Credentials of fall 2005 freshmen:** 24% ranked in the top 10 percent of their high school class; 25% were in the top 25 percent, and 80% were in the top half. (Proportion submitting class standing: 50%.) **Average high school grade point average:** 3.1. **First-year students who submitted SAT scores:** 95%. Scores (25/75 percentile): Verbal: 400-520, Math: 400-520, Combined: 800-1040. **First-year students submitting ACT scores:** 5%. Scores (25/75 percentile): English: N/A, Math: N/A, Composite: N/A.

ACADEMICS

Year founded: 1884. **Academic calendar:** Semester. **Degrees offered:** bachelor's, master's. **Most popular majors:** 25% architecture (B.Arch., B.A./B.S., M.Arch., M.A./M.S., Ph.D.), 24% business administration and management, 7% organizational behavior studies, 6% commercial and advertising art, 6% fashion/apparel design. **Major fields of study:** architecture and related services; business, management, marketing, and related support services; communication, journalism, and related programs; computer and information sciences and support services; history; liberal arts and sciences studies, and humanities; psychology; visual and performing arts. **Areas of required coursework:** arts/fine arts, humanities, computer literacy, mathematics, English (including composition), sciences (biological or physical), history, social science. **Special academic programs:** accelerated program, double major, internships, liberal arts/career combination, weekend college. **Faculty and instruction (2005-2006):** Total instructional faculty: 44 full-time, 161 part-time (63% men; 37% women; 19% minorities). Full-time faculty with Ph.D. or other terminal degree: 89%. Student/faculty ratio: 12/1. Classes of fewer than 20 students: 81%; of 20 to 49 students: 19%. **Advanced Placement and International Baccalaureate credit:** AP tests may be used for: Credit and/or placement. Scores accepted: 3, 4, 5. International Baccalaureate exams may be used for: Credit and/or placement. **Freshmen returning for sophomore year:** 81%. **Graduation rates:** Four-year: 23%; five-year: 47%; six-year: 50%. **Graduate study:** 25% of students pursue further study immediately upon graduation; 10% within one year; 25% within five years. Fields in which graduates pursue further study: Master of Business Administration (MBA), 15%; law, 5%; education, 5%.

COSTS AND FINANCIAL AID

Financial aid office: (818) 767-0888. **Expenses (2006-2007):** Tuition and fees 2006-2007: $23,474; room/board: $8,198. Estimated books and supplies: $1,314; transportation: $774; personal expenses: $2,088. **Financial aid:** Priority filing date for institution's financial aid form: March 2. In 2005-2006, 79% of undergraduates applied for financial aid. Of those, 74% were determined to have financial need; 5% had their need fully met. Average financial aid package (proportion receiving): $17,132 (73%). Average amount of gift aid, such as scholarships or grants (proportion receiving): $13,499 (70%). Average amount of self-help aid, such as work study or loans (proportion receiving): $4,652 (66%). Average need-based loan (excluding PLUS or other private loans): $4,521. Among students who received need-based aid, the average percentage of need met: 60%. Among students who received aid based on merit, the average award (and the proportion receiving): $13,031 (12%). The average athletic scholarship (and the proportion receiving): $0 (0%). Average amount of debt of borrowers graduating in 2005: $20,134. Proportion who borrowed: 91%.

CAMPUS LIFE AND EXTRACURRICULAR ACTIVITIES

Campus housing available (% using): coed dorms (94%), apartment for single students (6%), other housing options. Students who live in college-owned, operated, or affiliated housing: 24%. **Student employment:** During the 2005-2006 academic year, 8% of undergraduates worked on campus.

Average per-year earnings: $2,000. **Clubs and organizations:** Number of student organizations: 25. Activities include: literary magazine, student government, student newspaper, student film society. Number of fraternities: 2; sororities: 3. Proportion of men in fraternities: 15%; of women in sororities: 15%. Average proportion of students who stay on campus on weekends: 60%.

SERVICES AND FACILITIES

Basic services: nonremedial tutoring, placement service, health service, health insurance. **Remedial assistance:** math, writing. **Counseling services:** career, academic, psychological. **For learning-disabled students:** School does not offer a structured program with separate admission and additional fees. Total undergraduates in learning-disabled program or receiving services: 10. Services include: remedial math, remedial English, tape recorders, untimed tests, note-taking services, learning center, extended time for tests, tutors, priority registration, texts on tape, other testing accomodations. **Library:** Number of titles: 66,636; number of current serial subscriptions: 292. **Information technology resources:** Students are required to lease or own a computer. Number of campus computers available to all students: 210. School has a wireless network. Approximate number of users that can be accommodated: 200. Proportion of college-owned housing units wired for high-speed internet access: 0%. **Campus safety:** Security services offered: 24-hour foot-and-vehicle patrols, late-night transport/escort service, 24-hour emergency telephones, lighted pathways/sidewalks, controlled dormitory access (key, security card, etc).

TRANSFER AND INTERNATIONAL STUDENTS

Transfer students: May apply for admission for the following academic terms: Fall, Spring, Summer. Applicants do not need a minimum number of credits to apply. For fall 2005: Transfer applications received: 287. Transfer applicants offered admission: 164. Transfer applicants enrolled: 150. **International students:** Number of foreign undergraduates: 76 (6% of student body). Number of countries represented: 35. Minimum TOEFL score required: 500 (paper); 173 (computer). Average TOEFL score: 527 (paper).

Colorado

Adams State College

- **Address:** 208 Edgemont Boulevard, Alamosa, CO 81102
- **Website:** http://www.adams.edu
- **Public**
- **Enrollment:** N/A

KEY STATS
- ✔ **U.S News College Ranking:** fourth tier, Universities–Master's (West)
- ✔ **SAT Score (25th/75th percentile):** 830-1100
- ✔ **Tuition:** N/A

Selectivity: Less selective	**Room/board:** N/A
Acceptance rate: 63%	**Average debt:** N/A
Student/faculty ratio: N/A	**Proportion who borrowed:** N/A

Colorado Christian University

- **Address:** 180 S. Garrison Street, Lakewood, CO 80226
- **Website:** http://www.ccu.edu
- **Private; Religious affiliation:** Christian nondenominational
- **Enrollment:** N/A

KEY STATS
- ✔ **U.S News College Ranking:** fourth tier, Universities–Master's (West)
- ✔ **SAT or ACT Score (25th/75th percentile):** N/A
- ✔ **Tuition:** N/A

Selectivity: Less selective	**Room/board:** N/A
Acceptance rate: N/A	**Average debt:** N/A
Student/faculty ratio: N/A	**Proportion who borrowed:** N/A

Colorado College

- **Address:** 14 E. Cache La Poudre Street, Colorado Springs, CO 80903
- **Website:** http://www.ColoradoCollege.edu
- **Private**
- **Enrollment:** 1,928 full-time; 49 part-time

KEY STATS
- ✔ **U.S News College Ranking:** 26, Liberal Arts Colleges
- ✔ **SAT Score (25th/75th percentile):** 1220-1400
- ✔ **Tuition:** 2006-2007: $32,124

Selectivity: Most selective	**Room/board:** $8,052
Acceptance rate: 38%	**Average debt:** $16,300
Student/faculty ratio: 9/1	**Proportion who borrowed:** 46%

UNDERGRADUATE STUDENT BODY STATS
2005-2006 enrollment: 1,928 full-time; 49 part-time. Men: 46%; women: 54%. **Ethnic makeup:** African American: 2%; American-Indian: 1%; Asian American: 4%; Hispanic: 7%; White: 83%; International: 2%.

ADMISSIONS FACTS AND FIGURES
Phone: (719) 389-6344. **Email:** admission@ColoradoCollege.edu. **Website:** http://www.ColoradoCollege.edu. **Application deadlines for fall 2007:** Regular decision: January 15; decision sent by April 1. Early decision: Not offered. Early action: Send application by: November 15; Decision sent by: December 20. Admission can be deferred. **Application fee:** $50. Common application is accepted. **To apply online, go to:** http://www.ColoradoCollege.edu/Admission/Apply/. **Admissions requirements/recommendations:** High school units required (recommended): English: 4 (4); Total units: 16 (20). Tests: The college uses SAT or ACT

scores in admissions decisions. Either SAT or ACT required. For admission to the fall 2007 entering class, the school will accept: ACT with writing, ACT without writing. Campus visit: Recommended. Admissions interview: Neither required nor recommended. Off-campus interview: May be arranged. **Factors that count in admissions decisions:** *Academic:* Secondary school record: Very important. Class rank: Important. Letters of recommendation: Important. Standardized test scores: Important. Essay: Important. *Nonacademic:* Interview: Important. Extracurricular activities: Important. Talent/ability: Considered. Character/personal qualities: Considered. Alumni/ae relationship: Considered. Geographical residence: Not considered. State residency: Not considered. Religious affiliation/commitment: Not considered. Minority status: Considered. Volunteer work: Considered. Work experience: Considered. **Other schools with the greatest overlap in applicants:** Lewis and Clark College; University of Colorado–Boulder; University of Denver; University of Puget Sound; Whitman College. **Admissions statistics for the fall 2005 entering class:** Total applicants: 4,089. Total accepted: 1,535. Freshmen enrolled: 476; 99% were from out of state. Accepted through early-decision or early-action plans: 45%. Overall acceptance rate: 38%. Non-early acceptance rate: 33%. **Size of waiting list:** 695 applicants; enrolled from waiting list: 0. **Credentials of fall 2005 freshmen:** 66% ranked in the top 10 percent of their high school class; 90% were in the top 25 percent, and 99% were in the top half. (Proportion submitting class standing: 53%.) **First-year students who submitted SAT scores:** 62%. Scores (25/75 percentile): Verbal: 610-710, Math: 610-690, Combined: 1220-1400. **First-year students submitting ACT scores:** 38%. Scores (25/75 percentile): English: 27-32, Math: 25-30, Composite: 27-31.

ACADEMICS
Year founded: 1874. **Academic calendar:** Semester. **Degrees offered:** bachelor's, master's. **Most popular majors:** 11% biology/biological sciences, 8% sociology, 7% economics, 7% psychology, 6% English language and literature. **Major fields of study:** area, ethnic, cultural, and gender studies; biological and biomedical sciences; English language and literature/letters; foreign languages, literatures, and linguistics; history; liberal arts and sciences studies, and humanities; mathematics and statistics; multi/interdisciplinary studies; natural resources and conservation; philosophy and religious studies; physical sciences; psychology; social sciences; visual and performing arts. **Areas of required coursework:** humanities, foreign languages, sciences (biological or physical), social science. **Pre-professional programs:** pre-medicine. **Special academic programs (% participation):** cooperative (work-study plan) program, double major (4.7%), English as a Second Language (ESL), independent study, internships, student-designed major, study abroad, teacher certificate program. **Teacher certification offered in:** elementary, secondary. **Cooperative education programs:** engineering. **Reserve Officers Training Corps (ROTC):** Army ROTC: Offered at cooperating institution (University of Colorado at Colorado Springs). **Faculty and instruction (2005-2006):** Total instructional faculty: 176 full-time, 30 part-time. Full-time faculty with Ph.D. or other terminal degree: 93%. Student/faculty ratio: 9/1. Classes of fewer than 20 students: 67%; of 20 to 49 students: 33%. **Advanced Placement and International Baccalaureate credit:** AP tests may be used for: Credit and/or placement. Scores accepted: 3, 4, 5. International Baccalaureate exams may be used for: Credit and/or placement. **Freshmen returning for sophomore year:** 91%. **Graduation rates:** Four-year: 77%; five-year: 82%; six-year: 83%. **Graduate study:** 29% of students pursue further study immediately upon graduation; 19% within one year. Fields in which graduates pursue further study: law, 13%; medicine, 4%; arts and sciences, 44%.

COSTS AND FINANCIAL AID
Financial aid office: (719) 389-6651. **Expenses (2006-2007):** Tuition and fees 2006-2007: $32,124; room/board: $8,052. Estimated books and supplies: $904; transportation: $0; personal expenses: $920. **Financial aid:** Priority filing date for institution's financial aid form: February 15; deadline: February 15. In 2005-2006, 50% of undergraduates applied for financial aid. Of those, 46% were determined to have financial need; 67% had their need fully met. Average financial aid package (proportion receiving): $27,522 (45%). Average amount of gift aid, such as scholarships or grants (proportion receiving): $23,717 (41%). Average amount of self-help aid, such as work study or loans (proportion receiving): $5,347 (39%). Average need-

based loan (excluding PLUS or other private loans): $4,835. Among students who received need-based aid, the average percentage of need met: 91%. Among students who received aid based on merit, the average award (and the proportion receiving): $15,144 (11%). The average athletic scholarship (and the proportion receiving): $29,592 (2%). Average amount of debt of borrowers graduating in 2005: $16,300. Proportion who borrowed: 46%.

CAMPUS LIFE AND EXTRACURRICULAR ACTIVITIES

Campus housing available: coed dorms, women's dorms, men's dorms, fraternity housing, apartment for single students, special housing for disabled students, other housing options. Students who live in college-owned, operated, or affiliated housing: 75%. **Clubs and organizations:** Number of student organizations: 40. Activities include: choral groups, concert band, dance, drama/theater, jazz band, literary magazine, music ensembles, musical theater, radio station, student government, student newspaper, student film society, yearbook. Number of fraternities: 3; sororities: 3. **Sports program (2005-2006):** Member of NCAA III. *Men's intercollegiate varsity sports:* basketball, cross-country, football, ice hockey, lacrosse, soccer, swimming and diving, tennis, track and field (outdoor). *Women's intercollegiate varsity sports:* basketball, cross-country, lacrosse, soccer, softball, swimming and diving, tennis, track and field (indoor), track and field (outdoor), volleyball, water polo.

SERVICES AND FACILITIES

Basic services: nonremedial tutoring, women's center, day care, health service, health insurance. **Remedial assistance:** writing, study skills. **Counseling services:** minority student, career, personal, academic, psychological, birth control, religious. **For learning-disabled students:** School does not offer a structured program with separate admission and additional fees. Total undergraduates in learning-disabled program or receiving services: 117. Services include: tape recorders, note-taking services, learning center, readers, extended time for tests, tutors, priority seating, texts on tape, other testing accomodations. **Library:** Number of titles: 499,596; number of current serial subscriptions: 2,567. **Information technology resources:** Students are not required to lease or own a computer. Number of campus computers available to all students: 436. School has a wireless network. Approximate number of users that can be accommodated: 2,500. Proportion of college-owned housing units wired for high-speed internet access: 100%. **Campus safety:** Security services offered: 24-hour foot-and-vehicle patrols, late-night transport/escort service, 24-hour emergency telephones, lighted pathways/sidewalks, student patrols, controlled dormitory access (key, security card, etc).

TRANSFER AND INTERNATIONAL STUDENTS

Transfer students: May apply for admission for the following academic terms: Fall, Spring. Applicants do not need a minimum number of credits to apply. For fall 2005: Transfer applications received: 152. Transfer applicants offered admission: 48. Transfer applicants enrolled: 28. **International students:** Number of foreign undergraduates: 33 (2% of student body). Number of countries represented: 21. Minimum TOEFL score required: 550 (paper); 213 (computer). Average TOEFL score: 600 (paper).

Colorado School of Mines

- **Address:** 1600 Maple Street, Golden, CO 80401
- **Website:** http://www.mines.edu
- **Public**
- **Enrollment:** 2,909 full-time; 189 part-time

KEY STATS

✔ **U.S News College Ranking:** Unranked Specialty School–Engineering
✔ **ACT Score (25th/75th percentile):** 25-29
✔ **Tuition:** 2006-2007: $9,010 in state, $21,546 out of state

Selectivity: More selective	**Room/board:** $6,880
Acceptance rate: 80%	**Average debt:** $18,500
Student/faculty ratio: 14/1	**Proportion who borrowed:** 70%

UNDERGRADUATE STUDENT BODY STATS

2005-2006 enrollment: 2,909 full-time; 189 part-time. Men: 79%; women: 21%. **Ethnic makeup:** African American: 1%; American-Indian: 1%; Asian American: 5%; Hispanic: 7%; White: 83%; International: 3%. **Religious pref-**

erence: Roman Catholic: 13%; Protestant: 39%; Jewish: 15%; Muslim: 8%; Hindu: 2%; Buddhist: 1%; No preference: 19%; Unknown: 3%.

ADMISSIONS FACTS AND FIGURES

Phone: (303) 273-3220. **Email:** admit@mines.edu. **Website:** http://www.mines.edu. **Application deadlines for fall 2007:** Regular decision: May 1. Early decision: Not offered. Early action: Not offered. Admission can be deferred. **Application fee:** $45. Common application is not accepted. **Admissions requirements/recommendations:** High school units required (recommended): English: 4; Mathematics: 4; Science: 3; Social studies: 2; Academic electives: 3; Total units: 16. Tests: The college uses SAT or ACT scores in admissions decisions. Either SAT or ACT required. For admission to the fall 2007 entering class, the school will accept: ACT with writing, ACT without writing. Campus visit: Recommended. Admissions interview: Recommended. Off-campus interview: Not available. **Factors that count in admissions decisions:** *Academic:* Secondary school record: Very important. Class rank: Very important. Letters of recommendation: Considered. Standardized test scores: Important. Essay: Considered. *Nonacademic:* Interview: Not considered. Extracurricular activities: Considered. Talent/ability: Considered. Character/personal qualities: Not considered. Alumni/ae relationship: Considered. Geographical residence: Not considered. State residency: Not considered. Religious affiliation/commitment: Not considered. Minority status: Not considered. Volunteer work: Not considered. Work experience: Not considered. **Other schools with the greatest overlap in applicants:** Colorado State University; Stanford University; Texas A&M University–College Station; University of Colorado–Boulder; University of Denver. **Admissions statistics for the fall 2005 entering class:** Total applicants: 3,215. Total accepted: 2,556. Freshmen enrolled: 816; 25% were from out of state. Overall acceptance rate: 80%. **Credentials of fall 2005 freshmen:** 48% ranked in the top 10 percent of their high school class; 81% were in the top 25 percent, and 100% were in the top half. (Proportion submitting class standing: 85%.) **Average high school grade point average:** 3.7. **First-year students who submitted SAT scores:** 50%. Scores (25/75 percentile): Verbal: 540-650, Math: 630-690, Combined: 1170-1340. **First-year students submitting ACT scores:** 70%. Scores (25/75 percentile): English: 23-29, Math: 25-31, Composite: 25-29.

ACADEMICS

Year founded: 1874. **Academic calendar:** Semester. **Degrees offered:** bachelor's, master's, doctorate. **Most popular majors:** 72% engineering, 15% mathematics and statistics, 7% physics, 5% economics, 1% chemistry. **Major fields of study:** engineering; mathematics and statistics; physical sciences; social sciences. **Areas of required coursework:** arts/fine arts, humanities, computer literacy, mathematics, English (including composition), sciences (biological or physical). **Special academic programs (% participation):** accelerated program (2%), cooperative (work-study plan) program (2%), double major (8%), dual enrollment, English as a Second Language (ESL) (1%), honors program (3%), independent study (4%), internships (20%), study abroad (7%). **Cooperative education programs:** business, computer science, engineering. **Reserve Officers Training Corps (ROTC):** Army ROTC: Offered on campus; Air Force ROTC: Offered on campus. **Faculty and instruction (2005-2006):** Total instructional faculty: 204 full-time, 133 part-time (79% men; 21% women; 10% minorities). Full-time faculty with Ph.D. or other terminal degree: 94%. Student/faculty ratio: 14/1. Classes of fewer than 20 students: 42%; of 20 to 49 students: 49%; of 50 or more students: 10%. **Advanced Placement and International Baccalaureate credit:** AP tests may be used for: Credit and/or placement. Scores accepted: 4, 5. International Baccalaureate exams may be used for: Credit and/or placement. **Freshmen returning for sophomore year:** 84%. **Graduation rates:** Four-year: 39%; five-year: 65%; six-year: 65%. **Graduate study:** 15% of students pursue further study immediately upon graduation; 1% within one year; 1% within five years. Fields in which graduates pursue further study: Master of Business Administration (MBA), 20%; law, 10%; medicine, 3%; engineering, 67%.

COSTS AND FINANCIAL AID

Financial aid office: (303) 273-3220. **Expenses (2006-2007):** Tuition and fees 2006-2007: $9,010 in state, $21,546 out of state; room/board: $6,880. Estimated books and supplies: $1,300; transportation: $0; personal expenses: $1,800. **Financial aid:** Priority filing date for institution's financial aid form: March 1. In 2005-2006, 75% of undergraduates applied for financial aid. Of those, 68% were determined to have financial need; 82% had their need fully met. Average financial aid package (proportion receiving): $13,800 (68%). Average amount of gift aid, such as scholarships or grants (proportion receiving): $7,100 (60%). Average amount of self-help aid, such as work study or loans (proportion receiving): $6,700 (68%). Average need-based loan (excluding PLUS or other private loans): $5,200. Among students who received need-based aid, the average percentage of need met: 93%. Among students who received aid based on merit, the average award (and the proportion receiving): $5,100 (10%). The average athletic scholarship (and the proportion receiving): $4,500 (6%). Average amount of debt of borrowers graduating in 2005: $18,500. Proportion who borrowed: 70%.

CAMPUS LIFE AND EXTRACURRICULAR ACTIVITIES

Campus housing available (% using): coed dorms (43%), sorority housing (4%), fraternity housing (17%), apartments for married students (3%), apartment for single students (23%), special housing for disabled students (0%), other housing options (10%). Students who live in college-owned, operated, or affiliated housing: 35%. **Student employment:** During the 2005-2006 academic year, 50% of undergraduates worked on campus. Average per-year earnings: $1,200. **Clubs and organizations:** Number of student organizations: 135. Activities include: choral groups, concert band, dance, drama/theater, jazz band, literary magazine, marching band, music ensembles, musical theater, pep band, student government, student newspaper, yearbook. Number of fraternities: 7; sororities: 3. Proportion of men in fraternities: 20%; of women in sororities: 20%. Average proportion of students who stay on campus on weekends: 40%. **Sports program (2005-2006):** Member of NCAA II. *Men's intercollegiate varsity sports:* baseball, basketball, cross-country, football, golf, soccer, swimming and diving, tennis, track and field (indoor), track and field (outdoor), wrestling. *Women's intercollegiate varsity sports:* basketball, cross-country, soccer, softball, swimming and diving, track and field (indoor), track and field (outdoor), volleyball.

SERVICES AND FACILITIES

Basic services: nonremedial tutoring, women's center, placement service, health service, health insurance. **Remedial assistance:** math, writing, study skills. **Counseling services:** minority student, career, military, personal, veteran student, academic, older student, psychological, birth control. **For learning-disabled students:** School does not offer a structured program with separate admission and additional fees. Total undergraduates in learning-disabled program or receiving services: 27. Services include: untimed tests, note-taking services, readers, extended time for tests, tutors, priority seating, typist/scribe. **Library:** Number of titles: 150,000; number of current serial subscriptions: 4,883. **Information technology resources:** Students are not required to lease or own a computer. Number of campus computers available to all students: 350. School has a wireless network. Approximate number of users that can be accommodated: 200. Proportion of college-owned housing units wired for high-speed internet access: 100%. **Campus safety:** Security services offered: 24-hour foot-and-vehicle patrols, late-night transport/escort service, 24-hour emergency telephones, lighted pathways/sidewalks, student patrols, controlled dormitory access (key, security card, etc).

TRANSFER AND INTERNATIONAL STUDENTS

Transfer students: May apply for admission for the following academic terms: Fall, Spring, Summer. Applicants need a minimum number of credits to apply. For fall 2005: Transfer applications received: 227. Transfer applicants offered admission: 165. Transfer applicants enrolled: 96. **International students:** Number of foreign undergraduates: 86 (3% of student body). Number of countries represented: 52. Minimum TOEFL score required: 550 (paper); 213 (computer). Average TOEFL score: 550 (paper).

Colorado State University

- Address: 8020 Campus Delivery, Fort Collins, CO 80523
- Website: http://www.colostate.edu
- Public
- Enrollment: 18,995 full-time; 2,511 part-time

KEY STATS

✔ **U.S News College Ranking:** 124, National Universities
✔ **ACT Score (25th/75th percentile):** 22-26
✔ **Tuition:** 2006-2007: $4,716 in state, $16,244 out of state

Selectivity: Selective	Room/board: $6,930
Acceptance rate: 88%	Average debt: $16,887
Student/faculty ratio: 18/1	Proportion who borrowed: 52%

UNDERGRADUATE STUDENT BODY STATS

2005-2006 enrollment: 18,995 full-time; 2,511 part-time. Men: 48%; women: 52%. **Ethnic makeup:** African American: 2%; American-Indian: 1%; Asian American: 3%; Hispanic: 6%; White: 87%; International: 1%.

ADMISSIONS FACTS AND FIGURES

Phone: (970) 491-6909. **Email:** admissions@colostate.edu. **Website:** http://www.colostate.edu. **Application deadlines for fall 2007:** Regular decision: July 1. Early decision: Not offered. Early action: Not offered. Admission can be deferred. **Application fee:** $50. Common application is not accepted. **To apply online, go to:** http://admissions.colostate.edu/admissions/dsp_apply.cfm. **Admissions requirements/recommendations:** High school units required (recommended): English: 4 (4); Mathematics: 3 (4); Science: 2 (3); Foreign language: 2 (3); Social studies: 2 (3); Academic electives: 3 (2); Total units: 15 (18). Tests: The college uses SAT or ACT scores in admissions decisions. Either SAT or ACT required. For admission to the fall 2007 entering class, the school will accept: ACT with writing, ACT without writing. Campus visit: Recommended. Admissions interview: Neither required nor recommended. Off-campus interview: Not available. **Factors that count in admissions decisions:** *Academic:* Secondary school record: Very important. Class rank: Very important. Letters of recommendation: Important. Standardized test scores: Very important. Essay: Important. *Nonacademic:* Interview: Considered. Extracurricular activities: Considered. Talent/ability: Considered. Character/personal qualities: Considered. Alumni/ae relationship: Considered. Geographical residence: Considered. State residency: Considered. Religious affiliation/commitment: Not considered. Minority status: Considered. Volunteer work: Considered. **Other schools with the greatest overlap in applicants:** Arizona State University; Colorado School of Mines; Cornell University; University of Colorado–Boulder; University of Denver. **Admissions statistics for the fall 2005 entering class:** Total applicants: 10,770. Total accepted: 9,516. Freshmen enrolled: 3,893; 19% were from out of state. Overall acceptance rate: 88%. **Credentials of fall 2005 freshmen:** 17% ranked in the top 10 percent of their high school class; 46% were in the top 25 percent, and 84% were in the top half. (Proportion submitting class standing: 90%.) **Average high school grade point average:** 3.5. **First-year students who submitted SAT scores:** 43%. Scores (25/75 percentile): Verbal: 500-610, Math: 510-620, Combined: 1010-1230. **First-year students submitting ACT scores:** 90%. Scores (25/75 percentile): English: 21-26, Math: 20-26, Composite: 22-26.

ACADEMICS

Year founded: 1870. **Academic calendar:** Semester. **Degrees offered:** bachelor's, master's, first professional, doctorate. **Most popular majors:** 17% business administration and management, 8% human development and family studies, 8% social sciences, 7% biology/biological sciences, 7% engineering. **Major fields of study:** agriculture, agriculture operations, and related sciences; architecture and related services; biological and biomedical sciences; business, management, marketing, and related support services; communication, journalism, and related programs; computer and information sciences and support services; education; engineering; English language and literature/letters; family and consumer sciences/human sciences; foreign languages, literatures, and linguistics; health professions and related clinical sciences; history; liberal arts and sciences studies, and humanities; mathematics and statistics; natural resources and conservation; parks, recreation, leisure, and fitness studies; philosophy and religious studies; physical sciences; psychology; public administration and social service professions; social sciences; visual and performing arts. **Areas of required coursework:** arts/fine arts, humanities, mathematics, English (including composition), sciences (biological or physical), history, social science, other. **Pre-professional programs:** pre-law, pre-dentistry, pre-medicine, pre-veterinary science, pre-optometry, pre-pharmacy, other. **Special academic programs:** accelerated program, cooperative (work-study plan) program, distance learning, double major, dual enrollment, English as a Second Language (ESL), exchange student program (domestic), honors program, independent study, internships, liberal arts/career combination, study abroad, teacher certificate program. **Teacher certification offered in:** early childhood, vo-tech, secondary, bilingual/bicultural. **Cooperative education programs:** computer science, engineering. **Reserve Officers Training Corps (ROTC):** Army ROTC: Offered on campus; Air Force ROTC: Offered on campus. **Faculty and instruction (2005-2006):** Total instructional faculty: 851 full-time, 30 part-time (72% men; 28% women; 12% minorities). Full-time faculty with Ph.D. or other terminal degree: 99%. Student/faculty ratio: 18/1. Classes of fewer than 20 students: 38%; of 20 to 49 students: 45%; of 50 or more students: 17%. **Advanced Placement and International Baccalaureate credit:** AP tests may be used for: Credit and/or placement. Scores accepted: 3, 4, 5. International

Baccalaureate exams may be used for: Credit and/or placement. **Freshmen returning for sophomore year:** 82%. **Graduation rates:** Four-year: 34%; five-year; 58%; six-year: 63%.

COSTS AND FINANCIAL AID

Financial aid office: (970) 491-6321. **Expenses (2006-2007):** Tuition and fees 2006-2007: $4,716 in state, $16,244 out of state; room/board: $6,930. Estimated books and supplies: $900; transportation: $665; personal expenses: $1,000. **Financial aid:** Priority filing date for institution's financial aid form: March 1. In 2005-2006, 56% of undergraduates applied for financial aid. Of those, 39% were determined to have financial need; 50% had their need fully met. Average financial aid package (proportion receiving): $8,188 (39%). Average amount of gift aid, such as scholarships or grants (proportion receiving): $4,914 (27%). Average amount of self-help aid, such as work study or loans (proportion receiving): $5,456 (33%). Average need-based loan (excluding PLUS or other private loans): $5,355. Among students who received need-based aid, the average percentage of need met: 82%. Among students who received aid based on merit, the average award (and the proportion receiving): $2,275 (5%). The average athletic scholarship (and the proportion receiving): $13,084 (1%). Average amount of debt of borrowers graduating in 2005: $16,887. Proportion who borrowed: 52%.

CAMPUS LIFE AND EXTRACURRICULAR ACTIVITIES

Campus housing available: coed dorms, apartments for married students, apartment for single students, special housing for disabled students, special housing for international students. Students who live in college-owned, operated, or affiliated housing: 30%. **Student employment:** During the 2005-2006 academic year, 30% of undergraduates worked on campus. **Clubs and organizations:** Number of student organizations: 275. Activities include: choral groups, concert band, dance, drama/theater, jazz band, literary magazine, marching band, music ensembles, musical theater, opera, pep band, radio station, student government, student newspaper, symphony orchestra, television station, yearbook. Number of fraternities: 17; sororities: 8. Proportion of men in fraternities: 8%; of women in sororities: 9%. **Sports program (2005-2006):** Member of NCAA I. *Men's intercollegiate varsity sports:* basketball, cross-country, football, golf, track and field (indoor), track and field (outdoor). *Women's intercollegiate varsity sports:* basketball, cross-country, golf, softball, swimming and diving, tennis, track and field (indoor), track and field (outdoor), volleyball, water polo.

SERVICES AND FACILITIES

Basic services: nonremedial tutoring, women's center, day care, health service, health insurance. **Counseling services:** minority student, career, military, personal, veteran student, academic, older student, psychological, birth control, religious. **For learning-disabled students:** School does not offer a structured program with separate admission and additional fees. Total undergraduates in learning-disabled program or receiving services: 473. Services include: reading machines, tape recorders, diagnostic testing service, note-taking services, readers, extended time for tests, tutors, priority registration, substitution of courses, texts on tape, exams on tape or computer, other testing accomodations, other. **Library:** Number of titles: 2,001,655; number of current serial subscriptions: 28,837. **Information technology resources:** Students are not required to lease or own a computer. Number of campus computers available to all students: 2,700. School has a wireless network. **Campus safety:** Security services offered: 24-hour foot-and-vehicle patrols, late-night transport/escort service, 24-hour emergency telephones, lighted pathways/sidewalks, controlled dormitory access (key, security card, etc).

TRANSFER AND INTERNATIONAL STUDENTS

Transfer students: May apply for admission for the following academic terms: Fall, Spring, Summer. Applicants need a minimum number of credits to apply. For fall 2005: Transfer applications received: 2,393. Transfer applicants offered admission: 2,044. Transfer applicants enrolled: 1,436. **International students:** Number of foreign undergraduates: 197 (1% of student body). Number of countries represented: 85. Minimum TOEFL score required: 525 (paper); 197 (computer). Average TOEFL score: 581 (paper).

Colorado State University–Pueblo

- ■ **Address:** 2200 Bonforte Boulevard, Pueblo, CO 81001
- ■ **Website:** http://www.colostate-pueblo.edu
- ■ **Public**
- ■ **Enrollment:** 3,298 full-time; 1,791 part-time

KEY STATS

✔ **U.S News College Ranking:** fourth tier, Universities–Master's (West)
✔ **ACT Score (25th/75th percentile):** 18-22
✔ **Tuition:** 2006-2007: $6,783 in state, $15,435 out of state
  Selectivity: Less selective **Room/board:** $6,088
  Acceptance rate: 96% **Average debt:** $14,590
  Student/faculty ratio: 18/1 **Proportion who borrowed:** 81%

UNDERGRADUATE STUDENT BODY STATS

2005-2006 enrollment: 3,298 full-time; 1,791 part-time. Men: 40%; women: 60%. **Ethnic makeup:** African American: 5%; American-Indian: 2%; Asian American: 3%; Hispanic: 25%; White: 64%; International: 2%.

ADMISSIONS FACTS AND FIGURES

Phone: (719) 549-2461. **Email:** info@colostate-pueblo.edu. **Website:** http://www.colostate-pueblo.edu. **Application deadlines for fall 2007:** Regular decision: August 1. Early decision: Not offered. Early action: Not offered. Admission can be deferred. **Application fee:** $25. Common application is accepted. **To apply online, go to:** http://www.colostate-pueblo.edu/admissions/apply/ApplyNow.asp. **Admissions requirements/recommendations:** High school units required (recommended): English: 4 (4); Mathematics: 3 (3); Science: 3 (3); Foreign language: 2 (2); Social studies: 2 (2); History: 1 (1); Total units: 15 (4). Tests: The college uses SAT or ACT scores in admissions decisions. Either SAT or ACT required. For admission to the fall 2007 entering class, the school will accept: ACT with writing, ACT without writing. Campus visit: Recommended. Admissions interview: Neither required nor recommended. Off-campus interview: Not available. **Factors that count in admissions decisions:** *Academic:* Secondary school record: Very important. Class rank: Important. Letters of recommendation: Considered. Standardized test scores: Very important. Essay: Considered. *Nonacademic:* Interview: Considered. Extracurricular activities: Not considered. Talent/ability: Considered. Character/personal qualities: Considered. Alumni/ae relationship: Not considered. Geographical residence: Not considered. State residency: Not considered. Religious affiliation/commitment: Not considered. Minority status: Considered. Volunteer work: Considered. Work experience: Considered. **Admissions statistics for the fall 2005 entering class:** Total applicants: 1,771. Total accepted: 1,695. Freshmen enrolled: 683; 10% were from out of state. Overall acceptance rate: 96%. **Credentials of fall 2005 freshmen:** 2% ranked in the top 10 percent of their high school class; 9% were in the top 25 percent, and 37% were in the top half. (Proportion submitting class standing: 71%.) **Average high school grade point average:** 3.1. **First-year students who submitted SAT scores:** 13%. Scores (25/75 percentile): Verbal: 450-540, Math: 460-550, Combined: 910-1090. **First-year students submitting ACT scores:** 80%. Scores (25/75 percentile): English: 16-22, Math: 17-22, Composite: 18-22.

ACADEMICS

Year founded: 1933. **Academic calendar:** Semester. **Degrees offered:** bachelor's, master's. **Most popular majors:** 17% sociology, 14% business/commerce, 8% mass communication/media studies, 6% liberal arts and sciences/liberal studies, 6% nursing/registered nurse training (R.N., A.S.N., B.S.N., M.S.N.). **Major fields of study:** biological and biomedical sciences; business, management, marketing, and related support services; communication, journalism, and related programs; computer and information sciences and support services; engineering; engineering technologies/technicians; English language and literature/letters; foreign languages, literatures, and linguistics; health professions and related clinical sciences; history; liberal arts and sciences studies, and humanities; mathematics and statistics; parks, recreation, leisure, and fitness studies; physical sciences; psychology; public administration and social service professions; social sciences; visual and performing arts. **Areas of required coursework:** arts/fine arts, humanities, mathematics, English (including composition), sciences (biological or physical), history, social science. **Pre-professional programs:** pre-law, pre-dentistry, pre-medicine, pre-veterinary science, pre-optometry, pre-pharmacy. **Special academic programs:** accelerated program, cooperative (work-study plan) program, cross-registration, distance learning, double major, dual enrollment, English as a Second Language (ESL), exchange student program (domestic), external degree program, honors program, independent study, internships, study abroad, teacher certificate program, weekend college. **Teacher certification offered in:** elementary, secondary. **Cooperative education programs:** art, business, computer science, engineering, humanities, technologies. **Reserve Officers Training Corps (ROTC):** Army ROTC: Offered on campus. **Faculty and instruction (2005-2006):** Total instructional faculty: 155 full-time, 146 part-time (53% men; 47% women; 18% minorities). Full-time faculty with Ph.D. or other terminal degree: 66%. Student/faculty ratio: 18/1. Classes of fewer than 20 students: 43%; of 20 to 49 students: 48%; of 50 or more students: 9%. **Advanced Placement and International Baccalaureate credit:** AP tests may be used for: Credit only. Scores accepted: 3, 4, 5. International Baccalaureate exams may be used for: Credit only. **Freshmen returning for sophomore year:** 62%. **Graduation rates:** Four-year: 13%; five-year: 26%; six-year: 31%.

COSTS AND FINANCIAL AID

Financial aid office: (719) 549-2753. **Expenses (2006-2007):** Tuition and fees 2006-2007: $6,783 in state, $15,435 out of state; room/board: $6,088. Estimated books and supplies: $1,698; transportation: $676; personal expenses: $2,908. **Financial aid:** Priority filing date for institution's financial aid form: March 1. In 2005-2006, 76% of undergraduates applied for financial aid. Of those, 64% were determined to have financial need; 7% had their need fully met. Average financial aid package (proportion receiving): $7,247 (63%). Average amount of gift aid, such as scholarships or grants (proportion receiving): $4,517 (52%). Average amount of self-help aid, such as work study or loans (proportion receiving): $3,720 (59%). Average need-based loan (excluding PLUS or other private loans): $3,252. Among students who received need-based aid, the average percentage of need met: 59%. Among students who received aid based on merit, the average award (and the proportion receiving): $7,876 (20%). The average athletic scholarship (and the proportion receiving): $3,069 (4%). Average amount of debt of borrowers graduating in 2005: $14,590. Proportion who borrowed: 81%.

CAMPUS LIFE AND EXTRACURRICULAR ACTIVITIES

Campus housing available (% using): coed dorms (100%), apartment for single students, special housing for disabled students. Students who live in college-owned, operated, or affiliated housing: 12%. **Student employment:** During the 2005-2006 academic year, 13% of undergraduates worked on campus. Average per-year earnings: $1,309. **Clubs and organizations:** Number of student organizations: 69. Activities include: choral groups, concert band, dance, jazz band, literary magazine, music ensembles, pep band, radio station, student government, student newspaper, symphony orchestra, television station. Number of fraternities: 3; sororities: 1. Proportion of men in fraternities: 3%; of women in sororities: 2%. **Sports program (2005-2006):** Member of NCAA II. *Men's intercollegiate varsity sports:* baseball, basketball, golf, soccer, tennis. *Women's intercollegiate varsity sports:* basketball, cross-country, golf, soccer, softball, tennis, volleyball, .

SERVICES AND FACILITIES

Basic services: women's center, day care, health service. **Remedial assistance:** reading, math, writing. **Counseling services:** minority student, personal, academic, older student, psychological. **For learning-disabled students:** School does not offer a structured program with separate admission and additional fees. Total undergraduates in learning-disabled program or receiving services: 30. Services include: tape recorders, note-taking services, readers, extended time for tests, other. **Library:** Number of titles: 263,038; number of current serial subscriptions: 869. **Information technology resources:** Students are not required to lease or own a computer. Number of campus computers available to all students: 746. School has a wireless network. Approximate number of users that can be accommodated: 600. Proportion of college-owned housing units wired for high-speed internet access: 100%. **Campus safety:** Security services offered: 24-hour foot-and-vehicle patrols, late-night transport/escort service, 24-hour emergency telephones, lighted pathways/sidewalks, student patrols, controlled dormitory access (key, security card, etc).

TRANSFER AND INTERNATIONAL STUDENTS

Transfer students: May apply for admission for the following academic terms: Fall, Spring, Summer. Applicants need a minimum number of credits to apply. For fall 2005: Transfer applications received: 583. Transfer applicants offered admission: 581. Transfer applicants enrolled: 386. **International students:** Number of foreign undergraduates: 60 (2% of student body). Number of countries represented: 19. Minimum TOEFL score required: 500 (paper); 173 (computer). Average TOEFL score: 533 (paper).

- **Address:** 1000 Rim Drive, Durango, CO 81301
- **Website:** http://www.fortlewis.edu
- **Public**
- **Enrollment:** 3,637 full-time; 309 part-time

KEY STATS
- ✔ **U.S News College Ranking:** fourth tier, Liberal Arts Colleges
- ✔ **ACT Score (25th/75th percentile):** 18-23
- ✔ **Tuition:** 2006-2007: $5,973 in state, $14,061 out of state

Selectivity: Selective	**Room/board:** $6,468
Acceptance rate: 74%	**Average debt:** $16,966
Student/faculty ratio: 18/1	**Proportion who borrowed:** 60%

UNDERGRADUATE STUDENT BODY STATS

2005-2006 enrollment: 3,637 full-time; 309 part-time. Men: 52%; women: 48%. **Ethnic makeup:** African American: 1%; American-Indian: 19%; Asian American: 1%; Hispanic: 6%; White: 73%; International: 1%.

ADMISSIONS FACTS AND FIGURES

Phone: (970) 247-7184. **Email:** admission@fortlewis.edu. **Website:** http://www.fortlewis.edu. **Application deadlines for fall 2007:** Regular decision: August 1. Early decision: Not offered. Early action: Not offered. Admission can be deferred. **Application fee:** $30. Common application is accepted. **To apply online, go to:** http://www.fortlewis.edu/prospective_students/admission/main_apply.asp. **Admissions requirements/recommendations:** High school units required (recommended): English: (4); Mathematics: (4); Science: (3); Foreign language: (2); Social studies: (3); Academic electives: (2); Total units: (15). Tests: The college uses SAT or ACT scores in admissions decisions. Either SAT or ACT required. For admission to the fall 2007 entering class, the school will accept: ACT with writing, ACT without writing. Campus visit: Recommended. Admissions interview: Recommended. Off-campus interview: May not be arranged. **Factors that count in admissions decisions:** *Academic:* Secondary school record: Important. Class rank: Very important. Letters of recommendation: Considered. Standardized test scores: Very important. Essay: Considered. *Nonacademic:* Interview: Considered. Extracurricular activities: Considered. Talent/ability: Considered. Character/personal qualities: Considered. Alumni/ae relationship: Considered. Geographical residence: Considered. State residency: Considered. Religious affiliation/commitment: Considered. Minority status: Considered. Volunteer work: Considered. Work experience: Considered. **Other schools with the greatest overlap in applicants:** Colorado State University; Mesa State College; University of Colorado–Boulder; University of Northern Colorado; Western State College of Colorado. **Admissions statistics for the fall 2005 entering class:** Total applicants: 2,765. Total accepted: 2,042. Freshmen enrolled: 910; 27% were from out of state. Overall acceptance rate: 74%. **Credentials of fall 2005 freshmen:** 4% ranked in the top 10 percent of their high school class; 20% were in the top 25 percent, and 53% were in the top half. (Proportion submitting class standing: 72%.) **Average high school grade point average:** 3.0. **First-year students who submitted SAT scores:** 26%. Scores (25/75 percentile): Verbal: 458-560, Math: 450-550, Combined: 908-1110. **First-year students submitting ACT scores:** 91%. Scores (25/75 percentile): English: 17-23, Math: 17-23, Composite: 18-23.

ACADEMICS

Year founded: 1911. **Academic calendar:** Semester. **Degrees offered:** bachelor's. **Most popular majors:** 23% business, management, marketing, and related support services, 13% liberal arts and sciences studies, and humanities, 13% social sciences, 10% English language and literature/letters, 8% visual and performing arts. **Major fields of study:** agriculture, agriculture operations, and related sciences; area, ethnic, cultural, and gender studies; biological and biomedical sciences; business, management, marketing, and related support services; communication, journalism, and related programs; computer and information sciences and support services; education; engineering; English language and literature/letters; foreign languages, literatures, and linguistics; health professions and related clinical sciences; history; liberal arts and sciences studies, and humanities; mathematics and statistics; multi/interdisciplinary studies; parks, recreation, leisure, and fitness studies; philosophy and religious studies; physical sciences; psychology; social sciences; visual and performing arts. **Areas of required coursework:** computer literacy, English (including composition), sciences (biological or physical), social science, other. **Pre-professional programs:** pre-law, pre-medicine. **Special academic programs:** accelerated program, cooperative (work-study plan) program, distance learning, double major, dual enrollment, English as a Second Language (ESL), exchange student program (domestic), honors program, independent study, internships, liberal arts/career combination, student-designed major, study abroad, teacher certificate program. **Teacher certification offered in:** early childhood, elementary, secondary. **Cooperative education programs:** agriculture, art, business, computer science, education, engineering, health professions, humanities, natural science, social/behavioral science, technologies. **Faculty and instruction (2005-2006):** Total instructional faculty: 177 full-time, 64 part-time (52% men; 48% women; 11% minorities). Full-time faculty with Ph.D. or other terminal degree: 78%. Student/faculty ratio: 18/1. Classes of fewer than 20 students: 47%; of 20 to 49 students: 51%; of 50 or more students: 2%. **Advanced Placement and International Baccalaureate credit:** AP tests may be used for: Credit and/or placement. Scores accepted: 3, 4, 5. International Baccalaureate exams may be used for: Credit only. **Freshmen returning for sophomore year:** 57%. **Graduation rates:** Four-year: 10%; five-year: 24%; six-year: 28%. **Graduate study:** 16% of students pursue further study immediately upon graduation; 21% within one year; 29% within five years.

COSTS AND FINANCIAL AID
Financial aid office: (970) 247-7142. **Expenses (2006-2007):** Tuition and fees 2006-2007: $5,973 in state, $14,061 out of state; room/board: $6,468. Estimated books and supplies: $850; transportation: $1,026; personal expenses: $2,508. **Financial aid:** Priority filing date for institution's financial aid form: February 15. In 2005-2006, 62% of undergraduates applied for financial aid. Of those, 48% were determined to have financial need; 19% had their need fully met. Average financial aid package (proportion receiving): $7,050 (47%). Average amount of gift aid, such as scholarships or grants (proportion receiving): $4,097 (29%). Average amount of self-help aid, such as work study or loans (proportion receiving): $3,847 (42%). Average need-based loan (excluding PLUS or other private loans): $3,673. Among students who received need-based aid, the average percentage of need met: 72%. Among students who received aid based on merit, the average award (and the proportion receiving): $1,916 (6%). The average athletic scholarship (and the proportion receiving): $2,828 (4%). Average amount of debt of borrowers graduating in 2005: $16,966. Proportion who borrowed: 60%.

CAMPUS LIFE AND EXTRACURRICULAR ACTIVITIES
Campus housing available (% using): coed dorms (70%), apartments for married students (4%), apartment for single students (25%), special housing for disabled students (1%), other housing options. Students who live in college-owned, operated, or affiliated housing: 33%. **Student employment:** During the 2005-2006 academic year, 5% of undergraduates worked on campus. Average per-year earnings: $1,780. **Clubs and organizations:** Number of student organizations: 70. Activities include: choral groups, concert band, drama/theater, jazz band, literary magazine, music ensembles, pep band, radio station, student government, student newspaper. Number of fraternities: 0; sororities: 0. Average proportion of students who stay on campus on weekends: 33%. **Sports program (2005-2006):** Member of NCAA II. *Men's intercollegiate varsity sports:* basketball, cross-country, football, golf, soccer. *Women's intercollegiate varsity sports:* basketball, cross-country, soccer, softball, volleyball.

SERVICES AND FACILITIES
Basic services: nonremedial tutoring, placement service, day care, health service, health insurance. **Remedial assistance:** reading, math, writing. **Counseling services:** minority student, career, personal, veteran student, academic, older student, psychological, birth control, religious. **For learning-disabled students:** School does not offer a structured program with separate admission and additional fees. Total undergraduates in learning-disabled program or receiving services: 200. Services include: tape recorders, note-taking services, oral tests, readers, extended time for tests. **Library:** Number of titles: 194,889; number of current serial subscriptions: 15,882. **Information technology resources:** Students are not required to lease or own a computer. Number of campus computers available to all students: 633. School has a wireless network. Approximate number of users that can be accommodated: 200. Proportion of college-owned housing units wired for high-speed internet access: 100%. **Campus safety:** Security services offered: 24-hour foot-and-vehicle patrols, late-night transport/escort service, 24-hour emergency telephones, lighted pathways/sidewalks, controlled dormitory access (key, security card, etc.).

TRANSFER AND INTERNATIONAL STUDENTS
Transfer students: May apply for admission for the following academic terms: Fall, Winter, Spring, Summer. Applicants need a minimum number of credits to apply. For fall 2005: Transfer applications received: 879. Transfer applicants offered admission: 569. Transfer applicants enrolled: 319. **International students:** Number of foreign undergraduates: 36 (1% of student body). Number of countries represented: 14. Minimum TOEFL score required: 500 (paper); 173 (computer). Average TOEFL score: 500 (paper).

Mesa State College

- **Address:** 1100 North Avenue, Grand Junction, CO 81501-3122
- **Website:** http://www.mesastate.edu
- **Public**
- **Enrollment:** 4,521 full-time; 1,513 part-time

KEY STATS
✔ **U.S News College Ranking:** fourth tier, Liberal Arts Colleges
✔ **ACT Score (25th/75th percentile):** 18-23
✔ **Tuition:** 2006-2007: $4,163 in state, $11,381 out of state

Selectivity: Less selective	**Room/board:** $7,054
Acceptance rate: 94%	**Average debt:** $17,634
Student/faculty ratio: 19/1	**Proportion who borrowed:** 53%

UNDERGRADUATE STUDENT BODY STATS
2005-2006 enrollment: 4,521 full-time; 1,513 part-time. Men: 41%; women: 59%. **Ethnic makeup:** African American: 2%; American-Indian: 2%; Asian American: 2%; Hispanic: 8%; White: 86%; International: 1%.

ADMISSIONS FACTS AND FIGURES
Phone: (800) 982-6372. **Email:** admissions@mesastate.edu. **Website:** http://www.mesastate.edu. **Application deadlines for fall 2007:** Regular decision: August 15. Early decision: Not offered. Early action: Not offered. Admission can be deferred. **Application fee:** $30. Common application is not accepted. **Admissions requirements/recommendations:** High school units required (recommended): English: (4); Mathematics: (3); Science: (3); Foreign language: (0); Social studies: (3); History: (2); Academic electives: (2); Total units: (15). Tests: The college uses SAT or ACT scores in admissions decisions. Either SAT or ACT required. For admission to the fall 2007 entering class, the school will accept: ACT with writing, ACT without writing. Campus visit: Recommended. Admissions interview: Neither required nor recommended. Off-campus interview: May be arranged. **Factors that count in admissions decisions:** *Academic:* Secondary school record: Important. Class rank: Important. Letters of recommendation: Considered. Standardized test scores: Important. Essay: Considered. *Nonacademic:* Interview: Considered. Extracurricular activities: Considered. Talent/ability: Considered. Character/personal qualities: Considered. Alumni/ae relationship: Considered. Geographical residence: Considered. State residency: Considered. Religious affiliation/commitment: Not considered. Minority status: Considered. Volunteer work: Considered. Work experience: Considered. **Other schools with the greatest overlap in applicants:** Colorado State University; Fort Lewis College; University of Colorado–Boulder; University of Northern Colorado; Western State College of Colorado. **Admissions statistics for the fall 2005 entering class:** Total applicants: 3,988. Total accepted: 3,767. Freshmen enrolled: 1,288; 8% were from out of state. Overall acceptance rate: 94%. **Credentials of fall 2005 freshmen:** 6% ranked in the top 10 percent of their high school class; 20% were in the top 25 percent, and 47% were in the top half. (Proportion submitting class standing: 80%.) **Average high school grade point average:** 3.0. **First-year students who submitted SAT scores:** 15%. Scores (25/75 percentile): Verbal: 430-540, Math: 430-540, Combined: 860-1080. **First-year students submitting ACT scores:** 90%. Scores (25/75 percentile): English: 17-23, Math: 17-23, Composite: 18-23.

ACADEMICS
Year founded: 1925. **Academic calendar:** Semester. **Degrees offered:** certificate, associate, transfer-associate, terminal-associate, bachelor's, master's. **Most popular majors:** 19% business/commerce, 9% liberal arts and sciences/liberal studies, 8% visual and performing arts, 6% nursing/registered nurse training (R.N., A.S.N., B.S.N., M.S.N.), 5% biology/biological sciences. **Major fields of study:** agriculture, agriculture operations, and related

sciences; biological and biomedical sciences; business, management, marketing, and related support services; communication, journalism, and related programs; construction trades; education; engineering technologies/technicians; English language and literature/letters; health professions and related clinical sciences; history; liberal arts and sciences studies, and humanities; mathematics and statistics; mechanic and repair technologies/technicians; natural resources and conservation; parks, recreation, leisure, and fitness studies; precision production; psychology; security and protective services; social sciences; visual and performing arts. **Areas of required coursework:** arts/fine arts, humanities, computer literacy, mathematics, English (including composition), philosophy, foreign languages, sciences (biological or physical), history, social science. **Special academic programs:** accelerated program, cooperative (work-study plan) program, cross-registration, distance learning, double major, dual enrollment, English as a Second Language (ESL), exchange student program (domestic), honors program, independent study, internships, teacher certificate program, other. **Teacher certification offered in:** elementary, middle/junior high, secondary. **Cooperative education programs:** art, business, computer science, education, health professions, natural science, social/behavioral science. **Faculty and instruction (2005-2006):** Total instructional faculty: 206 full-time, 190 part-time (56% men; 44% women; 5% minorities). Full-time faculty with Ph.D. or other terminal degree: 82%. Student/faculty ratio: 19/1. Classes of fewer than 20 students: 53%; of 20 to 49 students: 41%; of 50 or more students: 6%. **Advanced Placement and International Baccalaureate credit:** AP tests may be used for: Credit and/or placement. Scores accepted: 3, 4, 5. International Baccalaureate exams may be used for: Credit and/or placement. **Freshmen returning for sophomore year:** 59%. **Graduation rates:** Four-year: 9%; five-year: 21%; six-year: 27%.

COSTS AND FINANCIAL AID

Financial aid office: (970) 248-1396. **Expenses (2006-2007):** Tuition and fees 2006-2007: $4,163 in state, $11,381 out of state; room/board: $7,054. Estimated books and supplies: $1,306; transportation: $750; personal expenses: $1,760. **Financial aid:** Priority filing date for institution's financial aid form: March 1. In 2005-2006, 72% of undergraduates applied for financial aid. Of those, 60% were determined to have financial need; 16% had their need fully met. Average financial aid package (proportion receiving): $5,206 (58%). Average amount of gift aid, such as scholarships or grants (proportion receiving): $3,546 (43%). Average amount of self-help aid, such as work study or loans (proportion receiving): $3,323 (46%). Average need-based loan (excluding PLUS or other private loans): $3,188. Among students who received need-based aid, the average percentage of need met: 60%. Among students who received aid based on merit, the average award (and the proportion receiving): $1,893 (4%). The average athletic scholarship (and the proportion receiving): $2,570 (4%). Average amount of debt of borrowers graduating in 2005: $17,634. Proportion who borrowed: 53%.

CAMPUS LIFE AND EXTRACURRICULAR ACTIVITIES

Campus housing available (% using): coed dorms (16%), apartments for married students, other housing options (84%). Students who live in college-owned, operated, or affiliated housing: 16%. **Student employment:** During the 2005-2006 academic year, 8% of undergraduates worked on campus. Average per-year earnings: $3,500. Activities include: choral groups, concert band, dance, drama/theater, jazz band, literary magazine, music ensembles, musical theater, pep band, radio station, student government, student newspaper, student film society, symphony orchestra, television station. Number of fraternities: 0; sororities: 0. Average proportion of students who stay on campus on weekends: 80%. **Sports program (2005-2006):** Member of NCAA II. *Men's intercollegiate varsity sports:* baseball, basketball, football, tennis. *Women's intercollegiate varsity sports:* basketball, cross-country, golf, soccer, softball, swimming and diving, tennis, track and field (indoor), track and field (outdoor), volleyball.

SERVICES AND FACILITIES

Basic services: nonremedial tutoring, placement service, day care, health service, health insurance, other. **Remedial assistance:** reading, math, writing, study skills. **Counseling services:** minority student, career, military, personal, veteran student, academic, older student. **For learning-disabled students:** School does not offer a structured program with separate admission and additional fees. Total undergraduates in learning-disabled program or receiving services: 62. Services include: remedial math, remedial English, reading machines, remedial reading, tape recorders, note-taking services, oral tests, learning center, readers, extended time for tests, tutors, priority registration, priority seating, substitution of courses, texts on tape, typist/scribe, exams on tape or computer. **Library:** Number of titles: 247,338; number of current serial subscriptions: 31,992. **Information technology**

resources: Students are not required to lease or own a computer. Number of campus computers available to all students: 250. School has a wireless network. Approximate number of users that can be accommodated: 100. Proportion of college-owned housing units wired for high-speed internet access: 100%. **Campus safety:** Security services offered: 24-hour foot-and-vehicle patrols, late-night transport/escort service, 24-hour emergency telephones, lighted pathways/sidewalks, student patrols, controlled dormitory access (key, security card, etc).

TRANSFER AND INTERNATIONAL STUDENTS

Transfer students: May apply for admission for the following academic terms: Fall, Spring, Summer. Applicants need a minimum number of credits to apply. For fall 2005: Transfer applications received: 1,012. Transfer applicants offered admission: 918. Transfer applicants enrolled: 587. **International students:** Number of foreign undergraduates: 28 (1% of student body). Number of countries represented: 15. Minimum TOEFL score required: 525 (paper); 190 (computer).

Metropolitan State College of Denver

- **Address:** 1201 Fifth Street, Denver, CO 80217-3362
- **Website:** http://www.mscd.edu
- **Public**
- **Enrollment:** N/A

KEY STATS

✔ **U.S News College Ranking:** fourth tier, Comp. Colleges–Bachelor's (West)
✔ **ACT Score (25th/75th percentile):** 17-22
✔ **Tuition:** 2005-2006: $2,779 in state, $10,007 out of state

Selectivity: Less selective	**Room/board:** $0
Acceptance rate: 85%	**Average debt:** N/A
Student/faculty ratio: N/A	**Proportion who borrowed:** N/A

Regis University

- **Address:** 3333 Regis Boulevard, B-20, Denver, CO 80221
- **Website:** http://www.regis.edu
- **Private; Religious affiliation:** Roman Catholic (Jesuit)
- **Enrollment:** 2,469 full-time; 3,669 part-time

KEY STATS

✔ **U.S News College Ranking:** 20, Universities–Master's (West)
✔ **ACT Score (25th/75th percentile):** 20-26
✔ **Tuition:** 2006-2007: $25,200

Selectivity: More selective	**Room/board:** $8,470
Acceptance rate: 81%	**Average debt:** N/A
Student/faculty ratio: 13/1	**Proportion who borrowed:** N/A

UNDERGRADUATE STUDENT BODY STATS

2005-2006 enrollment: 2,469 full-time; 3,669 part-time. Men: 37%; women: 63%. **Ethnic makeup:** African American: 5%; American-Indian: 1%; Asian American: 4%; Hispanic: 10%; White: 80%; International: 1%. **Religious preference:** Roman Catholic: 33%; Protestant: 20%; Jewish: 1%; Buddhist: 1%; No preference: 5%; Unknown: 24%; Other: 2%.

ADMISSIONS FACTS AND FIGURES

Phone: (303) 458-4900. **Email:** regisadm@regis.edu. **Website:** http://www.regis.edu. **Application deadlines for fall 2007:** Regular decision: August 1. Early decision: Not offered. Early action: Not offered. Admission can be deferred. **Application fee:** $40. Common application is accepted. **To apply online, go to:** http://www.regis.edu/rc.asp?page=applications.downloadapp. **Admissions requirements/recommendations:** High school units required (recommended): English: (4); Mathematics: (2); Science: (2); Foreign language: (2); Social studies: (3); History: (2); Total units: 15. Tests: The college uses SAT or ACT scores in admissions decisions. Either SAT or ACT required. For admission to the fall 2007 entering class, the school will accept: ACT with writing, ACT without writing. Campus visit: Recommended. Admissions interview: Recommended. Off-campus interview: May be arranged. **Factors that count in admissions decisions:**

Academic: Secondary school record: Very important. Class rank: Not considered. Letters of recommendation: Very important. Standardized test scores: Very important. Essay: Very important. *Nonacademic:* Interview: Considered. Extracurricular activities: Considered. Talent/ability: Considered. Character/personal qualities: Considered. Alumni/ae relationship: Considered. Geographical residence: Not considered. State residency: Not considered. Religious affiliation/commitment: Not considered. Minority status: Not considered. Volunteer work: Considered. Work experience: Considered. **Other schools with the greatest overlap in applicants:** Creighton University; Gonzaga University. **Admissions statistics for the fall 2005 entering class:** Total applicants: 1,833. Total accepted: 1,493. Freshmen enrolled: 402; 40% were from out of state. Overall acceptance rate: 81%. **Size of waiting list:** 165 applicants; enrolled from waiting list: 0. **Credentials of fall 2005 freshmen:** 24% ranked in the top 10 percent of their high school class; 55% were in the top 25 percent, and 83% were in the top half. (Proportion submitting class standing: 63%.) **Average high school grade point average:** 3.4. **First-year students who submitted SAT scores:** 51%. Scores (25/75 percentile): Verbal: 470-600, Math: 470-590, Combined: 940-1190. **First-year students submitting ACT scores:** 82%. Scores (25/75 percentile): English: N/A, Math: N/A, Composite: 20-26.

ACADEMICS

Year founded: 1877. **Academic calendar:** Semester. **Degrees offered:** bachelor's, master's, doctorate. **Most popular majors:** 40% business, management, marketing, and related support services, 18% health professions and related clinical sciences, 13% computer and information sciences and support services, 13% multi/interdisciplinary studies, 6% communications technologies/technicians and support services. **Major fields of study:** area, ethnic, cultural, and gender studies; biological and biomedical sciences; business, management, marketing, and related support services; communication, journalism, and related programs; computer and information sciences and support services; education; engineering; engineering technologies/technicians; English language and literature/letters; foreign languages, literatures, and linguistics; health professions and related clinical sciences; legal professions and studies; liberal arts and sciences studies, and humanities; mathematics and statistics; multi/interdisciplinary studies; philosophy and religious studies; physical sciences; psychology; public administration and social service professions; science technologies/technicians; security and protective services; social sciences; theology and religious vocations; visual and performing arts. **Areas of required coursework:** arts/fine arts, mathematics, English (including composition), philosophy, foreign languages, sciences (biological or physical), history, social science, other. **Preprofessional programs:** pre-law, pre-dentistry, pre-medicine, pre-theology, pre-veterinary science, pre-optometry, pre-pharmacy, other. **Special academic programs (% participation):** accelerated program (74%), distance learning (16%), double major (13%), dual enrollment, honors program (5%), independent study, internships, student-designed major (2%), study abroad, teacher certificate program (6%). **Teacher certification offered in:** early childhood, special education, elementary, middle/junior high, secondary, bilingual/bicultural. **Reserve Officers Training Corps (ROTC):** Army ROTC: Offered at cooperating institution (University of Colorado); Navy ROTC: Offered at cooperating institution (University of Colorado); Air Force ROTC: Offered at cooperating institution (University of Colorado). **Faculty and instruction (2005-2006):** Total instructional faculty: 223 full-time, 1,119 part-time (47% men; 53% women; 9% minorities). Full-time faculty with Ph.D. or other terminal degree: 63%. Student/faculty ratio: 13/1. Classes of fewer than 20 students: 90%; of 20 to 49 students: 10%; of 50 or more students: 1%. **Advanced Placement and International Baccalaureate credit:** AP tests may be used for: Credit and/or placement. Scores accepted: 3, 4. International Baccalaureate exams may be used for: Credit and/or placement. **Freshmen returning for sophomore year:** 82%. **Graduation rates:** Four-year: 46%; five-year: 57%; six-year: 59%. **Graduate study:** 30% of students pursue further study immediately upon graduation; 29% within one year.

COSTS AND FINANCIAL AID

Financial aid office: (303) 458-4066. **Expenses (2006-2007):** Tuition and fees 2006-2007: $25,200; room/board: $8,470. Estimated books and supplies: $1,698; transportation: $675. **Financial aid:** Priority filing date for institution's financial aid form: March 1. In 2005-2006, 89% of undergraduates applied for financial aid. Of those, 59% were determined to have financial need; 37% had their need fully met. Average financial aid package (proportion receiving): $15,599 (59%). Average amount of gift aid, such as scholarships or grants (proportion receiving): $11,003 (49%). Average amount of self-help aid, such as work study or loans (proportion receiving): $4,596 (50%). Average need-based loan (excluding PLUS or other private loans): $2,417. Among students who received need-based aid, the average percent-age of need met: 50%. Among students who received aid based on merit, the average award (and the proportion receiving): $7,858 (8%). The average athletic scholarship (and the proportion receiving): $5,898 (5%).

CAMPUS LIFE AND EXTRACURRICULAR ACTIVITIES

Campus housing available (% using): coed dorms (83%), apartment for single students (16%), special housing for disabled students (1%). Students who live in college-owned, operated, or affiliated housing: 11%. **Student employment:** During the 2005-2006 academic year, 55% of undergraduates worked on campus. Average per-year earnings: $1,900. **Clubs and organizations:** Number of student organizations: 30. Activities include: choral groups, dance, drama/theater, jazz band, literary magazine, music ensembles, musical theater, radio station, student government, student newspaper, yearbook. Number of fraternities: 0; sororities: 0. Average proportion of students who stay on campus on weekends: 70%. **Sports program (2005-2006):** Member of NCAA II. *Men's intercollegiate varsity sports:* baseball, basketball, cross-country, golf, soccer. *Women's intercollegiate varsity sports:* basketball, cross-country, golf, lacrosse, soccer, softball, volleyball.

SERVICES AND FACILITIES

Basic services: nonremedial tutoring, placement service, health service, health insurance, other. **Remedial assistance:** reading, math, writing, study skills. **Counseling services:** career, personal, academic, older student, psychological, religious, other. **For learning-disabled students:** School does not offer a structured program with separate admission and additional fees. Total undergraduates in learning-disabled program or receiving services: 140. Services include: reading machines, tape recorders, note-taking services, oral tests, learning center, readers, extended time for tests, texts on tape, exams on tape or computer, other. **Library:** Number of titles: 300,000; number of current serial subscriptions: 800. **Information technology resources:** Students are not required to lease or own a computer. Number of campus computers available to all students: 337. School has a wireless network. Approximate number of users that can be accommodated: 2,500. Proportion of college-owned housing units wired for high-speed internet access: 100%. **Campus safety:** Security services offered: 24-hour foot-and-vehicle patrols, late-night transport/escort service, 24-hour emergency telephones, lighted pathways/sidewalks, controlled dormitory access (key, security card, etc).

TRANSFER AND INTERNATIONAL STUDENTS

Transfer students: May apply for admission for the following academic terms: Fall, Spring, Summer. Applicants need a minimum number of credits to apply. For fall 2005: Transfer applications received: 156. Transfer applicants offered admission: 103. Transfer applicants enrolled: 67. **International students:** Number of foreign undergraduates: 54 (1% of student body). Number of countries represented: 38. Minimum TOEFL score required: 550 (paper); 213 (computer). Average TOEFL score: 600 (paper).

United States Air Force Academy

- **Address:** HQ USAFA/RRS, 2304 Cadet Drive, Suite 200, USAF Academy, CO 80840
- **Website:** http://www.usafa.edu
- **Public**
- **Enrollment:** 4,316 full-time

KEY STATS

✔ **U.S News College Ranking:** Unranked Specialty School–Military Academies
✔ **SAT Score (25th/75th percentile):** 1200-1370
✔ **Tuition:** N/A

Selectivity: More selective	Room/board: N/A
Acceptance rate: 18%	Average debt: N/A
Student/faculty ratio: 8/1	Proportion who borrowed: N/A

UNDERGRADUATE STUDENT BODY STATS

2005-2006 enrollment: 4,316 full-time. Men: 82%; women: 18%. **Ethnic makeup:** African American: 5%; American-Indian: 2%; Asian American: 8%; Hispanic: 7%; White: 77%; International: 1%. **Religious preference:** Roman Catholic: 24%; Protestant: 65%; Jewish: 1%; No preference: 6%; Other: 4%.

ADMISSIONS FACTS AND FIGURES

Phone: (800) 443-9266. **Email:** rr_webmail@usafa.af.mil. **Website:** http://www.usafa.edu. **Application deadlines for fall 2007:** Regular decision: January 31. Early decision: Not offered. Early action: Not offered. Admission cannot be deferred. **Application fee:** None. Common application is not accepted. **To apply online, go to:** https://admissions.usafa.af.mil/secure/Online/Eligibility.htm. **Admissions requirements/recommendations:** High school units required (recommended): English: (4); Mathematics: (4); Science: (4); Foreign language: (2); Social studies: (3); History: (3). Tests: The college uses SAT or ACT scores in admissions decisions. Either SAT or ACT required. For admission to the fall 2007 entering class, the school will accept: ACT with writing. Campus visit: Recommended. Admissions interview: Required. Off-campus interview: Not available. **Factors that count in admissions decisions:** *Academic:* Secondary school record: Very important. Class rank: Important. Letters of recommendation: Considered. Standardized test scores: Very important. Essay: Very important. *Nonacademic:* Interview: Very important. Extracurricular activities: Very important. Talent/ability: Very important. Character/personal qualities: Very important. Alumni/ae relationship: Considered. Geographical residence: Not considered. State residency: Not considered. Religious affiliation/commitment: Not considered. Minority status: Considered. Volunteer work: Very important. Work experience: Very important. **Other schools with the greatest overlap in applicants:** United States Coast Guard Academy; United States Merchant Marine Academy; United States Military Academy; United States Naval Academy. **Admissions statistics for the fall 2005 entering class:** Total applicants: 9,601. Total accepted: 1,746. Freshmen enrolled: 1,402; Overall acceptance rate: 18%. **Size of waiting list:** 0 applicants; enrolled from waiting list: 0. **Credentials of fall 2005 freshmen:** 57% ranked in the top 10 percent of their high school class; 85% were in the top 25 percent, and 98% were in the top half. **Average high school grade point average:** 3.6. **First-year students who submitted SAT scores:** 55%. Scores (25/75 percentile): Verbal: 590-670, Math: 610-700, Combined: 1200-1370. **First-year students submitting ACT scores:** 33%. Scores (25/75 percentile): English: 26-31, Math: 27-32, Composite: 27-32.

ACADEMICS

Year founded: 1954. **Academic calendar:** Semester. **Degrees offered:** bachelor's. **Most popular majors:** Information not available. **Major fields of study:** biological and biomedical sciences; business, management, marketing, and related support services; computer and information sciences and support services; engineering; English language and literature/letters; history; legal professions and studies; liberal arts and sciences studies, and humanities; multi/interdisciplinary studies; physical sciences; social sciences. **Areas of required coursework:** humanities, computer literacy, mathematics, English (including composition), philosophy, foreign languages, sciences (biological or physical), history, social science, other. **Special academic programs:** double major, exchange student program (domestic), study abroad. **Faculty and instruction (2005-2006):** Total instructional faculty: 559 (81% men; 19% women). Full-time faculty with Ph.D. or other terminal degree: 52%. Student/faculty ratio: 8/1. **Advanced Placement and International Baccalaureate credit:** AP tests may be used for: Placement only. **Freshmen returning for sophomore year:** 90%. **Graduation rates:** Four-year: 83%; five-year: 85%; six-year: 81%.

COSTS AND FINANCIAL AID

Financial aid office: (719) 333-3160.

CAMPUS LIFE AND EXTRACURRICULAR ACTIVITIES

Campus housing available: coed dorms. Activities include: concert band, marching band, music ensembles, musical theater, pep band, student newspaper, yearbook. Number of fraternities: 0; sororities: 0. Average proportion of students who stay on campus on weekends: 100%. **Sports program (2005-2006):** Member of NCAA I. *Men's intercollegiate varsity sports:* baseball, basketball, cross-country, fencing, football, golf, gymnastics, ice hockey, lacrosse, sailing, swimming and diving, tennis, track and field (indoor), track and field (outdoor), water polo, wrestling, mixed rifle. *Women's intercollegiate varsity sports:* basketball, cross-country, fencing, gymnastics, soccer, swimming and diving, tennis, track and field (indoor), track and field (outdoor), volleyball, mixed rifle.

SERVICES AND FACILITIES

Basic services: nonremedial tutoring, health service, health insurance. **Counseling services:** military, personal, academic, religious, other. **Information technology resources:** Students are required to lease or own a computer. School has a wireless network. Proportion of college-owned hous-

ing units wired for high-speed internet access: 100%. **Campus safety:** Security services offered: 24-hour foot-and-vehicle patrols, late-night transport/escort service, 24-hour emergency telephones, lighted pathways/sidewalks, controlled dormitory access (key, security card, etc).

TRANSFER AND INTERNATIONAL STUDENTS

International students: Number of foreign undergraduates: 48 (1% of student body). Number of countries represented: 24.

University of Colorado—Boulder

■ **Address:** Regent Administration Center, Room 125, 552 UCB, Boulder, - CO 80309-0552
■ **Website:** http://www.colorado.edu
■ **Public**
■ **Enrollment:** 23,539 full-time; 2,303 part-time

KEY STATS

✔ **U.S News College Ranking:** 77, National Universities
✔ **ACT Score (25th/75th percentile):** 23-28
✔ **Tuition:** 2006-2007: $5,643 in state, $22,989 out of state
  Selectivity: More selective   **Room/board:** $8,300
  Acceptance rate: 88%   **Average debt:** $17,225
  Student/faculty ratio: 16/1   **Proportion who borrowed:** 44%

UNDERGRADUATE STUDENT BODY STATS

2005-2006 enrollment: 23,539 full-time; 2,303 part-time. Men: 53%; women: 47%. **Ethnic makeup:** African American: 2%; American-Indian: 1%; Asian American: 6%; Hispanic: 6%; White: 84%; International: 1%.

ADMISSIONS FACTS AND FIGURES

Phone: (303) 492-6301. **Email:** apply@colorado.edu. **Website:** http://www.colorado.edu. **Application deadlines for fall 2007:** Regular decision: January 15. Early decision: Not offered. Early action: Not offered. Admission can be deferred. **Application fee:** $50. Common application is not accepted. **To apply online, go to:** http://www.colorado.edu/prospective/freshman/apply.html. **Admissions requirements/recommendations:** High school units required (recommended): English: 4; Mathematics: 3; Science: 3; Foreign language: 3; Social studies: 3; History: 1; Total units: 16. Tests: The college uses SAT or ACT scores in admissions decisions. Either SAT or ACT required. For admission to the fall 2007 entering class, the school will accept: ACT with writing, ACT without writing. Campus visit: Recommended. Admissions interview: Neither required nor recommended. Off-campus interview: Not available. **Factors that count in admissions decisions:** *Academic:* Secondary school record: Very important. Class rank: Very important. Letters of recommendation: Important. Standardized test scores: Very important. Essay: Important. *Nonacademic:* Interview: Not considered. Extracurricular activities: Considered. Talent/ability: Considered. Character/personal qualities: Important. Alumni/ae relationship: Considered. Geographical residence: Considered. State residency: Important. Religious affiliation/commitment: Not considered. Minority status: Important. Volunteer work: Considered. Work experience: Considered. **Other schools with the greatest overlap in applicants:** Colorado State University; University of Arizona; University of California—Los Angeles; University of Illinois—Urbana-Champaign; University of Minnesota—Twin Cities. **Admissions statistics for the fall 2005 entering class:** Total applicants: 17,111. Total accepted: 15,003. Freshmen enrolled: 5,047; 37% were from out of state. Overall acceptance rate: 88%. **Size of waiting list:** 59 applicants; enrolled from waiting list: 3. **Credentials of fall 2005 freshmen:** 22% ranked in the top 10 percent of their high school class; 54% were in the top 25 percent, and 89% were in the top half. (Proportion submitting class standing: 75%.) **Average high school grade point average:** 3.5. **First-year students who submitted SAT scores:** 67%. Scores (25/75 percentile): Verbal: 530-630, Math: 550-650, Combined: 1080-1280. **First-year students submitting ACT scores:** 76%. Scores (25/75 percentile): English: 22-28, Math: 23-28, Composite: 23-28.

ACADEMICS

Year founded: 1876. **Academic calendar:** Semester. **Degrees offered:** bachelor's, master's, first professional, doctorate. **Most popular majors:** 16% social sciences, 15% business, management, marketing, and related support services, 10% communication, journalism, and related programs, 9% biological and biomedical sciences, 9% psychology. **Major fields of study:** architecture and related services; area, ethnic, cultural, and gender studies; biological and biomedical sciences; business, management, marketing, and related support services; communication, journalism, and related programs; computer and information sciences and support services; education; engineering; English language and literature/letters; foreign languages, literatures, and linguistics; health professions and related clinical sciences; history; liberal arts and sciences studies, and humanities; mathematics and statistics; multi/interdisciplinary studies; natural resources and conservation; philosophy and religious studies; physical sciences; psychology; social sciences; visual and performing arts. **Areas of required coursework:** humanities, mathematics, English (including composition), foreign languages, sciences (biological or physical), history, social science, other. **Pre-professional programs:** pre-law, pre-dentistry, pre-medicine, pre-veterinary science, pre-pharmacy, other. **Special academic programs (% participation):** accelerated program (5%), cooperative (work-study plan) program, cross-registration, distance learning (38%), double major (13%), dual enrollment (3%), English as a Second Language (ESL), exchange student program (domestic), honors program (16%), independent study (13%), internships (14%), liberal arts/career combination (2%), student-designed major, study abroad (26%), teacher certificate program (5%), other. **Teacher certification offered in:** elementary, secondary. **Cooperative education programs:** engineering. **Reserve Officers Training Corps (ROTC):** Army ROTC: Offered on campus; Navy ROTC: Offered on campus; Air Force ROTC: Offered on campus. **Faculty and instruction (2005-2006):** Total instructional faculty: 1,227 full-time, 559 part-time (61% men; 39% women; 12% minorities). Full-time faculty with Ph.D. or other terminal degree: 91%. Student/faculty ratio: 16/1. Classes of fewer than 20 students: 47%; of 20 to 49 students: 38%; of 50 or more students: 15%. **Advanced Placement and International Baccalaureate credit:** AP tests may be used for: Credit and/or placement. Scores accepted: 4, 5. International Baccalaureate exams may be used for: Credit and/or placement. **Freshmen returning for sophomore year:** 83%. **Graduation rates:** Four-year: 38%; five-year: 61%; six-year: 66%. **Graduate study:** 38% of students pursue further study within one year. Fields in which graduates pursue further study: Master of Business Administration (MBA), 9%; law, 3%; medicine, 5%; engineering, 2%; education, 8%; arts and sciences, 8%.

COSTS AND FINANCIAL AID

Financial aid office: (303) 492-5091. **Expenses (2006-2007):** Tuition and fees 2006-2007: $5,643 in state, $22,989 out of state; room/board: $8,300. **Financial aid:** Priority filing date for institution's financial aid form: April 1. In 2005-2006, 78% of undergraduates applied for financial aid. Of those, 33% were determined to have financial need; 65% had their need fully met. Average financial aid package (proportion receiving): $9,973 (32%). Average amount of gift aid, such as scholarships or grants (proportion receiving): $4,411 (30%). Average amount of self-help aid, such as work study or loans (proportion receiving): $5,455 (30%). Average need-based loan (excluding PLUS or other private loans): $5,039. Among students who received need-based aid, the average percentage of need met: 90%. Among students who received aid based on merit, the average award (and the proportion receiving): $2,667 (37%). The average athletic scholarship (and the proportion receiving): $16,770 (1%). Average amount of debt of borrowers graduating in 2005: $17,225. Proportion who borrowed: 44%.

CAMPUS LIFE AND EXTRACURRICULAR ACTIVITIES

Campus housing available: coed dorms, sorority housing, apartments for married students, apartment for single students, special housing for disabled students, other housing options. Students who live in college-owned, operated, or affiliated housing: 22%. **Student employment:** During the 2005-2006 academic year, 14% of undergraduates worked on campus. Average per-year earnings: $3,200. **Clubs and organizations:** Number of student organizations: 293. Activities include: choral groups, concert band, dance, drama/theater, jazz band, literary magazine, marching band, music ensembles, musical theater, opera, pep band, radio station, student government, student newspaper, student film society, symphony orchestra, television station, yearbook. Number of fraternities: 14; sororities: 11. Proportion of men in fraternities: 7%; of women in sororities: 9%. **Sports program (2005-2006):** Member of NCAA I. *Men's intercollegiate varsity sports:* alpine skiing, basketball, cross-country, football, golf, nordic skiing, tennis, track and field (indoor), track and field (outdoor). *Women's intercollegiate varsity sports:* alpine skiing, basketball, cross-country, golf, nordic skiing, soccer, tennis, track and field (indoor), track and field (outdoor), volleyball.

SERVICES AND FACILITIES

Basic services: nonremedial tutoring, women's center, placement service, day care, health service, health insurance, other. **Counseling services:** minor-

ity student, career, personal, veteran student, academic, older student, psychological, birth control, other. **For learning-disabled students:** School does not offer a structured program with separate admission and additional fees. Total undergraduates in learning-disabled program or receiving services: 220. Services include: reading machines, diagnostic testing service, learning center, proofreading services, texts on tape, other. **Library:** Number of titles: 3,554,826; number of current serial subscriptions: 26,152. **Information technology resources:** Students are not required to lease or own a computer. Number of campus computers available to all students: 2,300. School has a wireless network. Approximate number of users that can be accommodated: 4,000. Proportion of college-owned housing units wired for high-speed internet access: 100%. **Campus safety:** Security services offered: 24-hour foot-and-vehicle patrols, late-night transport/escort service, 24-hour emergency telephones, lighted pathways/sidewalks, student patrols, controlled dormitory access (key, security card, etc).

TRANSFER AND INTERNATIONAL STUDENTS

Transfer students: May apply for admission for the following academic terms: Fall, Spring, Summer. Applicants do not need a minimum number of credits to apply. For fall 2005: Transfer applications received: 2,974. Transfer applicants offered admission: 2,025. Transfer applicants enrolled: 1,219. **International students:** Number of foreign undergraduates: 341 (1% of student body). Number of countries represented: 87. Minimum TOEFL score required: 500 (paper); 173 (computer). Average TOEFL score: 582 (paper).

University of Colorado–Colorado Springs

- **Address:** 1420 Austin Bluffs Parkway, Colorado Springs, CO 80918
- **Website:** http://www.uccs.edu
- **Public**
- **Enrollment:** 4,827 full-time; 1,444 part-time

KEY STATS

✔ **U.S News College Ranking:** 34, Universities–Master's (West)
✔ **ACT Score (25th/75th percentile):** 21-25
✔ **Tuition:** 2006-2007: $5,384 in state, $16,622 out of state

Selectivity: Selective	**Room/board:** $7,642
Acceptance rate: 67%	**Average debt:** $12,438
Student/faculty ratio: 18/1	**Proportion who borrowed:** 48%

UNDERGRADUATE STUDENT BODY STATS

2005-2006 enrollment: 4,827 full-time; 1,444 part-time. Men: 39%; women: 61%. **Ethnic makeup:** African American: 4%; American-Indian: 1%; Asian American: 5%; Hispanic: 9%; White: 81%.

ADMISSIONS FACTS AND FIGURES

Phone: (719) 262-3383. **Email:** admrecor@uccs.edu. **Website:** http://www.uccs.edu. **Application deadlines for fall 2007:** Regular decision: July 1. Early decision: Not offered. Early action: Not offered. Admission can be deferred. **Application fee:** $50. Common application is not accepted. **To apply online, go to:** http://www.uccs.edu/appintro.htm. **Admissions requirements/recommendations:** High school units required (recommended): English: 4 (4); Mathematics: 3 (4); Science: 3 (3); Foreign language: 2 (3); Social studies: 2 (3); History: 0 (1); Academic electives: 1 (1); Total units: 15 (16). Tests: The college uses SAT or ACT scores in admissions decisions. Either SAT or ACT required. For admission to the fall 2007 entering class, the school will accept: ACT with writing, ACT without writing. Campus visit: Neither required nor recommended. Admissions interview: Neither required nor recommended. Off-campus interview: May be arranged. **Factors that count in admissions decisions:** *Academic:* Secondary school record: Very important. Class rank: Very important. Letters of recommendation: Important. Standardized test scores: Very important. Essay: Considered. *Nonacademic:* Interview: Not considered. Extracurricular activities: Considered. Talent/ability: Considered. Character/personal qualities: Considered. Alumni/ae relationship: Considered. Geographical residence: Considered. State residency: Considered. Religious affiliation/commitment: Not considered. Minority status: Not considered. Volunteer work: Considered. Work experience: Not considered. **Other schools with the greatest overlap in applicants:** Colorado State University; Colorado State University–Pueblo; University of Colorado–Boulder; University of Colorado–Denver and Health Sciences Center; University of Northern

Colorado. **Admissions statistics for the fall 2005 entering class:** Total applicants: 2,572. Total accepted: 1,724. Freshmen enrolled: 1,048; 6% were from out of state. Overall acceptance rate: 67%. **Credentials of fall 2005 freshmen:** 15% ranked in the top 10 percent of their high school class; 42% were in the top 25 percent, and 78% were in the top half. (Proportion submitting class standing: 91%.) **Average high school grade point average:** 3.4. **First-year students who submitted SAT scores:** 36%. Scores (25/75 percentile): Verbal: 490-600, Math: 480-590, Combined: 970-1190. **First-year students submitting ACT scores:** 91%. Scores (25/75 percentile): English: 20-25, Math: 19-25, Composite: 21-25.

ACADEMICS

Year founded: 1965. **Academic calendar:** Semester. **Degrees offered:** certificate, bachelor's, master's, doctorate. **Most popular majors:** 19% business administration and management, 11% communication studies/speech communication and rhetoric, 10% psychology, 9% nursing/registered nurse training (R.N., A.S.N., B.S.N., M.S.N.), 7% biology/biological sciences. **Major fields of study:** biological and biomedical sciences; business, management, marketing, and related support services; communication, journalism, and related programs; computer and information sciences and support services; engineering; English language and literature/letters; foreign languages, literatures, and linguistics; health professions and related clinical sciences; history; liberal arts and sciences studies, and humanities; mathematics and statistics; natural resources and conservation; philosophy and religious studies; physical sciences; psychology; social sciences; visual and performing arts. **Areas of required coursework:** humanities, mathematics, English (including composition), sciences (biological or physical), history, social science. **Pre-professional programs:** pre-law, pre-dentistry, pre-medicine, pre-veterinary science, pre-pharmacy, other. **Special academic programs (% participation):** accelerated program (1%), cooperative (work-study plan) program (20%), distance learning (8%), double major (3%), independent study (15%), internships (36%), study abroad (1%), teacher certificate program (4%). **Teacher certification offered in:** special education, elementary, middle/junior high, secondary. **Cooperative education programs:** art, business, computer science, education, engineering, health professions, natural science, social/behavioral science. **Reserve Officers Training Corps (ROTC):** Army ROTC: Offered on campus. **Faculty and instruction (2005-2006):** Total instructional faculty: 200 full-time, 356 part-time (51% men; 49% women; 11% minorities). Full-time faculty with Ph.D. or other terminal degree: 100%. Student/faculty ratio: 18/1. Classes of fewer than 20 students: 36%; of 20 to 49 students: 51%; of 50 or more students: 12%. **Advanced Placement and International Baccalaureate credit:** AP tests may be used for: Credit only. Scores accepted: 4. **Freshmen returning for sophomore year:** 68%. **Graduation rates:** Four-year: 16%; five-year: 34%; six-year: 39%. **Graduate study:** 30% of students pursue further study immediately upon graduation; 32% within one year. Fields in which graduates pursue further study: Master of Business Administration (MBA), 12%; law, 1%; dentistry, 1%; education, 7%; arts and sciences, 50%.

COSTS AND FINANCIAL AID

Financial aid office: (719) 262-3460. **Expenses (2006-2007):** Tuition and fees 2006-2007: $5,384 in state, $16,622 out of state; room/board: $7,642. Estimated books and supplies: $1,296; transportation: $1,072; personal expenses: $2,908. **Financial aid:** Priority filing date for institution's financial aid form: April 1. In 2005-2006, 80% of undergraduates applied for financial aid. Of those, 54% were determined to have financial need; 11% had their need fully met. Average financial aid package (proportion receiving): $6,508 (51%). Average amount of gift aid, such as scholarships or grants (proportion receiving): $4,960 (34%). Average amount of self-help aid, such as work study or loans (proportion receiving): $3,823 (41%). Average need-based loan (excluding PLUS or other private loans): $3,603. Among students who received need-based aid, the average percentage of need met: 53%. Among students who received aid based on merit, the average award (and the proportion receiving): $1,709 (8%). The average athletic scholarship (and the proportion receiving): $2,438 (1%). Average amount of debt of borrowers graduating in 2005: $12,438. Proportion who borrowed: 48%.

CAMPUS LIFE AND EXTRACURRICULAR ACTIVITIES

Campus housing available (% using): coed dorms, women's dorms (40%), men's dorms (30%), apartment for single students (30%), special housing for disabled students. Students who live in college-owned, operated, or affiliated housing: 13%. **Student employment:** During the 2005-2006 academic year, 16% of undergraduates worked on campus. Average per-year earnings: $4,300. **Clubs and organizations:** Number of student organizations: 79. Activities include: choral groups, dance, drama/theater, jazz band, literary magazine, music ensembles, musical theater, radio station, student govern-

ment, student newspaper, student film society. ; sororities: 1. of women in sororities: 1%. **Sports program (2005-2006):** Member of NCAA II. *Men's intercollegiate varsity sports:* basketball, cross-country, golf, soccer, tennis, track and field (indoor), track and field (outdoor). *Women's intercollegiate varsity sports:* basketball, cross-country, softball, tennis, track and field (indoor), track and field (outdoor), volleyball.

SERVICES AND FACILITIES

Basic services: nonremedial tutoring, placement service, day care, health service, health insurance. **Remedial assistance:** reading, math, writing, other. **Counseling services:** minority student, career, military, personal, veteran student, academic, older student, psychological. **For learning-disabled students:** School does not offer a structured program with separate admission and additional fees. Services include: remedial math, remedial English, reading machines, remedial reading, tape recorders, other special classes, videotaped classes, diagnostic testing service, untimed tests, note-taking services, oral tests, learning center, readers, extended time for tests, tutors, priority seating, other testing accomodations, other. **Library:** Number of titles: 714,027; number of current serial subscriptions: 4,649. **Information technology resources:** Students are not required to lease or own a computer. School has a wireless network. Proportion of college-owned housing units wired for high-speed internet access: 100%. **Campus safety:** Security services offered: 24-hour foot-and-vehicle patrols, late-night transport/escort service, 24-hour emergency telephones, lighted pathways/sidewalks, student patrols, controlled dormitory access (key, security card, etc).

TRANSFER AND INTERNATIONAL STUDENTS

Transfer students: May apply for admission for the following academic terms: Fall, Spring, Summer. Applicants need a minimum number of credits to apply. For fall 2005: Transfer applications received: 1,377. Transfer applicants offered admission: 931. Transfer applicants enrolled: 581. **International students:** Number of foreign undergraduates: 23. Number of countries represented: 48. Minimum TOEFL score required: 550 (paper); 220 (computer). Average TOEFL score: 596 (paper).

University of Denver

- **Address:** 2199 S. University Boulevard, Denver, CO 80208
- **Website:** http://www.du.edu
- **Private**
- **Enrollment:** 4,431 full-time; 148 part-time

KEY STATS

✔ **U.S News College Ranking:** 88, National Universities
✔ **ACT Score (25th/75th percentile):** 23-28
✔ **Tuition:** 2006-2007: $30,372

Selectivity: More selective	**Room/board:** $9,228
Acceptance rate: 82%	**Average debt:** $22,663
Student/faculty ratio: 9/1	**Proportion who borrowed:** 43%

UNDERGRADUATE STUDENT BODY STATS

2005-2006 enrollment: 4,431 full-time; 148 part-time. Men: 48%; women: 52%. **Ethnic makeup:** African American: 2%; American-Indian: 1%; Asian American: 5%; Hispanic: 6%; White: 82%; International: 4%.

ADMISSIONS FACTS AND FIGURES

Phone: (303) 871-2036. **Email:** admission@du.edu. **Website:** http://www.du.edu. **Application deadlines for fall 2007:** Regular decision: January 15; decision sent by March 15. Early decision: Not offered. Early action: Send application by: November 1; Decision sent by: January 15. Admission can be deferred. **Application fee:** $50. Common application is accepted. **To apply online, go to:** http://www.du.edu/admission/app.html. **Admissions requirements/recommendations:** High school units required (recommended): English: (4); Mathematics: (4); Science: (4); Foreign language: (3); Social studies: (2); History: (2); Total units: (21). Tests: The college uses SAT or ACT scores in admissions decisions. Either SAT or ACT required. For admission to the fall 2007 entering class, the school will accept ACT with writing, ACT without writing. Campus visit: Recommended. Admissions interview: Required. Off-campus interview: May be arranged. **Factors that count in admissions decisions:** *Academic:* Secondary school record: Very important. Class rank: Not considered. Letters of recommendation: Important. Standardized test scores: Very important. Essay: Important. *Nonacademic:* Interview: Very important. Extracurricular activities: Important. Talent/ability: Important. Character/personal qualities: Very important. Alumni/ae relationship: Not considered. Geographical residence: Not considered. State residency: Not considered. Religious affiliation/commitment: Not considered. Minority status: Not considered. Volunteer work: Important. Work experience: Important. **Other schools with the greatest overlap in applicants:** Boston University; Colorado College; Colorado State University; University of Colorado–Boulder; University of Vermont. **Admissions statistics for the fall 2005 entering class:** Total applicants: 4,038. Total accepted: 3,304. Freshmen enrolled: 1,092; 55% were from out of state. Accepted through early-decision or early-action plans: 40%. Overall acceptance rate: 82%. Non-early acceptance rate: 78%. **Size of waiting list:** 123 applicants; enrolled from waiting list: 14. **Credentials of fall 2005 freshmen:** 36% ranked in the top 10 percent of their high school class; 69% were in the top 25 percent, and 90% were in the top half. (Proportion submitting class standing: 60%.) **Average high school grade point average:** 3.6. **First-year students who submitted SAT scores:** 70%. Scores (25/75 percentile): Verbal: 530-630, Math: 530-640, Combined: 1060-1270. **First-year students submitting ACT scores:** 71%. Scores (25/75 percentile): English: 23-29, Math: 23-28, Composite: 23-28.

ACADEMICS

Year founded: 1864. **Academic calendar:** Quarter. **Degrees offered:** certificate, bachelor's, post-bachelor's certificate, master's, post-master's certificate, first professional, doctorate. **Most popular majors:** 44% business, management, marketing, and related support services, 11% communication, journalism, and related programs, 10% social sciences, 6% biological and biomedical sciences, 6% visual and performing arts. **Major fields of study:** agriculture, agriculture operations, and related sciences; area, ethnic, cultural, and gender studies; biological and biomedical sciences; business, management, marketing, and related support services; communication, journalism, and related programs; computer and information sciences and support services; education; engineering; English language and literature/letters; foreign languages, literatures, and linguistics; history; mathematics and statistics; multi/interdisciplinary studies; natural resources and conservation; philosophy and religious studies; physical sciences; psychology; public administration and social service professions; social sciences; visual and performing arts. **Areas of required coursework:** humanities, mathematics, English (including composition), foreign languages, sciences (biological or physical), social science. **Pre-professional programs:** pre-law, pre-dentistry, pre-medicine, pre-theology, pre-veterinary science, pre-optometry, pre-pharmacy. **Special academic programs (% participation):** accelerated program, cooperative (work-study plan) program, double major (7%), dual enrollment, English as a Second Language (ESL), honors program (7%), independent study (35%), internships (29%), student-designed major, study abroad (37%), teacher certificate program, weekend college, other. **Teacher certification offered in:** elementary, middle/junior high, secondary. **Reserve Officers Training Corps (ROTC):** Army ROTC: Offered at cooperating institution (Univ of Colorado (Boulder)); Air Force ROTC: Offered at cooperating institution (Univ of Colorado (Boulder)). **Faculty and instruction (2005-2006):** Total instructional faculty: 386 full-time, 274 part-time. Full-time faculty with Ph.D. or other terminal degree: 90%. Student/faculty ratio: 9/1. Classes of fewer than 20 students: 60%; of 20 to 49 students: 36%; of 50 or more students: 4%. **Advanced Placement and International Baccalaureate credit:** AP tests may be used for: Credit and/or placement. Scores accepted: 3, 4, 5. International Baccalaureate exams may be used for: Credit and/or placement. **Freshmen returning for sophomore year:** 86%. **Graduation rates:** Four-year: 52%; five-year: 67%; six-year: 70%. **Graduate study:** 20% of students pursue further study immediately upon graduation; 15% within one year; 47% within five years.

COSTS AND FINANCIAL AID

Financial aid office: (303) 871-4020. **Expenses (2006-2007):** Tuition and fees 2006-2007: $30,372; room/board: $9,228. Estimated books and supplies: $1,698; transportation: $675; personal expenses: $1,161. **Financial aid:** Priority filing date for institution's financial aid form: March 1. In 2005-2006, 53% of undergraduates applied for financial aid. Of those, 42% were determined to have financial need; 13% had their need fully met. Average financial aid package (proportion receiving): $20,508 (42%). Average amount of gift aid, such as scholarships or grants (proportion receiving): $16,365 (41%). Average amount of self-help aid, such as work study or loans (proportion receiving): $4,250 (37%). Average need-based loan (excluding PLUS or other private loans): $3,745. Among students who received need-based aid, the average percentage of need met: 71%. Among students who received aid based on merit, the average award (and the proportion receiving): $8,313 (33%). The average athletic scholarship (and the proportion

receiving): $24,969 (4%). Average amount of debt of borrowers graduating in 2005: $22,663. Proportion who borrowed: 43%.

CAMPUS LIFE AND EXTRACURRICULAR ACTIVITIES

Campus housing available (% using): coed dorms (79%), sorority housing (7%), fraternity housing (5%), apartments for married students (1%), apartment for single students (7%), special housing for disabled students (1%). Students who live in college-owned, operated, or affiliated housing: 45%. **Student employment:** During the 2005-2006 academic year, 11% of undergraduates worked on campus. Average per-year earnings: $2,000. **Clubs and organizations:** Number of student organizations: 82. Activities include: choral groups, concert band, dance, drama/theater, jazz band, literary magazine, music ensembles, musical theater, opera, pep band, radio station, student government, student newspaper, student film society, symphony orchestra. Number of fraternities: 8; sororities: 5. Proportion of men in fraternities: 20%; of women in sororities: 19%. Average proportion of students who stay on campus on weekends: 55%. **Sports program (2005-2006):** Member of NCAA I. *Men's intercollegiate varsity sports:* alpine skiing, basketball, golf, ice hockey, lacrosse, nordic skiing, skiing, soccer, swimming and diving, tennis. *Women's intercollegiate varsity sports:* alpine skiing, basketball, golf, gymnastics, lacrosse, nordic skiing, skiing, soccer, swimming and diving, tennis, volleyball.

SERVICES AND FACILITIES

Basic services: nonremedial tutoring, women's center, placement service, health service, health insurance. **Counseling services:** minority student, career, military, personal, veteran student, academic, older student, psychological, birth control, religious. **For learning-disabled students:** School does not offer a structured program with separate admission and additional fees. Total undergraduates in learning-disabled program or receiving services: 205. Services include: reading machines, tape recorders, videotaped classes, diagnostic testing service, note-taking services, oral tests, learning center, readers, extended time for tests, tutors, priority registration, texts on tape, other. **Library:** Number of titles: 2,172,470; number of current serial subscriptions: 6,890. **Information technology resources:** Students are required to lease or own a computer. Number of campus computers available to all students: 108. School has a wireless network. Approximate number of users that can be accommodated: 14,000. Proportion of college-owned housing units wired for high-speed internet access: 95%. **Campus safety:** Security services offered: 24-hour foot-and-vehicle patrols, late-night transport/escort service, 24-hour emergency telephones, lighted pathways/sidewalks, controlled dormitory access (key, security card, etc).

TRANSFER AND INTERNATIONAL STUDENTS

Transfer students: May apply for admission for the following academic terms: Fall, Winter, Spring, Summer. Applicants do not need a minimum number of credits to apply. For fall 2005: Transfer applications received: 645. Transfer applicants offered admission: 387. Transfer applicants enrolled: 220. **International students:** Number of foreign undergraduates: 188 (4% of student body). Number of countries represented: 48. Minimum TOEFL score required: 525 (paper); 193 (computer). Average TOEFL score: 580 (paper).

University of Northern Colorado

- **Address:** Greeley, CO 80639
- **Website:** http://www.unco.edu
- **Public**
- **Enrollment:** 9,929 full-time; 1,220 part-time

KEY STATS

✔ **U.S News College Ranking:** fourth tier, National Universities
✔ **ACT Score (25th/75th percentile):** 20-24
✔ **Tuition:** 2006-2007: $6,014 in state, $12,530 out of state

Selectivity: Selective	**Room/board:** $6,832
Acceptance rate: 82%	**Average debt:** N/A
Student/faculty ratio: 24/1	**Proportion who borrowed:** N/A

UNDERGRADUATE STUDENT BODY STATS

2005-2006 enrollment: 9,929 full-time; 1,220 part-time. Men: 39%; women: 61%. **Ethnic makeup:** African American: 3%; American-Indian: 1%; Asian American: 3%; Hispanic: 8%; White: 84%.

ADMISSIONS FACTS AND FIGURES

Phone: (970) 351-2881. **Email:** admissions.help@unco.edu. **Website:** http://www.unco.edu. **Application deadlines for fall 2007:** Regular decision: August 1. Early decision: Not offered. Early action: Not offered. Admission can be deferred. **Application fee:** $40. Common application is not accepted. **To apply online, go to:** http://www.unco.edu/decide.html. **Admissions requirements/recommendations:** High school units required (recommended): English: (4); Mathematics: 3; Science: (3); Social studies: (3); Total units: 15. Tests: The college uses SAT or ACT scores in admissions decisions. Either SAT or ACT required. For admission to the fall 2007 entering class, the school will accept: ACT with writing, ACT without writing. Campus visit: Recommended. Admissions interview: Neither required nor recommended. Off-campus interview: May be arranged. **Factors that count in admissions decisions:** *Academic:* Secondary school record: Considered. Class rank: Very important. Letters of recommendation: Important. Standardized test scores: Very important. Essay: Not considered. *Nonacademic:* Interview: Considered. Extracurricular activities: Considered. Talent/ability: Considered. Character/personal qualities: Considered. Alumni/ae relationship: Not considered. Geographical residence: Not considered. State residency: Considered. Religious affiliation/commitment: Not considered. Minority status: Considered. Volunteer work: Not considered. Work experience: Considered. **Other schools with the greatest overlap in applicants:** Colorado State University; Mesa State College; Metropolitan State College of Denver; University of Denver. **Admissions statistics for the fall 2005 entering class:** Total applicants: 7,318. Total accepted: 6,025. Freshmen enrolled: 2,494; 10% were from out of state. Overall acceptance rate: 82%. **Credentials of fall 2005 freshmen:** 10% ranked in the top 10 percent of their high school class; 32% were in the top 25 percent, and 68% were in the top half. (Proportion submitting class standing: 87%.) **Average high school grade point average:** 3.2. **First-year students who submitted SAT scores:** 27%. Scores (25/75 percentile): Verbal: 480-580, Math: 470-580, Combined: 950-1160. **First-year students submitting ACT scores:** 93%. Scores (25/75 percentile): English: 19-25, Math: 18-24, Composite: 20-24.

ACADEMICS

Year founded: 1890. **Academic calendar:** Semester. **Degrees offered:** bachelor's, master's, post-master's certificate, doctorate. **Most popular majors:** 15% multi/interdisciplinary studies, 13% business administration and management, 11% social sciences, 10% health professions and related clinical sciences, 9% communication, journalism, and related programs. **Major fields of study:** area, ethnic, cultural, and gender studies; biological and biomedical sciences; business, management, marketing, and related support services; communication, journalism, and related programs; education; English language and literature/letters; family and consumer sciences/human sciences; foreign languages, literatures, and linguistics; health professions and related clinical sciences; history; mathematics and statistics; multi/interdisciplinary studies; parks, recreation, leisure, and fitness studies; philosophy and religious studies; physical sciences; psychology; public administration and social service professions; security and protective services; social sciences; visual and performing arts. **Areas of required coursework:** arts/fine arts, mathematics, English (including composition), sciences (biological or physical), history, social science. **Pre-professional programs:** pre-law, pre-dentistry, pre-medicine, pre-veterinary science, pre-optometry, pre-pharmacy, other. **Special academic programs:** cooperative (work-study plan) program, cross-registration, distance learning, double major, dual enrollment, English as a Second Language (ESL), exchange student program (domestic), external degree program, honors program, independent study, internships, student-designed major, study abroad, teacher certificate program. **Teacher certification offered in:** early childhood, special education, elementary, middle/junior high, secondary, bilingual/bicultural. **Reserve Officers Training Corps (ROTC):** Army ROTC: Offered on campus; Air Force ROTC: Offered on campus. **Faculty and instruction (2005-2006):** Total instructional faculty: 400 full-time, 201 part-time (47% men; 53% women; 9% minorities). Full-time faculty with Ph.D. or other terminal degree: 81%. Student/faculty ratio: 24/1. Classes of fewer than 20 students: 26%; of 20 to 49 students: 58%; of 50 or more students: 16%. **Advanced Placement and International Baccalaureate credit:** AP tests may be used for: Credit only. Scores accepted: 3, 4, 5. International Baccalaureate exams may be used for: Credit only. **Freshmen returning for sophomore year:** 70%. **Graduation rates:** Four-year: 26%; five-year: 42%; six-year: 46%. **Graduate study:** 5% of students pursue further study within one year.

COSTS AND FINANCIAL AID

Financial aid office: (970) 351-2502. **Expenses (2006-2007):** Tuition and fees 2006-2007: $6,014 in state, $12,530 out of state; room/board: $6,832. **Financial aid:** Priority filing date for institution's financial aid form: March 1.

In 2005-2006, 79% of undergraduates applied for financial aid. Of those, 45% were determined to have financial need; 53% had their need fully met. Average financial aid package (proportion receiving): $9,529 (44%). Average amount of gift aid, such as scholarships or grants (proportion receiving): $3,747 (23%). Average amount of self-help aid, such as work study or loans (proportion receiving): $4,169 (39%). Average need-based loan (excluding PLUS or other private loans): $3,618. Among students who received need-based aid, the average percentage of need met: 100%. Among students who received aid based on merit, the average award (and the proportion receiving): $2,632 (9%). The average athletic scholarship (and the proportion receiving): $5,067 (1%).

CAMPUS LIFE AND EXTRACURRICULAR ACTIVITIES

Campus housing available (% using): coed dorms (85%), women's dorms (2%), sorority housing (2%), fraternity housing (2%), apartments for married students (2%), apartment for single students (4%), special housing for disabled students (3%). Students who live in college-owned, operated, or affiliated housing: 32%. **Student employment:** During the 2005-2006 academic year, 15% of undergraduates worked on campus. Average per-year earnings: $1,631. **Clubs and organizations:** Number of student organizations: 137. Activities include: choral groups, concert band, dance, drama/theater, jazz band, literary magazine, marching band, music ensembles, musical theater, opera, pep band, radio station, student government, student newspaper, student film society, symphony orchestra. Number of fraternities: 9; sororities: 8. Proportion of men in fraternities: 6%; of women in sororities: 4%. Average proportion of students who stay on campus on weekends: 64%. **Sports program (2005-2006):** Member of NCAA I. *Men's intercollegiate varsity sports:* baseball, basketball, football, golf, tennis, track and field (outdoor), wrestling. *Women's intercollegiate varsity sports:* basketball, cross-country, golf, soccer, softball, swimming and diving, tennis, track and field (outdoor), volleyball.

SERVICES AND FACILITIES

Basic services: nonremedial tutoring, women's center, placement service, health service, health insurance. **Remedial assistance:** study skills. **Counseling services:** career, personal, psychological, birth control. **For learning-disabled students:** School does not offer a structured program with separate admission and additional fees. Services include: tape recorders, note-taking services, readers, extended time for tests, texts on tape, other testing accomodations. **Library:** Number of titles: 1,035,975; number of current serial subscriptions: 2,713. **Information technology resources:** Students are not required to lease or own a computer. Number of campus computers available to all students: 836. School has a wireless network. Approximate number of users that can be accommodated: 11,500. Proportion of college-owned housing units wired for high-speed internet access: 100%. **Campus safety:** Security services offered: 24-hour foot-and-vehicle patrols, late-night transport/escort service, 24-hour emergency telephones, lighted pathways/sidewalks, student patrols, controlled dormitory access (key, security card, etc).

TRANSFER AND INTERNATIONAL STUDENTS

Transfer students: May apply for admission for the following academic terms: Fall, Spring, Summer. Applicants do not need a minimum number of credits to apply. For fall 2005: Transfer applications received: 2,100. Transfer applicants offered admission: 1,515. Transfer applicants enrolled: 907. **International students:** Number of foreign undergraduates: 34. Number of countries represented: 48. Minimum TOEFL score required: 520 (paper). Average TOEFL score: 532 (paper).

Univ. of CO–Denver & Health Sci. Center

- **Address:** Campus Box 167 PO Box 173364, Denver, CO 80217-3364
- **Website:** http://www.cudenver.edu
- **Public**
- **Enrollment:** 5,900 full-time; 4,487 part-time

KEY STATS

✔ **U.S News College Ranking:** third tier, National Universities
✔ **ACT Score (25th/75th percentile):** 20-25
✔ **Tuition:** 2006-2007: $5,021 in state, $16,191 out of state

Selectivity: Selective	**Room/board:** N/A
Acceptance rate: 69%	**Average debt:** $20,444
Student/faculty ratio: 15/1	**Proportion who borrowed:** 51%

UNDERGRADUATE STUDENT BODY STATS

2005-2006 enrollment: 5,900 full-time; 4,487 part-time. Men: 43%; women: 57%. **Ethnic makeup:** African American: 4%; American-Indian: 1%; Asian American: 10%; Hispanic: 11%; White: 72%; International: 2%.

ADMISSIONS FACTS AND FIGURES

Phone: (303) 556-2704. **Email:** admissions@carbon.cudenver.edu. **Website:** http://www.cudenver.edu. **Application deadlines for fall 2007:** Regular decision: Rolling. Early decision: Not offered. Early action: Not offered. Admission can be deferred. **Application fee:** $50. Common application is not accepted. **Admissions requirements/recommendations:** High school units required (recommended): English: 4 (4); Mathematics: 3 (3); Science: 3 (3); Foreign language: 2 (3); Social studies: 2 (2); History: 1 (1); Academic electives: 1 (1); Total units: 16 (16). Tests: The college uses SAT or ACT scores in admissions decisions. Either SAT or ACT required. For admission to the fall 2007 entering class, the school will accept: ACT with writing, ACT without writing. Campus visit: Recommended. Admissions interview: Neither required nor recommended. Off-campus interview: May be arranged. **Factors that count in admissions decisions:** *Academic:* Secondary school record: Very important. Class rank: Very important. Letters of recommendation: Important. Standardized test scores: Very important. Essay: Important. *Nonacademic:* Interview: Not considered. Extracurricular activities: Considered. Talent/ability: Considered. Character/personal qualities: Considered. Alumni/ae relationship: Not considered. Geographical residence: Not considered. State residency: Not considered. Religious affiliation/commitment: Not considered. Minority status: Not considered. Volunteer work: Not considered. Work experience: Not considered. **Admissions statistics for the fall 2005 entering class:** Total applicants: 2,681. Total accepted: 1,852. Freshmen enrolled: 787; 5% were from out of state. Overall acceptance rate: 69%. **Credentials of fall 2005 freshmen:** 13% ranked in the top 10 percent of their high school class; 37% were in the top 25 percent, and 74% were in the top half. (Proportion submitting class standing: 92%.) **Average high school grade point average:** 3.3. **First-year students who submitted SAT scores:** 27%. Scores (25/75 percentile): Verbal: 490-590, Math: 490-600, Combined: 980-1190. **First-year students submitting ACT scores:** 94%. Scores (25/75 percentile): English: 19-25, Math: 19-25, Composite: 20-25.

ACADEMICS

Year founded: 1912. **Academic calendar:** Semester. **Degrees offered:** bachelor's, master's, post-master's certificate, first professional, doctorate. **Most popular majors:** 23% business, management, marketing, and related support services, 14% social sciences, 12% health professions and related clinical sciences, 10% visual and performing arts, 8% communication, journalism, and related programs. **Major fields of study:** biological and biomedical sciences; business, management, marketing, and related support services; communication, journalism, and related programs; computer and information sciences and support services; engineering; English language and literature/letters; foreign languages, literatures, and linguistics; health professions and related clinical sciences; history; mathematics and statistics; multi/interdisciplinary studies; philosophy and religious studies; physical sciences; psychology; social sciences; visual and performing arts. **Areas of required coursework:** arts/fine arts, humanities, mathematics, English (including composition), sciences (biological or physical), social science, other. **Pre-professional programs:** pre-dentistry, pre-medicine, pre-veterinary science, pre-pharmacy, other. **Special academic programs:** accelerated program, cooperative (work-study plan) program, cross-registration, distance learning, double major, English as a Second Language (ESL), honors program, independent study, internships, student-designed major, study abroad, teacher certificate program, weekend college. **Teacher certification offered in:** early childhood, special education, elementary, secondary. **Cooperative education programs:** art, business, computer science, education, engineering, humanities, natural science, social/behavioral science. **Reserve Officers Training Corps (ROTC):** Army ROTC: Offered at cooperating institution (CU-Boulder); Air Force ROTC: Offered at cooperating institution (CU-Boulder). **Faculty and instruction (2005-2006):** Total instructional faculty: 579 full-time, 783 part-time (52% men; 48% women; 10% minorities). Full-time faculty with Ph.D. or other terminal degree: 82%. Student/faculty ratio: 15/1. Classes of fewer than 20 students: 41%; of 20 to 49 students: 53%; of 50 or more students: 7%. **Advanced Placement and International Baccalaureate credit:** AP tests may be used for: Credit only. Scores accepted: 4, 5. **Freshmen returning for sophomore year:** 69%. **Graduation rates:** Four-year: 16%; five-year: 32%; six-year: 42%. **Graduate study:** 9% of students pursue further study within one year.

COSTS AND FINANCIAL AID

Financial aid office: (303) 556-2886. **Expenses (2006-2007):** Tuition and fees 2006-2007: $5,021 in state, $16,191 out of state; room/board: N/A. **Financial aid:** Priority filing date for institution's financial aid form: April 1. In 2005-2006, 63% of undergraduates applied for financial aid. Of those, 52% were determined to have financial need; 3% had their need fully met. Average financial aid package (proportion receiving): $9,163 (48%). Average amount of gift aid, such as scholarships or grants (proportion receiving): $5,138 (31%). Average amount of self-help aid, such as work study or loans (proportion receiving): $4,547 (40%). Average need-based loan (excluding PLUS or other private loans): $4,306. Among students who received need-based aid, the average percentage of need met: 73%. Among students who received aid based on merit, the average award (and the proportion receiving): $1,524 (3%). The average athletic scholarship (and the proportion receiving): $0 (0%). Average amount of debt of borrowers graduating in 2005: $20,444. Proportion who borrowed: 51%.

CAMPUS LIFE AND EXTRACURRICULAR ACTIVITIES

Students who live in college-owned, operated, or affiliated housing: 0%. **Clubs and organizations:** Number of student organizations: 57. Activities include: choral groups, dance, drama/theater, jazz band, music ensembles, musical theater, student government, student newspaper. Number of fraternities: 0; sororities: 0.

SERVICES AND FACILITIES

Basic services: nonremedial tutoring, placement service, day care, health service, health insurance. **Counseling services:** minority student, career, personal, veteran student, academic. **For learning-disabled students:** School does not offer a structured program with separate admission and additional fees. Services include: reading machines, diagnostic testing service, note-taking services, oral tests, readers, extended time for tests, tutors. **Library:** Number of titles: 761,846; number of current serial subscriptions: 5,306. **Information technology resources:** Students are not required to lease or own a computer. Number of campus computers available to all students: 150. School has a wireless network. Approximate number of users that can be accommodated: 2,000. **Campus safety:** Security services offered: 24-hour foot-and-vehicle patrols, late-night transport/escort service, 24-hour emergency telephones, lighted pathways/sidewalks.

TRANSFER AND INTERNATIONAL STUDENTS

Transfer students: May apply for admission for the following academic terms: Fall, Spring, Summer. Applicants need a minimum number of credits to apply. For fall 2005: Transfer applications received: 2,036. Transfer applicants offered admission: 1,482. Transfer applicants enrolled: 987. **International students:** Number of foreign undergraduates: 119 (2% of student body). Number of countries represented: 60. Minimum TOEFL score required: 525 (paper); 197 (computer). Average TOEFL score: 589 (paper).

Western State College of Colorado

- **Address:** 600 N. Adams Street, Gunnison, CO 81231
- **Website:** http://www.western.edu
- **Public**
- **Enrollment:** 2,034 full-time; 143 part-time

KEY STATS

✔ **U.S News College Ranking:** fourth tier, Liberal Arts Colleges
✔ **ACT Score (25th/75th percentile):** 18-23
✔ **Tuition:** 2006-2007: $3,350 in state, $11,909 out of state

Selectivity: Less selective	**Room/board:** $6,976
Acceptance rate: 95%	**Average debt:** $16,000
Student/faculty ratio: 18/1	**Proportion who borrowed:** 67%

UNDERGRADUATE STUDENT BODY STATS

2005-2006 enrollment: 2,034 full-time; 143 part-time. Men: 60%; women: 40%. **Ethnic makeup:** African American: 2%; American-Indian: 1%; Asian American: 1%; Hispanic: 5%; White: 91%.

ADMISSIONS FACTS AND FIGURES

Phone: (800) 876-5309. **Email:** discover@western.edu. **Website:** http://www.western.edu. **Application deadlines for fall 2007:** Regular decision: August 1; decision sent by November 1. Early decision: Not offered.

Early action: Not offered. Admission can be deferred. **Application fee:** $30. Common application is accepted. **Admissions requirements/recommendations:** High school units required (recommended): English: 4 (4); Mathematics: 3 (4); Science: 2 (3); Foreign language: (2); Social studies: 2 (3); History: 2 (3); Academic electives: 3. Tests: The college uses SAT or ACT scores in admissions decisions. Either SAT or ACT required. For admission to the fall 2007 entering class, the school will accept: ACT with writing, ACT without writing. Campus visit: Recommended. Admissions interview: Neither required nor recommended. **Factors that count in admissions decisions:** *Academic:* Secondary school record: Very important. Class rank: Very important. Letters of recommendation: Considered. Standardized test scores: Very important. Essay: Considered. *Nonacademic:* Interview: Considered. Extracurricular activities: Important. Talent/ability: Important. Character/personal qualities: Important. Alumni/ae relationship: Considered. Geographical residence: Not considered. State residency: Not considered. Religious affiliation/commitment: Not considered. Minority status: Not considered. Volunteer work: Not considered. Work experience: Not considered. **Admissions statistics for the fall 2005 entering class:** Total applicants: 1,424. Total accepted: 1,355. Freshmen enrolled: 478; 21% were from out of state. Overall acceptance rate: 95%. **Credentials of fall 2005 freshmen:** 4% ranked in the top 10 percent of their high school class; 16% were in the top 25 percent, and 50% were in the top half. (Proportion submitting class standing: 86%.) **Average high school grade point average:** 3.0. **First-year students who submitted SAT scores:** 29%. Scores (25/75 percentile): Verbal: 460-570, Math: 450-550, Combined: 910-1120. **First-year students submitting ACT scores:** 85%. Scores (25/75 percentile): English: N/A, Math: N/A, Composite: 18-23.

ACADEMICS

Year founded: 1901. **Academic calendar:** Semester. **Degrees offered:** bachelor's. **Most popular majors:** 28% business, management, marketing, and related support services, 12% parks, recreation, leisure, and fitness studies, 9% psychology, 9% visual and performing arts, 8% biological and biomedical sciences. **Major fields of study:** biological and biomedical sciences; business, management, marketing, and related support services; communication, journalism, and related programs; computer and information sciences and support services; education; English language and literature/letters; foreign languages, literatures, and linguistics; history; mathematics and statistics; multi/interdisciplinary studies; natural resources and conservation; parks, recreation, leisure, and fitness studies; philosophy and religious studies; physical sciences; psychology; social sciences; visual and performing arts. **Areas of required coursework:** arts/fine arts, humanities, mathematics, English (including composition), sciences (biological or physical), history, social science. **Pre-professional programs:** pre-law, pre-medicine. **Special academic programs (% participation):** cooperative (work-study plan) program, distance learning (5%), double major (25%), dual enrollment (5%), exchange student program (domestic) (1%), honors program (5%), independent study, internships, liberal arts/career combination, study abroad, teacher certificate program (8%). **Teacher certification offered in:** special education, elementary, middle/junior high, secondary. **Cooperative education programs:** art, business, computer science, education, humanities, natural science, social/behavioral science. **Faculty and instruction (2005-2006):** Total instructional faculty: 104 full-time, 25 part-time (62% men; 38% women; 2% minorities). Full-time faculty with Ph.D. or other terminal degree: 80%. Student/faculty ratio: 18/1. Classes of fewer than 20 students: 46%; of 20 to 49 students: 52%; of 50 or more students: 1%. **Advanced Placement and International Baccalaureate credit:** AP tests may be used for: Credit only. International Baccalaureate exams may be used for: Credit and/or placement. **Freshmen returning for sophomore year:** 59%. **Graduation rates:** Six-year: 36%.

COSTS AND FINANCIAL AID

Financial aid office: (970) 943-3085. **Expenses (2006-2007):** Tuition and fees 2006-2007: $3,350 in state, $11,909 out of state; room/board: $6,976. Estimated books and supplies: $1,306; transportation: $1,075; personal expenses: $1,361. **Financial aid:** Priority filing date for institution's financial aid form: April 1. In 2005-2006, 67% of undergraduates applied for financial aid. Of those, 44% were determined to have financial need; 8% had their need fully met. Average financial aid package (proportion receiving): $8,800 (37%). Average amount of gift aid, such as scholarships or grants (proportion receiving): $2,500 (19%). Average amount of self-help aid, such as work study or loans (proportion receiving): $1,790 (33%). Average need-based loan (excluding PLUS or other private loans): $5,000. Among students who received need-based aid, the average percentage of need met: 40%. Among students who received aid based on merit, the average award (and the proportion receiving): $1,500 (25%). The average athletic scholarship (and the proportion receiving): $1,750 (7%). Average amount of debt of borrowers graduating in 2005: $16,000. Proportion who borrowed: 67%.

CAMPUS LIFE AND EXTRACURRICULAR ACTIVITIES

Campus housing available: coed dorms, women's dorms, men's dorms, apartments for married students, apartment for single students. Students who live in college-owned, operated, or affiliated housing: 30%. **Student employment:** During the 2005-2006 academic year, 30% of undergraduates worked on campus. Average per-year earnings: $1,500. **Clubs and organizations:** Number of student organizations: 45. Activities include: choral groups, concert band, dance, drama/theater, jazz band, literary magazine, music ensembles, pep band, radio station, student government, student newspaper, symphony orchestra, television station. Average proportion of students who stay on campus on weekends: 60%. **Sports program (2005-2006):** Member of NCAA II. *Men's intercollegiate varsity sports:* basketball, cross-country, football, skiing, track and field (indoor), track and field (outdoor), wrestling. *Women's intercollegiate varsity sports:* basketball, cross-country, skiing, track and field (indoor), track and field (outdoor), volleyball.

SERVICES AND FACILITIES

Basic services: nonremedial tutoring, placement service, day care, health service, health insurance. **Remedial assistance:** reading, math, writing, study skills. **Counseling services:** minority student, career, personal, veteran student, academic, older student, psychological, birth control. **For learning-disabled students:** School does not offer a structured program with separate admission and additional fees. Services include: remedial math, remedial English, remedial reading, diagnostic testing service, extended time for tests. **Library:** Number of titles: 158,698; number of current serial subscriptions: 719. **Information technology resources:** Students are not required to lease or own a computer. Number of campus computers available to all students: 425. Proportion of college-owned housing units wired for high-speed internet access: 100%. **Campus safety:** Security services offered: 24-hour foot-and-vehicle patrols, late-night transport/escort service, lighted pathways/sidewalks, controlled dormitory access (key, security card, etc).

TRANSFER AND INTERNATIONAL STUDENTS

Transfer students: May apply for admission for the following academic terms: Fall, Spring, Summer. Applicants do not need a minimum number of credits to apply. For fall 2005: Transfer applications received: 407. Transfer applicants offered admission: 388. Transfer applicants enrolled: 224. **International students:** Number of foreign undergraduates: 0. Minimum TOEFL score required: 550 (paper); 213 (computer). Average TOEFL score: 600 (paper).

Connecticut

Albertus Magnus College

- **Address:** 700 Prospect Street, New Haven, CT 06511
- **Website:** http://www.albertus.edu
- **Private; Religious affiliation:** Roman Catholic
- **Enrollment:** 1,695 full-time; 87 part-time

KEY STATS

✔ **U.S News College Ranking:** 24, Comp. Colleges–Bachelor's (North)
✔ **SAT Score (25th/75th percentile):** 770-1020
✔ **Tuition:** 2006-2007: $19,390

Selectivity: Less selective	**Room/board:** $8,403
Acceptance rate: 89%	**Average debt:** $15,530
Student/faculty ratio: 15/1	**Proportion who borrowed:** 92%

UNDERGRADUATE STUDENT BODY STATS

2005-2006 enrollment: 1,695 full-time; 87 part-time. Men: 28%; women: 72%. **Ethnic makeup:** African American: 27%; Asian American: 1%; Hispanic: 11%; White: 60%.

ADMISSIONS FACTS AND FIGURES

Phone: (800) 578-9160. **Email:** admissions@albertus.edu. **Website:** http://www.albertus.edu. **Application deadlines for fall 2007:** Regular decision: August 15. Early decision: Not offered. Early action: Not offered. Admission can be deferred. **Application fee:** $35. Common application is accepted. **Admissions requirements/recommendations:** High school units required (recommended): English: 4 (4); Mathematics: 3 (3); Science: 1 (1); Foreign language: 3 (3); History: 1 (1); Academic electives: 3 (3); Total units: 16 (16). Tests: The college uses SAT or ACT scores in admissions decisions. Neither SAT nor ACT required. Campus visit: Recommended. Admissions interview: Recommended. Off-campus interview: May be arranged. **Factors that count in admissions decisions:** *Academic:* Secondary school record: Important. Class rank: Important. Letters of recommendation: Very important. Standardized test scores: Important. Essay: Important. *Nonacademic:* Interview: Important. Extracurricular activities: Important. Talent/ability: Considered. Character/personal qualities: Important. Alumni/ae relationship: Not considered. Geographical residence: Not considered. State residency: Not considered. Religious affiliation/commitment: Not considered. Minority status: Not considered. Volunteer work: Considered. Work experience: Not considered. **Admissions statistics for the fall 2005 entering class:** Total applicants: 613. Total accepted: 545. Freshmen enrolled: 484; Overall acceptance rate: 89%. **Credentials of fall 2005 freshmen:** 4% ranked in the top 10 percent of their high school class; 49% were in the top 25 percent, and 95% were in the top half. (Proportion submitting class standing: 92%.) **Average high school grade point average:** 2.7. **First-year students who submitted SAT scores:** 96%. Scores (25/75 percentile): Verbal: 390-520, Math: 380-500, Combined: 770-1020. **First-year students submitting ACT scores:** 3%. Scores (25/75 percentile): English: N/A, Math: N/A, Composite: N/A.

ACADEMICS

Year founded: 1925. **Academic calendar:** Semester. **Degrees offered:** associate, bachelor's, master's. **Most popular majors:** 36% business, management, marketing, and related support services, 16% sociology, 14% psychology, 6% English language and literature, 5% biological and biomedical sciences. **Major fields of study:** biological and biomedical sciences; business, management, marketing, and related support services; communication, journalism, and related programs; computer and information sciences and support services; education; English language and literature/letters; foreign languages, literatures, and linguistics; health professions and related clinical sciences; history; liberal arts and sciences studies, and humanities; mathematics and statistics; multi/interdisciplinary studies; physical sciences; psychology; public administration and social service professions; security and protective services; social sciences; visual and performing arts. **Areas of required coursework:** arts/fine arts, humanities, computer literacy, mathematics, English (including composition), philosophy, sciences (biological or physi-

cal), history, social science, other. **Pre-professional programs:** pre-law, pre-dentistry, pre-medicine, pre-veterinary science, pre-optometry, pre-pharmacy. **Special academic programs (% participation):** accelerated program (82%), distance learning (30%), double major (2%), honors program (2%), internships (35%), teacher certificate program (20%). **Teacher certification offered in:** middle/junior high, secondary. **Faculty and instruction (2005-2006):** Total instructional faculty: 34 full-time, 137 part-time (55% men; 45% women; 11% minorities). Full-time faculty with Ph.D. or other terminal degree: 74%. Student/faculty ratio: 15/1. Classes of fewer than 20 students: 79%; of 20 to 49 students: 21%; of 50 or more students: 0%. **Advanced Placement and International Baccalaureate credit:** AP tests may be used for: Credit and/or placement. **Freshmen returning for sophomore year:** 73%. **Graduation rates:** Four-year: 46%; five-year: 56%; six-year: 54%. **Graduate study:** 20% of students pursue further study immediately upon graduation; 30% within one year; 5% within five years. Fields in which graduates pursue further study: Master of Business Administration (MBA), 25%; law, 5%; medicine, 5%; dentistry, 2%; education, 10%; arts and sciences, 5%; veterinary medicine, 1%.

COSTS AND FINANCIAL AID

Financial aid office: (203) 773-8508. **Expenses (2006-2007):** Tuition and fees 2006-2007: $19,390; room/board: $8,403. Estimated books and supplies: $1,070; transportation: $1,823; personal expenses: $2,781. **Financial aid:** Priority filing date for institution's financial aid form: February 15. In 2005-2006, 66% of undergraduates applied for financial aid. Of those, 62% were determined to have financial need; 59% had their need fully met. Average financial aid package (proportion receiving): $6,335 (62%). Average amount of gift aid, such as scholarships or grants (proportion receiving): $4,815 (32%). Average amount of self-help aid, such as work study or loans (proportion receiving): $3,895 (62%). Average need-based loan (excluding PLUS or other private loans): $3,638. Among students who received need-based aid, the average percentage of need met: 50%. Among students who received aid based on merit, the average award (and the proportion receiving): $4,500 (1%). Average amount of debt of borrowers graduating in 2005: $15,530. Proportion who borrowed: 92%.

CAMPUS LIFE AND EXTRACURRICULAR ACTIVITIES

Campus housing available (% using): coed dorms (85%), women's dorms (15%). **Student employment:** During the 2005-2006 academic year, 20% of undergraduates worked on campus. **Clubs and organizations:** Number of student organizations: 10. Activities include: drama/theater, literary magazine, student government. Number of fraternities: 0; sororities: 0. Average proportion of students who stay on campus on weekends: 60%. **Sports program (2005-2006):** Member of NCAA III. *Men's intercollegiate varsity sports:* baseball, basketball, cross-country, soccer, tennis. *Women's intercollegiate varsity sports:* basketball, cross-country, soccer, softball, swimming and diving, tennis, volleyball.

SERVICES AND FACILITIES

Basic services: placement service, health service, health insurance. **Remedial assistance:** reading, math, writing, study skills. **Counseling services:** career, personal, academic, religious. **For learning-disabled students:** School does not offer a structured program with separate admission and additional fees. Services include: remedial math, remedial English, remedial reading, tape recorders, untimed tests, learning center, extended time for tests. **Library:** Number of titles: 79,118; number of current serial subscriptions: 9,578. **Information technology resources:** Students are not required to lease or own a computer. Number of campus computers available to all students: 190. School has a wireless network. Proportion of college-owned housing units wired for high-speed internet access: 100%. **Campus safety:** Security services offered: 24-hour foot-and-vehicle patrols, late-night transport/escort service, 24-hour emergency telephones, lighted pathways/sidewalks, controlled dormitory access (key, security card, etc).

TRANSFER AND INTERNATIONAL STUDENTS

Transfer students: May apply for admission for the following academic terms: Fall, Spring, Summer. Applicants do not need a minimum number of credits to apply. For fall 2005: Transfer applications received: 79. Transfer applicants offered admission: 28. Transfer applicants enrolled: 28. **International students:** Number of foreign undergraduates: 6. Minimum TOEFL score required: 550 (paper).

Central Connecticut State University

- **Address:** 1615 Stanley Street, New Britain, CT 06050
- **Website:** http://www.ccsu.edu
- **Public**
- **Enrollment:** 7,445 full-time; 2,233 part-time

KEY STATS

✔ **U.S News College Ranking:** third tier, Universities–Master's (North)
✔ **SAT Score (25th/75th percentile):** 940-1130
✔ **Tuition:** 2006-2007: $6,442 in state, $13,570 out of state

Selectivity: Selective	**Room/board:** $7,890
Acceptance rate: 62%	**Average debt:** $13,000
Student/faculty ratio: 19/1	**Proportion who borrowed:** 50%

UNDERGRADUATE STUDENT BODY STATS

2005-2006 enrollment: 7,445 full-time; 2,233 part-time. Men: 49%; women: 51%. **Ethnic makeup:** African American: 8%; American-Indian: 1%; Asian American: 3%; Hispanic: 6%; White: 82%; International: 1%.

ADMISSIONS FACTS AND FIGURES

Phone: (860) 832-2278. **Email:** admissions@ccsu.edu. **Website:** http://www.ccsu.edu. **Application deadlines for fall 2007:** Regular decision: June 1. Early decision: Not offered. Early action: Not offered. Admission cannot be deferred. **Application fee:** $50. Common application is not accepted. **To apply online, go to:** http://www.ccsu.edu/admission/applying.htm. **Admissions requirements/recommendations:** High school units required (recommended): English: 4; Mathematics: 3 (1); Science: 2; Foreign language: (3); Social studies: 2; History: 1; Total units: 13 (4). Tests: The college uses SAT or ACT scores in admissions decisions. Either SAT or ACT required. For admission to the fall 2007 entering class, the school will accept: ACT with writing, ACT without writing. Campus visit: Neither required nor recommended. Admissions interview: Recommended. Off-campus interview: May be arranged. **Factors that count in admissions decisions:** *Academic:* Secondary school record: Very important. Class rank: Important. Letters of recommendation: Considered. Standardized test scores: Important. Essay: Considered. *Nonacademic:* Interview: Considered. Extracurricular activities: Considered. Talent/ability: Considered. Character/personal qualities: Not considered. Alumni/ae relationship: Not considered. Geographical residence: Not considered. State residency: Considered. Religious affiliation/commitment: Not considered. Minority status: Considered. Volunteer work: Not considered. Work experience: Not considered. **Admissions statistics for the fall 2005 entering class:** Total applicants: 5,549. Total accepted: 3,421. Freshmen enrolled: 1,356; 7% were from out of state. Overall acceptance rate: 62%. **Credentials of fall 2005 freshmen:** 7% ranked in the top 10 percent of their high school class; 27% were in the top 25 percent, and 68% were in the top half. (Proportion submitting class standing: 73%.) **First-year students who submitted SAT scores:** 99%. Scores (25/75 percentile): Verbal: 470-560, Math: 470-570, Combined: 940-1130.

ACADEMICS

Year founded: 1849. **Academic calendar:** Semester. **Degrees offered:** certificate, bachelor's, post-bachelor's certificate, master's, post-master's certificate, doctorate. **Most popular majors:** 28% business administration and management, 12% sociology, 8% psychology, 5% English language and literature, 5% communication studies/speech communication and rhetoric. **Major fields of study:** biological and biomedical sciences; business, management, marketing, and related support services; communication, journalism, and related programs; computer and information sciences and support services; construction trades; education; engineering; engineering technologies/technicians; English language and literature/letters; foreign languages, literatures, and linguistics; health professions and related clinical sciences; history; mathematics and statistics; multi/interdisciplinary studies; parks, recreation, leisure, and fitness studies; philosophy and religious studies; physical sciences; psychology; public administration and social service professions; social sciences; visual and performing arts. **Areas of required coursework:** arts/fine arts, humanities, computer literacy, mathematics, English (including composition), philosophy, foreign languages, sciences

(biological or physical), history, social science. **Special academic programs:** cooperative (work-study plan) program, distance learning, double major, English as a Second Language (ESL), exchange student program (domestic), honors program, independent study, internships, student-designed major, study abroad, teacher certificate program. **Teacher certification offered in:** early childhood, elementary, middle/junior high. **Cooperative education programs:** business, computer science, technologies, other. **Reserve Officers Training Corps (ROTC):** Army ROTC: Offered at cooperating institution (UCONN); Air Force ROTC: Offered at cooperating institution (UCONN). **Faculty and instruction (2005-2006):** Total instructional faculty: 416 full-time, 434 part-time (59% men; 41% women; 11% minorities). Full-time faculty with Ph.D. or other terminal degree: 78%. Student/faculty ratio: 19/1. Classes of fewer than 20 students: 41%; of 20 to 49 students: 58%; of 50 or more students: 1%. **Advanced Placement and International Baccalaureate credit:** AP tests may be used for: Credit only. Scores accepted: 3, 4, 5. **Freshmen returning for sophomore year:** 77%. **Graduation rates:** Four-year: 11%; five-year: 34%; six-year: 42%.

COSTS AND FINANCIAL AID

Financial aid office: (860) 832-2200. **Expenses (2006-2007):** Tuition and fees 2006-2007: $6,442 in state, $13,570 out of state; room/board: $7,890. Estimated books and supplies: $1,010; transportation: $588; personal expenses: $1,744. **Financial aid:** Priority filing date for institution's financial aid form: February 15; deadline: September 24. In 2005-2006, 71% of undergraduates applied for financial aid. Of those, 54% were determined to have financial need; 11% had their need fully met. Average financial aid package (proportion receiving): $6,820 (52%). Average amount of gift aid, such as scholarships or grants (proportion receiving): $2,254 (37%). Average amount of self-help aid, such as work study or loans (proportion receiving): $3,244 (44%). Average need-based loan (excluding PLUS or other private loans): $3,294. Among students who received need-based aid, the average percentage of need met: 72%. Among students who received aid based on merit, the average award (and the proportion receiving): $2,243 (1%). The average athletic scholarship (and the proportion receiving): $7,814 (1%). Average amount of debt of borrowers graduating in 2005: $13,000. Proportion who borrowed: 50%.

CAMPUS LIFE AND EXTRACURRICULAR ACTIVITIES

Campus housing available: coed dorms, women's dorms, men's dorms. Students who live in college-owned, operated, or affiliated housing: 21%. **Clubs and organizations:** Number of student organizations: 100. Activities include: choral groups, concert band, dance, drama/theater, jazz band, literary magazine, music ensembles, pep band, radio station, student government, student newspaper, television station, yearbook. Number of fraternities: 3; sororities: 2. Proportion of men in fraternities: 1%; of women in sororities: 1%. **Sports program (2005-2006):** Member of NCAA I. *Men's intercollegiate varsity sports:* baseball, basketball, cross-country, football, golf, soccer, track and field (indoor), track and field (outdoor). *Women's intercollegiate varsity sports:* basketball, cross-country, golf, lacrosse, soccer, softball, swimming and diving, track and field (indoor), track and field (outdoor), volleyball.

SERVICES AND FACILITIES

Basic services: nonremedial tutoring, women's center, placement service, day care, health service, health insurance. **Remedial assistance:** reading, math. **Counseling services:** minority student, career, personal, veteran student, academic, psychological, religious. **For learning-disabled students:** School does not offer a structured program with separate admission and additional fees. Total undergraduates in learning-disabled program or receiving services: 304. Services include: remedial math, remedial English, reading machines, tape recorders, note-taking services, oral tests, learning center, readers, extended time for tests, tutors. **Library:** Number of titles: 688,604; number of current serial subscriptions: 2,705. **Information technology resources:** Students are not required to lease or own a computer. Number of campus computers available to all students: 750. School has a wireless network. Approximate number of users that can be accommodated: 1,000. Proportion of college-owned housing units wired for high-speed internet access: 100%. **Campus safety:** Security services offered: 24-hour foot-and-vehicle patrols, late-night transport/escort service, 24-hour emergency telephones, lighted pathways/sidewalks, student patrols, controlled dormitory access (key, security card, etc).

TRANSFER AND INTERNATIONAL STUDENTS

Transfer students: May apply for admission for the following academic terms: Fall, Spring. Applicants need a minimum number of credits to apply. For fall 2005: Transfer applications received: 1,474. Transfer applicants offered admission: 1,127. Transfer applicants enrolled: 701. **International students:** Number of foreign undergraduates: 124 (1% of student body). Minimum TOEFL score required: 500 (paper); 177 (computer). Average TOEFL score: 500 (paper).

Connecticut College

- ■ **Address:** 270 Mohegan Avenue, New London, CT 06320-4196
- ■ **Website:** http://www.conncoll.edu
- ■ **Private**
- ■ **Enrollment:** 1,808 full-time; 79 part-time

KEY STATS

✔ **U.S News College Ranking:** 39, Liberal Arts Colleges
✔ **SAT Score (25th/75th percentile):** 1250-1390
✔ **Tuition:** N/A

Selectivity: More selective	**Room/board:** N/A
Acceptance rate: 35%	**Average debt:** $22,542
Student/faculty ratio: 10/1	**Proportion who borrowed:** 44%

UNDERGRADUATE STUDENT BODY STATS

2005-2006 enrollment: 1,808 full-time; 79 part-time. Men: 40%; women: 60%. **Ethnic makeup:** African American: 4%; Asian American: 4%; Hispanic: 5%; White: 82%; International: 5%. **Religious preference:** Roman Catholic: 20%; Protestant: 15%; Jewish: 15%; Muslim: 1%; Hindu: 1%; Buddhist: 1%; No preference: 30%; Other: 17%.

ADMISSIONS FACTS AND FIGURES

Phone: (860) 439-2200. **Email:** admission@conncoll.edu. **Website:** http://www.conncoll.edu. **Application deadlines for fall 2007:** Regular decision: January 1; decision sent by March 31. Early decision: Send application by: November 15; Decision sent by: December 15. Early action: Not offered. Admission can be deferred. **Application fee:** $60. Common application is accepted. **To apply online, go to:** http://www.conncoll.edu/admissions/applying/. **Admissions requirements/recommendations:** High school units required (recommended): English: (4); Mathematics: (4); Science: (4); Foreign language: (2); Social studies: (2); History: (3); Academic electives: (3). Tests: The college uses SAT or ACT scores in admissions decisions. Neither SAT nor ACT required. For admission to the fall 2007 entering class, the school will accept: ACT with writing, ACT without writing. Campus visit: Recommended. Admissions interview: Recommended. Off-campus interview: May be arranged. **Factors that count in admissions decisions:** *Academic:* Secondary school record: Very important. Class rank: Important. Letters of recommendation: Important. Standardized test scores: Considered. Essay: Very important. *Nonacademic:* Interview: Very important. Extracurricular activities: Very important. Talent/ability: Very important. Character/personal qualities: Very important. Alumni/ae relationship: Important. Geographical residence: Important. State residency: Considered. Religious affiliation/commitment: Considered. Minority status: Very important. Volunteer work: Important. Work experience: Important. **Other schools with the greatest overlap in applicants:** Bowdoin College; Brown University; Skidmore College; Tufts University; Vassar College. **Admissions statistics for the fall 2005 entering class:** Total applicants: 4,183. Total accepted: 1,477. Freshmen enrolled: 492; 85% were from out of state. Accepted through early-decision or early-action plans: 42%. Overall acceptance rate: 35%. Early-decision acceptance rate: 67%. Non-early acceptance rate: 33%. **Size of waiting list:** 1061 applicants; enrolled from waiting list: 80. **Credentials of fall 2005 freshmen:** 54% ranked in the top 10 percent of their high school class; 83% were in the top 25 percent, and 99% were in the top half. (Proportion submitting class standing: 36%.) **First-year students who submitted SAT scores:** 52%. Scores (25/75 percentile): Verbal: 630-700, Math: 620-690, Combined: 1250-1390. **First-year students submitting ACT scores:** 28%. Scores (25/75 percentile): English: N/A, Math: N/A, Composite: 26-29.

ACADEMICS

Year founded: 1911. **Academic calendar:** Semester. **Degrees offered:** bachelor's, master's. **Most popular majors:** 12% political science and government, 10% economics, 9% psychology, 8% English language and literature, 7% international relations and affairs. **Major fields of study:** architecture and related services; area, ethnic, cultural, and gender studies; biological and biomedical sciences; computer and information sciences and support services; education; engineering; English language and literature/letters; family and consumer sciences/human sciences; foreign languages, literatures, and linguistics; history; mathematics and statistics; multi/interdisciplinary studies; philosophy and religious studies; physical sciences; psychology; social sciences; visual and performing arts. **Areas of required coursework:** arts/fine arts, humanities, mathematics, foreign languages, sciences (biological or physical), history, social science, other. **Pre-professional programs:** other. **Special academic programs (% participation):** cross-registration (1%), double major (27%), exchange student program (domestic) (2%), honors program (18%), independent study (40%), internships (75%), student-designed major (3%), study abroad (54%), teacher certificate program (5%). **Teacher certification offered in:** early childhood, elementary, middle/junior high, secondary. **Faculty and instruction (2005-2006):** Total instructional faculty: 162 full-time, 80 part-time (57% men; 43% women; 14% minorities). Full-time faculty with Ph.D. or other terminal degree: 91%. Student/faculty ratio: 10/1. Classes of fewer than 20 students: 65%; of 20 to 49 students: 33%; of 50 or more students: 2%. **Advanced Placement and International Baccalaureate credit:** AP tests may be used for: Placement only. Scores accepted: 4, 5. International Baccalaureate exams may be used for: Credit and/or placement. **Freshmen returning for sophomore year:** 91%. **Graduation rates:** Four-year: 84%; five-year: 87%; six-year: 87%. **Graduate study:** 20% of students pursue further study immediately upon graduation.

COSTS AND FINANCIAL AID

Financial aid office: (860) 439-2058. **Financial aid:** In 2005-2006, 49% of undergraduates applied for financial aid. Of those, 42% were determined to have financial need; 100% had their need fully met. Average financial aid package (proportion receiving) $26,014 (42%). Average amount of gift aid, such as scholarships or grants (proportion receiving): $23,748 (38%). Average amount of self-help aid, such as work study or loans (proportion receiving): $4,848 (37%). Average need-based loan (excluding PLUS or other private loans): $4,076. Among students who received need-based aid, the average percentage of need met: 100%. Average amount of debt of borrowers graduating in 2005: $22,542. Proportion who borrowed: 44%.

CAMPUS LIFE AND EXTRACURRICULAR ACTIVITIES

Campus housing available (% using): coed dorms (95%), apartment for single students (4%), cooperative housing (1%). Students who live in college-owned, operated, or affiliated housing: 99%. **Student employment:** During the 2005-2006 academic year, 45% of undergraduates worked on campus. **Clubs and organizations:** Number of student organizations: 55. Activities include: choral groups, concert band, dance, drama/theater, jazz band, literary magazine, music ensembles, musical theater, radio station, student government, student newspaper, student film society, symphony orchestra, yearbook. Number of fraternities: 0; sororities: 0. **Sports program (2005-2006):** Member of NCAA III. *Men's intercollegiate varsity sports:* basketball, cross-country, ice hockey, lacrosse, soccer, swimming and diving, tennis, track and field (indoor), track and field (outdoor), water polo. *Women's intercollegiate varsity sports:* basketball, cross-country, field hockey, ice hockey, lacrosse, soccer, squash, swimming and diving, tennis, track and field (indoor), track and field (outdoor), volleyball, water polo, rowing.

SERVICES AND FACILITIES

Basic services: nonremedial tutoring, placement service, health service, health insurance, other. **Counseling services:** minority student, career, personal, academic, older student, psychological, birth control, religious, other. **For learning-disabled students:** School does not offer a structured program with separate admission and additional fees. Services include: note-taking services, extended time for tests, early syllabus, exams on tape or computer, other testing accomodations, other. **Library:** Number of titles: 582,562; number of current serial subscriptions: 4,272. **Information technology resources:** Students are not required to lease or own a computer. Number of campus computers available to all students: 400. School has a wireless network. Approximate number of users that can be accommodated: 1,650. Proportion of college-owned housing units wired for high-speed internet access: 100%. **Campus safety:** Security services offered: 24-hour foot-and-vehicle patrols, late-night transport/escort service, 24-hour emergency telephones, lighted pathways/sidewalks, student patrols, controlled dormitory access (key, security card, etc).

TRANSFER AND INTERNATIONAL STUDENTS

Transfer students: May apply for admission for the following academic terms: Fall, Spring. Applicants need a minimum number of credits to apply. For fall 2005: Transfer applications received: 148. Transfer applicants offered admission: 34. Transfer applicants enrolled: 10. **International**

students: Number of foreign undergraduates: 86 (5% of student body). Number of countries represented: 41. Minimum TOEFL score required: 600 (paper); 250 (computer). Average TOEFL score: 637 (paper).

Eastern Connecticut State University

- ■ **Address:** 83 Windham Street, Willimantic, CT 06226
- ■ **Website:** http://www.easternct.edu
- ■ **Public**
- ■ **Enrollment:** 3,751 full-time; 994 part-time

KEY STATS
- ✔ **U.S News College Ranking:** third tier, Universities–Master's (North)
- ✔ **SAT Score (25th/75th percentile):** 920-1110
- ✔ **Tuition:** 2006-2007: $6,442 in state, $13,570 out of state

Selectivity: Less selective   **Room/board:** $7,964
Acceptance rate: 71%   **Average debt:** $16,899
Student/faculty ratio: 17/1   **Proportion who borrowed:** 71%

UNDERGRADUATE STUDENT BODY STATS
2005-2006 enrollment: 3,751 full-time; 994 part-time. Men: 44%; women: 56%. **Ethnic makeup:** African American: 7%; American-Indian: 1%; Asian American: 2%; Hispanic: 5%; White: 85%; International: 1%.

ADMISSIONS FACTS AND FIGURES
Phone: (860) 465-5286. **Email:** admissions@easternct.edu. **Website:** http://www.easternct.edu. **Application deadlines for fall 2007:** Regular decision: Rolling. Early decision: Not offered. Early action: Not offered. Admission can be deferred. **Application fee:** $50. Common application is accepted. **To apply online, go to:** http://www.easternct.edu/admis/online_admiss.html. **Admissions requirements/recommendations:** High school units required (recommended): English: 4; Mathematics: 3; Science: 2; Foreign language: 2; Social studies: 2; History: 3. Tests: The college uses SAT or ACT scores in admissions decisions. Either SAT or ACT required. For admission to the fall 2007 entering class, the school will accept: ACT with writing. Campus visit: Recommended. Admissions interview: Neither required nor recommended. **Factors that count in admissions decisions:** *Academic:* Secondary school record: Important. Class rank: Very important. Letters of recommendation: Important. Standardized test scores: Very important. Essay: Considered. *Nonacademic:* Interview: Important. Extracurricular activities: Considered. Talent/ability: Considered. Character/personal qualities: Considered. Alumni/ae relationship: Not considered. Geographical residence: Considered. State residency: Considered. Religious affiliation/commitment: Not considered. Minority status: Not considered. Volunteer work: Considered. Work experience: Considered. **Other schools with the greatest overlap in applicants:** Central Connecticut State University; Southern Connecticut State University; University of Connecticut; Western Connecticut State University. **Admissions statistics for the fall 2005 entering class:** Total applicants: 3,678. Total accepted: 2,613. Freshmen enrolled: 925; 11% were from out of state. Overall acceptance rate: 71%. **Size of waiting list:** 82 applicants; enrolled from waiting list: 40. **Credentials of fall 2005 freshmen:** 5% ranked in the top 10 percent of their high school class; 21% were in the top 25 percent, and 68% were in the top half. (Proportion submitting class standing: 72%.) **First-year students who submitted SAT scores:** 100%. Scores (25/75 percentile): Verbal: 460-560, Math: 460-550, Combined: 920-1110.

ACADEMICS
Year founded: 1889. **Academic calendar:** Semester. **Degrees offered:** associate, bachelor's, master's. **Most popular majors:** 14% psychology, 9% business/commerce, 9% sociology, 8% communication studies/speech communication and rhetoric, 7% general studies. **Major fields of study:** biological and biomedical sciences; business, management, marketing, and related support services; communication, journalism, and related programs; computer and information sciences and support services; education; English language and literature/letters; foreign languages, literatures, and linguistics; history; liberal arts and sciences studies, and humanities; mathematics and statistics; multi/interdisciplinary studies; parks, recreation, leisure, and fitness studies; physical sciences; psychology; public administration and social service professions; social sciences; visual and performing arts. **Areas of required coursework:** arts/fine arts, humanities, computer lit-

eracy, mathematics, English (including composition), foreign languages, sciences (biological or physical), social science, other. **Special academic programs (% participation):** accelerated program (.6%), cooperative (work-study plan) program (2.2%), cross-registration, distance learning (2.6%), double major (4.7%), dual enrollment (.3%), exchange student program (domestic) (.2%), honors program (3.8%), independent study (20.5%), internships (33.2%), student-designed major (7.6%), study abroad (.8%), teacher certificate program (10.7%), weekend college (14.3%). **Teacher certification offered in:** early childhood, elementary, secondary. **Cooperative education programs:** business, computer science, education, engineering, natural science, technologies, other. **Reserve Officers Training Corps (ROTC):** Army ROTC: Offered at cooperating institution (University of Connecticut); Air Force ROTC: Offered at cooperating institution (University of Connecticut). **Faculty and instruction (2005-2006):** Total instructional faculty: 188 full-time, 209 part-time (56% men; 44% women; 17% minorities). Full-time faculty with Ph.D. or other terminal degree: 93%. Student/faculty ratio: 17/1. Classes of fewer than 20 students: 35%; of 20 to 49 students: 65%; of 50 or more students: 0%. **Advanced Placement and International Baccalaureate credit:** AP tests may be used for: Credit only. **Freshmen returning for sophomore year:** 76%. **Graduation rates:** Four-year: 25%; five-year: 39%; six-year: 42%.

COSTS AND FINANCIAL AID
Financial aid office: (860) 465-5205. **Expenses (2006-2007):** Tuition and fees 2006-2007: $6,442 in state, $13,570 out of state; room/board: $7,964. Estimated books and supplies: $1,112; transportation: $1,110; personal expenses: $2,522. **Financial aid:** Priority filing date for institution's financial aid form: March 15. In 2005-2006, 87% of undergraduates applied for financial aid. Of those, 69% were determined to have financial need; 18% had their need fully met. Average financial aid package (proportion receiving): $11,279 (66%). Average amount of gift aid, such as scholarships or grants (proportion receiving): $5,742 (47%). Average amount of self-help aid, such as work study or loans (proportion receiving): $5,889 (59%). Average need-based loan (excluding PLUS or other private loans): $6,217. Among students who received need-based aid, the average percentage of need met: 60%. Among students who received aid based on merit, the average award (and the proportion receiving): $2,762 (5%). Average amount of debt of borrowers graduating in 2005: $16,899. Proportion who borrowed: 71%.

CAMPUS LIFE AND EXTRACURRICULAR ACTIVITIES
Campus housing available (% using): coed dorms (10%), women's dorms (4%), apartment for single students (86%). Students who live in college-owned, operated, or affiliated housing: 62%. **Clubs and organizations:** Number of student organizations: 67. Activities include: choral groups, concert band, dance, drama/theater, literary magazine, music ensembles, musical theater, radio station, student government, student newspaper, television station, yearbook. Number of fraternities: 0; sororities: 0. **Sports program (2005-2006):** Member of NCAA III. *Men's intercollegiate varsity sports:* baseball, basketball, cross-country, lacrosse, soccer, track and field (indoor), track and field (outdoor). *Women's intercollegiate varsity sports:* basketball, cross-country, field hockey, lacrosse, soccer, softball, swimming and diving, track and field (indoor), track and field (outdoor), volleyball.

SERVICES AND FACILITIES
Basic services: women's center, health service. **Remedial assistance:** math. **Counseling services:** career, academic, religious. **For learning-disabled students:** School does not offer a structured program with separate admission and additional fees. Total undergraduates in learning-disabled program or receiving services: 111. Services include: remedial math, reading machines, tape recorders, note-taking services, oral tests, learning center, readers, extended time for tests, tutors, priority registration, priority seating, texts on tape, other testing accomodations. **Library:** Number of titles: 331,451; number of current serial subscriptions: 3,186. **Information technology resources:** Students are not required to lease or own a computer. School does not have a wireless network. Proportion of college-owned housing units wired for high-speed internet access: 100%. **Campus safety:** Security services offered: 24-hour foot-and-vehicle patrols.

TRANSFER AND INTERNATIONAL STUDENTS
Transfer students: May apply for admission for the following academic terms: Fall, Spring. Applicants do not need a minimum number of credits to apply. For fall 2005: Transfer applications received: 612. Transfer applicants offered admission: 483. Transfer applicants enrolled: 346. **International students:** Number of foreign undergraduates: 33 (1% of student body). Minimum TOEFL score required: 550 (paper); 213 (computer). Average TOEFL score: 557 (paper).

Fairfield University

- **Address:** 1073 N. Benson Road, Fairfield, CT 06824-5195
- **Website:** http://www.fairfield.edu
- **Private; Religious affiliation:** Roman Catholic (Jesuit)
- **Enrollment:** 3,485 full-time; 588 part-time

KEY STATS

- ✔ **U.S News College Ranking:** 4, Universities–Master's (North)
- ✔ **SAT Score (25th/75th percentile):** 1110-1270
- ✔ **Tuition:** 2006-2007: $31,955

Selectivity: More selective	**Room/board:** $9,980
Acceptance rate: 74%	**Average debt:** $25,081
Student/faculty ratio: 13/1	**Proportion who borrowed:** 63%

UNDERGRADUATE STUDENT BODY STATS

2005-2006 enrollment: 3,485 full-time; 588 part-time. Men: 43%; women: 57%. **Ethnic makeup:** African American: 2%; Asian American: 3%; Hispanic: 5%; White: 89%; International: 1%. **Religious preference:** Roman Catholic: 80%; Protestant: 17%; Jewish: 1%; No preference: 1%; Unknown: 1%.

ADMISSIONS FACTS AND FIGURES

Phone: (203) 254-4100. **Email:** admis@mail.fairfield.edu. **Website:** http://www.fairfield.edu. **Application deadlines for fall 2007:** Regular decision: January 15; decision sent by April 1. Early decision: Not offered. Early action: Send application by: November 15; Decision sent by: December 15. Admission can be deferred. **Application fee:** $55. Common application is accepted. **To apply online, go to:** http://www.fairfield.edu/admission/application.htm. **Admissions requirements/recommendations:** High school units required (recommended): English: 4 (4); Mathematics: 3 (4); Science: 3 (4); Foreign language: 2 (4); Social studies: 3 (4); History: 0 (1); Academic electives: 0; Total units: 15 (18). Tests: The college uses SAT or ACT scores in admissions decisions. Either SAT or ACT required. For admission to the fall 2007 entering class, the school will accept: ACT without writing. Campus visit: Recommended. Admissions interview: Recommended. Off-campus interview: May be arranged. **Factors that count in admissions decisions:** *Academic:* Secondary school record: Very important. Class rank: Very important. Letters of recommendation: Very important. Standardized test scores: Very important. Essay: Very important. *Nonacademic:* Interview: Considered. Extracurricular activities: Important. Talent/ability: Important. Character/personal qualities: Important. Alumni/ae relationship: Considered. Geographical residence: Considered. State residency: Not considered. Religious affiliation/commitment: Not considered. Minority status: Considered. Volunteer work: Important. Work experience: Considered. **Other schools with the greatest overlap in applicants:** Boston College; College of the Holy Cross; Loyola College in Maryland; Providence College; Villanova University. **Admissions statistics for the fall 2005 entering class:** Total applicants: 6,895. Total accepted: 5,130. Freshmen enrolled: 940; 81% were from out of state. Overall acceptance rate: 74%. Non-early acceptance rate: 74%. **Size of waiting list:** 918 applicants; enrolled from waiting list: 64. **Credentials of fall 2005 freshmen:** 31% ranked in the top 10 percent of their high school class; 69% were in the top 25 percent, and 93% were in the top half. (Proportion submitting class standing: 36%.) **Average high school grade point average:** 3.4. First-year students who submitted SAT scores: 96%. Scores (25/75 percentile): Verbal: 550-630, Math: 560-640, Combined: 1110-1270. **First-year students submitting ACT scores:** 20%. Scores (25/75 percentile): English: N/A, Math: N/A, Composite: 23-27.

ACADEMICS

Year founded: 1942. **Academic calendar:** Semester. **Degrees offered:** associate, bachelor's, master's, post-master's certificate. **Most popular majors:** 34% marketing, 12% social sciences, 9% communication and media studies, 8% English language and literature, 7% nursing. **Major fields of study:** area, ethnic, cultural, and gender studies; biological and biomedical sciences; business, management, marketing, and related support services; communication, journalism, and related programs; computer and information sciences and support services; engineering; engineering technologies/technicians; English language and literature/letters; foreign languages, literatures, and linguistics; health professions and related clinical sciences; history; liberal arts and sciences studies, and humanities; mathematics and statistics; multi/interdisciplinary studies; philosophy and religious studies; physical sciences; psychology; social sciences; visual and performing arts. **Areas of required coursework:** arts/fine arts, mathematics, English (including composition), philosophy, foreign languages, sciences (biological or physical), history, social science, other. **Special academic programs (% participation):** double major (15%), exchange student program (domestic) (1%), honors program (6%), independent study (24%), internships (50%), student-designed major (.1%), study abroad (21%), teacher certificate program (3%). **Teacher certification offered in:** middle/junior high, secondary. **Cooperative education programs:** engineering. **Reserve Officers Training Corps (ROTC):** Army ROTC: Offered at cooperating institution (Sacred Heart University). **Faculty and instruction (2005-2006):** Total instructional faculty: 226 full-time, 197 part-time (52% men; 48% women; 4% minorities). Full-time faculty with Ph.D. or other terminal degree: 93%. Student/faculty ratio: 13/1. Classes of fewer than 20 students: 34%; of 20 to 49 students: 65%; of 50 or more students: 1%. **Advanced Placement and International Baccalaureate credit:** AP tests may be used for: Credit and/or placement. Scores accepted: 4, 5. International Baccalaureate exams may be used for: Credit and/or placement. **Freshmen returning for sophomore year:** 89%. **Graduation rates:** Four-year: 79%; five-year: 81%; six-year: 79%. **Graduate study:** 20% of students pursue further study immediately upon graduation; 2% within one year; 5% within five years. Fields in which graduates pursue further study: Master of Business Administration (MBA), 19%; law, 17%; medicine, 18%; dentistry, 3%; engineering, 2%; education, 19%; arts and sciences, 23%; veterinary medicine, 1%.

COSTS AND FINANCIAL AID

Financial aid office: (203) 254-4125. **Expenses (2006-2007):** Tuition and fees 2006-2007: $31,955; room/board: $9,980. Estimated books and supplies: $500; transportation: $1,000; personal expenses: $900. **Financial aid:** Priority filing date for institution's financial aid form: February 15; deadline: February 15. In 2005-2006, 59% of undergraduates applied for financial aid. Of those, 48% were determined to have financial need; 26% had their need fully met. Average financial aid package (proportion receiving): $17,079 (47%). Average amount of gift aid, such as scholarships or grants (proportion receiving): $11,906 (42%). Average amount of self-help aid, such as work study or loans (proportion receiving): $4,595 (40%). Average need-based loan (excluding PLUS or other private loans): $4,111. Among students who received need-based aid, the average percentage of need met: 65%. Among students who received aid based on merit, the average award (and the proportion receiving): $10,723 (7%). The average athletic scholarship (and the proportion receiving): $18,332 (5%). Average amount of debt of borrowers graduating in 2005: $25,081. Proportion who borrowed: 63%.

CAMPUS LIFE AND EXTRACURRICULAR ACTIVITIES

Campus housing available (% using): coed dorms (58%), apartment for single students (30%), special housing for disabled students (2%), other housing options (10%). Students who live in college-owned, operated, or affiliated housing: 85%. **Student employment:** During the 2005-2006 academic year, 13% of undergraduates worked on campus. Average per-year earnings: $1,000. **Clubs and organizations:** Number of student organizations: 95. Activities include: choral groups, concert band, dance, drama/theater, jazz band, literary magazine, music ensembles, pep band, radio station, student government, student newspaper, student film society, symphony orchestra, television station, yearbook. Number of fraternities: 0; sororities: 0. Average proportion of students who stay on campus on weekends: 90%. **Sports program (2005-2006):** Member of NCAA I. *Men's intercollegiate varsity sports:* baseball, basketball, cross-country, golf, lacrosse, soccer, swimming and diving, tennis. *Women's intercollegiate varsity sports:* basketball, cross-country, field hockey, golf, lacrosse, rowing, soccer, softball, swimming and diving, tennis, volleyball.

SERVICES AND FACILITIES

Basic services: nonremedial tutoring, women's center, placement service, health service, health insurance. **Counseling services:** minority student, career, personal, academic, psychological, religious. **For learning-disabled students:** School does not offer a structured program with separate admission and additional fees. Total undergraduates in learning-disabled program or receiving services: 123. Services include: reading machines, tape recorders, note-taking services, oral tests, readers, extended time for tests, tutors, priority registration, priority seating, substitution of courses, texts on tape, typist/scribe, other testing accomodations, other. **Library:** Number of titles: 333,251; number of current serial subscriptions: 1,762. **Information technology resources:** Students are not required to lease or own a computer. Number of campus computers available to all students: 230. School has a wireless network. Approximate number of users that can be accommodated: 500. Proportion of college-owned housing units wired for high-speed internet access: 100%. **Campus safety:** Security services offered: 24-hour foot-

and-vehicle patrols, late-night transport/escort service, 24-hour emergency telephones, lighted pathways/sidewalks, controlled dormitory access (key, security card, etc).

TRANSFER AND INTERNATIONAL STUDENTS

Transfer students: May apply for admission for the following academic terms: Fall, Spring. Applicants need a minimum number of credits to apply. For fall 2005: Transfer applications received: 195. Transfer applicants offered admission: 81. Transfer applicants enrolled: 41. **International students:** Number of foreign undergraduates: 26 (1% of student body). Number of countries represented: 41. Minimum TOEFL score required: 550 (paper); 213 (computer). Average TOEFL score: 613 (paper).

Post University

- ■ **Address:** 800 Country Club Road, PO Box 2540, Waterbury, CT 06723
- ■ **Website:** http://www.post.edu
- ■ **N/A**
- ■ **Enrollment:** 664 full-time; 437 part-time

KEY STATS

✔ **U.S News College Ranking:** fourth tier, Comp. Coll.–Bachelor's (North)

✔ **SAT Score (25th/75th percentile):** 956

✔ **Tuition:** 2006-2007: $750 in state; $750 out of state

Selectivity: Less selective	**Room/board:** $8,400
Acceptance rate: 62%	**Average debt:** $17,500
Student/faculty ratio: 13/1	**Proportion who borrowed:** 92%

UNDERGRADUATE STUDENT BODY STATS

2005-2006 enrollment: 664 full-time; 437 part-time. Men: 40%; women: 60%. **Ethnic makeup:** African American: 22%; Asian American: 2%; Hispanic: 10%; White: 62%; International: 3%.

ADMISSIONS FACTS AND FIGURES

Phone: (203) 596-4520. **Email:** admissions@post.edu. **Website:** http://www.post.edu. **Application deadlines for fall 2007:** Regular decision: Rolling. Early decision: Not offered. Early action: Not offered. Admission can be deferred. **Application fee:** $40. Common application is accepted. **Admissions requirements/recommendations:** High school units required (recommended): English: 4 (4); Mathematics: 2 (2); Science: 2 (2); Foreign language: 2 (2); Social studies: 1 (1); History: 2 (2); Academic electives: 2 (2); Total units: 16 (16). Tests: The college uses SAT or ACT scores in admissions decisions. Neither SAT nor ACT required. For admission to the fall 2007 entering class, the school will accept: ACT with writing, ACT without writing. Campus visit: Recommended. Admissions interview: Recommended. Off-campus interview: May be arranged. **Factors that count in admissions decisions:** *Academic:* Secondary school record: Important. Class rank: Considered. Letters of recommendation: Important. Standardized test scores: Important. Essay: Important. *Nonacademic:* Interview: Important. Extracurricular activities: Considered. Talent/ability: Considered. Character/personal qualities: Important. Alumni/ae relationship: Considered. Geographical residence: Not considered. State residency: Not considered. Religious affiliation/commitment: Not considered. Minority status: Not considered. Volunteer work: Considered. Work experience: Considered. **Other schools with the greatest overlap in applicants:** Central Connecticut State University; Quinnipiac University; Southern Connecticut State University; University of Bridgeport; University of New Haven. **Admissions statistics for the fall 2005 entering class:** Total applicants: 1,254. Total accepted: 782. Freshmen enrolled: 205; 33% were from out of state. Overall acceptance rate: 62%. **Credentials of fall 2005 freshmen:** 8% ranked in the top 10 percent of their high school class; 27% were in the top 25 percent, and 51% were in the top half. (Proportion submitting class standing: 70%.) **Average high school grade point average:** 2.7. **First-year students who submitted SAT scores:** 100%. Scores (25/75 percentile): Verbal: N/A, Math: N/A, Combined: N/A.

ACADEMICS

Year founded: 1890. **Academic calendar:** Semester. **Degrees offered:** certificate, associate, transfer-associate, terminal-associate, bachelor's, post-bachelor's certificate. **Most popular majors:** 25% business administration and management, 16% general studies, 6% accounting, 6% marketing/marketing management, 5% computer and information sciences. **Major fields of study:** agriculture, agriculture operations, and related sciences; biological and biomedical sciences; business, management, marketing, and related support services; computer and information sciences and support services; English language and literature/letters; history; legal professions and studies; liberal arts and sciences studies, and humanities; natural resources and conservation; psychology; public administration and social service professions; security and protective services; social sciences. **Areas of required coursework:** humanities, computer literacy, mathematics, English (including composition), sciences (biological or physical), history, social science. **Special academic programs (% participation):** accelerated program (45%), cooperative (work-study plan) program, cross-registration, distance learning (25%), double major (2%), English as a Second Language (ESL), independent study, internships (5%), study abroad (3%), weekend college (5%). **Cooperative education programs:** business, computer science, social/behavioral science. **Faculty and instruction (2005-2006):** Total instructional faculty: 30 full-time, 92 part-time (60% men; 40% women; 0% minorities). Full-time faculty with Ph.D. or other terminal degree: 67%. Student/faculty ratio: 13/1. Classes of fewer than 20 students: 75%; of 20 to 49 students: 25%; of 50 or more students: 0%. **Advanced Placement and International Baccalaureate credit:** AP tests may be used for: Credit and/or placement. Scores accepted: 3, 4, 5. International Baccalaureate exams may be used for: Credit and/or placement. **Freshmen returning for sophomore year:** 73%. **Graduation rates:** Four-year: 17%; five-year: 25%; six-year: 37%. **Graduate study:** 45% of students pursue further study immediately upon graduation; 10% within one year; 13% within five years. Fields in which graduates pursue further study: Master of Business Administration (MBA), 5%; law, 10%; medicine, 1%; education, 13%; arts and sciences, 40%; veterinary medicine, 1%.

COSTS AND FINANCIAL AID

Financial aid office: (203) 596-4526. **Expenses (2006-2007):** Tuition and fees 2006-2007: $750 in state, $750 out of state; room/board: $8,400. Estimated books and supplies: $1,000; transportation: $750; personal expenses: $3,000. **Financial aid:** Priority filing date for institution's financial aid form: March 1. In 2005-2006, 90% of undergraduates applied for financial aid. Of those, 78% were determined to have financial need; Average financial aid package (proportion receiving): $15,600 (78%). Average amount of gift aid, such as scholarships or grants (proportion receiving): $10,000 (78%). Average amount of self-help aid, such as work study or loans (proportion receiving): $6,000 (59%). Average need-based loan (excluding PLUS or other private loans): $4,500. Among students who received need-based aid, the average percentage of need met: 80%. Among students who received aid based on merit, the average award (and the proportion receiving): $3,500 (7%). The average athletic scholarship (and the proportion receiving): $7,500 (2%). Average amount of debt of borrowers graduating in 2005: $17,500. Proportion who borrowed: 92%.

CAMPUS LIFE AND EXTRACURRICULAR ACTIVITIES

Campus housing available (% using): coed dorms (100%). Students who live in college-owned, operated, or affiliated housing: 52%. **Student employment:** During the 2005-2006 academic year, 10% of undergraduates worked on campus. Average per-year earnings: $2,000. **Clubs and organizations:** Number of student organizations: 26. Activities include: dance, literary magazine, student government. Number of fraternities: 0; sororities: 0. Average proportion of students who stay on campus on weekends: 35%. **Sports program (2005-2006):** Member of NCAA II. *Men's intercollegiate varsity sports:* baseball, basketball, cross-country, golf, soccer, tennis. *Women's intercollegiate varsity sports:* basketball, soccer, softball, tennis, volleyball.

SERVICES AND FACILITIES

Basic services: nonremedial tutoring, placement service, health service, health insurance. **Remedial assistance:** reading, math, writing, study skills. **Counseling services:** minority student, career, personal, veteran student, academic, psychological. **For learning-disabled students:** School does not offer a structured program with separate admission and additional fees. Total undergraduates in learning-disabled program or receiving services: 32. Services include: remedial math, remedial English, remedial reading, untimed tests, learning center, extended time for tests, tutors, other testing accomodations. **Library:** Number of titles: 101,210; number of current serial subscriptions: 457. **Information technology resources:** Students are not required to lease or own a computer. Number of campus computers available to all students: 75. School does not have a wireless network. Proportion of college-owned housing units wired for high-speed internet access: 100%. **Campus safety:** Security services offered: late-night transport/escort service, 24-hour emergency telephones, lighted pathways/sidewalks, controlled dormitory access (key, security card, etc).

TRANSFER AND INTERNATIONAL STUDENTS

Transfer students: May apply for admission for the following academic terms: Fall, Spring, Summer. Applicants do not need a minimum number of credits to apply. For fall 2005: Transfer applications received: 226. Transfer applicants offered admission: 101. Transfer applicants enrolled: 60. **International students:** Number of foreign undergraduates: 30 (3% of student body). Number of countries represented: 14. Minimum TOEFL score required: 500 (paper); 170 (computer).

Quinnipiac University

- ■ **Address:** 275 Mount Carmel Avenue, Hamden, CT 06518
- ■ **Website:** http://www.quinnipiac.edu
- ■ **Private**
- ■ **Enrollment:** 5,286 full-time; 420 part-time

KEY STATS

- ✔ **U.S News College Ranking:** 12, Universities–Master's (North)
- ✔ **SAT Score (25th/75th percentile):** 1070-1225
- ✔ **Tuition:** 2006-2007: $26,280

Selectivity: More selective	**Room/board:** $10,700
Acceptance rate: 51%	**Average debt:** $25,794
Student/faculty ratio: 15/1	**Proportion who borrowed:** 70%

UNDERGRADUATE STUDENT BODY STATS

2005-2006 enrollment: 5,286 full-time; 420 part-time. Men: 39%; women: 61%. **Ethnic makeup:** African American: 2%; Asian American: 2%; Hispanic: 4%; White: 89%; International: 1%. **Religious preference:** Roman Catholic: 45%; Protestant: 30%; Jewish: 11%; Unknown: 14%.

ADMISSIONS FACTS AND FIGURES

Phone: (800) 462-1944. **Email:** admissions@quinnipiac.edu. **Website:** http://www.quinnipiac.edu. **Application deadlines for fall 2007:** Regular decision: February 1. Early decision: Not offered. Early action: Not offered. Admission can be deferred. **Application fee:** $45. Common application is accepted. **To apply online, go to:** http://www.quinnipiac.edu/x76.xml. **Admissions requirements/recommendations:** High school units required (recommended): English: 4 (4); Mathematics: 3 (3); Science: 2 (3); Foreign language: 2 (2); Social studies: 3 (3); Academic electives: 2 (2); Total units: 16 (16). Tests: The college uses SAT or ACT scores in admissions decisions. Either SAT or ACT required. For admission to the fall 2007 entering class, the school will accept: ACT without writing. Campus visit: Recommended. Admissions interview: Recommended. Off-campus interview: May be arranged. **Factors that count in admissions decisions:** *Academic:* Secondary school record: Very important. Class rank: Important. Letters of recommendation: Important. Standardized test scores: Very important. Essay: Important. *Nonacademic:* Interview: Important. Extracurricular activities: Important. Talent/ability: Not considered. Character/personal qualities: Important. Alumni/ae relationship: Considered. Geographical residence: Not considered. State residency: Not considered. Religious affiliation/commitment: Not considered. Minority status: Considered. Volunteer work: Considered. Work experience: Considered. **Other schools with the greatest overlap in applicants:** Boston University; Fairfield University; Ithaca College; Northeastern University; University of Connecticut. **Admissions statistics for the fall 2005 entering class:** Total applicants: 11,397. Total accepted: 5,811. Freshmen enrolled: 1,361; 78% were from out of state. Overall acceptance rate: 51%. **Size of waiting list:** 1120 applicants; enrolled from waiting list: 85. **Credentials of fall 2005 freshmen:** 30% ranked in the top 10 percent of their high school class; 60% were in the top 25 percent, and 95% were in the top half. (Proportion submitting class standing: 68%.) **Average high school grade point average:** 3.5. **First-year students who submitted SAT scores:** 95%. Scores (25/75 percentile): Verbal: 525-605, Math: 545-620, Combined: 1070-1225. **First-year students submitting ACT scores:** 30%. Scores (25/75 percentile): English: N/A, Math: N/A, Composite: 24-28.

ACADEMICS

Year founded: 1929. **Academic calendar:** Semester. **Degrees offered:** certificate, bachelor's, post-bachelor's certificate, master's, first professional, first professional certificate, doctorate. **Most popular majors:** 24% business, management, marketing, and related support services, 20% health professions and related clinical sciences, 16% communication, journalism, and related programs, 7% psychology, 6% social sciences. **Major fields of study:** biological and biomedical sciences; business, management, marketing, and related support services; communication, journalism, and related programs; computer and information sciences and support services; English language and literature/letters; family and consumer sciences/human sciences; foreign languages, literatures, and linguistics; health professions and related clinical sciences; history; legal professions and studies; liberal arts and sciences studies, and humanities; mathematics and statistics; multi/interdisciplinary studies; physical sciences; psychology; security and protective services; social sciences; visual and performing arts. **Areas of required coursework:** arts/fine arts, humanities, mathematics, English (including composition), philosophy, foreign languages, sciences (biological or physical), history, social science, other. **Pre-professional programs:** pre-law, pre-dentistry, pre-medicine, pre-veterinary science. **Special academic programs (% participation):** distance learning (4%), double major (2%), honors program (3%), internships (40%), liberal arts/career combination (28%), student-designed major (1%), study abroad (5%), teacher certificate program (12%). **Teacher certification offered in:** elementary, middle/junior high, secondary. **Reserve Officers Training Corps (ROTC):** Army ROTC: Offered at cooperating institution (Southern Connecticut State University); Air Force ROTC: Offered at cooperating institution (University of Connecticut). **Faculty and instruction (2005-2006):** Total instructional faculty: 286 full-time, 262 part-time. Full-time faculty with Ph.D. or other terminal degree: 86%. Student/faculty ratio: 15/1. Classes of fewer than 20 students: 55%; of 20 to 49 students: 45%; of 50 or more students: 0%. **Advanced Placement and International Baccalaureate credit:** AP tests may be used for: Credit and/or placement. Scores accepted: 3, 4, 5. International Baccalaureate exams may be used for: Credit and/or placement. **Freshmen returning for sophomore year:** 87%. **Graduation rates:** Four-year: 64%; five-year: 71%; six-year: 68%. **Graduate study:** 32% of students pursue further study immediately upon graduation; 6% within one year; 8% within five years. Fields in which graduates pursue further study: Master of Business Administration (MBA), 5%; law, 2%; medicine, 2%; dentistry, 1%; education, 9%; arts and sciences, 3%; veterinary medicine, 2%.

COSTS AND FINANCIAL AID

Financial aid office: (203) 582-8750. **Expenses (2006-2007):** Tuition and fees 2006-2007: $26,280; room/board: $10,700. Estimated books and supplies: $800; transportation: $300; personal expenses: $900. **Financial aid:** Priority filing date for institution's financial aid form: March 1; deadline: April 15. In 2005-2006, 70% of undergraduates applied for financial aid. Of those, 57% were determined to have financial need; 13% had their need fully met. Average financial aid package (proportion receiving): $14,511 (57%). Average amount of gift aid, such as scholarships or grants (proportion receiving): $9,613 (55%). Average amount of self-help aid, such as work study or loans (proportion receiving): $5,232 (50%). Average need-based loan (excluding PLUS or other private loans): $4,207. Among students who received need-based aid, the average percentage of need met: 65%. Among students who received aid based on merit, the average award (and the proportion receiving): $6,625 (10%). The average athletic scholarship (and the proportion receiving): $20,348 (5%). Average amount of debt of borrowers graduating in 2005: $25,794. Proportion who borrowed: 70%.

CAMPUS LIFE AND EXTRACURRICULAR ACTIVITIES

Campus housing available (% using): coed dorms (71%), apartment for single students (26%), other housing options (3%). Students who live in college-owned, operated, or affiliated housing: 75%. **Student employment:** During the 2005-2006 academic year, 20% of undergraduates worked on campus. Average per-year earnings: $2,100. **Clubs and organizations:** Number of student organizations: 72. Activities include: choral groups, dance, drama/theater, literary magazine, pep band, radio station, student government, student newspaper, television station, yearbook. Number of fraternities: 2; sororities: 3. Proportion of men in fraternities: 4%; of women in sororities: 4%. Average proportion of students who stay on campus on weekends: 75%. **Sports program (2005-2006):** Member of NCAA I. *Men's intercollegiate varsity sports:* baseball, basketball, cross-country, field hockey, golf, ice hockey, lacrosse, soccer, tennis, track and field (indoor), track and field (outdoor). *Women's intercollegiate varsity sports:* basketball, cross-country, field hockey, ice hockey, lacrosse, soccer, softball, tennis, track and field (indoor), track and field (outdoor), volleyball.

SERVICES AND FACILITIES

Basic services: nonremedial tutoring, placement service, health service. **Counseling services:** minority student, career, personal, veteran student, academic, older student, psychological, religious. **For learning-disabled students:** School does not offer a structured program with separate admission and additional fees. Services include: learning center, tutors. **Library:**

Number of titles: 285,000; number of current serial subscriptions: 21,000. **Information technology resources:** Students are required to lease or own a computer. Number of campus computers available to all students: 440. School has a wireless network. Approximate number of users that can be accommodated: 5,200. Proportion of college-owned housing units wired for high-speed internet access: 100%. **Campus safety:** Security services offered: 24-hour foot-and-vehicle patrols, late-night transport/escort service, 24-hour emergency telephones, lighted pathways/sidewalks, controlled dormitory access (key, security card, etc).

TRANSFER AND INTERNATIONAL STUDENTS
Transfer students: May apply for admission for the following academic terms: Fall, Spring. Applicants need a minimum number of credits to apply. For fall 2005: Transfer applications received: 763. Transfer applicants offered admission: 534. Transfer applicants enrolled: 195. **International students:** Number of foreign undergraduates: 66 (1% of student body). Number of countries represented: 18. Minimum TOEFL score required: 550 (paper); 213 (computer). Average TOEFL score: 555 (paper).

Sacred Heart University

- **Address:** 5151 Park Avenue, Fairfield, CT 06825
- **Website:** http://www.sacredheart.edu
- **Private; Religious affiliation:** Roman Catholic
- **Enrollment:** 3,244 full-time; 860 part-time

KEY STATS
- ✔ **U.S News College Ranking:** 44, Universities–Master's (North)
- ✔ **SAT Score (25th/75th percentile):** 990-1160
- ✔ **Tuition:** 2006-2007: $25,300

Selectivity: Selective	**Room/board:** $10,320
Acceptance rate: 64%	**Average debt:** $19,926
Student/faculty ratio: 13/1	**Proportion who borrowed:** 93%

UNDERGRADUATE STUDENT BODY STATS
2005-2006 enrollment: 3,244 full-time; 860 part-time. Men: 39%; women: 61%. **Ethnic makeup:** African American: 5%; Asian American: 1%; Hispanic: 6%; White: 86%; International: 1%. **Religious preference:** Protestant: 16%; Jewish: 1%; No preference: 7%; Roman Catholic: 72%; Other: 4%.

ADMISSIONS FACTS AND FIGURES
Phone: (203) 371-7880. **Email:** enroll@sacredheart.edu. **Website:** http://www.sacredheart.edu. **Application deadlines for fall 2007:** Regular decision: Rolling. Early decision: Send application by: October 1; Decision sent by: October 15. Early action: Not offered. Admission can be deferred. **Application fee:** $50. Common application is accepted. **To apply online, go to:** http://www.sacredheart.edu/apply.cfm. **Admissions requirements/recommendations:** High school units required (recommended): English: 4 (4); Mathematics: 3 (4); Science: 3 (4); Foreign language: 2 (4); Social studies: 3 (4); History: 3 (4); Academic electives: 3 (4); Total units: 22 (30). Tests: The college uses SAT or ACT scores in admissions decisions. Either SAT or ACT required. For admission to the fall 2007 entering class, the school will accept: ACT with writing. Campus visit: Recommended. Admissions interview: Recommended. Off-campus interview: May be arranged. **Factors that count in admissions decisions:** *Academic:* Secondary school record: Very important. Class rank: Important. Letters of recommendation: Important. Standardized test scores: Important. Essay: Important. *Nonacademic:* Interview: Important. Extracurricular activities: Important. Talent/ability: Important. Character/personal qualities: Important. Alumni/ae relationship: Considered. Geographical residence: Considered. State residency: Considered. Religious affiliation/commitment: Considered. Minority status: Considered. Volunteer work: Important. Work experience: Considered. **Other schools with the greatest overlap in applicants:** Fairfield University; Marist College; Providence College; Quinnipiac University; University of Connecticut. **Admissions statistics for the fall 2005 entering class:** Total applicants: 5,856. Total accepted: 3,731. Freshmen enrolled: 886; 70% were from out of state. Accepted through early-decision or early-action plans: 19%. Overall acceptance rate: 64%. Early-decision acceptance rate: 64%. Non-early acceptance rate: 64%. **Credentials of fall 2005 freshmen:** 8% ranked in the top 10 percent of their high school class; 37% were in the top 25 percent, and 91% were in the top half. (Proportion submitting class standing: 62%.) **Average high school grade point average:** 3.3. First-year stu-

dents who submitted SAT scores: 99%. Scores (25/75 percentile): Verbal: 490-580, Math: 500-580, Combined: 990-1160. **First-year students submitting ACT scores:** 15%. Scores (25/75 percentile): English: N/A, Math: N/A, Composite: N/A.

ACADEMICS
Year founded: 1963. **Academic calendar:** Semester. **Degrees offered:** certificate, associate, transfer-associate, terminal-associate, bachelor's, master's, post-master's certificate, doctorate. **Most popular majors:** 19% business, management, marketing, and related support services; 16% psychology, 7% finance, 6% communication, journalism, and related programs, 5% accounting. **Major fields of study:** biological and biomedical sciences; business, management, marketing, and related support services; communication, journalism, and related programs; computer and information sciences and support services; English language and literature/letters; foreign languages, literatures, and linguistics; health professions and related clinical sciences; history; legal professions and studies; liberal arts and sciences studies, and humanities; mathematics and statistics; natural resources and conservation; parks, recreation, leisure, and fitness studies; philosophy and religious studies; physical sciences; psychology; public administration and social service professions; security and protective services; social sciences; visual and performing arts. **Areas of required coursework:** arts/fine arts, humanities, computer literacy, mathematics, English (including composition), philosophy, sciences (biological or physical), history, social science. **Pre-professional programs:** pre-law, pre-dentistry, pre-medicine, pre-theology, pre-veterinary science, pre-optometry, pre-pharmacy, other. **Special academic programs (% participation):** distance learning (47%), double major (7%), English as a Second Language (ESL) (2%), honors program (6%), independent study (23%), internships (50%), study abroad (5%), teacher certificate program (9%). **Teacher certification offered in:** elementary, middle/junior high, secondary. **Reserve Officers Training Corps (ROTC):** Army ROTC: Offered on campus. **Faculty and instruction (2005-2006):** Total instructional faculty: 186 full-time, 286 part-time (52% men; 48% women; 10% minorities). Full-time faculty with Ph.D. or other terminal degree: 78%. Student/faculty ratio: 13/1. Classes of fewer than 20 students: 53%; of 20 to 49 students: 47%. **Advanced Placement and International Baccalaureate credit:** AP tests may be used for: Credit and/or placement. Scores accepted: 3, 4, 5. International Baccalaureate exams may be used for: Credit and/or placement. **Freshmen returning for sophomore year:** 80%. **Graduation rates:** Four-year: 56%; five-year: 63%; six-year: 58%. **Graduate study:** 45% of students pursue further study within one year. Fields in which graduates pursue further study: Master of Business Administration (MBA), 8%; law, 4%; medicine, 2%; dentistry, 1%; education, 43%; arts and sciences, 28%.

COSTS AND FINANCIAL AID
Financial aid office: (203) 371-7980. **Expenses (2006-2007):** Tuition and fees 2006-2007: $25,300; room/board: $10,320. Estimated books and supplies: $700; transportation: $700; personal expenses: $700. **Financial aid:** Priority filing date for institution's financial aid form: February 15. In 2005-2006, 86% of undergraduates applied for financial aid. Of those, 69% were determined to have financial need; 30% had their need fully met. Average financial aid package (proportion receiving): $14,943 (67%). Average amount of gift aid, such as scholarships or grants (proportion receiving): $9,436 (66%). Average amount of self-help aid, such as work study or loans (proportion receiving): $6,671 (58%). Average need-based loan (excluding PLUS or other private loans): $6,190. Among students who received need-based aid, the average percentage of need met: 70%. Among students who received aid based on merit, the average award (and the proportion receiving): $11,498 (19%). The average athletic scholarship (and the proportion receiving): $14,753 (4%). Average amount of debt of borrowers graduating in 2005: $19,926. Proportion who borrowed: 93%.

CAMPUS LIFE AND EXTRACURRICULAR ACTIVITIES
Campus housing available (% using): coed dorms (62%), apartment for single students (37%), special housing for disabled students (1%). Students who live in college-owned, operated, or affiliated housing: 68%. **Student employment:** During the 2005-2006 academic year, 28% of undergraduates worked on campus. Average per-year earnings: $1,157. **Clubs and organizations:** Number of student organizations: 65. Activities include: choral groups, concert band, dance, drama/theater, jazz band, literary magazine, marching band, music ensembles, musical theater, pep band, radio station, student government, student newspaper, student film society, television station, yearbook. Number of fraternities: 4; sororities: 6. Proportion of men in fraternities: 5%; of women in sororities: 5%. Average proportion of students who stay on campus on weekends: 75%. **Sports program (2005-2006):**

Member of NCAA I. *Men's intercollegiate varsity sports:* baseball, basketball, bowling, cross-country, fencing, football, golf, ice hockey, lacrosse, soccer, tennis, track and field (indoor), track and field (outdoor), volleyball, wrestling. *Women's intercollegiate varsity sports:* basketball, bowling, crew, cross-country, equestrian sports, fencing, field hockey, golf, ice hockey, lacrosse, rowing, soccer, softball, swimming and diving, tennis, track and field (indoor), track and field (outdoor), volleyball.

SERVICES AND FACILITIES

Basic services: nonremedial tutoring, health service, health insurance. **Counseling services:** minority student, career, personal, academic, older student, psychological, religious. **For learning-disabled students:** School does not offer a structured program with separate admission and additional fees. Total undergraduates in learning-disabled program or receiving services: 234. Services include: remedial math, reading machines, remedial reading, tape recorders, untimed tests, note-taking services, oral tests, learning center, readers, extended time for tests, tutors, substitution of courses, typist/scribe, other testing accomodations. **Library:** Number of titles: 131,237; number of current serial subscriptions: 871. **Information technology resources:** Students are required to lease or own a computer. Number of campus computers available to all students: 330. School has a wireless network. Approximate number of users that can be accommodated: 7,000. Proportion of college-owned housing units wired for high-speed internet access: 100%. **Campus safety:** Security services offered: 24-hour foot-and-vehicle patrols, late-night transport/escort service, 24-hour emergency telephones, lighted pathways/sidewalks, controlled dormitory access (key, security card, etc).

TRANSFER AND INTERNATIONAL STUDENTS

Transfer students: May apply for admission for the following academic terms: Fall, Spring. Applicants do not need a minimum number of credits to apply. For fall 2005: Transfer applications received: 435. Transfer applicants offered admission: 355. Transfer applicants enrolled: 190. **International students:** Number of foreign undergraduates: 38 (1% of student body). Number of countries represented: 37. Minimum TOEFL score required: 550 (paper); 213 (computer).

Southern Connecticut State University

- **Address:** 501 Crescent Street, New Haven, CT 06515-1355
- **Website:** http://www.southernct.edu/
- **Public**
- **Enrollment:** 6,697 full-time; 1,612 part-time

KEY STATS

✔ **U.S News College Ranking:** fourth tier, Universities–Master's (North)
✔ **SAT Score (25th/75th percentile):** 850-1050
✔ **Tuition:** 2006-2007: $7,323 in state, $14,451 out of state
Selectivity: Less selective **Room/board:** $8,031
Acceptance rate: 54% **Average debt:** N/A
Student/faculty ratio: 17/1 **Proportion who borrowed:** N/A

UNDERGRADUATE STUDENT BODY STATS

2005-2006 enrollment: 6,697 full-time; 1,612 part-time. Men: 38%; women: 62%. **Ethnic makeup:** African American: 12%; Asian American: 2%; Hispanic: 6%; White: 78%; International: 1%.

ADMISSIONS FACTS AND FIGURES

Phone: (203) 392-5656. **Email:** adminfo@southernct.edu. **Website:** http://www.southernct.edu/. **Application deadlines for fall 2007:** Regular decision: July 1. Early decision: Not offered. Early action: Not offered. Admission can be deferred. **Application fee:** $50. Common application is accepted. **Admissions requirements/recommendations:** High school units required (recommended): English: 4; Mathematics: 3 (4); Science: 2; Foreign language: 2 (3); Social studies: 2; History: 2; Academic electives: 1. Tests: The college uses SAT or ACT scores in admissions decisions. Either SAT or ACT required. For admission to the fall 2007 entering class, the school will accept: ACT with writing. Campus visit: Recommended. Admissions interview: Neither required nor recommended. Off-campus interview: Not available. **Factors that count in admissions decisions:** *Academic:* Secondary school record: Very important. Class rank: Considered. Letters of recommendation: Important. Standardized test scores: Important.

Essay: Important. *Nonacademic:* Interview: Not considered. Extracurricular activities: Considered. Talent/ability: Considered. Character/personal qualities: Considered. Alumni/ae relationship: Considered. Geographical residence: Not considered. State residency: Not considered. Religious affiliation/commitment: Not considered. Minority status: Considered. Volunteer work: Considered. Work experience: Considered. **Admissions statistics for the fall 2005 entering class:** Total applicants: 5,037. Total accepted: 2,722. Freshmen enrolled: 1,340; 7% were from out of state. Overall acceptance rate: 54%. **Credentials of fall 2005 freshmen:** 5% ranked in the top 10 percent of their high school class; 22% were in the top 25 percent, and 57% were in the top half. (Proportion submitting class standing: 77%.) **First-year students who submitted SAT scores:** 97%. Scores (25/75 percentile): Verbal: 430-530, Math: 420-520, Combined: 850-1050. **First-year students submitting ACT scores:** 3%. Scores (25/75 percentile): English: N/A, Math: N/A, Composite: N/A.

ACADEMICS

Year founded: 1893. **Academic calendar:** Semester. **Degrees offered:** bachelor's, master's, post-master's certificate, doctorate. **Most popular majors:** 14% psychology, 8% communication studies/speech communication and rhetoric, 8% liberal arts and sciences/liberal studies, 6% nursing/registered nurse training (R.N., A.S.N., B.S.N., M.S.N.), 5% business administration and management. **Major fields of study:** agriculture, agriculture operations, and related sciences; biological and biomedical sciences; business, management, marketing, and related support services; communication, journalism, and related programs; computer and information sciences and support services; education; English language and literature/letters; foreign languages, literatures, and linguistics; health professions and related clinical sciences; history; liberal arts and sciences studies, and humanities; library science; mathematics and statistics; parks, recreation, leisure, and fitness studies; philosophy and religious studies; physical sciences; psychology; public administration and social service professions; visual and performing arts. **Areas of required coursework:** arts/fine arts, humanities, mathematics, English (including composition), philosophy, foreign languages, sciences (biological or physical), history, social science. **Pre-professional programs:** pre-law, pre-dentistry, pre-medicine, pre-veterinary science, other. **Special academic programs:** accelerated program, cooperative (work-study plan) program, distance learning, double major, dual enrollment, exchange student program (domestic), external degree program, honors program, independent study, internships, liberal arts/career combination, student-designed major, study abroad, teacher certificate program. **Teacher certification offered in:** early childhood, special education, elementary, middle/junior high, secondary, bilingual/bicultural. **Cooperative education programs:** art, business, computer science, education, health professions, humanities, natural science, social/behavioral science, other. **Reserve Officers Training Corps (ROTC):** Army ROTC: Offered at cooperating institution (University of Connecticut); Air Force ROTC: Offered at cooperating institution (University of Connecticut). **Faculty and instruction (2005-2006):** Total instructional faculty: 403 full-time, 555 part-time (49% men; 51% women; 15% minorities). Full-time faculty with Ph.D. or other terminal degree: 90%. Student/faculty ratio: 17/1. Classes of fewer than 20 students: 32%; of 20 to 49 students: 67%; of 50 or more students: 1%. **Freshmen returning for sophomore year:** 72%. **Graduation rates:** Four-year: 12%; five-year: 30%; six-year: 36%.

COSTS AND FINANCIAL AID

Financial aid office: (203) 392-5222. **Expenses (2006-2007):** Tuition and fees 2006-2007: $7,323 in state, $14,451 out of state; room/board: $8,031. Estimated books and supplies: $1,300; transportation: $500; personal expenses: $150. **Financial aid:** Priority filing date for institution's financial aid form: March 10. In 2005-2006, 82% of undergraduates applied for financial aid. Of those, 49% were determined to have financial need; 32% had their need fully met. Average financial aid package (proportion receiving): $6,629 (46%). Average amount of gift aid, such as scholarships or grants (proportion receiving): $4,409 (33%). Average amount of self-help aid, such as work study or loans (proportion receiving): $3,469 (38%). Average need-based loan (excluding PLUS or other private loans): $3,383. Among students who received need-based aid, the average percentage of need met: 79%. Among students who received aid based on merit, the average award (and the proportion receiving): $2,935 (5%). The average athletic scholarship (and the proportion receiving): $5,206 (3%).

CAMPUS LIFE AND EXTRACURRICULAR ACTIVITIES

Campus housing available: coed dorms, apartment for single students, special housing for disabled students. Students who live in college-owned, operated, or affiliated housing: 31%. **Student employment:** During the 2005-

2006 academic year, 2% of undergraduates worked on campus. Average per-year earnings: $3,500. **Clubs and organizations:** Number of student organizations: 94. Activities include: choral groups, concert band, drama/theater, jazz band, literary magazine, marching band, music ensembles, musical theater, pep band, radio station, student government, student newspaper, yearbook. Number of fraternities: 5; sororities: 3. Proportion of men in fraternities: 1%; of women in sororities: 1%. Average proportion of students who stay on campus on weekends: 25%. **Sports program (2005-2006):** Member of NCAA II. *Men's intercollegiate varsity sports:* baseball, basketball, cross-country, football, gymnastics, soccer, swimming and diving, track and field (indoor), track and field (outdoor). *Women's intercollegiate varsity sports:* basketball, cross-country, field hockey, gymnastics, lacrosse, soccer, softball, swimming and diving, track and field (indoor), track and field (outdoor), volleyball.

SERVICES AND FACILITIES

Basic services: nonremedial tutoring, women's center, placement service, health service, health insurance. **Remedial assistance:** reading, math, writing, study skills. **Counseling services:** career, personal, academic, psychological. **For learning-disabled students:** School does not offer a structured program with separate admission and additional fees. Total undergraduates in learning-disabled program or receiving services: 239. Services include: remedial math, remedial English, reading machines, tape recorders, other special classes, note-taking services, special bookstore section, oral tests, learning center, readers, extended time for tests, tutors, early syllabus, priority registration, priority seating, substitution of courses, texts on tape, typist/scribe, exams on tape or computer, waiver of foreign language degree requirement, other. **Information technology resources:** Students are not required to lease or own a computer. Number of campus computers available to all students: 700. School has a wireless network. Approximate number of users that can be accommodated: 600. Proportion of college-owned housing units wired for high-speed internet access: 100%. **Campus safety:** Security services offered: 24-hour foot-and-vehicle patrols, late-night transport/escort service, 24-hour emergency telephones, lighted pathways/sidewalks, controlled dormitory access (key, security card, etc).

TRANSFER AND INTERNATIONAL STUDENTS

Transfer students: May apply for admission for the following academic terms: Fall, Spring. Applicants need a minimum number of credits to apply. For fall 2005: Transfer applications received: 1,692. Transfer applicants offered admission: 1,057. Transfer applicants enrolled: 608. **International students:** Number of foreign undergraduates: 70 (1% of student body). Number of countries represented: 40. Minimum TOEFL score required: 525 (paper); 197 (computer). Average TOEFL score: 550 (paper).

St. Joseph College

- **Address:** 1678 Asylum Avenue, West Hartford, CT 06117
- **Website:** http://www.sjc.edu
- **Private; Religious affiliation:** Roman Catholic
- **Enrollment:** 871 full-time; 288 part-time

KEY STATS

✔ **U.S News College Ranking:** 46, Universities–Master's (North)
✔ **SAT Score (25th/75th percentile):** 890-1110
✔ **Tuition:** 2006-2007: $23,490

Selectivity: Less selective	**Room/board:** $10,260
Acceptance rate: 72%	**Average debt:** $36,606
Student/faculty ratio: 12/1	**Proportion who borrowed:** 93%

UNDERGRADUATE STUDENT BODY STATS

2005-2006 enrollment: 871 full-time; 288 part-time. Men: 1%; women: 99%. **Ethnic makeup:** African American: 14%; Asian American: 2%; Hispanic: 8%; White: 76%.

ADMISSIONS FACTS AND FIGURES

Phone: (860) 231-5216. **Email:** admissions@sjc.edu. **Website:** http://www.sjc.edu. **Application deadlines for fall 2007:** Regular decision: Rolling. Early decision: Not offered. Early action: Not offered. Admission can be deferred. **Application fee:** $35. Common application is accepted. **Admissions requirements/recommendations:** High school units required (recommended): English: (4); Mathematics: (3); Science: (3); Foreign language: (2); Social studies: (2); History: (2); Total units: (16). Tests: The college uses SAT or ACT scores in admissions decisions. Either SAT or ACT required. Campus visit: Recommended. Admissions interview: Recommended. Off-campus interview: May be arranged. **Factors that count in admissions decisions:** *Academic:* Secondary school record: Very important. Letters of recommendation: Considered. Standardized test scores: Very important. Essay: Considered. *Nonacademic:* Interview: Considered. Extracurricular activities: Considered. Talent/ability: Considered. Character/personal qualities: Considered. Alumni/ae relationship: Considered. Geographical residence: Not considered. State residency: Not considered. Religious affiliation/commitment: Not considered. Minority status: Not considered. Volunteer work: Considered. Work experience: Considered. **Other schools with the greatest overlap in applicants:** Central Connecticut State University; Quinnipiac University; Southern Connecticut State University; University of Connecticut; University of Hartford. **Admissions statistics for the fall 2005 entering class:** Total applicants: 1,051. Total accepted: 755. Freshmen enrolled: 251; 20% were from out of state. Overall acceptance rate: 72%. **Credentials of fall 2005 freshmen:** 15% ranked in the top 10 percent of their high school class; 43% were in the top 25 percent, and 78% were in the top half. (Proportion submitting class standing: 73%.) **Average high school grade point average:** 3.1. **First-year students who submitted SAT scores:** 100%. Scores (25/75 percentile): Verbal: 450-570, Math: 440-540, Combined: 890-1110.

ACADEMICS

Year founded: 1932. **Academic calendar:** Semester. **Degrees offered:** certificate, bachelor's, master's. **Most popular majors:** 19% health professions and related clinical sciences, 17% human services, 14% psychology, 12% social work, 6% education. **Major fields of study:** biological and biomedical sciences; business, management, marketing, and related support services; education; English language and literature/letters; family and consumer sciences/human sciences; foreign languages, literatures, and linguistics; health professions and related clinical sciences; liberal arts and sciences studies, and humanities; mathematics and statistics; philosophy and religious studies; physical sciences; psychology; public administration and social service professions; social sciences; visual and performing arts. **Areas of required coursework:** arts/fine arts, humanities, computer literacy, mathematics, English (including composition), philosophy, foreign languages, sciences (biological or physical), history, social science, other. **Pre-professional programs:** pre-law, pre-dentistry, pre-medicine, pre-veterinary science. **Special academic programs:** distance learning, double major, English as a Second Language (ESL), honors program, independent study, internships, student-designed major, study abroad, teacher certificate program, weekend college. **Teacher certification offered in:** special education, elementary, middle/junior high, secondary. **Faculty and instruction (2005-2006):** Total instructional faculty: 77 full-time, 11 part-time (28% men; 72% women; 14% minorities). Full-time faculty with Ph.D. or other terminal degree: 88%. Student/faculty ratio: 12/1. Classes of fewer than 20 students: 71%; of 20 to 49 students: 28%; of 50 or more students: 1%. **Freshmen returning for sophomore year:** 73%. **Graduation rates:** Four-year: 43%; five-year: 53%; six-year: 56%. **Graduate study:** 30% of students pursue further study immediately upon graduation; 15% within one year; 25% within five years.

COSTS AND FINANCIAL AID

Financial aid office: (860) 231-5223. **Expenses (2006-2007):** Tuition and fees 2006-2007: $23,490; room/board: $10,260. Estimated books and supplies: $850; transportation: $2,000; personal expenses: $700. **Financial aid:** Priority filing date for institution's financial aid form: February 15; deadline: February 15. In 2005-2006, 90% of undergraduates applied for financial aid. Of those, 86% were determined to have financial need; 25% had their need fully met. Average financial aid package (proportion receiving): $17,997 (86%). Average amount of gift aid, such as scholarships or grants (proportion receiving): $11,289 (84%). Average amount of self-help aid, such as work study or loans (proportion receiving): $7,564 (78%). Average need-based loan (excluding PLUS or other private loans): $7,335. Among students who received need-based aid, the average percentage of need met: 70%. Among students who received aid based on merit, the average award (and the proportion receiving): $11,492 (13%). The average athletic scholarship (and the proportion receiving): $0 (0%). Average amount of debt of borrowers graduating in 2005: $36,606. Proportion who borrowed: 93%.

CAMPUS LIFE AND EXTRACURRICULAR ACTIVITIES

Campus housing available (% using): women's dorms (99%), special housing for disabled students. Students who live in college-owned, operated, or affiliated housing: 46%. **Student employment:** During the 2005-2006 academic year, 26% of undergraduates worked on campus. Average per-year earnings: $1,250. **Clubs and organizations:** Number of student organizations: 20. Activities include: choral groups, concert band, dance, drama/theater, literary magazine, music ensembles, student government, yearbook. Number of fraternities: 0; sororities: 0. Average proportion of students who stay on campus on weekends: 60%. **Sports program (2005-2006):** Member of NCAA III. *Women's intercollegiate varsity sports:* basketball, cross-country, soccer, softball, swimming and diving, tennis, volleyball.

SERVICES AND FACILITIES

Basic services: placement service, day care, health service, health insurance. **Remedial assistance:** reading, math, writing, study skills. **Counseling services:** career, personal, academic, older student, psychological. **For learning-disabled students:** School does not offer a structured program with separate admission and additional fees. Total undergraduates in learning-disabled program or receiving services: 30. Services include: tape recorders, untimed tests, note-taking services, oral tests, learning center, readers, extended time for tests, tutors, priority registration, priority seating, texts on tape, other testing accomodations. **Library:** Number of titles: 120,500; number of current serial subscriptions: 479. **Information technology resources:** Students are not required to lease or own a computer. Number of campus computers available to all students: 150. School has a wireless network. Approximate number of users that can be accommodated: 1,200. Proportion of college-owned housing units wired for high-speed internet access: 100%. **Campus safety:** Security services offered: 24-hour foot-and-vehicle patrols, late-night transport/escort service, 24-hour emergency telephones, lighted pathways/sidewalks, controlled dormitory access (key, security card, etc).

TRANSFER AND INTERNATIONAL STUDENTS

Transfer students: May apply for admission for the following academic terms: Fall, Spring, Summer. Applicants do not need a minimum number of credits to apply. For fall 2005: Transfer applications received: 477. Transfer applicants offered admission: 212. Transfer applicants enrolled: 109. **International students:** Number of foreign undergraduates: 1. Minimum TOEFL score required: 500 (paper); 250 (computer).

Trinity College

- **Address:** 300 Summit Street, Hartford, CT 06106
- **Website:** http://www.trincoll.edu
- **Private**
- **Enrollment:** 2,165 full-time; 178 part-time

KEY STATS

✔ **U.S News College Ranking:** 30, Liberal Arts Colleges
✔ **SAT Score (25th/75th percentile):** 1220-1400
✔ **Tuition:** 2006-2007: $35,130

Selectivity: More selective	**Room/board:** $8,970
Acceptance rate: 39%	**Average debt:** $14,283
Student/faculty ratio: 10/1	**Proportion who borrowed:** 44%

UNDERGRADUATE STUDENT BODY STATS

2005-2006 enrollment: 2,165 full-time; 178 part-time. Men: 49%; women: 51%. **Ethnic makeup:** African American: 5%; Asian American: 6%; Hispanic: 5%; White: 82%; International: 2%. **Religious preference:** Roman Catholic: 24%; Protestant: 25%; Jewish: 9%; Muslim: 1%; Hindu: 1%; Buddhist: 1%; No preference: 24%; Unknown: 7%; Other Christian: 7%; Other: 1%.

ADMISSIONS FACTS AND FIGURES

Phone: (860) 297-2180. **Email:** admissions.office@trincoll.edu. **Website:** http://www.trincoll.edu. **Application deadlines for fall 2007:** Regular decision: January 1; decision sent by April 1. Early decision: Send application by: November 15; Decision sent by: December 15. Early action: Not offered. Admission can be deferred. **Application fee:** $60. Common application is accepted. **To apply online, go to:** http://www.trincoll.edu/depts/admissio/commonapp/. **Admissions requirements/recommendations:** High school units required (recommended): English: 4; Mathematics: 3; Science: 2; Foreign language: 3; History: 2; Total units: 16. Tests: The college uses SAT or ACT scores in admissions decisions. Either SAT or ACT required. For admission to the fall 2007 entering class, the school will accept: ACT with writing, ACT without writing. Campus visit: Recommended. Admissions interview: Recommended. Off-

campus interview: May be arranged. **Factors that count in admissions decisions:** *Academic:* Secondary school record: Very important. Class rank: Important. Letters of recommendation: Important. Standardized test scores: Important. Essay: Important. *Nonacademic:* Interview: Considered. Extracurricular activities: Important. Talent/ability: Important. Character/personal qualities: Important. Alumni/ae relationship: Considered. Geographical residence: Considered. State residency: Not considered. Religious affiliation/commitment: Not considered. Minority status: Important. Volunteer work: Considered. Work experience: Considered. **Other schools with the greatest overlap in applicants:** Boston College; Brown University; Georgetown University; Middlebury College; Tufts University. **Admissions statistics for the fall 2005 entering class:** Total applicants: 5,744. Total accepted: 2,265. Freshmen enrolled: 573; 84% were from out of state. Accepted through early-decision or early-action plans: 40%. Overall acceptance rate: 39%. Early-decision acceptance rate: 64%. Non-early acceptance rate: 38%. **Size of waiting list:** 1259 applicants; enrolled from waiting list: 49. **Credentials of fall 2005 freshmen:** 53% ranked in the top 10 percent of their high school class; 89% were in the top 25 percent, and 99% were in the top half. (Proportion submitting class standing: 20%.) **First-year students who submitted SAT scores:** 56%. Scores (25/75 percentile): Verbal: 610-700, Math: 610-700, Combined: 1220-1400. **First-year students submitting ACT scores:** 20%. Scores (25/75 percentile): English: 24-31, Math: 25-29, Composite: 25-29.

ACADEMICS

Year founded: 1823. **Academic calendar:** Semester. **Degrees offered:** bachelor's, master's. **Most popular majors:** 14% economics, 10% political science and government, 8% English language and literature, 8% history, 7% psychology. **Major fields of study:** area, ethnic, cultural, and gender studies; biological and biomedical sciences; computer and information sciences and support services; education; engineering; English language and literature/letters; foreign languages, literatures, and linguistics; history; mathematics and statistics; natural resources and conservation; philosophy and religious studies; physical sciences; psychology; public administration and social service professions; social sciences; visual and performing arts. **Areas of required coursework:** arts/fine arts, humanities, sciences (biological or physical), social science, other. **Pre-professional programs:** pre-law, pre-medicine. **Special academic programs (% participation):** accelerated program (.2%), cross-registration (4%), double major (11%), exchange student program (domestic) (0%), honors program (27%), independent study (60%), internships (32%), student-designed major (1.4%), study abroad (51%), teacher certificate program (0%), other (0%). **Reserve Officers Training Corps (ROTC):** Army ROTC: Offered at cooperating institution (Univ. of Connecticut). **Faculty and instruction (2005-2006):** Total instructional faculty: 183 full-time, 75 part-time (59% men; 41% women; 16% minorities). Full-time faculty with Ph.D. or other terminal degree: 92%. Student/faculty ratio: 10/1. Classes of fewer than 20 students: 63%; of 20 to 49 students: 33%; of 50 or more students: 4%. **Advanced Placement and International Baccalaureate credit:** AP tests may be used for: Credit and/or placement. Scores accepted: 4, 5. International Baccalaureate exams may be used for: Credit and/or placement. **Freshmen returning for sophomore year:** 92%. **Graduation rates:** Four-year: 78%; five-year: 84%; six-year: 85%. **Graduate study:** 18% of students pursue further study immediately upon graduation; 60% within five years. Fields in which graduates pursue further study: Master of Business Administration (MBA), 18%; law, 11%; medicine, 4%; dentistry, 1%; engineering, 3%; theology (or the seminary), 1%; education, 6%; arts and sciences, 33%.

COSTS AND FINANCIAL AID

Financial aid office: (860) 297-2046. **Expenses (2006-2007):** Tuition and fees 2006-2007: $35,130; room/board: $8,970. **Financial aid:** In 2005-2006, 45% of undergraduates applied for financial aid. Of those, 40% were determined to have financial need; 100% had their need fully met. Average financial aid package (proportion receiving): $27,920 (40%). Average amount of gift aid, such as scholarships or grants (proportion receiving): N/A (37%). Average amount of self-help aid, such as work study or loans (proportion receiving): N/A (35%). Among students who received need-based aid, the average percentage of need met: 100%. Among students who received aid based on merit, the average award (and the proportion receiving): $16,807 (0%). Average amount of debt of borrowers graduating in 2005: $14,283. Proportion who borrowed: 44%.

CAMPUS LIFE AND EXTRACURRICULAR ACTIVITIES

Campus housing available (% using): coed dorms (98%), fraternity housing (2%). Students who live in college-owned, operated, or affiliated housing: 91%. **Student employment:** During the 2005-2006 academic year, 16% of undergraduates worked on campus. Average per-year earnings: $1,485. **Clubs and organizations:** Number of student organizations: 81. Activities include: choral groups, dance, drama/theater, jazz band, literary magazine, music ensembles, musical theater, radio station, student government, student newspaper, student film society, television station, yearbook. Number of fraternities: 7; sororities: 7. Proportion of men in fraternities: 20%; of women in sororities: 16%. **Sports program (2005-2006):** Member of NCAA III. *Men's intercollegiate varsity sports:* baseball, basketball, cross-country, football, golf, ice hockey, lacrosse, soccer, swimming and diving, tennis, track and field (indoor), track and field (outdoor), wrestling. *Women's intercollegiate varsity sports:* basketball, cross-country, field hockey, ice hockey, lacrosse, soccer, softball, squash, swimming and diving, tennis, track and field (indoor), track and field (outdoor), volleyball, rowing.

SERVICES AND FACILITIES

Basic services: nonremedial tutoring, women's center, health service. **Counseling services:** minority student, career, personal, academic, older student, psychological, birth control, religious. **For learning-disabled students:** School does not offer a structured program with separate admission and additional fees. Total undergraduates in learning-disabled program or receiving services: 180. Services include: other testing accommodations, tape recorders, note-taking services, oral tests, readers, extended time for tests, tutors, priority seating, texts on tape, other testing accomodations. **Library:** Number of titles: 1,003,933; number of current serial subscriptions: 12,957. **Information technology resources:** Students are not required to lease or own a computer. Number of campus computers available to all students: 349. School has a wireless network. Approximate number of users that can be accommodated: 2,000. Proportion of college-owned housing units wired for high-speed internet access: 100%. **Campus safety:** Security services offered: 24-hour foot-and-vehicle patrols, late-night transport/escort service, 24-hour emergency telephones, lighted pathways/sidewalks, controlled dormitory access (key, security card, etc).

TRANSFER AND INTERNATIONAL STUDENTS

Transfer students: May apply for admission for the following academic terms: Fall, Winter. Applicants do not need a minimum number of credits to apply. For fall 2005: Transfer applications received: 164. Transfer applicants offered admission: 35. Transfer applicants enrolled: 22. **International students:** Number of foreign undergraduates: 47 (2% of student body). Number of countries represented: 20.

United States Coast Guard Academy

- **Address:** 15 Mohegan Avenue, New London, CT 06320
- **Website:** http://www.uscga.edu
- **Public**
- **Enrollment:** 1,012 full-time

KEY STATS

✔ **U.S News College Ranking:** Unranked Specialty School–Military Academies

✔ **SAT Score (25th/75th percentile):** 1210-1370

✔ **Tuition:** 2006-2007: $3,000 in state, $3,000 out of state

Selectivity: More selective	**Room/board:** $0
Acceptance rate: 26%	**Average debt:** N/A
Student/faculty ratio: 9/1	**Proportion who borrowed:** N/A

UNDERGRADUATE STUDENT BODY STATS

2005-2006 enrollment: 1,012 full-time. Men: 72%; women: 28%. **Ethnic makeup:** African American: 3%; American-Indian: 1%; Asian American: 5%; Hispanic: 4%; White: 87%; International: 1%. **Religious preference:** Roman Catholic: 39%; Protestant: 43%; Jewish: 2%; Buddhist: 1%; No preference: 12%; Other: 3%.

ADMISSIONS FACTS AND FIGURES

Phone: (800) 883-8724. **Email:** admissions@cga.uscg.mil. **Website:** http://www.uscga.edu. **Application deadlines for fall 2007:** Regular decision: March 1. Early decision: Not offered. Early action: Send application by: November 1; Decision sent by: December 15. Admission cannot be deferred. Common application is not accepted. **To apply online, go to:** http://admissions.uscga.edu/i2e/academy_admission/app_process.asp. **Admissions requirements/recommendations:** High school units required (recom-

mended): English: 4; Mathematics: 4; Science: 3. Tests: The college uses SAT or ACT scores in admissions decisions. Either SAT or ACT required. For admission to the fall 2007 entering class, the school will accept: ACT with writing. Campus visit: Recommended. Admissions interview: Recommended. Off-campus interview: May be arranged. **Factors that count in admissions decisions:** *Academic:* Secondary school record: Very important. Class rank: Very important. Letters of recommendation: Important. Standardized test scores: Very important. Essay: Important. *Nonacademic:* Interview: Considered. Extracurricular activities: Very important. Talent/ability: Important. Character/personal qualities: Very important. Alumni/ae relationship: Considered. Geographical residence: Not considered. State residency: Not considered. Religious affiliation/commitment: Not considered. Minority status: Considered. Volunteer work: Considered. Work experience: Considered. **Other schools with the greatest overlap in applicants:** United States Air Force Academy; United States Merchant Marine Academy; United States Military Academy; United States Naval Academy. **Admissions statistics for the fall 2005 entering class:** Total applicants: 1,597. Total accepted: 422. Freshmen enrolled: 307; 93% were from out of state. Accepted through early-decision or early-action plans: 39%. Overall acceptance rate: 26%. Non-early acceptance rate: 25%. **Credentials of fall 2005 freshmen:** 47% ranked in the top 10 percent of their high school class; 86% were in the top 25 percent, and 100% were in the top half. (Proportion submitting class standing: 99%.) **Average high school grade point average:** 3.7. **First-year students who submitted SAT scores:** 92%. Scores (25/75 percentile): Verbal: 590-680, Math: 620-690, Combined: 1210-1370. **First-year students submitting ACT scores:** 38%. Scores (25/75 percentile): English: 25-30, Math: 26-31, Composite: 25-29.

ACADEMICS

Year founded: 1931. **Academic calendar:** Semester. **Degrees offered:** bachelor's. **Most popular majors:** 35% engineering, 18% chemical and physical oceanography, 18% political science and government, 16% business administration and management, 14% mathematics and statistics. **Major fields of study:** business, management, marketing, and related support services; engineering; mathematics and statistics; physical sciences; social sciences. **Areas of required coursework:** humanities, computer literacy, mathematics, English (including composition), philosophy, foreign languages, sciences (biological or physical), history, social science, other. **Special academic programs:** double major, exchange student program (domestic), honors program, independent study, internships. **Faculty and instruction (2005-2006):** Total instructional faculty: 100 full-time, 18 part-time (76% men; 24% women; 8% minorities). Full-time faculty with Ph.D. or other terminal degree: 49%. Student/faculty ratio: 9/1. Classes of fewer than 20 students: 63%; of 20 to 49 students: 37%. **Freshmen returning for sophomore year:** 86%. **Graduation rates:** Four-year: 68%; five-year: 72%; six-year: 69%.

COSTS AND FINANCIAL AID

Expenses (2006-2007): Tuition and fees 2006-2007: $3,000 in state, $3,000 out of state; room/board: $0.

CAMPUS LIFE AND EXTRACURRICULAR ACTIVITIES

Campus housing available (% using): coed dorms (100%). Students who live in college-owned, operated, or affiliated housing: 100%. **Student employment:** During the 2005-2006 academic year, 0% of undergraduates worked on campus. Activities include: choral groups, concert band, drama/theater, jazz band, marching band, music ensembles, musical theater, pep band, student government, yearbook. Number of fraternities: 0; sororities: 0. Average proportion of students who stay on campus on weekends: 100%. **Sports program (2005-2006):** Member of NCAA III. *Men's intercollegiate varsity sports:* baseball, basketball, cross-country, football, riflery, soccer, swimming and diving, tennis, track and field (indoor), track and field (outdoor), wrestling. *Women's intercollegiate varsity sports:* basketball, cross-country, soccer, softball, swimming and diving, track and field (indoor), track and field (outdoor), volleyball, rowing.

SERVICES AND FACILITIES

Basic services: nonremedial tutoring, health service, health insurance. **Remedial assistance:** reading, math, writing. **Counseling services:** minority student, career, military, personal, academic, psychological, birth control, religious. **Library:** Number of titles: 155,734; number of current serial subscriptions: 514. **Information technology resources:** Students are required to lease or own a computer. Number of campus computers available to all students: 323. School has a wireless network. Approximate number of users that can be accommodated: 315. Proportion of college-owned housing units wired for high-speed internet access: 100%. **Campus safety:** Security services offered: 24-hour foot-and-vehicle patrols, lighted pathways/sidewalks.

International students: Number of foreign undergraduates: 13 (1% of student body). Number of countries represented: 7. Minimum TOEFL score required: 560 (paper); 220 (computer). Average TOEFL score: 585 (paper).

University of Bridgeport

- ■ **Address:** 126 Park Avenue, Bridgeport, CT 06604
- ■ **Website:** http://www.bridgeport.edu
- ■ **Private**
- ■ **Enrollment:** 1,247 full-time; 429 part-time

KEY STATS

✔ **U.S News College Ranking:** fourth tier, National Universities
✔ **SAT Score (25th/75th percentile):** 770-980
✔ **Tuition:** 2005-2006: $20,595

Selectivity: Less selective	**Room/board:** $9,000
Acceptance rate: 73%	**Average debt:** N/A
Student/faculty ratio: 15/1	**Proportion who borrowed:** N/A

UNDERGRADUATE STUDENT BODY STATS

2005-2006 enrollment: 1,247 full-time; 429 part-time. Men: 36%; women: 64%. **Ethnic makeup:** African American: 33%; Asian American: 4%; Hispanic: 14%; White: 35%; International: 13%.

ADMISSIONS FACTS AND FIGURES

Phone: (203) 576-4552. **Email:** admit@bridgeport.edu. **Website:** http://www.bridgeport.edu. **Application deadlines for fall 2007:** Regular decision: Rolling. Early decision: Not offered. Early action: Not offered. Admission can be deferred. **Application fee:** $25. Common application is not accepted. **Admissions requirements/recommendations:** High school units required (recommended): English: 4 (4); Mathematics: 3 (3); Science: 2 (2); Social studies: 2 (2); Academic electives: 5 (5); Total units: 16 (16). Tests: The college uses SAT or ACT scores in admissions decisions. Either SAT or ACT required. For admission to the fall 2007 entering class, the school will accept: ACT with writing, ACT without writing. Campus visit: Recommended. Admissions interview: Recommended. Off-campus interview: May be arranged. **Factors that count in admissions decisions:** *Academic:* Secondary school record: Very important. Class rank: Important. Letters of recommendation: Important. Standardized test scores: Very important. Essay: Important. *Nonacademic:* Interview: Considered. Extracurricular activities: Considered. Talent/ability: Important. Character/personal qualities: Important. Alumni/ae relationship: Not considered. Geographical residence: Not considered. State residency: Not considered. Religious affiliation/commitment: Not considered. Minority status: Not considered. Volunteer work: Considered. Work experience: Considered. **Admissions statistics for the fall 2005 entering class:** Total applicants: 2,332. Total accepted: 1,709. Freshmen enrolled: 365; 58% were from out of state. Overall acceptance rate: 73%. **Credentials of fall 2005 freshmen:** 8% ranked in the top 10 percent of their high school class; 25% were in the top 25 percent, and 52% were in the top half. (Proportion submitting class standing: 55%.) **Average high school grade point average:** 2.8. **First-year students who submitted SAT scores:** 87%. Scores (25/75 percentile): Verbal: 380-490, Math: 390-490, Combined: 770-980. **First-year students submitting ACT scores:** 7%. Scores (25/75 percentile): English: 14-20, Math: 15-19, Composite: 15-20.

ACADEMICS

Year founded: 1927. **Academic calendar:** Semester. **Degrees offered:** associate, bachelor's, master's, post-master's certificate, first professional, doctorate. **Most popular majors:** 24% general studies, 8% psychology, 7% dental hygiene/hygienist, 6% community organization and advocacy, 5% business/commerce. **Major fields of study:** architecture and related services; area, ethnic, cultural, and gender studies; biological and biomedical sciences; business, management, marketing, and related support services; communication, journalism, and related programs; computer and information sciences and support services; engineering; health professions and related clinical sciences; liberal arts and sciences studies, and humanities; mathematics and statistics; multi/interdisciplinary studies; philosophy and religious studies; psychology; public administration and social service professions; social sciences; visual and performing arts. **Areas of required coursework:** arts/fine arts, humanities, computer literacy, mathematics,

English (including composition), philosophy, foreign languages, sciences (biological or physical), history, social science. **Pre-professional programs:** pre-law, pre-dentistry, pre-medicine, pre-veterinary science. **Special academic programs (% participation):** accelerated program (15%), cooperative (work-study plan) program (10%), cross-registration (1%), distance learning (5%), double major (10%), English as a Second Language (ESL) (5%), honors program (2%), independent study (5%), internships (5%), liberal arts/career combination (20%), student-designed major (5%), study abroad (5%), teacher certificate program (5%), weekend college (5%). **Teacher certification offered in:** elementary, middle/junior high, secondary. **Cooperative education programs:** art, business, computer science, education, engineering, health professions, humanities, natural science, social/behavioral science, technologies. **Reserve Officers Training Corps (ROTC):** Army ROTC: Offered at cooperating institution (UCONN). **Faculty and instruction (2005-2006):** Total instructional faculty: 89 full-time, 260 part-time (59% men; 41% women; 13% minorities). Full-time faculty with Ph.D. or other terminal degree: 84%. Student/faculty ratio: 15/1. Classes of fewer than 20 students: 65%; of 20 to 49 students: 34%; of 50 or more students: 1%. **Advanced Placement and International Baccalaureate credit:** AP tests may be used for: Placement only. Scores accepted: 3, 4, 5. International Baccalaureate exams may be used for: Credit and/or placement. **Freshmen returning for sophomore year:** 67%. **Graduation rates:** Four-year: 21%; five-year: 31%; six-year: 34%. **Graduate study:** 15% of students pursue further study immediately upon graduation; 25% within one year; 40% within five years. Fields in which graduates pursue further study: Master of Business Administration (MBA), 20%; law, 10%; medicine, 25%; engineering, 20%; education, 25%.

COSTS AND FINANCIAL AID

Financial aid office: (203) 576-4568. **Expenses (2005-2006):** Tuition and fees 2005-2006: $20,595; room/board: $9,000. Estimated books and supplies: $1,200; transportation: $1,000; personal expenses: $2,147. **Financial aid:** Priority filing date for institution's financial aid form: April 1.

CAMPUS LIFE AND EXTRACURRICULAR ACTIVITIES

Campus housing available (% using): coed dorms (100%). Students who live in college-owned, operated, or affiliated housing: 45%. **Student employment:** During the 2005-2006 academic year, 50% of undergraduates worked on campus. Average per-year earnings: $2,000. **Clubs and organizations:** Number of student organizations: 30. Activities include: choral groups, literary magazine, music ensembles, student government, student newspaper, yearbook. Number of fraternities: 3; sororities: 3. Proportion of men in fraternities: 2%; of women in sororities: 2%. Average proportion of students who stay on campus on weekends: 75%. **Sports program (2005-2006):** Member of NCAA II. *Men's intercollegiate varsity sports:* baseball, basketball, cross-country, soccer. *Women's intercollegiate varsity sports:* basketball, cross-country, gymnastics, soccer, softball, swimming and diving, volleyball.

SERVICES AND FACILITIES

Basic services: nonremedial tutoring, placement service, health service, health insurance. **Remedial assistance:** reading, math, writing, study skills. **Counseling services:** minority student, career, personal, veteran student, academic, older student, psychological, birth control, religious. **For learning-disabled students:** School does not offer a structured program with separate admission and additional fees. Services include: remedial math, remedial English, remedial reading, untimed tests, learning center, extended time for tests, tutors. **Library:** Number of titles: 270,000; number of current serial subscriptions: 1,800. **Information technology resources:** Students are not required to lease or own a computer. Number of campus computers available to all students: 600. School has a wireless network. Proportion of college-owned housing units wired for high-speed internet access: 100%. **Campus safety:** Security services offered: 24-hour foot-and-vehicle patrols, late-night transport/escort service, 24-hour emergency telephones, lighted pathways/sidewalks, student patrols, controlled dormitory access (key, security card, etc).

TRANSFER AND INTERNATIONAL STUDENTS

Transfer students: May apply for admission for the following academic terms: Fall, Spring, Summer. Applicants need a minimum number of credits to apply. For fall 2005: Transfer applications received: 806. Transfer applicants offered admission: 410. Transfer applicants enrolled: 174. **International students:** Number of foreign undergraduates: 221 (13% of student body). Number of countries represented: 74. Minimum TOEFL score required: 500 (paper). Average TOEFL score: 550 (paper).

University of Connecticut

- **Address:** 2131 Hillside Road, Unit 3088, Storrs, CT 06269-3088
- **Website:** http://www.uconn.edu
- **Public**
- **Enrollment:** 15,296 full-time; 816 part-time

KEY STATS

✔ **U.S News College Ranking:** 67, National Universities
✔ **SAT Score (25th/75th percentile):** 1090-1280
✔ **Tuition:** 2006-2007: $8,362 in state, $21,562 out of state

Selectivity: More selective	**Room/board:** $8,266
Acceptance rate: 51%	**Average debt:** $19,410
Student/faculty ratio: 17/1	**Proportion who borrowed:** 60%

UNDERGRADUATE STUDENT BODY STATS

2005-2006 enrollment: 15,296 full-time; 816 part-time. Men: 48%; women: 52%. **Ethnic makeup:** African American: 5%; Asian American: 7%; Hispanic: 5%; White: 82%; International: 1%.

ADMISSIONS FACTS AND FIGURES

Phone: (860) 486-3137. **Email:** beahusky@uconn.edu. **Website:** http://www.uconn.edu. **Application deadlines for fall 2007:** Regular decision: February 1. Early decision: Not offered. Early action: Send application by: December 1; Decision sent by: January 15. Admission can be deferred. **Application fee:** $70. Common application is not accepted. **Admissions requirements/recommendations:** High school units required (recommended): English: 4; Mathematics: 3; Science: 2; Foreign language: 2 (3); Social studies: 2; Academic electives: 3; Total units: 16. Tests: The college uses SAT or ACT scores in admissions decisions. Either SAT or ACT required. For admission to the fall 2007 entering class, the school will accept: ACT with writing. Campus visit: Recommended. Admissions interview: Neither required nor recommended. Off-campus interview: Not available. **Factors that count in admissions decisions:** *Academic:* Secondary school record: Very important. Class rank: Very important. Letters of recommendation: Important. Standardized test scores: Very important. Essay: Important. *Nonacademic:* Interview: Not considered. Extracurricular activities: Important. Talent/ability: Very important. Character/personal qualities: Important. Alumni/ae relationship: Considered. Geographical residence: Considered. State residency: Considered. Religious affiliation/commitment: Not considered. Minority status: Important. Volunteer work: Important. Work experience: Considered. **Other schools with the greatest overlap in applicants:** Boston College; Boston University; Northeastern University; University of Delaware; University of Massachusetts–Amherst. **Admissions statistics for the fall 2005 entering class:** Total applicants: 18,608. Total accepted: 9,498. Freshmen enrolled: 3,260; 28% were from out of state. Accepted through early-decision or early-action plans: 55%. Overall acceptance rate: 51%. Non-early acceptance rate: 40%. **Size of waiting list:** 3287 applicants; enrolled from waiting list: 325. **Credentials of fall 2005 freshmen:** 37% ranked in the top 10 percent of their high school class; 80% were in the top 25 percent, and 98% were in the top half. (Proportion submitting class standing: 71%.) **First-year students who submitted SAT scores:** 98%. Scores (25/75 percentile): Verbal: 540-630, Math: 550-650, Combined: 1090-1280. **First-year students submitting ACT scores:** 11%. Scores (25/75 percentile): English: N/A, Math: N/A, Composite: 23-27.

ACADEMICS

Year founded: 1881. **Academic calendar:** Semester. **Degrees offered:** associate, transfer-associate, terminal-associate, bachelor's, post-bachelor's certificate, master's, post-master's certificate, first professional, doctorate. **Most popular majors:** 15% business, management, marketing, and related support services, 15% social sciences, 8% psychology, 7% health professions and related clinical sciences, 6% engineering. **Major fields of study:** agriculture, agriculture operations, and related sciences; architecture and related services; area, ethnic, cultural, and gender studies; biological and biomedical sciences; business, management, marketing, and related support services; communication, journalism, and related programs; computer and information sciences and support services; education; engineering; English language and literature/letters; family and consumer sciences/human sciences; foreign languages, literatures, and linguistics; health professions and related clinical sciences; history; liberal arts and sciences studies, and humanities; mathematics and statistics; multi/interdisciplinary studies; natural resources and conservation; parks, recreation, leisure, and fitness studies; philosophy and religious studies; physical sciences; psychology; social sciences; visual and performing arts. **Areas of required coursework:** arts/fine arts, humanities, computer literacy, mathematics, English (including composition), foreign languages, sciences (biological or physical), history, social science. **Pre-professional programs:** pre-law, pre-dentistry, pre-medicine, pre-veterinary science, pre-pharmacy, other. **Special academic programs (% participation):** accelerated program (3%), cooperative (work-study plan) program (3%), distance learning (10%), double major (7%), dual enrollment, English as a Second Language (ESL) (0%), exchange student program (domestic) (1%), honors program (10%), independent study (20%), internships (20%), liberal arts/career combination (25%), student-designed major (2%), study abroad (12%), teacher certificate program (3%), other. **Teacher certification offered in:** special education, elementary, adult education, secondary. **Cooperative education programs:** art, computer science, social/behavioral science, other. **Reserve Officers Training Corps (ROTC):** Army ROTC: Offered on campus; Air Force ROTC: Offered on campus. **Faculty and instruction (2005-2006):** Total instructional faculty: 975 full-time, 290 part-time (62% men; 38% women; 14% minorities). Full-time faculty with Ph.D. or other terminal degree: 93%. Student/faculty ratio: 17/1. Classes of fewer than 20 students: 42%; of 20 to 49 students: 42%; of 50 or more students: 16%. **Advanced Placement and International Baccalaureate credit:** AP tests may be used for: Credit and/or placement. Scores accepted: 4, 5. International Baccalaureate exams may be used for: Credit and/or placement. **Freshmen returning for sophomore year:** 90%. **Graduation rates:** Four-year: 50%; five-year: 69%; six-year: 72%. **Graduate study:** 29% of students pursue further study within one year. Fields in which graduates pursue further study: Master of Business Administration (MBA), 10%; law, 6%; medicine, 2%; dentistry, 1%; engineering, 4%; education, 37%; arts and sciences, 16%; veterinary medicine, 1%.

COSTS AND FINANCIAL AID

Financial aid office: (860) 486-2819. **Expenses (2006-2007):** Tuition and fees 2006-2007: $8,362 in state, $21,562 out of state; room/board: $8,266. Estimated books and supplies: $726; transportation: $726; personal expenses: $1,500. **Financial aid:** Priority filing date for institution's financial aid form: March 1. In 2005-2006, 68% of undergraduates applied for financial aid. Of those, 49% were determined to have financial need; 17% had their need fully met. Average financial aid package (proportion receiving): $9,070 (47%). Average amount of gift aid, such as scholarships or grants (proportion receiving): $5,958 (36%). Average amount of self-help aid, such as work study or loans (proportion receiving): $4,289 (37%). Average need-based loan (excluding PLUS or other private loans): $5,122. Among students who received need-based aid, the average percentage of need met: 69%. Among students who received aid based on merit, the average award (and the proportion receiving): $5,951 (7%). The average athletic scholarship (and the proportion receiving): $18,774 (2%). Average amount of debt of borrowers graduating in 2005: $19,410. Proportion who borrowed: 60%.

CAMPUS LIFE AND EXTRACURRICULAR ACTIVITIES

Campus housing available (% using): coed dorms (73%), women's dorms (2%), men's dorms (1%), sorority housing (1%), fraternity housing (1%), apartment for single students (14%), special housing for disabled students (4%), special housing for international students (0%), other housing options (4%). Students who live in college-owned, operated, or affiliated housing: 72%. **Student employment:** During the 2005-2006 academic year, 48% of undergraduates worked on campus. Average per-year earnings: $2,200. **Clubs and organizations:** Number of student organizations: 334. Activities include: choral groups, concert band, dance, drama/theater, jazz band, literary magazine, marching band, music ensembles, musical theater, opera, pep band, radio station, student government, student newspaper, student film society, symphony orchestra, television station, yearbook. Number of fraternities: 15; sororities: 11. Proportion of men in fraternities: 8%; of women in sororities: 7%. Average proportion of students who stay on campus on weekends: 72%. **Sports program (2005-2006):** Member of NCAA I. *Men's intercollegiate varsity sports:* baseball, basketball, cross-country, football, golf, ice hockey, soccer, swimming and diving, tennis, track and field (indoor), track and field (outdoor). *Women's intercollegiate varsity sports:* basketball, crew, cross-country, field hockey, ice hockey, lacrosse, soccer, softball, swimming and diving, tennis, track and field (indoor), track and field (outdoor), volleyball.

SERVICES AND FACILITIES

Basic services: nonremedial tutoring, women's center, placement service, day care, health service, other. **Remedial assistance:** other. **Counseling services:** minority student, career, military, personal, veteran student, academic, older student, psychological, birth control, religious. **For learning-disabled**

students: School does not offer a structured program with separate admission and additional fees. Total undergraduates in learning-disabled program or receiving services: 119. Services include: reading machines, tape recorders, note-taking services, readers, extended time for tests, priority registration, substitution of courses, texts on tape, typist/scribe, exams on tape or computer, other testing accomodations, other. **Library:** Number of titles: 2,428,752; number of current serial subscriptions: 35,230. **Information technology resources:** Students are not required to lease or own a computer. Number of campus computers available to all students: 100. School has a wireless network. Proportion of college-owned housing units wired for high-speed internet access: 95%. **Campus safety:** Security services offered: 24-hour foot-and-vehicle patrols, late-night transport/escort service, 24-hour emergency telephones, lighted pathways/sidewalks, student patrols, controlled dormitory access (key, security card, etc).

TRANSFER AND INTERNATIONAL STUDENTS

Transfer students: May apply for admission for the following academic terms: Fall, Spring. Applicants need a minimum number of credits to apply. For fall 2005: Transfer applications received: 1,910. Transfer applicants offered admission: 1,004. Transfer applicants enrolled: 636. **International students:** Number of foreign undergraduates: 134 (1% of student body). Number of countries represented: 65. Minimum TOEFL score required: 550 (paper); 213 (computer).

University of Hartford

- **Address:** 200 Bloomfield Avenue, West Hartford, CT 06117-1599
- **Website:** http://www.hartford.edu
- **Private**
- **Enrollment:** 4,657 full-time; 935 part-time

KEY STATS

- ✔ **U.S News College Ranking:** fourth tier, National Universities
- ✔ **SAT Score (25th/75th percentile):** 970-1170
- ✔ **Tuition:** 2006-2007: $25,766

Selectivity: Selective	**Room/board:** $9,922
Acceptance rate: 66%	**Average debt:** N/A
Student/faculty ratio: 13/1	**Proportion who borrowed:** N/A

UNDERGRADUATE STUDENT BODY STATS

2005-2006 enrollment: 4,657 full-time; 935 part-time. Men: 49%; women: 51%. **Ethnic makeup:** African American: 10%; Asian American: 3%; Hispanic: 5%; White: 79%; International: 3%.

ADMISSIONS FACTS AND FIGURES

Phone: (860) 768-4296. **Email:** admission@hartford.edu. **Website:** http://www.hartford.edu. **Application deadlines for fall 2007:** Regular decision: Rolling. Early decision: Not offered. Early action: Send application by: November 15; Decision sent by: December 1. Admission can be deferred. **Application fee:** $35. Common application is accepted. **Admissions requirements/recommendations:** High school units required (recommended): English: 4; Mathematics: 2 (3); Science: 2 (3); Foreign language: (2); Social studies: 2 (3); History: 2; Academic electives: 4; Total units: 16. Tests: The college uses SAT or ACT scores in admissions decisions. Either SAT or ACT required. Campus visit: Recommended. Admissions interview: Recommended. Off-campus interview: May not be arranged. **Factors that count in admissions decisions:** *Academic:* Secondary school record: Very important. Class rank: Important. Letters of recommendation: Considered. Standardized test scores: Important. Essay: Considered. *Nonacademic:* Interview: Considered. Extracurricular activities: Considered. Talent/ability: Considered. Character/personal qualities: Considered. Alumni/ae relationship: Not considered. Geographical residence: Not considered. State residency: Not considered. Religious affiliation/commitment: Not considered. Minority status: Not considered. Volunteer work: Not considered. Work experience: Not considered. **Other schools with the greatest overlap in applicants:** Boston University; Hofstra University; Ithaca College; Northeastern State University; Quinnipiac University. **Admissions statistics for the fall 2005 entering class:** Total applicants: 12,065. Total accepted: 7,973. Freshmen enrolled: 1,489; 69% were from out of state. Overall acceptance rate: 66%. Non-early acceptance rate: 66%. **First-year students who submitted SAT scores:** 97%. Scores (25/75 percentile): Verbal: 480-580, Math: 490-

590, Combined: 970-1170. **First-year students submitting ACT scores:** 9%. Scores (25/75 percentile): English: N/A, Math: N/A, Composite: 21-25.

ACADEMICS

Year founded: 1877. **Academic calendar:** Semester. **Degrees offered:** certificate, diploma, associate, bachelor's, post-bachelor's certificate, master's, post-master's certificate, doctorate. **Most popular majors:** 19% visual and performing arts, 18% business, management, marketing, and related support services, 10% health professions and related clinical sciences, 9% education, 6% engineering. **Major fields of study:** area, ethnic, cultural, and gender studies; biological and biomedical sciences; business, management, marketing, and related support services; communication, journalism, and related programs; computer and information sciences and support services; education; engineering; engineering technologies/technicians; English language and literature/letters; foreign languages, literatures, and linguistics; health professions and related clinical sciences; history; legal professions and studies; liberal arts and sciences studies, and humanities; mathematics and statistics; multi/interdisciplinary studies; philosophy and religious studies; physical sciences; psychology; security and protective services; social sciences; visual and performing arts. **Areas of required coursework:** arts/fine arts, humanities, computer literacy, mathematics, English (including composition), philosophy, foreign languages, sciences (biological or physical), history, social science, other. **Pre-professional programs:** pre-law, pre-dentistry, pre-medicine, pre-veterinary science, pre-optometry, other. **Special academic programs:** cooperative (work-study plan) program, cross-registration, double major, dual enrollment, English as a Second Language (ESL), exchange student program (domestic), honors program, independent study, internships, liberal arts/career combination, student-designed major, study abroad, teacher certificate program, weekend college. **Teacher certification offered in:** early childhood, special education, elementary, secondary. **Cooperative education programs:** engineering. **Reserve Officers Training Corps (ROTC):** Army ROTC: Offered at cooperating institution (University of Connecticut); Air Force ROTC: Offered at cooperating institution (University of Connecticut). **Faculty and instruction (2005-2006):** Total instructional faculty: 325 full-time, 428 part-time (57% men; 43% women; 7% minorities). Full-time faculty with Ph.D. or other terminal degree: 72%. Student/faculty ratio: 13/1. Classes of fewer than 20 students: 60%; of 20 to 49 students: 40%; of 50 or more students: 1%. **Advanced Placement and International Baccalaureate credit:** AP tests may be used for: Credit and/or placement. Scores accepted: 3, 4, 5. International Baccalaureate exams may be used for: Credit only. **Freshmen returning for sophomore year:** 75%. **Graduation rates:** Four-year: 45%; five-year: 53%; six-year: 54%. **Graduate study:** 20% of students pursue further study immediately upon graduation; 79% within five years.

COSTS AND FINANCIAL AID

Financial aid office: (860) 768-4296. **Expenses (2006-2007):** Tuition and fees 2006-2007: $25,766; room/board: $9,922. Estimated books and supplies: $860; transportation: $1,000; personal expenses: $1,620. **Financial aid:** Priority filing date for institution's financial aid form: February 1. In 2005-2006, 67% of undergraduates applied for financial aid. Of those, 62% were determined to have financial need; 26% had their need fully met. Average financial aid package (proportion receiving): $16,790 (62%). Average amount of gift aid, such as scholarships or grants (proportion receiving): $12,322 (46%). Average amount of self-help aid, such as work study or loans (proportion receiving): $4,242 (53%). Average need-based loan (excluding PLUS or other private loans): $4,504. Among students who received need-based aid, the average percentage of need met: 72%. Among students who received aid based on merit, the average award (and the proportion receiving): $7,169 (30%). The average athletic scholarship (and the proportion receiving): $27,736 (2%).

CAMPUS LIFE AND EXTRACURRICULAR ACTIVITIES

Campus housing available: coed dorms, women's dorms, men's dorms, apartment for single students, special housing for disabled students, other housing options. Students who live in college-owned, operated, or affiliated housing: 66%. **Clubs and organizations:** Number of student organizations: 46. Activities include: choral groups, concert band, dance, drama/theater, jazz band, literary magazine, music ensembles, musical theater, opera, pep band, radio station, student government, student newspaper, symphony orchestra, television station, yearbook. Number of fraternities: 7; sororities: 7. Average proportion of students who stay on campus on weekends: 85%. **Sports program (2005-2006):** Member of NCAA I. *Men's intercollegiate varsity sports:* baseball, basketball, cross-country, golf, lacrosse, soccer, tennis, track and field (indoor), track and field (outdoor). *Women's intercollegiate*

varsity sports: basketball, cross-country, golf, soccer, softball, tennis, track and field (indoor), track and field (outdoor), volleyball.

SERVICES AND FACILITIES

Basic services: nonremedial tutoring, women's center, placement service, health service, health insurance. **Remedial assistance:** reading, math, writing, study skills. **Counseling services:** minority student, career, personal, veteran student, academic, psychological, birth control, religious, other. **For learning-disabled students:** School does not offer a structured program with separate admission and additional fees. Services include: reading machines, tape recorders, note-taking services, learning center, readers, extended time for tests, priority registration, texts on tape, typist/scribe, other. **Library:** Number of titles: 473,115; number of current serial subscriptions: 3,903. **Information technology resources:** Students are not required to lease or own a computer. Number of campus computers available to all students: 500. School has a wireless network. Approximate number of users that can be accommodated: 600. Proportion of college-owned housing units wired for high-speed internet access: 100%. **Campus safety:** Security services offered: 24-hour foot-and-vehicle patrols, late-night transport/escort service, 24-hour emergency telephones, controlled dormitory access (key, security card, etc).

TRANSFER AND INTERNATIONAL STUDENTS

Transfer students: May apply for admission for the following academic terms: Fall, Spring. Applicants need a minimum number of credits to apply. For fall 2005: Transfer applications received: 666. Transfer applicants offered admission: 331. Transfer applicants enrolled: 232. **International students:** Number of foreign undergraduates: 134 (3% of student body). Number of countries represented: 50. Minimum TOEFL score required: 550 (paper); 213 (computer).

University of New Haven

- **Address:** 300 Boston Post Road, West Haven, CT 06516
- **Website:** http://www.newhaven.edu
- **Private**
- **Enrollment:** 2,301 full-time; 487 part-time

KEY STATS

✔ **U.S News College Ranking:** third tier, Universities–Master's (North)
✔ **SAT Score (25th/75th percentile):** 930-1150
✔ **Tuition:** 2006-2007: $24,645

Selectivity: Selective	**Room/board:** $10,130
Acceptance rate: 73%	**Average debt:** N/A
Student/faculty ratio: 15/1	**Proportion who borrowed:** 62%

UNDERGRADUATE STUDENT BODY STATS

2005-2006 enrollment: 2,301 full-time; 487 part-time. Men: 51%; women: 49%. **Ethnic makeup:** African American: 8%; Asian American: 2%; Hispanic: 6%; White: 81%; International: 2%.

ADMISSIONS FACTS AND FIGURES

Phone: (203) 932-7319. **Email:** adminfo@newhaven.edu. **Website:** http://www.newhaven.edu. **Application deadlines for fall 2007:** Regular decision: Rolling. Early decision: Not offered. Early action: Not offered. Admission cannot be deferred. **Application fee:** $50. Common application is accepted. **To apply online, go to:** https://admissions.newhaven.edu/APPLY/ugrad/index.cfm?CFID=9182261&CFTOKEN=93106544. **Admissions requirements/recommendations:** High school units required (recommended): English: 4; Mathematics: 3; Science: 2; Foreign language: 2; Social studies: 2; History: 0; Academic electives: 0; Total units: 13. Tests: The college uses SAT or ACT scores in admissions decisions. Either SAT or ACT required. For admission to the fall 2007 entering class, the school will accept: ACT with writing, ACT without writing. Campus visit: Recommended. Admissions interview: Neither required nor recommended. Off-campus interview: Not available. **Factors that count in admissions decisions:** *Academic:* Secondary school record: Considered. Class rank: Not considered. Letters of recommendation: Important. Standardized test scores: Very important. Essay: Important. *Nonacademic:* Interview: Not considered. Extracurricular activities: Not considered. Talent/ability: Not considered. Character/personal qualities: Not considered. Alumni/ae relationship: Not considered. Geographical residence: Not considered. State residency: Not considered. Religious affiliation/commitment:

Not considered. Minority status: Not considered. Volunteer work: Not considered. Work experience: Not considered. **Admissions statistics for the fall 2005 entering class:** Total applicants: 3,051. Total accepted: 2,233. Freshmen enrolled: 664; 54% were from out of state. Overall acceptance rate: 73%. **Credentials of fall 2005 freshmen:** 16% ranked in the top 10 percent of their high school class; 41% were in the top 25 percent, and 77% were in the top half. (Proportion submitting class standing: 57%.) **Average high school grade point average:** 3.1. **First-year students who submitted SAT scores:** 96%. Scores (25/75 percentile): Verbal: 460-570, Math: 470-580, Combined: 930-1150.

ACADEMICS

Year founded: 1920. **Academic calendar:** 4-1-4. **Degrees offered:** certificate, associate, bachelor's, post-bachelor's certificate, master's, post-master's certificate. **Most popular majors:** 25% criminal justice/law enforcement administration, 10% business administration and management, 9% fire protection and safety technology/technician, 7% music, 5% forensic science and technology. **Major fields of study:** architecture and related services; biological and biomedical sciences; business, management, marketing, and related support services; communication, journalism, and related programs; computer and information sciences and support services; engineering; engineering technologies/technicians; English language and literature/letters; health professions and related clinical sciences; history; legal professions and studies; liberal arts and sciences studies, and humanities; mathematics and statistics; physical sciences; psychology; public administration and social service professions; science technologies/technicians; security and protective services; social sciences; visual and performing arts. **Areas of required coursework:** arts/fine arts, humanities, computer literacy, mathematics, English (including composition), philosophy, sciences (biological or physical), history, social science. **Pre-professional programs:** pre-law, pre-dentistry, pre-medicine, pre-veterinary science, other. **Special academic programs:** accelerated program, cooperative (work-study plan) program, distance learning, double major, honors program, independent study, internships, study abroad, teacher certificate program. **Teacher certification offered in:** elementary, secondary. **Cooperative education programs:** business, computer science, engineering, natural science, social/behavioral science, technologies. **Faculty and instruction (2005-2006):** Total instructional faculty: 162 full-time, 255 part-time. Full-time faculty with Ph.D. or other terminal degree: 85%. Student/faculty ratio: 15/1. Classes of fewer than 20 students: 44%; of 20 to 49 students: 55%; of 50 or more students: 0%. **Advanced Placement and International Baccalaureate credit:** AP tests may be used for: Credit and/or placement. Scores accepted: 3, 4, 5. International Baccalaureate exams may be used for: Credit and/or placement. **Freshmen returning for sophomore year:** 75%. **Graduation rates:** Four-year: 23%; five-year: 34%; six-year: 43%.

COSTS AND FINANCIAL AID

Financial aid office: (203) 932-7315. **Expenses (2006-2007):** Tuition and fees 2006-2007: $24,645; room/board: $10,130. **Financial aid:** Priority filing date for institution's financial aid form: March 1; deadline: March 1. In 2005-2006, 83% of undergraduates applied for financial aid. Of those, 74% were determined to have financial need; 18% had their need fully met. Average financial aid package (proportion receiving): $14,751 (74%). Average amount of gift aid, such as scholarships or grants (proportion receiving): $11,257 (71%). Average amount of self-help aid, such as work study or loans (proportion receiving): $4,294 (68%). Average need-based loan (excluding PLUS or other private loans): $4,174. Among students who received need-based aid, the average percentage of need met: 67%. Among students who received aid based on merit, the average award (and the proportion receiving): $15,347 (13%). The average athletic scholarship (and the proportion receiving): $16,099 (2%). Proportion who borrowed: 62%.

CAMPUS LIFE AND EXTRACURRICULAR ACTIVITIES

Campus housing available: coed dorms, apartment for single students, other housing options. Students who live in college-owned, operated, or affiliated housing: 54%. **Clubs and organizations:** Number of student organizations: 50. Activities include: choral groups, dance, drama/theater, literary magazine, marching band, pep band, radio station, student government, student newspaper, yearbook. Number of fraternities: 5; sororities: 3. Proportion of men in fraternities: 3%; of women in sororities: 4%. **Sports program (2005-2006):** Member of NCAA II. *Men's intercollegiate varsity sports:* baseball, basketball, cross-country, football, golf, lacrosse, soccer, track and field (indoor), track and field (outdoor), volleyball. *Women's intercollegiate varsity sports:* basketball, cross-country, golf, lacrosse, soccer, softball, tennis, track and field (indoor), track and field (outdoor), volleyball.

SERVICES AND FACILITIES

Basic services: nonremedial tutoring, placement service, health service, health insurance. **Remedial assistance:** reading, math, writing, study skills. **Counseling services:** minority student, career, personal, academic, psychological. **For learning-disabled students:** School does not offer a structured program with separate admission and additional fees. Total undergraduates in learning-disabled program or receiving services: 124. Services include: remedial math, remedial English, reading machines, remedial reading, tape recorders, diagnostic testing service, note-taking services, learning center, readers, extended time for tests, tutors, priority seating, texts on tape, exams on tape or computer, other testing accomodations, other. **Library:** Number of titles: 403,729; number of current serial subscriptions: 5,525. **Information technology resources:** Students are not required to lease or own a computer. Number of campus computers available to all students: 300. School has a wireless network. Approximate number of users that can be accommodated: 2,000. Proportion of college-owned housing units wired for high-speed internet access: 100%. **Campus safety:** Security services offered: 24-hour foot-and-vehicle patrols, late-night transport/escort service, 24-hour emergency telephones, lighted pathways/sidewalks, student patrols, controlled dormitory access (key, security card, etc).

TRANSFER AND INTERNATIONAL STUDENTS

Transfer students: May apply for admission for the following academic terms: Fall, Spring, Summer. Applicants do not need a minimum number of credits to apply. For fall 2005: Transfer applications received: 754. Transfer applicants offered admission: 444. Transfer applicants enrolled: 223. **International students:** Number of foreign undergraduates: 60 (2% of student body). Number of countries represented: 33.

Wesleyan University

- **Address:** 237 High Street, Middletown, CT 06459
- **Website:** http://www.wesleyan.edu
- **Private**
- **Enrollment:** 2,750 full-time; 14 part-time

KEY STATS

✔ **U.S News College Ranking:** 10, Liberal Arts Colleges
✔ **SAT Score (25th/75th percentile):** 1300-1490
✔ **Tuition:** 2006-2007: $35,023

Selectivity: Most selective	**Room/board:** $9,540
Acceptance rate: 28%	**Average debt:** $24,338
Student/faculty ratio: 9/1	**Proportion who borrowed:** 35%

UNDERGRADUATE STUDENT BODY STATS

2005-2006 enrollment: 2,750 full-time; 14 part-time. Men: 48%; women: 52%. **Ethnic makeup:** African American: 7%; Asian American: 10%; Hispanic: 7%; White: 69%; International: 6%.

ADMISSIONS FACTS AND FIGURES

Phone: (860) 685-3000. **Email:** admissions@wesleyan.edu. **Website:** http://www.wesleyan.edu. **Application deadlines for fall 2007:** Regular decision: January 1; decision sent by April 1. Early decision: Send application by: November 15; Decision sent by: December 15. Early action: Not offered. Admission can be deferred. **Application fee:** $55. Common application is accepted. **To apply online, go to:** http://www.admiss.wesleyan.edu. **Admissions requirements/recommendations:** High school units required (recommended): English: 4 (4); Mathematics: 3 (4); Science: 3 (4); Foreign language: 3 (4); Social studies: 3 (4); Total units: 16 (20). Tests: The college uses SAT or ACT scores in admissions decisions. Either SAT or ACT required. For admission to the fall 2007 entering class, the school will accept: ACT with writing, ACT without writing. Campus visit: Recommended. Admissions interview: Recommended. Off-campus interview: May be arranged. **Factors that count in admissions decisions:** *Academic:* Secondary school record: Very important. Class rank: Very important. Letters of recommendation: Important. Standardized test scores: Important. Essay: Important. *Nonacademic:* Interview: Considered. Extracurricular activities: Important. Talent/ability: Important. Character/personal qualities: Important. Alumni/ae relationship: Considered. Geographical residence: Considered. State residency: Not considered. Religious affiliation/commitment: Not considered. Minority status: Considered. Volunteer work: Considered. Work experience: Considered.

Admissions statistics for the fall 2005 entering class: Total applicants: 6,879. Total accepted: 1,902. Freshmen enrolled: 717; 90% were from out of state. Overall acceptance rate: 28%. Non-early acceptance rate: 28%. **Size of waiting list:** 1200 applicants; enrolled from waiting list: 90. **Credentials of fall 2005 freshmen:** 71% ranked in the top 10 percent of their high school class; 93% were in the top 25 percent, and 99% were in the top half. (Proportion submitting class standing: 51%.) **First-year students who submitted SAT scores:** 94%. Scores (25/75 percentile): Verbal: 650-750, Math: 650-740, Combined: 1300-1490. **First-year students submitting ACT scores:** 18%. Scores (25/75 percentile): English: N/A, Math: N/A, Composite: 28-32.

ACADEMICS

Year founded: 1831. **Academic calendar:** Semester. **Degrees offered:** bachelor's, master's, post-master's certificate, doctorate. **Most popular majors:** 9% political science and government, 9% psychology, 8% English language and literature, 5% American/United States studies/civilization, 5% sociology. **Major fields of study:** agriculture, agriculture operations, and related sciences; area, ethnic, cultural, and gender studies; biological and biomedical sciences; computer and information sciences and support services; foreign languages, literatures, and linguistics; history; mathematics and statistics; multi/interdisciplinary studies; natural resources and conservation; philosophy and religious studies; physical sciences; psychology; social sciences; visual and performing arts. **Pre-professional programs:** pre-law, pre-dentistry, pre-medicine, pre-veterinary science. **Special academic programs (% participation):** cross-registration (1%), double major (20%), dual enrollment (0%), exchange student program (domestic) (1%), honors program (1%), independent study (50%), internships (38%), student-designed major (0%), study abroad (46%). **Faculty and instruction (2005-2006):** Total instructional faculty: 325 full-time, 43 part-time (61% men; 39% women; 17% minorities). Full-time faculty with Ph.D. or other terminal degree: 91%. Student/faculty ratio: 9/1. Classes of fewer than 20 students: 66%; of 20 to 49 students: 29%; of 50 or more students: 5%. **Advanced Placement and International Baccalaureate credit:** AP tests may be used for: Credit and/or placement. Scores accepted: 4, 5. International Baccalaureate exams may be used for: Credit and/or placement. **Freshmen returning for sophomore year:** 96%. **Graduation rates:** Four-year: 83%; five-year: 89%; six-year: 90%. **Graduate study:** 15% of students pursue further study immediately upon graduation; 20% within one year; 60% within five years. Fields in which graduates pursue further study: law, 15%; medicine, 20%; education, 10%; arts and sciences, 50%.

COSTS AND FINANCIAL AID

Financial aid office: (860) 685-2800. **Expenses (2006-2007):** Tuition and fees 2006-2007: $35,023; room/board: $9,540. Estimated books and supplies: $2,310; transportation: $275; personal expenses: $130. **Financial aid:** In 2005-2006, 53% of undergraduates applied for financial aid. Of those, 48% were determined to have financial need; 100% had their need fully met. Average financial aid package (proportion receiving): $29,341 (48%). Average amount of gift aid, such as scholarships or grants (proportion receiving): $24,335 (45%). Average amount of self-help aid, such as work study or loans (proportion receiving): $6,238 (48%). Average need-based loan (excluding PLUS or other private loans): $4,429. Among students who received need-based aid, the average percentage of need met: 100%. Among students who received aid based on merit, the average award (and the proportion receiving): $0 (0%). The average athletic scholarship (and the proportion receiving): $0 (0%). Average amount of debt of borrowers graduating in 2005: $24,338. Proportion who borrowed: 35%.

CAMPUS LIFE AND EXTRACURRICULAR ACTIVITIES

Campus housing available (% using): coed dorms (49%), women's dorms (2%), men's dorms (2%), fraternity housing (3%), apartments for married students (0%), apartment for single students (20%), special housing for disabled students (2%), special housing for international students (1%), other housing options (21%). Students who live in college-owned, operated, or affiliated housing: 98%. **Student employment:** During the 2005-2006 academic year, 79% of undergraduates worked on campus. Average per-year earnings: $2,025. **Clubs and organizations:** Number of student organizations: 231. Activities include: choral groups, concert band, dance, drama/theater, jazz band, literary magazine, music ensembles, musical theater, pep band, radio station, student government, student newspaper, student film society, symphony orchestra, yearbook. Number of fraternities: 9; sororities: 4. Proportion of men in fraternities: 2%; of women in sororities: 2%. Average proportion of students who stay on campus on weekends: 98%. **Sports program (2005-2006):** Member of NCAA III. *Men's intercollegiate varsity sports:* baseball, basketball, cross-country, football, golf, ice hockey, lacrosse, soccer, swimming and diving, tennis, track and field (indoor), track and field (outdoor), wrestling. *Women's intercollegiate varsity sports:* basketball, cross-country, field hockey, ice hockey, lacrosse, soccer, softball, squash, swimming and diving, tennis, track and field (indoor), track and field (outdoor), volleyball, rowing.

SERVICES AND FACILITIES
Basic services: nonremedial tutoring, women's center, placement service, day care, health service, health insurance. **Remedial assistance:** other. **Counseling services:** minority student, career, personal, veteran student, academic, older student, psychological, birth control, religious. **For learning-disabled students:** School does not offer a structured program with separate admission and additional fees. Total undergraduates in learning-disabled program or receiving services: 114. Services include: note-taking services, extended time for tests, tutors, priority registration, texts on tape. **Library:** Number of titles: 1,324,647; number of current serial subscriptions: 7,217. **Information technology resources:** Students are not required to lease or own a computer. Number of campus computers available to all students: 185. School has a wireless network. Approximate number of users that can be accommodated: 3,000. Proportion of college-owned housing units wired for high-speed internet access: 100%. **Campus safety:** Security services offered: 24-hour foot-and-vehicle patrols, late-night transport/escort service, 24-hour emergency telephones, lighted pathways/sidewalks, controlled dormitory access (key, security card, etc).

TRANSFER AND INTERNATIONAL STUDENTS
Transfer students: May apply for admission for the following academic terms: Fall. Applicants need a minimum number of credits to apply. For fall 2005: Transfer applications received: 311. Transfer applicants offered admission: 126. Transfer applicants enrolled: 64. **International students:** Number of foreign undergraduates: 170 (6% of student body). Minimum TOEFL score required: 600 (paper); 273 (computer). Average TOEFL score: 628 (paper).

Western Connecticut State University

- **Address:** 181 White Street, Danbury, CT 06810
- **Website:** http://www.wcsu.edu
- **Public**
- **Enrollment:** 4,002 full-time; 1,193 part-time

KEY STATS
✔ **U.S News College Ranking:** fourth tier, Universities–Master's (North)
✔ **SAT Score (25th/75th percentile):** 890-1090
✔ **Tuition:** 2006-2007: $6,106 in state, $13,234 out of state

Selectivity: Less selective	**Room/board:** $7,749
Acceptance rate: 58%	**Average debt:** N/A
Student/faculty ratio: 15/1	**Proportion who borrowed:** N/A

UNDERGRADUATE STUDENT BODY STATS
2005-2006 enrollment: 4,002 full-time; 1,193 part-time. Men: 44%; women: 56%. **Ethnic makeup:** African American: 4%; Asian American: 4%; Hispanic: 6%; White: 86%; International: 1%.

ADMISSIONS FACTS AND FIGURES
Phone: (203) 837-9000. **Website:** http://www.wcsu.edu. **Application deadlines for fall 2007:** Regular decision: May 1. Early decision: Not offered. Early action: Not offered. Admission can be deferred. **Application fee:** $40. Common application is accepted. **To apply online, go to:** http://www.wcsu.edu/admissions/application/. **Admissions requirements/recommendations:** High school units required (recommended): English: 4; Mathematics: 3; Science: 2; Foreign language: 2 (3); Social studies: 1; History: 1; Total units: 13. Tests: The college uses SAT or ACT scores in admissions decisions. Either SAT or ACT required. For admission to the fall 2007 entering class, the school will accept: ACT with writing, ACT without writing. Campus visit: Neither required nor recommended. Admissions interview: Neither required nor recommended. Off-campus interview: May not be arranged. **Factors that count in admissions decisions:** *Academic:* Secondary school record: Very important. Class rank: Important. Letters of recommendation: Considered. Standardized test scores: Very important. Essay: Considered. *Nonacademic:* Interview: Considered. Extracurricular activities: Important. Talent/ability: Very important. Character/personal qualities: Considered. Alumni/ae relationship:

Considered. Geographical residence: Not considered. State residency: Considered. Religious affiliation/commitment: Not considered. Minority status: Considered. Volunteer work: Considered. Work experience: Considered. **Other schools with the greatest overlap in applicants:** Central Connecticut State University; Southern Connecticut State University; University of Connecticut. **Admissions statistics for the fall 2005 entering class:** Total applicants: 3,469. Total accepted: 2,029. Freshmen enrolled: 787; 10% were from out of state. Overall acceptance rate: 58%. **Credentials of fall 2005 freshmen:** 7% ranked in the top 10 percent of their high school class; 26% were in the top 25 percent, and 62% were in the top half. (Proportion submitting class standing: 67%.) **Average high school grade point average:** 3.0. **First-year students who submitted SAT scores:** 99%. Scores (25/75 percentile): Verbal: 450-550, Math: 440-540, Combined: 890-1090.

ACADEMICS
Year founded: 1903. **Academic calendar:** Semester. **Degrees offered:** certificate, associate, bachelor's, post-bachelor's certificate, master's, post-master's certificate, doctorate. **Most popular majors:** 28% business, management, marketing, and related support services, 13% education, 9% security and protective services, 7% communication, journalism, and related programs, 6% health professions and related clinical sciences. **Major fields of study:** area, ethnic, cultural, and gender studies; biological and biomedical sciences; business, management, marketing, and related support services; communication, journalism, and related programs; computer and information sciences and support services; education; English language and literature/letters; foreign languages, literatures, and linguistics; health professions and related clinical sciences; history; liberal arts and sciences studies, and humanities; mathematics and statistics; multi/interdisciplinary studies; physical sciences; psychology; public administration and social service professions; security and protective services; social sciences; visual and performing arts. **Areas of required coursework:** humanities, mathematics, English (including composition), sciences (biological or physical). **Special academic programs:** cooperative (work-study plan) program, cross-registration, distance learning, double major, dual enrollment, English as a Second Language (ESL), honors program, independent study, internships, student-designed major, study abroad, teacher certificate program. **Teacher certification offered in:** elementary, secondary. **Reserve Officers Training Corps (ROTC):** Army ROTC: Offered at cooperating institution (University of Connecticut); Air Force ROTC: Offered at cooperating institution (University of Connecticut). **Faculty and instruction (2005-2006):** Total instructional faculty: 197 full-time, 288 part-time (58% men; 42% women; 11% minorities). Full-time faculty with Ph.D. or other terminal degree: 86%. Student/faculty ratio: 15/1. Classes of fewer than 20 students: 41%; of 20 to 49 students: 58%; of 50 or more students: 1%. **Advanced Placement and International Baccalaureate credit:** AP tests may be used for: Credit and/or placement. International Baccalaureate exams may be used for: Placement only. **Freshmen returning for sophomore year:** 71%. **Graduation rates:** Four-year: 15%; five-year: 33%; six-year: 34%.

COSTS AND FINANCIAL AID
Financial aid office: (203) 837-8580. **Expenses (2006-2007):** Tuition and fees 2006-2007: $6,106 in state, $13,234 out of state; room/board: $7,749. Estimated books and supplies: $1,000 personal expenses: $3,592. **Financial aid:** In 2005-2006, 66% of undergraduates applied for financial aid. Of those, 45% were determined to have financial need; 24% had their need fully met. Average financial aid package (proportion receiving): $3,012 (41%). Average amount of gift aid, such as scholarships or grants (proportion receiving): $2,701 (32%). Average amount of self-help aid, such as work study or loans (proportion receiving): $3,503 (10%). Average need-based loan (excluding PLUS or other private loans): $3,503. Among students who received need-based aid, the average percentage of need met: 73%. Among students who received aid based on merit, the average award (and the proportion receiving): N/A (1%).

CAMPUS LIFE AND EXTRACURRICULAR ACTIVITIES
Campus housing available (% using): coed dorms, women's dorms, apartment for single students. Students who live in college-owned, operated, or affiliated housing: 30%. Activities include: choral groups, concert band, dance, drama/theater, jazz band, literary magazine, music ensembles, musical theater, opera, pep band, radio station, student government, student newspaper, symphony orchestra, yearbook. Number of fraternities: 0; sororities: 0. **Sports program (2005-2006):** Member of NCAA III. *Men's intercollegiate varsity sports:* baseball, basketball, football, lacrosse, soccer, tennis. *Women's intercollegiate varsity sports:* basketball, lacrosse, soccer, softball, swimming and diving, tennis, volleyball.

SERVICES AND FACILITIES

Basic services: day care. **Remedial assistance:** reading, math, writing, study skills. **Counseling services:** minority student, career, personal, veteran student, academic, older student, psychological, birth control, religious. **Library:** Number of titles: 286,621; number of current serial subscriptions: 25,262. **Information technology resources:** Students are not required to lease or own a computer. School has a wireless network. Approximate number of users that can be accommodated: 253. Proportion of college-owned housing units wired for high-speed internet access: 100%. **Campus safety:** Security services offered: 24-hour emergency telephones, lighted pathways/sidewalks, controlled dormitory access (key, security card, etc).

TRANSFER AND INTERNATIONAL STUDENTS

Transfer students: May apply for admission for the following academic terms: Fall, Spring. Applicants need a minimum number of credits to apply. For fall 2005: Transfer applications received: 855. Transfer applicants offered admission: 581. Transfer applicants enrolled: 382. **International students:** Number of foreign undergraduates: 38 (1% of student body). Minimum TOEFL score required: 213 (paper).

Yale University

- **Address:** PO Box 208234, New Haven, CT 06520
- **Website:** http://www.yale.edu/
- **Private**
- **Enrollment:** 5,350 full-time; 59 part-time

KEY STATS

✔ **U.S News College Ranking:** 3, National Universities
✔ **SAT Score (25th/75th percentile):** 1400-1580
✔ **Tuition:** 2006-2007: $33,030

Selectivity: Most selective	**Room/board:** $10,020
Acceptance rate: 10%	**Average debt:** $14,306
Student/faculty ratio: 6/1	**Proportion who borrowed:** 43%

UNDERGRADUATE STUDENT BODY STATS

2005-2006 enrollment: 5,350 full-time; 59 part-time. Men: 51%; women: 49%. **Ethnic makeup:** African American: 8%; American-Indian: 1%; Asian American: 14%; Hispanic: 7%; White: 62%; International: 8%.

ADMISSIONS FACTS AND FIGURES

Phone: (203) 432-9316. **Email:** student.questions@yale.edu. **Website:** http://www.yale.edu/. **Application deadlines for fall 2007:** Regular decision: December 31; decision sent by April 1. Early decision: Not offered. Early action: Send application by: November 1; Decision sent by: December 15. Admission can be deferred. **Application fee:** $75. Common application is accepted. **To apply online, go to:** http://www.yale.edu/admit/freshmen/application/index.html. **Admissions requirements/recommendations:** Tests: The college uses SAT or ACT scores in admissions decisions. Either SAT or ACT required. For admission to the fall 2007 entering class, the school will accept ACT with writing. Campus visit: Recommended. Admissions interview: Recommended. Off-campus interview: May be arranged. **Factors that count in admissions decisions:** *Academic:* Secondary school record: Very important. Class rank: Very important. Letters of recommendation: Very important. Standardized test scores: Very important. Essay: Very important. *Nonacademic:* Interview: Considered. Extracurricular activities: Very important. Talent/ability: Very important. Character/personal qualities: Very important. Alumni/ae relationship: Considered. Geographical residence: Considered. State residency: Considered. Religious affiliation/commitment: Not considered. Minority status: Considered. Volunteer work: Considered. Work experience: Considered. **Other schools with the greatest overlap in applicants:** Columbia University; Harvard University; Princeton University; Stanford University; University of Pennsylvania. **Admissions statistics for the fall 2005 entering class:** Total applicants: 19,451. Total accepted: 1,880. Freshmen enrolled: 1,321; 93% were from out of state. Accepted through early-decision or early-action plans: 47%. Overall acceptance rate: 10%. Non-early acceptance rate: 8%. **Size of waiting list:** 1094 applicants; enrolled from waiting list: 0. **Credentials of fall 2005 freshmen:** 95% ranked in the top 10 percent of their high school class; 99% were in the top 25 percent, and 100% were in the top half. (Proportion submitting class standing: 50%.) **First-year students who submitted SAT scores:** 96%.

Scores (25/75 percentile): Verbal: 700-790, Math: 700-790, Combined: 1400-1580. **First-year students submitting ACT scores:** 22%. Scores (25/75 percentile): English: N/A, Math: N/A, Composite: 31-34.

ACADEMICS

Year founded: 1701. **Academic calendar:** Semester. **Degrees offered:** bachelor's, master's, post-master's certificate, first professional, doctorate. **Most popular majors:** 14% history, 12% political science and government, 9% economics, 7% English language and literature, 6% psychology. **Major fields of study:** architecture and related services; area, ethnic, cultural, and gender studies; biological and biomedical sciences; computer and information sciences and support services; engineering; English language and literature/letters; foreign languages, literatures, and linguistics; history; liberal arts and sciences studies, and humanities; mathematics and statistics; multi/interdisciplinary studies; natural resources and conservation; philosophy and religious studies; physical sciences; psychology; social sciences; visual and performing arts. **Areas of required coursework:** humanities, foreign languages, sciences (biological or physical), social science. **Pre-professional programs:** pre-law, pre-medicine. **Special academic programs:** accelerated program, double major, English as a Second Language (ESL), honors program, independent study, internships, liberal arts/career combination, student-designed major, study abroad, teacher certificate program. **Teacher certification offered in:** early childhood, elementary, middle/junior high, secondary. **Reserve Officers Training Corps (ROTC):** Army ROTC: Offered at cooperating institution (University of Connecticut); Air Force ROTC: Offered at cooperating institution (University of Connecticut). **Faculty and instruction (2005-2006):** Total instructional faculty: 1,067 full-time, 414 part-time (66% men; 34% women; 15% minorities). Full-time faculty with Ph.D. or other terminal degree: 91%. Student/faculty ratio: 6/1. Classes of fewer than 20 students: 76%; of 20 to 49 students: 16%; of 50 or more students: 8%. **Advanced Placement and International Baccalaureate credit:** AP tests may be used for: Credit and/or placement. Scores accepted: 4, 5. International Baccalaureate exams may be used for: Credit and/or placement. **Freshmen returning for sophomore year:** 98%. **Graduation rates:** Four-year: 90%; five-year: 95%; six-year: 96%. **Graduate study:** 27% of students pursue further study within one year. Fields in which graduates pursue further study: Master of Business Administration (MBA), 1%; law, 6%; medicine, 7%; engineering, 1%; theology (or the seminary), 1%; education, 1%; arts and sciences, 9%.

COSTS AND FINANCIAL AID

Financial aid office: (203) 432-2700. **Expenses (2006-2007):** Tuition and fees 2006-2007: $33,030; room/board: $10,020. Estimated books and supplies: $950; transportation: $500; personal expenses: $1,850. **Financial aid:** Priority filing date for institution's financial aid form: March 1; deadline: March 1. In 2005-2006, 47% of undergraduates applied for financial aid. Of those, 42% were determined to have financial need; 100% had their need fully met. Average financial aid package (proportion receiving): $30,219 (42%). Average amount of gift aid, such as scholarships or grants (proportion receiving): $27,932 (42%). Average amount of self-help aid, such as work study or loans (proportion receiving): $2,956 (42%). Average need-based loan (excluding PLUS or other private loans): $1,994. Among students who received need-based aid, the average percentage of need met: 100%. Average amount of debt of borrowers graduating in 2005: $14,306. Proportion who borrowed: 43%.

CAMPUS LIFE AND EXTRACURRICULAR ACTIVITIES

Campus housing available: coed dorms, special housing for disabled students, other housing options. Students who live in college-owned, operated, or affiliated housing: 88%. **Student employment:** During the 2005-2006 academic year, 56% of undergraduates worked on campus. Average per-year earnings: $2,650. **Clubs and organizations:** Number of student organizations: 500. Activities include: choral groups, concert band, dance, drama/theater, jazz band, literary magazine, marching band, music ensembles, musical theater, opera, pep band, radio station, student government, student newspaper, student film society, symphony orchestra, television station, yearbook. Average proportion of students who stay on campus on weekends: 90%. **Sports program (2005-2006):** Member of NCAA I. *Men's intercollegiate varsity sports:* baseball, basketball, crew, cross-country, fencing, football, golf, heavyweight crew, ice hockey, lacrosse, lightweight crew, sailing, soccer, squash, swimming and diving, tennis, track and field (indoor), track and field (outdoor). *Women's intercollegiate varsity sports:* basketball, crew, cross-country, fencing, field hockey, golf, gymnastics, ice hockey, lacrosse, sailing, soccer, softball, squash, swimming and diving, tennis, track and field (indoor), track and field (outdoor), volleyball.

SERVICES AND FACILITIES

Basic services: nonremedial tutoring, women's center, placement service, health service, health insurance. **Counseling services:** minority student, career, military, personal, academic, older student, psychological, birth control, religious. **For learning-disabled students:** School does not offer a structured program with separate admission and additional fees. Total undergraduates in learning-disabled program or receiving services: 67. **Library:** Number of titles: 12,025,695; number of current serial subscriptions: 76,022. **Information technology resources:** Students are not required to lease or own a computer. Number of campus computers available to all students: 400. School has a wireless network. Approximate number of users that can be accommodated: 8,000. Proportion of college-owned housing units wired for high-speed internet access: 100%. **Campus safety:** Security services offered: 24-hour foot-and-vehicle patrols, late-night transport/escort service, 24-hour emergency telephones, lighted pathways/sidewalks, controlled dormitory access (key, security card, etc).

TRANSFER AND INTERNATIONAL STUDENTS

Transfer students: May apply for admission for the following academic terms: Fall. Applicants need a minimum number of credits to apply. For fall 2005: Transfer applications received: 681. Transfer applicants offered admission: 30. Transfer applicants enrolled: 25. **International students:** Number of foreign undergraduates: 437 (8% of student body). Number of countries represented: 72. Minimum TOEFL score required: 600 (paper); 250 (computer).

Delaware

Delaware State University

- **Address:** 1200 N. Dupont Highway, Dover, DE 19901
- **Website:** http://www.desu.edu
- **Public**
- **Enrollment:** 2,946 full-time; 494 part-time

KEY STATS
✔ **U.S News College Ranking:** fourth tier, Universities–Master's (North)
✔ **SAT Score (25th/75th percentile):** 720-900
✔ **Tuition:** 2005-2006: $5,975 in state, $12,219 out of state

Selectivity: Least selective	**Room/board:** $8,298
Acceptance rate: 64%	**Average debt:** N/A
Student/faculty ratio: 21/1	**Proportion who borrowed:** N/A

UNDERGRADUATE STUDENT BODY STATS
2005-2006 enrollment: 2,946 full-time; 494 part-time. Men: 42%; women: 58%. **Ethnic makeup:** African American: 80%; Asian American: 1%; Hispanic: 2%; White: 17%.

ADMISSIONS FACTS AND FIGURES
Phone: (302) 857-6353. **Email:** admissions@desu.edu. **Website:** http://www.desu.edu. **Application deadlines for fall 2007:** Regular decision: April 1. Early decision: Not offered. Early action: Not offered. Admission can be deferred. **Application fee:** $25. Common application is accepted. **Admissions requirements/recommendations:** High school units required (recommended): English: 4; Mathematics: 3; Science: 3; Social studies: 2; Academic electives: 4; Total units: 16. Tests: The college uses SAT or ACT scores in admissions decisions. Either SAT or ACT required. Campus visit: Recommended. Admissions interview: Neither required nor recommended. Off-campus interview: Not available. **Factors that count in admissions decisions:** *Academic:* Secondary school record: Very important. Class rank: Considered. Letters of recommendation: Important. Standardized test scores: Important. Essay: Important. *Nonacademic:* Interview: Considered. Extracurricular activities: Considered. Talent/ability: Considered. Character/personal qualities: Important. Alumni/ae relationship: Considered. Geographical residence: Not considered. State residency: Considered. Religious affiliation/commitment: Not considered. Minority status: Not considered. Volunteer work: Considered. Work experience: Considered. **Other schools with the greatest overlap in applicants:** Hampton University; Howard University; Morgan State University; Rutgers–New Brunswick; University of Delaware. **Admissions statistics for the fall 2005 entering class:** Total applicants: 3,692. Total accepted: 2,366. Freshmen enrolled: 940; Overall acceptance rate: 64%. **Credentials of fall 2005 freshmen:** 5% ranked in the top 10 percent of their high school class; 12% were in the top 25 percent, and 48% were in the top half. (Proportion submitting class standing: 69%.) **Average high school grade point average:** 2.6. **First-year students who submitted SAT scores:** 87%. Scores (25/75 percentile): Verbal: 360-450, Math: 360-450, Combined: 720-900. **First-year students submitting ACT scores:** 9%. Scores (25/75 percentile): English: 12-17, Math: 14-16, Composite: 14-17.

ACADEMICS
Year founded: 1891. **Academic calendar:** Semester. **Degrees offered:** bachelor's, master's, doctorate. **Most popular majors:** Information not available. **Major fields of study:** agriculture, agriculture operations, and related sciences; biological and biomedical sciences; business, management, marketing, and related support services; communication, journalism, and related programs; computer and information sciences and support services; education; English language and literature/letters; family and consumer sciences/human sciences; health professions and related clinical sciences; mathematics and statistics; multi/interdisciplinary studies; natural resources and conservation; parks, recreation, leisure, and fitness studies; physical sciences; psychology; public administration and social service professions; social sciences; transportation and materials moving; visual and

performing arts. **Areas of required coursework:** arts/fine arts, English (including composition), foreign languages, history, other. **Pre-professional programs:** pre-law, pre-veterinary science. **Special academic programs:** accelerated program, cooperative (work-study plan) program, distance learning, double major, dual enrollment, English as a Second Language (ESL), exchange student program (domestic), honors program, independent study, internships, study abroad, teacher certificate program, weekend college. **Teacher certification offered in:** early childhood, special education, elementary, vo-tech, middle/junior high, secondary. **Reserve Officers Training Corps (ROTC):** Army ROTC: Offered on campus; Air Force ROTC: Offered at cooperating institution (University of Delaware). **Faculty and instruction (2005-2006):** Total instructional faculty: 182 full-time, 182 part-time. Full-time faculty with Ph.D. or other terminal degree: 77%. Student/faculty ratio: 21/1. Classes of fewer than 20 students: 54%; of 20 to 49 students: 42%; of 50 or more students: 4%. **Advanced Placement and International Baccalaureate credit:** International Baccalaureate exams may be used for: Credit and/or placement. **Freshmen returning for sophomore year:** 66%. **Graduation rates:** Four-year: 21%; five-year: 32%; six-year: 33%.

COSTS AND FINANCIAL AID
Financial aid office: (302) 857-6250. **Expenses (2005-2006):** Tuition and fees 2005-2006: $5,975 in state, $12,219 out of state; room/board: $8,298. Estimated books and supplies: $1,400; transportation: $1,769; personal expenses: $1,020. **Financial aid:** Priority filing date for institution's financial aid form: March 1. In 2005-2006, 92% of undergraduates applied for financial aid. Of those, 84% were determined to have financial need; 31% had their need fully met. Average financial aid package (proportion receiving): $6,919 (83%). Average amount of gift aid, such as scholarships or grants (proportion receiving): $2,298 (54%). Average amount of self-help aid, such as work study or loans (proportion receiving): $3,023 (71%). Average need-based loan (excluding PLUS or other private loans): $2,950. Among students who received need-based aid, the average percentage of need met: 63%. Among students who received aid based on merit, the average award (and the proportion receiving): $8,071 (14%). The average athletic scholarship (and the proportion receiving): $13,313 (2%).

CAMPUS LIFE AND EXTRACURRICULAR ACTIVITIES
Campus housing available: women's dorms, men's dorms, apartments for married students, apartment for single students, special housing for disabled students, other housing options. Average per-year earnings: $2,000. **Clubs and organizations:** Number of student organizations: 79. Activities include: choral groups, concert band, dance, jazz band, marching band, music ensembles, pep band, radio station, student government, student newspaper, television station, yearbook. Number of fraternities: 3; sororities: 4. Average proportion of students who stay on campus on weekends: 55%. **Sports program (2005-2006):** Member of NCAA I. *Men's intercollegiate varsity sports:* baseball, basketball, cross-country, football, tennis, track and field (indoor), track and field (outdoor), wrestling. *Women's intercollegiate varsity sports:* basketball, bowling, cross-country, soccer, softball, tennis, track and field (indoor), track and field (outdoor), volleyball.

SERVICES AND FACILITIES
Basic services: nonremedial tutoring, placement service, health service. **Counseling services:** minority student, career, military, personal, veteran student, academic, older student, psychological, birth control, religious. **For learning-disabled students:** School does not offer a structured program with separate admission and additional fees. Total undergraduates in learning-disabled program or receiving services: 50. Services include: remedial math, remedial English, remedial reading, tape recorders, untimed tests, note-taking services, oral tests, learning center, readers, extended time for tests, tutors, substitution of courses, typist/scribe, other. **Library:** Number of titles: 401,639; number of current serial subscriptions: 32,436. **Information technology resources:** Students are not required to lease or own a computer. Number of campus computers available to all students: 1,200. School has a wireless network. Approximate number of users that can be accommodated: 500. Proportion of college-owned housing units wired for high-speed internet access: 100%. **Campus safety:** Security services offered: 24-hour foot-and-vehicle patrols, late-night transport/escort service, 24-hour emergency

telephones, lighted pathways/sidewalks, student patrols, controlled dormitory access (key, security card, etc).

TRANSFER AND INTERNATIONAL STUDENTS

Transfer students: May apply for admission for the following academic terms: Fall, Spring. Applicants need a minimum number of credits to apply. For fall 2005: Transfer applications received: 680. Transfer applicants offered admission: 387. Transfer applicants enrolled: 113. **International students:** Number of foreign undergraduates: 5. Minimum TOEFL score required: 560 (paper); 270 (computer). Average TOEFL score: 570 (paper).

Goldey Beacom College

- ■ **Address:** 4701 Limestone Road, Wilmington, DE 19808
- ■ **Website:** http://gbc.edu
- ■ **Private**
- ■ **Enrollment:** N/A

KEY STATS

✔ **U.S News College Ranking:** Unranked Specialty School–Business
✔ **SAT or ACT Score (25th/75th percentile):** N/A
✔ **Tuition:** 2006-2007: $15,368

Selectivity: Least selective	**Room/board:** N/A
Acceptance rate: N/A	**Average debt:** $15,711
Student/faculty ratio: N/A	**Proportion who borrowed:** N/A

University of Delaware

- ■ **Address:** Newark, DE 19716
- ■ **Website:** http://www.udel.edu/
- ■ **Public**
- ■ **Enrollment:** 14,899 full-time; 2,040 part-time

KEY STATS

✔ **U.S News College Ranking:** 67, National Universities
✔ **SAT Score (25th/75th percentile):** 1110-1300
✔ **Tuition:** 2006-2007: $7,740 in state, $18,450 out of state

Selectivity: More selective	**Room/board:** $7,366
Acceptance rate: 47%	**Average debt:** $15,200
Student/faculty ratio: 13/1	**Proportion who borrowed:** 40%

UNDERGRADUATE STUDENT BODY STATS

2005-2006 enrollment: 14,899 full-time; 2,040 part-time. Men: 42%; women: 58%. **Ethnic makeup:** African American: 6%; Asian American: 3%; Hispanic: 4%; White: 86%; International: 1%.

ADMISSIONS FACTS AND FIGURES

Phone: (302) 831-8123. **Email:** admissions@udel.edu. **Website:** http://www.udel.edu/. **Application deadlines for fall 2007:** Regular decision: January 15; decision sent by March 15. Early decision: Send application by: November 1; Decision sent by: December 15. Early action: Not offered. Admission can be deferred. **Application fee:** $60. Common application is accepted. **To apply online, go to:** http://www.udel.edu/admissions/viewbook/apply/. **Admissions requirements/recommendations:** High school units required (recommended): English: 4 (4); Mathematics: 3 (4); Science: 3 (4); Foreign language: 2 (4); Social studies: 2 (2); History: 2 (2); Academic electives: 2 (2); Total units: 18 (22). Tests: The college uses SAT or ACT scores in admissions decisions. Either SAT or ACT required. For admission to the fall 2007 entering class, the school will accept: ACT with writing. Campus visit: Recommended. Admissions interview: Neither required nor recommended. Off-campus interview: Not available. **Factors that count in admissions decisions:** *Academic:* Secondary school record: Very important. Class rank: Considered. Letters of recommendation: Important. Standardized test scores: Important. Essay: Very important. *Nonacademic:* Interview: Considered. Extracurricular activities: Important. Talent/ability: Important. Character/personal qualities: Important. Alumni/ae relationship: Considered. Geographical residence: Important. State residency: Very important. Religious affiliation/commitment: Not considered. Minority status: Considered. Volunteer work: Considered. Work experience: Considered.

Other schools with the greatest overlap in applicants: Pennsylvania State University–University Park; Rutgers–New Brunswick; University of Connecticut; University of Maryland–College Park; Villanova University. **Admissions statistics for the fall 2005 entering class:** Total applicants: 21,617. Total accepted: 10,256. Freshmen enrolled: 3,522; 67% were from out of state. Overall acceptance rate: 47%. Early-decision acceptance rate: 43%. Non-early acceptance rate: 48%. **Size of waiting list:** 3176 applicants; enrolled from waiting list: 142. **Credentials of fall 2005 freshmen:** 37% ranked in the top 10 percent of their high school class; 76% were in the top 25 percent, and 96% were in the top half. (Proportion submitting class standing: 63%.) **Average high school grade point average:** 3.6. **First-year students who submitted SAT scores:** 99%. Scores (25/75 percentile): Verbal: 550-640, Math: 560-660, Combined: 1110-1300. **First-year students submitting ACT scores:** 9%. Scores (25/75 percentile): English: 24-28, Math: 24-29, Composite: 24-29.

ACADEMICS

Year founded: 1743. **Academic calendar:** 4-1-4. **Degrees offered:** associate, bachelor's, master's, doctorate. **Most popular majors:** 17% business, management, marketing, and related support services, 14% social sciences, 12% education, 6% health professions and related clinical sciences, 6% psychology. **Major fields of study:** agriculture, agriculture operations, and related sciences; area, ethnic, cultural, and gender studies; biological and biomedical sciences; business, management, marketing, and related support services; computer and information sciences and support services; education; engineering technologies/technicians; English language and literature/letters; family and consumer sciences/human sciences; foreign languages, literatures, and linguistics; health professions and related clinical sciences; history; liberal arts and sciences studies, and humanities; mathematics and statistics; multi/interdisciplinary studies; natural resources and conservation; parks, recreation, leisure, and fitness studies; philosophy and religious studies; physical sciences; social sciences; visual and performing arts. **Areas of required coursework:** humanities, mathematics, English (including composition), foreign languages, sciences (biological or physical), social science, other. **Pre-professional programs:** pre-law, pre-dentistry, pre-medicine, pre-veterinary science, pre-optometry, pre-pharmacy, other. **Special academic programs (% participation):** accelerated program, cooperative (work-study plan) program, distance learning, double major (7%), dual enrollment (1%), English as a Second Language (ESL) (1%), honors program (12%), independent study, internships, liberal arts/career combination, student-designed major (2%), study abroad (38.4%), teacher certificate program (10%). **Teacher certification offered in:** early childhood, special education, elementary, middle/junior high, secondary. **Reserve Officers Training Corps (ROTC):** Army ROTC: Offered on campus; Air Force ROTC: Offered on campus. **Faculty and instruction (2005-2006):** Total instructional faculty: 1,126 full-time, 244 part-time (61% men; 39% women; 14% minorities). Full-time faculty with Ph.D. or other terminal degree: 84%. Student/faculty ratio: 13/1. Classes of fewer than 20 students: 34%; of 20 to 49 students: 49%; of 50 or more students: 17%. **Advanced Placement and International Baccalaureate credit:** AP tests may be used for: Credit and/or placement. Scores accepted: 2. International Baccalaureate exams may be used for: Credit only. **Freshmen returning for sophomore year:** 89%. **Graduation rates:** Four-year: 62%; five-year: 75%; six-year: 76%. **Graduate study:** 23% of students pursue further study immediately upon graduation; 48% within five years. Fields in which graduates pursue further study: Master of Business Administration (MBA), 4%; law, 12%; medicine, 7%; dentistry, 2%; engineering, 3%; theology (or the seminary), 1%; education, 8%; arts and sciences, 15%; veterinary medicine, 1%.

COSTS AND FINANCIAL AID

Financial aid office: (302) 831-8761. **Expenses (2006-2007):** Tuition and fees 2006-2007: $7,740 in state, $18,450 out of state; room/board: $7,366. **Financial aid:** Priority filing date for institution's financial aid form: February 1; deadline: March 15. In 2005-2006, 60% of undergraduates applied for financial aid. Of those, 38% were determined to have financial need; 51% had their need fully met. Average financial aid package (proportion receiving): $11,100 (38%). Average amount of gift aid, such as scholarships or grants (proportion receiving): $6,300 (28%). Average amount of self-help aid, such as work study or loans (proportion receiving): $5,400 (28%). Average need-based loan (excluding PLUS or other private loans): $4,900. Among students who received need-based aid, the average percentage of need met: 79%. Among students who received aid based on merit, the average award (and the proportion receiving): $4,400 (22%). The average athletic scholarship (and the proportion receiving): $13,200 (2%). Average amount of debt of borrowers graduating in 2005: $15,200. Proportion who borrowed: 40%.

CAMPUS LIFE AND EXTRACURRICULAR ACTIVITIES

Campus housing available (% using): coed dorms (76%), women's dorms (1%), sorority housing (2%), fraternity housing (0%), apartments for married students (1%), apartment for single students (16%), special housing for disabled students (1%), special housing for international students (1%), other housing options (2%). Students who live in college-owned, operated, or affiliated housing: 47%. **Clubs and organizations:** Number of student organizations: 254. Activities include: choral groups, concert band, dance, drama/theater, jazz band, literary magazine, marching band, music ensembles, musical theater, opera, pep band, radio station, student government, student newspaper, student film society, symphony orchestra, television station. Number of fraternities: 18; sororities: 5. Proportion of men in fraternities: 13%; of women in sororities: 13%. Average proportion of students who stay on campus on weekends: 67%. **Sports program (2005-2006):** Member of NCAA I. *Men's intercollegiate varsity sports:* baseball, basketball, cross-country, football, golf, lacrosse, soccer, swimming and diving, tennis, track and field (indoor), track and field (outdoor). *Women's intercollegiate varsity sports:* basketball, cross-country, field hockey, lacrosse, rowing, soccer, softball, swimming and diving, tennis, track and field (indoor), track and field (outdoor), volleyball.

SERVICES AND FACILITIES

Basic services: nonremedial tutoring, placement service, day care, health service, health insurance. **Remedial assistance:** reading, math, writing, study skills, other. **Counseling services:** minority student, career, personal, academic, older student, psychological, birth control, religious. **For learning-disabled students:** School does not offer a structured program with separate admission and additional fees. Total undergraduates in learning-disabled program or receiving services: 183. **Library:** Number of titles: 2,667,242; number of current serial subscriptions: 12,530. **Information technology resources:** Students are not required to lease or own a computer. Number of campus computers available to all students: 1,013. School has a wireless network. Approximate number of users that can be accommodated: 5,000. Proportion of college-owned housing units wired for high-speed internet access: 100%. **Campus safety:** Security services offered: 24-hour foot-and-vehicle patrols, late-night transport/escort service, 24-hour emergency telephones, lighted pathways/sidewalks, student patrols, controlled dormitory access (key, security card, etc).

TRANSFER AND INTERNATIONAL STUDENTS

Transfer students: May apply for admission for the following academic terms: Fall, Spring. Applicants need a minimum number of credits to apply. For fall 2005: Transfer applications received: 1,662. Transfer applicants offered admission: 796. Transfer applicants enrolled: 490. **International students:** Number of foreign undergraduates: 122 (1% of student body). Minimum TOEFL score required: 550 (paper); 213 (computer).

Wesley College

- **Address:** 120 N. State Street, Dover, DE 19901-3875
- **Website:** http://www.wesley.edu
- **Private; Religious affiliation:** United Methodist
- **Enrollment:** 1,745 full-time; 371 part-time

KEY STATS

✔ **U.S News College Ranking:** 24, Comp. Colleges–Bachelor's (North)

✔ **SAT Score (25th/75th percentile):** 880-1040

✔ **Tuition:** 2006-2007: $16,579

Selectivity: Selective	**Room/board:** $7,450
Acceptance rate: 71%	**Average debt:** $18,800
Student/faculty ratio: 20/1	**Proportion who borrowed:** 90%

UNDERGRADUATE STUDENT BODY STATS

2005-2006 enrollment: 1,745 full-time; 371 part-time. Men: 47%; women: 53%. **Ethnic makeup:** African American: 26%; Asian American: 2%; Hispanic: 2%; White: 69%; International: 1%. **Religious preference:** Roman Catholic: 39%; Protestant: 25%; Jewish: 1%; Unknown: 15%; United Methodist: 19%; Other: 1%.

ADMISSIONS FACTS AND FIGURES

Phone: (302) 736-2400. **Email:** admissions@wesley.edu. **Website:** http://www.wesley.edu. **Application deadlines for fall 2007:** Regular decision:

April 30. Early decision: Send application by: November 1; Decision sent by: November 15. Early action: Not offered. Admission can be deferred. **Application fee:** $25. Common application is accepted. **Admissions requirements/recommendations:** High school units required (recommended): English: 0 (4); Mathematics: 0 (3); Science: 0 (2); Foreign language: (2); Social studies: 0 (2); History: 0 (2); Academic electives: 0 (2); Total units: 16. Tests: The college uses SAT or ACT scores in admissions decisions. Either SAT or ACT required. Campus visit: Recommended. Admissions interview: Recommended. Off-campus interview: May be arranged. **Factors that count in admissions decisions:** *Academic:* Secondary school record: Very important. Class rank: Important. Letters of recommendation: Important. Standardized test scores: Important. Essay: Considered. *Nonacademic:* Interview: Important. Extracurricular activities: Important. Talent/ability: Important. Character/personal qualities: Important. Alumni/ae relationship: Considered. Geographical residence: Not considered. State residency: Not considered. Religious affiliation/commitment: Not considered. Minority status: Not considered. Volunteer work: Considered. Work experience: Considered. **Other schools with the greatest overlap in applicants:** Alvernia College; College Misericordia; Gwynedd-Mercy College; University of Delaware; Villa Julie College. **Admissions statistics for the fall 2005 entering class:** Total applicants: 2,266. Total accepted: 1,601. Freshmen enrolled: 528; 74% were from out of state. Overall acceptance rate: 71%. Non-early acceptance rate: 71%. **Credentials of fall 2005 freshmen:** 24% ranked in the top 10 percent of their high school class; 56% were in the top 25 percent, and 78% were in the top half. **Average high school grade point average:** 2.9. **First-year students who submitted SAT scores:** 73%. Scores (25/75 percentile): Verbal: 440-520, Math: 440-520, Combined: 880-1040.

ACADEMICS

Year founded: 1873. **Academic calendar:** Semester. **Degrees offered:** certificate, associate, bachelor's, post-bachelor's certificate, master's, post-master's certificate. **Most popular majors:** 40% business/commerce, 13% education, 12% social sciences, 11% liberal arts and sciences studies, and humanities, 8% psychology. **Major fields of study:** area, ethnic, cultural, and gender studies; biological and biomedical sciences; business, management, marketing, and related support services; communication, journalism, and related programs; education; English language and literature/letters; health professions and related clinical sciences; history; legal professions and studies; liberal arts and sciences studies, and humanities; parks, recreation, leisure, and fitness studies; psychology; social sciences. **Areas of required coursework:** arts/fine arts, humanities, mathematics, English (including composition), sciences (biological or physical), history, social science. **Pre-professional programs:** pre-law, pre-dentistry, pre-medicine, pre-theology. **Special academic programs (% participation):** accelerated program (23%), double major (1%), English as a Second Language (ESL) (.05%), independent study (8%), internships (4%), liberal arts/career combination (1%), study abroad (3%), teacher certificate program (13%). **Teacher certification offered in:** elementary. **Reserve Officers Training Corps (ROTC):** Army ROTC: Offered at cooperating institution (Delaware State University). **Faculty and instruction (2005-2006):** Total instructional faculty: 63 full-time, 88 part-time (52% men; 48% women; 8% minorities). Full-time faculty with Ph.D. or other terminal degree: 86%. Student/faculty ratio: 20/1. Classes of fewer than 20 students: 55%; of 20 to 49 students: 45%. **Advanced Placement and International Baccalaureate credit:** AP tests may be used for: Credit and/or placement. Scores accepted: 3, 4, 5. **Freshmen returning for sophomore year:** 58%. **Graduation rates:** Four-year: 28%; five-year: 38%; six-year: 44%.

COSTS AND FINANCIAL AID

Financial aid office: (302) 736-2321. **Expenses (2006-2007):** Tuition and fees 2006-2007: $16,579; room/board: $7,450. Estimated books and supplies: $1,000; transportation: $700; personal expenses: $750. **Financial aid:** Priority filing date for institution's financial aid form: April 15. In 2005-2006, 97% of undergraduates applied for financial aid. Of those, 88% were determined to have financial need; Average financial aid package (proportion receiving): $14,600 (88%). Average amount of gift aid, such as scholarships or grants (proportion receiving): $5,500 (73%). Average amount of self-help aid, such as work study or loans (proportion receiving): $2,225 (88%). Average need-based loan (excluding PLUS or other private loans): $4,700. Among students who received need-based aid, the average percentage of need met: 80%. Among students who received aid based on merit, the average award (and the proportion receiving): $2,500 (5%). The average athletic scholarship (and the proportion receiving): $0 (0%). Average amount of debt of borrowers graduating in 2005: $18,800. Proportion who borrowed: 90%.

CAMPUS LIFE AND EXTRACURRICULAR ACTIVITIES

Campus housing available (% using): coed dorms (67%), apartment for single students (32%), other housing options (1%). Students who live in college-owned, operated, or affiliated housing: 66%. **Student employment:** During the 2005-2006 academic year, 14% of undergraduates worked on campus. Average per-year earnings: $2,650. **Clubs and organizations:** Number of student organizations: 30. Activities include: choral groups, drama/theater, jazz band, literary magazine, music ensembles, radio station, student government, student newspaper, television station, yearbook. Number of fraternities: 1; sororities: 3. Proportion of men in fraternities: 1%; of women in sororities: 5%. Average proportion of students who stay on campus on weekends: 25%. **Sports program (2005-2006):** Member of NCAA III. *Men's intercollegiate varsity sports:* baseball, basketball, cross-country, football, golf, lacrosse, soccer, tennis. *Women's intercollegiate varsity sports:* basketball, cross-country, field hockey, lacrosse, soccer, softball, tennis.

SERVICES AND FACILITIES

Basic services: nonremedial tutoring, placement service, health service, health insurance. **Remedial assistance:** reading, math, writing, study skills, other. **Counseling services:** career, personal, veteran student, academic, older student, psychological, birth control, religious. **For learning-disabled students:** School does not offer a structured program with separate admission and additional fees. Total undergraduates in learning-disabled program or receiving services: 50. Services include: remedial math, remedial English, tape recorders, untimed tests, note-taking services, extended time for tests, tutors, priority registration, priority seating. **Library:** Number of titles: 104,636; number of current serial subscriptions: 252. **Information technology resources:** Students are not required to lease or own a computer. Number of campus computers available to all students: 204. School has a wireless network. Approximate number of users that can be accommodated: 500. Proportion of college-owned housing units wired for high-speed internet access: 100%. **Campus safety:** Security services offered: 24-hour foot-and-vehicle patrols, 24-hour emergency telephones, lighted pathways/sidewalks, student patrols, controlled dormitory access (key, security card, etc).

TRANSFER AND INTERNATIONAL STUDENTS

Transfer students: May apply for admission for the following academic terms: Fall, Spring, Summer. Applicants need a minimum number of credits to apply. For fall 2005: Transfer applications received: 149. Transfer applicants offered admission: 169. Transfer applicants enrolled: 87. **International students:** Number of foreign undergraduates: 16 (1% of student body). Minimum TOEFL score required: 500 (paper); 200 (computer). Average TOEFL score: 525 (paper).

Wilmington College

- **Address:** 320 Dupont Highway, New Castle, DE 19720
- **Website:** http://www.wilmcoll.edu
- **Private**
- **Enrollment:** 2,548 full-time; 2,422 part-time

KEY STATS
✔ **U.S News College Ranking:** fourth tier, National Universities
✔ **SAT or ACT Score (25th/75th percentile):** N/A
✔ **Tuition:** 2006-2007: $20,656

Selectivity: Selective	**Room/board:** $7,506
Acceptance rate: 100%	**Average debt:** N/A
Student/faculty ratio: N/A	**Proportion who borrowed:** N/A

UNDERGRADUATE STUDENT BODY STATS

2005-2006 enrollment: 2,548 full-time; 2,422 part-time. Men: 35%; women: 65%. **Ethnic makeup:** African American: 15%; Asian American: 1%; Hispanic: 2%; White: 81%.

ADMISSIONS FACTS AND FIGURES

Phone: (302) 328-9407. **Email:** inquire@wilmcoll.edu. **Website:** http://www.wilmcoll.edu. **Application deadlines for fall 2007:** Regular decision: Rolling. Early decision: Not offered. Early action: Not offered. Admission can be deferred. **Application fee:** $25. Common application is not accepted. **Admissions requirements/recommendations:** Tests: The college does not use SAT or ACT scores in admissions decisions. Neither SAT nor ACT required. Campus visit: Neither required nor recommended. Admissions interview: Recommended. **Factors that count in admissions decisions:** *Academic:* Standardized test scores: Not considered. **Other schools with the greatest overlap in applicants:** Delaware State University; Wesley College. **Admissions statistics for the fall 2005 entering class:** Overall acceptance rate: 100%.

ACADEMICS

Year founded: 1967. **Academic calendar:** Trimester. **Degrees offered:** certificate, associate, bachelor's, master's, doctorate. **Most popular majors:** Information not available. **Major fields of study:** business, management, marketing, and related support services; computer and information sciences and support services; education; health professions and related clinical sciences; legal professions and studies; liberal arts and sciences studies, and humanities; multi/interdisciplinary studies; parks, recreation, leisure, and fitness studies; psychology; security and protective services; transportation and materials moving; visual and performing arts. **Areas of required coursework:** arts/fine arts, humanities, computer literacy, mathematics, English (including composition), sciences (biological or physical), social science. **Special academic programs:** accelerated program, distance learning, independent study, internships. **Teacher certification offered in:** early childhood, special education, elementary, middle/junior high. **Reserve Officers Training Corps (ROTC):** Army ROTC: Offered at cooperating institution (University of Delaware). **Freshmen returning for sophomore year:** 73%. **Graduation rates:** Six-year: 41%.

COSTS AND FINANCIAL AID

Financial aid office: (302) 328-9437. **Expenses (2006-2007):** Tuition and fees 2006-2007: $20,656; room/board: $7,506.

CAMPUS LIFE AND EXTRACURRICULAR ACTIVITIES

Activities include: student government, yearbook. Number of fraternities: 0; sororities: 0. **Sports program (2005-2006):** Member of NCAA II. *Men's intercollegiate varsity sports:* baseball, basketball, cross-country, golf, soccer. *Women's intercollegiate varsity sports:* basketball, cross-country, lacrosse, soccer, softball, volleyball.

SERVICES AND FACILITIES

Remedial assistance: math; writing. **For learning-disabled students:** School does not offer a structured program with separate admission and additional fees. **Information technology resources:** Students are not required to lease or own a computer. **Campus safety:** Security services offered: 24-hour foot-and-vehicle patrols, 24-hour emergency telephones, lighted pathways/sidewalks.

TRANSFER AND INTERNATIONAL STUDENTS

Transfer students: May apply for admission for the following academic terms: Fall, Winter, Spring, Summer. Applicants need a minimum number of credits to apply. **International students:** Minimum TOEFL score required: 550 (paper).

U.S.NEWS & WORLD REPORT

District of Columbia

American University

- **Address:** 4400 Massachusetts Avenue NW, Washington, DC 20016
- **Website:** http://www.american.edu
- **Private; Religious affiliation:** United Methodist
- **Enrollment:** 5,624 full-time; 297 part-time

KEY STATS

✔ **U.S News College Ranking:** 86, National Universities
✔ **SAT Score (25th/75th percentile):** 1180-1360
✔ **Tuition:** 2006-2007: $29,673
  Selectivity: More selective   **Room/board:** $11,240
  Acceptance rate: 51%   **Average debt:** $19,766
  Student/faculty ratio: 14/1   **Proportion who borrowed:** 50%

UNDERGRADUATE STUDENT BODY STATS

2005-2006 enrollment: 5,624 full-time; 297 part-time. Men: 38%; women: 62%. **Ethnic makeup:** African American: 6%; Asian American: 5%; Hispanic: 5%; White: 78%; International: 6%.

ADMISSIONS FACTS AND FIGURES

Phone: (202) 885-6000. **Email:** admissions@american.edu. **Website:** http://www.american.edu. **Application deadlines for fall 2007:** Regular decision: January 15; decision sent by April 1. Early decision: Send application by: November 15; Decision sent by: December 31. Early action: Not offered. Admission can be deferred. **Application fee:** $45. Common application is accepted. **To apply online, go to:** http://admissions.american.edu. **Admissions requirements/recommendations:** High school units required (recommended): English: 4 (4); Mathematics: 3 (4); Science: 2 (4); Foreign language: 2 (3); Social studies: 2 (4); Academic electives: 3 (1); Total units: 16 (20). Tests: The college uses SAT or ACT scores in admissions decisions. Either SAT or ACT required. For admission to the fall 2007 entering class, the school will accept: ACT with writing. Campus visit: Recommended. Admissions interview: Recommended. Off-campus interview: May be arranged. **Factors that count in admissions decisions:** *Academic:* Secondary school record: Very important. Class rank: Important. Letters of recommendation: Important. Standardized test scores: Very important. Essay: Important. *Nonacademic:* Interview: Considered. Extracurricular activities: Important. Talent/ability: Considered. Character/personal qualities: Considered. Alumni/ae relationship: Considered. Geographical residence: Considered. State residency: Not considered. Religious affiliation/commitment: Not considered. Minority status: Considered. Volunteer work: Important. Work experience: Considered. **Other schools with the greatest overlap in applicants:** Boston College; George Washington University; Georgetown University; New York University; University of Maryland–College Park. **Admissions statistics for the fall 2005 entering class:** Total applicants: 13,583. Total accepted: 6,973. Freshmen enrolled: 1,223; 99% were from out of state. Accepted through early-decision or early-action plans: 19%. Overall acceptance rate: 51%. Early-decision acceptance rate: 60%. Non-early acceptance rate: 51%. **Size of waiting list:** 0 applicants; enrolled from waiting list: 0. **Credentials of fall 2005 freshmen:** 47% ranked in the top 10 percent of their high school class; 82% were in the top 25 percent, and 98% were in the top half. (Proportion submitting class standing: 48%.) **Average high school grade point average:** 3.5. **First-year students who submitted SAT scores:** 92%. Scores (25/75 percentile): Verbal: 600-690, Math: 580-670, Combined: 1180-1360. **First-year students submitting ACT scores:** 29%. Scores (25/75 percentile): English: N/A, Math: N/A, Composite: 26-30.

ACADEMICS

Year founded: 1893. **Academic calendar:** Semester. **Degrees offered:** certificate, associate, bachelor's, post-bachelor's certificate, master's, first professional, doctorate. **Most popular majors:** 19% international relations and affairs, 17% business/commerce, 9% political science and government, 7% communication studies/speech communication and rhetoric, 5% psychol-

ogy. **Major fields of study:** area, ethnic, cultural, and gender studies; biological and biomedical sciences; business, management, marketing, and related support services; communication, journalism, and related programs; communications technologies/technicians and support services; computer and information sciences and support services; education; English language and literature/letters; foreign languages, literatures, and linguistics; history; liberal arts and sciences studies, and humanities; mathematics and statistics; multi/interdisciplinary studies; natural resources and conservation; parks, recreation, leisure, and fitness studies; philosophy and religious studies; physical sciences; psychology; security and protective services; social sciences; visual and performing arts. **Areas of required coursework:** arts/fine arts, humanities, mathematics, English (including composition), sciences (biological or physical), social science, other. **Pre-professional programs:** pre-law, pre-dentistry, pre-medicine, pre-veterinary science, pre-optometry, pre-pharmacy. **Special academic programs (% participation):** accelerated program, cooperative (work-study plan) program (75.8%), cross-registration, double major, exchange student program (domestic), honors program (18.2%), independent study, internships (75.8%), student-designed major, study abroad (45%), teacher certificate program, weekend college. **Teacher certification offered in:** special education, elementary, secondary, bilingual/bicultural. **Cooperative education programs:** other. **Reserve Officers Training Corps (ROTC):** Army ROTC: Offered at cooperating institution (Georgetown University); Air Force ROTC: Offered at cooperating institution (Howard University). **Faculty and instruction (2005-2006):** Total instructional faculty: 513 full-time, 428 part-time (56% men; 44% women). Full-time faculty with Ph.D. or other terminal degree: 96%. Student/faculty ratio: 14/1. Classes of fewer than 20 students: 44%; of 20 to 49 students: 52%; of 50 or more students: 4%. **Advanced Placement and International Baccalaureate credit:** AP tests may be used for: Credit and/or placement. Scores accepted: 4, 5. International Baccalaureate exams may be used for: Credit and/or placement. **Freshmen returning for sophomore year:** 88%. **Graduation rates:** Four-year: 63%; five-year: 69%; six-year: 71%. **Graduate study:** 29% of students pursue further study immediately upon graduation; 14% within one year.

COSTS AND FINANCIAL AID

Financial aid office: (202) 885-6100. **Expenses (2006-2007):** Tuition and fees 2006-2007: $29,673; room/board: $11,240. Estimated books and supplies: $600; transportation: $700; personal expenses: $600. **Financial aid:** In 2005-2006, 61% of undergraduates applied for financial aid. Of those, 48% were determined to have financial need; 49% had their need fully met. Average financial aid package (proportion receiving): $26,534 (47%). Average amount of gift aid, such as scholarships or grants (proportion receiving): $13,534 (37%). Average amount of self-help aid, such as work study or loans (proportion receiving): $9,758 (43%). Average need-based loan (excluding PLUS or other private loans): $8,191. Among students who received need-based aid, the average percentage of need met: 75%. Among students who received aid based on merit, the average award (and the proportion receiving): $15,708 (13%). The average athletic scholarship (and the proportion receiving): $17,275 (3%). Average amount of debt of borrowers graduating in 2005: $19,766. Proportion who borrowed: 50%.

CAMPUS LIFE AND EXTRACURRICULAR ACTIVITIES

Campus housing available: coed dorms, apartments for married students, apartment for single students, special housing for disabled students, special housing for international students, other housing options. Students who live in college-owned, operated, or affiliated housing: 75%. **Student employment:** During the 2005-2006 academic year, 7% of undergraduates worked on campus. **Clubs and organizations:** Number of student organizations: 160. Activities include: choral groups, dance, drama/theater, jazz band, literary magazine, music ensembles, musical theater, opera, pep band, radio station, student government, student newspaper, student film society, symphony orchestra, television station, yearbook. Number of fraternities: 11; sororities: 11. Proportion of men in fraternities: 14%; of women in sororities: 16%. **Sports program (2005-2006):** Member of NCAA I. *Men's intercollegiate varsity sports:* basketball, cross-country, golf, soccer, swimming and diving, tennis, track and field (indoor), track and field (outdoor), wrestling. *Women's intercollegiate varsity sports:* basketball, cross-country, field hockey, lacrosse, soccer, swimming and diving, tennis, track and field (indoor), track and field (outdoor), volleyball.

SERVICES AND FACILITIES

Basic services: nonremedial tutoring, day care, health service, health insurance. **Counseling services:** minority student, career, personal, academic, psychological, religious. **For learning-disabled students:** Total undergraduates in learning-disabled program or receiving services: 240. Services include: tape recorders, other special classes, note-taking services, learning center, readers, extended time for tests, tutors, priority registration, texts on tape, typist/scribe, exams on tape or computer, other testing accomodations, waiver of foreign language degree requirement. **Library:** Number of titles: 1,002,900; number of current serial subscriptions: 65. **Information technology resources:** Students are not required to lease or own a computer. Number of campus computers available to all students: 600. School has a wireless network. Proportion of college-owned housing units wired for high-speed internet access: 100%. **Campus safety:** Security services offered: 24-hour foot-and-vehicle patrols, late-night transport/escort service, 24-hour emergency telephones, lighted pathways/sidewalks, controlled dormitory access (key, security card, etc).

TRANSFER AND INTERNATIONAL STUDENTS

Transfer students: May apply for admission for the following academic terms: Fall, Spring, Summer. Applicants need a minimum number of credits to apply. For fall 2005: Transfer applications received: 1,477. Transfer applicants offered admission: 1,015. Transfer applicants enrolled: 422. **International students:** Number of foreign undergraduates: 334 (6% of student body). Number of countries represented: 87. Minimum TOEFL score required: 550 (paper); 213 (computer). Average TOEFL score: 597 (paper).

Catholic University of America

- ■ **Address:** 620 Michigan Avenue NE, Washington, DC 20064
- ■ **Website:** http://www.cua.edu
- ■ **Private; Religious affiliation:** Roman Catholic
- ■ **Enrollment:** 2,802 full-time; 251 part-time

KEY STATS

✔ **U.S News College Ranking:** 120, National Universities
✔ **SAT Score (25th/75th percentile):** 1040-1250
✔ **Tuition:** 2006-2007: $27,440

Selectivity: Selective	**Room/board:** $10,330
Acceptance rate: 81%	**Average debt:** N/A
Student/faculty ratio: 9/1	**Proportion who borrowed:** N/A

UNDERGRADUATE STUDENT BODY STATS

2005-2006 enrollment: 2,802 full-time; 251 part-time. Men: 44%; women: 56%. **Ethnic makeup:** African American: 7%; Asian American: 3%; Hispanic: 5%; White: 82%; International: 2%. **Religious preference:** Protestant: 4%; No preference: 6%; Unknown: 16%; Roman Catholic: 74%.

ADMISSIONS FACTS AND FIGURES

Phone: (800) 673-2772. **Email:** cua-admissions@cua.edu. **Website:** http://www.cua.edu. **Application deadlines for fall 2007:** Regular decision: February 1; decision sent by March 1. Early decision: Not offered. Early action: Send application by: November 15; Decision sent by: December 15. Admission can be deferred. **Application fee:** $55. Common application is accepted. **To apply online, go to:** http://admissions.cua.edu/application/. **Admissions requirements/recommendations:** High school units required (recommended): English: (4); Mathematics: (3); Science: (3); Foreign language: (2); Social studies: (4); History: (1); Total units: (17). Tests: The college uses SAT or ACT scores in admissions decisions. Either SAT or ACT required. For admission to the fall 2007 entering class, the school will accept: ACT with writing. Campus visit: Recommended. Admissions interview: Recommended. Off-campus interview: May be arranged. **Factors that count in admissions decisions:** *Academic:* Secondary school record: Very important. Class rank: Important. Letters of recommendation: Very important. Standardized test scores: Very important. Essay: Very important. *Nonacademic:* Interview: Important. Extracurricular activities: Important. Talent/ability: Important. Character/personal qualities: Very important. Alumni/ae relationship: Considered. Geographical residence: Not considered. State residency: Not considered. Religious affiliation/commitment:

Not considered. Minority status: Considered. Volunteer work: Very important. Work experience: Considered. **Other schools with the greatest overlap in applicants:** American University; Boston College; George Washington University; Georgetown College; Loyola College in Maryland. **Admissions statistics for the fall 2005 entering class:** Total applicants: 3,152. Total accepted: 2,561. Freshmen enrolled: 792; 98% were from out of state. Overall acceptance rate: 81%. Non-early acceptance rate: 81%. **Credentials of fall 2005 freshmen:** 23% ranked in the top 10 percent of their high school class; 54% were in the top 25 percent, and 84% were in the top half. (Proportion submitting class standing: 27%.) **Average high school grade point average:** 3.3. **First-year students who submitted SAT scores:** 95%. Scores (25/75 percentile): Verbal: 530-630, Math: 510-620, Combined: 1040-1250. **First-year students submitting ACT scores:** 19%. Scores (25/75 percentile): English: N/A, Math: N/A, Composite: 21-27.

ACADEMICS

Year founded: 1887. **Academic calendar:** Semester. **Degrees offered:** bachelor's, master's, post-master's certificate, first professional, doctorate. **Most popular majors:** 12% architecture (B.Arch., B.A./B.S., M.Arch., M.A./M.S., Ph.D.), 9% communication studies/speech communication and rhetoric, 9% political science and government, 9% psychology, 7% business, management, marketing, and related support services. **Major fields of study:** architecture and related services; biological and biomedical sciences; business, management, marketing, and related support services; communication, journalism, and related programs; computer and information sciences and support services; education; engineering; English language and literature/letters; foreign languages, literatures, and linguistics; health professions and related clinical sciences; history; liberal arts and sciences studies, and humanities; mathematics and statistics; multi/interdisciplinary studies; philosophy and religious studies; physical sciences; psychology; public administration and social service professions; social sciences; visual and performing arts. **Areas of required coursework:** humanities, mathematics, English (including composition), philosophy, foreign languages, social science, other. **Pre-professional programs:** pre-law, pre-dentistry, pre-medicine, pre-theology, pre-veterinary science, pre-optometry. **Special academic programs:** accelerated program, cross-registration, double major, dual enrollment, English as a Second Language (ESL), honors program, independent study, internships, study abroad, teacher certificate program. **Teacher certification offered in:** early childhood, special education, elementary, secondary. **Cooperative education programs:** business, computer science, education, engineering, humanities, natural science, social/behavioral science, other. **Reserve Officers Training Corps (ROTC):** Army ROTC: Offered at cooperating institution (Georgetown University); Navy ROTC: Offered at cooperating institution (George Washington University); Air Force ROTC: Offered at cooperating institution (Howard University). **Faculty and instruction (2005-2006):** Total instructional faculty: 344 full-time, 370 part-time (63% men; 37% women; 6% minorities). Full-time faculty with Ph.D. or other terminal degree: 98%. Student/faculty ratio: 9/1. Classes of fewer than 20 students: 57%; of 20 to 49 students: 39%; of 50 or more students: 4%. **Advanced Placement and International Baccalaureate credit:** AP tests may be used for: Credit only. Scores accepted: 4, 5. International Baccalaureate exams may be used for: Credit only. **Freshmen returning for sophomore year:** 84%. **Graduation rates:** Four-year: 60%; five-year: 67%; six-year: 70%. **Graduate study:** 41% of students pursue further study within one year. Fields in which graduates pursue further study: Master of Business Administration (MBA), 2%; law, 13%; medicine, 6%; engineering, 12%; theology (or the seminary), 2%; education, 10%; arts and sciences, 13%.

COSTS AND FINANCIAL AID

Financial aid office: (202) 319-5307. **Expenses (2006-2007):** Tuition and fees 2006-2007: $27,440; room/board: $10,330. Estimated books and supplies: $1,000; transportation: $800; personal expenses: $1,500. **Financial aid:** Priority filing date for institution's financial aid form: February 1; deadline: April 15. In 2005-2006, 65% of undergraduates applied for financial aid. Of those, 52% were determined to have financial need; 53% had their need fully met. Average financial aid package (proportion receiving): $16,279 (52%). Average amount of gift aid, such as scholarships or grants (proportion receiving): $12,399 (50%). Average amount of self-help aid, such as work study or loans (proportion receiving): $4,790 (45%). Average need-based loan (excluding PLUS or other private loans): $4,793. Among students who received need-based aid, the average percentage of need met: 83%. Among students who received aid based on merit, the average award (and the proportion receiving): $8,962 (40%).

CAMPUS LIFE AND EXTRACURRICULAR ACTIVITIES

Campus housing available: coed dorms, women's dorms, men's dorms, apartment for single students, other housing options. Students who live in college-owned, operated, or affiliated housing: 68%. **Clubs and organizations:** Number of student organizations: 116. Activities include: choral groups, dance, drama/theater, jazz band, literary magazine, music ensembles, musical theater, opera, pep band, radio station, student government, student newspaper, student film society, symphony orchestra, yearbook. Number of fraternities: 1; sororities: 1. Proportion of men in fraternities: 1%; of women in sororities: 1%. **Sports program (2005-2006):** Member of NCAA III. **Men's intercollegiate varsity sports:** baseball, basketball, cross-country, football, lacrosse, soccer, swimming and diving, tennis, track and field (indoor), track and field (outdoor). **Women's intercollegiate varsity sports:** basketball, cross-country, field hockey, lacrosse, soccer, softball, swimming and diving, tennis, track and field (indoor), track and field (outdoor), volleyball.

SERVICES AND FACILITIES

Basic services: nonremedial tutoring, placement service, health service, health insurance. **Remedial assistance:** writing, study skills. **Counseling services:** minority student, career, military, personal, veteran student, academic, older student, psychological, religious. **For learning-disabled students:** School does not offer a structured program with separate admission and additional fees. Total undergraduates in learning-disabled program or receiving services: 300. Services include: remedial math, reading machines, tape recorders, videotaped classes, untimed tests, note-taking services, oral tests, learning center, readers, extended time for tests, tutors, early syllabus, priority registration, priority seating, substitution of courses, texts on tape, exams on tape or computer, other testing accomodations, other. **Library:** Number of titles: 1,595,284; number of current serial subscriptions: 10,448. **Information technology resources:** Students are not required to lease or own a computer. Number of campus computers available to all students: 500. School has a wireless network. Approximate number of users that can be accommodated: 1,000. Proportion of college-owned housing units wired for high-speed internet access: 100%. **Campus safety:** Security services offered: 24-hour foot-and-vehicle patrols, late-night transport/escort service, 24-hour emergency telephones, lighted pathways/sidewalks, student patrols, controlled dormitory access (key, security card, etc).

TRANSFER AND INTERNATIONAL STUDENTS

Transfer students: May apply for admission for the following academic terms: Fall, Spring. Applicants need a minimum number of credits to apply. For fall 2005: Transfer applications received: 519. Transfer applicants offered admission: 199. Transfer applicants enrolled: 99. **International students:** Number of foreign undergraduates: 62 (2% of student body). Number of countries represented: 65. Minimum TOEFL score required: 550 (paper); 213 (computer).

Corcoran College of Art and Design

- Address: 500 17th Street NW, Washington, DC 20006-4804
- Website: http://www.corcoran.edu
- Private
- Enrollment: 348 full-time; 172 part-time

KEY STATS

✔ **U.S News College Ranking:** Unranked Specialty School–Fine Arts
✔ **SAT Score (25th/75th percentile):** 960-1160
✔ **Tuition:** 2006-2007: $24,489
Selectivity: Selective **Room/board:** $10,795
Acceptance rate: 61% **Average debt:** $30,135
Student/faculty ratio: 4/1 **Proportion who borrowed:** 82%

UNDERGRADUATE STUDENT BODY STATS

2005-2006 enrollment: 348 full-time; 172 part-time. Men: 33%; women: 67%. **Ethnic makeup:** African American: 8%; Asian American: 10%; Hispanic: 8%; White: 75%.

ADMISSIONS FACTS AND FIGURES

Phone: (202) 639-1814. **Email:** admissions@corcoran.org. **Website:** http://www.corcoran.edu. **Application deadlines for fall 2007:** Regular decision: Rolling. Early decision: Not offered. Early action: Not offered.

Admission can be deferred. **Application fee:** $40. Common application is accepted. **Admissions requirements/recommendations:** High school units required (recommended): English: 4 (4); History: 4 (4). Tests: The college uses SAT or ACT scores in admissions decisions. Either SAT or ACT required. For admission to the fall 2007 entering class, the school will accept: ACT with writing, ACT without writing. Campus visit: Recommended. Admissions interview: Recommended. Off-campus interview: May be arranged. **Factors that count in admissions decisions:** *Academic:* Secondary school record: Very important. Class rank: Important. Letters of recommendation: Considered. Standardized test scores: Considered. Essay: Considered. *Nonacademic:* Interview: Important. Extracurricular activities: Considered. Talent/ability: Very important. Character/personal qualities: Considered. Alumni/ae relationship: Considered. Geographical residence: Not considered. State residency: Not considered. Religious affiliation/commitment: Not considered. Minority status: Not considered. Volunteer work: Considered. Work experience: Considered. **Other schools with the greatest overlap in applicants:** Maryland Institute College of Art; Pratt Institute; Savannah College of Art and Design; Virginia Commonwealth University. **Admissions statistics for the fall 2005 entering class:** Total applicants: 233. Total accepted: 143. Freshmen enrolled: 52; 90% were from out of state. Overall acceptance rate: 61%. **Credentials of fall 2005 freshmen:** 20% ranked in the top 10 percent of their high school class; 35% were in the top 25 percent, and 75% were in the top half. (Proportion submitting class standing: 38%.) **Average high school grade point average:** 3.4. **First-year students who submitted SAT scores:** 90%. Scores (25/75 percentile): Verbal: 490-620, Math: 470-540, Combined: 960-1160. **First-year students submitting ACT scores:** 19%. Scores (25/75 percentile): English: 14-26, Math: 18-27, Composite: 14-23.

ACADEMICS

Year founded: 1890. **Academic calendar:** Semester. **Degrees offered:** certificate, associate, bachelor's, master's. **Most popular majors:** 36% fine/studio arts, 29% graphic design, 18% photography, 11% digital communication and media/multimedia, 6% photojournalism. **Major fields of study:** communication, journalism, and related programs; education; visual and performing arts. **Areas of required coursework:** arts/fine arts, humanities, computer literacy, English (including composition), other. **Special academic programs (% participation):** exchange student program (domestic) (2%), internships (45%), study abroad (4%). **Faculty and instruction (2005-2006):** Total instructional faculty: 32 full-time, 255 part-time (45% men; 55% women). Full-time faculty with Ph.D. or other terminal degree: 59%. Student/faculty ratio: 4/1. Classes of fewer than 20 students: 94%; of 20 to 49 students: 6%. **Advanced Placement and International Baccalaureate credit:** AP tests may be used for: Credit only. Scores accepted: 4, 5. International Baccalaureate exams may be used for: Credit only. **Freshmen returning for sophomore year:** 74%. **Graduation rates:** Four-year: 66%; five-year: 66%; six-year: 58%. **Graduate study:** 15% of students pursue further study immediately upon graduation; 20% within one year; 25% within five years. Fields in which graduates pursue further study: law, 1%; education, 4%; arts and sciences, 95%.

COSTS AND FINANCIAL AID

Financial aid office: (202) 639-1818. **Expenses (2006-2007):** Tuition and fees 2006-2007: $24,489; room/board: $10,795. Estimated books and supplies: $2,500; transportation: $1,100; personal expenses: $2,174. **Financial aid:** Priority filing date for institution's financial aid form: April 15. In 2005-2006, 77% of undergraduates applied for financial aid. Of those, 77% were determined to have financial need; Average financial aid package (proportion receiving): $9,437 (77%). Average amount of gift aid, such as scholarships or grants (proportion receiving): $5,948 (61%). Average amount of self-help aid, such as work study or loans (proportion receiving): $9,437 (77%). Average need-based loan (excluding PLUS or other private loans): $4,749. Among students who received need-based aid, the average percentage of need met: 26%. Among students who received aid based on merit, the average award (and the proportion receiving): $4,257 (20%). The average athletic scholarship (and the proportion receiving): $0 (0%). Average amount of debt of borrowers graduating in 2005: $30,135. Proportion who borrowed: 82%.

CAMPUS LIFE AND EXTRACURRICULAR ACTIVITIES

Campus housing available (% using): coed dorms (100%), apartment for single students. Students who live in college-owned, operated, or affiliated housing: 27%. **Student employment:** During the 2005-2006 academic year, 10% of undergraduates worked on campus. Average per-year earnings: $1,000. Activities include: student government. Number of fraternities: 0;

sororities: o. Average proportion of students who stay on campus on weekends: 76%.

SERVICES AND FACILITIES
Basic services: nonremedial tutoring, health insurance. **Remedial assistance:** other. **Counseling services:** personal, academic, psychological. **For learning-disabled students:** School does not offer a structured program with separate admission and additional fees. Services include: learning center, extended time for tests, tutors. **Library:** Number of titles: 36,800; number of current serial subscriptions: 170. **Information technology resources:** Students are not required to lease or own a computer. Number of campus computers available to all students: 117. School has a wireless network. Approximate number of users that can be accommodated: 300. Proportion of college-owned housing units wired for high-speed internet access: 100%. **Campus safety:** Security services offered: 24-hour foot-and-vehicle patrols, controlled dormitory access (key, security card, etc).

TRANSFER AND INTERNATIONAL STUDENTS
Transfer students: May apply for admission for the following academic terms: Fall, Spring. Applicants need a minimum number of credits to apply. For fall 2005: Transfer applications received: 147. Transfer applicants offered admission: 94. Transfer applicants enrolled: 54. **International students:** Number of countries represented: 12. Minimum TOEFL score required: 550 (paper); 213 (computer). Average TOEFL score: 491 (paper).

Gallaudet University

- **Address:** 800 Florida Avenue NE, Washington, DC 20002
- **Website:** http://www.gallaudet.edu
- **Private**
- **Enrollment:** 1,174 full-time; 100 part-time

KEY STATS
✔ **U.S News College Ranking:** 23, Universities–Master's (North)
✔ **ACT Score (25th/75th percentile):** 14-18
✔ **Tuition:** 2006-2007: $10,562

Selectivity: Least selective	**Room/board:** $8,760
Acceptance rate: 76%	**Average debt:** $14,071
Student/faculty ratio: 8/1	**Proportion who borrowed:** 59%

UNDERGRADUATE STUDENT BODY STATS
2005-2006 enrollment: 1,174 full-time; 100 part-time. Men: 47%; women: 53%. **Ethnic makeup:** African American: 12%; American-Indian: 4%; Asian American: 5%; Hispanic: 9%; White: 61%; International: 10%.

ADMISSIONS FACTS AND FIGURES
Phone: (202) 651-5750. **Email:** admissions.office@gallaudet.edu. **Website:** http://www.gallaudet.edu. **Application deadlines for fall 2007:** Regular decision: Rolling. Early decision: Not offered. Early action: Not offered. Admission can be deferred. **Application fee:** $50. Common application is accepted. **To apply online, go to:** http://bison.gallaudet.edu/onlineapplication.html. **Admissions requirements/recommendations:** High school units required (recommended): English: 4 (4); Mathematics: 4 (4); Science: 4 (4); Foreign language: 0 (0); Social studies: 4 (4); History: 4 (4); Academic electives: 0 (0); Total units: 20 (20). Tests: The college uses SAT or ACT scores in admissions decisions. Either SAT or ACT required. For admission to the fall 2007 entering class, the school will accept: ACT with writing; ACT without writing. Campus visit: Recommended. Admissions interview: Required. Off-campus interview: May be arranged. **Factors that count in admissions decisions:** *Academic:* Secondary school record: Very important. Class rank: Considered. Letters of recommendation: Very important. Standardized test scores: Very important. Essay: Very important. *Nonacademic:* Interview: Considered. Extracurricular activities: Important. Talent/ability: Important. Character/personal qualities: Important. Alumni/ae relationship: Not considered. Geographical residence: Not considered. State residency: Not considered. Religious affiliation/commitment: Not considered. Minority status: Not considered. Volunteer work: Considered. Work experience: Considered. **Admissions statistics for the fall 2005 entering class:** Total applicants: 478. Total accepted: 361. Freshmen enrolled: 280; 92% were from out of state. Overall acceptance rate: 76%. **First-year students who submitted SAT scores:** 13%. Scores (25/75 percentile): Verbal: 320-550, Math: 355-520, Combined: 675-1070. **First-year**

---

students submitting ACT scores: 87%. Scores (25/75 percentile): English: N/A, Math: N/A, Composite: 14-18.

ACADEMICS
Year founded: 1864. **Academic calendar:** Semester. **Degrees offered:** certificate, bachelor's, master's, doctorate. **Most popular majors:** 12% communication, journalism, and related programs; 9% public administration and social service professions, 8% family and consumer sciences/human sciences, 7% psychology, 7% visual and performing arts. **Major fields of study:** area, ethnic, cultural, and gender studies; biological and biomedical sciences; business, management, marketing, and related support services; communication, journalism, and related programs; computer and information sciences and support services; education; English language and literature/letters; family and consumer sciences/human sciences; foreign languages, literatures, and linguistics; health professions and related clinical sciences; history; mathematics and statistics; parks, recreation, leisure, and fitness studies; philosophy and religious studies; physical sciences; psychology; public administration and social service professions; social sciences; visual and performing arts. **Areas of required coursework:** humanities, mathematics, English (including composition), philosophy, foreign languages, sciences (biological or physical), history, social science. **Special academic programs:** distance learning, double major, English as a Second Language (ESL), exchange student program (domestic), honors program, independent study, internships, student-designed major, study abroad, teacher certificate program. **Teacher certification offered in:** early childhood, special education, elementary, secondary. **Faculty and instruction (2005-2006):** Total instructional faculty: 235 (39% men; 61% women; 17% minorities). Full-time faculty with Ph.D. or other terminal degree: 78%. Student/faculty ratio: 8/1. Classes of fewer than 20 students: 89%; of 20 to 49 students: 11%; of 50 or more students: 0%. **Freshmen returning for sophomore year:** 69%. **Graduation rates:** Four-year: 6%; five-year: 17%; six-year: 30%. **Graduate study:** 38% of students pursue further study within one year.

COSTS AND FINANCIAL AID
Financial aid office: (202) 651-5290. **Expenses (2006-2007):** Tuition and fees 2006-2007: $10,562; room/board: $8,760. Estimated books and supplies: $870; transportation: $1,262; personal expenses: $3,056. **Financial aid:** Priority filing date for institution's financial aid form: July 1. In 2005-2006, 79% of undergraduates applied for financial aid. Of those, 71% were determined to have financial need; 32% had their need fully met. Average financial aid package (proportion receiving): $14,284 (67%). Average amount of gift aid, such as scholarships or grants (proportion receiving): $12,091 (65%). Average amount of self-help aid, such as work study or loans (proportion receiving): $2,936 (31%). Average need-based loan (excluding PLUS or other private loans): $2,926. Among students who received need-based aid, the average percentage of need met: 75%. Among students who received aid based on merit, the average award (and the proportion receiving): $4,323 (1%). The average athletic scholarship (and the proportion receiving): $0 (0%). Average amount of debt of borrowers graduating in 2005: $14,071. Proportion who borrowed: 59%.

CAMPUS LIFE AND EXTRACURRICULAR ACTIVITIES
Campus housing available (% using): coed dorms (94%), apartments for married students (2%), special housing for disabled students (4%). **Clubs and organizations:** Number of student organizations: 31. Activities include: dance, drama/theater, student government, student newspaper, student film society, yearbook. Number of fraternities: 4; sororities: 4. **Sports program (2005-2006):** Member of NCAA III. *Men's intercollegiate varsity sports:* baseball, basketball, cross-country, football, soccer, swimming and diving, tennis, track and field (indoor), track and field (outdoor), wrestling, mixed cross country. *Women's intercollegiate varsity sports:* basketball, cross-country, soccer, softball, swimming and diving, tennis, track and field (indoor), track and field (outdoor), volleyball, mixed cross country.

SERVICES AND FACILITIES
Basic services: nonremedial tutoring, placement service, day care, health service, health insurance. **Remedial assistance:** reading, math, writing, study skills. **Counseling services:** minority student, career, personal, academic, older student, psychological, religious. **For learning-disabled students:** School does not offer a structured program with separate admission and additional fees. Total undergraduates in learning-disabled program or receiving services: 60. Services include: remedial math, remedial English, reading machines, tape recorders, other special classes, diagnostic testing service, note-taking services, learning center, readers, extended time for tests, tutors, priority seating, substitution of courses, texts on tape, exams on tape or computer. **Library:** Number of titles: 244,494; number of current

serial subscriptions: 1,543. **Information technology resources:** Students are not required to lease or own a computer. School has a wireless network. Approximate number of users that can be accommodated: 2,208. Proportion of college-owned housing units wired for high-speed internet access: 100%. **Campus safety:** Security services offered: 24-hour foot-and-vehicle patrols, late-night transport/escort service, lighted pathways/sidewalks, controlled dormitory access (key, security card, etc.).

TRANSFER AND INTERNATIONAL STUDENTS
Transfer students: May apply for admission for the following academic terms: Fall, Spring. Applicants do not need a minimum number of credits to apply. For fall 2005: Transfer applications received: 126. Transfer applicants offered admission: 89. Transfer applicants enrolled: 71. **International students:** Number of foreign undergraduates: 116 (10% of student body). Number of countries represented: 28. Minimum TOEFL score required: 390 (paper). Average TOEFL score: 557 (paper).

Georgetown University

- **Address:** 37th and O Streets NW, Washington, DC 20057
- **Website:** http://www.georgetown.edu
- **Private; Religious affiliation:** Roman Catholic (Jesuit)
- **Enrollment:** 6,504 full-time; 215 part-time

KEY STATS
✔ **U.S News College Ranking:** 23, National Universities
✔ **SAT Score (25th/75th percentile):** 1290-1490
✔ **Tuition:** 2006-2007: $34,110

Selectivity: Most selective	**Room/board:** $11,210
Acceptance rate: 22%	**Average debt:** $23,724
Student/faculty ratio: 11/1	**Proportion who borrowed:** 45%

UNDERGRADUATE STUDENT BODY STATS
2005-2006 enrollment: 6,504 full-time; 215 part-time. Men: 46%; women: 54%. **Ethnic makeup:** African American: 7%; Asian American: 9%; Hispanic: 6%; White: 73%; International: 4%. **Religious preference:** Roman Catholic: 53%; Protestant: 24%; Jewish: 5%; Muslim: 2%; Hindu: 2%; Buddhist: 1%; No preference: 11%.

ADMISSIONS FACTS AND FIGURES
Phone: (202) 687-3600. **Email:** guadmiss@georgetown.edu. **Website:** http://www.georgetown.edu. **Application deadlines for fall 2007:** Regular decision: January 10; decision sent by April 1. Early decision: Not offered. Early action: Send application by: November 1; Decision sent by: December 15. Admission can be deferred. **Application fee:** $60. Common application is not accepted. **Admissions requirements/recommendations:** High school units required (recommended): English: 4 (4); Mathematics: 2 (4); Science: 1 (4); Foreign language: 2 (4); Social studies: 2 (4); History: 2 (2). Tests: The college uses SAT or ACT scores in admissions decisions. Either SAT or ACT required. For admission to the fall 2007 entering class, the school will accept: ACT with writing, ACT without writing. Campus visit: Recommended. Admissions interview: Required. Off-campus interview: May be arranged. **Factors that count in admissions decisions:** *Academic:* Secondary school record: Very important. Class rank: Very important. Letters of recommendation: Very important. Standardized test scores: Very important. Essay: Very important. *Nonacademic:* Interview: Important. Extracurricular activities: Important. Talent/ability: Very important. Character/personal qualities: Very important. Alumni/ae relationship: Considered. Geographical residence: Considered. State residency: Considered. Religious affiliation/commitment: Not considered. Minority status: Considered. Volunteer work: Important. Work experience: Considered. **Other schools with the greatest overlap in applicants:** Boston College; Duke University; George Washington University; New York University; University of Pennsylvania. **Admissions statistics for the fall 2005 entering class:** Total applicants: 15,285. Total accepted: 3,286. Freshmen enrolled: 1,551; 99% were from out of state. Accepted through early-decision or early-action plans: 37%. Overall acceptance rate: 22%. Non-early acceptance rate: 20%. **Size of waiting list:** 1832 applicants; enrolled from waiting list: 65. **Credentials of fall 2005 freshmen:** 86% ranked in the top 10 percent of their high school class; 97% were in the top 25 percent, and 100% were in the top half. (Proportion submitting class standing: 70%.) **Average high school grade point average:** 3.8. **First-year students who**

submitted SAT scores: 95%. Scores (25/75 percentile): Verbal: 640-750, Math: 650-740, Combined: 1290-1490. **First-year students submitting ACT scores:** 7%. Scores (25/75 percentile): English: 28-34, Math: 27-31, Composite: 27-32.

ACADEMICS
Year founded: 1789. **Academic calendar:** Semester. **Degrees offered:** certificate, bachelor's, master's, first professional, doctorate. **Most popular majors:** 16% international relations and affairs, 10% political science and government, 9% English language and literature, 8% finance, 5% nursing/registered nurse training (R.N., A.S.N., B.S.N., M.S.N.). **Major fields of study:** area, ethnic, cultural, and gender studies; biological and biomedical sciences; business, management, marketing, and related support services; computer and information sciences and support services; English language and literature/letters; foreign languages, literatures, and linguistics; health professions and related clinical sciences; history; liberal arts and sciences studies, and humanities; mathematics and statistics; multi/interdisciplinary studies; philosophy and religious studies; physical sciences; psychology; social sciences; visual and performing arts. **Areas of required coursework:** English (including composition), philosophy, other. **Pre-professional programs:** pre-law, pre-medicine. **Special academic programs (% participation):** cross-registration (3%), double major (25%), English as a Second Language (ESL) (2%), honors program, independent study (25%), internships, student-designed major, study abroad (50%). **Reserve Officers Training Corps (ROTC):** Army ROTC: Offered on campus; Navy ROTC: Offered at cooperating institution (George Washington University); Air Force ROTC: Offered at cooperating institution (Howard University). **Faculty and instruction (2005-2006):** Total instructional faculty: 752 full-time, 506 part-time (65% men; 35% women; 13% minorities). Full-time faculty with Ph.D. or other terminal degree: 92%. Student/faculty ratio: 11/1. Classes of fewer than 20 students: 57%; of 20 to 49 students: 35%; of 50 or more students: 8%. **Advanced Placement and International Baccalaureate credit:** AP tests may be used for: Credit and/or placement. Scores accepted: 4, 5. International Baccalaureate exams may be used for: Credit and/or placement. **Freshmen returning for sophomore year:** 97%. **Graduation rates:** Four-year: 88%; five-year: 92%; six-year: 93%. **Graduate study:** 29% of students pursue further study immediately upon graduation. Fields in which graduates pursue further study: Master of Business Administration (MBA), 3%; law, 10%; medicine, 5%; arts and sciences, 11%.

COSTS AND FINANCIAL AID
Financial aid office: (202) 687-4547. **Expenses (2006-2007):** Tuition and fees 2006-2007: $34,110; room/board: $11,210. Estimated books and supplies: $1,000; transportation: $440; personal expenses: $1,560. **Financial aid:** Priority filing date for institution's financial aid form: February 1. In 2005-2006, 49% of undergraduates applied for financial aid. Of those, 42% were determined to have financial need; 99% had their need fully met. Average financial aid package (proportion receiving): $25,600 (42%). Average amount of gift aid, such as scholarships or grants (proportion receiving): $19,300 (37%). Average amount of self-help aid, such as work study or loans (proportion receiving): $5,700 (37%). Average need-based loan (excluding PLUS or other private loans): $3,600. Among students who received need-based aid, the average percentage of need met: 100%. Among students who received aid based on merit, the average award (and the proportion receiving): $30,730 (0%). The average athletic scholarship (and the proportion receiving): $19,500 (2%). Average amount of debt of borrowers graduating in 2005: $23,724. Proportion who borrowed: 45%.

CAMPUS LIFE AND EXTRACURRICULAR ACTIVITIES
Campus housing available (% using): coed dorms (81%), apartment for single students (16%), other housing options (3%). Students who live in college-owned, operated, or affiliated housing: 72%. **Student employment:** During the 2005-2006 academic year, 50% of undergraduates worked on campus. Average per-year earnings: $2,850. **Clubs and organizations:** Number of student organizations: 172. Activities include: choral groups, concert band, dance, drama/theater, jazz band, literary magazine, music ensembles, musical theater, pep band, radio station, student government, student newspaper, student film society, symphony orchestra, television station, yearbook. Number of fraternities: 0; sororities: 0. Average proportion of students who stay on campus on weekends: 95%. **Sports program (2005-2006):** Member of NCAA I. *Men's intercollegiate varsity sports:* baseball, basketball, cross-country, football, golf, lacrosse, soccer, swimming and diving, tennis, track and field (indoor), track and field (outdoor). *Women's intercollegiate varsity sports:* basketball, cross-country, field hockey, golf, lacrosse, soccer, swimming and diving, tennis, track and field (indoor), track and field (outdoor), volleyball, rowing.

SERVICES AND FACILITIES

Basic services: nonremedial tutoring, women's center, placement service, health service. **Counseling services:** minority student, career, personal, academic, psychological, religious. **For learning-disabled students:** School does not offer a structured program with separate admission and additional fees. Services include: note-taking services, learning center, extended time for tests, tutors, exams on tape or computer, other. **Library:** Number of titles: 2,473,208; number of current serial subscriptions: 29,254. **Information technology resources:** Students are not required to lease or own a computer. Number of campus computers available to all students: 266. School has a wireless network. Approximate number of users that can be accommodated: 11,335. Proportion of college-owned housing units wired for high-speed internet access: 99%. **Campus safety:** Security services offered: 24-hour foot-and-vehicle patrols, late-night transport/escort service, 24-hour emergency telephones, lighted pathways/sidewalks, controlled dormitory access (key, security card, etc).

TRANSFER AND INTERNATIONAL STUDENTS

Transfer students: May apply for admission for the following academic terms: Fall. Applicants need a minimum number of credits to apply. For fall 2005: Transfer applications received: 1,447. Transfer applicants offered admission: 410. Transfer applicants enrolled: 238. **International students:** Number of foreign undergraduates: 262 (4% of student body). Number of countries represented: 81.

George Washington University

- **Address:** 2121 I Street NW, Washington, DC 20052
- **Website:** http://www.gwu.edu
- **Private**
- **Enrollment:** 9,741 full-time; 1,020 part-time

KEY STATS
✔ **U.S News College Ranking:** 52, National Universities
✔ **SAT Score (25th/75th percentile):** 1200-1390
✔ **Tuition:** 2006-2007: $35,630

Selectivity: More selective	**Room/board:** $11,100
Acceptance rate: 37%	**Average debt:** $27,041
Student/faculty ratio: 14/1	**Proportion who borrowed:** 50%

UNDERGRADUATE STUDENT BODY STATS

2005-2006 enrollment: 9,741 full-time; 1,020 part-time. Men: 44%; women: 56%. **Ethnic makeup:** African American: 6%; Asian American: 9%; Hispanic: 5%; White: 75%; International: 4%.

ADMISSIONS FACTS AND FIGURES

Phone: (202) 994-6040. **Email:** gwadm@gwu.edu. **Website:** http://www.gwu.edu. **Application deadlines for fall 2007:** Regular decision: January 10. Early decision: Send application by: December 1; Decision sent by: December 15. Early action: Not offered. Admission can be deferred. **Application fee:** $60. Common application is accepted. **To apply online, go to:** http://gwired.gwu.edu/adm/apply/index.html. **Admissions requirements/recommendations:** High school units required (recommended): English: 4 (4); Mathematics: 2 (4); Science: 2 (4); Foreign language: 2 (4); Social studies: 2 (4); Total units: 13 (20). Tests: The college uses SAT or ACT scores in admissions decisions. Either SAT or ACT required. For admission to the fall 2007 entering class, the school will accept: ACT with writing, ACT without writing. Campus visit: Recommended. Admissions interview: Recommended. Off-campus interview: May be arranged. **Factors that count in admissions decisions:** *Academic:* Secondary school record: Very important. Class rank: Important. Letters of recommendation: Important. Standardized test scores: Important. Essay: Important. *Nonacademic:* Interview: Important. Extracurricular activities: Important. Talent/ability: Important. Character/personal qualities: Considered. Alumni/ae relationship: Considered. Geographical residence: Considered. State residency: Not considered. Religious affiliation/commitment: Not considered. Minority status: Considered. Volunteer work: Important. Work experience: Considered. **Other schools with the greatest overlap in applicants:** Boston University; Emory University; Georgetown University; New York University. **Admissions statistics for the fall 2005 entering class:** Total applicants: 19,406. Total accepted: 7,275. Freshmen enrolled: 2,411; 99% were from out of state. Accepted through early-decision or early-action plans: 38%. Overall

acceptance rate: 37%. Early-decision acceptance rate: 58%. Non-early acceptance rate: 36%. **Size of waiting list:** 2082 applicants; enrolled from waiting list: 97. **Credentials of fall 2005 freshmen:** 63% ranked in the top 10 percent of their high school class; 88% were in the top 25 percent, and 99% were in the top half. (Proportion submitting class standing: 53%.) **First-year students who submitted SAT scores:** 95%. Scores (25/75 percentile): Verbal: 600-700, Math: 600-690, Combined: 1200-1390. **First-year students submitting ACT scores:** 21%. Scores (25/75 percentile): English: N/A, Math: N/A, Composite: 25-29.

ACADEMICS

Year founded: 1821. **Academic calendar:** Semester. **Degrees offered:** certificate, associate, bachelor's, post-bachelor's certificate, master's, post-master's certificate, first professional, doctorate. **Most popular majors:** 33% social sciences, 17% business, management, marketing, and related support services, 8% psychology, 6% English language and literature/letters, 4% biological and biomedical sciences. **Major fields of study:** area, ethnic, cultural, and gender studies; biological and biomedical sciences; business, management, marketing, and related support services; communication, journalism, and related programs; computer and information sciences and support services; education; engineering; English language and literature/letters; foreign languages, literatures, and linguistics; health professions and related clinical sciences; history; liberal arts and sciences studies, and humanities; mathematics and statistics; multi/interdisciplinary studies; philosophy and religious studies; physical sciences; psychology; security and protective services; social sciences; visual and performing arts. **Areas of required coursework:** humanities, mathematics, English (including composition), sciences (biological or physical), social science. **Pre-professional programs:** pre-law, premedicine. **Special academic programs (% participation):** accelerated program, cooperative (work-study plan) program (1%), cross-registration (3%), distance learning (7%), double major (17%), dual enrollment, honors program (11%), independent study, internships (64%), liberal arts/career combination, student-designed major (1%), study abroad (34%). **Cooperative education programs:** art, business, computer science, engineering, humanities, natural science, social/behavioral science, technologies. **Reserve Officers Training Corps (ROTC):** Army ROTC: Offered at cooperating institution (Georgetown University, Howard University); Navy ROTC: Offered on campus; Air Force ROTC: Offered at cooperating institution (University of Maryland, Howard University). **Faculty and instruction (2005-2006):** Total instructional faculty: 826 full-time, 1,210 part-time (61% men; 39% women; 16% minorities). Full-time faculty with Ph.D. or other terminal degree: 92%. Student/faculty ratio: 14/1. Classes of fewer than 20 students: 54%; of 20 to 49 students: 34%; of 50 or more students: 12%. **Advanced Placement and International Baccalaureate credit:** AP tests may be used for: Credit and/or placement. Scores accepted: 4, 5. International Baccalaureate exams may be used for: Credit and/or placement. **Freshmen returning for sophomore year:** 92%. **Graduation rates:** Four-year: 72%; five-year: 77%; six-year: 78%. **Graduate study:** 16% of students pursue further study immediately upon graduation; 25% within one year. Fields in which graduates pursue further study: Master of Business Administration (MBA), 2%; law, 28%; medicine, 16%; arts and sciences, 43%.

COSTS AND FINANCIAL AID

Financial aid office: (202) 994-6620. **Expenses (2006-2007):** Tuition and fees 2006-2007: $35,630; room/board: $11,100. Estimated books and supplies: $1,000 personal expenses: $1,350. **Financial aid:** Priority filing date for institution's financial aid form: February 1; deadline: February 1. In 2005-2006, 51% of undergraduates applied for financial aid. Of those, 44% were determined to have financial need; 63% had their need fully met. Average financial aid package (proportion receiving): $33,196 (43%). Average amount of gift aid, such as scholarships or grants (proportion receiving): $19,828 (41%). Average amount of self-help aid, such as work study or loans (proportion receiving): $7,727 (35%). Average need-based loan (excluding PLUS or other private loans): $6,806. Among students who received need-based aid, the average percentage of need met: 91%. Among students who received aid based on merit, the average award (and the proportion receiving): $19,290 (24%). The average athletic scholarship (and the proportion receiving): $20,921 (2%). Average amount of debt of borrowers graduating in 2005: $27,041. Proportion who borrowed: 50%.

CAMPUS LIFE AND EXTRACURRICULAR ACTIVITIES

Campus housing available (% using): coed dorms (95%), women's dorms (2%), sorority housing (2%), fraternity housing (1%), apartment for single students. Students who live in college-owned, operated, or affiliated housing: 67%. **Clubs and organizations:** Number of student organizations: 378. Activities include: choral groups, concert band, dance, drama/theater, jazz band, literary magazine, marching band, music ensembles, musical theater, pep band, radio station, student government, student newspaper, student film society, television station, yearbook. Number of fraternities: 17; sororities: 14. Proportion of men in fraternities: 16%; of women in sororities: 13%. Average proportion of students who stay on campus on weekends: 95%. **Sports program (2005-2006):** Member of NCAA I. **Men's intercollegiate varsity sports:** baseball, basketball, cross-country, golf, soccer, swimming and diving, tennis, water polo. **Women's intercollegiate varsity sports:** basketball, cross-country, gymnastics, lacrosse, soccer, softball, squash, swimming and diving, tennis, volleyball, water polo, rowing.

SERVICES AND FACILITIES

Basic services: nonremedial tutoring, placement service, health service, health insurance. **Counseling services:** minority student, career, personal, veteran student, academic, older student, psychological, birth control, religious, other. **For learning-disabled students:** School does not offer a structured program with separate admission and additional fees. Total undergraduates in learning-disabled program or receiving services: 272. Services include: reading machines, tape recorders, untimed tests, note-taking services, readers, extended time for tests, tutors, priority registration, priority seating, substitution of courses, texts on tape, typist/scribe, other testing accomodations. **Library:** Number of titles: 2,129,332; number of current serial subscriptions: 12,055. **Information technology resources:** Students are not required to lease or own a computer. Number of campus computers available to all students: 550. School has a wireless network. Proportion of college-owned housing units wired for high-speed internet access: 100%. **Campus safety:** Security services offered: 24-hour foot-and-vehicle patrols, late-night transport/escort service, 24-hour emergency telephones, lighted pathways/sidewalks, controlled dormitory access (key, security card, etc).

TRANSFER AND INTERNATIONAL STUDENTS

Transfer students: May apply for admission for the following academic terms: Fall, Spring, Summer. Applicants do not need a minimum number of credits to apply. For fall 2005: Transfer applications received: 2,090. Transfer applicants offered admission: 793. Transfer applicants enrolled: 383. **International students:** Number of foreign undergraduates: 431 (4% of student body). Number of countries represented: 80. Minimum TOEFL score required: 550 (paper); 213 (computer).

Howard University

- **Address:** 2400 Sixth Street NW, Washington, DC 20059
- **Website:** http://www.howard.edu
- **Private**
- **Enrollment:** 6,766 full-time; 398 part-time

KEY STATS

✔ **U.S News College Ranking:** 88, National Universities
✔ **SAT Score (25th/75th percentile):** 910-1370
✔ **Tuition:** 2006-2007: $12,985

Selectivity: Selective	**Room/board:** $6,522
Acceptance rate: 44%	**Average debt:** $16,546
Student/faculty ratio: 8/1	**Proportion who borrowed:** 80%

UNDERGRADUATE STUDENT BODY STATS

2005-2006 enrollment: 6,766 full-time; 398 part-time. Men: 33%; women: 67%. **Ethnic makeup:** African American: 90%; Asian American: 1%; Hispanic: 1%; International: 9%.

ADMISSIONS FACTS AND FIGURES

Phone: (202) 806-2700. **Email:** admission@howard.edu. **Website:** http://www.howard.edu. **Application deadlines for fall 2007:** Regular decision: February 15. Early decision: Send application by: November 1; Decision sent by: December 24. Early action: Send application by: November 1; Decision sent by: N/A. Admission can be deferred. **Application fee:** $45. Common application is not accepted. **Admissions requirements/recommendations:** High school units required (recommended): English: 4 (4); Mathematics: 2 (3); Science: 2 (4); Foreign language: 2 (2); Social studies: 2 (2); History: 2 (2); Total units: 14 (21). Tests: The college uses SAT or ACT scores in admissions decisions. Either SAT or ACT required. For admission to the fall 2007 entering class, the school will accept: ACT with writing. Campus visit: Recommended. Admissions interview: Neither required nor

recommended. Off-campus interview: Not available. **Factors that count in admissions decisions:** *Academic:* Secondary school record: Very important. Class rank: Very important. Letters of recommendation: Important. Standardized test scores: Very important. Essay: Considered. *Nonacademic:* Interview: Not considered. Extracurricular activities: Considered. Talent/ability: Considered. Character/personal qualities: Important. Alumni/ae relationship: Considered. Geographical residence: Not considered. State residency: Not considered. Religious affiliation/commitment: Not considered. Minority status: Not considered. Volunteer work: Considered. Work experience: Considered. **Other schools with the greatest overlap in applicants:** Hampton University; Morehouse College; Spelman College; University of Maryland–College Park. **Admissions statistics for the fall 2005 entering class:** Total applicants: 9,542. Total accepted: 4,227. Freshmen enrolled: 1,415; 98% were from out of state. Overall acceptance rate: 44%. Non-early acceptance rate: 44%. **Credentials of fall 2005 freshmen:** 21% ranked in the top 10 percent of their high school class; 54% were in the top 25 percent, and 84% were in the top half. (Proportion submitting class standing: 46%.) **Average high school grade point average:** 3.2. **First-year students who submitted SAT scores:** 84%. Scores (25/75 percentile): Verbal: 460-680, Math: 450-690, Combined: 910-1370. **First-year students submitting ACT scores:** 41%. Scores (25/75 percentile): English: N/A, Math: N/A, Composite: 19-28.

ACADEMICS

Year founded: 1867. **Academic calendar:** Semester. **Degrees offered:** certificate, bachelor's, master's, post-master's certificate, first professional, first professional certificate, doctorate. **Most popular majors:** 8% biology, 8% journalism, 7% radio and television, 6% marketing, 6% psychology. **Major fields of study:** architecture and related services; area, ethnic, cultural, and gender studies; biological and biomedical sciences; business, management, marketing, and related support services; communication, journalism, and related programs; education; engineering; English language and literature/letters; family and consumer sciences/human sciences; foreign languages, literatures, and linguistics; health professions and related clinical sciences; history; mathematics and statistics; multi/interdisciplinary studies; parks, recreation, leisure, and fitness studies; philosophy and religious studies; physical sciences; psychology; security and protective services; social sciences; visual and performing arts. **Areas of required coursework:** arts/fine arts, humanities, computer literacy, mathematics, English (including composition), philosophy, foreign languages, sciences (biological or physical), history, social science, other. **Pre-professional programs:** pre-law, pre-dentistry, pre-medicine, pre-veterinary science, pre-optometry, pre-pharmacy, other. **Special academic programs (% participation):** accelerated program (3%), cooperative (work-study plan) program (10%), cross-registration (2%), distance learning (2%), double major (2%), exchange student program (domestic) (19%), honors program (18%), independent study (10%), internships (23%), student-designed major (3%), study abroad (12%), teacher certificate program (5%). **Teacher certification offered in:** early childhood, special education, elementary, middle/junior high, secondary. **Cooperative education programs:** business, computer science, engineering, other. **Reserve Officers Training Corps (ROTC):** Army ROTC: Offered on campus; Air Force ROTC: Offered on campus. **Faculty and instruction (2005-2006):** Total instructional faculty: 1,069 full-time, 604 part-time (59% men; 41% women; 73% minorities). Full-time faculty with Ph.D. or other terminal degree: 90%. Student/faculty ratio: 8/1. Classes of fewer than 20 students: 64%; of 20 to 49 students: 32%; of 50 or more students: 4%. **Advanced Placement and International Baccalaureate credit:** AP tests may be used for: Credit and/or placement. Scores accepted: 3, 4, 5. International Baccalaureate exams may be used for: Credit and/or placement. **Freshmen returning for sophomore year:** 89%. **Graduation rates:** Four-year: 43%; five-year: 63%; six-year: 67%. **Graduate study:** 21% of students pursue further study immediately upon graduation; 13% within one year; 10% within five years. Fields in which graduates pursue further study: Master of Business Administration (MBA), 22%; law, 11%; medicine, 9%; dentistry, 9%; engineering, 14%; theology (or the seminary), 2%; education, 15%; arts and sciences, 27%.

COSTS AND FINANCIAL AID

Financial aid office: (202) 806-2762. **Expenses (2006-2007):** Tuition and fees 2006-2007: $12,985; room/board: $6,522. Estimated books and supplies: $1,200; transportation: $1,638; personal expenses: $900. **Financial aid:** Priority filing date for institution's financial aid form: February 15; deadline: August 15. In 2005-2006, 68% of undergraduates applied for financial aid. Of those, 65% were determined to have financial need; 20% had their need fully met. Average financial aid package (proportion receiving): $17,077 (63%). Average amount of gift aid, such as scholarships or grants (proportion receiving): $9,559 (36%). Average amount of self-help aid, such as work study or loans (proportion receiving): $3,636 (43%). Average need-based loan (excluding PLUS or other private loans): $3,636. Among students who received need-based aid, the average percentage of need met: 84%. Among students who received aid based on merit, the average award (and the proportion receiving): $10,755 (13%). The average athletic scholarship (and the proportion receiving): $0 (0%). Average amount of debt of borrowers graduating in 2005: $16,546. Proportion who borrowed: 80%.

CAMPUS LIFE AND EXTRACURRICULAR ACTIVITIES

Campus housing available (% using): coed dorms (10%), women's dorms (16%), men's dorms (14%), apartments for married students (3%), apartment for single students (15%), special housing for disabled students, other housing options (42%). Students who live in college-owned, operated, or affiliated housing: 55%. **Student employment:** During the 2005-2006 academic year, 10% of undergraduates worked on campus. Average per-year earnings: $4,500. **Clubs and organizations:** Number of student organizations: 225. Activities include: choral groups, concert band, dance, drama/theater, jazz band, literary magazine, marching band, music ensembles, musical theater, opera, pep band, radio station, student government, student newspaper, student film society, television station, yearbook. Number of fraternities: 10; sororities: 8. Proportion of men in fraternities: 2%; of women in sororities: 1%. Average proportion of students who stay on campus on weekends: 40%. **Sports program (2005-2006):** Member of NCAA I. *Men's intercollegiate varsity sports:* basketball, cross-country, football, soccer, swimming and diving, tennis, track and field (indoor), track and field (outdoor). *Women's intercollegiate varsity sports:* basketball, bowling, cross-country, lacrosse, soccer, softball, swimming and diving, tennis, track and field (indoor), track and field (outdoor), volleyball.

SERVICES AND FACILITIES

Basic services: nonremedial tutoring, women's center, placement service, health service, health insurance. **Remedial assistance:** reading, math, writing, study skills. **Counseling services:** minority student, career, personal, veteran student, academic, older student, psychological, birth control, religious. **For learning-disabled students:** School does not offer a structured program with separate admission and additional fees. Total undergraduates in learning-disabled program or receiving services: 380. Services include: reading machines, tape recorders, note-taking services, readers, extended time for tests, tutors, priority seating, texts on tape, other testing accomodations, other. **Library:** Number of titles: 2,162,556; number of current serial subscriptions: 12,216. **Information technology resources:** Students are not required to lease or own a computer. Number of campus computers available to all students: 2,319. School has a wireless network. Approximate number of users that can be accommodated: 5,000. Proportion of college-owned housing units wired for high-speed internet access: 100%. **Campus safety:** Security services offered: 24-hour foot-and-vehicle patrols, late-night transport/escort service, 24-hour emergency telephones, lighted pathways/sidewalks, student patrols, controlled dormitory access (key, security card, etc).

TRANSFER AND INTERNATIONAL STUDENTS

Transfer students: May apply for admission for the following academic terms: Fall, Spring, Summer. Applicants need a minimum number of credits to apply. For fall 2005: Transfer applications received: 1,923. Transfer applicants offered admission: 735. Transfer applicants enrolled: 375. **International students:** Number of foreign undergraduates: 580 (9% of student body). Number of countries represented: 91. Minimum TOEFL score required: 550 (paper); 213 (computer).

Southeastern University

- **Address:** 501 I Street SW, Washington, DC 20024
- **Website:** http://www.seu.edu
- **Private**
- **Enrollment:** N/A

KEY STATS

✔ **U.S News College Ranking:** fourth tier, Universities–Master's (North)
✔ **SAT or ACT Score (25th/75th percentile):** N/A
✔ **Tuition:** N/A

Selectivity: Less selective	**Room/board:** N/A
Acceptance rate: N/A	**Average debt:** N/A
Student/faculty ratio: N/A	**Proportion who borrowed:** N/A

Trinity University

- **Address:** 125 Michigan Avenue NE, Washington, DC 20017
- **Website:** http://www.trinitydc.edu
- **Private; Religious affiliation:** Roman Catholic
- **Enrollment:** N/A

KEY STATS

✔ **U.S News College Ranking:** third tier, Universities–Master's (North)
✔ **ACT Score (25th/75th percentile):** 13-18
✔ **Tuition:** 2006-2007: $17,875

Selectivity: Least selective	**Room/board:** $7,800
Acceptance rate: 86%	**Average debt:** $23,540
Student/faculty ratio: N/A	**Proportion who borrowed:** 87%

University of the District of Columbia

- **Address:** 4200 Connecticut Avenue NW, Washington, DC 20008
- **Website:** http://www.udc.edu/
- **Public**
- **Enrollment:** 1,966 full-time; 3,204 part-time

KEY STATS

✔ **U.S News College Ranking:** fourth tier, Universities–Master's (North)
✔ **SAT or ACT Score (25th/75th percentile):** N/A
✔ **Tuition:** 2006-2007: $3,210 in state, $6,510 out of state

Selectivity: Less selective	**Room/board:** N/A
Acceptance rate: 79%	**Average debt:** $18,700
Student/faculty ratio: 12/1	**Proportion who borrowed:** 60%

UNDERGRADUATE STUDENT BODY STATS

2005-2006 enrollment: 1,966 full-time; 3,204 part-time. Men: 35%; women: 65%. **Ethnic makeup:** African American: 81%; Asian American: 3%; Hispanic: 6%; White: 11%.

ADMISSIONS FACTS AND FIGURES

Phone: (202) 274-5010. **Website:** http://www.udc.edu/. **Application deadlines for fall 2007:** Regular decision: June 15. Early decision: Send application by: N/A; Decision sent by: N/A. Early action: Not offered. Admission can be deferred. **Application fee:** $20. Common application is not accepted. **Admissions requirements/recommendations:** High school units required (recommended): English: 4 (0); Mathematics: 2 (0); Science: 2 (0); Foreign language: 2 (0); Social studies: 0 (0); History: 0 (0); Academic electives: 0 (0); Total units: 14 (0). Tests: The college does not use SAT or ACT scores in admissions decisions. Neither SAT nor ACT required. Campus visit: Recommended. Admissions interview: Neither required nor recommended. Off-campus interview: Not available. **Factors that count in admissions decisions:** *Academic:* Secondary school record: Very important. Class rank: Not considered. Letters of recommendation: Not considered. Standardized test scores: Considered. Essay: Not considered. *Nonacademic:* Interview: Not considered. Extracurricular activities: Not considered. Talent/ability: Considered. Character/personal qualities: Not considered. Geographical residence: Not considered. State residency: Not considered. Religious affiliation/commitment: Not considered. Minority status: Not considered. Volunteer work: Not considered. Work experience: Not considered. **Admissions statistics for the fall 2005 entering class:** Total applicants: 2,147. Total accepted: 1,700. Freshmen enrolled: 1,137; 27% were from out of state. Overall acceptance rate: 79%. Non-early acceptance rate: 79%.

ACADEMICS

Year founded: 1976. **Academic calendar:** Semester. **Degrees offered:** associate, bachelor's, master's. **Most popular majors:** 10% business administration, management, and operations, 8% accounting, 5% computer and information sciences, 5% social work, 3% computer science. **Major fields of study:** architecture and related services; biological and biomedical sciences; business, management, marketing, and related support services; computer and information sciences and support services; construction trades; education; engineering; engineering technologies/technicians; English language and literature/letters; family and consumer sciences/human sciences; foreign languages, literatures, and linguistics; health professions and related clinical sciences; history; mathematics and statistics; natural resources and conservation; parks, recreation, leisure, and fitness studies; physical sciences; psychology; public administration and social service professions; security and protective services; social sciences; transportation and materials moving; visual and performing arts. **Areas of required coursework:** computer literacy, mathematics, English (including composition), foreign languages, sciences (biological or physical), social science. **Special academic programs (% participation):** cooperative (work-study plan) program (26%), English as a Second Language (ESL) (28%), honors program (16%), independent study (26%), internships (27%), teacher certificate program (15%). **Teacher certification offered in:** early childhood, special education, elementary, middle/junior high, adult education, secondary. **Cooperative education programs:** computer science, health professions, vocational arts, other. **Reserve Officers Training Corps (ROTC):** Army ROTC: Offered at cooperating institution (Howard University); Navy ROTC: Offered at cooperating institution (George Washington University); Air Force ROTC: Offered at cooperating institution (Howard University). **Faculty and instruction (2005-2006):** Total instructional faculty: 216 full-time, 236 part-time (55% men; 45% women). Full-time faculty with Ph.D. or other terminal degree: 61%. Student/faculty ratio: 12/1. Classes of fewer than 20 students: 52%; of 20 to 49 students: 27%; of 50 or more students: 21%. **Freshmen returning for sophomore year:** 55%. **Graduation rates:** Six-year: 13%.

COSTS AND FINANCIAL AID

Financial aid office: (202) 274-5060. **Expenses (2006-2007):** Tuition and fees 2006-2007: $3,210 in state, $6,510 out of state; room/board: N/A. Estimated books and supplies: $1,500; transportation: $1,500; personal expenses: $2,000. **Financial aid:** Priority filing date for institution's financial aid form: May 5. Average financial aid package (proportion receiving): $1,350 (N/A). Average amount of gift aid, such as scholarships or grants (proportion receiving): $950 (N/A). Among students who received need-based aid, the average percentage of need met: 37%. The average athletic scholarship (and the proportion receiving): $6,500 (N/A). Average amount of debt of borrowers graduating in 2005: $18,700. Proportion who borrowed: 60%.

CAMPUS LIFE AND EXTRACURRICULAR ACTIVITIES

Students who live in college-owned, operated, or affiliated housing: 0%. **Student employment:** During the 2005-2006 academic year, 3% of undergraduates worked on campus. Average per-year earnings: $4,000. **Clubs and organizations:** Number of student organizations: 54. Activities include: choral groups, concert band, dance, drama/theater, jazz band, music ensembles, musical theater, opera, pep band, student government, student newspaper, symphony orchestra, television station, yearbook. Number of fraternities: 4; sororities: 3. Proportion of men in fraternities: 3%; of women in sororities: 5%. Average proportion of students who stay on campus on weekends: 15%. **Sports program (2005-2006):** Member of NCAA II. *Men's intercollegiate varsity sports:* basketball, cross-country, soccer, tennis. *Women's intercollegiate varsity sports:* basketball, cross-country, soccer, tennis, volleyball.

SERVICES AND FACILITIES

Basic services: nonremedial tutoring, placement service, day care, health service, health insurance. **Remedial assistance:** reading, math, writing, study skills. **Counseling services:** minority student, career, military, veteran student, academic, older student. **For learning-disabled students:** School does not offer a structured program with separate admission and additional fees. Services include: remedial math, remedial English, reading machines, remedial reading, tape recorders, other special classes, diagnostic testing service, untimed tests, note-taking services, oral tests, learning center, readers, extended time for tests, tutors, other. **Information technology resources:** Students are not required to lease or own a computer. Number of campus computers available to all students: 265. School does not have a wireless network. **Campus safety:** Security services offered: 24-hour foot-and-vehicle patrols, late-night transport/escort service, 24-hour emergency telephones.

TRANSFER AND INTERNATIONAL STUDENTS

Transfer students: May apply for admission for the following academic terms: Fall, Spring, Summer. Applicants need a minimum number of credits to apply. **International students:** Number of foreign undergraduates: 0. Minimum TOEFL score required: 500 (paper); 213 (computer).

Florida

Barry University

- **Address:** 11300 N.E. Second Avenue, Miami Shores, FL 33161-6695
- **Website:** http://www.barry.edu
- **Private; Religious affiliation:** Roman Catholic
- **Enrollment:** 4,583 full-time; 1,333 part-time

KEY STATS

✔ **U.S News College Ranking:** 54, Universities–Master's (South)
✔ **SAT Score (25th/75th percentile):** 960-1070
✔ **Tuition:** 2006-2007: $24,000

Selectivity: Less selective	**Room/board:** $7,850
Acceptance rate: 72%	**Average debt:** $24,091
Student/faculty ratio: 14/1	**Proportion who borrowed:** 72%

UNDERGRADUATE STUDENT BODY STATS

2005-2006 enrollment: 4,583 full-time; 1,333 part-time. Men: 31%; women: 69%. **Ethnic makeup:** African American: 23%; Asian American: 1%; Hispanic: 33%; White: 38%; International: 5%.

ADMISSIONS FACTS AND FIGURES

Phone: (305) 899-3100. **Email:** admissions@mail.barry.edu. **Website:** http://www.barry.edu. **Application deadlines for fall 2007:** Regular decision: Rolling. Early decision: Not offered. Early action: Not offered. Admission can be deferred. **Application fee:** $30. Common application is accepted. **To apply online, go to:** http://www.barry.edu/undergrad-apply. **Admissions requirements/recommendations:** High school units required (recommended): English: (4); Mathematics: (3); Science: (3); Social studies: (3); Total units: (12). **Tests:** The college uses SAT or ACT scores in admissions decisions. Either SAT or ACT required. Campus visit: Recommended. Admissions interview: Recommended. **Factors that count in admissions decisions:** *Academic:* Secondary school record: Very important. Class rank: Considered. Letters of recommendation: Considered. Standardized test scores: Very important. Essay: Considered. *Nonacademic:* Interview: Important. Extracurricular activities: Considered. Talent/ability: Important. Character/personal qualities: Important. Alumni/ae relationship: Not considered. Geographical residence: Not considered. State residency: Not considered. Religious affiliation/commitment: Not considered. Minority status: Not considered. Volunteer work: Considered. Work experience: Considered. **Admissions statistics for the fall 2005 entering class:** Total applicants: 3,802. Total accepted: 2,728. Freshmen enrolled: 563; 54% were from out of state. Overall acceptance rate: 72%. **Average high school grade point average:** 3.1. **First-year students who submitted SAT scores:** 86%. Scores (25/75 percentile): Verbal: 480-540, Math: 480-530, Combined: 960-1070. **First-year students submitting ACT scores:** 31%. Scores (25/75 percentile): English: 16-22, Math: 16-22, Composite: 18-22.

ACADEMICS

Year founded: 1940. **Academic calendar:** Semester. **Degrees offered:** certificate, bachelor's, post-bachelor's certificate, master's, post-master's certificate, first professional, doctorate. **Most popular majors:** 22% education, 19% business, management, marketing, and related support services, 14% liberal arts and sciences studies, and humanities, 12% health professions and related clinical sciences, 8% computer and information sciences and support services. **Major fields of study:** biological and biomedical sciences; business, management, marketing, and related support services; communication, journalism, and related programs; computer and information sciences and support services; education; English language and literature/letters; foreign languages, literatures, and linguistics; health professions and related clinical sciences; history; legal professions and studies; liberal arts and sciences studies, and humanities; mathematics and statistics; natural resources and conservation; parks, recreation, leisure, and fitness studies; philosophy and religious studies; physical sciences; psychology; public administration and social service professions; security and protective services; social sciences; theology and religious vocations; visual and performing arts. **Areas of required coursework:** arts/fine arts, humanities, computer literacy, mathematics, English (including composition), philosophy, sciences (biological or physical), social science, other. **Pre-professional programs:** pre-law, pre-dentistry, pre-medicine, pre-veterinary science, pre-pharmacy. **Special academic programs:** accelerated program, distance learning, double major, dual enrollment, English as a Second Language (ESL), honors program, independent study, internships, study abroad, teacher certificate program. **Teacher certification offered in:** early childhood, elementary, middle/junior high, secondary. **Reserve Officers Training Corps (ROTC):** Army ROTC: Offered at cooperating institution (University of Miami); Air Force ROTC: Offered at cooperating institution. **Faculty and instruction (2005-2006):** Total instructional faculty: 353 full-time, 518 part-time. Full-time faculty with Ph.D. or other terminal degree: 85%. Student/faculty ratio: 14/1. Classes of fewer than 20 students: 68%; of 20 to 49 students: 31%; of 50 or more students: 1%. **Freshmen returning for sophomore year:** 65%. **Graduation rates:** Four-year: 21%; five-year: 34%; six-year: 45%.

COSTS AND FINANCIAL AID

Financial aid office: (800) 899-3673. **Expenses (2006-2007):** Tuition and fees 2006-2007: $24,000; room/board: $7,850. **Financial aid:** In 2005-2006, 81% of undergraduates applied for financial aid. Of those, 74% were determined to have financial need; 9% had their need fully met. Average financial aid package (proportion receiving): $14,124 (74%). Average amount of gift aid, such as scholarships or grants (proportion receiving): $6,639 (56%). Average amount of self-help aid, such as work study or loans (proportion receiving): $5,612 (68%). Average need-based loan (excluding PLUS or other private loans): $4,302. Among students who received need-based aid, the average percentage of need met: 62%. Among students who received aid based on merit, the average award (and the proportion receiving): $5,499 (7%). The average athletic scholarship (and the proportion receiving): $14,820 (3%). Average amount of debt of borrowers graduating in 2005: $24,091. Proportion who borrowed: 72%.

CAMPUS LIFE AND EXTRACURRICULAR ACTIVITIES

Campus housing available: coed dorms, women's dorms, men's dorms. **Clubs and organizations:** Number of student organizations: 88. Activities include: choral groups, dance, drama/theater, literary magazine, music ensembles, musical theater, radio station, student government, student newspaper, television station. Number of fraternities: 3; sororities: 2. **Sports program (2005-2006):** Member of NCAA II. *Men's intercollegiate varsity sports:* baseball, basketball, cheerleading, golf, soccer, tennis. *Women's intercollegiate varsity sports:* basketball, cheerleading, crew, golf, soccer, softball, tennis, volleyball.

SERVICES AND FACILITIES

Basic services: health service, health insurance. **Remedial assistance:** reading, math, writing, study skills. **Counseling services:** career, personal, academic. **For learning-disabled students:** School does not offer a structured program with separate admission and additional fees. Services include: remedial math, remedial English, reading machines, remedial reading, tape recorders, other special classes, note-taking services, oral tests, learning center, readers, extended time for tests, tutors, other. **Information technology resources:** Students are not required to lease or own a computer. Number of campus computers available to all students: 368. School has a wireless network. Proportion of college-owned housing units wired for high-speed internet access: 100%. **Campus safety:** Security services offered: 24-hour foot-and-vehicle patrols, late-night transport/escort service, 24-hour emergency telephones, lighted pathways/sidewalks, controlled dormitory access (key, security card, etc).

TRANSFER AND INTERNATIONAL STUDENTS

Transfer students: May apply for admission for the following academic terms: Fall, Winter, Spring, Summer. Applicants need a minimum number of credits to apply. For fall 2005: Transfer applications received: 2,277. Transfer applicants offered admission: 1,600. Transfer applicants enrolled: 621. **International students:** Number of foreign undergraduates: 257 (5% of student body). Minimum TOEFL score required: 550 (paper); 213 (computer).

Bethune-Cookman College

- **Address:** 640 Dr. Mary McLeod Bethune Boulevard, Daytona Beach, FL 32114
- **Website:** http://www.bethune.cookman.edu
- **Private; Religious affiliation:** Methodist
- **Enrollment:** 2,795 full-time; 295 part-time

KEY STATS

✔ **U.S News College Ranking:** third tier, Comp. Colleges–Bachelor's (South)
✔ **SAT Score (25th/75th percentile):** 720-920
✔ **Tuition:** 2006-2007: $11,230

Selectivity: Least selective	**Room/board:** $6,692
Acceptance rate: 74%	**Average debt:** $26,740
Student/faculty ratio: 17/1	**Proportion who borrowed:** 83%

UNDERGRADUATE STUDENT BODY STATS

2005-2006 enrollment: 2,795 full-time; 295 part-time. Men: 41%; women: 59%. **Ethnic makeup:** African American: 91%; Hispanic: 1%; White: 3%; International: 4%. **Religious preference:** Roman Catholic: 4%; Protestant: 60%; No preference: 19%; Unknown: 7%; Methodist: 8%; Other: 2%.

ADMISSIONS FACTS AND FIGURES

Phone: (800) 448-0228. **Email:** admissions@cookman.edu. **Website:** http://www.bethune.cookman.edu. **Application deadlines for fall 2007:** Regular decision: Rolling. Early decision: Not offered. Early action: Not offered. Admission can be deferred. **Application fee:** $25. Common application is not accepted. **To apply online, go to:** http://www.cookman.edu/admissions/download_bcc_application.htm. **Admissions requirements/recommendations:** High school units required (recommended): English: 4; Mathematics: 3; Science: 3; Foreign language: (2); Social studies: 1; History: 2; Academic electives: 6; Total units: 19 (3). **Tests:** The college uses SAT or ACT scores in admissions decisions. Either SAT or ACT required. For admission to the fall 2007 entering class, the school will accept: ACT with writing, ACT without writing. Campus visit: Neither required nor recommended. Admissions interview: Neither required nor recommended. Off-campus interview: May be arranged. **Factors that count in admissions decisions:** *Academic:* Secondary school record: Very important. Class rank: Considered. Letters of recommendation: Important. Standardized test scores: Very important. Essay: Considered. *Nonacademic:* Interview: Considered. Extracurricular activities: Considered. Talent/ability: Considered. Character/personal qualities: Important. Alumni/ae relationship: Considered. Geographical residence: Not considered. State residency: Not considered. Religious affiliation/commitment: Not considered. Minority status: Not considered. Volunteer work: Considered. Work experience: Considered. **Other schools with the greatest overlap in applicants:** Florida A&M University; Savannah State University; South Carolina State University; University of Central Florida; University of Florida. **Admissions statistics for the fall 2005 entering class:** Total applicants: 3,974. Total accepted: 2,925. Freshmen enrolled: 949; 35% were from out of state. Overall acceptance rate: 74%. **Credentials of fall 2005 freshmen:** 6% ranked in the top 10 percent of their high school class; 22% were in the top 25 percent, and 54% were in the top half. (Proportion submitting class standing: 61%.) **Average high school grade point average:** 2.8. **First-year students who submitted SAT scores:** 74%. Scores (25/75 percentile): Verbal: 360-460; Math: 360-460, Combined: 720-920. **First-year students submitting ACT scores:** 26%. Scores (25/75 percentile): English: N/A, Math: N/A, Composite: 14-16.

ACADEMICS

Year founded: 1904. **Academic calendar:** Semester. **Degrees offered:** bachelor's. **Most popular majors:** 20% business administration and management, 17% elementary education and teaching, 13% corrections and criminal justice, 11% psychology, 6% nursing/registered nurse training (R.N., A.S.N., B.S.N., M.S.N.). **Major fields of study:** biological and biomedical sciences; business, management, marketing, and related support services; communication, journalism, and related programs; computer and information sciences and support services; education; engineering; English language and literature/letters; health professions and related clinical sciences; history; liberal arts and sciences studies, and humanities; mathematics and statistics; multi/interdisciplinary studies; philosophy and religious studies; physical sciences; psychology; security and protective services; social sciences; visual and performing arts. **Areas of required coursework:** arts/fine arts, humanities, computer literacy, mathematics, English (including composition), philosophy, foreign languages, sciences (biological or physical), history, social science, other. **Special academic programs (% participation):** cooperative (work-study plan) program (15%), distance learning (1%), double major (0%), honors program (1%), internships (5%), study abroad (1%), weekend college (2%). **Teacher certification offered in:** special education, elementary, middle/junior high, secondary. **Cooperative education programs:** business, computer science, education, engineering, health professions, humanities, natural science, social/behavioral science. **Reserve Officers Training Corps (ROTC):** Army ROTC: Offered at cooperating institution (Embry-Riddle Aeronautical Univ); Air Force ROTC: Offered at cooperating institution (Embry-Riddle Aeronautical Univ). **Faculty and instruction (2005-2006):** Total instructional faculty: 147 full-time, 56 part-time (49% men; 51% women; 54% minorities). Full-time faculty with Ph.D. or other terminal degree: 54%. Student/faculty ratio: 17/1. Classes of fewer than 20 students: 47%; of 20 to 49 students: 51%; of 50 or more students: 1%. **Advanced Placement and International Baccalaureate credit:** AP tests may be used for: Credit only. Scores accepted: 3. International Baccalaureate exams may be used for: Credit only. **Freshmen returning for sophomore year:** 73%. **Graduation rates:** Four-year: 20%; five-year: 32%; six-year: 35%. **Graduate study:** 12% of students pursue further study immediately upon graduation; 31% within one year; 35% within five years. Fields in which graduates pursue further study: Master of Business Administration (MBA), 12%; law, 1%; medicine, 1%; dentistry, 1%; engineering, 2%; education, 10%; arts and sciences, 4%.

COSTS AND FINANCIAL AID

Financial aid office: (386) 481-2620. **Expenses (2006-2007):** Tuition and fees 2006-2007: $11,230; room/board: $6,692. Estimated books and supplies: $850; transportation: $830; personal expenses: $2,800. **Financial aid:** Priority filing date for institution's financial aid form: April 1. In 2005-2006, 99% of undergraduates applied for financial aid. Of those, 89% were determined to have financial need; 20% had their need fully met. Average financial aid package (proportion receiving): $13,981 (87%). Average amount of gift aid, such as scholarships or grants (proportion receiving): $6,510 (71%). Average amount of self-help aid, such as work study or loans (proportion receiving): $3,622 (79%). Average need-based loan (excluding PLUS or other private loans): $3,412. Among students who received need-based aid, the average percentage of need met: 66%. Among students who received aid based on merit, the average award (and the proportion receiving): $7,880 (3%). The average athletic scholarship (and the proportion receiving): $12,545 (9%). Average amount of debt of borrowers graduating in 2005: $26,740. Proportion who borrowed: 83%.

CAMPUS LIFE AND EXTRACURRICULAR ACTIVITIES

Campus housing available (% using): women's dorms (57%), men's dorms (43%). Students who live in college-owned, operated, or affiliated housing: 58%. **Student employment:** During the 2005-2006 academic year, 5% of undergraduates worked on campus. Average per-year earnings: $3,200. **Clubs and organizations:** Number of student organizations: 60. Activities include: choral groups, concert band, drama/theater, jazz band, marching band, music ensembles, radio station, student government, student newspaper, yearbook. Number of fraternities: 5; sororities: 4. Proportion of men in fraternities: 3%; of women in sororities: 5%. Average proportion of students who stay on campus on weekends: 80%. **Sports program (2005-2006):** Member of NCAA I. *Men's intercollegiate varsity sports:* baseball, basketball, cross-country, football, golf, tennis, track and field (indoor), track and field (outdoor). *Women's intercollegiate varsity sports:* basketball, bowling, cross-country, golf, softball, tennis, track and field (indoor), track and field (outdoor), volleyball.

SERVICES AND FACILITIES

Basic services: nonremedial tutoring, placement service, health service, health insurance. **Remedial assistance:** reading, math, writing, study skills. **Counseling services:** minority student, career, military, personal, veteran student, academic, older student, psychological, birth control, religious. **For learning-disabled students:** School does not offer a structured program with separate admission and additional fees. Total undergraduates in learning-disabled program or receiving services: 29. Services include: remedial math, remedial English, remedial reading, tape recorders, untimed tests, note-taking services, oral tests, learning center, readers, extended time for tests, tutors, priority registration, priority seating, exams on tape or computer, other testing accomodations. **Library:** Number of titles: 187,908; number of current serial subscriptions: 700. **Information technology resources:** Students are not required to lease or own a computer. Number of campus computers available to all students: 459. School has a wireless network.

Approximate number of users that can be accommodated: 900. Proportion of college-owned housing units wired for high-speed internet access: 100%. **Campus safety:** Security services offered: 24-hour foot-and-vehicle patrols, late-night transport/escort service, 24-hour emergency telephones, lighted pathways/sidewalks, controlled dormitory access (key, security card, etc.).

TRANSFER AND INTERNATIONAL STUDENTS

Transfer students: May apply for admission for the following academic terms: Fall, Spring, Summer. Applicants need a minimum number of credits to apply. For fall 2005: Transfer applications received: 340. Transfer applicants offered admission: 222. Transfer applicants enrolled: 101. **International students:** Number of foreign undergraduates: 109 (4% of student body). Minimum TOEFL score required: 550 (paper); 213 (computer). Average TOEFL score: 600 (paper).

Clearwater Christian College

- **Address:** 3400 Gulf-to-Bay Boulevard, Clearwater, FL 33759-4595
- **Website:** http://www.clearwater.edu
- **Private; Religious affiliation:** Christian nondenominational
- **Enrollment:** 548 full-time; 34 part-time

KEY STATS

✔ **U.S News College Ranking:** third tier, Comp. Colleges–Bachelor's (South)
✔ **SAT Score (25th/75th percentile):** 950-1150
✔ **Tuition:** 2006-2007: $12,500

Selectivity: Selective	**Room/board:** $5,330
Acceptance rate: 90%	**Average debt:** $16,300
Student/faculty ratio: 18/1	**Proportion who borrowed:** 64%

UNDERGRADUATE STUDENT BODY STATS

2005-2006 enrollment: 548 full-time; 34 part-time. Men: 51%; women: 49%. **Ethnic makeup:** African American: 2%; Asian American: 1%; Hispanic: 5%; White: 91%.

ADMISSIONS FACTS AND FIGURES

Phone: (800) 348-4463. **Email:** admissions@clearwater.edu. **Website:** http://www.clearwater.edu. **Application deadlines for fall 2007:** Regular decision: July 1. Early decision: Not offered. Early action: Not offered. Admission can be deferred. **Application fee:** $35. Common application is not accepted. **Admissions requirements/recommendations:** High school units required (recommended): English: (4); Mathematics: (3); Science: (3); Foreign language: (2); Social studies: (2); History: (1); Total units: (15). The college uses SAT or ACT scores in admissions decisions. Either SAT or ACT required. For admission to the fall 2007 entering class, the school will accept: ACT with writing, ACT without writing. Campus visit: Recommended. Admissions interview: Neither required nor recommended. Off-campus interview: May be arranged. **Factors that count in admissions decisions:** *Academic:* Secondary school record: Important. Class rank: Considered. Letters of recommendation: Important. Standardized test scores: Important. Essay: Important. *Nonacademic:* Interview: Considered. Extracurricular activities: Considered. Talent/ability: Considered. Character/personal qualities: Not considered. Alumni/ae relationship: Not considered. Geographical residence: Not considered. Religious affiliation/commitment: Not considered. Minority status: Not considered. Volunteer work: Not considered. Work experience: Not considered. **Other schools with the greatest overlap in applicants:** Cedarville University; Liberty University; University of South Florida. **Admissions statistics for the fall 2005 entering class:** Total applicants: 339. Total accepted: 305. Freshmen enrolled: 149; 57% were from out of state. Overall acceptance rate: 90%. **Size of waiting list:** 0 applicants; enrolled from waiting list: 0. **Credentials of fall 2005 freshmen:** 12% ranked in the top 10 percent of their high school class; 27% were in the top 25 percent, and 60% were in the top half. (Proportion submitting class standing: 55%.) **Average high school grade point average:** 3.5. **First-year students who submitted SAT scores:** 65%. Scores (25/75 percentile): Verbal: 490-590, Math: 460-560, Combined: 950-1150. **First-year students submitting ACT scores:** 59%. Scores (25/75 percentile): English: 20-26, Math: 17-23, Composite: 20-25.

ACADEMICS

Year founded: 1966. **Academic calendar:** Semester. **Degrees offered:** certificate, associate, bachelor's. **Most popular majors:** 16% business administration and management, 12% biology/biological sciences, 10% general studies, 8% elementary education and teaching, 7% psychology. **Major fields of study:** biological and biomedical sciences; business, management, marketing, and related support services; communication, journalism, and related programs; education; English language and literature/letters; health professions and related clinical sciences; history; legal professions and studies; liberal arts and sciences studies, and humanities; mathematics and statistics; multi/interdisciplinary studies; parks, recreation, leisure, and fitness studies; psychology; theology and religious vocations; visual and performing arts. **Areas of required coursework:** arts/fine arts, humanities, computer literacy, mathematics, English (including composition), sciences (biological or physical), history, social science. **Pre-professional programs:** pre-law, pre-medicine. **Special academic programs (% participation):** double major (1%), dual enrollment (1%), internships (5%), teacher certificate program (16%). **Teacher certification offered in:** special education, elementary, secondary. **Reserve Officers Training Corps (ROTC):** Army ROTC: Offered at cooperating institution (University of South Florida); Navy ROTC: Offered at cooperating institution (University of South Florida); Air Force ROTC: Offered at cooperating institution (University of South Florida). **Faculty and instruction (2005-2006):** Total instructional faculty: 31 full-time, 13 part-time (66% men; 34% women; 0% minorities). Full-time faculty with Ph.D. or other terminal degree: 58%. Student/faculty ratio: 18/1. Classes of fewer than 20 students: 70%; of 20 to 49 students: 27%; of 50 or more students: 3%. **Advanced Placement and International Baccalaureate credit:** AP tests may be used for: Credit and/or placement. Scores accepted: 3, 4, 5. International Baccalaureate exams may be used for: Credit and/or placement. **Freshmen returning for sophomore year:** 56%. **Graduation rates:** Four-year: 36%; five-year: 41%; six-year: 43%.

COSTS AND FINANCIAL AID

Financial aid office: (727) 726-1153. **Expenses (2006-2007):** Tuition and fees 2006-2007: $12,500; room/board: $5,330. Estimated books and supplies: $800; transportation: $1,500; personal expenses: $1,000. **Financial aid:** Priority filing date for institution's financial aid form: March 15. In 2005-2006, 100% of undergraduates applied for financial aid. Of those, 100% were determined to have financial need; 3% had their need fully met. Average financial aid package (proportion receiving): $8,245 (89%). Average amount of gift aid, such as scholarships or grants (proportion receiving): $3,694 (44%). Average amount of self-help aid, such as work study or loans (proportion receiving): $3,592 (40%). Average need-based loan (excluding PLUS or other private loans): $3,923. Among students who received need-based aid, the average percentage of need met: 47%. Among students who received aid based on merit, the average award (and the proportion receiving): $0 (0%). The average athletic scholarship (and the proportion receiving): $0 (0%). Average amount of debt of borrowers graduating in 2005: $16,300. Proportion who borrowed: 64%.

CAMPUS LIFE AND EXTRACURRICULAR ACTIVITIES

Campus housing available (% using): women's dorms (50%), men's dorms (50%). Students who live in college-owned, operated, or affiliated housing: 77%. **Student employment:** During the 2005-2006 academic year, 40% of undergraduates worked on campus. Average per-year earnings: $1,600. **Clubs and organizations:** Number of student organizations: 9. Activities include: choral groups, drama/theater, music ensembles, student government, student newspaper, symphony orchestra, yearbook. Number of fraternities: 6; sororities: 6. Proportion of men in fraternities: 100%; of women in sororities: 100%. Average proportion of students who stay on campus on weekends: 30%. **Sports program (2005-2006):** Member of NCAA II. *Men's intercollegiate varsity sports:* baseball, basketball, golf, soccer. *Women's intercollegiate varsity sports:* basketball, golf, soccer, volleyball.

SERVICES AND FACILITIES

Basic services: nonremedial tutoring, placement service, health insurance. **Remedial assistance:** math. **Counseling services:** career, personal, academic, religious. **For learning-disabled students:** School does not offer a structured program with separate admission and additional fees. Total undergraduates in learning-disabled program or receiving services: 4. Services include: remedial math, remedial English, tape recorders, videotaped classes, untimed tests, oral tests, readers, extended time for tests, tutors. **Library:** Number of titles: 105,013; number of current serial subscriptions: 3,409. **Information technology resources:** Students are not required to lease or own a computer. Number of campus computers available to all students: 40. School has a wireless network. Approximate number of users that can be accommodated: 50. Proportion of college-owned housing units wired for high-speed internet access: 100%. **Campus safety:** Security services offered: 24-hour foot-and-vehicle patrols, lighted pathways/sidewalks, student patrols.

TRANSFER AND INTERNATIONAL STUDENTS

Transfer students: May apply for admission for the following academic terms: Fall, Spring, Summer. Applicants do not need a minimum number of credits to apply. For fall 2005: Transfer applications received: 114. Transfer applicants offered admission: 81. Transfer applicants enrolled: 37. **International students:** Number of foreign undergraduates: 0. Number of countries represented: 5. Minimum TOEFL score required: 500 (paper); 173 (computer).

Eckerd College

- **Address:** 4200 54th Avenue S, St. Petersburg, FL 33711
- **Website:** http://www.eckerd.edu
- **Private; Religious affiliation:** Presbyterian
- **Enrollment:** 1,755 full-time; 24 part-time

KEY STATS

✔ **U.S News College Ranking:** third tier, Liberal Arts Colleges
✔ **SAT Score (25th/75th percentile):** 1020-1240
✔ **Tuition:** 2006-2007: $27,618

Selectivity: Selective	**Room/board:** $7,868
Acceptance rate: 72%	**Average debt:** $17,290
Student/faculty ratio: 13/1	**Proportion who borrowed:** 55%

UNDERGRADUATE STUDENT BODY STATS

2005-2006 enrollment: 1,755 full-time; 24 part-time. Men: 43%; women: 57%. **Ethnic makeup:** African American: 3%; Asian American: 2%; Hispanic: 4%; White: 86%; International: 5%. **Religious preference:** Roman Catholic: 20%; Protestant: 25%; Jewish: 4%; Hindu: 1%; Buddhist: 3%; No preference: 33%; Presbyterian: 7%; Other: 3%.

ADMISSIONS FACTS AND FIGURES

Phone: (727) 864-8331. **Email:** admissions@eckerd.edu. **Website:** http://www.eckerd.edu. **Application deadlines for fall 2007:** Regular decision: Rolling. Early decision: Not offered. Early action: Not offered. Admission can be deferred. **Application fee:** $35. Common application is accepted. **Admissions requirements/recommendations:** High school units required (recommended): English: 4; Mathematics: 3 (4); Science: 3 (4); Foreign language: 2 (3); Social studies: 2; History: 1 (2); Academic electives: 3; Total units: 18 (22). Tests: The college uses SAT or ACT scores in admissions decisions. Either SAT or ACT required. For admission to the fall 2007 entering class, the school will accept: ACT with writing, ACT without writing. Campus visit: Recommended. Admissions interview: Recommended. Off-campus interview: May be arranged. **Factors that count in admissions decisions:** *Academic:* Secondary school record: Very important. Class rank: Considered. Letters of recommendation: Important. Standardized test scores: Important. Essay: Important. *Nonacademic:* Interview: Important. Extracurricular activities: Important. Talent/ability: Important. Character/personal qualities: Important. Alumni/ae relationship: Considered. Geographical residence: Not considered. State residency: Not considered. Religious affiliation/commitment: Not considered. Minority status: Not considered. Volunteer work: Considered. Work experience: Considered. **Other schools with the greatest overlap in applicants:** Rollins College; Stetson University; University of Florida; University of Miami; University of Tampa. **Admissions statistics for the fall 2005 entering class:** Total applicants: 2,740. Total accepted: 1,962. Freshmen enrolled: 505; 78% were from out of state. Overall acceptance rate: 72%. **Size of waiting list:** 127 applicants; enrolled from waiting list: 40. **Credentials of fall 2005 freshmen:** 19% ranked in the top 10 percent of their high school class; 46% were in the top 25 percent, and 83% were in the top half. (Proportion submitting class standing: 54%.) **Average high school grade point average:** 3.3. **First-year students who submitted SAT scores:** 86%. Scores (25/75 percentile): Verbal: 510-630, Math: 510-610, Combined: 1020-1240. **First-year students submitting ACT scores:** 37%. Scores (25/75 percentile): English: 21-28, Math: 21-26, Composite: 22-27.

ACADEMICS

Year founded: 1958. **Academic calendar:** 4-1-4. **Degrees offered:** bachelor's. **Most popular majors:** 11% marine biology and biological oceanography, 9% business administration and management, 8% environmental studies, 7%

psychology, 6% international business/trade/commerce. **Major fields of study:** area, ethnic, cultural, and gender studies; biological and biomedical sciences; business, management, marketing, and related support services; communication, journalism, and related programs; computer and information sciences and support services; English language and literature/letters; family and consumer sciences/human sciences; foreign languages, literatures, and linguistics; history; liberal arts and sciences studies, and humanities; mathematics and statistics; multi/interdisciplinary studies; natural resources and conservation; philosophy and religious studies; physical sciences; psychology; social sciences; visual and performing arts. **Areas of required coursework:** arts/fine arts, humanities, mathematics, foreign languages, sciences (biological or physical), social science, other. **Pre-professional programs:** pre-law, pre-dentistry, pre-medicine, pre-veterinary science, pre-pharmacy. **Special academic programs (% participation):** accelerated program (2%), double major (19%), honors program (8%), independent study (35%), internships (65%), liberal arts/career combination (0%), student-designed major (19%), study abroad (19%). **Reserve Officers Training Corps (ROTC):** Army ROTC: Offered at cooperating institution (University of South Florida); Air Force ROTC: Offered at cooperating institution (University of South Florida). **Faculty and instruction (2005-2006):** Total instructional faculty: 107 full-time, 54 part-time (66% men; 34% women). Full-time faculty with Ph.D. or other terminal degree: 93%. Student/faculty ratio: 13/1. Classes of fewer than 20 students: 46%; of 20 to 49 students: 53%; of 50 or more students: 1%. **Advanced Placement and International Baccalaureate credit:** AP tests may be used for: Credit and/or placement. Scores accepted: 4, 5. International Baccalaureate exams may be used for: Credit and/or placement. **Freshmen returning for sophomore year:** 83%. **Graduation rates:** Four-year: 58%; five-year: 63%; six-year: 63%. **Graduate study:** 35% of students pursue further study within one year; 57% within five years. Fields in which graduates pursue further study: Master of Business Administration (MBA), 10%; law, 10%; medicine, 2%; education, 7%; arts and sciences, 71%.

COSTS AND FINANCIAL AID

Financial aid office: (727) 864-8334. **Expenses (2006-2007):** Tuition and fees 2006-2007: $27,618; room/board: $7,868. Estimated books and supplies: $1,000; transportation: $1,650; personal expenses: $1,400. **Financial aid:** Priority filing date for institution's financial aid form: March 1. In 2005-2006, 69% of undergraduates applied for financial aid. Of those, 57% were determined to have financial need; 30% had their need fully met. Average financial aid package (proportion receiving): $21,718 (57%). Average amount of gift aid, such as scholarships or grants (proportion receiving): $14,207 (56%). Average amount of self-help aid, such as work study or loans (proportion receiving): $4,675 (56%). Average need-based loan (excluding PLUS or other private loans): $3,237. Among students who received need-based aid, the average percentage of need met: 90%. Among students who received aid based on merit, the average award (and the proportion receiving): $9,330 (35%). The average athletic scholarship (and the proportion receiving): $15,110 (1%). Average amount of debt of borrowers graduating in 2005: $17,290. Proportion who borrowed: 55%.

CAMPUS LIFE AND EXTRACURRICULAR ACTIVITIES

Campus housing available (% using): coed dorms (90%), women's dorms (9%), men's dorms (0%), apartment for single students (0%), special housing for disabled students (1%). Students who live in college-owned, operated, or affiliated housing: 80%. **Student employment:** During the 2005-2006 academic year, 11% of undergraduates worked on campus. Average per-year earnings: $1,200. **Clubs and organizations:** Number of student organizations: 52. Activities include: choral groups, dance, drama/theater, literary magazine, music ensembles, musical theater, radio station, student government, student newspaper, student film society, television station. Number of fraternities: 0; sororities: 0. Average proportion of students who stay on campus on weekends: 80%. **Sports program (2005-2006):** Member of NCAA II. *Men's intercollegiate varsity sports:* baseball, basketball, golf, soccer, tennis. *Women's intercollegiate varsity sports:* basketball, cross-country, soccer, softball, tennis, volleyball.

SERVICES AND FACILITIES

Basic services: nonremedial tutoring, women's center, placement service, health service, health insurance. **Counseling services:** minority student, career, personal, academic, psychological, birth control, religious. **For learning-disabled students:** School does not offer a structured program with separate admission and additional fees. **Library:** Number of titles: 168,415; number of current serial subscriptions: 1,958. **Information technology resources:** Students are not required to lease or own a computer. Number of campus computers available to all students: 320. School has a wireless network. Approximate number of users that can be accommodated: 2,000. Proportion of college-owned housing units wired for high-speed internet access: 100%. **Campus safety:** Security services offered: 24-hour foot-and-vehicle patrols, late-night transport/escort service, 24-hour emergency telephones, lighted pathways/sidewalks, student patrols, controlled dormitory access (key, security card, etc).

TRANSFER AND INTERNATIONAL STUDENTS

Transfer students: May apply for admission for the following academic terms: Fall, Winter. Applicants do not need a minimum number of credits to apply. For fall 2005: Transfer applications received: 314. Transfer applicants offered admission: 153. Transfer applicants enrolled: 62. **International students:** Number of foreign undergraduates: 90 (5% of student body). Number of countries represented: 39. Minimum TOEFL score required: 550 (paper); 213 (computer). Average TOEFL score: 590 (paper).

Edward Waters College

- **Address:** 1658 Kings Road, Jacksonville, FL 32209
- **Website:** http://www.ewc.edu
- **Private; Religious affiliation:** African Methodist Episcopal
- **Enrollment:** 818 full-time; 21 part-time

KEY STATS

✔ **U.S News College Ranking:** fourth tier, Comp. Coll.–Bachelor's (South)
✔ **SAT or ACT Score (25th/75th percentile):** N/A
✔ **Tuition:** 2006-2007: $9,176

Selectivity: Less selective	**Room/board:** $3,124
Acceptance rate: 70%	**Average debt:** N/A
Student/faculty ratio: 19/1	**Proportion who borrowed:** N/A

UNDERGRADUATE STUDENT BODY STATS

2005-2006 enrollment: 818 full-time; 21 part-time. Men: 52%; women: 48%. **Ethnic makeup:** African American: 93%; Hispanic: 1%; White: 6%.

ADMISSIONS FACTS AND FIGURES

Phone: (904) 470-8200. **Email:** admissions@ewc.edu. **Website:** http://www.ewc.edu. **Application deadlines for fall 2007:** Regular decision: Rolling. Early decision: Not offered. Early action: Not offered. Admission cannot be deferred. **Application fee:** $25. Common application is accepted. **To apply online, go to:** http://admissions.ewc.edu/Application.php3. **Admissions requirements/recommendations:** High school units required (recommended): English: 4 (4); Mathematics: 3 (3); Science: 3 (3); Foreign language: 0 (0); Social studies: 3 (3); History: 0 (0); Academic electives: 0 (0); Total units: 13 (13). Tests: The college does not use SAT or ACT scores in admissions decisions. Neither SAT nor ACT required. Campus visit: Recommended. Admissions interview: Recommended. Off-campus interview: May be arranged. **Factors that count in admissions decisions:** *Academic:* Secondary school record: Very important. Class rank: Considered. Letters of recommendation: Very important. Standardized test scores: Considered. Essay: Not considered. *Nonacademic:* Interview: Not considered. Extracurricular activities: Considered. Talent/ability: Considered. Character/personal qualities: Considered. Alumni/ae relationship: Considered. Geographical residence: Not considered. State residency: Not considered. Religious affiliation/commitment: Not considered. Minority status: Not considered. Volunteer work: Considered. Work experience: Considered. **Admissions statistics for the fall 2005 entering class:** 29% were from out of state. Overall acceptance rate: 70%. **Size of waiting list:** 0 applicants; enrolled from waiting list: 0. **Credentials of fall 2005 freshmen:** 3% ranked in the top 10 percent of their high school class; 5% were in the top 25 percent, and 30% were in the top half. (Proportion submitting class standing: 100%.) **Average high school grade point average:** 2.5. **First-year students who submitted SAT scores:** 38%. Scores (25/75 percentile): Verbal: N/A, Math: N/A, Combined: N/A. **First-year students submitting ACT scores:** 18%. Scores (25/75 percentile): English: N/A, Math: N/A, Composite: N/A.

ACADEMICS

Year founded: 1866. **Academic calendar:** Semester. **Degrees offered:** bachelor's. **Most popular majors:** Information not available. **Major fields of study:** biological and biomedical sciences; business, management, marketing, and related support services; communication, journalism, and related programs; computer and information sciences and support services; education; English lan-

guage and literature/letters; health professions and related clinical sciences; mathematics and statistics; multi/interdisciplinary studies; psychology; science technologies/technicians; security and protective services; social sciences; visual and performing arts. **Areas of required coursework:** arts/fine arts, humanities, computer literacy, mathematics, English (including composition), philosophy, foreign languages, sciences (biological or physical), history, social science. **Pre-professional programs:** pre-law, pre-dentistry, pre-medicine. **Special academic programs:** accelerated program, cooperative (work-study plan) program, double major, dual enrollment, internships, teacher certificate program. **Reserve Officers Training Corps (ROTC):** Army ROTC: Offered on campus. **Faculty and instruction (2005-2006):** Total instructional faculty: 45. Student/faculty ratio: 19/1. **Freshmen returning for sophomore year:** 43%. **Graduation rates:** Four-year: 3%; five-year: 8%; six-year: 13%.

COSTS AND FINANCIAL AID

Financial aid office: (904) 470-8192. **Expenses (2006-2007):** Tuition and fees 2006-2007: $9,176; room/board: $3,124. Estimated books and supplies: $1,260 personal expenses: $3,904. **Financial aid:** Priority filing date for institution's financial aid form: May 15; deadline: June 30.

CAMPUS LIFE AND EXTRACURRICULAR ACTIVITIES

Campus housing available: women's dorms, men's dorms, other housing options. Students who live in college-owned, operated, or affiliated housing: 43%. **Student employment:** During the 2005-2006 academic year, 50% of undergraduates worked on campus. Average per-year earnings: $16,000. **Clubs and organizations:** Number of student organizations: 41. Activities include: choral groups, concert band, dance, drama/theater, jazz band, marching band, music ensembles, pep band, student government, student newspaper, symphony orchestra, yearbook. Number of fraternities: 4; sororities: 4. Proportion of men in fraternities: 3%; of women in sororities: 6%. Average proportion of students who stay on campus on weekends: 85%. **Sports program (2005-2006):** Member of NAIA. *Men's intercollegiate varsity sports:* baseball, basketball, cross-country, football, golf, track and field (indoor), track and field (outdoor). *Women's intercollegiate varsity sports:* basketball, cross-country, golf, softball, track and field (indoor), track and field (outdoor), volleyball.

SERVICES AND FACILITIES

Basic services: health insurance. **Remedial assistance:** reading, math, writing, study skills. **Counseling services:** career, military, veteran student, academic, religious. **For learning-disabled students:** School does not offer a structured program with separate admission and additional fees. Services include: remedial math, remedial English, remedial reading, tape recorders, untimed tests, note-taking services, oral tests, readers, extended time for tests, tutors. **Information technology resources:** Students are not required to lease or own a computer. Number of campus computers available to all students: 145. School has a wireless network. **Campus safety:** Security services offered: 24-hour foot-and-vehicle patrols, lighted pathways/sidewalks, controlled dormitory access (key, security card, etc).

TRANSFER AND INTERNATIONAL STUDENTS

Transfer students: May apply for admission for the following academic terms: Fall, Winter, Spring, Summer. Applicants need a minimum number of credits to apply. For fall 2005: Transfer applications received: 236. Transfer applicants offered admission: 92. Transfer applicants enrolled: 36. **International students:** Number of foreign undergraduates: 0. Minimum TOEFL score required: 500 (paper). Average TOEFL score: 500 (paper).

Embry Riddle Aeronautical University

- **Address:** 600 S. Clyde Morris Boulevard, Daytona Beach, FL 32114
- **Website:** http://www.embryriddle.edu
- **Private**
- **Enrollment:** 4,093 full-time; 289 part-time

KEY STATS

✔ **U.S News College Ranking:** 13, Universities–Master's (South)
✔ **SAT Score (25th/75th percentile):** 990-1230
✔ **Tuition:** 2006-2007: $25,490

Selectivity: Selective	**Room/board:** $8,100
Acceptance rate: 84%	**Average debt:** $52,276
Student/faculty ratio: 16/1	**Proportion who borrowed:** 68%

UNDERGRADUATE STUDENT BODY STATS

2005-2006 enrollment: 4,093 full-time; 289 part-time. Men: 83%; women: 17%. **Ethnic makeup:** African American: 5%; Asian American: 5%; Hispanic: 7%; White: 76%; International: 8%.

ADMISSIONS FACTS AND FIGURES

Phone: (800) 862-2416. **Email:** dbadmit@erau.edu. **Website:** http://www.embryriddle.edu. **Application deadlines for fall 2007:** Regular decision: Rolling. Early decision: Not offered. Early action: Not offered. Admission can be deferred. **Application fee:** $50. Common application is accepted. **Admissions requirements/recommendations:** High school units required (recommended): English: 4 (4); Mathematics: 3 (4); Science: 2 (3); Foreign language: 0 (1); Social studies: 2 (2); History: 1 (2); Academic electives: 3 (3); Total units: 15 (19). Tests: The college uses SAT or ACT scores in admissions decisions. Either SAT or ACT required. For admission to the fall 2007 entering class, the school will accept: ACT with writing, ACT without writing. Campus visit: Recommended. Admissions interview: Neither required nor recommended. Off-campus interview: Not available. **Factors that count in admissions decisions:** *Academic:* Secondary school record: Considered. Class rank: Considered. Letters of recommendation: Important. Standardized test scores: Very important. Essay: Considered. *Nonacademic:* Interview: Considered. Extracurricular activities: Considered. Talent/ability: Not considered. Character/personal qualities: Considered. Alumni/ae relationship: Considered. Geographical residence: Not considered. State residency: Not considered. Religious affiliation/commitment: Not considered. Minority status: Not considered. Volunteer work: Considered. Work experience: Considered. **Admissions statistics for the fall 2005 entering class:** Total applicants: 3,527. Total accepted: 2,978. Freshmen enrolled: 977; 73% were from out of state. Overall acceptance rate: 84%. **Credentials of fall 2005 freshmen:** 20% ranked in the top 10 percent of their high school class; 48% were in the top 25 percent, and 77% were in the top half. (Proportion submitting class standing: 69%.) **Average high school grade point average:** 3.3. **First-year students who submitted SAT scores:** 84%. Scores (25/75 percentile): Verbal: 480-600, Math: 510-630, Combined: 990-1230. **First-year students submitting ACT scores:** 41%. Scores (25/75 percentile): English: 19-25, Math: 21-27, Composite: 21-27.

ACADEMICS

Year founded: 1926. **Academic calendar:** Semester. **Degrees offered:** bachelor's, master's. **Most popular majors:** 29% airline/commercial/professional pilot and flight crew, 19% aerospace, aeronautical, and astronautical engineering, 8% air traffic controller, 8% business administration, management, and operations, 7% aeronautics/aviation/aerospace science and technology. **Major fields of study:** business, management, marketing, and related support services; communication, journalism, and related programs; engineering; engineering technologies/technicians; physical sciences; psychology; transportation and materials moving. **Areas of required coursework:** computer literacy, English (including composition). **Special academic programs:** cooperative (work-study plan) program, double major, dual enrollment, English as a Second Language (ESL), independent study, internships, study abroad. **Cooperative education programs:** business, computer science, engineering, other. **Reserve Officers Training Corps (ROTC):** Army ROTC: Offered on campus; Navy ROTC: Offered on campus; Air Force ROTC: Offered on campus. **Faculty and instruction (2005-2006):** Total instructional faculty: 227 full-time, 87 part-time (75% men; 25% women; 10% minorities). Full-time faculty with Ph.D. or other terminal degree: 65%. Student/faculty ratio: 16/1. Classes of fewer than 20 students: 23%; of 20 to 49 students: 74%; of 50 or more students: 3%. **Advanced Placement and International Baccalaureate credit:** AP tests may be used for: Credit and/or placement. Scores accepted: 3, 4, 5. **Freshmen returning for sophomore year:** 77%. **Graduation rates:** Four-year: 33%; five-year: 56%; six-year: 54%. **Graduate study:** 9% of students pursue further study immediately upon graduation; 6% within one year. Fields in which graduates pursue further study: Master of Business Administration (MBA), 25%; law, 1%; medicine, 2%; engineering, 14%; theology (or the seminary), 1%; education, 1%; arts and sciences, 8%.

COSTS AND FINANCIAL AID

Financial aid office: (800) 943-6279. **Expenses (2006-2007):** Tuition and fees 2006-2007: $25,490; room/board: $8,100. Estimated books and supplies: $950; transportation: $2,260; personal expenses: $1,340. **Financial aid:** In 2005-2006, 69% of undergraduates applied for financial aid. Of those, 60% were determined to have financial need; Average financial aid package (proportion receiving): $13,221 (60%). Average amount of gift aid, such as scholarships or grants (proportion receiving): $7,070 (55%). Average amount of self-help aid, such as work study or loans (proportion receiving): $5,245 (53%). Average need-based loan (excluding PLUS or other private

loans): $4,510. Average amount of debt of borrowers graduating in 2005: $52,276. Proportion who borrowed: 68%.

CAMPUS LIFE AND EXTRACURRICULAR ACTIVITIES

Campus housing available: coed dorms, apartment for single students, special housing for disabled students, other housing options. Students who live in college-owned, operated, or affiliated housing: 42%. **Student employment:** During the 2005-2006 academic year, 22% of undergraduates worked on campus. Average per-year earnings: $1,800. **Clubs and organizations:** Number of student organizations: 164. Activities include: choral groups, dance, drama/theater, pep band, radio station, student government, student newspaper, yearbook. Number of fraternities: 15; sororities: 5. Proportion of men in fraternities: 10%; of women in sororities: 14%. Average proportion of students who stay on campus on weekends: 75%. **Sports program (2005-2006):** Member of NAIA. *Men's intercollegiate varsity sports:* baseball, basketball, cheerleading, cross-country, golf, soccer, tennis. *Women's intercollegiate varsity sports:* cheerleading, cross-country, golf, soccer, tennis, volleyball.

SERVICES AND FACILITIES

Basic services: nonremedial tutoring, placement service, health service. **Remedial assistance:** math, other. **Counseling services:** minority student, career, personal, veteran student, academic. **For learning-disabled students:** School does not offer a structured program with separate admission and additional fees. Services include: reading machines, tape recorders, untimed tests, note-taking services, tutors. **Library:** Number of titles: 103,153; number of current serial subscriptions: 835. **Information technology resources:** Students are not required to lease or own a computer. Number of campus computers available to all students: 955. School has a wireless network. Approximate number of users that can be accommodated: 1,500. Proportion of college-owned housing units wired for high-speed internet access: 95%. **Campus safety:** Security services offered: 24-hour foot-and-vehicle patrols, late-night transport/escort service, 24-hour emergency telephones, lighted pathways/sidewalks, controlled dormitory access (key, security card, etc).

TRANSFER AND INTERNATIONAL STUDENTS

Transfer students: May apply for admission for the following academic terms: Fall, Spring, Summer. Applicants do not need a minimum number of credits to apply. For fall 2005: Transfer applications received: 793. Transfer applicants offered admission: 534. Transfer applicants enrolled: 260. **International students:** Number of foreign undergraduates: 329 (8% of student body). Number of countries represented: 85. Minimum TOEFL score required: 500 (paper); 173 (computer). Average TOEFL score: 567 (paper).

Flagler College

- **Address:** 74 King Street, St. Augustine, FL 32084
- **Website:** http://www.flagler.edu
- **Private**
- **Enrollment:** 2,089 full-time; 68 part-time

KEY STATS

✔ **U.S News College Ranking:** 15, Comp. Colleges–Bachelor's (South)
✔ **SAT Score (25th/75th percentile):** 1040-1220
✔ **Tuition:** 2006-2007: $9,450

Selectivity: More selective	**Room/board:** $5,760
Acceptance rate: 25%	**Average debt:** $15,037
Student/faculty ratio: 20/1	**Proportion who borrowed:** 55%

UNDERGRADUATE STUDENT BODY STATS

2005-2006 enrollment: 2,089 full-time; 68 part-time. Men: 38%; women: 62%. **Ethnic makeup:** African American: 2%; Asian American: 1%; Hispanic: 4%; White: 92%; International: 1%.

ADMISSIONS FACTS AND FIGURES

Phone: (800) 304-4208. **Email:** admiss@flagler.edu. **Website:** http://www.flagler.edu. **Application deadlines for fall 2007:** Regular decision: March 1; decision sent by March 30. Early decision: Send application by: December 1; Decision sent by: December 15. Early action: Not offered. Admission can be deferred. **Application fee:** $30. Common application is accepted. **To apply online, go to:** https://www.applyweb.com/aw?flagler. **Admissions requirements/recommendations:** High school units required (recommended): English: 4 (4); Mathematics: 3 (4); Science: 2 (3); Foreign language: o (2); Social studies: 3 (4); History: 1 (2); Academic electives: 3 (3); Total units: 16 (21). Tests: The college uses SAT or ACT scores in admissions decisions. Either SAT or ACT required. For admission to the fall 2007 entering class, the school will accept: ACT with writing, ACT without writing. Campus visit: Recommended. Admissions interview: Recommended. Off-campus interview: Not available. **Factors that count in admissions decisions:** *Academic:* Secondary school record: Very important. Class rank: Considered. Letters of recommendation: Important. Standardized test scores: Very important. Essay: Important. *Nonacademic:* Interview: Considered. Extracurricular activities: Important. Talent/ability: Considered. Character/personal qualities: Important. Alumni/ae relationship: Important. Geographical residence: Considered. State residency: Considered. Religious affiliation/commitment: Not considered. Minority status: Not considered. Volunteer work: Considered. Work experience: Considered. **Other schools with the greatest overlap in applicants:** Florida State University; University of Central Florida; University of Florida; University of North Florida; University of South Florida. **Admissions statistics for the fall 2005 entering class:** Total applicants: 2,248. Total accepted: 560. Freshmen enrolled: 458; 32% were from out of state. Accepted through early-decision or early-action plans: 78%. Overall acceptance rate: 25%. Early-decision acceptance rate: 56%. Non-early acceptance rate: 12%. **Size of waiting list:** 439 applicants; enrolled from waiting list: 31. **Credentials of fall 2005 freshmen:** 16% ranked in the top 10 percent of their high school class; 51% were in the top 25 percent, and 88% were in the top half. (Proportion submitting class standing: 76%.) **Average high school grade point average:** 3.4. **First-year students who submitted SAT scores:** 82%. Scores (25/75 percentile): Verbal: 530-620, Math: 510-600, Combined: 1040-1220. **First-year students submitting ACT scores:** 48%. Scores (25/75 percentile): English: 21-26, Math: 20-25, Composite: 22-26.

ACADEMICS

Year founded: 1968. **Academic calendar:** Semester. **Degrees offered:** bachelor's. **Most popular majors:** 23% business administration and management, 15% communication, journalism, and related programs, 14% visual and performing arts, 10% education, 8% social sciences. **Major fields of study:** area, ethnic, cultural, and gender studies; business, management, marketing, and related support services; communication, journalism, and related programs; education; English language and literature/letters; foreign languages, literatures, and linguistics; history; liberal arts and sciences studies, and humanities; parks, recreation, leisure, and fitness studies; philosophy and religious studies; psychology; social sciences; visual and performing arts. **Areas of required coursework:** humanities, computer literacy, mathematics, English (including composition), social science. **Pre-professional programs:** pre-law. **Special academic programs (% participation):** double major (8%), independent study (15%), internships (45%), study abroad (2%), other (18%). **Teacher certification offered in:** special education, elementary, middle/junior high, secondary. **Faculty and instruction (2005-2006):** Total instructional faculty: 74 full-time, 91 part-time (56% men; 44% women; 8% minorities). Full-time faculty with Ph.D. or other terminal degree: 64%. Student/faculty ratio: 20/1. Classes of fewer than 20 students: 36%; of 20 to 49 students: 63%; of 50 or more students: 0%. **Advanced Placement and International Baccalaureate credit:** AP tests may be used for: Credit only. Scores accepted: 4, 5. International Baccalaureate exams may be used for: Credit only. **Freshmen returning for sophomore year:** 74%. **Graduation rates:** Four-year: 44%; five-year: 55%; six-year: 54%. **Graduate study:** Fields in which graduates pursue further study: Master of Business Administration (MBA), 25%; law, 16%; theology (or the seminary), 2%; education, 28%; arts and sciences, 3%.

COSTS AND FINANCIAL AID

Financial aid office: (904) 819-6225. **Expenses (2006-2007):** Tuition and fees 2006-2007: $9,450; room/board: $5,760. Estimated books and supplies: $900; transportation: $1,600; personal expenses: $2,300. **Financial aid:** Priority filing date for institution's financial aid form: April 1. In 2005-2006, 64% of undergraduates applied for financial aid. Of those, 46% were determined to have financial need; 33% had their need fully met. Average financial aid package (proportion receiving): $10,752 (46%). Average amount of gift aid, such as scholarships or grants (proportion receiving): $3,060 (21%). Average amount of self-help aid, such as work study or loans (proportion receiving): $3,800 (38%). Average need-based loan (excluding PLUS or other private loans): $3,787. Among students who received need-based aid, the average percentage of need met: 79%. Among students who received aid based on merit, the average award (and the proportion receiving): $2,293 (3%). The average athletic scholarship (and the proportion receiving): $3,420 (6%). Average amount of debt of borrowers graduating in 2005: $15,037. Proportion who borrowed: 55%.

CAMPUS LIFE AND EXTRACURRICULAR ACTIVITIES

Campus housing available (% using): women's dorms (65%), men's dorms (35%). Students who live in college-owned, operated, or affiliated housing: 35%. **Student employment:** During the 2005-2006 academic year, 6% of undergraduates worked on campus. Average per-year earnings: $900. **Clubs and organizations:** Number of student organizations: 25. Activities include: choral groups, drama/theater, literary magazine, radio station, student government, student newspaper, television station. Number of fraternities: 0; sororities: 0. Average proportion of students who stay on campus on weekends: 35%. **Sports program (2005-2006):** Member of NAIA. *Men's intercollegiate varsity sports:* baseball, basketball, cross-country, golf, soccer, tennis. *Women's intercollegiate varsity sports:* basketball, cross-country, golf, soccer, tennis, volleyball.

SERVICES AND FACILITIES

Basic services: health service, health insurance. **Remedial assistance:** reading, math, writing. **Counseling services:** career, personal, academic, psychological. **For learning-disabled students:** School does not offer a structured program with separate admission and additional fees. Total undergraduates in learning-disabled program or receiving services: 53. Services include: remedial math, remedial English, reading machines, remedial reading, tape recorders, note-taking services, oral tests, readers, extended time for tests, tutors, priority registration, texts on tape, exams on tape or computer, other testing accomodations. **Library:** Number of titles: 86,679; number of current serial subscriptions: 493. **Information technology resources:** Students are not required to lease or own a computer. Number of campus computers available to all students: 210. School has a wireless network. Approximate number of users that can be accommodated: 150. Proportion of college-owned housing units wired for high-speed internet access: 100%. **Campus safety:** Security services offered: 24-hour foot-and-vehicle patrols, 24-hour emergency telephones, controlled dormitory access (key, security card, etc).

TRANSFER AND INTERNATIONAL STUDENTS

Transfer students: May apply for admission for the following academic terms: Fall, Spring. Applicants need a minimum number of credits to apply. For fall 2005: Transfer applications received: 581. Transfer applicants offered admission: 119. Transfer applicants enrolled: 103. **International students:** Number of foreign undergraduates: 27 (1% of student body). Number of countries represented: 34. Minimum TOEFL score required: 500 (paper); 213 (computer). Average TOEFL score: 603 (paper).

Florida A&M University

- **Address:** Tallahassee, FL 32307
- **Website:** http://www.famu.edu
- **Public**
- **Enrollment:** N/A

KEY STATS

✔ **U.S News College Ranking:** third tier, Universities–Master's (South)
✔ **ACT Score (25th/75th percentile):** 17-22
✔ **Tuition:** 2005-2006: $222 in state, $16,884 out of state

Selectivity: Less selective	**Room/board:** $5,686
Acceptance rate: 71%	**Average debt:** N/A
Student/faculty ratio: N/A	**Proportion who borrowed:** N/A

Florida Atlantic University

- **Address:** 777 Glades Road, PO Box 3091, Boca Raton, FL 33431
- **Website:** http://www.fau.edu
- **Public**
- **Enrollment:** 11,810 full-time; 9,695 part-time

KEY STATS

✔ **U.S News College Ranking:** fourth tier, National Universities
✔ **SAT Score (25th/75th percentile):** 960-1140
✔ **Tuition:** 2005-2006: $3,259 in state, $16,391 out of state

Selectivity: Selective	**Room/board:** $7,962
Acceptance rate: 55%	**Average debt:** N/A
Student/faculty ratio: 18/1	**Proportion who borrowed:** N/A

UNDERGRADUATE STUDENT BODY STATS

2005-2006 enrollment: 11,810 full-time; 9,695 part-time. Men: 40%; women: 60%. **Ethnic makeup:** African American: 18%; Asian American: 4%; Hispanic: 17%; White: 56%; International: 4%.

ADMISSIONS FACTS AND FIGURES

Phone: (561) 297-3040. **Email:** admisweb@fau.edu. **Website:** http://www.fau.edu. **Application deadlines for fall 2007:** Regular decision: June 1. Early decision: Not offered. Early action: Not offered. Admission can be deferred. **Application fee:** $30. Common application is not accepted. **To apply online, go to:** http://fauapps.fau.edu/uapp/. **Admissions requirements/recommendations:** High school units required (recommended): English: 4 (4); Mathematics: 3 (4); Science: 3 (3); Foreign language: 2 (2); Social studies: 3 (3); History: 0 (0); Academic electives: 3 (3); Total units: 20 (21). Tests: The college uses SAT or ACT scores in admissions decisions. Either SAT or ACT required. For admission to the fall 2007 entering class, the school will accept: ACT without writing. Campus visit: Recommended. Admissions interview: Neither required nor recommended. Off-campus interview: Not available. **Factors that count in admissions decisions:** *Academic:* Secondary school record: Important. Class rank: Important. Letters of recommendation: Considered. Standardized test scores: Very important. Essay: Not considered. *Nonacademic:* Interview: Not considered. Extracurricular activities: Considered. Talent/ability: Considered. Character/personal qualities: Not considered. Alumni/ae relationship: Not considered. Geographical residence: Not considered. State residency: Not considered. Religious affiliation/commitment: Not considered. Minority status: Not considered. Volunteer work: Considered. Work experience: Not considered. **Other schools with the greatest overlap in applicants:** Florida International University; Florida State University; University of Central Florida; University of Florida; University of South Florida. **Admissions statistics for the fall 2005 entering class:** Total applicants: 11,698. Total accepted: 6,396. Freshmen enrolled: 2,304; 9% were from out of state. Overall acceptance rate: 55%. **Credentials of fall 2005 freshmen:** 14% ranked in the top 10 percent of their high school class; 43% were in the top 25 percent, and 80% were in the top half. (Proportion submitting class standing: 57%.) **Average high school grade point average:** 3.4. **First-year students who submitted SAT scores:** 96%. Scores (25/75 percentile): Verbal: 480-570; Math: 480-570, Combined: 960-1140. **First-year students submitting ACT scores:** 42%. Scores (25/75 percentile): English: N/A, Math: N/A, Composite: 19-24.

ACADEMICS

Year founded: 1961. **Academic calendar:** Semester. **Degrees offered:** certificate, associate, bachelor's, master's, post-master's certificate, doctorate. **Most popular majors:** 8% elementary education and teaching, 7% biology/biological sciences, 5% accounting, 5% business administration and management, 5% nursing/registered nurse training (R.N., A.S.N., B.S.N., M.S.N.). **Major fields of study:** architecture and related services; biological and biomedical sciences; business, management, marketing, and related support services; communication, journalism, and related programs; computer and information sciences and support services; education; engineering; English language and literature/letters; foreign languages, literatures, and linguistics; health professions and related clinical sciences; history; liberal arts and sciences studies, and humanities; mathematics and statistics; parks, recreation, leisure, and fitness studies; philosophy and religious studies; physical sciences; psychology; public administration and social service professions; security and protective services; social sciences; visual and performing arts. **Areas of required coursework:** arts/fine arts, humanities, mathematics, English (including composition), foreign languages, sciences (biological or physical), history, social science. **Pre-professional programs:** pre-law, pre-dentistry, pre-medicine, pre-veterinary science. **Special academic programs:** accelerated program, cooperative (work-study plan) program, distance learning, double major, dual enrollment, English as a Second Language (ESL), honors program, independent study, internships, liberal arts/career combination, study abroad, teacher certificate program, weekend college. **Teacher certification offered in:** early childhood, special education, elementary, adult education, bilingual/bicultural. **Cooperative education programs:** art, business, computer science, education, engineering, health professions, humanities, natural science, social/behavioral science. **Reserve Officers Training Corps (ROTC):** Army ROTC: Offered on campus. **Faculty and instruction (2005-2006):** Total instructional faculty: 767 full-time, 619 part-time (57% men; 43% women; 16% minorities). Full-time faculty with Ph.D. or other terminal degree: 88%. Student/faculty ratio: 18/1. Classes of fewer than 20 students: 38%; of 20 to 49 students: 52%; of 50 or more students: 10%. **Advanced Placement and International Baccalaureate credit:** International Baccalaureate exams may be used for: Credit only. **Freshmen**

returning for sophomore year: 69%. **Graduation rates:** Four-year: 14%; five-year: 30%; six-year: 36%. **Graduate study:** 34% of students pursue further study immediately upon graduation.

COSTS AND FINANCIAL AID

Financial aid office: (561) 297-3530. **Expenses (2005-2006):** Tuition and fees 2005-2006: $3,259 in state, $16,391 out of state; room/board: $7,962. Estimated books and supplies: $700; transportation: $1,626; personal expenses: $1,410. **Financial aid:** Priority filing date for institution's financial aid form: March 1. In 2005-2006, 73% of undergraduates applied for financial aid. Of those, 48% were determined to have financial need; 13% had their need fully met. Average financial aid package (proportion receiving): $7,012 (46%). Average amount of gift aid, such as scholarships or grants (proportion receiving): $5,796 (39%). Average amount of self-help aid, such as work study or loans (proportion receiving): $3,864 (32%). Average need-based loan (excluding PLUS or other private loans): $3,741. Among students who received need-based aid, the average percentage of need met: 74%. Among students who received aid based on merit, the average award (and the proportion receiving): $2,315 (4%). The average athletic scholarship (and the proportion receiving): $8,192 (2%).

CAMPUS LIFE AND EXTRACURRICULAR ACTIVITIES

Campus housing available (% using): coed dorms (75%), women's dorms (1%), apartment for single students (24%). Students who live in college-owned, operated, or affiliated housing: 5%. **Clubs and organizations:** Number of student organizations: 178. Activities include: choral groups, dance, drama/theater, jazz band, literary magazine, marching band, music ensembles, musical theater, opera, radio station, student government, student newspaper, student film society, television station. Number of fraternities: 12; sororities: 9. Proportion of men in fraternities: 2%; of women in sororities: 2%. Average proportion of students who stay on campus on weekends: 80%. **Sports program (2005-2006):** Member of NCAA I. *Men's intercollegiate varsity sports:* baseball, basketball, cross-country, football, golf, soccer, swimming and diving, tennis. *Women's intercollegiate varsity sports:* basketball, cross-country, golf, soccer, softball, swimming and diving, tennis, track and field (outdoor), volleyball.

SERVICES AND FACILITIES

Basic services: nonremedial tutoring, women's center, placement service, health service, health insurance. **Counseling services:** minority student, career, military, personal, veteran student, academic, older student, psychological, birth control. **For learning-disabled students:** School does not offer a structured program with separate admission and additional fees. Total undergraduates in learning-disabled program or receiving services: 367. Services include: reading machines, tape recorders, other. **Library:** Number of titles: 1,765,142; number of current serial subscriptions: 12,549. **Information technology resources:** Students are not required to lease or own a computer. Number of campus computers available to all students: 1,722. School has a wireless network. Proportion of college-owned housing units wired for high-speed internet access: 98%. **Campus safety:** Security services offered: 24-hour foot-and-vehicle patrols, late-night transport/escort service, 24-hour emergency telephones, lighted pathways/sidewalks, student patrols, controlled dormitory access (key, security card, etc).

TRANSFER AND INTERNATIONAL STUDENTS

Transfer students: May apply for admission for the following academic terms: Fall, Spring, Summer. Applicants need a minimum number of credits to apply. For fall 2005: Transfer applications received: 6,303. Transfer applicants offered admission: 4,776. Transfer applicants enrolled: 2,484. **International students:** Number of foreign undergraduates: 787 (4% of student body). Number of countries represented: 136. Minimum TOEFL score required: 550 (paper); 213 (computer).

Florida Gulf Coast University

- **Address:** 10501 FGCU Boulevard S, Fort Myers, FL 33965-6565
- **Website:** http://www.fgcu.edu
- **Public**
- **Enrollment:** 4,601 full-time; 1,537 part-time

KEY STATS

✔ **U.S News College Ranking:** third tier, Universities–Master's (South)
✔ **SAT Score (25th/75th percentile):** 940-1130
✔ **Tuition:** 2006-2007: $3,559 in state, $2,704 out of state

Selectivity: Selective	**Room/board:** $7,798
Acceptance rate: 76%	**Average debt:** $13,245
Student/faculty ratio: 18/1	**Proportion who borrowed:** 47%

UNDERGRADUATE STUDENT BODY STATS

2005-2006 enrollment: 4,601 full-time; 1,537 part-time. Men: 38%; women: 62%. **Ethnic makeup:** African American: 6%; Asian American: 2%; Hispanic: 10%; White: 82%; International: 1%.

ADMISSIONS FACTS AND FIGURES

Phone: (239) 590-7878. **Email:** admissions@fgcu.edu. **Website:** http://www.fgcu.edu. **Application deadlines for fall 2007:** Regular decision: August 1. Early decision: Not offered. Early action: Not offered. Admission can be deferred. **Application fee:** $30. Common application is not accepted. **To apply online, go to:** http://enrollment.fgcu.edu/admissions/applyonline.htm. **Admissions requirements/recommendations:** High school units required (recommended): English: 4; Mathematics: 3; Science: 3; Foreign language: 2; Social studies: 3; Academic electives: 3; Total units: 18. Tests: The college uses SAT or ACT scores in admissions decisions. Either SAT or ACT required. For admission to the fall 2007 entering class, the school will accept: ACT with writing. Campus visit: Recommended. Admissions interview: Neither required nor recommended. Off-campus interview: May be arranged. **Factors that count in admissions decisions:** *Academic:* Secondary school record: Very important. Class rank: Considered. Letters of recommendation: Considered. Standardized test scores: Very important. Essay: Considered. *Nonacademic:* Interview: Not considered. Extracurricular activities: Considered. Talent/ability: Considered. Character/personal qualities: Considered. Alumni/ae relationship: Not considered. Geographical residence: Not considered. State residency: Not considered. Religious affiliation/commitment: Not considered. Minority status: Not considered. Volunteer work: Not considered. Work experience: Not considered. **Other schools with the greatest overlap in applicants:** Florida Atlantic University; Florida International University; University of Central Florida; University of South Florida. **Admissions statistics for the fall 2005 entering class:** Total applicants: 3,449. Total accepted: 2,617. Freshmen enrolled: 1,343; 10% were from out of state. Overall acceptance rate: 76%. **Credentials of fall 2005 freshmen:** 20% ranked in the top 10 percent of their high school class; 49% were in the top 25 percent, and 84% were in the top half. (Proportion submitting class standing: 80%.) **Average high school grade point average:** 3.4. **First-year students who submitted SAT scores:** 91%. Scores (25/75 percentile): Verbal: 470-560, Math: 470-570, Combined: 940-1130. **First-year students submitting ACT scores:** 53%. Scores (25/75 percentile): English: N/A, Math: N/A, Composite: 19-23.

ACADEMICS

Year founded: 1991. **Academic calendar:** Semester. **Degrees offered:** certificate, associate, transfer-associate, bachelor's, master's. **Most popular majors:** Information not available. **Major fields of study:** biological and biomedical sciences; business, management, marketing, and related support services; computer and information sciences and support services; education; health professions and related clinical sciences; legal professions and studies; liberal arts and sciences studies, and humanities; parks, recreation, leisure, and fitness studies; public administration and social service professions; security and protective services; social sciences. **Areas of required coursework:** humanities, mathematics, English (including composition), foreign languages, other. **Special academic program:** accelerated program, cooperative (work-study plan) program, cross-registration, distance learning, double major, dual enrollment, honors program, independent study, internships, study abroad, teacher certificate program. **Teacher certification offered in:** early childhood, special education, elementary, secondary. **Faculty and instruction (2005-2006):** Total instructional faculty: 253 full-time, 188 part-time (53%

men; 47% women; 13% minorities). Full-time faculty with Ph.D. or other terminal degree: 78%. Student/faculty ratio: 18/1. Classes of fewer than 20 students: 33%; of 20 to 49 students: 62%; of 50 or more students: 4%. **Advanced Placement and International Baccalaureate credit:** AP tests may be used for: Credit only. Scores accepted: 3, 4, 5. International Baccalaureate exams may be used for: Credit only. **Freshmen returning for sophomore year:** 71%. **Graduation rates:** Four-year: 14%; five-year: 34%; six-year: 37%.

COSTS AND FINANCIAL AID

Financial aid office: (239) 590-7920. **Expenses (2006-2007):** Tuition and fees 2006-2007: $3,559 in state, $2,704 out of state; room/board: $7,798. Estimated books and supplies: $700. **Financial aid:** Priority filing date for institution's financial aid form: February 1; deadline: March 15. Average amount of debt of borrowers graduating in 2005: $13,245. Proportion who borrowed: 47%.

CAMPUS LIFE AND EXTRACURRICULAR ACTIVITIES

Campus housing available: coed dorms, apartment for single students, special housing for disabled students. Students who live in college-owned, operated, or affiliated housing: 30%. Average per-year earnings: $6,000. **Clubs and organizations:** Number of student organizations: 42. Activities include: choral groups, dance, drama/theater, literary magazine, radio station, student government, student newspaper. Number of fraternities: 2; sororities: 3. Proportion of men in fraternities: 1%; of women in sororities: 1%. Average proportion of students who stay on campus on weekends: 50%. **Sports program (2005-2006):** Member of NCAA II. *Men's intercollegiate varsity sports:* baseball, basketball, cross-country, golf, tennis. *Women's intercollegiate varsity sports:* basketball, cross-country, golf, softball, tennis, volleyball.

SERVICES AND FACILITIES

Basic services: nonremedial tutoring, day care, health service. **Remedial assistance:** reading, math, writing, study skills. **Counseling services:** career, personal, academic, psychological. **For learning-disabled students:** School does not offer a structured program with separate admission and additional fees. Total undergraduates in learning-disabled program or receiving services: 240. Services include: remedial math, remedial English, reading machines, remedial reading, tape recorders, diagnostic testing service, untimed tests, note-taking services, learning center, readers, extended time for tests, tutors, priority registration, priority seating, texts on tape, other testing accomodations. **Library:** Number of titles: 176,898; number of current serial subscriptions: 2,638. **Information technology resources:** Students are not required to lease or own a computer. Number of campus computers available to all students: 372. School has a wireless network. Approximate number of users that can be accommodated: 32. Proportion of college-owned housing units wired for high-speed internet access: 100%. **Campus safety:** Security services offered: 24-hour foot-and-vehicle patrols, late-night transport/escort service, 24-hour emergency telephones, lighted pathways/sidewalks.

TRANSFER AND INTERNATIONAL STUDENTS

Transfer students: May apply for admission for the following academic terms: Fall, Spring, Summer. Applicants need a minimum number of credits to apply. For fall 2005: Transfer applications received: 1,675. Transfer applicants offered admission: 1,490. Transfer applicants enrolled: 966. **International students:** Number of foreign undergraduates: 58 (1% of student body). Number of countries represented: 36. Minimum TOEFL score required: 550 (paper); 213 (computer).

Florida Institute of Technology

- **Address:** 150 W. University Boulevard, Melbourne, FL 32901-6975
- **Website:** http://www.fit.edu
- **Private**
- **Enrollment:** 2,264 full-time; 94 part-time

KEY STATS

✔ **U.S News College Ranking:** third tier, National Universities
✔ **SAT Score (25th/75th percentile):** 1060-1290
✔ **Tuition:** 2006-2007: $27,540

Selectivity: More selective	**Room/board:** $7,400
Acceptance rate: 83%	**Average debt:** $24,535
Student/faculty ratio: 13/1	**Proportion who borrowed:** 54%

UNDERGRADUATE STUDENT BODY STATS

2005-2006 enrollment: 2,264 full-time; 94 part-time. Men: 69%; women: 31%. **Ethnic makeup:** African American: 4%; Asian American: 3%; Hispanic: 7%; White: 72%; International: 14%.

ADMISSIONS FACTS AND FIGURES

Phone: (800) 888-4348. **Email:** admission@fit.edu. **Website:** http://www.fit.edu. **Application deadlines for fall 2007:** Regular decision: Rolling. Early decision: Not offered. Early action: Not offered. Admission can be deferred. **Application fee:** $50. Common application is accepted. **To apply online, go to:** http://www.fit.edu/ugrad/apply.htm. **Admissions requirements/recommendations:** High school units required (recommended): English: 4; Mathematics: 4; Science: 3 (4); Total units: 12. Tests: The college uses SAT or ACT scores in admissions decisions. Either SAT or ACT required. For admission to the fall 2007 entering class, the school will accept: ACT with writing, ACT without writing. Campus visit: Recommended. Admissions interview: Recommended. Off-campus interview: May be arranged. **Factors that count in admissions decisions:** *Academic:* Secondary school record: Very important. Class rank: Important. Letters of recommendation: Considered. Standardized test scores: Important. Essay: Considered. *Nonacademic:* Interview: Not considered. Extracurricular activities: Not considered. Talent/ability: Not considered. Character/personal qualities: Considered. Alumni/ae relationship: Not considered. Geographical residence: Not considered. State residency: Not considered. Religious affiliation/commitment: Not considered. Minority status: Not considered. Volunteer work: Not considered. Work experience: Considered. **Other schools with the greatest overlap in applicants:** Embry Riddle Aeronautical University; Massachusetts Institute of Technology; University of Central Florida; University of Florida; University of Miami. **Admissions statistics for the fall 2005 entering class:** Total applicants: 2,463. Total accepted: 2,051. Freshmen enrolled: 604; 69% were from out of state. Overall acceptance rate: 83%. **Credentials of fall 2005 freshmen:** 32% ranked in the top 10 percent of their high school class; 66% were in the top 25 percent, and 92% were in the top half. (Proportion submitting class standing: 55%.) **Average high school grade point average:** 3.5. **First-year students who submitted SAT scores:** 92%. Scores (25/75 percentile): Verbal: 510-630, Math: 550-660, Combined: 1060-1290. **First-year students submitting ACT scores:** 36%. Scores (25/75 percentile): English: 21-29, Math: 23-29, Composite: 22-29.

ACADEMICS

Year founded: 1958. **Academic calendar:** Semester. **Degrees offered:** bachelor's, master's, post-master's certificate, doctorate. **Most popular majors:** 10% computer engineering, 9% electrical, electronics, and communications engineering, 8% computer science, 7% aviation/airway management and operations, 5% aerospace, aeronautical, and astronautical engineering. **Major fields of study:** biological and biomedical sciences; business, management, marketing, and related support services; communication, journalism, and related programs; computer and information sciences and support services; education; engineering; liberal arts and sciences studies, and humanities; mathematics and statistics; multi/interdisciplinary studies; natural resources and conservation; physical sciences; psychology; transportation and materials moving. **Areas of required coursework:** humanities, computer literacy, mathematics, English (including composition), sciences (biological or physical), social science. **Pre-professional programs:** pre-dentistry, pre-medicine, pre-veterinary science, pre-optometry, pre-pharmacy, other. **Special academic programs (% participation):** cooperative (work-study plan) program (10%), double major (1%), English as a Second Language (ESL) (4%), internships (35%), study abroad (15%), teacher certificate program (6%). **Teacher certification offered in:** secondary. **Cooperative education programs:** business, computer science, education, engineering, humanities, natural science, social/behavioral science, technologies, other. **Reserve Officers Training Corps (ROTC):** Army ROTC: Offered on campus. **Faculty and instruction (2005-2006):** Total instructional faculty: 202 full-time, 65 part-time (79% men; 21% women; 9% minorities). Full-time faculty with Ph.D. or other terminal degree: 91%. Student/faculty ratio: 13/1. Classes of fewer than 20 students: 54%; of 20 to 49 students: 43%; of 50 or more students: 4%. **Advanced Placement and International Baccalaureate credit:** AP tests may be used for: Credit and/or placement. Scores accepted: 4, 5. International Baccalaureate exams may be used for: Credit and/or placement. **Freshmen returning for sophomore year:** 78%. **Graduation rates:** Four-year: 35%; five-year: 50%; six-year: 52%. **Graduate study:** 29% of students pursue further study immediately upon graduation. Fields in which graduates pursue further study: Master of Business Administration (MBA), 5%; law, 3%; medicine, 5%; engineering, 39%; arts and sciences, 48%.

COSTS AND FINANCIAL AID

Financial aid office: (321) 674-8070. **Expenses (2006-2007):** Tuition and fees 2006-2007: $27,540; room/board: $7,400. Estimated books and supplies: $2,200; transportation: $800; personal expenses: $0. **Financial aid:** Priority filing date for institution's financial aid form: March 15. In 2005-2006, 71% of undergraduates applied for financial aid. Of those, 64% were determined to have financial need; 31% had their need fully met. Average financial aid package (proportion receiving): $21,102 (64%). Average amount of gift aid, such as scholarships or grants (proportion receiving): $14,095 (55%). Average amount of self-help aid, such as work study or loans (proportion receiving): $5,351 (52%). Average need-based loan (excluding PLUS or other private loans): $4,724. Among students who received need-based aid, the average percentage of need met: 84%. Among students who received aid based on merit, the average award (and the proportion receiving): $7,526 (26%). The average athletic scholarship (and the proportion receiving): $21,149 (2%). Average amount of debt of borrowers graduating in 2005: $24,535. Proportion who borrowed: 54%.

CAMPUS LIFE AND EXTRACURRICULAR ACTIVITIES

Campus housing available (% using): coed dorms (54%), women's dorms (6%), men's dorms (17%), apartment for single students (23%), special housing for disabled students (0%). Students who live in college-owned, operated, or affiliated housing: 55%. **Student employment:** During the 2005-2006 academic year, 12% of undergraduates worked on campus. Average per-year earnings: $9,894. **Clubs and organizations:** Number of student organizations: 112. Activities include: choral groups, dance, drama/theater, literary magazine, pep band, radio station, student government, student newspaper, student film society, television station. Number of fraternities: 7; sororities: 3. Proportion of men in fraternities: 16%; of women in sororities: 10%. Average proportion of students who stay on campus on weekends: 75%. **Sports program (2005-2006):** Member of NCAA II. *Men's intercollegiate varsity sports:* baseball, basketball, cheerleading, crew, cross-country, lightweight crew, soccer, tennis. *Women's intercollegiate varsity sports:* basketball, cross-country, golf, soccer, softball, tennis, volleyball, rowing.

SERVICES AND FACILITIES

Basic services: nonremedial tutoring, placement service, health service, health insurance. **Remedial assistance:** reading, math, writing, study skills. **Counseling services:** minority student, career, military, personal, veteran student, academic, psychological, religious. **For learning-disabled students:** School does not offer a structured program with separate admission and additional fees. Total undergraduates in learning-disabled program or receiving services: 41. Services include: remedial math, remedial English, tape recorders, diagnostic testing service, untimed tests, note-taking services, learning center, extended time for tests, tutors, priority seating, other. **Library:** Number of titles: 285,090; number of current serial subscriptions: 3,916. **Information technology resources:** Students are not required to lease or own a computer. Number of campus computers available to all students: 400. School has a wireless network. Approximate number of users that can be accommodated: 150. Proportion of college-owned housing units wired for high-speed internet access: 100%. **Campus safety:** Security services offered: 24-hour foot-and-vehicle patrols, late-night transport/escort service, 24-hour emergency telephones, lighted pathways/sidewalks, controlled dormitory access (key, security card, etc).

TRANSFER AND INTERNATIONAL STUDENTS

Transfer students: May apply for admission for the following academic terms: Fall, Spring, Summer. Applicants need a minimum number of credits to apply. For fall 2005: Transfer applications received: 391. Transfer applicants offered admission: 275. Transfer applicants enrolled: 114. **International students:** Number of foreign undergraduates: 338 (14% of student body). Number of countries represented: 79. Minimum TOEFL score required: 550 (paper); 213 (computer).

Florida International University

- **Address:** University Park, Miami, FL 33199
- **Website:** http://www.fiu.edu
- **Public**
- **Enrollment:** 18,697 full-time; 11,987 part-time

KEY STATS
- ✔ **U.S News College Ranking:** fourth tier, National Universities
- ✔ **SAT Score (25th/75th percentile):** 1030-1180
- ✔ **Tuition:** N/A

Selectivity: Selective	**Room/board:** N/A
Acceptance rate: 47%	**Average debt:** N/A
Student/faculty ratio: 17/1	**Proportion who borrowed:** N/A

UNDERGRADUATE STUDENT BODY STATS
2005-2006 enrollment: 18,697 full-time; 11,987 part-time. Men: 44%; women: 56%. **Ethnic makeup:** African American: 13%; Asian American: 4%; Hispanic: 60%; White: 17%; International: 7%.

ADMISSIONS FACTS AND FIGURES
Phone: (305) 348-2363. **Email:** admiss@fiu.edu. **Website:** http://www.fiu.edu. **Application deadlines for fall 2007:** Regular decision: September 4. Early decision: Not offered. Early action: Not offered. Admission can be deferred. **Application fee:** $25. Common application is not accepted. **Admissions requirements/recommendations:** High school units required (recommended): English: 4; Mathematics: 3; Science: 3; Foreign language: 2; Social studies: 3; History: 0; Academic electives: 3; Total units: 18. Tests: The college uses SAT or ACT scores in admissions decisions. Either SAT or ACT required. For admission to the fall 2007 entering class, the school will accept: ACT without writing. Campus visit: Recommended. Admissions interview: Neither required nor recommended. Off-campus interview: Not available. **Factors that count in admissions decisions:** *Academic:* Secondary school record: Very important. Class rank: Very important. Letters of recommendation: Considered. Standardized test scores: Very important. Essay: Not considered. *Nonacademic:* Interview: Considered. Extracurricular activities: Considered. Talent/ability: Considered. Character/personal qualities: Considered. Alumni/ae relationship: Not considered. Geographical residence: Not considered. State residency: Not considered. Religious affiliation/commitment: Not considered. Minority status: Not considered. Volunteer work: Considered. Work experience: Not considered. **Admissions statistics for the fall 2005 entering class:** Total applicants: 10,223. Total accepted: 4,833. Freshmen enrolled: 2,506; 14% were from out of state. Overall acceptance rate: 47%. **Average high school grade point average:** 3.6. **First-year students who submitted SAT scores:** 93%. Scores (25/75 percentile): Verbal: 520-590, Math: 510-590, Combined: 1030-1180. **First-year students submitting ACT scores:** 41%. Scores (25/75 percentile): English: N/A, Math: N/A, Composite: 21-25.

ACADEMICS
Year founded: 1965. **Academic calendar:** Semester. **Degrees offered:** bachelor's, master's, first professional, doctorate. **Most popular majors:** 35% business, management, marketing, and related support services, 9% health professions and related clinical sciences, 8% psychology, 7% social sciences, 6% communication, journalism, and related programs. **Major fields of study:** architecture and related services; area, ethnic, cultural, and gender studies; biological and biomedical sciences; business, management, marketing, and related support services; communication, journalism, and related programs; computer and information sciences and support services; education; engineering; engineering technologies/technicians; English language and literature/letters; foreign languages, literatures, and linguistics; health professions and related clinical sciences; history; liberal arts and sciences studies, and humanities; mathematics and statistics; natural resources and conservation; parks, recreation, leisure, and fitness studies; philosophy and religious studies; physical sciences; psychology; public administration and social service professions; security and protective services; social sciences; visual and performing arts. **Areas of required coursework:** mathematics, English (including composition), foreign languages, sciences (biological or physical), social science. **Pre-professional programs:** pre-law, pre-medicine. **Special academic programs:** distance learning, double major, dual enrollment, exchange student program (domestic), honors program, independent study, internships, study abroad, teacher certificate program, weekend college. **Teacher certification offered in:** early childhood, special education, ele-mentary, adult education, secondary. **Reserve Officers Training Corps (ROTC):** Army ROTC: Offered on campus; Air Force ROTC: Offered on campus. **Faculty and instruction (2005-2006):** Total instructional faculty: 757; full-time, 681 part-time (61% men; 39% women; 41% minorities). Full-time faculty with Ph.D. or other terminal degree: 84%. Student/faculty ratio: 17/1. Classes of fewer than 20 students: 26%; of 20 to 49 students: 53%; of 50 or more students: 21%. **Advanced Placement and International Baccalaureate credit:** AP tests may be used for: Credit and/or placement. Scores accepted: 3. International Baccalaureate exams may be used for: Credit only. **Freshmen returning for sophomore year:** 83%. **Graduation rates:** Four-year: 21%; five-year: 39%; six-year: 48%.

COSTS AND FINANCIAL AID
Financial aid office: (305) 348-2431.

CAMPUS LIFE AND EXTRACURRICULAR ACTIVITIES
Campus housing available (% using): coed dorms (18%), fraternity housing (3%), apartments for married students, apartment for single students (79%). Students who live in college-owned, operated, or affiliated housing: 7%. **Clubs and organizations:** Number of student organizations: 102. Activities include: drama/theater, jazz band, marching band, music ensembles, radio station, student government, student newspaper, yearbook. Number of fraternities: 10; sororities: 10. Proportion of men in fraternities: 14%; of women in sororities: 14%. Average proportion of students who stay on campus on weekends: 40%. **Sports program (2005-2006):** Member of NCAA I. *Men's intercollegiate varsity sports:* baseball, basketball, cross-country, football, soccer, track and field (indoor), track and field (outdoor). *Women's intercollegiate varsity sports:* basketball, cross-country, golf, soccer, softball, swimming and diving, tennis, track and field (indoor), track and field (outdoor), volleyball.

SERVICES AND FACILITIES
Basic services: nonremedial tutoring, women's center, placement service, day care, health service, health insurance. **Counseling services:** minority student, career, personal, academic, psychological. **For learning-disabled students:** Services include: remedial math, reading machines, tape recorders, other special classes, videotaped classes, diagnostic testing service, untimed tests, note-taking services, oral tests, learning center, readers, extended time for tests, tutors. **Library:** Number of titles: 1,939,102; number of current serial subscriptions: 53,510. **Information technology resources:** Students are not required to lease or own a computer. School has a wireless network. **Campus safety:** Security services offered: 24-hour foot-and-vehicle patrols, late-night transport/escort service, lighted pathways/sidewalks, student patrols.

TRANSFER AND INTERNATIONAL STUDENTS
Transfer students: May apply for admission for the following academic terms: Fall, Spring, Summer. Applicants need a minimum number of credits to apply. For fall 2005: Transfer applications received: 5,499. Transfer applicants offered admission: 4,233. Transfer applicants enrolled: 2,561. **International students:** Number of foreign undergraduates: 1967 (7% of student body). Minimum TOEFL score required: 500 (paper); 173 (computer).

Florida Memorial College

- **Address:** 15800 N.W. 42nd Avenue, Miami, FL 33054
- **Website:** http://www.fmc.edu/
- **Private; Religious affiliation:** Baptist
- **Enrollment:** N/A

KEY STATS
- ✔ **U.S News College Ranking:** third tier, Comp. Colleges–Bachelor's (South)
- ✔ **SAT or ACT Score (25th/75th percentile):** N/A
- ✔ **Tuition:** N/A

Selectivity: Less selective	**Room/board:** N/A
Acceptance rate: N/A	**Average debt:** N/A
Student/faculty ratio: N/A	**Proportion who borrowed:** N/A

Florida Southern College

- **Address:** 111 Lake Hollingsworth Drive, Lakeland, FL 33801-5698
- **Website:** http://www.flsouthern.edu
- **Private; Religious affiliation:** Methodist
- **Enrollment:** 1,759 full-time; 57 part-time

KEY STATS
✔ **U.S News College Ranking:** 8, Comp. Colleges–Bachelor's (South)
✔ **SAT Score (25th/75th percentile):** 950-1170
✔ **Tuition:** 2006-2007: $20,175

Selectivity: Selective	**Room/board:** $7,140
Acceptance rate: 73%	**Average debt:** $16,072
Student/faculty ratio: 13/1	**Proportion who borrowed:** 67%

UNDERGRADUATE STUDENT BODY STATS
2005-2006 enrollment: 1,759 full-time; 57 part-time. Men: 39%; women: 61%. **Ethnic makeup:** African American: 6%; Asian American: 1%; Hispanic: 6%; White: 83%; International: 4%. **Religious preference:** Roman Catholic: 17%; Protestant: 24%; Jewish: 1%; No preference: 30%; Methodist: 18%; Other: 10%.

ADMISSIONS FACTS AND FIGURES
Phone: (863) 680-4131. **Email:** fscadm@flsouthern.edu. **Website:** http://www.flsouthern.edu. **Application deadlines for fall 2007:** Regular decision: April 1. Early decision: Send application by: December 1; Decision sent by: December 15. Early action: Not offered. Admission can be deferred. **Application fee:** $30. Common application is accepted. **To apply online, go to:** http://www.applyweb.com/aw?fsc. **Admissions requirements/recommendations:** High school units required (recommended): English: 4; Mathematics: 3; Science: 3; Foreign language: (2); Social studies: 3; History: 3; Academic electives: 2; Total units: 18. Tests: The college uses SAT or ACT scores in admissions decisions. Either SAT or ACT required. For admission to the fall 2007 entering class, the school will accept: ACT with writing, ACT without writing. Campus visit: Recommended. Admissions interview: Recommended. Off-campus interview: May be arranged. **Factors that count in admissions decisions:** *Academic:* Secondary school record: Very important. Class rank: Considered. Letters of recommendation: Important. Standardized test scores: Important. Essay: Important. *Nonacademic:* Interview: Considered. Extracurricular activities: Important. Talent/ability: Considered. Character/personal qualities: Important. Alumni/ae relationship: Considered. Geographical residence: Not considered. State residency: Not considered. Religious affiliation/commitment: Not considered. Minority status: Considered. Volunteer work: Considered. Work experience: Considered. **Other schools with the greatest overlap in applicants:** Eckerd College; Florida State University; University of Central Florida; University of Florida; University of Tampa. **Admissions statistics for the fall 2005 entering class:** Total applicants: 1,829. Total accepted: 1,343. Freshmen enrolled: 464; 34% were from out of state. Accepted through early-decision or early-action plans: 9%. Overall acceptance rate: 73%. Early-decision acceptance rate: 98%. Non-early acceptance rate: 73%. **Credentials of fall 2005 freshmen:** 23% ranked in the top 10 percent of their high school class; 47% were in the top 25 percent, and 77% were in the top half. (Proportion submitting class standing: 75%.) **Average high school grade point average:** 3.5. **First-year students who submitted SAT scores:** 69%. Scores (25/75 percentile): Verbal: 470-580; Math: 480-590, Combined: 950-1170. **First-year students submitting ACT scores:** 30%. Scores (25/75 percentile): English: 19-27, Math: 19-26, Composite: 20-26.

ACADEMICS
Year founded: 1885. **Academic calendar:** Semester. **Degrees offered:** bachelor's, master's. **Most popular majors:** 35% business, management, marketing, and related support services, 11% education, 9% communication, journalism, and related programs, 6% biological and biomedical sciences, 6% psychology. **Major fields of study:** agriculture, agriculture operations, and related sciences; biological and biomedical sciences; business, management, marketing, and related support services; communication, journalism, and related programs; computer and information sciences and support services; education; English language and literature/letters; foreign languages, literatures, and linguistics; health professions and related clinical sciences; history; liberal arts and sciences studies, and humanities; mathematics and statistics; parks, recreation, leisure, and fitness studies; philosophy and religious studies; physical sciences; psychology; security and protective services;

social sciences; theology and religious vocations; visual and performing arts. **Areas of required coursework:** arts/fine arts, humanities, computer literacy, mathematics, English (including composition), sciences (biological or physical), history, social science, other. **Pre-professional programs:** pre-law, pre-dentistry, pre-medicine, pre-theology, pre-veterinary science, pre-pharmacy, other. **Special academic programs (% participation):** cross-registration (10%), double major (25%), dual enrollment (1%), exchange student program (domestic) (1%), honors program (10%), independent study (2%), internships (55%), liberal arts/career combination, study abroad (25%), teacher certificate program (11%). **Teacher certification offered in:** early childhood, special education, elementary, middle/junior high, secondary. **Reserve Officers Training Corps (ROTC):** Army ROTC: Offered on campus; Air Force ROTC: Offered at cooperating institution (USF Tampa). **Faculty and instruction (2005-2006):** Total instructional faculty: 107 full-time, 76 part-time (63% men; 37% women; 9% minorities). Full-time faculty with Ph.D. or other terminal degree: 83%. Student/faculty ratio: 13/1. Classes of fewer than 20 students: 64%; of 20 to 49 students: 36%; of 50 or more students: 0%. **Advanced Placement and International Baccalaureate credit:** AP tests may be used for: Credit and/or placement. Scores accepted: 3, 4, 5. International Baccalaureate exams may be used for: Credit and/or placement. **Freshmen returning for sophomore year:** 70%. **Graduation rates:** Four-year: 49%; five-year: 55%; six-year: 57%. **Graduate study:** 20% of students pursue further study immediately upon graduation. Fields in which graduates pursue further study: Master of Business Administration (MBA), 1%; law, 1%; medicine, 3%; arts and sciences, 15%.

COSTS AND FINANCIAL AID
Financial aid office: (863) 680-4140. **Expenses (2006-2007):** Tuition and fees 2006-2007: $20,175; room/board: $7,140. Estimated books and supplies: $1,150; transportation: $535; personal expenses: $500. **Financial aid:** Priority filing date for institution's financial aid form: April 1; deadline: August 1. In 2005-2006, 86% of undergraduates applied for financial aid. Of those, 72% were determined to have financial need; 34% had their need fully met. Average financial aid package (proportion receiving): $16,993 (72%). Average amount of gift aid, such as scholarships or grants (proportion receiving): $13,078 (68%). Average amount of self-help aid, such as work study or loans (proportion receiving): $5,938 (59%). Average need-based loan (excluding PLUS or other private loans): $5,199. Among students who received need-based aid, the average percentage of need met: 64%. Among students who received aid based on merit, the average award (and the proportion receiving): $13,443 (13%). The average athletic scholarship (and the proportion receiving): $6,552 (3%). Average amount of debt of borrowers graduating in 2005: $16,072. Proportion who borrowed: 67%.

CAMPUS LIFE AND EXTRACURRICULAR ACTIVITIES
Campus housing available (% using): women's dorms (41%), men's dorms (24%), sorority housing (21%), fraternity housing (14%), apartments for married students, special housing for disabled students. Students who live in college-owned, operated, or affiliated housing: 66%. **Student employment:** During the 2005-2006 academic year, 34% of undergraduates worked on campus. Average per-year earnings: $1,200. **Clubs and organizations:** Number of student organizations: 87. Activities include: choral groups, concert band, dance, drama/theater, jazz band, literary magazine, music ensembles, musical theater, opera, pep band, student government, student newspaper, symphony orchestra, yearbook. Number of fraternities: 5; sororities: 5. Proportion of men in fraternities: 5%; of women in sororities: 10%. Average proportion of students who stay on campus on weekends: 65%. **Sports program (2005-2006):** Member of NCAA II. *Men's intercollegiate varsity sports:* baseball, basketball, cross-country, golf, soccer, swimming and diving, tennis, track and field (indoor). *Women's intercollegiate varsity sports:* basketball, cross-country, golf, soccer, softball, swimming and diving, tennis, track and field (indoor), track and field (outdoor), volleyball.

SERVICES AND FACILITIES
Basic services: nonremedial tutoring, placement service, health service, health insurance. **Counseling services:** minority student, career, personal, academic, psychological, religious, other. **For learning-disabled students:** School does not offer a structured program with separate admission and additional fees. Total undergraduates in learning-disabled program or receiving services: 45. Services include: extended time for tests, other. **Library:** Number of titles: 180,805; number of current serial subscriptions: 687. **Information technology resources:** Students are not required to lease or own a computer. Number of campus computers available to all students: 350. School has a wireless network. Approximate number of users that can be accommodated: 75. Proportion of college-owned housing units wired for high-speed internet access: 100%. **Campus safety:** Security services offered:

24-hour foot-and-vehicle patrols, late-night transport/escort service, 24-hour emergency telephones, lighted pathways/sidewalks, student patrols, controlled dormitory access (key, security card, etc).

TRANSFER AND INTERNATIONAL STUDENTS

Transfer students: May apply for admission for the following academic terms: Fall, Spring, Summer. Applicants need a minimum number of credits to apply. For fall 2005: Transfer applications received: 262. Transfer applicants offered admission: 178. Transfer applicants enrolled: 111. **International students:** Number of foreign undergraduates: 75 (4% of student body). Number of countries represented: 34. Minimum TOEFL score required: 550 (paper); 213 (computer). Average TOEFL score: 571 (paper).

Florida State University

- **Address:** Tallahassee, FL 32306
- **Website:** http://www.fsu.edu
- **Public**
- **Enrollment:** 27,203 full-time; 3,580 part-time

KEY STATS

✔ **U.S News College Ranking:** 110, National Universities
✔ **SAT Score (25th/75th percentile):** 1070-1250
✔ **Tuition:** 2005-2006: $3,175 in state, $16,306 out of state
  Selectivity: More selective | **Room/board:** $7,774
  Acceptance rate: 62% | **Average debt:** $16,597
  Student/faculty ratio: 22/1 | **Proportion who borrowed:** 52%

UNDERGRADUATE STUDENT BODY STATS

2005-2006 enrollment: 27,203 full-time; 3,580 part-time. Men: 43%; women: 57%. **Ethnic makeup:** African American: 12%; Asian American: 3%; Hispanic: 11%; White: 74%; International: 1%.

ADMISSIONS FACTS AND FIGURES

Phone: (850) 644-6200. **Email:** admissions@admin.fsu.edu. **Website:** http://www.fsu.edu. **Application deadlines for fall 2007:** Regular decision: March 1. Early decision: Not offered. Early action: Not offered. Admission cannot be deferred. **Application fee:** $30. Common application is accepted. **To apply online, go to:** http://admissions.fsu.edu/online/. **Admissions requirements/recommendations:** High school units required (recommended): English: 4 (4); Mathematics: 3 (4); Science: 3 (4); Foreign language: 2 (4); Social studies: 1 (1); History: 2 (2); Academic electives: 3 (3); Total units: 18 (22). Tests: The college uses SAT or ACT scores in admissions decisions. Either SAT or ACT required. For admission to the fall 2007 entering class, the school will accept ACT with writing. Campus visit: Recommended. Admissions interview: Neither required nor recommended. Off-campus interview: Not available. **Factors that count in admissions decisions:** *Academic:* Secondary school record: Very important. Class rank: Important. Letters of recommendation: Considered. Standardized test scores: Important. Essay: Considered. *Nonacademic:* Interview: Not considered. Extracurricular activities: Considered. Talent/ability: Important. Character/personal qualities: Considered. Alumni/ae relationship: Considered. Geographical residence: Considered. State residency: Important. Religious affiliation/commitment: Not considered. Minority status: Not considered. Volunteer work: Considered. Work experience: Considered. **Other schools with the greatest overlap in applicants:** Florida International University; University of Central Florida; University of Florida; University of Miami; University of South Florida. **Admissions statistics for the fall 2005 entering class:** Total applicants: 22,450. Total accepted: 14,016. Freshmen enrolled: 6,067; 13% were from out of state. Overall acceptance rate: 62%. **Size of waiting list:** 300 applicants; enrolled from waiting list: N/A. **Credentials of fall 2005 freshmen:** 26% ranked in the top 10 percent of their high school class; 61% were in the top 25 percent, and 94% were in the top half. (Proportion submitting class standing: 81%.) **Average high school grade point average:** 3.6. **First-year students who submitted SAT scores:** 66%. Scores (25/75 percentile): Verbal: 530-620, Math: 540-630, Combined: 1070-1250. **First-year students submitting ACT scores:** 34%. Scores (25/75 percentile): English: 23-28, Math: 23-27, Composite: 23-27.

ACADEMICS

Year founded: 1851. **Academic calendar:** Semester. **Degrees offered:** certificate, associate, transfer-associate, bachelor's, post-bachelor's certificate,

master's, post-master's certificate, first professional, doctorate. **Most popular majors:** 6% criminal justice/safety studies, 5% English language and literature, 5% communication and media studies, 5% finance, 5% psychology. **Major fields of study:** area, ethnic, cultural, and gender studies; biological and biomedical sciences; business, management, marketing, and related support services; communication, journalism, and related programs; computer and information sciences and support services; education; engineering; English language and literature/letters; family and consumer sciences/human sciences; foreign languages, literatures, and linguistics; health professions and related clinical sciences; history; liberal arts and sciences studies, and humanities; mathematics and statistics; parks, recreation, leisure, and fitness studies; philosophy and religious studies; physical sciences; psychology; public administration and social service professions; security and protective services; social sciences; visual and performing arts. **Areas of required coursework:** arts/fine arts, humanities, computer literacy, mathematics, English (including composition), sciences (biological or physical), history, social science, other. **Pre-professional programs:** pre-law, pre-dentistry, pre-medicine, pre-theology, pre-veterinary science, pre-optometry, pre-pharmacy, other. **Special academic programs:** accelerated program, cooperative (work-study plan) program, cross-registration, distance learning, double major, dual enrollment, English as a Second Language (ESL), honors program, independent study, internships, study abroad, teacher certificate program. **Teacher certification offered in:** early childhood, special education, elementary, middle/junior high, adult education, secondary, bilingual/bicultural. **Cooperative education programs:** business, computer science, education, engineering, natural science, social/behavioral science, other. **Reserve Officers Training Corps (ROTC):** Army ROTC: Offered on campus; Navy ROTC: Offered at cooperating institution (Florida A&M); Air Force ROTC: Offered on campus. **Faculty and instruction (2005-2006):** Total instructional faculty: 1,265 full-time, 327 part-time (61% men; 39% women; 13% minorities). Full-time faculty with Ph.D. or other terminal degree: 92%. Student/faculty ratio: 22/1. Classes of fewer than 20 students: 36%; of 20 to 49 students: 50%; of 50 or more students: 15%. **Advanced Placement and International Baccalaureate credit:** AP tests may be used for: Credit and/or placement. Scores accepted: 3, 4, 5. International Baccalaureate exams may be used for: Credit and/or placement. **Freshmen returning for sophomore year:** 87%. **Graduation rates:** Four-year: 44%; five-year: 63%; six-year: 66%.

COSTS AND FINANCIAL AID

Financial aid office: (850) 644-1993. **Expenses (2005-2006):** Tuition and fees 2005-2006: $3,175 in state, $16,306 out of state; room/board: $7,774. Estimated books and supplies: $856; transportation: $1,070; personal expenses: $1,180. **Financial aid:** Priority filing date for institution's financial aid form: February 15. In 2005-2006, 57% of undergraduates applied for financial aid. Of those, 32% were determined to have financial need; Average financial aid package (proportion receiving): $8,752 (32%). Average amount of gift aid, such as scholarships or grants (proportion receiving): $3,003 (21%). Average amount of self-help aid, such as work study or loans (proportion receiving): $3,042 (24%). Average need-based loan (excluding PLUS or other private loans): $3,122. Among students who received need-based aid, the average percentage of need met: 70%. Among students who received aid based on merit, the average award (and the proportion receiving): $1,797 (4%). The average athletic scholarship (and the proportion receiving): $464 (3%). Average amount of debt of borrowers graduating in 2005: $16,597. Proportion who borrowed: 52%.

CAMPUS LIFE AND EXTRACURRICULAR ACTIVITIES

Campus housing available: coed dorms, women's dorms, sorority housing, fraternity housing, apartments for married students, apartment for single students, special housing for disabled students, other housing options. Students who live in college-owned, operated, or affiliated housing: 14%. **Student employment:** During the 2005-2006 academic year, 9% of undergraduates worked on campus. Average per-year earnings: $4,014. **Clubs and organizations:** Number of student organizations: 417. Activities include: choral groups, concert band, dance, drama/theater, jazz band, literary magazine, marching band, music ensembles, musical theater, opera, pep band, radio station, student government, student newspaper, student film society, symphony orchestra, television station, yearbook. Number of fraternities: 28; sororities: 24. Proportion of men in fraternities: 14%; of women in sororities: 14%. **Sports program (2005-2006):** Member of NCAA I. *Men's intercollegiate varsity sports:* baseball, basketball, cross-country, football, golf, swimming and diving, tennis, track and field (indoor), track and field (outdoor). *Women's intercollegiate varsity sports:* basketball, cross-country, golf, soccer, softball, swimming and diving, tennis, track and field (indoor), track and field (outdoor), volleyball.

SERVICES AND FACILITIES

Basic services: nonremedial tutoring, women's center, placement service, day care, health service, health insurance. **Remedial assistance:** reading, math, writing, study skills. **Counseling services:** minority student, career, military, personal, veteran student, academic, older student, psychological, birth control, religious. **For learning-disabled students:** School does not offer a structured program with separate admission and additional fees. Total undergraduates in learning-disabled program or receiving services: 615. Services include: remedial math, reading machines, remedial reading; tape recorders, diagnostic testing service, note-taking services, oral tests, readers, extended time for tests, priority registration, priority seating, substitution of courses, texts on tape, typist/scribe, exams on tape or computer, other testing accomodations, waiver of foreign language degree requirement, other. **Library:** Number of titles: 2,889,810; number of current serial subscriptions: 42,076. **Information technology resources:** Students are required to lease or own a computer. Number of campus computers available to all students: 2,958. School has a wireless network. Approximate number of users that can be accommodated: 3,000. Proportion of college-owned housing units wired for high-speed internet access: 100%. **Campus safety:** Security services offered: 24-hour foot-and-vehicle patrols, late-night transport/escort service, 24-hour emergency telephones, lighted pathways/sidewalks, controlled dormitory access (key, security card, etc).

TRANSFER AND INTERNATIONAL STUDENTS

Transfer students: May apply for admission for the following academic terms: Fall, Spring, Summer. Applicants need a minimum number of credits to apply. For fall 2005: Transfer applications received: 6,693. Transfer applicants offered admission: 3,375. Transfer applicants enrolled: 2,066. **International students:** Number of foreign undergraduates: 156 (1% of student body). Number of countries represented: 56. Minimum TOEFL score required: 550 (paper); 213 (computer). Average TOEFL score: 595 (paper).

International College

- **Address:** 2655 Northbrooke Drive, Naples, FL 34119
- **Website:** http://www.internationalcollege.edu
- **Private**
- **Enrollment:** 1,054 full-time; 417 part-time

KEY STATS
- ✔ **U.S News College Ranking:** fourth tier, Comp. Coll.–Bachelor's (South)
- ✔ **SAT or ACT Score (25th/75th percentile):** N/A
- ✔ **Tuition:** 2005-2006: $8,830

Selectivity: Less selective	**Room/board:** $0
Acceptance rate: 88%	**Average debt:** N/A
Student/faculty ratio: 19/1	**Proportion who borrowed:** N/A

UNDERGRADUATE STUDENT BODY STATS

2005-2006 enrollment: 1,054 full-time; 417 part-time. Men: 31%; women: 69%. **Ethnic makeup:** African American: 18%; American-Indian: 1%; Asian American: 1%; Hispanic: 18%; White: 62%.

ADMISSIONS FACTS AND FIGURES

Phone: (239) 513-1122. **Email:** admit@internationalcollege.edu. **Website:** http://www.internationalcollege.edu. **Application deadlines for fall 2007:** Regular decision: Rolling. Early decision: Not offered. Early action: Not offered. Admission cannot be deferred. **Application fee:** $20. Common application is accepted. **Admissions requirements/recommendations:** Tests: The college uses SAT or ACT scores in admissions decisions. Neither SAT nor ACT required. Campus visit: Recommended. Admissions interview: Recommended. Off-campus interview: Not available. **Factors that count in admissions decisions:** *Academic:* Secondary school record: Not considered. Class rank: Not considered. Letters of recommendation: Important. Standardized test scores: Important. Essay: Important. *Nonacademic:* Interview: Important. Extracurricular activities: Not considered. Talent/ability: Not considered. Character/personal qualities: Not considered. Alumni/ae relationship: Not considered. Geographical residence: Not considered. State residency: Not considered. Religious affiliation/commitment: Not considered. Minority status: Not considered. Volunteer work: Not considered. Work experience: Not considered. **Admissions statistics for the fall 2005 entering class:** Total applicants: 680. Total accepted: 595. Freshmen enrolled: 55; Overall acceptance rate: 88%.

ACADEMICS

Year founded: 1990. **Academic calendar:** Trimester. **Degrees offered:** certificate, associate, bachelor's, master's. **Most popular majors:** 58% business administration, management, and operations, 12% multi/interdisciplinary studies, 9% criminal justice/safety studies, 6% information technology, 5% business administration and management. **Major fields of study:** business, management, marketing, and related support services; computer and information sciences and support services; health professions and related clinical sciences; legal professions and studies; multi/interdisciplinary studies; psychology; security and protective services. **Areas of required coursework:** humanities, computer literacy, mathematics, English (including composition), social science. **Special academic programs (% participation):** accelerated program (20%), distance learning (30%). **Faculty and instruction (2005-2006):** Total instructional faculty: 53 full-time, 54 part-time (62% men; 38% women; 18% minorities). Full-time faculty with Ph.D. or other terminal degree: 62%. Student/faculty ratio: 19/1. Classes of fewer than 20 students: 84%; of 20 to 49 students: 16%. **Advanced Placement and International Baccalaureate credit:** AP tests may be used for: Credit and/or placement. Scores accepted: 3, 4, 5. International Baccalaureate exams may be used for: Credit and/or placement. **Freshmen returning for sophomore year:** 37%. **Graduation rates:** Four-year: 13%; five-year: 13%; six-year: 31%.

COSTS AND FINANCIAL AID

Financial aid office: (239) 513-1122. **Expenses (2005-2006):** Tuition and fees 2005-2006: $8,830; room/board: $0. Estimated books and supplies: $1,000; transportation: $1,984; personal expenses: $1,320. **Financial aid:** Priority filing date for institution's financial aid form: September 1.

CAMPUS LIFE AND EXTRACURRICULAR ACTIVITIES

Activities include: literary magazine. Number of fraternities: 0; sororities: 0.

SERVICES AND FACILITIES

Remedial assistance: math, writing. **Counseling services:** career, academic. **For learning-disabled students:** School does not offer a structured program with separate admission and additional fees. **Information technology resources:** Students are not required to lease or own a computer. Number of campus computers available to all students: 400. School has a wireless network. Proportion of college-owned housing units wired for high-speed internet access: 100%.

TRANSFER AND INTERNATIONAL STUDENTS

Transfer students: May apply for admission for the following academic terms: Fall, Winter, Summer. Applicants do not need a minimum number of credits to apply. For fall 2005: Transfer applicants enrolled: 414. **International students:** Number of foreign undergraduates: 0. Minimum TOEFL score required: 500 (paper); 273 (computer).

Jacksonville University

- **Address:** 2800 University Boulevard N, Jacksonville, FL 32211
- **Website:** http://www.jacksonville.edu
- **Private**
- **Enrollment:** 1,912 full-time; 698 part-time

KEY STATS
- ✔ **U.S News College Ranking:** 59, Universities–Master's (South)
- ✔ **SAT Score (25th/75th percentile):** 900-1120
- ✔ **Tuition:** 2006-2007: $21,200

Selectivity: Selective	**Room/board:** $6,780
Acceptance rate: 67%	**Average debt:** $21,483
Student/faculty ratio: 14/1	**Proportion who borrowed:** 53%

UNDERGRADUATE STUDENT BODY STATS

2005-2006 enrollment: 1,912 full-time; 698 part-time. Men: 42%; women: 58%. **Ethnic makeup:** African American: 16%; American-Indian: 1%; Asian American: 2%; Hispanic: 5%; White: 73%; International: 3%. **Religious preference:** Roman Catholic: 16%; Protestant: 18%; Jewish: 1%; No preference: 35%; Unknown: 19%; Other: 11%.

ADMISSIONS FACTS AND FIGURES

Phone: (800) 225-2027. **Email:** admissions@ju.edu. **Website:** http://www.jacksonville.edu. **Application deadlines for fall 2007:** Regular decision: Rolling. Early decision: Not offered. Early action: Not offered. Admission can be deferred. **Application fee:** $30. Common application is accepted. **To apply online, go to:** http://www.jacksonville.edu/admissions/index.asp. **Admissions requirements/recommendations:** High school units required (recommended): English: 4 (4); Mathematics: 3 (3); Science: 3 (3); Foreign language: 0 (2); Social studies: 3 (3); Total units: 13 (15). Tests: The college uses SAT or ACT scores in admissions decisions. Either SAT or ACT required. For admission to the fall 2007 entering class, the school will accept: ACT with writing, ACT without writing. Campus visit: Recommended. Admissions interview: Recommended. Off-campus interview: May be arranged. **Factors that count in admissions decisions:** *Academic:* Secondary school record: Important. Class rank: Not considered. Letters of recommendation: Considered. Standardized test scores: Very important. Essay: Considered. *Nonacademic:* Interview: Considered. Extracurricular activities: Considered. Talent/ability: Important. Character/personal qualities: Considered. Alumni/ae relationship: Not considered. Geographical residence: Not considered. State residency: Not considered. Religious affiliation/commitment: Not considered. Minority status: Not considered. Volunteer work: Considered. Work experience: Considered. **Other schools with the greatest overlap in applicants:** Florida State University; University of Central Florida; University of Florida; University of North Florida; University of South Florida. **Admissions statistics for the fall 2005 entering class:** Total applicants: 2,621. Total accepted: 1,753. Freshmen enrolled: 536; 44% were from out of state. Overall acceptance rate: 67%. **Credentials of fall 2005 freshmen:** 21% ranked in the top 10 percent of their high school class; 47% were in the top 25 percent, and 79% were in the top half. (Proportion submitting class standing: 78%.) **Average high school grade point average:** 3.2. **First-year students who submitted SAT scores:** 89%. Scores (25/75 percentile): Verbal: 450-560, Math: 450-560, Combined: 900-1120. **First-year students submitting ACT scores:** 42%. Scores (25/75 percentile): English: N/A, Math: N/A, Composite: 18-24.

ACADEMICS

Year founded: 1934. **Academic calendar:** Semester. **Degrees offered:** bachelor's, master's, first professional certificate. **Most popular majors:** 28% health professions and related clinical sciences, 26% business, management, marketing, and related support services, 7% visual and performing arts, 6% social sciences, 6% transportation and materials moving. **Major fields of study:** biological and biomedical sciences; business, management, marketing, and related support services; communication, journalism, and related programs; computer and information sciences and support services; education; English language and literature/letters; foreign languages, literatures, and linguistics; health professions and related clinical sciences; history; liberal arts and sciences studies, and humanities; mathematics and statistics; parks, recreation, leisure, and fitness studies; philosophy and religious studies; physical sciences; psychology; social sciences; theology and religious vocations; transportation and materials moving; visual and performing arts. **Areas of required coursework:** arts/fine arts, humanities, computer literacy, mathematics, English (including composition), philosophy, sciences (biological or physical), history, social science, other. **Pre-professional programs:** pre-law, pre-dentistry, pre-medicine, pre-veterinary science, pre-pharmacy. **Special academic programs (% participation):** accelerated program (20%), cooperative (work-study plan) program, distance learning (20%), double major (7%), dual enrollment, honors program, independent study, internships, liberal arts/career combination, student-designed major (0%), study abroad, teacher certificate program (3%). **Teacher certification offered in:** early childhood, elementary, secondary. **Reserve Officers Training Corps (ROTC):** Navy ROTC: Offered on campus. **Faculty and instruction (2005-2006):** Total instructional faculty: 135 full-time, 89 part-time (56% men; 44% women; 6% minorities). Full-time faculty with Ph.D. or other terminal degree: 81%. Student/faculty ratio: 14/1. Classes of fewer than 20 students: 61%; of 20 to 49 students: 38%; of 50 or more students: 1%. **Advanced Placement and International Baccalaureate credit:** AP tests may be used for: Credit only. Scores accepted: 3, 4. International Baccalaureate exams may be used for: Credit only. **Freshmen returning for sophomore year:** 68%. **Graduation rates:** Four-year: 29%; five-year: 41%; six-year: 42%. **Graduate study:** 17% of students pursue further study immediately upon graduation.

COSTS AND FINANCIAL AID

Financial aid office: (904) 256-7060. **Expenses (2006-2007):** Tuition and fees 2006-2007: $21,200; room/board: $6,780. Estimated books and supplies: $600; transportation: $800; personal expenses: $600. **Financial aid:** Priority filing date for institution's financial aid form: February 1; deadline: March 15. In 2005-2006, 86% of undergraduates applied for financial aid. Of those, 71% were determined to have financial need; 27% had their need

fully met. Average financial aid package (proportion receiving): $16,571 (71%). Average amount of gift aid, such as scholarships or grants (proportion receiving): $5,331 (48%). Average amount of self-help aid, such as work study or loans (proportion receiving): $4,511 (56%). Average need-based loan (excluding PLUS or other private loans): $3,963. Among students who received need-based aid, the average percentage of need met: 82%. Among students who received aid based on merit, the average award (and the proportion receiving): $5,066 (16%). The average athletic scholarship (and the proportion receiving): $7,672 (2%). Average amount of debt of borrowers graduating in 2005: $21,483. Proportion who borrowed: 53%.

CAMPUS LIFE AND EXTRACURRICULAR ACTIVITIES

Campus housing available (% using): coed dorms (10%), women's dorms (12%), men's dorms (28%), sorority housing (9%), fraternity housing (11%), apartment for single students (30%). Students who live in college-owned, operated, or affiliated housing: 59%. **Clubs and organizations:** Number of student organizations: 67. Activities include: choral groups, concert band, dance, drama/theater, jazz band, literary magazine, music ensembles, musical theater, pep band, radio station, student government, student newspaper, symphony orchestra, television station, yearbook. Number of fraternities: 7; sororities: 6. Proportion of men in fraternities: 18%; of women in sororities: 15%. Average proportion of students who stay on campus on weekends: 60%. **Sports program (2005-2006):** Member of NCAA I. *Men's intercollegiate varsity sports:* baseball, basketball, crew, cross-country, football, golf, soccer, tennis. *Women's intercollegiate varsity sports:* basketball, crew, cross-country, golf, rowing, soccer, softball, tennis, track and field (indoor), track and field (outdoor), volleyball.

SERVICES AND FACILITIES

Basic services: nonremedial tutoring, placement service, health service, health insurance. **Remedial assistance:** reading, math, writing, study skills. **Counseling services:** career, personal, academic, psychological. **For learning-disabled students:** School does not offer a structured program with separate admission and additional fees. Services include: remedial math, remedial English, reading machines, remedial reading, tape recorders, other special classes, videotaped classes, untimed tests, note-taking services, special bookstore section, oral tests, learning center, readers, extended time for tests, tutors, priority seating, texts on tape, other testing accomodations. **Library:** Number of titles: 325,781; number of current serial subscriptions: 324. **Information technology resources:** Students are not required to lease or own a computer. Number of campus computers available to all students: 150. School has a wireless network. Proportion of college-owned housing units wired for high-speed internet access: 100%. **Campus safety:** Security services offered: 24-hour foot-and-vehicle patrols, late-night transport/escort service, 24-hour emergency telephones, lighted pathways/sidewalks, controlled dormitory access (key, security card, etc).

TRANSFER AND INTERNATIONAL STUDENTS

Transfer students: May apply for admission for the following academic terms: Fall, Spring, Summer. Applicants need a minimum number of credits to apply. For fall 2005: Transfer applications received: 901. Transfer applicants offered admission: 572. Transfer applicants enrolled: 241. **International students:** Number of foreign undergraduates: 78 (3% of student body). Number of countries represented: 45. Minimum TOEFL score required: 540 (paper); 207 (computer). Average TOEFL score: 542 (paper).

Lynn University

- **Address:** 3601 N. Military Trail, Boca Raton, FL 33431
- **Website:** http://www.lynn.edu
- **Private**
- **Enrollment:** 1,951 full-time; 332 part-time

KEY STATS

✔ **U.S News College Ranking:** fourth tier, Universities–Master's (South)
✔ **SAT Score (25th/75th percentile):** 810-1030
✔ **Tuition:** 2006-2007: $27,700

Selectivity: Less selective	**Room/board:** $9,650
Acceptance rate: 80%	**Average debt:** $15,154
Student/faculty ratio: 17/1	**Proportion who borrowed:** 68%

UNDERGRADUATE STUDENT BODY STATS

2005-2006 enrollment: 1,951 full-time; 332 part-time. Men: 50%; women: 50%. **Ethnic makeup:** African American: 5%; Asian American: 1%; Hispanic: 7%; White: 74%; International: 13%.

ADMISSIONS FACTS AND FIGURES

Phone: (800) 888-5966. **Email:** admission@lynn.edu. **Website:** http://www.lynn.edu. **Application deadlines for fall 2007:** Regular decision: Rolling. Early decision: Not offered. Early action: Not offered. Admission can be deferred. **Application fee:** $35. Common application is accepted. **To apply online, go to:** http://www.lynn.edu/onlineapps. **Admissions requirements/recommendations:** High school units required (recommended): English: 4 (4); Mathematics: 4 (2); Science: 4 (2); Foreign language: 0; Social studies: 2 (2); History: 2; Academic electives: (4); Total units: 16. Tests: The college uses SAT or ACT scores in admissions decisions. Either SAT or ACT required. For admission to the fall 2007 entering class, the school will accept: ACT with writing, ACT without writing. Campus visit: Recommended. Admissions interview: Recommended. **Factors that count in admissions decisions: Academic:** Secondary school record: Very important. Class rank: Important. Letters of recommendation: Important. Standardized test scores: Very important. Essay: Important. **Nonacademic:** Interview: Considered. Extracurricular activities: Considered. Talent/ability: Considered. Character/personal qualities: Important. Alumni/ae relationship: Considered. Geographical residence: Not considered. State residency: Considered. Religious affiliation/commitment: Not considered. Minority status: Not considered. Volunteer work: Considered. Work experience: Considered. **Other schools with the greatest overlap in applicants:** Barry University; Florida Southern College; Rollins College; University of Tampa. **Admissions statistics for the fall 2005 entering class:** Total applicants: 2,939. Total accepted: 2,339. Freshmen enrolled: 655; 72% were from out of state. Overall acceptance rate: 80%. **Size of waiting list:** 0 applicants; enrolled from waiting list: 0. **Credentials of fall 2005 freshmen:** 8% ranked in the top 10 percent of their high school class; 33% were in the top 25 percent, and 65% were in the top half. (Proportion submitting class standing: 28%.) **First-year students who submitted SAT scores:** 81%. Scores (25/75 percentile): Verbal: 410-510, Math: 400-520, Combined: 810-1030. **First-year students submitting ACT scores:** 24%. Scores (25/75 percentile): English: N/A, Math: N/A, Composite: 16-21.

ACADEMICS

Year founded: 1962. **Academic calendar:** Semester. **Degrees offered:** certificate, bachelor's, post-bachelor's certificate, master's, post-master's certificate, doctorate. **Most popular majors:** 45% business, management, marketing, and related support services, 17% public administration and social service professions, 12% communication, journalism, and related programs, 7% psychology, 6% visual and performing arts. **Major fields of study:** biological and biomedical sciences; business, management, marketing, and related support services; communication, journalism, and related programs; education; health professions and related clinical sciences; liberal arts and sciences studies, and humanities; parks, recreation, leisure, and fitness studies; psychology; public administration and social service professions; security and protective services; social sciences; visual and performing arts. **Areas of required coursework:** arts/fine arts, humanities, computer literacy, mathematics, English (including composition), sciences (biological or physical), history, social science, other. **Special academic programs (% participation):** accelerated program, cooperative (work-study plan) program, distance learning (49%), double major (0%), dual enrollment, English as a Second Language (ESL) (8%), honors program (2%), independent study (15%), internships (30%), liberal arts/career combination, study abroad (18%), teacher certificate program. **Teacher certification offered in:** elementary, secondary. **Reserve Officers Training Corps (ROTC):** Air Force ROTC: Offered at cooperating institution (University of Miami). **Faculty and instruction (2005-2006):** Total instructional faculty: 74 full-time, 178 part-time (49% men; 51% women; 67% minorities). Full-time faculty with Ph.D. or other terminal degree: 78%. Student/faculty ratio: 17/1. Classes of fewer than 20 students: 53%; of 20 to 49 students: 47%; of 50 or more students: 0%. **Advanced Placement and International Baccalaureate credit:** AP tests may be used for: Placement only. International Baccalaureate exams may be used for: Credit and/or placement. **Freshmen returning for sophomore year:** 60%. **Graduation rates:** Four-year: 31%; five-year: 40%; six-year: 37%.

COSTS AND FINANCIAL AID

Financial aid office: (800) 544-8035. **Expenses (2006-2007):** Tuition and fees 2006-2007: $27,700; room/board: $9,650. **Financial aid:** Priority filing date for institution's financial aid form: March 1. In 2005-2006, 44% of undergraduates applied for financial aid. Of those, 37% were determined to have

financial need; 12% had their need fully met. Average financial aid package (proportion receiving): $16,051 (36%). Average amount of gift aid, such as scholarships or grants (proportion receiving): $12,320 (36%). Average amount of self-help aid, such as work study or loans (proportion receiving): $4,736 (31%). Average need-based loan (excluding PLUS or other private loans): $4,304. Among students who received need-based aid, the average percentage of need met: 55%. Among students who received aid based on merit, the average award (and the proportion receiving): $12,527 (29%). The average athletic scholarship (and the proportion receiving): $20,318 (4%). Average amount of debt of borrowers graduating in 2005: $15,154. Proportion who borrowed: 68%.

CAMPUS LIFE AND EXTRACURRICULAR ACTIVITIES

Campus housing available (% using): coed dorms (99%), women's dorms, special housing for disabled students (1%), special housing for international students. Students who live in college-owned, operated, or affiliated housing: 55%. **Student employment:** During the 2005-2006 academic year, 2% of undergraduates worked on campus. Average per-year earnings: $3,400. **Clubs and organizations:** Number of student organizations: 31. Activities include: choral groups, dance, drama/theater, literary magazine, music ensembles, radio station, student government, student newspaper, student film society, symphony orchestra, television station, yearbook. Number of fraternities: 1; sororities: 1. Average proportion of students who stay on campus on weekends: 95%. **Sports program (2005-2006):** Member of NCAA II. **Men's intercollegiate varsity sports:** baseball, basketball, golf, soccer, tennis. **Women's intercollegiate varsity sports:** basketball, golf, soccer, softball, tennis, volleyball, rowing.

SERVICES AND FACILITIES

Basic services: nonremedial tutoring, health service, health insurance. **Remedial assistance:** math, writing, study skills. **Counseling services:** career, personal, academic. **For learning-disabled students:** School does not offer a structured program with separate admission and additional fees. Services include: remedial math, remedial English, reading machines, tape recorders, other special classes, untimed tests, oral tests, learning center, readers, extended time for tests, tutors. **Library:** Number of titles: 110,000; number of current serial subscriptions: 400. **Information technology resources:** Students are not required to lease or own a computer. Number of campus computers available to all students: 235. School has a wireless network. Approximate number of users that can be accommodated: 50. Proportion of college-owned housing units wired for high-speed internet access: 100%. **Campus safety:** Security services offered: late-night transport/escort service, lighted pathways/sidewalks.

TRANSFER AND INTERNATIONAL STUDENTS

Transfer students: May apply for admission for the following academic terms: Fall, Spring. Applicants need a minimum number of credits to apply. For fall 2005: Transfer applications received: 405. Transfer applicants offered admission: 214. Transfer applicants enrolled: 129. **International students:** Number of foreign undergraduates: 301 (13% of student body). Minimum TOEFL score required: 500 (paper); 173 (computer). Average TOEFL score: 580 (paper).

New College of Florida

- **Address:** 5700 North Tamiami Trail, Sarasota, FL 34243-2197
- **Website:** http://www.ncf.edu
- **Public**
- **Enrollment:** 761 full-time

KEY STATS

✔ **U.S News College Ranking:** 86, Liberal Arts Colleges
✔ **SAT Score (25th/75th percentile):** 1210-1390
✔ **Tuition:** 2006-2007: $3,800 in state, $20,500 out of state

Selectivity: More selective	**Room/board:** $6,750
Acceptance rate: 60%	**Average debt:** $12,252
Student/faculty ratio: 11/1	**Proportion who borrowed:** 38%

UNDERGRADUATE STUDENT BODY STATS

2005-2006 enrollment: 761 full-time. Men: 39%; women: 61%. **Ethnic makeup:** African American: 2%; Asian American: 3%; Hispanic: 9%; White:

84%; International: 2%. **Religious preference:** Roman Catholic: 13%; Protestant: 25%; Jewish: 6%; Buddhist: 3%; No preference: 46%.

ADMISSIONS FACTS AND FIGURES

Phone: (941) 359-4269. **Email:** admissions@ncf.edu. **Website:** http://www.ncf.edu. **Application deadlines for fall 2007:** Regular decision: May 1. Early decision: Not offered. Early action: Not offered. Admission can be deferred. **Application fee:** $30. Common application is accepted. **Admissions requirements/recommendations:** High school units required (recommended): English: 4 (4); Mathematics: 3 (3); Science: 3 (3); Foreign language: 2 (2); Social studies: 3 (3); Academic electives: 3 (5); Total units: 18 (20). Tests: The college uses SAT or ACT scores in admissions decisions. Either SAT or ACT required. For admission to the fall 2007 entering class, the school will accept: ACT with writing, ACT without writing. Campus visit: Recommended. Admissions interview: Recommended. Off-campus interview: May be arranged. **Factors that count in admissions decisions:** *Academic:* Secondary school record: Very important. Class rank: Considered. Letters of recommendation: Important. Standardized test scores: Very important. Essay: Very important. *Nonacademic:* Interview: Considered. Extracurricular activities: Considered. Talent/ability: Considered. Character/personal qualities: Important. Alumni/ae relationship: Considered. Geographical residence: Considered. State residency: Considered. Religious affiliation/commitment: Not considered. Minority status: Not considered. Volunteer work: Considered. Work experience: Considered. **Other schools with the greatest overlap in applicants:** Florida State University; Hampshire College; University of Central Florida; University of Florida; University of Miami. **Admissions statistics for the fall 2005 entering class:** Total applicants: 684. Total accepted: 408. Freshmen enrolled: 218; 25% were from out of state. Overall acceptance rate: 60%. **Size of waiting list:** 19 applicants; enrolled from waiting list: 0. **Credentials of fall 2005 freshmen:** 44% ranked in the top 10 percent of their high school class; 80% were in the top 25 percent, and 97% were in the top half. (Proportion submitting class standing: 84%.) **Average high school grade point average:** 4.0. **First-year students who submitted SAT scores:** 95%. Scores (25/75 percentile): Verbal: 630-720, Math: 580-670, Combined: 1210-1390. **First-year students submitting ACT scores:** 44%. Scores (25/75 percentile): English: 26-31, Math: 24-27, Composite: 25-29.

ACADEMICS

Year founded: 2001. **Academic calendar:** 4-1-4. **Degrees offered:** bachelor's. **Most popular majors:** 100% liberal arts and sciences, general studies, and humanities. **Major fields of study:** liberal arts and sciences studies, and humanities. **Areas of required coursework:** humanities, sciences (biological or physical), social science. **Special academic programs (% participation):** cross-registration (20%), double major (4%), exchange student program (domestic) (21%), honors program (100%), independent study (100%), internships (49%), student-designed major (100%), study abroad (28%). **Faculty and instruction (2005-2006):** Total instructional faculty: 65 full-time, 10 part-time (51% men; 49% women; 13% minorities). Full-time faculty with Ph.D. or other terminal degree: 97%. Student/faculty ratio: 11/1. Classes of fewer than 20 students: 64%; of 20 to 49 students: 35%; of 50 or more students: 1%. **Freshmen returning for sophomore year:** 81%. **Graduation rates:** Four-year: 57%; five-year: 67%; six-year: 69%. **Graduate study:** 18% of students pursue further study immediately upon graduation; 19% within one year; 46% within five years. Fields in which graduates pursue further study: Master of Business Administration (MBA), 5%; law, 13%; medicine, 9%; engineering, 2%; theology (or the seminary), 2%; education, 6%; arts and sciences, 60%.

COSTS AND FINANCIAL AID

Financial aid office: (941) 359-4255. **Expenses (2006-2007):** Tuition and fees 2006-2007: $3,800 in state, $20,500 out of state; room/board: $6,750. Estimated books and supplies: $800; transportation: $1,100; personal expenses: $2,600. **Financial aid:** Priority filing date for institution's financial aid form: March 1. In 2005-2006, 55% of undergraduates applied for financial aid. Of those, 36% were determined to have financial need; 69% had their need fully met. Average financial aid package (proportion receiving): $11,792 (36%). Average amount of gift aid, such as scholarships or grants (proportion receiving): $7,549 (35%). Average amount of self-help aid, such as work study or loans (proportion receiving): $4,405 (28%). Average need-based loan (excluding PLUS or other private loans): $3,764. Among students who received need-based aid, the average percentage of need met: 94%. Among students who received aid based on merit, the average award (and the proportion receiving): $3,580 (49%). The average athletic scholarship (and the proportion receiving): $0 (0%). Average amount of debt of borrowers graduating in 2005: $12,252. Proportion who borrowed: 38%.

CAMPUS LIFE AND EXTRACURRICULAR ACTIVITIES

Campus housing available (% using): coed dorms (69%), apartment for single students (30%), special housing for disabled students (1%). Students who live in college-owned, operated, or affiliated housing: 68%. **Student employment:** During the 2005-2006 academic year, 20% of undergraduates worked on campus. Average per-year earnings: $2,240. **Clubs and organizations:** Number of student organizations: 45. Activities include: choral groups, dance, drama/theater, literary magazine, music ensembles, musical theater, radio station, student government, student newspaper, student film society. Number of fraternities: 0; sororities: 0. Average proportion of students who stay on campus on weekends: 90%.

SERVICES AND FACILITIES

Counseling services: minority student, career, military, personal, veteran student, academic, older student, psychological, birth control, religious. **For learning-disabled students:** School does not offer a structured program with separate admission and additional fees. Total undergraduates in learning-disabled program or receiving services: 15. Services include: tape recorders, note-taking services, oral tests, readers, extended time for tests, tutors, priority seating. **Library:** Number of titles: 259,886; number of current serial subscriptions: 1,012. **Information technology resources:** Students are not required to lease or own a computer. Number of campus computers available to all students: 50. School has a wireless network. Approximate number of users that can be accommodated: 1,000. Proportion of college-owned housing units wired for high-speed internet access: 100%. **Campus safety:** Security services offered: 24-hour foot-and-vehicle patrols, late-night transport/escort service, 24-hour emergency telephones, lighted pathways/sidewalks, controlled dormitory access (key, security card, etc).

TRANSFER AND INTERNATIONAL STUDENTS

Transfer students: May apply for admission for the following academic terms: Fall, Spring. Applicants do not need a minimum number of credits to apply. For fall 2005: Transfer applications received: 153. Transfer applicants offered admission: 46. Transfer applicants enrolled: 28. **International students:** Number of foreign undergraduates: 15 (2% of student body). Number of countries represented: 15. Minimum TOEFL score required: 560 (paper); 220 (computer).

Nova Southeastern University

- **Address:** 3301 College Avenue, Ft. Lauderdale, FL 33314
- **Website:** http://www.nova.edu
- **Private**
- **Enrollment:** 3,379 full-time; 2,074 part-time

KEY STATS

✔ **U.S News College Ranking:** fourth tier, National Universities
✔ **SAT Score (25th/75th percentile):** 940-1140
✔ **Tuition:** 2006-2007: $17,800

Selectivity: Selective	**Room/board:** $6,520
Acceptance rate: 54%	**Average debt:** $26,658
Student/faculty ratio: 18/1	**Proportion who borrowed:** 62%

UNDERGRADUATE STUDENT BODY STATS

2005-2006 enrollment: 3,379 full-time; 2,074 part-time. Men: 27%; women: 73%. **Ethnic makeup:** African American: 27%; Asian American: 5%; Hispanic: 25%; White: 37%; International: 6%.

ADMISSIONS FACTS AND FIGURES

Phone: (954) 262-8000. **Email:** ncsinfo@nova.edu. **Website:** http://www.nova.edu. **Application deadlines for fall 2007:** Regular decision: Rolling. Early decision: Not offered. Early action: Not offered. Admission can be deferred. **Application fee:** $50. Common application is not accepted. **To apply online, go to:** http://www.undergrad.nova.edu/admissions/. **Admissions requirements/recommendations:** High school units required (recommended): English: 4; Mathematics: 3; Science: 3; Foreign language: (2); Social studies: 1; History: 2; Academic electives: (1). Tests: The college uses SAT or ACT scores in admissions decisions. Either SAT or ACT required. Campus visit: Recommended. Admissions interview: Recommended. Off-campus interview: Not available. **Factors that count in admissions decisions:** *Academic:* Secondary school record: Very important. Class rank: Not considered. Letters of recommendation: Considered.

Standardized test scores: Very important. Essay: Considered. **Nonacademic:** Interview: Considered. Extracurricular activities: Considered. Talent/ability: Considered. Character/personal qualities: Considered. Alumni/ae relationship: Not considered. Geographical residence: Not considered. State residency: Not considered. Religious affiliation/commitment: Not considered. Minority status: Not considered. Volunteer work: Considered. Work experience: Considered. **Admissions statistics for the fall 2005 entering class:** Total applicants: 2,429. Total accepted: 1,315. Freshmen enrolled: 457; 18% were from out of state. Overall acceptance rate: 54%. **Credentials of fall 2005 freshmen:** 17% ranked in the top 10 percent of their high school class; 43% were in the top 25 percent, and 82% were in the top half. (Proportion submitting class standing: 69%.) **First-year students who submitted SAT scores:** 93%. Scores (25/75 percentile): Verbal: 470-560, Math: 470-580, Combined: 940-1140. **First-year students submitting ACT scores:** 43%. Scores (25/75 percentile): English: N/A, Math: N/A, Composite: 18-23.

ACADEMICS

Year founded: 1964. **Academic calendar:** Trimester. **Degrees offered:** certificate, associate, bachelor's, post-bachelor's certificate, master's, post-master's certificate, first professional, first professional certificate, doctorate. **Most popular majors:** 41% business, management, marketing, and related support services, 13% health professions and related clinical sciences, 12% education, 12% psychology, 8% liberal arts and sciences studies, and humanities. **Major fields of study:** biological and biomedical sciences; business, management, marketing, and related support services; communication, journalism, and related programs; computer and information sciences and support services; education; English language and literature/letters; health professions and related clinical sciences; history; legal professions and studies; liberal arts and sciences studies, and humanities; natural resources and conservation; parks, recreation, leisure, and fitness studies; psychology; security and protective services; social sciences. **Areas of required coursework:** mathematics, English (including composition), sciences (biological or physical), social science, other. **Pre-professional programs:** pre-law, pre-dentistry, pre-medicine, pre-optometry, pre-pharmacy. **Special academic programs:** accelerated program, cooperative (work-study plan) program, distance learning, double major, dual enrollment, honors program, internships, study abroad, teacher certificate program, other. **Teacher certification offered in:** early childhood, special education, elementary. **Cooperative education programs:** business, computer science, education, health professions, humanities, natural science, social/behavioral science, other. **Faculty and instruction (2005-2006):** Total instructional faculty: 582 full-time, 1,033 part-time. Full-time faculty with Ph.D. or other terminal degree: 89%. Student/faculty ratio: 18/1. Classes of fewer than 20 students: 69%; of 20 to 49 students: 30%; of 50 or more students: 0%. **Advanced Placement and International Baccalaureate credit:** AP tests may be used for: Credit and/or placement. Scores accepted: 3, 4, 5. International Baccalaureate exams may be used for: Credit only. **Freshmen returning for sophomore year:** 67%. **Graduation rates:** Six-year: 41%.

COSTS AND FINANCIAL AID

Financial aid office: (954) 262-3380. **Expenses (2006-2007):** Tuition and fees 2006-2007: $17,800; room/board: $6,520. Estimated books and supplies: $1,200; transportation: $2,540; personal expenses: $4,340. **Financial aid:** Priority filing date for institution's financial aid form: April 15. In 2005-2006, 100% of undergraduates applied for financial aid. Of those, 94% were determined to have financial need; 8% had their need fully met. Average financial aid package (proportion receiving): $13,662 (94%). Average amount of gift aid, such as scholarships or grants (proportion receiving): $7,125 (92%). Average amount of self-help aid, such as work study or loans (proportion receiving): $6,172 (85%). Average need-based loan (excluding PLUS or other private loans): $4,717. Among students who received need-based aid, the average percentage of need met: 64%. Among students who received aid based on merit, the average award (and the proportion receiving): $11,534 (6%). The average athletic scholarship (and the proportion receiving): $6,894 (1%). Average amount of debt of borrowers graduating in 2005: $26,658. Proportion who borrowed: 62%.

CAMPUS LIFE AND EXTRACURRICULAR ACTIVITIES

Campus housing available (% using): coed dorms (100%), apartments for married students, apartment for single students, special housing for disabled students, special housing for international students. Students who live in college-owned, operated, or affiliated housing: 9%. **Clubs and organizations:** Number of student organizations: 8. Activities include: choral groups, drama/theater, literary magazine, radio station, student government, student newspaper. Number of fraternities: 3; sororities: 2. Average proportion of students who stay on campus on weekends: 65%. **Sports pro-**

gram (2005-2006): Member of NCAA II. **Men's intercollegiate varsity sports:** baseball, basketball, cross-country, golf, soccer. **Women's intercollegiate varsity sports:** basketball, cross-country, golf, rowing, soccer, softball, tennis, volleyball.

SERVICES AND FACILITIES

Basic services: nonremedial tutoring, women's center, health service, health insurance. **Remedial assistance:** reading, math, writing, study skills. **Counseling services:** career, veteran student, academic, older student, psychological. **For learning-disabled students:** School does not offer a structured program with separate admission and additional fees. Total undergraduates in learning-disabled program or receiving services: 21. Services include: reading machines, tape recorders, note-taking services, oral tests, learning center, readers, extended time for tests, tutors, priority seating, texts on tape, other. **Library:** Number of titles: 668,738; number of current serial subscriptions: 22,837. **Information technology resources:** Students are not required to lease or own a computer. Number of campus computers available to all students: 1,713. School has a wireless network. Approximate number of users that can be accommodated: 2,000. Proportion of college-owned housing units wired for high-speed internet access: 20%. **Campus safety:** Security services offered: 24-hour foot-and-vehicle patrols, late-night transport/escort service, 24-hour emergency telephones, lighted pathways/sidewalks, controlled dormitory access (key, security card, etc).

TRANSFER AND INTERNATIONAL STUDENTS

Transfer students: May apply for admission for the following academic terms: Fall, Winter, Spring, Summer. Applicants need a minimum number of credits to apply. For fall 2005: Transfer applications received: 1,022. Transfer applicants offered admission: 510. Transfer applicants enrolled: 270. **International students:** Number of foreign undergraduates: 329 (6% of student body). Number of countries represented: 98. Minimum TOEFL score required: 550 (paper); 213 (computer).

Palm Beach Atlantic University

- **Address:** 901 S. Flagler Drive, West Palm Beach, FL 33416-4708
- **Website:** http://www.pba.edu
- **Private; Religious affiliation:** Christian nondenominational
- **Enrollment:** 2,216 full-time; 207 part-time

KEY STATS

✔ **U.S News College Ranking:** third tier, Universities–Master's (South)
✔ **SAT Score (25th/75th percentile):** 910-1110
✔ **Tuition:** 2006-2007: $18,740

Selectivity: More selective	**Room/board:** $7,237
Acceptance rate: 56%	**Average debt:** $24,393
Student/faculty ratio: 13/1	**Proportion who borrowed:** 80%

UNDERGRADUATE STUDENT BODY STATS

2005-2006 enrollment: 2,216 full-time; 207 part-time. Men: 35%; women: 65%. **Ethnic makeup:** African American: 15%; Asian American: 2%; Hispanic: 8%; White: 72%; International: 4%. **Religious preference:** Roman Catholic: 9%; Protestant: 50%; No preference: 4%; Unknown: 2%; Christian nondenominational: 31%; Jehovah's Witness, Mormon, Unity: 3%; Other: 1%.

ADMISSIONS FACTS AND FIGURES

Phone: (888) 468-6722. **Email:** admit@pba.edu. **Website:** http://www.pba.edu. **Application deadlines for fall 2007:** Regular decision: Rolling. Early decision: Not offered. Early action: Send application by: December 1; Decision sent by: December 15. Admission can be deferred. **Application fee:** $25. Common application is accepted. **Admissions requirements/recommendations:** High school units required (recommended): English: (4); Mathematics: (3); Science: (3); Social studies: (3); Total units: (18). Tests: The college uses SAT or ACT scores in admissions decisions. Either SAT or ACT required. For admission to the fall 2007 entering class, the school will accept: ACT with writing, ACT without writing. Campus visit: Recommended. Admissions interview: Required. Off-campus interview: May be arranged. **Factors that count in admissions decisions:** *Academic:* Secondary school record: Very important. Class rank: Important. Letters of recommendation: Considered. Standardized test scores: Important. Essay: Very important. **Nonacademic:** Interview: Very important.

Extracurricular activities: Considered. Talent/ability: Important. Character/personal qualities: Important. Alumni/ae relationship: Considered. Geographical residence: Considered. State residency: Not considered. Religious affiliation/commitment: Considered. Minority status: Considered. Volunteer work: Considered. Work experience: Considered. **Other schools with the greatest overlap in applicants:** Florida Atlantic University; Florida State University; University of Central Florida; University of Florida; University of South Florida. **Admissions statistics for the fall 2005 entering class:** Total applicants: 2,221. Total accepted: 1,242. Freshmen enrolled: 626; 44% were from out of state. Accepted through early-decision or early-action plans: 5%. Overall acceptance rate: 56%. **Credentials of fall 2005 freshmen:** 21% ranked in the top 10 percent of their high school class; 47% were in the top 25 percent, and 82% were in the top half. (Proportion submitting class standing: 52%.) **Average high school grade point average:** 3.5. **First-year students who submitted SAT scores:** 55%. Scores (25/75 percentile): Verbal: 450-540, Math: 460-570, Combined: 910-1110. **First-year students submitting ACT scores:** 32%. Scores (25/75 percentile): English: 19-25, Math: 17-24, Composite: 19-24.

ACADEMICS

Year founded: 1968. **Academic calendar:** Semester. **Degrees offered:** associate, bachelor's, master's, first professional. **Most popular majors:** 41% business, management, marketing, and related support services, 9% communication, journalism, and related programs, 9% education, 9% psychology, 8% theology and religious vocations. **Major fields of study:** biological and biomedical sciences; business, management, marketing, and related support services; communication, journalism, and related programs; computer and information sciences and support services; education; English language and literature/letters; health professions and related clinical sciences; history; legal professions and studies; liberal arts and sciences studies, and humanities; mathematics and statistics; philosophy and religious studies; psychology; social sciences; theology and religious vocations; visual and performing arts. **Areas of required coursework:** arts/fine arts, humanities, mathematics, English (including composition), sciences (biological or physical), social science. **Pre-professional programs:** pre-law, pre-pharmacy, other. **Special academic programs:** accelerated program, double major, dual enrollment, honors program, independent study, internships, study abroad, teacher certificate program. **Teacher certification offered in:** early childhood, special education, elementary, middle/junior high, secondary. **Faculty and instruction (2005-2006):** Total instructional faculty: 138 full-time, 130 part-time (58% men; 42% women; 8% minorities). Full-time faculty with Ph.D. or other terminal degree: 72%. Student/faculty ratio: 13/1. Classes of fewer than 20 students: 57%; of 20 to 49 students: 39%; of 50 or more students: 3%. **Advanced Placement and International Baccalaureate credit:** AP tests may be used for: Credit only. Scores accepted: 3, 4, 5. International Baccalaureate exams may be used for: Credit only. **Freshmen returning for sophomore year:** 71%. **Graduation rates:** Four-year: 37%; five-year: 43%; six-year: 42%.

COSTS AND FINANCIAL AID

Financial aid office: (561) 803-2000. **Expenses (2006-2007):** Tuition and fees 2006-2007: $18,740; room/board: $7,237. Estimated books and supplies: $1,000; transportation: $1,500; personal expenses: $1,500. **Financial aid:** Priority filing date for institution's financial aid form: February 1; deadline: August 1. In 2005-2006, 87% of undergraduates applied for financial aid. Of those, 38% were determined to have financial need; Among students who received need-based aid, the average percentage of need met: 32%. Among students who received aid based on merit, the average award (and the proportion receiving): $1,846 (15%). Average amount of debt of borrowers graduating in 2005: $24,393. Proportion who borrowed: 80%.

CAMPUS LIFE AND EXTRACURRICULAR ACTIVITIES

Campus housing available (% using): women's dorms (23%), men's dorms (13%), other housing options (64%). Students who live in college-owned, operated, or affiliated housing: 47%. **Student employment:** During the 2005-2006 academic year, 15% of undergraduates worked on campus. **Clubs and organizations:** Number of student organizations: 55. Activities include: choral groups, concert band, dance, drama/theater, jazz band, music ensembles, musical theater, pep band, student government, student newspaper, student film society, symphony orchestra, yearbook. Number of fraternities: 0; sororities: 0. Average proportion of students who stay on campus on weekends: 75%. **Sports program (2005-2006):** Member of NCAA II. *Men's intercollegiate varsity sports:* baseball, basketball, cross-country, soccer, tennis. *Women's intercollegiate varsity sports:* basketball, cross-country, soccer, softball, tennis, volleyball.

SERVICES AND FACILITIES

Basic services: health service, health insurance. **Remedial assistance:** math, writing. **Counseling services:** minority student, career, personal, veteran student, academic, older student, psychological, religious. **For learning-disabled students:** School does not offer a structured program with separate admission and additional fees. **Library:** Number of titles: 106,736; number of current serial subscriptions: 1,146. **Information technology resources:** Students are not required to lease or own a computer. Number of campus computers available to all students: 150. School has a wireless network. Approximate number of users that can be accommodated: 5,000. Proportion of college-owned housing units wired for high-speed internet access: 100%. **Campus safety:** Security services offered: 24-hour foot-and-vehicle patrols, late-night transport/escort service, 24-hour emergency telephones, lighted pathways/sidewalks, controlled dormitory access (key, security card, etc).

TRANSFER AND INTERNATIONAL STUDENTS

Transfer students: May apply for admission for the following academic terms: Fall, Winter, Spring, Summer. Applicants do not need a minimum number of credits to apply. For fall 2005: Transfer applications received: 909. Transfer applicants offered admission: 408. Transfer applicants enrolled: 217. **International students:** Number of foreign undergraduates: 90 (4% of student body). Minimum TOEFL score required: 550 (paper); 213 (computer). Average TOEFL score: 600 (paper).

Ringling School of Art and Design

- **Address:** 2700 N. Tamiami Trail, Sarasota, FL 34234-5895
- **Website:** http://www.ringling.edu
- **Private**
- **Enrollment:** 1,050 full-time; 38 part-time

KEY STATS

✔ **U.S News College Ranking:** Unranked Specialty School–Fine Arts
✔ **SAT or ACT Score (25th/75th percentile):** N/A
✔ **Tuition:** 2006-2007: $22,700

Selectivity: Least selective	**Room/board:** N/A
Acceptance rate: 73%	**Average debt:** $30,536
Student/faculty ratio: 13/1	**Proportion who borrowed:** 72%

UNDERGRADUATE STUDENT BODY STATS

2005-2006 enrollment: 1,050 full-time; 38 part-time. Men: 51%; women: 49%. **Ethnic makeup:** African American: 3%; American-Indian: 1%; Asian American: 4%; Hispanic: 11%; White: 77%; International: 5%.

ADMISSIONS FACTS AND FIGURES

Phone: (800) 255-7695. **Email:** admissions@ringling.edu. **Website:** http://www.ringling.edu. **Application deadlines for fall 2007:** Regular decision: Rolling. Early decision: Not offered. Early action: Not offered. Admission can be deferred. **Application fee:** $35. Common application is not accepted. **To apply online, go to:** https://saffron.ringling.edu/cgi-bin/admissions/app.cgi. **Admissions requirements/recommendations:** Tests: The college does not use SAT or ACT scores in admissions decisions. Neither SAT nor ACT required. Campus visit: Recommended. Admissions interview: Recommended. Off-campus interview: May be arranged. **Factors that count in admissions decisions:** *Academic:* Secondary school record: Very important. Class rank: Not considered. Letters of recommendation: Important. Standardized test scores: Not considered. Essay: Important. *Nonacademic:* Interview: Considered. Extracurricular activities: Considered. Talent/ability: Very important. Character/personal qualities: Important. Alumni/ae relationship: Considered. Geographical residence: Considered. State residency: Not considered. Religious affiliation/commitment: Not considered. Minority status: Considered. Volunteer work: Considered. Work experience: Considered. **Other schools with the greatest overlap in applicants:** Maryland Institute College of Art; Pratt Institute; Rhode Island School of Design; Savannah College of Art and Design; School of Visual Arts. **Admissions statistics for the fall 2005 entering class:** Total applicants: 1,058. Total accepted: 774. Freshmen enrolled: 217; 46% were from out of state. Overall acceptance rate: 73%. **Size of waiting list:** 45 applicants; enrolled from waiting list: 13. **Average high school grade point average:** 3.0.

ACADEMICS

Year founded: 1931. **Academic calendar:** Semester. **Degrees offered:** bachelor's. **Most popular majors:** 41% illustration, 18% design and applied arts, 16% graphic design. **Major fields of study:** visual and performing arts. **Areas of required coursework:** arts/fine arts, humanities, computer literacy, mathematics, English (including composition), philosophy, history, social science, other. **Special academic programs (% participation):** dual enrollment, exchange student program (domestic) (1%), independent study (25%), internships (6%), study abroad (1%). **Faculty and instruction (2005-2006):** Total instructional faculty: 59 full-time, 54 part-time (64% men; 36% women; 1% minorities). Full-time faculty with Ph.D. or other terminal degree: 69%. Student/faculty ratio: 13/1. Classes of fewer than 20 students: 56%; of 20 to 49 students: 43%; of 50 or more students: 1%. **Advanced Placement and International Baccalaureate credit:** International Baccalaureate exams may be used for: Credit only. **Freshmen returning for sophomore year:** 82%. **Graduation rates:** Four-year: 67%; five-year: 69%; six-year: 68%. **Graduate study:** 8% of students pursue further study within one year.

COSTS AND FINANCIAL AID

Financial aid office: (941) 351-5100. **Expenses (2006-2007):** Tuition and fees 2006-2007: $22,700; room/board: N/A. **Financial aid:** Priority filing date for institution's financial aid form: March 1; deadline: May 1. In 2005-2006, 95% of undergraduates applied for financial aid. Of those, 84% were determined to have financial need; 2% had their need fully met. Average financial aid package (proportion receiving): $9,533 (83%). Average amount of gift aid, such as scholarships or grants (proportion receiving): $6,659 (70%). Average amount of self-help aid, such as work study or loans (proportion receiving): $4,098 (79%). Average need-based loan (excluding PLUS or other private loans): $3,774. Among students who received need-based aid, the average percentage of need met: 29%. Among students who received aid based on merit, the average award (and the proportion receiving): $15,759 (15%). The average athletic scholarship (and the proportion receiving): $0 (0%). Average amount of debt of borrowers graduating in 2005: $30,536. Proportion who borrowed: 72%.

CAMPUS LIFE AND EXTRACURRICULAR ACTIVITIES

Campus housing available (% using): coed dorms (9%), women's dorms (16%), men's dorms (10%), apartments for married students (1%), apartment for single students (63%), special housing for disabled students (1%). Students who live in college-owned, operated, or affiliated housing: 48%. **Student employment:** During the 2005-2006 academic year, 11% of undergraduates worked on campus. Average per-year earnings: $4,128. **Clubs and organizations:** Number of student organizations: 14. Activities include: dance, drama/theater, student government, student film society. Number of fraternities: 2; sororities: 1. Proportion of men in fraternities: 3%; of women in sororities: 2%. Average proportion of students who stay on campus on weekends: 80%.

SERVICES AND FACILITIES

Basic services: nonremedial tutoring, placement service, health service, health insurance. **Remedial assistance:** reading, math, writing, study skills. **Counseling services:** minority student, career, personal, veteran student, academic, older student, psychological, religious, other. **For learning-disabled students:** School does not offer a structured program with separate admission and additional fees. Total undergraduates in learning-disabled program or receiving services: 109. Services include: remedial math, remedial English, reading machines, tape recorders, other special classes, note-taking services, learning center, extended time for tests, tutors, priority seating, proofreading services, texts on tape. **Library:** Number of titles: 48,608; number of current serial subscriptions: 340. **Information technology resources:** Students are not required to lease or own a computer. Number of campus computers available to all students: 800. School has a wireless network. Approximate number of users that can be accommodated: 3,010. Proportion of college-owned housing units wired for high-speed internet access: 100%. **Campus safety:** Security services offered: 24-hour foot-and-vehicle patrols, late-night transport/escort service, 24-hour emergency telephones, lighted pathways/sidewalks, controlled dormitory access (key, security card, etc).

TRANSFER AND INTERNATIONAL STUDENTS

Transfer students: May apply for admission for the following academic terms: Fall, Spring. Applicants do not need a minimum number of credits to apply. For fall 2005: Transfer applications received: 558. Transfer applicants offered admission: 170. Transfer applicants enrolled: 142. **International students:** Number of foreign undergraduates: 54 (5% of student body).

Number of countries represented: 28. Minimum TOEFL score required: 500 (paper); 173 (computer).

Rollins College

■ **Address:** 1000 Holt Avenue, Winter Park, FL 32789-4499
■ **Website:** http://www.rollins.edu
■ **Private**
■ **Enrollment:** 1,719 full-time

KEY STATS

✔ **U.S News College Ranking:** 1, Universities–Master's (South)
✔ **SAT Score (25th/75th percentile):** 1080-1290
✔ **Tuition:** 2006-2007: $30,860
  Selectivity: More selective   **Room/board:** $9,626
  Acceptance rate: 53%   **Average debt:** $15,438
  Student/faculty ratio: 11/1   **Proportion who borrowed:** 50%

UNDERGRADUATE STUDENT BODY STATS

2005-2006 enrollment: 1,719 full-time. Men: 40%; women: 60%. **Ethnic makeup:** African American: 5%; American-Indian: 1%; Asian American: 4%; Hispanic: 8%; White: 80%; International: 2%.

ADMISSIONS FACTS AND FIGURES

Phone: (407) 646-2161. **Email:** admission@rollins.edu. **Website:** http://www.rollins.edu. **Application deadlines for fall 2007:** Regular decision: February 15; decision sent by April 1. Early decision: Send application by: November 15; Decision sent by: December 15. Early action: Not offered. Admission can be deferred. **Application fee:** $40. Common application is accepted. **To apply online, go to:** http://www.rollins.edu/admission/application.shtml. **Admissions requirements/recommendations:** High school units required (recommended): English: 4 (4); Mathematics: 3 (4); Science: 2 (4); Foreign language: 2 (3); Social studies: 2 (3); History: 2 (3); Academic electives: 2 (3); Total units: 17 (24). Tests: The college uses SAT or ACT scores in admissions decisions. Either SAT or ACT required. For admission to the fall 2007 entering class, the school will accept: ACT without writing. Campus visit: Recommended. Admissions interview: Recommended. Off-campus interview: Not available. **Factors that count in admissions decisions:** *Academic:* Secondary school record: Very important. Class rank: Considered. Letters of recommendation: Important. Standardized test scores: Important. Essay: Important. *Nonacademic:* Interview: Considered. Extracurricular activities: Important. Talent/ability: Important. Character/personal qualities: Considered. Alumni/ae relationship: Considered. Geographical residence: Not considered. State residency: Not considered. Religious affiliation/commitment: Not considered. Minority status: Considered. Volunteer work: Considered. Work experience: Considered. **Other schools with the greatest overlap in applicants:** Stetson University; University of Central Florida; University of Florida; University of Miami; University of Richmond. **Admissions statistics for the fall 2005 entering class:** Total applicants: 2,958. Total accepted: 1,578. Freshmen enrolled: 464; 52% were from out of state. Accepted through early-decision or early-action plans: 36%. Overall acceptance rate: 53%. Early-decision acceptance rate: 66%. Non-early acceptance rate: 52%. **Size of waiting list:** 350 applicants; enrolled from waiting list: 40. **Credentials of fall 2005 freshmen:** 34% ranked in the top 10 percent of their high school class; 67% were in the top 25 percent, and 94% were in the top half. (Proportion submitting class standing: 50%.) **Average high school grade point average:** 3.4. **First-year students who submitted SAT scores:** 93%. Scores (25/75 percentile): Verbal: 540-650, Math: 540-640, Combined: 1080-1290. **First-year students submitting ACT scores:** 37%. Scores (25/75 percentile): English: N/A, Math: N/A, Composite: 22-27.

ACADEMICS

Year founded: 1885. **Academic calendar:** Semester. **Degrees offered:** bachelor's, master's. **Most popular majors:** 18% psychology, 10% economics, 7% English language and literature, 6% international business/trade/commerce, 4% political science and government. **Major fields of study:** area, ethnic, cultural, and gender studies; biological and biomedical sciences; business, management, marketing, and related support services; computer and information sciences and support services; education; English language and literature/letters; foreign languages, literatures, and linguistics; history; mathematics and statistics; multi/interdisciplinary studies; philosophy and religious studies; physical sciences; psychology; social sciences; visual and performing arts. **Areas of required coursework:** arts/fine arts, humanities, computer literacy, mathematics, English (including composition), philosophy, foreign languages, sciences (biological or physical), history, social science. **Pre-professional programs:** pre-law, pre-dentistry, pre-medicine. **Special academic programs:** accelerated program, cross-registration, double major, dual enrollment, honors program, independent study, internships, student-designed major, study abroad, teacher certificate program. **Teacher certification offered in:** elementary, secondary. **Faculty and instruction (2005-2006):** Total instructional faculty: 185 full-time, 32 part-time (61% men; 39% women; 11% minorities). Full-time faculty with Ph.D. or other terminal degree: 94%. Student/faculty ratio: 11/1. Classes of fewer than 20 students: 65%; of 20 to 49 students: 35%; of 50 or more students: 0%. **Advanced Placement and International Baccalaureate credit:** AP tests may be used for: Credit and/or placement. Scores accepted: 4, 5. International Baccalaureate exams may be used for: Credit and/or placement. **Freshmen returning for sophomore year:** 85%. **Graduation rates:** Four-year: 49%; five-year: 62%; six-year: 62%. **Graduate study:** 21% of students pursue further study immediately upon graduation; 30% within one year. Fields in which graduates pursue further study: Master of Business Administration (MBA), 6%; law, 7%; arts and sciences, 3%.

COSTS AND FINANCIAL AID

Financial aid office: (407) 646-2395. **Expenses (2006-2007):** Tuition and fees 2006-2007: $30,860; room/board: $9,626. Estimated books and supplies: $676; transportation: $750; personal expenses: $2,636. **Financial aid:** Priority filing date for institution's financial aid form: February 15; deadline: March 1. In 2005-2006, 47% of undergraduates applied for financial aid. Of those, 42% were determined to have financial need; 35% had their need fully met. Average financial aid package (proportion receiving): $27,679 (42%). Average amount of gift aid, such as scholarships or grants (proportion receiving): $23,591 (41%). Average amount of self-help aid, such as work study or loans (proportion receiving): $5,477 (39%). Average need-based loan (excluding PLUS or other private loans): $3,986. Among students who received need-based aid, the average percentage of need met: 90%. Among students who received aid based on merit, the average award (and the proportion receiving): $10,122 (13%). The average athletic scholarship (and the proportion receiving): $19,094 (5%). Average amount of debt of borrowers graduating in 2005: $15,438. Proportion who borrowed: 50%.

CAMPUS LIFE AND EXTRACURRICULAR ACTIVITIES

Campus housing available: coed dorms, women's dorms, men's dorms, sorority housing, fraternity housing, apartment for single students, special housing for disabled students. Students who live in college-owned, operated, or affiliated housing: 65%. **Student employment:** During the 2005-2006 academic year, 30% of undergraduates worked on campus. Average per-year earnings: $1,354. **Clubs and organizations:** Number of student organizations: 73. Activities include: choral groups, dance, drama/theater, literary magazine, music ensembles, musical theater, pep band, radio station, student government, student newspaper, student film society, television station, yearbook. Number of fraternities: 7; sororities: 5. Proportion of men in fraternities: 35%; of women in sororities: 37%. Average proportion of students who stay on campus on weekends: 58%. **Sports program (2005-2006):** Member of NCAA II. *Men's intercollegiate varsity sports:* baseball, basketball, crew, cross-country, golf, sailing, soccer, swimming and diving, tennis, water skiing. *Women's intercollegiate varsity sports:* basketball, cheerleading, crew, cross-country, golf, sailing, soccer, softball, swimming and diving, tennis, volleyball, water skiing.

SERVICES AND FACILITIES

Basic services: nonremedial tutoring, women's center, placement service, health service, health insurance. **Remedial assistance:** reading, math, writing. **Counseling services:** minority student, career, military, personal, veteran student, academic, older student, psychological, birth control, religious. **For learning-disabled students:** School does not offer a structured program with separate admission and additional fees. Services include: other testing accommodations, reading machines, tape recorders, untimed tests, note-taking services, learning center, readers, extended time for tests, tutors. **Library:** Number of titles: 342,536; number of current serial subscriptions: 15,749. **Information technology resources:** Students are not required to lease or own a computer. Number of campus computers available to all students: 210. School has a wireless network. Approximate number of users that can be accommodated: 2,000. Proportion of college-owned housing units wired for high-speed internet access: 100%. **Campus safety:** Security services offered: 24-hour foot-and-vehicle patrols, late-night transport/escort service, 24-hour emergency telephones, lighted pathways/sidewalks, controlled dormitory access (key, security card, etc).

TRANSFER AND INTERNATIONAL STUDENTS

Transfer students: May apply for admission for the following academic terms: Fall, Spring. Applicants need a minimum number of credits to apply. For fall 2005: Transfer applications received: 275. Transfer applicants offered admission: 123. Transfer applicants enrolled: 59. **International students:** Number of foreign undergraduates: 27 (2% of student body). Number of countries represented: 35. Minimum TOEFL score required: 550 (paper); 213 (computer). Average TOEFL score: 600 (paper).

Southeastern University

- ■ **Address:** 1000 Longfellow Boulevard, Lakeland, FL 33801
- ■ **Website:** http://www.seuniversity.edu
- ■ **Private; Religious affiliation:** Assemblies of God
- ■ **Enrollment:** 2,174 full-time; 123 part-time

KEY STATS

✔ **U.S News College Ranking:** fourth tier, Comp. Coll.–Bachelor's (South)
✔ **SAT Score (25th/75th percentile):** 860-1130
✔ **Tuition:** 2006-2007: $12,280

Selectivity: Less selective	**Room/board:** $6,178
Acceptance rate: 80%	**Average debt:** $18,933
Student/faculty ratio: 27/1	**Proportion who borrowed:** 93%

UNDERGRADUATE STUDENT BODY STATS

2005-2006 enrollment: 2,174 full-time; 123 part-time. Men: 43%; women: 57%. **Ethnic makeup:** African American: 7%; Asian American: 1%; Hispanic: 12%; White: 79%. **Religious preference:** Roman Catholic: 1%; Protestant: 28%; Jewish: 1%; Unknown: 11%; Assemblies of God: 59%.

ADMISSIONS FACTS AND FIGURES

Phone: (863) 667-5018. **Email:** admission@seuniversity.edu. **Website:** http://www.seuniversity.edu. **Application deadlines for fall 2007:** Regular decision: Rolling. Early decision: Not offered. Early action: Not offered. Admission can be deferred. **Application fee:** $40. Common application is not accepted. **To apply online, go to:** https://www.seuniversity.edu/forms/app.html. **Admissions requirements/recommendations:** High school units required (recommended): English: 3 (4); Mathematics: 3 (3); Science: 3 (3); Foreign language: (2); Social studies: 3 (3). Tests: The college uses SAT or ACT scores in admissions decisions. Either SAT or ACT required. For admission to the fall 2007 entering class, the school will accept: ACT with writing, ACT without writing. Campus visit: Recommended. Admissions interview: Neither required nor recommended. **Factors that count in admissions decisions:** *Academic:* Secondary school record: Important. Class rank: Not considered. Letters of recommendation: Very important. Standardized test scores: Important. Essay: Important. *Nonacademic:* Interview: Considered. Extracurricular activities: Considered. Talent/ability: Considered. Character/personal qualities: Very important. Alumni/ae relationship: Not considered. Geographical residence: Not considered. State residency: Not considered. Religious affiliation/commitment: Very important. Minority status: Not considered. Volunteer work: Considered. Work experience: Not considered. **Other schools with the greatest overlap in applicants:** Evangel University; Florida State University; Palm Beach Atlantic University; University of Florida; University of South Florida. **Admissions statistics for the fall 2005 entering class:** Total applicants: 939. Total accepted: 754. Freshmen enrolled: 521; 42% were from out of state. Overall acceptance rate: 80%. **First-year students who submitted SAT scores:** 73%. Scores (25/75 percentile): Verbal: 440-580, Math: 420-550, Combined: 860-1130. **First-year students submitting ACT scores:** 49%. Scores (25/75 percentile): English: N/A, Math: N/A, Composite: 18-23.

ACADEMICS

Year founded: 1935. **Academic calendar:** Semester. **Degrees offered:** bachelor's, master's. **Most popular majors:** 19% theology and religious vocations, 13% elementary education and teaching, 9% psychology, 6% business/commerce, 6% music. **Major fields of study:** biological and biomedical sciences; business, management, marketing, and related support services; communication, journalism, and related programs; computer and information sciences and support services; education; English language and literature/letters; legal professions and studies; mathematics and statistics; parks, recreation, leisure, and fitness studies; psychology; public administration and social service professions; theology and religious vocations; visual and performing arts. **Areas of required coursework:** humanities, mathematics, English (including composition), philosophy, sciences (biological or physical), history, social science, other. **Pre-professional programs:** pre-law, pre-medicine, pre-theology. **Special academic programs (% participation):** accelerated program (10%), distance learning (0%), double major (0%), dual enrollment (0%), honors program (0%), independent study (5%), internships (35%), study abroad (0%), teacher certificate program (19%). **Teacher certification offered in:** elementary, middle/junior high, secondary. **Reserve Officers Training Corps (ROTC):** Army ROTC: Offered at cooperating institution (Florida Southern College). **Faculty and instruction (2005-2006):** Total instructional faculty: 54 full-time, 83 part-time (61% men; 39% women; 8% minorities). Full-time faculty with Ph.D. or other terminal degree: 65%. Student/faculty ratio: 27/1. Classes of fewer than 20 students: 35%; of 20 to 49 students: 49%; of 50 or more students: 16%. **Advanced Placement and International Baccalaureate credit:** AP tests may be used for: Credit and/or placement. Scores accepted: 3. International Baccalaureate exams may be used for: Credit and/or placement. **Freshmen returning for sophomore year:** 67%. **Graduation rates:** Four-year: 34%; five-year: 47%; six-year: 40%.

COSTS AND FINANCIAL AID

Financial aid office: (863) 667-5026. **Expenses (2006-2007):** Tuition and fees 2006-2007: $12,280; room/board: $6,178. Estimated books and supplies: $900; transportation: $1,000; personal expenses: $900. **Financial aid:** Priority filing date for institution's financial aid form: April 15. In 2005-2006, 87% of undergraduates applied for financial aid. Of those, 71% were determined to have financial need; 11% had their need fully met. Average financial aid package (proportion receiving): $7,005 (69%). Average amount of gift aid, such as scholarships or grants (proportion receiving): $4,839 (64%). Average amount of self-help aid, such as work study or loans (proportion receiving): $3,008 (59%). Average need-based loan (excluding PLUS or other private loans): $575. Among students who received need-based aid, the average percentage of need met: 53%. Among students who received aid based on merit, the average award (and the proportion receiving): $10,455 (25%). The average athletic scholarship (and the proportion receiving): $0 (0%). Average amount of debt of borrowers graduating in 2005: $18,933. Proportion who borrowed: 93%.

CAMPUS LIFE AND EXTRACURRICULAR ACTIVITIES

Campus housing available (% using): women's dorms (58%), men's dorms (42%). Students who live in college-owned, operated, or affiliated housing: 67%. **Student employment:** During the 2005-2006 academic year, 17% of undergraduates worked on campus. Average per-year earnings: $2,100. **Clubs and organizations:** Number of student organizations: 23. Activities include: choral groups, concert band, drama/theater, jazz band, literary magazine, music ensembles, musical theater, opera, radio station, student government, student newspaper, television station, yearbook. Number of fraternities: 0; sororities: 0. Average proportion of students who stay on campus on weekends: 60%.

SERVICES AND FACILITIES

Basic services: placement service, health service. **Remedial assistance:** reading, math, writing. **Counseling services:** career, personal, veteran student, academic, religious. **For learning-disabled students:** School does not offer a structured program with separate admission and additional fees. Total undergraduates in learning-disabled program or receiving services: 31. Services include: remedial math, remedial English, reading machines, remedial reading, tape recorders, diagnostic testing service, untimed tests, note-taking services, special bookstore section, oral tests, learning center, readers, extended time for tests, tutors, priority registration, proofreading services, texts on tape, exams on tape or computer, other testing accomodations. **Library:** Number of titles: 94,308; number of current serial subscriptions: 665. **Information technology resources:** Students are not required to lease or own a computer. Number of campus computers available to all students: 68. School has a wireless network. Approximate number of users that can be accommodated: 336. Proportion of college-owned housing units wired for high-speed internet access: 100%. **Campus safety:** Security services offered: 24-hour foot-and-vehicle patrols, lighted pathways/sidewalks.

TRANSFER AND INTERNATIONAL STUDENTS

Transfer students: May apply for admission for the following academic terms: Fall, Spring, Summer. Applicants do not need a minimum number of credits to apply. For fall 2005: Transfer applications received: 398. Transfer applicants offered admission: 306. Transfer applicants enrolled: 237. **International students:** Number of foreign undergraduates: 4. Number

of countries represented: 20. Minimum TOEFL score required: 500 (paper); 221 (computer).

Stetson University

- **Address:** 421 N. Woodland Boulevard, Deland, FL 32723
- **Website:** http://www.stetson.edu
- **Private**
- **Enrollment:** 2,160 full-time; 74 part-time

KEY STATS

✔ **U.S News College Ranking:** 5, Universities–Master's (South)
✔ **SAT Score (25th/75th percentile):** 1040-1235
✔ **Tuition:** 2006-2007: $26,905
  Selectivity: More selective   **Room/board:** $7,632
  Acceptance rate: 69%   **Average debt:** $21,500
  Student/faculty ratio: 11/1   **Proportion who borrowed:** 55%

UNDERGRADUATE STUDENT BODY STATS

2005-2006 enrollment: 2,160 full-time; 74 part-time. Men: 42%; women: 58%. **Ethnic makeup:** African American: 4%; Asian American: 2%; Hispanic: 7%; White: 83%; International: 3%. **Religious preference:** Roman Catholic: 14%; Protestant: 24%; Jewish: 2%; No preference: 18%; Unknown: 34%; Other: 8%.

ADMISSIONS FACTS AND FIGURES

Phone: (800) 688-0101. **Email:** admissions@stetson.edu. **Website:** http://www.stetson.edu. **Application deadlines for fall 2007:** Regular decision: March 15. Early decision: Send application by: November 1; Decision sent by: November 25. Early action: Not offered. Admission can be deferred. **Application fee:** $40. Common application is accepted. **To apply online, go to:** http://www.stetson.edu/apply. **Admissions requirements/recommendations:** High school units required (recommended): English: 4; Mathematics: 3; Science: 3; Foreign language: 2; Social studies: 2; Total units: 14. Tests: The college uses SAT or ACT scores in admissions decisions. Either SAT or ACT required. For admission to the fall 2007 entering class, the school will accept: ACT with writing, ACT without writing. Campus visit: Recommended. Admissions interview: Recommended. Off-campus interview: May be arranged. **Factors that count in admissions decisions:** *Academic:* Secondary school record: Very important. Class rank: Important. Letters of recommendation: Important. Standardized test scores: Important. Essay: Important. *Nonacademic:* Interview: Important. Extracurricular activities: Important. Talent/ability: Important. Character/personal qualities: Important. Alumni/ae relationship: Considered. Geographical residence: Considered. State residency: Considered. Religious affiliation/commitment: Not considered. Minority status: Considered. Volunteer work: Important. Work experience: Important. **Other schools with the greatest overlap in applicants:** Florida State University; Rollins College; University of Central Florida; University of Florida; University of Miami. **Admissions statistics for the fall 2005 entering class:** Total applicants: 2,782. Total accepted: 1,918. Freshmen enrolled: 550; 22% were from out of state. Accepted through early-decision or early-action plans: 6%. Overall acceptance rate: 69%. Early-decision acceptance rate: 86%. Non-early acceptance rate: 69%. **Credentials of fall 2005 freshmen:** 27% ranked in the top 10 percent of their high school class; 57% were in the top 25 percent, and 88% were in the top half. (Proportion submitting class standing: 74%.) **Average high school grade point average:** 3.8. **First-year students who submitted SAT scores:** 92%. Scores (25/75 percentile): Verbal: 520-620, Math: 520-615, Combined: 1040-1235. **First-year students submitting ACT scores:** 45%. Scores (25/75 percentile): English: 21-27, Math: 21-26, Composite: 22-27.

ACADEMICS

Year founded: 1883. **Academic calendar:** Semester. **Degrees offered:** bachelor's, master's, post-master's certificate, first professional, first professional certificate. **Most popular majors:** 36% business, management, marketing, and related support services, 9% visual and performing arts, 7% biological and biomedical sciences, 7% social sciences, 6% education. **Major fields of study:** area, ethnic, cultural, and gender studies; biological and biomedical sciences; business, management, marketing, and related support services; communication, journalism, and related programs; computer and information sciences and support services; education; English language and literature/letters; foreign languages, literatures, and linguistics; health professions and related clinical sciences; history; liberal arts and sciences studies, and humanities; mathematics and statistics; natural resources and conservation; parks, recreation, leisure, and fitness studies; philosophy and religious studies; physical sciences; psychology; social sciences; visual and performing arts. **Areas of required coursework:** arts/fine arts, humanities, computer literacy, mathematics, English (including composition), foreign languages, sciences (biological or physical), history, social science, other. **Pre-professional programs:** pre-law, pre-dentistry, pre-medicine, pre-veterinary science. **Special academic programs:** accelerated program, double major, honors program, independent study, internships, liberal arts/career combination, student-designed major, study abroad, teacher certificate program. **Teacher certification offered in:** elementary, middle/junior high, secondary. **Cooperative education programs:** engineering, health professions, other. **Reserve Officers Training Corps (ROTC):** Army ROTC: Offered at cooperating institution (Embry Riddle). **Faculty and instruction (2005-2006):** Total instructional faculty: 233 full-time, 123 part-time (58% men; 42% women; 10% minorities). Full-time faculty with Ph.D. or other terminal degree: 92%. Student/faculty ratio: 11/1. Classes of fewer than 20 students: 59%; of 20 to 49 students: 40%; of 50 or more students: 1%. **Advanced Placement and International Baccalaureate credit:** AP tests may be used for: Credit and/or placement. Scores accepted: 4, 5. International Baccalaureate exams may be used for: Credit only. **Freshmen returning for sophomore year:** 78%. **Graduation rates:** Four-year: 57%; five-year: 64%; six-year: 64%. **Graduate study:** 47% of students pursue further study immediately upon graduation. Fields in which graduates pursue further study: Master of Business Administration (MBA), 23%; law, 20%; medicine, 16%; theology (or the seminary), 3%; education, 5%; arts and sciences, 33%.

COSTS AND FINANCIAL AID
Financial aid office: (386) 822-7120. **Expenses (2006-2007):** Tuition and fees 2006-2007: $26,905; room/board: $7,632. Estimated books and supplies: $1,000; transportation: $660; personal expenses: $960. **Financial aid:** Priority filing date for institution's financial aid form: March 15. In 2005-2006, 63% of undergraduates applied for financial aid. Of those, 54% were determined to have financial need; 38% had their need fully met. Average financial aid package (proportion receiving): $21,991 (54%). Average amount of gift aid, such as scholarships or grants (proportion receiving): $16,755 (53%). Average amount of self-help aid, such as work study or loans (proportion receiving): $6,200 (42%). Average need-based loan (excluding PLUS or other private loans): $4,983. Among students who received need-based aid, the average percentage of need met: 86%. Among students who received aid based on merit, the average award (and the proportion receiving): $9,975 (35%). The average athletic scholarship (and the proportion receiving): $16,126 (8%). Average amount of debt of borrowers graduating in 2005: $21,500. Proportion who borrowed: 55%.

CAMPUS LIFE AND EXTRACURRICULAR ACTIVITIES
Campus housing available (% using): coed dorms (56%), women's dorms (25%), men's dorms (4%), sorority housing (6%), fraternity housing (7%), apartment for single students, other housing options (2%). Students who live in college-owned, operated, or affiliated housing: 63%. **Student employment:** During the 2005-2006 academic year, 13% of undergraduates worked on campus. Average per-year earnings: $2,400. **Clubs and organizations:** Number of student organizations: 113. Activities include: choral groups, concert band, dance, drama/theater, jazz band, literary magazine, music ensembles, musical theater, opera, pep band, radio station, student government, student newspaper, student film society, symphony orchestra. Number of fraternities: 7; sororities: 6. Proportion of men in fraternities: 23%; of women in sororities: 22%. Average proportion of students who stay on campus on weekends: 60%. **Sports program (2005-2006):** Member of NCAA I. *Men's intercollegiate varsity sports:* baseball, basketball, crew, cross-country, golf, soccer, tennis. *Women's intercollegiate varsity sports:* basketball, crew, cross-country, golf, soccer, softball, tennis, volleyball.

SERVICES AND FACILITIES
Basic services: nonremedial tutoring, placement service, health service, other. **Remedial assistance:** math, writing, study skills, other. **Counseling services:** minority student, career, personal, academic, psychological, religious. **For learning-disabled students:** School does not offer a structured program with separate admission and additional fees. Total undergraduates in learning-disabled program or receiving services: 61. Services include: tape recorders, note-taking services, oral tests, learning center, readers, extended time for tests, tutors. **Library:** Number of titles: 392,218; number of current serial subscriptions: 17,000. **Information technology resources:** Students are not required to lease or own a computer. Number of campus computers available to all students: 380. School has a wireless network. Proportion of

college-owned housing units wired for high-speed internet access: 100%. **Campus safety:** Security services offered: 24-hour foot-and-vehicle patrols, late-night transport/escort service, 24-hour emergency telephones, lighted pathways/sidewalks, controlled dormitory access (key, security card, etc).

TRANSFER AND INTERNATIONAL STUDENTS
Transfer students: May apply for admission for the following academic terms: Fall, Spring, Summer. Applicants do not need a minimum number of credits to apply. For fall 2005: Transfer applications received: 325. Transfer applicants offered admission: 200. Transfer applicants enrolled: 99. **International students:** Number of foreign undergraduates: 73 (3% of student body). Number of countries represented: 40. Minimum TOEFL score required: 550 (paper); 213 (computer).

St. Leo University

- **Address:** PO Box 6665, Saint Leo, FL 33574-6665
- **Website:** http://www.saintleo.edu
- **Private; Religious affiliation:** Roman Catholic
- **Enrollment:** 1,335 full-time; 49 part-time

KEY STATS
✔ **U.S News College Ranking:** third tier, Universities–Master's (South)
✔ **SAT Score (25th/75th percentile):** 920-1090
✔ **Tuition:** 2006-2007: $15,226

Selectivity: Selective	**Room/board:** $7,618
Acceptance rate: 43%	**Average debt:** $15,300
Student/faculty ratio: 16/1	**Proportion who borrowed:** 67%

UNDERGRADUATE STUDENT BODY STATS
2005-2006 enrollment: 1,335 full-time; 49 part-time. Men: 45%; women: 55%. **Ethnic makeup:** African American: 8%; American-Indian: 1%; Asian American: 1%; Hispanic: 9%; White: 74%; International: 8%. **Religious preference:** Protestant: 30%; No preference: 20%; Roman Catholic: 48%; Other: 2%.

ADMISSIONS FACTS AND FIGURES
Phone: (800) 334-5532. **Email:** admission@saintleo.edu. **Website:** http://www.saintleo.edu. **Application deadlines for fall 2007:** Regular decision: August 15. Early decision: Not offered. Early action: Not offered. Admission can be deferred. **Application fee:** $35. Common application is accepted. **To apply online, go to:** http://www.slu4u.net. **Admissions requirements/recommendations:** High school units required (recommended): English: (4); Mathematics: (3); Science: (2); Foreign language: (2); Social studies: (3); Academic electives: (2); Total units: (16). Tests: The college uses SAT or ACT scores in admissions decisions. Either SAT or ACT required. For admission to the fall 2007 entering class, the school will accept: ACT with writing, ACT without writing. Campus visit: Recommended. Admissions interview: Recommended. Off-campus interview: May be arranged. **Factors that count in admissions decisions:** *Academic:* Secondary school record: Very important. Class rank: Considered. Letters of recommendation: Very important. Standardized test scores: Very important. Essay: Considered. *Nonacademic:* Interview: Important. Extracurricular activities: Important. Talent/ability: Important. Character/personal qualities: Very important. Alumni/ae relationship: Important. Geographical residence: Not considered. State residency: Not considered. Religious affiliation/commitment: Not considered. Minority status: Considered. Volunteer work: Important. Work experience: Considered. **Other schools with the greatest overlap in applicants:** Florida Southern College; University of Central Florida; University of Florida; University of South Florida; University of Tampa. **Admissions statistics for the fall 2005 entering class:** Total applicants: 3,248. Total accepted: 1,409. Freshmen enrolled: 454; 40% were from out of state. Overall acceptance rate: 43%. **Credentials of fall 2005 freshmen:** 8% ranked in the top 10 percent of their high school class; 30% were in the top 25 percent, and 67% were in the top half. (Proportion submitting class standing: 67%.) **Average high school grade point average:** 3.2. **First-year students who submitted SAT scores:** 69%. Scores (25/75 percentile): Verbal: 460-540, Math: 460-550, Combined: 920-1090. **First-year students submitting ACT scores:** 26%. Scores (25/75 percentile): English: 18-24, Math: 17-22, Composite: 19-24.

ACADEMICS

Year founded: 1889. **Academic calendar:** Semester. **Degrees offered:** associate, bachelor's, master's. **Most popular majors:** 33% business, management, marketing, and related support services, 14% education, 13% social sciences, 9% psychology, 7% history. **Major fields of study:** biological and biomedical sciences; business, management, marketing, and related support services; communication, journalism, and related programs; education; English language and literature/letters; health professions and related clinical sciences; history; mathematics and statistics; natural resources and conservation; parks, recreation, leisure, and fitness studies; psychology; public administration and social service professions; security and protective services; social sciences; theology and religious vocations. **Areas of required coursework:** arts/fine arts, humanities, computer literacy, mathematics, English (including composition), philosophy, sciences (biological or physical), history, social science, other. **Pre-professional programs:** pre-law, pre-dentistry, pre-medicine, pre-veterinary science, pre-optometry, pre-pharmacy, other. **Special academic programs (% participation):** distance learning (68%), double major (3%), dual enrollment (7%), honors program (12%), independent study (25%), internships (51%), liberal arts/career combination (0%), study abroad (7%), teacher certificate program (14%), weekend college (46%). **Teacher certification offered in:** elementary, middle/junior high. **Reserve Officers Training Corps (ROTC):** Army ROTC: Offered on campus; Air Force ROTC: Offered at cooperating institution (University of South Florida). **Faculty and instruction (2005-2006):** Total instructional faculty: 66 full-time, 56 part-time (63% men; 37% women; 7% minorities). Full-time faculty with Ph.D. or other terminal degree: 82%. Student/faculty ratio: 16/1. Classes of fewer than 20 students: 53%; of 20 to 49 students: 47%. **Advanced Placement and International Baccalaureate credit:** AP tests may be used for: Credit and/or placement. Scores accepted: 3. International Baccalaureate exams may be used for: Credit and/or placement. **Freshmen returning for sophomore year:** 69%. **Graduation rates:** Four-year: 25%; five-year: 39%; six-year: 41%.

COSTS AND FINANCIAL AID

Financial aid office: (352) 588-8270. **Expenses (2006-2007):** Tuition and fees 2006-2007: $15,226; room/board: $7,618. Estimated books and supplies: $1,200; transportation: $1,100; personal expenses: $900. **Financial aid:** Priority filing date for institution's financial aid form: April 1. In 2005-2006, 88% of undergraduates applied for financial aid. Of those, 69% were determined to have financial need; 40% had their need fully met. Average financial aid package (proportion receiving): $15,485 (68%). Average amount of gift aid, such as scholarships or grants (proportion receiving): $10,666 (68%). Average amount of self-help aid, such as work study or loans (proportion receiving): $5,375 (54%). Average need-based loan (excluding PLUS or other private loans): $3,684. Among students who received need-based aid, the average percentage of need met: 86%. Among students who received aid based on merit, the average award (and the proportion receiving): $5,845 (2%). The average athletic scholarship (and the proportion receiving): $8,898 (3%). Average amount of debt of borrowers graduating in 2005: $15,300. Proportion who borrowed: 67%.

CAMPUS LIFE AND EXTRACURRICULAR ACTIVITIES

Campus housing available: coed dorms, women's dorms, men's dorms, sorority housing, fraternity housing, apartment for single students, special housing for disabled students. Students who live in college-owned, operated, or affiliated housing: 75%. **Student employment:** During the 2005-2006 academic year, 15% of undergraduates worked on campus. Average per-year earnings: $2,500. **Clubs and organizations:** Number of student organizations: 50. Activities include: choral groups, concert band, dance, drama/theater, literary magazine, music ensembles, radio station, student government, student newspaper, television station, yearbook. Number of fraternities: 8; sororities: 4. Proportion of men in fraternities: 26%; of women in sororities: 14%. Average proportion of students who stay on campus on weekends: 80%. **Sports program (2005-2006):** Member of NCAA II. *Men's intercollegiate varsity sports:* baseball, basketball, cross-country, golf, lacrosse, soccer, swimming and diving, tennis. *Women's intercollegiate varsity sports:* basketball, cheerleading, cross-country, golf, soccer, softball, tennis, volleyball.

SERVICES AND FACILITIES

Basic services: nonremedial tutoring, health service, health insurance. **Remedial assistance:** math, writing, study skills. **Counseling services:** minority student, career, personal, veteran student, academic, older student, psychological, religious. **For learning-disabled students:** School does not offer a structured program with separate admission and additional fees. Services include: remedial math, remedial English, reading machines, tape

recorders, note-taking services, oral tests, learning center, readers, extended time for tests, tutors, other. **Library:** Number of titles: 141,521; number of current serial subscriptions: 700. **Information technology resources:** Students are not required to lease or own a computer. Number of campus computers available to all students: 1,230. School has a wireless network. Approximate number of users that can be accommodated: 1,300. Proportion of college-owned housing units wired for high-speed internet access: 100%. **Campus safety:** Security services offered: 24-hour foot-and-vehicle patrols, late-night transport/escort service, 24-hour emergency telephones, lighted pathways/sidewalks, student patrols, controlled dormitory access (key, security card, etc).

TRANSFER AND INTERNATIONAL STUDENTS

Transfer students: May apply for admission for the following academic terms: Fall, Spring. Applicants need a minimum number of credits to apply. For fall 2005: Transfer applications received: 353. Transfer applicants offered admission: 187. Transfer applicants enrolled: 111. **International students:** Number of foreign undergraduates: 112 (8% of student body). Number of countries represented: 42. Minimum TOEFL score required: 550 (paper); 213 (computer). Average TOEFL score: 550 (paper).

St. Thomas University

- **Address:** 16401 N.W. 37th Avenue, Miami Gardens, FL 33054
- **Website:** http://www.stu.edu
- **Private; Religious affiliation:** Roman Catholic
- **Enrollment:** 1,096 full-time; 62 part-time

KEY STATS

✔ **U.S News College Ranking:** fourth tier, Universities–Master's (South)
✔ **SAT Score (25th/75th percentile):** 780-1010
✔ **Tuition:** 2006-2007: $18,750

Selectivity: Less selective	**Room/board:** $5,912
Acceptance rate: 91%	**Average debt:** $16,000
Student/faculty ratio: 17/1	**Proportion who borrowed:** N/A

UNDERGRADUATE STUDENT BODY STATS

2005-2006 enrollment: 1,096 full-time; 62 part-time. Men: 42%; women: 58%. **Ethnic makeup:** African American: 26%; Asian American: 1%; Hispanic: 43%; White: 19%; International: 11%. **Religious preference:** Unknown: 62%; Roman Catholic: 28%; Other: 10%.

ADMISSIONS FACTS AND FIGURES

Phone: (305) 628-6546. **Email:** signup@stu.edu. **Website:** http://www.stu.edu. **Application deadlines for fall 2007:** Regular decision: Rolling. Early decision: Not offered. Early action: Not offered. Admission can be deferred. **Application fee:** $40. Common application is accepted. **To apply online, go to:** http://www.stu.edu/Admission/apply-now-article-1240.html. **Admissions requirements/recommendations:** High school units required (recommended): English: 4; Mathematics: 3; Science: 2; Social studies: 3; Academic electives: 6. Tests: The college uses SAT or ACT scores in admissions decisions. Either SAT or ACT required. For admission to the fall 2007 entering class, the school will accept: ACT without writing. Campus visit: Recommended. Admissions interview: Recommended. Off-campus interview: May be arranged. **Factors that count in admissions decisions:** *Academic:* Secondary school record: Important. Class rank: Very important. Letters of recommendation: Important. Standardized test scores: Very important. Essay: Important. *Nonacademic:* Interview: Not considered. Extracurricular activities: Considered. Talent/ability: Considered. Character/personal qualities: Considered. Alumni/ae relationship: Important. Geographical residence: Not considered. State residency: Not considered. Religious affiliation/commitment: Not considered. Minority status: Not considered. Volunteer work: Considered. Work experience: Considered. **Other schools with the greatest overlap in applicants:** Barry University; Florida International University; Florida Memorial College; Johnson and Wales University; University of Miami. **Admissions statistics for the fall 2005 entering class:** Total applicants: 551. Total accepted: 499. Freshmen enrolled: 206; 17% were from out of state. Overall acceptance rate: 91%. **Average high school grade point average:** 3.0. **First-year students who submitted SAT scores:** 68%. Scores (25/75 percentile): Verbal: 400-500, Math: 380-510, Combined: 780-1010.

First-year students submitting ACT scores: 32%. Scores (25/75 percentile): English: N/A, Math: N/A, Composite: 16-22.

ACADEMICS
Year founded: 1961. **Academic calendar:** Semester. **Degrees offered:** bachelor's, post-bachelor's certificate, master's, post-master's certificate, first professional, doctorate. **Most popular majors:** 50% business, management, marketing, and related support services, 11% health professions and related clinical sciences, 8% communication, journalism, and related programs, 6% security and protective services, 5% psychology. **Major fields of study:** biological and biomedical sciences; business, management, marketing, and related support services; communication, journalism, and related programs; computer and information sciences and support services; education; English language and literature/letters; health professions and related clinical sciences; history; liberal arts and sciences studies, and humanities; parks, recreation, leisure, and fitness studies; philosophy and religious studies; psychology; public administration and social service professions; security and protective services; social sciences. **Areas of required coursework:** computer literacy, mathematics, English (including composition), philosophy, sciences (biological or physical), history, social science, other. **Pre-professional programs:** pre-law, pre-dentistry, pre-medicine. **Special academic programs:** distance learning, double major, dual enrollment, honors program, independent study, internships, liberal arts/career combination, teacher certificate program. **Teacher certification offered in:** elementary, secondary. **Faculty and instruction (2005-2006):** Total instructional faculty: 95 full-time, 156 part-time (61% men; 39% women; 38% minorities). Full-time faculty with Ph.D. or other terminal degree: 87%. Student/faculty ratio: 17/1. Classes of fewer than 20 students: 63%; of 20 to 49 students: 36%; of 50 or more students: 0%. **Advanced Placement and International Baccalaureate credit:** AP tests may be used for: Credit only. Scores accepted: 3, 4, 5. International Baccalaureate exams may be used for: Credit only. **Freshmen returning for sophomore year:** 66%. **Graduation rates:** Four-year: 24%; five-year: 34%; six-year: 34%.

COSTS AND FINANCIAL AID
Financial aid office: (305) 474-6960. **Expenses (2006-2007):** Tuition and fees 2006-2007: $18,750; room/board: $5,912. Estimated books and supplies: $1,000; transportation: $1,968; personal expenses: $2,020. **Financial aid:** Priority filing date for institution's financial aid form: April 1. In 2005-2006, 84% of undergraduates applied for financial aid. Of those, 69% were determined to have financial need; 74% had their need fully met. Average financial aid package (proportion receiving): N/A (69%). Average amount of gift aid, such as scholarships or grants (proportion receiving): $1,910 (55%). Average amount of self-help aid, such as work study or loans (proportion receiving): $3,210 (58%). Average need-based loan (excluding PLUS or other private loans): $3,350. Among students who received aid based on merit, the average award (and the proportion receiving): $6,332 (13%). The average athletic scholarship (and the proportion receiving): $9,438 (7%). Average amount of debt of borrowers graduating in 2005: $16,000.

CAMPUS LIFE AND EXTRACURRICULAR ACTIVITIES
Campus housing available: women's dorms, men's dorms. Students who live in college-owned, operated, or affiliated housing: 10%. **Student employment:** During the 2005-2006 academic year, 6% of undergraduates worked on campus. Average per-year earnings: $3,000. **Clubs and organizations:** Number of student organizations: 14. Activities include: choral groups, literary magazine, music ensembles, student government, student newspaper, television station, yearbook. Number of fraternities: 0; sororities: 0. Average proportion of students who stay on campus on weekends: 65%. **Sports program (2005-2006):** Member of NAIA. *Men's intercollegiate varsity sports:* baseball, cross-country, golf, soccer, tennis, track and field (outdoor). *Women's intercollegiate varsity sports:* cross-country, soccer, softball, tennis, track and field (outdoor), volleyball.

SERVICES AND FACILITIES
Basic services: nonremedial tutoring, health insurance. **Remedial assistance:** reading, math, writing, study skills. **Counseling services:** career, personal, academic, psychological, religious. **For learning-disabled students:** School does not offer a structured program with separate admission and additional fees. Services include: remedial math, remedial English, remedial reading, tape recorders, untimed tests, note-taking services, learning center, extended time for tests, tutors. **Library:** Number of titles: 228,795; number of current serial subscriptions: 3,894. **Information technology resources:** Students are not required to lease or own a computer. Number of campus computers available to all students: 250. School has a wireless network. Approximate number of users that can be accommodated: 100. **Campus safety:** Security services offered: 24-hour foot-and-vehicle patrols, late-night transport/escort service, 24-hour emergency telephones, lighted pathways/sidewalks, controlled dormitory access (key, security card, etc).

TRANSFER AND INTERNATIONAL STUDENTS
Transfer students: May apply for admission for the following academic terms: Fall, Spring, Summer. Applicants need a minimum number of credits to apply. For fall 2005: Transfer applications received: 399. Transfer applicants offered admission: 321. Transfer applicants enrolled: 127. **International students:** Number of foreign undergraduates: 103 (11% of student body). Number of countries represented: 49. Minimum TOEFL score required: 525 (paper); 193 (computer). Average TOEFL score: 562 (paper).

University of Central Florida

- **Address:** 4000 Central Florida Boulevard, Orlando, FL 32816
- **Website:** http://www.ucf.edu
- **Public**
- **Enrollment:** 28,584 full-time; 9,212 part-time

KEY STATS
- ✔ **U.S News College Ranking:** fourth tier, National Universities
- ✔ **SAT Score (25th/75th percentile):** 1050-1230
- ✔ **Tuition:** 2005-2006: $3,339 in state, $16,470 out of state

Selectivity: More selective	**Room/board:** $7,400
Acceptance rate: 62%	**Average debt:** $13,095
Student/faculty ratio: 27/1	**Proportion who borrowed:** 44%

UNDERGRADUATE STUDENT BODY STATS
2005-2006 enrollment: 28,584 full-time; 9,212 part-time. Men: 45%; women: 55%. **Ethnic makeup:** African American: 9%; Asian American: 5%; Hispanic: 13%; White: 72%; International: 1%.

ADMISSIONS FACTS AND FIGURES
Phone: (407) 823-3000. **Email:** admission@mail.ucf.edu. **Website:** http://www.ucf.edu. **Application deadlines for fall 2007:** Regular decision: May 1. Early decision: Not offered. Early action: Not offered. Admission cannot be deferred. **Application fee:** $30. Common application is accepted. **To apply online, go to:** http://admissions.sdes.ucf.edu/. **Admissions requirements/recommendations:** High school units required (recommended): English: 4; Mathematics: 3; Science: 3; Foreign language: 2; Social studies: 3; Academic electives: 4; Total units: 19. **Tests:** The college uses SAT or ACT scores in admissions decisions. Either SAT or ACT required. For admission to the fall 2007 entering class, the school will accept ACT with writing. Campus visit: Recommended. Admissions interview: Recommended. Off-campus interview: Not available. **Factors that count in admissions decisions:** *Academic:* Secondary school record: Very important. Class rank: Considered. Letters of recommendation: Considered. Standardized test scores: Very important. Essay: Important. *Nonacademic:* Interview: Considered. Extracurricular activities: Considered. Talent/ability: Considered. Character/personal qualities: Considered. Alumni/ae relationship: Considered. Geographical residence: Considered. State residency: Considered. Religious affiliation/commitment: Not considered. Minority status: Not considered. Volunteer work: Considered. Work experience: Considered. **Other schools with the greatest overlap in applicants:** Florida State University; Georgia Institute of Technology; University of Florida; University of Georgia; University of South Florida. **Admissions statistics for the fall 2005 entering class:** Total applicants: 20,265. Total accepted: 12,542. Freshmen enrolled: 6,359; 7% were from out of state. Overall acceptance rate: 62%. **Size of waiting list:** 400 applicants; enrolled from waiting list: 0. **Credentials of fall 2005 freshmen:** 35% ranked in the top 10 percent of their high school class; 75% were in the top 25 percent, and 91% were in the top half. (Proportion submitting class standing: 85%.) **Average high school grade point average:** 3.5. **First-year students who submitted SAT scores:** 68%. Scores (25/75 percentile): Verbal: 520-610, Math: 530-620, Combined: 1050-1230. **First-year students submitting ACT scores:** 32%. Scores (25/75 percentile): English: N/A, Math: N/A, Composite: 22-26.

ACADEMICS
Year founded: 1963. **Academic calendar:** Semester. **Degrees offered:** certificate, associate, bachelor's, post-bachelor's certificate, master's, doctorate.

Most popular majors: 27% business, management, marketing, and related support services, 10% psychology, 9% education, 8% health professions and related clinical sciences, 6% engineering. **Major fields of study:** biological and biomedical sciences; business, management, marketing, and related support services; communication, journalism, and related programs; computer and information sciences and support services; education; engineering; engineering technologies/technicians; English language and literature/letters; foreign languages, literatures, and linguistics; health professions and related clinical sciences; history; legal professions and studies; liberal arts and sciences studies, and humanities; mathematics and statistics; philosophy and religious studies; physical sciences; psychology; public administration and social service professions; security and protective services; social sciences; visual and performing arts. **Areas of required coursework:** humanities, mathematics, English (including composition), sciences (biological or physical), history, social science. **Pre-professional programs:** pre-law, pre-medicine. **Special academic programs (% participation):** cooperative (work-study plan) program (7.2%), distance learning (72.8%), double major (2.1%), dual enrollment (.1%), honors program (6.3%), independent study (13.9%), internships (31.1%), study abroad (.2%), teacher certificate program (9.2%). **Teacher certification offered in:** early childhood, special education, elementary, vo-tech, middle/junior high, secondary. **Cooperative education programs:** art, business, computer science, education, engineering, health professions, humanities, natural science, social/behavioral science, technologies. **Reserve Officers Training Corps (ROTC):** Army ROTC: Offered on campus; Air Force ROTC: Offered on campus. **Faculty and instruction (2005-2006):** Total instructional faculty: 1,192 full-time, 445 part-time (59% men; 41% women; 20% minorities). Full-time faculty with Ph.D. or other terminal degree: 79%. Student/faculty ratio: 27/1. Classes of fewer than 20 students: 27%; of 20 to 49 students: 52%; of 50 or more students: 21%. **Advanced Placement and International Baccalaureate credit:** AP tests may be used for: Credit and/or placement. Scores accepted: 3, 4, 5. International Baccalaureate exams may be used for: Credit only. **Freshmen returning for sophomore year:** 82%. **Graduation rates:** Four-year: 30%; five-year: 52%; six-year: 57%. **Graduate study:** 21% of students pursue further study immediately upon graduation; 30% within one year; 47% within five years. Fields in which graduates pursue further study: Master of Business Administration (MBA), 22%; law, 5%; medicine, 8%; engineering, 8%; theology (or the seminary), 1%; education, 14%; arts and sciences, 34%.

COSTS AND FINANCIAL AID
Financial aid office: (407) 823-2827. **Expenses (2005-2006):** Tuition and fees 2005-2006: $3,339 in state, $16,470 out of state; room/board: $7,400. Estimated books and supplies: $860; transportation: $1,540; personal expenses: $2,136. **Financial aid:** Priority filing date for institution's financial aid form: March 1; deadline: June 30. In 2005-2006, 58% of undergraduates applied for financial aid. Of those, 51% were determined to have financial need; 36% had their need fully met. Average financial aid package (proportion receiving): $5,448 (48%). Average amount of gift aid, such as scholarships or grants (proportion receiving): $3,118 (18%). Average amount of self-help aid, such as work study or loans (proportion receiving): $4,238 (20%). Average need-based loan (excluding PLUS or other private loans): $4,106. Among students who received need-based aid, the average percentage of need met: 74%. Among students who received aid based on merit, the average award (and the proportion receiving): $1,816 (12%). The average athletic scholarship (and the proportion receiving): $4,726 (1%). Average amount of debt of borrowers graduating in 2005: $13,095. Proportion who borrowed: 44%.

CAMPUS LIFE AND EXTRACURRICULAR ACTIVITIES
Campus housing available (% using): coed dorms (27%), sorority housing (3%), fraternity housing (2%), apartment for single students (68%). Students who live in college-owned, operated, or affiliated housing: 23%. Average per-year earnings: $5,180. **Clubs and organizations:** Number of student organizations: 302. Activities include: choral groups, concert band, drama/theater, jazz band, literary magazine, marching band, music ensembles, musical theater, pep band, radio station, student government, student newspaper, student film society, symphony orchestra, television station. Number of fraternities: 24; sororities: 20. Proportion of men in fraternities: 11%; of women in sororities: 9%. **Sports program (2005-2006):** Member of NCAA I. *Men's intercollegiate varsity sports:* baseball, basketball, cross-country, football, golf, soccer, tennis. *Women's intercollegiate varsity sports:* basketball, cheerleading, crew, cross-country, golf, lightweight crew, rowing, soccer, softball, tennis, track and field (indoor), track and field (outdoor), volleyball.

SERVICES AND FACILITIES
Basic services: nonremedial tutoring, women's center, day care, health service, health insurance. **Counseling services:** minority student, career, personal, veteran student, academic, psychological, birth control. **For learning-disabled students:** School does not offer a structured program with separate admission and additional fees. Total undergraduates in learning-disabled program or receiving services: 556. Services include: reading machines, tape recorders, videotaped classes, note-taking services, readers, extended time for tests, tutors, priority registration, substitution of courses, other. **Library:** Number of titles: 1,623,277; number of current serial subscriptions: 16,530. **Information technology resources:** Students are not required to lease or own a computer. Number of campus computers available to all students: 3,147. School has a wireless network. Approximate number of users that can be accommodated: 10,000. Proportion of college-owned housing units wired for high-speed internet access: 100%. **Campus safety:** Security services offered: 24-hour foot-and-vehicle patrols, late-night transport/escort service, 24-hour emergency telephones, lighted pathways/sidewalks, controlled dormitory access (key, security card, etc).

TRANSFER AND INTERNATIONAL STUDENTS
Transfer students: May apply for admission for the following academic terms: Fall, Spring, Summer. Applicants need a minimum number of credits to apply. For fall 2005: Transfer applications received: 9,356. Transfer applicants offered admission: 5,724. Transfer applicants enrolled: 3,959. **International students:** Number of foreign undergraduates: 443 (1% of student body). Number of countries represented: 111. Minimum TOEFL score required: 550 (paper); 213 (computer).

University of Florida

- **Address:** 201 Criser Hall, Gainesville, FL 32611
- **Website:** http://www.ufl.edu
- **Public**
- **Enrollment:** 31,950 full-time; 2,662 part-time

KEY STATS
- ✔ **U.S News College Ranking:** 47, National Universities
- ✔ **SAT Score (25th/75th percentile):** 1160-1360
- ✔ **Tuition:** 2005-2006: $3,094 in state, $16,579 out of state

Selectivity: Most selective	**Room/board:** $6,260
Acceptance rate: 57%	**Average debt:** $14,830
Student/faculty ratio: 21/1	**Proportion who borrowed:** 41%

UNDERGRADUATE STUDENT BODY STATS
2005-2006 enrollment: 31,950 full-time; 2,662 part-time. Men: 46%; women: 54%. **Ethnic makeup:** African American: 9%; Asian American: 7%; Hispanic: 13%; White: 70%; International: 1%.

ADMISSIONS FACTS AND FIGURES
Phone: (352) 392-1365. **Website:** http://www.ufl.edu. **Application deadlines for fall 2007:** Regular decision: January 17. Early decision: Send application by: October 1; Decision sent by: December 1. Early action: Not offered. Admission cannot be deferred. **Application fee:** $30. Common application is accepted. **To apply online, go to:** http://admissions.ufl.edu. **Admissions requirements/recommendations:** High school units required (recommended): English: 4; Mathematics: 3; Science: 3; Foreign language: 2; Social studies: 3; History: 0; Academic electives: 0. Tests: The college uses SAT or ACT scores in admissions decisions. Either SAT or ACT required. For admission to the fall 2007 entering class, the school will accept: ACT with writing. Campus visit: Recommended. Admissions interview: Neither required nor recommended. Off-campus interview: Not available. **Factors that count in admissions decisions:** *Academic:* Secondary school record: Very important. Class rank: Considered. Letters of recommendation: Considered. Standardized test scores: Important. Essay: Important. *Nonacademic:* Interview: Not considered. Extracurricular activities: Important. Talent/ability: Important. Character/personal qualities: Important. Alumni/ae relationship: Considered. Geographical residence: Considered. State residency: Considered. Religious affiliation/commitment: Not considered. Minority status: Not considered. Volunteer work: Important. Work experience: Important. **Other schools with the greatest overlap in applicants:** Florida International University; Florida State University; University of Central Florida; University of Miami; University of South Florida. **Admissions statis-**

tics for the fall 2005 entering class: Total applicants: 21,151. Total accepted: 12,100. Freshmen enrolled: 7,241; 7% were from out of state. Accepted through early-decision or early-action plans: 31%. Overall acceptance rate: 57%. Early-decision acceptance rate: 50%. Non-early acceptance rate: 59%. **Credentials of fall 2005 freshmen:** 85% ranked in the top 10 percent of their high school class; 90% were in the top 25 percent, and 97% were in the top half. (Proportion submitting class standing: 70%.) **Average high school grade point average:** 4.0. **First-year students who submitted SAT scores:** 77%. Scores (25/75 percentile): Verbal: 570-670, Math: 590-690, Combined: 1160-1360. **First-year students submitting ACT scores:** 23%. Scores (25/75 percentile): English: N/A, Math: N/A, Composite: 25-29.

ACADEMICS

Year founded: 1853. **Academic calendar:** Semester. **Degrees offered:** bachelor's, master's, first professional, doctorate. **Most popular majors:** 19% business, management, marketing, and related support services, 13% social sciences, 10% engineering, 9% communication, journalism, and related programs, 7% health professions and related clinical sciences. **Major fields of study:** agriculture, agriculture operations, and related sciences; architecture and related services; area, ethnic, cultural, and gender studies; biological and biomedical sciences; business, management, marketing, and related support services; communication, journalism, and related programs; computer and information sciences and support services; education; engineering; engineering technologies/technicians; English language and literature/letters; family and consumer sciences/human sciences; foreign languages, literatures, and linguistics; health professions and related clinical sciences; history; mathematics and statistics; multi/interdisciplinary studies; natural resources and conservation; parks, recreation, leisure, and fitness studies; philosophy and religious studies; physical sciences; psychology; security and protective services; social sciences; visual and performing arts. **Areas of required coursework:** humanities, mathematics, English (including composition), sciences (biological or physical), social science. **Pre-professional programs:** pre-law, pre-dentistry, pre-medicine, pre-veterinary science, pre-pharmacy. **Special academic programs:** accelerated program, cooperative (work-study plan) program, cross-registration, distance learning, double major, dual enrollment, English as a Second Language (ESL), exchange student program (domestic), external degree program, honors program, independent study, internships, liberal arts/career combination, student-designed major, study abroad, teacher certificate program, weekend college, other. **Teacher certification offered in:** early childhood, special education, elementary, secondary. **Cooperative education programs:** agriculture, business, computer science, engineering, natural science. **Reserve Officers Training Corps (ROTC):** Army ROTC: Offered on campus; Navy ROTC: Offered on campus; Air Force ROTC: Offered on campus. **Faculty and instruction (2005-2006):** Total instructional faculty: 2,229 full-time, 82 part-time (70% men; 30% women; 17% minorities). Full-time faculty with Ph.D. or other terminal degree: 86%. Student/faculty ratio: 21/1. Classes of fewer than 20 students: 39%; of 20 to 49 students: 41%; of 50 or more students: 20%. **Advanced Placement and International Baccalaureate credit:** AP tests may be used for: Credit and/or placement. Scores accepted: 3, 4, 5. International Baccalaureate exams may be used for: Credit and/or placement. **Freshmen returning for sophomore year:** 94%. **Graduation rates:** Four-year: 53%; five-year: 75%; six-year: 79%.

COSTS AND FINANCIAL AID

Financial aid office: (352) 392-1271. **Expenses (2005-2006):** Tuition and fees 2005-2006: $3,094 in state, $16,579 out of state; room/board: $6,260. Estimated books and supplies: $930; transportation: $400; personal expenses: $2,820. **Financial aid:** Priority filing date for institution's financial aid form: March 15. In 2005-2006, 50% of undergraduates applied for financial aid. Of those, 38% were determined to have financial need; 33% had their need fully met. Average financial aid package (proportion receiving): $10,227 (38%). Average amount of gift aid, such as scholarships or grants (proportion receiving): $4,604 (24%). Average amount of self-help aid, such as work study or loans (proportion receiving): $3,783 (22%). Average need-based loan (excluding PLUS or other private loans): $3,707. Among students who received need-based aid, the average percentage of need met: 83%. Among students who received aid based on merit, the average award (and the proportion receiving): $4,427 (54%). The average athletic scholarship (and the proportion receiving): $9,871 (1%). Average amount of debt of borrowers graduating in 2005: $14,830. Proportion who borrowed: 41%.

CAMPUS LIFE AND EXTRACURRICULAR ACTIVITIES

Campus housing available (% using): coed dorms (41%), sorority housing (7%), fraternity housing (8%), apartments for married students (10%),

apartment for single students (17%), special housing for disabled students (0%), special housing for international students (2%), other housing options (15%). Students who live in college-owned, operated, or affiliated housing: 22%. **Student employment:** During the 2005-2006 academic year, 15% of undergraduates worked on campus. Average per-year earnings: $1,870. **Clubs and organizations:** Number of student organizations: 740. Activities include: choral groups, concert band, dance, drama/theater, jazz band, literary magazine, marching band, music ensembles, musical theater, pep band, radio station, student government, student newspaper, student film society, symphony orchestra, television station, yearbook. Number of fraternities: 35; sororities: 26. Proportion of men in fraternities: 15%; of women in sororities: 15%. **Sports program (2005-2006):** Member of NCAA I. *Men's intercollegiate varsity sports:* baseball, basketball, cross-country, football, golf, swimming and diving, tennis, track and field (indoor), track and field (outdoor). *Women's intercollegiate varsity sports:* basketball, cross-country, golf, gymnastics, soccer, softball, swimming and diving, tennis, track and field (indoor), track and field (outdoor), volleyball.

SERVICES AND FACILITIES

Basic services: nonremedial tutoring, women's center, placement service, day care, health service, health insurance. **Counseling services:** minority student, career, military, personal, veteran student, academic, older student, psychological, birth control, religious, other. **For learning-disabled students:** School does not offer a structured program with separate admission and additional fees. Total undergraduates in learning-disabled program or receiving services: 768. Services include: reading machines, tape recorders, diagnostic testing service, note-taking services, readers, extended time for tests. **Library:** Number of titles: 4,075,290; number of current serial subscriptions: 27,856. **Information technology resources:** Students are required to lease or own a computer. Number of campus computers available to all students: 1,120. School has a wireless network. Approximate number of users that can be accommodated: 14,150. Proportion of college-owned housing units wired for high-speed internet access: 98%. **Campus safety:** Security services offered: 24-hour foot-and-vehicle patrols, late-night transport/escort service, 24-hour emergency telephones, lighted pathways/sidewalks, student patrols, controlled dormitory access (key, security card, etc).

TRANSFER AND INTERNATIONAL STUDENTS

Transfer students: May apply for admission for the following academic terms: Fall, Spring, Summer. Applicants need a minimum number of credits to apply. For fall 2005: Transfer applications received: 5,456. Transfer applicants offered admission: 2,148. Transfer applicants enrolled: 1,774. **International students:** Number of foreign undergraduates: 286 (1% of student body). Number of countries represented: 133. Minimum TOEFL score required: 550 (paper); 213 (computer).

University of Miami

- ■ **Address:** PO Box 248025, Coral Gables, FL 33124
- ■ **Website:** http://www.miami.edu
- ■ **Private**
- ■ **Enrollment:** 9,766 full-time; 771 part-time

KEY STATS
✔ **U.S News College Ranking:** 54, National Universities
✔ **SAT Score (25th/75th percentile):** 1160-1360
✔ **Tuition:** 2006-2007: $31,232

Selectivity: More selective	**Room/board:** $9,278
Acceptance rate: 46%	**Average debt:** $19,140
Student/faculty ratio: 13/1	**Proportion who borrowed:** 56%

UNDERGRADUATE STUDENT BODY STATS

2005-2006 enrollment: 9,766 full-time; 771 part-time. Men: 43%; women: 57%. **Ethnic makeup:** African American: 9%; Asian American: 5%; Hispanic: 23%; White: 56%; International: 6%. **Religious preference:** Roman Catholic: 26%; Protestant: 16%; Jewish: 9%; Muslim: 1%; Hindu: 1%; Unknown: 44%; Other: 3%.

ADMISSIONS FACTS AND FIGURES

Phone: (305) 284-4323. **Email:** admission@miami.edu. **Website:** http://www.miami.edu. **Application deadlines for fall 2007:** Regular decision: February 1; decision sent by April 15. Early decision: Send application by:

November 1; Decision sent by: December 15. Early action: Send application by: November 1; Decision sent by: February 1. Admission can be deferred. **Application fee:** $65. Common application is accepted. **To apply online, go to:** http://www.miami.edu/apply/. **Admissions requirements/recommendations:** High school units required (recommended): English: (4); Mathematics: (4); Science: (3); Foreign language: (2); Social studies: (3); History: (2); Total units: (16). Tests: The college uses SAT or ACT scores in admissions decisions. Either SAT or ACT required. For admission to the fall 2007 entering class, the school will accept: ACT with writing, ACT without writing. Campus visit: Recommended. Admissions interview: Neither required nor recommended. Off-campus interview: May be arranged. **Factors that count in admissions decisions:** *Academic:* Secondary school record: Very important. Class rank: Very important. Letters of recommendation: Very important. Standardized test scores: Very important. Essay: Very important. *Nonacademic:* Interview: Not considered. Extracurricular activities: Very important. Talent/ability: Considered. Character/personal qualities: Considered. Alumni/ae relationship: Considered. Geographical residence: Considered. State residency: Not considered. Religious affiliation/commitment: Not considered. Minority status: Considered. Volunteer work: Important. Work experience: Considered. **Other schools with the greatest overlap in applicants:** Boston University; Duke University; New York University; University of Florida; University of Southern California. **Admissions statistics for the fall 2005 entering class:** Total applicants: 18,807. Total accepted: 8,679. Freshmen enrolled: 2,277; 56% were from out of state. Overall acceptance rate: 46%. Early-decision acceptance rate: 39%. Non-early acceptance rate: 47%. **Credentials of fall 2005 freshmen:** 62% ranked in the top 10 percent of their high school class; 89% were in the top 25 percent, and 98% were in the top half. (Proportion submitting class standing: 57%.) **Average high school grade point average:** 4.0. **First-year students who submitted SAT scores:** 78%. Scores (25/75 percentile): Verbal: 570-670, Math: 590-690, Combined: 1160-1360. **First-year students submitting ACT scores:** 20%. Scores (25/75 percentile): English: 25-31, Math: 24-30, Composite: 26-30.

ACADEMICS
Year founded: 1925. **Academic calendar:** Semester. **Degrees offered:** certificate, bachelor's, post-bachelor's certificate, master's, post-master's certificate, first professional, doctorate. **Most popular majors:** 22% business, management, marketing, and related support services, 10% communication, journalism, and related programs, 9% biological and biomedical sciences, 9% visual and performing arts, 8% social sciences. **Major fields of study:** architecture and related services; area, ethnic, cultural, and gender studies; biological and biomedical sciences; business, management, marketing, and related support services; communication, journalism, and related programs; computer and information sciences and support services; education; engineering; English language and literature/letters; foreign languages, literatures, and linguistics; health professions and related clinical sciences; history; legal professions and studies; liberal arts and sciences studies, and humanities; mathematics and statistics; multi/interdisciplinary studies; parks, recreation, leisure, and fitness studies; philosophy and religious studies; physical sciences; psychology; social sciences; visual and performing arts. **Areas of required coursework:** arts/fine arts, humanities, mathematics, English (including composition), sciences (biological or physical), history, social science. **Pre-professional programs:** pre-law, pre-dentistry, pre-medicine, pre-veterinary science, pre-pharmacy, other. **Special academic programs (% participation):** accelerated program (13%), distance learning, double major (28%), dual enrollment, English as a Second Language (ESL), honors program (28%), independent study (32%), internships, student-designed major, study abroad, teacher certificate program (5%), weekend college. **Teacher certification offered in:** early childhood, special education, elementary, secondary, bilingual/bicultural. **Reserve Officers Training Corps (ROTC):** Army ROTC: Offered on campus; Air Force ROTC: Offered on campus. **Faculty and instruction (2005-2006):** Total instructional faculty: 872 full-time, 403 part-time (63% men; 37% women; 24% minorities). Full-time faculty with Ph.D. or other terminal degree: 92%. Student/faculty ratio: 13/1. Classes of fewer than 20 students: 45%; of 20 to 49 students: 48%; of 50 or more students: 7%. **Advanced Placement and International Baccalaureate credit:** AP tests may be used for: Credit only. Scores accepted: 3, 4, 5. International Baccalaureate exams may be used for: Credit only. **Freshmen returning for sophomore year:** 88%. **Graduation rates:** Four-year: 56%; five-year: 68%; six-year: 71%. **Graduate study:** 37% of students pursue further study immediately upon graduation; 60% within five years. Fields in which graduates pursue further study: Master of Business Administration (MBA), 12%; law, 19%; medicine, 17%; arts and sciences, 28%.

COSTS AND FINANCIAL AID
Financial aid office: (305) 284-5212. **Expenses (2006-2007):** Tuition and fees 2006-2007: $31,232; room/board: $9,278. Estimated books and supplies: $870; transportation: $1,380; personal expenses: $1,250. **Financial aid:** Priority filing date for institution's financial aid form: February 1. In 2005-2006, 60% of undergraduates applied for financial aid. Of those, 52% were determined to have financial need; 30% had their need fully met. Average financial aid package (proportion receiving): $23,709 (52%). Average amount of gift aid, such as scholarships or grants (proportion receiving): $17,257 (51%). Average amount of self-help aid, such as work study or loans (proportion receiving): $6,259 (43%). Average need-based loan (excluding PLUS or other private loans): $5,104. Among students who received need-based aid, the average percentage of need met: 78%. Among students who received aid based on merit, the average award (and the proportion receiving): $14,784 (22%). The average athletic scholarship (and the proportion receiving): $24,072 (2%). Average amount of debt of borrowers graduating in 2005: $19,140. Proportion who borrowed: 56%.

CAMPUS LIFE AND EXTRACURRICULAR ACTIVITIES
Campus housing available (% using): coed dorms (86%), fraternity housing (3%), apartment for single students (10%), special housing for disabled students (1%). Students who live in college-owned, operated, or affiliated housing: 41%. **Student employment:** During the 2005-2006 academic year, 15% of undergraduates worked on campus. Average per-year earnings: $2,500. **Clubs and organizations:** Number of student organizations: 260. Activities include: choral groups, concert band, dance, drama/theater, jazz band, literary magazine, marching band, music ensembles, musical theater, opera, pep band, radio station, student government, student newspaper, student film society, symphony orchestra, television station, yearbook. Number of fraternities: 15; sororities: 13. Proportion of men in fraternities: 12%; of women in sororities: 14%. Average proportion of students who stay on campus on weekends: 75%. **Sports program (2005-2006):** Member of NCAA I. *Men's intercollegiate varsity sports:* baseball, basketball, cross-country, football, swimming and diving, tennis, track and field (indoor), track and field (outdoor). *Women's intercollegiate varsity sports:* basketball, cross-country, golf, soccer, swimming and diving, tennis, track and field (indoor), track and field (outdoor), volleyball, rowing.

SERVICES AND FACILITIES
Basic services: nonremedial tutoring, placement service, health service, health insurance. **Remedial assistance:** reading, math, writing, study skills. **Counseling services:** minority student, career, military, personal, academic, older student, psychological, religious. **For learning-disabled students:** School does not offer a structured program with separate admission and additional fees. Services include: tape recorders, learning center, readers, extended time for tests, tutors. **Library:** Number of titles: 2,571,045; number of current serial subscriptions: 38,432. **Information technology resources:** Students are not required to lease or own a computer. Number of campus computers available to all students: 1,800. School has a wireless network. Approximate number of users that can be accommodated: 10,000. Proportion of college-owned housing units wired for high-speed internet access: 100%. **Campus safety:** Security services offered: 24-hour foot-and-vehicle patrols, late-night transport/escort service, 24-hour emergency telephones, lighted pathways/sidewalks, controlled dormitory access (key, security card, etc).

TRANSFER AND INTERNATIONAL STUDENTS
Transfer students: May apply for admission for the following academic terms: Fall, Spring, Summer. Applicants do not need a minimum number of credits to apply. For fall 2005: Transfer applications received: 2,905. Transfer applicants offered admission: 1,324. Transfer applicants enrolled: 651. **International students:** Number of foreign undergraduates: 560 (6% of student body). Number of countries represented: 114. Minimum TOEFL score required: 550 (paper); 213 (computer).

University of North Florida

- **Address:** 4567 St. Johns Bluff Road S, Jacksonville, FL 32224-2645
- **Website:** http://www.unf.edu
- **Public**
- **Enrollment:** 9,540 full-time; 3,870 part-time

KEY STATS
- ✔ **U.S News College Ranking:** 47, Universities–Master's (South)
- ✔ **SAT Score (25th/75th percentile):** 1010-1210
- ✔ **Tuition:** 2006-2007: $3,352 in state, $15,105 out of state

Selectivity: Selective	**Room/board:** $6,773
Acceptance rate: 62%	**Average debt:** $16,707
Student/faculty ratio: 22/1	**Proportion who borrowed:** 46%

UNDERGRADUATE STUDENT BODY STATS
2005-2006 enrollment: 9,540 full-time; 3,870 part-time. Men: 42%; women: 58%. **Ethnic makeup:** African American: 10%; Asian American: 5%; Hispanic: 6%; White: 77%; International: 1%. **Religious preference:** Roman Catholic: 2%; Protestant: 2%; No preference: 95%; Other: 1%.

ADMISSIONS FACTS AND FIGURES
Phone: (904) 620-2624. **Email:** admissions@unf.edu. **Website:** http://www.unf.edu. **Application deadlines for fall 2007:** Regular decision: July 2. Early decision: Not offered. Early action: Send application by: November 15; Decision sent by: December 2. Admission can be deferred. **Application fee:** $30. Common application is accepted. **To apply online, go to:** http://csdweb.unf.edu/access/htdocs/onlineapp.htm. **Admissions requirements/recommendations:** High school units required (recommended): English: 4; Mathematics: 3; Science: 3; Foreign language: 2; Social studies: 3; Academic electives: 4; Total units: 19. Tests: The college uses SAT or ACT scores in admissions decisions. Either SAT or ACT required. For admission to the fall 2007 entering class, the school will accept: ACT with writing. Campus visit: Recommended. Admissions interview: Recommended. Off-campus interview: Not available. **Factors that count in admissions decisions:** *Academic:* Secondary school record: Very important. Class rank: Considered. Letters of recommendation: Considered. Standardized test scores: Very important. Essay: Considered. *Nonacademic:* Interview: Not considered. Extracurricular activities: Considered. Talent/ability: Considered. Character/personal qualities: Not considered. Alumni/ae relationship: Not considered. Geographical residence: Not considered. State residency: Not considered. Religious affiliation/commitment: Not considered. Minority status: Not considered. Volunteer work: Considered. Work experience: Considered. **Other schools with the greatest overlap in applicants:** Florida Atlantic University; Florida State University; University of Central Florida; University of Florida; University of South Florida. **Admissions statistics for the fall 2005 entering class:** Total applicants: 9,147. Total accepted: 5,668. Freshmen enrolled: 2,388; 3% were from out of state. Accepted through early-decision or early-action plans: 7%. Overall acceptance rate: 62%. Non-early acceptance rate: 60%. **Credentials of fall 2005 freshmen:** 23% ranked in the top 10 percent of their high school class; 55% were in the top 25 percent, and 87% were in the top half. (Proportion submitting class standing: 72%.) **Average high school grade point average:** 3.5. **First-year students who submitted SAT scores:** 52%. Scores (25/75 percentile): Verbal: 510-610, Math: 500-600, Combined: 1010-1210. **First-year students submitting ACT scores:** 48%. Scores (25/75 percentile): English: N/A, Math: N/A, Composite: 20-24.

ACADEMICS
Year founded: 1965. **Academic calendar:** Semester. **Degrees offered:** associate, transfer-associate, terminal-associate, bachelor's, post-bachelor's certificate, master's, post-master's certificate, doctorate. **Most popular majors:** 27% business, management, marketing, and related support services; 11% health professions and related clinical sciences; 10% education, 9% communication, journalism, and related programs, 7% security and protective services. **Major fields of study:** biological and biomedical sciences; business, management, marketing, and related support services; communication, journalism, and related programs; computer and information sciences and support services; education; engineering; engineering technologies/technicians; English language and literature/letters; foreign languages, literatures, and linguistics; health professions and related clinical sciences; history; liberal arts and sciences studies, and humanities; mathematics and statistics; multi/interdisciplinary studies; philosophy and religious studies; physical sciences; psychology; security and protective services; social sciences; visual and performing arts. **Areas of required coursework:** arts/fine arts, humanities, computer literacy, mathematics, English (including composition), philosophy, foreign languages, sciences (biological or physical), history, social science, other. **Pre-professional programs:** pre-law, pre-dentistry, pre-medicine. **Special academic programs (% participation):** accelerated program (35%), cooperative (work-study plan) program (3%), distance learning (10%), double major (6%), dual enrollment (1%), English as a Second Language (ESL), honors program (6%), independent study (20%), internships (39%), student-designed major, study abroad (6%), teacher certificate program, weekend college. **Teacher certification offered in:** special education, elementary, middle/junior high, secondary. **Cooperative education programs:** business, computer science, engineering, health professions, natural science, social/behavioral science. **Reserve Officers Training Corps (ROTC):** Navy ROTC: Offered at cooperating institution (Jacksonville University). **Faculty and instruction (2005-2006):** Total instructional faculty: 448 full-time, 252 part-time (54% men; 46% women; 14% minorities). Full-time faculty with Ph.D. or other terminal degree: 93%. Student/faculty ratio: 22/1. Classes of fewer than 20 students: 23%; of 20 to 49 students: 65%; of 50 or more students: 12%. **Advanced Placement and International Baccalaureate credit:** AP tests may be used for: Credit and/or placement. Scores accepted: 3, 4, 5. International Baccalaureate exams may be used for: Credit and/or placement. **Freshmen returning for sophomore year:** 77%. **Graduation rates:** Four-year: 25%; five-year: 44%; six-year: 47%.

COSTS AND FINANCIAL AID
Financial aid office: (904) 620-2604. **Expenses (2006-2007):** Tuition and fees 2006-2007: $3,352 in state, $15,105 out of state; room/board: $6,773. Estimated books and supplies: $800; transportation: $2,522; personal expenses: $961. **Financial aid:** Priority filing date for institution's financial aid form: April 1. In 2005-2006, 52% of undergraduates applied for financial aid. Of those, 15% were determined to have financial need; 28% had their need fully met. Average financial aid package (proportion receiving): $1,485 (15%). Average amount of gift aid, such as scholarships or grants (proportion receiving): $1,052 (9%). Average amount of self-help aid, such as work study or loans (proportion receiving): $1,773 (9%). Average need-based loan (excluding PLUS or other private loans): $1,561. Among students who received need-based aid, the average percentage of need met: 88%. Among students who received aid based on merit, the average award (and the proportion receiving): $1,297 (9%). The average athletic scholarship (and the proportion receiving): $2,578 (2%). Average amount of debt of borrowers graduating in 2005: $16,707. Proportion who borrowed: 46%.

CAMPUS LIFE AND EXTRACURRICULAR ACTIVITIES
Campus housing available: coed dorms, sorority housing, fraternity housing, apartments for married students, apartment for single students, special housing for disabled students, other housing options. Students who live in college-owned, operated, or affiliated housing: 18%. **Student employment:** During the 2005-2006 academic year, 5% of undergraduates worked on campus. Average per-year earnings: $7,274. **Clubs and organizations:** Number of student organizations: 172. Activities include: choral groups, concert band, dance, drama/theater, jazz band, literary magazine, music ensembles, pep band, radio station, student government, student newspaper, television station. Number of fraternities: 8; sororities: 7. Proportion of men in fraternities: 8%; of women in sororities: 6%. Average proportion of students who stay on campus on weekends: 60%. **Sports program (2005-2006):** Member of NCAA II. *Men's intercollegiate varsity sports:* baseball, basketball, cross-country, golf, soccer, tennis, track and field (indoor), track and field (outdoor). *Women's intercollegiate varsity sports:* basketball, cross-country, soccer, softball, swimming and diving, tennis, track and field (indoor), track and field (outdoor), volleyball.

SERVICES AND FACILITIES
Basic services: nonremedial tutoring, women's center, day care, health service, health insurance. **Remedial assistance:** reading, math, writing, study skills, other. **Counseling services:** minority student, career, personal, psychological, birth control, religious. **For learning-disabled students:** School does not offer a structured program with separate admission and additional fees. Total undergraduates in learning-disabled program or receiving services: 177. Services include: reading machines, tape recorders, untimed tests, note-taking services, oral tests, learning center, readers, extended time for tests, tutors, other. **Library:** Number of titles: 777,860; number of current serial subscriptions: 3,089. **Information technology resources:** Students are not required to lease or own a computer. Number of campus computers available to all students: 1,406. School has a wireless network. Approximate number of users that can be accommodated: 1,500. Proportion of college-

owned housing units wired for high-speed internet access: 100%. **Campus safety:** Security services offered: 24-hour foot-and-vehicle patrols, 24-hour emergency telephones, lighted pathways/sidewalks, controlled dormitory access (key, security card, etc).

TRANSFER AND INTERNATIONAL STUDENTS

Transfer students: May apply for admission for the following academic terms: Fall, Spring, Summer. Applicants need a minimum number of credits to apply. For fall 2005: Transfer applications received: 3,385. Transfer applicants offered admission: 2,107. Transfer applicants enrolled: 959. **International students:** Number of foreign undergraduates: 162 (1% of student body). Number of countries represented: 54. Minimum TOEFL score required: 500 (paper); 173 (computer). Average TOEFL score: 617 (paper).

University of South Florida

- **Address:** 4202 E. Fowler Avenue, Tampa, FL 33620-9951
- **Website:** http://www.usf.edu
- **Public**
- **Enrollment:** 23,945 full-time; 9,760 part-time

KEY STATS

✔ **U.S News College Ranking:** third tier, National Universities
✔ **SAT Score (25th/75th percentile):** 1030-1210
✔ **Tuition:** 2005-2006: $3,384 in state, $16,150 out of state
  Selectivity: More selective   **Room/board:** $6,900
  Acceptance rate: 58%   **Average debt:** $17,546
  Student/faculty ratio: 18/1   **Proportion who borrowed:** 53%

UNDERGRADUATE STUDENT BODY STATS

2005-2006 enrollment: 23,945 full-time; 9,760 part-time. Men: 41%; women: 59%. **Ethnic makeup:** African American: 13%; Asian American: 6%; Hispanic: 11%; White: 68%; International: 3%.

ADMISSIONS FACTS AND FIGURES

Phone: (813) 974-3350. **Email:** admission@admin.usf.edu. **Website:** http://www.usf.edu. **Application deadlines for fall 2007:** Regular decision: April 15; decision sent by April 15. Early decision: Not offered. Early action: Not offered. Admission cannot be deferred. **Application fee:** $30. Common application is accepted. **To apply online, go to:** http://usfweb.usf.edu/enroll/admiss/admiss.htm. **Admissions requirements/recommendations:** High school units required (recommended): English: 4; Mathematics: 3; Science: 3; Foreign language: 2; Social studies: 3; History: 0; Academic electives: 3; Total units: 19. Tests: The college uses SAT or ACT scores in admissions decisions. Either SAT or ACT required. For admission to the fall 2007 entering class, the school will accept: ACT with writing, ACT without writing. Campus visit: Recommended. Admissions interview: Neither required nor recommended. Off-campus interview: Not available. **Factors that count in admissions decisions:** *Academic:* Secondary school record: Very important. Class rank: Important. Letters of recommendation: Considered. Standardized test scores: Very important. Essay: Considered. *Nonacademic:* Interview: Not considered. Extracurricular activities: Considered. Talent/ability: Important. Character/personal qualities: Considered. Alumni/ae relationship: Not considered. Geographical residence: Considered. State residency: Considered. Religious affiliation/commitment: Not considered. Minority status: Not considered. Volunteer work: Considered. Work experience: Considered. **Other schools with the greatest overlap in applicants:** Florida State University; University of Central Florida; University of Florida. **Admissions statistics for the fall 2005 entering class:** Total applicants: 18,307. Total accepted: 10,664. Freshmen enrolled: 4,311; 6% were from out of state. Overall acceptance rate: 58%. **Credentials of fall 2005 freshmen:** 23% ranked in the top 10 percent of their high school class; 59% were in the top 25 percent, and 90% were in the top half. (Proportion submitting class standing: 91%.) **Average high school grade point average:** 3.5. **First-year students who submitted SAT scores:** 72%. Scores (25/75 percentile): Verbal: 510-600, Math: 520-610, Combined: 1030-1210. **First-year students submitting ACT scores:** 28%. Scores (25/75 percentile): English: 20-26, Math: 21-26, Composite: 21-26.

ACADEMICS

Year founded: 1956. **Academic calendar:** Semester. **Degrees offered:** certificate, diploma, associate, bachelor's, post-bachelor's certificate, master's, first

professional, doctorate. **Most popular majors:** 8% elementary education and teaching, 8% psychology, 7% criminal justice/safety studies, 5% management information systems, 4% business administration and management. **Major fields of study:** area, ethnic, cultural, and gender studies; biological and biomedical sciences; business, management, marketing, and related support services; communication, journalism, and related programs; computer and information sciences and support services; education; engineering; English language and literature/letters; foreign languages, literatures, and linguistics; health professions and related clinical sciences; history; liberal arts and sciences studies, and humanities; mathematics and statistics; multi/interdisciplinary studies; natural resources and conservation; philosophy and religious studies; physical sciences; psychology; public administration and social service professions; social sciences; visual and performing arts. **Areas of required coursework:** arts/fine arts, humanities, mathematics, English (including composition), sciences (biological or physical), history, social science, other. **Pre-professional programs:** pre-medicine. **Special academic programs:** accelerated program, cooperative (work-study plan) program, cross-registration, distance learning, double major, dual enrollment, exchange student program (domestic), honors program, internships, study abroad, teacher certificate program, weekend college. **Teacher certification offered in:** early childhood, special education, elementary, vo-tech, middle/junior high, adult education, secondary. **Cooperative education programs:** art, business, computer science, health professions, technologies. **Reserve Officers Training Corps (ROTC):** Army ROTC: Offered on campus; Navy ROTC: Offered on campus; Air Force ROTC: Offered on campus. **Faculty and instruction (2005-2006):** Total instructional faculty: 1,692 full-time, 241 part-time (61% men; 39% women; 22% minorities). Full-time faculty with Ph.D. or other terminal degree: 89%. Student/faculty ratio: 18/1. Classes of fewer than 20 students: 30%; of 20 to 49 students: 58%; of 50 or more students: 12%. **Advanced Placement and International Baccalaureate credit:** AP tests may be used for: Credit only. Scores accepted: 3, 4, 5. International Baccalaureate exams may be used for: Credit and/or placement. **Freshmen returning for sophomore year:** 81%. **Graduation rates:** Four-year: 22%; five-year: 40%; six-year: 48%. **Graduate study:** 20% of students pursue further study immediately upon graduation.

COSTS AND FINANCIAL AID

Financial aid office: (813) 974-4700. **Expenses (2005-2006):** Tuition and fees 2005-2006: $3,384 in state, $16,150 out of state; room/board: $6,900. Estimated books and supplies: $800 personal expenses: $3,670. **Financial aid:** Priority filing date for institution's financial aid form: March 1. In 2005-2006, 59% of undergraduates applied for financial aid. Of those, 47% were determined to have financial need; 10% had their need fully met. Average financial aid package (proportion receiving): $9,237 (46%). Average amount of gift aid, such as scholarships or grants (proportion receiving): $4,324 (27%). Average amount of self-help aid, such as work study or loans (proportion receiving): $4,676 (21%). Average need-based loan (excluding PLUS or other private loans): $4,340. Among students who received need-based aid, the average percentage of need met: 25%. Among students who received aid based on merit, the average award (and the proportion receiving): $2,503 (8%). The average athletic scholarship (and the proportion receiving): $4,082 (2%). Average amount of debt of borrowers graduating in 2005: $17,546. Proportion who borrowed: 53%.

CAMPUS LIFE AND EXTRACURRICULAR ACTIVITIES

Campus housing available (% using): coed dorms (43%), women's dorms (8%), sorority housing (4%), fraternity housing (4%), apartments for married students (1%), apartment for single students (40%), special housing for disabled students. Students who live in college-owned, operated, or affiliated housing: 13%. **Student employment:** During the 2005-2006 academic year, 15% of undergraduates worked on campus. **Clubs and organizations:** Number of student organizations: 225. Activities include: choral groups, concert band, dance, drama/theater, jazz band, literary magazine, marching band, music ensembles, musical theater, opera, pep band, radio station, student government, student newspaper, student film society, symphony orchestra, television station. Number of fraternities: 18; sororities: 14. Proportion of men in fraternities: 8%; of women in sororities: 6%. Average proportion of students who stay on campus on weekends: 15%. **Sports program (2005-2006):** Member of NCAA I. *Men's intercollegiate varsity sports:* baseball, basketball, cross-country, football, golf, soccer, tennis, track and field (outdoor). *Women's intercollegiate varsity sports:* basketball, cross-country, golf, sailing, soccer, softball, tennis, track and field (indoor), track and field (outdoor), volleyball.

SERVICES AND FACILITIES

Basic services: nonremedial tutoring, placement service, day care, health service, health insurance. **Remedial assistance:** reading, math, writing, study skills. **Counseling services:** minority student, career, military, personal, veteran student, academic, older student, psychological. **For learning-disabled students:** School does not offer a structured program with separate admission and additional fees. Services include: reading machines, tape recorders, note-taking services, oral tests, readers, extended time for tests, other. **Library:** Number of titles: 2,133,767; number of current serial subscriptions: 20,440. **Information technology resources:** Students are not required to lease or own a computer. Number of campus computers available to all students: 550. School has a wireless network. Approximate number of users that can be accommodated: 1,500. Proportion of college-owned housing units wired for high-speed internet access: 100%. **Campus safety:** Security services offered: 24-hour foot-and-vehicle patrols, late-night transport/escort service, 24-hour emergency telephones, lighted pathways/sidewalks, student patrols, controlled dormitory access (key, security card, etc).

TRANSFER AND INTERNATIONAL STUDENTS

Transfer students: May apply for admission for the following academic terms: Fall, Spring, Summer. Applicants do not need a minimum number of credits to apply. For fall 2005: Transfer applications received: 8,853. Transfer applicants offered admission: 6,851. Transfer applicants enrolled: 4,009. **International students:** Number of foreign undergraduates: 867 (3% of student body). Number of countries represented: 124. Minimum TOEFL score required: 550 (paper); 213 (computer).

University of Tampa

■ **Address:** 401 W. Kennedy Boulevard, Tampa, FL 33606-1490
■ **Website:** http://www.ut.edu
■ **Private**
■ **Enrollment:** 4,169 full-time; 467 part-time

KEY STATS

✔ **U.S News College Ranking:** 36, Universities–Master's (South)
✔ **SAT Score (25th/75th percentile):** 990-1170
✔ **Tuition:** 2006-2007: $19,628

Selectivity: Selective	**Room/board:** $7,254
Acceptance rate: 50%	**Average debt:** $23,051
Student/faculty ratio: 15/1	**Proportion who borrowed:** 71%

UNDERGRADUATE STUDENT BODY STATS

2005-2006 enrollment: 4,169 full-time; 467 part-time. Men: 38%; women: 62%. **Ethnic makeup:** African American: 6%; Asian American: 2%; Hispanic: 9%; White: 77%; International: 5%.

ADMISSIONS FACTS AND FIGURES

Phone: (888) 646-2738. **Email:** admissions@ut.edu. **Website:** http://www.ut.edu. **Application deadlines for fall 2007:** Regular decision: Rolling. Early decision: Not offered. Early action: Not offered. Admission can be deferred. **Application fee:** $40. Common application is accepted. **To apply online, go to:** http://www.ut.edu/direct.cfm?loc_type=app. **Admissions requirements/recommendations:** High school units required (recommended): English: 4; Mathematics: 3; Science: 3; Foreign language: 2; Social studies: 3; Academic electives: 3; Total units: 18. Tests: The college uses SAT or ACT scores in admissions decisions. Either SAT or ACT required. For admission to the fall 2007 entering class, the school will accept: ACT without writing. Campus visit: Recommended. Admissions interview: Recommended. Off-campus interview: May be arranged. **Factors that count in admissions decisions:** *Academic:* Secondary school record: Very important. Class rank: Considered. Letters of recommendation: Very important. Standardized test scores: Important. Essay: Important. *Nonacademic:* Interview: Considered. Extracurricular activities: Considered. Talent/ability: Considered. Character/personal qualities: Considered. Alumni/ae relationship: Considered. Geographical residence: Considered. State residency: Considered. Religious affiliation/commitment: Not considered. Minority status: Not considered. Volunteer work: Considered. Work experience: Considered. **Admissions statistics for the fall 2005 entering class:** Total applicants: 6,365. Total accepted: 3,202. Freshmen enrolled: 1,010; 68% were from out of state. Overall acceptance rate: 50%. **Credentials of fall 2005 freshmen:** 20% ranked in the top 10 percent of their high school class; 50%

were in the top 25 percent, and 84% were in the top half. (Proportion submitting class standing: 62%.) **Average high school grade point average:** 3.3. **First-year students who submitted SAT scores:** 86%. Scores (25/75 percentile): Verbal: 490-580, Math: 500-590, Combined: 990-1170. **First-year students submitting ACT scores:** 35%. Scores (25/75 percentile): English: 19-25, Math: 19-25, Composite: 20-25.

ACADEMICS

Year founded: 1931. **Academic calendar:** Semester. **Degrees offered:** certificate, associate, bachelor's, master's. **Most popular majors:** 28% business administration and management, 15% social sciences, 11% communication and media studies, 7% biology/biological sciences, 7% psychology. **Major fields of study:** biological and biomedical sciences; business, management, marketing, and related support services; communication, journalism, and related programs; computer and information sciences and support services; education; English language and literature/letters; foreign languages, literatures, and linguistics; health professions and related clinical sciences; history; liberal arts and sciences studies, and humanities; mathematics and statistics; multi/interdisciplinary studies; natural resources and conservation; physical sciences; psychology; social sciences; visual and performing arts. **Areas of required coursework:** arts/fine arts, humanities, computer literacy, mathematics, English (including composition), sciences (biological or physical), social science. **Pre-professional programs:** pre-law, pre-dentistry, pre-medicine, pre-veterinary science. **Special academic programs (% participation):** double major (3%), honors program (20%), independent study (37%), internships (30%), study abroad (4%), teacher certificate program (4%). **Teacher certification offered in:** early childhood, elementary, middle/junior high, secondary. **Reserve Officers Training Corps (ROTC):** Army ROTC: Offered on campus; Navy ROTC: Offered at cooperating institution (University of South Florida); Air Force ROTC: Offered at cooperating institution (University of South Florida). **Faculty and instruction (2005-2006):** Total instructional faculty: 208 full-time, 217 part-time (51% men; 49% women; 8% minorities). Full-time faculty with Ph.D. or other terminal degree: 94%. Student/faculty ratio: 15/1. Classes of fewer than 20 students: 41%; of 20 to 49 students: 58%; of 50 or more students: 1%. **Advanced Placement and International Baccalaureate credit:** AP tests may be used for: Credit only. Scores accepted: 3, 4, 5. International Baccalaureate exams may be used for: Credit only. **Freshmen returning for sophomore year:** 74%. **Graduation rates:** Four-year: 45%; five-year: 54%; six-year: 52%.

COSTS AND FINANCIAL AID

Financial aid office: (813) 253-6219. **Expenses (2006-2007):** Tuition and fees 2006-2007: $19,628; room/board: $7,254. Estimated books and supplies: $904; transportation: $691; personal expenses: $1,294. **Financial aid:** Priority filing date for institution's financial aid form: March 1. In 2005-2006, 66% of undergraduates applied for financial aid. Of those, 55% were determined to have financial need; 21% had their need fully met. Average financial aid package (proportion receiving): $14,640 (55%). Average amount of gift aid, such as scholarships or grants (proportion receiving): $6,758 (51%). Average amount of self-help aid, such as work study or loans (proportion receiving): $5,485 (45%). Average need-based loan (excluding PLUS or other private loans): $5,036. Among students who received need-based aid, the average percentage of need met: 81%. Among students who received aid based on merit, the average award (and the proportion receiving): $6,037 (9%). The average athletic scholarship (and the proportion receiving): $5,125 (0%). Average amount of debt of borrowers graduating in 2005: $23,051. Proportion who borrowed: 71%.

CAMPUS LIFE AND EXTRACURRICULAR ACTIVITIES

Campus housing available (% using): coed dorms (100%), special housing for disabled students (0%). Students who live in college-owned, operated, or affiliated housing: 58%. **Student employment:** During the 2005-2006 academic year, 22% of undergraduates worked on campus. Average per-year earnings: $2,000. **Clubs and organizations:** Number of student organizations: 120. Activities include: choral groups, concert band, dance, drama/theater, jazz band, literary magazine, music ensembles, musical theater, pep band, radio station, student government, student newspaper, student film society, symphony orchestra, television station, yearbook. Number of fraternities: 8; sororities: 10. Proportion of men in fraternities: 19%; of women in sororities: 19%. Average proportion of students who stay on campus on weekends: 90%. **Sports program (2005-2006):** Member of NCAA II. *Men's intercollegiate varsity sports:* baseball, basketball, cheerleading, cross-country, golf, soccer, swimming and diving, track and field (outdoor). *Women's intercollegiate varsity sports:* basketball, cheerleading, crew, cross-country, soccer, softball, swimming and diving, tennis, track and field (outdoor), volleyball.

SERVICES AND FACILITIES

Basic services: nonremedial tutoring, placement service, health service, health insurance. **Remedial assistance:** reading, math, study skills. **Counseling services:** career, personal, academic. **For learning-disabled students:** School does not offer a structured program with separate admission and additional fees. Total undergraduates in learning-disabled program or receiving services: 104. Services include: remedial math, remedial English, note-taking services, learning center, extended time for tests, tutors. **Library:** Number of titles: 288,857; number of current serial subscriptions: 24,122. **Information technology resources:** Students are not required to lease or own a computer. Number of campus computers available to all students: 472. School has a wireless network. Approximate number of users that can be accommodated: 600. Proportion of college-owned housing units wired for high-speed internet access: 100%. **Campus safety:** Security services offered: 24-hour foot-and-vehicle patrols, late-night transport/escort service, 24-hour emergency telephones, lighted pathways/sidewalks, student patrols, controlled dormitory access (key, security card, etc).

TRANSFER AND INTERNATIONAL STUDENTS

Transfer students: May apply for admission for the following academic terms: Fall, Spring, Summer. Applicants need a minimum number of credits to apply. For fall 2005: Transfer applications received: 2,026. Transfer applicants offered admission: 885. Transfer applicants enrolled: 409. **International students:** Number of foreign undergraduates: 240 (5% of student body). Number of countries represented: 87. Minimum TOEFL score required: 550 (paper); 213 (computer). Average TOEFL score: 630 (paper).

University of West Florida

- **Address:** 11000 University Parkway, Pensacola, FL 32514-5750
- **Website:** http://uwf.edu
- **Public**
- **Enrollment:** 5,771 full-time; 2,397 part-time

KEY STATS

- ✔ **U.S News College Ranking:** 56, Universities–Master's (South)
- ✔ **ACT Score (25th/75th percentile):** 21-26
- ✔ **Tuition:** 2006-2007: $3,311 in state, $15,818 out of state

Selectivity: Selective	**Room/board:** $6,600
Acceptance rate: 68%	**Average debt:** N/A
Student/faculty ratio: 19/1	**Proportion who borrowed:** N/A

UNDERGRADUATE STUDENT BODY STATS

2005-2006 enrollment: 5,771 full-time; 2,397 part-time. Men: 41%; women: 59%. **Ethnic makeup:** African American: 9%; American-Indian: 1%; Asian American: 4%; Hispanic: 5%; White: 80%; International: 1%.

ADMISSIONS FACTS AND FIGURES

Phone: (850) 474-2230. **Email:** admissions@uwf.edu. **Website:** http://uwf.edu. **Application deadlines for fall 2007:** Regular decision: June 30. Early decision: Not offered. Early action: Not offered. Admission can be deferred. **Application fee:** $30. Common application is not accepted. **Admissions requirements/recommendations:** High school units required (recommended): English: 4; Mathematics: 3; Science: 3; Foreign language: 2; Social studies: 3; Academic electives: 4; Total units: 19. **Tests:** The college uses SAT or ACT scores in admissions decisions. Either SAT or ACT required. For admission to the fall 2007 entering class, the school will accept: ACT with writing. Campus visit: Recommended. **Factors that count in admissions decisions:** *Academic:* Secondary school record: Very important. Class rank: Considered. Letters of recommendation: Considered. Standardized test scores: Very important. Essay: Considered. *Nonacademic:* Interview: Considered. Extracurricular activities: Considered. Talent/ability: Very important. Character/personal qualities: Considered. Alumni/ae relationship: Considered. Geographical residence: Considered. State residency: Considered. Religious affiliation/commitment: Not considered. Minority status: Considered. Volunteer work: Considered. Work experience: Considered. **Other schools with the greatest overlap in applicants:** Faulkner University; Florida State University; Troy State University–Dothan; Troy State University–Montgomery; University of South Alabama. **Admissions statistics for the fall 2005 entering class:** Total applicants: 3,401. Total accepted: 2,316. Freshmen enrolled: 924; 14% were from out of state. Overall acceptance rate: 68%. **Average high school grade point average:** 3.6.

First-year students who submitted SAT scores: 42%. Scores (25/75 percentile): Verbal: 500-600, Math: 490-600, Combined: 990-1200. **First-year students submitting ACT scores:** 58%. Scores (25/75 percentile): English: 20-26, Math: 19-25, Composite: 21-26.

ACADEMICS

Year founded: 1963. **Academic calendar:** Semester. **Degrees offered:** diploma, associate, bachelor's, master's, doctorate. **Most popular majors:** 18% business/commerce, 11% education, 10% mass communication/media studies, 9% psychology, 7% criminal justice/safety studies. **Major fields of study:** biological and biomedical sciences; business, management, marketing, and related support services; communication, journalism, and related programs; computer and information sciences and support services; education; engineering; English language and literature/letters; health professions and related clinical sciences; history; legal professions and studies; liberal arts and sciences studies, and humanities; mathematics and statistics; multi/interdisciplinary studies; natural resources and conservation; parks, recreation, leisure, and fitness studies; philosophy and religious studies; physical sciences; psychology; public administration and social service professions; security and protective services; social sciences; visual and performing arts. **Areas of required coursework:** mathematics, English (including composition). **Pre-professional programs:** pre-law, pre-dentistry, other. **Special academic programs:** cooperative (work-study plan) program, distance learning, double major, dual enrollment, exchange student program (domestic), honors program, independent study, internships, study abroad, teacher certificate program, other. **Teacher certification offered in:** early childhood, special education, elementary, middle/junior high, secondary. **Reserve Officers Training Corps (ROTC):** Army ROTC: Offered on campus; Air Force ROTC: Offered on campus. **Faculty and instruction (2005-2006):** Total instructional faculty: 308 full-time, 219 part-time (56% men; 44% women; 13% minorities). Full-time faculty with Ph.D. or other terminal degree: 85%. Student/faculty ratio: 19/1. Classes of fewer than 20 students: 37%; of 20 to 49 students: 56%; of 50 or more students: 8%. **Advanced Placement and International Baccalaureate credit:** AP tests may be used for: Credit only. **Freshmen returning for sophomore year:** 73%. **Graduation rates:** Four-year: 21%; five-year: 37%; six-year: 40%.

COSTS AND FINANCIAL AID

Financial aid office: (850) 474-3127. **Expenses (2005-2006):** Tuition and fees 2005-2006: $3,198 in state, $15,705 out of state; room/board: $6,600. Estimated books and supplies: $1,000; transportation: $850; personal expenses: $2,000.

CAMPUS LIFE AND EXTRACURRICULAR ACTIVITIES

Campus housing available: coed dorms, sorority housing, fraternity housing, special housing for disabled students, other housing options. Students who live in college-owned, operated, or affiliated housing: 16%. **Clubs and organizations:** Number of student organizations: 114. Activities include: choral groups, concert band, dance, drama/theater, jazz band, music ensembles, musical theater, radio station, student government, student newspaper, symphony orchestra, television station. Number of fraternities: 5; sororities: 6. Proportion of men in fraternities: 5%; of women in sororities: 5%. Average proportion of students who stay on campus on weekends: 15%. **Sports program (2005-2006):** Member of NCAA II. *Men's intercollegiate varsity sports:* baseball, basketball, cross-country, golf, soccer, tennis, track and field (outdoor). *Women's intercollegiate varsity sports:* basketball, cross-country, golf, soccer, softball, tennis, track and field (outdoor), volleyball.

SERVICES AND FACILITIES

Basic services: nonremedial tutoring, placement service, day care, health service, health insurance. **Counseling services:** minority student, career, military, personal, veteran student, academic, religious. **For learning-disabled students:** School does not offer a structured program with separate admission and additional fees. Total undergraduates in learning-disabled program or receiving services: 121. Services include: reading machines, note-taking services, learning center, readers, extended time for tests, tutors, other. **Library:** Number of titles: 730,732; number of current serial subscriptions: 5,120. **Information technology resources:** Students are not required to lease or own a computer. School has a wireless network. Approximate number of users that can be accommodated: 2,500. Proportion of college-owned housing units wired for high-speed internet access: 76%. **Campus safety:** Security services offered: 24-hour foot-and-vehicle patrols, late-night transport/escort service, 24-hour emergency telephones, lighted pathways/sidewalks, student patrols, controlled dormitory access (key, security card, etc).

TRANSFER AND INTERNATIONAL STUDENTS

Transfer students: May apply for admission for the following academic terms: Fall, Spring, Summer. Applicants do not need a minimum number of credits to apply. For fall 2005: Transfer applications received: 2,247. Transfer applicants offered admission: 1,696. Transfer applicants enrolled: 1,119. **International students:** Number of foreign undergraduates: 53 (1% of student body). Number of countries represented: 35. Minimum TOEFL score required: 525 (paper); 193 (computer).

Warner Southern College

- **Address:** 13895 US 27, Lake Wales, FL 33859
- **Website:** http://www.warner.edu
- **Private; Religious affiliation:** Church of God
- **Enrollment:** 778 full-time; 143 part-time

KEY STATS
- ✔ **U.S News College Ranking:** third tier, Comp. Colleges–Bachelor's (South)
- ✔ **SAT Score (25th/75th percentile):** 710-1180
- ✔ **Tuition:** 2006-2007: $13,315

Selectivity: Less selective	**Room/board:** $5,756
Acceptance rate: 58%	**Average debt:** $7,869
Student/faculty ratio: 16/1	**Proportion who borrowed:** 42%

UNDERGRADUATE STUDENT BODY STATS

2005-2006 enrollment: 778 full-time; 143 part-time. Men: 42%; women: 58%. **Ethnic makeup:** African American: 21%; Asian American: 1%; Hispanic: 10%; White: 66%; International: 2%. **Religious preference:** Roman Catholic: 9%; Protestant: 53%; Unknown: 21%; Church of God: 17%.

ADMISSIONS FACTS AND FIGURES

Phone: (800) 309-9563. **Email:** admissions@warner.edu. **Website:** http://www.warner.edu. **Application deadlines for fall 2007:** Regular decision: Rolling. Early decision: Not offered. Early action: Not offered. Admission can be deferred. **Application fee:** $20. Common application is not accepted. **To apply online, go to:** http://www.warner.edu/apply/. **Admissions requirements/recommendations:** High school units required (recommended): English: 0 (4); Mathematics: 0 (3); Science: 0 (2); Foreign language: 0 (1); Social studies: 0 (1); History: 0 (1); Academic electives: 0 (1); Total units: 0 (13). Tests: The college uses SAT or ACT scores in admissions decisions. Either SAT or ACT required. For admission to the fall 2007 entering class, the school will accept: ACT with writing, ACT without writing. Campus visit: Recommended. Admissions interview: Recommended. Off-campus interview: May be arranged. **Factors that count in admissions decisions:** *Academic:* Secondary school record: Very important. Class rank: Very important. Letters of recommendation: Important. Standardized test scores: Very important. Essay: Considered. *Nonacademic:* Interview: Considered. Extracurricular activities: Considered. Talent/ability: Considered. Character/personal qualities: Important. Alumni/ae relationship: Considered. Geographical residence: Not considered. State residency: Not considered. Religious affiliation/commitment: Not considered. Minority status: Not considered. Volunteer work: Not considered. Work experience: Not considered. **Other schools with the greatest overlap in applicants:** Anderson University; Florida Southern College; University of Central Florida; University of South Florida; Webber International University. **Admissions statistics for the fall 2005 entering class:** Total applicants: 391. Total accepted: 226. Freshmen enrolled: 109; 9% were from out of state. Overall acceptance rate: 58%. **Size of waiting list:** 0 applicants; enrolled from waiting list: 0. **Credentials of fall 2005 freshmen:** 11% ranked in the top 10 percent of their high school class; 28% were in the top 25 percent. **Average high school grade point average:** 3.2. **First-year students who submitted SAT scores:** 70%. Scores (25/75 percentile): Verbal: 340-600, Math: 370-580, Combined: 710-1180. **First-year students submitting ACT scores:** 57%. Scores (25/75 percentile): English: N/A, Math: N/A, Composite: 14-23.

ACADEMICS

Year founded: 1968. **Academic calendar:** Semester. **Degrees offered:** certificate, associate, bachelor's, master's. **Most popular majors:** Information not available. **Major fields of study:** biological and biomedical sciences; business, management, marketing, and related support services; communication, journalism, and related programs; education; English language and literature/letters; history; parks, recreation, leisure, and fitness studies; psychol-

ogy; public administration and social service professions; social sciences; theology and religious vocations. **Areas of required coursework:** arts/fine arts, humanities, computer literacy, mathematics, English (including composition), foreign languages, sciences (biological or physical), history, social science, other. **Pre-professional programs:** pre-law, pre-theology, other. **Special academic programs (% participation):** accelerated program (70%), distance learning (60%), double major (1%), dual enrollment (1%), independent study (10%), internships (20%), teacher certificate program (13%). **Teacher certification offered in:** special education, elementary, middle/junior high, secondary. **Faculty and instruction (2005-2006):** Total instructional faculty: 35 full-time, 64 part-time (63% men; 37% women; 8% minorities). Full-time faculty with Ph.D. or other terminal degree: 54%. Student/faculty ratio: 16/1. Classes of fewer than 20 students: 72%; of 20 to 49 students: 28%; of 50 or more students: 0%. **Advanced Placement and International Baccalaureate credit:** AP tests may be used for: Credit and/or placement. Scores accepted: 3, 4, 5. International Baccalaureate exams may be used for: Credit and/or placement. **Freshmen returning for sophomore year:** 66%. **Graduation rates:** Six-year: 40%.

COSTS AND FINANCIAL AID

Financial aid office: (863) 638-7202. **Expenses (2006-2007):** Tuition and fees 2006-2007: $13,315; room/board: $5,756. Estimated books and supplies: $1,000; transportation: $910; personal expenses: $1,792. **Financial aid:** Priority filing date for institution's financial aid form: May 1; deadline: January 15. In 2005-2006, 99% of undergraduates applied for financial aid. Of those, 65% were determined to have financial need; Average financial aid package (proportion receiving): N/A (65%). Average amount of gift aid, such as scholarships or grants (proportion receiving): $3,229 (42%). Average amount of self-help aid, such as work study or loans (proportion receiving): $4,661 (58%). Average need-based loan (excluding PLUS or other private loans): $4,654. Among students who received aid based on merit, the average award (and the proportion receiving): $3,608 (16%). The average athletic scholarship (and the proportion receiving): $4,064 (34%). Average amount of debt of borrowers graduating in 2005: $7,869. Proportion who borrowed: 42%.

CAMPUS LIFE AND EXTRACURRICULAR ACTIVITIES

Campus housing available (% using): women's dorms (51%), men's dorms (49%). Students who live in college-owned, operated, or affiliated housing: 23%. **Student employment:** During the 2005-2006 academic year, 16% of undergraduates worked on campus. Average per-year earnings: $1,000. **Clubs and organizations:** Number of student organizations: 0. Activities include: choral groups, music ensembles, student government, student newspaper. Number of fraternities: 2; sororities: 2. Average proportion of students who stay on campus on weekends: 65%. **Sports program (2005-2006):** Member of NAIA. *Men's intercollegiate varsity sports:* baseball, basketball, cross-country, golf, soccer, tennis, track and field (indoor), track and field (outdoor). *Women's intercollegiate varsity sports:* basketball, cross-country, golf, soccer, softball, tennis, track and field (indoor), track and field (outdoor), volleyball.

SERVICES AND FACILITIES

Basic services: nonremedial tutoring. **Remedial assistance:** reading, math, writing, study skills. **Counseling services:** academic, religious. **For learning-disabled students:** School does not offer a structured program with separate admission and additional fees. Services include: remedial math, remedial English, reading machines, remedial reading, oral tests, learning center, readers, extended time for tests, tutors. **Library:** Number of titles: 83,260; number of current serial subscriptions: 223. **Information technology resources:** Students are not required to lease or own a computer. Number of campus computers available to all students: 80. School does not have a wireless network. Proportion of college-owned housing units wired for high-speed internet access: 0%. **Campus safety:** Security services offered: 24-hour foot-and-vehicle patrols.

TRANSFER AND INTERNATIONAL STUDENTS

Transfer students: May apply for admission for the following academic terms: Fall, Spring, Summer. Applicants need a minimum number of credits to apply. For fall 2005: Transfer applications received: 144. Transfer applicants offered admission: 77. Transfer applicants enrolled: 65. **International students:** Number of foreign undergraduates: 14 (2% of student body). Number of countries represented: 17. Minimum TOEFL score required: 500 (paper); 173 (computer). Average TOEFL score: 500 (paper).

Webber International University

- **Address:** PO Box 96, Babson Park, FL 33827
- **Website:** http://www.webber.edu
- **Private**
- **Enrollment:** 506 full-time; 51 part-time

KEY STATS

- ✔ **U.S News College Ranking:** Unranked Specialty School–Business
- ✔ **SAT Score (25th/75th percentile):** 815-995
- ✔ **Tuition:** 2006-2007: $15,900

Selectivity: Less selective	**Room/board:** $4,990
Acceptance rate: 79%	**Average debt:** $16,329
Student/faculty ratio: 17/1	**Proportion who borrowed:** 64%

UNDERGRADUATE STUDENT BODY STATS

2005-2006 enrollment: 506 full-time; 51 part-time. Men: 63%; women: 37%. **Ethnic makeup:** African American: 23%; Hispanic: 6%; White: 56%; International: 15%.

ADMISSIONS FACTS AND FIGURES

Phone: (800) 741-1844. **Email:** admissions@webber.edu. **Website:** http://www.webber.edu. **Application deadlines for fall 2007:** Regular decision: August 1. Early decision: Not offered. Early action: Send application by: N/A; Decision sent by: N/A. Admission can be deferred. **Application fee:** $35. Common application is accepted. **Admissions requirements/recommendations:** High school units required (recommended): English: 4; Mathematics: 2 (3); Science: 1 (3); Foreign language: (1); Social studies: 2; History: (2); Academic electives: (4); Total units: (15). Tests: The college uses SAT or ACT scores in admissions decisions. Either SAT or ACT required. For admission to the fall 2007 entering class, the school will accept: ACT with writing, ACT without writing. Campus visit: Required. Admissions interview: Required. Off-campus interview: Not available. **Factors that count in admissions decisions:** *Academic:* Secondary school record: Very important. Class rank: Important. Letters of recommendation: Important. Standardized test scores: Very important. Essay: Important. *Nonacademic:* Interview: Important. Extracurricular activities: Considered. Talent/ability: Not considered. Character/personal qualities: Important. Alumni/ae relationship: Important. Geographical residence: Not considered. State residency: Not considered. Religious affiliation/commitment: Not considered. Minority status: Not considered. Volunteer work: Considered. Work experience: Considered. **Other schools with the greatest overlap in applicants:** Flagler College; Florida Southern College; Jacksonville University; Lynn University. **Admissions statistics for the fall 2005 entering class:** Overall acceptance rate: 79%. **Credentials of fall 2005 freshmen:** 4% ranked in the top 10 percent of their high school class; 29% were in the top 25 percent. **Average high school grade point average:** 3.0. **First-year students who submitted SAT scores:** 70%. Scores (25/75 percentile): Verbal: 400-480, Math: 415-515, Combined: 815-995. **First-year students submitting ACT scores:** 39%. Scores (25/75 percentile): English: N/A, Math: N/A, Composite: 16-19.

ACADEMICS

Year founded: 1927. **Academic calendar:** Semester. **Degrees offered:** associate, bachelor's, master's. **Most popular majors:** 25% business administration and management, 19% marketing/marketing management, 14% parks, recreation, and leisure facilities management, 11% accounting, 8% hospitality administration/management. **Major fields of study:** business, management, marketing, and related support services; computer and information sciences and support services; legal professions and studies; parks, recreation, leisure, and fitness studies. **Areas of required coursework:** humanities, computer literacy, mathematics, English (including composition), sciences (biological or physical), social science, other. **Pre-professional programs:** pre-law. **Special academic programs (% participation):** internships (80%), study abroad. **Faculty and instruction (2005-2006):** Total instructional faculty: 25 full-time, 20 part-time (62% men; 38% women). Full-time faculty with Ph.D. or other terminal degree: 72%. Student/faculty ratio: 17/1. **Advanced Placement and International Baccalaureate credit:** International Baccalaureate exams may be used for: Credit only. **Freshmen returning for sophomore year:** 60%. **Graduation rates:** Four-year: 36%; five-year: 44%; six-year: 42%. **Graduate study:** 22% of students pursue further study immediately upon graduation; 22% within one year. Fields in which graduates pursue further study: Master of Business Administration (MBA), 90%; law, 5%; education, 5%.

COSTS AND FINANCIAL AID

Financial aid office: (863) 638-2930. **Expenses (2006-2007):** Tuition and fees 2006-2007: $15,900; room/board: $4,990. Estimated books and supplies: $700; transportation: $1,064; personal expenses: $2,944. **Financial aid:** Priority filing date for institution's financial aid form: May 1; deadline: August 1. In 2005-2006, 70% of undergraduates applied for financial aid. Of those, 59% were determined to have financial need; 22% had their need fully met. Average financial aid package (proportion receiving): $12,660 (59%). Average amount of gift aid, such as scholarships or grants (proportion receiving): $9,515 (59%). Average amount of self-help aid, such as work study or loans (proportion receiving): $3,701 (54%). Average need-based loan (excluding PLUS or other private loans): $3,531. Among students who received need-based aid, the average percentage of need met: 68%. Among students who received aid based on merit, the average award (and the proportion receiving): $5,266 (35%). The average athletic scholarship (and the proportion receiving): $3,727 (27%). Average amount of debt of borrowers graduating in 2005: $16,329. Proportion who borrowed: 64%.

CAMPUS LIFE AND EXTRACURRICULAR ACTIVITIES

Campus housing available: women's dorms, men's dorms. Students who live in college-owned, operated, or affiliated housing: 100%. **Student employment:** During the 2005-2006 academic year, 15% of undergraduates worked on campus. Average per-year earnings: $1,000. **Clubs and organizations:** Number of student organizations: 9. Activities include: student government, student newspaper. Number of fraternities: 0; sororities: 0. Average proportion of students who stay on campus on weekends: 65%. **Sports program (2005-2006):** Member of NAIA. *Men's intercollegiate varsity sports:* baseball, basketball, cross-country, football, golf, soccer, tennis, track and field (outdoor). *Women's intercollegiate varsity sports:* basketball, cross-country, golf, soccer, softball, tennis, track and field (outdoor), volleyball.

SERVICES AND FACILITIES

Basic services: nonremedial tutoring, placement service, health service, health insurance. **Remedial assistance:** reading, math, writing. **Counseling services:** career, personal, academic. **For learning-disabled students:** School does not offer a structured program with separate admission and additional fees. **Information technology resources:** Students are not required to lease or own a computer. Number of campus computers available to all students: 100. School does not have a wireless network. Proportion of college-owned housing units wired for high-speed internet access: 100%. **Campus safety:** Security services offered: 24-hour foot-and-vehicle patrols, lighted pathways/sidewalks.

TRANSFER AND INTERNATIONAL STUDENTS

Transfer students: May apply for admission for the following academic terms: Fall, Spring, Summer. Applicants need a minimum number of credits to apply. **International students:** Number of foreign undergraduates: 84 (15% of student body). Number of countries represented: 25. Minimum TOEFL score required: 500 (paper); 173 (computer).

Georgia

Agnes Scott College

- **Address:** 141 E. College Avenue, Decatur, GA 30030
- **Website:** http://www.agnesscott.edu
- **Private; Religious affiliation:** Presbyterian (U.S.A.)
- **Enrollment:** 879 full-time; 124 part-time

KEY STATS
- ✔ **U.S News College Ranking:** 61, Liberal Arts Colleges
- ✔ **SAT Score (25th/75th percentile):** 1110-1335
- ✔ **Tuition:** 2006-2007: $25,785

Selectivity: More selective	**Room/board:** $8,990
Acceptance rate: 53%	**Average debt:** $22,018
Student/faculty ratio: 10/1	**Proportion who borrowed:** 71%

UNDERGRADUATE STUDENT BODY STATS
2005-2006 enrollment: 879 full-time; 124 part-time. Men: 1%; women: 99%. **Ethnic makeup:** African American: 19%; Asian American: 5%; Hispanic: 3%; White: 65%; International: 7%. **Religious preference:** Roman Catholic: 6%; Protestant: 21%; Jewish: 1%; Muslim: 2%; Hindu: 1%; No preference: 3%; Unknown: 62%; Presbyterian (U.S.A.): 2%; Other: 1%.

ADMISSIONS FACTS AND FIGURES
Phone: (800) 868-8602. **Email:** admission@agnesscott.edu. **Website:** http://www.agnesscott.edu. **Application deadlines for fall 2007:** Regular decision: May 1. Early decision: Send application by: November 15; Decision sent by: December 15. Early action: Not offered. Admission can be deferred. **Application fee:** $35. Common application is accepted. **To apply online, go to:** http://www.agnesscott.edu/onlineapplication/login.asp. **Admissions requirements/recommendations:** High school units required (recommended): English: (4); Mathematics: (3); Science: (2); Foreign language: (2); Social studies: (2); Total units: (16). Tests: The college uses SAT or ACT scores in admissions decisions. Either SAT or ACT required. For admission to the fall 2007 entering class, the school will accept: ACT without writing. Campus visit: Recommended. Admissions interview: Recommended. Off-campus interview: May be arranged. **Factors that count in admissions decisions:** **Academic:** Secondary school record: Very important. Class rank: Very important. Letters of recommendation: Very important. Standardized test scores: Very important. Essay: Very important. **Nonacademic:** Interview: Considered. Extracurricular activities: Important. Talent/ability: Very important. Character/personal qualities: Very important. Alumni/ae relationship: Considered. Geographical residence: Considered. State residency: Considered. Religious affiliation/commitment: Not considered. Minority status: Considered. Volunteer work: Important. Work experience: Important. **Other schools with the greatest overlap in applicants:** Emory University; Rhodes College; Tulane University; University of Georgia; University of Virginia. **Admissions statistics for the fall 2005 entering class:** Total applicants: 1,526. Total accepted: 812. Freshmen enrolled: 229; 52% were from out of state. Accepted through early-decision or early-action plans: 5%. Overall acceptance rate: 53%. Early-decision acceptance rate: 17%. Non-early acceptance rate: 55%. **Size of waiting list:** 51 applicants; enrolled from waiting list: 2. **Credentials of fall 2005 freshmen:** 48% ranked in the top 10 percent of their high school class; 75% were in the top 25 percent, and 96% were in the top half. (Proportion submitting class standing: 69%.) **Average high school grade point average:** 3.7. **First-year students who submitted SAT scores:** 91%. Scores (25/75 percentile): Verbal: 570-685, Math: 540-650, Combined: 1110-1335. **First-year students submitting ACT scores:** 45%. Scores (25/75 percentile): English: N/A, Math: N/A, Composite: 24-29.

ACADEMICS
Year founded: 1889. **Academic calendar:** Semester. **Degrees offered:** bachelor's, post-bachelor's certificate, master's. **Most popular majors:** 35% social sciences, 15% psychology, 10% visual and performing arts, 9% foreign languages, literatures, and linguistics, 8% history. **Major fields of study:** area, ethnic, cultural, and gender studies; biological and biomedical sciences;

English language and literature/letters; foreign languages, literatures, and linguistics; history; mathematics and statistics; multi/interdisciplinary studies; philosophy and religious studies; physical sciences; psychology; social sciences; visual and performing arts. **Areas of required coursework:** arts/fine arts, humanities, mathematics, English (including composition), philosophy, foreign languages, sciences (biological or physical), history, social science, other. **Pre-professional programs:** pre-law, pre-dentistry, pre-medicine, pre-veterinary science, other. **Special academic programs (% participation):** accelerated program (.5%), cross-registration (8.7%), double major (18%), dual enrollment, exchange student program (domestic), independent study (23.7%), internships (33%), student-designed major (.5%), study abroad (37.1%), teacher certificate program (3.2%). **Teacher certification offered in:** early childhood, elementary, middle/junior high, secondary. **Reserve Officers Training Corps (ROTC):** Army ROTC: Offered at cooperating institution (Georgia Institute of Technology); Air Force ROTC: Offered at cooperating institution (Georgia Institute of Technology). **Faculty and instruction (2005-2006):** Total instructional faculty: 81 full-time, 29 part-time (38% men; 62% women; 21% minorities). Full-time faculty with Ph.D. or other terminal degree: 96%. Student/faculty ratio: 10/1. Classes of fewer than 20 students: 73%; of 20 to 49 students: 27%; of 50 or more students: 0%. **Advanced Placement and International Baccalaureate credit:** AP tests may be used for: Credit and/or placement. Scores accepted: 4, 5. International Baccalaureate exams may be used for: Credit and/or placement. **Freshmen returning for sophomore year:** 83%. **Graduation rates:** Four-year: 60%; five-year: 63%; six-year: 66%. **Graduate study:** 25% of students pursue further study immediately upon graduation; 33% within one year; 40% within five years. Fields in which graduates pursue further study: Master of Business Administration (MBA), 3%; law, 16%; medicine, 11%; theology (or the seminary), 2%; education, 5%; arts and sciences, 34%; veterinary medicine, 2%.

COSTS AND FINANCIAL AID
Financial aid office: (404) 471-6395. **Expenses (2006-2007):** Tuition and fees 2006-2007: $25,785; room/board: $8,990. Estimated books and supplies: $700; transportation: $950; personal expenses: $900. **Financial aid:** Priority filing date for institution's financial aid form: February 15; deadline: May 1. In 2005-2006, 74% of undergraduates applied for financial aid. Of those, 63% were determined to have financial need; 70% had their need fully met. Average financial aid package (proportion receiving): $24,314 (63%). Average amount of gift aid, such as scholarships or grants (proportion receiving): $17,866 (63%). Average amount of self-help aid, such as work study or loans (proportion receiving): $5,712 (55%). Average need-based loan (excluding PLUS or other private loans): $3,923. Among students who received need-based aid, the average percentage of need met: 97%. Among students who received aid based on merit, the average award (and the proportion receiving): $12,976 (33%). Average amount of debt of borrowers graduating in 2005: $22,018. Proportion who borrowed: 71%.

CAMPUS LIFE AND EXTRACURRICULAR ACTIVITIES
Campus housing available (% using): women's dorms (79%), apartment for single students (18%), other housing options (3%). Students who live in college-owned, operated, or affiliated housing: 92%. **Student employment:** During the 2005-2006 academic year, 15% of undergraduates worked on campus. Average per-year earnings: $2,000. **Clubs and organizations:** Number of student organizations: 92. Activities include: choral groups, dance, drama/theater, jazz band, literary magazine, music ensembles, musical theater, pep band, student government, student newspaper, symphony orchestra, television station, yearbook. Number of fraternities: 0; sororities: 0. **Sports program (2005-2006):** Member of NCAA III. **Women's intercollegiate varsity sports:** basketball, cross-country, soccer, softball, swimming and diving, tennis, volleyball.

SERVICES AND FACILITIES
Basic services: nonremedial tutoring, placement service, health service, health insurance. **Counseling services:** minority student, career, personal, academic, older student, psychological, birth control, religious. **For learning-disabled students:** School does not offer a structured program with separate admission and additional fees. Total undergraduates in learning-disabled program or receiving services: 20. Services include: reading machines, tape

recorders, untimed tests, note-taking services, oral tests, readers, extended time for tests, tutors, early syllabus, priority registration, priority seating, substitution of courses, typist/scribe, exams on tape or computer, take home exams, other testing accomodations, waiver of foreign language degree requirement, waiver of math degree requirement, other. **Library:** Number of titles: 221,991; number of current serial subscriptions: 1,396. **Information technology resources:** Students are not required to lease or own a computer. Number of campus computers available to all students: 429. School has a wireless network. Approximate number of users that can be accommodated: 265. Proportion of college-owned housing units wired for high-speed internet access: 10%. **Campus safety:** Security services offered: 24-hour foot-and-vehicle patrols, late-night transport/escort service, 24-hour emergency telephones, lighted pathways/sidewalks, controlled dormitory access (key, security card, etc).

TRANSFER AND INTERNATIONAL STUDENTS

Transfer students: May apply for admission for the following academic terms: Fall, Spring. Applicants do not need a minimum number of credits to apply. For fall 2005: Transfer applications received: 156. Transfer applicants offered admission: 23. Transfer applicants enrolled: 10. **International students:** Number of foreign undergraduates: 64 (7% of student body). Number of countries represented: 30. Minimum TOEFL score required: 577 (paper); 233 (computer). Average TOEFL score: 610 (paper).

Albany State University

- **Address:** 504 College Drive, Albany, GA 31705
- **Website:** http://asuweb.asurams.edu/asu/
- **Public**
- **Enrollment:** N/A

....

KEY STATS

✔ **U.S News College Ranking:** fourth tier, Universities–Master's (South)
✔ **SAT or ACT Score (25th/75th percentile):** N/A
✔ **Tuition:** N/A
   Selectivity: Less selective   **Room/board:** N/A
   Acceptance rate: N/A   **Average debt:** N/A
   Student/faculty ratio: N/A   **Proportion who borrowed:** N/A

Armstrong Atlantic State University

- **Address:** 11935 Abercorn Street, Savannah, GA 31419
- **Website:** http://www.armstrong.edu
- **Public**
- **Enrollment:** 3,677 full-time; 2,238 part-time

....

KEY STATS

✔ **U.S News College Ranking:** fourth tier, Universities–Master's (South)
✔ **SAT Score (25th/75th percentile):** 910-1100
✔ **Tuition:** 2006-2007: $2,560 in state, $0 out of state
   Selectivity: Less selective   **Room/board:** N/A
   Acceptance rate: 100%   **Average debt:** $5,500
   Student/faculty ratio: 17/1   **Proportion who borrowed:** 40%

UNDERGRADUATE STUDENT BODY STATS

2005-2006 enrollment: 3,677 full-time; 2,238 part-time. Men: 32%; women: 68%. **Ethnic makeup:** African American: 21%; Asian American: 3%; Hispanic: 3%; White: 71%; International: 2%.

ADMISSIONS FACTS AND FIGURES

Phone: (912) 927-5277. **Email:** adm-info@mail.armstrong.edu. **Website:** http://www.armstrong.edu. **Application deadlines for fall 2007:** Regular decision: June 30. Early decision: Not offered. Early action: Not offered. Admission can be deferred. **Application fee:** $20. Common application is not accepted. **To apply online, go to:** https://www.applyweb.com/apply/aasu/. **Admissions requirements/recommendations:** High school units required (recommended): English: 4; Mathematics: 4; Science: 3; Foreign language: 2; Social studies: 3. Tests: The college uses SAT or ACT scores in admissions decisions. Either SAT or ACT required. For admission to the fall 2007 entering class, the school will accept: ACT with writing. Campus visit: Neither required nor recommended. Admissions interview: Neither required nor recommended. Off-campus interview: May not be arranged. **Factors that count in admissions decisions: Academic:** Secondary school record: Important. Class rank: Not considered. Letters of recommendation: Not considered. Standardized test scores: Very important. Essay: Not considered. **Nonacademic:** Interview: Not considered. Extracurricular activities: Considered. Talent/ability: Not considered. Character/personal qualities: Not considered. Alumni/ae relationship: Not considered. Geographical residence: Considered. State residency: Considered. Religious affiliation/commitment: Not considered. Minority status: Not considered. Volunteer work: Considered. Work experience: Considered. **Other schools with the greatest overlap in applicants:** Georgia Southern University; Savannah College of Art and Design; Savannah State University; University of Georgia; Valdosta State University. **Admissions statistics for the fall 2005 entering class:** Total applicants: 800. Total accepted: 799. Freshmen enrolled: 799; 5% were from out of state. Overall acceptance rate: 100%. **Average high school grade point average:** 3.1. **First-year students who submitted SAT scores:** 79%. Scores (25/75 percentile): Verbal: 460-550, Math: 450-550, Combined: 910-1100. **First-year students submitting ACT scores:** 22%. Scores (25/75 percentile): English: 18-22, Math: 17-22, Composite: 18-22.

ACADEMICS

Year founded: 1935. **Academic calendar:** Semester. **Degrees offered:** certificate, associate, bachelor's, post-bachelor's certificate, master's, doctorate. **Most popular majors:** 31% health professions and related clinical sciences, 18% education, 14% liberal arts and sciences studies, and humanities, 5% security and protective services, 4% social sciences. **Major fields of study:** biological and biomedical sciences; computer and information sciences and support services; education; English language and literature/letters; foreign languages, literatures, and linguistics; health professions and related clinical sciences; history; liberal arts and sciences studies, and humanities; mathematics and statistics; physical sciences; psychology; security and protective services; social sciences; visual and performing arts. **Areas of required coursework:** arts/fine arts, humanities, computer literacy, mathematics, English (including composition), sciences (biological or physical), history, social science. **Pre-professional programs:** pre-law, pre-dentistry, pre-medicine, pre-veterinary science, pre-pharmacy, other. **Special academic programs:** cooperative (work-study plan) program, distance learning, double major, dual enrollment, honors program, independent study, internships, study abroad, teacher certificate program, weekend college. **Teacher certification offered in:** early childhood, special education, elementary, middle/junior high, adult education, secondary. **Cooperative education programs:** computer science, engineering, other. **Reserve Officers Training Corps (ROTC):** Army ROTC: Offered on campus; Navy ROTC: Offered at cooperating institution (Savannah State University). **Faculty and instruction (2005-2006):** Total instructional faculty: 224 full-time, 200 part-time (41% men; 59% women; 15% minorities). Full-time faculty with Ph.D. or other terminal degree: 59%. Student/faculty ratio: 17/1. Classes of fewer than 20 students: 52%; of 20 to 49 students: 45%; of 50 or more students: 2%. **Advanced Placement and International Baccalaureate credit:** AP tests may be used for: Credit and/or placement. Scores accepted: 3, 4, 5. International Baccalaureate exams may be used for: Credit and/or placement. **Freshmen returning for sophomore year:** 66%. **Graduation rates:** Four-year: 6%; five-year: 17%; six-year: 20%.

COSTS AND FINANCIAL AID

Financial aid office: (912) 921-5990. **Expenses (2006-2007):** Tuition and fees 2006-2007: $2,560 in state, $0 out of state; room/board: N/A. **Financial aid:** Priority filing date for institution's financial aid form: March 15. Average amount of debt of borrowers graduating in 2005: $5,500. Proportion who borrowed: 40%.

CAMPUS LIFE AND EXTRACURRICULAR ACTIVITIES

Campus housing available: apartment for single students. **Clubs and organizations:** Number of student organizations: 61. Activities include: choral groups, concert band, drama/theater, jazz band, music ensembles, musical theater, pep band, student government, student newspaper, symphony orchestra. Number of fraternities: 4; sororities: 5. **Sports program (2005-2006):** Member of NCAA II. *Men's intercollegiate varsity sports:* baseball, basketball, golf, tennis. *Women's intercollegiate varsity sports:* basketball, golf, soccer, softball, tennis, volleyball.

SERVICES AND FACILITIES

Basic services: nonremedial tutoring, health service. **Remedial assistance:** reading, math, writing. **Counseling services:** minority student, career, veteran student, academic, older student, psychological. **For learning-disabled students:** School does not offer a structured program with separate admission and additional fees. Services include: remedial math, remedial English, reading machines, remedial reading, tape recorders, other special classes, diagnostic testing service, note-taking services, learning center, readers, extended time for tests, tutors, exams on tape or computer. **Library:** Number of titles: 232,791; number of current serial subscriptions: 1,145. **Information technology resources:** Students are not required to lease or own a computer. Number of campus computers available to all students: 500. School does not have a wireless network. Proportion of college-owned housing units wired for high-speed internet access: 100%. **Campus safety:** Security services offered: 24-hour foot-and-vehicle patrols, late-night transport/escort service, 24-hour emergency telephones, lighted pathways/sidewalks, controlled dormitory access (key, security card, etc).

TRANSFER AND INTERNATIONAL STUDENTS

Transfer students: May apply for admission for the following academic terms: Fall, Spring, Summer. Applicants need a minimum number of credits to apply. For fall 2005: Transfer applications received: 1,250. Transfer applicants offered admission: 988. Transfer applicants enrolled: 549. **International students:** Number of foreign undergraduates: 96 (2% of student body). Number of countries represented: 71. Minimum TOEFL score required: 523 (paper); 193 (computer).

Atlanta College of Art

- **Address:** 1280 Peachtree Street NE, Atlanta, GA 30309
- **Website:** http://www.aca.edu
- **Private**
- **Enrollment:** N/A

KEY STATS

✔ **U.S News College Ranking:** Unranked Specialty School–Fine Arts
✔ **ACT Score (25th/75th percentile):** 17-23
✔ **Tuition:** 2005-2006: $18,500

Selectivity: Less selective	**Room/board:** $6,975
Acceptance rate: 70%	**Average debt:** N/A
Student/faculty ratio: N/A	**Proportion who borrowed:** N/A

Augusta State University

- **Address:** 2500 Walton Way, Augusta, GA 30904-2200
- **Website:** http://www.aug.edu
- **Public**
- **Enrollment:** 3,686 full-time; 1,775 part-time

KEY STATS

✔ **U.S News College Ranking:** fourth tier, Universities–Master's (South)
✔ **SAT Score (25th/75th percentile):** 860-1080
✔ **Tuition:** 2006-2007: $3,042 in state, $10,650 out of state

Selectivity: Less selective	**Room/board:** $7,266
Acceptance rate: 63%	**Average debt:** $16,092
Student/faculty ratio: 19/1	**Proportion who borrowed:** 64%

UNDERGRADUATE STUDENT BODY STATS

2005-2006 enrollment: 3,686 full-time; 1,775 part-time. Men: 36%; women: 64%. **Ethnic makeup:** African American: 26%; Asian American: 3%; Hispanic: 3%; White: 67%; International: 1%.

ADMISSIONS FACTS AND FIGURES

Phone: (706) 737-1632. **Email:** admissions@aug.edu. **Website:** http://www.aug.edu. **Application deadlines for fall 2007:** Regular decision: Rolling. Early decision: Not offered. Early action: Not offered. Admission can be deferred. **Application fee:** $20. Common application is not accepted. **To apply online, go to:** http://www.aug.edu/admissions/. **Admissions requirements/recommendations:** High school units required (recommended): English: 4; Mathematics: 4; Science: 3; Foreign language: 2; Social studies: 3; Total units: 18. Tests: The college uses SAT or ACT scores in admissions decisions. Either SAT or ACT required. For admission to the fall

2007 entering class, the school will accept: ACT with writing, ACT without writing. Campus visit: Recommended. Admissions interview: Neither required nor recommended. **Factors that count in admissions decisions:** *Academic:* Secondary school record: Important. Class rank: Not considered. Letters of recommendation: Considered. Standardized test scores: Important. Essay: Not considered. *Nonacademic:* Interview: Not considered. Extracurricular activities: Not considered. Talent/ability: Not considered. Character/personal qualities: Not considered. Alumni/ae relationship: Not considered. Geographical residence: Not considered. State residency: Not considered. Religious affiliation/commitment: Not considered. Minority status: Not considered. Volunteer work: Not considered. Work experience: Not considered. **Admissions statistics for the fall 2005 entering class:** Total applicants: 1,939. Total accepted: 1,215. Freshmen enrolled: 988; 9% were from out of state. Overall acceptance rate: 63%. **Average high school grade point average:** 2.9. **First-year students who submitted SAT scores:** 89%. Scores (25/75 percentile): Verbal: 430-540, Math: 430-540, Combined: 860-1080. **First-year students submitting ACT scores:** 17%. Scores (25/75 percentile): English: N/A, Math: N/A, Composite: 16-21.

ACADEMICS

Year founded: 1925. **Academic calendar:** Semester. **Degrees offered:** associate, transfer-associate, terminal-associate, bachelor's, master's, post-master's certificate. **Most popular majors:** 9% business administration and management, 9% elementary education and teaching, 9% psychology, 8% sociology, 7% accounting. **Major fields of study:** biological and biomedical sciences; business, management, marketing, and related support services; communication, journalism, and related programs; computer and information sciences and support services; education; English language and literature/letters; foreign languages, literatures, and linguistics; history; mathematics and statistics; physical sciences; psychology; public administration and social service professions; security and protective services; social sciences; visual and performing arts. **Areas of required coursework:** humanities, mathematics, English (including composition), foreign languages, sciences (biological or physical), history, social science. **Special academic programs:** cooperative (work-study plan) program, cross-registration, distance learning, double major, dual enrollment, English as a Second Language (ESL), honors program, independent study, internships, study abroad, teacher certificate program. **Teacher certification offered in:** special education, elementary, middle/junior high, secondary. **Cooperative education programs:** business, computer science, technologies, other. **Reserve Officers Training Corps (ROTC):** Army ROTC: Offered on campus. **Faculty and instruction (2005-2006):** Total instructional faculty: 215 full-time, 115 part-time (50% men; 50% women; 15% minorities). Full-time faculty with Ph.D. or other terminal degree: 67%. Student/faculty ratio: 19/1. Classes of fewer than 20 students: 34%; of 20 to 49 students: 65%; of 50 or more students: 1%. **Advanced Placement and International Baccalaureate credit:** AP tests may be used for: Credit only. Scores accepted: 3, 4, 5. **Freshmen returning for sophomore year:** 66%. **Graduation rates:** Four-year: 5%; five-year: 14%; six-year: 20%.

COSTS AND FINANCIAL AID

Financial aid office: (706) 737-1431. **Expenses (2006-2007):** Tuition and fees 2006-2007: $3,042 in state, $10,650 out of state; room/board: $7,266. **Financial aid:** Priority filing date for institution's financial aid form: April 15; deadline: June 1. Average amount of debt of borrowers graduating in 2005: $16,092. Proportion who borrowed: 64%.

CAMPUS LIFE AND EXTRACURRICULAR ACTIVITIES

Campus housing available: apartment for single students. **Student employment:** During the 2005-2006 academic year, 5% of undergraduates worked on campus. Average per-year earnings: $5,000. **Clubs and organizations:** Number of student organizations: 66. Activities include: choral groups, concert band, drama/theater, jazz band, literary magazine, pep band, radio station, student government, student newspaper. Number of fraternities: 2; sororities: 4. Proportion of men in fraternities: 1%; of women in sororities: 1%. **Sports program (2005-2006):** Member of NCAA II. *Men's intercollegiate varsity sports:* baseball, basketball, golf, tennis. *Women's intercollegiate varsity sports:* basketball, cross-country, golf, softball, tennis, volleyball.

SERVICES AND FACILITIES

Basic services: placement service. **Remedial assistance:** reading, math, writing, study skills. **Counseling services:** minority student, career, military, personal, veteran student, academic. **For learning-disabled students:** School does not offer a structured program with separate admission and additional fees. Total undergraduates in learning-disabled program or receiving services: 23. Services include: remedial math, remedial English, reading machines, remedial reading, tape recorders, diagnostic testing service, note-taking services, oral tests, learning center, readers, extended time for tests, priority registration, priority seating, texts on tape, other testing accomodations. **Library:** Number of titles: 727,845; number of current serial subscriptions: 7,414. **Information technology resources:** Students are not required to lease or own a computer. Number of campus computers available to all students: 800. School has a wireless network. Approximate number of users that can be accommodated: 350. Proportion of college-owned housing units wired for high-speed internet access: 100%. **Campus safety:** Security services offered: 24-hour foot-and-vehicle patrols, late-night transport/escort service, 24-hour emergency telephones, lighted pathways/sidewalks.

TRANSFER AND INTERNATIONAL STUDENTS
Transfer students: May apply for admission for the following academic terms: Fall, Spring, Summer. Applicants need a minimum number of credits to apply. For fall 2005: Transfer applications received: 1,005. Transfer applicants offered admission: 567. Transfer applicants enrolled: 445. **International students:** Number of foreign undergraduates: 56 (1% of student body). Number of countries represented: 35. Minimum TOEFL score required: 500 (paper); 173 (computer).

Berry College

- **Address:** PO Box 490279, Mount Berry, GA 30149
- **Website:** http://www.berry.edu
- **Private**
- **Enrollment:** 1,829 full-time; 35 part-time

KEY STATS
✔ **U.S News College Ranking:** 2, Comp. Colleges–Bachelor's (South)
✔ **SAT Score (25th/75th percentile):** 1040-1250
✔ **Tuition:** 2006-2007: $18,950
  Selectivity: More selective   **Room/board:** $7,164
  Acceptance rate: 83%   **Average debt:** $12,028
  Student/faculty ratio: 13/1   **Proportion who borrowed:** 50%

UNDERGRADUATE STUDENT BODY STATS
2005-2006 enrollment: 1,829 full-time; 35 part-time. Men: 36%; women: 64%. **Ethnic makeup:** African American: 3%; Asian American: 2%; Hispanic: 2%; White: 92%; International: 2%. **Religious preference:** Roman Catholic: 15%; Protestant: 75%; Jewish: 1%; No preference: 4%; Muslim, Buddhist, Hindu, Orthodox Christian, indigenous religion: 5%.

ADMISSIONS FACTS AND FIGURES
Phone: (706) 236-2215. **Email:** admissions@berry.edu. **Website:** http://www.berry.edu. **Application deadlines for fall 2007:** Regular decision: July 21. Early decision: Not offered. Early action: Not offered. Admission can be deferred. **Application fee:** $50. Common application is accepted. **To apply online, go to:** http://www2.berry.edu/admissions/apply/index.asp?bhcp=1. **Admissions requirements/recommendations:** High school units required (recommended): English: 4; Mathematics: 4; Science: 3; Foreign language: 2; Social studies: 3; Total units: 20. Tests: The college uses SAT or ACT scores in admissions decisions. Either SAT or ACT required. For admission to the fall 2007 entering class, the school will accept: ACT with writing. Campus visit: Recommended. Admissions interview: Recommended. Off-campus interview: Not available. **Factors that count in admissions decisions:** *Academic:* Secondary school record: Very important. Class rank: Considered. Letters of recommendation: Considered. Standardized test scores: Very important. *Nonacademic:* Interview: Not considered. Extracurricular activities: Important. Character/personal qualities: Not considered. Alumni/ae relationship: Not considered. Volunteer work: Considered. Work experience: Considered. **Other schools with the greatest overlap in applicants:** Auburn University; Georgia Institute of Technology; Georgia Southern University; Mercer University. **Admissions statistics for the fall 2005 entering class:** Total applicants: 1,827. Total accepted: 1,517. Freshmen enrolled: 514; 15% were from out of state. Overall acceptance rate: 83%. **Credentials of fall 2005 freshmen:** 28% ranked in the top 10 percent of their high school class; 59% were in the top 25 percent, and 89% were in the top half. (Proportion submitting class standing: 65%.) **Average high school grade point average:** 3.5. **First-year students who submitted SAT scores:** 78%. Scores (25/75 percentile): Verbal: 520-630, Math: 520-620, Combined: 1040-1250. **First-year**

students submitting ACT scores: 22%. Scores (25/75 percentile): English: 23-29, Math: 20-26, Composite: 23-28.

ACADEMICS
Year founded: 1902. **Academic calendar:** Semester. **Degrees offered:** bachelor's, master's, post-master's certificate. **Most popular majors:** 14% business, management, marketing, and related support services, 12% education, 12% psychology, 10% social sciences, 9% communication, journalism, and related programs. **Major fields of study:** agriculture, agriculture operations, and related sciences; biological and biomedical sciences; business, management, marketing, and related support services; communication, journalism, and related programs; computer and information sciences and support services; education; engineering technologies/technicians; English language and literature/letters; foreign languages, literatures, and linguistics; health professions and related clinical sciences; history; mathematics and statistics; multi/interdisciplinary studies; natural resources and conservation; philosophy and religious studies; physical sciences; psychology; social sciences; visual and performing arts. **Areas of required coursework:** arts/fine arts, humanities, computer literacy, mathematics, English (including composition), sciences (biological or physical), history, social science. **Special academic programs:** cooperative (work-study plan) program, cross-registration, double major, dual enrollment, honors program, independent study, internships, liberal arts/career combination, student-designed major, study abroad, teacher certificate program, other. **Teacher certification offered in:** early childhood, elementary, middle/junior high, secondary, bilingual/bicultural. **Cooperative education programs:** business, computer science, humanities, natural science, social/behavioral science. **Faculty and instruction (2005-2006):** Total instructional faculty: 134 full-time, 62 part-time (64% men; 36% women; 5% minorities). Full-time faculty with Ph.D. or other terminal degree: 88%. Student/faculty ratio: 13/1. Classes of fewer than 20 students: 60%; of 20 to 49 students: 40%; of 50 or more students: 0%. **Advanced Placement and International Baccalaureate credit:** AP tests may be used for: Placement only. Scores accepted: 3, 4, 5. International Baccalaureate exams may be used for: Credit and/or placement. **Freshmen returning for sophomore year:** 78%. **Graduation rates:** Four-year: 49%; five-year: 63%; six-year: 61%. **Graduate study:** 24% of students pursue further study within one year; 34% within five years.

COSTS AND FINANCIAL AID
Financial aid office: (706) 236-1714. **Expenses (2006-2007):** Tuition and fees 2006-2007: $18,950; room/board: $7,164. Estimated books and supplies: $900; transportation: $500; personal expenses: $1,870. **Financial aid:** Priority filing date for institution's financial aid form: April 1. In 2005-2006, 74% of undergraduates applied for financial aid. Of those, 58% were determined to have financial need; 23% had their need fully met. Average financial aid package (proportion receiving): $14,794 (57%). Average amount of gift aid, such as scholarships or grants (proportion receiving): $11,398 (57%). Average amount of self-help aid, such as work study or loans (proportion receiving): $4,494 (45%). Average need-based loan (excluding PLUS or other private loans): $2,826. Among students who received need-based aid, the average percentage of need met: 82%. Among students who received aid based on merit, the average award (and the proportion receiving): $12,112 (42%). The average athletic scholarship (and the proportion receiving): $10,170 (6%). Average amount of debt of borrowers graduating in 2005: $12,028. Proportion who borrowed: 50%.

CAMPUS LIFE AND EXTRACURRICULAR ACTIVITIES
Campus housing available (% using): coed dorms (12%), women's dorms (51%), men's dorms (28%), apartment for single students (9%), special housing for disabled students (0%). Students who live in college-owned, operated, or affiliated housing: 74%. **Student employment:** During the 2005-2006 academic year, 67% of undergraduates worked on campus. Average per-year earnings: $1,560. **Clubs and organizations:** Number of student organizations: 77. Activities include: choral groups, concert band, dance, drama/theater, jazz band, literary magazine, music ensembles, musical theater, student government, student newspaper, television station, yearbook. Number of fraternities: 0; sororities: 0. Average proportion of students who stay on campus on weekends: 60%. **Sports program (2005-2006):** Member of NAIA. **Men's intercollegiate varsity sports:** baseball, basketball, cross-country, golf, soccer, tennis, track and field (indoor), track and field (outdoor). **Women's intercollegiate varsity sports:** basketball, cross-country, golf, soccer, tennis, track and field (indoor), track and field (outdoor), volleyball.

SERVICES AND FACILITIES
Basic services: nonremedial tutoring, placement service, health service. **Remedial assistance:** study skills. **Counseling services:** minority student,

career, personal, veteran student, academic, older student, psychological, religious. **For learning-disabled students:** School does not offer a structured program with separate admission and additional fees. Total undergraduates in learning-disabled program or receiving services: 41. Services include: remedial English, tape recorders, note-taking services, oral tests, readers, extended time for tests, tutors, priority seating, exams on tape or computer. **Library:** Number of titles: 321,335; number of current serial subscriptions: 1,792. **Information technology resources:** Students are not required to lease or own a computer. Number of campus computers available to all students: 158. School has a wireless network. Approximate number of users that can be accommodated: 600. Proportion of college-owned housing units wired for high-speed internet access: 100%. **Campus safety:** Security services offered: 24-hour foot-and-vehicle patrols, 24-hour emergency telephones, lighted pathways/sidewalks.

TRANSFER AND INTERNATIONAL STUDENTS

Transfer students: May apply for admission for the following academic terms: Fall, Spring, Summer. Applicants need a minimum number of credits to apply. For fall 2005: Transfer applications received: 214. Transfer applicants offered admission: 116. Transfer applicants enrolled: 69. **International students:** Number of foreign undergraduates: 29 (2% of student body). Number of countries represented: 18. Minimum TOEFL score required: 550 (paper); 213 (computer). Average TOEFL score: 579 (paper).

Brenau University

- **Address:** 500 Washington Street SE, Gainesville, GA 30501
- **Website:** http://www.brenau.edu
- **Private**
- **Enrollment:** 670 full-time; 41 part-time

KEY STATS

✔ **U.S News College Ranking:** 41, Universities–Master's (South)
✔ **SAT Score (25th/75th percentile):** 910-1100
✔ **Tuition:** 2006-2007: $16,590

Selectivity: Selective	**Room/board:** $8,850
Acceptance rate: 38%	**Average debt:** $17,953
Student/faculty ratio: 9/1	**Proportion who borrowed:** 65%

UNDERGRADUATE STUDENT BODY STATS

2005-2006 enrollment: 670 full-time; 41 part-time. Men: 0%; women: 100%. **Ethnic makeup:** African American: 16%; American-Indian: 1%; Asian American: 2%; Hispanic: 3%; White: 74%; International: 4%.

ADMISSIONS FACTS AND FIGURES

Phone: (770) 534-6100. **Email:** wcadmissions@lib.brenau.edu. **Website:** http://www.brenau.edu. **Application deadlines for fall 2007:** Regular decision: Rolling. Early decision: Not offered. Early action: Not offered. Admission can be deferred. **Application fee:** $35. Common application is accepted. **To apply online, go to:** https://secure.brenau.edu/WCApp.htm. **Admissions requirements/recommendations:** High school units required (recommended): English: 4; Mathematics: 3; Science: 2; Foreign language: 3. Tests: The college uses SAT or ACT scores in admissions decisions. Either SAT or ACT required. For admission to the fall 2007 entering class, the school will accept: ACT without writing. Campus visit: Recommended. Admissions interview: Recommended. Off-campus interview: May be arranged. **Factors that count in admissions decisions:** *Academic:* Secondary school record: Very important. Class rank: Important. Letters of recommendation: Considered. Standardized test scores: Important. Essay: Considered. *Nonacademic:* Interview: Considered. Extracurricular activities: Considered. Talent/ability: Considered. Character/personal qualities: Considered. Alumni/ae relationship: Not considered. Geographical residence: Not considered. State residency: Not considered. Religious affiliation/commitment: Not considered. Minority status: Not considered. Volunteer work: Considered. Work experience: Not considered. **Other schools with the greatest overlap in applicants:** Agnes Scott College; Berry College; Georgia Southern University; North Georgia College and State University; University of Georgia. **Admissions statistics for the fall 2005 entering class:** Total applicants: 2,063. Total accepted: 778. Freshmen enrolled: 176; 14% were from out of state. Overall acceptance rate: 38%. **Size of waiting list:** 0 applicants; enrolled from waiting list: 0. **First-year students who submitted SAT scores:** 88%. Scores (25/75 percentile): Verbal: 460-560, Math: 450-540, Combined:

910-1100. **First-year students submitting ACT scores:** 33%. Scores (25/75 percentile): English: N/A, Math: N/A, Composite: 18-23.

ACADEMICS

Year founded: 1878. **Academic calendar:** Semester. **Degrees offered:** bachelor's, master's, post-master's certificate. **Most popular majors:** 30% health professions and related clinical sciences, 21% visual and performing arts, 13% education, 10% business, management, marketing, and related support services, 8% psychology. **Major fields of study:** area, ethnic, cultural, and gender studies; biological and biomedical sciences; business, management, marketing, and related support services; communication, journalism, and related programs; education; English language and literature/letters; health professions and related clinical sciences; history; legal professions and studies; liberal arts and sciences studies, and humanities; mathematics and statistics; natural resources and conservation; parks, recreation, leisure, and fitness studies; psychology; public administration and social service professions; social sciences; visual and performing arts. **Areas of required coursework:** arts/fine arts, humanities, computer literacy, mathematics, English (including composition), philosophy, foreign languages, sciences (biological or physical), history, social science, other. **Pre-professional programs:** prelaw. **Special academic programs:** accelerated program, cross-registration, distance learning, double major, dual enrollment, exchange student program (domestic), honors program, independent study, internships, liberal arts/career combination, student-designed major, study abroad, teacher certificate program, weekend college. **Teacher certification offered in:** early childhood, special education, middle/junior high. **Faculty and instruction (2005-2006):** Total instructional faculty: 72 full-time, 33 part-time (31% men; 69% women; 7% minorities). Full-time faculty with Ph.D. or other terminal degree: 86%. Student/faculty ratio: 9/1. Classes of fewer than 20 students: 77%; of 20 to 49 students: 23%. **Advanced Placement and International Baccalaureate credit:** AP tests may be used for: Credit and/or placement. Scores accepted: 3, 4, 5. International Baccalaureate exams may be used for: Credit only. **Freshmen returning for sophomore year:** 73%. **Graduation rates:** Four-year: 42%; five-year: 51%; six-year: 42%.

COSTS AND FINANCIAL AID

Financial aid office: (770) 534-6176. **Expenses (2006-2007):** Tuition and fees 2006-2007: $16,590; room/board: $8,850. Estimated books and supplies: $875; transportation: $850; personal expenses: $1,250. **Financial aid:** Priority filing date for institution's financial aid form: April 15. In 2005-2006, 81% of undergraduates applied for financial aid. Of those, 73% were determined to have financial need; 33% had their need fully met. Average financial aid package (proportion receiving): $14,861 (73%). Average amount of gift aid, such as scholarships or grants (proportion receiving): $12,411 (73%). Average amount of self-help aid, such as work study or loans (proportion receiving): $3,523 (50%). Average need-based loan (excluding PLUS or other private loans): $3,439. Among students who received need-based aid, the average percentage of need met: 80%. Among students who received aid based on merit, the average award (and the proportion receiving): $7,643 (18%). The average athletic scholarship (and the proportion receiving): $7,542 (3%). Average amount of debt of borrowers graduating in 2005: $17,953. Proportion who borrowed: 65%.

CAMPUS LIFE AND EXTRACURRICULAR ACTIVITIES

Campus housing available (% using): women's dorms (62%), sorority housing (32%), apartment for single students (5%), special housing for disabled students (0%), special housing for international students (1%). Students who live in college-owned, operated, or affiliated housing: 55%. **Student employment:** During the 2005-2006 academic year, 25% of undergraduates worked on campus. Average per-year earnings: $1,600. **Clubs and organizations:** Number of student organizations: 44. Activities include: choral groups, dance, drama/theater, literary magazine, musical theater, opera, radio station, student government, student newspaper, yearbook. Number of fraternities: 0; sororities: 8. of women in sororities: 30%. Average proportion of students who stay on campus on weekends: 50%. **Sports program (2005-2006):** Member of NAIA. **Women's intercollegiate varsity sports:** cross-country, soccer, softball, tennis, volleyball.

SERVICES AND FACILITIES

Basic services: nonremedial tutoring, women's center, placement service, health service. **Remedial assistance:** reading, math, writing, study skills, other. **Counseling services:** minority student, career, personal, academic, older student, psychological, birth control, religious. **For learning-disabled students:** School does not offer a structured program with separate admission and additional fees. Total undergraduates in learning-disabled program or receiving services: 50. Services include: remedial math, remedial English, reading machines, remedial reading, tape recorders, other special classes, diagnostic testing service, untimed tests, note-taking services, oral tests, learning center, readers, extended time for tests, tutors, priority registration, priority seating, texts on tape. **Library:** Number of titles: 78,400; number of current serial subscriptions: 181. **Information technology resources:** Students are not required to lease or own a computer. Number of campus computers available to all students: 250. School has a wireless network. Approximate number of users that can be accommodated: 750. Proportion of college-owned housing units wired for high-speed internet access: 99%. **Campus safety:** Security services offered: 24-hour foot-and-vehicle patrols, late-night transport/escort service, 24-hour emergency telephones, lighted pathways/sidewalks, controlled dormitory access (key, security card, etc).

TRANSFER AND INTERNATIONAL STUDENTS
Transfer students: May apply for admission for the following academic terms: Fall, Spring, Summer. Applicants need a minimum number of credits to apply. For fall 2005: Transfer applications received: 409. Transfer applicants offered admission: 265. Transfer applicants enrolled: 92. **International students:** Number of foreign undergraduates: 29 (4% of student body). Number of countries represented: 14. Minimum TOEFL score required: 500 (paper); 173 (computer).

Brewton-Parker College

- **Address:** PO Box 197, Mount Vernon, GA 30445
- **Website:** http://www.bpc.edu
- **Private; Religious affiliation:** Baptist
- **Enrollment:** 846 full-time; 248 part-time

KEY STATS
✔ **U.S News College Ranking:** fourth tier, Comp. Coll.–Bachelor's (South) ·
✔ **SAT Score (25th/75th percentile):** 840-1080
✔ **Tuition:** 2005-2006: $11,584

Selectivity: Less selective	**Room/board:** $4,820
Acceptance rate: 97%	**Average debt:** $19,230
Student/faculty ratio: 6/1	**Proportion who borrowed:** 83%

Clark Atlanta University

- **Address:** 223 James P. Brawley Drive SW, Atlanta, GA 30314
- **Website:** http://www.cau.edu
- **Private; Religious affiliation:** Methodist
- **Enrollment:** 3,516 full-time; 151 part-time

KEY STATS
✔ **U.S News College Ranking:** fourth tier, National Universities
✔ **SAT Score (25th/75th percentile):** 690-1173
✔ **Tuition:** 2006-2007: $15,360

Selectivity: Less selective	**Room/board:** $6,888
Acceptance rate: 47%	**Average debt:** N/A
Student/faculty ratio: 18/1	**Proportion who borrowed:** N/A

UNDERGRADUATE STUDENT BODY STATS
2005-2006 enrollment: 3,516 full-time; 151 part-time. Men: 27%; women: 73%. **Ethnic makeup:** African American: 90%; White: 9%.

ADMISSIONS FACTS AND FIGURES
Phone: (800) 688-3228. **Email:** jdodds@cau.edu. **Website:** http://www.cau.edu. **Application deadlines for fall 2007:** Regular decision: June 1. Early decision: Not offered. Early action: Send application by: N/A; Decision sent by: N/A. Admission can be deferred. **Application fee:** $35. Common application is accepted. **Admissions requirements/recommendations:** High school units required (recommended): English: 4; Mathematics: 3; Science: 2; Foreign language: 2; Social studies: 3; Academic electives: 3; Total units: 17. Tests: The college uses SAT or ACT scores in admissions decisions. Either SAT or ACT required. For admission to the fall 2007 entering class, the school will accept: ACT with writing, ACT without writing. Campus visit: Recommended. Admissions interview: Neither required nor recommended. Off-campus interview: Not available. **Factors that count**

in admissions decisions: *Academic:* Secondary school record: Very important. Class rank: Considered. Letters of recommendation: Very important. Standardized test scores: Very important. Essay: Important. *Nonacademic:* Interview: Considered. Extracurricular activities: Considered. Talent/ability: Considered. Character/personal qualities: Considered. Alumni/ae relationship: Considered. Geographical residence: Not considered. State residency: Not considered. Religious affiliation/commitment: Not considered. Minority status: Not considered. Volunteer work: Considered. Work experience: Considered. **Admissions statistics for the fall 2005 entering class:** Total applicants: 8,150. Total accepted: 3,796. Freshmen enrolled: 881; 81% were from out of state. Overall acceptance rate: 47%. Non-early acceptance rate: 47%. **Average high school grade point average:** 3.0. **First-year students who submitted SAT scores:** 75%. Scores (25/75 percentile): Verbal: 330-593, Math: 360-580, Combined: 690-1173. **First-year students submitting ACT scores:** 41%. Scores (25/75 percentile): English: N/A, Math: N/A, Composite: 14-25.

ACADEMICS
Year founded: 1988. **Academic calendar:** Semester. **Degrees offered:** certificate, bachelor's, post-bachelor's certificate, master's, doctorate. **Most popular majors:** 27% business, management, marketing, and related support services, 14% communication, journalism, and related programs, 9% security and protective services, 7% biological and biomedical sciences, 7% psychology. **Major fields of study:** biological and biomedical sciences; business, management, marketing, and related support services; communication, journalism, and related programs; computer and information sciences and support services; education; engineering; English language and literature/letters; foreign languages, literatures, and linguistics; health professions and related clinical sciences; history; liberal arts and sciences studies, and humanities; mathematics and statistics; philosophy and religious studies; physical sciences; psychology; public administration and social service professions; security and protective services; social sciences; visual and performing arts. **Areas of required coursework:** arts/fine arts, computer literacy, mathematics, English (including composition), philosophy, foreign languages, sciences (biological or physical), history, social science, other. **Special academic programs:** accelerated program, cooperative (work-study plan) program, cross-registration, distance learning, double major, dual enrollment, honors program, independent study, internships, student-designed major, study abroad, teacher certificate program, weekend college. **Teacher certification offered in:** early childhood, special education, elementary, middle/junior high, secondary. **Cooperative education programs:** other. **Reserve Officers Training Corps (ROTC):** Army ROTC: Offered on campus; Navy ROTC: Offered on campus; Air Force ROTC: Offered on campus. **Faculty and instruction (2005-2006):** Total instructional faculty: 244 full-time, 3 part-time (63% men; 37% women; 0% minorities). Full-time faculty with Ph.D. or other terminal degree: 18%. Student/faculty ratio: 18/1. Classes of fewer than 20 students: 43%; of 20 to 49 students: 51%; of 50 or more students: 6%. **Advanced Placement and International Baccalaureate credit:** International Baccalaureate exams may be used for: Credit only. **Freshmen returning for sophomore year:** 71%. **Graduation rates:** Four-year: 19%; five-year: 30%; six-year: 32%. **Graduate study:** 29% of students pursue further study immediately upon graduation; 10% within one year. Fields in which graduates pursue further study: law, 3%; medicine, 2%.

COSTS AND FINANCIAL AID
Financial aid office: (404) 880-8111. **Expenses (2006-2007):** Tuition and fees 2006-2007: $15,360; room/board: $6,888. **Financial aid:** Priority filing date for institution's financial aid form: March 1; deadline: March 1. In 2005-2006, 95% of undergraduates applied for financial aid. Of those, 86% were determined to have financial need; Average financial aid package (proportion receiving): N/A (86%). Average amount of gift aid, such as scholarships or grants (proportion receiving): N/A (77%).

CAMPUS LIFE AND EXTRACURRICULAR ACTIVITIES
Campus housing available (% using): coed dorms (39%), women's dorms (16%), men's dorms (10%), apartment for single students (35%), other housing options. **Student employment:** During the 2005-2006 academic year, 6% of undergraduates worked on campus. Average per-year earnings: $8,237. **Clubs and organizations:** Number of student organizations: 80. Activities include: choral groups, concert band, dance, drama/theater, jazz band, literary magazine, marching band, music ensembles, musical theater, radio station, student government, student newspaper, student film society, symphony orchestra, television station, yearbook. Number of fraternities: 5; sororities: 4. **Sports program (2005-2006):** Member of NCAA II. *Men's intercollegiate varsity sports:* baseball, basketball, cross-country, football, golf, track and field (outdoor). *Women's intercollegiate varsity sports:* basketball, cross-country, golf, softball, tennis, track and field (outdoor), volleyball.

SERVICES AND FACILITIES

Basic services: nonremedial tutoring, placement service, health service. **Remedial assistance:** reading, math, writing, study skills, other. **Counseling services:** minority student, career, personal, veteran student, academic, older student, psychological, religious, other. **For learning-disabled students:** School does not offer a structured program with separate admission and additional fees. Total undergraduates in learning-disabled program or receiving services: 51. Services include: tape recorders, untimed tests, readers, extended time for tests, tutors, substitution of courses, other testing accomodations. **Library:** Number of titles: 520,727; number of current serial subscriptions: 17,356. **Information technology resources:** Students are not required to lease or own a computer. Number of campus computers available to all students: 640. School has a wireless network. Proportion of college-owned housing units wired for high-speed internet access: 100%. **Campus safety:** Security services offered: 24-hour foot-and-vehicle patrols, late-night transport/escort service, 24-hour emergency telephones, lighted pathways/sidewalks, controlled dormitory access (key, security card, etc).

TRANSFER AND INTERNATIONAL STUDENTS

Transfer students: May apply for admission for the following academic terms: Fall, Spring. Applicants need a minimum number of credits to apply. For fall 2005: Transfer applications received: 1,311. Transfer applicants offered admission: 560. Transfer applicants enrolled: 196. **International students:** Number of foreign undergraduates: 0. Minimum TOEFL score required: 500 (paper); 173 (computer).

Clayton State University

- **Address:** 5900 N. Lee Street, Morrow, GA 30260
- **Website:** http://www.clayton.edu
- **Public**
- **Enrollment:** 3,351 full-time; 2,861 part-time

KEY STATS

✔ **U.S News College Ranking:** third tier, Comp. Colleges–Bachelor's (South)
✔ **SAT Score (25th/75th percentile):** 880-1070
✔ **Tuition:** 2006-2007: $2,932 in state, $10,248 out of state

Selectivity: Less selective	**Room/board:** N/A
Acceptance rate: 37%	**Average debt:** $13,400
Student/faculty ratio: 17/1	**Proportion who borrowed:** 27%

UNDERGRADUATE STUDENT BODY STATS

2005-2006 enrollment: 3,351 full-time; 2,861 part-time. Men: 30%; women: 70%. **Ethnic makeup:** African American: 50%; Asian American: 4%; Hispanic: 2%; White: 40%; International: 2%.

ADMISSIONS FACTS AND FIGURES

Phone: (770) 961-3500. **Email:** ccsu-info@mail.clayton.edu. **Website:** http://www.clayton.edu. **Application deadlines for fall 2007:** Regular decision: July 1. Early decision: Not offered. Early action: Not offered. Admission can be deferred. **Application fee:** $40. Common application is not accepted. **To apply online, go to:** http://www.clayton.edu/futurestudents.htm. **Admissions requirements/recommendations:** High school units required (recommended): English: 4 (4); Mathematics: 4 (4); Science: 3 (4); Foreign language: 2 (3); Social studies: 3 (3); History: (2); Academic electives: (2); Total units: 16 (22). Tests: The college uses SAT or ACT scores in admissions decisions. SAT required. For admission to the fall 2007 entering class, the school will accept: ACT with writing, ACT without writing. Campus visit: Recommended. Admissions interview: Neither required nor recommended. Off-campus interview: Not available. **Factors that count in admissions decisions:** *Academic:* Secondary school record: Very important. Class rank: Considered. Letters of recommendation: Considered. Standardized test scores: Very important. Essay: Important. *Nonacademic:* Interview: Not considered. Extracurricular activities: Considered. Talent/ability: Considered. Character/personal qualities: Not considered. Alumni/ae relationship: Not considered. Geographical residence: Not considered. State residency: Not considered. Religious affiliation/commitment: Not considered. Minority status: Not considered. Volunteer work: Not considered. Work experience: Not considered. **Other schools with the greatest overlap in applicants:** Georgia College and State University; Georgia State University; Kennesaw State University; Southern Polytechnic State University; University of West Georgia. **Admissions statistics for the fall 2005 entering**

class: Total applicants: 4,273. Total accepted: 1,571. Freshmen enrolled: 1,255; 2% were from out of state. Overall acceptance rate: 37%. **Average high school grade point average:** 3.0. **First-year students who submitted SAT scores:** 79%. Scores (25/75 percentile): Verbal: 450-540, Math: 430-530, Combined: 880-1070. **First-year students submitting ACT scores:** 25%. Scores (25/75 percentile): English: 17-21, Math: 17-22, Composite: 17-21.

ACADEMICS

Year founded: 1969. **Academic calendar:** Semester. **Degrees offered:** certificate, associate, transfer-associate, terminal-associate, bachelor's. **Most popular majors:** 38% business, management, marketing, and related support services, 24% health professions and related clinical sciences, 11% psychology, 7% computer and information sciences and support services, 6% education. **Major fields of study:** biological and biomedical sciences; business, management, marketing, and related support services; communication, journalism, and related programs; computer and information sciences and support services; education; health professions and related clinical sciences; history; liberal arts and sciences studies, and humanities; psychology; security and protective services; visual and performing arts. **Areas of required coursework:** arts/fine arts, humanities, computer literacy, mathematics, English (including composition), philosophy, foreign languages, sciences (biological or physical), history, social science, other. **Pre-professional programs:** pre-law, pre-dentistry, pre-medicine, pre-veterinary science, pre-pharmacy, other. **Special academic programs (% participation):** cross-registration (1%), distance learning (10%), double major (10%), dual enrollment (1%), honors program (2%), independent study (26%), internships (71%), student-designed major (3%), study abroad (12%), teacher certificate program (2%). **Teacher certification offered in:** middle/junior high. **Reserve Officers Training Corps (ROTC):** Army ROTC: Offered at cooperating institution (Georgia State University); Navy ROTC: Offered at cooperating institution (Georgia Institute of Technology); Air Force ROTC: Offered at cooperating institution (Georgia Institute of Technology). **Faculty and instruction (2005-2006):** Total instructional faculty: 197 full-time, 170 part-time (46% men; 54% women; 29% minorities). Full-time faculty with Ph.D. or other terminal degree: 74%. Student/faculty ratio: 17/1. Classes of fewer than 20 students: 51%; of 20 to 49 students: 45%; of 50 or more students: 4%. **Advanced Placement and International Baccalaureate credit:** AP tests may be used for: Credit only. Scores accepted: 3, 4, 5. International Baccalaureate exams may be used for: Credit only. **Freshmen returning for sophomore year:** 61%. **Graduation rates:** Four-year: 11%; five-year: 18%; six-year: 20%. **Graduate study:** 12% of students pursue further study immediately upon graduation; 20% within one year; 35% within five years. Fields in which graduates pursue further study: Master of Business Administration (MBA), 5%; law, 3%; medicine, 2%; dentistry, 1%; engineering, 2%; education, 5%; arts and sciences, 25%.

COSTS AND FINANCIAL AID

Financial aid office: (678) 466-4185. **Expenses (2006-2007):** Tuition and fees 2006-2007: $2,932 in state, $10,248 out of state; room/board: N/A. **Financial aid:** Priority filing date for institution's financial aid form: July 23. In 2005-2006, 73% of undergraduates applied for financial aid. Of those, 65% were determined to have financial need; 4% had their need fully met. Average financial aid package (proportion receiving): $2,425 (63%). Average amount of gift aid, such as scholarships or grants (proportion receiving): $1,611 (37%). Average amount of self-help aid, such as work study or loans (proportion receiving): $1,900 (51%). Average need-based loan (excluding PLUS or other private loans): $1,856. Among students who received need-based aid, the average percentage of need met: 46%. Among students who received aid based on merit, the average award (and the proportion receiving): $730 (4%). The average athletic scholarship (and the proportion receiving): $1,477 (2%). Average amount of debt of borrowers graduating in 2005: $13,400. Proportion who borrowed: 27%.

CAMPUS LIFE AND EXTRACURRICULAR ACTIVITIES

Student employment: During the 2005-2006 academic year, 4% of undergraduates worked on campus. Average per-year earnings: $7,000. **Clubs and organizations:** Number of student organizations: 42. Activities include: choral groups, concert band, drama/theater, jazz band, literary magazine, music ensembles, musical theater, opera, pep band, student government, student newspaper, student film society. Number of fraternities: 4; sororities: 3. Average proportion of students who stay on campus on weekends: 5%. **Sports program (2005-2006):** Member of NCAA II. *Men's intercollegiate varsity sports:* basketball, cross-country, golf, soccer, track and field (indoor), track and field (outdoor). *Women's intercollegiate varsity sports:* basketball, cross-country, soccer, tennis, track and field (indoor), track and field (outdoor).

SERVICES AND FACILITIES
Basic services: nonremedial tutoring, placement service, health service. **Remedial assistance:** reading, math, writing, study skills. **Counseling services:** minority student, career, military, personal, veteran student, academic, older student. **For learning-disabled students:** School does not offer a structured program with separate admission and additional fees. Total undergraduates in learning-disabled program or receiving services: 12. Services include: reading machines, tape recorders, note-taking services, readers, extended time for tests, priority registration, priority seating, texts on tape, other testing accomodations. **Library:** Number of titles: 103,645; number of current serial subscriptions: 1,713. **Information technology resources:** Students are required to lease or own a computer. Number of campus computers available to all students: 64. School has a wireless network. Approximate number of users that can be accommodated: 1,500. Proportion of college-owned housing units wired for high-speed internet access: 100%. **Campus safety:** Security services offered: 24-hour foot-and-vehicle patrols, late-night transport/escort service, 24-hour emergency telephones, lighted pathways/sidewalks.

TRANSFER AND INTERNATIONAL STUDENTS
Transfer students: May apply for admission for the following academic terms: Fall, Spring, Summer. Applicants need a minimum number of credits to apply. For fall 2005: Transfer applications received: 2,102. Transfer applicants offered admission: 1,614. Transfer applicants enrolled: 889. **International students:** Number of foreign undergraduates: 151 (2% of student body). Number of countries represented: 82. Minimum TOEFL score required: 550 (paper); 210 (computer). Average TOEFL score: 573 (paper).

Columbus State University

- **Address:** 4225 University Avenue, Columbus, GA 31907
- **Website:** http://www.colstate.edu
- **Public**
- **Enrollment:** 4,414 full-time; 2,210 part-time

KEY STATS
✔ **U.S News College Ranking:** fourth tier, Universities–Master's (South)
✔ **SAT Score (25th/75th percentile):** 880-1110
✔ **Tuition:** 2006-2007: $3,164 in state, $10,772 out of state
  Selectivity: Less selective **Room/board:** $6,284
  Acceptance rate: 64% **Average debt:** $24,675
  Student/faculty ratio: 20/1 **Proportion who borrowed:** 71%

UNDERGRADUATE STUDENT BODY STATS
2005-2006 enrollment: 4,414 full-time; 2,210 part-time. Men: 38%; women: 62%. **Ethnic makeup:** African American: 32%; Asian American: 2%; Hispanic: 3%; White: 62%; International: 1%.

ADMISSIONS FACTS AND FIGURES
Phone: (706) 568-2035. **Email:** admissions@colstate.edu. **Website:** http://www.colstate.edu. **Application deadlines for fall 2007:** Regular decision: July 1. Early decision: Not offered. Early action: Not offered. Admission can be deferred. **Application fee:** $25. Common application is not accepted. **To apply online, go to:** http://admissions.colstate.edu/howtoapply.htm. **Admissions requirements/recommendations:** High school classes required (recommended): English: 4; Mathematics: 4; Science: 3; Foreign language: 2; Social studies: 3; Total units: 16. Tests: The college uses SAT or ACT scores in admissions decisions. Either SAT or ACT required. For admission to the fall 2007 entering class, the school will accept: ACT with writing, ACT without writing. Campus visit: Recommended. Admissions interview: Neither required nor recommended. Off-campus interview: May not be arranged. **Factors that count in admissions decisions:** *Academic:* Secondary school record: Important. Class rank: Not considered. Letters of recommendation: Not considered. Standardized test scores: Important. Essay: Not considered. *Nonacademic:* Interview: Considered. Extracurricular activities: Considered. Talent/ability: Considered. Character/personal qualities: Not considered. Alumni/ae relationship: Not considered. Geographical residence: Considered. State residency: Not considered. Religious affiliation/commitment: Not considered. Minority status: Not considered. Volunteer work: Not considered. Work experience: Not considered. **Admissions statistics for the fall 2005 entering class:** Total applicants: 3,005. Total accepted: 1,921. Freshmen enrolled: 1,184; Overall acceptance rate:

64%. **Average high school grade point average:** 3.0. **First-year students who submitted SAT scores:** 80%. Scores (25/75 percentile): Verbal: 450-560, Math: 430-550, Combined: 880-1110. **First-year students submitting ACT scores:** 30%. Scores (25/75 percentile): English: 16-23, Math: 16-21, Composite: 17-22.

ACADEMICS
Year founded: 1958. **Academic calendar:** Semester. **Degrees offered:** certificate, associate, bachelor's, post-bachelor's certificate, master's, post-master's certificate. **Most popular majors:** 22% business, management, marketing, and related support services, 15% education, 11% computer and information sciences and support services, 9% security and protective services, 8% biological and biomedical sciences. **Major fields of study:** biological and biomedical sciences; business, management, marketing, and related support services; communication, journalism, and related programs; education; English language and literature/letters; foreign languages, literatures, and linguistics; health professions and related clinical sciences; history; mathematics and statistics; physical sciences; psychology; social sciences; visual and performing arts. **Areas of required coursework:** arts/fine arts, humanities, computer literacy, mathematics, English (including composition), sciences (biological or physical), history, social science. **Pre-professional programs:** pre-medicine, other. **Special academic programs:** accelerated program, cooperative (work-study plan) program, distance learning, double major, dual enrollment, English as a Second Language (ESL), honors program, independent study, internships, liberal arts/career combination, study abroad, teacher certificate program. **Teacher certification offered in:** early childhood, special education, middle/junior high, secondary. **Reserve Officers Training Corps (ROTC):** Army ROTC: Offered on campus. **Faculty and instruction (2005-2006):** Total instructional faculty: 216 full-time, 195 part-time (51% men; 49% women; 17% minorities). Full-time faculty with Ph.D. or other terminal degree: 76%. Student/faculty ratio: 20/1. Classes of fewer than 20 students: 30%; of 20 to 49 students: 64%; of 50 or more students: 6%. **Freshmen returning for sophomore year:** 71%. **Graduation rates:** Four-year: 8%; five-year: 22%; six-year: 26%.

COSTS AND FINANCIAL AID
Financial aid office: (706) 568-2036. **Expenses (2006-2007):** Tuition and fees 2006-2007: $3,164 in state, $10,772 out of state; room/board: $6,284. **Financial aid:** Priority filing date for institution's financial aid form: May 1. In 2005-2006, 61% of undergraduates applied for financial aid. Of those, 50% were determined to have financial need; 63% had their need fully met. Average financial aid package (proportion receiving): $3,988 (47%). Average amount of gift aid, such as scholarships or grants (proportion receiving): $3,214 (47%). Average amount of self-help aid, such as work study or loans (proportion receiving): $3,645 (36%). Average need-based loan (excluding PLUS or other private loans): $3,456. Among students who received need-based aid, the average percentage of need met: 64%. Among students who received aid based on merit, the average award (and the proportion receiving): $1,672 (27%). The average athletic scholarship (and the proportion receiving): $2,491 (4%). Average amount of debt of borrowers graduating in 2005: $24,675. Proportion who borrowed: 71%.

CAMPUS LIFE AND EXTRACURRICULAR ACTIVITIES
Campus housing available: coed dorms, apartment for single students, special housing for disabled students, special housing for international students. **Student employment:** During the 2005-2006 academic year, 4% of undergraduates worked on campus. Average per-year earnings: $6. **Clubs and organizations:** Number of student organizations: 62. Activities include: choral groups, concert band, dance, drama/theater, jazz band, literary magazine, music ensembles, musical theater, opera, pep band, student government, student newspaper, symphony orchestra. Number of fraternities: 5; sororities: 6. **Sports program (2005-2006):** Member of NCAA II. *Men's intercollegiate varsity sports:* baseball, basketball, cross-country, golf, gymnastics, tennis. *Women's intercollegiate varsity sports:* basketball, cross-country, soccer, softball, tennis.

SERVICES AND FACILITIES
Basic services: nonremedial tutoring, placement service, health service, other. **Remedial assistance:** reading, math, writing, study skills. **Counseling services:** minority student, career, military, personal, veteran student, academic, older student, psychological. **For learning-disabled students:** School does not offer a structured program with separate admission and additional fees. Services include: remedial math, remedial English, reading machines, remedial reading, tape recorders, videotaped classes, diagnostic testing service, untimed tests, note-taking services, oral tests, learning center, readers, extended time for tests, tutors. **Library:** Number of titles: 376,622; number

of current serial subscriptions: 1,450. **Information technology resources:** Students are not required to lease or own a computer. School has a wireless network. Proportion of college-owned housing units wired for high-speed internet access: 100%. **Campus safety:** Security services offered: 24-hour foot-and-vehicle patrols, late-night transport/escort service, 24-hour emergency telephones, lighted pathways/sidewalks, controlled dormitory access (key, security card, etc).

TRANSFER AND INTERNATIONAL STUDENTS

Transfer students: May apply for admission for the following academic terms: Fall, Spring, Summer. Applicants need a minimum number of credits to apply. For fall 2005: Transfer applications received: 1,293. Transfer applicants offered admission: 882. Transfer applicants enrolled: 512. **International students:** Number of foreign undergraduates: 83 (1% of student body). Minimum TOEFL score required: 550 (paper); 213 (computer). Average TOEFL score: 564 (paper).

Covenant College

- **Address:** 14049 Scenic Highway, Lookout Mountain, GA 30750
- **Website:** http://www.covenant.edu
- **Private; Religious affiliation:** Presbyterian Church in America
- **Enrollment:** 893 full-time; 25 part-time

KEY STATS

✔ **U.S News College Ranking:** 9, Comp. Colleges–Bachelor's (South)
✔ **SAT Score (25th/75th percentile):** 1050-1280
✔ **Tuition:** 2006-2007: $22,040

Selectivity: Selective	**Room/board:** $5,680
Acceptance rate: 66%	**Average debt:** $14,980
Student/faculty ratio: 14/1	**Proportion who borrowed:** 58%

UNDERGRADUATE STUDENT BODY STATS

2005-2006 enrollment: 893 full-time; 25 part-time. Men: 44%; women: 56%. **Ethnic makeup:** African American: 3%; Asian American: 1%; Hispanic: 2%; White: 93%; International: 1%. **Religious preference:** Presbyterian Church in America: 63%; Other: 37%.

ADMISSIONS FACTS AND FIGURES

Phone: (706) 820-2398. **Email:** admissions@covenant.edu. **Website:** http://www.covenant.edu. **Application deadlines for fall 2007:** Regular decision: Rolling; decision sent by May 31. Early decision: Not offered. Early action: Not offered. Admission can be deferred. **Application fee:** $35. Common application is not accepted. **Admissions requirements/recommendations:** High school units required (recommended): English: 4 (4); Mathematics: 3 (3); Science: 2 (2); Foreign language: 2 (2); Social studies: 2 (2); Academic electives: 3 (3); Total units: 16 (16). Tests: The college uses SAT or ACT scores in admissions decisions. Either SAT or ACT required. For admission to the fall 2007 entering class, the school will accept: ACT with writing. Campus visit: Recommended. Admissions interview: Required. Off-campus interview: May be arranged. **Factors that count in admissions decisions:** *Academic:* Secondary school record: Very important. Class rank: Considered. Letters of recommendation: Very important. Standardized test scores: Very important. Essay: Considered. *Nonacademic:* Interview: Not considered. Extracurricular activities: Not considered. Talent/ability: Not considered. Character/personal qualities: Very important. Alumni/ae relationship: Considered. Geographical residence: Not considered. State residency: Not considered. Religious affiliation/commitment: Considered. Minority status: Not considered. Volunteer work: Not considered. Work experience: Not considered. **Other schools with the greatest overlap in applicants:** Belhaven College; Berry College; Erskine College; University of Georgia; Wheaton College. **Admissions statistics for the fall 2005 entering class:** Total applicants: 817. Total accepted: 543. Freshmen enrolled: 263; 77% were from out of state. Overall acceptance rate: 66%. **Size of waiting list:** 0 applicants; enrolled from waiting list: 0. **Credentials of fall 2005 freshmen:** 15% ranked in the top 10 percent of their high school class; 42% were in the top 25 percent, and 78% were in the top half. (Proportion submitting class standing: 47%.) **Average high school grade point average:** 3.6. **First-year students who submitted SAT scores:** 75%. Scores (25/75 percentile): Verbal: 540-640, Math: 510-640, Combined: 1050-1280. **First-year students submitting ACT scores:** 45%. Scores (25/75 percentile): English: 21-29, Math: 19-26, Composite: 21-28.

ACADEMICS

Year founded: 1955. **Academic calendar:** Semester. **Degrees offered:** associate, transfer-associate, bachelor's, master's. **Most popular majors:** 15% English language and literature/letters, 13% psychology, 11% history, 9% philosophy and religious studies, 8% social sciences. **Major fields of study:** business, management, marketing, and related support services; computer and information sciences and support services; education; English language and literature/letters; health professions and related clinical sciences; history; mathematics and statistics; multi/interdisciplinary studies; philosophy and religious studies; physical sciences; psychology; social sciences; theology and religious vocations; visual and performing arts. **Areas of required coursework:** arts/fine arts, humanities, computer literacy, mathematics, English (including composition), philosophy, sciences (biological or physical), history, social science. **Pre-professional programs:** pre-law, pre-medicine, other. **Special academic programs (% participation):** double major (10%), dual enrollment (0%), exchange student program (domestic) (1%), independent study (100%), internships (10%), student-designed major (5%), study abroad (100%), teacher certificate program (10%). **Teacher certification offered in:** early childhood, elementary, middle/junior high, secondary. **Faculty and instruction (2005-2006):** Total instructional faculty: 58 full-time, 19 part-time (79% men; 21% women; 4% minorities). Full-time faculty with Ph.D. or other terminal degree: 83%. Student/faculty ratio: 14/1. Classes of fewer than 20 students: 60%; of 20 to 49 students: 38%; of 50 or more students: 2%. **Advanced Placement and International Baccalaureate credit:** AP tests may be used for: Credit and/or placement. Scores accepted: 3. International Baccalaureate exams may be used for: Credit and/or placement. **Freshmen returning for sophomore year:** 72%. **Graduation rates:** Four-year: 56%; five-year: 65%; six-year: 63%.

COSTS AND FINANCIAL AID

Financial aid office: (706) 419-1126. **Expenses (2006-2007):** Tuition and fees 2006-2007: $22,040; room/board: $5,680. **Financial aid:** Priority filing date for institution's financial aid form: March 1. In 2005-2006, 81% of undergraduates applied for financial aid. Of those, 71% were determined to have financial need; 24% had their need fully met. Average financial aid package (proportion receiving): $15,096 (71%). Average amount of gift aid, such as scholarships or grants (proportion receiving): $11,054 (68%). Average amount of self-help aid, such as work study or loans (proportion receiving): $4,241 (61%). Average need-based loan (excluding PLUS or other private loans): $4,218. Among students who received need-based aid, the average percentage of need met: 84%. Among students who received aid based on merit, the average award (and the proportion receiving): $6,042 (22%). The average athletic scholarship (and the proportion receiving): $4,453 (5%). Average amount of debt of borrowers graduating in 2005: $14,980. Proportion who borrowed: 58%.

CAMPUS LIFE AND EXTRACURRICULAR ACTIVITIES

Campus housing available (% using): women's dorms (56%), men's dorms (36%), apartment for single students (8%). Students who live in college-owned, operated, or affiliated housing: 88%. **Student employment:** During the 2005-2006 academic year, 1% of undergraduates worked on campus. Average per-year earnings: $1,500. **Clubs and organizations:** Number of student organizations: 28. Activities include: choral groups, concert band, drama/theater, literary magazine, music ensembles, student government, student newspaper, yearbook. Number of fraternities: 0; sororities: 0. Average proportion of students who stay on campus on weekends: 90%. **Sports program (2005-2006):** Member of NAIA. *Men's intercollegiate varsity sports:* basketball, cross-country, golf, soccer. *Women's intercollegiate varsity sports:* basketball, cross-country, soccer, volleyball.

SERVICES AND FACILITIES

Basic services: placement service, health service, health insurance. **Remedial assistance:** study skills, other. **Counseling services:** career, personal, psychological, religious, other. **For learning-disabled students:** School does not offer a structured program with separate admission and additional fees. Total undergraduates in learning-disabled program or receiving services: 5. Services include: remedial math, remedial English, diagnostic testing service, extended time for tests, tutors. **Library:** Number of titles: 90,000; number of current serial subscriptions: 1,300. **Information technology resources:** Students are not required to lease or own a computer. Number of campus computers available to all students: 137. School has a wireless network. Approximate number of users that can be accommodated: 600. Proportion of college-owned housing units wired for high-speed internet access: 98%. **Campus safety:** Security services offered: late-night transport/escort service, lighted pathways/sidewalks, controlled dormitory access (key, security card, etc).

TRANSFER AND INTERNATIONAL STUDENTS

Transfer students: May apply for admission for the following academic terms: Fall, Spring. Applicants need a minimum number of credits to apply. For fall 2005: Transfer applications received: 116. Transfer applicants offered admission: 61. Transfer applicants enrolled: 36. **International students:** Number of foreign undergraduates: 10 (1% of student body). Number of countries represented: 6. Minimum TOEFL score required: 540 (paper); 207 (computer).

Emmanuel College

- **Address:** PO Box 129, Franklin Springs, GA 30639
- **Website:** http://www.emmanuelcollege.edu
- **Private; Religious affiliation:** International Pentecostal Holiness
- **Enrollment:** 594 full-time; 113 part-time

KEY STATS

✔ **U.S News College Ranking:** third tier, Comp. Colleges–Bachelor's (South)
✔ **SAT Score (25th/75th percentile):** 870-1100
✔ **Tuition:** 2006-2007: $10,590

Selectivity: Less selective	**Room/board:** $4,970
Acceptance rate: 38%	**Average debt:** $18,700
Student/faculty ratio: 10/1	**Proportion who borrowed:** N/A

UNDERGRADUATE STUDENT BODY STATS

2005-2006 enrollment: 594 full-time; 113 part-time. Men: 43%; women: 57%. **Ethnic makeup:** African American: 15%; Asian American: 1%; Hispanic: 1%; White: 82%; International: 1%. **Religious preference:** Protestant: 79%; International Pentecostal Holiness: 21%.

ADMISSIONS FACTS AND FIGURES

Phone: (800) 860-8800. **Email:** admissions@eclions.net. **Website:** http://www.emmanuelcollege.edu. **Application deadlines for fall 2007:** Regular decision: August 1. Early decision: Not offered. Early action: Not offered. Admission can be deferred. **Application fee:** $25. Common application is not accepted. **Admissions requirements/recommendations:** Tests: The college uses SAT or ACT scores in admissions decisions. Either SAT or ACT required. For admission to the fall 2007 entering class, the school will accept: ACT with writing, ACT without writing. Campus visit: Recommended. Admissions interview: Neither required nor recommended. Off-campus interview: May be arranged. **Factors that count in admissions decisions:** *Academic:* Secondary school record: Very important. Class rank: Not considered. Letters of recommendation: Considered. Standardized test scores: Very important. Essay: Not considered. *Nonacademic:* Interview: Considered. Extracurricular activities: Not considered. Talent/ability: Not considered. Character/personal qualities: Not considered. Alumni/ae relationship: Not considered. Geographical residence: Not considered. State residency: Not considered. Religious affiliation/commitment: Considered. Minority status: Not considered. Volunteer work: Not considered. Work experience: Not considered. **Other schools with the greatest overlap in applicants:** Piedmont College; University of Georgia. **Admissions statistics for the fall 2005 entering class:** Total applicants: 1,039. Total accepted: 391. Freshmen enrolled: 231; 23% were from out of state. Overall acceptance rate: 38%. **First-year students who submitted SAT scores:** 82%. Scores (25/75 percentile): Verbal: 440-570, Math: 430-530, Combined: 870-1100. **First-year students submitting ACT scores:** 3%. Scores (25/75 percentile): English: N/A, Math: N/A, Composite: N/A.

ACADEMICS

Year founded: 1919. **Academic calendar:** Semester. **Degrees offered:** associate, bachelor's. **Most popular majors:** 28% teacher education and professional development, 19% business administration, management, and operations, 16% theological and ministerial studies. **Major fields of study:** biological and biomedical sciences; business, management, marketing, and related support services; communication, journalism, and related programs; computer and information sciences and support services; education; English language and literature/letters; health professions and related clinical sciences; history; legal professions and studies; mathematics and statistics; parks, recreation, leisure, and fitness studies; psychology; theology and religious vocations; visual and performing arts. **Areas of required coursework:** humanities, mathematics, English (including composition), philosophy, sciences (biological or physical), history, social science. **Pre-professional**

programs: pre-law, pre-medicine, pre-pharmacy. **Special academic programs (% participation):** distance learning (5%), honors program (5%), independent study (5%), internships (15%), teacher certificate program (15%). **Teacher certification offered in:** early childhood, middle/junior high, secondary. **Faculty and instruction (2005-2006):** Total instructional faculty: 44 full-time, 24 part-time (66% men; 34% women; 3% minorities). Full-time faculty with Ph.D. or other terminal degree: 70%. Student/faculty ratio: 10/1. Classes of fewer than 20 students: 69%; of 20 to 49 students: 29%; of 50 or more students: 1%. **Advanced Placement and International Baccalaureate credit:** AP tests may be used for: Credit only. Scores accepted: 3, 4, 5. **Freshmen returning for sophomore year:** 67%. **Graduation rates:** Four-year: 24%; five-year: 37%; six-year: 33%. **Graduate study:** 50% of students pursue further study immediately upon graduation.

COSTS AND FINANCIAL AID

Financial aid office: (706) 245-2843. **Expenses (2006-2007):** Tuition and fees 2006-2007: $10,590; room/board: $4,970. Estimated books and supplies: $911; transportation: $1,878; personal expenses: $1,509. **Financial aid:** Priority filing date for institution's financial aid form: March 15; deadline: May 1. In 2005-2006, 99% of undergraduates applied for financial aid. Of those, 96% were determined to have financial need; 59% had their need fully met. Average financial aid package (proportion receiving): $8,650 (96%). Average amount of gift aid, such as scholarships or grants (proportion receiving): $2,900 (96%). Average amount of self-help aid, such as work study or loans (proportion receiving): $3,870 (93%). Average need-based loan (excluding PLUS or other private loans): $3,502. Among students who received need-based aid, the average percentage of need met: 48%. Among students who received aid based on merit, the average award (and the proportion receiving): $3,413 (23%). The average athletic scholarship (and the proportion receiving): $4,478 (15%). Average amount of debt of borrowers graduating in 2005: $18,700.

CAMPUS LIFE AND EXTRACURRICULAR ACTIVITIES

Campus housing available (% using): women's dorms (40%), men's dorms (40%), apartments for married students (20%). Students who live in college-owned, operated, or affiliated housing: 44%. **Clubs and organizations:** Number of student organizations: 20. Activities include: choral groups, drama/theater, literary magazine, music ensembles, musical theater, student government, student newspaper, yearbook. Number of fraternities: 0; sororities: 0. Average proportion of students who stay on campus on weekends: 30%. **Sports program (2005-2006):** Member of NAIA. *Men's intercollegiate varsity sports:* baseball, basketball, soccer, track and field (indoor). *Women's intercollegiate varsity sports:* basketball, soccer, softball, tennis.

SERVICES AND FACILITIES

Basic services: nonremedial tutoring, health insurance. **Remedial assistance:** reading, math, writing. **Counseling services:** minority student, career, personal, veteran student, academic, religious. **For learning-disabled students:** School does not offer a structured program with separate admission and additional fees. Total undergraduates in learning-disabled program or receiving services: 20. Services include: remedial math, remedial English, remedial reading. **Library:** Number of titles: 83,700; number of current serial subscriptions: 74. **Information technology resources:** Students are not required to lease or own a computer. Number of campus computers available to all students: 60. School has a wireless network. Approximate number of users that can be accommodated: 200. Proportion of college-owned housing units wired for high-speed internet access: 100%. **Campus safety:** Security services offered: 24-hour foot-and-vehicle patrols, lighted pathways/sidewalks, student patrols, controlled dormitory access (key, security card, etc).

TRANSFER AND INTERNATIONAL STUDENTS

Transfer students: May apply for admission for the following academic terms: Fall, Spring, Summer. Applicants do not need a minimum number of credits to apply. For fall 2005: Transfer applicants enrolled: 54. **International students:** Number of foreign undergraduates: 5 (1% of student body). Number of countries represented: 3. Minimum TOEFL score required: 550 (paper); 213 (computer).

Emory University

- **Address:** 201 Dowman Drive, Atlanta, GA 30322
- **Website:** http://www.emory.edu
- **Private; Religious affiliation:** Methodist
- **Enrollment:** 6,421 full-time; 89 part-time

KEY STATS

- ✔ **U.S News College Ranking:** 18, National Universities
- ✔ **SAT Score (25th/75th percentile):** 1300-1470
- ✔ **Tuition:** 2006-2007: $32,506

Selectivity: Most selective	**Room/board:** $9,938
Acceptance rate: 37%	**Average debt:** $22,175
Student/faculty ratio: 7/1	**Proportion who borrowed:** 40%

UNDERGRADUATE STUDENT BODY STATS

2005-2006 enrollment: 6,421 full-time; 89 part-time. Men: 42%; women: 58%. **Ethnic makeup:** African American: 9%; Asian American; 16%; Hispanic: 3%; White: 67%; International: 4%. **Religious preference:** Roman Catholic: 13%; Jewish: 25%; Muslim: 2%; Hindu: 6%; Buddhist: 1%; No preference: 22%; Methodist: 6%; Other Christian: 23%; Other: 2%.

ADMISSIONS FACTS AND FIGURES

Phone: (404) 727-6036. **Email:** admiss@emory.edu. **Website:** http://www.emory.edu. **Application deadlines for fall 2007:** Regular decision: January 15; decision sent by April 1. Early decision: Send application by: November 1; Decision sent by: December 15. Early action: Not offered. Admission can be deferred. **Application fee:** $50. Common application is accepted. **To apply online, go to:** http://www.emory.edu/ADMISSIONS/admission-aid/application.htm. **Admissions requirements/recommendations:** High school units required (recommended): English: 4; Mathematics: 3 (4); Science: 2 (3); Foreign language: 2 (3); Social studies: 2; History: 2; Academic electives: 2; Total units: 16. Tests: The college uses SAT or ACT scores in admissions decisions. Either SAT or ACT required. For admission to the fall 2007 entering class, the school will accept: ACT with writing. Campus visit: Neither required nor recommended. Admissions interview: Neither required nor recommended. **Factors that count in admissions decisions:** *Academic:* Secondary school record: Very important. Class rank: Considered. Letters of recommendation: Very important. Standardized test scores: Very important. Essay: Very important. *Nonacademic:* Interview: Not considered. Extracurricular activities: Very important. Talent/ability: Important. Character/personal qualities: Important. Alumni/ae relationship: Important. Geographical residence: Considered. State residency: Considered. Religious affiliation/commitment: Not considered. Minority status: Considered. Volunteer work: Considered. Work experience: Considered. **Other schools with the greatest overlap in applicants:** Duke University; Georgetown University; University of Pennsylvania; Vanderbilt University; Washington University in St. Louis. **Admissions statistics for the fall 2005 entering class:** Total applicants: 12,011. Total accepted: 4,395. Freshmen enrolled: 1,259; 83% were from out of state. Overall acceptance rate: 37%. Early-decision acceptance rate: 52%. Non-early acceptance rate: 35%. **Size of waiting list:** 1500 applicants; enrolled from waiting list: 25. **Credentials of fall 2005 freshmen:** 90% ranked in the top 10 percent of their high school class; 98% were in the top 25 percent, and 100% were in the top half. (Proportion submitting class standing: 41%.) **Average high school grade point average:** 3.8. **First-year students who submitted SAT scores:** 93%. Scores (25/75 percentile): Verbal: 640-730, Math: 660-740, Combined: 1300-1470. **First-year students submitting ACT scores:** 36%. Scores (25/75 percentile): English: N/A, Math: N/A, Composite: 29-33.

ACADEMICS

Year founded: 1836. **Academic calendar:** Semester. **Degrees offered:** associate, bachelor's, master's, first professional, doctorate. **Most popular majors:** 12% business administration and management, 9% economics, 9% political science and government, 8% psychology, 7% biology/biological sciences. **Major fields of study:** area, ethnic, cultural, and gender studies; biological and biomedical sciences; business, management, marketing, and related support services; computer and information sciences and support services; education; English language and literature/letters; foreign languages, literatures, and linguistics; health professions and related clinical sciences; history; mathematics and statistics; natural resources and conservation; philosophy and religious studies; physical sciences; psychology; social sciences; visual and performing arts. **Areas of required coursework:** humanities, mathemat-

ics, English (including composition), foreign languages, sciences (biological or physical), history, social science, other. **Special academic programs (% participation):** accelerated program, cooperative (work-study plan) program (29%), double major, exchange student program (domestic), honors program, independent study (29%), internships (49%), study abroad (41%), teacher certificate program, other. **Teacher certification offered in:** middle/junior high, secondary. **Cooperative education programs:** business, education. **Reserve Officers Training Corps (ROTC):** Army ROTC: Offered at cooperating institution (Georgia Institute of Technology); Navy ROTC: Offered at cooperating institution (Georgia Institute of Technology); Air Force ROTC: Offered at cooperating institution (Georgia Institute of Technology). **Faculty and instruction (2005-2006):** Total instructional faculty: 1,236 full-time, 199 part-time (59% men; 41% women; 18% minorities). Full-time faculty with Ph.D. or other terminal degree: 100%. Student/faculty ratio: 7/1. Classes of fewer than 20 students: 64%; of 20 to 49 students: 29%; of 50 or more students: 8%. **Advanced Placement and International Baccalaureate credit:** AP tests may be used for: Credit and/or placement. Scores accepted: 4, 5. International Baccalaureate exams may be used for: Credit and/or placement. **Freshmen returning for sophomore year:** 94%. **Graduation rates:** Four-year: 84%; five-year: 88%; six-year: 89%. **Graduate study:** 42% of students pursue further study immediately upon graduation. Fields in which graduates pursue further study: Master of Business Administration (MBA), 3%; law, 22%; medicine, 25%; arts and sciences, 37%.

COSTS AND FINANCIAL AID

Financial aid office: (404) 727-6039. **Expenses (2006-2007):** Tuition and fees 2006-2007: $32,506; room/board: $9,938. Estimated books and supplies: $1,000; transportation: $600; personal expenses: $800. **Financial aid:** Priority filing date for institution's financial aid form: February 15; deadline: April 1. In 2005-2006, 46% of undergraduates applied for financial aid. Of those, 38% were determined to have financial need; 100% had their need fully met. Average financial aid package (proportion receiving): $27,599 (38%). Average amount of gift aid, such as scholarships or grants (proportion receiving): $21,236 (35%). Average amount of self-help aid, such as work study or loans (proportion receiving): $6,734 (32%). Average need-based loan (excluding PLUS or other private loans): $5,355. Among students who received need-based aid, the average percentage of need met: 100%. Among students who received aid based on merit, the average award (and the proportion receiving): $17,985 (6%). Average amount of debt of borrowers graduating in 2005: $22,175. Proportion who borrowed: 40%.

CAMPUS LIFE AND EXTRACURRICULAR ACTIVITIES

Campus housing available: coed dorms, women's dorms, sorority housing, fraternity housing, apartments for married students, apartment for single students, special housing for disabled students, special housing for international students. Students who live in college-owned, operated, or affiliated housing: 66%. **Student employment:** During the 2005-2006 academic year, 28% of undergraduates worked on campus. Average per-year earnings: $1,505. **Clubs and organizations:** Number of student organizations: 252. Activities include: choral groups, concert band, dance, drama/theater, jazz band, literary magazine, music ensembles, musical theater, pep band, radio station, student government, student newspaper, student film society, symphony orchestra, television station. Number of fraternities: 14; sororities: 11. Proportion of men in fraternities: 31%; of women in sororities: 33%. **Sports program (2005-2006):** Member of NCAA III. *Men's intercollegiate varsity sports:* baseball, basketball, cross-country, golf, soccer, swimming and diving, tennis, track and field (indoor), track and field (outdoor). *Women's intercollegiate varsity sports:* basketball, cross-country, soccer, softball, swimming and diving, tennis, track and field (indoor), track and field (outdoor), volleyball.

SERVICES AND FACILITIES

Basic services: nonremedial tutoring, women's center, placement service, day care, health service, health insurance. **Counseling services:** career, personal, academic, psychological. **For learning-disabled students:** School does not offer a structured program with separate admission and additional fees. Services include: other special classes, note-taking services, oral tests, readers, extended time for tests, tutors. **Library:** Number of titles: 3,166,654; number of current serial subscriptions: 55,411. **Information technology resources:** Students are not required to lease or own a computer. Number of campus computers available to all students: 650. School has a wireless network. Proportion of college-owned housing units wired for high-speed internet access: 100%. **Campus safety:** Security services offered: 24-hour foot-and-vehicle patrols, late-night transport/escort service, 24-hour emergency telephones, lighted pathways/sidewalks, student patrols, controlled dormitory access (key, security card, etc).

TRANSFER AND INTERNATIONAL STUDENTS
Transfer students: May apply for admission for the following academic terms: Fall, Spring. Applicants need a minimum number of credits to apply. For fall 2005: Transfer applications received: 351. Transfer applicants offered admission: 120. Transfer applicants enrolled: 72. **International students:** Number of foreign undergraduates: 266 (4% of student body). Number of countries represented: 73.

Fort Valley State University

- **Address:** 1005 State University Drive, Fort Valley, GA 31030-4313
- **Website:** http://www.fvsu.edu
- **Public**
- **Enrollment:** N/A

KEY STATS
✔ **U.S News College Ranking:** fourth tier, Universities–Master's (South)
✔ **ACT Score (25th/75th percentile):** 15-24
✔ **Tuition:** 2006-2007: $2,861 in state, $10,469 out of state
  Selectivity: Selective   **Room/board:** $4,720
  Acceptance rate: 54%   **Average debt:** N/A
  Student/faculty ratio: N/A   **Proportion who borrowed:** N/A

Georgia College and State University

- **Address:** 231 W. Hancock Street, Milledgeville, GA 31061
- **Website:** http://www.gcsu.edu
- **Public**
- **Enrollment:** 4,246 full-time; 555 part-time

KEY STATS
✔ **U.S News College Ranking:** 50, Universities–Master's (South)
✔ **SAT Score (25th/75th percentile):** 1030-1200
✔ **Tuition:** 2006-2007: $4,356 in state, $15,078 out of state
  Selectivity: Selective   **Room/board:** $7,116
  Acceptance rate: 60%   **Average debt:** $15,082
  Student/faculty ratio: 16/1   **Proportion who borrowed:** 57%

UNDERGRADUATE STUDENT BODY STATS
2005-2006 enrollment: 4,246 full-time; 555 part-time. Men: 41%; women: 59%. **Ethnic makeup:** African American: 8%; Asian American: 1%; Hispanic: 1%; White: 88%; International: 2%. **Religious preference:** Roman Catholic: 16%; Jewish: 1%; No preference: 11%; Baptist: 29%; Other: 43%.

ADMISSIONS FACTS AND FIGURES
Phone: (478) 445-5779. **Email:** info@gcsu.edu. **Website:** http://www.gcsu.edu. **Application deadlines for fall 2007:** Regular decision: April 1. Early decision: Not offered. Early action: Send application by: November 1; Decision sent by: December 15. Admission can be deferred. **Application fee:** $25. Common application is not accepted. **To apply online, go to:** http://www.applyweb.com/aw?gcsu. **Admissions requirements/recommendations:** High school units required (recommended): English: 4; Mathematics: 4; Science: 3; Foreign language: 2; Social studies: 3; Total units: 16. Tests: The college uses SAT or ACT scores in admissions decisions. Either SAT or ACT required. For admission to the fall 2007 entering class, the school will accept: ACT with writing. Campus visit: Recommended. Admissions interview: Neither required nor recommended. Off-campus interview: Not available. **Factors that count in admissions decisions:** *Academic:* Secondary school record: Very important. Class rank: Important. Letters of recommendation: Important. Standardized test scores: Very important. Essay: Very important. *Nonacademic:* Interview: Considered. Extracurricular activities: Important. Talent/ability: Important. Character/personal qualities: Considered. Alumni/ae relationship: Considered. Geographical residence: Considered. State residency: Considered. Religious affiliation/commitment: Not considered. Minority status: Considered. Volunteer work: Considered. Work experience:

Considered. **Other schools with the greatest overlap in applicants:** Georgia Southern University; Georgia State University; Kennesaw State University; University of Georgia; Valdosta State University. **Admissions statistics for the fall 2005 entering class:** Total applicants: 3,236. Total accepted: 1,954. Freshmen enrolled: 1,036; 4% were from out of state. Accepted through early-decision or early-action plans: 28%. Overall acceptance rate: 60%. Non-early acceptance rate: 60%. **Size of waiting list:** 139 applicants; enrolled from waiting list: 16. **Credentials of fall 2005 freshmen:** 16% ranked in the top 10 percent of their high school class; 46% were in the top 25 percent, and 86% were in the top half. (Proportion submitting class standing: 63%.) **Average high school grade point average:** 3.5. **First-year students who submitted SAT scores:** 92%. Scores (25/75 percentile): Verbal: 520-600, Math: 510-600, Combined: 1030-1200. **First-year students submitting ACT scores:** 30%. Scores (25/75 percentile): English: 20-25, Math: 20-24, Composite: 20-24.

ACADEMICS
Year founded: 1889. **Academic calendar:** Semester. **Degrees offered:** bachelor's, master's, post-master's certificate. **Most popular majors:** 12% business administration and management, 10% nursing/registered nurse training (R.N., A.S.N., B.S.N., M.S.N.), 9% psychology, 8% early childhood education and teaching, 6% mass communication/media studies. **Major fields of study:** biological and biomedical sciences; business, management, marketing, and related support services; communication, journalism, and related programs; computer and information sciences and support services; education; English language and literature/letters; foreign languages, literatures, and linguistics; health professions and related clinical sciences; history; liberal arts and sciences studies, and humanities; mathematics and statistics; natural resources and conservation; parks, recreation, leisure, and fitness studies; philosophy and religious studies; physical sciences; psychology; security and protective services; social sciences; visual and performing arts. **Areas of required coursework:** arts/fine arts, humanities, mathematics, English (including composition), foreign languages, sciences (biological or physical), history, social science. **Pre-professional programs:** pre-law, pre-dentistry, pre-medicine, pre-veterinary science, pre-optometry, pre-pharmacy, other. **Special academic programs (% participation):** accelerated program (0%), distance learning (15.5%), double major (2.9%), dual enrollment (0%), English as a Second Language (ESL) (.4%), exchange student program (domestic), honors program (1.1%), independent study (22.4%), internships (50.32%), student-designed major (.26%), study abroad (11.08%), teacher certificate program (13%). **Teacher certification offered in:** early childhood, special education, elementary, middle/junior high, secondary. **Reserve Officers Training Corps (ROTC):** Army ROTC: Offered at cooperating institution (Georgia Military College). **Faculty and instruction (2005-2006):** Total instructional faculty: 268 full-time, 134 part-time (49% men; 51% women; 11% minorities). Full-time faculty with Ph.D. or other terminal degree: 75%. Student/faculty ratio: 16/1. Classes of fewer than 20 students: 37%; of 20 to 49 students: 61%; of 50 or more students: 1%. **Advanced Placement and International Baccalaureate credit:** AP tests may be used for: Credit and/or placement. Scores accepted: 3, 4, 5. International Baccalaureate exams may be used for: Credit only. **Freshmen returning for sophomore year:** 79%. **Graduation rates:** Four-year: 21%; five-year: 40%; six-year: 38%. **Graduate study:** 31% of students pursue further study within one year. Fields in which graduates pursue further study: Master of Business Administration (MBA), 21%; law, 8%; medicine, 3%; dentistry, 2%; engineering, 1%; theology (or the seminary), 2%; education, 19%; arts and sciences, 44%.

COSTS AND FINANCIAL AID
Financial aid office: (478) 445-5149. **Expenses (2006-2007):** Tuition and fees 2006-2007: $4,356 in state, $15,078 out of state; room/board: $7,116. Estimated books and supplies: $800; transportation: $1,024; personal expenses: $2,024. **Financial aid:** Priority filing date for institution's financial aid form: March 1. In 2005-2006, 93% of undergraduates applied for financial aid. Of those, 38% were determined to have financial need; 1% had their need fully met. Average financial aid package (proportion receiving): $5,338 (37%). Average amount of gift aid, such as scholarships or grants (proportion receiving): $2,859 (16%). Average amount of self-help aid, such as work study or loans (proportion receiving): $2,320 (24%). Average need-based loan (excluding PLUS or other private loans): $2,291. Among students who received need-based aid, the average percentage of need met: 41%. Among students who received aid based on merit, the average award (and the proportion receiving): $1,439 (2%). The average athletic scholarship (and the proportion receiving): $3,494 (3%). Average amount of debt of borrowers graduating in 2005: $15,082. Proportion who borrowed: 57%.

CAMPUS LIFE AND EXTRACURRICULAR ACTIVITIES

Campus housing available (% using): coed dorms (57%), apartment for single students (41%), special housing for international students (1%). Students who live in college-owned, operated, or affiliated housing: 40%. **Student employment:** During the 2005-2006 academic year, 6% of undergraduates worked on campus. Average per-year earnings: $2,600. **Clubs and organizations:** Number of student organizations: 126. Activities include: choral groups, concert band, dance, drama/theater, jazz band, literary magazine, music ensembles, musical theater, pep band, radio station, student government, student newspaper, television station. Number of fraternities: 5; sororities: 6. Proportion of men in fraternities: 9%; of women in sororities: 13%. Average proportion of students who stay on campus on weekends: 35%. **Sports program (2005-2006):** Member of NCAA II. *Men's intercollegiate varsity sports:* baseball, basketball, cross-country, golf, tennis. *Women's intercollegiate varsity sports:* basketball, cross-country, soccer, softball, tennis.

SERVICES AND FACILITIES

Basic services: nonremedial tutoring, women's center, health service, health insurance. **Remedial assistance:** reading, math, writing, study skills. **Counseling services:** minority student, career, personal, veteran student, academic. **For learning-disabled students:** School does not offer a structured program with separate admission and additional fees. Total undergraduates in learning-disabled program or receiving services: 116. Services include: tape recorders, diagnostic testing service, untimed tests, oral tests, readers, extended time for tests, tutors, priority registration. **Library:** Number of titles: 172,770; number of current serial subscriptions: 23,849. **Information technology resources:** Students are not required to lease or own a computer. Number of campus computers available to all students: 180. School has a wireless network. Approximate number of users that can be accommodated: 263. Proportion of college-owned housing units wired for high-speed internet access: 100%. **Campus safety:** Security services offered: 24-hour foot-and-vehicle patrols, late-night transport/escort service, 24-hour emergency telephones, lighted pathways/sidewalks, student patrols, controlled dormitory access (key, security card, etc).

TRANSFER AND INTERNATIONAL STUDENTS

Transfer students: May apply for admission for the following academic terms: Fall, Spring, Summer. Applicants need a minimum number of credits to apply. For fall 2005: Transfer applications received: 1,048. Transfer applicants offered admission: 665. Transfer applicants enrolled: 361. **International students:** Number of foreign undergraduates: 78 (2% of student body). Number of countries represented: 32. Minimum TOEFL score required: 500 (paper); 173 (computer). Average TOEFL score: 573 (paper).

Georgia Institute of Technology

■ **Address:** 225 North Avenue NW, Atlanta, GA 30332
■ **Website:** http://www.admission.gatech.edu
■ **Public**
■ **Enrollment:** 10,992 full-time; 849 part-time

KEY STATS

✔ **U.S News College Ranking:** 38, National Universities
✔ **SAT Score (25th/75th percentile):** 1250-1440
✔ **Tuition:** 2006-2007: $4,854 in state, $19,914 out of state

Selectivity: Most selective	**Room/board:** $6,800
Acceptance rate: 68%	**Average debt:** $16,399
Student/faculty ratio: 14/1	**Proportion who borrowed:** 44%

UNDERGRADUATE STUDENT BODY STATS

2005-2006 enrollment: 10,992 full-time; 849 part-time. Men: 72%; women: 28%. **Ethnic makeup:** African American: 7%; Asian American: 15%; Hispanic: 4%; White: 69%; International: 5%.

ADMISSIONS FACTS AND FIGURES

Phone: (404) 894-4154. **Email:** admission@gatech.edu. **Website:** http://www.admission.gatech.edu. **Application deadlines for fall 2007:** Regular decision: January 15; decision sent by March 15. Early decision: Not offered. Early action: Not offered. Admission cannot be deferred. **Application fee:** $50. Common application is accepted. **To apply online, go to:** http://www.apply.gatech.edu. **Admissions requirements/recommenda-**

tions: High school units required (recommended): English: 4; Mathematics: 4; Science: 3; Foreign language: 2; Social studies: 3; Total units: 16. Tests: The college uses SAT or ACT scores in admissions decisions. Either SAT or ACT required. For admission to the fall 2007 entering class, the school will accept: ACT with writing. Campus visit: Recommended. Admissions interview: Neither required nor recommended. Off-campus interview: Not available. **Factors that count in admissions decisions:** *Academic:* Secondary school record: Important. Class rank: Not considered. Letters of recommendation: Not considered. Standardized test scores: Important. Essay: Important. *Nonacademic:* Interview: Not considered. Extracurricular activities: Important. Talent/ability: Important. Character/personal qualities: Not considered. Alumni/ae relationship: Not considered. Geographical residence: Considered. State residency: Considered. Religious affiliation/commitment: Not considered. Minority status: Not considered. Volunteer work: Important. Work experience: Important. **Other schools with the greatest overlap in applicants:** Duke University; Massachusetts Institute of Technology; University of Florida; University of Georgia; Virginia Tech. **Admissions statistics for the fall 2005 entering class:** Total applicants: 9,172. Total accepted: 6,191. Freshmen enrolled: 2,425; 31% were from out of state. Overall acceptance rate: 68%. **Size of waiting list:** 426 applicants; enrolled from waiting list: 102. **Credentials of fall 2005 freshmen:** 66% ranked in the top 10 percent of their high school class; 96% were in the top 25 percent, and 99% were in the top half. (Proportion submitting class standing: 63%.) **Average high school grade point average:** 3.7. **First-year students who submitted SAT scores:** 97%. Scores (25/75 percentile): Verbal: 600-700, Math: 650-740, Combined: 1250-1440. **First-year students submitting ACT scores:** 34%. Scores (25/75 percentile): English: 25-30, Math: 27-32, Composite: 26-30.

ACADEMICS

Year founded: 1885. **Academic calendar:** Semester. **Degrees offered:** bachelor's, master's, doctorate. **Most popular majors:** 54% engineering, 14% business, management, marketing, and related support services, 12% computer and information sciences and support services, 3% architecture and related services, 3% physical sciences. **Major fields of study:** architecture and related services; biological and biomedical sciences; business, management, marketing, and related support services; communication, journalism, and related programs; computer and information sciences and support services; engineering; history; mathematics and statistics; multi/interdisciplinary studies; physical sciences; psychology; public administration and social service professions; social sciences; visual and performing arts. **Areas of required coursework:** humanities, computer literacy, mathematics, English (including composition), sciences (biological or physical), history, social science, other. **Pre-professional programs:** pre-law, pre-dentistry, pre-medicine, pre-veterinary science, pre-optometry, pre-pharmacy. **Special academic programs (% participation):** accelerated program, cooperative (work-study plan) program (25%), cross-registration (3%), distance learning, double major (3%), dual enrollment (3%), English as a Second Language (ESL), honors program, independent study, internships (2%), student-designed major, study abroad (24%), other. **Cooperative education programs:** business, computer science, engineering, other. **Reserve Officers Training Corps (ROTC):** Army ROTC: Offered on campus; Navy ROTC: Offered on campus; Air Force ROTC: Offered on campus. **Faculty and instruction (2005-2006):** Total instructional faculty: 810 full-time, 27 part-time (82% men; 18% women; 24% minorities). Full-time faculty with Ph.D. or other terminal degree: 97%. Student/faculty ratio: 14/1. Classes of fewer than 20 students: 39%; of 20 to 49 students: 41%; of 50 or more students: 20%. **Advanced Placement and International Baccalaureate credit:** AP tests may be used for: Credit and/or placement. Scores accepted: 4, 5. International Baccalaureate exams may be used for: Credit only. **Freshmen returning for sophomore year:** 91%. **Graduation rates:** Four-year: 29%; five-year: 68%; six-year: 76%. **Graduate study:** 19% of students pursue further study immediately upon graduation; 38% within five years. Fields in which graduates pursue further study: Master of Business Administration (MBA), 4%; law, 7%; medicine, 15%; dentistry, 2%; engineering, 47%; theology (or the seminary), 1%; education, 5%; arts and sciences, 11%; veterinary medicine, 1%.

COSTS AND FINANCIAL AID

Financial aid office: (404) 894-4582. **Expenses (2006-2007):** Tuition and fees 2006-2007: $4,854 in state, $19,914 out of state; room/board: $6,800. Estimated books and supplies: $1,000; transportation: $0; personal expenses: $1,500. **Financial aid:** Priority filing date for institution's financial aid form: March 1; deadline: March 1. In 2005-2006, 57% of undergraduates applied for financial aid. Of those, 31% were determined to have financial need; 32% had their need fully met. Average financial aid package (proportion receiving): $5,461 (30%). Average amount of gift aid, such as scholarships or grants (proportion receiving): $4,334 (17%). Average amount of self-help aid, such as work study or loans (proportion receiving): $4,185 (23%). Average need-based loan (excluding PLUS or other private loans): $3,995. Among students who received need-based aid, the average percentage of need met: 42%. Among students who received aid based on merit, the average award (and the proportion receiving): $2,964 (7%). The average athletic scholarship (and the proportion receiving): $13,760 (2%). Average amount of debt of borrowers graduating in 2005: $16,399. Proportion who borrowed: 44%.

CAMPUS LIFE AND EXTRACURRICULAR ACTIVITIES

Campus housing available (% using): coed dorms (19%), women's dorms (8%), men's dorms (25%), sorority housing (1%), fraternity housing (15%), apartments for married students (4%), apartment for single students (26%), special housing for disabled students (1%), special housing for international students (1%). Students who live in college-owned, operated, or affiliated housing: 64%. **Clubs and organizations:** Number of student organizations: 391. Activities include: choral groups, concert band, dance, drama/theater, jazz band, literary magazine, marching band, music ensembles, musical theater, opera, pep band, radio station, student government, student newspaper, student film society, symphony orchestra, television station, yearbook. Number of fraternities: 34; sororities: 14. Proportion of men in fraternities: 21%; of women in sororities: 24%. Average proportion of students who stay on campus on weekends: 67%. **Sports program (2005-2006):** Member of NCAA I. **Men's intercollegiate varsity sports:** baseball, basketball, cross-country, football, golf, swimming and diving, tennis, track and field (indoor), track and field (outdoor). **Women's intercollegiate varsity sports:** basketball, cross-country, softball, swimming and diving, tennis, track and field (indoor), track and field (outdoor), volleyball.

SERVICES AND FACILITIES

Basic services: nonremedial tutoring, women's center, placement service, day care, health service, health insurance. **Remedial assistance:** reading, math, writing, study skills. **Counseling services:** minority student, career, military, personal, veteran student, academic, older student, psychological, birth control, other. **For learning-disabled students:** School does not offer a structured program with separate admission and additional fees. Total undergraduates in learning-disabled program or receiving services: 215. Services include: tape recorders, videotaped classes, diagnostic testing service, note-taking services, oral tests, learning center, readers, extended time for tests, tutors, priority registration, priority seating, texts on tape, typist/scribe, exams on tape or computer, other testing accomodations, waiver of foreign language degree requirement, other. **Library:** Number of titles: 2,410,964; number of current serial subscriptions: 30,799. **Information technology resources:** Students are required to lease or own a computer. Number of campus computers available to all students: 300. School has a wireless network. Approximate number of users that can be accommodated: 5,000. Proportion of college-owned housing units wired for high-speed internet access: 100%. **Campus safety:** Security services offered: 24-hour foot-and-vehicle patrols, late-night transport/escort service, 24-hour emergency telephones, lighted pathways/sidewalks, controlled dormitory access (key, security card, etc).

TRANSFER AND INTERNATIONAL STUDENTS

Transfer students: May apply for admission for the following academic terms: Fall, Spring, Summer. Applicants need a minimum number of credits to apply. For fall 2005: Transfer applications received: 1,199. Transfer applicants offered admission: 494. Transfer applicants enrolled: 407. **International students:** Number of foreign undergraduates: 539 (5% of student body). Number of countries represented: 85. Minimum TOEFL score required: 600 (paper); 250 (computer).

Georgia Southern University

- **Address:** PO Box 8033, Statesboro, GA 30460
- **Website:** http://www.georgiasouthern.edu/
- **Public**
- **Enrollment:** 13,119 full-time; 1,531 part-time

KEY STATS

✔ **U.S News College Ranking:** 53, Universities–Master's (South)
✔ **SAT Score (25th/75th percentile):** 1020-1170
✔ **Tuition:** 2006-2007: $3,612 in state, $11,196 out of state
  Selectivity: Selective   **Room/board:** $6,500
  Acceptance rate: 55%   **Average debt:** $17,913
  Student/faculty ratio: 20/1 **Proportion who borrowed:** 70%

UNDERGRADUATE STUDENT BODY STATS

2005-2006 enrollment: 13,119 full-time; 1,531 part-time. Men: 51%; women: 49%. **Ethnic makeup:** African American: 22%; Asian American: 1%; Hispanic: 1%; White: 74%; International: 1%.

ADMISSIONS FACTS AND FIGURES

Phone: (912) 681-5391. **Email:** admissions@georgiasouthern.edu. **Website:** http://www.georgiasouthern.edu/. **Application deadlines for fall 2007:** Regular decision: May 1. Early decision: Not offered. Early action: Not offered. Admission can be deferred. **Application fee:** $50. Common application is accepted. **To apply online, go to:** http://admissions.georgiasouthern.edu/. **Admissions requirements/recommendations:** High school units required (recommended): English: 4; Mathematics: 4; Science: 3; Foreign language: 2; Social studies: 3; Total units: 16. Tests: The college uses SAT or ACT scores in admissions decisions. Either SAT or ACT required. For admission to the fall 2007 entering class, the school will accept ACT without writing. Campus visit: Recommended. Admissions interview: Neither required nor recommended. Off-campus interview: May not be arranged. **Factors that count in admissions decisions: Academic:** Secondary school record: Very important. Class rank: Considered. Letters of recommendation: Not considered. Standardized test scores: Very important. Essay: Not considered. **Nonacademic:** Interview: Not considered. Extracurricular activities: Not considered. Talent/ability: Not considered. Character/personal qualities: Not considered. Alumni/ae relationship: Not considered. Geographical residence: Not considered. State residency: Not considered. Religious affiliation/commitment: Not considered. Minority status: Not considered. Volunteer work: Not considered. Work experience: Not considered. **Other schools with the greatest overlap in applicants:** Georgia College and State University; Georgia Institute of Technology; Georgia State University; Kennesaw State University; University of Georgia. **Admissions statistics for the fall 2005 entering class:** Total applicants: 8,302. Total accepted: 4,585. Freshmen enrolled: 3,145; Overall acceptance rate: 55%. **Average high school grade point average:** 3.1. **First-year students who submitted SAT scores:** 85%. Scores (25/75 percentile): Verbal: 510-580, Math: 510-590, Combined: 1020-1170. **First-year students submitting ACT scores:** 28%. Scores (25/75 percentile): English: 19-23, Math: 18-24, Composite: 20-23.

ACADEMICS

Year founded: 1906. **Academic calendar:** Semester. **Degrees offered:** bachelor's, master's, post-master's certificate, doctorate. **Most popular majors:** 29% business, management, marketing, and related support services, 11% education, 7% health professions and related clinical sciences, 7% parks, recreation, leisure, and fitness studies, 6% communication, journalism, and related programs. **Major fields of study:** biological and biomedical sciences; business, management, marketing, and related support services; communication, journalism, and related programs; communications technologies/technicians and support services; computer and information sciences and support services; education; engineering technologies/technicians; English language and literature/letters; family and consumer sciences/human sciences; foreign languages, literatures, and linguistics; health professions and related clinical sciences; history; liberal arts and sciences studies, and humanities; mathematics and statistics; parks, recreation, leisure, and fitness studies; philosophy and religious studies; physical sciences; psychology; security and protective services; social sciences; visual and performing arts. **Areas of required coursework:** arts/fine arts, humanities, computer literacy, mathematics, English (including composition), sciences (biological or physical), history, social science, other. **Pre-professional**

programs: pre-law, pre-dentistry, pre-medicine, pre-veterinary science, pre-optometry, pre-pharmacy. **Special academic programs (% participation):** accelerated program (86.5%), cooperative (work-study plan) program (1.2%), cross-registration (0%), distance learning (14.5%), double major (.2%), dual enrollment (1.1%), English as a Second Language (ESL) (.3%), external degree program (0%), honors program (2.7%), independent study (14%), internships (55%), student-designed major (1.5%), study abroad (6.2%), teacher certification program (11%), weekend college (5.1%). **Teacher certification offered in:** early childhood, special education, middle/junior high, secondary. **Cooperative education programs:** business, computer science, engineering, health professions, natural science, technologies, other. **Reserve Officers Training Corps (ROTC):** Army ROTC: Offered on campus. **Faculty and instruction (2005-2006):** Total instructional faculty: 660 full-time, 53 part-time (53% men; 47% women; 14% minorities). Full-time faculty with Ph.D. or other terminal degree: 76%. Student/faculty ratio: 20/1. Classes of fewer than 20 students: 28%; of 20 to 49 students: 61%; of 50 or more students: 11%. **Advanced Placement and International Baccalaureate credit:** AP tests may be used for: Credit and/or placement. Scores accepted: 3, 4, 5. International Baccalaureate exams may be used for: Credit and/or placement. **Freshmen returning for sophomore year:** 78%. **Graduation rates:** Four-year: 12%; five-year: 34%; six-year: 38%. **Graduate study:** 9% of students pursue further study immediately upon graduation; 11% within one year; 19% within five years. Fields in which graduates pursue further study: Master of Business Administration (MBA), 3%; education, 2%.

COSTS AND FINANCIAL AID
Financial aid office: (912) 681-5413. **Expenses (2006-2007):** Tuition and fees 2006-2007: $3,612 in state, $11,196 out of state; room/board: $6,500. **Financial aid:** Priority filing date for institution's financial aid form: March 31. In 2005-2006, 86% of undergraduates applied for financial aid. Of those, 50% were determined to have financial need; 17% had their need fully met. Average financial aid package (proportion receiving): $6,625 (48%). Average amount of gift aid, such as scholarships or grants (proportion receiving): $4,406 (39%). Average amount of self-help aid, such as work study or loans (proportion receiving): $3,893 (38%). Average need-based loan (excluding PLUS or other private loans): $3,849. Among students who received need-based aid, the average percentage of need met: 63%. Among students who received aid based on merit, the average award (and the proportion receiving): $1,448 (2%). The average athletic scholarship (and the proportion receiving): $4,614 (1%). Average amount of debt of borrowers graduating in 2005: $17,913. Proportion who borrowed: 70%.

CAMPUS LIFE AND EXTRACURRICULAR ACTIVITIES
Campus housing available (% using): coed dorms (70%), sorority housing (2%), fraternity housing (3%), apartment for single students (20%), special housing for disabled students (5%). **Student employment:** During the 2005-2006 academic year, 12% of undergraduates worked on campus. Average per-year earnings: $1,432. **Clubs and organizations:** Number of student organizations: 213. Activities include: choral groups, concert band, dance, drama/theater, jazz band, literary magazine, marching band, music ensembles, musical theater, opera, pep band, radio station, student government, student newspaper, student film society, symphony orchestra. Number of fraternities: 19; sororities: 6. Average proportion of students who stay on campus on weekends: 65%. **Sports program (2005-2006):** Member of NCAA I. *Men's intercollegiate varsity sports:* baseball, basketball, football, golf, soccer, tennis. *Women's intercollegiate varsity sports:* basketball, cross-country, soccer, softball, swimming and diving, tennis, track and field (indoor), track and field (outdoor), volleyball.

SERVICES AND FACILITIES
Basic services: nonremedial tutoring, health service, health insurance, other. **Remedial assistance:** reading, math, writing, study skills, other. **Counseling services:** minority student, career, personal, veteran student, academic, older student, psychological, birth control. **For learning-disabled students:** School does not offer a structured program with separate admission and additional fees. Total undergraduates in learning-disabled program or receiving services: 429. Services include: remedial math, remedial English, reading machines, remedial reading, tape recorders, other special classes, diagnostic testing service, note-taking services, oral tests, learning center, readers, extended time for tests, tutors, priority registration, priority seating, substitution of courses, texts on tape, exams on tape or computer, other testing accomodations. **Library:** Number of titles: 577,172; number of current serial subscriptions: 2,687. **Information technology resources:** Students are not required to lease or own a computer. Number of campus computers available to all students: 1,675. School has a wireless network. Approximate number of users that can be accommodated: 1,500. Proportion of college-owned housing units wired for high-speed internet access: 90%. **Campus safety:** Security services offered: 24-hour foot-and-vehicle patrols, late-night transport/escort service, 24-hour emergency telephones, lighted pathways/sidewalks, student patrols, controlled dormitory access (key, security card, etc).

TRANSFER AND INTERNATIONAL STUDENTS
Transfer students: May apply for admission for the following academic terms: Fall, Spring, Summer. Applicants need a minimum number of credits to apply. For fall 2005: Transfer applications received: 1,348. Transfer applicants offered admission: 1,001. Transfer applicants enrolled: 853. **International students:** Number of foreign undergraduates: 107 (1% of student body). Number of countries represented: 67. Minimum TOEFL score required: 500 (paper); 173 (computer). Average TOEFL score: 571 (paper).

Georgia Southwestern State University

- **Address:** 800 Wheatley Street, Americus, GA 31709
- **Website:** http://www.gsw.edu
- **Public**
- **Enrollment:** 1,699 full-time; 539 part-time

KEY STATS
✔ **U.S News College Ranking:** fourth tier, Universities–Master's (South)
✔ **SAT Score (25th/75th percentile):** 890-1090
✔ **Tuition:** 2006-2007: $3,162 in state, $10,770 out of state

Selectivity: Selective	**Room/board:** $4,956
Acceptance rate: 74%	**Average debt:** $15,346
Student/faculty ratio: 17/1	**Proportion who borrowed:** 68%

UNDERGRADUATE STUDENT BODY STATS
2005-2006 enrollment: 1,699 full-time; 539 part-time. Men: 35%; women: 65%. **Ethnic makeup:** African American: 34%; American-Indian: 1%; Asian American: 1%; Hispanic: 1%; White: 62%; International: 2%.

ADMISSIONS FACTS AND FIGURES
Phone: (229) 928-1273. **Email:** gswapps@canes.gsw.edu. **Website:** http://www.gsw.edu. **Application deadlines for fall 2007:** Regular decision: July 21. Early decision: Send application by: N/A; Decision sent by: N/A. Early action: Not offered. Admission can be deferred. **Application fee:** $25. Common application is not accepted. **To apply online, go to:** https://www.ganet.org/gsw. **Admissions requirements/recommendations:** High school units required (recommended): English: 4; Mathematics: 4; Science: 3; Foreign language: 2; Social studies: 1; History: 2; Academic electives: (2); Total units: 16. Tests: The college uses SAT or ACT scores in admissions decisions. Either SAT or ACT required. For admission to the fall 2007 entering class, the school will accept: ACT with writing, ACT without writing. Campus visit: Recommended. Admissions interview: Recommended. **Factors that count in admissions decisions:** *Academic:* Secondary school record: Very important. Class rank: Important. Letters of recommendation: Considered. Standardized test scores: Very important. Essay: Considered. *Nonacademic:* Interview: Considered. Extracurricular activities: Considered. Talent/ability: Considered. **Admissions statistics for the fall 2005 entering class:** Total applicants: 1,083. Total accepted: 797. Freshmen enrolled: 385; 2% were from out of state. Overall acceptance rate: 74%. Non-early acceptance rate: 74%. **Credentials of fall 2005 freshmen:** 14% ranked in the top 10 percent of their high school class; 40% were in the top 25 percent, and 77% were in the top half. (Proportion submitting class standing: 52%.) **Average high school grade point average:** 3.1. **First-year students who submitted SAT scores:** 72%. Scores (25/75 percentile): Verbal: 450-540, Math: 440-550, Combined: 890-1090. **First-year students submitting ACT scores:** 13%. Scores (25/75 percentile): English: N/A, Math: N/A, Composite: 17-20.

ACADEMICS
Year founded: 1906. **Academic calendar:** Semester. **Degrees offered:** certificate, associate, bachelor's, master's, post-master's certificate. **Most popular majors:** 18% elementary education and teaching, 9% business administration and management, 8% psychology, 7% accounting, 6% nursing/registered nurse training (R.N., A.S.N., B.S.N., M.S.N.). **Major fields of study:** biological and biomedical sciences; business, management, marketing, and related support services; computer and information sciences and support

services; education; engineering technologies/technicians; English language and literature/letters; health professions and related clinical sciences; history; mathematics and statistics; physical sciences; psychology; social sciences; visual and performing arts. **Areas of required coursework:** arts/fine arts, humanities, mathematics, English (including composition), foreign languages, sciences (biological or physical), history, social science. **Pre-professional programs:** pre-dentistry, pre-medicine, pre-veterinary science, pre-pharmacy. **Special academic programs:** accelerated program, cooperative (work-study plan) program, distance learning, double major, dual enrollment, English as a Second Language (ESL), honors program, independent study, internships, study abroad, teacher certificate program. **Teacher certification offered in:** early childhood, special education, middle/junior high. **Faculty and instruction (2005-2006):** Total instructional faculty: 95 full-time, 55 part-time (51% men; 49% women; 13% minorities). Full-time faculty with Ph.D. or other terminal degree: 79%. Student/faculty ratio: 17/1. Classes of fewer than 20 students: 49%; of 20 to 49 students: 49%; of 50 or more students: 1%. **Advanced Placement and International Baccalaureate credit:** AP tests may be used for: Credit and/or placement. Scores accepted: 3, 4, 5. **Freshmen returning for sophomore year:** 68%. **Graduation rates:** Four-year: 16%; five-year: 28%; six-year: 32%.

COSTS AND FINANCIAL AID

Financial aid office: (229) 928-1378. **Expenses (2006-2007):** Tuition and fees 2006-2007: $3,162 in state, $10,770 out of state; room/board: $4,956. **Financial aid:** Priority filing date for institution's financial aid form: April 1. In 2005-2006, 76% of undergraduates applied for financial aid. Of those, 63% were determined to have financial need; 9% had their need fully met. Average financial aid package (proportion receiving): $6,219 (62%). Average amount of gift aid, such as scholarships or grants (proportion receiving): $3,018 (43%). Average amount of self-help aid, such as work study or loans (proportion receiving): $3,341 (44%). Average need-based loan (excluding PLUS or other private loans): $3,249. Among students who received need-based aid, the average percentage of need met: 55%. Among students who received aid based on merit, the average award (and the proportion receiving): $2,961 (8%). The average athletic scholarship (and the proportion receiving): $2,535 (3%). Average amount of debt of borrowers graduating in 2005: $15,346. Proportion who borrowed: 68%.

CAMPUS LIFE AND EXTRACURRICULAR ACTIVITIES

Campus housing available: coed dorms, women's dorms, men's dorms. Students who live in college-owned, operated, or affiliated housing: 27%. **Clubs and organizations:** Number of student organizations: 75. Activities include: choral groups, concert band, dance, drama/theater, jazz band, literary magazine, student government, student newspaper, television station. Number of fraternities: 7; sororities: 6. Proportion of men in fraternities: 17%; of women in sororities: 10%. **Sports program (2005-2006):** Member of NAIA. **Men's intercollegiate varsity sports:** baseball, basketball, golf, soccer, tennis. **Women's intercollegiate varsity sports:** basketball, golf, soccer, softball, tennis, volleyball.

SERVICES AND FACILITIES

Basic services: nonremedial tutoring, health service, health insurance. **Remedial assistance:** reading, math, writing, study skills. **Counseling services:** minority student, career, personal, academic. **Library:** Number of titles: 428,197; number of current serial subscriptions: 516. **Information technology resources:** Students are not required to lease or own a computer. Number of campus computers available to all students: 562. **Campus safety:** Security services offered: 24-hour foot-and-vehicle patrols, late-night transport/escort service, 24-hour emergency telephones, lighted pathways/sidewalks, controlled dormitory access (key, security card, etc).

TRANSFER AND INTERNATIONAL STUDENTS

Transfer students: May apply for admission for the following academic terms: Fall, Spring, Summer. Applicants need a minimum number of credits to apply. For fall 2005: Transfer applications received: 506. Transfer applicants offered admission: 385. Transfer applicants enrolled: 267. **International students:** Number of foreign undergraduates: 44 (2% of student body). Number of countries represented: 22. Minimum TOEFL score required: 523 (paper); 193 (computer).

Georgia State University

- **Address:** University Plaza, Atlanta, GA 30303-3083
- **Website:** http://www.gsu.edu
- **Public**
- **Enrollment:** 13,752 full-time; 5,208 part-time

KEY STATS

✔ **U.S News College Ranking:** fourth tier, National Universities
✔ **SAT Score (25th/75th percentile):** 990-1180
✔ **Tuition:** 2006-2007: $4,646 in state, $16,106 out of state
   Selectivity: Selective   **Room/board:** $6,980
   Acceptance rate: 50%   **Average debt:** $13,886
   Student/faculty ratio: 20/1 **Proportion who borrowed:** 48%

UNDERGRADUATE STUDENT BODY STATS

2005-2006 enrollment: 13,752 full-time; 5,208 part-time. Men: 39%; women: 61%. **Ethnic makeup:** African American: 31%; Asian American: 10%; Hispanic: 3%; White: 52%; International: 3%.

ADMISSIONS FACTS AND FIGURES

Phone: (404) 651-2365. **Email:** admissions@gsu.edu. **Website:** http://www.gsu.edu. **Application deadlines for fall 2007:** Regular decision: March 1. Early decision: Not offered. Early action: Not offered. Admission can be deferred. **Application fee:** $50. Common application is not accepted. **To apply online, go to:** http://www.gsu.edu/~wwwadm/adm30.html. **Admissions requirements/recommendations:** High school units required (recommended): English: 4; Mathematics: 4; Science: 3; Foreign language: 2; Social studies: 2; History: 1; Total units: 16. Tests: The college uses SAT or ACT scores in admissions decisions. Either SAT or ACT required. For admission to the fall 2007 entering class, the school will accept: ACT with writing. Campus visit: Required. Admissions interview: Neither required nor recommended. Off-campus interview: Not available. **Factors that count in admissions decisions:** *Academic:* Secondary school record: Very important. Class rank: Not considered. Letters of recommendation: Considered. Standardized test scores: Very important. Essay: Considered. *Nonacademic:* Interview: Considered. Extracurricular activities: Considered. Talent/ability: Considered. Character/personal qualities: Considered. Alumni/ae relationship: Considered. Geographical residence: Considered. State residency: Considered. Religious affiliation/commitment: Not considered. Minority status: Not considered. Volunteer work: Considered. Work experience: Considered. **Other schools with the greatest overlap in applicants:** Georgia Institute of Technology; Georgia Southern University; Kennesaw State University; University of Georgia. **Admissions statistics for the fall 2005 entering class:** Total applicants: 8,313. Total accepted: 4,117. Freshmen enrolled: 2,291; 3% were from out of state. Overall acceptance rate: 50%. **Average high school grade point average:** 3.3. **First-year students who submitted SAT scores:** 96%. Scores (25/75 percentile): Verbal: 490-590, Math: 500-590, Combined: 990-1180. **First-year students submitting ACT scores:** 31%. Scores (25/75 percentile): English: 19-24, Math: 19-24, Composite: 19-24.

ACADEMICS

Year founded: 1913. **Academic calendar:** Semester. **Degrees offered:** certificate, bachelor's, post-bachelor's certificate, master's, post-master's certificate, first professional, doctorate. **Most popular majors:** 31% business, management, marketing, and related support services, 13% social sciences, 9% psychology, 7% visual and performing arts, 6% communication, journalism, and related programs. **Major fields of study:** area, ethnic, cultural, and gender studies; biological and biomedical sciences; business, management, marketing, and related support services; communication, journalism, and related programs; computer and information sciences and support services; education; English language and literature/letters; family and consumer sciences/human sciences; foreign languages, literatures, and linguistics; health professions and related clinical sciences; history; mathematics and statistics; multi/interdisciplinary studies; parks, recreation, leisure, and fitness studies; philosophy and religious studies; physical sciences; psychology; public administration and social service professions; security and protective services; social sciences; visual and performing arts. **Areas of required coursework:** humanities, mathematics, English (including composition), philosophy, sciences (biological or physical), history, social science. **Pre-professional programs:** pre-law, pre-medicine. **Special academic programs:** accelerated program, cooperative (work-study plan) program, cross-registration, distance learning, double major, dual enrollment, English as a Second Language (ESL), exchange student program (domestic), honors program, independent study, internships, student-designed major, study abroad, teacher certificate program, other. **Teacher certification offered in:** early childhood, special education, elementary, middle/junior high, secondary, bilingual/bicultural. **Cooperative education programs:** art, business, computer science, education, health professions, humanities, natural science, social/behavioral science, other. **Reserve Officers Training Corps (ROTC):** Army ROTC: Offered on campus; Navy ROTC: Offered at cooperating institution (Georgia Institute of Technology); Air Force ROTC: Offered at cooperating institution (Georgia Institute of Technology). **Faculty and instruction (2005-2006):** Total instructional faculty: 1,054 full-time, 376 part-time. Full-time faculty with Ph.D. or other terminal degree: 85%. Student/faculty ratio: 20/1. Classes of fewer than 20 students: 16%; of 20 to 49 students: 70%; of 50 or more students: 14%. **Advanced Placement and International Baccalaureate credit:** AP tests may be used for: Credit only. Scores accepted: 3, 4, 5. International Baccalaureate exams may be used for: Credit only. **Freshmen returning for sophomore year:** 82%. **Graduation rates:** Four-year: 13%; five-year: 32%; six-year: 39%.

COSTS AND FINANCIAL AID

Financial aid office: (404) 651-2227. **Expenses (2005-2006):** Tuition and fees 2005-2006: $4,464 in state, $15,360 out of state; room/board: $6,980. Estimated books and supplies: $1,000; transportation: $1,740; personal expenses: $2,166. **Financial aid:** Priority filing date for institution's financial aid form: April 1; deadline: November 1. In 2005-2006, 68% of undergraduates applied for financial aid. Of those, 54% were determined to have financial need; 17% had their need fully met. Average financial aid package (proportion receiving): $8,671 (54%). Average amount of gift aid, such as scholarships or grants (proportion receiving): $4,309 (41%). Average amount of self-help aid, such as work study or loans (proportion receiving): $4,077 (36%). Average need-based loan (excluding PLUS or other private loans): $4,002. Among students who received need-based aid, the average percentage of need met: 76%. Among students who received aid based on merit, the average award (and the proportion receiving): $4,270 (21%). The average athletic scholarship (and the proportion receiving): $2,661 (0%). Average amount of debt of borrowers graduating in 2005: $13,886. Proportion who borrowed: 48%.

CAMPUS LIFE AND EXTRACURRICULAR ACTIVITIES

Campus housing available (% using): coed dorms (82%), apartments for married students (5%), apartment for single students (1%), special housing for disabled students (3%), special housing for international students (8%), other housing options (1%). Students who live in college-owned, operated, or affiliated housing: 10%. **Student employment:** During the 2005-2006 academic year, 7% of undergraduates worked on campus. Average per-year earnings: $5,000. **Clubs and organizations:** Number of student organizations: 201. Activities include: choral groups, concert band, dance, drama/theater, jazz band, literary magazine, music ensembles, pep band, radio station, student government, student newspaper, student film society, television station. Number of fraternities: 10; sororities: 11. Proportion of men in fraternities: 3%; of women in sororities: 4%. Average proportion of students who stay on campus on weekends: 60%. **Sports program (2005-2006):** Member of NCAA I. *Men's intercollegiate varsity sports:* baseball, basketball, cross-country, golf, soccer, tennis, track and field (indoor), track and field (outdoor). *Women's intercollegiate varsity sports:* basketball, cheerleading, cross-country, golf, soccer, softball, tennis, track and field (indoor), track and field (outdoor), volleyball.

SERVICES AND FACILITIES

Basic services: nonremedial tutoring, placement service, day care, health service, health insurance. **Remedial assistance:** reading, math, writing, study skills. **Counseling services:** minority student, career, personal, veteran student, academic, psychological. **For learning-disabled students:** School does not offer a structured program with separate admission and additional fees. Total undergraduates in learning-disabled program or receiving services: 150. Services include: tape recorders, diagnostic testing service, extended time for tests, tutors, priority registration, priority seating, texts on tape, other testing accomodations, other. **Library:** Number of titles: 1,420,068; number of current serial subscriptions: 7,788. **Information technology resources:** Students are not required to lease or own a computer. Number of campus computers available to all students: 733. School has a wireless network. Approximate number of users that can be accommodated: 2,800. Proportion of college-owned housing units wired for high-speed internet access: 100%. **Campus safety:** Security services offered: 24-hour foot-and-vehicle patrols, late-night transport/escort service, 24-hour emergency tele-

phones, lighted pathways/sidewalks, controlled dormitory access (key, security card, etc).

TRANSFER AND INTERNATIONAL STUDENTS

Transfer students: May apply for admission for the following academic terms: Fall, Spring, Summer. Applicants need a minimum number of credits to apply. For fall 2005: Transfer applications received: 5,591. Transfer applicants offered admission: 3,060. Transfer applicants enrolled: 1,962. **International students:** Number of foreign undergraduates: 552 (3% of student body). Number of countries represented: 103. Minimum TOEFL score required: 550 (paper); 213 (computer). Average TOEFL score: 503 (paper).

Kennesaw State University

- **Address:** 1000 Chastain Road, Kennesaw, GA 30144-5591
- **Website:** http://www.kennesaw.edu
- **Public**
- **Enrollment:** 11,411 full-time; 5,328 part-time

KEY STATS

✔ **U.S News College Ranking:** third tier, Universities–Master's (South)
✔ **SAT Score (25th/75th percentile):** 980-1130
✔ **Tuition:** 2006-2007: $3,242 in state, $10,850 out of state
Selectivity: Selective   **Room/board:** $8,877
Acceptance rate: 62%   **Average debt:** $15,346
Student/faculty ratio: 20/1 **Proportion who borrowed:** 45%

UNDERGRADUATE STUDENT BODY STATS

2005-2006 enrollment: 11,411 full-time; 5,328 part-time. Men: 39%; women: 61%. **Ethnic makeup:** African American: 8%; Asian American: 2%; Hispanic: 2%; White: 80%; International: 8%.

ADMISSIONS FACTS AND FIGURES

Phone: (770) 423-6300. **Email:** ksuadmit@kennesaw.edu. **Website:** http://www.kennesaw.edu. **Application deadlines for fall 2007:** Regular decision: May 27. Early decision: Not offered. Early action: Not offered. Admission can be deferred. **Application fee:** $40. Common application is not accepted. **To apply online, go to:** http://www.kennesaw.edu/admissions/. **Admissions requirements/recommendations:** High school units required (recommended): English: 4; Mathematics: 4; Science: 3; Foreign language: 2; Social studies: 3; Total units: 16. Tests: The college uses SAT or ACT scores in admissions decisions. Either SAT or ACT required. For admission to the fall 2007 entering class, the school will accept: ACT with writing. Campus visit: Recommended. Admissions interview: Neither required nor recommended. Off-campus interview: Not available. **Factors that count in admissions decisions:** *Academic:* Secondary school record: Very important. Class rank: Not considered. Letters of recommendation: Not considered. Standardized test scores: Very important. Essay: Not considered. *Nonacademic:* Interview: Not considered. Extracurricular activities: Not considered. Talent/ability: Not considered. Character/personal qualities: Not considered. Alumni/ae relationship: Not considered. Geographical residence: Not considered. State residency: Not considered. Religious affiliation/commitment: Not considered. Minority status: Not considered. Volunteer work: Not considered. Work experience: Not considered. **Other schools with the greatest overlap in applicants:** Georgia Institute of Technology; Georgia Southern University; Georgia State University; University of Georgia; University of West Georgia. **Admissions statistics for the fall 2005 entering class:** Total applicants: 6,658. Total accepted: 4,119. Freshmen enrolled: 2,348; Overall acceptance rate: 62%. **Credentials of fall 2005 freshmen:** 21% ranked in the top 10 percent of their high school class; 53% were in the top 25 percent, and 81% were in the top half. (Proportion submitting class standing: 50%.) **First-year students who submitted SAT scores:** 86%. Scores (25/75 percentile): Verbal: 490-570, Math: 490-560, Combined: 980-1130. **First-year students submitting ACT scores:** 7%. Scores (25/75 percentile): English: N/A, Math: N/A, Composite: 20-23.

ACADEMICS

Year founded: 1963. **Academic calendar:** Semester. **Degrees offered:** certificate, bachelor's, post-bachelor's certificate, master's. **Most popular majors:** Information not available. **Major fields of study:** area, ethnic, cultural, and gender studies; biological and biomedical sciences; business, management, marketing, and related support services; communication, journalism, and related programs; computer and information sciences and support services; education; English language and literature/letters; foreign languages, literatures, and linguistics; health professions and related clinical sciences; history; mathematics and statistics; parks, recreation, leisure, and fitness studies; physical sciences; psychology; public administration and social service professions; security and protective services; social sciences; visual and performing arts. **Areas of required coursework:** arts/fine arts, humanities, mathematics, English (including composition), foreign languages, sciences (biological or physical), history, social science, other. **Pre-professional programs:** pre-law, pre-dentistry, pre-medicine, pre-veterinary science, pre-optometry, pre-pharmacy, other. **Special academic programs (% participation):** accelerated program (5%), cooperative (work-study plan) program (5%), cross-registration (1%), distance learning (1%), double major (1%), dual enrollment (1%), English as a Second Language (ESL) (2%), honors program (5%), independent study (3%), internships (30%), liberal arts/career combination (10%), study abroad (2%), teacher certificate program (21%), weekend college (3%). **Teacher certification offered in:** early childhood, elementary, middle/junior high, secondary. **Cooperative education programs:** art, business, computer science, health professions, humanities, natural science, social/behavioral science. **Reserve Officers Training Corps (ROTC):** Army ROTC: Offered at cooperating institution (Georgia Institute of Technology); Air Force ROTC: Offered at cooperating institution (Georgia Institute of Technology). **Faculty and instruction (2005-2006):** Total instructional faculty: 578 full-time, 351 part-time (46% men; 54% women; 13% minorities). Full-time faculty with Ph.D. or other terminal degree: 72%. Student/faculty ratio: 20/1. Classes of fewer than 20 students: 21%; of 20 to 49 students: 68%; of 50 or more students: 11%. **Advanced Placement and International Baccalaureate credit:** AP tests may be used for: Credit only. Scores accepted: 3, 4, 5. International Baccalaureate exams may be used for: Credit only. **Freshmen returning for sophomore year:** 75%. **Graduation rates:** Six-year: 29%.

COSTS AND FINANCIAL AID
Financial aid office: (770) 423-6074. **Expenses (2006-2007):** Tuition and fees 2006-2007: $3,242 in state, $10,850 out of state; room/board: $8,877. Estimated books and supplies: $1,000; transportation: $961; personal expenses: $1,421. **Financial aid:** Priority filing date for institution's financial aid form: April 1. In 2005-2006, 80% of undergraduates applied for financial aid. Of those, 39% were determined to have financial need; 16% had their need fully met. Average financial aid package (proportion receiving): $9,524 (38%). Average amount of gift aid, such as scholarships or grants (proportion receiving): $2,690 (19%). Average amount of self-help aid, such as work study or loans (proportion receiving): $3,380 (34%). Average need-based loan (excluding PLUS or other private loans): $3,402. Among students who received need-based aid, the average percentage of need met: 22%. Among students who received aid based on merit, the average award (and the proportion receiving): $1,672 (30%). The average athletic scholarship (and the proportion receiving): $3,064 (1%). Average amount of debt of borrowers graduating in 2005: $15,346. Proportion who borrowed: 45%.

CAMPUS LIFE AND EXTRACURRICULAR ACTIVITIES
Campus housing available (% using): apartment for single students (100%). Students who live in college-owned, operated, or affiliated housing: 11%. **Student employment:** During the 2005-2006 academic year, 20% of undergraduates worked on campus. Average per-year earnings: $3,750. **Clubs and organizations:** Number of student organizations: 115. Activities include: choral groups, concert band, dance, drama/theater, jazz band, literary magazine, music ensembles, musical theater, student government, student newspaper, symphony orchestra. Number of fraternities: 5; sororities: 5. Average proportion of students who stay on campus on weekends: 30%. **Sports program (2005-2006):** Member of NCAA II. *Men's intercollegiate varsity sports:* baseball, basketball, cross-country, golf, track and field (indoor), track and field (outdoor). *Women's intercollegiate varsity sports:* basketball, cross-country, golf, soccer, softball, tennis, track and field (indoor), track and field (outdoor).

SERVICES AND FACILITIES
Basic services: nonremedial tutoring, placement service, health service, health insurance. **Remedial assistance:** reading, math, writing, study skills. **Counseling services:** minority student, career, military, personal, veteran student, academic, older student, psychological, birth control. **For learning-disabled students:** School does not offer a structured program with separate admission and additional fees. Total undergraduates in learning-disabled program or receiving services: 53. Services include: remedial math, remedial English, reading machines, remedial reading, tape recorders, diagnostic testing service, oral tests, extended time for tests, priority registration, prior-

ity seating, texts on tape. **Library:** Number of titles: 617,881; number of current serial subscriptions: 2,995. **Information technology resources:** Students are not required to lease or own a computer. Number of campus computers available to all students: 1,300. School has a wireless network. Approximate number of users that can be accommodated: 2,000. Proportion of college-owned housing units wired for high-speed internet access: 100%. **Campus safety:** Security services offered: 24-hour foot-and-vehicle patrols, late-night transport/escort service, 24-hour emergency telephones, lighted pathways/sidewalks, student patrols, controlled dormitory access (key, security card, etc).

TRANSFER AND INTERNATIONAL STUDENTS
Transfer students: May apply for admission for the following academic terms: Fall, Spring, Summer. Applicants need a minimum number of credits to apply. **International students:** Number of foreign undergraduates: 1309 (8% of student body). Number of countries represented: 132. Minimum TOEFL score required: 527 (paper); 197 (computer). Average TOEFL score: 560 (paper).

LaGrange College

- **Address:** 601 Broad Street, LaGrange, GA 30240
- **Website:** http://www.lagrange.edu
- **Private; Religious affiliation:** United Methodist
- **Enrollment:** 898 full-time; 88 part-time

KEY STATS
✔ **U.S News College Ranking:** 7, Comp. Colleges–Bachelor's (South)
✔ **SAT Score (25th/75th percentile):** 930-1140
✔ **Tuition:** 2006-2007: $17,253

Selectivity: Selective	**Room/board:** $7,182
Acceptance rate: 48%	**Average debt:** $17,074
Student/faculty ratio: 10/1	**Proportion who borrowed:** 79%

UNDERGRADUATE STUDENT BODY STATS
2005-2006 enrollment: 898 full-time; 88 part-time. Men: 39%; women: 61%. **Ethnic makeup:** African American: 20%; American-Indian: 1%; Asian American: 1%; Hispanic: 1%; White: 74%; International: 3%. **Religious preference:** Roman Catholic: 5%; Protestant: 29%; No preference: 33%; United Methodist: 19%.

ADMISSIONS FACTS AND FIGURES
Phone: (706) 880-8005. **Email:** admission@lagrange.edu. **Website:** http://www.lagrange.edu. **Application deadlines for fall 2007:** Regular decision: August 1. Early decision: Not offered. Early action: Not offered. Admission can be deferred. **Application fee:** $30. Common application is accepted. **To apply online, go to:** https://www.applyweb.com/apply/lgc/index.html. **Admissions requirements/recommendations:** High school units required (recommended): English: 4 (4); Mathematics: 4 (4); Science: 3 (3); Foreign language: (2); Social studies: 3 (3); Total units: 14 (16). Tests: The college uses SAT or ACT scores in admissions decisions. Either SAT or ACT required. For admission to the fall 2007 entering class, the school will accept: ACT with writing. Campus visit: Recommended. Admissions interview: Recommended. Off-campus interview: May be arranged. **Factors that count in admissions decisions:** *Academic:* Secondary school record: Very important. Class rank: Important. Letters of recommendation: Important. Standardized test scores: Important. Essay: Important. *Nonacademic:* Interview: Important. Extracurricular activities: Considered. Talent/ability: Considered. Character/personal qualities: Very important. Alumni/ae relationship: Considered. Geographical residence: Considered. State residency: Not considered. Religious affiliation/commitment: Not considered. Minority status: Not considered. Volunteer work: Considered. Work experience: Considered. **Other schools with the greatest overlap in applicants:** Berry College; Georgia College and State University; Mercer University; University of Georgia. **Admissions statistics for the fall 2005 entering class:** Total applicants: 1,247. Total accepted: 604. Freshmen enrolled: 204; 8% were from out of state. Overall acceptance rate: 48%. **Credentials of fall 2005 freshmen:** 21% ranked in the top 10 percent of their high school class; 40% were in the top 25 percent, and 76% were in the top half. (Proportion submitting class standing: 48%.) **Average high school grade point average:** 3.5. **First-year students who submitted SAT scores:** 83%. Scores (25/75 percentile): Verbal: 460-570,

Math: 470-570, Combined: 930-1140. **First-year students submitting ACT scores:** 39%. Scores (25/75 percentile): English: 18-23, Math: 18-23, Composite: 18-24.

ACADEMICS

Year founded: 1831. **Academic calendar:** 4-1-4. **Degrees offered:** associate, bachelor's, master's. **Most popular majors:** 41% business administration and management, 11% visual and performing arts, 7% biomedical sciences, 7% education, 7% psychology. **Major fields of study:** biological and biomedical sciences; business, management, marketing, and related support services; computer and information sciences and support services; education; English language and literature/letters; foreign languages, literatures, and linguistics; health professions and related clinical sciences; history; mathematics and statistics; philosophy and religious studies; physical sciences; psychology; social sciences; visual and performing arts. **Areas of required coursework:** arts/fine arts, humanities, computer literacy, mathematics, English (including composition), philosophy, foreign languages, sciences (biological or physical), history, social science. **Pre-professional programs:** pre-law, pre-dentistry, pre-medicine, pre-theology, pre-veterinary science, pre-optometry, pre-pharmacy, other. **Special academic programs (% participation):** accelerated program (16%), double major (3%), dual enrollment (2%), independent study (46%), internships (81%), liberal arts/career combination, study abroad (21%), teacher certificate program (6%). **Teacher certification offered in:** early childhood, elementary, middle/junior high, secondary. **Faculty and instruction (2005-2006):** Total instructional faculty: 65 full-time, 53 part-time (54% men; 46% women; 8% minorities). Full-time faculty with Ph.D. or other terminal degree: 82%. Student/faculty ratio: 10/1. Classes of fewer than 20 students: 86%; of 20 to 49 students: 13%; of 50 or more students: 0%. **Advanced Placement and International Baccalaureate credit:** AP tests may be used for: Credit and/or placement. International Baccalaureate exams may be used for: Credit and/or placement. **Freshmen returning for sophomore year:** 76%. **Graduation rates:** Four-year: 29%; five-year: 39%; six-year: 45%. **Graduate study:** 41% of students pursue further study within one year. Fields in which graduates pursue further study: Master of Business Administration (MBA), 13%; law, 13%; medicine, 3%; theology (or the seminary), 3%; education, 28%; arts and sciences, 34%; veterinary medicine, 6%.

COSTS AND FINANCIAL AID

Financial aid office: (706) 880-8229. **Expenses (2006-2007):** Tuition and fees 2006-2007: $17,253; room/board: $7,182. Estimated books and supplies: $1,000 personal expenses: $2,000. **Financial aid:** In 2005-2006, 98% of undergraduates applied for financial aid. Of those, 73% were determined to have financial need; 32% had their need fully met. Average financial aid package (proportion receiving): $14,651 (73%). Average amount of gift aid, such as scholarships or grants (proportion receiving): $9,241 (73%). Average amount of self-help aid, such as work study or loans (proportion receiving): $4,165 (57%). Average need-based loan (excluding PLUS or other private loans): $3,889. Among students who received need-based aid, the average percentage of need met: 81%. Among students who received aid based on merit, the average award (and the proportion receiving): $5,803 (24%). The average athletic scholarship (and the proportion receiving): $0 (0%). Average amount of debt of borrowers graduating in 2005: $17,074. Proportion who borrowed: 79%.

CAMPUS LIFE AND EXTRACURRICULAR ACTIVITIES

Campus housing available (% using): coed dorms (25%), women's dorms (18%), men's dorms (14%), apartment for single students (43%). Students who live in college-owned, operated, or affiliated housing: 71%. **Clubs and organizations:** Number of student organizations: 52. Activities include: choral groups, dance, drama/theater, jazz band, literary magazine, music ensembles, musical theater, student government, student newspaper, yearbook. Number of fraternities: 4; sororities: 6. Proportion of men in fraternities: 37%; of women in sororities: 28%. Average proportion of students who stay on campus on weekends: 70%. **Sports program (2005-2006):** Member of NCAA III. *Men's intercollegiate varsity sports:* baseball, basketball, cross-country, golf, soccer, swimming and diving, tennis. *Women's intercollegiate varsity sports:* basketball, cross-country, soccer, softball, swimming and diving, tennis, volleyball.

SERVICES AND FACILITIES

Basic services: nonremedial tutoring, placement service, health service, health insurance. **Remedial assistance:** study skills. **Counseling services:** minority student, career, personal, veteran student, academic, older student, psychological, birth control, religious. **For learning-disabled students:** School does not offer a structured program with separate admission and additional

fees. Total undergraduates in learning-disabled program or receiving services: 15. Services include: tape recorders, untimed tests, note-taking services, oral tests, readers, extended time for tests, tutors. **Library:** Number of titles: 116,300; number of current serial subscriptions: 374. **Information technology resources:** Students are not required to lease or own a computer. Number of campus computers available to all students: 184. School has a wireless network. Proportion of college-owned housing units wired for high-speed internet access: 100%. **Campus safety:** Security services offered: 24-hour foot-and-vehicle patrols, late-night transport/escort service, 24-hour emergency telephones, lighted pathways/sidewalks, controlled dormitory access (key, security card, etc).

TRANSFER AND INTERNATIONAL STUDENTS

Transfer students: May apply for admission for the following academic terms: Fall, Winter, Spring, Summer. Applicants need a minimum number of credits to apply. For fall 2005: Transfer applications received: 135. Transfer applicants offered admission: 98. Transfer applicants enrolled: 47. **International students:** Number of foreign undergraduates: 26 (3% of student body). Number of countries represented: 18. Minimum TOEFL score required: 500 (paper); 173 (computer).

Mercer University

- **Address:** 1400 Coleman Avenue, Macon, GA 31207-0003
- **Website:** http://www.mercer.edu
- **Private; Religious affiliation:** Baptist
- **Enrollment:** 3,796 full-time; 702 part-time

KEY STATS

✔ **U.S News College Ranking:** 9, Universities–Master's (South)
✔ **SAT Score (25th/75th percentile):** 1080-1280
✔ **Tuition:** 2006-2007: $25,256

Selectivity: More selective	**Room/board:** $7,710
Acceptance rate: 80%	**Average debt:** $11,075
Student/faculty ratio: 13/1	**Proportion who borrowed:** 63%

UNDERGRADUATE STUDENT BODY STATS

2005-2006 enrollment: 3,796 full-time; 702 part-time. Men: 31%; women: 69%. **Ethnic makeup:** African American: 27%; Asian American: 4%; Hispanic: 2%; White: 64%; International: 3%. **Religious preference:** Roman Catholic: 8%; Protestant: 21%; Muslim: 1%; Hindu: 1%; No preference: 12%; Baptist: 43%; Other: 14%.

ADMISSIONS FACTS AND FIGURES

Phone: (478) 301-2650. **Email:** admissions@mercer.edu. **Website:** http://www.mercer.edu. **Application deadlines for fall 2007:** Regular decision: July 1. Early decision: Not offered. Early action: Send application by: November 1; Decision sent by: November 15. Admission can be deferred. **Application fee:** $50. Common application is accepted. **To apply online, go to:** http://www.collegenet.com. **Admissions requirements/recommendations:** High school units required (recommended): English: 4; Mathematics: 4; Science: 3; Foreign language: 2; Social studies: 1; History: 2; Total units: 16. Tests: The college uses SAT or ACT scores in admissions decisions. Either SAT or ACT required. For admission to the fall 2007 entering class, the school will accept: ACT without writing. Campus visit: Recommended. Admissions interview: Recommended. Off-campus interview: May be arranged. **Factors that count in admissions decisions:** *Academic:* Secondary school record: Very important. Class rank: Considered. Letters of recommendation: Considered. Standardized test scores: Very important. Essay: Not considered. *Nonacademic:* Interview: Considered. Extracurricular activities: Important. Talent/ability: Important. Character/personal qualities: Important. Alumni/ae relationship: Considered. Geographical residence: Not considered. State residency: Not considered. Religious affiliation/commitment: Not considered. Minority status: Not considered. Volunteer work: Important. Work experience: Considered. **Other schools with the greatest overlap in applicants:** Emory University; Furman University; Samford University; University of Georgia; Vanderbilt University. **Admissions statistics for the fall 2005 entering class:** Total applicants: 3,108. Total accepted: 2,486. Freshmen enrolled: 616; 25% were from out of state. Accepted through early-decision or early-action plans: 50%. Overall acceptance rate: 80%. Non-early acceptance rate: 74%. **Size of waiting list:** 20 applicants; enrolled from waiting list: 10. **Credentials of fall 2005 freshmen:** 48% ranked in the top 10 percent of their high school class; 74% were in the top 25 percent, and 94% were in the top half. (Proportion submitting class standing: 29%.) **Average high school grade point average:** 3.6. **First-year students who submitted SAT scores:** 95%. Scores (25/75 percentile): Verbal: 530-640, Math: 550-640, Combined: 1080-1280. **First-year students submitting ACT scores:** 43%. Scores (25/75 percentile): English: 22-28, Math: 22-27, Composite: 22-27.

ACADEMICS

Year founded: 1833. **Academic calendar:** Semester. **Degrees offered:** bachelor's, master's, post-master's certificate, first professional, doctorate. **Most popular majors:** 22% business, management, marketing, and related support services, 18% engineering, 10% social sciences, 8% communication, journalism, and related programs, 7% education. **Major fields of study:** area, ethnic, cultural, and gender studies; biological and biomedical sciences; business, management, marketing, and related support services; communication, journalism, and related programs; computer and information sciences and support services; education; engineering; English language and literature/letters; foreign languages, literatures, and linguistics; health professions and related clinical sciences; history; liberal arts and sciences studies, and humanities; mathematics and statistics; multi/interdisciplinary studies; natural resources and conservation; philosophy and religious studies; physical sciences; psychology; public administration and social service professions; security and protective services; social sciences; visual and performing arts. **Areas of required coursework:** arts/fine arts, humanities, computer literacy, mathematics, English (including composition), philosophy, foreign languages, sciences (biological or physical), history, social science, other. **Pre-professional programs:** pre-law, pre-dentistry, pre-medicine, pretheology, pre-veterinary science, pre-pharmacy, other. **Special academic programs:** accelerated program, cooperative (work-study plan) program, cross-registration, double major, dual enrollment, honors program, independent study, internships, liberal arts/career combination, student-designed major, study abroad, teacher certificate program. **Teacher certification offered in:** elementary, middle/junior high, secondary. **Cooperative education programs:** art, business, computer science, engineering, humanities, natural science, social/behavioral science, other. **Reserve Officers Training Corps (ROTC):** Army ROTC: Offered on campus. **Faculty and instruction (2005-2006):** Total instructional faculty: 345 full-time, 269 part-time (56% men; 44% women; 16% minorities). Full-time faculty with Ph.D. or other terminal degree: 86%. Student/faculty ratio: 13/1. Classes of fewer than 20 students: 56%; of 20 to 49 students: 42%; of 50 or more students: 3%. **Advanced Placement and International Baccalaureate credit:** AP tests may be used for: Credit and/or placement. Scores accepted: 3, 4, 5. International Baccalaureate exams may be used for: Credit only. **Freshmen returning for sophomore year:** 79%. **Graduation rates:** Four-year: 35%; five-year: 49%; six-year: 51%. **Graduate study:** 20% of students pursue further study within one year.

COSTS AND FINANCIAL AID

Financial aid office: (478) 301-2670. **Expenses (2006-2007):** Tuition and fees 2006-2007: $25,256; room/board: $7,710. **Financial aid:** Priority filing date for institution's financial aid form: April 1. In 2005-2006, 79% of undergraduates applied for financial aid. Of those, 64% were determined to have financial need; 51% had their need fully met. Average financial aid package (proportion receiving): $23,102 (64%). Average amount of gift aid, such as scholarships or grants (proportion receiving): $14,556 (64%). Average amount of self-help aid, such as work study or loans (proportion receiving): $7,328 (41%). Average need-based loan (excluding PLUS or other private loans): $6,668. Among students who received need-based aid, the average percentage of need met: 91%. Among students who received aid based on merit, the average award (and the proportion receiving): $15,854 (33%). The average athletic scholarship (and the proportion receiving): $14,906 (6%). Average amount of debt of borrowers graduating in 2005: $11,075. Proportion who borrowed: 63%.

CAMPUS LIFE AND EXTRACURRICULAR ACTIVITIES

Campus housing available (% using): coed dorms (32%), women's dorms (21%), men's dorms (13%), sorority housing (3%), fraternity housing (6%), apartments for married students, apartment for single students (25%), special housing for disabled students, special housing for international students. Students who live in college-owned, operated, or affiliated housing: 66%. **Student employment:** During the 2005-2006 academic year, 21% of undergraduates worked on campus. Average per-year earnings: $1,953. **Clubs and organizations:** Number of student organizations: 90. Activities include: choral groups, concert band, dance, drama/theater, jazz band, literary magazine, music ensembles, opera, pep band, radio station, student

government, student newspaper, student film society. Number of fraternities: 10; sororities: 6. Proportion of men in fraternities: 24%; of women in sororities: 25%. Average proportion of students who stay on campus on weekends: 65%. **Sports program (2005-2006):** Member of NCAA I. *Men's intercollegiate varsity sports:* baseball, basketball, cross-country, golf, soccer, tennis, volleyball, mixed rifle. *Women's intercollegiate varsity sports:* basketball, cross-country, golf, soccer, softball, team handball, tennis, volleyball, mixed rifle.

SERVICES AND FACILITIES

Basic services: nonremedial tutoring, placement service, health service, health insurance. **Counseling services:** minority student, career, military, personal, veteran student, academic, older student, psychological, religious. **For learning-disabled students:** School does not offer a structured program with separate admission and additional fees. Total undergraduates in learning-disabled program or receiving services: 28. Services include: reading machines, tape recorders, note-taking services, oral tests, learning center, readers, extended time for tests, tutors, early syllabus, priority registration, priority seating, substitution of courses, texts on tape, typist/scribe, exams on tape or computer, other. **Library:** Number of titles: 713,609; number of current serial subscriptions: 236,974. **Information technology resources:** Students are not required to lease or own a computer. Number of campus computers available to all students: 930. School has a wireless network. Approximate number of users that can be accommodated: 460. Proportion of college-owned housing units wired for high-speed internet access: 100%. **Campus safety:** Security services offered: 24-hour foot-and-vehicle patrols, late-night transport/escort service, 24-hour emergency telephones, lighted pathways/sidewalks, student patrols, controlled dormitory access (key, security card, etc).

TRANSFER AND INTERNATIONAL STUDENTS

Transfer students: May apply for admission for the following academic terms: Fall, Spring, Summer. Applicants need a minimum number of credits to apply. For fall 2005: Transfer applications received: 319. Transfer applicants offered admission: 305. Transfer applicants enrolled: 114. **International students:** Number of foreign undergraduates: 112 (3% of student body). Number of countries represented: 567. Minimum TOEFL score required: 550 (paper); 213 (computer).

Morehouse College

- **Address:** 830 Westview Drive SW, Atlanta, GA 30314
- **Website:** http://www.morehouse.edu
- **Private**
- **Enrollment:** 2,857 full-time; 172 part-time

KEY STATS

✔ **U.S News College Ranking:** third tier, Liberal Arts Colleges
✔ **SAT Score (25th/75th percentile):** 980-1200
✔ **Tuition:** 2006-2007: $16,830

Selectivity: Selective	**Room/board:** $9,454
Acceptance rate: 53%	**Average debt:** $22,625
Student/faculty ratio: 16/1	**Proportion who borrowed:** 90%

UNDERGRADUATE STUDENT BODY STATS

2005-2006 enrollment: 2,857 full-time; 172 part-time. Men: 100%; women: 0%. **Ethnic makeup:** African American: 95%; White: 4%; International: 1%. **Religious preference:** Roman Catholic: 5%; Protestant: 1%; No preference: 16%; Unknown: 20%; Other: 58%.

ADMISSIONS FACTS AND FIGURES

Phone: (800) 851-1254. **Email:** admissions@morehouse.edu. **Website:** http://www.morehouse.edu. **Application deadlines for fall 2007:** Regular decision: February 15; decision sent by April 1. Early decision: Not offered. Early action: Send application by: November 1; Decision sent by: December 1. Admission can be deferred. **Application fee:** $45. Common application is accepted. **Admissions requirements/recommendations:** High school units required (recommended): English: 4 (4); Mathematics: 3 (3); Science: 2 (2); Foreign language: 2 (2); Social studies: 2 (2); History: (0); Academic electives: (0); Total units: 13 (13). Tests: The college uses SAT or ACT scores in admissions decisions. Either SAT or ACT required. For admission to the fall 2007 entering class, the school will accept: ACT with writing. Campus visit:

Recommended. Admissions interview: Recommended. Off-campus interview: May be arranged. **Factors that count in admissions decisions:** *Academic:* Secondary school record: Very important. Class rank: Important. Letters of recommendation: Important. Standardized test scores: Very important. Essay: Very important. *Nonacademic:* Interview: Considered. Extracurricular activities: Considered. Talent/ability: Considered. Character/personal qualities: Considered. Alumni/ae relationship: Considered. Geographical residence: Considered. State residency: Not considered. Religious affiliation/commitment: Not considered. Minority status: Considered. Volunteer work: Considered. Work experience: Not considered. **Other schools with the greatest overlap in applicants:** Duke University; Harvard University; Howard University; University of North Carolina–Chapel Hill; Washington State University. **Admissions statistics for the fall 2005 entering class:** Total applicants: 2,520. Total accepted: 1,327. Freshmen enrolled: 661; 73% were from out of state. Overall acceptance rate: 53%. Non-early acceptance rate: 53%. **Size of waiting list:** 0 applicants; enrolled from waiting list: 0. **Credentials of fall 2005 freshmen:** 18% ranked in the top 10 percent of their high school class; 41% were in the top 25 percent, and 72% were in the top half. (Proportion submitting class standing: 42%.) **Average high school grade point average:** 3.2. **First-year students who submitted SAT scores:** 80%. Scores (25/75 percentile): Verbal: 490-600, Math: 490-600, Combined: 980-1200. **First-year students submitting ACT scores:** 20%. Scores (25/75 percentile): English: 19-26, Math: 18-24, Composite: 17-25.

ACADEMICS

Year founded: 1867. **Academic calendar:** Semester. **Degrees offered:** bachelor's. **Most popular majors:** 35% business administration and management, 19% social sciences, 7% psychology, 6% English language and literature, 6% mathematics. **Major fields of study:** area, ethnic, cultural, and gender studies; biological and biomedical sciences; business, management, marketing, and related support services; communication, journalism, and related programs; computer and information sciences and support services; education; engineering; English language and literature/letters; foreign languages, literatures, and linguistics; history; mathematics and statistics; parks, recreation, leisure, and fitness studies; philosophy and religious studies; physical sciences; psychology; social sciences; visual and performing arts. **Areas of required coursework:** arts/fine arts, humanities, mathematics, English (including composition), philosophy, foreign languages, sciences (biological or physical), history, social science. **Special academic programs (% participation):** cross-registration (61%), double major (2%), dual enrollment (.46%), exchange student program (domestic) (0%), honors program (5%), independent study (23%), internships (89%), study abroad (7%), teacher certificate program (2%). **Teacher certification offered in:** early childhood. **Cooperative education programs:** business, computer science, education, engineering, social/behavioral science. **Reserve Officers Training Corps (ROTC):** Army ROTC: Offered on campus; Navy ROTC: Offered on campus; Air Force ROTC: Offered at cooperating institution (Georgia Institute of Technology). **Faculty and instruction (2005-2006):** Total instructional faculty: 167 full-time, 56 part-time (68% men; 32% women; 61% minorities). Full-time faculty with Ph.D. or other terminal degree: 86%. Student/faculty ratio: 16/1. Classes of fewer than 20 students: 41%; of 20 to 49 students: 56%; of 50 or more students: 3%. **Advanced Placement and International Baccalaureate credit:** AP tests may be used for: Credit and/or placement. Scores accepted: 3. International Baccalaureate exams may be used for: Credit and/or placement. **Freshmen returning for sophomore year:** 85%. **Graduation rates:** Four-year: 43%; five-year: 56%; six-year: 61%. **Graduate study:** 53% of students pursue further study immediately upon graduation.

COSTS AND FINANCIAL AID

Financial aid office: (404) 681-2800. **Expenses (2006-2007):** Tuition and fees 2006-2007: $16,830; room/board: $9,454. Estimated books and supplies: $850; transportation: $3,800; personal expenses: $3,800. **Financial aid:** In 2005-2006, 99% of undergraduates applied for financial aid. Of those, 99% were determined to have financial need; 2% had their need fully met. Average financial aid package (proportion receiving): $7,859 (99%). Average amount of gift aid, such as scholarships or grants (proportion receiving): $6,125 (50%). Average amount of self-help aid, such as work study or loans (proportion receiving): $5,028 (98%). Average need-based loan (excluding PLUS or other private loans): $4,250. Among students who received need-based aid, the average percentage of need met: 49%. Among students who received aid based on merit, the average award (and the proportion receiving): $7,544 (68%). The average athletic scholarship (and the proportion receiving): $9,864 (42%). Average amount of debt of borrowers graduating in 2005: $22,625. Proportion who borrowed: 90%.

CAMPUS LIFE AND EXTRACURRICULAR ACTIVITIES

Campus housing available (% using): men's dorms (100%), apartment for single students. Students who live in college-owned, operated, or affiliated housing: 55%. **Student employment:** During the 2005-2006 academic year, 20% of undergraduates worked on campus. Average per-year earnings: $1,500. **Clubs and organizations:** Number of student organizations: 78. Activities include: choral groups, concert band, drama/theater, jazz band, literary magazine, marching band, music ensembles, pep band, student government, student newspaper, yearbook. Number of fraternities: 8; sororities: 0. Proportion of men in fraternities: 3%; Average proportion of students who stay on campus on weekends: 60%. **Sports program (2005-2006):** Member of NCAA II. *Men's intercollegiate varsity sports:* baseball, basketball, cross-country, football, golf, soccer, tennis, track and field (indoor), track and field (outdoor).

SERVICES AND FACILITIES

Basic services: nonremedial tutoring, placement service, health service, health insurance. **Remedial assistance:** reading, math, writing, study skills. **Counseling services:** career, personal, academic, older student, psychological. **For learning-disabled students:** School does not offer a structured program with separate admission and additional fees. Total undergraduates in learning-disabled program or receiving services: 42. Services include: remedial math, remedial English, remedial reading, tape recorders, diagnostic testing service, untimed tests, note-taking services, special bookstore section, oral tests, learning center, readers, extended time for tests, tutors, priority seating, other testing accomodations. **Library:** Number of titles: 743,801; number of current serial subscriptions: 1,060. **Information technology resources:** Students are not required to lease or own a computer. Number of campus computers available to all students: 400. School has a wireless network. Proportion of college-owned housing units wired for high-speed internet access: 100%. **Campus safety:** Security services offered: 24-hour foot-and-vehicle patrols, late-night transport/escort service, 24-hour emergency telephones, lighted pathways/sidewalks, controlled dormitory access (key, security card, etc.).

TRANSFER AND INTERNATIONAL STUDENTS

Transfer students: May apply for admission for the following academic terms: Fall, Spring. Applicants need a minimum number of credits to apply. **International students:** Number of foreign undergraduates: 17 (1% of student body). Number of countries represented: 15. Minimum TOEFL score required: 500 (paper). Average TOEFL score: 550 (paper).

North Georgia College and State University

- **Address:** College Circle, Dahlonega, GA 30597
- **Website:** http://www.ngcsu.edu
- **Public**
- **Enrollment:** 3,353 full-time; 837 part-time

KEY STATS

✔ **U.S News College Ranking:** 56, Universities–Master's (South)
✔ **SAT Score (25th/75th percentile):** 990-1160
✔ **Tuition:** 2006-2007: $2,536 in state, $10,144 out of state

Selectivity: Selective	Room/board: $4,780
Acceptance rate: 68%	Average debt: N/A
Student/faculty ratio: 15/1	Proportion who borrowed: N/A

UNDERGRADUATE STUDENT BODY STATS

2005-2006 enrollment: 3,353 full-time; 837 part-time. Men: 38%; women: 62%. **Ethnic makeup:** African American: 3%; Asian American: 1%; Hispanic: 3%; White: 93%; International: 1%.

ADMISSIONS FACTS AND FIGURES

Phone: (800) 498-9581. **Email:** admissions@ngcsu.edu. **Website:** http://www.ngcsu.edu. **Application deadlines for fall 2007:** Regular decision: July 1. Early decision: Not offered. Early action: Not offered. Admission cannot be deferred. **Application fee:** $25. Common application is not accepted. **To apply online, go to:** http://www.applyweb.com/aw?ngcsu. **Admissions requirements/recommendations:** High school units required (recommended): English: 4; Mathematics: 4; Science: 3; Foreign language: 2; Social studies: 3; Academic electives: 0; Total units: 17. Tests: The college uses SAT or ACT scores in admissions decisions. Either SAT or ACT required. For admission to the fall 2007 entering class, the school will accept: ACT with writing, ACT without writing. **Campus visit:** Recommended. **Admissions interview:** Neither required nor recommended. **Off-campus interview:** Not available. **Factors that count in admissions decisions:** *Academic:* Secondary school record: Considered. Class rank: Considered. Letters of recommendation: Considered. Standardized test scores: Very important. Essay: Not considered. *Nonacademic:* Interview: Not considered. Extracurricular activities: Considered. Talent/ability: Considered. Character/personal qualities: Considered. Alumni/ae relationship: Considered. Geographical residence: Not considered. State residency: Not considered. Religious affiliation/commitment: Not considered. Minority status: Not considered. Volunteer work: Considered. Work experience: Considered. **Other schools with the greatest overlap in applicants:** Berry College; Georgia Southern University; Georgia State University; University of Georgia; University of West Georgia. **Admissions statistics for the fall 2005 entering class:** Total applicants: 2,115. Total accepted: 1,429. Freshmen enrolled: 731; 7% were from out of state. Overall acceptance rate: 68%. **Size of waiting list:** 64 applicants; enrolled from waiting list: 29. **Credentials of fall 2005 freshmen:** 24% ranked in the top 10 percent of their high school class; 57% were in the top 25 percent, and 85% were in the top half. (Proportion submitting class standing: 86%.) **Average high school grade point average:** 3.1. **First-year students who submitted SAT scores:** 87%. Scores (25/75 percentile): Verbal: 500-590, Math: 490-570, Combined: 990-1160. **First-year students submitting ACT scores:** 22%. Scores (25/75 percentile): English: 19-24, Math: 18-24, Composite: 20-24.

ACADEMICS

Year founded: 1873. **Academic calendar:** Semester. **Degrees offered:** certificate, associate, bachelor's, master's, post-master's certificate. **Most popular majors:** 6% business administration and management, 6% special education and teaching, 5% biology/biological sciences, 5% marketing/marketing management, 4% criminal justice/safety studies. **Major fields of study:** biological and biomedical sciences; business, management, marketing, and related support services; computer and information sciences and support services; education; English language and literature/letters; foreign languages, literatures, and linguistics; health professions and related clinical sciences; history; mathematics and statistics; physical sciences; psychology; public administration and social service professions; security and protective services; social sciences; visual and performing arts. **Areas of required coursework:** arts/fine arts, humanities, computer literacy, mathematics, English (including composition), philosophy, foreign languages, sciences (biological or physical), history, social science. **Pre-professional programs:** pre-law, pre-dentistry, pre-medicine, pre-veterinary science, pre-pharmacy, other. **Special academic programs (% participation):** cooperative (work-study plan) program (10%), distance learning (21%), double major (5%), dual enrollment (1%), external degree program (1%), honors program (2%), independent study (5%), internships (25%), study abroad (3%), teacher certificate program (19%), other (5%). **Teacher certification offered in:** early childhood, special education, elementary, middle/junior high, secondary. **Reserve Officers Training Corps (ROTC):** Army ROTC: Offered on campus. **Faculty and instruction (2005-2006):** Total instructional faculty: 199 full-time, 123 part-time (47% men; 53% women; 4% minorities). Full-time faculty with Ph.D. or other terminal degree: 68%. Student/faculty ratio: 15/1. Classes of fewer than 20 students: 37%; of 20 to 49 students: 61%; of 50 or more students: 2%. **Advanced Placement and International Baccalaureate credit:** AP tests may be used for: Credit only. Scores accepted: 3, 4, 5. International Baccalaureate exams may be used for: Credit only. **Freshmen returning for sophomore year:** 76%. **Graduation rates:** Four-year: 22%; five-year: 41%; six-year: 47%. **Graduate study:** 20% of students pursue further study immediately upon graduation; 23% within one year; 26% within five years. Fields in which graduates pursue further study: Master of Business Administration (MBA), 5%; law, 3%; medicine, 2%; dentistry, 2%; engineering, 1%; theology (or the seminary), 1%; education, 75%; arts and sciences, 10%; veterinary medicine, 1%.

COSTS AND FINANCIAL AID

Financial aid office: (706) 864-1412. **Expenses (2006-2007):** Tuition and fees 2006-2007: $2,536 in state, $10,144 out of state; room/board: $4,780. **Financial aid:** Priority filing date for institution's financial aid form: May 1; deadline: May 1.

CAMPUS LIFE AND EXTRACURRICULAR ACTIVITIES

Campus housing available (% using): women's dorms (50%), men's dorms (30%), apartment for single students (20%). Students who live in college-owned, operated, or affiliated housing: 29%. **Student employment:** During the 2005-2006 academic year, 12% of undergraduates worked on campus. Average per-year earnings: $3,000. **Clubs and organizations:** Number of student organizations: 140. Activities include: choral groups, concert band, dance, drama/theater, jazz band, literary magazine, marching band, music ensembles, pep band, student government, student newspaper, symphony orchestra, yearbook. Number of fraternities: 8; sororities: 4. Proportion of men in fraternities: 1%; of women in sororities: 3%. Average proportion of students who stay on campus on weekends: 50%. **Sports program (2005-2006):** Member of NCAA II. *Men's intercollegiate varsity sports:* baseball, basketball, cross-country, soccer, tennis. *Women's intercollegiate varsity sports:* basketball, cross-country, soccer, softball, tennis.

SERVICES AND FACILITIES

Basic services: nonremedial tutoring, placement service, health service, health insurance. **Remedial assistance:** reading, math, writing, study skills. **Counseling services:** minority student, career, military, personal, veteran student, academic, older student, psychological, birth control. **For learning-disabled students:** School does not offer a structured program with separate admission and additional fees. Total undergraduates in learning-disabled program or receiving services: 100. Services include: remedial math, remedial English, reading machines, remedial reading, tape recorders, diagnostic testing service, untimed tests, note-taking services, readers, extended time for tests, tutors, priority registration, priority seating. **Library:** Number of titles: 175,330; number of current serial subscriptions: 650. **Information technology resources:** Students are not required to lease or own a computer. Number of campus computers available to all students: 470. School has a wireless network. Approximate number of users that can be accommodated: 200. Proportion of college-owned housing units wired for high-speed internet access: 98%. **Campus safety:** Security services offered: 24-hour foot-and-vehicle patrols, 24-hour emergency telephones, lighted pathways/sidewalks, controlled dormitory access (key, security card, etc).

TRANSFER AND INTERNATIONAL STUDENTS

Transfer students: May apply for admission for the following academic terms: Fall, Spring, Summer. Applicants need a minimum number of credits to apply. For fall 2005: Transfer applications received: 1,154. Transfer applicants offered admission: 874. Transfer applicants enrolled: 420. **International students:** Number of foreign undergraduates: 23 (1% of student body). Number of countries represented: 28. Minimum TOEFL score required: 550 (paper); 213 (computer). Average TOEFL score: 610 (paper).

Oglethorpe University

- **Address:** 4484 Peachtree Road NE, Atlanta, GA 30319-2797
- **Website:** http://www.oglethorpe.edu
- **Private**
- **Enrollment:** 886 full-time; 132 part-time

KEY STATS

✔ **U.S News College Ranking:** third tier, Liberal Arts Colleges
✔ **SAT Score (25th/75th percentile):** 970-1240
✔ **Tuition:** 2006-2007: $23,510

Selectivity: Selective	Room/board: $8,000
Acceptance rate: 64%	Average debt: N/A
Student/faculty ratio: N/A	Proportion who borrowed: N/A

UNDERGRADUATE STUDENT BODY STATS

2005-2006 enrollment: 886 full-time; 132 part-time. Men: 36%; women: 64%. **Ethnic makeup:** African American: 21%; Asian American: 4%; Hispanic: 1%; White: 72%; International: 2%.

ADMISSIONS FACTS AND FIGURES

Phone: (404) 364-8307. **Email:** admission@oglethorpe.edu. **Website:** http://www.oglethorpe.edu. **Application deadlines for fall 2007:** Regular decision: Rolling. Early decision: Not offered. Early action: Send application by: N/A; Decision sent by: N/A. **Application fee:** $30. Common application is accepted. **Admissions requirements/recommendations:** High school units required (recommended): English: 4; Mathematics: 3; Science: 2; Foreign language: (2); Social studies: 3. Tests: The college uses SAT or ACT scores in admissions decisions. Either SAT or ACT required. For admission to the fall 2007 entering class, the school will accept: ACT without writing. **Factors that count in admissions decisions:** *Academic:* Secondary school record: Very important. Class rank: Considered. Letters of recommendation: Considered. Standardized test scores: Important. Essay: Very important. *Nonacademic:*

Interview: Very important. Extracurricular activities: Considered. Talent/ability: Considered. Character/personal qualities: Considered. Alumni/ae relationship: Considered. Geographical residence: Not considered. State residency: Not considered. Religious affiliation/commitment: Not considered. Minority status: Not considered. Volunteer work: Considered. Work experience: Considered. **Admissions statistics for the fall 2005 entering class:** Total applicants: 1,236. Total accepted: 794. Freshmen enrolled: 233; 29% were from out of state. Overall acceptance rate: 64%. Non-early acceptance rate: 64%. **Credentials of fall 2005 freshmen:** 27% ranked in the top 10 percent of their high school class; 57% were in the top 25 percent, and 84% were in the top half. (Proportion submitting class standing: 48%.) **Average high school grade point average:** 3.5. **First-year students who submitted SAT scores:** 83%. Scores (25/75 percentile): Verbal: 500-630, Math: 470-610, Combined: 970-1240. **First-year students submitting ACT scores:** 29%. Scores (25/75 percentile): English: N/A, Math: N/A, Composite: 21-27.

ACADEMICS

Year founded: 1835. **Academic calendar:** Semester. **Degrees offered:** bachelor's, master's. **Most popular majors:** 32% business, management, marketing, and related support services, 21% English language and literature/letters, 11% psychology, 9% social sciences, 8% biological and biomedical sciences. **Major fields of study:** area, ethnic, cultural, and gender studies; biological and biomedical sciences; business, management, marketing, and related support services; communication, journalism, and related programs; English language and literature/letters; history; liberal arts and sciences studies, and humanities; mathematics and statistics; multi/interdisciplinary studies; philosophy and religious studies; physical sciences; psychology; public administration and social service professions; social sciences; visual and performing arts. **Areas of required coursework:** arts/fine arts, humanities, computer literacy, mathematics, English (including composition), philosophy, foreign languages, sciences (biological or physical), history, social science. **Pre-professional programs:** pre-law, pre-dentistry, pre-medicine, pre-theology, pre-veterinary science, pre-optometry, pre-pharmacy. **Special academic programs:** accelerated program, cooperative (work-study plan) program, cross-registration, double major, dual enrollment, exchange student program (domestic), honors program, independent study, internships, liberal arts/career combination, student-designed major, study abroad, teacher certificate program. **Faculty and instruction (2005-2006):** Total instructional faculty: N/A. Classes of fewer than 20 students: 79%; of 20 to 49 students: 21%; of 50 or more students: 0%. **Advanced Placement and International Baccalaureate credit:** AP tests may be used for: Credit and/or placement. Scores accepted: 4, 5. International Baccalaureate exams may be used for: Credit only. **Freshmen returning for sophomore year:** 84%. **Graduation rates:** Four-year: 53%; five-year: 60%; six-year: 60%.

COSTS AND FINANCIAL AID

Financial aid office: (404) 364-8356. **Expenses (2006-2007):** Tuition and fees 2006-2007: $23,510; room/board: $8,000. **Financial aid:** Priority filing date for institution's financial aid form: March 1; deadline: September 1.

CAMPUS LIFE AND EXTRACURRICULAR ACTIVITIES

Campus housing available: coed dorms, women's dorms, men's dorms, sorority housing, fraternity housing. Students who live in college-owned, operated, or affiliated housing: 60%. Activities include: choral groups, dance, drama/theater, literary magazine, musical theater, radio station, student government, student newspaper, student film society, yearbook. Number of fraternities: 4; sororities: 3. Proportion of men in fraternities: 33%; of women in sororities: 25%. **Sports program (2005-2006):** Member of NCAA III. *Men's intercollegiate varsity sports:* baseball, basketball, cross-country, golf, soccer, tennis, track and field (indoor), track and field (outdoor). *Women's intercollegiate varsity sports:* basketball, cross-country, golf, soccer, tennis, track and field (indoor), track and field (outdoor), volleyball.

SERVICES AND FACILITIES

Basic services: nonremedial tutoring, placement service, health service, health insurance. **Counseling services:** psychological. **Information technology resources:** Students are not required to lease or own a computer. School has a wireless network. Proportion of college-owned housing units wired for high-speed internet access: 100%. **Campus safety:** Security services offered: 24-hour foot-and-vehicle patrols, 24-hour emergency telephones, lighted pathways/sidewalks, controlled dormitory access (key, security card, etc).

TRANSFER AND INTERNATIONAL STUDENTS

Transfer students: May apply for admission for the following academic terms: Fall, Spring, Summer. Applicants need a minimum number of credits to apply. For fall 2005: Transfer applications received: 199. Transfer

applicants offered admission: 92. Transfer applicants enrolled: 72. **International students:** Number of foreign undergraduates: 18 (2% of student body). Minimum TOEFL score required: 500 (paper).

Paine College

- Address: 1235 15th Street, Augusta, GA 30901-3182
- Website: http://www.paine.edu
- Private; Religious affiliation: CME and UM
- Enrollment: 760 full-time; 68 part-time

KEY STATS

✔ **U.S News College Ranking:** fourth tier, Liberal Arts Colleges
✔ **SAT Score (25th/75th percentile):** 730-910
✔ **Tuition:** 2006-2007: $10,184

Selectivity: Less selective	**Room/board:** $4,966
Acceptance rate: 29%	**Average debt:** $21,661
Student/faculty ratio: 9/1	**Proportion who borrowed:** 95%

UNDERGRADUATE STUDENT BODY STATS

2005-2006 enrollment: 760 full-time; 68 part-time. Men: 30%; women: 70%. **Ethnic makeup:** African American: 98%; White: 1%. **Religious preference:** Roman Catholic: 1%; Protestant: 29%; No preference: 50%; Unknown: 14%; CME and UM: 3%; Other: 1%.

ADMISSIONS FACTS AND FIGURES

Phone: (706) 821-8320. **Email:** tinsleyj@mail.paine.edu. **Website:** http://www.paine.edu. **Application deadlines for fall 2007:** Regular decision: August 1. Early decision: Not offered. Early action: Not offered. Admission can be deferred. **Application fee:** $20. Common application is not accepted. **Admissions requirements/recommendations:** High school units required (recommended): English: 4 (4); Mathematics: 3 (3); Science: 3 (3); Foreign language: (1); Social studies: 3 (3); History: 1 (1); Academic electives: 3 (3); Total units: 16 (16). **Tests:** The college uses SAT or ACT scores in admissions decisions. Either SAT or ACT required. For admission to the fall 2007 entering class, the school will accept: ACT with writing, ACT without writing. Campus visit: Neither required nor recommended. Admissions interview: Neither required nor recommended. Off-campus interview: May be arranged. **Factors that count in admissions decisions:** *Academic:* Secondary school record: Very important. Class rank: Not considered. Letters of recommendation: Very important. Standardized test scores: Very important. Essay: Considered. *Nonacademic:* Interview: Considered. Extracurricular activities: Considered. Talent/ability: Important. Character/personal qualities: Very important. Alumni/ae relationship: Considered. Geographical residence: Not considered. State residency: Not considered. Religious affiliation/commitment: Not considered. Minority status: Not considered. Volunteer work: Not considered. Work experience: Not considered. **Admissions statistics for the fall 2005 entering class:** Total applicants: 3,683. Total accepted: 1,081. Freshmen enrolled: 198; 18% were from out of state. Overall acceptance rate: 29%. **Average high school grade point average:** 2.9. **First-year students who submitted SAT scores:** 75%. Scores (25/75 percentile): Verbal: 370-460, Math: 360-450, Combined: 730-910. **First-year students submitting ACT scores:** 34%. Scores (25/75 percentile): English: N/A, Math: N/A, Composite: 14-17.

ACADEMICS

Year founded: 1882. **Academic calendar:** Semester. **Degrees offered:** bachelor's. **Most popular majors:** 26% sociology, 12% business administration and management, 11% biology/biological sciences, 8% accounting, 5% criminology. **Major fields of study:** biological and biomedical sciences; business, management, marketing, and related support services; communication, journalism, and related programs; education; English language and literature/letters; history; mathematics and statistics; multi/interdisciplinary studies; natural resources and conservation; philosophy and religious studies; physical sciences; psychology; social sciences; visual and performing arts. **Areas of required coursework:** arts/fine arts, humanities, computer literacy, mathematics, English (including composition), philosophy, foreign languages, sciences (biological or physical), history, social science, other. **Pre-professional programs:** other. **Special academic programs (% participation):** cross-registration (9%), dual enrollment (0%), honors program (9%), independent study (1%), internships (18.4%), liberal arts/career combination (29.6%), study abroad (2%), teacher certificate program (4%). **Teacher certification offered in: early childhood, elementary, middle/junior high, secondary. **Reserve Officers Training Corps (ROTC):** Army ROTC: Offered at cooperating institution (Augusta State University). **Faculty and instruction (2005-2006):** Total instructional faculty: 74 full-time, 27 part-time (68% men; 32% women; 79% minorities). Full-time faculty with Ph.D. or other terminal degree: 51%. Student/faculty ratio: 9/1. Classes of fewer than 20 students: 78%; of 20 to 49 students: 22%. **Advanced Placement and International Baccalaureate credit:** AP tests may be used for: Credit only. **Freshmen returning for sophomore year:** 65%. **Graduation rates:** Four-year: 8%; five-year: 23%; six-year: 28%. **Graduate study:** 5% of students pursue further study immediately upon graduation; 7% within one year; 30% within five years. Fields in which graduates pursue further study: Master of Business Administration (MBA), 10%; law, 5%; medicine, 5%; dentistry, 5%; engineering, 5%; theology (or the seminary), 5%; education, 15%; arts and sciences, 50%.

COSTS AND FINANCIAL AID

Financial aid office: (706) 821-8262. **Expenses (2006-2007):** Tuition and fees 2006-2007: $10,184; room/board: $4,966. **Financial aid:** Priority filing date for institution's financial aid form: March 1. In 2005-2006, 100% of undergraduates applied for financial aid. Of those, 94% were determined to have financial need; 10% had their need fully met. Average financial aid package (proportion receiving): $8,964 (93%). Average amount of gift aid, such as scholarships or grants (proportion receiving): $6,054 (89%). Average amount of self-help aid, such as work study or loans (proportion receiving): $3,585 (82%). Average need-based loan (excluding PLUS or other private loans): $2,887. Among students who received need-based aid, the average percentage of need met: 60%. Among students who received aid based on merit, the average award (and the proportion receiving): $10,442 (5%). The average athletic scholarship (and the proportion receiving): $4,105 (2%). Average amount of debt of borrowers graduating in 2005: $21,661. Proportion who borrowed: 95%.

CAMPUS LIFE AND EXTRACURRICULAR ACTIVITIES

Campus housing available (% using): women's dorms (70%), men's dorms (30%), other housing options. Students who live in college-owned, operated, or affiliated housing: 57%. **Clubs and organizations:** Number of student organizations: 32. Activities include: choral groups, dance, drama/theater, literary magazine, marching band, music ensembles, pep band, student government, student newspaper, yearbook. Number of fraternities: 4; sororities: 4. Proportion of men in fraternities: 10%; of women in sororities: 10%. Average proportion of students who stay on campus on weekends: 25%. **Sports program (2005-2006):** Member of NCAA II. *Men's intercollegiate varsity sports:* baseball, basketball, cross-country, golf, track and field (outdoor). *Women's intercollegiate varsity sports:* basketball, cross-country, softball, track and field (outdoor), volleyball.

SERVICES AND FACILITIES

Basic services: nonremedial tutoring, placement service, health service, health insurance. **Remedial assistance:** reading, math, writing, study skills. **Counseling services:** career, military, personal, veteran student, academic, religious. **For learning-disabled students:** School does not offer a structured program with separate admission and additional fees. Total undergraduates in learning-disabled program or receiving services: 0. Services include: remedial math, remedial English, remedial reading, tutors. **Library:** Number of titles: 56,628; number of current serial subscriptions: 7,951. **Information technology resources:** Students are not required to lease or own a computer. Number of campus computers available to all students: 220. School has a wireless network. Proportion of college-owned housing units wired for high-speed internet access: 100%. **Campus safety:** Security services offered: 24-hour foot-and-vehicle patrols, late-night transport/escort service, 24-hour emergency telephones, lighted pathways/sidewalks, controlled dormitory access (key, security card, etc).

TRANSFER AND INTERNATIONAL STUDENTS

Transfer students: May apply for admission for the following academic terms: Fall, Winter, Spring, Summer. Applicants do not need a minimum number of credits to apply. For fall 2005: Transfer applications received: 129. Transfer applicants offered admission: 47. Transfer applicants enrolled: 24. **International students:** Number of foreign undergraduates: 3. Number of countries represented: 3. Minimum TOEFL score required: 500 (paper).

Piedmont College

- **Address:** PO Box 10, Demorest, GA 30535
- **Website:** http://www.piedmont.edu
- **Private; Religious affiliation:** United Church of Christ
- **Enrollment:** 845 full-time; 94 part-time

KEY STATS

✔ **U.S News College Ranking:** third tier, Universities–Master's (South)
✔ **SAT Score (25th/75th percentile):** 940-1140
✔ **Tuition:** 2006-2007: $15,500

Selectivity: Selective	**Room/board:** $5,000
Acceptance rate: 66%	**Average debt:** $14,408
Student/faculty ratio: 13/1	**Proportion who borrowed:** 66%

UNDERGRADUATE STUDENT BODY STATS

2005-2006 enrollment: 845 full-time; 94 part-time. Men: 36%; women: 64%. **Ethnic makeup:** African American: 6%; Asian American: 1%; Hispanic: 2%; White: 90%.

ADMISSIONS FACTS AND FIGURES

Phone: (800) 277-7020. **Email:** ugrad@piedmont.edu. **Website:** http://www.piedmont.edu. **Application deadlines for fall 2007:** Regular decision: July 1. Early decision: Not offered. Early action: Not offered. Admission can be deferred. Common application is not accepted. **Admissions requirements/recommendations:** High school units required (recommended): English: (4); Mathematics: (3); Science: (3); Foreign language: (2); Social studies: (1); History: (2); Total units: 21 (21). Tests: The college uses SAT or ACT scores in admissions decisions. Either SAT or ACT required. Campus visit: Recommended. Admissions interview: Recommended. Off-campus interview: May be arranged. **Factors that count in admissions decisions:** *Academic:* Secondary school record: Very important. Class rank: Important. Letters of recommendation: Important. Standardized test scores: Very important. Essay: Important. *Nonacademic:* Interview: Important. Extracurricular activities: Important. Talent/ability: Important. Character/personal qualities: Important. Alumni/ae relationship: Considered. Geographical residence: Considered. State residency: Considered. Religious affiliation/commitment: Not considered. Minority status: Not considered. Volunteer work: Considered. Work experience: Considered. **Other schools with the greatest overlap in applicants:** Berry College; LaGrange College; North Georgia College and State University; Shorter College. **Admissions statistics for the fall 2005 entering class:** Total applicants: 485. Total accepted: 322. Freshmen enrolled: 166; 1% were from out of state. Overall acceptance rate: 66%. **Size of waiting list:** 0 applicants; enrolled from waiting list: 0. **Credentials of fall 2005 freshmen:** 18% ranked in the top 10 percent of their high school class; 41% were in the top 25 percent, and 79% were in the top half. (Proportion submitting class standing: 66%.) **Average high school grade point average:** 3.4. **First-year students who submitted SAT scores:** 81%. Scores (25/75 percentile): Verbal: 480-570, Math: 460-570, Combined: 940-1140. **First-year students submitting ACT scores:** 27%. Scores (25/75 percentile): English: N/A, Math: N/A, Composite: 18-23.

ACADEMICS

Year founded: 1897. **Academic calendar:** Semester. **Degrees offered:** bachelor's, master's. **Most popular majors:** 32% teacher education and professional development, 23% business administration, management, and operations, 11% social sciences, 7% nursing, 6% psychology. **Major fields of study:** biological and biomedical sciences; business, management, marketing, and related support services; communication, journalism, and related programs; education; English language and literature/letters; foreign languages, literatures, and linguistics; history; multi/interdisciplinary studies; philosophy and religious studies; physical sciences; psychology; security and protective services; social sciences; visual and performing arts. **Areas of required coursework:** arts/fine arts, humanities, computer literacy, mathematics, English (including composition), philosophy, foreign languages, sciences (biological or physical), history, social science. **Special academic programs (% participation):** accelerated program, distance learning (1%), double major (1%), dual enrollment (1%), teacher certificate program (1%). **Teacher certification offered in:** early childhood, special education, middle/junior high, secondary. **Faculty and instruction (2005-2006):** Total instructional faculty: 98 full-time, 100 part-time (50% men; 50% women; 6% minorities). Full-time faculty with Ph.D. or other terminal degree: 77%.

Student/faculty ratio: 13/1. Classes of fewer than 20 students: 83%; of 20 to 49 students: 17%; of 50 or more students: 0%. **Freshmen returning for sophomore year:** 69%. **Graduation rates:** Four-year: 26%; five-year: 36%; six-year: 37%.

COSTS AND FINANCIAL AID

Financial aid office: (706) 776-0114. **Expenses (2006-2007):** Tuition and fees 2006-2007: $15,500; room/board: $5,000. Estimated books and supplies: $1,250; transportation: $1,400; personal expenses: $0. **Financial aid:** Priority filing date for institution's financial aid form: May 5. In 2005-2006, 91% of undergraduates applied for financial aid. Of those, 74% were determined to have financial need; 58% had their need fully met. Average financial aid package (proportion receiving): $14,989 (71%). Average amount of gift aid, such as scholarships or grants (proportion receiving): $2,312 (52%). Average amount of self-help aid, such as work study or loans (proportion receiving): $4,869 (48%). Average need-based loan (excluding PLUS or other private loans): $4,921. Among students who received need-based aid, the average percentage of need met: 60%. Among students who received aid based on merit, the average award (and the proportion receiving): $3,094 (11%). Average amount of debt of borrowers graduating in 2005: $14,408. Proportion who borrowed: 66%.

CAMPUS LIFE AND EXTRACURRICULAR ACTIVITIES

Campus housing available: coed dorms, women's dorms, men's dorms, apartments for married students, special housing for international students. Students who live in college-owned, operated, or affiliated housing: 39%. **Clubs and organizations:** Number of student organizations: 21. Activities include: choral groups, dance, drama/theater, music ensembles, radio station, student government, student newspaper, television station, yearbook. Number of fraternities: 0; sororities: 0. Average proportion of students who stay on campus on weekends: 20%. **Sports program (2005-2006):** Member of NCAA III. *Men's intercollegiate varsity sports:* baseball, basketball, cross-country, golf, soccer, tennis. *Women's intercollegiate varsity sports:* basketball, cross-country, golf, soccer, softball, tennis, volleyball.

SERVICES AND FACILITIES

For learning-disabled students: Total undergraduates in learning-disabled program or receiving services: 17. Services include: tape recorders, untimed tests, oral tests, learning center, tutors. **Library:** Number of titles: 124,777; number of current serial subscriptions: 8,578. **Information technology resources:** Students are not required to lease or own a computer. Number of campus computers available to all students: 100. Proportion of college-owned housing units wired for high-speed internet access: 100%.

TRANSFER AND INTERNATIONAL STUDENTS

Transfer students: May apply for admission for the following academic terms: Fall, Spring, Summer. Applicants do not need a minimum number of credits to apply. For fall 2005: Transfer applications received: 158. Transfer applicants offered admission: 107. Transfer applicants enrolled: 52. **International students:** Number of foreign undergraduates: 2. Number of countries represented: 23. Minimum TOEFL score required: 550 (paper); 213 (computer). Average TOEFL score: 230 (paper).

Reinhardt College

- **Address:** 7300 Reinhardt College Circle, Waleska, GA 30183-0128
- **Website:** http://www.reinhardt.edu/
- **Private; Religious affiliation:** United Methodist
- **Enrollment:** 881 full-time; 129 part-time

KEY STATS

✔ **U.S News College Ranking:** third tier, Comp. Colleges–Bachelor's (South)
✔ **SAT Score (25th/75th percentile):** 850-1070
✔ **Tuition:** 2006-2007: $14,120

Selectivity: Less selective	**Room/board:** $6,126
Acceptance rate: 39%	**Average debt:** $5,500
Student/faculty ratio: 10/1	**Proportion who borrowed:** 69%

UNDERGRADUATE STUDENT BODY STATS

2005-2006 enrollment: 881 full-time; 129 part-time. Men: 42%; women: 58%. **Ethnic makeup:** African American: 7%; Asian American: 1%; Hispanic: 2%; White: 89%; International: 1%. **Religious preference:** Roman

---

Catholic: 7%; Protestant: 48%; Jewish: 1%; No preference: 23%; United Methodist: 21%.

ADMISSIONS FACTS AND FIGURES

Phone: (770) 720-5526. **Email:** admissions@reinhardt.edu. **Website:** http://www.reinhardt.edu/. **Application deadlines for fall 2007:** Regular decision: August 15. Early decision: Not offered. Early action: Not offered. Admission can be deferred. **Application fee:** $25. Common application is not accepted. **To apply online, go to:** http://www.reinhardt.edu/Admissions/application.htm. **Admissions requirements/recommendations:** High school units required (recommended): English: 4; Mathematics: 4; Science: 3; Foreign language: (2); Social studies: 4; Total units: 15 (2). Tests: The college uses SAT or ACT scores in admissions decisions. Either SAT or ACT required. For admission to the fall 2007 entering class, the school will accept: ACT with writing, ACT without writing. Campus visit: Recommended. Admissions interview: Neither required nor recommended. Off-campus interview: May be arranged. **Factors that count in admissions decisions:** *Academic:* Secondary school record: Very important. Class rank: Important. Letters of recommendation: Considered. Standardized test scores: Very important. Essay: Considered. *Nonacademic:* Interview: Important. Extracurricular activities: Considered. Talent/ability: Important. Character/personal qualities: Important. Alumni/ae relationship: Important. Geographical residence: Not considered. State residency: Not considered. Religious affiliation/commitment: Not considered. Minority status: Considered. Volunteer work: Considered. Work experience: Not considered. **Other schools with the greatest overlap in applicants:** Berry College; Georgia State University; Kennesaw State University; Shorter College; University of Georgia. **Admissions statistics for the fall 2005 entering class:** Total applicants: 836. Total accepted: 330. Freshmen enrolled: 222; 4% were from out of state. Overall acceptance rate: 39%. **Credentials of fall 2005 freshmen:** 12% ranked in the top 10 percent of their high school class; 27% were in the top 25 percent, and 59% were in the top half. (Proportion submitting class standing: 51%.) **Average high school grade point average:** 3.0. **First-year students who submitted SAT scores:** 86%. Scores (25/75 percentile): Verbal: 430-540, Math: 420-530, Combined: 850-1070. **First-year students submitting ACT scores:** 32%. Scores (25/75 percentile): English: N/A, Math: N/A, Composite: 17-21.

ACADEMICS

Year founded: 1883. **Academic calendar:** Semester. **Degrees offered:** associate, transfer-associate, bachelor's. **Most popular majors:** 39% business administration, management, and operations, 34% education, 6% biology, 5% liberal arts and sciences studies, and humanities, 4% psychology. **Major fields of study:** biological and biomedical sciences; business, management, marketing, and related support services; communication, journalism, and related programs; education; English language and literature/letters; history; liberal arts and sciences studies, and humanities; philosophy and religious studies; psychology; social sciences; visual and performing arts. **Areas of required coursework:** arts/fine arts, humanities, mathematics, English (including composition), philosophy, sciences (biological or physical), history, social science. **Special academic programs (% participation):** accelerated program (5%), honors program (8%), independent study (7%), internships (4%), study abroad (2%), teacher certificate program (12%), weekend college (4%). **Teacher certification offered in:** early childhood, middle/junior high, secondary. **Faculty and instruction (2005-2006):** Total instructional faculty: 54 full-time, 63 part-time (58% men; 42% women; 2% minorities). Full-time faculty with Ph.D. or other terminal degree: 43%. Student/faculty ratio: 10/1. Classes of fewer than 20 students: 74%; of 20 to 49 students: 25%; of 50 or more students: 0%. **Advanced Placement and International Baccalaureate credit:** AP tests may be used for: Credit and/or placement. Scores accepted: 3. International Baccalaureate exams may be used for: Credit only. **Freshmen returning for sophomore year:** 58%. **Graduation rates:** Four-year: 16%; five-year: 26%; six-year: 27%. **Graduate study:** 8% of students pursue further study immediately upon graduation; 12% within one year; 15% within five years. Fields in which graduates pursue further study: Master of Business Administration (MBA), 20%; medicine, 1%; theology (or the seminary), 5%; education, 15%.

COSTS AND FINANCIAL AID

Financial aid office: (770) 720-5667. **Expenses (2006-2007):** Tuition and fees 2006-2007: $14,120; room/board: $6,126. Estimated books and supplies: $1,100; transportation: $2,000; personal expenses: $1,000. **Financial aid:** Priority filing date for institution's financial aid form: May 1. In 2005-2006, 96% of undergraduates applied for financial aid. Of those, 80% were determined to have financial need; Average financial aid package (proportion receiving): $9,943 (80%). Average amount of gift aid, such as scholarships or grants (proportion receiving): $2,000 (38%). Average amount of self-help aid, such as work study or loans (proportion receiving): $4,000 (58%). Average need-based loan (excluding PLUS or other private loans): $4,670. Among students who received need-based aid, the average percentage of need met: 37%. Among students who received aid based on merit, the average award (and the proportion receiving): $3,613 (71%). The average athletic scholarship (and the proportion receiving): $4,000 (14%). Average amount of debt of borrowers graduating in 2005: $5,500. Proportion who borrowed: 69%.

CAMPUS LIFE AND EXTRACURRICULAR ACTIVITIES

Campus housing available (% using): women's dorms (44%), men's dorms (26%), apartment for single students (30%), other housing options. Students who live in college-owned, operated, or affiliated housing: 45%. **Student employment:** During the 2005-2006 academic year, 19% of undergraduates worked on campus. Average per-year earnings: $2,300. **Clubs and organizations:** Number of student organizations: 15. Activities include: choral groups, drama/theater, literary magazine, radio station, student government, television station, yearbook. Number of fraternities: 0; sororities: 0. Average proportion of students who stay on campus on weekends: 15%. **Sports program (2005-2006):** Member of NAIA. *Men's intercollegiate varsity sports:* baseball, basketball, cross-country, golf, soccer, tennis. *Women's intercollegiate varsity sports:* basketball, cross-country, soccer, softball, tennis, volleyball.

SERVICES AND FACILITIES

Basic services: nonremedial tutoring, placement service, health service, health insurance. **Remedial assistance:** reading, math, writing, study skills. **Counseling services:** career, veteran student, academic, religious. **For learning-disabled students:** School does not offer a structured program with separate admission and additional fees. Total undergraduates in learning-disabled program or receiving services: 115. Services include: tape recorders, note-taking services, oral tests, learning center, readers, extended time for tests, tutors, priority registration, priority seating, texts on tape, other testing accomodations. **Library:** Number of titles: 51,556; number of current serial subscriptions: 340. **Information technology resources:** Students are not required to lease or own a computer. Number of campus computers available to all students: 180. School has a wireless network. Approximate number of users that can be accommodated: 150. Proportion of college-owned housing units wired for high-speed internet access: 100%. **Campus safety:** Security services offered: 24-hour foot-and-vehicle patrols, 24-hour emergency telephones, lighted pathways/sidewalks.

TRANSFER AND INTERNATIONAL STUDENTS

Transfer students: May apply for admission for the following academic terms: Fall, Spring, Summer. Applicants need a minimum number of credits to apply. For fall 2005: Transfer applications received: 99. Transfer applicants offered admission: 91. Transfer applicants enrolled: 72. **International students:** Number of foreign undergraduates: 8 (1% of student body). Number of countries represented: 9. Minimum TOEFL score required: 500 (paper); 173 (computer).

Savannah College of Art and Design

- **Address:** 342 Bull Street, PO Box 3146, Savannah, GA 31402-3146
- **Website:** http://www.scad.edu
- **Private**
- **Enrollment:** 5,528 full-time; 608 part-time

KEY STATS

- ✔ **U.S News College Ranking:** Unranked Specialty School–Fine Arts
- ✔ **SAT Score (25th/75th percentile):** 970-1180
- ✔ **Tuition:** 2006-2007: $22,950

Selectivity: Less selective	**Room/board:** $9,595
Acceptance rate: 68%	**Average debt:** $24,700
Student/faculty ratio: 18/1	**Proportion who borrowed:** 93%

UNDERGRADUATE STUDENT BODY STATS

2005-2006 enrollment: 5,528 full-time; 608 part-time. Men: 48%; women: 52%. **Ethnic makeup:** African American: 5%; Asian American: 2%; Hispanic: 4%; White: 85%; International: 4%.

ADMISSIONS FACTS AND FIGURES

Phone: (912) 525-5100. **Email:** admission@scad.edu. **Website:** http://www.scad.edu. **Application deadlines for fall 2007:** Regular decision: Rolling. Early decision: Not offered. Early action: Not offered. Admission can be deferred. **Application fee:** $50. Common application is not accepted. **Admissions requirements/recommendations:** Tests: The college uses SAT or ACT scores in admissions decisions. Either SAT or ACT required. For admission to the fall 2007 entering class, the school will accept: ACT with writing, ACT without writing. Campus visit: Recommended. Admissions interview: Recommended. Off-campus interview: May be arranged. **Factors that count in admissions decisions:** *Academic:* Secondary school record: Important. Class rank: Important. Letters of recommendation: Very important. Standardized test scores: Important. Essay: Not considered. *Nonacademic:* Interview: Very important. Extracurricular activities: Considered. Talent/ability: Very important. Character/personal qualities: Important. Alumni/ae relationship: Considered. Geographical residence: Not considered. State residency: Not considered. Religious affiliation/commitment: Not considered. Minority status: Not considered. Volunteer work: Not considered. Work experience: Considered. **Admissions statistics for the fall 2005 entering class:** Total applicants: 4,782. Total accepted: 3,251. Freshmen enrolled: 1,407; 85% were from out of state. Overall acceptance rate: 68%. **First-year students who submitted SAT scores:** 73%. Scores (25/75 percentile): Verbal: 490-600, Math: 480-580, Combined: 970-1180. **First-year students submitting ACT scores:** 25%. Scores (25/75 percentile): English: N/A, Math: N/A, Composite: 20-26.

ACADEMICS

Year founded: 1978. **Academic calendar:** Quarter. **Degrees offered:** certificate, bachelor's, post-bachelor's certificate, master's. **Most popular majors:** 14% illustration, 12% graphic design, 10% computer graphics, 10% photography, 8% animation, interactive technology, video graphics, and special effects. **Major fields of study:** architecture and related services; communication, journalism, and related programs; communications technologies/technicians and support services; computer and information sciences and support services; English language and literature/letters; multi/interdisciplinary studies; visual and performing arts. **Areas of required coursework:** arts/fine arts, humanities, computer literacy, mathematics, English (including composition), sciences (biological or physical), social science. **Special academic programs:** distance learning, double major, dual enrollment, English as a Second Language (ESL), independent study, internships, study abroad. **Faculty and instruction (2005-2006):** Total instructional faculty: 366 full-time, 53 part-time (58% men; 42% women; 10% minorities). Full-time faculty with Ph.D. or other terminal degree: 79%. Student/faculty ratio: 18/1. Classes of fewer than 20 students: 75%; of 20 to 49 students: 25%; of 50 or more students: 0%. **Advanced Placement and International Baccalaureate credit:** AP tests may be used for: Credit and/or placement. Scores accepted: 3, 4, 5. International Baccalaureate exams may be used for: Credit and/or placement. **Freshmen returning for sophomore year:** 81%. **Graduation rates:** Four-year: 42%; five-year: 58%; six-year: 59%. **Graduate study:** 10% of students pursue further study immediately upon graduation.

COSTS AND FINANCIAL AID

Financial aid office: (912) 525-6104. **Expenses (2006-2007):** Tuition and fees 2006-2007: $22,950; room/board: $9,595. Estimated books and supplies: $1,500; transportation: $1,200; personal expenses: $1,500. **Financial aid:** Priority filing date for institution's financial aid form: April 1. In 2005-2006, 65% of undergraduates applied for financial aid. Of those, 52% were determined to have financial need; 39% had their need fully met. Average financial aid package (proportion receiving): $9,476 (51%). Average amount of gift aid, such as scholarships or grants (proportion receiving): $3,490 (15%). Average amount of self-help aid, such as work study or loans (proportion receiving): $3,932 (45%). Average need-based loan (excluding PLUS or other private loans): $3,893. Among students who received need-based aid, the average percentage of need met: 13%. Among students who received aid based on merit, the average award (and the proportion receiving): $4,426 (28%). The average athletic scholarship (and the proportion receiving): $13,172 (4%). Average amount of debt of borrowers graduating in 2005: $24,700. Proportion who borrowed: 93%.

CAMPUS LIFE AND EXTRACURRICULAR ACTIVITIES

Campus housing available (% using): coed dorms (92%), women's dorms (3%), apartment for single students (5%). Students who live in college-owned, operated, or affiliated housing: 37%. **Student employment:** During the 2005-2006 academic year, 20% of undergraduates worked on campus. Average per-year earnings: $3,200. **Clubs and organizations:** Number of student organizations: 49. Activities include: choral groups, dance, drama/theater, literary magazine, music ensembles, musical theater, radio station, student government, student newspaper, television station. Number of fraternities: 0; sororities: 0. Average proportion of students who stay on campus on weekends: 35%. **Sports program (2005-2006):** Member of NCAA III. *Men's intercollegiate varsity sports:* baseball, basketball, cross-country, equestrian Sports, golf, soccer, swimming and diving, tennis, rowing. *Women's intercollegiate varsity sports:* basketball, cross-country, equestrian sports, golf, soccer, softball, swimming and diving, tennis, volleyball, rowing.

SERVICES AND FACILITIES

Basic services: nonremedial tutoring, health service, other. **Remedial assistance:** other. **Counseling services:** personal, academic, other. **For learning-disabled students:** School does not offer a structured program with separate admission and additional fees. Total undergraduates in learning-disabled program or receiving services: 340. Services include: reading machines, tape recorders, note-taking services, oral tests, learning center, readers, extended time for tests, tutors, priority registration, priority seating, typist/scribe, exams on tape or computer, other testing accomodations, other. **Library:** Number of titles: 128,574; number of current serial subscriptions: 1,051. **Information technology resources:** Students are not required to lease or own a computer. Number of campus computers available to all students: 1,800. School has a wireless network. Approximate number of users that can be accommodated: 5,000. Proportion of college-owned housing units wired for high-speed internet access: 100%. **Campus safety:** Security services offered: 24-hour foot-and-vehicle patrols, late-night transport/escort service, 24-hour emergency telephones, lighted pathways/sidewalks, student patrols, controlled dormitory access (key, security card, etc).

TRANSFER AND INTERNATIONAL STUDENTS

Transfer students: May apply for admission for the following academic terms: Fall, Winter, Spring, Summer. Applicants do not need a minimum number of credits to apply. For fall 2005: Transfer applications received: 1,796. Transfer applicants offered admission: 968. Transfer applicants enrolled: 492. **International students:** Number of foreign undergraduates: 248 (4% of student body). Number of countries represented: 80. Minimum TOEFL score required: 450 (paper); 133 (computer). Average TOEFL score: 400 (paper).

Savannah State University

- ■ **Address:** PO Box 20482, Savannah, GA 31404
- ■ **Website:** http://www.savstate.edu/
- ■ **Public**
- ■ **Enrollment:** 2,374 full-time; 601 part-time

KEY STATS

✔ **U.S News College Ranking:** fourth tier, Universities–Master's (South)
✔ **SAT Score (25th/75th percentile):** 800-960
✔ **Tuition:** 2006-2007: $3,178 in state, $10,860 out of state

Selectivity: Less selective	**Room/board:** $5,010
Acceptance rate: 36%	**Average debt:** N/A
Student/faculty ratio: 19/1	**Proportion who borrowed:** N/A

UNDERGRADUATE STUDENT BODY STATS

2005-2006 enrollment: 2,374 full-time; 601 part-time. Men: 44%; women: 56%. **Ethnic makeup:** African American: 96%; Asian American: 1%; White: 3%.

ADMISSIONS FACTS AND FIGURES

Phone: (912) 356-2181. **Email:** admissions@savstate.edu. **Website:** http://www.savstate.edu/. **Application deadlines for fall 2007:** Regular decision: September 1. Early decision: Not offered. Early action: Not offered. **Application fee:** $20. **To apply online, go to:** https://www.applyweb.com/aw?ssu. **Admissions requirements/recommendations:** High school units required (recommended): English: 4; Mathematics: 3; Science: 3; Foreign language: 2; Social studies: 3; Total units: 16. Tests: The college uses SAT or ACT scores in admissions decisions. Either SAT or ACT required. **Factors that count in admissions decisions:** *Academic:* Secondary school record: Very important. Class rank: Not considered. Letters of recommendation: Not considered. Standardized test scores: Very important. Essay: Not considered. *Nonacademic:* Interview: Not considered. Extracurricular activities: Not considered. Talent/ability: Not considered.

Character/personal qualities: Not considered. Alumni/ae relationship: Not considered. Geographical residence: Not considered. State residency: Not considered. Religious affiliation/commitment: Not considered. Minority status: Not considered. Volunteer work: Not considered. Work experience: Not considered. **Admissions statistics for the fall 2005 entering class:** Overall acceptance rate: 36%. **Average high school grade point average:** 2.7. **First-year students who submitted SAT scores:** 82%. Scores (25/75 percentile): Verbal: 400-480, Math: 400-480, Combined: 800-960.

ACADEMICS

Year founded: 1890. **Academic calendar:** Semester. **Degrees offered:** bachelor's, master's. **Most popular majors:** Information not available. **Major fields of study:** area, ethnic, cultural, and gender studies; biological and biomedical sciences; business, management, marketing, and related support services; communication, journalism, and related programs; computer and information sciences and support services; engineering; engineering technologies/technicians; English language and literature/letters; history; mathematics and statistics; parks, recreation, leisure, and fitness studies; physical sciences; public administration and social service professions; security and protective services; social sciences; visual and performing arts. **Reserve Officers Training Corps (ROTC):** Army ROTC: Offered on campus; Navy ROTC: Offered on campus. **Faculty and instruction (2005-2006):** Total instructional faculty: 123 full-time, 38 part-time (55% men; 45% women; 47% minorities). Student/faculty ratio: 19/1. Classes of fewer than 20 students: 43%; of 20 to 49 students: 56%; of 50 or more students: 1%. **Freshmen returning for sophomore year:** 72%. **Graduation rates:** Four-year: 6%; five-year: 19%; six-year: 24%.

COSTS AND FINANCIAL AID

Financial aid office: (912) 356-2253. **Expenses (2006-2007):** Tuition and fees 2006-2007: $3,178 in state, $10,860 out of state; room/board: $5,010.

CAMPUS LIFE AND EXTRACURRICULAR ACTIVITIES

Campus housing available: women's dorms, men's dorms. **Sports program (2005-2006):** Member of NCAA I. *Men's intercollegiate varsity sports:* baseball, basketball, cross-country, football, golf, tennis, track and field (indoor), track and field (outdoor). *Women's intercollegiate varsity sports:* basketball, bowling, cross-country, golf, softball, tennis, track and field (indoor), track and field (outdoor), volleyball.

SERVICES AND FACILITIES

Basic services: placement service, health service, health insurance. **Remedial assistance:** reading, math, writing, study skills. **Counseling services:** minority student, career, military, personal, academic. **Information technology resources:** Students are not required to lease or own a computer. School has a wireless network. **Campus safety:** Security services offered: 24-hour foot-and-vehicle patrols, 24-hour emergency telephones, lighted pathways/sidewalks.

TRANSFER AND INTERNATIONAL STUDENTS

Transfer students: May apply for admission for the following academic terms: Fall, Spring, Summer. Applicants need a minimum number of credits to apply. **International students:** Number of foreign undergraduates: 0.

Shorter College

- ■ **Address:** 315 Shorter Avenue, Rome, GA 30165-4298
- ■ **Website:** http://www.shorter.edu
- ■ **Private; Religious affiliation:** Baptist
- ■ **Enrollment:** 929 full-time; 38 part-time

KEY STATS

✔ **U.S News College Ranking:** 21, Comp. Colleges–Bachelor's (South)
✔ **SAT Score (25th/75th percentile):** 920-1130
✔ **Tuition:** 2006-2007: $14,300

Selectivity: Selective	**Room/board:** $6,600
Acceptance rate: 75%	**Average debt:** $16,193
Student/faculty ratio: 11/1	**Proportion who borrowed:** 59%

UNDERGRADUATE STUDENT BODY STATS

2005-2006 enrollment: 929 full-time; 38 part-time. Men: 49%; women: 51%. **Ethnic makeup:** African American: 9%; Asian American: 1%; Hispanic: 2%;

White: 84%; International: 4%. **Religious preference:** Roman Catholic: 6%; Protestant: 27%; No preference: 10%; Baptist: 56%; Other: 1%.

ADMISSIONS FACTS AND FIGURES

Phone: (800) 868-6980. **Email:** admissions@shorter.edu. **Website:** http://www.shorter.edu. **Application deadlines for fall 2007:** Regular decision: August 17. Early decision: Not offered. Early action: Not offered. Admission can be deferred. **Application fee:** $25. Common application is not accepted. **To apply online, go to:** http://www.shorter.edu/coming/hr_application.asp#on. **Admissions requirements/recommendations:** High school units required (recommended): English: 4; Mathematics: 4; Science: 3; Foreign language: 2; Social studies: 0; History: 3; Academic electives: 0; Total units: 16. Tests: The college uses SAT or ACT scores in admissions decisions. Either SAT or ACT required. For admission to the fall 2007 entering class, the school will accept: ACT with writing. Campus visit: Recommended. Admissions interview: Recommended. Off-campus interview: May be arranged. **Factors that count in admissions decisions:** *Academic:* Secondary school record: Important. Class rank: Important. Letters of recommendation: Considered. Standardized test scores: Very important. Essay: Important. *Nonacademic:* Interview: Considered. Extracurricular activities: Considered. Talent/ability: Important. Character/personal qualities: Considered. Alumni/ae relationship: Considered. Geographical residence: Not considered. State residency: Not considered. Religious affiliation/commitment: Not considered. Minority status: Not considered. Volunteer work: Considered. Work experience: Considered. **Other schools with the greatest overlap in applicants:** Berry College; Kennesaw State University; University of Georgia. **Admissions statistics for the fall 2005 entering class:** Total applicants: 1,031. Total accepted: 769. Freshmen enrolled: 291; 9% were from out of state. Overall acceptance rate: 75%. **Credentials of fall 2005 freshmen:** 19% ranked in the top 10 percent of their high school class; 46% were in the top 25 percent, and 75% were in the top half. (Proportion submitting class standing: 71%.) **Average high school grade point average:** 3.3. **First-year students who submitted SAT scores:** 88%. Scores (25/75 percentile): Verbal: 460-570, Math: 460-560, Combined: 920-1130. **First-year students submitting ACT scores:** 40%. Scores (25/75 percentile): English: 17-24, Math: 17-23, Composite: 17-23.

ACADEMICS

Year founded: 1873. **Academic calendar:** Semester. **Degrees offered:** bachelor's. **Most popular majors:** 21% business, management, marketing, and related support services, 19% education, 13% biological and biomedical sciences, 10% visual and performing arts, 10% communication, journalism, and related programs. **Major fields of study:** biological and biomedical sciences; business, management, marketing, and related support services; communication, journalism, and related programs; computer and information sciences and support services; education; English language and literature/letters; foreign languages, literatures, and linguistics; history; liberal arts and sciences studies, and humanities; mathematics and statistics; multi/interdisciplinary studies; natural resources and conservation; parks, recreation, leisure, and fitness studies; philosophy and religious studies; physical sciences; psychology; social sciences; theology and religious vocations; visual and performing arts. **Areas of required coursework:** arts/fine arts, computer literacy, mathematics, English (including composition), sciences (biological or physical), history, social science, other. **Special academic programs (% participation):** cross-registration (1%), double major (4%), dual enrollment (1%), honors program (8%), independent study (21%), internships (37%), student-designed major (2%), study abroad (7%), teacher certification program (25%), weekend college. **Teacher certification offered in:** early childhood, elementary, middle/junior high, secondary. **Faculty and instruction (2005-2006):** Total instructional faculty: 65 full-time, 55 part-time (57% men; 43% women; 3% minorities). Full-time faculty with Ph.D. or other terminal degree: 77%. Student/faculty ratio: 11/1. Classes of fewer than 20 students: 62%; of 20 to 49 students: 37%; of 50 or more students: 1%. **Advanced Placement and International Baccalaureate credit:** AP tests may be used for: Credit and/or placement. Scores accepted: 3. International Baccalaureate exams may be used for: Placement only. **Freshmen returning for sophomore year:** 73%. **Graduation rates:** Four-year: 39%; five-year: 51%; six-year: 48%. **Graduate study:** 40% of students pursue further study within one year; 47% within five years. Fields in which graduates pursue further study: Master of Business Administration (MBA), 13%; medicine, 14%; theology (or the seminary), 12%; education, 25%; arts and sciences, 25%.

COSTS AND FINANCIAL AID

Financial aid office: (706) 233-7227. **Expenses (2006-2007):** Tuition and fees 2006-2007: $14,300; room/board: $6,600. Estimated books and supplies: $1,100; transportation: $2,500; personal expenses: $3,250. **Financial aid:**

Priority filing date for institution's financial aid form: April 15. In 2005-2006, 81% of undergraduates applied for financial aid. Of those, 68% were determined to have financial need; 21% had their need fully met. Average financial aid package (proportion receiving): $11,105 (68%). Average amount of gift aid, such as scholarships or grants (proportion receiving): $8,424 (67%). Average amount of self-help aid, such as work study or loans (proportion receiving): $3,865 (47%). Average need-based loan (excluding PLUS or other private loans): $3,525. Among students who received need-based aid, the average percentage of need met: 61%. Among students who received aid based on merit, the average award (and the proportion receiving): $8,685 (31%). The average athletic scholarship (and the proportion receiving): $5,986 (12%). Average amount of debt of borrowers graduating in 2005: $16,193. Proportion who borrowed: 59%.

CAMPUS LIFE AND EXTRACURRICULAR ACTIVITIES

Campus housing available (% using): women's dorms (45%), men's dorms (35%), apartment for single students (20%). Students who live in college-owned, operated, or affiliated housing: 62%. **Student employment:** During the 2005-2006 academic year, 20% of undergraduates worked on campus. Average per-year earnings: $1,200. **Clubs and organizations:** Number of student organizations: 29. Activities include: choral groups, concert band, drama/theater, literary magazine, music ensembles, musical theater, opera, radio station, student government, student newspaper, student film society, television station, yearbook. Number of fraternities: 2; sororities: 2. Proportion of men in fraternities: 7%; of women in sororities: 32%. Average proportion of students who stay on campus on weekends: 20%. **Sports program (2005-2006):** Member of NAIA. *Men's intercollegiate varsity sports:* baseball, basketball, golf, soccer, tennis. *Women's intercollegiate varsity sports:* basketball, golf, soccer, softball, tennis, volleyball.

SERVICES AND FACILITIES

Basic services: nonremedial tutoring, placement service, health service, health insurance. **Remedial assistance:** math, writing. **Counseling services:** career, personal, academic, religious. **For learning-disabled students:** School does not offer a structured program with separate admission and additional fees. **Library:** Number of titles: 135,806; number of current serial subscriptions: 582. **Information technology resources:** Students are not required to lease or own a computer. Number of campus computers available to all students: 75. School has a wireless network. Approximate number of users that can be accommodated: 1,200. Proportion of college-owned housing units wired for high-speed internet access: 100%. **Campus safety:** Security services offered: 24-hour foot-and-vehicle patrols, lighted pathways/sidewalks, controlled dormitory access (key, security card, etc.).

TRANSFER AND INTERNATIONAL STUDENTS

Transfer students: May apply for admission for the following academic terms: Fall, Spring, Summer. Applicants need a minimum number of credits to apply. For fall 2005: Transfer applications received: 257. Transfer applicants offered admission: 196. Transfer applicants enrolled: 115. **International students:** Number of foreign undergraduates: 42 (4% of student body). Number of countries represented: 25. Minimum TOEFL score required: 500 (paper); 173 (computer). Average TOEFL score: 521 (paper).

Southern Polytechnic State University

- **Address:** 1100 S. Marietta Parkway, Marietta, GA 30060-2896
- **Website:** http://www.spsu.edu
- **Public**
- **Enrollment:** 2,193 full-time; 1,137 part-time

KEY STATS

✔ **U.S News College Ranking:** Unranked Specialty School–Engineering
✔ **SAT Score (25th/75th percentile):** 1030-1220
✔ **Tuition:** 2006-2007: $3,322 in state, $11,578 out of state

Selectivity: Selective	**Room/board:** $5,610
Acceptance rate: 66%	**Average debt:** $12,706
Student/faculty ratio: 15/1	**Proportion who borrowed:** 60%

UNDERGRADUATE STUDENT BODY STATS

2005-2006 enrollment: 2,193 full-time; 1,137 part-time. Men: 83%; women: 17%. **Ethnic makeup:** African American: 21%; Asian American: 6%; Hispanic: 3%; White: 65%; International: 6%.

ADMISSIONS FACTS AND FIGURES

Phone: (678) 915-4188. **Email:** admissions@spsu.edu. **Website:** http://www.spsu.edu. **Application deadlines for fall 2007:** Regular decision: August 1. Early decision: Not offered. Early action: Not offered. Admission can be deferred. **Application fee:** $20. Common application is not accepted. **To apply online, go to:** https://www.applyweb.com/apply/spsu/menu.html. **Admissions requirements/recommendations:** High school units required (recommended): English: 4; Mathematics: 4; Science: 3; Foreign language: 2; Social studies: 3; History: 2; Academic electives: 2; Total units: 18. Tests: The college uses SAT or ACT scores in admissions decisions. Either SAT or ACT required. For admission to the fall 2007 entering class, the school will accept: ACT with writing. Campus visit: Recommended. Admissions interview: Neither required nor recommended. Off-campus interview: Not available. **Factors that count in admissions decisions:** *Academic:* Secondary school record: Very important. Class rank: Not considered. Letters of recommendation: Not considered. Standardized test scores: Very important. Essay: Not considered. *Nonacademic:* Interview: Not considered. Extracurricular activities: Not considered. Talent/ability: Not considered. Character/personal qualities: Not considered. Alumni/ae relationship: Not considered. Geographical residence: Not considered. State residency: Not considered. Religious affiliation/commitment: Not considered. Minority status: Not considered. Volunteer work: Not considered. Work experience: Not considered. **Other schools with the greatest overlap in applicants:** Georgia Institute of Technology; Georgia Southern University; Georgia State University; Kennesaw State University; University of Georgia. **Admissions statistics for the fall 2005 entering class:** Total applicants: 1,056. Total accepted: 701. Freshmen enrolled: 448; 1% were from out of state. Overall acceptance rate: 66%. **Size of waiting list:** 0 applicants; enrolled from waiting list: 0. **Average high school grade point average:** 3.2. **First-year students who submitted SAT scores:** 85%. Scores (25/75 percentile): Verbal: 500-600, Math: 530-620, Combined: 1030-1220. **First-year students submitting ACT scores:** 15%. Scores (25/75 percentile): English: 19-23, Math: 20-24, Composite: 20-24.

ACADEMICS

Year founded: 1948. **Academic calendar:** Semester. **Degrees offered:** certificate, transfer-associate, bachelor's, post-bachelor's certificate, master's, post-master's certificate. **Most popular majors:** 41% engineering technologies/technicians, 26% computer and information sciences and support services, 19% business, management, marketing, and related support services, 6% architecture (B.Arch., B.A./B.S., M.Arch., M.A./M.S., Ph.D.), 4% communication, journalism, and related programs. **Major fields of study:** architecture and related services; biological and biomedical sciences; business, management, marketing, and related support services; communication, journalism, and related programs; computer and information sciences and support services; engineering; engineering technologies/technicians; mathematics and statistics; physical sciences; social sciences. **Areas of required coursework:** arts/fine arts, humanities, mathematics, English (including composition), sciences (biological or physical), social science. **Pre-professional programs:** pre-law, pre-dentistry, pre-medicine, pre-veterinary science, pre-optometry, pre-pharmacy. **Special academic programs (% participation):** cross-registration, distance learning, double major, dual enrollment, honors program (2.4%); independent study, internships, study abroad. **Cooperative education programs:** business, computer science, engineering, technologies. **Reserve Officers Training Corps (ROTC):** Army ROTC: Offered at cooperating institution (Georgia Institute of Technology); Navy ROTC: Offered at cooperating institution (Georgia Institute of Technology); Air Force ROTC: Offered at cooperating institution (Georgia Institute of Technology). **Faculty and instruction (2005-2006):** Total instructional faculty: 131 full-time, 78 part-time (77% men; 23% women; 23% minorities). Full-time faculty with Ph.D. or other terminal degree: 55%. Student/faculty ratio: 15/1. Classes of fewer than 20 students: 47%; of 20 to 49 students: 52%; of 50 or more students: 1%. **Advanced Placement and International Baccalaureate credit:** AP tests may be used for: Credit and/or placement. Scores accepted: 3, 4, 5. International Baccalaureate exams may be used for: Credit and/or placement. **Freshmen returning for sophomore year:** 69%. **Graduation rates:** Four-year: 6%; five-year: 19%; six-year: 24%.

COSTS AND FINANCIAL AID

Financial aid office: (678) 915-7290. **Expenses (2006-2007):** Tuition and fees 2006-2007: $3,322 in state, $11,578 out of state; room/board: $5,610. Estimated books and supplies: $1,500; transportation: $2,400; personal expenses: $1,500. **Financial aid:** Priority filing date for institution's financial aid form: April 1. In 2005-2006, 62% of undergraduates applied for financial aid. Of those, 46% were determined to have financial need; 46% had their need fully met. Average financial aid package (proportion receiving): $2,667 (44%). Average amount of gift aid, such as scholarships or grants

(proportion receiving): $2,352 (26%). Average amount of self-help aid, such as work study or loans (proportion receiving): $3,908 (31%). Average need-based loan (excluding PLUS or other private loans): $3,950. Among students who received need-based aid, the average percentage of need met: 74%. Among students who received aid based on merit, the average award (and the proportion receiving): $4,097 (1%). The average athletic scholarship (and the proportion receiving): $3,761 (2%). Average amount of debt of borrowers graduating in 2005: $12,706. Proportion who borrowed: 60%.

CAMPUS LIFE AND EXTRACURRICULAR ACTIVITIES

Campus housing available (% using): coed dorms (28%), apartment for single students (72%). Students who live in college-owned, operated, or affiliated housing: 27%. **Student employment:** During the 2005-2006 academic year, 18% of undergraduates worked on campus. Average per-year earnings: $3,000. **Clubs and organizations:** Number of student organizations: 70. Activities include: jazz band, pep band, radio station, student government, student newspaper. Number of fraternities: 7; sororities: 3. Proportion of men in fraternities: 5%; of women in sororities: 5%. Average proportion of students who stay on campus on weekends: 70%. **Sports program (2005-2006):** Member of NAIA. *Men's intercollegiate varsity sports:* baseball, basketball, tennis. *Women's intercollegiate varsity sports:* basketball.

SERVICES AND FACILITIES

Basic services: nonremedial tutoring, placement service, health service, health insurance. **Remedial assistance:** study skills. **Counseling services:** minority student, career, personal, veteran student, academic, psychological. **For learning-disabled students:** School does not offer a structured program with separate admission and additional fees. Total undergraduates in learning-disabled program or receiving services: 50. Services include: untimed tests, note-taking services, oral tests, learning center, readers, extended time for tests, tutors, priority registration. **Library:** Number of titles: 120,764; number of current serial subscriptions: 1,124. **Information technology resources:** Students are not required to lease or own a computer. Number of campus computers available to all students: 800. School has a wireless network. Proportion of college-owned housing units wired for high-speed internet access: 100%. **Campus safety:** Security services offered: 24-hour foot-and-vehicle patrols, late-night transport/escort service, 24-hour emergency telephones, lighted pathways/sidewalks, student patrols, controlled dormitory access (key, security card, etc).

TRANSFER AND INTERNATIONAL STUDENTS

Transfer students: May apply for admission for the following academic terms: Fall, Spring, Summer. Applicants need a minimum number of credits to apply. For fall 2005: Transfer applications received: 763. Transfer applicants offered admission: 557. Transfer applicants enrolled: 427. **International students:** Number of foreign undergraduates: 187 (6% of student body). Number of countries represented: 28. Minimum TOEFL score required: 550 (paper); 213 (computer). Average TOEFL score: 560 (paper).

Spelman College

- **Address:** 350 Spelman Lane SW, Atlanta, GA 30314-4399
- **Website:** http://www.spelman.edu
- **Private**
- **Enrollment:** 2,221 full-time; 97 part-time

KEY STATS

✔ **U.S News College Ranking:** 74, Liberal Arts Colleges
✔ **SAT Score (25th/75th percentile):** 1010-1180
✔ **Tuition:** 2006-2007: $17,005

Selectivity: More selective	**Room/board:** $8,750
Acceptance rate: 39%	**Average debt:** $23,500
Student/faculty ratio: 12/1	**Proportion who borrowed:** 75%

UNDERGRADUATE STUDENT BODY STATS

2005-2006 enrollment: 2,221 full-time; 97 part-time. Men: 1%; women: 99%. **Ethnic makeup:** African American: 95%; White: 3%; International: 2%. **Religious preference:** Roman Catholic: 7%; Protestant: 68%; Muslim: 2%; No preference: 6%; Other: 17%.

ADMISSIONS FACTS AND FIGURES

Phone: (800) 982-2411. **Email:** admiss@spelman.edu. **Website:** http://www.spelman.edu. **Application deadlines for fall 2007:** Regular decision: February 1; decision sent by April 1. Early decision: Send application by: November 1; Decision sent by: December 15. Early action: Send application by: November 15; Decision sent by: December 31. Admission can be deferred. **Application fee:** $35. Common application is accepted. **Admissions requirements/recommendations:** High school units required (recommended): English: 4 (4); Mathematics: 3 (4); Science: 3 (4); Foreign language: 2 (4); Social studies: 3 (4); History: 2 (3); Academic electives: 2 (2); Total units: 15 (19). Tests: The college uses SAT or ACT scores in admissions decisions. Either SAT or ACT required. For admission to the fall 2007 entering class, the school will accept: ACT with writing, ACT without writing. Campus visit: Recommended. Admissions interview: Neither required nor recommended. Off-campus interview: May be arranged. **Factors that count in admissions decisions:** *Academic:* Secondary school record: Very important. Class rank: Considered. Letters of recommendation: Important. Standardized test scores: Very important. Essay: Very important. *Nonacademic:* Interview: Not considered. Extracurricular activities: Important. Talent/ability: Considered. Character/personal qualities: Very important. Alumni/ae relationship: Considered. Geographical residence: Not considered. State residency: Not considered. Religious affiliation/commitment: Not considered. Minority status: Not considered. Volunteer work: Important. Work experience: Important. **Other schools with the greatest overlap in applicants:** Duke University; Florida A&M University; Hampton University; Howard University; Smith College. **Admissions statistics for the fall 2005 entering class:** Total applicants: 4,534. Total accepted: 1,771. Freshmen enrolled: 531; 83% were from out of state. Overall acceptance rate: 39%. Non-early acceptance rate: 39%. **Size of waiting list:** 102 applicants; enrolled from waiting list: 2. **Credentials of fall 2005 freshmen:** 33% ranked in the top 10 percent of their high school class; 71% were in the top 25 percent, and 91% were in the top half. (Proportion submitting class standing: 65%.) **Average high school grade point average:** 3.6. **First-year students who submitted SAT scores:** 85%. Scores (25/75 percentile): Verbal: 510-600, Math: 500-580, Combined: 1010-1180. **First-year students submitting ACT scores:** 48%. Scores (25/75 percentile): English: N/A, Math: N/A, Composite: 21-25.

ACADEMICS

Year founded: 1881. **Academic calendar:** Semester. **Degrees offered:** bachelor's. **Most popular majors:** 28% social sciences, 19% psychology, 13% biological and biomedical sciences, 11% English language and literature/letters, 5% visual and performing arts. **Major fields of study:** area, ethnic, cultural, and gender studies; biological and biomedical sciences; computer and information sciences and support services; education; engineering; English language and literature/letters; foreign languages, literatures, and linguistics; legal professions and studies; mathematics and statistics; multi/interdisciplinary studies; natural resources and conservation; philosophy and religious studies; physical sciences; psychology; public administration and social service professions; social sciences; visual and performing arts. **Areas of required coursework:** arts/fine arts, humanities, computer literacy, mathematics, English (including composition), philosophy, foreign languages, sciences (biological or physical), history, social science, other. **Pre-professional programs:** pre-law, pre-dentistry, pre-medicine, other. **Special academic programs (% participation):** cross-registration (35%), double major (8%), dual enrollment (1%), exchange student program (domestic) (2%), honors program (15%), independent study (2%), internships (20%), liberal arts/career combination (100%), student-designed major (5%), study abroad (5%), teacher certificate program (7%). **Teacher certification offered in:** early childhood, elementary, secondary. **Reserve Officers Training Corps (ROTC):** Army ROTC: Offered at cooperating institution (Morehouse College); Navy ROTC: Offered at cooperating institution (Morehouse College); Air Force ROTC: Offered at cooperating institution (Morehouse College). **Faculty and instruction (2005-2006):** Total instructional faculty: 169 full-time, 76 part-time (36% men; 64% women; 77% minorities). Full-time faculty with Ph.D. or other terminal degree: 85%. Student/faculty ratio: 12/1. Classes of fewer than 20 students: 56%; of 20 to 49 students: 42%; of 50 or more students: 1%. **Advanced Placement and International Baccalaureate credit:** AP tests may be used for: Credit only. Scores accepted: 3, 4, 5. International Baccalaureate exams may be used for: Credit only. **Freshmen returning for sophomore year:** 90%. **Graduation rates:** Four-year: 62%; five-year: 73%; six-year: 74%. **Graduate study:** 38% of students pursue further study immediately upon graduation. Fields in which graduates pursue further study: Master of Business Administration (MBA), 2%; law, 22%; medicine, 6%; dentistry, 5%; engineering, 1%; theology (or the seminary), 2%; education, 20%; arts and sciences, 29%.

COSTS AND FINANCIAL AID

Financial aid office: (404) 270-5212. **Expenses (2006-2007):** Tuition and fees 2006-2007: $17,005; room/board: $8,750. **Financial aid:** Priority filing date for institution's financial aid form: March 1. In 2005-2006, 92% of undergraduates applied for financial aid. Of those, 75% were determined to have financial need; 3% had their need fully met. Average financial aid package (proportion receiving): $10,500 (75%). Average amount of gift aid, such as scholarships or grants (proportion receiving): N/A (57%). Average amount of self-help aid, such as work study or loans (proportion receiving): N/A (75%). Among students who received need-based aid, the average percentage of need met: 67%. Among students who received aid based on merit, the average award (and the proportion receiving): $24,000 (0%). The average athletic scholarship (and the proportion receiving): $0 (0%). Average amount of debt of borrowers graduating in 2005: $23,500. Proportion who borrowed: 75%.

CAMPUS LIFE AND EXTRACURRICULAR ACTIVITIES

Campus housing available (% using): women's dorms (96%), other housing options (4%). Students who live in college-owned, operated, or affiliated housing: 62%. **Student employment:** During the 2005-2006 academic year, 10% of undergraduates worked on campus. Average per-year earnings: $2,500. **Clubs and organizations:** Number of student organizations: 82. Activities include: choral groups, dance, drama/theater, jazz band, literary magazine, marching band, music ensembles, student government, student newspaper, student film society, yearbook. ; sororities: 4. of women in sororities: 5%. Average proportion of students who stay on campus on weekends: 70%. **Sports program (2005-2006):** Member of NCAA II. *Women's intercollegiate varsity sports:* basketball, cross-country, golf, soccer, tennis, track and field (indoor), track and field (outdoor), volleyball.

SERVICES AND FACILITIES

Basic services: nonremedial tutoring, women's center, placement service, health service, health insurance. **Counseling services:** career, personal, academic, birth control. **For learning-disabled students:** School does not offer a structured program with separate admission and additional fees. Total undergraduates in learning-disabled program or receiving services: 15. Services include: tape recorders, note-taking services, oral tests, learning center, readers, extended time for tests, tutors, priority registration, priority seating, texts on tape, other testing accomodations, other. **Library:** Number of titles: 752,499; number of current serial subscriptions: 1,419. **Information technology resources:** Students are not required to lease or own a computer. Number of campus computers available to all students: 550. School has a wireless network. Approximate number of users that can be accommodated: 3,000. Proportion of college-owned housing units wired for high-speed internet access: 85%. **Campus safety:** Security services offered: 24-hour foot-and-vehicle patrols, late-night transport/escort service, 24-hour emergency telephones, lighted pathways/sidewalks, controlled dormitory access (key, security card, etc).

TRANSFER AND INTERNATIONAL STUDENTS

Transfer students: May apply for admission for the following academic terms: Fall, Spring. Applicants do not need a minimum number of credits to apply. For fall 2005: Transfer applications received: 263. Transfer applicants offered admission: 76. Transfer applicants enrolled: 47. **International students:** Number of foreign undergraduates: 34 (2% of student body). Number of countries represented: 21. Minimum TOEFL score required: 500 (paper); 250 (computer).

Thomas University

- **Address:** 1501 Millpond Road, Thomasville, GA 31792
- **Website:** http://www.thomasu.edu
- **Private**
- **Enrollment:** N/A

KEY STATS

✔ **U.S News College Ranking:** fourth tier, Comp. Coll.–Bachelor's (South)
✔ **SAT or ACT Score (25th/75th percentile):** N/A
✔ **Tuition:** 2005-2006: $10,310

Selectivity: Less selective	**Room/board:** $4,800
Acceptance rate: N/A	**Average debt:** N/A
Student/faculty ratio: N/A	**Proportion who borrowed:** N/A

Toccoa Falls College

- **Address:** 325 Chapel Drive, Toccoa Falls, GA 30598
- **Website:** http://www.tfc.edu
- **Private; Religious affiliation:** Christian and Missionary
- **Enrollment:** 863 full-time; 59 part-time

KEY STATS

✔ **U.S News College Ranking:** third tier, Comp. Colleges–Bachelor's (South)

✔ **SAT Score (25th/75th percentile):** 880-1160

✔ **Tuition:** 2006-2007: $13,375

Selectivity: Selective	**Room/board:** $4,800
Acceptance rate: 61%	**Average debt:** $17,273
Student/faculty ratio: 16/1	**Proportion who borrowed:** 71%

UNDERGRADUATE STUDENT BODY STATS

2005-2006 enrollment: 863 full-time; 59 part-time. Men: 43%; women: 57%. **Ethnic makeup:** African American: 3%; Asian American: 7%; Hispanic: 2%; White: 86%; International: 2%.

ADMISSIONS FACTS AND FIGURES

Phone: (706) 886-6831. **Email:** admissions@tfc.edu. **Website:** http://www.tfc.edu. **Application deadlines for fall 2007:** Regular decision: Rolling. Early decision: Not offered. Early action: Not offered. Admission can be deferred. **Application fee:** $20. Common application is not accepted. **To apply online, go to:** http://www.tfc.edu/adm/application/undergrad_application.htm. **Admissions requirements/recommendations:** High school units required (recommended): English: 4 (4); Mathematics: 3 (3); Science: 3 (3); Foreign language: 0 (0); Social studies: 3 (3); History: 0 (0); Academic electives: 6 (6); Total units: 19 (19). Tests: The college uses SAT or ACT scores in admissions decisions. Either SAT or ACT required. For admission to the fall 2007 entering class, the school will accept: ACT with writing, ACT without writing. Campus visit: Recommended. Admissions interview: Neither required nor recommended. Off-campus interview: May be arranged. **Factors that count in admissions decisions:** *Academic:* Secondary school record: Very important. Class rank: Not considered. Letters of recommendation: Very important. Standardized test scores: Very important. Essay: Very important. *Nonacademic:* Interview: Considered. Extracurricular activities: Considered. Talent/ability: Considered. Character/personal qualities: Very important. Alumni/ae relationship: Not considered. Geographical residence: Not considered. State residency: Not considered. Religious affiliation/commitment: Very important. Minority status: Not considered. Volunteer work: Considered. Work experience: Considered. **Admissions statistics for the fall 2005 entering class:** Total applicants: 815. Total accepted: 496. Freshmen enrolled: 271; 43% were from out of state. Overall acceptance rate: 61%. **Credentials of fall 2005 freshmen:** 18% ranked in the top 10 percent of their high school class; 40% were in the top 25 percent, and 69% were in the top half. (Proportion submitting class standing: 63%.) **Average high school grade point average:** 3.4. **First-year students who submitted SAT scores:** 80%. Scores (25/75 percentile): Verbal: 450-590, Math: 430-570, Combined: 880-1160. **First-year students submitting ACT scores:** 37%. Scores (25/75 percentile): English: N/A, Math: N/A, Composite: 19-26.

ACADEMICS

Year founded: 1907. **Academic calendar:** 4-1-4. **Degrees offered:** associate, bachelor's. **Most popular majors:** 45% theology and religious vocations, 19% psychology, 15% education, 7% business, management, marketing, and related support services, 5% communication, journalism, and related programs. **Major fields of study:** biological and biomedical sciences; business, management, marketing, and related support services; communication, journalism, and related programs; education; English language and literature/letters; legal professions and studies; philosophy and religious studies; psychology; theology and religious vocations; visual and performing arts. **Areas of required coursework:** humanities, computer literacy, mathematics, English (including composition), history, social science, other. **Pre-professional programs:** pre-law, pre-medicine. **Special academic programs (% participation):** distance learning, double major (1%), independent study (35%), internships (46%), teacher certificate program (18%). **Teacher certification offered in:** early childhood, middle/junior high, secondary. **Faculty and instruction (2005-2006):** Total instructional faculty: 43 full-time, 35 part-time

(71% men; 29% women; 1% minorities). Full-time faculty with Ph.D. or other terminal degree: 56%. Student/faculty ratio: 16/1. Classes of fewer than 20 students: 60%; of 20 to 49 students: 33%; of 50 or more students: 7%. **Advanced Placement and International Baccalaureate credit:** International Baccalaureate exams may be used for: Credit and/or placement. **Freshmen returning for sophomore year:** 70%. **Graduation rates:** Four-year: 32%; five-year: 43%; six-year: 45%.

COSTS AND FINANCIAL AID

Financial aid office: (706) 886-6831. **Expenses (2006-2007):** Tuition and fees 2006-2007: $13,375; room/board: $4,800. Estimated books and supplies: $855; transportation: $2,188; personal expenses: $2,327. **Financial aid:** Priority filing date for institution's financial aid form: May 1. In 2005-2006, 88% of undergraduates applied for financial aid. Of those, 78% were determined to have financial need; 12% had their need fully met. Average financial aid package (proportion receiving): $9,653 (78%). Average amount of gift aid, such as scholarships or grants (proportion receiving): $6,486 (77%). Average amount of self-help aid, such as work study or loans (proportion receiving): $4,018 (62%). Average need-based loan (excluding PLUS or other private loans): $3,110. Among students who received need-based aid, the average percentage of need met: 60%. Among students who received aid based on merit, the average award (and the proportion receiving): $7,595 (20%). The average athletic scholarship (and the proportion receiving): $0 (0%). Average amount of debt of borrowers graduating in 2005: $17,273. Proportion who borrowed: 71%.

CAMPUS LIFE AND EXTRACURRICULAR ACTIVITIES

Campus housing available (% using): women's dorms (55%), men's dorms (36%), apartments for married students (5%), apartment for single students (1%), special housing for international students (2%), other housing options (1%). Students who live in college-owned, operated, or affiliated housing: 61%. **Student employment:** During the 2005-2006 academic year, 12% of undergraduates worked on campus. Average per-year earnings: $1,875. **Clubs and organizations:** Number of student organizations: 10. Activities include: choral groups, concert band, drama/theater, jazz band, music ensembles, radio station, student government, student newspaper, yearbook. Number of fraternities: 0; sororities: 0. Average proportion of students who stay on campus on weekends: 60%.

SERVICES AND FACILITIES

Basic services: nonremedial tutoring, placement service, health service, health insurance. **Counseling services:** career, personal, academic, older student, psychological, religious. **For learning-disabled students:** School does not offer a structured program with separate admission and additional fees. Services include: untimed tests, note-taking services, oral tests, learning center, readers, extended time for tests, tutors, priority seating, other testing accomodations, other. **Library:** Number of titles: 139,082; number of current serial subscriptions: 18,134. **Information technology resources:** Students are not required to lease or own a computer. Number of campus computers available to all students: 60. School does not have a wireless network. Proportion of college-owned housing units wired for high-speed internet access: 90%. **Campus safety:** Security services offered: 24-hour foot-and-vehicle patrols, lighted pathways/sidewalks, controlled dormitory access (key, security card, etc).

TRANSFER AND INTERNATIONAL STUDENTS

Transfer students: May apply for admission for the following academic terms: Fall, Winter, Spring, Summer. Applicants need a minimum number of credits to apply. For fall 2005: Transfer applicants enrolled: 135. **International students:** Number of foreign undergraduates: 14 (2% of student body). Number of countries represented: 11. Minimum TOEFL score required: 550 (paper); 213 (computer). Average TOEFL score: 566 (paper).

University of Georgia

- **Address:** Terrell Hall, Athens, GA 30602
- **Website:** http://www.uga.edu
- **Public**
- **Enrollment:** 22,730 full-time; 2,474 part-time

KEY STATS

✔ **U.S News College Ranking:** 60, National Universities
✔ **SAT Score (25th/75th percentile):** 1130-1330
✔ **Tuition:** 2006-2007: $4,892 in state, $17,722 out of state
  Selectivity: More selective **Room/board:** $6,848
  Acceptance rate: 65% **Average debt:** $13,422
  Student/faculty ratio: 18/1 **Proportion who borrowed:** 43%

UNDERGRADUATE STUDENT BODY STATS

2005-2006 enrollment: 22,730 full-time; 2,474 part-time. Men: 43%; women: 57%. **Ethnic makeup:** African American: 5%; Asian American: 5%; Hispanic: 2%; White: 86%; International: 1%. **Religious preference:** Roman Catholic: 11%; Protestant: 43%; Jewish: 2%; No preference: 37%; Other: 7%.

ADMISSIONS FACTS AND FIGURES

Phone: (706) 542-8776. **Email:** undergrad@admissions.uga.edu. **Website:** http://www.uga.edu. **Application deadlines for fall 2007:** Regular decision: January 15; decision sent by March 31. Early decision: Not offered. Early action: Send application by: October 15; Decision sent by: December 15. Admission can be deferred. **Application fee:** $50. Common application is not accepted. **To apply online, go to:** http://www.admissions.uga.edu/apply_now.html. **Admissions requirements/recommendations:** High school units required (recommended): English: 4 (4); Mathematics: 4 (4); Science: 3 (3); Foreign language: 2 (3); Social studies: 1 (1); History: 2 (2); Total units: 16 (17). Tests: The college uses SAT or ACT scores in admissions decisions. Either SAT or ACT required. For admission to the fall 2007 entering class, the school will accept: ACT with writing. Campus visit: Recommended. Admissions interview: Neither required nor recommended. Off-campus interview: Not available. **Factors that count in admissions decisions:** *Academic:* Secondary school record: Very important. Class rank: Considered. Letters of recommendation: Considered. Standardized test scores: Important. Essay: Considered. *Nonacademic:* Interview: Not considered. Extracurricular activities: Considered. Talent/ability: Considered. Character/personal qualities: Considered. Alumni/ae relationship: Not considered. Geographical residence: Not considered. State residency: Not considered. Religious affiliation/commitment: Not considered. Minority status: Not considered. Volunteer work: Considered. Work experience: Considered. **Other schools with the greatest overlap in applicants:** Auburn University; Emory University; Georgia Institute of Technology; University of North Carolina–Chapel Hill; Vanderbilt University. **Admissions statistics for the fall 2005 entering class:** Total applicants: 12,326. Total accepted: 7,982. Freshmen enrolled: 4,712; 12% were from out of state. Accepted through early-decision or early-action plans: 62%. Overall acceptance rate: 65%. Non-early acceptance rate: 52%. **Size of waiting list:** 493 applicants; enrolled from waiting list: 13. **Credentials of fall 2005 freshmen:** 52% ranked in the top 10 percent of their high school class; 84% were in the top 25 percent, and 98% were in the top half. (Proportion submitting class standing: 82%.) **Average high school grade point average:** 3.7. **First-year students who submitted SAT scores:** 97%. Scores (25/75 percentile): Verbal: 560-660; Math: 570-670, Combined: 1130-1330. **First-year students submitting ACT scores:** 37%. Scores (25/75 percentile): English: 23-29, Math: 23-28, Composite: 24-28.

ACADEMICS

Year founded: 1785. **Academic calendar:** Semester. **Degrees offered:** certificate, bachelor's, post-bachelor's certificate, master's, post-master's certificate, first professional, first professional certificate, doctorate. **Most popular majors:** 10% psychology, 8% political science and government, 4% biology/biological sciences, 3% finance, 3% marketing/management. **Major fields of study:** agriculture, agriculture operations, and related sciences; architecture and related services; area, ethnic, cultural, and gender studies; biological and biomedical sciences; business, management, marketing, and related support services; communication, journalism, and related programs; communications technologies/technicians and support services; computer and information sciences and support services; education; engineering; English language and literature/letters; family and consumer sciences/human sciences; foreign languages, literatures, and linguistics; health professions and related clinical sciences; history; liberal arts and sciences studies, and humanities; mathematics and statistics; multi/interdisciplinary studies; natural resources and conservation; parks, recreation, leisure, and fitness studies; philosophy and religious studies; physical sciences; psychology; public administration and social service professions; security and protective services; social sciences; visual and performing arts. **Areas of required coursework:** arts/fine arts, humanities, computer literacy, mathematics, English (including composition), foreign languages, sciences (biological or physical), history, social science, other. **Pre-professional programs:** pre-law, pre-dentistry, pre-medicine, pre-theology, pre-veterinary science, pre-optometry, pre-pharmacy. **Special academic programs (% participation):** accelerated program, cooperative (work-study plan) program, cross-registration, distance learning, double major (10%), dual enrollment, exchange student program (domestic) (1%), external degree program, honors program (15%), independent study (6%), internships (27%), liberal arts/career combination, student-designed major, study abroad (21%), teacher certificate program (8%). **Teacher certification offered in:** early childhood, special education, elementary, vo-tech, middle/junior high, secondary, bilingual/bicultural. **Cooperative education programs:** agriculture, business, natural science. **Reserve Officers Training Corps (ROTC):** Army ROTC: Offered on campus; Air Force ROTC: Offered on campus. **Faculty and instruction (2005-2006):** Total instructional faculty: 1,691 full-time, 420 part-time (67% men; 33% women; 14% minorities). Full-time faculty with Ph.D. or other terminal degree: 93%. Student/faculty ratio: 18/1. Classes of fewer than 20 students: 35%; of 20 to 49 students: 55%; of 50 or more students: 10%. **Advanced Placement and International Baccalaureate credit:** AP tests may be used for: Credit and/or placement. Scores accepted: 3, 4, 5. International Baccalaureate exams may be used for: Credit and/or placement. **Freshmen returning for sophomore year:** 93%. **Graduation rates:** Four-year: 41%; five-year: 68%; six-year: 74%. **Graduate study:** 18% of students pursue further study immediately upon graduation; 42% within five years. Fields in which graduates pursue further study: Master of Business Administration (MBA), 9%; law, 19%; medicine, 10%; theology (or the seminary), 1%; education, 8%; arts and sciences, 11%; veterinary medicine, 2%.

COSTS AND FINANCIAL AID

Financial aid office: (706) 542-6147. **Expenses (2006-2007):** Tuition and fees 2006-2007: $4,892 in state, $17,722 out of state; room/board: $6,848. Estimated personal expenses: $2,200. **Financial aid:** Priority filing date for institution's financial aid form: March 1. In 2005-2006, 45% of undergraduates applied for financial aid. Of those, 26% were determined to have financial need; 32% had their need fully met. Average financial aid package (proportion receiving): $7,320 (25%). Average amount of gift aid, such as scholarships or grants (proportion receiving): $5,731 (21%). Average amount of self-help aid, such as work study or loans (proportion receiving): $3,825 (17%). Average need-based loan (excluding PLUS or other private loans): $3,683. Among students who received need-based aid, the average percentage of need met: 74%. Among students who received aid based on merit, the average award (and the proportion receiving): $1,870 (6%). The average athletic scholarship (and the proportion receiving): $9,315 (2%). Average amount of debt of borrowers graduating in 2005: $13,422. Proportion who borrowed: 43%.

CAMPUS LIFE AND EXTRACURRICULAR ACTIVITIES

Campus housing available (% using): coed dorms (69%), women's dorms (18%), sorority housing (2%), fraternity housing (3%), apartments for married students (4%), apartment for single students (4%), special housing for disabled students, special housing for international students, other housing options. Students who live in college-owned, operated, or affiliated housing: 27%. **Student employment:** During the 2005-2006 academic year, 8% of undergraduates worked on campus. Average per-year earnings: $3,520. **Clubs and organizations:** Number of student organizations: 450. Activities include: choral groups, concert band, dance, drama/theater, jazz band, literary magazine, marching band, music ensembles, musical theater, opera, pep band, radio station, student government, student newspaper, student film society, symphony orchestra, television station, yearbook. Number of fraternities: 32; sororities: 22. Proportion of men in fraternities: 18%; of women in sororities: 23%. Average proportion of students who stay on campus on weekends: 75%. **Sports program (2005-2006):** Member of NCAA I. *Men's intercollegiate varsity sports:* baseball, basketball, cross-country, football, golf, swimming and diving, tennis, track and field (indoor), track and field (outdoor). *Women's intercollegiate varsity sports:* basketball, cross-country, equestrian sports, golf, gymnastics, soccer, softball, swimming and diving, tennis, track and field (indoor), track and field (outdoor), volleyball.

SERVICES AND FACILITIES

Basic services: nonremedial tutoring, women's center, placement service, day care, health service, health insurance. **Remedial assistance:** reading, math, writing, study skills. **Counseling services:** minority student, career, military, personal, veteran student, academic, older student, psychological, birth control, religious. **For learning-disabled students:** School does not offer a structured program with separate admission and additional fees. Total undergraduates in learning-disabled program or receiving services: 192. Services include: remedial math, remedial English, reading machines, remedial reading, tape recorders, diagnostic testing service, note-taking services, oral tests, learning center, readers, extended time for tests, tutors, priority registration, texts on tape, typist/scribe. **Library:** Number of titles: 4,114,611; number of current serial subscriptions: 48,227. **Information technology resources:** Students are not required to lease or own a computer. Number of campus computers available to all students: 3,100. School has a wireless network. Approximate number of users that can be accommodated: 15,000. Proportion of college-owned housing units wired for high-speed internet access: 100%. **Campus safety:** Security services offered: 24-hour foot-and-vehicle patrols, late-night transport/escort service, 24-hour emergency telephones, lighted pathways/sidewalks, controlled dormitory access (key, security card, etc).

TRANSFER AND INTERNATIONAL STUDENTS

Transfer students: May apply for admission for the following academic terms: Fall, Spring, Summer. Applicants need a minimum number of credits to apply. For fall 2005: Transfer applications received: 2,326. Transfer applicants offered admission: 1,316. Transfer applicants enrolled: 843. **International students:** Number of foreign undergraduates: 187 (1% of student body). Number of countries represented: 61. Minimum TOEFL score required: 213 (computer).

University of West Georgia

■ **Address:** 1601 Maple Street, Carrollton, GA 30118
■ **Website:** http://www.westga.edu
■ **Public**
■ **Enrollment:** 6,921 full-time; 1,425 part-time

KEY STATS

✔ **U.S News College Ranking:** fourth tier, Universities–Master's (South)
✔ **SAT Score (25th/75th percentile):** 930-1110
✔ **Tuition:** 2005-2006: $3,270 in state, $10,586 out of state

Selectivity: Selective	**Room/board:** $5,568
Acceptance rate: 55%	**Average debt:** $14,555
Student/faculty ratio: 19/1	**Proportion who borrowed:** 61%

UNDERGRADUATE STUDENT BODY STATS

2005-2006 enrollment: 6,921 full-time; 1,425 part-time. Men: 40%; women: 60%. **Ethnic makeup:** African American: 23%; Asian American: 1%; Hispanic: 2%; White: 73%; International: 1%.

ADMISSIONS FACTS AND FIGURES

Phone: (678) 839-4000. **Email:** admiss@westga.edu. **Website:** http://www.westga.edu. **Application deadlines for fall 2007:** Regular decision: July 1. Early decision: Not offered. Early action: Not offered. Admission cannot be deferred. **Application fee:** $20. Common application is not accepted. **To apply online, go to:** http://www.westga.edu/~admiss/. **Admissions requirements/recommendations:** High school units required (recommended): English: 4 (4); Mathematics: 4 (4); Science: 3 (3); Foreign language: 2 (2); Social studies: 3 (1); History: (2); Total units: 16 (16). Tests: The college uses SAT or ACT scores in admissions decisions. Either SAT or ACT required. For admission to the fall 2007 entering class, the school will accept: ACT with writing. Campus visit: Recommended. Admissions interview: Recommended. **Factors that count in admissions decisions:** *Academic:* Secondary school record: Very important. Class rank: Not considered. Letters of recommendation: Not considered. Standardized test scores: Very important. Essay: Not considered. *Nonacademic:* Interview: Not considered. Extracurricular activities: Not considered. Talent/ability: Not considered. Character/personal qualities: Not considered. Alumni/ae relationship: Not considered. Geographical residence: Not considered. State residency: Not considered. Religious affiliation/commitment: Not considered. Minority status: Not considered. Volunteer work: Not considered. Work experience: Not

considered. **Other schools with the greatest overlap in applicants:** Georgia Southern University; Georgia State University; Kennesaw State University; University of Georgia; Valdosta State University. **Admissions statistics for the fall 2005 entering class:** Total applicants: 5,175. Total accepted: 2,859. Freshmen enrolled: 1,983; 2% were from out of state. Overall acceptance rate: 55%. **Average high school grade point average:** 3.0. **First-year students who submitted SAT scores:** 85%. Scores (25/75 percentile): Verbal: 470-560, Math: 460-550, Combined: 930-1110. **First-year students submitting ACT scores:** 27%. Scores (25/75 percentile): English: 18-22, Math: 18-22, Composite: 18-22.

ACADEMICS

Year founded: 1906. **Academic calendar:** Semester. **Degrees offered:** bachelor's, master's, post-master's certificate, doctorate. **Most popular majors:** 26% business, management, marketing, and related support services, 22% education, 14% social sciences, 7% health professions and related clinical sciences, 6% psychology. **Major fields of study:** biological and biomedical sciences; business, management, marketing, and related support services; communication, journalism, and related programs; computer and information sciences and support services; education; English language and literature/letters; foreign languages, literatures, and linguistics; health professions and related clinical sciences; history; mathematics and statistics; natural resources and conservation; parks, recreation, leisure, and fitness studies; philosophy and religious studies; physical sciences; psychology; social sciences; visual and performing arts. **Areas of required coursework:** arts/fine arts, humanities, computer literacy, mathematics, English (including composition), foreign languages, sciences (biological or physical), history, social science. **Pre-professional programs:** pre-law, pre-dentistry, pre-medicine, pre-veterinary science, pre-pharmacy, other. **Special academic programs:** accelerated program, cooperative (work-study plan) program, distance learning, double major, dual enrollment, external degree program, honors program, independent study, study abroad, teacher certificate program. **Teacher certification offered in:** early childhood, special education, elementary, middle/junior high, secondary. **Cooperative education programs:** other. **Reserve Officers Training Corps (ROTC):** Army ROTC: Offered on campus. **Faculty and instruction (2005-2006):** Total instructional faculty: 383 full-time, 135 part-time (48% men; 52% women; 14% minorities). Full-time faculty with Ph.D. or other terminal degree: 78%. Student/faculty ratio: 19/1. Classes of fewer than 20 students: 39%; of 20 to 49 students: 50%; of 50 or more students: 11%. **Advanced Placement and International Baccalaureate credit:** AP tests may be used for: Credit and/or placement. Scores accepted: 3, 4, 5. **Freshmen returning for sophomore year:** 71%. **Graduation rates:** Four-year: 9%; five-year: 25%; six-year: 31%.

COSTS AND FINANCIAL AID

Financial aid office: (678) 839-6421. **Expenses (2005-2006):** Tuition and fees 2005-2006: $3,270 in state, $10,586 out of state; room/board: $5,568. Estimated books and supplies: $900. **Financial aid:** Priority filing date for institution's financial aid form: April 1. In 2005-2006, 70% of undergraduates applied for financial aid. Of those, 50% were determined to have financial need; 22% had their need fully met. Average financial aid package (proportion receiving): $6,441 (49%). Average amount of gift aid, such as scholarships or grants (proportion receiving): $4,346 (39%). Average amount of self-help aid, such as work study or loans (proportion receiving): $3,393 (43%). Average need-based loan (excluding PLUS or other private loans): $3,025. Among students who received need-based aid, the average percentage of need met: 78%. Among students who received aid based on merit, the average award (and the proportion receiving): $1,635 (2%). The average athletic scholarship (and the proportion receiving): $4,193 (1%). Average amount of debt of borrowers graduating in 2005: $14,555. Proportion who borrowed: 61%.

CAMPUS LIFE AND EXTRACURRICULAR ACTIVITIES

Campus housing available: coed dorms, women's dorms, men's dorms. Students who live in college-owned, operated, or affiliated housing: 30%. **Student employment:** During the 2005-2006 academic year, 20% of undergraduates worked on campus. Average per-year earnings: $4,320. **Clubs and organizations:** Number of student organizations: 71. Activities include: choral groups, concert band, dance, drama/theater, jazz band, literary magazine, marching band, music ensembles, musical theater, opera, pep band, radio station, student government, student newspaper, television station. Number of fraternities: 12; sororities: 8. Proportion of men in fraternities: 3%; of women in sororities: 3%. Average proportion of students who stay on campus on weekends: 25%. **Sports program (2005-2006):** Member of NCAA II. *Men's intercollegiate varsity sports:* baseball, basketball, cross-country, football, track and field (indoor), track and field (outdoor). *Women's intercol-*

legiate varsity sports: basketball, cross-country, softball, track and field (indoor), track and field (outdoor), volleyball.

SERVICES AND FACILITIES
Basic services: nonremedial tutoring, placement service, health service. **Remedial assistance:** reading, math, writing, study skills. **Counseling services:** minority student, career, military, personal, veteran student, academic, older student, psychological. **For learning-disabled students:** School does not offer a structured program with separate admission and additional fees. Total undergraduates in learning-disabled program or receiving services: 100. Services include: remedial math, remedial English, reading machines, remedial reading, tape recorders, untimed tests, note-taking services, oral tests, readers, extended time for tests, tutors, priority registration, other. **Library:** Number of titles: 521,039; number of current serial subscriptions: 65,517. **Information technology resources:** Students are not required to lease or own a computer. Number of campus computers available to all students: 745. School has a wireless network. Approximate number of users that can be accommodated: 250. Proportion of college-owned housing units wired for high-speed internet access: 100%. **Campus safety:** Security services offered: 24-hour foot-and-vehicle patrols, 24-hour emergency telephones, lighted pathways/sidewalks, controlled dormitory access (key, security card, etc).

TRANSFER AND INTERNATIONAL STUDENTS
Transfer students: May apply for admission for the following academic terms: Fall, Spring, Summer. Applicants need a minimum number of credits to apply. For fall 2005: Transfer applications received: 1,501. Transfer applicants offered admission: 912. Transfer applicants enrolled: 571. **International students:** Number of foreign undergraduates: 104 (1% of student body). Number of countries represented: 38. Minimum TOEFL score required: 523 (paper); 193 (computer).

Valdosta State University

- **Address:** 1500 N. Patterson Street, Valdosta, GA 31698
- **Website:** http://www.valdosta.edu
- **Public**
- **Enrollment:** 7,557 full-time; 1,536 part-time

KEY STATS
✔ **U.S News College Ranking:** third tier, Universities–Master's (South)
✔ **SAT Score (25th/75th percentile):** 950-1130
✔ **Tuition:** 2006-2007: $3,278 in state, $10,594 out of state

Selectivity: Less selective	**Room/board:** $5,524
Acceptance rate: 63%	**Average debt:** $16,220
Student/faculty ratio: 20/1	**Proportion who borrowed:** 61%

UNDERGRADUATE STUDENT BODY STATS
2005-2006 enrollment: 7,557 full-time; 1,536 part-time. Men: 41%; women: 59%. **Ethnic makeup:** African American: 22%; Asian American: 1%; Hispanic: 2%; White: 74%; International: 1%.

ADMISSIONS FACTS AND FIGURES
Phone: (229) 333-5791. **Email:** admissions@valdosta.edu. **Website:** http://www.valdosta.edu. **Application deadlines for fall 2007:** Regular decision: July 15. Early decision: Not offered. Early action: Not offered. Admission can be deferred. **Application fee:** $20. Common application is not accepted. **To apply online, go to:** https://www.applyweb.com/aw?valdosta. **Admissions requirements/recommendations:** High school units required (recommended): English: 4; Mathematics: 4; Science: 3; Foreign language: 2; Social studies: 3; Total units: 16. Tests: The college uses SAT or ACT scores in admissions decisions. Either SAT or ACT required. For admission to the fall 2007 entering class, the school will accept: ACT with writing, ACT without writing. Campus visit: Recommended. Admissions interview: Neither required nor recommended. Off-campus interview: Not available. **Factors that count in admissions decisions:** *Academic:* Secondary school record: Very important. Class rank: Important. Letters of recommendation: Not considered. Standardized test scores: Important. Essay: Not considered. *Nonacademic:* Interview: Not considered. Extracurricular activities: Not considered. Talent/ability: Considered. Character/personal qualities: Not considered. Alumni/ae relationship: Not considered. Geographical residence: Not considered. State residency: Not considered. Religious affilia-

tion/commitment: Not considered. Minority status: Not considered. Volunteer work: Not considered. Work experience: Not considered. **Other schools with the greatest overlap in applicants:** Georgia College and State University; Georgia Southern University; Georgia State University; University of Georgia; University of West Georgia. **Admissions statistics for the fall 2005 entering class:** Total applicants: 5,782. Total accepted: 3,643. Freshmen enrolled: 1,757; 1% were from out of state. Overall acceptance rate: 63%. **Average high school grade point average:** 3.0. **First-year students who submitted SAT scores:** 86%. Scores (25/75 percentile): Verbal: 480-560, Math: 470-570, Combined: 950-1130. **First-year students submitting ACT scores:** 12%. Scores (25/75 percentile): English: 20-23, Math: 19-23, Composite: 20-23.

ACADEMICS
Year founded: 1906. **Academic calendar:** Semester. **Degrees offered:** associate, bachelor's, master's, post-master's certificate, doctorate. **Most popular majors:** 23% education, 22% business, management, marketing, and related support services, 8% health professions and related clinical sciences, 7% social sciences. **Major fields of study:** biological and biomedical sciences; business, management, marketing, and related support services; communication, journalism, and related programs; computer and information sciences and support services; education; engineering technologies/technicians; English language and literature/letters; foreign languages, literatures, and linguistics; health professions and related clinical sciences; history; legal professions and studies; liberal arts and sciences studies, and humanities; mathematics and statistics; natural resources and conservation; parks, recreation, leisure, and fitness studies; philosophy and religious studies; physical sciences; psychology; security and protective services; social sciences; visual and performing arts. **Areas of required coursework:** humanities, mathematics, English (including composition), sciences (biological or physical), history, social science, other. **Pre-professional programs:** pre-medicine, pre-pharmacy. **Special academic programs:** cooperative (work-study plan) program, distance learning, double major, dual enrollment, English as a Second Language (ESL), external degree program, honors program, independent study, internships, liberal arts/career combination, study abroad, teacher certificate program, weekend college. **Teacher certification offered in:** early childhood, special education, middle/junior high, adult education, secondary. **Cooperative education programs:** art, business, computer science, education, engineering, health professions, humanities, natural science, social/behavioral science, technologies, other. **Reserve Officers Training Corps (ROTC):** Air Force ROTC: Offered on campus. **Faculty and instruction (2005-2006):** Total instructional faculty: 435 full-time, 110 part-time (52% men; 48% women; 19% minorities). Full-time faculty with Ph.D. or other terminal degree: 78%. Student/faculty ratio: 20/1. Classes of fewer than 20 students: 29%; of 20 to 49 students: 65%; of 50 or more students: 5%. **Advanced Placement and International Baccalaureate credit:** International Baccalaureate exams may be used for: Credit and/or placement. **Freshmen returning for sophomore year:** 75%. **Graduation rates:** Four-year: 18%; five-year: 35%; six-year: 36%.

COSTS AND FINANCIAL AID
Financial aid office: (229) 333-5935. **Expenses (2006-2007):** Tuition and fees 2006-2007: $3,278 in state, $10,594 out of state; room/board: $5,524. Estimated books and supplies: $1,000; transportation: $2,100; personal expenses: $2,400. **Financial aid:** Priority filing date for institution's financial aid form: May 1. In 2005-2006, 88% of undergraduates applied for financial aid. Of those, 58% were determined to have financial need; 60% had their need fully met. Average financial aid package (proportion receiving): $6,501 (57%). Average amount of gift aid, such as scholarships or grants (proportion receiving): $4,631 (42%). Average amount of self-help aid, such as work study or loans (proportion receiving): $1,090 (48%). Average need-based loan (excluding PLUS or other private loans): $3,873. Among students who received need-based aid, the average percentage of need met: 91%. Among students who received aid based on merit, the average award (and the proportion receiving): $1,445 (25%). The average athletic scholarship (and the proportion receiving): $3,361 (3%). Average amount of debt of borrowers graduating in 2005: $16,220. Proportion who borrowed: 61%.

CAMPUS LIFE AND EXTRACURRICULAR ACTIVITIES
Campus housing available (% using): coed dorms (43%), women's dorms (10%), men's dorms (14%), apartments for married students (0%), apartment for single students (29%), special housing for disabled students (0%), special housing for international students (1%), other housing options (3%). Students who live in college-owned, operated, or affiliated housing: 20%. **Student employment:** During the 2005-2006 academic year, 11% of under-

graduates worked on campus. Average per-year earnings: $5,300. **Clubs and organizations:** Number of student organizations: 148. Activities include: choral groups, dance, drama/theater, jazz band, literary magazine, marching band, musical theater, radio station, student government, student newspaper, symphony orchestra, television station. Number of fraternities: 12; sororities: 8. Proportion of men in fraternities: 10%; of women in sororities: 8%. Average proportion of students who stay on campus on weekends: 50%. **Sports program (2005-2006):** Member of NCAA II. *Men's intercollegiate varsity sports:* baseball, basketball, cross-country, football, golf, tennis, track and field (outdoor). *Women's intercollegiate varsity sports:* basketball, cross-country, golf, softball, tennis, track and field (outdoor), volleyball.

SERVICES AND FACILITIES

Basic services: nonremedial tutoring, placement service, health service, health insurance. **Remedial assistance:** reading, math, writing. **Counseling services:** minority student, career, personal, veteran student, academic, psychological, other. **For learning-disabled students:** School does not offer a structured program with separate admission and additional fees. Total undergraduates in learning-disabled program or receiving services: 50. Services include: remedial math, remedial English, reading machines, remedial reading, tape recorders, note-taking services, readers, extended time for tests, tutors, priority registration, priority seating, substitution of courses, texts on tape, exams on tape or computer, other testing accomodations. **Library:** Number of titles: 578,855; number of current serial subscriptions: 2,788. **Information technology resources:** Students are not required to lease or own a computer. Number of campus computers available to all students: 1,800. School has a wireless network. Approximate number of users that can be accommodated: 2,500. Proportion of college-owned housing units wired for high-speed internet access: 100%. **Campus safety:** Security services offered: 24-hour foot-and-vehicle patrols, late-night transport/escort service, 24-hour emergency telephones, lighted pathways/sidewalks, controlled dormitory access (key, security card, etc).

TRANSFER AND INTERNATIONAL STUDENTS

Transfer students: May apply for admission for the following academic terms: Fall, Spring, Summer. Applicants need a minimum number of credits to apply. For fall 2005: Transfer applications received: 1,420. Transfer applicants offered admission: 1,015. Transfer applicants enrolled: 575. **International students:** Number of foreign undergraduates: 100 (1% of student body). Number of countries represented: 63. Minimum TOEFL score required: 523 (paper); 193 (computer). Average TOEFL score: 600 (paper).

Wesleyan College

- **Address:** 4760 Forsyth Road, Macon, GA 31210-4462
- **Website:** http://www.wesleyancollege.edu
- **Private; Religious affiliation:** United Methodist
- **Enrollment:** 400 full-time; 151 part-time

KEY STATS

✔ **U.S News College Ranking:** third tier, Liberal Arts Colleges
✔ **SAT Score (25th/75th percentile):** 990-1230
✔ **Tuition:** 2006-2007: $14,500

Selectivity: More selective	**Room/board:** $7,500
Acceptance rate: 55%	**Average debt:** $20,988
Student/faculty ratio: 8/1	**Proportion who borrowed:** 80%

UNDERGRADUATE STUDENT BODY STATS

2005-2006 enrollment: 400 full-time; 151 part-time. Men: 1%; women: 99%. **Ethnic makeup:** African American: 25%; Asian American: 3%; Hispanic: 3%; White: 50%; International: 19%. **Religious preference:** Roman Catholic: 8%; Protestant: 40%; Jewish: 1%; Muslim: 1%; Hindu: 2%; Buddhist: 1%; No preference: 28%; United Methodist: 14%.

ADMISSIONS FACTS AND FIGURES

Phone: (800) 447-6610. **Email:** admissions@wesleyancollege.edu. **Website:** http://www.wesleyancollege.edu. **Application deadlines for fall 2007:** Regular decision: August 1. Early decision: Send application by: November 15; Decision sent by: December 15. Early action: Send application by: February 15; Decision sent by: March 15. Admission can be deferred. **Application fee:** $30. Common application is accepted. **To apply online, go to:** http://www.wesleyancollege.edu/admissions/. **Admissions**

requirements/recommendations: High school units required (recommended): English: 4 (4); Mathematics: 3 (4); Science: 3 (4); Foreign language: 2 (3); Social studies: 3 (3); History: 0 (0); Academic electives: 0 (0); Total units: 15 (21). Tests: The college uses SAT or ACT scores in admissions decisions. Either SAT or ACT required. For admission to the fall 2007 entering class, the school will accept: ACT with writing, ACT without writing. Campus visit: Recommended. Admissions interview: Recommended. Off-campus interview: May be arranged. **Factors that count in admissions decisions: Academic:** Secondary school record: Very important. Class rank: Considered. Letters of recommendation: Important. Standardized test scores: Very important. Essay: Important. **Nonacademic:** Interview: Important. Extracurricular activities: Important. Talent/ability: Important. Character/personal qualities: Important. Alumni/ae relationship: Important. Geographical residence: Not considered. State residency: Not considered. Religious affiliation/commitment: Not considered. Minority status: Not considered. Volunteer work: Important. Work experience: Important. **Other schools with the greatest overlap in applicants:** Agnes Scott College; Berry College; Georgia College and State University; Mercer University; University of Georgia. **Admissions statistics for the fall 2005 entering class:** Total applicants: 483. Total accepted: 267. Freshmen enrolled: 113; Overall acceptance rate: 55%. Non-early acceptance rate: 55%. **Size of waiting list:** 0 applicants; enrolled from waiting list: N/A. **Credentials of fall 2005 freshmen:** 34% ranked in the top 10 percent of their high school class; 66% were in the top 25 percent, and 85% were in the top half. (Proportion submitting class standing: 73%.) **Average high school grade point average:** 3.5. **First-year students who submitted SAT scores:** 92%. Scores (25/75 percentile): Verbal: 500-630, Math: 490-600, Combined: 990-1230. **First-year students submitting ACT scores:** 36%. Scores (25/75 percentile): English: N/A, Math: N/A, Composite: 21-26.

ACADEMICS

Year founded: 1836. **Academic calendar:** Semester. **Degrees offered:** bachelor's, master's. **Most popular majors:** 28% business administration, management, and operations, 17% psychology, 11% elementary education and teaching, 9% communication, journalism, and related programs, 8% biology/biological sciences. **Major fields of study:** area, ethnic, cultural, and gender studies; biological and biomedical sciences; business, management, marketing, and related support services; communication, journalism, and related programs; computer and information sciences and support services; education; engineering; English language and literature/letters; foreign languages, literatures, and linguistics; history; liberal arts and sciences studies, and humanities; mathematics and statistics; multi/interdisciplinary studies; philosophy and religious studies; physical sciences; psychology; social sciences; visual and performing arts. **Areas of required coursework:** arts/fine arts, humanities, mathematics, English (including composition), foreign languages, sciences (biological or physical), social science. **Pre-professional programs:** pre-law, pre-dentistry, pre-medicine, pre-veterinary science, pre-pharmacy, other. **Special academic programs:** accelerated program, cross-registration, double major, dual enrollment, exchange student program (domestic), honors program, independent study, internships, student-designed major, study abroad, teacher certificate program, weekend college. **Teacher certification offered in:** early childhood, middle/junior high. **Cooperative education programs:** education, engineering. **Faculty and instruction (2005-2006):** Total instructional faculty: 46 full-time, 37 part-time (40% men; 60% women; 11% minorities). Full-time faculty with Ph.D. or other terminal degree: 96%. Student/faculty ratio: 8/1. Classes of fewer than 20 students: 90%; of 20 to 49 students: 10%. **Advanced Placement and International Baccalaureate credit:** AP tests may be used for: Credit only. Scores accepted: 4, 5. International Baccalaureate exams may be used for: Credit only. **Freshmen returning for sophomore year:** 69%. **Graduation rates:** Four-year: 40%; five-year: 44%; six-year: 45%. **Graduate study:** 27% of students pursue further study immediately upon graduation; 32% within one year; 22% within five years.

COSTS AND FINANCIAL AID

Financial aid office: (888) 665-5723. **Expenses (2006-2007):** Tuition and fees 2006-2007: $14,500; room/board: $7,500. Estimated books and supplies: $900; transportation: $500; personal expenses: $1,000. **Financial aid:** Priority filing date for institution's financial aid form: April 1; deadline: June 30. In 2005-2006, 75% of undergraduates applied for financial aid. Of those, 62% were determined to have financial need; 27% had their need fully met. Average financial aid package (proportion receiving): $10,758 (62%). Average amount of gift aid, such as scholarships or grants (proportion receiving): $7,913 (60%). Average amount of self-help aid, such as work study or loans (proportion receiving): $4,079 (47%). Average need-based loan (excluding PLUS or other private loans): $3,799. Among students who received need-based aid, the average percentage of need met: 79%. Among students who received aid based on merit, the average award (and the proportion receiving): $13,943 (38%). The average athletic scholarship (and the proportion receiving): $0 (0%). Average amount of debt of borrowers graduating in 2005: $20,988. Proportion who borrowed: 80%.

CAMPUS LIFE AND EXTRACURRICULAR ACTIVITIES

Campus housing available (% using): women's dorms (72%), apartment for single students (28%). Students who live in college-owned, operated, or affiliated housing: 89%. **Student employment:** During the 2005-2006 academic year, 45% of undergraduates worked on campus. Average per-year earnings: $1,000. **Clubs and organizations:** Number of student organizations: 44. Activities include: choral groups, dance, drama/theater, literary magazine, music ensembles, student government, student newspaper, yearbook. Number of fraternities: 0; sororities: 0. Average proportion of students who stay on campus on weekends: 70%. **Sports program (2005-2006):** Member of NCAA III. *Women's intercollegiate varsity sports:* basketball, equestrian sports, soccer, softball, tennis, volleyball.

SERVICES AND FACILITIES

Basic services: nonremedial tutoring, placement service, health service, health insurance. **Remedial assistance:** reading, math, writing, study skills.

Counseling services: career, personal, academic, psychological, birth control, religious. **For learning-disabled students:** School does not offer a structured program with separate admission and additional fees. Total undergraduates in learning-disabled program or receiving services: 7. Services include: notetaking services, learning center, extended time for tests, tutors, priority seating. **Library:** Number of titles: 143,071; number of current serial subscriptions: 615. **Information technology resources:** Students are required to lease or own a computer. Number of campus computers available to all students: 100. School has a wireless network. Proportion of college-owned housing units wired for high-speed internet access: 100%. **Campus safety:** Security services offered: 24-hour foot-and-vehicle patrols, late-night transport/escort service, 24-hour emergency telephones, lighted pathways/sidewalks, controlled dormitory access (key, security card, etc).

TRANSFER AND INTERNATIONAL STUDENTS

Transfer students: May apply for admission for the following academic terms: Fall, Spring. Applicants need a minimum number of credits to apply. For fall 2005: Transfer applications received: 60. Transfer applicants offered admission: 28. Transfer applicants enrolled: 14. **International students:** Number of foreign undergraduates: 77 (19% of student body). Number of countries represented: 24. Minimum TOEFL score required: 550 (paper); 213 (computer). Average TOEFL score: 597 (paper).

Hawaii

Brigham Young University–Hawaii

- **Address:** 55-220 Kulanui Street, Laie Oahu, HI 96762-1294
- **Website:** http://www.byuh.edu
- **Private; Religious affiliation:** Church of Jesus Christ of Latter-day Saints
- **Enrollment:** 2,246 full-time; 245 part-time

KEY STATS

- ✔ **U.S News College Ranking:** 4, Comp. Coll.–Bachelor's (West)
- ✔ **ACT Score (25th/75th percentile):** 20-26
- ✔ **Tuition:** 2006-2007: $3,040

Selectivity: More selective	**Room/board:** $5,170
Acceptance rate: 11%	**Average debt:** $9,794
Student/faculty ratio: 15/1	**Proportion who borrowed:** 25%

UNDERGRADUATE STUDENT BODY STATS

2005-2006 enrollment: 2,246 full-time; 245 part-time. Men: 42%; women: 58%. **Ethnic makeup:** African American: 1%; American-Indian: 1%; Asian American: 22%; Hispanic: 2%; White: 28%; International: 47%.

ADMISSIONS FACTS AND FIGURES

Phone: (808) 293-3738. **Email:** admissions@byuh.edu. **Website:** http://www.byuh.edu. **Application deadlines for fall 2007:** Regular decision: February 15; decision sent by April 1. Early decision: Not offered. Early action: Not offered. Admission can be deferred. **Application fee:** $30. Common application is not accepted. **Admissions requirements/recommendations:** High school units required (recommended): English: (4); Mathematics: (4); Science: (2); Foreign language: (2); Social studies: (0); History: (2); Academic electives: (0); Total units: (0). Tests: The college uses SAT or ACT scores in admissions decisions. Neither SAT nor ACT required. For admission to the fall 2007 entering class, the school will accept: ACT without writing. Campus visit: Neither required nor recommended. Admissions interview: Neither required nor recommended. Off-campus interview: May be arranged. **Factors that count in admissions decisions:** *Academic:* Secondary school record: Very important. Class rank: Important. Letters of recommendation: Very important. Standardized test scores: Very important. Essay: Very important. *Nonacademic:* Interview: Very important. Extracurricular activities: Very important. Talent/ability: Important. Character/personal qualities: Very important. Alumni/ae relationship: Important. Geographical residence: Very important. State residency: Considered. Religious affiliation/commitment: Very important. Minority status: Not considered. Volunteer work: Important. Work experience: Important. **Other schools with the greatest overlap in applicants:** Brigham Young University–Provo. **Admissions statistics for the fall 2005 entering class:** Total applicants: 2,128. Total accepted: 243. Freshmen enrolled: 220; 61% were from out of state. Overall acceptance rate: 11%. **Credentials of fall 2005 freshmen:** 25% ranked in the top 10 percent of their high school class; 61% were in the top 25 percent, and 90% were in the top half. (Proportion submitting class standing: 33%.) **Average high school grade point average:** 3.3. **First-year students who submitted SAT scores:** 6%. Scores (25/75 percentile): Verbal: 505-630, Math: 555-630, Combined: 1060-1260. **First-year students submitting ACT scores:** 41%. Scores (25/75 percentile): English: 19-26, Math: 20-26, Composite: 20-26.

ACADEMICS

Year founded: 1955. **Academic calendar:** Semester. **Degrees offered:** associate, bachelor's. **Most popular majors:** 13% international business/trade/commerce, 10% information science/studies, 8% psychology, 7% accounting, 6% social work. **Major fields of study:** area, ethnic, cultural, and gender studies; biological and biomedical sciences; business, management, marketing, and related support services; computer and information sciences and support services; education; English language and literature/letters; history; liberal arts and sciences studies, and humanities; mathematics and statistics; multi/interdisciplinary studies; parks, recreation, leisure, and fitness studies; psychology; public administration and social service professions; social sciences; visual and performing arts. **Areas of required coursework:** arts/fine arts, humanities, mathematics, English (including composition), foreign languages, sciences (biological or physical), history, social science, other. **Pre-professional programs:** pre-law, pre-dentistry, pre-medicine. **Special academic programs (% participation):** cooperative (work-study plan) program (10%), double major (3%), English as a Second Language (ESL) (16%), honors program (1%), internships (30%), student-designed major (3%), study abroad (1%), teacher certificate program (3%). **Teacher certification offered in:** special education, elementary, secondary. **Cooperative education programs:** business, computer science, education, social/behavioral science, technologies. **Reserve Officers Training Corps (ROTC):** Army ROTC: Offered at cooperating institution (University of Hawaii-Manoa); Air Force ROTC: Offered at cooperating institution (University of Hawaii-Manoa). **Faculty and instruction (2005-2006):** Total instructional faculty: 117 full-time, 116 part-time (64% men; 36% women; 33% minorities). Full-time faculty with Ph.D. or other terminal degree: 80%. Student/faculty ratio: 15/1. Classes of fewer than 20 students: 54%; of 20 to 49 students: 42%; of 50 or more students: 4%. **Advanced Placement and International Baccalaureate credit:** AP tests may be used for: Credit only. Scores accepted: 3, 4, 5. International Baccalaureate exams may be used for: Credit only. **Freshmen returning for sophomore year:** 73%. **Graduation rates:** Four-year: 23%; five-year: 32%; six-year: 39%. **Graduate study:** 13% of students pursue further study immediately upon graduation.

COSTS AND FINANCIAL AID

Financial aid office: (808) 293-3530. **Expenses (2006-2007):** Tuition and fees 2006-2007: $3,040; room/board: $5,170. **Financial aid:** Priority filing date for institution's financial aid form: March 1; deadline: March 31. In 2005-2006, 85% of undergraduates applied for financial aid. Of those, 76% were determined to have financial need; 71% had their need fully met. Average financial aid package (proportion receiving): $7,900 (71%). Average amount of gift aid, such as scholarships or grants (proportion receiving): $4,000 (67%). Average amount of self-help aid, such as work study or loans (proportion receiving): $4,500 (54%). Average need-based loan (excluding PLUS or other private loans): $2,000. Among students who received need-based aid, the average percentage of need met: 80%. Among students who received aid based on merit, the average award (and the proportion receiving): $1,400 (5%). The average athletic scholarship (and the proportion receiving): $4,400 (3%). Average amount of debt of borrowers graduating in 2005: $9,794. Proportion who borrowed: 25%.

CAMPUS LIFE AND EXTRACURRICULAR ACTIVITIES

Campus housing available (% using): women's dorms (48%), men's dorms (34%), apartments for married students (18%). Students who live in college-owned, operated, or affiliated housing: 65%. **Student employment:** During the 2005-2006 academic year, 65% of undergraduates worked on campus. Average per-year earnings: $7,834. **Clubs and organizations:** Number of student organizations: 52. Activities include: choral groups, concert band, dance, drama/theater, jazz band, literary magazine, music ensembles, pep band, student government, student newspaper, student film society, yearbook. Number of fraternities: 0; sororities: 0. Average proportion of students who stay on campus on weekends: 95%. **Sports program (2005-2006):** Member of NCAA II. *Men's intercollegiate varsity sports:* basketball, cross-country, golf, tennis, water polo. *Women's intercollegiate varsity sports:* cross-country, golf, softball, tennis, volleyball.

SERVICES AND FACILITIES

Basic services: nonremedial tutoring, placement service, health service, health insurance. **Remedial assistance:** reading, math, writing, study skills. **Counseling services:** minority student, career, personal, academic, older student, psychological, religious, other. **For learning-disabled students:** School does not offer a structured program with separate admission and additional fees. Total undergraduates in learning-disabled program or receiving services: 58. Services include: remedial math, reading machines, tape recorders, videotaped classes, diagnostic testing service, untimed tests, note-taking services, oral tests, learning center, readers, extended time for tests, tutors, priority registration, other. **Library:** Number of titles: 208,474; number of current serial subscriptions: 17,000. **Information technology resources:**

Students are not required to lease or own a computer. Number of campus computers available to all students: 571. School has a wireless network. Approximate number of users that can be accommodated: 2,000. Proportion of college-owned housing units wired for high-speed internet access: 95%. **Campus safety:** Security services offered: 24-hour foot and vehicle patrols, late-night transport/escort service, 24-hour emergency telephones, lighted pathways/sidewalks, student patrols, controlled dormitory access (key, security card, etc.).

TRANSFER AND INTERNATIONAL STUDENTS

Transfer students: May apply for admission for the following academic terms: Fall, Winter, Spring, Summer. Applicants need a minimum number of credits to apply. For fall 2005: Transfer applications received: 670. Transfer applicants offered admission: 173. Transfer applicants enrolled: 144. **International students:** Number of foreign undergraduates: 1120 (47% of student body). Number of countries represented: 69. Minimum TOEFL score required: 475 (paper); 153 (computer). Average TOEFL score: 488 (paper).

Chaminade University of Honolulu

- **Address:** 3140 Waialae Avenue, Honolulu, HI 96816-1578
- **Website:** http://www.chaminade.edu
- **Private; Religious affiliation:** Roman Catholic
- **Enrollment:** 1,058 full-time; 48 part-time

KEY STATS

✔ **U.S News College Ranking:** third tier, Universities–Master's (West)
✔ **SAT Score (25th/75th percentile):** 840-1060
✔ **Tuition:** 2006-2007: $14,960

Selectivity: Less selective	**Room/board:** $9,210
Acceptance rate: 96%	**Average debt:** $22,263
Student/faculty ratio: N/A	**Proportion who borrowed:** 56%

UNDERGRADUATE STUDENT BODY STATS

2005-2006 enrollment: 1,058 full-time; 48 part-time. Men: 31%; women: 69%. **Ethnic makeup:** African American: 4%; American-Indian: 1%; Asian American: 64%; Hispanic: 7%; White: 23%; International: 2%. **Religious preference:** Roman Catholic: 41%; Protestant: 32%; Buddhist: 1%; No preference: 25%; Other: 1%.

ADMISSIONS FACTS AND FIGURES

Phone: (808) 735-4735. **Email:** admissions@chaminade.edu. **Website:** http://www.chaminade.edu. **Application deadlines for fall 2007:** Regular decision: Rolling. Early decision: Not offered. Early action: Not offered. Admission can be deferred. **Application fee:** $50. Common application is accepted. **Admissions requirements/recommendations:** High school units required (recommended): English: 4 (4); Mathematics: 3 (3); Science: 2 (2); Social studies: 3 (3). Tests: The college uses SAT or ACT scores in admissions decisions. Either SAT or ACT required. For admission to the fall 2007 entering class, the school will accept: ACT with writing, ACT without writing. Campus visit: Recommended. Admissions interview: Recommended. Off-campus interview: May be arranged. **Factors that count in admissions decisions:** *Academic:* Secondary school record: Very important. Class rank: Not considered. Letters of recommendation: Considered. Standardized test scores: Very important. Essay: Important. *Nonacademic:* Interview: Important. Extracurricular activities: Important. Talent/ability: Important. Character/personal qualities: Important. Alumni/ae relationship: Not considered. Geographical residence: Not considered. State residency: Not considered. Religious affiliation/commitment: Not considered. Minority status: Not considered. Volunteer work: Important. Work experience: Considered. **Admissions statistics for the fall 2005 entering class:** Total applicants: 904. Total accepted: 870. Freshmen enrolled: 266; 57% were from out of state. Overall acceptance rate: 96%. **Credentials of fall 2005 freshmen:** 11% ranked in the top 10 percent of their high school class; 35% were in the top 25 percent, and 62% were in the top half. (Proportion submitting class standing: 63%.) **Average high school grade point average:** 3.1. **First-year students who submitted SAT scores:** 83%. Scores (25/75 percentile): Verbal: 430-530, Math: 410-530, Combined: 840-1060. **First-year students submitting ACT scores:** 17%. Scores (25/75 percentile): English: 18-24, Math: 18-24, Composite: 18-23.

ACADEMICS

Year founded: 1955. **Academic calendar:** Semester. **Degrees offered:** associate, bachelor's, post-bachelor's certificate, master's. **Most popular majors:** Information not available. **Major fields of study:** biological and biomedical sciences; business, management, marketing, and related support services; communication, journalism, and related programs; computer and information sciences and support services; education; English language and literature/letters; history; multi/interdisciplinary studies; philosophy and religious studies; psychology; security and protective services; social sciences; visual and performing arts. **Areas of required coursework:** arts/fine arts, humanities, mathematics, English (including composition), philosophy, foreign languages, sciences (biological or physical), history, social science, other. **Pre-professional programs:** pre-medicine. **Special academic programs:** distance learning, double major, exchange student program (domestic), internships, student-designed major, teacher certificate program. **Teacher certification offered in:** early childhood, special education, elementary, middle/junior high, secondary. **Cooperative education programs:** education, social/behavioral science. **Reserve Officers Training Corps (ROTC):** Army ROTC: Offered at cooperating institution (University of Hawaii at Manoa); Air Force ROTC: Offered at cooperating institution (University of Hawaii at Manoa). **Faculty and instruction (2005-2006):** Total instructional faculty: N/A. Classes of fewer than 20 students: 63%; of 20 to 49 students: 37%. **Advanced Placement and International Baccalaureate credit:** AP tests may be used for: Credit only. Scores accepted: 3, 4, 5. International Baccalaureate exams may be used for: Credit only. **Freshmen returning for sophomore year:** 65%. **Graduation rates:** Four-year: 20%; five-year: 37%; six-year: 39%.

COSTS AND FINANCIAL AID

Financial aid office: (808) 735-4780. **Expenses (2006-2007):** Tuition and fees 2006-2007: $14,960; room/board: $9,210. Estimated books and supplies: $1,200; transportation: $864; personal expenses: $1,254. **Financial aid:** Priority filing date for institution's financial aid form: March 1. In 2005-2006, 76% of undergraduates applied for financial aid. Of those, 66% were determined to have financial need; 16% had their need fully met. Average financial aid package (proportion receiving): $12,642 (66%). Average amount of gift aid, such as scholarships or grants (proportion receiving): $8,312 (66%). Average amount of self-help aid, such as work study or loans (proportion receiving): $5,362 (57%). Average need-based loan (excluding PLUS or other private loans): $4,128. Among students who received need-based aid, the average percentage of need met: 65%. Among students who received aid based on merit, the average award (and the proportion receiving): $4,840 (23%). The average athletic scholarship (and the proportion receiving): $7,560 (1%). Average amount of debt of borrowers graduating in 2005: $22,263. Proportion who borrowed: 56%.

CAMPUS LIFE AND EXTRACURRICULAR ACTIVITIES

Campus housing available: coed dorms, women's dorms. Students who live in college-owned, operated, or affiliated housing: 32%. **Student employment:** During the 2005-2006 academic year, 5% of undergraduates worked on campus. Average per-year earnings: $2,000. **Clubs and organizations:** Number of student organizations: 38. Activities include: choral groups, drama/theater, literary magazine, musical theater, student government, student newspaper, yearbook. Number of fraternities: 0; sororities: 0. **Sports program (2005-2006):** Member of NCAA II. *Men's intercollegiate varsity sports:* basketball, cross-country, golf, tennis, water polo. *Women's intercollegiate varsity sports:* cross-country, golf, softball, tennis, volleyball, water polo.

SERVICES AND FACILITIES

Basic services: nonremedial tutoring, placement service, health insurance. **Remedial assistance:** reading, math, writing, study skills. **Counseling services:** career, personal, veteran student, academic, psychological, religious, other. **For learning-disabled students:** School does not offer a structured program with separate admission and additional fees. **Library:** Number of titles: 68,256; number of current serial subscriptions: 273. **Information technology resources:** Students are not required to lease or own a computer. Number of campus computers available to all students: 90. School has a wireless network. Approximate number of users that can be accommodated: 3,000. Proportion of college-owned housing units wired for high-speed internet access: 100%. **Campus safety:** Security services offered: 24-hour foot and vehicle patrols, late-night transport/escort service, 24-hour emergency telephones, lighted pathways/sidewalks, controlled dormitory access (key, security card, etc.).

TRANSFER AND INTERNATIONAL STUDENTS

Transfer students: May apply for admission for the following academic terms: Fall, Spring. Applicants need a minimum number of credits to apply. For fall 2005: Transfer applications received: 212. Transfer applicants offered admission: 211. Transfer applicants enrolled: 102. **International students:** Number of foreign undergraduates: 20 (2% of student body). Number of countries represented: 9. Minimum TOEFL score required: 450 (paper); 133 (computer).

Hawaii Pacific University

- **Address:** 1164 Bishop Street, Honolulu, HI 96813
- **Website:** http://www.hpu.edu
- **Private**
- **Enrollment:** 4,240 full-time; 2,671 part-time

KEY STATS

✔ **U.S News College Ranking:** third tier, Universities–Master's (West)
✔ **SAT Score (25th/75th percentile):** 860-1130
✔ **Tuition:** 2006-2007: $12,312

Selectivity: Selective	**Room/board:** $9,340
Acceptance rate: 82%	**Average debt:** $17,125
Student/faculty ratio: 17/1	**Proportion who borrowed:** 36%

UNDERGRADUATE STUDENT BODY STATS

2005-2006 enrollment: 4,240 full-time; 2,671 part-time. Men: 41%; women: 59%. **Ethnic makeup:** African American: 7%; American-Indian: 1%; Asian American: 35%; Hispanic: 7%; White: 39%; International: 11%.

ADMISSIONS FACTS AND FIGURES

Phone: (808) 544-0238. **Email:** admissions@hpu.edu. **Website:** http://www.hpu.edu. **Application deadlines for fall 2007:** Regular decision: August 15. Early decision: Not offered. Early action: Not offered. Admission can be deferred. **Application fee:** $50. Common application is accepted. **To apply online, go to:** http://web1.hpu.edu/index.cfm?section=admissions. **Admissions requirements/recommendations:** High school units required (recommended): English: (4); Mathematics: (3); Science: (2); Foreign language: (1); Social studies: (2); History: (2); Total units: (14). Tests: The college uses SAT or ACT scores in admissions decisions. Either SAT or ACT required. For admission to the fall 2007 entering class, the school will accept: ACT with writing, ACT without writing. Campus visit: Recommended. Admissions interview: Recommended. Off-campus interview: May be arranged. **Factors that count in admissions decisions:** *Academic:* Secondary school record: Very important. Class rank: Not considered. Letters of recommendation: Considered. Standardized test scores: Very important. Essay: Considered. *Nonacademic:* Interview: Important. Extracurricular activities: Important. Talent/ability: Very important. Character/personal qualities: Considered. Alumni/ae relationship: Not considered. Geographical residence: Not considered. State residency: Not considered. Religious affiliation/commitment: Not considered. Minority status: Not considered. Volunteer work: Considered. Work experience: Considered. **Other schools with the greatest overlap in applicants:** Boston University; New York University; University of Hawaii–Manoa; University of Southern California; University of Washington. **Admissions statistics for the fall 2005 entering class:** Total applicants: 3,094. Total accepted: 2,541. Freshmen enrolled: 657; 60% were from out of state. Overall acceptance rate: 82%. **Credentials of fall 2005 freshmen:** 22% ranked in the top 10 percent of their high school class; 50% were in the top 25 percent, and 79% were in the top half. (Proportion submitting class standing: 66%.) **Average high school grade point average:** 3.3. **First-year students who submitted SAT scores:** 79%. Scores (25/75 percentile): Verbal: 420-560, Math: 440-570, Combined: 860-1130. **First-year students submitting ACT scores:** 31%. Scores (25/75 percentile): English: 17-24, Math: 17-24, Composite: 17-24.

ACADEMICS

Year founded: 1965. **Academic calendar:** Semester. **Degrees offered:** certificate, associate, bachelor's, post-bachelor's certificate, master's, post-master's certificate. **Most popular majors:** 44% business, management, marketing, and related support services, 14% health professions and related clinical sciences, 9% computer and information sciences and support services, 9% security and protective services, 6% legal professions and studies. **Major fields of study:** area, ethnic, cultural, and gender studies; biological and bio-

medical sciences; business, management, marketing, and related support services; communication, journalism, and related programs; computer and information sciences and support services; education; English language and literature/letters; health professions and related clinical sciences; liberal arts and sciences studies, and humanities; mathematics and statistics; multi/interdisciplinary studies; natural resources and conservation; physical sciences; psychology; public administration and social service professions; security and protective services; social sciences. **Areas of required coursework:** humanities, computer literacy, mathematics, English (including composition), sciences (biological or physical), history, social science, other. **Pre-professional programs:** pre-law, pre-medicine. **Special academic programs (% participation):** accelerated program (30%), cooperative (work-study plan) program (6%), distance learning (25%), double major (2%), English as a Second Language (ESL) (3%), honors program (8%), internships (25%), student-designed major (.1%), study abroad (1%). **Teacher certification offered in:** secondary. **Cooperative education programs:** business, computer science, education, health professions, humanities, natural science, social/behavioral science. **Reserve Officers Training Corps (ROTC):** Army ROTC: Offered at cooperating institution (University of Hawaii); Air Force ROTC: Offered at cooperating institution (University of Hawaii, Manoa). **Faculty and instruction (2005-2006):** Total instructional faculty: 238 full-time, 374 part-time (54% men; 46% women; 31% minorities). Full-time faculty with Ph.D. or other terminal degree: 65%. Student/faculty ratio: 17/1. Classes of fewer than 20 students: 47%; of 20 to 49 students: 53%. **Advanced Placement and International Baccalaureate credit:** AP tests may be used for: Credit and/or placement. Scores accepted: 2, 3, 4. International Baccalaureate exams may be used for: Credit and/or placement. **Freshmen returning for sophomore year:** 67%. **Graduation rates:** Four-year: 23%; five-year: 32%; six-year: 38%. **Graduate study:** 46% of students pursue further study immediately upon graduation; 75% within one year; 88% within five years. Fields in which graduates pursue further study: Master of Business Administration (MBA), 40%; law, 5%; medicine, 2%; education, 12%; arts and sciences, 25%.

COSTS AND FINANCIAL AID

Financial aid office: (808) 544-0253. **Expenses (2006-2007):** Tuition and fees 2006-2007: $12,312; room/board: $9,340. Estimated books and supplies: $1,040; transportation: $440; personal expenses: $950. **Financial aid:** Priority filing date for institution's financial aid form: March 1. In 2005-2006, 66% of undergraduates applied for financial aid. Of those, 37% were determined to have financial need; 20% had their need fully met. Average financial aid package (proportion receiving): $10,465 (36%). Average amount of gift aid, such as scholarships or grants (proportion receiving): $3,915 (19%). Average amount of self-help aid, such as work study or loans (proportion receiving): $4,613 (35%). Average need-based loan (excluding PLUS or other private loans): $4,145. Among students who received need-based aid, the average percentage of need met: 71%. Among students who received aid based on merit, the average award (and the proportion receiving): $6,543 (24%). The average athletic scholarship (and the proportion receiving): $6,411 (4%). Average amount of debt of borrowers graduating in 2005: $17,125. Proportion who borrowed: 36%.

CAMPUS LIFE AND EXTRACURRICULAR ACTIVITIES

Campus housing available: coed dorms, women's dorms, apartment for single students. Students who live in college-owned, operated, or affiliated housing: 4%. **Student employment:** During the 2005-2006 academic year, 5% of undergraduates worked on campus. Average per-year earnings: $4,200. **Clubs and organizations:** Number of student organizations: 97. Activities include: choral groups, drama/theater, literary magazine, music ensembles, musical theater, pep band, student government, student newspaper. Number of fraternities: 0; sororities: 0. Average proportion of students who stay on campus on weekends: 25%. **Sports program (2005-2006):** Member of NCAA II. *Men's intercollegiate varsity sports:* baseball, basketball, cross-country, tennis. *Women's intercollegiate varsity sports:* cross-country, softball, tennis, volleyball.

SERVICES AND FACILITIES

Basic services: nonremedial tutoring, placement service, health insurance. **Remedial assistance:** reading, math, writing, study skills. **Counseling services:** career, military, personal, veteran student, academic, older student, religious. **For learning-disabled students:** School does not offer a structured program with separate admission and additional fees. Total undergraduates in learning-disabled program or receiving services: 59. Services include: remedial math, remedial English, remedial reading, tape recorders, untimed tests, oral tests, learning center, readers, extended time for tests, tutors, early syllabus, priority registration, priority seating, texts on tape, other testing accomodations. **Library:** Number of titles: 108,000; number of current serial subscriptions: 284,000. **Information technology resources:** Students are not required to lease or own a computer. Number of campus computers available to all students: 650. School has a wireless network. Approximate number of users that can be accommodated: 400. Proportion of college-owned housing units wired for high-speed internet access: 100%. **Campus safety:** Security services offered: 24-hour foot and vehicle patrols, lighted pathways/sidewalks, controlled dormitory access (key, security card, etc).

TRANSFER AND INTERNATIONAL STUDENTS
Transfer students: May apply for admission for the following academic terms: Fall, Winter, Spring, Summer. Applicants need a minimum number of credits to apply. For fall 2005: Transfer applications received: 2,302. Transfer applicants offered admission: 2,015. Transfer applicants enrolled: 934. **International students:** Number of foreign undergraduates: 690 (11% of student body). Number of countries represented: 92. Minimum TOEFL score required: 550 (paper); 213 (computer). Average TOEFL score: 569 (paper).

University of Hawaii–Hilo

- **Address:** 200 W. Kawili Street, Hilo, HI 96720-4091
- **Website:** http://www.uhh.hawaii.edu
- **Public**
- **Enrollment:** 2,628 full-time; 606 part-time

KEY STATS
✔ **U.S News College Ranking:** fourth tier, Liberal Arts Colleges
✔ **SAT Score (25th/75th percentile):** 880-1190
✔ **Tuition:** 2005-2006: $2,610 in state, $8,178 out of state

Selectivity: Selective	**Room/board:** $5,472
Acceptance rate: 59%	**Average debt:** N/A
Student/faculty ratio: N/A	**Proportion who borrowed:** N/A

UNDERGRADUATE STUDENT BODY STATS
2005-2006 enrollment: 2,628 full-time; 606 part-time. Men: 41%; women: 59%. **Ethnic makeup:** African American: 1%; American-Indian: 1%; Asian American: 39%; Hispanic: 3%; White: 48%; International: 8%.

ADMISSIONS FACTS AND FIGURES
Phone: (800) 897-4456. **Email:** uhhadm@hawaii.edu. **Website:** http://www.uhh.hawaii.edu. **Application deadlines for fall 2007:** Regular decision: July 1; decision sent by July 15. Early decision: Not offered. Early action: Not offered. Admission can be deferred. **Application fee:** $40. Common application is not accepted. **To apply online, go to:** http://www.uhh.hawaii.edu/studentaffairs/admissions/. **Admissions requirements/recommendations:** High school units required (recommended): English: 4 (4); Mathematics: 3 (4); Science: 3 (4); Foreign language: 0 (2); Social studies: 2 (2); History: 2 (2); Academic electives: 3 (1); Total units: 17 (19). Tests: The college uses SAT or ACT scores in admissions decisions. Either SAT or ACT required. For admission to the fall 2007 entering class, the school will accept: ACT with writing, ACT without writing. Campus visit: Recommended. Admissions interview: Neither required nor recommended. Off-campus interview: Not available. **Factors that count in admissions decisions:** *Academic:* Secondary school record: Very important. Class rank: Important. Letters of recommendation: Considered. Standardized test scores: Important. Essay: Considered. *Nonacademic:* Interview: Not considered. Extracurricular activities: Not considered. Talent/ability: Not considered. Character/personal qualities: Not considered. Alumni/ae relationship: Not considered. Geographical residence: Considered. State residency: Considered. Religious affiliation/commitment: Not considered. Minority status: Not considered. Volunteer work: Not considered. Work experience: Not considered. **Admissions statistics for the fall 2005 entering class:** Total applicants: 1,480. Total accepted: 866. Freshmen enrolled: 439; 28% were from out of state. Overall acceptance rate: 59%. **Credentials of fall 2005 freshmen:** 17% ranked in the top 10 percent of their high school class; 46% were in the top 25 percent, and 83% were in the top half. (Proportion submitting class standing: 67%.) **Average high school grade point average:** 3.3. **First-year students who submitted SAT scores:** 74%. Scores (25/75 percentile): Verbal: 440-590, Math: 440-600, Combined: 880-1190. **First-year students submitting ACT scores:** 4%. Scores (25/75 percentile): English: 16-24, Math: 16-24, Composite: 17-24.

ACADEMICS
Year founded: 1970. **Academic calendar:** Semester. **Degrees offered:** certificate, bachelor's, post-bachelor's certificate, master's. **Most popular majors:** 16% psychology, 8% business, management, marketing, and related support services, 7% communication, journalism, and related programs, 6% social sciences, 5% aquaculture. **Major fields of study:** agriculture, agriculture operations, and related sciences; area, ethnic, cultural, and gender studies; biological and biomedical sciences; business, management, marketing, and related support services; communication, journalism, and related programs; computer and information sciences and support services; education; English language and literature/letters; foreign languages, literatures, and linguistics; health professions and related clinical sciences; history; mathematics and statistics; parks, recreation, leisure, and fitness studies; philosophy and religious studies; physical sciences; psychology; social sciences; visual and performing arts. **Areas of required coursework:** humanities, mathematics, English (including composition), sciences (biological or physical), social science, other. **Pre-professional programs:** pre-law, pre-medicine, pre-veterinary science, pre-pharmacy. **Special academic programs:** cross-registration, distance learning, double major, English as a Second Language (ESL), exchange student program (domestic), honors program, independent study, internships, study abroad, teacher certificate program. **Teacher certification offered in:** elementary, secondary. **Advanced Placement and International Baccalaureate credit:** AP tests may be used for: Credit and/or placement. Scores accepted: 3, 4, 5. International Baccalaureate exams may be used for: Credit and/or placement. **Freshmen returning for sophomore year:** 66%. **Graduation rates:** Four-year: 11%; five-year: 27%; six-year: 31%. **Graduate study:** Fields in which graduates pursue further study: Master of Business Administration (MBA), 1%; law, 1%; medicine, 4%; dentistry, 4%.

COSTS AND FINANCIAL AID
Financial aid office: (808) 974-7323. **Expenses (2005-2006):** Tuition and fees 2005-2006: $2,610 in state, $8,178 out of state; room/board: $5,472. Estimated books and supplies: $1,048; transportation: $360; personal expenses: $1,318. **Financial aid:** Priority filing date for institution's financial aid form: March 1.

CAMPUS LIFE AND EXTRACURRICULAR ACTIVITIES
Campus housing available (% using): coed dorms (47%), apartments for married students (2%), apartment for single students (51%). **Student employment:** During the 2005-2006 academic year, 23% of undergraduates worked on campus. Average per-year earnings: $1,832. **Clubs and organizations:** Number of student organizations: 40. Activities include: choral groups, dance, drama/theater, jazz band, literary magazine, music ensembles, pep band, radio station, student government, student newspaper. Number of fraternities: 0; sororities: 0. Average proportion of students who stay on campus on weekends: 18%. **Sports program (2005-2006):** Member of NCAA II. *Men's intercollegiate varsity sports:* baseball, basketball, cross-country, golf, tennis. *Women's intercollegiate varsity sports:* cross-country, golf, softball, tennis, volleyball.

SERVICES AND FACILITIES
Basic services: nonremedial tutoring, women's center, placement service, health service, health insurance. **Remedial assistance:** reading, math, writing, study skills. **Counseling services:** minority student, career, personal, academic, older student. **For learning-disabled students:** Services include: remedial math, remedial English, reading machines, remedial reading, tape recorders, other special classes, videotaped classes, note-taking services, oral tests, learning center, readers, extended time for tests, tutors, other. **Information technology resources:** Students are not required to lease or own a computer. Number of campus computers available to all students: 600. School has a wireless network. Proportion of college-owned housing units wired for high-speed internet access: 25%. **Campus safety:** Security services offered: 24-hour foot and vehicle patrols, late-night transport/escort service, 24-hour emergency telephones, lighted pathways/sidewalks, controlled dormitory access (key, security card, etc).

TRANSFER AND INTERNATIONAL STUDENTS
Transfer students: May apply for admission for the following academic terms: Fall, Spring. Applicants need a minimum number of credits to apply. For fall 2005: Transfer applications received: 998. Transfer applicants offered admission: 867. Transfer applicants enrolled: 633. **International students:** Number of foreign undergraduates: 250 (8% of student body). Minimum TOEFL score required: 500 (paper); 173 (computer).

University of Hawaii–Manoa

- **Address:** 2500 Campus Road, Honolulu, HI 96822
- **Website:** http://www.manoa.hawaii.edu/
- **Public**
- **Enrollment:** 11,857 full-time; 2,495 part-time

KEY STATS
- ✔ **U.S News College Ranking:** third tier, National Universities
- ✔ **SAT Score (25th/75th percentile):** 1000-1200
- ✔ **Tuition:** 2006-2007: $4,522 in state, $12,394 out of state

Selectivity: Selective	**Room/board:** $7,185
Acceptance rate: 68%	**Average debt:** $12,579
Student/faculty ratio: 12/1	**Proportion who borrowed:** 33%

UNDERGRADUATE STUDENT BODY STATS
2005-2006 enrollment: 11,857 full-time; 2,495 part-time. Men: 44%; women: 56%. **Ethnic makeup:** African American: 1%; Asian American: 65%; Hispanic: 2%; White: 28%; International: 3%.

ADMISSIONS FACTS AND FIGURES
Phone: (808) 956-8975. **Email:** ar-info@hawaii.edu. **Website:** http://www.manoa.hawaii.edu/. **Application deadlines for fall 2007:** Regular decision: May 1. Early decision: Not offered. Early action: Not offered. Admission cannot be deferred. **Application fee:** $50. Common application is not accepted. **To apply online, go to:** http://www.hawaii.edu/admrec/. **Admissions requirements/recommendations:** High school units required (recommended): English: 4; Mathematics: 3; Science: 3; Foreign language: (2); Social studies: 3; Academic electives: 4; Total units: 22. Tests: The college uses SAT or ACT scores in admissions decisions. Either SAT or ACT required. For admission to the fall 2007 entering class, the school will accept: ACT with writing. Campus visit: Neither required nor recommended. Admissions interview: Neither required nor recommended. Off-campus interview: Not available. **Factors that count in admissions decisions:** *Academic:* Secondary school record: Very important. Class rank: Considered. Letters of recommendation: Considered. Standardized test scores: Very important. Essay: Considered. *Nonacademic:* Interview: Considered. Extracurricular activities: Considered. Talent/ability: Considered. Character/personal qualities: Not considered. Alumni/ae relationship: Not considered. Geographical residence: Considered. State residency: Important. Religious affiliation/commitment: Not considered. Minority status: Not considered. Volunteer work: Not considered. Work experience: Not considered. **Other schools with the greatest overlap in applicants:** Colorado State University; Hawaii Pacific University; University of Colorado–Boulder; University of Hawaii–Hilo; University of Washington. **Admissions statistics for the fall 2005 entering class:** Total applicants: 6,896. Total accepted: 4,679. Freshmen enrolled: 2,022; 25% were from out of state. Overall acceptance rate: 68%. **Credentials of fall 2005 freshmen:** 25% ranked in the top 10 percent of their high school class; 61% were in the top 25 percent, and 91% were in the top half. (Proportion submitting class standing: 68%.) **Average high school grade point average:** 3.4. **First-year students who submitted SAT scores:** 88%. Scores (25/75 percentile): Verbal: 480-580, Math: 520-620, Combined: 1000-1200. **First-year students submitting ACT scores:** 15%. Scores (25/75 percentile): English: 20-25, Math: 21-26, Composite: 21-25.

ACADEMICS
Year founded: 1907. **Academic calendar:** Semester. **Degrees offered:** certificate, bachelor's, post-bachelor's certificate, master's, first professional, doctorate. **Most popular majors:** 7% psychology, 5% marketing, 4% finance and financial management services, 4% liberal arts and sciences studies, and humanities, 4% sociology. **Major fields of study:** agriculture, agriculture operations, and related sciences; area, ethnic, cultural, and gender studies; biological and biomedical sciences; business, management, marketing, and related support services; communication, journalism, and related programs; computer and information sciences and support services; education; engineering; English language and literature/letters; family and consumer sciences/human sciences; foreign languages, literatures, and linguistics; health professions and related clinical sciences; history; liberal arts and sciences studies, and humanities; mathematics and statistics; multi/interdisciplinary studies; natural resources and conservation; parks, recreation, leisure, and fitness studies; philosophy and religious studies; physical sciences; psychology; public administration and social service professions; social sciences; visual and performing arts. **Areas of required coursework:**

arts/fine arts, humanities, English (including composition), foreign languages, sciences (biological or physical), social science, other. **Pre-professional programs:** pre-law, pre-dentistry, pre-medicine, pre-veterinary science, pre-optometry, pre-pharmacy. **Special academic programs (% participation):** accelerated program, cooperative (work-study plan) program, distance learning, double major (6%), English as a Second Language (ESL), exchange student program (domestic), honors program, independent study, internships, student-designed major (4.4%), study abroad, teacher certificate program (10%). **Teacher certification offered in:** early childhood, special education, elementary, vo-tech, secondary. **Cooperative education programs:** agriculture, art, business, computer science, education, engineering, health professions, humanities, natural science, social/behavioral science, technologies, other. **Reserve Officers Training Corps (ROTC):** Army ROTC: Offered on campus; Air Force ROTC: Offered on campus. **Faculty and instruction (2005-2006):** Total instructional faculty: 1,086 full-time, 83 part-time (61% men; 39% women; 32% minorities). Full-time faculty with Ph.D. or other terminal degree: 80%. Student/faculty ratio: 12/1. Classes of fewer than 20 students: 46%; of 20 to 49 students: 45%; of 50 or more students: 9%. **Advanced Placement and International Baccalaureate credit:** AP tests may be used for: Credit and/or placement. Scores accepted: 4, 5. International Baccalaureate exams may be used for: Credit and/or placement. **Freshmen returning for sophomore year:** 77%. **Graduation rates:** Four-year: 12%; five-year: 43%; six-year: 51%. **Graduate study:** 53% of students pursue further study within five years. Fields in which graduates pursue further study: Master of Business Administration (MBA), 9%; law, 4%; medicine, 6%; engineering, 3%; education, 27%; arts and sciences, 22%.

COSTS AND FINANCIAL AID
Financial aid office: (808) 956-7251. **Expenses (2006-2007):** Tuition and fees 2006-2007: $4,522 in state, $12,394 out of state; room/board: $7,185. Estimated books and supplies: $1,145; transportation: $360; personal expenses: $1,244. **Financial aid:** Priority filing date for institution's financial aid form: March 1. In 2005-2006, 57% of undergraduates applied for financial aid. Of those, 35% were determined to have financial need; 23% had their need fully met. Average financial aid package (proportion receiving): $6,039 (32%). Average amount of gift aid, such as scholarships or grants (proportion receiving): $3,617 (24%). Average amount of self-help aid, such as work study or loans (proportion receiving): $4,096 (23%). Average need-based loan (excluding PLUS or other private loans): $3,664. Among students who received need-based aid, the average percentage of need met: 66%. Among students who received aid based on merit, the average award (and the proportion receiving): $2,393 (8%). The average athletic scholarship (and the proportion receiving): $11,897 (2%). Average amount of debt of borrowers graduating in 2005: $12,579. Proportion who borrowed: 33%.

CAMPUS LIFE AND EXTRACURRICULAR ACTIVITIES
Campus housing available (% using): coed dorms (56%), women's dorms (4%), apartments for married students (1%), apartment for single students (39%), special housing for disabled students. Students who live in college-owned, operated, or affiliated housing: 15%. **Student employment:** During the 2005-2006 academic year, 32% of undergraduates worked on campus. Average per-year earnings: $4,961. **Clubs and organizations:** Number of student organizations: 150. Activities include: choral groups, concert band, dance, drama/theater, jazz band, literary magazine, marching band, music ensembles, pep band, radio station, student government, student newspaper, symphony orchestra, television station, yearbook. Number of fraternities: 4; sororities: 2. Proportion of men in fraternities: 1%; of women in sororities: 1%. Average proportion of students who stay on campus on weekends: 70%. **Sports program (2005-2006):** Member of NCAA I. *Men's intercollegiate varsity sports:* baseball, basketball, cheerleading, football, golf, swimming and diving, tennis, volleyball, co-ed sailing. *Women's intercollegiate varsity sports:* basketball, cheerleading, cross-country, golf, sailing, soccer, softball, swimming and diving, tennis, track and field (indoor), track and field (outdoor), volleyball, water polo, coed sailing.

SERVICES AND FACILITIES
Basic services: nonremedial tutoring, women's center, placement service, day care, health service, health insurance, other. **Remedial assistance:** study skills. **Counseling services:** career, military, personal, academic, psychological, birth control. **For learning-disabled students:** School does not offer a structured program with separate admission and additional fees. Total undergraduates in learning-disabled program or receiving services: 300. Services include: reading machines, tape recorders, note-taking services, readers, extended time for tests, tutors, priority registration, texts on tape, typist/scribe, exams on tape or computer. **Library:** Number of titles: 3,356,031; number of current serial subscriptions: 26,605. **Information tech-**

nology resources: Students are not required to lease or own a computer. Number of campus computers available to all students: 200. School has a wireless network. Approximate number of users that can be accommodated: 2,000. Proportion of college-owned housing units wired for high-speed internet access: 100%. **Campus safety:** Security services offered: 24-hour foot and vehicle patrols, late-night transport/escort service, 24-hour emergency telephones, lighted pathways/sidewalks, student patrols, controlled dormitory access (key, security card, etc).

TRANSFER AND INTERNATIONAL STUDENTS

Transfer students: May apply for admission for the following academic terms: Fall, Spring. Applicants need a minimum number of credits to apply. For fall 2005: Transfer applications received: 5,518. Transfer applicants offered admission: 3,644. Transfer applicants enrolled: 2,310. **International students:** Number of foreign undergraduates: 406 (3% of student body). Number of countries represented: 97. Minimum TOEFL score required: 500 (paper); 173 (computer).

Idaho

Albertson College

- **Address:** 2112 Cleveland Boulevard, Caldwell, ID 83605
- **Website:** http://www.albertson.edu
- **Private; Religious affiliation:** APCU
- **Enrollment:** 761 full-time; 39 part-time

KEY STATS
- ✔ **U.S News College Ranking:** fourth tier, Liberal Arts Colleges
- ✔ **ACT Score (25th/75th percentile):** 23-28
- ✔ **Tuition:** 2006-2007: $16,425

Selectivity: More selective	**Room/board:** $5,926
Acceptance rate: 84%	**Average debt:** $25,343
Student/faculty ratio: 9/1	**Proportion who borrowed:** 94%

UNDERGRADUATE STUDENT BODY STATS
2005-2006 enrollment: 761 full-time; 39 part-time. Men: 42%; women: 58%. **Ethnic makeup:** African American: 1%; American-Indian: 1%; Asian American: 3%; Hispanic: 5%; White: 89%; International: 2%.

ADMISSIONS FACTS AND FIGURES
Phone: (800) 224-3246. **Email:** admission@albertson.edu. **Website:** http://www.albertson.edu. **Application deadlines for fall 2007:** Regular decision: June 1. Early decision: Not offered. Early action: Send application by: July 15; Decision sent by: October 30. Admission can be deferred. **Application fee:** $50. Common application is accepted. **Admissions requirements/recommendations:** High school units required (recommended): English: 4 (4); Mathematics: 3 (4); Science: 2 (3); Foreign language: 0 (2); Social studies: 0 (2); History: 3 (3); Academic electives: 3 (3); Total units: 15 (21). Tests: The college uses SAT or ACT scores in admissions decisions. Either SAT or ACT required. For admission to the fall 2007 entering class, the school will accept: ACT with writing. Campus visit: Recommended. Admissions interview: Recommended. Off-campus interview: May be arranged. **Factors that count in admissions decisions:** *Academic:* Secondary school record: Very important. Class rank: Considered. Letters of recommendation: Very important. Standardized test scores: Very important. Essay: Important. *Nonacademic:* Interview: Important. Extracurricular activities: Important. Talent/ability: Important. Character/personal qualities: Important. Alumni/ae relationship: Considered. Geographical residence: Considered. State residency: Not considered. Religious affiliation/commitment: Not considered. Minority status: Considered. Volunteer work: Important. Work experience: Important. **Other schools with the greatest overlap in applicants:** Boise State University; Idaho State University; University of Idaho. **Admissions statistics for the fall 2005 entering class:** Total applicants: 923. Total accepted: 777. Freshmen enrolled: 196; 28% were from out of state. Overall acceptance rate: 84%. Non-early acceptance rate: 84%. **Credentials of fall 2005 freshmen:** 34% ranked in the top 10 percent of their high school class; 70% were in the top 25 percent, and 92% were in the top half. (Proportion submitting class standing: 80%.) **Average high school grade point average:** 3.6. **First-year students who submitted SAT scores:** 65%. Scores (25/75 percentile): Verbal: 520-643, Math: 530-640, Combined: 1050-1283. **First-year students submitting ACT scores:** 75%. Scores (25/75 percentile): English: 22-29, Math: 22-27, Composite: 23-28.

ACADEMICS
Year founded: 1891. **Academic calendar:** Other. **Degrees offered:** bachelor's, master's. **Most popular majors:** 21% business, management, marketing, and related support services, 13% history, 12% social sciences, 9% psychology, 8% biology/biological sciences. **Major fields of study:** biological and biomedical sciences; business, management, marketing, and related support services; education; engineering; English language and literature/letters; foreign languages, literatures, and linguistics; health professions and related clinical sciences; history; liberal arts and sciences studies, and humanities; mathematics and statistics; multi/interdisciplinary studies; natural resources and conservation; parks, recreation, leisure, and fitness studies; philosophy and religious studies; physical sciences; psychology; social sciences; visual and performing arts. **Areas of required coursework:** arts/fine arts, humanities, mathematics, English (including composition), philosophy, sciences (biological or physical), history, social science, other. **Pre-professional programs:** pre-law, pre-dentistry, pre-medicine, pre-theology, pre-veterinary science, pre-optometry, pre-pharmacy, other. **Special academic programs (% participation):** cross-registration, double major (17%), dual enrollment, English as a Second Language (ESL), exchange student program (domestic), honors program, independent study (100%), internships, liberal arts/career combination, student-designed major, study abroad, teacher certificate program. **Teacher certification offered in:** elementary, middle/junior high, secondary. **Cooperative education programs:** business, computer science, engineering, health professions, natural science. **Reserve Officers Training Corps (ROTC):** Army ROTC: Offered on campus. **Faculty and instruction (2005-2006):** Total instructional faculty: 66 full-time, 55 part-time (60% men; 40% women; 4% minorities). Full-time faculty with Ph.D. or other terminal degree: 83%. Student/faculty ratio: 9/1. Classes of fewer than 20 students: 78%; of 20 to 49 students: 21%; of 50 or more students: 2%. **Advanced Placement and International Baccalaureate credit:** AP tests may be used for: Credit and/or placement. Scores accepted: 3, 4, 5. International Baccalaureate exams may be used for: Credit and/or placement. **Freshmen returning for sophomore year:** 77%. **Graduation rates:** Four-year: 48%; five-year: 55%; six-year: 55%.

COSTS AND FINANCIAL AID
Financial aid office: (208) 459-5308. **Expenses (2006-2007):** Tuition and fees 2006-2007: $16,425; room/board: $5,926. Estimated books and supplies: $900; transportation: $550; personal expenses: $700. **Financial aid:** Priority filing date for institution's financial aid form: February 15. In 2005-2006, 69% of undergraduates applied for financial aid. Of those, 64% were determined to have financial need; 15% had their need fully met. Average financial aid package (proportion receiving): $13,993 (64%). Average amount of gift aid, such as scholarships or grants (proportion receiving): $4,060 (39%). Average amount of self-help aid, such as work study or loans (proportion receiving): $4,449 (53%). Average need-based loan (excluding PLUS or other private loans): $4,444. Among students who received need-based aid, the average percentage of need met: 83%. Among students who received aid based on merit, the average award (and the proportion receiving): $7,791 (32%). The average athletic scholarship (and the proportion receiving): $4,725 (23%). Average amount of debt of borrowers graduating in 2005: $25,343. Proportion who borrowed: 94%.

CAMPUS LIFE AND EXTRACURRICULAR ACTIVITIES
Campus housing available (% using): coed dorms (78%), fraternity housing, apartment for single students (11%), special housing for disabled students, other housing options (11%). Students who live in college-owned, operated, or affiliated housing: 52%. **Student employment:** During the 2005-2006 academic year, 8% of undergraduates worked on campus. Average per-year earnings: $1,050. **Clubs and organizations:** Number of student organizations: 29. Activities include: choral groups, concert band, dance, drama/theater, jazz band, literary magazine, music ensembles, musical theater, opera, pep band, radio station, student government, student newspaper, student film society, symphony orchestra, yearbook. Number of fraternities: 3; sororities: 4. Proportion of men in fraternities: 12%; of women in sororities: 13%. Average proportion of students who stay on campus on weekends: 65%. **Sports program (2005-2006):** Member of NAIA. *Men's intercollegiate varsity sports:* baseball, basketball, cross-country, golf, skiing, soccer, swimming and diving, tennis, track and field (indoor), track and field (outdoor), ultimate frisbee. *Women's intercollegiate varsity sports:* basketball, cross-country, golf, skiing, soccer, softball, swimming and diving, tennis, track and field (indoor), track and field (outdoor), volleyball.

SERVICES AND FACILITIES
Basic services: nonremedial tutoring, placement service, health service, health insurance, other. **Remedial assistance:** reading, math, writing, study skills. **Counseling services:** minority student, career, military, personal, academic, older student, psychological, birth control, religious, other. **For learning-disabled students:** School does not offer a structured program with separate admission and additional fees. Total undergraduates in learn-

ing-disabled program or receiving services: 26. Services include: remedial math, tape recorders, diagnostic testing service, untimed tests, note-taking services, oral tests, learning center, readers, extended time for tests, tutors, early syllabus, priority seating, texts on tape, exams on tape or computer, other testing accomodations, other. **Library:** Number of titles: 198,201; number of current serial subscriptions: 1,142. **Information technology resources:** Students are not required to lease or own a computer. Number of campus computers available to all students: 240. School has a wireless network. Approximate number of users that can be accommodated: 40,000. Proportion of college-owned housing units wired for high-speed internet access: 100%. **Campus safety:** Security services offered: 24-hour foot and vehicle patrols, late-night transport/escort service, 24-hour emergency telephones, lighted pathways/sidewalks, student patrols, controlled dormitory access (key, security card, etc.).

TRANSFER AND INTERNATIONAL STUDENTS

Transfer students: May apply for admission for the following academic terms: Fall, Winter, Spring. Applicants need a minimum number of credits to apply. For fall 2005: Transfer applicants enrolled: 52. **International students:** Number of foreign undergraduates: 12 (2% of student body). Number of countries represented: 10. Minimum TOEFL score required: 550 (paper); 213 (computer).

Boise State University

■ **Address:** 1910 University Drive, Boise, ID 83725
■ **Website:** http://www.BoiseState.edu
■ **Public**
■ **Enrollment:** 10,840 full-time; 6,085 part-time

KEY STATS

✔ **U.S News College Ranking:** third tier, Universities–Master's (West)
✔ **ACT Score (25th/75th percentile):** 17-26
✔ **Tuition:** 2006-2007: $4,154 in state, $11,932 out of state

Selectivity: Selective	**Room/board:** $5,778
Acceptance rate: 90%	**Average debt:** $14,765
Student/faculty ratio: 20/1	**Proportion who borrowed:** 59%

UNDERGRADUATE STUDENT BODY STATS

2005-2006 enrollment: 10,840 full-time; 6,085 part-time. Men: 46%; women: 54%. **Ethnic makeup:** African American: 1%; American-Indian: 1%; Asian American: 3%; Hispanic: 6%; White: 88%; International: 1%.

ADMISSIONS FACTS AND FIGURES

Phone: (208) 426-1156. **Email:** bsuinfo@boisestate.edu. **Website:** http://www.BoiseState.edu. **Application deadlines for fall 2007:** Regular decision: July 12. Early decision: Not offered. Early action: Not offered. Admission cannot be deferred. **Application fee:** $30. Common application is not accepted. **To apply online, go to:** http://admissions.boisestate.edu/applying.htm /applicat.htm. **Admissions requirements/recommendations:** High school units required (recommended): English: 8 (8); Mathematics: 6 (6); Science: 6 (6); Foreign language: 0 (0); Social studies: 5 (5); History: 2 (2); Academic electives: 3 (2); Total units: 30 (30). Tests: The college uses SAT or ACT scores in admissions decisions. Either SAT or ACT required. For admission to the fall 2007 entering class, the school will accept: ACT with writing, ACT without writing. Campus visit: Neither required nor recommended. Admissions interview: Neither required nor recommended. Off-campus interview: Not available. **Factors that count in admissions decisions:** *Academic:* Secondary school record: Very important. Class rank: Not considered. Letters of recommendation: Not considered. Standardized test scores: Very important. Essay: Not considered. *Nonacademic:* Interview: Not considered. Extracurricular activities: Not considered. Talent/ability: Not considered. Character/personal qualities: Not considered. Alumni/ae relationship: Not considered. Geographical residence: Not considered. State residency: Not considered. Religious affiliation/commitment: Not considered. Minority status: Not considered. Volunteer work: Not considered. Work experience: Not considered. **Other schools with the greatest overlap in applicants:** Albertson College; Brigham Young University–Provo; Idaho State University; Lewis-Clark State College; University of Idaho. **Admissions statistics for the fall 2005 entering class:** Total applicants: 3,339. Total accepted: 2,991. Freshmen enrolled: 2,501; 9% were from out of state. Overall acceptance rate: 90%. **Credentials of fall 2005 freshmen:** 9% ranked in the top 10

percent of their high school class; 28% were in the top 25 percent, and 64% were in the top half. (Proportion submitting class standing: 89%.) **Average high school grade point average:** 3.3. **First-year students who submitted SAT scores:** 45%. Scores (25/75 percentile): Verbal: 460-590, Math: 480-575, Combined: 940-1165. **First-year students submitting ACT scores:** 72%. Scores (25/75 percentile): English: 16-26, Math: 17-27, Composite: 17-26.

ACADEMICS

Year founded: 1932. **Academic calendar:** Semester. **Degrees offered:** certificate, diploma, associate, bachelor's, master's, doctorate. **Most popular majors:** 5% accounting, 5% business/commerce, 5% criminal justice/law enforcement administration, 5% education, 5% nursing/registered nurse training (R.N., A.S.N., B.S.N., M.S.N.). **Major fields of study:** agriculture, agriculture operations, and related sciences; area, ethnic, cultural, and gender studies; biological and biomedical sciences; business, management, marketing, and related support services; computer and information sciences and support services; construction trades; education; engineering; engineering technologies/technicians; English language and literature/letters; family and consumer sciences/human sciences; foreign languages, literatures, and linguistics; health professions and related clinical sciences; history; mathematics and statistics; mechanic and repair technologies/technicians; multi/interdisciplinary studies; parks, recreation, leisure, and fitness studies; philosophy and religious studies; physical sciences; precision production; psychology; public administration and social service professions; security and protective services; social sciences; visual and performing arts. **Areas of required coursework:** arts/fine arts, humanities, computer literacy, mathematics, English (including composition), sciences (biological or physical), history, social science. **Pre-professional programs:** pre-law, pre-dentistry, pre-medicine, pre-veterinary science, pre-optometry, pre-pharmacy. **Special academic programs (% participation):** accelerated program (1%), cooperative (work-study plan) program (3%), distance learning (5%), double major (10%), dual enrollment (2%), English as a Second Language (ESL) (1%), honors program (1%), internships (8%), liberal arts/career combination (2%), study abroad (1%), teacher certificate program (5%), weekend college (2%). **Teacher certification offered in:** early childhood, special education, elementary, middle/junior high, secondary, bilingual/bicultural. **Reserve Officers Training Corps (ROTC):** Army ROTC: Offered on campus. **Faculty and instruction (2005-2006):** Total instructional faculty: 578 full-time, 549 part-time (57% men; 43% women; 7% minorities). Full-time faculty with Ph.D. or other terminal degree: 85%. Student/faculty ratio: 20/1. Classes of fewer than 20 students: 46%; of 20 to 49 students: 48%; of 50 or more students: 6%. **Advanced Placement and International Baccalaureate credit:** AP tests may be used for: Credit only. **Freshmen returning for sophomore year:** 61%. **Graduation rates:** Four-year: 6%; five-year: 18%; six-year: 27%. **Graduate study:** 5% of students pursue further study immediately upon graduation; 10% within one year; 15% within five years. Fields in which graduates pursue further study: Master of Business Administration (MBA), 3%; law, 1%; engineering, 1%; education, 10%.

COSTS AND FINANCIAL AID

Financial aid office: (208) 426-1540. **Expenses (2006-2007):** Tuition and fees 2006-2007: $4,154 in state, $11,932 out of state; room/board: $5,778. Estimated books and supplies: $1,050; transportation: $1,424; personal expenses: $2,052. **Financial aid:** Priority filing date for institution's financial aid form: April 1. In 2005-2006, 69% of undergraduates applied for financial aid. Of those, 56% were determined to have financial need; 15% had their need fully met. Average financial aid package (proportion receiving): $8,348 (54%). Average amount of gift aid, such as scholarships or grants (proportion receiving): $3,299 (42%). Average amount of self-help aid, such as work study or loans (proportion receiving): $4,622 (42%). Average need-based loan (excluding PLUS or other private loans): $3,938. Among students who received need-based aid, the average percentage of need met: 65%. Among students who received aid based on merit, the average award (and the proportion receiving): $2,207 (1%). The average athletic scholarship (and the proportion receiving): $11,887 (3%). Average amount of debt of borrowers graduating in 2005: $14,765. Proportion who borrowed: 59%.

CAMPUS LIFE AND EXTRACURRICULAR ACTIVITIES

Campus housing available (% using): coed dorms (50%), women's dorms (15%), men's dorms (10%), apartments for married students (10%), apartment for single students (15%), special housing for disabled students. Students who live in college-owned, operated, or affiliated housing: 8%. **Student employment:** During the 2005-2006 academic year, 8% of undergraduates worked on campus. Average per-year earnings: $2,000. Activities include: choral groups, dance, drama/theater, marching band, music ensembles, musical theater, pep band, radio station, student government, student newspaper. Number of fraternities: 2; sororities: 0. Proportion of men in fraternities: 1%; of women in sororities: 1%. Average proportion of students who stay on campus on weekends: 9%. **Sports program (2005-2006):** Member of NCAA I. *Men's intercollegiate varsity sports:* basketball, cross-country, football, golf, tennis, track and field (indoor), track and field (outdoor), wrestling. *Women's intercollegiate varsity sports:* basketball, cross-country, golf, gymnastics, skiing, soccer, tennis, track and field (indoor), track and field (outdoor), volleyball.

SERVICES AND FACILITIES

Basic services: nonremedial tutoring, women's center, placement service, day care, health service, health insurance. **Remedial assistance:** reading, math, writing. **Counseling services:** minority student, career, personal, veteran student, academic. **For learning-disabled students:** School does not offer a structured program with separate admission and additional fees. Services include: remedial math, remedial English, remedial reading, tape recorders, diagnostic testing service, oral tests, learning center, tutors. **Library:** Number of titles: 615,000; number of current serial subscriptions: 4,800. **Information technology resources:** Students are not required to lease or own a computer. Number of campus computers available to all students: 700. School does not have a wireless network. Proportion of college-owned housing units wired for high-speed internet access: 100%. **Campus safety:** Security services offered: 24-hour foot and vehicle patrols, late-night transport/escort service, 24-hour emergency telephones, lighted pathways/sidewalks, controlled dormitory access (key, security card, etc).

TRANSFER AND INTERNATIONAL STUDENTS

Transfer students: May apply for admission for the following academic terms: Fall, Spring, Summer. Applicants do not need a minimum number of credits to apply. For fall 2005: Transfer applications received: 2,241. Transfer applicants offered admission: 1,783. Transfer applicants enrolled: 1,057. **International students:** Number of foreign undergraduates: 113 (1% of student body). Number of countries represented: 65. Minimum TOEFL score required: 500 (paper); 173 (computer).

Idaho State University

- **Address:** 741 S. Seventh Avenue, Pocatello, ID 83209
- **Website:** http://www.isu.edu
- **Public**
- **Enrollment:** 7,745 full-time; 3,907 part-time

KEY STATS

✔ **U.S News College Ranking:** fourth tier, National Universities
✔ **ACT Score (25th/75th percentile):** 18-24
✔ **Tuition:** 2006-2007: $4,190 in state, $8,270 out of state

Selectivity: Selective	Room/board: $4,950
Acceptance rate: 77%	Average debt: $19,299
Student/faculty ratio: 15/1	Proportion who borrowed: 71%

UNDERGRADUATE STUDENT BODY STATS

2005-2006 enrollment: 7,745 full-time; 3,907 part-time. Men: 43%; women: 57%. **Ethnic makeup:** African American: 1%; American-Indian: 2%; Asian American: 1%; Hispanic: 5%; White: 89%; International: 2%. **Religious preference:** Roman Catholic: 6%; Protestant: 4%; Jewish: 1%; Unknown: 42%; Church of Jesus Christ of Latter-day Saints: 36%; Other: 11%.

ADMISSIONS FACTS AND FIGURES

Phone: (208) 282-2475. **Email:** info@isu.edu. **Website:** http://www.isu.edu. **Application deadlines for fall 2007:** Regular decision: Rolling. Early decision: Not offered. Early action: Not offered. Admission can be deferred. **Application fee:** $40. Common application is accepted. **To apply online, go to:** http://www.isu.edu/departments/enroll/admis.shtml. **Admissions requirements/recommendations:** High school units required (recommended): English: 4; Mathematics: 3 (4); Science: 3; Foreign language: 1; Social studies: 3; History: 0; Academic electives: 0; Total units: 16. Tests: The college uses SAT or ACT scores in admissions decisions. Either SAT or ACT required. For admission to the fall 2007 entering class, the school will accept: ACT with writing, ACT without writing. Campus visit: Recommended. Admissions interview: Neither required nor recommended. Off-campus interview: Not available. **Factors that count in admissions decisions:** *Academic:* Secondary school record: Not considered. Class rank: Not considered. Letters of recommendation: Not considered. Standardized test scores: Considered. Essay: Not considered. *Nonacademic:* Interview: Not considered. Extracurricular activities: Not considered. Talent/ability: Not considered. Character/personal qualities: Not considered. Alumni/ae relationship: Not considered. Geographical residence: Not considered. State residency: Not considered. Religious affiliation/commitment: Not considered. Minority status: Not considered. Volunteer work: Not considered. Work experience: Not considered. **Other schools with the greatest overlap in applicants:** Boise State University; University of Idaho; Utah State University. **Admissions statistics for the fall 2005 entering class:** Total applicants: 3,566. Total accepted: 2,731. Freshmen enrolled: 2,490; 4% were from out of state. Overall acceptance rate: 77%. **Credentials of fall 2005 freshmen:** 13% ranked in the top 10 percent of their high school class; 32% were in the top 25 percent, and 61% were in the top half. (Proportion submitting class standing: 44%.) **Average high school grade point average:** 3.3. **First-year students who submitted SAT scores:** 6%. Scores (25/75 percentile): Verbal: 440-570, Math: 470-610, Combined: 910-1180. **First-year students submitting ACT scores:** 57%. Scores (25/75 percentile): English: 17-23, Math: 17-23, Composite: 18-24.

ACADEMICS

Year founded: 1901. **Academic calendar:** Semester. **Degrees offered:** certificate, associate, bachelor's, post-bachelor's certificate, master's, post-master's certificate, first professional, first professional certificate, doctorate. **Most popular majors:** 9% nursing/registered nurse training (R.N., A.S.N., B.S.N., M.S.N.), 6% elementary education and teaching, 6% secondary education and teaching, 5% biology/biological sciences, 5% human resources management/personnel administration. **Major fields of study:** area, ethnic, cultural, and gender studies; biological and biomedical sciences; business, management, marketing, and related support services; communication, journalism, and related programs; computer and information sciences and support services; education; engineering; engineering technologies/technicians; English language and literature/letters; family and consumer sciences/human sciences; foreign languages, literatures, and linguistics; health professions and related clinical sciences; history; liberal arts and sciences studies, and humanities; mathematics and statistics; multi/interdisciplinary studies; philosophy and religious studies; physical sciences; psychology; public administration and social service professions; social sciences; visual and performing arts. **Areas of required coursework:** arts/fine arts, humanities, mathematics, English (including composition), philosophy, sciences (biological or physical), history, social science, other. **Pre-professional programs:** pre-law, pre-dentistry, pre-medicine, pre-veterinary science, pre-optometry, pre-pharmacy, other. **Special academic programs (% participation):** cross-registration (1%), distance learning (19%), double major (5%), dual enrollment (6%), English as a Second Language (ESL) (2%), exchange student program (domestic) (1%), honors program (1%), independent study (1%), internships (20%), student-designed major (1%), study abroad (2%), teacher certificate program (12%). **Teacher certification offered in:** early childhood, special education, elementary, vo-tech, secondary. **Cooperative education programs:** health professions, natural science, other. **Reserve Officers Training Corps (ROTC):** Army ROTC: Offered on campus. **Faculty and instruction (2005-2006):** Total instructional faculty: 651 full-time, 257 part-time (54% men; 46% women; 6% minorities). Full-time faculty with Ph.D. or other terminal degree: 57%. Student/faculty ratio: 15/1. Classes of fewer than 20 students: 62%; of 20 to 49 students: 34%; of 50 or more students: 4%. **Advanced Placement and International Baccalaureate credit:** AP tests may be used for: Credit only. Scores accepted: 3, 4, 5. **Freshmen returning for sophomore year:** 58%. **Graduation rates:** Four-year: 8%; five-year: 21%; six-year: 29%.

COSTS AND FINANCIAL AID

Financial aid office: (208) 282-2756. **Expenses (2006-2007):** Tuition and fees 2006-2007: $4,190 in state, $8,270 out of state; room/board: $4,950. Estimated books and supplies: $900; transportation: $1,012; personal expenses: $1,840. **Financial aid:** Priority filing date for institution's financial aid form: March 1. In 2005-2006, 81% of undergraduates applied for financial aid. Of those, 72% were determined to have financial need; 15% had their need fully met. Average financial aid package (proportion receiving): $7,494 (70%). Average amount of gift aid, such as scholarships or grants (proportion receiving): $3,044 (52%). Average amount of self-help aid, such as work study or loans (proportion receiving): $3,853 (56%). Average need-based loan (excluding PLUS or other private loans): $3,560. Among students who received need-based aid, the average percentage of need met: 67%. Among students who received aid based on merit, the average award (and the proportion receiving): $2,243 (13%). The average athletic scholarship (and the proportion receiving): $8,313 (4%). The average amount of debt of borrowers graduating in 2005: $19,299. Proportion who borrowed: 71%.

CAMPUS LIFE AND EXTRACURRICULAR ACTIVITIES

Campus housing available (% using): coed dorms (32%), women's dorms (5%), men's dorms (5%), apartments for married students (24%), apartment for single students (34%), special housing for disabled students (0%), other housing options. Students who live in college-owned, operated, or affiliated housing: 6%. **Student employment:** During the 2005-2006 academic year, 16% of undergraduates worked on campus. Average per-year earnings: $4,480. **Clubs and organizations:** Number of student organizations: 146. Activities include: choral groups, concert band, dance, drama/theater, literary magazine, marching band, music ensembles, musical theater, pep band, radio station, student government, student newspaper, symphony orchestra, television station, yearbook. Number of fraternities: 3; sororities: 3. Proportion of men in fraternities: 1%; of women in sororities: 1%. **Sports program (2005-2006):** Member of NCAA I. *Men's intercollegiate varsity sports:* basketball, cross-country, football, golf, tennis, track and field (indoor), track and field (outdoor). *Women's intercollegiate varsity sports:* basketball, cross-country, golf, soccer, tennis, track and field (indoor), track and field (outdoor), volleyball.

SERVICES AND FACILITIES

Basic services: nonremedial tutoring, placement service, day care, health service, health insurance, other. **Remedial assistance:** reading, math, writing, study skills. **Counseling services:** minority student, career, personal, academic, other. **For learning-disabled students:** School does not offer a structured program with separate admission and additional fees. Services include: remedial math, remedial English, reading machines, remedial reading, tape recorders, diagnostic testing service, untimed tests, note-taking services, oral tests, learning center, readers, extended time for tests, tutors, priority registration, other testing accomodations. **Library:** Number of titles: 942,314; number of current serial subscriptions: 16,345. **Information technology resources:** Students are not required to lease or own a computer. Number of campus computers available to all students: 786. School has a wireless network. Approximate number of users that can be accommodated: 500. Proportion of college-owned housing units wired for high-speed internet access: 42%. **Campus safety:** Security services offered: 24-hour foot and vehicle patrols, late-night transport/escort service, 24-hour emergency telephones, lighted pathways/sidewalks, controlled dormitory access (key, security card, etc).

TRANSFER AND INTERNATIONAL STUDENTS

Transfer students: May apply for admission for the following academic terms: Fall, Spring, Summer. Applicants need a minimum number of credits to apply. For fall 2005: Transfer applications received: 1,316. Transfer applicants offered admission: 1,073. Transfer applicants enrolled: 1,166. **International students:** Number of foreign undergraduates: 207 (2% of student body). Number of countries represented: 71. Minimum TOEFL score required: 500 (paper); 173 (computer). Average TOEFL score: 550 (paper).

Lewis-Clark State College

- **Address:** 500 Eighth Avenue, Lewiston, ID 83501
- **Website:** http://www.lcsc.edu
- **Public**
- **Enrollment:** 2,281 full-time; 1,170 part-time

KEY STATS

✔ **U.S News College Ranking:** 20, Comp. Coll.–Bachelor's (West)
✔ **ACT Score (25th/75th percentile):** 17-22
✔ **Tuition:** 2006-2007: $3,897 in state, $10,841 out of state

Selectivity: Selective	**Room/board:** $4,500
Acceptance rate: 59%	**Average debt:** N/A
Student/faculty ratio: 15/1	**Proportion who borrowed:** 61%

UNDERGRADUATE STUDENT BODY STATS

2005-2006 enrollment: 2,281 full-time; 1,170 part-time. Men: 39%; women: 61%. **Ethnic makeup:** African American: 1%; American-Indian: 5%; Asian American: 1%; Hispanic: 5%; White: 85%; International: 4%.

ADMISSIONS FACTS AND FIGURES

Phone: (208) 792-2210. **Email:** admissions@lcsc.edu. **Website:** http://www.lcsc.edu. **Application deadlines for fall 2007:** Regular decision: Rolling. Early decision: Not offered. Early action: Send application by: N/A;

Decision sent by: N/A. Admission can be deferred. **Application fee:** $35. Common application is not accepted. **To apply online, go to:** http://www.lcsc.edu/Admissions/forms.htm. **Admissions requirements/recommendations:** High school units required (recommended): English: 4; Mathematics: 3; Science: 3; Foreign language: (1); Academic electives: 2; Total units: 15. Tests: The college uses SAT or ACT scores in admissions decisions. Neither SAT nor ACT required. For admission to the fall 2007 entering class, the school will accept: ACT with writing, ACT without writing. Campus visit: Recommended. Admissions interview: Neither required nor recommended. Off-campus interview: Not available. **Factors that count in admissions decisions:** *Academic:* Secondary school record: Very important. Class rank: Not considered. Letters of recommendation: Not considered. Standardized test scores: Very important. Essay: Not considered. *Nonacademic:* Interview: Not considered. Extracurricular activities: Not considered. Talent/ability: Not considered. Character/personal qualities: Not considered. Alumni/ae relationship: Not considered. Geographical residence: Not considered. State residency: Not considered. Religious affiliation/commitment: Not considered. Minority status: Not considered. Volunteer work: Not considered. Work experience: Not considered. **Other schools with the greatest overlap in applicants:** Boise State University; University of Idaho. **Admissions statistics for the fall 2005 entering class:** Total applicants: 1,100. Total accepted: 650. Freshmen enrolled: 509; 21% were from out of state. Overall acceptance rate: 59%. Non-early acceptance rate: 59%. **Credentials of fall 2005 freshmen:** 9% ranked in the top 10 percent of their high school class; 26% were in the top 25 percent, and 55% were in the top half. (Proportion submitting class standing: 65%.) **Average high school grade point average:** 3.0. **First-year students who submitted SAT scores:** 21%. Scores (25/75 percentile): Verbal: 420-540, Math: 440-570, Combined: 860-1110. **First-year students submitting ACT scores:** 56%. Scores (25/75 percentile): English: 15-22, Math: 16-21, Composite: 17-22.

ACADEMICS

Year founded: 1893. **Academic calendar:** Semester. **Degrees offered:** certificate, associate, transfer-associate, terminal-associate, bachelor's. **Most popular majors:** 23% business, management, marketing, and related support services, 15% health professions and related clinical sciences, 13% education, 13% public administration and social service professions, 4% psychology. **Major fields of study:** biological and biomedical sciences; business, management, marketing, and related support services; communication, journalism, and related programs; communications technologies/technicians and support services; computer and information sciences and support services; education; engineering technologies/technicians; English language and literature/letters; family and consumer sciences/human sciences; health professions and related clinical sciences; legal professions and studies; mathematics and statistics; mechanic and repair technologies/technicians; multi/interdisciplinary studies; parks, recreation, leisure, and fitness studies; physical sciences; precision production; psychology; public administration and social service professions; security and protective services; social sciences. **Areas of required coursework:** arts/fine arts, humanities, mathematics, English (including composition), sciences (biological or physical), social science, other. **Pre-professional programs:** pre-dentistry, pre-medicine, pre-veterinary science, pre-pharmacy, other. **Special academic programs:** accelerated program, cooperative (work-study plan) program, distance learning, double major, dual enrollment, English as a Second Language (ESL), honors program, independent study, internships, liberal arts/career combination, student-designed major, study abroad, teacher certificate program, weekend college. **Teacher certification offered in:** elementary, secondary. **Cooperative education programs:** business, computer science, education, health professions, humanities, natural science, social/behavioral science, technologies. **Reserve Officers Training Corps (ROTC):** Army ROTC: Offered on campus; Navy ROTC: Offered at cooperating institution (University of Idaho); Air Force ROTC: Offered at cooperating institution (University of Idaho). **Faculty and instruction (2005-2006):** Total instructional faculty: 158 full-time, 71 part-time (55% men; 45% women; 4% minorities). Full-time faculty with Ph.D. or other terminal degree: 65%. Student/faculty ratio: 15/1. Classes of fewer than 20 students: 70%; of 20 to 49 students: 30%; of 50 or more students: 0%. **Advanced Placement and International Baccalaureate credit:** AP tests may be used for: Credit only. Scores accepted: 3, 4, 5. International Baccalaureate exams may be used for: Credit only. **Freshmen returning for sophomore year:** 57%. **Graduation rates:** Four-year: 10%; five-year: 21%; six-year: 25%. **Graduate study:** 6% of students pursue further study immediately upon graduation.

COSTS AND FINANCIAL AID

Financial aid office: (208) 792-2224. **Expenses (2006-2007):** Tuition and fees 2006-2007: $3,897 in state, $10,841 out of state; room/board: $4,500.

Estimated books and supplies: $1,500; transportation: $1,800; personal expenses: $2,000. **Financial aid:** Priority filing date for institution's financial aid form: March 1. In 2005-2006, 80% of undergraduates applied for financial aid. Of those, 72% were determined to have financial need; 11% had their need fully met. Average financial aid package (proportion receiving): $5,452 (70%). Average amount of gift aid, such as scholarships or grants (proportion receiving): $3,125 (53%). Average amount of self-help aid, such as work study or loans (proportion receiving): $3,611 (61%). Average need-based loan (excluding PLUS or other private loans): $3,552. Among students who received need-based aid, the average percentage of need met: 11%. Among students who received aid based on merit, the average award (and the proportion receiving): $2,478 (7%). The average athletic scholarship (and the proportion receiving): $5,793 (6%). Proportion who borrowed: 61%.

CAMPUS LIFE AND EXTRACURRICULAR ACTIVITIES

Campus housing available: coed dorms, apartments for married students, apartment for single students. Students who live in college-owned, operated, or affiliated housing: 8%. Average per-year earnings: $2,000. **Clubs and organizations:** Number of student organizations: 52. Activities include: choral groups, dance, drama/theater, jazz band, literary magazine, radio station, student government, student newspaper. Number of fraternities: 0; sororities: 0. Average proportion of students who stay on campus on weekends: 8%. **Sports program (2005-2006):** Member of NAIA. *Men's intercollegiate varsity sports:* baseball, basketball, cross-country, golf, tennis, track and field (outdoor). *Women's intercollegiate varsity sports:* basketball, cross-country, golf, tennis, track and field (outdoor), volleyball.

SERVICES AND FACILITIES

Basic services: nonremedial tutoring, placement service, day care, health service, health insurance. **Remedial assistance:** reading, math, writing, study skills. **Counseling services:** minority student, career, military, personal, veteran student, academic, older student, psychological, birth control. **For learning-disabled students:** School does not offer a structured program with separate admission and additional fees. Services include: remedial math, remedial English, reading machines, remedial reading, tape recorders, learning center, readers, extended time for tests, tutors, texts on tape, other testing accomodations. **Information technology resources:** Students are not required to lease or own a computer. Number of campus computers available to all students: 472. School has a wireless network. Proportion of college-owned housing units wired for high-speed internet access: 60%. **Campus safety:** Security services offered: 24-hour foot and vehicle patrols, late-night transport/escort service, 24-hour emergency telephones, lighted pathways/sidewalks, controlled dormitory access (key, security card, etc).

TRANSFER AND INTERNATIONAL STUDENTS

Transfer students: May apply for admission for the following academic terms: Fall, Spring, Summer. Applicants need a minimum number of credits to apply. For fall 2005: Transfer applications received: 625. Transfer applicants offered admission: 484. Transfer applicants enrolled: 328. **International students:** Number of foreign undergraduates: 105 (4% of student body). Number of countries represented: 35. Minimum TOEFL score required: 500 (paper); 173 (computer). Average TOEFL score: 533 (paper).

Northwest Nazarene University

- **Address:** 623 Holly Street, Nampa, ID 83686
- **Website:** http://www.nnu.edu
- **Private; Religious affiliation:** Church of the Nazarene
- **Enrollment:** 1,073 full-time; 91 part-time

KEY STATS

✔ **U.S News College Ranking:** 34, Universities–Master's (West)
✔ **ACT Score (25th/75th percentile):** 19-25
✔ **Tuition:** 2006-2007: $18,770

Selectivity: Selective	**Room/board:** $4,860
Acceptance rate: 52%	**Average debt:** $24,405
Student/faculty ratio: 11/1	**Proportion who borrowed:** 94%

UNDERGRADUATE STUDENT BODY STATS

2005-2006 enrollment: 1,073 full-time; 91 part-time. Men: 39%; women: 61%. **Ethnic makeup:** African American: 1%; American-Indian: 1%; Asian American: 1%; Hispanic: 2%; White: 94%; International: 1%.

ADMISSIONS FACTS AND FIGURES

Phone: (208) 467-8000. **Email:** Admissions@nnu.edu. **Website:** http://www.nnu.edu. **Application deadlines for fall 2007:** Regular decision: August 8. Early decision: Not offered. Early action: Send application by: December 15; Decision sent by: January 15. Admission can be deferred. **Application fee:** $25. Common application is accepted. **Admissions requirements/recommendations:** High school units required (recommended): English: 4 (4); Mathematics: 3 (3); Science: 3 (3); Foreign language: 2 (2); Social studies: 3 (2); History: (1); Total units: (15). Tests: The college uses SAT or ACT scores in admissions decisions. ACT required. For admission to the fall 2007 entering class, the school will accept: ACT with writing, ACT without writing. Campus visit: Recommended. Admissions interview: Recommended. Off-campus interview: May be arranged. **Factors that count in admissions decisions:** *Academic:* Secondary school record: Considered. Class rank: Very important. Letters of recommendation: Very important. Standardized test scores: Very important. Essay: Considered. *Nonacademic:* Interview: Not considered. Extracurricular activities: Considered. Talent/ability: Considered. Character/personal qualities: Considered. Alumni/ae relationship: Considered. Geographical residence: Not considered. State residency: Not considered. Religious affiliation/commitment: Considered. Minority status: Not considered. Volunteer work: Not considered. Work experience: Not considered. **Other schools with the greatest overlap in applicants:** Albertson College; Boise State University; Idaho State University; Point Loma Nazarene University; University of Idaho. **Admissions statistics for the fall 2005 entering class:** Total applicants: 923. Total accepted: 476. Freshmen enrolled: 264; 62% were from out of state. Overall acceptance rate: 52%. Non-early acceptance rate: 52%. **Credentials of fall 2005 freshmen:** 24% ranked in the top 10 percent of their high school class; 49% were in the top 25 percent, and 80% were in the top half. (Proportion submitting class standing: 66%.) **Average high school grade point average:** 3.4. **First-year students who submitted SAT scores:** 39%. Scores (25/75 percentile): Verbal: 470-570, Math: 440-580, Combined: 910-1150. **First-year students submitting ACT scores:** 100%. Scores (25/75 percentile): English: 19-26, Math: 18-25, Composite: 19-25.

ACADEMICS

Year founded: 1913. **Academic calendar:** Semester. **Degrees offered:** bachelor's, master's. **Most popular majors:** 20% business, management, marketing, and related support services, 20% education, 9% theology and religious vocations, 8% public administration and social service professions, 6% health professions and related clinical sciences. **Major fields of study:** biological and biomedical sciences; business, management, marketing, and related support services; communication, journalism, and related programs; computer and information sciences and support services; education; engineering; English language and literature/letters; foreign languages, literatures, and linguistics; health professions and related clinical sciences; history; liberal arts and sciences studies, and humanities; parks, recreation, leisure, and fitness studies; philosophy and religious studies; physical sciences; psychology; public administration and social service professions; social sciences; theology and religious vocations; visual and performing arts. **Areas of required coursework:** arts/fine arts, humanities, mathematics, English (including composition), philosophy, sciences (biological or physical), history, social science, other. **Pre-professional programs:** pre-law, pre-dentistry, pre-medicine, pre-theology, pre-veterinary science, pre-optometry, pre-pharmacy, other. **Special academic programs (% participation):** accelerated program (.1%), cross-registration (0%), distance learning (0%), double major (.06%), exchange student program (domestic) (0%), honors program (.01%), independent study (.2%), internships (.15%), liberal arts/career combination (100%), student-designed major (.008%), study abroad (.024%), teacher certificate program (.22%). **Teacher certification offered in:** special education, elementary, middle/junior high, secondary. **Cooperative education programs:** education, health professions. **Reserve Officers Training Corps (ROTC):** Army ROTC: Offered on campus. **Faculty and instruction (2005-2006):** Total instructional faculty: 98 full-time, 5 part-time (62% men; 38% women; 3% minorities). Full-time faculty with Ph.D. or other terminal degree: 71%. Student/faculty ratio: 11/1. Classes of fewer than 20 students: 63%; of 20 to 49 students: 32%; of 50 or more students: 5%. **Advanced Placement and International Baccalaureate credit:** AP tests may be used for: Credit and/or placement. Scores accepted: 3, 4, 5. International Baccalaureate exams may be used for: Credit only. **Freshmen returning for**

sophomore year: 70%. **Graduation rates:** Four-year: 30%; five-year: 39%; six-year: 47%.

COSTS AND FINANCIAL AID

Financial aid office: (208) 467-8347. **Expenses (2006-2007):** Tuition and fees 2006-2007: $18,770; room/board: $4,860. Estimated books and supplies: $900; transportation: $850; personal expenses: $900. **Financial aid:** Priority filing date for institution's financial aid form: March 1. In 2005-2006, 82% of undergraduates applied for financial aid. Of those, 72% were determined to have financial need; 22% had their need fully met. Average financial aid package (proportion receiving): $13,254 (72%). Average amount of gift aid, such as scholarships or grants (proportion receiving): $2,920 (51%). Average amount of self-help aid, such as work study or loans (proportion receiving): $5,279 (60%). Average need-based loan (excluding PLUS or other private loans): $4,798. Among students who received need-based aid, the average percentage of need met: 74%. Among students who received aid based on merit, the average award (and the proportion receiving): $8,446 (10%). The average athletic scholarship (and the proportion receiving): $3,826 (1%). Average amount of debt of borrowers graduating in 2005: $24,405. Proportion who borrowed: 94%.

CAMPUS LIFE AND EXTRACURRICULAR ACTIVITIES

Campus housing available (% using): coed dorms (35%), women's dorms (40%), men's dorms (20%), apartments for married students (5%), apartment for single students, other housing options (1%). Students who live in college-owned, operated, or affiliated housing: 61%. **Student employment:** During the 2005-2006 academic year, 29% of undergraduates worked on campus. Average per-year earnings: $3,337. **Clubs and organizations:** Number of student organizations: 31. Activities include: choral groups, concert band, drama/theater, jazz band, literary magazine, music ensembles, musical theater, pep band, student government, student newspaper, symphony orchestra, yearbook. Number of fraternities: 0; sororities: 0. Average proportion of students who stay on campus on weekends: 60%. **Sports program (2005-2006):** Member of NCAA II. *Men's intercollegiate varsity sports:* baseball, basketball, cross-country, golf, track and field (indoor), track and field (outdoor). *Women's intercollegiate varsity sports:* basketball, cross-country, soccer, softball, track and field (indoor), track and field (outdoor), volleyball.

SERVICES AND FACILITIES

Basic services: nonremedial tutoring, health service, health insurance. **Remedial assistance:** reading, math, writing, study skills, other. **Counseling services:** minority student, career, military, personal, veteran student, academic, older student, psychological, birth control, religious. **For learning-disabled students:** School does not offer a structured program with separate admission and additional fees. Total undergraduates in learning-disabled program or receiving services: 13. Services include: remedial math, remedial English, remedial reading, tape recorders, other special classes, untimed tests, note-taking services, oral tests, learning center, readers, extended time for tests, tutors, early syllabus, priority registration, priority seating, proofreading services, texts on tape, exams on tape or computer, other testing accomodations. **Library:** Number of titles: 181,235; number of current serial subscriptions: 841. **Information technology resources:** Students are not required to lease or own a computer. Number of campus computers available to all students: 275. School has a wireless network. Approximate number of users that can be accommodated: 255. Proportion of college-owned housing units wired for high-speed internet access: 100%. **Campus safety:** Security services offered: late-night transport/escort service, 24-hour emergency telephones, lighted pathways/sidewalks, student patrols, controlled dormitory access (key, security card, etc).

TRANSFER AND INTERNATIONAL STUDENTS

Transfer students: May apply for admission for the following academic terms: Fall, Spring, Summer. Applicants need a minimum number of credits to apply. For fall 2005: Transfer applications received: 276. Transfer applicants offered admission: 114. Transfer applicants enrolled: 76. **International students:** Number of foreign undergraduates: 9 (1% of student body). Number of countries represented: 8. Minimum TOEFL score required: 500 (paper); 173 (computer).

University of Idaho

- **Address:** 875 Perimeter Drive, PO Box 442282, Moscow, ID 83844-2282
- **Website:** http://www.its.uidaho.edu/uihome/
- **Public**
- **Enrollment:** 8,380 full-time; 1,123 part-time

KEY STATS

✔ **U.S News College Ranking:** third tier, National Universities
✔ **ACT Score (25th/75th percentile):** 20-26
✔ **Tuition:** 2006-2007: $4,200 in state, $13,800 out of state
  Selectivity: Selective   **Room/board:** $5,696
  Acceptance rate: 82%   **Average debt:** $20,002
  Student/faculty ratio: 20/1   **Proportion who borrowed:** 69%

UNDERGRADUATE STUDENT BODY STATS

2005-2006 enrollment: 8,380 full-time; 1,123 part-time. Men: 54%; women: 46%. **Ethnic makeup:** African American: 1%; American-Indian: 1%; Asian American: 2%; Hispanic: 4%; White: 89%; International: 2%.

ADMISSIONS FACTS AND FIGURES

Phone: (888) 884-3246. **Email:** admappl@uidaho.edu. **Website:** http://www.its.uidaho.edu/uihome/. **Application deadlines for fall 2007:** Regular decision: August 1; decision sent by August 15. Early decision: Not offered. Early action: Not offered. Admission can be deferred. **Application fee:** $40. Common application is accepted. **To apply online, go to:** http://www.students.uidaho.edu/default.aspx?pid=15568. **Admissions requirements/recommendations:** High school units required (recommended): English: 4; Mathematics: 3; Science: 3; Foreign language: 1; Social studies: 3; Academic electives: 2; Total units: 15. Tests: The college uses SAT or ACT scores in admissions decisions. Either SAT or ACT required. For admission to the fall 2007 entering class, the school will accept: ACT with writing, ACT without writing. Campus visit: Recommended. Admissions interview: Neither required nor recommended. Off-campus interview: May be arranged. **Factors that count in admissions decisions:** *Academic:* Secondary school record: Very important. Class rank: Not considered. Letters of recommendation: Not considered. Standardized test scores: Very important. Essay: Not considered. *Nonacademic:* Interview: Not considered. Extracurricular activities: Not considered. Talent/ability: Not considered. Character/personal qualities: Not considered. Alumni/ae relationship: Not considered. Geographical residence: Not considered. State residency: Not considered. Religious affiliation/commitment: Not considered. Minority status: Not considered. Volunteer work: Not considered. Work experience: Not considered. **Admissions statistics for the fall 2005 entering class:** Total applicants: 4,444. Total accepted: 3,660. Freshmen enrolled: 1,745; 34% were from out of state. Overall acceptance rate: 82%. **Credentials of fall 2005 freshmen:** 20% ranked in the top 10 percent of their high school class; 46% were in the top 25 percent, and 77% were in the top half. (Proportion submitting class standing: 75%.) **Average high school grade point average:** 3.4. **First-year students who submitted SAT scores:** 60%. Scores (25/75 percentile): Verbal: 490-610, Math: 490-610, Combined: 980-1220. **First-year students submitting ACT scores:** 67%. Scores (25/75 percentile): English: 19-26, Math: 19-26, Composite: 20-26.

ACADEMICS

Year founded: 1889. **Academic calendar:** Semester. **Degrees offered:** certificate, bachelor's, master's, post-master's certificate, first professional, doctorate. **Most popular majors:** 13% business, management, marketing, and related support services, 11% education, 9% engineering, 9% social sciences, 7% communication, journalism, and related programs. **Major fields of study:** agriculture, agriculture operations, and related sciences; architecture and related services; area, ethnic, cultural, and gender studies; biological and biomedical sciences; business, management, marketing, and related support services; communications technologies/technicians and support services; computer and information sciences and support services; construction trades; education; engineering technologies/technicians; English language and literature/letters; family and consumer sciences/human sciences; foreign languages, literatures, and linguistics; legal professions and studies; liberal arts and sciences studies, and humanities; library science; mathematics and statistics; mechanic and repair technologies/technicians; military technologies; multi/interdisciplinary studies; natural resources and conservation; parks, recreation, leisure, and fitness studies; personal and culinary services; philosophy and religious studies; physical sciences; precision production; psychology; security and protective services; social sciences; theology and religious vocations; transportation and materials moving; visual and performing arts. **Areas of required coursework:** mathematics, English (including composition), foreign languages, sciences (biological or physical), social science, other. **Pre-professional programs:** pre-medicine, pre-veterinary science. **Special academic programs:** accelerated program, cooperative (work-study plan) program, cross-registration, distance learning, double major, dual enrollment, English as a Second Language (ESL), exchange student program (domestic), honors program, independent study, internships, student-designed major, study abroad, teacher certificate program. **Teacher certification offered in:** early childhood, special education, elementary, vo-tech, middle/junior high, adult education, secondary. **Cooperative education programs:** agriculture, art, business, computer science, education, engineering, health professions, home economics, humanities, natural science, social/behavioral science, technologies, vocational arts. **Reserve Officers Training Corps (ROTC):** Army ROTC: Offered on campus; Navy ROTC: Offered on campus; Air Force ROTC: Offered at cooperating institution (Washington State University). **Faculty and instruction (2005-2006):** Total instructional faculty: 564 full-time, 22 part-time (74% men; 26% women; 9% minorities). Full-time faculty with Ph.D. or other terminal degree: 80%. Student/faculty ratio: 20/1. Classes of fewer than 20 students: 50%; of 20 to 49 students: 42%; of 50 or more students: 8%. **Advanced Placement and International Baccalaureate credit:** AP tests may be used for: Placement only. Scores accepted: 3, 4, 5. International Baccalaureate exams may be used for: Credit and/or placement. **Freshmen returning for sophomore year:** 80%. **Graduation rates:** Four-year: 23%; five-year: 52%; six-year: 60%.

COSTS AND FINANCIAL AID

Financial aid office: (208) 885-6312. **Expenses (2006-2007):** Tuition and fees 2006-2007: $4,200 in state, $13,800 out of state; room/board: $5,696. Estimated books and supplies: $1,388; transportation: $1,554; personal expenses: $2,682. **Financial aid:** Priority filing date for institution's financial aid form: February 15. In 2005-2006, 74% of undergraduates applied for financial aid. Of those, 59% were determined to have financial need; 26% had their need fully met. Average financial aid package (proportion receiving): $9,287 (58%). Average amount of gift aid, such as scholarships or grants (proportion receiving): $3,133 (37%). Average amount of self-help aid, such as work study or loans (proportion receiving): $5,843 (50%). Average need-based loan (excluding PLUS or other private loans): $5,733. Among students who received need-based aid, the average percentage of need met: 76%. Among students who received aid based on merit, the average award (and the proportion receiving): $3,562 (26%). The average athletic scholarship (and the proportion receiving): $12,959 (3%). Average amount of debt of borrowers graduating in 2005: $20,002. Proportion who borrowed: 69%.

CAMPUS LIFE AND EXTRACURRICULAR ACTIVITIES

Campus housing available: coed dorms, women's dorms, men's dorms, sorority housing, fraternity housing, apartments for married students, apartment for single students, special housing for disabled students, special housing for international students, cooperative housing. **Student employment:** During the 2005-2006 academic year, 35% of undergraduates worked on campus. Average per-year earnings: $1,500. **Clubs and organizations:** Number of student organizations: 181. Activities include: choral groups, concert band, dance, drama/theater, jazz band, literary magazine, marching band, music ensembles, musical theater, opera, pep band, radio station, student government, student newspaper, student film society, symphony orchestra, television station, yearbook. Number of fraternities: 18; sororities: 9. Average proportion of students who stay on campus on weekends: 90%. **Sports program (2005-2006):** Member of NCAA I. *Men's intercollegiate varsity sports:* basketball, cross-country, football, golf, tennis, track and field (indoor), track and field (outdoor). *Women's intercollegiate varsity sports:* basketball, cross-country, golf, soccer, swimming and diving, tennis, track and field (indoor), track and field (outdoor), volleyball.

SERVICES AND FACILITIES

Basic services: nonremedial tutoring, women's center, placement service, day care, health service, health insurance. **Remedial assistance:** reading, math, writing, study skills. **Counseling services:** minority student, career, military, personal, veteran student, academic, older student, psychological, birth control. **For learning-disabled students:** School does not offer a structured program with separate admission and additional fees. Services include: reading machines, tape recorders, videotaped classes, note-taking services, oral tests, learning center, readers, extended time for tests, tutors, other. **Information technology resources:** Students are not required to lease or own a computer. Number of campus computers available to all students: 700. School has a wireless network. Proportion of college-owned housing units wired for high-speed internet access: 100%. **Campus safety:** Security services offered: 24-hour foot and vehicle patrols, late-night transport/escort service, 24-hour emergency telephones, lighted pathways/sidewalks, controlled dormitory access (key, security card, etc).

TRANSFER AND INTERNATIONAL STUDENTS

Transfer students: May apply for admission for the following academic terms: Fall, Spring, Summer. Applicants need a minimum number of credits to apply. For fall 2005: Transfer applications received: 1,629. Transfer applicants offered admission: 1,169. Transfer applicants enrolled: 751. **International students:** Number of foreign undergraduates: 182 (2% of student body). Number of countries represented: 39. Minimum TOEFL score required: 525 (paper); 193 (computer). Average TOEFL score: 550 (paper).

Illinois

Augustana College

- **Address:** 639 38th Street, Rock Island, IL 61201-2296
- **Website:** http://www.augustana.edu
- **Private; Religious affiliation:** Evangelical Lutheran Church in America
- **Enrollment:** 2,363 full-time; 23 part-time

KEY STATS
- ✔ **U.S News College Ranking:** 104, Liberal Arts Colleges
- ✔ **ACT Score (25th/75th percentile):** 24-29
- ✔ **Tuition:** 2006-2007: $24,924
  - **Selectivity:** More selective   **Room/board:** $6,807
  - **Acceptance rate:** 84%   **Average debt:** $18,098
  - **Student/faculty ratio:** 12/1   **Proportion who borrowed:** 71%

UNDERGRADUATE STUDENT BODY STATS
2005-2006 enrollment: 2,363 full-time; 23 part-time. Men: 42%; women: 58%. **Ethnic makeup:** African American: 2%; Asian American: 2%; Hispanic: 3%; White: 91%; International: 1%. **Religious preference:** Roman Catholic: 35%; Protestant: 17%; Jewish: 1%; No preference: 2%; Unknown: 12%; Evangelical Lutheran Church in America: 22%; Other: 1%.

ADMISSIONS FACTS AND FIGURES
Phone: (800) 798-8100. **Email:** admissions@augustana.edu. **Website:** http://www.augustana.edu. **Application deadlines for fall 2007:** Regular decision: Rolling. Early decision: Not offered. Early action: Not offered. Admission can be deferred. **Application fee:** $25. Common application is accepted. **To apply online, go to:** http://www.augustana.edu/admission/app/application.htm. **Admissions requirements/recommendations:** High school units required (recommended): English: 4 (4); Mathematics: 3 (3); Science: 2 (2); Foreign language: 1 (1); Social studies: 1 (1); History: 1 (1); Academic electives: 4 (4); Total units: 16 (16). Tests: The college uses SAT or ACT scores in admissions decisions. Either SAT or ACT required. For admission to the fall 2007 entering class, the school will accept: ACT with writing, ACT without writing. Campus visit: Recommended. Admissions interview: Recommended. Off-campus interview: Not available. **Factors that count in admissions decisions: Academic:** Secondary school record: Very important. Class rank: Very important. Letters of recommendation: Important. Standardized test scores: Important. Essay: Important. **Nonacademic:** Interview: Important. Extracurricular activities: Important. Talent/ability: Important. Character/personal qualities: Important. Alumni/ae relationship: Considered. Geographical residence: Considered. State residency: Not considered. Religious affiliation/commitment: Considered. Minority status: Considered. Volunteer work: Considered. Work experience: Considered. **Admissions statistics for the fall 2005 entering class:** Total applicants: 2,921. Total accepted: 2,462. Freshmen enrolled: 679; 11% were from out of state. Overall acceptance rate: 84%. **Credentials of fall 2005 freshmen:** 29% ranked in the top 10 percent of their high school class; 63% were in the top 25 percent, and 94% were in the top half. (Proportion submitting class standing: 90%.) **Average high school grade point average:** 3.5. **First-year students who submitted SAT scores:** 6%. Scores (25/75 percentile): Verbal: N/A, Math: N/A, Combined: N/A. **First-year students submitting ACT scores:** 99%. Scores (25/75 percentile): English: N/A, Math: N/A, Composite: 24-29.

ACADEMICS
Year founded: 1860. **Academic calendar:** Quarter. **Degrees offered:** bachelor's. **Most popular majors:** 20% business/commerce, 15% biology, 11% social sciences, 8% English composition, 8% physiological psychology/psychobiology. **Major fields of study:** area, ethnic, cultural, and gender studies; biological and biomedical sciences; business, management, marketing, and related support services; computer and information sciences and support services; education; engineering; English language and literature/letters; foreign languages, literatures, and linguistics; health professions and related clinical sciences; history; mathematics and statistics; multi/interdis-

ciplinary studies; natural resources and conservation; philosophy and religious studies; physical sciences; psychology; public administration and social service professions; social sciences; visual and performing arts. **Areas of required coursework:** arts/fine arts, humanities, mathematics, English (including composition), foreign languages, sciences (biological or physical), social science, other. **Pre-professional programs:** pre-law, pre-dentistry, pre-medicine, pre-veterinary science, pre-optometry, pre-pharmacy, other. **Special academic programs (% participation):** accelerated program, cooperative (work-study plan) program, double major (31%), honors program (11%), independent study (49%), internships, liberal arts/career combination, study abroad (30%), teacher certificate program (12%). **Teacher certification offered in:** elementary, middle/junior high, secondary. **Faculty and instruction (2005-2006):** Total instructional faculty: 149 full-time, 86 part-time (57% men; 43% women; 9% minorities). Full-time faculty with Ph.D. or other terminal degree: 96%. Student/faculty ratio: 12/1. Classes of fewer than 20 students: 49%; of 20 to 49 students: 48%; of 50 or more students: 3%. **Advanced Placement and International Baccalaureate credit:** AP tests may be used for: Credit and/or placement. Scores accepted: 3, 4, 5. International Baccalaureate exams may be used for: Credit and/or placement. **Freshmen returning for sophomore year:** 86%. **Graduation rates:** Four-year: 71%; five-year: 76%; six-year: 76%. **Graduate study:** 35% of students pursue further study immediately upon graduation. Fields in which graduates pursue further study: Master of Business Administration (MBA), 5%; law, 3%; medicine, 4%; dentistry, 1%; engineering, 1%; education, 2%; arts and sciences, 18%; veterinary medicine, 1%.

COSTS AND FINANCIAL AID
Financial aid office: (309) 794-7207. **Expenses (2006-2007):** Tuition and fees 2006-2007: $24,924; room/board: $6,807. Estimated books and supplies: $675; transportation: $400; personal expenses: $800. **Financial aid:** Priority filing date for institution's financial aid form: April 1. In 2005-2006, 81% of undergraduates applied for financial aid. Of those, 68% were determined to have financial need; 27% had their need fully met. Average financial aid package (proportion receiving): $17,229 (68%). Average amount of gift aid, such as scholarships or grants (proportion receiving): $11,882 (67%). Average amount of self-help aid, such as work study or loans (proportion receiving): $4,909 (62%). Average need-based loan (excluding PLUS or other private loans): $4,541. Among students who received need-based aid, the average percentage of need met: 86%. Among students who received aid based on merit, the average award (and the proportion receiving): $8,087 (13%). Average amount of debt of borrowers graduating in 2005: $18,098. Proportion who borrowed: 71%.

CAMPUS LIFE AND EXTRACURRICULAR ACTIVITIES
Campus housing available: coed dorms, women's dorms, men's dorms, apartment for single students. Students who live in college-owned, operated, or affiliated housing: 70%. **Student employment:** During the 2005-2006 academic year, 60% of undergraduates worked on campus. Average per-year earnings: $1,500. **Clubs and organizations:** Number of student organizations: 153. Activities include: choral groups, concert band, dance, drama/theater, jazz band, literary magazine, music ensembles, musical theater, opera, pep band, radio station, student government, student newspaper, symphony orchestra, yearbook. Number of fraternities: 7; sororities: 6. Proportion of men in fraternities: 19%; of women in sororities: 26%. Average proportion of students who stay on campus on weekends: 80%. **Sports program (2005-2006):** Member of NCAA III. **Men's intercollegiate varsity sports:** baseball, basketball, cross-country, football, golf, soccer, swimming and diving, tennis, track and field (indoor), track and field (outdoor), wrestling. **Women's intercollegiate varsity sports:** basketball, cross-country, golf, soccer, softball, swimming and diving, tennis, track and field (indoor), track and field (outdoor), volleyball.

SERVICES AND FACILITIES
Basic services: nonremedial tutoring, women's center, placement service, health service, health insurance, other. **Counseling services:** minority student, career, personal, academic, psychological, religious. **For learning-disabled students:** School does not offer a structured program with separate admission and additional fees. Total undergraduates in learning-disabled

program or receiving services: 14. Services include: tape recorders, untimed tests, note-taking services, oral tests, learning center, tutors, early syllabus, priority registration, priority seating, substitution of courses, texts on tape, exams on tape or computer, take home exams, other testing accomodations, waiver of foreign language degree requirement, waiver of math degree requirement, other. **Information technology resources:** Students are not required to lease or own a computer. Number of campus computers available to all students: 450. School has a wireless network. Proportion of college-owned housing units wired for high-speed internet access: 95%. **Campus safety:** Security services offered: 24-hour foot and vehicle patrols, late-night transport/escort service, 24-hour emergency telephones, lighted pathways/sidewalks, controlled dormitory access (key, security card, etc).

TRANSFER AND INTERNATIONAL STUDENTS
Transfer students: May apply for admission for the following academic terms: Fall, Winter, Spring, Summer. Applicants need a minimum number of credits to apply. For fall 2005: Transfer applications received: 186. Transfer applicants offered admission: 146. Transfer applicants enrolled: 63. **International students:** Number of foreign undergraduates: 32 (1% of student body). Minimum TOEFL score required: 550 (paper); 203 (computer).

Aurora University

- ■ **Address:** 347 S. Gladstone Avenue, Aurora, IL 60506-4892
- ■ **Website:** http://www.aurora.edu
- ■ **Private**
- ■ **Enrollment:** 1,686 full-time; 221 part-time

KEY STATS
- ✔ **U.S News College Ranking:** third tier, Universities–Master's (Midwest)
- ✔ **ACT Score (25th/75th percentile):** 19-23
- ✔ **Tuition:** 2006-2007: $16,190

Selectivity: Selective	**Room/board:** $6,680
Acceptance rate: 74%	**Average debt:** $18,374
Student/faculty ratio: 17/1	**Proportion who borrowed:** 74%

UNDERGRADUATE STUDENT BODY STATS
2005-2006 enrollment: 1,686 full-time; 221 part-time. Men: 34%; women: 66%. **Ethnic makeup:** African American: 13%; Asian American: 2%; Hispanic: 12%; White: 72%.

ADMISSIONS FACTS AND FIGURES
Phone: (800) 742-5281. **Email:** admission@aurora.edu. **Website:** http://www.aurora.edu. **Application deadlines for fall 2007:** Regular decision: Rolling. Early decision: Not offered. Early action: Send application by: N/A; Decision sent by: N/A. Admission can be deferred. **Application fee:** $25. Common application is accepted. **To apply online, go to:** http://www.aurora.edu/prospective/apply.htm. **Admissions requirements/recommendations:** High school units required (recommended): English: (4); Mathematics: (3); Science: (3); Social studies: (3); Academic electives: (3); Total units: (16). Tests: The college uses SAT or ACT scores in admissions decisions. Either SAT or ACT required. For admission to the fall 2007 entering class, the school will accept: ACT with writing, ACT without writing. Campus visit: Recommended. Admissions interview: Recommended. Off-campus interview: May be arranged. **Factors that count in admissions decisions:** *Academic:* Secondary school record: Very important. Class rank: Very important. Letters of recommendation: Very important. Standardized test scores: Very important. Essay: Considered. *Nonacademic:* Interview: Very important. Extracurricular activities: Considered. Talent/ability: Considered. Character/personal qualities: Important. Alumni/ae relationship: Not considered. Geographical residence: Not considered. State residency: Not considered. Religious affiliation/commitment: Not considered. Minority status: Not considered. Volunteer work: Not considered. Work experience: Not considered. **Other schools with the greatest overlap in applicants:** Eastern Illinois University; Elmhurst College; Illinois State University; North Central College; Northern Illinois University. **Admissions statistics for the fall 2005 entering class:** Total applicants: 1,405. Total accepted: 1,036. Freshmen enrolled: 383; 8% were from out of state. Overall acceptance rate: 74%. Non-early acceptance rate: 74%. **Credentials of fall 2005 freshmen:** 10% ranked in the top 10 percent of their high school class; 36% were in the top 25 percent, and 70% were in the top half. (Proportion submitting class standing: 96%.) **Average**

high school grade point average: 3.2. **First-year students who submitted SAT scores:** 3%. Scores (25/75 percentile): Verbal: 450-530, Math: 430-540, Combined: 880-1070. **First-year students submitting ACT scores:** 97%. Scores (25/75 percentile): English: 19-24, Math: 18-23, Composite: 19-23.

ACADEMICS
Year founded: 1893. **Academic calendar:** Semester. **Degrees offered:** bachelor's, post-bachelor's certificate, master's, post-master's certificate, doctorate. **Most popular majors:** 26% business, management, marketing, and related support services, 20% education, 10% health professions and related clinical sciences, 8% public administration and social service professions, 8% security and protective services. **Major fields of study:** biological and biomedical sciences; business, management, marketing, and related support services; communication, journalism, and related programs; computer and information sciences and support services; education; engineering; English language and literature/letters; health professions and related clinical sciences; history; liberal arts and sciences studies, and humanities; mathematics and statistics; natural resources and conservation; parks, recreation, leisure, and fitness studies; physical sciences; psychology; public administration and social service professions; security and protective services; social sciences. **Areas of required coursework:** arts/fine arts, humanities, computer literacy, mathematics, English (including composition), philosophy, sciences (biological or physical), history, social science. **Pre-professional programs:** pre-law, pre-dentistry, pre-medicine, pre-veterinary science, other. **Special academic programs:** accelerated program, cross-registration, double major, dual enrollment, honors program, independent study, internships, liberal arts/career combination, student-designed major, study abroad, teacher certificate program, weekend college. **Teacher certification offered in:** elementary, middle/junior high, secondary. **Reserve Officers Training Corps (ROTC):** Army ROTC: Offered at cooperating institution (Wheaton College). **Faculty and instruction (2005-2006):** Total instructional faculty: 95 full-time, 176 part-time (44% men; 56% women; 12% minorities). Full-time faculty with Ph.D. or other terminal degree: 84%. Student/faculty ratio: 17/1. Classes of fewer than 20 students: 34%; of 20 to 49 students: 66%; of 50 or more students: 0%. **Advanced Placement and International Baccalaureate credit:** AP tests may be used for: Credit only. Scores accepted: 3. **Freshmen returning for sophomore year:** 70%. **Graduation rates:** Four-year: 33%; five-year: 51%; six-year: 49%.

COSTS AND FINANCIAL AID
Financial aid office: (630) 844-5533. **Expenses (2006-2007):** Tuition and fees 2006-2007: $16,190; room/board: $6,680. Estimated books and supplies: $1,000; transportation: $1,022; personal expenses: $1,100. **Financial aid:** Priority filing date for institution's financial aid form: April 15. In 2005-2006, 99% of undergraduates applied for financial aid. Of those, 76% were determined to have financial need; 41% had their need fully met. Average financial aid package (proportion receiving): $17,348 (76%). Average amount of gift aid, such as scholarships or grants (proportion receiving): $5,855 (53%). Average amount of self-help aid, such as work study or loans (proportion receiving): $4,412 (62%). Average need-based loan (excluding PLUS or other private loans): $3,811. Among students who received need-based aid, the average percentage of need met: 89%. Among students who received aid based on merit, the average award (and the proportion receiving): $8,703 (21%). The average athletic scholarship (and the proportion receiving): $0 (0%). Average amount of debt of borrowers graduating in 2005: $18,374. Proportion who borrowed: 74%.

CAMPUS LIFE AND EXTRACURRICULAR ACTIVITIES
Campus housing available (% using): coed dorms (100%), special housing for disabled students. Students who live in college-owned, operated, or affiliated housing: 31%. **Student employment:** During the 2005-2006 academic year, 18% of undergraduates worked on campus. Average per-year earnings: $4,160. **Clubs and organizations:** Number of student organizations: 27. Activities include: choral groups, dance, drama/theater, literary magazine, student government, student newspaper. Number of fraternities: 1; sororities: 7. Proportion of men in fraternities: 1%; of women in sororities: 3%. Average proportion of students who stay on campus on weekends: 30%. **Sports program (2005-2006):** Member of NCAA III. *Men's intercollegiate varsity sports:* baseball, basketball, cross-country, football, golf, soccer, tennis, track and field (indoor), track and field (outdoor). *Women's intercollegiate varsity sports:* basketball, cross-country, golf, soccer, softball, tennis, track and field (indoor), track and field (outdoor), volleyball.

SERVICES AND FACILITIES
Basic services: nonremedial tutoring, health service, health insurance. **Remedial assistance:** math, writing, study skills, other. **Counseling services:**

career, personal, academic, psychological. **For learning-disabled students:** School does not offer a structured program with separate admission and additional fees. Total undergraduates in learning-disabled program or receiving services: 42. Services include: remedial math, remedial English, reading machines, tape recorders, note-taking services, oral tests, learning center, readers, extended time for tests, tutors, priority seating, texts on tape, other testing accomodations, other. **Library:** Number of titles: 92,025; number of current serial subscriptions: 210. **Information technology resources:** Students are not required to lease or own a computer. Number of campus computers available to all students: 125. School has a wireless network. Approximate number of users that can be accommodated: 1,000. Proportion of college-owned housing units wired for high-speed internet access: 100%. **Campus safety:** Security services offered: 24-hour foot and vehicle patrols, late-night transport/escort service, 24-hour emergency telephones, lighted pathways/sidewalks, student patrols, controlled dormitory access (key, security card, etc).

TRANSFER AND INTERNATIONAL STUDENTS

Transfer students: May apply for admission for the following academic terms: Fall, Spring. Applicants need a minimum number of credits to apply. For fall 2005: Transfer applications received: 753. Transfer applicants offered admission: 713. Transfer applicants enrolled: 320. **International students:** Number of foreign undergraduates: 2. Minimum TOEFL score required: 550 (paper); 213 (computer).

Benedictine University

- **Address:** 5700 College Road, Lisle, IL 60532
- **Website:** http://www.ben.edu
- **Private; Religious affiliation:** Roman Catholic
- **Enrollment:** 1,518 full-time; 802 part-time

KEY STATS

- ✔ **U.S News College Ranking:** 30, Universities–Master's (Midwest)
- ✔ **ACT Score (25th/75th percentile):** 20-25
- ✔ **Tuition:** 2006-2007: $20,310

Selectivity: Selective	**Room/board:** $6,250
Acceptance rate: 82%	**Average debt:** N/A
Student/faculty ratio: 13/1	**Proportion who borrowed:** N/A

UNDERGRADUATE STUDENT BODY STATS

2005-2006 enrollment: 1,518 full-time; 802 part-time. Men: 40%; women: 60%. **Ethnic makeup:** African American: 10%; Asian American: 14%; Hispanic: 7%; White: 67%; International: 1%.

ADMISSIONS FACTS AND FIGURES

Phone: (630) 829-6300. **Email:** admissions@ben.edu. **Website:** http://www.ben.edu. **Application deadlines for fall 2007:** Regular decision: Rolling. Early decision: Not offered. Early action: Not offered. Admission can be deferred. **Application fee:** $40. Common application is accepted. **Admissions requirements/recommendations:** High school units required (recommended): English: 4; Mathematics: 3 (4); Science: 2 (3); Foreign language: 2; History: 1; Total units: 16. Tests: The college uses SAT or ACT scores in admissions decisions. Either SAT or ACT required. For admission to the fall 2007 entering class, the school will accept: ACT with writing, ACT without writing. Campus visit: Recommended. Admissions interview: Neither required nor recommended. Off-campus interview: May be arranged. **Factors that count in admissions decisions:** Academic: Secondary school record: Considered. Class rank: Very important. Letters of recommendation: Considered. Standardized test scores: Very important. Essay: Considered. *Nonacademic:* Interview: Considered. Extracurricular activities: Considered. Talent/ability: Considered. **Admissions statistics for the fall 2005 entering class:** Total applicants: 972. Total accepted: 800. Freshmen enrolled: 311; 4% were from out of state. Overall acceptance rate: 82%. **Credentials of fall 2005 freshmen:** 20% ranked in the top 10 percent of their high school class; 45% were in the top 25 percent, and 74% were in the top half. (Proportion submitting class standing: 87%.) **Average high school grade point average:** 3.4. **First-year students submitting ACT scores:** 100%. Scores (25/75 percentile): English: 19-25, Math: 20-25, Composite: 20-25.

ACADEMICS

Year founded: 1887. **Academic calendar:** Semester. **Degrees offered:** certificate, associate, bachelor's, post-bachelor's certificate, master's, doctorate. **Most popular majors:** 35% business, management, marketing, and related support services, 9% health professions and related clinical sciences, 9% psychology, 8% biological and biomedical sciences, 8% social sciences. **Major fields of study:** biological and biomedical sciences; business, management, marketing, and related support services; communication, journalism, and related programs; computer and information sciences and support services; education; engineering; English language and literature/letters; family and consumer sciences/human sciences; foreign languages, literatures, and linguistics; health professions and related clinical sciences; history; legal professions and studies; liberal arts and sciences studies, and humanities; mathematics and statistics; multi/interdisciplinary studies; natural resources and conservation; philosophy and religious studies; physical sciences; psychology; social sciences; visual and performing arts. **Areas of required coursework:** arts/fine arts, humanities, mathematics, English (including composition), philosophy, sciences (biological or physical), social science. **Pre-professional programs:** pre-law, pre-dentistry, pre-medicine, pre-veterinary science, pre-optometry, pre-pharmacy. **Special academic programs:** accelerated program, cooperative (work-study plan) program, cross-registration, distance learning, double major, exchange student program (domestic), honors program, independent study, internships, study abroad, teacher certificate program, weekend college. **Teacher certification offered in:** special education, elementary, middle/junior high, secondary. **Reserve Officers Training Corps (ROTC):** Army ROTC: Offered at cooperating institution (Wheaton College). **Faculty and instruction (2005-2006):** Total instructional faculty: 88 full-time, 266 part-time (55% men; 45% women; 12% minorities). Full-time faculty with Ph.D. or other terminal degree: 91%. Student/faculty ratio: 13/1. Classes of fewer than 20 students: 61%; of 20 to 49 students: 39%; of 50 or more students: 0%. **Advanced Placement and International Baccalaureate credit:** International Baccalaureate exams may be used for: Credit only. **Freshmen returning for sophomore year:** 76%. **Graduation rates:** Four-year: 29%; five-year: 44%; six-year: 51%.

COSTS AND FINANCIAL AID

Financial aid office: (630) 829-6108. **Expenses (2006-2007):** Tuition and fees 2006-2007: $20,310; room/board: $6,250. **Financial aid:** In 2005-2006, 75% of undergraduates applied for financial aid. Of those, 74% were determined to have financial need; 40% had their need fully met. Average financial aid package (proportion receiving): $11,980 (73%). Average amount of gift aid, such as scholarships or grants (proportion receiving): $6,350 (42%). Average amount of self-help aid, such as work study or loans (proportion receiving): $4,344 (50%). Average need-based loan (excluding PLUS or other private loans): $4,170. Among students who received need-based aid, the average percentage of need met: 85%. Among students who received aid based on merit, the average award (and the proportion receiving): $6,720 (18%). The average athletic scholarship (and the proportion receiving): $0 (0%).

CAMPUS LIFE AND EXTRACURRICULAR ACTIVITIES

Campus housing available: coed dorms, women's dorms, men's dorms, apartments for married students, apartment for single students. Students who live in college-owned, operated, or affiliated housing: 22%. **Student employment:** During the 2005-2006 academic year, 26% of undergraduates worked on campus. **Clubs and organizations:** Number of student organizations: 30. Activities include: choral groups, concert band, jazz band, literary magazine, music ensembles, pep band, student government, student newspaper, student film society, symphony orchestra, television station. Number of fraternities: 0; sororities: 0. **Sports program (2005-2006):** Member of NCAA III. *Men's intercollegiate varsity sports:* baseball, basketball, cross-country, football, golf, soccer, swimming and diving, track and field (indoor), track and field (outdoor). *Women's intercollegiate varsity sports:* basketball, cross-country, soccer, softball, swimming and diving, tennis, track and field (indoor), track and field (outdoor), volleyball.

SERVICES AND FACILITIES

Basic services: nonremedial tutoring, placement service, health service. **Counseling services:** career, military, personal, academic, psychological, religious. **For learning-disabled students:** School does not offer a structured program with separate admission and additional fees. Services include: reading machines, tape recorders, videotaped classes, untimed tests, note-taking services, oral tests, learning center, readers, extended time for tests, tutors, priority seating, proofreading services, texts on tape, other testing accomodations. **Library:** Number of titles: 166,537; number of current serial subscriptions: 16,186. **Information technology resources:** Students are not required to lease or own a computer. Number of campus computers available to all students: 200. School does not have a wireless network. Proportion of college-owned housing units wired for high-speed internet access: 100%. **Campus safety:** Security services offered: 24-hour foot and vehicle patrols, late-night transport/escort service, 24-hour emergency telephones, lighted pathways/sidewalks, controlled dormitory access (key, security card, etc).

TRANSFER AND INTERNATIONAL STUDENTS

Transfer students: May apply for admission for the following academic terms: Fall, Spring, Summer. Applicants do not need a minimum number of credits to apply. For fall 2005: Transfer applications received: 634. Transfer applicants offered admission: 525. Transfer applicants enrolled: 235. **International students:** Number of foreign undergraduates: 23 (1% of student body). Number of countries represented: 9. Minimum TOEFL score required: 550 (paper); 213 (computer).

Blackburn College

- **Address:** 700 College Avenue, Carlinville, IL 62626
- **Website:** http://www.blackburn.edu
- **Private; Religious affiliation:** Presbyterian
- **Enrollment:** 589 full-time; 16 part-time

KEY STATS

✔ **U.S News College Ranking:** fourth tier, Liberal Arts Colleges
✔ **ACT Score (25th/75th percentile):** 19-24
✔ **Tuition:** 2006-2007: $15,700

Selectivity: Selective	**Room/board:** $3,880
Acceptance rate: 62%	**Average debt:** $12,120
Student/faculty ratio: 17/1	**Proportion who borrowed:** 84%

UNDERGRADUATE STUDENT BODY STATS

2005-2006 enrollment: 589 full-time; 16 part-time. Men: 47%; women: 53%. **Ethnic makeup:** African American: 7%; Asian American: 1%; Hispanic: 1%; White: 89%; International: 1%. **Religious preference:** Roman Catholic: 15%; Protestant: 1%; Unknown: 55%; Presbyterian: 2%; Other: 27%.

ADMISSIONS FACTS AND FIGURES

Phone: (800) 233-3550. **Email:** admit@mail.blackburn.edu. **Website:** http://www.blackburn.edu. **Application deadlines for fall 2007:** Regular decision: Rolling. Early decision: Not offered. Early action: Not offered. Admission can be deferred. **Application fee:** None. Common application is not accepted. **Admissions requirements/recommendations:** High school units required (recommended): English: 4 (4); Mathematics: 3 (3); Science: 2 (3); Foreign language: 2 (2); Social studies: 2 (2); History: 2 (2); Academic electives: 3; Total units: 18 (16). Tests: The college uses SAT or ACT scores in admissions decisions. Either SAT or ACT required. For admission to the fall 2007 entering class, the school will accept: ACT with writing, ACT without writing. Campus visit: Recommended. Admissions interview: Recommended. Off-campus interview: May be arranged. **Factors that count in admissions decisions:** *Academic:* Secondary school record: Very important. Class rank: Very important. Letters of recommendation: Considered. Standardized test scores: Very important. Essay: Considered. *Nonacademic:* Interview: Considered. Extracurricular activities: Considered. Talent/ability: Considered. Character/personal qualities: Very important. Alumni/ae relationship: Considered. Geographical residence: Not considered. State residency: Not considered. Religious affiliation/commitment: Not considered. Minority status: Not considered. Volunteer work: Considered. Work experience: Important. **Other schools with the greatest overlap in applicants:** Illinois College; Millikin University; Southern Illinois University–Edwardsville; University of Illinois–Springfield; University of Illinois–Urbana-Champaign. **Admissions statistics for the fall 2005 entering class:** Total applicants: 937. Total accepted: 583. Freshmen enrolled: 211; Overall acceptance rate: 62%. **Size of waiting list:** 0 applicants; enrolled from waiting list: 0. **Credentials of fall 2005 freshmen:** 17% ranked in the top 10 percent of their high school class; 44% were in the top 25 percent, and 80% were in the top half. (Proportion submitting class standing: 97%.) **First-year students who submitted SAT scores:** 3%. Scores (25/75 percentile): Verbal: N/A, Math: N/A, Combined: N/A. **First-year students submitting ACT scores:** 97%. Scores (25/75 percentile): English: 18-24, Math: 17-25, Composite: 19-24.

ACADEMICS

Year founded: 1837. **Academic calendar:** Semester. **Degrees offered:** bachelor's. **Most popular majors:** 17% elementary education and teaching, 9% biology/biological sciences, 7% accounting, 7% business administration, management, and operations, 7% communication studies/speech communication and rhetoric. **Major fields of study:** biological and biomedical sciences; communication, journalism, and related programs; computer and information sciences and support services; education; English language and literature/letters; mathematics and statistics; multi/interdisciplinary studies. **Areas of required coursework:** arts/fine arts, humanities, mathematics, English (including composition), philosophy, sciences (biological or physical), history, social science. **Pre-professional programs:** pre-law, pre-dentistry, pre-medicine, pre-theology, pre-veterinary science. **Special academic programs (% participation):** cooperative (work-study plan) program, double major (16.5%), independent study (36.3%), internships (28.9%), study abroad (2.4%), teacher certificate program (28.9%). **Teacher certification offered in:** elementary, middle/junior high, secondary. **Faculty and instruction (2005-2006):** Total instructional faculty: N/A. Student/faculty ratio: 17/1. Classes of fewer than 20 students: 65%; of 20 to 49 students: 34%; of 50 or more students: 1%. **Advanced Placement and International Baccalaureate credit:** AP tests may be used for: Credit and/or placement. Scores accepted: 3, 4, 5. **Freshmen returning for sophomore year:** 61%. **Graduation rates:** Six-year: 38%.

COSTS AND FINANCIAL AID

Financial aid office: (800) 233-3550. **Expenses (2006-2007):** Tuition and fees 2006-2007: $15,700; room/board: $3,880. Estimated books and supplies: $700; transportation: $50; personal expenses: $800. **Financial aid:** Priority filing date for institution's financial aid form: April 1. In 2005-2006, 96% of undergraduates applied for financial aid. Of those, 85% were determined to have financial need; 38% had their need fully met. Average financial aid package (proportion receiving): $9,808 (85%). Average amount of gift aid, such as scholarships or grants (proportion receiving): $6,179 (82%). Average amount of self-help aid, such as work study or loans (proportion receiving): $5,325 (80%). Average need-based loan (excluding PLUS or other private loans): $3,030. Among students who received need-based aid, the average percentage of need met: 91%. Among students who received aid based on merit, the average award (and the proportion receiving): $6,499 (10%). The average athletic scholarship (and the proportion receiving): $0 (0%). Average amount of debt of borrowers graduating in 2005: $12,120. Proportion who borrowed: 84%.

CAMPUS LIFE AND EXTRACURRICULAR ACTIVITIES

Campus housing available (% using): coed dorms (70%), women's dorms (19%), men's dorms (11%). **Student employment:** During the 2005-2006 academic year, 85% of undergraduates worked on campus. Average per-year earnings: $4,450. **Clubs and organizations:** Number of student organizations: 22. Activities include: choral groups, concert band, drama/theater, literary magazine, student government, student newspaper, yearbook. Number of fraternities: 0; sororities: 0. Average proportion of students who stay on campus on weekends: 65%. **Sports program (2005-2006):** Member of NCAA III. *Men's intercollegiate varsity sports:* baseball, basketball, cross-country, football, golf, soccer. *Women's intercollegiate varsity sports:* basketball, cross-country, soccer, softball, tennis, volleyball.

SERVICES AND FACILITIES

Basic services: placement service. **Remedial assistance:** math, writing, study skills. **Counseling services:** minority student, career, academic, psychological, religious. **For learning-disabled students:** School does not offer a structured program with separate admission and additional fees. Total undergraduates in learning-disabled program or receiving services: 6. Services include: remedial English, reading machines, tape recorders, videotaped classes, untimed tests, note-taking services, oral tests, learning center, readers, extended time for tests, tutors, priority seating, proofreading services, texts on tape, typist/scribe, exams on tape or computer. **Library:** Number of titles: 61,586; number of current serial subscriptions: 79. **Information technology resources:** Students are not required to lease or own a computer. Number of campus computers available to all students: 58. School does not have a wireless network. Proportion of college-owned housing units wired for high-speed internet access: 100%. **Campus safety:** Security services offered: late-night transport/escort service, 24-hour emergency telephones, lighted pathways/sidewalks, student patrols.

TRANSFER AND INTERNATIONAL STUDENTS

Transfer students: May apply for admission for the following academic terms: Fall, Spring, Summer. Applicants do not need a minimum number of credits to apply. For fall 2005: Transfer applications received: 165. Transfer applicants offered admission: 81. Transfer applicants enrolled: 47. **International students:** Number of foreign undergraduates: 7 (1% of student body). Minimum TOEFL score required: 525 (paper); 197 (computer). Average TOEFL score: 540 (paper).

Bradley University

- **Address:** 1501 W. Bradley Avenue, Peoria, IL 61625
- **Website:** http://www.bradley.edu
- **Private**
- **Enrollment:** 5,055 full-time; 314 part-time

KEY STATS
✔ **U.S News College Ranking:** 7, Universities–Master's (Midwest)
✔ **ACT Score (25th/75th percentile):** 23-27
✔ **Tuition:** 2006-2007: $19,830

Selectivity: More selective	**Room/board:** $6,750
Acceptance rate: 89%	**Average debt:** $15,105
Student/faculty ratio: 14/1	**Proportion who borrowed:** 74%

UNDERGRADUATE STUDENT BODY STATS
2005-2006 enrollment: 5,055 full-time; 314 part-time. Men: 45%; women: 55%. **Ethnic makeup:** African American: 6%; Asian American: 3%; Hispanic: 2%; White: 88%; International: 1%.

ADMISSIONS FACTS AND FIGURES
Phone: (800) 447-6460. **Email:** admissions@bradley.edu. **Website:** http://www.bradley.edu. **Application deadlines for fall 2007:** Regular decision: Rolling. Early decision: Not offered. Early action: Not offered. Admission can be deferred. **Application fee:** $35. Common application is accepted. **To apply online, go to:** http://www.bradley.edu/admissions/student/application.html. **Admissions requirements/recommendations:** High school units required (recommended): English: 4 (5); Mathematics: 3 (4); Science: 2 (3); Foreign language: (2); Social studies: 2 (3); Total units: 11 (17). Tests: The college uses SAT or ACT scores in admissions decisions. Either SAT or ACT required. For admission to the fall 2007 entering class, the school will accept: ACT with writing, ACT without writing. Campus visit: Recommended. Admissions interview: Recommended. Off-campus interview: May be arranged. **Factors that count in admissions decisions: Academic:** Secondary school record: Very important. Class rank: Considered. Letters of recommendation: Considered. Standardized test scores: Important. Essay: Considered. **Nonacademic:** Interview: Considered. Extracurricular activities: Important. Talent/ability: Considered. Character/personal qualities: Considered. Alumni/ae relationship: Considered. Geographical residence: Considered. State residency: Not considered. Religious affiliation/commitment: Not considered. Minority status: Considered. Volunteer work: Considered. Work experience: Not considered. **Other schools with the greatest overlap in applicants:** DePaul University; Illinois State University; Marquette University; Northern Illinois University; University of Illinois–Urbana-Champaign. **Admissions statistics for the fall 2005 entering class:** Total applicants: 4,186. Total accepted: 3,715. Freshmen enrolled: 1,136; 15% were from out of state. Overall acceptance rate: 89%. **Size of waiting list:** 46 applicants; enrolled from waiting list: 13. **Credentials of fall 2005 freshmen:** 30% ranked in the top 10 percent of their high school class; 61% were in the top 25 percent, and 92% were in the top half. (Proportion submitting class standing: 88%.) **Average high school grade point average:** 3.6. **First-year students who submitted SAT scores:** 10%. Scores (25/75 percentile): Verbal: 510-650, Math: 540-650, Combined: 1050-1300. **First-year students submitting ACT scores:** 95%. Scores (25/75 percentile): English: 22-28, Math: 22-28, Composite: 23-27.

ACADEMICS
Year founded: 1897. **Academic calendar:** Semester. **Degrees offered:** bachelor's, master's, doctorate. **Most popular majors:** 7% elementary education and teaching, 5% advertising, 5% psychology, 4% English language and literature, 4% mechanical engineering. **Major fields of study:** agriculture, agriculture operations, and related sciences; biological and biomedical sciences; business, management, marketing, and related support services; communication, journalism, and related programs; communications technologies/technicians and support services; computer and information sciences and support services; education; engineering; engineering technologies/technicians; English language and literature/letters; family and consumer sciences/human sciences; foreign languages, literatures, and linguistics; health professions and related clinical sciences; history; mathematics and statistics; natural resources and conservation; philosophy and religious studies; physical sciences; psychology; public administration and social service professions; security and protective services; social sciences; visual and performing arts. **Areas of required coursework:** arts/fine arts, humanities, computer literacy, mathematics, English (including composition), sciences (biological or physical), social science, other. **Pre-professional programs:** other. **Special academic programs (% participation):** cooperative (work-study plan) program (3%), double major (8%), honors program (8%), independent study, internships (26%), student-designed major, study abroad (20%), teacher certificate program (19%). **Teacher certification offered in:** early childhood, special education, elementary, secondary. **Cooperative education programs:** art, business, computer science, education, engineering, health professions, home economics, humanities, natural science, social/behavioral science. **Reserve Officers Training Corps (ROTC):** Army ROTC: Offered at cooperating institution (Illinois State University). **Faculty and instruction (2005-2006):** Total instructional faculty: 321 full-time, 224 part-time (58% men; 42% women; 12% minorities). Full-time faculty with Ph.D. or other terminal degree: 85%. Student/faculty ratio: 14/1. Classes of fewer than 20 students: 46%; of 20 to 49 students: 50%; of 50 or more students: 4%. **Advanced Placement and International Baccalaureate credit:** AP tests may be used for: Credit only. Scores accepted: 4, 5. International Baccalaureate exams may be used for: Credit only. **Freshmen returning for sophomore year:** 88%. **Graduation rates:** Four-year: 53%; five-year: 71%; six-year: 72%. **Graduate study:** 17% of students pursue further study immediately upon graduation. Fields in which graduates pursue further study: Master of Business Administration (MBA), 8%; law, 7%; medicine, 3%; engineering, 9%; education, 4%; arts and sciences, 33%.

COSTS AND FINANCIAL AID
Financial aid office: (309) 677-3089. **Expenses (2006-2007):** Tuition and fees 2006-2007: $19,830; room/board: $6,750. Estimated books and supplies: $1,000; transportation: $250; personal expenses: $1,870. **Financial aid:** Priority filing date for institution's financial aid form: March 1. In 2005-2006, 88% of undergraduates applied for financial aid. Of those, 73% were determined to have financial need; 37% had their need fully met. Average financial aid package (proportion receiving): $13,098 (73%). Average amount of gift aid, such as scholarships or grants (proportion receiving): $8,755 (69%). Average amount of self-help aid, such as work study or loans (proportion receiving): $6,397 (52%). Average need-based loan (excluding PLUS or other private loans): $5,757. Among students who received need-based aid, the average percentage of need met: 82%. Among students who received aid based on merit, the average award (and the proportion receiving): $10,015 (23%). The average athletic scholarship (and the proportion receiving): $12,918 (2%). Average amount of debt of borrowers graduating in 2005: $15,105. Proportion who borrowed: 74%.

CAMPUS LIFE AND EXTRACURRICULAR ACTIVITIES
Campus housing available (% using): coed dorms (74%), sorority housing (8%), fraternity housing (15%), apartments for married students, apartment for single students (3%). Students who live in college-owned, operated, or affiliated housing: 70%. **Student employment:** During the 2005-2006 academic year, 18% of undergraduates worked on campus. Average per-year earnings: $1,050. **Clubs and organizations:** Number of student organizations: 215. Activities include: choral groups, concert band, dance, drama/theater, jazz band, literary magazine, music ensembles, pep band, radio station, student government, student newspaper, student film society, symphony orchestra, yearbook. Number of fraternities: 17; sororities: 12. Proportion of men in fraternities: 28%; of women in sororities: 25%. Average proportion of students who stay on campus on weekends: 75%. **Sports program (2005-2006):** Member of NCAA I. *Men's intercollegiate varsity sports:* baseball, basketball, cross-country, golf, soccer, tennis. *Women's intercollegiate varsity sports:* basketball, cross-country, golf, softball, tennis, track and field (indoor), track and field (outdoor), volleyball.

SERVICES AND FACILITIES
Basic services: nonremedial tutoring, placement service, health service, health insurance. **Remedial assistance:** study skills, other. **Counseling services:** minority student, career, academic, psychological. **For learning-disabled students:** School does not offer a structured program with separate admission and additional fees. Total undergraduates in learning-disabled program or receiving services: 100. Services include: tape recorders, videotaped classes, untimed tests, learning center, extended time for tests, tutors,

exams on tape or computer. **Library:** Number of titles: 531,292; number of current serial subscriptions: 19,000. **Information technology resources:** Students are not required to lease or own a computer. Number of campus computers available to all students: 900. School has a wireless network. Approximate number of users that can be accommodated: 1,600. Proportion of college-owned housing units wired for high-speed internet access: 100%. **Campus safety:** Security services offered: 24-hour foot and vehicle patrols, late-night transport/escort service, 24-hour emergency telephones, lighted pathways/sidewalks, controlled dormitory access (key, security card, etc).

TRANSFER AND INTERNATIONAL STUDENTS

Transfer students: May apply for admission for the following academic terms: Fall, Winter, Spring, Summer. Applicants need a minimum number of credits to apply. For fall 2005: Transfer applications received: 1,228. Transfer applicants offered admission: 704. Transfer applicants enrolled: 354. **International students:** Number of foreign undergraduates: 58 (1% of student body). Number of countries represented: 31. Minimum TOEFL score required: 550 (paper); 197 (computer). Average TOEFL score: 510 (paper).

Chicago State University

- ■ **Address:** 9501 S. King Drive, Chicago, IL 60628
- ■ **Website:** http://www.csu.edu
- ■ **Public**
- ■ **Enrollment:** 3,456 full-time; 1,704 part-time

KEY STATS

✔ **U.S News College Ranking:** fourth tier, Universities–Master's (Midwest)
✔ **ACT Score (25th/75th percentile):** 17-20
✔ **Tuition:** 2006-2007: $7,138 in state, $12,748 out of state

Selectivity: Less selective	**Room/board:** $6,492
Acceptance rate: 51%	**Average debt:** N/A
Student/faculty ratio: 14/1	**Proportion who borrowed:** N/A

UNDERGRADUATE STUDENT BODY STATS

2005-2006 enrollment: 3,456 full-time; 1,704 part-time. Men: 28%; women: 72%. **Ethnic makeup:** African American: 87%; Asian American: 1%; Hispanic: 6%; White: 6%; International: 1%.

ADMISSIONS FACTS AND FIGURES

Phone: (773) 995-2513. **Email:** ug-admissions@csu.edu. **Website:** http://www.csu.edu. **Application deadlines for fall 2007:** Regular decision: Rolling. Early decision: Not offered. Early action: Not offered. Admission can be deferred. **Application fee:** $25. Common application is accepted. **Admissions requirements/recommendations:** High school units required (recommended): English: 4; Mathematics: 3; Science: 3; Foreign language: (2); History: (2); Academic electives: 2 (2); Total units: 15. Tests: The college uses SAT or ACT scores in admissions decisions. ACT required. For admission to the fall 2007 entering class, the school will accept: ACT with writing, ACT without writing. Campus visit: Recommended. Admissions interview: Neither required nor recommended. Off-campus interview: Not available. **Factors that count in admissions decisions:** *Academic:* Secondary school record: Very important. Class rank: Not considered. Letters of recommendation: Considered. Standardized test scores: Very important. Essay: Not considered. *Nonacademic:* Interview: Considered. Extracurricular activities: Considered. Talent/ability: Considered. Character/personal qualities: Not considered. Alumni/ae relationship: Not considered. Geographical residence: Not considered. State residency: Not considered. Religious affiliation/commitment: Not considered. Minority status: Not considered. Volunteer work: Not considered. Work experience: Not considered. **Other schools with the greatest overlap in applicants:** Northeastern Illinois University; Northern Illinois University; Southern Illinois University–Carbondale; Southern Illinois University–Edwardsville; University of Illinois–Chicago. **Admissions statistics for the fall 2005 entering class:** Total applicants: 2,997. Total accepted: 1,518. Freshmen enrolled: 451; 7% were from out of state. Overall acceptance rate: 51%. **Credentials of fall 2005 freshmen:** 11% ranked in the top 10 percent of their high school class; 32% were in the top 25 percent, and 63% were in the top half. (Proportion submitting class standing: 85%.) **Average high school grade**

point average: 2.6. **First-year students submitting ACT scores:** 90%. Scores (25/75 percentile): English: 16-20, Math: 16-18, Composite: 17-20.

ACADEMICS

Year founded: 1867. **Academic calendar:** Semester. **Degrees offered:** certificate, bachelor's, post-bachelor's certificate, master's, doctorate. **Most popular majors:** 36% liberal arts and sciences/liberal studies, 15% business administration and management, 9% psychology, 6% criminal justice/safety studies, 4% elementary education and teaching. **Major fields of study:** area, ethnic, cultural, and gender studies; biological and biomedical sciences; business, management, marketing, and related support services; communication, journalism, and related programs; computer and information sciences and support services; education; English language and literature/letters; foreign languages, literatures, and linguistics; health professions and related clinical sciences; history; liberal arts and sciences studies, and humanities; mathematics and statistics; parks, recreation, leisure, and fitness studies; physical sciences; psychology; security and protective services; social sciences; visual and performing arts. **Areas of required coursework:** arts/fine arts, humanities, computer literacy, mathematics, English (including composition), philosophy, foreign languages, sciences (biological or physical), history, social science, other. **Pre-professional programs:** pre-law, pre-dentistry, pre-medicine, pre-pharmacy. **Special academic programs:** cooperative (work-study plan) program, distance learning, double major, English as a Second Language (ESL), honors program, independent study, internships, liberal arts/career combination, student-designed major, study abroad, teacher certificate program, weekend college. **Teacher certification offered in:** early childhood, special education, elementary, vo-tech, middle/junior high, secondary, bilingual/bicultural. **Reserve Officers Training Corps (ROTC):** Army ROTC: Offered on campus. **Faculty and instruction (2005-2006):** Total instructional faculty: 307 full-time, 155 part-time (48% men; 52% women; 66% minorities). Full-time faculty with Ph.D. or other terminal degree: 64%. Student/faculty ratio: 14/1. Classes of fewer than 20 students: 43%; of 20 to 49 students: 55%; of 50 or more students: 1%. **Advanced Placement and International Baccalaureate credit:** AP tests may be used for: Credit only. Scores accepted: 3. International Baccalaureate exams may be used for: Credit and/or placement. **Freshmen returning for sophomore year:** 57%. **Graduation rates:** Four-year: 2%; five-year: 9%; six-year: 16%. **Graduate study:** 12% of students pursue further study immediately upon graduation; 17% within one year; 43% within five years.

COSTS AND FINANCIAL AID

Financial aid office: (773) 995-2304. **Expenses (2006-2007):** Tuition and fees 2006-2007: $7,138 in state, $12,748 out of state; room/board: $6,492. Estimated books and supplies: $1,400; transportation: $800; personal expenses: $2,500. **Financial aid:** Priority filing date for institution's financial aid form: January 15. In 2005-2006, 93% of undergraduates applied for financial aid. Of those, 84% were determined to have financial need; 1% had their need fully met. Average financial aid package (proportion receiving): $3,912 (80%). Average amount of gift aid, such as scholarships or grants (proportion receiving): $3,012 (72%). Average amount of self-help aid, such as work study or loans (proportion receiving): $2,046 (48%). Average need-based loan (excluding PLUS or other private loans): $1,993. Among students who received need-based aid, the average percentage of need met: 47%. Among students who received aid based on merit, the average award (and the proportion receiving): $2,573 (1%). The average athletic scholarship (and the proportion receiving): $5,002 (3%).

CAMPUS LIFE AND EXTRACURRICULAR ACTIVITIES

Campus housing available (% using): coed dorms (95%), special housing for disabled students (5%). Students who live in college-owned, operated, or affiliated housing: 6%. **Clubs and organizations:** Number of student organizations: 48. Activities include: choral groups, dance, drama/theater, jazz band, literary magazine, music ensembles, opera, radio station, student government, student newspaper, student film society, television station. Number of fraternities: 4; sororities: 4. Average proportion of students who stay on campus on weekends: 7%. **Sports program (2005-2006):** Member of NCAA I. *Men's intercollegiate varsity sports:* baseball, basketball, cross-country, golf, tennis, track and field (indoor), track and field (outdoor). *Women's intercollegiate varsity sports:* basketball, cross-country, golf, tennis, track and field (indoor), track and field (outdoor), volleyball.

SERVICES AND FACILITIES

Basic services: nonremedial tutoring, women's center, placement service, day care, health service, health insurance. **Remedial assistance:** reading, math, writing, study skills. **Counseling services:** minority student, career, military, personal, veteran student, academic, older student, psychological, birth control. **For learning-disabled students:** School does not offer a structured program with separate admission and additional fees. Total undergraduates in learning-disabled program or receiving services: 17. Services include: remedial math, remedial English, reading machines, remedial reading, tape recorders, diagnostic testing service, note-taking services, oral tests, learning center, readers, extended time for tests, tutors, early syllabus, priority registration, priority seating, texts on tape, typist/scribe, other testing accomodations. **Library:** Number of titles: 423,697; number of current serial subscriptions: 19,005. **Information technology resources:** Students are not required to lease or own a computer. Number of campus computers available to all students: 754. School has a wireless network. Proportion of college-owned housing units wired for high-speed internet access: 100%. **Campus safety:** Security services offered: late-night transport/escort service, 24-hour emergency telephones, lighted pathways/sidewalks, student patrols, controlled dormitory access (key, security card, etc).

TRANSFER AND INTERNATIONAL STUDENTS

Transfer students: May apply for admission for the following academic terms: Fall, Spring, Summer. Applicants need a minimum number of credits to apply. For fall 2005: Transfer applications received: 2,997. Transfer applicants offered admission: 1,518. Transfer applicants enrolled: 794. **International students:** Number of foreign undergraduates: 35 (1% of student body). Number of countries represented: 19. Minimum TOEFL score required: 525 (paper); 195 (computer).

Columbia College

- **Address:** 600 S. Michigan Avenue, Chicago, IL 60605-1996
- **Website:** http://www.colum.edu
- **Private**
- **Enrollment:** 8,728 full-time; 1,416 part-time

KEY STATS

✔ **U.S News College Ranking:** fourth tier, Universities–Master's (Midwest)
✔ **ACT Score (25th/75th percentile):** 17-24
✔ **Tuition:** 2006-2007: $16,788

Selectivity: Less selective	**Room/board:** $9,765
Acceptance rate: 91%	**Average debt:** N/A
Student/faculty ratio: 14/1	**Proportion who borrowed:** N/A

UNDERGRADUATE STUDENT BODY STATS

2005-2006 enrollment: 8,728 full-time; 1,416 part-time. Men: 49%; women: 51%. **Ethnic makeup:** African American: 14%; American-Indian: 1%; Asian American: 3%; Hispanic: 9%; White: 71%; International: 2%.

ADMISSIONS FACTS AND FIGURES

Phone: (312) 344-7130. **Email:** admissions@colum.edu. **Website:** http://www.colum.edu. **Application deadlines for fall 2007:** Regular decision: Rolling. Early decision: Not offered. Early action: Not offered. Admission can be deferred. **Application fee:** $35. Common application is not accepted. **Admissions requirements/recommendations:** High school units required (recommended): English: 0 (4); Mathematics: 0 (2); Science: 0 (3); Foreign language: 0 (0); Social studies: 0 (3); History: 0 (3); Academic electives: 0 (0); Total units: 0 (15). Tests: The college does not use SAT or ACT scores in admissions decisions. Neither SAT nor ACT required. Campus visit: Recommended. Admissions interview: Recommended. Off-campus interview: Not available. **Factors that count in admissions decisions:** *Academic:* Secondary school record: Not considered. Class rank: Not considered. Letters of recommendation: Not considered. Standardized test scores: Not considered. Essay: Not considered. *Nonacademic:* Interview: Not considered. Extracurricular activities: Not considered. Talent/ability: Not considered. Character/personal qualities: Not considered. Alumni/ae relationship: Not considered. Geographical residence: Not considered. State residency: Not considered. Religious affiliation/commitment: Not considered. Minority status: Not considered. Volunteer work: Not considered. Work experience: Not considered. **Other schools with the greatest overlap in applicants:** DePaul University; Illinois Institute of Art at Chicago; Illinois State University; Northern Illinois University; University of Illinois–Chicago. **Admissions statistics for the fall 2005 entering class:** Total applicants: 3,428. Total accepted: 3,111. Freshmen enrolled: 1,829; 39% were from out of state. Overall acceptance rate: 91%. **Credentials of fall 2005 freshmen:** 7% ranked in the top 10 percent of their high school class; 23% were in the top 25 percent, and 50%

were in the top half. (Proportion submitting class standing: 77%:) **Average high school grade point average:** 2.9. **First-year students submitting ACT scores:** 72%. Scores (25/75 percentile): English: N/A, Math: N/A, Composite: 17-24.

ACADEMICS

Year founded: 1890. **Academic calendar:** Semester. **Degrees offered:** bachelor's, post-bachelor's certificate, master's. **Most popular majors:** 43% visual and performing arts, 19% business, management, marketing, and related support services, 6% liberal arts and sciences studies, and humanities, 6% communication, journalism, and related programs, 4% English language and literature/letters. **Major fields of study:** area, ethnic, cultural, and gender studies; business, management, marketing, and related support services; communication, journalism, and related programs; communications technologies/technicians and support services; computer and information sciences and support services; education; English language and literature/letters; foreign languages, literatures, and linguistics; liberal arts and sciences studies, and humanities; multi/interdisciplinary studies; visual and performing arts. **Areas of required coursework:** arts/fine arts, humanities, computer literacy, mathematics, English (including composition), sciences (biological or physical), history, social science. **Special academic programs:** cooperative (work-study plan) program, distance learning, dual enrollment, English as a Second Language (ESL), independent study, internships, liberal arts/career combination, student-designed major, study abroad, teacher certificate program. **Teacher certification offered in:** early childhood, elementary, middle/junior high, secondary, bilingual/bicultural. **Faculty and instruction (2005-2006):** Total instructional faculty: 299 full-time, 1,327 part-time (54% men; 46% women; 14% minorities). Full-time faculty with Ph.D. or other terminal degree: 0%. Student/faculty ratio: 14/1. Classes of fewer than 20 students: 77%; of 20 to 49 students: 23%; of 50 or more students: 0%. **Advanced Placement and International Baccalaureate credit:** AP tests may be used for: Credit and/or placement. Scores accepted: 3, 4, 5. International Baccalaureate exams may be used for: Credit and/or placement. **Freshmen returning for sophomore year:** 61%. **Graduation rates:** Four-year: 20%; five-year: 28%; six-year: 29%. **Graduate study:** 13% of students pursue further study within one year.

COSTS AND FINANCIAL AID

Financial aid office: (312) 344-7054. **Expenses (2006-2007):** Tuition and fees 2006-2007: $16,788; room/board: $9,765. Estimated books and supplies: $1,300. **Financial aid:** Priority filing date for institution's financial aid form: August 1.

CAMPUS LIFE AND EXTRACURRICULAR ACTIVITIES

Campus housing available: coed dorms. Students who live in college-owned, operated, or affiliated housing: 20%. Average per-year earnings: $2,240. **Clubs and organizations:** Number of student organizations: 53. Activities include: choral groups, concert band, dance, drama/theater, jazz band, literary magazine, music ensembles, musical theater, radio station, student government, student newspaper, student film society, television station. Number of fraternities: 0; sororities: 0. Average proportion of students who stay on campus on weekends: 11%.

SERVICES AND FACILITIES

Basic services: nonremedial tutoring, placement service, health service, health insurance, other. **Remedial assistance:** reading, math, writing, study skills. **Counseling services:** minority student, career, personal, veteran student, academic, psychological. **For learning-disabled students:** School does not offer a structured program with separate admission and additional fees. Services include: remedial math, remedial English, remedial reading, note-taking services, extended time for tests, other. **Library:** Number of titles: 247,974; number of current serial subscriptions: 1,226. **Information technology resources:** Students are not required to lease or own a computer. Number of campus computers available to all students: 730. School has a wireless network. **Campus safety:** Security services offered: late-night transport/escort service, controlled dormitory access (key, security card, etc).

TRANSFER AND INTERNATIONAL STUDENTS

Transfer students: May apply for admission for the following academic terms: Fall, Spring, Summer. Applicants do not need a minimum number of credits to apply. For fall 2005: Transfer applications received: 2,099. Transfer applicants offered admission: 1,828. Transfer applicants enrolled: 1,468. **International students:** Number of foreign undergraduates: 170 (2% of student body). Minimum TOEFL score required: 533 (paper); 200 (computer). Average TOEFL score: 525 (paper).

Concordia University–River Forest

- **Address:** 7400 Augusta Street, River Forest, IL 60305-1499
- **Website:** http://www.curf.edu
- **Private; Religious affiliation:** Lutheran
- **Enrollment:** 961 full-time; 71 part-time

KEY STATS

✔ **U.S News College Ranking:** 51, Universities–Master's (Midwest)
✔ **ACT Score (25th/75th percentile):** 19-25
✔ **Tuition:** 2006-2007: $20,300

Selectivity: More selective	**Room/board:** $6,600
Acceptance rate: 62%	**Average debt:** $17,470
Student/faculty ratio: 17/1	**Proportion who borrowed:** 76%

UNDERGRADUATE STUDENT BODY STATS

2005-2006 enrollment: 961 full-time; 71 part-time. Men: 36%; women: 64%. **Ethnic makeup:** African American: 8%; Asian American: 1%; Hispanic: 7%; White: 83%.

ADMISSIONS FACTS AND FIGURES

Phone: (708) 209-3100. **Email:** crfadmis@curf.edu. **Website:** http://www.curf.edu. **Application deadlines for fall 2007:** Regular decision: Rolling. Early decision: Not offered. Early action: Not offered. Admission can be deferred. Common application is not accepted. **To apply online, go to:** http://www.curf.edu/admission/apply_online_now.asp. **Admissions requirements/recommendations:** High school units required (recommended): English: 4 (4); Mathematics: 3 (3); Science: 2 (4); Foreign language: (2); Social studies: 2 (2); History: (2); Total units: 15. Tests: The college uses SAT or ACT scores in admissions decisions. Either SAT or ACT required. For admission to the fall 2007 entering class, the school will accept: ACT without writing. Campus visit: Recommended. Admissions interview: Recommended. **Factors that count in admissions decisions:** *Academic:* Secondary school record: Important. Class rank: Important. Letters of recommendation: Considered. Standardized test scores: Important. Essay: Considered. *Nonacademic:* Interview: Considered. Extracurricular activities: Considered. Talent/ability: Not considered. Character/personal qualities: Considered. Alumni/ae relationship: Not considered. Geographical residence: Not considered. State residency: Not considered. Religious affiliation/commitment: Not considered. Minority status: Not considered. Volunteer work: Not considered. Work experience: Not considered. **Admissions statistics for the fall 2005 entering class:** Total applicants: 1,005. Total accepted: 628. Freshmen enrolled: 210; 35% were from out of state. Overall acceptance rate: 62%. **Credentials of fall 2005 freshmen:** 25% ranked in the top 10 percent of their high school class; 50% were in the top 25 percent, and 72% were in the top half. (Proportion submitting class standing: 93%.) **Average high school grade point average:** 3.2. **First-year students who submitted SAT scores:** 15%. Scores (25/75 percentile): Verbal: N/A, Math: N/A, Combined: N/A. **First-year students submitting ACT scores:** 93%. Scores (25/75 percentile): English: N/A, Math: N/A, Composite: 19-25.

ACADEMICS

Year founded: 1864. **Academic calendar:** Semester. **Degrees offered:** bachelor's, post-bachelor's certificate, master's, post-master's certificate, doctorate. **Most popular majors:** 35% elementary education and teaching, 24% business, management, marketing, and related support services; 6% philosophy and religious studies, 6% psychology, 5% nursing/registered nurse training (R.N., A.S.N., B.S.N., M.S.N.). **Major fields of study:** biological and biomedical sciences; business, management, marketing, and related support services; computer and information sciences and support services; education; English language and literature/letters; health professions and related clinical sciences; history; liberal arts and sciences studies, and humanities; mathematics and statistics; multi/interdisciplinary studies; physical sciences; psychology; public administration and social service professions; social sciences; theology and religious vocations. **Areas of required coursework:** arts/fine arts, humanities, computer literacy, mathematics, English (including composition), foreign languages, sciences (biological or physical), history, social science. **Pre-professional programs:** pre-law, pre-dentistry, pre-medicine, pre-theology. **Special academic programs:** distance learning, double major, exchange student program (domestic), honors program, independent study, internships, study abroad, teacher certificate program. **Teacher certification offered in:** early childhood, special education, elemen-

tary, middle/junior high, secondary. **Faculty and instruction (2005-2006):** Total instructional faculty: 87. Full-time faculty with Ph.D. or other terminal degree: 74%. Student/faculty ratio: 17/1. Classes of fewer than 20 students: 66%; of 20 to 49 students: 33%; of 50 or more students: 1%. **Advanced Placement and International Baccalaureate credit:** AP tests may be used for: Credit only. **Freshmen returning for sophomore year:** 72%. **Graduation rates:** Four-year: 27%; five-year: 48%; six-year: 52%. **Graduate study:** 23% of students pursue further study immediately upon graduation. Fields in which graduates pursue further study: theology (or the seminary), 30%.

COSTS AND FINANCIAL AID

Financial aid office: (708) 209-3113. **Expenses (2006-2007):** Tuition and fees 2006-2007: $20,300; room/board: $6,600. Estimated books and supplies: $900; transportation: $600; personal expenses: $600. **Financial aid:** Priority filing date for institution's financial aid form: April 1; deadline: April 1. In 2005-2006, 90% of undergraduates applied for financial aid. Of those, 76% were determined to have financial need; 37% had their need fully met. Average financial aid package (proportion receiving): $18,080 (76%). Average amount of gift aid, such as scholarships or grants (proportion receiving): $9,034 (68%). Average amount of self-help aid, such as work study or loans (proportion receiving): $6,862 (61%). Average need-based loan (excluding PLUS or other private loans): $6,573. Among students who received need-based aid, the average percentage of need met: 80%. Among students who received aid based on merit, the average award (and the proportion receiving): $8,348 (19%). The average athletic scholarship (and the proportion receiving): $0 (0%). Average amount of debt of borrowers graduating in 2005: $17,470. Proportion who borrowed: 76%.

CAMPUS LIFE AND EXTRACURRICULAR ACTIVITIES

Campus housing available: coed dorms, women's dorms, men's dorms, special housing for disabled students. Students who live in college-owned, operated, or affiliated housing: 70%. **Clubs and organizations:** Number of student organizations: 43. Activities include: choral groups, concert band, dance, drama/theater, jazz band, literary magazine, music ensembles, musical theater, radio station, student government, student newspaper, yearbook. Number of fraternities: 0; sororities: 0. **Sports program (2005-2006):** Member of NCAA III. *Men's intercollegiate varsity sports:* baseball, basketball, cheerleading, cross-country, football, soccer, tennis, track and field (indoor), track and field (outdoor). *Women's intercollegiate varsity sports:* basketball, cheerleading, cross-country, soccer, softball, tennis, track and field (indoor), track and field (outdoor), volleyball.

SERVICES AND FACILITIES

Basic services: nonremedial tutoring, placement service, day care, health insurance. **Remedial assistance:** writing. **Counseling services:** career, personal, academic, psychological, religious. **Library:** Number of titles: 140,000; number of current serial subscriptions: 235. **Information technology resources:** Students are not required to lease or own a computer. Number of campus computers available to all students: 95. School does not have a wireless network. **Campus safety:** Security services offered: 24-hour foot and vehicle patrols, late-night transport/escort service, 24-hour emergency telephones, lighted pathways/sidewalks, student patrols, controlled dormitory access (key, security card, etc).

TRANSFER AND INTERNATIONAL STUDENTS

Transfer students: May apply for admission for the following academic terms: Fall, Spring, Summer. Applicants need a minimum number of credits to apply. For fall 2005: Transfer applications received: 410. Transfer applicants offered admission: 198. Transfer applicants enrolled: 93. **International students:** Number of foreign undergraduates: 0. Minimum TOEFL score required: 525 (paper); 195 (computer).

DePaul University

- **Address:** 1 E. Jackson Boulevard, Chicago, IL 60604-2287
- **Website:** http://www.depaul.edu
- **Private; Religious affiliation:** Roman Catholic
- **Enrollment:** 11,381 full-time; 3,359 part-time

KEY STATS

✔ **U.S News College Ranking:** third tier, National Universities
✔ **ACT Score (25th/75th percentile):** 22-27
✔ **Tuition:** 2006-2007: $21,425

Selectivity: Selective	**Room/board:** $9,864
Acceptance rate: 71%	**Average debt:** $21,061
Student/faculty ratio: 17/1	**Proportion who borrowed:** 65%

UNDERGRADUATE STUDENT BODY STATS

2005-2006 enrollment: 11,381 full-time; 3,359 part-time. Men: 43%; women: 57%. **Ethnic makeup:** African American: 10%; Asian American: 9%; Hispanic: 13%; White: 65%; International: 2%. **Religious preference:** Roman Catholic: 36%; Protestant: 15%; Jewish: 2%; Muslim: 2%; Hindu: 1%; No preference: 4%; Unknown: 16%; Other: 24%.

ADMISSIONS FACTS AND FIGURES

Phone: (312) 362-8300. **Email:** admitdpu@depaul.edu. **Website:** http://www.depaul.edu. **Application deadlines for fall 2007:** Regular decision: Rolling. Early decision: Not offered. Early action: Send application by: November 15; Decision sent by: January 1. Admission can be deferred. **Application fee:** $40. Common application is accepted. **To apply online, go to:** http://www.depaul.edu/admission/admfin/onlineap/welcome.htm. **Admissions requirements/recommendations:** High school units required (recommended): English: 4 (4); Mathematics: 2 (2); Science: 2 (2); Social studies: 2 (2); Academic electives: 4 (4); Total units: 14 (16). Tests: The college uses SAT or ACT scores in admissions decisions. Either SAT or ACT required. For admission to the fall 2007 entering class, the school will accept: ACT with writing, ACT without writing. Campus visit: Recommended. Admissions interview: Neither required nor recommended. Off-campus interview: May be arranged. **Factors that count in admissions decisions:** *Academic:* Secondary school record: Very important. Class rank: Important. Letters of recommendation: Important. Standardized test scores: Important. Essay: Important. *Nonacademic:* Interview: Considered. Extracurricular activities: Important. Talent/ability: Important. Character/personal qualities: Very important. Alumni/ae relationship: Considered. Geographical residence: Considered. State residency: Considered. Religious affiliation/commitment: Considered. Minority status: Considered. Volunteer work: Important. Work experience: Important. **Admissions statistics for the fall 2005 entering class:** Total applicants: 9,779. Total accepted: 6,963. Freshmen enrolled: 2,400; 29% were from out of state. Accepted through early-decision or early-action plans: 51%. Overall acceptance rate: 71%. Non-early acceptance rate: 63%. **Credentials of fall 2005 freshmen:** 19% ranked in the top 10 percent of their high school class; 43% were in the top 25 percent, and 76% were in the top half. (Proportion submitting class standing: 71%.) **Average high school grade point average:** 3.4. **First-year students who submitted SAT scores:** 28%. Scores (25/75 percentile): Verbal: 530-630, Math: 510-620, Combined: 1040-1250. **First-year students submitting ACT scores:** 84%. Scores (25/75 percentile): English: 22-28, Math: 20-26, Composite: 22-27.

ACADEMICS

Year founded: 1898. **Academic calendar:** Quarter. **Degrees offered:** certificate, bachelor's, post-bachelor's certificate, master's, post-master's certificate, first professional, first professional certificate, doctorate. **Most popular majors:** 31% business, management, marketing, and related support services, 14% liberal arts and sciences studies, and humanities, 11% computer and information sciences and support services, 10% social sciences, 7% communications technologies/technicians and support services. **Major fields of study:** area, ethnic, cultural, and gender studies; biological and biomedical sciences; business, management, marketing, and related support services; communication, journalism, and related programs; computer and information sciences and support services; education; English language and literature/letters; foreign languages, literatures, and linguistics; health professions and related clinical sciences; liberal arts and sciences studies, and humanities; mathematics and statistics; natural resources and conservation; philosophy and religious studies; physical sciences; psychology; public

administration and social service professions; social sciences; visual and performing arts. **Areas of required coursework:** arts/fine arts, humanities, computer literacy, mathematics, English (including composition), philosophy, foreign languages, sciences (biological or physical), history, social science, other. **Pre-professional programs:** pre-law, pre-dentistry, pre-medicine, pre-theology, pre-veterinary science, pre-optometry, pre-pharmacy, other. **Special academic programs:** accelerated program, cooperative (work-study plan) program, distance learning, double major, English as a Second Language (ESL), honors program, independent study, internships, study abroad, teacher certificate program, weekend college. **Teacher certification offered in:** early childhood, elementary, middle/junior high, secondary, bilingual/bicultural. **Reserve Officers Training Corps (ROTC):** Army ROTC: Offered on campus. **Faculty and instruction (2005-2006):** Total instructional faculty: 834 full-time, 644 part-time (56% men; 44% women; 17% minorities). Full-time faculty with Ph.D. or other terminal degree: 80%. Student/faculty ratio: 17/1. Classes of fewer than 20 students: 39%; of 20 to 49 students: 60%; of 50 or more students: 1%. **Advanced Placement and International Baccalaureate credit:** AP tests may be used for: Credit and/or placement. Scores accepted: 3, 4, 5. International Baccalaureate exams may be used for: Credit only. **Freshmen returning for sophomore year:** 84%. **Graduation rates:** Four-year: 40%; five-year: 58%; six-year: 64%. **Graduate study:** 14% of students pursue further study immediately upon graduation. Fields in which graduates pursue further study: Master of Business Administration (MBA), 18%; law, 10%; medicine, 5%; dentistry, 2%; engineering, 4%; theology (or the seminary), 3%; education, 17%; arts and sciences, 41%.

COSTS AND FINANCIAL AID

Financial aid office: (312) 362-8091. **Expenses (2006-2007):** Tuition and fees 2006-2007: $21,425; room/board: $9,864. Estimated books and supplies: $1,000; transportation: $169. **Financial aid:** Priority filing date for institution's financial aid form: May 1; deadline: May 1. In 2005-2006, 71% of undergraduates applied for financial aid. Of those, 62% were determined to have financial need; 5% had their need fully met. Average financial aid package (proportion receiving): $16,309 (59%). Average amount of gift aid, such as scholarships or grants (proportion receiving): $10,461 (49%). Average amount of self-help aid, such as work study or loans (proportion receiving): $6,170 (53%). Average need-based loan (excluding PLUS or other private loans): $4,581. Among students who received need-based aid, the average percentage of need met: 66%. Among students who received aid based on merit, the average award (and the proportion receiving): $8,144 (7%). The average athletic scholarship (and the proportion receiving): $18,522 (2%). Average amount of debt of borrowers graduating in 2005: $21,061. Proportion who borrowed: 65%.

CAMPUS LIFE AND EXTRACURRICULAR ACTIVITIES

Campus housing available (% using): coed dorms (73%), apartment for single students (27%), other housing options. Students who live in college-owned, operated, or affiliated housing: 22%. **Student employment:** During the 2005-2006 academic year, 23% of undergraduates worked on campus. Average per-year earnings: $5,670. **Clubs and organizations:** Number of student organizations: 184. Activities include: choral groups, concert band, dance, drama/theater, jazz band, music ensembles, musical theater, opera, pep band, radio station, student government, student newspaper, student film society, symphony orchestra. Number of fraternities: 12; sororities: 12. Proportion of men in fraternities: 4%; of women in sororities: 4%. Average proportion of students who stay on campus on weekends: 90%. **Sports program (2005-2006):** Member of NCAA I. *Men's intercollegiate varsity sports:* basketball, cross-country, golf, soccer, tennis, track and field (indoor), track and field (outdoor). *Women's intercollegiate varsity sports:* basketball, cross-country, soccer, softball, tennis, track and field (indoor), track and field (outdoor), volleyball.

SERVICES AND FACILITIES

Basic services: nonremedial tutoring, women's center, placement service, health service, health insurance. **Remedial assistance:** reading, math, writing. **Counseling services:** minority student, career, military, personal, veteran student, academic, older student, psychological, birth control, religious. **For learning-disabled students:** School does not offer a structured program with separate admission and additional fees. Total undergraduates in learning-disabled program or receiving services: 215. Services include: remedial math, remedial English, remedial reading, tape recorders, diagnostic testing service, untimed tests, readers, extended time for tests, tutors, priority registration, texts on tape, waiver of foreign language degree requirement, other. **Library:** Number of titles: 877,858; number of current serial subscriptions: 28,864. **Information technology resources:** Students are not required to lease or own a computer. Number of campus computers available to all students: 1,800. School has a wireless network. Approximate number of users that can be accommodated: 3,575. Proportion of college-owned housing units wired for high-speed internet access: 100%. **Campus safety:** Security services offered: 24-hour foot and vehicle patrols, late-night transport/escort service, 24-hour emergency telephones, lighted pathways/sidewalks, controlled dormitory access (key, security card, etc).

TRANSFER AND INTERNATIONAL STUDENTS

Transfer students: May apply for admission for the following academic terms: Fall, Winter, Spring, Summer. Applicants need a minimum number of credits to apply. For fall 2005: Transfer applications received: 3,135. Transfer applicants offered admission: 1,798. Transfer applicants enrolled: 1,229. **International students:** Number of foreign undergraduates: 179 (2% of student body). Number of countries represented: 65. Minimum TOEFL score required: 550 (paper); 213 (computer).

Dominican University

- **Address:** 7900 W. Division, River Forest, IL 60305
- **Website:** http://www.dom.edu
- **Private; Religious affiliation:** Roman Catholic
- **Enrollment:** 1,146 full-time; 191 part-time

KEY STATS

✔ **U.S News College Ranking:** 18, Universities–Master's (Midwest)
✔ **ACT Score (25th/75th percentile):** 20-25
✔ **Tuition:** 2006-2007: $21,250
  Selectivity: More selective **Room/board:** $7,300
  Acceptance rate: 81% **Average debt:** $14,923
  Student/faculty ratio: 12/1 **Proportion who borrowed:** 60%

UNDERGRADUATE STUDENT BODY STATS

2005-2006 enrollment: 1,146 full-time; 191 part-time. Men: 31%; women: 69%. **Ethnic makeup:** African American: 7%; Asian American: 3%; Hispanic: 19%; White: 69%; International: 1%. **Religious preference:** Roman Catholic: 66%; Protestant: 1%; Jewish: 1%; Muslim: 1%; Buddhist: 1%; No preference: 16%; Unknown: 2%; Christian: 6%; Other: 6%.

ADMISSIONS FACTS AND FIGURES

Phone: (708) 524-6800. **Email:** domadmis@dom.edu. **Website:** http://www.dom.edu. **Application deadlines for fall 2007:** Regular decision: Rolling. Early decision: Not offered. Early action: Not offered. Admission can be deferred. **Application fee:** $25. Common application is accepted. **Admissions requirements/recommendations:** High school units required (recommended): English: (4); Mathematics: (3); Science: (3); Foreign language: (2); Social studies: (1); History: (2); Total units: 16. Tests: The college uses SAT or ACT scores in admissions decisions. Either SAT or ACT required. For admission to the fall 2007 entering class, the school will accept: ACT with writing, ACT without writing. Campus visit: Recommended. Admissions interview: Recommended. Off-campus interview: May be arranged. **Factors that count in admissions decisions:** *Academic:* Secondary school record: Very important. Class rank: Important. Letters of recommendation: Considered. Standardized test scores: Important. Essay: Important. *Nonacademic:* Interview: Considered. Extracurricular activities: Considered. Talent/ability: Considered. Character/personal qualities: Important. Alumni/ae relationship: Considered. Geographical residence: Not considered. State residency: Not considered. Religious affiliation/commitment: Not considered. Minority status: Not considered. Volunteer work: Considered. Work experience: Considered. **Other schools with the greatest overlap in applicants:** DePaul University; Elmhurst College; Loyola University Chicago; University of Illinois–Chicago; University of Illinois–Urbana-Champaign. **Admissions statistics for the fall 2005 entering class:** Total applicants: 993. Total accepted: 808. Freshmen enrolled: 271; 11% were from out of state. Overall acceptance rate: 81%. **Credentials of fall 2005 freshmen:** 24% ranked in the top 10 percent of their high school class; 52% were in the top 25 percent, and 85% were in the top half. (Proportion submitting class standing: 86%.) **Average high school grade point average:** 3.5. **First-year students who submitted SAT scores:** 10%. Scores (25/75 percentile): Verbal: 470-580, Math: 480-570, Combined: 950-1150. **First-year students submitting ACT scores:** 97%. Scores (25/75 percentile): English: 19-25, Math: 18-24, Composite: 20-25.

ACADEMICS

Year founded: 1901. **Academic calendar:** Semester. **Degrees offered:** certificate, bachelor's, post-bachelor's certificate, master's, post-master's certificate. **Most popular majors:** 16% business administration and management, 11% psychology, 7% organizational behavior studies, 6% sociology, 5% accounting. **Major fields of study:** area, ethnic, cultural, and gender studies; biological and biomedical sciences; business, management, marketing, and related support services; communication, journalism, and related programs; computer and information sciences and support services; English language and literature/letters; family and consumer sciences/human sciences; foreign languages, literatures, and linguistics; health professions and related clinical sciences; history; liberal arts and sciences studies, and humanities; mathematics and statistics; multi/interdisciplinary studies; natural resources and conservation; philosophy and religious studies; physical sciences; psychology; social sciences; theology and religious vocations; visual and performing arts. **Areas of required coursework:** arts/fine arts, humanities, computer literacy, mathematics, English (including composition), philosophy, foreign languages, sciences (biological or physical), history, social science, other. **Pre-professional programs:** pre-law, pre-dentistry, pre-medicine, pre-veterinary science, pre-optometry, pre-pharmacy, other. **Special academic programs (% participation):** accelerated program (7%), cross-registration, distance learning, double major (16%), dual enrollment, exchange student program (domestic), honors program (3%), independent study (35%), internships (35%), liberal arts/career combination, student-designed major, study abroad (12%), teacher certificate program. **Teacher certification offered in:** early childhood, special education, elementary, middle/junior high, secondary. **Faculty and instruction (2005-2006):** Total instructional faculty: 109 full-time, 200 part-time (40% men; 60% women). Full-time faculty with Ph.D. or other terminal degree: 85%. Student/faculty ratio: 12/1. Classes of fewer than 20 students: 70%; of 20 to 49 students: 30%; of 50 or more students: 0%. **Advanced Placement and International Baccalaureate credit:** AP tests may be used for: Credit only. Scores accepted: 3, 4, 5. International Baccalaureate exams may be used for: Credit and/or placement. **Freshmen returning for sophomore year:** 81%. **Graduation rates:** Four-year: 54%; five-year: 61%; six-year: 63%. **Graduate study:** 25% of students pursue further study immediately upon graduation; 35% within one year; 50% within five years. Fields in which graduates pursue further study: Master of Business Administration (MBA), 30%; law, 5%; medicine, 5%; dentistry, 1%; engineering, 1%; theology (or the seminary), 1%; education, 30%; arts and sciences, 15%.

COSTS AND FINANCIAL AID

Financial aid office: (708) 524-6809. **Expenses (2006-2007):** Tuition and fees 2006-2007: $21,250; room/board: $7,300. Estimated books and supplies: $1,000; transportation: $100; personal expenses: $900. **Financial aid:** Priority filing date for institution's financial aid form: April 15. In 2005-2006, 91% of undergraduates applied for financial aid. Of those, 81% were determined to have financial need; 27% had their need fully met. Average financial aid package (proportion receiving): $15,046 (81%). Average amount of gift aid, such as scholarships or grants (proportion receiving): $11,237 (80%). Average amount of self-help aid, such as work study or loans (proportion receiving): $4,661 (69%). Average need-based loan (excluding PLUS or other private loans): $3,763. Among students who received need-based aid, the average percentage of need met: 80%. Among students who received aid based on merit, the average award (and the proportion receiving): $11,282 (18%). The average athletic scholarship (and the proportion receiving): $0 (0%). Average amount of debt of borrowers graduating in 2005: $14,923. Proportion who borrowed: 60%.

CAMPUS LIFE AND EXTRACURRICULAR ACTIVITIES

Campus housing available (% using): coed dorms (99%), special housing for disabled students (1%). Students who live in college-owned, operated, or affiliated housing: 38%. **Student employment:** During the 2005-2006 academic year, 30% of undergraduates worked on campus. Average per-year earnings: $2,200. **Clubs and organizations:** Number of student organizations: 30. Activities include: dance, drama/theater, literary magazine, musical theater, student government, student newspaper. Number of fraternities: 0; sororities: 0. Average proportion of students who stay on campus on weekends: 50%. **Sports program (2005-2006):** Member of NCAA III. *Men's intercollegiate varsity sports:* baseball, basketball, cross-country, soccer, tennis. *Women's intercollegiate varsity sports:* basketball, cross-country, soccer, softball, tennis, volleyball.

SERVICES AND FACILITIES

Basic services: nonremedial tutoring, placement service, day care, health service, health insurance. **Remedial assistance:** math, writing, study skills, other. **Counseling services:** minority student, career, personal, veteran student, academic, psychological, religious. **For learning-disabled students:** School does not offer a structured program with separate admission and additional fees. Total undergraduates in learning-disabled program or receiving services: 12. **Library:** Number of titles: 297,000; number of current serial subscriptions: 950. **Information technology resources:** Students are not required to lease or own a computer. Number of campus computers available to all students: 398. School has a wireless network. Approximate number of users that can be accommodated: 120. Proportion of college-owned housing units wired for high-speed internet access: 100%. **Campus safety:** Security services offered: 24-hour foot and vehicle patrols, late-night transport/escort service, 24-hour emergency telephones, lighted pathways/sidewalks, controlled dormitory access (key, security card, etc).

TRANSFER AND INTERNATIONAL STUDENTS
Transfer students: May apply for admission for the following academic terms: Fall, Spring, Summer. Applicants need a minimum number of credits to apply. For fall 2005: Transfer applications received: 273. Transfer applicants offered admission: 254. Transfer applicants enrolled: 142. **International students:** Number of foreign undergraduates: 17 (1% of student body). Number of countries represented: 19. Minimum TOEFL score required: 550 (paper); 213 (computer). Average TOEFL score: 560 (paper).

Eastern Illinois University

- **Address:** 600 Lincoln Avenue, Charleston, IL 61920-3099
- **Website:** http://www.eiu.edu
- **Public**
- **Enrollment:** 9,293 full-time; 1,082 part-time

KEY STATS
✔ **U.S News College Ranking:** 47; Universities–Master's (Midwest)
✔ **ACT Score (25th/75th percentile):** 19-24
✔ **Tuition:** 2006-2007: $7,069 in state, $17,482 out of state
   Selectivity: Selective   **Room/board:** $6,660
   Acceptance rate: 78%   **Average debt:** $15,538
   Student/faculty ratio: 16/1   **Proportion who borrowed:** 63%

UNDERGRADUATE STUDENT BODY STATS
2005-2006 enrollment: 9,293 full-time; 1,082 part-time. Men: 42%; women: 58%. **Ethnic makeup:** African American: 7%; Asian American: 1%; Hispanic: 2%; White: 89%.

ADMISSIONS FACTS AND FIGURES
Phone: (800) 252-5711. **Email:** admissns@eiu.edu. **Website:** http://www.eiu.edu. **Application deadlines for fall 2007:** Regular decision: Rolling. Early decision: Not offered. Early action: Not offered. Admission cannot be deferred. **Application fee:** $30. Common application is not accepted. **To apply online, go to:** http://www.applyweb.com/apply/eiu/menu.html. **Admissions requirements/recommendations:** High school units required (recommended): English: 4; Mathematics: 3; Science: 3; Foreign language: (2); Social studies: 3; Academic electives: 2; Total units: 15 (22). **Tests:** The college uses SAT or ACT scores in admissions decisions. Either SAT or ACT required. For admission to the fall 2007 entering class, the school will accept: ACT with writing, ACT without writing. Campus visit: Recommended. Admissions interview: Recommended. Off-campus interview: May be arranged. **Factors that count in admissions decisions:** *Academic:* Secondary school record: Very important. Class rank: Very important. Letters of recommendation: Considered. Standardized test scores: Very important. Essay: Considered. *Nonacademic:* Interview: Not considered. Extracurricular activities: Not considered. Talent/ability: Not considered. Character/personal qualities: Not considered. Alumni/ae relationship: Not considered. Geographical residence: Not considered. State residency: Not considered. Religious affiliation/commitment: Not considered. Minority status: Not considered. Volunteer work: Not considered. Work experience: Not considered. **Other schools with the greatest overlap in applicants:** Illinois State University; Lakeland College; Southern Illinois University–Carbondale; University of Illinois–Urbana-Champaign; Western Illinois University. **Admissions statistics for the fall 2005 entering class:** Total applicants: 7,682. Total accepted: 5,975. Freshmen enrolled: 1,668; 1% were from out of state. Overall acceptance rate: 78%. **Credentials of fall 2005 freshmen:** 7% ranked in the top 10

percent of their high school class; 24% were in the top 25 percent, and 60% were in the top half. (Proportion submitting class standing: 90%.) **Average high school grade point average:** 3.0. **First-year students who submitted SAT scores:** 2%. Scores (25/75 percentile): Verbal: N/A, Math: N/A, Combined: N/A. **First-year students submitting ACT scores:** 98%. Scores (25/75 percentile): English: 19-24, Math: 18-24, Composite: 19-24.

ACADEMICS
Year founded: 1895. **Academic calendar:** Semester. **Degrees offered:** bachelor's, post-bachelor's certificate, master's, post-master's certificate. **Most popular majors:** 26% education, 14% business, management, marketing, and related support services, 10% English language and literature/letters, 8% liberal arts and sciences studies, and humanities, 8% social sciences. **Major fields of study:** area, ethnic, cultural, and gender studies; biological and biomedical sciences; business, management, marketing, and related support services; communication, journalism, and related programs; computer and information sciences and support services; education; engineering; engineering technologies/technicians; English language and literature/letters; family and consumer sciences/human sciences; foreign languages, literatures, and linguistics; health professions and related clinical sciences; history; liberal arts and sciences studies, and humanities; mathematics and statistics; multi/interdisciplinary studies; parks, recreation, leisure, and fitness studies; philosophy and religious studies; physical sciences; psychology; social sciences; visual and performing arts. **Areas of required coursework:** arts/fine arts, humanities, computer literacy, mathematics, English (including composition), foreign languages, sciences (biological or physical), history, social science, other. **Pre-professional programs:** pre-law, pre-dentistry, pre-medicine, pre-veterinary science, pre-optometry, pre-pharmacy, other. **Special academic programs:** distance learning, double major, honors program, independent study, internships, study abroad, teacher certificate program. **Teacher certification offered in:** early childhood, special education, elementary, vo-tech, middle/junior high, secondary. **Cooperative education programs:** business, engineering, health professions. **Reserve Officers Training Corps (ROTC):** Army ROTC: Offered on campus. **Faculty and instruction (2005-2006):** Total instructional faculty: 610 full-time, 145 part-time (53% men; 47% women; 10% minorities). Full-time faculty with Ph.D. or other terminal degree: 70%. Student/faculty ratio: 16/1. Classes of fewer than 20 students: 30%; of 20 to 49 students: 65%; of 50 or more students: 5%. **Advanced Placement and International Baccalaureate credit:** AP tests may be used for: Credit only. Scores accepted: 3, 4, 5. **Freshmen returning for sophomore year:** 80%. **Graduation rates:** Four-year: 33%; five-year: 56%; six-year: 62%.

COSTS AND FINANCIAL AID
Financial aid office: (217) 581-3713. **Expenses (2006-2007):** Tuition and fees 2006-2007: $7,069 in state, $17,482 out of state; room/board: $6,660. **Financial aid:** Priority filing date for institution's financial aid form: March 1. In 2005-2006, 68% of undergraduates applied for financial aid. Of those, 53% were determined to have financial need; 64% had their need fully met. Average financial aid package (proportion receiving): $9,783 (47%). Average amount of gift aid, such as scholarships or grants (proportion receiving): $2,886 (22%). Average amount of self-help aid, such as work study or loans (proportion receiving): $3,150 (30%). Average need-based loan (excluding PLUS or other private loans): $3,461. Among students who received need-based aid, the average percentage of need met: 19%. Among students who received aid based on merit, the average award (and the proportion receiving): $7,140 (3%). The average athletic scholarship (and the proportion receiving): $4,357 (0%). Average amount of debt of borrowers graduating in 2005: $15,538. Proportion who borrowed: 63%.

CAMPUS LIFE AND EXTRACURRICULAR ACTIVITIES
Campus housing available (% using): coed dorms (18%), women's dorms (38%), men's dorms (23%), sorority housing (7%), fraternity housing (4%), apartments for married students (3%), apartment for single students (7%), special housing for disabled students. Students who live in college-owned, operated, or affiliated housing: 43%. Average per-year earnings: $1,372. **Clubs and organizations:** Number of student organizations: 114. Activities include: choral groups, concert band, dance, drama/theater, jazz band, literary magazine, marching band, music ensembles, musical theater, pep band, radio station, student government, student newspaper, symphony orchestra, television station, yearbook. Number of fraternities: 12; sororities: 13. Proportion of men in fraternities: 16%; of women in sororities: 17%. Average proportion of students who stay on campus on weekends: 65%. **Sports program (2005-2006):** Member of NCAA I. *Men's intercollegiate varsity sports:* baseball, basketball, cross-country, football, golf, soccer, swimming and diving, tennis, track and field (indoor), track and field (outdoor),

wrestling. **Women's intercollegiate varsity sports:** basketball, cross-country, golf, rugby, soccer, softball, swimming and diving, tennis, track and field (indoor), track and field (outdoor), volleyball.

SERVICES AND FACILITIES

Basic services: nonremedial tutoring, women's center, placement service, health service, health insurance, other. **Remedial assistance:** reading, math, writing, study skills, other. **Counseling services:** minority student, career, personal, academic, psychological, birth control, other. **For learning-disabled students:** School does not offer a structured program with separate admission and additional fees. Total undergraduates in learning-disabled program or receiving services: 30. Services include: remedial math, remedial English, reading machines, remedial reading, tape recorders, other special classes, note-taking services, oral tests, learning center, readers, extended time for tests, tutors, priority registration, priority seating, texts on tape, other testing accomodations. **Library:** Number of titles: 1,044,728; number of current serial subscriptions: 5,292. **Information technology resources:** Students are not required to lease or own a computer. Number of campus computers available to all students: 859. School has a wireless network. Approximate number of users that can be accommodated: 5,200. Proportion of college-owned housing units wired for high-speed internet access: 100%. **Campus safety:** Security services offered: 24-hour foot and vehicle patrols, late-night transport/escort service, 24-hour emergency telephones, lighted pathways/sidewalks, controlled dormitory access (key, security card, etc).

TRANSFER AND INTERNATIONAL STUDENTS

Transfer students: May apply for admission for the following academic terms: Fall, Spring, Summer. Applicants need a minimum number of credits to apply. For fall 2005: Transfer applications received: 2,065. Transfer applicants offered admission: 1,659. Transfer applicants enrolled: 1,130. **International students:** Number of foreign undergraduates: 46. Number of countries represented: 28. Minimum TOEFL score required: 500 (paper); 173 (computer).

East-West University

- **Address:** 816 S. Michigan Avenue, Chicago, IL 60605
- **Website:** http://www.eastwest.edu
- **Private**
- **Enrollment:** N/A

KEY STATS
- ✔ **U.S News College Ranking:** fourth tier, Comp. Coll.–Bachelor's (Midwest)
- ✔ **SAT or ACT Score (25th/75th percentile):** N/A
- ✔ **Tuition:** N/A

Selectivity: Less selective	**Room/board:** N/A
Acceptance rate: N/A	**Average debt:** N/A
Student/faculty ratio: N/A	**Proportion who borrowed:** N/A

Elmhurst College

- **Address:** 190 Prospect Avenue, Elmhurst, IL 60126
- **Website:** http://www.elmhurst.edu
- **Private; Religious affiliation:** United Church of Christ
- **Enrollment:** 2,362 full-time; 329 part-time

KEY STATS
- ✔ **U.S News College Ranking:** 9, Comp. Coll.–Bachelor's (Midwest)
- ✔ **ACT Score (25th/75th percentile):** 20-27
- ✔ **Tuition:** 2006-2007: $23,160

Selectivity: More selective	**Room/board:** $6,822
Acceptance rate: 75%	**Average debt:** $16,080
Student/faculty ratio: 13/1	**Proportion who borrowed:** 75%

UNDERGRADUATE STUDENT BODY STATS

2005-2006 enrollment: 2,362 full-time; 329 part-time. Men: 35%; women: 65%. **Ethnic makeup:** African American: 6%; Asian American: 3%; Hispanic: 6%; White: 84%; International: 1%. **Religious preference:** Roman Catholic: 43%; Protestant: 20%; Jewish: 1%; Muslim: 1%; No preference: 16%; Unknown: 1%; United Church of Christ: 6%; Other: 12%.

ADMISSIONS FACTS AND FIGURES

Phone: (630) 617-3400. **Email:** admit@elmhurst.edu. **Website:** http://www.elmhurst.edu. **Application deadlines for fall 2007:** Regular decision: July 15. Early decision: Not offered. Early action: Not offered. Admission can be deferred. Common application is not accepted. **Admissions requirements/recommendations:** High school units required (recommended): English: 4 (4); Mathematics: 2 (3); Science: 2 (3); Foreign language: 1 (2); Social studies: 2 (3); History: 1 (2); Academic electives: 4 (4); Total units: 16 (21). Tests: The college uses SAT or ACT scores in admissions decisions. Either SAT or ACT required. For admission to the fall 2007 entering class, the school will accept: ACT with writing, ACT without writing. Campus visit: Recommended. Admissions interview: Recommended. Off-campus interview: Not available. **Factors that count in admissions decisions:** *Academic:* Secondary school record: Very important. Class rank: Very important. Letters of recommendation: Important. Standardized test scores: Very important. Essay: Important. *Nonacademic:* Interview: Important. Extracurricular activities: Considered. Talent/ability: Considered. Character/personal qualities: Considered. Alumni/ae relationship: Considered. Geographical residence: Not considered. State residency: Not considered. Religious affiliation/commitment: Not considered. Minority status: Not considered. Volunteer work: Not considered. Work experience: Not considered. **Other schools with the greatest overlap in applicants:** Augustana College; DePaul University; North Central College; Northern Illinois University; University of Illinois–Chicago. **Admissions statistics for the fall 2005 entering class:** Total applicants: 1,700. Total accepted: 1,278. Freshmen enrolled: 466; 13% were from out of state. Overall acceptance rate: 75%. **Credentials of fall 2005 freshmen:** 23% ranked in the top 10 percent of their high school class; 49% were in the top 25 percent, and 82% were in the top half. (Proportion submitting class standing: 93%.) **Average high school grade point average:** 3.4. **First-year students who submitted SAT scores:** 6%. Scores (25/75 percentile): Verbal: 500-640, Math: 500-620, Combined: 1000-1260. **First-year students submitting ACT scores:** 98%. Scores (25/75 percentile): English: 20-27, Math: 19-26, Composite: 20-27.

ACADEMICS

Year founded: 1871. **Academic calendar:** 4-1-4. **Degrees offered:** bachelor's, master's. **Most popular majors:** 27% business, management, marketing, and related support services, 19% education, 9% health professions and related clinical sciences, 5% psychology, 5% visual and performing arts. **Major fields of study:** area, ethnic, cultural, and gender studies; biological and biomedical sciences; business, management, marketing, and related support services; communication, journalism, and related programs; computer and information sciences and support services; education; English language and literature/letters; foreign languages, literatures, and linguistics; health professions and related clinical sciences; history; liberal arts and sciences studies, and humanities; mathematics and statistics; multi/interdisciplinary studies; natural resources and conservation; parks, recreation, leisure, and fitness studies; philosophy and religious studies; physical sciences; psychology; public administration and social service professions; social sciences; theology and religious vocations; visual and performing arts. **Areas of required coursework:** arts/fine arts, humanities, mathematics, English (including composition), philosophy, foreign languages, sciences (biological or physical), history, social science. **Pre-professional programs:** pre-law, pre-dentistry, pre-medicine, pre-theology, pre-veterinary science, pre-optometry, pre-pharmacy. **Special academic programs (% participation):** accelerated program (12%), double major (10%), dual enrollment (1%), honors program (10%), independent study (5%), internships (24%), liberal arts/career combination (75%), student-designed major (1%), study abroad (19%), teacher certificate program (20%). **Teacher certification offered in:** early childhood, special education, elementary, middle/junior high, secondary. **Reserve Officers Training Corps (ROTC):** Army ROTC: Offered at cooperating institution (Wheaton College); Air Force ROTC: Offered at cooperating institution (Illinois Institute of Technology). **Faculty and instruction (2005-2006):** Total instructional faculty: 117 full-time, 180 part-time (51% men; 49% women; 7% minorities). Full-time faculty with Ph.D. or other terminal degree: 89%. Student/faculty ratio: 13/1. Classes of fewer than 20 students: 62%; of 20 to 49 students: 38%; of 50 or more students: 0%. **Advanced Placement and International Baccalaureate credit:** AP tests may be used for: Credit and/or placement. Scores accepted: 3, 4, 5. International Baccalaureate exams may be used for: Credit and/or placement. **Freshmen returning for sophomore year:** 81%. **Graduation rates:** Four-year: 59%; five-year: 68%; six-year: 72%. **Graduate study:** 10% of students pursue further study immediately upon graduation; 20% within one year; 50% within five years. Fields in which graduates pursue further study: Master of Business Administration (MBA), 30%; law, 2%; medicine, 5%; dentistry, 2%; theology (or the seminary), 5%; education, 50%; arts and sciences, 6%.

COSTS AND FINANCIAL AID

Financial aid office: (630) 617-3075. **Expenses (2006-2007):** Tuition and fees 2006-2007: $23,160; room/board: $6,822. Estimated books and supplies: $1,000; transportation: $518; personal expenses: $1,200. **Financial aid:** Priority filing date for institution's financial aid form: April 15. In 2005-2006, 81% of undergraduates applied for financial aid. Of those, 70% were determined to have financial need; 29% had their need fully met. Average financial aid package (proportion receiving): $15,512 (70%). Average amount of gift aid, such as scholarships or grants (proportion receiving): $11,156 (70%). Average amount of self-help aid, such as work study or loans (proportion receiving): $4,119 (59%). Average need-based loan (excluding PLUS or other private loans): $3,745. Among students who received need-based aid, the average percentage of need met: 91%. Among students who received aid based on merit, the average award (and the proportion receiving): $8,374 (20%). Average amount of debt of borrowers graduating in 2005: $16,080. Proportion who borrowed: 75%.

CAMPUS LIFE AND EXTRACURRICULAR ACTIVITIES

Campus housing available (% using): coed dorms (97%), apartment for single students (3%). Students who live in college-owned, operated, or affiliated housing: 37%. **Student employment:** During the 2005-2006 academic year, 26% of undergraduates worked on campus. Average per-year earnings: $1,250. **Clubs and organizations:** Number of student organizations: 106. Activities include: choral groups, concert band, drama/theater, jazz band, literary magazine, music ensembles, musical theater, radio station, student government, student newspaper, yearbook. Number of fraternities: 4; sororities: 5. Proportion of men in fraternities: 11%; of women in sororities: 10%. Average proportion of students who stay on campus on weekends: 25%. **Sports program (2005-2006):** Member of NCAA III. *Men's intercollegiate varsity sports:* baseball, basketball, cross-country, football, golf, soccer, tennis, track and field (indoor), track and field (outdoor), wrestling. *Women's intercollegiate varsity sports:* basketball, bowling, cross-country, golf, soccer, softball, tennis, track and field (indoor), track and field (outdoor), volleyball.

SERVICES AND FACILITIES

Basic services: nonremedial tutoring, placement service, health service, health insurance. **Remedial assistance:** reading, math, writing, study skills. **Counseling services:** minority student, career, personal, academic, psychological, birth control, religious. **For learning-disabled students:** School does not offer a structured program with separate admission and additional fees. **Library:** Number of titles: 221,570; number of current serial subscriptions: 1,202. **Information technology resources:** Students are not required to lease or own a computer. Number of campus computers available to all students: 440. School has a wireless network. Approximate number of users that can be accommodated: 1,000. Proportion of college-owned housing units wired for high-speed internet access: 100%. **Campus safety:** Security services offered: 24-hour foot and vehicle patrols, late-night transport/escort service, 24-hour emergency telephones, lighted pathways/sidewalks, controlled dormitory access (key, security card, etc).

TRANSFER AND INTERNATIONAL STUDENTS

Transfer students: May apply for admission for the following academic terms: Fall, Winter, Spring. Applicants do not need a minimum number of credits to apply. For fall 2005: Transfer applications received: 889. Transfer applicants offered admission: 732. Transfer applicants enrolled: 405. **International students:** Number of foreign undergraduates: 20 (1% of student body). Number of countries represented: 13. Minimum TOEFL score required: 550 (paper); 213 (computer). Average TOEFL score: 600 (paper).

Eureka College

- **Address:** 300 E. College Avenue, Eureka, IL 61530-1500
- **Website:** http://www.eureka.edu
- **Private; Religious affiliation:** Christian Church (Disciples of Christ)
- **Enrollment:** 503 full-time; 33 part-time

KEY STATS
✔ **U.S News College Ranking:** 42, Comp. Coll.–Bachelor's (Midwest)
✔ **ACT Score (25th/75th percentile):** 19-25
✔ **Tuition:** 2006-2007: $14,180

Selectivity: Selective	**Room/board:** $6,270
Acceptance rate: 74%	**Average debt:** $15,352
Student/faculty ratio: 12/1	**Proportion who borrowed:** 89%

UNDERGRADUATE STUDENT BODY STATS

2005-2006 enrollment: 503 full-time; 33 part-time. Men: 44%; women: 56%. **Ethnic makeup:** African American: 5%; Asian American: 1%; Hispanic: 1%; White: 90%; International: 2%. **Religious preference:** Roman Catholic: 3%; Protestant: 7%; No preference: 14%; Unknown: 73%; Christian Church (Disciples of Christ): 2%.

ADMISSIONS FACTS AND FIGURES

Phone: (309) 467-6345. **Email:** admissions@eureka.edu. **Website:** http://www.eureka.edu. **Application deadlines for fall 2007:** Regular decision: August 1. Early decision: Not offered. Early action: Not offered. Admission can be deferred. **Application fee:** None. Common application is accepted. **To apply online, go to:** http://www.eureka.edu/admissions/adprocess.asp. **Admissions requirements/recommendations:** High school units required (recommended): English: 4 (4); Mathematics: 3 (3); Science: 3 (3); Foreign language: 2 (2); Social studies: 3 (3); History: 2 (2); Academic electives: 0 (0); Total units: 14 (14). Tests: The college uses SAT or ACT scores in admissions decisions. Either SAT or ACT required. For admission to the fall 2007 entering class, the school will accept: ACT with writing, ACT without writing. Campus visit: Recommended. Admissions interview: Recommended. Off-campus interview: Not available. **Factors that count in admissions decisions:** *Academic:* Secondary school record: Very important. Class rank: Very important. Letters of recommendation: Very important. Standardized test scores: Very important. Essay: Considered. *Nonacademic:* Interview: Considered. Extracurricular activities: Important. Talent/ability: Important. Character/personal qualities: Very important. Alumni/ae relationship: Not considered. Geographical residence: Not considered. State residency: Not considered. Religious affiliation/commitment: Not considered. Minority status: Not considered. Volunteer work: Considered. Work experience: Not considered. **Other schools with the greatest overlap in applicants:** Augustana College; Bradley University; Illinois College; Illinois State University; Monmouth College. **Admissions statistics for the fall 2005 entering class:** Total applicants: 846. Total accepted: 625. Freshmen enrolled: 138; 9% were from out of state. Overall acceptance rate: 74%. **Size of waiting list:** 0 applicants; enrolled from waiting list: 0. **Credentials of fall 2005 freshmen:** 13% ranked in the top 10 percent of their high school class; 41% were in the top 25 percent, and 76% were in the top half. (Proportion submitting class standing: 96%.) **Average high school grade point average:** 3.3. **First-year students who submitted SAT scores:** 2%. Scores (25/75 percentile): Verbal: N/A, Math: N/A, Combined: N/A. **First-year students submitting ACT scores:** 98%. Scores (25/75 percentile): English: N/A, Math: N/A, Composite: 19-25.

ACADEMICS

Year founded: 1855. **Academic calendar:** Semester. **Degrees offered:** bachelor's. **Most popular majors:** 13% business administration and management, 12% elementary education and teaching, 7% psychology, 6% history, 6% sport and fitness administration/management. **Major fields of study:** biological and biomedical sciences; business, management, marketing, and related support services; communication, journalism, and related programs; computer and information sciences and support services; education; English language and literature/letters; history; mathematics and statistics; philosophy and religious studies; physical sciences; psychology; security and protective services; social sciences; visual and performing arts. **Areas of required coursework:** arts/fine arts, humanities, mathematics, English (including composition), philosophy, sciences (biological or physical), history, social science, other. **Pre-professional programs:** pre-law, pre-dentistry, pre-medicine, pre-theology, pre-veterinary science. **Special academic pro-**

grams (% participation): double major (5%), dual enrollment (0%), honors program (5%), independent study (19%), internships (32%), student-designed major (1%), study abroad (5%), teacher certificate program (23%). Teacher certification offered in: elementary, middle/junior high, secondary. Cooperative education programs: health professions. Faculty and instruction (2005-2006): Total instructional faculty: 36 full-time, 1 part-time (59% men; 41% women; 3% minorities). Full-time faculty with Ph.D. or other terminal degree: 47%. Student/faculty ratio: 12/1. Classes of fewer than 20 students: 68%; of 20 to 49 students: 32%; of 50 or more students: 0%. Advanced Placement and International Baccalaureate credit: International Baccalaureate exams may be used for: Credit and/or placement. Freshmen returning for sophomore year: 66%. Graduation rates: Four-year: 47%; five-year: 55%; six-year: 54%.

COSTS AND FINANCIAL AID

Financial aid office: (309) 467-6311. Expenses (2006-2007): Tuition and fees 2006-2007: $14,180; room/board: $6,270. Estimated books and supplies: $750; transportation: $100; personal expenses: $150. Financial aid: Priority filing date for institution's financial aid form: April 15; deadline: April 15. In 2005-2006, 89% of undergraduates applied for financial aid. Of those, 78% were determined to have financial need; 79% had their need fully met. Average financial aid package (proportion receiving): $15,467 (78%). Average amount of gift aid, such as scholarships or grants (proportion receiving): $10,666 (73%). Average amount of self-help aid, such as work study or loans (proportion receiving): $4,073 (66%). Average need-based loan (excluding PLUS or other private loans): $3,798. Among students who received need-based aid, the average percentage of need met: 81%. Among students who received aid based on merit, the average award (and the proportion receiving): $4,125 (2%). The average athletic scholarship (and the proportion receiving): $0 (0%). Average amount of debt of borrowers graduating in 2005: $15,352. Proportion who borrowed: 89%.

CAMPUS LIFE AND EXTRACURRICULAR ACTIVITIES

Campus housing available (% using): coed dorms (21%), women's dorms (31%), men's dorms (25%), sorority housing (13%), fraternity housing (10%), special housing for disabled students (0%). Students who live in college-owned, operated, or affiliated housing: 66%. Student employment: During the 2005-2006 academic year, 14% of undergraduates worked on campus. Average per-year earnings: $1,734. Clubs and organizations: Number of student organizations: 37. Activities include: choral groups, drama/theater, literary magazine, student government, student newspaper, yearbook. Number of fraternities: 3; sororities: 3. Proportion of men in fraternities: 9%; of women in sororities: 10%. Average proportion of students who stay on campus on weekends: 70%. Sports program (2005-2006): Member of NCAA III. Men's intercollegiate varsity sports: baseball, basketball, football, golf, swimming and diving, tennis. Women's intercollegiate varsity sports: basketball, softball, swimming and diving, tennis, volleyball.

SERVICES AND FACILITIES

Basic services: nonremedial tutoring, placement service, health service, health insurance. Remedial assistance: math, writing, study skills. Counseling services: career, academic. For learning-disabled students: School does not offer a structured program with separate admission and additional fees. Total undergraduates in learning-disabled program or receiving services: 5. Services include: learning center, tutors. Library: Number of titles: 89,872; number of current serial subscriptions: 250. Information technology resources: Students are not required to lease or own a computer. Number of campus computers available to all students: 90. School has a wireless network. Approximate number of users that can be accommodated: 30. Proportion of college-owned housing units wired for high-speed internet access: 100%.

TRANSFER AND INTERNATIONAL STUDENTS

Transfer students: May apply for admission for the following academic terms: Fall, Spring, Summer. Applicants need a minimum number of credits to apply. For fall 2005: Transfer applications received: 266. Transfer applicants offered admission: 173. Transfer applicants enrolled: 83. International students: Number of foreign undergraduates: 7 (2% of student body). Minimum TOEFL score required: 550 (paper); 210 (computer).

Greenville College

- ■ **Address:** 315 E. College Avenue, Greenville, IL 62246-0159
- ■ **Website:** http://www.greenville.edu
- ■ **Private; Religious affiliation:** Free Methodist
- ■ **Enrollment:** 1,175 full-time; 40 part-time

KEY STATS

✔ **U.S News College Ranking:** 46, Comp. Coll.–Bachelor's (Midwest)
✔ **ACT Score (25th/75th percentile):** 19-25
✔ **Tuition:** 2006-2007: $17,932

Selectivity: Selective	**Room/board:** $6,300
Acceptance rate: 90%	**Average debt:** $19,820
Student/faculty ratio: 15/1	**Proportion who borrowed:** 85%

UNDERGRADUATE STUDENT BODY STATS

2005-2006 enrollment: 1,175 full-time; 40 part-time. Men: 46%; women: 54%. Ethnic makeup: African American: 8%; American-Indian: 1%; Asian American: 1%; Hispanic: 2%; White: 88%; International: 1%. Religious preference: Roman Catholic: 5%; Protestant: 75%; Unknown: 9%; Free Methodist: 11%.

ADMISSIONS FACTS AND FIGURES

Phone: (618) 664-7100. Email: admissions@greenville.edu. Website: http://www.greenville.edu. Application deadlines for fall 2007: Regular decision: August 1; decision sent by September 1. Early decision: Not offered. Early action: Not offered. Admission can be deferred. Application fee: $25. Common application is not accepted. To apply online, go to: http://www.greenville.edu/admissions/application. Admissions requirements/recommendations: High school units required (recommended): English: (4); Mathematics: (2); Science: (1); Foreign language: (2); History: (1); Total units: (11). Tests: The college uses SAT or ACT scores in admissions decisions. Either SAT or ACT required. For admission to the fall 2007 entering class, the school will accept: ACT with writing, ACT without writing. Campus visit: Recommended. Admissions interview: Recommended. Off-campus interview: Not available. Factors that count in admissions decisions: Academic: Secondary school record: Very important. Class rank: Very important. Letters of recommendation: Considered. Standardized test scores: Very important. Essay: Very important. Nonacademic: Interview: Not considered. Extracurricular activities: Considered. Talent/ability: Considered. Character/personal qualities: Very important. Alumni/ae relationship: Considered. Geographical residence: Not considered. State residency: Not considered. Religious affiliation/commitment: Very important. Minority status: Not considered. Volunteer work: Not considered. Work experience: Not considered. Other schools with the greatest overlap in applicants: Eastern Illinois University; Millikin University; Olivet Nazarene University; Southern Illinois University–Carbondale; Spring Arbor University. Admissions statistics for the fall 2005 entering class: Total applicants: 633. Total accepted: 570. Freshmen enrolled: 252; 46% were from out of state. Overall acceptance rate: 90%. Credentials of fall 2005 freshmen: 16% ranked in the top 10 percent of their high school class; 37% were in the top 25 percent, and 71% were in the top half. (Proportion submitting class standing: 84%.) Average high school grade point average: 3.3. First-year students who submitted SAT scores: 16%. Scores (25/75 percentile): Verbal: 450-590, Math: 430-555, Combined: 880-1145. First-year students submitting ACT scores: 84%. Scores (25/75 percentile): English: 18-27, Math: 17-25, Composite: 19-25.

ACADEMICS

Year founded: 1892. Academic calendar: 4-1-4. Degrees offered: bachelor's, master's. Most popular majors: 40% business, management, marketing, and related support services, 12% education, 8% visual and performing arts, 4% communications technologies/technicians and support services, 4% liberal arts and sciences studies, and humanities. Major fields of study: biological and biomedical sciences; business, management, marketing, and related support services; communication, journalism, and related programs; communications technologies/technicians and support services; computer and information sciences and support services; education; English language and literature/letters; foreign languages, literatures, and linguistics; history; liberal arts and sciences studies, and humanities; mathematics and statistics; multi/interdisciplinary studies; parks, recreation, leisure, and fitness studies; philosophy and religious studies; physical sciences; psychology; public administration and social service professions; security and protective services; social sciences; theology and religious vocations; visual and performing arts. **Areas of required coursework:** humanities, mathematics, English (including composition), philosophy, foreign languages, sciences (biological or physical), history, social science, other. **Pre-professional programs:** pre-law, pre-dentistry, pre-medicine, pre-veterinary science, pre-pharmacy. **Special academic programs (% participation):** cooperative (work-study plan) program (4%), double major (10%), honors program (1%), independent study (8%), internships (75%), liberal arts/career combination (100%), student-designed major (5%), study abroad (1%), teacher certificate program (12%). **Teacher certification offered in:** early childhood, special education, elementary, secondary. **Faculty and instruction (2005-2006):** Total instructional faculty: 59 full-time, 71 part-time (65% men; 35% women; 5% minorities). Full-time faculty with Ph.D. or other terminal degree: 64%. Student/faculty ratio: 15/1. Classes of fewer than 20 students: 58%; of 20 to 49 students: 36%; of 50 or more students: 6%. **Advanced Placement and International Baccalaureate credit:** AP tests may be used for: Credit and/or placement. Scores accepted: 3, 4, 5. International Baccalaureate exams may be used for: Credit and/or placement. **Freshmen returning for sophomore year:** 72%. **Graduation rates:** Four-year: 38%; five-year: 50%; six-year: 54%.

COSTS AND FINANCIAL AID

Financial aid office: (618) 664-7110. **Expenses (2006-2007):** Tuition and fees 2006-2007: $17,932; room/board: $6,300. Estimated books and supplies: $900; transportation: $800; personal expenses: $1,400. **Financial aid:** Priority filing date for institution's financial aid form: May 1. In 2005-2006, 92% of undergraduates applied for financial aid. Of those, 85% were determined to have financial need; 15% had their need fully met. Average financial aid package (proportion receiving): $14,260 (85%). Average amount of gift aid, such as scholarships or grants (proportion receiving): $9,875 (85%). Average amount of self-help aid, such as work study or loans (proportion receiving): $4,826 (77%). Average need-based loan (excluding PLUS or other private loans): $3,987. Among students who received need-based aid, the average percentage of need met: 76%. Among students who received aid based on merit, the average award (and the proportion receiving): $8,163 (15%). The average athletic scholarship (and the proportion receiving): $0 (0%). Average amount of debt of borrowers graduating in 2005: $19,820. Proportion who borrowed: 85%.

CAMPUS LIFE AND EXTRACURRICULAR ACTIVITIES

Campus housing available (% using): women's dorms (32%), men's dorms (36%), apartment for single students (19%), other housing options (13%). Students who live in college-owned, operated, or affiliated housing: 66%. **Student employment:** During the 2005-2006 academic year, 25% of undergraduates worked on campus. Average per-year earnings: $1,000. **Clubs and organizations:** Number of student organizations: 25. Activities include: choral groups, concert band, drama/theater, jazz band, music ensembles, pep band, radio station, student government, student newspaper, yearbook. Number of fraternities: 0; sororities: 0. Average proportion of students who stay on campus on weekends: 70%. **Sports program (2005-2006):** Member of NCAA III. *Men's intercollegiate varsity sports:* baseball, basketball, cross-country, football, soccer, tennis, track and field (indoor), track and field (outdoor). *Women's intercollegiate varsity sports:* basketball, cross-country, soccer, softball, tennis, track and field (indoor), track and field (outdoor), volleyball.

SERVICES AND FACILITIES

Basic services: nonremedial tutoring, health insurance. **Remedial assistance:** math, study skills, other. **Counseling services:** career, personal, academic, older student, psychological, religious. **For learning-disabled students:** School does not offer a structured program with separate admission and additional fees. Services include: remedial math, remedial English, extended time for tests, tutors, early syllabus, priority seating. **Library:** Number of titles: 131,425; number of current serial subscriptions: 1,990. **Information technology resources:** Students are not required to lease or own a computer. Number of campus computers available to all students: 65. School has a wireless network. Approximate number of users that can be accommodated: 2,000. Proportion of college-owned housing units wired for high-speed internet access: 100%. **Campus safety:** Security services offered: late-night transport/escort service, 24-hour emergency telephones, lighted pathways/sidewalks, student patrols, controlled dormitory access (key, security card, etc).

TRANSFER AND INTERNATIONAL STUDENTS

Transfer students: May apply for admission for the following academic terms: Fall, Winter, Spring, Summer. Applicants do not need a minimum number of credits to apply. For fall 2005: Transfer applications received:

162. Transfer applicants offered admission: 156. Transfer applicants enrolled: 84. **International students:** Number of foreign undergraduates: 13 (1% of student body). Number of countries represented: 12. Minimum TOEFL score required: 525 (paper); 197 (computer). Average TOEFL score: 530 (paper).

Illinois College

- **Address:** 1101 W. College Avenue, Jacksonville, IL 62650-2299
- **Website:** http://www.ic.edu
- **Private; Religious affiliation:** Presbyterian/United Church of Christ
- **Enrollment:** 1,010 full-time; 20 part-time

KEY STATS

✔ **U.S News College Ranking:** 14, Comp. Coll.–Bachelor's (Midwest)
✔ **ACT Score (25th/75th percentile):** 21-27
✔ **Tuition:** 2006-2007: $16,120

Selectivity: More selective **Room/board:** $6,730
Acceptance rate: 64% **Average debt:** $11,105
Student/faculty ratio: 12/1 **Proportion who borrowed:** 95%

UNDERGRADUATE STUDENT BODY STATS

2005-2006 enrollment: 1,010 full-time; 20 part-time. Men: 46%; women: 54%. **Ethnic makeup:** African American: 3%; Asian American: 1%; Hispanic: 1%; White: 94%; International: 2%. **Religious preference:** Roman Catholic: 23%; Protestant: 44%; No preference: 12%; Unknown: 3%; Presbyterian/United Church of Christ: 6%; Methodist: 12%.

ADMISSIONS FACTS AND FIGURES

Phone: (217) 245-3030. **Email:** admissions@ic.edu. **Website:** http://www.ic.edu. **Application deadlines for fall 2007:** Regular decision: August 1. Early decision: Not offered. Early action: Not offered. Admission can be deferred. **Application fee:** $25. Common application is accepted. **To apply online, go to:** http://www.ic.edu/Admissions/onlineapp.htm. **Admissions requirements/recommendations:** High school units required (recommended): English: 3 (4); Mathematics: 1 (2); Science: 1 (2); Foreign language: (2); Social studies: 1 (2); History: 1 (2); Total units: 15 (15). Tests: The college uses SAT or ACT scores in admissions decisions. Either SAT or ACT required. For admission to the fall 2007 entering class, the school will accept: ACT with writing, ACT without writing. Campus visit: Recommended. Admissions interview: Recommended. Off-campus interview: May be arranged. **Factors that count in admissions decisions:** *Academic:* Secondary school record: Very important. Class rank: Important. Letters of recommendation: Very important. Standardized test scores: Important. Essay: Important. *Nonacademic:* Interview: Considered. Extracurricular activities: Important. Talent/ability: Important. Character/personal qualities: Important. Alumni/ae relationship: Considered. Geographical residence: Considered. State residency: Considered. Religious affiliation/commitment: Not considered. Minority status: Not considered. Volunteer work: Considered. Work experience: Considered. **Other schools with the greatest overlap in applicants:** Illinois State University; Millikin University; Southern Illinois University–Carbondale; Southern Illinois University–Edwardsville; University of Illinois–Urbana-Champaign. **Admissions statistics for the fall 2005 entering class:** Total applicants: 1,149. Total accepted: 740. Freshmen enrolled: 256; 5% were from out of state. Overall acceptance rate: 64%. **Size of waiting list:** 0 applicants; enrolled from waiting list: 0. **Credentials of fall 2005 freshmen:** 23% ranked in the top 10 percent of their high school class; 53% were in the top 25 percent, and 82% were in the top half. (Proportion submitting class standing: 95%.) **Average high school grade point average:** 3.4. **First-year students who submitted SAT scores:** 8%. Scores (25/75 percentile): Verbal: 540-650, Math: 560-640, Combined: 1100-1290. **First-year students submitting ACT scores:** 96%. Scores (25/75 percentile): English: 20-27, Math: 20-26, Composite: 21-27.

ACADEMICS

Year founded: 1829. **Academic calendar:** Semester. **Degrees offered:** bachelor's. **Most popular majors:** 13% business/managerial economics, 8% biology/biological sciences, 6% elementary education and teaching, 6% psychology, 6% sociology. **Major fields of study:** biological and biomedical sciences; business, management, marketing, and related support services; computer and information sciences and support services; education; engineering; English language and literature/letters; foreign languages, literatures, and linguistics; health professions and related clinical sciences; history; mathematics and statistics; multi/interdisciplinary studies; parks, recreation, leisure, and fitness studies; philosophy and religious studies; physical sciences; psychology; social sciences; visual and performing arts. **Areas of required coursework:** arts/fine arts, humanities, mathematics, English (including composition), philosophy, foreign languages, sciences (biological or physical), social science, other. **Special academic programs (% participation):** cross-registration (2.7%), double major (13%), dual enrollment (0%), independent study (26.6%), internships (24.5%), liberal arts/career combination (3.8%), student-designed major (0%), study abroad (15.2%), teacher certificate program (15.8%). **Teacher certification offered in:** early childhood, elementary, middle/junior high, secondary. **Faculty and instruction (2005-2006):** Total instructional faculty: 71 full-time, 34 part-time (59% men; 41% women; 10% minorities). Full-time faculty with Ph.D. or other terminal degree: 86%. Student/faculty ratio: 12/1. Classes of fewer than 20 students: 63%; of 20 to 49 students: 36%; of 50 or more students: 1%. **Advanced Placement and International Baccalaureate credit:** AP tests may be used for: Credit only. Scores accepted: 3, 4, 5. International Baccalaureate exams may be used for: Credit only. **Freshmen returning for sophomore year:** 75%. **Graduation rates:** Four-year: 40%; five-year: 54%; six-year: 58%. **Graduate study:** 19% of students pursue further study immediately upon graduation; 25% within one year; 30% within five years. Fields in which graduates pursue further study: Master of Business Administration (MBA), 19%; law, 10%; medicine, 20%; dentistry, 4%; engineering, 3%; theology (or the seminary), 4%; education, 7%; arts and sciences, 30%; veterinary medicine, 3%.

COSTS AND FINANCIAL AID

Financial aid office: (217) 245-3035. **Expenses (2006-2007):** Tuition and fees 2006-2007: $16,120; room/board: $6,730. Estimated books and supplies: $900; transportation: $400; personal expenses: $900. **Financial aid:** Priority filing date for institution's financial aid form: March 1. In 2005-2006, 88% of undergraduates applied for financial aid. Of those, 75% were determined to have financial need; 35% had their need fully met. Average financial aid package (proportion receiving): $13,570 (75%). Average amount of gift aid, such as scholarships or grants (proportion receiving): $6,292 (62%). Average amount of self-help aid, such as work study or loans (proportion receiving): $5,543 (63%). Average need-based loan (excluding PLUS or other private loans): $4,307. Among students who received need-based aid, the average percentage of need met: 85%. Among students who received aid based on merit, the average award (and the proportion receiving): $5,587 (18%). The average athletic scholarship (and the proportion receiving): $0 (0%). Average amount of debt of borrowers graduating in 2005: $11,105. Proportion who borrowed: 95%.

CAMPUS LIFE AND EXTRACURRICULAR ACTIVITIES

Campus housing available (% using): coed dorms (40%), women's dorms (28%), men's dorms (22%), apartment for single students (8%), special housing for disabled students (1%), other housing options (1%). Students who live in college-owned, operated, or affiliated housing: 71%. **Student employment:** During the 2005-2006 academic year, 48% of undergraduates worked on campus. Average per-year earnings: $1,920. **Clubs and organizations:** Number of student organizations: 72. Activities include: choral groups, concert band, dance, drama/theater, literary magazine, music ensembles, musical theater, pep band, student government, student newspaper, yearbook. Number of fraternities: 0; sororities: 0. Average proportion of students who stay on campus on weekends: 65%. **Sports program (2005-2006):** Member of NCAA III. *Men's intercollegiate varsity sports:* baseball, basketball, cross-country, football, golf, soccer, tennis, track and field (indoor), track and field (outdoor), wrestling. *Women's intercollegiate varsity sports:* basketball, cross-country, golf, soccer, softball, tennis, track and field (indoor), track and field (outdoor), volleyball.

SERVICES AND FACILITIES

Basic services: nonremedial tutoring, placement service, health service. **Counseling services:** career, personal, academic, psychological, birth control, religious. **For learning-disabled students:** School does not offer a structured program with separate admission and additional fees. Total undergraduates in learning-disabled program or receiving services: 16. Services include: reading machines, tape recorders, diagnostic testing service, untimed tests, note-taking services, oral tests, readers, extended time for tests, tutors, early syllabus, priority registration, priority seating, proofreading services, substitution of courses, texts on tape, typist/scribe, take home exams, other testing accomodations, waiver of foreign language degree requirement, waiver of math degree requirement, other. **Library:** Number of titles: 166,968;

number of current serial subscriptions: 648. **Information technology resources:** Students are not required to lease or own a computer. Number of campus computers available to all students: 158. School has a wireless network. Approximate number of users that can be accommodated: 1,000. Proportion of college-owned housing units wired for high-speed internet access: 99%. **Campus safety:** Security services offered: 24-hour foot and vehicle patrols, late-night transport/escort service, 24-hour emergency telephones, lighted pathways/sidewalks, student patrols, controlled dormitory access (key, security card, etc).

TRANSFER AND INTERNATIONAL STUDENTS

Transfer students: May apply for admission for the following academic terms: Fall, Spring, Summer. Applicants do not need a minimum number of credits to apply. For fall 2005: Transfer applications received: 137. Transfer applicants offered admission: 63. Transfer applicants enrolled: 38. **International students:** Number of foreign undergraduates: 17 (2% of student body). Number of countries represented: 13. Minimum TOEFL score required: 550 (paper); 213 (computer). Average TOEFL score: 578 (paper).

Illinois Institute of Technology

- **Address:** 3300 S. Federal Street, Chicago, IL 60616-3793
- **Website:** http://www.iit.edu
- **Private**
- **Enrollment:** 1,988 full-time; 228 part-time

KEY STATS

✔ **U.S News College Ranking:** 105, National Universities
✔ **ACT Score (25th/75th percentile):** 25-30
✔ **Tuition:** 2006-2007: $24,113

Selectivity: More selective	**Room/board:** $8,049
Acceptance rate: 63%	**Average debt:** $19,483
Student/faculty ratio: N/A	**Proportion who borrowed:** 54%

UNDERGRADUATE STUDENT BODY STATS

2005-2006 enrollment: 1,988 full-time; 228 part-time. Men: 74%; women: 26%. **Ethnic makeup:** African American: 5%; Asian American: 14%; Hispanic: 7%; White: 58%; International: 16%.

ADMISSIONS FACTS AND FIGURES

Phone: (800) 448-2329. **Email:** admission@iit.edu. **Website:** http://www.iit.edu. **Application deadlines for fall 2007:** Regular decision: Rolling. Early decision: Not offered. Early action: Not offered. Admission can be deferred. **Application fee:** $30. Common application is accepted. **To apply online, go to:** http://www.iit.edu/admission/undergrad. **Admissions requirements/recommendations:** High school units required (recommended): English: 4 (4); Mathematics: 4 (4); Science: 3 (3); Social studies: 2 (2); History: 2 (2). Tests: The college uses SAT or ACT scores in admissions decisions. Either SAT or ACT required. For admission to the fall 2007 entering class, the school will accept: ACT with writing, ACT without writing. Campus visit: Recommended. Admissions interview: Recommended. Off-campus interview: May be arranged. **Factors that count in admissions decisions:** *Academic:* Secondary school record: Considered. Class rank: Considered. Letters of recommendation: Important. Standardized test scores: Very important. Essay: Important. *Nonacademic:* Interview: Considered. Extracurricular activities: Considered. Talent/ability: Considered. Character/personal qualities: Considered. Alumni/ae relationship: Considered. Geographical residence: Not considered. State residency: Not considered. Religious affiliation/commitment: Not considered. Minority status: Not considered. Volunteer work: Considered. Work experience: Considered. **Other schools with the greatest overlap in applicants:** Northwestern University; Purdue University–West Lafayette; Rose-Hulman Institute of Technology; University of Illinois–Chicago; University of Illinois–Urbana-Champaign. **Admissions statistics for the fall 2005 entering class:** Total applicants: 2,514. Total accepted: 1,588. Freshmen enrolled: 415; 36% were from out of state. Overall acceptance rate: 63%. **Credentials of fall 2005 freshmen:** 38% ranked in the top 10 percent of their high school class; 69% were in the top 25 percent, and 94% were in the top half. (Proportion submitting class standing: 77%.) **Average high school grade point average:** 3.9. **First-year students who submitted SAT scores:** 42%. Scores (25/75 percentile): Verbal: 560-660, Math: 620-720, Combined: 1180-1380. **First-year**

students submitting ACT scores: 74%. Scores (25/75 percentile): English: 24-30, Math: 27-32, Composite: 25-30.

ACADEMICS
Year founded: 1890. Academic calendar: Semester. Degrees offered: certificate, bachelor's, post-bachelor's certificate, master's, first professional, doctorate. Most popular majors: Information not available. Major fields of study: architecture and related services; biological and biomedical sciences; business, management, marketing, and related support services; communication, journalism, and related programs; computer and information sciences and support services; engineering; engineering technologies/technicians; English language and literature/letters; mathematics and statistics; multi/interdisciplinary studies; physical sciences; psychology. Areas of required coursework: humanities, computer literacy, mathematics, social science. Pre-professional programs: pre-law, pre-medicine, pre-pharmacy. Special academic programs (% participation): cooperative (work-study plan) program (11%), distance learning (32%), double major (8%), English as a Second Language (ESL) (4%), independent study (39%), liberal arts/career combination (0%), study abroad (4%), teacher certificate program (0%). Teacher certification offered in: secondary. Cooperative education programs: computer science, engineering. Reserve Officers Training Corps (ROTC): Army ROTC: Offered on campus; Navy ROTC: Offered on campus; Air Force ROTC: Offered on campus. Faculty and instruction (2005-2006): Total instructional faculty: 298. Classes of fewer than 20 students: 68%; of 20 to 49 students: 29%; of 50 or more students: 3%. Advanced Placement and International Baccalaureate credit: AP tests may be used for: Credit only. Scores accepted: 3, 4, 5. International Baccalaureate exams may be used for: Credit only. Freshmen returning for sophomore year: 82%. Graduation rates: Four-year: 64%; five-year: 67%; six-year: 69%.

COSTS AND FINANCIAL AID
Financial aid office: (312) 567-7219. Expenses (2006-2007): Tuition and fees 2006-2007: $24,113; room/board: $8,049. Financial aid: Priority filing date for institution's financial aid form: April 15. In 2005-2006, 66% of undergraduates applied for financial aid. Of those, 58% were determined to have financial need; 20% had their need fully met. Average financial aid package (proportion receiving): $20,610 (58%). Average amount of gift aid, such as scholarships or grants (proportion receiving): $13,484 (57%). Average amount of self-help aid, such as work study or loans (proportion receiving): $5,168 (44%). Average need-based loan (excluding PLUS or other private loans): $4,594. Among students who received need-based aid, the average percentage of need met: 85%. Among students who received aid based on merit, the average award (and the proportion receiving): $10,259 (39%). The average athletic scholarship (and the proportion receiving): $5,958 (5%). Average amount of debt of borrowers graduating in 2005: $19,483. Proportion who borrowed: 54%.

CAMPUS LIFE AND EXTRACURRICULAR ACTIVITIES
Campus housing available: coed dorms, women's dorms, men's dorms, sorority housing, fraternity housing, apartments for married students, apartment for single students. Students who live in college-owned, operated, or affiliated housing: 54%. Student employment: During the 2005-2006 academic year, 21% of undergraduates worked on campus. Average per-year earnings: $2,300. Clubs and organizations: Number of student organizations: 98. Activities include: choral groups, concert band, drama/theater, jazz band, literary magazine, music ensembles, musical theater, radio station, student government, student newspaper, student film society. Number of fraternities: 6; sororities: 4. Proportion of men in fraternities: 17%; of women in sororities: 17%. Average proportion of students who stay on campus on weekends: 80%. Sports program (2005-2006): Member of NAIA. Men's intercollegiate varsity sports: baseball, basketball, cross-country, soccer, swimming and diving. Women's intercollegiate varsity sports: basketball, cross-country, soccer, swimming and diving, volleyball.

SERVICES AND FACILITIES
Basic services: nonremedial tutoring, women's center, health service, health insurance. Remedial assistance: math. Counseling services: minority student, career, military, personal, veteran student, academic, psychological, birth control, religious, other. For learning-disabled students: School does not offer a structured program with separate admission and additional fees. Services include: tape recorders, videotaped classes, untimed tests, note-taking services, oral tests, learning center, readers, extended time for tests, tutors, other. Information technology resources: Students are not required to lease or own a computer. Number of campus computers available to all students: 560. School has a wireless network. Proportion of college-owned housing units wired for high-speed internet access: 100%. Campus safety:

Security services offered: 24-hour foot and vehicle patrols, late-night transport/escort service, 24-hour emergency telephones, lighted pathways/sidewalks, controlled dormitory access (key, security card, etc).

TRANSFER AND INTERNATIONAL STUDENTS
Transfer students: May apply for admission for the following academic terms: Fall, Spring. Applicants need a minimum number of credits to apply. For fall 2005: Transfer applications received: 540. Transfer applicants offered admission: 288. Transfer applicants enrolled: 209. International students: Number of foreign undergraduates: 339 (16% of student body). Minimum TOEFL score required: 550 (paper); 213 (computer). Average TOEFL score: 590 (paper).

Illinois State University

- **Address:** Campus Box 2200, Normal, IL 61790-2200
- **Website:** http://www.ilstu.edu
- **Public**
- **Enrollment:** 16,635 full-time; 1,223 part-time

KEY STATS
✔ U.S News College Ranking: third tier, National Universities
✔ ACT Score (25th/75th percentile): 22-26
✔ Tuition: 2006-2007: $8,040 in state, $14,730 out of state

Selectivity: Selective	Room/board: $6,194
Acceptance rate: 77%	Average debt: $15,616
Student/faculty ratio: 19/1	Proportion who borrowed: 59%

UNDERGRADUATE STUDENT BODY STATS
2005-2006 enrollment: 16,635 full-time; 1,223 part-time. Men: 42%; women: 58%. Ethnic makeup: African American: 6%; Asian American: 2%; Hispanic: 3%; White: 88%; International: 1%.

ADMISSIONS FACTS AND FIGURES
Phone: (309) 438-2181. Email: admissions@ilstu.edu. Website: http://www.ilstu.edu. Application deadlines for fall 2007: Regular decision: March 1. Early decision: Not offered. Early action: Not offered. Admission cannot be deferred. Application fee: $30. Common application is not accepted. To apply online, go to: http://www.admissions.ilstu.edu/apply/. Admissions requirements/recommendations: High school units required (recommended): English: 4; Mathematics: 3; Science: 2; Foreign language: 2; Social studies: 2; Academic electives: 2; Total units: 15. Tests: The college uses SAT or ACT scores in admissions decisions. Either SAT or ACT required. For admission to the fall 2007 entering class, the school will accept: ACT with writing, ACT without writing. Campus visit: Required. Admissions interview: Neither required nor recommended. Factors that count in admissions decisions: Academic: Secondary school record: Important. Class rank: Important. Letters of recommendation: Not considered. Standardized test scores: Important. Essay: Considered. Nonacademic: Interview: Not considered. Extracurricular activities: Considered. Talent/ability: Considered. Character/personal qualities: Considered. Alumni/ae relationship: Not considered. Geographical residence: Not considered. State residency: Not considered. Religious affiliation/commitment: Not considered. Minority status: Not considered. Volunteer work: Not considered. Work experience: Not considered. Other schools with the greatest overlap in applicants: Eastern Illinois University; Northern Illinois University; Southern Illinois University–Carbondale; University of Illinois–Urbana-Champaign; Western Illinois University. Admissions statistics for the fall 2005 entering class: Total applicants: 10,414. Total accepted: 8,030. Freshmen enrolled: 3,179; 1% were from out of state. Overall acceptance rate: 77%. Size of waiting list: 473 applicants; enrolled from waiting list: 31. Credentials of fall 2005 freshmen: 11% ranked in the top 10 percent of their high school class; 36% were in the top 25 percent, and 83% were in the top half. (Proportion submitting class standing: 95%.) First-year students submitting ACT scores: 99%. Scores (25/75 percentile): English: 21-26, Math: 20-26, Composite: 22-26.

ACADEMICS
Year founded: 1857. Academic calendar: Semester. Degrees offered: bachelor's, post-bachelor's certificate, master's, post-master's certificate, doctorate. Most popular majors: 21% education, 20% business, management, marketing, and related support services, 7% health professions and related clinical

sciences, 7% social sciences, 6% communication, journalism, and related programs. **Major fields of study:** agriculture, agriculture operations, and related sciences; biological and biomedical sciences; business, management, marketing, and related support services; communication, journalism, and related programs; computer and information sciences and support services; education; engineering technologies/technicians; English language and literature/letters; family and consumer sciences/human sciences; foreign languages, literatures, and linguistics; health professions and related clinical sciences; history; liberal arts and sciences studies, and humanities; mathematics and statistics; parks, recreation, leisure, and fitness studies; philosophy and religious studies; physical sciences; psychology; public administration and social service professions; security and protective services; social sciences; visual and performing arts. **Areas of required coursework:** arts/fine arts, humanities, computer literacy, mathematics, English (including composition), philosophy, sciences (biological or physical), history, social science. **Pre-professional programs:** pre-law, pre-medicine, pre-veterinary science. **Special academic programs (% participation):** distance learning (20%), double major (6.3%), exchange student program (domestic) (.3%), honors program (12%), independent study (28%), internships (39%), student-designed major (1%), study abroad (6%), teacher certificate program (25%). **Cooperative education programs:** agriculture, health professions, home economics, natural science, social/behavioral science, technologies. **Reserve Officers Training Corps (ROTC):** Army ROTC: Offered on campus. **Faculty and instruction (2005-2006):** Total instructional faculty: 829 full-time, 274 part-time (54% men; 46% women; 10% minorities). Full-time faculty with Ph.D. or other terminal degree: 84%. Student/faculty ratio: 19/1. Classes of fewer than 20 students: 32%; of 20 to 49 students: 56%; of 50 or more students: 12%. **Freshmen returning for sophomore year:** 83%. **Graduation rates:** Four-year: 35%; five-year: 58%; six-year: 63%. **Graduate study:** 36% of students pursue further study within one year.

COSTS AND FINANCIAL AID

Financial aid office: (309) 438-2231. **Expenses (2006-2007):** Tuition and fees 2006-2007: $8,040 in state, $14,730 out of state; room/board: $6,194. **Financial aid:** Priority filing date for institution's financial aid form: March 1. In 2005-2006, 66% of undergraduates applied for financial aid. Of those, 45% were determined to have financial need; 45% had their need fully met. Average financial aid package (proportion receiving): $9,056 (44%). Average amount of gift aid, such as scholarships or grants (proportion receiving): $6,844 (29%). Average amount of self-help aid, such as work study or loans (proportion receiving): $5,026 (39%). Average need-based loan (excluding PLUS or other private loans): $4,921. Among students who received need-based aid, the average percentage of need met: 84%. Among students who received aid based on merit, the average award (and the proportion receiving): $4,230 (2%). The average athletic scholarship (and the proportion receiving): $9,041 (1%). Average amount of debt of borrowers graduating in 2005: $15,616. Proportion who borrowed: 59%.

CAMPUS LIFE AND EXTRACURRICULAR ACTIVITIES

Campus housing available: coed dorms, men's dorms, sorority housing, fraternity housing, apartments for married students, apartment for single students, special housing for disabled students, special housing for international students. Students who live in college-owned, operated, or affiliated housing: 35%. **Student employment:** During the 2005-2006 academic year, 18% of undergraduates worked on campus. Average per-year earnings: $2,250. **Clubs and organizations:** Number of student organizations: 250. Activities include: choral groups, concert band, dance, drama/theater, jazz band, literary magazine, marching band, music ensembles, musical theater, pep band, radio station, student government, student newspaper, student film society, symphony orchestra, television station. Number of fraternities: 17; sororities: 15. Proportion of men in fraternities: 7%; of women in sororities: 8%. **Sports program (2005-2006):** Member of NCAA I. **Men's intercollegiate varsity sports:** baseball, basketball, cross-country, football, golf, tennis, track and field (indoor), track and field (outdoor). **Women's intercollegiate varsity sports:** basketball, cross-country, golf, gymnastics, soccer, softball, swimming and diving, tennis, track and field (indoor), track and field (outdoor), volleyball.

SERVICES AND FACILITIES

Basic services: placement service, day care, health service, health insurance, other. **Remedial assistance:** reading, math, study skills. **Counseling services:** minority student, career, military, personal, veteran student, academic, older student, psychological, birth control, religious. **For learning-disabled students:** School does not offer a structured program with separate admission and additional fees. Total undergraduates in learning-disabled program or receiving services: 92. Services include: reading machines, diagnostic test-

ing service, note-taking services, learning center, readers, extended time for tests, tutors, other testing accomodations. **Library:** Number of titles: 1,519,687; number of current serial subscriptions: 8,878. **Information technology resources:** Students are not required to lease or own a computer. Number of campus computers available to all students: 2,530. School has a wireless network. Approximate number of users that can be accommodated: 1,100. Proportion of college-owned housing units wired for high-speed internet access: 90%. **Campus safety:** Security services offered: 24-hour foot and vehicle patrols, late-night transport/escort service, 24-hour emergency telephones, lighted pathways/sidewalks, student patrols, controlled dormitory access (key, security card, etc).

TRANSFER AND INTERNATIONAL STUDENTS

Transfer students: May apply for admission for the following academic terms: Fall, Spring, Summer. Applicants need a minimum number of credits to apply. For fall 2005: Transfer applications received: 3,660. Transfer applicants offered admission: 3,035. Transfer applicants enrolled: 1,754. **International students:** Number of foreign undergraduates: 137 (1% of student body). Number of countries represented: 47. Minimum TOEFL score required: 550 (paper); 213 (computer). Average TOEFL score: 619 (paper).

Illinois Wesleyan University

- **Address:** Box 2900, Bloomington, IL 61702-2900
- **Website:** http://www.iwu.edu
- **Private**
- **Enrollment:** 2,140 full-time; 6 part-time

KEY STATS

✔ **U.S News College Ranking:** 61, Liberal Arts Colleges
✔ **ACT Score (25th/75th percentile):** 26-31
✔ **Tuition:** 2006-2007: $29,136

Selectivity: More selective	**Room/board:** $6,714
Acceptance rate: 57%	**Average debt:** $21,846
Student/faculty ratio: 12/1	**Proportion who borrowed:** 67%

UNDERGRADUATE STUDENT BODY STATS

2005-2006 enrollment: 2,140 full-time; 6 part-time. Men: 43%; women: 57%. **Ethnic makeup:** African American: 4%; Asian American: 3%; Hispanic: 3%; White: 88%; International: 2%.

ADMISSIONS FACTS AND FIGURES

Phone: (800) 332-2498. **Email:** iwuadmit@iwu.edu. **Website:** http://www.iwu.edu. **Application deadlines for fall 2007:** Regular decision: Rolling. Early decision: Not offered. Early action: Not offered. Admission can be deferred. Common application is accepted. **Admissions requirements/recommendations:** High school units required (recommended): English: (4); Mathematics: (3); Science: (3); Foreign language: (3); Social studies: (2); Total units: (15). Tests: The college uses SAT or ACT scores in admissions decisions. Either SAT or ACT required. For admission to the fall 2007 entering class, the school will accept: ACT with writing, ACT without writing. Campus visit: Recommended. Admissions interview: Recommended. Off-campus interview: Not available. **Factors that count in admissions decisions:** *Academic:* Secondary school record: Very important. Class rank: Important. Letters of recommendation: Considered. Standardized test scores: Important. Essay: Important. *Nonacademic:* Interview: Very important. Extracurricular activities: Important. Talent/ability: Important. Character/personal qualities: Important. Alumni/ae relationship: Considered. Geographical residence: Considered. State residency: Considered. Religious affiliation/commitment: Not considered. Minority status: Considered. Volunteer work: Considered. Work experience: Considered. **Other schools with the greatest overlap in applicants:** Augustana College; Northwestern University; University of Illinois–Urbana-Champaign; University of Notre Dame; Washington University in St. Louis. **Admissions statistics for the fall 2005 entering class:** Total applicants: 2,770. Total accepted: 1,580. Freshmen enrolled: 565; 15% were from out of state. Overall acceptance rate: 57%. **Size of waiting list:** 459 applicants; enrolled from waiting list: 44. **Credentials of fall 2005 freshmen:** 47% ranked in the top 10 percent of their high school class; 81% were in the top 25 percent, and 99% were in the top half. (Proportion submitting class standing: 85%.) **First-year students who submitted SAT scores:** 32%. Scores (25/75 percentile): Verbal: 600-690, Math: 590-690, Combined: 1190-1380. **First-year**

students submitting ACT scores: 90%. Scores (25/75 percentile): English: 26-32, Math: 26-31, Composite: 26-31.

ACADEMICS

Year founded: 1850. **Academic calendar:** Other. **Degrees offered:** bachelor's. **Most popular majors:** 17% business/commerce, 8% psychology, 7% English language and literature, 7% biology/biological sciences, 7% history. **Major fields of study:** area, ethnic, cultural, and gender studies; biological and biomedical sciences; business, management, marketing, and related support services; computer and information sciences and support services; education; English language and literature/letters; foreign languages, literatures, and linguistics; health professions and related clinical sciences; history; mathematics and statistics; multi/interdisciplinary studies; natural resources and conservation; philosophy and religious studies; physical sciences; psychology; social sciences; visual and performing arts. **Areas of required coursework:** arts/fine arts, humanities, mathematics, English (including composition), foreign languages, sciences (biological or physical), history, social science, other. **Pre-professional programs:** pre-law, pre-dentistry, pre-medicine, pre-theology, pre-veterinary science, pre-optometry, pre-pharmacy. **Special academic programs (% participation):** double major (18%), honors program (6%), independent study (28%), internships (25%), student-designed major (1%), study abroad (24%), teacher certificate program (14%). **Teacher certification offered in:** elementary, middle/junior high, secondary. **Reserve Officers Training Corps (ROTC):** Army ROTC: Offered at cooperating institution (Illinois State University). **Faculty and instruction (2005-2006):** Total instructional faculty: 161 full-time, 61 part-time (55% men; 45% women; 14% minorities). Full-time faculty with Ph.D. or other terminal degree: 93%. Student/faculty ratio: 12/1. Classes of fewer than 20 students: 60%; of 20 to 49 students: 38%; of 50 or more students: 2%. **Advanced Placement and International Baccalaureate credit:** AP tests may be used for: Credit only. Scores accepted: 4, 5. International Baccalaureate exams may be used for: Credit only. **Freshmen returning for sophomore year:** 93%. **Graduation rates:** Four-year: 77%; five-year: 81%; six-year: 82%. **Graduate study:** 32% of students pursue further study within one year. Fields in which graduates pursue further study: Master of Business Administration (MBA), 3%; law, 9%; medicine, 19%; dentistry, 3%; engineering, 3%; education, 3%; arts and sciences, 60%; veterinary medicine, 1%.

COSTS AND FINANCIAL AID

Financial aid office: (309) 556-3096. **Expenses (2006-2007):** Tuition and fees 2006-2007: $29,136; room/board: $6,714. Estimated books and supplies: $650; transportation: $0; personal expenses: $780. **Financial aid:** Priority filing date for institution's financial aid form: March 1; deadline: March 1. In 2005-2006, 61% of undergraduates applied for financial aid. Of those, 54% were determined to have financial need; 49% had their need fully met. Average financial aid package (proportion receiving): $18,285 (54%). Average amount of gift aid, such as scholarships or grants (proportion receiving): $13,565 (54%). Average amount of self-help aid, such as work study or loans (proportion receiving): $6,617 (47%). Average need-based loan (excluding PLUS or other private loans): $4,935. Among students who received need-based aid, the average percentage of need met: 93%. Among students who received aid based on merit, the average award (and the proportion receiving): $8,691 (31%). The average athletic scholarship (and the proportion receiving): $0 (0%). Average amount of debt of borrowers graduating in 2005: $21,846. Proportion who borrowed: 67%.

CAMPUS LIFE AND EXTRACURRICULAR ACTIVITIES

Campus housing available (% using): coed dorms (79%), sorority housing (11%), fraternity housing (10%). Students who live in college-owned, operated, or affiliated housing: 75%. **Student employment:** During the 2005-2006 academic year, 44% of undergraduates worked on campus. Average per-year earnings: $1,655. **Clubs and organizations:** Number of student organizations: 180. Activities include: choral groups, concert band, dance, drama/theater, jazz band, literary magazine, music ensembles, musical theater, opera, pep band, radio station, student government, student newspaper, student film society, symphony orchestra, television station, yearbook. Number of fraternities: 6; sororities: 5. Proportion of men in fraternities: 33%; of women in sororities: 25%. Average proportion of students who stay on campus on weekends: 85%. **Sports program (2005-2006):** Member of NCAA III. *Men's intercollegiate varsity sports:* baseball, basketball, cross-country, football, golf, soccer, swimming and diving, tennis, track and field (indoor), track and field (outdoor). *Women's intercollegiate varsity sports:* basketball, cross-country, golf, soccer, softball, swimming and diving, tennis, track and field (indoor), track and field (outdoor), volleyball.

SERVICES AND FACILITIES

Basic services: nonremedial tutoring, placement service, health service, health insurance. **Counseling services:** minority student, career, personal, academic, psychological, birth control, religious. **For learning-disabled students:** School does not offer a structured program with separate admission and additional fees. Services include: tape recorders, oral tests, extended time for tests, tutors, substitution of courses, other. **Library:** Number of titles: 321,241; number of current serial subscriptions: 9,812. **Information technology resources:** Students are not required to lease or own a computer. Number of campus computers available to all students: 430. School has a wireless network. Approximate number of users that can be accommodated: 250. Proportion of college-owned housing units wired for high-speed internet access: 100%. **Campus safety:** Security services offered: 24-hour foot and vehicle patrols, late-night transport/escort service, 24-hour emergency telephones, lighted pathways/sidewalks, controlled dormitory access (key, security card, etc).

TRANSFER AND INTERNATIONAL STUDENTS

Transfer students: May apply for admission for the following academic terms: Fall, Spring. Applicants do not need a minimum number of credits to apply. For fall 2005: Transfer applications received: 130. Transfer applicants offered admission: 48. Transfer applicants enrolled: 27. **International students:** Number of foreign undergraduates: 39 (2% of student body). Number of countries represented: 17. Minimum TOEFL score required: 550 (paper); 213 (computer). Average TOEFL score: 590 (paper).

Judson College

- **Address:** 1151 N. State Street, Elgin, IL 60123-1498
- **Website:** http://www.judsoncollege.edu
- **Private; Religious affiliation:** American Baptist
- **Enrollment:** 915 full-time; 278 part-time

KEY STATS

✔ **U.S News College Ranking:** 44, Comp. Coll.–Bachelor's (Midwest)
✔ **ACT Score (25th/75th percentile):** 20-25
✔ **Tuition:** 2006-2007: $19,450

Selectivity: Selective	**Room/board:** $6,900
Acceptance rate: 76%	**Average debt:** $19,216
Student/faculty ratio: 14/1	**Proportion who borrowed:** 92%

UNDERGRADUATE STUDENT BODY STATS

2005-2006 enrollment: 915 full-time; 278 part-time. Men: 42%; women: 58%. **Ethnic makeup:** African American: 4%; Asian American: 1%; Hispanic: 5%; White: 87%; International: 3%. **Religious preference:** Roman Catholic: 6%; Protestant: 58%; American Baptist: 4%; Other: 32%.

ADMISSIONS FACTS AND FIGURES

Phone: (800) 879-5376. **Email:** admissions@judsoncollege.edu. **Website:** http://www.judsoncollege.edu. **Application deadlines for fall 2007:** Regular decision: Rolling. Early decision: Not offered. Early action: Not offered. Admission can be deferred. **Application fee:** $35. Common application is accepted. **To apply online, go to:** http://application.judsoncollege.edu. **Admissions requirements/recommendations:** High school units required (recommended): English: (4); Mathematics: (3); Science: (2); Social studies: (2); Total units: (11). Tests: The college uses SAT or ACT scores in admissions decisions. Either SAT or ACT required. For admission to the fall 2007 entering class, the school will accept: ACT without writing. Campus visit: Recommended. Admissions interview: Neither required nor recommended. Off-campus interview: Not available. **Factors that count in admissions decisions:** *Academic:* Secondary school record: Very important. Class rank: Considered. Letters of recommendation: Considered. Standardized test scores: Very important. Essay: Considered. *Nonacademic:* Interview: Not considered. Extracurricular activities: Not considered. Talent/ability: Considered. Character/personal qualities: Not considered. Alumni/ae relationship: Not considered. Geographical residence: Not considered. State residency: Not considered. Religious affiliation/commitment: Not considered. Minority status: Not considered. Volunteer work: Not considered. Work experience: Not considered. **Admissions statistics for the fall 2005 entering class:** Total applicants: 457. Total accepted: 347. Freshmen enrolled: 135; 39% were from out of state. Overall acceptance rate: 76%. **Average high school grade point average:** 3.2. **First-year students who submitted SAT**

scores: 26%. Scores (25/75 percentile): Verbal: 470-610, Math: 450-600, Combined: 920-1210. **First-year students submitting ACT scores:** 83%. Scores (25/75 percentile): English: N/A, Math: N/A, Composite: 20-25.

ACADEMICS
Year founded: 1963. **Academic calendar:** Semester. **Degrees offered:** certificate, bachelor's, master's. **Most popular majors:** 45% business, management, marketing, and related support services, 19% security and protective services, 9% education, 6% architecture and related services, 5% philosophy and religious studies. **Major fields of study:** architecture and related services; biological and biomedical sciences; business, management, marketing, and related support services; communication, journalism, and related programs; education; English language and literature/letters; history; mathematics and statistics; multi/interdisciplinary studies; parks, recreation, leisure, and fitness studies; physical sciences; psychology; public administration and social service professions; security and protective services; social sciences; theology and religious vocations; visual and performing arts. **Areas of required coursework:** arts/fine arts, humanities, mathematics, English (including composition), sciences (biological or physical), history, social science, other. **Pre-professional programs:** pre-law, pre-dentistry, pre-medicine. **Special academic programs (% participation):** accelerated program (58%), distance learning, double major, honors program, independent study, internships, student-designed major, study abroad, teacher certificate program. **Teacher certification offered in:** early childhood, elementary, secondary. **Faculty and instruction (2005-2006):** Total instructional faculty: 55 full-time, 56 part-time (59% men; 41% women; 11% minorities). Full-time faculty with Ph.D. or other terminal degree: 76%. Student/faculty ratio: 14/1. Classes of fewer than 20 students: 82%; of 20 to 49 students: 18%; of 50 or more students: 0%. **Advanced Placement and International Baccalaureate credit:** AP tests may be used for: Credit and/or placement. Scores accepted: 3, 4, 5. International Baccalaureate exams may be used for: Credit only. **Freshmen returning for sophomore year:** 73%. **Graduation rates:** Four-year: 32%; five-year: 50%; six-year: 50%. **Graduate study:** 46% of students pursue further study immediately upon graduation. Fields in which graduates pursue further study: Master of Business Administration (MBA), 20%; law, 5%; theology (or the seminary), 10%; education, 15%; arts and sciences, 50%.

COSTS AND FINANCIAL AID
Financial aid office: (847) 628-2532. **Expenses (2006-2007):** Tuition and fees 2006-2007: $19,450; room/board: $6,900. Estimated books and supplies: $1,000; transportation: $500; personal expenses: $1,000. **Financial aid:** In 2005-2006, 91% of undergraduates applied for financial aid. Of those, 75% were determined to have financial need; 27% had their need fully met. Average financial aid package (proportion receiving): $8,846 (75%). Average amount of gift aid, such as scholarships or grants (proportion receiving): $6,691 (63%). Average amount of self-help aid, such as work study or loans (proportion receiving): $8,224 (57%). Among students who received need-based aid, the average percentage of need met: 33%. Among students who received aid based on merit, the average award (and the proportion receiving): $1,523 (9%). The average athletic scholarship (and the proportion receiving): $2,214 (1%). Average amount of debt of borrowers graduating in 2005: $19,216. Proportion who borrowed: 92%.

CAMPUS LIFE AND EXTRACURRICULAR ACTIVITIES
Campus housing available: coed dorms, women's dorms, men's dorms, apartments for married students, special housing for disabled students. Students who live in college-owned, operated, or affiliated housing: 65%. **Clubs and organizations:** Number of student organizations: 15. Activities include: choral groups, concert band, drama/theater, jazz band, music ensembles, student government, student newspaper, student film society, symphony orchestra. Number of fraternities: 0; sororities: 0. Average proportion of students who stay on campus on weekends: 40%. **Sports program (2005-2006):** Member of NAIA. *Men's intercollegiate varsity sports:* baseball, basketball, soccer. *Women's intercollegiate varsity sports:* basketball, soccer, softball, volleyball.

SERVICES AND FACILITIES
Basic services: nonremedial tutoring, placement service, health service. **Remedial assistance:** reading, math, writing, study skills. **Counseling services:** minority student, career, personal, academic, older student, psychological, religious. **For learning-disabled students:** School does not offer a structured program with separate admission and additional fees. Services include: remedial math, remedial English, remedial reading, tape recorders, videotaped classes, untimed tests, note-taking services, oral tests, learning center, readers, extended time for tests, tutors, early syllabus, priority seating, proofreading services, texts on tape, typist/scribe, exams on tape or

computer, other testing accomodations, other. **Library:** Number of titles: 103,433; number of current serial subscriptions: 461. **Information technology resources:** Students are not required to lease or own a computer. Number of campus computers available to all students: 220. School has a wireless network. Approximate number of users that can be accommodated: 600. Proportion of college-owned housing units wired for high-speed internet access: 100%. **Campus safety:** Security services offered: 24-hour foot and vehicle patrols, late-night transport/escort service, 24-hour emergency telephones, lighted pathways/sidewalks, student patrols, controlled dormitory access (key, security card, etc).

TRANSFER AND INTERNATIONAL STUDENTS
Transfer students: May apply for admission for the following academic terms: Fall, Spring. Applicants need a minimum number of credits to apply. For fall 2005: Transfer applications received: 334. Transfer applicants offered admission: 289. Transfer applicants enrolled: 242. **International students:** Number of foreign undergraduates: 30 (3% of student body). Number of countries represented: 15. Minimum TOEFL score required: 550 (paper); 213 (computer). Average TOEFL score: 533 (paper).

Kendall College

- **Address:** 900 N. North Branch Street, Chicago, IL 60622
- **Website:** http://www.kendall.edu
- **Private; Religious affiliation:** Methodist
- **Enrollment:** 497 full-time; 283 part-time

KEY STATS
✔ **U.S News College Ranking:** fourth tier, Comp. Coll.–Bachelor's (Midwest)
✔ **ACT Score (25th/75th percentile):** 19-24
✔ **Tuition:** 2006-2007: $20,700

Selectivity: Selective	**Room/board:** $7,650
Acceptance rate: 30%	**Average debt:** $20,271
Student/faculty ratio: 19/1	**Proportion who borrowed:** 78%

UNDERGRADUATE STUDENT BODY STATS
2005-2006 enrollment: 497 full-time; 283 part-time. Men: 41%; women: 59%. **Ethnic makeup:** African American: 2%; Asian American: 1%; Hispanic: 3%; White: 83%; International: 9%.

ADMISSIONS FACTS AND FIGURES
Phone: (877) 588-8860. **Email:** admissions@kendall.edu. **Website:** http://www.kendall.edu. **Application deadlines for fall 2007:** Regular decision: Rolling. Early decision: Send application by: N/A; Decision sent by: N/A. Early action: Not offered. Admission can be deferred. **Application fee:** $75. Common application is not accepted. **Admissions requirements/recommendations:** High school units required (recommended): English: 4 (4); Mathematics: 2 (2); Science: 2 (2); Foreign language: 2 (2); Social studies: 2 (2); History: 0 (0); Academic electives: 0 (0); Total units: 12 (12). Tests: The college uses SAT or ACT scores in admissions decisions. Either SAT or ACT required. For admission to the fall 2007 entering class, the school will accept: ACT with writing, ACT without writing. Campus visit: Recommended. Admissions interview: Recommended. Off-campus interview: Not available. **Factors that count in admissions decisions:** *Academic:* Secondary school record: Very important. Class rank: Very important. Letters of recommendation: Very important. Standardized test scores: Very important. Essay: Considered. *Nonacademic:* Interview: Considered. Extracurricular activities: Considered. Talent/ability: Considered. Character/personal qualities: Important. Alumni/ae relationship: Not considered. Geographical residence: Considered. State residency: Not considered. Religious affiliation/commitment: Not considered. Minority status: Not considered. Volunteer work: Not considered. Work experience: Considered. **Other schools with the greatest overlap in applicants:** Johnson and Wales University. **Admissions statistics for the fall 2005 entering class:** Total applicants: 605. Total accepted: 180. Overall acceptance rate: 30%. Non-early acceptance rate: 30%. **Average high school grade point average:** 3.0. **First-year students who submitted SAT scores:** 17%. Scores (25/75 percentile): Verbal: N/A, Math: N/A, Combined: N/A. **First-year students submitting ACT scores:** 100%. Scores (25/75 percentile): English: N/A, Math: N/A, Composite: N/A.

ACADEMICS

Year founded: 1934. **Academic calendar:** Quarter. **Degrees offered:** certificate, associate, transfer-associate, bachelor's. **Most popular majors:** Information not available. **Major fields of study:** business, management, marketing, and related support services; education; personal and culinary services. **Areas of required coursework:** humanities, mathematics, English (including composition), foreign languages, social science. **Special academic programs (% participation):** accelerated program, cooperative (work-study plan) program, double major, honors program, internships (63%), student-designed major (6%), study abroad (2%), teacher certificate program (2%). **Teacher certification offered in:** early childhood. **Faculty and instruction (2005-2006):** Total instructional faculty: 37 full-time, 43 part-time (54% men; 46% women; 23% minorities). Student/faculty ratio: 19/1. **Advanced Placement and International Baccalaureate credit:** International Baccalaureate exams may be used for: Credit and/or placement. **Graduation rates:** Six-year: 29%.

COSTS AND FINANCIAL AID

Financial aid office: (312) 752-2028. **Expenses (2006-2007):** Tuition and fees 2006-2007: $20,700; room/board: $7,650. Estimated books and supplies: $600; transportation: $400; personal expenses: $300. **Financial aid:** In 2005-2006, 97% of undergraduates applied for financial aid. Of those, 85% were determined to have financial need; 3% had their need fully met. Average financial aid package (proportion receiving): $7,572 (85%). Average amount of gift aid, such as scholarships or grants (proportion receiving): $6,088 (71%). Average amount of self-help aid, such as work study or loans (proportion receiving): $2,664 (79%). Average need-based loan (excluding PLUS or other private loans): $2,560. Among students who received need-based aid, the average percentage of need met: 31%. Among students who received aid based on merit, the average award (and the proportion receiving): $18,229 (15%). The average athletic scholarship (and the proportion receiving): $0 (0%). Average amount of debt of borrowers graduating in 2005: $20,271. Proportion who borrowed: 78%.

CAMPUS LIFE AND EXTRACURRICULAR ACTIVITIES

Campus housing available: women's dorms, men's dorms. Students who live in college-owned, operated, or affiliated housing: 18%. **Student employment:** During the 2005-2006 academic year, 15% of undergraduates worked on campus. Average per-year earnings: $4,500. **Clubs and organizations:** Number of student organizations: 8. Activities include: student government, student newspaper, yearbook. Number of fraternities: 0; sororities: 0. Average proportion of students who stay on campus on weekends: 18%. **Sports program (2005-2006):** Member of NAIA. *Men's intercollegiate varsity sports:* basketball, soccer, volleyball. *Women's intercollegiate varsity sports:* basketball, volleyball.

SERVICES AND FACILITIES

Basic services: nonremedial tutoring, health insurance. **Remedial assistance:** reading, math, writing, study skills. **Counseling services:** career, academic, psychological. **For learning-disabled students:** Services include: remedial math, remedial English, remedial reading, tutors. **Information technology resources:** Students are not required to lease or own a computer. Number of campus computers available to all students: 100. School has a wireless network. **Campus safety:** Security services offered: 24-hour emergency telephones, lighted pathways/sidewalks, student patrols, controlled dormitory access (key, security card, etc).

TRANSFER AND INTERNATIONAL STUDENTS

Transfer students: May apply for admission for the following academic terms: Fall, Winter, Spring, Summer. Applicants need a minimum number of credits to apply. **International students:** Number of foreign undergraduates: 38 (9% of student body). Minimum TOEFL score required: 500 (paper).

Knox College

- **Address:** 2 E. South Street, Galesburg, IL 61401
- **Website:** http://www.knox.edu
- **Private**
- **Enrollment:** 1,218 full-time; 27 part-time

KEY STATS

✔ **U.S News College Ranking:** 79, Liberal Arts Colleges
✔ **ACT Score (25th/75th percentile):** 25-30
✔ **Tuition:** 2006-2007: $27,900
  Selectivity: More selective **Room/board:** $5,925
  Acceptance rate: 76% **Average debt:** $19,642
  Student/faculty ratio: 12/1 **Proportion who borrowed:** 68%

UNDERGRADUATE STUDENT BODY STATS

2005-2006 enrollment: 1,218 full-time; 27 part-time. Men: 46%; women: 54%. **Ethnic makeup:** African American: 4%; Asian American: 5%; Hispanic: 4%; White: 80%; International: 7%.

ADMISSIONS FACTS AND FIGURES

Phone: (800) 678-5669. **Email:** admission@knox.edu. **Website:** http://www.knox.edu. **Application deadlines for fall 2007:** Regular decision: February 1; decision sent by March 31. Early decision: Not offered. Early action: Send application by: December 1; Decision sent by: December 31. Admission can be deferred. **Application fee:** $40. Common application is accepted. **To apply online, go to:** http://www.knox.edu/apply. **Admissions requirements/recommendations:** High school units required (recommended): English: (4); Mathematics: (4); Science: (3); Foreign language: (3); Social studies: (2); History: (2); Total units: 15 (18). Tests: The college uses SAT or ACT scores in admissions decisions. Neither SAT nor ACT required. For admission to the fall 2007 entering class, the school will accept: ACT with writing, ACT without writing. Campus visit: Recommended. Admissions interview: Recommended. Off-campus interview: May be arranged. **Factors that count in admissions decisions:** *Academic:* Secondary school record: Very important. Class rank: Important. Letters of recommendation: Important. Standardized test scores: Considered. Essay: Important. *Nonacademic:* Interview: Considered. Extracurricular activities: Considered. Talent/ability: Considered. Character/personal qualities: Considered. Alumni/ae relationship: Considered. Geographical residence: Not considered. State residency: Not considered. Religious affiliation/commitment: Not considered. Minority status: Considered. Volunteer work: Considered. Work experience: Not considered. **Other schools with the greatest overlap in applicants:** Beloit College; Grinnell College; Illinois Wesleyan University; Lawrence University; University of Illinois–Urbana-Champaign. **Admissions statistics for the fall 2005 entering class:** Total applicants: 1,771. Total accepted: 1,338. Freshmen enrolled: 325; 49% were from out of state. Accepted through early-decision or early-action plans: 54%. Overall acceptance rate: 76%. Non-early acceptance rate: 63%. **Size of waiting list:** 69 applicants; enrolled from waiting list: 11. **Credentials of fall 2005 freshmen:** 33% ranked in the top 10 percent of their high school class; 61% were in the top 25 percent, and 97% were in the top half. (Proportion submitting class standing: 69%.) First-year students who submitted SAT scores: 50%. Scores (25/75 percentile): Verbal: 580-700, Math: 540-660, Combined: 1120-1360. **First-year students submitting ACT scores:** 79%. Scores (25/75 percentile): English: 25-31, Math: 24-29, Composite: 25-30.

ACADEMICS

Year founded: 1837. **Academic calendar:** Trimester. **Degrees offered:** bachelor's. **Most popular majors:** 10% psychology, 7% economics, 7% political science and government, 7% social sciences, 6% education. **Major fields of study:** area, ethnic, cultural, and gender studies; biological and biomedical sciences; computer and information sciences and support services; education; English language and literature/letters; foreign languages, literatures, and linguistics; history; liberal arts and sciences studies, and humanities; mathematics and statistics; multi/interdisciplinary studies; natural resources and conservation; philosophy and religious studies; physical sciences; psychology; social sciences; visual and performing arts. **Areas of required coursework:** arts/fine arts, humanities, mathematics, foreign languages, sciences (biological or physical), social science. **Pre-professional programs:** pre-law, pre-medicine, pre-optometry. **Special academic programs (% participation):** double major (28%), dual enrollment (0%), honors program

(11%), independent study (75%), internships (70%), liberal arts/career combination (2%), student-designed major (4%), study abroad (26%), teacher certificate program (8%). **Teacher certification offered in:** elementary, middle/junior high, secondary. **Faculty and instruction (2005-2006):** Total instructional faculty: 95 full-time, 22 part-time (56% men; 44% women; 11% minorities). Full-time faculty with Ph.D. or other terminal degree: 94%. Student/faculty ratio: 12/1. Classes of fewer than 20 students: 66%; of 20 to 49 students: 34%; of 50 or more students: 1%. **Advanced Placement and International Baccalaureate credit:** AP tests may be used for: Credit and/or placement. Scores accepted: 4, 5. International Baccalaureate exams may be used for: Credit only. **Freshmen returning for sophomore year:** 87%. **Graduation rates:** Four-year: 67%; five-year: 74%; six-year: 75%. **Graduate study:** 29% of students pursue further study immediately upon graduation. Fields in which graduates pursue further study: law, 8%; medicine, 14%; engineering, 2%; theology (or the seminary), 1%; arts and sciences, 75%.

COSTS AND FINANCIAL AID
Financial aid office: (309) 341-7130. **Expenses (2006-2007):** Tuition and fees 2006-2007: $27,900; room/board: $5,925. Estimated books and supplies: $900; transportation: $450; personal expenses: $600. **Financial aid:** Priority filing date for institution's financial aid form: February 15. In 2005-2006, 79% of undergraduates applied for financial aid. Of those, 67% were determined to have financial need; 47% had their need fully met. Average financial aid package (proportion receiving): $21,317 (67%). Average amount of gift aid, such as scholarships or grants (proportion receiving): $16,117 (67%). Average amount of self-help aid, such as work study or loans (proportion receiving): $5,997 (58%). Average need-based loan (excluding PLUS or other private loans): $5,138. Among students who received need-based aid, the average percentage of need met: 95%. Among students who received aid based on merit, the average award (and the proportion receiving): $10,011 (29%). Average amount of debt of borrowers graduating in 2005: $19,642. Proportion who borrowed: 68%.

CAMPUS LIFE AND EXTRACURRICULAR ACTIVITIES
Campus housing available (% using): coed dorms (54%), women's dorms (9%), men's dorms (7%), fraternity housing (10%), apartment for single students (14%). Students who live in college-owned, operated, or affiliated housing: 95%. **Student employment:** During the 2005-2006 academic year, 37% of undergraduates worked on campus. Average per-year earnings: $890. **Clubs and organizations:** Number of student organizations: 99. Activities include: choral groups, concert band, dance, drama/theater, jazz band, literary magazine, music ensembles, radio station, student government, student newspaper, symphony orchestra, yearbook. Number of fraternities: 4; sororities: 2. Proportion of men in fraternities: 24%; of women in sororities: 11%. Average proportion of students who stay on campus on weekends: 75%. **Sports program (2005-2006):** Member of NCAA III. *Men's intercollegiate varsity sports:* baseball, basketball, cross-country, football, golf, soccer, swimming and diving, tennis, track and field (indoor), track and field (outdoor), wrestling. *Women's intercollegiate varsity sports:* basketball, cross-country, golf, soccer, softball, swimming and diving, tennis, track and field (indoor), track and field (outdoor), volleyball.

SERVICES AND FACILITIES
Basic services: nonremedial tutoring. **Remedial assistance:** reading, math, writing, study skills. **Counseling services:** minority student, career, personal, academic, psychological. **For learning-disabled students:** School does not offer a structured program with separate admission and additional fees. Total undergraduates in learning-disabled program or receiving services: 47. Services include: remedial math, remedial English, remedial reading, tape recorders, untimed tests, note-taking services, oral tests, learning center, readers, extended time for tests, tutors. **Library:** Number of titles: 311,715; number of current serial subscriptions: 12,782. **Information technology resources:** Students are not required to lease or own a computer. Number of campus computers available to all students: 300. School has a wireless network. Approximate number of users that can be accommodated: 2,900. Proportion of college-owned housing units wired for high-speed internet access: 100%. **Campus safety:** Security services offered: 24-hour foot and vehicle patrols, late-night transport/escort service, 24-hour emergency telephones, lighted pathways/sidewalks, controlled dormitory access (key, security card, etc.).

TRANSFER AND INTERNATIONAL STUDENTS
Transfer students: May apply for admission for the following academic terms: Fall, Winter, Spring. Applicants need a minimum number of credits to apply. For fall 2005: Transfer applications received: 99. Transfer applicants offered admission: 61. Transfer applicants enrolled: 38. **International**

students: Number of foreign undergraduates: 88 (7% of student body). Number of countries represented: 46. Minimum TOEFL score required: 550 (paper); 213 (computer).

Lake Forest College

- **Address:** 555 N. Sheridan Road, Lake Forest, IL 60045
- **Website:** http://www.lakeforest.edu
- **Private; Religious affiliation:** Presbyterian
- **Enrollment:** 1,398 full-time; 20 part-time

KEY STATS
✔ **U.S News College Ranking:** 95, Liberal Arts Colleges
✔ **ACT Score (25th/75th percentile):** 23-28
✔ **Tuition:** 2006-2007: $29,034
  Selectivity: More selective   **Room/board:** $6,960
  Acceptance rate: 63%   **Average debt:** $18,306
  Student/faculty ratio: 12/1   **Proportion who borrowed:** 53%

UNDERGRADUATE STUDENT BODY STATS
2005-2006 enrollment: 1,398 full-time; 20 part-time. Men: 42%; women: 58%. **Ethnic makeup:** African American: 5%; Asian American: 3%; Hispanic: 6%; White: 77%; International: 8%.

ADMISSIONS FACTS AND FIGURES
Phone: (847) 735-5000. **Email:** admissions@lakeforest.edu. **Website:** http://www.lakeforest.edu. **Application deadlines for fall 2007:** Regular decision: May 1; decision sent by April 1. Early decision: Send application by: December 1; Decision sent by: December 20. Early action: Send application by: December 1; Decision sent by: January 15. Admission can be deferred. **Application fee:** $40. Common application is accepted. **To apply online, go to:** http://www.lakeforest.edu/admissions/application/default.asp. **Admissions requirements/recommendations:** High school units required (recommended): English: 4 (4); Mathematics: 3 (4); Science: 2 (4); Foreign language: 2 (4); Social studies: 1 (2); History: 1 (2); Academic electives: 3; Total units: 16 (20). Tests: The college uses SAT or ACT scores in admissions decisions. Either SAT or ACT required. For admission to the fall 2007 entering class, the school will accept: ACT with writing, ACT without writing. Campus visit: Recommended. Admissions interview: Recommended. Off-campus interview: May be arranged. **Factors that count in admissions decisions:** *Academic:* Secondary school record: Very important. Class rank: Considered. Letters of recommendation: Very important. Standardized test scores: Important. Essay: Important. *Nonacademic:* Interview: Very important. Extracurricular activities: Important. Talent/ability: Important. Character/personal qualities: Important. Alumni/ae relationship: Considered. Geographical residence: Considered. State residency: Not considered. Religious affiliation/commitment: Not considered. Minority status: Not considered. Volunteer work: Considered. Work experience: Considered. **Other schools with the greatest overlap in applicants:** American University; Boston University; Northwestern University; Skidmore College; University of Denver. **Admissions statistics for the fall 2005 entering class:** Total applicants: 2,195. Total accepted: 1,377. Freshmen enrolled: 358; 60% were from out of state. Accepted through early-decision or early-action plans: 50%. Overall acceptance rate: 63%. Early-decision acceptance rate: 60%. Non-early acceptance rate: 53%. **Size of waiting list:** 46 applicants; enrolled from waiting list: 22. **Credentials of fall 2005 freshmen:** 32% ranked in the top 10 percent of their high school class; 54% were in the top 25 percent, and 90% were in the top half. (Proportion submitting class standing: 64%.) **Average high school grade point average:** 3.4. **First-year students who submitted SAT scores:** 48%. Scores (25/75 percentile): Verbal: 540-640, Math: 530-650, Combined: 1070-1290. **First-year students submitting ACT scores:** 64%. Scores (25/75 percentile): English: 22-29, Math: 21-27, Composite: 23-28.

ACADEMICS
Year founded: 1857. **Academic calendar:** Semester. **Degrees offered:** bachelor's, master's. **Most popular majors:** 16% communication studies/speech communication and rhetoric, 11% business/commerce, 8% economics, 7% English language and literature, 7% psychology. **Major fields of study:** area, ethnic, cultural, and gender studies; biological and biomedical sciences; business, management, marketing, and related support services; communication, journalism, and related programs; computer and information sciences and support services; education; English language and

literature/letters; foreign languages, literatures, and linguistics; history; liberal arts and sciences studies, and humanities; mathematics and statistics; natural resources and conservation; philosophy and religious studies; physical sciences; psychology; social sciences; visual and performing arts. **Areas of required coursework:** humanities, mathematics, English (including composition), sciences (biological or physical), social science. **Special academic programs (% participation):** accelerated program (2%), double major (37%), honors program (9%), independent study (44%), internships (35%), student-designed major (1%), study abroad (22%), teacher certificate program (4%). **Teacher certification offered in:** elementary, middle/junior high, secondary, bilingual/bicultural. **Cooperative education programs:** engineering. **Faculty and instruction (2005-2006):** Total instructional faculty: 88 full-time, 60 part-time (59% men; 41% women; 9% minorities). Full-time faculty with Ph.D. or other terminal degree: 95%. Student/faculty ratio: 12/1. Classes of fewer than 20 students: 59%; of 20 to 49 students: 41%; of 50 or more students: 0%. **Advanced Placement and International Baccalaureate credit:** AP tests may be used for: Credit and/or placement. Scores accepted: 3, 4, 5. International Baccalaureate exams may be used for: Credit and/or placement. **Freshmen returning for sophomore year:** 80%. **Graduation rates:** Four-year: 63%; five-year: 69%; six-year: 70%. **Graduate study:** 35% of students pursue further study immediately upon graduation; 40% within one year; 50% within five years. Fields in which graduates pursue further study: Master of Business Administration (MBA), 2%; law, 17%; medicine, 27%; dentistry, 1%; education, 13%; arts and sciences, 42%; veterinary medicine, 1%.

COSTS AND FINANCIAL AID

Financial aid office: (847) 735-5104. **Expenses (2006-2007):** Tuition and fees 2006-2007: $29,034; room/board: $6,960. Estimated books and supplies: $700; transportation: $0; personal expenses: $806. **Financial aid:** Priority filing date for institution's financial aid form: February 15; deadline: May 1. In 2005-2006, 93% of undergraduates applied for financial aid. Of those, 78% were determined to have financial need; 100% had their need fully met. Average financial aid package (proportion receiving): $21,562 (78%). Average amount of gift aid, such as scholarships or grants (proportion receiving): $17,771 (78%). Average amount of self-help aid, such as work study or loans (proportion receiving): $5,896 (49%). Average need-based loan (excluding PLUS or other private loans): $4,821. Among students who received need-based aid, the average percentage of need met: 100%. Among students who received aid based on merit, the average award (and the proportion receiving): $10,967 (15%). The average athletic scholarship (and the proportion receiving): $0 (0%). Average amount of debt of borrowers graduating in 2005: $18,306. Proportion who borrowed: 53%.

CAMPUS LIFE AND EXTRACURRICULAR ACTIVITIES

Campus housing available (% using): coed dorms (90%), women's dorms (8%), apartment for single students (2%). Students who live in college-owned, operated, or affiliated housing: 78%. **Student employment:** During the 2005-2006 academic year, 55% of undergraduates worked on campus. Average per-year earnings: $2,000. **Clubs and organizations:** Number of student organizations: 82. Activities include: choral groups, concert band, dance, drama/theater, jazz band, literary magazine, music ensembles, musical theater, radio station, student government, student newspaper, student film society. Number of fraternities: 3; sororities: 5. Proportion of men in fraternities: 9%; of women in sororities: 19%. Average proportion of students who stay on campus on weekends: 80%. **Sports program (2005-2006):** Member of NCAA III. *Men's intercollegiate varsity sports:* basketball, cross-country, football, handball, ice hockey, soccer, swimming and diving, tennis. *Women's intercollegiate varsity sports:* basketball, cross-country, handball, ice hockey, soccer, softball, swimming and diving, tennis, volleyball.

SERVICES AND FACILITIES

Basic services: nonremedial tutoring, placement service, health service, health insurance, other. **Counseling services:** minority student, career, personal, veteran student, academic, older student, psychological, birth control, religious. **For learning-disabled students:** School does not offer a structured program with separate admission and additional fees. Services include: reading machines, tape recorders, untimed tests, note-taking services, oral tests, learning center, readers, extended time for tests, tutors, texts on tape, typist/scribe, take home exams. **Library:** Number of titles: 277,438; number of current serial subscriptions: 1,769. **Information technology resources:** Students are not required to lease or own a computer. Number of campus computers available to all students: 175. School has a wireless network. Approximate number of users that can be accommodated: 1,500. Proportion of college-owned housing units wired for high-speed internet access: 100%. **Campus safety:** Security services offered: 24-hour foot and vehicle patrols,

late-night transport/escort service, 24-hour emergency telephones, lighted pathways/sidewalks, student patrols, controlled dormitory access (key, security card, etc).

TRANSFER AND INTERNATIONAL STUDENTS

Transfer students: May apply for admission for the following academic terms: Fall, Spring. Applicants do not need a minimum number of credits to apply. For fall 2005: Transfer applications received: 266. Transfer applicants offered admission: 110. Transfer applicants enrolled: 61. **International students:** Number of foreign undergraduates: 117 (8% of student body). Number of countries represented: 31. Minimum TOEFL score required: 550 (paper); 220 (computer). Average TOEFL score: 625 (paper).

Lewis University

- **Address:** 1 University Parkway, Romeoville, IL 60446-2200
- **Website:** http://www.lewisu.edu
- **Private; Religious affiliation:** Roman Catholic
- **Enrollment:** 2,662 full-time; 931 part-time

KEY STATS

✔ **U.S News College Ranking:** 47, Universities–Master's (Midwest)
✔ **ACT Score (25th/75th percentile):** 19-25
✔ **Tuition:** 2006-2007: $19,200

Selectivity: Selective	**Room/board:** $7,600
Acceptance rate: 69%	**Average debt:** $14,328
Student/faculty ratio: 14/1	**Proportion who borrowed:** 71%

UNDERGRADUATE STUDENT BODY STATS

2005-2006 enrollment: 2,662 full-time; 931 part-time. Men: 39%; women: 61%. **Ethnic makeup:** African American: 12%; Asian American: 4%; Hispanic: 9%; White: 72%; International: 3%. **Religious preference:** Unknown: 9%; Roman Catholic: 61%; Other: 30%.

ADMISSIONS FACTS AND FIGURES

Phone: (800) 897-9000. **Email:** admissions@lewisu.edu. **Website:** http://www.lewisu.edu. **Application deadlines for fall 2007:** Regular decision: Rolling. Early decision: Not offered. Early action: Not offered. Admission can be deferred. **Application fee:** $40. Common application is accepted. **Admissions requirements/recommendations:** High school units required (recommended): English: 3 (4); Mathematics: 2 (3); Science: 2 (2); Foreign language: 0 (2); Social studies: 2 (2); History: 1 (1); Academic electives: 8 (4); Total units: 18 (18). Tests: The college uses SAT or ACT scores in admissions decisions. Either SAT or ACT required. For admission to the fall 2007 entering class, the school will accept: ACT with writing, ACT without writing. Campus visit: Recommended. Admissions interview: Recommended. Off-campus interview: Not available. **Factors that count in admissions decisions:** *Academic:* Secondary school record: Very important. Class rank: Considered. Letters of recommendation: Considered. Standardized test scores: Important. Essay: Considered. *Nonacademic:* Interview: Considered. Extracurricular activities: Considered. Talent/ability: Considered. Character/personal qualities: Considered. Alumni/ae relationship: Considered. Geographical residence: Not considered. State residency: Not considered. Religious affiliation/commitment: Not considered. Minority status: Not considered. Volunteer work: Considered. Work experience: Considered. **Other schools with the greatest overlap in applicants:** Benedictine University; DePaul University; North Central College; Northern Illinois University; St. Xavier University. **Admissions statistics for the fall 2005 entering class:** Total applicants: 2,014. Total accepted: 1,398. Freshmen enrolled: 561; 7% were from out of state. Overall acceptance rate: 69%. **Credentials of fall 2005 freshmen:** 15% ranked in the top 10 percent of their high school class; 40% were in the top 25 percent, and 74% were in the top half. (Proportion submitting class standing: 90%.) **Average high school grade point average:** 3.2. **First-year students who submitted SAT scores:** 4%. Scores (25/75 percentile): Verbal: 500-570, Math: 510-570, Combined: 1010-1140. **First-year students submitting ACT scores:** 96%. Scores (25/75 percentile): English: 19-25, Math: 19-25, Composite: 19-25.

ACADEMICS

Year founded: 1932. **Academic calendar:** Semester. **Degrees offered:** certificate, associate, bachelor's, master's, post-master's certificate, doctorate. **Most popular majors:** 24% business/commerce, 16% nursing/registered nurse training (R.N., A.S.N., B.S.N., M.S.N.), 12% criminal justice/safety studies, 8% aviation/airway management and operations, 6% education. **Major fields of study:** agriculture, agriculture operations, and related sciences; area, ethnic, cultural, and gender studies; biological and biomedical sciences; business, management, marketing, and related support services; communication, journalism, and related programs; communications technologies/technicians and support services; computer and information sciences and support services; education; English language and literature/letters; health professions and related clinical sciences; liberal arts and sciences studies, and humanities; mathematics and statistics; natural resources and conservation; parks, recreation, leisure, and fitness studies; philosophy and religious studies; physical sciences; psychology; public administration and social service professions; security and protective services; social sciences; transportation and materials moving; visual and performing arts. **Areas of required coursework:** arts/fine arts, humanities, computer literacy, mathematics, English (including composition), philosophy, sciences (biological or physical), history, social science. **Pre-professional programs:** pre-law, pre-dentistry, pre-medicine, pre-veterinary science, pre-optometry, pre-pharmacy, other. **Special academic programs (% participation):** accelerated program (17%), distance learning, double major (14%), dual enrollment, English as a Second Language (ESL) (1%), honors program (5%), independent study (9%), internships (20%), liberal arts/career combination (75%), student-designed major, study abroad (5%), teacher certificate program (10%). **Teacher certification offered in:** special education, elementary, middle/junior high, secondary. **Reserve Officers Training Corps (ROTC):** Army ROTC: Offered at cooperating institution (Wheaton College); Air Force ROTC: Offered at cooperating institution (Illinois Institute of Technology). **Faculty and instruction (2005-2006):** Total instructional faculty: 164 full-time, 340 part-time (47% men; 53% women; 10% minorities). Full-time faculty with Ph.D. or other terminal degree: 62%. Student/faculty ratio: 14/1. Classes of fewer than 20 students: 66%; of 20 to 49 students: 33%; of 50 or more students: 1%. **Advanced Placement and International Baccalaureate credit:** AP tests may be used for: Credit and/or placement. Scores accepted: 3, 4, 5. International Baccalaureate exams may be used for: Credit and/or placement. **Freshmen returning for sophomore year:** 77%. **Graduation rates:** Four-year: 26%; five-year: 46%; six-year: 53%.

COSTS AND FINANCIAL AID
Financial aid office: (815) 836-5263. **Expenses (2006-2007):** Tuition and fees 2006-2007: $19,200; room/board: $7,600. Estimated books and supplies: $500; transportation: $570; personal expenses: $1,320. **Financial aid:** Priority filing date for institution's financial aid form: May 1; deadline: May 1. In 2005-2006, 80% of undergraduates applied for financial aid. Of those, 79% were determined to have financial need; 38% had their need fully met. Average financial aid package (proportion receiving): $12,416 (79%). Average amount of gift aid, such as scholarships or grants (proportion receiving): $5,862 (46%). Average amount of self-help aid, such as work study or loans (proportion receiving): $4,736 (62%). Average need-based loan (excluding PLUS or other private loans): $4,495. Among students who received need-based aid, the average percentage of need met: 76%. Among students who received aid based on merit, the average award (and the proportion receiving): $5,388 (13%). The average athletic scholarship (and the proportion receiving): $6,902 (8%). Average amount of debt of borrowers graduating in 2005: $14,328. Proportion who borrowed: 71%.

CAMPUS LIFE AND EXTRACURRICULAR ACTIVITIES
Campus housing available (% using): coed dorms (100%). Students who live in college-owned, operated, or affiliated housing: 38%. **Student employment:** During the 2005-2006 academic year, 25% of undergraduates worked on campus. Average per-year earnings: $3,000. **Clubs and organizations:** Number of student organizations: 42. Activities include: choral groups, concert band, dance, drama/theater, jazz band, literary magazine, music ensembles, musical theater, pep band, radio station, student government, student newspaper, symphony orchestra, television station, yearbook. Number of fraternities: 7; sororities: 5. Proportion of men in fraternities: 4%; of women in sororities: 7%. Average proportion of students who stay on campus on weekends: 60%. **Sports program (2005-2006):** Member of NCAA II. **Men's intercollegiate varsity sports:** baseball, basketball, cross-country, golf, soccer, swimming and diving, tennis, track and field (indoor), track and field (outdoor), volleyball. **Women's intercollegiate varsity sports:** basketball, cross-country, golf, soccer, softball, swimming and diving, tennis, track and field (indoor), track and field (outdoor), volleyball.

SERVICES AND FACILITIES
Basic services: nonremedial tutoring, health service, health insurance. **Remedial assistance:** reading, math, writing, study skills. **Counseling serv-**

ices: minority student, career, military, personal, academic, older student, psychological, religious. **For learning-disabled students:** School does not offer a structured program with separate admission and additional fees. Total undergraduates in learning-disabled program or receiving services: 55. Services include: diagnostic testing service, untimed tests, note-taking services, oral tests, learning center, readers, extended time for tests, tutors, priority registration, priority seating, other testing accomodations. **Library:** Number of titles: 152,214; number of current serial subscriptions: 1,238. **Information technology resources:** Students are not required to lease or own a computer. Number of campus computers available to all students: 270. School has a wireless network. Approximate number of users that can be accommodated: 6,500. Proportion of college-owned housing units wired for high-speed internet access: 100%. **Campus safety:** Security services offered: 24-hour foot and vehicle patrols, late-night transport/escort service, 24-hour emergency telephones, lighted pathways/sidewalks, student patrols, controlled dormitory access (key, security card, etc).

TRANSFER AND INTERNATIONAL STUDENTS
Transfer students: May apply for admission for the following academic terms: Fall, Spring, Summer. Applicants need a minimum number of credits to apply. For fall 2005: Transfer applications received: 1,105. Transfer applicants offered admission: 619. Transfer applicants enrolled: 409. **International students:** Number of foreign undergraduates: 123 (3% of student body). Number of countries represented: 31. Minimum TOEFL score required: 500 (paper); 173 (computer). Average TOEFL score: 515 (paper).

Loyola University Chicago

- **Address:** 820 N. Michigan Avenue, Chicago, IL 60611-9810
- **Website:** http://www.luc.edu
- **Private; Religious affiliation:** Roman Catholic
- **Enrollment:** 8,318 full-time; 922 part-time

KEY STATS
✔ **U.S News College Ranking:** 112, National Universities
✔ **ACT Score (25th/75th percentile):** 22-27
✔ **Tuition:** 2006-2007: $26,122

Selectivity: More selective	**Room/board:** $9,614
Acceptance rate: 81%	**Average debt:** $24,299
Student/faculty ratio: 14/1	**Proportion who borrowed:** 68%

UNDERGRADUATE STUDENT BODY STATS
2005-2006 enrollment: 8,318 full-time; 922 part-time. Men: 35%; women: 65%. **Ethnic makeup:** African American: 6%; Asian American: 11%; Hispanic: 10%; White: 71%; International: 2%. **Religious preference:** Roman Catholic: 65%; Protestant: 6%; Jewish: 2%; Muslim: 4%; Hindu: 2%; No preference: 7%; Orthodox: 3%; Other: 11%.

ADMISSIONS FACTS AND FIGURES
Phone: (312) 915-6500. **Email:** admission@luc.edu. **Website:** http://www.luc.edu. **Application deadlines for fall 2007:** Regular decision: Rolling. Early decision: Not offered. Early action: Not offered. Admission cannot be deferred. **Application fee:** $25. Common application is not accepted. **Admissions requirements/recommendations:** High school units required (recommended): English: 4 (4); Mathematics: 2 (4); Science: 2 (3); Foreign language: 0 (2); Social studies: 2 (3); History: 1 (2); Academic electives: 3 (1); Total units: 15 (20). Tests: The college uses SAT or ACT scores in admissions decisions. Either SAT or ACT required. For admission to the fall 2007 entering class, the school will accept: ACT with writing, ACT without writing. Campus visit: Recommended. Admissions interview: Recommended. Off-campus interview: May be arranged. **Factors that count in admissions decisions:** *Academic:* Secondary school record: Very important. Class rank: Important. Letters of recommendation: Important. Standardized test scores: Very important. Essay: Important. *Nonacademic:* Interview: Considered. Extracurricular activities: Important. Talent/ability: Considered. Character/personal qualities: Important. Alumni/ae relationship: Considered. Geographical residence: Considered. State residency: Considered. Religious affiliation/commitment: Not considered. Minority status: Not considered. Volunteer work: Important. Work experience: Considered. **Other schools with the greatest overlap in applicants:** DePaul University; Marquette University; Northwestern University; University of Illinois–Chicago; University of Illinois–Urbana-Champaign. **Admissions**

statistics for the fall 2005 entering class: Total applicants: 13,163. Total accepted: 10,722. Freshmen enrolled: 2,080; 39% were from out of state. Overall acceptance rate: 81%. **Size of waiting list:** 88 applicants; enrolled from waiting list: N/A. **Credentials of fall 2005 freshmen:** 30% ranked in the top 10 percent of their high school class; 63% were in the top 25 percent, and 94% were in the top half. (Proportion submitting class standing: 72%.) **Average high school grade point average:** 3.5. **First-year students who submitted SAT scores:** 37%. Scores (25/75 percentile): Verbal: 540-640, Math: 530-640, Combined: 1070-1280. **First-year students submitting ACT scores:** 89%. Scores (25/75 percentile): English: 22-29, Math: 21-27, Composite: 22-27.

ACADEMICS

Year founded: 1870. **Academic calendar:** Semester. **Degrees offered:** certificate, bachelor's, post-bachelor's certificate, master's, post-master's certificate, first professional, doctorate. **Most popular majors:** 23% business, management, marketing, and related support services, 12% psychology, 11% biological and biomedical sciences, 10% social sciences, 7% health professions and related clinical sciences. **Major fields of study:** biological and biomedical sciences; business, management, marketing, and related support services; communication, journalism, and related programs; computer and information sciences and support services; education; English language and literature/letters; foreign languages, literatures, and linguistics; health professions and related clinical sciences; history; liberal arts and sciences studies, and humanities; mathematics and statistics; multi/interdisciplinary studies; natural resources and conservation; philosophy and religious studies; physical sciences; psychology; public administration and social service professions; security and protective services; social sciences; theology and religious vocations; visual and performing arts. **Areas of required coursework:** arts/fine arts, humanities, mathematics, English (including composition), philosophy, foreign languages, sciences (biological or physical), history, social science. **Pre-professional programs:** pre-law, pre-dentistry, pre-medicine, pre-theology, pre-veterinary science, pre-optometry, pre-pharmacy. **Special academic programs:** accelerated program, double major, dual enrollment, exchange student program (domestic), honors program, independent study, internships, study abroad, teacher certificate program. **Teacher certification offered in:** special education, elementary, middle/junior high, secondary, bilingual/bicultural. **Reserve Officers Training Corps (ROTC):** Army ROTC: Offered at cooperating institution (University of Illinois-Chicago); Navy ROTC: Offered at cooperating institution (Northwestern University); Air Force ROTC: Offered at cooperating institution (Illinois Institute of Technology). **Faculty and instruction (2005-2006):** Total instructional faculty: 523 full-time, 583 part-time (51% men; 49% women; 11% minorities). Full-time faculty with Ph.D. or other terminal degree: 98%. Student/faculty ratio: 14/1. Classes of fewer than 20 students: 37%; of 20 to 49 students: 56%; of 50 or more students: 7%. **Advanced Placement and International Baccalaureate credit:** AP tests may be used for: Credit only. Scores accepted: 3, 4, 5. International Baccalaureate exams may be used for: Credit and/or placement. **Freshmen returning for sophomore year:** 84%. **Graduation rates:** Four-year: 51%; five-year: 65%; six-year: 67%.

COSTS AND FINANCIAL AID

Financial aid office: (773) 508-3155. **Expenses (2006-2007):** Tuition and fees 2006-2007: $26,122; room/board: $9,614. Estimated books and supplies: $1,200; transportation: $450; personal expenses: $1,600. **Financial aid:** Priority filing date for institution's financial aid form: March 1. In 2005-2006, 81% of undergraduates applied for financial aid. Of those, 71% were determined to have financial need; 12% had their need fully met. Average financial aid package (proportion receiving): $20,367 (70%). Average amount of gift aid, such as scholarships or grants (proportion receiving): $11,760 (67%). Average amount of self-help aid, such as work study or loans (proportion receiving): $5,147 (61%). Average need-based loan (excluding PLUS or other private loans): $3,971. Among students who received need-based aid, the average percentage of need met: 79%. Among students who received aid based on merit, the average award (and the proportion receiving): $7,205 (7%). The average athletic scholarship (and the proportion receiving): $20,468 (1%). Average amount of debt of borrowers graduating in 2005: $24,299. Proportion who borrowed: 68%.

CAMPUS LIFE AND EXTRACURRICULAR ACTIVITIES

Campus housing available (% using): coed dorms (57%), women's dorms (6%), sorority housing, fraternity housing, apartment for single students (35%), special housing for disabled students (1%), special housing for international students (1%). Students who live in college-owned, operated, or affiliated housing: 38%. **Student employment:** During the 2005-2006 academic year, 5% of undergraduates worked on campus. **Clubs and organiza-**

tions: Number of student organizations: 136. Activities include: choral groups, concert band, drama/theater, jazz band, literary magazine, music ensembles, pep band, radio station, student government, student newspaper, student film society, symphony orchestra, yearbook. Number of fraternities: 6; sororities: 6. Proportion of men in fraternities: 5%; of women in sororities: 5%. Average proportion of students who stay on campus on weekends: 65%. **Sports program (2005-2006):** Member of NCAA I. *Men's intercollegiate varsity sports:* basketball, cheerleading, cross-country, golf, soccer, track and field (indoor), track and field (outdoor), volleyball. *Women's intercollegiate varsity sports:* basketball, cheerleading, cross-country, golf, soccer, softball, track and field (indoor), track and field (outdoor), volleyball.

SERVICES AND FACILITIES

Basic services: nonremedial tutoring, women's center, placement service, day care, health service, health insurance. **Remedial assistance:** reading, math, writing, study skills. **Counseling services:** minority student, career, personal, academic, older student, psychological, religious. **For learning-disabled students:** School does not offer a structured program with separate admission and additional fees. Total undergraduates in learning-disabled program or receiving services: 76. Services include: reading machines, tape recorders, note-taking services, oral tests, learning center, readers, extended time for tests, tutors, priority registration, priority seating, texts on tape, other. **Library:** Number of titles: 1,787,209; number of current serial subscriptions: 8,462. **Information technology resources:** Students are not required to lease or own a computer. Number of campus computers available to all students: 503. School has a wireless network. Approximate number of users that can be accommodated: 300. Proportion of college-owned housing units wired for high-speed internet access: 100%. **Campus safety:** Security services offered: 24-hour foot and vehicle patrols, late-night transport/escort service, 24-hour emergency telephones, lighted pathways/sidewalks, controlled dormitory access (key, security card, etc).

TRANSFER AND INTERNATIONAL STUDENTS

Transfer students: May apply for admission for the following academic terms: Fall, Spring, Summer. Applicants need a minimum number of credits to apply. For fall 2005: Transfer applications received: 1,974. Transfer applicants offered admission: 1,578. Transfer applicants enrolled: 683. **International students:** Number of foreign undergraduates: 143 (2% of student body). Number of countries represented: 50. Minimum TOEFL score required: 550 (paper); 79 (computer). Average TOEFL score: 606 (paper).

MacMurray College

- **Address:** 447 E. College, Jacksonville, IL 62650
- **Website:** http://www.mac.edu
- **Private; Religious affiliation:** Methodist
- **Enrollment:** 642 full-time; 57 part-time

KEY STATS

✔ **U.S News College Ranking:** third tier, Comp. Coll.–Bachelor's (Midwest)
✔ **ACT Score (25th/75th percentile):** 20-24
✔ **Tuition:** 2006-2007: $15,825

Selectivity: Selective	**Room/board:** $5,998
Acceptance rate: 57%	**Average debt:** $12,440
Student/faculty ratio: 13/1	**Proportion who borrowed:** 91%

UNDERGRADUATE STUDENT BODY STATS

2005-2006 enrollment: 642 full-time; 57 part-time. Men: 40%; women: 60%. **Ethnic makeup:** African American: 11%; American-Indian: 1%; Hispanic: 3%; White: 84%; International: 1%. **Religious preference:** Roman Catholic: 18%; Protestant: 78%; Jewish: 1%; Unknown: 3%.

ADMISSIONS FACTS AND FIGURES

Phone: (217) 479-7056. **Email:** admissions@mac.edu. **Website:** http://www.mac.edu. **Application deadlines for fall 2007:** Regular decision: Rolling. Early decision: Not offered. Early action: Not offered. Admission can be deferred. Common application is accepted. **To apply online, go to:** http://www.mac.edu/admissions/app.html. **Admissions requirements/recommendations:** High school units required (recommended): English: (4); Mathematics: (3); Science: (2); Foreign language: (2); Social studies: (2); Total units: (13). Tests: The college uses SAT or ACT scores in admissions decisions. Either SAT or ACT required. For admission to the fall 2007 entering class, the school will accept: ACT with writing, ACT without writing. Campus visit: Recommended. Admissions interview: Neither required nor recommended. Off-campus interview: Not available. **Factors that count in admissions decisions: Academic:** Secondary school record: Very important. Class rank: Important. Letters of recommendation: Considered. Standardized test scores: Very important. Essay: Considered. **Nonacademic:** Interview: Considered. Extracurricular activities: Important. Talent/ability: Important. Character/personal qualities: Important. Alumni/ae relationship: Important. Geographical residence: Considered. State residency: Considered. Religious affiliation/commitment: Considered. Minority status: Not considered. Volunteer work: Considered. Work experience: Not considered. **Other schools with the greatest overlap in applicants:** Aurora University; Blackburn College; Eureka College; Knox College; Millikin University. **Admissions statistics for the fall 2005 entering class:** Total applicants: 1,421. Total accepted: 806. Freshmen enrolled: 320; 3% were from out of state. Overall acceptance rate: 57%. **Size of waiting list:** 0 applicants; enrolled from waiting list: 0. **Credentials of fall 2005 freshmen:** 13% ranked in the top 10 percent of their high school class; 28% were in the top 25 percent, and 91% were in the top half. (Proportion submitting class standing: 93%.) **Average high school grade point average:** 2.8. **First-year students who submitted SAT scores:** 8%. Scores (25/75 percentile): Verbal: 430-710, Math: 450-590, Combined: 880-1300. **First-year students submitting ACT scores:** 92%. Scores (25/75 percentile): English: 19-23, Math: 18-24, Composite: 20-24.

ACADEMICS

Year founded: 1846. **Academic calendar:** Semester. **Degrees offered:** associate, bachelor's. **Most popular majors:** 22% education, 13% psychology, 9% health professions and related clinical sciences, 9% security and protective services, 8% business, management, marketing, and related support services. **Major fields of study:** biological and biomedical sciences; business, management, marketing, and related support services; communication, journalism, and related programs; computer and information sciences and support services; education; English language and literature/letters; foreign languages, literatures, and linguistics; health professions and related clinical sciences; history; legal professions and studies; liberal arts and sciences studies, and humanities; mathematics and statistics; parks, recreation, leisure, and fitness studies; philosophy and religious studies; psychology; public administration and social service professions; security and protective services; social sciences; theology and religious vocations; visual and performing arts. **Areas of required coursework:** arts/fine arts, humanities, mathematics, English (including composition), sciences (biological or physical), social science. **Pre-professional programs:** pre-law, pre-dentistry, pre-medicine, pre-veterinary science, other. **Special academic programs (% participation):** cooperative (work-study plan) program (2%), cross-registration (2%), double major (15%), dual enrollment (4%), independent study (32%), internships (90%), liberal arts/career combination (100%), study abroad (5%), teacher certificate program (30%). **Teacher certification offered in:** special education, elementary, middle/junior high, secondary. **Faculty and instruction (2005-2006):** Total instructional faculty: 38 full-time, 41 part-time (41% men; 59% women; 1% minorities). Full-time faculty with Ph.D. or other terminal degree: 71%. Student/faculty ratio: 13/1. Classes of fewer than 20 students: 66%; of 20 to 49 students: 33%; of 50 or more students: 2%. **Advanced Placement and International Baccalaureate credit:** AP tests may be used for: Credit only. International Baccalaureate exams may be used for: Credit only. **Freshmen returning for sophomore year:** 57%. **Graduation rates:** Six-year: 47%. **Graduate study:** 16% of students pursue further study immediately upon graduation; 12% within one year. Fields in which graduates pursue further study: Master of Business Administration (MBA), 75%; law, 5%; medicine, 1%; engineering, 2%; education, 17%.

COSTS AND FINANCIAL AID

Financial aid office: (217) 479-7041. **Expenses (2006-2007):** Tuition and fees 2006-2007: $15,825; room/board: $5,998. Estimated books and supplies: $875; transportation: $500; personal expenses: $800. **Financial aid:** Priority filing date for institution's financial aid form: March 1. In 2005-2006, 100% of undergraduates applied for financial aid. Of those, 90% were determined to have financial need; 15% had their need fully met. Average financial aid package (proportion receiving): $13,591 (90%). Average amount of gift aid, such as scholarships or grants (proportion receiving): $9,942 (89%). Average amount of self-help aid, such as work study or loans (proportion receiving): $4,308 (77%). Average need-based loan (excluding PLUS or other private loans): $4,184. Among students who received need-based aid, the average percentage of need met: 75%. Among students who received aid based on merit, the average award (and the proportion receiving): $12,548 (9%). The average athletic scholarship (and the proportion receiving): $0

(0%). Average amount of debt of borrowers graduating in 2005: $12,440. Proportion who borrowed: 91%.

CAMPUS LIFE AND EXTRACURRICULAR ACTIVITIES

Campus housing available (% using): coed dorms (90%), women's dorms (10%). Students who live in college-owned, operated, or affiliated housing: 54%. **Student employment:** During the 2005-2006 academic year, 22% of undergraduates worked on campus. Average per-year earnings: $941. **Clubs and organizations:** Number of student organizations: 32. Activities include: choral groups, dance, drama/theater, literary magazine, music ensembles, student government, student newspaper, yearbook. Number of fraternities: 2; sororities: 1. Proportion of men in fraternities: 9%; of women in sororities: 15%. Average proportion of students who stay on campus on weekends: 45%. **Sports program (2005-2006):** Member of NCAA III. **Men's intercollegiate varsity sports:** baseball, basketball, cross-country, football, golf, soccer, tennis, wrestling. **Women's intercollegiate varsity sports:** basketball, cross-country, golf, soccer, softball, tennis, volleyball.

SERVICES AND FACILITIES

Basic services: nonremedial tutoring, placement service, health service, health insurance. **Remedial assistance:** study skills. **Counseling services:** career, personal, academic, older student, psychological, religious. **For learning-disabled students:** School does not offer a structured program with separate admission and additional fees. Services include: untimed tests, note-taking services, oral tests, learning center, readers, tutors, proofreading services, texts on tape. **Library:** Number of titles: 1,817,284; number of current serial subscriptions: 130. **Information technology resources:** Students are not required to lease or own a computer. Number of campus computers available to all students: 150. School has a wireless network. Proportion of college-owned housing units wired for high-speed internet access: 100%. **Campus safety:** Security services offered: 24-hour foot and vehicle patrols, late-night transport/escort service, 24-hour emergency telephones, lighted pathways/sidewalks, student patrols, controlled dormitory access (key, security card, etc).

TRANSFER AND INTERNATIONAL STUDENTS

Transfer students: May apply for admission for the following academic terms: Fall, Spring, Summer. Applicants need a minimum number of credits to apply. For fall 2005: Transfer applications received: 323. Transfer applicants offered admission: 186. Transfer applicants enrolled: 96. **International students:** Number of foreign undergraduates: 4 (1% of student body). Number of countries represented: 4. Minimum TOEFL score required: 550 (paper); 213 (computer). Average TOEFL score: 565 (paper).

McKendree College

- **Address:** 701 College Road, Lebanon, IL 62254-1299
- **Website:** http://www.mckendree.edu
- **Private; Religious affiliation:** Methodist
- **Enrollment:** 1,617 full-time; 640 part-time

KEY STATS
✔ **U.S News College Ranking:** 23, Comp. Coll.–Bachelor's (Midwest)
✔ **ACT Score (25th/75th percentile):** 21-26
✔ **Tuition:** 2006-2007: $18,900

Selectivity: More selective	**Room/board:** $7,380
Acceptance rate: 62%	**Average debt:** $16,322
Student/faculty ratio: 14/1	**Proportion who borrowed:** 57%

UNDERGRADUATE STUDENT BODY STATS

2005-2006 enrollment: 1,617 full-time; 640 part-time. Men: 44%; women: 56%. **Ethnic makeup:** African American: 13%; Asian American: 1%; Hispanic: 2%; White: 82%; International: 2%. **Religious preference:** Roman Catholic: 23%; Protestant: 38%; No preference: 2%; Unknown: 29%; Methodist: 6%; Other: 2%.

ADMISSIONS FACTS AND FIGURES

Phone: (618) 537-6831. **Email:** inquiry@mckendree.edu. **Website:** http://www.mckendree.edu. **Application deadlines for fall 2007:** Regular decision: Rolling; decision sent by March 1. Early decision: Not offered. Early action: Not offered. Admission can be deferred. **Application fee:** $40. Common application is accepted. **Admissions requirements/recommenda-**

tions: High school units required (recommended): English: 4 (4); Mathematics: 3 (3); Science: 3 (3); Foreign language: 2 (2); Social studies: 2 (2); History: 2 (2); Total units: 14 (14). Tests: The college uses SAT or ACT scores in admissions decisions. Either SAT or ACT required. For admission to the fall 2007 entering class, the school will accept: ACT with writing, ACT without writing. Campus visit: Recommended. Admissions interview: Recommended. Off-campus interview: Not available. **Factors that count in admissions decisions:** *Academic:* Secondary school record: Very important. Class rank: Very important. Letters of recommendation: Important. Standardized test scores: Important. Essay: Important. **Nonacademic:** Interview: Important. Extracurricular activities: Important. Talent/ability: Very important. Character/personal qualities: Very important. Alumni/ae relationship: Considered. Geographical residence: Not considered. State residency: Not considered. Religious affiliation/commitment: Not considered. Minority status: Not considered. Volunteer work: Important. Work experience: Important. **Other schools with the greatest overlap in applicants:** Illinois College; Millikin University; Southern Illinois University–Edwardsville; University of Illinois–Urbana-Champaign. **Admissions statistics for the fall 2005 entering class:** Total applicants: 1,465. Total accepted: 914. Freshmen enrolled: 273; 19% were from out of state. Overall acceptance rate: 62%. **Credentials of fall 2005 freshmen:** 22% ranked in the top 10 percent of their high school class; 52% were in the top 25 percent, and 76% were in the top half. (Proportion submitting class standing: 92%.) **Average high school grade point average:** 3.3. **First-year students who submitted SAT scores:** 8%. Scores (25/75 percentile): Verbal: 410-520, Math: 470-570. Combined: 880-1090. **First-year students submitting ACT scores:** 92%. Scores (25/75 percentile): English: 17-24, Math: 18-25, Composite: 21-26.

ACADEMICS

Year founded: 1828. **Academic calendar:** Semester. **Degrees offered:** associate, bachelor's, master's. **Most popular majors:** 10% business administration and management, 10% elementary education and teaching, 10% management science, 7% psychology, 6% accounting. **Major fields of study:** biological and biomedical sciences; business, management, marketing, and related support services; communication, journalism, and related programs; computer and information sciences and support services; education; English language and literature/letters; health professions and related clinical sciences; history; liberal arts and sciences studies, and humanities; mathematics and statistics; philosophy and religious studies; physical sciences; psychology; social sciences; visual and performing arts. **Areas of required coursework:** arts/fine arts, humanities, computer literacy, mathematics, English (including composition), philosophy, foreign languages, sciences (biological or physical), history, social science, other. **Pre-professional programs:** pre-medicine, pre-theology. **Special academic programs (% participation):** cross-registration (4%), distance learning (2%), double major (.5%), external degree program (1%), honors program (1%), independent study (12.8%), internships (24.5%), liberal arts/career combination (100%), student-designed major (0%), study abroad (1%), teacher certificate program (21.5%). **Teacher certification offered in:** special education, elementary, secondary. **Cooperative education programs:** business, engineering, health professions. **Reserve Officers Training Corps (ROTC):** Army ROTC: Offered at cooperating institution (Southern Illinois University- Edwardsville); Air Force ROTC: Offered at cooperating institution (Southern Illinois University- Edwardsville). **Faculty and instruction (2005-2006):** Total instructional faculty: 70 full-time, 179 part-time (53% men; 47% women; 7% minorities). Full-time faculty with Ph.D. or other terminal degree: 81%. Student/faculty ratio: 14/1. Classes of fewer than 20 students: 72%; of 20 to 49 students: 28%. **Advanced Placement and International Baccalaureate credit:** AP tests may be used for: Credit and/or placement. Scores accepted: 3, 4, 5. International Baccalaureate exams may be used for: Credit only. **Freshmen returning for sophomore year:** 76%. **Graduation rates:** Four-year: 41%; five-year: 60%; six-year: 58%. **Graduate study:** 20% of students pursue further study immediately upon graduation; 24% within one year; 30% within five years. Fields in which graduates pursue further study: Master of Business Administration (MBA), 3%; law, 5%; medicine, 1%; theology (or the seminary), 2%; education, 2%; arts and sciences, 5%; veterinary medicine, 2%.

COSTS AND FINANCIAL AID

Financial aid office: (618) 537-6828. **Expenses (2006-2007):** Tuition and fees 2006-2007: $18,900; room/board: $7,380. Estimated books and supplies: $1,200; transportation: $820; personal expenses: $1,000. **Financial aid:** Priority filing date for institution's financial aid form: May 31. In 2005-2006, 87% of undergraduates applied for financial aid. Of those, 78% were determined to have financial need; 24% had their need fully met. Average

financial aid package (proportion receiving): $15,473 (78%). Average amount of gift aid, such as scholarships or grants (proportion receiving): $12,144 (77%). Average amount of self-help aid, such as work study or loans (proportion receiving): $4,398 (60%). Average need-based loan (excluding PLUS or other private loans): $3,627. Among students who received need-based aid, the average percentage of need met: 81%. Among students who received aid based on merit, the average award (and the proportion receiving): $11,327 (21%). The average athletic scholarship (and the proportion receiving): $6,624 (13%). Average amount of debt of borrowers graduating in 2005: $16,322. Proportion who borrowed: 57%.

CAMPUS LIFE AND EXTRACURRICULAR ACTIVITIES

Campus housing available (% using): coed dorms (42%), apartment for single students (58%). Students who live in college-owned, operated, or affiliated housing: 40%. **Student employment:** During the 2005-2006 academic year, 24% of undergraduates worked on campus. Average per-year earnings: $2,000. **Clubs and organizations:** Number of student organizations: 62. Activities include: choral groups, concert band, dance, drama/theater, jazz band, literary magazine, marching band, music ensembles, musical theater, pep band, student government, student newspaper, student film society, yearbook. Number of fraternities: 4; sororities: 3. Proportion of men in fraternities: 11%; of women in sororities: 9%. Average proportion of students who stay on campus on weekends: 60%. **Sports program (2005-2006):** Member of NAIA. *Men's intercollegiate varsity sports:* baseball, basketball, cross-country, football, golf, soccer, tennis, track and field (indoor), track and field (outdoor). *Women's intercollegiate varsity sports:* basketball, cross-country, golf, soccer, softball, tennis, track and field (indoor), track and field (outdoor), volleyball.

SERVICES AND FACILITIES

Basic services: nonremedial tutoring, placement service, health service, health insurance. **Remedial assistance:** reading, math, writing, study skills. **Counseling services:** minority student, career, personal, veteran student, academic, psychological, religious. **For learning-disabled students:** School does not offer a structured program with separate admission and additional fees. Total undergraduates in learning-disabled program or receiving services: 2. Services include: remedial math, remedial English, reading machines, tape recorders, untimed tests, oral tests, learning center, extended time for tests, tutors, priority seating, texts on tape. **Library:** Number of titles: 96,265; number of current serial subscriptions: 545. **Information technology resources:** Students are not required to lease or own a computer. Number of campus computers available to all students: 160. School has a wireless network. Approximate number of users that can be accommodated: 50. Proportion of college-owned housing units wired for high-speed internet access: 100%. **Campus safety:** Security services offered: 24-hour foot and vehicle patrols, late-night transport/escort service, lighted pathways/sidewalks, controlled dormitory access (key, security card, etc).

TRANSFER AND INTERNATIONAL STUDENTS

Transfer students: May apply for admission for the following academic terms: Fall, Spring, Summer. Applicants do not need a minimum number of credits to apply. For fall 2005: Transfer applications received: 521. Transfer applicants offered admission: 338. Transfer applicants enrolled: 336. **International students:** Number of foreign undergraduates: 47 (2% of student body). Number of countries represented: 24. Minimum TOEFL score required: 520 (paper); 190 (computer). Average TOEFL score: 525 (paper).

Millikin University

- **Address:** 1184 W. Main Street, Decatur, IL 62522-2084
- **Website:** http://www.millikin.edu
- **Private; Religious affiliation:** Presbyterian
- **Enrollment:** 2,438 full-time; 178 part-time

KEY STATS

✔ **U.S News College Ranking:** 18, Comp. Coll.–Bachelor's (Midwest)
✔ **ACT Score (25th/75th percentile):** 20-26
✔ **Tuition:** 2006-2007: $22,069

Selectivity: Selective	**Room/board:** $6,926
Acceptance rate: 70%	**Average debt:** $18,418
Student/faculty ratio: 13/1	**Proportion who borrowed:** 79%

UNDERGRADUATE STUDENT BODY STATS

2005-2006 enrollment: 2,438 full-time; 178 part-time. Men: 41%; women: 59%. **Ethnic makeup:** African American: 9%; Asian American: 1%; Hispanic: 2%; White: 87%.

ADMISSIONS FACTS AND FIGURES

Phone: (217) 424-6210. **Email:** admis@millikin.edu. **Website:** http://www.millikin.edu. **Application deadlines for fall 2007:** Regular decision: August 15. Early decision: Not offered. Early action: Not offered. Admission can be deferred. Common application is accepted. **To apply online, go to:** http://www.millikin.edu/admission/applications/. **Admissions requirements/recommendations:** High school units required (recommended): English: 4 (4); Mathematics: 3 (3); Science: 3 (3); Foreign language: 2 (2); Social studies: 2 (2); History: 2 (2); Academic electives: 0 (0); Total units: 16 (16). Tests: The college uses SAT or ACT scores in admissions decisions. Either SAT or ACT required. For admission to the fall 2007 entering class, the school will accept: ACT with writing, ACT without writing. Campus visit: Recommended. Admissions interview: Recommended. Off-campus interview: May be arranged. **Factors that count in admissions decisions:** *Academic:* Secondary school record: Very important. Class rank: Important. Letters of recommendation: Important. Standardized test scores: Important. Essay: Not considered. *Nonacademic:* Interview: Important. Extracurricular activities: Considered. Talent/ability: Considered. Character/personal qualities: Considered. Alumni/ae relationship: Considered. Geographical residence: Not considered. State residency: Not considered. Religious affiliation/commitment: Not considered. Minority status: Considered. Volunteer work: Considered. Work experience: Considered. **Admissions statistics for the fall 2005 entering class:** Total applicants: 2,917. Total accepted: 2,033. Freshmen enrolled: 573; 4% were from out of state. Overall acceptance rate: 70%. **Credentials of fall 2005 freshmen:** 17% ranked in the top 10 percent of their high school class; 44% were in the top 25 percent, and 79% were in the top half. (Proportion submitting class standing: 94%.) **First-year students who submitted SAT scores:** 15%. Scores (25/75 percentile): Verbal: 450-610, Math: 450-580, Combined: 900-1190. **First-year students submitting ACT scores:** 94%. Scores (25/75 percentile): English: 20-27, Math: 19-26, Composite: 20-26.

ACADEMICS

Year founded: 1901. **Academic calendar:** Semester. **Degrees offered:** bachelor's, master's. **Most popular majors:** 27% business, management, marketing, and related support services, 18% visual and performing arts, 15% education, 7% health professions and related clinical sciences, 4% parks, recreation, leisure, and fitness studies. **Major fields of study:** area, ethnic, cultural, and gender studies; biological and biomedical sciences; business, management, marketing, and related support services; communication, journalism, and related programs; computer and information sciences and support services; education; English language and literature/letters; foreign languages, literatures, and linguistics; health professions and related clinical sciences; history; mathematics and statistics; multi/interdisciplinary studies; parks, recreation, leisure, and fitness studies; philosophy and religious studies; physical sciences; psychology; public administration and social service professions; social sciences; visual and performing arts. **Areas of required coursework:** arts/fine arts, mathematics, English (including composition), sciences (biological or physical), other. **Pre-professional programs:** pre-law, pre-dentistry, pre-medicine, pre-veterinary science, pre-optometry, pre-pharmacy, other. **Special academic programs (% participation):** accelerated program (17%), double major (7%), exchange student program (domestic) (.1%), honors program (5%), independent study (24%), internships (72%), student-designed major (4%), study abroad (4%), teacher certificate program (17%), other (53%). **Teacher certification offered in:** early childhood, elementary, middle/junior high, secondary. **Faculty and instruction (2005-2006):** Total instructional faculty: 145 full-time, 137 part-time (52% men; 48% women; 9% minorities). Full-time faculty with Ph.D. or other terminal degree: 74%. Student/faculty ratio: 13/1. Classes of fewer than 20 students: 54%; of 20 to 49 students: 44%; of 50 or more students: 2%. **Advanced Placement and International Baccalaureate credit:** AP tests may be used for: Credit only. Scores accepted: 3, 4, 5. International Baccalaureate exams may be used for: Credit only. **Freshmen returning for sophomore year:** 79%. **Graduation rates:** Four-year: 54%; five-year: 61%; six-year: 61%. **Graduate study:** 19% of students pursue further study immediately upon graduation. Fields in which graduates pursue further study: Master of Business Administration (MBA), 6%; law, 8%; medicine, 8%; theology (or the seminary), 5%; education, 2%; arts and sciences, 67%; veterinary medicine, 1%.

COSTS AND FINANCIAL AID

Financial aid office: (217) 424-6343. **Expenses (2006-2007):** Tuition and fees 2006-2007: $22,069; room/board: $6,926. Estimated books and supplies: $1,000; transportation: $300; personal expenses: $1,550. **Financial aid:** Priority filing date for institution's financial aid form: March 15. In 2005-2006, 89% of undergraduates applied for financial aid. Of those, 75% were determined to have financial need; 55% had their need fully met. Average financial aid package (proportion receiving): $15,927 (75%). Average amount of gift aid, such as scholarships or grants (proportion receiving): $7,189 (65%). Average amount of self-help aid, such as work study or loans (proportion receiving): $4,472 (62%). Average need-based loan (excluding PLUS or other private loans): $4,230. Among students who received need-based aid, the average percentage of need met: 91%. Among students who received aid based on merit, the average award (and the proportion receiving): $7,126 (10%). The average athletic scholarship (and the proportion receiving): $0 (0%). Average amount of debt of borrowers graduating in 2005: $18,418. Proportion who borrowed: 79%.

CAMPUS LIFE AND EXTRACURRICULAR ACTIVITIES

Campus housing available (% using): coed dorms (33%), women's dorms (11%), men's dorms (6%), sorority housing (6%), fraternity housing (3%), apartments for married students (0%), apartment for single students (41%), special housing for disabled students (0%). Students who live in college-owned, operated, or affiliated housing: 62%. **Student employment:** During the 2005-2006 academic year, 6% of undergraduates worked on campus. Average per-year earnings: $2,000. **Clubs and organizations:** Number of student organizations: 83. Activities include: choral groups, concert band, dance, drama/theater, jazz band, literary magazine, music ensembles, musical theater, opera, pep band, radio station, student government, student newspaper, student film society, symphony orchestra. Number of fraternities: 4; sororities: 3. Proportion of men in fraternities: 19%; of women in sororities: 15%. Average proportion of students who stay on campus on weekends: 75%. **Sports program (2005-2006):** Member of NCAA III. *Men's intercollegiate varsity sports:* baseball, basketball, cross-country, football, golf, soccer, swimming and diving, track and field (indoor), track and field (outdoor), wrestling. *Women's intercollegiate varsity sports:* basketball, cross-country, golf, soccer, softball, swimming and diving, tennis, track and field (indoor), track and field (outdoor), volleyball.

SERVICES AND FACILITIES

Basic services: nonremedial tutoring, placement service, health service. **Remedial assistance:** math, writing, study skills. **Counseling services:** personal, psychological, birth control. **For learning-disabled students:** School does not offer a structured program with separate admission and additional fees. Services include: remedial math, remedial English, tape recorders, other special classes, untimed tests, note-taking services, oral tests, learning center, readers, extended time for tests, tutors, other. **Library:** Number of titles: 212,145; number of current serial subscriptions: 580. **Information technology resources:** Students are not required to lease or own a computer. Number of campus computers available to all students: 280. School has a wireless network. Approximate number of users that can be accommodated: 500. Proportion of college-owned housing units wired for high-speed internet access: 100%. **Campus safety:** Security services offered: 24-hour foot and vehicle patrols, late-night transport/escort service, 24-hour emergency telephones, lighted pathways/sidewalks, controlled dormitory access (key, security card, etc).

TRANSFER AND INTERNATIONAL STUDENTS

Transfer students: May apply for admission for the following academic terms: Fall, Spring, Summer. Applicants need a minimum number of credits to apply. For fall 2005: Transfer applications received: 517. Transfer applicants offered admission: 254. Transfer applicants enrolled: 124. **International students:** Number of foreign undergraduates: 7. Number of countries represented: 5. Minimum TOEFL score required: 550 (paper); 213 (computer). Average TOEFL score: 643 (paper).

Monmouth College

- **Address:** 700 E. Broadway, Monmouth, IL 61462
- **Website:** http://www.monm.edu
- **Private; Religious affiliation:** Presbyterian
- **Enrollment:** 1,329 full-time; 16 part-time

KEY STATS
- ✔ **U.S News College Ranking:** third tier, Liberal Arts Colleges
- ✔ **ACT Score (25th/75th percentile):** 20-26
- ✔ **Tuition:** 2006-2007: $21,100

Selectivity: Selective	**Room/board:** $6,150
Acceptance rate: 72%	**Average debt:** $18,901
Student/faculty ratio: 13/1	**Proportion who borrowed:** 82%

UNDERGRADUATE STUDENT BODY STATS
2005-2006 enrollment: 1,329 full-time; 16 part-time. Men: 47%; women: 53%. **Ethnic makeup:** African American: 3%; Asian American: 1%; Hispanic: 3%; White: 91%; International: 1%.

ADMISSIONS FACTS AND FIGURES
Phone: (800) 747-2687. **Email:** admit@monm.edu. **Website:** http://www.monm.edu. **Application deadlines for fall 2007:** Early decision: Not offered. Early action: Not offered. **Admissions requirements/recommendations:** High school units required (recommended): English: 4 (4); Mathematics: 3 (3); Science: 2 (3); Foreign language: 2 (3); Social studies: 2 (3); History: 1 (2); Total units: 14 (22). Tests: The college uses SAT or ACT scores in admissions decisions. Either SAT or ACT required. For admission to the fall 2007 entering class, the school will accept: ACT with writing, ACT without writing. Campus visit: Recommended. Admissions interview: Recommended. Off-campus interview: May be arranged. **Factors that count in admissions decisions:** *Academic:* Secondary school record: Very important. Class rank: Important. Letters of recommendation: Considered. Standardized test scores: Important. Essay: Considered. *Nonacademic:* Interview: Important. Extracurricular activities: Important. Talent/ability: Important. Character/personal qualities: Important. Alumni/ae relationship: Considered. Geographical residence: Considered. State residency: Considered. Religious affiliation/commitment: Not considered. Minority status: Not considered. Volunteer work: Considered. Work experience: Considered. **Other schools with the greatest overlap in applicants:** Augustana College; Illinois Wesleyan University; Illinois Wesleyan University; Knox College; Knox College; University of Illinois–Urbana-Champaign; University of Illinois–Urbana-Champaign; Western Illinois University; Western Illinois University. **Admissions statistics for the fall 2005 entering class:** 10% were from out of state. Overall acceptance rate: 72%. **Credentials of fall 2005 freshmen:** 14% ranked in the top 10 percent of their high school class; 40% were in the top 25 percent.

ACADEMICS
Year founded: 1853. **Academic calendar:** Semester. **Degrees offered:** bachelor's. **Most popular majors:** 22% education, 19% business, management, marketing, and related support services, 12% English language and literature/letters, 10% biological and biomedical sciences, 10% psychology. **Major fields of study:** biological and biomedical sciences; business, management, marketing, and related support services; computer and information sciences and support services; education; engineering; English language and literature/letters; foreign languages, literatures, and linguistics; health professions and related clinical sciences; history; legal professions and studies; mathematics and statistics; philosophy and religious studies; physical sciences; psychology; social sciences; visual and performing arts. **Areas of required coursework:** arts/fine arts, humanities, mathematics, English (including composition), foreign languages, sciences (biological or physical), social science, other. **Pre-professional programs:** pre-law, pre-dentistry, pre-medicine, pre-theology, pre-veterinary science, pre-optometry. **Special academic programs (% participation):** double major (20%), honors program (4%), independent study (5%), internships (17%), liberal arts/career combination (4%), student-designed major (2%), study abroad (7%), teacher certificate program (31%). **Teacher certification offered in:** elementary, middle/junior high, secondary, bilingual/bicultural. **Reserve Officers Training Corps (ROTC):** Army ROTC: Offered at cooperating institution (Western Illinois University). **Faculty and instruction (2005-2006):** Total instructional faculty: 87 full-time, 46 part-time (55% men; 45% women; 8% minorities). Full-time faculty with Ph.D. or other terminal degree: 76%.

Student/faculty ratio: 13/1. Classes of fewer than 20 students: 51%; of 20 to 49 students: 49%. **Advanced Placement and International Baccalaureate credit:** AP tests may be used for: Credit and/or placement. Scores accepted: 3, 4, 5. International Baccalaureate exams may be used for: Credit and/or placement. **Freshmen returning for sophomore year:** 81%. **Graduation rates:** Six-year: 60%. **Graduate study:** 27% of students pursue further study immediately upon graduation. Fields in which graduates pursue further study: Master of Business Administration (MBA), 15%; law, 3%; medicine, 20%; dentistry, 1%; engineering, 3%; theology (or the seminary), 3%; education, 10%; arts and sciences, 44%; veterinary medicine, 1%.

COSTS AND FINANCIAL AID
Financial aid office: (309) 457-2129. **Expenses (2006-2007):** Tuition and fees 2006-2007: $21,100; room/board: $6,150. Estimated books and supplies: $650; transportation: $350; personal expenses: $400. **Financial aid:** Priority filing date for institution's financial aid form: March 1. Average amount of debt of borrowers graduating in 2005: $18,901. Proportion who borrowed: 82%.

CAMPUS LIFE AND EXTRACURRICULAR ACTIVITIES
Campus housing available (% using): coed dorms (13%), women's dorms (42%), men's dorms (28%), fraternity housing (10%), special housing for disabled students, other housing options (7%). **Student employment:** During the 2005-2006 academic year, 33% of undergraduates worked on campus. Average per-year earnings: $1,400. **Clubs and organizations:** Number of student organizations: 60. Activities include: choral groups, concert band, dance, drama/theater, jazz band, literary magazine, music ensembles, musical theater, pep band, radio station, student government, student newspaper, student film society, television station. Number of fraternities: 3; sororities: 3. Average proportion of students who stay on campus on weekends: 75%. **Sports program (2005-2006):** Member of NCAA III. *Men's intercollegiate varsity sports:* baseball, basketball, cross-country, football, golf, soccer, swimming and diving, tennis, track and field (indoor), track and field (outdoor). *Women's intercollegiate varsity sports:* basketball, cross-country, golf, soccer, softball, swimming and diving, tennis, track and field (indoor), track and field (outdoor), volleyball.

SERVICES AND FACILITIES
Basic services: nonremedial tutoring, placement service, health service, health insurance. **Counseling services:** minority student, career, personal, veteran student, academic, older student, psychological, religious. **For learning-disabled students:** School does not offer a structured program with separate admission and additional fees. Services include: tape recorders, untimed tests, note-taking services, oral tests, learning center, readers, extended time for tests, tutors, priority seating, other testing accomodations, other. **Library:** Number of titles: 185,771; number of current serial subscriptions: 1,251. **Information technology resources:** Students are not required to lease or own a computer. Number of campus computers available to all students: 350. School has a wireless network. Approximate number of users that can be accommodated: 500. Proportion of college-owned housing units wired for high-speed internet access: 100%. **Campus safety:** Security services offered: late-night transport/escort service, 24-hour emergency telephones, lighted pathways/sidewalks, controlled dormitory access (key, security card, etc).

TRANSFER AND INTERNATIONAL STUDENTS
Transfer students: May apply for admission for the following academic terms: Fall, Spring. Applicants need a minimum number of credits to apply. **International students:** Number of foreign undergraduates: 18 (1% of student body). Number of countries represented: 12. Minimum TOEFL score required: 500 (paper); 173 (computer). Average TOEFL score: 565 (paper).

National-Louis University

- **Address:** 122 S. Michigan Avenue, Chicago, IL 60603
- **Website:** http://www.nl.edu
- **Private**
- **Enrollment:** 1,588 full-time; 572 part-time

KEY STATS
✔ **U.S News College Ranking:** fourth tier, National Universities
✔ **SAT or ACT Score (25th/75th percentile):** N/A
✔ **Tuition:** 2006-2007: $17,805

Selectivity: Selective	**Room/board:** N/A
Acceptance rate: 98%	**Average debt:** $15,000
Student/faculty ratio: N/A	**Proportion who borrowed:** 59%

UNDERGRADUATE STUDENT BODY STATS
2005-2006 enrollment: 1,588 full-time; 572 part-time. Men: 26%; women: 74%. **Ethnic makeup:** African American: 26%; Asian American: 2%; Hispanic: 8%; White: 64%.

ADMISSIONS FACTS AND FIGURES
Phone: (888) 658-8632. **Email:** nluinfo@nl.edu. **Website:** http://www.nl.edu. **Application deadlines for fall 2007:** Regular decision: Rolling. Early decision: Not offered. Early action: Send application by: N/A; Decision sent by: N/A. Admission can be deferred. **Application fee:** $40. Common application is not accepted. **To apply online, go to:** http://www.nl.edu/nlu_admissions/index.html. **Admissions requirements/recommendations:** High school units required (recommended): English: 0 (0); Mathematics: 0 (0); Science: 0 (0); Foreign language: 0 (0); Social studies: 0 (0); History: 0 (0); Academic electives: 0 (0); Total units: 0 (0). Tests: The college uses SAT or ACT scores in admissions decisions. Either SAT or ACT required. Campus visit: Recommended. Admissions interview: Recommended. Off-campus interview: May be arranged. **Factors that count in admissions decisions: Academic:** Secondary school record: Very important. Class rank: Considered. Letters of recommendation: Considered. Standardized test scores: Very important. Essay: Considered. **Nonacademic:** Interview: Not considered. Extracurricular activities: Not considered. Talent/ability: Not considered. Character/personal qualities: Not considered. Alumni/ae relationship: Not considered. Geographical residence: Not considered. State residency: Not considered. Religious affiliation/commitment: Not considered. Minority status: Not considered. Volunteer work: Not considered. Work experience: Not considered. **Admissions statistics for the fall 2005 entering class:** Total applicants: 60. Total accepted: 59. Freshmen enrolled: 34; 0% were from out of state. Overall acceptance rate: 98%. Non-early acceptance rate: 98%. **Size of waiting list:** 0 applicants; enrolled from waiting list: 0.

ACADEMICS
Year founded: 1886. **Academic calendar:** Quarter. **Degrees offered:** certificate, bachelor's, post-bachelor's certificate, master's, post-master's certificate, doctorate. **Most popular majors:** 49% business, management, marketing, and related support services, 27% multi/interdisciplinary studies, 9% education, 8% health professions and related clinical sciences, 2% psychology. **Major fields of study:** biological and biomedical sciences; business, management, marketing, and related support services; computer and information sciences and support services; education; English language and literature/letters; health professions and related clinical sciences; mathematics and statistics; multi/interdisciplinary studies; psychology; public administration and social service professions; social sciences; visual and performing arts. **Areas of required coursework:** arts/fine arts, humanities, computer literacy, mathematics, English (including composition), philosophy, sciences (biological or physical), history, social science. **Special academic programs:** accelerated program, cross-registration, distance learning, double major, dual enrollment, English as a Second Language (ESL), independent study, internships, study abroad, teacher certificate program, weekend college. **Teacher certification offered in:** early childhood, special education, elementary, middle/junior high, adult education, secondary, bilingual/bicultural. **Cooperative education programs:** art, business, computer science, education, health professions, humanities, natural science, social/behavioral science, technologies. **Faculty and instruction (2005-2006):** Total instructional faculty: 253 full-time, 829 part-time (34% men; 66% women; 12% minorities). Full-time faculty with Ph.D. or other terminal degree: 71%. Classes of fewer than 20 students: 92%; of 20 to 49 students:

8%. **Advanced Placement and International Baccalaureate credit:** AP tests may be used for: Credit only. International Baccalaureate exams may be used for: Credit only. **Freshmen returning for sophomore year:** 42%. **Graduation rates:** Four-year: 13%; five-year: 23%; six-year: 31%.

COSTS AND FINANCIAL AID
Financial aid office: (847) 465-5350. **Expenses (2006-2007):** Tuition and fees 2006-2007: $17,805; room/board: N/A. Estimated books and supplies: $875. **Financial aid:** In 2005-2006, 72% of undergraduates applied for financial aid. Of those, 65% were determined to have financial need; 5% had their need fully met. Average financial aid package (proportion receiving): $9,559 (64%). Average amount of gift aid, such as scholarships or grants (proportion receiving): N/A (57%). Average amount of self-help aid, such as work study or loans (proportion receiving): N/A (55%). Among students who received need-based aid, the average percentage of need met: 49%. Among students who received aid based on merit, the average award (and the proportion receiving): $1,863 (8%). The average athletic scholarship (and the proportion receiving): $0 (0%). Average amount of debt of borrowers graduating in 2005: $15,000. Proportion who borrowed: 59%.

CAMPUS LIFE AND EXTRACURRICULAR ACTIVITIES
Campus housing available: coed dorms, special housing for disabled students, special housing for international students. **Student employment:** During the 2005-2006 academic year, 2% of undergraduates worked on campus. Average per-year earnings: $2,600. **Clubs and organizations:** Number of student organizations: 14. Number of fraternities: 0; sororities: 0. Average proportion of students who stay on campus on weekends: 55%.

SERVICES AND FACILITIES
Basic services: nonremedial tutoring, health service. **Remedial assistance:** reading, math, writing, study skills. **Counseling services:** minority student, career, military, personal, veteran student, academic, older student, psychological, birth control. **For learning-disabled students:** Services include: remedial math, remedial English, reading machines, remedial reading, tape recorders, other special classes, videotaped classes, diagnostic testing service, oral tests, learning center, readers, tutors. **Information technology resources:** Students are not required to lease or own a computer. Number of campus computers available to all students: 165. **Campus safety:** Security services offered: late-night transport/escort service, 24-hour emergency telephones, lighted pathways/sidewalks, student patrols, controlled dormitory access (key, security card, etc.).

TRANSFER AND INTERNATIONAL STUDENTS
Transfer students: May apply for admission for the following academic terms: Fall, Winter, Spring, Summer. Applicants need a minimum number of credits to apply. **International students:** Number of foreign undergraduates: 0. Minimum TOEFL score required: 500 (paper); 173 (computer).

North Central College

- **Address:** 30 N. Brainard Street, PO Box 3063, Naperville, IL 60540
- **Website:** http://www.noctrl.edu
- **Private; Religious affiliation:** United Methodist
- **Enrollment:** 1,910 full-time; 223 part-time

KEY STATS
✔ **U.S News College Ranking:** 16, Universities–Master's (Midwest)
✔ **ACT Score (25th/75th percentile):** 22-27
✔ **Tuition:** 2006-2007: $22,890

Selectivity: More selective	**Room/board:** $7,440
Acceptance rate: 70%	**Average debt:** $14,608
Student/faculty ratio: 15/1	**Proportion who borrowed:** 70%

UNDERGRADUATE STUDENT BODY STATS
2005-2006 enrollment: 1,910 full-time; 223 part-time. Men: 42%; women: 58%. **Ethnic makeup:** African American: 4%; Asian American: 3%; Hispanic: 5%; White: 87%; International: 2%. **Religious preference:** Roman Catholic: 26%; Protestant: 27%; Jewish: 1%; Muslim: 1%; No preference: 2%; Unknown: 34%; United Methodist: 8%; Other: 1%.

ADMISSIONS FACTS AND FIGURES

Phone: (630) 637-5800. **Email:** ncadm@noctrl.edu. **Website:** http://www.noctrl.edu. **Application deadlines for fall 2007:** Regular decision: Rolling. Early decision: Not offered. Early action: Not offered. Admission can be deferred. **Application fee:** $25. Common application is accepted. **To apply online, go to:** https://www2.noctrl.edu/cgi-bin/applogin.pl. **Admissions requirements/recommendations:** High school units required (recommended): English: 4 (4); Mathematics: 3 (3); Science: 3 (3); Foreign language: 0 (3); Social studies: 2 (2); History: 1 (1); Academic electives: 3 (3); Total units: 16 (19). Tests: The college uses SAT or ACT scores in admissions decisions. Either SAT or ACT required. For admission to the fall 2007 entering class, the school will accept: ACT with writing, ACT without writing. Campus visit: Recommended. Admissions interview: Recommended. Off-campus interview: May be arranged. **Factors that count in admissions decisions:** *Academic:* Secondary school record: Very important. Class rank: Considered. Letters of recommendation: Considered. Standardized test scores: Very important. Essay: Considered. *Nonacademic:* Interview: Considered. Extracurricular activities: Important. Talent/ability: Important. Character/personal qualities: Very important. Alumni/ae relationship: Considered. Geographical residence: Not considered. State residency: Not considered. Religious affiliation/commitment: Not considered. Minority status: Not considered. Volunteer work: Important. Work experience: Important. **Other schools with the greatest overlap in applicants:** Augustana College; Elmhurst College; Illinois State University; Millikin University; Northern Illinois University. **Admissions statistics for the fall 2005 entering class:** Total applicants: 1,936. Total accepted: 1,348. Freshmen enrolled: 425; 12% were from out of state. Overall acceptance rate: 70%. **Credentials of fall 2005 freshmen:** 20% ranked in the top 10 percent of their high school class; 50% were in the top 25 percent. **Average high school grade point average:** 3.5. **First-year students who submitted SAT scores:** 13%. Scores (25/75 percentile): Verbal: 510-630, Math: 510-650, Combined: 1020-1280. **First-year students submitting ACT scores:** 95%. Scores (25/75 percentile): English: 21-28, Math: 21-28, Composite: 22-27.

ACADEMICS

Year founded: 1861. **Academic calendar:** Quarter. **Degrees offered:** bachelor's, post-bachelor's certificate, master's. **Most popular majors:** 11% elementary education and teaching, 9% business administration, management, and operations, 8% psychology, 5% accounting, 5% organizational communication. **Major fields of study:** area, ethnic, cultural, and gender studies; biological and biomedical sciences; business, management, marketing, and related support services; communication, journalism, and related programs; communications technologies/technicians and support services; computer and information sciences and support services; education; English language and literature/letters; foreign languages, literatures, and linguistics; health professions and related clinical sciences; history; liberal arts and sciences studies, and humanities; mathematics and statistics; multi/interdisciplinary studies; parks, recreation, leisure, and fitness studies; philosophy and religious studies; physical sciences; psychology; social sciences; visual and performing arts. **Areas of required coursework:** humanities, mathematics, English (including composition), sciences (biological or physical), social science, other. **Pre-professional programs:** pre-law, pre-dentistry, pre-medicine, pre-theology, pre-veterinary science, pre-pharmacy. **Special academic programs (% participation):** accelerated program (1%), cross-registration (1%), double major (14%), English as a Second Language (ESL), exchange student program (domestic), honors program (26%), independent study (23%), internships (27%), student-designed major, study abroad (10%), teacher certificate program (21%), weekend college. **Teacher certification offered in:** elementary, middle/junior high, secondary. **Reserve Officers Training Corps (ROTC):** Army ROTC: Offered at cooperating institution (Wheaton College); Air Force ROTC: Offered at cooperating institution (Illinois Institute of Technology). **Faculty and instruction (2005-2006):** Total instructional faculty: 111 full-time, 92 part-time (50% men; 50% women; 7% minorities). Full-time faculty with Ph.D. or other terminal degree: 86%. Student/faculty ratio: 15/1. Classes of fewer than 20 students: 45%; of 20 to 49 students: 55%; of 50 or more students: 0%. **Advanced Placement and International Baccalaureate credit:** AP tests may be used for: Credit and/or placement. Scores accepted: 3, 4, 5. International Baccalaureate exams may be used for: Credit and/or placement. **Freshmen returning for sophomore year:** 77%. **Graduation rates:** Four-year: 55%; five-year: 63%; six-year: 64%. **Graduate study:** 15% of students pursue further study immediately upon graduation. Fields in which graduates pursue further study: law, 12%; education, 10%; arts and sciences, 78%.

COSTS AND FINANCIAL AID

Financial aid office: (630) 637-5600. **Expenses (2006-2007):** Tuition and fees 2006-2007: $22,890; room/board: $7,440. Estimated books and supplies: $750; transportation: $318; personal expenses: $1,182. **Financial aid:** In 2005-2006, 79% of undergraduates applied for financial aid. Of those, 68% were determined to have financial need; 42% had their need fully met. Average financial aid package (proportion receiving): $19,796 (67%). Average amount of gift aid, such as scholarships or grants (proportion receiving): $11,941 (66%). Average amount of self-help aid, such as work study or loans (proportion receiving): $6,784 (56%). Average need-based loan (excluding PLUS or other private loans): $6,531. Among students who received need-based aid, the average percentage of need met: 86%. Among students who received aid based on merit, the average award (and the proportion receiving): $8,669 (23%). The average athletic scholarship (and the proportion receiving): $0 (0%). Average amount of debt of borrowers graduating in 2005: $14,608. Proportion who borrowed: 70%.

CAMPUS LIFE AND EXTRACURRICULAR ACTIVITIES

Campus housing available (% using): coed dorms (80%), women's dorms (20%), special housing for disabled students, other housing options. Students who live in college-owned, operated, or affiliated housing: 48%. **Student employment:** During the 2005-2006 academic year, 26% of undergraduates worked on campus. Average per-year earnings: $1,530. **Clubs and organizations:** Number of student organizations: 55. Activities include: choral groups, concert band, drama/theater, jazz band, literary magazine, music ensembles, musical theater, pep band, radio station, student government, student newspaper. Number of fraternities: 0; sororities: 0. Average proportion of students who stay on campus on weekends: 70%. **Sports program (2005-2006):** Member of NCAA III. *Men's intercollegiate varsity sports:* baseball, basketball, cross-country, football, golf, soccer, swimming and diving, tennis, track and field (indoor), track and field (outdoor), wrestling. *Women's intercollegiate varsity sports:* basketball, cross-country, golf, soccer, softball, swimming and diving, tennis, track and field (indoor), track and field (outdoor), volleyball.

SERVICES AND FACILITIES

Basic services: nonremedial tutoring, placement service, health service, health insurance. **Remedial assistance:** math, writing, study skills. **Counseling services:** career, academic, psychological, birth control, religious. **For learning-disabled students:** School does not offer a structured program with separate admission and additional fees. Total undergraduates in learning-disabled program or receiving services: 47. Services include: remedial math, other testing accommodations, reading machines, tape recorders, diagnostic testing service, untimed tests, note-taking services, oral tests, learning center, readers, extended time for tests, tutors, early syllabus, priority seating, texts on tape, typist/scribe, exams on tape or computer, other testing accomodations, other. **Library:** Number of titles: 159,076; number of current serial subscriptions: 1,871. **Information technology resources:** Students are not required to lease or own a computer. Number of campus computers available to all students: 325. School has a wireless network. Approximate number of users that can be accommodated: 200. Proportion of college-owned housing units wired for high-speed internet access: 100%. **Campus safety:** Security services offered: 24-hour foot and vehicle patrols, late-night transport/escort service, 24-hour emergency telephones, lighted pathways/sidewalks, controlled dormitory access (key, security card, etc).

TRANSFER AND INTERNATIONAL STUDENTS

Transfer students: May apply for admission for the following academic terms: Fall, Winter, Spring, Summer. Applicants need a minimum number of credits to apply. For fall 2005: Transfer applications received: 715. Transfer applicants offered admission: 467. Transfer applicants enrolled: 268. **International students:** Number of foreign undergraduates: 32 (2% of student body). Number of countries represented: 24. Minimum TOEFL score required: 520 (paper); 190 (computer).

Northeastern Illinois University

- **Address:** 5500 N. St. Louis Avenue, Chicago, IL 60625
- **Website:** http://www.neiu.edu
- **Public**
- **Enrollment:** 5,207 full-time; 4,211 part-time

KEY STATS

- ✔ **U.S News College Ranking:** fourth tier, Universities–Master's (Midwest)
- ✔ **ACT Score (25th/75th percentile):** 16-21
- ✔ **Tuition:** 2006-2007: $5,549 in state, $9,629 out of state
- **Selectivity:** Less selective   **Room/board:** N/A
- **Acceptance rate:** 75%   **Average debt:** $12,284
- **Student/faculty ratio:** 16/1   **Proportion who borrowed:** 34%

UNDERGRADUATE STUDENT BODY STATS

2005-2006 enrollment: 5,207 full-time; 4,211 part-time. Men: 38%; women: 62%. **Ethnic makeup:** African American: 12%; Asian American: 11%; Hispanic: 29%; White: 47%; International: 2%.

ADMISSIONS FACTS AND FIGURES

Phone: (773) 442-4000. **Email:** admrec@neiu.edu. **Website:** http://www.neiu.edu. **Application deadlines for fall 2007:** Regular decision: July 1. Early decision: Not offered. Early action: Not offered. Admission can be deferred. **Application fee:** $25. Common application is not accepted. **To apply online, go to:** https://apply.embark.com/ugrad/neiu/51. **Admissions requirements/recommendations:** High school units required (recommended): English: 4; Mathematics: 3; Science: 3; Social studies: 3; Total units: 15. Tests: The college uses SAT or ACT scores in admissions decisions. ACT required. For admission to the fall 2007 entering class, the school will accept: ACT with writing, ACT without writing. Campus visit: Recommended. Admissions interview: Neither required nor recommended. Off-campus interview: Not available. **Factors that count in admissions decisions:** *Academic:* Secondary school record: Very important. Class rank: Very important. Letters of recommendation: Not considered. Standardized test scores: Very important. Essay: Not considered. *Nonacademic:* Interview: Not considered. Extracurricular activities: Not considered. Talent/ability: Not considered. Character/personal qualities: Not considered. Alumni/ae relationship: Not considered. Geographical residence: Not considered. State residency: Not considered. Religious affiliation/commitment: Not considered. Minority status: Not considered. Volunteer work: Not considered. Work experience: Not considered. **Admissions statistics for the fall 2005 entering class:** Total applicants: 3,071. Total accepted: 2,298. Freshmen enrolled: 1,058; 1% were from out of state. Overall acceptance rate: 75%. **Credentials of fall 2005 freshmen:** 7% ranked in the top 10 percent of their high school class; 16% were in the top 25 percent, and 55% were in the top half. (Proportion submitting class standing: 78%.) **Average high school grade point average:** 2.8. **First-year students submitting ACT scores:** 90%. Scores (25/75 percentile): English: 14-21, Math: 15-20, Composite: 16-21.

ACADEMICS

Year founded: 1867. **Academic calendar:** Semester. **Degrees offered:** bachelor's, master's. **Most popular majors:** 17% education, 16% liberal arts and sciences studies, and humanities, 14% business, management, marketing, and related support services, 9% social sciences, 7% computer and information sciences and support services. **Major fields of study:** area, ethnic, cultural, and gender studies; biological and biomedical sciences; computer and information sciences and support services; English language and literature/letters; foreign languages, literatures, and linguistics; history; mathematics and statistics; natural resources and conservation; philosophy and religious studies; physical sciences; psychology; public administration and social service professions; science technologies/technicians; security and protective services; social sciences; visual and performing arts. **Areas of required coursework:** arts/fine arts, humanities, mathematics, English (including composition), sciences (biological or physical), social science. **Pre-professional programs:** pre-law, pre-dentistry, pre-medicine, pre-veterinary science, pre-pharmacy. **Special academic programs:** accelerated program, cooperative (work-study plan) program, distance learning, double major, dual enrollment, exchange student program (domestic), honors program, independent study, internships, student-designed major, study abroad, teacher certificate program. **Teacher certification offered in:** early childhood, special education, elementary, middle/junior high, secondary, bilingual/bicultural. **Reserve Officers Training Corps (ROTC):** Army ROTC: Offered at cooperating institution (University of Illinois at Chicago); Air Force ROTC: Offered at cooperating institution (Illinois Institute of Technology). **Faculty and instruction (2005-2006):** Total instructional faculty: 415 full-time, 265 part-time (52% men; 48% women; 26% minorities). Full-time faculty with Ph.D. or other terminal degree: 72%. Student/faculty ratio: 16/1. Classes of fewer than 20 students: 45%; of 20 to 49 students: 52%; of 50 or more students: 3%. **Advanced Placement and International Baccalaureate credit:** AP tests may be used for: Credit only. Scores accepted: 4, 5. International Baccalaureate exams may be used for: Credit only. **Freshmen returning for sophomore year:** 69%. **Graduation rates:** Four-year: 2%; five-year: 10%; six-year: 16%. **Graduate study:** 25% of students pursue further study within one year. Fields in which graduates pursue further study: Master of Business Administration (MBA), 21%; law, 2%; medicine, 2%.

COSTS AND FINANCIAL AID

Financial aid office: (773) 442-5000. **Expenses (2006-2007):** Tuition and fees 2006-2007: $5,549 in state, $9,629 out of state; room/board: N/A. **Financial aid:** Priority filing date for institution's financial aid form: March 1. In 2005-2006, 62% of undergraduates applied for financial aid. Of those, 50% were determined to have financial need; 14% had their need fully met. Average financial aid package (proportion receiving): $6,870 (49%). Average amount of gift aid, such as scholarships or grants (proportion receiving): $5,302 (43%). Average amount of self-help aid, such as work study or loans (proportion receiving): $3,968 (18%). Average need-based loan (excluding PLUS or other private loans): $3,849. Among students who received need-based aid, the average percentage of need met: 64%. Among students who received aid based on merit, the average award (and the proportion receiving): $1,377 (3%). The average athletic scholarship (and the proportion receiving): $0 (0%). Average amount of debt of borrowers graduating in 2005: $12,284. Proportion who borrowed: 34%.

CAMPUS LIFE AND EXTRACURRICULAR ACTIVITIES

Clubs and organizations: Number of student organizations: 66. Activities include: dance, drama/theater, jazz band, literary magazine, music ensembles, radio station, student government, student newspaper. Number of fraternities: 1; sororities: 4.

SERVICES AND FACILITIES

Basic services: nonremedial tutoring, women's center, placement service, day care, health service, health insurance. **Remedial assistance:** reading, math, writing, study skills. **Counseling services:** minority student, career, military, personal, veteran student, academic, older student, psychological, birth control, religious. **For learning-disabled students:** School does not offer a structured program with separate admission and additional fees. Total undergraduates in learning-disabled program or receiving services: 312. Services include: remedial math, remedial English, reading machines, remedial reading, tape recorders, other special classes, untimed tests, note-taking services, oral tests, learning center, readers, extended time for tests, tutors, priority registration, priority seating, proofreading services, texts on tape, typist/scribe, exams on tape or computer. **Library:** Number of titles: 716,357; number of current serial subscriptions: 5,587. **Information technology resources:** Students are not required to lease or own a computer. Number of campus computers available to all students: 430. School does not have a wireless network. **Campus safety:** Security services offered: 24-hour foot and vehicle patrols, late-night transport/escort service, 24-hour emergency telephones, lighted pathways/sidewalks.

TRANSFER AND INTERNATIONAL STUDENTS

Transfer students: May apply for admission for the following academic terms: Fall, Spring, Summer. Applicants need a minimum number of credits to apply. For fall 2005: Transfer applications received: 2,011. Transfer applicants offered admission: 1,541. Transfer applicants enrolled: 1,200. **International students:** Number of foreign undergraduates: 142 (2% of student body). Minimum TOEFL score required: 500 (paper); 173 (computer).

Northern Illinois University

- **Address:** PO Box 3001, DeKalb, IL 60115
- **Website:** http://www.niu.edu/
- **Public**
- **Enrollment:** 16,609 full-time; 1,858 part-time

KEY STATS

✔ **U.S News College Ranking:** fourth tier, National Universities
✔ **ACT Score (25th/75th percentile):** 19-24
✔ **Tuition:** 2006-2007: $7,871 in state, $13,421 out of state

Selectivity: Selective	**Room/board:** $7,500
Acceptance rate: 66%	**Average debt:** $17,773
Student/faculty ratio: 17/1	**Proportion who borrowed:** 60%

UNDERGRADUATE STUDENT BODY STATS

2005-2006 enrollment: 16,609 full-time; 1,858 part-time. Men: 48%; women: 52%. **Ethnic makeup:** Asian American: 13%; White: 88%.

ADMISSIONS FACTS AND FIGURES

Phone: (815) 753-0446. **Email:** admission-info@niu.edu. **Website:** http://www.niu.edu/. **Application deadlines for fall 2007:** Regular decision: August 1. Early decision: Not offered. Early action: Not offered. Admission can be deferred. Common application is not accepted. **Admissions requirements/recommendations:** High school units required (recommended): English: 4; Mathematics: 2 (4); Science: 2 (4); Foreign language: 1 (2); Social studies: 2 (3); History: 1; Total units: 15. Tests: The college uses SAT or ACT scores in admissions decisions. Either SAT or ACT required. For admission to the fall 2007 entering class, the school will accept: ACT with writing, ACT without writing. Campus visit: Recommended. Admissions interview: Neither required nor recommended. Off-campus interview: Not available. **Factors that count in admissions decisions:** *Academic:* Secondary school record: Very important. Class rank: Very important. Letters of recommendation: Considered. Standardized test scores: Very important. Essay: Considered. *Nonacademic:* Interview: Considered. Extracurricular activities: Considered. Talent/ability: Considered. Character/personal qualities: Not considered. Alumni/ae relationship: Not considered. Geographical residence: Not considered. State residency: Not considered. Religious affiliation/commitment: Not considered. Minority status: Considered. Volunteer work: Not considered. Work experience: Not considered. **Admissions statistics for the fall 2005 entering class:** Total applicants: 15,007. Total accepted: 9,917. Freshmen enrolled: 3,179; 3% were from out of state. Overall acceptance rate: 66%. **Size of waiting list:** 800 applicants; enrolled from waiting list: 0. **Credentials of fall 2005 freshmen:** 9% ranked in the top 10 percent of their high school class; 31% were in the top 25 percent, and 71% were in the top half. (Proportion submitting class standing: 96%.) **First-year students who submitted SAT scores:** 3%. Scores (25/75 percentile): Verbal: N/A, Math: N/A, Combined: N/A. **First-year students submitting ACT scores:** 99%. Scores (25/75 percentile): English: 19-25, Math: 18-25, Composite: 19-24.

ACADEMICS

Year founded: 1895. **Academic calendar:** Semester. **Degrees offered:** bachelor's, master's, first professional, doctorate. **Most popular majors:** 7% elementary education and teaching, 5% accounting, 5% management science, 5% marketing/marketing management, 5% psychology. **Major fields of study:** biological and biomedical sciences; business, management, marketing, and related support services; communication, journalism, and related programs; computer and information sciences and support services; education; engineering; engineering technologies/technicians; English language and literature/letters; family and consumer sciences/human sciences; foreign languages, literatures, and linguistics; health professions and related clinical sciences; history; liberal arts and sciences studies, and humanities; mathematics and statistics; philosophy and religious studies; physical sciences; psychology; social sciences; visual and performing arts. **Areas of required coursework:** humanities, mathematics, English (including composition), philosophy, foreign languages, history, social science. **Pre-professional programs:** pre-law, pre-dentistry, pre-medicine. **Special academic programs:** accelerated program, cooperative (work-study plan) program, cross-registration, distance learning, double major, external degree program, honors program, independent study, internships, liberal arts/career combination, student-designed major, study abroad, teacher certificate program. **Teacher certification offered in:** early childhood, special education, elementary, middle/junior high, adult education, secondary. **Reserve Officers Training Corps**

(ROTC): Army ROTC: Offered on campus. **Faculty and instruction (2005-2006):** Total instructional faculty: 894 full-time, 299 part-time (54% men; 46% women; 12% minorities). Full-time faculty with Ph.D. or other terminal degree: 83%. Student/faculty ratio: 17/1. Classes of fewer than 20 students: 39%; of 20 to 49 students: 49%; of 50 or more students: 12%. **Advanced Placement and International Baccalaureate credit:** AP tests may be used for: Credit and/or placement. **Freshmen returning for sophomore year:** 78%. **Graduation rates:** Four-year: 25%; five-year: 48%; six-year: 53%. **Graduate study:** 10% of students pursue further study immediately upon graduation.

COSTS AND FINANCIAL AID

Financial aid office: (815) 753-1300. **Expenses (2006-2007):** Tuition and fees 2006-2007: $7,871 in state, $13,421 out of state; room/board: $7,500. Estimated books and supplies: $1,200; transportation: $500; personal expenses: $1,684. **Financial aid:** Priority filing date for institution's financial aid form: March 1. In 2005-2006, 76% of undergraduates applied for financial aid. Of those, 54% were determined to have financial need; 18% had their need fully met. Average financial aid package (proportion receiving): $9,489 (52%). Average amount of gift aid, such as scholarships or grants (proportion receiving): $5,859 (33%). Average amount of self-help aid, such as work study or loans (proportion receiving): $3,679 (46%). Average need-based loan (excluding PLUS or other private loans): $3,968. Among students who received need-based aid, the average percentage of need met: 70%. Among students who received aid based on merit, the average award (and the proportion receiving): $1,230 (2%). The average athletic scholarship (and the proportion receiving): $11,571 (2%). Average amount of debt of borrowers graduating in 2005: $17,773. Proportion who borrowed: 60%.

CAMPUS LIFE AND EXTRACURRICULAR ACTIVITIES

Campus housing available: coed dorms, sorority housing, fraternity housing, apartments for married students, special housing for disabled students, special housing for international students. Students who live in college-owned, operated, or affiliated housing: 33%. **Student employment:** During the 2005-2006 academic year, 24% of undergraduates worked on campus. Average per-year earnings: $1,700. **Clubs and organizations:** Number of student organizations: 400. Activities include: choral groups, concert band, dance, drama/theater, jazz band, marching band, music ensembles, musical theater, radio station, student government, student newspaper, student film society, symphony orchestra, television station. Number of fraternities: 21; sororities: 16. Proportion of men in fraternities: 11%; of women in sororities: 7%. Average proportion of students who stay on campus on weekends: 60%. **Sports program (2005-2006):** Member of NCAA I. *Men's intercollegiate varsity sports:* baseball, basketball, football, golf, soccer, tennis, wrestling. *Women's intercollegiate varsity sports:* basketball, cross-country, golf, gymnastics, soccer, softball, tennis, track and field (indoor), track and field (outdoor), volleyball.

SERVICES AND FACILITIES

Basic services: nonremedial tutoring, women's center, placement service, day care, health service, health insurance. **Remedial assistance:** reading, math, writing, study skills. **Counseling services:** minority student, career, personal, veteran student, academic, older student, psychological, birth control, religious. **For learning-disabled students:** School does not offer a structured program with separate admission and additional fees. Total undergraduates in learning-disabled program or receiving services: 163. Services include: reading machines, tape recorders, note-taking services, learning center, readers, extended time for tests, tutors, priority registration, priority seating, substitution of courses, texts on tape, exams on tape or computer. **Library:** Number of titles: 2,181,108; number of current serial subscriptions: 26,971. **Information technology resources:** Students are not required to lease or own a computer. School has a wireless network. Approximate number of users that can be accommodated: 1,000. Proportion of college-owned housing units wired for high-speed internet access: 100%. **Campus safety:** Security services offered: 24-hour foot and vehicle patrols, late-night transport/escort service, 24-hour emergency telephones, lighted pathways/sidewalks, controlled dormitory access (key, security card, etc).

TRANSFER AND INTERNATIONAL STUDENTS

Transfer students: May apply for admission for the following academic terms: Fall, Spring, Summer. Applicants need a minimum number of credits to apply. For fall 2005: Transfer applications received: 5,576. Transfer applicants offered admission: 3,858. Transfer applicants enrolled: 2,229. **International students:** Number of foreign undergraduates: 0. Number of countries represented: 100. Minimum TOEFL score required: 550 (paper); 197 (computer). Average TOEFL score: 560 (paper).

North Park University

- **Address:** 3225 W. Foster Avenue, Chicago, IL 60625-4895
- **Website:** http://www.northpark.edu
- **Private; Religious affiliation:** Evangelical Covenant Church
- **Enrollment:** 1,575 full-time; 325 part-time

KEY STATS
✔ **U.S News College Ranking:** 44, Universities–Master's (Midwest)
✔ **ACT Score (25th/75th percentile):** 19-26
✔ **Tuition:** 2006-2007: $15,100

Selectivity: Selective	**Room/board:** $7,550
Acceptance rate: 69%	**Average debt:** $14,978
Student/faculty ratio: 12/1	**Proportion who borrowed:** 68%

UNDERGRADUATE STUDENT BODY STATS
2005-2006 enrollment: 1,575 full-time; 325 part-time. Men: 36%; women: 64%. **Ethnic makeup:** African American: 12%; American-Indian: 1%; Asian American: 10%; Hispanic: 9%; White: 63%; International: 5%. **Religious preference:** Roman Catholic: 14%; Protestant: 32%; Jewish: 1%; No preference: 10%; Unknown: 12%; Evangelical Covenant Church: 24%.

ADMISSIONS FACTS AND FIGURES
Phone: (773) 244-5500. **Email:** admissions@northpark.edu. **Website:** http://www.northpark.edu. **Application deadlines for fall 2007:** Regular decision: June 1. Early decision: Not offered. Early action: Not offered. Admission can be deferred. **Application fee:** $40. Common application is not accepted. **Admissions requirements/recommendations:** High school units required (recommended): English: 3 (3); Mathematics: 3 (3); Foreign language: 1 (1); Social studies: 1 (1); Total units: 4 (4). Tests: The college uses SAT or ACT scores in admissions decisions. Either SAT or ACT required. For admission to the fall 2007 entering class, the school will accept ACT without writing. Campus visit: Recommended. Admissions interview: Recommended. Off-campus interview: May be arranged. **Factors that count in admissions decisions: Academic:** Secondary school record: Very important. Class rank: Very important. Letters of recommendation: Very important. Standardized test scores: Very important. Essay: Very important. *Nonacademic:* Interview: Considered. Extracurricular activities: Important. Talent/ability: Important. Character/personal qualities: Important. Alumni/ae relationship: Considered. Geographical residence: Considered. State residency: Not considered. Religious affiliation/commitment: Not considered. Minority status: Considered. Volunteer work: Important. Work experience: Important. **Other schools with the greatest overlap in applicants:** Bethel University; DePaul University; Loyola University Chicago; Northern Illinois University; University of Illinois–Chicago. **Admissions statistics for the fall 2005 entering class:** Total applicants: 1,386. Total accepted: 957. Freshmen enrolled: 359; 45% were from out of state. Overall acceptance rate: 69%. **Credentials of fall 2005 freshmen:** 16% ranked in the top 10 percent of their high school class; 42% were in the top 25 percent, and 77% were in the top half. (Proportion submitting class standing: 82%.) **Average high school grade point average:** 3.2. **First-year students who submitted SAT scores:** 24%. Scores (25/75 percentile): Verbal: 520-640, Math: 490-650, Combined: 1010-1290. **First-year students submitting ACT scores:** 79%. Scores (25/75 percentile): English: 18-26, Math: 17-24, Composite: 19-26.

ACADEMICS
Year founded: 1891. **Academic calendar:** Semester. **Degrees offered:** certificate, bachelor's, post-bachelor's certificate, master's, doctorate. **Most popular majors:** 14% nursing/registered nurse training (R.N., A.S.N., B.S.N., M.S.N.), 7% biology/biological sciences, 7% communication studies/speech communication and rhetoric, 7% management science, 5% elementary education and teaching. **Major fields of study:** area, ethnic, cultural, and gender studies; biological and biomedical sciences; business, management, marketing, and related support services; communication, journalism, and related programs; education; English language and literature/letters; foreign languages, literatures, and linguistics; health professions and related clinical sciences; history; mathematics and statistics; multi/interdisciplinary studies; philosophy and religious studies; physical sciences; psychology; social sciences; theology and religious vocations; visual and performing arts. **Areas of required coursework:** arts/fine arts, mathematics, English (including composition), foreign languages, sciences (biological or physical). **Pre-professional programs:** pre-law, pre-dentistry, pre-medicine, pre-theology, pre-veterinary science, pre-pharmacy. **Special academic programs:** double major, English as

a Second Language (ESL), honors program, independent study, internships, student-designed major, study abroad, teacher certificate program. **Teacher certification offered in:** early childhood, elementary, middle/junior high, secondary. **Faculty and instruction (2005-2006):** Total instructional faculty: 122 full-time, 217 part-time (50% men; 50% women; 16% minorities). Full-time faculty with Ph.D. or other terminal degree: 73%. Student/faculty ratio: 12/1. Classes of fewer than 20 students: 56%; of 20 to 49 students: 43%; of 50 or more students: 2%. **Advanced Placement and International Baccalaureate credit:** AP tests may be used for: Credit and/or placement. Scores accepted: 3, 4, 5. International Baccalaureate exams may be used for: Credit and/or placement. **Freshmen returning for sophomore year:** 71%. **Graduation rates:** Four-year: 41%; five-year: 54%; six-year: 53%. **Graduate study:** 12% of students pursue further study immediately upon graduation; 15% within five years. Fields in which graduates pursue further study: Master of Business Administration (MBA), 15%; law, 1%; medicine, 3%; dentistry, 1%; theology (or the seminary), 5%.

COSTS AND FINANCIAL AID
Financial aid office: (773) 244-5526. **Expenses (2006-2007):** Tuition and fees 2006-2007: $15,100; room/board: $7,550. Estimated books and supplies: $950; transportation: $300; personal expenses: $1,350. **Financial aid:** Priority filing date for institution's financial aid form: April 1; deadline: June 1. Average amount of debt of borrowers graduating in 2005: $14,978. Proportion who borrowed: 68%.

CAMPUS LIFE AND EXTRACURRICULAR ACTIVITIES
Campus housing available: women's dorms, men's dorms, apartment for single students. Students who live in college-owned, operated, or affiliated housing: 63%. **Student employment:** During the 2005-2006 academic year, 29% of undergraduates worked on campus. Average per-year earnings: $2,200. Activities include: choral groups, concert band, drama/theater, jazz band, literary magazine, music ensembles, musical theater, opera, pep band, student government, student newspaper, symphony orchestra, yearbook. Number of fraternities: 0; sororities: 0. Average proportion of students who stay on campus on weekends: 80%. **Sports program (2005-2006):** Member of NCAA III. *Men's intercollegiate varsity sports:* baseball, basketball, cross-country, football, golf, soccer, track and field (indoor), track and field (outdoor). *Women's intercollegiate varsity sports:* basketball, cross-country, golf, soccer, softball, tennis, track and field (indoor), track and field (outdoor), volleyball.

SERVICES AND FACILITIES
Basic services: nonremedial tutoring, placement service, health service, health insurance. **Remedial assistance:** reading, math, writing, study skills. **Counseling services:** career, personal, academic, psychological, religious. **For learning-disabled students:** School does not offer a structured program with separate admission and additional fees. Total undergraduates in learning-disabled program or receiving services: 35. Services include: remedial math, remedial English, remedial reading, tape recorders, untimed tests, note-taking services, oral tests, learning center, extended time for tests, tutors, texts on tape, other testing accomodations. **Library:** Number of titles: 225,000; number of current serial subscriptions: 975. **Information technology resources:** Students are not required to lease or own a computer. School has a wireless network. Proportion of college-owned housing units wired for high-speed internet access: 100%. **Campus safety:** Security services offered: 24-hour foot and vehicle patrols, 24-hour emergency telephones, lighted pathways/sidewalks, controlled dormitory access (key, security card, etc).

TRANSFER AND INTERNATIONAL STUDENTS
Transfer students: May apply for admission for the following academic terms: Fall, Spring, Summer. Applicants need a minimum number of credits to apply. For fall 2005: Transfer applications received: 632. Transfer applicants offered admission: 394. Transfer applicants enrolled: 246. **International students:** Number of foreign undergraduates: 46 (5% of student body). Number of countries represented: 28. Minimum TOEFL score required: 550 (paper); 213 (computer).

Northwestern University

- **Address:** 633 Clark Street, Evanston, IL 60208
- **Website:** http://www.northwestern.edu
- **Private**
- **Enrollment:** 7,872 full-time; 151 part-time

KEY STATS

- ✔ **U.S News College Ranking:** 14, National Universities
- ✔ **SAT Score (25th/75th percentile):** 1320-1500
- ✔ **Tuition:** 2006-2007: $33,559
  - **Selectivity:** Most selective
  - **Acceptance rate:** 30%
  - **Student/faculty ratio:** 7/1
  - **Room/board:** $10,266
  - **Average debt:** $18,362
  - **Proportion who borrowed:** 46%

UNDERGRADUATE STUDENT BODY STATS

2005-2006 enrollment: 7,872 full-time; 151 part-time. Men: 47%; women: 53%. **Ethnic makeup:** African American: 5%; Asian American: 17%; Hispanic: 6%; White: 66%; International: 5%. **Religious preference:** Roman Catholic: 22%; Protestant: 25%; Jewish: 13%; Muslim: 1%; Hindu: 3%; Buddhist: 1%; No preference: 25%; Other: 10%.

ADMISSIONS FACTS AND FIGURES

Phone: (847) 491-7271. **Email:** ug-admission@northwestern.edu. **Website:** http://www.northwestern.edu. **Application deadlines for fall 2007:** Regular decision: January 1; decision sent by April 15. Early decision: Send application by: November 1; Decision sent by: December 15. Early action: Not offered. Admission can be deferred. **Application fee:** $65. Common application is accepted. **To apply online, go to:** http://www.ugadm.northwestern.edu. **Admissions requirements/recommendations:** High school units required (recommended): English: (4); Mathematics: (3); Science: (2); Foreign language: (2); Social studies: (2); Academic electives: (1); Total units: (16). Tests: The college uses SAT or ACT scores in admissions decisions. Either SAT or ACT required. For admission to the fall 2007 entering class, the school will accept: ACT with writing, the new SAT. Campus visit: Recommended. Admissions interview: Neither required nor recommended. Off-campus interview: May be arranged. **Factors that count in admissions decisions:** *Academic:* Secondary school record: Very important. Class rank: Very important. Letters of recommendation: Important. Standardized test scores: Very important. Essay: Very important. *Nonacademic:* Interview: Considered. Extracurricular activities: Important. Talent/ability: Important. Character/personal qualities: Important. Alumni/ae relationship: Considered. Geographical residence: Not considered. State residency: Not considered. Religious affiliation/commitment: Not considered. Minority status: Considered. Volunteer work: Considered. Work experience: Considered. **Other schools with the greatest overlap in applicants:** Cornell University; Duke University; University of Michigan–Ann Arbor; University of Pennsylvania; Washington University in St. Louis. **Admissions statistics for the fall 2005 entering class:** Total applicants: 16,221. Total accepted: 4,819. Freshmen enrolled: 1,952; 75% were from out of state. Accepted through early-decision or early-action plans: 26%. Overall acceptance rate: 30%. Early-decision acceptance rate: 49%. Non-early acceptance rate: 28%. **Size of waiting list:** 1272 applicants; enrolled from waiting list: 12. **Credentials of fall 2005 freshmen:** 82% ranked in the top 10 percent of their high school class; 96% were in the top 25 percent, and 100% were in the top half. (Proportion submitting class standing: 53%.) **First-year students who submitted SAT scores:** 84%. Scores (25/75 percentile): Verbal: 650-740, Math: 670-760, Combined: 1320-1500. **First-year students submitting ACT scores:** 51%. Scores (25/75 percentile): English: 29-34, Math: 28-34, Composite: 29-33.

ACADEMICS

Year founded: 1851. **Academic calendar:** Quarter. **Degrees offered:** certificate, bachelor's, master's, post-master's certificate, first professional, doctorate. **Most popular majors:** 19% communication, journalism, and related programs, 14% engineering, 10% visual and performing arts, 9% economics, 9% psychology. **Major fields of study:** area, ethnic, cultural, and gender studies; biological and biomedical sciences; business, management, marketing, and related support services; communication, journalism, and related programs; computer and information sciences and support services; education; engineering; English language and literature/letters; foreign languages, literatures, and linguistics; health professions and related clinical sciences; history; legal professions and studies; liberal arts and sciences studies, and humanities; mathematics and statistics; multi/interdisciplinary studies; natural resources and conservation; philosophy and religious studies; physical sciences; psychology; public administration and social service professions; social sciences; visual and performing arts. **Areas of required coursework:** arts/fine arts, humanities, mathematics, English (including composition), foreign languages, sciences (biological or physical), social science. **Pre-professional programs:** pre-law, pre-medicine. **Special academic programs:** accelerated program, cooperative (work-study plan) program, double major, honors program, independent study, internships, liberal arts/career combination, student-designed major, study abroad, teacher certificate program. **Teacher certification offered in:** secondary. **Cooperative education programs:** engineering. **Reserve Officers Training Corps (ROTC):** Army ROTC: Offered at cooperating institution (University of Illinois, Chicago); Navy ROTC: Offered on campus; Air Force ROTC: Offered at cooperating institution (Illinois Institute of Technology). **Faculty and instruction (2005-2006):** Total instructional faculty: 938 full-time, 207 part-time (69% men; 31% women; 14% minorities). Full-time faculty with Ph.D. or other terminal degree: 100%. Student/faculty ratio: 7/1. Classes of fewer than 20 students: 72%; of 20 to 49 students: 19%; of 50 or more students: 9%. **Advanced Placement and International Baccalaureate credit:** AP tests may be used for: Credit and/or placement. Scores accepted: 4, 5. International Baccalaureate exams may be used for: Credit and/or placement. **Freshmen returning for sophomore year:** 97%. **Graduation rates:** Four-year: 85%; five-year: 93%; six-year: 93%. **Graduate study:** 22% of students pursue further study within one year. Fields in which graduates pursue further study: law, 4%; medicine, 6%.

COSTS AND FINANCIAL AID

Financial aid office: (847) 491-7400. **Expenses (2006-2007):** Tuition and fees 2006-2007: $33,559; room/board: $10,266. Estimated books and supplies: $1,488; transportation: $400; personal expenses: $1,698. **Financial aid:** Priority filing date for institution's financial aid form: February 1; deadline: February 1. In 2005-2006, 49% of undergraduates applied for financial aid. Of those, 43% were determined to have financial need; 100% had their need fully met. Average financial aid package (proportion receiving): $25,831 (43%). Average amount of gift aid, such as scholarships or grants (proportion receiving): $21,489 (42%). Average amount of self-help aid, such as work study or loans (proportion receiving): $6,066 (40%). Average need-based loan (excluding PLUS or other private loans): $4,503. Among students who received need-based aid, the average percentage of need met: 100%. Among students who received aid based on merit, the average award (and the proportion receiving): $2,353 (2%). The average athletic scholarship (and the proportion receiving): $27,876 (5%). Average amount of debt of borrowers graduating in 2005: $18,362. Proportion who borrowed: 46%.

CAMPUS LIFE AND EXTRACURRICULAR ACTIVITIES

Campus housing available: coed dorms, women's dorms, men's dorms, sorority housing, fraternity housing, other housing options. Students who live in college-owned, operated, or affiliated housing: 65%. **Student employment:** During the 2005-2006 academic year, 49% of undergraduates worked on campus. Average per-year earnings: $1,257. **Clubs and organizations:** Number of student organizations: 415. Activities include: choral groups, concert band, dance, drama/theater, jazz band, literary magazine, marching band, music ensembles, musical theater, opera, pep band, radio station, student government, student newspaper, student film society, symphony orchestra, television station, yearbook. Number of fraternities: 23; sororities: 19. Proportion of men in fraternities: 32%; of women in sororities: 38%. **Sports program (2005-2006):** Member of NCAA I. *Men's intercollegiate varsity sports:* baseball, basketball, football, golf, soccer, swimming and diving, tennis, wrestling. *Women's intercollegiate varsity sports:* basketball, cross-country, fencing, field hockey, golf, lacrosse, soccer, softball, swimming and diving, tennis, volleyball.

SERVICES AND FACILITIES

Basic services: nonremedial tutoring, women's center, placement service, health service, health insurance. **Counseling services:** minority student, career, personal, academic, psychological, birth control, religious. **For learning-disabled students:** School does not offer a structured program with separate admission and additional fees. Services include: reading machines, tape recorders, diagnostic testing service, note-taking services, oral tests, readers, extended time for tests, priority registration, priority seating, texts on tape, other testing accomodations, other. **Library:** Number of titles: 4,603,824; number of current serial subscriptions: 41,693. **Information technology resources:** Students are not required to lease or own a computer. Number of campus computers available to all students: 725. School has a wireless network. Proportion of college-owned housing units wired for high-speed internet access: 100%. **Campus safety:** Security services offered: 24-hour foot and vehicle patrols, late-night transport/escort service, 24-hour emergency telephones, lighted pathways/sidewalks, student patrols, controlled dormitory access (key, security card, etc.).

TRANSFER AND INTERNATIONAL STUDENTS
Transfer students: May apply for admission for the following academic terms: Fall, Winter, Spring, Summer. Applicants need a minimum number of credits to apply. For fall 2005: Transfer applications received: 774. Transfer applicants offered admission: 137. Transfer applicants enrolled: 76. **International students:** Number of foreign undergraduates: 410 (5% of student body). Number of countries represented: 48. Minimum TOEFL score required: 600 (paper); 250 (computer). Average TOEFL score: 626 (paper).

Olivet Nazarene University

- **Address:** 1 University Avenue, Bourbonnais, IL 60914
- **Website:** http://www.olivet.edu
- **Private; Religious affiliation:** Church of the Nazarene
- **Enrollment:** 2,582 full-time; 320 part-time

KEY STATS
✔ **U.S News College Ranking:** 53, Universities–Master's (Midwest)
✔ **ACT Score (25th/75th percentile):** 21-27
✔ **Tuition:** 2006-2007: $17,590

Selectivity: More selective	**Room/board:** $6,400
Acceptance rate: 59%	**Average debt:** $20,062
Student/faculty ratio: 22/1	**Proportion who borrowed:** 75%

UNDERGRADUATE STUDENT BODY STATS
2005-2006 enrollment: 2,582 full-time; 320 part-time. Men: 37%; women: 63%. **Ethnic makeup:** African American: 7%; Asian American: 1%; Hispanic: 3%; White: 88%; International: 1%. **Religious preference:** Roman Catholic: 6%; Protestant: 44%; Unknown: 3%; Church of the Nazarene: 47%.

ADMISSIONS FACTS AND FIGURES
Phone: (815) 939-5011. **Email:** admissions@olivet.edu. **Website:** http://www.olivet.edu. **Application deadlines for fall 2007:** Regular decision: May 15. Early decision: Not offered. Early action: Send application by: December 10; Decision sent by: February 1. Admission cannot be deferred. Common application is not accepted. **To apply online, go to:** http://www.olivet.edu/admissions/application/adm_undergrad_apply.asp. **Admissions requirements/recommendations:** High school units required (recommended): English: 4 (4); Mathematics: 3 (3); Science: 3 (3); Foreign language: 0 (2); Social studies: 3 (3); History: 2 (2); Academic electives: 0 (0); Total units: 15 (17). Tests: The college uses SAT or ACT scores in admissions decisions. ACT required. For admission to the fall 2007 entering class, the school will accept: ACT with writing, ACT without writing. Campus visit: Recommended. Admissions interview: Recommended. Off-campus interview: May be arranged. **Factors that count in admissions decisions:** *Academic:* Secondary school record: Very important. Class rank: Very important. Letters of recommendation: Very important. Standardized test scores: Very important. Essay: Important. *Nonacademic:* Interview: Very important. Extracurricular activities: Important. Talent/ability: Important. Character/personal qualities: Very important. Alumni/ae relationship: Not considered. Geographical residence: Not considered. State residency: Not considered. Religious affiliation/commitment: Considered. Minority status: Not considered. Volunteer work: Considered. Work experience: Considered. **Other schools with the greatest overlap in applicants:** Calvin College; Taylor University; University of Illinois–Urbana-Champaign; Wheaton College. **Admissions statistics for the fall 2005 entering class:** Total applicants: 2,543. Total accepted: 1,493. Freshmen enrolled: 671; 52% were from out of state. Overall acceptance rate: 59%. Non-early acceptance rate: 59%. **Credentials of fall 2005 freshmen:** 25% ranked in the top 10 percent of their high school class; 53% were in the top 25 percent, and 80% were in the top half. (Proportion submitting class standing: 74%.) **Average high school grade point average:** 3.5. **First-year students who submitted SAT scores:** 20%. Scores (25/75 percentile): Verbal: 500-620, Math: 480-580, Combined: 980-1200. **First-year students submitting ACT scores:** 98%. Scores (25/75 percentile): English: 20-27, Math: 20-26, Composite: 21-27.

ACADEMICS
Year founded: 1907. **Academic calendar:** Semester. **Degrees offered:** associate, bachelor's, master's. **Most popular majors:** 15% business, management, marketing, and related support services; 15% education, 11% philosophy and religious studies, 9% health professions and related clinical sciences, 7% psychology. **Major fields of study:** architecture and related services; biological and biomedical sciences; business, management, marketing, and related support services; communication, journalism, and related programs; computer and information sciences and support services; education; English language and literature/letters; foreign languages, literatures, and linguistics; health professions and related clinical sciences; history; liberal arts and sciences studies, and humanities; mathematics and statistics; parks, recreation, leisure, and fitness studies; philosophy and religious studies; physical sciences; psychology; public administration and social service professions; security and protective services; social sciences; theology and religious vocations; visual and performing arts. **Areas of required coursework:** arts/fine arts, humanities, mathematics, English (including composition), foreign languages, sciences (biological or physical), history, social science, other. **Pre-professional programs:** pre-law, pre-dentistry, pre-medicine, pre-veterinary science, pre-optometry, pre-pharmacy, other. **Special academic programs (% participation):** accelerated program (18%), distance learning (5%), double major (15%), honors program (12%), independent study (40%), internships (85%), student-designed major (4%), study abroad (25%), teacher certificate program (17%). **Teacher certification offered in:** early childhood, elementary, middle/junior high, secondary. **Reserve Officers Training Corps (ROTC):** Army ROTC: Offered at cooperating institution (Wheaton College). **Faculty and instruction (2005-2006):** Total instructional faculty: 105 full-time, 37 part-time (59% men; 41% women; 3% minorities). Full-time faculty with Ph.D. or other terminal degree: 60%. Student/faculty ratio: 22/1. Classes of fewer than 20 students: 38%; of 20 to 49 students: 49%; of 50 or more students: 13%. **Advanced Placement and International Baccalaureate credit:** AP tests may be used for: Credit and/or placement. Scores accepted: 3, 4, 5. International Baccalaureate exams may be used for: Credit only. **Freshmen returning for sophomore year:** 79%. **Graduation rates:** Four-year: 40%; five-year: 56%; six-year: 54%. **Graduate study:** 24% of students pursue further study immediately upon graduation; 39% within one year; 55% within five years. Fields in which graduates pursue further study: Master of Business Administration (MBA), 13%; law, 3%; medicine, 9%; engineering, 2%; theology (or the seminary), 11%; education, 26%; arts and sciences, 27%.

COSTS AND FINANCIAL AID
Financial aid office: (815) 939-5249. **Expenses (2006-2007):** Tuition and fees 2006-2007: $17,590; room/board: $6,400. Estimated books and supplies: $900; transportation: $400; personal expenses: $1,300. **Financial aid:** Priority filing date for institution's financial aid form: March 1. In 2005-2006, 80% of undergraduates applied for financial aid. Of those, 71% were determined to have financial need; 36% had their need fully met. Average financial aid package (proportion receiving): $12,033 (70%). Average amount of gift aid, such as scholarships or grants (proportion receiving): $9,075 (68%). Average amount of self-help aid, such as work study or loans (proportion receiving): $4,343 (55%). Average need-based loan (excluding PLUS or other private loans): $4,056. Among students who received need-based aid, the average percentage of need met: 84%. Among students who received aid based on merit, the average award (and the proportion receiving): $6,361 (25%). The average athletic scholarship (and the proportion receiving): $5,004 (12%). Average amount of debt of borrowers graduating in 2005: $20,062. Proportion who borrowed: 75%.

CAMPUS LIFE AND EXTRACURRICULAR ACTIVITIES
Campus housing available (% using): women's dorms (30%), men's dorms (30%), apartments for married students (5%), apartment for single students (35%), special housing for disabled students (0%). Students who live in college-owned, operated, or affiliated housing: 80%. **Student employment:** During the 2005-2006 academic year, 41% of undergraduates worked on campus. Average per-year earnings: $1,000. **Clubs and organizations:** Number of student organizations: 79. Activities include: choral groups, concert band, dance, drama/theater, jazz band, literary magazine, marching band, music ensembles, musical theater, opera, pep band, radio station, student government, student newspaper, student film society, symphony orchestra, television station, yearbook. Number of fraternities: 0; sororities: 0. Average proportion of students who stay on campus on weekends: 75%. **Sports program (2005-2006):** Member of NAIA. *Men's intercollegiate varsity sports:* baseball, basketball, cross-country, football, golf, soccer, tennis, track and field (indoor), track and field (outdoor). *Women's intercollegiate varsity*

sports: basketball, cross-country, soccer, softball, tennis, track and field (indoor), track and field (outdoor), volleyball.

SERVICES AND FACILITIES
Basic services: health service. **Remedial assistance:** math, writing, study skills. **Counseling services:** career, personal, veteran student, academic, psychological, religious. **For learning-disabled students:** School does not offer a structured program with separate admission and additional fees. Total undergraduates in learning-disabled program or receiving services: 74. Services include: remedial math, remedial English, reading machines, tape recorders, diagnostic testing service, untimed tests, note-taking services, oral tests, learning center, readers, extended time for tests, tutors, priority seating, other testing accomodations, other. **Library:** Number of titles: 213,051; number of current serial subscriptions: 2,896. **Information technology resources:** Students are not required to lease or own a computer. Number of campus computers available to all students: 500. School has a wireless network. Approximate number of users that can be accommodated: 8,000. Proportion of college-owned housing units wired for high-speed internet access: 100%. **Campus safety:** Security services offered: 24-hour foot and vehicle patrols, late-night transport/escort service, 24-hour emergency telephones, lighted pathways/sidewalks, student patrols, controlled dormitory access (key, security card, etc).

TRANSFER AND INTERNATIONAL STUDENTS
Transfer students: May apply for admission for the following academic terms: Fall, Spring, Summer. Applicants need a minimum number of credits to apply. For fall 2005: Transfer applications received: 472. Transfer applicants offered admission: 304. Transfer applicants enrolled: 272. **International students:** Number of foreign undergraduates: 31 (1% of student body). Number of countries represented: 18. Minimum TOEFL score required: 500 (paper); 173 (computer).

Principia College

- **Address:** 1 Maybeck Place, Elsah, IL 62028
- **Website:** http://www.prin.edu/college
- **Private; Religious affiliation:** Christian Science
- **Enrollment:** 536 full-time; 6 part-time

KEY STATS
- ✔ **U.S News College Ranking:** 86, Liberal Arts Colleges
- ✔ **SAT Score (25th/75th percentile):** 1010-1270
- ✔ **Tuition:** 2005-2006: $20,415

Selectivity: More selective	**Room/board:** $7,350
Acceptance rate: 89%	**Average debt:** N/A
Student/faculty ratio: 8/1	**Proportion who borrowed:** N/A

UNDERGRADUATE STUDENT BODY STATS
2005-2006 enrollment: 536 full-time; 6 part-time. Men: 48%; women: 52%. **Ethnic makeup:** African American: 1%; Asian American: 1%; Hispanic: 1%; White: 84%; International: 13%.

ADMISSIONS FACTS AND FIGURES
Phone: (618) 374-5181. **Email:** collegeadmissions@prin.edu. **Website:** http://www.prin.edu/college. **Application deadlines for fall 2007:** Regular decision: March 1. Early decision: Not offered. Early action: Send application by: November 15; Decision sent by: December 1. Admission can be deferred. **Application fee:** None. Common application is not accepted. **Admissions requirements/recommendations:** High school units required (recommended): English: 4 (4); Mathematics: 4 (4); Science: 3 (3); Foreign language: 2 (3); Social studies: 2 (2); History: 1 (2); Academic electives: 2 (2); Total units: 16 (20). Tests: The college uses SAT or ACT scores in admissions decisions. Either SAT or ACT required. For admission to the fall 2007 entering class, the school will accept: ACT with writing. Campus visit: Recommended. Admissions interview: Recommended. Off-campus interview: May be arranged. **Factors that count in admissions decisions:** *Academic:* Secondary school record: Very important. Class rank: Important. Letters of recommendation: Important. Standardized test scores: Important. Essay: Very important. *Nonacademic:* Interview: Important. Extracurricular activities: Important. Talent/ability: Important. Character/personal qualities: Very important. Alumni/ae relationship: Considered. Geographical residence: Not considered. State residency: Not considered. Religious affilia-

tion/commitment: Very important. Minority status: Considered. Volunteer work: Considered. Work experience: Considered. **Other schools with the greatest overlap in applicants:** Ball State University; Indiana University–Bloomington; University of California–Santa Barbara; University of Chicago; University of Puget Sound. **Admissions statistics for the fall 2005 entering class:** Total applicants: 242. Total accepted: 216. Freshmen enrolled: 139; 90% were from out of state. Accepted through early-decision or early-action plans: 16%. Overall acceptance rate: 89%. Non-early acceptance rate: 88%. **Size of waiting list:** 0 applicants; enrolled from waiting list: 0. **Credentials of fall 2005 freshmen:** 38% ranked in the top 10 percent of their high school class; 63% were in the top 25 percent, and 79% were in the top half. (Proportion submitting class standing: 49%.) **Average high school grade point average:** 3.4. **First-year students who submitted SAT scores:** 85%. Scores (25/75 percentile): Verbal: 510-650, Math: 500-620, Combined: 1010-1270. **First-year students submitting ACT scores:** 46%. Scores (25/75 percentile): English: 20-30, Math: 21-29, Composite: 21-30.

ACADEMICS
Year founded: 1910. **Academic calendar:** Quarter. **Degrees offered:** bachelor's. **Most popular majors:** 20% business administration and management, 13% fine/studio arts, 10% mass communication/media studies, 8% environmental science, 7% social sciences. **Major fields of study:** biological and biomedical sciences; business, management, marketing, and related support services; communication, journalism, and related programs; computer and information sciences and support services; education; engineering; English language and literature/letters; foreign languages, literatures, and linguistics; history; mathematics and statistics; natural resources and conservation; parks, recreation, leisure, and fitness studies; philosophy and religious studies; physical sciences; social sciences; visual and performing arts. **Areas of required coursework:** arts/fine arts, humanities, mathematics, English (including composition), philosophy, foreign languages, sciences (biological or physical), history, social science, other. **Special academic programs (% participation):** double major (21%), independent study (2%), internships (7%), student-designed major (1%), study abroad (17%). **Teacher certification offered in:** elementary. **Faculty and instruction (2005-2006):** Total instructional faculty: 55 full-time, 11 part-time (61% men; 39% women; 2% minorities). Full-time faculty with Ph.D. or other terminal degree: 45%. Student/faculty ratio: 8/1. Classes of fewer than 20 students: 96%; of 20 to 49 students: 4%. **Advanced Placement and International Baccalaureate credit:** AP tests may be used for: Credit and/or placement. Scores accepted: 3, 4, 5. International Baccalaureate exams may be used for: Credit and/or placement. **Freshmen returning for sophomore year:** 86%. **Graduation rates:** Four-year: 73%; five-year: 83%; six-year: 85%. **Graduate study:** 5% of students pursue further study immediately upon graduation; 6% within one year; 12% within five years. Fields in which graduates pursue further study: Master of Business Administration (MBA), 10%; law, 10%; engineering, 2%; theology (or the seminary), 1%; education, 8%.

COSTS AND FINANCIAL AID
Financial aid office: (618) 374-5186. **Expenses (2005-2006):** Tuition and fees 2005-2006: $20,415; room/board: $7,350. Estimated books and supplies: $750; transportation: $700; personal expenses: $750.

CAMPUS LIFE AND EXTRACURRICULAR ACTIVITIES
Campus housing available (% using): women's dorms (49%), men's dorms (49%), apartments for married students (2%). Students who live in college-owned, operated, or affiliated housing: 99%. **Student employment:** During the 2005-2006 academic year, 50% of undergraduates worked on campus. Average per-year earnings: $3,000. **Clubs and organizations:** Number of student organizations: 28. Activities include: choral groups, dance, drama/theater, music ensembles, pep band, radio station, student government, student newspaper, television station, yearbook. Number of fraternities: 0; sororities: 0. Average proportion of students who stay on campus on weekends: 100%. **Sports program (2005-2006):** Member of NCAA III. ***Men's intercollegiate varsity sports:*** baseball, basketball, cross-country, football, golf, soccer, swimming and diving, tennis, track and field (indoor), track and field (outdoor). ***Women's intercollegiate varsity sports:*** basketball, cross-country, soccer, swimming and diving, tennis, track and field (indoor), track and field (outdoor), volleyball.

SERVICES AND FACILITIES
Basic services: day care, health service, other. **Remedial assistance:** reading, writing, study skills. **Counseling services:** career, personal, academic, other. **For learning-disabled students:** Total undergraduates in learning-disabled program or receiving services: 0. **Library:** Number of titles: 210,000; number of current serial subscriptions: 12,000. **Information technology**

resources: Students are not required to lease or own a computer. Number of campus computers available to all students: 250. School does not have a wireless network. Proportion of college-owned housing units wired for high-speed internet access: 100%. **Campus safety:** Security services offered: 24-hour foot and vehicle patrols, 24-hour emergency telephones, lighted pathways/sidewalks, controlled dormitory access (key, security card, etc).

TRANSFER AND INTERNATIONAL STUDENTS

Transfer students: May apply for admission for the following academic terms: Fall, Winter, Spring. Applicants do not need a minimum number of credits to apply. For fall 2005: Transfer applications received: 23. Transfer applicants offered admission: 21. Transfer applicants enrolled: 17. **International students:** Number of foreign undergraduates: 69 (13% of student body). Minimum TOEFL score required: 550 (paper); 213 (computer). Average TOEFL score: 563 (paper).

Quincy University

- **Address:** 1800 College Avenue, Quincy, IL 62301
- **Website:** http://www.quincy.edu
- **Private; Religious affiliation:** Catholic
- **Enrollment:** 927 full-time; 148 part-time

KEY STATS

✔ **U.S News College Ranking:** third tier, Universities–Master's (Midwest)
✔ **ACT Score (25th/75th percentile):** 19-24
✔ **Tuition:** 2006-2007: $19,010

Selectivity: Selective	**Room/board:** $6,980
Acceptance rate: 94%	**Average debt:** $16,134
Student/faculty ratio: 13/1	**Proportion who borrowed:** 80%

UNDERGRADUATE STUDENT BODY STATS

2005-2006 enrollment: 927 full-time; 148 part-time. Men: 43%; women: 57%. **Ethnic makeup:** African American: 6%; Asian American: 1%; Hispanic: 3%; White: 89%; International: 1%. **Religious preference:** Roman Catholic: 50%; Protestant: 23%; Muslim: 1%; No preference: 25%.

ADMISSIONS FACTS AND FIGURES

Phone: (217) 228-5210. **Email:** admissions@quincy.edu. **Website:** http://www.quincy.edu. **Application deadlines for fall 2007:** Regular decision: Rolling. Early decision: Not offered. Early action: Not offered. Admission can be deferred. **Application fee:** $25. Common application is accepted. **To apply online, go to:** http://www.quincy.edu/admissions/applying/. **Admissions requirements/recommendations:** High school units required (recommended): English: 4 (4); Mathematics: (3); Science: (3); Foreign language: (2); Social studies: (2); History: (2); Total units: (16). Tests: The college uses SAT or ACT scores in admissions decisions. Either SAT or ACT required. For admission to the fall 2007 entering class, the school will accept: ACT with writing, ACT without writing. Campus visit: Recommended. Admissions interview: Recommended. Off-campus interview: May be arranged. **Factors that count in admissions decisions:** *Academic:* Secondary school record: Very important. Class rank: Considered. Letters of recommendation: Very important. Standardized test scores: Very important. Essay: Very important. *Nonacademic:* Interview: Important. Extracurricular activities: Considered. Talent/ability: Considered. Character/personal qualities: Considered. Alumni/ae relationship: Considered. Geographical residence: Considered. State residency: Considered. Religious affiliation/commitment: Considered. Minority status: Considered. Volunteer work: Considered. Work experience: Considered. **Other schools with the greatest overlap in applicants:** Augustana College; Bradley University; Illinois Wesleyan University; St. Louis University; Truman State University. **Admissions statistics for the fall 2005 entering class:** Total applicants: 986. Total accepted: 926. Freshmen enrolled: 202; 32% were from out of state. Overall acceptance rate: 94%. **Credentials of fall 2005 freshmen:** 5% ranked in the top 10 percent of their high school class; 28% were in the top 25 percent, and 62% were in the top half. (Proportion submitting class standing: 93%.) **Average high school grade point average:** 3.1. **First-year students who submitted SAT scores:** 9%. Scores (25/75 percentile): Verbal: 440-520, Math: 470-550, Combined: 910-1070. **First-year students submitting ACT scores:** 91%. Scores (25/75 percentile): English: 18-24, Math: 18-24, Composite: 19-24.

ACADEMICS

Year founded: 1860. **Academic calendar:** Semester. **Degrees offered:** associate, bachelor's, master's. **Most popular majors:** 22% business, management, marketing, and related support services, 19% education, 10% health professions and related clinical sciences, 6% psychology, 6% security and protective services. **Major fields of study:** biological and biomedical sciences; business, management, marketing, and related support services; communication, journalism, and related programs; computer and information sciences and support services; education; English language and literature/letters; foreign languages, literatures, and linguistics; health professions and related clinical sciences; history; liberal arts and sciences studies, and humanities; mathematics and statistics; parks, recreation, leisure, and fitness studies; philosophy and religious studies; physical sciences; psychology; public administration and social service professions; security and protective services; social sciences; transportation and materials moving; visual and performing arts. **Areas of required coursework:** arts/fine arts, humanities, computer literacy, mathematics, English (including composition), philosophy, sciences (biological or physical), history, social science, other. **Pre-professional programs:** pre-law, pre-dentistry, pre-medicine, pre-veterinary science, pre-pharmacy. **Special academic programs:** accelerated program, cooperative (work-study plan) program, distance learning, double major, dual enrollment, English as a Second Language (ESL), honors program, independent study, internships, liberal arts/career combination, student-designed major, study abroad, teacher certificate program. **Teacher certification offered in:** special education, elementary, secondary. **Cooperative education programs:** engineering. **Faculty and instruction (2005-2006):** Total instructional faculty: 54 full-time, 73 part-time (57% men; 43% women; 2% minorities). Full-time faculty with Ph.D. or other terminal degree: 83%. Student/faculty ratio: 13/1. Classes of fewer than 20 students: 71%; of 20 to 49 students: 29%; of 50 or more students: 0%. **Advanced Placement and International Baccalaureate credit:** AP tests may be used for: Credit and/or placement. Scores accepted: 3, 4, 5. International Baccalaureate exams may be used for: Credit only. **Freshmen returning for sophomore year:** 68%. **Graduation rates:** Six-year: 49%. **Graduate study:** 25% of students pursue further study within one year. Fields in which graduates pursue further study: Master of Business Administration (MBA), 2%; law, 3%; medicine, 2%.

COSTS AND FINANCIAL AID

Financial aid office: (217) 228-5260. **Expenses (2006-2007):** Tuition and fees 2006-2007: $19,010; room/board: $6,980. Estimated books and supplies: $1,250; transportation: $1,000; personal expenses: $1,500. **Financial aid:** Priority filing date for institution's financial aid form: April 15. In 2005-2006, 85% of undergraduates applied for financial aid. Of those, 73% were determined to have financial need; 26% had their need fully met. Average financial aid package (proportion receiving): $14,835 (72%). Average amount of gift aid, such as scholarships or grants (proportion receiving): $9,365 (71%). Average amount of self-help aid, such as work study or loans (proportion receiving): $4,940 (65%). Average need-based loan (excluding PLUS or other private loans): $4,373. Among students who received need-based aid, the average percentage of need met: 85%. Among students who received aid based on merit, the average award (and the proportion receiving): $3,867 (21%). The average athletic scholarship (and the proportion receiving): $8,506 (9%). Average amount of debt of borrowers graduating in 2005: $16,134. Proportion who borrowed: 80%.

CAMPUS LIFE AND EXTRACURRICULAR ACTIVITIES

Campus housing available (% using): coed dorms (27%), women's dorms (32%), men's dorms (23%), sorority housing (2%), fraternity housing (1%), apartment for single students (3%), other housing options (12%). Students who live in college-owned, operated, or affiliated housing: 62%. **Student employment:** During the 2005-2006 academic year, 17% of undergraduates worked on campus. Average per-year earnings: $1,000. **Clubs and organizations:** Number of student organizations: 42. Activities include: choral groups, concert band, dance, drama/theater, jazz band, literary magazine, music ensembles, musical theater, opera, pep band, radio station, student government, student newspaper, symphony orchestra, television station, yearbook. Number of fraternities: 1; sororities: 2. Proportion of men in fraternities: 4%; of women in sororities: 11%. Average proportion of students who stay on campus on weekends: 75%. **Sports program (2005-2006):** Member of NCAA II. **Men's intercollegiate varsity sports:** baseball, basketball, football, golf, soccer, tennis, volleyball. **Women's intercollegiate varsity sports:** basketball, golf, soccer, softball, tennis, volleyball.

SERVICES AND FACILITIES

Basic services: nonremedial tutoring, placement service, health service, health insurance. **Remedial assistance:** writing, study skills. **Counseling services:** minority student, career, personal, academic, older student, religious. **For learning-disabled students:** School does not offer a structured program with separate admission and additional fees. Services include: remedial English, reading machines, tape recorders, untimed tests, note-taking services, oral tests, learning center, readers, extended time for tests, tutors. **Library:** Number of titles: 388,016; number of current serial subscriptions: 524. **Information technology resources:** Students are not required to lease or own a computer. Number of campus computers available to all students: 240. School has a wireless network. Proportion of college-owned housing units wired for high-speed internet access: 85%. **Campus safety:** Security services offered: 24-hour foot and vehicle patrols, late-night transport/escort service, 24-hour emergency telephones, lighted pathways/sidewalks, controlled dormitory access (key, security card, etc).

TRANSFER AND INTERNATIONAL STUDENTS

Transfer students: May apply for admission for the following academic terms: Fall, Spring, Summer. Applicants need a minimum number of credits to apply. For fall 2005: Transfer applications received: 180. Transfer applicants offered admission: 177. Transfer applicants enrolled: 97. **International students:** Number of foreign undergraduates: 10 (1% of student body). Number of countries represented: 6. Minimum TOEFL score required: 500 (paper). Average TOEFL score: 550 (paper).

Robert Morris College

- **Address:** 401 S. State Street, Chicago, IL 60605
- **Website:** http://www.robertmorris.edu/
- **Private**
- **Enrollment:** 4,706 full-time; 712 part-time

KEY STATS

✔ **U.S News College Ranking:** Unranked Specialty School–Business
✔ **SAT or ACT Score (25th/75th percentile):** N/A
✔ **Tuition:** 2006-2007: $15,900

Selectivity: Least selective	**Room/board:** $8,979
Acceptance rate: 80%	**Average debt:** $18,479
Student/faculty ratio: 26/1	**Proportion who borrowed:** 93%

UNDERGRADUATE STUDENT BODY STATS

2005-2006 enrollment: 4,706 full-time; 712 part-time. Men: 34%; women: 66%. **Ethnic makeup:** African American: 39%; Asian American: 2%; Hispanic: 24%; White: 34%.

ADMISSIONS FACTS AND FIGURES

Phone: (312) 935-4400. **Email:** enroll@robertmorris.edu. **Website:** http://www.robertmorris.edu/. **Application deadlines for fall 2007:** Regular decision: Rolling. Early decision: Not offered. Early action: Not offered. Admission can be deferred. **Application fee:** $30. Common application is accepted. **Admissions requirements/recommendations:** Tests: The college does not use SAT or ACT scores in admissions decisions. Neither SAT nor ACT required. Campus visit: Recommended. Admissions interview: Recommended. Off-campus interview: May be arranged. **Factors that count in admissions decisions:** *Academic:* Secondary school record: Very important. Class rank: Very important. Letters of recommendation: Considered. Standardized test scores: Considered. Essay: Considered. *Nonacademic:* Interview: Very important. Extracurricular activities: Considered. Talent/ability: Considered. Character/personal qualities: Considered. Alumni/ae relationship: Not considered. Geographical residence: Not considered. State residency: Not considered. Religious affiliation/commitment: Not considered. Minority status: Not considered. Volunteer work: Considered. Work experience: Considered. **Admissions statistics for the fall 2005 entering class:** Total applicants: 2,714. Total accepted: 2,167. Freshmen enrolled: 977; 1% were from out of state. Overall acceptance rate: 80%. **Credentials of fall 2005 freshmen:** 7% ranked in the top 10 percent of their high school class; 23% were in the top 25 percent, and 50% were in the top half. (Proportion submitting class standing: 83%.) **Average high school grade point average:** 2.6.

ACADEMICS

Year founded: 1913. **Academic calendar:** Other. **Degrees offered:** diploma, associate, bachelor's, master's. **Most popular majors:** 79% business, management, marketing, and related support services, 13% computer and information sciences and support services, 8% visual and performing arts. **Major fields of study:** business, management, marketing, and related support services; computer and information sciences and support services; visual and performing arts. **Areas of required coursework:** arts/fine arts, humanities, computer literacy, mathematics, English (including composition), philosophy, sciences (biological or physical), history, social science, other. **Special academic programs:** accelerated program, cooperative (work-study plan) program, distance learning, dual enrollment, honors program, internships, study abroad. **Cooperative education programs:** art, business, health professions, other. **Reserve Officers Training Corps (ROTC):** Army ROTC: Offered at cooperating institution (U of I Chicago). **Faculty and instruction (2005-2006):** Total instructional faculty: 133 full-time, 235 part-time (56% men; 44% women; 25% minorities). Full-time faculty with Ph.D. or other terminal degree: 20%. Student/faculty ratio: 26/1. Classes of fewer than 20 students: 41%; of 20 to 49 students: 58%; of 50 or more students: 1%. **Freshmen returning for sophomore year:** 61%. **Graduation rates:** Four-year: 40%; five-year: 60%; six-year: 53%.

COSTS AND FINANCIAL AID

Financial aid office: (312) 935-4408. **Expenses (2006-2007):** Tuition and fees 2006-2007: $15,900; room/board: $8,979. Estimated books and supplies: $1,350; transportation: $1,405; personal expenses: $1,883. **Financial aid:** In 2005-2006, 96% of undergraduates applied for financial aid. Of those, 93% were determined to have financial need; 4% had their need fully met. Average financial aid package (proportion receiving): $11,059 (92%). Average amount of gift aid, such as scholarships or grants (proportion receiving): $8,262 (90%). Average amount of self-help aid, such as work study or loans (proportion receiving): $3,656 (75%). Average need-based loan (excluding PLUS or other private loans): $3,620. Among students who received need-based aid, the average percentage of need met: 47%. Among students who received aid based on merit, the average award (and the proportion receiving): $9,897 (3%). The average athletic scholarship (and the proportion receiving): $6,171 (1%). Average amount of debt of borrowers graduating in 2005: $18,479. Proportion who borrowed: 93%.

CAMPUS LIFE AND EXTRACURRICULAR ACTIVITIES

Campus housing available: coed dorms. Students who live in college-owned, operated, or affiliated housing: 3%. **Clubs and organizations:** Number of student organizations: 20. Activities include: choral groups, dance, drama/theater, literary magazine, student newspaper. Number of fraternities: 0; sororities: 0. Average proportion of students who stay on campus on weekends: 70%. **Sports program (2005-2006):** Member of NAIA. *Men's intercollegiate varsity sports:* baseball, basketball, cross-country, football, golf, soccer. *Women's intercollegiate varsity sports:* basketball, cross-country, golf, soccer, softball, tennis, volleyball.

SERVICES AND FACILITIES

Basic services: nonremedial tutoring, placement service. **Remedial assistance:** study skills. **Counseling services:** career, personal, veteran student, academic, psychological. **For learning-disabled students:** School does not offer a structured program with separate admission and additional fees. Total undergraduates in learning-disabled program or receiving services: 17. Services include: tape recorders, note-taking services, oral tests, learning center, readers, extended time for tests, tutors, texts on tape, other testing accomodations, other. **Library:** Number of titles: 128,604; number of current serial subscriptions: 94. **Information technology resources:** Students are not required to lease or own a computer. Number of campus computers available to all students: 1,809. School has a wireless network. **Campus safety:** Security services offered: late-night transport/escort service, lighted pathways/sidewalks, controlled dormitory access (key, security card, etc).

TRANSFER AND INTERNATIONAL STUDENTS

Transfer students: May apply for admission for the following academic terms: Fall, Winter, Spring, Summer. Applicants need a minimum number of credits to apply. For fall 2005: Transfer applications received: 1,268. Transfer applicants offered admission: 1,101. Transfer applicants enrolled: 711. **International students:** Number of foreign undergraduates: 22. Number of countries represented: 12. Minimum TOEFL score required: 500 (paper); 173 (computer). Average TOEFL score: 500 (paper).

Rockford College

- **Address:** 5050 E. State Street, Rockford, IL 61108-2393
- **Website:** http://www.rockford.edu
- **Private**
- **Enrollment:** 731 full-time; 141 part-time

KEY STATS
✔ **U.S News College Ranking:** third tier, Universities–Master's (Midwest)
✔ **ACT Score (25th/75th percentile):** 21-29
✔ **Tuition:** 2006-2007: $22,460

Selectivity: Selective	**Room/board:** $7,190
Acceptance rate: 49%	**Average debt:** $30,125
Student/faculty ratio: N/A	**Proportion who borrowed:** 85%

UNDERGRADUATE STUDENT BODY STATS
2005-2006 enrollment: 731 full-time; 141 part-time. Men: 36%; women: 64%. **Ethnic makeup:** African American: 7%; Asian American: 2%; Hispanic: 5%; White: 84%; International: 2%.

ADMISSIONS FACTS AND FIGURES
Phone: (815) 226-4050. **Email:** rcadmissions@rockford.edu. **Website:** http://www.rockford.edu. **Application deadlines for fall 2007:** Regular decision: August 1. Early decision: Not offered. Early action: Not offered. Admission can be deferred. **Application fee:** $35. Common application is accepted. **Admissions requirements/recommendations:** High school units required (recommended): English: 4 (4); Mathematics: 3 (3); Science: 3 (3); Foreign language: 2 (2); Social studies: 3 (3); History: 3 (3); Academic electives: 2 (2); Total units: 15 (15). Tests: The college uses SAT or ACT scores in admissions decisions. ACT required. For admission to the fall 2007 entering class, the school will accept: ACT with writing, ACT without writing. Campus visit: Recommended. Admissions interview: Required. Off-campus interview: May be arranged. **Factors that count in admissions decisions:** **Academic:** Secondary school record: Important. Class rank: Important. Letters of recommendation: Important. Standardized test scores: Important. Essay: Important. **Nonacademic:** Interview: Important. Extracurricular activities: Very important. Talent/ability: Very important. Character/personal qualities: Very important. Alumni/ae relationship: Important. Geographical residence: Important. State residency: Important. Religious affiliation/commitment: Considered. Minority status: Important. Volunteer work: Very important. Work experience: Very important. **Admissions statistics for the fall 2005 entering class:** Total applicants: 749. Total accepted: 370. Freshmen enrolled: 270; 12% were from out of state. Overall acceptance rate: 49%. **Size of waiting list:** 0 applicants; enrolled from waiting list: 0. **Credentials of fall 2005 freshmen:** 16% ranked in the top 10 percent of their high school class; 35% were in the top 25 percent, and 57% were in the top half. **Average high school grade point average:** 3.1. **First-year students submitting ACT scores:** 100%. Scores (25/75 percentile): English: 20-31, Math: 20-30, Composite: 21-29.

ACADEMICS
Year founded: 1847. **Academic calendar:** Semester. **Degrees offered:** bachelor's, master's. **Most popular majors:** 24% elementary education and teaching, 13% business administration and management, 8% nursing/registered nurse training (R.N., A.S.N., B.S.N., M.S.N.), 6% physical education teaching and coaching, 6% psychology. **Major fields of study:** biological and biomedical sciences; business, management, marketing, and related support services; computer and information sciences and support services; education; engineering; English language and literature/letters; family and consumer sciences/human sciences; foreign languages, literatures, and linguistics; health professions and related clinical sciences; history; mathematics and statistics; parks, recreation, leisure, and fitness studies; philosophy and religious studies; physical sciences; psychology; public administration and social service professions; social sciences; visual and performing arts. **Areas of required coursework:** arts/fine arts, humanities, mathematics, English (including composition), sciences (biological or physical), social science. **Pre-professional programs:** pre-law, pre-dentistry, pre-medicine, pre-veterinary science, pre-pharmacy. **Special academic programs (% participation):** accelerated program, cooperative (work-study plan) program, double major (8.3%), English as a Second Language (ESL), honors program (2.4%), independent study, internships, liberal arts/career combination, student-designed major, study abroad, teacher certificate program (20.6%). **Teacher certification offered in:** special education, elementary, middle/junior high, secondary, bilingual/bicultural. **Reserve Officers Training Corps (ROTC):** Army ROTC: Offered at cooperating institution (Northern Illinois University). **Faculty and instruction (2005-2006):** Total instructional faculty: N/A. Classes of fewer than 20 students: 80%; of 20 to 49 students: 20%; of 50 or more students: 0%. **Advanced Placement and International Baccalaureate credit:** AP tests may be used for: Credit and/or placement. Scores accepted: 3, 4, 5. International Baccalaureate exams may be used for: Credit and/or placement. **Freshmen returning for sophomore year:** 51%. **Graduation rates:** Four-year: 32%; five-year: 43%; six-year: 46%.

COSTS AND FINANCIAL AID
Financial aid office: (815) 226-3396. **Expenses (2006-2007):** Tuition and fees 2006-2007: $22,460; room/board: $7,190. Estimated books and supplies: $1,020; transportation: $1,190; personal expenses: $2,190. **Financial aid:** Priority filing date for institution's financial aid form: March 15. In 2005-2006, 97% of undergraduates applied for financial aid. Of those, 89% were determined to have financial need; 35% had their need fully met. Average financial aid package (proportion receiving): $11,679 (78%). Average amount of gift aid, such as scholarships or grants (proportion receiving): $8,939 (72%). Average amount of self-help aid, such as work study or loans (proportion receiving): $5,002 (47%). Average need-based loan (excluding PLUS or other private loans): $4,060. Among students who received need-based aid, the average percentage of need met: 35%. Among students who received aid based on merit, the average award (and the proportion receiving): $6,053 (16%). The average athletic scholarship (and the proportion receiving): $0 (0%). Average amount of debt of borrowers graduating in 2005: $30,125. Proportion who borrowed: 85%.

CAMPUS LIFE AND EXTRACURRICULAR ACTIVITIES
Campus housing available: coed dorms, special housing for disabled students. **Student employment:** During the 2005-2006 academic year, 16% of undergraduates worked on campus. Average per-year earnings: $2,300. **Clubs and organizations:** Number of student organizations: 25. Activities include: choral groups, dance, drama/theater, literary magazine, music ensembles, musical theater, radio station, student government, student newspaper. Number of fraternities: 0; sororities: 0. Average proportion of students who stay on campus on weekends: 70%. **Sports program (2005-2006):** Member of NCAA III. **Men's intercollegiate varsity sports:** baseball, basketball, cross-country, football, golf, soccer, tennis, track and field (indoor), track and field (outdoor). **Women's intercollegiate varsity sports:** basketball, cross-country, soccer, softball, tennis, track and field (indoor), track and field (outdoor), volleyball.

SERVICES AND FACILITIES
Basic services: nonremedial tutoring, placement service, health service, health insurance. **Remedial assistance:** reading, math, writing, study skills. **Counseling services:** minority student, career, personal, veteran student, academic, older student, psychological, birth control, religious. **For learning-disabled students:** School does not offer a structured program with separate admission and additional fees. Total undergraduates in learning-disabled program or receiving services: 29. Services include: remedial math, remedial English, reading machines, remedial reading, tape recorders, diagnostic testing service, untimed tests, note-taking services, special bookstore section, oral tests, learning center, readers, extended time for tests, tutors, priority registration, priority seating, proofreading services, texts on tape, typist/scribe, exams on tape or computer, take home exams, other testing accomodations, other. **Library:** Number of titles: 144,453; number of current serial subscriptions: 475. **Information technology resources:** Students are not required to lease or own a computer. Number of campus computers available to all students: 100. School has a wireless network. Approximate number of users that can be accommodated: 400. Proportion of college-owned housing units wired for high-speed internet access: 100%. **Campus safety:** Security services offered: 24-hour foot and vehicle patrols, late-night transport/escort service, 24-hour emergency telephones, lighted pathways/sidewalks, student patrols, controlled dormitory access (key, security card, etc).

TRANSFER AND INTERNATIONAL STUDENTS
Transfer students: May apply for admission for the following academic terms: Fall, Winter, Spring, Summer. Applicants need a minimum number of credits to apply. **International students:** Number of foreign undergraduates: 17 (2% of student body). Minimum TOEFL score required: 525 (paper); 195 (computer). Average TOEFL score: 530 (paper).

Roosevelt University

■ **Address:** 430 S. Michigan Avenue, Chicago, IL 60605
■ **Website:** http://www.roosevelt.edu
■ **Private**
■ **Enrollment:** 2,041 full-time; 2,032 part-time

KEY STATS

✔ **U.S News College Ranking:** third tier, Universities–Master's (Midwest)
✔ **ACT Score (25th/75th percentile):** 19-25
✔ **Tuition:** 2006-2007: $15,564

Selectivity: Selective	**Room/board:** $10,366
Acceptance rate: 68%	**Average debt:** N/A
Student/faculty ratio: 12/1	**Proportion who borrowed:** N/A

UNDERGRADUATE STUDENT BODY STATS

2005-2006 enrollment: 2,041 full-time; 2,032 part-time. Men: 33%; women: 67%. **Ethnic makeup:** African American: 24%; Asian American: 5%; Hispanic: 11%; White: 58%; International: 2%.

ADMISSIONS FACTS AND FIGURES

Phone: (312) 341-3515. **Email:** applyRU@roosevelt.edu. **Website:** http://www.roosevelt.edu. **Application deadlines for fall 2007:** Regular decision: September 1. Early decision: Not offered. Early action: Not offered. Admission can be deferred. **Application fee:** $25. Common application is accepted. **Admissions requirements/recommendations:** High school units required (recommended): English: 4 (4); Mathematics: 3 (4); Science: 3 (3); Foreign language: 0 (2); Social studies: 2 (2); History: 1 (2); Academic electives: 2 (2); Total units: 15 (19). Tests: The college uses SAT or ACT scores in admissions decisions. Either SAT or ACT required. For admission to the fall 2007 entering class, the school will accept: ACT with writing, ACT without writing. Campus visit: Recommended. Admissions interview: Recommended. Off-campus interview: May be arranged. **Factors that count in admissions decisions: Academic:** Secondary school record: Very important. Class rank: Important. Letters of recommendation: Important. Standardized test scores: Important. Essay: Important. **Nonacademic:** Interview: Important. Extracurricular activities: Considered. Talent/ability: Considered. Character/personal qualities: Important. Alumni/ae relationship: Considered. Geographical residence: Not considered. State residency: Not considered. Religious affiliation/commitment: Not considered. Minority status: Considered. Volunteer work: Considered. Work experience: Considered. **Other schools with the greatest overlap in applicants:** DePaul University; Loyola University Chicago; Northern Illinois University; University of Illinois–Chicago. **Admissions statistics for the fall 2005 entering class:** Total applicants: 1,347. Total accepted: 915. Freshmen enrolled: 326; 29% were from out of state. Overall acceptance rate: 68%. **Size of waiting list:** 0 applicants; enrolled from waiting list: 0. **Credentials of fall 2005 freshmen:** 3% ranked in the top 10 percent of their high school class; 11% were in the top 25 percent, and 33% were in the top half. (Proportion submitting class standing: 70%.) **Average high school grade point average:** 3.1. **First-year students who submitted SAT scores:** 17%. Scores (25/75 percentile): Verbal: 500-630, Math: 470-590, Combined: 970-1220. **First-year students submitting ACT scores:** 66%. Scores (25/75 percentile): English: 20-27, Math: 17-24, Composite: 19-25.

ACADEMICS

Year founded: 1945. **Academic calendar:** Semester. **Degrees offered:** certificate, bachelor's, post-bachelor's certificate, master's, post-master's certificate, doctorate. **Most popular majors:** 32% business, management, marketing, and related support services, 12% psychology, 9% computer and information sciences and support services, 8% education, 8% social sciences. **Major fields of study:** area, ethnic, cultural, and gender studies; biological and biomedical sciences; business, management, marketing, and related support services; communication, journalism, and related programs; computer and information sciences and support services; education; engineering; engineering technologies/technicians; English language and literature/letters; foreign languages, literatures, and linguistics; health professions and related clinical sciences; legal professions and studies; liberal arts and sciences studies, and humanities; mathematics and statistics; multi/interdisciplinary studies; natural resources and conservation; philosophy and religious studies; physical sciences; psychology; public administration and social service professions; security and protective services; social sciences; visual and performing arts. **Areas of required coursework:** humani-

ties, mathematics, English (including composition), sciences (biological or physical), history, social science. **Pre-professional programs:** pre-medicine, pre-pharmacy. **Special academic programs:** accelerated program, distance learning, double major, dual enrollment, English as a Second Language (ESL), honors program, independent study, internships, student-designed major, study abroad, teacher certificate program, weekend college. **Teacher certification offered in:** early childhood, special education, elementary, secondary. **Faculty and instruction (2005-2006):** Total instructional faculty: 212 full-time, 409 part-time (60% men; 40% women). Full-time faculty with Ph.D. or other terminal degree: 82%. Student/faculty ratio: 12/1. Classes of fewer than 20 students: 63%; of 20 to 49 students: 36%; of 50 or more students: 1%. **Advanced Placement and International Baccalaureate credit:** International Baccalaureate exams may be used for: Credit and/or placement. **Freshmen returning for sophomore year:** 65%. **Graduation rates:** Four-year: 20%; five-year: 31%; six-year: 32%. **Graduate study:** 23% of students pursue further study immediately upon graduation; 25% within one year; 22% within five years.

COSTS AND FINANCIAL AID

Financial aid office: (312) 341-3565. **Expenses (2006-2007):** Tuition and fees 2006-2007: $15,564; room/board: $10,366. Estimated books and supplies: $1,200; transportation: $1,200; personal expenses: $1,500. **Financial aid:** Priority filing date for institution's financial aid form: April 1. In 2005-2006, 88% of undergraduates applied for financial aid. Of those, 71% were determined to have financial need; 28% had their need fully met. Average financial aid package (proportion receiving): $14,500 (69%). Average amount of gift aid, such as scholarships or grants (proportion receiving): $6,000 (49%). Average amount of self-help aid, such as work study or loans (proportion receiving): N/A (47%). Among students who received need-based aid, the average percentage of need met: 75%.

CAMPUS LIFE AND EXTRACURRICULAR ACTIVITIES

Campus housing available (% using): coed dorms (100%), other housing options. Students who live in college-owned, operated, or affiliated housing: 11%. **Student employment:** During the 2005-2006 academic year, 25% of undergraduates worked on campus. Average per-year earnings: $2,200. **Clubs and organizations:** Number of student organizations: 38. Activities include: choral groups, concert band, dance, drama/theater, jazz band, literary magazine, music ensembles, musical theater, opera, radio station, student government, student newspaper, symphony orchestra. Number of fraternities: 2; sororities: 4. Proportion of men in fraternities: 1%; of women in sororities: 1%. Average proportion of students who stay on campus on weekends: 75%.

SERVICES AND FACILITIES

Basic services: nonremedial tutoring, placement service, day care, health insurance. **Remedial assistance:** reading, math, writing, study skills. **Counseling services:** minority student, career, personal, veteran student, academic, older student, psychological. **For learning-disabled students:** Services include: remedial math, remedial English, remedial reading, diagnostic testing service, untimed tests, note-taking services, learning center, extended time for tests, tutors. **Library:** Number of titles: 176,135; number of current serial subscriptions: 1,126. **Information technology resources:** Students are not required to lease or own a computer. Number of campus computers available to all students: 646. School has a wireless network. Proportion of college-owned housing units wired for high-speed internet access: 50%. **Campus safety:** Security services offered: 24-hour foot and vehicle patrols, late-night transport/escort service, 24-hour emergency telephones, lighted pathways/sidewalks, controlled dormitory access (key, security card, etc).

TRANSFER AND INTERNATIONAL STUDENTS

Transfer students: May apply for admission for the following academic terms: Fall, Spring, Summer. Applicants need a minimum number of credits to apply. For fall 2005: Transfer applications received: 1,237. Transfer applicants offered admission: 1,080. Transfer applicants enrolled: 686. **International students:** Number of foreign undergraduates: 84 (2% of student body). Number of countries represented: 42. Minimum TOEFL score required: 525 (paper); 213 (computer). Average TOEFL score: 550 (paper).

School of the Art Institute of Chicago

- **Address:** 37 S. Wabash, Chicago, IL 60603
- **Website:** http://www.artic.edu/saic
- **Private**
- **Enrollment:** 1,889 full-time; 210 part-time

KEY STATS

✔ **U.S News College Ranking:** Unranked Specialty School–Fine Arts
✔ **SAT or ACT Score (25th/75th percentile):** N/A
✔ **Tuition:** 2006-2007: $29,220

Selectivity: Least selective	**Room/board:** N/A
Acceptance rate: 84%	**Average debt:** $28,959
Student/faculty ratio: 11/1	**Proportion who borrowed:** 63%

UNDERGRADUATE STUDENT BODY STATS

2005-2006 enrollment: 1,889 full-time; 210 part-time. Men: 34%; women: 66%. **Ethnic makeup:** African American: 3%; American-Indian: 1%; Asian American: 10%; Hispanic: 7%; White: 62%; International: 16%.

ADMISSIONS FACTS AND FIGURES

Phone: (312) 899-5219. **Email:** admiss@artic.edu. **Website:** http://www.artic.edu/saic. **Application deadlines for fall 2007:** Regular decision: September 1. Early decision: Not offered. Early action: Send application by: January 2; Decision sent by: N/A. Admission can be deferred. **Application fee:** $65. Common application is not accepted. **To apply online, go to:** http://www.artic.edu/saic/ugapp. **Admissions requirements/recommendations:** Tests: The college uses SAT or ACT scores in admissions decisions. Either SAT or ACT required. For admission to the fall 2007 entering class, the school will accept: ACT with writing, ACT without writing. Campus visit: Recommended. Admissions interview: Recommended. Off-campus interview: May be arranged. **Factors that count in admissions decisions:** *Academic:* Secondary school record: Considered. Class rank: Important. Letters of recommendation: Very important. Standardized test scores: Important. Essay: Very important. *Nonacademic:* Interview: Important. Extracurricular activities: Important. Talent/ability: Very important. Character/personal qualities: Very important. Alumni/ae relationship: Considered. Geographical residence: Considered. State residency: Considered. Religious affiliation/commitment: Not considered. Minority status: Important. Volunteer work: Considered. Work experience: Considered. **Other schools with the greatest overlap in applicants:** Kansas City Art Institute; Maryland Institute College of Art; Pratt Institute; Rhode Island School of Design; University of Illinois–Chicago. **Admissions statistics for the fall 2005 entering class:** Total applicants: 1,354. Total accepted: 1,136. Freshmen enrolled: 356; 69% were from out of state. Overall acceptance rate: 84%. Non-early acceptance rate: 84%.

ACADEMICS

Year founded: 1866. **Academic calendar:** Semester. **Degrees offered:** bachelor's, post-bachelor's certificate, master's. **Most popular majors:** Information not available. **Major fields of study:** architecture and related services; education; English language and literature/letters; visual and performing arts. **Areas of required coursework:** arts/fine arts, humanities, English (including composition), sciences (biological or physical), social science, other. **Special academic programs:** cooperative (work-study plan) program, cross-registration, double major, English as a Second Language (ESL), exchange student program (domestic), independent study, internships, student-designed major, study abroad, teacher certificate program. **Teacher certification offered in:** elementary, middle/junior high, secondary. **Cooperative education programs:** art, business, computer science, technologies. **Faculty and instruction (2005-2006):** Total instructional faculty: 124 full-time, 344 part-time (55% men; 45% women; 3% minorities). Full-time faculty with Ph.D. or other terminal degree: 90%. Student/faculty ratio: 11/1. Classes of fewer than 20 students: 76%; of 20 to 49 students: 22%; of 50 or more students: 2%. **Advanced Placement and International Baccalaureate credit:** AP tests may be used for: Credit only. Scores accepted: 3, 4, 5. International Baccalaureate exams may be used for: Credit only. **Freshmen returning for sophomore year:** 79%. **Graduation rates:** Four-year: 38%; five-year: 52%; six-year: 54%.

COSTS AND FINANCIAL AID

Financial aid office: (312) 899-5106. **Expenses (2006-2007):** Tuition and fees 2006-2007: $29,220; room/board: N/A. Estimated books and supplies: $2,340; transportation: $910; personal expenses: $2,460. **Financial aid:**

Priority filing date for institution's financial aid form: March 15. In 2005-2006, 77% of undergraduates applied for financial aid. Of those, 57% were determined to have financial need; Average financial aid package (proportion receiving): $20,027 (56%). Average amount of gift aid, such as scholarships or grants (proportion receiving): $10,963 (48%). Average amount of self-help aid, such as work study or loans (proportion receiving): $6,731 (54%). Average need-based loan (excluding PLUS or other private loans): $4,854. Among students who received aid based on merit, the average award (and the proportion receiving): $5,249 (37%). The average athletic scholarship (and the proportion receiving): $0 (0%). Average amount of debt of borrowers graduating in 2005: $28,959. Proportion who borrowed: 63%.

CAMPUS LIFE AND EXTRACURRICULAR ACTIVITIES

Campus housing available (% using): coed dorms (100%), special housing for disabled students. Students who live in college-owned, operated, or affiliated housing: 36%. **Student employment:** During the 2005-2006 academic year, 20% of undergraduates worked on campus. Average per-year earnings: $3,000. **Clubs and organizations:** Number of student organizations: 46. Activities include: dance, drama/theater, literary magazine, music ensembles, radio station, student government, student newspaper, student film society, television station. Number of fraternities: 0; sororities: 0.

SERVICES AND FACILITIES

Basic services: nonremedial tutoring, placement service, health service, health insurance, other. **Remedial assistance:** reading, math, writing, study skills, other. **Counseling services:** minority student, career, personal, veteran student, academic, psychological, birth control. **For learning-disabled students:** School does not offer a structured program with separate admission and additional fees. Total undergraduates in learning-disabled program or receiving services: 92. Services include: remedial English, remedial reading, tape recorders, untimed tests, note-taking services, oral tests, learning center, readers, extended time for tests, tutors, priority registration, texts on tape, other testing accomodations, other. **Library:** Number of titles: 78,028; number of current serial subscriptions: 355. **Information technology resources:** Students are not required to lease or own a computer. Number of campus computers available to all students: 450. School has a wireless network. Approximate number of users that can be accommodated: 1,625. Proportion of college-owned housing units wired for high-speed internet access: 100%. **Campus safety:** Security services offered: 24-hour foot and vehicle patrols, late-night transport/escort service, 24-hour emergency telephones, lighted pathways/sidewalks, controlled dormitory access (key, security card, etc).

TRANSFER AND INTERNATIONAL STUDENTS

Transfer students: May apply for admission for the following academic terms: Fall, Spring. Applicants do not need a minimum number of credits to apply. For fall 2005: Transfer applications received: 617. Transfer applicants offered admission: 512. Transfer applicants enrolled: 279. **International students:** Number of foreign undergraduates: 326 (16% of student body). Minimum TOEFL score required: 550 (paper); 213 (computer).

Shimer College

- **Address:** PO Box 500; 414 N. Sheridan, Waukegan, IL 60079
- **Website:** http://www.shimer.edu
- **Private**
- **Enrollment:** N/A

KEY STATS

✔ **U.S News College Ranking:** Unranked, Liberal Arts Colleges
✔ **SAT or ACT Score (25th/75th percentile):** N/A
✔ **Tuition:** 2005-2006: $19,525

Selectivity: N/A	**Room/board:** $3,000
Acceptance rate: 94%	**Average debt:** N/A
Student/faculty ratio: N/A	**Proportion who borrowed:** N/A

Southern Illinois University–Carbondale

- **Address:** Carbondale, IL 62901-6899
- **Website:** http://www.siuc.edu
- **Public**
- **Enrollment:** 14,962 full-time; 1,735 part-time

KEY STATS

- ✔ **U.S News College Ranking:** third tier, National Universities
- ✔ **ACT Score (25th/75th percentile):** 19-24
- ✔ **Tuition:** 2006-2007: $7,291 in state, $15,257 out of state

Selectivity: Selective	**Room/board:** $6,138
Acceptance rate: 77%	**Average debt:** $14,708
Student/faculty ratio: 17/1	**Proportion who borrowed:** 39%

UNDERGRADUATE STUDENT BODY STATS

2005-2006 enrollment: 14,962 full-time; 1,735 part-time. Men: 57%; women: 43%. **Ethnic makeup:** African American: 16%; American-Indian: 1%; Asian American: 2%; Hispanic: 4%; White: 76%; International: 2%.

ADMISSIONS FACTS AND FIGURES

Phone: (618) 536-4405. **Email:** joinsiuc@siu.edu. **Website:** http://www.siuc.edu. **Application deadlines for fall 2007:** Regular decision: August 17. Early decision: Not offered. Early action: Not offered. Admission can be deferred. **Application fee:** $30. Common application is not accepted. **To apply online, go to:** http://admissions.siu.edu/admpp.htm. **Admissions requirements/recommendations:** High school units required (recommended): English: 4; Mathematics: 3; Science: 3; Foreign language: (2); Social studies: 3; Academic electives: 2; Total units: 15. Tests: The college uses SAT or ACT scores in admissions decisions. Either SAT or ACT required. For admission to the fall 2007 entering class, the school will accept: ACT without writing. Campus visit: Recommended. Admissions interview: Neither required nor recommended. Off-campus interview: Not available. **Factors that count in admissions decisions:** *Academic:* Secondary school record: Important. Class rank: Very important. Letters of recommendation: Considered. Standardized test scores: Very important. Essay: Considered. *Nonacademic:* Interview: Not considered. Extracurricular activities: Not considered. Talent/ability: Not considered. Character/personal qualities: Not considered. Alumni/ae relationship: Not considered. Geographical residence: Not considered. State residency: Not considered. Religious affiliation/commitment: Not considered. Minority status: Not considered. Volunteer work: Not considered. Work experience: Not considered. **Other schools with the greatest overlap in applicants:** Illinois State University; Northern Illinois University; University of Illinois–Urbana-Champaign; Western Illinois University. **Admissions statistics for the fall 2005 entering class:** Total applicants: 9,285. Total accepted: 7,173. Freshmen enrolled: 2,470; 8% were from out of state. Overall acceptance rate: 77%. **Credentials of fall 2005 freshmen:** 9% ranked in the top 10 percent of their high school class; 27% were in the top 25 percent, and 60% were in the top half. (Proportion submitting class standing: 92%.) **First-year students who submitted SAT scores:** 4%. Scores (25/75 percentile): Verbal: 450-590, Math: 460-580, Combined: 910-1170. **First-year students submitting ACT scores:** 90%. Scores (25/75 percentile): English: 18-24, Math: 17-24, Composite: 19-24.

ACADEMICS

Year founded: 1869. **Academic calendar:** Semester. **Degrees offered:** associate, bachelor's, post-bachelor's certificate, master's, first professional, first professional certificate, doctorate. **Most popular majors:** 22% education, 9% engineering technologies/technicians, 8% business, management, marketing, and related support services, 8% health professions and related clinical sciences, 6% visual and performing arts. **Major fields of study:** agriculture, agriculture operations, and related sciences; architecture and related services; biological and biomedical sciences; business, management, marketing, and related support services; communication, journalism, and related programs; computer and information sciences and support services; education; engineering; engineering technologies/technicians; English language and literature/letters; family and consumer sciences/human sciences; foreign languages, literatures, and linguistics; health professions and related clinical sciences; history; legal professions and studies; liberal arts and sciences studies, and humanities; mathematics and statistics; mechanic and repair technologies/technicians; multi/interdisciplinary studies; natural resources and conservation; parks, recreation, leisure, and fitness studies; philosophy and religious studies; physical sciences; psychology; public administration and social service professions; security and protective services; social sciences; transportation and materials moving; visual and performing arts. **Areas of required coursework:** arts/fine arts, mathematics, English (including composition), sciences (biological or physical), social science, other. **Pre-professional programs:** pre-law, pre-dentistry, pre-medicine, pre-veterinary science, pre-optometry, pre-pharmacy, other. **Special academic programs:** cooperative (work-study plan) program, distance learning, double major, English as a Second Language (ESL), honors program, independent study, internships, student-designed major, study abroad, teacher certificate program. **Teacher certification offered in:** early childhood, special education, elementary, middle/junior high, secondary. **Cooperative education programs:** agriculture, art, business, education, engineering, health professions, home economics, humanities, natural science, social/behavioral science, technologies, vocational arts. **Reserve Officers Training Corps (ROTC):** Army ROTC: Offered on campus; Air Force ROTC: Offered on campus. **Faculty and instruction (2005-2006):** Total instructional faculty: 901 full-time, 180 part-time (64% men; 36% women; 13% minorities). Full-time faculty with Ph.D. or other terminal degree: 84%. Student/faculty ratio: 17/1. Classes of fewer than 20 students: 47%; of 20 to 49 students: 47%; of 50 or more students: 6%. **Advanced Placement and International Baccalaureate credit:** AP tests may be used for: Credit and/or placement. Scores accepted: 3, 4, 5. **Freshmen returning for sophomore year:** 69%. **Graduation rates:** Four-year: 19%; five-year: 37%; six-year: 41%. **Graduate study:** 44% of students pursue further study within five years. Fields in which graduates pursue further study: law, 4%; medicine, 1%.

COSTS AND FINANCIAL AID

Financial aid office: (618) 453-4334. **Expenses (2006-2007):** Tuition and fees 2006-2007: $7,291 in state, $15,257 out of state; room/board: $6,138. Estimated books and supplies: $900 personal expenses: $2,397. **Financial aid:** Priority filing date for institution's financial aid form: April 1. In 2005-2006, 70% of undergraduates applied for financial aid. Of those, 56% were determined to have financial need; 87% had their need fully met. Average financial aid package (proportion receiving): $10,016 (55%). Average amount of gift aid, such as scholarships or grants (proportion receiving): $6,185 (42%). Average amount of self-help aid, such as work study or loans (proportion receiving): $4,637 (47%). Average need-based loan (excluding PLUS or other private loans): $3,884. Among students who received need-based aid, the average percentage of need met: 98%. Among students who received aid based on merit, the average award (and the proportion receiving): $3,280 (7%). The average athletic scholarship (and the proportion receiving): $10,251 (1%). Average amount of debt of borrowers graduating in 2005: $14,708. Proportion who borrowed: 39%.

CAMPUS LIFE AND EXTRACURRICULAR ACTIVITIES

Campus housing available: coed dorms, women's dorms, men's dorms, sorority housing, fraternity housing, apartments for married students, apartment for single students, special housing for disabled students. Students who live in college-owned, operated, or affiliated housing: 30%. **Student employment:** During the 2005-2006 academic year, 25% of undergraduates worked on campus. Average per-year earnings: $1,736. **Clubs and organizations:** Number of student organizations: 450. Activities include: choral groups, concert band, dance, drama/theater, jazz band, literary magazine, marching band, music ensembles, musical theater, opera, pep band, radio station, student government, student newspaper, student film society, symphony orchestra, television station, yearbook. Number of fraternities: 17; sororities: 11. Proportion of men in fraternities: 5%; of women in sororities: 5%. Average proportion of students who stay on campus on weekends: 75%. **Sports program (2005-2006):** Member of NCAA I. *Men's intercollegiate varsity sports:* baseball, basketball, cross-country, football, golf, swimming and diving, tennis, track and field (indoor), track and field (outdoor). *Women's intercollegiate varsity sports:* basketball, cross-country, golf, softball, swimming and diving, tennis, track and field (indoor), track and field (outdoor), volleyball.

SERVICES AND FACILITIES

Basic services: nonremedial tutoring, women's center, placement service, day care, health service, health insurance. **Remedial assistance:** reading, math, writing, study skills. **Counseling services:** minority student, career, military, personal, veteran student, academic, older student, psychological, birth control, religious. **For learning-disabled students:** School does not offer a structured program with separate admission and additional fees. Total undergraduates in learning-disabled program or receiving services: 150. Services include: reading machines, tape recorders, other special classes, videotaped classes, diagnostic testing service, note-taking services, oral tests, learning center, readers, extended time for tests, priority registration, substitution of courses, texts on tape, typist/scribe, exams on tape or computer, other testing accomodations, waiver of foreign language degree requirement, waiver of math degree requirement, other. **Library:** Number of titles: 2,840,324; number of current serial subscriptions: 40,411. **Information technology resources:** Students are not required to lease or own a computer. Number of campus computers available to all students: 1,827. School has a wireless network. Approximate number of users that can be accommodated: 8,000. Proportion of college-owned housing units wired for high-speed internet access: 90%. **Campus safety:** Security services offered: 24-hour foot and vehicle patrols, late-night transport/escort service, 24-hour emergency telephones, lighted pathways/sidewalks, student patrols, controlled dormitory access (key, security card, etc).

TRANSFER AND INTERNATIONAL STUDENTS

Transfer students: May apply for admission for the following academic terms: Fall, Spring, Summer. Applicants need a minimum number of credits to apply. For fall 2005: Transfer applications received: 5,051. Transfer applicants offered admission: 4,250. Transfer applicants enrolled: 3,027. **International students:** Number of foreign undergraduates: 322 (2% of student body). Number of countries represented: 109. Minimum TOEFL score required: 520 (paper); 190 (computer).

Southern Illinois University–Edwardsville

- **Address:** Box 1600, Edwardsville, IL 62026
- **Website:** http://www.siue.edu
- **Public**
- **Enrollment:** 9,232 full-time; 1,713 part-time

KEY STATS

✔ **U.S News College Ranking:** 55, Universities–Master's (Midwest)
✔ **ACT Score (25th/75th percentile):** 20-25
✔ **Tuition:** 2005-2006: $5,209 in state, $11,734 out of state

Selectivity: Selective	Room/board: $5,819
Acceptance rate: 77%	Average debt: $17,290
Student/faculty ratio: N/A	Proportion who borrowed: 20%

UNDERGRADUATE STUDENT BODY STATS

2005-2006 enrollment: 9,232 full-time; 1,713 part-time. Men: 45%; women: 55%. **Ethnic makeup:** African American: 10%; Asian American: 2%; Hispanic: 2%; White: 85%; International: 1%.

ADMISSIONS FACTS AND FIGURES

Phone: (618) 650-3705. **Email:** admissions@siue.edu. **Website:** http://www.siue.edu. **Application deadlines for fall 2007:** Regular decision: May 1. Early decision: Not offered. Early action: Not offered. Admission can be deferred. **Application fee:** $30. Common application is not accepted. **To apply online, go to:** http://www.admissions.siue.edu. **Admissions requirements/recommendations:** High school units required (recommended): English: 4; Mathematics: 3; Science: 3; Foreign language: (2); Social studies: 3 (0); History: (2); Academic electives: 2; Total units: 15. Tests: The college uses SAT or ACT scores in admissions decisions. ACT required. For admission to the fall 2007 entering class, the school will accept: ACT with writing, ACT without writing. Campus visit: Recommended. Admissions interview: Neither required nor recommended. Off-campus interview: Not available. **Factors that count in admissions decisions:** *Academic:* Secondary school record: Important. Class rank: Very important. Letters of recommendation: Not considered. Standardized test scores: Very important. Essay: Not considered. *Nonacademic:* Interview: Not considered. Extracurricular activities: Not considered. Talent/ability: Not considered. Character/personal qualities: Not considered. Alumni/ae relationship: Not considered. Geographical residence: Not considered. State residency: Not considered. Religious affiliation/commitment: Not considered. Minority status: Not considered. Volunteer work: Not considered. Work experience: Not considered. **Other schools with the greatest overlap in applicants:** Lewis and Clark College. **Admissions statistics for the fall 2005 entering class:** Total applicants: 5,379. Total accepted: 4,149. Freshmen enrolled: 1,748; 9% were from out of state. Overall acceptance rate: 77%. **Credentials of fall 2005 freshmen:** 16% ranked in the top 10 percent of their high school class; 43% were in the top 25 percent, and 78% were in the top half. (Proportion submitting

class standing: 96%.) **First-year students submitting ACT scores:** 98%. Scores (25/75 percentile): English: 19-26, Math: 18-25, Composite: 20-25.

ACADEMICS

Year founded: 1957. **Academic calendar:** Semester. **Degrees offered:** bachelor's, post-bachelor's certificate, master's, post-master's certificate, first professional, first professional certificate. **Most popular majors:** 26% business, management, marketing, and related support services, 11% education, 7% psychology, 6% engineering, 6% visual and performing arts. **Major fields of study:** biological and biomedical sciences; business, management, marketing, and related support services; communication, journalism, and related programs; computer and information sciences and support services; education; engineering; engineering technologies/technicians; English language and literature/letters; foreign languages, literatures, and linguistics; health professions and related clinical sciences; history; liberal arts and sciences studies, and humanities; mathematics and statistics; parks, recreation, leisure, and fitness studies; philosophy and religious studies; physical sciences; psychology; public administration and social service professions; security and protective services; social sciences; visual and performing arts. **Areas of required coursework:** arts/fine arts, humanities, computer literacy, mathematics, English (including composition), philosophy, sciences (biological or physical), history, social science. **Pre-professional programs:** pre-law, pre-dentistry, pre-medicine, pre-veterinary science, pre-pharmacy. **Special academic programs:** accelerated program, cooperative (work-study plan) program, cross-registration, distance learning, double major, English as a Second Language (ESL), honors program, independent study, internships, student-designed major, study abroad, teacher certificate program, weekend college. **Teacher certification offered in:** early childhood, special education, elementary, middle/junior high, secondary. **Cooperative education programs:** business, computer science, engineering, natural science, social/behavioral science. **Reserve Officers Training Corps (ROTC):** Army ROTC: Offered on campus; Air Force ROTC: Offered on campus. **Faculty and instruction (2005-2006):** Total instructional faculty: 556 full-time, 263 part-time (55% men; 45% women; 12% minorities). Full-time faculty with Ph.D. or other terminal degree: 83%. Classes of fewer than 20 students: 38%; of 20 to 49 students: 50%; of 50 or more students: 12%. **Advanced Placement and International Baccalaureate credit:** International Baccalaureate exams may be used for: Credit and/or placement. **Freshmen returning for sophomore year:** 74%. **Graduation rates:** Four-year: 19%; five-year: 37%; six-year: 43%. **Graduate study:** 30% of students pursue further study within one year; 24% within five years.

COSTS AND FINANCIAL AID

Financial aid office: (618) 650-3839. **Expenses (2005-2006):** Tuition and fees 2005-2006: $5,209 in state, $11,734 out of state; room/board: $5,819. Estimated books and supplies: $652; transportation: $1,823; personal expenses: $1,404. **Financial aid:** Priority filing date for institution's financial aid form: March 1; deadline: June 1. In 2005-2006, 70% of undergraduates applied for financial aid. Of those, 52% were determined to have financial need; 24% had their need fully met. Average financial aid package (proportion receiving): $9,050 (50%). Average amount of gift aid, such as scholarships or grants (proportion receiving): $5,560 (36%). Average amount of self-help aid, such as work study or loans (proportion receiving): $4,502 (41%). Average need-based loan (excluding PLUS or other private loans): $3,700. Among students who received need-based aid, the average percentage of need met: 76%. Among students who received aid based on merit, the average award (and the proportion receiving): $3,926 (10%). The average athletic scholarship (and the proportion receiving): $2,196 (1%). Average amount of debt of borrowers graduating in 2005: $17,290. Proportion who borrowed: 20%.

CAMPUS LIFE AND EXTRACURRICULAR ACTIVITIES

Campus housing available (% using): coed dorms (51%), fraternity housing, apartments for married students (5%), apartment for single students (44%), other housing options. Students who live in college-owned, operated, or affiliated housing: 27%. **Student employment:** During the 2005-2006 academic year, 14% of undergraduates worked on campus. Average per-year earnings: $2,812. **Clubs and organizations:** Number of student organizations: 140. Activities include: choral groups, concert band, dance, drama/theater, jazz band, literary magazine, music ensembles, musical theater, opera, pep band, radio station, student government, student newspaper, symphony orchestra. Number of fraternities: 9; sororities: 7. **Sports program (2005-2006):** Member of NCAA II. *Men's intercollegiate varsity sports:* baseball, basketball, cross-country, golf, soccer, tennis, track and field (indoor), track and field (outdoor), wrestling. *Women's intercollegiate varsity sports:* basketball, cross-country, golf, soccer, softball, tennis, track and field (indoor), track and field (outdoor), volleyball.

SERVICES AND FACILITIES

Basic services: nonremedial tutoring, day care, health service, health insurance. **Remedial assistance:** reading, math, writing, study skills. **Counseling services:** minority student, career, military, personal, veteran student, academic, older student, psychological, birth control, religious, other. **For learning-disabled students:** School does not offer a structured program with separate admission and additional fees. Total undergraduates in learning-disabled program or receiving services: 133. Services include: remedial math, remedial English, reading machines, remedial reading, tape recorders, other special classes, diagnostic testing service, untimed tests, note-taking services, oral tests, learning center, readers, extended time for tests, tutors, priority registration, priority seating, other. **Library:** Number of titles: 839,239; number of current serial subscriptions: 24,601. **Information technology resources:** Students are not required to lease or own a computer. Number of campus computers available to all students: 800. School does not have a wireless network. Proportion of college-owned housing units wired for high-speed internet access: 100%. **Campus safety:** Security services offered: 24-hour foot and vehicle patrols, late-night transport/escort service, 24-hour emergency telephones, lighted pathways/sidewalks, controlled dormitory access (key, security card, etc).

TRANSFER AND INTERNATIONAL STUDENTS

Transfer students: May apply for admission for the following academic terms: Fall, Spring, Summer. Applicants need a minimum number of credits to apply. For fall 2005: Transfer applications received: 2,580. Transfer applicants offered admission: 2,146. Transfer applicants enrolled: 1,300. **International students:** Number of foreign undergraduates: 112 (1% of student body). Minimum TOEFL score required: 550 (paper); 213 (computer).

St. Xavier University

- **Address:** 3700 W. 103rd Street, Chicago, IL 60655
- **Website:** http://www.sxu.edu
- **Private; Religious affiliation:** Roman Catholic
- **Enrollment:** 2,391 full-time; 791 part-time

KEY STATS

✔ **U.S News College Ranking:** 36, Universities–Master's (Midwest)
✔ **ACT Score (25th/75th percentile):** 20-25
✔ **Tuition:** 2006-2007: $19,860

Selectivity: Selective	**Room/board:** $7,414
Acceptance rate: 69%	**Average debt:** $20,470
Student/faculty ratio: 15/1	**Proportion who borrowed:** 81%

UNDERGRADUATE STUDENT BODY STATS

2005-2006 enrollment: 2,391 full-time; 791 part-time. Men: 28%; women: 72%. **Ethnic makeup:** African American: 18%; Asian American: 2%; Hispanic: 13%; White: 67%. **Religious preference:** Roman Catholic: 60%; Protestant: 20%; Muslim: 2%; Other: 11%.

ADMISSIONS FACTS AND FIGURES

Phone: (773) 298-3050. **Email:** admission@sxu.edu. **Website:** http://www.sxu.edu. **Application deadlines for fall 2007:** Regular decision: Rolling. Early decision: Not offered. Early action: Not offered. Admission can be deferred. **Application fee:** $25. Common application is accepted. **To apply online, go to:** http://www.sxu.edu/admission. **Admissions requirements/recommendations:** High school units required (recommended): English: 4 (4); Mathematics: 3 (3); Science: 2 (2); Foreign language: 2 (2); Social studies: 2 (2); History: 2 (2); Academic electives: 3 (3); Total units: 16 (16). Tests: The college uses SAT or ACT scores in admissions decisions. Either SAT or ACT required. For admission to the fall 2007 entering class, the school will accept: ACT with writing, ACT without writing. Campus visit: Recommended. Admissions interview: Recommended. Off-campus interview: Not available. **Factors that count in admissions decisions:** *Academic:* Secondary school record: Important. Class rank: Not considered. Letters of recommendation: Considered. Standardized test scores: Very important. Essay: Very important. *Nonacademic:* Interview: Considered. Extracurricular activities: Considered. Talent/ability: Considered. Character/personal qualities: Considered. Alumni/ae relationship: Not considered. Geographical residence: Not considered. State residency: Not considered. Religious affiliation/commitment: Not considered. Minority status: Not considered. Volunteer work: Considered. Work experience: Considered.

Other schools with the greatest overlap in applicants: DePaul University; Loyola University Chicago; Northern Illinois University; University of Illinois–Chicago; University of Illinois–Urbana-Champaign. **Admissions statistics for the fall 2005 entering class:** Total applicants: 1,998. Total accepted: 1,385. Freshmen enrolled: 422; 9% were from out of state. Overall acceptance rate: 69%. **Credentials of fall 2005 freshmen:** 14% ranked in the top 10 percent of their high school class; 43% were in the top 25 percent, and 73% were in the top half. (Proportion submitting class standing: 80%.) **Average high school grade point average:** 3.2. **First-year students who submitted SAT scores:** 6%. Scores (25/75 percentile): Verbal: 471-590, Math: 480-590, Combined: 951-1180. **First-year students submitting ACT scores:** 96%. Scores (25/75 percentile): English: 20-26, Math: 18-24, Composite: 20-25.

ACADEMICS

Year founded: 1846. **Academic calendar:** Semester. **Degrees offered:** bachelor's, post-bachelor's certificate, master's, post-master's certificate. **Most popular majors:** 21% business, management, marketing, and related support services, 20% education, 16% health professions and related clinical sciences, 9% liberal arts and sciences studies, and humanities, 7% psychology. **Major fields of study:** area, ethnic, cultural, and gender studies; biological and biomedical sciences; business, management, marketing, and related support services; communication, journalism, and related programs; computer and information sciences and support services; education; English language and literature/letters; foreign languages, literatures, and linguistics; health professions and related clinical sciences; history; liberal arts and sciences studies, and humanities; mathematics and statistics; multi/interdisciplinary studies; philosophy and religious studies; physical sciences; psychology; security and protective services; social sciences; visual and performing arts. **Areas of required coursework:** humanities, mathematics, English (including composition), philosophy, sciences (biological or physical), history, social science, other. **Pre-professional programs:** pre-pharmacy. **Special academic programs (% participation):** accelerated program (20%), cooperative (work-study plan) program (5%), distance learning (5%), double major (5%), English as a Second Language (ESL), exchange student program (domestic), honors program, independent study, internships, liberal arts/career combination, student-designed major, study abroad, teacher certificate program (14.3%). **Teacher certification offered in:** early childhood, elementary, middle/junior high, secondary, bilingual/bicultural. **Faculty and instruction (2005-2006):** Total instructional faculty: 168 full-time, 258 part-time (39% men; 61% women; 7% minorities). Full-time faculty with Ph.D. or other terminal degree: 85%. Student/faculty ratio: 15/1. Classes of fewer than 20 students: 48%; of 20 to 49 students: 52%; of 50 or more students: 1%. **Advanced Placement and International Baccalaureate credit:** AP tests may be used for: Credit and/or placement. Scores accepted: 3, 4, 5. International Baccalaureate exams may be used for: Credit only. **Freshmen returning for sophomore year:** 77%. **Graduation rates:** Four-year: 30%; five-year: 50%; six-year: 53%. **Graduate study:** 24% of students pursue further study within one year. Fields in which graduates pursue further study: Master of Business Administration (MBA), 20%; law, 1%; medicine, 1%; dentistry, 1%; theology (or the seminary), 1%; education, 19%; arts and sciences, 57%.

COSTS AND FINANCIAL AID

Financial aid office: (773) 298-3070. **Expenses (2006-2007):** Tuition and fees 2006-2007: $19,860; room/board: $7,414. Estimated books and supplies: $900; transportation: $417; personal expenses: $973. **Financial aid:** Priority filing date for institution's financial aid form: March 1. In 2005-2006, 90% of undergraduates applied for financial aid. Of those, 80% were determined to have financial need; 22% had their need fully met. Average financial aid package (proportion receiving): $15,408 (80%). Average amount of gift aid, such as scholarships or grants (proportion receiving): $9,018 (79%). Average amount of self-help aid, such as work study or loans (proportion receiving): $8,568 (74%). Average need-based loan (excluding PLUS or other private loans): $3,885. Among students who received need-based aid, the average percentage of need met: 83%. Among students who received aid based on merit, the average award (and the proportion receiving): $4,135 (18%). The average athletic scholarship (and the proportion receiving): $8,502 (8%). Average amount of debt of borrowers graduating in 2005: $20,470. Proportion who borrowed: 81%.

CAMPUS LIFE AND EXTRACURRICULAR ACTIVITIES

Campus housing available (% using): coed dorms (100%). Students who live in college-owned, operated, or affiliated housing: 19%. **Student employment:** During the 2005-2006 academic year, 22% of undergraduates worked on campus. Average per-year earnings: $3,000. **Clubs and organizations:**

Number of student organizations: 33. Activities include: choral groups, concert band, dance, drama/theater, jazz band, literary magazine, marching band, music ensembles, radio station, student government, student newspaper, symphony orchestra. Number of fraternities: 0; sororities: 0. Average proportion of students who stay on campus on weekends: 50%. **Sports program (2005-2006):** Member of NAIA. *Men's intercollegiate varsity sports:* baseball, basketball, cross-country, football, soccer. *Women's intercollegiate varsity sports:* basketball, cross-country, soccer, softball, volleyball.

SERVICES AND FACILITIES

Basic services: nonremedial tutoring, placement service, day care, health service, health insurance. **Remedial assistance:** reading, math, writing, study skills. **Counseling services:** career, personal. **For learning-disabled students:** School does not offer a structured program with separate admission and additional fees. Total undergraduates in learning-disabled program or receiving services: 85. Services include: remedial math, tape recorders, note-taking services, oral tests, learning center, extended time for tests, tutors, texts on tape, other. **Library:** Number of titles: 174,000; number of current serial subscriptions: 15,000. **Information technology resources:** Students are not required to lease or own a computer. Number of campus computers available to all students: 500. School has a wireless network. Approximate number of users that can be accommodated: 1,500. Proportion of college-owned housing units wired for high-speed internet access: 100%. **Campus safety:** Security services offered: 24-hour foot and vehicle patrols, late-night transport/escort service, 24-hour emergency telephones, lighted pathways/sidewalks, student patrols, controlled dormitory access (key, security card, etc).

TRANSFER AND INTERNATIONAL STUDENTS

Transfer students: May apply for admission for the following academic terms: Fall, Spring, Summer. Applicants do not need a minimum number of credits to apply. For fall 2005: Transfer applications received: 1,770. Transfer applicants offered admission: 961. Transfer applicants enrolled: 543. **International students:** Number of foreign undergraduates: 14. Number of countries represented: 12. Minimum TOEFL score required: 550 (paper); 213 (computer).

Trinity Christian College

■ **Address:** 6601 W. College Drive, Palos Heights, IL 60463
■ **Website:** http://www.trnty.edu
■ **Private; Religious affiliation:** Reformed
■ **Enrollment:** 1,049 full-time; 231 part-time

KEY STATS

✔ **U.S News College Ranking:** 35, Comp. Coll.–Bachelor's (Midwest)
✔ **ACT Score (25th/75th percentile):** 19-25
✔ **Tuition:** 2006-2007: $17,920

Selectivity: Selective	**Room/board:** $6,810
Acceptance rate: 89%	**Average debt:** $18,956
Student/faculty ratio: 12/1	**Proportion who borrowed:** 80%

UNDERGRADUATE STUDENT BODY STATS

2005-2006 enrollment: 1,049 full-time; 231 part-time. Men: 34%; women: 66%. **Ethnic makeup:** African American: 8%; Asian American: 2%; Hispanic: 5%; White: 84%; International: 1%. **Religious preference:** Roman Catholic: 8%; No preference: 1%; Reformed: 50%; Baptist: 5%; Other: 36%.

ADMISSIONS FACTS AND FIGURES

Phone: (800) 748-0085. **Email:** admissions@trnty.edu. **Website:** http://www.trnty.edu. **Application deadlines for fall 2007:** Regular decision: August 31. Early decision: Not offered. Early action: Not offered. Admission can be deferred. **Application fee:** $20. Common application is not accepted. **Admissions requirements/recommendations:** High school units required (recommended): English: 3 (4); Mathematics: 3 (3); Science: 2 (3); Foreign language: (2); Social studies: 2 (3); History: (2); Total units: 16 (18). **Tests:** The college uses SAT or ACT scores in admissions decisions. Either SAT or ACT required. For admission to the fall 2007 entering class, the school will accept: ACT with writing, ACT without writing. Campus visit: Recommended. Admissions interview: Recommended. Off-campus interview: May be arranged. **Factors that count in admissions decisions:** *Academic:* Secondary school record: Very important. Class rank: Important.

Letters of recommendation: Important. Standardized test scores: Very important. Essay: Important. *Nonacademic:* Interview: Important. Extracurricular activities: Important. Talent/ability: Important. Character/personal qualities: Important. Alumni/ae relationship: Considered. Geographical residence: Not considered. State residency: Not considered. Religious affiliation/commitment: Important. Minority status: Not considered. Volunteer work: Considered. Work experience: Considered. **Other schools with the greatest overlap in applicants:** Calvin College; Dordt College; Hope College; Northwestern College. **Admissions statistics for the fall 2005 entering class:** Total applicants: 600. Total accepted: 535. Freshmen enrolled: 229; 52% were from out of state. Overall acceptance rate: 89%. **Credentials of fall 2005 freshmen:** 14% ranked in the top 10 percent of their high school class; 33% were in the top 25 percent, and 64% were in the top half. (Proportion submitting class standing: 86%.) **Average high school grade point average:** 3.3. **First-year students who submitted SAT scores:** 10%. Scores (25/75 percentile): Verbal: 470-600, Math: 440-570, Combined: 910-1170. **First-year students submitting ACT scores:** 90%. Scores (25/75 percentile): English: 19-25, Math: 17-25, Composite: 19-25.

ACADEMICS

Year founded: 1959. **Academic calendar:** Semester. **Degrees offered:** bachelor's. **Most popular majors:** 34% education, 17% business, management, marketing, and related support services, 8% theology and religious vocations, 6% health professions and related clinical sciences, 6% psychology. **Major fields of study:** biological and biomedical sciences; business, management, marketing, and related support services; communication, journalism, and related programs; computer and information sciences and support services; education; English language and literature/letters; foreign languages, literatures, and linguistics; health professions and related clinical sciences; history; mathematics and statistics; parks, recreation, leisure, and fitness studies; philosophy and religious studies; physical sciences; psychology; public administration and social service professions; social sciences; theology and religious vocations; visual and performing arts. **Areas of required coursework:** arts/fine arts, humanities, mathematics, English (including composition), philosophy, sciences (biological or physical), history, social science, other. **Pre-professional programs:** pre-law, pre-dentistry, pre-medicine, pre-theology, pre-veterinary science, pre-optometry, pre-pharmacy. **Special academic programs (% participation):** cooperative (work-study plan) program (40%), double major (8%), honors program (10%), independent study (5%), internships (90%), liberal arts/career combination (100%), study abroad (5%), teacher certificate program (36%). **Teacher certification offered in:** special education, elementary, middle/junior high, secondary, bilingual/bicultural. **Faculty and instruction (2005-2006):** Total instructional faculty: 76 full-time, 51 part-time (59% men; 41% women; 16% minorities). Full-time faculty with Ph.D. or other terminal degree: 62%. Student/faculty ratio: 12/1. Classes of fewer than 20 students: 64%; of 20 to 49 students: 36%; of 50 or more students: 0%. **Advanced Placement and International Baccalaureate credit:** AP tests may be used for: Credit and/or placement. Scores accepted: 3, 4, 5. **Freshmen returning for sophomore year:** 78%. **Graduation rates:** Four-year: 43%; five-year: 52%; six-year: 56%. **Graduate study:** 9% of students pursue further study immediately upon graduation. Fields in which graduates pursue further study: Master of Business Administration (MBA), 1%; law, 7%; medicine, 14%; dentistry, 1%; theology (or the seminary), 42%; arts and sciences, 35%.

COSTS AND FINANCIAL AID

Financial aid office: (708) 239-4706. **Expenses (2006-2007):** Tuition and fees 2006-2007: $17,920; room/board: $6,810. Estimated books and supplies: $925; transportation: $1,419; personal expenses: $1,426. **Financial aid:** Priority filing date for institution's financial aid form: February 1; deadline: April 15. In 2005-2006, 86% of undergraduates applied for financial aid. Of those, 80% were determined to have financial need; Average financial aid package (proportion receiving): $7,806 (80%). Average amount of gift aid, such as scholarships or grants (proportion receiving): $5,600 (71%). Average amount of self-help aid, such as work study or loans (proportion receiving): $3,100 (64%). Average need-based loan (excluding PLUS or other private loans): $3,966. Among students who received need-based aid, the average percentage of need met: 68%. Average amount of debt of borrowers graduating in 2005: $18,956. Proportion who borrowed: 80%.

CAMPUS LIFE AND EXTRACURRICULAR ACTIVITIES

Campus housing available (% using): coed dorms (87%), apartment for single students (13%). Students who live in college-owned, operated, or affiliated housing: 52%. **Student employment:** During the 2005-2006 academic year, 38% of undergraduates worked on campus. Average per-year earnings: $1,400. **Clubs and organizations:** Number of student organizations: 20.

Activities include: choral groups, concert band, dance, drama/theater, jazz band, literary magazine, music ensembles, student government, student newspaper, yearbook. Number of fraternities: 0; sororities: 0. Average proportion of students who stay on campus on weekends: 50%. **Sports program (2005-2006):** Member of NAIA. **Men's intercollegiate varsity sports:** baseball, basketball, cross-country, soccer, track and field (indoor), track and field (outdoor). **Women's intercollegiate varsity sports:** basketball, cross-country, soccer, softball, track and field (indoor), track and field (outdoor), volleyball.

SERVICES AND FACILITIES

Basic services: nonremedial tutoring, placement service, health insurance. **Remedial assistance:** reading, math, writing, study skills. **Counseling services:** minority student, career, personal, academic, older student, psychological, religious. **For learning-disabled students:** School does not offer a structured program with separate admission and additional fees. Total undergraduates in learning-disabled program or receiving services: 156. Services include: remedial English, tape recorders, untimed tests, note-taking services, oral tests, learning center, readers, extended time for tests, tutors, priority registration, priority seating, proofreading services, texts on tape, typist/scribe, other. **Library:** Number of titles: 79,375; number of current serial subscriptions: 435. **Information technology resources:** Students are not required to lease or own a computer. Number of campus computers available to all students: 150. School has a wireless network. Proportion of college-owned housing units wired for high-speed internet access: 100%. **Campus safety:** Security services offered: 24-hour foot and vehicle patrols, late-night transport/escort service, 24-hour emergency telephones, lighted pathways/sidewalks, student patrols, controlled dormitory access (key, security card, etc.).

TRANSFER AND INTERNATIONAL STUDENTS

Transfer students: May apply for admission for the following academic terms: Fall, Spring. Applicants need a minimum number of credits to apply. For fall 2005: Transfer applications received: 246. Transfer applicants offered admission: 203. Transfer applicants enrolled: 93. **International students:** Number of foreign undergraduates: 16 (1% of student body). Number of countries represented: 13. Minimum TOEFL score required: 550 (paper); 213 (computer).

University of Chicago

- **Address:** 5801 S. Ellis Avenue, Chicago, IL 60637
- **Website:** http://www.uchicago.edu
- **Private**
- **Enrollment:** 4,614 full-time; 57 part-time

KEY STATS

✔ **U.S News College Ranking:** 9, National Universities
✔ **SAT Score (25th/75th percentile):** 1350-1530
✔ **Tuition:** 2006-2007: $34,005

Selectivity: Most selective	**Room/board:** $10,608
Acceptance rate: 40%	**Average debt:** $17,651
Student/faculty ratio: 7/1	**Proportion who borrowed:** 51%

UNDERGRADUATE STUDENT BODY STATS

2005-2006 enrollment: 4,614 full-time; 57 part-time. Men: 50%; women: 50%. **Ethnic makeup:** African American: 4%; Asian American: 14%; Hispanic: 8%; White: 66%; International: 7%.

ADMISSIONS FACTS AND FIGURES

Phone: (773) 702-8650. **Email:** collegeadmissions@uchicago.edu. **Website:** http://www.uchicago.edu. **Application deadlines for fall 2007:** Regular decision: January 2; decision sent by April 1. Early decision: Not offered. Early action: Send application by: November 1; Decision sent by: December 15. Admission can be deferred. **Application fee:** $60. Common application is not accepted. **To apply online, go to:** http://uncommonapplication.uchicago.edu. **Admissions requirements/recommendations:** High school units required (recommended): English: (4); Mathematics: (4); Science: (4); Foreign language: (3); Social studies: (2); History: (2); Total units: (19). Tests: The college uses SAT or ACT scores in admissions decisions. Either SAT or ACT required. For admission to the fall 2007 entering class, the school will accept: ACT with writing, ACT without writing. Campus visit: Recommended. Admissions interview:

Recommended. Off-campus interview: May be arranged. **Factors that count in admissions decisions:** *Academic:* Secondary school record: Very important. Class rank: Important. Letters of recommendation: Very important. Standardized test scores: Considered. Essay: Very important. *Nonacademic:* Interview: Considered. Extracurricular activities: Important. Talent/ability: Very important. Character/personal qualities: Very important. Alumni/ae relationship: Considered. Geographical residence: Not considered. State residency: Not considered. Religious affiliation/commitment: Not considered. Minority status: Considered. Volunteer work: Important. Work experience: Considered. **Other schools with the greatest overlap in applicants:** Columbia University; Harvard University; Northwestern University; University of Pennsylvania; Yale University. **Admissions statistics for the fall 2005 entering class:** Total applicants: 9,011. Total accepted: 3,628. Freshmen enrolled: 1,203; 83% were from out of state. Accepted through early-decision or early-action plans: 35%. Overall acceptance rate: 40%. Non-early acceptance rate: 40%. **Size of waiting list:** 1545 applicants; enrolled from waiting list: 42. **Credentials of fall 2005 freshmen:** 79% ranked in the top 10 percent of their high school class; 95% were in the top 25 percent, and 98% were in the top half. (Proportion submitting class standing: 59%.) **First-year students who submitted SAT scores:** 84%. Scores (25/75 percentile): Verbal: 680-770, Math: 670-760, Combined: 1350-1530. **First-year students submitting ACT scores:** 39%. Scores (25/75 percentile): English: 29-33, Math: 29-33, Composite: 29-33.

ACADEMICS

Year founded: 1892. **Academic calendar:** Quarter. **Degrees offered:** bachelor's, master's, first professional, doctorate. **Most popular majors:** 39% social sciences, 11% biological and biomedical sciences, 7% mathematics and statistics, 7% psychology, 6% history. **Major fields of study:** area, ethnic, cultural, and gender studies; biological and biomedical sciences; computer and information sciences and support services; English language and literature/letters; foreign languages, literatures, and linguistics; history; liberal arts and sciences studies, and humanities; mathematics and statistics; multi/interdisciplinary studies; natural resources and conservation; philosophy and religious studies; physical sciences; psychology; public administration and social service professions; social sciences; theology and religious vocations; visual and performing arts. **Areas of required coursework:** arts/fine arts, humanities, mathematics, English (including composition), foreign languages, sciences (biological or physical), history, social science. **Pre-professional programs:** pre-law, pre-medicine. **Special academic programs (% participation):** accelerated program, double major (20%), exchange student program (domestic), independent study (50%), internships, student-designed major, study abroad (10%), teacher certificate program. **Teacher certification offered in:** elementary. **Reserve Officers Training Corps (ROTC):** Army ROTC: Offered at cooperating institution (University of Illinois Chicago); Air Force ROTC: Offered at cooperating institution (Illiniois Institute of Technology). **Faculty and instruction (2005-2006):** Total instructional faculty: 1,040 full-time, 547 part-time (70% men; 30% women; 15% minorities). Full-time faculty with Ph.D. or other terminal degree: 100%. Student/faculty ratio: 7/1. Classes of fewer than 20 students: 66%; of 20 to 49 students: 29%; of 50 or more students: 5%. **Advanced Placement and International Baccalaureate credit:** AP tests may be used for: Credit and/or placement. Scores accepted: 4, 5. International Baccalaureate exams may be used for: Credit and/or placement. **Freshmen returning for sophomore year:** 96%. **Graduation rates:** Four-year: 85%; five-year: 90%; six-year: 91%.

COSTS AND FINANCIAL AID

Financial aid office: (773) 702-8666. **Expenses (2006-2007):** Tuition and fees 2006-2007: $34,005; room/board: $10,608. Estimated books and supplies: $1,000 personal expenses: $1,829. **Financial aid:** In 2005-2006, 54% of undergraduates applied for financial aid. Of those, 45% were determined to have financial need; 100% had their need fully met. Average financial aid package (proportion receiving): $29,176 (45%). Average amount of gift aid, such as scholarships or grants (proportion receiving): $23,078 (45%). Average amount of self-help aid, such as work study or loans (proportion receiving): $7,451 (39%). Average need-based loan (excluding PLUS or other private loans): $5,494. Among students who received need-based aid, the average percentage of need met: 100%. Among students who received aid based on merit, the average award (and the proportion receiving): $11,579 (11%). The average athletic scholarship (and the proportion receiving): $0 (0%). Average amount of debt of borrowers graduating in 2005: $17,651. Proportion who borrowed: 51%.

CAMPUS LIFE AND EXTRACURRICULAR ACTIVITIES

Campus housing available: coed dorms, fraternity housing, apartments for married students. **Clubs and organizations:** Number of student organizations: 350. Activities include: choral groups, concert band, dance, drama/theater, jazz band, literary magazine, music ensembles, musical theater, pep band, radio station, student government, student newspaper, student film society, symphony orchestra. Number of fraternities: 11; sororities: 4. Average proportion of students who stay on campus on weekends: 95%.
Sports program (2005-2006): Member of NCAA III. *Men's intercollegiate varsity sports:* baseball, basketball, cross-country, football, soccer, swimming and diving, tennis, track and field (indoor), track and field (outdoor), wrestling. *Women's intercollegiate varsity sports:* basketball, cross-country, soccer, softball, swimming and diving, tennis, track and field (indoor), track and field (outdoor), volleyball.

SERVICES AND FACILITIES

Basic services: nonremedial tutoring, health service, health insurance. **Counseling services:** minority student, career, personal, academic, psychological, birth control, religious. **Library:** Number of titles: 7,600,347; number of current serial subscriptions: 41,790. **Information technology resources:** Students are not required to lease or own a computer. School has a wireless network. Proportion of college-owned housing units wired for high-speed internet access: 100%. **Campus safety:** Security services offered: 24-hour foot and vehicle patrols, late-night transport/escort service, 24-hour emergency telephones, lighted pathways/sidewalks, controlled dormitory access (key, security card, etc).

TRANSFER AND INTERNATIONAL STUDENTS

Transfer students: May apply for admission for the following academic terms: Fall. Applicants need a minimum number of credits to apply. For fall 2005: Transfer applications received: 524. Transfer applicants offered admission: 157. Transfer applicants enrolled: 68. **International students:** Number of foreign undergraduates: 339 (7% of student body). Number of countries represented: 55. Minimum TOEFL score required: 600 (paper); 250 (computer).

University of Illinois–Chicago

- **Address:** 601 S. Morgan M/C 102, Chicago, IL 60607
- **Website:** http://www.uic.edu
- **Public**
- **Enrollment:** 13,733 full-time; 1,417 part-time

KEY STATS

✔ **U.S News College Ranking:** third tier, National Universities
✔ **ACT Score (25th/75th percentile):** 20-26
✔ **Tuition:** 2006-2007: $9,742 in state, $22,132 out of state
  Selectivity: More selective   Room/board: $7,446
  Acceptance rate: 58%   Average debt: $18,800
  Student/faculty ratio: 16/1   Proportion who borrowed: 46%

UNDERGRADUATE STUDENT BODY STATS

2005-2006 enrollment: 13,733 full-time; 1,417 part-time. Men: 47%; women: 53%. **Ethnic makeup:** African American: 9%; Asian American: 25%; Hispanic: 17%; White: 49%; International: 1%.

ADMISSIONS FACTS AND FIGURES

Phone: (312) 996-4350. **Email:** uicadmit@uic.edu. **Website:** http://www.uic.edu. **Application deadlines for fall 2007:** Regular decision: January 15. Early decision: Not offered. Early action: Not offered. Admission cannot be deferred. **Application fee:** $40. Common application is not accepted. **To apply online, go to:** http://www.uic.edu/depts/oar/dloadapp.htm. **Admissions requirements/recommendations:** High school units required (recommended): English: 4; Mathematics: 3 (4); Science: 3; Foreign language: 2 (4); Social studies: 3; Academic electives: 1; Total units: 16. Tests: The college uses SAT or ACT scores in admissions decisions. Either SAT or ACT required. For admission to the fall 2007 entering class, the school will accept: ACT without writing. Campus visit: Recommended. Admissions interview: Neither required nor recommended. Off-campus interview: Not available. **Factors that count in admissions decisions:** *Academic:* Secondary school record: Considered. Class rank: Very important. Letters of recommendation: Considered.

Standardized test scores: Very important. Essay: Considered. *Nonacademic:* Interview: Not considered. Extracurricular activities: Not considered. Talent/ability: Considered. Character/personal qualities: Considered. Alumni/ae relationship: Not considered. Geographical residence: Not considered. State residency: Not considered. Religious affiliation/commitment: Not considered. Minority status: Not considered. Volunteer work: Not considered. Work experience: Not considered. **Admissions statistics for the fall 2005 entering class:** Total applicants: 12,692. Total accepted: 7,418. Freshmen enrolled: 2,776; 4% were from out of state. Overall acceptance rate: 58%. **Size of waiting list:** 0 applicants; enrolled from waiting list: 0. **Credentials of fall 2005 freshmen:** 25% ranked in the top 10 percent of their high school class; 57% were in the top 25 percent, and 91% were in the top half. (Proportion submitting class standing: 100%.) **First-year students who submitted SAT scores:** 11%. Scores (25/75 percentile): Verbal: N/A, Math: N/A, Combined: N/A. **First-year students submitting ACT scores:** 97%. Scores (25/75 percentile): English: 20-27, Math: 20-27, Composite: 20-26.

ACADEMICS

Year founded: 1965. **Academic calendar:** Semester. **Degrees offered:** bachelor's, master's, first professional, first professional certificate, doctorate. **Most popular majors:** 20% business, management, marketing, and related support services, 11% biological and biomedical sciences, 10% engineering, 9% psychology, 8% health professions and related clinical sciences. **Major fields of study:** architecture and related services; area, ethnic, cultural, and gender studies; biological and biomedical sciences; business, management, marketing, and related support services; communication, journalism, and related programs; computer and information sciences and support services; education; engineering; engineering technologies/technicians; English language and literature/letters; foreign languages, literatures, and linguistics; health professions and related clinical sciences; history; liberal arts and sciences studies, and humanities; mathematics and statistics; multi/interdisciplinary studies; parks, recreation, leisure, and fitness studies; philosophy and religious studies; physical sciences; psychology; public administration and social service professions; security and protective services; social sciences; visual and performing arts. **Areas of required coursework:** humanities, English (including composition), sciences (biological or physical), social science. **Pre-professional programs:** pre-law, pre-dentistry, pre-medicine, pre-veterinary science, pre-pharmacy, other. **Special academic programs:** accelerated program, cooperative (work-study plan) program, distance learning, double major, English as a Second Language (ESL), exchange student program (domestic), honors program, independent study, internships, student-designed major, study abroad, teacher certificate program. **Teacher certification offered in:** elementary, middle/junior high, secondary, bilingual/bicultural. **Cooperative education programs:** business, engineering, other. **Reserve Officers Training Corps (ROTC):** Army ROTC: Offered on campus; Navy ROTC: Offered at cooperating institution (Illinois Institute of Technology); Air Force ROTC: Offered at cooperating institution (Illinois Institute of Technology). **Faculty and instruction (2005-2006):** Total instructional faculty: 1,163 full-time, 362 part-time (55% men; 45% women; 20% minorities). Full-time faculty with Ph.D. or other terminal degree: 76%. Student/faculty ratio: 16/1. Classes of fewer than 20 students: 36%; of 20 to 49 students: 47%; of 50 or more students: 18%. **Advanced Placement and International Baccalaureate credit:** AP tests may be used for: Credit and/or placement. Scores accepted: 3, 4, 5. International Baccalaureate exams may be used for: Credit only. **Freshmen returning for sophomore year:** 78%. **Graduation rates:** Four-year: 20%; five-year: 42%; six-year: 50%. **Graduate study:** 34% of students pursue further study immediately upon graduation. Fields in which graduates pursue further study: law, 3%; medicine, 8%.

COSTS AND FINANCIAL AID

Financial aid office: (312) 996-3126. **Expenses (2006-2007):** Tuition and fees 2006-2007: $9,742 in state, $22,132 out of state; room/board: $7,446. Estimated books and supplies: $900; transportation: $190; personal expenses: $2,000. **Financial aid:** Priority filing date for institution's financial aid form: March 1. In 2005-2006, 69% of undergraduates applied for financial aid. Of those, 54% were determined to have financial need; 59% had their need fully met. Average financial aid package (proportion receiving): $10,753 (54%). Average amount of gift aid, such as scholarships or grants (proportion receiving): $8,389 (42%). Average amount of self-help aid, such as work study or loans (proportion receiving): $4,330 (42%). Average need-based loan (excluding PLUS or other private loans): $3,665. Among students who received need-based aid, the average percentage of need met: 91%. Among students who received aid based on merit, the average award (and the proportion receiving): $3,665 (7%). The average athletic scholarship (and the proportion receiving): $10,610 (1%). Average amount of debt of borrowers graduating in 2005: $18,800. Proportion who borrowed: 46%.

CAMPUS LIFE AND EXTRACURRICULAR ACTIVITIES

Campus housing available: coed dorms, apartments for married students, apartment for single students, special housing for disabled students, other housing options. Students who live in college-owned, operated, or affiliated housing: 12%. **Student employment:** During the 2005-2006 academic year, 28% of undergraduates worked on campus. Average per-year earnings: $5,530. **Clubs and organizations:** Number of student organizations: 259. Activities include: choral groups, concert band, dance, drama/theater, jazz band, literary magazine, music ensembles, musical theater, pep band, radio station, student government, student newspaper. Number of fraternities: 14; sororities: 13. Proportion of men in fraternities: 1%; of women in sororities: 1%. Average proportion of students who stay on campus on weekends: 50%. **Sports program (2005-2006):** Member of NCAA I. *Men's intercollegiate varsity sports:* baseball, basketball, cross-country, gymnastics, soccer, swimming and diving, tennis, track and field (indoor), track and field (outdoor). *Women's intercollegiate varsity sports:* basketball, cross-country, gymnastics, softball, swimming and diving, tennis, track and field (indoor), track and field (outdoor), volleyball.

SERVICES AND FACILITIES

Basic services: nonremedial tutoring, women's center, placement service, day care, health service, health insurance. **Remedial assistance:** reading, math, writing, study skills. **Counseling services:** minority student, career, military, personal, veteran student, academic, psychological, birth control, religious, other. **For learning-disabled students:** School does not offer a structured program with separate admission and additional fees. Total undergraduates in learning-disabled program or receiving services: 55. Services include: remedial math, remedial English, reading machines, remedial reading, tape recorders, note-taking services, oral tests, learning center, readers, extended time for tests, tutors, priority registration, priority seating, texts on tape, typist/scribe, exams on tape or computer, waiver of foreign language degree requirement. **Library:** Number of titles: 2,284,649; number of current serial subscriptions: 39,350. **Information technology resources:** Students are not required to lease or own a computer. Number of campus computers available to all students: 1,100. School has a wireless network. Approximate number of users that can be accommodated: 3,500. Proportion of college-owned housing units wired for high-speed internet access: 100%. **Campus safety:** Security services offered: 24-hour foot and vehicle patrols, late-night transport/escort service, 24-hour emergency telephones, lighted pathways/sidewalks, student patrols, controlled dormitory access (key, security card, etc).

TRANSFER AND INTERNATIONAL STUDENTS

Transfer students: May apply for admission for the following academic terms: Fall, Spring, Summer. Applicants need a minimum number of credits to apply. For fall 2005: Transfer applications received: 5,872. Transfer applicants offered admission: 2,117. Transfer applicants enrolled: 1,320. **International students:** Number of foreign undergraduates: 117 (1% of student body). Minimum TOEFL score required: 520 (paper); 190 (computer).

University of Illinois–Springfield

- **Address:** 1 University Plaza, Springfield, IL 62703-5407
- **Website:** http://www.uis.edu
- **Public**
- **Enrollment:** 1,561 full-time; 1,073 part-time

KEY STATS

✔ **U.S News College Ranking:** Unranked, Universities–Master's (Midwest)
✔ **ACT Score (25th/75th percentile):** 22-27
✔ **Tuition:** 2006-2007: $6,412 in state, $17,572 out of state

Selectivity: N/A	Room/board: N/A
Acceptance rate: 63%	Average debt: $10,486
Student/faculty ratio: 13/1	Proportion who borrowed: 46%

UNDERGRADUATE STUDENT BODY STATS

2005-2006 enrollment: 1,561 full-time; 1,073 part-time. Men: 40%; women: 60%. **Ethnic makeup:** African American: 9%; Asian American: 3%; Hispanic: 2%; White: 85%; International: 1%.

ADMISSIONS FACTS AND FIGURES

Phone: (217) 206-4847. **Email:** admissions@uis.edu. **Website:** http://www.uis.edu. **Application deadlines for fall 2007:** Regular decision: Rolling. Early decision: Not offered. Early action: Not offered. Admission cannot be deferred. **Application fee:** $40. Common application is not accepted. **To apply online, go to:** http://www.uis.edu/admissions/apply.html. **Admissions requirements/recommendations:** High school units required (recommended): English: 4; Mathematics: 3 (4); Science: 3 (4); Foreign language: 2 (4); Social studies: 3 (4). Tests: The college uses SAT or ACT scores in admissions decisions. Either SAT or ACT required. For admission to the fall 2007 entering class, the school will accept: ACT with writing, ACT without writing. Campus visit: Recommended. Admissions interview: Recommended. Off-campus interview: May be arranged. **Factors that count in admissions decisions:** *Academic:* Secondary school record: Important. Class rank: Important. Letters of recommendation: Considered. Standardized test scores: Important. Essay: Important. *Nonacademic:* Interview: Not considered. Extracurricular activities: Considered. Talent/ability: Considered. Character/personal qualities: Considered. Alumni/ae relationship: Not considered. Geographical residence: Not considered. State residency: Not considered. Religious affiliation/commitment: Not considered. Minority status: Not considered. Volunteer work: Considered. Work experience: Not considered. **Admissions statistics for the fall 2005 entering class:** Total applicants: 493. Total accepted: 311. Freshmen enrolled: 138; 4% were from out of state. Overall acceptance rate: 63%. **Size of waiting list:** 21 applicants; enrolled from waiting list: 14. **Credentials of fall 2005 freshmen:** 20% ranked in the top 10 percent of their high school class; 52% were in the top 25 percent, and 90% were in the top half. (Proportion submitting class standing: 90%.) **First-year students submitting ACT scores:** 100%. Scores (25/75 percentile): English: 22-28, Math: 21-27, Composite: 22-27.

ACADEMICS

Year founded: 1969. **Academic calendar:** Semester. **Degrees offered:** bachelor's, post-bachelor's certificate, master's, post-master's certificate, doctorate. **Most popular majors:** 15% business administration, management, and operations, 12% psychology, 9% business administration and management, 9% liberal arts and sciences/liberal studies, 8% communication and media studies. **Major fields of study:** biological and biomedical sciences; business, management, marketing, and related support services; communication, journalism, and related programs; computer and information sciences and support services; English language and literature/letters; health professions and related clinical sciences; history; legal professions and studies; liberal arts and sciences studies, and humanities; mathematics and statistics; philosophy and religious studies; physical sciences; psychology; public administration and social service professions; security and protective services; social sciences; visual and performing arts. **Areas of required coursework:** arts/fine arts, humanities, mathematics, English (including composition), sciences (biological or physical), social science, other. **Pre-professional programs:** pre-law, pre-medicine, pre-veterinary science. **Special academic programs:** distance learning, independent study, internships, study abroad, teacher certificate program. **Teacher certification offered in:** elementary, secondary. **Faculty and instruction (2005-2006):** Total instructional faculty: 179 full-time, 152 part-time (53% men; 47% women; 14% minorities). Full-time faculty with Ph.D. or other terminal degree: 92%. Student/faculty ratio: 13/1. Classes of fewer than 20 students: 65%; of 20 to 49 students: 35%; of 50 or more students: 0%. **Advanced Placement and International Baccalaureate credit:** AP tests may be used for: Credit and/or placement. **Freshmen returning for sophomore year:** 84%.

COSTS AND FINANCIAL AID

Financial aid office: (217) 206-6724. **Expenses (2006-2007):** Tuition and fees 2006-2007: $6,412 in state, $17,572 out of state; room/board: N/A. Estimated books and supplies: $1,200; transportation: $900; personal expenses: $1,800. **Financial aid:** Priority filing date for institution's financial aid form: April 1; deadline: November 15. In 2005-2006, 78% of undergraduates applied for financial aid. Of those, 61% were determined to have financial need; 37% had their need fully met. Average financial aid package (proportion receiving): $7,814 (60%). Average amount of gift aid, such as scholarships or grants (proportion receiving): $5,136 (43%). Average amount of self-help aid, such as work study or loans (proportion receiving): $3,941 (47%). Average need-based loan (excluding PLUS or other private loans): $3,841. Among students who received need-based aid, the average percentage of need met: 84%. Among students who received aid based on merit, the average award (and the proportion receiving): $3,216 (15%). The average athletic scholarship (and the proportion receiving): $2,941 (1%). Average amount of debt of borrowers graduating in 2005: $10,486. Proportion who borrowed: 46%.

CAMPUS LIFE AND EXTRACURRICULAR ACTIVITIES

Campus housing available (% using): coed dorms (26%), apartments for married students (4%), apartment for single students (45%), special housing for disabled students (5%), special housing for international students (20%). **Clubs and organizations:** Number of student organizations: 64. Activities include: choral groups, concert band, dance, drama/theater, jazz band, music ensembles, musical theater, pep band, student government, student newspaper, student film society. Number of fraternities: 0; sororities: 0. Average proportion of students who stay on campus on weekends: 65%. **Sports program (2005-2006):** Member of NAIA. *Men's intercollegiate varsity sports:* basketball, soccer, tennis. *Women's intercollegiate varsity sports:* basketball, softball, tennis, volleyball.

SERVICES AND FACILITIES

Basic services: women's center, day care, health service, health insurance. **Remedial assistance:** reading, math, writing, study skills. **Counseling services:** minority student, career, personal, academic, psychological. **For learning-disabled students:** School does not offer a structured program with separate admission and additional fees. Services include: tape recorders, note-taking services, oral tests, learning center, readers, extended time for tests, tutors, priority registration, priority seating, proofreading services, substitution of courses, texts on tape, exams on tape or computer, other testing accomodations, other. **Library:** Number of titles: 536,743; number of current serial subscriptions: 6,661. **Information technology resources:** Students are not required to lease or own a computer. School has a wireless network. Proportion of college-owned housing units wired for high-speed internet access: 100%. **Campus safety:** Security services offered: 24-hour foot and vehicle patrols, 24-hour emergency telephones, lighted pathways/sidewalks, controlled dormitory access (key, security card, etc).

TRANSFER AND INTERNATIONAL STUDENTS

Transfer students: May apply for admission for the following academic terms: Fall, Spring, Summer. Applicants need a minimum number of credits to apply. For fall 2005: Transfer applications received: 1,318. Transfer applicants offered admission: 844. Transfer applicants enrolled: 578. **International students:** Number of foreign undergraduates: 17 (1% of student body). Number of countries represented: 16. Minimum TOEFL score required: 500 (paper); 173 (computer). Average TOEFL score: 500 (paper).

University of Illinois—Urbana-Champaign

- ■ **Address:** 601 E. John Street, Champaign, IL 61820-5711
- ■ **Website:** http://www.uiuc.edu
- ■ **Public**
- ■ **Enrollment:** 29,912 full-time; 997 part-time

KEY STATS

✔ **U.S News College Ranking:** 41, National Universities
✔ **ACT Score (25th/75th percentile):** 26-31
✔ **Tuition:** 2006-2007: $8,716 in state, $22,802 out of state

Selectivity: More selective	**Room/board:** $7,716
Acceptance rate: 75%	**Average debt:** $15,825
Student/faculty ratio: 14/1	**Proportion who borrowed:** 44%

UNDERGRADUATE STUDENT BODY STATS

2005-2006 enrollment: 29,912 full-time; 997 part-time. Men: 53%; women: 47%. **Ethnic makeup:** African American: 7%; Asian American: 13%; Hispanic: 6%; White: 70%; International: 4%.

ADMISSIONS FACTS AND FIGURES

Phone: (217) 333-0302. **Email:** ugradadmissions@uiuc.edu. **Website:** http://www.uiuc.edu. **Application deadlines for fall 2007:** Regular decision: January 2. Early decision: Not offered. Early action: Not offered. Admission can be deferred. **Application fee:** $40. Common application is not accepted. **To apply online, go to:** http://www.apply.uiuc.edu. **Admissions requirements/recommendations:** High school units required (recommended): English: 4; Mathematics: 3; Science: 2; Foreign language: 2; Social studies: 2; History: 0; Academic electives: 2; Total units: 15. Tests: The college uses SAT or ACT scores in admissions decisions. Either SAT or ACT required. For admission to the fall 2007 entering class, the school will accept: ACT without writing. Campus visit: Recommended. Admissions interview: Neither required nor recommended. Off-campus interview: May be arranged. **Factors that count in admissions decisions:** *Academic:* Secondary school record: Very important. Class rank: Very important. Letters of recommendation: Considered. Standardized test scores: Very important. Essay: Very important. *Nonacademic:* Interview: Considered. Extracurricular activities: Important. Talent/ability: Important. Character/personal qualities: Important. Alumni/ae relationship: Considered. Geographical residence: Considered. State residency: Considered. Religious affiliation/commitment: Not considered. Minority status: Considered. Volunteer work: Important. Work experience: Important. **Other schools with the greatest overlap in applicants:** Illinois Wesleyan University; Northwestern University; Purdue University–West Lafayette; University of Michigan–Ann Arbor; University of Wisconsin–Madison. **Admissions statistics for the fall 2005 entering class:** Total applicants: 18,987. Total accepted: 14,326. Freshmen enrolled: 7,582; 7% were from out of state. Overall acceptance rate: 75%. **Size of waiting list:** 503 applicants; enrolled from waiting list: 0. **Credentials of fall 2005 freshmen:** 48% ranked in the top 10 percent of their high school class; 86% were in the top 25 percent, and 99% were in the top half. (Proportion submitting class standing: 83%.) **First-year students who submitted SAT scores:** 27%. Scores (25/75 percentile): Verbal: 560-670, Math: 620-730, Combined: 1180-1400. **First-year students submitting ACT scores:** 100%. Scores (25/75 percentile): English: 25-31, Math: 25-32, Composite: 26-31.

ACADEMICS

Year founded: 1867. **Academic calendar:** Semester. **Degrees offered:** certificate, bachelor's, post-bachelor's certificate, master's, post-master's certificate, first professional, doctorate. **Most popular majors:** 15% business, management, marketing, and related support services; 15% engineering; 10% social sciences; 7% biological and biomedical sciences; 7% psychology. **Major fields of study:** agriculture, agriculture operations, and related sciences; architecture and related services; area, ethnic, cultural, and gender studies; biological and biomedical sciences; business, management, marketing, and related support services; communication, journalism, and related programs; computer and information sciences and support services; education; engineering; English language and literature/letters; family and consumer sciences/human sciences; foreign languages, literatures, and linguistics; health professions and related clinical sciences; history; liberal arts and sciences studies, and humanities; mathematics and statistics; multi/interdisciplinary studies; natural resources and conservation; parks, recreation, leisure, and fitness studies; philosophy and religious studies; physical sciences; psychology; social sciences; transportation and materials moving; visual and performing arts. **Areas of required coursework:** humanities, mathematics, English (including composition), philosophy, foreign languages, sciences (biological or physical), history, social science, other. **Pre-professional programs:** pre-law, pre-dentistry, pre-medicine, pre-veterinary science, pre-optometry, pre-pharmacy. **Special academic programs (% participation):** accelerated program (13%), cooperative (work-study plan) program (2%), cross-registration (1%), distance learning (5%), double major (10%), dual enrollment (1%), English as a Second Language (ESL) (2%), exchange student program (domestic) (1%), honors program (25%), independent study (72%), internships (30%), liberal arts/career combination (20%), student-designed major (1%), study abroad (21%), teacher certificate program (6%), other (100%). **Teacher certification offered in:** early childhood, special education, elementary, secondary. **Cooperative education programs:** computer science, engineering, other. **Reserve Officers Training Corps (ROTC):** Army ROTC: Offered on campus; Navy ROTC: Offered on campus; Air Force ROTC: Offered on campus. **Faculty and instruction (2005-2006):** Total instructional faculty: 2,271 full-time, 430 part-time (67% men; 33% women; 19% minorities). Full-time faculty with Ph.D. or other terminal degree: 87%. Student/faculty ratio: 14/1. Classes of fewer than 20 students: 34%; of 20 to 49 students: 48%; of 50 or more students: 18%. **Advanced Placement and International Baccalaureate credit:** AP tests may be used for: Credit and/or placement. Scores accepted: 4, 5. International Baccalaureate exams may be used for: Credit and/or placement. **Freshmen returning for sophomore year:** 92%. **Graduation rates:** Four-year: 60%; five-year: 80%; six-year: 83%. **Graduate study:** 23% of students pursue further study immediately upon graduation; 33% within one year; 45% within five years. Fields in which graduates pursue further study: Master of Business Administration (MBA), 18%; law, 14%; medicine, 11%; dentistry, 3%; engineering, 29%; theology (or the seminary), 2%; education, 25%; arts and sciences, 57%; veterinary medicine, 3%.

COSTS AND FINANCIAL AID

Financial aid office: (217) 333-0100. **Expenses (2006-2007):** Tuition and fees 2006-2007: $8,716 in state, $22,802 out of state; room/board: $7,716. Estimated books and supplies: $1,000; transportation: $470; personal expenses: $2,230. **Financial aid:** Priority filing date for institution's financial aid form: March 15. In 2005-2006, 57% of undergraduates applied for financial aid. Of those, 40% were determined to have financial need; 46% had their need fully met. Average financial aid package (proportion receiving): $9,939 (39%). Average amount of gift aid, such as scholarships or grants (proportion receiving): $7,519 (31%). Average amount of self-help aid, such as work study or loans (proportion receiving): $4,596 (34%). Average need-based loan (excluding PLUS or other private loans): $4,487. Among students who received need-based aid, the average percentage of need met: 84%. Among students who received aid based on merit, the average award (and the proportion receiving): $3,713 (15%). The average athletic scholarship (and the proportion receiving): $12,569 (1%). Average amount of debt of borrowers graduating in 2005: $15,825. Proportion who borrowed: 44%.

CAMPUS LIFE AND EXTRACURRICULAR ACTIVITIES

Campus housing available (% using): coed dorms (46%), women's dorms (6%), men's dorms (1%), sorority housing (8%), fraternity housing (17%), apartments for married students (6%), apartment for single students (0%), special housing for disabled students (1%), special housing for international students (0%), other housing options (14%). Students who live in college-owned, operated, or affiliated housing: 52%. **Student employment:** During the 2005-2006 academic year, 24% of undergraduates worked on campus. Average per-year earnings: $1,007. **Clubs and organizations:** Number of student organizations: 999. Activities include: choral groups, concert band, dance, drama/theater, jazz band, literary magazine, marching band, music ensembles, musical theater, opera, pep band, radio station, student government, student newspaper, symphony orchestra, television station, yearbook. Number of fraternities: 58; sororities: 33. Proportion of men in fraternities: 20%; of women in sororities: 22%. Average proportion of students who stay on campus on weekends: 75%. **Sports program (2005-2006):** Member of NCAA I. *Men's intercollegiate varsity sports:* baseball, basketball, cross-country, football, golf, gymnastics, tennis, track and field (indoor), track and field (outdoor), wrestling. *Women's intercollegiate varsity sports:* basketball, cross-country, golf, gymnastics, soccer, softball, swimming and diving, tennis, track and field (indoor), track and field (outdoor), volleyball.

SERVICES AND FACILITIES

Basic services: nonremedial tutoring, women's center, placement service, day care, health service, health insurance, other. **Remedial assistance:** reading, math, writing, study skills. **Counseling services:** minority student, career, military, personal, veteran student, academic, older student, psychological, birth control, other. **For learning-disabled students:** School does not offer a structured program with separate admission and additional fees. Total undergraduates in learning-disabled program or receiving services: 182. Services include: reading machines, tape recorders, other special classes, note-taking services, special bookstore section, oral tests, learning center, readers, extended time for tests, early syllabus, priority registration, priority seating, proofreading services, substitution of courses, texts on tape, typist/scribe, exams on tape or computer, other testing accomodations, other. **Library:** Number of titles: 10,015,321; number of current serial subscriptions: 89,444. **Information technology resources:** Students are not required to lease or own a computer. Number of campus computers available to all students: 4,500. School has a wireless network. Approximate number of users that can be accommodated: 9,000. Proportion of college-owned housing units wired for high-speed internet access: 100%. **Campus safety:** Security services offered: 24-hour foot and vehicle patrols, late-night transport/escort service, 24-hour emergency telephones, lighted pathways/sidewalks, student patrols, controlled dormitory access (key, security card, etc).

TRANSFER AND INTERNATIONAL STUDENTS

Transfer students: May apply for admission for the following academic terms: Fall, Spring, Summer. Applicants need a minimum number of credits to apply. For fall 2005: Transfer applications received: 2,533. Transfer applicants offered admission: 1,356. Transfer applicants enrolled: 1,094. **International students:** Number of foreign undergraduates: 1226 (4% of student body). Number of countries represented: 65. Minimum TOEFL score required: 550 (paper); 213 (computer).

University of St. Francis

- **Address:** 500 Wilcox Street, Joliet, IL 60435
- **Website:** http://www.stfrancis.edu
- **Private; Religious affiliation:** Roman Catholic
- **Enrollment:** 1,138 full-time; 138 part-time

KEY STATS

✔ **U.S News College Ranking:** 40, Universities–Master's (Midwest)
✔ **ACT Score (25th/75th percentile):** 20-24
✔ **Tuition:** 2006-2007: $19,540

Selectivity: Selective	**Room/board:** $7,280
Acceptance rate: 57%	**Average debt:** $14,650
Student/faculty ratio: 12/1	**Proportion who borrowed:** 88%

UNDERGRADUATE STUDENT BODY STATS

2005-2006 enrollment: 1,138 full-time; 138 part-time. Men: 31%; women: 69%. **Ethnic makeup:** African American: 9%; Asian American: 4%; Hispanic: 7%; White: 78%; International: 1%. **Religious preference:** Protestant: 26%; Roman Catholic: 54%; Other: 20%.

ADMISSIONS FACTS AND FIGURES

Phone: (800) 735-7500. **Email:** information@stfrancis.edu. **Website:** http://www.stfrancis.edu. **Application deadlines for fall 2007:** Regular decision: August 1. Early decision: Not offered. Early action: Not offered. Admission can be deferred. **Application fee:** $30. Common application is not accepted. **To apply online, go to:** http://www.stfrancis.edu/admissions/apply.htm. **Admissions requirements/recommendations:** High school units required (recommended): English: 4; Mathematics: 2; Science: 2; Foreign language: (1); Social studies: 2; Academic electives: 3; Total units: 16. Tests: The college uses SAT or ACT scores in admissions decisions. Either SAT or ACT required. For admission to the fall 2007 entering class, the school will accept: ACT with writing, ACT without writing. Campus visit: Recommended. Admissions interview: Recommended. Off-campus interview: May be arranged. **Factors that count in admissions decisions:** *Academic:* Secondary school record: Very important. Class rank: Very important. Letters of recommendation: Considered. Standardized test scores: Very important. Essay: Considered. *Nonacademic:* Interview: Considered. Extracurricular activities: Considered. Talent/ability: Considered. Character/personal qualities: Not considered. Alumni/ae relationship: Not considered. Geographical residence: Not considered. State residency: Not considered. Religious affiliation/commitment: Not considered. Minority status: Not considered. Volunteer work: Considered. Work experience: Not considered. **Other schools with the greatest overlap in applicants:** Lewis University; Millikin University; Northern Illinois University; St. Xavier University. **Admissions statistics for the fall 2005 entering class:** Total applicants: 759. Total accepted: 429. Freshmen enrolled: 190; 2% were from out of state. Overall acceptance rate: 57%. **Credentials of fall 2005 freshmen:** 18% ranked in the top 10 percent of their high school class; 43% were in the top 25 percent, and 84% were in the top half. (Proportion submitting class standing: 93%.) **Average high school grade point average:** 3.2. **First-year students submitting ACT scores:** 100%. Scores (25/75 percentile): English: 19-24, Math: 18-25, Composite: 20-24.

ACADEMICS

Year founded: 1920. **Academic calendar:** Semester. **Degrees offered:** bachelor's, master's. **Most popular majors:** 25% elementary education and teaching, 19% business administration and management, 15% nursing/registered nurse training (R.N., A.S.N., B.S.N., M.S.N.), 5% mass communication/media studies, 5% visual and performing arts. **Major fields of study:** biological and biomedical sciences; business, management, marketing, and related support services; communication, journalism, and related programs; computer and information sciences and support services; education; English language and literature/letters; health professions and related clinical sciences; history; liberal arts and sciences studies, and humanities; mathematics and statistics; multi/interdisciplinary studies; natural resources and conservation; parks, recreation, leisure, and fitness studies; psychology; public administration and social service professions; social sciences; theology and religious vocations; visual and performing arts. **Areas of required coursework:** arts/fine arts, computer literacy, mathematics, English (including composition), philosophy, sciences (biological or physical), history, social science, other. **Pre-professional programs:** pre-dentistry, pre-medicine, pre-veterinary science. **Special academic programs (% participation):** accelerated program, distance learning (19%), double major (4%), honors program, independent study (1%), internships (32%), student-designed major, study abroad (1%), teacher certificate program (32%). **Teacher certification offered in:** special education, elementary, secondary. **Faculty and instruction (2005-2006):** Total instructional faculty: 74 full-time, 145 part-time (46% men; 54% women; 7% minorities). Full-time faculty with Ph.D. or other terminal degree: 59%. Student/faculty ratio: 12/1. Classes of fewer than 20 students: 68%; of 20 to 49 students: 32%; of 50 or more students: 0%. **Advanced Placement and International Baccalaureate credit:** AP tests may be used for: Credit and/or placement. Scores accepted: 3, 4, 5. International Baccalaureate exams may be used for: Credit only. **Freshmen returning for sophomore year:** 76%. **Graduation rates:** Four-year: 32%; five-year: 52%; six-year: 53%. **Graduate study:** 28% of students pursue further study immediately upon graduation. Fields in which graduates pursue further study: Master of Business Administration (MBA), 10%; law, 10%; medicine, 20%; arts and sciences, 60%.

COSTS AND FINANCIAL AID

Financial aid office: (815) 740-3403. **Expenses (2006-2007):** Tuition and fees 2006-2007: $19,540; room/board: $7,280. Estimated books and supplies: $800; transportation: $500; personal expenses: $1,000. **Financial aid:** Priority filing date for institution's financial aid form: April 1. In 2005-2006, 84% of undergraduates applied for financial aid. Of those, 71% were determined to have financial need; 72% had their need fully met. Average financial aid package (proportion receiving): $15,359 (71%). Average amount of gift aid, such as scholarships or grants (proportion receiving): $6,894 (47%). Average amount of self-help aid, such as work study or loans (proportion receiving): $5,077 (53%). Average need-based loan (excluding PLUS or other private loans): $4,413. Among students who received need-based aid, the average percentage of need met: 73%. Among students who received aid based on merit, the average award (and the proportion receiving): $5,793 (12%). The average athletic scholarship (and the proportion receiving): $8,845 (4%). Average amount of debt of borrowers graduating in 2005: $14,650. Proportion who borrowed: 88%.

CAMPUS LIFE AND EXTRACURRICULAR ACTIVITIES

Campus housing available (% using): coed dorms (100%). Students who live in college-owned, operated, or affiliated housing: 23%. **Student employment:** During the 2005-2006 academic year, 28% of undergraduates worked on campus. Average per-year earnings: $1,685. **Clubs and organizations:** Number of student organizations: 38. Activities include: choral groups, dance, drama/theater, literary magazine, music ensembles, musical theater, radio station, student government, student newspaper, symphony orchestra, television station. Number of fraternities: 0; sororities: 0. Average proportion of students who stay on campus on weekends: 50%. **Sports program (2005-2006):** Member of NAIA. *Men's intercollegiate varsity sports:* baseball, basketball, cross-country, football, golf, soccer, track and field (indoor), track and field (outdoor). *Women's intercollegiate varsity sports:* basketball, cross-country, golf, soccer, softball, tennis, track and field (indoor), track and field (outdoor), volleyball.

SERVICES AND FACILITIES

Basic services: nonremedial tutoring, health insurance, other. **Remedial assistance:** math, writing, study skills, other. **Counseling services:** career, personal, academic, older student, psychological, religious. **For learning-disabled students:** School does not offer a structured program with separate admission and additional fees. Total undergraduates in learning-disabled program or receiving services: 15. Services include: remedial math, remedial English, tape recorders, untimed tests, note-taking services, oral tests, learning center, readers, extended time for tests, tutors, priority seating, texts on tape, other testing accomodations. **Library:** Number of titles: 107,457; number of current serial subscriptions: 8,000. **Information technology resources:** Students are not required to lease or own a computer. Number of campus computers available to all students: 362. School has a wireless network. Approximate number of users that can be accommodated: 250. Proportion of college-owned housing units wired for high-speed internet access: 100%. **Campus safety:** Security services offered: 24-hour foot and vehicle patrols, late-night transport/escort service, 24-hour emergency telephones, lighted pathways/sidewalks, student patrols, controlled dormitory access (key, security card, etc).

TRANSFER AND INTERNATIONAL STUDENTS

Transfer students: May apply for admission for the following academic terms: Fall, Spring, Summer. Applicants need a minimum number of credits to apply. For fall 2005: Transfer applications received: 765. Transfer applicants offered admission: 504. Transfer applicants enrolled: 204. **International students:** Number of foreign undergraduates: 11 (1% of student body). Minimum TOEFL score required: 550 (paper); 213 (computer).

VanderCook College of Music

- **Address:** 3140 S. Federal Street, Chicago, IL 60616
- **Website:** http://www.vandercook.edu
- **Private**
- **Enrollment:** N/A

KEY STATS

✔ **U.S News College Ranking:** Unranked Specialty School—Fine Arts
✔ **SAT Score (25th/75th percentile):** 930-1080
✔ **Tuition:** 2005-2006: $16,610

Selectivity: Less selective	**Room/board:** $7,200
Acceptance rate: 89%	**Average debt:** N/A
Student/faculty ratio: N/A	**Proportion who borrowed:** N/A

Western Illinois University

- **Address:** 1 University Circle, Macomb, IL 61455
- **Website:** http://www.wiu.edu
- **Public**
- **Enrollment:** 10,317 full-time; 967 part-time

KEY STATS

✔ **U.S News College Ranking:** 55, Universities—Master's (Midwest)
✔ **ACT Score (25th/75th percentile):** 19-23
✔ **Tuition:** 2006-2007: $6,899 in state, $9,383 out of state

Selectivity: Selective	**Room/board:** $6,143
Acceptance rate: 72%	**Average debt:** $14,850
Student/faculty ratio: 17/1	**Proportion who borrowed:** 62%

UNDERGRADUATE STUDENT BODY STATS

2005-2006 enrollment: 10,317 full-time; 967 part-time. Men: 51%; women: 49%. **Ethnic makeup:** African American: 7%; Asian American: 1%; Hispanic: 4%; White: 87%; International: 1%.

ADMISSIONS FACTS AND FIGURES

Phone: (309) 298-3157. **Email:** admissions@wiu.edu. **Website:** http://www.wiu.edu. **Application deadlines for fall 2007:** Regular decision: May 15. Early decision: Not offered. Early action: Not offered. Admission can be deferred. **Application fee:** $30. Common application is not accepted. **To apply online, go to:** http://www.student.services.wiu.edu/admissions/application/. **Admissions requirements/recommendations:** High school units required (recommended): English: (4); Mathematics: (3); Science: (3); Social studies: (3); Academic electives: (2); Total units: (15). Tests: The college uses SAT or ACT scores in admissions decisions. Either SAT or ACT required. For admission to the fall 2007 entering class, the school will accept: ACT with writing, ACT without writing. Campus visit: Recommended. Admissions interview: Neither required nor recommended. Off-campus interview: May be arranged. **Factors that count in admissions decisions:** *Academic:* Secondary school record: Very important. Class rank: Very important. Letters of recommendation: Not considered. Standardized test scores: Very important. Essay: Not considered. *Nonacademic:* Interview: Not considered. Extracurricular activities: Not considered. Talent/ability: Not considered. Character/personal qualities: Not considered. Alumni/ae relationship: Not considered. Geographical residence: Not considered. State residency: Not considered. Religious affiliation/commitment: Not considered. Minority status: Not considered. Volunteer work: Not considered. Work experience: Not considered. **Other schools with the greatest overlap in applicants:** Eastern Illinois University; Eastern Illinois University; Eastern Illinois University; Illinois State University; Illinois State University; Illinois State University; Illinois State University; Northern Illinois University; Northern Illinois University; Northern Illinois University; Northern Illinois University. **Admissions statistics for the fall 2005 entering class:** Total applicants: 7,286. Total accepted: 5,224. Freshmen enrolled: 1,816; 7% were from out of state. Overall acceptance rate: 72%. **Credentials of fall 2005 freshmen:** 5% ranked in the top 10 percent of their high school class; 22% were in the top 25 percent, and 55% were in the top half. (Proportion submitting class standing: 92%.) **Average high school grade point average:** 3.0. **First-year students submitting ACT scores:** 97%. Scores (25/75 percentile): English: N/A, Math: N/A, Composite: 19-23.

ACADEMICS

Year founded: 1899. **Academic calendar:** Semester. **Degrees offered:** bachelor's, post-bachelor's certificate, master's, post-master's certificate, doctorate. **Most popular majors:** 13% business, management, marketing, and related support services, 13% criminal justice/law enforcement administration, 13% education, 13% liberal arts and sciences/liberal studies, 5% psychology. **Major fields of study:** agriculture, agriculture operations, and related sciences; area, ethnic, cultural, and gender studies; biological and biomedical sciences; business, management, marketing, and related support services; communication, journalism, and related programs; communications technologies/technicians and support services; computer and information sciences and support services; education; engineering technologies/technicians; English language and literature/letters; family and consumer sciences/human sciences; foreign languages, literatures, and linguistics; health professions and related clinical sciences; history; liberal arts and sciences studies, and humanities; mathematics and statistics; parks, recreation, leisure, and fitness studies; philosophy and religious studies; physical sciences; psychology; public administration and social service professions; security and protective services; social sciences; visual and performing arts. **Areas of required coursework:** humanities, mathematics, English (including composition), sciences (biological or physical), history, social science, other. **Pre-professional programs:** pre-law, pre-dentistry, pre-medicine, pre-veterinary science, pre-optometry, pre-pharmacy, other. **Special academic programs (% participation):** distance learning (36.9%), double major (3.1%), dual enrollment, English as a Second Language (ESL) (1.1%), external degree program (9.9%), honors program (8.9%), independent study (19.7%), internships (1.9%), student-designed major (2%), study abroad (.9%), teacher certificate program (13.4%), weekend college (.4%). **Teacher certification offered in:** early childhood, special education, elementary, middle/junior high, secondary, bilingual/bicultural. **Reserve Officers Training Corps (ROTC):** Army ROTC: Offered on campus. **Faculty and instruction (2005-2006):** Total instructional faculty: 649 full-time, 82 part-time (59% men; 41% women; 14% minorities). Full-time faculty with Ph.D. or other terminal degree: 71%. Student/faculty ratio: 17/1. Classes of fewer than 20 students: 34%; of 20 to 49 students: 58%; of 50 or more students: 8%. **Advanced Placement and International Baccalaureate credit:** AP tests may be used for: Credit and/or placement. Scores accepted: 2, 3, 4, 5. International Baccalaureate exams may be used for: Credit only. **Freshmen returning for sophomore year:** 77%. **Graduation rates:** Four-year: 32%; five-year: 52%; six-year: 54%. **Graduate study:** 25% of students pursue further study within one year. Fields in which graduates pursue further study: law, 4%; medicine, 1%.

COSTS AND FINANCIAL AID

Financial aid office: (309) 298-2446. **Expenses (2006-2007):** Tuition and fees 2006-2007: $6,899 in state, $9,383 out of state; room/board: $6,143. Estimated books and supplies: $1,050; transportation: $1,090; personal expenses: $1,610. **Financial aid:** Priority filing date for institution's financial aid form: February 15. In 2005-2006, 70% of undergraduates applied for financial aid. Of those, 56% were determined to have financial need; 36% had their need fully met. Average financial aid package (proportion receiving): $7,891 (54%). Average amount of gift aid, such as scholarships or grants (proportion receiving): $5,776 (38%). Average amount of self-help aid, such as work study or loans (proportion receiving): $3,710 (49%). Average need-based loan (excluding PLUS or other private loans): $3,573. Among students who received need-based aid, the average percentage of need met: 67%. Among students who received aid based on merit, the average award (and the proportion receiving): $2,306 (5%). The average athletic scholarship (and the proportion receiving): $6,204 (3%). Average amount of debt of borrowers graduating in 2005: $14,850. Proportion who borrowed: 62%.

CAMPUS LIFE AND EXTRACURRICULAR ACTIVITIES

Campus housing available (% using): coed dorms (73%), women's dorms (6%), men's dorms (6%), sorority housing (3%), fraternity housing (3%), apartments for married students (2%), apartment for single students (5%), special housing for disabled students (1%), special housing for international students (1%). Students who live in college-owned, operated, or affiliated housing: 55%. **Student employment:** During the 2005-2006 academic year,

20% of undergraduates worked on campus. Average per-year earnings: $1,350. **Clubs and organizations:** Number of student organizations: 198. Activities include: choral groups, concert band, dance, drama/theater, jazz band, marching band, music ensembles, musical theater, pep band, radio station, student government, student newspaper, television station, yearbook. Number of fraternities: 15; sororities: 10. Proportion of men in fraternities: 9%; of women in sororities: 8%. **Sports program (2005-2006):** Member of NCAA I. *Men's intercollegiate varsity sports:* baseball, basketball, cross-country, football, golf, soccer, swimming and diving, tennis, track and field (indoor), track and field (outdoor). *Women's intercollegiate varsity sports:* basketball, cross-country, golf, soccer, softball, swimming and diving, tennis, track and field (indoor), track and field (outdoor), volleyball.

SERVICES AND FACILITIES

Basic services: nonremedial tutoring, women's center, placement service, day care, health service, health insurance. **Remedial assistance:** math, writing. **Counseling services:** personal, academic, psychological. **For learning-disabled students:** School does not offer a structured program with separate admission and additional fees. Services include: remedial math, remedial English, remedial reading, tape recorders, oral tests, readers, extended time for tests, tutors. **Library:** Number of titles: 718,241; number of current serial subscriptions: 3,445. **Information technology resources:** Students are not required to lease or own a computer. Number of campus computers available to all students: 1,000. School has a wireless network. Proportion of college-owned housing units wired for high-speed internet access: 100%. **Campus safety:** Security services offered: 24-hour foot and vehicle patrols, late-night transport/escort service, 24-hour emergency telephones, lighted pathways/sidewalks, controlled dormitory access (key, security card, etc).

TRANSFER AND INTERNATIONAL STUDENTS

Transfer students: May apply for admission for the following academic terms: Fall, Spring, Summer. Applicants need a minimum number of credits to apply. For fall 2005: Transfer applications received: 2,966. Transfer applicants offered admission: 2,170. Transfer applicants enrolled: 1,403. **International students:** Number of foreign undergraduates: 120 (1% of student body). Number of countries represented: 46. Minimum TOEFL score required: 550 (paper); 213 (computer).

Wheaton College

- **Address:** 501 College Avenue, Wheaton, IL 60187
- **Website:** http://www.wheaton.edu
- **Private; Religious affiliation:** Christian nondenominational
- **Enrollment:** 2,342 full-time; 75 part-time

KEY STATS

✔ **U.S News College Ranking:** 61, Liberal Arts Colleges
✔ **SAT Score (25th/75th percentile):** 1250-1440
✔ **Tuition:** 2006-2007: $22,450

Selectivity: More selective	**Room/board:** $7,040
Acceptance rate: 51%	**Average debt:** $17,936
Student/faculty ratio: 12/1	**Proportion who borrowed:** 55%

UNDERGRADUATE STUDENT BODY STATS

2005-2006 enrollment: 2,342 full-time; 75 part-time. Men: 49%; women: 51%. **Ethnic makeup:** African American: 2%; Asian American: 7%; Hispanic: 3%; White: 87%; International: 1%.

ADMISSIONS FACTS AND FIGURES

Phone: (630) 752-5005. **Email:** admissions@wheaton.edu. **Website:** http://www.wheaton.edu. **Application deadlines for fall 2007:** Regular decision: January 15; decision sent by April 1. Early decision: Not offered. Early action: Send application by: November 1; Decision sent by: December 31. Admission cannot be deferred. **Application fee:** $50. Common application is not accepted. **To apply online, go to:** http://www.wheaton.edu/admissions/UndGrad/applying/forms.htm. **Admissions requirements/recommendations:** High school units required (recommended): English: (4); Mathematics: (4); Science: (4); Foreign language: (3); Social studies: (4); Total units: 15 (18). Tests: The college uses SAT or ACT scores in admissions decisions. Either SAT or ACT required. For admission to the fall 2007 entering class, the school will accept: ACT with writing. Campus visit: Recommended. Admissions interview:

Recommended. Off-campus interview: May be arranged. **Factors that count in admissions decisions:** *Academic:* Secondary school record: Very important. Class rank: Considered. Letters of recommendation: Very important. Standardized test scores: Very important. Essay: Very important. *Nonacademic:* Interview: Considered. Extracurricular activities: Considered. Talent/ability: Considered. Character/personal qualities: Important. Alumni/ae relationship: Important. Geographical residence: Considered. State residency: Considered. Religious affiliation/commitment: Very important. Minority status: Important. Volunteer work: Important. Work experience: Not considered. **Other schools with the greatest overlap in applicants:** Calvin College; Gordon College; Grove City College; Taylor University; Westmont College. **Admissions statistics for the fall 2005 entering class:** Total applicants: 2,163. Total accepted: 1,097. Freshmen enrolled: 578; 82% were from out of state. Accepted through early-decision or early-action plans: 49%. Overall acceptance rate: 51%. Non-early acceptance rate: 58%. Size of waiting list: 349 applicants; enrolled from waiting list: 39. **Credentials of fall 2005 freshmen:** 54% ranked in the top 10 percent of their high school class; 81% were in the top 25 percent, and 97% were in the top half. (Proportion submitting class standing: 63%.) **Average high school grade point average:** 3.7. **First-year students who submitted SAT scores:** 76%. Scores (25/75 percentile): Verbal: 630-730, Math: 620-710, Combined: 1250-1440. **First-year students submitting ACT scores:** 60%. Scores (25/75 percentile): English: N/A, Math: N/A, Composite: 27-31.

ACADEMICS
Year founded: 1860. **Academic calendar:** Semester. **Degrees offered:** bachelor's, post-bachelor's certificate, master's, doctorate. **Most popular majors:** 15% social sciences, 9% education, 9% theology and religious vocations, 8% English language and literature/letters, 8% business, management, marketing, and related support services. **Major fields of study:** biological and biomedical sciences; business, management, marketing, and related support services; communication, journalism, and related programs; computer and information sciences and support services; education; engineering; English language and literature/letters; foreign languages, literatures, and linguistics; health professions and related clinical sciences; history; mathematics and statistics; multi/interdisciplinary studies; natural resources and conservation; parks, recreation, leisure, and fitness studies; philosophy and religious studies; physical sciences; psychology; social sciences; theology and religious vocations; visual and performing arts. **Areas of required coursework:** arts/fine arts, humanities, mathematics, English (including composition), philosophy, foreign languages, sciences (biological or physical), history, social science, other. **Pre-professional programs:** pre-law, pre-dentistry, pre-medicine, pre-theology. **Special academic programs (% participation):** cross-registration, double major, exchange student program (domestic), independent study, internships, liberal arts/career combination (1%), student-designed major (2.4%), study abroad, teacher certificate program (17%). **Teacher certification offered in:** elementary, middle/junior high, secondary. **Reserve Officers Training Corps (ROTC):** Army ROTC: Offered on campus; Air Force ROTC: Offered at cooperating institution (Illinois Institute of Technology). **Faculty and instruction (2005-2006):** Total instructional faculty: 191 full-time, 98 part-time (67% men; 33% women; 9% minorities). Full-time faculty with Ph.D. or other terminal degree: 93%. Student/faculty ratio: 12/1. Classes of fewer than 20 students: 51%; of 20 to 49 students: 47%; of 50 or more students: 2%. **Advanced Placement and International Baccalaureate credit:** AP tests may be used for: Credit and/or placement. Scores accepted: 3, 4, 5. International Baccalaureate exams may be used for: Credit and/or placement. **Freshmen returning for sophomore year:** 94%. **Graduation rates:** Four-year: 77%; five-year: 85%; six-year: 86%. **Graduate study:** 33% of students pursue further study within one year; 55% within five years. Fields in which graduates pursue further study: Master of Business Administration (MBA), 2%; law, 7%; medicine, 13%; engineering, 2%; theology (or the seminary), 18%; education, 20%; arts and sciences, 37%.

COSTS AND FINANCIAL AID
Financial aid office: (630) 752-5021. **Expenses (2006-2007):** Tuition and fees 2006-2007: $22,450; room/board: $7,040. Estimated books and supplies: $744 personal expenses: $1,900. **Financial aid:** Priority filing date for institution's financial aid form: February 15. In 2005-2006, 73% of undergraduates applied for financial aid. Of those, 50% were determined to have financial need; 22% had their need fully met. Average financial aid package (proportion receiving): $18,555 (49%). Average amount of gift aid, such as scholarships or grants (proportion receiving): $12,710 (41%). Average amount of self-help aid, such as work study or loans (proportion receiving): $5,952 (47%). Average need-based loan (excluding PLUS or other private loans): $5,523. Among students who received need-based aid, the average percentage of need met: 85%. Among students who received aid based on merit, the average award (and the proportion receiving): $3,658 (19%). The average athletic scholarship (and the proportion receiving): $0 (0%). Average amount of debt of borrowers graduating in 2005: $17,936. Proportion who borrowed: 55%.

CAMPUS LIFE AND EXTRACURRICULAR ACTIVITIES
Campus housing available: women's dorms, men's dorms, apartments for married students, apartment for single students, cooperative housing, other housing options. Students who live in college-owned, operated, or affiliated housing: 90%. **Student employment:** During the 2005-2006 academic year, 48% of undergraduates worked on campus. Average per-year earnings: $1,000. **Clubs and organizations:** Number of student organizations: 102. Activities include: choral groups, concert band, drama/theater, jazz band, literary magazine, music ensembles, musical theater, opera, pep band, radio station, student government, student newspaper, symphony orchestra, television station, yearbook. Number of fraternities: 0; sororities: 0. Average proportion of students who stay on campus on weekends: 90%. **Sports program (2005-2006):** Member of NCAA III. *Men's intercollegiate varsity sports:* baseball, basketball, cross-country, football, golf, soccer, swimming and diving, tennis, track and field (indoor), track and field (outdoor), wrestling. *Women's intercollegiate varsity sports:* basketball, cross-country, golf, soccer, softball, swimming and diving, tennis, track and field (indoor), track and field (outdoor), volleyball, water polo.

SERVICES AND FACILITIES
Basic services: health service, health insurance, other. **Counseling services:** minority student, career, military, personal, veteran student, academic, psychological, birth control, religious. **For learning-disabled students:** School does not offer a structured program with separate admission and additional fees. Total undergraduates in learning-disabled program or receiving services: 6. **Library:** Number of titles: 398,796; number of current serial subscriptions: 3,810. **Information technology resources:** Students are not required to lease or own a computer. Number of campus computers available to all students: 201. School has a wireless network. Approximate number of users that can be accommodated: 800. Proportion of college-owned housing units wired for high-speed internet access: 100%. **Campus safety:** Security services offered: 24-hour foot and vehicle patrols, late-night transport/escort service, 24-hour emergency telephones, lighted pathways/sidewalks, student patrols, controlled dormitory access (key, security card, etc).

TRANSFER AND INTERNATIONAL STUDENTS
Transfer students: May apply for admission for the following academic terms: Fall, Spring. Applicants need a minimum number of credits to apply. For fall 2005: Transfer applications received: 180. Transfer applicants offered admission: 110. Transfer applicants enrolled: 75. **International students:** Number of foreign undergraduates: 21 (1% of student body). Number of countries represented: 12. Minimum TOEFL score required: 550 (paper); 213 (computer).

Indiana

Anderson University

- **Address:** 1100 E. Fifth Street, Anderson, IN 46012
- **Website:** http://www.anderson.edu
- **Private; Religious affiliation:** Church of God
- **Enrollment:** 2,149 full-time; 188 part-time

KEY STATS

✔ **U.S News College Ranking:** 37, Universities–Master's (Midwest)
✔ **SAT Score (25th/75th percentile):** 940-1180
✔ **Tuition:** 2005-2006: $18,900

Selectivity: Selective	**Room/board:** $6,150
Acceptance rate: 91%	**Average debt:** N/A
Student/faculty ratio: 15/1	**Proportion who borrowed:** N/A

UNDERGRADUATE STUDENT BODY STATS

2005-2006 enrollment: 2,149 full-time; 188 part-time. Men: 41%; women: 59%. **Ethnic makeup:** African American: 5%; American-Indian: 1%; Hispanic: 1%; White: 91%; International: 2%. **Religious preference:** Roman Catholic: 3%; Protestant: 54%; No preference: 16%; Unknown: 1%; Church of God: 26%.

ADMISSIONS FACTS AND FIGURES

Phone: (765) 641-4080. **Email:** info@anderson.edu. **Website:** http://www.anderson.edu. **Application deadlines for fall 2007:** Regular decision: July 1. Early decision: Not offered. Early action: Not offered. Admission can be deferred. **Application fee:** $25. Common application is not accepted. **Admissions requirements/recommendations:** High school units required (recommended): English: 4 (4); Mathematics: 3 (4); Science: 3 (4); Foreign language: 2 (3); Social studies: 2 (3); History: 1 (2); Academic electives: (5); Total units: 17 (28). Tests: The college uses SAT or ACT scores in admissions decisions. Either SAT or ACT required. For admission to the fall 2007 entering class, the school will accept: ACT with writing. Campus visit: Recommended. Admissions interview: Recommended. Off-campus interview: May be arranged. **Factors that count in admissions decisions:** *Academic:* Secondary school record: Very important. Class rank: Important. Letters of recommendation: Important. Standardized test scores: Important. Essay: Considered. *Nonacademic:* Interview: Important. Extracurricular activities: Important. Talent/ability: Considered. Character/personal qualities: Important. Alumni/ae relationship: Considered. Geographical residence: Not considered. State residency: Not considered. Religious affiliation/commitment: Very important. Minority status: Considered. Volunteer work: Important. Work experience: Not considered. **Other schools with the greatest overlap in applicants:** Ball State University; Huntington University; Indiana University–Bloomington; Indiana Wesleyan University; Taylor University. **Admissions statistics for the fall 2005 entering class:** Total applicants: 1,968. Total accepted: 1,792. Freshmen enrolled: 580; 40% were from out of state. Overall acceptance rate: 91%. **Credentials of fall 2005 freshmen:** 23% ranked in the top 10 percent of their high school class; 50% were in the top 25 percent, and 77% were in the top half. (Proportion submitting class standing: 88%.) **Average high school grade point average:** 3.4. **First-year students who submitted SAT scores:** 55%. Scores (25/75 percentile): Verbal: 470-590, Math: 470-590, Combined: 940-1180. **First-year students submitting ACT scores:** 54%. Scores (25/75 percentile): English: 20-26, Math: 19-26, Composite: 21-26.

ACADEMICS

Year founded: 1917. **Academic calendar:** Semester. **Degrees offered:** associate, bachelor's, master's, first professional, doctorate. **Most popular majors:** 22% business, management, marketing, and related support services, 13% education, 7% health professions and related clinical sciences, 7% visual and performing arts, 6% public administration and social service professions. **Major fields of study:** biological and biomedical sciences; business, management, marketing, and related support services; communication, journalism, and related programs; computer and information sciences and support serv-

ices; education; English language and literature/letters; family and consumer sciences/human sciences; foreign languages, literatures, and linguistics; health professions and related clinical sciences; history; liberal arts and sciences studies, and humanities; mathematics and statistics; multi/interdisciplinary studies; parks, recreation, leisure, and fitness studies; philosophy and religious studies; physical sciences; psychology; public administration and social service professions; security and protective services; social sciences; theology and religious vocations; visual and performing arts. **Areas of required coursework:** arts/fine arts, humanities, mathematics, English (including composition), philosophy, foreign languages, sciences (biological or physical), history, social science. **Pre-professional programs:** pre-law, pre-dentistry, pre-medicine, pre-theology, pre-veterinary science, pre-optometry, pre-pharmacy. **Special academic programs (% participation):** accelerated program (5%), cross-registration (21%), double major (11%), honors program (0%), independent study (57%), internships (17%), student-designed major (1%), study abroad (3%), teacher certificate program (14%). **Teacher certification offered in:** elementary, secondary. **Faculty and instruction (2005-2006):** Total instructional faculty: 137 full-time, 91 part-time (57% men; 43% women; 4% minorities). Full-time faculty with Ph.D. or other terminal degree: 66%. Student/faculty ratio: 15/1. Classes of fewer than 20 students: 52%; of 20 to 49 students: 45%; of 50 or more students: 4%. **Advanced Placement and International Baccalaureate credit:** AP tests may be used for: Credit and/or placement. Scores accepted: 3, 4, 5. International Baccalaureate exams may be used for: Credit and/or placement. **Freshmen returning for sophomore year:** 75%. **Graduation rates:** Four-year: 42%; five-year: 57%; six-year: 57%. **Graduate study:** 17% of students pursue further study immediately upon graduation; 20% within one year; 30% within five years.

COSTS AND FINANCIAL AID

Financial aid office: (765) 641-4180. **Expenses (2005-2006):** Tuition and fees 2005-2006: $18,900; room/board: $6,150. Estimated books and supplies: $850; transportation: $750; personal expenses: $1,350. **Financial aid:** Priority filing date for institution's financial aid form: March 1.

CAMPUS LIFE AND EXTRACURRICULAR ACTIVITIES

Campus housing available (% using): coed dorms (7%), women's dorms (40%), men's dorms (27%), apartment for single students (25%), other housing options (1%). Students who live in college-owned, operated, or affiliated housing: 69%. **Student employment:** During the 2005-2006 academic year, 49% of undergraduates worked on campus. Average per-year earnings: $2,600. **Clubs and organizations:** Number of student organizations: 33. Activities include: choral groups, concert band, dance, drama/theater, jazz band, literary magazine, music ensembles, musical theater, opera, pep band, radio station, student government, student newspaper, symphony orchestra, yearbook. Number of fraternities: 0; sororities: 0. Average proportion of students who stay on campus on weekends: 60%. **Sports program (2005-2006):** Member of NCAA III. *Men's intercollegiate varsity sports:* baseball, basketball, cheerleading, cross-country, football, golf, soccer, tennis, track and field (indoor), track and field (outdoor). *Women's intercollegiate varsity sports:* basketball, cheerleading, cross-country, golf, soccer, softball, tennis, track and field (indoor), track and field (outdoor), volleyball.

SERVICES AND FACILITIES

Basic services: nonremedial tutoring, health service. **Remedial assistance:** writing, study skills. **Counseling services:** minority student, career, personal, veteran student, academic, older student, psychological, religious, other. **For learning-disabled students:** School does not offer a structured program with separate admission and additional fees. Total undergraduates in learning-disabled program or receiving services: 46. Services include: reading machines, tape recorders, other special classes, untimed tests, note-taking services, oral tests, learning center, readers, extended time for tests, tutors, proofreading services, texts on tape, typist/scribe, other. **Library:** Number of titles: 327,192; number of current serial subscriptions: 683. **Information technology resources:** Students are not required to lease or own a computer. Number of campus computers available to all students: 250. School has a wireless network. Approximate number of users that can be accommodated: 500. Proportion of college-owned housing units wired for high-speed internet access: 100%. **Campus safety:** Security services offered: 24-hour foot and vehicle patrols, late-night transport/escort service, 24-hour emergency telephones, lighted pathways/sidewalks, student patrols, controlled dormitory access (key, security card, etc).

TRANSFER AND INTERNATIONAL STUDENTS

Transfer students: May apply for admission for the following academic terms: Fall, Spring, Summer. Applicants need a minimum number of credits to apply. For fall 2005: Transfer applications received: 284. Transfer applicants offered admission: 250. Transfer applicants enrolled: 90. **International students:** Number of foreign undergraduates: 50 (2% of student body). Number of countries represented: 21. Minimum TOEFL score required: 515 (paper); 187 (computer). Average TOEFL score: 560 (paper).

Ball State University

- ■ **Address:** 2000 University Avenue, Muncie, IN 47306
- ■ **Website:** http://www.bsu.edu
- ■ **Public**
- ■ **Enrollment:** 16,063 full-time; 1,363 part-time

KEY STATS

✔ **U.S News College Ranking:** third tier, National Universities
✔ **SAT Score (25th/75th percentile):** 940-1140
✔ **Tuition:** 2005-2006: $6,160 in state, $15,336 out of state

Selectivity: Selective	**Room/board:** $6,328
Acceptance rate: 80%	**Average debt:** N/A
Student/faculty ratio: 17/1	**Proportion who borrowed:** N/A

UNDERGRADUATE STUDENT BODY STATS

2005-2006 enrollment: 16,063 full-time; 1,363 part-time. Men: 48%; women: 52%. **Ethnic makeup:** African American: 7%; Asian American: 1%; Hispanic: 2%; White: 91%.

ADMISSIONS FACTS AND FIGURES

Phone: (765) 285-8300. **Email:** askus@bsu.edu. **Website:** http://www.bsu.edu. **Application deadlines for fall 2007:** Regular decision: Rolling. Early decision: Not offered. Early action: Not offered. Admission can be deferred. **Application fee:** $25. Common application is accepted. **To apply online, go to:** http://www.bsu.edu/admissions. **Admissions requirements/recommendations:** High school units required (recommended): English: 4; Mathematics: 3; Science: 3; Foreign language: (3); Social studies: 3; Total units: 15 (3). **Tests:** The college uses SAT or ACT scores in admissions decisions. Either SAT or ACT required. For admission to the fall 2007 entering class, the school will accept: ACT with writing. Campus visit: Recommended. Admissions interview: Neither required nor recommended. Off-campus interview: Not available. **Factors that count in admissions decisions:** *Academic:* Secondary school record: Very important. Class rank: Not considered. Letters of recommendation: Considered. Standardized test scores: Important. Essay: Considered. *Nonacademic:* Interview: Considered. Extracurricular activities: Considered. Talent/ability: Considered. Character/personal qualities: Considered. Alumni/ae relationship: Considered. Geographical residence: Not considered. State residency: Not considered. Religious affiliation/commitment: Not considered. Minority status: Not considered. Volunteer work: Considered. Work experience: Considered. **Other schools with the greatest overlap in applicants:** Indiana University–Bloomington; Purdue University–West Lafayette. **Admissions statistics for the fall 2005 entering class:** Total applicants: 9,889. Total accepted: 7,944. Freshmen enrolled: 3,692; 8% were from out of state. Overall acceptance rate: 80%. **Credentials of fall 2005 freshmen:** 14% ranked in the top 10 percent of their high school class; 41% were in the top 25 percent, and 79% were in the top half. (Proportion submitting class standing: 86%.) **First-year students who submitted SAT scores:** 80%. Scores (25/75 percentile): Verbal: 470-570, Math: 470-570, Combined: 940-1140. **First-year students submitting ACT scores:** 18%. Scores (25/75 percentile): English: 19-24, Math: 19-25, Composite: 19-25.

ACADEMICS

Year founded: 1918. **Academic calendar:** Semester. **Degrees offered:** associate, bachelor's, post-bachelor's certificate, master's, post-master's certificate, doctorate. **Most popular majors:** 16% education, 14% business, management, marketing, and related support services, 11% communication, jour-

nalism, and related programs, 11% liberal arts and sciences studies, and humanities, 6% health professions and related clinical sciences. **Major fields of study:** architecture and related services; area, ethnic, cultural, and gender studies; biological and biomedical sciences; business, management, marketing, and related support services; communication, journalism, and related programs; computer and information sciences and support services; education; engineering; engineering technologies/technicians; English language and literature/letters; family and consumer sciences/human sciences; foreign languages, literatures, and linguistics; health professions and related clinical sciences; history; legal professions and studies; liberal arts and sciences studies, and humanities; library science; mathematics and statistics; natural resources and conservation; parks, recreation, leisure, and fitness studies; philosophy and religious studies; physical sciences; psychology; public administration and social service professions; security and protective services; social sciences; visual and performing arts. **Areas of required coursework:** arts/fine arts, humanities, mathematics, English (including composition), sciences (biological or physical), history, social science. **Pre-professional programs:** pre-law, pre-dentistry, pre-medicine, pre-pharmacy, other. **Special academic programs:** accelerated program, cooperative (work-study plan) program, distance learning, double major, dual enrollment, English as a Second Language (ESL), exchange student program (domestic), honors program, independent study, internships, liberal arts/career combination, student-designed major, study abroad, teacher certificate program. **Teacher certification offered in:** early childhood, special education, elementary, vo-tech, middle/junior high, secondary. **Cooperative education programs:** computer science. **Reserve Officers Training Corps (ROTC):** Army ROTC: Offered on campus. **Faculty and instruction (2005-2006):** Total instructional faculty: 910 full-time, 239 part-time (58% men; 42% women; 9% minorities). Full-time faculty with Ph.D. or other terminal degree: 76%. Student/faculty ratio: 17/1. Classes of fewer than 20 students: 32%; of 20 to 49 students: 58%; of 50 or more students: 10%. **Advanced Placement and International Baccalaureate credit:** AP tests may be used for: Credit and/or placement. Scores accepted: 3, 4, 5. International Baccalaureate exams may be used for: Credit and/or placement. **Freshmen returning for sophomore year:** 78%. **Graduation rates:** Four-year: 27%; five-year: 49%; six-year: 54%. **Graduate study:** 22% of students pursue further study within one year.

COSTS AND FINANCIAL AID

Financial aid office: (765) 285-5600. **Expenses (2005-2006):** Tuition and fees 2005-2006: $6,160 in state, $15,336 out of state; room/board: $6,328. Estimated books and supplies: $880; transportation: $762; personal expenses: $1,370. **Financial aid:** Priority filing date for institution's financial aid form: March 10.

CAMPUS LIFE AND EXTRACURRICULAR ACTIVITIES

Campus housing available: coed dorms, women's dorms, men's dorms, sorority housing, fraternity housing, apartments for married students, apartment for single students, special housing for disabled students, special housing for international students, cooperative housing. Students who live in college-owned, operated, or affiliated housing: 37%. **Student employment:** During the 2005-2006 academic year, 30% of undergraduates worked on campus. Average per-year earnings: $1,241. **Clubs and organizations:** Number of student organizations: 312. Activities include: choral groups, concert band, dance, drama/theater, jazz band, literary magazine, marching band, music ensembles, musical theater, pep band, radio station, student government, student newspaper, student film society, symphony orchestra, television station. Number of fraternities: 12; sororities: 15. Proportion of men in fraternities: 7%; of women in sororities: 10%. **Sports program (2005-2006):** Member of NCAA I. *Men's intercollegiate varsity sports:* baseball, basketball, football, golf, swimming and diving, track and field (outdoor), volleyball. *Women's intercollegiate varsity sports:* basketball, cross-country, field hockey, golf, gymnastics, soccer, softball, swimming and diving, tennis, track and field (indoor), track and field (outdoor), volleyball.

SERVICES AND FACILITIES

Basic services: nonremedial tutoring, placement service, day care, health service. **Remedial assistance:** reading, writing, study skills. **Counseling services:** minority student, career, military, personal, veteran student, academic, older student, psychological, birth control, other. **For learning-disabled students:** School does not offer a structured program with separate admission and additional fees. Total undergraduates in learning-disabled program or receiving services: 250. Services include: reading machines, tape recorders, note-taking services, oral tests, learning center, readers, extended time for tests, tutors, priority registration. **Library:** Number of titles: 1,500,000; number of current serial subscriptions: 2,660. **Information technology resources:** Students are not required to lease or own a computer. Number of campus computers available to all students: 750. School has a wireless network. Proportion of college-owned housing units wired for high-speed internet access: 100%. **Campus safety:** Security services offered: 24-hour foot and vehicle patrols, late-night transport/escort service, 24-hour emergency telephones, lighted pathways/sidewalks, student patrols, controlled dormitory access (key, security card, etc).

TRANSFER AND INTERNATIONAL STUDENTS

Transfer students: May apply for admission for the following academic terms: Fall, Spring, Summer. Applicants need a minimum number of credits to apply. For fall 2005: Transfer applications received: 1,453. Transfer applicants offered admission: 873. Transfer applicants enrolled: 677. **International students:** Number of foreign undergraduates: 5. Number of countries represented: 84. Minimum TOEFL score required: 550 (paper); 213 (computer). Average TOEFL score: 516 (paper).

Bethel College

- **Address:** 1001 W. McKinley Avenue, Mishawaka, IN 46545
- **Website:** http://www.bethelcollege.edu
- **Private; Religious affiliation:** Missionary Church
- **Enrollment:** N/A

KEY STATS

- ✔ **U.S News College Ranking:** 38, Comp. Coll.–Bachelor's (Midwest)
- ✔ **ACT Score (25th/75th percentile):** 18-26
- ✔ **Tuition:** 2006-2007: $17,450

Selectivity: Selective	**Room/board:** $5,630
Acceptance rate: 71%	**Average debt:** $16,204
Student/faculty ratio: N/A	**Proportion who borrowed:** 77%

Butler University

- **Address:** 4600 Sunset Avenue, Indianapolis, IN 46208
- **Website:** http://www.butler.edu
- **Private**
- **Enrollment:** 3,576 full-time; 75 part-time

KEY STATS

- ✔ **U.S News College Ranking:** 5, Universities–Master's (Midwest)
- ✔ **SAT Score (25th/75th percentile):** 1080-1280
- ✔ **Tuition:** 2006-2007: $25,414

Selectivity: More selective	**Room/board:** $8,530
Acceptance rate: 72%	**Average debt:** N/A
Student/faculty ratio: 12/1	**Proportion who borrowed:** 70%

UNDERGRADUATE STUDENT BODY STATS

2005-2006 enrollment: 3,576 full-time; 75 part-time. Men: 38%; women: 62%. **Ethnic makeup:** African American: 3%; Asian American: 2%; Hispanic: 1%; White: 90%; International: 3%. **Religious preference:** Roman Catholic: 32%; Protestant: 48%; Jewish: 2%; No preference: 11%; Unknown: 3%; Other: 4%.

ADMISSIONS FACTS AND FIGURES

Phone: (888) 940-8100. **Email:** admission@butler.edu. **Website:** http://www.butler.edu. **Application deadlines for fall 2007:** Regular decision: Rolling. Early decision: Not offered. Early action: Send application by: December 1; Decision sent by: December 20. Admission can be deferred. **Application fee:** $35. Common application is accepted. **Admissions requirements/recommendations:** High school units required (recommended): English: 4; Mathematics: 3; Science: 3; Foreign language: 2; History: 2; Academic electives: 2; Total units: 16. Tests: The college uses SAT or ACT scores in admissions decisions. Either SAT or ACT required. For admission to the fall 2007 entering class, the school will accept: ACT with writing. Campus visit: Recommended. Admissions interview: Recommended. Off-campus interview: Not available. **Factors that count in admissions decisions:**

Academic: Secondary school record: Very important. Class rank: Important. Letters of recommendation: Considered. Standardized test scores: Important. Essay: Important. **Nonacademic:** Interview: Not considered. Extracurricular activities: Considered. Talent/ability: Not considered. Character/personal qualities: Not considered. Alumni/ae relationship: Considered. Geographical residence: Considered. State residency: Considered. Religious affiliation/commitment: Not considered. Minority status: Not considered. Volunteer work: Considered. Work experience: Considered. **Other schools with the greatest overlap in applicants:** Ball State University; DePauw University; Indiana University–Bloomington; Miami University–Oxford; Purdue University–West Lafayette. **Admissions statistics for the fall 2005 entering class:** Total applicants: 4,782. Total accepted: 3,458. Freshmen enrolled: 867; 43% were from out of state. Accepted through early-decision or early-action plans: 100%. Overall acceptance rate: 72%. Non-early acceptance rate: 500%. **Credentials of fall 2005 freshmen:** 47% ranked in the top 10 percent of their high school class; 78% were in the top 25 percent, and 95% were in the top half. (Proportion submitting class standing: 84%.) **Average high school grade point average:** 3.6. **First-year students who submitted SAT scores:** 57%. Scores (25/75 percentile): Verbal: 540-630, Math: 540-650, Combined: 1080-1280. **First-year students submitting ACT scores:** 43%. Scores (25/75 percentile): English: 23-29, Math: 23-28, Composite: 24-29.

ACADEMICS

Year founded: 1855. **Academic calendar:** Semester. **Degrees offered:** associate, bachelor's, master's, first professional. **Most popular majors:** 16% business, management, marketing, and related support services, 16% health professions and related clinical sciences, 13% communication, journalism, and related programs, 10% education, 8% visual and performing arts. **Major fields of study:** biological and biomedical sciences; business, management, marketing, and related support services; communication, journalism, and related programs; computer and information sciences and support services; education; English language and literature/letters; foreign languages, literatures, and linguistics; health professions and related clinical sciences; history; liberal arts and sciences studies, and humanities; mathematics and statistics; multi/interdisciplinary studies; philosophy and religious studies; physical sciences; psychology; security and protective services; social sciences; visual and performing arts. **Areas of required coursework:** arts/fine arts, humanities, mathematics, English (including composition), sciences (biological or physical), social science, other. **Pre-professional programs:** pre-law, pre-dentistry, pre-medicine, pre-theology, pre-veterinary science, pre-pharmacy, other. **Special academic programs (% participation):** cross-registration (1%), double major (15%), dual enrollment (1%), exchange student program (domestic) (1%), honors program (17%), independent study (68%), internships (75%), student-designed major (1%), study abroad (20%), teacher certificate program (8%). **Teacher certification offered in:** early childhood, elementary, middle/junior high, secondary. **Cooperative education programs:** business, engineering, health professions, other. **Reserve Officers Training Corps (ROTC):** Army ROTC: Offered on campus; Air Force ROTC: Offered at cooperating institution (Indiana University (Bloomington)). **Faculty and instruction (2005-2006):** Total instructional faculty: 279 full-time, 155 part-time (58% men; 42% women; 9% minorities). Full-time faculty with Ph.D. or other terminal degree: 85%. Student/faculty ratio: 12/1. Classes of fewer than 20 students: 56%; of 20 to 49 students: 41%; of 50 or more students: 3%. **Advanced Placement and International Baccalaureate credit:** AP tests may be used for: Credit only. Scores accepted: 3, 4, 5. International Baccalaureate exams may be used for: Credit only. **Freshmen returning for sophomore year:** 87%. **Graduation rates:** Four-year: 55%; five-year: 63%; six-year: 69%. **Graduate study:** 21% of students pursue further study immediately upon graduation; 25% within one year; 31% within five years. Fields in which graduates pursue further study: Master of Business Administration (MBA), 5%; law, 8%; medicine, 10%; dentistry, 1%; education, 6%; arts and sciences, 67%.

COSTS AND FINANCIAL AID

Financial aid office: (317) 940-8200. **Expenses (2006-2007):** Tuition and fees 2006-2007: $25,414; room/board: $8,530. Estimated books and supplies: $800; transportation: $600; personal expenses: $1,450. **Financial aid:** Priority filing date for institution's financial aid form: March 1; deadline: August 1. In 2005-2006, 91% of undergraduates applied for financial aid. Of those, 60% were determined to have financial need; 21% had their need fully met. Average financial aid package (proportion receiving): $17,500 (60%). Average amount of gift aid, such as scholarships or grants (proportion receiving): $12,800 (57%). Average amount of self-help aid, such as work study or loans (proportion receiving): $5,700 (48%). Average need-based loan (excluding PLUS or other private loans): $5,200. Among students who received need-based aid, the average percentage of need met: 78%. Among students who received aid based on merit, the average award (and the proportion receiving): $9,400 (26%). The average athletic scholarship (and the proportion receiving): $18,000 (3%). Proportion who borrowed: 70%.

CAMPUS LIFE AND EXTRACURRICULAR ACTIVITIES

Campus housing available (% using): coed dorms (47%), women's dorms (19%), sorority housing (18%), fraternity housing (11%), apartment for single students (4%), other housing options (1%). Students who live in college-owned, operated, or affiliated housing: 56%. **Student employment:** During the 2005-2006 academic year, 25% of undergraduates worked on campus. Average per-year earnings: $1,000. **Clubs and organizations:** Number of student organizations: 100. Activities include: choral groups, concert band, dance, drama/theater, jazz band, literary magazine, marching band, music ensembles, opera, pep band, student government, student newspaper, symphony orchestra, television station, yearbook. Number of fraternities: 8; sororities: 8. Proportion of men in fraternities: 24%; of women in sororities: 29%. Average proportion of students who stay on campus on weekends: 75%. **Sports program (2005-2006):** Member of NCAA I. *Men's intercollegiate varsity sports:* baseball, basketball, cross-country, football, golf, lacrosse, soccer, swimming and diving, tennis, track and field (indoor), track and field (outdoor). *Women's intercollegiate varsity sports:* basketball, cross-country, golf, soccer, softball, swimming and diving, tennis, track and field (indoor), track and field (outdoor), volleyball.

SERVICES AND FACILITIES

Basic services: placement service, day care, health service. **Counseling services:** career, personal, academic, psychological. **For learning-disabled students:** School does not offer a structured program with separate admission and additional fees. Total undergraduates in learning-disabled program or receiving services: 50. Services include: reading machines, tape recorders, note-taking services, learning center, readers, extended time for tests, tutors, priority registration, priority seating, texts on tape, other testing accomodations, other. **Library:** Number of titles: 348,542; number of current serial subscriptions: 1,741. **Information technology resources:** Students are not required to lease or own a computer. Number of campus computers available to all students: 430. School has a wireless network. Proportion of college-owned housing units wired for high-speed internet access: 100%. **Campus safety:** Security services offered: 24-hour foot and vehicle patrols, late-night transport/escort service, 24-hour emergency telephones, lighted pathways/sidewalks, controlled dormitory access (key, security card, etc).

TRANSFER AND INTERNATIONAL STUDENTS

Transfer students: May apply for admission for the following academic terms: Fall, Spring, Summer. Applicants need a minimum number of credits to apply. For fall 2005: Transfer applications received: 704. Transfer applicants offered admission: 261. Transfer applicants enrolled: 112. **International students:** Number of foreign undergraduates: 103 (3% of student body). Number of countries represented: 53. Minimum TOEFL score required: 550 (paper); 213 (computer). Average TOEFL score: 596 (paper).

Calumet College of St. Joseph

- **Address:** 2400 New York Avenue, Whiting, IN 46394
- **Website:** http://www.ccsj.edu
- **Private; Religious affiliation:** Roman Catholic
- **Enrollment:** 468 full-time; 709 part-time

KEY STATS

✔ **U.S News College Ranking:** fourth tier, Comp. Coll.–Bachelor's (Midwest)
✔ **SAT Score:** 841
✔ **Tuition:** 2006-2007: $10,650

Selectivity: Less selective	**Room/board:** N/A
Acceptance rate: 27%	**Average debt:** $16,040
Student/faculty ratio: 8/1	**Proportion who borrowed:** 65%

UNDERGRADUATE STUDENT BODY STATS

2005-2006 enrollment: 468 full-time; 709 part-time. Men: 43%; women: 57%. **Ethnic makeup:** African American: 29%; Asian American: 1%; Hispanic: 20%; White: 50%. **Religious preference:** Roman Catholic: 45%; Unknown: 3%; Other: 52%.

ADMISSIONS FACTS AND FIGURES

Phone: (219) 473-4215. **Email:** admissions@ccsj.edu. **Website:** http://www.ccsj.edu. **Application deadlines for fall 2007:** Regular decision: Rolling. Early decision: Not offered. Early action: Not offered. Admission can be deferred. Common application is accepted. **Admissions requirements/recommendations:** High school units required (recommended): English: 4 (4); Mathematics: 3 (3); Science: 3 (3); Foreign language: 2 (2); Social studies: 3 (3); History: 1 (1). Tests: The college uses SAT or ACT scores in admissions decisions: Neither SAT nor ACT required. For admission to the fall 2007 entering class, the school will accept: ACT with writing, ACT without writing. Campus visit: Recommended. Admissions interview: Recommended. Off-campus interview: May be arranged. **Factors that count in admissions decisions:** *Academic:* Secondary school record: Important. Class rank: Important. Letters of recommendation: Considered. Standardized test scores: Important. Essay: Important. *Nonacademic:* Interview: Considered. Extracurricular activities: Considered. Talent/ability: Considered. Character/personal qualities: Considered. Alumni/ae relationship: Considered. Geographical residence: Not considered. State residency: Not considered. Religious affiliation/commitment: Considered. Minority status: Not considered. Volunteer work: Important. Work experience: Considered. **Other schools with the greatest overlap in applicants:** Indiana University Northwest; Purdue University–Calumet. **Admissions statistics for the fall 2005 entering class:** Total applicants: 221. Total accepted: 60. Freshmen enrolled: 60; Overall acceptance rate: 27%. **Credentials of fall 2005 freshmen:** 10% ranked in the top 10 percent of their high school class; 26% were in the top 25 percent, and 50% were in the top half. (Proportion submitting class standing: 92%.) **Average high school grade point average:** 2.6. **First-year students who submitted SAT scores:** 38%. Scores (25/75 percentile): Verbal: N/A, Math: N/A, Combined: N/A. **First-year students submitting ACT scores:** 30%. Scores (25/75 percentile): English: N/A, Math: N/A, Composite: N/A.

ACADEMICS

Year founded: 1951. **Academic calendar:** Trimester. **Degrees offered:** certificate, diploma, associate, bachelor's, post-bachelor's certificate, master's. **Most popular majors:** 48% securities services administration/management, 20% management science. **Major fields of study:** business, management, marketing, and related support services; education; English language and literature/letters; legal professions and studies; liberal arts and sciences studies, and humanities; philosophy and religious studies; psychology; public administration and social service professions; security and protective services. **Areas of required coursework:** arts/fine arts, humanities, computer literacy, mathematics, English (including composition), sciences (biological or physical), history. **Special academic programs (% participation):** accelerated program (30%), cooperative (work-study plan) program (5%), cross-registration (5%), distance learning (5%), double major (2%), independent study (5%), internships (5%), teacher certificate program (10%), weekend college (10%). **Teacher certification offered in:** elementary, middle/junior high, secondary. **Cooperative education programs:** agriculture, art, business, computer science, education, engineering, health professions, humanities, natural science, social/behavioral science, technologies, vocational arts. **Faculty and instruction (2005-2006):** Total instructional faculty: 38 full-time, 119 part-time (62% men; 38% women; 12% minorities). Full-time faculty with Ph.D. or other terminal degree: 79%. Student/faculty ratio: 8/1. Classes of fewer than 20 students: 81%; of 20 to 49 students: 19%; of 50 or more students: 0%. **Freshmen returning for sophomore year:** 57%. **Graduation rates:** Six-year: 13%.

COSTS AND FINANCIAL AID

Financial aid office: (219) 473-4213. **Expenses (2006-2007):** Tuition and fees 2006-2007: $10,650; room/board: N/A. **Financial aid:** Priority filing date for institution's financial aid form: March 1. In 2005-2006, 97% of undergraduates applied for financial aid. Of those, 84% were determined to have financial need; Average financial aid package (proportion receiving): N/A (56%). Average amount of self-help aid, such as work study or loans (proportion receiving): N/A (32%). Average amount of debt of borrowers graduating in 2005: $16,040. Proportion who borrowed: 65%.

CAMPUS LIFE AND EXTRACURRICULAR ACTIVITIES

Students who live in college-owned, operated, or affiliated housing: 0%. **Student employment:** During the 2005-2006 academic year, 10% of undergraduates worked on campus. **Clubs and organizations:** Number of student organizations: 9. Activities include: choral groups, drama/theater, literary magazine, music ensembles, musical theater, student government, student newspaper. Number of fraternities: 0; sororities: 1. **Sports program (2005-2006):** Member of NAIA. *Men's intercollegiate varsity sports:* baseball, basketball, soccer. *Women's intercollegiate varsity sports:* basketball, soccer, softball, volleyball.

SERVICES AND FACILITIES

Basic services: nonremedial tutoring, placement service, day care. **Remedial assistance:** reading, math, writing, study skills. **Counseling services:** career, personal, academic, religious. **For learning-disabled students:** Services include: remedial math, remedial English, tape recorders, untimed tests, note-taking services, oral tests, learning center, readers, extended time for tests, tutors, texts on tape. **Library:** Number of titles: 93,841; number of current serial subscriptions: 251. **Information technology resources:** Students are not required to lease or own a computer. Number of campus computers available to all students: 125. School has a wireless network. Approximate number of users that can be accommodated: 40. **Campus safety:** Security services offered: 24-hour emergency telephones, lighted pathways/sidewalks.

TRANSFER AND INTERNATIONAL STUDENTS

Transfer students: May apply for admission for the following academic terms: Fall, Winter, Spring, Summer. Applicants need a minimum number of credits to apply. **International students:** Number of foreign undergraduates: 2.

DePauw University

- **Address:** 313 S. Locust Street, Greencastle, IN 46135
- **Website:** http://www.depauw.edu
- **Private; Religious affiliation:** United Methodist
- **Enrollment:** 2,351 full-time; 46 part-time

KEY STATS

✔ **U.S News College Ranking:** 48, Liberal Arts Colleges
✔ **SAT Score (25th/75th percentile):** 1130-1330
✔ **Tuition:** 2006-2007: $27,780

Selectivity: More selective	**Room/board:** $7,800
Acceptance rate: 66%	**Average debt:** $15,635
Student/faculty ratio: 10/1	**Proportion who borrowed:** 55%

UNDERGRADUATE STUDENT BODY STATS

2005-2006 enrollment: 2,351 full-time; 46 part-time. Men: 45%; women: 55%. **Ethnic makeup:** African American: 6%; Asian American: 2%; Hispanic: 3%; White: 88%; International: 2%. **Religious preference:** Roman Catholic: 23%; Protestant: 31%; Jewish: 1%; No preference: 13%; Unknown: 17%; United Methodist: 11%; Orthodox (Eastern), Mennonite, Quaker, Unitarian, B'hai: 2%; Other: 2%.

ADMISSIONS FACTS AND FIGURES

Phone: (765) 658-4006. **Email:** admission@depauw.edu. **Website:** http://www.depauw.edu. **Application deadlines for fall 2007:** Regular decision: February 1; decision sent by April 1. Early decision: Send application by: November 1; Decision sent by: January 1. Early action: Send application by: December 1; Decision sent by: February 15. Admission can be deferred. **Application fee:** $40. Common application is accepted. **To apply online, go to:** http://www.depauw.edu/admission/applying/index.asp. **Admissions requirements/recommendations:** High school units required (recommended): English: (4); Mathematics: (4); Science: (4); Foreign language: (2); Social studies: (3); History: (3); Academic electives: (10); Total units: (32). Tests: The college uses SAT or ACT scores in admissions decisions. Either SAT or ACT required. For admission to the fall 2007 entering class, the school will accept: ACT with writing. Campus visit: Recommended. Admissions interview: Recommended. Off-campus interview: May be arranged. **Factors that count in admissions decisions:** *Academic:* Secondary school record: Very important. Class rank: Important. Letters of recommendation: Important. Standardized test scores: Very important. Essay: Important. *Nonacademic:* Interview: Important. Extracurricular activities: Considered. Talent/ability: Considered. Character/personal qualities: Considered. Alumni/ae relationship: Considered. Geographical residence: Considered. State residency: Not considered. Religious affiliation/commitment: Not considered. Minority status: Considered. Volunteer work: Considered. Work experience: Considered. **Other schools with the greatest overlap in applicants:** Indiana University–Bloomington; Miami University–Oxford; Purdue University–West Lafayette; University of Notre Dame; Vanderbilt University. **Admissions statistics for the fall 2005 entering class:** Total applicants: 3,440. Total accepted: 2,269. Freshmen enrolled: 586; 53% were from out of state. Accepted through early-decision or early-action plans: 61%. Overall acceptance rate: 66%. Early-decision acceptance rate: 89%. Non-early acceptance rate: 64%. **Size of waiting list:** 80 applicants; enrolled from waiting list: 6. **Credentials of fall 2005 freshmen:** 55% ranked in the top 10 percent of their high school class; 87% were in the top 25 percent, and 98% were in the top half. (Proportion submitting class standing: 73%.) **Average high school grade point average:** 3.7. **First-year students who submitted SAT scores:** 79%. Scores (25/75 percentile): Verbal: 560-660, Math: 570-670, Combined: 1130-1330. **First-year students submitting ACT scores:** 65%. Scores (25/75 percentile): English: 24-30, Math: 24-29, Composite: 24-29.

ACADEMICS

Year founded: 1837. **Academic calendar:** 4-1-4. **Degrees offered:** bachelor's, master's. **Most popular majors:** 10% economics, 10% mass communication/media studies, 9% English composition, 7% computer and information sciences, 6% Spanish language and literature. **Major fields of study:** area, ethnic, cultural, and gender studies; biological and biomedical sciences; communication, journalism, and related programs; computer and information sciences and support services; education; English language and literature/letters; foreign languages, literatures, and linguistics; health professions and related clinical sciences; history; mathematics and statistics; multi/interdisciplinary studies; natural resources and conservation; parks, recreation, leisure, and fitness studies; philosophy and religious studies; physical sciences; psychology; social sciences; visual and performing arts. **Areas of required coursework:** arts/fine arts, humanities, mathematics, English (including composition), philosophy, foreign languages, sciences (biological or physical), history, social science. **Pre-professional programs:** other. **Special academic programs (% participation):** double major (15.1%), dual enrollment (6%), honors program (21%), independent study (9%), internships (63.4%), student-designed major (0%), study abroad (60%), teacher certificate program (5.2%). **Teacher certification offered in:** early childhood, elementary, middle/junior high, secondary. **Reserve Officers Training Corps (ROTC):** Army ROTC: Offered at cooperating institution (Rose-Hulman Institute of Technology); Air Force ROTC: Offered at cooperating institution (Indiana University). **Faculty and instruction (2005-2006):** Total instructional faculty: 212 full-time, 41 part-time (56% men; 44% women; 14% minorities). Full-time faculty with Ph.D. or other terminal degree: 97%. Student/faculty ratio: 10/1. Classes of fewer than 20 students: 67%; of 20 to 49 students: 33%; of 50 or more students: 0%. **Advanced Placement and International Baccalaureate credit:** AP tests may be used for: Credit and/or placement. Scores accepted: 4, 5. International Baccalaureate exams may be used for: Credit and/or placement. **Freshmen returning for sophomore year:** 92%. **Graduation rates:** Four-year: 75%; five-year: 78%; six-year: 79%. **Graduate study:** 23% of students pursue further study immediately upon graduation; 50% within five years. Fields in which graduates pursue further study: Master of Business Administration (MBA), 2%; law, 21%; medicine, 9%; theology (or the seminary), 5%; education, 21%; arts and sciences, 41%.

COSTS AND FINANCIAL AID

Financial aid office: (765) 658-4030. **Expenses (2006-2007):** Tuition and fees 2006-2007: $27,780; room/board: $7,800. Estimated books and supplies: $700; transportation: $300; personal expenses: $1,000. **Financial aid:** In 2005-2006, 57% of undergraduates applied for financial aid. Of those, 47% were determined to have financial need; 99% had their need fully met. Average financial aid package (proportion receiving): $24,873 (47%). Average amount of gift aid, such as scholarships or grants (proportion receiving): $14,486 (47%). Average amount of self-help aid, such as work study or loans (proportion receiving): $6,226 (34%). Average need-based loan (excluding PLUS or other private loans): $4,637. Among students who received need-based aid, the average percentage of need met: 98%. Among students who received aid based on merit, the average award (and the proportion receiving): $12,245 (49%). The average athletic scholarship (and the proportion receiving): $0 (0%). Average amount of debt of borrowers graduating in 2005: $15,635. Proportion who borrowed: 55%.

CAMPUS LIFE AND EXTRACURRICULAR ACTIVITIES

Campus housing available (% using): coed dorms (44%), sorority housing (19%), fraternity housing (21%), apartment for single students (16%). Students who live in college-owned, operated, or affiliated housing: 99%. **Student employment:** During the 2005-2006 academic year, 13% of undergraduates worked on campus. Average per-year earnings: $524. **Clubs and organizations:** Number of student organizations: 102. Activities include:

choral groups, concert band, dance, drama/theater, jazz band, literary magazine, music ensembles, musical theater, opera, pep band, radio station, student government, student newspaper, student film society, symphony orchestra, television station, yearbook. Number of fraternities: 13; sororities: 11. Proportion of men in fraternities: 72%; of women in sororities: 68%. **Sports program (2005-2006):** Member of NCAA III. *Men's intercollegiate varsity sports:* baseball, basketball, cross-country, football, golf, soccer, swimming and diving, tennis, track and field (indoor), track and field (outdoor). *Women's intercollegiate varsity sports:* basketball, cross-country, field hockey, golf, soccer, softball, swimming and diving, tennis, track and field (indoor), track and field (outdoor), volleyball.

SERVICES AND FACILITIES

Basic services: nonremedial tutoring, women's center, placement service, health service. **Remedial assistance:** reading, math, writing, study skills. **Counseling services:** minority student, career, personal, academic, psychological, birth control, religious. **For learning-disabled students:** School does not offer a structured program with separate admission and additional fees. Total undergraduates in learning-disabled program or receiving services: 50. Services include: remedial math, remedial English, reading machines, remedial reading, tape recorders, diagnostic testing service, untimed tests, note-taking services, oral tests, learning center, readers, extended time for tests, tutors, priority registration, priority seating, texts on tape, other testing accomodations. **Library:** Number of titles: 783,190; number of current serial subscriptions: 2,859. **Information technology resources:** Students are required to lease or own a computer. Number of campus computers available to all students: 424. School has a wireless network. Approximate number of users that can be accommodated: 1,000. Proportion of college-owned housing units wired for high-speed internet access: 100%. **Campus safety:** Security services offered: 24-hour foot and vehicle patrols, late-night transport/escort service, 24-hour emergency telephones, lighted pathways/sidewalks, student patrols, controlled dormitory access (key, security card, etc).

TRANSFER AND INTERNATIONAL STUDENTS

Transfer students: May apply for admission for the following academic terms: Fall, Spring. Applicants do not need a minimum number of credits to apply. For fall 2005: Transfer applications received: 51. Transfer applicants offered admission: 28. Transfer applicants enrolled: 12. **International students:** Number of foreign undergraduates: 36 (2% of student body). Number of countries represented: 22. Minimum TOEFL score required: 560 (paper); 225 (computer).

Earlham College

- **Address:** 801 National Road W, Richmond, IN 47374
- **Website:** http://www.earlham.edu
- **Private; Religious affiliation:** Quaker
- **Enrollment:** 1,201 full-time; 25 part-time

KEY STATS

✔ **U.S News College Ranking:** 65, Liberal Arts Colleges
✔ **SAT Score (25th/75th percentile):** 1100-1350
✔ **Tuition:** 2006-2007: $29,320

Selectivity: More selective	**Room/board:** $6,200
Acceptance rate: 70%	**Average debt:** $19,000
Student/faculty ratio: 12/1	**Proportion who borrowed:** 70%

UNDERGRADUATE STUDENT BODY STATS

2005-2006 enrollment: 1,201 full-time; 25 part-time. Men: 42%; women: 58%. **Ethnic makeup:** African American: 7%; Asian American: 2%; Hispanic: 3%; White: 81%; International: 7%.

ADMISSIONS FACTS AND FIGURES

Phone: (765) 983-1600. **Email:** admission@earlham.edu. **Website:** http://www.earlham.edu. **Application deadlines for fall 2007:** Regular decision: February 15; decision sent by March 15. Early decision: Send application by: December 1; Decision sent by: December 15. Early action: Send application by: January 1; Decision sent by: February 1. Admission can be deferred. **Application fee:** $30. Common application is accepted. **To apply online, go to:** http://www.earlham.edu/~adm/apps.html. **Admissions requirements/recommendations:** High school units required (recommended): English: 4 (4); Mathematics: 3 (4); Science: 3 (4); Foreign lan-

guage: 2 (4); Social studies: 2 (3); History: 1 (1); Total units: 15 (20). Tests: The college uses SAT or ACT scores in admissions decisions. Either SAT or ACT required. For admission to the fall 2007 entering class, the school will accept: ACT with writing. Campus visit: Recommended. Admissions interview: Recommended. Off-campus interview: May be arranged. **Factors that count in admissions decisions: Academic:** Secondary school record: Very important. Class rank: Important. Letters of recommendation: Very important. Standardized test scores: Important. Essay: Very important. *Nonacademic:* Interview: Important. Extracurricular activities: Important. Talent/ability: Important. Character/personal qualities: Very important. Alumni/ae relationship: Considered. Geographical residence: Not considered. State residency: Not considered. Religious affiliation/commitment: Considered. Minority status: Important. Volunteer work: Important. Work experience: Considered. **Other schools with the greatest overlap in applicants:** Beloit College; Grinnell College; Kenyon College; Macalester College; Oberlin College. **Admissions statistics for the fall 2005 entering class:** Total applicants: 1,554. Total accepted: 1,092. Freshmen enrolled: 324; 75% were from out of state. Accepted through early-decision or early-action plans: 52%. Overall acceptance rate: 70%. Early-decision acceptance rate: 95%. Non-early acceptance rate: 60%. **Size of waiting list:** 72 applicants; enrolled from waiting list: 12. **Credentials of fall 2005 freshmen:** 30% ranked in the top 10 percent of their high school class; 61% were in the top 25 percent, and 87% were in the top half. (Proportion submitting class standing: 47%.) **Average high school grade point average:** 3.5. **First-year students who submitted SAT scores:** 85%. Scores (25/75 percentile): Verbal: 570-700, Math: 530-650, Combined: 1100-1350. **First-year students submitting ACT scores:** 36%. Scores (25/75 percentile): English: N/A, Math: N/A, Composite: 23-29.

ACADEMICS

Year founded: 1847. **Academic calendar:** Semester. **Degrees offered:** bachelor's, master's, first professional. **Most popular majors:** 15% biology/biological sciences, 10% art/art studies, 9% psychology, 8% multi/interdisciplinary studies, 7% sociology. **Major fields of study:** area, ethnic, cultural, and gender studies; biological and biomedical sciences; business, management, marketing, and related support services; computer and information sciences and support services; English language and literature/letters; foreign languages, literatures, and linguistics; history; mathematics and statistics; multi/interdisciplinary studies; natural resources and conservation; philosophy and religious studies; physical sciences; psychology; social sciences; visual and performing arts. **Areas of required coursework:** arts/fine arts, humanities, mathematics, English (including composition), foreign languages, sciences (biological or physical), other. **Pre-professional programs:** pre-law, pre-dentistry, pre-medicine, other. **Special academic programs (% participation):** accelerated program (3%), cross-registration (1%), double major (8%), English as a Second Language (ESL) (3%), independent study (60%), internships (10%), student-designed major (2%), study abroad (80%), teacher certificate program. **Teacher certification offered in:** middle/junior high, secondary. **Faculty and instruction (2005-2006):** Total instructional faculty: 93 full-time, 15 part-time (56% men; 44% women; 21% minorities). Full-time faculty with Ph.D. or other terminal degree: 97%. Student/faculty ratio: 12/1. Classes of fewer than 20 students: 71%; of 20 to 49 students: 25%; of 50 or more students: 4%. **Advanced Placement and International Baccalaureate credit:** AP tests may be used for: Credit and/or placement. Scores accepted: 4, 5. International Baccalaureate exams may be used for: Credit only. **Freshmen returning for sophomore year:** 85%. **Graduation rates:** Four-year: 54%; five-year: 67%; six-year: 68%. **Graduate study:** 36% of students pursue further study immediately upon graduation; 75% within five years. Fields in which graduates pursue further study: law, 4%; medicine, 3%; theology (or the seminary), 4%; education, 5%; arts and sciences, 13%; veterinary medicine, 1%.

COSTS AND FINANCIAL AID

Financial aid office: (765) 983-1217. **Expenses (2006-2007):** Tuition and fees 2006-2007: $29,320; room/board: $6,200. Estimated books and supplies: $850; transportation: $500; personal expenses: $1,000. **Financial aid:** Priority filing date for institution's financial aid form: March 1. In 2005-2006, 66% of undergraduates applied for financial aid. Of those, 59% were determined to have financial need; 43% had their need fully met. Average financial aid package (proportion receiving): $21,500 (59%). Average amount of gift aid, such as scholarships or grants (proportion receiving): $13,243 (52%). Average amount of self-help aid, such as work study or loans (proportion receiving): $5,845 (50%). Average need-based loan (excluding PLUS or other private loans): $4,783. Among students who received need-based aid, the average percentage of need met: 85%. Among students who received aid based on merit, the average award (and the proportion receiving): $6,916 (22%). Average amount of debt of borrowers graduating in 2005: $19,000. Proportion who borrowed: 70%.

CAMPUS LIFE AND EXTRACURRICULAR ACTIVITIES
Campus housing available (% using): coed dorms (70%). Students who live in college-owned, operated, or affiliated housing: 88%. **Student employment:** During the 2005-2006 academic year, 16% of undergraduates worked on campus. Average per-year earnings: $744. **Clubs and organizations:** Number of student organizations: 62. Activities include: choral groups, concert band, dance, drama/theater, jazz band, literary magazine, music ensembles, musical theater, radio station, student government, student newspaper, student film society, symphony orchestra, yearbook. Number of fraternities: 0; sororities: 0. Average proportion of students who stay on campus on weekends: 92%. **Sports program (2005-2006):** Member of NCAA III. *Men's intercollegiate varsity sports:* baseball, basketball, cross-country, football, soccer, tennis, track and field (indoor), track and field (outdoor). *Women's intercollegiate varsity sports:* basketball, cross-country, field hockey, soccer, tennis, track and field (indoor), track and field (outdoor), volleyball.

SERVICES AND FACILITIES
Basic services: nonremedial tutoring, women's center, placement service, day care, health service, health insurance. **Counseling services:** minority student, career, personal, veteran student, academic, older student, psychological, birth control, religious. **For learning-disabled students:** School does not offer a structured program with separate admission and additional fees. Total undergraduates in learning-disabled program or receiving services: 110. **Library:** Number of titles: 404,760; number of current serial subscriptions: 19,163. **Information technology resources:** Students are not required to lease or own a computer. Number of campus computers available to all students: 164. School has a wireless network. Proportion of college-owned housing units wired for high-speed internet access: 75%. **Campus safety:** Security services offered: 24-hour foot and vehicle patrols, late-night transport/escort service, 24-hour emergency telephones, lighted pathways/sidewalks, student patrols, controlled dormitory access (key, security card, etc.).

TRANSFER AND INTERNATIONAL STUDENTS
Transfer students: May apply for admission for the following academic terms: Fall, Spring. Applicants need a minimum number of credits to apply. For fall 2005: Transfer applications received: 76. Transfer applicants offered admission: 43. Transfer applicants enrolled: 24. **International students:** Number of foreign undergraduates: 83 (7% of student body). Number of countries represented: 42. Minimum TOEFL score required: 550 (paper); 213 (computer). Average TOEFL score: 620 (paper).

Franklin College

- **Address:** 101 Branigin Boulevard, Franklin, IN 46131-2623
- **Website:** http://www.franklincollege.edu
- **Private; Religious affiliation:** American Baptist
- **Enrollment:** 946 full-time; 57 part-time

KEY STATS
✔ **U.S News College Ranking:** 24, Comp. Coll.–Bachelor's (Midwest)
✔ **SAT Score (25th/75th percentile):** 920-1140
✔ **Tuition:** 2006-2007: $20,325

Selectivity: Selective	**Room/board:** $5,970
Acceptance rate: 78%	**Average debt:** $21,263
Student/faculty ratio: 16/1	**Proportion who borrowed:** 90%

UNDERGRADUATE STUDENT BODY STATS
2005-2006 enrollment: 946 full-time; 57 part-time. Men: 52%; women: 48%. **Ethnic makeup:** African American: 4%; Hispanic: 1%; White: 93%; International: 1%. **Religious preference:** Roman Catholic: 16%; Protestant: 45%; Hindu: 1%; No preference: 32%; American Baptist: 6%.

ADMISSIONS FACTS AND FIGURES
Phone: (317) 738-8062. **Email:** admissions@franklincollege.edu. **Website:** http://www.franklincollege.edu. **Application deadlines for fall 2007:** Regular decision: Rolling. Early decision: Not offered. Early action: Not offered. Admission can be deferred. **Application fee:** $30. Common application is accepted. **To apply online, go to:** https://www.applyweb.com/aw?fc. **Admissions requirements/recommendations:** High school units required

(recommended): English: 4; Mathematics: 3; Science: 2; Foreign language: (2); Social studies: 3. Tests: The college uses SAT or ACT scores in admissions decisions. Either SAT or ACT required. For admission to the fall 2007 entering class, the school will accept: ACT with writing. Campus visit: Recommended. Admissions interview: Recommended. Off-campus interview: May be arranged. **Factors that count in admissions decisions:** *Academic:* Secondary school record: Very important. Class rank: Very important. Letters of recommendation: Considered. Standardized test scores: Important. Essay: Important. *Nonacademic:* Interview: Considered. Extracurricular activities: Important. Talent/ability: Important. Character/personal qualities: Important. Alumni/ae relationship: Important. Geographical residence: Considered. State residency: Considered. Religious affiliation/commitment: Considered. Minority status: Important. Volunteer work: Important. Work experience: Considered. **Other schools with the greatest overlap in applicants:** Ball State University; Hanover College; Indiana University–Bloomington; Manchester College; Purdue University–West Lafayette. **Admissions statistics for the fall 2005 entering class:** Total applicants: 1,009. Total accepted: 790. Freshmen enrolled: 273; 3% were from out of state. Overall acceptance rate: 78%. **Size of waiting list:** 0 applicants; enrolled from waiting list: 0. **Credentials of fall 2005 freshmen:** 20% ranked in the top 10 percent of their high school class; 54% were in the top 25 percent, and 82% were in the top half. (Proportion submitting class standing: 3%.) **Average high school grade point average:** 3.2. **First-year students who submitted SAT scores:** 92%. Scores (25/75 percentile): Verbal: 460-560, Math: 460-580, Combined: 920-1140. **First-year students submitting ACT scores:** 29%. Scores (25/75 percentile): English: 18-25, Math: 19-26, Composite: 19-25.

ACADEMICS
Year founded: 1834. **Academic calendar:** 4-1-4. **Degrees offered:** bachelor's. **Most popular majors:** 22% journalism, 19% elementary education and teaching, 16% sociology, 11% business/commerce, 6% biology/biological sciences. **Major fields of study:** area, ethnic, cultural, and gender studies; biological and biomedical sciences; business, management, marketing, and related support services; communication, journalism, and related programs; computer and information sciences and support services; education; English language and literature/letters; foreign languages, literatures, and linguistics; health professions and related clinical sciences; history; mathematics and statistics; parks, recreation, leisure, and fitness studies; philosophy and religious studies; physical sciences; psychology; social sciences; visual and performing arts. **Areas of required coursework:** arts/fine arts, humanities, mathematics, English (including composition), foreign languages, sciences (biological or physical), history, social science, other. **Pre-professional programs:** pre-law, pre-dentistry, pre-medicine, pre-theology, pre-veterinary science, pre-optometry, pre-pharmacy, other. **Special academic programs (% participation):** cooperative (work-study plan) program (90%), cross-registration (1%), double major (11%), dual enrollment, independent study (20%), internships (64%), study abroad, teacher certificate program (27%). **Teacher certification offered in:** early childhood, elementary, middle/junior high, secondary. **Cooperative education programs:** engineering, health professions, technologies, other. **Reserve Officers Training Corps (ROTC):** Army ROTC: Offered at cooperating institution (IUPUI). **Faculty and instruction (2005-2006):** Total instructional faculty: 66 full-time, 45 part-time (59% men; 41% women; 4% minorities). Full-time faculty with Ph.D. or other terminal degree: 82%. Student/faculty ratio: 16/1. Classes of fewer than 20 students: 65%; of 20 to 49 students: 35%; of 50 or more students: 0%. **Advanced Placement and International Baccalaureate credit:** AP tests may be used for: Credit only. **Freshmen returning for sophomore year:** 74%. **Graduation rates:** Four-year: 47%; five-year: 54%; six-year: 58%. **Graduate study:** 15% of students pursue further study immediately upon graduation. Fields in which graduates pursue further study: law, 2%; medicine, 1%; arts and sciences, 10%; veterinary medicine, 1%.

COSTS AND FINANCIAL AID
Financial aid office: (317) 738-8075. **Expenses (2006-2007):** Tuition and fees 2006-2007: $20,325; room/board: $5,970. Estimated books and supplies: $1,000; transportation: $1,000; personal expenses: $1,000. **Financial aid:** Priority filing date for institution's financial aid form: March 1; deadline: March 1. In 2005-2006, 93% of undergraduates applied for financial aid. Of those, 81% were determined to have financial need; 26% had their need fully met. Average financial aid package (proportion receiving): $15,508 (81%). Average amount of gift aid, such as scholarships or grants (proportion receiving): $11,681 (81%). Average amount of self-help aid, such as work study or loans (proportion receiving): $4,837 (64%). Average need-based loan (excluding PLUS or other private loans): $4,021. Among students who received need-based aid, the average percentage of need met:

88%. Among students who received aid based on merit, the average award (and the proportion receiving): $11,692 (18%). The average athletic scholarship (and the proportion receiving): $0 (0%). Average amount of debt of borrowers graduating in 2005: $21,263. Proportion who borrowed: 90%.

CAMPUS LIFE AND EXTRACURRICULAR ACTIVITIES

Campus housing available (% using): coed dorms (65%), fraternity housing (35%), special housing for disabled students. Students who live in college-owned, operated, or affiliated housing: 74%. **Student employment:** During the 2005-2006 academic year, 53% of undergraduates worked on campus. Average per-year earnings: $1,398. **Clubs and organizations:** Number of student organizations: 62. Activities include: choral groups, dance, drama/theater, literary magazine, musical theater, pep band, radio station, student government, student newspaper, television station, yearbook. Number of fraternities: 4; sororities: 4. Proportion of men in fraternities: 31%; of women in sororities: 42%. **Sports program (2005-2006):** Member of NCAA III. *Men's intercollegiate varsity sports:* baseball, basketball, cross-country, football, golf, soccer, tennis, track and field (indoor), track and field (outdoor). *Women's intercollegiate varsity sports:* basketball, cross-country, golf, soccer, softball, tennis, track and field (indoor), track and field (outdoor), volleyball.

SERVICES AND FACILITIES

Basic services: nonremedial tutoring, placement service, health service, health insurance. **Remedial assistance:** reading, math, writing, study skills. **Counseling services:** minority student, career, personal, veteran student, academic, older student, psychological, birth control, religious. **For learning-disabled students:** School does not offer a structured program with separate admission and additional fees. Services include: remedial math, remedial English, remedial reading, tape recorders, other special classes, videotaped classes, untimed tests, note-taking services, oral tests, learning center, readers, extended time for tests, tutors, priority registration, texts on tape. **Library:** Number of titles: 127,878; number of current serial subscriptions: 349. **Information technology resources:** Students are not required to lease or own a computer. Number of campus computers available to all students: 400. School has a wireless network. Approximate number of users that can be accommodated: 1,500. Proportion of college-owned housing units wired for high-speed internet access: 100%. **Campus safety:** Security services offered: 24-hour foot and vehicle patrols, late-night transport/escort service, 24-hour emergency telephones, lighted pathways/sidewalks, controlled dormitory access (key, security card, etc).

TRANSFER AND INTERNATIONAL STUDENTS

Transfer students: May apply for admission for the following academic terms: Fall, Winter, Spring, Summer. Applicants do not need a minimum number of credits to apply. For fall 2005: Transfer applications received: 67. Transfer applicants offered admission: 41. Transfer applicants enrolled: 35. **International students:** Number of foreign undergraduates: 9 (1% of student body). Minimum TOEFL score required: 550 (paper); 213 (computer). Average TOEFL score: 570 (paper).

Goshen College

- **Address:** 1700 S. Main Street, Goshen, IN 46526
- **Website:** http://www.goshen.edu
- **Private; Religious affiliation:** Mennonite
- **Enrollment:** 825 full-time; 97 part-time

KEY STATS

✔ **U.S News College Ranking:** third tier, Liberal Arts Colleges
✔ **SAT Score (25th/75th percentile):** 1020-1310
✔ **Tuition:** 2006-2007: $20,300

Selectivity: More selective	**Room/board:** $6,700
Acceptance rate: 76%	**Average debt:** $18,680
Student/faculty ratio: 10/1	**Proportion who borrowed:** 69%

UNDERGRADUATE STUDENT BODY STATS

2005-2006 enrollment: 825 full-time; 97 part-time. Men: 40%; women: 60%. **Ethnic makeup:** African American: 3%; Asian American: 1%; Hispanic: 4%; White: 84%; International: 8%. **Religious preference:** Roman Catholic: 6%; Protestant: 22%; Hindu: 1%; No preference: 3%; Unknown: 13%; Mennonite: 54%.

ADMISSIONS FACTS AND FIGURES

Phone: (574) 535-7535. **Email:** admissions@goshen.edu. **Website:** http://www.goshen.edu. **Application deadlines for fall 2007:** Regular decision: August 15. Early decision: Not offered. Early action: Send application by: December 1; Decision sent by: December 15. Admission can be deferred. **Application fee:** $25. Common application is accepted. **To apply online, go to:** http://www.goshen.edu/apply. **Admissions requirements/recommendations:** High school units required (recommended): English: 4 (4); Mathematics: 3 (3); Science: 2 (3); Foreign language: 2 (2); Social studies: 2 (2); History: 2 (2); Total units: 15 (16). Tests: The college uses SAT or ACT scores in admissions decisions. Either SAT or ACT required. For admission to the fall 2007 entering class, the school will accept: ACT with writing, ACT without writing. Campus visit: Recommended. Admissions interview: Recommended. Off-campus interview: May be arranged. **Factors that count in admissions decisions:** *Academic:* Secondary school record: Important. Class rank: Considered. Letters of recommendation: Important. Standardized test scores: Important. Essay: Important. *Nonacademic:* Interview: Considered. Extracurricular activities: Considered. Talent/ability: Considered. Character/personal qualities: Important. Alumni/ae relationship: Considered. Geographical residence: Considered. State residency: Considered. Religious affiliation/commitment: Considered. Minority status: Considered. Volunteer work: Considered. Work experience: Considered. **Admissions statistics for the fall 2005 entering class:** Total applicants: 492. Total accepted: 375. Freshmen enrolled: 197; 60% were from out of state. Accepted through early-decision or early-action plans: 13%. Overall acceptance rate: 76%. Non-early acceptance rate: 75%. **Size of waiting list:** 0 applicants; enrolled from waiting list: 0. **Credentials of fall 2005 freshmen:** 30% ranked in the top 10 percent of their high school class; 63% were in the top 25 percent, and 90% were in the top half. (Proportion submitting class standing: 85%.) **Average high school grade point average:** 3.6. **First-year students who submitted SAT scores:** 69%. Scores (25/75 percentile): Verbal: 510-660, Math: 510-650, Combined: 1020-1310. **First-year students submitting ACT scores:** 40%. Scores (25/75 percentile): English: 23-30, Math: 21-28, Composite: 23-28.

ACADEMICS

Year founded: 1894. **Academic calendar:** Semester. **Degrees offered:** certificate, bachelor's. **Most popular majors:** 20% business, management, marketing, and related support services, 10% health professions and related clinical sciences, 8% computer and information sciences and support services, 8% visual and performing arts, 7% education. **Major fields of study:** area, ethnic, cultural, and gender studies; biological and biomedical sciences; business, management, marketing, and related support services; communication, journalism, and related programs; computer and information sciences and support services; education; English language and literature/letters; foreign languages, literatures, and linguistics; health professions and related clinical sciences; history; mathematics and statistics; multi/interdisciplinary studies; natural resources and conservation; philosophy and religious studies; physical sciences; psychology; public administration and social service professions; social sciences; visual and performing arts. **Areas of required coursework:** arts/fine arts, humanities, mathematics, English (including composition), philosophy, foreign languages, sciences (biological or physical), history, social science, other. **Pre-professional programs:** pre-dentistry, pre-medicine, pre-theology, pre-veterinary science. **Special academic programs (% participation):** cross-registration (1%), double major (6%), dual enrollment (1%), English as a Second Language (ESL) (2%), honors program (5%), independent study (3%), internships (97%), student-designed major (3%), study abroad (85%), teacher certificate program (8%), other (20%). **Teacher certification offered in:** special education, elementary, middle/junior high, secondary. **Faculty and instruction (2005-2006):** Total instructional faculty: 69 full-time, 31 part-time (49% men; 51% women; 7% minorities). Full-time faculty with Ph.D. or other terminal degree: 65%. Student/faculty ratio: 10/1. Classes of fewer than 20 students: 65%; of 20 to 49 students: 32%; of 50 or more students: 4%. **Advanced Placement and International Baccalaureate credit:** AP tests may be used for: Credit and/or placement. Scores accepted: 3. International Baccalaureate exams may be used for: Credit and/or placement. **Freshmen returning for sophomore year:** 81%. **Graduation rates:** Four-year: 46%; five-year: 58%; six-year: 60%. **Graduate study:** 12% of students pursue further study immediately upon graduation.

COSTS AND FINANCIAL AID

Financial aid office: (574) 535-7583. **Expenses (2006-2007):** Tuition and fees 2006-2007: $20,300; room/board: $6,700. Estimated books and supplies: $800; transportation: $700; personal expenses: $0. **Financial aid:** Priority filing date for institution's financial aid form: February 15. In 2005-2006,

100% of undergraduates applied for financial aid. Of those, 78% were determined to have financial need; 30% had their need fully met. Average financial aid package (proportion receiving): $16,555 (78%). Average amount of gift aid, such as scholarships or grants (proportion receiving): $11,680 (78%). Average amount of self-help aid, such as work study or loans (proportion receiving): $5,573 (57%). Average need-based loan (excluding PLUS or other private loans): $4,887. Among students who received need-based aid, the average percentage of need met: 86%. Among students who received aid based on merit, the average award (and the proportion receiving): $8,031 (7%). The average athletic scholarship (and the proportion receiving): $6,683 (2%). Average amount of debt of borrowers graduating in 2005: $18,680. Proportion who borrowed: 69%.

CAMPUS LIFE AND EXTRACURRICULAR ACTIVITIES

Campus housing available (% using): coed dorms (70%), apartment for single students (10%), other housing options (20%). Students who live in college-owned, operated, or affiliated housing: 68%. **Clubs and organizations:** Number of student organizations: 28. Activities include: choral groups, drama/theater, jazz band, music ensembles, musical theater, radio station, student government, student newspaper, symphony orchestra, television station, yearbook. Number of fraternities: 0; sororities: 0. **Sports program (2005-2006):** Member of NAIA. *Men's intercollegiate varsity sports:* baseball, basketball, cross-country, golf, soccer, tennis, track and field (indoor), track and field (outdoor). *Women's intercollegiate varsity sports:* basketball, cross-country, soccer, softball, tennis, track and field (indoor), track and field (outdoor), volleyball.

SERVICES AND FACILITIES

Basic services: placement service, day care, health service, health insurance. **Remedial assistance:** math, writing, study skills. **Counseling services:** minority student, career, personal, academic, older student, psychological, religious. **For learning-disabled students:** School does not offer a structured program with separate admission and additional fees. Total undergraduates in learning-disabled program or receiving services: 26. Services include: remedial math, remedial English, reading machines, tape recorders, untimed tests, note-taking services, special bookstore section, oral tests, learning center, readers, extended time for tests, tutors, early syllabus, priority seating, proofreading services, typist/scribe, exams on tape or computer, other testing accomodations, other. **Library:** Number of titles: 130,117; number of current serial subscriptions: 937. **Information technology resources:** Students are not required to lease or own a computer. Number of campus computers available to all students: 118. School has a wireless network. Approximate number of users that can be accommodated: 500. Proportion of college-owned housing units wired for high-speed internet access: 100%. **Campus safety:** Security services offered: 24-hour emergency telephones, lighted pathways/sidewalks, controlled dormitory access (key, security card, etc).

TRANSFER AND INTERNATIONAL STUDENTS

Transfer students: May apply for admission for the following academic terms: Fall, Spring, Summer. Applicants do not need a minimum number of credits to apply. For fall 2005: Transfer applications received: 172. Transfer applicants offered admission: 106. Transfer applicants enrolled: 75. **International students:** Number of foreign undergraduates: 70 (8% of student body). Number of countries represented: 26. Minimum TOEFL score required: 550 (paper); 213 (computer). Average TOEFL score: 580 (paper).

Grace College and Seminary

- **Address:** 200 Seminary Drive, Winona Lake, IN 46590
- **Website:** http://www.grace.edu
- **Private; Religious affiliation:** Grace Brethren Church
- **Enrollment:** 980 full-time; 148 part-time

KEY STATS

✔ **U.S News College Ranking:** third tier, Comp. Coll.–Bachelor's (Midwest)
✔ **SAT Score (25th/75th percentile):** 930-1180
✔ **Tuition:** 2006-2007: $17,350

Selectivity: Selective	**Room/board:** $6,360
Acceptance rate: 73%	**Average debt:** N/A
Student/faculty ratio: 16/1	**Proportion who borrowed:** 75%

UNDERGRADUATE STUDENT BODY STATS

2005-2006 enrollment: 980 full-time; 148 part-time. Men: 53%; women: 47%. **Ethnic makeup:** African American: 10%; American-Indian: 1%; Asian American: 1%; Hispanic: 2%; White: 86%; International: 1%.

ADMISSIONS FACTS AND FIGURES

Phone: (574) 372-5100. **Email:** enroll@grace.edu. **Website:** http://www.grace.edu. **Application deadlines for fall 2007:** Regular decision: August 15. Early decision: Not offered. Early action: Not offered. Admission can be deferred. **Application fee:** $20. Common application is not accepted. **Admissions requirements/recommendations:** High school units required (recommended): English: 4 (4); Mathematics: 2 (2); Science: 2 (2); Foreign language: 2 (2); Social studies: 2 (2); History: 1 (1); Total units: 14 (14). Tests: The college uses SAT or ACT scores in admissions decisions. Either SAT or ACT required. For admission to the fall 2007 entering class, the school will accept: ACT with writing, ACT without writing. Campus visit: Recommended. Admissions interview: Neither required nor recommended. Off-campus interview: Not available. **Factors that count in admissions decisions:** *Academic:* Secondary school record: Very important. Class rank: Considered. Letters of recommendation: Very important. Standardized test scores: Very important. Essay: Very important. *Nonacademic:* Interview: Considered. Extracurricular activities: Considered. Talent/ability: Considered. Character/personal qualities: Important. Alumni/ae relationship: Considered. Geographical residence: Not considered. State residency: Not considered. Religious affiliation/commitment: Very important. Minority status: Not considered. Volunteer work: Not considered. Work experience: Not considered. **Other schools with the greatest overlap in applicants:** Huntington University; Indiana Wesleyan University; Taylor University. **Admissions statistics for the fall 2005 entering class:** Total applicants: 837. Total accepted: 609. Freshmen enrolled: 218; 52% were from out of state. Overall acceptance rate: 73%. **Credentials of fall 2005 freshmen:** 24% ranked in the top 10 percent of their high school class; 53% were in the top 25 percent, and 76% were in the top half. (Proportion submitting class standing: 86%.) **Average high school grade point average:** 3.4. **First-year students who submitted SAT scores:** 67%. Scores (25/75 percentile): Verbal: 480-590, Math: 450-590, Combined: 930-1180. **First-year students submitting ACT scores:** 55%. Scores (25/75 percentile): English: 19-27, Math: 18-25, Composite: 20-25.

ACADEMICS

Year founded: 1948. **Academic calendar:** Semester. **Degrees offered:** certificate, diploma, associate, bachelor's, post-bachelor's certificate, master's, doctorate. **Most popular majors:** 24% elementary education and teaching, 19% business administration, management, and operations, 11% counseling psychology, 6% communication studies/speech communication and rhetoric, 5% Bible/biblical studies. **Major fields of study:** biological and biomedical sciences; business, management, marketing, and related support services; communication, journalism, and related programs; education; English language and literature/letters; foreign languages, literatures, and linguistics; mathematics and statistics; parks, recreation, leisure, and fitness studies; physical sciences; psychology; public administration and social service professions; security and protective services; social sciences; theology and religious vocations; visual and performing arts. **Areas of required coursework:** arts/fine arts, humanities, mathematics, English (including composition), philosophy, sciences (biological or physical), history, other. **Pre-professional programs:** pre-law, pre-dentistry, pre-medicine, pre-theology. **Special academic programs:** distance learning, double major, English as a Second Language (ESL), independent study, internships, study abroad. **Teacher certification offered in:** special education, elementary, middle/junior high, secondary. **Faculty and instruction (2005-2006):** Total instructional faculty: 43 full-time, 78 part-time (75% men; 25% women; 5% minorities). Full-time faculty with Ph.D. or other terminal degree: 70%. Student/faculty ratio: 16/1. Classes of fewer than 20 students: 57%; of 20 to 49 students: 41%; of 50 or more students: 2%. **Advanced Placement and International Baccalaureate credit:** AP tests may be used for: Placement only. International Baccalaureate exams may be used for: Credit and/or placement. **Freshmen returning for sophomore year:** 75%. **Graduation rates:** Four-year: 58%; five-year: 65%; six-year: 59%. **Graduate study:** 17% of students pursue further study immediately upon graduation. Fields in which graduates pursue further study: law, 1%; medicine, 4%; dentistry, 1%; theology (or the seminary), 6%; arts and sciences, 1%.

COSTS AND FINANCIAL AID

Financial aid office: (574) 372-5100. **Expenses (2006-2007):** Tuition and fees 2006-2007: $17,350; room/board: $6,360. Estimated books and supplies: $800; transportation: $600; personal expenses: $800. **Financial aid:** Priority filing date for institution's financial aid form: March 1. In 2005-2006, 89% of undergraduates applied for financial aid. Of those, 78% were determined to have financial need; 32% had their need fully met. Average financial aid package (proportion receiving): $12,941 (78%). Average amount of gift aid, such as scholarships or grants (proportion receiving): $8,034 (76%). Average amount of self-help aid, such as work study or loans (proportion receiving): $5,865 (68%). Average need-based loan (excluding PLUS or other private loans): $5,568. Among students who received need-based aid, the average percentage of need met: 83%. Among students who received aid based on merit, the average award (and the proportion receiving): $12,198 (20%). The average athletic scholarship (and the proportion receiving): $4,406 (9%). Proportion who borrowed: 75%.

CAMPUS LIFE AND EXTRACURRICULAR ACTIVITIES

Campus housing available: women's dorms, men's dorms. Students who live in college-owned, operated, or affiliated housing: 75%. **Student employment:** During the 2005-2006 academic year, 31% of undergraduates worked on campus. Average per-year earnings: $2,000. **Clubs and organizations:** Number of student organizations: 9. Activities include: choral groups, concert band, drama/theater, music ensembles, musical theater, opera, pep band, student government, student newspaper, symphony orchestra, yearbook. Number of fraternities: 0; sororities: 0. Average proportion of students who stay on campus on weekends: 65%. **Sports program (2005-2006):** Member of NAIA. *Men's intercollegiate varsity sports:* baseball, basketball, cross-country, golf, soccer, tennis, track and field (indoor), track and field (outdoor). *Women's intercollegiate varsity sports:* basketball, cross-country, soccer, softball, tennis, track and field (indoor), track and field (outdoor), volleyball.

SERVICES AND FACILITIES

Basic services: placement service, health service. **Remedial assistance:** math, writing, study skills. **Counseling services:** career, personal, academic, psychological, religious. **For learning-disabled students:** School does not offer a structured program with separate admission and additional fees. Total undergraduates in learning-disabled program or receiving services: 21. Services include: remedial math, remedial English, reading machines, tape recorders, untimed tests, note-taking services, oral tests, learning center, readers, extended time for tests, tutors, other testing accomodations. **Library:** Number of titles: 154,687; number of current serial subscriptions: 402. **Information technology resources:** Students are not required to lease or own a computer. Number of campus computers available to all students: 85. School has a wireless network. Approximate number of users that can be accommodated: 30. Proportion of college-owned housing units wired for high-speed internet access: 90%. **Campus safety:** Security services offered: 24-hour foot and vehicle patrols, late-night transport/escort service, 24-hour emergency telephones, lighted pathways/sidewalks, controlled dormitory access (key, security card, etc.).

TRANSFER AND INTERNATIONAL STUDENTS

Transfer students: May apply for admission for the following academic terms: Fall, Spring. Applicants need a minimum number of credits to apply. For fall 2005: Transfer applications received: 116. Transfer applicants offered admission: 67. Transfer applicants enrolled: 30. **International students:** Number of foreign undergraduates: 7 (1% of student body). Number of countries represented: 5. Minimum TOEFL score required: 500 (paper); 173 (computer).

Hanover College

- **Address:** Box 108, Hanover, IN 47243
- **Website:** http://www.hanover.edu
- **Private; Religious affiliation:** Presbyterian
- **Enrollment:** 1,004 full-time; 4 part-time

KEY STATS
- ✔ **U.S News College Ranking:** 86, Liberal Arts Colleges
- ✔ **SAT Score (25th/75th percentile):** 1090-1300
- ✔ **Tuition:** 2006-2007: $22,700

Selectivity: More selective	**Room/board:** $6,800
Acceptance rate: 70%	**Average debt:** $18,124
Student/faculty ratio: 10/1	**Proportion who borrowed:** 62%

UNDERGRADUATE STUDENT BODY STATS

2005-2006 enrollment: 1,004 full-time; 4 part-time. Men: 44%; women: 56%. **Ethnic makeup:** African American: 1%; Asian American: 3%; Hispanic: 1%; White: 89%; International: 5%. **Religious preference:** Roman Catholic: 14%; Protestant: 73%; Unknown: 8%; Presbyterian: 5%.

ADMISSIONS FACTS AND FIGURES

Phone: (812) 866-7021. **Email:** admission@hanover.edu. **Website:** http://www.hanover.edu. **Application deadlines for fall 2007:** Regular decision: March 1. Early decision: Not offered. Early action: Send application by: December 1; Decision sent by: December 20. Admission can be deferred. **Application fee:** $35. Common application is accepted. **Admissions requirements/recommendations:** High school units required (recommended): English: 4 (4); Mathematics: 3 (4); Science: 3 (4); Foreign language: 2 (4); Social studies: 2 (3); History: 2 (3); Academic electives: 2 (3); Total units: 20 (28). Tests: The college uses SAT or ACT scores in admissions decisions. Either SAT or ACT required. For admission to the fall 2007 entering class, the school will accept: ACT with writing. Campus visit: Recommended. Admissions interview: Recommended. Off-campus interview: May be arranged. **Factors that count in admissions decisions:** *Academic:* Secondary school record: Very important. Class rank: Very important. Letters of recommendation: Important. Standardized test scores: Considered. Essay: Important. *Nonacademic:* Interview: Considered. Extracurricular activities: Considered. Talent/ability: Important. Character/personal qualities: Considered. Alumni/ae relationship: Considered. Geographical residence: Considered. State residency: Considered. Religious affiliation/commitment: Not considered. Minority status: Considered. Volunteer work: Considered. Work experience: Considered. **Other schools with the greatest overlap in applicants:** DePauw University; Earlham College; Franklin College; Indiana University–Bloomington; Taylor University. **Admissions statistics for the fall 2005 entering class:** Total applicants: 1,680. Total accepted: 1,168. Freshmen enrolled: 265; 38% were from out of state. Accepted through early-decision or early-action plans: 72%. Overall acceptance rate: 70%. **Size of waiting list:** 54 applicants; enrolled from waiting list: 38. **Credentials of fall 2005 freshmen:** 44% ranked in the top 10 percent of their high school class; 80% were in the top 25 percent, and 96% were in the top half. (Proportion submitting class standing: 84%.) **First-year students who submitted SAT scores:** 63%. Scores (25/75 percentile): Verbal: 540-650, Math: 550-650, Combined: 1090-1300. **First-year students submitting ACT scores:** 37%. Scores (25/75 percentile): English: N/A, Math: N/A, Composite: 23-29.

ACADEMICS

Year founded: 1827. **Academic calendar:** Other. **Degrees offered:** bachelor's. **Most popular majors:** 10% business administration and management, 10% psychology, 9% biology, 9% sociology, 8% physical education teaching and coaching. **Major fields of study:** area, ethnic, cultural, and gender studies; biological and biomedical sciences; business, management, marketing, and related support services; communication, journalism, and related programs; computer and information sciences and support services; English language and literature/letters; foreign languages, literatures, and linguistics; history; mathematics and statistics; multi/interdisciplinary studies; parks, recreation, leisure, and fitness studies; philosophy and religious studies; physical sciences; psychology; social sciences; theology and religious vocations; visual and performing arts. **Areas of required coursework:** arts/fine arts, humanities, mathematics, English (including composition), philosophy, foreign languages, sciences (biological or physical), history, social science, other. **Special academic programs (% participation):** double major (7%), dual enrollment (0%), independent study (58%), internships (18%), student-designed major (0%), study abroad (17%), teacher certificate program (10%). **Teacher certification offered in:** early childhood, elementary, middle/junior high, secondary. **Faculty and instruction (2005-2006):** Total instructional faculty: 95 full-time, 8 part-time (64% men; 36% women; 10% minorities). Full-time faculty with Ph.D. or other terminal degree: 98%. Student/faculty ratio: 10/1. Classes of fewer than 20 students: 84%; of 20 to 49 students: 16%; of 50 or more students: 0%. **Advanced Placement and International Baccalaureate credit:** AP tests may be used for: Credit and/or placement. Scores accepted: 4, 5. International Baccalaureate exams may be used for: Credit and/or placement. **Freshmen returning for sophomore year:** 76%. **Graduation rates:** Four-year: 68%; five-year: 69%; six-year: 70%. **Graduate study:** 30% of students pursue further study immediately upon graduation. Fields in which graduates pursue further study: Master of Business Administration (MBA), 12%; law, 21%; medicine, 15%; theology (or the seminary), 8%; education, 7%; arts and sciences, 37%.

COSTS AND FINANCIAL AID

Financial aid office: (800) 213-2178. **Expenses (2006-2007):** Tuition and fees 2006-2007: $22,700; room/board: $6,800. Estimated books and supplies: $900; transportation: $600; personal expenses: $900. **Financial aid:** Priority filing date for institution's financial aid form: March 10. In 2005-2006, 89% of undergraduates applied for financial aid. Of those, 77% were determined to have financial need; 38% had their need fully met. Average financial aid package (proportion receiving): $17,526 (77%). Average amount of gift aid, such as scholarships or grants (proportion receiving): $14,918 (77%). Average amount of self-help aid, such as work study or loans (proportion receiving): $4,277 (47%). Average need-based loan (excluding PLUS or other private loans): $3,371. Among students who received need-based aid, the average percentage of need met: 78%. Among students who received aid based on merit, the average award (and the proportion receiving): $14,843 (21%). The average athletic scholarship (and the proportion receiving): $0 (0%). Average amount of debt of borrowers graduating in 2005: $18,124. Proportion who borrowed: 62%.

CAMPUS LIFE AND EXTRACURRICULAR ACTIVITIES

Campus housing available (% using): coed dorms (7%), women's dorms (26%), men's dorms (18%), sorority housing (16%), fraternity housing (15%), apartments for married students (1%), apartment for single students (11%), other housing options (6%). Students who live in college-owned, operated, or affiliated housing: 94%. **Student employment:** During the 2005-2006 academic year, 25% of undergraduates worked on campus. Average per-year earnings: $1,355. **Clubs and organizations:** Number of student organizations: 56. Activities include: choral groups, concert band, dance, drama/theater, jazz band, literary magazine, music ensembles, musical theater, pep band, radio station, student government, student newspaper, student film society, symphony orchestra, television station, yearbook. Number of fraternities: 5; sororities: 4. Proportion of men in fraternities: 35%; of women in sororities: 38%. **Sports program (2005-2006):** Member of NCAA III. *Men's intercollegiate varsity sports:* baseball, basketball, cross-country, football, golf, soccer, tennis, track and field (indoor), track and field (outdoor). *Women's intercollegiate varsity sports:* basketball, cross-country, field hockey, golf, soccer, softball, tennis, track and field (indoor), track and field (outdoor), volleyball.

SERVICES AND FACILITIES

Basic services: nonremedial tutoring, placement service, health service. **Counseling services:** career, personal, academic, psychological, religious. **For learning-disabled students:** School does not offer a structured program with separate admission and additional fees. Services include: tape recorders, untimed tests, note-taking services, extended time for tests. **Information technology resources:** Students are not required to lease or own a computer. Number of campus computers available to all students: 112. School has a wireless network. Approximate number of users that can be accommodated: 1,000. Proportion of college-owned housing units wired for high-speed internet access: 100%. **Campus safety:** Security services offered: 24-hour foot and vehicle patrols, late-night transport/escort service, 24-hour emergency telephones, lighted pathways/sidewalks, controlled dormitory access (key, security card, etc.).

TRANSFER AND INTERNATIONAL STUDENTS

Transfer students: May apply for admission for the following academic terms: Fall, Winter. Applicants do not need a minimum number of credits to apply. For fall 2005: Transfer applications received: 57. Transfer applicants offered admission: 30. Transfer applicants enrolled: 19. **International students:** Number of foreign undergraduates: 46 (5% of student body). Number of countries represented: 17. Minimum TOEFL score required: 550 (paper); 213 (computer). Average TOEFL score: 570 (paper).

Huntington University

- **Address:** 2303 College Avenue, Huntington, IN 46750
- **Website:** http://www.huntington.edu
- **Private; Religious affiliation:** United Brethren in Christ
- **Enrollment:** 830 full-time; 119 part-time

KEY STATS

✔ **U.S News College Ranking:** 16, Comp. Coll.–Bachelor's (Midwest)
✔ **SAT Score (25th/75th percentile):** 900-1250
✔ **Tuition:** 2006-2007: $18,860

Selectivity: Selective	**Room/board:** $6,530
Acceptance rate: 93%	**Average debt:** $18,290
Student/faculty ratio: 11/1	**Proportion who borrowed:** 62%

UNDERGRADUATE STUDENT BODY STATS

2005-2006 enrollment: 830 full-time; 119 part-time. Men: 44%; women: 56%. **Ethnic makeup:** African American: 1%; White: 95%; International: 4%. **Religious preference:** Roman Catholic: 3%; Protestant: 80%; United Brethren in Christ: 17%.

ADMISSIONS FACTS AND FIGURES

Phone: (800) 642-6493. **Email:** admissions@huntington.edu. **Website:** http://www.huntington.edu. **Application deadlines for fall 2007:** Regular decision: August 1. Early decision: Not offered. Early action: Not offered. Admission can be deferred. **Application fee:** $20. Common application is accepted. **To apply online, go to:** http://www.huntington.edu/admissions. **Admissions requirements/recommendations:** High school units required (recommended): English: 4 (4); Mathematics: 2 (3); Science: 2 (3); Foreign language: 2 (2); Social studies: 3 (3); History: 2 (2); Academic electives: 0 (0); Total units: 15 (17). Tests: The college uses SAT or ACT scores in admissions decisions. Either SAT or ACT required. For admission to the fall 2007 entering class, the school will accept: ACT with writing. Campus visit: Recommended. Admissions interview: Recommended. Off-campus interview: May be arranged. **Factors that count in admissions decisions:** *Academic:* Secondary school record: Important. Class rank: Important. Letters of recommendation: Considered. Standardized test scores: Very important. Essay: Considered. *Nonacademic:* Interview: Considered. Extracurricular activities: Considered. Talent/ability: Considered. Character/personal qualities: Important. Alumni/ae relationship: Considered. Geographical residence: Not considered. State residency: Not considered. Religious affiliation/commitment: Very important. Minority status: Considered. Volunteer work: Considered. Work experience: Considered. **Other schools with the greatest overlap in applicants:** Anderson University; Bethel College; Grace College and Seminary; Indiana Wesleyan University; Taylor University. **Admissions statistics for the fall 2005 entering class:** Total applicants: 692. Total accepted: 641. Freshmen enrolled: 229; 20% were from out of state. Overall acceptance rate: 93%. **Credentials of fall 2005 freshmen:** 28% ranked in the top 10 percent of their high school class; 54% were in the top 25 percent, and 87% were in the top half. (Proportion submitting class standing: 94%.) **Average high school grade point average:** 3.4. **First-year students who submitted SAT scores:** 81%. Scores (25/75 percentile): Verbal: 460-630, Math: 440-620, Combined: 900-1250. **First-year students submitting ACT scores:** 55%. Scores (25/75 percentile): English: 20-28, Math: 19-27, Composite: 19-27.

ACADEMICS

Year founded: 1897. **Academic calendar:** 4-1-4. **Degrees offered:** diploma, associate, transfer-associate, terminal-associate, bachelor's, master's. **Most popular majors:** 21% business administration and management, 20% elementary education and teaching, 11% religious education, 9% philosophy and religious studies, 9% psychology. **Major fields of study:** biological and biomedical sciences; business, management, marketing, and related support services; communication, journalism, and related programs; computer and information sciences and support services; education; English language and literature/letters; health professions and related clinical sciences; history; legal professions and studies; mathematics and statistics; natural resources and conservation; parks, recreation, leisure, and fitness studies; philosophy and religious studies; physical sciences; psychology; public administration and social service professions; social sciences; theology and religious vocations; visual and performing arts. **Areas of required coursework:** arts/fine arts, humanities, mathematics, English (including composition), philosophy, sciences (biological or physical), history, social science, other. **Pre-professional programs:** pre-law, pre-medicine. **Special academic programs (% participation):** accelerated program (11%), double major (11%), independent study (1%), internships (45%), study abroad (2%), teacher certificate program (15%). **Teacher certification offered in:** special education, elementary, middle/junior high, secondary. **Faculty and instruction (2005-2006):** Total instructional faculty: 59 full-time, 63 part-time (60% men; 40% women; 1% minorities). Full-time faculty with Ph.D. or other terminal degree: 90%. Student/faculty ratio: 11/1. Classes of fewer than 20 students: 72%; of 20 to 49 students: 28%; of 50 or more students: 0%. **Advanced Placement and International Baccalaureate credit:** AP tests may be used for: Credit only. Scores accepted: 3, 4, 5. International Baccalaureate exams may be used for: Placement only. **Freshmen returning for sophomore year:** 77%. **Graduation rates:** Four-year: 58%; five-year: 68%; six-year: 64%. **Graduate study:** 9% of students pursue further study immediately upon graduation. Fields in which graduates pursue further study: law, 12%; medicine, 12%; theology (or the seminary), 24%; education, 12%; arts and sciences, 41%.

COSTS AND FINANCIAL AID

Financial aid office: (260) 359-4015. **Expenses (2006-2007):** Tuition and fees 2006-2007: $18,860; room/board: $6,530. Estimated books and supplies: $800; transportation: $800; personal expenses: $1,200. **Financial aid:** Priority filing date for institution's financial aid form: March 1. In 2005-2006, 84% of undergraduates applied for financial aid. Of those, 73% were determined to have financial need; 17% had their need fully met. Average financial aid package (proportion receiving): $12,751 (73%). Average amount of gift aid, such as scholarships or grants (proportion receiving): $10,409 (66%). Average amount of self-help aid, such as work study or loans (proportion receiving): $4,718 (62%). Average need-based loan (excluding PLUS or other private loans): $4,118. Among students who received need-based aid, the average percentage of need met: 72%. Among students who received aid based on merit, the average award (and the proportion receiving): $6,328 (13%). The average athletic scholarship (and the proportion receiving): $5,065 (4%). Average amount of debt of borrowers graduating in 2005: $18,290. Proportion who borrowed: 62%.

CAMPUS LIFE AND EXTRACURRICULAR ACTIVITIES

Campus housing available (% using): women's dorms (51%), men's dorms (37%), apartment for single students (12%), special housing for disabled students (0%). Students who live in college-owned, operated, or affiliated housing: 69%. **Student employment:** During the 2005-2006 academic year, 63% of undergraduates worked on campus. Average per-year earnings: $1,003. Activities include: choral groups, concert band, dance, drama/theater, jazz band, literary magazine, music ensembles, musical theater, opera, pep band, radio station, student government, student newspaper, student film society, television station, yearbook. Number of fraternities: 0; sororities: 0. Average proportion of students who stay on campus on weekends: 65%. **Sports program (2005-2006):** Member of NAIA. *Men's intercollegiate varsity sports:* baseball, basketball, cross-country, golf, soccer, tennis, track and field (indoor), track and field (outdoor). *Women's intercollegiate varsity sports:* basketball, cross-country, soccer, softball, tennis, track and field (indoor), track and field (outdoor), volleyball.

SERVICES AND FACILITIES

Basic services: nonremedial tutoring, health service, health insurance. **Remedial assistance:** math, writing, study skills. **Counseling services:** career, personal, academic, psychological, religious. **For learning-disabled students:** School does not offer a structured program with separate admission and additional fees. Services include: remedial math, other testing accommodations, remedial English, note-taking services, oral tests, learning center, readers, extended time for tests, tutors, priority registration, priority seating, proofreading services, texts on tape, typist/scribe, exams on tape or computer, other testing accomodations, other. **Library:** Number of titles: 153,473; number of current serial subscriptions: 324. **Information technology resources:** Students are not required to lease or own a computer. Number of campus computers available to all students: 124. School has a wireless network. Approximate number of users that can be accommodated: 2,000. Proportion of college-owned housing units wired for high-speed internet access: 100%. **Campus safety:** Security services offered: late-night transport/escort service, 24-hour emergency telephones, lighted pathways/sidewalks, controlled dormitory access (key, security card, etc).

TRANSFER AND INTERNATIONAL STUDENTS

Transfer students: May apply for admission for the following academic terms: Fall, Spring. Applicants need a minimum number of credits to apply. For fall 2005: Transfer applications received: 91. Transfer applicants offered

admission: 74. Transfer applicants enrolled: 42. **International students:** Number of foreign undergraduates: 30 (4% of student body). Number of countries represented: 18. Minimum TOEFL score required: 525 (paper); 200 (computer). Average TOEFL score: 570 (paper).

Indiana Institute of Technology

■ **Address:** 1600 E. Washington Boulevard, Fort Wayne, IN 46803
■ **Website:** http://www.indianatech.edu
■ Private
■ **Enrollment:** 1,487 full-time; 1,334 part-time

KEY STATS

✔ **U.S News College Ranking:** Unranked Specialty School–Business
✔ **SAT Score (25th/75th percentile):** 908-971
✔ **Tuition:** 2005-2006: $17,850
   Selectivity: Less selective   **Room/board:** $6,750
   Acceptance rate: 54%   **Average debt:** N/A
   Student/faculty ratio: 20/1   **Proportion who borrowed:** N/A

UNDERGRADUATE STUDENT BODY STATS

2005-2006 enrollment: 1,487 full-time; 1,334 part-time. Men: 45%; women: 55%. **Ethnic makeup:** African American: 20%; American-Indian: 1%; Asian American: 1%; Hispanic: 3%; White: 76%.

ADMISSIONS FACTS AND FIGURES

Phone: (800) 937-2448. **Email:** admissions@indianatech.edu. **Website:** http://www.indianatech.edu. **Application deadlines for fall 2007:** Regular decision: September 1. Early decision: Not offered. Early action: Not offered. Admission can be deferred. **Application fee:** $25. Common application is not accepted. **Admissions requirements/recommendations:** High school units required (recommended): English: 4 (4); Mathematics: 2 (4); Science: 2 (3); Academic electives: 7 (4). Tests: The college uses SAT or ACT scores in admissions decisions. Either SAT or ACT required. Campus visit: Recommended. Admissions interview: Recommended. Off-campus interview: May be arranged. **Factors that count in admissions decisions:** *Academic:* Secondary school record: Very important. Class rank: Important. Letters of recommendation: Considered. Standardized test scores: Important. Essay: Considered. *Nonacademic:* Interview: Important. Extracurricular activities: Considered. Talent/ability: Considered. Character/personal qualities: Considered. Alumni/ae relationship: Very important. Geographical residence: Not considered. State residency: Not considered. Religious affiliation/commitment: Not considered. Minority status: Important. Volunteer work: Considered. Work experience: Considered. **Admissions statistics for the fall 2005 entering class:** Total applicants: 2,251. Total accepted: 1,213. Freshmen enrolled: 252; 16% were from out of state. Overall acceptance rate: 54%. **Credentials of fall 2005 freshmen:** 8% ranked in the top 10 percent of their high school class; 16% were in the top 25 percent, and 34% were in the top half. (Proportion submitting class standing: 84%.) **Average high school grade point average:** 2.7. **First-year students who submitted SAT scores:** 60%. Scores (25/75 percentile): Verbal: 441-468; Math: 467-503, Combined: 908-971. **First-year students submitting ACT scores:** 38%. Scores (25/75 percentile): English: 16-17, Math: 17-18, Composite: 17-18.

ACADEMICS

Year founded: 1930. **Academic calendar:** Semester. **Degrees offered:** associate, bachelor's, master's. **Most popular majors:** 85% business administration and management, 10% accounting, 2% computer and information sciences and support services, 2% industrial engineering, 1% computer science. **Major fields of study:** business, management, marketing, and related support services; computer and information sciences and support services; engineering; parks, recreation, leisure, and fitness studies. **Areas of required coursework:** humanities, computer literacy, mathematics, English (including composition), social science. **Special academic programs (% participation):** accelerated program (86%), cross-registration, double major (14%), dual enrollment, external degree program, independent study (13%), internships, student-designed major (0%). **Faculty and instruction (2005-2006):** Total instructional faculty: 36 full-time, 198 part-time (63% men; 37% women; 10% minorities). Full-time faculty with Ph.D. or other terminal degree: 33%. Student/faculty ratio: 20/1. Classes of fewer than 20 students: 86%; of 20 to 49 students: 14%. **Advanced Placement and International Baccalaureate**

credit: AP tests may be used for: Credit and/or placement. International Baccalaureate exams may be used for: Credit only. **Freshmen returning for sophomore year:** 62%. **Graduation rates:** Four-year: 0%; five-year: 0%; six-year: 25%.

COSTS AND FINANCIAL AID
Financial aid office: (260) 422-5561. **Expenses (2005-2006):** Tuition and fees 2005-2006: $17,850; room/board: $6,750. Estimated books and supplies: $0; transportation: $0; personal expenses: $3,000.

CAMPUS LIFE AND EXTRACURRICULAR ACTIVITIES
Campus housing available (% using): coed dorms (60%), fraternity housing (20%), apartment for single students (20%). Students who live in college-owned, operated, or affiliated housing: 40%. **Student employment:** During the 2005-2006 academic year, 4% of undergraduates worked on campus. Average per-year earnings: $1,800. **Clubs and organizations:** Number of student organizations: 15. Activities include: choral groups, dance, pep band, student government, student newspaper. Number of fraternities: 3; sororities: 1. Proportion of men in fraternities: 15%; of women in sororities: 5%. Average proportion of students who stay on campus on weekends: 30%. **Sports program (2005-2006):** Member of NAIA. *Men's intercollegiate varsity sports:* baseball, basketball, cheerleading, soccer. *Women's intercollegiate varsity sports:* basketball, cheerleading, soccer, softball.

SERVICES AND FACILITIES
Basic services: placement service. **Remedial assistance:** study skills. **Counseling services:** career, academic. **For learning-disabled students:** School does not offer a structured program with separate admission and additional fees. Total undergraduates in learning-disabled program or receiving services: 7. Services include: remedial math, remedial English, remedial reading, note-taking services, oral tests, extended time for tests, tutors, priority seating. **Library:** Number of titles: 32,000,000; number of current serial subscriptions: 167. **Information technology resources:** Students are required to lease or own a computer. Number of campus computers available to all students: 240. School has a wireless network. Approximate number of users that can be accommodated: 400. Proportion of college-owned housing units wired for high-speed internet access: 100%. **Campus safety:** Security services offered: 24-hour foot and vehicle patrols, lighted pathways/sidewalks, controlled dormitory access (key, security card, etc).

TRANSFER AND INTERNATIONAL STUDENTS
Transfer students: May apply for admission for the following academic terms: Fall, Spring, Summer. Applicants do not need a minimum number of credits to apply. For fall 2005: Transfer applications received: 169. Transfer applicants offered admission: 136. Transfer applicants enrolled: 40. **International students:** Number of foreign undergraduates: 9. Minimum TOEFL score required: 550 (paper). Average TOEFL score: 535 (paper).

Indiana State University

- **Address:** 200 N. Seventh Street, Terre Haute, IN 47809-9989
- **Website:** http://web.indstate.edu/
- **Public**
- **Enrollment:** 7,628 full-time; 1,042 part-time

KEY STATS
✔ **U.S News College Ranking:** fourth tier, National Universities
✔ **SAT Score (25th/75th percentile):** 840-1050
✔ **Tuition:** 2006-2007: $6,216 in state, $13,632 out of state

Selectivity: Less selective	**Room/board:** $5,938
Acceptance rate: 80%	**Average debt:** $20,494
Student/faculty ratio: 17/1	**Proportion who borrowed:** 65%

UNDERGRADUATE STUDENT BODY STATS
2005-2006 enrollment: 7,628 full-time; 1,042 part-time. Men: 48%; women: 52%. **Ethnic makeup:** African American: 11%; Asian American: 1%; Hispanic: 1%; White: 85%; International: 1%.

ADMISSIONS FACTS AND FIGURES
Phone: (812) 237-2121. **Email:** admisu@isugw.indstate.edu. **Website:** http://web.indstate.edu/. **Application deadlines for fall 2007:** Regular decision: August 15. Early decision: Not offered. Early action: Not offered.

Admission can be deferred. **Application fee:** $25. Common application is not accepted. **To apply online, go to:** http://web.indstate.edu/join_us/admissions.htm. **Admissions requirements/recommendations:** High school units required (recommended): English: 8 (8); Mathematics: 8 (8); Science: 6 (6); Foreign language: 2 (2); Social studies: 4 (4); History: 2 (2); Academic electives: 4 (4); Total units: 40 (40). Tests: The college uses SAT or ACT scores in admissions decisions. Either SAT or ACT required. For admission to the fall 2007 entering class, the school will accept: ACT with writing. Campus visit: Recommended. Admissions interview: Neither required nor recommended. Off-campus interview: Not available. **Factors that count in admissions decisions:** *Academic:* Secondary school record: Very important. Class rank: Very important. Letters of recommendation: Important. Standardized test scores: Important. Essay: Important. *Nonacademic:* Interview: Considered. Extracurricular activities: Considered. Talent/ability: Considered. Character/personal qualities: Considered. Alumni/ae relationship: Not considered. Geographical residence: Not considered. State residency: Not considered. Religious affiliation/commitment: Not considered. Minority status: Not considered. Volunteer work: Not considered. Work experience: Not considered. **Other schools with the greatest overlap in applicants:** Ball State University; Indiana University–Bloomington; Purdue University–West Lafayette. **Admissions statistics for the fall 2005 entering class:** Total applicants: 5,351. Total accepted: 4,279. Freshmen enrolled: 1,642; 9% were from out of state. Overall acceptance rate: 80%. **Credentials of fall 2005 freshmen:** 10% ranked in the top 10 percent of their high school class; 28% were in the top 25 percent, and 62% were in the top half. (Proportion submitting class standing: 90%.) **Average high school grade point average:** 3.0. **First-year students who submitted SAT scores:** 79%. Scores (25/75 percentile): Verbal: 420-530, Math: 420-520, Combined: 840-1050. **First-year students submitting ACT scores:** 23%. Scores (25/75 percentile): English: 16-23, Math: 16-23, Composite: 17-23.

ACADEMICS
Year founded: 1865. **Academic calendar:** Semester. **Degrees offered:** certificate, associate, transfer-associate, terminal-associate, bachelor's, post-bachelor's certificate, master's, post-master's certificate, doctorate. **Most popular majors:** 18% education, 17% business, management, marketing, and related support services, 12% social sciences, 8% engineering technologies/technicians, 6% health professions and related clinical sciences. **Major fields of study:** architecture and related services; area, ethnic, cultural, and gender studies; biological and biomedical sciences; business, management, marketing, and related support services; communication, journalism, and related programs; computer and information sciences and support services; education; engineering technologies/technicians; English language and literature/letters; family and consumer sciences/human sciences; foreign languages, literatures, and linguistics; health professions and related clinical sciences; history; liberal arts and sciences studies, and humanities; mathematics and statistics; parks, recreation, leisure, and fitness studies; philosophy and religious studies; physical sciences; psychology; public administration and social service professions; social sciences; transportation and materials moving; visual and performing arts. **Areas of required coursework:** arts/fine arts, computer literacy, mathematics, English (including composition), foreign languages, sciences (biological or physical), history, social science, other. **Pre-professional programs:** pre-law, pre-dentistry, pre-medicine, pre-theology, pre-veterinary science, pre-optometry, pre-pharmacy. **Special academic programs:** accelerated program, cooperative (work-study plan) program, distance learning, double major, dual enrollment, English as a Second Language (ESL), honors program, independent study, internships, study abroad, teacher certificate program. **Teacher certification offered in:** early childhood, special education, elementary, middle/junior high, secondary. **Cooperative education programs:** business, computer science, education, health professions, home economics, technologies, other. **Reserve Officers Training Corps (ROTC):** Army ROTC: Offered on campus; Air Force ROTC: Offered on campus. **Faculty and instruction (2005-2006):** Total instructional faculty: 489 full-time, 173 part-time (59% men; 41% women; 9% minorities). Full-time faculty with Ph.D. or other terminal degree: 77%. Student/faculty ratio: 17/1. Classes of fewer than 20 students: 50%; of 20 to 49 students: 44%; of 50 or more students: 6%. **Advanced Placement and International Baccalaureate credit:** AP tests may be used for: Credit only. Scores accepted: 3, 4, 5. **Freshmen returning for sophomore year:** 69%. **Graduation rates:** Four-year: 18%; five-year: 34%; six-year: 39%. **Graduate study:** 26% of students pursue further study immediately upon graduation. Fields in which graduates pursue further study: medicine, 3%; dentistry, 1%; engineering, 1%; arts and sciences, 4%.

COSTS AND FINANCIAL AID

Financial aid office: (812) 237-2215. **Expenses (2006-2007):** Tuition and fees 2006-2007: $6,216 in state, $13,632 out of state; room/board: $5,938. Estimated books and supplies: $1,140; transportation: $1,108; personal expenses: $1,794. **Financial aid:** Priority filing date for institution's financial aid form: March 1; deadline: March 1. In 2005-2006, 79% of undergraduates applied for financial aid. Of those, 59% were determined to have financial need; 18% had their need fully met. Average financial aid package (proportion receiving): $7,321 (56%). Average amount of gift aid, such as scholarships or grants (proportion receiving): $4,844 (35%). Average amount of self-help aid, such as work study or loans (proportion receiving): $3,920 (42%). Average need-based loan (excluding PLUS or other private loans): $3,786. Among students who received need-based aid, the average percentage of need met: 78%. Among students who received aid based on merit, the average award (and the proportion receiving): $2,889 (8%). The average athletic scholarship (and the proportion receiving): $9,010 (4%). Average amount of debt of borrowers graduating in 2005: $20,494. Proportion who borrowed: 65%.

CAMPUS LIFE AND EXTRACURRICULAR ACTIVITIES

Campus housing available: coed dorms, women's dorms, men's dorms, sorority housing, fraternity housing, apartments for married students, apartment for single students, special housing for disabled students. Students who live in college-owned, operated, or affiliated housing: 34%. **Student employment:** During the 2005-2006 academic year, 12% of undergraduates worked on campus. Average per-year earnings: $2,200. **Clubs and organizations:** Number of student organizations: 96. Activities include: choral groups, concert band, dance, drama/theater, jazz band, literary magazine, marching band, music ensembles, musical theater, pep band, radio station, student government, student newspaper, student film society, symphony orchestra, yearbook. Number of fraternities: 17; sororities: 13. Proportion of men in fraternities: 12%; of women in sororities: 11%. **Sports program (2005-2006):** Member of NCAA I. *Men's intercollegiate varsity sports:* baseball, basketball, cross-country, football, tennis, track and field (indoor), track and field (outdoor). *Women's intercollegiate varsity sports:* basketball, cross-country, soccer, softball, tennis, track and field (indoor), track and field (outdoor), volleyball.

SERVICES AND FACILITIES

Basic services: women's center, placement service, day care, health service, health insurance. **Remedial assistance:** reading, writing, study skills. **Counseling services:** minority student, career, personal, academic, psychological. **For learning-disabled students:** School does not offer a structured program with separate admission and additional fees. Total undergraduates in learning-disabled program or receiving services: 135. Services include: note-taking services, oral tests, learning center, readers, extended time for tests, tutors, other. **Library:** Number of titles: 1,326,337; number of current serial subscriptions: 43,464. **Information technology resources:** Students are not required to lease or own a computer. Number of campus computers available to all students: 415. School has a wireless network. Approximate number of users that can be accommodated: 10,375. Proportion of college-owned housing units wired for high-speed internet access: 100%. **Campus safety:** Security services offered: 24-hour foot and vehicle patrols, late-night transport/escort service, 24-hour emergency telephones, lighted pathways/sidewalks, controlled dormitory access (key, security card, etc.)

TRANSFER AND INTERNATIONAL STUDENTS

Transfer students: May apply for admission for the following academic terms: Fall, Spring, Summer. Applicants do not need a minimum number of credits to apply. For fall 2005: Transfer applications received: 1,962. Transfer applicants offered admission: 1,366. Transfer applicants enrolled: 675. **International students:** Number of foreign undergraduates: 123 (1% of student body). Minimum TOEFL score required: 500 (paper); 173 (computer). Average TOEFL score: 523 (paper).

Indiana University—Bloomington

- **Address:** 107 S. Indiana Ave., Bloomington, IN 47405-7000
- **Website:** http://www.iub.edu
- **Public**
- **Enrollment:** 27,974 full-time; 1,588 part-time

KEY STATS

✔ **U.S News College Ranking:** 70, National Universities
✔ **SAT Score (25th/75th percentile):** 990-1230
✔ **Tuition:** 2006-2007: $6,310 in state, $19,301 out of state

Selectivity: Selective	**Room/board:** $6,352
Acceptance rate: 85%	**Average debt:** $21,251
Student/faculty ratio: 18/1	**Proportion who borrowed:** 44%

UNDERGRADUATE STUDENT BODY STATS

2005-2006 enrollment: 27,974 full-time; 1,588 part-time. Men: 48%; women: 52%. **Ethnic makeup:** African American: 5%; Asian American: 3%; Hispanic: 2%; White: 86%; International: 4%.

ADMISSIONS FACTS AND FIGURES

Phone: (812) 855-0661. **Email:** iuadmit@indiana.edu. **Website:** http://www.iub.edu. **Application deadlines for fall 2007:** Regular decision: Rolling. Early decision: Not offered. Early action: Not offered. Admission can be deferred. **Application fee:** $50. Common application is not accepted. **To apply online, go to:** http://www.indiana.edu/~iuadmit/apply/index.shtml. **Admissions requirements/recommendations:** High school units required (recommended): English: 4; Mathematics: 3 (4); Science: 1 (3); Foreign language: (3); Social studies: 2 (3); Academic electives: 4; Total units: 14 (19). Tests: The college uses SAT or ACT scores in admissions decisions. Either SAT or ACT required. For admission to the fall 2007 entering class, the school will accept: ACT with writing. Campus visit: Recommended. Admissions interview: Neither required nor recommended. Off-campus interview: Not available. **Factors that count in admissions decisions:** *Academic:* Secondary school record: Very important. Class rank: Very important. Letters of recommendation: Considered. Standardized test scores: Important. Essay: Considered. *Nonacademic:* Interview: Considered. Extracurricular activities: Considered. Talent/ability: Considered. Character/personal qualities: Considered. Alumni/ae relationship: Considered. Geographical residence: Considered. State residency: Considered. Religious affiliation/commitment: Not considered. Minority status: Considered. Volunteer work: Considered. Work experience: Considered. **Other schools with the greatest overlap in applicants:** Ball State University; Miami University–Oxford; Purdue University–West Lafayette; University of Illinois–Urbana-Champaign; University of Iowa. **Admissions statistics for the fall 2005 entering class:** Total applicants: 21,974. Total accepted: 18,602. Freshmen enrolled: 6,949; 32% were from out of state. Overall acceptance rate: 85%. **Credentials of fall 2005 freshmen:** 25% ranked in the top 10 percent of their high school class; 57% were in the top 25 percent, and 94% were in the top half. (Proportion submitting class standing: 65%.) **Average high school grade point average:** 3.3. **First-year students who submitted SAT scores:** 84%. Scores (25/75 percentile): Verbal: 490-610, Math: 500-620, Combined: 990-1230. **First-year students submitting ACT scores:** 39%. Scores (25/75 percentile): English: 21-28, Math: 21-27, Composite: 21-27.

ACADEMICS

Year founded: 1820. **Academic calendar:** Semester. **Degrees offered:** certificate, diploma, associate, bachelor's, post-bachelor's certificate, master's, first professional, doctorate. **Most popular majors:** 20% business, management, marketing, and related support services, 16% education, 10% communication, journalism, and related programs, 7% public administration and social service professions, 7% social sciences. **Major fields of study:** biological and biomedical sciences; business, management, marketing, and related support services; communications technologies/technicians and support services; computer and information sciences and support services; education; English language and literature/letters; family and consumer sciences/human sciences; foreign languages, literatures, and linguistics; health professions and related clinical sciences; history; liberal arts and sciences studies, and humanities; mathematics and statistics; multi/interdisciplinary studies; parks, recreation, leisure, and fitness studies; philosophy and religious studies; physical sciences; psychology; public administration and social service professions; security and protective services; social sciences; visual and performing arts. **Areas of required coursework:** arts/fine arts, humanities, mathematics, English (including composition), sciences (biological or physical), social science. **Pre-professional programs:** pre-law, pre-dentistry, pre-medicine, pre-optometry. **Special academic programs:** accelerated program, cooperative (work-study plan) program, distance learning, double major, dual enrollment, English as a Second Language (ESL), external degree program, honors program, independent study, internships, liberal arts/career combination, student-designed major, study abroad, teacher certificate program. **Teacher certification offered in:** early childhood, special education, elementary, secondary. **Cooperative education programs:** business, computer science, education, health professions, humanities, natural science, social/behavioral science. **Reserve Officers Training Corps (ROTC):** Army ROTC: Offered on campus; Air Force ROTC: Offered on campus. **Faculty and instruction (2005-2006):** Total instructional faculty: 1,865 full-time, 309 part-time (63% men; 37% women; 14% minorities). Full-time faculty with Ph.D. or other terminal degree: 77%. Student/faculty ratio: 18/1. Classes of fewer than 20 students: 41%; of 20 to 49 students: 41%; of 50 or more students: 18%. **Advanced Placement and International Baccalaureate credit:** AP tests may be used for: Credit and/or placement. Scores accepted: 3, 4, 5. International Baccalaureate exams may be used for: Credit and/or placement. **Freshmen returning for sophomore year:** 88%. **Graduation rates:** Four-year: 49%; five-year: 68%; six-year: 72%.

COSTS AND FINANCIAL AID

Financial aid office: (812) 855-0321. **Expenses (2006-2007):** Tuition and fees 2006-2007: $6,310 in state, $19,301 out of state; room/board: $6,352. **Financial aid:** Priority filing date for institution's financial aid form: March 1. In 2005-2006, 73% of undergraduates applied for financial aid. Of those, 55% were determined to have financial need; 7% had their need fully met. Average financial aid package (proportion receiving): $6,940 (54%). Average amount of gift aid, such as scholarships or grants (proportion receiving): $5,546 (19%). Average amount of self-help aid, such as work study or loans (proportion receiving): $4,222 (31%). Average need-based loan (excluding PLUS or other private loans): $4,161. Among students who received need-based aid, the average percentage of need met: 59%. Among students who received aid based on merit, the average award (and the proportion receiving): $4,333 (6%). The average athletic scholarship (and the proportion receiving): $13,355 (2%). Average amount of debt of borrowers graduating in 2005: $21,251. Proportion who borrowed: 44%.

CAMPUS LIFE AND EXTRACURRICULAR ACTIVITIES

Campus housing available: coed dorms, women's dorms, men's dorms, sorority housing, fraternity housing, apartments for married students, apartment for single students, special housing for disabled students, special housing for international students, cooperative housing, other housing options. Students who live in college-owned, operated, or affiliated housing: 42%. Activities include: choral groups, concert band, dance, drama/theater, jazz band, literary magazine, marching band, music ensembles, musical theater, opera, pep band, radio station, student government, student newspaper, symphony orchestra, television station, yearbook. Number of fraternities: 33; sororities: 26. Proportion of men in fraternities: 16%; of women in sororities: 18%. **Sports program (2005-2006):** Member of NCAA I. *Men's intercollegiate varsity sports:* baseball, basketball, cheerleading, cross-country, football, golf, soccer, swimming and diving, tennis, track and field (indoor), track and field (outdoor), wrestling. *Women's intercollegiate varsity sports:* basketball, crew, cross-country, field hockey, golf, soccer, softball, swimming and diving, tennis, track and field (indoor), track and field (outdoor), volleyball, water polo.

SERVICES AND FACILITIES

Basic services: nonremedial tutoring, women's center, placement service, day care, health service. **Remedial assistance:** reading, math, writing, study skills. **Counseling services:** minority student, career, military, personal, veteran student, academic, older student, psychological, birth control, religious. **For learning-disabled students:** School does not offer a structured program with separate admission and additional fees. Total undergraduates in learning-disabled program or receiving services: 500. Services include: reading machines, tape recorders, note-taking services, oral tests, readers, extended time for tests, priority registration, priority seating, texts on tape, other testing accomodations, other. **Library:** Number of titles: 6,647,355; number of current serial subscriptions: 59,439. **Information technology resources:** Students are not required to lease or own a computer. Number of campus computers available to all students: 2,262. School has a wireless network. **Campus safety:** Security services offered: 24-hour foot and vehicle patrols, late-night transport/escort service, 24-hour emergency telephones, lighted pathways/sidewalks, controlled dormitory access (key, security card, etc).

TRANSFER AND INTERNATIONAL STUDENTS

Transfer students: May apply for admission for the following academic terms: Fall, Spring, Summer. Applicants need a minimum number of credits to apply. For fall 2005: Transfer applications received: 2,122. Transfer applicants offered admission: 1,441. Transfer applicants enrolled: 838. **International students:** Number of foreign undergraduates: 1183 (4% of student body).

Indiana University East

- **Address:** 2325 Chester Boulevard, Richmond, IN 47374-1289
- **Website:** http://www.iue.edu
- **Public**
- **Enrollment:** 1,292 full-time; 1,100 part-time

KEY STATS

✔ **U.S News College Ranking:** fourth tier, Comp. Coll.–Bachelor's (Midwest)
✔ **SAT Score (25th/75th percentile):** 790-1040
✔ **Tuition:** 2006-2007: $4,471 in state, $11,419 out of state

Selectivity: Less selective	**Room/board:** N/A
Acceptance rate: 88%	**Average debt:** $24,729
Student/faculty ratio: 13/1	**Proportion who borrowed:** 59%

UNDERGRADUATE STUDENT BODY STATS

2005-2006 enrollment: 1,292 full-time; 1,100 part-time. Men: 32%; women: 68%. **Ethnic makeup:** African American: 4%; Asian American: 1%; Hispanic: 1%; White: 94%.

ADMISSIONS FACTS AND FIGURES

Phone: (765) 973-8208. **Email:** eaadmit@indiana.edu. **Website:** http://www.iue.edu. **Application deadlines for fall 2007:** Regular decision: Rolling. Early decision: Not offered. Early action: Not offered. Admission can be deferred. **Application fee:** $25. Common application is not accepted. **To apply online, go to:** http://www.iue.edu/admissions/apps.shtml. **Admissions requirements/recommendations:** High school units required (recommended): English: 4; Mathematics: 3 (3); Science: 1; Social studies: 2; Academic electives: (4); Total units: 14 (16). Tests: The college uses SAT or ACT scores in admissions decisions. Neither SAT nor ACT required. For admission to the fall 2007 entering class, the school will accept: ACT with writing. Campus visit: Recommended. Admissions interview: Neither required nor recommended. Off-campus interview: May be arranged. **Factors that count in admissions decisions:** *Academic:* Secondary school record: Very important. Class rank: Important. Letters of recommendation: Not considered. Standardized test scores: Very important. Essay: Not considered. *Nonacademic:* Interview: Not considered. Extracurricular activities: Not considered. Talent/ability: Not considered. Character/personal qualities: Not considered. Alumni/ae relationship: Not considered. Geographical residence: Considered. State residency: Considered. Religious affiliation/commitment: Not considered. Minority status: Not considered. Volunteer work: Not considered. Work experience: Not considered. **Admissions statistics for the fall 2005 entering class:** Total applicants: 491. Total accepted: 434. Freshmen enrolled: 372; 18% were from out of state. Overall acceptance rate: 88%. **Credentials of fall 2005 freshmen:** 8% ranked in the top 10 percent of their high school class; 26% were in the top 25 percent, and 58% were in the top half. (Proportion submitting class standing: 48%.) First-year students who submitted SAT scores: 44%. Scores (25/75 percentile): Verbal: 400-530, Math: 390-510, Combined: 790-1040. **First-year students submitting ACT scores:** 19%. Scores (25/75 percentile): English: 15-21, Math: 16-20, Composite: 16-20.

ACADEMICS

Year founded: 1971. **Academic calendar:** Semester. **Degrees offered:** associate, bachelor's, post-bachelor's certificate. **Most popular majors:** 21% education, 18% health professions and related clinical sciences, 16% liberal arts and sciences studies, and humanities, 15% philosophy and religious studies, 6% public administration and social service professions. **Major fields of study:** biological and biomedical sciences; business, management, marketing, and related support services; communication, journalism, and related programs; computer and information sciences and support services; education; English language and literature/letters; health professions and related clinical sciences; history; liberal arts and sciences studies, and humanities; mathematics and statistics; multi/interdisciplinary studies; natural resources and conservation; psychology; public administration and social service professions; security and protective services; social sciences; visual and performing arts. **Areas of required coursework:** humanities, computer literacy, English (including composition), sciences (biological or physical), social science. **Special academic programs:** cooperative (work-study plan) program, cross-registration, distance learning, double major, dual enrollment, external degree program, independent study, internships, teacher certificate program, weekend college, other. **Teacher certification offered in:** elementary, secondary. **Faculty and instruction (2005-2006):** Total instructional faculty: 87 full-time, 117 part-time (47% men; 53% women; 5% minorities). Full-time faculty with Ph.D. or other terminal degree: 53%. Student/faculty ratio: 13/1. Classes of fewer than 20 students: 65%; of 20 to 49 students: 33%; of 50 or more students: 2%. **Advanced Placement and International Baccalaureate credit:** AP tests may be used for: Credit only. Scores accepted: 3, 4, 5. **Freshmen returning for sophomore year:** 57%. **Graduation rates:** Four-year: 6%; five-year: 17%; six-year: 24%.

COSTS AND FINANCIAL AID

Financial aid office: (765) 973-8206. **Expenses (2006-2007):** Tuition and fees 2006-2007: $4,471 in state, $11,419 out of state; room/board: N/A. **Financial aid:** Priority filing date for institution's financial aid form: March 1. In 2005-2006, 89% of undergraduates applied for financial aid. Of those, 72% were determined to have financial need; 7% had their need fully met. Average financial aid package (proportion receiving): $5,918 (70%). Average amount of gift aid, such as scholarships or grants (proportion receiving): $4,272 (52%). Average amount of self-help aid, such as work study or loans (proportion receiving): $3,361 (50%). Average need-based loan (excluding PLUS or other private loans): $3,240. Among students who received need-based aid, the average percentage of need met: 59%. Among students who received aid based on merit, the average award (and the proportion receiving): $1,737 (4%). Average amount of debt of borrowers graduating in 2005: $24,729. Proportion who borrowed: 59%.

CAMPUS LIFE AND EXTRACURRICULAR ACTIVITIES

Activities include: drama/theater, student government, student newspaper, television station. Number of fraternities: 1; sororities: 1.

SERVICES AND FACILITIES

Basic services: nonremedial tutoring, placement service, health service, health insurance, other. **Remedial assistance:** reading, math, writing, study skills. **Counseling services:** minority student, career, personal, veteran student, academic, older student, psychological. **For learning-disabled students:** Services include: remedial math, remedial English, reading machines, remedial reading, tape recorders, diagnostic testing service, untimed tests, note-taking services, oral tests, learning center, readers, tutors. **Information technology resources:** Students are not required to lease or own a computer. **Campus safety:** Security services offered: 24-hour foot and vehicle patrols, lighted pathways/sidewalks.

TRANSFER AND INTERNATIONAL STUDENTS

Transfer students: May apply for admission for the following academic terms: Fall, Spring, Summer. Applicants do not need a minimum number of credits to apply. For fall 2005: Transfer applications received: 220. Transfer applicants offered admission: 188. Transfer applicants enrolled: 177. **International students:** Number of foreign undergraduates: 2.

Indiana University–Kokomo

- **Address:** 2300 S. Washington Street, PO Box 9003, Kokomo, IN 46904-9003
- **Website:** http://www.iuk.edu
- **Public**
- **Enrollment:** 1,423 full-time; 1,314 part-time

KEY STATS

✔ **U.S News College Ranking:** fourth tier, Comp. Coll.–Bachelor's (Midwest)
✔ **SAT Score (25th/75th percentile):** 870-1080
✔ **Tuition:** 2006-2007: $4,502 in state, $11,447 out of state
Selectivity: Less selective   **Room/board:** N/A
Acceptance rate: 82%   **Average debt:** $15,195
Student/faculty ratio: 16/1   **Proportion who borrowed:** 38%

UNDERGRADUATE STUDENT BODY STATS

2005-2006 enrollment: 1,423 full-time; 1,314 part-time. Men: 29%; women: 71%. **Ethnic makeup:** African American: 3%; American-Indian: 1%; Asian American: 1%; Hispanic: 1%; White: 94%.

ADMISSIONS FACTS AND FIGURES

Phone: (765) 455-9531. **Email:** Iuadmiss@iuk.edu. **Website:** http://www.iuk.edu. **Application deadlines for fall 2007:** Early decision: Not offered. Early action: Not offered. Admission can be deferred. **Application fee:** $30. Common application is not accepted. **To apply online, go to:** http://www.iuk.edu/admission/onlineapp.htm. **Admissions requirements/recommendations:** High school units required (recommended): English: 4; Mathematics: 3; Science: 1; Foreign language: (2); Social studies: 2; History: (2); Total units: 14. Tests: The college uses SAT or ACT scores in admissions decisions. Either SAT or ACT required. Campus visit: Recommended. Admissions interview: Recommended. Off-campus interview: May be arranged. **Factors that count in admissions decisions:** *Academic:* Secondary school record: Very important. Class rank: Very important. Letters of recommendation: Considered. Standardized test scores: Important. Essay: Not considered. *Nonacademic:* Interview: Not considered. Extracurricular activities: Not considered. Talent/ability: Not considered. Character/personal qualities: Not considered. Alumni/ae relationship: Not considered. Geographical residence: Not considered. State residency: Not considered. Religious affiliation/commitment: Not considered. Minority status: Not considered. Volunteer work: Not considered. Work experience: Not considered. **Admissions statistics for the fall 2005 entering class:** Total applicants: 717. Total accepted: 587. Freshmen enrolled: 476; Overall acceptance rate: 82%. **Credentials of fall 2005 freshmen:** 5% ranked in the top 10 percent of their high school class; 20% were in the top 25 percent, and 57% were in the top half. (Proportion submitting class standing: 88%.) **Average high school grade point average:** 2.7. **First-year students who submitted SAT scores:** 69%. Scores (25/75 percentile): Verbal: 440-540, Math: 430-540, Combined: 870-1080. **First-year students submitting ACT scores:** 23%. Scores (25/75 percentile): English: 16-22, Math: 17-21, Composite: 17-22.

ACADEMICS

Year founded: 1945. **Academic calendar:** Semester. **Degrees offered:** certificate, associate, bachelor's, post-bachelor's certificate, master's. **Most popular majors:** 19% education, 18% health professions and related clinical sciences, 18% liberal arts and sciences studies, and humanities, 16% business, management, marketing, and related support services, 7% security and protective services. **Major fields of study:** biological and biomedical sciences; business, management, marketing, and related support services; communication, journalism, and related programs; computer and information sciences and support services; education; English language and literature/letters; health professions and related clinical sciences; liberal arts and sciences studies, and humanities; mathematics and statistics; multi/interdisciplinary studies; physical sciences; psychology; public administration and social service professions; security and protective services; social sciences. **Areas of required coursework:** computer literacy, mathematics, English (including composition). **Pre-professional programs:** pre-law, pre-dentistry, pre-medicine. **Special academic programs:** accelerated program, cross-registration, distance learning, double major, dual enrollment, external degree program, honors program, independent study, internships, study abroad, teacher certificate program. **Teacher certification offered in:** elementary, middle/junior high. **Faculty and instruction (2005-2006):** Total instructional faculty: 96 full-time, 76 part-time (43% men; 57% women; 9% minorities). Full-time faculty with Ph.D. or other terminal degree: 68%. Student/faculty ratio: 16/1. Classes of fewer than 20 students: 50%; of 20 to 49 students: 47%; of 50 or more students: 3%. **Advanced Placement and International Baccalaureate credit:** AP tests may be used for: Credit and/or placement. Scores accepted: 4, 5. **Freshmen returning for sophomore year:** 60%. **Graduation rates:** Four-year: 10%; five-year: 22%; six-year: 23%.

COSTS AND FINANCIAL AID

Financial aid office: (765) 455-9216. **Expenses (2006-2007):** Tuition and fees 2006-2007: $4,502 in state, $11,447 out of state; room/board: N/A. **Financial aid:** Priority filing date for institution's financial aid form: March 10. In 2005-2006, 76% of undergraduates applied for financial aid. Of those, 53% were determined to have financial need; 19% had their need fully met. Average financial aid package (proportion receiving): $6,081 (52%). Average amount of gift aid, such as scholarships or grants (proportion receiving): $4,288 (34%). Average amount of self-help aid, such as work study or loans (proportion receiving): $3,152 (42%). Average need-based loan (excluding PLUS or other private loans): $3,043. Among students who received need-based aid, the average percentage of need met:

73%. Among students who received aid based on merit, the average award (and the proportion receiving): $2,022 (6%). Average amount of debt of borrowers graduating in 2005: $15,195. Proportion who borrowed: 38%.

CAMPUS LIFE AND EXTRACURRICULAR ACTIVITIES
Clubs and organizations: Number of student organizations: 21. Activities include: choral groups, drama/theater, student government, student newspaper. ; sororities: 1. of women in sororities: 2%.

SERVICES AND FACILITIES
Basic services: placement service, day care. **Remedial assistance:** math, writing. **Counseling services:** minority student, career, personal, veteran student, academic, older student. **For learning-disabled students:** Services include: remedial math, remedial English, remedial reading, diagnostic testing service, untimed tests, note-taking services, oral tests, learning center, readers, tutors. **Information technology resources:** Students are not required to lease or own a computer. Number of campus computers available to all students: 182. School has a wireless network. **Campus safety:** Security services offered: 24-hour foot and vehicle patrols, late-night transport/escort service, 24-hour emergency telephones, lighted pathways/sidewalks.

TRANSFER AND INTERNATIONAL STUDENTS
Transfer students: May apply for admission for the following academic terms: Fall, Spring, Summer. Applicants need a minimum number of credits to apply. For fall 2005: Transfer applications received: 292. Transfer applicants offered admission: 243. Transfer applicants enrolled: 211. **International students:** Number of foreign undergraduates: 7. Minimum TOEFL score required: 550 (paper).

Indiana University Northwest

- **Address:** 3400 Broadway, Gary, IN 46408
- **Website:** http://www.iun.edu
- **Public**
- **Enrollment:** 2,469 full-time; 1,918 part-time

KEY STATS
✔ **U.S News College Ranking:** fourth tier, Universities–Master's (Midwest)
✔ **SAT Score (25th/75th percentile):** 790-1020
✔ **Tuition:** 2006-2007: $4,572 in state, $11,507 out of state

Selectivity: Less selective	**Room/board:** N/A
Acceptance rate: 75%	**Average debt:** $18,394
Student/faculty ratio: 13/1	**Proportion who borrowed:** 45%

UNDERGRADUATE STUDENT BODY STATS
2005-2006 enrollment: 2,469 full-time; 1,918 part-time. Men: 30%; women: 70%. **Ethnic makeup:** African American: 22%; Asian American: 1%; Hispanic: 12%; White: 64%.

ADMISSIONS FACTS AND FIGURES
Phone: (219) 980-6991. **Email:** admit@iun.edu. **Website:** http://www.iun.edu. **Application deadlines for fall 2007:** Regular decision: Rolling. Early decision: Not offered. Early action: Not offered. Admission can be deferred. **Application fee:** $25. Common application is not accepted. To apply online, go to: http://www.iun.edu/~admit/apps.shtml. **Admissions requirements/recommendations:** High school units required (recommended): English: 4; Mathematics: 3; Science: 1; Foreign language: (2); Social studies: 2; Academic electives: 4; Total units: 16. Tests: The college uses SAT or ACT scores in admissions decisions. Either SAT or ACT required. For admission to the fall 2007 entering class, the school will accept: ACT with writing. Campus visit: Recommended. Admissions interview: Neither required nor recommended. Off-campus interview: May be arranged. **Factors that count in admissions decisions:** *Academic:* Secondary school record: Very important. Class rank: Very important. Letters of recommendation: Considered. Standardized test scores: Very important. Essay: Not considered. *Nonacademic:* Interview: Not considered. Extracurricular activities: Not considered. Talent/ability: Not considered. Character/personal qualities: Not considered. Alumni/ae relationship: Not considered. Geographical residence: Not considered. State residency: Not considered. Religious affiliation/commitment: Not considered. Minority status: Not considered. Volunteer work: Not considered. Work experience: Not considered. **Other schools with the greatest overlap in applicants:** Purdue

University–Calumet; Purdue University–North Central. **Admissions statistics for the fall 2005 entering class:** Total applicants: 1,062. Total accepted: 795. Freshmen enrolled: 604; 1% were from out of state. Overall acceptance rate: 75%. **Credentials of fall 2005 freshmen:** 6% ranked in the top 10 percent of their high school class; 21% were in the top 25 percent, and 49% were in the top half. (Proportion submitting class standing: 86%.) **Average high school grade point average:** 2.6. **First-year students who submitted SAT scores:** 68%. Scores (25/75 percentile): Verbal: 400-510, Math: 390-510, Combined: 790-1020. **First-year students submitting ACT scores:** 11%. Scores (25/75 percentile): English: 15-22, Math: 15-22, Composite: 16-21.

ACADEMICS
Year founded: 1948. **Academic calendar:** Semester. **Degrees offered:** certificate, associate, bachelor's, post-bachelor's certificate, master's. **Most popular majors:** 16% business, management, marketing, and related support services, 15% education, 15% health professions and related clinical sciences, 12% liberal arts and sciences studies, and humanities, 12% security and protective services. **Major fields of study:** area, ethnic, cultural, and gender studies; biological and biomedical sciences; business, management, marketing, and related support services; communication, journalism, and related programs; computer and information sciences and support services; education; English language and literature/letters; foreign languages, literatures, and linguistics; health professions and related clinical sciences; history; liberal arts and sciences studies, and humanities; mathematics and statistics; multi/interdisciplinary studies; parks, recreation, leisure, and fitness studies; philosophy and religious studies; physical sciences; psychology; public administration and social service professions; security and protective services; social sciences; visual and performing arts. **Areas of required coursework:** humanities, computer literacy, mathematics, English (including composition), foreign languages, sciences (biological or physical), history, social science. **Pre-professional programs:** pre-law, pre-dentistry, pre-medicine, pre-veterinary science, pre-optometry, pre-pharmacy, other. **Special academic programs:** accelerated program, cooperative (work-study plan) program, distance learning, double major, dual enrollment, external degree program, independent study, internships, liberal arts/career combination, student-designed major, study abroad, teacher certificate program, weekend college, other. **Teacher certification offered in:** special education, elementary, middle/junior high, secondary. **Cooperative education programs:** business, computer science, humanities. **Reserve Officers Training Corps (ROTC):** Army ROTC: Offered on campus. **Faculty and instruction (2005-2006):** Total instructional faculty: 186 full-time, 196 part-time (48% men; 52% women; 21% minorities). Full-time faculty with Ph.D. or other terminal degree: 66%. Student/faculty ratio: 13/1. Classes of fewer than 20 students: 54%; of 20 to 49 students: 42%; of 50 or more students: 3%. **Advanced Placement and International Baccalaureate credit:** AP tests may be used for: Credit only. Scores accepted: 3, 4, 5. **Freshmen returning for sophomore year:** 62%. **Graduation rates:** Four-year: 11%; five-year: 22%; six-year: 24%.

COSTS AND FINANCIAL AID
Financial aid office: (877) 280-4593. **Expenses (2006-2007):** Tuition and fees 2006-2007: $4,572 in state, $11,507 out of state; room/board: N/A. **Financial aid:** Priority filing date for institution's financial aid form: March 1. In 2005-2006, 79% of undergraduates applied for financial aid. Of those, 63% were determined to have financial need; 10% had their need fully met. Average financial aid package (proportion receiving): $7,363 (62%). Average amount of gift aid, such as scholarships or grants (proportion receiving): $4,944 (43%). Average amount of self-help aid, such as work study or loans (proportion receiving): $3,963 (53%). Average need-based loan (excluding PLUS or other private loans): $3,264. Among students who received need-based aid, the average percentage of need met: 64%. Among students who received aid based on merit, the average award (and the proportion receiving): $2,983 (2%). The average athletic scholarship (and the proportion receiving): $840 (1%). Average amount of debt of borrowers graduating in 2005: $18,394. Proportion who borrowed: 45%.

CAMPUS LIFE AND EXTRACURRICULAR ACTIVITIES
Students who live in college-owned, operated, or affiliated housing: 0%. **Clubs and organizations:** Number of student organizations: 60. Activities include: choral groups, dance, drama/theater, literary magazine, radio station, student government, student newspaper. Number of fraternities: 2; sororities: 3. Proportion of men in fraternities: 1%; of women in sororities: 1%. **Sports program (2005-2006):** Member of NAIA. *Men's intercollegiate varsity sports:* baseball, basketball, golf. *Women's intercollegiate varsity sports:* basketball, golf, volleyball.

SERVICES AND FACILITIES

Basic services: nonremedial tutoring, placement service, day care, health insurance. **Remedial assistance:** reading, math, writing, study skills, other. **Counseling services:** minority student, career, military, veteran student, academic, older student, psychological. **For learning-disabled students:** School does not offer a structured program with separate admission and additional fees. Total undergraduates in learning-disabled program or receiving services: 13. Services include: remedial math, remedial English, remedial reading, tape recorders, diagnostic testing service, untimed tests, note-taking services, oral tests, learning center, readers, extended time for tests, tutors, early syllabus, priority seating, substitution of courses, texts on tape, typist/scribe, exams on tape or computer, take home exams, other testing accomodations, other. **Library:** Number of titles: 509,251; number of current serial subscriptions: 1,527. **Information technology resources:** Students are not required to lease or own a computer. Number of campus computers available to all students: 145. School has a wireless network. Approximate number of users that can be accommodated: 400. **Campus safety:** Security services offered: 24-hour foot and vehicle patrols, late-night transport/escort service, 24-hour emergency telephones, lighted pathways/sidewalks.

TRANSFER AND INTERNATIONAL STUDENTS

Transfer students: May apply for admission for the following academic terms: Fall, Spring, Summer. Applicants need a minimum number of credits to apply. For fall 2005: Transfer applications received: 507. Transfer applicants offered admission: 398. Transfer applicants enrolled: 350. **International students:** Number of foreign undergraduates: 7.

Indiana Univ.-Purdue Univ.—Fort Wayne

- **Address:** 2101 E. Coliseum Boulevard, Fort Wayne, IN 46805-1499
- **Website:** http://www.ipfw.edu
- **Public**
- **Enrollment:** 6,813 full-time; 4,215 part-time

KEY STATS

✔ **U.S News College Ranking:** fourth tier, Universities–Master's (Midwest)
✔ **SAT Score (25th/75th percentile):** 870-1090
✔ **Tuition:** 2006-2007: $6,041 in state, $13,763 out of state

Selectivity: Less selective	**Room/board:** $8,174
Acceptance rate: 96%	**Average debt:** $16,880
Student/faculty ratio: 17/1	**Proportion who borrowed:** 60%

UNDERGRADUATE STUDENT BODY STATS

2005-2006 enrollment: 6,813 full-time; 4,215 part-time. Men: 43%; women: 57%. **Ethnic makeup:** African American: 5%; Asian American: 2%; Hispanic: 3%; White: 89%; International: 1%.

ADMISSIONS FACTS AND FIGURES

Phone: (260) 481-6812. **Email:** ipfwadms@ipfw.edu. **Website:** http://www.ipfw.edu. **Application deadlines for fall 2007:** Regular decision: August 1. Early decision: Not offered. Early action: Not offered. Admission can be deferred. **Application fee:** $30. Common application is not accepted. **To apply online, go to:** http://www.ipfw.edu/admiss/. **Admissions requirements/recommendations:** High school units required (recommended): English: 4; Mathematics: 3; Science: 2 (1); Social studies: 5; Academic electives: 5; Total units: 20. Tests: The college uses SAT or ACT scores in admissions decisions. Either SAT or ACT required. For admission to the fall 2007 entering class, the school will accept: ACT with writing, ACT without writing. Campus visit: Recommended. Admissions interview: Neither required nor recommended. Off-campus interview: Not available. **Factors that count in admissions decisions:** *Academic:* Secondary school record: Very important. Class rank: Very important. Letters of recommendation: Considered. Standardized test scores: Very important. Essay: Not considered. *Nonacademic:* Interview: Not considered. Extracurricular activities: Not considered. Talent/ability: Considered. Character/personal qualities: Not considered. Alumni/ae relationship: Not considered. Geographical residence: Not considered. State residency: Considered. Religious affiliation/commitment: Not considered. Minority status: Not considered. Volunteer work: Not considered. Work experience: Not considered. **Other schools with the greatest overlap in applicants:** Ball State University; Indiana University–Bloomington; Purdue University–West Lafayette; Taylor University; University of St. Francis. **Admissions statistics for the fall 2005**

entering class: Total applicants: 2,786. Total accepted: 2,681. Freshmen enrolled: 1,895; 6% were from out of state. Overall acceptance rate: 96%. **Credentials of fall 2005 freshmen:** 9% ranked in the top 10 percent of their high school class; 28% were in the top 25 percent, and 62% were in the top half. (Proportion submitting class standing: 80%.) **Average high school grade point average:** 3.0. **First-year students who submitted SAT scores:** 84%. Scores (25/75 percentile): Verbal: 430-540, Math: 440-550, Combined: 870-1090. **First-year students submitting ACT scores:** 19%. Scores (25/75 percentile): English: 17-23, Math: 18-24, Composite: 18-24.

ACADEMICS

Year founded: 1964. **Academic calendar:** Semester. **Degrees offered:** certificate, associate, transfer-associate, terminal-associate, bachelor's, post-bachelor's certificate, master's. **Most popular majors:** 21% education, 19% business administration and management, 14% general studies, 6% engineering technology, 6% psychology. **Major fields of study:** area, ethnic, cultural, and gender studies; biological and biomedical sciences; business, management, marketing, and related support services; communication, journalism, and related programs; computer and information sciences and support services; education; engineering; engineering technologies/technicians; English language and literature/letters; foreign languages, literatures, and linguistics; health professions and related clinical sciences; history; legal professions and studies; liberal arts and sciences studies, and humanities; mathematics and statistics; philosophy and religious studies; physical sciences; psychology; public administration and social service professions; security and protective services; social sciences; visual and performing arts. **Areas of required coursework:** arts/fine arts, humanities, computer literacy, mathematics, English (including composition), sciences (biological or physical), social science, other. **Pre-professional programs:** pre-dentistry, pre-medicine, pre-veterinary science, pre-pharmacy. **Special academic programs:** cooperative (work-study plan) program, distance learning, double major, English as a Second Language (ESL), exchange student program (domestic), honors program, independent study, internships, liberal arts/career combination, study abroad, teacher certificate program, weekend college. **Teacher certification offered in:** early childhood, elementary, middle/junior high, secondary. **Cooperative education programs:** business, computer science, engineering, natural science, technologies. **Faculty and instruction (2005-2006):** Total instructional faculty: 372 full-time, 394 part-time (52% men; 48% women; 8% minorities). Full-time faculty with Ph.D. or other terminal degree: 88%. Student/faculty ratio: 17/1. Classes of fewer than 20 students: 46%; of 20 to 49 students: 50%; of 50 or more students: 4%. **Advanced Placement and International Baccalaureate credit:** AP tests may be used for: Credit only. Scores accepted: 4, 5. International Baccalaureate exams may be used for: Credit only. **Freshmen returning for sophomore year:** 63%. **Graduation rates:** Four-year: 4%; five-year: 14%; six-year: 19%. **Graduate study:** 15% of students pursue further study immediately upon graduation.

COSTS AND FINANCIAL AID

Financial aid office: (260) 481-6820. **Expenses (2006-2007):** Tuition and fees 2006-2007: $6,041 in state, $13,763 out of state; room/board: $8,174. Estimated transportation: $1,650; personal expenses: $1,602. **Financial aid:** Priority filing date for institution's financial aid form: March 10. In 2005-2006, 76% of undergraduates applied for financial aid. Of those, 58% were determined to have financial need; 12% had their need fully met. Average financial aid package (proportion receiving): $6,546 (55%). Average amount of gift aid, such as scholarships or grants (proportion receiving): $4,260 (36%). Average amount of self-help aid, such as work study or loans (proportion receiving): $3,173 (44%). Average need-based loan (excluding PLUS or other private loans): $3,112. Among students who received need-based aid, the average percentage of need met: 73%. Among students who received aid based on merit, the average award (and the proportion receiving): $1,860 (18%). The average athletic scholarship (and the proportion receiving): $6,365 (3%). Average amount of debt of borrowers graduating in 2005: $16,880. Proportion who borrowed: 60%.

CAMPUS LIFE AND EXTRACURRICULAR ACTIVITIES

Campus housing available (% using): apartment for single students (100%). Students who live in college-owned, operated, or affiliated housing: 5%. Average per-year earnings: $5,000. **Clubs and organizations:** Number of student organizations: 89. Activities include: choral groups, concert band, dance, drama/theater, jazz band, literary magazine, music ensembles, musical theater, opera, pep band, student government, student newspaper, symphony orchestra, television station. Number of fraternities: 2; sororities: 0. Proportion of men in fraternities: 1%; Average proportion of students who stay on campus on weekends: 20%. **Sports program (2005-2006):** Member of NCAA I. *Men's intercollegiate varsity sports:* baseball, basketball, cross-country, golf, soccer, tennis, track and field (indoor), track and field (outdoor), volleyball. *Women's intercollegiate varsity sports:* basketball, cross-country, golf, soccer, softball, tennis, track and field (indoor), track and field (outdoor), volleyball.

SERVICES AND FACILITIES

Basic services: nonremedial tutoring, women's center, placement service, day care, health service, health insurance. **Remedial assistance:** reading, math, writing, study skills. **Counseling services:** minority student, career, personal, veteran student, academic, older student, psychological, birth control, religious. **For learning-disabled students:** School does not offer a structured program with separate admission and additional fees. Services include: remedial math, remedial English, reading machines, remedial reading, tape recorders, note-taking services, learning center, readers, extended time for tests, tutors, other testing accomodations. **Library:** Number of titles: 474,802; number of current serial subscriptions: 22,782. **Information technology resources:** Students are not required to lease or own a computer. Number of campus computers available to all students: 274. School has a wireless network. Proportion of college-owned housing units wired for high-speed internet access: 100%. **Campus safety:** Security services offered: 24-hour foot and vehicle patrols, late-night transport/escort service, 24-hour emergency telephones, lighted pathways/sidewalks, controlled dormitory access (key, security card, etc).

TRANSFER AND INTERNATIONAL STUDENTS

Transfer students: May apply for admission for the following academic terms: Fall, Spring, Summer. Applicants do not need a minimum number of credits to apply. For fall 2005: Transfer applications received: 1,187. Transfer applicants offered admission: 1,147. Transfer applicants enrolled: 789. **International students:** Number of foreign undergraduates: 125 (1% of student body). Number of countries represented: 73. Minimum TOEFL score required: 550 (paper); 213 (computer).

Indiana Univ.-Purdue Univ.-Indianapolis

- **Address:** 425 N. University Boulevard, Indianapolis, IN 46202-5143
- **Website:** http://www.iupui.edu
- **Public**
- **Enrollment:** 13,736 full-time; 7,702 part-time

KEY STATS

✔ **U.S News College Ranking:** fourth tier, National Universities
✔ **SAT Score (25th/75th percentile):** 880-1110
✔ **Tuition:** 2006-2007: $5,608 in state, $16,432 out of state

Selectivity: Less selective	**Room/board:** N/A
Acceptance rate: 74%	**Average debt:** $23,041
Student/faculty ratio: 17/1	**Proportion who borrowed:** 52%

UNDERGRADUATE STUDENT BODY STATS

2005-2006 enrollment: 13,736 full-time; 7,702 part-time. Men: 41%; women: 59%. **Ethnic makeup:** African American: 11%; Asian American: 2%; Hispanic: 2%; White: 83%; International: 2%.

ADMISSIONS FACTS AND FIGURES

Phone: (317) 274-4591. **Email:** apply@iupui.edu. **Website:** http://www.iupui.edu. **Application deadlines for fall 2007:** Regular decision: Rolling. Early decision: Not offered. Early action: Not offered. Admission can be deferred. **Application fee:** $50. Common application is not accepted. **To apply online, go to:** http://www.enroll.iupui.edu/. **Admissions requirements/recommendations:** High school units required (recommended): English: 4 (4); Mathematics: 3 (4); Science: 3 (4); Foreign language: (3); Social studies: 1 (2); History: 2 (2); Academic electives: 4 (4); Total units: 17 (23). Tests: The college uses SAT or ACT scores in admissions decisions. Either SAT or ACT required. For admission to the fall 2007 entering class, the school will accept: ACT with writing. Campus visit: Recommended. Admissions interview: Recommended. Off-campus interview: Not available. **Factors that count in admissions decisions:** *Academic:* Secondary school record: Very important. Class rank: Considered. Letters of recommendation: Considered. Standardized test scores: Considered. Essay: Considered. *Nonacademic:* Interview: Not considered. Extracurricular activities: Not considered. Talent/ability: Not considered. Character/personal qualities: Considered. Alumni/ae relationship: Not considered. Geographical resi-

dence: Not considered. State residency: Not considered. Religious affiliation/commitment: Not considered. Minority status: Not considered. Volunteer work: Considered. Work experience: Considered. **Other schools with the greatest overlap in applicants:** Indiana University Northwest; Indiana University Southeast; Indiana University–Bloomington; Indiana University–Kokomo; Indiana University–South Bend. **Admissions statistics for the fall 2005 entering class:** Total applicants: 6,136. Total accepted: 4,525. Freshmen enrolled: 2,746; 2% were from out of state. Overall acceptance rate: 74%. **Credentials of fall 2005 freshmen:** 9% ranked in the top 10 percent of their high school class; 33% were in the top 25 percent, and 70% were in the top half. (Proportion submitting class standing: 83%.) **Average high school grade point average:** 3.0. First-year students who submitted SAT scores: 75%. Scores (25/75 percentile): Verbal: 440-550, Math: 440-560, Combined: 880-1110. **First-year students submitting ACT scores:** 27%. Scores (25/75 percentile): English: 16-23, Math: 17-23, Composite: 18-23.

ACADEMICS

Year founded: 1969. **Academic calendar:** Semester. **Degrees offered:** certificate, associate, bachelor's, post-bachelor's certificate, master's, first professional, doctorate. **Most popular majors:** 17% business, management, marketing, and related support services, 15% liberal arts and sciences studies, and humanities, 14% health professions and related clinical sciences, 10% education, 6% communication, journalism, and related programs. **Major fields of study:** area, ethnic, cultural, and gender studies; biological and biomedical sciences; business, management, marketing, and related support services; communication, journalism, and related programs; computer and information sciences and support services; education; engineering; engineering technologies/technicians; English language and literature/letters; foreign languages, literatures, and linguistics; health professions and related clinical sciences; history; liberal arts and sciences studies, and humanities; mathematics and statistics; multi/interdisciplinary studies; natural resources and conservation; philosophy and religious studies; physical sciences; psychology; public administration and social service professions; security and protective services; social sciences; visual and performing arts. **Areas of required coursework:** humanities, computer literacy, mathematics, English (including composition), sciences (biological or physical), social science. **Pre-professional programs:** pre-law, pre-dentistry, pre-medicine, pre-veterinary science, pre-optometry, pre-pharmacy, other. **Special academic programs:** accelerated program, cooperative (work-study plan) program, cross-registration, distance learning, double major, dual enrollment, English as a Second Language (ESL), external degree program, honors program, independent study, internships, liberal arts/career combination, student-designed major, study abroad, teacher certificate program, weekend college. **Teacher certification offered in:** special education, elementary, secondary. **Cooperative education programs:** art, business, computer science, education, engineering, health professions, humanities, natural science, social/behavioral science, technologies, vocational arts. **Reserve Officers Training Corps (ROTC):** Army ROTC: Offered on campus; Navy ROTC: Offered at cooperating institution (Purdue University); Air Force ROTC: Offered at cooperating institution (Indiana University South Bend). **Faculty and instruction (2005-2006):** Total instructional faculty: 2,132 full-time, 888 part-time (60% men; 40% women; 16% minorities). Full-time faculty with Ph.D. or other terminal degree: 82%. Student/faculty ratio: 17/1. Classes of fewer than 20 students: 39%; of 20 to 49 students: 52%; of 50 or more students: 9%. **Advanced Placement and International Baccalaureate credit:** AP tests may be used for: Credit and/or placement. Scores accepted: 3, 4, 5. **Freshmen returning for sophomore year:** 66%. **Graduation rates:** Four-year: 7%; five-year: 19%; six-year: 26%. **Graduate study:** 20% of students pursue further study within one year. Fields in which graduates pursue further study: Master of Business Administration (MBA), 2%; law, 1%; medicine, 1%; arts and sciences, 1%.

COSTS AND FINANCIAL AID

Financial aid office: (317) 274-4162. **Expenses (2006-2007):** Tuition and fees 2006-2007: $5,608 in state, $16,432 out of state; room/board: N/A. **Financial aid:** Priority filing date for institution's financial aid form: March 1. In 2005-2006, 79% of undergraduates applied for financial aid. Of those, 62% were determined to have financial need; 4% had their need fully met. Average financial aid package (proportion receiving): $6,929 (60%). Average amount of gift aid, such as scholarships or grants (proportion receiving): $4,829 (34%). Average amount of self-help aid, such as work study or loans (proportion receiving): $4,000 (46%). Average need-based loan (excluding PLUS or other private loans): $3,704. Among students who received need-based aid, the average percentage of need met: 51%. Among students who received aid based on merit, the average award (and the proportion receiving): $3,061 (4%). The average athletic scholarship (and the

proportion receiving): $6,676 (1%). Average amount of debt of borrowers graduating in 2005: $23,041. Proportion who borrowed: 52%.

CAMPUS LIFE AND EXTRACURRICULAR ACTIVITIES

Campus housing available: coed dorms, apartments for married students, apartment for single students, special housing for international students, other housing options. Students who live in college-owned, operated, or affiliated housing: 3%. **Clubs and organizations:** Number of student organizations: 162. Activities include: choral groups, concert band, dance, drama/theater, jazz band, literary magazine, music ensembles, pep band, student government, student newspaper. Number of fraternities: 3; sororities: 5. Proportion of men in fraternities: 1%; of women in sororities: 1%. **Sports program (2005-2006):** Member of NCAA I. *Men's intercollegiate varsity sports:* basketball, cross-country, golf, soccer, swimming and diving, tennis. *Women's intercollegiate varsity sports:* basketball, cross-country, golf, soccer, softball, swimming and diving, tennis, volleyball.

SERVICES AND FACILITIES

Basic services: nonremedial tutoring, women's center, placement service, day care, health service, health insurance, other. **Remedial assistance:** math, writing. **Counseling services:** minority student, career, military, personal, veteran student, academic, older student, psychological, birth control. **For learning-disabled students:** School does not offer a structured program with separate admission and additional fees. Total undergraduates in learning-disabled program or receiving services: 520. Services include: remedial math, remedial English, reading machines, remedial reading, tape recorders, videotaped classes, diagnostic testing service, untimed tests, note-taking services, oral tests, learning center, readers, extended time for tests, tutors, substitution of courses, texts on tape, typist/scribe, exams on tape or computer, take home exams, other testing accomodations. **Library:** Number of titles: 925,785; number of current serial subscriptions: 4,296.
Information technology resources: Students are not required to lease or own a computer. Number of campus computers available to all students: 2,500. School has a wireless network. Approximate number of users that can be accommodated: 13,500. Proportion of college-owned housing units wired for high-speed internet access: 95%. **Campus safety:** Security services offered: 24-hour foot and vehicle patrols, late-night transport/escort service, 24-hour emergency telephones, lighted pathways/sidewalks, controlled dormitory access (key, security card, etc).

TRANSFER AND INTERNATIONAL STUDENTS

Transfer students: May apply for admission for the following academic terms: Fall, Spring, Summer. Applicants do not need a minimum number of credits to apply. For fall 2005: Transfer applications received: 3,156. Transfer applicants offered admission: 2,566. Transfer applicants enrolled: 1,823. **International students:** Number of foreign undergraduates: 354 (2% of student body). Number of countries represented: 76. Minimum TOEFL score required: 550 (paper); 173 (computer).

Indiana University–South Bend

- **Address:** 1700 Mishawaka Avenue, PO Box 7111, South Bend, IN 46634-7111
- **Website:** http://www.iusb.edu
- **Public**
- **Enrollment:** 3,636 full-time; 2,688 part-time

KEY STATS

✔ **U.S News College Ranking:** fourth tier, Universities–Master's (Midwest)
✔ **SAT Score (25th/75th percentile):** 850-1070
✔ **Tuition:** 2006-2007: $4,659 in state, $12,433 out of state

Selectivity: Less selective	**Room/board:** N/A
Acceptance rate: 88%	**Average debt:** $20,199
Student/faculty ratio: 14/1	**Proportion who borrowed:** 53%

UNDERGRADUATE STUDENT BODY STATS

2005-2006 enrollment: 3,636 full-time; 2,688 part-time. Men: 38%; women: 62%. **Ethnic makeup:** African American: 7%; Asian American: 1%; Hispanic: 3%; White: 86%; International: 2%.

ADMISSIONS FACTS AND FIGURES

Phone: (574) 520-4839. **Email:** admissions@iusb.edu. **Website:** http://www.iusb.edu. **Application deadlines for fall 2007:** Regular decision: Rolling. Early decision: Not offered. Early action: Not offered. Admission can be deferred. **Application fee:** $45. Common application is not accepted. **To apply online, go to:** http://www.iusb.edu/~admissio/. **Admissions requirements/recommendations:** High school units required (recommended): English: 4 (8); Mathematics: 3 (6); Science: 1 (6); Foreign language: (2); Social studies: 2 (4); History: (2); Total units: 13. Tests: The college uses SAT or ACT scores in admissions decisions. Neither SAT nor ACT required. For admission to the fall 2007 entering class, the school will accept: ACT with writing. Campus visit: Recommended. Admissions interview: Recommended. Off-campus interview: May be arranged. **Factors that count in admissions decisions:** *Academic:* Secondary school record: Very important. Class rank: Important. Letters of recommendation: Considered. Standardized test scores: Considered. Essay: Not considered. *Nonacademic:* Interview: Considered. Extracurricular activities: Considered. Talent/ability: Not considered. Character/personal qualities: Not considered. Alumni/ae relationship: Not considered. Geographical residence: Not considered. State residency: Considered. Religious affiliation/commitment: Not considered. Minority status: Not considered. Volunteer work: Not considered. Work experience: Not considered. **Other schools with the greatest overlap in applicants:** Ball State University; Bethel College; Indiana University–Bloomington; Purdue University–West Lafayette. **Admissions statistics for the fall 2005 entering class:** Total applicants: 1,560. Total accepted: 1,374. Freshmen enrolled: 1,006; 2% were from out of state. Overall acceptance rate: 88%. **Credentials of fall 2005 freshmen:** 7% ranked in the top 10 percent of their high school class; 24% were in the top 25 percent, and 59% were in the top half. (Proportion submitting class standing: 75%.) **Average high school grade point average:** 2.8. **First-year students who submitted SAT scores:** 74%. Scores (25/75 percentile): Verbal: 430-540, Math: 420-530, Combined: 850-1070. **First-year students submitting ACT scores:** 9%. Scores (25/75 percentile): English: 16-22, Math: 17-21, Composite: 18-23.

ACADEMICS

Year founded: 1922. **Academic calendar:** Semester. **Degrees offered:** certificate, diploma, associate, bachelor's, post-bachelor's certificate, master's. **Most popular majors:** 22% education, 16% business, management, marketing, and related support services, 13% liberal arts and sciences studies, and humanities, 12% health professions and related clinical sciences, 7% security and protective services. **Major fields of study:** area, ethnic, cultural, and gender studies; biological and biomedical sciences; business, management, marketing, and related support services; communication, journalism, and related programs; computer and information sciences and support services; education; engineering technologies/technicians; English language and literature/letters; family and consumer sciences/human sciences; foreign languages, literatures, and linguistics; history; liberal arts and sciences studies, and humanities; mathematics and statistics; multi/interdisciplinary studies; natural resources and conservation; philosophy and religious studies; physical sciences; psychology; public administration and social service professions; social sciences; visual and performing arts. **Areas of required coursework:** arts/fine arts, humanities, computer literacy, mathematics, English (including composition), foreign languages, sciences (biological or physical), history, social science, other. **Pre-professional programs:** pre-law, pre-dentistry, pre-medicine, pre-optometry, pre-pharmacy. **Special academic programs:** accelerated program, cross-registration, distance learning, double major, English as a Second Language (ESL), external degree program, honors program, independent study, internships, liberal arts/career combination, study abroad, teacher certificate program, weekend college, other. **Teacher certification offered in:** early childhood, special education, elementary, secondary. **Reserve Officers Training Corps (ROTC):** Army ROTC: Offered at cooperating institution (Notre Dame); Navy ROTC: Offered at cooperating institution (Notre Dame); Air Force ROTC: Offered at cooperating institution (Notre Dame). **Faculty and instruction (2005-2006):** Total instructional faculty: 275 full-time, 278 part-time (49% men; 51% women; 13% minorities). Full-time faculty with Ph.D. or other terminal degree: 67%. Student/faculty ratio: 14/1. Classes of fewer than 20 students: 48%; of 20 to 49 students: 47%; of 50 or more students: 4%. **Advanced Placement and International Baccalaureate credit:** AP tests may be used for: Credit only. **Freshmen returning for sophomore year:** 67%. **Graduation rates:** Four-year: 6%; five-year: 19%; six-year: 24%.

COSTS AND FINANCIAL AID

Financial aid office: (574) 237-4357. **Expenses (2006-2007):** Tuition and fees 2006-2007: $4,659 in state, $12,433 out of state; room/board: N/A.

Financial aid: Priority filing date for institution's financial aid form: March 1. In 2005-2006, 80% of undergraduates applied for financial aid. Of those, 59% were determined to have financial need; 7% had their need fully met. Average financial aid package (proportion receiving): $6,050 (58%). Average amount of gift aid, such as scholarships or grants (proportion receiving): $4,153 (39%). Average amount of self-help aid, such as work study or loans (proportion receiving): $3,365 (44%). Average need-based loan (excluding PLUS or other private loans): $3,277. Among students who received need-based aid, the average percentage of need met: 58%. Among students who received aid based on merit, the average award (and the proportion receiving): $1,966 (4%). The average athletic scholarship (and the proportion receiving): $3,355 (1%). Average amount of debt of borrowers graduating in 2005: $20,199. Proportion who borrowed: 53%.

CAMPUS LIFE AND EXTRACURRICULAR ACTIVITIES
Campus housing available: special housing for international students, other housing options. **Clubs and organizations:** Number of student organizations: 55. Activities include: choral groups, drama/theater, jazz band, literary magazine, music ensembles, musical theater, opera, pep band, student government, student newspaper, student film society, symphony orchestra. Number of fraternities: 1; sororities: 1. **Sports program (2005-2006):** Member of NAIA. *Men's intercollegiate varsity sports:* basketball. *Women's intercollegiate varsity sports:* basketball, cheerleading.

SERVICES AND FACILITIES
Basic services: nonremedial tutoring, women's center, placement service, day care, other. **Remedial assistance:** reading, math, writing, study skills. **Counseling services:** minority student, career, personal, veteran student, academic, older student, psychological. **For learning-disabled students:** Services include: remedial math, remedial English, remedial reading, learning center, tutors, other. **Information technology resources:** Students are not required to lease or own a computer. Number of campus computers available to all students: 550. School has a wireless network. Approximate number of users that can be accommodated: 800. **Campus safety:** Security services offered: 24-hour foot and vehicle patrols, late-night transport/escort service, lighted pathways/sidewalks.

TRANSFER AND INTERNATIONAL STUDENTS
Transfer students: May apply for admission for the following academic terms: Fall, Spring, Summer. Applicants need a minimum number of credits to apply. For fall 2005: Transfer applications received: 717. Transfer applicants offered admission: 674. Transfer applicants enrolled: 529. **International students:** Number of foreign undergraduates: 105 (2% of student body). Number of countries represented: 58. Minimum TOEFL score required: 530 (paper); 197 (computer).

Indiana University Southeast

- **Address:** 4201 Grant Line Road, New Albany, IN 47150-6405
- **Website:** http://www.ius.edu
- **Public**
- **Enrollment:** 3,220 full-time; 2,080 part-time

KEY STATS
✔ **U.S News College Ranking:** fourth tier, Universities–Master's (Midwest)
✔ **SAT Score (25th/75th percentile):** 860-1070
✔ **Tuition:** 2006-2007: $4,550 in state, $11,498 out of state

Selectivity: Less selective	**Room/board:** N/A
Acceptance rate: 89%	**Average debt:** $18,570
Student/faculty ratio: 16/1	**Proportion who borrowed:** 42%

UNDERGRADUATE STUDENT BODY STATS
2005-2006 enrollment: 3,220 full-time; 2,080 part-time. Men: 36%; women: 64%. **Ethnic makeup:** African American: 4%; Asian American: 1%; Hispanic: 1%; White: 93%.

ADMISSIONS FACTS AND FIGURES
Phone: (812) 941-2212. **Email:** admissions@ius.edu. **Website:** http://www.ius.edu. **Application deadlines for fall 2007:** Regular decision: Rolling. Early decision: Not offered. Early action: Not offered. Admission can be deferred. **Application fee:** $30. Common application is not accepted. **To apply online, go to:** http://www.ius.edu/apply. **Admissions**

requirements/recommendations: High school units required (recommended): English: 4; Mathematics: 3 (4); Science: 1 (2); Foreign language: (2); Social studies: 2; History: (1); Academic electives: 4; Total units: 14 (19). Tests: The college uses SAT or ACT scores in admissions decisions. Either SAT or ACT required. For admission to the fall 2007 entering class, the school will accept: ACT with writing. Campus visit: Recommended. Admissions interview: Recommended. Off-campus interview: Not available. **Factors that count in admissions decisions:** *Academic:* Secondary school record: Very important. Class rank: Very important. Letters of recommendation: Considered. Standardized test scores: Important. Essay: Not considered. *Nonacademic:* Interview: Considered. Extracurricular activities: Not considered. Talent/ability: Not considered. Character/personal qualities: Not considered. Alumni/ae relationship: Not considered. Geographical residence: Not considered. State residency: Considered. Religious affiliation/commitment: Not considered. Minority status: Not considered. Volunteer work: Not considered. Work experience: Not considered. **Admissions statistics for the fall 2005 entering class:** Total applicants: 1,194. Total accepted: 1,066. Freshmen enrolled: 753; 14% were from out of state. Overall acceptance rate: 89%. **Credentials of fall 2005 freshmen:** 8% ranked in the top 10 percent of their high school class; 28% were in the top 25 percent, and 68% were in the top half. (Proportion submitting class standing: 66%.) **Average high school grade point average:** 2.9. **First-year students who submitted SAT scores:** 74%. Scores (25/75 percentile): Verbal: 430-540, Math: 430-530, Combined: 860-1070. **First-year students submitting ACT scores:** 29%. Scores (25/75 percentile): English: 16-22, Math: 16-22, Composite: 17-22.

ACADEMICS
Year founded: 1941. **Academic calendar:** Semester. **Degrees offered:** certificate, associate, bachelor's, post-bachelor's certificate, master's. **Most popular majors:** 24% business, management, marketing, and related support services, 23% education, 16% liberal arts and sciences studies, and humanities, 7% psychology, 6% health professions and related clinical sciences. **Major fields of study:** area, ethnic, cultural, and gender studies; biological and biomedical sciences; business, management, marketing, and related support services; communication, journalism, and related programs; computer and information sciences and support services; education; English language and literature/letters; foreign languages, literatures, and linguistics; health professions and related clinical sciences; history; liberal arts and sciences studies, and humanities; mathematics and statistics; philosophy and religious studies; physical sciences; psychology; security and protective services; social sciences; visual and performing arts. **Areas of required coursework:** humanities, computer literacy, mathematics, English (including composition), sciences (biological or physical), social science. **Pre-professional programs:** pre-law, pre-dentistry, pre-medicine, pre-optometry. **Special academic programs:** accelerated program, cross-registration, double major, dual enrollment, external degree program, independent study, internships, study abroad, teacher certificate program, weekend college, other. **Teacher certification offered in:** special education, elementary, secondary. **Reserve Officers Training Corps (ROTC):** Army ROTC: Offered at cooperating institution (University of Louisville); Air Force ROTC: Offered at cooperating institution (University of Louisville). **Faculty and instruction (2005-2006):** Total instructional faculty: 189 full-time, 245 part-time (51% men; 49% women; 10% minorities). Full-time faculty with Ph.D. or other terminal degree: 72%. Student/faculty ratio: 16/1. Classes of fewer than 20 students: 46%; of 20 to 49 students: 53%; of 50 or more students: 1%. **Advanced Placement and International Baccalaureate credit:** AP tests may be used for: Credit only. Scores accepted: 3, 4, 5. **Freshmen returning for sophomore year:** 67%. **Graduation rates:** Four-year: 8%; five-year: 24%; six-year: 29%.

COSTS AND FINANCIAL AID
Financial aid office: (812) 941-2246. **Expenses (2006-2007):** Tuition and fees 2006-2007: $4,550 in state, $11,498 out of state; room/board: N/A. **Financial aid:** Priority filing date for institution's financial aid form: March 1. In 2005-2006, 74% of undergraduates applied for financial aid. Of those, 59% were determined to have financial need; 5% had their need fully met. Average financial aid package (proportion receiving): $6,127 (58%). Average amount of gift aid, such as scholarships or grants (proportion receiving): $4,560 (33%). Average amount of self-help aid, such as work study or loans (proportion receiving): $3,945 (42%). Average need-based loan (excluding PLUS or other private loans): $3,772. Among students who received need-based aid, the average percentage of need met: 52%. Among students who received aid based on merit, the average award (and the proportion receiving): $2,376 (3%). The average athletic scholarship (and the proportion receiving): $1,074 (2%). Average amount of debt of borrowers graduating in 2005: $18,570. Proportion who borrowed: 42%.

CAMPUS LIFE AND EXTRACURRICULAR ACTIVITIES

Activities include: choral groups, concert band, drama/theater, literary magazine, music ensembles, student government, student newspaper, symphony orchestra. Number of fraternities: 2; sororities: 4. Proportion of men in fraternities: 3%; of women in sororities: 3%. **Sports program (2005-2006):** Member of NAIA. *Men's intercollegiate varsity sports:* baseball, basketball, cross-country, tennis. *Women's intercollegiate varsity sports:* basketball, cross-country, tennis, volleyball.

SERVICES AND FACILITIES

Basic services: placement service, day care. **Remedial assistance:** reading, math, writing, study skills, other. **Counseling services:** career, personal, academic, psychological. **For learning-disabled students:** Services include: remedial math, remedial English, reading machines, remedial reading, other special classes, untimed tests, note-taking services, special bookstore section, oral tests, tutors, other. **Information technology resources:** Students are not required to lease or own a computer. Number of campus computers available to all students: 830. **Campus safety:** Security services offered: 24-hour foot and vehicle patrols, 24-hour emergency telephones, lighted pathways/sidewalks.

TRANSFER AND INTERNATIONAL STUDENTS

Transfer students: May apply for admission for the following academic terms: Fall, Spring, Summer. Applicants need a minimum number of credits to apply. For fall 2005: Transfer applications received: 501. Transfer applicants offered admission: 448. Transfer applicants enrolled: 398. **International students:** Number of foreign undergraduates: 14.

Indiana Wesleyan University

- **Address:** 4201 S. Washington Street, Marion, IN 46953-4999
- **Website:** http://www.indwes.edu
- **Private; Religious affiliation:** Wesleyan Church
- **Enrollment:** 7,852 full-time; 595 part-time

KEY STATS

✔ **U.S News College Ranking:** 62, Universities–Master's (Midwest)
✔ **SAT Score (25th/75th percentile):** 870-1303
✔ **Tuition:** N/A

Selectivity: Selective	**Room/board:** N/A
Acceptance rate: 82%	**Average debt:** N/A
Student/faculty ratio: 16/1	**Proportion who borrowed:** N/A

UNDERGRADUATE STUDENT BODY STATS

2005-2006 enrollment: 7,852 full-time; 595 part-time. Men: 36%; women: 64%. **Ethnic makeup:** African American: 13%; Asian American: 1%; Hispanic: 2%; White: 84%. **Religious preference:** Roman Catholic: 10%; Protestant: 66%; No preference: 5%; Unknown: 8%; Wesleyan Church: 9%.

ADMISSIONS FACTS AND FIGURES

Phone: (800) 332-6901. **Email:** admissions@indwes.edu. **Website:** http://www.indwes.edu. **Application deadlines for fall 2007:** Regular decision: August 1. Early decision: Not offered. Early action: Not offered. Admission cannot be deferred. **Application fee:** $25. Common application is not accepted. **To apply online, go to:** http://www.indwes.edu/admissions. **Admissions requirements/recommendations:** High school units required (recommended): English: (4); Mathematics: (4); Science: (4); Foreign language: (2); Social studies: (2); History: (2); Academic electives: (3); Total units: 10 (21). Tests: The college uses SAT or ACT scores in admissions decisions. Either SAT or ACT required. For admission to the fall 2007 entering class, the school will accept: ACT without writing. Campus visit: Recommended. Admissions interview: Neither required nor recommended. Off-campus interview: Not available. **Factors that count in admissions decisions:** *Academic:* Secondary school record: Very important. Class rank: Important. Letters of recommendation: Very important. Standardized test scores: Very important. Essay: Not considered. *Nonacademic:* Interview: Considered. Extracurricular activities: Considered. Talent/ability: Considered. Character/personal qualities: Very important. Alumni/ae relationship: Considered. Geographical residence: Not considered. State residency: Not considered. Religious affiliation/commitment: Considered. Minority status: Not considered. Volunteer work: Not considered. Work experience: Not considered. **Other schools with the greatest overlap in appli-**

cants: Azusa Pacific University; Baylor University; Cedarville University; Taylor University; Wheaton College. **Admissions statistics for the fall 2005 entering class:** Total applicants: 2,105. Total accepted: 1,722. 36% were from out of state. Overall acceptance rate: 82%. Size of waiting list: 0 applicants; enrolled from waiting list: 0. **Credentials of fall 2005 freshmen:** 22% ranked in the top 10 percent of their high school class; 47% were in the top 25 percent, and 85% were in the top half. (Proportion submitting class standing: 87%.) **Average high school grade point average:** 3.5. **First-year students who submitted SAT scores:** 68%. Scores (25/75 percentile): Verbal: 440-655, Math: 430-648, Combined: 870-1303. **First-year students submitting ACT scores:** 63%. Scores (25/75 percentile): English: 18-30, Math: 17-28, Composite: 19-28.

ACADEMICS

Year founded: 1920. **Academic calendar:** Semester. **Degrees offered:** certificate, associate, bachelor's, post-bachelor's certificate, master's, doctorate. **Most popular majors:** 17% philosophy and religious studies, 13% nursing, 11% education, 11% psychology, 10% business administration and management. **Major fields of study:** area, ethnic, cultural, and gender studies; biological and biomedical sciences; business, management, marketing, and related support services; communication, journalism, and related programs; computer and information sciences and support services; education; English language and literature/letters; foreign languages, literatures, and linguistics; health professions and related clinical sciences; history; legal professions and studies; liberal arts and sciences studies, and humanities; mathematics and statistics; multi/interdisciplinary studies; parks, recreation, leisure, and fitness studies; philosophy and religious studies; physical sciences; psychology; public administration and social service professions; security and protective services; social sciences; theology and religious vocations; visual and performing arts. **Areas of required coursework:** arts/fine arts, humanities, computer literacy, mathematics, English (including composition), philosophy, sciences (biological or physical), history, social science. **Pre-professional programs:** pre-law, pre-medicine, pre-theology. **Special academic programs:** accelerated program, cooperative (work-study plan) program, cross-registration, distance learning, double major, dual enrollment, English as a Second Language (ESL), honors program, independent study, internships, liberal arts/career combination, student-designed major, study abroad, teacher certificate program, other. **Teacher certification offered in:** early childhood, special education, elementary, middle/junior high, adult education, secondary. **Cooperative education programs:** business, education, health professions, humanities, technologies. **Reserve Officers Training Corps (ROTC):** Army ROTC: Offered at cooperating institution (Ball State University). **Faculty and instruction (2005-2006):** Total instructional faculty: 156 full-time, 88 part-time (55% men; 45% women; 2% minorities). Full-time faculty with Ph.D. or other terminal degree: 56%. Student/faculty ratio: 16/1. Classes of fewer than 20 students: 60%; of 20 to 49 students: 36%; of 50 or more students: 5%. **Freshmen returning for sophomore year:** 80%. **Graduation rates:** Four-year: 57%; five-year: 66%; six-year: 62%.

COSTS AND FINANCIAL AID

Financial aid office: (765) 677-2116. **Financial aid:** Priority filing date for institution's financial aid form: March 1.

CAMPUS LIFE AND EXTRACURRICULAR ACTIVITIES

Campus housing available (% using): women's dorms (55%), men's dorms (40%), apartment for single students (2%), other housing options (3%). Students who live in college-owned, operated, or affiliated housing: 72%. **Student employment:** During the 2005-2006 academic year, 20% of undergraduates worked on campus. Average per-year earnings: $1,500. **Clubs and organizations:** Number of student organizations: 40. Activities include: choral groups, concert band, drama/theater, jazz band, literary magazine, music ensembles, musical theater, opera, pep band, radio station, student government, student newspaper, student film society, symphony orchestra, television station, yearbook. Number of fraternities: 0; sororities: 0. Average proportion of students who stay on campus on weekends: 60%. **Sports program (2005-2006):** Member of NAIA. *Men's intercollegiate varsity sports:* baseball, basketball, cross-country, golf, soccer, tennis, track and field (indoor), track and field (outdoor). *Women's intercollegiate varsity sports:* basketball, cross-country, soccer, softball, tennis, track and field (indoor), track and field (outdoor), volleyball.

SERVICES AND FACILITIES

Basic services: nonremedial tutoring, placement service, health service. **Remedial assistance:** reading, math, writing, study skills, other. **Counseling services:** minority student, career, personal, academic, older student, psychological, religious. **For learning-disabled students:** School does not offer a structured program with separate admission and additional fees. Total undergraduates in learning-disabled program or receiving services: 26. Services include: reading machines, tape recorders, videotaped classes, untimed tests, note-taking services, oral tests, learning center, readers, extended time for tests, tutors, priority registration, priority seating, texts on tape, exams on tape or computer, other testing accomodations. **Library:** Number of titles: 141,236; number of current serial subscriptions: 76,011. **Information technology resources:** Students are not required to lease or own a computer. Number of campus computers available to all students: 300. School has a wireless network. Approximate number of users that can be accommodated: 1,000. Proportion of college-owned housing units wired for high-speed internet access: 100%. **Campus safety:** Security services offered: 24-hour foot and vehicle patrols, late-night transport/escort service, 24-hour emergency telephones, lighted pathways/sidewalks, controlled dormitory access (key, security card, etc).

TRANSFER AND INTERNATIONAL STUDENTS
Transfer students: May apply for admission for the following academic terms: Fall, Spring, Summer. Applicants need a minimum number of credits to apply. For fall 2005: Transfer applicants enrolled: 122. **International students:** Number of foreign undergraduates: 12. Number of countries represented: 11. Minimum TOEFL score required: 550 (paper); 213 (computer). Average TOEFL score: 555 (paper).

Manchester College

- **Address:** 604 E. College Avenue, North Manchester, IN 46962
- **Website:** http://www.manchester.edu
- **Private; Religious affiliation:** Church of the Brethren
- **Enrollment:** 1,056 full-time; 38 part-time

KEY STATS
- ✔ **U.S News College Ranking:** 20, Comp. Coll.–Bachelor's (Midwest)
- ✔ **SAT Score (25th/75th percentile):** 930-1160
- ✔ **Tuition:** 2006-2007: $20,500

Selectivity: Selective	Room/board: $7,260
Acceptance rate: 73%	Average debt: $18,254
Student/faculty ratio: 14/1	Proportion who borrowed: 70%

UNDERGRADUATE STUDENT BODY STATS
2005-2006 enrollment: 1,056 full-time; 38 part-time. Men: 47%; women: 53%. **Ethnic makeup:** African American: 3%; Asian American: 1%; Hispanic: 2%; White: 87%; International: 6%. **Religious preference:** Roman Catholic: 11%; Protestant: 43%; Muslim: 1%; No preference: 15%; Unknown: 18%; Church of the Brethren: 12%.

ADMISSIONS FACTS AND FIGURES
Phone: (800) 852-3648. **Email:** admitinfo@manchester.edu. **Website:** http://www.manchester.edu. **Application deadlines for fall 2007:** Regular decision: Rolling. Early decision: Not offered. Early action: Not offered. Admission can be deferred. **Application fee:** $25. Common application is accepted. **To apply online, go to:** http://admissions.manchester.edu/apply/index.cfm. **Admissions requirements/recommendations:** High school units required (recommended): English: 4 (4); Mathematics: 2 (3); Science: 2 (3); Foreign language: 2 (2); Social studies: 2 (2); History: 1 (2); Academic electives: 1 (2); Total units: 14 (17). Tests: The college uses SAT or ACT scores in admissions decisions. Either SAT or ACT required. For admission to the fall 2007 entering class, the school will accept: ACT with writing, ACT without writing. Campus visit: Recommended. Admissions interview: Neither required nor recommended. **Factors that count in admissions decisions: *Academic:*** Secondary school record: Very important. Class rank: Considered. Letters of recommendation: Important. Standardized test scores: Important. Essay: Not considered. ***Nonacademic:*** Interview: Considered. Extracurricular activities: Not considered. Talent/ability: Considered. Character/personal qualities: Considered. Alumni/ae relationship: Considered. Geographical residence: Not considered. State residency: Not considered. Religious affiliation/commitment: Considered. Minority status: Not considered. Volunteer work: Not considered. Work experience: Not considered. **Admissions statistics for the fall 2005 entering class:** Total applicants: 1,487. Total accepted: 1,089. Freshmen enrolled: 330; 8% were from out of state. Overall acceptance rate: 73%. **Credentials of fall 2005 freshmen:** 22% ranked in the top 10 percent of their high school class; 50% were in the top 25 percent, and 85% were in the top half. (Proportion submitting class standing: 94%.) **First-year students who submitted SAT scores:** 82%. Scores (25/75 percentile): Verbal: 460-580, Math: 470-580, Combined: 930-1160. **First-year students submitting ACT scores:** 36%. Scores (25/75 percentile): English: N/A, Math: N/A, Composite: 18-24.

ACADEMICS
Year founded: 1889. **Academic calendar:** 4-1-4. **Degrees offered:** associate, bachelor's, master's. **Most popular majors:** 36% education, 24% business, management, marketing, and related support services, 6% psychology, 6% social sciences, 5% parks, recreation, leisure, and fitness studies. **Major fields of study:** biological and biomedical sciences; business, management, marketing, and related support services; communication, journalism, and related programs; computer and information sciences and support services; education; engineering; English language and literature/letters; foreign languages, literatures, and linguistics; health professions and related clinical sciences; history; mathematics and statistics; multi/interdisciplinary studies; natural resources and conservation; philosophy and religious studies; physical sciences; psychology; public administration and social service professions; social sciences; visual and performing arts. **Areas of required coursework:** arts/fine arts, humanities, mathematics, English (including composition), philosophy, sciences (biological or physical), history, social science. **Pre-professional programs:** pre-law, pre-dentistry, pre-medicine, pre-theology, pre-veterinary science, pre-optometry, pre-pharmacy. **Special academic programs:** cross-registration, double major, dual enrollment, exchange student program (domestic), honors program, independent study, internships, liberal arts/career combination, student-designed major, study abroad, teacher certificate program. **Teacher certification offered in:** early childhood, elementary, middle/junior high, secondary. **Faculty and instruction (2005-2006):** Total instructional faculty: 68 full-time, 21 part-time (62% men; 38% women; 7% minorities). Full-time faculty with Ph.D. or other terminal degree: 93%. Student/faculty ratio: 14/1. Classes of fewer than 20 students: 58%; of 20 to 49 students: 41%; of 50 or more students: 1%. **Advanced Placement and International Baccalaureate credit:** AP tests may be used for: Credit and/or placement. International Baccalaureate exams may be used for: Credit and/or placement. **Freshmen returning for sophomore year:** 70%. **Graduation rates:** Six-year: 52%.

COSTS AND FINANCIAL AID
Financial aid office: (260) 982-5066. **Expenses (2006-2007):** Tuition and fees 2006-2007: $20,500; room/board: $7,260. Estimated books and supplies: $550; transportation: $550; personal expenses: $900. **Financial aid:** Priority filing date for institution's financial aid form: March 1. In 2005-2006, 94% of undergraduates applied for financial aid. Of those, 86% were determined to have financial need; 43% had their need fully met. Average financial aid package (proportion receiving): $17,375 (85%). Average amount of gift aid, such as scholarships or grants (proportion receiving): $13,794 (85%). Average amount of self-help aid, such as work study or loans (proportion receiving): $3,633 (84%). Average need-based loan (excluding PLUS or other private loans): $3,202. Among students who received need-based aid, the average percentage of need met: 88%. Among students who received aid based on merit, the average award (and the proportion receiving): $8,648 (6%). Average amount of debt of borrowers graduating in 2005: $18,254. Proportion who borrowed: 70%.

CAMPUS LIFE AND EXTRACURRICULAR ACTIVITIES
Campus housing available: coed dorms, women's dorms, apartments for married students, apartment for single students, special housing for disabled students. Students who live in college-owned, operated, or affiliated housing: 74%. **Student employment:** During the 2005-2006 academic year, 25% of undergraduates worked on campus. Average per-year earnings: $1,500. **Clubs and organizations:** Number of student organizations: 55. Activities include: choral groups, concert band, dance, drama/theater, jazz band, literary magazine, music ensembles, musical theater, pep band, radio station, student government, student newspaper, symphony orchestra, yearbook. Number of fraternities: 0; sororities: 0. Average proportion of students who stay on campus on weekends: 75%. **Sports program (2005-2006):** Member of NCAA III. **Men's intercollegiate varsity sports:** baseball, basketball, cross-country, football, golf, soccer, tennis, track and field (indoor), track and field (outdoor), wrestling. **Women's intercollegiate varsity sports:** basketball, cross-country, golf, soccer, softball, tennis, track and field (indoor), track and field (outdoor), volleyball.

SERVICES AND FACILITIES

Basic services: nonremedial tutoring, placement service, health service, health insurance. **Remedial assistance:** study skills. **Counseling services:** minority student, career, personal, academic, psychological, birth control, religious. **For learning-disabled students:** School does not offer a structured program with separate admission and additional fees. Services include: tape recorders, untimed tests, note-taking services, oral tests, learning center, readers, extended time for tests, tutors. **Information technology resources:** Students are not required to lease or own a computer. Number of campus computers available to all students: 169. School does not have a wireless network. Proportion of college-owned housing units wired for high-speed internet access: 100%. **Campus safety:** Security services offered: 24-hour foot and vehicle patrols, late-night transport/escort service, 24-hour emergency telephones, lighted pathways/sidewalks, controlled dormitory access (key, security card, etc).

TRANSFER AND INTERNATIONAL STUDENTS

Transfer students: May apply for admission for the following academic terms: Fall, Winter, Spring, Summer. Applicants do not need a minimum number of credits to apply. For fall 2005: Transfer applications received: 73. Transfer applicants offered admission: 42. Transfer applicants enrolled: 30. **International students:** Number of foreign undergraduates: 66 (6% of student body). Minimum TOEFL score required: 550 (paper); 213 (computer).

Marian College

- **Address:** 3200 Cold Spring Road, Indianapolis, IN 46222
- **Website:** http://www.marian.edu
- **Private; Religious affiliation:** Roman Catholic
- **Enrollment:** 1,088 full-time; 578 part-time

KEY STATS

- ✔ **U.S News College Ranking:** 52, Comp. Coll.–Bachelor's (Midwest)
- ✔ **SAT Score (25th/75th percentile):** 910-1130
- ✔ **Tuition:** 2006-2007: $19,900

Selectivity: Selective	**Room/board:** $6,900
Acceptance rate: 85%	**Average debt:** $20,197
Student/faculty ratio: 14/1	**Proportion who borrowed:** 75%

UNDERGRADUATE STUDENT BODY STATS

2005-2006 enrollment: 1,088 full-time; 578 part-time. Men: 26%; women: 74%. **Ethnic makeup:** African American: 14%; American-Indian: 1%; Asian American: 1%; Hispanic: 1%; White: 81%; International: 2%. **Religious preference:** Protestant: 30%; Unknown: 30%; Roman Catholic: 39%; Other: 1%.

ADMISSIONS FACTS AND FIGURES

Phone: (317) 955-6300. **Email:** admissions@marian.edu. **Website:** http://www.marian.edu. **Application deadlines for fall 2007:** Regular decision: August 1. Early decision: Not offered. Early action: Not offered. Admission cannot be deferred. **Application fee:** $20. Common application is not accepted. **Admissions requirements/recommendations:** High school units required (recommended): English: 4 (4); Mathematics: 2 (3); Science: 2 (2); Foreign language: 1 (2); Social studies: 1 (1); History: 1 (1); Academic electives: 2 (2); Total units: 13 (15). Tests: The college uses SAT or ACT scores in admissions decisions. Either SAT or ACT required. For admission to the fall 2007 entering class, the school will accept: ACT with writing. Campus visit: Recommended. Admissions interview: Recommended. Off-campus interview: Not available. **Factors that count in admissions decisions:** *Academic:* Secondary school record: Considered. Class rank: Important. Letters of recommendation: Important. Standardized test scores: Very important. Essay: Considered. *Nonacademic:* Interview: Considered. Extracurricular activities: Considered. Talent/ability: Considered. Character/personal qualities: Considered. Alumni/ae relationship: Considered. Geographical residence: Not considered. State residency: Not considered. Religious affiliation/commitment: Not considered. Minority status: Not considered. Volunteer work: Considered. Work experience: Not considered. **Other schools with the greatest overlap in applicants:** Ball State University; Franklin College; Indiana University–Bloomington; Indiana University-Purdue University–Indianapolis; University of Indianapolis. **Admissions statistics for the fall 2005 entering class:** Total applicants: 657. Total accepted: 557. Freshmen enrolled: 191; 8% were from out of state. Overall acceptance rate: 85%. **Credentials of fall 2005 freshmen:** 15% ranked

in the top 10 percent of their high school class; 42% were in the top 25 percent, and 72% were in the top half. (Proportion submitting class standing: 89%.) **Average high school grade point average:** 3.2. **First-year students who submitted SAT scores:** 81%. Scores (25/75 percentile): Verbal: 460-560, Math: 450-570, Combined: 910-1130. **First-year students submitting ACT scores:** 40%. Scores (25/75 percentile): English: 17-23, Math: 16-23, Composite: 18-23.

ACADEMICS

Year founded: 1851. **Academic calendar:** Semester. **Degrees offered:** certificate, associate, bachelor's, master's. **Most popular majors:** 34% business, management, marketing, and related support services, 17% health professions and related clinical sciences, 9% education, 8% parks, recreation, leisure, and fitness studies, 6% psychology. **Major fields of study:** biological and biomedical sciences; business, management, marketing, and related support services; communication, journalism, and related programs; education; English language and literature/letters; foreign languages, literatures, and linguistics; health professions and related clinical sciences; history; mathematics and statistics; parks, recreation, leisure, and fitness studies; philosophy and religious studies; physical sciences; psychology; science technologies/technicians; social sciences; theology and religious vocations; visual and performing arts. **Areas of required coursework:** humanities, mathematics, English (including composition), philosophy, foreign languages, sciences (biological or physical), history, social science, other. **Pre-professional programs:** pre-law, pre-dentistry, pre-medicine, pre-theology, pre-veterinary science, pre-pharmacy. **Special academic programs (% participation):** accelerated program (5%), cooperative (work-study plan) program (1%), cross-registration (5%), double major (10%), dual enrollment,(2%), honors program (12%), independent study (10%), internships (25%), student-designed major (2%), study abroad (4%), teacher certificate program (20%). **Teacher certification offered in:** early childhood, special education, elementary, middle/junior high, secondary, bilingual/bicultural. **Cooperative education programs:** art, business, computer science, education, health professions, humanities, natural science, social/behavioral science. **Reserve Officers Training Corps (ROTC):** Army ROTC: Offered at cooperating institution (Indiana University-Purdue University-Indianapolis). **Faculty and instruction (2005-2006):** Total instructional faculty: 72 full-time, 61 part-time (47% men; 53% women; 6% minorities). Full-time faculty with Ph.D. or other terminal degree: 61%. Student/faculty ratio: 14/1. Classes of fewer than 20 students: 67%; of 20 to 49 students: 31%; of 50 or more students: 2%. **Advanced Placement and International Baccalaureate credit:** AP tests may be used for: Placement only. Scores accepted: 3, 4, 5. International Baccalaureate exams may be used for: Credit and/or placement. **Freshmen returning for sophomore year:** 69%. **Graduation rates:** Four-year: 35%; five-year: 48%; six-year: 49%. **Graduate study:** 10% of students pursue further study immediately upon graduation; 15% within one year. Fields in which graduates pursue further study: law, 13%; medicine, 6%; theology (or the seminary), 6%; education, 15%; arts and sciences, 60%.

COSTS AND FINANCIAL AID

Financial aid office: (317) 955-6040. **Expenses (2006-2007):** Tuition and fees 2006-2007: $19,900; room/board: $6,900. Estimated books and supplies: $700; transportation: $1,083; personal expenses: $2,474. **Financial aid:** Priority filing date for institution's financial aid form: March 10. In 2005-2006, 88% of undergraduates applied for financial aid. Of those, 79% were determined to have financial need; 33% had their need fully met. Average financial aid package (proportion receiving): $15,345 (79%). Average amount of gift aid, such as scholarships or grants (proportion receiving): $5,044 (49%). Average amount of self-help aid, such as work study or loans (proportion receiving): $4,046 (49%). Average need-based loan (excluding PLUS or other private loans): $3,302. Among students who received need-based aid, the average percentage of need met: 72%. Among students who received aid based on merit, the average award (and the proportion receiving): $6,901 (12%). The average athletic scholarship (and the proportion receiving): $6,749 (4%). Average amount of debt of borrowers graduating in 2005: $20,197. Proportion who borrowed: 75%.

CAMPUS LIFE AND EXTRACURRICULAR ACTIVITIES

Campus housing available (% using): coed dorms (41%), women's dorms (49%), apartments for married students (0%), apartment for single students (5%), cooperative housing (0%), other housing options (5%). Students who live in college-owned, operated, or affiliated housing: 42%. **Student employment:** During the 2005-2006 academic year, 25% of undergraduates worked on campus. Average per-year earnings: $2,000. **Clubs and organizations:** Number of student organizations: 35. Activities include: choral groups, concert band, dance, drama/theater, jazz band, literary magazine, music ensembles, musical theater, pep band, student government, student newspaper, yearbook. Number of fraternities: 0; sororities: 0. Average proportion of students who stay on campus on weekends: 70%. **Sports program (2005-2006):** Member of NAIA. *Men's intercollegiate varsity sports:* baseball, basketball, cheerleading, cross-country, golf, soccer, tennis, track and field (indoor), track and field (outdoor), cycling. *Women's intercollegiate varsity sports:* basketball, cheerleading, cross-country, cycling, golf, soccer, softball, tennis, track and field (indoor), track and field (outdoor), volleyball.

SERVICES AND FACILITIES

Basic services: nonremedial tutoring, placement service, health service. **Remedial assistance:** reading, math, writing, study skills. **Counseling services:** career, personal, academic, psychological, religious. **For learning-disabled students:** School does not offer a structured program with separate admission and additional fees. Total undergraduates in learning-disabled program or receiving services: 68. Services include: remedial math, remedial English, reading machines, remedial reading, tape recorders, other special classes, diagnostic testing service, untimed tests, note-taking services, learning center, readers, extended time for tests, tutors, substitution of courses, other testing accomodations, waiver of foreign language degree requirement. **Library:** Number of titles: 134,000; number of current serial subscriptions: 336. **Information technology resources:** Students are not required to lease or own a computer. Number of campus computers available to all students: 150. School does not have a wireless network. Proportion of college-owned housing units wired for high-speed internet access: 100%. **Campus safety:** Security services offered: 24-hour foot and vehicle patrols, late-night transport/escort service, lighted pathways/sidewalks, controlled dormitory access (key, security card, etc).

TRANSFER AND INTERNATIONAL STUDENTS

Transfer students: May apply for admission for the following academic terms: Fall, Spring, Summer. Applicants need a minimum number of credits to apply. For fall 2005: Transfer applications received: 630. Transfer applicants offered admission: 335. Transfer applicants enrolled: 122. **International students:** Number of foreign undergraduates: 22 (2% of student body). Number of countries represented: 5. Minimum TOEFL score required: 550 (paper); 213 (computer). Average TOEFL score: 550 (paper).

Martin University

- Address: PO Box 18567, 2171 Avondale Place, Indianapolis, IN 46218
- Website: http://www.martin.edu
- Private
- Enrollment: N/A

KEY STATS

✔ **U.S News College Ranking:** fourth tier, Comp. Coll.–Bachelor's (Midwest)
✔ **SAT or ACT Score (25th/75th percentile):** N/A
✔ **Tuition:** N/A

Selectivity: Less selective	Room/board: N/A
Acceptance rate: N/A	Average debt: N/A
Student/faculty ratio: N/A	Proportion who borrowed: N/A

Oakland City University

- Address: 138 N. Lucretia Street, Oakland City, IN 47660
- Website: http://www.oak.edu
- Private; Religious affiliation: General Baptist
- Enrollment: 1,275 full-time; 409 part-time

KEY STATS

✔ **U.S News College Ranking:** fourth tier, Universities–Master's (Midwest)
✔ **ACT Score (25th/75th percentile):** 17-23
✔ **Tuition:** N/A

Selectivity: Selective	Room/board: N/A
Acceptance rate: 52%	Average debt: N/A
Student/faculty ratio: N/A	Proportion who borrowed: N/A

UNDERGRADUATE STUDENT BODY STATS

2005-2006 enrollment: 1,275 full-time; 409 part-time. Men: 45%; women: 55%. **Ethnic makeup:** African American: 10%; Asian American: 1%; Hispanic: 2%; White: 85%; International: 2%.

ADMISSIONS FACTS AND FIGURES

Phone: (800) 737-5125. **Email:** ocuadmit@oak.edu. **Website:** http://www.oak.edu. **Application deadlines for fall 2007:** Regular decision: August 1. Early decision: Not offered. Early action: Not offered. Admission can be deferred. **Application fee:** $35. Common application is accepted. **Admissions requirements/recommendations:** High school units required (recommended): English: (4); Mathematics: (3); Science: (3); Foreign language: (0); Social studies: (2); History: (0); Academic electives: (0); Total units: (12). Tests: The college uses SAT or ACT scores in admissions decisions. SAT required. For admission to the fall 2007 entering class, the school will accept: ACT with writing, ACT without writing. Campus visit: Required. Admissions interview: Required. Off-campus interview: May be arranged. **Factors that count in admissions decisions:** *Academic:* Secondary school record: Very important. Class rank: Considered. Letters of recommendation: Considered. Standardized test scores: Very important. Essay: Considered. *Nonacademic:* Interview: Important. Extracurricular activities: Not considered. Talent/ability: Considered. Character/personal qualities: Important. Alumni/ae relationship: Not considered. Geographical residence: Not considered. State residency: Not considered. Religious affiliation/commitment: Not considered. Minority status: Not considered. Volunteer work: Considered. Work experience: Not considered. **Admissions statistics for the fall 2005 entering class:** Total applicants: 402. Total accepted: 208. Freshmen enrolled: 208; 10% were from out of state. Overall acceptance rate: 52%. **Size of waiting list:** 0 applicants; enrolled from waiting list: 0. **Credentials of fall 2005 freshmen:** 5% ranked in the top 10 percent of their high school class; 23% were in the top 25 percent, and 62% were in the top half. (Proportion submitting class standing: 100%.) **Average high school grade point average:** 3.0. **First-year students who submitted SAT scores:** 57%. Scores (25/75 percentile): Verbal: 430-580, Math: 440-600, Combined: 870-1180. **First-year students submitting ACT scores:** 61%. Scores (25/75 percentile): English: 15-21, Math: 18-23, Composite: 17-23.

ACADEMICS

Year founded: 1885. **Academic calendar:** Semester. **Degrees offered:** certificate, associate, bachelor's, master's, first professional certificate, doctorate. **Most popular majors:** 50% business, management, marketing, and related support services, 16% education, 10% history, 6% philosophy and religious studies, 5% liberal arts and sciences studies, and humanities. **Major fields of study:** biological and biomedical sciences; business, management, marketing, and related support services; computer and information sciences and support services; education; English language and literature/letters; liberal arts and sciences studies, and humanities; mathematics and statistics; philosophy and religious studies; security and protective services; social sciences; visual and performing arts. **Areas of required coursework:** arts/fine arts, humanities, computer literacy, mathematics, English (including composition), philosophy, sciences (biological or physical), history, social science. **Special academic programs:** accelerated program, cooperative (work-study plan) program, distance learning, double major, dual enrollment, external degree program, honors program, independent study, internships, liberal arts/career combination, teacher certificate program. **Teacher certification offered in:** early childhood, special education, elementary, secondary. **Faculty and instruction (2005-2006):** Total instructional faculty: 21 full-time, 22 part-time. Classes of fewer than 20 students: 69%; of 20 to 49 students: 30%; of 50 or more students: 1%. **Advanced Placement and International Baccalaureate credit:** AP tests may be used for: Credit only. Scores accepted: 3. **Freshmen returning for sophomore year:** 63%. **Graduation rates:** Four-year: 51%; five-year: 57%; six-year: 37%. **Graduate study:** 30% of students pursue further study immediately upon graduation.

COSTS AND FINANCIAL AID

Financial aid office: (812) 749-1224.

CAMPUS LIFE AND EXTRACURRICULAR ACTIVITIES

Campus housing available: women's dorms, men's dorms, apartments for married students, apartment for single students. Students who live in college-owned, operated, or affiliated housing: 47%. **Student employment:** During the 2005-2006 academic year, 5% of undergraduates worked on campus. Activities include: choral groups, drama/theater, music ensembles, pep band, student government, student newspaper, yearbook. Number of fraternities: 0; sororities: 0. Average proportion of students who stay on campus on weekends: 10%. **Sports program (2005-2006):** Member of NAIA.

Men's intercollegiate varsity sports: baseball, basketball, cross-country, golf, soccer. *Women's intercollegiate varsity sports:* basketball, cross-country, golf, soccer, softball, volleyball.

SERVICES AND FACILITIES
Remedial assistance: math, writing. **Counseling services:** academic. **Library:** Number of titles: 87,724; number of current serial subscriptions: 222. **Information technology resources:** Students are not required to lease or own a computer. Number of campus computers available to all students: 92. School does not have a wireless network. Proportion of college-owned housing units wired for high-speed internet access: 100%. **Campus safety:** Security services offered: lighted pathways/sidewalks, controlled dormitory access (key, security card, etc).

TRANSFER AND INTERNATIONAL STUDENTS
Transfer students: May apply for admission for the following academic terms: Fall, Spring, Summer. Applicants do not need a minimum number of credits to apply. For fall 2005: Transfer applications received: 229. Transfer applicants offered admission: 163. Transfer applicants enrolled: 115. **International students:** Number of foreign undergraduates: 35 (2% of student body). Minimum TOEFL score required: 500 (paper). Average TOEFL score: 510 (paper).

Purdue University–Calumet

- **Address:** 2200 169th Street, Hammond, IN 46323-2094
- **Website:** http://www.calumet.purdue.edu/
- **Public**
- **Enrollment:** 5,029 full-time; 3,330 part-time

KEY STATS
- ✔ **U.S News College Ranking:** fourth tier, Universities–Master's (Midwest)
- ✔ **SAT Score (25th/75th percentile):** 790-1020
- ✔ **Tuition:** 2006-2007: $5,043 in state, $11,290 out of state

Selectivity: Less selective	**Room/board:** $5,513
Acceptance rate: 80%	**Average debt:** $15,687
Student/faculty ratio: 18/1	**Proportion who borrowed:** 56%

UNDERGRADUATE STUDENT BODY STATS
2005-2006 enrollment: 5,029 full-time; 3,330 part-time. Men: 43%; women: 57%. **Ethnic makeup:** African American: 16%; Asian American: 1%; Hispanic: 14%; White: 67%; International: 1%.

ADMISSIONS FACTS AND FIGURES
Phone: (219) 989-2213. **Email:** adms@calumet.purdue.edu. **Website:** http://www.calumet.purdue.edu/. **Application deadlines for fall 2007:** Regular decision: September 1. Early decision: Not offered. Early action: Not offered. Admission can be deferred. Common application is accepted. **To apply online, go to:** http://www.calumet.purdue.edu/admissions/. **Admissions requirements/recommendations:** High school units required (recommended): English: 4 (4); Mathematics: 2 (2); Science: 1 (2); Foreign language: 2 (2); Social studies: 1 (1); History: 1 (1); Total units: 14 (14). Tests: The college uses SAT or ACT scores in admissions decisions. Neither SAT nor ACT required. For admission to the fall 2007 entering class, the school will accept: ACT with writing. Campus visit: Recommended. Admissions interview: Neither required nor recommended. Off-campus interview: Not available. **Factors that count in admissions decisions:** *Academic:* Secondary school record: Very important. Class rank: Important. Letters of recommendation: Not considered. Standardized test scores: Very important. Essay: Not considered. *Nonacademic:* Interview: Not considered. Extracurricular activities: Not considered. Talent/ability: Not considered. Character/personal qualities: Not considered. Alumni/ae relationship: Not considered. Geographical residence: Not considered. State residency: Not considered. Religious affiliation/commitment: Not considered. Minority status: Not considered. Volunteer work: Not considered. Work experience: Not considered. **Other schools with the greatest overlap in applicants:** Ball State University; Indiana University Northwest; Indiana University–Bloomington; Purdue University–West Lafayette; Valparaiso University. **Admissions statistics for the fall 2005 entering class:** Total applicants: 2,405. Total accepted: 1,916. Freshmen enrolled: 1,252; 11% were from out of state. Overall acceptance rate: 80%. **Credentials of fall 2005 freshmen:** 7% ranked in the top 10 percent of their high school class; 22% were in the top 25 percent, and 52%

were in the top half. (Proportion submitting class standing: 95%.) **First-year students who submitted SAT scores:** 71%. Scores (25/75 percentile): Verbal: 400-510, Math: 390-510, Combined: 790-1020. **First-year students submitting ACT scores:** 21%. Scores (25/75 percentile): English: N/A, Math: N/A, Composite: N/A.

ACADEMICS
Year founded: 1946. **Academic calendar:** Semester. **Degrees offered:** certificate, associate, transfer-associate, terminal-associate, bachelor's, post-bachelor's certificate, master's. **Most popular majors:** 16% business administration and management, 8% computer and information sciences and support services, 7% communication studies/speech communication and rhetoric, 7% elementary education and teaching, 7% engineering. **Major fields of study:** area, ethnic, cultural, and gender studies; biological and biomedical sciences; business, management, marketing, and related support services; communication, journalism, and related programs; communications technologies/technicians and support services; computer and information sciences and support services; education; engineering; engineering technologies/technicians; English language and literature/letters; family and consumer sciences/human sciences; foreign languages, literatures, and linguistics; health professions and related clinical sciences; history; mathematics and statistics; parks, recreation, leisure, and fitness studies; philosophy and religious studies; physical sciences; psychology; security and protective services; social sciences. **Areas of required coursework:** humanities, computer literacy, mathematics, English (including composition), sciences (biological or physical), social science, other. **Pre-professional programs:** pre-law, pre-dentistry, pre-medicine, pre-veterinary science, pre-optometry, pre-pharmacy. **Special academic programs (% participation):** accelerated program, cooperative (work-study plan) program (0%), cross-registration, distance learning, double major, dual enrollment, English as a Second Language (ESL), honors program (0%), independent study, internships (7%), study abroad, teacher certificate program (7%), other. **Teacher certification offered in:** special education, elementary, middle/junior high, secondary. **Cooperative education programs:** engineering, technologies. **Faculty and instruction (2005-2006):** Total instructional faculty: 275 full-time, 190 part-time (51% men; 49% women; 15% minorities). Full-time faculty with Ph.D. or other terminal degree: 63%. Student/faculty ratio: 18/1. Classes of fewer than 20 students: 25%; of 20 to 49 students: 70%; of 50 or more students: 6%. **Advanced Placement and International Baccalaureate credit:** AP tests may be used for: Credit only. Scores accepted: 3, 4, 5. International Baccalaureate exams may be used for: Credit and/or placement. **Freshmen returning for sophomore year:** 63%. **Graduation rates:** Four-year: 4%; five-year: 15%; six-year: 21%.

COSTS AND FINANCIAL AID
Financial aid office: (219) 989-2301. **Expenses (2006-2007):** Tuition and fees 2006-2007: $5,043 in state, $11,290 out of state; room/board: $5,513. Estimated books and supplies: $1,000; transportation: $1,797; personal expenses: $1,720. **Financial aid:** Priority filing date for institution's financial aid form: March 10. In 2005-2006, 71% of undergraduates applied for financial aid. Of those, 44% were determined to have financial need; Average financial aid package (proportion receiving): $5,886 (42%). Average amount of gift aid, such as scholarships or grants (proportion receiving): N/A (29%). Average amount of self-help aid, such as work study or loans (proportion receiving): N/A (31%). Among students who received need-based aid, the average percentage of need met: 24%. Among students who received aid based on merit, the average award (and the proportion receiving): $1,597 (4%). The average athletic scholarship (and the proportion receiving): $2,820 (0%). Average amount of debt of borrowers graduating in 2005: $15,687. Proportion who borrowed: 56%.

CAMPUS LIFE AND EXTRACURRICULAR ACTIVITIES
Campus housing available (% using): apartment for single students (100%). Students who live in college-owned, operated, or affiliated housing: 4%. **Student employment:** During the 2005-2006 academic year, 10% of undergraduates worked on campus. Average per-year earnings: $3,300. **Clubs and organizations:** Number of student organizations: 57. Activities include: choral groups, dance, drama/theater, literary magazine, musical theater, student government, student newspaper. Number of fraternities: 2; sororities: 1. Proportion of men in fraternities: 1%; of women in sororities: 1%. Average proportion of students who stay on campus on weekends: 4%. **Sports program (2005-2006):** Member of NAIA. *Men's intercollegiate varsity sports:* basketball. *Women's intercollegiate varsity sports:* basketball.

SERVICES AND FACILITIES

Basic services: nonremedial tutoring, placement service, day care, health service, health insurance. **Remedial assistance:** reading, math, writing, study skills, other. **Counseling services:** minority student, career, personal, veteran student, academic, older student, psychological, other. **For learning-disabled students:** School does not offer a structured program with separate admission and additional fees. Total undergraduates in learning-disabled program or receiving services: 50. Services include: reading machines, tape recorders, note-taking services, oral tests, readers, extended time for tests, tutors, priority seating, proofreading services, substitution of courses, texts on tape, typist/scribe, exams on tape or computer, other testing accomodations, other. **Library:** Number of titles: 266,432; number of current serial subscriptions: 1,228. **Information technology resources:** Students are not required to lease or own a computer. Number of campus computers available to all students: 1,300. School has a wireless network. Approximate number of users that can be accommodated: 250. Proportion of college-owned housing units wired for high-speed internet access: 100%. **Campus safety:** Security services offered: 24-hour foot and vehicle patrols, 24-hour emergency telephones, lighted pathways/sidewalks, student patrols, controlled dormitory access (key, security card, etc).

TRANSFER AND INTERNATIONAL STUDENTS

Transfer students: May apply for admission for the following academic terms: Fall, Spring, Summer. Applicants need a minimum number of credits to apply. **International students:** Number of foreign undergraduates: 73 (1% of student body). Number of countries represented: 27. Minimum TOEFL score required: 550 (paper); 213 (computer). Average TOEFL score: 562 (paper).

Purdue University–North Central

- **Address:** 1401 S. U.S. Highway 421, Westville, IN 46391
- **Website:** http://www.pnc.edu
- **Public**
- **Enrollment:** 2,053 full-time; 1,434 part-time

KEY STATS

✔ **U.S News College Ranking:** fourth tier, Comp. Coll.–Bachelor's (Midwest)
✔ **SAT Score (25th/75th percentile):** 850-1080
✔ **Tuition:** 2006-2007: $5,567 in state, $13,007 out of state

Selectivity: Less selective	**Room/board:** N/A
Acceptance rate: 96%	**Average debt:** $14,009
Student/faculty ratio: 17/1	**Proportion who borrowed:** 53%

UNDERGRADUATE STUDENT BODY STATS

2005-2006 enrollment: 2,053 full-time; 1,434 part-time. Men: 41%; women: 59%. **Ethnic makeup:** African American: 4%; American-Indian: 1%; Asian American: 1%; Hispanic: 4%; White: 89%.

ADMISSIONS FACTS AND FIGURES

Phone: (219) 785-5455. **Email:** admissions@pnc.edu. **Website:** http://www.pnc.edu. **Application deadlines for fall 2007:** Regular decision: Rolling. Early decision: Not offered. Early action: Not offered. Admission can be deferred. Common application is not accepted. **To apply online, go to:** http://www.pnc.edu/admissions/applying.html. **Admissions requirements/recommendations:** High school units required (recommended): English: 4 (4); Mathematics: 3 (4); Science: 2 (3); Foreign language: 0 (4); Social studies: 1 (2); History: 0 (1); Academic electives: 5 (5); Total units: 17 (26). Tests: The college uses SAT or ACT scores in admissions decisions. Neither SAT nor ACT required. For admission to the fall 2007 entering class, the school will accept: ACT with writing, ACT without writing. Campus visit: Recommended. Admissions interview: Recommended. Off-campus interview: May be arranged. **Factors that count in admissions decisions:** *Academic:* Secondary school record: Very important. Class rank: Important. Letters of recommendation: Considered. Standardized test scores: Important. Essay: Not considered. *Nonacademic:* Interview: Considered. Extracurricular activities: Considered. Talent/ability: Considered. Character/personal qualities: Considered. Alumni/ae relationship: Not considered. Geographical residence: Not considered. State residency: Not considered. Religious affiliation/commitment: Not considered. Minority status: Not considered. Volunteer work: Considered. Work experience: Considered. **Other schools with the greatest overlap in applicants:** Ball

State University; Indiana University Northwest; Indiana University–South Bend; Purdue University–Calumet; Purdue University–West Lafayette. **Admissions statistics for the fall 2005 entering class:** Total applicants: 998. Total accepted: 955. Freshmen enrolled: 683; 1% were from out of state. Overall acceptance rate: 96%. **Credentials of fall 2005 freshmen:** 4% ranked in the top 10 percent of their high school class; 17% were in the top 25 percent, and 49% were in the top half. (Proportion submitting class standing: 83%.) **Average high school grade point average:** 2.8. **First-year students who submitted SAT scores:** 60%. Scores (25/75 percentile): Verbal: 420-540, Math: 430-540, Combined: 850-1080. **First-year students submitting ACT scores:** 15%. Scores (25/75 percentile): English: 16-22, Math: 17-23, Composite: 18-22.

ACADEMICS

Year founded: 1946. **Academic calendar:** Semester. **Degrees offered:** certificate, associate, terminal-associate, bachelor's, master's. **Most popular majors:** 32% business, management, marketing, and related support services, 27% liberal arts and sciences/liberal studies, 14% engineering technologies/technicians, 10% elementary education and teaching, 7% computer and information sciences and support services. **Major fields of study:** biological and biomedical sciences; business, management, marketing, and related support services; communication, journalism, and related programs; computer and information sciences and support services; education; engineering technologies/technicians; English language and literature/letters; health professions and related clinical sciences; liberal arts and sciences studies, and humanities; social sciences. **Areas of required coursework:** humanities, computer literacy, mathematics, English (including composition), sciences (biological or physical), social science. **Special academic programs:** distance learning, dual enrollment, independent study, internships, teacher certificate program. **Teacher certification offered in:** elementary. **Faculty and instruction (2005-2006):** Total instructional faculty: 103 full-time, 150 part-time (53% men; 47% women; 12% minorities). Full-time faculty with Ph.D. or other terminal degree: 53%. Student/faculty ratio: 17/1. Classes of fewer than 20 students: 56%; of 20 to 49 students: 42%; of 50 or more students: 2%. **Advanced Placement and International Baccalaureate credit:** AP tests may be used for: Credit and/or placement. Scores accepted: 3, 4, 5. International Baccalaureate exams may be used for: Credit only. **Freshmen returning for sophomore year:** 53%. **Graduation rates:** Four-year: 2%; five-year: 9%; six-year: 11%.

COSTS AND FINANCIAL AID

Financial aid office: (219) 785-5279. **Expenses (2006-2007):** Tuition and fees 2006-2007: $5,567 in state, $13,007 out of state; room/board: N/A. Estimated books and supplies: $1,372; transportation: $2,000; personal expenses: $2,190. **Financial aid:** Priority filing date for institution's financial aid form: March 1. In 2005-2006, 77% of undergraduates applied for financial aid. Of those, 60% were determined to have financial need; 18% had their need fully met. Average financial aid package (proportion receiving): $6,808 (57%). Average amount of gift aid, such as scholarships or grants (proportion receiving): $4,335 (40%). Average amount of self-help aid, such as work study or loans (proportion receiving): $2,909 (42%). Average need-based loan (excluding PLUS or other private loans): $2,854. Among students who received need-based aid, the average percentage of need met: 51%. Among students who received aid based on merit, the average award (and the proportion receiving): $1,846 (5%). The average athletic scholarship (and the proportion receiving): $969 (1%). Average amount of debt of borrowers graduating in 2005: $14,009. Proportion who borrowed: 53%.

CAMPUS LIFE AND EXTRACURRICULAR ACTIVITIES

Students who live in college-owned, operated, or affiliated housing: 0%. **Student employment:** During the 2005-2006 academic year, 8% of undergraduates worked on campus. Average per-year earnings: $779. **Clubs and organizations:** Number of student organizations: 25. Activities include: student government, student newspaper. Number of fraternities: 0; sororities: 0. **Sports program (2005-2006):** Member of NAIA. *Men's intercollegiate varsity sports:* baseball, basketball. *Women's intercollegiate varsity sports:* softball.

SERVICES AND FACILITIES

Basic services: placement service, day care, health insurance. **Remedial assistance:** reading, math, writing, study skills. **Counseling services:** career, personal, academic. **For learning-disabled students:** School does not offer a structured program with separate admission and additional fees. Services include: remedial math, remedial English, remedial reading, tape recorders, note-taking services, oral tests, learning center, readers, extended time for tests, tutors, texts on tape, other testing accomodations. **Library:** Number of titles: 87,160; number of current serial subscriptions: 395. **Information technology resources:** Students are not required to lease or own a computer. Number of campus computers available to all students: 496. School has a wireless network. Approximate number of users that can be accommodated: 250. **Campus safety:** Security services offered: 24-hour foot and vehicle patrols, late-night transport/escort service, 24-hour emergency telephones, lighted pathways/sidewalks.

TRANSFER AND INTERNATIONAL STUDENTS

Transfer students: May apply for admission for the following academic terms: Fall, Spring, Summer. Applicants do not need a minimum number of credits to apply. For fall 2005: Transfer applications received: 276. Transfer applicants offered admission: 272. Transfer applicants enrolled: 189. **International students:** Number of foreign undergraduates: 8. Number of countries represented: 8. Minimum TOEFL score required: 550 (paper); 213 (computer).

Purdue University–West Lafayette

- **Address:** Schleman Hall, 475 Stadium Mall Drive, West Lafayette, IN 47907-2050
- **Website:** http://www.purdue.edu
- **Public**
- **Enrollment:** 29,196 full-time; 1,679 part-time

KEY STATS

✔ **U.S News College Ranking:** 64, National Universities
✔ **SAT Score (25th/75th percentile):** 1030-1260
✔ **Tuition:** 2006-2007: $7,096 in state, $21,266 out of state
  Selectivity: More selective   **Room/board:** $7,140
  Acceptance rate: 85%   **Average debt:** $18,978
  Student/faculty ratio: 14/1   **Proportion who borrowed:** 49%

UNDERGRADUATE STUDENT BODY STATS

2005-2006 enrollment: 29,196 full-time; 1,679 part-time. Men: 59%; women: 41%. **Ethnic makeup:** African American: 4%; Asian American: 5%; Hispanic: 3%; White: 82%; International: 6%.

ADMISSIONS FACTS AND FIGURES

Phone: (765) 494-1776. **Email:** admissions@purdue.edu. **Website:** http://www.purdue.edu. **Application deadlines for fall 2007:** Regular decision: Rolling. Early decision: Not offered. Early action: Not offered. Admission can be deferred. **Application fee:** $30. Common application is accepted. **To apply online, go to:** http://www.purdue.edu/Admissions/Undergrad/. **Admissions requirements/recommendations:** High school units required (recommended): English: 4 (4); Mathematics: 3 (3); Science: 2 (3); Foreign language: 2 (2); Total units: 11 (12). Tests: The college uses SAT or ACT scores in admissions decisions. Either SAT or ACT required. For admission to the fall 2007 entering class, the school will accept: ACT with writing. Campus visit: Recommended. Admissions interview: Neither required nor recommended. Off-campus interview: Not available. **Factors that count in admissions decisions:** *Academic:* Secondary school record: Very important. Class rank: Very important. Letters of recommendation: Considered. Standardized test scores: Very important. Essay: Considered. *Nonacademic:* Interview: Not considered. Extracurricular activities: Considered. Talent/ability: Not considered. Character/personal qualities: Considered. Alumni/ae relationship: Considered. Geographical residence: Considered. State residency: Considered. Religious affiliation/commitment: Not considered. Minority status: Considered. Volunteer work: Considered. Work experience: Considered. **Other schools with the greatest overlap in applicants:** Ball State University; Indiana University–Bloomington; Indiana University–Purdue University–Indianapolis; University of Illinois–Urbana-Champaign; University of Michigan–Ann Arbor. **Admissions statistics for the fall 2005 entering class:** Total applicants: 24,052. Total accepted: 20,432. Freshmen enrolled: 7,110; 29% were from out of state. Overall acceptance rate: 85%. **Credentials of fall 2005 freshmen:** 27% ranked in the top 10 percent of their high school class; 58% were in the top 25 percent, and 90% were in the top half. (Proportion submitting class standing: 78%.) **Average high school grade point average:** 3.4. **First-year students who submitted SAT scores:** 83%. Scores (25/75 percentile): Verbal: 500-610, Math: 530-650, Combined:

1030-1260. **First-year students submitting ACT scores:** 40%. Scores (25/75 percentile): English: 21-28, Math: 23-29, Composite: 23-28.

ACADEMICS

Year founded: 1869. **Academic calendar:** Semester. **Degrees offered:** certificate, associate, terminal-associate, bachelor's, post-bachelor's certificate, master's, first professional, doctorate. **Most popular majors:** 21% liberal arts and sciences studies, and humanities, 20% engineering, 16% business, management, marketing, and related support services, 8% engineering technologies/technicians, 7% agriculture, agriculture operations, and related sciences. **Major fields of study:** agriculture, agriculture operations, and related sciences; architecture and related services; area, ethnic, cultural, and gender studies; biological and biomedical sciences; business, management, marketing, and related support services; communication, journalism, and related programs; computer and information sciences and support services; education; engineering; engineering technologies/technicians; English language and literature/letters; family and consumer sciences/human sciences; foreign languages, literatures, and linguistics; health professions and related clinical sciences; history; liberal arts and sciences studies, and humanities; mathematics and statistics; multi/interdisciplinary studies; natural resources and conservation; philosophy and religious studies; physical sciences; psychology; social sciences; transportation and materials moving; visual and performing arts. **Areas of required coursework:** humanities, computer literacy, mathematics, English (including composition), philosophy, foreign languages, sciences (biological or physical), history, social science. **Pre-professional programs:** pre-law, pre-dentistry, pre-medicine, pre-veterinary science, pre-optometry, pre-pharmacy, other. **Special academic programs (% participation):** accelerated program, cooperative (work-study plan) program, cross-registration, distance learning, double major, dual enrollment, English as a Second Language (ESL), exchange student program (domestic), honors program, independent study, internships, liberal arts/career combination, study abroad (9.2%), teacher certificate program, weekend college. **Teacher certification offered in:** early childhood, special education, elementary, vo-tech, middle/junior high, secondary. **Cooperative education programs:** agriculture, art, business, computer science, education, engineering, health professions, home economics, humanities, natural science, social/behavioral science, technologies, vocational arts. **Reserve Officers Training Corps (ROTC):** Army ROTC: Offered on campus; Navy ROTC: Offered on campus; Air Force ROTC: Offered on campus. **Faculty and instruction (2005-2006):** Total instructional faculty: 1,960 full-time, 333 part-time (70% men; 30% women; 15% minorities). Full-time faculty with Ph.D. or other terminal degree: 98%. Student/faculty ratio: 14/1. Classes of fewer than 20 students: 33%; of 20 to 49 students: 49%; of 50 or more students: 19%. **Advanced Placement and International Baccalaureate credit:** AP tests may be used for: Credit and/or placement. Scores accepted: 3, 4, 5. International Baccalaureate exams may be used for: Credit and/or placement. **Freshmen returning for sophomore year:** 86%. **Graduation rates:** Four-year: 32%; five-year: 61%; six-year: 66%. **Graduate study:** 19% of students pursue further study immediately upon graduation. Fields in which graduates pursue further study: Master of Business Administration (MBA), 2%; law, 11%; medicine, 5%; dentistry, 1%; engineering, 21%; education, 3%; arts and sciences, 33%; veterinary medicine, 3%.

COSTS AND FINANCIAL AID

Financial aid office: (765) 494-5090. **Expenses (2006-2007):** Tuition and fees 2006-2007: $7,096 in state, $21,266 out of state; room/board: $7,140. Estimated books and supplies: $990; transportation: $270; personal expenses: $1,650. **Financial aid:** Priority filing date for institution's financial aid form: March 1. In 2005-2006, 61% of undergraduates applied for financial aid. Of those, 41% were determined to have financial need; 36% had their need fully met. Average financial aid package (proportion receiving): $11,256 (41%). Average amount of gift aid, such as scholarships or grants (proportion receiving): $8,293 (13%). Average amount of self-help aid, such as work study or loans (proportion receiving): $4,269 (36%). Average need-based loan (excluding PLUS or other private loans): $4,107. Among students who received need-based aid, the average percentage of need met: 92%. Among students who received aid based on merit, the average award (and the proportion receiving): $11,431 (14%). The average athletic scholarship (and the proportion receiving): $16,952 (1%). Average amount of debt of borrowers graduating in 2005: $18,978. Proportion who borrowed: 49%.

CAMPUS LIFE AND EXTRACURRICULAR ACTIVITIES

Campus housing available (% using): coed dorms (41%), women's dorms (5%), men's dorms (18%), sorority housing (6%), fraternity housing (8%), apartments for married students (7%), apartment for single students (9%), cooperative housing (2%), other housing options (4%). Students who live in college-owned, operated, or affiliated housing: 30%. **Student employment:** During the 2005-2006 academic year, 21% of undergraduates worked on campus. Average per-year earnings: $1,274. **Clubs and organizations:** Number of student organizations: 747. Activities include: choral groups, concert band, dance, drama/theater, jazz band, literary magazine, marching band, music ensembles, pep band, radio station, student government, student newspaper, student film society, symphony orchestra, yearbook. Number of fraternities: 50; sororities: 29. Proportion of men in fraternities: 18%; of women in sororities: 17%. Average proportion of students who stay on campus on weekends: 60%. **Sports program (2005-2006):** Member of NCAA I. *Men's intercollegiate varsity sports:* baseball, basketball, cross-country, football, golf, swimming and diving, tennis, track and field (indoor), track and field (outdoor), wrestling. *Women's intercollegiate varsity sports:* basketball, cross-country, golf, soccer, softball, swimming and diving, tennis, track and field (indoor), track and field (outdoor), volleyball.

SERVICES AND FACILITIES
Basic services: nonremedial tutoring, women's center, placement service, health service, health insurance. **Remedial assistance:** reading, math, writing, study skills. **Counseling services:** minority student, career, military, personal, veteran student, academic, older student, psychological, birth control. **For learning-disabled students:** School does not offer a structured program with separate admission and additional fees. Total undergraduates in learning-disabled program or receiving services: 164. Services include: reading machines, tape recorders, diagnostic testing service, note-taking services, oral tests, learning center, readers, extended time for tests, priority registration, priority seating, substitution of courses, texts on tape, typist/scribe, exams on tape or computer, other testing accomodations, other. **Library:** Number of titles: 2,475,242; number of current serial subscriptions: 21,598. **Information technology resources:** Students are not required to lease or own a computer. Number of campus computers available to all students: 5,477. School has a wireless network. Approximate number of users that can be accommodated: 30,000. Proportion of college-owned housing units wired for high-speed internet access: 100%. **Campus safety:** Security services offered: 24-hour foot and vehicle patrols, late-night transport/escort service, 24-hour emergency telephones, lighted pathways/sidewalks, student patrols, controlled dormitory access (key, security card, etc).

TRANSFER AND INTERNATIONAL STUDENTS
Transfer students: May apply for admission for the following academic terms: Fall, Spring, Summer. Applicants do not need a minimum number of credits to apply. For fall 2005: Transfer applications received: 2,446. Transfer applicants offered admission: 1,665. Transfer applicants enrolled: 1,046. **International students:** Number of foreign undergraduates: 1834 (6% of student body). Number of countries represented: 125. Minimum TOEFL score required: 550 (paper); 213 (computer). Average TOEFL score: 560 (paper).

Rose-Hulman Institute of Technology

- **Address:** 5500 Wabash Avenue, Terre Haute, IN 47803
- **Website:** http://www.rose-hulman.edu
- **Private**
- **Enrollment:** 1,766 full-time; 9 part-time

KEY STATS
✔ **U.S News College Ranking:** Unranked Specialty School–Engineering
✔ **SAT Score (25th/75th percentile):** 1210-1400
✔ **Tuition:** 2006-2007: $28,995

Selectivity: More selective	Room/board: $7,869
Acceptance rate: 69%	Average debt: $33,105
Student/faculty ratio: 12/1	Proportion who borrowed: 79%

UNDERGRADUATE STUDENT BODY STATS
2005-2006 enrollment: 1,766 full-time; 9 part-time. Men: 81%; women: 19%. **Ethnic makeup:** African American: 2%; Asian American: 4%; Hispanic: 1%; White: 91%; International: 1%.

ADMISSIONS FACTS AND FIGURES
Phone: (812) 877-8213. **Email:** admis.ofc@rose-hulman.edu. **Website:** http://www.rose-hulman.edu. **Application deadlines for fall 2007:** Regular decision: March 1. Early decision: Not offered. Early action: Not offered.

Admission can be deferred. **Application fee:** $40. Common application is accepted. **To apply online, go to:** http://www.rose-hulman.edu/admissions. **Admissions requirements/recommendations:** High school units required (recommended): English: 4; Mathematics: 4 (5); Science: 2 (3); Social studies: 2; Academic electives: 4; Total units: 16. Tests: The college uses SAT or ACT scores in admissions decisions. Either SAT or ACT required. For admission to the fall 2007 entering class, the school will accept: ACT with writing, ACT without writing. Campus visit: Recommended. Admissions interview: Recommended. Off-campus interview: May not be arranged. **Factors that count in admissions decisions:** *Academic:* Secondary school record: Very important. Class rank: Very important. Letters of recommendation: Important. Standardized test scores: Very important. Essay: Not considered. *Nonacademic:* Interview: Considered. Extracurricular activities: Considered. Talent/ability: Considered. Character/personal qualities: Important. Alumni/ae relationship: Considered. Geographical residence: Not considered. State residency: Not considered. Religious affiliation/commitment: Not considered. Minority status: Important. Volunteer work: Considered. Work experience: Considered. **Other schools with the greatest overlap in applicants:** Carnegie Mellon University; Georgia Institute of Technology; Massachusetts Institute of Technology; Purdue University–West Lafayette; University of Illinois–Urbana-Champaign. **Admissions statistics for the fall 2005 entering class:** Total applicants: 3,294. Total accepted: 2,288. Freshmen enrolled: 448; 58% were from out of state. Overall acceptance rate: 69%. **Credentials of fall 2005 freshmen:** 64% ranked in the top 10 percent of their high school class; 93% were in the top 25 percent, and 100% were in the top half. (Proportion submitting class standing: 82%.) **First-year students who submitted SAT scores:** 84%. Scores (25/75 percentile): Verbal: 570-680, Math: 640-720, Combined: 1210-1400. **First-year students submitting ACT scores:** 59%. Scores (25/75 percentile): English: 25-31, Math: 28-33, Composite: 27-32.

ACADEMICS
Year founded: 1874. **Academic calendar:** Quarter. **Degrees offered:** bachelor's, master's. **Most popular majors:** 31% mechanical engineering, 15% chemical engineering, 14% electrical, electronics, and communications engineering, 11% computer engineering, 10% computer science. **Major fields of study:** biological and biomedical sciences; computer and information sciences and support services; engineering; mathematics and statistics; physical sciences; social sciences. **Areas of required coursework:** humanities, computer literacy, mathematics, English (including composition), sciences (biological or physical), social science. **Pre-professional programs:** pre-law, pre-medicine. **Special academic programs (% participation):** accelerated program (12%), cooperative (work-study plan) program (10%), cross-registration, double major (8%), independent study (8%), study abroad (2%). **Cooperative education programs:** computer science, engineering, natural science. **Reserve Officers Training Corps (ROTC):** Army ROTC: Offered on campus; Air Force ROTC: Offered on campus. **Faculty and instruction (2005-2006):** Total instructional faculty: 148 full-time, 7 part-time (82% men; 18% women; 7% minorities). Full-time faculty with Ph.D. or other terminal degree: 100%. Student/faculty ratio: 12/1. Classes of fewer than 20 students: 38%; of 20 to 49 students: 62%; of 50 or more students: 0%. **Advanced Placement and International Baccalaureate credit:** AP tests may be used for: Credit and/or placement. Scores accepted: 4, 5. International Baccalaureate exams may be used for: Credit and/or placement. **Freshmen returning for sophomore year:** 92%. **Graduation rates:** Four-year: 73%; five-year: 81%; six-year: 80%. **Graduate study:** 19% of students pursue further study immediately upon graduation. Fields in which graduates pursue further study: Master of Business Administration (MBA), 10%; law, 2%; medicine, 2%; dentistry, 1%; engineering, 33%; arts and sciences, 2%.

COSTS AND FINANCIAL AID
Financial aid office: (812) 877-8259. **Expenses (2006-2007):** Tuition and fees 2006-2007: $28,995; room/board: $7,869. Estimated books and supplies: $1,500; transportation: $0; personal expenses: $1,500. **Financial aid:** Priority filing date for institution's financial aid form: March 1. In 2005-2006, 80% of undergraduates applied for financial aid. Of those, 69% were determined to have financial need; 12% had their need fully met. Average financial aid package (proportion receiving): $19,591 (69%). Average amount of gift aid, such as scholarships or grants (proportion receiving): $13,595 (68%). Average amount of self-help aid, such as work study or loans (proportion receiving): $7,394 (58%). Average need-based loan (excluding PLUS or other private loans): $6,671. Among students who received need-based aid, the average percentage of need met: 79%. Among students who received aid based on merit, the average award (and the proportion receiving): $6,771 (27%). Average amount of debt of borrowers graduating in 2005: $33,105. Proportion who borrowed: 79%.

CAMPUS LIFE AND EXTRACURRICULAR ACTIVITIES

Campus housing available (% using): coed dorms (38%), men's dorms (22%), sorority housing (2%), fraternity housing (18%), apartment for single students (20%). Students who live in college-owned, operated, or affiliated housing: 60%. **Student employment:** During the 2005-2006 academic year, 25% of undergraduates worked on campus. Average per-year earnings: $1,500. **Clubs and organizations:** Number of student organizations: 88. Activities include: choral groups, concert band, dance, drama/theater, jazz band, literary magazine, music ensembles, musical theater, pep band, radio station, student government, student newspaper, yearbook. Number of fraternities: 8; sororities: 2. Proportion of men in fraternities: 37%; of women in sororities: 43%. Average proportion of students who stay on campus on weekends: 60%. **Sports program (2005-2006):** Member of NCAA III. **Men's intercollegiate varsity sports:** baseball, basketball, cross-country, football, golf, riflery, soccer, swimming and diving, tennis, track and field (indoor), track and field (outdoor), wrestling. **Women's intercollegiate varsity sports:** basketball, cross-country, golf, riflery, soccer, softball, swimming and diving, tennis, track and field (indoor), track and field (outdoor), volleyball.

SERVICES AND FACILITIES

Basic services: nonremedial tutoring, placement service, health service, health insurance. **Remedial assistance:** study skills. **Counseling services:** career, personal, academic, psychological, birth control. **For learning-disabled students:** School does not offer a structured program with separate admission and additional fees. Total undergraduates in learning-disabled program or receiving services: 20. Services include: tape recorders, note-taking services, learning center, extended time for tests, tutors, texts on tape. **Library:** Number of titles: 301; number of current serial subscriptions: 301. **Information technology resources:** Students are required to lease or own a computer. Number of campus computers available to all students: 200. School has a wireless network. Approximate number of users that can be accommodated: 1,000. Proportion of college-owned housing units wired for high-speed internet access: 100%. **Campus safety:** Security services offered: 24-hour foot and vehicle patrols, late-night transport/escort service, 24-hour emergency telephones, lighted pathways/sidewalks, controlled dormitory access (key, security card, etc).

TRANSFER AND INTERNATIONAL STUDENTS

Transfer students: May apply for admission for the following academic terms: Fall. Applicants do not need a minimum number of credits to apply. For fall 2005: Transfer applications received: 91. Transfer applicants offered admission: 46. Transfer applicants enrolled: 21. **International students:** Number of foreign undergraduates: 25 (1% of student body). Number of countries represented: 16. Minimum TOEFL score required: 550 (paper); 210 (computer).

St. Joseph's College

- **Address:** PO Box 890, Rensselaer, IN 47978
- **Website:** http://www.saintjoe.edu
- **Private; Religious affiliation:** Roman Catholic
- **Enrollment:** 886 full-time; 117 part-time

KEY STATS

✔ **U.S News College Ranking:** 38, Comp. Coll.–Bachelor's (Midwest)
✔ **SAT Score (25th/75th percentile):** 880-1100
✔ **Tuition:** 2006-2007: $20,960

Selectivity: Less selective	**Room/board:** $6,720
Acceptance rate: 78%	**Average debt:** $23,417
Student/faculty ratio: 15/1	**Proportion who borrowed:** 74%

UNDERGRADUATE STUDENT BODY STATS

2005-2006 enrollment: 886 full-time; 117 part-time. Men: 38%; women: 62%. **Ethnic makeup:** African American: 6%; Hispanic: 3%; White: 89%; International: 1%. **Religious preference:** Protestant: 38%; No preference: 14%; Roman Catholic: 46%; Other: 2%.

ADMISSIONS FACTS AND FIGURES

Phone: (219) 866-6170. **Email:** admissions@saintjoe.edu. **Website:** http://www.saintjoe.edu. **Application deadlines for fall 2007:** Regular decision: Rolling. Early decision: Not offered. Early action: Not offered. Admission can be deferred. **Application fee:** $25. Common application is not accepted. **Admissions requirements/recommendations:** High school units required (recommended): English: (4); Mathematics: (3); Science: (3); Foreign language: (2); Social studies: (3); Total units: (15). Tests: The college uses SAT or ACT scores in admissions decisions. Either SAT or ACT required. For admission to the fall 2007 entering class, the school will accept: ACT with writing, ACT without writing. Campus visit: Recommended. Admissions interview: Neither required nor recommended. Off-campus interview: Not available. **Factors that count in admissions decisions:** *Academic:* Secondary school record: Very important. Class rank: Very important. Letters of recommendation: Important. Standardized test scores: Very important. Essay: Considered. *Nonacademic:* Interview: Important. Extracurricular activities: Considered. Talent/ability: Considered. Character/personal qualities: Important. Alumni/ae relationship: Considered. Geographical residence: Not considered. State residency: Not considered. Religious affiliation/commitment: Not considered. Minority status: Not considered. Volunteer work: Considered. Work experience: Considered. **Admissions statistics for the fall 2005 entering class:** Total applicants: 1,363. Total accepted: 1,061. Freshmen enrolled: 233; 34% were from out of state. Overall acceptance rate: 78%. **Credentials of fall 2005 freshmen:** 13% ranked in the top 10 percent of their high school class; 40% were in the top 25 percent, and 72% were in the top half. (Proportion submitting class standing: 91%.) **Average high school grade point average:** 3.1. **First-year students who submitted SAT scores:** 61%. Scores (25/75 percentile): Verbal: 430-550, Math: 450-550, Combined: 880-1100. **First-year students submitting ACT scores:** 39%. Scores (25/75 percentile): English: 19-24, Math: 18-24, Composite: 19-24.

ACADEMICS

Year founded: 1889. **Academic calendar:** Semester. **Degrees offered:** certificate, diploma, associate, bachelor's, master's. **Most popular majors:** 21% business, management, marketing, and related support services, 16% education, 11% security and protective services, 7% psychology, 6% social sciences. **Major fields of study:** biological and biomedical sciences; business, management, marketing, and related support services; communication, journalism, and related programs; computer and information sciences and support services; education; English language and literature/letters; health professions and related clinical sciences; history; mathematics and statistics; philosophy and religious studies; physical sciences; psychology; public administration and social service professions; security and protective services; social sciences; theology and religious vocations; visual and performing arts. **Areas of required coursework:** arts/fine arts, humanities, computer literacy, English (including composition), philosophy, sciences (biological or physical), history, social science. **Pre-professional programs:** pre-law, pre-dentistry, pre-medicine, pre-veterinary science, pre-optometry, pre-pharmacy. **Special academic programs (% participation):** accelerated program (7%), cross-registration (4%), double major (4%), dual enrollment (1%), honors program (11%), independent study (26%), internships (15%), liberal arts/career combination (100%), student-designed major (0%), study abroad (0%), teacher certificate program (16%). **Teacher certification offered in:** early childhood, elementary, middle/junior high, secondary. **Cooperative education programs:** education, health professions, social/behavioral science. **Faculty and instruction (2005-2006):** Total instructional faculty: 56 full-time, 21 part-time (58% men; 42% women; 6% minorities). Full-time faculty with Ph.D. or other terminal degree: 79%. Student/faculty ratio: 15/1. Classes of fewer than 20 students: 82%; of 20 to 49 students: 18%; of 50 or more students: 1%. **Advanced Placement and International Baccalaureate credit:** AP tests may be used for: Credit only. Scores accepted: 3. **Freshmen returning for sophomore year:** 70%. **Graduation rates:** Four-year: 42%; five-year: 50%; six-year: 55%. **Graduate study:** 12% of students pursue further study immediately upon graduation. Fields in which graduates pursue further study: law, 20%; medicine, 12%; theology (or the seminary), 4%; education, 20%; arts and sciences, 40%; veterinary medicine, 4%.

COSTS AND FINANCIAL AID

Financial aid office: (219) 866-6163. **Expenses (2006-2007):** Tuition and fees 2006-2007: $20,960; room/board: $6,720. Estimated books and supplies: $700; transportation: $470; personal expenses: $650. **Financial aid:** Priority filing date for institution's financial aid form: March 1. In 2005-2006, 86% of undergraduates applied for financial aid. Of those, 72% were determined to have financial need; 36% had their need fully met. Average financial aid package (proportion receiving): $18,976 (72%). Average amount of gift aid, such as scholarships or grants (proportion receiving): $12,234 (71%). Average amount of self-help aid, such as work study or loans (proportion receiving): $4,467 (50%). Average need-based loan (excluding PLUS or other private loans): $4,299. Among students who received need-based aid, the average percentage of need met: 84%. Among students who received aid based on merit, the average award (and the proportion receiving): $10,042 (14%). The average athletic scholarship (and the proportion receiving): $10,959 (6%). Average amount of debt of borrowers graduating in 2005: $23,417. Proportion who borrowed: 74%.

CAMPUS LIFE AND EXTRACURRICULAR ACTIVITIES

Campus housing available (% using): coed dorms (22%), women's dorms (33%), men's dorms (31%), apartment for single students (14%). Students who live in college-owned, operated, or affiliated housing: 68%. **Student employment:** During the 2005-2006 academic year, 33% of undergraduates worked on campus. Average per-year earnings: $1,500. **Clubs and organizations:** Number of student organizations: 46. Activities include: choral groups, concert band, dance, drama/theater, jazz band, literary magazine, marching band, music ensembles, musical theater, pep band, radio station, student government, student newspaper, student film society, television station. Number of fraternities: 0; sororities: 0. Average proportion of students who stay on campus on weekends: 70%. **Sports program (2005-2006):** Member of NCAA II. *Men's intercollegiate varsity sports:* baseball, basketball, cross-country, football, golf, soccer, tennis, track and field (indoor), track and field (outdoor). *Women's intercollegiate varsity sports:* basketball, cross-country, golf, soccer, softball, tennis, track and field (indoor), track and field (outdoor), volleyball.

SERVICES AND FACILITIES

Basic services: nonremedial tutoring. **Remedial assistance:** reading, writing, study skills. **Counseling services:** career, personal, academic, religious. **For learning-disabled students:** School does not offer a structured program with separate admission and additional fees. Total undergraduates in learning-disabled program or receiving services: 9. Services include: remedial English, tape recorders, other special classes, untimed tests, oral tests, extended time for tests, tutors. **Library:** Number of titles: 156,044; number of current serial subscriptions: 399. **Information technology resources:** Students are not required to lease or own a computer. Number of campus computers available to all students: 69. School has a wireless network. Approximate number of users that can be accommodated: 2,000. Proportion of college-owned housing units wired for high-speed internet access: 100%. **Campus safety:** Security services offered: 24-hour foot and vehicle patrols, late-night transport/escort service, 24-hour emergency telephones, student patrols, controlled dormitory access (key, security card, etc).

TRANSFER AND INTERNATIONAL STUDENTS

Transfer students: May apply for admission for the following academic terms: Fall, Spring. Applicants need a minimum number of credits to apply. For fall 2005: Transfer applications received: 153. Transfer applicants offered admission: 68. Transfer applicants enrolled: 34. **International students:** Number of foreign undergraduates: 9 (1% of student body). Number of countries represented: 4. Minimum TOEFL score required: 550 (paper); 213 (computer).

St. Mary-of-the-Woods College

- **Address:** St.Mary-of-the-Woods, IN 47876
- **Website:** http://www.smwc.edu
- **Private; Religious affiliation:** Roman Catholic
- **Enrollment:** 510 full-time; 1,116 part-time

KEY STATS

✔ **U.S News College Ranking:** 41, Comp. Coll.–Bachelor's (Midwest)
✔ **SAT or ACT Score (25th/75th percentile):** N/A
✔ **Tuition:** 2005-2006: $18,660

Selectivity: Less selective	**Room/board:** $6,820
Acceptance rate: N/A	**Average debt:** $19,113
Student/faculty ratio: N/A	**Proportion who borrowed:** 86%

UNDERGRADUATE STUDENT BODY STATS

2005-2006 enrollment: 510 full-time; 1,116 part-time. Men: 1%; women: 99%. **Ethnic makeup:** African American: 3%; American-Indian: 1%; Hispanic: 1%; White: 95%.

ADMISSIONS FACTS AND FIGURES

Phone: (800) 926-7692. **Email:** smwcadms@smwc.edu. **Website:** http://www.smwc.edu. **Application deadlines for fall 2007:** Regular decision: Rolling. Early decision: Not offered. Early action: Not offered. Admission cannot be deferred. **Application fee:** $30. Common application is not accepted. **Admissions requirements/recommendations:** High school units required (recommended): English: 4; Mathematics: 3; Science: 3; Foreign language: 2; Social studies: 3; History: 0; Academic electives: 0; Total units: 18. Tests: The college uses SAT or ACT scores in admissions decisions. Either SAT or ACT required. Campus visit: Recommended. Admissions interview: Recommended. Off-campus interview: May be arranged. **Factors that count in admissions decisions:** *Academic:* Secondary school record: Very important. Class rank: Important. Letters of recommendation: Important. Standardized test scores: Important. Essay: Important. *Nonacademic:* Interview: Considered. Extracurricular activities: Considered. Talent/ability: Considered. Character/personal qualities: Considered. Alumni/ae relationship: Considered. Geographical residence: Not considered. State residency: Not considered. Religious affiliation/commitment: Not considered. Minority status: Not considered. Volunteer work: Considered. Work experience: Not considered. **Other schools with the greatest overlap in applicants:** Indiana State University; Indiana University–Bloomington; St. Joseph's College. **Size of waiting list:** 0 applicants; enrolled from waiting list: 0.

ACADEMICS

Year founded: 1840. **Academic calendar:** Semester. **Degrees offered:** certificate, associate, bachelor's, post-bachelor's certificate, master's. **Most popular majors:** 33% education, 16% business, management, marketing, and related support services, 14% communication, journalism, and related programs, 5% legal professions and studies, 5% psychology. **Major fields of study:** agriculture, agriculture operations, and related sciences; business, management, marketing, and related support services; communication, journalism, and related programs; computer and information sciences and support services; education; English language and literature/letters; liberal arts and sciences studies, and humanities; psychology; social sciences; theology and religious vocations; visual and performing arts. **Areas of required coursework:** arts/fine arts, humanities, computer literacy, mathematics, English (including composition), philosophy, foreign languages, sciences (biological or physical), history, social science, other. **Pre-professional programs:** pre-law, pre-dentistry, pre-medicine, pre-veterinary science, pre-optometry, pre-pharmacy. **Special academic programs:** accelerated program, cross-registration, distance learning, double major, external degree program, independent study, internships, student-designed major, study abroad, teacher certificate program. **Teacher certification offered in:** early childhood, special education, elementary, middle/junior high, secondary. **Reserve Officers Training Corps (ROTC):** Army ROTC: Offered at cooperating institution (Rose Hulman Institute of Technology); Air Force ROTC: Offered at cooperating institution (Indiana State University). **Faculty and instruction (2005-2006):** Total instructional faculty: N/A. Classes of fewer than 20 students: 92%; of 20 to 49 students: 8%; of 50 or more students: 0%. **Advanced Placement and International Baccalaureate credit:** AP tests may be used for: Credit and/or placement. Scores accepted: 3. International Baccalaureate exams may be used for: Credit and/or placement. **Freshmen returning for sophomore year:** 68%. **Graduation rates:** Four-year: 46%; five-year: 52%; six-year: 54%. **Graduate study:** 25% of students pursue further study immediately upon graduation.

COSTS AND FINANCIAL AID

Financial aid office: (812) 535-5109. **Expenses (2005-2006):** Tuition and fees 2005-2006: $18,660; room/board: $6,820. Estimated books and supplies: $1,000; transportation: $1,000; personal expenses: $800. **Financial aid:** Priority filing date for institution's financial aid form: March 10. In 2005-2006, 100% of undergraduates applied for financial aid. Of those, 100% were determined to have financial need; Average financial aid package (proportion receiving): $12,733 (99%). Average amount of gift aid, such as scholarships or grants (proportion receiving): $9,720 (62%). Average amount of self-help aid, such as work study or loans (proportion receiving): $4,600 (91%). Average need-based loan (excluding PLUS or other private loans): $3,000. Among students who received need-based aid, the average percentage of need met: 79%. Among students who received aid based on merit, the average award (and the proportion receiving): $0 (0%). The average athletic scholarship (and the proportion receiving): $0 (0%). Average amount of debt of borrowers graduating in 2005: $19,113. Proportion who borrowed: 86%.

CAMPUS LIFE AND EXTRACURRICULAR ACTIVITIES

Campus housing available (% using): women's dorms (100%). **Student employment:** During the 2005-2006 academic year, 60% of undergraduates worked on campus. Average per-year earnings: $800. **Clubs and organizations:** Number of student organizations: 30. Activities include: choral groups, concert band, drama/theater, jazz band, literary magazine, music ensembles, musical theater, student government, student newspaper. Number of fraternities: 0; sororities: 0. Average proportion of students who stay on campus on weekends: 50%.

SERVICES AND FACILITIES

Basic services: nonremedial tutoring, placement service, day care. **Remedial assistance:** math, writing, study skills. **Counseling services:** career, personal, academic, psychological, religious. **For learning-disabled students:** School does not offer a structured program with separate admission and additional fees. Total undergraduates in learning-disabled program or receiving services: 13. Services include: remedial math, remedial English, remedial reading, tape recorders, other special classes, untimed tests, note-taking services, oral tests, learning center, readers, extended time for tests, tutors, other testing accomodations. **Library:** Number of titles: 149,705; number of current serial subscriptions: 50. **Information technology resources:** Students are not required to lease or own a computer. Number of campus computers available to all students: 200. School has a wireless network. Approximate number of users that can be accommodated: 500. Proportion of college-owned housing units wired for high-speed internet access: 100%. **Campus safety:** Security services offered: 24-hour foot and vehicle patrols, lighted pathways/sidewalks, controlled dormitory access (key, security card, etc).

TRANSFER AND INTERNATIONAL STUDENTS

Transfer students: May apply for admission for the following academic terms: Fall, Winter. Applicants do not need a minimum number of credits to apply. **International students:** Minimum TOEFL score required: 500 (paper); 173 (computer).

St. Mary's College

- **Address:** Notre Dame, IN 46556
- **Website:** http://www.saintmarys.edu
- **Private; Religious affiliation:** Roman Catholic
- **Enrollment:** 1,366 full-time; 31 part-time

KEY STATS

✔ **U.S News College Ranking:** 1, Comp. Coll.–Bachelor's (Midwest)
✔ **SAT Score (25th/75th percentile):** 1050-1240
✔ **Tuition:** 2006-2007: $25,580

Selectivity: More selective	**Room/board:** $8,425
Acceptance rate: 81%	**Average debt:** $24,617
Student/faculty ratio: 10/1	**Proportion who borrowed:** 68%

UNDERGRADUATE STUDENT BODY STATS

2005-2006 enrollment: 1,366 full-time; 31 part-time. Men: 0%; women: 100%. **Ethnic makeup:** African American: 1%; American-Indian: 1%; Asian American: 2%; Hispanic: 4%; White: 92%; International: 1%. **Religious preference:** Protestant: 14%; No preference: 3%; Roman Catholic: 82%; Other: 1%.

ADMISSIONS FACTS AND FIGURES

Phone: (574) 284-4587. **Email:** admission@saintmarys.edu. **Website:** http://www.saintmarys.edu. **Application deadlines for fall 2007:** Regular decision: Rolling. Early decision: Send application by: November 15; Decision sent by: December 15. Early action: Not offered. Admission can be deferred. **Application fee:** $30. Common application is accepted. **To apply online, go to:** http://www.saintmarys.edu/Considering/Application. **Admissions requirements/recommendations:** High school units required (recommended): English: 4 (4); Mathematics: 3 (4); Science: 2 (4); Foreign language: 2 (4); Academic electives: 3; Total units: 16. Tests: The college uses SAT or ACT scores in admissions decisions. Either SAT or ACT required. For admission to the fall 2007 entering class, the school will accept: ACT with writing, ACT without writing. Campus visit: Neither required nor recommended. Admissions interview: Neither required nor recommended. Off-campus interview: May be arranged. **Factors that count in admissions decisions:** *Academic:* Secondary school record: Very impor-

tant. Class rank: Important. Letters of recommendation: Important. Standardized test scores: Very important. Essay: Very important. *Nonacademic:* Interview: Considered. Extracurricular activities: Important. Talent/ability: Important. Character/personal qualities: Important. Alumni/ae relationship: Considered. Geographical residence: Considered. State residency: Not considered. Religious affiliation/commitment: Not considered. Minority status: Considered. Volunteer work: Considered. Work experience: Considered. **Other schools with the greatest overlap in applicants:** Indiana University–Bloomington; Loyola University Chicago; Purdue University–West Lafayette; University of Michigan–Ann Arbor; University of Notre Dame. **Admissions statistics for the fall 2005 entering class:** Total applicants: 997. Total accepted: 807. Freshmen enrolled: 377; 76% were from out of state. Accepted through early-decision or early-action plans: 19%. Overall acceptance rate: 81%. Early-decision acceptance rate: 85%. Non-early acceptance rate: 80%. **Credentials of fall 2005 freshmen:** 32% ranked in the top 10 percent of their high school class; 66% were in the top 25 percent, and 94% were in the top half. (Proportion submitting class standing: 73%.) **Average high school grade point average:** 3.7. **First-year students who submitted SAT scores:** 74%. Scores (25/75 percentile): Verbal: 530-630, Math: 520-610, Combined: 1050-1240. **First-year students submitting ACT scores:** 67%. Scores (25/75 percentile): English: 23-29, Math: 22-27, Composite: 23-27.

ACADEMICS

Year founded: 1844. **Academic calendar:** Semester. **Degrees offered:** bachelor's. **Most popular majors:** 22% communication studies/speech communication and rhetoric, 15% elementary education and teaching, 10% business administration and management, 7% nursing/registered nurse training (R.N., A.S.N., B.S.N., M.S.N.), 7% psychology. **Major fields of study:** biological and biomedical sciences; business, management, marketing, and related support services; communication, journalism, and related programs; education; English language and literature/letters; foreign languages, literatures, and linguistics; health professions and related clinical sciences; history; liberal arts and sciences studies, and humanities; mathematics and statistics; multi/interdisciplinary studies; philosophy and religious studies; physical sciences; psychology; public administration and social service professions; social sciences; visual and performing arts. **Areas of required coursework:** arts/fine arts, humanities, computer literacy, mathematics, English (including composition), philosophy, foreign languages, sciences (biological or physical), history, social science, other. **Pre-professional programs:** pre-dentistry, pre-medicine, other. **Special academic programs (% participation):** accelerated program (2%), cooperative (work-study plan) program (1%), cross-registration (33%), double major (12%), exchange student program (domestic) (1%), independent study (11%), internships (13%), liberal arts/career combination (0%), student-designed major (1%), study abroad (18%), teacher certificate program (15%). **Teacher certification offered in:** elementary, middle/junior high, secondary. **Cooperative education programs:** engineering, health professions. **Reserve Officers Training Corps (ROTC):** Army ROTC: Offered at cooperating institution (University of Notre Dame); Navy ROTC: Offered at cooperating institution (University of Notre Dame); Air Force ROTC: Offered at cooperating institution (University of Notre Dame). **Faculty and instruction (2005-2006):** Total instructional faculty: 125 full-time, 73 part-time (36% men; 64% women; 9% minorities). Full-time faculty with Ph.D. or other terminal degree: 89%. Student/faculty ratio: 10/1. Classes of fewer than 20 students: 63%; of 20 to 49 students: 35%; of 50 or more students: 2%. **Advanced Placement and International Baccalaureate credit:** AP tests may be used for: Credit and/or placement. Scores accepted: 3, 4, 5. International Baccalaureate exams may be used for: Credit and/or placement. **Freshmen returning for sophomore year:** 85%. **Graduation rates:** Four-year: 69%; five-year: 74%; six-year: 75%. **Graduate study:** 10% of students pursue further study immediately upon graduation; 17% within one year; 31% within five years. Fields in which graduates pursue further study: Master of Business Administration (MBA), 14%; law, 13%; medicine, 3%; dentistry, 1%; theology (or the seminary), 1%; education, 9%; arts and sciences, 31%.

COSTS AND FINANCIAL AID

Financial aid office: (574) 284-4557. **Expenses (2006-2007):** Tuition and fees 2006-2007: $25,580; room/board: $8,425. Estimated books and supplies: $1,000; transportation: $470; personal expenses: $1,200. **Financial aid:** Priority filing date for institution's financial aid form: March 1. In 2005-2006, 75% of undergraduates applied for financial aid. Of those, 70% were determined to have financial need; 19% had their need fully met. Average financial aid package (proportion receiving): $18,964 (70%). Average amount of gift aid, such as scholarships or grants (proportion receiving): $9,405 (61%). Average amount of self-help aid, such as work study or loans (proportion receiving): $4,848 (53%). Average need-based loan (excluding PLUS or other private loans): $2,961. Among students who received need-based aid, the average percentage of need met: 77%. Among students who received aid based on merit, the average award (and the proportion receiving): $7,845 (21%). The average athletic scholarship (and the proportion receiving): $0 (0%). Average amount of debt of borrowers graduating in 2005: $24,617. Proportion who borrowed: 68%.

CAMPUS LIFE AND EXTRACURRICULAR ACTIVITIES

Campus housing available (% using): women's dorms (94%), apartment for single students (6%). Students who live in college-owned, operated, or affiliated housing: 84%. **Student employment:** During the 2005-2006 academic year, 45% of undergraduates worked on campus. Average per-year earnings: $1,800. **Clubs and organizations:** Number of student organizations: 101. Activities include: choral groups, dance, drama/theater, literary magazine, marching band, music ensembles, musical theater, radio station, student government, student newspaper, television station, yearbook. Number of fraternities: 0; sororities: 0. Average proportion of students who stay on campus on weekends: 70%. **Sports program (2005-2006):** Member of NCAA III. *Women's intercollegiate varsity sports:* basketball, cross-country, golf, soccer, softball, swimming and diving, tennis, volleyball.

SERVICES AND FACILITIES

Basic services: women's center, day care, health service. **Remedial assistance:** writing. **Counseling services:** minority student, career, military, personal, academic, psychological, religious. **For learning-disabled students:** School does not offer a structured program with separate admission and additional fees. **Library:** Number of titles: 228,012; number of current serial subscriptions: 634. **Information technology resources:** Students are not required to lease or own a computer. Number of campus computers available to all students: 200. School has a wireless network. Approximate number of users that can be accommodated: 1,000. Proportion of college-owned housing units wired for high-speed internet access: 100%. **Campus safety:** Security services offered: 24-hour foot and vehicle patrols, late-night transport/escort service, 24-hour emergency telephones, lighted pathways/sidewalks, controlled dormitory access (key, security card, etc).

TRANSFER AND INTERNATIONAL STUDENTS

Transfer students: May apply for admission for the following academic terms: Fall, Spring. Applicants do not need a minimum number of credits to apply. For fall 2005: Transfer applications received: 90. Transfer applicants offered admission: 45. Transfer applicants enrolled: 30. **International students:** Number of foreign undergraduates: 8 (1% of student body). Number of countries represented: 9. Minimum TOEFL score required: 500 (paper). Average TOEFL score: 550 (paper).

Taylor University

- **Address:** 236 W. Reade Avenue, Upland, IN 46989-1002
- **Website:** http://www.taylor.edu
- **Private; Religious affiliation:** Christian interdenominational
- **Enrollment:** 1,794 full-time; 57 part-time

KEY STATS

✔ **U.S News College Ranking:** 3, Comp. Coll.–Bachelor's (Midwest)
✔ **ACT Score (25th/75th percentile):** 23-29
✔ **Tuition:** 2006-2007: $22,028

Selectivity: More selective	**Room/board:** $5,867
Acceptance rate: 82%	**Average debt:** $17,910
Student/faculty ratio: 12/1	**Proportion who borrowed:** 60%

UNDERGRADUATE STUDENT BODY STATS

2005-2006 enrollment: 1,794 full-time; 57 part-time. Men: 45%; women: 55%. **Ethnic makeup:** African American: 2%; Asian American: 1%; Hispanic: 2%; White: 94%; International: 1%.

ADMISSIONS FACTS AND FIGURES

Phone: (765) 998-5134. **Email:** admissions_u@taylor.edu. **Website:** http://www.taylor.edu. **Application deadlines for fall 2007:** Regular decision: September 1. Early decision: Not offered. Early action: Send application by: December 1; Decision sent by: December 20. Admission can be deferred. **Application fee:** $25. Common application is not accepted. **Admissions**

requirements/recommendations: High school units required (recommended): English: 4 (4); Mathematics: 3 (4); Science: 3 (4); Foreign language: (2); Social studies: 2; Total units: 15 (24). Tests: The college uses SAT or ACT scores in admissions decisions. Either SAT or ACT required. For admission to the fall 2007 entering class, the school will accept: ACT without writing. Campus visit: Recommended. Admissions interview: Required. Off-campus interview: May be arranged. **Factors that count in admissions decisions:** *Academic:* Secondary school record: Very important. Class rank: Important. Letters of recommendation: Very important. Standardized test scores: Very important. Essay: Very important. *Nonacademic:* Interview: Very important. Extracurricular activities: Important. Talent/ability: Considered. Character/personal qualities: Very important. Alumni/ae relationship: Considered. Geographical residence: Not considered. State residency: Considered. Religious affiliation/commitment: Very important. Minority status: Important. Volunteer work: Important. Work experience: Not considered. **Other schools with the greatest overlap in applicants:** Anderson University; Bethel University; Cedarville University; Indiana Wesleyan University; Wheaton College. **Admissions statistics for the fall 2005 entering class:** Total applicants: 1,517. Total accepted: 1,237. Freshmen enrolled: 461; 69% were from out of state. Accepted through early-decision or early-action plans: 78%. Overall acceptance rate: 82%. Non-early acceptance rate: 66%. **Size of waiting list:** 91 applicants; enrolled from waiting list: 31. **Credentials of fall 2005 freshmen:** 37% ranked in the top 10 percent of their high school class; 68% were in the top 25 percent, and 90% were in the top half. (Proportion submitting class standing: 100%.) **Average high school grade point average:** 3.8. First-year students who submitted SAT scores: 64%. Scores (25/75 percentile): Verbal: 540-660; Math: 550-660; Combined: 1090-1320. **First-year students submitting ACT scores:** 67%. Scores (25/75 percentile): English: 24-30, Math: 23-29, Composite: 23-29.

ACADEMICS

Year founded: 1846. **Academic calendar:** 4-1-4. **Degrees offered:** associate, bachelor's, master's. **Most popular majors:** 12% psychology, 11% business administration and management, 10% elementary education and teaching, 5% biology/biological sciences, 5% communication studies/speech communication and rhetoric. **Major fields of study:** biological and biomedical sciences; business, management, marketing, and related support services; communication, journalism, and related programs; computer and information sciences and support services; education; engineering; English language and literature/letters; foreign languages, literatures, and linguistics; history; mathematics and statistics; multi/interdisciplinary studies; natural resources and conservation; parks, recreation, leisure, and fitness studies; philosophy and religious studies; physical sciences; psychology; public administration and social service professions; social sciences; theology and religious vocations; visual and performing arts. **Areas of required coursework:** arts/fine arts, humanities, computer literacy, mathematics, English (including composition), philosophy, sciences (biological or physical), history, social science. **Pre-professional programs:** pre-medicine, other. **Special academic programs (% participation):** cross-registration (1%), distance learning (10%), double major (5%), dual enrollment (1%), English as a Second Language (ESL) (0%), exchange student program (domestic) (0%), honors program (10%), independent study (23%), internships (82%), student-designed major (1%), study abroad (43%), teacher certificate program (18%). **Teacher certification offered in:** early childhood, elementary, middle/junior high, secondary. **Faculty and instruction (2005-2006):** Total instructional faculty: 128 full-time, 59 part-time (64% men; 36% women; 3% minorities). Full-time faculty with Ph.D. or other terminal degree: 73%. Student/faculty ratio: 12/1. Classes of fewer than 20 students: 55%; of 20 to 49 students: 43%; of 50 or more students: 2%. **Advanced Placement and International Baccalaureate credit:** AP tests may be used for: Credit and/or placement. Scores accepted: 3, 4, 5. International Baccalaureate exams may be used for: Credit only. **Freshmen returning for sophomore year:** 88%. **Graduation rates:** Four-year: 73%; five-year: 78%; six-year: 79%. **Graduate study:** 16% of students pursue further study within one year; 17% within five years. Fields in which graduates pursue further study: law, 2%; medicine, 1%; dentistry, 1%; engineering, 1%; theology (or the seminary), 2%; education, 1%; arts and sciences, 2%.

COSTS AND FINANCIAL AID

Financial aid office: (765) 998-5358. **Expenses (2006-2007):** Tuition and fees 2006-2007: $22,028; room/board: $5,867. Estimated books and supplies: $800; transportation: $0; personal expenses: $1,600. **Financial aid:** In 2005-2006, 70% of undergraduates applied for financial aid. Of those, 57% were determined to have financial need; 26% had their need fully met. Average financial aid package (proportion receiving): $14,069 (57%). Average amount of gift aid, such as scholarships or grants (proportion receiving):

$10,631 (52%). Average amount of self-help aid, such as work study or loans (proportion receiving): $4,882 (50%). Average need-based loan (excluding PLUS or other private loans): $4,537. Among students who received need-based aid, the average percentage of need met: 78%. Among students who received aid based on merit, the average award (and the proportion receiving): $3,898 (23%). The average athletic scholarship (and the proportion receiving): $5,415 (3%). Average amount of debt of borrowers graduating in 2005: $17,910. Proportion who borrowed: 60%.

CAMPUS LIFE AND EXTRACURRICULAR ACTIVITIES

Campus housing available (% using): coed dorms (22%), women's dorms (34%), men's dorms (37%), apartments for married students (1%), apartment for single students (6%). Students who live in college-owned, operated, or affiliated housing: 91%. **Student employment:** During the 2005-2006 academic year, 10% of undergraduates worked on campus. Average per-year earnings: $700. **Clubs and organizations:** Number of student organizations: 62. Activities include: choral groups, concert band, drama/theater, jazz band, literary magazine, music ensembles, musical theater, pep band, radio station, student government, student newspaper, symphony orchestra, television station, yearbook. Number of fraternities: 0; sororities: 0. Average proportion of students who stay on campus on weekends: 80%. **Sports program (2005-2006):** Member of NAIA. *Men's intercollegiate varsity sports:* baseball, basketball, cross-country, football, golf, soccer, tennis, track and field (indoor), track and field (outdoor). *Women's intercollegiate varsity sports:* basketball, cross-country, soccer, softball, tennis, track and field (indoor), track and field (outdoor), volleyball.

SERVICES AND FACILITIES

Basic services: nonremedial tutoring, placement service, health service, health insurance. **Remedial assistance:** reading, math, writing, study skills. **Counseling services:** minority student, career, personal, academic, psychological, religious. **For learning-disabled students:** School does not offer a structured program with separate admission and additional fees. Total undergraduates in learning-disabled program or receiving services: 33. Services include: remedial math, remedial English, reading machines, remedial reading, tape recorders, note-taking services, oral tests, learning center, readers, extended time for tests, tutors, priority registration, texts on tape, exams on tape or computer, other testing accomodations, other. **Library:** Number of titles: 186,441; number of current serial subscriptions: 634. **Information technology resources:** Students are not required to lease or own a computer. Number of campus computers available to all students: 250. School has a wireless network. Approximate number of users that can be accommodated: 1,500. Proportion of college-owned housing units wired for high-speed internet access: 100%. **Campus safety:** Security services offered: 24-hour foot and vehicle patrols, late-night transport/escort service, 24-hour emergency telephones, lighted pathways/sidewalks, controlled dormitory access (key, security card, etc).

TRANSFER AND INTERNATIONAL STUDENTS

Transfer students: May apply for admission for the following academic terms: Fall, Winter, Spring, Summer. Applicants do not need a minimum number of credits to apply. For fall 2005: Transfer applications received: 131. Transfer applicants offered admission: 83. Transfer applicants enrolled: 45. **International students:** Number of foreign undergraduates: 18 (1% of student body). Number of countries represented: 22. Minimum TOEFL score required: 550 (paper); 213 (computer).

Tri-State University

- Address: 1 University Avenue, Angola, IN 46703
- Website: http://www.tristate.edu
- Private
- Enrollment: 1,000 full-time; 168 part-time

KEY STATS

- ✔ **U.S News College Ranking:** 46, Comp. Coll.–Bachelor's (Midwest)
- ✔ **SAT Score (25th/75th percentile):** 940-1170
- ✔ **Tuition:** 2006-2007: $21,210

Selectivity: Selective	**Room/board:** $6,240
Acceptance rate: 75%	**Average debt:** $15,400
Student/faculty ratio: 13/1	**Proportion who borrowed:** 61%

UNDERGRADUATE STUDENT BODY STATS

2005-2006 enrollment: 1,000 full-time; 168 part-time. Men: 66%; women: 34%. **Ethnic makeup:** African American: 3%; Asian American: 1%; Hispanic: 1%; White: 94%; International: 1%.

ADMISSIONS FACTS AND FIGURES

Phone: (260) 665-4132. **Email:** admit@tristate.edu. **Website:** http://www.tristate.edu. **Application deadlines for fall 2007:** Regular decision: June 1. Early decision: Not offered. Early action: Not offered. Admission can be deferred. Common application is accepted. **Admissions requirements/recommendations:** High school units required (recommended): English: 4; Mathematics: 3; Science: 2; Social studies: 2; History: 2; Academic electives: 5; Total units: 17. Tests: The college uses SAT or ACT scores in admissions decisions. Either SAT or ACT required. For admission to the fall 2007 entering class, the school will accept: ACT with writing, ACT without writing. Campus visit: Recommended. Admissions interview: Recommended. **Factors that count in admissions decisions: *Academic:*** Secondary school record: Very important. Class rank: Very important. Letters of recommendation: Considered. Standardized test scores: Important. Essay: Considered. *Nonacademic:* Interview: Important. Extracurricular activities: Important. Talent/ability: Considered. Character/personal qualities: Considered. Alumni/ae relationship: Considered. Geographical residence: Not considered. State residency: Not considered. Religious affiliation/commitment: Not considered. Minority status: Not considered. Volunteer work: Considered. Work experience: Considered. **Other schools with the greatest overlap in applicants:** Ball State University; Manchester College; Purdue University–West Lafayette; Rose-Hulman Institute of Technology; University of St. Francis. **Admissions statistics for the fall 2005 entering class:** Total applicants: 1,649. Total accepted: 1,229. Freshmen enrolled: 305; 34% were from out of state. Overall acceptance rate: 75%. **Credentials of fall 2005 freshmen:** 17% ranked in the top 10 percent of their high school class; 44% were in the top 25 percent, and 74% were in the top half. (Proportion submitting class standing: 92%.) **Average high school grade point average:** 3.3. **First-year students who submitted SAT scores:** 57%. Scores (25/75 percentile): Verbal: 450-570, Math: 490-600, Combined: 940-1170. **First-year students submitting ACT scores:** 43%. Scores (25/75 percentile): English: 18-24, Math: 19-26, Composite: 20-25.

ACADEMICS

Year founded: 1884. **Academic calendar:** Semester. **Degrees offered:** associate, bachelor's, master's. **Most popular majors:** 39% engineering, 17% education, 16% business/commerce, 10% criminal justice/law enforcement administration, 4% computer and information sciences. **Major fields of study:** biological and biomedical sciences; business, management, marketing, and related support services; communication, journalism, and related programs; computer and information sciences and support services; education; engineering; engineering technologies/technicians; English language and literature/letters; health professions and related clinical sciences; history; liberal arts and sciences studies, and humanities; mathematics and statistics; natural resources and conservation; parks, recreation, leisure, and fitness studies; physical sciences; psychology; security and protective services; social sciences. **Areas of required coursework:** humanities, computer literacy, mathematics, English (including composition), sciences (biological or physical), social science. **Pre-professional programs:** pre-medicine. **Special academic programs (% participation):** cooperative (work-study plan) program (10%), distance learning (10%), double major (5%), honors program (5%), internships (10%), teacher certificate program (10%). **Teacher certification offered in:** elementary, middle/junior high, secondary. **Cooperative education programs:** business, computer science, engineering, natural science, technologies. **Faculty and instruction (2005-2006):** Total instructional faculty: 69 full-time, 30 part-time (74% men; 26% women; 4% minorities). Full-time faculty with Ph.D. or other terminal degree: 65%. Student/faculty ratio: 13/1. Classes of fewer than 20 students: 60%; of 20 to 49 students: 40%; of 50 or more students: 0%. **Advanced Placement and International Baccalaureate credit:** AP tests may be used for: Credit and/or placement. Scores accepted: 3, 4, 5. **Freshmen returning for sophomore year:** 67%. **Graduation rates:** Four-year: 39%; five-year: 54%; six-year: 54%. **Graduate study:** 30% of students pursue further study immediately upon graduation; 10% within one year; 20% within five years. Fields in which graduates pursue further study: Master of Business Administration (MBA), 25%; law, 20%; medicine, 3%; dentistry, 2%; engineering, 20%; education, 10%; arts and sciences, 20%.

COSTS AND FINANCIAL AID

Financial aid office: (260) 665-4175. **Expenses (2006-2007):** Tuition and fees 2006-2007: $21,210; room/board: $6,240. Estimated books and supplies:

$1,200; transportation: $1,500; personal expenses: $2,100. **Financial aid:** Priority filing date for institution's financial aid form: March 10; deadline: June 1. In 2005-2006, 100% of undergraduates applied for financial aid. Of those, 73% were determined to have financial need; 100% had their need fully met. Average financial aid package (proportion receiving): $13,327 (73%). Average amount of gift aid, such as scholarships or grants (proportion receiving): $3,552 (34%). Average amount of self-help aid, such as work study or loans (proportion receiving): $3,157 (73%). Average need-based loan (excluding PLUS or other private loans): $3,753. Among students who received need-based aid, the average percentage of need met: 90%. Among students who received aid based on merit, the average award (and the proportion receiving): $6,758 (31%). The average athletic scholarship (and the proportion receiving): $0 (0%). Average amount of debt of borrowers graduating in 2005: $15,400. Proportion who borrowed: 61%.

CAMPUS LIFE AND EXTRACURRICULAR ACTIVITIES

Campus housing available (% using): coed dorms (91%), apartment for single students (9%). Students who live in college-owned, operated, or affiliated housing: 40%. **Student employment:** During the 2005-2006 academic year, 28% of undergraduates worked on campus. Average per-year earnings: $1,377. Activities include: choral groups, dance, drama/theater, pep band, radio station, student government, student newspaper, yearbook. Number of fraternities: 8; sororities: 4. Proportion of men in fraternities: 25%; of women in sororities: 15%. Average proportion of students who stay on campus on weekends: 60%. **Sports program (2005-2006):** Member of NCAA III. *Men's intercollegiate varsity sports:* baseball, basketball, cross-country, football, golf, soccer, swimming and diving, tennis, track and field (indoor), track and field (outdoor), wrestling. *Women's intercollegiate varsity sports:* basketball, cross-country, golf, soccer, softball, tennis, track and field (indoor), track and field (outdoor), volleyball.

SERVICES AND FACILITIES

Basic services: nonremedial tutoring, placement service. **Remedial assistance:** math, writing, study skills. **Counseling services:** career, personal, academic, older student, psychological. **Library:** Number of titles: 74,448; number of current serial subscriptions: 359. **Information technology resources:** Students are not required to lease or own a computer. Number of campus computers available to all students: 200. School has a wireless network. Approximate number of users that can be accommodated: 50. Proportion of college-owned housing units wired for high-speed internet access: 100%. **Campus safety:** Security services offered: 24-hour foot and vehicle patrols, late-night transport/escort service, 24-hour emergency telephones, lighted pathways/sidewalks, controlled dormitory access (key, security card, etc).

TRANSFER AND INTERNATIONAL STUDENTS

Transfer students: May apply for admission for the following academic terms: Fall, Spring, Summer. Applicants do not need a minimum number of credits to apply. For fall 2005: Transfer applications received: 199. Transfer applicants offered admission: 103. Transfer applicants enrolled: 46. **International students:** Number of foreign undergraduates: 10 (1% of student body). Number of countries represented: 13. Minimum TOEFL score required: 550 (paper); 217 (computer).

University of Evansville

- **Address:** 1800 Lincoln Avenue, Evansville, IN 47722
- **Website:** http://www.evansville.edu
- **Private; Religious affiliation:** Methodist
- **Enrollment:** 2,432 full-time; 335 part-time

KEY STATS

✔ **U.S News College Ranking:** 11, Universities–Master's (Midwest)
✔ **SAT Score (25th/75th percentile):** 1040-1270
✔ **Tuition:** 2006-2007: $22,980

Selectivity: More selective	**Room/board:** $7,310
Acceptance rate: 91%	**Average debt:** $21,142
Student/faculty ratio: 13/1	**Proportion who borrowed:** 67%

UNDERGRADUATE STUDENT BODY STATS

2005-2006 enrollment: 2,432 full-time; 335 part-time. Men: 38%; women: 62%. **Ethnic makeup:** African American: 2%; Asian American: 1%; Hispanic: 1%; White: 91%; International: 5%. **Religious preference:** Roman Catholic: 14%; Protestant: 18%; Unknown: 57%; Methodist: 10%; Other: 1%.

ADMISSIONS FACTS AND FIGURES

Phone: (812) 488-2468. **Email:** admission@evansville.edu. **Website:** http://www.evansville.edu. **Application deadlines for fall 2007:** Regular decision: February 1; decision sent by March 1. Early decision: Not offered. Early action: Send application by: December 1; Decision sent by: December 15. Admission can be deferred. **Application fee:** $35. Common application is accepted. **To apply online, go to:** http://www.evansville.edu/prospects/admission/applyonline/. **Admissions requirements/recommendations:** High school units required (recommended): English: 4 (4); Mathematics: 3 (4); Science: 2 (3); Foreign language: 0 (2); Social studies: 2 (2); History: 0 (0); Academic electives: 0 (0); Total units: 11 (15). Tests: The college uses SAT or ACT scores in admissions decisions. Either SAT or ACT required. For admission to the fall 2007 entering class, the school will accept: ACT with writing. Campus visit: Recommended. Admissions interview: Recommended. Off-campus interview: May be arranged. **Factors that count in admissions decisions:** *Academic:* Secondary school record: Very important. Class rank: Important. Letters of recommendation: Important. Standardized test scores: Very important. Essay: Not considered. *Nonacademic:* Interview: Important. Extracurricular activities: Important. Talent/ability: Important. Character/personal qualities: Important. Alumni/ae relationship: Considered. Geographical residence: Not considered. State residency: Not considered. Religious affiliation/commitment: Not considered. Minority status: Not considered. Volunteer work: Important. Work experience: Considered. **Other schools with the greatest overlap in applicants:** Ball State University; Butler University; Indiana University–Bloomington; Purdue University–West Lafayette; University of Southern Indiana. **Admissions statistics for the fall 2005 entering class:** Total applicants: 2,583. Total accepted: 2,339. Freshmen enrolled: 670; 38% were from out of state. Overall acceptance rate: 91%. Non-early acceptance rate: 91%. **Credentials of fall 2005 freshmen:** 35% ranked in the top 10 percent of their high school class; 65% were in the top 25 percent, and 92% were in the top half. (Proportion submitting class standing: 88%.) **Average high school grade point average:** 3.6. **First-year students who submitted SAT scores:** 77%. Scores (25/75 percentile): Verbal: 520-630, Math: 520-640, Combined: 1040-1270. **First-year students submitting ACT scores:** 54%. Scores (25/75 percentile): English: 22-28, Math: 21-27, Composite: 22-28.

ACADEMICS

Year founded: 1854. **Academic calendar:** Semester. **Degrees offered:** associate, bachelor's, master's. **Most popular majors:** 14% health professions and related clinical sciences, 12% visual and performing arts, 11% business, management, marketing, and related support services, 11% education, 11% engineering. **Major fields of study:** biological and biomedical sciences; business, management, marketing, and related support services; communication, journalism, and related programs; computer and information sciences and support services; education; engineering; engineering technologies/technicians; English language and literature/letters; foreign languages, literatures, and linguistics; health professions and related clinical sciences; history; legal professions and studies; liberal arts and sciences studies, and humanities; mathematics and statistics; multi/interdisciplinary studies; natural resources and conservation; parks, recreation, leisure, and fitness studies; philosophy and religious studies; physical sciences; psychology; public administration and social service professions; social sciences; visual and performing arts. **Areas of required coursework:** arts/fine arts, humanities, mathematics, philosophy, foreign languages, sciences (biological or physical), history, social science, other. **Pre-professional programs:** pre-law, pre-dentistry, pre-medicine, pre-theology, pre-veterinary science, pre-pharmacy, other. **Special academic programs (% participation):** accelerated program (7%), cooperative (work-study plan) program (6%), double major (11%), dual enrollment (3%), English as a Second Language (ESL) (1%), external degree program (3%), honors program (5%), independent study (39%), internships (44%), student-designed major (0%), study abroad (42%), teacher certificate program (11%). **Teacher certification offered in:** early childhood, special education, elementary, middle/junior high, secondary, bilingual/bicultural. **Cooperative education programs:** business, computer science, engineering, natural science, technologies, other. **Faculty and instruction (2005-2006):** Total instructional faculty: 175 full-time, 49 part-time (62% men; 38% women; 5% minorities). Full-time faculty with Ph.D. or other terminal degree: 88%. Student/faculty ratio: 13/1. Classes of fewer than 20 students: 57%; of 20 to 49 students: 41%; of 50 or more students: 2%. **Advanced Placement and International Baccalaureate credit:** AP tests may be used for: Credit and/or placement. Scores accepted: 4, 5. International Baccalaureate exams may be used for: Credit only. **Freshmen**

returning for sophomore year: 80%. **Graduation rates:** Four-year: 46%; five-year: 61%; six-year: 62%. **Graduate study:** 18% of students pursue further study within one year.

COSTS AND FINANCIAL AID

Financial aid office: (812) 488-2364. **Expenses (2006-2007):** Tuition and fees 2006-2007: $22,980; room/board: $7,310. Estimated books and supplies: $1,000; transportation: $700; personal expenses: $850. **Financial aid:** Priority filing date for institution's financial aid form: March 10; deadline: March 10. In 2005-2006, 84% of undergraduates applied for financial aid. Of those, 71% were determined to have financial need; 36% had their need fully met. Average financial aid package (proportion receiving): $19,847 (71%). Average amount of gift aid, such as scholarships or grants (proportion receiving): $15,028 (69%). Average amount of self-help aid, such as work study or loans (proportion receiving): $5,079 (50%). Average need-based loan (excluding PLUS or other private loans): $4,760. Among students who received need-based aid, the average percentage of need met: 93%. Among students who received aid based on merit, the average award (and the proportion receiving): $10,137 (23%). The average athletic scholarship (and the proportion receiving): $20,570 (3%). Average amount of debt of borrowers graduating in 2005: $21,142. Proportion who borrowed: 67%.

CAMPUS LIFE AND EXTRACURRICULAR ACTIVITIES

Campus housing available (% using): coed dorms (46%), women's dorms (20%), men's dorms (10%), fraternity housing (7%), apartment for single students (17%). Students who live in college-owned, operated, or affiliated housing: 71%. **Student employment:** During the 2005-2006 academic year, 7% of undergraduates worked on campus. Average per-year earnings: $1,300. **Clubs and organizations:** Number of student organizations: 170. Activities include: choral groups, concert band, dance, drama/theater, jazz band, literary magazine, music ensembles, musical theater, opera, pep band, radio station, student government, student newspaper, student film society, symphony orchestra, yearbook. Number of fraternities: 6; sororities: 5. Proportion of men in fraternities: 26%; of women in sororities: 23%. Average proportion of students who stay on campus on weekends: 65%.
Sports program (2005-2006): Member of NCAA I. *Men's intercollegiate varsity sports:* baseball, basketball, cross-country, golf, soccer, swimming and diving. *Women's intercollegiate varsity sports:* basketball, cross-country, golf, soccer, softball, swimming and diving, tennis, volleyball.

SERVICES AND FACILITIES

Basic services: nonremedial tutoring, placement service, health service, health insurance. **Counseling services:** minority student, career, personal, academic, psychological, religious. **For learning-disabled students:** School does not offer a structured program with separate admission and additional fees. Total undergraduates in learning-disabled program or receiving services: 30. Services include: tape recorders, note-taking services, extended time for tests, tutors, priority seating, texts on tape, other testing accomodations. **Library:** Number of titles: 282,820; number of current serial subscriptions: 1,000. **Information technology resources:** Students are not required to lease or own a computer. Number of campus computers available to all students: 325. School has a wireless network. Approximate number of users that can be accommodated: 1,000. Proportion of college-owned housing units wired for high-speed internet access: 100%. **Campus safety:** Security services offered: 24-hour foot and vehicle patrols, late-night transport/escort service, 24-hour emergency telephones, lighted pathways/sidewalks, controlled dormitory access (key, security card, etc).

TRANSFER AND INTERNATIONAL STUDENTS

Transfer students: May apply for admission for the following academic terms: Fall, Spring, Summer. Applicants do not need a minimum number of credits to apply. For fall 2005: Transfer applications received: 226. Transfer applicants offered admission: 102. Transfer applicants enrolled: 57. **International students:** Number of foreign undergraduates: 118 (5% of student body). Number of countries represented: 42. Minimum TOEFL score required: 500 (paper); 173 (computer). Average TOEFL score: 573 (paper).

University of Indianapolis

- **Address:** 1400 E. Hanna Avenue, Indianapolis, IN 46227-3697
- **Website:** http://www.uindy.edu
- **Private; Religious affiliation:** United Methodist
- **Enrollment:** 2,389 full-time; 972 part-time

KEY STATS

✔ **U.S News College Ranking:** 28, Universities–Master's (Midwest)
✔ **SAT Score (25th/75th percentile):** 910-1140
✔ **Tuition:** 2006-2007: $18,850

Selectivity: Selective	**Room/board:** $7,380
Acceptance rate: 83%	**Average debt:** $24,651
Student/faculty ratio: 12/1	**Proportion who borrowed:** 75%

UNDERGRADUATE STUDENT BODY STATS

2005-2006 enrollment: 2,389 full-time; 972 part-time. Men: 32%; women: 68%. **Ethnic makeup:** African American: 11%; Asian American: 1%; Hispanic: 2%; White: 84%; International: 2%. **Religious preference:** Roman Catholic: 24%; Protestant: 38%; Unknown: 20%; United Methodist: 17%; Other: 1%.

ADMISSIONS FACTS AND FIGURES

Phone: (317) 788-3216. **Email:** admissions@uindy.edu. **Website:** http://www.uindy.edu. **Application deadlines for fall 2007:** Regular decision: Rolling. Early decision: Not offered. Early action: Not offered. Admission can be deferred. **Application fee:** $20. Common application is not accepted. **To apply online, go to:** http://admissions.uindy.edu/app.html. **Admissions requirements/recommendations:** High school units required (recommended): English: 4 (4); Mathematics: 3 (4); Science: 2 (3); Foreign language: 0 (2); Social studies: 1 (1); History: 1 (1); Academic electives: 3 (3); Total units: 15 (15). Tests: The college uses SAT or ACT scores in admissions decisions. Either SAT or ACT required. For admission to the fall 2007 entering class, the school will accept ACT with writing, ACT without writing. Campus visit: Recommended. Admissions interview: Recommended. Off-campus interview: May be arranged. **Factors that count in admissions decisions:** *Academic:* Secondary school record: Very important. Class rank: Important. Letters of recommendation: Considered. Standardized test scores: Important. Essay: Not considered. *Nonacademic:* Interview: Not considered. Extracurricular activities: Considered. Talent/ability: Not considered. Character/personal qualities: Not considered. Alumni/ae relationship: Not considered. Geographical residence: Not considered. State residency: Not considered. Religious affiliation/commitment: Not considered. Minority status: Not considered. Volunteer work: Not considered. Work experience: Not considered. **Admissions statistics for the fall 2005 entering class:** Total applicants: 2,884. Total accepted: 2,404. Freshmen enrolled: 737; 9% were from out of state. Overall acceptance rate: 83%. **Size of waiting list:** 15 applicants; enrolled from waiting list: 15. **Credentials of fall 2005 freshmen:** 20% ranked in the top 10 percent of their high school class; 54% were in the top 25 percent, and 87% were in the top half. (Proportion submitting class standing: 91%.) **Average high school grade point average:** 3.1. **First-year students who submitted SAT scores:** 86%. Scores (25/75 percentile): Verbal: 450-570, Math: 460-570, Combined: 910-1140. **First-year students submitting ACT scores:** 42%. Scores (25/75 percentile): English: 18-25, Math: 18-24, Composite: 19-24.

ACADEMICS

Year founded: 1902. **Academic calendar:** Semester. **Degrees offered:** associate, bachelor's, master's, doctorate. **Most popular majors:** 25% business, management, marketing, and related support services, 17% education, 10% psychology, 7% nursing/registered nurse training (R.N., A.S.N., B.S.N., M.S.N.), 6% social sciences. **Major fields of study:** biological and biomedical sciences; business, management, marketing, and related support services; communication, journalism, and related programs; computer and information sciences and support services; education; engineering; English language and literature/letters; foreign languages, literatures, and linguistics; health professions and related clinical sciences; history; liberal arts and sciences studies, and humanities; mathematics and statistics; multi/interdisciplinary studies; natural resources and conservation; parks, recreation, leisure, and fitness studies; philosophy and religious studies; physical sciences; psychology; public administration and social service professions; security and protective services; social sciences; visual and performing arts. **Areas of required coursework:** arts/fine arts, humanities, computer literacy, mathematics, English (including composition), philosophy, foreign languages, sciences (biological or physical), history, social science, other. **Preprofessional programs:** pre-law, pre-dentistry, pre-medicine, pre-theology, pre-veterinary science, pre-optometry, other. **Special academic programs:** accelerated program, cross-registration, double major, dual enrollment, English as a Second Language (ESL), honors program, independent study, internships, liberal arts/career combination, student-designed major, study abroad, teacher certificate program, weekend college, other. **Teacher certification offered in:** elementary, middle/junior high, secondary. **Reserve Officers Training Corps (ROTC):** Army ROTC: Offered at cooperating institution (I.U.P.U.I.). **Faculty and instruction (2005-2006):** Total instructional faculty: 166 full-time, 250 part-time (52% men; 48% women; 8% minorities). Full-time faculty with Ph.D. or other terminal degree: 74%. Student/faculty ratio: 12/1. Classes of fewer than 20 students: 61%; of 20 to 49 students: 38%; of 50 or more students: 1%. **Advanced Placement and International Baccalaureate credit:** AP tests may be used for: Credit and/or placement. Scores accepted: 3, 4, 5. International Baccalaureate exams may be used for: Credit only. **Freshmen returning for sophomore year:** 78%. **Graduation rates:** Four-year: 42%; five-year: 52%; six-year: 53%. **Graduate study:** 25% of students pursue further study immediately upon graduation. Fields in which graduates pursue further study: Master of Business Administration (MBA), 14%; law, 6%; medicine, 6%; education, 3%; arts and sciences, 71%.

COSTS AND FINANCIAL AID

Financial aid office: (317) 788-3217. **Expenses (2006-2007):** Tuition and fees 2006-2007: $18,850; room/board: $7,380. Estimated books and supplies: $830; transportation: $660; personal expenses: $1,420. **Financial aid:** Priority filing date for institution's financial aid form: March 10. In 2005-2006, 87% of undergraduates applied for financial aid. Of those, 75% were determined to have financial need; 34% had their need fully met. Average financial aid package (proportion receiving): $16,861 (75%). Average amount of gift aid, such as scholarships or grants (proportion receiving): $8,442 (65%). Average amount of self-help aid, such as work study or loans (proportion receiving): $3,985 (57%). Average need-based loan (excluding PLUS or other private loans): $3,907. Among students who received need-based aid, the average percentage of need met: 85%. Among students who received aid based on merit, the average award (and the proportion receiving): $10,014 (13%). The average athletic scholarship (and the proportion receiving): $10,133 (12%). Average amount of debt of borrowers graduating in 2005: $24,651. Proportion who borrowed: 75%.

CAMPUS LIFE AND EXTRACURRICULAR ACTIVITIES

Campus housing available (% using): coed dorms (74%), women's dorms (13%), apartments for married students (0%), apartment for single students (13%). Students who live in college-owned, operated, or affiliated housing: 36%. **Student employment:** During the 2005-2006 academic year, 50% of undergraduates worked on campus. Average per-year earnings: $1,000. **Clubs and organizations:** Number of student organizations: 53. Activities include: choral groups, concert band, dance, drama/theater, jazz band, literary magazine, music ensembles, musical theater, opera, pep band, radio station, student government, student newspaper, television station. Number of fraternities: 0; sororities: 0. Average proportion of students who stay on campus on weekends: 50%. **Sports program (2005-2006):** Member of NCAA II. *Men's intercollegiate varsity sports:* baseball, basketball, cross-country, football, golf, soccer, swimming and diving, tennis, track and field (indoor), track and field (outdoor), wrestling. *Women's intercollegiate varsity sports:* basketball, cross-country, golf, soccer, softball, swimming and diving, tennis, track and field (indoor), track and field (outdoor), volleyball.

SERVICES AND FACILITIES

Basic services: nonremedial tutoring, placement service, day care, health service, health insurance. **Remedial assistance:** math, writing, study skills. **Counseling services:** minority student, career, personal, academic, psychological, religious, other. **For learning-disabled students:** School does not offer a structured program with separate admission and additional fees. Total undergraduates in learning-disabled program or receiving services: 60. Services include: remedial math, remedial English, reading machines, tape recorders, other special classes, diagnostic testing service, untimed tests, oral tests, learning center, readers, extended time for tests, tutors, priority seating, texts on tape, other testing accomodations, other. **Library:** Number of titles: 182,645; number of current serial subscriptions: 1,024. **Information technology resources:** Students are not required to lease or own a computer. Number of campus computers available to all students: 209. School has a wireless network. Approximate number of users that can be accommodated: 2,500. Proportion of college-owned housing units wired for high-speed internet access: 100%. **Campus safety:** Security services offered: 24-hour foot and vehicle patrols, late-night transport/escort service, 24-hour emergency telephones, lighted pathways/sidewalks, student patrols, controlled dormitory access (key, security card, etc).

TRANSFER AND INTERNATIONAL STUDENTS

Transfer students: May apply for admission for the following academic terms: Fall, Winter, Spring, Summer. Applicants do not need a minimum number of credits to apply. For fall 2005: Transfer applications received: 391. Transfer applicants offered admission: 261. Transfer applicants enrolled: 107. **International students:** Number of foreign undergraduates: 81 (2% of student body). Number of countries represented: 60. Minimum TOEFL score required: 500 (paper); 173 (computer). Average TOEFL score: 540 (paper).

University of Notre Dame

- **Address:** Notre Dame, IN 46556
- **Website:** http://www.nd.edu
- **Private; Religious affiliation:** Roman Catholic
- **Enrollment:** 8,260 full-time; 15 part-time

KEY STATS

✔ **U.S News College Ranking:** 20, National Universities
✔ **SAT Score (25th/75th percentile):** 1290-1470
✔ **Tuition:** 2005-2006: $31,542

Selectivity: Most selective	**Room/board:** $8,010
Acceptance rate: 32%	**Average debt:** N/A
Student/faculty ratio: 11/1	**Proportion who borrowed:** N/A

UNDERGRADUATE STUDENT BODY STATS

2005-2006 enrollment: 8,260 full-time; 15 part-time. Men: 53%; women: 47%. **Ethnic makeup:** African American: 4%; American-Indian: 1%; Asian American: 6%; Hispanic: 8%; White: 78%; International: 4%. **Religious preference:** Protestant: 7%; Roman Catholic: 82%; Other: 11%.

ADMISSIONS FACTS AND FIGURES

Phone: (574) 631-7505. **Email:** admissio.1@nd.edu. **Website:** http://www.nd.edu. **Application deadlines for fall 2007:** Regular decision: December 31; decision sent by April 10. Early decision: Not offered. Early action: Send application by: November 1; Decision sent by: December 20. Admission can be deferred. **Application fee:** $50. Common application is accepted. **To apply online, go to:** http://admissions.nd.edu/onlineapplication. **Admissions requirements/recommendations:** High school units required (recommended): English: 4 (4); Mathematics: 3 (4); Science: 2 (4); Foreign language: 2 (4); History: 2 (4); Academic electives: 3 (3); Total units: 16 (23). Tests: The college uses SAT or ACT scores in admissions decisions. Either SAT or ACT required. For admission to the fall 2007 entering class, the school will accept: ACT with writing, ACT without writing. Campus visit: Neither required nor recommended. Admissions interview: Neither required nor recommended. Off-campus interview: Not available. **Factors that count in admissions decisions:** *Academic:* Secondary school record: Very important. Class rank: Important. Letters of recommendation: Important. Standardized test scores: Important. Essay: Important. *Nonacademic:* Interview: Not considered. Extracurricular activities: Important. Talent/ability: Important. Character/personal qualities: Important. Alumni/ae relationship: Important. Geographical residence: Not considered. State residency: Not considered. Religious affiliation/commitment: Considered. Minority status: Considered. Volunteer work: Important. Work experience: Considered. **Admissions statistics for the fall 2005 entering class:** Total applicants: 11,317. Total accepted: 3,582. Freshmen enrolled: 1,966; 89% were from out of state. Overall acceptance rate: 32%. Non-early acceptance rate: 32%. **Size of waiting list:** 787 applicants; enrolled from waiting list: 98. **Credentials of fall 2005 freshmen:** 86% ranked in the top 10 percent of their high school class; 97% were in the top 25 percent, and 100% were in the top half. **First-year students who submitted SAT scores:** 68%. Scores (25/75 percentile): Verbal: 630-730, Math: 660-740, Combined: 1290-1470. **First-year students submitting ACT scores:** 32%. Scores (25/75 percentile): English: N/A, Math: N/A, Composite: 30-33.

ACADEMICS

Year founded: 1842. **Academic calendar:** Semester. **Degrees offered:** bachelor's, master's, first professional, doctorate. **Most popular majors:** 22% business/commerce, 9% political science and government, 8% engineering, 7% pre-medicine/pre-medical studies, 6% psychology. **Major fields of study:** architecture and related services; area, ethnic, cultural, and gender studies; biological and biomedical sciences; business, management, marketing, and related support services; computer and information sciences and support services; education; engineering; English language and literature/letters; foreign languages, literatures, and linguistics; health professions and related clinical sciences; history; liberal arts and sciences studies, and humanities; mathematics and statistics; multi/interdisciplinary studies; natural resources and conservation; philosophy and religious studies; physical sciences; psychology; social sciences; theology and religious vocations; visual and performing arts. **Areas of required coursework:** arts/fine arts, humanities, mathematics, English (including composition), philosophy, foreign languages, sciences (biological or physical), history, social science, other. **Pre-professional programs:** pre-dentistry, pre-medicine, pre-veterinary science, pre-optometry. **Special academic programs:** accelerated program, cross-registration, distance learning, double major, honors program, independent study, internships, liberal arts/career combination, student-designed major, study abroad, other. **Reserve Officers Training Corps (ROTC):** Army ROTC: Offered on campus; Navy ROTC: Offered on campus; Air Force ROTC: Offered on campus. **Faculty and instruction (2005-2006):** Total instructional faculty: 877 full-time, 396 part-time (72% men; 28% women; 12% minorities). Full-time faculty with Ph.D. or other terminal degree: 92%. Student/faculty ratio: 11/1. Classes of fewer than 20 students: 50%; of 20 to 49 students: 38%; of 50 or more students: 11%. **Advanced Placement and International Baccalaureate credit:** AP tests may be used for: Credit and/or placement. Scores accepted: 4, 5. International Baccalaureate exams may be used for: Credit and/or placement. **Freshmen returning for sophomore year:** 98%. **Graduation rates:** Four-year: 88%; five-year: 95%; six-year: 95%. **Graduate study:** 33% of students pursue further study immediately upon graduation. Fields in which graduates pursue further study: Master of Business Administration (MBA), 1%; law, 8%; medicine, 7%; engineering, 1%; education, 4%; arts and sciences, 8%.

COSTS AND FINANCIAL AID

Financial aid office: (574) 631-6436. **Expenses (2005-2006):** Tuition and fees 2005-2006: $31,542; room/board: $8,010. Estimated books and supplies: $850; transportation: $500; personal expenses: $900. **Financial aid:** Priority filing date for institution's financial aid form: February 15; deadline: February 15.

CAMPUS LIFE AND EXTRACURRICULAR ACTIVITIES

Campus housing available (% using): women's dorms (47%), men's dorms (53%). Students who live in college-owned, operated, or affiliated housing: 77%. **Clubs and organizations:** Number of student organizations: 305. Activities include: choral groups, concert band, dance, drama/theater, jazz band, literary magazine, marching band, music ensembles, musical theater, opera, pep band, radio station, student government, student newspaper, student film society, symphony orchestra, yearbook. Number of fraternities: 0; sororities: 0. **Sports program (2005-2006):** Member of NCAA I. *Men's intercollegiate varsity sports:* baseball, basketball, cheerleading, cross-country, fencing, football, golf, ice hockey, lacrosse, soccer, swimming and diving, tennis, track and field (indoor), track and field (outdoor). *Women's intercollegiate varsity sports:* basketball, crew, cross-country, fencing, golf, lacrosse, soccer, softball, swimming and diving, tennis, track and field (indoor), track and field (outdoor), volleyball.

SERVICES AND FACILITIES

Basic services: nonremedial tutoring, women's center, placement service, day care, health service, health insurance. **Counseling services:** career, personal, academic, psychological, religious. **For learning-disabled students:** School does not offer a structured program with separate admission and additional fees. Services include: reading machines, tape recorders, videotaped classes, diagnostic testing service, untimed tests, note-taking services, oral tests, learning center, readers, extended time for tests, tutors, texts on tape. **Library:** Number of titles: 2,794,991; number of current serial subscriptions: 24,932. **Information technology resources:** Students are not required to lease or own a computer. Number of campus computers available to all students: 600. School has a wireless network. **Campus safety:** Security services offered: 24-hour foot and vehicle patrols, late-night transport/escort service, 24-hour emergency telephones, lighted pathways/sidewalks, controlled dormitory access (key, security card, etc).

TRANSFER AND INTERNATIONAL STUDENTS

Transfer students: May apply for admission for the following academic terms: Fall, Spring. Applicants need a minimum number of credits to apply.

For fall 2005: Transfer applications received: 434. Transfer applicants offered admission: 142. Transfer applicants enrolled: 115. **International students:** Number of foreign undergraduates: 221 (4% of student body). Number of countries represented: 61.

University of Southern Indiana

- **Address:** 8600 University Boulevard, Evansville, IN 47712
- **Website:** http://www.usi.edu
- **Public**
- **Enrollment:** 7,477 full-time; 1,775 part-time

KEY STATS
- ✔ **U.S News College Ranking:** fourth tier, Universities–Master's (Midwest)
- ✔ **SAT Score (25th/75th percentile):** 840-1070
- ✔ **Tuition:** 2006-2007: $4,460 in state, $10,631 out of state

Selectivity: Less selective	**Room/board:** $6,492
Acceptance rate: 91%	**Average debt:** $15,724
Student/faculty ratio: 18/1	**Proportion who borrowed:** 60%

UNDERGRADUATE STUDENT BODY STATS

2005-2006 enrollment: 7,477 full-time; 1,775 part-time. Men: 40%; women: 60%. **Ethnic makeup:** African American: 5%; Asian American: 1%; Hispanic: 1%; White: 93%; International: 1%.

ADMISSIONS FACTS AND FIGURES

Phone: (812) 464-1765. **Email:** enroll@usi.edu. **Website:** http://www.usi.edu. **Application deadlines for fall 2007:** Regular decision: August 15. Early decision: Not offered. Early action: Not offered. Admission cannot be deferred. **Application fee:** $25. Common application is accepted. **To apply online, go to:** http://www.usi.edu/admissn/apply.asp. **Admissions requirements/recommendations:** High school units required (recommended): English: (4); Mathematics: (4); Science: (3); Foreign language: (2); Social studies: (2); History: (2); Academic electives: (2); Total units: (18). Tests: The college uses SAT or ACT scores in admissions decisions. Either SAT or ACT required. For admission to the fall 2007 entering class, the school will accept: ACT with writing. Campus visit: Recommended. Admissions interview: Neither required nor recommended. Off-campus interview: May be arranged. **Factors that count in admissions decisions:** *Academic:* Secondary school record: Considered. Class rank: Important. Letters of recommendation: Considered. Standardized test scores: Considered. Essay: Considered. *Nonacademic:* Interview: Considered. Extracurricular activities: Considered. Talent/ability: Considered. Character/personal qualities: Considered. Alumni/ae relationship: Considered. Geographical residence: Not considered. State residency: Not considered. Religious affiliation/commitment: Not considered. Minority status: Not considered. Volunteer work: Not considered. Work experience: Considered. **Admissions statistics for the fall 2005 entering class:** Total applicants: 4,807. Total accepted: 4,356. Freshmen enrolled: 2,148; 4% were from out of state. Overall acceptance rate: 91%. **Credentials of fall 2005 freshmen:** 7% ranked in the top 10 percent of their high school class; 25% were in the top 25 percent, and 56% were in the top half. (Proportion submitting class standing: 94%.) **Average high school grade point average:** 2.9. First-year students who submitted SAT scores: 77%. Scores (25/75 percentile): Verbal: 420-530, Math: 420-540, Combined: 840-1070. **First-year students submitting ACT scores:** 32%. Scores (25/75 percentile): English: 16-23, Math: 17-23, Composite: 18-23.

ACADEMICS

Year founded: 1965. **Academic calendar:** Semester. **Degrees offered:** certificate, associate, transfer-associate, terminal-associate, bachelor's, post-bachelor's certificate, master's. **Most popular majors:** 23% business/commerce, 16% health professions and related clinical sciences, 14% elementary education and teaching, 13% public relations, advertising, and applied communication, 6% sociology. **Major fields of study:** biological and biomedical sciences; business, management, marketing, and related support services; communication, journalism, and related programs; computer and information sciences and support services; education; engineering; engineering technologies/technicians; English language and literature/letters; foreign languages, literatures, and linguistics; health professions and related clinical sciences; history; liberal arts and sciences studies, and humanities; mathematics and statistics; multi/interdisciplinary studies; parks, recreation, leisure, and fitness studies; philosophy and religious studies; physical sciences; psychology; public administration and social service professions; social sciences; visual and performing arts. **Areas of required coursework:** arts/fine arts, humanities, computer literacy, mathematics, English (including composition), philosophy, sciences (biological or physical), history, social science. **Pre-professional programs:** pre-law, pre-dentistry, pre-medicine, pre-veterinary science, pre-optometry, pre-pharmacy, other. **Special academic programs (% participation):** cooperative (work-study plan) program (2.4%), cross-registration (.3%), distance learning (49.5%), double major (2.6%), dual enrollment (4.3%), English as a Second Language (ESL) (.3%), honors program (6.1%), independent study (7.2%), internships (10.4%), study abroad (0%), teacher certificate program (18.8%). **Teacher certification offered in:** early childhood, special education, elementary, middle/junior high, secondary. **Cooperative education programs:** business, computer science, engineering. **Reserve Officers Training Corps (ROTC):** Army ROTC: Offered on campus. **Faculty and instruction (2005-2006):** Total instructional faculty: 303 full-time, 316 part-time (46% men; 54% women; 7% minorities). Full-time faculty with Ph.D. or other terminal degree: 63%. Student/faculty ratio: 18/1. Classes of fewer than 20 students: 38%; of 20 to 49 students: 58%; of 50 or more students: 4%. **Advanced Placement and International Baccalaureate credit:** AP tests may be used for: Credit and/or placement. Scores accepted: 3, 4, 5. **Freshmen returning for sophomore year:** 62%. **Graduation rates:** Four-year: 5%; five-year: 18%; six-year: 31%. **Graduate study:** 16% of students pursue further study within one year.

COSTS AND FINANCIAL AID

Financial aid office: (812) 464-1767. **Expenses (2006-2007):** Tuition and fees 2006-2007: $4,460 in state, $10,631 out of state; room/board: $6,492. Estimated books and supplies: $900; transportation: $800; personal expenses: $1,822. **Financial aid:** Priority filing date for institution's financial aid form: March 1; deadline: March 1. In 2005-2006, 80% of undergraduates applied for financial aid. Of those, 59% were determined to have financial need; 13% had their need fully met. Average financial aid package (proportion receiving): $5,393 (52%). Average amount of gift aid, such as scholarships or grants (proportion receiving): $4,509 (37%). Average amount of self-help aid, such as work study or loans (proportion receiving): $3,281 (31%). Average need-based loan (excluding PLUS or other private loans): $3,260. Among students who received need-based aid, the average percentage of need met: 54%. Among students who received aid based on merit, the average award (and the proportion receiving): $2,140 (7%). The average athletic scholarship (and the proportion receiving): $5,409 (1%). Average amount of debt of borrowers graduating in 2005: $15,724. Proportion who borrowed: 60%.

CAMPUS LIFE AND EXTRACURRICULAR ACTIVITIES

Campus housing available (% using): coed dorms (21%), sorority housing (2%), fraternity housing (1%), other housing options (76%). Students who live in college-owned, operated, or affiliated housing: 32%. **Student employment:** During the 2005-2006 academic year, 14% of undergraduates worked on campus. Average per-year earnings: $1,281. **Clubs and organizations:** Number of student organizations: 82. Activities include: choral groups, dance, drama/theater, jazz band, literary magazine, pep band, radio station, student government, student newspaper. Number of fraternities: 5; sororities: 4. Proportion of men in fraternities: 2%; of women in sororities: 2%. Average proportion of students who stay on campus on weekends: 13%. **Sports program (2005-2006):** Member of NCAA II. *Men's intercollegiate varsity sports:* baseball, basketball, cross-country, golf, soccer, tennis. *Women's intercollegiate varsity sports:* basketball, cross-country, golf, soccer, softball, tennis, volleyball.

SERVICES AND FACILITIES

Basic services: nonremedial tutoring, placement service, day care, health service, health insurance. **Remedial assistance:** reading, math, writing, study skills. **Counseling services:** minority student, career, personal, academic, psychological, birth control. **For learning-disabled students:** School does not offer a structured program with separate admission and additional fees. Total undergraduates in learning-disabled program or receiving services: 206. Services include: remedial math, other testing accommodations, remedial English, remedial reading, note-taking services, oral tests, learning center, readers, extended time for tests, tutors, priority registration, priority seating, texts on tape, other testing accomodations. **Library:** Number of titles: 247,329; number of current serial subscriptions: 14,276. **Information technology resources:** Students are not required to lease or own a computer. Number of campus computers available to all students: 778. School has a wireless network. Proportion of college-owned housing units wired for high-speed internet access: 100%. **Campus safety:** Security services offered: 24-hour foot and vehicle patrols, late-night transport/escort service, 24-hour emergency telephones, lighted pathways/sidewalks, student patrols, controlled dormitory access (key, security card, etc).

TRANSFER AND INTERNATIONAL STUDENTS

Transfer students: May apply for admission for the following academic terms: Fall, Spring, Summer. Applicants do not need a minimum number of credits to apply. For fall 2005: Transfer applications received: 1,179. Transfer applicants offered admission: 968. Transfer applicants enrolled: 663. **International students:** Number of foreign undergraduates: 50 (1% of student body). Minimum TOEFL score required: 525 (paper); 197 (computer).

University of St. Francis

- **Address:** 2701 Spring Street, Fort Wayne, IN 46808
- **Website:** http://www.sf.edu
- **Private; Religious affiliation:** Roman Catholic
- **Enrollment:** 1,343 full-time; 425 part-time

KEY STATS

✔ **U.S News College Ranking:** third tier, Universities–Master's (Midwest)
✔ **SAT Score (25th/75th percentile):** 880-1160
✔ **Tuition:** 2006-2007: $18,508

Selectivity: Less selective	**Room/board:** $5,834
Acceptance rate: 59%	**Average debt:** $22,709
Student/faculty ratio: 11/1	**Proportion who borrowed:** 85%

UNDERGRADUATE STUDENT BODY STATS

2005-2006 enrollment: 1,343 full-time; 425 part-time. Men: 30%; women: 70%. **Ethnic makeup:** African American: 4%; American-Indian: 1%; Asian American: 1%; Hispanic: 2%; White: 93%. **Religious preference:** Roman Catholic: 21%; Protestant: 40%; Unknown: 31%; Roman Catholic: 7%.

ADMISSIONS FACTS AND FIGURES

Phone: (260) 434-3279. **Email:** admis@sf.edu. **Website:** http://www.sf.edu. **Application deadlines for fall 2007:** Regular decision: August 1. Early decision: Not offered. Early action: Not offered. Admission can be deferred. **Application fee:** $20. Common application is not accepted. **Admissions requirements/recommendations:** High school units required (recommended): English: 4 (4); Mathematics: 2 (3); Science: 2 (3); Foreign language: 0 (0); Social studies: 2 (3); History: 1 (1); Academic electives: 1 (4); Total units: 20 (26). Tests: The college uses SAT or ACT scores in admissions decisions. Either SAT or ACT required. For admission to the fall 2007 entering class, the school will accept: ACT with writing, ACT without writing. Campus visit: Recommended. Admissions interview: Neither required nor recommended. Off-campus interview: Not available. **Factors that count in admissions decisions:** *Academic:* Secondary school record: Very important. Class rank: Important. Letters of recommendation: Considered. Standardized test scores: Very important. Essay: Considered. *Nonacademic:* Interview: Considered. Extracurricular activities: Not considered. Talent/ability: Not considered. Character/personal qualities: Not considered. Alumni/ae relationship: Not considered. Geographical residence: Not considered. State residency: Not considered. Religious affiliation/commitment: Not considered. Minority status: Not considered. Volunteer work: Not considered. Work experience: Considered. **Admissions statistics for the fall 2005 entering class:** Total applicants: 1,129. Total accepted: 664. Freshmen enrolled: 319; 10% were from out of state. Overall acceptance rate: 59%. **Credentials of fall 2005 freshmen:** 10% ranked in the top 10 percent of their high school class; 34% were in the top 25 percent, and 67% were in the top half. (Proportion submitting class standing: 83%.) **Average high school grade point average:** 3.2. **First-year students who submitted SAT scores:** 84%. Scores (25/75 percentile): Verbal: 430-570, Math: 450-590, Combined: 880-1160. **First-year students submitting ACT scores:** 42%. Scores (25/75 percentile): English: 16-23, Math: 17-23, Composite: 18-23.

ACADEMICS

Year founded: 1890. **Academic calendar:** Semester. **Degrees offered:** certificate, associate, bachelor's, master's, post-master's certificate. **Most popular majors:** 21% business, management, marketing, and related support services, 21% health professions and related clinical sciences, 18% education, 13% visual and performing arts, 7% liberal arts and sciences studies, and humanities. **Major fields of study:** area, ethnic, cultural, and gender studies;

biological and biomedical sciences; business, management, marketing, and related support services; communication, journalism, and related programs; education; English language and literature/letters; health professions and related clinical sciences; history; legal professions and studies; liberal arts and sciences studies, and humanities; mathematics and statistics; multi/interdisciplinary studies; natural resources and conservation; philosophy and religious studies; physical sciences; psychology; public administration and social service professions; social sciences; theology and religious vocations; visual and performing arts. **Areas of required coursework:** arts/fine arts, humanities, computer literacy, mathematics, English (including composition), philosophy, sciences (biological or physical), history, social science, other. **Pre-professional programs:** pre-law, pre-dentistry, pre-medicine, pre-veterinary science, pre-pharmacy. **Special academic programs (% participation):** cross-registration (1%), distance learning (34%), double major (1%), dual enrollment (0%), exchange student program (domestic) (0%), honors program (4%), independent study (40%), internships (30%), liberal arts/career combination (0%), student-designed major (6%), teacher certificate program (18%). **Teacher certification offered in:** special education, elementary, middle/junior high, secondary. **Cooperative education programs:** business. **Faculty and instruction (2005-2006):** Total instructional faculty: 101 full-time, 122 part-time (39% men; 61% women; 6% minorities). Full-time faculty with Ph.D. or other terminal degree: 44%. Student/faculty ratio: 11/1. Classes of fewer than 20 students: 62%; of 20 to 49 students: 37%; of 50 or more students: 1%. **Advanced Placement and International Baccalaureate credit:** AP tests may be used for: Credit and/or placement. Scores accepted: 3. International Baccalaureate exams may be used for: Credit only. **Freshmen returning for sophomore year:** 72%. **Graduation rates:** Four-year: 30%; five-year: 48%; six-year: 47%. **Graduate study:** 14% of students pursue further study immediately upon graduation. Fields in which graduates pursue further study: law, 15%; medicine, 6%; education, 3%; arts and sciences, 9%.

COSTS AND FINANCIAL AID
Financial aid office: (260) 434-3283. **Expenses (2006-2007):** Tuition and fees 2006-2007: $18,508; room/board: $5,834. Estimated books and supplies: $1,000; transportation: $1,000; personal expenses: $1,100. **Financial aid:** Priority filing date for institution's financial aid form: March 10; deadline: June 30. In 2005-2006, 97% of undergraduates applied for financial aid. Of those, 86% were determined to have financial need; 26% had their need fully met. Average financial aid package (proportion receiving): $12,457 (86%). Average amount of gift aid, such as scholarships or grants (proportion receiving): $8,927 (85%). Average amount of self-help aid, such as work study or loans (proportion receiving): $4,064 (76%). Average need-based loan (excluding PLUS or other private loans): $3,130. Among students who received need-based aid, the average percentage of need met: 74%. Among students who received aid based on merit, the average award (and the proportion receiving): $9,793 (12%). The average athletic scholarship (and the proportion receiving): $4,538 (8%). Average amount of debt of borrowers graduating in 2005: $22,709. Proportion who borrowed: 85%.

CAMPUS LIFE AND EXTRACURRICULAR ACTIVITIES
Campus housing available (% using): coed dorms (61%), apartment for single students (38%), special housing for disabled students (1%). Students who live in college-owned, operated, or affiliated housing: 19%. **Student employment:** During the 2005-2006 academic year, 3% of undergraduates worked on campus. Average per-year earnings: $1,750. **Clubs and organizations:** Number of student organizations: 33. Activities include: choral groups, dance, drama/theater, jazz band, literary magazine, music ensembles, musical theater, pep band, student government, student newspaper, student film society. Number of fraternities: 0; sororities: 0. Average proportion of students who stay on campus on weekends: 30%. **Sports program (2005-2006):** Member of NAIA. *Men's intercollegiate varsity sports:* baseball, basketball, cross-country, football, golf, soccer, track and field (indoor), track and field (outdoor). *Women's intercollegiate varsity sports:* basketball, cross-country, soccer, softball, tennis, track and field (indoor), track and field (outdoor), volleyball.

SERVICES AND FACILITIES
Basic services: nonremedial tutoring. **Remedial assistance:** reading, math, writing. **Counseling services:** career, personal, academic, religious. **For learning-disabled students:** School does not offer a structured program with separate admission and additional fees. Total undergraduates in learning-disabled program or receiving services: 41. Services include: remedial math, remedial English, reading machines, remedial reading, tape recorders, untimed tests, note-taking services, oral tests, learning center, readers, extended time for tests, tutors, priority seating, proofreading serv-

ices, typist/scribe, exams on tape or computer, other testing accomodations, other. **Library:** Number of titles: 50,186; number of current serial subscriptions: 549. **Information technology resources:** Students are not required to lease or own a computer. Number of campus computers available to all students: 404. School has a wireless network. Proportion of college-owned housing units wired for high-speed internet access: 100%. **Campus safety:** Security services offered: 24-hour foot and vehicle patrols, late-night transport/escort service, 24-hour emergency telephones, lighted pathways/sidewalks, controlled dormitory access (key, security card, etc).

TRANSFER AND INTERNATIONAL STUDENTS
Transfer students: May apply for admission for the following academic terms: Fall, Spring, Summer. Applicants do not need a minimum number of credits to apply. For fall 2005: Transfer applications received: 607. Transfer applicants offered admission: 292. Transfer applicants enrolled: 165. **International students:** Number of foreign undergraduates: 0. Number of countries represented: 2. Minimum TOEFL score required: 550 (paper); 217 (computer).

Valparaiso University

- **Address:** Kretzmann Hall, 1700 Chapel Drive, Valparaiso, IN 46383
- **Website:** http://www.valpo.edu
- **Private; Religious affiliation:** Lutheran
- **Enrollment:** 2,825 full-time; 139 part-time

KEY STATS
✔ **U.S News College Ranking:** 3, Universities–Master's (Midwest)
✔ **ACT Score (25th/75th percentile):** 23-28
✔ **Tuition:** 2006-2007: $24,000

Selectivity: More selective	**Room/board:** $6,640
Acceptance rate: 83%	**Average debt:** $23,853
Student/faculty ratio: 13/1	**Proportion who borrowed:** 71%

UNDERGRADUATE STUDENT BODY STATS
2005-2006 enrollment: 2,825 full-time; 139 part-time. Men: 48%; women: 52%. **Ethnic makeup:** African American: 4%; Asian American: 2%; Hispanic: 3%; White: 90%; International: 2%. **Religious preference:** Roman Catholic: 21%; Protestant: 21%; Muslim: 1%; No preference: 6%; Unknown: 4%; Lutheran: 40%; Other Christian, Orthodox, Church of Jesus Christ Latter Day St: 7%.

ADMISSIONS FACTS AND FIGURES
Phone: (888) 468-2576. **Email:** undergrad.admissions@valpo.edu. **Website:** http://www.valpo.edu. **Application deadlines for fall 2007:** Regular decision: August 15. Early decision: Not offered. Early action: Send application by: November 1; Decision sent by: December 1. Admission can be deferred. **Application fee:** $30. Common application is accepted. **To apply online, go to:** http://www.valpo.edu/admissions/apply/. **Admissions requirements/recommendations:** High school units required (recommended): English: 4 (4); Mathematics: 3 (4); Science: 2 (3); Foreign language: (2); Social studies: 3 (3); Academic electives: 3 (3); Total units: 15 (19). Tests: The college uses SAT or ACT scores in admissions decisions. Either SAT or ACT required. For admission to the fall 2007 entering class, the school will accept: ACT with writing. Campus visit: Recommended. Admissions interview: Recommended. Off-campus interview: May be arranged. **Factors that count in admissions decisions:** *Academic:* Secondary school record: Very important. Class rank: Important. Letters of recommendation: Considered. Standardized test scores: Important. Essay: Considered. *Nonacademic:* Interview: Considered. Extracurricular activities: Important. Talent/ability: Important. Character/personal qualities: Considered. Alumni/ae relationship: Considered. Geographical residence: Not considered. State residency: Not considered. Religious affiliation/commitment: Considered. Minority status: Considered. Volunteer work: Considered. Work experience: Not considered. **Other schools with the greatest overlap in applicants:** Butler University; Indiana University–Bloomington; Marquette University; Purdue University–Calumet; Purdue University–West Lafayette. **Admissions statistics for the fall 2005 entering class:** Total applicants: 3,532. Total accepted: 2,931. Freshmen enrolled: 673; 67% were from out of state. Accepted through early-decision or early-action plans: 57%. Overall acceptance rate: 83%. Non-early acceptance rate: 77%. **Credentials of fall 2005 freshmen:** 34% ranked in the top 10 percent of their high school class; 60% were in the top

25 percent, and 85% were in the top half. (Proportion submitting class standing: 83%.) **Average high school grade point average:** 3.4. **First-year students who submitted SAT scores:** 55%. Scores (25/75 percentile): Verbal: 520-630, Math: 520-640, Combined: 1040-1270. **First-year students submitting ACT scores:** 67%. Scores (25/75 percentile): English: 22-29, Math: 23-29, Composite: 23-28.

ACADEMICS

Year founded: 1859. **Academic calendar:** Semester. **Degrees offered:** certificate, associate, terminal-associate, bachelor's, post-bachelor's certificate, master's, post-master's certificate, first professional. **Most popular majors:** 6% elementary education and teaching, 5% English language and literature, 5% nursing/registered nurse training (R.N., A.S.N., B.S.N., M.S.N.), 5% political science and government, 4% mechanical engineering. **Major fields of study:** area, ethnic, cultural, and gender studies; biological and biomedical sciences; business, management, marketing, and related support services; communication, journalism, and related programs; computer and information sciences and support services; education; engineering; English language and literature/letters; foreign languages, literatures, and linguistics; health professions and related clinical sciences; history; mathematics and statistics; multi/interdisciplinary studies; natural resources and conservation; parks, recreation, leisure, and fitness studies; philosophy and religious studies; physical sciences; psychology; public administration and social service professions; social sciences; theology and religious vocations; visual and performing arts. **Areas of required coursework:** humanities, foreign languages, sciences (biological or physical), social science, other. **Pre-professional programs:** pre-law, pre-dentistry, pre-medicine, pre-theology, pre-veterinary science, pre-optometry. **Special academic programs (% participation):** accelerated program (4%), cooperative (work-study plan) program (1%), distance learning (30%), double major (24%), English as a Second Language (ESL) (0%), exchange student program (domestic) (4%), honors program (12%), independent study (24%), internships (36%), liberal arts/career combination (1%), student-designed major (3%), study abroad (19%), teacher certificate program (11%). **Teacher certification offered in:** special education, elementary, middle/junior high, secondary. **Cooperative education programs:** business, computer science, engineering, health professions, humanities, natural science, social/behavioral science, other. **Reserve Officers Training Corps (ROTC):** Air Force ROTC: Offered on campus. **Faculty and instruction (2005-2006):** Total instructional faculty: 243 full-time, 119 part-time (60% men; 40% women; 5% minorities). Full-time faculty with Ph.D. or other terminal degree: 89%. Student/faculty ratio: 13/1. Classes of fewer than 20 students: 52%; of 20 to 49 students: 44%; of 50 or more students: 3%. **Advanced Placement and International Baccalaureate credit:** AP tests may be used for: Credit and/or placement. Scores accepted: 3, 4, 5. International Baccalaureate exams may be used for: Credit and/or placement. **Freshmen returning for sophomore year:** 86%. **Graduation rates:** Four-year: 59%; five-year: 70%; six-year: 73%. **Graduate study:** 27% of students pursue further study within one year. Fields in which graduates pursue further study: Master of Business Administration (MBA), 4%; law, 10%; medicine, 7%; engineering, 3%; theology (or the seminary), 7%; arts and sciences, 69%.

COSTS AND FINANCIAL AID

Financial aid office: (219) 464-5015. **Expenses (2006-2007):** Tuition and fees 2006-2007: $24,000; room/board: $6,640. Estimated books and supplies: $1,000; transportation: $500; personal expenses: $870. **Financial aid:** Priority filing date for institution's financial aid form: March 1. In 2005-2006, 81% of undergraduates applied for financial aid. Of those, 68% were determined to have financial need; 31% had their need fully met. Average financial aid package (proportion receiving): $17,707 (68%). Average amount of gift aid, such as scholarships or grants (proportion receiving): $12,137 (67%). Average amount of self-help aid, such as work study or loans (proportion receiving): $5,433 (62%). Average need-based loan (excluding PLUS or other private loans): $4,988. Among students who received need-based aid, the average percentage of need met: 90%. Among students who received aid based on merit, the average award (and the proportion receiving): $7,888 (25%). The average athletic scholarship (and the proportion receiving): $16,569 (3%). Average amount of debt of borrowers graduating in 2005: $23,853. Proportion who borrowed: 71%.

CAMPUS LIFE AND EXTRACURRICULAR ACTIVITIES

Campus housing available (% using): coed dorms (68%), women's dorms (19%), fraternity housing (7%), apartment for single students (5%), other housing options (1%). Students who live in college-owned, operated, or affiliated housing: 64%. **Student employment:** During the 2005-2006 academic year, 40% of undergraduates worked on campus. Average per-year earnings:

$1,000. **Clubs and organizations:** Number of student organizations: 74. Activities include: choral groups, concert band, dance, drama/theater, jazz band, literary magazine, music ensembles, musical theater, pep band, radio station, student government, student newspaper, student film society, symphony orchestra, yearbook. Number of fraternities: 9; sororities: 6. Proportion of men in fraternities: 26%; of women in sororities: 21%. **Sports program (2005-2006):** Member of NCAA I. *Men's intercollegiate varsity sports:* baseball, basketball, cross-country, football, soccer, swimming and diving, tennis, track and field (indoor), track and field (outdoor). *Women's intercollegiate varsity sports:* basketball, cross-country, soccer, softball, swimming and diving, tennis, track and field (indoor), track and field (outdoor), volleyball.

SERVICES AND FACILITIES

Basic services: nonremedial tutoring, placement service, health service, health insurance. **Remedial assistance:** writing, study skills. **Counseling services:** minority student, career, military, personal, academic, older student, psychological, religious. **For learning-disabled students:** School does not offer a structured program with separate admission and additional fees. Total undergraduates in learning-disabled program or receiving services: 25. Services include: reading machines, tape recorders, other special classes, videotaped classes, untimed tests, note-taking services, oral tests, readers, extended time for tests, tutors, priority registration, priority seating, other testing accomodations, other. **Library:** Number of titles: 1,362,598; number of current serial subscriptions: 25,463. **Information technology resources:** Students are not required to lease or own a computer. Number of campus computers available to all students: 820. School has a wireless network. Approximate number of users that can be accommodated: 2,100. Proportion of college-owned housing units wired for high-speed internet access: 100%. **Campus safety:** Security services offered: 24-hour foot and vehicle patrols, late-night transport/escort service, 24-hour emergency telephones, lighted pathways/sidewalks, controlled dormitory access (key, security card, etc).

TRANSFER AND INTERNATIONAL STUDENTS

Transfer students: May apply for admission for the following academic terms: Fall, Spring, Summer. Applicants do not need a minimum number of credits to apply. For fall 2005: Transfer applications received: 320. Transfer applicants offered admission: 195. Transfer applicants enrolled: 93. **International students:** Number of foreign undergraduates: 53 (2% of student body). Number of countries represented: 25. Minimum TOEFL score required: 550 (paper); 213 (computer).

Wabash College

■ **Address:** PO Box 352, Crawfordsville, IN 47933
■ **Website:** http://www.wabash.edu
■ **Private**
■ **Enrollment:** 871 full-time; 6 part-time

KEY STATS

✔ **U.S News College Ranking:** 51, Liberal Arts Colleges
✔ **SAT Score (25th/75th percentile):** 1080-1310
✔ **Tuition:** 2006-2007: $24,792

Selectivity: More selective	**Room/board:** $7,064
Acceptance rate: 51%	**Average debt:** $17,328
Student/faculty ratio: 10/1	**Proportion who borrowed:** 65%

UNDERGRADUATE STUDENT BODY STATS

2005-2006 enrollment: 871 full-time; 6 part-time. Men: 100%; women: 0%. **Ethnic makeup:** African American: 6%; Asian American: 3%; Hispanic: 4%; White: 83%; International: 4%.

ADMISSIONS FACTS AND FIGURES

Phone: (800) 345-5385. **Email:** admissions@wabash.edu. **Website:** http://www.wabash.edu. **Application deadlines for fall 2007:** Regular decision: Rolling. Early decision: Send application by: November 15; Decision sent by: December 15. Early action: Send application by: December 12; Decision sent by: January 31. Admission can be deferred. **Application fee:** $30. Common application is accepted. **To apply online, go to:** http://www.wabash.edu/admissions/apply/. **Admissions requirements/recommendations:** High school units required (recommended): English: (4); Mathematics: (4); Science: (2); Foreign language: (2); Social studies: (2); History: (0); Total units: (17). Tests: The college uses SAT or ACT scores in admissions decisions. Either SAT or ACT required. For admission to the fall 2007 entering class, the school will accept: ACT with writing, ACT without writing. Campus visit: Recommended. Admissions interview: Recommended. Off-campus interview: May be arranged. **Factors that count in admissions decisions:** *Academic:* Secondary school record: Very important. Class rank: Very important. Letters of recommendation: Important. Standardized test scores: Important. Essay: Considered. *Nonacademic:* Interview: Important. Extracurricular activities: Important. Talent/ability: Important. Character/personal qualities: Important. Alumni/ae relationship: Considered. Geographical residence: Considered. State residency: Not considered. Religious affiliation/commitment: Not considered. Minority status: Considered. Volunteer work: Considered. Work experience: Considered. **Other schools with the greatest overlap in applicants:** Butler University; DePauw University; Hanover College; Indiana University–Bloomington; Purdue University–West Lafayette. **Admissions statistics for the fall 2005 entering class:** Total applicants: 1,358. Total accepted: 691. Freshmen enrolled: 249; 29% were from out of state. Accepted through early-decision or early-action plans: 15%. Overall acceptance rate: 51%. Early-decision acceptance rate: 68%. Non-early acceptance rate: 50%. **Size of waiting list:** 71 applicants; enrolled from waiting list: 1. **Credentials of fall 2005 freshmen:** 29% ranked in the top 10 percent of their high school class; 69% were in the top 25 percent, and 93% were in the top half. (Proportion submitting class standing: 82%.) **Average high school grade point average:** 3.6. **First-year students who submitted SAT scores:** 89%. Scores (25/75 percentile): Verbal: 530-650, Math: 550-660, Combined: 1080-1310. **First-year students submitting ACT scores:** 44%. Scores (25/75 percentile): English: 22-28, Math: 23-29, Composite: 23-28.

ACADEMICS

Year founded: 1832. **Academic calendar:** Semester. **Degrees offered:** bachelor's. **Most popular majors:** 17% English language and literature, 14% history, 11% psychology, 10% economics, 8% biology/biological sciences. **Major fields of study:** biological and biomedical sciences; English language and literature/letters; foreign languages, literatures, and linguistics; mathematics and statistics; philosophy and religious studies; physical sciences; psychology; social sciences; visual and performing arts. **Areas of required coursework:** arts/fine arts, humanities, mathematics, English (including composition), foreign languages, sciences (biological or physical), social science. **Pre-professional programs:** pre-law, pre-dentistry, pre-medicine, other. **Special academic programs (% participation):** double major (15%), independent study (35%), internships (40%), student-designed major (0%), study abroad (29%), teacher certificate program (5%). **Teacher certification offered in:** secondary. **Reserve Officers Training Corps (ROTC):** Army ROTC: Offered at cooperating institution (Purdue). **Faculty and instruction (2005-2006):** Total instructional faculty: 87 full-time, 2 part-time (80% men; 20% women; 6% minorities). Full-time faculty with Ph.D. or other terminal degree: 97%. Student/faculty ratio: 10/1. Classes of fewer than 20 students: 77%; of 20 to 49 students: 22%; of 50 or more students: 1%. **Advanced Placement and International Baccalaureate credit:** AP tests may be used for: Credit and/or placement. Scores accepted: 4, 5. International Baccalaureate exams may be used for: Credit and/or placement. **Freshmen returning for sophomore year:** 86%. **Graduation rates:** Four-year: 66%; five-year: 69%; six-year: 70%. **Graduate study:** 36% of students pursue further study immediately upon graduation; 42% within one year; 75% within five years. Fields in which graduates pursue further study: law, 7%; medicine, 7%; engineering, 3%; theology (or the seminary), 2%; education, 1%; arts and sciences, 17%.

COSTS AND FINANCIAL AID

Financial aid office: (765) 361-6370. **Expenses (2006-2007):** Tuition and fees 2006-2007: $24,792; room/board: $7,064. Estimated books and supplies: $700 personal expenses: $1,000. **Financial aid:** Priority filing date for institution's financial aid form: February 15; deadline: March 1. In 2005-2006, 80% of undergraduates applied for financial aid. Of those, 70% were determined to have financial need; 100% had their need fully met. Average financial aid package (proportion receiving): $22,192 (70%). Average amount of gift aid, such as scholarships or grants (proportion receiving): $15,660 (70%). Average amount of self-help aid, such as work study or loans (proportion receiving): $4,683 (68%). Average need-based loan (excluding PLUS or other private loans): $2,353. Among students who received need-based aid, the average percentage of need met: 100%. Among students who received aid based on merit, the average award (and the proportion receiving): $11,150 (26%). Average amount of debt of borrowers graduating in 2005: $17,328. Proportion who borrowed: 65%.

CAMPUS LIFE AND EXTRACURRICULAR ACTIVITIES

Campus housing available (% using): men's dorms (30%), fraternity housing (65%), other housing options (5%). Students who live in college-owned, operated, or affiliated housing: 88%. **Student employment:** During the 2005-2006 academic year, 74% of undergraduates worked on campus. Average per-year earnings: $1,500. **Clubs and organizations:** Number of student organizations: 50. Activities include: choral groups, concert band, dance, drama/theater, jazz band, literary magazine, music ensembles, musical theater, pep band, radio station, student government, student newspaper, student film society, symphony orchestra, yearbook. Number of fraternities: 10 Proportion of men in fraternities: 65%; Average proportion of students who stay on campus on weekends: 65%. **Sports program (2005-2006):** Member of NCAA III. *Men's intercollegiate varsity sports:* baseball, basketball, cross-country, football, golf, soccer, swimming and diving, tennis, track and field (indoor), track and field (outdoor), wrestling.

SERVICES AND FACILITIES

Basic services: nonremedial tutoring, placement service, health service, health insurance. **Remedial assistance:** math, writing, study skills. **Counseling services:** minority student, career, personal, academic, psychological, religious. **For learning-disabled students:** School does not offer a structured program with separate admission and additional fees. Services include: tape recorders, untimed tests, learning center, extended time for tests, tutors, other. **Library:** Number of titles: 431,942; number of current serial subscriptions: 4,776. **Information technology resources:** Students are not required to lease or own a computer. Number of campus computers available to all students: 350. School has a wireless network. Proportion of college-owned housing units wired for high-speed internet access: 98%. **Campus safety:** Security services offered: 24-hour foot and vehicle patrols, late-night transport/escort service, 24-hour emergency telephones, lighted pathways/sidewalks.

TRANSFER AND INTERNATIONAL STUDENTS

Transfer students: May apply for admission for the following academic terms: Fall. Applicants do not need a minimum number of credits to apply. For fall 2005: Transfer applications received: 27. Transfer applicants offered admission: 2. Transfer applicants enrolled: 2. **International students:** Number of foreign undergraduates: 33 (4% of student body). Number of countries represented: 33. Minimum TOEFL score required: 550 (paper); 213 (computer). Average TOEFL score: 597 (paper).

Iowa

Briar Cliff University

- **Address:** 3303 Rebecca Street, Box 2100, Sioux City, IA 51104
- **Website:** http://www.briarcliff.edu
- **Private; Religious affiliation:** Roman Catholic
- **Enrollment:** 970 full-time; 126 part-time

KEY STATS

✔ **U.S News College Ranking:** third tier, Comp. Coll.–Bachelor's (Midwest)
✔ **ACT Score (25th/75th percentile):** 19-24
✔ **Tuition:** 2005-2006: $17,985

Selectivity: Selective	**Room/board:** $5,565
Acceptance rate: 76%	**Average debt:** N/A
Student/faculty ratio: 13/1	**Proportion who borrowed:** N/A

UNDERGRADUATE STUDENT BODY STATS

2005-2006 enrollment: 970 full-time; 126 part-time. Men: 40%; women: 60%. **Ethnic makeup:** African American: 2%; American-Indian: 1%; Asian American: 2%; Hispanic: 4%; White: 91%. **Religious preference:** Protestant: 15%; No preference: 1%; Unknown: 36%; Roman Catholic: 48%.

ADMISSIONS FACTS AND FIGURES

Phone: (712) 279-5200. **Email:** admissions@briarcliff.edu. **Website:** http://www.briarcliff.edu. **Application deadlines for fall 2007:** Regular decision: Rolling. Early decision: Not offered. Early action: Not offered. Admission can be deferred. **Application fee:** $20. Common application is accepted. **Admissions requirements/recommendations:** High school units required (recommended): English: 4 (4); Mathematics: 3 (3); Science: 3 (3); Foreign language: 2 (2); Social studies: 1 (1); History: 1 (2); Academic electives: 1 (1); Total units: 16 (16). Tests: The college uses SAT or ACT scores in admissions decisions. ACT required. For admission to the fall 2007 entering class, the school will accept: ACT with writing, ACT without writing. Campus visit: Recommended. Admissions interview: Recommended. Off-campus interview: May be arranged. **Factors that count in admissions decisions:** *Academic:* Secondary school record: Very important. Class rank: Important. Letters of recommendation: Important. Standardized test scores: Very important. Essay: Considered. *Nonacademic:* Interview: Considered. Extracurricular activities: Important. Talent/ability: Considered. Character/personal qualities: Considered. Alumni/ae relationship: Considered. Geographical residence: Not considered. State residency: Not considered. Religious affiliation/commitment: Not considered. Minority status: Not considered. Volunteer work: Not considered. Work experience: Not considered. **Other schools with the greatest overlap in applicants:** Buena Vista University; Iowa State University; Morningside College; University of Iowa. **Admissions statistics for the fall 2005 entering class:** Total applicants: 1,275. Total accepted: 971. Freshmen enrolled: 251; 49% were from out of state. Overall acceptance rate: 76%. **Size of waiting list:** 0 applicants; enrolled from waiting list: 0. **Credentials of fall 2005 freshmen:** 15% ranked in the top 10 percent of their high school class; 35% were in the top 25 percent, and 59% were in the top half. (Proportion submitting class standing: 96%.) **Average high school grade point average:** 3.2. **First-year students who submitted SAT scores:** 3%. Scores (25/75 percentile): Verbal: 420-560, Math: 387-650, Combined: 807-1210. **First-year students submitting ACT scores:** 97%. Scores (25/75 percentile): English: 18-24, Math: 18-24, Composite: 19-24.

ACADEMICS

Year founded: 1930. **Academic calendar:** Trimester. **Degrees offered:** associate, bachelor's, post-bachelor's certificate, master's. **Most popular majors:** 16% business administration and management, 12% elementary education and teaching, 11% nursing/registered nurse training (R.N., A.S.N., B.S.N., M.S.N.), 7% biology/biological sciences, 6% human resources management/personnel administration. **Major fields of study:** biological and biomedical sciences; business, management, marketing, and related support services; communication, journalism, and related programs; computer and information sciences and support services; education; English language and literature/letters; foreign languages, literatures, and linguistics; health professions and related clinical sciences; mathematics and statistics; natural resources and conservation; parks, recreation, leisure, and fitness studies; physical sciences; psychology; public administration and social service professions; security and protective services; social sciences; theology and religious vocations; visual and performing arts. **Areas of required coursework:** arts/fine arts, humanities, computer literacy, mathematics, English (including composition), philosophy, foreign languages, sciences (biological or physical), history, social science, other. **Pre-professional programs:** pre-law, pre-dentistry, pre-medicine, pre-veterinary science, pre-optometry, pre-pharmacy, other. **Special academic programs (% participation):** accelerated program (8%), distance learning (7%), double major (7%), dual enrollment (0%), honors program (0%), independent study (100%), internships (75%), study abroad (0%), teacher certificate program (13%). **Teacher certification offered in:** special education, elementary, middle/junior high, secondary. **Faculty and instruction (2005-2006):** Total instructional faculty: 56 full-time, 40 part-time (50% men; 50% women; 1% minorities). Full-time faculty with Ph.D. or other terminal degree: 61%. Student/faculty ratio: 13/1. Classes of fewer than 20 students: 62%; of 20 to 49 students: 37%; of 50 or more students: 1%. **Advanced Placement and International Baccalaureate credit:** AP tests may be used for: Credit only. Scores accepted: 3, 4, 5. International Baccalaureate exams may be used for: Credit only. **Freshmen returning for sophomore year:** 69%. **Graduation rates:** Four-year: 40%; five-year: 51%; six-year: 51%. **Graduate study:** 17% of students pursue further study within one year. Fields in which graduates pursue further study: Master of Business Administration (MBA), 11%; law, 1%; medicine, 5%; dentistry, 5%; education, 5%; arts and sciences, 26%; veterinary medicine, 10%.

COSTS AND FINANCIAL AID

Financial aid office: (712) 279-5239. **Expenses (2005-2006):** Tuition and fees 2005-2006: $17,985; room/board: $5,565. Estimated books and supplies: $825; transportation: $870; personal expenses: $1,935. **Financial aid:** Priority filing date for institution's financial aid form: March 15; deadline: August 29.

CAMPUS LIFE AND EXTRACURRICULAR ACTIVITIES

Campus housing available (% using): coed dorms (84%), other housing options (16%). Students who live in college-owned, operated, or affiliated housing: 55%. **Student employment:** During the 2005-2006 academic year, 25% of undergraduates worked on campus. Average per-year earnings: $700. **Clubs and organizations:** Number of student organizations: 36. Activities include: choral groups, dance, drama/theater, literary magazine, musical theater, opera, radio station, student government, student newspaper. Number of fraternities: 0; sororities: 0. Average proportion of students who stay on campus on weekends: 70%. **Sports program (2005-2006):** Member of NAIA. *Men's intercollegiate varsity sports:* baseball, basketball, cross-country, football, golf, soccer, track and field (indoor), track and field (outdoor), wrestling. *Women's intercollegiate varsity sports:* basketball, cross-country, golf, soccer, softball, track and field (indoor), track and field (outdoor), volleyball.

SERVICES AND FACILITIES

Basic services: nonremedial tutoring, placement service, health service. **Remedial assistance:** reading, math, writing, study skills. **Counseling services:** career, military, personal, veteran student, academic, older student, psychological, religious. **For learning-disabled students:** School does not offer a structured program with separate admission and additional fees. Total undergraduates in learning-disabled program or receiving services: 10. Services include: remedial math, reading machines, remedial reading, tape recorders, note-taking services, oral tests, extended time for tests, priority registration, exams on tape or computer, other testing accomodations. **Library:** Number of titles: 84,540; number of current serial subscriptions: 10,409. **Information technology resources:** Students are not required to lease or own a computer. Number of campus computers available to all students: 142. School has a wireless network. Approximate number of users that can be accommodated: 225. Proportion of college-owned housing units wired for high-speed internet access: 100%. **Campus safety:** Security services offered: 24-hour foot and vehicle patrols, late-night transport/escort service, 24-hour emergency telephones, lighted pathways/sidewalks, controlled dormitory access (key, security card, etc).

TRANSFER AND INTERNATIONAL STUDENTS

Transfer students: May apply for admission for the following academic terms: Fall, Winter, Spring, Summer. Applicants need a minimum number of credits to apply. For fall 2005: Transfer applications received: 294. Transfer applicants offered admission: 197. Transfer applicants enrolled: 102. **International students:** Number of foreign undergraduates: 2. Number of countries represented: 2. Minimum TOEFL score required: 500 (paper); 200 (computer). Average TOEFL score: 550 (paper).

Buena Vista University

- **Address:** 610 W. Fourth Street, Storm Lake, IA 50588
- **Website:** http://www.bvu.edu
- **Private; Religious affiliation:** Presbyterian
- **Enrollment:** 1,198 full-time; 16 part-time

KEY STATS

- ✔ **U.S News College Ranking:** 18, Comp. Coll.–Bachelor's (Midwest)
- ✔ **ACT Score (25th/75th percentile):** 19-25
- ✔ **Tuition:** 2006-2007: $22,556

Selectivity: Selective	**Room/board:** $6,296
Acceptance rate: 83%	**Average debt:** $29,059
Student/faculty ratio: 13/1	**Proportion who borrowed:** 92%

UNDERGRADUATE STUDENT BODY STATS

2005-2006 enrollment: 1,198 full-time; 16 part-time. Men: 48%; women: 52%. **Ethnic makeup:** African American: 3%; Asian American: 2%; Hispanic: 2%; White: 93%. **Religious preference:** Roman Catholic: 29%; Protestant: 45%; Unknown: 12%; Presbyterian: 5%; Other: 9%.

ADMISSIONS FACTS AND FIGURES

Phone: (800) 383-9600. **Email:** admissions@bvu.edu. **Website:** http://www.bvu.edu. **Application deadlines for fall 2007:** Regular decision: Rolling. Early decision: Not offered. Early action: Not offered. Admission can be deferred. Common application is accepted. **Admissions requirements/recommendations:** High school units required (recommended): English: 4; Mathematics: (4); Science: 2 (4); Foreign language: (2); Social studies: 2; History: (2); Total units: 15. **Tests:** The college uses SAT or ACT scores in admissions decisions. Either SAT or ACT required. For admission to the fall 2007 entering class, the school will accept: ACT with writing, ACT without writing. Campus visit: Recommended. Admissions interview: Recommended. Off-campus interview: May be arranged. **Factors that count in admissions decisions:** *Academic:* Secondary school record: Very important. Class rank: Very important. Letters of recommendation: Very important. Standardized test scores: Very important. Essay: Considered. *Nonacademic:* Interview: Considered. Extracurricular activities: Considered. Talent/ability: Considered. Character/personal qualities: Considered. Alumni/ae relationship: Considered. Geographical residence: Not considered. State residency: Not considered. Religious affiliation/commitment: Not considered. Minority status: Not considered. Volunteer work: Considered. Work experience: Considered. **Other schools with the greatest overlap in applicants:** Central College; Morningside College; Simpson University; University of Northern Iowa; Wartburg College. **Admissions statistics for the fall 2005 entering class:** Total applicants: 1,183. Total accepted: 984. Freshmen enrolled: 287; 23% were from out of state. Overall acceptance rate: 83%. **Credentials of fall 2005 freshmen:** 16% ranked in the top 10 percent of their high school class; 38% were in the top 25 percent, and 75% were in the top half. (Proportion submitting class standing: 98%.) **Average high school grade point average:** 3.3. **First-year students who submitted SAT scores:** 1%. Scores (25/75 percentile): Verbal: N/A, Math: N/A, Combined: N/A. **First-year students submitting ACT scores:** 99%. Scores (25/75 percentile): English: N/A, Math: N/A, Composite: 19-25.

ACADEMICS

Year founded: 1891. **Academic calendar:** 4-1-4. **Degrees offered:** bachelor's, master's. **Most popular majors:** 29% business, management, marketing, and related support services, 21% education, 13% multi/interdisciplinary studies, 13% psychology, 5% security and protective services. **Major fields of study:** biological and biomedical sciences; business, management, marketing, and related support services; communication, journalism, and related programs; computer and information sciences and support services; education; English language and literature/letters; foreign languages, literatures, and linguistics; health professions and related clinical sciences; history; mathematics and statistics; multi/interdisciplinary studies; parks, recreation, leisure, and fitness studies; philosophy and religious studies; physical sciences; psychology; public administration and social service professions; security and protective services; social sciences; visual and performing arts. **Areas of required coursework:** arts/fine arts, humanities, computer literacy, mathematics, English (including composition), sciences (biological or physical), social science. **Pre-professional programs:** pre-law, pre-dentistry, pre-medicine, pre-theology, pre-veterinary science, pre-optometry, pre-pharmacy, other. **Special academic programs:** distance learning, double major, dual enrollment, English as a Second Language (ESL), exchange student program (domestic), external degree program, honors program, independent study, internships, liberal arts/career combination, student-designed major, study abroad, teacher certificate program. **Teacher certification offered in:** special education, elementary, middle/junior high, secondary. **Faculty and instruction (2005-2006):** Total instructional faculty: 81 full-time, 35 part-time (53% men; 47% women; 4% minorities). Full-time faculty with Ph.D. or other terminal degree: 69%. Student/faculty ratio: 13/1. Classes of fewer than 20 students: 65%; of 20 to 49 students: 35%; of 50 or more students: 1%. **Advanced Placement and International Baccalaureate credit:** AP tests may be used for: Credit and/or placement. Scores accepted: 3, 4, 5. International Baccalaureate exams may be used for: Credit and/or placement. **Freshmen returning for sophomore year:** 75%. **Graduation rates:** Four-year: 45%; five-year: 55%; six-year: 57%. **Graduate study:** 17% of students pursue further study immediately upon graduation. Fields in which graduates pursue further study: Master of Business Administration (MBA), 2%; law, 2%; medicine, 44%; education, 2%; arts and sciences, 49%.

COSTS AND FINANCIAL AID

Financial aid office: (712) 749-2164. **Expenses (2006-2007):** Tuition and fees 2006-2007: $22,556; room/board: $6,296. Estimated books and supplies: $750 personal expenses: $1,500. **Financial aid:** Priority filing date for institution's financial aid form: June 1. In 2005-2006, 97% of undergraduates applied for financial aid. Of those, 92% were determined to have financial need; 28% had their need fully met. Average financial aid package (proportion receiving): $19,994 (92%). Average amount of gift aid, such as scholarships or grants (proportion receiving): $9,608 (90%). Average amount of self-help aid, such as work study or loans (proportion receiving): $5,324 (79%). Average need-based loan (excluding PLUS or other private loans): $4,689. Among students who received need-based aid, the average percentage of need met: 91%. Among students who received aid based on merit, the average award (and the proportion receiving): $6,550 (5%). The average athletic scholarship (and the proportion receiving): $0 (0%). Average amount of debt of borrowers graduating in 2005: $29,059. Proportion who borrowed: 92%.

CAMPUS LIFE AND EXTRACURRICULAR ACTIVITIES

Campus housing available (% using): coed dorms (62%), women's dorms (15%), men's dorms (23%). Students who live in college-owned, operated, or affiliated housing: 88%. **Clubs and organizations:** Number of student organizations: 75. Activities include: choral groups, concert band, drama/theater, jazz band, literary magazine, music ensembles, musical theater, pep band, radio station, student government, student newspaper, symphony orchestra, television station, yearbook. Number of fraternities: 0; sororities: 0. Average proportion of students who stay on campus on weekends: 60%. **Sports program (2005-2006):** Member of NCAA III. *Men's intercollegiate varsity sports:* baseball, basketball, cross-country, football, golf, soccer, swimming and diving, tennis, track and field (indoor), track and field (outdoor), wrestling. *Women's intercollegiate varsity sports:* basketball, cross-country, golf, soccer, softball, swimming and diving, tennis, track and field (indoor), track and field (outdoor), volleyball.

SERVICES AND FACILITIES

Basic services: nonremedial tutoring, placement service, health service. **Remedial assistance:** reading, math, writing, study skills. **Counseling services:** minority student, career, personal, veteran student, academic, psychological, birth control, religious. **For learning-disabled students:** School does not offer a structured program with separate admission and additional fees. Total undergraduates in learning-disabled program or receiving services: 32. Services include: remedial math, remedial English, tape recorders, learning center, tutors. **Library:** Number of titles: 139,101; number of current serial subscriptions: 654. **Information technology resources:** Students are not required to lease or own a computer. School has a wireless network. Approximate number of users that can be accommodated: 10,000. Proportion of college-owned housing units wired for high-speed internet access: 100%. **Campus safety:** Security services offered: late-night transport/escort service, 24-hour emergency telephones, lighted pathways/sidewalks, controlled dormitory access (key, security card, etc).

TRANSFER AND INTERNATIONAL STUDENTS
Transfer students: May apply for admission for the following academic terms: Fall, Winter, Spring. Applicants do not need a minimum number of credits to apply. For fall 2005: Transfer applications received: 196. Transfer applicants offered admission: 108. Transfer applicants enrolled: 56. **International students:** Number of foreign undergraduates: 0. Number of countries represented: 1. Minimum TOEFL score required: 550 (paper). Average TOEFL score: 525 (paper).

Central College

- ■ **Address:** 812 University Street, Pella, IA 50219
- ■ **Website:** http://www.central.edu
- ■ **Private; Religious affiliation:** Reformed Church
- ■ **Enrollment:** 1,601 full-time; 34 part-time

KEY STATS
- ✔ **U.S News College Ranking:** 10, Comp. Coll.–Bachelor's (Midwest)
- ✔ **ACT Score (25th/75th percentile):** 21-26
- ✔ **Tuition:** 2006-2007: $21,222
  - **Selectivity:** More selective   **Room/board:** $7,224
  - **Acceptance rate:** 84%   **Average debt:** $23,490
  - **Student/faculty ratio:** 16/1   **Proportion who borrowed:** 85%

UNDERGRADUATE STUDENT BODY STATS
2005-2006 enrollment: 1,601 full-time; 34 part-time. Men: 44%; women: 56%. **Ethnic makeup:** African American: 1%; Asian American: 1%; Hispanic: 1%; White: 95%; International: 2%. **Religious preference:** Roman Catholic: 16%; Protestant: 61%; No preference: 1%; Unknown: 12%; Reformed Church: 10%.

ADMISSIONS FACTS AND FIGURES
Phone: (641) 628-5286. **Email:** admissions@central.edu. **Website:** http://www.central.edu. **Application deadlines for fall 2007:** Regular decision: Rolling. Early decision: Not offered. Early action: Not offered. Admission can be deferred. **Application fee:** $25. Common application is accepted. **Admissions requirements/recommendations:** High school units required (recommended): English: 4 (4); Mathematics: 3 (3); Science: 3 (3); Foreign language: 3 (3); Social studies: 3 (3); History: 2 (2); Total units: 21. Tests: The college uses SAT or ACT scores in admissions decisions. Either SAT or ACT required. For admission to the fall 2007 entering class, the school will accept: ACT with writing, ACT without writing. Campus visit: Recommended. Admissions interview: Recommended. Off-campus interview: May be arranged. **Factors that count in admissions decisions:** *Academic:* Secondary school record: Very important. Class rank: Important. Letters of recommendation: Important. Standardized test scores: Very important. Essay: Considered. *Nonacademic:* Interview: Considered. Extracurricular activities: Considered. Talent/ability: Not considered. Character/personal qualities: Considered. Alumni/ae relationship: Not considered. Geographical residence: Not considered. State residency: Not considered. Religious affiliation/commitment: Not considered. Minority status: Not considered. Volunteer work: Considered. Work experience: Considered. **Other schools with the greatest overlap in applicants:** Buena Vista University; Iowa State University; Simpson College; University of Northern Iowa; Wartburg College. **Admissions statistics for the fall 2005 entering class:** Total applicants: 1,641. Total accepted: 1,375. Freshmen enrolled: 366; Overall acceptance rate: 84%. **Credentials of fall 2005 freshmen:** 25% ranked in the top 10 percent of their high school class; 53% were in the top 25 percent, and 78% were in the top half. (Proportion submitting class standing: 97%.) **Average high school grade point average:** 3.5. **First-year students who submitted SAT scores:** 4%. Scores (25/75 percentile): Verbal: 460-650, Math: 470-610, Combined: 930-1260. **First-year students submitting ACT scores:** 95%. Scores (25/75 percentile): English: 20-26, Math: 19-25, Composite: 21-26.

ACADEMICS
Year founded: 1853. **Academic calendar:** Semester. **Degrees offered:** bachelor's. **Most popular majors:** 13% business, management, marketing, and related support services, 12% education, 11% parks, recreation, leisure, and fitness studies, 6% communication studies/speech communication and rhetoric, 5% general studies. **Major fields of study:** area, ethnic, cultural, and gender studies; biological and biomedical sciences; communication, journalism, and related programs; computer and information sciences and support services; education; English language and literature/letters; foreign languages, literatures, and linguistics; history; liberal arts and sciences studies, and humanities; mathematics and statistics; multi/interdisciplinary studies; natural resources and conservation; philosophy and religious studies; physical sciences; psychology; social sciences; visual and performing arts. **Areas of required coursework:** arts/fine arts, humanities, mathematics, English (including composition), foreign languages, sciences (biological or physical), history, social science. **Pre-professional programs:** pre-law, pre-medicine, pre-veterinary science. **Special academic programs (% participation):** cooperative (work-study plan) program (1%), double major (7%), English as a Second Language (ESL) (1%), honors program (12%), independent study, internships (50%), liberal arts/career combination (100%), student-designed major (1%), study abroad (40%), teacher certificate program (20%). **Teacher certification offered in:** early childhood, special education, elementary, middle/junior high, secondary. **Cooperative education programs:** business. **Faculty and instruction (2005-2006):** Total instructional faculty: 87 full-time, 49 part-time (63% men; 38% women; 9% minorities). Full-time faculty with Ph.D. or other terminal degree: 100%. Student/faculty ratio: 16/1. Classes of fewer than 20 students: 62%; of 20 to 49 students: 38%; of 50 or more students: 0%. **Advanced Placement and International Baccalaureate credit:** AP tests may be used for: Credit and/or placement. Scores accepted: 3, 4, 5. International Baccalaureate exams may be used for: Credit and/or placement. **Freshmen returning for sophomore year:** 81%. **Graduation rates:** Four-year: 60%; five-year: 64%; six-year: 66%. **Graduate study:** 21% of students pursue further study immediately upon graduation; 19% within one year. Fields in which graduates pursue further study: business. Master of Business Administration (MBA), 2%; law, 11%; medicine, 9%; dentistry, 4%; engineering, 7%; theology (or the seminary), 3%; education, 2%; arts and sciences, 3%; veterinary medicine, 2%.

COSTS AND FINANCIAL AID
Financial aid office: (641) 628-5187. **Expenses (2006-2007):** Tuition and fees 2006-2007: $21,222; room/board: $7,224. Estimated books and supplies: $880; transportation: $600; personal expenses: $1,374. **Financial aid:** Priority filing date for institution's financial aid form: March 15. In 2005-2006, 89% of undergraduates applied for financial aid. Of those, 81% were determined to have financial need; 16% had their need fully met. Average financial aid package (proportion receiving): $16,987 (81%). Average amount of gift aid, such as scholarships or grants (proportion receiving): $11,542 (80%). Average amount of self-help aid, such as work study or loans (proportion receiving): $5,189 (68%). Average need-based loan (excluding PLUS or other private loans): $4,208. Among students who received need-based aid, the average percentage of need met: 81%. Among students who received aid based on merit, the average award (and the proportion receiving): $8,000 (19%). The average athletic scholarship (and the proportion receiving): $0 (0%). Average amount of debt of borrowers graduating in 2005: $23,490. Proportion who borrowed: 85%.

CAMPUS LIFE AND EXTRACURRICULAR ACTIVITIES
Campus housing available: coed dorms, women's dorms, men's dorms, sorority housing, fraternity housing, apartments for married students. **Student employment:** During the 2005-2006 academic year, 56% of undergraduates worked on campus. Average per-year earnings: $1,200. **Clubs and organizations:** Number of student organizations: 63. Activities include: choral groups, concert band, drama/theater, jazz band, literary magazine, music ensembles, musical theater, radio station, student government, student newspaper, symphony orchestra, yearbook. Number of fraternities: 4; sororities: 3. Average proportion of students who stay on campus on weekends: 75%. **Sports program (2005-2006):** Member of NCAA III. *Men's intercollegiate varsity sports:* baseball, basketball, cross-country, football, golf, soccer, tennis, track and field (indoor), track and field (outdoor), wrestling. *Women's intercollegiate varsity sports:* basketball, cross-country, golf, soccer, softball, tennis, track and field (indoor), track and field (outdoor), volleyball.

SERVICES AND FACILITIES
Basic services: nonremedial tutoring, health service, health insurance. **Counseling services:** minority student, career, personal, veteran student, academic, older student, psychological, birth control, religious. **For learning-dis-**

abled students: School does not offer a structured program with separate admission and additional fees. Services include: reading machines, tape recorders, videotaped classes, diagnostic testing service, untimed tests, note-taking services, oral tests, learning center, readers, extended time for tests, tutors, texts on tape. **Library:** Number of titles: 233,860; number of current serial subscriptions: 1,170. **Information technology resources:** Students are not required to lease or own a computer. Number of campus computers available to all students: 400. School has a wireless network. Approximate number of users that can be accommodated: 500. Proportion of college-owned housing units wired for high-speed internet access: 100%. **Campus safety:** Security services offered: 24-hour foot and vehicle patrols, late-night transport/escort service, 24-hour emergency telephones, lighted pathways/sidewalks, student patrols, controlled dormitory access (key, security card, etc).

TRANSFER AND INTERNATIONAL STUDENTS

Transfer students: May apply for admission for the following academic terms: Fall, Spring, Summer. Applicants do not need a minimum number of credits to apply. For fall 2005: Transfer applications received: 162. Transfer applicants offered admission: 95. Transfer applicants enrolled: 58. **International students:** Number of foreign undergraduates: 30 (2% of student body). Number of countries represented: 16. Minimum TOEFL score required: 530 (paper); 179 (computer).

Clarke College

- **Address:** 1550 Clarke Drive, Dubuque, IA 52001
- **Website:** http://www.clarke.edu
- **Private; Religious affiliation:** Roman Catholic
- **Enrollment:** 857 full-time; 164 part-time

KEY STATS

✔ **U.S News College Ranking:** 31, Comp. Coll.–Bachelor's (Midwest)
✔ **ACT Score (25th/75th percentile):** 20-25
✔ **Tuition:** 2006-2007: $20,297

Selectivity: Selective	**Room/board:** $6,574
Acceptance rate: 61%	**Average debt:** $19,492
Student/faculty ratio: 11/1	**Proportion who borrowed:** 72%

UNDERGRADUATE STUDENT BODY STATS

2005-2006 enrollment: 857 full-time; 164 part-time. Men: 29%; women: 71%. **Ethnic makeup:** African American: 3%; Asian American: 1%; Hispanic: 3%; White: 93%; International: 1%.

ADMISSIONS FACTS AND FIGURES

Phone: (563) 588-6316. **Email:** admissions@clarke.edu. **Website:** http://www.clarke.edu. **Application deadlines for fall 2007:** Regular decision: Rolling. Early decision: Not offered. Early action: Not offered. Admission can be deferred. **Application fee:** $25. Common application is accepted. **To apply online, go to:** http://www.clarke.edu/admissions/apply.htm. **Admissions requirements/recommendations:** High school units required (recommended): English: 4; Mathematics: 3 (4); Science: 3 (4); Foreign language: 2; Social studies: 3; Academic electives: 4; Total units: 21. Tests: The college uses SAT or ACT scores in admissions decisions. Either SAT or ACT required. For admission to the fall 2007 entering class, the school will accept: ACT with writing, ACT without writing. Campus visit: Recommended. Admissions interview: Recommended. Off-campus interview: May be arranged. **Factors that count in admissions decisions:** *Academic:* Secondary school record: Very important. Class rank: Important. Letters of recommendation: Not considered. Standardized test scores: Very important. Essay: Not considered. *Nonacademic:* Interview: Considered. Extracurricular activities: Considered. Talent/ability: Considered. Character/personal qualities: Not considered. Alumni/ae relationship: Not considered. Geographical residence: Not considered. State residency: Not considered. Religious affiliation/commitment: Not considered. Minority status: Considered. Volunteer work: Considered. Work experience: Not considered. **Other schools with the greatest overlap in applicants:** Coe College; Loras College; Luther College; St. Ambrose University; University of Dubuque. **Admissions statistics for the fall 2005 entering class:** Total applicants: 784. Total accepted: 478. Freshmen enrolled: 158; 50% were from out of state. Overall acceptance rate: 61%. **Credentials of fall 2005 freshmen:** 13% ranked in the top 10 percent of their high school class; 34% were in the top 25 percent, and 75% were in the top half. (Proportion submitting class standing: 87%.) **Average high school grade point average:** 3.3. First-year students who submitted SAT scores: 8%. Scores (25/75 percentile): Verbal: 473-628, Math: 473-643, Combined: 946-1271. **First-year students submitting ACT scores:** 96%. Scores (25/75 percentile): English: 19-25, Math: 18-25, Composite: 20-25.

ACADEMICS

Year founded: 1843. **Academic calendar:** Semester. **Degrees offered:** associate, bachelor's, master's, doctorate. **Most popular majors:** 22% elementary education and teaching, 17% business administration and management, 10% communication studies/speech communication and rhetoric, 10% computer and information sciences, 7% psychology. **Major fields of study:** biological and biomedical sciences; communication, journalism, and related programs; computer and information sciences and support services; education; English language and literature/letters; foreign languages, literatures, and linguistics; liberal arts and sciences studies, and humanities; mathematics and statistics; multi/interdisciplinary studies; philosophy and religious studies; physical sciences; psychology; public administration and social service professions; social sciences. **Areas of required coursework:** arts/fine arts, humanities, English (including composition), philosophy, sciences (biological or physical), social science. **Pre-professional programs:** pre-law, pre-dentistry, pre-medicine, pre-veterinary science, pre-pharmacy. **Special academic programs (% participation):** accelerated program (14%), cooperative (work-study plan) program (1%), cross-registration (1%), distance learning (1%), double major (1%), dual enrollment (1%), honors program (1%), independent study (1%), internships (1%), student-designed major (1%), study abroad (1%), teacher certificate program (1%). **Teacher certification offered in:** special education, elementary, middle/junior high, secondary. **Reserve Officers Training Corps (ROTC):** Army ROTC: Offered at cooperating institution (University of Dubuque). **Faculty and instruction (2005-2006):** Total instructional faculty: 83 full-time, 47 part-time (39% men; 61% women; 2% minorities). Full-time faculty with Ph.D. or other terminal degree: 57%. Student/faculty ratio: 11/1. Classes of fewer than 20 students: 81%; of 20 to 49 students: 18%; of 50 or more students: 0%. **Advanced Placement and International Baccalaureate credit:** AP tests may be used for: Credit and/or placement. Scores accepted: 2, 3, 4, 5. International Baccalaureate exams may be used for: Credit and/or placement. **Freshmen returning for sophomore year:** 79%. **Graduation rates:** Four-year: 45%; five-year: 56%; six-year: 61%. **Graduate study:** 23% of students pursue further study immediately upon graduation.

COSTS AND FINANCIAL AID

Financial aid office: (563) 588-6327. **Expenses (2006-2007):** Tuition and fees 2006-2007: $20,297; room/board: $6,574. Estimated books and supplies: $1,000; transportation: $300; personal expenses: $700. **Financial aid:** Priority filing date for institution's financial aid form: April 15. In 2005-2006, 94% of undergraduates applied for financial aid. Of those, 86% were determined to have financial need; 27% had their need fully met. Average financial aid package (proportion receiving): $16,631 (86%). Average amount of gift aid, such as scholarships or grants (proportion receiving): $12,897 (85%). Average amount of self-help aid, such as work study or loans (proportion receiving): $4,719 (71%). Average need-based loan (excluding PLUS or other private loans): $4,237. Among students who received need-based aid, the average percentage of need met: 100%. Among students who received aid based on merit, the average award (and the proportion receiving): $12,108 (11%). The average athletic scholarship (and the proportion receiving): $0 (0%). Average amount of debt of borrowers graduating in 2005: $19,492. Proportion who borrowed: 72%.

CAMPUS LIFE AND EXTRACURRICULAR ACTIVITIES

Campus housing available: coed dorms, women's dorms, men's dorms, apartment for single students. Students who live in college-owned, operated, or affiliated housing: 37%. Activities include: choral groups, drama/theater, jazz band, literary magazine, music ensembles, radio station, student government, student newspaper, yearbook. Number of fraternities: 0; sororities: 0. Average proportion of students who stay on campus on weekends: 60%. **Sports program (2005-2006):** Member of NCAA III. *Men's intercollegiate varsity sports:* baseball, basketball, cross-country, golf, soccer, tennis, volleyball. *Women's intercollegiate varsity sports:* basketball, bowling, cross-country, golf, soccer, softball, tennis, volleyball.

SERVICES AND FACILITIES

Basic services: placement service, health service. **Remedial assistance:** reading, math, writing, study skills. **Counseling services:** career, personal, academic, older student, psychological, religious. **For learning-disabled**

students: School does not offer a structured program with separate admission and additional fees. Services include: remedial math, remedial English, remedial reading, untimed tests, oral tests, learning center, readers, extended time for tests, tutors, other. **Library:** Number of titles: 129,563; number of current serial subscriptions: 133,587. **Information technology resources:** Students are not required to lease or own a computer. Number of campus computers available to all students: 237. School has a wireless network. **Campus safety:** Security services offered: 24-hour foot and vehicle patrols, 24-hour emergency telephones, lighted pathways/sidewalks, controlled dormitory access (key, security card, etc).

TRANSFER AND INTERNATIONAL STUDENTS

Transfer students: May apply for admission for the following academic terms: Fall, Spring, Summer. Applicants need a minimum number of credits to apply. For fall 2005: Transfer applications received: 251. Transfer applicants offered admission: 157. Transfer applicants enrolled: 123. **International students:** Number of foreign undergraduates: 9 (1% of student body). Minimum TOEFL score required: 525 (paper); 203 (computer).

Coe College

- **Address:** 1220 First Avenue NE, Cedar Rapids, IA 52402
- **Website:** http://www.coe.edu
- **Private; Religious affiliation:** Presbyterian
- **Enrollment:** 1,245 full-time; 86 part-time

KEY STATS

✔ **U.S News College Ranking:** 95, Liberal Arts Colleges
✔ **ACT Score (25th/75th percentile):** 23-28
✔ **Tuition:** 2006-2007: $25,120

Selectivity: More selective	**Room/board:** $6,550
Acceptance rate: 72%	**Average debt:** $20,237
Student/faculty ratio: 12/1	**Proportion who borrowed:** 76%

UNDERGRADUATE STUDENT BODY STATS

2005-2006 enrollment: 1,245 full-time; 86 part-time. Men: 43%; women: 57%. **Ethnic makeup:** African American: 2%; Asian American: 1%; Hispanic: 2%; White: 91%; International: 4%. **Religious preference:** Roman Catholic: 20%; Protestant: 6%; Jewish: 1%; No preference: 54%; Presbyterian: 5%; Lutheran: 9%; Other: 5%.

ADMISSIONS FACTS AND FIGURES

Phone: (319) 399-8500. **Email:** admission@coe.edu. **Website:** http://www.coe.edu. **Application deadlines for fall 2007:** Regular decision: March 1; decision sent by March 15. Early decision: Not offered. Early action: Send application by: December 10; Decision sent by: January 20. Admission can be deferred. **Application fee:** $30. Common application is accepted. **To apply online, go to:** http://www.coe.edu/admission/apply/. **Admissions requirements/recommendations:** High school units required (recommended): English: (4); Mathematics: (3); Science: (3); Foreign language: (2); Social studies: (3); History: (0); Academic electives: (2); Total units: (18). Tests: The college uses SAT or ACT scores in admissions decisions. Either SAT or ACT required. For admission to the fall 2007 entering class, the school will accept: ACT with writing, ACT without writing. Campus visit: Recommended. Admissions interview: Recommended. Off-campus interview: May be arranged. **Factors that count in admissions decisions:** *Academic:* Secondary school record: Very important. Class rank: Important. Letters of recommendation: Important. Standardized test scores: Very important. Essay: Important. *Nonacademic:* Interview: Considered. Extracurricular activities: Considered. Talent/ability: Considered. Character/personal qualities: Considered. Alumni/ae relationship: Considered. Geographical residence: Not considered. State residency: Not considered. Religious affiliation/commitment: Not considered. Minority status: Considered. Volunteer work: Considered. Work experience: Not considered. **Other schools with the greatest overlap in applicants:** Beloit College; Cornell College; Luther College; Macalester College; University of Iowa. **Admissions statistics for the fall 2005 entering class:** Total applicants: 1,278. Total accepted: 922. Freshmen enrolled: 316; 41% were from out of state. Accepted through early-decision or early-action plans: 65%. Overall acceptance rate: 72%. Non-early acceptance rate: 61%. **Credentials of fall 2005 freshmen:** 30% ranked in the top 10 percent of their high school class; 67% were in the top 25 percent, and 95% were in the top half. (Proportion submitting class standing: 94%.) **Average high school grade point average:** 3.7. **First-year students who submitted SAT scores:** 16%. Scores (25/75 percentile): Verbal: 540-660, Math: 540-650, Combined: 1080-1310. **First-year students submitting ACT scores:** 85%. Scores (25/75 percentile): English: 22-29, Math: 22-27, Composite: 23-28.

ACADEMICS

Year founded: 1851. **Academic calendar:** Semester. **Degrees offered:** bachelor's, master's. **Most popular majors:** 17% social sciences, 15% business, management, marketing, and related support services, 10% psychology, 10% visual and performing arts, 8% English language and literature/letters. **Major fields of study:** area, ethnic, cultural, and gender studies; biological and biomedical sciences; business, management, marketing, and related support services; communication, journalism, and related programs; computer and information sciences and support services; education; English language and literature/letters; foreign languages, literatures, and linguistics; health professions and related clinical sciences; history; mathematics and statistics; philosophy and religious studies; physical sciences; psychology; social sciences; visual and performing arts. **Areas of required coursework:** arts/fine arts, humanities, English (including composition), sciences (biological or physical), social science, other. **Pre-professional programs:** prelaw, pre-dentistry, pre-medicine, pre-veterinary science. **Special academic programs (% participation):** accelerated program (0%), cross-registration (3%), double major (36%), dual enrollment (0%), English as a Second Language (ESL) (0%), exchange student program (domestic), honors program (9%), independent study (24%), internships (35%), student-designed major (1%), study abroad, teacher certificate program (12%). **Teacher certification offered in:** elementary, middle/junior high, secondary. **Cooperative education programs:** other. **Reserve Officers Training Corps (ROTC):** Army ROTC: Offered at cooperating institution (University of Iowa); Air Force ROTC: Offered at cooperating institution (University of Iowa). **Faculty and instruction (2005-2006):** Total instructional faculty: 76 full-time, 49 part-time (57% men; 43% women; 5% minorities). Full-time faculty with Ph.D. or other terminal degree: 96%. Student/faculty ratio: 12/1. Classes of fewer than 20 students: 67%; of 20 to 49 students: 32%; of 50 or more students: 1%. **Advanced Placement and International Baccalaureate credit:** AP tests may be used for: Credit and/or placement. Scores accepted: 4, 5. International Baccalaureate exams may be used for: Credit and/or placement. **Freshmen returning for sophomore year:** 81%. **Graduation rates:** Four-year: 66%; five-year: 73%; six-year: 73%. **Graduate study:** 28% of students pursue further study immediately upon graduation; 30% within one year; 40% within five years. Fields in which graduates pursue further study: Master of Business Administration (MBA), 10%; law, 15%; medicine, 5%; dentistry, 2%; engineering, 5%; theology (or the seminary), 2%; education, 10%; arts and sciences, 50%; veterinary medicine, 1%.

COSTS AND FINANCIAL AID

Financial aid office: (319) 399-8540. **Expenses (2006-2007):** Tuition and fees 2006-2007: $25,120; room/board: $6,550. Estimated books and supplies: $700; transportation: $550; personal expenses: $1,350. **Financial aid:** Priority filing date for institution's financial aid form: March 1. In 2005-2006, 85% of undergraduates applied for financial aid. Of those, 77% were determined to have financial need; 20% had their need fully met. Average financial aid package (proportion receiving): $20,370 (77%). Average amount of gift aid, such as scholarships or grants (proportion receiving): $14,228 (75%). Average amount of self-help aid, such as work study or loans (proportion receiving): $6,864 (67%). Average need-based loan (excluding PLUS or other private loans): $6,229. Among students who received need-based aid, the average percentage of need met: 90%. Among students who received aid based on merit, the average award (and the proportion receiving): $11,287 (20%). The average athletic scholarship (and the proportion receiving): $0 (0%). Average amount of debt of borrowers graduating in 2005: $20,237. Proportion who borrowed: 76%.

CAMPUS LIFE AND EXTRACURRICULAR ACTIVITIES

Campus housing available: coed dorms, women's dorms, men's dorms, sorority housing, fraternity housing, apartment for single students, other housing options. Students who live in college-owned, operated, or affiliated housing: 84%. **Student employment:** During the 2005-2006 academic year, 5% of undergraduates worked on campus. Average per-year earnings: $600. **Clubs and organizations:** Number of student organizations: 60. Activities include: choral groups, concert band, drama/theater, jazz band, literary magazine, music ensembles, pep band, radio station, student government, student newspaper, symphony orchestra, yearbook. Number of fraternities: 5; sororities: 3. Proportion of men in fraternities: 26%; of women in sororities: 19%. Average proportion of students who stay on campus on weekends: 75%. **Sports program (2005-2006):** Member of NCAA III. ***Men's inter-collegiate varsity sports:*** baseball, basketball, cross-country, football, golf, soccer, swimming and diving, tennis, track and field (indoor), track and field (outdoor), wrestling. ***Women's intercollegiate varsity sports:*** basketball, cross-country, golf, soccer, softball, swimming and diving, tennis, track and field (indoor), track and field (outdoor), volleyball.

SERVICES AND FACILITIES

Basic services: nonremedial tutoring, placement service, health service. **Remedial assistance:** reading, math, writing, study skills. **Counseling services:** career, personal, academic, psychological, birth control, religious. **For learning-disabled students:** School does not offer a structured program with separate admission and additional fees. Services include: remedial reading, tape recorders, untimed tests, note-taking services, oral tests, learning center, extended time for tests, tutors, texts on tape, exams on tape or computer, other testing accomodations. **Library:** Number of titles: 218,881; number of current serial subscriptions: 1,626. **Information technology resources:** Students are not required to lease or own a computer. Number of campus computers available to all students: 460. School has a wireless network. Approximate number of users that can be accommodated: 600. Proportion of college-owned housing units wired for high-speed internet access: 100%. **Campus safety:** Security services offered: 24-hour foot and vehicle patrols, late-night transport/escort service, 24-hour emergency telephones, lighted pathways/sidewalks, controlled dormitory access (key, security card, etc).

TRANSFER AND INTERNATIONAL STUDENTS

Transfer students: May apply for admission for the following academic terms: Fall, Spring, Summer. Applicants do not need a minimum number of credits to apply. For fall 2005: Transfer applications received: 149. Transfer applicants offered admission: 118. Transfer applicants enrolled: 63. **International students:** Number of foreign undergraduates: 54 (4% of student body). Minimum TOEFL score required: 500 (paper); 173 (computer). Average TOEFL score: 593 (paper).

Cornell College

- **Address:** 600 First Street, Mount Vernon, IA 52314
- **Website:** http://www.cornellcollege.edu
- **Private; Religious affiliation:** United Methodist
- **Enrollment:** 1,166 full-time; 13 part-time

KEY STATS
✔ **U.S News College Ranking:** third tier, Liberal Arts Colleges
✔ **ACT Score (25th/75th percentile):** 23-29
✔ **Tuition:** 2006-2007: $24,800

Selectivity: More selective	**Room/board:** $6,660
Acceptance rate: 66%	**Average debt:** $23,185
Student/faculty ratio: 11/1	**Proportion who borrowed:** 78%

UNDERGRADUATE STUDENT BODY STATS

2005-2006 enrollment: 1,166 full-time; 13 part-time. Men: 45%; women: 55%. **Ethnic makeup:** African American: 4%; Asian American: 1%; Hispanic: 3%; White: 89%; International: 2%. **Religious preference:** Roman Catholic: 15%; Protestant: 26%; Jewish: 1%; No preference: 48%; United Methodist: 9%; Other: 1%.

ADMISSIONS FACTS AND FIGURES

Phone: (800) 747-1112. **Email:** admissions@cornellcollege.edu. **Website:** http://www.cornellcollege.edu. **Application deadlines for fall 2007:** Regular decision: March 1; decision sent by April 1. Early decision: Send application by: November 1; Decision sent by: December 1. Early action: Send application by: December 1; Decision sent by: December 20. Admission can be deferred. **Application fee:** $30. Common application is accepted. **Admissions requirements/recommendations:** High school units required (recommended): English: (4); Mathematics: (3); Science: (3); Foreign language: (2); Social studies: (1); History: (2); Academic electives: (0); Total units: (17). Tests: The college uses SAT or ACT scores in admissions decisions. Either SAT or ACT required. For admission to the fall 2007 entering class, the school will accept: ACT with writing, ACT without writing. Campus visit: Recommended. Admissions interview: Recommended. Off-campus interview: May be arranged. **Factors that count in admissions decisions:**

Academic: Secondary school record: Very important. Class rank: Important. Letters of recommendation: Very important. Standardized test scores: Important. Essay: Very important. **Nonacademic:** Interview: Considered. Extracurricular activities: Important. Talent/ability: Important. Character/personal qualities: Important. Alumni/ae relationship: Considered. Geographical residence: Considered. State residency: Considered. Religious affiliation/commitment: Considered. Minority status: Considered. Volunteer work: Important. Work experience: Important. **Other schools with the greatest overlap in applicants:** Beloit College; Coe College; Colorado College; Grinnell College; University of Iowa. **Admissions statistics for the fall 2005 entering class:** Total applicants: 1,653. Total accepted: 1,096. Freshmen enrolled: 319; 73% were from out of state. Accepted through early-decision or early-action plans: 77%. Overall acceptance rate: 66%. Early-decision acceptance rate: 84%. Non-early acceptance rate: 57%. **Size of waiting list:** 65 applicants; enrolled from waiting list: 11. **Credentials of fall 2005 freshmen:** 24% ranked in the top 10 percent of their high school class; 56% were in the top 25 percent, and 88% were in the top half. (Proportion submitting class standing: 83%.) **Average high school grade point average:** 3.5. **First-year students who submitted SAT scores:** 30%. Scores (25/75 percentile): Verbal: 560-680, Math: 550-680, Combined: 1110-1360. **First-year students submitting ACT scores:** 86%. Scores (25/75 percentile): English: 23-29, Math: 23-28, Composite: 23-29.

ACADEMICS

Year founded: 1853. **Academic calendar:** Other. **Degrees offered:** bachelor's. **Most popular majors:** 15% education, 13% psychology, 13% social sciences, 10% history, 10% multi/interdisciplinary studies. **Major fields of study:** agriculture, agriculture operations, and related sciences; area, ethnic, cultural, and gender studies; biological and biomedical sciences; business, management, marketing, and related support services; computer and information sciences and support services; education; English language and literature/letters; foreign languages, literatures, and linguistics; history; liberal arts and sciences studies, and humanities; mathematics and statistics; multi/interdisciplinary studies; natural resources and conservation; parks, recreation, leisure, and fitness studies; philosophy and religious studies; physical sciences; psychology; social sciences; visual and performing arts. **Areas of required coursework:** arts/fine arts, humanities, mathematics, English (including composition), foreign languages, sciences (biological or physical), social science. **Pre-professional programs:** pre-law, pre-dentistry, pre-medicine, pre-theology, pre-veterinary science, pre-optometry, pre-pharmacy. **Special academic programs (% participation):** double major (44%), English as a Second Language (ESL) (1%), independent study, internships, student-designed major (10%), study abroad (33%), teacher certificate program (13%). **Teacher certification offered in:** elementary, middle/junior high, secondary. **Cooperative education programs:** health professions. **Faculty and instruction (2005-2006):** Total instructional faculty: 94 full-time, 18 part-time (54% men; 46% women; 7% minorities). Full-time faculty with Ph.D. or other terminal degree: 89%. Student/faculty ratio: 11/1. Classes of fewer than 20 students: 59%; of 20 to 49 students: 41%. **Advanced Placement and International Baccalaureate credit:** AP tests may be used for: Credit and/or placement. Scores accepted: 3, 4, 5. International Baccalaureate exams may be used for: Credit only. **Freshmen returning for sophomore year:** 80%. **Graduation rates:** Four-year: 60%; five-year: 66%; six-year: 67%.

COSTS AND FINANCIAL AID

Financial aid office: (319) 895-4216. **Expenses (2006-2007):** Tuition and fees 2006-2007: $24,800; room/board: $6,660. Estimated books and supplies: $720; transportation: $1,160; personal expenses: $540. **Financial aid:** Priority filing date for institution's financial aid form: March 1; deadline: March 1. In 2005-2006, 89% of undergraduates applied for financial aid. Of those, 80% were determined to have financial need; 50% had their need fully met. Average financial aid package (proportion receiving): $18,510 (80%). Average amount of gift aid, such as scholarships or grants (proportion receiving): $15,005 (80%). Average amount of self-help aid, such as work study or loans (proportion receiving): $3,505 (57%). Average need-based loan (excluding PLUS or other private loans): $4,370. Among students who received need-based aid, the average percentage of need met: 91%. Among students who received aid based on merit, the average award (and the proportion receiving): $11,705 (25%). The average athletic scholarship (and the proportion receiving): $0 (0%). Average amount of debt of borrowers graduating in 2005: $23,185. Proportion who borrowed: 78%.

CAMPUS LIFE AND EXTRACURRICULAR ACTIVITIES

Campus housing available (% using): coed dorms (58%), women's dorms (19%), men's dorms (15%), apartment for single students (8%). Students who live in college-owned, operated, or affiliated housing: 90%. **Student**

employment: During the 2005-2006 academic year, 19% of undergraduates worked on campus. Average per-year earnings: $1,000. **Clubs and organizations:** Number of student organizations: 76. Activities include: choral groups, concert band, dance, drama/theater, jazz band, literary magazine, music ensembles, musical theater, opera, pep band, radio station, student government, student newspaper, symphony orchestra, yearbook. Number of fraternities: 8; sororities: 7. Proportion of men in fraternities: 30%; of women in sororities: 32%. Average proportion of students who stay on campus on weekends: 75%. **Sports program (2005-2006):** Member of NCAA III. *Men's intercollegiate varsity sports:* baseball, basketball, cross-country, football, golf, soccer, tennis, track and field (indoor), track and field (outdoor), wrestling. *Women's intercollegiate varsity sports:* basketball, cross-country, golf, soccer, softball, tennis, track and field (indoor), track and field (outdoor), volleyball.

SERVICES AND FACILITIES

Basic services: nonremedial tutoring, women's center, health service, health insurance. **Counseling services:** minority student, career, personal, academic, older student, psychological, birth control, religious. **For learning-disabled students:** School does not offer a structured program with separate admission and additional fees. Total undergraduates in learning-disabled program or receiving services: 41. Services include: tape recorders, untimed tests, oral tests, learning center, extended time for tests, tutors, early syllabus, priority registration, priority seating, substitution of courses, texts on tape, other testing accomodations, other. **Library:** Number of titles: 177,554; number of current serial subscriptions: 779. **Information technology resources:** Students are not required to lease or own a computer. Number of campus computers available to all students: 123. School has a wireless network. Proportion of college-owned housing units wired for high-speed internet access: 100%. **Campus safety:** Security services offered: 24-hour foot and vehicle patrols, 24-hour emergency telephones, lighted pathways/sidewalks.

TRANSFER AND INTERNATIONAL STUDENTS

Transfer students: May apply for admission for the following academic terms: Fall, Winter, Spring. Applicants do not need a minimum number of credits to apply. For fall 2005: Transfer applications received: 136. Transfer applicants offered admission: 76. Transfer applicants enrolled: 33.
International students: Number of foreign undergraduates: 28 (2% of student body). Number of countries represented: 16. Minimum TOEFL score required: 550 (paper); 213 (computer). Average TOEFL score: 595 (paper).

Dordt College

- **Address:** 498 Fourth Avenue NE, Sioux Center, IA 51250
- **Website:** http://www.dordt.edu
- **Private; Religious affiliation:** Christian Reformed
- **Enrollment:** 1,197 full-time; 62 part-time

KEY STATS
- ✔ **U.S News College Ranking:** 11, Comp. Coll.–Bachelor's (Midwest)
- ✔ **ACT Score (25th/75th percentile):** 21-27
- ✔ **Tuition:** 2006-2007: $18,660

Selectivity: Selective	**Room/board:** $5,160
Acceptance rate: 92%	**Average debt:** $16,610
Student/faculty ratio: 13/1	**Proportion who borrowed:** 80%

UNDERGRADUATE STUDENT BODY STATS
2005-2006 enrollment: 1,197 full-time; 62 part-time. Men: 46%; women: 54%. **Ethnic makeup:** African American: 1%; Asian American: 1%; White: 89%; International: 10%. **Religious preference:** Roman Catholic: 1%; Protestant: 34%; Christian Reformed: 65%.

ADMISSIONS FACTS AND FIGURES
Phone: (800) 343-6738. **Email:** admissions@dordt.edu. **Website:** http://www.dordt.edu. **Application deadlines for fall 2007:** Regular decision: August 1. Early decision: Not offered. Early action: Not offered. Admission cannot be deferred. **Application fee:** $25. Common application is not accepted. **To apply online, go to:** http://www.dordt.edu/offices/admissions/apply/. **Admissions requirements/recommendations:** High school units required (recommended): English: 3 (4); Mathematics: 2 (3); Science: 2 (4); Foreign language: 2 (3); Social studies: (1); History: 2; Academic electives: 6; Total units: 17 (25). Tests: The college uses SAT or

ACT scores in admissions decisions. Either SAT or ACT required. Campus visit: Recommended. Admissions interview: Neither required nor recommended. **Factors that count in admissions decisions:** *Academic:* Secondary school record: Very important. Class rank: Considered. Letters of recommendation: Not considered. Standardized test scores: Very important. Essay: Not considered. *Nonacademic:* Interview: Not considered. Extracurricular activities: Considered. Talent/ability: Considered. Character/personal qualities: Considered. Alumni/ae relationship: Considered. Geographical residence: Not considered. State residency: Not considered. Religious affiliation/commitment: Very important. Minority status: Not considered. Volunteer work: Not considered. Work experience: Not considered. **Other schools with the greatest overlap in applicants:** Calvin College; Northwestern College; Trinity Christian College; University of Sioux Falls. **Admissions statistics for the fall 2005 entering class:** Total applicants: 774. Total accepted: 712. Freshmen enrolled: 356; 39% were from out of state. Overall acceptance rate: 92%. **Size of waiting list:** 0 applicants; enrolled from waiting list: 0. **Credentials of fall 2005 freshmen:** 18% ranked in the top 10 percent of their high school class; 40% were in the top 25 percent, and 72% were in the top half. (Proportion submitting class standing: 88%.) **Average high school grade point average:** 3.4. **First-year students who submitted SAT scores:** 19%. Scores (25/75 percentile): Verbal: 490-637, Math: 510-650, Combined: 1000-1287. **First-year students submitting ACT scores:** 81%. Scores (25/75 percentile): English: 20-27, Math: 21-27, Composite: 21-27.

ACADEMICS
Year founded: 1955. **Academic calendar:** Semester. **Degrees offered:** associate, bachelor's, master's. **Most popular majors:** 23% elementary education and teaching, 18% business/commerce, 6% agriculture, 6% social work, 4% engineering. **Major fields of study:** agriculture, agriculture operations, and related sciences; biological and biomedical sciences; business, management, marketing, and related support services; communication, journalism, and related programs; computer and information sciences and support services; education; engineering; English language and literature/letters; foreign languages, literatures, and linguistics; health professions and related clinical sciences; history; liberal arts and sciences studies, and humanities; mathematics and statistics; natural resources and conservation; parks, recreation, leisure, and fitness studies; philosophy and religious studies; physical sciences; psychology; public administration and social service professions; social sciences; theology and religious vocations; visual and performing arts. **Areas of required coursework:** arts/fine arts, humanities, English (including composition), philosophy, sciences (biological or physical), history, social science, other. **Pre-professional programs:** pre-law, pre-dentistry, pre-medicine, pre-theology, pre-veterinary science, pre-optometry, pre-pharmacy. **Special academic programs (% participation):** double major (10%), English as a Second Language (ESL) (1%), independent study (9%), internships (15%), student-designed major (1%), study abroad (7%). **Teacher certification offered in:** elementary, middle/junior high, secondary. **Cooperative education programs:** health professions. **Faculty and instruction (2005-2006):** Total instructional faculty: 80 full-time, 42 part-time (74% men; 26% women; 3% minorities). Full-time faculty with Ph.D. or other terminal degree: 76%. Student/faculty ratio: 13/1. Classes of fewer than 20 students: 64%; of 20 to 49 students: 31%; of 50 or more students: 4%. **Advanced Placement and International Baccalaureate credit:** International Baccalaureate exams may be used for: Credit and/or placement. **Freshmen returning for sophomore year:** 82%. **Graduation rates:** Four-year: 59%; five-year: 65%; six-year: 66%. **Graduate study:** 9% of students pursue further study immediately upon graduation. Fields in which graduates pursue further study: Master of Business Administration (MBA), 7%; law, 7%; medicine, 4%; engineering, 11%; theology (or the seminary), 22%; education, 4%; arts and sciences, 37%; veterinary medicine, 7%.

COSTS AND FINANCIAL AID
Financial aid office: (712) 722-6087. **Expenses (2006-2007):** Tuition and fees 2006-2007: $18,660; room/board: $5,160. Estimated books and supplies: $780. **Financial aid:** Priority filing date for institution's financial aid form: April 1. In 2005-2006, 86% of undergraduates applied for financial aid. Of those, 76% were determined to have financial need; 13% had their need fully met. Average financial aid package (proportion receiving): $15,719 (76%). Average amount of gift aid, such as scholarships or grants (proportion receiving): $8,731 (76%). Average amount of self-help aid, such as work study or loans (proportion receiving): $6,987 (75%). Average need-based loan (excluding PLUS or other private loans): $4,487. Among students who received need-based aid, the average percentage of need met: 86%. Among students who received aid based on merit, the average award (and the proportion receiving): $8,179 (20%). The average athletic scholarship (and the

proportion receiving): $2,862 (4%). Average amount of debt of borrowers graduating in 2005: $16,610. Proportion who borrowed: 80%.

CAMPUS LIFE AND EXTRACURRICULAR ACTIVITIES
Campus housing available (% using): coed dorms (33%), women's dorms (12%), men's dorms (14%), apartment for single students (41%). Students who live in college-owned, operated, or affiliated housing: 85%. **Student employment:** During the 2005-2006 academic year, 38% of undergraduates worked on campus. Average per-year earnings: $1,300. **Clubs and organizations:** Number of student organizations: 37. Activities include: choral groups, concert band, dance, drama/theater, jazz band, literary magazine, music ensembles, radio station, student government, student newspaper, yearbook. Number of fraternities: 0; sororities: 0. Average proportion of students who stay on campus on weekends: 75%. **Sports program (2005-2006):** Member of NAIA. **Men's intercollegiate varsity sports:** baseball, basketball, cross-country, golf, soccer, tennis, track and field (indoor), track and field (outdoor). **Women's intercollegiate varsity sports:** basketball, cross-country, soccer, softball, tennis, track and field (indoor), track and field (outdoor), volleyball.

SERVICES AND FACILITIES
Basic services: nonremedial tutoring, placement service, health service, health insurance. **Remedial assistance:** reading, math, writing, study skills. **Counseling services:** minority student, career, personal, academic, religious. **For learning-disabled students:** School does not offer a structured program with separate admission and additional fees. Total undergraduates in learning-disabled program or receiving services: 24. Services include: remedial math, remedial English, tape recorders, untimed tests, note-taking services, oral tests, learning center, readers, extended time for tests, tutors, priority seating, texts on tape, exams on tape or computer, other testing accomodations, other. **Library:** Number of titles: 141,619; number of current serial subscriptions: 920. **Information technology resources:** Students are not required to lease or own a computer. Number of campus computers available to all students: 207. School has a wireless network. Approximate number of users that can be accommodated: 100. Proportion of college-owned housing units wired for high-speed internet access: 100%. **Campus safety:** Security services offered: late-night transport/escort service, lighted pathways/sidewalks, student patrols, controlled dormitory access (key, security card, etc).

TRANSFER AND INTERNATIONAL STUDENTS
Transfer students: May apply for admission for the following academic terms: Fall, Spring. Applicants need a minimum number of credits to apply. For fall 2005: Transfer applications received: 71. Transfer applicants offered admission: 49. Transfer applicants enrolled: 33. **International students:** Number of foreign undergraduates: 118 (10% of student body). Number of countries represented: 11. Minimum TOEFL score required: 550 (paper); 213 (computer). Average TOEFL score: 585 (paper).

Drake University

- **Address:** 2507 University Avenue, Des Moines, IA 50311
- **Website:** http://www.drake.edu
- **Private**
- **Enrollment:** 2,913 full-time; 228 part-time

KEY STATS
✔ **U.S News College Ranking:** 4, Universities–Master's (Midwest)
✔ **ACT Score (25th/75th percentile):** 24-29
✔ **Tuition:** 2006-2007: $22,682

Selectivity: More selective	**Room/board:** $6,500
Acceptance rate: 82%	**Average debt:** $25,800
Student/faculty ratio: 14/1	**Proportion who borrowed:** 70%

UNDERGRADUATE STUDENT BODY STATS
2005-2006 enrollment: 2,913 full-time; 228 part-time. Men: 43%; women: 57%. **Ethnic makeup:** African American: 4%; Asian American: 4%; Hispanic: 1%; White: 86%; International: 5%.

ADMISSIONS FACTS AND FIGURES
Phone: (515) 271-3181. **Email:** admission@drake.edu. **Website:** http://www.drake.edu. **Application deadlines for fall 2007:** Regular decision:

Rolling. Early decision: Not offered. Early action: Not offered. Admission can be deferred. **Application fee:** $25. Common application is accepted. **Admissions requirements/recommendations:** High school units required (recommended): English: 4 (4); Mathematics: 3 (3); Science: 2 (2); Foreign language: 0 (2); Social studies: 4 (4); History: 0 (0); Academic electives: 0 (0); Total units: 16 (16). Tests: The college uses SAT or ACT scores in admissions decisions. Either SAT or ACT required. For admission to the fall 2007 entering class, the school will accept: ACT with writing, ACT without writing. Campus visit: Recommended. Admissions interview: Recommended. Off-campus interview: May be arranged. **Factors that count in admissions decisions:** *Academic:* Secondary school record: Very important. Class rank: Important. Letters of recommendation: Important. Standardized test scores: Important. Essay: Considered. *Nonacademic:* Interview: Considered. Extracurricular activities: Considered. Talent/ability: Considered. Character/personal qualities: Considered. Alumni/ae relationship: Not considered. Geographical residence: Not considered. State residency: Not considered. Religious affiliation/commitment: Not considered. Minority status: Not considered. Volunteer work: Considered. Work experience: Considered. **Other schools with the greatest overlap in applicants:** Butler University; Creighton University; Iowa State University; Marquette University; University of Iowa. **Admissions statistics for the fall 2005 entering class:** Total applicants: 3,668. Total accepted: 3,006. Freshmen enrolled: 809; 68% were from out of state. Overall acceptance rate: 82%. **Size of waiting list:** 0 applicants; enrolled from waiting list: 0. **Credentials of fall 2005 freshmen:** 37% ranked in the top 10 percent of their high school class; 73% were in the top 25 percent, and 93% were in the top half. (Proportion submitting class standing: 85%.) Average high school grade point average: 3.7. **First-year students who submitted SAT scores:** 20%. Scores (25/75 percentile): Verbal: 520-660, Math: 510-650, Combined: 1030-1310. **First-year students submitting ACT scores:** 94%. Scores (25/75 percentile): English: 24-30, Math: 23-28, Composite: 24-29.

ACADEMICS
Year founded: 1881. **Academic calendar:** Semester. **Degrees offered:** certificate, bachelor's, master's, post-master's certificate, first professional, first professional certificate, doctorate. **Most popular majors:** 28% business, management, marketing, and related support services, 20% communication, journalism, and related programs, 10% education, 9% visual and performing arts, 8% biological and biomedical sciences. **Major fields of study:** biological and biomedical sciences; business, management, marketing, and related support services; communication, journalism, and related programs; education; English language and literature/letters; history; legal professions and studies; mathematics and statistics; multi/interdisciplinary studies; natural resources and conservation; philosophy and religious studies; physical sciences; psychology; social sciences; visual and performing arts. **Areas of required coursework:** arts/fine arts, humanities, computer literacy, mathematics, English (including composition), sciences (biological or physical), history, social science, other. **Pre-professional programs:** pre-law, pre-dentistry, pre-medicine, pre-theology, pre-veterinary science, pre-optometry, pre-pharmacy, other. **Special academic programs (% participation):** accelerated program (5%), cooperative (work-study plan) program (0%), cross-registration (4%), distance learning (35%), double major (18%), dual enrollment (0%), English as a Second Language (ESL) (4%), exchange student program (domestic) (0%), honors program (6%), independent study (25%), internships (68%), liberal arts/career combination (1%), student-designed major (0%), study abroad (17%), teacher certificate program (7%). **Teacher certification offered in:** early childhood, special education, elementary, middle/junior high, secondary. **Cooperative education programs:** computer science, education. **Reserve Officers Training Corps (ROTC):** Army ROTC: Offered on campus; Air Force ROTC: Offered at cooperating institution (Iowa State University). **Faculty and instruction (2005-2006):** Total instructional faculty: 246 full-time, 143 part-time (58% men; 42% women; 7% minorities). Full-time faculty with Ph.D. or other terminal degree: 96%. Student/faculty ratio: 14/1. Classes of fewer than 20 students: 44%; of 20 to 49 students: 47%; of 50 or more students: 9%. **Advanced Placement and International Baccalaureate credit:** AP tests may be used for: Placement only. Scores accepted: 3, 4. International Baccalaureate exams may be used for: Credit and/or placement. **Freshmen returning for sophomore year:** 84%. **Graduation rates:** Four-year: 55%; five-year: 65%; six-year: 70%. **Graduate study:** 22% of students pursue further study immediately upon graduation. Fields in which graduates pursue further study: Master of Business Administration (MBA), 14%; law, 21%; medicine, 15%; education, 12%; arts and sciences, 37%.

COSTS AND FINANCIAL AID

Financial aid office: (515) 271-2905. **Expenses (2006-2007):** Tuition and fees 2006-2007: $22,682; room/board: $6,500. Estimated books and supplies: $900; transportation: $1,550; personal expenses: $1,950. **Financial aid:** Priority filing date for institution's financial aid form: March 1. In 2005-2006, 75% of undergraduates applied for financial aid. Of those, 62% were determined to have financial need; 34% had their need fully met. Average financial aid package (proportion receiving): $17,453 (62%). Average amount of gift aid, such as scholarships or grants (proportion receiving): $10,719 (61%). Average amount of self-help aid, such as work study or loans (proportion receiving): $6,715 (53%). Average need-based loan (excluding PLUS or other private loans): $5,472. Among students who received need-based aid, the average percentage of need met: 84%. Among students who received aid based on merit, the average award (and the proportion receiving): $9,026 (31%). The average athletic scholarship (and the proportion receiving): $17,703 (3%). Average amount of debt of borrowers graduating in 2005: $25,800. Proportion who borrowed: 70%.

CAMPUS LIFE AND EXTRACURRICULAR ACTIVITIES

Campus housing available (% using): coed dorms (52%), sorority housing (11%), fraternity housing (9%), other housing options (28%). Students who live in college-owned, operated, or affiliated housing: 61%. **Student employment:** During the 2005-2006 academic year, 15% of undergraduates worked on campus. Average per-year earnings: $1,600. **Clubs and organizations:** Number of student organizations: 187. Activities include: choral groups, concert band, dance, drama/theater, jazz band, literary magazine, marching band, music ensembles, musical theater, opera, pep band, radio station, student government, student newspaper, symphony orchestra, television station. Number of fraternities: 9; sororities: 6. Proportion of men in fraternities: 30%; of women in sororities: 22%. Average proportion of students who stay on campus on weekends: 80%. **Sports program (2005-2006):** Member of NCAA I. **Men's intercollegiate varsity sports:** basketball, cross-country, football, golf, soccer, tennis, track and field (indoor), track and field (outdoor). **Women's intercollegiate varsity sports:** basketball, cross-country, soccer, softball, tennis, track and field (indoor), track and field (outdoor), volleyball, rowing.

SERVICES AND FACILITIES

Basic services: nonremedial tutoring, women's center, placement service, health service, health insurance. **Counseling services:** minority student, career, military, personal, veteran student, academic, older student, psychological, birth control, other. **For learning-disabled students:** School does not offer a structured program with separate admission and additional fees. Total undergraduates in learning-disabled program or receiving services: 54. Services include: reading machines, tape recorders, note-taking services, readers, extended time for tests, priority seating, texts on tape, other testing accomodations. **Library:** Number of titles: 721,210; number of current serial subscriptions: 32,994. **Information technology resources:** Students are not required to lease or own a computer. Number of campus computers available to all students: 400. School has a wireless network. Approximate number of users that can be accommodated: 2,000. Proportion of college-owned housing units wired for high-speed internet access: 100%. **Campus safety:** Security services offered: 24-hour foot and vehicle patrols, late-night transport/escort service, 24-hour emergency telephones, lighted pathways/sidewalks, controlled dormitory access (key, security card, etc).

TRANSFER AND INTERNATIONAL STUDENTS

Transfer students: May apply for admission for the following academic terms: Fall, Spring, Summer. Applicants need a minimum number of credits to apply. For fall 2005: Transfer applications received: 382. Transfer applicants offered admission: 237. Transfer applicants enrolled: 125. **International students:** Number of foreign undergraduates: 111 (5% of student body). Number of countries represented: 61. Minimum TOEFL score required: 530 (paper); 197 (computer). Average TOEFL score: 597 (paper).

Graceland University

- **Address:** 1 University Place, Lamoni, IA 50140-1698
- **Website:** http://www.graceland.edu
- **Private; Religious affiliation:** Community of Christ
- **Enrollment:** N/A

KEY STATS

✔ **U.S News College Ranking:** fourth tier, Comp. Coll.–Bachelor's (Midwest)
✔ **SAT or ACT Score (25th/75th percentile):** N/A
✔ **Tuition:** N/A

Selectivity: Less selective	**Room/board:** N/A
Acceptance rate: N/A	**Average debt:** N/A
Student/faculty ratio: N/A	**Proportion who borrowed:** N/A

Grand View College

- **Address:** 1200 Grandview Avenue, Des Moines, IA 50316
- **Website:** http://www.gvc.edu
- **Private; Religious affiliation:** Evangelical Lutheran Church in America
- **Enrollment:** 1,305 full-time; 454 part-time

KEY STATS

✔ **U.S News College Ranking:** fourth tier, Comp. Coll.–Bachelor's (Midwest)
✔ **ACT Score (25th/75th percentile):** 18-22
✔ **Tuition:** 2006-2007: $16,890

Selectivity: Selective	**Room/board:** $5,856
Acceptance rate: 95%	**Average debt:** $18,463
Student/faculty ratio: 12/1	**Proportion who borrowed:** 94%

UNDERGRADUATE STUDENT BODY STATS

2005-2006 enrollment: 1,305 full-time; 454 part-time. Men: 31%; women: 69%. **Ethnic makeup:** African American: 3%; Asian American: 2%; Hispanic: 1%; White: 93%; International: 1%.

ADMISSIONS FACTS AND FIGURES

Phone: (515) 263-2810. **Email:** admissions@gvc.edu. **Website:** http://www.gvc.edu. **Application deadlines for fall 2007:** Regular decision: August 15. Early decision: Not offered. Early action: Not offered. Admission can be deferred. **Application fee:** $35. Common application is accepted. **Admissions requirements/recommendations:** High school units required (recommended): English: (4); Mathematics: (3); Science: (3); Foreign language: (2); Social studies: (3); Total units: (15). Tests: The college uses SAT or ACT scores in admissions decisions. Either SAT or ACT required. For admission to the fall 2007 entering class, the school will accept: ACT without writing. Campus visit: Recommended. Admissions interview: Recommended. **Factors that count in admissions decisions:** *Academic:* Secondary school record: Very important. Class rank: Very important. Letters of recommendation: Not considered. Standardized test scores: Important. Essay: Not considered. *Nonacademic:* Interview: Not considered. Extracurricular activities: Considered. Talent/ability: Considered. Character/personal qualities: Very important. Alumni/ae relationship: Considered. Geographical residence: Not considered. State residency: Not considered. Religious affiliation/commitment: Not considered. Minority status: Not considered. Volunteer work: Not considered. Work experience: Not considered. **Other schools with the greatest overlap in applicants:** Central College; Drake University; Iowa State University; Simpson College. **Admissions statistics for the fall 2005 entering class:** Total applicants: 442. Total accepted: 421. Freshmen enrolled: 221; 15% were from out of state. Overall acceptance rate: 95%. **Credentials of fall 2005 freshmen:** 11% ranked in the top 10 percent of their high school class; 32% were in the top 25 percent, and 67% were in the top half. (Proportion submitting class standing: 93%.) **Average high school grade point average:** 3.1. **First-year students who submitted SAT scores:** 4%. Scores (25/75 percentile): Verbal: 400-520, Math: 410-500, Combined: 810-1020. **First-year students submitting ACT scores:** 95%. Scores (25/75 percentile): English: 17-22, Math: 17-22, Composite: 18-22.

ACADEMICS

Year founded: 1896. **Academic calendar:** Semester. **Degrees offered:** certificate, associate, bachelor's, post-bachelor's certificate. **Most popular majors:** Information not available. **Major fields of study:** biological and biomedical sciences; business, management, marketing, and related support services; communication, journalism, and related programs; communications technologies/technicians and support services; computer and information sciences and support services; education; English language and literature/letters; health professions and related clinical sciences; liberal arts and sciences studies, and humanities; mathematics and statistics; philosophy and religious studies; physical sciences; psychology; public administration and social service professions; security and protective services; social sciences; visual and performing arts. **Areas of required coursework:** arts/fine arts, humanities, computer literacy, mathematics, English (including composition), sciences (biological or physical), history, social science. **Pre-professional programs:** pre-law, pre-dentistry, pre-medicine, pre-optometry, pre-pharmacy. **Special academic programs:** accelerated program, cooperative (work-study plan) program, cross-registration, distance learning, double major, dual enrollment, honors program, independent study, internships, liberal arts/career combination, student-designed major, study abroad, teacher certificate program, weekend college. **Teacher certification offered in:** elementary, secondary. **Reserve Officers Training Corps (ROTC):** Army ROTC: Offered at cooperating institution (Drake University); Air Force ROTC: Offered at cooperating institution (Drake University). **Faculty and instruction (2005-2006):** Total instructional faculty: 86 full-time, 116 part-time (44% men; 56% women; 5% minorities). Full-time faculty with Ph.D. or other terminal degree: 58%. Student/faculty ratio: 12/1. Classes of fewer than 20 students: 80%; of 20 to 49 students: 20%; of 50 or more students: 0%. **Freshmen returning for sophomore year:** 69%. **Graduation rates:** Four-year: 25%; five-year: 35%; six-year: 35%.

COSTS AND FINANCIAL AID

Financial aid office: (515) 263-2820. **Expenses (2006-2007):** Tuition and fees 2006-2007: $16,890; room/board: $5,856. Estimated books and supplies: $800; transportation: $600; personal expenses: $2,002. **Financial aid:** Priority filing date for institution's financial aid form: March 1. In 2005-2006, 94% of undergraduates applied for financial aid. Of those, 81% were determined to have financial need; 17% had their need fully met. Average financial aid package (proportion receiving): $12,144 (80%). Average amount of gift aid, such as scholarships or grants (proportion receiving): $8,448 (80%). Average amount of self-help aid, such as work study or loans (proportion receiving): $4,187 (72%). Average need-based loan (excluding PLUS or other private loans): $3,867. Among students who received need-based aid, the average percentage of need met: 74%. Among students who received aid based on merit, the average award (and the proportion receiving): $11,108 (18%). The average athletic scholarship (and the proportion receiving): $4,111 (4%). Average amount of debt of borrowers graduating in 2005: $18,463. Proportion who borrowed: 94%.

CAMPUS LIFE AND EXTRACURRICULAR ACTIVITIES

Campus housing available (% using): coed dorms (67%), apartment for single students (26%), other housing options (7%). Students who live in college-owned, operated, or affiliated housing: 34%. **Student employment:** During the 2005-2006 academic year, 15% of undergraduates worked on campus. Average per-year earnings: $1,500. Activities include: choral groups, dance, drama/theater, literary magazine, music ensembles, radio station, student government, student newspaper, yearbook. Number of fraternities: 0; sororities: 0. **Sports program (2005-2006):** Member of NAIA. **Men's intercollegiate varsity sports:** baseball, basketball, cross-country, gymnastics, soccer. **Women's intercollegiate varsity sports:** basketball, cross-country, golf, soccer, softball, volleyball.

SERVICES AND FACILITIES

Basic services: nonremedial tutoring, placement service, health service, health insurance. **Remedial assistance:** reading, math, writing, study skills. **Counseling services:** minority student, career, personal, academic, birth control, religious. **For learning-disabled students:** School does not offer a structured program with separate admission and additional fees. Services include: remedial math, remedial English, reading machines, remedial reading, tape recorders, videotaped classes, untimed tests, note-taking services, oral tests, learning center, readers, extended time for tests, tutors. **Library:** Number of titles: 105,146; number of current serial subscriptions: 8,141. **Information technology resources:** Students are not required to lease or own a computer. Number of campus computers available to all students: 185. School has a wireless network. Proportion of college-owned housing units wired for high-speed internet access: 98%. **Campus safety:** Security

services offered: 24-hour foot and vehicle patrols, late-night transport/escort service, 24-hour emergency telephones, lighted pathways/sidewalks, controlled dormitory access (key, security card, etc).

TRANSFER AND INTERNATIONAL STUDENTS

Transfer students: May apply for admission for the following academic terms: Fall, Spring, Summer. Applicants need a minimum number of credits to apply. For fall 2005: Transfer applications received: 445. Transfer applicants offered admission: 432. Transfer applicants enrolled: 327. **International students:** Number of foreign undergraduates: 12 (1% of student body). Minimum TOEFL score required: 550 (paper); 210 (computer).

Grinnell College

- **Address:** Grinnell, IA 50112-1690
- **Website:** http://www.grinnell.edu
- **Private**
- **Enrollment:** 1,546 full-time; 31 part-time

KEY STATS

✔ **U.S News College Ranking:** 14, Liberal Arts Colleges
✔ **SAT Score (25th/75th percentile):** 1280-1480
✔ **Tuition:** 2006-2007: $29,030

Selectivity: Most selective	**Room/board:** $7,700
Acceptance rate: 45%	**Average debt:** $16,744
Student/faculty ratio: 9/1	**Proportion who borrowed:** 61%

UNDERGRADUATE STUDENT BODY STATS

2005-2006 enrollment: 1,546 full-time; 31 part-time. Men: 45%; women: 55%. **Ethnic makeup:** African American: 4%; Asian American: 6%; Hispanic: 4%; White: 75%; International: 11%. **Religious preference:** Roman Catholic: 14%; Protestant: 22%; Jewish: 6%; Muslim: 1%; Hindu: 1%; Buddhist: 1%; No preference: 46%; Other: 9%.

ADMISSIONS FACTS AND FIGURES

Phone: (800) 247-0113. **Email:** askgrin@grinnell.edu. **Website:** http://www.grinnell.edu. **Application deadlines for fall 2007:** Regular decision: January 20; decision sent by April 1. Early decision: Send application by: November 20; Decision sent by: December 20. Early action: Not offered. Admission can be deferred. **Application fee:** $30. Common application is accepted. **To apply online, go to:** http://www.grinnell.edu/admission/applying/. **Admissions requirements/recommendations:** High school units required (recommended): English: (4); Mathematics: (4); Science: (4); Foreign language: (4); Social studies: (4); History: (0); Academic electives: (0); Total units: (20). Tests: The college uses SAT or ACT scores in admissions decisions. Either SAT or ACT required. For admission to the fall 2007 entering class, the school will accept: ACT with writing, ACT without writing. Campus visit: Recommended. Admissions interview: Recommended. Off-campus interview: May be arranged. **Factors that count in admissions decisions:** *Academic:* Secondary school record: Very important. Class rank: Very important. Letters of recommendation: Very important. Standardized test scores: Very important. Essay: Important. *Nonacademic:* Interview: Important. Extracurricular activities: Very important. Talent/ability: Very important. Character/personal qualities: Considered. Alumni/ae relationship: Considered. Geographical residence: Considered. State residency: Considered. Religious affiliation/commitment: Not considered. Minority status: Important. Volunteer work: Considered. Work experience: Considered. **Other schools with the greatest overlap in applicants:** Carleton College; Macalester College; Oberlin College; University of Chicago; Washington University in St. Louis. **Admissions statistics for the fall 2005 entering class:** Total applicants: 3,121. Total accepted: 1,398. Freshmen enrolled: 387; 81% were from out of state. Accepted through early-decision or early-action plans: 24%. Overall acceptance rate: 45%. Early-decision acceptance rate: 70%. Non-early acceptance rate: 44%. **Size of waiting list:** 598 applicants; enrolled from waiting list: 30. **Credentials of fall 2005 freshmen:** 73% ranked in the top 10 percent of their high school class; 93% were in the top 25 percent, and 99% were in the top half. (Proportion submitting class standing: 72%.) **First-year students who submitted SAT scores:** 61%. Scores (25/75 percentile): Verbal: 640-750, Math: 640-730, Combined: 1280-1480. **First-year students submitting ACT scores:** 38%. Scores (25/75 percentile): English: 28-34, Math: 27-32, Composite: 29-33.

ACADEMICS

Year founded: 1846. **Academic calendar:** Semester. **Degrees offered:** bachelor's. **Most popular majors:** 10% economics, 8% biology/biological sciences, 8% history, 7% English language and literature, 7% political science and government. **Major fields of study:** biological and biomedical sciences; computer and information sciences and support services; English language and literature/letters; foreign languages, literatures, and linguistics; history; mathematics and statistics; multi/interdisciplinary studies; philosophy and religious studies; physical sciences; psychology; social sciences; visual and performing arts. **Special academic programs (% participation):** accelerated program (12%), double major (16%), exchange student program (domestic) (0%), independent study (52%), internships (18%), liberal arts/career combination (1%), student-designed major (2%), study abroad (52%), teacher certificate program (2%). **Teacher certification offered in:** elementary, middle/junior high, secondary. **Faculty and instruction (2005-2006):** Total instructional faculty: 156 full-time, 43 part-time (53% men; 47% women; 13% minorities). Full-time faculty with Ph.D. or other terminal degree: 96%. Student/faculty ratio: 9/1. Classes of fewer than 20 students: 63%; of 20 to 49 students: 37%; of 50 or more students: 0%. **Advanced Placement and International Baccalaureate credit:** AP tests may be used for: Credit and/or placement. Scores accepted: 3, 4, 5. International Baccalaureate exams may be used for: Credit and/or placement. **Freshmen returning for sophomore year:** 92%. **Graduation rates:** Four-year: 83%; five-year: 87%; six-year: 87%. **Graduate study:** 25% of students pursue further study immediately upon graduation; 35% within one year; 65% within five years. Fields in which graduates pursue further study: law, 10%; medicine, 10%; theology (or the seminary), 2%; education, 10%; arts and sciences, 60%; veterinary medicine, 1%.

COSTS AND FINANCIAL AID

Financial aid office: (641) 269-3250. **Expenses (2006-2007):** Tuition and fees 2006-2007: $29,030; room/board: $7,700. Estimated books and supplies: $600; transportation: $500; personal expenses: $400. **Financial aid:** Priority filing date for institution's financial aid form: February 1; deadline: February 1. In 2005-2006, 62% of undergraduates applied for financial aid. Of those, 55% were determined to have financial need; 100% had their need fully met. Average financial aid package (proportion receiving): $23,921 (55%). Average amount of gift aid, such as scholarships or grants (proportion receiving): $17,919 (54%). Average amount of self-help aid, such as work study or loans (proportion receiving): $5,752 (45%). Average need-based loan (excluding PLUS or other private loans): $5,131. Among students who received need-based aid, the average percentage of need met: 100%. Among students who received aid based on merit, the average award (and the proportion receiving): $10,564 (34%). Average amount of debt of borrowers graduating in 2005: $16,744. Proportion who borrowed: 61%.

CAMPUS LIFE AND EXTRACURRICULAR ACTIVITIES

Campus housing available (% using): coed dorms (87%), cooperative housing (13%). Students who live in college-owned, operated, or affiliated housing: 87%. **Student employment:** During the 2005-2006 academic year, 60% of undergraduates worked on campus. Average per-year earnings: $1,800. **Clubs and organizations:** Number of student organizations: 178. Activities include: choral groups, concert band, dance, drama/theater, jazz band, literary magazine, music ensembles, musical theater, radio station, student government, student newspaper, student film society, symphony orchestra, yearbook. Number of fraternities: 0; sororities: 0. Average proportion of students who stay on campus on weekends: 100%. **Sports program (2005-2006):** Member of NCAA III. *Men's intercollegiate varsity sports:* baseball, basketball, cross-country, football, golf, soccer, swimming and diving, tennis, track and field (indoor), track and field (outdoor). *Women's intercollegiate varsity sports:* basketball, cross-country, golf, soccer, softball, swimming and diving, tennis, track and field (indoor), track and field (outdoor), volleyball.

SERVICES AND FACILITIES

Basic services: nonremedial tutoring, health service, health insurance. **Counseling services:** minority student, career, personal, veteran student, academic, psychological, birth control, religious. **For learning-disabled students:** School does not offer a structured program with separate admission and additional fees. Total undergraduates in learning-disabled program or receiving services: 35. Services include: tape recorders, untimed tests, notetaking services, oral tests, readers, extended time for tests, tutors, other. **Library:** Number of titles: 1,091,023; number of current serial subscriptions: 16,039. **Information technology resources:** Students are not required to lease or own a computer. Number of campus computers available to all students: 400. School has a wireless network. Approximate number of users that can

be accommodated: 300. Proportion of college-owned housing units wired for high-speed internet access: 100%. **Campus safety:** Security services offered: 24-hour foot and vehicle patrols, late-night transport/escort service, 24-hour emergency telephones, lighted pathways/sidewalks, student patrols, controlled dormitory access (key, security card, etc).

TRANSFER AND INTERNATIONAL STUDENTS

Transfer students: May apply for admission for the following academic terms: Fall, Spring. Applicants need a minimum number of credits to apply. For fall 2005: Transfer applications received: 122. Transfer applicants offered admission: 37. Transfer applicants enrolled: 19. **International students:** Number of foreign undergraduates: 164 (11% of student body). Number of countries represented: 49. Minimum TOEFL score required: 550 (paper); 220 (computer). Average TOEFL score: 635 (paper).

Iowa State University

- **Address:** 100 Alumni Hall, Ames, IA 50011
- **Website:** http://www.iastate.edu
- **Public**
- **Enrollment:** 19,433 full-time; 1,299 part-time

KEY STATS

✔ **U.S News College Ranking:** 81, National Universities
✔ **ACT Score (25th/75th percentile):** 22-27
✔ **Tuition:** 2006-2007: $5,830 in state, $16,324 out of state

Selectivity: More selective	**Room/board:** $6,445
Acceptance rate: 90%	**Average debt:** $25,851
Student/faculty ratio: 15/1	**Proportion who borrowed:** 67%

UNDERGRADUATE STUDENT BODY STATS

2005-2006 enrollment: 19,433 full-time; 1,299 part-time. Men: 56%; women: 44%. **Ethnic makeup:** African American: 3%; Asian American: 3%; Hispanic: 2%; White: 89%; International: 3%.

ADMISSIONS FACTS AND FIGURES

Phone: (800) 262-3810. **Email:** admissions@iastate.edu. **Website:** http://www.iastate.edu. **Application deadlines for fall 2007:** Regular decision: August 1. Early decision: Not offered. Early action: Not offered. Admission can be deferred. **Application fee:** $30. Common application is accepted. **To apply online, go to:** http://www.iastate.edu/~adm_info/. **Admissions requirements/recommendations:** High school units required (recommended): English: 4; Mathematics: 3 (4); Science: 3 (4); Foreign language: 2 (4); Social studies: 3 (4). Tests: The college uses SAT or ACT scores in admissions decisions. Either SAT or ACT required. For admission to the fall 2007 entering class, the school will accept: ACT with writing, ACT without writing. Campus visit: Recommended. Admissions interview: Neither required nor recommended. Off-campus interview: Not available. **Factors that count in admissions decisions:** *Academic:* Secondary school record: Very important. Class rank: Very important. Letters of recommendation: Considered. Standardized test scores: Very important. Essay: Considered. *Nonacademic:* Interview: Considered. Extracurricular activities: Considered. Talent/ability: Considered. Character/personal qualities: Considered. Alumni/ae relationship: Not considered. Geographical residence: Considered. State residency: Considered. Religious affiliation/commitment: Not considered. Minority status: Not considered. Volunteer work: Considered. Work experience: Considered. **Other schools with the greatest overlap in applicants:** Purdue University–West Lafayette; University of Illinois–Urbana-Champaign; University of Iowa; University of Minnesota–Twin Cities; University of Wisconsin–Madison. **Admissions statistics for the fall 2005 entering class:** Total applicants: 9,101. Total accepted: 8,216. Freshmen enrolled: 3,769; 26% were from out of state. Overall acceptance rate: 90%. **Credentials of fall 2005 freshmen:** 24% ranked in the top 10 percent of their high school class; 52% were in the top 25 percent, and 92% were in the top half. (Proportion submitting class standing: 100%.) **Average high school grade point average:** 3.5. **First-year students who submitted SAT scores:** 13%. Scores (25/75 percentile): Verbal: 530-660, Math: 550-690, Combined: 1080-1350. **First-year students submitting ACT scores:** 95%. Scores (25/75 percentile): English: 21-27, Math: 21-28, Composite: 22-27.

ACADEMICS

Year founded: 1858. **Academic calendar:** Semester. **Degrees offered:** bachelor's, master's, post-master's certificate, first professional, doctorate. **Most popular majors:** 21% business, management, marketing, and related support services, 18% engineering, 9% agriculture, agriculture operations, and related sciences, 7% education, 7% visual and performing arts. **Major fields of study:** agriculture, agriculture operations, and related sciences; architecture and related services; area, ethnic, cultural, and gender studies; biological and biomedical sciences; business, management, marketing, and related support services; communication, journalism, and related programs; computer and information sciences and support services; education; engineering; English language and literature/letters; family and consumer sciences/human sciences; foreign languages, literatures, and linguistics; health professions and related clinical sciences; history; liberal arts and sciences studies, and humanities; mathematics and statistics; multi/interdisciplinary studies; natural resources and conservation; parks, recreation, leisure, and fitness studies; philosophy and religious studies; physical sciences; psychology; public administration and social service professions; social sciences; visual and performing arts. **Areas of required coursework:** humanities, mathematics, English (including composition), sciences (biological or physical), social science, other. **Pre-professional programs:** pre-law, pre-dentistry, pre-medicine, pre-theology, pre-veterinary science, pre-optometry, pre-pharmacy, other. **Special academic programs:** accelerated program, cooperative (work-study plan) program, cross-registration, distance learning, double major, dual enrollment, English as a Second Language (ESL), exchange student program (domestic), external degree program, honors program, independent study, internships, liberal arts/career combination, student-designed major, study abroad, teacher certificate program, weekend college. **Teacher certification offered in:** early childhood, special education, elementary, vo-tech, middle/junior high, adult education, secondary, bilingual/bicultural. **Cooperative education programs:** agriculture, business, computer science, education, engineering, home economics, humanities, natural science, social/behavioral science, technologies, other. **Reserve Officers Training Corps (ROTC):** Army ROTC: Offered on campus; Navy ROTC: Offered on campus; Air Force ROTC: Offered on campus. **Faculty and instruction (2005-2006):** Total instructional faculty: 1,419 full-time, 217 part-time (67% men; 33% women; 16% minorities). Full-time faculty with Ph.D. or other terminal degree: 91%. Student/faculty ratio: 15/1. Classes of fewer than 20 students: 36%; of 20 to 49 students: 47%; of 50 or more students: 17%. **Advanced Placement and International Baccalaureate credit:** AP tests may be used for: Credit and/or placement. Scores accepted: 3, 4, 5. International Baccalaureate exams may be used for: Credit and/or placement. **Freshmen returning for sophomore year:** 85%. **Graduation rates:** Four-year: 31%; five-year: 63%; six-year: 68%. **Graduate study:** 20% of students pursue further study within one year.

COSTS AND FINANCIAL AID

Financial aid office: (515) 294-2223. **Expenses (2006-2007):** Tuition and fees 2006-2007: $5,830 in state, $16,324 out of state; room/board: $6,445. Estimated books and supplies: $892; transportation: $594; personal expenses: $2,675. **Financial aid:** Priority filing date for institution's financial aid form: March 1. In 2005-2006, 75% of undergraduates applied for financial aid. Of those, 57% were determined to have financial need; 45% had their need fully met. Average financial aid package (proportion receiving): $9,181 (56%). Average amount of gift aid, such as scholarships or grants (proportion receiving): $4,235 (56%). Average amount of self-help aid, such as work study or loans (proportion receiving): $4,451 (48%). Average need-based loan (excluding PLUS or other private loans): $4,328. Among students who received need-based aid, the average percentage of need met: 81%. Among students who received aid based on merit, the average award (and the proportion receiving): $1,880 (27%). The average athletic scholarship (and the proportion receiving): $12,917 (2%). Average amount of debt of borrowers graduating in 2005: $25,851. Proportion who borrowed: 67%.

CAMPUS LIFE AND EXTRACURRICULAR ACTIVITIES

Campus housing available: coed dorms, women's dorms, men's dorms, sorority housing, fraternity housing, apartments for married students, apartment for single students, special housing for disabled students, special housing for international students, other housing options. Students who live in college-owned, operated, or affiliated housing: 34%. **Student employment:** During the 2005-2006 academic year, 31% of undergraduates worked on campus. Average per-year earnings: $3,060. **Clubs and organizations:** Number of student organizations: 687. Activities include: choral groups, concert band, dance, drama/theater, jazz band, literary magazine, marching band, music ensembles, musical theater, opera, pep band, radio station, student government, student newspaper, student film society, symphony

orchestra, television station. Number of fraternities: 30; sororities: 16. Proportion of men in fraternities: 12%; of women in sororities: 14%. Average proportion of students who stay on campus on weekends: 60%. **Sports program (2005-2006):** Member of NCAA I. *Men's intercollegiate varsity sports:* basketball, cross-country, football, golf, track and field (indoor), track and field (outdoor), wrestling. *Women's intercollegiate varsity sports:* basketball, cross-country, golf, gymnastics, soccer, softball, swimming and diving, tennis, track and field (indoor), track and field (outdoor), volleyball.

SERVICES AND FACILITIES

Basic services: nonremedial tutoring, women's center, placement service, day care, health service, health insurance, other. **Remedial assistance:** study skills. **Counseling services:** minority student, career, military, personal, veteran student, academic, older student, psychological, birth control, religious. **For learning-disabled students:** School does not offer a structured program with separate admission and additional fees. Total undergraduates in learning-disabled program or receiving services: 212. Services include: reading machines, tape recorders, videotaped classes, note-taking services, learning center, readers, extended time for tests, priority registration, priority seating, texts on tape, other testing accomodations, other. **Library:** Number of titles: 2,444,263; number of current serial subscriptions: 33,914. **Information technology resources:** Students are not required to lease or own a computer. Number of campus computers available to all students: 3,000. School has a wireless network. Approximate number of users that can be accommodated: 12,000. Proportion of college-owned housing units wired for high-speed internet access: 100%. **Campus safety:** Security services offered: 24-hour foot and vehicle patrols, late-night transport/escort service, 24-hour emergency telephones, lighted pathways/sidewalks, controlled dormitory access (key, security card, etc).

TRANSFER AND INTERNATIONAL STUDENTS

Transfer students: May apply for admission for the following academic terms: Fall, Spring, Summer. Applicants need a minimum number of credits to apply. For fall 2005: Transfer applications received: 2,485. Transfer applicants offered admission: 2,006. Transfer applicants enrolled: 1,417. **International students:** Number of foreign undergraduates: 543 (3% of student body). Number of countries represented: 110. Minimum TOEFL score required: 500 (paper); 173 (computer). Average TOEFL score: 550 (paper).

Iowa Wesleyan College

- **Address:** 601 N. Main Street, Mount Pleasant, IA 52641
- **Website:** http://www.iwc.edu
- **Private; Religious affiliation:** United Methodist
- **Enrollment:** 614 full-time; 235 part-time

KEY STATS

✔ **U.S News College Ranking:** fourth tier, Comp. Coll.–Bachelor's (Midwest)
✔ **ACT Score (25th/75th percentile):** 16-21
✔ **Tuition:** 2006-2007: $17,800

Selectivity: Less selective	**Room/board:** $5,530
Acceptance rate: 59%	**Average debt:** $22,907
Student/faculty ratio: 12/1	**Proportion who borrowed:** 78%

UNDERGRADUATE STUDENT BODY STATS

2005-2006 enrollment: 614 full-time; 235 part-time. Men: 39%; women: 61%. **Ethnic makeup:** African American: 10%; Asian American: 2%; Hispanic: 7%; White: 71%; International: 9%. **Religious preference:** Roman Catholic: 22%; Protestant: 21%; No preference: 44%; United Methodist: 12%; Other: 1%.

ADMISSIONS FACTS AND FIGURES

Phone: (319) 385-6231. **Email:** admit@iwc.edu. **Website:** http://www.iwc.edu. **Application deadlines for fall 2007:** Regular decision: August 15. Early decision: Not offered. Early action: Not offered. Admission can be deferred. Common application is accepted. **Admissions requirements/recommendations:** High school units required (recommended): English: 4 (4); Mathematics: 3 (3); Science: 2 (2); Foreign language: 0 (0); Social studies: 3 (3); History: 0; Academic electives: 0 (4); Total units: 14 (16). Tests: The college uses SAT or ACT scores in admissions decisions. Either SAT or ACT required. For admission to the fall 2007 entering class, the school will accept: ACT with writing, ACT without writing. Campus visit:

Recommended. Admissions interview: Recommended. Off-campus interview: May be arranged. **Factors that count in admissions decisions:** **Academic:** Secondary school record: Very important. Class rank: Very important. Letters of recommendation: Considered. Standardized test scores: Very important. Essay: Considered. **Nonacademic:** Interview: Important. Extracurricular activities: Considered. Talent/ability: Considered. Character/personal qualities: Important. Alumni/ae relationship: Considered. Geographical residence: Not considered. State residency: Considered. Religious affiliation/commitment: Considered. Minority status: Not considered. Volunteer work: Not considered. Work experience: Not considered. **Other schools with the greatest overlap in applicants:** Culver-Stockton College; Simpson College; St. Ambrose University; University of Iowa. **Admissions statistics for the fall 2005 entering class:** Total applicants: 727. Total accepted: 426. Freshmen enrolled: 135; 48% were from out of state. Overall acceptance rate: 59%. **Credentials of fall 2005 freshmen:** 5% ranked in the top 10 percent of their high school class; 7% were in the top 25 percent, and 45% were in the top half. (Proportion submitting class standing: 78%.) **Average high school grade point average:** 2.8. **First-year students who submitted SAT scores:** 10%. Scores (25/75 percentile): Verbal: 410-500, Math: 410-520, Combined: 820-1020. **First-year students submitting ACT scores:** 76%. Scores (25/75 percentile): English: 15-21, Math: 15-20, Composite: 16-21.

ACADEMICS

Year founded: 1842. **Academic calendar:** Semester. **Degrees offered:** bachelor's. **Most popular majors:** 29% adult and continuing education and teaching, 16% business/commerce, 9% psychology, 7% nursing/registered nurse training (R.N., A.S.N., B.S.N., M.S.N.), 4% sociology. **Major fields of study:** biological and biomedical sciences; business, management, marketing, and related support services; communication, journalism, and related programs; computer and information sciences and support services; education; English language and literature/letters; health professions and related clinical sciences; history; liberal arts and sciences studies, and humanities; mathematics and statistics; philosophy and religious studies; physical sciences; psychology; social sciences; visual and performing arts. **Areas of required coursework:** arts/fine arts, humanities, computer literacy, mathematics, English (including composition), sciences (biological or physical), social science. **Pre-professional programs:** pre-law, pre-medicine, pre-theology, pre-veterinary science, pre-pharmacy. **Special academic programs (% participation):** distance learning (5%), double major (10%), dual enrollment (10%), independent study (10%), internships (100%), liberal arts/career combination (50%), student-designed major (.5%), teacher certificate program (25%), other (100%). **Teacher certification offered in:** early childhood, special education, elementary, secondary. **Cooperative education programs:** health professions. **Faculty and instruction (2005-2006):** Total instructional faculty: 42 full-time, 60 part-time (64% men; 36% women; 2% minorities). Full-time faculty with Ph.D. or other terminal degree: 62%. Student/faculty ratio: 12/1. Classes of fewer than 20 students: 72%; of 20 to 49 students: 28%; of 50 or more students: 0%. **Advanced Placement and International Baccalaureate credit:** AP tests may be used for: Placement only. Scores accepted: 3, 4, 5. International Baccalaureate exams may be used for: Placement only. **Freshmen returning for sophomore year:** 51%. **Graduation rates:** Four-year: 22%; five-year: 32%; six-year: 35%. **Graduate study:** 25% of students pursue further study immediately upon graduation; 53% within one year; 76% within five years. Fields in which graduates pursue further study: Master of Business Administration (MBA), 35%; law, 15%; medicine, 10%; dentistry, 5%; theology (or the seminary), 20%; education, 10%; arts and sciences, 5%.

COSTS AND FINANCIAL AID

Financial aid office: (319) 385-6242. **Expenses (2006-2007):** Tuition and fees 2006-2007: $17,800; room/board: $5,530. Estimated books and supplies: $800; transportation: $1,025; personal expenses: $1,810. **Financial aid:** Priority filing date for institution's financial aid form: April 1. In 2005-2006, 95% of undergraduates applied for financial aid. Of those, 92% were determined to have financial need; 46% had their need fully met. Average financial aid package (proportion receiving): $14,852 (92%). Average amount of gift aid, such as scholarships or grants (proportion receiving): $7,833 (92%). Average amount of self-help aid, such as work study or loans (proportion receiving): $5,200 (92%). Average need-based loan (excluding PLUS or other private loans): $5,000. Among students who received need-based aid, the average percentage of need met: 89%. Among students who received aid based on merit, the average award (and the proportion receiving): $7,564 (5%). Average amount of debt of borrowers graduating in 2005: $22,907. Proportion who borrowed: 78%.

CAMPUS LIFE AND EXTRACURRICULAR ACTIVITIES

Campus housing available (% using): women's dorms (34%), men's dorms (50%), apartment for single students (10%), other housing options (6%). Students who live in college-owned, operated, or affiliated housing: 38%. **Student employment:** During the 2005-2006 academic year, 10% of undergraduates worked on campus. Average per-year earnings: $1,200. **Clubs and organizations:** Number of student organizations: 28. Activities include: choral groups, concert band, dance, drama/theater, jazz band, literary magazine, music ensembles, pep band, radio station, student government, student newspaper, symphony orchestra. Number of fraternities: 1; sororities: 1. Proportion of men in fraternities: 1%; of women in sororities: 2%. Average proportion of students who stay on campus on weekends: 85%. **Sports program (2005-2006):** Member of NAIA. **Men's intercollegiate varsity sports:** baseball, basketball, football, golf, soccer, track and field (indoor), track and field (outdoor). **Women's intercollegiate varsity sports:** basketball, golf, soccer, softball, track and field (indoor), track and field (outdoor), volleyball.

SERVICES AND FACILITIES

Basic services: nonremedial tutoring, placement service, health service, health insurance. **Remedial assistance:** reading, math, writing, study skills. **Counseling services:** minority student, career, military, personal, academic, older student, psychological, religious. **For learning-disabled students:** School does not offer a structured program with separate admission and additional fees. Total undergraduates in learning-disabled program or receiving services: 26. Services include: remedial math, remedial English, reading machines, remedial reading, tape recorders, other special classes, diagnostic testing service, untimed tests, note-taking services, oral tests, learning center, readers, extended time for tests, tutors, other testing accomodations, other. **Library:** Number of titles: 107,313; number of current serial subscriptions: 397. **Information technology resources:** Students are not required to lease or own a computer. Number of campus computers available to all students: 80. School does not have a wireless network. Proportion of college-owned housing units wired for high-speed internet access: 100%. **Campus safety:** Security services offered: 24-hour foot and vehicle patrols, late-night transport/escort service, lighted pathways/sidewalks, controlled dormitory access (key, security card, etc).

TRANSFER AND INTERNATIONAL STUDENTS

Transfer students: May apply for admission for the following academic terms: Fall, Spring, Summer. Applicants need a minimum number of credits to apply. For fall 2005: Transfer applications received: 413. Transfer applicants offered admission: 232. Transfer applicants enrolled: 131. **International students:** Number of foreign undergraduates: 76 (9% of student body). Number of countries represented: 16. Minimum TOEFL score required: 500 (paper). Average TOEFL score: 500 (paper).

Loras College

- **Address:** 1450 Alta Vista, Dubuque, IA 52004-0178
- **Website:** http://www.loras.edu
- **Private; Religious affiliation:** Roman Catholic
- **Enrollment:** 1,512 full-time; 82 part-time

KEY STATS

✔ **U.S News College Ranking:** 25, Comp. Coll.–Bachelor's (Midwest)
✔ **ACT Score (25th/75th percentile):** 20-25
✔ **Tuition:** 2006-2007: $22,053

Selectivity: Selective	**Room/board:** $6,305
Acceptance rate: 82%	**Average debt:** $24,320
Student/faculty ratio: 13/1	**Proportion who borrowed:** 94%

UNDERGRADUATE STUDENT BODY STATS

2005-2006 enrollment: 1,512 full-time; 82 part-time. Men: 50%; women: 50%. **Ethnic makeup:** African American: 1%; Asian American: 1%; Hispanic: 1%; White: 94%; International: 3%.

ADMISSIONS FACTS AND FIGURES

Phone: (800) 245-6727. **Email:** adms@loras.edu. **Website:** http://www.loras.edu. **Application deadlines for fall 2007:** Regular decision: Rolling. Early decision: Not offered. Early action: Not offered. Admission can be deferred. **Application fee:** $25. Common application is not accepted.

To apply online, go to: http://www.loras.edu/~ADMISS/apply.shtml. **Admissions requirements/recommendations:** High school units required (recommended): English: 4; Mathematics: 3; Science: 4; Social studies: 3; History: 3; Total units: 16. Tests: The college uses SAT or ACT scores in admissions decisions. Neither SAT nor ACT required. For admission to the fall 2007 entering class, the school will accept: ACT with writing, ACT without writing. Campus visit: Recommended. Admissions interview: Recommended. Off-campus interview: May be arranged. **Factors that count in admissions decisions:** *Academic:* Secondary school record: Very important. Class rank: Important. Letters of recommendation: Considered. Standardized test scores: Very important. Essay: Considered. *Nonacademic:* Interview: Not considered. Extracurricular activities: Considered. Talent/ability: Not considered. Character/personal qualities: Considered. Alumni/ae relationship: Not considered. Geographical residence: Not considered. State residency: Not considered. Religious affiliation/commitment: Not considered. Minority status: Considered. Volunteer work: Considered. Work experience: Considered. **Other schools with the greatest overlap in applicants:** Clarke College; St. Ambrose University; University of Iowa; University of Northern Iowa; Wartburg College. **Admissions statistics for the fall 2005 entering class:** Total applicants: 1,402. Total accepted: 1,152. Freshmen enrolled: 366; 48% were from out of state. Overall acceptance rate: 82%. **Credentials of fall 2005 freshmen:** 13% ranked in the top 10 percent of their high school class; 34% were in the top 25 percent; and 65% were in the top half. (Proportion submitting class standing: 9%.) **Average high school grade point average:** 3.2. **First-year students who submitted SAT scores:** 5%. Scores (25/75 percentile): Verbal: 453-575, Math: 503-625, Combined: 956-1200. **First-year students submitting ACT scores:** 89%. Scores (25/75 percentile): English: 19-25, Math: 18-25, Composite: 20-25.

ACADEMICS

Year founded: 1839. **Academic calendar:** Semester. **Degrees offered:** associate, bachelor's, master's. **Most popular majors:** 10% physical education teaching and coaching, 9% elementary education and teaching, 8% criminal justice/safety studies, 7% marketing/marketing management, 6% business administration and management. **Major fields of study:** biological and biomedical sciences; business, management, marketing, and related support services; communication, journalism, and related programs; computer and information sciences and support services; education; engineering; English language and literature/letters; foreign languages, literatures, and linguistics; history; philosophy and religious studies; physical sciences; psychology; public administration and social service professions; social sciences; visual and performing arts. **Areas of required coursework:** arts/fine arts, humanities, mathematics, English (including composition), sciences (biological or physical), social science. **Special academic programs (% participation):** cooperative (work-study plan) program (6%), cross-registration (12%), double major (23%), dual enrollment (5%), English as a Second Language (ESL) (0%), honors program (7%), independent study (15%), internships (20%), student-designed major (.3%), study abroad (3%), teacher certificate program (6%). **Teacher certification offered in:** early childhood, special education, elementary, middle/junior high, secondary. **Reserve Officers Training Corps (ROTC):** Army ROTC: Offered at cooperating institution (University of Dubuque). **Faculty and instruction (2005-2006):** Total instructional faculty: 114 full-time, 29 part-time (64% men; 36% women; 3% minorities). Full-time faculty with Ph.D. or other terminal degree: 93%. Student/faculty ratio: 13/1. Classes of fewer than 20 students: 56%; of 20 to 49 students: 44%. **Advanced Placement and International Baccalaureate credit:** AP tests may be used for: Credit only. Scores accepted: 3, 4, 5. International Baccalaureate exams may be used for: Credit only. **Freshmen returning for sophomore year:** 79%. **Graduation rates:** Four-year: 55%; five-year: 64%; six-year: 66%. **Graduate study:** 20% of students pursue further study immediately upon graduation. Fields in which graduates pursue further study: Master of Business Administration (MBA), 4%; law, 6%; medicine, 19%; dentistry, 4%; education, 17%.

COSTS AND FINANCIAL AID

Financial aid office: (563) 588-7136. **Expenses (2006-2007):** Tuition and fees 2006-2007: $22,053; room/board: $6,305. Estimated books and supplies: $1,100; transportation: $750; personal expenses: $600. **Financial aid:** Priority filing date for institution's financial aid form: April 15; deadline: August 1. In 2005-2006, 85% of undergraduates applied for financial aid. Of those, 77% were determined to have financial need; 33% had their need fully met. Average financial aid package (proportion receiving): $18,374 (76%). Average amount of gift aid, such as scholarships or grants (proportion receiving): $8,170 (68%). Average amount of self-help aid, such as work study or loans (proportion receiving): $4,988 (68%). Average need-based loan (excluding PLUS or other private loans): $4,230. Among students who received need-based aid, the average percentage of need met: 88%. Among students who received aid based on merit, the average award (and the proportion receiving): $8,289 (32%). The average athletic scholarship (and the proportion receiving): $0 (0%). Average amount of debt of borrowers graduating in 2005: $24,320. Proportion who borrowed: 94%.

CAMPUS LIFE AND EXTRACURRICULAR ACTIVITIES

Campus housing available (% using): coed dorms (50%), women's dorms (15%), apartment for single students (28%), other housing options (7%). Students who live in college-owned, operated, or affiliated housing: 60%. **Student employment:** During the 2005-2006 academic year, 40% of undergraduates worked on campus. Average per-year earnings: $1,500. **Clubs and organizations:** Number of student organizations: 55. Activities include: choral groups, concert band, dance, drama/theater, jazz band, music ensembles, musical theater, radio station, student government, student newspaper, television station, yearbook. Number of fraternities: 1; sororities: 1. Proportion of men in fraternities: 2%; Average proportion of students who stay on campus on weekends: 50%. **Sports program (2005-2006):** Member of NCAA III. *Men's intercollegiate varsity sports:* baseball, basketball, cross-country, football, golf, soccer, swimming and diving, tennis, track and field (indoor), track and field (outdoor), wrestling. *Women's intercollegiate varsity sports:* basketball, cross-country, golf, soccer, softball, swimming and diving, tennis, track and field (indoor), track and field (outdoor), volleyball.

SERVICES AND FACILITIES

Basic services: nonremedial tutoring, health insurance. **Remedial assistance:** reading, math, writing, study skills. **Counseling services:** minority student, career, military, personal, veteran student, academic, older student, psychological, religious. **For learning-disabled students:** School does not offer a structured program with separate admission and additional fees. Total undergraduates in learning-disabled program or receiving services: 73. Services include: reading machines, tape recorders, other special classes, untimed tests, note-taking services, learning center, extended time for tests, tutors, other. **Library:** Number of titles: 347,351; number of current serial subscriptions: 11,032. **Information technology resources:** Students are required to lease or own a computer. Number of campus computers available to all students: 20. School has a wireless network. **Campus safety:** Security services offered: 24-hour foot and vehicle patrols, late-night transport/escort service, 24-hour emergency telephones, lighted pathways/sidewalks, controlled dormitory access (key, security card, etc).

TRANSFER AND INTERNATIONAL STUDENTS

Transfer students: May apply for admission for the following academic terms: Fall, Spring, Summer. Applicants need a minimum number of credits to apply. For fall 2005: Transfer applications received: 175. Transfer applicants offered admission: 117. Transfer applicants enrolled: 67. **International students:** Number of foreign undergraduates: 47 (3% of student body). Number of countries represented: 7. Minimum TOEFL score required: 550 (paper); 213 (computer). Average TOEFL score: 525 (paper).

Luther College

- **Address:** 700 College Drive, Decorah, IA 52101-1045
- **Website:** http://www.luther.edu
- **Private; Religious affiliation:** Lutheran
- **Enrollment:** 2,476 full-time; 69 part-time

KEY STATS

✔ **U.S News College Ranking:** 95, Liberal Arts Colleges
✔ **ACT Score (25th/75th percentile):** 22-28
✔ **Tuition:** 2006-2007: $26,380

Selectivity: More selective	**Room/board:** $4,290
Acceptance rate: 75%	**Average debt:** $18,504
Student/faculty ratio: 13/1	**Proportion who borrowed:** 76%

UNDERGRADUATE STUDENT BODY STATS

2005-2006 enrollment: 2,476 full-time; 69 part-time. Men: 42%; women: 58%. **Ethnic makeup:** African American: 1%; Asian American: 2%; Hispanic: 1%; White: 93%; International: 3%. **Religious preference:** Roman Catholic: 15%; Protestant: 14%; Unknown: 12%; Lutheran: 52%; Other: 7%.

ADMISSIONS FACTS AND FIGURES

Phone: (563) 387-1287. **Email:** admissions@luther.edu. **Website:** http://www.luther.edu. **Application deadlines for fall 2007:** Regular decision: Rolling. Early decision: Not offered. Early action: Not offered. Admission can be deferred. **Application fee:** $25. Common application is accepted. **To apply online, go to:** http://www.luther.edu/admis/apply.html. **Admissions requirements/recommendations:** High school units required (recommended): English: (4); Mathematics: (3); Science: (2); Foreign language: (2); Social studies: (3); Total units: (14). Tests: The college uses SAT or ACT scores in admissions decisions. Either SAT or ACT required. For admission to the fall 2007 entering class, the school will accept: ACT with writing, ACT without writing. Campus visit: Recommended. Admissions interview: Recommended. Off-campus interview: May be arranged. **Factors that count in admissions decisions:** *Academic:* Secondary school record: Very important. Class rank: Very important. Letters of recommendation: Very important. Standardized test scores: Very important. Essay: Important. *Nonacademic:* Interview: Considered. Extracurricular activities: Important. Talent/ability: Important. Character/personal qualities: Important. Alumni/ae relationship: Considered. Geographical residence: Considered. State residency: Not considered. Religious affiliation/commitment: Considered. Minority status: Considered. Volunteer work: Important. Work experience: Not considered. **Other schools with the greatest overlap in applicants:** Concordia College–Moorhead; Gustavus Adolphus College; St. Olaf College; University of Iowa; Wartburg College. **Admissions statistics for the fall 2005 entering class:** Total applicants: 2,121. Total accepted: 1,593. Freshmen enrolled: 631; 63% were from out of state. Overall acceptance rate: 75%. **Credentials of fall 2005 freshmen:** 32% ranked in the top 10 percent of their high school class; 61% were in the top 25 percent, and 84% were in the top half. (Proportion submitting class standing: 95%.) **Average high school grade point average:** 3.6. **First-year students who submitted SAT scores:** 15%. Scores (25/75 percentile): Verbal: 550-670, Math: 550-670, Combined: 1100-1340. **First-year students submitting ACT scores:** 93%. Scores (25/75 percentile): English: 22-29, Math: 22-28, Composite: 22-28.

ACADEMICS

Year founded: 1861. **Academic calendar:** 4-1-4. **Degrees offered:** bachelor's. **Most popular majors:** 13% biology/biological sciences, 12% business administration and management, 10% music, 10% psychology, 8% elementary education and teaching. **Major fields of study:** area, ethnic, cultural, and gender studies; biological and biomedical sciences; business, management, marketing, and related support services; communication, journalism, and related programs; computer and information sciences and support services; education; English language and literature/letters; foreign languages, literatures, and linguistics; health professions and related clinical sciences; history; mathematics and statistics; multi/interdisciplinary studies; parks, recreation, leisure, and fitness studies; philosophy and religious studies; physical sciences; psychology; public administration and social service professions; social sciences; visual and performing arts. **Areas of required coursework:** arts/fine arts, humanities, mathematics, English (including composition), philosophy, foreign languages, sciences (biological or physical), history, social science, other. **Pre-professional programs:** pre-law, pre-dentistry, pre-medicine, pre-theology, pre-veterinary science, pre-optometry, pre-pharmacy, other. **Special academic programs (% participation):** double major (25%), dual enrollment, honors program, independent study, internships, student-designed major, study abroad, teacher certificate program. **Teacher certification offered in:** early childhood, special education, elementary, middle/junior high, secondary, bilingual/bicultural. **Faculty and instruction (2005-2006):** Total instructional faculty: 179 full-time, 60 part-time (57% men; 43% women; 4% minorities). Full-time faculty with Ph.D. or other terminal degree: 88%. Student/faculty ratio: 13/1. Classes of fewer than 20 students: 50%; of 20 to 49 students: 48%; of 50 or more students: 2%. **Advanced Placement and International Baccalaureate credit:** AP tests may be used for: Credit and/or placement. Scores accepted: 4, 5. International Baccalaureate exams may be used for: Credit and/or placement. **Freshmen returning for sophomore year:** 85%. **Graduation rates:** Four-year: 65%; five-year: 74%; six-year: 75%. **Graduate study:** 23% of students pursue further study immediately upon graduation. Fields in which graduates pursue further study: Master of Business Administration (MBA), 3%; law, 6%; medicine, 17%; engineering, 3%; theology (or the seminary), 6%; arts and sciences, 65%.

COSTS AND FINANCIAL AID

Financial aid office: (563) 387-1018. **Expenses (2006-2007):** Tuition and fees 2006-2007: $26,380; room/board: $4,290. Estimated books and supplies: $830; transportation: $1,020; personal expenses: $1,510. **Financial aid:** Priority filing date for institution's financial aid form: March 1. In 2005-2006, 85% of undergraduates applied for financial aid. Of those, 71% were determined to have financial need; 36% had their need fully met. Average financial aid package (proportion receiving): $19,374 (71%). Average amount of gift aid, such as scholarships or grants (proportion receiving): $12,386 (71%). Average amount of self-help aid, such as work study or loans (proportion receiving): $6,229 (61%). Average need-based loan (excluding PLUS or other private loans): $5,150. Among students who received need-based aid, the average percentage of need met: 88%. Among students who received aid based on merit, the average award (and the proportion receiving): $6,301 (29%). Average amount of debt of borrowers graduating in 2005: $18,504. Proportion who borrowed: 76%.

CAMPUS LIFE AND EXTRACURRICULAR ACTIVITIES

Campus housing available (% using): coed dorms (90%), apartments for married students (1%), apartment for single students (2%), other housing options (7%). Students who live in college-owned, operated, or affiliated housing: 84%. **Student employment:** During the 2005-2006 academic year, 76% of undergraduates worked on campus. Average per-year earnings: $1,684. **Clubs and organizations:** Number of student organizations: 139. Activities include: choral groups, concert band, dance, drama/theater, jazz band, literary magazine, music ensembles, musical theater, pep band, radio station, student government, student newspaper, student film society, symphony orchestra, yearbook. Number of fraternities: 2; sororities: 3. Proportion of men in fraternities: 7%; of women in sororities: 9%. Average proportion of students who stay on campus on weekends: 90%. **Sports program (2005-2006):** Member of NCAA III. *Men's intercollegiate varsity sports:* baseball, basketball, cross-country, football, golf, soccer, swimming and diving, tennis, track and field (indoor), track and field (outdoor), wrestling. *Women's intercollegiate varsity sports:* basketball, cross-country, golf, soccer, softball, swimming and diving, tennis, track and field (indoor), track and field (outdoor), volleyball.

SERVICES AND FACILITIES

Basic services: nonremedial tutoring, placement service, health service, health insurance. **Remedial assistance:** reading, writing, study skills. **Counseling services:** minority student, career, personal, academic, older student, psychological, birth control, religious. **For learning-disabled students:** School does not offer a structured program with separate admission and additional fees. Total undergraduates in learning-disabled program or receiving services: 20. Services include: tape recorders, note-taking services, oral tests, learning center, extended time for tests, tutors, priority registration, texts on tape, other testing accomodations, other. **Library:** Number of titles: 339,206; number of current serial subscriptions: 882. **Information technology resources:** Students are not required to lease or own a computer. Number of campus computers available to all students: 500. School has a wireless network. Approximate number of users that can be accommodated: 5,000. Proportion of college-owned housing units wired for high-speed internet access: 100%. **Campus safety:** Security services offered: 24-hour foot and vehicle patrols, late-night transport/escort service, 24-hour emergency telephones, lighted pathways/sidewalks, controlled dormitory access (key, security card, etc).

TRANSFER AND INTERNATIONAL STUDENTS

Transfer students: May apply for admission for the following academic terms: Fall, Winter, Spring, Summer. Applicants do not need a minimum number of credits to apply. For fall 2005: Transfer applications received: 149. Transfer applicants offered admission: 95. Transfer applicants enrolled: 56. **International students:** Number of foreign undergraduates: 64 (3% of student body). Number of countries represented: 25. Minimum TOEFL score required: 550 (paper); 213 (computer). Average TOEFL score: 550 (paper).

Maharishi University of Management

- **Address:** Fairfield, IA 52557
- **Website:** http://www.mum.edu
- **Private**
- **Enrollment:** N/A

KEY STATS

✔ **U.S News College Ranking:** fourth tier, Universities–Master's (Midwest)
✔ **ACT Score (25th/75th percentile):** 19-25
✔ **Tuition:** 2006-2007: $24,430

Selectivity: Selective	**Room/board:** $6,000
Acceptance rate: 67%	**Average debt:** $19,545
Student/faculty ratio: N/A	**Proportion who borrowed:** 93%

Morningside College

- **Address:** 1501 Morningside Avenue, Sioux City, IA 51106
- **Website:** http://www.morningside.edu
- **Private; Religious affiliation:** United Methodist
- **Enrollment:** 1,066 full-time; 83 part-time

KEY STATS

✔ **U.S News College Ranking:** 42, Comp. Coll.–Bachelor's (Midwest)
✔ **ACT Score (25th/75th percentile):** 19-25
✔ **Tuition:** 2006-2007: $18,940

Selectivity: Selective	**Room/board:** $5,930
Acceptance rate: 83%	**Average debt:** $26,816
Student/faculty ratio: 16/1	**Proportion who borrowed:** 91%

UNDERGRADUATE STUDENT BODY STATS

2005-2006 enrollment: 1,066 full-time; 83 part-time. Men: 46%; women: 54%. **Ethnic makeup:** African American: 2%; Asian American: 1%; Hispanic: 3%; White: 91%; International: 2%. **Religious preference:** Roman Catholic: 21%; Protestant: 29%; No preference: 30%; United Methodist: 20%.

ADMISSIONS FACTS AND FIGURES

Phone: (712) 274-5111. **Email:** mscadm@morningside.edu. **Website:** http://www.morningside.edu. **Application deadlines for fall 2007:** Regular decision: Rolling. Early decision: Not offered. Early action: Not offered. Admission can be deferred. **Application fee:** $25. Common application is not accepted. **To apply online, go to:** http://www.morningside.edu/admissions/OurApplication.htm. **Admissions requirements/recommendations:** High school units required (recommended): English: 3 (3); Mathematics: 2 (2); Science: 2 (2); Social studies: 3 (3); Total units: 10 (10). Tests: The college uses SAT or ACT scores in admissions decisions. Either SAT or ACT required. For admission to the fall 2007 entering class, the school will accept: ACT with writing, ACT without writing. Campus visit: Recommended. Admissions interview: Recommended. Off-campus interview: Not available. **Factors that count in admissions decisions:** *Academic:* Secondary school record: Very important. Class rank: Very important. Letters of recommendation: Very important. Standardized test scores: Very important. Essay: Considered. *Nonacademic:* Interview: Important. Extracurricular activities: Important. Talent/ability: Important. Character/personal qualities: Not considered. Alumni/ae relationship: Not considered. Geographical residence: Not considered. State residency: Not considered. Religious affiliation/commitment: Not considered. Minority status: Not considered. Volunteer work: Not considered. Work experience: Not considered. **Other schools with the greatest overlap in applicants:** Briar Cliff University; Buena Vista University; Iowa State University; University of Iowa; University of Northern Iowa. **Admissions statistics for the fall 2005 entering class:** Total applicants: 1,160. Total accepted: 957. Freshmen enrolled: 309; 34% were from out of state. Overall acceptance rate: 83%. **Credentials of fall 2005 freshmen:** 17% ranked in the top 10 percent of their high school class; 39% were in the top 25 percent, and 74% were in the top half. (Proportion submitting class standing: 97%.) **Average high school grade point average:** 3.3. **First-year students who submitted SAT scores:** 6%. Scores (25/75 percentile): Verbal: N/A, Math: N/A, Combined: N/A. **First-**year students submitting ACT scores:** 95%. Scores (25/75 percentile): English: 18-24, Math: 18-25, Composite: 19-25.

ACADEMICS

Year founded: 1894. **Academic calendar:** Semester. **Degrees offered:** bachelor's, master's. **Most popular majors:** 15% elementary education and teaching, 10% nursing/registered nurse training (R.N., A.S.N., B.S.N., M.S.N.), 8% marketing/marketing management, 6% finance, 6% human resources management/personnel administration. **Major fields of study:** biological and biomedical sciences; business, management, marketing, and related support services; communication, journalism, and related programs; computer and information sciences and support services; education; engineering; English language and literature/letters; foreign languages, literatures, and linguistics; health professions and related clinical sciences; history; mathematics and statistics; multi/interdisciplinary studies; philosophy and religious studies; physical sciences; psychology; social sciences; visual and performing arts. **Areas of required coursework:** arts/fine arts, humanities, mathematics, English (including composition), sciences (biological or physical). **Pre-professional programs:** pre-law, pre-dentistry, pre-medicine, pre-theology, pre-veterinary science, pre-optometry, pre-pharmacy. **Special academic programs (% participation):** double major (16%), English as a Second Language (ESL) (0%), honors program (9%), independent study (20%), internships (36%), student-designed major (0%), study abroad (0%), teacher certificate program (29%). **Teacher certification offered in:** special education, elementary, secondary. **Cooperative education programs:** health professions. **Reserve Officers Training Corps (ROTC):** Army ROTC: Offered at cooperating institution (University of South Dakota). **Faculty and instruction (2005-2006):** Total instructional faculty: 64 full-time, 66 part-time (47% men; 53% women; 2% minorities). Full-time faculty with Ph.D. or other terminal degree: 80%. Student/faculty ratio: 16/1. Classes of fewer than 20 students: 47%; of 20 to 49 students: 53%; of 50 or more students: 1%. **Advanced Placement and International Baccalaureate credit:** AP tests may be used for: Credit and/or placement. Scores accepted: 3, 4, 5. International Baccalaureate exams may be used for: Credit and/or placement. **Freshmen returning for sophomore year:** 66%. **Graduation rates:** Four-year: 39%; five-year: 54%; six-year: 55%. **Graduate study:** 12% of students pursue further study immediately upon graduation. Fields in which graduates pursue further study: law, 15%; medicine, 15%; education, 8%; arts and sciences, 62%.

COSTS AND FINANCIAL AID

Financial aid office: (712) 274-5159. **Expenses (2006-2007):** Tuition and fees 2006-2007: $18,940; room/board: $5,930. Estimated books and supplies: $800; transportation: $800; personal expenses: $1,500. **Financial aid:** Priority filing date for institution's financial aid form: March 1. In 2005-2006, 95% of undergraduates applied for financial aid. Of those, 87% were determined to have financial need; 62% had their need fully met. Average financial aid package (proportion receiving): $16,302 (87%). Average amount of gift aid, such as scholarships or grants (proportion receiving): $5,702 (69%). Average amount of self-help aid, such as work study or loans (proportion receiving): $4,394 (76%). Average need-based loan (excluding PLUS or other private loans): $3,585. Among students who received need-based aid, the average percentage of need met: 77%. Among students who received aid based on merit, the average award (and the proportion receiving): $6,130 (12%). The average athletic scholarship (and the proportion receiving): $2,647 (45%). Average amount of debt of borrowers graduating in 2005: $26,816. Proportion who borrowed: 91%.

CAMPUS LIFE AND EXTRACURRICULAR ACTIVITIES

Campus housing available (% using): coed dorms (90%), apartments for married students (1%), apartment for single students (8%), special housing for disabled students (1%). Students who live in college-owned, operated, or affiliated housing: 66%. **Student employment:** During the 2005-2006 academic year, 25% of undergraduates worked on campus. Average per-year earnings: $1,400. **Clubs and organizations:** Number of student organizations: 39. Activities include: choral groups, concert band, dance, drama/theater, jazz band, literary magazine, music ensembles, musical theater, pep band, radio station, student government, student newspaper, television station, yearbook. Number of fraternities: 2; sororities: 1. Proportion of men in fraternities: 7%; of women in sororities: 3%. Average proportion of students who stay on campus on weekends: 60%. **Sports program (2005-2006):** Member of NAIA. *Men's intercollegiate varsity sports:* baseball, basketball, cheerleading, cross-country, football, golf, soccer, swimming and diving, tennis, track and field (indoor), track and field (outdoor), wrestling. *Women's intercollegiate varsity sports:* basketball, cross-country, golf, soccer, softball, swimming and diving, tennis, volleyball.

SERVICES AND FACILITIES

Basic services: nonremedial tutoring, placement service, health service, health insurance. **Remedial assistance:** reading, math, writing, study skills. **Counseling services:** minority student, career, personal, academic, older student, psychological, birth control, religious. **For learning-disabled students:** School does not offer a structured program with separate admission and additional fees. Total undergraduates in learning-disabled program or receiving services: 22. Services include: remedial math, remedial English, reading machines, remedial reading, tape recorders, diagnostic testing service, untimed tests, note-taking services, oral tests, learning center, readers, extended time for tests, tutors, priority seating, proofreading services, substitution of courses, texts on tape. **Library:** Number of titles: 104,424; number of current serial subscriptions: 450. **Information technology resources:** Students are required to lease or own a computer. Number of campus computers available to all students: 150. School has a wireless network. Approximate number of users that can be accommodated: 1,000. Proportion of college-owned housing units wired for high-speed internet access: 100%. **Campus safety:** Security services offered: late-night transport/escort service, 24-hour emergency telephones, lighted pathways/sidewalks, student patrols, controlled dormitory access (key, security card, etc.).

TRANSFER AND INTERNATIONAL STUDENTS

Transfer students: May apply for admission for the following academic terms: Fall, Spring, Summer. Applicants need a minimum number of credits to apply. For fall 2005: Transfer applications received: 180. Transfer applicants offered admission: 104. Transfer applicants enrolled: 73. **International students:** Number of foreign undergraduates: 25 (2% of student body). Number of countries represented: 8. Minimum TOEFL score required: 425 (paper); 113 (computer).

Mount Mercy College

- **Address:** 1330 Elmhurst Drive NE, Cedar Rapids, IA 52402
- **Website:** http://www.mtmercy.edu
- **Private; Religious affiliation:** Roman Catholic
- **Enrollment:** 1,019 full-time; 471 part-time

KEY STATS

✔ **U.S News College Ranking:** 33, Comp. Coll.–Bachelor's (Midwest)
✔ **ACT Score (25th/75th percentile):** 20-24
✔ **Tuition:** 2006-2007: $18,930

Selectivity: Selective	**Room/board:** $5,970
Acceptance rate: 79%	**Average debt:** $22,530
Student/faculty ratio: 12/1	**Proportion who borrowed:** 72%

UNDERGRADUATE STUDENT BODY STATS

2005-2006 enrollment: 1,019 full-time; 471 part-time. Men: 27%; women: 73%. **Ethnic makeup:** African American: 2%; Asian American: 1%; Hispanic: 1%; White: 96%. **Religious preference:** Protestant: 26%; No preference: 39%; Roman Catholic: 34%.

ADMISSIONS FACTS AND FIGURES

Phone: (319) 368-6460. **Email:** admission@mtmercy.edu. **Website:** http://www.mtmercy.edu. **Application deadlines for fall 2007:** Regular decision: August 25. Early decision: Not offered. Early action: Not offered. Admission can be deferred. **Application fee:** $20. Common application is accepted. **To apply online, go to:** http://www.mtmercy.edu/forms2/frapplic.htm. **Admissions requirements/recommendations:** High school units required (recommended): English: 4 (4); Mathematics: 3 (3); Science: 2 (2); Foreign language: 2 (2); Social studies: 3 (3); History: 2 (2); Total units: 16 (16). Tests: The college uses SAT or ACT scores in admissions decisions. Either SAT or ACT required. For admission to the fall 2007 entering class, the school will accept: ACT with writing, ACT without writing. Campus visit: Recommended. Admissions interview: Recommended. Off-campus interview: May be arranged. **Factors that count in admissions decisions:** *Academic:* Secondary school record: Very important. Class rank: Very important. Letters of recommendation: Considered. Standardized test scores: Very important. Essay: Considered. *Nonacademic:* Interview: Considered. Extracurricular activities: Considered. Talent/ability: Considered. Character/personal qualities: Considered. Alumni/ae relationship: Considered. Geographical residence: Not considered. State residency: Not

considered. Religious affiliation/commitment: Not considered. Minority status: Not considered. Volunteer work: Considered. Work experience: Not considered. **Other schools with the greatest overlap in applicants:** Coe College; Iowa State University; St. Ambrose University; University of Iowa; University of Northern Iowa. **Admissions statistics for the fall 2005 entering class:** Total applicants: 478. Total accepted: 376. Freshmen enrolled: 181; 9% were from out of state. Overall acceptance rate: 79%. **Credentials of fall 2005 freshmen:** 13% ranked in the top 10 percent of their high school class; 42% were in the top 25 percent, and 76% were in the top half. (Proportion submitting class standing: 99%.) **Average high school grade point average:** 3.4. **First-year students who submitted SAT scores:** 1%. Scores (25/75 percentile): Verbal: N/A, Math: N/A, Combined: N/A. **First-year students submitting ACT scores:** 99%. Scores (25/75 percentile): English: 19-25, Math: 18-24, Composite: 20-24.

ACADEMICS

Year founded: 1928. **Academic calendar:** 4-1-4. **Degrees offered:** bachelor's. **Most popular majors:** 22% business administration, management, and operations, 12% elementary education and teaching, 12% nursing/registered nurse training (R.N., A.S.N., B.S.N., M.S.N.), 10% business administration and management, 6% computer science. **Major fields of study:** biological and biomedical sciences; business, management, marketing, and related support services; communication, journalism, and related programs; computer and information sciences and support services; education; English language and literature/letters; health professions and related clinical sciences; history; legal professions and studies; mathematics and statistics; multi/interdisciplinary studies; philosophy and religious studies; psychology; public administration and social service professions; social sciences; visual and performing arts. **Areas of required coursework:** arts/fine arts, humanities, mathematics, English (including composition), philosophy, sciences (biological or physical), history, social science, other. **Pre-professional programs:** pre-law, pre-dentistry, pre-medicine, pre-veterinary science, other. **Special academic programs (% participation):** accelerated program (25.49%), cooperative (work-study plan) program (0%), cross-registration (0%), double major (10.3%), dual enrollment (1.9%), honors program (2.9%), independent study (5%), internships (35%), liberal arts/career combination (4%), teacher certificate program (14.4%). **Teacher certification offered in:** early childhood, special education, elementary, middle/junior high, secondary. **Faculty and instruction (2005-2006):** Total instructional faculty: 73 full-time, 78 part-time (36% men; 64% women; 2% minorities). Full-time faculty with Ph.D. or other terminal degree: 58%. Student/faculty ratio: 12/1. Classes of fewer than 20 students: 75%; of 20 to 49 students: 23%; of 50 or more students: 2%. **Advanced Placement and International Baccalaureate credit:** AP tests may be used for: Credit only. Scores accepted: 3, 4, 5. International Baccalaureate exams may be used for: Credit only. **Freshmen returning for sophomore year:** 75%. **Graduation rates:** Four-year: 50%; five-year: 60%; six-year: 63%. **Graduate study:** 14% of students pursue further study immediately upon graduation; 14% within one year; 24% within five years.

COSTS AND FINANCIAL AID

Financial aid office: (319) 368-6467. **Expenses (2006-2007):** Tuition and fees 2006-2007: $18,930; room/board: $5,970. Estimated books and supplies: $840; transportation: $960; personal expenses: $1,800. **Financial aid:** Priority filing date for institution's financial aid form: March 1. In 2005-2006, 96% of undergraduates applied for financial aid. Of those, 84% were determined to have financial need; 39% had their need fully met. Average financial aid package (proportion receiving): $14,744 (84%). Average amount of gift aid, such as scholarships or grants (proportion receiving): $9,678 (84%). Average amount of self-help aid, such as work study or loans (proportion receiving): $5,803 (74%). Average need-based loan (excluding PLUS or other private loans): $5,041. Among students who received need-based aid, the average percentage of need met: 81%. Among students who received aid based on merit, the average award (and the proportion receiving): $11,522 (16%). The average athletic scholarship (and the proportion receiving): $0 (0%). Average amount of debt of borrowers graduating in 2005: $22,530. Proportion who borrowed: 72%.

CAMPUS LIFE AND EXTRACURRICULAR ACTIVITIES

Campus housing available (% using): coed dorms (66%), apartment for single students (9%), other housing options (25%). Students who live in college-owned, operated, or affiliated housing: 26%. **Student employment:** During the 2005-2006 academic year, 28% of undergraduates worked on campus. Average per-year earnings: $1,500. **Clubs and organizations:** Number of student organizations: 31. Activities include: choral groups, drama/theater, literary magazine, student government, student newspaper. Number of fraternities: 0; sororities: 0. Average proportion of students who stay on campus on weekends: 30%. **Sports program (2005-2006):** Member of NAIA. *Men's intercollegiate varsity sports:* baseball, basketball, cross-country, golf, soccer, track and field (indoor), track and field (outdoor). *Women's intercollegiate varsity sports:* basketball, cross-country, golf, soccer, softball, track and field (indoor), track and field (outdoor), volleyball.

SERVICES AND FACILITIES

Basic services: nonremedial tutoring, placement service, health service. **Remedial assistance:** reading, math, writing, study skills. **Counseling services:** minority student, career, personal, veteran student, academic, older student, psychological, religious. **For learning-disabled students:** School does not offer a structured program with separate admission and additional fees. Total undergraduates in learning-disabled program or receiving services: 70. Services include: remedial math, remedial English, reading machines, remedial reading, tape recorders, videotaped classes, note-taking services, oral tests, learning center, readers, extended time for tests, tutors, priority registration, priority seating, other testing accomodations. **Library:** Number of titles: 124,335; number of current serial subscriptions: 711. **Information technology resources:** Students are not required to lease or own a computer. Number of campus computers available to all students: 100. School has a wireless network. Approximate number of users that can be accommodated: 500. Proportion of college-owned housing units wired for high-speed internet access: 100%. **Campus safety:** Security services offered: 24-hour foot and vehicle patrols, late-night transport/escort service, 24-hour emergency telephones, lighted pathways/sidewalks, controlled dormitory access (key, security card, etc).

TRANSFER AND INTERNATIONAL STUDENTS

Transfer students: May apply for admission for the following academic terms: Fall, Winter, Spring, Summer. Applicants do not need a minimum number of credits to apply. For fall 2005: Transfer applications received: 452. Transfer applicants offered admission: 325. Transfer applicants enrolled: 240. **International students:** Number of foreign undergraduates: 5. Number of countries represented: 0.

Northwestern College

- ■ **Address:** 101 Seventh Street SW, Orange City, IA 51041
- ■ **Website:** http://www.nwciowa.edu
- ■ **Private; Religious affiliation:** Reformed Church in America
- ■ **Enrollment:** 1,226 full-time; 47 part-time

KEY STATS

- ✔ **U.S News College Ranking:** 20, Comp. Coll.–Bachelor's (Midwest)
- ✔ **ACT Score (25th/75th percentile):** 21-27
- ✔ **Tuition:** 2006-2007: $18,296

Selectivity: More selective	**Room/board:** $5,210
Acceptance rate: 93%	**Average debt:** $22,286
Student/faculty ratio: 15/1	**Proportion who borrowed:** 85%

UNDERGRADUATE STUDENT BODY STATS

2005-2006 enrollment: 1,226 full-time; 47 part-time. Men: 38%; women: 62%. **Ethnic makeup:** African American: 1%; Asian American: 1%; Hispanic: 1%; White: 95%; International: 2%. **Religious preference:** Roman Catholic: 3%; Protestant: 93%; Unknown: 2%.

ADMISSIONS FACTS AND FIGURES

Phone: (712) 707-7130. **Email:** admissions@nwciowa.edu. **Website:** http://www.nwciowa.edu. **Application deadlines for fall 2007:** Regular decision: August 15. Early decision: Not offered. Early action: Not offered. Admission can be deferred. **Application fee:** $25. Common application is accepted. **Admissions requirements/recommendations:** High school units required (recommended): English: (4); Mathematics: (3); Science: (3); Foreign language: (3); Social studies: (3); Total units: (16). Tests: The college uses SAT or ACT scores in admissions decisions. Either SAT or ACT required. For admission to the fall 2007 entering class, the school will accept: ACT with writing, ACT without writing. Campus visit: Recommended. Admissions interview: Neither required nor recommended. Off-campus interview: May be arranged. **Factors that count in admissions decisions:** *Academic:* Secondary school record: Very important. Class rank: Important. Letters of recommendation: Important. Standardized test scores: Very important. Essay: Considered. *Nonacademic:* Interview: Considered.

Extracurricular activities: Not considered. Talent/ability: Considered. Character/personal qualities: Important. Alumni/ae relationship: Not considered. Geographical residence: Not considered. State residency: Not considered. Religious affiliation/commitment: Considered. Minority status: Not considered. Volunteer work: Not considered. Work experience: Not considered. **Other schools with the greatest overlap in applicants:** Bethel College; Northwestern College; University of Nebraska–Omaha; University of Northern Iowa; University of Sioux Falls. **Admissions statistics for the fall 2005 entering class:** Total applicants: 1,185. Total accepted: 1,101. Freshmen enrolled: 374; 49% were from out of state. Overall acceptance rate: 93%. **Credentials of fall 2005 freshmen:** 26% ranked in the top 10 percent of their high school class; 58% were in the top 25 percent, and 83% were in the top half. (Proportion submitting class standing: 90%.) **Average high school grade point average:** 3.5. **First-year students submitting ACT scores:** 95%. Scores (25/75 percentile): English: 21-29, Math: 20-26, Composite: 21-27.

ACADEMICS

Year founded: 1882. **Academic calendar:** Semester. **Degrees offered:** certificate, bachelor's. **Most popular majors:** 22% business, management, marketing, and related support services, 20% education, 7% biological and biomedical sciences, 6% visual and performing arts, 5% theology and religious vocations. **Major fields of study:** agriculture, agriculture operations, and related sciences; biological and biomedical sciences; business, management, marketing, and related support services; communication, journalism, and related programs; computer and information sciences and support services; education; English language and literature/letters; foreign languages, literatures, and linguistics; health professions and related clinical sciences; history; liberal arts and sciences studies, and humanities; mathematics and statistics; parks, recreation, leisure, and fitness studies; philosophy and religious studies; physical sciences; psychology; public administration and social service professions; social sciences; theology and religious vocations; visual and performing arts. **Areas of required coursework:** arts/fine arts, mathematics, English (including composition), philosophy, foreign languages, sciences (biological or physical), history, social science, other. **Pre-professional programs:** pre-law, pre-dentistry, pre-medicine, pre-veterinary science, pre-optometry, pre-pharmacy, other. **Special academic programs (% participation):** double major (1%), English as a Second Language (ESL) (1%), honors program (1%), internships (5%), student-designed major (1%), study abroad (5%), teacher certificate program (25%). **Teacher certification offered in:** early childhood, special education, elementary, middle/junior high, secondary. **Faculty and instruction (2005-2006):** Total instructional faculty: 78 full-time, 50 part-time (55% men; 45% women; 2% minorities). Full-time faculty with Ph.D. or other terminal degree: 79%. Student/faculty ratio: 15/1. Classes of fewer than 20 students: 57%; of 20 to 49 students: 42%; of 50 or more students: 2%. **Advanced Placement and International Baccalaureate credit:** AP tests may be used for: Credit and/or placement. Scores accepted: 3, 4, 5. International Baccalaureate exams may be used for: Credit and/or placement. **Freshmen returning for sophomore year:** 76%. **Graduation rates:** Four-year: 49%; five-year: 59%; six-year: 58%. **Graduate study:** 20% of students pursue further study immediately upon graduation.

COSTS AND FINANCIAL AID

Financial aid office: (712) 707-7131. **Expenses (2006-2007):** Tuition and fees 2006-2007: $18,296; room/board: $5,210. Estimated books and supplies: $900; transportation: $1,400; personal expenses: $1,994. **Financial aid:** Priority filing date for institution's financial aid form: April 1. In 2005-2006, 78% of undergraduates applied for financial aid. Of those, 78% were determined to have financial need; 51% had their need fully met. Average financial aid package (proportion receiving): $13,700 (78%). Average amount of gift aid, such as scholarships or grants (proportion receiving): $4,995 (69%). Average amount of self-help aid, such as work study or loans (proportion receiving): $4,529 (69%). Average need-based loan (excluding PLUS or other private loans): $4,155. Among students who received aid based on merit, the average award (and the proportion receiving): $4,908 (20%). The average athletic scholarship (and the proportion receiving): $2,898 (23%). Average amount of debt of borrowers graduating in 2005: $22,286. Proportion who borrowed: 85%.

CAMPUS LIFE AND EXTRACURRICULAR ACTIVITIES

Campus housing available: women's dorms, men's dorms, apartment for single students. Students who live in college-owned, operated, or affiliated housing: 87%. **Student employment:** During the 2005-2006 academic year, 55% of undergraduates worked on campus. Average per-year earnings: $1,050. Activities include: choral groups, concert band, dance, drama/theater, jazz band, literary magazine, music ensembles, musical theater, pep band, radio station, student government, student newspaper, symphony orchestra, television station, yearbook. Average proportion of students who stay on campus on weekends: 80%. **Sports program (2005-2006):** Member of NAIA. *Men's intercollegiate varsity sports:* baseball, basketball, cross-country, football, golf, soccer, track and field (indoor), track and field (outdoor), wrestling. *Women's intercollegiate varsity sports:* basketball, cross-country, golf, soccer, softball, track and field (indoor), track and field (outdoor), volleyball.

SERVICES AND FACILITIES

Basic services: nonremedial tutoring, placement service, health service, health insurance. **Remedial assistance:** reading, math, writing, study skills. **Counseling services:** career, personal, academic, psychological, religious. **For learning-disabled students:** School does not offer a structured program with separate admission and additional fees. Total undergraduates in learning-disabled program or receiving services: 20. Services include: remedial math, remedial English, tape recorders, untimed tests, note-taking services, oral tests, learning center, extended time for tests, tutors. **Library:** Number of titles: 120,328; number of current serial subscriptions: 578. **Information technology resources:** Students are not required to lease or own a computer. Number of campus computers available to all students: 250. School has a wireless network. Approximate number of users that can be accommodated: 1,000. Proportion of college-owned housing units wired for high-speed internet access: 100%. **Campus safety:** Security services offered: lighted pathways/sidewalks, controlled dormitory access (key, security card, etc).

TRANSFER AND INTERNATIONAL STUDENTS

Transfer students: May apply for admission for the following academic terms: Fall, Spring. Applicants do not need a minimum number of credits to apply. For fall 2005: Transfer applications received: 1,185. Transfer applicants offered admission: 1,101. Transfer applicants enrolled: 374.
International students: Number of foreign undergraduates: 21 (2% of student body). Minimum TOEFL score required: 550 (paper); 213 (computer).

Simpson College

- **Address:** 701 N. C Street, Indianola, IA 50125
- **Website:** http://www.simpson.edu
- **Private; Religious affiliation:** United Methodist
- **Enrollment:** 1,507 full-time; 528 part-time

KEY STATS

✔ **U.S News College Ranking:** 8, Comp. Coll.–Bachelor's (Midwest)
✔ **ACT Score (25th/75th percentile):** 22-27
✔ **Tuition:** 2006-2007: $22,266

Selectivity: More selective	**Room/board:** $6,278
Acceptance rate: 87%	**Average debt:** $24,403
Student/faculty ratio: 15/1	**Proportion who borrowed:** 87%

UNDERGRADUATE STUDENT BODY STATS

2005-2006 enrollment: 1,507 full-time; 528 part-time. Men: 41%; women: 59%. **Ethnic makeup:** African American: 2%; Asian American: 1%; Hispanic: 1%; White: 94%; International: 1%. **Religious preference:** Roman Catholic: 22%; Protestant: 37%; No preference: 16%; United Methodist: 23%; Jewish, Muslim, Hindu, Buddhist, Unknown: 1%; Other: 1%.

ADMISSIONS FACTS AND FIGURES

Phone: (800) 362-2454. **Email:** admiss@simpson.edu. **Website:** http://www.simpson.edu. **Application deadlines for fall 2007:** Regular decision: August 15. Early decision: Not offered. Early action: Not offered. Admission can be deferred. Common application is not accepted. **Admissions requirements/recommendations:** High school units required (recommended): English: 4 (4); Mathematics: 3 (3); Science: 3 (3); Foreign language: 3 (3); Social studies: 3 (3); Total units: 16 (16). Tests: The college uses SAT or ACT scores in admissions decisions. Either SAT or ACT required. For admission to the fall 2007 entering class, the school will accept: ACT with writing, ACT without writing. Campus visit: Recommended. Admissions interview: Recommended. Off-campus interview: May be arranged. **Factors that count in admissions decisions:** *Academic:* Secondary school record: Very important. Class rank: Very important. Letters of recommendation: Important. Standardized test scores: Very important. Essay: Not considered. *Nonacademic:* Interview: Considered. Extracurricular activities: Considered. Talent/ability: Not considered.

Character/personal qualities: Important. Alumni/ae relationship: Considered. Geographical residence: Not considered. State residency: Not considered. Religious affiliation/commitment: Not considered. Minority status: Not considered. Volunteer work: Considered. Work experience: Not considered. **Admissions statistics for the fall 2005 entering class:** Total applicants: 1,216. Total accepted: 1,055. Freshmen enrolled: 336; 12% were from out of state. Overall acceptance rate: 87%. **Credentials of fall 2005 freshmen:** 30% ranked in the top 10 percent of their high school class; 61% were in the top 25 percent, and 90% were in the top half. (Proportion submitting class standing: 98%.) **First-year students submitting ACT scores:** 98%. Scores (25/75 percentile): English: N/A, Math: N/A, Composite: 22-27.

ACADEMICS

Year founded: 1860. **Academic calendar:** Other. **Degrees offered:** bachelor's. **Most popular majors:** 30% business, management, marketing, and related support services, 9% liberal arts and sciences studies, and humanities, 9% social sciences, 7% biological and biomedical sciences, 6% communication, journalism, and related programs. **Major fields of study:** biological and biomedical sciences; business, management, marketing, and related support services; communication, journalism, and related programs; computer and information sciences and support services; education; English language and literature/letters; foreign languages, literatures, and linguistics; history; liberal arts and sciences studies, and humanities; mathematics and statistics; natural resources and conservation; parks, recreation, leisure, and fitness studies; philosophy and religious studies; physical sciences; psychology; security and protective services; social sciences; visual and performing arts. **Areas of required coursework:** arts/fine arts, humanities, mathematics, English (including composition), philosophy, foreign languages, sciences (biological or physical), history, social science. **Pre-professional programs:** pre-law, pre-dentistry, pre-medicine, pre-theology, pre-veterinary science, pre-optometry, pre-pharmacy, other. **Special academic programs (% participation):** accelerated program (30%), cooperative (work-study plan) program (40%), double major (25%), external degree program (1%), honors program (2%), independent study (16%), internships (48%), study abroad (42%), teacher certificate program (10%), weekend college (5%). **Teacher certification offered in:** early childhood, special education, elementary, middle/junior high, secondary. **Cooperative education programs:** computer science, engineering. **Faculty and instruction (2005-2006):** Total instructional faculty: 87 full-time, 63 part-time (49% men; 51% women; 7% minorities). Full-time faculty with Ph.D. or other terminal degree: 90%. Student/faculty ratio: 15/1. Classes of fewer than 20 students: 68%; of 20 to 49 students: 32%; of 50 or more students: 1%. **Advanced Placement and International Baccalaureate credit:** AP tests may be used for: Credit and/or placement. Scores accepted: 3, 4, 5. International Baccalaureate exams may be used for: Credit only. **Freshmen returning for sophomore year:** 79%. **Graduation rates:** Four-year: 58%; five-year: 69%; six-year: 66%. **Graduate study:** 19% of students pursue further study within one year. Fields in which graduates pursue further study: Master of Business Administration (MBA), 4%; law, 12%; medicine, 9%; theology (or the seminary), 12%; arts and sciences, 44%; veterinary medicine, 2%.

COSTS AND FINANCIAL AID

Financial aid office: (515) 961-1630. **Expenses (2006-2007):** Tuition and fees 2006-2007: $22,266; room/board: $6,278. Estimated books and supplies: $900; transportation: $700; personal expenses: $1,300. **Financial aid:** Priority filing date for institution's financial aid form: April 1. In 2005-2006, 99% of undergraduates applied for financial aid. Of those, 85% were determined to have financial need; 26% had their need fully met. Average financial aid package (proportion receiving): $18,989 (85%). Average amount of gift aid, such as scholarships or grants (proportion receiving): $12,633 (85%). Average amount of self-help aid, such as work study or loans (proportion receiving): $4,212 (73%). Average need-based loan (excluding PLUS or other private loans): $3,994. Among students who received need-based aid, the average percentage of need met: 87%. Among students who received aid based on merit, the average award (and the proportion receiving): $9,198 (14%). The average athletic scholarship (and the proportion receiving): $0 (0%). Average amount of debt of borrowers graduating in 2005: $24,403. Proportion who borrowed: 87%.

CAMPUS LIFE AND EXTRACURRICULAR ACTIVITIES

Campus housing available (% using): coed dorms (48%), women's dorms (3%), men's dorms (0%), sorority housing (9%), fraternity housing (9%), apartment for single students (27%), other housing options (4%). Students who live in college-owned, operated, or affiliated housing: 70%. **Student employment:** During the 2005-2006 academic year, 32% of undergraduates worked on campus. Average per-year earnings: $960. **Clubs and organiza-**

tions: Number of student organizations: 60. Activities include: choral groups, concert band, drama/theater, jazz band, literary magazine, music ensembles, opera, pep band, radio station, student government, student newspaper, yearbook. Number of fraternities: 4; sororities: 4. Proportion of men in fraternities: 14%; of women in sororities: 16%. Average proportion of students who stay on campus on weekends: 75%. **Sports program (2005-2006):** Member of NCAA III. *Men's intercollegiate varsity sports:* baseball, basketball, cross-country, football, golf, soccer, tennis, track and field (indoor), track and field (outdoor), wrestling. *Women's intercollegiate varsity sports:* basketball, cross-country, golf, soccer, softball, swimming and diving, tennis, track and field (indoor), track and field (outdoor), volleyball.

SERVICES AND FACILITIES

Basic services: nonremedial tutoring, placement service, health service, health insurance. **Remedial assistance:** study skills. **Counseling services:** minority student, career, personal, academic, birth control. **For learning-disabled students:** School does not offer a structured program with separate admission and additional fees. Services include: tape recorders, untimed tests, note-taking services, oral tests, learning center, readers, extended time for tests, tutors, substitution of courses. **Library:** Number of titles: 152,451; number of current serial subscriptions: 531. **Information technology resources:** Students are not required to lease or own a computer. Number of campus computers available to all students: 275. School has a wireless network. Approximate number of users that can be accommodated: 384. Proportion of college-owned housing units wired for high-speed internet access: 100%. **Campus safety:** Security services offered: 24-hour foot and vehicle patrols, late-night transport/escort service, 24-hour emergency telephones, lighted pathways/sidewalks, student patrols, controlled dormitory access (key, security card, etc.).

TRANSFER AND INTERNATIONAL STUDENTS

Transfer students: May apply for admission for the following academic terms: Fall, Spring, Summer. Applicants do not need a minimum number of credits to apply. For fall 2005: Transfer applications received: 150. Transfer applicants offered admission: 130. Transfer applicants enrolled: 70. **International students:** Number of foreign undergraduates: 27 (1% of student body). Number of countries represented: 12. Minimum TOEFL score required: 550 (paper); 213 (computer).

St. Ambrose University

- **Address:** 518 W. Locust Street, Davenport, IA 52803-2898
- **Website:** http://www.sau.edu
- **Private; Religious affiliation:** Roman Catholic
- **Enrollment:** 2,200 full-time; 498 part-time

KEY STATS

✔ **U.S News College Ranking:** 40, Universities–Master's (Midwest)
✔ **ACT Score (25th/75th percentile):** 19-25
✔ **Tuition:** 2006-2007: $19,535

Selectivity: Selective	**Room/board:** $7,240
Acceptance rate: 84%	**Average debt:** $24,728
Student/faculty ratio: 15/1	**Proportion who borrowed:** 79%

UNDERGRADUATE STUDENT BODY STATS

2005-2006 enrollment: 2,200 full-time; 498 part-time. Men: 40%; women: 60%. **Ethnic makeup:** African American: 3%; Asian American: 1%; Hispanic: 3%; White: 91%; International: 1%.

ADMISSIONS FACTS AND FIGURES

Phone: (563) 333-6300. **Email:** admit@sau.edu. **Website:** http://www.sau.edu. **Application deadlines for fall 2007:** Regular decision: Rolling. Early decision: Not offered. Early action: Not offered. Admission can be deferred. **Application fee:** $25. Common application is accepted. **To apply online, go to:** http://www.sau.edu/administration/newstudent/admit-form.htm. **Admissions requirements/recommendations:** High school units required (recommended): English: 4 (4); Mathematics: 3 (3); Science: 2 (2); Foreign language: 1 (1); Social studies: 1 (1); History: 1 (1); Academic electives: 4 (4); Total units: 18 (18). Tests: The college uses SAT or ACT scores in admissions decisions. Either SAT or ACT required. For admission to the fall 2007 entering class, the school will accept: ACT with writing. Campus visit: Recommended. Admissions interview: Recommended. Off-campus

interview: May be arranged. **Factors that count in admissions decisions:** *Academic:* Secondary school record: Very important. Class rank: Very important. Letters of recommendation: Important. Standardized test scores: Very important. Essay: Considered. *Nonacademic:* Interview: Considered. Extracurricular activities: Considered. Talent/ability: Considered. Character/personal qualities: Important. Alumni/ae relationship: Important. Geographical residence: Not considered. State residency: Not considered. Religious affiliation/commitment: Not considered. Minority status: Not considered. Volunteer work: Considered. Work experience: Not considered. **Other schools with the greatest overlap in applicants:** Clarke College; Drake University; Loras College; University of Dubuque; University of Iowa. **Admissions statistics for the fall 2005 entering class:** Total applicants: 1,634. Total accepted: 1,373. Freshmen enrolled: 474; 53% were from out of state. Overall acceptance rate: 84%. **Size of waiting list:** 0 applicants; enrolled from waiting list: 0. **Credentials of fall 2005 freshmen:** 16% ranked in the top 10 percent of their high school class; 36% were in the top 25 percent, and 65% were in the top half. (Proportion submitting class standing: 94%.) **Average high school grade point average:** 3.2. **First-year students submitting ACT scores:** 99%. Scores (25/75 percentile): English: 19-25, Math: 18-25, Composite: 19-25.

ACADEMICS

Year founded: 1882. **Academic calendar:** 4-1-4. **Degrees offered:** certificate, bachelor's, post-bachelor's certificate, master's, post-master's certificate, doctorate. **Most popular majors:** 28% business, management, marketing, and related support services, 15% education, 11% psychology, 7% communication, journalism, and related programs, 5% computer and information sciences and support services. **Major fields of study:** biological and biomedical sciences; business, management, marketing, and related support services; communication, journalism, and related programs; computer and information sciences and support services; education; engineering; English language and literature/letters; foreign languages, literatures, and linguistics; health professions and related clinical sciences; history; legal professions and studies; mathematics and statistics; multi/interdisciplinary studies; philosophy and religious studies; physical sciences; psychology; public administration and social service professions; security and protective services; social sciences; theology and religious vocations; visual and performing arts. **Areas of required coursework:** arts/fine arts, humanities, mathematics, English (including composition), philosophy, foreign languages, sciences (biological or physical), history, social science, other. **Pre-professional programs:** pre-law, pre-medicine. **Special academic programs (% participation):** accelerated program (12%), cooperative (work-study plan) program, distance learning (2%), double major (13%), independent study (24%), internships (33%), liberal arts/career combination (9%), student-designed major (3%), study abroad (3%), teacher certificate program (15%). **Teacher certification offered in:** early childhood, special education, elementary, middle/junior high, secondary. **Cooperative education programs:** art, business, computer science, engineering, health professions, humanities, natural science, social/behavioral science. **Faculty and instruction (2005-2006):** Total instructional faculty: 157 full-time, 133 part-time (55% men; 45% women; 6% minorities). Full-time faculty with Ph.D. or other terminal degree: 71%. Student/faculty ratio: 15/1. Classes of fewer than 20 students: 60%; of 20 to 49 students: 40%; of 50 or more students: 0%. **Advanced Placement and International Baccalaureate credit:** AP tests may be used for: Credit only. Scores accepted: 3, 4, 5. International Baccalaureate exams may be used for: Credit only. **Freshmen returning for sophomore year:** 79%. **Graduation rates:** Four-year: 53%; five-year: 63%; six-year: 62%. **Graduate study:** 24% of students pursue further study within one year. Fields in which graduates pursue further study: Master of Business Administration (MBA), 15%; law, 1%; medicine, 2%; theology (or the seminary), 1%; education, 15%; arts and sciences, 2%.

COSTS AND FINANCIAL AID

Financial aid office: (563) 333-6314. **Expenses (2006-2007):** Tuition and fees 2006-2007: $19,535; room/board: $7,240. Estimated books and supplies: $1,000; transportation: $1,020; personal expenses: $1,125. **Financial aid:** Priority filing date for institution's financial aid form: March 15. In 2005-2006, 97% of undergraduates applied for financial aid. Of those, 71% were determined to have financial need; 31% had their need fully met. Average financial aid package (proportion receiving): $15,159 (70%). Average amount of gift aid, such as scholarships or grants (proportion receiving): $8,630 (69%). Average amount of self-help aid, such as work study or loans (proportion receiving): $4,849 (62%). Average need-based loan (excluding PLUS or other private loans): $4,049. Among students who received need-based aid, the average percentage of need met: 16%. Among students who received aid based on merit, the average award (and the proportion receiv-

ing): $7,603 (26%). The average athletic scholarship (and the proportion receiving): $3,335 (7%). Average amount of debt of borrowers graduating in 2005: $24,728. Proportion who borrowed: 79%.

CAMPUS LIFE AND EXTRACURRICULAR ACTIVITIES

Campus housing available (% using): coed dorms (44%), women's dorms (10%), men's dorms (2%), apartment for single students (15%), other housing options (29%). Students who live in college-owned, operated, or affiliated housing: 50%. **Student employment:** During the 2005-2006 academic year, 31% of undergraduates worked on campus. Average per-year earnings: $1,600. **Clubs and organizations:** Number of student organizations: 43. Activities include: choral groups, concert band, dance, drama/theater, jazz band, literary magazine, music ensembles, musical theater, opera, pep band, radio station, student government, student newspaper, symphony orchestra, television station. Number of fraternities: 0; sororities: 0. Average proportion of students who stay on campus on weekends: 40%. **Sports program (2005-2006):** Member of NAIA. *Men's intercollegiate varsity sports:* baseball, basketball, cross-country, football, golf, soccer, tennis, track and field (indoor), track and field (outdoor), volleyball. *Women's intercollegiate varsity sports:* basketball, cross-country, golf, soccer, softball, tennis, track and field (indoor), track and field (outdoor), volleyball.

SERVICES AND FACILITIES

Basic services: nonremedial tutoring, women's center, placement service, day care, health service. **Remedial assistance:** reading, math, writing, study skills. **Counseling services:** career, personal, veteran student, academic, psychological, religious. **For learning-disabled students:** School does not offer a structured program with separate admission and additional fees. Total undergraduates in learning-disabled program or receiving services: 143. Services include: remedial math, remedial English, remedial reading, tape recorders, diagnostic testing service, untimed tests, oral tests, learning center, extended time for tests, tutors, other testing accomodations. **Library:** Number of titles: 147,083; number of current serial subscriptions: 751. **Information technology resources:** Students are not required to lease or own a computer. Number of campus computers available to all students: 215. School has a wireless network. Proportion of college-owned housing units wired for high-speed internet access: 90%. **Campus safety:** Security services offered: 24-hour foot and vehicle patrols, late-night transport/escort service, 24-hour emergency telephones, lighted pathways/sidewalks, student patrols, controlled dormitory access (key, security card, etc.).

TRANSFER AND INTERNATIONAL STUDENTS

Transfer students: May apply for admission for the following academic terms: Fall, Winter, Spring, Summer. Applicants need a minimum number of credits to apply. For fall 2005: Transfer applications received: 571. Transfer applicants offered admission: 399. Transfer applicants enrolled: 298. **International students:** Number of foreign undergraduates: 35 (1% of student body). Number of countries represented: 17. Minimum TOEFL score required: 500 (paper); 213 (computer). Average TOEFL score: 535 (paper).

University of Dubuque

- **Address:** 2000 University Avenue, Dubuque, IA 52001
- **Website:** http://www.dbq.edu
- **Private; Religious affiliation:** Presbyterian
- **Enrollment:** 1,124 full-time; 55 part-time

KEY STATS

✔ **U.S News College Ranking:** third tier, Universities–Master's (Midwest)
✔ **ACT Score (25th/75th percentile):** 18-22
✔ **Tuition:** 2006-2007: $18,260

Selectivity: Less selective	**Room/board:** $6,200
Acceptance rate: 77%	**Average debt:** $26,000
Student/faculty ratio: 15/1	**Proportion who borrowed:** N/A

UNDERGRADUATE STUDENT BODY STATS

2005-2006 enrollment: 1,124 full-time; 55 part-time. Men: 62%; women: 38%. **Ethnic makeup:** African American: 11%; American-Indian: 2%; Asian American: 1%; Hispanic: 4%; White: 80%; International: 1%. **Religious preference:** Roman Catholic: 25%; Protestant: 22%; No preference: 1%; Unknown: 49%; Presbyterian: 3%.

ADMISSIONS FACTS AND FIGURES

Phone: (800) 722-5583. **Email:** admssns@univ.dbq.edu. **Website:** http://www.dbq.edu. **Application deadlines for fall 2007:** Regular decision: August 15. Early decision: Not offered. Early action: Not offered. Admission can be deferred. **Application fee:** $25. Common application is accepted. **Admissions requirements/recommendations:** High school units required (recommended): English: 4; Mathematics: 3; Science: 3; Foreign language: 0; Social studies: 3; History: 0; Academic electives: 3; Total units: 16. Tests: The college uses SAT or ACT scores in admissions decisions. Either SAT or ACT required. For admission to the fall 2007 entering class, the school will accept: ACT with writing, ACT without writing. Campus visit: Recommended. Admissions interview: Recommended. Off-campus interview: May be arranged. **Factors that count in admissions decisions:** *Academic:* Secondary school record: Very important. Class rank: Very important. Letters of recommendation: Very important. Standardized test scores: Very important. Essay: Very important. *Nonacademic:* Interview: Considered. Extracurricular activities: Considered. Talent/ability: Considered. Character/personal qualities: Very important. Alumni/ae relationship: Considered. Geographical residence: Not considered. State residency: Not considered. Religious affiliation/commitment: Not considered. Minority status: Not considered. Volunteer work: Considered. Work experience: Considered. **Other schools with the greatest overlap in applicants:** Clarke College; Loras College; Mount Mercy College; Purdue University–West Lafayette; St. Ambrose University. **Admissions statistics for the fall 2005 entering class:** Total applicants: 885. Total accepted: 681. Freshmen enrolled: 309; 60% were from out of state. Overall acceptance rate: 77%. **Credentials of fall 2005 freshmen:** 6% ranked in the top 10 percent of their high school class; 21% were in the top 25 percent, and 52% were in the top half. (Proportion submitting class standing: 94%.) **Average high school grade point average:** 3.0. **First-year students who submitted SAT scores:** 18%. Scores (25/75 percentile): Verbal: 400-540, Math: 430-560, Combined: 830-1100. **First-year students submitting ACT scores:** 87%. Scores (25/75 percentile): English: 16-21, Math: 17-22, Composite: 18-22.

ACADEMICS

Year founded: 1852. **Academic calendar:** Semester. **Degrees offered:** certificate, bachelor's, master's, doctorate. **Most popular majors:** 27% computer and information sciences, 13% business administration and management, 9% airline/commercial/professional pilot and flight crew, 8% elementary education and teaching, 7% health and physical education. **Major fields of study:** biological and biomedical sciences; business, management, marketing, and related support services; computer and information sciences and support services; education; English language and literature/letters; health professions and related clinical sciences; natural resources and conservation; parks, recreation, leisure, and fitness studies; philosophy and religious studies; psychology; security and protective services; social sciences; transportation and materials moving. **Areas of required coursework:** arts/fine arts, humanities, computer literacy, mathematics, English (including composition), foreign languages, sciences (biological or physical), social science. **Preprofessional programs:** pre-medicine. **Special academic programs (% participation):** cooperative (work-study plan) program, cross-registration (10%), double major (50%), dual enrollment (5%), exchange student program (domestic), independent study (10%), internships (85%), liberal arts/career combination, student-designed major (1%), study abroad, teacher certificate program. **Teacher certification offered in:** special education, elementary, middle/junior high, secondary. **Cooperative education programs:** business, computer science, education, natural science, social/behavioral science, technologies, vocational arts. **Reserve Officers Training Corps (ROTC):** Army ROTC: Offered on campus. **Faculty and instruction (2005-2006):** Total instructional faculty: 69 full-time, 58 part-time (50% men; 50% women; 3% minorities). Full-time faculty with Ph.D. or other terminal degree: 58%. Student/faculty ratio: 15/1. Classes of fewer than 20 students: 58%; of 20 to 49 students: 41%; of 50 or more students: 1%. **Advanced Placement and International Baccalaureate credit:** AP tests may be used for: Credit and/or placement. Scores accepted: 3. International Baccalaureate exams may be used for: Credit and/or placement. **Freshmen returning for sophomore year:** 67%. **Graduation rates:** Four-year: 44%; five-year: 51%; six-year: 41%. **Graduate study:** 10% of students pursue further study immediately upon graduation; 5% within one year; 10% within five years. Fields in which graduates pursue further study: Master of Business Administration (MBA), 50%; law, 2%; medicine, 1%; theology (or the seminary), 3%; education, 10%; arts and sciences, 2%.

COSTS AND FINANCIAL AID

Financial aid office: (563) 589-3396. **Expenses (2006-2007):** Tuition and fees 2006-2007: $18,260; room/board: $6,200. Estimated books and supplies:

$850; transportation: $900; personal expenses: $3,790. **Financial aid:** Priority filing date for institution's financial aid form: April 1. In 2005-2006, 99% of undergraduates applied for financial aid. Of those, 90% were determined to have financial need; 52% had their need fully met. Average financial aid package (proportion receiving): $17,080 (90%). Average amount of gift aid, such as scholarships or grants (proportion receiving): $8,879 (87%). Average amount of self-help aid, such as work study or loans (proportion receiving): $9,485 (80%). Average need-based loan (excluding PLUS or other private loans): $9,143. Among students who received need-based aid, the average percentage of need met: 85%. Among students who received aid based on merit, the average award (and the proportion receiving): $15,378 (10%). The average athletic scholarship (and the proportion receiving): $0 (0%). Average amount of debt of borrowers graduating in 2005: $26,000.

CAMPUS LIFE AND EXTRACURRICULAR ACTIVITIES

Campus housing available (% using): coed dorms (70%), apartment for single students (30%). Students who live in college-owned, operated, or affiliated housing: 85%. **Student employment:** During the 2005-2006 academic year, 50% of undergraduates worked on campus. Average per-year earnings: $1,500. **Clubs and organizations:** Number of student organizations: 40. Activities include: choral groups, dance, drama/theater, jazz band, pep band, student government, student newspaper, yearbook. Number of fraternities: 5; sororities: 5. Proportion of men in fraternities: 13%; of women in sororities: 25%. Average proportion of students who stay on campus on weekends: 75%. **Sports program (2005-2006):** Member of NCAA III. *Men's intercollegiate varsity sports:* baseball, basketball, cross-country, football, golf, soccer, tennis, track and field (indoor), track and field (outdoor), wrestling. *Women's intercollegiate varsity sports:* basketball, cross-country, golf, soccer, softball, tennis, track and field (indoor), track and field (outdoor), volleyball.

SERVICES AND FACILITIES

Basic services: nonremedial tutoring, placement service, health service, health insurance. **Remedial assistance:** reading, math, writing, study skills. **Counseling services:** minority student, career, military, personal, veteran student, academic, psychological, religious. **For learning-disabled students:** School does not offer a structured program with separate admission and additional fees. Total undergraduates in learning-disabled program or receiving services: 28. Services include: remedial math, remedial English, remedial reading, tape recorders, other special classes, untimed tests, note-taking services, special bookstore section, oral tests, learning center, extended time for tests, tutors, other. **Library:** Number of titles: 172,864; number of current serial subscriptions: 20,000. **Information technology resources:** Students are not required to lease or own a computer. Number of campus computers available to all students: 150. School does not have a wireless network. Proportion of college-owned housing units wired for high-speed internet access: 100%. **Campus safety:** Security services offered: 24-hour foot and vehicle patrols, late-night transport/escort service, 24-hour emergency telephones, lighted pathways/sidewalks, controlled dormitory access (key, security card, etc.).

TRANSFER AND INTERNATIONAL STUDENTS

Transfer students: May apply for admission for the following academic terms: Fall, Spring. Applicants need a minimum number of credits to apply. For fall 2005: Transfer applications received: 235. Transfer applicants offered admission: 186. Transfer applicants enrolled: 128. **International students:** Number of foreign undergraduates: 11 (1% of student body). Minimum TOEFL score required: 500 (paper); 170 (computer). Average TOEFL score: 525 (paper).

University of Iowa

■ **Address:** 107 Calvin Hall, Iowa City, IA 52242-1396
■ **Website:** http://www.uiowa.edu
■ **Public**
■ **Enrollment:** 18,194 full-time; 2,106 part-time

KEY STATS

✔ **U.S News College Ranking:** 64, National Universities
✔ **ACT Score (25th/75th percentile):** 22-27
✔ **Tuition:** 2006-2007: $5,935 in state, $18,195 out of state
Selectivity: More selective **Room/board:** $6,912
Acceptance rate: 84% **Average debt:** $19,886
Student/faculty ratio: 15/1 **Proportion who borrowed:** 58%

UNDERGRADUATE STUDENT BODY STATS

2005-2006 enrollment: 18,194 full-time; 2,106 part-time. Men: 47%; women: 53%. **Ethnic makeup:** African American: 2%; Asian American: 4%; Hispanic: 2%; White: 90%; International: 1%.

ADMISSIONS FACTS AND FIGURES

Phone: (800) 553-4692. **Email:** admissions@uiowa.edu. **Website:** http://www.uiowa.edu. **Application deadlines for fall 2007:** Regular decision: April 1. Early decision: Not offered. Early action: Not offered. Admission cannot be deferred. **Application fee:** $40. Common application is not accepted. **Admissions requirements/recommendations:** High school units required (recommended): English: 4; Mathematics: 3; Science: 3; Foreign language: 2; Social studies: 3; Total units: 15. Tests: The college uses SAT or ACT scores in admissions decisions. Either SAT or ACT required. For admission to the fall 2007 entering class, the school will accept: ACT without writing. Campus visit: Recommended. Admissions interview: Neither required nor recommended. **Factors that count in admissions decisions:** *Academic:* Secondary school record: Very important. Class rank: Very important. Letters of recommendation: Considered. Standardized test scores: Very important. Essay: Not considered. *Nonacademic:* Interview: Not considered. Extracurricular activities: Not considered. Talent/ability: Considered. Character/personal qualities: Considered. Alumni/ae relationship: Not considered. Geographical residence: Not considered. State residency: Considered. Religious affiliation/commitment: Not considered. Minority status: Not considered. Volunteer work: Not considered. Work experience: Not considered. **Other schools with the greatest overlap in applicants:** Indiana University–Bloomington; Iowa State University; University of Illinois–Urbana-Champaign; University of Northern Iowa; University of Wisconsin–Madison. **Admissions statistics for the fall 2005 entering class:** Total applicants: 13,241. Total accepted: 11,122. Freshmen enrolled: 3,849; 39% were from out of state. Overall acceptance rate: 84%. **Size of waiting list:** 149 applicants; enrolled from waiting list: 142. **Credentials of fall 2005 freshmen:** 22% ranked in the top 10 percent of their high school class; 53% were in the top 25 percent, and 92% were in the top half. (Proportion submitting class standing: 89%.) **Average high school grade point average:** 3.6. **First-year students who submitted SAT scores:** 13%. Scores (25/75 percentile): Verbal: 520-650, Math: 540-660, Combined: 1060-1310. **First-year students submitting ACT scores:** 95%. Scores (25/75 percentile): English: 21-28, Math: 21-27, Composite: 22-27.

ACADEMICS

Year founded: 1847. **Academic calendar:** Semester. **Degrees offered:** certificate, bachelor's, post-bachelor's certificate, master's, post-master's certificate, first professional, first professional certificate, doctorate. **Most popular majors:** 19% business, management, marketing, and related support services, 15% social sciences, 10% communication, journalism, and related programs, 8% psychology, 7% visual and performing arts. **Major fields of study:** area, ethnic, cultural, and gender studies; biological and biomedical sciences; business, management, marketing, and related support services; communication, journalism, and related programs; computer and information sciences and support services; education; engineering; English language and literature/letters; foreign languages, literatures, and linguistics; health professions and related clinical sciences; history; legal professions and studies; liberal arts and sciences studies, and humanities; mathematics and statistics; multi/interdisciplinary studies; natural resources and conservation; parks, recreation, leisure, and fitness studies; philosophy and religious studies; physical sciences; psychology; public administration and social service professions; social sciences; visual and performing arts. **Areas**

of required coursework: humanities, mathematics, English (including composition), foreign languages, sciences (biological or physical), history, social science. **Pre-professional programs:** pre-law, pre-dentistry, pre-medicine, pre-veterinary science, pre-optometry, pre-pharmacy, other. **Special academic programs:** accelerated program, cooperative (work-study plan) program, distance learning, double major, dual enrollment, English as a Second Language (ESL), exchange student program (domestic), external degree program, honors program, independent study, internships, student-designed major, study abroad, teacher certificate program. **Teacher certification offered in:** early childhood, special education, elementary, middle/junior high, secondary, bilingual/bicultural. **Cooperative education programs:** business, engineering. **Reserve Officers Training Corps (ROTC):** Army ROTC: Offered on campus; Air Force ROTC: Offered on campus. **Faculty and instruction (2005-2006):** Total instructional faculty: 1,595 full-time, 98 part-time (72% men; 28% women; 14% minorities). Full-time faculty with Ph.D. or other terminal degree: 96%. Student/faculty ratio: 15/1. Classes of fewer than 20 students: 49%; of 20 to 49 students: 41%; of 50 or more students: 10%. **Advanced Placement and International Baccalaureate credit:** AP tests may be used for: Credit and/or placement. Scores accepted: 3, 4, 5. International Baccalaureate exams may be used for: Credit and/or placement. **Freshmen returning for sophomore year:** 83%. **Graduation rates:** Four-year: 38%; five-year: 62%; six-year: 66%.

COSTS AND FINANCIAL AID

Financial aid office: (319) 335-1450. **Expenses (2006-2007):** Tuition and fees 2006-2007: $5,935 in state, $18,195 out of state; room/board: $6,912. Estimated books and supplies: $840; transportation: $860; personal expenses: $2,400. **Financial aid:** In 2005-2006, 72% of undergraduates applied for financial aid. Of those, 54% were determined to have financial need; 92% had their need fully met. Average financial aid package (proportion receiving): $7,445 (51%). Average amount of gift aid, such as scholarships or grants (proportion receiving): $4,459 (30%). Average amount of self-help aid, such as work study or loans (proportion receiving): $4,436 (43%). Average need-based loan (excluding PLUS or other private loans): $3,847. Among students who received need-based aid, the average percentage of need met: 97%. Among students who received aid based on merit, the average award (and the proportion receiving): $1,950 (14%). The average athletic scholarship (and the proportion receiving): $13,978 (2%). Average amount of debt of borrowers graduating in 2005: $19,886. Proportion who borrowed: 58%.

CAMPUS LIFE AND EXTRACURRICULAR ACTIVITIES

Campus housing available: coed dorms, apartments for married students, apartment for single students, special housing for disabled students. Students who live in college-owned, operated, or affiliated housing: 27%. **Student employment:** During the 2005-2006 academic year, 30% of undergraduates worked on campus. **Clubs and organizations:** Number of student organizations: 400. Activities include: choral groups, concert band, dance, drama/theater, jazz band, literary magazine, marching band, music ensembles, musical theater, opera, pep band, radio station, student government, student newspaper, student film society, symphony orchestra, yearbook. Number of fraternities: 16; sororities: 17. Proportion of men in fraternities: 7%; of women in sororities: 12%. Average proportion of students who stay on campus on weekends: 95%. **Sports program (2005-2006):** Member of NCAA I. *Men's intercollegiate varsity sports:* baseball, basketball, cross-country, football, golf, gymnastics, swimming and diving, tennis, track and field (indoor), track and field (outdoor), wrestling. *Women's intercollegiate varsity sports:* basketball, cross-country, field hockey, golf, gymnastics, soccer, softball, swimming and diving, tennis, track and field (indoor), track and field (outdoor), volleyball, rowing.

SERVICES AND FACILITIES

Basic services: nonremedial tutoring, women's center, placement service, day care, health service, health insurance. **Remedial assistance:** reading, math, writing, study skills. **Counseling services:** minority student, career, personal, veteran student, academic, older student, psychological, birth control. **For learning-disabled students:** School does not offer a structured program with separate admission and additional fees. Total undergraduates in learning-disabled program or receiving services: 429. Services include: reading machines, tape recorders, diagnostic testing service, note-taking services, readers, extended time for tests, tutors, priority registration, priority seating, substitution of courses, texts on tape, typist/scribe, exams on tape or computer, other testing accomodations. **Library:** Number of titles: 4,551,217; number of current serial subscriptions: 50,214. **Information technology resources:** Students are not required to lease or own a computer. Number of campus computers available to all students: 1,200. School has a wireless network. Approximate number of users that can be accommodated: 30,000. Proportion of college-owned housing units wired for high-speed internet access: 100%. **Campus safety:** Security services offered: 24-hour foot and vehicle patrols, 24-hour emergency telephones, lighted pathways/sidewalks, controlled dormitory access (key, security card, etc).

TRANSFER AND INTERNATIONAL STUDENTS

Transfer students: May apply for admission for the following academic terms: Fall, Winter, Spring, Summer. Applicants need a minimum number of credits to apply. For fall 2005: Transfer applications received: 2,879. Transfer applicants offered admission: 2,097. Transfer applicants enrolled: 1,338. **International students:** Number of foreign undergraduates: 247 (1% of student body). Number of countries represented: 60. Minimum TOEFL score required: 530 (paper); 197 (computer). Average TOEFL score: 560 (paper).

University of Northern Iowa

- **Address:** 1227 W. 27th Street, Cedar Falls, IA 50614
- **Website:** http://www.uni.edu/
- **Public**
- **Enrollment:** 9,753 full-time; 1,241 part-time

KEY STATS

✔ **U.S News College Ranking:** 18, Universities–Master's (Midwest)
✔ **ACT Score (25th/75th percentile):** 20-25
✔ **Tuition:** 2006-2007: $5,912 in state, $13,828 out of state
   Selectivity: Selective   **Room/board:** $5,752
   Acceptance rate: 78%   **Average debt:** $20,239
   Student/faculty ratio: 16/1   **Proportion who borrowed:** 77%

UNDERGRADUATE STUDENT BODY STATS

2005-2006 enrollment: 9,753 full-time; 1,241 part-time. Men: 43%; women: 57%. **Ethnic makeup:** African American: 3%; Asian American: 1%; Hispanic: 1%; White: 92%; International: 2%.

ADMISSIONS FACTS AND FIGURES

Phone: (800) 772-2037. **Email:** admissions@uni.edu. **Website:** http://www.uni.edu/. **Application deadlines for fall 2007:** Regular decision: August 15. Early decision: Not offered. Early action: Not offered. Admission can be deferred. **Application fee:** $30. Common application is not accepted. **To apply online, go to:** http://access.uni.edu/stdt/ugapinst.htm. **Admissions requirements/recommendations:** High school units required (recommended): English: 4; Mathematics: 3; Science: 3; Foreign language: (2); Social studies: 3; Academic electives: 2; Total units: 15. Tests: The college uses SAT or ACT scores in admissions decisions. Either SAT or ACT required. For admission to the fall 2007 entering class, the school will accept: ACT with writing, ACT without writing. Campus visit: Recommended. Admissions interview: Neither required nor recommended. Off-campus interview: Not available. **Factors that count in admissions decisions:** *Academic:* Secondary school record: Very important. Class rank: Very important. Letters of recommendation: Considered. Standardized test scores: Very important. Essay: Not considered. *Nonacademic:* Interview: Considered. Extracurricular activities: Not considered. Talent/ability: Considered. Character/personal qualities: Not considered. Alumni/ae relationship: Not considered. Geographical residence: Not considered. State residency: Considered. Religious affiliation/commitment: Not considered. Minority status: Considered. Volunteer work: Not considered. Work experience: Not considered. **Other schools with the greatest overlap in applicants:** Iowa State University; University of Iowa; Wartburg College. **Admissions statistics for the fall 2005 entering class:** Total applicants: 4,360. Total accepted: 3,422. Freshmen enrolled: 1,737; 8% were from out of state. **Overall acceptance rate:** 78%. **Credentials of fall 2005 freshmen:** 19% ranked in the top 10 percent of their high school class; 48% were in the top 25 percent, and 90% were in the top half. (Proportion submitting class standing: 93%.) **First-year students who submitted SAT scores:** 5%. Scores (25/75 percentile): Verbal: 473-590, Math: 490-638, Combined: 963-1228. **First-year students submitting ACT scores:** 97%. Scores (25/75 percentile): English: 19-25, Math: 19-25, Composite: 20-25.

ACADEMICS

Year founded: 1876. **Academic calendar:** Semester. **Degrees offered:** bachelor's, master's, doctorate. **Most popular majors:** 13% elementary education and teaching, 6% business administration and management, 6% liberal arts and sciences/liberal studies, 5% accounting, 4% marketing/marketing management. **Major fields of study:** area, ethnic, cultural, and gender studies; biological and biomedical sciences; business, management, marketing, and related support services; communication, journalism, and related programs; communications technologies/technicians and support services; computer and information sciences and support services; education; engineering; engineering technologies/technicians; English language and literature/letters; family and consumer sciences/human sciences; foreign languages, literatures, and linguistics; health professions and related clinical sciences; history; liberal arts and sciences studies, and humanities; mathematics and statistics; multi/interdisciplinary studies; natural resources and conservation; parks, recreation, leisure, and fitness studies; philosophy and religious studies; physical sciences; psychology; public administration and social service professions; social sciences; visual and performing arts. **Areas of required coursework:** arts/fine arts, humanities, mathematics, English (including composition), philosophy, foreign languages, sciences (biological or physical), history, social science, other. **Pre-professional programs:** pre-law, pre-dentistry, pre-medicine, pre-theology, pre-veterinary science, pre-optometry, pre-pharmacy, other. **Special academic programs (% participation):** accelerated program, cooperative (work-study plan) program (.5%), distance learning, double major (15%), dual enrollment (.1%), English as a Second Language (ESL) (.4%), exchange student program (domestic), external degree program, honors program, independent study (.5%), internships (.5%), student-designed major (.2%), study abroad (.3%), teacher certification program (26%), other. **Teacher certification offered in:** early childhood, special education, elementary, middle/junior high, secondary, bilingual/bicultural. **Cooperative education programs:** art, business, computer science, education, health professions, home economics, humanities, natural science, social/behavioral science, technologies, other. **Reserve Officers Training Corps (ROTC):** Army ROTC: Offered on campus. **Faculty and instruction (2005-2006):** Total instructional faculty: 641 full-time, 188 part-time (55% men; 45% women; 10% minorities). Full-time faculty with Ph.D. or other terminal degree: 81%. Student/faculty ratio: 16/1. Classes of fewer than 20 students: 33%; of 20 to 49 students: 58%; of 50 or more students: 9%. **Advanced Placement and International Baccalaureate credit:** AP tests may be used for: Credit only. Scores accepted: 3, 4, 5. International Baccalaureate exams may be used for: Credit and/or placement. **Freshmen returning for sophomore year:** 81%. **Graduation rates:** Four-year: 34%; five-year: 61%; six-year: 65%. **Graduate study:** 14% of students pursue further study immediately upon graduation.

COSTS AND FINANCIAL AID

Financial aid office: (319) 273-2700. **Expenses (2006-2007):** Tuition and fees 2006-2007: $5,912 in state, $13,828 out of state; room/board: $5,752. Estimated books and supplies: $878; transportation: $602; personal expenses: $2,660. **Financial aid:** In 2005-2006, 78% of undergraduates applied for financial aid. Of those, 57% were determined to have financial need; 21% had their need fully met. Average financial aid package (proportion receiving): $6,738 (55%). Average amount of gift aid, such as scholarships or grants (proportion receiving): $2,690 (34%). Average amount of self-help aid, such as work study or loans (proportion receiving): $4,310 (49%). Average need-based loan (excluding PLUS or other private loans): $4,121. Among students who received need-based aid, the average percentage of need met: 66%. Among students who received aid based on merit, the average award (and the proportion receiving): $2,900 (9%). The average athletic scholarship (and the proportion receiving): $9,456 (3%). Average amount of debt of borrowers graduating in 2005: $20,239. Proportion who borrowed: 77%.

CAMPUS LIFE AND EXTRACURRICULAR ACTIVITIES

Campus housing available (% using): coed dorms (67%), women's dorms (17%), men's dorms (0%), sorority housing, fraternity housing, apartments for married students (9%), apartment for single students (6%), special housing for disabled students (1%), other housing options. Students who live in college-owned, operated, or affiliated housing: 36%. **Student employment:** During the 2005-2006 academic year, 24% of undergraduates worked on campus. Average per-year earnings: $1,408. **Clubs and organizations:** Number of student organizations: 314. Activities include: choral groups, concert band, dance, drama/theater, jazz band, literary magazine, marching band, music ensembles, musical theater, opera, pep band, radio station, student government, student newspaper, student film society, symphony orchestra. Number of fraternities: 8; sororities: 4. Proportion of men

in fraternities: 4%; of women in sororities: 3%. Average proportion of students who stay on campus on weekends: 30%. **Sports program (2005-2006):** Member of NCAA I. *Men's intercollegiate varsity sports:* baseball, basketball, cross-country, football, golf, track and field (indoor), track and field (outdoor), wrestling. *Women's intercollegiate varsity sports:* basketball, cross-country, golf, soccer, softball, swimming and diving, tennis, track and field (indoor), track and field (outdoor), volleyball.

SERVICES AND FACILITIES

Basic services: nonremedial tutoring, placement service, day care, health service, health insurance. **Remedial assistance:** reading, math, writing, study skills. **Counseling services:** minority student, career, military, personal, veteran student, academic, older student, psychological, birth control. **For learning-disabled students:** School does not offer a structured program with separate admission and additional fees. Total undergraduates in learning-disabled program or receiving services: 98. Services include: reading machines, tape recorders, diagnostic testing service, note-taking services, readers, extended time for tests, tutors, early syllabus, priority registration, priority seating, substitution of courses, texts on tape, typist/scribe, exams on tape or computer, other testing accomodations. **Library:** Number of titles: 1,214,845; number of current serial subscriptions: 6,379. **Information technology resources:** Students are not required to lease or own a computer. Number of campus computers available to all students: 1,900. School has a wireless network. Approximate number of users that can be accommodated: 1,000. Proportion of college-owned housing units wired for high-speed internet access: 100%. **Campus safety:** Security services offered: 24-hour foot and vehicle patrols, late-night transport/escort service, 24-hour emergency telephones, lighted pathways/sidewalks, student patrols, controlled dormitory access (key, security card, etc).

TRANSFER AND INTERNATIONAL STUDENTS

Transfer students: May apply for admission for the following academic terms: Fall, Spring, Summer. Applicants need a minimum number of credits to apply. For fall 2005: Transfer applications received: 2,019. Transfer applicants offered admission: 1,577. Transfer applicants enrolled: 1,201. **International students:** Number of foreign undergraduates: 238 (2% of student body). Number of countries represented: 76. Minimum TOEFL score required: 550 (paper); 213 (computer).

Upper Iowa University

- **Address:** Box 1857, Fayette, IA 52142
- **Website:** http://www.uiu.edu
- Private
- **Enrollment:** N/A

KEY STATS
- ✔ **U.S News College Ranking:** fourth tier, Comp. Coll.–Bachelor's (Midwest)
- ✔ **SAT or ACT Score (25th/75th percentile):** N/A
- ✔ **Tuition:** 2006-2007: $18,056

Selectivity: Selective	Room/board: N/A
Acceptance rate: 56%	Average debt: N/A
Student/faculty ratio: N/A	Proportion who borrowed: N/A

Waldorf College

- **Address:** 106 S. Sixth Street, Forest City, IA 50436
- **Website:** http://www.waldorf.edu
- Private; **Religious affiliation:** Lutheran
- **Enrollment:** 568 full-time; 81 part-time

KEY STATS
- ✔ **U.S News College Ranking:** third tier, Comp. Coll.–Bachelor's (Midwest)
- ✔ **ACT Score (25th/75th percentile):** 14-24
- ✔ **Tuition:** 2006-2007: $16,670

Selectivity: Less selective	Room/board: $5,270
Acceptance rate: 58%	Average debt: $14,782
Student/faculty ratio: 12/1	Proportion who borrowed: 63%

UNDERGRADUATE STUDENT BODY STATS

2005-2006 enrollment: 568 full-time; 81 part-time. Men: 49%; women: 51%. **Ethnic makeup:** African American: 4%; Asian American: 1%; Hispanic: 1%; White: 87%; International: 7%. **Religious preference:** Roman Catholic: 16%; Protestant: 29%; Buddhist: 1%; No preference: 4%; Unknown: 10%; Lutheran: 40%.

ADMISSIONS FACTS AND FIGURES

Phone: (641) 585-8112. **Email:** admissions@waldorf.edu. **Website:** http://www.waldorf.edu. **Application deadlines for fall 2007:** Regular decision: Rolling. Early decision: Not offered. Early action: Not offered. Admission can be deferred. **Application fee:** None. Common application is accepted. **To apply online, go to:** http://www.waldorf.edu/admissions/apply.htm. **Admissions requirements/recommendations:** High school units required (recommended): English: (4); Mathematics: (3); Science: (3); Foreign language: (2); Social studies: (4); History: (0); Academic electives: (0); Total units: (16). Tests: The college uses SAT or ACT scores in admissions decisions. Either SAT or ACT required. For admission to the fall 2007 entering class, the school will accept: ACT with writing, ACT without writing. Campus visit: Recommended. Admissions interview: Neither required nor recommended. Off-campus interview: Not available. **Factors that count in admissions decisions: Academic:** Secondary school record: Very important. Class rank: Important. Letters of recommendation: Important. Standardized test scores: Very important. Essay: Not considered. **Nonacademic:** Interview: Considered. Extracurricular activities: Not considered. Talent/ability: Not considered. Character/personal qualities: Considered. Alumni/ae relationship: Not considered. Geographical residence: Not considered. State residency: Not considered. Religious affiliation/commitment: Not considered. Minority status: Not considered. Volunteer work: Not considered. Work experience: Not considered. **Other schools with the greatest overlap in applicants:** Buena Vista University; Central College; Minnesota State University–Mankato; University of Northern Iowa; Wartburg College. **Admissions statistics for the fall 2005 entering class:** Total applicants: 646. Total accepted: 377. Freshmen enrolled: 161; 49% were from out of state. Overall acceptance rate: 58%. **Credentials of fall 2005 freshmen:** 10% ranked in the top 10 percent of their high school class; 15% were in the top 25 percent, and 43% were in the top half. (Proportion submitting class standing: 100%.) **Average high school grade point average:** 3.0. **First-year students submitting ACT scores:** 100%. Scores (25/75 percentile): English: 13-26, Math: 15-24, Composite: 14-24.

ACADEMICS

Year founded: 1903. **Academic calendar:** Semester. **Degrees offered:** associate, bachelor's. **Most popular majors:** 31% business/commerce, 21% communication studies/speech communication and rhetoric, 10% foods, nutrition, and wellness studies, 8% education, 8% elementary education and teaching. **Major fields of study:** business, management, marketing, and related support services; communication, journalism, and related programs; computer and information sciences and support services; education; English language and literature/letters; health professions and related clinical sciences; history; liberal arts and sciences studies, and humanities; visual and performing arts. **Areas of required coursework:** arts/fine arts, humanities, mathematics, English (including composition), philosophy, sciences (biological or physical), history, social science, other. **Pre-professional programs:** pre-law. **Special academic programs (% participation):** accelerated program (8%), double major (4%), English as a Second Language (ESL) (1%), honors program (9%), internships (100%), teacher certificate program (14%). **Teacher certification offered in:** special education, elementary, middle/junior high, secondary. **Faculty and instruction (2005-2006):** Total instructional faculty: 35 (54% men; 46% women; 0% minorities). Full-time faculty with Ph.D. or other terminal degree: 63%. Student/faculty ratio: 12/1. Classes of fewer than 20 students: 59%; of 20 to 49 students: 41%; of 50 or more students: 1%. **Advanced Placement and International Baccalaureate credit:** International Baccalaureate exams may be used for: Credit and/or placement. **Freshmen returning for sophomore year:** 64%. **Graduation rates:** Four-year: 28%; five-year: 28%; six-year: 32%. **Graduate study:** 11% of students pursue further study immediately upon graduation; 11% within one year; 0% within five years. Fields in which graduates pursue further study: theology (or the seminary), 25%; arts and sciences, 83%.

COSTS AND FINANCIAL AID

Financial aid office: (641) 585-8120. **Expenses (2006-2007):** Tuition and fees 2006-2007: $16,670; room/board: $5,270. Estimated books and supplies: $880; transportation: $1,060; personal expenses: $1,535. **Financial aid:** Priority filing date for institution's financial aid form: March 1. In 2005-2006, 88% of undergraduates applied for financial aid. Of those, 83% were determined to have financial need; 34% had their need fully met. Average

financial aid package (proportion receiving): $14,532 (83%). Average amount of gift aid, such as scholarships or grants (proportion receiving): $9,868 (83%). Average amount of self-help aid, such as work study or loans (proportion receiving): $5,278 (73%). Average need-based loan (excluding PLUS or other private loans): $4,846. Among students who received need-based aid, the average percentage of need met: 86%. Among students who received aid based on merit, the average award (and the proportion receiving): $10,207 (16%). The average athletic scholarship (and the proportion receiving): $2,655 (10%). Average amount of debt of borrowers graduating in 2005: $14,782. Proportion who borrowed: 63%.

CAMPUS LIFE AND EXTRACURRICULAR ACTIVITIES

Campus housing available (% using): coed dorms (53%), women's dorms (18%), men's dorms (28%), special housing for disabled students (1%). Students who live in college-owned, operated, or affiliated housing: 70%. **Student employment:** During the 2005-2006 academic year, 34% of undergraduates worked on campus. Average per-year earnings: $428. **Clubs and organizations:** Number of student organizations: 23. Activities include: choral groups, concert band, drama/theater, jazz band, literary magazine, music ensembles, musical theater, pep band, radio station, student government, student newspaper, symphony orchestra, television station, yearbook. Number of fraternities: 0; sororities: 0. Average proportion of students who stay on campus on weekends: 50%. **Sports program (2005-2006):** Member of NAIA. **Men's intercollegiate varsity sports:** baseball, basketball, football, golf, soccer, wrestling. **Women's intercollegiate varsity sports:** basketball, golf, soccer, softball, volleyball.

SERVICES AND FACILITIES

Basic services: nonremedial tutoring, placement service, health service, health insurance. **Remedial assistance:** reading, math, writing, study skills. **Counseling services:** minority student, career, military, personal, veteran student, academic, older student, psychological, birth control, religious. **For learning-disabled students:** School does not offer a structured program with separate admission and additional fees. Total undergraduates in learning-disabled program or receiving services: 20. Services include: remedial math, remedial English, tape recorders, other special classes, untimed tests, note-taking services, oral tests, learning center, readers, extended time for tests, tutors, texts on tape, other testing accomodations. **Library:** Number of titles: 53,958; number of current serial subscriptions: 221. **Information technology resources:** Students are required to lease or own a computer. Number of campus computers available to all students: 650. School has a wireless network. Approximate number of users that can be accommodated: 240. Proportion of college-owned housing units wired for high-speed internet access: 100%. **Campus safety:** Security services offered: late-night transport/escort service, lighted pathways/sidewalks, controlled dormitory access (key, security card, etc.).

TRANSFER AND INTERNATIONAL STUDENTS

Transfer students: May apply for admission for the following academic terms: Fall, Winter, Spring, Summer. Applicants do not need a minimum number of credits to apply. For fall 2005: Transfer applications received: 638. Transfer applicants offered admission: 429. Transfer applicants enrolled: 202. **International students:** Number of foreign undergraduates: 29 (7% of student body). Number of countries represented: 13. Minimum TOEFL score required: 500 (paper); 173 (computer). Average TOEFL score: 520 (paper).

Wartburg College

- **Address:** PO Box 1003, Waverly, IA 50677-0903
- **Website:** http://www.wartburg.edu
- **Private; Religious affiliation:** Lutheran
- **Enrollment:** 1,732 full-time; 79 part-time

KEY STATS

✔ **U.S News College Ranking:** 6, Comp. Coll.–Bachelor's (Midwest)
✔ **ACT Score (25th/75th percentile):** 21-26
✔ **Tuition:** 2006-2007: $22,410

Selectivity: More selective	**Room/board:** $6,715
Acceptance rate: 88%	**Average debt:** $22,122
Student/faculty ratio: 12/1	**Proportion who borrowed:** 84%

UNDERGRADUATE STUDENT BODY STATS

2005-2006 enrollment: 1,732 full-time; 79 part-time. Men: 47%; women: 53%. **Ethnic makeup:** African American: 3%; Asian American: 1%; Hispanic: 1%; White: 89%; International: 5%. **Religious preference:** Roman Catholic: 23%; Protestant: 21%; No preference: 1%; Unknown: 13%; Lutheran: 37%.

ADMISSIONS FACTS AND FIGURES

Phone: (319) 352-8264. **Email:** admissions@wartburg.edu. **Website:** http://www.wartburg.edu. **Application deadlines for fall 2007:** Regular decision: Rolling. Early decision: Not offered. Early action: Send application by: December 1; Decision sent by: N/A. Admission can be deferred. **Application fee:** $20. Common application is accepted. **To apply online, go to:** http://www.wartburg.edu/admissions/online.html. **Admissions requirements/recommendations:** High school units required (recommended): English: (4); Mathematics: (3); Science: (3); Foreign language: (2); Social studies: (2); Total units: (15). Tests: The college uses SAT or ACT scores in admissions decisions. Either SAT or ACT required. For admission to the fall 2007 entering class, the school will accept: ACT with writing, ACT without writing. Campus visit: Recommended. Admissions interview: Neither required nor recommended. Off-campus interview: May be arranged. **Factors that count in admissions decisions:** *Academic:* Secondary school record: Very important. Class rank: Very important. Letters of recommendation: Very important. Standardized test scores: Very important. Essay: Not considered. *Nonacademic:* Interview: Important. Extracurricular activities: Considered. Talent/ability: Considered. Character/personal qualities: Important. Alumni/ae relationship: Not considered. Geographical residence: Not considered. State residency: Not considered. Religious affiliation/commitment: Not considered. Minority status: Considered. Volunteer work: Considered. Work experience: Considered. **Other schools with the greatest overlap in applicants:** Central College. **Admissions statistics for the fall 2005 entering class:** Total applicants: 1,681. Total accepted: 1,472. Freshmen enrolled: 519; 25% were from out of state. Overall acceptance rate: 88%. Non-early acceptance rate: 88%. **Size of waiting list:** 0 applicants; enrolled from waiting list: 0. **Credentials of fall 2005 freshmen:** 31% ranked in the top 10 percent of their high school class; 62% were in the top 25 percent, and 89% were in the top half. (Proportion submitting class standing: 92%.) **Average high school grade point average:** 3.6. **First-year students who submitted SAT scores:** 6%. Scores (25/75 percentile): Verbal: 500-600, Math: 500-650, Combined: 1000-1250. **First-year students submitting ACT scores:** 94%. Scores (25/75 percentile): English: 20-27, Math: 20-26, Composite: 21-26.

ACADEMICS

Year founded: 1852. **Academic calendar:** Other. **Degrees offered:** bachelor's. **Most popular majors:** 19% business/commerce, 15% elementary education and teaching, 11% communication studies/speech communication and rhetoric, 10% biology/biological sciences, 6% social sciences. **Major fields of study:** biological and biomedical sciences; business, management, marketing, and related support services; communication, journalism, and related programs; computer and information sciences and support services; education; engineering; English language and literature/letters; foreign languages, literatures, and linguistics; health professions and related clinical sciences; history; mathematics and statistics; parks, recreation, leisure, and fitness studies; philosophy and religious studies; physical sciences; psychology; public administration and social service professions; social sciences; theology and religious vocations; visual and performing arts. **Areas of required coursework:** humanities, mathematics, English (including composition), philosophy, foreign languages, sciences (biological or physical), social science, other. **Pre-professional programs:** pre-law, pre-dentistry, pre-medicine, pre-veterinary science, pre-optometry, pre-pharmacy. **Special academic programs:** accelerated program, double major, dual enrollment, honors program, independent study, internships, student-designed major, study abroad, teacher certificate program. **Teacher certification offered in:** early childhood, special education, elementary, middle/junior high, secondary. **Faculty and instruction (2005-2006):** Total instructional faculty: 106 full-time, 73 part-time (51% men; 49% women; 6% minorities). Full-time faculty with Ph.D. or other terminal degree: 80%. Student/faculty ratio: 12/1. Classes of fewer than 20 students: 43%; of 20 to 49 students: 54%; of 50 or more students: 2%. **Advanced Placement and International Baccalaureate credit:** AP tests may be used for: Credit and/or placement. Scores accepted: 3, 4. **Freshmen returning for sophomore year:** 78%. **Graduation rates:** Four-year: 62%; five-year: 67%; six-year: 69%. **Graduate study:** 24% of students pursue further study within one year. Fields in which graduates pursue further study: Master of Business

Administration (MBA), 2%; law, 9%; medicine, 19%; dentistry, 2%; engineering, 6%; theology (or the seminary), 8%; education, 18%; arts and sciences, 19%.

COSTS AND FINANCIAL AID

Financial aid office: (319) 352-8262. **Expenses (2006-2007):** Tuition and fees 2006-2007: $22,410; room/board: $6,715. Estimated books and supplies: $800; transportation: $500; personal expenses: $900. **Financial aid:** Priority filing date for institution's financial aid form: March 1. In 2005-2006, 91% of undergraduates applied for financial aid. Of those, 78% were determined to have financial need; 29% had their need fully met. Average financial aid package (proportion receiving): $17,098 (78%). Average amount of gift aid, such as scholarships or grants (proportion receiving): $12,455 (78%). Average amount of self-help aid, such as work study or loans (proportion receiving): $5,370 (68%). Average need-based loan (excluding PLUS or other private loans): $4,786. Among students who received need-based aid, the average percentage of need met: 85%. Among students who received aid based on merit, the average award (and the proportion receiving): $12,721 (23%). The average athletic scholarship (and the proportion receiving): $0 (0%). Average amount of debt of borrowers graduating in 2005: $22,122. Proportion who borrowed: 84%.

CAMPUS LIFE AND EXTRACURRICULAR ACTIVITIES

Campus housing available (% using): coed dorms (75%), women's dorms (16%), men's dorms (9%). Students who live in college-owned, operated, or affiliated housing: 80%. **Student employment:** During the 2005-2006 academic year, 30% of undergraduates worked on campus. Average per-year earnings: $1,500. **Clubs and organizations:** Number of student organizations: 90. Activities include: choral groups, concert band, dance, drama/theater, jazz band, literary magazine, music ensembles, musical theater, opera, pep band, radio station, student government, student newspaper, student film society, symphony orchestra, television station, yearbook. Number of fraternities: 0; sororities: 0. Average proportion of students who stay on campus on weekends: 60%. **Sports program (2005-2006):** Member of NCAA III. *Men's intercollegiate varsity sports:* baseball, basketball, cross-country, football, golf, soccer, tennis, track and field (indoor), track and field (outdoor), wrestling. *Women's intercollegiate varsity sports:* basketball, cross-country, golf, soccer, softball, tennis, track and field (indoor), track and field (outdoor), volleyball.

SERVICES AND FACILITIES

Basic services: health service. **Remedial assistance:** reading, math, writing, study skills. **Counseling services:** career, personal, academic, religious. **For learning-disabled students:** School does not offer a structured program with separate admission and additional fees. Total undergraduates in learning-disabled program or receiving services: 4. Services include: tape recorders, oral tests, readers, extended time for tests, tutors. **Library:** Number of titles: 186,089; number of current serial subscriptions: 12,473. **Information technology resources:** Students are not required to lease or own a computer. Number of campus computers available to all students: 275. School has a wireless network. Proportion of college-owned housing units wired for high-speed internet access: 100%. **Campus safety:** Security services offered: 24-hour foot and vehicle patrols, late-night transport/escort service, 24-hour emergency telephones, lighted pathways/sidewalks, student patrols, controlled dormitory access (key, security card, etc).

TRANSFER AND INTERNATIONAL STUDENTS

Transfer students: May apply for admission for the following academic terms: Fall, Winter, Spring, Summer. Applicants need a minimum number of credits to apply. For fall 2005: Transfer applications received: 113. Transfer applicants offered admission: 82. Transfer applicants enrolled: 42. **International students:** Number of foreign undergraduates: 92 (5% of student body). Number of countries represented: 36. Minimum TOEFL score required: 480 (paper); 157 (computer). Average TOEFL score: 550 (paper).

William Penn University

- **Address:** 201 Trueblood Avenue, Oskaloosa, IA 52577
- **Website:** http://www.wmpenn.edu
- **Private; Religious affiliation:** Quaker
- **Enrollment:** 1,768 full-time; 27 part-time

KEY STATS

- ✔ **U.S News College Ranking:** fourth tier, Comp. Coll.–Bachelor's (Midwest)
- ✔ **ACT Score (25th/75th percentile):** 17-22
- ✔ **Tuition:** 2005-2006: $15,334

Selectivity: Selective	**Room/board:** $4,896
Acceptance rate: 60%	**Average debt:** N/A
Student/faculty ratio: 15/1	**Proportion who borrowed:** N/A

UNDERGRADUATE STUDENT BODY STATS

2005-2006 enrollment: 1,768 full-time; 27 part-time. Men: 45%; women: 55%. **Ethnic makeup:** African American: 8%; American-Indian: 1%; Asian American: 2%; Hispanic: 3%; White: 86%. **Religious preference:** Roman Catholic: 8%; Protestant: 36%; No preference: 4%; Unknown: 45%; Quaker: 1%.

ADMISSIONS FACTS AND FIGURES

Phone: (641) 673-1012. **Email:** admissions@wmpenn.edu. **Website:** http://www.wmpenn.edu. **Application deadlines for fall 2007:** Regular decision: August 27. Early decision: Not offered. Early action: Not offered. Admission cannot be deferred. **Application fee:** $20. Common application is accepted. **Admissions requirements/recommendations:** High school units required (recommended): English: 0 (4); Mathematics: 0 (4); Science: 0 (4); Foreign language: 0 (0); Social studies: 0 (3); History: 0 (4); Academic electives: 0 (4); Total units: 0 (23). **Tests:** The college uses SAT or ACT scores in admissions decisions. ACT required. For admission to the fall 2007 entering class, the school will accept: ACT with writing, ACT without writing. Campus visit: Recommended. Admissions interview: Recommended. Off-campus interview: May be arranged. **Factors that count in admissions decisions:** *Academic:* Secondary school record: Very important. Class rank: Very important. Letters of recommendation: Considered. Standardized test scores: Very important. Essay: Considered. *Nonacademic:* Interview: Considered. Extracurricular activities: Important. Talent/ability: Important. Character/personal qualities: Very important. Alumni/ae relationship: Very important. Geographical residence: Important. State residency: Important. Religious affiliation/commitment: Not considered. Minority status: Not considered. Volunteer work: Considered. Work experience: Considered. **Other schools with the greatest overlap in applicants:** Central College; Graceland University; Grand View College; Iowa Wesleyan College; Simpson University. **Admissions statistics for the fall 2005 entering class:** Total applicants: 586. Total accepted: 352. Freshmen enrolled: 168; 50% were from out of state. Overall acceptance rate: 60%. **Credentials of fall 2005 freshmen:** 9% ranked in the top 10 percent of their high school class; 22% were in the top 25 percent, and 51% were in the top half. (Proportion submitting class standing: 95%.) **Average high school grade point average:** 2.7. **First-year students who submitted SAT scores:** 18%. Scores (25/75 percentile): Verbal: 340-510, Math: 340-520, Combined: 680-1030. **First-year students submitting ACT scores:** 82%. Scores (25/75 percentile): English: 16-21, Math: 17-22, Composite: 17-22.

ACADEMICS

Year founded: 1873. **Academic calendar:** Semester. **Degrees offered:** associate, transfer-associate, bachelor's. **Most popular majors:** 53% business, management, marketing, and related support services, 18% education, 12% social sciences, 7% communication, journalism, and related programs, 4% parks, recreation, leisure, and fitness studies. **Major fields of study:** biological and biomedical sciences; business, management, marketing, and related support services; communication, journalism, and related programs; computer and information sciences and support services; education; engineering; history; mathematics and statistics; parks, recreation, leisure, and fitness studies; psychology; public administration and social service professions; social

sciences. **Areas of required coursework:** arts/fine arts, computer literacy, mathematics, English (including composition), sciences (biological or physical), history, social science, other. **Pre-professional programs:** pre-law, pre-dentistry, pre-medicine, pre-veterinary science. **Special academic programs (% participation):** distance learning (5%), double major (3%), English as a Second Language (ESL) (2%), independent study (18%), internships (20%), study abroad (0%), teacher certificate program (21%). **Teacher certification offered in:** special education, elementary, secondary. **Faculty and instruction (2005-2006):** Total instructional faculty: 36 full-time, 149 part-time (55% men; 45% women; 6% minorities). Full-time faculty with Ph.D. or other terminal degree: 47%. Student/faculty ratio: 15/1. Classes of fewer than 20 students: 72%; of 20 to 49 students: 25%; of 50 or more students: 2%. **Advanced Placement and International Baccalaureate credit:** AP tests may be used for: Placement only. **Freshmen returning for sophomore year:** 45%. **Graduation rates:** Four-year: 22%; five-year: 45%; six-year: 32%. **Graduate study:** 52% of students pursue further study immediately upon graduation; 36% within one year; 10% within five years. Fields in which graduates pursue further study: Master of Business Administration (MBA), 65%; law, 3%; medicine, 7%; dentistry, 3%; engineering, 10%; theology (or the seminary), 2%; education, 10%.

COSTS AND FINANCIAL AID

Financial aid office: (641) 673-1040. **Expenses (2005-2006):** Tuition and fees 2005-2006: $15,334; room/board: $4,896. Estimated books and supplies: $800; transportation: $1,000; personal expenses: $1,242.

CAMPUS LIFE AND EXTRACURRICULAR ACTIVITIES

Campus housing available (% using): coed dorms (79%), women's dorms (8%), apartments for married students (5%), apartment for single students (8%). Students who live in college-owned, operated, or affiliated housing: 19%. **Student employment:** During the 2005-2006 academic year, 40% of undergraduates worked on campus. Average per-year earnings: $1,000. **Clubs and organizations:** Number of student organizations: 33. Activities include: choral groups, dance, drama/theater, jazz band, literary magazine, music ensembles, pep band, radio station, student government, student newspaper, yearbook. Number of fraternities: 2; sororities: 3. Proportion of men in fraternities: 8%; of women in sororities: 5%. Average proportion of students who stay on campus on weekends: 70%. **Sports program (2005-2006):** Member of NAIA. *Men's intercollegiate varsity sports:* baseball, basketball, cheerleading, cross-country, football, golf, soccer, track and field (indoor), track and field (outdoor), wrestling. *Women's intercollegiate varsity sports:* basketball, cheerleading, cross-country, soccer, softball, track and field (indoor), track and field (outdoor), volleyball.

SERVICES AND FACILITIES

Basic services: nonremedial tutoring, placement service, health insurance. **Remedial assistance:** reading, math, writing, study skills. **Counseling services:** career, personal, academic, psychological, religious. **For learning-disabled students:** School does not offer a structured program with separate admission and additional fees. Total undergraduates in learning-disabled program or receiving services: 21. Services include: remedial math, remedial English, remedial reading, tape recorders, untimed tests, note-taking services, extended time for tests, tutors. **Library:** Number of titles: 76,327; number of current serial subscriptions: 205. **Information technology resources:** Students are not required to lease or own a computer. Number of campus computers available to all students: 67. School has a wireless network. Approximate number of users that can be accommodated: 400. Proportion of college-owned housing units wired for high-speed internet access: 5%. **Campus safety:** Security services offered: 24-hour foot and vehicle patrols, late-night transport/escort service, 24-hour emergency telephones, lighted pathways/sidewalks, student patrols, controlled dormitory access (key, security card, etc).

TRANSFER AND INTERNATIONAL STUDENTS

Transfer students: May apply for admission for the following academic terms: Fall, Spring, Summer. Applicants need a minimum number of credits to apply. For fall 2005: Transfer applications received: 271. Transfer applicants offered admission: 195. Transfer applicants enrolled: 129. **International students:** Number of foreign undergraduates: 1. Number of countries represented: 13. Minimum TOEFL score required: 500 (paper); 173 (computer).

Kansas

Baker University

- **Address:** PO Box 65, Baldwin City, KS 66006
- **Website:** http://www.bakeru.edu
- **Private; Religious affiliation:** United Methodist
- **Enrollment:** 991 full-time; 860 part-time

KEY STATS
- ✔ **U.S News College Ranking:** 44, Universities–Master's (Midwest)
- ✔ **ACT Score (25th/75th percentile):** 21-26
- ✔ **Tuition:** 2006-2007: $17,580

Selectivity: More selective	**Room/board:** $5,850
Acceptance rate: 63%	**Average debt:** $19,602
Student/faculty ratio: 12/1	**Proportion who borrowed:** 86%

UNDERGRADUATE STUDENT BODY STATS
2005-2006 enrollment: 991 full-time; 860 part-time. Men: 42%; women: 58%. **Ethnic makeup:** African American: 8%; American-Indian: 1%; Asian American: 1%; Hispanic: 4%; White: 86%.

ADMISSIONS FACTS AND FIGURES
Phone: (800) 873-4282. **Email:** admission@bakeru.edu. **Website:** http://www.bakeru.edu. **Application deadlines for fall 2007:** Regular decision: Rolling. Early decision: Not offered. Early action: Not offered. Admission can be deferred. Common application is accepted. **To apply online, go to:** http://www.bakeru.edu/admissions/app/. **Admissions requirements/recommendations:** High school units required (recommended): English: (4); Mathematics: (3); Science: (3); Foreign language: (2); Social studies: (3); Total units: (17). Tests: The college uses SAT or ACT scores in admissions decisions. Either SAT or ACT required. For admission to the fall 2007 entering class, the school will accept: ACT with writing, ACT without writing. Campus visit: Recommended. Admissions interview: Recommended. Off-campus interview: May be arranged. **Factors that count in admissions decisions:** *Academic:* Secondary school record: Very important. Class rank: Important. Letters of recommendation: Very important. Standardized test scores: Very important. Essay: Considered. *Nonacademic:* Interview: Considered. Extracurricular activities: Considered. Talent/ability: Considered. Character/personal qualities: Considered. Alumni/ae relationship: Considered. Geographical residence: Considered. State residency: Not considered. Religious affiliation/commitment: Not considered. Minority status: Not considered. Volunteer work: Considered. Work experience: Considered. **Other schools with the greatest overlap in applicants:** Hendrix College; Kansas State University; Rockhurst University; University of Kansas; William Jewell College. **Admissions statistics for the fall 2005 entering class:** Total applicants: 1,051. Total accepted: 666. Freshmen enrolled: 239; 26% were from out of state. Overall acceptance rate: 63%. **Size of waiting list:** 0 applicants; enrolled from waiting list: 0. **Credentials of fall 2005 freshmen:** 25% ranked in the top 10 percent of their high school class; 52% were in the top 25 percent, and 81% were in the top half. (Proportion submitting class standing: 90%.) **Average high school grade point average:** 3.5. **First-year students who submitted SAT scores:** 14%. Scores (25/75 percentile): Verbal: 460-570, Math: 443-588, Combined: 903-1158. **First-year students submitting ACT scores:** 96%. Scores (25/75 percentile): English: 20-26, Math: 20-26, Composite: 21-26.

ACADEMICS
Year founded: 1858. **Academic calendar:** 4-1-4. **Degrees offered:** associate, bachelor's, master's, doctorate. **Most popular majors:** 18% business/commerce, 9% biology/biological sciences, 9% elementary education and teaching, 9% mass communication/media studies, 7% health and physical education. **Major fields of study:** biological and biomedical sciences; business, management, marketing, and related support services; communication, journalism, and related programs; computer and information sciences and support services; education; English language and literature/letters; foreign languages, literatures, and linguistics; health professions and related clinical sciences; history; mathematics and statistics; multi/interdisciplinary studies; parks, recreation, leisure, and fitness studies; philosophy and religious studies; physical sciences; psychology; social sciences; visual and performing arts. **Areas of required coursework:** arts/fine arts, humanities, mathematics, English (including composition), sciences (biological or physical), history, social science, other. **Pre-professional programs:** pre-law, pre-dentistry, pre-medicine, pre-theology, pre-veterinary science, pre-optometry, pre-pharmacy, other. **Special academic programs (% participation):** accelerated program, distance learning, double major (10%), honors program (10%), independent study (20%), internships (30%), student-designed major (2%), study abroad (8%), teacher certificate program (12%). **Teacher certification offered in:** special education, elementary, middle/junior high, secondary. **Reserve Officers Training Corps (ROTC):** Army ROTC: Offered at cooperating institution (University of Kansas); Air Force ROTC: Offered at cooperating institution (University of Kansas). **Faculty and instruction (2005-2006):** Total instructional faculty: 81 full-time, 365 part-time (57% men; 43% women; 6% minorities). Full-time faculty with Ph.D. or other terminal degree: 72%. Student/faculty ratio: 12/1. Classes of fewer than 20 students: 75%; of 20 to 49 students: 24%; of 50 or more students: 1%. **Advanced Placement and International Baccalaureate credit:** AP tests may be used for: Credit only. Scores accepted: 3, 4, 5. International Baccalaureate exams may be used for: Credit only. **Freshmen returning for sophomore year:** 74%. **Graduation rates:** Four-year: 39%; five-year: 59%; six-year: 59%. **Graduate study:** 30% of students pursue further study immediately upon graduation. Fields in which graduates pursue further study: Master of Business Administration (MBA), 3%; law, 14%; medicine, 22%; dentistry, 3%; engineering, 5%; education, 11%; arts and sciences, 40%.

COSTS AND FINANCIAL AID
Financial aid office: (785) 594-4595. **Expenses (2006-2007):** Tuition and fees 2006-2007: $17,580; room/board: $5,850. Estimated books and supplies: $1,200; transportation: $2,230; personal expenses: $1,400. **Financial aid:** Priority filing date for institution's financial aid form: March 1. In 2005-2006, 94% of undergraduates applied for financial aid. Of those, 78% were determined to have financial need; 34% had their need fully met. Average financial aid package (proportion receiving): $20,977 (78%). Average amount of gift aid, such as scholarships or grants (proportion receiving): $5,114 (77%). Average amount of self-help aid, such as work study or loans (proportion receiving): $14,810 (78%). Average need-based loan (excluding PLUS or other private loans): $3,637. Among students who received need-based aid, the average percentage of need met: 85%. Among students who received aid based on merit, the average award (and the proportion receiving): $5,809 (22%). The average athletic scholarship (and the proportion receiving): $1,606 (22%). Average amount of debt of borrowers graduating in 2005: $19,602. Proportion who borrowed: 86%.

CAMPUS LIFE AND EXTRACURRICULAR ACTIVITIES
Campus housing available (% using): coed dorms (15%), women's dorms (20%), men's dorms (17%), sorority housing (20%), fraternity housing (14%), apartment for single students (14%), special housing for disabled students. Students who live in college-owned, operated, or affiliated housing: 84%. **Student employment:** During the 2005-2006 academic year, 1% of undergraduates worked on campus. Average per-year earnings: $260. **Clubs and organizations:** Number of student organizations: 57. Activities include: choral groups, concert band, drama/theater, jazz band, literary magazine, music ensembles, radio station, student government, student newspaper, television station, yearbook. Number of fraternities: 4; sororities: 4. Proportion of men in fraternities: 39%; of women in sororities: 45%. Average proportion of students who stay on campus on weekends: 50%. **Sports program (2005-2006):** Member of NAIA. *Men's intercollegiate varsity sports:* baseball, basketball, cheerleading, cross-country, football, golf, soccer, tennis, track and field (indoor), track and field (outdoor). *Women's intercollegiate varsity sports:* basketball, cheerleading, cross-country, golf, soccer, softball, tennis, track and field (indoor), track and field (outdoor), volleyball.

SERVICES AND FACILITIES
Basic services: nonremedial tutoring, placement service, health service. **Remedial assistance:** reading, math, writing, study skills. **Counseling serv-**

ices: minority student, career, personal, veteran student, academic, older student, psychological, birth control, religious. **For learning-disabled students:** School does not offer a structured program with separate admission and additional fees. Total undergraduates in learning-disabled program or receiving services: 11. Services include: tape recorders, note-taking services, oral tests, learning center, readers, extended time for tests, tutors, priority seating, exams on tape or computer. **Library:** Number of titles: 132,325; number of current serial subscriptions: 678. **Information technology resources:** Students are not required to lease or own a computer. Number of campus computers available to all students: 237. School has a wireless network. Approximate number of users that can be accommodated: 25. Proportion of college-owned housing units wired for high-speed internet access: 100%. **Campus safety:** Security services offered: 24-hour foot and vehicle patrols, lighted pathways/sidewalks, controlled dormitory access (key, security card, etc).

TRANSFER AND INTERNATIONAL STUDENTS

Transfer students: May apply for admission for the following academic terms: Fall, Winter, Spring, Summer. Applicants need a minimum number of credits to apply. For fall 2005: Transfer applications received: 166. Transfer applicants offered admission: 65. Transfer applicants enrolled: 52. **International students:** Number of foreign undergraduates: 6. Number of countries represented: 6. Minimum TOEFL score required: 525 (paper); 195 (computer).

Benedictine College

- **Address:** 1020 N. Second Street, Atchison, KS 66002
- **Website:** http://www.benedictine.edu
- **Private; Religious affiliation:** Roman Catholic
- **Enrollment:** 1,176 full-time; 280 part-time

KEY STATS

✔ **U.S News College Ranking:** third tier, Universities–Master's (Midwest)
✔ **ACT Score (25th/75th percentile):** 19-26
✔ **Tuition:** 2005-2006: $15,760

Selectivity: Selective	**Room/board:** $6,278
Acceptance rate: 90%	**Average debt:** $22,333
Student/faculty ratio: 17/1	**Proportion who borrowed:** 62%

UNDERGRADUATE STUDENT BODY STATS

2005-2006 enrollment: 1,176 full-time; 280 part-time. Men: 48%; women: 52%. **Ethnic makeup:** African American: 4%; Asian American: 2%; Hispanic: 9%; White: 82%; International: 3%. **Religious preference:** Protestant: 12%; Unknown: 14%; Roman Catholic: 72%; Other: 2%.

ADMISSIONS FACTS AND FIGURES

Phone: (800) 467-5340. **Email:** bcadmiss@benedictine.edu. **Website:** http://www.benedictine.edu. **Application deadlines for fall 2007:** Regular decision: Rolling. Early decision: Not offered. Early action: Not offered. Admission can be deferred. **Application fee:** $25. Common application is accepted. **To apply online, go to:** http://www.benedictine.edu. **Admissions requirements/recommendations:** High school units required (recommended): English: 4; Mathematics: 3 (4); Science: 2 (4); Foreign language: 2 (4); Social studies: 2; History: 1. Tests: The college uses SAT or ACT scores in admissions decisions. Either SAT or ACT required. For admission to the fall 2007 entering class, the school will accept: ACT with writing, ACT without writing. Campus visit: Recommended. Admissions interview: Recommended. Off-campus interview: May be arranged. **Factors that count in admissions decisions:** *Academic:* Secondary school record: Very important. Class rank: Very important. Letters of recommendation: Considered. Standardized test scores: Very important. Essay: Considered. *Nonacademic:* Interview: Considered. Extracurricular activities: Considered. Talent/ability: Considered. Character/personal qualities: Considered. Alumni/ae relationship: Considered. Geographical residence: Not considered. State residency: Not considered. Religious affiliation/commitment: Not considered. Minority status: Considered. Volunteer work: Considered. Work experience: Considered. **Other schools with the greatest overlap in applicants:** Creighton University; Kansas State University; Rockhurst University; St. Louis University; University of Kansas. **Admissions statistics for the fall 2005 entering class:** Total applicants: 708. Total accepted: 634. Freshmen enrolled: 304; 34% were from out of state. Overall acceptance rate: 90%.

Credentials of fall 2005 freshmen: 10% ranked in the top 10 percent of their high school class; 30% were in the top 25 percent, and 65% were in the top half. (Proportion submitting class standing: 76%.) **Average high school grade point average:** 3.3. **First-year students who submitted SAT scores:** 11%. Scores (25/75 percentile): Verbal: 440-575, Math: 450-575, Combined: 890-1150. **First-year students submitting ACT scores:** 89%. Scores (25/75 percentile): English: 19-26, Math: 19-26, Composite: 19-26.

ACADEMICS

Year founded: 1859. **Academic calendar:** Semester. **Degrees offered:** associate, bachelor's, master's. **Most popular majors:** 20% business, management, marketing, and related support services, 15% social sciences, 12% philosophy and religious studies, 10% area, ethnic, cultural, and gender studies, 7% psychology. **Major fields of study:** biological and biomedical sciences; business, management, marketing, and related support services; communication, journalism, and related programs; computer and information sciences and support services; education; English language and literature/letters; foreign languages, literatures, and linguistics; health professions and related clinical sciences; history; liberal arts and sciences studies, and humanities; mathematics and statistics; multi/interdisciplinary studies; philosophy and religious studies; physical sciences; psychology; social sciences; visual and performing arts. **Areas of required coursework:** arts/fine arts, humanities, mathematics, English (including composition), philosophy, foreign languages, sciences (biological or physical), history, social science, other. **Pre-professional programs:** pre-law. **Special academic programs (% participation):** cooperative (work-study plan) program (0%), double major (24%), dual enrollment (40%), English as a Second Language (ESL) (3%), independent study (11%), internships (44%), liberal arts/career combination (3%), student-designed major (3%), study abroad (5%), teacher certificate program (11%). **Teacher certification offered in:** special education, elementary, middle/junior high, secondary. **Cooperative education programs:** other. **Reserve Officers Training Corps (ROTC):** Army ROTC: Offered on campus. **Faculty and instruction (2005-2006):** Total instructional faculty: 66 full-time, 46 part-time (63% men; 38% women; 4% minorities). Full-time faculty with Ph.D. or other terminal degree: 76%. Student/faculty ratio: 17/1. Classes of fewer than 20 students: 49%; of 20 to 49 students: 51%; of 50 or more students: 0%. **Advanced Placement and International Baccalaureate credit:** AP tests may be used for: Credit and/or placement. Scores accepted: 3, 4, 5. International Baccalaureate exams may be used for: Credit and/or placement. Freshmen returning for sophomore year: 81%. **Graduation rates:** Four-year: 31%; five-year: 44%; six-year: 49%. **Graduate study:** 15% of students pursue further study immediately upon graduation. Fields in which graduates pursue further study: Master of Business Administration (MBA), 21%; law, 11%; medicine, 26%; theology (or the seminary), 16%; education, 11%; arts and sciences, 16%.

COSTS AND FINANCIAL AID

Financial aid office: (913) 360-7484. **Expenses (2005-2006):** Tuition and fees 2005-2006: $15,760; room/board: $6,278. Estimated books and supplies: $2,400; transportation: $2,000; personal expenses: $2,800. **Financial aid:** Priority filing date for institution's financial aid form: March 15. In 2005-2006, 99% of undergraduates applied for financial aid. Of those, 77% were determined to have financial need; 44% had their need fully met. Average financial aid package (proportion receiving): $13,973 (77%). Average amount of gift aid, such as scholarships or grants (proportion receiving): $11,150 (74%). Average amount of self-help aid, such as work study or loans (proportion receiving): $6,107 (35%). Average need-based loan (excluding PLUS or other private loans): $6,418. Among students who received need-based aid, the average percentage of need met: 67%. Among students who received aid based on merit, the average award (and the proportion receiving): $4,680 (17%). The average athletic scholarship (and the proportion receiving): $6,900 (37%). Average amount of debt of borrowers graduating in 2005: $22,333. Proportion who borrowed: 62%.

CAMPUS LIFE AND EXTRACURRICULAR ACTIVITIES

Campus housing available (% using): coed dorms (20%), women's dorms (35%), men's dorms (40%), other housing options (5%). Students who live in college-owned, operated, or affiliated housing: 72%. **Student employment:** During the 2005-2006 academic year, 16% of undergraduates worked on campus. **Clubs and organizations:** Number of student organizations: 45. Activities include: choral groups, concert band, dance, drama/theater, jazz band, literary magazine, music ensembles, musical theater, pep band, student government, student newspaper, symphony orchestra, yearbook. Number of fraternities: 0; sororities: 0. Average proportion of students who stay on campus on weekends: 60%. **Sports program (2005-2006):** Member of NAIA. *Men's intercollegiate varsity sports:* baseball, basketball, cross-country, football, golf, soccer, tennis, track and field (indoor), track and field (outdoor). *Women's intercollegiate varsity sports:* basketball, cross-country, golf, soccer, softball, tennis, track and field (indoor), track and field (outdoor), volleyball.

SERVICES AND FACILITIES
Basic services: nonremedial tutoring, placement service, health service. **Remedial assistance:** reading, study skills. **Counseling services:** career, personal, psychological, religious. **For learning-disabled students:** School does not offer a structured program with separate admission and additional fees. Total undergraduates in learning-disabled program or receiving services: 80. Services include: tape recorders, untimed tests, note-taking services, oral tests, learning center, readers, extended time for tests, tutors. **Library:** Number of titles: 369,624; number of current serial subscriptions: 515. **Information technology resources:** Students are not required to lease or own a computer. Number of campus computers available to all students: 83. School has a wireless network. Proportion of college-owned housing units wired for high-speed internet access: 100%. **Campus safety:** Security services offered: 24-hour foot and vehicle patrols, late-night transport/escort service, 24-hour emergency telephones, lighted pathways/sidewalks, controlled dormitory access (key, security card, etc).

TRANSFER AND INTERNATIONAL STUDENTS
Transfer students: May apply for admission for the following academic terms: Fall, Spring, Summer. Applicants do not need a minimum number of credits to apply. For fall 2005: Transfer applications received: 114. Transfer applicants offered admission: 57. Transfer applicants enrolled: 55. **International students:** Number of foreign undergraduates: 29 (3% of student body). Number of countries represented: 18. Minimum TOEFL score required: 535 (paper); 200 (computer).

Bethany College

- **Address:** 421 N. First Street, Lindsborg, KS 67456-1897
- **Website:** http://www.bethanylb.edu
- **Private; Religious affiliation:** Evangelical Lutheran Church in America
- **Enrollment:** 552 full-time; 36 part-time

KEY STATS
✔ **U.S News College Ranking:** third tier, Comp. Coll.–Bachelor's (Midwest)
✔ **ACT Score (25th/75th percentile):** 19-25
✔ **Tuition:** 2006-2007: $16,210

Selectivity: Selective	**Room/board:** $5,270
Acceptance rate: 63%	**Average debt:** $16,925
Student/faculty ratio: 11/1	**Proportion who borrowed:** 82%

UNDERGRADUATE STUDENT BODY STATS
2005-2006 enrollment: 552 full-time; 36 part-time. Men: 55%; women: 45%. **Ethnic makeup:** African American: 8%; American-Indian: 1%; Asian American: 1%; Hispanic: 5%; White: 81%; International: 4%. **Religious preference:** Roman Catholic: 14%; Protestant: 19%; Jewish: 1%; Muslim: 1%; No preference: 2%; Unknown: 25%; Evangelical Lutheran Church in America: 23%; Christian: 15%.

ADMISSIONS FACTS AND FIGURES
Phone: (800) 826-2281. **Email:** admissions@bethanylb.edu. **Website:** http://www.bethanylb.edu. **Application deadlines for fall 2007:** Regular decision: Rolling. Early decision: Not offered. Early action: Not offered. Admission cannot be deferred. **Application fee:** $20. Common application is accepted. **Admissions requirements/recommendations:** High school units required (recommended): English: (4); Mathematics: (3); Science: (3); Foreign language: (2); Social studies: (3). Tests: The college uses SAT or ACT scores in admissions decisions. Either SAT or ACT required. For admission to the fall 2007 entering class, the school will accept: ACT with writing, ACT without writing. Campus visit: Recommended. Admissions interview: Recommended. Off-campus interview: May be arranged. **Factors that count in admissions decisions:** *Academic:* Secondary school record: Important. Class rank: Very important. Letters of recommendation: Considered. Standardized test scores: Very important. Essay: Considered. *Nonacademic:* Interview: Considered. Extracurricular activities: Considered. Talent/ability: Considered. Character/personal qualities: Considered. Alumni/ae relationship: Considered. Geographical residence: Not consid-

ered. State residency: Not considered. Religious affiliation/commitment: Not considered. Minority status: Not considered. Volunteer work: Not considered. Work experience: Not considered. **Other schools with the greatest overlap in applicants:** Fort Hays State University; Kansas State University; University of Kansas. **Admissions statistics for the fall 2005 entering class:** Total applicants: 868. Total accepted: 548. Freshmen enrolled: 148; 44% were from out of state. Overall acceptance rate: 63%. **Credentials of fall 2005 freshmen:** 17% ranked in the top 10 percent of their high school class; 41% were in the top 25 percent, and 78% were in the top half. (Proportion submitting class standing: 87%.) **Average high school grade point average:** 3.4. **First-year students who submitted SAT scores:** 22%. Scores (25/75 percentile): Verbal: 380-520, Math: 410-590, Combined: 790-1110. **First-year students submitting ACT scores:** 73%. Scores (25/75 percentile): English: 18-25, Math: 17-24, Composite: 19-25.

ACADEMICS
Year founded: 1881. **Academic calendar:** 4-1-4. **Degrees offered:** bachelor's. **Most popular majors:** 25% education, 17% business/commerce, 13% biology, 12% visual and performing arts, 11% criminal justice and corrections. **Major fields of study:** biological and biomedical sciences; business, management, marketing, and related support services; communication, journalism, and related programs; education; English language and literature/letters; history; mathematics and statistics; physical sciences; psychology; public administration and social service professions; security and protective services; theology and religious vocations; visual and performing arts. **Areas of required coursework:** humanities, mathematics, English (including composition), philosophy, sciences (biological or physical), history, social science. **Pre-professional programs:** pre-law, pre-medicine, pre-theology, pre-veterinary science, pre-pharmacy. **Special academic programs (% participation):** accelerated program (3%), cross-registration (5%), double major (2%), dual enrollment (0%), exchange student program (domestic) (1%), independent study (5%), internships (19%), student-designed major (1%), teacher certificate program (14%). **Teacher certification offered in:** early childhood, special education, elementary, middle/junior high, secondary. **Cooperative education programs:** education, engineering. **Faculty and instruction (2005-2006):** Total instructional faculty: 40 full-time, 30 part-time (54% men; 46% women; 0% minorities). Full-time faculty with Ph.D. or other terminal degree: 60%. Student/faculty ratio: 11/1. Classes of fewer than 20 students: 81%; of 20 to 49 students: 19%; of 50 or more students: 0%. **Freshmen returning for sophomore year:** 64%. **Graduation rates:** Four-year: 32%; five-year: 46%; six-year: 43%. **Graduate study:** 20% of students pursue further study immediately upon graduation. Fields in which graduates pursue further study: Master of Business Administration (MBA), 13%; law, 13%; medicine, 13%; engineering, 6%; theology (or the seminary), 13%; veterinary medicine, 6%.

COSTS AND FINANCIAL AID
Financial aid office: (785) 227-3311. **Expenses (2006-2007):** Tuition and fees 2006-2007: $16,210; room/board: $5,270. Estimated books and supplies: $1,000; transportation: $900; personal expenses: $1,900. **Financial aid:** Priority filing date for institution's financial aid form: March 15. In 2005-2006, 97% of undergraduates applied for financial aid. Of those, 82% were determined to have financial need; 46% had their need fully met. Average financial aid package (proportion receiving): $16,612 (82%). Average amount of gift aid, such as scholarships or grants (proportion receiving): $5,404 (67%). Average amount of self-help aid, such as work study or loans (proportion receiving): $5,655 (69%). Average need-based loan (excluding PLUS or other private loans): $4,822. Among students who received need-based aid, the average percentage of need met: 96%. Among students who received aid based on merit, the average award (and the proportion receiving): $6,189 (5%). The average athletic scholarship (and the proportion receiving): $4,420 (8%). Average amount of debt of borrowers graduating in 2005: $16,925. Proportion who borrowed: 82%.

CAMPUS LIFE AND EXTRACURRICULAR ACTIVITIES
Campus housing available (% using): coed dorms (80%), women's dorms (16%), other housing options (4%). Students who live in college-owned, operated, or affiliated housing: 72%. **Student employment:** During the 2005-2006 academic year, 23% of undergraduates worked on campus. Average per-year earnings: $1,500. **Clubs and organizations:** Number of student organizations: 40. Activities include: choral groups, concert band, dance, drama/theater, jazz band, music ensembles, musical theater, pep band, student government, student newspaper, symphony orchestra, yearbook. Number of fraternities: 3; sororities: 3. Proportion of men in fraternities: 15%; of women in sororities: 18%. Average proportion of students who stay on campus on weekends: 60%. **Sports program (2005-2006):** Member of

NAIA. Men's intercollegiate varsity sports: baseball, basketball, cross-country, football, golf, soccer, tennis, track and field (indoor), track and field (outdoor). **Women's intercollegiate varsity sports:** basketball, cross-country, soccer, softball, tennis, track and field (indoor), track and field (outdoor), volleyball.

SERVICES AND FACILITIES
Basic services: nonremedial tutoring, health service, health insurance. **Remedial assistance:** math, writing, study skills. **Counseling services:** minority student, career, personal, academic, religious. **For learning-disabled students:** Services include: tape recorders, other special classes, diagnostic testing service, untimed tests, note-taking services, oral tests, learning center, readers, extended time for tests, tutors. **Information technology resources:** Students are not required to lease or own a computer. Number of campus computers available to all students: 75. School does not have a wireless network. Proportion of college-owned housing units wired for high-speed internet access: 56%. **Campus safety:** Security services offered: late-night transport/escort service, 24-hour emergency telephones, lighted pathways/sidewalks, controlled dormitory access (key, security card, etc).

TRANSFER AND INTERNATIONAL STUDENTS
Transfer students: May apply for admission for the following academic terms: Fall, Winter, Spring, Summer. Applicants do not need a minimum number of credits to apply. For fall 2005: Transfer applications received: 202. Transfer applicants offered admission: 118. Transfer applicants enrolled: 77. **International students:** Number of foreign undergraduates: 23 (4% of student body). Minimum TOEFL score required: 525 (paper); 195 (computer).

Bethel College

- ■ **Address:** 300 E. 27th Street, North Newton, KS 67117-0531
- ■ **Website:** http://www.bethelks.edu
- ■ **Private; Religious affiliation:** Mennonite Church U.S.A.
- ■ **Enrollment:** 476 full-time; 38 part-time

KEY STATS
✔ **U.S News College Ranking:** 29, Comp. Coll.–Bachelor's (Midwest)
✔ **ACT Score (25th/75th percentile):** 20-25
✔ **Tuition:** 2006-2007: $16,700

Selectivity: Selective	**Room/board:** $6,100
Acceptance rate: 72%	**Average debt:** $18,584
Student/faculty ratio: 9/1	**Proportion who borrowed:** 86%

UNDERGRADUATE STUDENT BODY STATS
2005-2006 enrollment: 476 full-time; 38 part-time. Men: 49%; women: 51%. **Ethnic makeup:** African American: 6%; American-Indian: 1%; Asian American: 2%; Hispanic: 4%; White: 82%; International: 5%. **Religious preference:** Roman Catholic: 10%; Protestant: 34%; No preference: 2%; Unknown: 19%; Mennonite Church U.S.A.: 35%.

ADMISSIONS FACTS AND FIGURES
Phone: (800) 522-1887. **Email:** admissions@bethelks.edu. **Website:** http://www.bethelks.edu. **Application deadlines for fall 2007:** Regular decision: Rolling. Early decision: Not offered. Early action: Not offered. Admission can be deferred. **Application fee:** $20. Common application is not accepted. **To apply online, go to:** http://www.bethelks.edu/admissions/application/app_intro.php. **Admissions requirements/recommendations:** High school units required (recommended): English: 4 (4); Mathematics: 4 (4); Science: 3 (3); Foreign language: 2 (2); Social studies: 3 (3); History: 1 (1); Total units: 18 (18). **Tests:** The college uses SAT or ACT scores in admissions decisions. Either SAT or ACT required. For admission to the fall 2007 entering class, the school will accept: ACT with writing, ACT without writing. Campus visit: Recommended. Admissions interview: Required. Off-campus interview: May be arranged. **Factors that count in admissions decisions:** *Academic:* Secondary school record: Considered. Class rank: Considered. Letters of recommendation: Considered. Standardized test scores: Very important. Essay: Considered. *Nonacademic:* Interview: Considered. Extracurricular activities: Not considered. Talent/ability: Considered. Character/personal qualities: Considered. Alumni/ae relationship: Considered. Geographical residence: Not considered. State residency: Not considered. Religious affiliation/commitment: Not considered. Minority status: Not considered. Volunteer work: Not considered. Work experience: Not considered. **Other schools with the greatest overlap in applicants:** Kansas State University; Pittsburg State University; University of Kansas; Wichita State University. **Admissions statistics for the fall 2005 entering class:** Total applicants: 581. Total accepted: 418. Freshmen enrolled: 96; 29% were from out of state. Overall acceptance rate: 72%. **Credentials of fall 2005 freshmen:** 17% ranked in the top 10 percent of their high school class; 46% were in the top 25 percent, and 79% were in the top half. (Proportion submitting class standing: 94%.) **Average high school grade point average:** 3.5. **First-year students who submitted SAT scores:** 9%. Scores (25/75 percentile): Verbal: 410-630, Math: 450-650, Combined: 860-1280. **First-year students submitting ACT scores:** 91%. Scores (25/75 percentile): English: 19-26, Math: 20-26, Composite: 20-25.

ACADEMICS
Year founded: 1887. **Academic calendar:** 4-1-4. **Degrees offered:** certificate, bachelor's. **Most popular majors:** 24% nursing/registered nurse training (R.N., A.S.N., B.S.N., M.S.N.), 8% business/commerce, 7% social work, 7% visual and performing arts, 6% elementary education and teaching. **Major fields of study:** biological and biomedical sciences; business, management, marketing, and related support services; communication, journalism, and related programs; computer and information sciences and support services; education; English language and literature/letters; foreign languages, literatures, and linguistics; health professions and related clinical sciences; history; mathematics and statistics; multi/interdisciplinary studies; parks, recreation, leisure, and fitness studies; philosophy and religious studies; physical sciences; psychology; public administration and social service professions; visual and performing arts. **Areas of required coursework:** arts/fine arts, humanities, computer literacy, mathematics, English (including composition), philosophy, foreign languages, sciences (biological or physical), history, social science, other. **Pre-professional programs:** pre-law, pre-dentistry, pre-medicine, pre-veterinary science, pre-optometry, pre-pharmacy. **Special academic programs (% participation):** cross-registration (23%), double major (12%), dual enrollment (2%), exchange student program (domestic) (1%), independent study (36%), internships (25%), liberal arts/career combination (30%), study abroad (4%), teacher certificate program (12%). **Teacher certification offered in:** special education, elementary, middle/junior high, secondary. **Faculty and instruction (2005-2006):** Total instructional faculty: 47 full-time, 19 part-time (52% men; 48% women; 0% minorities). Full-time faculty with Ph.D. or other terminal degree: 57%. Student/faculty ratio: 9/1. Classes of fewer than 20 students: 75%; of 20 to 49 students: 23%; of 50 or more students: 1%. **Advanced Placement and International Baccalaureate credit:** AP tests may be used for: Credit and/or placement. Scores accepted: 4, 5. International Baccalaureate exams may be used for: Credit and/or placement. **Freshmen returning for sophomore year:** 72%. **Graduation rates:** Four-year: 43%; five-year: 52%; six-year: 47%.

COSTS AND FINANCIAL AID
Financial aid office: (316) 284-5232. **Expenses (2006-2007):** Tuition and fees 2006-2007: $16,700; room/board: $6,100. Estimated books and supplies: $800; transportation: $700; personal expenses: $1,915. **Financial aid:** Priority filing date for institution's financial aid form: August 15. In 2005-2006, 87% of undergraduates applied for financial aid. Of those, 87% were determined to have financial need; 35% had their need fully met. Average financial aid package (proportion receiving): $16,297 (87%). Average amount of gift aid, such as scholarships or grants (proportion receiving): $4,798 (66%). Average amount of self-help aid, such as work study or loans (proportion receiving): $6,128 (68%). Average need-based loan (excluding PLUS or other private loans): $5,242. Among students who received need-based aid, the average percentage of need met: 90%. Among students who received aid based on merit, the average award (and the proportion receiving): $8,648 (9%). The average athletic scholarship (and the proportion receiving): $2,914 (37%). Average amount of debt of borrowers graduating in 2005: $18,584. Proportion who borrowed: 86%.

CAMPUS LIFE AND EXTRACURRICULAR ACTIVITIES
Campus housing available (% using): coed dorms (99%), apartments for married students, apartment for single students (1%), special housing for disabled students. Students who live in college-owned, operated, or affiliated housing: 67%. **Student employment:** During the 2005-2006 academic year, 39% of undergraduates worked on campus. Average per-year earnings: $1,200. **Clubs and organizations:** Number of student organizations: 34. Activities include: choral groups, concert band, dance, drama/theater, jazz band, literary magazine, music ensembles, musical theater, opera, pep band, radio station, student government, student newspaper, symphony orchestra, yearbook. Number of fraternities: 0; sororities: 0. Average propor-

tion of students who stay on campus on weekends: 80%. **Sports program (2005-2006):** Member of NAIA. *Men's intercollegiate varsity sports:* basketball, cross-country, football, golf, soccer, tennis, track and field (indoor), track and field (outdoor). *Women's intercollegiate varsity sports:* basketball, cross-country, golf, soccer, tennis, track and field (indoor), track and field (outdoor), volleyball.

SERVICES AND FACILITIES

Basic services: nonremedial tutoring, health service, health insurance. **Remedial assistance:** reading, math, writing, study skills. **Counseling services:** minority student, career, personal, academic, psychological, birth control, religious. **For learning-disabled students:** School does not offer a structured program with separate admission and additional fees. Total undergraduates in learning-disabled program or receiving services: 8. Services include: tape recorders, videotaped classes, untimed tests, note-taking services, oral tests, learning center, readers, extended time for tests, tutors, other. **Library:** Number of titles: 140,408; number of current serial subscriptions: 537. **Information technology resources:** Students are not required to lease or own a computer. Number of campus computers available to all students: 60. School has a wireless network. Approximate number of users that can be accommodated: 30. Proportion of college-owned housing units wired for high-speed internet access: 97%. **Campus safety:** Security services offered: 24-hour emergency telephones, lighted pathways/sidewalks, controlled dormitory access (key, security card, etc).

TRANSFER AND INTERNATIONAL STUDENTS

Transfer students: May apply for admission for the following academic terms: Fall, Winter, Spring, Summer. Applicants do not need a minimum number of credits to apply. For fall 2005: Transfer applications received: 202. Transfer applicants offered admission: 120. Transfer applicants enrolled: 76. **International students:** Number of foreign undergraduates: 27 (5% of student body). Number of countries represented: 15. Minimum TOEFL score required: 540 (paper); 207 (computer). Average TOEFL score: 620 (paper).

Central Christian College

- **Address:** 1200 S. Main, PO Box 1403, McPherson, KS 67460-5799
- **Website:** http://www.centralchristian.edu/index.html
- **Private; Religious affiliation:** Free Methodist
- **Enrollment:** 306 full-time; 20 part-time

KEY STATS

- ✔ **U.S News College Ranking:** fourth tier, Comp. Coll.–Bachelor's (Midwest)
- ✔ **ACT Score (25th/75th percentile):** 20-26
- ✔ **Tuition:** 2006-2007: $14,500

Selectivity: Selective	**Room/board:** $5,000
Acceptance rate: 45%	**Average debt:** $20,000
Student/faculty ratio: 16/1	**Proportion who borrowed:** 73%

UNDERGRADUATE STUDENT BODY STATS

2005-2006 enrollment: 306 full-time; 20 part-time. Men: 47%; women: 53%. **Ethnic makeup:** African American: 9%; American-Indian: 2%; Hispanic: 7%; White: 78%; International: 3%. **Religious preference:** Roman Catholic: 3%; Protestant: 70%; No preference: 4%; Free Methodist: 21%; Other: 2%.

ADMISSIONS FACTS AND FIGURES

Phone: (800) 835-0078. **Email:** david.ferrell@centralchristian.edu. **Website:** http://www.centralchristian.edu/index.html. **Application deadlines for fall 2007:** Regular decision: July 1. Early decision: Not offered. Early action: Not offered. Admission can be deferred. **Application fee:** $20. Common application is accepted. **Admissions requirements/recommendations:** High school units required (recommended): English: (4); Mathematics: (2); Science: (1); Foreign language: (0); Social studies: (2); History: (1); Academic electives: (10); Total units: (22). Tests: The college uses SAT or ACT scores in admissions decisions. Either SAT or ACT required. For admission to the fall 2007 entering class, the school will accept: ACT without writing. Campus visit: Recommended. Admissions interview: Neither required nor recommended. Off-campus interview: Not available. **Factors that count in admissions decisions:** *Academic:* Secondary school record: Very important. Class rank: Important. Letters of recommendation: Very important. Standardized test scores: Important. Essay: Important. *Nonacademic:* Interview: Not consid-

ered. Extracurricular activities: Considered. Talent/ability: Not considered. Character/personal qualities: Important. Alumni/ae relationship: Considered. Geographical residence: Not considered. State residency: Not considered. Religious affiliation/commitment: Important. Minority status: Not considered. Volunteer work: Not considered. Work experience: Not considered. **Other schools with the greatest overlap in applicants:** Azusa Pacific University; Greenville College; Indiana Wesleyan University; Oklahoma Wesleyan University; Spring Arbor University. **Admissions statistics for the fall 2005 entering class:** Total applicants: 626. Total accepted: 283. Freshmen enrolled: 97; 42% were from out of state. Overall acceptance rate: 45%. **Credentials of fall 2005 freshmen:** 15% ranked in the top 10 percent of their high school class; 42% were in the top 25 percent, and 80% were in the top half. (Proportion submitting class standing: 87%.) **Average high school grade point average:** 3.4. **First-year students who submitted SAT scores:** 14%. Scores (25/75 percentile): Verbal: 450-610, Math: 400-560, Combined: 850-1170. **First-year students submitting ACT scores:** 76%. Scores (25/75 percentile): English: 17-26, Math: 17-25, Composite: 20-26.

ACADEMICS

Year founded: 1884. **Academic calendar:** 4-1-4. **Degrees offered:** associate, transfer-associate, bachelor's. **Most popular majors:** 42% business, management, marketing, and related support services, 31% liberal arts and sciences studies, and humanities, 20% theological and ministerial studies, 7% health professions and related clinical sciences. **Major fields of study:** biological and biomedical sciences; business, management, marketing, and related support services; communication, journalism, and related programs; health professions and related clinical sciences; legal professions and studies; liberal arts and sciences studies, and humanities; mathematics and statistics; parks, recreation, leisure, and fitness studies; physical sciences; psychology; security and protective services; social sciences; theology and religious vocations; visual and performing arts. **Areas of required coursework:** arts/fine arts, humanities, computer literacy, mathematics, English (including composition), philosophy, sciences (biological or physical), history, social science, other. **Pre-professional programs:** pre-law, pre-medicine, pre-theology. **Special academic programs (% participation):** cooperative (work-study plan) program (13%), double major (.5%), independent study (15%), internships (12%), student-designed major (55%). **Cooperative education programs:** business, health professions, social/behavioral science, other. **Faculty and instruction (2005-2006):** Total instructional faculty: 12 full-time, 25 part-time (49% men; 51% women; 0% minorities). Full-time faculty with Ph.D. or other terminal degree: 17%. Student/faculty ratio: 16/1. Classes of fewer than 20 students: 75%; of 20 to 49 students: 22%; of 50 or more students: 3%. **Advanced Placement and International Baccalaureate credit:** AP tests may be used for: Credit and/or placement. Scores accepted: 3, 4, 5. International Baccalaureate exams may be used for: Credit only. **Freshmen returning for sophomore year:** 58%. **Graduation rates:** Four-year: 15%; five-year: 18%; six-year: 24%. **Graduate study:** 1% of students pursue further study immediately upon graduation; 2% within one year; 3% within five years. Fields in which graduates pursue further study: Master of Business Administration (MBA), 4%; law, 3%; medicine, 3%; dentistry, 3%; theology (or the seminary), 5%; education, 3%.

COSTS AND FINANCIAL AID

Financial aid office: (620) 241-0723. **Expenses (2006-2007):** Tuition and fees 2006-2007: $14,500; room/board: $5,000. Estimated books and supplies: $1,000; transportation: $1,000; personal expenses: $1,000. **Financial aid:** Priority filing date for institution's financial aid form: March 1. In 2005-2006, 92% of undergraduates applied for financial aid. Of those, 85% were determined to have financial need; Average financial aid package (proportion receiving): $12,372 (84%). Average amount of gift aid, such as scholarships or grants (proportion receiving): $3,815 (57%). Average amount of self-help aid, such as work study or loans (proportion receiving): $4,560 (69%). Average need-based loan (excluding PLUS or other private loans): $4,560. Among students who received need-based aid, the average percentage of need met: 61%. Among students who received aid based on merit, the average award (and the proportion receiving): $5,460 (7%). The average athletic scholarship (and the proportion receiving): $1,521 (43%). Average amount of debt of borrowers graduating in 2005: $20,000. Proportion who borrowed: 73%.

CAMPUS LIFE AND EXTRACURRICULAR ACTIVITIES

Campus housing available (% using): coed dorms (28%), women's dorms (31%), men's dorms (34%), apartments for married students (4%), apartment for single students (3%). Students who live in college-owned, operated, or affiliated housing: 85%. **Student employment:** During the 2005-2006 academic year, 67% of undergraduates worked on campus.

Average per-year earnings: $1,300. Activities include: choral groups, concert band, drama/theater, jazz band, music ensembles, musical theater, pep band, radio station, student government, student newspaper, yearbook. Number of fraternities: 0; sororities: 0. Average proportion of students who stay on campus on weekends: 75%. **Sports program (2005-2006):** Member of NAIA. *Men's intercollegiate varsity sports:* baseball, basketball, cross-country, golf, soccer, tennis. *Women's intercollegiate varsity sports:* basketball, cross-country, golf, soccer, softball, tennis, volleyball.

SERVICES AND FACILITIES

Basic services: nonremedial tutoring, health service, health insurance. **Remedial assistance:** math, writing, study skills, other. **Counseling services:** minority student, career, personal, academic, older student, psychological, religious. **For learning-disabled students:** School does not offer a structured program with separate admission and additional fees. Total undergraduates in learning-disabled program or receiving services: 6. Services include: remedial math, remedial English, other special classes, untimed tests, note-taking services, oral tests, readers, extended time for tests, tutors. **Library:** Number of titles: 37,339; number of current serial subscriptions: 95. **Information technology resources:** Students are not required to lease or own a computer. Number of campus computers available to all students: 38. School has a wireless network. Approximate number of users that can be accommodated: 20. Proportion of college-owned housing units wired for high-speed internet access: 1%. **Campus safety:** Security services offered: 24-hour emergency telephones, lighted pathways/sidewalks, controlled dormitory access (key, security card, etc).

TRANSFER AND INTERNATIONAL STUDENTS

Transfer students: May apply for admission for the following academic terms: Fall, Winter, Spring. Applicants need a minimum number of credits to apply. For fall 2005: Transfer applications received: 85. Transfer applicants offered admission: 31. Transfer applicants enrolled: 37. **International students:** Number of foreign undergraduates: 10 (3% of student body). Number of countries represented: 3. Minimum TOEFL score required: 500 (paper). Average TOEFL score: 525 (paper).

Emporia State University

- **Address:** 1200 Commercial, Emporia, KS 66801-5087
- **Website:** http://www.emporia.edu
- **Public**
- **Enrollment:** 3,797 full-time; 554 part-time

KEY STATS

✔ **U.S News College Ranking:** third tier, Universities–Master's (Midwest)
✔ **ACT Score (25th/75th percentile):** 19-24
✔ **Tuition:** 2006-2007: $3,586 in state, $10,938 out of state

Selectivity: Selective	**Room/board:** $5,170
Acceptance rate: 78%	**Average debt:** $17,435
Student/faculty ratio: 18/1	**Proportion who borrowed:** 72%

UNDERGRADUATE STUDENT BODY STATS

2005-2006 enrollment: 3,797 full-time; 554 part-time. Men: 38%; women: 62%. **Ethnic makeup:** African American: 4%; American-Indian: 1%; Asian American: 1%; Hispanic: 5%; White: 87%; International: 2%.

ADMISSIONS FACTS AND FIGURES

Phone: (620) 341-5465. **Email:** go2esu@emporia.edu. **Website:** http://www.emporia.edu. **Application deadlines for fall 2007:** Regular decision: Rolling. Early decision: Not offered. Early action: Not offered. Admission can be deferred. **Application fee:** $30. Common application is not accepted. **To apply online, go to:** http://www.applyweb.com/apply/emporia/index2.html. **Admissions requirements/recommendations:** High school units required (recommended): English: 4 (4); Mathematics: 3 (3); Science: 3 (3); Social studies: 3 (3). Tests: The college uses SAT or ACT scores in admissions decisions. Either SAT or ACT required. For admission to the fall 2007 entering class, the school will accept: ACT with writing, ACT without writing. Campus visit: Recommended. Admissions interview: Neither required nor recommended. Off-campus interview: Not available. **Factors that count in admissions decisions:** *Academic:* Secondary school record: Not considered. Class rank: Very important. Letters of recommendation: Not considered. Standardized test scores: Very important. Essay: Considered.

Nonacademic: Interview: Not considered. Extracurricular activities: Considered. Talent/ability: Important. Character/personal qualities: Not considered. Alumni/ae relationship: Not considered. Geographical residence: Not considered. State residency: Not considered. Religious affiliation/commitment: Not considered. Minority status: Not considered. Volunteer work: Not considered. Work experience: Not considered. **Other schools with the greatest overlap in applicants:** Kansas State University; Pittsburg State University; University of Kansas; Washburn University; Wichita State University. **Admissions statistics for the fall 2005 entering class:** Total applicants: 1,188. Total accepted: 931. Freshmen enrolled: 739; 7% were from out of state. Overall acceptance rate: 78%. **Credentials of fall 2005 freshmen:** 11% ranked in the top 10 percent of their high school class; 31% were in the top 25 percent, and 65% were in the top half. (Proportion submitting class standing: 77%.) **Average high school grade point average:** 3.2. **First-year students submitting ACT scores:** 93%. Scores (25/75 percentile): English: 18-24, Math: 18-24, Composite: 19-24.

ACADEMICS

Year founded: 1863. **Academic calendar:** Semester. **Degrees offered:** certificate, bachelor's, post-bachelor's certificate, master's, post-master's certificate, doctorate. **Most popular majors:** 29% education, 19% business, management, marketing, and related support services, 12% social sciences, 8% health professions and related clinical sciences, 5% communication, journalism, and related programs. **Major fields of study:** biological and biomedical sciences; business, management, marketing, and related support services; communication, journalism, and related programs; computer and information sciences and support services; education; English language and literature/letters; foreign languages, literatures, and linguistics; health professions and related clinical sciences; history; liberal arts and sciences studies, and humanities; mathematics and statistics; multi/interdisciplinary studies; parks, recreation, leisure, and fitness studies; physical sciences; psychology; social sciences; visual and performing arts. **Areas of required coursework:** arts/fine arts, humanities, computer literacy, mathematics, English (including composition), sciences (biological or physical), history, social science, other. **Pre-professional programs:** pre-law, pre-dentistry, pre-medicine, pre-veterinary science, pre-optometry, pre-pharmacy, other. **Special academic programs:** distance learning, double major, dual enrollment, English as a Second Language (ESL), honors program, independent study, internships, student-designed major, study abroad, teacher certificate program. **Teacher certification offered in:** early childhood, special education, elementary, middle/junior high, secondary, bilingual/bicultural. **Faculty and instruction (2005-2006):** Total instructional faculty: 252 full-time, 30 part-time (57% men; 43% women; 8% minorities). Full-time faculty with Ph.D. or other terminal degree: 82%. Student/faculty ratio: 18/1. Classes of fewer than 20 students: 46%; of 20 to 49 students: 48%; of 50 or more students: 6%. **Advanced Placement and International Baccalaureate credit:** AP tests may be used for: Credit and/or placement. Scores accepted: 3, 4, 5. International Baccalaureate exams may be used for: Credit and/or placement. **Freshmen returning for sophomore year:** 68%. **Graduation rates:** Four-year: 22%; five-year: 39%; six-year: 44%. **Graduate study:** 18% of students pursue further study within one year.

COSTS AND FINANCIAL AID

Financial aid office: (620) 341-5457. **Expenses (2006-2007):** Tuition and fees 2006-2007: $3,586 in state, $10,938 out of state; room/board: $5,170. Estimated books and supplies: $900; transportation: $910; personal expenses: $1,800. **Financial aid:** Priority filing date for institution's financial aid form: March 15. In 2005-2006, 77% of undergraduates applied for financial aid. Of those, 58% were determined to have financial need; 26% had their need fully met. Average financial aid package (proportion receiving): $5,955 (58%). Average amount of gift aid, such as scholarships or grants (proportion receiving): $2,192 (38%). Average amount of self-help aid, such as work study or loans (proportion receiving): $1,691 (52%). Average need-based loan (excluding PLUS or other private loans): $2,765. Among students who received need-based aid, the average percentage of need met: 67%. Among students who received aid based on merit, the average award (and the proportion receiving): $849 (9%). The average athletic scholarship (and the proportion receiving): $1,393 (1%). Average amount of debt of borrowers graduating in 2005: $17,435. Proportion who borrowed: 72%.

CAMPUS LIFE AND EXTRACURRICULAR ACTIVITIES

Campus housing available (% using): coed dorms (76%), sorority housing (8%), fraternity housing (6%), apartments for married students (10%), special housing for disabled students, special housing for international students. Students who live in college-owned, operated, or affiliated housing:

19%. **Student employment:** During the 2005-2006 academic year, 19% of undergraduates worked on campus. Average per-year earnings: $2,655. **Clubs and organizations:** Number of student organizations: 131. Activities include: choral groups, concert band, dance, drama/theater, jazz band, literary magazine, marching band, music ensembles, musical theater, opera, pep band, student government, student newspaper, student film society, symphony orchestra, yearbook. Number of fraternities: 6; sororities: 4. Proportion of men in fraternities: 13%; of women in sororities: 9%. **Sports program (2005-2006):** Member of NCAA II. *Men's intercollegiate varsity sports:* baseball, basketball, cross-country, football, tennis, track and field (indoor), track and field (outdoor). *Women's intercollegiate varsity sports:* basketball, cross-country, soccer, softball, tennis, track and field (indoor), track and field (outdoor), volleyball.

SERVICES AND FACILITIES

Basic services: nonremedial tutoring, women's center, placement service, day care, health service, health insurance. **Remedial assistance:** reading, math, writing. **Counseling services:** minority student, career, military, personal, veteran student, academic, older student, psychological, birth control, religious, other. **For learning-disabled students:** School does not offer a structured program with separate admission and additional fees. Total undergraduates in learning-disabled program or receiving services: 193. Services include: remedial math, remedial English, reading machines, remedial reading, tape recorders, diagnostic testing service, note-taking services, oral tests, readers, extended time for tests, tutors, priority registration, priority seating, texts on tape, other testing accomodations, other. **Library:** Number of titles: 2,398,893; number of current serial subscriptions: 12,086. **Information technology resources:** Students are not required to lease or own a computer. Number of campus computers available to all students: 410. School has a wireless network. Approximate number of users that can be accommodated: 130. Proportion of college-owned housing units wired for high-speed internet access: 91%. **Campus safety:** Security services offered: 24-hour foot and vehicle patrols, late-night transport/escort service, 24-hour emergency telephones, lighted pathways/sidewalks, student patrols, controlled dormitory access (key, security card, etc).

TRANSFER AND INTERNATIONAL STUDENTS

Transfer students: May apply for admission for the following academic terms: Fall, Spring, Summer. Applicants need a minimum number of credits to apply. For fall 2005: Transfer applications received: 985. Transfer applicants offered admission: 861. Transfer applicants enrolled: 426. **International students:** Number of foreign undergraduates: 87 (2% of student body). Number of countries represented: 47. Minimum TOEFL score required: 450 (paper); 133 (computer). Average TOEFL score: 550 (paper).

Fort Hays State University

■ **Address:** 600 Park Street, Hays, KS 67601-4099
■ **Website:** http://www.fhsu.edu
■ **Public**
■ **Enrollment:** 4,270 full-time; 3,564 part-time

KEY STATS

✔ **U.S News College Ranking:** fourth tier, Universities–Master's (Midwest)
✔ **ACT Score (25th/75th percentile):** 18-24
✔ **Tuition:** 2006-2007: $3,192 in state, $10,032 out of state

Selectivity: Less selective	**Room/board:** $5,553
Acceptance rate: 91%	**Average debt:** N/A
Student/faculty ratio: 17/1	**Proportion who borrowed:** N/A

UNDERGRADUATE STUDENT BODY STATS

2005-2006 enrollment: 4,270 full-time; 3,564 part-time. Men: 45%; women: 55%. **Ethnic makeup:** African American: 2%; Hispanic: 2%; White: 64%; International: 31%.

ADMISSIONS FACTS AND FIGURES

Phone: (800) 628-3478. **Email:** tigers@fhsu.edu. **Website:** http://www.fhsu.edu. **Application deadlines for fall 2007:** Regular decision: Rolling. Early decision: Not offered. Early action: Send application by: N/A; Decision sent by: N/A. Admission can be deferred. **Application fee:** $30. Common application is not accepted. **To apply online, go to:** http://www.fhsu.edu/admissions. **Admissions requirements/recommenda-**

tions: High school units required (recommended): English: (4); Mathematics: (3); Science: (3); Social studies: (2); History: (1); Total units: (14). Tests: The college uses SAT or ACT scores in admissions decisions. Either SAT or ACT required. For admission to the fall 2007 entering class, the school will accept: ACT with writing, ACT without writing. Campus visit: Recommended. Admissions interview: Neither required nor recommended. Off-campus interview: Not available. **Factors that count in admissions decisions:** *Academic:* Secondary school record: Considered. Class rank: Considered. Letters of recommendation: Not considered. Standardized test scores: Considered. Essay: Not considered. *Nonacademic:* Interview: Not considered. Extracurricular activities: Not considered. Talent/ability: Not considered. Character/personal qualities: Not considered. Alumni/ae relationship: Not considered. Geographical residence: Not considered. State residency: Not considered. Religious affiliation/commitment: Not considered. Minority status: Not considered. Volunteer work: Not considered. Work experience: Not considered. **Admissions statistics for the fall 2005 entering class:** Total applicants: 1,533. Total accepted: 1,393. Freshmen enrolled: 811; 10% were from out of state. Overall acceptance rate: 91%. Non-early acceptance rate: 91%. **Credentials of fall 2005 freshmen:** 9% ranked in the top 10 percent of their high school class; 31% were in the top 25 percent, and 63% were in the top half. (Proportion submitting class standing: 88%.) **Average high school grade point average:** 3.3. **First-year students submitting ACT scores:** 93%. Scores (25/75 percentile): English: 16-24, Math: 17-24, Composite: 18-24.

ACADEMICS

Year founded: 1902. **Academic calendar:** Semester. **Degrees offered:** certificate, associate, bachelor's, master's, post-master's certificate. **Most popular majors:** Information not available. **Major fields of study:** agriculture, agriculture operations, and related sciences; biological and biomedical sciences; business, management, marketing, and related support services; communication, journalism, and related programs; communications technologies/technicians and support services; computer and information sciences and support services; education; English language and literature/letters; foreign languages, literatures, and linguistics; health professions and related clinical sciences; history; liberal arts and sciences studies, and humanities; mathematics and statistics; multi/interdisciplinary studies; philosophy and religious studies; physical sciences; psychology; public administration and social service professions; security and protective services; social sciences; visual and performing arts. **Areas of required coursework:** arts/fine arts, humanities, computer literacy, mathematics, English (including composition), sciences (biological or physical), social science. **Special academic programs:** distance learning, double major, dual enrollment, English as a Second Language (ESL), exchange student program (domestic), external degree program, honors program, independent study, internships, liberal arts/career combination, student-designed major, study abroad, teacher certificate program. **Teacher certification offered in:** special education, elementary, secondary. **Faculty and instruction (2005-2006):** Total instructional faculty: 265 full-time, 82 part-time (57% men; 43% women; 5% minorities). Full-time faculty with Ph.D. or other terminal degree: 62%. Student/faculty ratio: 17/1. Classes of fewer than 20 students: 49%; of 20 to 49 students: 48%; of 50 or more students: 4%. **Freshmen returning for sophomore year:** 70%. **Graduation rates:** Four-year: 24%; five-year: 44%; six-year: 48%. **Graduate study:** 16% of students pursue further study immediately upon graduation; 16% within one year.

COSTS AND FINANCIAL AID

Financial aid office: (785) 628-4408. **Expenses (2006-2007):** Tuition and fees 2006-2007: $3,192 in state, $10,032 out of state; room/board: $5,553. **Financial aid:** Priority filing date for institution's financial aid form: March 15.

CAMPUS LIFE AND EXTRACURRICULAR ACTIVITIES

Campus housing available (% using): coed dorms (12%), women's dorms (40%), men's dorms (39%), sorority housing (1%), fraternity housing (1%), apartments for married students (3%), apartment for single students (4%). Students who live in college-owned, operated, or affiliated housing: 12%. **Clubs and organizations:** Number of student organizations: 105. Activities include: choral groups, concert band, dance, drama/theater, jazz band, marching band, music ensembles, musical theater, pep band, radio station, student government, student newspaper, television station, yearbook. Number of fraternities: 3; sororities: 3. Proportion of men in fraternities: 1%; of women in sororities: 1%. **Sports program (2005-2006):** Member of NCAA II. *Men's intercollegiate varsity sports:* baseball, basketball, cross-country, football, golf, track and field (indoor), track and field (outdoor), wrestling. *Women's intercollegiate varsity sports:* basketball, cross-country, golf, softball, tennis, track and field (indoor), track and field (outdoor), volleyball.

SERVICES AND FACILITIES

Basic services: placement service, day care, health service, health insurance. **Counseling services:** career, academic, psychological, birth control. **For learning-disabled students:** School does not offer a structured program with separate admission and additional fees. Services include: diagnostic testing service, note-taking services, oral tests, readers, extended time for tests, tutors, priority seating, other testing accomodations. **Library:** Number of titles: 2,249,022; number of current serial subscriptions: 1,463. **Information technology resources:** Students are not required to lease or own a computer. Proportion of college-owned housing units wired for high-speed internet access: 100%. **Campus safety:** Security services offered: 24-hour foot and vehicle patrols, late-night transport/escort service, 24-hour emergency telephones, lighted pathways/sidewalks, student patrols, controlled dormitory access (key, security card, etc).

TRANSFER AND INTERNATIONAL STUDENTS

Transfer students: May apply for admission for the following academic terms: Fall, Spring, Summer. Applicants do not need a minimum number of credits to apply. For fall 2005: Transfer applications received: 1,733. Transfer applicants offered admission: 1,704. Transfer applicants enrolled: 1,271. **International students:** Number of foreign undergraduates: 2373 (31% of student body). Number of countries represented: 24. Minimum TOEFL score required: 500 (paper); 173 (computer).

Friends University

- **Address:** 2100 W. University Street, Wichita, KS 67213
- **Website:** http://www.friends.edu
- **Private**
- **Enrollment:** 1,756 full-time; 484 part-time

KEY STATS

✔ **U.S News College Ranking:** fourth tier, Universities–Master's (Midwest)
✔ **ACT Score (25th/75th percentile):** 18-24
✔ **Tuition:** 2006-2007: $16,170

Selectivity: Selective	**Room/board:** $4,970
Acceptance rate: 86%	**Average debt:** $17,750
Student/faculty ratio: 13/1	**Proportion who borrowed:** 100%

UNDERGRADUATE STUDENT BODY STATS

2005-2006 enrollment: 1,756 full-time; 484 part-time. Men: 41%; women: 59%. **Ethnic makeup:** African American: 9%; American-Indian: 2%; Asian American: 1%; Hispanic: 4%; White: 83%; International: 1%. **Religious preference:** Roman Catholic: 15%; Protestant: 68%; Unknown: 17%.

ADMISSIONS FACTS AND FIGURES

Phone: (316) 295-5100. **Email:** learn@friends.edu. **Website:** http://www.friends.edu. **Application deadlines for fall 2007:** Regular decision: Rolling. Early decision: Not offered. Early action: Not offered. Admission cannot be deferred. **Application fee:** $20. Common application is not accepted. **Admissions requirements/recommendations:** High school units required (recommended): English: (3); Mathematics: (3); Science: (1); Foreign language: (2); Social studies: (2); History: (2); Academic electives: (5); Total units: (19). Tests: The college uses SAT or ACT scores in admissions decisions. ACT required. For admission to the fall 2007 entering class, the school will accept: ACT with writing, ACT without writing. Campus visit: Recommended. Admissions interview: Neither required nor recommended. Off-campus interview: May be arranged. **Factors that count in admissions decisions:** *Academic:* Secondary school record: Very important. Class rank: Considered. Letters of recommendation: Considered. Standardized test scores: Very important. Essay: Considered. *Nonacademic:* Interview: Considered. Extracurricular activities: Important. Talent/ability: Considered. Character/personal qualities: Considered. Alumni/ae relationship: Important. Geographical residence: Not considered. State residency: Not considered. Religious affiliation/commitment: Not considered. Minority status: Not considered. Volunteer work: Not considered. Work experience: Not considered. **Other schools with the greatest overlap in applicants:** Emporia State University; Kansas State University; Newman University; Washburn University; Wichita State University. **Admissions statistics for the**

fall 2005 entering class: Total applicants: 914. Total accepted: 782. Freshmen enrolled: 174; 22% were from out of state. Overall acceptance rate: 86%. **Credentials of fall 2005 freshmen:** 15% ranked in the top 10 percent of their high school class; 34% were in the top 25 percent, and 65% were in the top half. (Proportion submitting class standing: 84%.) **Average high school grade point average:** 3.2. **First-year students who submitted SAT scores:** 6%. Scores (25/75 percentile): Verbal: 420-590, Math: 420-640, Combined: 840-1230. **First-year students submitting ACT scores:** 89%. Scores (25/75 percentile): English: 17-25, Math: 17-24, Composite: 18-24.

ACADEMICS

Year founded: 1898. **Academic calendar:** Semester. **Degrees offered:** associate, transfer-associate, terminal-associate, bachelor's, master's, post-master's certificate. **Most popular majors:** 22% education, 11% business/commerce, 10% visual and performing arts, 9% psychology, 6% biology/biological sciences. **Major fields of study:** biological and biomedical sciences; business, management, marketing, and related support services; communication, journalism, and related programs; computer and information sciences and support services; education; English language and literature/letters; foreign languages, literatures, and linguistics; history; liberal arts and sciences studies, and humanities; mathematics and statistics; multi/interdisciplinary studies; parks, recreation, leisure, and fitness studies; philosophy and religious studies; physical sciences; psychology; security and protective services; social sciences; visual and performing arts. **Areas of required coursework:** arts/fine arts, humanities, computer literacy, mathematics, English (including composition), philosophy, foreign languages, sciences (biological or physical), history, social science, other. **Pre-professional programs:** pre-law, pre-dentistry, pre-medicine, pre-theology, pre-veterinary science, pre-optometry, pre-pharmacy. **Special academic programs (% participation):** cross-registration (1%), double major (2%), dual enrollment (.5%), honors program (5%), independent study (5%), internships (15%), liberal arts/career combination (15%), student-designed major (2%), study abroad (1%), teacher certificate program (24%). **Teacher certification offered in:** elementary, middle/junior high, secondary. **Faculty and instruction (2005-2006):** Total instructional faculty: 75 full-time, 78 part-time (48% men; 52% women; 9% minorities). Full-time faculty with Ph.D. or other terminal degree: 64%. Student/faculty ratio: 13/1. Classes of fewer than 20 students: 59%; of 20 to 49 students: 39%; of 50 or more students: 2%. **Advanced Placement and International Baccalaureate credit:** AP tests may be used for: Credit and/or placement. Scores accepted: 4, 5. International Baccalaureate exams may be used for: Credit and/or placement. **Freshmen returning for sophomore year:** 63%. **Graduation rates:** Four-year: 20%; five-year: 39%; six-year: 42%. **Graduate study:** Fields in which graduates pursue further study: Master of Business Administration (MBA), 39%; law, 3%; medicine, 3%; theology (or the seminary), 5%; education, 3%; arts and sciences, 25%.

COSTS AND FINANCIAL AID

Financial aid office: (316) 295-5200. **Expenses (2006-2007):** Tuition and fees 2006-2007: $16,170; room/board: $4,970. Estimated books and supplies: $900; transportation: $1,860; personal expenses: $1,400. **Financial aid:** Priority filing date for institution's financial aid form: March 15. In 2005-2006, 94% of undergraduates applied for financial aid. Of those, 86% were determined to have financial need; 38% had their need fully met. Average financial aid package (proportion receiving): $9,673 (85%). Average amount of gift aid, such as scholarships or grants (proportion receiving): $3,453 (59%). Average amount of self-help aid, such as work study or loans (proportion receiving): $6,214 (85%). Average need-based loan (excluding PLUS or other private loans): $3,480. Among students who received need-based aid, the average percentage of need met: 45%. Among students who received aid based on merit, the average award (and the proportion receiving): $1,427 (12%). The average athletic scholarship (and the proportion receiving): $1,174 (4%). Average amount of debt of borrowers graduating in 2005: $17,750. Proportion who borrowed: 100%.

CAMPUS LIFE AND EXTRACURRICULAR ACTIVITIES

Campus housing available (% using): coed dorms (54%), apartments for married students (0%), apartment for single students (29%), special housing for disabled students (0%), other housing options (17%). Students who live in college-owned, operated, or affiliated housing: 32%. **Student employment:** During the 2005-2006 academic year, 30% of undergraduates worked on campus. Average per-year earnings: $2,040. **Clubs and organizations:** Number of student organizations: 36. Activities include: choral groups, concert band, dance, drama/theater, jazz band, literary magazine, music ensembles, musical theater, pep band, student government, student newspaper, symphony orchestra, yearbook. Number of fraternities: 1; sororities: 0. Proportion of men in fraternities: 10%; Average proportion of students who stay on campus on weekends: 32%. **Sports program (2005-2006):** Member of NAIA. *Men's intercollegiate varsity sports:* baseball, basketball, cheerleading, cross-country, football, golf, soccer, tennis, track and field (indoor), track and field (outdoor). *Women's intercollegiate varsity sports:* basketball, cheerleading, cross-country, soccer, softball, tennis, track and field (indoor), track and field (outdoor), volleyball.

SERVICES AND FACILITIES

Basic services: nonremedial tutoring, placement service, health service, health insurance. **Remedial assistance:** math, writing, study skills. **Counseling services:** career, personal, veteran student, academic, older student, psychological, religious, other. **For learning-disabled students:** School does not offer a structured program with separate admission and additional fees. Total undergraduates in learning-disabled program or receiving services: 23. Services include: remedial math, remedial English, reading machines, tape recorders, other special classes, videotaped classes, untimed tests, note-taking services, oral tests, learning center, readers, extended time for tests, tutors, priority seating, texts on tape, typist/scribe, exams on tape or computer, take home exams, other testing accomodations. **Library:** Number of titles: 68,782; number of current serial subscriptions: 352. **Information technology resources:** Students are not required to lease or own a computer. Number of campus computers available to all students: 346. School has a wireless network. Approximate number of users that can be accommodated: 350. Proportion of college-owned housing units wired for high-speed internet access: 80%. **Campus safety:** Security services offered: 24-hour foot and vehicle patrols, late-night transport/escort service, 24-hour emergency telephones, lighted pathways/sidewalks, student patrols, controlled dormitory access (key, security card, etc).

TRANSFER AND INTERNATIONAL STUDENTS

Transfer students: May apply for admission for the following academic terms: Fall, Spring. Applicants need a minimum number of credits to apply. For fall 2005: Transfer applications received: 309. Transfer applicants offered admission: 257. Transfer applicants enrolled: 147. **International students:** Number of foreign undergraduates: 18 (1% of student body). Number of countries represented: 22. Minimum TOEFL score required: 500 (paper); 173 (computer). Average TOEFL score: 501 (paper).

Kansas State University

- ■ **Address:** Anderson Hall, Manhattan, KS 66506
- ■ **Website:** http://www.ksu.edu
- ■ **Public**
- ■ **Enrollment:** 16,519 full-time; 2,319 part-time

KEY STATS

- ✔ **U.S News College Ranking:** 124, National Universities
- ✔ **ACT Score (25th/75th percentile):** 21-27
- ✔ **Tuition:** 2006-2007: $5,779 in state, $15,514 out of state

Selectivity: More selective	**Room/board:** $6,324
Acceptance rate: 62%	**Average debt:** $19,000
Student/faculty ratio: 21/1	**Proportion who borrowed:** 55%

UNDERGRADUATE STUDENT BODY STATS

2005-2006 enrollment: 16,519 full-time; 2,319 part-time. Men: 51%; women: 49%. **Ethnic makeup:** African American: 3%; American-Indian: 1%; Asian American: 1%; Hispanic: 3%; White: 91%; International: 1%.

ADMISSIONS FACTS AND FIGURES

Phone: (785) 532-6250. **Email:** kstate@ksu.edu. **Website:** http://www.ksu.edu. **Application deadlines for fall 2007:** Regular decision: Rolling. Early decision: Not offered. Early action: Not offered. Admission cannot be deferred. **Application fee:** $30. Common application is not accepted. **To apply online, go to:** http://www.ksu.edu/admit/. **Admissions requirements/recommendations:** High school units required (recommended): English: (4); Mathematics: (3); Science: (3); Social studies: (2); History: (1); Total units: (14). Tests: The college uses SAT or ACT scores in admissions decisions. Either SAT or ACT required. For admission to the fall 2007 entering class, the school will accept: ACT with writing, ACT without writing. Campus visit: Recommended. Admissions interview: Neither required nor recommended. Off-campus interview: Not available. **Factors that count in admissions decisions:** *Academic:* Secondary school record: Very

important. Class rank: Very important. Letters of recommendation: Considered. Standardized test scores: Very important. Essay: Not considered. *Nonacademic:* Interview: Not considered. Extracurricular activities: Not considered. Talent/ability: Not considered. Character/personal qualities: Not considered. Alumni/ae relationship: Not considered. Geographical residence: Not considered. State residency: Not considered. Religious affiliation/commitment: Not considered. Minority status: Not considered. Volunteer work: Not considered. Work experience: Not considered. **Admissions statistics for the fall 2005 entering class:** Total applicants: 7,705. Total accepted: 4,788. Freshmen enrolled: 3,309; Overall acceptance rate: 62%. **Credentials of fall 2005 freshmen:** 32% ranked in the top 10 percent of their high school class; 60% were in the top 25 percent, and 90% were in the top half. (Proportion submitting class standing: 78%.) **First-year students submitting ACT scores:** 88%. Scores (25/75 percentile): English: 20-26, Math: 20-27, Composite: 21-27.

ACADEMICS

Year founded: 1863. **Academic calendar:** Semester. **Degrees offered:** certificate, associate, bachelor's, master's, post-master's certificate, first professional, doctorate. **Most popular majors:** 17% business, management, marketing, and related support services, 11% education, 10% social sciences, 9% agriculture, agriculture operations, and related sciences, 9% engineering. **Major fields of study:** agriculture, agriculture operations, and related sciences; architecture and related services; area, ethnic, cultural, and gender studies; biological and biomedical sciences; business, management, marketing, and related support services; communication, journalism, and related programs; computer and information sciences and support services; education; engineering; engineering technologies/technicians; English language and literature/letters; family and consumer sciences/human sciences; foreign languages, literatures, and linguistics; health professions and related clinical sciences; history; liberal arts and sciences studies, and humanities; mathematics and statistics; mechanic and repair technologies/technicians; multi/interdisciplinary studies; parks, recreation, leisure, and fitness studies; philosophy and religious studies; physical sciences; psychology; public administration and social service professions; social sciences; transportation and materials moving; visual and performing arts. **Areas of required coursework:** humanities, computer literacy, mathematics, English (including composition), sciences (biological or physical), history, social science. **Pre-professional programs:** pre-law, pre-dentistry, pre-medicine, pre-veterinary science, pre-optometry, pre-pharmacy, other. **Special academic programs:** accelerated program, cooperative (work-study plan) program, distance learning, double major, English as a Second Language (ESL), exchange student program (domestic), honors program, independent study, internships, study abroad, teacher certificate program, other. **Teacher certification offered in:** early childhood, special education, elementary, middle/junior high, secondary. **Reserve Officers Training Corps (ROTC):** Army ROTC: Offered on campus; Air Force ROTC: Offered on campus. **Faculty and instruction (2005-2006):** Total instructional faculty: 888 full-time, 159 part-time (63% men; 37% women; 12% minorities). Full-time faculty with Ph.D. or other terminal degree: 85%. Student/faculty ratio: 21/1. Classes of fewer than 20 students: 50%; of 20 to 49 students: 41%; of 50 or more students: 9%. **Advanced Placement and International Baccalaureate credit:** AP tests may be used for: Credit only. Scores accepted: 3, 4, 5. International Baccalaureate exams may be used for: Credit only. **Freshmen returning for sophomore year:** 80%. **Graduation rates:** Four-year: 22%; five-year: 52%; six-year: 56%. **Graduate study:** 17% of students pursue further study within one year.

COSTS AND FINANCIAL AID

Financial aid office: (785) 532-6420. **Expenses (2006-2007):** Tuition and fees 2006-2007: $5,779 in state, $15,514 out of state; room/board: $6,324. Estimated books and supplies: $1,061; transportation: $212; personal expenses: $3,183. **Financial aid:** Priority filing date for institution's financial aid form: March 1. In 2005-2006, 67% of undergraduates applied for financial aid. Of those, 52% were determined to have financial need; 15% had their need fully met. Average financial aid package (proportion receiving): $5,850 (49%). Average amount of gift aid, such as scholarships or grants (proportion receiving): $2,442 (41%). Average amount of self-help aid, such as work study or loans (proportion receiving): $3,620 (48%). Average need-based loan (excluding PLUS or other private loans): $3,505. Among students who received need-based aid, the average percentage of need met: 76%. Among students who received aid based on merit, the average award (and the proportion receiving): $1,918 (6%). The average athletic scholarship (and the proportion receiving): $5,689 (3%). Average amount of debt of borrowers graduating in 2005: $19,000. Proportion who borrowed: 55%.

CAMPUS LIFE AND EXTRACURRICULAR ACTIVITIES

Campus housing available (% using): coed dorms (34%), women's dorms (17%), men's dorms (10%), sorority housing (12%), fraternity housing (18%), apartments for married students (7%), apartment for single students (1%), cooperative housing (1%). Students who live in college-owned, operated, or affiliated housing: 28%. **Student employment:** During the 2005-2006 academic year, 31% of undergraduates worked on campus. Average per-year earnings: $4,467. **Clubs and organizations:** Number of student organizations: 418. Activities include: choral groups, concert band, dance, drama/theater, jazz band, marching band, music ensembles, musical theater, pep band, radio station, student government, student newspaper, symphony orchestra, television station, yearbook. Number of fraternities: 28; sororities: 13. Proportion of men in fraternities: 20%; of women in sororities: 20%. Average proportion of students who stay on campus on weekends: 65%. **Sports program (2005-2006):** Member of NCAA I. *Men's intercollegiate varsity sports:* baseball, basketball, cross-country, football, golf, track and field (indoor), track and field (outdoor). *Women's intercollegiate varsity sports:* basketball, cross-country, equestrian sports, golf, rowing, tennis, track and field (indoor), track and field (outdoor), volleyball.

SERVICES AND FACILITIES

Basic services: nonremedial tutoring, women's center, placement service, day care, health service, health insurance. **Remedial assistance:** math, study skills, other. **Counseling services:** minority student, career, personal, veteran student, academic, psychological. **For learning-disabled students:** School does not offer a structured program with separate admission and additional fees. Total undergraduates in learning-disabled program or receiving services: 216. Services include: remedial math, reading machines, note-taking services, oral tests, readers, extended time for tests, tutors, priority registration, proofreading services, substitution of courses, texts on tape, exams on tape or computer, other testing accomodations. **Library:** Number of titles: 1,775,141; number of current serial subscriptions: 12,247. **Information technology resources:** Students are not required to lease or own a computer. Number of campus computers available to all students: 489. School has a wireless network. Approximate number of users that can be accommodated: 3,750. Proportion of college-owned housing units wired for high-speed internet access: 100%. **Campus safety:** Security services offered: 24-hour foot and vehicle patrols, late-night transport/escort service, 24-hour emergency telephones, lighted pathways/sidewalks, controlled dormitory access (key, security card, etc).

TRANSFER AND INTERNATIONAL STUDENTS

Transfer students: May apply for admission for the following academic terms: Fall, Spring, Summer. Applicants need a minimum number of credits to apply. For fall 2005: Transfer applications received: 2,232. Transfer applicants offered admission: 1,631. Transfer applicants enrolled: 1,723. **International students:** Number of foreign undergraduates: 200 (1% of student body). Number of countries represented: 62. Minimum TOEFL score required: 550 (paper); 213 (computer).

Kansas Wesleyan University

- **Address:** 100 E. Claflin, Salina, KS 67401
- **Website:** http://www.kwu.edu
- **Private; Religious affiliation:** United Methodist
- **Enrollment:** N/A

KEY STATS

✔ **U.S News College Ranking:** third tier, Comp. Coll.–Bachelor's (Midwest)
✔ **ACT Score (25th/75th percentile):** 19-23
✔ **Tuition:** N/A

Selectivity: Selective	Room/board: N/A
Acceptance rate: 96%	Average debt: N/A
Student/faculty ratio: N/A	Proportion who borrowed: N/A

McPherson College

- **Address:** PO Box 1402, McPherson, KS 67460
- **Website:** http://www.mcpherson.edu
- **Private; Religious affiliation:** Church of the Brethren
- **Enrollment:** 426 full-time; 58 part-time

KEY STATS

✔ **U.S News College Ranking:** third tier, Comp. Coll.–Bachelor's (Midwest)
✔ **ACT Score (25th/75th percentile):** 19-24
✔ **Tuition:** 2006-2007: $15,775

Selectivity: Selective	Room/board: $6,050
Acceptance rate: 85%	Average debt: $18,010
Student/faculty ratio: 12/1	Proportion who borrowed: 83%

UNDERGRADUATE STUDENT BODY STATS

2005-2006 enrollment: 426 full-time; 58 part-time. Men: 62%; women: 38%. **Ethnic makeup:** African American: 6%; American-Indian: 1%; Hispanic: 6%; White: 86%. **Religious preference:** Roman Catholic: 13%; Protestant: 1%; Church of the Brethren: 10%; Baptist: 8%; Other: 67%.

ADMISSIONS FACTS AND FIGURES

Phone: (800) 365-7402. **Email:** admiss@mcpherson.edu. **Website:** http://www.mcpherson.edu. **Application deadlines for fall 2007:** Regular decision: Rolling. Early decision: Not offered. Early action: Not offered. Admission can be deferred. **Application fee:** $25. Common application is not accepted. **To apply online, go to:** http://www.mcpherson.edu/admissions/howtoapply/index.asp. **Admissions requirements/recommendations:** Tests: The college uses SAT or ACT scores in admissions decisions. Either SAT or ACT required. For admission to the fall 2007 entering class, the school will accept: ACT with writing, ACT without writing. Campus visit: Recommended. Admissions interview: Neither required nor recommended. Off-campus interview: Not available. **Factors that count in admissions decisions:** *Academic:* Secondary school record: Very important. Class rank: Considered. Letters of recommendation: Considered. Standardized test scores: Very important. Essay: Not considered. *Nonacademic:* Interview: Considered. Extracurricular activities: Considered. Talent/ability: Considered. Character/personal qualities: Considered. Alumni/ae relationship: Considered. Geographical residence: Not considered. State residency: Not considered. Religious affiliation/commitment: Not considered. Minority status: Not considered. Volunteer work: Considered. Work experience: Considered. **Other schools with the greatest overlap in applicants:** Bethany College; Bethel College; Kansas Wesleyan University; Sterling College; Tabor College. **Admissions statistics for the fall 2005 entering class:** Total applicants: 495. Total accepted: 421. Freshmen enrolled: 109; 48% were from out of state. Overall acceptance rate: 85%. **Average high school grade point average:** 3.3. **First-year students who submitted SAT scores:** 23%. Scores (25/75 percentile): Verbal: 410-560, Math: 410-580, Combined: 820-1140. **First-year students submitting ACT scores:** 85%. Scores (25/75 percentile): English: N/A, Math: N/A, Composite: 19-24.

ACADEMICS

Year founded: 1887. **Academic calendar:** 4-1-4. **Degrees offered:** bachelor's. **Most popular majors:** 25% business, management, marketing, and related support services, 11% visual and performing arts, 9% education, 8% biological and biomedical sciences, 7% engineering technologies/technicians. **Major fields of study:** biological and biomedical sciences; business, management, marketing, and related support services; computer and information sciences and support services; education; engineering technologies/technicians; English language and literature/letters; foreign languages, literatures, and linguistics; history; multi/interdisciplinary studies; parks, recreation, leisure, and fitness studies; philosophy and religious studies; physical sciences; psychology; social sciences; visual and performing arts. **Areas of required coursework:** arts/fine arts, computer literacy, mathematics, English (including composition), sciences (biological or physical), history, social science. **Pre-professional programs:** pre-law, pre-dentistry, pre-medicine, pre-veterinary science, pre-optometry, pre-pharmacy, other. **Special academic programs:** cross-registration, double major, dual enrollment, English as a Second Language (ESL), exchange student program (domestic), independent study, internships, student-designed major, study abroad, teacher certificate program. **Teacher certification offered in:** early childhood, special education, elementary, middle/junior high, secondary. **Cooperative education programs:** business, computer science, education, health professions, humanities, natural science, social/behavioral science, technologies, other. **Faculty and instruction (2005-2006):** Total instructional faculty: 35 full-time, 12 part-time (70% men; 30% women; 2% minorities). Full-time faculty with Ph.D. or other terminal degree: 63%. Student/faculty ratio: 12/1. Classes of fewer than 20 students: 80%; of 20 to 49 students: 19%; of 50 or more students: 1%. **Advanced Placement and International Baccalaureate credit:** AP tests may be used for: Credit and/or placement. Scores accepted: 3, 4, 5. International Baccalaureate exams may be used for: Credit and/or placement. **Freshmen returning for sophomore year:** 83%. **Graduation rates:** Four-year: 19%; five-year: 25%; six-year: 32%.

COSTS AND FINANCIAL AID

Financial aid office: (620) 241-0731. **Expenses (2006-2007):** Tuition and fees 2006-2007: $15,775; room/board: $6,050. **Financial aid:** Priority filing date for institution's financial aid form: March 1; deadline: April 1. In 2005-2006, 95% of undergraduates applied for financial aid. Of those, 84% were determined to have financial need; 32% had their need fully met. Average financial aid package (proportion receiving): $16,893 (84%). Average amount of gift aid, such as scholarships or grants (proportion receiving): $5,077 (69%). Average amount of self-help aid, such as work study or loans (proportion receiving): $6,275 (73%). Average need-based loan (excluding PLUS or other private loans): $5,858. Among students who received need-based aid, the average percentage of need met: 88%. Among students who received aid based on merit, the average award (and the proportion receiving): $4,240 (13%). Average amount of debt of borrowers graduating in 2005: $18,010. Proportion who borrowed: 83%.

CAMPUS LIFE AND EXTRACURRICULAR ACTIVITIES

Campus housing available (% using): coed dorms (44%), women's dorms (7%), men's dorms (49%), special housing for disabled students (0%). Students who live in college-owned, operated, or affiliated housing: 72%. **Student employment:** During the 2005-2006 academic year, 24% of undergraduates worked on campus. Average per-year earnings: $1,000. **Clubs and organizations:** Number of student organizations: 13. Activities include: choral groups, concert band, drama/theater, jazz band, music ensembles, musical theater, pep band, student government, student newspaper, yearbook. Number of fraternities: 0; sororities: 0. Average proportion of students who stay on campus on weekends: 60%. **Sports program (2005-2006):** Member of NAIA. **Men's intercollegiate varsity sports:** basketball, cross-country, football, soccer, track and field (indoor), track and field (outdoor). **Women's intercollegiate varsity sports:** basketball, cross-country, soccer, softball, track and field (indoor), track and field (outdoor), volleyball.

SERVICES AND FACILITIES

Basic services: nonremedial tutoring, other. **Remedial assistance:** reading, math, writing, study skills. **Counseling services:** minority student, career, personal, academic, religious. **For learning-disabled students:** Services include: reading machines, note-taking services, oral tests, learning center, extended time for tests, tutors. **Library:** Number of titles: 89,946; number of current serial subscriptions: 4,056. **Information technology resources:** Students are not required to lease or own a computer. Number of campus computers available to all students: 96. School has a wireless network. Proportion of college-owned housing units wired for high-speed internet access: 100%. **Campus safety:** Security services offered: lighted pathways/sidewalks, controlled dormitory access (key, security card, etc).

TRANSFER AND INTERNATIONAL STUDENTS

Transfer students: May apply for admission for the following academic terms: Fall, Winter, Spring. Applicants need a minimum number of credits to apply. For fall 2005: Transfer applications received: 597. Transfer applicants offered admission: 523. Transfer applicants enrolled: 60. **International students:** Number of foreign undergraduates: 2. Number of countries represented: 1. Minimum TOEFL score required: 550 (paper); 213 (computer).

MidAmerica Nazarene University

- **Address:** 2030 E. College Way, Olathe, KS 66062
- **Website:** http://www.mnu.edu
- **Private; Religious affiliation:** Nazarene
- **Enrollment:** 1,198 full-time; 159 part-time

KEY STATS

✔ **U.S News College Ranking:** third tier, Universities–Master's (Midwest)
✔ **ACT Score (25th/75th percentile):** 18-25
✔ **Tuition:** 2006-2007: $15,968

Selectivity: Selective	**Room/board:** $5,830
Acceptance rate: 69%	**Average debt:** $19,222
Student/faculty ratio: 18/1	**Proportion who borrowed:** 80%

UNDERGRADUATE STUDENT BODY STATS

2005-2006 enrollment: 1,198 full-time; 159 part-time. Men: 47%; women: 53%. **Ethnic makeup:** African American: 7%; American-Indian: 1%; Asian American: 1%; Hispanic: 4%; White: 86%; International: 1%. **Religious preference:** Roman Catholic: 8%; Protestant: 36%; No preference: 16%; Nazarene: 38%; Other: 1%.

ADMISSIONS FACTS AND FIGURES

Phone: (913) 791-3380. **Email:** admissions@mnu.edu. **Website:** http://www.mnu.edu. **Application deadlines for fall 2007:** Regular decision: August 1. Early decision: Not offered. Early action: Not offered. Admission can be deferred. **Application fee:** $25. Common application is not accepted. **To apply online, go to:** http://www.mnu.edu/admissions/application.html. **Admissions requirements/recommendations:** High school units required (recommended): English: 4 (4); Mathematics: 3 (3); Science: 3 (3); Foreign language: 1 (1); Social studies: 3 (3); Total units: 14 (14). Tests: The college uses SAT or ACT scores in admissions decisions. Either SAT or ACT required. For admission to the fall 2007 entering class, the school will accept: ACT with writing, ACT without writing. Campus visit: Recommended. Admissions interview: Neither required nor recommended. Off-campus interview: May be arranged. **Factors that count in admissions decisions:** *Academic:* Secondary school record: Very important. Class rank: Very important. Letters of recommendation: Important. Standardized test scores: Very important. Essay: Considered. *Nonacademic:* Interview: Considered. Extracurricular activities: Considered. Talent/ability: Considered. Character/personal qualities: Very important. Alumni/ae relationship: Not considered. Geographical residence: Not considered. State residency: Not considered. Religious affiliation/commitment: Not considered. Minority status: Not considered. Volunteer work: Not considered. Work experience: Not considered. **Other schools with the greatest overlap in applicants:** Kansas State University; Olivet Nazarene University; Southern Nazarene University; University of Kansas. **Admissions statistics for the fall 2005 entering class:** Total applicants: 750. Total accepted: 519. Freshmen enrolled: 216; 34% were from out of state. Overall acceptance rate: 69%. **Credentials of fall 2005 freshmen:** 12% ranked in the top 10 percent of their high school class; 34% were in the top 25 percent, and 65% were in the top half. (Proportion submitting class standing: 84%.) **Average high school grade point average:** 3.4. **First-year students who submitted SAT scores:** 9%. Scores (25/75 percentile): Verbal: 330-560, Math: 340-520, Combined: 670-1080. **First-year students submitting ACT scores:** 100%. Scores (25/75 percentile): English: 18-25, Math: N/A, Composite: 18-25.

ACADEMICS

Year founded: 1966. **Academic calendar:** Semester. **Degrees offered:** associate, bachelor's, master's. **Most popular majors:** 40% human resources management/personnel administration, 8% nursing/registered nurse training (R.N., A.S.N., B.S.N., M.S.N.), 6% business administration and management, 6% elementary education and teaching, 5% psychology. **Major fields of study:** communication, journalism, and related programs; computer and information sciences and support services; education. **Areas of required coursework:** arts/fine arts, humanities, computer literacy, mathematics, English (including composition), philosophy, foreign languages, sciences (biological or physical), history, social science, other. **Pre-professional programs:** pre-law, pre-dentistry, pre-medicine, pre-theology, pre-veterinary science, pre-pharmacy. **Special academic programs:** accelerated program, cross-registration, distance learning, double major, dual enrollment, independent study, internships, study abroad, teacher certificate program. **Teacher certification offered in:** elementary, middle/junior high, secondary.

Reserve Officers Training Corps (ROTC): Army ROTC: Offered at cooperating institution (University of Kansas); Air Force ROTC: Offered at cooperating institution (University of Kansas). **Faculty and instruction (2005-2006):** Total instructional faculty: 71 full-time, 102 part-time (55% men; 45% women; 3% minorities). Full-time faculty with Ph.D. or other terminal degree: 38%. Student/faculty ratio: 18/1. Classes of fewer than 20 students: 62%; of 20 to 49 students: 37%; of 50 or more students: 2%. **Advanced Placement and International Baccalaureate credit:** AP tests may be used for: Credit and/or placement. Scores accepted: 3, 4, 5. International Baccalaureate exams may be used for: Credit and/or placement. **Freshmen returning for sophomore year:** 71%. **Graduation rates:** Six-year: 49%. **Graduate study:** 9% of students pursue further study immediately upon graduation.

COSTS AND FINANCIAL AID

Financial aid office: (913) 791-3298. **Expenses (2006-2007):** Tuition and fees 2006-2007: $15,968; room/board: $5,830. Estimated books and supplies: $1,300; transportation: $1,427; personal expenses: $1,306. **Financial aid:** Priority filing date for institution's financial aid form: March 1. In 2005-2006, 82% of undergraduates applied for financial aid. Of those, 70% were determined to have financial need; Average financial aid package (proportion receiving): $10,028 (70%). Average amount of gift aid, such as scholarships or grants (proportion receiving): $6,260 (61%). Average amount of self-help aid, such as work study or loans (proportion receiving): $5,053 (60%). Average need-based loan (excluding PLUS or other private loans): $5,861. Among students who received need-based aid, the average percentage of need met: 60%. Among students who received aid based on merit, the average award (and the proportion receiving): $2,921 (15%). The average athletic scholarship (and the proportion receiving): $4,293 (5%). Average amount of debt of borrowers graduating in 2005: $19,222. Proportion who borrowed: 80%.

CAMPUS LIFE AND EXTRACURRICULAR ACTIVITIES

Campus housing available (% using): women's dorms (44%), men's dorms (36%), apartment for single students (17%), special housing for disabled students (3%). Students who live in college-owned, operated, or affiliated housing: 53%. **Student employment:** During the 2005-2006 academic year, 34% of undergraduates worked on campus. Average per-year earnings: $1,086. **Clubs and organizations:** Number of student organizations: 26. Activities include: choral groups, concert band, drama/theater, jazz band, music ensembles, pep band, radio station, student government, student newspaper, television station, yearbook. Average proportion of students who stay on campus on weekends: 40%. **Sports program (2005-2006):** Member of NAIA. *Men's intercollegiate varsity sports:* baseball, basketball, cross-country, football, track and field (indoor), track and field (outdoor). *Women's intercollegiate varsity sports:* basketball, cross-country, soccer, softball, track and field (indoor), track and field (outdoor), volleyball.

SERVICES AND FACILITIES

Basic services: nonremedial tutoring, health service. **Remedial assistance:** reading, math, writing, study skills. **Counseling services:** career, personal, psychological. **For learning-disabled students:** School does not offer a structured program with separate admission and additional fees. Total undergraduates in learning-disabled program or receiving services: 20. Services include: remedial math, remedial English, remedial reading, tape recorders, videotaped classes, diagnostic testing service, untimed tests, note-taking services, oral tests, learning center, readers, extended time for tests, tutors, priority seating, texts on tape, exams on tape or computer, other testing accomodations. **Library:** Number of titles: 120,520; number of current serial subscriptions: 1,250. **Information technology resources:** Students are not required to lease or own a computer. Number of campus computers available to all students: 100. School has a wireless network. Approximate number of users that can be accommodated: 1,000. Proportion of college-owned housing units wired for high-speed internet access: 100%. **Campus safety:** Security services offered: 24-hour foot and vehicle patrols, late-night transport/escort service, 24-hour emergency telephones, lighted pathways/sidewalks, student patrols, controlled dormitory access (key, security card, etc).

TRANSFER AND INTERNATIONAL STUDENTS

Transfer students: May apply for admission for the following academic terms: Fall, Winter, Spring, Summer. Applicants need a minimum number of credits to apply. For fall 2005: Transfer applications received: 69. Transfer applicants offered admission: 69. Transfer applicants enrolled: 69. **International students:** Number of foreign undergraduates: 19 (1% of student body). Minimum TOEFL score required: 550 (paper); 214 (computer).

Newman University

- **Address:** 3100 McCormick Avenue, Wichita, KS 67213
- **Website:** http://www.newmanu.edu
- **Private; Religious affiliation:** Roman Catholic
- **Enrollment:** N/A

KEY STATS

- ✔ **U.S News College Ranking:** fourth tier, Universities–Master's (Midwest)
- ✔ **SAT or ACT Score (25th/75th percentile):** N/A
- ✔ **Tuition:** 2006-2007: $17,008

Selectivity: Less selective	Room/board: $5,372
Acceptance rate: N/A	Average debt: $19,054
Student/faculty ratio: N/A	Proportion who borrowed: 70%

Ottawa University

- **Address:** 1001 S. Cedar Street, Ottawa, KS 66067-3399
- **Website:** http://www.ottawa.edu
- **Private; Religious affiliation:** American Baptist
- **Enrollment:** N/A

KEY STATS

- ✔ **U.S News College Ranking:** fourth tier, Comp. Coll.–Bachelor's (Midwest)
- ✔ **SAT or ACT Score (25th/75th percentile):** N/A
- ✔ **Tuition:** N/A

Selectivity: Less selective	Room/board: N/A
Acceptance rate: N/A	Average debt: N/A
Student/faculty ratio: N/A	Proportion who borrowed: N/A

Pittsburg State University

- **Address:** 1701 S. Broadway, Pittsburg, KS 66762
- **Website:** http://www.pittstate.edu
- **Public**
- **Enrollment:** 5,133 full-time; 410 part-time

KEY STATS

- ✔ **U.S News College Ranking:** third tier, Universities–Master's (Midwest)
- ✔ **ACT Score (25th/75th percentile):** 19-24
- ✔ **Tuition:** 2006-2007: $1,765 in state, $4,944 out of state

Selectivity: Selective	Room/board: $4,550
Acceptance rate: 90%	Average debt: $10,742
Student/faculty ratio: 18/1	Proportion who borrowed: 93%

UNDERGRADUATE STUDENT BODY STATS

2005-2006 enrollment: 5,133 full-time; 410 part-time. Men: 52%; women: 48%. **Ethnic makeup:** African American: 2%; American-Indian: 2%; Hispanic: 2%; White: 90%; International: 4%.

ADMISSIONS FACTS AND FIGURES

Phone: (800) 854-7488. **Email:** psuadmit@pittstate.edu. **Website:** http://www.pittstate.edu. **Application deadlines for fall 2007:** Regular decision: Rolling. Early decision: Not offered. Early action: Not offered. Admission can be deferred. **Application fee:** $30. Common application is not accepted. **To apply online, go to:** http://www.pittstate.edu/admit/applyingforms.html. **Admissions requirements/recommendations:** High school units required (recommended): English: 4 (4); Mathematics: 3 (3); Science: 3 (3); Foreign language: 0 (0); Social studies: 2 (2); History: 1 (1); Total units: 14 (14). Tests: The college uses SAT or ACT scores in admissions decisions. ACT required. For admission to the fall 2007 entering class, the school will accept: ACT with writing, ACT without writing. Campus visit: Recommended. Admissions interview: Neither required nor recommended. **Factors that count in admissions decisions:** *Academic:* Secondary school record: Important. Class rank: Important. Standardized test scores:

Important. *Nonacademic:* Interview: Not considered. Extracurricular activities: Not considered. Talent/ability: Not considered. Character/personal qualities: Not considered. Alumni/ae relationship: Not considered. Geographical residence: Not considered. State residency: Considered. Religious affiliation/commitment: Not considered. Minority status: Not considered. Volunteer work: Not considered. Work experience: Not considered. **Other schools with the greatest overlap in applicants:** Emporia State University; Kansas State University; Missouri Southern State University; University of Kansas; Wichita State University. **Admissions statistics for the fall 2005 entering class:** Total applicants: 1,935. Total accepted: 1,738. Freshmen enrolled: 1,003; 25% were from out of state. Overall acceptance rate: 90%. **Credentials of fall 2005 freshmen:** 13% ranked in the top 10 percent of their high school class; 35% were in the top 25 percent, and 70% were in the top half. (Proportion submitting class standing: 89%.) **First-year students submitting ACT scores:** 94%. Scores (25/75 percentile): English: 18-25, Math: 18-24, Composite: 19-24.

ACADEMICS

Year founded: 1903. **Academic calendar:** Semester. **Degrees offered:** certificate, diploma, associate, transfer-associate, bachelor's, master's, post-master's certificate. **Most popular majors:** 10% elementary education and teaching, 7% psychology, 6% automotive engineering technology/technician, 6% nursing/registered nurse training (R.N., A.S.N., B.S.N., M.S.N.), 5% graphic design. **Major fields of study:** biological and biomedical sciences; business, management, marketing, and related support services; communication, journalism, and related programs; communications technologies/technicians and support services; computer and information sciences and support services; education; engineering technologies/technicians; English language and literature/letters; family and consumer sciences/human sciences; foreign languages, literatures, and linguistics; health professions and related clinical sciences; history; liberal arts and sciences studies, and humanities; mathematics and statistics; multi/interdisciplinary studies; parks, recreation, leisure, and fitness studies; physical sciences; psychology; public administration and social service professions; security and protective services; social sciences; visual and performing arts. **Areas of required coursework:** arts/fine arts, humanities, computer literacy, mathematics, English (including composition), sciences (biological or physical), history, social science, other. **Pre-professional programs:** pre-law, pre-dentistry, pre-medicine, pre-pharmacy. **Special academic programs:** accelerated program, cooperative (work-study plan) program, cross-registration, distance learning, double major, dual enrollment, English as a Second Language (ESL), exchange student program (domestic), external degree program, honors program, internships, liberal arts/career combination, study abroad, teacher certificate program. **Teacher certification offered in:** early childhood, special education, elementary, middle/junior high, bilingual/bicultural. **Cooperative education programs:** business, education, engineering, health professions, social/behavioral science, technologies, vocational arts. **Reserve Officers Training Corps (ROTC):** Army ROTC: Offered on campus. **Faculty and instruction (2005-2006):** Total instructional faculty: 291 full-time, 100 part-time (58% men; 42% women; 7% minorities). Full-time faculty with Ph.D. or other terminal degree: 76%. Student/faculty ratio: 18/1. Classes of fewer than 20 students: 36%; of 20 to 49 students: 53%; of 50 or more students: 11%. **Advanced Placement and International Baccalaureate credit:** AP tests may be used for: Placement only. Scores accepted: 3, 4, 5. International Baccalaureate exams may be used for: Credit only. **Freshmen returning for sophomore year:** 75%. **Graduation rates:** Four-year: 51%; five-year: 52%; six-year: 49%. **Graduate study:** 16% of students pursue further study within one year.

COSTS AND FINANCIAL AID

Financial aid office: (620) 235-4240. **Expenses (2006-2007):** Tuition and fees 2006-2007: $1,765 in state, $4,944 out of state; room/board: $4,550. Estimated books and supplies: $800; transportation: $780; personal expenses: $1,980. **Financial aid:** Priority filing date for institution's financial aid form: March 1. In 2005-2006, 73% of undergraduates applied for financial aid. Of those, 59% were determined to have financial need; 13% had their need fully met. Average financial aid package (proportion receiving): $6,890 (57%). Average amount of gift aid, such as scholarships or grants (proportion receiving): $3,365 (45%). Average amount of self-help aid, such as work study or loans (proportion receiving): $3,593 (46%). Average need-based loan (excluding PLUS or other private loans): $3,657. Among students who received need-based aid, the average percentage of need met: 87%. Among students who received aid based on merit, the average award (and the proportion receiving): $1,849 (13%). The average athletic scholarship (and the proportion receiving): $3,834 (3%). Average amount of debt of borrowers graduating in 2005: $10,742. Proportion who borrowed: 93%.

CAMPUS LIFE AND EXTRACURRICULAR ACTIVITIES

Campus housing available (% using): coed dorms (16%), sorority housing (1%), fraternity housing (1%), apartments for married students (0%), other housing options (82%). **Student employment:** During the 2005-2006 academic year, 12% of undergraduates worked on campus. Average per-year earnings: $1,150. **Clubs and organizations:** Number of student organizations: 147. Activities include: choral groups, concert band, dance, drama/theater, jazz band, literary magazine, marching band, music ensembles, musical theater, pep band, radio station, student government, student newspaper, symphony orchestra, television station, yearbook. Number of fraternities: 7; sororities: 3. Proportion of men in fraternities: 6%; of women in sororities: 7%. **Sports program (2005-2006):** Member of NCAA II. *Men's intercollegiate varsity sports:* baseball, basketball, cross-country, football, golf, track and field (indoor), track and field (outdoor). *Women's intercollegiate varsity sports:* basketball, cross-country, softball, track and field (indoor), track and field (outdoor), volleyball.

SERVICES AND FACILITIES

Basic services: placement service, health service. **Counseling services:** minority student, career, military, personal, veteran student, academic, older student, psychological, birth control, religious. **For learning-disabled students:** School does not offer a structured program with separate admission and additional fees. Total undergraduates in learning-disabled program or receiving services: 133. Services include: tape recorders, diagnostic testing service, untimed tests, note-taking services, oral tests, learning center, readers, extended time for tests, tutors, priority seating, texts on tape, typist/scribe, other testing accomodations. **Library:** Number of titles: 862,417; number of current serial subscriptions: 6,722. **Information technology resources:** Students are not required to lease or own a computer. School has a wireless network. Proportion of college-owned housing units wired for high-speed internet access: 100%. **Campus safety:** Security services offered: 24-hour foot and vehicle patrols, 24-hour emergency telephones, lighted pathways/sidewalks, controlled dormitory access (key, security card, etc).

TRANSFER AND INTERNATIONAL STUDENTS

Transfer students: May apply for admission for the following academic terms: Fall, Spring, Summer. Applicants need a minimum number of credits to apply. For fall 2005: Transfer applications received: 842. Transfer applicants offered admission: 751. Transfer applicants enrolled: 539. **International students:** Number of foreign undergraduates: 218 (4% of student body). Number of countries represented: 217. Minimum TOEFL score required: 520 (paper); 190 (computer). Average TOEFL score: 520 (paper).

Southwestern College

- **Address:** 100 College Street, Winfield, KS 67156-2499
- **Website:** http://www.sckans.edu
- **Private; Religious affiliation:** United Methodist
- **Enrollment:** 569 full-time; 694 part-time

KEY STATS
✔ **U.S News College Ranking:** 35, Comp. Coll.–Bachelor's (Midwest)
✔ **ACT Score (25th/75th percentile):** 19-26
✔ **Tuition:** 2006-2007: $16,900

Selectivity: More selective	**Room/board:** $5,438
Acceptance rate: 34%	**Average debt:** $17,858
Student/faculty ratio: 13/1	**Proportion who borrowed:** 65%

UNDERGRADUATE STUDENT BODY STATS

2005-2006 enrollment: 569 full-time; 694 part-time. Men: 50%; women: 50%. **Ethnic makeup:** African American: 8%; American-Indian: 2%; Asian American: 1%; Hispanic: 4%; White: 83%; International: 2%. **Religious preference:** Roman Catholic: 3%; Protestant: 15%; No preference: 28%; Unknown: 41%; United Methodist: 11%.

ADMISSIONS FACTS AND FIGURES

Phone: (620) 229-6236. **Email:** scadmit@sckans.edu. **Website:** http://www.sckans.edu. **Application deadlines for fall 2007:** Regular decision: August 1. Early decision: Not offered. Early action: Not offered. Admission can be deferred. **Application fee:** $20. Common application is accepted. **To apply online, go to:** http://www.sckans.edu/campus/admission/apply.html. **Admissions requirements/recommendations:** High school units required (recommended): English: 4; Mathematics: 3; Science: 2; Foreign language: (1); Social studies: 1; History: 1; Total units: 12 (1). Tests: The college uses SAT or ACT scores in admissions decisions. Either SAT or ACT required. For admission to the fall 2007 entering class, the school will accept: ACT with writing, ACT without writing. Campus visit: Recommended. Admissions interview: Required. Off-campus interview: May be arranged. **Factors that count in admissions decisions: *Academic:*** Secondary school record: Very important. Class rank: Considered. Letters of recommendation: Considered. Standardized test scores: Very important. Essay: Very important. ***Nonacademic:*** Interview: Important. Extracurricular activities: Considered. Talent/ability: Considered. Character/personal qualities: Important. Alumni/ae relationship: Considered. Geographical residence: Not considered. State residency: Not considered. Religious affiliation/commitment: Not considered. Minority status: Not considered. Volunteer work: Considered. Work experience: Considered. **Other schools with the greatest overlap in applicants:** Emporia State University; Kansas State University; University of Kansas; Wichita State University. **Admissions statistics for the fall 2005 entering class:** Total applicants: 494. Total accepted: 167. Freshmen enrolled: 136; 40% were from out of state. Overall acceptance rate: 34%. **Credentials of fall 2005 freshmen:** 21% ranked in the top 10 percent of their high school class; 45% were in the top 25 percent, and 75% were in the top half. (Proportion submitting class standing: 92%.) **Average high school grade point average:** 3.4. **First-year students who submitted SAT scores:** 14%. Scores (25/75 percentile): Verbal: 440-550, Math: 410-590, Combined: 850-1140. **First-year students submitting ACT scores:** 91%. Scores (25/75 percentile): English: 19-25, Math: 18-25, Composite: 19-26.

ACADEMICS

Year founded: 1885. **Academic calendar:** Semester. **Degrees offered:** bachelor's, master's. **Most popular majors:** 16% business administration and management, 13% elementary education and teaching, 13% nursing/registered nurse training (R.N., A.S.N., B.S.N., M.S.N.), 10% biology/biological sciences, 10% music. **Major fields of study:** biological and biomedical sciences; business, management, marketing, and related support services; communication, journalism, and related programs; computer and information sciences and support services; education; engineering; English language and literature/letters; health professions and related clinical sciences; history; liberal arts and sciences studies, and humanities; mathematics and statistics; parks, recreation, leisure, and fitness studies; philosophy and religious studies; physical sciences; psychology; social sciences; visual and performing arts. **Areas of required coursework:** English (including composition), other. **Special academic programs (% participation):** distance learning (61%), double major (19%), dual enrollment (0%), exchange student program (domestic) (0%), honors program (6%), independent study (10%), internships (4%), student-designed major (0%), study abroad (0%), teacher certificate program (7%). **Teacher certification offered in:** early childhood, elementary, middle/junior high, secondary. **Faculty and instruction (2005-2006):** Total instructional faculty: 46 full-time, 98 part-time (58% men; 42% women; 8% minorities). Full-time faculty with Ph.D. or other terminal degree: 52%. Student/faculty ratio: 13/1. Classes of fewer than 20 students: 83%; of 20 to 49 students: 16%; of 50 or more students: 2%. **Advanced Placement and International Baccalaureate credit:** International Baccalaureate exams may be used for: Credit only. **Freshmen returning for sophomore year:** 69%. **Graduation rates:** Four-year: 42%; five-year: 53%; six-year: 55%.

COSTS AND FINANCIAL AID

Financial aid office: (620) 229-6215. **Expenses (2006-2007):** Tuition and fees 2006-2007: $16,900; room/board: $5,438. Estimated books and supplies: $600; transportation: $2,208; personal expenses: $2,679. **Financial aid:** Priority filing date for institution's financial aid form: April 1; deadline: August 1. In 2005-2006, 86% of undergraduates applied for financial aid. Of those, 77% were determined to have financial need; 43% had their need fully met. Average financial aid package (proportion receiving): $16,151 (75%). Average amount of gift aid, such as scholarships or grants (proportion receiving): $9,175 (75%). Average amount of self-help aid, such as work study or loans (proportion receiving): $6,499 (61%). Average need-based loan (excluding PLUS or other private loans): $5,899. Among students who received need-based aid, the average percentage of need met: 81%. Among students who received aid based on merit, the average award (and the proportion receiving): $6,356 (20%). The average athletic scholarship (and the proportion receiving): $2,718 (9%). Average amount of debt of borrowers graduating in 2005: $17,858. Proportion who borrowed: 65%.

CAMPUS LIFE AND EXTRACURRICULAR ACTIVITIES

Campus housing available (% using): coed dorms (13%), women's dorms (21%), men's dorms (26%), apartments for married students (0%), apartment for single students (40%), special housing for disabled students (0%). Students who live in college-owned, operated, or affiliated housing: 30%. **Student employment:** During the 2005-2006 academic year, 20% of undergraduates worked on campus. Average per-year earnings: $900. **Clubs and organizations:** Number of student organizations: 18. Activities include: choral groups, concert band, dance, drama/theater, jazz band, literary magazine, music ensembles, musical theater, pep band, radio station, student government, student newspaper, student film society, symphony orchestra, television station, yearbook. Number of fraternities: 2; sororities: 1. Proportion of men in fraternities: 15%; of women in sororities: 12%. Average proportion of students who stay on campus on weekends: 60%. **Sports program (2005-2006):** Member of NAIA. ***Men's intercollegiate varsity sports:*** basketball, cross-country, football, golf, soccer, tennis, track and field (indoor), track and field (outdoor). ***Women's intercollegiate varsity sports:*** basketball, cross-country, golf, soccer, softball, tennis, track and field (indoor), track and field (outdoor), volleyball.

SERVICES AND FACILITIES

Basic services: nonremedial tutoring, placement service, health service. **Remedial assistance:** reading, math, writing, study skills, other. **Counseling services:** career, personal, academic, psychological, birth control, religious. **For learning-disabled students:** School does not offer a structured program with separate admission and additional fees. **Library:** Number of titles: 66,540; number of current serial subscriptions: 138. **Information technology resources:** Students are required to lease or own a computer. Number of campus computers available to all students: 600. School has a wireless network. Approximate number of users that can be accommodated: 500. Proportion of college-owned housing units wired for high-speed internet access: 100%. **Campus safety:** Security services offered: 24-hour foot and vehicle patrols, late-night transport/escort service, 24-hour emergency telephones, lighted pathways/sidewalks, controlled dormitory access (key, security card, etc).

TRANSFER AND INTERNATIONAL STUDENTS

Transfer students: May apply for admission for the following academic terms: Fall, Spring. Applicants need a minimum number of credits to apply. **International students:** Number of foreign undergraduates: 20 (2% of student body). Number of countries represented: 11. Minimum TOEFL score required: 550 (paper); 213 (computer). Average TOEFL score: 570 (paper).

Sterling College

- **Address:** PO Box 98, Sterling, KS 67579
- **Website:** http://www.sterling.edu
- **Private; Religious affiliation:** Presbyterian
- **Enrollment:** 433 full-time; 61 part-time

KEY STATS

✔ **U.S News College Ranking:** third tier, Comp. Coll.–Bachelor's (Midwest)
✔ **ACT Score (25th/75th percentile):** 19-25
✔ **Tuition:** 2005-2006: $13,806

Selectivity: Selective	**Room/board:** $6,086
Acceptance rate: 56%	**Average debt:** N/A
Student/faculty ratio: 10/1	**Proportion who borrowed:** N/A

UNDERGRADUATE STUDENT BODY STATS

2005-2006 enrollment: 433 full-time; 61 part-time. Men: 52%; women: 48%. **Ethnic makeup:** African American: 9%; American-Indian: 2%; Asian American: 1%; Hispanic: 6%; White: 82%; International: 1%. **Religious preference:** Roman Catholic: 9%; Protestant: 53%; No preference: 29%; Presbyterian: 9%.

ADMISSIONS FACTS AND FIGURES

Phone: (800) 346-1017. **Email:** admissions@sterling.edu. **Website:** http://www.sterling.edu. **Application deadlines for fall 2007:** Regular decision: Rolling. Early decision: Not offered. Early action: Send application by: November 15; Decision sent by: December 1. Admission cannot be deferred. **Application fee:** $25. Common application is accepted. **Admissions requirements/recommendations:** High school units required (recommended):

English: 4 (4); Mathematics: 3 (3); Science: 3 (3); Foreign language: 2 (2); Social studies: 1 (1); History: 2 (2); Academic electives: 1 (1); Total units: 18 (18). **Tests:** The college uses SAT or ACT scores in admissions decisions. Either SAT or ACT required. For admission to the fall 2007 entering class, the school will accept: ACT with writing, ACT without writing. Campus visit: Recommended. Admissions interview: Recommended. Off-campus interview: May be arranged. **Factors that count in admissions decisions: *Academic:*** Secondary school record: Very important. Class rank: Considered. Letters of recommendation: Important. Standardized test scores: Very important. Essay: Important. ***Nonacademic:*** Interview: Important. Extracurricular activities: Important. Talent/ability: Considered. Character/personal qualities: Very important. Alumni/ae relationship: Considered. Geographical residence: Not considered. State residency: Not considered. Religious affiliation/commitment: Important. Minority status: Not considered. Volunteer work: Important. Work experience: Considered. **Other schools with the greatest overlap in applicants:** Bethany College; Kansas State University; Kansas Wesleyan University; McPherson College; Tabor College. **Admissions statistics for the fall 2005 entering class:** Total applicants: 541. Total accepted: 305. Freshmen enrolled: 127; 48% were from out of state. Overall acceptance rate: 56%. Non-early acceptance rate: 56%. **Credentials of fall 2005 freshmen:** 11% ranked in the top 10 percent of their high school class; 31% were in the top 25 percent, and 67% were in the top half. (Proportion submitting class standing: 87%.) **Average high school grade point average:** 3.3. **First-year students who submitted SAT scores:** 17%. Scores (25/75 percentile): Verbal: 420-510, Math: 430-520, Combined: 850-1030. **First-year students submitting ACT scores:** 83%. Scores (25/75 percentile): English: 17-24, Math: 18-24, Composite: 19-25.

ACADEMICS

Year founded: 1887. **Academic calendar:** 4-1-4. **Degrees offered:** bachelor's. **Most popular majors:** 21% elementary education and teaching, 10% business administration and management, 8% biology/biological sciences, 7% health and physical education, 7% religious education. **Major fields of study:** biological and biomedical sciences; business, management, marketing, and related support services; communication, journalism, and related programs; computer and information sciences and support services; education; English language and literature/letters; health professions and related clinical sciences; history; mathematics and statistics; multi/interdisciplinary studies; parks, recreation, leisure, and fitness studies; philosophy and religious studies; physical sciences; theology and religious vocations; visual and performing arts. **Areas of required coursework:** arts/fine arts, humanities, computer literacy, mathematics, English (including composition), philosophy, sciences (biological or physical), history, social science, other. **Pre-professional programs:** pre-dentistry, pre-medicine, pre-theology, pre-veterinary science. **Special academic programs (% participation):** cross-registration (1%), double major (9%), dual enrollment, independent study (15%), internships (73%), student-designed major (5%), study abroad (1%), teacher certificate program (25%). **Teacher certification offered in:** special education, elementary, middle/junior high, secondary. **Faculty and instruction (2005-2006):** Total instructional faculty: 40 full-time, 21 part-time (64% men; 36% women; 2% minorities). Full-time faculty with Ph.D. or other terminal degree: 50%. Student/faculty ratio: 10/1. Classes of fewer than 20 students: 76%; of 20 to 49 students: 24%; of 50 or more students: 1%. **Advanced Placement and International Baccalaureate credit:** AP tests may be used for: Credit and/or placement. Scores accepted: 3, 4, 5. International Baccalaureate exams may be used for: Credit and/or placement. **Freshmen returning for sophomore year:** 64%. **Graduation rates:** Four-year: 55%; five-year: 62%; six-year: 46%.

COSTS AND FINANCIAL AID

Financial aid office: (620) 278-4207. **Expenses (2005-2006):** Tuition and fees 2005-2006: $13,806; room/board: $6,086. Estimated books and supplies: $600; transportation: $1,100; personal expenses: $500. **Financial aid:** Priority filing date for institution's financial aid form: April 1.

CAMPUS LIFE AND EXTRACURRICULAR ACTIVITIES

Campus housing available (% using): women's dorms (49%), men's dorms (51%). Students who live in college-owned, operated, or affiliated housing: 71%. **Student employment:** During the 2005-2006 academic year, 42% of undergraduates worked on campus. Average per-year earnings: $1,100. **Clubs and organizations:** Number of student organizations: 15. Activities include: choral groups, concert band, drama/theater, jazz band, literary magazine, music ensembles, musical theater, pep band, radio station, student government, student newspaper, yearbook. Number of fraternities: 0; sororities: 0. Average proportion of students who stay on campus on weekends: 65%. **Sports program (2005-2006):** Member of NAIA. ***Men's intercolle-***

giate varsity sports: baseball, basketball, cross-country, football, soccer, track and field (indoor), track and field (outdoor). ***Women's intercollegiate varsity sports:*** basketball, cross-country, soccer, softball, track and field (indoor), track and field (outdoor), volleyball.

SERVICES AND FACILITIES

Basic services: nonremedial tutoring, health insurance. **Remedial assistance:** math, writing, study skills. **Counseling services:** personal, academic, religious. **For learning-disabled students:** School does not offer a structured program with separate admission and additional fees. Total undergraduates in learning-disabled program or receiving services: 10. Services include: remedial math, remedial English, tape recorders, diagnostic testing service, untimed tests, note-taking services, oral tests, learning center, readers, extended time for tests, tutors. **Library:** Number of titles: 77,536; number of current serial subscriptions: 270. **Information technology resources:** Students are not required to lease or own a computer. Number of campus computers available to all students: 125. School has a wireless network. Approximate number of users that can be accommodated: 250. Proportion of college-owned housing units wired for high-speed internet access: 100%. **Campus safety:** Security services offered: lighted pathways/sidewalks, controlled dormitory access (key, security card, etc).

TRANSFER AND INTERNATIONAL STUDENTS

Transfer students: May apply for admission for the following academic terms: Fall, Winter, Spring. Applicants do not need a minimum number of credits to apply. For fall 2005: Transfer applications received: 143. Transfer applicants offered admission: 95. Transfer applicants enrolled: 46. **International students:** Number of foreign undergraduates: 4 (1% of student body). Number of countries represented: 5. Minimum TOEFL score required: 520 (paper); 190 (computer).

Tabor College

- **Address:** 400 S. Jefferson, Hillsboro, KS 67063
- **Website:** http://www.tabor.edu
- **Private; Religious affiliation:** Mennonite Brethren
- **Enrollment:** 483 full-time; 115 part-time

KEY STATS

✔ **U.S News College Ranking:** 50, Comp. Coll.–Bachelor's (Midwest)
✔ **ACT Score (25th/75th percentile):** 20-27
✔ **Tuition:** 2006-2007: $16,744

Selectivity: Selective	**Room/board:** $5,910
Acceptance rate: 100%	**Average debt:** $20,180
Student/faculty ratio: 11/1	**Proportion who borrowed:** 82%

UNDERGRADUATE STUDENT BODY STATS

2005-2006 enrollment: 483 full-time; 115 part-time. Men: 52%; women: 48%. **Ethnic makeup:** African American: 5%; American-Indian: 1%; Asian American: 1%; Hispanic: 4%; White: 88%; International: 1%. **Religious preference:** Roman Catholic: 5%; Protestant: 55%; Unknown: 7%; Mennonite Brethren: 31%.

ADMISSIONS FACTS AND FIGURES

Phone: (620) 947-3121. **Email:** admissions@tabor.edu. **Website:** http://www.tabor.edu. **Application deadlines for fall 2007:** Regular decision: Rolling. Early decision: Send application by: December 31; Decision sent by: N/A. Early action: Not offered. Admission cannot be deferred. **Application fee:** $20. Common application is accepted. **To apply online, go to:** http://www.tabor.edu/admissions/apply.php. **Admissions requirements/recommendations:** High school units required (recommended): English: (4); Mathematics: (3); Science: (3); Foreign language: (1); Social studies: (2); History: (2); Total units: (17). **Tests:** The college uses SAT or ACT scores in admissions decisions. Either SAT or ACT required. For admission to the fall 2007 entering class, the school will accept: ACT with writing, ACT without writing. Campus visit: Recommended. Admissions interview: Recommended. Off-campus interview: May be arranged. **Factors that count in admissions decisions: *Academic:*** Secondary school record: Very important. Class rank: Not considered. Letters of recommendation: Very important. Standardized test scores: Very important. Essay: Important. ***Nonacademic:*** Interview: Important. Extracurricular activities: Not considered. Talent/ability: Not considered. Character/personal qualities: Very important. Alumni/ae relationship: Considered. Geographical residence: Considered. State residency: Considered. Religious affiliation/commitment: Important. Minority status: Not considered. Volunteer work: Considered. Work experience: Not considered. **Other schools with the greatest overlap in applicants:** Bethel College; John Brown University; MidAmerica Nazarene University; Sterling College. **Admissions statistics for the fall 2005 entering class:** Total applicants: 234. Total accepted: 234. Freshmen enrolled: 124; 41% were from out of state. Accepted through early-decision or early-action plans: 63%. Overall acceptance rate: 100%. Early-decision acceptance rate: 56%. **Credentials of fall 2005 freshmen:** 24% ranked in the top 10 percent of their high school class; 53% were in the top 25 percent, and 74% were in the top half. (Proportion submitting class standing: 91%.) **Average high school grade point average:** 3.5. **First-year students who submitted SAT scores:** 6%. Scores (25/75 percentile): Verbal: N/A, Math: N/A, Combined: N/A. **First-year students submitting ACT scores:** 94%. Scores (25/75 percentile): English: 19-28, Math: 19-27, Composite: 20-27.

ACADEMICS
Year founded: 1908. **Academic calendar:** 4-1-4. **Degrees offered:** associate, bachelor's, master's. **Most popular majors:** 19% business, management, marketing, and related support services, 19% philosophy and religious studies, 16% education, 12% health professions and related clinical sciences, 7% visual and performing arts. **Major fields of study:** biological and biomedical sciences; business, management, marketing, and related support services; communication, journalism, and related programs; computer and information sciences and support services; education; English language and literature/letters; health professions and related clinical sciences; history; liberal arts and sciences studies, and humanities; mathematics and statistics; multi/interdisciplinary studies; parks, recreation, leisure, and fitness studies; philosophy and religious studies; physical sciences; psychology; social sciences; theology and religious vocations; visual and performing arts. **Areas of required coursework:** arts/fine arts, humanities, computer literacy, mathematics, English (including composition), philosophy, sciences (biological or physical), history, social science, other. **Pre-professional programs:** pre-law, pre-dentistry, pre-medicine, pre-theology, pre-veterinary science, pre-optometry, pre-pharmacy. **Special academic programs (% participation):** accelerated program (33%), cross-registration (2%), double major (13%), dual enrollment (24%), independent study (53%), internships (52%), student-designed major (1%), study abroad (4%), teacher certificate program (17%). **Teacher certification offered in:** early childhood, special education, elementary, secondary. **Faculty and instruction (2005-2006):** Total instructional faculty: 34 full-time, 22 part-time (68% men; 32% women; 2% minorities). Full-time faculty with Ph.D. or other terminal degree: 65%. Student/faculty ratio: 11/1. Classes of fewer than 20 students: 76%; of 20 to 49 students: 24%; of 50 or more students: 1%. **Advanced Placement and International Baccalaureate credit:** AP tests may be used for: Credit and/or placement. Scores accepted: 3, 4, 5. International Baccalaureate exams may be used for: Credit and/or placement. **Freshmen returning for sophomore year:** 72%. **Graduation rates:** Four-year: 40%; five-year: 46%; six-year: 46%. **Graduate study:** 15% of students pursue further study within one year; 20% within five years. Fields in which graduates pursue further study: Master of Business Administration (MBA), 8%; law, 5%; medicine, 15%; dentistry, 2%; theology (or the seminary), 8%; education, 20%; arts and sciences, 30%; veterinary medicine, 12%.

COSTS AND FINANCIAL AID
Financial aid office: (620) 947-3121. **Expenses (2006-2007):** Tuition and fees 2006-2007: $16,744; room/board: $5,910. Estimated books and supplies: $700; transportation: $2,000; personal expenses: $3,000. **Financial aid:** Priority filing date for institution's financial aid form: March 1. In 2005-2006, 95% of undergraduates applied for financial aid. Of those, 74% were determined to have financial need; 35% had their need fully met. Average financial aid package (proportion receiving): $15,794 (74%). Average amount of gift aid, such as scholarships or grants (proportion receiving): $3,482 (59%). Average amount of self-help aid, such as work study or loans (proportion receiving): $7,072 (67%). Average need-based loan (excluding PLUS or other private loans): $7,072. Among students who received need-based aid, the average percentage of need met: 89%. Among students who received aid based on merit, the average award (and the proportion receiving): $5,086 (20%). The average athletic scholarship (and the proportion receiving): $3,081 (53%). Average amount of debt of borrowers graduating in 2005: $20,180. Proportion who borrowed: 82%.

CAMPUS LIFE AND EXTRACURRICULAR ACTIVITIES
Campus housing available (% using): women's dorms (43%), men's dorms (57%). Students who live in college-owned, operated, or affiliated housing:

80%. **Student employment:** During the 2005-2006 academic year, 62% of undergraduates worked on campus. Average per-year earnings: $550. **Clubs and organizations:** Number of student organizations: 9. Activities include: choral groups, concert band, drama/theater, music ensembles, musical theater, pep band, student government, student newspaper, yearbook. Number of fraternities: 0; sororities: 0. Average proportion of students who stay on campus on weekends: 70%. **Sports program (2005-2006):** Member of NAIA. **Men's intercollegiate varsity sports:** baseball, basketball, cheerleading, cross-country, football, soccer, tennis, track and field (indoor), track and field (outdoor). **Women's intercollegiate varsity sports:** basketball, cheerleading, cross-country, soccer, softball, tennis, track and field (indoor), track and field (outdoor), volleyball.

SERVICES AND FACILITIES
Basic services: nonremedial tutoring, placement service, health insurance, other. **Remedial assistance:** reading, math, writing, study skills. **Counseling services:** minority student, career, personal, academic, older student, religious. **For learning-disabled students:** School does not offer a structured program with separate admission and additional fees. Total undergraduates in learning-disabled program or receiving services: 5. Services include: remedial math, remedial English, remedial reading, tape recorders, other special classes, untimed tests, note-taking services, oral tests, learning center, readers, extended time for tests, tutors, proofreading services, typist/scribe, other testing accomodations. **Library:** Number of titles: 81,384; number of current serial subscriptions: 146. **Information technology resources:** Students are not required to lease or own a computer. Number of campus computers available to all students: 55. School has a wireless network. Proportion of college-owned housing units wired for high-speed internet access: 100%. **Campus safety:** Security services offered: lighted pathways/sidewalks, controlled dormitory access (key, security card, etc).

TRANSFER AND INTERNATIONAL STUDENTS
Transfer students: May apply for admission for the following academic terms: Fall, Winter, Spring. Applicants need a minimum number of credits to apply. For fall 2005: Transfer applications received: 57. Transfer applicants offered admission: 57. Transfer applicants enrolled: 44. **International students:** Number of foreign undergraduates: 5 (1% of student body). Number of countries represented: 6. Minimum TOEFL score required: 525 (paper); 195 (computer).

University of Kansas

■ **Address:** 1502 Iowa Street, Lawrence, KS 66045-7576
■ **Website:** http://www.ku.edu
■ **Public**
■ **Enrollment:** 18,888 full-time; 2,503 part-time

KEY STATS
✔ **U.S News College Ranking:** 88, National Universities
✔ **ACT Score (25th/75th percentile):** 22-27
✔ **Tuition:** 2005-2006: $5,413 in state, $13,866 out of state

Selectivity: More selective	**Room/board:** $5,502
Acceptance rate: 74%	**Average debt:** $17,243
Student/faculty ratio: 20/1	**Proportion who borrowed:** 42%

UNDERGRADUATE STUDENT BODY STATS
2005-2006 enrollment: 18,888 full-time; 2,503 part-time. Men: 49%; women: 51%. **Ethnic makeup:** African American: 4%; American-Indian: 1%; Asian American: 4%; Hispanic: 3%; White: 85%; International: 3%.

ADMISSIONS FACTS AND FIGURES
Phone: (785) 864-3911. **Email:** adm@ku.edu. **Website:** http://www.ku.edu. **Application deadlines for fall 2007:** Regular decision: April 1. Early decision: Not offered. Early action: Not offered. Admission cannot be deferred. **Application fee:** $30. Common application is not accepted. **To apply online, go to:** http://www.admissions.ku.edu. **Admissions requirements/recommendations:** High school units required (recommended): English: 4 (4); Mathematics: 3 (4); Science: 3 (3); Foreign language: (2); Social studies: 3 (3); Total units: 14 (17). Tests: The college uses SAT or ACT scores in admissions decisions. Either SAT or ACT required. For admission to the fall 2007 entering class, the school will accept: ACT with writing, ACT without writing. Campus visit: Recommended. Admissions interview: Neither required

nor recommended. Off-campus interview: Not available. **Factors that count in admissions decisions: Academic:** Secondary school record: Very important. Class rank: Very important. Letters of recommendation: Not considered. Standardized test scores: Very important. Essay: Not considered. *Nonacademic:* Interview: Not considered. Extracurricular activities: Not considered. Talent/ability: Not considered. Character/personal qualities: Not considered. Alumni/ae relationship: Not considered. Geographical residence: Not considered. State residency: Not considered. Religious affiliation/commitment: Not considered. Minority status: Not considered. Volunteer work: Not considered. Work experience: Not considered. **Other schools with the greatest overlap in applicants:** Kansas State University; University of Colorado–Boulder; University of Missouri–Columbia; University of Oklahoma; University of Texas–Austin. **Admissions statistics for the fall 2005 entering class:** Total applicants: 10,030. Total accepted: 7,435. Freshmen enrolled: 4,201; 27% were from out of state. Overall acceptance rate: 74%. **Size of waiting list:** 202 applicants; enrolled from waiting list: 141. **Credentials of fall 2005 freshmen:** 28% ranked in the top 10 percent of their high school class; 55% were in the top 25 percent, and 88% were in the top half. (Proportion submitting class standing: 74%.) **Average high school grade point average:** 3.4. **First-year students submitting ACT scores:** 99%. Scores (25/75 percentile): English: N/A, Math: N/A, Composite: 22-27.

ACADEMICS

Year founded: 1866. **Academic calendar:** Semester. **Degrees offered:** bachelor's, master's, post-master's certificate, first professional, doctorate. **Most popular majors:** 11% business, management, marketing, and related support services, 7% biological and biomedical sciences, 7% journalism, 7% psychology, 6% speech and rhetorical studies. **Major fields of study:** architecture and related services; area, ethnic, cultural, and gender studies; biological and biomedical sciences; business, management, marketing, and related support services; communication, journalism, and related programs; computer and information sciences and support services; education; engineering; English language and literature/letters; foreign languages, literatures, and linguistics; health professions and related clinical sciences; history; liberal arts and sciences studies, and humanities; mathematics and statistics; multi/interdisciplinary studies; natural resources and conservation; parks, recreation, leisure, and fitness studies; philosophy and religious studies; physical sciences; psychology; public administration and social service professions; social sciences; visual and performing arts. **Areas of required coursework:** humanities, mathematics, English (including composition), foreign languages, sciences (biological or physical), history, social science, other. **Pre-professional programs:** pre-law, pre-dentistry, pre-medicine, pre-veterinary science, pre-optometry. **Special academic programs (% participation):** accelerated program, cooperative (work-study plan) program, distance learning (2%), double major (10%), dual enrollment, English as a Second Language (ESL) (4%), honors program (18%), independent study, internships, liberal arts/career combination, student-designed major, study abroad (20%), teacher certificate program (4%). **Teacher certification offered in:** early childhood, special education, elementary, middle/junior high, secondary. **Cooperative education programs:** engineering. **Reserve Officers Training Corps (ROTC):** Army ROTC: Offered on campus; Navy ROTC: Offered on campus; Air Force ROTC: Offered on campus. **Faculty and instruction (2005-2006):** Total instructional faculty: 1,192 full-time, 91 part-time (64% men; 36% women; 15% minorities). Full-time faculty with Ph.D. or other terminal degree: 96%. Student/faculty ratio: 20/1. Classes of fewer than 20 students: 35%; of 20 to 49 students: 54%; of 50 or more students: 11%. **Advanced Placement and International Baccalaureate credit:** AP tests may be used for: Credit and/or placement. Scores accepted: 3, 4, 5. International Baccalaureate exams may be used for: Credit and/or placement. **Freshmen returning for sophomore year:** 82%. **Graduation rates:** Four-year: 31%; five-year: 54%; six-year: 59%. **Graduate study:** 28% of students pursue further study within one year.

COSTS AND FINANCIAL AID

Financial aid office: (785) 864-4700. **Expenses (2005-2006):** Tuition and fees 2005-2006: $5,413 in state, $13,866 out of state; room/board: $5,502. Estimated books and supplies: $750; transportation: $1,344; personal expenses: $2,094. **Financial aid:** Priority filing date for institution's financial aid form: March 1. In 2005-2006, 61% of undergraduates applied for financial aid. Of those, 42% were determined to have financial need; 21% had their need fully met. Average financial aid package (proportion receiving): $6,401 (40%). Average amount of gift aid, such as scholarships or grants (proportion receiving): $5,708 (30%). Average amount of self-help aid, such as work study or loans (proportion receiving): $4,588 (34%). Average need-based loan (excluding PLUS or other private loans): $4,284. Among students who received need-based aid, the average percentage of need met:

56%. Among students who received aid based on merit, the average award (and the proportion receiving): $4,032 (1%). The average athletic scholarship (and the proportion receiving): $5,799 (0%). Average amount of debt of borrowers graduating in 2005: $17,243. Proportion who borrowed: 42%.

CAMPUS LIFE AND EXTRACURRICULAR ACTIVITIES

Campus housing available (% using): coed dorms (56%), women's dorms (13%), apartments for married students (5%), apartment for single students (15%), cooperative housing (11%). Students who live in college-owned, operated, or affiliated housing: 22%. **Student employment:** During the 2005-2006 academic year, 14% of undergraduates worked on campus. Average per-year earnings: $4,160. **Clubs and organizations:** Number of student organizations: 400. Activities include: choral groups, concert band, dance, drama/theater, jazz band, literary magazine, marching band, music ensembles, musical theater, opera, pep band, radio station, student government, student newspaper, symphony orchestra, television station, yearbook. Number of fraternities: 21; sororities: 17. Proportion of men in fraternities: 12%; of women in sororities: 18%. Average proportion of students who stay on campus on weekends: 15%. **Sports program (2005-2006):** Member of NCAA I. *Men's intercollegiate varsity sports:* baseball, basketball, cross-country, football, golf, track and field (indoor), track and field (outdoor). *Women's intercollegiate varsity sports:* basketball, cross-country, golf, rowing, soccer, softball, swimming and diving, tennis, track and field (indoor), track and field (outdoor), volleyball.

SERVICES AND FACILITIES

Basic services: nonremedial tutoring, women's center, placement service, day care, health service, health insurance, other. **Remedial assistance:** math. **Counseling services:** minority student, career, military, personal, veteran student, academic, older student, psychological, birth control. **For learning-disabled students:** School does not offer a structured program with separate admission and additional fees. Total undergraduates in learning-disabled program or receiving services: 185. Services include: remedial math, reading machines, tape recorders, diagnostic testing service, note-taking services, learning center, readers, extended time for tests, tutors, priority registration, priority seating, texts on tape, exams on tape or computer, other testing accomodations, other. **Library:** Number of titles: 4,853,631; number of current serial subscriptions: 50,992. **Information technology resources:** Students are not required to lease or own a computer. Number of campus computers available to all students: 1,680. School has a wireless network. Approximate number of users that can be accommodated: 4,250. Proportion of college-owned housing units wired for high-speed internet access: 100%. **Campus safety:** Security services offered: 24-hour foot and vehicle patrols, late-night transport/escort service, 24-hour emergency telephones, lighted pathways/sidewalks, controlled dormitory access (key, security card, etc).

TRANSFER AND INTERNATIONAL STUDENTS

Transfer students: May apply for admission for the following academic terms: Fall, Spring, Summer. Applicants do not need a minimum number of credits to apply. For fall 2005: Transfer applications received: 2,808. Transfer applicants offered admission: 2,111. Transfer applicants enrolled: 1,475. **International students:** Number of foreign undergraduates: 550 (3% of student body). Number of countries represented: 78.

University of St. Mary

■ **Address:** 4100 S. Fourth Street Trafficway, Leavenworth, KS 66048
■ **Website:** http://www.stmary.edu
■ **Private; Religious affiliation:** Roman Catholic
■ **Enrollment:** 376 full-time; 152 part-time

KEY STATS

✔ **U.S News College Ranking:** fourth tier, Universities–Master's (Midwest)
✔ **ACT Score (25th/75th percentile):** 17-22
✔ **Tuition:** 2006-2007: $16,410

Selectivity: Selective	Room/board: $6,100
Acceptance rate: 45%	Average debt: $17,125
Student/faculty ratio: 10/1	Proportion who borrowed: 72%

UNDERGRADUATE STUDENT BODY STATS

2005-2006 enrollment: 376 full-time; 152 part-time. Men: 42%; women: 58%. **Ethnic makeup:** African American: 13%; Asian American: 3%; Hispanic: 11%; White: 72%; International: 1%.

ADMISSIONS FACTS AND FIGURES

Phone: (913) 758-6118. **Email:** admiss@stmary.edu. **Website:** http://www.stmary.edu. **Application deadlines for fall 2007:** Regular decision: Rolling. Early decision: Not offered. Early action: Not offered. Admission can be deferred. **Application fee:** $25. Common application is accepted. **Admissions requirements/recommendations:** High school units required (recommended): English: 4 (4); Mathematics: 2 (4); Science: 2 (4); Foreign language: (2); Social studies: (2); History: 2 (4); Academic electives: 2 (2); Total units: 12 (24). Tests: The college uses SAT or ACT scores in admissions decisions. Either SAT or ACT required. For admission to the fall 2007 entering class, the school will accept: ACT without writing. Campus visit: Recommended. Admissions officers interview: Recommended. Off-campus interview: May be arranged. **Factors that count in admissions decisions:** *Academic:* Secondary school record: Very important. Class rank: Important. Letters of recommendation: Considered. Standardized test scores: Very important. Essay: Considered. *Nonacademic:* Interview: Important. Extracurricular activities: Important. Talent/ability: Important. Character/personal qualities: Very important. Alumni/ae relationship: Considered. Geographical residence: Not considered. State residency: Not considered. Religious affiliation/commitment: Not considered. Minority status: Not considered. Volunteer work: Considered. Work experience: Considered. **Other schools with the greatest overlap in applicants:** Baker University; Kansas State University; MidAmerica Nazarene University; Ottawa University; University of Kansas. **Admissions statistics for the fall 2005 entering class:** Total applicants: 570. Total accepted: 255. Freshmen enrolled: 83; 50% were from out of state. Overall acceptance rate: 45%. **Credentials of fall 2005 freshmen:** 6% ranked in the top 10 percent of their high school class; 23% were in the top 25 percent, and 70% were in the top half. (Proportion submitting class standing: 85%.) **First-year students who submitted SAT scores:** 11%. Scores (25/75 percentile): Verbal: 370-490, Math: 310-500, Combined: 680-990. **First-year students submitting ACT scores:** 89%. Scores (25/75 percentile): English: 16-23, Math: 16-21, Composite: 17-22.

ACADEMICS

Year founded: 1923. **Academic calendar:** Semester. **Degrees offered:** associate, bachelor's, master's. **Most popular majors:** 22% psychology, 20% business administration and management, 16% elementary education and teaching, 7% information technology, 5% biology/biological sciences. **Major fields of study:** biological and biomedical sciences; business, management, marketing, and related support services; communication, journalism, and related programs; computer and information sciences and support services; education; English language and literature/letters; family and consumer sciences/human sciences; health professions and related clinical sciences; history; liberal arts and sciences studies, and humanities; mathematics and statistics; multi/interdisciplinary studies; parks, recreation, leisure, and fitness studies; physical sciences; psychology; social sciences; theology and religious vocations; visual and performing arts. **Areas of required coursework:** arts/fine arts, computer literacy, mathematics, English (including composition), philosophy, sciences (biological or physical), history, social science, other. **Pre-professional programs:** pre-law, pre-medicine. **Special academic programs (% participation):** accelerated program (0%), distance learning (0%), double major (6%), dual enrollment (14%), exchange student program (domestic) (0%), honors program (10%), independent study (28%), internships (3%), student-designed major (5%), study abroad (0%), teacher certificate program (13%). **Teacher certification offered in:** elementary, secondary. **Reserve Officers Training Corps (ROTC):** Army ROTC: Offered at cooperating institution (University of Kansas); Air Force ROTC: Offered at cooperating institution (University of Kansas). **Faculty and instruction (2005-2006):** Total instructional faculty: 39 full-time, 50 part-time (43% men; 57% women; 6% minorities). Full-time faculty with Ph.D. or other terminal degree: 72%. Student/faculty ratio: 10/1. Classes of fewer than 20 students: 76%; of 20 to 49 students: 24%; of 50 or more students: 1%. **Advanced Placement and International Baccalaureate credit:** International Baccalaureate exams may be used for: Credit only. **Freshmen returning for sophomore year:** 59%. **Graduation rates:** Four-year: 28%; five-year: 39%; six-year: 44%. **Graduate study:** 20% of students pursue further study immediately upon graduation. Fields in which graduates pursue further study: Master of Business Administration (MBA), 4%; law, 1%; education, 4%; arts and sciences, 5%.

COSTS AND FINANCIAL AID

Financial aid office: (800) 752-7043. **Expenses (2006-2007):** Tuition and fees 2006-2007: $16,410; room/board: $6,100. Estimated books and supplies: $1,000; transportation: $1,410; personal expenses: $1,650. **Financial aid:** Priority filing date for institution's financial aid form: April 1. In 2005-2006, 70% of undergraduates applied for financial aid. Of those, 43% were determined to have financial need; 9% had their need fully met. Average financial aid package (proportion receiving): $10,420 (43%). Average amount of gift aid, such as scholarships or grants (proportion receiving): $6,653 (43%). Average amount of self-help aid, such as work study or loans (proportion receiving): $4,579 (43%). Average need-based loan (excluding PLUS or other private loans): $4,124. Among students who received need-based aid, the average percentage of need met: 86%. Among students who received aid based on merit, the average award (and the proportion receiving): $4,500 (39%). The average athletic scholarship (and the proportion receiving): $7,000 (56%). Average amount of debt of borrowers graduating in 2005: $17,125. Proportion who borrowed: 72%.

CAMPUS LIFE AND EXTRACURRICULAR ACTIVITIES

Campus housing available (% using): coed dorms (100%). Students who live in college-owned, operated, or affiliated housing: 42%. **Clubs and organizations:** Number of student organizations: 21. Activities include: choral groups, concert band, drama/theater, literary magazine, music ensembles, musical theater, opera, student government, student newspaper. Number of fraternities: 0; sororities: 0. Average proportion of students who stay on campus on weekends: 45%. **Sports program (2005-2006):** Member of NAIA. *Men's intercollegiate varsity sports:* baseball, basketball, football, soccer. *Women's intercollegiate varsity sports:* basketball, soccer, softball, volleyball.

SERVICES AND FACILITIES

Basic services: nonremedial tutoring, placement service, day care, health service, health insurance. **Remedial assistance:** reading, math, writing, study skills. **Counseling services:** veteran student, academic, psychological, religious. **For learning-disabled students:** School does not offer a structured program with separate admission and additional fees. Total undergraduates in learning-disabled program or receiving services: 12. Services include: remedial math, tape recorders, untimed tests, learning center, extended time for tests, tutors, priority seating, other testing accomodations. **Information technology resources:** Students are not required to lease or own a computer. Number of campus computers available to all students: 315. School has a wireless network. Approximate number of users that can be accommodated: 1,200. Proportion of college-owned housing units wired for high-speed internet access: 100%. **Campus safety:** Security services offered: 24-hour foot and vehicle patrols, 24-hour emergency telephones, lighted pathways/sidewalks, controlled dormitory access (key, security card, etc).

TRANSFER AND INTERNATIONAL STUDENTS

Transfer students: May apply for admission for the following academic terms: Fall, Spring, Summer. Applicants need a minimum number of credits to apply. For fall 2005: Transfer applications received: 178. Transfer applicants offered admission: 84. Transfer applicants enrolled: 51. **International students:** Number of foreign undergraduates: 4 (1% of student body). Number of countries represented: 4. Minimum TOEFL score required: 500 (paper); 173 (computer).

Washburn University

- **Address:** 1700 S.W. College, Topeka, KS 66621
- **Website:** http://www.washburn.edu
- **Public**
- **Enrollment:** 4,151 full-time; 2,273 part-time

KEY STATS

✔ **U.S News College Ranking:** 30, Universities–Master's (Midwest)
✔ **ACT Score (25th/75th percentile):** 19-24
✔ **Tuition:** 2005-2006: $4,982 in state, $11,192 out of state

Selectivity: Selective	**Room/board:** $4,752
Acceptance rate: 99%	**Average debt:** $13,125
Student/faculty ratio: 16/1	**Proportion who borrowed:** 60%

UNDERGRADUATE STUDENT BODY STATS

2005-2006 enrollment: 4,151 full-time; 2,273 part-time. Men: 38%; women: 62%. **Ethnic makeup:** African American: 4%; American-Indian: 1%; Asian American: 1%; Hispanic: 2%; White: 91%; International: 1%.

ADMISSIONS FACTS AND FIGURES

Phone: (785) 670-1030. **Email:** admissions@washburn.edu. **Website:** http://www.washburn.edu. **Application deadlines for fall 2007:** Regular decision: August 1. Early decision: Not offered. Early action: Not offered. Admission cannot be deferred. **Application fee:** $20. Common application is not accepted. **To apply online, go to:** http://www.washburn.edu/future/admissions/apply-online/. **Admissions requirements/recommendations:** High school units required (recommended): English: (4); Mathematics: (3); Science: (3); Foreign language: (2); Social studies: (3); History: (1). Tests: The college uses SAT or ACT scores in admissions decisions. ACT required. For admission to the fall 2007 entering class, the school will accept: ACT with writing, ACT without writing. Campus visit: Recommended. Admissions interview: Neither required nor recommended. Off-campus interview: May be arranged. **Factors that count in admissions decisions:** *Academic:* Secondary school record: Very important. Class rank: Not considered. Letters of recommendation: Not considered. Standardized test scores: Very important. Essay: Not considered. *Nonacademic:* Interview: Not considered. Extracurricular activities: Not considered. Talent/ability: Not considered. Character/personal qualities: Not considered. Alumni/ae relationship: Not considered. Geographical residence: Not considered. State residency: Not considered. Religious affiliation/commitment: Not considered. Minority status: Not considered. Volunteer work: Not considered. Work experience: Not considered. **Admissions statistics for the fall 2005 entering class:** Total applicants: 1,576. Total accepted: 1,565. Freshmen enrolled: 863; 6% were from out of state. Overall acceptance rate: 99%. **Credentials of fall 2005 freshmen:** 23% ranked in the top 10 percent of their high school class; 39% were in the top 25 percent, and 74% were in the top half. (Proportion submitting class standing: 76%.) **Average high school grade point average:** 3.2. **First-year students submitting ACT scores:** 80%. Scores (25/75 percentile): English: 18-24, Math: 18-24, Composite: 19-24.

ACADEMICS

Year founded: 1865. **Academic calendar:** Semester. **Degrees offered:** certificate, associate, bachelor's, post-bachelor's certificate, master's, first professional, first professional certificate. **Most popular majors:** 23% business/commerce, 20% health professions and related clinical sciences, 12% criminal justice/law enforcement administration, 8% education, 6% communication studies/speech communication and rhetoric. **Major fields of study:** biological and biomedical sciences; business, management, marketing, and related support services; communication, journalism, and related programs; computer and information sciences and support services; education; English language and literature/letters; foreign languages, literatures, and linguistics; health professions and related clinical sciences; history; legal professions and studies; liberal arts and sciences studies, and humanities; mathematics and statistics; multi/interdisciplinary studies; parks, recreation, leisure, and fitness studies; philosophy and religious studies; physical sciences; psychology; public administration and social service professions; security and protective services; social sciences; visual and performing arts. **Areas of required coursework:** arts/fine arts, humanities, mathematics, English (including composition), foreign languages, sciences (biological or physical), social science, other. **Pre-professional programs:** pre-law, pre-dentistry, pre-medicine, pre-theology, pre-veterinary science, pre-optometry, pre-pharmacy, other. **Special academic programs (% participation):** cooperative (work-study plan) program (3%), cross-registration (2%), distance learning (13%), double major (10%), dual enrollment (1%), English as a Second Language (ESL) (1%), honors program (5%), independent study (10%), internships (10%), liberal arts/career combination (5%), student-designed major (1%), study abroad (1%), teacher certificate program (20%). **Teacher certification offered in:** early childhood, special education, elementary, middle/junior high, secondary. **Cooperative education programs:** computer science, education, engineering, health professions, social/behavioral science. **Reserve Officers Training Corps (ROTC):** Army ROTC: Offered on campus; Navy ROTC: Offered at cooperating institution (University of Kansas); Air Force ROTC: Offered at cooperating institution (University of Kansas, Kansas State University). **Faculty and instruction (2005-2006):** Total instructional faculty: 258 full-time, 252 part-time (55% men; 45% women; 10% minorities). Full-time faculty with Ph.D. or other terminal degree: 87%. Student/faculty ratio: 16/1. Classes of fewer than 20 students: 40%; of 20 to 49 students: 58%; of 50 or more students: 2%. **Advanced Placement and International Baccalaureate credit:** AP tests may be used for: Credit and/or placement. Scores accepted: 3, 4, 5. **Freshmen return-**

ing for sophomore year: 71%. **Graduation rates:** Four-year: 30%; five-year: 53%; six-year: 64%. **Graduate study:** 39% of students pursue further study immediately upon graduation; 64% within five years. Fields in which graduates pursue further study: Master of Business Administration (MBA), 25%; law, 15%; medicine, 6%; dentistry, 5%; engineering, 6%; theology (or the seminary), 2%; education, 15%; arts and sciences, 25%; veterinary medicine, 1%.

COSTS AND FINANCIAL AID

Financial aid office: (785) 670-1151. **Expenses (2005-2006):** Tuition and fees 2005-2006: $4,982 in state, $11,192 out of state; room/board: $4,752. Estimated books and supplies: $976; transportation: $1,804; personal expenses: $1,332. **Financial aid:** Priority filing date for institution's financial aid form: February 15. In 2005-2006, 88% of undergraduates applied for financial aid. Of those, 59% were determined to have financial need; 18% had their need fully met. Average financial aid package (proportion receiving): $7,426 (58%). Average amount of gift aid, such as scholarships or grants (proportion receiving): $3,264 (34%). Average amount of self-help aid, such as work study or loans (proportion receiving): $4,001 (51%). Average need-based loan (excluding PLUS or other private loans): $3,846. Among students who received need-based aid, the average percentage of need met: 36%. Among students who received aid based on merit, the average award (and the proportion receiving): $1,900 (20%). The average athletic scholarship (and the proportion receiving): $4,199 (3%). Average amount of debt of borrowers graduating in 2005: $13,125. Proportion who borrowed: 60%.

CAMPUS LIFE AND EXTRACURRICULAR ACTIVITIES

Campus housing available (% using): coed dorms (51%), sorority housing (14%), fraternity housing (14%), apartment for single students (21%). Students who live in college-owned, operated, or affiliated housing: 16%. **Student employment:** During the 2005-2006 academic year, 8% of undergraduates worked on campus. Average per-year earnings: $3,700. **Clubs and organizations:** Number of student organizations: 90. Activities include: choral groups, concert band, dance, drama/theater, jazz band, literary magazine, marching band, music ensembles, musical theater, pep band, student government, student newspaper, student film society, symphony orchestra, television station, yearbook. Number of fraternities: 4; sororities: 5. Proportion of men in fraternities: 9%; of women in sororities: 7%. Average proportion of students who stay on campus on weekends: 35%. **Sports program (2005-2006):** Member of NCAA II. *Men's intercollegiate varsity sports:* baseball, basketball, football, golf, tennis. *Women's intercollegiate varsity sports:* basketball, soccer, softball, tennis, volleyball.

SERVICES AND FACILITIES

Basic services: nonremedial tutoring, placement service, day care, health service, health insurance. **Remedial assistance:** math, writing, study skills. **Counseling services:** minority student, career, military, personal, veteran student, academic, older student, psychological, birth control. **For learning-disabled students:** School does not offer a structured program with separate admission and additional fees. Total undergraduates in learning-disabled program or receiving services: 35. Services include: reading machines, tape recorders, note-taking services, oral tests, learning center, readers, extended time for tests, tutors, other testing accomodations. **Library:** Number of titles: 338,794; number of current serial subscriptions: 1,634. **Information technology resources:** Students are not required to lease or own a computer. Number of campus computers available to all students: 400. School has a wireless network. Approximate number of users that can be accommodated: 1,200. Proportion of college-owned housing units wired for high-speed internet access: 100%. **Campus safety:** Security services offered: 24-hour foot and vehicle patrols, late-night transport/escort service, 24-hour emergency telephones, lighted pathways/sidewalks, student patrols, controlled dormitory access (key, security card, etc).

TRANSFER AND INTERNATIONAL STUDENTS

Transfer students: May apply for admission for the following academic terms: Fall, Spring, Summer. Applicants need a minimum number of credits to apply. For fall 2005: Transfer applications received: 1,160. Transfer applicants offered admission: 1,160. Transfer applicants enrolled: 633. **International students:** Number of foreign undergraduates: 65 (1% of student body). Minimum TOEFL score required: 520 (paper); 193 (computer).

Wichita State University

- **Address:** 1845 Fairmount, Wichita, KS 67260
- **Website:** http://www.wichita.edu
- **Public**
- **Enrollment:** 7,198 full-time; 3,777 part-time

KEY STATS
✔ **U.S News College Ranking:** fourth tier, National Universities
✔ **ACT Score (25th/75th percentile):** 20-25
✔ **Tuition:** 2006-2007: $4,517 in state, $11,864 out of state
  Selectivity: Selective **Room/board:** $5,276
  Acceptance rate: 84% **Average debt:** $18,068
  Student/faculty ratio: 18/1 **Proportion who borrowed:** 59%

UNDERGRADUATE STUDENT BODY STATS
2005-2006 enrollment: 7,198 full-time; 3,777 part-time. Men: 44%; women: 56%. **Ethnic makeup:** African American: 7%; American-Indian: 1%; Asian American: 7%; Hispanic: 5%; White: 75%; International: 5%.

ADMISSIONS FACTS AND FIGURES
Phone: (316) 978-3085. **Email:** admissions@wichita.edu. **Website:** http://www.wichita.edu. **Application deadlines for fall 2007:** Regular decision: Rolling. Early decision: Not offered. Early action: Not offered. Admission can be deferred. **Application fee:** $30. Common application is not accepted. **Admissions requirements/recommendations:** High school units required (recommended): English: 4; Mathematics: 3; Science: 3; Social studies: 3; Total units: 14. Tests: The college uses SAT or ACT scores in admissions decisions. Neither SAT nor ACT required. For admission to the fall 2007 entering class, the school will accept: ACT with writing, ACT without writing. Campus visit: Recommended. Admissions interview: Neither required nor recommended. Off-campus interview: Not available. **Factors that count in admissions decisions:** *Academic:* Secondary school record: Very important. Class rank: Very important. Letters of recommendation: Not considered. Standardized test scores: Very important. Essay: Not considered. *Nonacademic:* Interview: Not considered. Extracurricular activities: Not considered. Talent/ability: Not considered. Character/personal qualities: Not considered. Alumni/ae relationship: Not considered. Geographical residence: Not considered. State residency: Not considered. Religious affiliation/commitment: Not considered. Minority status: Not considered. Volunteer work: Not considered. Work experience: Not considered. **Other schools with the greatest overlap in applicants:** Kansas State University; University of Kansas. **Admissions statistics for the fall 2005 entering class:** Total applicants: 2,066. Total accepted: 1,734. Freshmen enrolled: 1,241; 6% were from out of state. Overall acceptance rate: 84%. **Credentials of fall 2005 freshmen:** 19% ranked in the top 10 percent of their high school class; 47% were in the top 25 percent, and 76% were in the top half. (Proportion submitting class standing: 82%.) **Average high school grade point average:** 3.3. **First-year students who submitted SAT scores:** 8%. Scores (25/75 percentile): Verbal: 470-590, Math: 480-610, Combined: 950-1200. **First-year students submitting ACT scores:** 86%. Scores (25/75 percentile): English: 19-26, Math: 18-25, Composite: 20-25.

ACADEMICS
Year founded: 1895. **Academic calendar:** Semester. **Degrees offered:** certificate, associate, bachelor's, post-bachelor's certificate, master's, post-master's certificate, doctorate. **Most popular majors:** 23% business, management, marketing, and related support services, 12% education, 12% health professions and related clinical sciences, 10% engineering, 6% social sciences. **Major fields of study:** area, ethnic, cultural, and gender studies; biological and biomedical sciences; business, management, marketing, and related support services; communication, journalism, and related programs; computer and information sciences and support services; education; engineering; engineering technologies/technicians; English language and literature/letters; foreign languages, literatures, and linguistics; health professions and related clinical sciences; history; liberal arts and sciences studies, and humanities; mathematics and statistics; multi/interdisciplinary studies; parks, recreation, leisure, and fitness studies; philosophy and religious studies; physical sciences; psychology; public administration and social service professions; security and protective services; social sciences; visual and performing arts. **Pre-professional programs:** pre-law, pre-medicine. **Special academic programs:** accelerated program, cooperative (work-study plan) program, distance learning, double major, dual enrollment,

English as a Second Language (ESL), exchange student program (domestic), honors program, independent study, internships, liberal arts/career combination, student-designed major, study abroad, teacher certificate program. **Cooperative education programs:** art, business, computer science, education, engineering, health professions, humanities, natural science, social/behavioral science. **Faculty and instruction (2005-2006):** Total instructional faculty: 467 full-time, 48 part-time (60% men; 40% women; 12% minorities). Full-time faculty with Ph.D. or other terminal degree: 81%. Student/faculty ratio: 18/1. Classes of fewer than 20 students: 52%; of 20 to 49 students: 41%; of 50 or more students: 7%. **Advanced Placement and International Baccalaureate credit:** AP tests may be used for: Credit only. International Baccalaureate exams may be used for: Credit and/or placement. **Freshmen returning for sophomore year:** 69%. **Graduation rates:** Four-year: 15%; five-year: 31%; six-year: 37%.

COSTS AND FINANCIAL AID
Financial aid office: (316) 978-3430. **Expenses (2006-2007):** Tuition and fees 2006-2007: $4,517 in state, $11,864 out of state; room/board: $5,276. Estimated books and supplies: $900; transportation: $1,300; personal expenses: $1,545. **Financial aid:** Priority filing date for institution's financial aid form: March 15. In 2005-2006, 68% of undergraduates applied for financial aid. Of those, 67% were determined to have financial need; 9% had their need fully met. Average financial aid package (proportion receiving): $5,924 (62%). Average amount of gift aid, such as scholarships or grants (proportion receiving): $2,754 (32%). Average amount of self-help aid, such as work study or loans (proportion receiving): $3,137 (42%). Average need-based loan (excluding PLUS or other private loans): $2,856. Among students who received need-based aid, the average percentage of need met: 46%. Among students who received aid based on merit, the average award (and the proportion receiving): $4,209 (14%). The average athletic scholarship (and the proportion receiving): $5,842 (2%). Average amount of debt of borrowers graduating in 2005: $18,068. Proportion who borrowed: 59%.

CAMPUS LIFE AND EXTRACURRICULAR ACTIVITIES
Campus housing available: coed dorms, fraternity housing, apartments for married students, apartment for single students, special housing for disabled students. Students who live in college-owned, operated, or affiliated housing: 7%. **Student employment:** During the 2005-2006 academic year, 13% of undergraduates worked on campus. Average per-year earnings: $6,042. **Clubs and organizations:** Number of student organizations: 174. Activities include: choral groups, concert band, dance, drama/theater, jazz band, literary magazine, music ensembles, musical theater, opera, pep band, radio station, student government, student newspaper, student film society, symphony orchestra, television station. Number of fraternities: 7; sororities: 7. Proportion of men in fraternities: 7%; of women in sororities: 5%. **Sports program (2005-2006):** Member of NCAA I. *Men's intercollegiate varsity sports:* baseball, basketball, cross-country, golf, tennis, track and field (indoor), track and field (outdoor). *Women's intercollegiate varsity sports:* basketball, cross-country, golf, softball, track and field (indoor), track and field (outdoor), volleyball.

SERVICES AND FACILITIES
Basic services: nonremedial tutoring, placement service, day care, health service, health insurance. **Remedial assistance:** reading, math, writing, study skills. **Counseling services:** minority student, career, military, personal, veteran student, academic, older student, psychological, birth control, religious. **For learning-disabled students:** School does not offer a structured program with separate admission and additional fees. Services include: remedial math, remedial English, reading machines, tape recorders, videotaped classes, diagnostic testing service, untimed tests, note-taking services, oral tests, readers, extended time for tests, tutors. **Library:** Number of titles: 1,680,529; number of current serial subscriptions: 20,361. **Information technology resources:** Students are not required to lease or own a computer. Number of campus computers available to all students: 1,500. School has a wireless network. **Campus safety:** Security services offered: 24-hour foot and vehicle patrols, late-night transport/escort service, 24-hour emergency telephones, lighted pathways/sidewalks, student patrols, controlled dormitory access (key, security card, etc).

TRANSFER AND INTERNATIONAL STUDENTS
Transfer students: May apply for admission for the following academic terms: Fall, Spring, Summer. Applicants do not need a minimum number of credits to apply. For fall 2005: Transfer applications received: 2,226. Transfer applicants offered admission: 2,074. Transfer applicants enrolled: 1,240. **International students:** Number of foreign undergraduates: 458 (5% of student body). Number of countries represented: 59. Minimum TOEFL score required: 530 (paper); 197 (computer). Average TOEFL score: 541 (paper).

Kentucky

Alice Lloyd College

- **Address:** 100 Purpose Road, Pippa Passes, KY 41844
- **Website:** http://www.alc.edu
- **Private**
- **Enrollment:** 589 full-time; 23 part-time

KEY STATS
✔ **U.S News College Ranking:** third tier, Comp. Coll.–Bachelor's (South)
✔ **ACT Score (25th/75th percentile):** 18-24
✔ **Tuition:** 2006-2007: $7,560

Selectivity: Selective	**Room/board:** $3,900
Acceptance rate: 59%	**Average debt:** $3,495
Student/faculty ratio: 18/1	**Proportion who borrowed:** 56%

UNDERGRADUATE STUDENT BODY STATS
2005-2006 enrollment: 589 full-time; 23 part-time. Men: 48%; women: 52%. **Ethnic makeup:** African American: 2%; Hispanic: 1%; White: 97%.

ADMISSIONS FACTS AND FIGURES
Phone: (888) 280-4252. **Email:** admissions@alc.edu. **Website:** http://www.alc.edu. **Application deadlines for fall 2007:** Regular decision: July 1. Early decision: Not offered. Early action: Not offered. Admission can be deferred. **Application fee:** None. Common application is not accepted. **Admissions requirements/recommendations:** High school units required (recommended): English: 4; Mathematics: 3; Science: 3; History: 2. Tests: The college uses SAT or ACT scores in admissions decisions. Either SAT or ACT required. For admission to the fall 2007 entering class, the school will accept: ACT with writing, ACT without writing. Campus visit: Recommended. Admissions interview: Recommended. Off-campus interview: May be arranged. **Factors that count in admissions decisions:** *Academic:* Secondary school record: Very important. Class rank: Important. Letters of recommendation: Considered. Standardized test scores: Very important. Essay: Considered. *Nonacademic:* Interview: Considered. Extracurricular activities: Considered. Talent/ability: Considered. Character/personal qualities: Important. Alumni/ae relationship: Considered. Geographical residence: Very important. State residency: Not considered. Religious affiliation/commitment: Not considered. Minority status: Considered. Volunteer work: Considered. Work experience: Considered. **Other schools with the greatest overlap in applicants:** Eastern Kentucky University; Georgetown College; Morehead State University; Pikeville College. **Admissions statistics for the fall 2005 entering class:** Total applicants: 1,014. Total accepted: 603. Freshmen enrolled: 188; 17% were from out of state. Overall acceptance rate: 59%. **Size of waiting list:** 42 applicants; enrolled from waiting list: 30. **Credentials of fall 2005 freshmen:** 28% ranked in the top 10 percent of their high school class; 48% were in the top 25 percent, and 83% were in the top half. (Proportion submitting class standing: 78%.) **Average high school grade point average:** 3.4. **First-year students who submitted SAT scores:** 3%. Scores (25/75 percentile): Verbal: 440-460, Math: 440-480, Combined: 880-940. **First-year students submitting ACT scores:** 97%. Scores (25/75 percentile): English: 17-23, Math: 17-22, Composite: 18-24.

ACADEMICS
Year founded: 1923. **Academic calendar:** Semester. **Degrees offered:** bachelor's. **Most popular majors:** 28% education, 19% history, 18% business, management, marketing, and related support services, 17% biological and biomedical sciences, 7% English language and literature/letters. **Major fields of study:** biological and biomedical sciences; business, management, marketing, and related support services; education; English language and literature/letters; multi/interdisciplinary studies; parks, recreation, leisure, and fitness studies; social sciences. **Areas of required coursework:** humanities, computer literacy, mathematics, English (including composition), sciences (biological or physical), history, social science, other. **Pre-professional programs:** pre-law, pre-dentistry, pre-medicine, pre-optometry, pre-pharmacy. **Special academic programs (% participation):** cooperative (work-study plan)

program (100%), double major (2%), independent study, internships, liberal arts/career combination, student-designed major, study abroad, teacher certificate program (57%), other. **Teacher certification offered in:** elementary, middle/junior high, secondary. **Faculty and instruction (2005-2006):** Total instructional faculty: 29 full-time, 9 part-time (66% men; 34% women; 5% minorities). Full-time faculty with Ph.D. or other terminal degree: 55%. Student/faculty ratio: 18/1. Classes of fewer than 20 students: 49%; of 20 to 49 students: 51%; of 50 or more students: 0%. **Freshmen returning for sophomore year:** 61%. **Graduation rates:** Four-year: 14%; five-year: 27%; six-year: 30%. **Graduate study:** 98% of students pursue further study immediately upon graduation; 2% within one year. Fields in which graduates pursue further study: Master of Business Administration (MBA), 1%; law, 2%; medicine, 91%; dentistry, 2%; engineering, 1%; theology (or the seminary), 1%; education, 1%; arts and sciences, 2%.

COSTS AND FINANCIAL AID
Financial aid office: (606) 368-6059. **Expenses (2006-2007):** Tuition and fees 2006-2007: $7,560; room/board: $3,900. Estimated books and supplies: $850; transportation: $1,800; personal expenses: $1,300. **Financial aid:** Priority filing date for institution's financial aid form: March 15; deadline: August 15. In 2005-2006, 100% of undergraduates applied for financial aid. Of those, 54% were determined to have financial need; 31% had their need fully met. Average financial aid package (proportion receiving): $8,678 (54%). Average amount of gift aid, such as scholarships or grants (proportion receiving): $7,087 (54%). Average amount of self-help aid, such as work study or loans (proportion receiving): $1,591 (54%). Average need-based loan (excluding PLUS or other private loans): $501. Among students who received need-based aid, the average percentage of need met: 60%. Among students who received aid based on merit, the average award (and the proportion receiving): $4,970 (41%). The average athletic scholarship (and the proportion receiving): $7,317 (5%). Average amount of debt of borrowers graduating in 2005: $3,495. Proportion who borrowed: 56%.

CAMPUS LIFE AND EXTRACURRICULAR ACTIVITIES
Campus housing available (% using): women's dorms (50%), men's dorms (50%). Students who live in college-owned, operated, or affiliated housing: 77%. **Student employment:** During the 2005-2006 academic year, 100% of undergraduates worked on campus. Average per-year earnings: $1,751. **Clubs and organizations:** Number of student organizations: 18. Activities include: choral groups, drama/theater, literary magazine, pep band, radio station, student government, student newspaper, television station, yearbook. Number of fraternities: 0; sororities: 0. Average proportion of students who stay on campus on weekends: 10%. **Sports program (2005-2006):** Member of NAIA. *Men's intercollegiate varsity sports:* baseball, basketball, cross-country, golf, tennis, track and field (outdoor). *Women's intercollegiate varsity sports:* basketball, cross-country, golf, softball, tennis, track and field (indoor).

SERVICES AND FACILITIES
Basic services: placement service, day care, health service. **Remedial assistance:** math, writing, other. **Counseling services:** career, personal, academic. **Library:** Number of titles: 74,281; number of current serial subscriptions: 158. **Information technology resources:** Students are not required to lease or own a computer. Number of campus computers available to all students: 98. School has a wireless network. Approximate number of users that can be accommodated: 25. Proportion of college-owned housing units wired for high-speed internet access: 100%. **Campus safety:** Security services offered: 24-hour foot and vehicle patrols, late-night transport/escort service, lighted pathways/sidewalks.

TRANSFER AND INTERNATIONAL STUDENTS
Transfer students: May apply for admission for the following academic terms: Fall, Spring. Applicants need a minimum number of credits to apply. For fall 2005: Transfer applications received: 123. Transfer applicants offered admission: 71. Transfer applicants enrolled: 35. **International students:** Number of foreign undergraduates: 2. Number of countries represented: 2. Minimum TOEFL score required: 550 (paper); 213 (computer). Average TOEFL score: 570 (paper).

Asbury College

- **Address:** One Macklem Drive, Wilmore, KY 40390
- **Website:** http://www.asbury.edu
- **Private**
- **Enrollment:** 1,124 full-time; 105 part-time

KEY STATS

✔ **U.S News College Ranking:** 3, Comp. Coll.–Bachelor's (South)
✔ **ACT Score (25th/75th percentile):** 21-28
✔ **Tuition:** 2006-2007: $20,184

Selectivity: More selective	**Room/board:** $4,974
Acceptance rate: 74%	**Average debt:** $22,016
Student/faculty ratio: 11/1	**Proportion who borrowed:** 69%

UNDERGRADUATE STUDENT BODY STATS

2005-2006 enrollment: 1,124 full-time; 105 part-time. Men: 41%; women: 59%. **Ethnic makeup:** African American: 1%; Asian American: 1%; Hispanic: 1%; White: 95%; International: 1%.

ADMISSIONS FACTS AND FIGURES

Phone: (800) 888-1818. **Email:** admissions@asbury.edu. **Website:** http://www.asbury.edu. **Application deadlines for fall 2007:** Regular decision: Rolling. Early decision: Not offered. Early action: Not offered. Admission can be deferred. **Application fee:** $30. Common application is not accepted. **Admissions requirements/recommendations:** High school units required (recommended): English: (4); Mathematics: (4); Science: (3); Foreign language: (2); Social studies: (1); History: (1); Total units: (15). Tests: The college uses SAT or ACT scores in admissions decisions. Either SAT or ACT required. For admission to the fall 2007 entering class, the school will accept: ACT with writing, ACT without writing. Campus visit: Recommended. Admissions interview: Neither required nor recommended. Off-campus interview: Not available. **Factors that count in admissions decisions:** *Academic:* Secondary school record: Important. Class rank: Considered. Letters of recommendation: Important. Standardized test scores: Very important. Essay: Not considered. *Nonacademic:* Interview: Not considered. Extracurricular activities: Considered. Talent/ability: Considered. Character/personal qualities: Important. Alumni/ae relationship: Not considered. Geographical residence: Not considered. State residency: Not considered. Religious affiliation/commitment: Not considered. Minority status: Not considered. Volunteer work: Not considered. Work experience: Not considered. **Other schools with the greatest overlap in applicants:** Cedarville University; Georgetown College; Indiana Wesleyan University; Taylor University; Wheaton College. **Admissions statistics for the fall 2005 entering class:** Total applicants: 797. Total accepted: 589. Freshmen enrolled: 277; 65% were from out of state. Overall acceptance rate: 74%. **Size of waiting list:** 0 applicants; enrolled from waiting list: 0. **Credentials of fall 2005 freshmen:** 35% ranked in the top 10 percent of their high school class; 64% were in the top 25 percent, and 85% were in the top half. (Proportion submitting class standing: 71%.) **Average high school grade point average:** 3.6. **First-year students who submitted SAT scores:** 56%. Scores (25/75 percentile): Verbal: 530-660, Math: 500-630, Combined: 1030-1290. **First-year students submitting ACT scores:** 69%. Scores (25/75 percentile): English: 21-29, Math: 19-26, Composite: 21-28.

ACADEMICS

Year founded: 1890. **Academic calendar:** Semester. **Degrees offered:** bachelor's, master's. **Most popular majors:** 12% radio and television broadcasting technology/technician, 8% speech and rhetorical studies, 7% psychology, 6% elementary education and teaching, 6% social work. **Major fields of study:** biological and biomedical sciences; business, management, marketing, and related support services; communication, journalism, and related programs; communications technologies/technicians and support services; education; English language and literature/letters; foreign languages, literatures, and linguistics; health professions and related clinical sciences; history; mathematics and statistics; parks, recreation, leisure, and fitness studies; philosophy and religious studies; physical sciences; psychology; public administration and social service professions; social sciences; theology and religious vocations; visual and performing arts. **Areas of required coursework:** arts/fine arts, humanities, computer literacy, mathematics, English (including composition), philosophy, foreign languages, sciences (biological or physical), history, social science, other. **Pre-professional programs:** pre-law, pre-dentistry, pre-medicine, pre-theology, pre-veterinary science. **Special academic programs:** double major, English as a Second Language (ESL), internships, study abroad, teacher certificate program. **Teacher certification offered in:** elementary, middle/junior high, secondary. **Reserve Officers Training Corps (ROTC):** Army ROTC: Offered at cooperating institution (University of Kentucky); Air Force ROTC: Offered at cooperating institution (University of Kentucky). **Faculty and instruction (2005-2006):** Total instructional faculty: 86 full-time, 65 part-time (64% men; 36% women; 3% minorities). Full-time faculty with Ph.D. or other terminal degree: 80%. Student/faculty ratio: 11/1. Classes of fewer than 20 students: 61%; of 20 to 49 students: 39%; of 50 or more students: 0%. **Advanced Placement and International Baccalaureate credit:** International Baccalaureate exams may be used for: Credit only. **Freshmen returning for sophomore year:** 80%. **Graduation rates:** Four-year: 61%; five-year: 69%; six-year: 65%.

COSTS AND FINANCIAL AID

Financial aid office: (800) 888-1818. **Expenses (2006-2007):** Tuition and fees 2006-2007: $20,184; room/board: $4,974. Estimated books and supplies: $730; transportation: $1,100; personal expenses: $1,110. **Financial aid:** Priority filing date for institution's financial aid form: March 1. In 2005-2006, 82% of undergraduates applied for financial aid. Of those, 71% were determined to have financial need; 24% had their need fully met. Average financial aid package (proportion receiving): $13,506 (71%). Average amount of gift aid, such as scholarships or grants (proportion receiving): $8,075 (69%). Average amount of self-help aid, such as work study or loans (proportion receiving): $4,405 (64%). Average need-based loan (excluding PLUS or other private loans): $3,737. Among students who received need-based aid, the average percentage of need met: 78%. Among students who received aid based on merit, the average award (and the proportion receiving): $10,356 (9%). The average athletic scholarship (and the proportion receiving): $1,412 (0%). Average amount of debt of borrowers graduating in 2005: $22,016. Proportion who borrowed: 69%.

CAMPUS LIFE AND EXTRACURRICULAR ACTIVITIES

Campus housing available (% using): women's dorms (48%), men's dorms (37%), apartments for married students (3%), apartment for single students (11%), other housing options (1%). Students who live in college-owned, operated, or affiliated housing: 84%. **Student employment:** During the 2005-2006 academic year, 58% of undergraduates worked on campus. Average per-year earnings: $1,154. **Clubs and organizations:** Number of student organizations: 34. Activities include: choral groups, concert band, drama/theater, jazz band, literary magazine, music ensembles, musical theater, opera, radio station, student government, student newspaper, symphony orchestra, television station, yearbook. Number of fraternities: 0; sororities: 0. Average proportion of students who stay on campus on weekends: 75%. **Sports program (2005-2006):** Member of NAIA. *Men's intercollegiate varsity sports:* basketball, cross-country, soccer, swimming and diving, tennis, track and field (outdoor). *Women's intercollegiate varsity sports:* basketball, cross-country, soccer, swimming and diving, tennis, track and field (outdoor), volleyball.

SERVICES AND FACILITIES

Basic services: nonremedial tutoring, placement service, health service, health insurance. **Remedial assistance:** math, writing, study skills. **Counseling services:** minority student, career, military, personal, veteran student, academic, older student, psychological, birth control, religious. **Library:** Number of titles: 146,708; number of current serial subscriptions: 511. **Information technology resources:** Students are not required to lease or own a computer. Number of campus computers available to all students: 189. School does not have a wireless network. Proportion of college-owned housing units wired for high-speed internet access: 100%. **Campus safety:** Security services offered: 24-hour foot and vehicle patrols, late-night transport/escort service, lighted pathways/sidewalks, controlled dormitory access (key, security card, etc).

TRANSFER AND INTERNATIONAL STUDENTS

Transfer students: May apply for admission for the following academic terms: Fall, Spring, Summer. Applicants need a minimum number of credits to apply. For fall 2005: Transfer applications received: 163. Transfer applicants offered admission: 91. Transfer applicants enrolled: 55. **International students:** Number of foreign undergraduates: 16 (1% of student body). Number of countries represented: 11. Minimum TOEFL score required: 550 (paper); 213 (computer).

Bellarmine University

- **Address:** 2001 Newburg Road, Louisville, KY 40205
- **Website:** http://www.bellarmine.edu
- **Private; Religious affiliation:** Roman Catholic
- **Enrollment:** 1,766 full-time; 530 part-time

KEY STATS

✔ **U.S News College Ranking:** 18, Universities–Master's (South)
✔ **ACT Score (25th/75th percentile):** 21-26
✔ **Tuition:** 2006-2007: $24,150

Selectivity: More selective	Room/board: $6,880
Acceptance rate: 70%	Average debt: $12,263
Student/faculty ratio: 13/1	Proportion who borrowed: 68%

UNDERGRADUATE STUDENT BODY STATS

2005-2006 enrollment: 1,766 full-time; 530 part-time. Men: 35%; women: 65%. **Ethnic makeup:** African American: 3%; Asian American: 2%; Hispanic: 2%; White: 92%; International: 1%. **Religious preference:** Protestant: 20%; Jewish: 1%; No preference: 1%; Unknown: 32%; Roman Catholic: 43%; Unitarian: 2%; Other: 1%.

ADMISSIONS FACTS AND FIGURES

Phone: (502) 452-8131. **Email:** admissions@bellarmine.edu. **Website:** http://www.bellarmine.edu. **Application deadlines for fall 2007:** Regular decision: August 15. Early decision: Not offered. Early action: Send application by: November 1; Decision sent by: December 15. Admission can be deferred. **Application fee:** $25. Common application is accepted. **Admissions requirements/recommendations:** High school units required (recommended): English: 4; Mathematics: 3 (4); Science: 2 (4); Foreign language: 0 (2); Social studies: 2 (3); History: 1 (2); Academic electives: 0 (0); Total units: 20. Tests: The college uses SAT or ACT scores in admissions decisions. Either SAT or ACT required. For admission to the fall 2007 entering class, the school will accept: ACT with writing, ACT without writing. Campus visit: Recommended. Admissions interview: Recommended. Off-campus interview: May be arranged. **Factors that count in admissions decisions:** *Academic:* Secondary school record: Very important. Class rank: Considered. Letters of recommendation: Very important. Standardized test scores: Very important. Essay: Important. *Nonacademic:* Interview: Considered. Extracurricular activities: Important. Talent/ability: Considered. Character/personal qualities: Important. Alumni/ae relationship: Considered. Geographical residence: Considered. State residency: Considered. Religious affiliation/commitment: Not considered. Minority status: Considered. Volunteer work: Considered. Work experience: Considered. **Other schools with the greatest overlap in applicants:** Centre College; Transylvania University; University of Kentucky; University of Louisville; Xavier University. **Admissions statistics for the fall 2005 entering class:** Total applicants: 2,043. Total accepted: 1,430. Freshmen enrolled: 436; 31% were from out of state. Accepted through early-decision or early-action plans: 55%. Overall acceptance rate: 70%. Non-early acceptance rate: 67%. **Credentials of fall 2005 freshmen:** 22% ranked in the top 10 percent of their high school class; 50% were in the top 25 percent, and 76% were in the top half. (Proportion submitting class standing: 67%.) **Average high school grade point average:** 3.5. **First-year students who submitted SAT scores:** 31%. Scores (25/75 percentile): Verbal: 480-590, Math: 490-600, Combined: 970-1190. **First-year students submitting ACT scores:** 84%. Scores (25/75 percentile): English: 20-27, Math: 19-26, Composite: 21-26.

ACADEMICS

Year founded: 1950. **Academic calendar:** Semester. **Degrees offered:** certificate, bachelor's, post-bachelor's certificate, master's, doctorate. **Most popular majors:** 24% nursing/registered nurse training (R.N., A.S.N., B.S.N., M.S.N.), 11% business/commerce, 8% liberal arts and sciences/liberal studies, 8% psychology, 7% English language and literature. **Major fields of study:** agriculture, agriculture operations, and related sciences; biological and biomedical sciences; business, management, marketing, and related support services; communication, journalism, and related programs; computer and information sciences and support services; education; engineering; English language and literature/letters; health professions and related clinical sciences; history; liberal arts and sciences studies, and humanities; mathematics and statistics; multi/interdisciplinary studies; philosophy and religious studies; physical sciences; psychology; security and protective services; social sciences; theology and religious vocations; visual and performing arts. **Areas of required coursework:** arts/fine arts, humanities, mathematics, English (including composition), philosophy, sciences (biological or physical), history, social science, other. **Pre-professional programs:** pre-law, pre-dentistry, pre-medicine, pre-veterinary science, pre-pharmacy, other. **Special academic programs (% participation):** accelerated program (15%), cross-registration (1%), distance learning (0%), double major (12%), dual enrollment (5%), exchange student program (domestic) (0%), honors program (5%), independent study (3%), internships (29%), liberal arts/career combination (1%), student-designed major (0%), study abroad (20%), teacher certificate program (8%), weekend college (0%). **Teacher certification offered in:** special education, elementary, middle/junior high, secondary. **Reserve Officers Training Corps (ROTC):** Army ROTC: Offered at cooperating institution (University of Louisville); Air Force ROTC: Offered at cooperating institution (University of Louisville). **Faculty and instruction (2005-2006):** Total instructional faculty: 114 full-time, 122 part-time (46% men; 54% women; 6% minorities). Full-time faculty with Ph.D. or other terminal degree: 79%. Student/faculty ratio: 13/1. Classes of fewer than 20 students: 60%; of 20 to 49 students: 39%; of 50 or more students: 1%. **Advanced Placement and International Baccalaureate credit:** AP tests may be used for: Credit and/or placement. Scores accepted: 3, 4, 5. International Baccalaureate exams may be used for: Credit and/or placement. **Freshmen returning for sophomore year:** 81%. **Graduation rates:** Four-year: 56%; five-year: 65%; six-year: 58%. **Graduate study:** 18% of students pursue further study immediately upon graduation; 23% within one year. Fields in which graduates pursue further study: Master of Business Administration (MBA), 18%; law, 7%; medicine, 3%; dentistry, 1%; theology (or the seminary), 3%; education, 5%; arts and sciences, 64%.

COSTS AND FINANCIAL AID

Financial aid office: (502) 452-8124. **Expenses (2006-2007):** Tuition and fees 2006-2007: $24,150; room/board: $6,880. Estimated books and supplies: $644; transportation: $2,166; personal expenses: $2,474. **Financial aid:** Priority filing date for institution's financial aid form: March 1. In 2005-2006, 77% of undergraduates applied for financial aid. Of those, 67% were determined to have financial need; 28% had their need fully met. Average financial aid package (proportion receiving): $15,600 (67%). Average amount of gift aid, such as scholarships or grants (proportion receiving): $11,714 (65%). Average amount of self-help aid, such as work study or loans (proportion receiving): N/A (47%). Among students who received need-based aid, the average percentage of need met: 83%. Average amount of debt of borrowers graduating in 2005: $12,263. Proportion who borrowed: 68%.

CAMPUS LIFE AND EXTRACURRICULAR ACTIVITIES

Campus housing available (% using): coed dorms (66%), women's dorms (22%), men's dorms (10%), apartment for single students (1%), special housing for disabled students (1%), other housing options (0%). Students who live in college-owned, operated, or affiliated housing: 40%. **Student employment:** During the 2005-2006 academic year, 10% of undergraduates worked on campus. Average per-year earnings: $2,000. **Clubs and organizations:** Number of student organizations: 61. Activities include: choral groups, dance, drama/theater, jazz band, literary magazine, music ensembles, musical theater, pep band, radio station, student government, student newspaper, yearbook. Number of fraternities: 1; sororities: 1. Average proportion of students who stay on campus on weekends: 45%. **Sports program (2005-2006):** Member of NCAA II. *Men's intercollegiate varsity sports:* baseball, basketball, cross-country, golf, lacrosse, soccer, tennis, track and field (indoor), track and field (outdoor). *Women's intercollegiate varsity sports:* basketball, cross-country, field hockey, golf, soccer, softball, tennis, track and field (indoor), track and field (outdoor), volleyball.

SERVICES AND FACILITIES

Basic services: nonremedial tutoring, placement service. **Counseling services:** career, personal, academic, psychological, religious. **For learning-disabled students:** School does not offer a structured program with separate admission and additional fees. Total undergraduates in learning-disabled program or receiving services: 120. Services include: reading machines, tape recorders, videotaped classes, untimed tests, note-taking services, oral tests, learning center, readers, extended time for tests, tutors, texts on tape, typist/scribe, exams on tape or computer, other testing accomodations, other. **Library:** Number of titles: 115,719; number of current serial subscriptions: 550. **Information technology resources:** Students are not required to lease or own a computer. Number of campus computers available to all students: 600. School has a wireless network. Approximate number of users that can be accommodated: 1,500. Proportion of college-owned housing units wired for high-speed internet access: 100%. **Campus safety:** Security services offered: 24-hour foot and vehicle patrols, late-night transport/escort service, 24-hour emergency telephones, lighted pathways/sidewalks, controlled dormitory access (key, security card, etc).

TRANSFER AND INTERNATIONAL STUDENTS

Transfer students: May apply for admission for the following academic terms: Fall, Spring, Summer. Applicants do not need a minimum number of credits to apply. For fall 2005: Transfer applications received: 271. Transfer applicants offered admission: 218. Transfer applicants enrolled: 152. **International students:** Number of foreign undergraduates: 20 (1% of student body). Number of countries represented: 12. Minimum TOEFL score required: 550 (paper); 213 (computer).

Berea College

- **Address:** CPO Box 2142, Berea, KY 40404
- **Website:** http://www.berea.edu
- **Private**
- **Enrollment:** 1,529 full-time; 66 part-time

KEY STATS

✔ **U.S News College Ranking:** 1, Comp. Coll.–Bachelor's (South)
✔ **ACT Score (25th/75th percentile):** 21-25
✔ **Tuition:** 2006-2007: $520

Selectivity: More selective	**Room/board:** $5,230
Acceptance rate: 27%	**Average debt:** $7,299
Student/faculty ratio: 11/1	**Proportion who borrowed:** 79%

UNDERGRADUATE STUDENT BODY STATS

2005-2006 enrollment: 1,529 full-time; 66 part-time. Men: 41%; women: 59%. **Ethnic makeup:** African American: 19%; American-Indian: 1%; Asian American: 1%; Hispanic: 2%; White: 70%; International: 7%.

ADMISSIONS FACTS AND FIGURES

Phone: (859) 985-3500. **Email:** admissions@berea.edu. **Website:** http://www.berea.edu. **Application deadlines for fall 2007:** Regular decision: April 30. Early decision: Not offered. Early action: Not offered. Admission cannot be deferred. **Application fee:** None. Common application is not accepted. **To apply online, go to:** http://www.berea.edu/futurestudents/domestic/admissions/applyonline.asp. **Admissions requirements/recommendations:** High school units required (recommended): English: 4 (4); Mathematics: 3 (3); Science: 2 (2); Foreign language: 2 (2); Social studies: 1 (1); History: 1 (1); Total units: 13 (13). Tests: The college uses SAT or ACT scores in admissions decisions. Either SAT or ACT required. For admission to the fall 2007 entering class, the school will accept: ACT with writing, ACT without writing. Campus visit: Recommended. Admissions interview: Required. Off-campus interview: May be arranged. **Factors that count in admissions decisions:** *Academic:* Secondary school record: Very important. Class rank: Very important. Letters of recommendation: Considered. Standardized test scores: Very important. Essay: Important. *Nonacademic:* Interview: Important. Extracurricular activities: Important. Talent/ability: Important. Character/personal qualities: Important. Alumni/ae relationship: Not considered. Geographical residence: Very important. State residency: Considered. Religious affiliation/commitment: Not considered. Minority status: Important. Volunteer work: Important. Work experience: Considered. **Other schools with the greatest overlap in applicants:** Eastern Kentucky University; Morehead State University; University of Kentucky; University of Louisville; University of Tennessee. **Admissions statistics for the fall 2005 entering class:** Total applicants: 1,908. Total accepted: 511. Freshmen enrolled: 378; 56% were from out of state. Overall acceptance rate: 27%. **Credentials of fall 2005 freshmen:** 30% ranked in the top 10 percent of their high school class; 66% were in the top 25 percent, and 91% were in the top half. (Proportion submitting class standing: 84%.) **Average high school grade point average:** 3.5. **First-year students who submitted SAT scores:** 25%. Scores (25/75 percentile): Verbal: 510-638, Math: 503-618, Combined: 1013-1256. **First-year students submitting ACT scores:** 73%. Scores (25/75 percentile): English: 21-26, Math: 18-24, Composite: 21-25.

ACADEMICS

Year founded: 1855. **Academic calendar:** 4-1-4. **Degrees offered:** bachelor's. **Most popular majors:** 10% business/commerce, 9% industrial technology/technician, 8% family and consumer sciences/human sciences,

7% psychology, 6% biology/biological sciences. **Major fields of study:** agriculture, agriculture operations, and related sciences; area, ethnic, cultural, and gender studies; biological and biomedical sciences; business, management, marketing, and related support services; communication, journalism, and related programs; education; engineering technologies/technicians; English language and literature/letters; family and consumer sciences/human sciences; foreign languages, literatures, and linguistics; health professions and related clinical sciences; mathematics and statistics; multi/interdisciplinary studies; philosophy and religious studies; physical sciences; psychology; social sciences; visual and performing arts. **Areas of required coursework:** arts/fine arts, humanities, mathematics, English (including composition), sciences (biological or physical), history, social science, other. **Pre-professional programs:** pre-law, pre-medicine, pre-veterinary science. **Special academic programs:** double major, exchange student program (domestic), honors program, independent study, internships, student-designed major, study abroad, teacher certificate program, other. **Teacher certification offered in:** early childhood, elementary, middle/junior high, secondary. **Reserve Officers Training Corps (ROTC):** Army ROTC: Offered at cooperating institution (Eastern KY Univ). **Faculty and instruction (2005-2006):** Total instructional faculty: 130 full-time, 29 part-time (59% men; 41% women; 11% minorities). Full-time faculty with Ph.D. or other terminal degree: 92%. Student/faculty ratio: 11/1. Classes of fewer than 20 students: 66%; of 20 to 49 students: 34%; of 50 or more students: 0%. **Advanced Placement and International Baccalaureate credit:** AP tests may be used for: Credit and/or placement. Scores accepted: 3, 4, 5. International Baccalaureate exams may be used for: Credit only. **Freshmen returning for sophomore year:** 81%. **Graduation rates:** Four-year: 35%; five-year: 61%; six-year: 56%.

COSTS AND FINANCIAL AID

Financial aid office: (859) 985-3310. **Expenses (2006-2007):** Tuition and fees 2006-2007: $520; room/board: $5,230. Estimated books and supplies: $750; transportation: $400; personal expenses: $1,350. **Financial aid:** Priority filing date for institution's financial aid form: April 15; deadline: August 1. In 2005-2006, 100% of undergraduates applied for financial aid. Of those, 100% were determined to have financial need; 23% had their need fully met. Average financial aid package (proportion receiving): $26,299 (100%). Average amount of gift aid, such as scholarships or grants (proportion receiving): $24,062 (100%). Average amount of self-help aid, such as work study or loans (proportion receiving): $1,712 (100%). Average need-based loan (excluding PLUS or other private loans): $1,190. Among students who received need-based aid, the average percentage of need met: 92%. Among students who received aid based on merit, the average award (and the proportion receiving): $0 (0%). The average athletic scholarship (and the proportion receiving): $0 (0%). Average amount of debt of borrowers graduating in 2005: $7,299. Proportion who borrowed: 79%.

CAMPUS LIFE AND EXTRACURRICULAR ACTIVITIES

Campus housing available (% using): women's dorms (54%), men's dorms (41%), apartments for married students (3%), cooperative housing (1%), other housing options (1%). Students who live in college-owned, operated, or affiliated housing: 84%. **Student employment:** During the 2005-2006 academic year, 100% of undergraduates worked on campus. Average per-year earnings: $1,713. **Clubs and organizations:** Number of student organizations: 77. Activities include: choral groups, dance, drama/theater, jazz band, literary magazine, music ensembles, pep band, student government, student newspaper, yearbook. Number of fraternities: 0; sororities: 0. Average proportion of students who stay on campus on weekends: 65%. **Sports program (2005-2006):** Member of NAIA. *Men's intercollegiate varsity sports:* baseball, basketball, cheerleading, cross-country, golf, soccer, swimming and diving, tennis, track and field (indoor), track and field (outdoor). *Women's intercollegiate varsity sports:* basketball, cheerleading, cross-country, soccer, softball, swimming and diving, tennis, track and field (indoor), track and field (outdoor), volleyball.

SERVICES AND FACILITIES

Basic services: nonremedial tutoring, placement service, day care, health service, health insurance. **Remedial assistance:** math, other. **Counseling services:** minority student, career, personal, academic, older student, psychological, birth control, religious. **For learning-disabled students:** School does not offer a structured program with separate admission and additional fees. Total undergraduates in learning-disabled program or receiving services: 45. Services include: remedial math, tape recorders, diagnostic testing service, note-taking services, oral tests, learning center, extended time for tests, tutors, priority seating, texts on tape, other testing accomodations. **Library:**

Number of titles: 363,566; number of current serial subscriptions: 998. **Information technology resources:** Students are not required to lease or own a computer. Number of campus computers available to all students: 1,600. School has a wireless network. Approximate number of users that can be accommodated: 575. Proportion of college-owned housing units wired for high-speed internet access: 100%. **Campus safety:** Security services offered: 24-hour foot and vehicle patrols, 24-hour emergency telephones, lighted pathways/sidewalks, controlled dormitory access (key, security card, etc).

TRANSFER AND INTERNATIONAL STUDENTS

Transfer students: May apply for admission for the following academic terms: Fall, Spring. Applicants do not need a minimum number of credits to apply. For fall 2005: Transfer applications received: 120. Transfer applicants offered admission: 32. Transfer applicants enrolled: 27. **International students:** Number of foreign undergraduates: 109 (7% of student body). Number of countries represented: 67. Minimum TOEFL score required: 500 (paper); 173 (computer). Average TOEFL score: 600 (paper).

Brescia University

- **Address:** 717 Frederica Street, Owensboro, KY 42301
- **Website:** http://www.brescia.edu
- **Private; Religious affiliation:** Roman Catholic
- **Enrollment:** 428 full-time; 216 part-time

KEY STATS

✔ **U.S News College Ranking:** 34, Comp. Coll.–Bachelor's (South)
✔ **ACT Score (25th/75th percentile):** 18-23
✔ **Tuition:** 2006-2007: $13,620

Selectivity: Selective	**Room/board:** $5,800
Acceptance rate: 75%	**Average debt:** N/A
Student/faculty ratio: 9/1	**Proportion who borrowed:** N/A

UNDERGRADUATE STUDENT BODY STATS

2005-2006 enrollment: 428 full-time; 216 part-time. Men: 45%; women: 55%. **Ethnic makeup:** African American: 4%; Hispanic: 1%; White: 84%; International: 10%. **Religious preference:** Protestant: 31%; Unknown: 25%; Roman Catholic: 43%; Greek Orthodox: 0%; Other: 1%.

ADMISSIONS FACTS AND FIGURES

Phone: (270) 686-4241. **Email:** admissions@brescia.edu. **Website:** http://www.brescia.edu. **Application deadlines for fall 2007:** Regular decision: Rolling. Early decision: Not offered. Early action: Not offered. Admission can be deferred. **Application fee:** $25. Common application is accepted. **To apply online, go to:** http://www.brescia.edu/admissions/application/index.asp. **Admissions requirements/recommendations:** High school units required (recommended): English: 4; Mathematics: 3; Science: 2; Foreign language: (2); Social studies: 2; Total units: (17). Tests: The college uses SAT or ACT scores in admissions decisions. Either SAT or ACT required. For admission to the fall 2007 entering class, the school will accept: ACT with writing, ACT without writing. Campus visit: Recommended. Admissions interview: Recommended. Off-campus interview: May be arranged. **Factors that count in admissions decisions:** *Academic:* Secondary school record: Not considered. Class rank: Not considered. Letters of recommendation: Not considered. Standardized test scores: Very important. Essay: Not considered. *Nonacademic:* Interview: Not considered. Extracurricular activities: Not considered. Talent/ability: Not considered. Character/personal qualities: Not considered. Alumni/ae relationship: Not considered. Geographical residence: Not considered. State residency: Not considered. Religious affiliation/commitment: Not considered. Minority status: Not considered. Volunteer work: Not considered. Work experience: Not considered. **Other schools with the greatest overlap in applicants:** University of Louisville; Western Kentucky University. **Admissions statistics for the fall 2005 entering class:** Total applicants: 126. Total accepted: 94. Freshmen enrolled: 48; 13% were from out of state. Overall acceptance rate: 75%. **Average high school grade point average:** 3.3. **First-year students who submitted SAT scores:** 16%. Scores (25/75 percentile): Verbal: 410-600; Math: 320-570, Combined: 730-1170. **First-year students submitting ACT scores:** 84%. Scores (25/75 percentile): English: 18-23, Math: 17-23, Composite: 18-23.

ACADEMICS

Year founded: 1950. **Academic calendar:** Semester. **Degrees offered:** associate, bachelor's, post-bachelor's certificate, master's. **Most popular majors:** 25% business, management, marketing, and related support services; 17% education; 12% public administration and social service professions; 11% biological and biomedical sciences; 9% liberal arts and sciences studies, and humanities. **Major fields of study:** biological and biomedical sciences; business, management, marketing, and related support services; education; English language and literature/letters; foreign languages, literatures, and linguistics; health professions and related clinical sciences; history; liberal arts and sciences studies, and humanities; mathematics and statistics; multi/interdisciplinary studies; physical sciences; psychology; public administration and social service professions; social sciences; theology and religious vocations; visual and performing arts. **Areas of required coursework:** arts/fine arts, humanities, computer literacy, mathematics, English (including composition), philosophy, foreign languages, sciences (biological or physical), history, social science, other. **Pre-professional programs:** pre-law, pre-dentistry, pre-medicine, pre-veterinary science, pre-optometry, pre-pharmacy, other. **Special academic programs:** cross-registration, distance learning, double major, English as a Second Language (ESL), exchange student program (domestic), honors program, independent study, internships, liberal arts/career combination, student-designed major, teacher certificate program, weekend college. **Teacher certification offered in:** special education, elementary, middle/junior high, secondary. **Faculty and instruction (2005-2006):** Total instructional faculty: 44 full-time, 33 part-time (55% men; 45% women; 6% minorities). Full-time faculty with Ph.D. or other terminal degree: 57%. Student/faculty ratio: 9/1. Classes of fewer than 20 students: 84%; of 20 to 49 students: 16%; of 50 or more students: 0%. **Advanced Placement and International Baccalaureate credit:** AP tests may be used for: Credit and/or placement. Scores accepted: 3, 4, 5. International Baccalaureate exams may be used for: Credit and/or placement. **Freshmen returning for sophomore year:** 80%. **Graduation rates:** Four-year: 32%; five-year: 43%; six-year: 47%.

COSTS AND FINANCIAL AID

Financial aid office: (270) 686-4253. **Expenses (2006-2007):** Tuition and fees 2006-2007: $13,620; room/board: $5,800. Estimated books and supplies: $1,000; transportation: $1,000; personal expenses: $1,000. **Financial aid:** Priority filing date for institution's financial aid form: August 1. In 2005-2006, 85% of undergraduates applied for financial aid. Of those, 72% were determined to have financial need; 33% had their need fully met. Average financial aid package (proportion receiving): $13,927 (72%). Average amount of gift aid, such as scholarships or grants (proportion receiving): $4,085 (49%). Average amount of self-help aid, such as work study or loans (proportion receiving): $1,316 (28%). Average need-based loan (excluding PLUS or other private loans): $768. Among students who received need-based aid, the average percentage of need met: 75%. Among students who received aid based on merit, the average award (and the proportion receiving): $8,293 (8%). The average athletic scholarship (and the proportion receiving): $7,037 (7%).

CAMPUS LIFE AND EXTRACURRICULAR ACTIVITIES

Campus housing available: coed dorms, women's dorms, men's dorms, apartment for single students, special housing for disabled students, other housing options. Students who live in college-owned, operated, or affiliated housing: 41%. **Clubs and organizations:** Number of student organizations: 36. Activities include: choral groups, dance, drama/theater, literary magazine, student government, student newspaper. Number of fraternities: 0; sororities: 0. Average proportion of students who stay on campus on weekends: 90%. **Sports program (2005-2006):** Member of NAIA. *Men's intercollegiate varsity sports:* baseball, basketball, golf, soccer. *Women's intercollegiate varsity sports:* basketball, golf, soccer, softball, volleyball.

SERVICES AND FACILITIES

Basic services: nonremedial tutoring, women's center, placement service, health insurance. **Remedial assistance:** reading, math, writing, study skills. **Counseling services:** minority student, career, personal, academic, psychological, religious, other. **For learning-disabled students:** School does not offer a structured program with separate admission and additional fees. **Information technology resources:** Students are not required to lease or own a computer. School has a wireless network. **Campus safety:** Security services offered: lighted pathways/sidewalks, controlled dormitory access (key, security card, etc).

TRANSFER AND INTERNATIONAL STUDENTS

Transfer students: May apply for admission for the following academic terms: Fall, Spring. Applicants do not need a minimum number of credits to apply. For fall 2005: Transfer applications received: 89. Transfer applicants offered admission: 64. Transfer applicants enrolled: 45. **International students:** Number of foreign undergraduates: 49 (10% of student body). Number of countries represented: 22. Minimum TOEFL score required: 550 (paper); 213 (computer).

Campbellsville University

- **Address:** 1 University Drive, Campbellsville, KY 42718
- **Website:** http://www.campbellsville.edu
- **Private; Religious affiliation:** Baptist
- **Enrollment:** 1,266 full-time; 570 part-time

KEY STATS

✔ **U.S News College Ranking:** third tier, Universities–Master's (South)
✔ **ACT Score (25th/75th percentile):** 18-24
✔ **Tuition:** 2006-2007: $16,340

Selectivity: Selective	Room/board: $5,932
Acceptance rate: 68%	Average debt: $18,437
Student/faculty ratio: 12/1	Proportion who borrowed: 80%

UNDERGRADUATE STUDENT BODY STATS

2005-2006 enrollment: 1,266 full-time; 570 part-time. Men: 44%; women: 56%. **Ethnic makeup:** African American: 5%; Asian American: 1%; Hispanic: 1%; White: 91%; International: 3%.

ADMISSIONS FACTS AND FIGURES

Phone: (270) 789-5220. **Email:** admissions@campbellsville.edu. **Website:** http://www.campbellsville.edu. **Application deadlines for fall 2007:** Regular decision: August 1. Early decision: Not offered. Early action: Not offered. Admission can be deferred. **Application fee:** $20. Common application is accepted. **Admissions requirements/recommendations:** High school units required (recommended): English: 4 (4); Mathematics: 3 (3); Science: 3 (3); Social studies: 2 (2); History: 1 (1); Academic electives: 6 (6); Total units: 21 (21). Tests: The college uses SAT or ACT scores in admissions decisions. Either SAT or ACT required. For admission to the fall 2007 entering class, the school will accept: ACT with writing, ACT without writing. Campus visit: Recommended. Admissions interview: Recommended. Off-campus interview: May be arranged. **Factors that count in admissions decisions:** *Academic:* Secondary school record: Very important. Class rank: Important. Letters of recommendation: Important. Standardized test scores: Important. Essay: Considered. *Nonacademic:* Interview: Important. Extracurricular activities: Considered. Talent/ability: Considered. Character/personal qualities: Important. Alumni/ae relationship: Considered. Geographical residence: Not considered. State residency: Not considered. Religious affiliation/commitment: Considered. Minority status: Not considered. Volunteer work: Considered. Work experience: Considered. **Other schools with the greatest overlap in applicants:** Eastern Kentucky University; Georgetown College; Lindsey Wilson College; University of the Cumberlands; Western Kentucky University. **Admissions statistics for the fall 2005 entering class:** Total applicants: 1,351. Total accepted: 922. Freshmen enrolled: 356; 16% were from out of state. Overall acceptance rate: 68%. **Credentials of fall 2005 freshmen:** 16% ranked in the top 10 percent of their high school class; 38% were in the top 25 percent. **First-year students who submitted SAT scores:** 6%. Scores (25/75 percentile): Verbal: 430-560, Math: 440-560, Combined: 870-1120. **First-year students submitting ACT scores:** 86%. Scores (25/75 percentile): English: N/A, Math: N/A, Composite: 18-24.

ACADEMICS

Year founded: 1906. **Academic calendar:** Semester. **Degrees offered:** certificate, associate, bachelor's, master's. **Most popular majors:** 19% business, management, marketing, and related support services, 16% education, 12% theology and religious vocations, 10% public administration and social service professions, 8% social sciences. **Major fields of study:** biological and biomedical sciences; business, management, marketing, and related support services; communication, journalism, and related programs; computer and information sciences and support services; education; English language and literature/letters; mathematics and statistics; parks, recreation, leisure, and fitness studies; physical sciences; psychology; social sciences; theology and religious vocations; visual and performing arts. **Areas of required coursework:** arts/fine arts, humanities, computer literacy, mathematics, English (including composition), philosophy, sciences (biological or physical), history, social science, other. **Pre-professional programs:** pre-law, pre-dentistry, pre-medicine, pre-theology, pre-veterinary science, pre-optometry, pre-pharmacy. **Special academic programs:** accelerated program, distance learning, double major, dual enrollment, English as a Second Language (ESL), honors program, independent study, internships, study abroad, teacher certificate program, weekend college. **Teacher certification offered in:** early childhood, special education, elementary, middle/junior high, secondary. **Faculty and instruction (2005-2006):** Total instructional faculty: 86 full-time, 131 part-time (48% men; 52% women; 8% minorities). Full-time faculty with Ph.D. or other terminal degree: 66%. Student/faculty ratio: 12/1. Classes of fewer than 20 students: 76%; of 20 to 49 students: 24%. **Advanced Placement and International Baccalaureate credit:** AP tests may be used for: Credit only. Scores accepted: 3. **Freshmen returning for sophomore year:** 63%. **Graduation rates:** Four-year: 27%; five-year: 32%; six-year: 37%.

COSTS AND FINANCIAL AID

Financial aid office: (270) 789-5013. **Expenses (2006-2007):** Tuition and fees 2006-2007: $16,340; room/board: $5,932. Estimated books and supplies: $1,000; transportation: $1,100; personal expenses: $1,900. **Financial aid:** In 2005-2006, 86% of undergraduates applied for financial aid. Of those, 78% were determined to have financial need; 25% had their need fully met. Average financial aid package (proportion receiving): $11,897 (77%). Average amount of gift aid, such as scholarships or grants (proportion receiving): $8,953 (76%). Average amount of self-help aid, such as work study or loans (proportion receiving): $3,935 (60%). Average need-based loan (excluding PLUS or other private loans): $3,447. Among students who received need-based aid, the average percentage of need met: 72%. Among students who received aid based on merit, the average award (and the proportion receiving): $7,860 (16%). The average athletic scholarship (and the proportion receiving): $6,480 (6%). Average amount of debt of borrowers graduating in 2005: $18,437. Proportion who borrowed: 80%.

CAMPUS LIFE AND EXTRACURRICULAR ACTIVITIES

Campus housing available: women's dorms, men's dorms, apartments for married students. Students who live in college-owned, operated, or affiliated housing: 52%. **Student employment:** During the 2005-2006 academic year, 12% of undergraduates worked on campus. Average per-year earnings: $1,500. **Clubs and organizations:** Number of student organizations: 40. Activities include: choral groups, concert band, dance, drama/theater, jazz band, literary magazine, marching band, music ensembles, musical theater, pep band, radio station, student government, student newspaper, television station, yearbook. Average proportion of students who stay on campus on weekends: 30%. **Sports program (2005-2006):** Member of NAIA. *Men's intercollegiate varsity sports:* baseball, basketball, cross-country, football, golf, soccer, tennis, track and field (outdoor), wrestling. *Women's intercollegiate varsity sports:* basketball, cross-country, golf, soccer, softball, tennis, track and field (outdoor), volleyball.

SERVICES AND FACILITIES

Basic services: nonremedial tutoring, placement service, health service, health insurance. **Remedial assistance:** reading, math, writing, study skills. **Counseling services:** career, personal, academic, psychological, religious. **Library:** Number of titles: 89,441; number of current serial subscriptions: 338. **Information technology resources:** Students are not required to lease or own a computer. Number of campus computers available to all students: 160. School does not have a wireless network. **Campus safety:** Security services offered: 24-hour foot and vehicle patrols, late-night transport/escort service, 24-hour emergency telephones, lighted pathways/sidewalks, controlled dormitory access (key, security card, etc).

TRANSFER AND INTERNATIONAL STUDENTS

Transfer students: May apply for admission for the following academic terms: Fall, Spring, Summer. Applicants do not need a minimum number of credits to apply. For fall 2005: Transfer applications received: 274. Transfer applicants offered admission: 196. Transfer applicants enrolled: 128. **International students:** Number of foreign undergraduates: 46 (3% of student body). Minimum TOEFL score required: 500 (paper); 177 (computer).

Centre College

- **Address:** 600 W. Walnut Street, Danville, KY 40422
- **Website:** http://www.centre.edu
- **Private; Religious affiliation:** Presbyterian (U.S.A.)
- **Enrollment:** 1,127 full-time; 3 part-time

KEY STATS
✔ **U.S News College Ranking:** 44, Liberal Arts Colleges
✔ **ACT Score (25th/75th percentile):** 25-29
✔ **Tuition:** 2005-2006: $23,110
  Selectivity: More selective   **Room/board:** $7,700
  Acceptance rate: 63%   **Average debt:** $13,700
  Student/faculty ratio: 11/1   **Proportion who borrowed:** 58%

UNDERGRADUATE STUDENT BODY STATS
2005-2006 enrollment: 1,127 full-time; 3 part-time. Men: 49%; women: 51%. **Ethnic makeup:** African American: 2%; Asian American: 2%; Hispanic: 1%; White: 93%; International: 2%. **Religious preference:** Roman Catholic: 21%; Protestant: 47%; Jewish: 1%; Muslim: 1%; Buddhist: 1%; No preference: 18%; Unknown: 1%; Presbyterian (U.S.A.): 9%.

ADMISSIONS FACTS AND FIGURES
Phone: (859) 238-5350. **Email:** admission@centre.edu. **Website:** http://www.centre.edu. **Application deadlines for fall 2007:** Regular decision: February 1; decision sent by March 1. Early decision: Not offered. Early action: Send application by: December 1; Decision sent by: January 15. Admission can be deferred. **Application fee:** $40. Common application is accepted. **To apply online, go to:** http://www.centre.edu/web/admission/howtoapply.html. **Admissions requirements/recommendations:** High school units required (recommended): English: 4 (4); Mathematics: 4 (4); Science: 2 (3); Foreign language: 2 (3); Social studies: 2 (3); Academic electives: 2 (2); Total units: 16 (19). Tests: The college uses SAT or ACT scores in admissions decisions. Either SAT or ACT required. For admission to the fall 2007 entering class, the school will accept: ACT with writing, ACT without writing. Campus visit: Recommended. Admissions interview: Recommended. Off-campus interview: May be arranged. **Factors that count in admissions decisions:** *Academic:* Secondary school record: Very important. Class rank: Important. Letters of recommendation: Considered. Standardized test scores: Very important. Essay: Important. *Nonacademic:* Interview: Considered. Extracurricular activities: Important. Talent/ability: Important. Character/personal qualities: Important. Alumni/ae relationship: Considered. Geographical residence: Considered. State residency: Not considered. Religious affiliation/commitment: Not considered. Minority status: Considered. Volunteer work: Considered. Work experience: Considered. **Other schools with the greatest overlap in applicants:** Furman University; Rhodes College; Transylvania University; University of Kentucky; Vanderbilt University. **Admissions statistics for the fall 2005 entering class:** Total applicants: 1,983. Total accepted: 1,259. Freshmen enrolled: 316; 36% were from out of state. Accepted through early-decision or early-action plans: 55%. Overall acceptance rate: 63%. Non-early acceptance rate: 54%. **Size of waiting list:** 102 applicants; enrolled from waiting list: 5. **Credentials of fall 2005 freshmen:** 56% ranked in the top 10 percent of their high school class; 85% were in the top 25 percent, and 97% were in the top half. (Proportion submitting class standing: 72%.) **First-year students who submitted SAT scores:** 71%. Scores (25/75 percentile): Verbal: 580-690, Math: 600-680, Combined: 1180-1370. **First-year students submitting ACT scores:** 90%. Scores (25/75 percentile): English: 25-31, Math: 24-28, Composite: 25-29.

ACADEMICS
Year founded: 1819. **Academic calendar:** 4-1-4. **Degrees offered:** bachelor's. **Most popular majors:** 14% history, 10% English language and literature, 10% economics, 9% biology/biological sciences, 9% political science and government. **Major fields of study:** biological and biomedical sciences; computer and information sciences and support services; education; English language and literature/letters; foreign languages, literatures, and linguistics; history; mathematics and statistics; multi/interdisciplinary studies; philosophy and religious studies; physical sciences; psychology; social sciences; visual and performing arts. **Areas of required coursework:** humanities, mathematics, philosophy, foreign languages, sciences (biological or physical), history, social science. **Special academic programs (% participation):** cross-registration (1%), double major (22%), honors program (3%), independent study (36%), internships (28%), student-designed major (0%), study abroad (70%), teacher certificate program (5%). **Teacher certification offered in:** elementary, secondary. **Reserve Officers Training Corps (ROTC):** Army ROTC: Offered at cooperating institution (University of Kentucky); Air Force ROTC: Offered at cooperating institution (University of Kentucky). **Faculty and instruction (2005-2006):** Total instructional faculty: 96 full-time, 27 part-time (63% men; 37% women; 5% minorities). Full-time faculty with Ph.D. or other terminal degree: 98%. Student/faculty ratio: 11/1. Classes of fewer than 20 students: 54%; of 20 to 49 students: 46%; of 50 or more students: 0%. **Advanced Placement and International Baccalaureate credit:** AP tests may be used for: Credit and/or placement. Scores accepted: 4, 5. International Baccalaureate exams may be used for: Credit and/or placement. **Freshmen returning for sophomore year:** 89%. **Graduation rates:** Four-year: 77%; five-year: 78%; six-year: 79%. **Graduate study:** 32% of students pursue further study immediately upon graduation; 37% within one year. Fields in which graduates pursue further study: Master of Business Administration (MBA), 2%; law, 19%; medicine, 6%; theology (or the seminary), 2%; education, 3%; arts and sciences, 67%; veterinary medicine, 1%.

COSTS AND FINANCIAL AID
Financial aid office: (859) 238-5365. **Expenses (2005-2006):** Tuition and fees 2005-2006: $23,110; room/board: $7,700. Estimated books and supplies: $890; transportation: $300; personal expenses: $700. **Financial aid:** Priority filing date for institution's financial aid form: March 1; deadline: March 1. In 2005-2006, 74% of undergraduates applied for financial aid. Of those, 61% were determined to have financial need; 38% had their need fully met. Average financial aid package (proportion receiving): $18,526 (61%). Average amount of gift aid, such as scholarships or grants (proportion receiving): $15,809 (60%). Average amount of self-help aid, such as work study or loans (proportion receiving): $4,632 (43%). Average need-based loan (excluding PLUS or other private loans): $4,110. Among students who received need-based aid, the average percentage of need met: 88%. Among students who received aid based on merit, the average award (and the proportion receiving): $10,381 (34%). The average athletic scholarship (and the proportion receiving): $0 (0%). Average amount of debt of borrowers graduating in 2005: $13,700. Proportion who borrowed: 58%.

CAMPUS LIFE AND EXTRACURRICULAR ACTIVITIES
Campus housing available (% using): coed dorms (31%), women's dorms (34%), men's dorms (19%), sorority housing (4%), fraternity housing (5%), apartment for single students (6%), special housing for disabled students (0%), special housing for international students (1%). Students who live in college-owned, operated, or affiliated housing: 93%. **Student employment:** During the 2005-2006 academic year, 24% of undergraduates worked on campus. Average per-year earnings: $500. **Clubs and organizations:** Number of student organizations: 81. Activities include: choral groups, concert band, dance, drama/theater, jazz band, literary magazine, music ensembles, musical theater, pep band, student government, student newspaper, student film society, yearbook. Number of fraternities: 5; sororities: 4. Proportion of men in fraternities: 49%; of women in sororities: 55%. Average proportion of students who stay on campus on weekends: 70%. **Sports program (2005-2006):** Member of NCAA III. *Men's intercollegiate varsity sports:* baseball, basketball, cross-country, football, golf, soccer, swimming and diving, tennis, track and field (outdoor). *Women's intercollegiate varsity sports:* basketball, cross-country, field hockey, golf, soccer, softball, swimming and diving, tennis, track and field (outdoor), volleyball.

SERVICES AND FACILITIES
Basic services: nonremedial tutoring, placement service, health service. **Remedial assistance:** writing. **Counseling services:** minority student, career, personal, academic, psychological, birth control, religious. **For learning-disabled students:** School does not offer a structured program with separate admission and additional fees. Total undergraduates in learning-disabled program or receiving services: 29. Services include: tape recorders, other special classes, videotaped classes, note-taking services, oral tests, learning center, readers, extended time for tests, tutors, early syllabus, priority registration, priority seating, proofreading services, texts on tape, other testing accomodations. **Library:** Number of titles: 221,636; number of current serial subscriptions: 2,360. **Information technology resources:** Students are not required to lease or own a computer. Number of campus computers available to all students: 260. School has a wireless network. Approximate number of users that can be accommodated: 800. Proportion of college-owned housing units wired for high-speed internet access: 100%. **Campus safety:** Security services offered: 24-hour foot and vehicle patrols, late-night trans-

port/escort service, 24-hour emergency telephones, lighted pathways/sidewalks, controlled dormitory access (key, security card, etc).

TRANSFER AND INTERNATIONAL STUDENTS
Transfer students: May apply for admission for the following academic terms: Fall, Winter, Spring. Applicants do not need a minimum number of credits to apply. For fall 2005: Transfer applications received: 51. Transfer applicants offered admission: 21. Transfer applicants enrolled: 13. **International students:** Number of foreign undergraduates: 22 (2% of student body). Minimum TOEFL score required: 580 (paper); 237 (computer). Average TOEFL score: 604 (paper).

Eastern Kentucky University

- **Address:** 521 Lancaster Avenue, Richmond, KY 40475
- **Website:** http://www.eku.edu
- **Public**
- **Enrollment:** 10,919 full-time; 3,023 part-time

KEY STATS
✔ **U.S News College Ranking:** third tier, Universities–Master's (South)
✔ **ACT Score (25th/75th percentile):** 18-23
✔ **Tuition:** 2006-2007: $5,120 in state, $13,530 out of state
  Selectivity: Selective   **Room/board:** $5,257
  Acceptance rate: 73%   **Average debt:** $16,906
  Student/faculty ratio: 17/1   **Proportion who borrowed:** 48%

UNDERGRADUATE STUDENT BODY STATS
2005-2006 enrollment: 10,919 full-time; 3,023 part-time. Men: 39%; women: 61%. **Ethnic makeup:** African American: 4%; Asian American: 1%; Hispanic: 1%; White: 93%; International: 1%.

ADMISSIONS FACTS AND FIGURES
Phone: (800) 465-9191. **Email:** admissions@eku.edu. **Website:** http://www.eku.edu. **Application deadlines for fall 2007:** Regular decision: August 1. Early decision: Not offered. Early action: Not offered. Admission can be deferred. **Application fee:** $30. Common application is not accepted. **To apply online, go to:** http://www.admissions.eku.edu/. **Admissions requirements/recommendations:** High school units required (recommended): English: 4; Mathematics: 3; Science: 3; Foreign language: 2; Social studies: 3; History: 0; Academic electives: 7; Total units: 25. Tests: The college uses SAT or ACT scores in admissions decisions. ACT required. For admission to the fall 2007 entering class, the school will accept: ACT without writing. Campus visit: Neither required nor recommended. Admissions interview: Neither required nor recommended. Off-campus interview: Not available. **Factors that count in admissions decisions:** *Academic:* Secondary school record: Very important. Class rank: Not considered. Letters of recommendation: Not considered. Standardized test scores: Very important. Essay: Not considered. *Nonacademic:* Interview: Not considered. Extracurricular activities: Not considered. Talent/ability: Not considered. Character/personal qualities: Not considered. Alumni/ae relationship: Not considered. Geographical residence: Not considered. State residency: Not considered. Religious affiliation/commitment: Not considered. Minority status: Not considered. Volunteer work: Not considered. Work experience: Not considered. **Other schools with the greatest overlap in applicants:** Morehead State University; Northern Kentucky University; University of Kentucky; Western Kentucky University. **Admissions statistics for the fall 2005 entering class:** Total applicants: 6,208. Total accepted: 4,552. Freshmen enrolled: 2,500; 3% were from out of state. Overall acceptance rate: 73%. **Credentials of fall 2005 freshmen:** 13% ranked in the top 10 percent of their high school class; 35% were in the top 25 percent. **Average high school grade point average:** 3.2. **First-year students who submitted SAT scores:** 11%. Scores (25/75 percentile): Verbal: 450-560, Math: 440-580, Combined: 890-1140. **First-year students submitting ACT scores:** 98%. Scores (25/75 percentile): English: 17-23, Math: 17-22, Composite: 18-23.

ACADEMICS
Year founded: 1906. **Academic calendar:** Semester. **Degrees offered:** certificate, associate, bachelor's, post-bachelor's certificate, master's, post-master's certificate. **Most popular majors:** 8% elementary education and teaching, 6% criminal justice/law enforcement administration, 6% nursing/registered nurse training (R.N., A.S.N., B.S.N., M.S.N.), 4% occupational ther-

apy/therapist, 4% psychology. **Major fields of study:** agriculture, agriculture operations, and related sciences; biological and biomedical sciences; business, management, marketing, and related support services; communication, journalism, and related programs; communications technologies/technicians and support services; computer and information sciences and support services; education; engineering technologies/technicians; English language and literature/letters; family and consumer sciences/human sciences; foreign languages, literatures, and linguistics; health professions and related clinical sciences; history; legal professions and studies; liberal arts and sciences studies, and humanities; mathematics and statistics; natural resources and conservation; parks, recreation, leisure, and fitness studies; philosophy and religious studies; physical sciences; psychology; public administration and social service professions; security and protective services; social sciences; transportation and materials moving; visual and performing arts. **Areas of required coursework:** arts/fine arts, humanities, computer literacy, mathematics, English (including composition), foreign languages, sciences (biological or physical), history, social science, other. **Pre-professional programs:** pre-law, pre-dentistry, pre-medicine, pre-veterinary science, pre-optometry, pre-pharmacy. **Special academic programs:** cooperative (work-study plan) program, distance learning, double major, dual enrollment, English as a Second Language (ESL), honors program, independent study, internships, student-designed major, study abroad, teacher certificate program. **Teacher certification offered in:** early childhood, special education, elementary, vo-tech, middle/junior high, secondary. **Cooperative education programs:** agriculture, business, computer science, education, health professions, home economics, humanities, natural science, social/behavioral science, technologies, vocational arts, other. **Reserve Officers Training Corps (ROTC):** Army ROTC: Offered on campus; Air Force ROTC: Offered at cooperating institution (University of Kentucky). **Faculty and instruction (2005-2006):** Total instructional faculty: 556 full-time, 454 part-time (49% men; 51% women; 8% minorities). Full-time faculty with Ph.D. or other terminal degree: 75%. Student/faculty ratio: 17/1. Classes of fewer than 20 students: 52%; of 20 to 49 students: 45%; of 50 or more students: 3%. **Advanced Placement and International Baccalaureate credit:** AP tests may be used for: Credit only. Scores accepted: 3, 4, 5. International Baccalaureate exams may be used for: Credit only. **Freshmen returning for sophomore year:** 67%. **Graduation rates:** Four-year: 13%; five-year: 31%; six-year: 36%. **Graduate study:** 46% of students pursue further study within one year.

COSTS AND FINANCIAL AID
Financial aid office: (859) 622-2361. **Expenses (2006-2007):** Tuition and fees 2006-2007: $5,120 in state, $13,530 out of state; room/board: $5,257. Estimated books and supplies: $800 personal expenses: $1,550. **Financial aid:** Priority filing date for institution's financial aid form: April 1. In 2005-2006, 74% of undergraduates applied for financial aid. Of those, 57% were determined to have financial need; 10% had their need fully met. Average financial aid package (proportion receiving): $7,185 (56%). Average amount of gift aid, such as scholarships or grants (proportion receiving): $4,823 (36%). Average amount of self-help aid, such as work study or loans (proportion receiving): $3,620 (47%). Average need-based loan (excluding PLUS or other private loans): $3,108. Among students who received need-based aid, the average percentage of need met: 85%. Among students who received aid based on merit, the average award (and the proportion receiving): $2,014 (24%). The average athletic scholarship (and the proportion receiving): $9,382 (3%). Average amount of debt of borrowers graduating in 2005: $16,906. Proportion who borrowed: 48%.

CAMPUS LIFE AND EXTRACURRICULAR ACTIVITIES
Campus housing available (% using): coed dorms (50%), women's dorms (33%), men's dorms (17%), apartments for married students, apartment for single students, special housing for disabled students. Students who live in college-owned, operated, or affiliated housing: 31%. **Student employment:** During the 2005-2006 academic year, 10% of undergraduates worked on campus. Average per-year earnings: $2,000. **Clubs and organizations:** Number of student organizations: 192. Activities include: choral groups, concert band, dance, drama/theater, jazz band, literary magazine, marching band, music ensembles, musical theater, pep band, radio station, student government, student newspaper, symphony orchestra. Number of fraternities: 12; sororities: 13. Proportion of men in fraternities: 8%; of women in sororities: 6%. Average proportion of students who stay on campus on weekends: 40%. **Sports program (2005-2006):** Member of NCAA I. *Men's intercollegiate varsity sports:* baseball, basketball, cross-country, football, golf, tennis, track and field (indoor), track and field (outdoor). *Women's intercollegiate varsity sports:* basketball, cross-country, golf, soccer, softball, tennis, track and field (indoor), track and field (outdoor), volleyball.

SERVICES AND FACILITIES

Basic services: nonremedial tutoring, health service. **Remedial assistance:** reading, math, writing, study skills. **Counseling services:** minority student, career, personal, academic, psychological, religious. **For learning-disabled students:** School does not offer a structured program with separate admission and additional fees. Total undergraduates in learning-disabled program or receiving services: 280. Services include: remedial math, remedial English, reading machines, remedial reading, tape recorders, other special classes, diagnostic testing service, note-taking services, oral tests, learning center, readers, extended time for tests, tutors, other. **Library:** Number of titles: 659,448; number of current serial subscriptions: 3,206. **Information technology resources:** Students are not required to lease or own a computer. Number of campus computers available to all students: 532. School has a wireless network. Approximate number of users that can be accommodated: 3,500. Proportion of college-owned housing units wired for high-speed internet access: 98%. **Campus safety:** Security services offered: 24-hour foot and vehicle patrols, late-night transport/escort service, 24-hour emergency telephones, lighted pathways/sidewalks, controlled dormitory access (key, security card, etc).

TRANSFER AND INTERNATIONAL STUDENTS

Transfer students: May apply for admission for the following academic terms: Fall, Spring, Summer. Applicants do not need a minimum number of credits to apply. For fall 2005: Transfer applications received: 2,426. Transfer applicants offered admission: 1,522. Transfer applicants enrolled: 1,018. **International students:** Number of foreign undergraduates: 115 (1% of student body). Number of countries represented: 38. Minimum TOEFL score required: 500 (paper); 173 (computer). Average TOEFL score: 525 (paper).

Georgetown College

- **Address:** 400 E. College Street, Georgetown, KY 40324
- **Website:** http://www.georgetowncollege.edu
- **Private; Religious affiliation:** Baptist
- **Enrollment:** 1,310 full-time; 55 part-time

KEY STATS

✔ **U.S News College Ranking:** third tier, Liberal Arts Colleges
✔ **ACT Score (25th/75th percentile):** 21-26
✔ **Tuition:** 2006-2007: $20,700

Selectivity: More selective	**Room/board:** $6,070
Acceptance rate: 95%	**Average debt:** $15,018
Student/faculty ratio: 11/1	**Proportion who borrowed:** 69%

UNDERGRADUATE STUDENT BODY STATS

2005-2006 enrollment: 1,310 full-time; 55 part-time. Men: 45%; women: 55%. **Ethnic makeup:** African American: 4%; Asian American: 1%; Hispanic: 1%; White: 94%; International: 1%. **Religious preference:** Roman Catholic: 12%; Protestant: 30%; No preference: 6%; Unknown: 3%; Baptist: 41%; Disciples of Christ: 3%; Other: 5%.

ADMISSIONS FACTS AND FIGURES

Phone: (502) 863-8009. **Email:** admissions@georgetowncollege.edu. **Website:** http://www.georgetowncollege.edu. **Application deadlines for fall 2007:** Regular decision: August 1. Early decision: Not offered. Early action: Not offered. Admission can be deferred. **Application fee:** $30. Common application is not accepted. **Admissions requirements/recommendations:** High school units required (recommended): English: 4 (4); Mathematics: 3 (3); Science: 3 (3); Foreign language: 2 (2); Social studies: 2 (2); Total units: 20 (20). Tests: The college uses SAT or ACT scores in admissions decisions. Either SAT or ACT required. For admission to the fall 2007 entering class, the school will accept: ACT with writing, ACT without writing. Campus visit: Recommended. Admissions interview: Recommended. Off-campus interview: May be arranged. **Factors that count in admissions decisions:** *Academic:* Secondary school record: Very important. Class rank: Important. Letters of recommendation: Important. Standardized test scores: Important. Essay: Very important. *Nonacademic:* Interview: Considered. Extracurricular activities: Important. Talent/ability: Important. Character/personal qualities: Important. Alumni/ae relationship: Considered. Geographical residence: Considered. State residency: Considered. Religious affiliation/commitment: Considered. Minority status: Not considered. Volunteer work: Considered.

Work experience: Not considered. **Other schools with the greatest overlap in applicants:** Centre College; Eastern Kentucky University; Transylvania University; University of Kentucky; Western Kentucky University. **Admissions statistics for the fall 2005 entering class:** Total applicants: 1,063. Total accepted: 1,009. Freshmen enrolled: 416; 14% were from out of state. Overall acceptance rate: 95%. **Size of waiting list:** 0 applicants; enrolled from waiting list: 0. **Credentials of fall 2005 freshmen:** 31% ranked in the top 10 percent of their high school class; 58% were in the top 25 percent, and 86% were in the top half. (Proportion submitting class standing: 87%.) **Average high school grade point average:** 3.5. **First-year students who submitted SAT scores:** 20%. Scores (25/75 percentile): Verbal: 480-590, Math: 470-590, Combined: 950-1180. **First-year students submitting ACT scores:** 94%. Scores (25/75 percentile): English: 20-27, Math: 19-26, Composite: 21-26.

ACADEMICS

Year founded: 1787. **Academic calendar:** Semester. **Degrees offered:** bachelor's, master's. **Most popular majors:** 12% biology/biological sciences, 12% business/commerce, 11% communication studies/speech communication and rhetoric, 10% psychology, 8% elementary education and teaching. **Major fields of study:** area, ethnic, cultural, and gender studies; biological and biomedical sciences; business, management, marketing, and related support services; communication, journalism, and related programs; computer and information sciences and support services; education; English language and literature/letters; foreign languages, literatures, and linguistics; health professions and related clinical sciences; history; liberal arts and sciences studies, and humanities; mathematics and statistics; multi/interdisciplinary studies; parks, recreation, leisure, and fitness studies; philosophy and religious studies; physical sciences; psychology; social sciences; visual and performing arts. **Areas of required coursework:** arts/fine arts, humanities, computer literacy, mathematics, English (including composition), philosophy, foreign languages, sciences (biological or physical), history, social science. **Special academic programs:** accelerated program, cooperative (work-study plan) program, double major, dual enrollment, honors program, independent study, internships, liberal arts/career combination, student-designed major, study abroad, teacher certificate program. **Teacher certification offered in:** early childhood, special education, elementary, middle/junior high, secondary. **Reserve Officers Training Corps (ROTC):** Army ROTC: Offered at cooperating institution (University of Kentucky); Air Force ROTC: Offered at cooperating institution (University of Kentucky). **Faculty and instruction (2005-2006):** Total instructional faculty: 101 full-time, 72 part-time (53% men; 47% women; 5% minorities). Full-time faculty with Ph.D. or other terminal degree: 88%. Student/faculty ratio: 11/1. Classes of fewer than 20 students: 58%; of 20 to 49 students: 42%; of 50 or more students: 0%. **Advanced Placement and International Baccalaureate credit:** AP tests may be used for: Credit only. Scores accepted: 3. International Baccalaureate exams may be used for: Credit only. **Freshmen returning for sophomore year:** 79%. **Graduation rates:** Four-year: 46%; five-year: 57%; six-year: 58%. **Graduate study:** 50% of students pursue further study immediately upon graduation; 60% within one year; 60% within five years. Fields in which graduates pursue further study: Master of Business Administration (MBA), 10%; law, 15%; medicine, 15%; dentistry, 3%; engineering, 3%; theology (or the seminary), 15%; education, 20%; arts and sciences, 15%; veterinary medicine, 4%.

COSTS AND FINANCIAL AID

Financial aid office: (502) 863-8027. **Expenses (2006-2007):** Tuition and fees 2006-2007: $20,700; room/board: $6,070. Estimated books and supplies: $1,250; transportation: $700; personal expenses: $1,350. **Financial aid:** Priority filing date for institution's financial aid form: March 15; deadline: August 1. In 2005-2006, 80% of undergraduates applied for financial aid. Of those, 66% were determined to have financial need; 59% had their need fully met. Average financial aid package (proportion receiving): $17,844 (66%). Average amount of gift aid, such as scholarships or grants (proportion receiving): $13,703 (66%). Average amount of self-help aid, such as work study or loans (proportion receiving): $4,452 (44%). Average need-based loan (excluding PLUS or other private loans): $4,145. Among students who received need-based aid, the average percentage of need met: 92%. Among students who received aid based on merit, the average award (and the proportion receiving): $8,581 (32%). The average athletic scholarship (and the proportion receiving): $6,399 (6%). Average amount of debt of borrowers graduating in 2005: $15,018. Proportion who borrowed: 69%.

CAMPUS LIFE AND EXTRACURRICULAR ACTIVITIES

Campus housing available: women's dorms, men's dorms, sorority housing, fraternity housing, apartment for single students. Students who live in college-owned, operated, or affiliated housing: 86%. **Student employment:**

During the 2005-2006 academic year, 50% of undergraduates worked on campus. Average per-year earnings: $1,400. **Clubs and organizations:** Number of student organizations: 100. Activities include: choral groups, concert band, dance, drama/theater, literary magazine, music ensembles, pep band, radio station, student government, student newspaper, yearbook. Number of fraternities: 5; sororities: 4. Proportion of men in fraternities: 25%; of women in sororities: 35%. Average proportion of students who stay on campus on weekends: 70%. **Sports program (2005-2006):** Member of NAIA. *Men's intercollegiate varsity sports:* baseball, basketball, cross-country, football, golf, soccer, tennis, track and field (indoor), track and field (outdoor). *Women's intercollegiate varsity sports:* basketball, cross-country, golf, soccer, softball, tennis, track and field (indoor), track and field (outdoor), volleyball.

SERVICES AND FACILITIES

Basic services: nonremedial tutoring, placement service, health service, health insurance. **Remedial assistance:** study skills. **Counseling services:** minority student, career, personal, academic, psychological, religious. **For learning-disabled students:** School does not offer a structured program with separate admission and additional fees. Services include: reading machines, tape recorders, untimed tests, note-taking services, readers, extended time for tests, tutors, proofreading services, texts on tape, other testing accomodations. **Library:** Number of titles: 163,950; number of current serial subscriptions: 555. **Information technology resources:** Students are not required to lease or own a computer. Number of campus computers available to all students: 250. School has a wireless network. Proportion of college-owned housing units wired for high-speed internet access: 100%. **Campus safety:** Security services offered: 24-hour foot and vehicle patrols, late-night transport/escort service, 24-hour emergency telephones, lighted pathways/sidewalks, controlled dormitory access (key, security card, etc).

TRANSFER AND INTERNATIONAL STUDENTS

Transfer students: May apply for admission for the following academic terms: Fall, Spring, Summer. Applicants do not need a minimum number of credits to apply. For fall 2005: Transfer applications received: 66. Transfer applicants offered admission: 59. Transfer applicants enrolled: 29. **International students:** Number of foreign undergraduates: 11 (1% of student body). Number of countries represented: 8. Minimum TOEFL score required: 520 (paper); 190 (computer).

Kentucky Christian University

- **Address:** 100 Academic Parkway, Grayson, KY 41143
- **Website:** http://www.kcu.edu
- **Private; Religious affiliation:** Christian Church/Church of Christ
- **Enrollment:** 555 full-time; 25 part-time

KEY STATS

✔ **U.S News College Ranking:** 49, Comp. Coll.–Bachelor's (South)
✔ **ACT Score (25th/75th percentile):** 19-24
✔ **Tuition:** 2006-2007: $12,630

Selectivity: Selective	**Room/board:** $4,624
Acceptance rate: 70%	**Average debt:** $25,731
Student/faculty ratio: 15/1	**Proportion who borrowed:** 84%

UNDERGRADUATE STUDENT BODY STATS

2005-2006 enrollment: 555 full-time; 25 part-time. Men: 42%; women: 58%. **Ethnic makeup:** African American: 2%; Asian American: 2%; White: 95%; International: 1%.

ADMISSIONS FACTS AND FIGURES

Phone: (800) 522-3181. **Email:** knights@kcu.edu. **Website:** http://www.kcu.edu. **Application deadlines for fall 2007:** Regular decision: August 1. Early decision: Not offered. Early action: Not offered. Admission cannot be deferred. **Application fee:** $25. Common application is accepted. **Admissions requirements/recommendations:** High school units required (recommended): English: 4; Mathematics: (4); Science: (4); Foreign language: (2); Social studies: 4; History: 4; Academic electives: (2). Tests: The college uses SAT or ACT scores in admissions decisions. Either SAT or ACT required. For admission to the fall 2007 entering class, the school will accept: ACT with writing, ACT without writing. Campus visit: Recommended. Admissions interview: Recommended. Off-campus inter-

view: Not available. **Factors that count in admissions decisions:** *Academic:* Secondary school record: Very important. Class rank: Considered. Letters of recommendation: Considered. Standardized test scores: Very important. Essay: Important. *Nonacademic:* Character/personal qualities: Very important. Religious affiliation/commitment: Considered. **Other schools with the greatest overlap in applicants:** Cincinnati Christian University; Johnson Bible College; Lincoln Christian College and Seminary; Ozark Christian College. **Admissions statistics for the fall 2005 entering class:** Total applicants: 335. Total accepted: 235. Freshmen enrolled: 138; Overall acceptance rate: 70%. **Credentials of fall 2005 freshmen:** 18% ranked in the top 10 percent of their high school class; 36% were in the top 25 percent, and 75% were in the top half. (Proportion submitting class standing: 81%.) **Average high school grade point average:** 3.0. **First-year students who submitted SAT scores:** 18%. Scores (25/75 percentile): Verbal: 450-560, Math: 430-560, Combined: 880-1120. **First-year students submitting ACT scores:** 76%. Scores (25/75 percentile): English: N/A, Math: N/A, Composite: 19-24.

ACADEMICS

Year founded: 1919. **Academic calendar:** Semester. **Degrees offered:** bachelor's, master's. **Most popular majors:** 35% religion/religious studies, 17% business/commerce, 17% education, 9% history, 6% social work. **Major fields of study:** business, management, marketing, and related support services; education; health professions and related clinical sciences; history; liberal arts and sciences studies, and humanities; multi/interdisciplinary studies; natural resources and conservation; philosophy and religious studies; psychology; public administration and social service professions. **Areas of required coursework:** humanities, computer literacy, mathematics, English (including composition), philosophy, sciences (biological or physical), history, social science, other. **Pre-professional programs:** pre-law. **Special academic programs (% participation):** distance learning (20%), double major (94%), English as a Second Language (ESL) (1%), independent study (5%), internships, study abroad (3%), teacher certificate program (25%). **Teacher certification offered in:** elementary, middle/junior high, secondary. **Cooperative education programs:** health professions. **Faculty and instruction (2005-2006):** Total instructional faculty: 34 full-time, 18 part-time (62% men; 38% women; 4% minorities). Full-time faculty with Ph.D. or other terminal degree: 76%. Student/faculty ratio: 15/1. Classes of fewer than 20 students: 76%; of 20 to 49 students: 21%; of 50 or more students: 4%. **Advanced Placement and International Baccalaureate credit:** AP tests may be used for: Placement only. Scores accepted: 3, 4. **Freshmen returning for sophomore year:** 72%. **Graduation rates:** Four-year: 20%; five-year: 34%; six-year: 39%. **Graduate study:** 40% of students pursue further study within one year.

COSTS AND FINANCIAL AID

Financial aid office: (606) 474-3226. **Expenses (2006-2007):** Tuition and fees 2006-2007: $12,630; room/board: $4,624. Estimated books and supplies: $900; transportation: $1,558; personal expenses: $2,130. **Financial aid:** Priority filing date for institution's financial aid form: April 1. In 2005-2006, 93% of undergraduates applied for financial aid. Of those, 81% were determined to have financial need; 21% had their need fully met. Average financial aid package (proportion receiving): $11,728 (81%). Average amount of gift aid, such as scholarships or grants (proportion receiving): $4,743 (62%). Average amount of self-help aid, such as work study or loans (proportion receiving): $4,697 (70%). Average need-based loan (excluding PLUS or other private loans): $3,656. Among students who received need-based aid, the average percentage of need met: 74%. Among students who received aid based on merit, the average award (and the proportion receiving): $2,919 (13%). The average athletic scholarship (and the proportion receiving): $0 (0%). Average amount of debt of borrowers graduating in 2005: $25,731. Proportion who borrowed: 84%.

CAMPUS LIFE AND EXTRACURRICULAR ACTIVITIES

Campus housing available (% using): women's dorms (47%), men's dorms (39%), apartments for married students (7%), apartment for single students (2%), other housing options (5%). **Student employment:** During the 2005-2006 academic year, 10% of undergraduates worked on campus. Average per-year earnings: $1,860. Activities include: choral groups, concert band, drama/theater, jazz band, music ensembles, musical theater, pep band, student government, yearbook. Number of fraternities: 0; sororities: 0. Average proportion of students who stay on campus on weekends: 65%. **Sports program (2005-2006):** Member of NCAA II. *Men's intercollegiate varsity sports:* basketball, cross-country, soccer. *Women's intercollegiate varsity sports:* basketball, cross-country, soccer, volleyball.

SERVICES AND FACILITIES

Basic services: nonremedial tutoring, health service, health insurance. **Remedial assistance:** reading, math, writing. **Counseling services:** personal, academic, psychological, religious. **For learning-disabled students:** School does not offer a structured program with separate admission and additional fees. Services include: remedial math, remedial English, untimed tests, note-taking services, oral tests, learning center, readers, extended time for tests, tutors. **Library:** Number of titles: 102,889; number of current serial subscriptions: 378. **Information technology resources:** Students are not required to lease or own a computer. Number of campus computers available to all students: 74. School has a wireless network. Proportion of college-owned housing units wired for high-speed internet access: 38%. **Campus safety:** Security services offered: 24-hour foot and vehicle patrols, 24-hour emergency telephones, lighted pathways/sidewalks, controlled dormitory access (key, security card, etc).

TRANSFER AND INTERNATIONAL STUDENTS

Transfer students: May apply for admission for the following academic terms: Fall, Spring. Applicants do not need a minimum number of credits to apply. For fall 2005: Transfer applications received: 101. Transfer applicants offered admission: 73. Transfer applicants enrolled: 53. **International students:** Number of foreign undergraduates: 6 (1% of student body). Number of countries represented: 11. Minimum TOEFL score required: 500 (paper); 173 (computer). Average TOEFL score: 550 (paper).

Kentucky State University

- **Address:** 400 E. Main Street, Frankfort, KY 40601
- **Website:** http://www.kysu.edu
- **Public**
- **Enrollment:** 1,619 full-time; 608 part-time

KEY STATS

✔ **U.S News College Ranking:** third tier, Universities–Master's (South)
✔ **ACT Score (25th/75th percentile):** 15-19
✔ **Tuition:** 2005-2006: $4,468 in state, $10,910 out of state

Selectivity: Less selective	**Room/board:** $5,620
Acceptance rate: 33%	**Average debt:** N/A
Student/faculty ratio: 15/1	**Proportion who borrowed:** N/A

UNDERGRADUATE STUDENT BODY STATS

2005-2006 enrollment: 1,619 full-time; 608 part-time. Men: 43%; women: 57%. **Ethnic makeup:** African American: 64%; Asian American: 1%; White: 35%.

ADMISSIONS FACTS AND FIGURES

Phone: (800) 325-1716. **Email:** james.burrell@kysu.edu. **Website:** http://www.kysu.edu. **Application deadlines for fall 2007:** Regular decision: August 10. Early decision: Not offered. Early action: Not offered. Admission can be deferred. **Application fee:** $22. Common application is accepted. **Admissions requirements/recommendations:** High school units required (recommended): English: 4; Mathematics: 3; Science: 3; Foreign language: 2; Social studies: 3; History: 1; Academic electives: 7; Total units: 23. Tests: The college uses SAT or ACT scores in admissions decisions. Either SAT or ACT required. For admission to the fall 2007 entering class, the school will accept: ACT with writing, ACT without writing. Campus visit: Neither required nor recommended. Admissions interview: Neither required nor recommended. **Factors that count in admissions decisions:** *Academic:* Secondary school record: Very important. Class rank: Not considered. Letters of recommendation: Considered. Standardized test scores: Very important. Essay: Not considered. *Nonacademic:* Interview: Not considered. Extracurricular activities: Considered. Talent/ability: Not considered. Character/personal qualities: Not considered. Geographical residence: Not considered. State residency: Important. Religious affiliation/commitment: Not considered. Minority status: Not considered. Volunteer work: Not considered. Work experience: Not considered. **Admissions statistics for the fall 2005 entering class:** Total applicants: 5,681. Total accepted: 1,891. Freshmen enrolled: 825; 49% were from out of state. Overall acceptance rate: 33%. **Size of waiting list:** 0 applicants; enrolled from waiting list: 0. **First-year students who submitted SAT scores:** 16%. Scores (25/75 percentile): Verbal: 370-470, Math: 360-480, Combined: 730-950. **First-year students submitting**

ACT scores: 89%. Scores (25/75 percentile): English: 13-19, Math: 15-18, Composite: 15-19.

ACADEMICS

Year founded: 1886. **Academic calendar:** Semester. **Degrees offered:** certificate, associate, bachelor's, master's. **Most popular majors:** 22% business/commerce, 11% computer and information sciences, 10% criminal justice/police science, 8% psychology, 7% biology/biological sciences. **Major fields of study:** biological and biomedical sciences; business, management, marketing, and related support services; computer and information sciences and support services; education; engineering; English language and literature/letters; family and consumer sciences/human sciences; health professions and related clinical sciences; history; liberal arts and sciences studies, and humanities; mathematics and statistics; physical sciences; psychology; public administration and social service professions; security and protective services; social sciences; visual and performing arts. **Areas of required coursework:** arts/fine arts, humanities, computer literacy, mathematics, English (including composition), foreign languages, sciences (biological or physical), history, social science. **Special academic programs:** distance learning, double major, honors program, independent study. **Reserve Officers Training Corps (ROTC):** Army ROTC: Offered at cooperating institution (University of Kentucky). **Faculty and instruction (2005-2006):** Total instructional faculty: 153 full-time, 5 part-time (40% men; 60% women; 47% minorities). Student/faculty ratio: 15/1. **Freshmen returning for sophomore year:** 64%. **Graduation rates:** Four-year: 13%; five-year: 22%; six-year: 32%.

COSTS AND FINANCIAL AID

Financial aid office: (502) 597-5960. **Expenses (2005-2006):** Tuition and fees 2005-2006: $4,468 in state, $10,910 out of state; room/board: $5,620. Estimated books and supplies: $1,000; transportation: $352; personal expenses: $1,500.

CAMPUS LIFE AND EXTRACURRICULAR ACTIVITIES

Campus housing available (% using): women's dorms (58%), men's dorms (42%). Students who live in college-owned, operated, or affiliated housing: 43%. Activities include: choral groups, concert band, dance, drama/theater, jazz band, marching band, music ensembles, musical theater, opera, pep band, student government, student newspaper, yearbook. Number of fraternities: 6; sororities: 5. **Sports program (2005-2006):** Member of NCAA II. *Men's intercollegiate varsity sports:* baseball, basketball, cross-country, football, golf, tennis, track and field (indoor), track and field (outdoor). *Women's intercollegiate varsity sports:* basketball, cross-country, softball, tennis, track and field (indoor), track and field (outdoor), volleyball.

SERVICES AND FACILITIES

Basic services: health insurance. **Remedial assistance:** reading, math, writing, study skills. **Counseling services:** career, academic. **Library:** Number of titles: 457,841; number of current serial subscriptions: 846. **Information technology resources:** Students are not required to lease or own a computer. Number of campus computers available to all students: 300. School has a wireless network. Approximate number of users that can be accommodated: 200. Proportion of college-owned housing units wired for high-speed internet access: 100%. **Campus safety:** Security services offered: 24-hour emergency telephones, lighted pathways/sidewalks, controlled dormitory access (key, security card, etc).

TRANSFER AND INTERNATIONAL STUDENTS

Transfer students: May apply for admission for the following academic terms: Fall, Spring, Summer. Applicants need a minimum number of credits to apply. For fall 2005: Transfer applications received: 268. Transfer applicants offered admission: 130. Transfer applicants enrolled: 123. **International students:** Number of foreign undergraduates: 1. Number of countries represented: 66. Minimum TOEFL score required: 525 (paper).

Kentucky Wesleyan College

- **Address:** 3000 Frederica Street, PO Box 1039, Owensboro, KY 42302
- **Website:** http://www.kwc.edu
- **Private; Religious affiliation:** United Methodist
- **Enrollment:** 717 full-time; 38 part-time

KEY STATS

✔ **U.S News College Ranking:** 25, Comp. Coll.–Bachelor's (South)
✔ **ACT Score (25th/75th percentile):** 18-25
✔ **Tuition:** 2006-2007: $13,600

Selectivity: Selective	**Room/board:** $5,750
Acceptance rate: 77%	**Average debt:** $11,191
Student/faculty ratio: 16/1	**Proportion who borrowed:** 69%

UNDERGRADUATE STUDENT BODY STATS

2005-2006 enrollment: 717 full-time; 38 part-time. Men: 51%; women: 49%. **Ethnic makeup:** African American: 10%; Hispanic: 2%; White: 86%; International: 1%. **Religious preference:** Roman Catholic: 18%; Protestant: 45%; No preference: 3%; Unknown: 19%; United Methodist: 14%; Other: 1%.

ADMISSIONS FACTS AND FIGURES

Phone: (800) 999-0592. **Email:** admitme@kwc.edu. **Website:** http://www.kwc.edu. **Application deadlines for fall 2007:** Regular decision: August 21. Early decision: Not offered. Early action: Not offered. Admission can be deferred. **Application fee:** None. Common application is accepted. **Admissions requirements/recommendations:** High school units required (recommended): English: 4; Mathematics: 3; Science: 3; Foreign language: (2); Social studies: 3; Total units: 13 (2). Tests: The college uses SAT or ACT scores in admissions decisions. Either SAT or ACT required. For admission to the fall 2007 entering class, the school will accept: ACT with writing, ACT without writing. Campus visit: Recommended. Admissions interview: Recommended. Off-campus interview: May be arranged. **Factors that count in admissions decisions:** *Academic:* Secondary school record: Very important. Class rank: Important. Letters of recommendation: Considered. Standardized test scores: Important. Essay: Not considered. *Nonacademic:* Interview: Considered. Extracurricular activities: Important. Talent/ability: Important. Character/personal qualities: Important. Alumni/ae relationship: Considered. Geographical residence: Not considered. State residency: Not considered. Religious affiliation/commitment: Not considered. Minority status: Considered. Volunteer work: Considered. Work experience: Considered. **Admissions statistics for the fall 2005 entering class:** Total applicants: 1,074. Total accepted: 828. Freshmen enrolled: 209; 26% were from out of state. Overall acceptance rate: 77%. **Credentials of fall 2005 freshmen:** 19% ranked in the top 10 percent of their high school class; 44% were in the top 25 percent, and 75% were in the top half. (Proportion submitting class standing: 90%.) **Average high school grade point average:** 3.3. **First-year students who submitted SAT scores:** 18%. Scores (25/75 percentile): Verbal: 400-570, Math: 460-580, Combined: 860-1150. **First-year students submitting ACT scores:** 88%. Scores (25/75 percentile): English: 18-27, Math: 18-25, Composite: 18-25.

ACADEMICS

Year founded: 1858. **Academic calendar:** Semester. **Degrees offered:** bachelor's. **Most popular majors:** 20% business/commerce, 14% communication studies/speech communication and rhetoric, 13% education, 8% criminal justice/safety studies, 7% English language and literature. **Major fields of study:** biological and biomedical sciences; business, management, marketing, and related support services; communication, journalism, and related programs; computer and information sciences and support services; education; English language and literature/letters; foreign languages, literatures, and linguistics; history; mathematics and statistics; multi/interdisciplinary studies; parks, recreation, leisure, and fitness studies; philosophy and religious studies; physical sciences; psychology; public administration and social service professions; security and protective services; social sciences; visual and performing arts. **Areas of required coursework:** arts/fine arts, humanities, computer literacy, mathematics, English (including composition), philosophy, foreign languages, sciences (biological or physical), history, social science. **Pre-professional programs:** pre-law, pre-dentistry, pre-medicine, pre-veterinary science, pre-optometry, pre-pharmacy, other. **Special academic programs (% participation):** accelerated program, cooperative (work-study plan) program (22%), double major (10%), independent

study (58%), internships (39%), liberal arts/career combination (100%), student-designed major (0%), study abroad (0%), teacher certificate program (11%). **Teacher certification offered in:** early childhood, elementary, middle/junior high, secondary, bilingual/bicultural. **Cooperative education programs:** business, computer science, natural science, social/behavioral science. **Faculty and instruction (2005-2006):** Total instructional faculty: 34 full-time, 34 part-time (53% men; 47% women; 3% minorities). Full-time faculty with Ph.D. or other terminal degree: 79%. Student/faculty ratio: 16/1. Classes of fewer than 20 students: 70%; of 20 to 49 students: 30%; of 50 or more students: 0%. **Advanced Placement and International Baccalaureate credit:** AP tests may be used for: Credit only. Scores accepted: 3, 4, 5. International Baccalaureate exams may be used for: Credit and/or placement. **Freshmen returning for sophomore year:** 65%. **Graduation rates:** Four-year: 31%; five-year: 45%; six-year: 44%. **Graduate study:** 20% of students pursue further study immediately upon graduation; 40% within one year. Fields in which graduates pursue further study: Master of Business Administration (MBA), 8%; arts and sciences, 7%.

COSTS AND FINANCIAL AID

Financial aid office: (270) 926-3111. **Expenses (2006-2007):** Tuition and fees 2006-2007: $13,600; room/board: $5,750. Estimated books and supplies: $1,250; transportation: $2,000; personal expenses: $2,000. **Financial aid:** Priority filing date for institution's financial aid form: March 15. In 2005-2006, 96% of undergraduates applied for financial aid. Of those, 84% were determined to have financial need; 23% had their need fully met. Average financial aid package (proportion receiving): $12,214 (84%). Average amount of gift aid, such as scholarships or grants (proportion receiving): $9,766 (84%). Average amount of self-help aid, such as work study or loans (proportion receiving): $3,330 (62%). Average need-based loan (excluding PLUS or other private loans): $2,902. Among students who received need-based aid, the average percentage of need met: 75%. Among students who received aid based on merit, the average award (and the proportion receiving): $10,887 (16%). The average athletic scholarship (and the proportion receiving): $2,565 (24%). Average amount of debt of borrowers graduating in 2005: $11,191. Proportion who borrowed: 69%.

CAMPUS LIFE AND EXTRACURRICULAR ACTIVITIES

Campus housing available (% using): coed dorms (30%), women's dorms (31%), men's dorms (39%), sorority housing, fraternity housing. Students who live in college-owned, operated, or affiliated housing: 49%. **Student employment:** During the 2005-2006 academic year, 20% of undergraduates worked on campus. Average per-year earnings: $475. **Clubs and organizations:** Number of student organizations: 32. Activities include: choral groups, dance, drama/theater, jazz band, literary magazine, marching band, music ensembles, pep band, radio station, student government, student newspaper, yearbook. Proportion of men in fraternities: 13%; of women in sororities: 21%. Average proportion of students who stay on campus on weekends: 49%. **Sports program (2005-2006):** Member of NCAA II. *Men's intercollegiate varsity sports:* baseball, basketball, football, golf, soccer. *Women's intercollegiate varsity sports:* basketball, golf, soccer, softball, tennis, volleyball.

SERVICES AND FACILITIES

Basic services: nonremedial tutoring, placement service, health service, health insurance. **Remedial assistance:** reading, math, writing, study skills. **Counseling services:** career, veteran student, academic, psychological, religious. **For learning-disabled students:** School does not offer a structured program with separate admission and additional fees. Services include: note-taking services, learning center, tutors, other. **Library:** Number of titles: 108,356; number of current serial subscriptions: 322. **Information technology resources:** Students are not required to lease or own a computer. Number of campus computers available to all students: 125. School has a wireless network. Approximate number of users that can be accommodated: 1,000. Proportion of college-owned housing units wired for high-speed internet access: 100%. **Campus safety:** Security services offered: late-night transport/escort service, 24-hour emergency telephones, lighted pathways/sidewalks, controlled dormitory access (key, security card, etc).

TRANSFER AND INTERNATIONAL STUDENTS

Transfer students: May apply for admission for the following academic terms: Fall, Spring, Summer. Applicants need a minimum number of credits to apply. For fall 2005: Transfer applications received: 207. Transfer applicants offered admission: 121. Transfer applicants enrolled: 76. **International students:** Number of foreign undergraduates: 7 (1% of student body). Number of countries represented: 6. Minimum TOEFL score required: 500 (paper); 173 (computer).

Lindsey Wilson College

- **Address:** 210 Lindsey Wilson Street, Columbia, KY 42728
- **Website:** http://www.lindsey.edu
- **Private; Religious affiliation:** United Methodist
- **Enrollment:** 1,457 full-time; 165 part-time

KEY STATS

✔ **U.S News College Ranking:** fourth tier, Liberal Arts Colleges
✔ **ACT Score (25th/75th percentile):** 17-22
✔ **Tuition:** 2005-2006: $13,814

Selectivity: Less selective	**Room/board:** $5,926
Acceptance rate: 80%	**Average debt:** $9,389
Student/faculty ratio: N/A	**Proportion who borrowed:** 99%

UNDERGRADUATE STUDENT BODY STATS

2005-2006 enrollment: 1,457 full-time; 165 part-time. Men: 35%; women: 65%. **Ethnic makeup:** African American: 7%; Asian American: 1%; Hispanic: 1%; White: 86%; International: 4%. **Religious preference:** Roman Catholic: 5%; Protestant: 33%; No preference: 4%; Unknown: 36%; United Methodist: 11%.

ADMISSIONS FACTS AND FIGURES

Phone: (270) 384-8100. **Email:** admissions@lindsey.edu. **Website:** http://www.lindsey.edu. **Application deadlines for fall 2007:** Regular decision: Rolling. Early decision: Not offered. Early action: Not offered. Admission cannot be deferred. Common application is accepted. **Admissions requirements/recommendations:** Tests: The college uses SAT or ACT scores in admissions decisions. Neither SAT nor ACT required. For admission to the fall 2007 entering class, the school will accept: ACT with writing, ACT without writing. Campus visit: Recommended. Admissions interview: Recommended. Off-campus interview: May be arranged. **Factors that count in admissions decisions:** *Academic:* Secondary school record: Very important. Class rank: Important. Letters of recommendation: Considered. Standardized test scores: Important. Essay: Considered. *Nonacademic:* Interview: Very important. Extracurricular activities: Considered. Talent/ability: Considered. Character/personal qualities: Very important. Alumni/ae relationship: Considered. Geographical residence: Considered. State residency: Considered. Religious affiliation/commitment: Considered. Minority status: Considered. Volunteer work: Considered. Work experience: Considered. **Admissions statistics for the fall 2005 entering class:** Total applicants: 1,621. Total accepted: 1,303. Freshmen enrolled: 414; Overall acceptance rate: 80%. **Credentials of fall 2005 freshmen:** 12% ranked in the top 10 percent of their high school class; 34% were in the top 25 percent, and 67% were in the top half. (Proportion submitting class standing: 73%.) **Average high school grade point average:** 3.1. **First-year students submitting ACT scores:** 82%. Scores (25/75 percentile): English: 16-22, Math: 16-22, Composite: 17-22.

ACADEMICS

Year founded: 1903. **Academic calendar:** Semester. **Degrees offered:** associate, bachelor's, master's. **Most popular majors:** Information not available. **Major fields of study:** area, ethnic, cultural, and gender studies; biological and biomedical sciences; business, management, marketing, and related support services; communication, journalism, and related programs; education; English language and literature/letters; history; liberal arts and sciences studies, and humanities; mathematics and statistics; philosophy and religious studies; psychology; public administration and social service professions; security and protective services; social sciences; visual and performing arts. **Areas of required coursework:** humanities, mathematics, English (including composition), sciences (biological or physical), social science. **Pre-professional programs:** pre-law, pre-medicine, pre-pharmacy. **Special academic programs (% participation):** double major (1%), English as a Second Language (ESL), student-designed major, study abroad, teacher certificate program (19%), weekend college (22%). **Teacher certification offered in:** early childhood, elementary, middle/junior high, secondary. **Faculty and instruction (2005-2006):** Total instructional faculty: 70 full-time, 41 part-time (52% men; 48% women; 6% minorities). Full-time faculty with Ph.D. or other terminal degree: 71%. **Advanced Placement and International Baccalaureate credit:** International Baccalaureate exams may be used for: Credit and/or placement. **Freshmen returning for sophomore year:** 52%. **Graduation rates:** Four-year: 12%; five-year: 22%; six-year: 23%. **Graduate study:** 8% of students pursue further study immediately upon graduation.

COSTS AND FINANCIAL AID

Financial aid office: (270) 384-8022. **Expenses (2005-2006):** Tuition and fees 2005-2006: $13,814; room/board: $5,926. Estimated books and supplies: $600; transportation: $500; personal expenses: $1,050. **Financial aid:** Priority filing date for institution's financial aid form: March 15. In 2005-2006, 99% of undergraduates applied for financial aid. Of those, 91% were determined to have financial need; 26% had their need fully met. Average financial aid package (proportion receiving): $10,491 (91%). Average amount of gift aid, such as scholarships or grants (proportion receiving): N/A (89%). Average amount of self-help aid, such as work study or loans (proportion receiving): N/A (72%). Average amount of debt of borrowers graduating in 2005: $9,389. Proportion who borrowed: 99%.

CAMPUS LIFE AND EXTRACURRICULAR ACTIVITIES

Campus housing available (% using): women's dorms (33%), men's dorms (34%), special housing for disabled students (1%), other housing options (32%). **Student employment:** During the 2005-2006 academic year, 11% of undergraduates worked on campus. Average per-year earnings: $1,040. **Clubs and organizations:** Number of student organizations: 29. Activities include: choral groups, dance, drama/theater, literary magazine, music ensembles, student government, student newspaper, yearbook. Number of fraternities: 0; sororities: 0. Average proportion of students who stay on campus on weekends: 60%. **Sports program (2005-2006):** Member of NAIA. *Men's intercollegiate varsity sports:* baseball, basketball, cross-country, golf, soccer, tennis, track and field (indoor), track and field (outdoor). *Women's intercollegiate varsity sports:* basketball, cross-country, golf, soccer, softball, tennis, track and field (indoor), track and field (outdoor), volleyball.

SERVICES AND FACILITIES

Basic services: placement service, health service, other. **Remedial assistance:** reading, math, writing, study skills. **Counseling services:** career, personal, academic, religious. **For learning-disabled students:** School does not offer a structured program with separate admission and additional fees. Total undergraduates in learning-disabled program or receiving services: 15. Services include: remedial math, remedial English, reading machines, remedial reading, tape recorders, untimed tests, note-taking services, oral tests, learning center, readers, extended time for tests, tutors, priority seating. **Library:** Number of titles: 50,261; number of current serial subscriptions: 13,000. **Information technology resources:** Students are not required to lease or own a computer. Number of campus computers available to all students: 200. School has a wireless network. Approximate number of users that can be accommodated: 50. Proportion of college-owned housing units wired for high-speed internet access: 100%. **Campus safety:** Security services offered: 24-hour foot and vehicle patrols, late-night transport/escort service, 24-hour emergency telephones, lighted pathways/sidewalks, controlled dormitory access (key, security card, etc).

TRANSFER AND INTERNATIONAL STUDENTS

Transfer students: May apply for admission for the following academic terms: Fall, Spring, Summer. Applicants do not need a minimum number of credits to apply. For fall 2005: Transfer applications received: 377. Transfer applicants offered admission: 188. Transfer applicants enrolled: 143. **International students:** Number of foreign undergraduates: 43 (4% of student body). Number of countries represented: 34. Minimum TOEFL score required: 450 (paper); 133 (computer). Average TOEFL score: 468 (paper).

Mid-Continent University

- **Address:** 99 Powell Road E, Mayfield, KY 42066
- **Website:** http://www.midcontinent.edu
- **Private; Religious affiliation:** Southern Baptist
- **Enrollment:** 587 full-time; 62 part-time

KEY STATS

✔ **U.S News College Ranking:** fourth tier, Comp. Coll.–Bachelor's (South)
✔ **ACT Score (25th/75th percentile):** 17-21
✔ **Tuition:** 2006-2007: $11,000

Selectivity: Less selective	**Room/board:** $5,860
Acceptance rate: 39%	**Average debt:** $7,000
Student/faculty ratio: 15/1	**Proportion who borrowed:** 77%

UNDERGRADUATE STUDENT BODY STATS
2005-2006 enrollment: 587 full-time; 62 part-time. Men: 53%; women: 47%. **Ethnic makeup:** African American: 31%; Asian American: 1%; Hispanic: 2%; White: 58%; International: 8%. **Religious preference:** Southern Baptist: 90%; Other: 10%.

ADMISSIONS FACTS AND FIGURES
Phone: (270) 247-8521. **Email:** admissions@midcontinent.edu. **Website:** http://www.midcontinent.edu. **Application deadlines for fall 2007:** Regular decision: Rolling; decision sent by August 1. Early decision: Not offered. Early action: Not offered. Admission can be deferred. **Application fee:** $20. Common application is not accepted. **Admissions requirements/recommendations:** High school units required (recommended): English: 4 (4); Mathematics: 2 (2); Science: 2 (2); Foreign language: 1 (1); Social studies: 2 (2); History: 1 (1); Total units: 13 (13). Tests: The college uses SAT or ACT scores in admissions decisions. Either SAT or ACT required. Campus visit: Recommended. Admissions interview: Recommended. Off-campus interview: May be arranged. **Factors that count in admissions decisions:** *Academic:* Secondary school record: Very important. Class rank: Important. Letters of recommendation: Important. Standardized test scores: Very important. Essay: Important. *Nonacademic:* Interview: Important. Extracurricular activities: Considered. Talent/ability: Considered. Character/personal qualities: Very important. Alumni/ae relationship: Important. Geographical residence: Important. State residency: Not considered. Religious affiliation/commitment: Very important. Minority status: Important. Volunteer work: Considered. Work experience: Considered. **Admissions statistics for the fall 2005 entering class:** Total applicants: 285. Total accepted: 112. Freshmen enrolled: 94; 16% were from out of state. Overall acceptance rate: 39%. **Size of waiting list:** 0 applicants; enrolled from waiting list: 0. **Credentials of fall 2005 freshmen:** 10% ranked in the top 10 percent of their high school class; 22% were in the top 25 percent, and 60% were in the top half. (Proportion submitting class standing: 100%.) **Average high school grade point average:** 2.8. **First-year students who submitted SAT scores:** 9%. Scores (25/75 percentile): Verbal: 450-490, Math: 510-590, Combined: 960-1080. **First-year students submitting ACT scores:** 57%. Scores (25/75 percentile): English: 15-21, Math: 16-20, Composite: 17-21.

ACADEMICS
Year founded: 1949. **Academic calendar:** Semester. **Degrees offered:** associate, bachelor's. **Most popular majors:** 47% organizational behavior studies, 15% counseling psychology, 15% missions/missionary studies and missiology, 12% education, 11% Bible/biblical studies. **Major fields of study:** business, management, marketing, and related support services; education; foreign languages, literatures, and linguistics; psychology; social sciences; theology and religious vocations. **Areas of required coursework:** computer literacy, mathematics, English (including composition), philosophy, sciences (biological or physical), history, social science. **Special academic programs (% participation):** distance learning (43%), double major (2%), independent study (15%), student-designed major (2%). **Teacher certification offered in:** elementary. **Faculty and instruction (2005-2006):** Total instructional faculty: 20 full-time, 36 part-time (79% men; 21% women; 14% minorities). Full-time faculty with Ph.D. or other terminal degree: 70%. Student/faculty ratio: 15/1. Classes of fewer than 20 students: 87%; of 20 to 49 students: 13%; of 50 or more students: 0%. **Advanced Placement and International Baccalaureate credit:** AP tests may be used for: Credit only. Scores accepted: 4. **Freshmen returning for sophomore year:** 58%. **Graduation rates:** Four-year: 9%; five-year: 9%; six-year: 25%. **Graduate study:** 15% of students pursue further study immediately upon graduation; 10% within one year; 3% within five years. Fields in which graduates pursue further study: theology (or the seminary), 10%.

COSTS AND FINANCIAL AID
Financial aid office: (270) 247-8521. **Expenses (2006-2007):** Tuition and fees 2006-2007: $11,000; room/board: $5,860. **Financial aid:** Priority filing date for institution's financial aid form: March 15. In 2005-2006, 98% of undergraduates applied for financial aid. Of those, 74% were determined to have financial need; 13% had their need fully met. Average financial aid package (proportion receiving): $7,198 (73%). Average amount of gift aid, such as scholarships or grants (proportion receiving): $5,309 (67%). Average amount of self-help aid, such as work study or loans (proportion receiving): $3,426 (59%). Average need-based loan (excluding PLUS or other private loans): $2,782. Among students who received need-based aid, the average percentage of need met: 60%. Among students who received aid based on merit, the average award (and the proportion receiving): $6,248 (5%). The average athletic scholarship (and the proportion receiving): $0 (0%).

Average amount of debt of borrowers graduating in 2005: $7,000. Proportion who borrowed: 77%.

CAMPUS LIFE AND EXTRACURRICULAR ACTIVITIES
Campus housing available (% using): women's dorms (18%), men's dorms (12%). **Student employment:** During the 2005-2006 academic year, 10% of undergraduates worked on campus. Average per-year earnings: $800. **Clubs and organizations:** Number of student organizations: 5. Activities include: music ensembles, student government, student newspaper. Number of fraternities: 0; sororities: 0. Average proportion of students who stay on campus on weekends: 20%. **Sports program (2005-2006):** Member of NAIA. *Men's intercollegiate varsity sports:* baseball, cross-country, soccer. *Women's intercollegiate varsity sports:* cross-country, softball, volleyball.

SERVICES AND FACILITIES
Basic services: nonremedial tutoring. **Remedial assistance:** reading, math, writing, study skills. **Counseling services:** career, personal, psychological, religious. **For learning-disabled students:** School does not offer a structured program with separate admission and additional fees. Services include: remedial math, remedial English, remedial reading, tape recorders, video-taped classes, untimed tests, note-taking services, oral tests, readers, extended time for tests, tutors. **Library:** Number of titles: 45,973; number of current serial subscriptions: 14. **Information technology resources:** Students are not required to lease or own a computer. Number of campus computers available to all students: 29. School does not have a wireless network. Proportion of college-owned housing units wired for high-speed internet access: 100%. **Campus safety:** Security services offered: 24-hour emergency telephones, lighted pathways/sidewalks, controlled dormitory access (key, security card, etc).

TRANSFER AND INTERNATIONAL STUDENTS
Transfer students: May apply for admission for the following academic terms: Fall, Spring, Summer. Applicants do not need a minimum number of credits to apply. For fall 2005: Transfer applications received: 50. Transfer applicants offered admission: 40. Transfer applicants enrolled: 31. **International students:** Number of foreign undergraduates: 37 (8% of student body). Minimum TOEFL score required: 500 (paper); 173 (computer). Average TOEFL score: 567 (paper).

Midway College

- **Address:** 512 E. Stephens Street, Midway, KY 40347
- **Website:** http://www.Midway.edu
- **Private; Religious affiliation:** Disciples of Christ
- **Enrollment:** 876 full-time; 403 part-time

KEY STATS
✔ **U.S News College Ranking:** fourth tier, Comp. Coll.–Bachelor's (South)
✔ **ACT Score (25th/75th percentile):** 17-22
✔ **Tuition:** 2006-2007: $14,850

Selectivity: Selective	**Room/board:** $6,000
Acceptance rate: 75%	**Average debt:** $15,407
Student/faculty ratio: 12/1	**Proportion who borrowed:** 80%

UNDERGRADUATE STUDENT BODY STATS
2005-2006 enrollment: 876 full-time; 403 part-time. Men: 14%; women: 86%. **Ethnic makeup:** African American: 6%; White: 93%; International: 1%.

ADMISSIONS FACTS AND FIGURES
Phone: (800) 755-0031. **Email:** admissions@midway.edu. **Website:** http://www.Midway.edu. **Application deadlines for fall 2007:** Regular decision: Rolling. Early decision: Not offered. Early action: Not offered. Admission cannot be deferred. **Application fee:** $25. Common application is accepted. **Admissions requirements/recommendations:** High school units required (recommended): English: 4; Mathematics: (3); Science: (2); Foreign language: (1); Social studies: (1); Total units: 15. Tests: The college does not use SAT or ACT scores in admissions decisions. Neither SAT nor ACT required. For admission to the fall 2007 entering class, the school will accept: ACT with writing, ACT without writing. Campus visit: Recommended. Admissions interview: Recommended. Off-campus interview: May be arranged. **Factors that count in admissions decisions:**

Academic: Secondary school record: Very important. Class rank: Considered. Letters of recommendation: Considered. Standardized test scores: Very important. Essay: Considered. *Nonacademic:* Interview: Considered. Extracurricular activities: Considered. Talent/ability: Considered. Character/personal qualities: Considered. Alumni/ae relationship: Considered. Geographical residence: Considered. State residency: Considered. Religious affiliation/commitment: Not considered. Minority status: Not considered. Volunteer work: Considered. Work experience: Considered. **Admissions statistics for the fall 2005 entering class:** Total applicants: 423. Total accepted: 319. Freshmen enrolled: 161; 16% were from out of state. Overall acceptance rate: 75%. **Credentials of fall 2005 freshmen:** 15% ranked in the top 10 percent of their high school class; 35% were in the top 25 percent, and 61% were in the top half. (Proportion submitting class standing: 84%.) **Average high school grade point average:** 3.1. **First-year students who submitted SAT scores:** 13%. Scores (25/75 percentile): Verbal: 470-660, Math: 440-630, Combined: 910-1290. **First-year students submitting ACT scores:** 54%. Scores (25/75 percentile): English: 17-22, Math: 16-21, Composite: 17-22.

ACADEMICS

Year founded: 1847. **Academic calendar:** Semester. **Degrees offered:** associate, bachelor's. **Most popular majors:** 39% business, management, marketing, and related support services, 35% education, 12% health professions and related clinical sciences, 11% agriculture, agriculture operations, and related sciences, 3% biological and biomedical sciences. **Major fields of study:** agriculture, agriculture operations, and related sciences; biological and biomedical sciences; business, management, marketing, and related support services; education; English language and literature/letters; health professions and related clinical sciences; mathematics and statistics; physical sciences; psychology. **Areas of required coursework:** humanities, computer literacy, mathematics, English (including composition), sciences (biological or physical), history. **Pre-professional programs:** pre-veterinary science. **Special academic programs:** accelerated program, distance learning, double major, dual enrollment, study abroad, teacher certificate program, weekend college. **Teacher certification offered in:** special education, elementary, middle/junior high, secondary. **Cooperative education programs:** education. **Reserve Officers Training Corps (ROTC):** Army ROTC: Offered at cooperating institution (University of Kentucky). **Faculty and instruction (2005-2006):** Total instructional faculty: 50 full-time, 99 part-time (37% men; 63% women). Full-time faculty with Ph.D. or other terminal degree: 44%. Student/faculty ratio: 12/1. Classes of fewer than 20 students: 78%; of 20 to 49 students: 22%; of 50 or more students: 0%. **Freshmen returning for sophomore year:** 51%. **Graduation rates:** Four-year: 24%; five-year: 24%; six-year: 27%.

COSTS AND FINANCIAL AID

Financial aid office: (859) 846-5745. **Expenses (2006-2007):** Tuition and fees 2006-2007: $14,850; room/board: $6,000. **Financial aid:** Priority filing date for institution's financial aid form: March 15; deadline: April 15. In 2005-2006, 88% of undergraduates applied for financial aid. Of those, 81% were determined to have financial need; 26% had their need fully met. Average financial aid package (proportion receiving): $12,196 (81%). Average amount of gift aid, such as scholarships or grants (proportion receiving): $5,792 (75%). Average amount of self-help aid, such as work study or loans (proportion receiving): $3,772 (73%). Average need-based loan (excluding PLUS or other private loans): $3,658. Among students who received need-based aid, the average percentage of need met: 59%. Among students who received aid based on merit, the average award (and the proportion receiving): $3,756 (1%). The average athletic scholarship (and the proportion receiving): $1,250 (0%). Average amount of debt of borrowers graduating in 2005: $15,407. Proportion who borrowed: 80%.

CAMPUS LIFE AND EXTRACURRICULAR ACTIVITIES

Campus housing available (% using): women's dorms (100%). Students who live in college-owned, operated, or affiliated housing: 13%. Activities include: choral groups, student government, student newspaper, yearbook. Average proportion of students who stay on campus on weekends: 20%. **Sports program (2005-2006):** Member of NAIA. *Women's intercollegiate varsity sports:* basketball, soccer, softball, tennis.

SERVICES AND FACILITIES

Basic services: nonremedial tutoring, health service. **Remedial assistance:** math, writing. **Counseling services:** career, academic. **For learning-disabled students:** Services include: remedial math, remedial English, tape recorders, untimed tests, oral tests, extended time for tests, tutors, priority seating, texts on tape, other testing accomodations. **Information technology**

resources: Students are not required to lease or own a computer. Number of campus computers available to all students: 60. Proportion of college-owned housing units wired for high-speed internet access: 100%. **Campus safety:** Security services offered: 24-hour foot and vehicle patrols, late-night transport/escort service, lighted pathways/sidewalks, controlled dormitory access (key, security card, etc).

TRANSFER AND INTERNATIONAL STUDENTS

Transfer students: May apply for admission for the following academic terms: Fall, Spring, Summer. Applicants do not need a minimum number of credits to apply. For fall 2005: Transfer applications received: 700. Transfer applicants offered admission: 538. Transfer applicants enrolled: 307. **International students:** Number of foreign undergraduates: 8 (1% of student body).

Morehead State University

- **Address:** 150 University Boulevard, Morehead, KY 40351
- **Website:** http://www.moreheadstate.edu
- **Public**
- **Enrollment:** 5,964 full-time; 1,580 part-time

KEY STATS

✔ **U.S News College Ranking:** 63, Universities–Master's (South)
✔ **ACT Score (25th/75th percentile):** 17-22
✔ **Tuition:** 2006-2007: $4,870 in state, $12,950 out of state

Selectivity: Selective	**Room/board:** $5,208
Acceptance rate: 69%	**Average debt:** $16,995
Student/faculty ratio: 17/1	**Proportion who borrowed:** 59%

UNDERGRADUATE STUDENT BODY STATS

2005-2006 enrollment: 5,964 full-time; 1,580 part-time. Men: 38%; women: 62%. **Ethnic makeup:** African American: 4%; Hispanic: 1%; White: 95%.

ADMISSIONS FACTS AND FIGURES

Phone: (606) 783-2000. **Email:** admissions@moreheadstate.edu. **Website:** http://www.moreheadstate.edu. **Application deadlines for fall 2007:** Regular decision: Rolling. Early decision: Not offered. Early action: Not offered. Admission can be deferred. Common application is not accepted. **To apply online, go to:** http://www.moreheadstate.edu/prospects/web01.html. **Admissions requirements/recommendations:** High school units required (recommended): English: 4; Mathematics: 3; Science: 3; Foreign language: (2); Social studies: 3; Academic electives: 7; Total units: 22. Tests: The college uses SAT or ACT scores in admissions decisions. Either SAT or ACT required. For admission to the fall 2007 entering class, the school will accept: ACT with writing, ACT without writing. Campus visit: Recommended. Admissions interview: Neither required nor recommended. **Factors that count in admissions decisions:** *Academic:* Secondary school record: Very important. Class rank: Considered. Letters of recommendation: Considered. Standardized test scores: Very important. Essay: Not considered. *Nonacademic:* Interview: Considered. Extracurricular activities: Considered. Talent/ability: Important. Character/personal qualities: Important. Alumni/ae relationship: Not considered. Geographical residence: Not considered. State residency: Not considered. Religious affiliation/commitment: Not considered. Minority status: Not considered. Volunteer work: Considered. Work experience: Considered. **Admissions statistics for the fall 2005 entering class:** Total applicants: 5,092. Total accepted: 3,528. Freshmen enrolled: 1,300; 18% were from out of state. Overall acceptance rate: 69%. **Credentials of fall 2005 freshmen:** 17% ranked in the top 10 percent of their high school class; 39% were in the top 25 percent, and 71% were in the top half. (Proportion submitting class standing: 77%.) **Average high school grade point average:** 3.2. **First-year students who submitted SAT scores:** 3%. Scores (25/75 percentile): Verbal: N/A, Math: N/A, Combined: N/A. **First-year students submitting ACT scores:** 97%. Scores (25/75 percentile): English: 16-22, Math: 16-21, Composite: 17-22.

ACADEMICS

Year founded: 1922. **Academic calendar:** Semester. **Degrees offered:** associate, bachelor's, post-bachelor's certificate, master's, post-master's certificate. **Most popular majors:** 11% elementary education and teaching, 10% general studies, 7% communication studies/speech communication and rhetoric, 6% manufacturing technology/technician, 5% business administration and management. **Major fields of study:** agriculture, agriculture operations, and related sciences; biological and biomedical sciences; business, management, marketing, and related support services; communication, journalism, and related programs; computer and information sciences and support services; education; engineering technologies/technicians; English language and literature/letters; family and consumer sciences/human sciences; foreign languages, literatures, and linguistics; health professions and related clinical sciences; history; legal professions and studies; liberal arts and sciences studies, and humanities; mathematics and statistics; parks, recreation, leisure, and fitness studies; philosophy and religious studies; physical sciences; psychology; public administration and social service professions; social sciences; visual and performing arts. **Areas of required coursework:** humanities, computer literacy, mathematics, English (including composition), sciences (biological or physical), history, social science. **Pre-professional programs:** pre-law, pre-dentistry, pre-medicine, pre-veterinary science, pre-optometry, pre-pharmacy, other. **Special academic programs:** accelerated program, cooperative (work-study plan) program, distance learning, double major, dual enrollment, exchange student program (domestic), honors program, independent study, internships, student-designed major, study abroad, teacher certificate program, weekend college. **Teacher certification offered in:** early childhood, special education, elementary, vo-tech, middle/junior high, secondary. **Cooperative education programs:** business, computer science, engineering, home economics, natural science. **Reserve Officers Training Corps (ROTC):** Army ROTC: Offered on campus. **Faculty and instruction (2005-2006):** Total instructional faculty: 378 full-time, 156 part-time (51% men; 49% women; 8% minorities). Student/faculty ratio: 17/1. Classes of fewer than 20 students: 50%; of 20 to 49 students: 47%; of 50 or more students: 3%. **Advanced Placement and International Baccalaureate credit:** AP tests may be used for: Credit and/or placement. Scores accepted: 3, 4, 5. **Freshmen returning for sophomore year:** 64%. **Graduation rates:** Four-year: 16%; five-year: 36%; six-year: 42%.

COSTS AND FINANCIAL AID
Financial aid office: (606) 783-2011. **Expenses (2006-2007):** Tuition and fees 2006-2007: $4,870 in state, $12,950 out of state; room/board: $5,208. Estimated books and supplies: $900; transportation: $600; personal expenses: $1,200. **Financial aid:** Priority filing date for institution's financial aid form: March 15. In 2005-2006, 82% of undergraduates applied for financial aid. Of those, 68% were determined to have financial need; 38% had their need fully met. Average financial aid package (proportion receiving): $7,826 (67%). Average amount of gift aid, such as scholarships or grants (proportion receiving): $4,263 (49%). Average amount of self-help aid, such as work study or loans (proportion receiving): $3,467 (49%). Average need-based loan (excluding PLUS or other private loans): $3,329. Among students who received need-based aid, the average percentage of need met: 86%. Among students who received aid based on merit, the average award (and the proportion receiving): $3,261 (18%). The average athletic scholarship (and the proportion receiving): $5,457 (3%). Average amount of debt of borrowers graduating in 2005: $16,995. Proportion who borrowed: 59%.

CAMPUS LIFE AND EXTRACURRICULAR ACTIVITIES
Campus housing available (% using): coed dorms (52%), women's dorms (19%), men's dorms (16%), sorority housing (2%), fraternity housing (1%), apartments for married students (4%), apartment for single students (4%), special housing for disabled students (1%), special housing for international students (1%). Students who live in college-owned, operated, or affiliated housing: 36%. **Student employment:** During the 2005-2006 academic year, 11% of undergraduates worked on campus. Average per-year earnings: $1,433. Activities include: choral groups, concert band, dance, drama/theater, jazz band, literary magazine, marching band, music ensembles, musical theater, opera, pep band, radio station, student government, student newspaper, symphony orchestra, television station, yearbook. Number of fraternities: 12; sororities: 10. Average proportion of students who stay on campus on weekends: 40%. **Sports program (2005-2006):** Member of NCAA I. *Men's intercollegiate varsity sports:* baseball, basketball, cross-country, football, golf, tennis, track and field (indoor), track and field (outdoor), mixed rifle. *Women's intercollegiate varsity sports:* basketball, cross-country, riflery, soccer, softball, tennis, track and field (indoor), track and field (outdoor), volleyball, mixed rifle.

SERVICES AND FACILITIES
Basic services: nonremedial tutoring, day care, health service, health insurance. **Remedial assistance:** reading, math, writing, study skills. **Counseling services:** career, personal, veteran student, academic, older student, birth control. **For learning-disabled students:** School does not offer a structured

program with separate admission and additional fees. Total undergraduates in learning-disabled program or receiving services: 29. Services include: remedial math, remedial English, reading machines, remedial reading, tape recorders, note-taking services, extended time for tests, tutors, other testing accomodations, other. **Library:** Number of titles: 522,673; number of current serial subscriptions: 3,046. **Information technology resources:** Students are not required to lease or own a computer. Number of campus computers available to all students: 1,000. School has a wireless network. Proportion of college-owned housing units wired for high-speed internet access: 100%. **Campus safety:** Security services offered: 24-hour foot and vehicle patrols, late-night transport/escort service, 24-hour emergency telephones, lighted pathways/sidewalks, controlled dormitory access (key, security card, etc).

TRANSFER AND INTERNATIONAL STUDENTS
Transfer students: May apply for admission for the following academic terms: Fall, Spring, Summer. Applicants need a minimum number of credits to apply. For fall 2005: Transfer applications received: 876. Transfer applicants offered admission: 531. Transfer applicants enrolled: 379. **International students:** Number of foreign undergraduates: 28. Number of countries represented: 15. Minimum TOEFL score required: 500 (paper); 173 (computer).

Murray State University

- **Address:** 113 Sparks Hall, Murray, KY 42071
- **Website:** http://www.murraystate.edu
- **Public**
- **Enrollment:** 7,155 full-time; 1,422 part-time

KEY STATS
✔ **U.S News College Ranking:** 15, Universities–Master's (South)
✔ **ACT Score (25th/75th percentile):** 21-26
✔ **Tuition:** 2006-2007: $4,998 in state, $6,788 out of state
Selectivity: More selective **Room/board:** $5,226
Acceptance rate: 64% **Average debt:** $17,617
Student/faculty ratio: 17/1 **Proportion who borrowed:** 52%

UNDERGRADUATE STUDENT BODY STATS
2005-2006 enrollment: 7,155 full-time; 1,422 part-time. Men: 43%; women: 57%. **Ethnic makeup:** African American: 6%; Asian American: 1%; Hispanic: 1%; White: 91%; International: 2%.

ADMISSIONS FACTS AND FIGURES
Phone: (270) 762-3741. **Email:** admissions@murraystate.edu. **Website:** http://www.murraystate.edu. **Application deadlines for fall 2007:** Regular decision: August 1. Early decision: Not offered. Early action: Not offered. Admission can be deferred. **Application fee:** $30. Common application is accepted. **Admissions requirements/recommendations:** High school units required (recommended): English: 4; Mathematics: 3 (4); Science: 3 (4); Foreign language: 2; Social studies: 3; Academic electives: 6; Total units: 22. Tests: The college uses SAT or ACT scores in admissions decisions. ACT required. For admission to the fall 2007 entering class, the school will accept: ACT without writing. Campus visit: Recommended. Admissions interview: Recommended. Off-campus interview: May be arranged. **Factors that count in admissions decisions:** *Academic:* Secondary school record: Very important. Class rank: Very important. Letters of recommendation: Considered. Standardized test scores: Very important. Essay: Not considered. *Nonacademic:* Interview: Considered. Extracurricular activities: Considered. Talent/ability: Considered. Character/personal qualities: Considered. Alumni/ae relationship: Considered. Geographical residence: Considered. State residency: Considered. Religious affiliation/commitment: Not considered. Minority status: Not considered. Volunteer work: Not considered. Work experience: Not considered. **Other schools with the greatest overlap in applicants:** Austin Peay State University; Southern Illinois University–Carbondale; University of Kentucky; University of Louisville; Western Kentucky University. **Admissions statistics for the fall 2005 entering class:** Total applicants: 3,057. Total accepted: 1,944. Freshmen enrolled: 1,030; 32% were from out of state. Overall acceptance rate: 64%. **Credentials of fall 2005 freshmen:** 28% ranked in the top 10 percent of their high school class; 65% were in the top 25 percent, and 99% were in the top half. (Proportion submitting class standing: 91%.) **Average high school grade**

point average: 3.6. **First-year students submitting ACT scores:** 100%. Scores (25/75 percentile): English: 20-26, Math: 19-25, Composite: 21-26.

ACADEMICS

Year founded: 1922. **Academic calendar:** Semester. **Degrees offered:** associate, bachelor's, master's. **Most popular majors:** 18% education, 15% business, management, marketing, and related support services, 12% communication, journalism, and related programs, 10% health professions and related clinical sciences, 5% engineering technologies/technicians. **Major fields of study:** agriculture, agriculture operations, and related sciences; biological and biomedical sciences; business, management, marketing, and related support services; communication, journalism, and related programs; communications technologies/technicians and support services; computer and information sciences and support services; education; engineering; engineering technologies/technicians; English language and literature/letters; family and consumer sciences/human sciences; foreign languages, literatures, and linguistics; health professions and related clinical sciences; history; liberal arts and sciences studies, and humanities; mathematics and statistics; natural resources and conservation; parks, recreation, leisure, and fitness studies; philosophy and religious studies; physical sciences; psychology; public administration and social service professions; security and protective services; social sciences; visual and performing arts. **Areas of required coursework:** arts/fine arts, humanities, computer literacy, mathematics, English (including composition), sciences (biological or physical), history, social science, other. **Pre-professional programs:** pre-law, pre-dentistry, pre-medicine, pre-theology, pre-veterinary science, pre-optometry, pre-pharmacy. **Special academic programs:** cooperative (work-study plan) program, cross-registration, distance learning, double major, dual enrollment, English as a Second Language (ESL), exchange student program (domestic), external degree program, honors program, independent study, internships, liberal arts/career combination, study abroad, teacher certificate program, weekend college, other. **Teacher certification offered in:** early childhood, special education, elementary, vo-tech, middle/junior high, secondary, bilingual/bicultural. **Cooperative education programs:** agriculture, art, business, computer science, education, engineering, health professions, home economics, humanities, natural science, social/behavioral science, technologies, other. **Reserve Officers Training Corps (ROTC):** Army ROTC: Offered on campus. **Faculty and instruction (2005-2006):** Total instructional faculty: 386 full-time, 151 part-time (59% men; 41% women; 8% minorities). Full-time faculty with Ph.D. or other terminal degree: 78%. Student/faculty ratio: 17/1. Classes of fewer than 20 students: 50%; of 20 to 49 students: 45%; of 50 or more students: 5%. **Advanced Placement and International Baccalaureate credit:** AP tests may be used for: Credit only. Scores accepted: 3, 4, 5. International Baccalaureate exams may be used for: Credit only. **Freshmen returning for sophomore year:** 77%. **Graduation rates:** Four-year: 38%; five-year: 55%; six-year: 57%.

COSTS AND FINANCIAL AID

Financial aid office: (270) 809-2546. **Expenses (2006-2007):** Tuition and fees 2006-2007: $4,998 in state, $6,788 out of state; room/board: $5,226. **Financial aid:** Priority filing date for institution's financial aid form: April 1. In 2005-2006, 86% of undergraduates applied for financial aid. Of those, 48% were determined to have financial need; 90% had their need fully met. Average financial aid package (proportion receiving): $4,613 (44%). Average amount of gift aid, such as scholarships or grants (proportion receiving): $2,182 (30%). Average amount of self-help aid, such as work study or loans (proportion receiving): $2,432 (43%). Average need-based loan (excluding PLUS or other private loans): $1,955. Among students who received need-based aid, the average percentage of need met: 88%. Among students who received aid based on merit, the average award (and the proportion receiving): $2,552 (33%). The average athletic scholarship (and the proportion receiving): $7,320 (3%). Average amount of debt of borrowers graduating in 2005: $17,617. Proportion who borrowed: 52%.

CAMPUS LIFE AND EXTRACURRICULAR ACTIVITIES

Campus housing available (% using): coed dorms (79%), women's dorms (8%), men's dorms (0%), fraternity housing (2%), apartments for married students (1%), apartment for single students (9%), special housing for disabled students (1%). Students who live in college-owned, operated, or affiliated housing: 38%. **Student employment:** During the 2005-2006 academic year, 18% of undergraduates worked on campus. Average per-year earnings: $3,000. **Clubs and organizations:** Number of student organizations: 210. Activities include: choral groups, concert band, dance, drama/theater, jazz band, literary magazine, marching band, music ensembles, musical theater, pep band, radio station, student government, student newspaper, student film society, symphony orchestra, television station, yearbook. Number of

fraternities: 14; sororities: 7. Proportion of men in fraternities: 16%; of women in sororities: 12%. Average proportion of students who stay on campus on weekends: 40%. **Sports program (2005-2006):** Member of NCAA I. **Men's intercollegiate varsity sports:** baseball, basketball, cross-country, football, golf, riflery, tennis, track and field (indoor), track and field (outdoor). **Women's intercollegiate varsity sports:** basketball, cross-country, golf, rowing, soccer, tennis, track and field (indoor), track and field (outdoor), volleyball, mixed rifle.

SERVICES AND FACILITIES

Basic services: nonremedial tutoring, women's center, placement service, health service, health insurance, other. **Remedial assistance:** reading, math, writing, study skills, other. **Counseling services:** minority student, career, military, personal, veteran student, academic, older student, psychological, birth control, religious. **For learning-disabled students:** School does not offer a structured program with separate admission and additional fees. Total undergraduates in learning-disabled program or receiving services: 321. Services include: remedial math, remedial English, reading machines, remedial reading, tape recorders, other special classes, diagnostic testing service, untimed tests, note-taking services, special bookstore section, oral tests, learning center, readers, extended time for tests, tutors, texts on tape. **Library:** Number of titles: 454,300; number of current serial subscriptions: 1,250. **Information technology resources:** Students are not required to lease or own a computer. Number of campus computers available to all students: 1,800. School has a wireless network. Approximate number of users that can be accommodated: 2,000. Proportion of college-owned housing units wired for high-speed internet access: 100%. **Campus safety:** Security services offered: 24-hour foot and vehicle patrols, late-night transport/escort service, 24-hour emergency telephones, lighted pathways/sidewalks, student patrols, controlled dormitory access (key, security card, etc).

TRANSFER AND INTERNATIONAL STUDENTS

Transfer students: May apply for admission for the following academic terms: Fall, Spring, Summer. Applicants need a minimum number of credits to apply. For fall 2005: Transfer applications received: 1,058. Transfer applicants offered admission: 866. Transfer applicants enrolled: 662. **International students:** Number of foreign undergraduates: 122 (2% of student body). Number of countries represented: 56. Minimum TOEFL score required: 500 (paper); 173 (computer).

Northern Kentucky University

- **Address:** Nunn Drive, Highland Heights, KY 41099
- **Website:** http://www.nku.edu
- **Public**
- **Enrollment:** 9,154 full-time; 2,932 part-time

KEY STATS

✔ **U.S News College Ranking:** third tier, Universities–Master's (South)
✔ **ACT Score (25th/75th percentile):** 18-23
✔ **Tuition:** 2006-2007: $5,448 in state, $10,200 out of state

Selectivity: Selective	**Room/board:** $5,020
Acceptance rate: 75%	**Average debt:** N/A
Student/faculty ratio: 16/1	**Proportion who borrowed:** 32%

UNDERGRADUATE STUDENT BODY STATS

2005-2006 enrollment: 9,154 full-time; 2,932 part-time. Men: 42%; women: 58%. **Ethnic makeup:** African American: 5%; Asian American: 1%; Hispanic: 1%; White: 91%; International: 2%.

ADMISSIONS FACTS AND FIGURES

Phone: (800) 637-9948. **Email:** admitnku@nku.edu. **Website:** http://www.nku.edu. **Application deadlines for fall 2007:** Regular decision: August 1. Early decision: Not offered. Early action: Not offered. Admission cannot be deferred. **Application fee:** $30. Common application is not accepted. **Admissions requirements/recommendations:** High school units required (recommended): English: 4; Mathematics: 3; Science: 3; Foreign language: 2; Social studies: 3; Academic electives: 5; Total units: 22. Tests: The college uses SAT or ACT scores in admissions decisions. Either SAT or ACT required. For admission to the fall 2007 entering class, the school will accept: ACT without writing. Campus visit: Recommended. Admissions interview: Neither required nor recommended. Off-campus interview: May be arranged. **Factors that count in admissions decisions:** *Academic:* Secondary school record: Important. Class rank: Considered. Letters of recommendation: Not considered. Standardized test scores: Important. Essay: Not considered. *Nonacademic:* Interview: Not considered. Extracurricular activities: Not considered. Talent/ability: Not considered. Character/personal qualities: Not considered. Alumni/ae relationship: Not considered. Geographical residence: Not considered. State residency: Not considered. Religious affiliation/commitment: Not considered. Minority status: Not considered. Volunteer work: Not considered. Work experience: Not considered. **Other schools with the greatest overlap in applicants:** Eastern Kentucky University; Morehead State University; University of Cincinnati; University of Kentucky; University of Louisville. **Admissions statistics for the fall 2005 entering class:** Total applicants: 4,317. Total accepted: 3,242. Freshmen enrolled: 1,843; 28% were from out of state. Overall acceptance rate: 75%. **First-year students who submitted SAT scores:** 13%. Scores (25/75 percentile): Verbal: 440-540, Math: 440-560, Combined: 880-1100. **First-year students submitting ACT scores:** 81%. Scores (25/75 percentile): English: 17-23, Math: 17-23, Composite: 18-23.

ACADEMICS

Year founded: 1968. **Academic calendar:** Semester. **Degrees offered:** certificate, associate, bachelor's, post-bachelor's certificate, master's, post-master's certificate, first professional. **Most popular majors:** 24% business, management, marketing, and related support services, 13% education, 8% English language and literature/letters, 8% social sciences, 7% health professions and related clinical sciences. **Major fields of study:** biological and biomedical sciences; business, management, marketing, and related support services; communication, journalism, and related programs; computer and information sciences and support services; education; engineering technologies/technicians; English language and literature/letters; foreign languages, literatures, and linguistics; health professions and related clinical sciences; history; liberal arts and sciences studies, and humanities; mathematics and statistics; natural resources and conservation; parks, recreation, leisure, and fitness studies; philosophy and religious studies; physical sciences; psychology; public administration and social service professions; security and protective services; social sciences; visual and performing arts. **Areas of required coursework:** arts/fine arts, humanities, mathematics, English (including composition), foreign languages, sciences (biological or physical), history, social science, other. **Pre-professional programs:** pre-law, pre-dentistry, pre-medicine, pre-veterinary science, pre-optometry, pre-pharmacy, other. **Special academic programs (% participation):** cooperative (work-study plan) program (5%), cross-registration, distance learning (18%), double major (55%), dual enrollment (1%), exchange student program (domestic), honors program (2%), independent study (9%), internships (26%), liberal arts/career combination, study abroad, teacher certificate program (13%). **Teacher certification offered in:** early childhood, special education, elementary, middle/junior high, secondary. **Cooperative education programs:** art, business, computer science, education, humanities, natural science, social/behavioral science, technologies, other. **Reserve Officers Training Corps (ROTC):** Army ROTC: Offered on campus; Air Force ROTC: Offered at cooperating institution (University of Cincinnati). **Faculty and instruction (2005-2006):** Total instructional faculty: 544 full-time, 429 part-time (49% men; 51% women; 8% minorities). Full-time faculty with Ph.D. or other terminal degree: 70%. Student/faculty ratio: 16/1. Classes of fewer than 20 students: 35%; of 20 to 49 students: 62%; of 50 or more students: 3%. **Advanced Placement and International Baccalaureate credit:** AP tests may be used for: Credit only. Scores accepted: 3, 4, 5. International Baccalaureate exams may be used for: Credit only. **Freshmen returning for sophomore year:** 69%. **Graduation rates:** Four-year: 10%; five-year: 30%; six-year: 38%. **Graduate study:** 42% of students pursue further study within five years.

COSTS AND FINANCIAL AID

Financial aid office: (859) 572-5143. **Expenses (2006-2007):** Tuition and fees 2006-2007: $5,448 in state, $10,200 out of state; room/board: $5,020. Estimated books and supplies: $800; transportation: $1,460; personal expenses: $800. **Financial aid:** Priority filing date for institution's financial aid form: March 1. Proportion who borrowed: 32%.

CAMPUS LIFE AND EXTRACURRICULAR ACTIVITIES

Campus housing available (% using): coed dorms (100%), women's dorms, men's dorms, apartment for single students, special housing for disabled students, cooperative housing, other housing options. Students who live in college-owned, operated, or affiliated housing: 11%. **Student employment:** During the 2005-2006 academic year, 11% of undergraduates worked on campus. Average per-year earnings: $1,800. **Clubs and organizations:**

Number of student organizations: 179. Activities include: choral groups, concert band, dance, drama/theater, jazz band, literary magazine, music ensembles, musical theater, pep band, radio station, student government, student newspaper, student film society, symphony orchestra, television station. Number of fraternities: 8; sororities: 8. Proportion of men in fraternities: 4%; of women in sororities: 4%. Average proportion of students who stay on campus on weekends: 20%. **Sports program (2005-2006):** Member of NCAA II. *Men's intercollegiate varsity sports:* baseball, basketball, cross-country, golf, soccer, tennis, track and field (indoor), track and field (outdoor). *Women's intercollegiate varsity sports:* basketball, cross-country, golf, soccer, softball, tennis, track and field (indoor), track and field (outdoor), volleyball.

SERVICES AND FACILITIES

Basic services: nonremedial tutoring, placement service, day care, health service, health insurance. **Remedial assistance:** reading, math, writing, study skills. **Counseling services:** minority student, career, personal, academic, older student, psychological, birth control, religious. **For learning-disabled students:** School does not offer a structured program with separate admission and additional fees. Total undergraduates in learning-disabled program or receiving services: 110. Services include: remedial math, remedial English, reading machines, remedial reading, tape recorders, other special classes, learning center, readers, extended time for tests, tutors, priority registration, priority seating, exams on tape or computer, other. **Library:** Number of titles: 300,258; number of current serial subscriptions: 1,886. **Information technology resources:** Students are not required to lease or own a computer. Number of campus computers available to all students: 1,300. School has a wireless network. Approximate number of users that can be accommodated: 3,000. Proportion of college-owned housing units wired for high-speed internet access: 98%. **Campus safety:** Security services offered: 24-hour foot and vehicle patrols, late-night transport/escort service, 24-hour emergency telephones, lighted pathways/sidewalks, student patrols, controlled dormitory access (key, security card, etc).

TRANSFER AND INTERNATIONAL STUDENTS

Transfer students: May apply for admission for the following academic terms: Fall, Winter, Spring, Summer. Applicants need a minimum number of credits to apply. For fall 2005: Transfer applications received: 1,186. Transfer applicants offered admission: 892. Transfer applicants enrolled: 627. **International students:** Number of foreign undergraduates: 202 (2% of student body). Number of countries represented: 63. Minimum TOEFL score required: 500 (paper); 173 (computer). Average TOEFL score: 558 (paper).

Pikeville College

- **Address:** 147 Sycamore Street, Pikeville, KY 41501-1194
- **Website:** http://www.pc.edu/
- **Private; Religious affiliation:** Presbyterian (U.S.A.)
- **Enrollment:** 778 full-time; 66 part-time

KEY STATS
- ✔ **U.S News College Ranking:** 46, Comp. Coll.–Bachelor's (South)
- ✔ **ACT Score (25th/75th percentile):** 17-22
- ✔ **Tuition:** 2006-2007: $12,750

Selectivity: Less selective	**Room/board:** $5,000
Acceptance rate: 100%	**Average debt:** $15,208
Student/faculty ratio: 14/1	**Proportion who borrowed:** 73%

UNDERGRADUATE STUDENT BODY STATS

2005-2006 enrollment: 778 full-time; 66 part-time. Men: 48%; women: 52%. **Ethnic makeup:** African American: 8%; Hispanic: 1%; White: 90%; International: 1%. **Religious preference:** Roman Catholic: 3%; Protestant: 57%; No preference: 34%; Presbyterian (U.S.A.): 1%; Other: 5%.

ADMISSIONS FACTS AND FIGURES

Phone: (606) 218-5251. **Email:** wewantyou@pc.edu. **Website:** http://www.pc.edu/. **Application deadlines for fall 2007:** Regular decision: August 16. Early decision: Not offered. Early action: Not offered. Admission can be deferred. Common application is not accepted. **Admissions requirements/recommendations:** High school units required (recommended): English: (4); Mathematics: (3); Science: (3); Social studies: (2); History: (1);

Total units: (13). Tests: The college does not use SAT or ACT scores in admissions decisions. Neither SAT nor ACT required. For admission to the fall 2007 entering class, the school will accept: ACT with writing, ACT without writing. Campus visit: Neither required nor recommended. Admissions interview: Neither required nor recommended. Off-campus interview: May be arranged. **Factors that count in admissions decisions: Academic:** Secondary school record: Not considered. Class rank: Not considered. Letters of recommendation: Not considered. Standardized test scores: Not considered. Essay: Not considered. **Nonacademic:** Interview: Not considered. Extracurricular activities: Not considered. Talent/ability: Not considered. Character/personal qualities: Not considered. Alumni/ae relationship: Not considered. Geographical residence: Not considered. State residency: Not considered. Religious affiliation/commitment: Not considered. Minority status: Not considered. Volunteer work: Not considered. Work experience: Not considered. **Other schools with the greatest overlap in applicants:** Alice Lloyd College; Eastern Kentucky University; Morehead State University; University of Kentucky; University of Louisville. **Admissions statistics for the fall 2005 entering class:** Total applicants: 520. Total accepted: 520. Freshmen enrolled: 208; 21% were from out of state. Overall acceptance rate: 100%. **Credentials of fall 2005 freshmen:** 40% were in the top 25 percent, and 81% were in the top half. (Proportion submitting class standing: 73%.) **Average high school grade point average:** 3.1. **First-year students submitting ACT scores:** 100%. Scores (25/75 percentile): English: 15-22, Math: 15-21, Composite: 17-22.

ACADEMICS

Year founded: 1889. **Academic calendar:** Semester. **Degrees offered:** associate, transfer-associate, terminal-associate, bachelor's, post-bachelor's certificate, first professional. **Most popular majors:** 20% psychology, 19% business, management, marketing, and related support services, 16% education, 9% security and protective services, 7% biological and biomedical sciences. **Major fields of study:** biological and biomedical sciences; business, management, marketing, and related support services; communication, journalism, and related programs; computer and information sciences and support services; education; English language and literature/letters; history; mathematics and statistics; philosophy and religious studies; physical sciences; psychology; security and protective services; social sciences; visual and performing arts. **Areas of required coursework:** humanities, computer literacy, mathematics, English (including composition), sciences (biological or physical), history, social science, other. **Pre-professional programs:** pre-law, pre-dentistry, pre-medicine, pre-theology, pre-pharmacy. **Special academic programs (% participation):** double major (8%), independent study (17%), internships (4%), liberal arts/career combination, study abroad (1%), teacher certificate program. **Teacher certification offered in:** elementary, middle/junior high, secondary. **Faculty and instruction (2005-2006):** Total instructional faculty: 54 full-time, 7 part-time (44% men; 56% women; 0% minorities). Full-time faculty with Ph.D. or other terminal degree: 52%. Student/faculty ratio: 14/1. Classes of fewer than 20 students: 47%; of 20 to 49 students: 53%; of 50 or more students: 0%. **Advanced Placement and International Baccalaureate credit:** AP tests may be used for: Credit only. **Freshmen returning for sophomore year:** 58%. **Graduation rates:** Four-year: 22%; five-year: 36%; six-year: 34%. **Graduate study:** 22% of students pursue further study within one year; 40% within five years. Fields in which graduates pursue further study: Master of Business Administration (MBA), 21%; law, 3%; medicine, 6%; dentistry, 5%; theology (or the seminary), 1%; arts and sciences, 50%.

COSTS AND FINANCIAL AID

Financial aid office: (606) 218-5253. **Expenses (2006-2007):** Tuition and fees 2006-2007: $12,750; room/board: $5,000. Estimated books and supplies: $1,600; transportation: $2,000; personal expenses: $2,000. **Financial aid:** Priority filing date for institution's financial aid form: March 15. In 2005-2006, 97% of undergraduates applied for financial aid. Of those, 96% were determined to have financial need; 70% had their need fully met. Average financial aid package (proportion receiving): $12,119 (96%). Average amount of gift aid, such as scholarships or grants (proportion receiving): $9,978 (95%). Average amount of self-help aid, such as work study or loans (proportion receiving): $3,628 (59%). Average need-based loan (excluding PLUS or other private loans): $3,462. Among students who received need-based aid, the average percentage of need met: 90%. Among students who received aid based on merit, the average award (and the proportion receiving): $3,094 (1%). The average athletic scholarship (and the proportion receiving): $9,416 (1%). Average amount of debt of borrowers graduating in 2005: $15,208. Proportion who borrowed: 73%.

CAMPUS LIFE AND EXTRACURRICULAR ACTIVITIES

Campus housing available (% using): coed dorms (19%), women's dorms (31%), men's dorms (50%). Students who live in college-owned, operated, or affiliated housing: 34%. **Student employment:** During the 2005-2006 academic year, 1% of undergraduates worked on campus. Average per-year earnings: $1,500. **Clubs and organizations:** Number of student organizations: 40. Activities include: choral groups, concert band, dance, drama/theater, jazz band, pep band, student government, student newspaper, yearbook. Number of fraternities: 0; sororities: 0. Average proportion of students who stay on campus on weekends: 30%. **Sports program (2005-2006):** Member of NAIA. **Men's intercollegiate varsity sports:** baseball, basketball, cross-country, football, golf, tennis. **Women's intercollegiate varsity sports:** basketball, cross-country, golf, softball, tennis, volleyball.

SERVICES AND FACILITIES

Basic services: nonremedial tutoring, health service, health insurance. **Remedial assistance:** reading, math, writing. **Counseling services:** career, personal, veteran student, academic, religious. **For learning-disabled students:** School does not offer a structured program with separate admission and additional fees. Total undergraduates in learning-disabled program or receiving services: 5. Services include: remedial math, remedial English, remedial reading, untimed tests, oral tests, readers, extended time for tests, tutors. **Library:** Number of titles: 72,673; number of current serial subscriptions: 219. **Information technology resources:** Students are not required to lease or own a computer. Number of campus computers available to all students: 162. School has a wireless network. Approximate number of users that can be accommodated: 1,416. Proportion of college-owned housing units wired for high-speed internet access: 75%. **Campus safety:** Security services offered: 24-hour foot and vehicle patrols, 24-hour emergency telephones, controlled dormitory access (key, security card, etc).

TRANSFER AND INTERNATIONAL STUDENTS

Transfer students: May apply for admission for the following academic terms: Fall, Spring, Summer. Applicants need a minimum number of credits to apply. For fall 2005: Transfer applications received: 171. Transfer applicants offered admission: 171. Transfer applicants enrolled: 106. **International students:** Number of foreign undergraduates: 12 (1% of student body). Number of countries represented: 7. Minimum TOEFL score required: 500 (paper); 175 (computer).

Spalding University

- **Address:** 851 S. Fourth Street, Louisville, KY 40203-2188
- **Website:** http://www.spalding.edu
- **Private; Religious affiliation:** Roman Catholic
- **Enrollment:** N/A

KEY STATS
✔ **U.S News College Ranking:** third tier, Universities–Master's (South)
✔ **ACT Score (25th/75th percentile):** 17-21
✔ **Tuition:** 2005-2006: $14,400

Selectivity: Less selective	**Room/board:** $3,858
Acceptance rate: 62%	**Average debt:** N/A
Student/faculty ratio: N/A	**Proportion who borrowed:** N/A

Thomas More College

- **Address:** 333 Thomas More Parkway, Crestview Hills, KY 41017-3495
- **Website:** http://www.thomasmore.edu
- **Private; Religious affiliation:** Roman Catholic
- **Enrollment:** 1,128 full-time; 215 part-time

KEY STATS
✔ **U.S News College Ranking:** 25, Comp. Coll.–Bachelor's (South)
✔ **ACT Score (25th/75th percentile):** 19-24
✔ **Tuition:** 2006-2007: $19,380

Selectivity: Selective	**Room/board:** $6,250
Acceptance rate: 63%	**Average debt:** $25,779
Student/faculty ratio: 14/1	**Proportion who borrowed:** 70%

UNDERGRADUATE STUDENT BODY STATS

2005-2006 enrollment: 1,128 full-time; 215 part-time. Men: 49%; women: 51%. **Ethnic makeup:** African American: 6%; Asian American: 1%; White: 92%. **Religious preference:** Roman Catholic: 25%; Protestant: 21%; No preference: 5%; Unknown: 49%.

ADMISSIONS FACTS AND FIGURES

Phone: (800) 825-4557. **Email:** admissions@thomasmore.edu. **Website:** http://www.thomasmore.edu. **Application deadlines for fall 2007:** Regular decision: August 15. Early decision: Not offered. Early action: Not offered. Admission can be deferred. **Application fee:** $25. Common application is accepted. **Admissions requirements/recommendations:** High school units required (recommended): English: 4; Mathematics: 3; Science: 3; Foreign language: 2; Social studies: 3; Academic electives: (2); Total units: 15. Tests: The college uses SAT or ACT scores in admissions decisions. Either SAT or ACT required. For admission to the fall 2007 entering class, the school will accept: ACT with writing, ACT without writing. Campus visit: Recommended. Admissions interview: Recommended. Off-campus interview: May be arranged. **Factors that count in admissions decisions:** *Academic:* Secondary school record: Very important. Class rank: Important. Letters of recommendation: Important. Standardized test scores: Important. Essay: Considered. *Nonacademic:* Interview: Considered. Extracurricular activities: Considered. Talent/ability: Considered. Character/personal qualities: Considered. Alumni/ae relationship: Not considered. Geographical residence: Not considered. State residency: Not considered. Religious affiliation/commitment: Not considered. Minority status: Not considered. Volunteer work: Considered. Work experience: Not considered. **Other schools with the greatest overlap in applicants:** Bellarmine University; College of Mount St. Joseph; Northern Kentucky University; University of Kentucky; Xavier University. **Admissions statistics for the fall 2005 entering class:** Total applicants: 1,007. Total accepted: 637. Freshmen enrolled: 227; 32% were from out of state. Overall acceptance rate: 63%. **Credentials of fall 2005 freshmen:** 14% ranked in the top 10 percent of their high school class; 37% were in the top 25 percent, and 70% were in the top half. (Proportion submitting class standing: 85%.) **Average high school grade point average:** 3.3. **First-year students who submitted SAT scores:** 29%. Scores (25/75 percentile): Verbal: 450-610, Math: 460-590, Combined: 910-1200. **First-year students submitting ACT scores:** 90%. Scores (25/75 percentile): English: 17-29, Math: 23-27, Composite: 19-24.

ACADEMICS

Year founded: 1921. **Academic calendar:** Semester. **Degrees offered:** certificate, associate, bachelor's, master's. **Most popular majors:** 50% business, management, marketing, and related support services, 6% education, 5% communication, journalism, and related programs, 5% history, 5% social sciences. **Major fields of study:** biological and biomedical sciences; business, management, marketing, and related support services; communication, journalism, and related programs; computer and information sciences and support services; education; English language and literature/letters; health professions and related clinical sciences; history; liberal arts and sciences studies, and humanities; mathematics and statistics; parks, recreation, leisure, and fitness studies; philosophy and religious studies; physical sciences; psychology; security and protective services; social sciences; visual and performing arts. **Areas of required coursework:** arts/fine arts, humanities, computer literacy, mathematics, English (including composition), philosophy, foreign languages, sciences (biological or physical), history, social science. **Pre-professional programs:** pre-law, pre-dentistry, pre-medicine, pre-veterinary science, pre-pharmacy. **Special academic programs:** accelerated program, cooperative (work-study plan) program, cross-registration, double major, dual enrollment, honors program, independent study, internships, liberal arts/career combination, student-designed major, study abroad, weekend college. **Teacher certification offered in:** early childhood, elementary, middle/junior high, secondary. **Cooperative education programs:** art, business, computer science, education, humanities, natural science, social/behavioral science, technologies. **Reserve Officers Training Corps (ROTC):** Army ROTC: Offered at cooperating institution (Xavier University); Air Force ROTC: Offered at cooperating institution (University of Cincinnati). **Faculty and instruction (2005-2006):** Total instructional faculty: 71 full-time, 63 part-time (54% men; 46% women; 6% minorities). Full-time faculty with Ph.D. or other terminal degree: 70%. Student/faculty ratio: 14/1. Classes of fewer than 20 students: 81%; of 20 to 49 students: 19%; of 50 or more students: 0%. **Advanced Placement and International Baccalaureate credit:** AP tests may be used for: Credit and/or placement. Scores accepted: 3, 4, 5. International Baccalaureate exams may be used for: Credit only. **Freshmen returning for sophomore year:** 63%. **Graduation rates:** Four-year: 39%; five-year: 51%; six-year: 55%. **Graduate study:** 20% of stu-

dents pursue further study immediately upon graduation; 44% within one year; 26% within five years. Fields in which graduates pursue further study: Master of Business Administration (MBA), 41%; law, 8%; medicine, 3%; engineering, 3%; theology (or the seminary), 5%; education, 7%; arts and sciences, 28%; veterinary medicine, 5%.

COSTS AND FINANCIAL AID

Financial aid office: (859) 344-3319. **Expenses (2006-2007):** Tuition and fees 2006-2007: $19,380; room/board: $6,250. Estimated books and supplies: $800; transportation: $500; personal expenses: $2,300. **Financial aid:** Priority filing date for institution's financial aid form: March 15; deadline: March 15. In 2005-2006, 74% of undergraduates applied for financial aid. Of those, 74% were determined to have financial need; 100% had their need fully met. Average financial aid package (proportion receiving): $17,432 (73%). Average amount of gift aid, such as scholarships or grants (proportion receiving): $4,608 (65%). Average amount of self-help aid, such as work study or loans (proportion receiving): $4,112 (36%). Average need-based loan (excluding PLUS or other private loans): $2,281. Among students who received need-based aid, the average percentage of need met: 82%. Among students who received aid based on merit, the average award (and the proportion receiving): $6,804 (13%). The average athletic scholarship (and the proportion receiving): $0 (0%). Average amount of debt of borrowers graduating in 2005: $25,779. Proportion who borrowed: 70%.

CAMPUS LIFE AND EXTRACURRICULAR ACTIVITIES

Campus housing available (% using): coed dorms (47%), women's dorms (20%), men's dorms (33%). Students who live in college-owned, operated, or affiliated housing: 21%. **Student employment:** During the 2005-2006 academic year, 17% of undergraduates worked on campus. Average per-year earnings: $2,100. **Clubs and organizations:** Number of student organizations: 37. Activities include: choral groups, drama/theater, literary magazine, student government. Number of fraternities: 0; sororities: 0. Average proportion of students who stay on campus on weekends: 25%. **Sports program (2005-2006):** Member of NCAA III. *Men's intercollegiate varsity sports:* baseball, basketball, cross-country, football, golf, soccer, tennis. *Women's intercollegiate varsity sports:* basketball, cross-country, golf, soccer, softball, tennis, volleyball.

SERVICES AND FACILITIES

Basic services: nonremedial tutoring, placement service. **Remedial assistance:** reading, math, writing, study skills. **Counseling services:** minority student, career, personal, veteran student, academic, older student, psychological, religious. **For learning-disabled students:** School does not offer a structured program with separate admission and additional fees. Total undergraduates in learning-disabled program or receiving services: 12. Services include: remedial math, remedial English, remedial reading, tape recorders, other special classes, untimed tests, note-taking services, oral tests, learning center, readers, extended time for tests, tutors, priority seating, texts on tape, other. **Library:** Number of titles: 112,836; number of current serial subscriptions: 505. **Information technology resources:** Students are not required to lease or own a computer. Number of campus computers available to all students: 109. School has a wireless network. Proportion of college-owned housing units wired for high-speed internet access: 100%. **Campus safety:** Security services offered: 24-hour foot and vehicle patrols, late-night transport/escort service, lighted pathways/sidewalks, student patrols, controlled dormitory access (key, security card, etc).

TRANSFER AND INTERNATIONAL STUDENTS

Transfer students: May apply for admission for the following academic terms: Fall, Spring, Summer. Applicants do not need a minimum number of credits to apply. For fall 2005: Transfer applications received: 102. Transfer applicants offered admission: 61. Transfer applicants enrolled: 36. **International students:** Number of foreign undergraduates: 5. Number of countries represented: 6. Minimum TOEFL score required: 515 (paper); 187 (computer). Average TOEFL score: 600 (paper).

Transylvania University

- **Address:** 300 N. Broadway, Lexington, KY 40508-1797
- **Website:** http://www.transy.edu
- **Private; Religious affiliation:** Christian Church (Disciples of Christ)
- **Enrollment:** 1,135 full-time; 16 part-time

KEY STATS

✔ **U.S News College Ranking:** 95, Liberal Arts Colleges
✔ **ACT Score (25th/75th percentile):** 23-28
✔ **Tuition:** 2006-2007: $20,950

Selectivity: More selective	**Room/board:** $6,850
Acceptance rate: 84%	**Average debt:** $15,673
Student/faculty ratio: 13/1	**Proportion who borrowed:** 59%

UNDERGRADUATE STUDENT BODY STATS

2005-2006 enrollment: 1,135 full-time; 16 part-time. Men: 40%; women: 60%. **Ethnic makeup:** African American: 2%; Asian American: 2%; Hispanic: 1%; White: 95%. **Religious preference:** Roman Catholic: 18%; Protestant: 51%; Jewish: 1%; No preference: 21%; Christian Church (Disciples of Christ): 9%.

ADMISSIONS FACTS AND FIGURES

Phone: (859) 233-8242. **Email:** admissions@transy.edu. **Website:** http://www.transy.edu. **Application deadlines for fall 2007:** Regular decision: February 1; decision sent by March 15. Early decision: Not offered. Early action: Send application by: December 1; Decision sent by: January 15. Admission can be deferred. **Application fee:** $30. Common application is accepted. **To apply online, go to:** http://www.transy.edu/apply.html. **Admissions requirements/recommendations:** High school units required (recommended): English: 4 (4); Mathematics: 3 (4); Science: 3 (3); Foreign language: 0 (2); Social studies: 2 (2); History: 1 (1); Academic electives: 0 (1); Total units: 12 (16). Tests: The college uses SAT or ACT scores in admissions decisions. Either SAT or ACT required. For admission to the fall 2007 entering class, the school will accept: ACT with writing, ACT without writing. Campus visit: Recommended. Admissions interview: Recommended. Off-campus interview: May be arranged. **Factors that count in admissions decisions:** *Academic:* Secondary school record: Very important. Class rank: Important. Letters of recommendation: Important. Standardized test scores: Very important. Essay: Important. *Nonacademic:* Interview: Considered. Extracurricular activities: Important. Talent/ability: Important. Character/personal qualities: Considered. Alumni/ae relationship: Considered. Geographical residence: Considered. State residency: Considered. Religious affiliation/commitment: Not considered. Minority status: Not considered. Volunteer work: Considered. Work experience: Considered. **Other schools with the greatest overlap in applicants:** Centre College; Denison University; Hanover College; University of Kentucky; Vanderbilt University. **Admissions statistics for the fall 2005 entering class:** Total applicants: 1,222. Total accepted: 1,032. Freshmen enrolled: 326; 15% were from out of state. Overall acceptance rate: 84%. **Credentials of fall 2005 freshmen:** 42% ranked in the top 10 percent of their high school class; 77% were in the top 25 percent, and 96% were in the top half. (Proportion submitting class standing: 87%.) **Average high school grade point average:** 3.6. **First-year students who submitted SAT scores:** 5%. Scores (25/75 percentile): Verbal: 500-580, Math: 460-590, Combined: 960-1170. **First-year students submitting ACT scores:** 96%. Scores (25/75 percentile): English: 24-29, Math: 22-27, Composite: 23-28.

ACADEMICS

Year founded: 1780. **Academic calendar:** Other. **Degrees offered:** bachelor's. **Most popular majors:** 17% business/commerce, 13% biology/biological sciences, 10% psychology, 7% history, 6% accounting. **Major fields of study:** biological and biomedical sciences; business, management, marketing, and related support services; computer and information sciences and support services; education; engineering; English language and literature/letters; foreign languages, literatures, and linguistics; history; liberal arts and sciences studies, and humanities; mathematics and statistics; parks, recreation, leisure, and fitness studies; philosophy and religious studies; physical sciences; psychology; social sciences; visual and performing arts. **Areas of required coursework:** arts/fine arts, humanities, mathematics, English (including composition), foreign languages, sciences (biological or physical), social science, other. **Special academic programs (% participation):** double major (10%), independent study (2%), internships (33%), liberal arts/career

combination (0%), student-designed major (1%), study abroad (62%), teacher certificate program (3%). **Teacher certification offered in:** elementary, middle/junior high, secondary. **Reserve Officers Training Corps (ROTC):** Army ROTC: Offered at cooperating institution (University of Kentucky); Air Force ROTC: Offered at cooperating institution (University of Kentucky). **Faculty and instruction (2005-2006):** Total instructional faculty: 81 full-time, 15 part-time (63% men; 38% women; 5% minorities). Full-time faculty with Ph.D. or other terminal degree: 91%. Student/faculty ratio: 13/1. Classes of fewer than 20 students: 67%; of 20 to 49 students: 33%; of 50 or more students: 0%. **Advanced Placement and International Baccalaureate credit:** AP tests may be used for: Credit and/or placement. Scores accepted: 4, 5. International Baccalaureate exams may be used for: Credit and/or placement. **Freshmen returning for sophomore year:** 85%. **Graduation rates:** Four-year: 60%; five-year: 64%; six-year: 65%. **Graduate study:** 40% of students pursue further study immediately upon graduation; 15% within one year. Fields in which graduates pursue further study: Master of Business Administration (MBA), 5%; law, 20%; medicine, 8%; dentistry, 5%; theology (or the seminary), 5%; arts and sciences, 51%.

COSTS AND FINANCIAL AID

Financial aid office: (859) 233-8239. **Expenses (2006-2007):** Tuition and fees 2006-2007: $20,950; room/board: $6,850. Estimated books and supplies: $900; transportation: $750; personal expenses: $1,250. **Financial aid:** Priority filing date for institution's financial aid form: March 1. In 2005-2006, 72% of undergraduates applied for financial aid. Of those, 60% were determined to have financial need; 27% had their need fully met. Average financial aid package (proportion receiving): $16,537 (60%). Average amount of gift aid, such as scholarships or grants (proportion receiving): $12,598 (60%). Average amount of self-help aid, such as work study or loans (proportion receiving): $4,887 (48%). Average need-based loan (excluding PLUS or other private loans): $3,829. Among students who received need-based aid, the average percentage of need met: 87%. Among students who received aid based on merit, the average award (and the proportion receiving): $11,584 (38%). The average athletic scholarship (and the proportion receiving): $0 (0%). Average amount of debt of borrowers graduating in 2005: $15,673. Proportion who borrowed: 59%.

CAMPUS LIFE AND EXTRACURRICULAR ACTIVITIES

Campus housing available (% using): coed dorms (20%), women's dorms (47%), men's dorms (32%), apartment for single students, special housing for disabled students (1%). Students who live in college-owned, operated, or affiliated housing: 77%. **Student employment:** During the 2005-2006 academic year, 36% of undergraduates worked on campus. Average per-year earnings: $1,500. **Clubs and organizations:** Number of student organizations: 40. Activities include: choral groups, concert band, dance, drama/theater, jazz band, literary magazine, music ensembles, musical theater, opera, pep band, radio station, student government, student newspaper, symphony orchestra, yearbook. Number of fraternities: 4; sororities: 4. Proportion of men in fraternities: 50%; of women in sororities: 50%. Average proportion of students who stay on campus on weekends: 66%. **Sports program (2005-2006):** Member of NCAA III. *Men's intercollegiate varsity sports:* baseball, basketball, cheerleading, cross-country, golf, soccer, swimming and diving, tennis. *Women's intercollegiate varsity sports:* basketball, cheerleading, cross-country, field hockey, golf, soccer, softball, swimming and diving, tennis, volleyball.

SERVICES AND FACILITIES

Basic services: placement service, health service. **Remedial assistance:** writing. **Counseling services:** minority student, career, personal, academic, psychological, birth control, religious. **For learning-disabled students:** Services include: untimed tests, note-taking services, extended time for tests, tutors, priority registration, priority seating. **Library:** Number of titles: 124,949; number of current serial subscriptions: 500. **Information technology resources:** Students are not required to lease or own a computer. Number of campus computers available to all students: 250. School has a wireless network. Approximate number of users that can be accommodated: 250. Proportion of college-owned housing units wired for high-speed internet access: 100%. **Campus safety:** Security services offered: 24-hour foot and vehicle patrols, late-night transport/escort service, 24-hour emergency telephones, lighted pathways/sidewalks, controlled dormitory access (key, security card, etc).

TRANSFER AND INTERNATIONAL STUDENTS

Transfer students: May apply for admission for the following academic terms: Fall, Winter. Applicants do not need a minimum number of credits to apply. For fall 2005: Transfer applications received: 54. Transfer applicants offered admission: 33. Transfer applicants enrolled: 18. **International students:** Number of foreign undergraduates: 0. Number of countries represented: 0. Minimum TOEFL score required: 550 (paper); 220 (computer). Average TOEFL score: 525 (paper).

University of Kentucky

- ■ **Address:** 101 Main Building, Lexington, KY 40506
- ■ **Website:** http://www.uky.edu
- ■ **Public**
- ■ **Enrollment:** 17,050 full-time; 1,652 part-time

KEY STATS
✔ **U.S News College Ranking:** 112, National Universities
✔ **ACT Score (25th/75th percentile):** 22-27
✔ **Tuition 2006-2007:** $6,510 in state, $13,970 out of state
Selectivity: More selective   **Room/board:** $5,510
Acceptance rate: 77%   **Average debt:** $17,692
Student/faculty ratio: 18/1   **Proportion who borrowed:** 68%

UNDERGRADUATE STUDENT BODY STATS
2005-2006 enrollment: 17,050 full-time; 1,652 part-time. Men: 48%; women: 52%. **Ethnic makeup:** African American: 5%; Asian American: 2%; Hispanic: 1%; White: 91%; International: 1%.

ADMISSIONS FACTS AND FIGURES
Phone: (859) 257-2000. **Website:** http://www.uky.edu. **Application deadlines for fall 2007:** Regular decision: February 15. Early decision: Not offered. Early action: Not offered. Admission can be deferred. **Application fee:** $40. Common application is not accepted. **To apply online, go to:** http://www.uky.edu/Admissions/application.html. **Admissions requirements/recommendations:** High school units required (recommended): English: 4 (4); Mathematics: 3 (4); Science: 3 (4); Foreign language: 2 (2); Social studies: 3 (3); Academic electives: 5 (3); Total units: 22 (22). Tests: The college uses SAT or ACT scores in admissions decisions. Either SAT or ACT required. For admission to the fall 2007 entering class, the school will accept: ACT with writing, ACT without writing. Campus visit: Recommended. Admissions interview: Neither required nor recommended. **Factors that count in admissions decisions: *Academic:*** Secondary school record: Very important. Class rank: Considered. Letters of recommendation: Considered. Standardized test scores: Very important. Essay: Considered. *Nonacademic:* Interview: Considered. Extracurricular activities: Considered. Talent/ability: Considered. Character/personal qualities: Considered. Alumni/ae relationship: Considered. Geographical residence: Considered. State residency: Not considered. Religious affiliation/commitment: Not considered. Minority status: Considered. Volunteer work: Considered. Work experience: Not considered. **Admissions statistics for the fall 2005 entering class:** Total applicants: 10,516. Total accepted: 8,124. Freshmen enrolled: 3,835; 24% were from out of state. Overall acceptance rate: 77%. **Credentials of fall 2005 freshmen:** 28% ranked in the top 10 percent of their high school class; 57% were in the top 25 percent, and 86% were in the top half. (Proportion submitting class standing: 75%.) **Average high school grade point average:** 3.6. **First-year students who submitted SAT scores:** 34%. Scores (25/75 percentile): Verbal: 510-630, Math: 520-640, Combined: 1030-1270. **First-year students submitting ACT scores:** 90%. Scores (25/75 percentile): English: 22-28, Math: 21-27, Composite: 22-27.

ACADEMICS
Year founded: 1865. **Academic calendar:** Semester. **Degrees offered:** bachelor's, master's, post-master's certificate, first professional, doctorate. **Most popular majors:** 5% finance, 5% marketing/marketing management, 5% psychology, 4% accounting, 4% business/commerce. **Major fields of study:** agriculture, agriculture operations, and related sciences; architecture and related services; area, ethnic, cultural, and gender studies; biological and biomedical sciences; business, management, marketing, and related support services; communication, journalism, and related programs; computer and information sciences and support services; education; engineering; English language and literature/letters; family and consumer sciences/human sciences; foreign languages, literatures, and linguistics; health professions and related clinical sciences; history; liberal arts and sciences studies, and humanities; mathematics and statistics; multi/interdisciplinary studies; natural resources and conservation; philosophy and

religious studies; physical sciences; psychology; public administration and social service professions; social sciences; visual and performing arts. **Areas of required coursework:** humanities, mathematics, English (including composition), foreign languages, sciences (biological or physical), social science. **Pre-professional programs:** pre-dentistry, pre-medicine, pre-veterinary science, pre-optometry, pre-pharmacy. **Special academic programs:** accelerated program, cooperative (work-study plan) program, distance learning, double major, English as a Second Language (ESL), exchange student program (domestic), honors program, independent study, internships, study abroad, teacher certificate program, weekend college. **Teacher certification offered in:** early childhood, special education, elementary, middle/junior high, secondary. **Reserve Officers Training Corps (ROTC):** Army ROTC: Offered on campus; Air Force ROTC: Offered on campus. **Faculty and instruction (2005-2006):** Total instructional faculty: 1,211 full-time, 513 part-time (65% men; 35% women; 12% minorities). Full-time faculty with Ph.D. or other terminal degree: 91%. Student/faculty ratio: 18/1. Classes of fewer than 20 students: 27%; of 20 to 49 students: 57%; of 50 or more students: 16%. **Advanced Placement and International Baccalaureate credit:** AP tests may be used for: Placement only. **Freshmen returning for sophomore year:** 78%. **Graduation rates:** Four-year: 29%; five-year: 54%; six-year: 60%.

COSTS AND FINANCIAL AID
Financial aid office: (859) 257-3172. **Expenses (2006-2007):** Tuition and fees 2006-2007: $6,510 in state, $13,970 out of state; room/board: $5,510. Estimated books and supplies: $800; transportation: $630; personal expenses: $1,366. **Financial aid:** Priority filing date for institution's financial aid form: February 15. In 2005-2006, 53% of undergraduates applied for financial aid. Of those, 39% were determined to have financial need; 44% had their need fully met. Average financial aid package (proportion receiving): $7,861 (38%). Average amount of gift aid, such as scholarships or grants (proportion receiving): $4,854 (24%). Average amount of self-help aid, such as work study or loans (proportion receiving): $3,897 (29%). Average need-based loan (excluding PLUS or other private loans): $3,765. Among students who received need-based aid, the average percentage of need met: 81%. Among students who received aid based on merit, the average award (and the proportion receiving): $2,821 (3%). The average athletic scholarship (and the proportion receiving): $13,034 (2%). Average amount of debt of borrowers graduating in 2005: $17,692. Proportion who borrowed: 68%.

CAMPUS LIFE AND EXTRACURRICULAR ACTIVITIES
Campus housing available (% using): coed dorms (52%), women's dorms (14%), men's dorms (14%), sorority housing (9%), fraternity housing (6%), apartment for single students (5%), special housing for disabled students, special housing for international students. Students who live in college-owned, operated, or affiliated housing: 29%. **Clubs and organizations:** Number of student organizations: 348. Activities include: choral groups, concert band, dance, drama/theater, jazz band, literary magazine, marching band, music ensembles, musical theater, opera, pep band, radio station, student government, student newspaper, symphony orchestra, yearbook. Number of fraternities: 26; sororities: 17. Proportion of men in fraternities: 15%; of women in sororities: 19%. Average proportion of students who stay on campus on weekends: 32%. **Sports program (2005-2006):** Member of NCAA I. ***Men's intercollegiate varsity sports:*** baseball, basketball, cross-country, football, golf, riflery, soccer, swimming and diving, tennis, track and field (indoor), track and field (outdoor). ***Women's intercollegiate varsity sports:*** basketball, cross-country, golf, gymnastics, riflery, soccer, softball, swimming and diving, tennis, track and field (indoor), track and field (outdoor), volleyball.

SERVICES AND FACILITIES
Basic services: nonremedial tutoring, women's center, placement service, health service, health insurance. **Counseling services:** minority student, career, military, academic, psychological. **For learning-disabled students:** School does not offer a structured program with separate admission and additional fees. Total undergraduates in learning-disabled program or receiving services: 495. Services include: remedial math, reading machines, tape recorders, diagnostic testing service, oral tests, readers, extended time for tests, priority registration, substitution of courses, texts on tape, exams on tape or computer, other testing accomodations. **Library:** Number of titles: 3,286,731; number of current serial subscriptions: 28,350. **Information technology resources:** Students are not required to lease or own a computer. Number of campus computers available to all students: 810. School has a wireless network. Proportion of college-owned housing units wired for high-speed internet access: 100%. **Campus safety:** Security services offered: 24-hour foot and vehicle patrols, late-night transport/escort service, 24-hour

emergency telephones, lighted pathways/sidewalks, controlled dormitory access (key, security card, etc).

TRANSFER AND INTERNATIONAL STUDENTS

Transfer students: May apply for admission for the following academic terms: Fall, Spring, Summer. Applicants need a minimum number of credits to apply. For fall 2005: Transfer applications received: 2,270. Transfer applicants offered admission: 1,614. Transfer applicants enrolled: 1,214. **International students:** Number of foreign undergraduates: 148 (1% of student body). Number of countries represented: 52. Minimum TOEFL score required: 527 (paper); 197 (computer).

University of Louisville

- **Address:** 2301 S. Third Street, Louisville, KY 40292
- **Website:** http://www.louisville.edu
- **Public**
- **Enrollment:** 11,441 full-time; 3,492 part-time

KEY STATS

✔ **U.S News College Ranking:** third tier, National Universities
✔ **ACT Score (25th/75th percentile):** 21-27
✔ **Tuition:** 2006-2007: $6,252 in state, $16,072 out of state

Selectivity: More selective	**Room/board:** $5,096
Acceptance rate: 79%	**Average debt:** $15,128
Student/faculty ratio: 17/1	**Proportion who borrowed:** 42%

UNDERGRADUATE STUDENT BODY STATS

2005-2006 enrollment: 11,441 full-time; 3,492 part-time. Men: 47%; women: 53%. **Ethnic makeup:** African American: 14%; Asian American: 3%; Hispanic: 1%; White: 81%; International: 1%.

ADMISSIONS FACTS AND FIGURES

Phone: (502) 852-6531. **Email:** admitme@gwise.louisville.edu. **Website:** http://www.louisville.edu. **Application deadlines for fall 2007:** Regular decision: August 22. Early decision: Not offered. Early action: Not offered. Admission can be deferred. **Application fee:** $30. Common application is not accepted. **To apply online, go to:** http://admissions.louisville.edu/app/ugrd.html. **Admissions requirements/recommendations:** High school units required (recommended): English: 4; Mathematics: 3 (4); Science: 3 (4); Foreign language: 2; Social studies: 3; Academic electives: 5; Total units: 21 (8). Tests: The college uses SAT or ACT scores in admissions decisions. Either SAT or ACT required. For admission to the fall 2007 entering class, the school will accept: ACT with writing, ACT without writing. Campus visit: Recommended. Admissions interview: Neither required nor recommended. Off-campus interview: Not available. **Factors that count in admissions decisions:** *Academic:* Secondary school record: Very important. Class rank: Considered. Letters of recommendation: Considered. Standardized test scores: Very important. Essay: Considered. *Nonacademic:* Interview: Not considered. Extracurricular activities: Considered. Talent/ability: Considered. Character/personal qualities: Not considered. Alumni/ae relationship: Not considered. Geographical residence: Not considered. State residency: Considered. Religious affiliation/commitment: Not considered. Minority status: Considered. Volunteer work: Considered. Work experience: Considered. **Other schools with the greatest overlap in applicants:** Bellarmine University; Eastern Kentucky University; Murray State University; University of Kentucky; Western Kentucky University. **Admissions statistics for the fall 2005 entering class:** Total applicants: 5,712. Total accepted: 4,515. Freshmen enrolled: 2,313; 18% were from out of state. Overall acceptance rate: 79%. **Credentials of fall 2005 freshmen:** 22% ranked in the top 10 percent of their high school class; 51% were in the top 25 percent, and 80% were in the top half. (Proportion submitting class standing: 36%.) **Average high school grade point average:** 3.0. **First-year students who submitted SAT scores:** 31%. Scores (25/75 percentile): Verbal: 500-620, Math: 510-640; Combined: 1010-1260. **First-year students submitting ACT scores:** 91%. Scores (25/75 percentile): English: 21-27, Math: 20-27, Composite: 21-27.

ACADEMICS

Year founded: 1798. **Academic calendar:** Semester. **Degrees offered:** certificate, associate, transfer-associate, terminal-associate, bachelor's, post-bachelor's certificate, master's, post-master's certificate, first professional, doctorate. **Most popular majors:** 22% business, management, marketing, and related support services, 10% social sciences, 9% engineering, 8% psychology, 7% communication, journalism, and related programs. **Major fields of study:** area, ethnic, cultural, and gender studies; biological and biomedical sciences; business, management, marketing, and related support services; communication, journalism, and related programs; education; engineering; English language and literature/letters; foreign languages, literatures, and linguistics; health professions and related clinical sciences; history; liberal arts and sciences studies, and humanities; mathematics and statistics; parks, recreation, leisure, and fitness studies; philosophy and religious studies; physical sciences; psychology; security and protective services; social sciences; visual and performing arts. **Areas of required coursework:** arts/fine arts, humanities, mathematics, English (including composition), sciences (biological or physical), history, social science, other. **Pre-professional programs:** pre-law, pre-dentistry, pre-medicine, pre-optometry, pre-pharmacy. **Special academic programs:** cooperative (work-study plan) program, distance learning, double major, dual enrollment, English as a Second Language (ESL), honors program, independent study, internships, student-designed major, study abroad, teacher certificate program. **Teacher certification offered in:** early childhood, special education, elementary, vo-tech. **Cooperative education programs:** business, computer science, education, engineering. **Reserve Officers Training Corps (ROTC):** Army ROTC: Offered on campus; Air Force ROTC: Offered on campus. **Faculty and instruction (2005-2006):** Total instructional faculty: 802 full-time, 511 part-time (59% men; 41% women; 16% minorities). Full-time faculty with Ph.D. or other terminal degree: 89%. Student/faculty ratio: 17/1. Classes of fewer than 20 students: 27%; of 20 to 49 students: 60%; of 50 or more students: 13%. **Advanced Placement and International Baccalaureate credit:** International Baccalaureate exams may be used for: Credit and/or placement. **Freshmen returning for sophomore year:** 76%. **Graduation rates:** Four-year: 13%; five-year: 30%; six-year: 37%.

COSTS AND FINANCIAL AID

Financial aid office: (502) 852-5511. **Expenses (2006-2007):** Tuition and fees 2006-2007: $6,252 in state, $16,072 out of state; room/board: $5,096. Estimated books and supplies: $800; transportation: $3,090; personal expenses: $4,914. **Financial aid:** Priority filing date for institution's financial aid form: March 15. In 2005-2006, 60% of undergraduates applied for financial aid. Of those, 52% were determined to have financial need; 12% had their need fully met. Average financial aid package (proportion receiving): $8,175 (51%). Average amount of gift aid, such as scholarships or grants (proportion receiving): $5,473 (43%). Average amount of self-help aid, such as work study or loans (proportion receiving): $3,035 (35%). Average need-based loan (excluding PLUS or other private loans): $3,976. Among students who received need-based aid, the average percentage of need met: 55%. Among students who received aid based on merit, the average award (and the proportion receiving): $5,184 (16%). The average athletic scholarship (and the proportion receiving): $11,777 (3%). Average amount of debt of borrowers graduating in 2005: $15,128. Proportion who borrowed: 42%.

CAMPUS LIFE AND EXTRACURRICULAR ACTIVITIES

Campus housing available: coed dorms, sorority housing, fraternity housing, apartments for married students, apartment for single students, special housing for disabled students, other housing options. Students who live in college-owned, operated, or affiliated housing: 15%. **Clubs and organizations:** Number of student organizations: 220. Activities include: choral groups, concert band, drama/theater, jazz band, marching band, radio station, student government, student newspaper, student film society. Number of fraternities: 13; sororities: 9. Proportion of men in fraternities: 3%; of women in sororities: 3%. **Sports program (2005-2006):** Member of NCAA I. *Men's intercollegiate varsity sports:* baseball, basketball, cheerleading, cross-country, football, golf, soccer, swimming and diving, tennis, track and field (indoor), track and field (outdoor). *Women's intercollegiate varsity sports:* basketball, cheerleading, crew, cross-country, field hockey, golf, soccer, softball, swimming and diving, tennis, track and field (indoor), track and field (outdoor), volleyball.

SERVICES AND FACILITIES

Basic services: health service. **Remedial assistance:** other. **Counseling services:** career, personal, academic. **For learning-disabled students:** School does not offer a structured program with separate admission and additional fees. Services include: reading machines, tape recorders, note-taking services, oral tests, readers, extended time for tests, other. **Library:** Number of titles: 2,016,208; number of current serial subscriptions: 24,720. **Information technology resources:** Students are not required to lease or own a computer.

Number of campus computers available to all students: 350. School has a wireless network. Approximate number of users that can be accommodated: 3,500. Proportion of college-owned housing units wired for high-speed internet access: 100%. **Campus safety:** Security services offered: 24-hour foot and vehicle patrols, late-night transport/escort service, 24-hour emergency telephones, lighted pathways/sidewalks.

TRANSFER AND INTERNATIONAL STUDENTS

Transfer students: May apply for admission for the following academic terms: Fall, Spring, Summer. Applicants need a minimum number of credits to apply. For fall 2005: Transfer applications received: 1,652. Transfer applicants offered admission: 1,483. Transfer applicants enrolled: 1,046. **International students:** Number of foreign undergraduates: 166 (1% of student body). Number of countries represented: 58. Minimum TOEFL score required: 550 (paper); 213 (computer). Average TOEFL score: 550 (paper).

University of the Cumberlands

- **Address:** 6178 College Station Drive, Williamsburg, KY 40769
- **Website:** http://www.ucumberlands.edu
- **Private; Religious affiliation:** Kentucky Baptist Convention
- **Enrollment:** 1,411 full-time; 222 part-time

KEY STATS
✔ **U.S News College Ranking:** third tier, Universities–Master's (South)
✔ **ACT Score (25th/75th percentile):** 18-23
✔ **Tuition:** 2006-2007: $13,658

Selectivity: Selective	**Room/board:** $6,326
Acceptance rate: 83%	**Average debt:** $16,083
Student/faculty ratio: 16/1	**Proportion who borrowed:** 58%

UNDERGRADUATE STUDENT BODY STATS

2005-2006 enrollment: 1,411 full-time; 222 part-time. Men: 48%; women: 52%. **Ethnic makeup:** African American: 7%; Asian American: 1%; Hispanic: 2%; White: 88%; International: 2%. **Religious preference:** Roman Catholic: 5%; Protestant: 28%; No preference: 9%; Unknown: 2%; Kentucky Baptist Convention: 53%; Other: 3%.

ADMISSIONS FACTS AND FIGURES

Phone: (800) 343-1609. **Email:** admiss@ucumberlands.edu. **Website:** http://www.ucumberlands.edu. **Application deadlines for fall 2007:** Regular decision: August 15. Early decision: Not offered. Early action: Not offered. Admission can be deferred. **Application fee:** $30. Common application is accepted. **To apply online, go to:** http://www.gohigherky.org/Applications/University_of_the_Cumberlands/apply.html. **Admissions requirements/recommendations:** High school units required (recommended): English: 4 (4); Mathematics: 3 (3); Science: 2 (3); Foreign language: (1); Social studies: 1 (2). Tests: The college uses SAT or ACT scores in admissions decisions. Either SAT or ACT required. For admission to the fall 2007 entering class, the school will accept: ACT with writing, ACT without writing. Campus visit: Recommended. Admissions interview: Neither required nor recommended. Off-campus interview: Not available. **Factors that count in admissions decisions: Academic:** Secondary school record: Very important. Class rank: Considered. Letters of recommendation: Considered. Standardized test scores: Considered. Essay: Considered. **Nonacademic:** Interview: Considered. Extracurricular activities: Considered. Talent/ability: Considered. Character/personal qualities: Considered. Alumni/ae relationship: Not considered. Geographical residence: Not considered. State residency: Not considered. Religious affiliation/commitment: Not considered. Minority status: Not considered. Volunteer work: Considered. Work experience: Not considered. **Other schools with the greatest overlap in applicants:** Campbellsville University; Carson-Newman College; Eastern Kentucky University; University of Kentucky; University of Tennessee. **Admissions statistics for the fall 2005 entering class:** Total applicants: 984. Total accepted: 818. Freshmen enrolled: 433; 43% were from out of state. Overall acceptance rate: 83%. **Credentials of fall 2005 freshmen:** 16% ranked in the top 10 percent of their high school class; 42% were in the top 25 percent, and 70% were in the top half. (Proportion submitting class standing: 92%.) **Average high school grade point average:** 3.3. **First-year students who submitted SAT scores:** 28%. Scores (25/75 percentile): Verbal: 430-550; Math: 450-550, Combined: 880-1100. **First-year students submitting ACT**

scores: 86%. Scores (25/75 percentile): English: 17-24, Math: 17-23, Composite: 18-23.

ACADEMICS

Year founded: 1888. **Academic calendar:** Semester. **Degrees offered:** bachelor's, post-bachelor's certificate, master's, post-master's certificate. **Most popular majors:** 18% business/commerce, 18% education, 12% biology/biological sciences, 8% psychology, 7% community health services/liaison/counseling. **Major fields of study:** biological and biomedical sciences; business, management, marketing, and related support services; communication, journalism, and related programs; computer and information sciences and support services; education; English language and literature/letters; health professions and related clinical sciences; history; mathematics and statistics; philosophy and religious studies; physical sciences; psychology; public administration and social service professions; social sciences; theology and religious vocations; visual and performing arts. **Areas of required coursework:** arts/fine arts, humanities, computer literacy, mathematics, English (including composition), philosophy, sciences (biological or physical), history, social science, other. **Pre-professional programs:** pre-law, pre-dentistry, pre-medicine, pre-veterinary science, pre-optometry, pre-pharmacy. **Special academic programs (% participation):** distance learning (18%), double major (14%), dual enrollment (9%), honors program (0%), independent study (1%), internships (44%), student-designed major (0%), study abroad (1%), teacher certificate program (21%). **Teacher certification offered in:** special education, elementary, middle/junior high, secondary. **Cooperative education programs:** computer science, education, health professions, social/behavioral science. **Reserve Officers Training Corps (ROTC):** Army ROTC: Offered on campus. **Faculty and instruction (2005-2006):** Total instructional faculty: 86 full-time, 26 part-time (60% men; 40% women; 4% minorities). Full-time faculty with Ph.D. or other terminal degree: 72%. Student/faculty ratio: 16/1. Classes of fewer than 20 students: 66%; of 20 to 49 students: 32%; of 50 or more students: 3%. **Advanced Placement and International Baccalaureate credit:** AP tests may be used for: Credit and/or placement. Scores accepted: 3, 4, 5. International Baccalaureate exams may be used for: Credit only. **Freshmen returning for sophomore year:** 62%. **Graduation rates:** Four-year: 21%; five-year: 32%; six-year: 37%. **Graduate study:** 20% of students pursue further study immediately upon graduation; 29% within one year; 65% within five years. Fields in which graduates pursue further study: Master of Business Administration (MBA), 2%; law, 1%; medicine, 3%; dentistry, 1%; engineering, 1%; theology (or the seminary), 2%; education, 15%; arts and sciences, 3%; veterinary medicine, 1%.

COSTS AND FINANCIAL AID

Financial aid office: (800) 532-0828. **Expenses (2006-2007):** Tuition and fees 2006-2007: $13,658; room/board: $6,326. Estimated books and supplies: $900; transportation: $800; personal expenses: $1,500. **Financial aid:** Priority filing date for institution's financial aid form: March 1. In 2005-2006, 91% of undergraduates applied for financial aid. Of those, 83% were determined to have financial need; 60% had their need fully met. Average financial aid package (proportion receiving): $13,277 (83%). Average amount of gift aid, such as scholarships or grants (proportion receiving): $6,032 (61%). Average amount of self-help aid, such as work study or loans (proportion receiving): $4,298 (58%). Average need-based loan (excluding PLUS or other private loans): $3,796. Among students who received need-based aid, the average percentage of need met: 94%. Among students who received aid based on merit, the average award (and the proportion receiving): $6,136 (4%). The average athletic scholarship (and the proportion receiving): $4,480 (4%). Average amount of debt of borrowers graduating in 2005: $16,083. Proportion who borrowed: 58%.

CAMPUS LIFE AND EXTRACURRICULAR ACTIVITIES

Campus housing available (% using): women's dorms (55%), men's dorms (45%). Students who live in college-owned, operated, or affiliated housing: 67%. **Student employment:** During the 2005-2006 academic year, 12% of undergraduates worked on campus. Average per-year earnings: $2,992. **Clubs and organizations:** Number of student organizations: 45. Activities include: choral groups, concert band, dance, drama/theater, jazz band, literary magazine, marching band, music ensembles, musical theater, pep band, radio station, student government, student newspaper, television station. Number of fraternities: 0; sororities: 0. Average proportion of students who stay on campus on weekends: 40%. **Sports program (2005-2006):** Member of NAIA. **Men's intercollegiate varsity sports:** baseball, basketball, cheerleading, cross-country, football, golf, soccer, swimming and diving, tennis, track and field (indoor), track and field (outdoor), wrestling, judo. **Women's intercollegiate varsity sports:** basketball, cross-country, golf, soccer, softball, swimming and diving, tennis, track and field (indoor), track and field (outdoor), volleyball.

SERVICES AND FACILITIES
Basic services: nonremedial tutoring. **Counseling services:** career, academic. **For learning-disabled students:** School does not offer a structured program with separate admission and additional fees. Services include: tutors. **Library:** Number of titles: 201,423; number of current serial subscriptions: 24,793. **Information technology resources:** Students are not required to lease or own a computer. Number of campus computers available to all students: 400. School has a wireless network. Approximate number of users that can be accommodated: 150. Proportion of college-owned housing units wired for high-speed internet access: 100%. **Campus safety:** Security services offered: 24-hour foot and vehicle patrols, late-night transport/escort service, lighted pathways/sidewalks.

TRANSFER AND INTERNATIONAL STUDENTS
Transfer students: May apply for admission for the following academic terms: Fall, Spring, Summer. Applicants do not need a minimum number of credits to apply. For fall 2005: Transfer applications received: 147. Transfer applicants offered admission: 109. Transfer applicants enrolled: 66. **International students:** Number of foreign undergraduates: 25 (2% of student body). Number of countries represented: 27. Minimum TOEFL score required: 550 (paper); 213 (computer).

Western Kentucky University

- **Address:** 1 Big Red Way, Bowling Green, KY 42101-3576
- **Website:** http://www.wku.edu
- **Public**
- **Enrollment:** 13,053 full-time; 2,914 part-time

KEY STATS
- ✔ **U.S News College Ranking:** 41, Universities–Master's (South)
- ✔ **ACT Score (25th/75th percentile):** 18-23
- ✔ **Tuition:** 2006-2007: $5,860 in state, $14,400 out of state

Selectivity: Selective	**Room/board:** $5,426
Acceptance rate: 92%	**Average debt:** N/A
Student/faculty ratio: 19/1	**Proportion who borrowed:** N/A

UNDERGRADUATE STUDENT BODY STATS
2005-2006 enrollment: 13,053 full-time; 2,914 part-time. Men: 42%; women: 58%. **Ethnic makeup:** African American: 9%; Asian American: 1%; Hispanic: 1%; White: 87%; International: 1%.

ADMISSIONS FACTS AND FIGURES
Phone: (270) 745-2551. **Email:** admission@wku.edu. **Website:** http://www.wku.edu. **Application deadlines for fall 2007:** Regular decision: August 1. Early decision: Not offered. Early action: Not offered. Admission cannot be deferred. **Application fee:** $35. Common application is not accepted. **To apply online, go to:** http://www.wku.edu/Info/Admissions/. **Admissions requirements/recommendations:** High school units required (recommended): English: 4; Mathematics: 3; Science: 3; Foreign language: 2; Social studies: 3; Total units: 22. Tests: The college uses SAT or ACT scores in admissions decisions. Either SAT or ACT required. For admission to the fall 2007 entering class, the school will accept: ACT with writing, ACT without writing. Campus visit: Neither required nor recommended. Admissions interview: Neither required nor recommended. Off-campus interview: Not available. **Factors that count in admissions decisions:** *Academic:* Secondary school record: Not considered. Class rank: Not considered. Letters of recommendation: Not considered. Standardized test scores: Very important. Essay: Not considered. *Nonacademic:* Interview: Not considered. Extracurricular activities: Not considered. Talent/ability: Not considered. Character/personal qualities: Not considered. Alumni/ae relationship: Not considered. Geographical residence: Not considered. State residency: Not considered. Religious affiliation/commitment: Not considered. Minority status: Not considered. Volunteer work: Not considered. Work experience: Not considered. **Admissions statistics for the fall 2005 entering class:** Total applicants: 6,781. Total accepted: 6,220. Freshmen enrolled: 3,150; 16% were from out of state. Overall acceptance rate: 92%. **Credentials of fall 2005 freshmen:** 15% ranked in the top 10 percent of their high school class; 36% were in the top 25 percent, and 67% were in the top half. (Proportion sub-

mitting class standing: 75%.) **Average high school grade point average:** 3.1. **First-year students who submitted SAT scores:** 4%. Scores (25/75 percentile): Verbal: 450-550, Math: 440-560, Combined: 890-1110. **First-year students submitting ACT scores:** 96%. Scores (25/75 percentile): English: 17-24, Math: 17-23, Composite: 18-23.

ACADEMICS
Year founded: 1906. **Academic calendar:** Semester. **Degrees offered:** certificate, diploma, associate, transfer-associate, terminal-associate, bachelor's, post-bachelor's certificate, master's, post-master's certificate. **Most popular majors:** 19% education, 16% business, management, marketing, and related support services, 11% communication, journalism, and related programs, 9% liberal arts and sciences studies, and humanities, 9% social sciences. **Major fields of study:** agriculture, agriculture operations, and related sciences; biological and biomedical sciences; business, management, marketing, and related support services; communication, journalism, and related programs; computer and information sciences and support services; education; engineering; engineering technologies/technicians; English language and literature/letters; family and consumer sciences/human sciences; foreign languages, literatures, and linguistics; health professions and related clinical sciences; history; liberal arts and sciences studies, and humanities; mathematics and statistics; multi/interdisciplinary studies; parks, recreation, leisure, and fitness studies; philosophy and religious studies; physical sciences; psychology; public administration and social service professions; social sciences; visual and performing arts. **Areas of required coursework:** arts/fine arts, humanities, mathematics, English (including composition), foreign languages, sciences (biological or physical), history, social science, other. **Pre-professional programs:** pre-law, pre-dentistry, pre-medicine, pre-theology, pre-veterinary science, pre-optometry, pre-pharmacy, other. **Special academic programs:** cooperative (work-study plan) program, distance learning, double major, dual enrollment, English as a Second Language (ESL), exchange student program (domestic), external degree program, honors program, independent study, internships, student-designed major, study abroad, teacher certificate program. **Teacher certification offered in:** early childhood, special education, elementary, vo-tech, middle/junior high, secondary. **Cooperative education programs:** agriculture, art, business, computer science, education, engineering, health professions, home economics, humanities, natural science, social/behavioral science, technologies, other. **Reserve Officers Training Corps (ROTC):** Army ROTC: Offered on campus; Air Force ROTC: Offered at cooperating institution (Tennessee State University). **Faculty and instruction (2005-2006):** Total instructional faculty: 694 full-time, 413 part-time (53% men; 47% women; 7% minorities). Full-time faculty with Ph.D. or other terminal degree: 74%. Student/faculty ratio: 19/1. Classes of fewer than 20 students: 39%; of 20 to 49 students: 55%; of 50 or more students: 6%. **Advanced Placement and International Baccalaureate credit:** AP tests may be used for: Credit only. Scores accepted: 3, 4, 5. International Baccalaureate exams may be used for: Credit only. **Freshmen returning for sophomore year:** 74%. **Graduation rates:** Four-year: 27%; five-year: 43%; six-year: 44%.

COSTS AND FINANCIAL AID
Financial aid office: (270) 745-2755. **Expenses (2006-2007):** Tuition and fees 2006-2007: $5,860 in state, $14,400 out of state; room/board: $5,426. **Financial aid:** Priority filing date for institution's financial aid form: April 1.

CAMPUS LIFE AND EXTRACURRICULAR ACTIVITIES
Campus housing available (% using): coed dorms (53%), women's dorms (32%), men's dorms (15%), special housing for disabled students, special housing for international students. Students who live in college-owned, operated, or affiliated housing: 32%. **Student employment:** During the 2005-2006 academic year, 6% of undergraduates worked on campus. Average per-year earnings: $1,365. **Clubs and organizations:** Number of student organizations: 251. Activities include: choral groups, concert band, dance, drama/theater, jazz band, literary magazine, marching band, music ensembles, musical theater, opera, pep band, radio station, student government, student newspaper, student film society, symphony orchestra, television station, yearbook. Number of fraternities: 16; sororities: 12. Proportion of men in fraternities: 9%; of women in sororities: 7%. Average proportion of students who stay on campus on weekends: 60%. **Sports program (2005-2006):** Member of NCAA I. *Men's intercollegiate varsity sports:* baseball, basketball, cross-country, football, golf, soccer, swimming and diving, tennis, track and field (indoor), track and field (outdoor). *Women's intercollegiate varsity sports:* basketball, cross-country, golf, soccer, softball, swimming and diving, tennis, track and field (indoor), track and field (outdoor), volleyball.

SERVICES AND FACILITIES

Basic services: nonremedial tutoring, women's center, placement service, day care, health service, health insurance. **Remedial assistance:** reading, math, writing, study skills, other. **Counseling services:** minority student, career, military, personal, veteran student, academic, older student, psychological, birth control. **For learning-disabled students:** School does not offer a structured program with separate admission and additional fees. Total undergraduates in learning-disabled program or receiving services: 214. Services include: remedial math, remedial English, reading machines, remedial reading, tape recorders, videotaped classes, diagnostic testing service, note-taking services, oral tests, learning center, readers, extended time for tests, tutors, priority registration, priority seating, texts on tape, other. **Library:** Number of titles: 1,681,876; number of current serial subscriptions: 3,912. **Information technology resources:** Students are not required to lease or own a computer. Number of campus computers available to all students: 1,350. School has a wireless network. Approximate number of users that can be accommodated: 3,000. Proportion of college-owned housing units wired for high-speed internet access: 100%. **Campus safety:** Security services offered: 24-hour foot and vehicle patrols, late-night transport/escort service, 24-hour emergency telephones, lighted pathways/sidewalks, controlled dormitory access (key, security card, etc).

TRANSFER AND INTERNATIONAL STUDENTS

Transfer students: May apply for admission for the following academic terms: Fall, Winter, Spring, Summer. Applicants do not need a minimum number of credits to apply. For fall 2005: Transfer applications received: 1,954. Transfer applicants offered admission: 1,650. Transfer applicants enrolled: 865. **International students:** Number of foreign undergraduates: 225 (1% of student body). Number of countries represented: 44. Minimum TOEFL score required: 525 (paper); 197 (computer).

Louisiana

Centenary College of Louisiana

- **Address:** PO Box 41188, Shreveport, LA 71134-1188
- **Website:** http://www.centenary.edu
- **Private; Religious affiliation:** United Methodist
- **Enrollment:** 882 full-time; 22 part-time

KEY STATS
✔ **U.S News College Ranking:** 13, Universities–Master's (South)
✔ **ACT Score (25th/75th percentile):** 22-27
✔ **Tuition:** 2006-2007: $19,760

Selectivity: More selective	**Room/board:** $6,990
Acceptance rate: 64%	**Average debt:** $17,300
Student/faculty ratio: 10/1	**Proportion who borrowed:** 53%

UNDERGRADUATE STUDENT BODY STATS

2005-2006 enrollment: 882 full-time; 22 part-time. Men: 38%; women: 62%. **Ethnic makeup:** African American: 7%; American-Indian: 1%; Asian American: 2%; Hispanic: 4%; White: 84%; International: 2%. **Religious preference:** Roman Catholic: 20%; Protestant: 38%; Jewish: 1%; No preference: 14%; Unknown: 5%; United Methodist: 21%; Other: 1%.

ADMISSIONS FACTS AND FIGURES

Phone: (800) 234-4448. **Email:** admissions@centenary.edu. **Website:** http://www.centenary.edu. **Application deadlines for fall 2007:** Regular decision: August 1; decision sent by November 15. Early decision: Send application by: December 1; Decision sent by: January 1. Early action: Send application by: January 15; Decision sent by: February 1. Admission can be deferred. **Application fee:** $30. Common application is accepted. **Admissions requirements/recommendations:** High school units required (recommended): English: 4 (4); Mathematics: 3 (3); Science: 3 (3); Foreign language: 2 (2); Social studies: 3 (3); Total units: 15 (15). Tests: The college uses SAT or ACT scores in admissions decisions. Either SAT or ACT required. For admission to the fall 2007 entering class, the school will accept: ACT without writing. Campus visit: Recommended. Admissions interview: Recommended. Off-campus interview: May be arranged. **Factors that count in admissions decisions:** *Academic:* Secondary school record: Very important. Class rank: Considered. Letters of recommendation: Considered. Standardized test scores: Important. Essay: Considered. *Nonacademic:* Interview: Important. Extracurricular activities: Important. Talent/ability: Important. Character/personal qualities: Important. Alumni/ae relationship: Important. Geographical residence: Considered. State residency: Not considered. Religious affiliation/commitment: Considered. Minority status: Considered. Volunteer work: Important. Work experience: Considered. **Other schools with the greatest overlap in applicants:** Baylor University; Louisiana State University–Baton Rouge; Louisiana Tech University; Loyola University New Orleans; Tulane University. **Admissions statistics for the fall 2005 entering class:** Total applicants: 1,348. Total accepted: 856. Freshmen enrolled: 233; 57% were from out of state. Accepted through early-decision or early-action plans: 72%. Overall acceptance rate: 64%. Early-decision acceptance rate: 64%. Non-early acceptance rate: 57%. **Credentials of fall 2005 freshmen:** 40% ranked in the top 10 percent of their high school class; 70% were in the top 25 percent, and 91% were in the top half. (Proportion submitting class standing: 89%.) **Average high school grade point average:** 3.3. **First-year students who submitted SAT scores:** 49%. Scores (25/75 percentile): Verbal: 510-650, Math: 500-630, Combined: 1010-1280. **First-year students submitting ACT scores:** 83%. Scores (25/75 percentile): English: 22-29, Math: 20-27, Composite: 22-27.

ACADEMICS

Year founded: 1825. **Academic calendar:** Other. **Degrees offered:** bachelor's, master's. **Most popular majors:** 11% business administration and management, 10% psychology, 9% mass communication/media studies, 8% biology/biological sciences, 8% health and physical education. **Major fields of study:** area, ethnic, cultural, and gender studies; biological and biomedical sciences; business, management, marketing, and related support services; communication, journalism, and related programs; education; English language and literature/letters; foreign languages, literatures, and linguistics; health professions and related clinical sciences; history; liberal arts and sciences studies, and humanities; mathematics and statistics; multi/interdisciplinary studies; parks, recreation, leisure, and fitness studies; philosophy and religious studies; physical sciences; psychology; social sciences; visual and performing arts. **Areas of required coursework:** arts/fine arts, humanities, computer literacy, mathematics, English (including composition), sciences (biological or physical), history, social science. **Pre-professional programs:** pre-law, pre-dentistry, pre-medicine, pre-veterinary science, pre-pharmacy, other. **Special academic programs:** cooperative (work-study plan) program, cross-registration, double major, dual enrollment, exchange student program (domestic), independent study, internships, liberal arts/career combination, student-designed major, study abroad, teacher certificate program. **Teacher certification offered in:** elementary, middle/junior high, secondary. **Cooperative education programs:** business, engineering, health professions, social/behavioral science. **Faculty and instruction (2005-2006):** Total instructional faculty: 72 full-time, 50 part-time (60% men; 40% women; 6% minorities). Full-time faculty with Ph.D. or other terminal degree: 94%. Student/faculty ratio: 10/1. Classes of fewer than 20 students: 69%; of 20 to 49 students: 31%; of 50 or more students: 0%. **Advanced Placement and International Baccalaureate credit:** AP tests may be used for: Credit and/or placement. Scores accepted: 4, 5. International Baccalaureate exams may be used for: Credit only. **Freshmen returning for sophomore year:** 78%. **Graduation rates:** Four-year: 43%; five-year: 51%; six-year: 54%. **Graduate study:** 50% of students pursue further study immediately upon graduation.

COSTS AND FINANCIAL AID

Financial aid office: (318) 869-5137. **Expenses (2006-2007):** Tuition and fees 2006-2007: $19,760; room/board: $6,990. Estimated books and supplies: $1,100; transportation: $950; personal expenses: $1,600. **Financial aid:** Priority filing date for institution's financial aid form: February 15. In 2005-2006, 83% of undergraduates applied for financial aid. Of those, 62% were determined to have financial need; 38% had their need fully met. Average financial aid package (proportion receiving): $13,618 (60%). Average amount of gift aid, such as scholarships or grants (proportion receiving): $11,289 (60%). Average amount of self-help aid, such as work study or loans (proportion receiving): $4,124 (34%). Average need-based loan (excluding PLUS or other private loans): $3,631. Among students who received need-based aid, the average percentage of need met: 75%. Among students who received aid based on merit, the average award (and the proportion receiving): $10,270 (28%). The average athletic scholarship (and the proportion receiving): $12,220 (21%). Average amount of debt of borrowers graduating in 2005: $17,300. Proportion who borrowed: 53%.

CAMPUS LIFE AND EXTRACURRICULAR ACTIVITIES

Campus housing available (% using): coed dorms (70%), women's dorms (30%), fraternity housing. Students who live in college-owned, operated, or affiliated housing: 67%. **Student employment:** During the 2005-2006 academic year, 25% of undergraduates worked on campus. Average per-year earnings: $1,500. **Clubs and organizations:** Number of student organizations: 51. Activities include: choral groups, concert band, dance, drama/theater, jazz band, literary magazine, music ensembles, musical theater, opera, pep band, radio station, student government, student newspaper, student film society, symphony orchestra, yearbook. Number of fraternities: 4; sororities: 2. of women in sororities: 26%. Average proportion of students who stay on campus on weekends: 70%. **Sports program (2005-2006):** Member of NCAA I. *Men's intercollegiate varsity sports:* baseball, basketball, cross-country, golf, soccer, swimming and diving, tennis. *Women's intercollegiate varsity sports:* basketball, cross-country, golf, gymnastics, soccer, softball, swimming and diving, tennis, volleyball.

SERVICES AND FACILITIES

Basic services: nonremedial tutoring, placement service, health service, health insurance. **Remedial assistance:** writing, study skills. **Counseling services:** minority student, career, personal, veteran student, academic, psychological, religious. **For learning-disabled students:** School does not offer a structured program with separate admission and additional fees. Total undergraduates in learning-disabled program or receiving services: 16. Services include: reading machines, tape recorders, untimed tests, note-taking services, oral tests, learning center, readers, extended time for tests, tutors, priority seating, texts on tape. **Library:** Number of titles: 208,128; number of current serial subscriptions: 55,961. **Information technology resources:** Students are not required to lease or own a computer. Number of campus computers available to all students: 400. School has a wireless network. Approximate number of users that can be accommodated: 225. Proportion of college-owned housing units wired for high-speed internet access: 100%. **Campus safety:** Security services offered: 24-hour foot and vehicle patrols, late-night transport/escort service, 24-hour emergency telephones, lighted pathways/sidewalks, student patrols, controlled dormitory access (key, security card, etc).

TRANSFER AND INTERNATIONAL STUDENTS

Transfer students: May apply for admission for the following academic terms: Fall, Spring, Summer. Applicants do not need a minimum number of credits to apply. For fall 2005: Transfer applications received: 102. Transfer applicants offered admission: 43. Transfer applicants enrolled: 26. **International students:** Number of foreign undergraduates: 17 (2% of student body). Number of countries represented: 13. Minimum TOEFL score required: 550 (paper); 220 (computer).

Dillard University

■ **Address:** 2601 Gentilly Boulevard, New Orleans, LA 70122
■ **Website:** http://www.dillard.edu
■ **Private; Religious affiliation:** United Methodist/United Church of Christ
■ **Enrollment:** N/A

KEY STATS

✔ **U.S News College Ranking:** 17, Comp. Coll.–Bachelor's (South)
✔ **ACT Score (25th/75th percentile):** 19-22
✔ **Tuition:** N/A

Selectivity: Selective	**Room/board:** N/A
Acceptance rate: 47%	**Average debt:** N/A
Student/faculty ratio: N/A	**Proportion who borrowed:** N/A

Grambling State University

■ **Address:** Box 607, Grambling, LA 71245
■ **Website:** http://www.gram.edu/
■ **Public**
■ **Enrollment:** N/A

KEY STATS

✔ **U.S News College Ranking:** fourth tier, Universities–Master's (South)
✔ **SAT or ACT Score (25th/75th percentile):** N/A
✔ **Tuition:** 2006-2007: $3,606 in state, $8,956 out of state

Selectivity: Less selective	**Room/board:** $4,718
Acceptance rate: N/A	**Average debt:** N/A
Student/faculty ratio: N/A	**Proportion who borrowed:** N/A

Louisiana College

■ **Address:** 1140 College Drive, Pineville, LA 71360
■ **Website:** http://www.lacollege.edu
■ **Private; Religious affiliation:** Southern Baptist Convention
■ **Enrollment:** N/A

KEY STATS

✔ **U.S News College Ranking:** 30, Comp. Coll.–Bachelor's (South)
✔ **ACT Score (25th/75th percentile):** 20-26
✔ **Tuition:** 2005-2006: $10,930

Selectivity: Selective	**Room/board:** $4,060
Acceptance rate: 73%	**Average debt:** N/A
Student/faculty ratio: N/A	**Proportion who borrowed:** N/A

Louisiana State University–Baton Rouge

■ **Address:** 156 Thomas Boyd Hall, Baton Rouge, LA 70803
■ **Website:** http://www.lsu.edu
■ **Public**
■ **Enrollment:** 23,766 full-time; 1,939 part-time

KEY STATS

✔ **U.S News College Ranking:** third tier, National Universities
✔ **ACT Score (25th/75th percentile):** 22-27
✔ **Tuition:** 2005-2006: $4,419 in state, $12,719 out of state

Selectivity: More selective	**Room/board:** $6,330
Acceptance rate: 73%	**Average debt:** N/A
Student/faculty ratio: 22/1	**Proportion who borrowed:** N/A

UNDERGRADUATE STUDENT BODY STATS

2005-2006 enrollment: 23,766 full-time; 1,939 part-time. Men: 48%; women: 52%. **Ethnic makeup:** African American: 9%; Asian American: 3%; Hispanic: 3%; White: 83%; International: 2%. **Religious preference:** Roman Catholic: 39%; Protestant: 29%; No preference: 28%; Other: 1%.

ADMISSIONS FACTS AND FIGURES

Phone: (225) 578-1175. **Email:** admissions@lsu.edu. **Website:** http://www.lsu.edu. **Application deadlines for fall 2007:** Regular decision: April 15. Early decision: Not offered. Early action: Not offered. Admission can be deferred. **Application fee:** $40. Common application is not accepted. **To apply online, go to:** http://appl003.lsu.edu/slas/ugadmissions.nsf/index. **Admissions requirements/recommendations:** High school units required (recommended): English: 4; Mathematics: 3 (4); Science: 3; Foreign language: 2; Social studies: 2; History: 1; Academic electives: 3; Total units: 18. Tests: The college does not use SAT or ACT scores in admissions decisions. Neither SAT nor ACT required. For admission to the fall 2007 entering class, the school will accept: ACT with writing. Campus visit: Recommended. Admissions interview: Neither required nor recommended. Off-campus interview: Not available. **Factors that count in admissions decisions:** *Academic:* Secondary school record: Very important. Class rank: Important. Letters of recommendation: Not considered. Standardized test scores: Very important. Essay: Not considered. *Nonacademic:* Interview: Not considered. Extracurricular activities: Considered. Talent/ability: Considered. Character/personal qualities: Not considered. Alumni/ae relationship: Not considered. Geographical residence: Not considered. State residency: Not considered. Religious affiliation/commitment: Not considered. Minority status: Not considered. Volunteer work: Not considered. Work experience: Not considered. **Other schools with the greatest overlap in applicants:** Florida State University; Texas A&M University–College Station; Tulane University; University of Florida; University of Georgia. **Admissions statistics for the fall 2005 entering class:** Total applicants: 10,825. Total accepted: 7,927. Freshmen enrolled: 4,970; 17% were from out of state. Overall acceptance rate: 73%. **Credentials of fall 2005 freshmen:** 25% ranked in the top 10 percent of their high school class; 53% were in the top 25 percent, and 83% were in the top half. (Proportion submitting class standing: 93%.) **Average high school grade point average:** 3.5. **First-year students who submitted SAT scores:** 14%. Scores (25/75 percentile): Verbal: 520-630; Math: 540-660, Combined: 1060-1290. **First-year students submitting ACT**

scores: 86%. Scores (25/75 percentile): English: 23-29, Math: 21-26, Composite: 22-27.

ACADEMICS

Year founded: 1860. **Academic calendar:** Semester. **Degrees offered:** bachelor's, master's, post-master's certificate, first professional, doctorate. **Most popular majors:** 21% business, management, marketing, and related support services, 10% education, 9% engineering, 9% liberal arts and sciences studies, and humanities, 9% social sciences. **Major fields of study:** agriculture, agriculture operations, and related sciences; architecture and related services; area, ethnic, cultural, and gender studies; biological and biomedical sciences; business, management, marketing, and related support services; communication, journalism, and related programs; computer and information sciences and support services; education; engineering; English language and literature/letters; family and consumer sciences/human sciences; foreign languages, literatures, and linguistics; health professions and related clinical sciences; history; liberal arts and sciences studies, and humanities; mathematics and statistics; multi/interdisciplinary studies; natural resources and conservation; philosophy and religious studies; physical sciences; psychology; social sciences; visual and performing arts. **Areas of required coursework:** arts/fine arts, humanities, computer literacy, mathematics, English (including composition), foreign languages, sciences (biological or physical), social science. **Pre-professional programs:** pre-law, pre-dentistry, pre-medicine, pre-veterinary science, pre-pharmacy. **Special academic programs:** accelerated program, cooperative (work-study plan) program, cross-registration, distance learning, double major, dual enrollment, English as a Second Language (ESL), exchange student program (domestic), honors program, independent study, internships, student-designed major, study abroad, teacher certificate program. **Teacher certification offered in:** early childhood, elementary, vo-tech, secondary. **Cooperative education programs:** agriculture, business, computer science, engineering, natural science, technologies, other. **Reserve Officers Training Corps (ROTC):** Army ROTC: Offered on campus; Navy ROTC: Offered at cooperating institution (Southern University A&M College); Air Force ROTC: Offered on campus. **Faculty and instruction (2005-2006):** Total instructional faculty: 1,277 full-time, 190 part-time (66% men; 34% women; 12% minorities). Full-time faculty with Ph.D. or other terminal degree: 85%. Student/faculty ratio: 22/1. Classes of fewer than 20 students: 31%; of 20 to 49 students: 49%; of 50 or more students: 20%. **Advanced Placement and International Baccalaureate credit:** AP tests may be used for: Credit and/or placement. Scores accepted: 3, 4, 5. International Baccalaureate exams may be used for: Credit only. **Freshmen returning for sophomore year:** 84%. **Graduation rates:** Four-year: 26%; five-year: 51%; six-year: 59%. **Graduate study:** 20% of students pursue further study immediately upon graduation. Fields in which graduates pursue further study: Master of Business Administration (MBA), 5%; law, 13%; medicine, 11%; dentistry, 2%; engineering, 3%; education, 7%; arts and sciences, 11%; veterinary medicine, 2%.

COSTS AND FINANCIAL AID

Financial aid office: (225) 578-3103. **Expenses (2005-2006):** Tuition and fees 2005-2006: $4,419 in state, $12,719 out of state; room/board: $6,330. Estimated books and supplies: $1,500; transportation: $908; personal expenses: $1,574. **Financial aid:** In 2005-2006, 69% of undergraduates applied for financial aid. Of those, 44% were determined to have financial need; 16% had their need fully met. Average financial aid package (proportion receiving): $7,070 (43%). Average amount of gift aid, such as scholarships or grants (proportion receiving): $4,664 (37%). Average amount of self-help aid, such as work study or loans (proportion receiving): $3,963 (30%). Average need-based loan (excluding PLUS or other private loans): $3,885. Among students who received need-based aid, the average percentage of need met: 57%. Among students who received aid based on merit, the average award (and the proportion receiving): $3,603 (10%). The average athletic scholarship (and the proportion receiving): $11,545 (2%).

CAMPUS LIFE AND EXTRACURRICULAR ACTIVITIES

Campus housing available (% using): coed dorms (36%), women's dorms (18%), men's dorms (12%), sorority housing, fraternity housing, apartments for married students (4%), apartment for single students (29%), special housing for disabled students (1%). Students who live in college-owned, operated, or affiliated housing: 23%. **Student employment:** During the 2005-2006 academic year, 25% of undergraduates worked on campus. Average per-year earnings: $2,200. **Clubs and organizations:** Number of student organizations: 335. Activities include: choral groups, concert band, dance, drama/theater, jazz band, literary magazine, marching band, music ensembles, musical theater, opera, pep band, radio station, student government, student newspaper, student film society, symphony orchestra, television sta-

tion, yearbook. Number of fraternities: 20; sororities: 15. Proportion of men in fraternities: 10%; of women in sororities: 17%. Average proportion of students who stay on campus on weekends: 50%. **Sports program (2005-2006):** Member of NCAA I. *Men's intercollegiate varsity sports:* baseball, basketball, cross-country, football, golf, swimming and diving, tennis, track and field (indoor), track and field (outdoor). *Women's intercollegiate varsity sports:* basketball, cross-country, golf, gymnastics, soccer, softball, swimming and diving, tennis, track and field (indoor), track and field (outdoor), volleyball.

SERVICES AND FACILITIES

Basic services: nonremedial tutoring, women's center, placement service, day care, health service, health insurance. **Counseling services:** minority student, career, military, personal, veteran student, academic, older student, psychological. **For learning-disabled students:** School does not offer a structured program with separate admission and additional fees. Total undergraduates in learning-disabled program or receiving services: 175. Services include: tape recorders, other special classes, note-taking services, oral tests, readers, extended time for tests, priority registration, texts on tape. **Library:** Number of titles: 3,233,034; number of current serial subscriptions: 58,918. **Information technology resources:** Students are not required to lease or own a computer. Number of campus computers available to all students: 5,000. School has a wireless network. Approximate number of users that can be accommodated: 12,000. Proportion of college-owned housing units wired for high-speed internet access: 95%. **Campus safety:** Security services offered: 24-hour foot and vehicle patrols, late-night transport/escort service, 24-hour emergency telephones, lighted pathways/sidewalks, controlled dormitory access (key, security card, etc).

TRANSFER AND INTERNATIONAL STUDENTS

Transfer students: May apply for admission for the following academic terms: Fall, Spring, Summer. Applicants need a minimum number of credits to apply. For fall 2005: Transfer applications received: 2,005. Transfer applicants offered admission: 1,148. Transfer applicants enrolled: 788. **International students:** Number of foreign undergraduates: 448 (2% of student body). Number of countries represented: 83. Minimum TOEFL score required: 550 (paper); 213 (computer). Average TOEFL score: 586 (paper).

Louisiana State University–Shreveport

- **Address:** 1 University Place, Shreveport, LA 71115
- **Website:** http://www.lsus.edu
- **Public**
- **Enrollment:** 2,672 full-time; 1,268 part-time

KEY STATS

✔ **U.S News College Ranking:** fourth tier, Universities–Master's (South)
✔ **ACT Score (25th/75th percentile):** 19-24
✔ **Tuition:** N/A

Selectivity: Less selective	**Room/board:** N/A
Acceptance rate: 89%	**Average debt:** N/A
Student/faculty ratio: N/A	**Proportion who borrowed:** N/A

UNDERGRADUATE STUDENT BODY STATS

2005-2006 enrollment: 2,672 full-time; 1,268 part-time. Men: 37%; women: 63%. **Ethnic makeup:** African American: 23%; American-Indian: 1%; Asian American: 2%; Hispanic: 2%; White: 72%.

ADMISSIONS FACTS AND FIGURES

Phone: (318) 797-5061. **Email:** admissions@pilot.lsus.edu. **Website:** http://www.lsus.edu. **Application deadlines for fall 2007:** Regular decision: August 1. Early decision: Not offered. Early action: Not offered. Admission cannot be deferred. **Application fee:** $10. Common application is not accepted. **Admissions requirements/recommendations:** High school units required (recommended): English: (4); Mathematics: (3); Science: (3); Social studies: (3). Tests: The college uses SAT or ACT scores in admissions decisions. Either SAT or ACT required. Campus visit: Recommended. Admissions interview: Neither required nor recommended. Off-campus interview: Not available. **Factors that count in admissions decisions:** *Academic:* Secondary school record: Considered. Class rank: Not considered. Letters of recommendation: Not considered. Standardized test scores: Considered. Essay: Not considered. *Nonacademic:* Interview: Not considered. Extracurricular activities: Not considered.

Talent/ability: Not considered. Character/personal qualities: Not considered. Alumni/ae relationship: Not considered. Geographical residence: Not considered. State residency: Not considered. Religious affiliation/commitment: Not considered. Minority status: Not considered. Volunteer work: Not considered. Work experience: Not considered. **Admissions statistics for the fall 2005 entering class:** Total applicants: 809. Total accepted: 717. Freshmen enrolled: 459; Overall acceptance rate: 89%. **Size of waiting list:** 0 applicants; enrolled from waiting list: 0.

ACADEMICS
Year founded: 1967. **Academic calendar:** Semester. **Degrees offered:** bachelor's, master's, post-master's certificate. **Most popular majors:** Information not available. **Major fields of study:** biological and biomedical sciences; business, management, marketing, and related support services; communication, journalism, and related programs; computer and information sciences and support services; education; English language and literature/letters; foreign languages, literatures, and linguistics; health professions and related clinical sciences; liberal arts and sciences studies, and humanities; mathematics and statistics; natural resources and conservation; physical sciences; psychology; security and protective services; social sciences. **Areas of required coursework:** arts/fine arts, humanities, mathematics, English (including composition), sciences (biological or physical), social science. **Pre-professional programs:** pre-law, pre-dentistry, pre-medicine, pre-pharmacy. **Special academic programs:** cooperative (work-study plan) program, study abroad, teacher certificate program. **Teacher certification offered in:** early childhood, special education, elementary, middle/junior high, secondary. **Cooperative education programs:** health professions. **Reserve Officers Training Corps (ROTC):** Army ROTC: Offered at cooperating institution (Northwestern State University). **Advanced Placement and International Baccalaureate credit:** AP tests may be used for: Credit only. Scores accepted: 2, 3. **Freshmen returning for sophomore year:** 56%. **Graduation rates:** Four-year: 4%; five-year: 10%; six-year: 18%.

COSTS AND FINANCIAL AID
Financial aid office: (318) 797-5363.

CAMPUS LIFE AND EXTRACURRICULAR ACTIVITIES
Campus housing available: apartment for single students. Average per-year earnings: $6,240. **Clubs and organizations:** Number of student organizations: 52. Activities include: jazz band, radio station, student government, student newspaper. Number of fraternities: 1; sororities: 3. Average proportion of students who stay on campus on weekends: 40%. **Sports program (2005-2006):** Member of NAIA. *Men's intercollegiate varsity sports:* baseball, basketball. *Women's intercollegiate varsity sports:* basketball.

SERVICES AND FACILITIES
Remedial assistance: reading, math, writing, study skills. **Counseling services:** career, personal, academic, psychological. **For learning-disabled students:** School does not offer a structured program with separate admission and additional fees. Services include: remedial math, remedial English. **Library:** Number of titles: 183,133; number of current serial subscriptions: 64,909. **Information technology resources:** Students are not required to lease or own a computer. Number of campus computers available to all students: 110. School has a wireless network. **Campus safety:** Security services offered: 24-hour foot and vehicle patrols, lighted pathways/sidewalks.

TRANSFER AND INTERNATIONAL STUDENTS
Transfer students: May apply for admission for the following academic terms: Fall, Spring, Summer. Applicants need a minimum number of credits to apply. For fall 2005: Transfer applications received: 669. Transfer applicants offered admission: 463. Transfer applicants enrolled: 435. **International students:** Number of foreign undergraduates: 1. Minimum TOEFL score required: 500 (paper).

Louisiana Tech University

- **Address:** 700 West California Avenue, Ruston, LA 71272
- **Website:** http://www.latech.edu
- **Public**
- **Enrollment:** 7,618 full-time; 1,658 part-time

KEY STATS
✔ **U.S News College Ranking:** fourth tier, National Universities
✔ **ACT Score (25th/75th percentile):** 19-26
✔ **Tuition:** 2006-2007: $3,921 in state, $9,362 out of state
   Selectivity: Selective   **Room/board:** $4,155
   Acceptance rate: 83%   **Average debt:** $17,234
   Student/faculty ratio: 23/1   **Proportion who borrowed:** 82%

UNDERGRADUATE STUDENT BODY STATS
2005-2006 enrollment: 7,618 full-time; 1,658 part-time. Men: 52%; women: 48%. **Ethnic makeup:** African American: 15%; American-Indian: 1%; Asian American: 1%; Hispanic: 1%; White: 79%; International: 3%.

ADMISSIONS FACTS AND FIGURES
Phone: (318) 257-3036. **Email:** bulldog@latech.edu. **Website:** http://www.latech.edu. **Application deadlines for fall 2007:** Regular decision: July 31. Early decision: Not offered. Early action: Not offered. Admission cannot be deferred. **Application fee:** $20. Common application is not accepted. **To apply online, go to:** https://secure.latech.edu/admissions/application.php. **Admissions requirements/recommendations:** High school units required (recommended): English: 4; Mathematics: 3; Science: 3; Foreign language: 2; Social studies: 3; Total units: 17. Tests: The college uses SAT or ACT scores in admissions decisions. Either SAT or ACT required. For admission to the fall 2007 entering class, the school will accept: ACT with writing, ACT without writing. Campus visit: Neither required nor recommended. Admissions interview: Neither required nor recommended. Off-campus interview: Not available. **Factors that count in admissions decisions:** *Academic:* Secondary school record: Very important. Class rank: Very important. Letters of recommendation: Considered. Standardized test scores: Very important. Essay: Not considered. *Nonacademic:* Interview: Not considered. Extracurricular activities: Considered. Talent/ability: Important. Character/personal qualities: Not considered. Alumni/ae relationship: Considered. Geographical residence: Not considered. State residency: Not considered. Religious affiliation/commitment: Not considered. Minority status: Not considered. Volunteer work: Not considered. Work experience: Not considered. **Other schools with the greatest overlap in applicants:** Louisiana State University–Baton Rouge; Northwestern State University of Louisiana; Southeastern Louisiana University; University of Louisiana–Monroe; University of New Orleans. **Admissions statistics for the fall 2005 entering class:** Total applicants: 3,519. Total accepted: 2,932. Freshmen enrolled: 1,797; 12% were from out of state. Overall acceptance rate: 83%. **Credentials of fall 2005 freshmen:** 21% ranked in the top 10 percent of their high school class; 46% were in the top 25 percent, and 77% were in the top half. (Proportion submitting class standing: 83%.) **Average high school grade point average:** 3.3. **First-year students submitting ACT scores:** 91%. Scores (25/75 percentile): English: N/A, Math: N/A, Composite: 19-26.

ACADEMICS
Year founded: 1894. **Academic calendar:** Quarter. **Degrees offered:** associate, bachelor's, post-bachelor's certificate, master's, doctorate. **Most popular majors:** 22% business, management, marketing, and related support services, 12% engineering, 6% education, 5% biological and biomedical sciences, 5% social sciences. **Major fields of study:** agriculture, agriculture operations, and related sciences; architecture and related services; biological and biomedical sciences; business, management, marketing, and related support services; communication, journalism, and related programs; computer and information sciences and support services; education; engineering; engineering technologies/technicians; English language and literature/letters; family and consumer sciences/human sciences; foreign languages, literatures, and linguistics; health professions and related clinical sciences; history; liberal arts and sciences studies, and humanities; mathematics and statistics; natural resources and conservation; parks, recreation, leisure, and fitness studies; physical sciences; psychology; social sciences; transportation and materials moving; visual and performing arts. **Areas of required coursework:** arts/fine arts, humanities, computer literacy, mathematics, English (including composition), sciences (biological or physical),

social science. **Special academic programs:** distance learning, double major, dual enrollment, honors program, independent study, internships, study abroad, teacher certificate program. **Teacher certification offered in:** early childhood, special education, elementary, middle/junior high, secondary. **Cooperative education programs:** agriculture, engineering, natural science, other. **Reserve Officers Training Corps (ROTC):** Army ROTC: Offered at cooperating institution (Grambling State University); Air Force ROTC: Offered on campus. **Faculty and instruction (2005-2006):** Total instructional faculty: 378 full-time, 100 part-time (61% men; 39% women; 5% minorities). Full-time faculty with Ph.D. or other terminal degree: 82%. Student/faculty ratio: 23/1. Classes of fewer than 20 students: 44%; of 20 to 49 students: 46%; of 50 or more students: 10%. **Freshmen returning for sophomore year:** 72%. **Graduation rates:** Four-year: 28%; five-year: 45%; six-year: 49%.

COSTS AND FINANCIAL AID

Financial aid office: (318) 257-2643. **Expenses (2006-2007):** Tuition and fees 2006-2007: $3,921 in state, $9,362 out of state; room/board: $4,155. Estimated books and supplies: $1,200; transportation: $1,347; personal expenses: $1,500. **Financial aid:** Priority filing date for institution's financial aid form: April 15. In 2005-2006, 70% of undergraduates applied for financial aid. Of those, 45% were determined to have financial need; 16% had their need fully met. Average financial aid package (proportion receiving): $6,406 (42%). Average amount of gift aid, such as scholarships or grants (proportion receiving): $4,641 (37%). Average amount of self-help aid, such as work study or loans (proportion receiving): $3,296 (30%). Average need-based loan (excluding PLUS or other private loans): $3,037. Among students who received need-based aid, the average percentage of need met: 60%. Among students who received aid based on merit, the average award (and the proportion receiving): $2,165 (14%). The average athletic scholarship (and the proportion receiving): $6,563 (0%). Average amount of debt of borrowers graduating in 2005: $17,234. Proportion who borrowed: 82%.

CAMPUS LIFE AND EXTRACURRICULAR ACTIVITIES

Campus housing available (% using): women's dorms (42%), men's dorms (48%), fraternity housing (1%), apartments for married students (1%), apartment for single students (7%), special housing for disabled students (1%). Students who live in college-owned, operated, or affiliated housing: 32%. **Student employment:** During the 2005-2006 academic year, 12% of undergraduates worked on campus. Average per-year earnings: $2,500. **Clubs and organizations:** Number of student organizations: 157. Activities include: choral groups, concert band, dance, drama/theater, jazz band, marching band, music ensembles, musical theater, pep band, radio station, student government, student newspaper, yearbook. Number of fraternities: 8; sororities: 4. Proportion of men in fraternities: 7%; of women in sororities: 9%. **Sports program (2005-2006):** Member of NCAA I. *Men's intercollegiate varsity sports:* baseball, basketball, cross-country, football, golf, track and field (indoor), track and field (outdoor). *Women's intercollegiate varsity sports:* basketball, bowling, cross-country, curling, soccer, softball, tennis, track and field (indoor), track and field (outdoor), volleyball.

SERVICES AND FACILITIES

Basic services: women's center, health service, health insurance, other. **Counseling services:** minority student, career, military, personal, veteran student, academic, psychological. **Library:** Number of titles: 2,945,155; number of current serial subscriptions: 2,803. **Information technology resources:** Students are not required to lease or own a computer. Number of campus computers available to all students: 145. School has a wireless network. Approximate number of users that can be accommodated: 3,000. Proportion of college-owned housing units wired for high-speed internet access: 100%. **Campus safety:** Security services offered: 24-hour foot and vehicle patrols, late-night transport/escort service, 24-hour emergency telephones, lighted pathways/sidewalks, student patrols, controlled dormitory access (key, security card, etc).

TRANSFER AND INTERNATIONAL STUDENTS

Transfer students: May apply for admission for the following academic terms: Fall, Winter, Spring, Summer. Applicants need a minimum number of credits to apply. For fall 2005: Transfer applicants enrolled: 520. **International students:** Number of foreign undergraduates: 190 (3% of student body). Number of countries represented: 61. Minimum TOEFL score required: 500 (paper); 173 (computer).

Loyola University New Orleans

- **Address:** 6363 St. Charles Avenue, New Orleans, LA 70118-6195
- **Website:** http://www.loyno.edu
- **Private; Religious affiliation:** Roman Catholic (Jesuit)
- **Enrollment:** N/A

KEY STATS

✔ **U.S News College Ranking:** 7, Universities–Master's (South)
✔ **ACT Score (25th/75th percentile):** 24-29
✔ **Tuition:** 2005-2006: $23,200

Selectivity: More selective	**Room/board:** $8,262
Acceptance rate: 68%	**Average debt:** N/A
Student/faculty ratio: N/A	**Proportion who borrowed:** N/A

McNeese State University

- **Address:** 4100 Ryan Street, Lake Charles, LA 70609
- **Website:** http://www.mcneese.edu
- **Public**
- **Enrollment:** 6,507 full-time; 1,340 part-time

KEY STATS

✔ **U.S News College Ranking:** fourth tier, Universities–Master's (South)
✔ **ACT Score:** 21
✔ **Tuition:** 2005-2006: $3,159 in state, $9,225 out of state

Selectivity: Selective	**Room/board:** $4,637
Acceptance rate: 82%	**Average debt:** N/A
Student/faculty ratio: N/A	**Proportion who borrowed:** N/A

UNDERGRADUATE STUDENT BODY STATS

2005-2006 enrollment: 6,507 full-time; 1,340 part-time. Men: 40%; women: 60%. **Ethnic makeup:** African American: 19%; American-Indian: 1%; Asian American: 1%; Hispanic: 1%; White: 76%; International: 2%.

ADMISSIONS FACTS AND FIGURES

Phone: (337) 475-5356. **Email:** info@mcneese.edu. **Website:** http://www.mcneese.edu. **Application deadlines for fall 2007:** Regular decision: Rolling. Early decision: Not offered. Early action: Not offered. Admission can be deferred. **Application fee:** $20. Common application is not accepted. **Admissions requirements/recommendations:** High school units required (recommended): English: (4); Mathematics: (3); Science: (3); Foreign language: (2); Social studies: (1); History: (2); Academic electives: (0); Total units: (17). Tests: The college uses SAT or ACT scores in admissions decisions. Either SAT or ACT required. Campus visit: Recommended. Admissions interview: Neither required nor recommended. Off-campus interview: May be arranged. **Factors that count in admissions decisions:** *Academic:* Secondary school record: Very important. Class rank: Not considered. Letters of recommendation: Considered. Standardized test scores: Very important. Essay: Not considered. *Nonacademic:* Interview: Not considered. Extracurricular activities: Considered. Talent/ability: Considered. Character/personal qualities: Considered. Alumni/ae relationship: Not considered. Geographical residence: Not considered. State residency: Not considered. Religious affiliation/commitment: Not considered. Minority status: Considered. Volunteer work: Not considered. Work experience: Not considered. **Admissions statistics for the fall 2005 entering class:** Total applicants: 1,985. Total accepted: 1,629. Freshmen enrolled: 1,405; 8% were from out of state. Overall acceptance rate: 82%. **Credentials of fall 2005 freshmen:** 14% ranked in the top 10 percent of their high school class; 37% were in the top 25 percent, and 68% were in the top half. (Proportion submitting class standing: 93%.) **Average high school grade point average:** 3.1. **First-year students submitting ACT scores:** 93%. Scores (25/75 percentile): English: N/A, Math: N/A, Composite: N/A.

ACADEMICS

Year founded: 1939. **Academic calendar:** Semester. **Degrees offered:** associate, transfer-associate, terminal-associate, bachelor's, post-bachelor's certificate, master's, post-master's certificate. **Most popular majors:** 17% general studies, 9% business administration and management, 7% nursing/registered nurse training (R.N., A.S.N., B.S.N., M.S.N.), 5% engineering, 4% accounting. **Major fields of study:** agriculture, agriculture operations, and related sciences; biological and biomedical sciences; business, management, marketing, and related support services; communication, journalism, and related programs; computer and information sciences and support services; education; engineering; engineering technologies/technicians; English language and literature/letters; family and consumer sciences/human sciences; foreign languages, literatures, and linguistics; health professions and related clinical sciences; history; liberal arts and sciences studies, and humanities; natural resources and conservation; physical sciences; psychology; security and protective services; social sciences; visual and performing arts. **Areas of required coursework:** arts/fine arts, humanities, computer literacy, mathematics, English (including composition), sciences (biological or physical), social science. **Pre-professional programs:** pre-law, pre-dentistry, pre-medicine. **Special academic programs:** accelerated program, cooperative (work-study plan) program, distance learning, double major, dual enrollment, English as a Second Language (ESL), honors program, independent study, internships, teacher certificate program. **Teacher certification offered in:** early childhood, special education, elementary, secondary. **Cooperative education programs:** engineering, technologies. **Faculty and instruction (2005-2006):** Total instructional faculty: 305 full-time, 104 part-time (53% men; 47% women; 13% minorities). Full-time faculty with Ph.D. or other terminal degree: 67%. **Advanced Placement and International Baccalaureate credit:** AP tests may be used for: Credit and/or placement. Scores accepted: 2, 3, 4, 5. **Freshmen returning for sophomore year:** 67%. **Graduation rates:** Four-year: 11%; five-year: 26%; six-year: 29%.

COSTS AND FINANCIAL AID
Financial aid office: (337) 475-5065. **Expenses (2005-2006):** Tuition and fees 2005-2006: $3,159 in state, $9,225 out of state; room/board: $4,637. **Financial aid:** Priority filing date for institution's financial aid form: May 1.

CAMPUS LIFE AND EXTRACURRICULAR ACTIVITIES
Campus housing available: coed dorms, fraternity housing, apartments for married students, apartment for single students, other housing options. **Clubs and organizations:** Number of student organizations: 93. Activities include: choral groups, concert band, dance, drama/theater, jazz band, literary magazine, marching band, music ensembles, musical theater, opera, student government, student newspaper, symphony orchestra, yearbook. Number of fraternities: 7; sororities: 6. **Sports program (2005-2006):** Member of NCAA I. *Men's intercollegiate varsity sports:* baseball, basketball, cross-country, football, golf, track and field (indoor), track and field (outdoor). *Women's intercollegiate varsity sports:* basketball, cross-country, golf, soccer, softball, tennis, track and field (indoor), track and field (outdoor), volleyball.

SERVICES AND FACILITIES
Basic services: nonremedial tutoring, women's center, placement service, health service, health insurance. **Remedial assistance:** reading, math, writing, study skills. **Counseling services:** minority student, career, military, personal, veteran student, academic, older student, psychological, birth control, religious. **For learning-disabled students:** Services include: remedial math, remedial English, reading machines, remedial reading, other special classes, note-taking services, oral tests, learning center, readers, extended time for tests, tutors, other. **Information technology resources:** Students are not required to lease or own a computer. Number of campus computers available to all students: 700. School does not have a wireless network. **Campus safety:** Security services offered: 24-hour foot and vehicle patrols, late-night transport/escort service, 24-hour emergency telephones, lighted pathways/sidewalks, controlled dormitory access (key, security card, etc).

TRANSFER AND INTERNATIONAL STUDENTS
Transfer students: May apply for admission for the following academic terms: Fall, Spring, Summer. Applicants need a minimum number of credits to apply. For fall 2005: Transfer applicants enrolled: 338. **International students:** Number of foreign undergraduates: 142 (2% of student body). Minimum TOEFL score required: 500 (paper); 173 (computer).

Nicholls State University

■ **Address:** PO Box 2004, University Station, Thibodaux, LA 70310
■ **Website:** http://www.nicholls.edu
■ **Public**
■ **Enrollment:** 5,501 full-time; 1,385 part-time

KEY STATS
✔ **U.S News College Ranking:** fourth tier, Universities–Master's (South)
✔ **ACT Score (25th/75th percentile):** 18-22
✔ **Tuition:** 2005-2006: $3,390 in state, $8,838 out of state
Selectivity: Selective   **Room/board:** N/A
Acceptance rate: 67%   **Average debt:** $12,738
Student/faculty ratio: 22/1   **Proportion who borrowed:** 48%

UNDERGRADUATE STUDENT BODY STATS
2005-2006 enrollment: 5,501 full-time; 1,385 part-time. Men: 37%; women: 63%. **Ethnic makeup:** African American: 20%; American-Indian: 2%; Asian American: 1%; Hispanic: 1%; White: 74%; International: 1%. **Religious preference:** Roman Catholic: 23%; Protestant: 10%; Unknown: 65%; Other: 2%.

ADMISSIONS FACTS AND FIGURES
Phone: (985) 448-4507. **Email:** nicholls@nicholls.edu. **Website:** http://www.nicholls.edu. **Application deadlines for fall 2007:** Regular decision: Rolling. Early decision: Not offered. Early action: Not offered. Admission can be deferred. **Application fee:** $20. Common application is not accepted. **Admissions requirements/recommendations:** High school units required (recommended): English: 4 (4); Mathematics: 3 (3); Science: 3 (3); Foreign language: 2 (2); Social studies: 1 (1); History: 2 (2); Academic electives: (7); Total units: 17 (23). Tests: The college uses SAT or ACT scores in admissions decisions. Either SAT or ACT required. For admission to the fall 2007 entering class, the school will accept: ACT with writing, ACT without writing. Campus visit: Required. Admissions interview: Neither required nor recommended. **Factors that count in admissions decisions:** *Academic:* Secondary school record: Considered. Class rank: Considered. Letters of recommendation: Not considered. Standardized test scores: Very important. Essay: Not considered. *Nonacademic:* Interview: Not considered. Extracurricular activities: Not considered. Talent/ability: Not considered. Character/personal qualities: Not considered. Alumni/ae relationship: Not considered. Geographical residence: Not considered. State residency: Not considered. Religious affiliation/commitment: Not considered. Minority status: Not considered. Volunteer work: Not considered. Work experience: Not considered. **Admissions statistics for the fall 2005 entering class:** Total applicants: 2,339. Total accepted: 1,566. Freshmen enrolled: 1,301; 4% were from out of state. Overall acceptance rate: 67%. **Size of waiting list:** 2339 applicants; enrolled from waiting list: 1566. **Credentials of fall 2005 freshmen:** 17% ranked in the top 10 percent of their high school class; 41% were in the top 25 percent, and 72% were in the top half. (Proportion submitting class standing: 92%.) **Average high school grade point average:** 3.1. **First-year students submitting ACT scores:** 98%. Scores (25/75 percentile): English: 18-24, Math: 17-23, Composite: 18-22.

ACADEMICS
Year founded: 1948. **Academic calendar:** Semester. **Degrees offered:** associate, transfer-associate, terminal-associate, bachelor's, master's, post-master's certificate. **Most popular majors:** 21% health professions and related clinical sciences, 20% business, management, marketing, and related support services, 16% education, 7% liberal arts and sciences studies, and humanities, 5% family and consumer sciences/human sciences. **Major fields of study:** agriculture, agriculture operations, and related sciences; biological and biomedical sciences; business, management, marketing, and related support services; communication, journalism, and related programs; computer and information sciences and support services; education; engineering technologies/technicians; English language and literature/letters; family and consumer sciences/human sciences; foreign languages, literatures, and linguistics; health professions and related clinical sciences; history; liberal arts and sciences studies, and humanities; mathematics and statistics; personal and culinary services; physical sciences; psychology; social sciences; visual and performing arts. **Areas of required coursework:** arts/fine arts, humanities, computer literacy, mathematics, English (including composition), sciences (biological or physical), social science. **Pre-professional programs:** pre-law, pre-dentistry, pre-medicine, pre-veterinary science, pre-pharmacy. **Special academic programs:** cross-registration, distance learn-

ing, dual enrollment, honors program, independent study, internships, study abroad, teacher certificate program. **Teacher certification offered in:** early childhood, elementary, middle/junior high, secondary. **Faculty and instruction (2005-2006):** Total instructional faculty: 289 full-time, 1 part-time (49% men; 51% women; 11% minorities). Full-time faculty with Ph.D. or other terminal degree: 55%. Student/faculty ratio: 22/1. Classes of fewer than 20 students: 39%; of 20 to 49 students: 48%; of 50 or more students: 13%. **Freshmen returning for sophomore year:** 63%. **Graduation rates:** Four-year: 10%; five-year: 19%; six-year: 27%.

COSTS AND FINANCIAL AID

Financial aid office: (985) 448-4048. **Expenses (2005-2006):** Tuition and fees 2005-2006: $3,390 in state, $8,838 out of state; room/board: N/A. Estimated books and supplies: $1,000; transportation: $907; personal expenses: $1,574. **Financial aid:** Priority filing date for institution's financial aid form: April 8; deadline: April 19. In 2005-2006, 81% of undergraduates applied for financial aid. Of those, 54% were determined to have financial need; 63% had their need fully met. Average financial aid package (proportion receiving): $5,506 (53%). Average amount of gift aid, such as scholarships or grants (proportion receiving): $3,107 (44%). Average amount of self-help aid, such as work study or loans (proportion receiving): $312 (41%). Average need-based loan (excluding PLUS or other private loans): $2,973. Among students who received need-based aid, the average percentage of need met: 87%. Among students who received aid based on merit, the average award (and the proportion receiving): $2,811 (2%). The average athletic scholarship (and the proportion receiving): $3,896 (2%). Average amount of debt of borrowers graduating in 2005: $12,738. Proportion who borrowed: 48%.

CAMPUS LIFE AND EXTRACURRICULAR ACTIVITIES

Campus housing available: coed dorms, women's dorms, men's dorms, apartments for married students, special housing for disabled students, special housing for international students, other housing options. Students who live in college-owned, operated, or affiliated housing: 15%. **Student employment:** During the 2005-2006 academic year, 9% of undergraduates worked on campus. Average per-year earnings: $2,000. **Clubs and organizations:** Number of student organizations: 76. Activities include: choral groups, concert band, dance, drama/theater, jazz band, literary magazine, marching band, music ensembles, musical theater, pep band, radio station, student government, student newspaper, student film society, television station, yearbook. Number of fraternities: 9; sororities: 7. Proportion of men in fraternities: 5%; of women in sororities: 4%. Average proportion of students who stay on campus on weekends: 20%. **Sports program (2005-2006):** Member of NCAA I. *Men's intercollegiate varsity sports:* baseball, basketball, cross-country, football, golf, tennis. *Women's intercollegiate varsity sports:* basketball, cross-country, golf, soccer, softball, tennis, track and field (indoor), track and field (outdoor), volleyball.

SERVICES AND FACILITIES

Basic services: nonremedial tutoring, women's center, placement service, health service, health insurance. **Remedial assistance:** math, writing. **Counseling services:** minority student, career, military, personal, veteran student, academic, older student, psychological, birth control. **For learning-disabled students:** School does not offer a structured program with separate admission and additional fees. Services include: remedial math, remedial English, tape recorders, untimed tests, note-taking services, oral tests, learning center, extended time for tests, tutors, other. **Library:** Number of titles: 438,495; number of current serial subscriptions: 1,999. **Information technology resources:** Students are not required to lease or own a computer. Number of campus computers available to all students: 1,000. School has a wireless network. Approximate number of users that can be accommodated: 7,250. Proportion of college-owned housing units wired for high-speed internet access: 50%. **Campus safety:** Security services offered: 24-hour foot and vehicle patrols, late-night transport/escort service, 24-hour emergency telephones, lighted pathways/sidewalks, student patrols, controlled dormitory access (key, security card, etc).

TRANSFER AND INTERNATIONAL STUDENTS

Transfer students: May apply for admission for the following academic terms: Fall, Spring, Summer. Applicants need a minimum number of credits to apply. For fall 2005: Transfer applicants enrolled: 237. **International students:** Number of foreign undergraduates: 74 (1% of student body). Number of countries represented: 25. Minimum TOEFL score required: 500 (paper); 173 (computer).

Northwestern State University of Louisiana

■ **Address:** College Avenue, Natchitoches, LA 71497
■ **Website:** http://www.nsula.edu
■ **Public**
■ **Enrollment:** 6,460 full-time; 2,328 part-time

KEY STATS
✔ **U.S News College Ranking:** fourth tier, Universities–Master's (South)
✔ **ACT Score (25th/75th percentile):** 17-22
✔ **Tuition:** 2005-2006: $3,393 in state, $9,471 out of state
  Selectivity: Selective   **Room/board:** $3,626
  Acceptance rate: 77%   **Average debt:** $17,442
  Student/faculty ratio: 18/1 **Proportion who borrowed:** 68%

UNDERGRADUATE STUDENT BODY STATS
2005-2006 enrollment: 6,460 full-time; 2,328 part-time. Men: 33%; women: 67%. **Ethnic makeup:** African American: 31%; American-Indian: 2%; Asian American: 1%; Hispanic: 2%; White: 63%.

ADMISSIONS FACTS AND FIGURES
Phone: (800) 426-3754. **Email:** admissions@nsula.edu. **Website:** http://www.nsula.edu. **Application deadlines for fall 2007:** Regular decision: July 6. Early decision: Not offered. Early action: Not offered. Admission can be deferred. **Application fee:** $20. Common application is accepted. **Admissions requirements/recommendations:** High school units required (recommended): English: 4; Mathematics: 3; Science: 3; Foreign language: 2; Social studies: 1; History: 2; Academic electives: 1; Total units: 17. Tests: The college uses SAT or ACT scores in admissions decisions. Either SAT or ACT required. For admission to the fall 2007 entering class, the school will accept: ACT with writing, ACT without writing. Campus visit: Recommended. Admissions interview: Recommended. Off-campus interview: May be arranged. **Factors that count in admissions decisions:** *Academic:* Secondary school record: Very important. Class rank: Important. Letters of recommendation: Not considered. Standardized test scores: Very important. Essay: Not considered. *Nonacademic:* Interview: Not considered. Extracurricular activities: Considered. Talent/ability: Considered. Character/personal qualities: Not considered. Alumni/ae relationship: Considered. Geographical residence: Considered. State residency: Considered. Religious affiliation/commitment: Not considered. Minority status: Important. Volunteer work: Not considered. Work experience: Not considered. **Other schools with the greatest overlap in applicants:** Louisiana State University–Baton Rouge; Louisiana Tech University; McNeese State University; Southeastern Louisiana University; University of Louisiana–Lafayette. **Admissions statistics for the fall 2005 entering class:** Total applicants: 2,852. Total accepted: 2,206. Freshmen enrolled: 1,539; 11% were from out of state. Overall acceptance rate: 77%. **Credentials of fall 2005 freshmen:** 14% ranked in the top 10 percent of their high school class; 35% were in the top 25 percent, and 66% were in the top half. (Proportion submitting class standing: 93%.) **Average high school grade point average:** 3.1. **First-year students who submitted SAT scores:** 9%. Scores (25/75 percentile): Verbal: 445-570, Math: 450-570, Combined: 895-1140. **First-year students submitting ACT scores:** 89%. Scores (25/75 percentile): English: 17-24, Math: 16-21, Composite: 17-22.

ACADEMICS
Year founded: 1884. **Academic calendar:** Semester. **Degrees offered:** associate, bachelor's, master's, post-master's certificate. **Most popular majors:** 16% health professions and related clinical sciences, 15% liberal arts and sciences studies, and humanities, 14% business, management, marketing, and related support services, 10% education, 9% psychology. **Major fields of study:** biological and biomedical sciences; business, management, marketing, and related support services; communication, journalism, and related programs; computer and information sciences and support services; education; engineering technologies/technicians; English language and literature/letters; family and consumer sciences/human sciences; health professions and related clinical sciences; history; liberal arts and sciences studies, and humanities; mathematics and statistics; multi/interdisciplinary studies; physical sciences; psychology; public administration and social service professions; security and protective services; social sciences; visual and performing arts. **Areas of required coursework:** arts/fine arts, humanities, computer literacy, mathematics, English (including composition), sciences (biological or physical), history, social science, other. **Pre-professional pro-**

grams: pre-dentistry, pre-medicine, pre-veterinary science, pre-optometry, pre-pharmacy. **Special academic programs:** cooperative (work-study plan) program, distance learning, double major, dual enrollment, honors program, independent study, internships, liberal arts/career combination, study abroad, teacher certificate program. **Teacher certification offered in:** early childhood, special education, elementary, middle/junior high, adult education, secondary. **Cooperative education programs:** other. **Reserve Officers Training Corps (ROTC):** Army ROTC: Offered on campus. **Faculty and instruction (2005-2006):** Total instructional faculty: 309 full-time, 237 part-time. Full-time faculty with Ph.D. or other terminal degree: 57%. Student/faculty ratio: 18/1. Classes of fewer than 20 students: 38%; of 20 to 49 students: 50%; of 50 or more students: 11%. **Advanced Placement and International Baccalaureate credit:** AP tests may be used for: Credit and/or placement. Scores accepted: 3, 4, 5. **Freshmen returning for sophomore year:** 69%. **Graduation rates:** Four-year: 14%; five-year: 27%; six-year: 29%.

COSTS AND FINANCIAL AID

Financial aid office: (318) 357-5961. **Expenses (2005-2006):** Tuition and fees 2005-2006: $3,393 in state, $9,471 out of state; room/board: $3,626. Estimated books and supplies: $1,000; transportation: $907; personal expenses: $1,574. **Financial aid:** Priority filing date for institution's financial aid form: May 1. In 2005-2006, 80% of undergraduates applied for financial aid. Of those, 56% were determined to have financial need; 1% had their need fully met. Average financial aid package (proportion receiving): $5,208 (56%). Average amount of gift aid, such as scholarships or grants (proportion receiving): N/A (45%). Average amount of self-help aid, such as work study or loans (proportion receiving): $3,261 (46%). Average need-based loan (excluding PLUS or other private loans): $4,913. Among students who received need-based aid, the average percentage of need met: 48%. Among students who received aid based on merit, the average award (and the proportion receiving): $3,711 (23%). The average athletic scholarship (and the proportion receiving): $6,895 (2%). Average amount of debt of borrowers graduating in 2005: $17,442. Proportion who borrowed: 68%.

CAMPUS LIFE AND EXTRACURRICULAR ACTIVITIES

Campus housing available (% using): coed dorms (66%), sorority housing, fraternity housing, apartments for married students (2%), apartment for single students (32%), special housing for disabled students, other housing options. Students who live in college-owned, operated, or affiliated housing: 20%. **Student employment:** During the 2005-2006 academic year, 11% of undergraduates worked on campus. Average per-year earnings: $1,207. **Clubs and organizations:** Number of student organizations: 78. Activities include: choral groups, concert band, dance, drama/theater, jazz band, literary magazine, marching band, music ensembles, musical theater, opera, pep band, radio station, student government, student newspaper, symphony orchestra, television station, yearbook. Number of fraternities: 10; sororities: 8. Proportion of men in fraternities: 9%; of women in sororities: 5%. **Sports program (2005-2006):** Member of NCAA I. *Men's intercollegiate varsity sports:* baseball, basketball, cross-country, football, track and field (indoor), track and field (outdoor). *Women's intercollegiate varsity sports:* basketball, cross-country, soccer, softball, tennis, track and field (indoor), track and field (outdoor), volleyball.

SERVICES AND FACILITIES

Basic services: nonremedial tutoring, placement service, health service, health insurance. **Remedial assistance:** reading, math, writing, study skills. **Counseling services:** minority student, career, personal, veteran student, academic, older student, psychological. **For learning-disabled students:** School does not offer a structured program with separate admission and additional fees. Total undergraduates in learning-disabled program or receiving services: 180. Services include: remedial math, remedial English, reading machines, tape recorders, other special classes, untimed tests, note-taking services, oral tests, learning center, readers, extended time for tests, tutors, priority registration, priority seating, substitution of courses, exams on tape or computer. **Library:** Number of titles: 765,833; number of current serial subscriptions: 1,446. **Information technology resources:** Students are not required to lease or own a computer. School has a wireless network. **Campus safety:** Security services offered: 24-hour foot and vehicle patrols, late-night transport/escort service, 24-hour emergency telephones, lighted pathways/sidewalks, student patrols, controlled dormitory access (key, security card, etc).

TRANSFER AND INTERNATIONAL STUDENTS

Transfer students: May apply for admission for the following academic terms: Fall, Spring, Summer. Applicants need a minimum number of credits to apply. For fall 2005: Transfer applications received: 882. Transfer applicants offered admission: 688. Transfer applicants enrolled: 458. **International students:** Number of foreign undergraduates: 33. Number of countries represented: 22. Minimum TOEFL score required: 500 (paper); 173 (computer).

Our Lady of Holy Cross College

- **Address:** 4123 Woodland Drive, New Orleans, LA 70131
- **Website:** http://www.olhcc.edu
- **Private; Religious affiliation:** Roman Catholic
- **Enrollment:** N/A

KEY STATS

✔ **U.S News College Ranking:** third tier, Comp. Coll.–Bachelor's (South)
✔ **ACT Score:** 20
✔ **Tuition:** 2006-2007: $7,008
  Selectivity: Less selective   **Room/board:** N/A
  Acceptance rate: N/A   **Average debt:** N/A
  Student/faculty ratio: N/A   **Proportion who borrowed:** 88%

Southeastern Louisiana University

- **Address:** SLU 10752, Hammond, LA 70402
- **Website:** http://www.selu.edu
- **Public**
- **Enrollment:** 11,644 full-time; 2,719 part-time

KEY STATS

✔ **U.S News College Ranking:** fourth tier, Universities–Master's (South)
✔ **ACT Score (25th/75th percentile):** 19-23
✔ **Tuition:** 2005-2006: $3,341 in state, $8,669 out of state
  Selectivity: Selective   **Room/board:** $5,180
  Acceptance rate: 95%   **Average debt:** $15,793
  Student/faculty ratio: 27/1   **Proportion who borrowed:** 61%

UNDERGRADUATE STUDENT BODY STATS

2005-2006 enrollment: 11,644 full-time; 2,719 part-time. Men: 38%; women: 62%. **Ethnic makeup:** African American: 18%; Asian American: 1%; Hispanic: 2%; White: 78%; International: 1%.

ADMISSIONS FACTS AND FIGURES

Phone: (985) 549-2066. **Email:** admissions@selu.edu. **Website:** http://www.selu.edu. **Application deadlines for fall 2007:** Regular decision: August 15. Early decision: Not offered. Early action: Not offered. Admission can be deferred. **Application fee:** $20. Common application is not accepted. **To apply online, go to:** http://www2.selu.edu/ProspectiveStudents.html. **Admissions requirements/recommendations:** High school units required (recommended): English: 4; Mathematics: 3; Science: 3; Foreign language: 2; Social studies: 3; Total units: 17. Tests: The college uses SAT or ACT scores in admissions decisions. Either SAT or ACT required. For admission to the fall 2007 entering class, the school will accept: ACT with writing, ACT without writing. Campus visit: Recommended. Admissions interview: Neither required nor recommended. Off-campus interview: Not available. **Factors that count in admissions decisions:** *Academic:* Secondary school record: Very important. Class rank: Considered. Letters of recommendation: Not considered. Standardized test scores: Very important. Essay: Not considered. *Nonacademic:* Interview: Not considered. Extracurricular activities: Not considered. Talent/ability: Not considered. Character/personal qualities: Not considered. Alumni/ae relationship: Not considered. Geographical residence: Not considered. State residency: Not considered. Religious affiliation/commitment: Not considered. Minority status: Not considered. Volunteer work: Not considered. Work experience: Not considered. **Admissions statistics for the fall 2005 entering class:** Total applicants: 3,286. Total accepted: 3,111. Freshmen enrolled: 2,578; 1% were from out of state. Overall acceptance rate: 95%. **Credentials of fall 2005 freshmen:** 9% ranked in the top 10 percent of their high school class; 28% were in the top 25 percent, and 61% were in the top half. (Proportion submitting class standing: 93%.) **Average high school grade point average:** 3.0. **First-year students sub-**

mitting ACT scores: 100%. Scores (25/75 percentile): English: 19-24, Math: 18-22, Composite: 19-23.

ACADEMICS
Year founded: 1925. **Academic calendar:** Semester. **Degrees offered:** associate, bachelor's, master's. **Most popular majors:** 20% business administration and management, 9% general studies, 8% nursing/registered nurse training (R.N., A.S.N., B.S.N., M.S.N.), 6% accounting, 6% marketing/marketing management. **Major fields of study:** agriculture, agriculture operations, and related sciences; biological and biomedical sciences; business, management, marketing, and related support services; communication, journalism, and related programs; computer and information sciences and support services; education; engineering technologies/technicians; English language and literature/letters; family and consumer sciences/human sciences; foreign languages, literatures, and linguistics; health professions and related clinical sciences; history; liberal arts and sciences studies, and humanities; mathematics and statistics; physical sciences; psychology; public administration and social service professions; security and protective services; social sciences; visual and performing arts. **Areas of required coursework:** arts/fine-arts, humanities, computer literacy, mathematics, English (including composition), sciences (biological or physical), history, social science. **Pre-professional programs:** pre-law, pre-dentistry, pre-medicine, pre-veterinary science, pre-optometry, pre-pharmacy, other. **Special academic programs:** cross-registration, distance learning, double major, dual enrollment, honors program, independent study, internships, liberal arts/career combination, study abroad, teacher certificate program. **Teacher certification offered in:** early childhood, special education, elementary, middle/junior high, secondary. **Cooperative education programs:** art, business, computer science, education, health professions, home economics, humanities, natural science, social/behavioral science, technologies, vocational arts. **Reserve Officers Training Corps (ROTC):** Army ROTC: Offered at cooperating institution (Louisiana State University). **Faculty and instruction (2005-2006):** Total instructional faculty: 496 full-time, 197 part-time (45% men; 55% women; 10% minorities). Full-time faculty with Ph.D. or other terminal degree: 61%. Student/faculty ratio: 27/1. Classes of fewer than 20 students: 31%; of 20 to 49 students: 60%; of 50 or more students: 9%. **Advanced Placement and International Baccalaureate credit:** AP tests may be used for: Credit only. Scores accepted: 3. **Freshmen returning for sophomore year:** 68%. **Graduation rates:** Four-year: 8%; five-year: 21%; six-year: 24%.

COSTS AND FINANCIAL AID
Financial aid office: (985) 549-2244. **Expenses (2005-2006):** Tuition and fees 2005-2006: $3,341 in state, $8,669 out of state; room/board: $5,180. Estimated books and supplies: $1,000; transportation: $906; personal expenses: $1,574. **Financial aid:** Priority filing date for institution's financial aid form: May 1. Average amount of debt of borrowers graduating in 2005: $15,793. Proportion who borrowed: 61%.

CAMPUS LIFE AND EXTRACURRICULAR ACTIVITIES
Campus housing available (% using): coed dorms (77%), sorority housing (5%), fraternity housing (3%), apartment for single students (15%). Students who live in college-owned, operated, or affiliated housing: 15%. **Clubs and organizations:** Number of student organizations: 95. Activities include: choral groups, concert band, dance, drama/theater, jazz band, marching band, music ensembles, musical theater, opera, pep band, radio station, student government, student newspaper, symphony orchestra, television station, yearbook. Number of fraternities: 9; sororities: 9. Proportion of men in fraternities: 3%; of women in sororities: 5%. Average proportion of students who stay on campus on weekends: 10%. **Sports program (2005-2006):** Member of NCAA I. *Men's intercollegiate varsity sports:* baseball, basketball, cross-country, football, golf, tennis, track and field (indoor), track and field (outdoor). *Women's intercollegiate varsity sports:* basketball, cross-country, soccer, softball, tennis, track and field (indoor), track and field (outdoor), volleyball.

SERVICES AND FACILITIES
Basic services: placement service, health service, health insurance, other. **Remedial assistance:** reading, math, writing, study skills, other. **Counseling services:** minority student, career, personal, veteran student, academic, older student, psychological, birth control, other. **For learning-disabled students:** School does not offer a structured program with separate admission and additional fees. Total undergraduates in learning-disabled program or receiving services: 250. Services include: remedial math, remedial English, reading machines, remedial reading, tape recorders, note-taking services, oral tests, extended time for tests, tutors, priority registration, substitution of courses, typist/scribe, exams on tape or computer, other testing accommo-

dations, other. **Library:** Number of titles: 613,998; number of current serial subscriptions: 2,901. **Information technology resources:** Students are not required to lease or own a computer. Number of campus computers available to all students: 1,453. School has a wireless network. Approximate number of users that can be accommodated: 650. Proportion of college-owned housing units wired for high-speed internet access: 100%. **Campus safety:** Security services offered: 24-hour foot and vehicle patrols, late-night transport/escort service, 24-hour emergency telephones, lighted pathways/sidewalks, controlled dormitory access (key, security card, etc).

TRANSFER AND INTERNATIONAL STUDENTS
Transfer students: May apply for admission for the following academic terms: Fall, Spring, Summer. Applicants need a minimum number of credits to apply. For fall 2005: Transfer applications received: 1,097. Transfer applicants offered admission: 986. Transfer applicants enrolled: 812. **International students:** Number of foreign undergraduates: 122 (1% of student body). Number of countries represented: 56. Minimum TOEFL score required: 500 (paper); 173 (computer).

Southern University and A&M College

- **Address:** PO Box 9374, Baton Rouge, LA 70813
- **Website:** http://www.subr.edu/
- **Public**
- **Enrollment:** 7,931 full-time; 1,033 part-time

KEY STATS
- ✔ **U.S News College Ranking:** fourth tier, Universities–Master's (South)
- ✔ **ACT Score (25th/75th percentile):** 16-19
- ✔ **Tuition:** 2005-2006: $3,592 in state, $9,384 out of state

Selectivity: Less selective	**Room/board:** $4,646
Acceptance rate: 53%	**Average debt:** $23,000
Student/faculty ratio: 20/1	**Proportion who borrowed:** 90%

UNDERGRADUATE STUDENT BODY STATS
2005-2006 enrollment: 7,931 full-time; 1,033 part-time. Men: 39%; women: 61%. **Ethnic makeup:** African American: 92%; White: 2%; International: 6%.

ADMISSIONS FACTS AND FIGURES
Phone: (225) 771-2430. **Email:** admit@subr.edu. **Website:** http://www.subr.edu/. **Application deadlines for fall 2007:** Regular decision: July 1. Early decision: Not offered. Early action: Not offered. Admission can be deferred. **Application fee:** $20. Common application is not accepted. **Admissions requirements/recommendations:** High school units required (recommended): English: 4; Mathematics: 3; Science: 3; Foreign language: 2; Social studies: 2; History: 1; Total units: 17. Tests: The college uses SAT or ACT scores in admissions decisions. Either SAT or ACT required. For admission to the fall 2007 entering class, the school will accept: ACT with writing, ACT without writing. Campus visit: Recommended. Admissions interview: Neither required nor recommended. Off-campus interview: Not available. **Factors that count in admissions decisions:** *Academic:* Secondary school record: Very important. Class rank: Very important. Letters of recommendation: Not considered. Standardized test scores: Very important. Essay: Not considered. *Nonacademic:* Interview: Not considered. Extracurricular activities: Not considered. Talent/ability: Considered. Character/personal qualities: Not considered. Alumni/ae relationship: Not considered. Geographical residence: Not considered. State residency: Not considered. Religious affiliation/commitment: Not considered. Minority status: Not considered. Volunteer work: Not considered. Work experience: Not considered. **Other schools with the greatest overlap in applicants:** Grambling State University; Louisiana State University–Baton Rouge; Louisiana State University–Baton Rouge; McNeese State University; McNeese State University; Southeastern Louisiana University; Southeastern Louisiana University; University of Louisiana–Lafayette; University of Louisiana–Lafayette. **Admissions statistics for the fall 2005 entering class:** Total applicants: 4,703. Total accepted: 2,479. Freshmen enrolled: 1,502; 28% were from out of state. Overall acceptance rate: 53%. **Credentials of fall 2005 freshmen:** 11% ranked in the top 10 percent of their high school class; 26% were in the top 25 percent, and 61% were in the top half. (Proportion submitting class standing: 98%.) **Average high school grade point average:** 2.8. **First-year students who submitted SAT scores:** 12%. Scores (25/75 per-

centile): Verbal: 380-480, Math: 370-480, Combined: 750-960. **First-year students submitting ACT scores:** 88%. Scores (25/75 percentile): English: 15-20, Math: 15-18, Composite: 16-19.

ACADEMICS
Year founded: 1880. **Academic calendar:** Semester. **Degrees offered:** associate, bachelor's, master's, post-master's certificate, doctorate. **Most popular majors:** 17% business, management, marketing, and related support services, 17% health professions and related clinical sciences, 8% engineering, 7% computer and information sciences and support services, 5% social sciences. **Major fields of study:** agriculture, agriculture operations, and related sciences; architecture and related services; biological and biomedical sciences; business, management, marketing, and related support services; communication, journalism, and related programs; computer and information sciences and support services; education; engineering; engineering technologies/technicians; English language and literature/letters; family and consumer sciences/human sciences; foreign languages, literatures, and linguistics; health professions and related clinical sciences; history; mathematics and statistics; natural resources and conservation; parks, recreation, leisure, and fitness studies; physical sciences; psychology; public administration and social service professions; security and protective services; social sciences; visual and performing arts. **Areas of required coursework:** arts/fine arts, humanities, computer literacy, mathematics, English (including composition), foreign languages, sciences (biological or physical), history, social science, other. **Pre-professional programs:** pre-law, pre-medicine. **Special academic programs:** cooperative (work-study plan) program, cross-registration, distance learning, double major, dual enrollment, exchange student program (domestic), honors program, independent study, internships, study abroad, teacher certificate program, weekend college. **Teacher certification offered in:** early childhood, special education, elementary, middle/junior high, secondary. **Cooperative education programs:** engineering. **Reserve Officers Training Corps (ROTC):** Army ROTC: Offered on campus; Navy ROTC: Offered on campus; Air Force ROTC: Offered at cooperating institution (Louisiana State University). **Faculty and instruction (2005-2006):** Total instructional faculty: 406 full-time, 167 part-time (51% men; 49% women; 83% minorities). Full-time faculty with Ph.D. or other terminal degree: 67%. Student/faculty ratio: 20/1. Classes of fewer than 20 students: 30%; of 20 to 49 students: 60%; of 50 or more students: 11%. **Advanced Placement and International Baccalaureate credit:** International Baccalaureate exams may be used for: Credit and/or placement. **Freshmen returning for sophomore year:** 70%. **Graduation rates:** Four-year: 7%; five-year: 19%; six-year: 26%. **Graduate study:** 15% of students pursue further study immediately upon graduation. Fields in which graduates pursue further study: engineering, 2%; education, 31%; arts and sciences, 66%.

COSTS AND FINANCIAL AID
Financial aid office: (225) 771-2790. **Expenses (2005-2006):** Tuition and fees 2005-2006: $3,592 in state, $9,384 out of state; room/board: $4,646. Estimated books and supplies: $1,680; transportation: $1,761; personal expenses: $2,027. **Financial aid:** Priority filing date for institution's financial aid form: May 15. In 2005-2006, 90% of undergraduates applied for financial aid. Of those, 82% were determined to have financial need; 20% had their need fully met. Average financial aid package (proportion receiving): $9,516 (79%). Average amount of gift aid, such as scholarships or grants (proportion receiving): $1,808 (52%). Average amount of self-help aid, such as work study or loans (proportion receiving): $4,779 (67%). Average need-based loan (excluding PLUS or other private loans): $3,997. Among students who received need-based aid, the average percentage of need met: 78%. Among students who received aid based on merit, the average award (and the proportion receiving): $2,746 (13%). The average athletic scholarship (and the proportion receiving): $4,433 (3%). Average amount of debt of borrowers graduating in 2005: $23,000. Proportion who borrowed: 90%.

CAMPUS LIFE AND EXTRACURRICULAR ACTIVITIES
Campus housing available (% using): women's dorms (72%), men's dorms (28%). Students who live in college-owned, operated, or affiliated housing: 34%. **Student employment:** During the 2005-2006 academic year, 15% of undergraduates worked on campus. Average per-year earnings: $4,400. **Clubs and organizations:** Number of student organizations: 79. Activities include: choral groups, concert band, dance, drama/theater, jazz band, literary magazine, marching band, music ensembles, musical theater, pep band, student government, student newspaper, yearbook. Number of fraternities: 5; sororities: 4. Proportion of men in fraternities: 1%; of women in sororities: 2%. Average proportion of students who stay on campus on weekends: 66%. **Sports program (2005-2006):** Member of NCAA I. **Men's intercollegiate varsity sports:** baseball, basketball, cross-country, football, golf, tennis,

track and field (indoor), track and field (outdoor). **Women's intercollegiate varsity sports:** basketball, bowling, cross-country, golf, soccer, softball, tennis, track and field (indoor), track and field (outdoor), volleyball.

SERVICES AND FACILITIES
Basic services: nonremedial tutoring, women's center, health service, health insurance. **Remedial assistance:** math, writing, study skills. **Counseling services:** minority student, career, military, personal, veteran student, academic, older student, psychological, birth control, religious. **For learning-disabled students:** School does not offer a structured program with separate admission and additional fees. Total undergraduates in learning-disabled program or receiving services: 257. Services include: tape recorders, note-taking services, oral tests, learning center, readers, extended time for tests, tutors, priority registration, priority seating, texts on tape, exams on tape or computer, other testing accomodations. **Library:** Number of titles: 807,728; number of current serial subscriptions: 1,689. **Information technology resources:** Students are not required to lease or own a computer. Number of campus computers available to all students: 1,300. School has a wireless network. Proportion of college-owned housing units wired for high-speed internet access: 100%. **Campus safety:** Security services offered: 24-hour foot and vehicle patrols, late-night transport/escort service, 24-hour emergency telephones, lighted pathways/sidewalks, controlled dormitory access (key, security card, etc).

TRANSFER AND INTERNATIONAL STUDENTS
Transfer students: May apply for admission for the following academic terms: Fall, Spring, Summer. Applicants need a minimum number of credits to apply. For fall 2005: Transfer applications received: 849. Transfer applicants offered admission: 406. Transfer applicants enrolled: 290. **International students:** Number of foreign undergraduates: 523 (6% of student body). Minimum TOEFL score required: 500 (paper); 125 (computer). Average TOEFL score: 525 (paper).

Southern University–New Orleans

- **Address:** 6400 Press Drive, New Orleans, LA 70126
- **Website:** http://www.suno.edu
- **Public**
- **Enrollment:** N/A

KEY STATS
✔ **U.S News College Ranking:** fourth tier, Universities–Master's (South)
✔ **SAT or ACT Score (25th/75th percentile):** N/A
✔ **Tuition:** N/A

Selectivity: Less selective	**Room/board:** N/A
Acceptance rate: N/A	**Average debt:** N/A
Student/faculty ratio: N/A	**Proportion who borrowed:** N/A

Tulane University

- **Address:** 6823 St. Charles Avenue, 218 Gibson Hall, New Orleans, LA 70118
- **Website:** http://www.tulane.edu
- **Private**
- **Enrollment:** N/A

KEY STATS
✔ **U.S News College Ranking:** 44, National Universities
✔ **ACT Score (25th/75th percentile):** 28-32
✔ **Tuition:** 2006-2007: $34,696

Selectivity: Most selective	**Room/board:** $8,667
Acceptance rate: 45%	**Average debt:** $21,379
Student/faculty ratio: N/A	**Proportion who borrowed:** 49%

University of Louisiana–Lafayette

- **Address:** PO Drawer 41008, Lafayette, LA 70504-1008
- **Website:** http://www.louisiana.edu
- **Public**
- **Enrollment:** 12,926 full-time; 2,638 part-time

KEY STATS

✔ **U.S News College Ranking:** fourth tier, National Universities
✔ **ACT Score (25th/75th percentile):** 19-24
✔ **Tuition:** 2006-2007: $3,360 in state, $9,540 out of state

Selectivity: Selective	**Room/board:** $3,770
Acceptance rate: 76%	**Average debt:** N/A
Student/faculty ratio: 27/1	**Proportion who borrowed:** N/A

UNDERGRADUATE STUDENT BODY STATS

2005-2006 enrollment: 12,926 full-time; 2,638 part-time. Men: 41%; women: 59%. **Ethnic makeup:** African American: 19%; Asian American: 2%; Hispanic: 2%; White: 75%; International: 2%. **Religious preference:** Roman Catholic: 50%; Protestant: 12%; Unknown: 31%; Other: 7%.

ADMISSIONS FACTS AND FIGURES

Phone: (337) 482-6467. **Email:** enroll@louisiana.edu. **Website:** http://www.louisiana.edu. **Application deadlines for fall 2007:** Regular decision: Rolling. Early decision: Not offered. Early action: Not offered. Admission can be deferred. **Application fee:** $25. Common application is not accepted. **To apply online, go to:** http://admissions.louisiana.edu/.
Admissions requirements/recommendations: High school units required (recommended): English: 4; Mathematics: 3; Science: 3; Social studies: 2; History: 1; Academic electives: 5. Tests: The college uses SAT or ACT scores in admissions decisions. Either SAT or ACT required. For admission to the fall 2007 entering class, the school will accept: ACT with writing, ACT without writing. Campus visit: Neither required nor recommended. Admissions interview: Neither required nor recommended. Off-campus interview: Not available. **Factors that count in admissions decisions:** *Academic:* Secondary school record: Very important. Class rank: Very important. Letters of recommendation: Not considered. Standardized test scores: Very important. Essay: Not considered. *Nonacademic:* Interview: Not considered. Extracurricular activities: Not considered. Talent/ability: Not considered. Character/personal qualities: Not considered. Alumni/ae relationship: Not considered. Geographical residence: Not considered. State residency: Considered. Religious affiliation/commitment: Not considered. Minority status: Not considered. Volunteer work: Not considered. Work experience: Not considered. **Other schools with the greatest overlap in applicants:** Louisiana State University–Baton Rouge; McNeese State University; Nicholls State University; Northwestern State University of Louisiana; Southeastern Louisiana University. **Admissions statistics for the fall 2005 entering class:** Total applicants: 6,309. Total accepted: 4,782. Freshmen enrolled: 2,819; 4% were from out of state. Overall acceptance rate: 76%. **Credentials of fall 2005 freshmen:** 15% ranked in the top 10 percent of their high school class; 38% were in the top 25 percent, and 71% were in the top half. (Proportion submitting class standing: 89%.) **Average high school grade point average:** 3.2. **First-year students submitting ACT scores:** 95%. Scores (25/75 percentile): English: 19-26, Math: 18-24, Composite: 19-24.

ACADEMICS

Year founded: 1898. **Academic calendar:** Semester. **Degrees offered:** bachelor's, master's, post-master's certificate, doctorate. **Most popular majors:** 11% general studies, 8% business administration and management, 6% elementary education and teaching, 4% marketing/marketing management, 3% finance. **Major fields of study:** agriculture, agriculture operations, and related sciences; architecture and related services; biological and biomedical sciences; business, management, marketing, and related support services; communication, journalism, and related programs; computer and information sciences and support services; education; engineering; engineering technologies/technicians; English language and literature/letters; family and consumer sciences/human sciences; foreign languages, literatures, and linguistics; health professions and related clinical sciences; history; liberal arts and sciences studies, and humanities; mathematics and statistics; natural resources and conservation; philosophy and religious studies; physical sciences; psychology; security and protective services; social sciences; visual and performing arts. **Areas of required coursework:** arts/fine arts, computer literacy, mathematics, English (including composition), sciences (biological or physical), history, social science. **Pre-professional programs:** pre-veterinary science, pre-pharmacy, other. **Special academic programs:** accelerated program, cooperative (work-study plan) program, cross-registration, distance learning, double major, dual enrollment, exchange student program (domestic), honors program, independent study, internships, study abroad, teacher certificate program. **Teacher certification offered in:** early childhood, special education, elementary, vo-tech, middle/junior high, secondary. **Reserve Officers Training Corps (ROTC):** Army ROTC: Offered on campus. **Faculty and instruction (2005-2006):** Total instructional faculty: 564 full-time, 153 part-time (58% men; 42% women; 14% minorities). Full-time faculty with Ph.D. or other terminal degree: 69%. Student/faculty ratio: 27/1. Classes of fewer than 20 students: 29%; of 20 to 49 students: 61%; of 50 or more students: 10%. **Advanced Placement and International Baccalaureate credit:** AP tests may be used for: Credit and/or placement. Scores accepted: 3, 4, 5. **Freshmen returning for sophomore year:** 72%. **Graduation rates:** Four-year: 12%; five-year: 31%; six-year: 38%.

COSTS AND FINANCIAL AID

Financial aid office: (337) 482-6506. **Expenses (2006-2007):** Tuition and fees 2006-2007: $3,360 in state, $9,540 out of state; room/board: $3,770. Estimated books and supplies: $1,000; transportation: $940; personal expenses: $1,631. **Financial aid:** Priority filing date for institution's financial aid form: May 1. In 2005-2006, 76% of undergraduates applied for financial aid. Of those, 53% were determined to have financial need; 8% had their need fully met. Average financial aid package (proportion receiving): $5,627 (51%). Average amount of gift aid, such as scholarships or grants (proportion receiving): $3,733 (43%). Average amount of self-help aid, such as work study or loans (proportion receiving): $3,670 (34%). Average need-based loan (excluding PLUS or other private loans): $3,656. Among students who received need-based aid, the average percentage of need met: 56%. Among students who received aid based on merit, the average award (and the proportion receiving): $1,763 (12%). The average athletic scholarship (and the proportion receiving): $4,669 (2%).

CAMPUS LIFE AND EXTRACURRICULAR ACTIVITIES

Campus housing available (% using): women's dorms (43%), men's dorms (16%), fraternity housing (3%), apartments for married students (4%), apartment for single students (22%), other housing options (12%). Students who live in college-owned, operated, or affiliated housing: 12%. **Student employment:** During the 2005-2006 academic year, 9% of undergraduates worked on campus. Average per-year earnings: $1,854. **Clubs and organizations:** Number of student organizations: 139. Activities include: choral groups, concert band, dance, drama/theater, jazz band, literary magazine, marching band, music ensembles, musical theater, opera, pep band, radio station, student government, student newspaper, symphony orchestra, yearbook. Number of fraternities: 11; sororities: 9. Proportion of men in fraternities: 2%; of women in sororities: 5%. Average proportion of students who stay on campus on weekends: 10%. **Sports program (2005-2006):** Member of NCAA I. *Men's intercollegiate varsity sports:* baseball, basketball, cross-country, football, golf, tennis, track and field (indoor), track and field (outdoor). *Women's intercollegiate varsity sports:* basketball, cross-country, soccer, softball, tennis, track and field (indoor), track and field (outdoor), volleyball.

SERVICES AND FACILITIES

Basic services: nonremedial tutoring, placement service, day care, health service, health insurance. **Remedial assistance:** reading, math, writing, study skills. **Counseling services:** career, personal, academic. **For learning-disabled students:** School does not offer a structured program with separate admission and additional fees. Total undergraduates in learning-disabled program or receiving services: 135. Services include: remedial math, remedial English, reading machines, remedial reading, tape recorders, other special classes, diagnostic testing service, untimed tests, note-taking services, oral tests, learning center, readers, extended time for tests, tutors. **Library:** Number of titles: 976,202; number of current serial subscriptions: 4,394. **Information technology resources:** Students are not required to lease or own a computer. Number of campus computers available to all students: 1,500. School has a wireless network. Approximate number of users that can be accommodated: 725. Proportion of college-owned housing units wired for high-speed internet access: 38%. **Campus safety:** Security services offered: 24-hour foot and vehicle patrols, late-night transport/escort service, 24-hour emergency telephones, lighted pathways/sidewalks, controlled dormitory access (key, security card, etc.).

TRANSFER AND INTERNATIONAL STUDENTS

Transfer students: May apply for admission for the following academic terms: Fall, Spring, Summer. Applicants do not need a minimum number of credits to apply. For fall 2005: Transfer applications received: 2,261. Transfer applicants offered admission: 1,489. Transfer applicants enrolled: 1,065. **International students:** Number of foreign undergraduates: 199 (2% of student body). Number of countries represented: 76. Minimum TOEFL score required: 450 (paper); 133 (computer). Average TOEFL score: 516 (paper).

University of Louisiana–Monroe

- **Address:** 700 University Avenue, Monroe, LA 71209
- **Website:** http://www.ulm.edu
- **Public**
- **Enrollment:** N/A

KEY STATS
✔ **U.S News College Ranking:** fourth tier, Universities–Master's (South)
✔ **ACT Score (25th/75th percentile):** 18-23
✔ **Tuition:** N/A

Selectivity: Selective	**Room/board:** N/A
Acceptance rate: 90%	**Average debt:** N/A
Student/faculty ratio: N/A	**Proportion who borrowed:** N/A

University of New Orleans

- **Address:** 2000 Lakeshore Drive, New Orleans, LA 70148
- **Website:** http://www.uno.edu
- **Public**
- **Enrollment:** N/A

KEY STATS
✔ **U.S News College Ranking:** fourth tier, National Universities
✔ **ACT Score (25th/75th percentile):** 18-23
✔ **Tuition:** 2005-2006: $3,810 in state, $10,854 out of state

Selectivity: Selective	**Room/board:** N/A
Acceptance rate: 63%	**Average debt:** N/A
Student/faculty ratio: N/A	**Proportion who borrowed:** N/A

Xavier University of Louisiana

- **Address:** 1 Drexel Drive, New Orleans, LA 70125
- **Website:** http://www.xula.edu
- **Private; Religious affiliation:** Roman Catholic
- **Enrollment:** N/A

KEY STATS
✔ **U.S News College Ranking:** 29, Universities–Master's (South)
✔ **ACT Score (25th/75th percentile):** 18-24
✔ **Tuition:** 2005-2006: $13,100

Selectivity: Selective	**Room/board:** $7,100
Acceptance rate: 83%	**Average debt:** N/A
Student/faculty ratio: N/A	**Proportion who borrowed:** N/A

Maine

■ **Address:** Two Andrews Road, Lewiston, ME 04240
■ **Website:** http://www.bates.edu
■ **Private**
■ **Enrollment:** 1,699 full-time; 31 part-time

KEY STATS

✔ **U.S News College Ranking:** 23, Liberal Arts Colleges
✔ **SAT Score (25th/75th percentile):** 1280-1410
✔ **Tuition:** N/A

Selectivity: Most selective	**Room/board:** N/A
Acceptance rate: 29%	**Average debt:** $13,636
Student/faculty ratio: 10/1	**Proportion who borrowed:** 46%

UNDERGRADUATE STUDENT BODY STATS

2005-2006 enrollment: 1,699 full-time; 31 part-time. Men: 49%; women: 51%. **Ethnic makeup:** African American: 3%; Asian American: 4%; Hispanic: 2%; White: 85%; International: 5%.

ADMISSIONS FACTS AND FIGURES

Phone: (207) 786-6000. **Email:** admissions@bates.edu. **Website:** http://www.bates.edu. **Application deadlines for fall 2007:** Regular decision: January 1; decision sent by March 31. Early decision: Send application by: November 15; Decision sent by: December 20. Early action: Not offered. Admission can be deferred. **Application fee:** $60. Common application is accepted. **To apply online, go to:** http://www.bates.edu/apply.xml. **Admissions requirements/recommendations:** High school units required (recommended): English: 4 (4); Mathematics: 3 (4); Science: 3 (4); Foreign language: 2 (4); Total units: 17 (23). Tests: The college uses SAT or ACT scores in admissions decisions. Neither SAT nor ACT required. For admission to the fall 2007 entering class, the school will accept: ACT with writing, ACT without writing. Campus visit: Recommended. Admissions interview: Recommended. Off-campus interview: May be arranged. **Factors that count in admissions decisions:** *Academic:* Secondary school record: Very important. Class rank: Very important. Letters of recommendation: Very important. Standardized test scores: Considered. Essay: Very important. *Nonacademic:* Interview: Very important. Extracurricular activities: Very important. Talent/ability: Very important. Character/personal qualities: Very important. Alumni/ae relationship: Considered. Geographical residence: Considered. State residency: Considered. Religious affiliation/commitment: Not considered. Minority status: Considered. Volunteer work: Considered. Work experience: Considered. **Other schools with the greatest overlap in applicants:** Bowdoin College; Colby College; Middlebury College; Tufts University; Williams College. **Admissions statistics for the fall 2005 entering class:** Total applicants: 4,356. Total accepted: 1,272. Freshmen enrolled: 490; 90% were from out of state. Overall acceptance rate: 29%. Non-early acceptance rate: 29%. **Credentials of fall 2005 freshmen:** 57% ranked in the top 10 percent of their high school class; 91% were in the top 25 percent, and 99% were in the top half. (Proportion submitting class standing: 41%.) **First-year students who submitted SAT scores:** 50%. Scores (25/75 percentile): Verbal: 640-710, Math: 640-700, Combined: 1280-1410.

ACADEMICS

Year founded: 1855. **Academic calendar:** Other. **Degrees offered:** bachelor's. **Most popular majors:** 29% social sciences, 12% psychology, 9% biological and biomedical sciences, 8% English language and literature/letters, 8% multi/interdisciplinary studies. **Major fields of study:** area, ethnic, cultural, and gender studies; biological and biomedical sciences; engineering; English language and literature/letters; foreign languages, literatures, and linguistics; history; mathematics and statistics; multi/interdisciplinary studies; natural resources and conservation; philosophy and religious studies; physical sciences; psychology; social sciences; visual and performing arts. **Areas of required coursework:** humanities, mathematics, sciences (biological or physical), social science. **Special academic programs (% participation):** accelerated program (1%), cooperative (work-study plan) program, double major (11%), exchange student program (domestic) (0%), honors program (12%), independent study (18%), internships, liberal arts/career combination (0%), student-designed major (3%), study abroad (60%), teacher certificate program (1.4%). **Teacher certification offered in:** middle/junior high, secondary. **Faculty and instruction (2005-2006):** Total instructional faculty: 164 full-time, 23 part-time (53% men; 47% women; 12% minorities). Full-time faculty with Ph.D. or other terminal degree: 94%. Student/faculty ratio: 10/1. Classes of fewer than 20 students: 63%; of 20 to 49 students: 32%; of 50 or more students: 5%. **Advanced Placement and International Baccalaureate credit:** AP tests may be used for: Credit and/or placement. Scores accepted: 4, 5. International Baccalaureate exams may be used for: Credit and/or placement. **Freshmen returning for sophomore year:** 94%. **Graduation rates:** Four-year: 84%; five-year: 88%; six-year: 89%.

COSTS AND FINANCIAL AID

Financial aid office: (207) 786-6096. **Financial aid:** In 2005-2006, 49% of undergraduates applied for financial aid. Of those, 44% were determined to have financial need; 87% had their need fully met. Average financial aid package (proportion receiving): $27,428 (40%). Average amount of gift aid, such as scholarships or grants (proportion receiving): $24,000 (39%). Average amount of self-help aid, such as work study or loans (proportion receiving): $4,360 (39%). Average need-based loan (excluding PLUS or other private loans): $3,877. Among students who received need-based aid, the average percentage of need met: 100%. Average amount of debt of borrowers graduating in 2005: $13,636. Proportion who borrowed: 46%.

CAMPUS LIFE AND EXTRACURRICULAR ACTIVITIES

Campus housing available (% using): coed dorms (72%), women's dorms (1%), men's dorms (1%), other housing options (26%). Students who live in college-owned, operated, or affiliated housing: 93%. **Student employment:** During the 2005-2006 academic year, 50% of undergraduates worked on campus. Average per-year earnings: $1,000. **Clubs and organizations:** Number of student organizations: 91. Activities include: choral groups, concert band, dance, drama/theater, jazz band, literary magazine, music ensembles, musical theater, pep band, radio station, student government, student newspaper, student film society, symphony orchestra, television station, yearbook. Number of fraternities: 0; sororities: 0. Average proportion of students who stay on campus on weekends: 95%. **Sports program (2005-2006):** Member of NCAA III. **Men's intercollegiate varsity sports:** baseball, basketball, cross-country, football, golf, lacrosse, skiing, soccer, swimming and diving, tennis, track and field (indoor), track and field (outdoor). **Women's intercollegiate varsity sports:** basketball, cross-country, field hockey, golf, lacrosse, rowing, skiing, soccer, softball, squash, swimming and diving, tennis, track and field (indoor), track and field (outdoor), volleyball.

SERVICES AND FACILITIES

Basic services: nonremedial tutoring, women's center, placement service, health service, health insurance. **Remedial assistance:** math, writing. **Counseling services:** minority student, career, personal, academic, older student, psychological, birth control, religious. **For learning-disabled students:** School does not offer a structured program with separate admission and additional fees. Total undergraduates in learning-disabled program or receiving services: 141. Services include: tape recorders, diagnostic testing service, untimed tests, note-taking services, oral tests, learning center, readers, extended time for tests, proofreading services, texts on tape. **Library:** Number of titles: 591,630; number of current serial subscriptions: 25,703. **Information technology resources:** Students are not required to lease or own a computer. Number of campus computers available to all students: 414. School has a wireless network. Approximate number of users that can be accommodated: 3,500. Proportion of college-owned housing units wired for high-speed internet access: 100%. **Campus safety:** Security services offered: 24-hour foot and vehicle patrols, late-night transport/escort service, 24-hour emergency telephones, lighted pathways/sidewalks, student patrols, controlled dormitory access (key, security card, etc).

TRANSFER AND INTERNATIONAL STUDENTS

Transfer students: May apply for admission for the following academic terms: Fall, Winter. Applicants need a minimum number of credits to apply. For fall 2005: Transfer applications received: 149. Transfer applicants offered admission: 41. Transfer applicants enrolled: 20. **International students:** Number of foreign undergraduates: 91 (5% of student body). Number of countries represented: 67. Minimum TOEFL score required: 0 (computer).

Bowdoin College

■ **Address:** 5700 College Station, Brunswick, ME 04011-8448
■ **Website:** http://www.bowdoin.edu
■ **Private**
■ **Enrollment:** 1,661 full-time; 5 part-time

KEY STATS

✔ **U.S News College Ranking:** 7, Liberal Arts Colleges
✔ **SAT Score (25th/75th percentile):** 1320-1470
✔ **Tuition:** 2006-2007: $34,640

Selectivity: Most selective	**Room/board:** $9,310
Acceptance rate: 25%	**Average debt:** $15,300
Student/faculty ratio: 10/1	**Proportion who borrowed:** 54%

UNDERGRADUATE STUDENT BODY STATS

2005-2006 enrollment: 1,661 full-time; 5 part-time. Men: 49%; women: 51%. **Ethnic makeup:** African American: 6%; American-Indian: 1%; Asian American: 12%; Hispanic: 7%; White: 71%; International: 3%. **Religious preference:** Roman Catholic: 23%; Protestant: 29%; Jewish: 8%; Muslim: 1%; Hindu: 1%; Buddhist: 1%; No preference: 34%; Other: 3%.

ADMISSIONS FACTS AND FIGURES

Phone: (207) 725-3100. **Email:** admissions@bowdoin.edu. **Website:** http://www.bowdoin.edu. **Application deadlines for fall 2007:** Regular decision: January 1. Early decision: Send application by: November 15; Decision sent by: December 31. Early action: Not offered. Admission can be deferred. **Application fee:** $60. Common application is accepted. **To apply online, go to:** http://www.bowdoin.edu/admissions/apply/. **Admissions requirements/recommendations:** High school units required (recommended): English: (4); Mathematics: (4); Science: (4); Foreign language: (4); Social studies: (4); Total units: (20). Tests: The college uses SAT or ACT scores in admissions decisions. Neither SAT nor ACT required. For admission to the fall 2007 entering class, the school will accept: ACT with writing, ACT without writing. Campus visit: Recommended. Admissions interview: Recommended. Off-campus interview: May be arranged. **Factors that count in admissions decisions:** *Academic:* Secondary school record: Very important. Class rank: Very important. Letters of recommendation: Very important. Standardized test scores: Considered. Essay: Very important. *Nonacademic:* Interview: Considered. Extracurricular activities: Very important. Talent/ability: Very important. Character/personal qualities: Very important. Alumni/ae relationship: Important. Geographical residence: Important. State residency: Considered. Religious affiliation/commitment: Not considered. Minority status: Important. Volunteer work: Important. Work experience: Important. **Other schools with the greatest overlap in applicants:** Brown University; Dartmouth College; Middlebury College; Williams College; Yale University. **Admissions statistics for the fall 2005 entering class:** Total applicants: 5,026. Total accepted: 1,232. Freshmen enrolled: 478; 88% were from out of state. Accepted through early-decision or early-action plans: 37%. Overall acceptance rate: 25%. Early-decision acceptance rate: 29%. Non-early acceptance rate: 24%. **Credentials of fall 2005 freshmen:** 78% ranked in the top 10 percent of their high school class; 96% were in the top 25 percent, and 100% were in the top half. (Proportion submitting class standing: 51%.) **First-year students who submitted SAT scores:** 76%. Scores (25/75 percentile): Verbal: 660-740, Math: 660-730, Combined: 1320-1470.

ACADEMICS

Year founded: 1794. **Academic calendar:** Semester. **Degrees offered:** bachelor's. **Most popular majors:** 19% political science and government, 13% economics, 10% history, 8% Spanish language and literature, 8% biology. **Major fields of study:** area, ethnic, cultural, and gender studies; biological and biomedical sciences; computer and information sciences and support services; English language and literature/letters; foreign languages, literatures, and linguistics; history; mathematics and statistics; multi/interdisciplinary studies; natural resources and conservation; philosophy and religious studies; physical sciences; psychology; social sciences; visual and performing arts. **Areas of required coursework:** arts/fine arts, humanities, mathematics, sciences (biological or physical), social science, other. **Special academic programs (% participation):** accelerated program (4.2%), double major (27.9%), exchange student program (domestic) (0%), independent study (62%), liberal arts/career combination (0%), student-designed major (.7%), study abroad (50.7%), teacher certificate program (1%). **Teacher certification offered in:** middle/junior high, secondary. **Faculty and instruction (2005-2006):** Total instructional faculty: 157 full-time, 33 part-time (52% men; 48% women; 11% minorities). Full-time faculty with Ph.D. or other terminal degree: 98%. Student/faculty ratio: 10/1. Classes of fewer than 20 students: 65%; of 20 to 49 students: 32%; of 50 or more students: 3%. **Advanced Placement and International Baccalaureate credit:** AP tests may be used for: Credit and/or placement. Scores accepted: 3, 4, 5. International Baccalaureate exams may be used for: Credit and/or placement. **Freshmen returning for sophomore year:** 98%. **Graduation rates:** Four-year: 90%; five-year: 94%; six-year: 94%. **Graduate study:** 11% of students pursue further study immediately upon graduation; 15% within one year; 20% within five years. Fields in which graduates pursue further study: Master of Business Administration (MBA), 20%; law, 10%; medicine, 13%; dentistry, 5%; engineering, 2%; theology (or the seminary), 1%; education, 15%; arts and sciences, 31%; veterinary medicine, 3%.

COSTS AND FINANCIAL AID

Financial aid office: (207) 725-3273. **Expenses (2006-2007):** Tuition and fees 2006-2007: $34,640; room/board: $9,310. Estimated books and supplies: $800 personal expenses: $1,200. **Financial aid:** In 2005-2006, 53% of undergraduates applied for financial aid. Of those, 45% were determined to have financial need; 100% had their need fully met. Average financial aid package (proportion receiving): $29,090 (45%). Average amount of gift aid, such as scholarships or grants (proportion receiving): $24,785 (44%). Average amount of self-help aid, such as work study or loans (proportion receiving): $4,731 (40%). Average need-based loan (excluding PLUS or other private loans): $3,285. Among students who received need-based aid, the average percentage of need met: 100%. Among students who received aid based on merit, the average award (and the proportion receiving): $1,000 (3%). The average athletic scholarship (and the proportion receiving): $0 (0%). Average amount of debt of borrowers graduating in 2005: $15,300. Proportion who borrowed: 54%.

CAMPUS LIFE AND EXTRACURRICULAR ACTIVITIES

Campus housing available (% using): coed dorms (63%), apartment for single students (22%), special housing for disabled students (0%), other housing options (15%). Students who live in college-owned, operated, or affiliated housing: 95%. **Student employment:** During the 2005-2006 academic year, 46% of undergraduates worked on campus. Average per-year earnings: $1,835. **Clubs and organizations:** Number of student organizations: 109. Activities include: choral groups, concert band, dance, drama/theater, jazz band, literary magazine, music ensembles, musical theater, radio station, student government, student newspaper, student film society, symphony orchestra, television station, yearbook. Number of fraternities: 0; sororities: 0. Average proportion of students who stay on campus on weekends: 90%. **Sports program (2005-2006):** Member of NCAA III. *Men's intercollegiate varsity sports:* baseball, basketball, cross-country, football, golf, ice hockey, lacrosse, skiing, soccer, swimming and diving, tennis, track and field (indoor), track and field (outdoor). *Women's intercollegiate varsity sports:* basketball, cross-country, field hockey, golf, ice hockey, lacrosse, rugby, skiing, soccer, softball, squash, swimming and diving, tennis, track and field (indoor), track and field (outdoor), volleyball.

SERVICES AND FACILITIES

Basic services: nonremedial tutoring, women's center, placement service, day care, health service, health insurance. **Counseling services:** minority student, career, personal, academic, psychological, birth control, religious. **For learning-disabled students:** School does not offer a structured program with separate admission and additional fees. Total undergraduates in learning-disabled program or receiving services: 81. Services include: reading machines, tape recorders, note-taking services, oral tests, learning center, readers, extended time for tests, tutors. **Library:** Number of titles: 995,507; number of current serial subscriptions: 6,300. **Information technology resources:** Students are not required to lease or own a computer. Number of campus computers available to all students: 450. School has a wireless network. Approximate number of users that can be accommodated: 2,500.

Proportion of college-owned housing units wired for high-speed internet access: 100%. **Campus safety:** Security services offered: 24-hour foot and vehicle patrols, late-night transport/escort service, 24-hour emergency telephones, lighted pathways/sidewalks, controlled dormitory access (key, security card, etc).

TRANSFER AND INTERNATIONAL STUDENTS

Transfer students: May apply for admission for the following academic terms: Fall. Applicants need a minimum number of credits to apply. For fall 2005: Transfer applications received: 113. Transfer applicants offered admission: 14. Transfer applicants enrolled: 3. **International students:** Number of foreign undergraduates: 47 (3% of student body). Number of countries represented: 24. Minimum TOEFL score required: 600 (paper); 250 (computer).

Colby College

- ■ **Address:** 4000 Mayflower Hill, Waterville, ME 04901-8840
- ■ **Website:** http://www.colby.edu
- ■ **Private**
- ■ **Enrollment:** 1,871 full-time

KEY STATS

✔ **U.S News College Ranking:** 20, Liberal Arts Colleges
✔ **SAT Score (25th/75th percentile):** 1280-1430
✔ **Tuition:** N/A

Selectivity: Most selective	**Room/board:** N/A
Acceptance rate: 38%	**Average debt:** $18,479
Student/faculty ratio: 10/1	**Proportion who borrowed:** 43%

UNDERGRADUATE STUDENT BODY STATS

2005-2006 enrollment: 1,871 full-time. Men: 46%; women: 54%. **Ethnic makeup:** African American: 2%; Asian American: 6%; Hispanic: 3%; White: 83%; International: 6%.

ADMISSIONS FACTS AND FIGURES

Phone: (800) 723-3032. **Email:** admissions@colby.edu. **Website:** http://www.colby.edu. **Application deadlines for fall 2007:** Regular decision: January 1; decision sent by April 1. Early decision: Send application by: November 15; Decision sent by: December 15. Early action: Not offered. Admission can be deferred. Common application is accepted. **To apply online, go to:** http://www.colby.edu/admissions. **Admissions requirements/recommendations:** High school units required (recommended): English: 4 (4); Mathematics: 3 (3); Science: 2 (2); Foreign language: 3 (3); Social studies: 2 (2); History: 0 (0); Academic electives: 2 (2); Total units: 16 (16). Tests: The college uses SAT or ACT scores in admissions decisions. Either SAT or ACT required. For admission to the fall 2007 entering class, the school will accept: ACT with writing, ACT without writing. Campus visit: Recommended. Admissions interview: Recommended. Off-campus interview: May be arranged. **Factors that count in admissions decisions:** *Academic:* Secondary school record: Very important. Class rank: Important. Letters of recommendation: Important. Standardized test scores: Important. Essay: Important. *Nonacademic:* Interview: Important. Extracurricular activities: Important. Talent/ability: Important. Character/personal qualities: Very important. Alumni/ae relationship: Considered. Geographical residence: Considered. State residency: Considered. Religious affiliation/commitment: Not considered. Minority status: Important. Volunteer work: Considered. Work experience: Considered. **Other schools with the greatest overlap in applicants:** Bates College; Bowdoin College; Dartmouth College; Middlebury College; Williams College. **Admissions statistics for the fall 2005 entering class:** Total applicants: 3,874. Total accepted: 1,454. Freshmen enrolled: 511; 89% were from out of state. Accepted through early-decision or early-action plans: 42%. Overall acceptance rate: 38%. Early-decision acceptance rate: 52%. Non-early acceptance rate: 36%. **Size of waiting list:** 624 applicants; enrolled from waiting list: 1. **Credentials of fall 2005 freshmen:** 67% ranked in the top 10 percent of their high school class; 92% were in the top 25 percent, and 99% were in the top half. (Proportion submitting class standing: 53%.) **First-year students who submitted SAT scores:** 84%. Scores (25/75 percentile): Verbal: 640-720, Math: 640-710, Combined: 1280-1430. **First-year students submitting ACT scores:** 26%. Scores (25/75 percentile): English: 27-33, Math: 26-30, Composite: 27-31.

ACADEMICS

Year founded: 1813. **Academic calendar:** 4-1-4. **Degrees offered:** bachelor's. **Most popular majors:** 16% biology/biological sciences, 13% English literature (British and Commonwealth), 13% political science and government, 11% economics, 7% history. **Major fields of study:** area, ethnic, cultural, and gender studies; biological and biomedical sciences; computer and information sciences and support services; English language and literature/letters; foreign languages, literatures, and linguistics; history; mathematics and statistics; multi/interdisciplinary studies; natural resources and conservation; philosophy and religious studies; physical sciences; psychology; social sciences; visual and performing arts. **Areas of required coursework:** arts/fine arts, humanities, mathematics, English (including composition), foreign languages, sciences (biological or physical), history, social science, other. **Pre-professional programs:** pre-law, pre-dentistry, pre-medicine, pre-veterinary science, other. **Special academic programs (% participation):** cross-registration (.2%), double major (23%), exchange student program (domestic) (2%), honors program (15%), independent study (55%), internships (45%), student-designed major (2%), study abroad (67%), teacher certificate program (.2%). **Teacher certification offered in:** secondary. **Reserve Officers Training Corps (ROTC):** Army ROTC: Offered at cooperating institution (University of Maine). **Faculty and instruction (2005-2006):** Total instructional faculty: 161 full-time, 64 part-time (51% men; 49% women; 12% minorities). Full-time faculty with Ph.D. or other terminal degree: 96%. Student/faculty ratio: 10/1. Classes of fewer than 20 students: 58%; of 20 to 49 students: 37%; of 50 or more students: 5%. **Advanced Placement and International Baccalaureate credit:** AP tests may be used for: Credit and/or placement. Scores accepted: 4, 5. International Baccalaureate exams may be used for: Credit and/or placement. **Freshmen returning for sophomore year:** 93%. **Graduation rates:** Four-year: 85%; five-year: 89%; six-year: 89%. **Graduate study:** 15% of students pursue further study immediately upon graduation; 21% within one year; 50% within five years. Fields in which graduates pursue further study: Master of Business Administration (MBA), 3%; law, 20%; medicine, 15%; education, 5%; arts and sciences, 57%.

COSTS AND FINANCIAL AID

Financial aid office: (800) 723-3032. **Financial aid:** In 2005-2006, 44% of undergraduates applied for financial aid. Of those, 38% were determined to have financial need; 100% had their need fully met. Average financial aid package (proportion receiving): $27,177 (38%). Average amount of gift aid, such as scholarships or grants (proportion receiving): $25,352 (36%). Average amount of self-help aid, such as work study or loans (proportion receiving): $3,812 (32%). Average need-based loan (excluding PLUS or other private loans): $3,306. Among students who received need-based aid, the average percentage of need met: 100%. Among students who received aid based on merit, the average award (and the proportion receiving): $0 (0%). The average athletic scholarship (and the proportion receiving): $0 (0%). Average amount of debt of borrowers graduating in 2005: $18,479. Proportion who borrowed: 43%.

CAMPUS LIFE AND EXTRACURRICULAR ACTIVITIES

Campus housing available (% using): coed dorms (74%), other housing options (26%). Students who live in college-owned, operated, or affiliated housing: 94%. **Student employment:** During the 2005-2006 academic year, 42% of undergraduates worked on campus. Average per-year earnings: $1,020. **Clubs and organizations:** Number of student organizations: 106. Activities include: choral groups, concert band, dance, drama/theater, jazz band, literary magazine, music ensembles, musical theater, radio station, student government, student newspaper, student film society, symphony orchestra, yearbook. Number of fraternities: 0; sororities: 0. Average proportion of students who stay on campus on weekends: 87%. **Sports program (2005-2006):** Member of NCAA III. *Men's intercollegiate varsity sports:* baseball, basketball, cross-country, football, golf, ice hockey, lacrosse, skiing, soccer, swimming and diving, tennis, track and field (indoor), track and field (outdoor). *Women's intercollegiate varsity sports:* basketball, cross-country, field hockey, golf, ice hockey, lacrosse, rowing, skiing, soccer, softball, squash, swimming and diving, tennis, track and field (indoor), track and field (outdoor), volleyball.

SERVICES AND FACILITIES

Basic services: nonremedial tutoring, women's center, placement service, health service, health insurance, other. **Counseling services:** minority student, career, military, personal, veteran student, academic, older student, psychological, birth control, religious. **For learning-disabled students:** School does not offer a structured program with separate admission and additional fees. Total undergraduates in learning-disabled program or receiving services: 120. Services include: reading machines, tape recorders, note-taking services, readers, extended time for tests, tutors, waiver of foreign language degree requirement. **Library:** Number of titles: 436,170; number of current serial subscriptions: 3,875. **Information technology resources:** Students are not required to lease or own a computer. Number of campus computers available to all students: 300. School has a wireless network. Approximate number of users that can be accommodated: 500. Proportion of college-owned housing units wired for high-speed internet access: 100%. **Campus safety:** Security services offered: 24-hour foot and vehicle patrols, late-night transport/escort service, 24-hour emergency telephones, lighted pathways/sidewalks, student patrols, controlled dormitory access (key, security card, etc.).

TRANSFER AND INTERNATIONAL STUDENTS

Transfer students: May apply for admission for the following academic terms: Fall, Spring. Applicants do not need a minimum number of credits to apply. For fall 2005: Transfer applications received: 106. Transfer applicants offered admission: 19. Transfer applicants enrolled: 11. **International students:** Number of foreign undergraduates: 121 (6% of student body). Number of countries represented: 66. Minimum TOEFL score required: 600 (paper); 240 (computer). Average TOEFL score: 643 (paper).

College of the Atlantic

- **Address:** 105 Eden Street, Bar Harbor, ME 04609
- **Website:** http://www.coa.edu/
- **Private**
- **Enrollment:** 296 full-time; 14 part-time

KEY STATS

- ✔ **U.S News College Ranking:** third tier, Liberal Arts Colleges
- ✔ **SAT Score (25th/75th percentile):** 1090-1300
- ✔ **Tuition:** 2006-2007: $28,140

Selectivity: More selective	**Room/board:** $7,710
Acceptance rate: 66%	**Average debt:** $16,705
Student/faculty ratio: 10/1	**Proportion who borrowed:** 57%

UNDERGRADUATE STUDENT BODY STATS

2005-2006 enrollment: 296 full-time; 14 part-time. Men: 36%; women: 64%. **Ethnic makeup:** White: 83%; International: 17%.

ADMISSIONS FACTS AND FIGURES

Phone: (800) 528-0025. **Email:** inquiry@ecology.coa.edu. **Website:** http://www.coa.edu/. **Application deadlines for fall 2007:** Regular decision: February 15; decision sent by April 1. Early decision: Send application by: December 1; Decision sent by: December 15. Early action: Not offered. Admission can be deferred. **Application fee:** $45. Common application is accepted. **To apply online, go to:** https://apply.embark.com/ugrad/coa/10/. **Admissions requirements/recommendations:** High school units required (recommended): English: 4; Mathematics: 3 (4); Science: 2 (3); Foreign language: 0 (2); Social studies: 2; History: 0 (2); Academic electives: 0 (1); Total units: 15 (19). Tests: The college uses SAT or ACT scores in admissions decisions. Neither SAT nor ACT required. For admission to the fall 2007 entering class, the school will accept: ACT with writing, ACT without writing. Campus visit: Recommended. Admissions interview: Recommended. Off-campus interview: May be arranged. **Factors that count in admissions decisions:** *Academic:* Secondary school record: Important. Class rank: Considered. Letters of recommendation: Very important. Standardized test scores: Considered. Essay: Very important. *Nonacademic:* Interview: Important. Extracurricular activities: Important. Talent/ability: Important. Character/personal qualities: Important. Alumni/ae relationship: Considered. Geographical residence: Considered. State residency: Considered. Religious affiliation/commitment: Not considered. Minority status: Considered. Volunteer work: Important. Work experience: Important. **Other schools with the greatest overlap in applicants:** Bard College; Bowdoin College; Colby College; Hampshire College; Reed College. **Admissions statistics for the fall 2005 entering class:** Total applicants: 284. Total accepted: 188. Freshmen enrolled: 82; 72% were from out of state. Accepted through early-decision or early-action plans: 39%. Overall acceptance rate: 66%. Early-decision acceptance rate: 73%. Non-early acceptance rate: 65%. **Size of waiting list:** 3 applicants; enrolled from waiting list: 1. **Credentials of fall 2005 freshmen:** 36% ranked in the top 10 percent of their high school class; 76% were in the top 25 percent, and 95% were in the top

half. (Proportion submitting class standing: 49%.) **Average high school grade point average:** 3.6. **First-year students who submitted SAT scores:** 89%. Scores (25/75 percentile): Verbal: 560-670, Math: 530-630, Combined: 1090-1300. **First-year students submitting ACT scores:** 40%. Scores (25/75 percentile): English: N/A, Math: N/A, Composite: 23-28.

ACADEMICS

Year founded: 1969. **Academic calendar:** Trimester. **Degrees offered:** bachelor's, master's. **Most popular majors:** Information not available. **Major fields of study:** multi/interdisciplinary studies. **Areas of required coursework:** arts/fine arts, humanities, mathematics, English (including composition), sciences (biological or physical), history, social science. **Pre-professional programs:** pre-law, pre-medicine, pre-theology, pre-veterinary science. **Special academic programs (% participation):** cross-registration (19%), exchange student program (domestic) (11%), independent study (85%), internships (100%), student-designed major (100%), study abroad (42%), teacher certificate program (10%). **Teacher certification offered in:** elementary, secondary. **Cooperative education programs:** education, engineering. **Faculty and instruction (2005-2006):** Total instructional faculty: 27 full-time, 13 part-time (65% men; 35% women; 8% minorities). Full-time faculty with Ph.D. or other terminal degree: 89%. Student/faculty ratio: 10/1. Classes of fewer than 20 students: 97%; of 20 to 49 students: 3%. **Advanced Placement and International Baccalaureate credit:** AP tests may be used for: Credit only. Scores accepted: 4, 5. International Baccalaureate exams may be used for: Credit only. **Freshmen returning for sophomore year:** 80%. **Graduation rates:** Four-year: 45%; five-year: 58%; six-year: 62%. **Graduate study:** 10% of students pursue further study immediately upon graduation; 18% within one year; 65% within five years. Fields in which graduates pursue further study: Master of Business Administration (MBA), 3%; law, 5%; medicine, 10%; engineering, 1%; theology (or the seminary), 1%; education, 13%; arts and sciences, 29%; veterinary medicine, 1%.

COSTS AND FINANCIAL AID

Financial aid office: (800) 528-0025. **Expenses (2006-2007):** Tuition and fees 2006-2007: $28,140; room/board: $7,710. Estimated books and supplies: $525; transportation: $200; personal expenses: $385. **Financial aid:** Priority filing date for institution's financial aid form: February 15; deadline: February 15. In 2005-2006, 95% of undergraduates applied for financial aid. Of those, 93% were determined to have financial need; 95% had their need fully met. Average financial aid package (proportion receiving): $24,478 (93%). Average amount of gift aid, such as scholarships or grants (proportion receiving): $20,849 (85%). Average amount of self-help aid, such as work study or loans (proportion receiving): $4,545 (79%). Average need-based loan (excluding PLUS or other private loans): $3,990. Among students who received need-based aid, the average percentage of need met: 95%. Among students who received aid based on merit, the average award (and the proportion receiving): $4,200 (6%). The average athletic scholarship (and the proportion receiving): $0 (0%). Average amount of debt of borrowers graduating in 2005: $16,705. Proportion who borrowed: 57%.

CAMPUS LIFE AND EXTRACURRICULAR ACTIVITIES

Campus housing available (% using): coed dorms (100%), special housing for disabled students (0%). Students who live in college-owned, operated, or affiliated housing: 35%. **Student employment:** During the 2005-2006 academic year, 25% of undergraduates worked on campus. Average per-year earnings: $930. **Clubs and organizations:** Number of student organizations: 8. Activities include: choral groups, dance, drama/theater, literary magazine, music ensembles, student government, student newspaper, yearbook. Number of fraternities: 0; sororities: 0. Average proportion of students who stay on campus on weekends: 40%.

SERVICES AND FACILITIES

Basic services: nonremedial tutoring, health service, health insurance. **Remedial assistance:** writing, study skills. **Counseling services:** minority student, career, personal, academic, psychological, birth control. **For learning-disabled students:** School does not offer a structured program with separate admission and additional fees. Total undergraduates in learning-disabled program or receiving services: 20. Services include: remedial English, remedial reading, tape recorders, other special classes, untimed tests, note-taking services, oral tests, readers, extended time for tests, tutors, proofreading services, texts on tape, other testing accomodations. **Library:** Number of titles: 40,300; number of current serial subscriptions: 550. **Information technology resources:** Students are not required to lease or own a computer. Number of campus computers available to all students: 50. School has a wireless network. Approximate number of users that can be accommodated: 150. Proportion of college-owned housing units wired for high-speed internet access: 100%. **Campus safety:** Security services offered: late-night transport/escort service, 24-hour emergency telephones, lighted pathways/sidewalks, controlled dormitory access (key, security card, etc).

TRANSFER AND INTERNATIONAL STUDENTS

Transfer students: May apply for admission for the following academic terms: Fall, Winter, Spring. Applicants do not need a minimum number of credits to apply. For fall 2005: Transfer applications received: 23. Transfer applicants offered admission: 18. Transfer applicants enrolled: 10.
International students: Number of foreign undergraduates: 51 (17% of student body). Number of countries represented: 42. Minimum TOEFL score required: 550 (paper); 217 (computer). Average TOEFL score: 600 (paper).

Husson College

- **Address:** 1 College Circle, Bangor, ME 04401
- **Website:** http://www.husson.edu
- **Private**
- **Enrollment:** 1,605 full-time; 372 part-time

KEY STATS

✔ **U.S News College Ranking:** fourth tier, Universities–Master's (North)
✔ **SAT Score (25th/75th percentile):** 810-1000
✔ **Tuition:** 2006-2007: $11,770

Selectivity: Less selective	**Room/board:** $6,240
Acceptance rate: 95%	**Average debt:** $16,940
Student/faculty ratio: 16/1	**Proportion who borrowed:** 90%

UNDERGRADUATE STUDENT BODY STATS

2005-2006 enrollment: 1,605 full-time; 372 part-time. Men: 38%; women: 62%. **Ethnic makeup:** African American: 3%; Asian American: 1%; White: 93%; International: 2%. **Religious preference:** Roman Catholic: 20%; Protestant: 26%; Jewish: 2%; Buddhist: 1%; No preference: 30%; Other: 21%.

ADMISSIONS FACTS AND FIGURES

Phone: (207) 941-7100. **Email:** admit@husson.edu. **Website:** http://www.husson.edu. **Application deadlines for fall 2007:** Regular decision: August 30. Early decision: Not offered. Early action: Send application by: December 15; Decision sent by: January 2. Admission can be deferred. **Application fee:** $25. Common application is accepted. **Admissions requirements/recommendations:** High school units required (recommended): English: (4); Mathematics: (3); Science: (3); Social studies: (1); History: (1). Tests: The college uses SAT or ACT scores in admissions decisions. Either SAT or ACT required. For admission to the fall 2007 entering class, the school will accept: ACT with writing. Campus visit: Recommended. Admissions interview: Recommended. Off-campus interview: May be arranged. **Factors that count in admissions decisions:** *Academic:* Secondary school record: Very important. Class rank: Important. Letters of recommendation: Very important. Standardized test scores: Important. Essay: Important. *Nonacademic:* Interview: Very important. Extracurricular activities: Important. Talent/ability: Not considered. Character/personal qualities: Important. Alumni/ae relationship: Considered. Geographical residence: Not considered. State residency: Not considered. Religious affiliation/commitment: Not considered. Minority status: Not considered. Volunteer work: Considered. Work experience: Considered. **Other schools with the greatest overlap in applicants:** St. Joseph's College; University of Maine–Farmington; University of Maine–Orono; University of New England; University of Southern Maine. **Admissions statistics for the fall 2005 entering class:** Total applicants: 677. Total accepted: 641. Freshmen enrolled: 327; 17% were from out of state. Overall acceptance rate: 95%. Non-early acceptance rate: 95%. **Size of waiting list:** 0 applicants; enrolled from waiting list: 0. **Credentials of fall 2005 freshmen:** 11% ranked in the top 10 percent of their high school class; 28% were in the top 25 percent, and 61% were in the top half. (Proportion submitting class standing: 94%.) **Average high school grade point average:** 3.2. **First-year students who submitted SAT scores:** 95%. Scores (25/75 percentile): Verbal: 410-490, Math: 400-510, Combined: 810-1000. **First-year students submitting ACT scores:** 9%. Scores (25/75 percentile): English: N/A, Math: N/A, Composite: 16-20.

ACADEMICS

Year founded: 1898. **Academic calendar:** Semester. **Degrees offered:** associate, bachelor's, master's, post-master's certificate, doctorate. **Most popular majors:** 62% business/commerce, 16% health professions and related clinical sciences, 6% computer and information sciences, 5% criminology, 3% legal assistant/paralegal. **Major fields of study:** biological and biomedical sciences; business, management, marketing, and related support services; computer and information sciences and support services; education; health professions and related clinical sciences; legal professions and studies; liberal arts and sciences studies, and humanities; psychology; security and protective services. **Areas of required coursework:** arts/fine arts, humanities, computer literacy, mathematics, English (including composition), philosophy, foreign languages, sciences (biological or physical), history, social science. **Pre-professional programs:** pre-dentistry, pre-medicine, pre-veterinary science, pre-pharmacy. **Special academic programs:** cooperative (work-study plan) program, double major, English as a Second Language (ESL), independent study, internships, liberal arts/career combination, student-designed major, teacher certificate program, weekend college. **Teacher certification offered in:** elementary, middle/junior high, secondary. **Cooperative education programs:** business, computer science, health professions. **Reserve Officers Training Corps (ROTC):** Army ROTC: Offered at cooperating institution (University of Maine Orono); Navy ROTC: Offered at cooperating institution (University of Maine Orono). **Faculty and instruction (2005-2006):** Total instructional faculty: 50 full-time, 4 part-time (48% men; 52% women; 7% minorities). Full-time faculty with Ph.D. or other terminal degree: 98%. Student/faculty ratio: 16/1. Classes of fewer than 20 students: 59%; of 20 to 49 students: 40%; of 50 or more students: 1%. **Advanced Placement and International Baccalaureate credit:** AP tests may be used for: Credit and/or placement. Scores accepted: 3, 4, 5. International Baccalaureate exams may be used for: Credit and/or placement. **Freshmen returning for sophomore year:** 66%. **Graduation rates:** Six-year: 47%. **Graduate study:** 2% of students pursue further study immediately upon graduation; 5% within one year; 10% within five years. Fields in which graduates pursue further study: Master of Business Administration (MBA), 17%.

COSTS AND FINANCIAL AID

Financial aid office: (207) 941-7156. **Expenses (2006-2007):** Tuition and fees 2006-2007: $11,770; room/board: $6,240. Estimated books and supplies: $930; transportation: $460; personal expenses: $1,030. **Financial aid:** Priority filing date for institution's financial aid form: April 15; deadline: April 15. In 2005-2006, 94% of undergraduates applied for financial aid. Of those, 69% were determined to have financial need; 18% had their need fully met. Average financial aid package (proportion receiving): $7,835 (65%). Average amount of gift aid, such as scholarships or grants (proportion receiving): $5,363 (61%). Average amount of self-help aid, such as work study or loans (proportion receiving): $3,771 (49%). Average need-based loan (excluding PLUS or other private loans): $3,252. Among students who received need-based aid, the average percentage of need met: 72%. Among students who received aid based on merit, the average award (and the proportion receiving): $6,286 (15%). The average athletic scholarship (and the proportion receiving): $0 (0%). Average amount of debt of borrowers graduating in 2005: $16,940. Proportion who borrowed: 90%.

CAMPUS LIFE AND EXTRACURRICULAR ACTIVITIES

Campus housing available (% using): coed dorms (100%). Students who live in college-owned, operated, or affiliated housing: 46%. **Student employment:** During the 2005-2006 academic year, 25% of undergraduates worked on campus. Average per-year earnings: $1,250. **Clubs and organizations:** Number of student organizations: 28. Activities include: choral groups, drama/theater, literary magazine, pep band, radio station, student government, student newspaper, yearbook. Number of fraternities: 3; sororities: 3. Proportion of men in fraternities: 3%; of women in sororities: 3%. Average proportion of students who stay on campus on weekends: 40%. **Sports program (2005-2006):** Member of NAIA. *Men's intercollegiate varsity sports:* baseball, basketball, cross-country, football, golf, soccer. *Women's intercollegiate varsity sports:* basketball, cross-country, field hockey, soccer, softball, volleyball.

SERVICES AND FACILITIES

Basic services: nonremedial tutoring, health service, health insurance. **Remedial assistance:** reading, math, writing, study skills. **Counseling services:** minority student, career, military, personal, academic, psychological, religious. **For learning-disabled students:** School does not offer a structured program with separate admission and additional fees. Services include: remedial math, reading machines, tape recorders, untimed tests, note-taking services, extended time for tests. **Library:** Number of titles: 37,916; number of current serial subscriptions: 490. **Information technology resources:** Students are not required to lease or own a computer. Number of campus computers available to all students: 110. School has a wireless network. Proportion of college-owned housing units wired for high-speed internet access: 100%. **Campus safety:** Security services offered: 24-hour foot and vehicle patrols, late-night transport/escort service, lighted pathways/sidewalks, controlled dormitory access (key, security card, etc.).

TRANSFER AND INTERNATIONAL STUDENTS
Transfer students: May apply for admission for the following academic terms: Fall, Winter, Spring, Summer. Applicants need a minimum number of credits to apply. For fall 2005: Transfer applications received: 188. Transfer applicants offered admission: 178. Transfer applicants enrolled: 117. **International students:** Number of foreign undergraduates: 32 (2% of student body). Minimum TOEFL score required: 500 (paper); 173 (computer).

Maine College of Art

- ■ **Address:** 97 Spring Street, Portland, ME 04101
- ■ **Website:** http://www.meca.edu
- ■ Private
- ■ **Enrollment:** 435 full-time; 23 part-time

KEY STATS
✔ **U.S News College Ranking:** Unranked Specialty School—Fine Arts
✔ **SAT Score (25th/75th percentile):** 930-1160
✔ **Tuition:** 2006-2007: $25,169

Selectivity: Less selective	**Room/board:** N/A
Acceptance rate: 69%	**Average debt:** N/A
Student/faculty ratio: 9/1	**Proportion who borrowed:** N/A

UNDERGRADUATE STUDENT BODY STATS
2005-2006 enrollment: 435 full-time; 23 part-time. Men: 34%; women: 66%. **Ethnic makeup:** African American: 1%; American-Indian: 1%; Hispanic: 3%; White: 94%; International: 1%.

ADMISSIONS FACTS AND FIGURES
Phone: (800) 639-4808. **Email:** admissions@meca.edu. **Website:** http://www.meca.edu. **Application deadlines for fall 2007:** Regular decision: Rolling. Early decision: Not offered. Early action: Not offered. Admission can be deferred. **Application fee:** $40. Common application is accepted. **Admissions requirements/recommendations:** High school units required (recommended): English: (4); Mathematics: (3); Science: (2); Foreign language: (2); Social studies: (2); Total units: (16). Tests: The college uses SAT or ACT scores in admissions decisions. Either SAT or ACT required. For admission to the fall 2007 entering class, the school will accept: ACT with writing, ACT without writing. Campus visit: Recommended. Admissions interview: Recommended. Off-campus interview: May be arranged. **Factors that count in admissions decisions:** *Academic:* Secondary school record: Important. Class rank: Considered. Letters of recommendation: Important. Standardized test scores: Considered. Essay: Important. *Nonacademic:* Interview: Important. Extracurricular activities: Considered. Talent/ability: Very important. Character/personal qualities: Important. Alumni/ae relationship: Considered. Geographical residence: Considered. State residency: Considered. Religious affiliation/commitment: Not considered. Minority status: Not considered. Volunteer work: Considered. Work experience: Considered. **Other schools with the greatest overlap in applicants:** Maryland Institute College of Art; Massachusetts College of Art; Montserrat College of Art; Rhode Island School of Design; University of Southern Maine. **Admissions statistics for the fall 2005 entering class:** Total applicants: 472. Total accepted: 324. Freshmen enrolled: 122; 66% were from out of state. Overall acceptance rate: 69%. **Credentials of fall 2005 freshmen:** 4% ranked in the top 10 percent of their high school class; 31% were in the top 25 percent, and 65% were in the top half. (Proportion submitting class standing: 59%.) **Average high school grade point average:** 3.2. **First-year students who submitted SAT scores:** 93%. Scores (25/75 percentile): Verbal: 480-590, Math: 450-570, Combined: 930-1160.

ACADEMICS
Year founded: 1882. **Academic calendar:** Semester. **Degrees offered:** bachelor's, post-bachelor's certificate, master's. **Most popular majors:** Information not available. **Major fields of study:** visual and performing arts. **Areas of**

required coursework: arts/fine arts, humanities, mathematics, English (including composition), philosophy, history, other. **Special academic programs (% participation):** cross-registration, double major, exchange student program (domestic), independent study, internships, student-designed major (3%), study abroad, teacher certificate program. **Teacher certification offered in:** elementary, middle/junior high, secondary. **Cooperative education programs:** art, education. **Faculty and instruction (2005-2006):** Total instructional faculty: 32 full-time, 43 part-time (52% men; 48% women; 3% minorities). Full-time faculty with Ph.D. or other terminal degree: 88%. Student/faculty ratio: 9/1. **Advanced Placement and International Baccalaureate credit:** International Baccalaureate exams may be used for: Credit only. **Freshmen returning for sophomore year:** 65%. **Graduation rates:** Six-year: 39%.

COSTS AND FINANCIAL AID
Financial aid office: (207) 775-3052. **Expenses (2006-2007):** Tuition and fees 2006-2007: $25,169; room/board: N/A. **Financial aid:** Priority filing date for institution's financial aid form: March 1; deadline: April 15. In 2005-2006, 89% of undergraduates applied for financial aid. Of those, 82% were determined to have financial need; 8% had their need fully met. Average financial aid package (proportion receiving): $13,102 (81%). Average amount of gift aid, such as scholarships or grants (proportion receiving): $9,426 (80%). Average amount of self-help aid, such as work study or loans (proportion receiving): $4,204 (72%). Average need-based loan (excluding PLUS or other private loans): $3,960. Among students who received need-based aid, the average percentage of need met: 55%. Among students who received aid based on merit, the average award (and the proportion receiving): $8,593 (18%). The average athletic scholarship (and the proportion receiving): $0 (0%).

CAMPUS LIFE AND EXTRACURRICULAR ACTIVITIES
Campus housing available (% using): coed dorms (100%). Students who live in college-owned, operated, or affiliated housing: 34%. **Student employment:** During the 2005-2006 academic year, 1% of undergraduates worked on campus. Average per-year earnings: $1,500. Activities include: student government. Number of fraternities: 0; sororities: 0. Average proportion of students who stay on campus on weekends: 90%.

SERVICES AND FACILITIES
Basic services: nonremedial tutoring, health service. **Counseling services:** career, personal, academic, psychological, birth control. **For learning-disabled students:** School does not offer a structured program with separate admission and additional fees. Total undergraduates in learning-disabled program or receiving services: 35. Services include: tape recorders, untimed tests, note-taking services, oral tests, learning center, readers, extended time for tests, early syllabus. **Library:** Number of titles: 25,000; number of current serial subscriptions: 100. **Information technology resources:** Students are not required to lease or own a computer. Number of campus computers available to all students: 77. School does not have a wireless network. Proportion of college-owned housing units wired for high-speed internet access: 0%. **Campus safety:** Security services offered: 24-hour emergency telephones, controlled dormitory access (key, security card, etc).

TRANSFER AND INTERNATIONAL STUDENTS
Transfer students: May apply for admission for the following academic terms: Fall, Spring. Applicants do not need a minimum number of credits to apply. For fall 2005: Transfer applications received: 87. Transfer applicants offered admission: 67. Transfer applicants enrolled: 38. **International students:** Number of foreign undergraduates: 4 (1% of student body). Number of countries represented: 1. Minimum TOEFL score required: 500 (paper); 173 (computer). Average TOEFL score: 539 (paper).

St. Joseph's College

- **Address:** 278 Whites Bridge Road, Standish, ME 04084
- **Website:** http://www.sjcme.edu
- **Private; Religious affiliation:** Roman Catholic
- **Enrollment:** 925 full-time; 30 part-time

KEY STATS

- ✔ **U.S News College Ranking:** third tier, Universities–Master's (North)
- ✔ **SAT Score (25th/75th percentile):** 920-1120
- ✔ **Tuition:** 2006-2007: $21,760

Selectivity: Selective	**Room/board:** $9,030
Acceptance rate: 79%	**Average debt:** $28,195
Student/faculty ratio: 15/1	**Proportion who borrowed:** 96%

UNDERGRADUATE STUDENT BODY STATS

2005-2006 enrollment: 925 full-time; 30 part-time. Men: 36%; women: 64%. **Ethnic makeup:** African American: 2%; Hispanic: 1%; White: 96%.

ADMISSIONS FACTS AND FIGURES

Phone: (207) 893-7746. **Email:** admission@sjcme.edu. **Website:** http://www.sjcme.edu. **Application deadlines for fall 2007:** Regular decision: August 1. Early decision: Not offered. Early action: Send application by: November 15; Decision sent by: December 15. Admission can be deferred. **Application fee:** $40. Common application is accepted. **To apply online, go to:** http://www.sjcme.edu/application. **Admissions requirements/recommendations:** High school units required (recommended): English: (4); Mathematics: (3); Science: (2); Foreign language: (2); Social studies: (1); History: (1); Total units: (16). Tests: The college uses SAT or ACT scores in admissions decisions. Either SAT or ACT required. For admission to the fall 2007 entering class, the school will accept: ACT with writing, ACT without writing. Campus visit: Recommended. Admissions interview: Recommended. Off-campus interview: May be arranged. **Factors that count in admissions decisions:** *Academic:* Secondary school record: Important. Class rank: Considered. Letters of recommendation: Important. Standardized test scores: Important. Essay: Important. *Nonacademic:* Interview: Considered. Extracurricular activities: Very important. Talent/ability: Important. Character/personal qualities: Important. Alumni/ae relationship: Not considered. Geographical residence: Not considered. State residency: Not considered. Religious affiliation/commitment: Not considered. Minority status: Not considered. Volunteer work: Very important. Work experience: Important. **Admissions statistics for the fall 2005 entering class:** Total applicants: 1,107. Total accepted: 874. Freshmen enrolled: 360; 46% were from out of state. Overall acceptance rate: 79%. Non-early acceptance rate: 79%. **Size of waiting list:** 50 applicants; enrolled from waiting list: 35. **Credentials of fall 2005 freshmen:** 19% ranked in the top 10 percent of their high school class; 45% were in the top 25 percent, and 75% were in the top half. (Proportion submitting class standing: 78%.) **Average high school grade point average:** 3.4. **First-year students who submitted SAT scores:** 69%. Scores (25/75 percentile): Verbal: 460-560, Math: 460-560, Combined: 920-1120.

ACADEMICS

Year founded: 1912. **Academic calendar:** Semester. **Degrees offered:** bachelor's. **Most popular majors:** 27% elementary education and teaching, 23% business administration and management, 15% nursing/registered nurse training (R.N., A.S.N., B.S.N., M.S.N.). **Major fields of study:** biological and biomedical sciences; business, management, marketing, and related support services; communication, journalism, and related programs; computer and information sciences and support services; education; English language and literature/letters; foreign languages, literatures, and linguistics; health professions and related clinical sciences; history; mathematics and statistics; natural resources and conservation; parks, recreation, leisure, and fitness studies; philosophy and religious studies; physical sciences; psychology; security and protective services; social sciences; theology and religious vocations. **Areas of required coursework:** humanities, mathematics, English (including composition), philosophy, foreign languages, sciences (biological or physical), history, other. **Pre-professional programs:** pre-medicine, pre-veterinary science, pre-optometry, pre-pharmacy, other. **Special academic programs:** cooperative (work-study plan) program, cross-registration, distance learning, double major, external degree program, honors program, independent study, internships, student-designed major, study abroad, teacher certificate program. **Teacher certification offered in:** elementary, middle/jun-

ior high, secondary. **Cooperative education programs:** education, health professions. **Reserve Officers Training Corps (ROTC):** Army ROTC: Offered at cooperating institution (University of New Hampshire). **Faculty and instruction (2005-2006):** Total instructional faculty: 64 full-time, 44 part-time (46% men; 54% women; 1% minorities). Full-time faculty with Ph.D. or other terminal degree: 84%. Student/faculty ratio: 15/1. Classes of fewer than 20 students: 53%; of 20 to 49 students: 46%; of 50 or more students: 0%. **Advanced Placement and International Baccalaureate credit:** AP tests may be used for: Credit only. Scores accepted: 3. International Baccalaureate exams may be used for: Credit only. **Freshmen returning for sophomore year:** 78%. **Graduation rates:** Four-year: 48%; five-year: 50%; six-year: 53%. **Graduate study:** 15% of students pursue further study immediately upon graduation; 13% within one year. Fields in which graduates pursue further study: Master of Business Administration (MBA), 3%; medicine, 2%; education, 3%; arts and sciences, 6%; veterinary medicine, 1%.

COSTS AND FINANCIAL AID

Financial aid office: (800) 752-1266. **Expenses (2006-2007):** Tuition and fees 2006-2007: $21,760; room/board: $9,030. Estimated books and supplies: $800; transportation: $420; personal expenses: $1,330. **Financial aid:** Priority filing date for institution's financial aid form: March 1. In 2005-2006, 90% of undergraduates applied for financial aid. Of those, 81% were determined to have financial need; 40% had their need fully met. Average financial aid package (proportion receiving): $16,472 (81%). Average amount of gift aid, such as scholarships or grants (proportion receiving): $10,328 (80%). Average amount of self-help aid, such as work study or loans (proportion receiving): $7,172 (70%). Average need-based loan (excluding PLUS or other private loans): $6,098. Among students who received need-based aid, the average percentage of need met: 83%. Among students who received aid based on merit, the average award (and the proportion receiving): $12,702 (18%). The average athletic scholarship (and the proportion receiving): $0 (0%). Average amount of debt of borrowers graduating in 2005: $28,195. Proportion who borrowed: 96%.

CAMPUS LIFE AND EXTRACURRICULAR ACTIVITIES

Campus housing available: coed dorms, women's dorms, men's dorms, other housing options. Students who live in college-owned, operated, or affiliated housing: 78%. **Student employment:** During the 2005-2006 academic year, 8% of undergraduates worked on campus. Average per-year earnings: $1,275. **Clubs and organizations:** Number of student organizations: 28. Activities include: choral groups, concert band, dance, drama/theater, literary magazine, music ensembles, musical theater, pep band, radio station, student government, student newspaper, yearbook. Number of fraternities: 0; sororities: 0. Average proportion of students who stay on campus on weekends: 65%. **Sports program (2005-2006):** Member of NCAA III. *Men's intercollegiate varsity sports:* baseball, basketball, cross-country, golf, soccer. *Women's intercollegiate varsity sports:* basketball, cross-country, field hockey, soccer, softball, volleyball.

SERVICES AND FACILITIES

Basic services: health service, health insurance. **Remedial assistance:** study skills, other. **Counseling services:** career, military, personal, veteran student, academic, psychological, religious, other. **For learning-disabled students:** School does not offer a structured program with separate admission and additional fees. Total undergraduates in learning-disabled program or receiving services: 37. Services include: reading machines, tape recorders, note-taking services, oral tests, readers, extended time for tests, tutors, other. **Library:** Number of titles: 98,626; number of current serial subscriptions: 11,461. **Information technology resources:** Students are not required to lease or own a computer. Number of campus computers available to all students: 102. School has a wireless network. Approximate number of users that can be accommodated: 300. Proportion of college-owned housing units wired for high-speed internet access: 100%. **Campus safety:** Security services offered: 24-hour foot and vehicle patrols, late-night transport/escort service, 24-hour emergency telephones, lighted pathways/sidewalks, controlled dormitory access (key, security card, etc).

TRANSFER AND INTERNATIONAL STUDENTS

Transfer students: May apply for admission for the following academic terms: Fall, Spring. Applicants do not need a minimum number of credits to apply. For fall 2005: Transfer applications received: 63. Transfer applicants offered admission: 35. Transfer applicants enrolled: 17. **International students:** Number of foreign undergraduates: 0. Number of countries represented: 0. Average TOEFL score: 500 (paper).

Thomas College

■ **Address:** 180 W. River Road, Waterville, ME 04901
■ **Website:** http://www.thomas.edu
■ **Private**
■ **Enrollment:** 598 full-time; 133 part-time

KEY STATS
✔ **U.S News College Ranking:** Unranked Specialty School–Business
✔ **SAT Score (25th/75th percentile):** 860-1060
✔ **Tuition:** 2006-2007: $17,730

Selectivity: Less selective	**Room/board:** $7,070
Acceptance rate: 73%	**Average debt:** $19,125
Student/faculty ratio: 17/1	**Proportion who borrowed:** 78%

UNDERGRADUATE STUDENT BODY STATS

2005-2006 enrollment: 598 full-time; 133 part-time. Men: 49%; women: 51%. **Ethnic makeup:** African American: 1%; American-Indian: 1%; Asian American: 1%; Hispanic: 1%; White: 97%.

ADMISSIONS FACTS AND FIGURES

Phone: (800) 339-7001. **Email:** admiss@thomas.edu. **Website:** http://www.thomas.edu. **Application deadlines for fall 2007:** Regular decision: Rolling. Early decision: Not offered. Early action: Send application by: December 15; Decision sent by: December 31. Admission can be deferred. **Application fee:** $50. Common application is accepted. **Admissions requirements/recommendations:** High school units required (recommended): English: (4); Mathematics: (3); Science: (3); Foreign language: (2); Social studies: (2); History: (0); Academic electives: (2); Total units: 16. Tests: The college uses SAT or ACT scores in admissions decisions. Neither SAT nor ACT required. For admission to the fall 2007 entering class, the school will accept: ACT with writing, ACT without writing. Campus visit: Recommended. Admissions interview: Recommended. Off-campus interview: Not available. **Factors that count in admissions decisions:** *Academic:* Secondary school record: Very important. Class rank: Important. Letters of recommendation: Important. Standardized test scores: Important. Essay: Important. *Nonacademic:* Interview: Considered. Extracurricular activities: Considered. Talent/ability: Considered. Character/personal qualities: Considered. Alumni/ae relationship: Considered. Geographical residence: Not considered. State residency: Not considered. Religious affiliation/commitment: Not considered. Minority status: Not considered. Volunteer work: Considered. Work experience: Considered. **Other schools with the greatest overlap in applicants:** Bentley College; Husson College; St. Joseph's College; University of Maine–Orono; University of Southern Maine. **Admissions statistics for the fall 2005 entering class:** Total applicants: 628. Total accepted: 458. Freshmen enrolled: 221; 24% were from out of state. Overall acceptance rate: 73%. Non-early acceptance rate: 73%. **Credentials of fall 2005 freshmen:** 12% ranked in the top 10 percent of their high school class; 30% were in the top 25 percent, and 60% were in the top half. (Proportion submitting class standing: 93%.) **Average high school grade point average:** 2.8. **First-year students who submitted SAT scores:** 90%. Scores (25/75 percentile): Verbal: 430-520, Math: 430-540, Combined: 860-1060. **First-year students submitting ACT scores:** 4%. Scores (25/75 percentile): English: N/A, Math: N/A, Composite: 17-N/A.

ACADEMICS

Year founded: 1894. **Academic calendar:** Semester. **Degrees offered:** associate, bachelor's, master's. **Most popular majors:** 62% accounting and business/management, 12% computer and information sciences, 8% criminal justice and corrections, 8% parks, recreation, and leisure facilities management, 7% elementary education and teaching. **Major fields of study:** business, management, marketing, and related support services; communication, journalism, and related programs; computer and information sciences and support services; education; parks, recreation, leisure, and fitness studies; psychology; security and protective services; social sciences. **Areas of required coursework:** humanities, computer literacy, mathematics, English (including composition), philosophy, history, social science. **Special academic programs (% participation):** cross-registration (1%), internships (20%), study abroad (1%), teacher certificate program (1%). **Teacher certification offered in:** elementary. **Faculty and instruction (2005-2006):** Total instructional faculty: 23 full-time, 55 part-time (65% men; 35% women). Full-time faculty with Ph.D. or other terminal degree: 52%. Student/faculty ratio: 17/1. Classes of fewer than 20 students: 45%; of 20 to 49 students:

55%. **Freshmen returning for sophomore year:** 65%. **Graduation rates:** Four-year: 40%; five-year: 44%; six-year: 53%. **Graduate study:** 11% of students pursue further study immediately upon graduation; 8% within five years. Fields in which graduates pursue further study: Master of Business Administration (MBA), 30%; law, 22%.

COSTS AND FINANCIAL AID

Financial aid office: (207) 859-1112. **Expenses (2006-2007):** Tuition and fees 2006-2007: $17,730; room/board: $7,070. Estimated books and supplies: $800; transportation: $1,000; personal expenses: $1,000. **Financial aid:** Priority filing date for institution's financial aid form: February 15. In 2005-2006, 97% of undergraduates applied for financial aid. Of those, 90% were determined to have financial need; 19% had their need fully met. Average financial aid package (proportion receiving): $15,198 (90%). Average amount of gift aid, such as scholarships or grants (proportion receiving): $9,382 (90%). Average amount of self-help aid, such as work study or loans (proportion receiving): $4,680 (86%). Average need-based loan (excluding PLUS or other private loans): $4,274. Among students who received need-based aid, the average percentage of need met: 85%. Among students who received aid based on merit, the average award (and the proportion receiving): $4,619 (14%). The average athletic scholarship (and the proportion receiving): $0 (0%). Average amount of debt of borrowers graduating in 2005: $19,125. Proportion who borrowed: 78%.

CAMPUS LIFE AND EXTRACURRICULAR ACTIVITIES

Campus housing available (% using): coed dorms (100%). Students who live in college-owned, operated, or affiliated housing: 65%. **Student employment:** During the 2005-2006 academic year, 3% of undergraduates worked on campus. Average per-year earnings: $1,200. Activities include: choral groups, dance, drama/theater, student government, student newspaper, yearbook. Number of fraternities: 1; sororities: 2. Proportion of men in fraternities: 2%; of women in sororities: 3%. Average proportion of students who stay on campus on weekends: 30%. **Sports program (2005-2006):** Member of NCAA III. *Men's intercollegiate varsity sports:* baseball, basketball, golf, lacrosse, soccer, tennis. *Women's intercollegiate varsity sports:* basketball, field hockey, lacrosse, soccer, softball, volleyball.

SERVICES AND FACILITIES

Basic services: nonremedial tutoring, placement service, health service, health insurance. **Remedial assistance:** reading, math, writing, study skills. **Counseling services:** career, personal, veteran student, academic, psychological. **For learning-disabled students:** School does not offer a structured program with separate admission and additional fees. Total undergraduates in learning-disabled program or receiving services: 16. Services include: tape recorders, note-taking services, oral tests, learning center, extended time for tests, tutors, priority registration, priority seating, texts on tape. **Library:** Number of titles: 21,250; number of current serial subscriptions: 24. **Information technology resources:** Students are not required to lease or own a computer. Number of campus computers available to all students: 138. School has a wireless network. Approximate number of users that can be accommodated: 400. Proportion of college-owned housing units wired for high-speed internet access: 100%. **Campus safety:** Security services offered: 24-hour foot and vehicle patrols, 24-hour emergency telephones, lighted pathways/sidewalks, controlled dormitory access (key, security card, etc).

TRANSFER AND INTERNATIONAL STUDENTS

Transfer students: May apply for admission for the following academic terms: Fall, Spring. Applicants do not need a minimum number of credits to apply. For fall 2005: Transfer applications received: 84. Transfer applicants offered admission: 50. Transfer applicants enrolled: 35. **International students:** Minimum TOEFL score required: 530 (paper); 197 (computer).

Unity College

- **Address:** 90 Quaker Hill Road, Unity, ME 04988
- **Website:** http://www.unity.edu
- **Private**
- **Enrollment:** 517 full-time; 5 part-time

KEY STATS

✔ **U.S News College Ranking:** third tier, Comp. Coll.–Bachelor's (North)
✔ **SAT Score (25th/75th percentile):** 980-1100
✔ **Tuition:** 2006-2007: $18,180

Selectivity: Less selective	**Room/board:** $6,960
Acceptance rate: 77%	**Average debt:** N/A
Student/faculty ratio: 15/1	**Proportion who borrowed:** N/A

UNDERGRADUATE STUDENT BODY STATS

2005-2006 enrollment: 517 full-time; 5 part-time. Men: 62%; women: 38%. **Ethnic makeup:** Hispanic: 1%; White: 98%.

ADMISSIONS FACTS AND FIGURES

Phone: (207) 948-3131. **Email:** admissions@unity.edu. **Website:** http://www.unity.edu. **Application deadlines for fall 2007:** Regular decision: August 1. Early decision: Not offered. Early action: Not offered. Admission can be deferred. **Application fee:** $25. Common application is accepted. **To apply online, go to:** http://www.unity.edu/ADMISSNS/adm_welcome0504.asp. **Admissions requirements/recommendations:** High school units required (recommended): English: 4 (4); Mathematics: 3 (4); Science: 2 (3); Social studies: 2 (2); History: 2 (2); Total units: 18 (19). Tests: The college uses SAT or ACT scores in admissions decisions. Neither SAT nor ACT required. For admission to the fall 2007 entering class, the school will accept: ACT with writing, ACT without writing. Campus visit: Recommended. Admissions interview: Recommended. Off-campus interview: May be arranged. **Factors that count in admissions decisions:** *Academic:* Secondary school record: Very important. Class rank: Considered. Letters of recommendation: Important. Standardized test scores: Considered. Essay: Important. *Nonacademic:* Interview: Important. Extracurricular activities: Important. Talent/ability: Considered. Character/personal qualities: Important. Alumni/ae relationship: Not considered. Geographical residence: Not considered. State residency: Not considered. Religious affiliation/commitment: Not considered. Minority status: Not considered. Volunteer work: Considered. Work experience: Considered. **Other schools with the greatest overlap in applicants:** Green Mountain College; Paul Smith's College; University of Maine–Machias; University of Maine–Orono; University of New Hampshire. **Admissions statistics for the fall 2005 entering class:** Total applicants: 459. Total accepted: 353. Freshmen enrolled: 153; 69% were from out of state. Overall acceptance rate: 77%. **Size of waiting list:** 0 applicants; enrolled from waiting list: 0. **Credentials of fall 2005 freshmen:** 6% ranked in the top 10 percent of their high school class; 29% were in the top 25 percent, and 64% were in the top half. (Proportion submitting class standing: 82%.) **Average high school grade point average:** 3.1. **First-year students who submitted SAT scores:** 77%. Scores (25/75 percentile): Verbal: 490-560, Math: 490-540, Combined: 980-1100. **First-year students submitting ACT scores:** 2%. Scores (25/75 percentile): English: N/A, Math: N/A, Composite: N/A.

ACADEMICS

Year founded: 1965. **Academic calendar:** Semester. **Degrees offered:** associate, bachelor's. **Most popular majors:** 25% natural resources management and policy, 11% wildlife biology, 9% aquaculture, 9% forestry. **Major fields of study:** agriculture, agriculture operations, and related sciences; biological and biomedical sciences; education; English language and literature/letters; health professions and related clinical sciences; liberal arts and sciences studies, and humanities; natural resources and conservation; parks, recreation, leisure, and fitness studies. **Areas of required coursework:** arts/fine arts, humanities, computer literacy, mathematics, English (including composition), sciences (biological or physical), social science. **Special academic programs (% participation):** cross-registration (1%), double major (5%), dual enrollment (1%), independent study (40%), internships (80%), student-designed major (5%), teacher certificate program (2%). **Faculty and instruction (2005-2006):** Total instructional faculty: 28 full-time, 13 part-time (68% men; 32% women; 5% minorities). Full-time faculty with Ph.D. or other terminal degree: 68%. Student/faculty ratio: 15/1. Classes of fewer than 20 students: 53%; of 20 to 49 students: 47%. **Advanced Placement and International Baccalaureate credit:** AP tests may be used for: Credit and/or placement. Scores accepted: 3, 4, 5. International Baccalaureate exams may be used for: Credit and/or placement. **Freshmen returning for sophomore year:** 63%. **Graduation rates:** Five-year: 43%; six-year: 47%. **Graduate study:** 17% of students pursue further study within one year.

COSTS AND FINANCIAL AID

Financial aid office: (207) 948-3131. **Expenses (2006-2007):** Tuition and fees 2006-2007: $18,180; room/board: $6,960. Estimated books and supplies: $450; transportation: $400; personal expenses: $550. **Financial aid:** Priority filing date for institution's financial aid form: April 15. In 2005-2006, 89% of undergraduates applied for financial aid. Of those, 79% were determined to have financial need; 27% had their need fully met. Average financial aid package (proportion receiving): $13,589 (79%). Average amount of gift aid, such as scholarships or grants (proportion receiving): $7,300 (78%). Average amount of self-help aid, such as work study or loans (proportion receiving): $6,615 (75%). Average need-based loan (excluding PLUS or other private loans): $5,751. Among students who received need-based aid, the average percentage of need met: 76%. Among students who received aid based on merit, the average award (and the proportion receiving): $8,753 (17%). The average athletic scholarship (and the proportion receiving): $0 (0%).

CAMPUS LIFE AND EXTRACURRICULAR ACTIVITIES

Campus housing available (% using): coed dorms (92%), special housing for disabled students (1%), cooperative housing (7%). Students who live in college-owned, operated, or affiliated housing: 65%. **Student employment:** During the 2005-2006 academic year, 5% of undergraduates worked on campus. Average per-year earnings: $4,882. **Clubs and organizations:** Number of student organizations: 35. Activities include: dance, drama/theater, literary magazine, musical theater, student government, student newspaper. Number of fraternities: 0; sororities: 0. Average proportion of students who stay on campus on weekends: 53%.

SERVICES AND FACILITIES

Basic services: nonremedial tutoring, placement service, health service, health insurance. **Remedial assistance:** reading, math, writing, study skills. **Counseling services:** career, personal, veteran student, academic, older student, psychological, birth control. **For learning-disabled students:** School does not offer a structured program with separate admission and additional fees. Total undergraduates in learning-disabled program or receiving services: 24. Services include: remedial math, remedial English, note-taking services, learning center, readers, extended time for tests, tutors, proofreading services, texts on tape, other testing accomodations. **Library:** Number of titles: 57,174; number of current serial subscriptions: 432. **Information technology resources:** Students are not required to lease or own a computer. Number of campus computers available to all students: 80. School has a wireless network. Proportion of college-owned housing units wired for high-speed internet access: 100%. **Campus safety:** Security services offered: 24-hour foot and vehicle patrols, late-night transport/escort service, 24-hour emergency telephones, controlled dormitory access (key, security card, etc).

TRANSFER AND INTERNATIONAL STUDENTS

Transfer students: May apply for admission for the following academic terms: Fall, Spring. Applicants need a minimum number of credits to apply. For fall 2005: Transfer applications received: 79. Transfer applicants offered admission: 52. Transfer applicants enrolled: 29. **International students:** Minimum TOEFL score required: 500 (paper); 170 (computer).

University of Maine–Augusta

- **Address:** 46 University Drive, Augusta, ME 04330
- **Website:** http://www.uma.edu
- **Public**
- **Enrollment:** 1,544 full-time; 3,950 part-time

KEY STATS
- ✔ **U.S News College Ranking:** fourth tier, Comp. Coll.–Bachelor's (North)
- ✔ **SAT Score:** 914
- ✔ **Tuition:** 2006-2007: $4,680 in state, $10,478 out of state

Selectivity: Less selective	**Room/board:** N/A
Acceptance rate: 94%	**Average debt:** $12,861
Student/faculty ratio: 16/1	**Proportion who borrowed:** 62%

UNDERGRADUATE STUDENT BODY STATS
2005-2006 enrollment: 1,544 full-time; 3,950 part-time. Men: 26%; women: 74%. **Ethnic makeup:** African American: 1%; American-Indian: 3%; White: 95%.

ADMISSIONS FACTS AND FIGURES
Phone: (207) 621-3185. **Email:** umaar@maine.edu. **Website:** http://www.uma.edu. **Application deadlines for fall 2007:** Regular decision: August 30. Early decision: Not offered. Early action: Not offered. Admission can be deferred. **Application fee:** $40. Common application is accepted. **To apply online, go to:** http://apply.maine.edu. **Admissions requirements/recommendations:** High school units required (recommended): English: (4); Mathematics: (2); Science: (2); Social studies: (2); History: (2). Tests: The college does not use SAT or ACT scores in admissions decisions. Neither SAT nor ACT required. Campus visit: Recommended. Admissions interview: Neither required nor recommended. Off-campus interview: May be arranged. **Factors that count in admissions decisions:** *Academic:* Secondary school record: Important. Class rank: Important. Letters of recommendation: Considered. Standardized test scores: Considered. Essay: Considered. *Nonacademic:* Interview: Considered. Extracurricular activities: Not considered. Talent/ability: Considered. Character/personal qualities: Considered. Alumni/ae relationship: Not considered. Geographical residence: Not considered. State residency: Not considered. Religious affiliation/commitment: Not considered. Minority status: Not considered. Volunteer work: Considered. Work experience: Considered. **Other schools with the greatest overlap in applicants:** Thomas College; University of Maine–Farmington; University of Maine–Orono; University of Southern Maine. **Admissions statistics for the fall 2005 entering class:** Total applicants: 637. Total accepted: 598. Freshmen enrolled: 596; Overall acceptance rate: 94%.

ACADEMICS
Year founded: 1965. **Academic calendar:** Semester. **Degrees offered:** certificate, associate, transfer-associate, terminal-associate, bachelor's, post-bachelor's certificate. **Most popular majors:** 31% health professions and related clinical sciences, 18% business/commerce, 13% liberal arts and sciences studies, and humanities, 8% criminal justice and corrections, 6% library science/librarianship. **Major fields of study:** biological and biomedical sciences; business, management, marketing, and related support services; computer and information sciences and support services; English language and literature/letters; health professions and related clinical sciences; library science; public administration and social service professions; security and protective services; social sciences; visual and performing arts. **Areas of required coursework:** arts/fine arts, humanities, computer literacy, mathematics, English (including composition), sciences (biological or physical), history, social science. **Special academic programs:** cross-registration, distance learning, dual enrollment, honors program, independent study, internships, liberal arts/career combination, student-designed major, study abroad. **Reserve Officers Training Corps (ROTC):** Army ROTC: Offered at cooperating institution (University of Maine); Navy ROTC: Offered at cooperating institution (University of Maine); Air Force ROTC: Offered at cooperating institution (University of Maine). **Faculty and instruction (2005-2006):** Total instructional faculty: 95 full-time, 229 part-time (51% men; 49% women). Full-time faculty with Ph.D. or other terminal degree: 38%. Student/faculty ratio: 16/1. Classes of fewer than 20 students: 69%; of 20 to 49 students: 29%; of 50 or more students: 1%. **Advanced Placement and International Baccalaureate credit:** AP tests may be used for: Credit and/or placement. Scores accepted: 3. International Baccalaureate exams may be used for: Credit and/or placement. **Freshmen returning for sophomore year:** 58%. **Graduation rates:** Four-year: 5%; five-year: 13%; six-year: 25%.

COSTS AND FINANCIAL AID
Financial aid office: (207) 621-3163. **Expenses (2006-2007):** Tuition and fees 2006-2007: $4,680 in state, $10,478 out of state; room/board: N/A. **Financial aid:** Priority filing date for institution's financial aid form: March 1. In 2005-2006, 92% of undergraduates applied for financial aid. Of those, 84% were determined to have financial need; 22% had their need fully met. Average financial aid package (proportion receiving): $7,929 (77%). Average amount of gift aid, such as scholarships or grants (proportion receiving): $4,742 (70%). Average amount of self-help aid, such as work study or loans (proportion receiving): $3,898 (64%). Average need-based loan (excluding PLUS or other private loans): $3,747. Among students who received need-based aid, the average percentage of need met: 72%. Among students who received aid based on merit, the average award (and the proportion receiving): $4,416 (8%). The average athletic scholarship (and the proportion receiving): $1,346 (0%). Average amount of debt of borrowers graduating in 2005: $12,861. Proportion who borrowed: 62%.

CAMPUS LIFE AND EXTRACURRICULAR ACTIVITIES
Students who live in college-owned, operated, or affiliated housing: 0%. **Student employment:** During the 2005-2006 academic year, 11% of undergraduates worked on campus. Average per-year earnings: $2,400. **Clubs and organizations:** Number of student organizations: 7. Activities include: concert band, jazz band, music ensembles, pep band, student government. Number of fraternities: 0; sororities: 0. **Sports program (2005-2006):** *Men's intercollegiate varsity sports:* basketball. *Women's intercollegiate varsity sports:* basketball, soccer.

SERVICES AND FACILITIES
Basic services: other. **Counseling services:** minority student, career, military, personal, veteran student, psychological, birth control, other. **For learning-disabled students:** School does not offer a structured program with separate admission and additional fees. Total undergraduates in learning-disabled program or receiving services: 42. Services include: remedial math, remedial English, remedial reading, extended time for tests, tutors. **Library:** Number of titles: 94,317; number of current serial subscriptions: 568. **Information technology resources:** Students are not required to lease or own a computer. Number of campus computers available to all students: 178. School has a wireless network. Approximate number of users that can be accommodated: 100. **Campus safety:** Security services offered: late-night transport/escort service, lighted pathways/sidewalks, student patrols.

TRANSFER AND INTERNATIONAL STUDENTS
Transfer students: May apply for admission for the following academic terms: Fall, Spring, Summer. Applicants do not need a minimum number of credits to apply. **International students:** Number of foreign undergraduates: 15. Minimum TOEFL score required: 500 (paper); 173 (computer). Average TOEFL score: 500 (paper).

University of Maine–Farmington

- **Address:** 111 South Street, Farmington, ME 04938
- **Website:** http://www.umf.maine.edu
- **Public**
- **Enrollment:** 2,123 full-time; 329 part-time

KEY STATS
- ✔ **U.S News College Ranking:** 19, Comp. Coll.–Bachelor's (North)
- ✔ **SAT Score (25th/75th percentile):** 900-1130
- ✔ **Tuition:** 2006-2007: $6,044 in state, $13,274 out of state

Selectivity: Selective	**Room/board:** $6,164
Acceptance rate: 74%	**Average debt:** $16,289
Student/faculty ratio: 16/1	**Proportion who borrowed:** 80%

UNDERGRADUATE STUDENT BODY STATS
2005-2006 enrollment: 2,123 full-time; 329 part-time. Men: 34%; women: 66%. **Ethnic makeup:** American-Indian: 1%; Asian American: 1%; Hispanic: 1%; White: 97%.

ADMISSIONS FACTS AND FIGURES
Phone: (207) 778-7050. **Email:** umfadmit@maine.edu. **Website:** http://www.umf.maine.edu. **Application deadlines for fall 2007:** Regular decision: Rolling. Early decision: Not offered. Early action: Send application

by: December 15; Decision sent by: N/A. Admission can be deferred. **Application fee:** $40. Common application is accepted. **To apply online, go to:** http://apply.maine.edu. **Admissions requirements/recommendations:** High school units required (recommended): English: 4; Mathematics: 3 (4); Science: 2 (3); Foreign language: 2 (3); Social studies: 2 (3); Academic electives: (3); Total units: 15 (19). Tests: The college does not use SAT or ACT scores in admissions decisions. Neither SAT nor ACT required. Campus visit: Recommended. Admissions interview: Recommended. Off-campus interview: May be arranged. **Factors that count in admissions decisions:** *Academic:* Secondary school record: Very important. Class rank: Very important. Letters of recommendation: Important. Standardized test scores: Not considered. Essay: Important. *Nonacademic:* Interview: Important. Extracurricular activities: Important. Talent/ability: Important. Character/personal qualities: Important. Alumni/ae relationship: Considered. Geographical residence: Considered. State residency: Not considered. Religious affiliation/commitment: Not considered. Minority status: Considered. Volunteer work: Important. Work experience: Important. **Other schools with the greatest overlap in applicants:** St. Joseph's College; University of Maine–Orono; University of New England; University of New Hampshire; University of Southern Maine. **Admissions statistics for the fall 2005 entering class:** Total applicants: 1,602. Total accepted: 1,190. Freshmen enrolled: 575; 23% were from out of state. Overall acceptance rate: 74%. Non-early acceptance rate: 74%. **Credentials of fall 2005 freshmen:** 12% ranked in the top 10 percent of their high school class; 38% were in the top 25 percent, and 80% were in the top half. (Proportion submitting class standing: 87%.) **First-year students who submitted SAT scores:** 60%. Scores (25/75 percentile): Verbal: 450-580, Math: 450-550, Combined: 900-1130.

ACADEMICS

Year founded: 1864. **Academic calendar:** Semester. **Degrees offered:** certificate, bachelor's. **Most popular majors:** 20% elementary education and teaching, 9% psychology, 8% theology and religious vocations, 6% early childhood education and teaching, 5% English language and literature. **Major fields of study:** area, ethnic, cultural, and gender studies; biological and biomedical sciences; business, management, marketing, and related support services; computer and information sciences and support services; education; English language and literature/letters; health professions and related clinical sciences; history; liberal arts and sciences studies, and humanities; mathematics and statistics; multi/interdisciplinary studies; natural resources and conservation; philosophy and religious studies; physical sciences; psychology; social sciences; visual and performing arts. **Areas of required coursework:** arts/fine arts, humanities, mathematics, English (including composition), sciences (biological or physical), social science, other. **Special academic programs (% participation):** cross-registration (5%), double major (3%), dual enrollment (1%), exchange student program (domestic) (4%), honors program (4%), independent study (2%), internships (14%), student-designed major (1%), study abroad (8%), teacher certificate program (48%). **Teacher certification offered in:** early childhood, special education, elementary, middle/junior high, secondary. **Faculty and instruction (2005-2006):** Total instructional faculty: 118 full-time, 57 part-time (49% men; 51% women; 3% minorities). Full-time faculty with Ph.D. or other terminal degree: 92%. Student/faculty ratio: 16/1. Classes of fewer than 20 students: 65%; of 20 to 49 students: 33%; of 50 or more students: 2%. **Advanced Placement and International Baccalaureate credit:** AP tests may be used for: Credit only. Scores accepted: 3, 4, 5. International Baccalaureate exams may be used for: Credit only. **Freshmen returning for sophomore year:** 72%. **Graduation rates:** Four-year: 42%; five-year: 61%; six-year: 58%. **Graduate study:** 15% of students pursue further study immediately upon graduation; 18% within one year; 25% within five years. Fields in which graduates pursue further study: Master of Business Administration (MBA), 6%; law, 3%; medicine, 1%; dentistry, 1%; engineering, 1%; theology (or the seminary), 2%; education, 65%; arts and sciences, 20%; veterinary medicine, 1%.

COSTS AND FINANCIAL AID

Financial aid office: (207) 778-7100. **Expenses (2006-2007):** Tuition and fees 2006-2007: $6,044 in state, $13,274 out of state; room/board: $6,164. Estimated books and supplies: $660; transportation: $545; personal expenses: $1,846. **Financial aid:** Priority filing date for institution's financial aid form: March 1. In 2005-2006, 84% of undergraduates applied for financial aid. Of those, 67% were determined to have financial need; 22% had their need fully met. Average financial aid package (proportion receiving): $8,156 (67%). Average amount of gift aid, such as scholarships or grants (proportion receiving): $4,007 (54%). Average amount of self-help aid, such as work study or loans (proportion receiving): $4,355 (59%). Average need-based loan (excluding PLUS or other private loans): $3,671. Among students who received need-based aid, the average percentage of need met: 79%. Among students who received aid based on merit, the average award (and the proportion receiving): $1,647 (4%). The average athletic scholarship (and the proportion receiving): $0 (0%). Average amount of debt of borrowers graduating in 2005: $16,289. Proportion who borrowed: 80%.

CAMPUS LIFE AND EXTRACURRICULAR ACTIVITIES

Campus housing available (% using): coed dorms (84%), women's dorms (14%), special housing for international students (1%). Students who live in college-owned, operated, or affiliated housing: 45%. **Student employment:** During the 2005-2006 academic year, 48% of undergraduates worked on campus. Average per-year earnings: $1,600. **Clubs and organizations:** Number of student organizations: 58. Activities include: choral groups, dance, drama/theater, literary magazine, music ensembles, radio station, student government, student newspaper, student film society, yearbook. Number of fraternities: 0; sororities: 0. Average proportion of students who stay on campus on weekends: 50%. **Sports program (2005-2006):** Member of NAIA. *Men's intercollegiate varsity sports:* baseball, basketball, cross-country, golf, soccer. *Women's intercollegiate varsity sports:* basketball, cross-country, field hockey, soccer, softball, volleyball.

SERVICES AND FACILITIES

Basic services: nonremedial tutoring, placement service, health service, health insurance. **Remedial assistance:** reading, math, writing, study skills. **Counseling services:** minority student, career, military, personal, veteran student, academic, older student, psychological, birth control. **For learning-disabled students:** School does not offer a structured program with separate admission and additional fees. Total undergraduates in learning-disabled program or receiving services: 37. Services include: remedial math, remedial English, tape recorders, note-taking services, learning center, extended time for tests, tutors, priority seating, texts on tape, other testing accomodations, other. **Library:** Number of titles: 100,464; number of current serial subscriptions: 610. **Information technology resources:** Students are not required to lease or own a computer. Number of campus computers available to all students: 180. School has a wireless network. Approximate number of users that can be accommodated: 3,000. Proportion of college-owned housing units wired for high-speed internet access: 100%. **Campus safety:** Security services offered: 24-hour foot and vehicle patrols, late-night transport/escort service, 24-hour emergency telephones, lighted pathways/sidewalks, controlled dormitory access (key, security card, etc).

TRANSFER AND INTERNATIONAL STUDENTS

Transfer students: May apply for admission for the following academic terms: Fall, Spring. Applicants do not need a minimum number of credits to apply. For fall 2005: Transfer applications received: 270. Transfer applicants offered admission: 161. Transfer applicants enrolled: 116. **International students:** Number of foreign undergraduates: 10. Minimum TOEFL score required: 550 (paper); 213 (computer).

University of Maine–Fort Kent

- **Address:** 23 University Drive, Fort Kent, ME 04743
- **Website:** http://www.umfk.maine.edu
- **Public**
- **Enrollment:** 762 full-time; 431 part-time

KEY STATS

✔ **U.S News College Ranking:** fourth tier, Comp. Coll.–Bachelor's (North)
✔ **SAT or ACT Score (25th/75th percentile):** N/A
✔ **Tuition:** 2006-2007: $5,213 in state, $11,783 out of state

Selectivity: Less selective	**Room/board:** $6,282
Acceptance rate: 81%	**Average debt:** N/A
Student/faculty ratio: N/A	**Proportion who borrowed:** N/A

UNDERGRADUATE STUDENT BODY STATS

2005-2006 enrollment: 762 full-time; 431 part-time. Men: 34%; women: 66%. **Ethnic makeup:** African American: 1%; American-Indian: 2%; Hispanic: 1%; White: 71%; International: 26%.

ADMISSIONS FACTS AND FIGURES

Phone: (207) 834-7600. **Email:** umfkadm@maine.edu. **Website:** http://www.umfk.maine.edu. **Application deadlines for fall 2007:** Regular decision: Rolling. Early decision: Not offered. Early action: Not offered. Admission can be deferred. **Application fee:** $40. Common application is accepted. **To apply online, go to:** http://www.umfk.maine.edu/admissions/apply.htm. **Admissions requirements/recommendations:** High school units required (recommended): English: 4; Mathematics: 2; Science: 2; Foreign language: (2); Social studies: 2; Total units: 16. Tests: The college uses SAT or ACT scores in admissions decisions. Neither SAT nor ACT required. Campus visit: Recommended. Admissions interview: Recommended. Off-campus interview: May be arranged. **Factors that count in admissions decisions:** *Academic:* Secondary school record: Very important. Class rank: Very important. Letters of recommendation: Important. Standardized test scores: Important. Essay: Important. *Nonacademic:* Interview: Important. Extracurricular activities: Considered. Talent/ability: Considered. Character/personal qualities: Considered. Alumni/ae relationship: Not considered. Geographical residence: Not considered. State residency: Not considered. Religious affiliation/commitment: Not considered. Minority status: Not considered. Volunteer work: Not considered. Work experience: Not considered. **Admissions statistics for the fall 2005 entering class:** Overall acceptance rate: 81%. **Credentials of fall 2005 freshmen:** 24% ranked in the top 10 percent of their high school class; 52% were in the top 25 percent.

ACADEMICS

Year founded: 1878. **Academic calendar:** Semester. **Degrees offered:** certificate, associate, bachelor's. **Most popular majors:** Information not available. **Major fields of study:** biological and biomedical sciences; business, management, marketing, and related support services; computer and information sciences and support services; education; English language and literature/letters; foreign languages, literatures, and linguistics; health professions and related clinical sciences; history; liberal arts and sciences studies, and humanities; natural resources and conservation; physical sciences; social sciences. **Areas of required coursework:** arts/fine arts, computer literacy, mathematics, English (including composition), foreign languages, sciences (biological or physical), history, social science, other. **Special academic programs (% participation):** accelerated program (0%), cooperative (work-study plan) program (10%), distance learning (3%), double major (4%), honors program (1%), independent study (13%), internships (15%), student-designed major (.01%), study abroad (.01%), teacher certificate program (52%). **Teacher certification offered in:** elementary, middle/junior high, secondary, bilingual/bicultural. **Cooperative education programs:** business, social/behavioral science. **Advanced Placement and International Baccalaureate credit:** AP tests may be used for: Placement only. **Freshmen returning for sophomore year:** 59%. **Graduation rates:** Four-year: 21%; five-year: 31%; six-year: 41%.

COSTS AND FINANCIAL AID

Financial aid office: (888) 879-8635. **Expenses (2006-2007):** Tuition and fees 2006-2007: $5,213 in state, $11,783 out of state; room/board: $6,282. **Financial aid:** Priority filing date for institution's financial aid form: March 15.

CAMPUS LIFE AND EXTRACURRICULAR ACTIVITIES

Campus housing available (% using): coed dorms (20%). Average per-year earnings: $1,500. Activities include: choral groups, drama/theater, music ensembles, musical theater, student government. Number of fraternities: 1; sororities: 1. Average proportion of students who stay on campus on weekends: 75%. **Sports program (2005-2006):** Member of NAIA. *Men's intercollegiate varsity sports:* basketball, skiing, soccer. *Women's intercollegiate varsity sports:* basketball, skiing, soccer.

SERVICES AND FACILITIES

Basic services: placement service, health service, health insurance. **Remedial assistance:** reading, math, writing, study skills. **Counseling services:** minority student, military, personal, veteran student, academic, older student. **For learning-disabled students:** School does not offer a structured program with separate admission and additional fees. Services include: remedial math, remedial English, remedial reading, tape recorders, videotaped classes, untimed tests, oral tests, readers, extended time for tests, tutors, other. **Library:** Number of titles: 69,189; number of current serial subscriptions: 335. **Information technology resources:** Students are not required to lease or own a computer. Number of campus computers available to all students: 99. School has a wireless network. Proportion of college-owned housing units wired for high-speed internet access: 100%. **Campus safety:** Security services offered: controlled dormitory access (key, security card, etc).

TRANSFER AND INTERNATIONAL STUDENTS

Transfer students: May apply for admission for the following academic terms: Fall, Spring. Applicants need a minimum number of credits to apply. **International students:** Number of foreign undergraduates: 305 (26% of student body). Minimum TOEFL score required: 500 (paper).

University of Maine—Machias

- **Address:** 9 O'Brien Avenue, Machias, ME 04654
- **Website:** http://www.umm.maine.edu
- **Public**
- **Enrollment:** 462 full-time; 687 part-time

KEY STATS

✔ **U.S News College Ranking:** third tier, Comp. Coll.–Bachelor's (North)
✔ **SAT Score (25th/75th percentile):** 830-1110
✔ **Tuition:** 2006-2007: $5,170 in state, $13,030 out of state
  Selectivity: Less selective   **Room/board:** $5,916
  Acceptance rate: 83%   **Average debt:** $15,062
  Student/faculty ratio: 14/1   **Proportion who borrowed:** 69%

UNDERGRADUATE STUDENT BODY STATS

2005-2006 enrollment: 462 full-time; 687 part-time. Men: 26%; women: 74%. **Ethnic makeup:** African American: 1%; American-Indian: 4%; Asian American: 1%; Hispanic: 2%; White: 87%; International: 5%.

ADMISSIONS FACTS AND FIGURES

Phone: (888) 468-6866. **Email:** ummadmissions@maine.edu. **Website:** http://www.umm.maine.edu. **Application deadlines for fall 2007:** Regular decision: August 15. Early decision: Not offered. Early action: Send application by: December 15; Decision sent by: N/A. Admission can be deferred. **Application fee:** $40. Common application is accepted. **To apply online, go to:** http://apply.maine.edu/. **Admissions requirements/recommendations:** High school units required (recommended): English: 4; Mathematics: 3; Science: 2; Foreign language: (2); Social studies: 2; Academic electives: (3); Total units: 11 (5). Tests: The college uses SAT or ACT scores in admissions decisions. Either SAT or ACT required. For admission to the fall 2007 entering class, the school will accept: ACT with writing, ACT without writing. Campus visit: Recommended. Admissions interview: Recommended. Off-campus interview: May be arranged. **Factors that count in admissions decisions:** *Academic:* Secondary school record: Very important. Class rank: Important. Letters of recommendation: Very important. Standardized test scores: Important. Essay: Very important. *Nonacademic:* Interview: Very important. Extracurricular activities: Important. Talent/ability: Considered. Character/personal qualities: Considered. Alumni/ae relationship: Not considered. Geographical residence: Not considered. State residency: Not considered. Religious affiliation/commitment: Not considered. Minority status: Not considered. Volunteer work: Considered. Work experience: Considered. **Other schools with the greatest overlap in applicants:** University of Maine–Farmington; University of Maine–Orono; University of New England. **Admissions statistics for the fall 2005 entering class:** Total applicants: 374. Total accepted: 312. Freshmen enrolled: 120; 28% were from out of state. Overall acceptance rate: 83%. Non-early acceptance rate: 83%. **Credentials of fall 2005 freshmen:** 9% ranked in the top 10 percent of their high school class; 25% were in the top 25 percent, and 64% were in the top half. (Proportion submitting class standing: 73%.) **Average high school grade point average:** 2.8. **First-year students who submitted SAT scores:** 72%. Scores (25/75 percentile): Verbal: 430-570, Math: 400-540, Combined: 830-1110. **First-year students submitting ACT scores:** 12%. Scores (25/75 percentile): English: 17-25, Math: 17-25, Composite: 18-25.

ACADEMICS

Year founded: 1909. **Academic calendar:** Semester. **Degrees offered:** bachelor's. **Most popular majors:** 20% business administration and management, 14% behavioral sciences, 13% biology/biological sciences, 13% liberal arts and sciences/liberal studies, 10% elementary education and teaching. **Major fields of study:** biological and biomedical sciences; business, management, marketing, and related support services; education; English language and literature/letters; history; liberal arts and sciences studies, and humanities; multi/interdisciplinary studies; natural resources and conservation; parks, recreation, leisure, and fitness studies; visual and performing arts. **Areas of required coursework:** arts/fine arts, humanities, mathematics, English (including composition), sciences (biological or physical), history, social science, other. **Pre-professional programs:** other. **Special academic programs:** cooperative (work-study plan) program, distance learning, double major, dual enrollment, honors program, independent study, internships, student-designed major, study abroad, teacher certificate program. **Teacher certification offered in:** elementary, middle/junior high, secondary. **Cooperative education programs:** business, natural science, social/behavioral science, other. **Faculty and instruction (2005-2006):** Total instructional faculty: 30 full-time, 58 part-time (55% men; 45% women; 1% minorities). Full-time faculty with Ph.D. or other terminal degree: 73%. Student/faculty ratio: 14/1. Classes of fewer than 20 students: 78%; of 20 to 49 students: 22%. **Advanced Placement and International Baccalaureate credit:** AP tests may be used for: Credit only. Scores accepted: 3, 4, 5. **Freshmen returning for sophomore year:** 71%. **Graduation rates:** Four-year: 21%; five-year: 36%; six-year: 46%. **Graduate study:** 10% of students pursue further study immediately upon graduation. Fields in which graduates pursue further study: arts and sciences, 100%.

COSTS AND FINANCIAL AID
Financial aid office: (207) 255-1203. **Expenses (2006-2007):** Tuition and fees 2006-2007: $5,170 in state, $13,030 out of state; room/board: $5,916. Estimated books and supplies: $800; transportation: $900; personal expenses: $1,600. **Financial aid:** Priority filing date for institution's financial aid form: March 1. In 2005-2006, 90% of undergraduates applied for financial aid. Of those, 83% were determined to have financial need; 24% had their need fully met. Average financial aid package (proportion receiving): $9,604 (80%). Average amount of gift aid, such as scholarships or grants (proportion receiving): $5,438 (71%). Average amount of self-help aid, such as work study or loans (proportion receiving): $4,507 (64%). Average need-based loan (excluding PLUS or other private loans): $4,172. Among students who received need-based aid, the average percentage of need met: 82%. Among students who received aid based on merit, the average award (and the proportion receiving): $6,118 (6%). The average athletic scholarship (and the proportion receiving): $0 (0%). Average amount of debt of borrowers graduating in 2005: $15,062. Proportion who borrowed: 69%.

CAMPUS LIFE AND EXTRACURRICULAR ACTIVITIES
Campus housing available (% using): coed dorms (100%). Students who live in college-owned, operated, or affiliated housing: 39%. **Student employment:** During the 2005-2006 academic year, 70% of undergraduates worked on campus. Average per-year earnings: $1,400. **Clubs and organizations:** Number of student organizations: 33. Activities include: choral groups, dance, drama/theater, literary magazine, music ensembles, musical theater, pep band, radio station, student government. Number of fraternities: 4; sororities: 4. Proportion of men in fraternities: 8%; of women in sororities: 4%. Average proportion of students who stay on campus on weekends: 50%. **Sports program (2005-2006):** Member of NAIA. *Men's intercollegiate varsity sports:* basketball, cross-country, soccer. *Women's intercollegiate varsity sports:* basketball, cross-country, soccer, volleyball.

SERVICES AND FACILITIES
Basic services: nonremedial tutoring, placement service, day care, health service, health insurance. **Remedial assistance:** reading, math, writing, study skills. **Counseling services:** career, personal, veteran student, academic. **For learning-disabled students:** School does not offer a structured program with separate admission and additional fees. Total undergraduates in learning-disabled program or receiving services: 63. Services include: remedial math, other testing accommodations, remedial English, reading machines, remedial reading, tape recorders, untimed tests, note-taking services, learning center, readers, extended time for tests, tutors, priority seating, texts on tape, typist/scribe, other testing accomodations, other. **Library:** Number of titles: 83,134; number of current serial subscriptions: 498. **Information technology resources:** Students are not required to lease or own a computer. Number of campus computers available to all students: 117. School has a wireless network. Approximate number of users that can be accommodated: 500. Proportion of college-owned housing units wired for high-speed internet access: 100%. **Campus safety:** Security services offered: late-night transport/escort service, lighted pathways/sidewalks, controlled dormitory access (key, security card, etc.).

TRANSFER AND INTERNATIONAL STUDENTS
Transfer students: May apply for admission for the following academic terms: Fall, Spring, Summer. Applicants do not need a minimum number of credits to apply. For fall 2005: Transfer applications received: 74. Transfer applicants offered admission: 56. Transfer applicants enrolled: 37. **International students:** Number of foreign undergraduates: 27 (5% of student body). Number of countries represented: 8. Minimum TOEFL score required: 500 (paper); 173 (computer).

University of Maine—Orono

- **Address:** 168 College Avenue, Orono, ME 04469
- **Website:** http://www.umaine.edu
- **Public**
- **Enrollment:** 7,617 full-time; 1,562 part-time

KEY STATS
✔ **U.S News College Ranking:** third tier, National Universities
✔ **SAT Score (25th/75th percentile):** 970-1190
✔ **Tuition:** 2006-2007: $7,464 in state, $18,414 out of state

Selectivity: Selective	**Room/board:** $7,125
Acceptance rate: 80%	**Average debt:** $20,930
Student/faculty ratio: 16/1	**Proportion who borrowed:** 75%

UNDERGRADUATE STUDENT BODY STATS
2005-2006 enrollment: 7,617 full-time; 1,562 part-time. Men: 48%; women: 52%. **Ethnic makeup:** African American: 1%; American-Indian: 2%; Asian American: 1%; Hispanic: 1%; White: 94%; International: 2%.

ADMISSIONS FACTS AND FIGURES
Phone: (877) 486-2364. **Email:** um-admit@maine.edu. **Website:** http://www.umaine.edu. **Application deadlines for fall 2007:** Regular decision: Rolling. Early decision: Not offered. Early action: Send application by: December 15; Decision sent by: January 15. Admission can be deferred. **Application fee:** $40. Common application is accepted. **To apply online, go to:** http://apply.maine.edu. **Admissions requirements/recommendations:** High school units required (recommended): English: 4 (4); Mathematics: 3 (4); Science: 2 (4); Foreign language: 2 (2); Social studies: 2 (3); History: (1); Academic electives: 4 (4); Total units: 17 (21). Tests: The college uses SAT or ACT scores in admissions decisions. Either SAT or ACT required. For admission to the fall 2007 entering class, the school will accept: ACT with writing, ACT without writing. Campus visit: Recommended. Admissions interview: Recommended. Off-campus interview: Not available. **Factors that count in admissions decisions:** *Academic:* Secondary school record: Very important. Class rank: Very important. Letters of recommendation: Important. Standardized test scores: Very important. Essay: Important. *Nonacademic:* Interview: Considered. Extracurricular activities: Considered. Talent/ability: Considered. Character/personal qualities: Considered. Alumni/ae relationship: Not considered. Geographical residence: Considered. State residency: Considered. Religious affiliation/commitment: Not considered. Minority status: Not considered. Volunteer work: Considered. Work experience: Considered. **Other schools with the greatest overlap in applicants:** University of Maine–Farmington; University of Massachusetts–Amherst; University of New Hampshire; University of Southern Maine; University of Vermont. **Admissions statistics for the fall 2005 entering class:** Total applicants: 5,702. Total accepted: 4,580. Freshmen enrolled: 1,800; 18% were from out of state. Overall acceptance rate: 80%. Non-early acceptance rate: 80%. **Size of waiting list:** 68 applicants; enrolled from waiting list: 26. **Credentials of fall 2005 freshmen:** 22% ranked in the top 10 percent of their high school class; 52% were in the top 25 percent, and 86% were in the top half. (Proportion submitting class standing: 76%.) **Average high school grade point average:** 3.3. **First-year students who submitted SAT scores:** 94%. Scores (25/75 percentile): Verbal: 480-590, Math: 490-600, Combined: 970-1190. **First-year students submitting ACT scores:** 10%. Scores (25/75 percentile): English: N/A, Math: N/A, Composite: 20-25.

ACADEMICS
Year founded: 1862. **Academic calendar:** Semester. **Degrees offered:** bachelor's, post-bachelor's certificate, master's, post-master's certificate, doctorate. **Most popular majors:** 11% business/commerce, 6% elementary education and teaching, 6% nursing/registered nurse training (R.N., A.S.N., B.S.N., M.S.N.), 5% psychology, 3% human development and family studies. **Major fields of study:** agriculture, agriculture operations, and related sciences; architecture and related services; area, ethnic, cultural, and gender studies; biological and biomedical sciences; business, management, marketing, and related support services; communication, journalism, and related programs; computer and information sciences and support services; education; engineering; engineering technologies/technicians; English language and litera-

ture/letters; family and consumer sciences/human sciences; foreign languages, literatures, and linguistics; health professions and related clinical sciences; history; liberal arts and sciences studies, and humanities; mathematics and statistics; multi/interdisciplinary studies; natural resources and conservation; parks, recreation, leisure, and fitness studies; philosophy and religious studies; physical sciences; psychology; public administration and social service professions; social sciences; visual and performing arts. **Areas of required coursework:** arts/fine arts, humanities, mathematics, English (including composition), sciences (biological or physical), social science. **Pre-professional programs:** pre-law, pre-dentistry, pre-medicine, pre-veterinary science, pre-optometry, pre-pharmacy. **Special academic programs:** accelerated program, cooperative (work-study plan) program, distance learning, double major, English as a Second Language (ESL), exchange student program (domestic), honors program, independent study, internships, liberal arts/career combination, study abroad, teacher certificate program. **Teacher certification offered in:** early childhood, special education, elementary, middle/junior high, adult education, secondary. **Cooperative education programs:** business, education, engineering, health professions, natural science, social/behavioral science. **Reserve Officers Training Corps (ROTC):** Army ROTC: Offered on campus; Navy ROTC: Offered at cooperating institution (Maine Maritime Academy). **Faculty and instruction (2005-2006):** Total instructional faculty: 515 full-time, 324 part-time (60% men; 40% women; 3% minorities). Full-time faculty with Ph.D. or other terminal degree: 85%. Student/faculty ratio: 16/1. Classes of fewer than 20 students: 45%; of 20 to 49 students: 43%; of 50 or more students: 12%. **Advanced Placement and International Baccalaureate credit:** AP tests may be used for: Credit and/or placement. Scores accepted: 3, 4, 5. International Baccalaureate exams may be used for: Credit only. **Freshmen returning for sophomore year:** 79%. **Graduation rates:** Four-year: 28%; five-year: 47%; six-year: 53%. **Graduate study:** 25% of students pursue further study within one year.

COSTS AND FINANCIAL AID

Financial aid office: (207) 581-1324. **Expenses (2006-2007):** Tuition and fees 2006-2007: $7,464 in state, $18,414 out of state; room/board: $7,125. Estimated books and supplies: $700; transportation: $500; personal expenses: $1,100. **Financial aid:** Priority filing date for institution's financial aid form: March 1. In 2005-2006, 81% of undergraduates applied for financial aid. Of those, 64% were determined to have financial need; 26% had their need fully met. Average financial aid package (proportion receiving): $9,460 (63%). Average amount of gift aid, such as scholarships or grants (proportion receiving): $5,075 (49%). Average amount of self-help aid, such as work study or loans (proportion receiving): $4,968 (56%). Average need-based loan (excluding PLUS or other private loans): $4,228. Among students who received need-based aid, the average percentage of need met: 83%. Among students who received aid based on merit, the average award (and the proportion receiving): $5,272 (21%). The average athletic scholarship (and the proportion receiving): $15,034 (1%). Average amount of debt of borrowers graduating in 2005: $20,930. Proportion who borrowed: 75%.

CAMPUS LIFE AND EXTRACURRICULAR ACTIVITIES

Campus housing available (% using): coed dorms (86%), sorority housing (1%), fraternity housing (1%), apartments for married students (3%), apartment for single students (9%), special housing for disabled students, special housing for international students. Students who live in college-owned, operated, or affiliated housing: 43%. **Student employment:** During the 2005-2006 academic year, 15% of undergraduates worked on campus. Average per-year earnings: $2,550. **Clubs and organizations:** Number of student organizations: 234. Activities include: choral groups, concert band, dance, drama/theater, jazz band, marching band, music ensembles, musical theater, opera, pep band, radio station, student government, student newspaper, student film society, symphony orchestra. Number of fraternities: 5; sororities: 1. Average proportion of students who stay on campus on weekends: 75%. **Sports program (2005-2006):** Member of NCAA I. **Men's intercollegiate varsity sports:** baseball, basketball, cross-country, football, ice hockey, soccer, swimming and diving, track and field (indoor), track and field (outdoor). **Women's intercollegiate varsity sports:** basketball, cross-country, field hockey, ice hockey, soccer, softball, swimming and diving, track and field (indoor), track and field (outdoor), volleyball.

SERVICES AND FACILITIES

Basic services: nonremedial tutoring, women's center, placement service, day care, health service, health insurance. **Remedial assistance:** math, writing; study skills. **Counseling services:** minority student, career, military, personal, veteran student, academic, older student, psychological, birth control, religious. **For learning-disabled students:** School does not offer a structured

program with separate admission and additional fees. Services include: remedial math, remedial English, remedial reading, tape recorders, note-taking services, oral tests, readers, extended time for tests, tutors, texts on tape, exams on tape or computer, other testing accomodations, waiver of foreign language degree requirement, waiver of math degree requirement. **Library:** Number of titles: 1,326,490; number of current serial subscriptions: 5,438. **Information technology resources:** Students are not required to lease or own a computer. Number of campus computers available to all students: 500. School has a wireless network. Approximate number of users that can be accommodated: 6,000. Proportion of college-owned housing units wired for high-speed internet access: 100%. **Campus safety:** Security services offered: 24-hour foot and vehicle patrols, late-night transport/escort service, 24-hour emergency telephones, lighted pathways/sidewalks, student patrols, controlled dormitory access (key, security card, etc).

TRANSFER AND INTERNATIONAL STUDENTS

Transfer students: May apply for admission for the following academic terms: Fall, Spring. Applicants need a minimum number of credits to apply. For fall 2005: Transfer applications received: 886. Transfer applicants offered admission: 678. Transfer applicants enrolled: 453. **International students:** Number of foreign undergraduates: 138 (2% of student body). Number of countries represented: 72. Minimum TOEFL score required: 530 (paper); 197 (computer). Average TOEFL score: 550 (paper).

University of Maine–Presque Isle

- **Address:** 181 Main Street, Presque Isle, ME 04769
- **Website:** http://www.umpi.maine.edu
- **Public**
- **Enrollment:** 1,112 full-time; 436 part-time

KEY STATS

✔ **U.S News College Ranking:** fourth tier, Liberal Arts Colleges
✔ **SAT Score (25th/75th percentile):** 780-1030
✔ **Tuition:** 2006-2007: $5,380 in state, $12,280 out of state
Selectivity: Less selective   **Room/board:** $5,658
Acceptance rate: 86%   **Average debt:** $11,181
Student/faculty ratio: 16/1   **Proportion who borrowed:** 33%

UNDERGRADUATE STUDENT BODY STATS

2005-2006 enrollment: 1,112 full-time; 436 part-time. Men: 34%; women: 66%. **Ethnic makeup:** African American: 1%; American-Indian: 4%; Asian American: 1%; Hispanic: 1%; White: 85%; International: 9%.

ADMISSIONS FACTS AND FIGURES

Phone: (207) 768-9532. **Email:** adventure@umpi.maine.edu. **Website:** http://www.umpi.maine.edu. **Application deadlines for fall 2007:** Regular decision: Rolling. Early decision: Not offered. Early action: Send application by: October 31; Decision sent by: April 1. Admission can be deferred. **Application fee:** $40. Common application is accepted. **To apply online, go to:** http://apply.maine.edu. **Admissions requirements/recommendations:** High school units required (recommended): English: 4; Mathematics: 3; Science: 2; Foreign language: 2; Social studies: 3; Academic electives: 2; Total units: 16. Tests: The college does not use SAT or ACT scores in admissions decisions. Neither SAT nor ACT required. Campus visit: Recommended. Admissions interview: Recommended. Off-campus interview: May be arranged. **Factors that count in admissions decisions:** *Academic:* Secondary school record: Very important. Class rank: Very important. Letters of recommendation: Very important. Standardized test scores: Considered. Essay: Very important. *Nonacademic:* Interview: Important. Extracurricular activities: Considered. Talent/ability: Considered. Character/personal qualities: Considered. Alumni/ae relationship: Considered. Geographical residence: Not considered. State residency: Considered. Religious affiliation/commitment: Not considered. Minority status: Considered. Volunteer work: Considered. Work experience: Considered. **Admissions statistics for the fall 2005 entering class:** Total applicants: 483. Total accepted: 417. Freshmen enrolled: 211; 4% were from out of state. Overall acceptance rate: 86%. Non-early acceptance rate: 86%. **Credentials of fall 2005 freshmen:** 8% ranked in the top 10 percent of their high school class; 23% were in the top 25 percent; and 51% were in the top half. (Proportion submitting class standing: 73%.) **Average high school grade point average:** 3.0. **First-year students who submitted SAT scores:**

56%. Scores (25/75 percentile): Verbal: 390-530, Math: 390-500, Combined: 780-1030.

ACADEMICS

Year founded: 1903. **Academic calendar:** Semester. **Degrees offered:** associate, bachelor's. **Most popular majors:** 46% liberal arts and sciences studies, and humanities, 17% education, 9% business, management, marketing, and related support services, 5% public administration and social service professions, 4% multi/interdisciplinary studies. **Major fields of study:** biological and biomedical sciences; education; foreign languages, literatures, and linguistics; liberal arts and sciences studies, and humanities; multi/interdisciplinary studies; natural resources and conservation; parks, recreation, leisure, and fitness studies; physical sciences; psychology; public administration and social service professions; security and protective services; social sciences; visual and performing arts. **Areas of required coursework:** arts/fine arts, humanities, mathematics, English (including composition), foreign languages, sciences (biological or physical), history, social science. **Pre-professional programs:** pre-medicine. **Special academic programs:** accelerated program, cooperative (work-study plan) program, cross-registration, distance learning, double major, exchange student program (domestic), honors program, independent study, internships, student-designed major, study abroad, teacher certificate program. **Teacher certification offered in:** elementary, middle/junior high, secondary. **Cooperative education programs:** business, education, health professions, other. **Faculty and instruction (2005-2006):** Total instructional faculty: 54 full-time, 62 part-time (55% men; 45% women; 3% minorities). Full-time faculty with Ph.D. or other terminal degree: 81%. Student/faculty ratio: 16/1. Classes of fewer than 20 students: 63%; of 20 to 49 students: 37%. **Advanced Placement and International Baccalaureate credit:** AP tests may be used for: Credit and/or placement. Scores accepted: 3, 4, 5. **Freshmen returning for sophomore year:** 61%. **Graduation rates:** Four-year: 16%; five-year: 34%; six-year: 39%.

COSTS AND FINANCIAL AID

Financial aid office: (207) 768-9511. **Expenses (2006-2007):** Tuition and fees 2006-2007: $5,380 in state, $12,280 out of state; room/board: $5,658. Estimated books and supplies: $800; transportation: $1,100. **Financial aid:** Priority filing date for institution's financial aid form: April 1. In 2005-2006, 73% of undergraduates applied for financial aid. Of those, 63% were determined to have financial need; 38% had their need fully met. Average financial aid package (proportion receiving): $7,248 (57%). Average amount of gift aid, such as scholarships or grants (proportion receiving): $4,509 (52%). Average amount of self-help aid, such as work study or loans (proportion receiving): $3,855 (43%). Average need-based loan (excluding PLUS or other private loans): $3,323. Among students who received need-based aid, the average percentage of need met: 89%. Among students who received aid based on merit, the average award (and the proportion receiving): $4,532 (8%). Average amount of debt of borrowers graduating in 2005: $11,181. Proportion who borrowed: 33%.

CAMPUS LIFE AND EXTRACURRICULAR ACTIVITIES

Campus housing available: coed dorms, apartments for married students. Students who live in college-owned, operated, or affiliated housing: 22%. **Student employment:** During the 2005-2006 academic year, 8% of undergraduates worked on campus. Average per-year earnings: $800. **Clubs and organizations:** Number of student organizations: 20. Activities include: drama/theater, radio station, student government, student newspaper. Number of fraternities: 1; sororities: 1. Proportion of men in fraternities: 1%; of women in sororities: 1%. Average proportion of students who stay on campus on weekends: 50%. **Sports program (2005-2006):** Member of NCAA III. *Men's intercollegiate varsity sports:* baseball, basketball, cross-country, golf, nordic skiing, soccer. *Women's intercollegiate varsity sports:* basketball, cross-country, nordic skiing, soccer, softball, volleyball.

SERVICES AND FACILITIES

Basic services: nonremedial tutoring, placement service, day care, health service, health insurance. **Remedial assistance:** reading, math, writing, study skills, other. **Counseling services:** minority student, career, personal, veteran student, academic, older student, psychological, birth control. **For learning-disabled students:** School does not offer a structured program with separate admission and additional fees. Total undergraduates in learning-disabled program or receiving services: 23. Services include: remedial math, remedial English, reading machines, remedial reading, tape recorders, diagnostic testing service, note-taking services, oral tests, readers, extended time for tests, tutors, early syllabus, priority registration, priority seating, proofreading services, texts on tape, typist/scribe, exams on tape or computer, other

testing accomodations. **Library:** Number of titles: 162,500; number of current serial subscriptions: 325. **Information technology resources:** Students are not required to lease or own a computer. Number of campus computers available to all students: 121. School has a wireless network. Approximate number of users that can be accommodated: 900. Proportion of college-owned housing units wired for high-speed internet access: 100%. **Campus safety:** Security services offered: 24-hour emergency telephones, lighted pathways/sidewalks, student patrols, controlled dormitory access (key, security card, etc).

TRANSFER AND INTERNATIONAL STUDENTS

Transfer students: May apply for admission for the following academic terms: Fall, Spring, Summer. Applicants need a minimum number of credits to apply. For fall 2005: Transfer applications received: 570. Transfer applicants offered admission: 393. Transfer applicants enrolled: 231. **International students:** Number of foreign undergraduates: 114 (9% of student body). Number of countries represented: 6. Minimum TOEFL score required: 550 (paper); 230 (computer). Average TOEFL score: 565 (paper).

University of New England

- **Address:** Hills Beach Road, Biddeford, ME 04005
- **Website:** http://www.une.edu
- **Private**
- **Enrollment:** 1,519 full-time; 217 part-time

KEY STATS

✔ **U.S News College Ranking:** 62, Universities–Master's (North)
✔ **SAT Score (25th/75th percentile):** 940-1150
✔ **Tuition:** 2006-2007: $23,790

Selectivity: Selective	**Room/board:** $9,255
Acceptance rate: 92%	**Average debt:** $37,606
Student/faculty ratio: 11/1	**Proportion who borrowed:** 88%

UNDERGRADUATE STUDENT BODY STATS

2005-2006 enrollment: 1,519 full-time; 217 part-time. Men: 24%; women: 76%. **Ethnic makeup:** African American: 1%; Asian American: 1%; Hispanic: 1%; White: 97%.

ADMISSIONS FACTS AND FIGURES

Phone: (207) 283-0171. **Email:** admissions@une.edu. **Website:** http://www.une.edu. **Application deadlines for fall 2007:** Regular decision: August 15. Early decision: Not offered. Early action: Not offered. Admission can be deferred. **Application fee:** $40. Common application is accepted. **Admissions requirements/recommendations:** High school units required (recommended): English: 4; Mathematics: 3 (4); Science: 2 (4); Foreign language: (2); Social studies: (2); History: (2); Academic electives: (4); Total units: 11 (20). Tests: The college uses SAT or ACT scores in admissions decisions. Neither SAT nor ACT required. Campus visit: Recommended. Admissions interview: Recommended. Off-campus interview: May be arranged. **Factors that count in admissions decisions:** *Academic:* Secondary school record: Very important. Class rank: Considered. Letters of recommendation: Considered. Standardized test scores: Considered. Essay: Considered. *Nonacademic:* Interview: Considered. Extracurricular activities: Considered. Talent/ability: Not considered. Character/personal qualities: Considered. Alumni/ae relationship: Considered. Geographical residence: Considered. State residency: Not considered. Religious affiliation/commitment: Not considered. Minority status: Not considered. Volunteer work: Considered. Work experience: Not considered. **Other schools with the greatest overlap in applicants:** Quinnipiac University; St. Joseph's College; University of Maine–Orono; University of New Hampshire; University of Southern Maine. **Admissions statistics for the fall 2005 entering class:** Total applicants: 2,055. Total accepted: 1,888. Freshmen enrolled: 468; 67% were from out of state. Overall acceptance rate: 92%. **Size of waiting list:** 17 applicants; enrolled from waiting list: 2. **Credentials of fall 2005 freshmen:** 17% ranked in the top 10 percent of their high school class; 49% were in the top 25 percent, and 86% were in the top half. (Proportion submitting class standing: 73%.) **Average high school grade point average:** 3.2. **First-year students who submitted SAT scores:** 93%. Scores (25/75 percentile): Verbal: 470-570, Math: 470-580, Combined: 940-1150.

ACADEMICS

Year founded: 1831. **Academic calendar:** Semester. **Degrees offered:** associate, bachelor's, post-bachelor's certificate, master's, post-master's certificate, first professional. **Most popular majors:** 39% health professions and related clinical sciences, 26% biological and biomedical sciences, 10% psychology, 7% natural resources and conservation, 4% education. **Major fields of study:** agriculture, agriculture operations, and related sciences; area, ethnic, cultural, and gender studies; biological and biomedical sciences; business, management, marketing, and related support services; education; English language and literature/letters; health professions and related clinical sciences; history; liberal arts and sciences studies, and humanities; mathematics and statistics; natural resources and conservation; parks, recreation, leisure, and fitness studies; physical sciences; psychology; social sciences. **Areas of required coursework:** arts/fine arts, humanities, mathematics, English (including composition), sciences (biological or physical), social science. **Pre-professional programs:** other. **Special academic programs:** cross-registration, double major, honors program, independent study, internships, student-designed major, study abroad, teacher certificate program. **Teacher certification offered in:** elementary, secondary. **Reserve Officers Training Corps (ROTC):** Army ROTC: Offered at cooperating institution (UNH). **Faculty and instruction (2005-2006):** Total instructional faculty: 137 full-time, 104 part-time (50% men; 50% women; 4% minorities). Full-time faculty with Ph.D. or other terminal degree: 85%. Student/faculty ratio: 11/1. Classes of fewer than 20 students: 49%; of 20 to 49 students: 48%; of 50 or more students: 3%. **Advanced Placement and International Baccalaureate credit:** AP tests may be used for: Credit only. Scores accepted: 3, 4, 5. International Baccalaureate exams may be used for: Credit only. **Freshmen returning for sophomore year:** 71%. **Graduation rates:** Four-year: 48%; five-year: 55%; six-year: 58%.

COSTS AND FINANCIAL AID

Financial aid office: (207) 602-2342. **Expenses (2006-2007):** Tuition and fees 2006-2007: $23,790; room/board: $9,255. Estimated books and supplies: $1,000; transportation: $1,025; personal expenses: $925. **Financial aid:** Priority filing date for institution's financial aid form: May 1. In 2005-2006, 91% of undergraduates applied for financial aid. Of those, 83% were determined to have financial need; 13% had their need fully met. Average financial aid package (proportion receiving): $15,659 (83%). Average amount of gift aid, such as scholarships or grants (proportion receiving): $10,052 (82%). Average amount of self-help aid, such as work study or loans (proportion receiving): $6,249 (76%). Average need-based loan (excluding PLUS or other private loans): $5,150. Among students who received need-based aid, the average percentage of need met: 67%. Among students who received aid based on merit, the average award (and the proportion receiving): $7,770 (16%). The average athletic scholarship (and the proportion receiving): $0 (0%). Average amount of debt of borrowers graduating in 2005: $37,606. Proportion who borrowed: 88%.

CAMPUS LIFE AND EXTRACURRICULAR ACTIVITIES

Campus housing available (% using): coed dorms (90%), women's dorms (10%). Students who live in college-owned, operated, or affiliated housing: 66%. **Student employment:** During the 2005-2006 academic year, 8% of undergraduates worked on campus. Average per-year earnings: $495. **Clubs and organizations:** Number of student organizations: 44. Activities include: dance, drama/theater, literary magazine, student government, yearbook. Number of fraternities: 0; sororities: 0. Average proportion of students who stay on campus on weekends: 60%. **Sports program (2005-2006):** Member of NCAA III. *Men's intercollegiate varsity sports:* basketball, cross-country, golf, lacrosse, soccer. *Women's intercollegiate varsity sports:* basketball, cross-country, field hockey, lacrosse, soccer, softball, swimming and diving, volleyball.

SERVICES AND FACILITIES

Basic services: nonremedial tutoring, health service, health insurance. **Remedial assistance:** math, writing, study skills. **Counseling services:** minority student, career, personal, veteran student, academic, older student, psychological, religious. **For learning-disabled students:** School does not offer a structured program with separate admission and additional fees. Total undergraduates in learning-disabled program or receiving services: 57. Services include: remedial math, remedial English, reading machines, tape recorders, note-taking services, learning center, readers, extended time for tests, tutors, priority registration, priority seating, texts on tape, other testing accomodations. **Library:** Number of titles: 143,278; number of current serial subscriptions: 25,063. **Information technology resources:** Students are not required to lease or own a computer. Number of campus computers available to all students: 170. School has a wireless network. Proportion of college-owned housing units wired for high-speed internet access: 100%. **Campus safety:** Security services offered: 24-hour foot and vehicle patrols, late-night transport/escort service, 24-hour emergency telephones, lighted pathways/sidewalks, controlled dormitory access (key, security card, etc).

TRANSFER AND INTERNATIONAL STUDENTS

Transfer students: May apply for admission for the following academic terms: Fall, Spring. Applicants need a minimum number of credits to apply. For fall 2005: Transfer applications received: 338. Transfer applicants offered admission: 294. Transfer applicants enrolled: 142. **International students:** Number of foreign undergraduates: 3. Number of countries represented: 3. Minimum TOEFL score required: 550 (paper); 213 (computer).

University of Southern Maine

- **Address:** 37 College Avenue, Gorham, ME 04038
- **Website:** http://www.usm.maine.edu
- **Public**
- **Enrollment:** 4,788 full-time; 3,834 part-time

KEY STATS

✔ **U.S News College Ranking:** third tier, Universities–Master's (North)
✔ **SAT Score (25th/75th percentile):** 900-1120
✔ **Tuition:** 2006-2007: $5,873 in state, $14,693 out of state
  Selectivity: Less selective **Room/board:** $7,499
  Acceptance rate: 79% **Average debt:** $21,800
  Student/faculty ratio: 16/1 **Proportion who borrowed:** 61%

UNDERGRADUATE STUDENT BODY STATS

2005-2006 enrollment: 4,788 full-time; 3,834 part-time. Men: 41%; women: 59%. **Ethnic makeup:** African American: 1%; American-Indian: 2%; Asian American: 1%; Hispanic: 1%; White: 95%. **Religious preference:** Roman Catholic: 50%; Protestant: 30%; Jewish: 3%; Muslim: 2%; Hindu: 1%; Buddhist: 2%; No preference: 10%; Pagan: 2%.

ADMISSIONS FACTS AND FIGURES

Phone: (207) 780-5670. **Email:** usmadm@usm.maine.edu. **Website:** http://www.usm.maine.edu. **Application deadlines for fall 2007:** Early decision: Not offered. Early action: Not offered. Admission can be deferred. **Application fee:** $40. Common application is accepted. **To apply online, go to:** http://apply.maine.edu. **Admissions requirements/recommendations:** High school units required (recommended): English: 4 (0); Mathematics: 3 (4); Science: 2 (3); Foreign language: 2 (3); Social studies: 2 (3); History: 2 (3); Academic electives: 0 (0); Total units: 16 (0). Tests: The college uses SAT or ACT scores in admissions decisions. Either SAT or ACT required. For admission to the fall 2007 entering class, the school will accept: ACT with writing, ACT without writing. Campus visit: Recommended. Admissions interview: Recommended. Off-campus interview: May be arranged. **Factors that count in admissions decisions:** *Academic:* Secondary school record: Very important. Class rank: Very important. Letters of recommendation: Important. Standardized test scores: Very important. Essay: Important. *Nonacademic:* Interview: Considered. Extracurricular activities: Considered. Talent/ability: Considered. Character/personal qualities: Considered. Alumni/ae relationship: Considered. Geographical residence: Considered. State residency: Considered. Religious affiliation/commitment: Not considered. Minority status: Considered. Volunteer work: Considered. Work experience: Considered. **Other schools with the greatest overlap in applicants:** St. Joseph's College; University of Maine–Farmington; University of Maine–Orono; University of New England; University of New Hampshire. **Admissions statistics for the fall 2005 entering class:** Total applicants: 3,599. Total accepted: 2,848. Freshmen enrolled: 1,010; 18% were from out of state. Overall acceptance rate: 79%. **Credentials of fall 2005 freshmen:** 10% ranked in the top 10 percent of their high school class; 31% were in the top 25 percent, and 71% were in the top half. (Proportion submitting class standing: 74%.) **Average high school grade point average:** 3.0. **First-year students who submitted SAT scores:** 93%. Scores (25/75 percentile): Verbal: 450-570, Math: 450-550, Combined: 900-1120. **First-year students submitting ACT scores:** 7%. Scores (25/75 percentile): English: N/A, Math: N/A, Composite: 17-22.

ACADEMICS

Year founded: 1878. **Academic calendar:** Semester. **Degrees offered:** associate, bachelor's, master's, post-master's certificate, first professional, doctorate. **Most popular majors:** 14% nursing/registered nurse training (R.N., A.S.N., B.S.N., M.S.N.), 9% business administration and management, 6% psychology, 5% social sciences, 5% communication studies/speech communication and rhetoric. **Major fields of study:** area, ethnic, cultural, and gender studies; biological and biomedical sciences; business, management, marketing, and related support services; communication, journalism, and related programs; computer and information sciences and support services; education; engineering; English language and literature/letters; foreign languages, literatures, and linguistics; health professions and related clinical sciences; liberal arts and sciences studies, and humanities; mathematics and statistics; natural resources and conservation; parks, recreation, leisure, and fitness studies; philosophy and religious studies; physical sciences; psychology; public administration and social service professions; social sciences; visual and performing arts. **Areas of required coursework:** arts/fine arts, humanities, mathematics, English (including composition), philosophy, sciences (biological or physical), history, social science. **Pre-professional programs:** pre-law, pre-dentistry, pre-medicine, pre-veterinary science. **Special academic programs:** cooperative (work-study plan) program, cross-registration, distance learning, double major, dual enrollment, English as a Second Language (ESL), exchange student program (domestic), honors program, independent study, internships, liberal arts/career combination, student-designed major, study abroad, teacher certificate program, weekend college, other. **Teacher certification offered in:** special education, elementary, middle/junior high, adult education, secondary. **Cooperative education programs:** art, business, computer science, education, engineering, health professions, humanities, natural science, social/behavioral science, technologies, vocational arts. **Reserve Officers Training Corps (ROTC):** Army ROTC: Offered at cooperating institution (UNH); Air Force ROTC: Offered at cooperating institution (UNH). **Faculty and instruction (2005-2006):** Total instructional faculty: 375 full-time, 287 part-time (51% men; 49% women; 4% minorities). Full-time faculty with Ph.D. or other terminal degree: 2%. Student/faculty ratio: 16/1. Classes of fewer than 20 students: 52%; of 20 to 49 students: 44%; of 50 or more students: 3%. **Advanced Placement and International Baccalaureate credit:** AP tests may be used for: Credit and/or placement. Scores accepted: 3, 4, 5. International Baccalaureate exams may be used for: Credit and/or placement. **Freshmen returning for sophomore year:** 68%. **Graduation rates:** Four-year: 12%; five-year: 30%; six-year: 32%.

COSTS AND FINANCIAL AID

Financial aid office: (207) 780-5250. **Expenses (2006-2007):** Tuition and fees 2006-2007: $5,873 in state, $14,693 out of state; room/board: $7,499. Estimated books and supplies: $870; transportation: $1,384; personal expenses: $1,845. **Financial aid:** Priority filing date for institution's financial aid form: February 15. In 2005-2006, 81% of undergraduates applied for financial aid. Of those, 67% were determined to have financial need; 27% had their need fully met. Average financial aid package (proportion receiving): $8,754 (65%). Average amount of gift aid, such as scholarships or grants (proportion receiving): $3,914 (50%). Average amount of self-help aid, such as work study or loans (proportion receiving): $5,173 (59%). Average need-based loan (excluding PLUS or other private loans): $4,085. Among students who received need-based aid, the average percentage of need met: 76%. Among students who received aid based on merit, the average award (and the proportion receiving): $4,409 (12%). The average athletic scholarship (and the proportion receiving): $0 (0%). Average amount of debt of borrowers graduating in 2005: $21,800. Proportion who borrowed: 61%.

CAMPUS LIFE AND EXTRACURRICULAR ACTIVITIES

Campus housing available (% using): coed dorms (95%), apartments for married students (1%), apartment for single students (0%), other housing options (4%). Students who live in college-owned, operated, or affiliated housing: 21%. **Clubs and organizations:** Number of student organizations: 100. Activities include: choral groups, concert band, dance, drama/theater, jazz band, literary magazine, music ensembles, musical theater, radio station, student government, student newspaper, symphony orchestra, television station. Number of fraternities: 4; sororities: 3. Average proportion of students who stay on campus on weekends: 80%. **Sports program (2005-2006):** Member of NCAA III. *Men's intercollegiate varsity sports:* baseball, basketball, cheerleading, cross-country, golf, ice hockey, lacrosse, soccer, tennis, track and field (indoor), track and field (outdoor), wrestling. *Women's intercollegiate varsity sports:* basketball, cheerleading, cross-country, field hockey, golf, ice hockey, lacrosse, soccer, softball, tennis, track and field (indoor), track and field (outdoor), volleyball.

SERVICES AND FACILITIES

Basic services: nonremedial tutoring, women's center, placement service, day care, health service, health insurance. **Remedial assistance:** reading, math, writing, study skills. **Counseling services:** minority student, career, military, personal, veteran student, academic, older student, psychological, birth control, religious. **For learning-disabled students:** School does not offer a structured program with separate admission and additional fees. Total undergraduates in learning-disabled program or receiving services: 53. Services include: remedial math, remedial English, reading machines, remedial reading, tape recorders, untimed tests, note-taking services, learning center, readers, extended time for tests, tutors, substitution of courses, texts on tape, typist/scribe, other testing accomodations, waiver of math degree requirement. **Library:** Number of titles: 561,006; number of current serial subscriptions: 2,040. **Information technology resources:** Students are not required to lease or own a computer. Number of campus computers available to all students: 850. School has a wireless network. Approximate number of users that can be accommodated: 1,000. Proportion of college-owned housing units wired for high-speed internet access: 100%. **Campus safety:** Security services offered: 24-hour foot and vehicle patrols, late-night transport/escort service, 24-hour emergency telephones, lighted pathways/sidewalks, student patrols, controlled dormitory access (key, security card, etc).

TRANSFER AND INTERNATIONAL STUDENTS

Transfer students: May apply for admission for the following academic terms: Fall, Spring. Applicants need a minimum number of credits to apply. For fall 2005: Transfer applications received: 1,534. Transfer applicants offered admission: 1,130. Transfer applicants enrolled: 784. **International students:** Number of foreign undergraduates: 1. Minimum TOEFL score required: 550 (paper); 213 (computer). Average TOEFL score: 558 (paper).

Maryland

Bowie State University

- **Address:** 14000 Jericho Park Road, Bowie, MD 20715-9465
- **Website:** http://www.bowiestate.edu
- **Public**
- **Enrollment:** 3,287 full-time; 733 part-time

KEY STATS
✔ **U.S News College Ranking:** fourth tier, Universities–Master's (North)
✔ **SAT Score (25th/75th percentile):** 981-1156
✔ **Tuition:** 2006-2007: $5,730 in state, $15,034 out of state

Selectivity: Selective	**Room/board:** $8,934
Acceptance rate: 46%	**Average debt:** N/A
Student/faculty ratio: 17/1	**Proportion who borrowed:** N/A

UNDERGRADUATE STUDENT BODY STATS
2005-2006 enrollment: 3,287 full-time; 733 part-time. Men: 37%; women: 63%. **Ethnic makeup:** African American: 91%; Asian American: 2%; Hispanic: 1%; White: 6%.

ADMISSIONS FACTS AND FIGURES
Phone: (301) 860-3415. **Email:** ugradadmissions@bowiestate.edu. **Website:** http://www.bowiestate.edu. **Application deadlines for fall 2007:** Early decision: Not offered. Early action: Not offered. Admission can be deferred. **Application fee:** $40. Common application is not accepted. **Admissions requirements/recommendations:** High school units required (recommended): English: 4; Mathematics: 3; Science: 3; Foreign language: 2; Social studies: 1; History: 2. Tests: The college uses SAT or ACT scores in admissions decisions. Either SAT or ACT required. For admission to the fall 2007 entering class, the school will accept: ACT with writing, ACT without writing. Campus visit: Neither required nor recommended. Admissions interview: Neither required nor recommended. Off-campus interview: Not available. **Factors that count in admissions decisions:** *Academic:* Secondary school record: Considered. Class rank: Not considered. Letters of recommendation: Considered. Standardized test scores: Very important. Essay: Considered. *Nonacademic:* Interview: Considered. Extracurricular activities: Considered. Talent/ability: Not considered. Character/personal qualities: Not considered. Alumni/ae relationship: Not considered. Geographical residence: Not considered. State residency: Not considered. Religious affiliation/commitment: Not considered. Minority status: Not considered. Volunteer work: Not considered. Work experience: Not considered. **Admissions statistics for the fall 2005 entering class:** Total applicants: 5,653. Total accepted: 2,605. Freshmen enrolled: 1,226; 13% were from out of state. Overall acceptance rate: 46%. **Size of waiting list:** 0 applicants; enrolled from waiting list: N/A. **First-year students who submitted SAT scores:** 98%. Scores (25/75 percentile): Verbal: 483-557, Math: 498-599, Combined: 981-1156. **First-year students submitting ACT scores:** 2%. Scores (25/75 percentile): English: 3-15, Math: 7-11, Composite: 5-13.

ACADEMICS
Year founded: 1865. **Academic calendar:** Semester. **Degrees offered:** bachelor's, post-bachelor's certificate, master's, doctorate. **Most popular majors:** 23% business administration and management, 12% sociology, 10% communication and media studies, 9% psychology, 8% nursing. **Major fields of study:** biological and biomedical sciences; business, management, marketing, and related support services; communication, journalism, and related programs; computer and information sciences and support services; education; English language and literature/letters; health professions and related clinical sciences; history; mathematics and statistics; multi/interdisciplinary studies; psychology; public administration and social service professions; social sciences; visual and performing arts. **Areas of required coursework:** arts/fine arts, humanities, computer literacy, mathematics, English (including composition), philosophy, sciences (biological or physical), history, social science, other. **Special academic programs:** cooperative (work-study plan) program, cross-registration, distance learning, double major, dual

enrollment, exchange student program (domestic), honors program, independent study, internships, liberal arts/career combination, study abroad, teacher certificate program. **Teacher certification offered in:** early childhood, elementary, secondary. **Reserve Officers Training Corps (ROTC):** Army ROTC: Offered on campus; Air Force ROTC: Offered at cooperating institution (University of Maryland–College Park). **Faculty and instruction (2005-2006):** Total instructional faculty: 192 full-time, 172 part-time (55% men; 45% women; 77% minorities). Student/faculty ratio: 17/1. Classes of fewer than 20 students: 34%; of 20 to 49 students: 66%. **Advanced Placement and International Baccalaureate credit:** AP tests may be used for: Credit only. Scores accepted: 3, 4, 5. International Baccalaureate exams may be used for: Credit only. **Freshmen returning for sophomore year:** 72%. **Graduation rates:** Six-year: 33%.

COSTS AND FINANCIAL AID
Financial aid office: (301) 860-3540. **Expenses (2006-2007):** Tuition and fees 2006-2007: $5,730 in state, $15,034 out of state; room/board: $8,934. Estimated books and supplies: $1,340; transportation: $1,912; personal expenses: $2,186. **Financial aid:** Priority filing date for institution's financial aid form: March 1; deadline: March 1.

CAMPUS LIFE AND EXTRACURRICULAR ACTIVITIES
Campus housing available (% using): coed dorms (24%), women's dorms (24%), men's dorms (15%), apartment for single students (37%), other housing options (0%). Students who live in college-owned, operated, or affiliated housing: 28%. **Clubs and organizations:** Number of student organizations: 71. Activities include: choral groups, concert band, dance, drama/theater, jazz band, literary magazine, marching band, musical theater, pep band, radio station, student government, student newspaper, television station, yearbook. Number of fraternities: 6; sororities: 5. Proportion of men in fraternities: 2%; of women in sororities: 2%. Average proportion of students who stay on campus on weekends: 50%. **Sports program (2005-2006):** Member of NCAA II. *Men's intercollegiate varsity sports:* basketball, crosscountry, football, track and field (indoor), track and field (outdoor). *Women's intercollegiate varsity sports:* basketball, bowling, cheerleading, cross-country, softball, tennis, track and field (indoor), track and field (outdoor), volleyball.

SERVICES AND FACILITIES
Basic services: nonremedial tutoring, placement service, health service. **Remedial assistance:** reading, math, writing, study skills. **Counseling services:** minority student, career, military, personal, academic. **For learning-disabled students:** School does not offer a structured program with separate admission and additional fees. Total undergraduates in learning-disabled program or receiving services: 26. Services include: reading machines, tape recorders, note-taking services, oral tests, learning center, extended time for tests, tutors, priority registration, priority seating, texts on tape, exams on tape or computer, other testing accomodations. **Library:** Number of titles: 266,203; number of current serial subscriptions: 460. **Information technology resources:** Students are not required to lease or own a computer. Number of campus computers available to all students: 3,144. School has a wireless network. Approximate number of users that can be accommodated: 500. **Campus safety:** Security services offered: 24-hour foot and vehicle patrols, 24-hour emergency telephones, lighted pathways/sidewalks, controlled dormitory access (key, security card, etc).

TRANSFER AND INTERNATIONAL STUDENTS
Transfer students: May apply for admission for the following academic terms: Fall, Spring. Applicants need a minimum number of credits to apply. **International students:** Minimum TOEFL score required: 500 (paper); 173 (computer).

Capitol College

- **Address:** 11301 Springfield Road, Laurel, MD 20708
- **Website:** http://www.capitol-college.edu
- **Private**
- **Enrollment:** 218 full-time; 124 part-time

KEY STATS

✔ **U.S News College Ranking:** Unranked Specialty School–Engineering
✔ **SAT Score (25th/75th percentile):** 840-1080
✔ **Tuition:** 2006-2007: $18,716

Selectivity: Less selective	**Room/board:** $4,198
Acceptance rate: 65%	**Average debt:** $23,772
Student/faculty ratio: 9/1	**Proportion who borrowed:** 63%

UNDERGRADUATE STUDENT BODY STATS

2005-2006 enrollment: 218 full-time; 124 part-time. Men: 81%; women: 19%. **Ethnic makeup:** African American: 42%; Asian American: 7%; Hispanic: 5%; White: 44%; International: 2%.

ADMISSIONS FACTS AND FIGURES

Phone: (800) 950-1992. **Email:** admissions@capitol-college.edu. **Website:** http://www.capitol-college.edu. **Application deadlines for fall 2007:** Regular decision: Rolling. Early decision: Not offered. Early action: Not offered. Admission cannot be deferred. **Application fee:** $25. Common application is not accepted. **Admissions requirements/recommendations:** High school units required (recommended): English: 4 (4); Mathematics: 3 (4); Science: 2 (3); Foreign language: 0 (0); Social studies: 2 (2); History: 1 (1); Academic electives: 0 (0); Total units: 14 (16). Tests: The college uses SAT or ACT scores in admissions decisions. SAT required. For admission to the fall 2007 entering class, the school will accept: ACT with writing. Campus visit: Recommended. Admissions interview: Recommended. Off-campus interview: May be arranged. **Factors that count in admissions decisions:** *Academic:* Secondary school record: Very important. Class rank: Not considered. Letters of recommendation: Considered. Standardized test scores: Important. Essay: Important. *Nonacademic:* Interview: Important. Extracurricular activities: Considered. Talent/ability: Not considered. Character/personal qualities: Considered. Alumni/ae relationship: Considered. Geographical residence: Not considered. State residency: Not considered. Religious affiliation/commitment: Not considered. Minority status: Not considered. Volunteer work: Considered. Work experience: Considered. **Admissions statistics for the fall 2005 entering class:** Total applicants: 565. Total accepted: 367. Freshmen enrolled: 71; 22% were from out of state. Overall acceptance rate: 65%. **First-year students who submitted SAT scores:** 94%. Scores (25/75 percentile): Verbal: 410-550, Math: 430-530, Combined: 840-1080.

ACADEMICS

Year founded: 1964. **Academic calendar:** Semester. **Degrees offered:** certificate, associate, bachelor's, post-bachelor's certificate, master's. **Most popular majors:** 26% electrical, electronics, and communications engineering, 22% computer and information sciences, 15% engineering technologies/technicians, 11% computer engineering, 11% electrical and electronic engineering technologies/technicians. **Major fields of study:** business, management, marketing, and related support services; computer and information sciences and support services; engineering; engineering technologies/technicians. **Areas of required coursework:** humanities, computer literacy, mathematics, English (including composition), sciences (biological or physical), history, social science. **Special academic programs:** double major (5%). **Faculty and instruction (2005-2006):** Total instructional faculty: 15 full-time, 46 part-time (84% men; 16% women; 20% minorities). Student/faculty ratio: 9/1. Classes of fewer than 20 students: 82%; of 20 to 49 students: 18%. **Freshmen returning for sophomore year:** 60%. **Graduation rates:** Four-year: 18%; five-year: 35%; six-year: 31%.

COSTS AND FINANCIAL AID

Financial aid office: (301) 369-2800. **Expenses (2006-2007):** Tuition and fees 2006-2007: $18,716; room/board: $4,198. Estimated books and supplies: $1,000; transportation: $1,100; personal expenses: $1,500. **Financial aid:** Priority filing date for institution's financial aid form: March 1. In 2005-2006, 83% of undergraduates applied for financial aid. Of those, 77% were determined to have financial need; 14% had their need fully met. Average financial aid package (proportion receiving): $9,155 (76%). Average amount of gift aid, such as scholarships or grants (proportion receiving): $6,797 (67%). Average amount of self-help aid, such as work study or loans (proportion receiving): $4,216 (61%). Average need-based loan (excluding PLUS or other private loans): $4,027. Among students who received need-based aid, the average percentage of need met: 45%. Among students who received aid based on merit, the average award (and the proportion receiving): $6,083 (3%). Average amount of debt of borrowers graduating in 2005: $23,772. Proportion who borrowed: 63%.

CAMPUS LIFE AND EXTRACURRICULAR ACTIVITIES

Campus housing available (% using): women's dorms (22%), men's dorms (77%), special housing for disabled students (1%). Students who live in college-owned, operated, or affiliated housing: 26%. **Student employment:** During the 2005-2006 academic year, 15% of undergraduates worked on campus. Average per-year earnings: $1,500. **Clubs and organizations:** Number of student organizations: 6. Activities include: student government. Number of fraternities: 0; sororities: 0. Average proportion of students who stay on campus on weekends: 45%.

SERVICES AND FACILITIES

Basic services: nonremedial tutoring, placement service, health insurance. **Remedial assistance:** reading, math, writing, study skills. **Counseling services:** career, personal, veteran student, academic, older student. **For learning-disabled students:** School does not offer a structured program with separate admission and additional fees. Services include: remedial math, remedial English, reading machines, tape recorders, videotaped classes, note-taking services, oral tests, extended time for tests, tutors, priority seating, proofreading services, texts on tape, typist/scribe, other testing accomodations. **Library:** Number of titles: 10,172; number of current serial subscriptions: 87. **Information technology resources:** Students are not required to lease or own a computer. Number of campus computers available to all students: 43. School has a wireless network. Approximate number of users that can be accommodated: 150. Proportion of college-owned housing units wired for high-speed internet access: 100%. **Campus safety:** Security services offered: late-night transport/escort service, lighted pathways/sidewalks, controlled dormitory access (key, security card, etc).

TRANSFER AND INTERNATIONAL STUDENTS

Transfer students: May apply for admission for the following academic terms: Fall, Spring, Summer. Applicants need a minimum number of credits to apply. For fall 2005: Transfer applications received: 78. Transfer applicants offered admission: 63. Transfer applicants enrolled: 32. **International students:** Number of foreign undergraduates: 7 (2% of student body). Minimum TOEFL score required: 500 (paper); 170 (computer).

College of Notre Dame of Maryland

- **Address:** 4701 N. Charles Street, Baltimore, MD 21210
- **Website:** http://www.ndm.edu
- **Private; Religious affiliation:** Roman Catholic
- **Enrollment:** 596 full-time; 1,131 part-time

KEY STATS

✔ **U.S News College Ranking:** 31, Universities–Master's (North)
✔ **SAT Score (25th/75th percentile):** 910-1140
✔ **Tuition:** 2006-2007: $23,000

Selectivity: Selective	**Room/board:** $8,300
Acceptance rate: 81%	**Average debt:** $19,211
Student/faculty ratio: 11/1	**Proportion who borrowed:** 71%

UNDERGRADUATE STUDENT BODY STATS

2005-2006 enrollment: 596 full-time; 1,131 part-time. Men: 6%; women: 94%. **Ethnic makeup:** African American: 25%; Asian American: 2%; Hispanic: 3%; White: 68%; International: 1%.

ADMISSIONS FACTS AND FIGURES

Phone: (410) 532-5330. **Email:** admiss@ndm.edu. **Website:** http://www.ndm.edu. **Application deadlines for fall 2007:** Regular decision: Rolling. Early decision: Not offered. Early action: Not offered. Admission can be deferred. **Application fee:** $40. Common application is accepted. **Admissions requirements/recommendations:** High school units required (recommended): English: 4 (4); Mathematics: 3 (3); Science: 2 (2); Foreign language: 3 (3); Social studies: 2 (2); History: 0 (0); Academic electives: 4 (4); Total units: 18 (18). **Tests:** The college uses SAT or ACT scores in admissions decisions. Either SAT or ACT required. For admission to the fall 2007 entering class, the school will accept: ACT with writing, ACT without writing. Campus visit: Recommended. Admissions interview: Recommended. Off-campus interview: May be arranged. **Factors that count in admissions decisions: Academic:** Secondary school record: Very important. Class rank: Considered. Letters of recommendation: Very important. Standardized test scores: Very important. Essay: Very important. **Nonacademic:** Interview: Very important. Extracurricular activities: Important. Talent/ability: Important. Character/personal qualities: Considered. Alumni/ae relationship: Considered. Geographical residence: Not considered. State residency: Not considered. Religious affiliation/commitment: Not considered. Minority status: Not considered. Volunteer work: Important. Work experience: Considered. **Other schools with the greatest overlap in applicants:** McDaniel College; Mount St. Mary's College; Towson University; University of Maryland–Baltimore County; Villa Julie College. **Admissions statistics for the fall 2005 entering class:** Total applicants: 477. Total accepted: 388. Freshmen enrolled: 147; 14% were from out of state. Overall acceptance rate: 81%. **Credentials of fall 2005 freshmen:** 24% ranked in the top 10 percent of their high school class; 40% were in the top 25 percent, and 72% were in the top half. (Proportion submitting class standing: 61%.) **Average high school grade point average:** 3.3. **First-year students who submitted SAT scores:** 92%. Scores (25/75 percentile): Verbal: 460-580, Math: 450-560, Combined: 910-1140. **First-year students submitting ACT scores:** 8%. Scores (25/75 percentile): English: N/A, Math: N/A, Composite: N/A.

ACADEMICS

Year founded: 1873. **Academic calendar:** Semester. **Degrees offered:** certificate, bachelor's, post-bachelor's certificate, master's, post-master's certificate, doctorate. **Most popular majors:** 21% business/commerce, 14% education, 11% liberal arts and sciences studies, and humanities, 7% communication and media studies, 7% nursing. **Major fields of study:** biological and biomedical sciences; business, management, marketing, and related support services; communication, journalism, and related programs; computer and information sciences and support services; education; engineering; English language and literature/letters; foreign languages, literatures, and linguistics; health professions and related clinical sciences; history; liberal arts and sciences studies, and humanities; mathematics and statistics; multi/interdisciplinary studies; philosophy and religious studies; physical sciences; psychology; public administration and social service professions; social sciences; visual and performing arts. **Areas of required coursework:** arts/fine arts, humanities, mathematics, English (including composition), philosophy, foreign languages, sciences (biological or physical), history, social science, other. **Pre-professional programs:** pre-law, pre-dentistry, pre-medicine, pre-veterinary science, pre-pharmacy. **Special academic programs:** accelerated program, cross-registration, double major, English as a Second Language (ESL), honors program, independent study, internships, liberal arts/career combination, student-designed major, study abroad, teacher certificate program, weekend college. **Teacher certification offered in:** early childhood, special education, elementary, middle/junior high, secondary, bilingual/bicultural. **Reserve Officers Training Corps (ROTC):** Army ROTC: Offered at cooperating institution (Loyola College). **Faculty and instruction (2005-2006):** Total instructional faculty: 78 full-time, 11 part-time (28% men; 72% women; 7% minorities). Full-time faculty with Ph.D. or other terminal degree: 82%. Student/faculty ratio: 11/1. Classes of fewer than 20 students: 82%; of 20 to 49 students: 18%; of 50 or more students: 0%. **Advanced Placement and International Baccalaureate credit:** AP tests may be used for: Credit and/or placement. Scores accepted: 3, 4, 5. International Baccalaureate exams may be used for: Credit and/or placement. **Freshmen returning for sophomore year:** 86%. **Graduation rates:** Four-year: 57%; five-year: 61%; six-year: 68%. **Graduate study:** 42% of students pursue further study within one year. Fields in which graduates pursue further study: Master of Business Administration (MBA), 24%; law, 14%; medicine, 29%; engineering, 4%; education, 19%; arts and sciences, 10%.

COSTS AND FINANCIAL AID

Financial aid office: (410) 532-5369. **Expenses (2006-2007):** Tuition and fees 2006-2007: $23,000; room/board: $8,300. Estimated books and supplies: $1,000; transportation: $400; personal expenses: $1,000. **Financial aid:** Priority filing date for institution's financial aid form: February 15. In 2005-2006, 84% of undergraduates applied for financial aid. Of those, 76% were determined to have financial need; 26% had their need fully met. Average financial aid package (proportion receiving): $18,061 (74%). Average

amount of gift aid, such as scholarships or grants (proportion receiving): $8,635 (65%). Average amount of self-help aid, such as work study or loans (proportion receiving): $4,470 (56%). Average need-based loan (excluding PLUS or other private loans): $4,221. Among students who received need-based aid, the average percentage of need met: 75%. Among students who received aid based on merit, the average award (and the proportion receiving): $9,055 (8%). The average athletic scholarship (and the proportion receiving): $0 (0%). Average amount of debt of borrowers graduating in 2005: $19,211. Proportion who borrowed: 71%.

CAMPUS LIFE AND EXTRACURRICULAR ACTIVITIES

Campus housing available (% using): women's dorms (100%). Students who live in college-owned, operated, or affiliated housing: 52%. Average per-year earnings: $1,500. **Clubs and organizations:** Number of student organizations: 30. Activities include: choral groups, dance, drama/theater, literary magazine, music ensembles, radio station, student government, student newspaper, student film society, television station, yearbook. Number of fraternities: 0; sororities: 0. **Sports program (2005-2006):** Member of NCAA III. **Women's intercollegiate varsity sports:** basketball, field hockey, lacrosse, soccer, swimming and diving, tennis, volleyball.

SERVICES AND FACILITIES

Basic services: nonremedial tutoring, health service, health insurance. **Counseling services:** career, personal, academic, older student, psychological. **For learning-disabled students:** School does not offer a structured program with separate admission and additional fees. Services include: reading machines, tape recorders, untimed tests, oral tests, extended time for tests, tutors, priority seating, proofreading services, substitution of courses, texts on tape, exams on tape or computer, take home exams, other testing accomodations, waiver of foreign language degree requirement. **Library:** Number of titles: 455,081; number of current serial subscriptions: 1,421. **Information technology resources:** Students are not required to lease or own a computer. Number of campus computers available to all students: 180. School has a wireless network. Proportion of college-owned housing units wired for high-speed internet access: 100%. **Campus safety:** Security services offered: 24-hour foot and vehicle patrols, late-night transport/escort service, 24-hour emergency telephones, lighted pathways/sidewalks, controlled dormitory access (key, security card, etc).

TRANSFER AND INTERNATIONAL STUDENTS

Transfer students: May apply for admission for the following academic terms: Fall, Spring. Applicants need a minimum number of credits to apply. For fall 2005: Transfer applications received: 117. Transfer applicants offered admission: 89. Transfer applicants enrolled: 44. **International students:** Number of foreign undergraduates: 21 (1% of student body). Number of countries represented: 11. Minimum TOEFL score required: 500 (paper); 173 (computer).

Columbia Union College

- **Address:** 7600 Flower Avenue, Takoma Park, MD 20912
- **Website:** http://www.cuc.edu
- **Private; Religious affiliation:** Seventh-day Adventist
- **Enrollment:** 730 full-time; 288 part-time

KEY STATS

✔ **U.S News College Ranking:** third tier, Comp. Coll.–Bachelor's (North)
✔ **SAT Score (25th/75th percentile):** 730-970
✔ **Tuition:** 2006-2007: $18,439

Selectivity: Less selective	**Room/board:** $6,247
Acceptance rate: 35%	**Average debt:** N/A
Student/faculty ratio: 12/1	**Proportion who borrowed:** N/A

UNDERGRADUATE STUDENT BODY STATS

2005-2006 enrollment: 730 full-time; 288 part-time. Men: 36%; women: 64%. **Ethnic makeup:** African American: 56%; Asian American: 6%; Hispanic: 8%; White: 27%; International: 4%. **Religious preference:** Roman Catholic: 6%; Protestant: 9%; Unknown: 21%; Seventh-day Adventist: 52%; Other: 12%.

ADMISSIONS FACTS AND FIGURES

Phone: (301) 891-4080. **Email:** enroll@cuc.edu. **Website:** http://www.cuc.edu. **Application deadlines for fall 2007:** Regular decision: August 1. Early decision: Not offered. Early action: Not offered. Admission can be deferred. **Application fee:** $25. Common application is not accepted. **Admissions requirements/recommendations:** High school units required (recommended): English: 4; Mathematics: 2; Science: 2; Foreign language: 2; Social studies: 2; History: 4; Total units: 16. Tests: The college uses SAT or ACT scores in admissions decisions. Either SAT or ACT required. For admission to the fall 2007 entering class, the school will accept: ACT with writing. Campus visit: Recommended. Admissions interview: Neither required nor recommended. Off-campus interview: May be arranged. **Factors that count in admissions decisions:** *Academic:* Secondary school record: Very important. Class rank: Not considered. Letters of recommendation: Important. Standardized test scores: Very important. Essay: Considered. *Nonacademic:* Interview: Not considered. Extracurricular activities: Considered. Talent/ability: Important. Character/personal qualities: Important. Alumni/ae relationship: Not considered. Geographical residence: Not considered. State residency: Not considered. Religious affiliation/commitment: Important. Minority status: Not considered. Volunteer work: Considered. Work experience: Considered. **Other schools with the greatest overlap in applicants:** Andrews University; Southern Adventist University; University of Maryland–College Park. **Admissions statistics for the fall 2005 entering class:** Total applicants: 1,351. Total accepted: 469. Freshmen enrolled: 172; 62% were from out of state. Overall acceptance rate: 35%. **Average high school grade point average:** 3.0. **First-year students who submitted SAT scores:** 67%. Scores (25/75 percentile): Verbal: 360-490, Math: 370-480, Combined: 730-970. **First-year students submitting ACT scores:** 22%. Scores (25/75 percentile): English: 15-21, Math: 16-21, Composite: 17-21.

ACADEMICS

Year founded: 1904. **Academic calendar:** Semester. **Degrees offered:** certificate, associate, bachelor's, master's. **Most popular majors:** 25% psychology, 21% business, management, marketing, and related support services, 20% health professions and related clinical sciences. **Major fields of study:** biological and biomedical sciences; business, management, marketing, and related support services; communication, journalism, and related programs; computer and information sciences and support services; education; English language and literature/letters; health professions and related clinical sciences; history; liberal arts and sciences studies, and humanities; mathematics and statistics; parks, recreation, leisure, and fitness studies; philosophy and religious studies; physical sciences; psychology; theology and religious vocations; visual and performing arts. **Areas of required coursework:** arts/fine arts, humanities, computer literacy, mathematics, English (including composition), sciences (biological or physical), history, social science, other. **Pre-professional programs:** pre-law, pre-dentistry, pre-medicine, pre-veterinary science, pre-optometry, pre-pharmacy. **Special academic programs (% participation):** accelerated program (48%), cooperative (work-study plan) program, distance learning, double major, English as a Second Language (ESL), external degree program, honors program, independent study, internships, student-designed major, study abroad, teacher certificate program. **Teacher certification offered in:** special education, elementary, secondary. **Cooperative education programs:** business, computer science, natural science. **Faculty and instruction (2005-2006):** Total instructional faculty: 53 full-time, 3 part-time (57% men; 43% women; 36% minorities). Full-time faculty with Ph.D. or other terminal degree: 47%. Student/faculty ratio: 12/1. Classes of fewer than 20 students: 81%; of 20 to 49 students: 19%; of 50 or more students: 1%. **Advanced Placement and International Baccalaureate credit:** AP tests may be used for: Credit only. Scores accepted: 3, 4, 5. **Freshmen returning for sophomore year:** 62%. **Graduation rates:** Four-year: 15%; five-year: 28%; six-year: 32%. **Graduate study:** 30% of students pursue further study within one year.

COSTS AND FINANCIAL AID

Financial aid office: (301) 891-4005. **Expenses (2006-2007):** Tuition and fees 2006-2007: $18,439; room/board: $6,247. Estimated books and supplies: $950; transportation: $0; personal expenses: $1,050. **Financial aid:** Priority filing date for institution's financial aid form: March 1.

CAMPUS LIFE AND EXTRACURRICULAR ACTIVITIES

Campus housing available: women's dorms, men's dorms, apartments for married students, apartment for single students. Students who live in college-owned, operated, or affiliated housing: 48%. **Student employment:** During the 2005-2006 academic year, 33% of undergraduates worked on campus. Average per-year earnings: $5,500. Activities include: choral groups, concert band, music ensembles, radio station, student government, student newspaper, symphony orchestra, yearbook. **Sports program (2005-2006):** Member of NCAA II. *Men's intercollegiate varsity sports:* baseball, basketball, cross-country, soccer, track and field (outdoor). *Women's intercollegiate varsity sports:* basketball, cross-country, soccer, softball, track and field (outdoor).

SERVICES AND FACILITIES

Basic services: nonremedial tutoring, health service, health insurance. **Remedial assistance:** math, writing, study skills. **Counseling services:** career, personal, academic, psychological, religious. **For learning-disabled students:** School does not offer a structured program with separate admission and additional fees. Services include: remedial math, remedial English, untimed tests, learning center, extended time for tests, tutors. **Library:** Number of titles: 141,152; number of current serial subscriptions: 382. **Information technology resources:** Students are not required to lease or own a computer. Number of campus computers available to all students: 75. School has a wireless network. Approximate number of users that can be accommodated: 300. Proportion of college-owned housing units wired for high-speed internet access: 90%. **Campus safety:** Security services offered: 24-hour foot and vehicle patrols, late-night transport/escort service, lighted pathways/sidewalks, controlled dormitory access (key, security card, etc).

TRANSFER AND INTERNATIONAL STUDENTS

Transfer students: May apply for admission for the following academic terms: Fall, Spring, Summer. Applicants need a minimum number of credits to apply. For fall 2005: Transfer applications received: 449. Transfer applicants offered admission: 219. Transfer applicants enrolled: 75. **International students:** Number of foreign undergraduates: 35 (4% of student body). Number of countries represented: 38. Minimum TOEFL score required: 550 (paper); 213 (computer).

Coppin State University

- **Address:** 2500 W. North Avenue, Baltimore, MD 21216-3698
- **Website:** http://www.coppin.edu
- Public
- **Enrollment:** 2,727 full-time; 724 part-time

KEY STATS

✔ **U.S News College Ranking:** fourth tier, Universities–Master's (North)
✔ **SAT Score (25th/75th percentile):** 770-930
✔ **Tuition:** 2006-2007: $4,910 in state, $11,934 out of state

Selectivity: Less selective	**Room/board:** $6,426
Acceptance rate: 49%	**Average debt:** $13,833
Student/faculty ratio: 17/1	**Proportion who borrowed:** 73%

UNDERGRADUATE STUDENT BODY STATS

2005-2006 enrollment: 2,727 full-time; 724 part-time. Men: 23%; women: 77%. **Ethnic makeup:** African American: 96%; White: 1%; International: 3%.

ADMISSIONS FACTS AND FIGURES

Phone: (410) 951-3600. **Email:** admissions@coppin.edu. **Website:** http://www.coppin.edu. **Application deadlines for fall 2007:** Regular decision: July 15. Early decision: Not offered. Early action: Not offered. Admission can be deferred. **Application fee:** $35. Common application is accepted. **To apply online, go to:** http://apply.usmd.edu. **Admissions requirements/recommendations:** High school units required (recommended): English: 4; Mathematics: 3; Science: 2; Foreign language: 2; Social studies: 3; Total units: 16. Tests: The college uses SAT or ACT scores in admissions decisions. Either SAT or ACT required. For admission to the fall 2007 entering class, the school will accept: ACT with writing, ACT without writing. Campus visit: Recommended. Admissions interview: Neither required nor recommended. Off-campus interview: Not available. **Factors that count in admissions decisions:** *Academic:* Secondary school record: Very important. Class rank: Considered. Letters of recommendation: Important. Standardized test scores: Important. Essay: Considered. *Nonacademic:* Interview: Considered. Extracurricular activities: Considered. Talent/ability: Important. Character/personal qualities: Considered. Alumni/ae relationship: Considered. Geographical residence:

Considered. State residency: Considered. Religious affiliation/commitment: Not considered. Minority status: Considered. Volunteer work: Considered. Work experience: Considered. **Other schools with the greatest overlap in applicants:** Frostburg State University; Morgan State University; Morgan State University; Towson University; Towson University; University of Maryland–Baltimore County; University of Maryland–Baltimore County; University of Maryland–Eastern Shore; University of Maryland–Eastern Shore. **Admissions statistics for the fall 2005 entering class:** Total applicants: 3,825. Total accepted: 1,855. Freshmen enrolled: 690; Overall acceptance rate: 49%. **Size of waiting list:** 0 applicants; enrolled from waiting list: 0. **First-year students who submitted SAT scores:** 82%. Scores (25/75 percentile): Verbal: 390-470, Math: 380-460, Combined: 770-930.

ACADEMICS

Year founded: 1900. **Academic calendar:** Semester. **Degrees offered:** certificate, bachelor's, master's. **Most popular majors:** 17% psychology, 16% business administration, management, and operations, 14% criminal justice/safety studies, 12% nursing, 9% liberal arts and sciences/liberal studies. **Major fields of study:** biological and biomedical sciences; business, management, marketing, and related support services; computer and information sciences and support services; education; English language and literature/letters; health professions and related clinical sciences; history; mathematics and statistics; multi/interdisciplinary studies; parks, recreation, leisure, and fitness studies; physical sciences; psychology; public administration and social service professions; security and protective services; social sciences; visual and performing arts. **Areas of required coursework:** arts/fine arts, humanities, computer literacy, mathematics, English (including composition), philosophy, sciences (biological or physical), history, social science. **Pre-professional programs:** pre-dentistry, pre-pharmacy, other. **Special academic programs:** accelerated program, cooperative (work-study plan) program, distance learning, double major, external degree program, honors program, independent study, internships, liberal arts/career combination, study abroad, teacher certificate program, weekend college, other. **Teacher certification offered in:** early childhood, special education, elementary, adult education, secondary. **Cooperative education programs:** business, computer science, natural science, social/behavioral science. **Reserve Officers Training Corps (ROTC):** Army ROTC: Offered on campus. **Faculty and instruction (2005-2006):** Total instructional faculty: 131 full-time, 128 part-time (48% men; 52% women; 88% minorities). Full-time faculty with Ph.D. or other terminal degree: 58%. Student/faculty ratio: 17/1. Classes of fewer than 20 students: 31%; of 20 to 49 students: 65%; of 50 or more students: 3%. **Advanced Placement and International Baccalaureate credit:** AP tests may be used for: Credit and/or placement. Scores accepted: 3. International Baccalaureate exams may be used for: Credit and/or placement. **Freshmen returning for sophomore year:** 67%. **Graduation rates:** Four-year: 9%; five-year: 16%; six-year: 24%.

COSTS AND FINANCIAL AID

Financial aid office: (410) 951-3636. **Expenses (2006-2007):** Tuition and fees 2006-2007: $4,910 in state, $11,934 out of state; room/board: $6,426. Estimated books and supplies: $800; transportation: $600; personal expenses: $2,786. **Financial aid:** Priority filing date for institution's financial aid form: March 1. In 2005-2006, 87% of undergraduates applied for financial aid. Of those, 87% were determined to have financial need; 15% had their need fully met. Average financial aid package (proportion receiving): $6,880 (80%). Average amount of gift aid, such as scholarships or grants (proportion receiving): $4,399 (65%). Average amount of self-help aid, such as work study or loans (proportion receiving): $3,802 (62%). Average need-based loan (excluding PLUS or other private loans): $4,034. Among students who received need-based aid, the average percentage of need met: 66%. Among students who received aid based on merit, the average award (and the proportion receiving): $2,427 (1%). The average athletic scholarship (and the proportion receiving): $14,456 (2%). Average amount of debt of borrowers graduating in 2005: $13,833. Proportion who borrowed: 73%.

CAMPUS LIFE AND EXTRACURRICULAR ACTIVITIES

Campus housing available: coed dorms, special housing for disabled students, other housing options. **Clubs and organizations:** Number of student organizations: 28. Activities include: choral groups, concert band, dance, drama/theater, music ensembles, radio station, student government, student newspaper, student film society, television station, yearbook. Number of fraternities: 3; sororities: 4. Average proportion of students who stay on campus on weekends: 40%. **Sports program (2005-2006):** Member of

NCAA I. **Men's intercollegiate varsity sports:** baseball, basketball, cheerleading, cross-country, tennis, track and field (indoor), track and field (outdoor). **Women's intercollegiate varsity sports:** basketball, bowling, cheerleading, cross-country, softball, tennis, track and field (indoor), track and field (outdoor), volleyball.

SERVICES AND FACILITIES

Basic services: nonremedial tutoring, health service, health insurance. **Remedial assistance:** reading, math, writing, study skills. **Counseling services:** career, personal, academic, psychological. **For learning-disabled students:** Services include: remedial math, remedial reading, untimed tests, extended time for tests. **Information technology resources:** Students are not required to lease or own a computer. Number of campus computers available to all students: 335. School has a wireless network. Proportion of college-owned housing units wired for high-speed internet access: 100%. **Campus safety:** Security services offered: 24-hour foot and vehicle patrols, late-night transport/escort service, 24-hour emergency telephones, lighted pathways/sidewalks, controlled dormitory access (key, security card, etc).

TRANSFER AND INTERNATIONAL STUDENTS

Transfer students: May apply for admission for the following academic terms: Fall, Spring. Applicants need a minimum number of credits to apply. For fall 2005: Transfer applications received: 1,232. Transfer applicants offered admission: 904. Transfer applicants enrolled: 271. **International students:** Number of foreign undergraduates: 22 (3% of student body). Number of countries represented: 23. Minimum TOEFL score required: 500 (paper); 173 (computer).

Frostburg State University

- **Address:** 101 Braddock Road, Frostburg, MD 21532
- **Website:** http://www.frostburg.edu
- **Public**
- **Enrollment:** 4,053 full-time; 268 part-time

KEY STATS

✔ **U.S News College Ranking:** third tier, Universities–Master's (North)
✔ **SAT Score (25th/75th percentile):** 900-1100
✔ **Tuition:** 2006-2007: $6,616 in state, $15,442 out of state

Selectivity: Less selective	**Room/board:** $6,800
Acceptance rate: 76%	**Average debt:** $15,678
Student/faculty ratio: 17/1	**Proportion who borrowed:** 61%

UNDERGRADUATE STUDENT BODY STATS

2005-2006 enrollment: 4,053 full-time; 268 part-time. Men: 51%; women: 49%. **Ethnic makeup:** African American: 15%; Asian American: 2%; Hispanic: 2%; White: 80%; International: 1%.

ADMISSIONS FACTS AND FIGURES

Phone: (301) 687-4201. **Email:** fsuadmissions@frostburg.edu. **Website:** http://www.frostburg.edu. **Application deadlines for fall 2007:** Regular decision: Rolling. Early decision: Send application by: December 15; Decision sent by: N/A. Early action: Not offered. **Application fee:** $30. Common application is not accepted. **To apply online, go to:** http://www.frostburg.edu/ungrad/admiss/onlineapproc.htm. **Admissions requirements/recommendations:** High school units required (recommended): English: 4; Mathematics: 3; Science: 3; Foreign language: 2; History: 3; Total units: 15. Tests: The college uses SAT or ACT scores in admissions decisions. Either SAT or ACT required. For admission to the fall 2007 entering class, the school will accept: ACT with writing, ACT without writing. Campus visit: Recommended. **Factors that count in admissions decisions:** *Academic:* Secondary school record: Very important. Standardized test scores: Very important. Essay: Considered. **Admissions statistics for the fall 2005 entering class:** Total applicants: 3,430. Total accepted: 2,596. Freshmen enrolled: 942; 11% were from out of state. Overall acceptance rate: 76%. Non-early acceptance rate: 76%. **Credentials of fall 2005 freshmen:** 10% ranked in the top 10 percent of their high school class; 32% were in the top 25 percent, and 73% were in the top half. (Proportion submitting class standing: 5%.) **Average high school grade point average:** 3.1. **First-year students who submitted SAT scores:** 97%. Scores (25/75 percentile): Verbal: 450-550, Math: 450-550, Combined: 900-

1100. **First-year students submitting ACT scores:** 12%. Scores (25/75 percentile): English: N/A, Math: N/A, Composite: 18-21.

ACADEMICS

Year founded: 1898. **Academic calendar:** Semester. **Degrees offered:** certificate, bachelor's, post-bachelor's certificate, master's, post-master's certificate. **Most popular majors:** 12% business administration and management, 10% elementary education and teaching, 7% psychology, 6% liberal arts and sciences/liberal studies, 6% visual and performing arts. **Major fields of study:** architecture and related services; biological and biomedical sciences; business, management, marketing, and related support services; communication, journalism, and related programs; computer and information sciences and support services; education; English language and literature/letters; foreign languages, literatures, and linguistics; health professions and related clinical sciences; history; liberal arts and sciences studies, and humanities; mathematics and statistics; multi/interdisciplinary studies; natural resources and conservation; parks, recreation, leisure, and fitness studies; philosophy and religious studies; physical sciences; psychology; public administration and social service professions; security and protective services; social sciences; visual and performing arts. **Areas of required coursework:** arts/fine arts, humanities, mathematics, English (including composition), sciences (biological or physical), social science. **Pre-professional programs:** pre-law, pre-dentistry, pre-medicine, pre-veterinary science, pre-optometry, pre-pharmacy. **Special academic programs:** distance learning, double major, dual enrollment, honors program, independent study, internships, study abroad, teacher certificate program. **Teacher certification offered in:** early childhood, special education, elementary, middle/junior high, secondary. **Cooperative education programs:** engineering. **Faculty and instruction (2005-2006):** Total instructional faculty: 233 full-time, 118 part-time (57% men; 43% women; 10% minorities). Full-time faculty with Ph.D. or other terminal degree: 86%. Student/faculty ratio: 17/1. Classes of fewer than 20 students: 52%; of 20 to 49 students: 45%; of 50 or more students: 3%. **Advanced Placement and International Baccalaureate credit:** AP tests may be used for: Credit only. Scores accepted: 3, 4, 5. International Baccalaureate exams may be used for: Credit only. **Freshmen returning for sophomore year:** 73%. **Graduation rates:** Four-year: 21%; five-year: 43%; six-year: 49%.

COSTS AND FINANCIAL AID

Financial aid office: (301) 687-4301. **Expenses (2006-2007):** Tuition and fees 2006-2007: $6,616 in state, $15,442 out of state; room/board: $6,800. Estimated books and supplies: $1,200; transportation: $500; personal expenses: $1,000. **Financial aid:** Priority filing date for institution's financial aid form: March 1. In 2005-2006, 70% of undergraduates applied for financial aid. Of those, 48% were determined to have financial need; 26% had their need fully met. Average financial aid package (proportion receiving): $6,906 (48%). Average amount of gift aid, such as scholarships or grants (proportion receiving): $4,075 (36%). Average amount of self-help aid, such as work study or loans (proportion receiving): $3,363 (37%). Average need-based loan (excluding PLUS or other private loans): $3,320. Among students who received need-based aid, the average percentage of need met: 71%. Among students who received aid based on merit, the average award (and the proportion receiving): $2,452 (10%). Average amount of debt of borrowers graduating in 2005: $15,678. Proportion who borrowed: 61%.

CAMPUS LIFE AND EXTRACURRICULAR ACTIVITIES

Campus housing available (% using): coed dorms (96%), women's dorms (4%). Students who live in college-owned, operated, or affiliated housing: 35%. **Student employment:** During the 2005-2006 academic year, 17% of undergraduates worked on campus. Average per-year earnings: $800. **Clubs and organizations:** Number of student organizations: 80. Activities include: choral groups, concert band, dance, drama/theater, jazz band, literary magazine, marching band, music ensembles, musical theater, pep band, radio station, student government, student newspaper, television station. Number of fraternities: 8; sororities: 8. Proportion of men in fraternities: 10%; of women in sororities: 10%. **Sports program (2005-2006):** Member of NCAA III. *Men's intercollegiate varsity sports:* baseball, basketball, cheerleading, cross-country, football, soccer, swimming and diving, tennis, track and field (indoor), track and field (outdoor). *Women's intercollegiate varsity sports:* basketball, cheerleading, cross-country, field hockey, golf, lacrosse, soccer, softball, swimming and diving, tennis, track and field (indoor), track and field (outdoor), volleyball.

SERVICES AND FACILITIES

Basic services: nonremedial tutoring, health service. **Remedial assistance:** math. **Counseling services:** career, personal, veteran student, psychological. **For learning-disabled students:** School does not offer a structured program with separate admission and additional fees. Total undergraduates in learning-disabled program or receiving services: 260. Services include: remedial math, tape recorders, untimed tests, note-taking services, readers, extended time for tests, tutors. **Library:** Number of titles: 362,799; number of current serial subscriptions: 939. **Information technology resources:** Students are not required to lease or own a computer. Number of campus computers available to all students: 668. School has a wireless network. Proportion of college-owned housing units wired for high-speed internet access: 100%. **Campus safety:** Security services offered: late-night transport/escort service, 24-hour emergency telephones.

TRANSFER AND INTERNATIONAL STUDENTS

Transfer students: May apply for admission for the following academic terms: Fall, Winter, Spring, Summer. Applicants need a minimum number of credits to apply. For fall 2005: Transfer applications received: 670. Transfer applicants offered admission: 490. Transfer applicants enrolled: 323. **International students:** Number of foreign undergraduates: 32 (1% of student body). Minimum TOEFL score required: 550 (paper); 213 (computer).

Goucher College

- **Address:** 1021 Dulaney Valley Road, Baltimore, MD 21204
- **Website:** http://www.goucher.edu
- **Private**
- **Enrollment:** 1,306 full-time; 40 part-time

KEY STATS

✔ **U.S News College Ranking:** 91, Liberal Arts Colleges
✔ **SAT Score (25th/75th percentile):** 1100-1310
✔ **Tuition:** 2006-2007: $29,325

Selectivity: More selective	**Room/board:** $9,225
Acceptance rate: 67%	**Average debt:** $15,468
Student/faculty ratio: 9/1	**Proportion who borrowed:** 50%

UNDERGRADUATE STUDENT BODY STATS

2005-2006 enrollment: 1,306 full-time; 40 part-time. Men: 33%; women: 67%. **Ethnic makeup:** African American: 4%; Asian American: 3%; Hispanic: 3%; White: 88%; International: 1%. **Religious preference:** Roman Catholic: 11%; Protestant: 28%; Jewish: 20%; No preference: 36%; Unknown: 5%.

ADMISSIONS FACTS AND FIGURES

Phone: (410) 337-6100. **Email:** admissions@goucher.edu. **Website:** http://www.goucher.edu. **Application deadlines for fall 2007:** Regular decision: February 1; decision sent by April 1. Early decision: Not offered. Early action: Send application by: December 15; Decision sent by: February 15. Admission can be deferred. **Application fee:** $40. Common application is accepted. **To apply online, go to:** http://www.goucher.edu/admissions. **Admissions requirements/recommendations:** High school units required (recommended): English: 4 (4); Mathematics: 3 (4); Science: 2 (3); Foreign language: 2 (4); Social studies: 3 (3); Academic electives: 2 (2); Total units: 16 (20). Tests: The college uses SAT or ACT scores in admissions decisions. Either SAT or ACT required. For admission to the fall 2007 entering class, the school will accept: ACT with writing. Campus visit: Recommended. Admissions interview: Recommended. Off-campus interview: May be arranged. **Factors that count in admissions decisions:** *Academic:* Secondary school record: Very important. Class rank: Considered. Letters of recommendation: Important. Standardized test scores: Important. Essay: Important. *Nonacademic:* Interview: Considered. Extracurricular activities: Considered. Talent/ability: Important. Character/personal qualities: Considered. Alumni/ae relationship: Considered. Geographical residence: Not considered. State residency: Not considered. Religious affiliation/commitment: Not considered. Minority status: Considered. Volunteer work: Considered. Work experience: Considered. **Other schools with the greatest overlap in applicants:** American University; Clark University; Dickinson College; Skidmore College; Towson University. **Admissions statistics for the fall 2005 entering**

class: Total applicants: 2,976. Total accepted: 1,991. Freshmen enrolled: 340; 76% were from out of state. Accepted through early-decision or early-action plans: 38%. Overall acceptance rate: 67%. Non-early acceptance rate: 61%. **Size of waiting list:** 264 applicants; enrolled from waiting list: 59. **Credentials of fall 2005 freshmen:** 26% ranked in the top 10 percent of their high school class; 63% were in the top 25 percent, and 83% were in the top half. (Proportion submitting class standing: 40%.) **Average high school grade point average:** 3.2. **First-year students who submitted SAT scores:** 94%. Scores (25/75 percentile): Verbal: 560-670, Math: 540-640, Combined: 1100-1310. **First-year students submitting ACT scores:** 23%. Scores (25/75 percentile): English: 22-28, Math: 20-26, Composite: 23-27.

ACADEMICS

Year founded: 1885. **Academic calendar:** Semester. **Degrees offered:** bachelor's, post-bachelor's certificate, master's. **Most popular majors:** 15% psychology, 14% visual and performing arts, 11% English language and literature, 8% business administration and management, 5% biology/biological sciences. **Major fields of study:** area, ethnic, cultural, and gender studies; biological and biomedical sciences; business, management, marketing, and related support services; communication, journalism, and related programs; computer and information sciences and support services; education; English language and literature/letters; foreign languages, literatures, and linguistics; history; mathematics and statistics; multi/interdisciplinary studies; philosophy and religious studies; physical sciences; psychology; social sciences; visual and performing arts. **Areas of required coursework:** arts/fine arts, humanities, computer literacy, mathematics, English (including composition), foreign languages, sciences (biological or physical), history, social science, other. **Pre-professional programs:** pre-law, pre-dentistry, pre-medicine, pre-veterinary science. **Special academic programs (% participation):** cross-registration (12%), double major (16.4%), dual enrollment, independent study, internships (82.1%), student-designed major (2.2%), study abroad (57%), teacher certificate program (5.8%). **Teacher certification offered in:** special education, elementary, secondary. **Reserve Officers Training Corps (ROTC):** Army ROTC: Offered at cooperating institution (Loyola College of Maryland). **Faculty and instruction (2005-2006):** Total instructional faculty: 113 full-time, 78 part-time (37% men; 63% women; 12% minorities). Full-time faculty with Ph.D. or other terminal degree: 89%. Student/faculty ratio: 9/1. Classes of fewer than 20 students: 76%; of 20 to 49 students: 24%; of 50 or more students: 1%. **Advanced Placement and International Baccalaureate credit:** AP tests may be used for: Credit and/or placement. Scores accepted: 4, 5. International Baccalaureate exams may be used for: Credit and/or placement. **Freshmen returning for sophomore year:** 82%. **Graduation rates:** Four-year: 57%; five-year: 62%; six-year: 64%. **Graduate study:** 37% of students pursue further study within one year. Fields in which graduates pursue further study: Master of Business Administration (MBA), 1%; law, 2%; medicine, 2%; engineering, 1%; education, 8%; arts and sciences, 18%.

COSTS AND FINANCIAL AID

Financial aid office: (410) 337-6141. **Expenses (2006-2007):** Tuition and fees 2006-2007: $29,325; room/board: $9,225. Estimated books and supplies: $800; transportation: $530; personal expenses: $800. **Financial aid:** Priority filing date for institution's financial aid form: February 15; deadline: February 15. In 2005-2006, 67% of undergraduates applied for financial aid. Of those, 55% were determined to have financial need; 23% had their need fully met. Average financial aid package (proportion receiving): $19,792 (55%). Average amount of gift aid, such as scholarships or grants (proportion receiving): $16,011 (52%). Average amount of self-help aid, such as work study or loans (proportion receiving): $5,337 (48%). Average need-based loan (excluding PLUS or other private loans): $4,827. Among students who received need-based aid, the average percentage of need met: 82%. Among students who received aid based on merit, the average award (and the proportion receiving): $13,652 (30%). The average athletic scholarship (and the proportion receiving): $0 (0%). Average amount of debt of borrowers graduating in 2005: $15,468. Proportion who borrowed: 50%.

CAMPUS LIFE AND EXTRACURRICULAR ACTIVITIES

Campus housing available (% using): coed dorms (77%), women's dorms (14%), other housing options (1%). Students who live in college-owned, operated, or affiliated housing: 81%. **Student employment:** During the 2005-2006 academic year, 52% of undergraduates worked on campus. **Clubs and organizations:** Number of student organizations: 60. Activities include: choral groups, dance, drama/theater, jazz band, literary magazine, music ensembles, opera, radio station, student government, student newspaper, student film society, symphony orchestra, television station, yearbook. Number of fraternities: 0; sororities: 0. Average proportion of students who stay on campus on weekends: 98%. **Sports program (2005-2006):** Member of NCAA III. *Men's intercollegiate varsity sports:* basketball, cross-country, lacrosse, soccer, swimming and diving, tennis, track and field (indoor), track and field (outdoor). *Women's intercollegiate varsity sports:* basketball, cross-country, equestrian sports, field hockey, lacrosse, soccer, swimming and diving, tennis, track and field (indoor), track and field (outdoor), volleyball.

SERVICES AND FACILITIES

Basic services: nonremedial tutoring, placement service, health service, health insurance. **Remedial assistance:** writing, study skills. **Counseling services:** minority student, career, personal, academic, older student, psychological, birth control, religious. **For learning-disabled students:** School does not offer a structured program with separate admission and additional fees. Services include: reading machines, tape recorders, note-taking services, learning center, extended time for tests. **Library:** Number of titles: 302,615; number of current serial subscriptions: 2,195. **Information technology resources:** Students are not required to lease or own a computer. Number of campus computers available to all students: 140. School has a wireless network. Approximate number of users that can be accommodated: 350. Proportion of college-owned housing units wired for high-speed internet access: 100%. **Campus safety:** Security services offered: 24-hour foot and vehicle patrols, late-night transport/escort service, 24-hour emergency telephones, lighted pathways/sidewalks, controlled dormitory access (key, security card, etc).

TRANSFER AND INTERNATIONAL STUDENTS

Transfer students: May apply for admission for the following academic terms: Fall, Spring. Applicants need a minimum number of credits to apply. For fall 2005: Transfer applications received: 150. Transfer applicants offered admission: 90. Transfer applicants enrolled: 40. **International students:** Number of foreign undergraduates: 12 (1% of student body). Number of countries represented: 9. Minimum TOEFL score required: 550 (paper); 230 (computer). Average TOEFL score: 557 (paper).

Hood College

- **Address:** 401 Rosemont Avenue, Frederick, MD 21701
- **Website:** http://www.hood.edu
- **Private; Religious affiliation:** United Church of Christ (historic affiliation)
- **Enrollment:** 1,007 full-time; 176 part-time

KEY STATS

✔ **U.S News College Ranking:** 18, Universities–Master's (North)
✔ **SAT Score (25th/75th percentile):** 1010-1200
✔ **Tuition:** 2006-2007: $23,655

Selectivity: More selective	**Room/board:** $8,135
Acceptance rate: 51%	**Average debt:** $16,295
Student/faculty ratio: 12/1	**Proportion who borrowed:** 74%

UNDERGRADUATE STUDENT BODY STATS

2005-2006 enrollment: 1,007 full-time; 176 part-time. Men: 25%; women: 75%. **Ethnic makeup:** African American: 12%; Asian American: 2%; Hispanic: 3%; White: 80%; International: 3%. **Religious preference:** Roman Catholic: 15%; Protestant: 18%; Jewish: 2%; Muslim: 1%; Hindu: 1%; Buddhist: 1%; No preference: 1%; Unknown: 41%; United Church of Christ (historic affiliation): 1%; Christian: 12%; Other: 7%.

ADMISSIONS FACTS AND FIGURES

Phone: (800) 922-1599. **Email:** admissions@hood.edu. **Website:** http://www.hood.edu. **Application deadlines for fall 2007:** Regular decision: Rolling. Early decision: Not offered. Early action: Send application by: October 1; Decision sent by: October 15. Admission can be deferred. **Application fee:** $35. Common application is accepted. **To apply online, go to:** http://www.hood.edu/admissions/index.cfm?pid=/admissions/app/_applyOnline.htm. **Admissions requirements/recommendations:** High school units required (recommended): English: 0 (4); Mathematics: 0 (3); Science: 0 (3); Foreign language: 0 (2); Social studies: 0 (3); History: 0 (0); Academic electives: 0 (1); Total units: 0 (16). Tests: The college uses

SAT or ACT scores in admissions decisions. Either SAT or ACT required. For admission to the fall 2007 entering class, the school will accept: ACT with writing, ACT without writing. Campus visit: Recommended. Admissions interview: Recommended. Off-campus interview: Not available. **Factors that count in admissions decisions:** *Academic:* Secondary school record: Very important. Class rank: Important. Letters of recommendation: Considered. Standardized test scores: Very important. Essay: Considered. *Nonacademic:* Interview: Considered. Extracurricular activities: Important. Talent/ability: Important. Character/personal qualities: Important. Alumni/ae relationship: Important. Geographical residence: Not considered. State residency: Not considered. Religious affiliation/commitment: Not considered. Minority status: Considered. Volunteer work: Considered. Work experience: Considered. **Other schools with the greatest overlap in applicants:** McDaniel College; Mount St. Mary's University; Salisbury University; Towson University; University of Maryland–College Park. **Admissions statistics for the fall 2005 entering class:** Total applicants: 1,852. Total accepted: 938. Freshmen enrolled: 237; 31% were from out of state. Accepted through early-decision or early-action plans: 24%. Overall acceptance rate: 51%. Non-early acceptance rate: 47%. **Credentials of fall 2005 freshmen:** 33% ranked in the top 10 percent of their high school class; 64% were in the top 25 percent, and 96% were in the top half. (Proportion submitting class standing: 73%.) **Average high school grade point average:** 3.3. **First-year students who submitted SAT scores:** 96%. Scores (25/75 percentile): Verbal: 510-600, Math: 500-600, Combined: 1010-1200. **First-year students submitting ACT scores:** 19%. Scores (25/75 percentile): English: N/A, Math: N/A, Composite: 20-25.

ACADEMICS

Year founded: 1893. **Academic calendar:** Semester. **Degrees offered:** bachelor's, post-bachelor's certificate, master's. **Most popular majors:** 12% education, 12% psychology, 12% social sciences, 10% English language and literature/letters, 9% biological and biomedical sciences. **Major fields of study:** area, ethnic, cultural, and gender studies; biological and biomedical sciences; business, management, marketing, and related support services; communication, journalism, and related programs; computer and information sciences and support services; education; English language and literature/letters; foreign languages, literatures, and linguistics; history; legal professions and studies; mathematics and statistics; multi/interdisciplinary studies; natural resources and conservation; philosophy and religious studies; physical sciences; psychology; public administration and social service professions; social sciences; visual and performing arts. **Areas of required coursework:** arts/fine arts, humanities, computer literacy, mathematics, English (including composition), philosophy, foreign languages, sciences (biological or physical), history, social science, other. **Pre-professional programs:** pre-law, pre-dentistry, pre-medicine, pre-veterinary science. **Special academic programs (% participation):** accelerated program (3%), distance learning (1%), double major (15%), dual enrollment (0%), honors program (16%), independent study (51%), internships (23%), liberal arts/career combination (5%), student-designed major (0%), study abroad (16%), teacher certificate program (10%). **Teacher certification offered in:** early childhood, special education, elementary, secondary. **Reserve Officers Training Corps (ROTC):** Army ROTC: Offered at cooperating institution (McDaniel College). **Faculty and instruction (2005-2006):** Total instructional faculty: 81 full-time, 121 part-time (48% men; 52% women; 8% minorities). Full-time faculty with Ph.D. or other terminal degree: 99%. Student/faculty ratio: 12/1. Classes of fewer than 20 students: 63%; of 20 to 49 students: 37%; of 50 or more students: 1%. **Advanced Placement and International Baccalaureate credit:** AP tests may be used for: Credit and/or placement. Scores accepted: 4, 5. International Baccalaureate exams may be used for: Credit and/or placement. **Freshmen returning for sophomore year:** 82%. **Graduation rates:** Four-year: 64%; five-year: 66%; six-year: 69%. **Graduate study:** 32% of students pursue further study immediately upon graduation; 35% within one year. Fields in which graduates pursue further study: Master of Business Administration (MBA), 3%; medicine, 16%; education, 5%; arts and sciences, 65%; veterinary medicine, 3%.

COSTS AND FINANCIAL AID

Financial aid office: (301) 696-3411. **Expenses (2006-2007):** Tuition and fees 2006-2007: $23,655; room/board: $8,135. Estimated books and supplies: $800; transportation: $400; personal expenses: $700. **Financial aid:** Priority filing date for institution's financial aid form: February 15. In 2005-2006, 92% of undergraduates applied for financial aid. Of those, 80% were determined to have financial need; 43% had their need fully met. Average financial aid package (proportion receiving): $18,020

(79%). Average amount of gift aid, such as scholarships or grants (proportion receiving): $14,814 (78%). Average amount of self-help aid, such as work study or loans (proportion receiving): $4,873 (54%). Average need-based loan (excluding PLUS or other private loans): $4,450. Among students who received need-based aid, the average percentage of need met: 87%. Among students who received aid based on merit, the average award (and the proportion receiving): $13,256 (20%). The average athletic scholarship (and the proportion receiving): $0 (0%). Average amount of debt of borrowers graduating in 2005: $16,295. Proportion who borrowed: 74%.

CAMPUS LIFE AND EXTRACURRICULAR ACTIVITIES

Campus housing available (% using): coed dorms (75%), women's dorms (20%), special housing for disabled students (0%), other housing options (5%). Students who live in college-owned, operated, or affiliated housing: 53%. **Student employment:** During the 2005-2006 academic year, 12% of undergraduates worked on campus. Average per-year earnings: $1,084. **Clubs and organizations:** Number of student organizations: 74. Activities include: choral groups, dance, drama/theater, jazz band, literary magazine, music ensembles, musical theater, radio station, student government, student newspaper, student film society, yearbook. Number of fraternities: 0; sororities: 0. Average proportion of students who stay on campus on weekends: 50%. **Sports program (2005-2006):** Member of NCAA III. *Men's intercollegiate varsity sports:* basketball, cross-country, golf, lacrosse, soccer, swimming and diving, tennis. *Women's intercollegiate varsity sports:* basketball, cross-country, field hockey, golf, lacrosse, soccer, softball, swimming and diving, tennis, volleyball.

SERVICES AND FACILITIES

Basic services: nonremedial tutoring, placement service, health service, health insurance. **Remedial assistance:** reading, math, writing, study skills, other. **Counseling services:** minority student, career, personal, veteran student, academic, older student, psychological, birth control, religious. **For learning-disabled students:** School does not offer a structured program with separate admission and additional fees. Total undergraduates in learning-disabled program or receiving services: 21. Services include: remedial math, remedial English, reading machines, tape recorders, other special classes, untimed tests, note-taking services, oral tests, extended time for tests, tutors, priority seating, other testing accomodations, other. **Library:** Number of titles: 207,285; number of current serial subscriptions: 457. **Information technology resources:** Students are not required to lease or own a computer. Number of campus computers available to all students: 252. School has a wireless network. Approximate number of users that can be accommodated: 3,200. Proportion of college-owned housing units wired for high-speed internet access: 100%. **Campus safety:** Security services offered: 24-hour foot and vehicle patrols, late-night transport/escort service, 24-hour emergency telephones, lighted pathways/sidewalks, controlled dormitory access (key, security card, etc).

TRANSFER AND INTERNATIONAL STUDENTS

Transfer students: May apply for admission for the following academic terms: Fall, Spring, Summer. Applicants need a minimum number of credits to apply. For fall 2005: Transfer applications received: 380. Transfer applicants offered admission: 209. Transfer applicants enrolled: 140. **International students:** Number of foreign undergraduates: 31 (3% of student body). Number of countries represented: 26. Minimum TOEFL score required: 550 (paper); 213 (computer). Average TOEFL score: 574 (paper).

Johns Hopkins University

- **Address:** 3400 N. Charles Street, Baltimore, MD 21218
- **Website:** http://www.jhu.edu
- **Private**
- **Enrollment:** 5,195 full-time; 483 part-time

KEY STATS

✔ **U.S News College Ranking:** 16, National Universities
✔ **SAT Score (25th/75th percentile):** 1290-1500
✔ **Tuition:** 2006-2007: $33,900

Selectivity: Most selective	**Room/board:** $10,622
Acceptance rate: 35%	**Average debt:** $15,177
Student/faculty ratio: 10/1	**Proportion who borrowed:** 51%

UNDERGRADUATE STUDENT BODY STATS

2005-2006 enrollment: 5,195 full-time; 483 part-time. Men: 49%; women: 51%. **Ethnic makeup:** African American: 6%; American-Indian: 1%; Asian American: 19%; Hispanic: 5%; White: 64%; International: 5%. **Religious preference:** Roman Catholic: 31%; Protestant: 32%; Jewish: 13%; Muslim: 2%; Hindu: 5%; Buddhist: 2%; No preference: 12%.

ADMISSIONS FACTS AND FIGURES

Phone: (410) 516-8171. **Email:** gotojhu@jhu.edu. **Website:** http://www.jhu.edu. **Application deadlines for fall 2007:** Regular decision: January 1; decision sent by April 1. Early decision: Send application by: November 15; Decision sent by: December 15. Early action: Not offered. Admission can be deferred. **Application fee:** $60. Common application is accepted. **To apply online, go to:** http://apply.jhu.edu. **Admissions requirements/recommendations:** High school units required (recommended): English: (4); Mathematics: (4); Science: (4); Foreign language: (3); Social studies: (2); History: (2); Total units: (19). Tests: The college uses SAT or ACT scores in admissions decisions. Either SAT or ACT required. For admission to the fall 2007 entering class, the school will accept: ACT with writing. Campus visit: Recommended. Admissions interview: Recommended. Off-campus interview: May be arranged. **Factors that count in admissions decisions:** *Academic:* Secondary school record: Very important. Class rank: Important. Letters of recommendation: Very important. Standardized test scores: Important. Essay: Important. *Nonacademic:* Interview: Considered. Extracurricular activities: Important. Talent/ability: Important. Character/personal qualities: Very important. Alumni/ae relationship: Considered. Geographical residence: Considered. State residency: Considered. Religious affiliation/commitment: Not considered. Minority status: Considered. Volunteer work: Important. Work experience: Important. **Other schools with the greatest overlap in applicants:** Cornell University; Duke University; Harvard University; University of Pennsylvania; Yale University. **Admissions statistics for the fall 2005 entering class:** Total applicants: 11,278. Total accepted: 3,910. Freshmen enrolled: 1,154; 85% were from out of state. Accepted through early-decision or early-action plans: 33%. Overall acceptance rate: 35%. Non-early acceptance rate: 28%. **Size of waiting list:** 2085 applicants; enrolled from waiting list: 4. **Credentials of fall 2005 freshmen:** 81% ranked in the top 10 percent of their high school class; 97% were in the top 25 percent, and 100% were in the top half. (Proportion submitting class standing: 42%.) **Average high school grade point average:** 3.7. **First-year students who submitted SAT scores:** 96%. Scores (25/75 percentile): Verbal: 630-740, Math: 660-760, Combined: 1290-1500. **First-year students submitting ACT scores:** 20%. Scores (25/75 percentile): English: 27-33, Math: 27-33, Composite: 28-32.

ACADEMICS

Year founded: 1876. **Academic calendar:** Semester. **Degrees offered:** certificate, diploma, bachelor's, post-bachelor's certificate, master's, post-master's certificate, first professional, doctorate. **Most popular majors:** 14% biomedical/medical engineering; 10% international relations and affairs, 6% economics, 6% neuroscience, 5% biology/biological sciences. **Major fields of study:** area, ethnic, cultural, and gender studies; biological and biomedical sciences; communications technologies/technicians and support services; computer and information sciences and support services; education; engineering; English language and literature/letters; foreign languages, literatures, and linguistics; health professions and related clinical sciences; history; liberal arts and sciences studies, and humanities; mathematics and statistics; multi/interdisciplinary studies; philosophy and religious studies;

physical sciences; psychology; social sciences; visual and performing arts. **Areas of required coursework:** humanities, mathematics, sciences (biological or physical), social science. **Pre-professional programs:** pre-law, pre-medicine. **Special academic programs (% participation):** cross-registration, double major (14%), independent study (49%), internships (59%), student-designed major (1%), study abroad (21%), teacher certificate program. **Teacher certification offered in:** special education, elementary, middle/junior high, secondary. **Reserve Officers Training Corps (ROTC):** Army ROTC: Offered on campus; Air Force ROTC: Offered at cooperating institution (University of Maryland, College Park). **Faculty and instruction (2005-2006):** Total instructional faculty: 2,927 full-time, 238 part-time (66% men; 34% women; 17% minorities). Full-time faculty with Ph.D. or other terminal degree: 94%. Student/faculty ratio: 10/1. Classes of fewer than 20 students: 51%; of 20 to 49 students: 30%; of 50 or more students: 19%. **Advanced Placement and International Baccalaureate credit:** AP tests may be used for: Credit only. Scores accepted: 4, 5. International Baccalaureate exams may be used for: Credit only. **Freshmen returning for sophomore year:** 95%. **Graduation rates:** Four-year: 81%; five-year: 89%; six-year: 90%. **Graduate study:** 49% of students pursue further study immediately upon graduation; 74% within five years. Fields in which graduates pursue further study: Master of Business Administration (MBA), 13%; law, 15%; medicine, 22%; engineering, 17%; arts and sciences, 34%.

COSTS AND FINANCIAL AID

Financial aid office: (410) 516-8028. **Expenses (2006-2007):** Tuition and fees 2006-2007: $33,900; room/board: $10,622. Estimated books and supplies: $1,000; transportation: $700; personal expenses: $800. **Financial aid:** Priority filing date for institution's financial aid form: February 1; deadline: February 15. In 2005-2006, 60% of undergraduates applied for financial aid. Of those, 50% were determined to have financial need; 98% had their need fully met. Average financial aid package (proportion receiving): $26,553 (49%). Average amount of gift aid, such as scholarships or grants (proportion receiving): $17,776 (41%). Average amount of self-help aid, such as work study or loans (proportion receiving): $4,155 (44%). Average need-based loan (excluding PLUS or other private loans): $4,087. Among students who received need-based aid, the average percentage of need met: 96%. Among students who received aid based on merit, the average award (and the proportion receiving): $12,609 (4%). The average athletic scholarship (and the proportion receiving): $26,268 (1%). Average amount of debt of borrowers graduating in 2005: $15,177. Proportion who borrowed: 51%.

CAMPUS LIFE AND EXTRACURRICULAR ACTIVITIES

Campus housing available (% using): coed dorms (78%), women's dorms (1%), men's dorms (1%), sorority housing (1%), apartment for single students (18%), special housing for disabled students (1%). Students who live in college-owned, operated, or affiliated housing: 51%. **Student employment:** During the 2005-2006 academic year, 37% of undergraduates worked on campus. Average per-year earnings: $5,208. **Clubs and organizations:** Number of student organizations: 270. Activities include: choral groups, concert band, dance, drama/theater, jazz band, literary magazine, music ensembles, musical theater, pep band, radio station, student government, student newspaper, student film society, symphony orchestra, yearbook. Number of fraternities: 13; sororities: 10. Proportion of men in fraternities: 21%; of women in sororities: 22%. Average proportion of students who stay on campus on weekends: 90%. **Sports program (2005-2006):** Member of NCAA III. **Men's intercollegiate varsity sports:** baseball, basketball, crew, cross-country, fencing, football, lacrosse, soccer, swimming and diving, tennis, track and field (indoor), track and field (outdoor), water polo, wrestling. **Women's intercollegiate varsity sports:** basketball, crew, cross-country, fencing, field hockey, lacrosse, soccer, swimming and diving, tennis, track and field (indoor), track and field (outdoor), volleyball.

SERVICES AND FACILITIES

Basic services: nonremedial tutoring, women's center, placement service, health service, health insurance. **Counseling services:** minority student, career, military, personal, academic, psychological, birth control, religious. **For learning-disabled students:** School does not offer a structured program with separate admission and additional fees. Total undergraduates in learning-disabled program or receiving services: 126. Services include: reading machines, tape recorders, untimed tests, note-taking services, oral tests, readers, extended time for tests, tutors, priority registration, priority seating, texts on tape, typist/scribe, exams on tape or computer, other testing accomodations. **Library:** Number of titles: 3,621,727; number of current serial subscriptions: 73,872. **Information technology resources:** Students are not required to lease or own a computer. Number of campus computers available to all students: 460. School has a wireless network. Approximate number of users that can be accommodated: 5,000. Proportion of college-owned housing units wired for high-speed internet access: 100%. **Campus safety:** Security services offered: 24-hour foot and vehicle patrols, late-night transport/escort service, 24-hour emergency telephones, lighted pathways/sidewalks, student patrols, controlled dormitory access (key, security card, etc).

TRANSFER AND INTERNATIONAL STUDENTS

Transfer students: May apply for admission for the following academic terms: Fall. Applicants need a minimum number of credits to apply. For fall 2005: Transfer applications received: 528. Transfer applicants offered admission: 76. Transfer applicants enrolled: 34. **International students:** Number of foreign undergraduates: 288 (5% of student body). Number of countries represented: 41. Minimum TOEFL score required: 600 (paper); 250 (computer).

Loyola College in Maryland

- **Address:** 4501 N. Charles Street, Baltimore, MD 21210
- **Website:** http://www.loyola.edu
- **Private; Religious affiliation:** Roman Catholic
- **Enrollment:** 3,501 full-time; 55 part-time

KEY STATS

✔ **U.S News College Ranking:** 2, Universities–Master's (North)
✔ **SAT Score (25th/75th percentile):** 1130-1310
✔ **Tuition:** 2006-2007: $31,500

Selectivity: More selective	**Room/board:** $9,560
Acceptance rate: 64%	**Average debt:** $15,680
Student/faculty ratio: 12/1	**Proportion who borrowed:** 74%

UNDERGRADUATE STUDENT BODY STATS

2005-2006 enrollment: 3,501 full-time; 55 part-time. Men: 42%; women: 58%. **Ethnic makeup:** African American: 5%; Asian American: 2%; Hispanic: 3%; White: 89%; International: 1%. **Religious preference:** Roman Catholic: 78%; Protestant: 9%; Jewish: 1%; Unknown: 3%.

ADMISSIONS FACTS AND FIGURES

Phone: (410) 617-5012. **Website:** http://www.loyola.edu. **Application deadlines for fall 2007:** Regular decision: January 15; decision sent by April 1. Early decision: Not offered. Early action: Send application by: November 15; Decision sent by: January 1. Admission can be deferred. **Application fee:** $50. Common application is accepted. **Admissions requirements/recommendations:** High school units required (recommended): English: 4 (4); Mathematics: 3 (4); Science: 3 (4); History: 2 (3); Total units: 16 (19). Tests: The college uses SAT or ACT scores in admissions decisions. Either SAT or ACT required. For admission to the fall 2007 entering class, the school will accept: ACT with writing, ACT without writing. Campus visit: Recommended. Admissions interview: Recommended. Off-campus interview: Not available. **Factors that count in admissions decisions:** *Academic:* Secondary school record: Very important. Class rank: Considered. Letters of recommendation: Considered. Standardized test scores: Important. Essay: Considered. *Nonacademic:* Interview: Not considered. Extracurricular activities: Considered. Talent/ability: Considered. Character/personal qualities: Considered. Alumni/ae relationship: Considered. Geographical residence: Not considered. State residency: Not considered. Religious affiliation/commitment: Not considered. Minority status: Considered. Volunteer work: Considered. Work experience: Considered. **Other schools with the greatest overlap in applicants:** Boston College; Fairfield University; Fordham University; Providence College; Villanova University. **Admissions statistics for the fall 2005 entering class:** Total applicants: 7,717. Total accepted: 4,913. Freshmen enrolled: 898; 83% were from out of state. Overall acceptance rate: 64%. Non-early acceptance rate: 64%. **Size of waiting list:** 1682 applicants; enrolled from waiting list: 484. **Credentials of fall 2005 freshmen:** 35% ranked in the top 10 percent of their high school class; 74% were in the top 25 percent, and 97% were in the top half. (Proportion submitting class standing: 40%.) **Average high school grade point average:** 3.5. **First-year students who submitted SAT scores:** 99%. Scores (25/75 percentile): Verbal: 560-650, Math: 570-660, Combined: 1130-1310. **First-year students submitting ACT scores:** 11%. Scores (25/75 percentile): English: 23-29, Math: 23-27, Composite: 24-28.

ACADEMICS

Year founded: 1852. **Academic calendar:** Semester. **Degrees offered:** bachelor's, master's, post-master's certificate, doctorate. **Most popular majors:** 34% business/commerce, 13% communication studies/speech communication and rhetoric, 9% psychology, 7% social sciences, 6% biology/biological sciences. **Major fields of study:** biological and biomedical sciences; business, management, marketing, and related support services; communication, journalism, and related programs; computer and information sciences and support services; education; engineering; English language and literature/letters; foreign languages, literatures, and linguistics; health professions and related clinical sciences; history; mathematics and statistics; multi/interdisciplinary studies; philosophy and religious studies; physical sciences; psychology; social sciences; visual and performing arts. **Areas of required coursework:** arts/fine arts, humanities, computer literacy, mathematics, English (including composition), philosophy, foreign languages, sciences (biological or physical), history, social science, other. **Pre-professional programs:** pre-law, pre-dentistry, pre-medicine, pre-veterinary science, pre-optometry, pre-pharmacy. **Special academic programs (% participation):** cooperative (work-study plan) program (27%), cross-registration (2%), double major (4%), honors program (6%), independent study, internships (31%), study abroad (59.7%), teacher certificate program (5%). **Teacher certification offered in:** special education, elementary, middle/junior high, secondary. **Reserve Officers Training Corps (ROTC):** Army ROTC: Offered on campus; Air Force ROTC: Offered at cooperating institution (University of Maryland-College Park). **Faculty and instruction (2005-2006):** Total instructional faculty: 305 full-time, 232 part-time (56% men; 44% women; 8% minorities). Full-time faculty with Ph.D. or other terminal degree: 84%. Student/faculty ratio: 12/1. Classes of fewer than 20 students: 39%; of 20 to 49 students: 61%; of 50 or more students: 0%. **Advanced Placement and International Baccalaureate credit:** International Baccalaureate exams may be used for: Credit only. **Freshmen returning for sophomore year:** 91%. **Graduation rates:** Four-year: 78%; five-year: 82%; six-year: 82%. **Graduate study:** 26% of students pursue further study within one year.

COSTS AND FINANCIAL AID

Financial aid office: (410) 617-2576. **Expenses (2006-2007):** Tuition and fees 2006-2007: $31,500; room/board: $9,560. Estimated books and supplies: $850; transportation: $350; personal expenses: $1,050. **Financial aid:** Priority filing date for institution's financial aid form: February 15; deadline: February 15. In 2005-2006, 57% of undergraduates applied for financial aid. Of those, 44% were determined to have financial need; 96% had their need fully met. Average financial aid package (proportion receiving): $20,465 (44%). Average amount of gift aid, such as scholarships or grants (proportion receiving): $12,785 (33%). Average amount of self-help aid, such as work study or loans (proportion receiving): $7,680 (38%). Average need-based loan (excluding PLUS or other private loans): $5,730. Among students who received need-based aid, the average percentage of need met: 98%. Among students who received aid based on merit, the average award (and the proportion receiving): $11,176 (11%). The average athletic scholarship (and the proportion receiving): $24,854 (5%). Average amount of debt of borrowers graduating in 2005: $15,680. Proportion who borrowed: 74%.

CAMPUS LIFE AND EXTRACURRICULAR ACTIVITIES

Campus housing available (% using): coed dorms (16%), apartment for single students (60%), special housing for disabled students (1%), other housing options (23%). Students who live in college-owned, operated, or affiliated housing: 79%. **Student employment:** During the 2005-2006 academic year, 46% of undergraduates worked on campus. Average per-year earnings: $1,950. **Clubs and organizations:** Number of student organizations: 139. Activities include: choral groups, dance, drama/theater, jazz band, literary magazine, music ensembles, musical theater, pep band, radio station, student government, student newspaper, television station, yearbook. Number of fraternities: 0; sororities: 0. Average proportion of students who stay on campus on weekends: 80%. **Sports program (2005-2006):** Member of NCAA I. *Men's intercollegiate varsity sports:* basketball, cross-country, golf, lacrosse, soccer, swimming and diving, tennis. *Women's intercollegiate varsity sports:* basketball, cross-country, lacrosse, soccer, swimming and diving, tennis, track and field (outdoor), volleyball, rowing.

SERVICES AND FACILITIES

Basic services: nonremedial tutoring, women's center, placement service, health service, health insurance, other. **Remedial assistance:** other. **Counseling services:** minority student, career, personal, academic, psychological, religious. **For learning-disabled students:** School does not offer a structured program with separate admission and additional fees. Total undergraduates in learning-disabled program or receiving services: 104. Services include: reading machines, tape recorders, note-taking services, oral tests, readers, extended time for tests, tutors, early syllabus, priority seating, exams on tape or computer, other testing accomodations, other. **Library:** Number of titles: 293,639; number of current serial subscriptions: 2,126. **Information technology resources:** Students are not required to lease or own a computer. Number of campus computers available to all students: 630. School has a wireless network. Approximate number of users that can be accommodated: 750. Proportion of college-owned housing units wired for high-speed internet access: 100%. **Campus safety:** Security services offered: 24-hour foot and vehicle patrols, late-night transport/escort service, 24-hour emergency telephones, lighted pathways/sidewalks, student patrols, controlled dormitory access (key, security card, etc).

TRANSFER AND INTERNATIONAL STUDENTS

Transfer students: May apply for admission for the following academic terms: Fall, Spring, Summer. Applicants do not need a minimum number of credits to apply. For fall 2005: Transfer applications received: 195. Transfer applicants offered admission: 94. Transfer applicants enrolled: 27. **International students:** Number of foreign undergraduates: 24 (1% of student body). Number of countries represented: 14. Minimum TOEFL score required: 550 (paper); 213 (computer).

Maryland Institute College of Art

- **Address:** 1300 Mount Royal Avenue, Baltimore, MD 21217-4134
- **Website:** http://www.mica.edu
- **Private**
- **Enrollment:** 1,478 full-time; 19 part-time

KEY STATS

✔ **U.S News College Ranking:** Unranked Specialty School–Fine Arts
✔ **SAT Score (25th/75th percentile):** 1050-1270
✔ **Tuition:** 2006-2007: $28,670

Selectivity: More selective	**Room/board:** $7,910
Acceptance rate: 45%	**Average debt:** N/A
Student/faculty ratio: 10/1	**Proportion who borrowed:** N/A

UNDERGRADUATE STUDENT BODY STATS

2005-2006 enrollment: 1,478 full-time; 19 part-time. Men: 38%; women: 62%. **Ethnic makeup:** African American: 4%; Asian American: 8%; Hispanic: 5%; White: 78%; International: 5%.

ADMISSIONS FACTS AND FIGURES

Phone: (410) 225-2222. **Email:** admissions@mica.edu. **Website:** http://www.mica.edu. **Application deadlines for fall 2007:** Regular decision: February 15; decision sent by March 15. Early decision: Send application by: November 15; Decision sent by: December 15. Early action: Not offered. Admission can be deferred. **Application fee:** $50. Common application is not accepted. **To apply online, go to:** http://www.mica.edu/ADM/index.cfm?id=1. **Admissions requirements/recommendations:** High school units required (recommended): English: 4 (4); Mathematics: 2 (3); Science: 2 (3); Foreign language: 0 (0); Social studies: 4 (4); History: 3 (4); Academic electives: 6 (0); Total units: 24 (24). Tests: The college uses SAT or ACT scores in admissions decisions. Either SAT or ACT required. For admission to the fall 2007 entering class, the school will accept: ACT with writing, ACT without writing. Campus visit: Recommended. Admissions interview: Neither required nor recommended. Off-campus interview: May be arranged. **Factors that count in admissions decisions:** *Academic:* Secondary school record: Very important. Class rank: Important. Letters of recommendation: Considered. Standardized test scores: Important. Essay: Important. *Nonacademic:* Interview: Important. Extracurricular activities: Important. Talent/ability: Very important. Character/personal qualities: Considered. Alumni/ae relationship: Considered. Geographical residence: Not considered. State residency: Not considered. Religious affiliation/commitment: Not considered. Minority status: Considered. Volunteer work: Considered. Work experience: Not considered. **Other schools with the greatest overlap in applicants:** Carnegie Mellon University; Pratt Institute; Rhode Island School of Design; School of the Art Institute of Chicago;

Syracuse University. **Admissions statistics for the fall 2005 entering class:** Total applicants: 2,487. Total accepted: 1,118. Freshmen enrolled: 396; 82% were from out of state. Overall acceptance rate: 45%. Non-early acceptance rate: 44%. **Size of waiting list:** 12 applicants; enrolled from waiting list: 3. **Credentials of fall 2005 freshmen:** 29% ranked in the top 10 percent of their high school class; 62% were in the top 25 percent, and 91% were in the top half. **Average high school grade point average:** 3.5. **First-year students who submitted SAT scores:** 94%. Scores (25/75 percentile): Verbal: 540-650, Math: 510-620, Combined: 1050-1270.

ACADEMICS

Year founded: 1826. **Academic calendar:** Semester. **Degrees offered:** bachelor's, post-bachelor's certificate, master's. **Most popular majors:** Information not available. **Major fields of study:** education; visual and performing arts. **Areas of required coursework:** arts/fine arts, humanities, English (including composition), sciences (biological or physical), history, social science. **Special academic programs:** accelerated program, cross-registration, distance learning, double major, dual enrollment, exchange student program (domestic), independent study, internships, student-designed major, study abroad, teacher certificate program, other. **Teacher certification offered in:** elementary, middle/junior high, secondary. **Reserve Officers Training Corps (ROTC):** Army ROTC: Offered at cooperating institution (Johns Hopkins University). **Faculty and instruction (2005-2006):** Total instructional faculty: 118 full-time, 149 part-time (51% men; 49% women). Full-time faculty with Ph.D. or other terminal degree: 86%. Student/faculty ratio: 10/1. Classes of fewer than 20 students: 71%; of 20 to 49 students: 29%. **Advanced Placement and International Baccalaureate credit:** AP tests may be used for: Credit and/or placement. Scores accepted: 4. **Freshmen returning for sophomore year:** 85%. **Graduation rates:** Four-year: 67%; five-year: 71%; six-year: 70%. **Graduate study:** 23% of students pursue further study immediately upon graduation.

COSTS AND FINANCIAL AID

Financial aid office: (410) 225-2285. **Expenses (2006-2007):** Tuition and fees 2006-2007: $28,670; room/board: $7,910. Estimated books and supplies: $1,400; transportation: $700; personal expenses: $600.

CAMPUS LIFE AND EXTRACURRICULAR ACTIVITIES

Campus housing available: coed dorms, apartments for married students, apartment for single students, special housing for disabled students, special housing for international students. Students who live in college-owned, operated, or affiliated housing: 88%. **Clubs and organizations:** Number of student organizations: 40. Activities include: choral groups, dance, drama/theater, literary magazine, student government, student film society, television station. Number of fraternities: 0; sororities: 0. Average proportion of students who stay on campus on weekends: 90%.

SERVICES AND FACILITIES

Basic services: nonremedial tutoring, health service, health insurance. **Remedial assistance:** writing, study skills. **Counseling services:** minority student, career, personal, academic, psychological. **For learning-disabled students:** School does not offer a structured program with separate admission and additional fees. **Library:** Number of titles: 76,500; number of current serial subscriptions: 315. **Information technology resources:** Students are not required to lease or own a computer. Number of campus computers available to all students: 350. School has a wireless network. Proportion of college-owned housing units wired for high-speed internet access: 100%. **Campus safety:** Security services offered: 24-hour foot and vehicle patrols, late-night transport/escort service, lighted pathways/sidewalks, student patrols, controlled dormitory access (key, security card, etc).

TRANSFER AND INTERNATIONAL STUDENTS

Transfer students: May apply for admission for the following academic terms: Fall, Spring. Applicants need a minimum number of credits to apply. For fall 2005: Transfer applications received: 230. Transfer applicants offered admission: 134. Transfer applicants enrolled: 62. **International students:** Number of foreign undergraduates: 75 (5% of student body). Minimum TOEFL score required: 550 (paper); 213 (computer).

McDaniel College

- **Address:** 2 College Hill, Westminster, MD 21157
- **Website:** http://www.mcdaniel.edu
- **Private**
- **Enrollment:** 1,643 full-time; 52 part-time

KEY STATS

- ✔ **U.S News College Ranking:** third tier, Liberal Arts Colleges
- ✔ **SAT Score (25th/75th percentile):** 990-1230
- ✔ **Tuition:** 2006-2007: $27,280

Selectivity: Selective
Room/board: $5,900
Acceptance rate: 79%
Average debt: $21,416
Student/faculty ratio: 13/1
Proportion who borrowed: 60%

UNDERGRADUATE STUDENT BODY STATS

2005-2006 enrollment: 1,643 full-time; 52 part-time. Men: 43%; women: 57%. **Ethnic makeup:** African American: 7%; American-Indian: 1%; Asian American: 2%; Hispanic: 2%; White: 88%; International: 1%.

ADMISSIONS FACTS AND FIGURES

Phone: (800) 638-5005. **Email:** admissions@mcdaniel.edu. **Website:** http://www.mcdaniel.edu. **Application deadlines for fall 2007:** Regular decision: February 1; decision sent by March 15. Early decision: Not offered. Early action: Send application by: December 1; Decision sent by: January 15. Admission can be deferred. **Application fee:** $50. Common application is accepted. **Admissions requirements/recommendations:** High school units required (recommended): English: 4 (4); Mathematics: 3 (4); Science: 3 (4); Foreign language: 3 (4); Social studies: 2 (3); History: 2 (3); Total units: 19 (24). Tests: The college uses SAT or ACT scores in admissions decisions. Neither SAT nor ACT required. For admission to the fall 2007 entering class, the school will accept: ACT with writing, ACT without writing. Campus visit: Recommended. Admissions interview: Recommended. Off-campus interview: May be arranged. **Factors that count in admissions decisions:** *Academic:* Secondary school record: Very important. Class rank: Considered. Letters of recommendation: Considered. Standardized test scores: Important. Essay: Important. *Nonacademic:* Interview: Important. Extracurricular activities: Considered. Talent/ability: Considered. Character/personal qualities: Not considered. Alumni/ae relationship: Important. Geographical residence: Not considered. State residency: Not considered. Religious affiliation/commitment: Not considered. Minority status: Important. Volunteer work: Important. Work experience: Important. **Admissions statistics for the fall 2005 entering class:** Total applicants: 2,256. Total accepted: 1,782. Freshmen enrolled: 448; 35% were from out of state. Overall acceptance rate: 79%. Non-early acceptance rate: 79%. **Size of waiting list:** 49 applicants; enrolled from waiting list: 10. **Credentials of fall 2005 freshmen:** 26% ranked in the top 10 percent of their high school class; 55% were in the top 25 percent, and 86% were in the top half. (Proportion submitting class standing: 59%.) **Average high school grade point average:** 3.4. **First-year students who submitted SAT scores:** 96%. Scores (25/75 percentile): Verbal: 490-610, Math: 500-620, Combined: 990-1230. **First-year students submitting ACT scores:** 13%. Scores (25/75 percentile): English: N/A, Math: N/A, Composite: N/A.

ACADEMICS

Year founded: 1867. **Academic calendar:** 4-1-4. **Degrees offered:** bachelor's, master's. **Most popular majors:** 13% business administration and management, 11% psychology, 10% sociology, 9% communication studies/speech communication and rhetoric, 8% biology/biological sciences. **Major fields of study:** biological and biomedical sciences; business, management, marketing, and related support services; communication, journalism, and related programs; computer and information sciences and support services; education; English language and literature/letters; foreign languages, literatures, and linguistics; history; mathematics and statistics; natural resources and conservation; philosophy and religious studies; physical sciences; psychology; public administration and social service professions; social sciences; visual and performing arts. **Areas of required coursework:** arts/fine arts, humanities, mathematics, English (including composition), philosophy, foreign languages, sciences (biological or physical), history, social science, other. **Pre-professional programs:** pre-law, pre-dentistry, pre-medicine, pre-veterinary science, pre-optometry, pre-pharmacy, other. **Special academic programs (% participation):** accelerated program (8%), double major (21%), dual enrollment (1%), exchange student program (domestic) (5%), honors program (10%), independent study (38%), internships (38%), student-designed major (1%), study abroad (23%), teacher certificate program (4%). **Teacher certification offered in:** elementary, secondary. **Reserve Officers Training Corps (ROTC):** Army ROTC: Offered on campus. **Faculty and instruction (2005-2006):** Total instructional faculty: 132 full-time, 72 part-time (52% men; 48% women; 9% minorities). Full-time faculty with Ph.D. or other terminal degree: 87%. Student/faculty ratio: 13/1. Classes of fewer than 20 students: 62%; of 20 to 49 students: 37%; of 50 or more students: 0%. **Advanced Placement and International Baccalaureate credit:** AP tests may be used for: Credit and/or placement. Scores accepted: 4, 5. International Baccalaureate exams may be used for: Credit and/or placement. **Freshmen returning for sophomore year:** 82%. **Graduation rates:** Four-year: 63%; five-year: 72%; six-year: 74%. **Graduate study:** 52% of students pursue further study within one year. Fields in which graduates pursue further study: Master of Business Administration (MBA), 10%; law, 10%; medicine, 10%; dentistry, 1%; education, 21%; arts and sciences, 47%; veterinary medicine, 1%.

COSTS AND FINANCIAL AID

Financial aid office: (410) 857-2233. **Expenses (2006-2007):** Tuition and fees 2006-2007: $27,280; room/board: $5,900. Estimated books and supplies: $900; transportation: $400; personal expenses: $170. **Financial aid:** Priority filing date for institution's financial aid form: March 1. In 2005-2006, 75% of undergraduates applied for financial aid. Of those, 62% were determined to have financial need; 30% had their need fully met. Average financial aid package (proportion receiving): $20,398 (62%). Average amount of gift aid, such as scholarships or grants (proportion receiving): $9,091 (61%). Average amount of self-help aid, such as work study or loans (proportion receiving): $5,383 (59%). Average need-based loan (excluding PLUS or other private loans): $4,505. Among students who received need-based aid, the average percentage of need met: 94%. Among students who received aid based on merit, the average award (and the proportion receiving): $10,326 (33%). The average athletic scholarship (and the proportion receiving): $0 (0%). Average amount of debt of borrowers graduating in 2005: $21,416. Proportion who borrowed: 60%.

CAMPUS LIFE AND EXTRACURRICULAR ACTIVITIES

Campus housing available (% using): coed dorms (30%), women's dorms (16%), men's dorms (15%), sorority housing (9%), fraternity housing (5%), apartment for single students (17%), other housing options (8%). Students who live in college-owned, operated, or affiliated housing: 77%. **Student employment:** During the 2005-2006 academic year, 5% of undergraduates worked on campus. Average per-year earnings: $486. **Clubs and organizations:** Number of student organizations: 119. Activities include: choral groups, concert band, dance, drama/theater, jazz band, literary magazine, music ensembles, musical theater, pep band, radio station, student government, student newspaper, student film society, television station, yearbook. Number of fraternities: 6; sororities: 4. Proportion of men in fraternities: 13%; of women in sororities: 11%. Average proportion of students who stay on campus on weekends: 75%. **Sports program (2005-2006):** Member of NCAA III. *Men's intercollegiate varsity sports:* baseball, basketball, cross-country, football, golf, lacrosse, soccer, swimming and diving, tennis, track and field (indoor), track and field (outdoor), wrestling. *Women's intercollegiate varsity sports:* basketball, cross-country, field hockey, golf, lacrosse, soccer, softball, swimming and diving, tennis, track and field (indoor), track and field (outdoor), volleyball.

SERVICES AND FACILITIES

Basic services: nonremedial tutoring, placement service, health service, health insurance. **Remedial assistance:** math, writing. **Counseling services:** minority student, career, personal, academic, birth control. **For learning-disabled students:** School does not offer a structured program with separate admission and additional fees. Total undergraduates in learning-disabled program or receiving services: 141. Services include: remedial math, remedial English, reading machines, tape recorders, note-taking services, learning center, readers, extended time for tests, tutors, texts on tape. **Library:** Number of titles: 581,691; number of current serial subscriptions: 14,218. **Information technology resources:** Students are not required to lease or own a computer. Number of campus computers available to all students: 171. School has a wireless network. Approximate number of users that can be accommodated: 300. Proportion of college-owned housing units wired for high-speed internet access: 100%. **Campus safety:** Security services offered: 24-hour foot and vehicle patrols, late-night transport/escort service, 24-hour emergency telephones, lighted pathways/sidewalks, controlled dormitory access (key, security card, etc).

TRANSFER AND INTERNATIONAL STUDENTS

Transfer students: May apply for admission for the following academic terms: Fall, Spring. Applicants need a minimum number of credits to apply. For fall 2005: Transfer applications received: 161. Transfer applicants offered admission: 109. Transfer applicants enrolled: 69. **International students:** Number of foreign undergraduates: 18 (1% of student body). Number of countries represented: 11. Minimum TOEFL score required: 550 (paper); 213 (computer). Average TOEFL score: 598 (paper).

Morgan State University

- **Address:** 1700 E. Cold Spring Lane, Baltimore, MD 21251
- **Website:** http://www.morgan.edu
- **Public**
- **Enrollment:** 5,101 full-time; 646 part-time

KEY STATS
- ✔ **U.S News College Ranking:** third tier, Universities–Master's (North)
- ✔ **SAT Score (25th/75th percentile):** 880-1050
- ✔ **Tuition:** 2006-2007: $3,209 in state, $6,982 out of state

Selectivity: Less selective	**Room/board:** $3,495
Acceptance rate: 19%	**Average debt:** N/A
Student/faculty ratio: 14/1	**Proportion who borrowed:** N/A

UNDERGRADUATE STUDENT BODY STATS

2005-2006 enrollment: 5,101 full-time; 646 part-time. Men: 44%; women: 56%. **Ethnic makeup:** African American: 92%; Hispanic: 1%; White: 5%; International: 1%.

ADMISSIONS FACTS AND FIGURES

Phone: (800) 332-6674. **Website:** http://www.morgan.edu. **Application deadlines for fall 2007:** Regular decision: Rolling. Early decision: Not offered. Early action: Send application by: N/A; Decision sent by: N/A. Admission can be deferred. **Application fee:** $25. Common application is accepted. **To apply online, go to:** http://www.morgan.edu/admin/admission/admission.asp. **Admissions requirements/recommendations:** High school units required (recommended): English: 4 (4); Mathematics: 3 (3); Science: 3 (3); Foreign language: 2 (2); Social studies: 3 (3); History: 3 (3); Academic electives: 3 (3); Total units: 21 (21). Tests: The college uses SAT or ACT scores in admissions decisions. Either SAT or ACT required. For admission to the fall 2007 entering class, the school will accept: ACT with writing, ACT without writing. Campus visit: Recommended. Admissions interview: Neither required nor recommended. Off-campus interview: May be arranged. **Factors that count in admissions decisions:** *Academic:* Secondary school record: Very important. Class rank: Considered. Letters of recommendation: Considered. Standardized test scores: Very important. Essay: Considered. *Nonacademic:* Interview: Not considered. Extracurricular activities: Considered. Talent/ability: Considered. Character/personal qualities: Considered. Alumni/ae relationship: Considered. Geographical residence: Considered. State residency: Considered. Religious affiliation/commitment: Not considered. Minority status: Considered. Volunteer work: Considered. Work experience: Considered. **Admissions statistics for the fall 2005 entering class:** Total applicants: 11,445. Total accepted: 2,122. Freshmen enrolled: 793; 31% were from out of state. Overall acceptance rate: 19%. Non-early acceptance rate: 19%. **Size of waiting list:** 1235 applicants; enrolled from waiting list: 345. **Average high school grade point average:** 2.8. **First-year students who submitted SAT scores:** 88%. Scores (25/75 percentile): Verbal: 440-520, Math: 440-530, Combined: 880-1050. **First-year students submitting ACT scores:** 3%. Scores (25/75 percentile): English: N/A, Math: N/A, Composite: N/A.

ACADEMICS

Year founded: 1867. **Academic calendar:** Semester. **Degrees offered:** bachelor's, master's, doctorate. **Most popular majors:** 11% communication, journalism, and related programs, 7% architectural engineering, 7% biology, 7% information science/studies, 7% psychology. **Major fields of study:** architecture and related services; area, ethnic, cultural, and gender studies; biological and biomedical sciences; business, management, marketing, and related support services; communication, journalism, and related programs; computer and information sciences and support services; education; engineering; English language and literature/letters; family and consumer sciences/human sciences; history; mathematics and statistics;

philosophy and religious studies; physical sciences; psychology; social sciences; visual and performing arts. **Areas of required coursework:** humanities, mathematics, English (including composition), sciences (biological or physical), history, social science. **Pre-professional programs:** pre-law, pre-dentistry, pre-medicine, pre-theology, pre-veterinary science, pre-optometry, pre-pharmacy. **Special academic programs:** cooperative (work-study plan) program, cross-registration, distance learning, double major, dual enrollment, honors program, independent study, internships, liberal arts/career combination, teacher certificate program, weekend college, other. **Teacher certification offered in:** elementary, secondary. **Cooperative education programs:** art, business, computer science, education, engineering, health professions, home economics, humanities, natural science, social/behavioral science, technologies. **Reserve Officers Training Corps (ROTC):** Army ROTC: Offered on campus. **Faculty and instruction (2005-2006):** Total instructional faculty: 388. Full-time faculty with Ph.D. or other terminal degree: 69%. Student/faculty ratio: 14/1. Classes of fewer than 20 students: 51%; of 20 to 49 students: 49%; of 50 or more students: 0%. **Advanced Placement and International Baccalaureate credit:** AP tests may be used for: Credit and/or placement. Scores accepted: 3, 4, 5. International Baccalaureate exams may be used for: Credit and/or placement. **Freshmen returning for sophomore year:** 72%. **Graduation rates:** Four-year: 24%; five-year: 40%; six-year: 40%. **Graduate study:** 42% of students pursue further study within one year.

COSTS AND FINANCIAL AID

Financial aid office: (443) 885-3170. **Expenses (2006-2007):** Tuition and fees 2006-2007: $3,209 in state, $6,982 out of state; room/board: $3,495. Estimated books and supplies: $1,000.

CAMPUS LIFE AND EXTRACURRICULAR ACTIVITIES

Campus housing available (% using): coed dorms (43%), women's dorms (29%), men's dorms (23%), apartment for single students, special housing for disabled students (5%). **Student employment:** During the 2005-2006 academic year, 6% of undergraduates worked on campus. Average per-year earnings: $2,500. **Clubs and organizations:** Number of student organizations: 61. Activities include: choral groups, concert band, dance, drama/theater, jazz band, marching band, music ensembles, musical theater, radio station, student government, student newspaper, student film society, yearbook. Number of fraternities: 4; sororities: 5. Average proportion of students who stay on campus on weekends: 55%. **Sports program (2005-2006):** Member of NCAA I. *Men's intercollegiate varsity sports:* basketball, cross-country, football, tennis, track and field (indoor), track and field (outdoor). *Women's intercollegiate varsity sports:* basketball, bowling, cross-country, softball, tennis, track and field (indoor), track and field (outdoor), volleyball.

SERVICES AND FACILITIES

Basic services: nonremedial tutoring, day care, health service, health insurance. **Remedial assistance:** reading, math, writing, study skills. **Counseling services:** minority student, career, personal, academic, psychological. **For learning-disabled students:** School does not offer a structured program with separate admission and additional fees. Total undergraduates in learning-disabled program or receiving services: 45. Services include: remedial math, remedial English, remedial reading, tape recorders, other special classes, note-taking services, oral tests, learning center, readers, extended time for tests, tutors, priority registration, priority seating, other testing accomodations. **Library:** Number of titles: 303,917; number of current serial subscriptions: 1,684. **Information technology resources:** Students are not required to lease or own a computer. School has a wireless network. Approximate number of users that can be accommodated: 1,500. Proportion of college-owned housing units wired for high-speed internet access: 100%. **Campus safety:** Security services offered: 24-hour foot and vehicle patrols, 24-hour emergency telephones, lighted pathways/sidewalks, controlled dormitory access (key, security card, etc).

TRANSFER AND INTERNATIONAL STUDENTS

Transfer students: May apply for admission for the following academic terms: Fall, Spring. Applicants need a minimum number of credits to apply. For fall 2005: Transfer applications received: 1,321. Transfer applicants offered admission: 521. Transfer applicants enrolled: 311. **International students:** Number of foreign undergraduates: 69 (1% of student body). Minimum TOEFL score required: 550 (paper).

Mount St. Mary's University

- **Address:** 16300 Old Emmitsburg Road, Emmitsburg, MD 21727
- **Website:** http://www.msmary.edu
- **Private; Religious affiliation:** Roman Catholic
- **Enrollment:** 1,485 full-time; 171 part-time

KEY STATS

✔ **U.S News College Ranking:** 25, Universities–Master's (North)
✔ **SAT Score (25th/75th percentile):** 1000-1200
✔ **Tuition:** 2006-2007: $24,030

Selectivity: Selective	Room/board: $8,690
Acceptance rate: 84%	Average debt: $15,964
Student/faculty ratio: 13/1	Proportion who borrowed: 75%

UNDERGRADUATE STUDENT BODY STATS

2005-2006 enrollment: 1,485 full-time; 171 part-time. Men: 39%; women: 61%. **Ethnic makeup:** African American: 7%; Asian American: 2%; Hispanic: 3%; White: 87%; International: 1%.

ADMISSIONS FACTS AND FIGURES

Phone: (800) 448-4347. **Email:** admissions@msmary.edu. **Website:** http://www.msmary.edu. **Application deadlines for fall 2007:** Regular decision: Rolling. Early decision: Not offered. Early action: Send application by: December 1; Decision sent by: December 15. Admission can be deferred. **Application fee:** $35. Common application is not accepted. **To apply online, go to:** http://www.msmary.edu/college/html/apply/applyundergraduate.htm. **Admissions requirements/recommendations:** High school units required (recommended): English: 4; Mathematics: 3; Science: 3; Foreign language: 2; Social studies: 3; Academic electives: 1; Total units: 16. Tests: The college uses SAT or ACT scores in admissions decisions. Either SAT or ACT required. For admission to the fall 2007 entering class, the school will accept: ACT with writing, ACT without writing. Campus visit: Recommended. Admissions interview: Recommended. Off-campus interview: May be arranged. **Factors that count in admissions decisions:** *Academic:* Secondary school record: Very important. Class rank: Considered. Letters of recommendation: Considered. Standardized test scores: Important. Essay: Not considered. *Nonacademic:* Interview: Not considered. Extracurricular activities: Considered. Talent/ability: Considered. Character/personal qualities: Considered. Alumni/ae relationship: Considered. Geographical residence: Not considered. State residency: Not considered. Religious affiliation/commitment: Not considered. Minority status: Not considered. Volunteer work: Considered. Work experience: Considered. **Other schools with the greatest overlap in applicants:** Loyola College in Maryland; McDaniel College; St. Joseph's University; Towson University; University of Maryland–College Park. **Admissions statistics for the fall 2005 entering class:** Total applicants: 2,190. Total accepted: 1,847. Freshmen enrolled: 439; 44% were from out of state. Accepted through early-decision or early-action plans: 19%. Overall acceptance rate: 84%. Non-early acceptance rate: 83%. **Credentials of fall 2005 freshmen:** 20% ranked in the top 10 percent of their high school class; 48% were in the top 25 percent, and 81% were in the top half. (Proportion submitting class standing: 55%.) **Average high school grade point average:** 3.2. **First-year students who submitted SAT scores:** 97%. Scores (25/75 percentile): Verbal: 500-600, Math: 500-600, Combined: 1000-1200.

ACADEMICS

Year founded: 1808. **Academic calendar:** Semester. **Degrees offered:** bachelor's, post-bachelor's certificate, master's, post-master's certificate, first professional. **Most popular majors:** 31% business administration and management, 11% elementary education and teaching, 8% sociology, 7% communication studies/speech communication and rhetoric, 5% accounting. **Major fields of study:** biological and biomedical sciences; business, management, marketing, and related support services; communication, journalism, and related programs; computer and information sciences and support services; education; English language and literature/letters; foreign languages, literatures, and linguistics; history; mathematics and statistics; multi/interdisciplinary studies; parks, recreation, leisure, and fitness studies; philosophy and religious studies; physical sciences; psychology; security and protective services; social sciences; theology and religious vocations; visual and performing arts. **Areas of required coursework:** arts/fine arts, humanities, computer literacy, mathematics, English (including composition), philosophy, foreign languages, sciences (biological or physical), history, social science, other. **Pre-professional programs:** pre-law, pre-medicine, pre-theology. **Special academic programs:** accelerated program, cross-registration, double major, dual enrollment, honors program, independent study, internships, liberal arts/career combination, student-designed major, study abroad, teacher certificate program, weekend college, other. **Teacher certification offered in:** special education, elementary, middle/junior high, secondary. **Reserve Officers Training Corps (ROTC):** Army ROTC: Offered at cooperating institution (McDaniel College). **Faculty and instruction (2005-2006):** Total instructional faculty: 105 full-time, 88 part-time (61% men; 39% women; 5% minorities). Full-time faculty with Ph.D. or other terminal degree: 90%. Student/faculty ratio: 13/1. Classes of fewer than 20 students: 42%; of 20 to 49 students: 58%; of 50 or more students: 1%. **Advanced Placement and International Baccalaureate credit:** AP tests may be used for: Credit only. Scores accepted: 3, 4, 5. International Baccalaureate exams may be used for: Credit only. **Freshmen returning for sophomore year:** 81%. **Graduation rates:** Four-year: 64%; five-year: 68%; six-year: 66%. **Graduate study:** 30% of students pursue further study within one year. Fields in which graduates pursue further study: Master of Business Administration (MBA), 7%; law, 3%; medicine, 2%; education, 5%; arts and sciences, 13%.

COSTS AND FINANCIAL AID

Financial aid office: (301) 447-5207. **Expenses (2006-2007):** Tuition and fees 2006-2007: $24,030; room/board: $8,690. Estimated books and supplies: $800; transportation: $300; personal expenses: $600. **Financial aid:** Priority filing date for institution's financial aid form: February 15; deadline: February 15. In 2005-2006, 75% of undergraduates applied for financial aid. Of those, 61% were determined to have financial need; 30% had their need fully met. Average financial aid package (proportion receiving): $15,181 (61%). Average amount of gift aid, such as scholarships or grants (proportion receiving): $11,892 (60%). Average amount of self-help aid, such as work study or loans (proportion receiving): $4,729 (46%). Average need-based loan (excluding PLUS or other private loans): $4,056. Among students who received need-based aid, the average percentage of need met: 77%. Among students who received aid based on merit, the average award (and the proportion receiving): $13,552 (33%). The average athletic scholarship (and the proportion receiving): $10,104 (8%). Average amount of debt of borrowers graduating in 2005: $15,964. Proportion who borrowed: 75%.

CAMPUS LIFE AND EXTRACURRICULAR ACTIVITIES

Campus housing available: coed dorms, apartment for single students, special housing for disabled students, other housing options. Students who live in college-owned, operated, or affiliated housing: 81%. **Student employment:** During the 2005-2006 academic year, 32% of undergraduates worked on campus. Average per-year earnings: $1,032. **Clubs and organizations:** Number of student organizations: 70. Activities include: choral groups, concert band, dance, drama/theater, jazz band, literary magazine, music ensembles, musical theater, radio station, student government, student newspaper, television station, yearbook. Number of fraternities: 0; sororities: 0. Average proportion of students who stay on campus on weekends: 80%. **Sports program (2005-2006):** Member of NCAA I. *Men's intercollegiate varsity sports:* baseball, basketball, cross-country, golf, lacrosse, soccer, tennis, track and field (indoor), track and field (outdoor). *Women's intercollegiate varsity sports:* basketball, cross-country, golf, lacrosse, soccer, softball, swimming and diving, tennis, track and field (indoor), track and field (outdoor).

SERVICES AND FACILITIES

Basic services: nonremedial tutoring, health service, health insurance. **Remedial assistance:** math. **Counseling services:** minority student, career, personal, academic, psychological, religious. **For learning-disabled students:** School does not offer a structured program with separate admission and additional fees. Services include: remedial math, reading machines, tape recorders, note-taking services, oral tests, learning center, readers, extended time for tests, tutors, texts on tape, other. **Library:** Number of titles: 209,770; number of current serial subscriptions: 935. **Information technology resources:** Students are not required to lease or own a computer. Number of campus computers available to all students: 150. School has a wireless network. Approximate number of users that can be accommodated: 2,500. Proportion of college-owned housing units wired for high-speed internet access: 100%. **Campus safety:** Security services offered: 24-hour foot and vehicle patrols, late-night transport/escort service, 24-hour emergency telephones, lighted pathways/sidewalks, controlled dormitory access (key, security card, etc).

TRANSFER AND INTERNATIONAL STUDENTS

Transfer students: May apply for admission for the following academic terms: Fall, Spring, Summer. Applicants do not need a minimum number of credits to apply. For fall 2005: Transfer applications received: 113. Transfer applicants offered admission: 70. Transfer applicants enrolled: 28. **International students:** Number of foreign undergraduates: 13 (1% of student body). Number of countries represented: 11. Minimum TOEFL score required: 550 (paper); 215 (computer).

Salisbury University

- **Address:** 1101 Camden Avenue, Salisbury, MD 21801
- **Website:** http://www.salisbury.edu/
- **Public**
- **Enrollment:** 5,798 full-time; 639 part-time

KEY STATS

✔ **U.S News College Ranking:** 38, Universities–Master's (North)
✔ **SAT Score (25th/75th percentile):** 1050-1210
✔ **Tuition:** 2006-2007: $6,412 in state, $14,306 out of state

Selectivity: More selective	**Room/board:** $7,058
Acceptance rate: 57%	**Average debt:** $15,831
Student/faculty ratio: 16/1	**Proportion who borrowed:** 63%

UNDERGRADUATE STUDENT BODY STATS

2005-2006 enrollment: 5,798 full-time; 639 part-time. Men: 44%; women: 56%. **Ethnic makeup:** African American: 9%; Asian American: 2%; Hispanic: 3%; White: 85%; International: 1%.

ADMISSIONS FACTS AND FIGURES

Phone: (410) 543-6161. **Email:** admissions@salisbury.edu. **Website:** http://www.salisbury.edu/. **Application deadlines for fall 2007:** Regular decision: January 15; decision sent by March 15. Early decision: Not offered. Early action: Send application by: December 1; Decision sent by: January 15. Admission cannot be deferred. **Application fee:** $45. Common application is not accepted. **To apply online, go to:** http://www.salisbury.edu/admissions/applications/welcome.html. **Admissions requirements/recommendations:** High school units required (recommended): English: 4 (4); Mathematics: 3 (4); Science: 3 (4); Foreign language: 2 (3); Social studies: 3 (3); Academic electives: (3); Total units: 15 (21). Tests: The college uses SAT or ACT scores in admissions decisions. Either SAT or ACT required. For admission to the fall 2007 entering class, the school will accept: ACT without writing. Campus visit: Recommended. Admissions interview: Neither required nor recommended. Off-campus interview: Not available. **Factors that count in admissions decisions:** *Academic:* Secondary school record: Very important. Class rank: Important. Letters of recommendation: Considered. Standardized test scores: Important. Essay: Considered. *Nonacademic:* Interview: Considered. Extracurricular activities: Important. Talent/ability: Important. Character/personal qualities: Considered. Alumni/ae relationship: Important. Geographical residence: Important. State residency: Not considered. Religious affiliation/commitment: Not considered. Minority status: Considered. Volunteer work: Considered. Work experience: Considered. **Other schools with the greatest overlap in applicants:** Frostburg State University; St. Mary's College of Maryland; Towson University; University of Maryland–Baltimore County; University of Maryland–College Park. **Admissions statistics for the fall 2005 entering class:** Total applicants: 5,296. Total accepted: 3,011. Freshmen enrolled: 958; 17% were from out of state. Overall acceptance rate: 57%. Non-early acceptance rate: 57%. **Credentials of fall 2005 freshmen:** 18% ranked in the top 10 percent of their high school class; 56% were in the top 25 percent, and 87% were in the top half. (Proportion submitting class standing: 49%.) **Average high school grade point average:** 3.5. **First-year students who submitted SAT scores:** 97%. Scores (25/75 percentile): Verbal: 520-600, Math: 530-610, Combined: 1050-1210. **First-year students submitting ACT scores:** 10%. Scores (25/75 percentile): English: N/A, Math: N/A, Composite: N/A.

ACADEMICS

Year founded: 1925. **Academic calendar:** 4-1-4. **Degrees offered:** bachelor's, post-bachelor's certificate, master's, post-master's certificate. **Most popular majors:** 17% business administration and management, 12% elementary education and teaching, 10% communication studies/speech communication and rhetoric, 10% nursing/registered nurse training (R.N., A.S.N.,

B.S.N., M.S.N.), 7% biology/biological sciences. **Major fields of study:** biological and biomedical sciences; business, management, marketing, and related support services; communication, journalism, and related programs; computer and information sciences and support services; education; engineering; English language and literature/letters; foreign languages, literatures, and linguistics; health professions and related clinical sciences; history; liberal arts and sciences studies, and humanities; mathematics and statistics; multi/interdisciplinary studies; natural resources and conservation; parks, recreation, leisure, and fitness studies; philosophy and religious studies; physical sciences; psychology; public administration and social service professions; social sciences; visual and performing arts. **Areas of required coursework:** arts/fine arts, humanities, computer literacy, mathematics, English (including composition), sciences (biological or physical), history, social science. **Pre-professional programs:** pre-law, pre-dentistry, premedicine, pre-veterinary science, pre-optometry, pre-pharmacy, other. **Special academic programs:** accelerated program, cooperative (work-study plan) program, cross-registration, distance learning, double major, dual enrollment, English as a Second Language (ESL), exchange student program (domestic), honors program, independent study, internships, liberal arts/career combination, student-designed major, study abroad, teacher certificate program. **Teacher certification offered in:** early childhood, elementary, secondary. **Cooperative education programs:** natural science, social/behavioral science. **Reserve Officers Training Corps (ROTC):** Army ROTC: Offered at cooperating institution (Delaware State University). **Faculty and instruction (2005-2006):** Total instructional faculty: 323 full-time, 171 part-time (49% men; 51% women; 10% minorities). Full-time faculty with Ph.D. or other terminal degree: 82%. Student/faculty ratio: 16/1. Classes of fewer than 20 students: 28%; of 20 to 49 students: 68%; of 50 or more students: 4%. **Advanced Placement and International Baccalaureate credit:** AP tests may be used for: Placement only. Scores accepted: 3. International Baccalaureate exams may be used for: Credit and/or placement. **Freshmen returning for sophomore year:** 81%. **Graduation rates:** Four-year: 52%; five-year: 68%; six-year: 67%. **Graduate study:** 28% of students pursue further study within one year; 50% within five years. Fields in which graduates pursue further study: Master of Business Administration (MBA), 3%; law, 2%; medicine, 2%.

COSTS AND FINANCIAL AID

Financial aid office: (410) 543-6165. **Expenses (2006-2007):** Tuition and fees 2006-2007: $6,412 in state, $14,306 out of state; room/board: $7,058. **Financial aid:** Priority filing date for institution's financial aid form: February 1. In 2005-2006, 65% of undergraduates applied for financial aid. Of those, 42% were determined to have financial need; 19% had their need fully met. Average financial aid package (proportion receiving): $6,052 (42%). Average amount of gift aid, such as scholarships or grants (proportion receiving): $4,351 (30%). Average amount of self-help aid, such as work study or loans (proportion receiving): $3,422 (36%). Average need-based loan (excluding PLUS or other private loans): $3,356. Among students who received need-based aid, the average percentage of need met: 57%. Among students who received aid based on merit, the average award (and the proportion receiving): $3,428 (13%). Average amount of debt of borrowers graduating in 2005: $15,831. Proportion who borrowed: 63%.

CAMPUS LIFE AND EXTRACURRICULAR ACTIVITIES

Campus housing available (% using): coed dorms (75%), women's dorms (14%), men's dorms (11%), apartment for single students. Students who live in college-owned, operated, or affiliated housing: 46%. **Student employment:** During the 2005-2006 academic year, 30% of undergraduates worked on campus. Average per-year earnings: $3,000. **Clubs and organizations:** Number of student organizations: 100. Activities include: choral groups, concert band, dance, drama/theater, jazz band, literary magazine, music ensembles, musical theater, pep band, radio station, student government, student newspaper, student film society, symphony orchestra, television station, yearbook. Number of fraternities: 6; sororities: 5. Proportion of men in fraternities: 6%; of women in sororities: 5%. Average proportion of students who stay on campus on weekends: 70%. **Sports program (2005-2006):** Member of NCAA III. *Men's intercollegiate varsity sports:* baseball, basketball, cross-country, football, lacrosse, soccer, swimming and diving, tennis, track and field (indoor), track and field (outdoor). *Women's intercollegiate varsity sports:* basketball, cross-country, field hockey, lacrosse, soccer, softball, swimming and diving, tennis, track and field (indoor), track and field (outdoor), volleyball.

SERVICES AND FACILITIES

Basic services: nonremedial tutoring, health service. **Counseling services:** minority student, career, personal, veteran student, academic, psychological. **For learning-disabled students:** School does not offer a structured program with separate admission and additional fees. Total undergraduates in learning-disabled program or receiving services: 165. Services include: note-taking services, oral tests, readers, extended time for tests, tutors. **Library:** Number of titles: 508,474; number of current serial subscriptions: 1,252. **Information technology resources:** Students are not required to lease or own a computer. Number of campus computers available to all students: 275. School has a wireless network. Approximate number of users that can be accommodated: 460. Proportion of college-owned housing units wired for high-speed internet access: 100%. **Campus safety:** Security services offered: 24-hour foot and vehicle patrols, late-night transport/escort service, 24-hour emergency telephones, lighted pathways/sidewalks, controlled dormitory access (key, security card, etc).

TRANSFER AND INTERNATIONAL STUDENTS

Transfer students: May apply for admission for the following academic terms: Fall, Spring. Applicants need a minimum number of credits to apply. For fall 2005: Transfer applications received: 1,569. Transfer applicants offered admission: 1,218. Transfer applicants enrolled: 716. **International students:** Number of foreign undergraduates: 33 (1% of student body). Number of countries represented: 27. Minimum TOEFL score required: 550 (paper); 213 (computer). Average TOEFL score: 595 (paper).

St. John's College

- **Address:** PO Box 2800, Annapolis, MD 21404
- **Website:** http://www.sjca.edu
- **Private**
- **Enrollment:** N/A

KEY STATS

✔ **U.S News College Ranking:** third tier, Liberal Arts Colleges
✔ **SAT or ACT Score (25th/75th percentile):** N/A
✔ **Tuition:** 2006-2007: $34,506

Selectivity: Selective	**Room/board:** $8,270
Acceptance rate: N/A	**Average debt:** N/A
Student/faculty ratio: N/A	**Proportion who borrowed:** N/A

St. Mary's College of Maryland

- **Address:** 18952 E. Fisher Road, St. Mary's City, MD 20686-3001
- **Website:** http://www.smcm.edu
- **Public**
- **Enrollment:** 1,849 full-time; 115 part-time

KEY STATS

✔ **U.S News College Ranking:** 95, Liberal Arts Colleges
✔ **SAT Score (25th/75th percentile):** 1130-1340
✔ **Tuition:** 2006-2007: $11,710 in state, $21,280 out of state

Selectivity: More selective	**Room/board:** $8,505
Acceptance rate: 68%	**Average debt:** $17,125
Student/faculty ratio: 12/1	**Proportion who borrowed:** 69%

UNDERGRADUATE STUDENT BODY STATS

2005-2006 enrollment: 1,849 full-time; 115 part-time. Men: 43%; women: 57%. **Ethnic makeup:** African American: 8%; Asian American: 4%; Hispanic: 3%; White: 84%; International: 1%. **Religious preference:** Roman Catholic: 28%; Protestant: 27%; Jewish: 3%; Muslim: 1%; Buddhist: 1%; No preference: 28%; Other: 12%.

ADMISSIONS FACTS AND FIGURES

Phone: (800) 492-7181. **Email:** admissions@smcm.edu. **Website:** http://www.smcm.edu. **Application deadlines for fall 2007:** Regular decision: January 15; decision sent by April 1. Early decision: Send application by: December 1; Decision sent by: January 1. Early action: Not offered. Admission cannot be deferred. **Application fee:** $40. Common application

is accepted. **To apply online, go to:** http://www.smcm.edu/admissions/application. **Admissions requirements/recommendations:** High school units required (recommended): English: 4 (4); Mathematics: 3 (3); Science: 3 (3); Foreign language: 0 (2); Social studies: 3 (3); History: 0 (1); Academic electives: 7 (8); Total units: 20 (28). Tests: The college uses SAT or ACT scores in admissions decisions. Either SAT or ACT required. For admission to the fall 2007 entering class, the school will accept: ACT with writing, ACT without writing. Campus visit: Recommended. Admissions interview: Recommended. Off-campus interview: Not available. **Factors that count in admissions decisions:** *Academic:* Secondary school record: Very important. Class rank: Not considered. Letters of recommendation: Important. Standardized test scores: Very important. Essay: Very important. *Nonacademic:* Interview: Considered. Extracurricular activities: Important. Talent/ability: Important. Character/personal qualities: Considered. Alumni/ae relationship: Considered. Geographical residence: Considered. State residency: Considered. Religious affiliation/commitment: Not considered. Minority status: Considered. Volunteer work: Considered. Work experience: Considered. **Other schools with the greatest overlap in applicants:** College of William and Mary; University of Mary Washington; University of Maryland–Baltimore County; University of Maryland–College Park; Washington College. **Admissions statistics for the fall 2005 entering class:** Total applicants: 2,200. Total accepted: 1,503. Freshmen enrolled: 488; 18% were from out of state. Accepted through early-decision or early-action plans: 25%. Overall acceptance rate: 68%. Early-decision acceptance rate: 52%. Non-early acceptance rate: 71%. **Size of waiting list:** 213 applicants; enrolled from waiting list: 6. **Credentials of fall 2005 freshmen:** 34% ranked in the top 10 percent of their high school class; 73% were in the top 25 percent, and 95% were in the top half. (Proportion submitting class standing: 39%.) **Average high school grade point average:** 3.4. **First-year students who submitted SAT scores:** 98%. Scores (25/75 percentile): Verbal: 570-690, Math: 560-650, Combined: 1130-1340. **First-year students submitting ACT scores:** 2%. Scores (25/75 percentile): English: N/A, Math: N/A, Composite: N/A.

ACADEMICS

Year founded: 1840. **Academic calendar:** Semester. **Degrees offered:** bachelor's, master's. **Most popular majors:** 14% psychology, 12% economics, 11% political science and government, 10% English language and literature, 10% biology/biological sciences. **Major fields of study:** biological and biomedical sciences; computer and information sciences and support services; English language and literature/letters; foreign languages, literatures, and linguistics; history; mathematics and statistics; multi/interdisciplinary studies; philosophy and religious studies; physical sciences; psychology; public administration and social service professions; social sciences; visual and performing arts. **Areas of required coursework:** arts/fine arts, humanities, mathematics, English (including composition), philosophy, foreign languages, sciences (biological or physical), history, social science. **Pre-professional programs:** pre-law, pre-dentistry, pre-medicine, pre-veterinary science, pre-optometry, pre-pharmacy. **Special academic programs (% participation):** cooperative (work-study plan) program, double major (14%), dual enrollment, exchange student program (domestic) (1%), honors program (5%), independent study (80%), internships (18%), student-designed major (3%), study abroad, teacher certificate program (4%). **Teacher certification offered in:** early childhood, elementary, middle/junior high, secondary. **Cooperative education programs:** computer science. **Faculty and instruction (2005-2006):** Total instructional faculty: 128 full-time, 81 part-time (54% men; 46% women; 13% minorities). Full-time faculty with Ph.D. or other terminal degree: 98%. Student/faculty ratio: 12/1. Classes of fewer than 20 students: 60%; of 20 to 49 students: 39%; of 50 or more students: 1%. **Advanced Placement and International Baccalaureate credit:** AP tests may be used for: Credit and/or placement. Scores accepted: 4, 5. International Baccalaureate exams may be used for: Credit and/or placement. **Freshmen returning for sophomore year:** 89%. **Graduation rates:** Four-year: 63%; five-year: 71%; six-year: 72%. **Graduate study:** 35% of students pursue further study within one year; 59% within five years. Fields in which graduates pursue further study: Master of Business Administration (MBA), 8%; law, 16%; medicine, 5%; engineering, 2%; theology (or the seminary), 1%; education, 21%; arts and sciences, 46%; veterinary medicine, 1%.

COSTS AND FINANCIAL AID

Financial aid office: (240) 895-3000. **Expenses (2006-2007):** Tuition and fees 2006-2007: $11,710 in state, $21,280 out of state; room/board: $8,505. Estimated books and supplies: $1,000; transportation: $1,292; personal expenses: $1,500. **Financial aid:** Priority filing date for institution's financial aid form: February 15; deadline: March 1. In 2005-2006, 62% of undergraduates applied for financial aid. Of those, 46% were determined to have financial need; Average financial aid package (proportion receiving): $6,250 (46%). Average amount of gift aid, such as scholarships or grants (proportion receiving): $4,000 (19%). Average amount of self-help aid, such as work study or loans (proportion receiving): $5,500 (19%). Average need-based loan (excluding PLUS or other private loans): $5,500. Among students who received need-based aid, the average percentage of need met: 62%. Among students who received aid based on merit, the average award (and the proportion receiving): $4,000 (24%). The average athletic scholarship (and the proportion receiving): $0 (0%). Average amount of debt of borrowers graduating in 2005: $17,125. Proportion who borrowed: 69%.

CAMPUS LIFE AND EXTRACURRICULAR ACTIVITIES

Campus housing available (% using): coed dorms (27%), women's dorms (10%), men's dorms (11%), apartment for single students (27%), special housing for disabled students (1%), other housing options (24%). Students who live in college-owned, operated, or affiliated housing: 84%. **Student employment:** During the 2005-2006 academic year, 30% of undergraduates worked on campus. Average per-year earnings: $1,100. **Clubs and organizations:** Number of student organizations: 76. Activities include: choral groups, dance, drama/theater, jazz band, literary magazine, music ensembles, musical theater, radio station, student government, student newspaper, student film society, symphony orchestra, television station, yearbook. Number of fraternities: 0; sororities: 0. Average proportion of students who stay on campus on weekends: 70%. **Sports program (2005-2006):** Member of NCAA III. *Men's intercollegiate varsity sports:* baseball, basketball, lacrosse, sailing, soccer, swimming and diving, tennis. *Women's intercollegiate varsity sports:* basketball, field hockey, lacrosse, sailing, soccer, swimming and diving, tennis, volleyball.

SERVICES AND FACILITIES

Basic services: nonremedial tutoring, placement service, health service, other. **Counseling services:** minority student, career, personal, veteran student, academic, psychological, birth control. **For learning-disabled students:** School does not offer a structured program with separate admission and additional fees. Total undergraduates in learning-disabled program or receiving services: 48. Services include: tape recorders, untimed tests, note-taking services, oral tests, extended time for tests, tutors, priority registration, priority seating, texts on tape, other testing accomodations, other. **Library:** Number of titles: 158,318; number of current serial subscriptions: 1,114. **Information technology resources:** Students are not required to lease or own a computer. Number of campus computers available to all students: 255. School has a wireless network. Approximate number of users that can be accommodated: 500. Proportion of college-owned housing units wired for high-speed internet access: 100%. **Campus safety:** Security services offered: 24-hour foot and vehicle patrols, late-night transport/escort service, 24-hour emergency telephones, lighted pathways/sidewalks, student patrols, controlled dormitory access (key, security card, etc).

TRANSFER AND INTERNATIONAL STUDENTS

Transfer students: May apply for admission for the following academic terms: Fall, Spring. Applicants need a minimum number of credits to apply. For fall 2005: Transfer applications received: 216. Transfer applicants offered admission: 110. Transfer applicants enrolled: 67. **International students:** Number of foreign undergraduates: 16 (1% of student body). Number of countries represented: 12. Minimum TOEFL score required: 550 (paper); 250 (computer).

Towson University

■ **Address:** 8000 York Road, Towson, MD 21252-0001
■ **Website:** http://www.towson.edu
■ **Public**
■ **Enrollment:** 12,812 full-time; 1,683 part-time

KEY STATS
✔ **U.S News College Ranking:** 40, Universities–Master's (North)
✔ **SAT Score (25th/75th percentile):** 1000-1180
✔ **Tuition:** 2006-2007: $7,398 in state, $16,522 out of state

Selectivity: Selective	**Room/board:** $7,112
Acceptance rate: 64%	**Average debt:** $14,808
Student/faculty ratio: 18/1	**Proportion who borrowed:** 53%

UNDERGRADUATE STUDENT BODY STATS

2005-2006 enrollment: 12,812 full-time; 1,683 part-time. Men: 39%; women: 61%. **Ethnic makeup:** African American: 11%; Asian American: 4%; Hispanic: 2%; White: 81%; International: 2%.

ADMISSIONS FACTS AND FIGURES

Phone: (410) 704-2113. **Email:** admissions@towson.edu. **Website:** http://www.towson.edu. **Application deadlines for fall 2007:** Regular decision: February 15. Early decision: Not offered. Early action: Not offered. Admission can be deferred. **Application fee:** $45. Common application is accepted. **To apply online, go to:** http://apply.usmd.edu. **Admissions requirements/recommendations:** High school units required (recommended): English: 4 (4); Mathematics: 3 (4); Science: 3 (3); Foreign language: 2 (4); Social studies: 3 (4); Academic electives: 6; Total units: 21. Tests: The college uses SAT or ACT scores in admissions decisions. Either SAT or ACT required. For admission to the fall 2007 entering class, the school will accept: ACT with writing. Campus visit: Recommended. Admissions interview: Neither required nor recommended. Off-campus interview: Not available. **Factors that count in admissions decisions:** *Academic:* Secondary school record: Important. Class rank: Considered. Letters of recommendation: Considered. Standardized test scores: Important. Essay: Considered. *Nonacademic:* Interview: Not considered. Extracurricular activities: Not considered. Talent/ability: Considered. Character/personal qualities: Not considered. Alumni/ae relationship: Not considered. Geographical residence: Not considered. State residency: Not considered. Religious affiliation/commitment: Not considered. Minority status: Not considered. Volunteer work: Not considered. Work experience: Not considered. **Admissions statistics for the fall 2005 entering class:** Total applicants: 11,746. Total accepted: 7,499. Freshmen enrolled: 2,327; 24% were from out of state. Overall acceptance rate: 64%. **Size of waiting list:** 2718 applicants; enrolled from waiting list: 921. **Credentials of fall 2005 freshmen:** 24% ranked in the top 10 percent of their high school class; 54% were in the top 25 percent, and 91% were in the top half. (Proportion submitting class standing: 62%.) **Average high school grade point average:** 3.5. **First-year students who submitted SAT scores:** 97%. Scores (25/75 percentile): Verbal: 490-580, Math: 510-600, Combined: 1000-1180. **First-year students submitting ACT scores:** 9%. Scores (25/75 percentile): English: 17-27, Math: 17-27, Composite: 19-26.

ACADEMICS

Year founded: 1866. **Academic calendar:** Semester. **Degrees offered:** bachelor's, post-bachelor's certificate, master's, post-master's certificate, doctorate. **Most popular majors:** 16% business administration and management, 8% psychology, 7% elementary education and teaching, 7% mass communication/media studies, 5% sociology. **Major fields of study:** area, ethnic, cultural, and gender studies; biological and biomedical sciences; business, management, marketing, and related support services; communication, journalism, and related programs; computer and information sciences and support services; education; English language and literature/letters; foreign languages, literatures, and linguistics; health professions and related clinical sciences; history; mathematics and statistics; multi/interdisciplinary studies; parks, recreation, leisure, and fitness studies; philosophy and religious studies; physical sciences; psychology; social sciences; visual and performing arts. **Areas of required coursework:** arts/fine arts, humanities, computer literacy, mathematics, English (including composition), sciences (biological or physical), history, social science, other. **Pre-professional programs:** pre-law, pre-dentistry, pre-medicine, pre-veterinary science, pre-optometry, pre-pharmacy. **Special academic programs:** cooperative (work-study plan) program, cross-registration, distance learning, double major, dual enrollment, English as a Second Language (ESL), exchange student program (domestic), honors program, independent study, internships, liberal arts/career combination, student-designed major, study abroad, teacher certificate program. **Teacher certification offered in:** early childhood, special education, elementary, middle/junior high, secondary, bilingual/bicultural. **Reserve Officers Training Corps (ROTC):** Army ROTC: Offered at cooperating institution (Loyola College); Air Force ROTC: Offered at cooperating institution (UMCP). **Faculty and instruction (2005-2006):** Total instructional faculty: 663 full-time, 582 part-time (50% men; 50% women; 12% minorities). Full-time faculty with Ph.D. or other terminal degree: 79%. Student/faculty ratio: 18/1. Classes of fewer than 20 students: 36%; of 20 to 49 students: 63%; of 50 or more students: 1%. **Advanced Placement and International Baccalaureate credit:** AP tests may be used for: Credit and/or placement. Scores accepted: 4. **Freshmen returning for sophomore year:** 85%. **Graduation rates:** Four-year: 31%; five-year: 53%; six-year: 58%.

COSTS AND FINANCIAL AID

Financial aid office: (410) 704-4236. **Expenses (2006-2007):** Tuition and fees 2006-2007: $7,398 in state, $16,522 out of state; room/board: $7,112. Estimated books and supplies: $912; transportation: $1,798; personal expenses: $1,596. **Financial aid:** Priority filing date for institution's financial aid form: January 31. In 2005-2006, 59% of undergraduates applied for financial aid. Of those, 43% were determined to have financial need; 16% had their need fully met. Average financial aid package (proportion receiving): $7,602 (42%). Average amount of gift aid, such as scholarships or grants (proportion receiving): $5,042 (28%). Average amount of self-help aid, such as work study or loans (proportion receiving): $3,795 (30%). Average need-based loan (excluding PLUS or other private loans): $3,707. Among students who received need-based aid, the average percentage of need met: 64%. Among students who received aid based on merit, the average award (and the proportion receiving): $3,906 (3%). The average athletic scholarship (and the proportion receiving): $9,553 (1%). Average amount of debt of borrowers graduating in 2005: $14,808. Proportion who borrowed: 53%.

CAMPUS LIFE AND EXTRACURRICULAR ACTIVITIES

Campus housing available: coed dorms, apartment for single students, special housing for disabled students, special housing for international students, other housing options. Students who live in college-owned, operated, or affiliated housing: 23%. Activities include: choral groups, concert band, dance, drama/theater, jazz band, literary magazine, marching band, music ensembles, musical theater, pep band, radio station, student government, student newspaper, symphony orchestra, television station, yearbook. Number of fraternities: 13; sororities: 14. Proportion of men in fraternities: 8%; of women in sororities: 6%. **Sports program (2005-2006):** Member of NCAA I. *Men's intercollegiate varsity sports:* baseball, basketball, cross-country, football, golf, lacrosse, soccer, swimming and diving, tennis, track and field (indoor), track and field (outdoor). *Women's intercollegiate varsity sports:* basketball, cross-country, field hockey, gymnastics, lacrosse, soccer, softball, swimming and diving, tennis, track and field (indoor), track and field (outdoor), volleyball.

SERVICES AND FACILITIES

Basic services: nonremedial tutoring, women's center, day care, health service. **Remedial assistance:** reading, math, writing. **Counseling services:** career, academic, psychological. **For learning-disabled students:** School does not offer a structured program with separate admission and additional fees. Total undergraduates in learning-disabled program or receiving services: 472. Services include: reading machines, tape recorders, note-taking services, oral tests, learning center, readers, extended time for tests, early syllabus, priority registration, priority seating, substitution of courses, texts on tape, typist/scribe, exams on tape or computer, other testing accomodations. **Library:** Number of titles: 574,096; number of current serial subscriptions: 4,154. **Information technology resources:** Students are not required to lease or own a computer. School has a wireless network. Approximate number of users that can be accommodated: 9,000. Proportion of college-owned housing units wired for high-speed internet access: 100%. **Campus safety:** Security services offered: 24-hour foot and vehicle patrols, late-night transport/escort service, 24-hour emergency telephones, lighted pathways/sidewalks, student patrols, controlled dormitory access (key, security card, etc).

TRANSFER AND INTERNATIONAL STUDENTS

Transfer students: May apply for admission for the following academic terms: Fall, Spring. Applicants need a minimum number of credits to apply. For fall 2005: Transfer applications received: 3,361. Transfer applicants

offered admission: 2,421. Transfer applicants enrolled: 1,480. **International students:** Number of foreign undergraduates: 270 (2% of student body). Number of countries represented: 101. Minimum TOEFL score required: 500 (paper); 173 (computer).

United States Naval Academy

- **Address:** 121 Blake Road, Annapolis, MD 21402
- **Website:** http://www.usna.edu
- **Public**
- **Enrollment:** 4,422 full-time

KEY STATS

✔ **U.S News College Ranking:** Unranked Specialty School–Military Academies

✔ **SAT Score (25th/75th percentile):** 1190-1380

✔ **Tuition:** N/A

Selectivity: More selective	**Room/board:** $0
Acceptance rate: 13%	**Average debt:** N/A
Student/faculty ratio: 8/1	**Proportion who borrowed:** N/A

UNDERGRADUATE STUDENT BODY STATS

2005-2006 enrollment: 4,422 full-time. Men: 82%; women: 18%. **Ethnic makeup:** African American: 6%; American-Indian: 2%; Asian American: 5%; Hispanic: 9%; White: 76%; International: 1%.

ADMISSIONS FACTS AND FIGURES

Phone: (410) 293-4361. **Email:** webmail@usna.edu. **Website:** http://www.usna.edu. **Application deadlines for fall 2007:** Regular decision: January 31. Early decision: Not offered. Early action: Send application by: N/A; Decision sent by: N/A. Admission cannot be deferred. Common application is not accepted. **Admissions requirements/recommendations:** High school units required (recommended): English: (4); Mathematics: (4); Science: (2); Foreign language: (2); History: (2). Tests: The college uses SAT or ACT scores in admissions decisions. Either SAT or ACT required. For admission to the fall 2007 entering class, the school will accept: ACT with writing. Campus visit: Recommended. Admissions interview: Required. Off-campus interview: May be arranged. **Factors that count in admissions decisions:** *Academic:* Secondary school record: Very important. Class rank: Very important. Letters of recommendation: Very important. Standardized test scores: Very important. Essay: Very important. *Nonacademic:* Interview: Very important. Extracurricular activities: Very important. Talent/ability: Important. Character/personal qualities: Very important. Alumni/ae relationship: Considered. Geographical residence: Important. State residency: Not considered. Religious affiliation/commitment: Not considered. Minority status: Considered. Volunteer work: Considered. Work experience: Considered. **Other schools with the greatest overlap in applicants:** United States Air Force Academy; United States Military Academy. **Admissions statistics for the fall 2005 entering class:** Total applicants: 11,259. Total accepted: 1,497. Freshmen enrolled: 1,227; 96% were from out of state. Overall acceptance rate: 13%. Non-early acceptance rate: 13%. **Credentials of fall 2005 freshmen:** 57% ranked in the top 10 percent of their high school class; 82% were in the top 25 percent, and 97% were in the top half. (Proportion submitting class standing: 77%.) **First-year students who submitted SAT scores:** 92%. Scores (25/75 percentile): Verbal: 570-680, Math: 620-700, Combined: 1190-1380. **First-year students submitting ACT scores:** 56%. Scores (25/75 percentile): English: 24-30, Math: 26-31, Composite: N/A.

ACADEMICS

Year founded: 1845. **Academic calendar:** Semester. **Degrees offered:** bachelor's. **Most popular majors:** 14% political science and government, 11% economics, 10% systems engineering, 9% history, 8% mechanical engineering. **Major fields of study:** computer and information sciences and support services; engineering; English language and literature/letters; history; mathematics and statistics; physical sciences; social sciences. **Areas of required coursework:** humanities, mathematics, English (including composition), sciences (biological or physical), history, social science, other. **Special academic programs (% participation):** exchange student program (domestic) (1%), honors program (1%), independent study (1%). **Faculty and instruction (2005-2006):** Total instructional faculty: 530 full-time, 56 part-time (79% men; 21% women; 10% minorities). Full-time faculty with

Ph.D. or other terminal degree: 67%. Student/faculty ratio: 8/1. Classes of fewer than 20 students: 52%; of 20 to 49 students: 48%. **Advanced Placement and International Baccalaureate credit:** AP tests may be used for: Credit and/or placement. Scores accepted: 4, 5. **Freshmen returning for sophomore year:** 96%. **Graduation rates:** Four-year: 86%; five-year: 86%; six-year: 86%. **Graduate study:** 2% of students pursue further study immediately upon graduation. Fields in which graduates pursue further study: medicine, 1%.

CAMPUS LIFE AND EXTRACURRICULAR ACTIVITIES

Campus housing available (% using): coed dorms (100%). Students who live in college-owned, operated, or affiliated housing: 100%. **Student employment:** During the 2005-2006 academic year, 0% of undergraduates worked on campus. Average per-year earnings: $0. **Clubs and organizations:** Number of student organizations: 90. Activities include: choral groups, literary magazine, marching band, music ensembles, musical theater, pep band, radio station, student government, yearbook. Number of fraternities: 0; sororities: 0. Average proportion of students who stay on campus on weekends: 50%. **Sports program (2005-2006):** Member of NCAA I. *Men's intercollegiate varsity sports:* baseball, basketball, cross-country, football, golf, gymnastics, heavyweight crew, lacrosse, lightweight crew, lightweight football, riflery, sailing, soccer, squash, swimming and diving, tennis, track and field (indoor), track and field (outdoor), volleyball, wrestling, lightweight crew, wrestling, golf. *Women's intercollegiate varsity sports:* basketball, crew, cross-country, riflery, sailing, soccer, swimming and diving, track and field (indoor), track and field (outdoor), volleyball.

SERVICES AND FACILITIES

Basic services: health service, health insurance. **Remedial assistance:** reading, math, writing, study skills. **Counseling services:** career, military, academic, psychological, religious. **Library:** Number of titles: 662,575; number of current serial subscriptions: 2,709. **Information technology resources:** Students are required to lease or own a computer. School does not have a wireless network. Proportion of college-owned housing units wired for high-speed internet access: 100%. **Campus safety:** Security services offered: 24-hour foot and vehicle patrols, lighted pathways/sidewalks, student patrols, controlled dormitory access (key, security card, etc).

TRANSFER AND INTERNATIONAL STUDENTS

International students: Number of foreign undergraduates: 42 (1% of student body). Number of countries represented: 23. Minimum TOEFL score required: 500 (paper); 173 (computer).

University of Maryland–Baltimore County

- **Address:** 1000 Hilltop Circle, Baltimore, MD 21250
- **Website:** http://www.umbc.edu
- **Public**
- **Enrollment:** 7,980 full-time; 1,426 part-time

KEY STATS

✔ **U.S News College Ranking:** third tier, National Universities
✔ **SAT Score (25th/75th percentile):** 1110-1320
✔ **Tuition:** 2006-2007: $8,622 in state, $17,354 out of state
  Selectivity: More selective   **Room/board:** N/A
  Acceptance rate: 71%   **Average debt:** $19,018
  Student/faculty ratio: 18/1   **Proportion who borrowed:** 48%

UNDERGRADUATE STUDENT BODY STATS

2005-2006 enrollment: 7,980 full-time; 1,426 part-time. Men: 54%; women: 46%. **Ethnic makeup:** African American: 14%; Asian American: 20%; Hispanic: 4%; White: 58%; International: 4%.

ADMISSIONS FACTS AND FIGURES

Phone: (410) 455-2291. **Email:** admissions@umbc.edu. **Website:** http://www.umbc.edu. **Application deadlines for fall 2007:** Regular decision: February 1. Early decision: Not offered. Early action: Send application by: November 1; Decision sent by: December 15. Admission cannot be deferred. **Application fee:** $50. Common application is accepted. **To apply online, go to:** http://www.umbc.edu/undergrad/index.html?l1=apply&. **Admissions requirements/recommendations:** High school units required (recommended): English: 4 (4); Mathematics: 3 (4); Science: 3 (3); Foreign language: 3 (2); Social studies: 0 (2); History: 0 (2); Academic electives: 0 (4); Total units: 22 (23). Tests: The college uses SAT or ACT scores in admissions decisions. Either SAT or ACT required. For admission to the fall 2007 entering class, the school will accept: ACT with writing, ACT without writing. Campus visit: Recommended. Admissions interview: Neither required nor recommended. Off-campus interview: Not available. **Factors that count in admissions decisions:** *Academic:* Secondary school record: Very important. Class rank: Important. Letters of recommendation: Important. Standardized test scores: Very important. Essay: Important. *Nonacademic:* Interview: Not considered. Extracurricular activities: Considered. Talent/ability: Considered. Character/personal qualities: Considered. Alumni/ae relationship: Not considered. Geographical residence: Not considered. State residency: Not considered. Religious affiliation/commitment: Not considered. Minority status: Not considered. Volunteer work: Considered. Work experience: Not considered. **Other schools with the greatest overlap in applicants:** Pennsylvania State University–University Park; St. Mary's College of Maryland; Towson University; University of Delaware; University of Maryland–College Park. **Admissions statistics for the fall 2005 entering class:** Total applicants: 5,229. Total accepted: 3,735. Freshmen enrolled: 1,429; 11% were from out of state. Accepted through early-decision or early-action plans: 14%. Overall acceptance rate: 71%. Non-early acceptance rate: 78%. **Size of waiting list:** 100 applicants; enrolled from waiting list: 25. **Credentials of fall 2005 freshmen:** 30% ranked in the top 10 percent of their high school class; 59% were in the top 25 percent, and 88% were in the top half. (Proportion submitting class standing: 51%.) **Average high school grade point average:** 3.5. **First-year students who submitted SAT scores:** 99%. Scores (25/75 percentile): Verbal: 540-650, Math: 570-670, Combined: 1110-1320. **First-year students submitting ACT scores:** 9%. Scores (25/75 percentile): English: 21-27, Math: 23-28, Composite: 23-27.

ACADEMICS

Year founded: 1963. **Academic calendar:** 4-1-4. **Degrees offered:** bachelor's, post-bachelor's certificate, master's, doctorate. **Most popular majors:** 24% computer and information sciences and support services, 14% social sciences, 11% biological and biomedical sciences, 11% psychology, 8% visual and performing arts. **Major fields of study:** area, ethnic, cultural, and gender studies; biological and biomedical sciences; computer and information sciences and support services; engineering; English language and literature/letters; foreign languages, literatures, and linguistics; health professions and related clinical sciences; history; mathematics and statistics; multi/interdisciplinary studies; natural resources and conservation; philosophy and religious studies; physical sciences; psychology; public administration and social service professions; social sciences; visual and performing arts. **Areas of required coursework:** arts/fine arts, humanities, mathematics, English (including composition), foreign languages, sciences (biological or physical), social science. **Pre-professional programs:** pre-law, pre-dentistry, pre-medicine, pre-veterinary science, pre-optometry, pre-pharmacy, other. **Special academic programs:** cooperative (work-study plan) program, cross-registration, distance learning, double major, dual enrollment, English as a Second Language (ESL), honors program, independent study, internships, liberal arts/career combination, student-designed major, study abroad, teacher certificate program. **Teacher certification offered in:** early childhood, elementary, secondary, bilingual/bicultural. **Cooperative education programs:** computer science, engineering, natural science, social/behavioral science, technologies. **Reserve Officers Training Corps (ROTC):** Army ROTC: Offered at cooperating institution (John's Hopkins). **Faculty and instruction (2005-2006):** Total instructional faculty: 458 full-time, 295 part-time (60% men; 40% women; 15% minorities). Full-time faculty with Ph.D. or other terminal degree: 90%. Student/faculty ratio: 18/1. Classes of fewer than 20 students: 43%; of 20 to 49 students: 45%; of 50 or more students: 12%. **Advanced Placement and International Baccalaureate credit:** AP tests may be used for: Credit and/or placement. Scores accepted: 3, 4, 5. International Baccalaureate exams may be used for: Credit and/or placement. **Freshmen returning for sophomore year:** 82%. **Graduation rates:** Four-year: 30%; five-year: 51%; six-year: 58%. **Graduate study:** 38% of students pursue further study within one year. Fields in which graduates pursue further study: Master of Business Administration (MBA), 5%; law, 7%; medicine, 5%; dentistry, 1%; engineering, 7%; theology (or the seminary), 1%; education, 9%; arts and sciences, 44%; veterinary medicine, 1%.

COSTS AND FINANCIAL AID

Financial aid office: (410) 455-2387. **Expenses (2006-2007):** Tuition and fees 2006-2007: $8,622 in state, $17,354 out of state; room/board: N/A. Estimated books and supplies: $1,100; transportation: $892; personal expenses: $1,450. **Financial aid:** Priority filing date for institution's financial aid form: February 14. In 2005-2006, 58% of undergraduates applied for financial aid. Of those, 44% were determined to have financial need; 37% had their need fully met. Average financial aid package (proportion receiving): $9,827 (44%). Average amount of gift aid, such as scholarships or grants (proportion receiving): $4,766 (33%). Average amount of self-help aid, such as work study or loans (proportion receiving): $4,390 (43%). Average need-based loan (excluding PLUS or other private loans): $4,315. Among students who received need-based aid, the average percentage of need met: 73%. Among students who received aid based on merit, the average award (and the proportion receiving): $3,667 (8%). The average athletic scholarship (and the proportion receiving): $4,007 (6%). Average amount of debt of borrowers graduating in 2005: $19,018. Proportion who borrowed: 48%.

CAMPUS LIFE AND EXTRACURRICULAR ACTIVITIES

Campus housing available: coed dorms, apartment for single students, special housing for disabled students, other housing options. Students who live in college-owned, operated, or affiliated housing: 34%. Average per-year earnings: $3,200. **Clubs and organizations:** Number of student organizations: 190. Activities include: choral groups, dance, drama/theater, literary magazine, music ensembles, pep band, radio station, student government, student newspaper, student film society. Number of fraternities: 13; sororities: 8. Proportion of men in fraternities: 2%; of women in sororities: 2%. Average proportion of students who stay on campus on weekends: 50%. **Sports program (2005-2006):** Member of NCAA I. **Men's intercollegiate varsity sports:** baseball, basketball, cross-country, lacrosse, soccer, swimming and diving, tennis, track and field (indoor), track and field (outdoor). **Women's intercollegiate varsity sports:** basketball, cross-country, field hockey, lacrosse, soccer, softball, swimming and diving, tennis, track and field (indoor), track and field (outdoor), volleyball.

SERVICES AND FACILITIES

Basic services: nonremedial tutoring, women's center, placement service, day care, health service, health insurance. **Remedial assistance:** reading, math, writing, study skills. **Counseling services:** career, academic, psychological, birth control. **For learning-disabled students:** School does not offer a structured program with separate admission and additional fees. Total undergraduates in learning-disabled program or receiving services: 100. Services include: remedial math, remedial English, remedial reading, tape recorders, videotaped classes, untimed tests, note-taking services, oral tests, learning center, readers, extended time for tests, tutors, priority registration, priority seating, other testing accomodations, other. **Library:** Number of titles: 988,005; number of current serial subscriptions: 4,193. **Information technology resources:** Students are not required to lease or own a computer. Number of campus computers available to all students: 875. School has a wireless network. Approximate number of users that can be accommodated: 5,000. Proportion of college-owned housing units wired for high-speed internet access: 100%. **Campus safety:** Security services offered: 24-hour foot and vehicle patrols, late-night transport/escort service, 24-hour emergency telephones, lighted pathways/sidewalks, controlled dormitory access (key, security card, etc).

TRANSFER AND INTERNATIONAL STUDENTS

Transfer students: May apply for admission for the following academic terms: Fall, Spring. Applicants need a minimum number of credits to apply. For fall 2005: Transfer applications received: 1,855. Transfer applicants offered admission: 1,496. Transfer applicants enrolled: 961. **International students:** Number of foreign undergraduates: 373 (4% of student body). Number of countries represented: 85. Minimum TOEFL score required: 550 (paper); 220 (computer).

University of Maryland–College Park

■ **Address:** College Park, MD 20742-5025
■ **Website:** http://www.maryland.edu
■ **Public**
■ **Enrollment:** 23,226 full-time; 2,147 part-time

KEY STATS

✔ **U.S News College Ranking:** 54, National Universities
✔ **SAT Score (25th/75th percentile):** 1180-1370
✔ **Tuition:** 2006-2007: $7,906 in state, $21,345 out of state
  Selectivity: More selective   **Room/board:** $8,562
  Acceptance rate: 49%   **Average debt:** $14,451
  Student/faculty ratio: 18/1   **Proportion who borrowed:** 46%

UNDERGRADUATE STUDENT BODY STATS

2005-2006 enrollment: 23,226 full-time; 2,147 part-time. Men: 51%; women: 49%. **Ethnic makeup:** African American: 13%; Asian American: 14%; Hispanic: 6%; White: 66%; International: 2%.

ADMISSIONS FACTS AND FIGURES

Phone: (301) 314-8385. **Email:** um-admit@uga.umd.edu. **Website:** http://www.maryland.edu. **Application deadlines for fall 2007:** Regular decision: January 20; decision sent by April 1. Early decision: Not offered. Early action: Send application by: December 1; Decision sent by: February 15. Admission can be deferred. **Application fee:** $55. Common application is not accepted. **To apply online, go to:** http://www.uga.umd.edu. **Admissions requirements/recommendations:** High school units required (recommended): English: 4; Mathematics: 3 (4); Science: 3; Foreign language: 2; Social studies: 3; Total units: 17 (18). Tests: The college uses SAT or ACT scores in admissions decisions. Either SAT or ACT required. For admission to the fall 2007 entering class, the school will accept: ACT with writing. Campus visit: Recommended. Admissions interview: Neither required nor recommended. Off-campus interview: Not available. **Factors that count in admissions decisions:** *Academic:* Secondary school record: Very important. Class rank: Important. Letters of recommendation: Important. Standardized test scores: Very important. Essay: Important. *Nonacademic:* Interview: Not considered. Extracurricular activities: Considered. Talent/ability: Important. Character/personal qualities: Considered. Alumni/ae relationship: Considered. Geographical residence: Considered. State residency: Important. Religious affiliation/commitment: Not considered. Minority status: Considered. Volunteer work: Considered. Work experience: Considered. **Other schools with the greatest overlap in applicants:** Cornell University; New York University; University of Maryland–Baltimore County. **Admissions statistics for the fall 2005 entering class:** Total applicants: 22,428. Total accepted: 11,002. Freshmen enrolled: 4,211; 34% were from out of state. Accepted through early-decision or early-action plans: 91%. Overall acceptance rate: 49%. Non-early acceptance rate: 32%. **Size of waiting list:** 2530 applicants; enrolled from waiting list: 1508. **Credentials of fall 2005 freshmen:** 64% ranked in the top 10 percent of their high school class; 86% were in the top 25 percent, and 99% were in the top half. (Proportion submitting class standing: 40%.) **Average high school grade point average:** 3.9. **First-year students who submitted SAT scores:** 98%. Scores (25/75 percentile): Verbal: 580-670, Math: 600-700, Combined: 1180-1370.

ACADEMICS

Year founded: 1856. **Academic calendar:** Semester. **Degrees offered:** certificate, bachelor's, post-bachelor's certificate, master's, post-master's certificate, first professional, doctorate. **Most popular majors:** 7% criminology, 6% political science and government, 5% economics, 5% finance, 5% psychology. **Major fields of study:** agriculture, agriculture operations, and related sciences; architecture and related services; area, ethnic, cultural, and gender studies; biological and biomedical sciences; business, management, marketing, and related support services; communication, journalism, and related programs; computer and information sciences and support services; education; engineering; English language and literature/letters; family and consumer sciences/human sciences; foreign languages, literatures, and linguistics; health professions and related clinical sciences; history; legal professions and studies; mathematics and statistics; multi/interdisciplinary studies; natural resources and conservation; parks, recreation, leisure, and fitness studies; philosophy and religious studies; physical sciences; psychology; social sciences; visual and performing arts. **Areas of required coursework:** arts/fine arts, mathematics, English (including composition), sciences (biological or physical), history, social science, other. **Pre-professional programs:** pre-law, pre-dentistry, pre-medicine, pre-veterinary science, pre-optometry, pre-pharmacy, other. **Special academic programs:** accelerated program, cooperative (work-study plan) program, cross-registration, distance learning, double major, dual enrollment, English as a Second Language (ESL), exchange student program (domestic), external degree program, honors program, independent study, internships, student-designed major, study abroad, teacher certificate program, other. **Teacher certification offered in:** early childhood, special education, elementary, middle/junior high, secondary. **Cooperative education programs:** engineering. **Reserve Officers Training Corps (ROTC):** Army ROTC: Offered on campus; Navy ROTC: Offered at cooperating institution (George Washington University); Air Force ROTC: Offered on campus. **Faculty and instruction (2005-2006):** Total instructional faculty: 1,536 full-time, 534 part-time (66% men; 34% women; 16% minorities). Full-time faculty with Ph.D. or other terminal degree: 94%. Student/faculty ratio: 18/1. Classes of fewer than 20 students: 34%; of 20 to 49 students: 51%; of 50 or more students: 15%. **Advanced Placement and International Baccalaureate credit:** AP tests may be used for: Credit and/or placement. Scores accepted: 3, 4, 5. International Baccalaureate exams may be used for: Credit and/or placement. **Freshmen returning for sophomore year:** 93%. **Graduation rates:** Four-year: 50%; five-year: 73%; six-year: 76%. **Graduate study:** 24% of students pursue further study immediately upon graduation.

COSTS AND FINANCIAL AID

Financial aid office: (301) 314-9000. **Expenses (2006-2007):** Tuition and fees 2006-2007: $7,906 in state, $21,345 out of state; room/board: $8,562. Estimated books and supplies: $952; transportation: $696; personal expenses: $2,089. **Financial aid:** Priority filing date for institution's financial aid form: February 15. In 2005-2006, 66% of undergraduates applied for financial aid. Of those, 40% were determined to have financial need; 29% had their need fully met. Average financial aid package (proportion receiving): $12,598 (37%). Average amount of gift aid, such as scholarships or grants (proportion receiving): $4,715 (26%). Average amount of self-help aid, such as work study or loans (proportion receiving): $3,925 (26%). Average need-based loan (excluding PLUS or other private loans): $3,794. Among students who received need-based aid, the average percentage of need met: 69%. Among students who received aid based on merit, the average award (and the proportion receiving): $6,129 (16%). The average athletic scholarship (and the proportion receiving): $11,377 (2%). Average amount of debt of borrowers graduating in 2005: $14,451. Proportion who borrowed: 46%.

CAMPUS LIFE AND EXTRACURRICULAR ACTIVITIES

Campus housing available (% using): coed dorms (72%), women's dorms (1%), sorority housing (5%), fraternity housing (7%), apartment for single students (15%), special housing for disabled students, special housing for international students, other housing options. Students who live in college-owned, operated, or affiliated housing: 43%. **Student employment:** During the 2005-2006 academic year, 28% of undergraduates worked on campus. Average per-year earnings: $5,600. **Clubs and organizations:** Number of student organizations: 535. Activities include: choral groups, concert band, dance, drama/theater, jazz band, literary magazine, marching band, music ensembles, musical theater, opera, pep band, radio station, student government, student newspaper, student film society, symphony orchestra, television station, yearbook. Number of fraternities: 23; sororities: 14. Proportion of men in fraternities: 9%; of women in sororities: 11%. Average proportion of students who stay on campus on weekends: 50%. **Sports program (2005-2006):** Member of NCAA I. *Men's intercollegiate varsity sports:* baseball, basketball, cross-country, football, golf, lacrosse, soccer, swimming and diving, tennis, track and field (indoor), track and field (outdoor), wrestling. *Women's intercollegiate varsity sports:* basketball, cheerleading, cross-country, field hockey, golf, gymnastics, lacrosse, soccer, softball, swimming and diving, tennis, track and field (indoor), track and field (outdoor), volleyball, water polo.

SERVICES AND FACILITIES

Basic services: nonremedial tutoring, day care, health service, health insurance. **Remedial assistance:** reading, math, writing, study skills, other. **Counseling services:** minority student, career, personal, veteran student, academic, older student, psychological, birth control. **For learning-disabled students:** School does not offer a structured program with separate admission and additional fees. Total undergraduates in learning-disabled program or receiving services: 482. Services include: reading machines, tape

recorders, other special classes, note-taking services, oral tests, learning center, readers, extended time for tests, priority registration, priority seating, substitution of courses, texts on tape, typist/scribe, other testing accomodations. **Library:** Number of titles: 3,182,973; number of current serial subscriptions: 33,477. **Information technology resources:** Students are not required to lease or own a computer. Number of campus computers available to all students: 1,800. School has a wireless network. Approximate number of users that can be accommodated: 5,000. Proportion of college-owned housing units wired for high-speed internet access: 100%. **Campus safety:** Security services offered: 24-hour foot and vehicle patrols, late-night transport/escort service, 24-hour emergency telephones, lighted pathways/sidewalks, student patrols, controlled dormitory access (key, security card, etc).

TRANSFER AND INTERNATIONAL STUDENTS

Transfer students: May apply for admission for the following academic terms: Fall, Spring. Applicants need a minimum number of credits to apply. For fall 2005: Transfer applications received: 6,059. Transfer applicants offered admission: 3,867. Transfer applicants enrolled: 2,371. **International students:** Number of foreign undergraduates: 517 (2% of student body). Number of countries represented: 142. Minimum TOEFL score required: 575 (paper); 233 (computer). Average TOEFL score: 589 (paper).

University of Maryland–Eastern Shore

- ■ **Address:** J.T. Williams Hall, Room 2106, Princess Anne, MD 21853
- ■ **Website:** http://www.umes.edu
- ■ **Public**
- ■ **Enrollment:** 3,158 full-time; 290 part-time

KEY STATS

✔ **U.S News College Ranking:** third tier, Universities–Master's (North)
✔ **SAT Score (25th/75th percentile):** 730-920
✔ **Tuition:** 2005-2006: $5,808 in state, $11,964 out of state
Selectivity: Least selective   **Room/board:** $6,130
Acceptance rate: 66%   **Average debt:** N/A
Student/faculty ratio: 17/1   **Proportion who borrowed:** N/A

UNDERGRADUATE STUDENT BODY STATS

2005-2006 enrollment: 3,158 full-time; 290 part-time. Men: 39%; women: 61%. **Ethnic makeup:** African American: 81%; Asian American: 1%; Hispanic: 1%; White: 14%; International: 3%.

ADMISSIONS FACTS AND FIGURES

Phone: (410) 651-6410. **Email:** umesadmissions@umes.edu. **Website:** http://www.umes.edu. **Application deadlines for fall 2007:** Regular decision: July 15. Early decision: Not offered. Early action: Send application by: November 15; Decision sent by: December 1. Admission can be deferred. **Application fee:** $25. Common application is accepted. **Admissions requirements/recommendations:** High school units required (recommended): English: 4; Mathematics: 3; Science: 2; Foreign language: 2; Social studies: 3; Academic electives: 6. Tests: The college uses SAT or ACT scores in admissions decisions. Either SAT or ACT required. For admission to the fall 2007 entering class, the school will accept: ACT with writing, ACT without writing. Campus visit: Recommended. Admissions interview: Recommended. Off-campus interview: Not available. **Factors that count in admissions decisions:** *Academic:* Secondary school record: Very important. Class rank: Very important. Letters of recommendation: Considered. Standardized test scores: Very important. Essay: Considered. *Nonacademic:* Interview: Considered. Extracurricular activities: Considered. Talent/ability: Considered. Character/personal qualities: Very important. Alumni/ae relationship: Not considered. Geographical residence: Not considered. State residency: Considered. Religious affiliation/commitment: Not considered. Minority status: Not considered. Volunteer work: Not considered. Work experience: Not considered. **Other schools with the greatest overlap in applicants:** Alabama Agricultural and Mechanical University; Albany State University; Alcorn State University; California State University–Bakersfield; Fort Valley State University. **Admissions statistics for the fall 2005 entering class:** Total applicants: 3,558. Total accepted: 2,365. Freshmen enrolled: 1,054; 24% were from out of state. Overall acceptance rate: 66%. Non-early acceptance rate: 66%. **Size of waiting list:** 0 applicants; enrolled from waiting list: 0. **First-year students who submitted SAT scores:** 82%. Scores (25/75 percentile): Verbal: 370-460, Math: 360-460, Combined: 730-920. **First-year students submitting ACT scores:** 12%. Scores (25/75 percentile): English: N/A, Math: N/A, Composite: 14-18.

ACADEMICS

Year founded: 1886. **Academic calendar:** Semester. **Degrees offered:** bachelor's, master's, doctorate. **Most popular majors:** 14% business administration and management, 12% criminal justice/law enforcement administration, 10% family and consumer sciences/human sciences, 9% sociology, 8% biology/biological sciences. **Major fields of study:** agriculture, agriculture operations, and related sciences; architecture and related services; area, ethnic, cultural, and gender studies; biological and biomedical sciences; business, management, marketing, and related support services; computer and information sciences and support services; construction trades; education; engineering; engineering technologies/technicians; English language and literature/letters; family and consumer sciences/human sciences; health professions and related clinical sciences; history; legal professions and studies; liberal arts and sciences studies, and humanities; mathematics and statistics; multi/interdisciplinary studies; natural resources and conservation; parks; recreation, leisure, and fitness studies; physical sciences; security and protective services; social sciences; transportation and materials moving; visual and performing arts. **Areas of required coursework:** mathematics, English (including composition), social science. **Pre-professional programs:** pre-law, pre-dentistry, pre-medicine, pre-veterinary science, pre-pharmacy. **Special academic programs (% participation):** cooperative (work-study plan) program, cross-registration (2.8%), distance learning (3.7%), dual enrollment (.1%), honors program (8.7%), independent study (2.8%), internships (1.2%), study abroad (.3%). **Cooperative education programs:** agriculture, art, business, computer science, education, engineering, health professions, home economics, humanities, natural science, social/behavioral science, technologies, vocational arts. **Faculty and instruction (2005-2006):** Total instructional faculty: 169 full-time, 98 part-time (52% men; 48% women; 52% minorities). Full-time faculty with Ph.D. or other terminal degree: 62%. Student/faculty ratio: 17/1. Classes of fewer than 20 students: 45%; of 20 to 49 students: 51%; of 50 or more students: 4%. **Advanced Placement and International Baccalaureate credit:** AP tests may be used for: Credit and/or placement. International Baccalaureate exams may be used for: Credit and/or placement. **Freshmen returning for sophomore year:** 68%. **Graduation rates:** Four-year: 25%; five-year: 38%; six-year: 42%.

COSTS AND FINANCIAL AID

Financial aid office: (410) 651-6172. **Expenses (2005-2006):** Tuition and fees 2005-2006: $5,808 in state, $11,964 out of state; room/board: $6,130. Estimated books and supplies: $1,400; transportation: $1,000; personal expenses: $1,600. **Financial aid:** Priority filing date for institution's financial aid form: March 1.

CAMPUS LIFE AND EXTRACURRICULAR ACTIVITIES

Campus housing available (% using): coed dorms (57%), women's dorms (27%), men's dorms (16%). Students who live in college-owned, operated, or affiliated housing: 55%. **Student employment:** During the 2005-2006 academic year, 12% of undergraduates worked on campus. Average per-year earnings: $4,760. **Clubs and organizations:** Number of student organizations: 75. Activities include: choral groups, concert band, dance, drama/theater, jazz band, music ensembles, radio station, student government, student newspaper, yearbook. Number of fraternities: 4; sororities: 4. Average proportion of students who stay on campus on weekends: 75%. **Sports program (2005-2006):** Member of NCAA I. *Men's intercollegiate varsity sports:* baseball, basketball, cross-country, tennis, track and field (indoor), track and field (outdoor). *Women's intercollegiate varsity sports:* basketball, bowling, cross-country, softball, tennis, track and field (indoor), track and field (outdoor), volleyball.

SERVICES AND FACILITIES

Basic services: nonremedial tutoring, placement service, day care, health service, health insurance. **Remedial assistance:** reading, math, writing, study skills, other. **Counseling services:** minority student, career, personal, veteran student, academic, psychological, religious. **For learning-disabled students:** Services include: remedial math, remedial English, remedial reading, tape recorders, untimed tests, note-taking services, extended time for tests, tutors, other. **Library:** Number of titles: 217,429; number of current serial subscriptions: 565. **Information technology resources:** Students are not required to lease or own a computer. Number of campus computers available to all students: 739. School has a wireless network. **Campus safety:** Security services offered: 24-hour foot and vehicle patrols, late-night trans-port/escort service, 24-hour emergency telephones, lighted pathways/sidewalks, student patrols, controlled dormitory access (key, security card, etc).

TRANSFER AND INTERNATIONAL STUDENTS

Transfer students: May apply for admission for the following academic terms: Fall, Winter, Spring, Summer. Applicants need a minimum number of credits to apply. For fall 2005: Transfer applications received: 501. Transfer applicants offered admission: 343. Transfer applicants enrolled: 199. **International students:** Number of foreign undergraduates: 98 (3% of student body). Number of countries represented: 98. Minimum TOEFL score required: 500 (paper); 173 (computer). Average TOEFL score: 550 (paper).

University of Maryland–University College

- ■ **Address:** 3501 University Boulevard E, Adelphi, MD 20783
- ■ **Website:** http://umuc.edu/
- ■ **Public**
- ■ **Enrollment:** 2,780 full-time; 16,220 part-time

KEY STATS

✔ **U.S News College Ranking:** Unranked, Universities–Master's (North)
✔ **SAT or ACT Score (25th/75th percentile):** N/A
✔ **Tuition:** 2006-2007: $7,020 in state, $13,440 out of state
  Selectivity: N/A   **Room/board:** N/A
  Acceptance rate: 100%   **Average debt:** N/A
  Student/faculty ratio: 18/1   **Proportion who borrowed:** N/A

UNDERGRADUATE STUDENT BODY STATS

2005-2006 enrollment: 2,780 full-time; 16,220 part-time. Men: 41%; women: 59%. **Ethnic makeup:** African American: 33%; American-Indian: 1%; Asian American: 5%; Hispanic: 5%; White: 55%; International: 1%.

ADMISSIONS FACTS AND FIGURES

Phone: (301) 985-7000. **Email:** umucinfo@umuc.edu. **Website:** http://umuc.edu/. **Application deadlines for fall 2007:** Regular decision: Rolling. Early decision: Not offered. Early action: Not offered. Admission can be deferred. **Application fee:** $30. Common application is not accepted. **To apply online, go to:** https://nova.umuc.edu/studserv/isis/ugradapp.html. **Admissions requirements/recommendations:** Tests: The college does not use SAT or ACT scores in admissions decisions. Neither SAT nor ACT required. Campus visit: Neither required nor recommended. Admissions interview: Neither required nor recommended. Off-campus interview: Not available. **Factors that count in admissions decisions:** *Academic:* Secondary school record: Not considered. Class rank: Not considered. Letters of recommendation: Not considered. Standardized test scores: Not considered. Essay: Not considered. *Nonacademic:* Interview: Not considered. Extracurricular activities: Not considered. Talent/ability: Not considered. Character/personal qualities: Not considered. Alumni/ae relationship: Not considered. Geographical residence: Not considered. State residency: Not considered. Religious affiliation/commitment: Not considered. Minority status: Not considered. Volunteer work: Not considered. Work experience: Not considered. **Admissions statistics for the fall 2005 entering class:** Total applicants: 1,599. Total accepted: 1,599. Freshmen enrolled: 974; 51% were from out of state. Overall acceptance rate: 100%.

ACADEMICS

Year founded: 1947. **Academic calendar:** Semester. **Degrees offered:** certificate, transfer-associate, bachelor's, post-bachelor's certificate, master's, doctorate. **Most popular majors:** 29% business, management, marketing, and related support services, 26% multi/interdisciplinary studies, 25% computer and information sciences and support services, 5% psychology, 4% legal professions and studies. **Major fields of study:** area, ethnic, cultural, and gender studies; biological and biomedical sciences; business, management, marketing, and related support services; communication, journalism, and related programs; computer and information sciences and support services; English language and literature/letters; history; legal professions and studies; liberal arts and sciences studies, and humanities; multi/interdisciplinary studies; natural resources and conservation; psychology; security and protective services; social sciences. **Areas of required coursework:** humanities, computer literacy, mathematics, English (including composition), sciences (biological or physical), social science. **Special**

academic programs: accelerated program, cooperative (work-study plan) program, cross-registration, distance learning, double major, dual enrollment, external degree program, teacher certificate program, weekend college. **Faculty and instruction (2005-2006):** Total instructional faculty: 221 full-time, 1,172 part-time (60% men; 40% women; 20% minorities). Full-time faculty with Ph.D. or other terminal degree: 63%. Student/faculty ratio: 18/1. Classes of fewer than 20 students: 51%; of 20 to 49 students: 49%. **Advanced Placement and International Baccalaureate credit:** AP tests may be used for: Placement only. Scores accepted: 3, 4, 5. International Baccalaureate exams may be used for: Credit only. **Graduation rates:** Six-year: 19%.

COSTS AND FINANCIAL AID

Financial aid office: (301) 985-7510. **Expenses (2006-2007):** Tuition and fees 2006-2007: $7,020 in state, $13,440 out of state; room/board: N/A. Estimated books and supplies: $1,362; transportation: $396; personal expenses: $4,099. **Financial aid:** Priority filing date for institution's financial aid form: June 1. In 2005-2006, 61% of undergraduates applied for financial aid. Of those, 58% were determined to have financial need; 3% had their need fully met. Average financial aid package (proportion receiving): $4,807 (49%). Average amount of gift aid, such as scholarships or grants (proportion receiving): $1,542 (27%). Average amount of self-help aid, such as work study or loans (proportion receiving): $2,276 (41%). Average need-based loan (excluding PLUS or other private loans): $2,126. Among students who received need-based aid, the average percentage of need met: 25%.

CAMPUS LIFE AND EXTRACURRICULAR ACTIVITIES

Number of fraternities: 0; sororities: 0.

SERVICES AND FACILITIES

Basic services: nonremedial tutoring. **Remedial assistance:** math, writing. **Counseling services:** minority student, career, military, veteran student, academic, older student. **For learning-disabled students:** School does not offer a structured program with separate admission and additional fees. Services include: remedial math, remedial English, tape recorders, untimed tests, note-taking services, oral tests, readers, tutors. **Information technology resources:** Students are not required to lease or own a computer. Number of campus computers available to all students: 375. School has a wireless network. **Campus safety:** Security services offered: 24-hour emergency telephones, lighted pathways/sidewalks.

TRANSFER AND INTERNATIONAL STUDENTS

Transfer students: May apply for admission for the following academic terms: Fall, Spring, Summer. Applicants do not need a minimum number of credits to apply. For fall 2005: Transfer applications received: 5,782. Transfer applicants offered admission: 5,782. Transfer applicants enrolled: 3,686. **International students:** Number of foreign undergraduates: 176 (1% of student body). Minimum TOEFL score required: 550 (paper); 213 (computer).

Villa Julie College

- **Address:** 1525 Greenspring Valley Road, Stevenson, MD 21153
- **Website:** http://www.vjc.edu
- **Private**
- **Enrollment:** 2,294 full-time; 512 part-time

KEY STATS

✔ **U.S News College Ranking:** 16, Comp. Coll.–Bachelor's (North)
✔ **SAT Score (25th/75th percentile):** 900-1120
✔ **Tuition:** 2006-2007: $16,770

Selectivity: Selective	**Room/board:** $9,188
Acceptance rate: 70%	**Average debt:** $15,580
Student/faculty ratio: 14/1	**Proportion who borrowed:** 68%

UNDERGRADUATE STUDENT BODY STATS

2005-2006 enrollment: 2,294 full-time; 512 part-time. Men: 29%; women: 71%. **Ethnic makeup:** African American: 15%; Asian American: 3%; Hispanic: 1%; White: 81%. **Religious preference:** Roman Catholic: 27%; Protestant: 30%; Jewish: 2%; Unknown: 38%; Other: 3%.

Phone: (410) 486-7001. **Email:** admissions@mail.vjc.edu. **Website:** http://www.vjc.edu. **Application deadlines for fall 2007:** Regular decision: March 1. Early decision: Not offered. Early action: Not offered. Admission can be deferred. **Application fee:** $25. Common application is not accepted. **To apply online, go to:** https://www14.vjc.edu/admissions/online_application_v4/. **Admissions requirements/recommendations:** High school units required (recommended): English: 4 (4); Mathematics: 3 (3); Science: 3 (3); Social studies: 2 (2); History: 1 (1); Academic electives: 4 (4); Total units: 17 (17). Tests: The college uses SAT or ACT scores in admissions decisions. Either SAT or ACT required. For admission to the fall 2007 entering class, the school will accept: ACT with writing, ACT without writing. Campus visit: Recommended. Admissions interview: Recommended. Off-campus interview: May be arranged. **Factors that count in admissions decisions:** *Academic:* Secondary school record: Very important. Class rank: Important. Letters of recommendation: Considered. Standardized test scores: Very important. Essay: Important. *Nonacademic:* Interview: Considered. Extracurricular activities: Important. Talent/ability: Important. Character/personal qualities: Considered. Alumni/ae relationship: Considered. Geographical residence: Not considered. State residency: Not considered. Religious affiliation/commitment: Not considered. Minority status: Not considered. Volunteer work: Considered. Work experience: Not considered. **Other schools with the greatest overlap in applicants:** Frostburg State University; Salisbury University; Towson University; University of Maryland–Baltimore County; University of Maryland–College Park. **Admissions statistics for the fall 2005 entering class:** Total applicants: 2,166. Total accepted: 1,509. Freshmen enrolled: 543; 5% were from out of state. Overall acceptance rate: 70%. **Credentials of fall 2005 freshmen:** 17% ranked in the top 10 percent of their high school class; 42% were in the top 25 percent, and 78% were in the top half. (Proportion submitting class standing: 84%.) **Average high school grade point average:** 3.3. **First-year students who submitted SAT scores:** 98%. Scores (25/75 percentile): Verbal: 450-560, Math: 450-560, Combined: 900-1120. **First-year students submitting ACT scores:** 12%. Scores (25/75 percentile): English: 17-24, Math: 17-21, Composite: 18-22.

ACADEMICS

Year founded: 1947. **Academic calendar:** Semester. **Degrees offered:** certificate, bachelor's, master's. **Most popular majors:** 19% nursing/registered nurse training (R.N., A.S.N., B.S.N., M.S.N.), 11% business administration and management, 10% management information systems, 8% legal assistant/paralegal, 6% design and visual communications. **Major fields of study:** biological and biomedical sciences; business, management, marketing, and related support services; computer and information sciences and support services; education; English language and literature/letters; family and consumer sciences/human sciences; health professions and related clinical sciences; history; legal professions and studies; mathematics and statistics; multi/interdisciplinary studies; physical sciences; psychology; visual and performing arts. **Areas of required coursework:** arts/fine arts, humanities, computer literacy, mathematics, English (including composition), philosophy, sciences (biological or physical), history, social science. **Pre-professional programs:** pre-law, pre-dentistry, pre-medicine, pre-veterinary science, pre-optometry, pre-pharmacy. **Special academic programs (% participation):** accelerated program, cooperative (work-study plan) program (12%), cross-registration, distance learning, double major (1%), dual enrollment, honors program, independent study (5%), internships (20%), liberal arts/career combination (100%), student-designed major (3%), study abroad, teacher certificate program (9%), weekend college. **Teacher certification offered in:** early childhood, elementary. **Cooperative education programs:** art, business, computer science, education, health professions, humanities, natural science, social/behavioral science, technologies, other. **Reserve Officers Training Corps (ROTC):** Army ROTC: Offered at cooperating institution (Johns Hopkins University). **Faculty and instruction (2005-2006):** Total instructional faculty: 93 full-time, 256 part-time (44% men; 56% women; 10% minorities). Full-time faculty with Ph.D. or other terminal degree: 67%. Student/faculty ratio: 14/1. Classes of fewer than 20 students: 64%; of 20 to 49 students: 36%; of 50 or more students: 0%. **Advanced Placement and International Baccalaureate credit:** AP tests may be used for: Credit and/or placement. Scores accepted: 3, 4, 5. International Baccalaureate exams may be used for: Credit and/or placement. **Freshmen returning for sophomore year:** 79%. **Graduation rates:** Four-year: 51%; five-year: 64%; six-year: 58%. **Graduate study:** 13% of students pursue further study within one year. Fields in which graduates pursue further study: Master of Business Administration (MBA), 25%; law, 25%; arts and sciences, 50%.

COSTS AND FINANCIAL AID

Financial aid office: (443) 334-2559. **Expenses (2006-2007):** Tuition and fees 2006-2007: $16,770; room/board: $9,188. Estimated books and supplies:

$1,200; transportation: $931; personal expenses: $2,025. **Financial aid:** Priority filing date for institution's financial aid form: February 15. In 2005-2006, 71% of undergraduates applied for financial aid. Of those, 57% were determined to have financial need; 27% had their need fully met. Average financial aid package (proportion receiving): $10,438 (56%). Average amount of gift aid, such as scholarships or grants (proportion receiving): $7,876 (53%). Average amount of self-help aid, such as work study or loans (proportion receiving): $3,662 (37%). Average need-based loan (excluding PLUS or other private loans): $3,586. Among students who received need-based aid, the average percentage of need met: 71%. Among students who received aid based on merit, the average award (and the proportion receiving): $5,720 (24%). The average athletic scholarship (and the proportion receiving): $0 (0%). Average amount of debt of borrowers graduating in 2005: $15,580. Proportion who borrowed: 68%.

CAMPUS LIFE AND EXTRACURRICULAR ACTIVITIES

Campus housing available (% using): apartment for single students (72%), other housing options (28%). Students who live in college-owned, operated, or affiliated housing: 27%. **Student employment:** During the 2005-2006 academic year, 10% of undergraduates worked on campus. Average per-year earnings: $1,727. Activities include: choral groups, dance, drama/theater, jazz band, literary magazine, music ensembles, pep band, student government, student newspaper, symphony orchestra. Number of fraternities: 0; sororities: 1. of women in sororities: 2%. Average proportion of students who stay on campus on weekends: 75%. **Sports program (2005-2006):** Member of NCAA III. *Men's intercollegiate varsity sports:* baseball, basketball, cross-country, field hockey, golf, lacrosse, soccer, tennis, track and field (indoor), volleyball. *Women's intercollegiate varsity sports:* basketball, cross-country, golf, lacrosse, soccer, softball, tennis, track and field (indoor), volleyball.

SERVICES AND FACILITIES

Basic services: nonremedial tutoring, placement service. **Remedial assistance:** reading, math, writing, study skills, other. **Counseling services:** minority student, career, military, personal, veteran student, academic, older student, psychological, birth control. **For learning-disabled students:** School does not offer a structured program with separate admission and additional fees. Total undergraduates in learning-disabled program or receiving services: 81. Services include: remedial math, remedial English, reading machines, remedial reading, tape recorders, untimed tests, note-taking services, oral tests, learning center, readers, extended time for tests, tutors, early syllabus, priority seating, typist/scribe, exams on tape or computer, other testing accomodations. **Library:** Number of titles: 79,248; number of current serial subscriptions: 1,058. **Information technology resources:** Students are not required to lease or own a computer. Number of campus computers available to all students: 550. School has a wireless network. Approximate number of users that can be accommodated: 400. Proportion of college-owned housing units wired for high-speed internet access: 100%. **Campus safety:** Security services offered: late-night transport/escort service, 24-hour emergency telephones, lighted pathways/sidewalks, controlled dormitory access (key, security card, etc).

TRANSFER AND INTERNATIONAL STUDENTS

Transfer students: May apply for admission for the following academic terms: Fall, Spring, Summer. Applicants do not need a minimum number of credits to apply. For fall 2005: Transfer applications received: 817. Transfer applicants offered admission: 511. Transfer applicants enrolled: 199. **International students:** Number of foreign undergraduates: 8. Number of countries represented: 9. Minimum TOEFL score required: 550 (paper); 213 (computer).

Washington College

- **Address:** 300 Washington Avenue, Chestertown, MD 21620
- **Website:** http://www.washcoll.edu
- **Private**
- **Enrollment:** 1,312 full-time; 29 part-time

KEY STATS

- ✔ **U.S News College Ranking:** third tier, Liberal Arts Colleges
- ✔ **SAT Score (25th/75th percentile):** 1050-1250
- ✔ **Tuition:** 2006-2007: $30,200

Selectivity: More selective	**Room/board:** $6,450
Acceptance rate: 59%	**Average debt:** $20,483
Student/faculty ratio: 12/1	**Proportion who borrowed:** 60%

UNDERGRADUATE STUDENT BODY STATS

2005-2006 enrollment: 1,312 full-time; 29 part-time. Men: 38%; women: 62%. **Ethnic makeup:** African American: 4%; Asian American: 1%; Hispanic: 1%; White: 91%; International: 3%.

ADMISSIONS FACTS AND FIGURES

Phone: (410) 778-7700. **Email:** ivictorius2@washcoll.edu. **Website:** http://www.washcoll.edu. **Application deadlines for fall 2007:** Regular decision: March 1. Early decision: Send application by: November 15; Decision sent by: December 15. Early action: Send application by: December 1; Decision sent by: December 20. Admission can be deferred. **Application fee:** $45. Common application is accepted. **To apply online, go to:** https://app.commonapp.org. **Admissions requirements/recommendations:** High school units required (recommended): English: 4 (4); Mathematics: 3 (4); Science: 3 (4); Foreign language: 2 (4); Social studies: 4 (4); Total units: 16 (20). Tests: The college uses SAT or ACT scores in admissions decisions. Either SAT or ACT required. For admission to the fall 2007 entering class, the school will accept: ACT without writing. Campus visit: Recommended. Off-campus interview: Not available. **Factors that count in admissions decisions: *Academic:*** Secondary school record: Very important. Class rank: Important. Letters of recommendation: Important. Standardized test scores: Important. Essay: Important. ***Nonacademic:*** Interview: Very important. Extracurricular activities: Important. Talent/ability: Important. Character/personal qualities: Important. Alumni/ae relationship: Considered. Geographical residence: Considered. State residency: Considered. Religious affiliation/commitment: Not considered. Minority status: Considered. Volunteer work: Considered. Work experience: Considered. **Admissions statistics for the fall 2005 entering class:** Total applicants: 2,223. Total accepted: 1,311. Freshmen enrolled: 343; 56% were from out of state. Accepted through early-decision or early-action plans: 11%. Overall acceptance rate: 59%. Non-early acceptance rate: 57%. **Size of waiting list:** 708 applicants; enrolled from waiting list: 48. **Credentials of fall 2005 freshmen:** 36% ranked in the top 10 percent of their high school class; 68% were in the top 25 percent. (Proportion submitting class standing: 57%.) **Average high school grade point average:** 3.4. **First-year students who submitted SAT scores:** 93%. Scores (25/75 percentile): Verbal: 530-630, Math: 520-620, Combined: 1050-1250. **First-year students submitting ACT scores:** 5%. Scores (25/75 percentile): English: N/A, Math: N/A, Composite: 22-27.

ACADEMICS

Year founded: 1782. **Academic calendar:** Semester. **Degrees offered:** bachelor's, master's. **Most popular majors:** 25% social sciences, 14% business, management, marketing, and related support services, 10% English language and literature/letters, 10% psychology, 8% foreign languages, literatures, and linguistics. **Major fields of study:** area, ethnic, cultural, and gender studies; biological and biomedical sciences; business, management, marketing, and related support services; computer and information sciences and support services; English language and literature/letters; foreign languages, literatures, and linguistics; history; liberal arts and sciences studies, and humanities; mathematics and statistics; multi/interdisciplinary studies; natural resources and conservation; philosophy and religious studies; physical sciences; psychology; social sciences; visual and performing arts. **Areas of required coursework:** arts/fine arts, humanities, mathematics, English (including composition), foreign languages, sciences (biological or physical), social science, other. **Pre-professional programs:** pre-law, pre-dentistry, pre-medicine, pre-veterinary science, pre-optometry, pre-pharmacy. **Special academic programs (% participation):** double major (19%), English as a Second

Language (ESL), exchange student program (domestic), independent study (10%), internships (10%), liberal arts/career combination, student-designed major, study abroad (30%), teacher certificate program (3%). **Teacher certification offered in:** elementary, middle/junior high, secondary. **Faculty and instruction (2005-2006):** Total instructional faculty: 93 full-time, 51 part-time (58% men; 42% women; 10% minorities). Full-time faculty with Ph.D. or other terminal degree: 90%. Student/faculty ratio: 12/1. Classes of fewer than 20 students: 69%; of 20 to 49 students: 30%; of 50 or more students: 1%. **Advanced Placement and International Baccalaureate credit:** International Baccalaureate exams may be used for: Placement only. **Freshmen returning for sophomore year:** 86%. **Graduation rates:** Four-year: 62%; five-year: 68%; six-year: 68%.

COSTS AND FINANCIAL AID

Financial aid office: (410) 778-7214. **Expenses (2006-2007):** Tuition and fees 2006-2007: $30,200; room/board: $6,450. Estimated books and supplies: $1,200; transportation: $0; personal expenses: $1,000. **Financial aid:** Priority filing date for institution's financial aid form: February 15. In 2005-2006, 60% of undergraduates applied for financial aid. Of those, 44% were determined to have financial need; 73% had their need fully met. Average financial aid package (proportion receiving): $16,314 (44%). Average amount of gift aid, such as scholarships or grants (proportion receiving): $14,939 (43%). Average amount of self-help aid, such as work study or loans (proportion receiving): $5,331 (32%). Average need-based loan (excluding PLUS or other private loans): $4,583. Among students who received need-based aid, the average percentage of need met: 90%. Among students who received aid based on merit, the average award (and the proportion receiving): $10,743 (40%). The average athletic scholarship (and the proportion receiving): $0 (0%). Average amount of debt of borrowers graduating in 2005: $20,483. Proportion who borrowed: 60%.

CAMPUS LIFE AND EXTRACURRICULAR ACTIVITIES

Campus housing available: coed dorms, women's dorms, men's dorms, sorority housing, fraternity housing, apartment for single students, special housing for disabled students, special housing for international students.

Students who live in college-owned, operated, or affiliated housing: 80%. **Student employment:** During the 2005-2006 academic year, 35% of undergraduates worked on campus. Average per-year earnings: $2,000. Activities include: choral groups, concert band, dance, drama/theater, jazz band, literary magazine, music ensembles, student government, student newspaper, student film society, symphony orchestra, yearbook. Number of fraternities: 3; sororities: 3. Proportion of men in fraternities: 20%; of women in sororities: 20%. Average proportion of students who stay on campus on weekends: 75%. **Sports program (2005-2006):** Member of NCAA III. *Men's intercollegiate varsity sports:* baseball, basketball, crew, lacrosse, sailing, soccer, swimming and diving, tennis. *Women's intercollegiate varsity sports:* basketball, crew, field hockey, lacrosse, sailing, soccer, softball, swimming and diving, tennis, volleyball.

SERVICES AND FACILITIES

Basic services: nonremedial tutoring, placement service, health service. **Remedial assistance:** math, writing, study skills. **Counseling services:** career, academic. **For learning-disabled students:** School does not offer a structured program with separate admission and additional fees. Services include: tape recorders, extended time for tests, tutors. **Information technology resources:** Students are not required to lease or own a computer. School has a wireless network. Approximate number of users that can be accommodated: 625. Proportion of college-owned housing units wired for high-speed internet access: 100%. **Campus safety:** Security services offered: 24-hour foot-and-vehicle patrols, 24-hour emergency telephones, lighted pathways/sidewalks, controlled dormitory access (key, security card, etc).

TRANSFER AND INTERNATIONAL STUDENTS

Transfer students: May apply for admission for the following academic terms: Fall, Spring. Applicants do not need a minimum number of credits to apply. For fall 2005: Transfer applications received: 29. Transfer applicants offered admission: 45. Transfer applicants enrolled: 24. **International students:** Number of foreign undergraduates: 37 (3% of student body). Minimum TOEFL score required: 500 (paper); 173 (computer). Average TOEFL score: 570 (paper).

Massachusetts

American International College

■ **Address:** 1000 State Street, Springfield, MA 01109
■ **Website:** http://www.aic.edu
■ **Private**
■ **Enrollment:** 1,214 full-time; 184 part-time

KEY STATS
✔ **U.S News College Ranking:** fourth tier, Universities–Master's (North)
✔ **SAT Score (25th/75th percentile):** 860-1100
✔ **Tuition:** 2006-2007: $20,990

Selectivity: Less selective	**Room/board:** $9,270
Acceptance rate: 84%	**Average debt:** $29,700
Student/faculty ratio: 17/1	**Proportion who borrowed:** 87%

UNDERGRADUATE STUDENT BODY STATS
2005-2006 enrollment: 1,214 full-time; 184 part-time. Men: 41%; women: 59%. **Ethnic makeup:** African American: 25%; Asian American: 2%; Hispanic: 9%; White: 62%; International: 1%.

ADMISSIONS FACTS AND FIGURES
Phone: (413) 205-3201. **Email:** inquiry@acad.aic.edu. **Website:** http://www.aic.edu. **Application deadlines for fall 2007:** Regular decision: Rolling. Early decision: Not offered. Early action: Not offered. Admission can be deferred. **Application fee:** $25. Common application is accepted. **Admissions requirements/recommendations:** High school units required (recommended): English: 4; Mathematics: 2 (3); Science: 2; Foreign language: (2); Social studies: 2; History: 2; Academic electives: 4; Total units: 16. Tests: The college uses SAT or ACT scores in admissions decisions. Either SAT or ACT required. For admission to the fall 2007 entering class, the school will accept: ACT with writing. Campus visit: Recommended. Admissions interview: Recommended. Off-campus interview: May be arranged. **Factors that count in admissions decisions:** *Academic:* Secondary school record: Very important. Class rank: Important. Letters of recommendation: Important. Standardized test scores: Important. Essay: Considered. *Nonacademic:* Interview: Considered. Extracurricular activities: Considered. Talent/ability: Considered. Character/personal qualities: Considered. Alumni/ae relationship: Considered. Geographical residence: Not considered. State residency: Not considered. Religious affiliation/commitment: Not considered. Minority status: Not considered. Volunteer work: Considered. Work experience: Not considered. **Other schools with the greatest overlap in applicants:** Quinnipiac University; Springfield College; University of Connecticut; Western New England College; Westfield State College. **Admissions statistics for the fall 2005 entering class:** Total applicants: 1,333. Total accepted: 1,118. Freshmen enrolled: 331; 45% were from out of state. Overall acceptance rate: 84%. **Credentials of fall 2005 freshmen:** 15% ranked in the top 10 percent of their high school class; 25% were in the top 25 percent, and 90% were in the top half. (Proportion submitting class standing: 71%.) **Average high school grade point average:** 2.8. **First-year students who submitted SAT scores:** 97%. Scores (25/75 percentile): Verbal: 430-520, Math: 430-580, Combined: 860-1100. **First-year students submitting ACT scores:** 1%. Scores (25/75 percentile): English: N/A, Math: N/A, Composite: N/A.

ACADEMICS
Year founded: 1885. **Academic calendar:** Semester. **Degrees offered:** associate, bachelor's, master's, post-master's certificate, doctorate. **Most popular majors:** 30% business, management, marketing, and related support services, 15% health professions and related clinical sciences, 11% psychology, 10% education, 8% security and protective services. **Major fields of study:** area, ethnic, cultural, and gender studies; biological and biomedical sciences; business, management, marketing, and related support services; communication, journalism, and related programs; computer and information sciences and support services; education; English language and literature/letters; foreign languages, literatures, and linguistics; health professions and related clinical sciences; history; liberal arts and sciences studies, and humanities; mathematics and statistics; parks, recreation, leisure, and fitness studies; philosophy and religious studies; psychology. **Areas of required coursework:** humanities, computer literacy, mathematics, English (including composition), sciences (biological or physical), social science. **Pre-professional programs:** pre-law, pre-dentistry, pre-medicine, pre-veterinary science, pre-optometry, pre-pharmacy. **Special academic programs (% participation):** double major (15%), English as a Second Language (ESL) (1%), independent study (20%), internships (85%), teacher certificate program (3%), weekend college (1%). **Teacher certification offered in:** early childhood, special education, elementary, middle/junior high, secondary. **Reserve Officers Training Corps (ROTC):** Army ROTC: Offered at cooperating institution (Western New England College); Air Force ROTC: Offered at cooperating institution (University of Massachusetts-Amherst). **Faculty and instruction (2005-2006):** Total instructional faculty: 69 full-time, 100 part-time (56% men; 44% women; 7% minorities). Full-time faculty with Ph.D. or other terminal degree: 55%. Student/faculty ratio: 17/1. Classes of fewer than 20 students: 53%; of 20 to 49 students: 45%; of 50 or more students: 2%. **Advanced Placement and International Baccalaureate credit:** AP tests may be used for: Credit and/or placement. Scores accepted: 3. International Baccalaureate exams may be used for: Credit and/or placement. **Freshmen returning for sophomore year:** 62%. **Graduation rates:** Four-year: 32%; five-year: 40%; six-year: 43%. **Graduate study:** 50% of students pursue further study immediately upon graduation; 10% within five years. Fields in which graduates pursue further study: Master of Business Administration (MBA), 25%; law, 2%; medicine, 2%; dentistry, 1%; education, 30%; veterinary medicine, 1%.

COSTS AND FINANCIAL AID
Financial aid office: (413) 205-3259. **Expenses (2006-2007):** Tuition and fees 2006-2007: $20,990; room/board: $9,270. Estimated books and supplies: $1,000; transportation: $500; personal expenses: $1,600. **Financial aid:** Priority filing date for institution's financial aid form: May 1. In 2005-2006, 100% of undergraduates applied for financial aid. Of those, 92% were determined to have financial need; 22% had their need fully met. Average financial aid package (proportion receiving): $20,200 (90%). Average amount of gift aid, such as scholarships or grants (proportion receiving): $10,813 (72%). Average amount of self-help aid, such as work study or loans (proportion receiving): $6,975 (67%). Average need-based loan (excluding PLUS or other private loans): $4,653. Among students who received need-based aid, the average percentage of need met: 82%. Among students who received aid based on merit, the average award (and the proportion receiving): $6,741 (15%). The average athletic scholarship (and the proportion receiving): $14,333 (13%). Average amount of debt of borrowers graduating in 2005: $29,700. Proportion who borrowed: 87%.

CAMPUS LIFE AND EXTRACURRICULAR ACTIVITIES
Campus housing available (% using): coed dorms (82%), women's dorms (18%). Students who live in college-owned, operated, or affiliated housing: 47%. **Student employment:** During the 2005-2006 academic year, 22% of undergraduates worked on campus. Average per-year earnings: $2,400. **Clubs and organizations:** Number of student organizations: 40. Activities include: choral groups, dance, drama/theater, radio station, student government, student newspaper, yearbook. Number of fraternities: 0; sororities: 0. Average proportion of students who stay on campus on weekends: 65%. **Sports program (2005-2006):** Member of NCAA II. *Men's intercollegiate varsity sports:* baseball, basketball, football, golf, ice hockey, lacrosse, soccer, tennis, wrestling. *Women's intercollegiate varsity sports:* basketball, field hockey, lacrosse, soccer, softball, tennis, volleyball.

SERVICES AND FACILITIES
Basic services: nonremedial tutoring, placement service, health service, health insurance. **Remedial assistance:** reading, math, writing, study skills. **Counseling services:** minority student, career, military, personal, veteran student, academic, psychological, birth control. **For learning-disabled students:** School does not offer a structured program with separate admission and additional fees. Total undergraduates in learning-disabled program or receiving services: 37. Services include: reading machines, tape recorders,

diagnostic testing service, untimed tests, note-taking services, oral tests, learning center, readers, extended time for tests, tutors, other testing accomodations. **Library:** Number of titles: 63,687; number of current serial subscriptions: 946. **Information technology resources:** Students are not required to lease or own a computer. Number of campus computers available to all students: 165. School has a wireless network. Approximate number of users that can be accommodated: 4,240. Proportion of college-owned housing units wired for high-speed internet access: 100%. **Campus safety:** Security services offered: 24-hour foot-and-vehicle patrols, late-night transport/escort service, 24-hour emergency telephones, lighted pathways/sidewalks, student patrols, controlled dormitory access (key, security card, etc).

TRANSFER AND INTERNATIONAL STUDENTS
Transfer students: May apply for admission for the following academic terms: Fall, Spring, Summer. Applicants do not need a minimum number of credits to apply. For fall 2005: Transfer applications received: 488. Transfer applicants offered admission: 351. Transfer applicants enrolled: 192. **International students:** Number of foreign undergraduates: 18 (1% of student body). Minimum TOEFL score required: 500 (paper); 173 (computer). Average TOEFL score: 590 (paper).

Amherst College

- **Address:** PO Box 5000, Amherst, MA 01002-5000
- **Website:** http://www.amherst.edu
- **Private**
- **Enrollment:** 1,623 full-time

KEY STATS
✔ **U.S News College Ranking:** 2, Liberal Arts Colleges
✔ **SAT Score (25th/75th percentile):** 1350-1560
✔ **Tuition:** 2006-2007: $34,916
  Selectivity: Most selective   **Room/board:** $9,080
  Acceptance rate: 19%   **Average debt:** $12,109
  Student/faculty ratio: 8/1   **Proportion who borrowed:** 47%

UNDERGRADUATE STUDENT BODY STATS
2005-2006 enrollment: 1,623 full-time. Men: 52%; women: 48%. **Ethnic makeup:** African American: 9%; Asian American: 13%; Hispanic: 6%; White: 64%; International: 7%.

ADMISSIONS FACTS AND FIGURES
Phone: (413) 542-2328. **Email:** admission@amherst.edu. **Website:** http://www.amherst.edu. **Application deadlines for fall 2007:** Regular decision: January 1; decision sent by April 5. Early decision: Send application by: November 15; Decision sent by: December 15. Early action: Not offered. Admission can be deferred. **Application fee:** $55. Common application is accepted. **To apply online, go to:** http://www.amherst.edu/admission/. **Admissions requirements/recommendations:** High school units required (recommended): English: (4); Mathematics: (4); Science: (3); Foreign language: (4); Social studies: (2); History: (2); Total units: (20). Tests: The college uses SAT or ACT scores in admissions decisions. Either SAT or ACT required. For admission to the fall 2007 entering class, the school will accept: ACT without writing. Campus visit: Recommended. Admissions interview: Neither required nor recommended. Off-campus interview: Not available. **Factors that count in admissions decisions:** *Academic:* Secondary school record: Very important. Class rank: Important. Letters of recommendation: Very important. Standardized test scores: Very important. Essay: Very important. *Nonacademic:* Interview: Not considered. Extracurricular activities: Very important. Talent/ability: Very important. Character/personal qualities: Very important. Alumni/ae relationship: Important. Geographical residence: Considered. State residency: Considered. Religious affiliation/commitment: Not considered. Minority status: Considered. Volunteer work: Important. Work experience: Considered. **Other schools with the greatest overlap in applicants:** Brown University; Harvard University; Princeton University; Williams College; Yale University. **Admissions statistics for the fall 2005 entering class:** Total applicants: 6,273. Total accepted: 1,175. Freshmen enrolled: 431; 87% were from out of state. Overall acceptance rate: 19%. Non-early acceptance rate: 19%. **Size of waiting list:** 1162 applicants; enrolled from waiting list: 0. **Credentials of fall 2005 freshmen:** 87% ranked in the top 10 percent of their high school class; 96% were in the top 25 percent, and 100% were in the top half. (Proportion

submitting class standing: 57%.) **First-year students who submitted SAT scores:** 87%. Scores (25/75 percentile): Verbal: 670-780, Math: 680-780, Combined: 1350-1560. **First-year students submitting ACT scores:** 13%. Scores (25/75 percentile): English: 29-34, Math: 28-33, Composite: 29-33.

ACADEMICS
Year founded: 1821. **Academic calendar:** Semester. **Degrees offered:** bachelor's. **Most popular majors:** 15% economics, 13% English language and literature, 12% history, 12% psychology, 10% political science and government. **Major fields of study:** area, ethnic, cultural, and gender studies; biological and biomedical sciences; computer and information sciences and support services; English language and literature/letters; foreign languages, literatures, and linguistics; history; legal professions and studies; mathematics and statistics; multi/interdisciplinary studies; philosophy and religious studies; physical sciences; psychology; social sciences; visual and performing arts. **Pre-professional programs:** pre-law, pre-dentistry, pre-medicine, pre-veterinary science. **Special academic programs (% participation):** cross-registration (52%), double major (30%), exchange student program (domestic) (5%), honors program (42%), independent study (16%), internships (60%), student-designed major (1%), study abroad (40%), teacher certificate program. **Teacher certification offered in:** secondary. **Faculty and instruction (2005-2006):** Total instructional faculty: 186 full-time, 28 part-time (61% men; 39% women; 15% minorities). Full-time faculty with Ph.D. or other terminal degree: 94%. Student/faculty ratio: 8/1. Classes of fewer than 20 students: 72%; of 20 to 49 students: 24%; of 50 or more students: 4%. **Advanced Placement and International Baccalaureate credit:** AP tests may be used for: Placement only. Scores accepted: 5. **Freshmen returning for sophomore year:** 97%. **Graduation rates:** Four-year: 89%; five-year: 95%; six-year: 96%. **Graduate study:** 28% of students pursue further study immediately upon graduation. Fields in which graduates pursue further study: Master of Business Administration (MBA), 9%; law, 16%; medicine, 12%; dentistry, 1%; engineering, 1%; theology (or the seminary), 2%; education, 4%; arts and sciences, 12%; veterinary medicine, 1%.

COSTS AND FINANCIAL AID
Financial aid office: (413) 542-2296. **Expenses (2006-2007):** Tuition and fees 2006-2007: $34,916; room/board: $9,080. Estimated books and supplies: $950; transportation: $650; personal expenses: $1,700. **Financial aid:** Priority filing date for institution's financial aid form: February 15. In 2005-2006, 58% of undergraduates applied for financial aid. Of those, 48% were determined to have financial need; 100% had their need fully met. Average financial aid package (proportion receiving): $31,048 (48%). Average amount of gift aid, such as scholarships or grants (proportion receiving): $28,713 (46%). Average amount of self-help aid, such as work study or loans (proportion receiving): $3,564 (45%). Average need-based loan (excluding PLUS or other private loans): $2,935. Among students who received need-based aid, the average percentage of need met: 100%. Among students who received aid based on merit, the average award (and the proportion receiving): $0 (0%). The average athletic scholarship (and the proportion receiving): $0 (0%). Average amount of debt of borrowers graduating in 2005: $12,109. Proportion who borrowed: 47%.

CAMPUS LIFE AND EXTRACURRICULAR ACTIVITIES
Campus housing available (% using): coed dorms (100%), special housing for disabled students, cooperative housing, other housing options. Students who live in college-owned, operated, or affiliated housing: 97%. **Student employment:** During the 2005-2006 academic year, 60% of undergraduates worked on campus. Average per-year earnings: $1,600. **Clubs and organizations:** Number of student organizations: 104. Activities include: choral groups, concert band, dance, drama/theater, jazz band, literary magazine, music ensembles, musical theater, opera, pep band, radio station, student government, student newspaper, student film society, symphony orchestra, yearbook. Number of fraternities: 0; sororities: 0. Average proportion of students who stay on campus on weekends: 100%. **Sports program (2005-2006):** Member of NCAA III. *Men's intercollegiate varsity sports:* baseball, basketball, cross-country, football, golf, ice hockey, lacrosse, soccer, swimming and diving, tennis, track and field (indoor), track and field (outdoor). *Women's intercollegiate varsity sports:* basketball, cross-country, field hockey, golf, ice hockey, lacrosse, soccer, softball, squash, swimming and diving, tennis, track and field (indoor), track and field (outdoor), volleyball.

SERVICES AND FACILITIES
Basic services: nonremedial tutoring, women's center, placement service, health service, health insurance. **Counseling services:** minority student, career, personal, veteran student, academic, psychological, birth control, religious, other. **For learning-disabled students:** School does not offer a

structured program with separate admission and additional fees. Services include: tape recorders, note-taking services, readers, extended time for tests, tutors, other. **Library:** Number of titles: 1,003,887; number of current serial subscriptions: 10,632. **Information technology resources:** Students are not required to lease or own a computer. Number of campus computers available to all students: 168. School has a wireless network. Proportion of college-owned housing units wired for high-speed internet access: 100%. **Campus safety:** Security services offered: 24-hour foot-and-vehicle patrols, late-night transport/escort service, 24-hour emergency telephones, lighted pathways/sidewalks, student patrols, controlled dormitory access (key, security card, etc).

TRANSFER AND INTERNATIONAL STUDENTS

Transfer students: May apply for admission for the following academic terms: Fall, Spring. Applicants need a minimum number of credits to apply. For fall 2005: Transfer applications received: 168. Transfer applicants offered admission: 25. Transfer applicants enrolled: 11. **International students:** Number of foreign undergraduates: 110 (7% of student body). Minimum TOEFL score required: 600 (paper); 250 (computer). Average TOEFL score: 650 (paper).

Anna Maria College

- **Address:** Sunset Lane, Paxton, MA 01612
- **Website:** http://www.annamaria.edu
- **Private; Religious affiliation:** Roman Catholic
- **Enrollment:** 540 full-time; 205 part-time

KEY STATS

- ✔ **U.S News College Ranking:** fourth tier, Universities–Master's (North)
- ✔ **SAT Score (25th/75th percentile):** 820-1030
- ✔ **Tuition:** 2006-2007: $23,034

Selectivity: Less selective	**Room/board:** $8,410
Acceptance rate: 90%	**Average debt:** $23,513
Student/faculty ratio: 9/1	**Proportion who borrowed:** 86%

UNDERGRADUATE STUDENT BODY STATS

2005-2006 enrollment: 540 full-time; 205 part-time. Men: 41%; women: 59%. **Ethnic makeup:** African American: 2%; Asian American: 1%; Hispanic: 3%; White: 93%; International: 1%. **Religious preference:** Roman Catholic: 13%; Protestant: 2%; Unknown: 85%.

ADMISSIONS FACTS AND FIGURES

Phone: (508) 849-3360. **Email:** admission@annamaria.edu. **Website:** http://www.annamaria.edu. **Application deadlines for fall 2007:** Regular decision: Rolling. Early decision: Not offered. Early action: Not offered. Admission can be deferred. **Application fee:** $40. Common application is accepted. **Admissions requirements/recommendations:** High school units required (recommended): English: 4; Mathematics: 3; Science: 3; Foreign language: 2; Social studies: 2; History: 2; Academic electives: 4; Total units: 19. Tests: The college uses SAT or ACT scores in admissions decisions. Either SAT or ACT required. For admission to the fall 2007 entering class, the school will accept: ACT with writing, ACT without writing. Campus visit: Neither required nor recommended. Admissions interview: Recommended. Off-campus interview: May be arranged. **Factors that count in admissions decisions:** *Academic:* Secondary school record: Important. Class rank: Considered. Letters of recommendation: Important. Standardized test scores: Important. Essay: Important. *Nonacademic:* Interview: Considered. Extracurricular activities: Important. Talent/ability: Considered. Character/personal qualities: Considered. Alumni/ae relationship: Considered. Geographical residence: Not considered. State residency: Not considered. Religious affiliation/commitment: Not considered. Minority status: Not considered. Volunteer work: Considered. Work experience: Considered. **Other schools with the greatest overlap in applicants:** Assumption College; Fitchburg State College; Worcester State College. **Admissions statistics for the fall 2005 entering class:** Total applicants: 557. Total accepted: 501. Freshmen enrolled: 161; 26% were from out of state. Overall acceptance rate: 90%. **Credentials of fall 2005 freshmen:** 4% ranked in the top 10 percent of their high school class; 15% were in the top 25 percent, and 47% were in the top half. (Proportion submitting class standing: 71%.) **Average high school grade point average:** 2.6. **First-year students who submitted SAT scores:** 96%. Scores (25/75 percentile): Verbal: 420-510,

Math: 400-520, Combined: 820-1030. **First-year students submitting ACT scores:** 8%. Scores (25/75 percentile): English: N/A, Math: N/A, Composite: 15-19.

ACADEMICS

Year founded: 1946. **Academic calendar:** Semester. **Degrees offered:** certificate, associate, bachelor's, post-bachelor's certificate, master's, post-master's certificate. **Most popular majors:** 39% security and protective services, 13% public administration and social service professions, 12% business, management, marketing, and related support services, 10% liberal arts and sciences studies, and humanities, 9% health professions and related clinical sciences. **Major fields of study:** business, management, marketing, and related support services; computer and information sciences and support services; education; English language and literature/letters; foreign languages, literatures, and linguistics; health professions and related clinical sciences; history; legal professions and studies; liberal arts and sciences studies, and humanities; natural resources and conservation; psychology; public administration and social service professions; security and protective services; social sciences; theology and religious vocations; visual and performing arts. **Areas of required coursework:** arts/fine arts, humanities, computer literacy, mathematics, English (including composition), philosophy, foreign languages, sciences (biological or physical), history, social science. **Pre-professional programs:** pre-law. **Special academic programs:** accelerated program, cooperative (work-study plan) program, cross-registration, double major, dual enrollment, English as a Second Language (ESL), exchange student program (domestic), honors program, independent study, internships, liberal arts/career combination, student-designed major, study abroad, teacher certificate program. **Teacher certification offered in:** early childhood, elementary, middle/junior high, secondary. **Reserve Officers Training Corps (ROTC):** Air Force ROTC: Offered at cooperating institution (Worcester Polytechnic Institute). **Faculty and instruction (2005-2006):** Total instructional faculty: 38 full-time, 133 part-time (53% men; 47% women). Full-time faculty with Ph.D. or other terminal degree: 47%. Student/faculty ratio: 9/1. Classes of fewer than 20 students: 83%; of 20 to 49 students: 17%; of 50 or more students: 0%. **Advanced Placement and International Baccalaureate credit:** AP tests may be used for: Credit and/or placement. Scores accepted: 3, 4, 5. International Baccalaureate exams may be used for: Credit only. **Freshmen returning for sophomore year:** 67%. **Graduation rates:** Four-year: 48%; five-year: 63%; six-year: 56%.

COSTS AND FINANCIAL AID

Financial aid office: (508) 849-3366. **Expenses (2006-2007):** Tuition and fees 2006-2007: $23,034; room/board: $8,410. Estimated personal expenses: $2,130. **Financial aid:** Priority filing date for institution's financial aid form: March 1. In 2005-2006, 89% of undergraduates applied for financial aid. Of those, 82% were determined to have financial need; 27% had their need fully met. Average financial aid package (proportion receiving): $15,242 (81%). Average amount of gift aid, such as scholarships or grants (proportion receiving): $10,958 (78%). Average amount of self-help aid, such as work study or loans (proportion receiving): $3,866 (78%). Average need-based loan (excluding PLUS or other private loans): $4,178. Among students who received need-based aid, the average percentage of need met: 75%. Among students who received aid based on merit, the average award (and the proportion receiving): $6,913 (14%). The average athletic scholarship (and the proportion receiving): $0 (0%). Average amount of debt of borrowers graduating in 2005: $23,513. Proportion who borrowed: 86%.

CAMPUS LIFE AND EXTRACURRICULAR ACTIVITIES

Campus housing available (% using): coed dorms (100%), special housing for disabled students (0%). Students who live in college-owned, operated, or affiliated housing: 68%. **Clubs and organizations:** Number of student organizations: 13. Activities include: choral groups, drama/theater, jazz band, music ensembles, student government, yearbook. Number of fraternities: 0; sororities: 0. **Sports program (2005-2006):** Member of NCAA III. *Men's intercollegiate varsity sports:* baseball, basketball, cross-country, golf, soccer. *Women's intercollegiate varsity sports:* basketball, field hockey, soccer, softball, volleyball.

SERVICES AND FACILITIES

Basic services: nonremedial tutoring, health service, health insurance. **Remedial assistance:** reading, math, writing, study skills. **Counseling services:** career, personal, academic, psychological, religious. **Library:** Number of titles: 83,570; number of current serial subscriptions: 101. **Information technology resources:** Students are not required to lease or own a computer. Number of campus computers available to all students: 42. School does not have a wireless network. Proportion of college-owned housing units wired for high-speed internet access: 100%. **Campus safety:** Security services offered: 24-hour foot-and-vehicle patrols, 24-hour emergency telephones, lighted pathways/sidewalks, controlled dormitory access (key, security card, etc).

TRANSFER AND INTERNATIONAL STUDENTS

Transfer students: May apply for admission for the following academic terms: Fall, Spring. Applicants need a minimum number of credits to apply. For fall 2005: Transfer applications received: 88. Transfer applicants offered admission: 49. Transfer applicants enrolled: 24. **International students:** Number of foreign undergraduates: 4 (1% of student body). Number of countries represented: 4. Minimum TOEFL score required: 470 (paper); 150 (computer).

Assumption College

- **Address:** 500 Salisbury Street, Worcester, MA 01609
- **Website:** http://www.assumption.edu
- **Private; Religious affiliation:** Roman Catholic
- **Enrollment:** 2,099 full-time; 25 part-time

KEY STATS

✔ **U.S News College Ranking:** 31, Universities–Master's (North)
✔ **SAT Score (25th/75th percentile):** 980-1170
✔ **Tuition:** 2006-2007: $26,060

Selectivity: Selective	**Room/board:** $9,170
Acceptance rate: 76%	**Average debt:** $21,773
Student/faculty ratio: 13/1	**Proportion who borrowed:** 76%

UNDERGRADUATE STUDENT BODY STATS

2005-2006 enrollment: 2,099 full-time; 25 part-time. Men: 40%; women: 60%. **Ethnic makeup:** African American: 1%; Asian American: 2%; Hispanic: 2%; White: 95%.

ADMISSIONS FACTS AND FIGURES

Phone: (888) 882-7786. **Email:** admiss@assumption.edu. **Website:** http://www.assumption.edu. **Application deadlines for fall 2007:** Regular decision: February 15. Early decision: Not offered. Early action: Send application by: November 15; Decision sent by: December 30. Admission can be deferred. **Application fee:** $50. Common application is accepted. **To apply online, go to:** http://www.assumption.edu/admiss/Applying/freshman.html. **Admissions requirements/recommendations:** High school units required (recommended): English: 4; Mathematics: 3; Science: 2; Foreign language: 2; History: 2; Academic electives: 5; Total units: 18. Tests: The college uses SAT or ACT scores in admissions decisions. Either SAT or ACT required. For admission to the fall 2007 entering class, the school will accept: ACT without writing. Campus visit: Recommended. Admissions interview: Recommended. Off-campus interview: Not available. **Factors that count in admissions decisions:** *Academic:* Secondary school record: Important. Class rank: Considered. Letters of recommendation: Important. Standardized test scores: Very important. Essay: Very important. *Nonacademic:* Interview: Important. Extracurricular activities: Considered. Talent/ability: Considered. Character/personal qualities: Considered. Alumni/ae relationship: Considered. Geographical residence: Not considered. State residency: Not considered. Religious affiliation/commitment: Not considered. Minority status: Considered. Volunteer work: Important. Work experience: Considered. **Other schools with the greatest overlap in applicants:** Merrimack College; Providence College; St. Anselm College; Stonehill College; University of Massachusetts–Amherst. **Admissions statistics for the fall 2005 entering class:** Total applicants: 3,357. Total accepted: 2,538. Freshmen enrolled: 565; 32% were from out of state. Overall acceptance rate: 76%. Non-early acceptance rate: 76%. **Size of waiting list:** 415 applicants; enrolled from waiting list: 55. **Credentials of fall 2005 freshmen:** 12% ranked in the top 10 percent of their high school class; 41% were in the top 25 percent, and 79% were in the top half. (Proportion submitting class standing: 70%.) **Average high school grade point average:** 3.2. **First-year students who submitted SAT scores:** 100%. Scores (25/75 percentile): Verbal: 490-580, Math: 490-590, Combined: 980-1170. **First-year students submitting ACT scores:** 21%. Scores (25/75 percentile): English: 18-24, Math: 18-24, Composite: 19-23.

ACADEMICS

Year founded: 1904. **Academic calendar:** Semester. **Degrees offered:** bachelor's, master's, post-master's certificate. **Most popular majors:** 14% business, management, marketing, and related support services, 14% psychology, 13% communication, journalism, and related programs, 12% English language and literature/letters, 9% social sciences. **Major fields of study:** area, ethnic, cultural, and gender studies; biological and biomedical sciences; business, management, marketing, and related support services; communication, journalism, and related programs; computer and information sciences and support services; English language and literature/letters; foreign languages, literatures, and linguistics; health professions and related clinical sciences; history; mathematics and statistics; multi/interdisciplinary studies; natural resources and conservation; philosophy and religious studies; physical sciences; psychology; social sciences; theology and religious vocations; visual and performing arts. **Areas of required coursework:** arts/fine arts, mathematics, English (including composition), philosophy, foreign languages, sciences (biological or physical), history, social science, other. **Pre-professional programs:** pre-optometry. **Special academic programs:** cross-registration, double major, honors program, independent study, internships, student-designed major, study abroad, teacher certificate program. **Teacher certification offered in:** elementary, middle/junior high, secondary. **Reserve Officers Training Corps (ROTC):** Army ROTC: Offered at cooperating institution (Worcester Polytechnic Institute); Air Force ROTC: Offered at cooperating institution (Worcester Polytechnic Institute). **Faculty and instruction (2005-2006):** Total instructional faculty: 129 full-time, 87 part-time (59% men; 41% women; 5% minorities). Full-time faculty with Ph.D. or other terminal degree: 95%. Student/faculty ratio: 13/1. Classes of fewer than 20 students: 42%; of 20 to 49 students: 58%. **Advanced Placement and International Baccalaureate credit:** AP tests may be used for: Credit and/or placement. Scores accepted: 3, 4, 5. International Baccalaureate exams may be used for: Credit and/or placement. **Freshmen returning for sophomore year:** 82%. **Graduation rates:** Four-year: 68%; five-year: 70%; six-year: 72%. **Graduate study:** 25% of students pursue further study within one year.

COSTS AND FINANCIAL AID

Financial aid office: (508) 767-7158. **Expenses (2006-2007):** Tuition and fees 2006-2007: $26,060; room/board: $9,170. Estimated books and supplies: $850; transportation: $400; personal expenses: $1,130. **Financial aid:** Priority filing date for institution's financial aid form: February 1. In 2005-2006, 82% of undergraduates applied for financial aid. Of those, 71% were determined to have financial need; 20% had their need fully met. Average financial aid package (proportion receiving): $15,462 (70%). Average amount of gift aid, such as scholarships or grants (proportion receiving): $11,400 (69%). Average amount of self-help aid, such as work study or loans (proportion receiving): $4,786 (62%). Average need-based loan (excluding PLUS or other private loans): $4,451. Among students who received need-based aid, the average percentage of need met: 72%. Among students who received aid based on merit, the average award (and the proportion receiving): $13,992 (23%). The average athletic scholarship (and the proportion receiving): $26,318 (1%). Average amount of debt of borrowers graduating in 2005: $21,773. Proportion who borrowed: 76%.

CAMPUS LIFE AND EXTRACURRICULAR ACTIVITIES

Campus housing available: coed dorms, women's dorms, special housing for disabled students, other housing options. Students who live in college-owned, operated, or affiliated housing: 89%. **Student employment:** During the 2005-2006 academic year, 17% of undergraduates worked on campus. Average per-year earnings: $1,038. **Clubs and organizations:** Number of student organizations: 50. Activities include: choral groups, concert band, drama/theater, literary magazine, musical theater, pep band, student government, student newspaper, student film society, television station, yearbook. Number of fraternities: 0; sororities: 0. Average proportion of students who stay on campus on weekends: 80%. **Sports program (2005-2006):** Member of NCAA II. *Men's intercollegiate varsity sports:* baseball, basketball, cross-country, football, golf, ice hockey, lacrosse, soccer, tennis, track and field (indoor), track and field (outdoor). *Women's intercollegiate varsity sports:* basketball, cross-country, field hockey, lacrosse, soccer, softball, tennis, track and field (indoor), track and field (outdoor), volleyball, rowing.

SERVICES AND FACILITIES

Basic services: nonremedial tutoring, placement service, health service, health insurance. **Counseling services:** minority student, career, personal, academic, psychological, religious. **For learning-disabled students:** School does not offer a structured program with separate admission and additional fees. Total undergraduates in learning-disabled program or receiving services: 160. Services include: reading machines, tape recorders, untimed tests, note-taking services, oral tests, learning center, readers, extended time for tests, tutors, priority registration, priority seating, exams on tape or computer. **Library:** Number of titles: 200,316; number of current serial subscriptions: 1,902. **Information technology resources:** Students are not required to lease or own a computer. Number of campus computers available to all students: 225. School has a wireless network. Approximate number of users that can be accommodated: 1,800. Proportion of college-owned housing units wired for high-speed internet access: 100%. **Campus safety:** Security services offered: 24-hour foot-and-vehicle patrols, late-night transport/escort service, 24-hour emergency telephones, lighted pathways/sidewalks, controlled dormitory access (key, security card, etc.).

TRANSFER AND INTERNATIONAL STUDENTS
Transfer students: May apply for admission for the following academic terms: Fall, Spring. Applicants do not need a minimum number of credits to apply. For fall 2005: Transfer applications received: 106. Transfer applicants offered admission: 53. Transfer applicants enrolled: 24. **International students:** Number of foreign undergraduates: 6. Number of countries represented: 5.

Atlantic Union College

- **Address:** PO Box 1000, South Lancaster, MA 01561
- **Website:** http://www.atlanticuc.edu
- **Private; Religious affiliation:** Seventh-day Adventist
- **Enrollment:** 422 full-time; 56 part-time

KEY STATS
✔ **U.S News College Ranking:** fourth tier, Comp. Coll.–Bachelor's (North)
✔ **SAT or ACT Score (25th/75th percentile):** N/A
✔ **Tuition:** 2006-2007: $14,260

Selectivity: Less selective	**Room/board:** $4,790
Acceptance rate: N/A	**Average debt:** $30,062
Student/faculty ratio: N/A	**Proportion who borrowed:** 100%

UNDERGRADUATE STUDENT BODY STATS
2005-2006 enrollment: 422 full-time; 56 part-time. Men: 39%; women: 61%. Ethnic makeup: African American: 51%; Asian American: 1%; Hispanic: 24%; White: 24%.

ADMISSIONS FACTS AND FIGURES
Phone: (978) 368-2235. **Email:** enroll@atlanticuc.edu. **Website:** http://www.atlanticuc.edu. **Application deadlines for fall 2007:** Regular decision: August 1. Early decision: Not offered. Early action: Not offered. **Application fee:** $25. Common application is not accepted. **Admissions requirements/recommendations:** Tests: The college uses SAT or ACT scores in admissions decisions. Neither SAT nor ACT required. Campus visit: Recommended. Admissions interview: Neither required nor recommended. Off-campus interview: Not available.

ACADEMICS
Year founded: 1882. **Academic calendar:** Semester. **Degrees offered:** certificate, associate, bachelor's, post-bachelor's certificate, master's. **Most popular majors:** Information not available. **Major fields of study:** biological and biomedical sciences; business, management, marketing, and related support services; computer and information sciences and support services; education; English language and literature/letters; health professions and related clinical sciences; history; liberal arts and sciences studies, and humanities; mathematics and statistics; parks, recreation, leisure, and fitness studies; philosophy and religious studies; psychology; public administration and social service professions; social sciences; theology and religious vocations; visual and performing arts. **Areas of required coursework:** arts/fine arts, humanities, computer literacy, mathematics, English (including composition), philosophy, foreign languages, sciences (biological or physical), history, social science. **Pre-professional programs:** pre-law, pre-dentistry, pre-medicine, pre-veterinary science, pre-pharmacy. **Special academic programs:** cross-registration, distance learning, double major, English as a Second Language (ESL), honors program, independent study, internships, study abroad, teacher certificate program. **Teacher certification offered in:** early childhood, elementary, secondary. **Advanced Placement and**

International Baccalaureate credit: International Baccalaureate exams may be used for: Credit only. **Graduation rates:** Six-year: 39%.

COSTS AND FINANCIAL AID
Financial aid office: (978) 368-2280. **Expenses (2006-2007):** Tuition and fees 2006-2007: $14,260; room/board: $4,790. Estimated books and supplies: $1,500; transportation: $0; personal expenses: $1,000. **Financial aid:** Priority filing date for institution's financial aid form: September 12; deadline: September 12. In 2005-2006, 76% of undergraduates applied for financial aid. Of those, 68% were determined to have financial need; 16% had their need fully met. Average financial aid package (proportion receiving): $10,995 (68%). Average amount of gift aid, such as scholarships or grants (proportion receiving): $6,608 (65%). Average amount of self-help aid, such as work study or loans (proportion receiving): $5,061 (63%). Average need-based loan (excluding PLUS or other private loans): $4,295. Among students who received need-based aid, the average percentage of need met: 75%. Among students who received aid based on merit, the average award (and the proportion receiving): $7,271 (31%). The average athletic scholarship (and the proportion receiving): $0 (0%). Average amount of debt of borrowers graduating in 2005: $30,062. Proportion who borrowed: 100%.

CAMPUS LIFE AND EXTRACURRICULAR ACTIVITIES
Campus housing available: women's dorms, men's dorms, apartments for married students. Activities include: choral groups, concert band, drama/theater, music ensembles, yearbook.

SERVICES AND FACILITIES
Basic services: health service, health insurance. **Remedial assistance:** reading, math, writing, study skills. **Counseling services:** personal, religious. **For learning-disabled students:** Services include: remedial math, remedial reading, diagnostic testing service, learning center, extended time for tests. **Information technology resources:** Students are not required to lease or own a computer.

TRANSFER AND INTERNATIONAL STUDENTS
Transfer students: May apply for admission for the following academic terms: Fall, Spring, Summer. Applicants do not need a minimum number of credits to apply. **International students:** Number of foreign undergraduates: 0. Minimum TOEFL score required: 525 (paper); 195 (computer).

Babson College

- **Address:** 231 Forest Street, Babson Park, MA 02457-0310
- **Website:** http://www.babson.edu
- **Private**
- **Enrollment:** 1,725 full-time

KEY STATS
✔ **U.S News College Ranking:** Unranked Specialty School–Business
✔ **SAT Score (25th/75th percentile):** 1180-1350
✔ **Tuition:** 2006-2007: $32,256

Selectivity: More selective	**Room/board:** $11,222
Acceptance rate: 37%	**Average debt:** $24,900
Student/faculty ratio: 13/1	**Proportion who borrowed:** 48%

UNDERGRADUATE STUDENT BODY STATS
2005-2006 enrollment: 1,725 full-time. Men: 61%; women: 39%. **Ethnic makeup:** African American: 3%; Asian American: 8%; Hispanic: 6%; White: 64%; International: 18%.

ADMISSIONS FACTS AND FIGURES
Phone: (781) 239-5522. **Email:** ugradadmission@babson.edu. **Website:** http://www.babson.edu. **Application deadlines for fall 2007:** Regular decision: January 15; decision sent by April 1. Early decision: Send application by: November 15; Decision sent by: December 15. Early action: Send application by: November 15; Decision sent by: January 1. Admission can be deferred. **Application fee:** $65. Common application is accepted. **To apply online, go to:** http://www3.babson.edu/UG/admission/applynow.cfm. **Admissions requirements/recommendations:** High school units required (recommended): English: 4 (4); Mathematics: 4 (4); Science: 3 (3); Foreign language: 2 (4); Social studies: 2 (3); History: 1 (1); Total units: 16. Tests: The college uses SAT or ACT scores in admissions decisions. Either SAT or

ACT required. For admission to the fall 2007 entering class, the school will accept: ACT with writing. Campus visit: Recommended. Admissions interview: Recommended. Off-campus interview: May be arranged. **Factors that count in admissions decisions: *Academic:*** Secondary school record: Very important. Class rank: Important. Letters of recommendation: Important. Standardized test scores: Very important. Essay: Important. ***Nonacademic:*** Interview: Considered. Extracurricular activities: Considered. Talent/ability: Considered. Character/personal qualities: Considered. Alumni/ae relationship: Considered. Geographical residence: Considered. State residency: Considered. Religious affiliation/commitment: Not considered. Minority status: Considered. Volunteer work: Considered. Work experience: Considered. **Other schools with the greatest overlap in applicants:** Bentley College; Boston College; Boston University; New York University; University of Pennsylvania. **Admissions statistics for the fall 2005 entering class:** Total applicants: 3,159. Total accepted: 1,164. Freshmen enrolled: 420; 80% were from out of state. Accepted through early-decision or early-action plans: 62%. Overall acceptance rate: 37%. Early-decision acceptance rate: 63%. Non-early acceptance rate: 29%. **Size of waiting list:** 320 applicants; enrolled from waiting list: 35. **Credentials of fall 2005 freshmen:** 52% ranked in the top 10 percent of their high school class; 85% were in the top 25 percent, and 99% were in the top half. (Proportion submitting class standing: 34%.) **First-year students who submitted SAT scores:** 92%. Scores (25/75 percentile): Verbal: 570-660, Math: 610-690, Combined: 1180-1350. **First-year students submitting ACT scores:** 8%. Scores (25/75 percentile): English: 24-27, Math: 27-29, Composite: 26-28.

ACADEMICS
Year founded: 1919. **Academic calendar:** Semester. **Degrees offered:** bachelor's, master's, post-master's certificate. **Most popular majors:** 100% business, management, marketing, and related support services. **Major fields of study:** business, management, marketing, and related support services; communication, journalism, and related programs; computer and information sciences and support services; history; legal professions and studies; mathematics and statistics; philosophy and religious studies; social sciences. **Areas of required coursework:** arts/fine arts, humanities, computer literacy, mathematics, English (including composition), sciences (biological or physical), history, social science, other. **Special academic programs:** accelerated program, cross-registration, exchange student program (domestic), honors program, independent study, internships, liberal arts/career combination, student-designed major, study abroad, other. **Reserve Officers Training Corps (ROTC):** Air Force ROTC: Offered at cooperating institution (Boston University). **Faculty and instruction (2005-2006):** Total instructional faculty: 151 full-time, 78 part-time (69% men; 31% women; 11% minorities). Full-time faculty with Ph.D. or other terminal degree: 91%. Student/faculty ratio: 13/1. Classes of fewer than 20 students: 21%; of 20 to 49 students: 76%; of 50 or more students: 3%. **Advanced Placement and International Baccalaureate credit:** AP tests may be used for: Credit and/or placement. Scores accepted: 4, 5. International Baccalaureate exams may be used for: Credit and/or placement. **Freshmen returning for sophomore year:** 93%. **Graduation rates:** Four-year: 80%; five-year: 85%; six-year: 85%. **Graduate study:** 6% of students pursue further study immediately upon graduation.

COSTS AND FINANCIAL AID
Financial aid office: (781) 239-4219. **Expenses (2006-2007):** Tuition and fees 2006-2007: $32,256; room/board: $11,222. Estimated books and supplies: $930; transportation: $575; personal expenses: $1,640. **Financial aid:** Priority filing date for institution's financial aid form: February 15; deadline: February 15. In 2005-2006, 45% of undergraduates applied for financial aid. Of those, 41% were determined to have financial need; 88% had their need fully met. Average financial aid package (proportion receiving): $26,018 (41%). Average amount of gift aid, such as scholarships or grants (proportion receiving): $20,807 (39%). Average amount of self-help aid, such as work study or loans (proportion receiving): $5,211 (41%). Average need-based loan (excluding PLUS or other private loans): $3,932. Among students who received need-based aid, the average percentage of need met: 97%. Among students who received aid based on merit, the average award (and the proportion receiving): $9,153 (8%). The average athletic scholarship (and the proportion receiving): $0 (0%). Average amount of debt of borrowers graduating in 2005: $24,900. Proportion who borrowed: 48%.

CAMPUS LIFE AND EXTRACURRICULAR ACTIVITIES
Campus housing available: coed dorms, women's dorms, men's dorms, sorority housing, fraternity housing, apartments for married students, special housing for disabled students, special housing for international students, other housing options. Students who live in college-owned, operated, or affiliated housing: 81%. **Student employment:** During the 2005-2006 aca-

demic year, 31% of undergraduates worked on campus. Average per-year earnings: $1,764. **Clubs and organizations:** Number of student organizations: 64. Activities include: choral groups, concert band, dance, drama/theater, jazz band, literary magazine, music ensembles, musical theater, radio station, student government, student newspaper, yearbook. Number of fraternities: 3; sororities: 3. Proportion of men in fraternities: 10%; of women in sororities: 12%. Average proportion of students who stay on campus on weekends: 75%. **Sports program (2005-2006):** Member of NCAA III. ***Men's intercollegiate varsity sports:*** alpine skiing, baseball, basketball, cross-country, golf, ice hockey, lacrosse, soccer, swimming and diving, tennis, track and field (outdoor). ***Women's intercollegiate varsity sports:*** alpine skiing, basketball, cross-country, field hockey, lacrosse, soccer, softball, swimming and diving, tennis, track and field (outdoor), volleyball.

SERVICES AND FACILITIES
Basic services: nonremedial tutoring, placement service, health service, other. **Remedial assistance:** study skills. **Counseling services:** minority student, career, personal, academic, psychological, birth control, religious. **For learning-disabled students:** School does not offer a structured program with separate admission and additional fees. Total undergraduates in learning-disabled program or receiving services: 100. Services include: reading machines, tape recorders, note-taking services, extended time for tests. **Library:** Number of titles: 131,436; number of current serial subscriptions: 65,951. **Information technology resources:** Students are required to lease or own a computer. Number of campus computers available to all students: 290. School has a wireless network. Approximate number of users that can be accommodated: 2,090. Proportion of college-owned housing units wired for high-speed internet access: 100%. **Campus safety:** Security services offered: 24-hour foot-and-vehicle patrols, late-night transport/escort service, 24-hour emergency telephones, lighted pathways/sidewalks, controlled dormitory access (key, security card, etc).

TRANSFER AND INTERNATIONAL STUDENTS
Transfer students: May apply for admission for the following academic terms: Fall, Spring. Applicants need a minimum number of credits to apply. For fall 2005: Transfer applications received: 203. Transfer applicants offered admission: 94. Transfer applicants enrolled: 47. **International students:** Number of foreign undergraduates: 304 (18% of student body). Number of countries represented: 60. Minimum TOEFL score required: 600 (paper); 250 (computer). Average TOEFL score: 610 (paper).

Bay Path College

- **Address:** 588 Longmeadow Street, Longmeadow, MA 01106
- **Website:** http://www.baypath.edu
- **Private**
- **Enrollment:** 1,109 full-time; 234 part-time

KEY STATS
✔ **U.S News College Ranking:** 31, Comp. Coll.–Bachelor's (North)
✔ **SAT Score (25th/75th percentile):** 900-1100
✔ **Tuition:** 2005-2006: $20,606

Selectivity: Less selective	**Room/board:** $8,756
Acceptance rate: 69%	**Average debt:** N/A
Student/faculty ratio: N/A	**Proportion who borrowed:** N/A

UNDERGRADUATE STUDENT BODY STATS
2005-2006 enrollment: 1,109 full-time; 234 part-time. Men: 0%; women: 100%. **Ethnic makeup:** African American: 12%; Asian American: 1%; Hispanic: 7%; White: 79%; International: 1%.

ADMISSIONS FACTS AND FIGURES
Phone: (413) 565-1331. **Email:** admiss@baypath.edu. **Website:** http://www.baypath.edu. **Application deadlines for fall 2007:** Regular decision: Rolling. Early decision: Not offered. Early action: Send application by: December 15; Decision sent by: January 2. Admission can be deferred. **Application fee:** $25. Common application is accepted. **Admissions requirements/recommendations:** High school units required (recommended): English: 4 (4); Mathematics: 3 (4); Science: 2 (3); Foreign language: 0 (2); Social studies: 2 (0); History: 2 (2); Total units: 15 (17). Tests: The college uses SAT or ACT scores in admissions decisions. Either SAT or ACT required. For admission to the fall 2007 entering class, the school will

accept: ACT with writing. Campus visit: Recommended. Admissions interview: Recommended. Off-campus interview: Not available. **Factors that count in admissions decisions:** *Academic:* Secondary school record: Very important. Class rank: Considered. Letters of recommendation: Considered. Standardized test scores: Very important. Essay: Considered. *Nonacademic:* Interview: Considered. Extracurricular activities: Important. Talent/ability: Considered. Character/personal qualities: Considered. Alumni/ae relationship: Not considered. Geographical residence: Not considered. State residency: Not considered. Religious affiliation/commitment: Not considered. Minority status: Not considered. Volunteer work: Considered. Work experience: Considered. **Other schools with the greatest overlap in applicants:** Elms College (College of Our Lady of the Elms); Framingham State College; University of New Haven; Western New England College; Westfield State College. **Admissions statistics for the fall 2005 entering class:** Total applicants: 599. Total accepted: 414. Freshmen enrolled: 132; Accepted through early-decision or early-action plans: 76%. Overall acceptance rate: 69%. Non-early acceptance rate: 62%. **Credentials of fall 2005 freshmen:** 11% ranked in the top 10 percent of their high school class; 25% were in the top 25 percent. **Average high school grade point average:** 3.1. **First-year students who submitted SAT scores:** 91%. Scores (25/75 percentile): Verbal: 460-560, Math: 440-540, Combined: 900-1100. **First-year students submitting ACT scores:** 9%. Scores (25/75 percentile): English: N/A, Math: N/A, Composite: 17-25.

ACADEMICS

Year founded: 1897. **Academic calendar:** Semester. **Degrees offered:** certificate, associate, bachelor's, master's. **Most popular majors:** Information not available. **Major fields of study:** biological and biomedical sciences; business, management, marketing, and related support services; education; health professions and related clinical sciences; legal professions and studies; liberal arts and sciences studies, and humanities; psychology; security and protective services. **Areas of required coursework:** arts/fine arts, humanities, computer literacy, mathematics, English (including composition), sciences (biological or physical), history, social science, other. **Pre-professional programs:** pre-law, pre-medicine, pre-veterinary science. **Special academic programs (% participation):** accelerated program, cooperative (work-study plan) program, cross-registration, double major, English as a Second Language (ESL), exchange student program (domestic), honors program, independent study, internships (25%), study abroad, teacher certificate program (7%), weekend college (27%). **Teacher certification offered in:** early childhood, elementary. **Cooperative education programs:** business. **Reserve Officers Training Corps (ROTC):** Army ROTC: Offered at cooperating institution (Western New England College); Air Force ROTC: Offered at cooperating institution (Western New England College). **Faculty and instruction (2005-2006):** Total instructional faculty: 38 full-time, 145 part-time (37% men; 63% women; 4% minorities). Full-time faculty with Ph.D. or other terminal degree: 11%. Classes of fewer than 20 students: 70%; of 20 to 49 students: 30%. **Advanced Placement and International Baccalaureate credit:** AP tests may be used for: Credit and/or placement. Scores accepted: 3, 4, 5. **Freshmen returning for sophomore year:** 69%. **Graduation rates:** Six-year: 64%. **Graduate study:** 5% of students pursue further study immediately upon graduation; 8% within one year; 10% within five years. Fields in which graduates pursue further study: Master of Business Administration (MBA), 10%; law, 14%; medicine, 2%; education, 10%; arts and sciences, 1%; veterinary medicine, 2%.

COSTS AND FINANCIAL AID

Financial aid office: (413) 565-1261. **Expenses (2005-2006):** Tuition and fees 2005-2006: $20,606; room/board: $8,756. Estimated books and supplies: $800; transportation: $400; personal expenses: $900. **Financial aid:** Priority filing date for institution's financial aid form: March 15.

CAMPUS LIFE AND EXTRACURRICULAR ACTIVITIES

Campus housing available: women's dorms. Students who live in college-owned, operated, or affiliated housing: 66%. **Clubs and organizations:** Number of student organizations: 36. Activities include: choral groups, dance, drama/theater, literary magazine, musical theater, radio station, student government, television station, yearbook. Number of fraternities: 0; sororities: 0. Average proportion of students who stay on campus on weekends: 55%. **Sports program (2005-2006):** Member of NCAA III. *Women's intercollegiate varsity sports:* basketball, cross-country, soccer, softball, tennis, volleyball.

SERVICES AND FACILITIES

Basic services: nonremedial tutoring, health service, health insurance, other. **Remedial assistance:** reading, math, writing, study skills, other. **Counseling**

services: career, personal, academic, older student, psychological, birth control, other. **For learning-disabled students:** School does not offer a structured program with separate admission and additional fees. Services include: tape recorders, untimed tests, note-taking services, learning center, extended time for tests, tutors, priority seating, texts on tape, other testing accomodations, other. **Library:** Number of titles: 47,415; number of current serial subscriptions: 132. **Information technology resources:** Students are not required to lease or own a computer. Number of campus computers available to all students: 200. School has a wireless network. Approximate number of users that can be accommodated: 750. Proportion of college-owned housing units wired for high-speed internet access: 100%. **Campus safety:** Security services offered: 24-hour foot-and-vehicle patrols, late-night transport/escort service, 24-hour emergency telephones, lighted pathways/sidewalks, controlled dormitory access (key, security card, etc).

TRANSFER AND INTERNATIONAL STUDENTS

Transfer students: May apply for admission for the following academic terms: Fall, Spring. Applicants need a minimum number of credits to apply. For fall 2005: Transfer applications received: 120. Transfer applicants offered admission: 72. Transfer applicants enrolled: 39. **International students:** Number of foreign undergraduates: 12 (1% of student body). Number of countries represented: 6. Minimum TOEFL score required: 500 (paper); 173 (computer). Average TOEFL score: 547 (paper).

Becker College

- **Address:** 61 Sever Street, Worcester, MA 01609
- **Website:** http://www.beckercollege.edu
- **Private**
- **Enrollment:** 1,120 full-time; 669 part-time

KEY STATS

✔ **U.S News College Ranking:** fourth tier, Comp. Coll.–Bachelor's (North)
✔ **SAT or ACT Score (25th/75th percentile):** N/A
✔ **Tuition:** 2006-2007: $21,055

Selectivity: Less selective	**Room/board:** $8,500
Acceptance rate: N/A	**Average debt:** $32,120
Student/faculty ratio: 18/1	**Proportion who borrowed:** 98%

UNDERGRADUATE STUDENT BODY STATS

2005-2006 enrollment: 1,120 full-time; 669 part-time. Men: 28%; women: 72%. **Ethnic makeup:** African American: 8%; Asian American: 1%; Hispanic: 4%; White: 87%.

ADMISSIONS FACTS AND FIGURES

Phone: (877) 523-2537. **Email:** admissions@beckercollege.edu. **Website:** http://www.beckercollege.edu. **Application deadlines for fall 2007:** Regular decision: Rolling. Early decision: Not offered. Early action: Not offered. Admission can be deferred. **Application fee:** $25. Common application is accepted. **Admissions requirements/recommendations:** Tests: The college uses SAT or ACT scores in admissions decisions. Either SAT or ACT required. Campus visit: Recommended. Admissions interview: Recommended. Off-campus interview: Not available. **Factors that count in admissions decisions:** *Academic:* Secondary school record: Very important. Class rank: Considered. Letters of recommendation: Considered. Standardized test scores: Important. Essay: Considered. *Nonacademic:* Interview: Considered. Extracurricular activities: Considered. Talent/ability: Considered. Character/personal qualities: Considered. Alumni/ae relationship: Considered. Geographical residence: Not considered. State residency: Not considered. Religious affiliation/commitment: Not considered. Minority status: Not considered. Volunteer work: Considered. Work experience: Considered.

ACADEMICS

Year founded: 1784. **Academic calendar:** Semester. **Degrees offered:** certificate, associate, bachelor's. **Most popular majors:** 52% business administration, management, and operations, 21% nursing/registered nurse training (R.N., A.S.N., B.S.N., M.S.N.), 16% veterinary sciences/veterinary clinical sciences (cert., M.S., Ph.D.), 6% psychology, 5% interior design. **Major fields of study:** business, management, marketing, and related support services; health professions and related clinical sciences; legal professions and studies; liberal arts and sciences studies, and humanities; parks, recreation, leisure, and fitness studies; psychology; security and protective services; visual and performing arts. **Areas of required coursework:** humanities, computer literacy, mathematics, English (including composition), sciences (biological or physical), history, social science. **Special academic programs:** accelerated program, cooperative (work-study plan) program, cross-registration, dual enrollment, internships, study abroad. **Cooperative education programs:** business, health professions. **Reserve Officers Training Corps (ROTC):** Army ROTC: Offered at cooperating institution (Worcester Polytechnic Institute). **Faculty and instruction (2005-2006):** Total instructional faculty: 39 full-time, 106 part-time (30% men; 70% women; 4% minorities). Full-time faculty with Ph.D. or other terminal degree: 41%. Student/faculty ratio: 18/1. Classes of fewer than 20 students: 36%; of 20 to 49 students: 60%; of 50 or more students: 4%. **Freshmen returning for sophomore year:** 62%. **Graduation rates:** Four-year: 38%; five-year: 38%; six-year: 42%.

COSTS AND FINANCIAL AID

Financial aid office: (508) 791-9241. **Expenses (2006-2007):** Tuition and fees 2006-2007: $21,055; room/board: $8,500. Estimated books and supplies: $1,000; transportation: $600. **Financial aid:** Priority filing date for institution's financial aid form: March 1. In 2005-2006, 95% of undergraduates applied for financial aid. Of those, 87% were determined to have financial need; 8% had their need fully met. Average financial aid package (proportion receiving): $9,286 (86%). Average amount of gift aid, such as scholarships or grants (proportion receiving): $6,642 (80%). Average amount of self-help aid, such as work study or loans (proportion receiving): $3,249 (82%). Average need-based loan (excluding PLUS or other private loans): $2,937. Among students who received need-based aid, the average percentage of need met: 46%. Among students who received aid based on merit, the average award (and the proportion receiving): $11,833 (13%). The average athletic scholarship (and the proportion receiving): $0 (0%). Average amount of debt of borrowers graduating in 2005: $32,120. Proportion who borrowed: 98%.

CAMPUS LIFE AND EXTRACURRICULAR ACTIVITIES

Campus housing available: coed dorms, women's dorms, men's dorms, apartment for single students. Average per-year earnings: $3,000. **Clubs and organizations:** Number of student organizations: 24. Activities include: dance, student government, student newspaper, yearbook. Number of fraternities: 0; sororities: 0. Average proportion of students who stay on campus on weekends: 70%. **Sports program (2005-2006):** Member of NCAA III. *Men's intercollegiate varsity sports:* baseball, basketball, football, golf, lacrosse; soccer, tennis. *Women's intercollegiate varsity sports:* basketball, equestrian sports, field hockey, soccer, softball, tennis, volleyball.

SERVICES AND FACILITIES

Basic services: nonremedial tutoring, placement service, health service, health insurance. **Remedial assistance:** reading, math, writing, study skills, other. **Counseling services:** career, personal, academic, older student, psychological. **For learning-disabled students:** School does not offer a structured program with separate admission and additional fees. Services include: tape recorders, note-taking services, oral tests, learning center, extended time for tests, tutors. **Information technology resources:** Students are not required to lease or own a computer. Number of campus computers available to all students: 75. **Campus safety:** Security services offered: 24-hour foot-and-vehicle patrols, late-night transport/escort service, 24-hour emergency telephones, lighted pathways/sidewalks, student patrols, controlled dormitory access (key, security card, etc).

TRANSFER AND INTERNATIONAL STUDENTS

Transfer students: May apply for admission for the following academic terms: Fall, Spring. Applicants do not need a minimum number of credits to apply. **International students:** Number of foreign undergraduates: 4. Minimum TOEFL score required: 500 (paper); 173 (computer).

Benjamin Franklin Institute of Technology

- **Address:** 41 Berkeley Street, Boston, MA 02116
- **Website:** http://www.bfit.edu
- **Private**
- **Enrollment:** N/A

KEY STATS

✔ **U.S News College Ranking:** Unranked Specialty School–Engineering
✔ **SAT or ACT Score (25th/75th percentile):** N/A
✔ **Tuition:** N/A
Selectivity: Least selective **Room/board:** N/A
Acceptance rate: N/A **Average debt:** N/A
Student/faculty ratio: N/A **Proportion who borrowed:** N/A

Bentley College

- **Address:** 175 Forest Street, Waltham, MA 02452-4705
- **Website:** http://www.bentley.edu
- **Private**
- **Enrollment:** 3,958 full-time; 336 part-time

KEY STATS

✔ **U.S News College Ranking:** 6, Universities–Master's (North)
✔ **SAT Score (25th/75th percentile):** 1150-1300
✔ **Tuition:** 2006-2007: $28,164
Selectivity: More selective **Room/board:** $10,530
Acceptance rate: 43% **Average debt:** $26,248
Student/faculty ratio: 12/1 **Proportion who borrowed:** 65%

UNDERGRADUATE STUDENT BODY STATS

2005-2006 enrollment: 3,958 full-time; 336 part-time. Men: 59%; women: 41%. **Ethnic makeup:** African American: 3%; Asian American: 8%; Hispanic: 4%; White: 78%; International: 8%.

ADMISSIONS FACTS AND FIGURES

Phone: (781) 891-2244. **Email:** ugadmission@bentley.edu. **Website:** http://www.bentley.edu. **Application deadlines for fall 2007:** Regular decision: February 1; decision sent by April 1. Early decision: Send application by: November 15; Decision sent by: December 22. Early action: Send application by: December 1; Decision sent by: January 30. Admission can be deferred. **Application fee:** $50. Common application is accepted. **To apply online, go to:** http://www.applyweb.com/aw?bentley. **Admissions requirements/recommendations:** High school units required (recommended): English: (4); Mathematics: (4); Science: (3); Foreign language: (3); History: (3); Total units: (19). Tests: The college uses SAT or ACT scores in admissions decisions. Either SAT or ACT required. For admission to the fall 2007 entering class, the school will accept: ACT with writing. Campus visit: Recommended. Admissions interview: Recommended. Off-campus interview: May be arranged. **Factors that count in admissions decisions:** *Academic:* Secondary school record: Very important. Class rank: Important. Letters of recommendation: Important. Standardized test scores: Very important. Essay: Important. *Nonacademic:* Interview: Considered. Extracurricular activities: Important. Talent/ability: Considered. Character/personal qualities: Important. Alumni/ae relationship: Considered. Geographical residence: Considered. State residency: Considered. Religious affiliation/commitment: Not considered. Minority status: Considered. Volunteer work: Important. Work experience: Important. **Other schools with the greatest overlap in applicants:** Babson College; Boston College; Boston University; Bryant University; Northeastern University. **Admissions statistics for the fall 2005 entering class:** Total applicants: 5,802. Total accepted: 2,516. Freshmen enrolled: 937; 52% were from out of state. Accepted through early-decision or early-action plans: 51%. Overall acceptance rate: 43%. Early-decision acceptance rate: 62%. Non-early acceptance rate: 37%. **Size of waiting list:** 923 applicants; enrolled from waiting list: 5. **Credentials of fall 2005 freshmen:** 39% ranked in the top 10 percent of their high school class; 82% were in the top 25 percent, and 99% were in the top half. (Proportion submitting class standing: 55%.) **First-year students who submitted SAT scores:** 93%. Scores (25/75 percentile): Verbal:

550-630, Math: 600-670, Combined: 1150-1300. **First-year students submitting ACT scores:** 15%. Scores (25/75 percentile): English: N/A, Math: N/A, Composite: 24-27.

ACADEMICS

Year founded: 1917. **Academic calendar:** Semester. **Degrees offered:** certificate, associate, transfer-associate, terminal-associate, bachelor's, post-bachelor's certificate, master's, post-master's certificate, doctorate. **Most popular majors:** 20% finance, 17% marketing/marketing management, 14% business administration and management, 11% accounting, 11% accounting and related services. **Major fields of study:** business, management, marketing, and related support services; computer and information sciences and support services; English language and literature/letters; history; legal professions and studies; liberal arts and sciences studies, and humanities; mathematics and statistics; multi/interdisciplinary studies; philosophy and religious studies; public administration and social service professions. **Areas of required coursework:** humanities, computer literacy, mathematics, English (including composition), philosophy, sciences (biological or physical), history, social science, other. **Pre-professional programs:** pre-law. **Special academic programs (% participation):** accelerated program (2.5%), cooperative (work-study plan) program, cross-registration, distance learning (.3%), double major (7%), honors program (11.3%), independent study (6.8%), internships (12.5%), liberal arts/career combination (3%), student-designed major, study abroad (7.8%). **Reserve Officers Training Corps (ROTC):** Army ROTC: Offered at cooperating institution (Boston University); Air Force ROTC: Offered at cooperating institution (Boston University). **Faculty and instruction (2005-2006):** Total instructional faculty: 270 full-time, 205 part-time (61% men; 39% women; 12% minorities). Full-time faculty with Ph.D. or other terminal degree: 82%. Student/faculty ratio: 12/1. Classes of fewer than 20 students: 24%; of 20 to 49 students: 76%; of 50 or more students: 0%. **Advanced Placement and International Baccalaureate credit:** AP tests may be used for: Credit and/or placement. Scores accepted: 4. International Baccalaureate exams may be used for: Credit and/or placement. **Freshmen returning for sophomore year:** 94%. **Graduation rates:** Four-year: 71%; five-year: 80%; six-year: 78%. **Graduate study:** 12% of students pursue further study immediately upon graduation. Fields in which graduates pursue further study: Master of Business Administration (MBA), 31%; law, 5%; arts and sciences, 64%.

COSTS AND FINANCIAL AID

Financial aid office: (781) 891-3441. **Expenses (2006-2007):** Tuition and fees 2006-2007: $28,164; room/board: $10,530. Estimated books and supplies: $980. **Financial aid:** In 2005-2006, 68% of undergraduates applied for financial aid. Of those, 52% were determined to have financial need; 30% had their need fully met. Average financial aid package (proportion receiving): $23,177 (52%). Average amount of gift aid, such as scholarships or grants (proportion receiving): $17,666 (43%). Average amount of self-help aid, such as work study or loans (proportion receiving): $6,123 (47%). Average need-based loan (excluding PLUS or other private loans): $5,018. Among students who received need-based aid, the average percentage of need met: 91%. Among students who received aid based on merit, the average award (and the proportion receiving): $12,262 (10%). The average athletic scholarship (and the proportion receiving): $26,522 (1%). Average amount of debt of borrowers graduating in 2005: $26,248. Proportion who borrowed: 65%.

CAMPUS LIFE AND EXTRACURRICULAR ACTIVITIES

Campus housing available (% using): coed dorms (31%), apartment for single students (32%), special housing for disabled students (0%), other housing options (37%). Students who live in college-owned, operated, or affiliated housing: 80%. **Student employment:** During the 2005-2006 academic year, 10% of undergraduates worked on campus. Average per-year earnings: $1,100. **Clubs and organizations:** Number of student organizations: 80. Activities include: choral groups, dance, drama/theater, jazz band, pep band, radio station, student government, student newspaper, yearbook. Number of fraternities: 7; sororities: 5. Average proportion of students who stay on campus on weekends: 85%. **Sports program (2005-2006):** Member of NCAA II. *Men's intercollegiate varsity sports:* baseball, basketball, cross-country, football, golf, ice hockey, lacrosse, soccer, swimming and diving, tennis, track and field (indoor), track and field (outdoor). *Women's intercollegiate varsity sports:* basketball, cross-country, field hockey, lacrosse, soccer, softball, swimming and diving, tennis, track and field (indoor), track and field (outdoor), volleyball.

SERVICES AND FACILITIES

Basic services: nonremedial tutoring, women's center, placement service, day care, health service, health insurance. **Remedial assistance:** reading, math, writing, study skills. **Counseling services:** minority student, career, personal, academic, older student, psychological, birth control, religious. **For learning-disabled students:** School does not offer a structured program with separate admission and additional fees. Total undergraduates in learning-disabled program or receiving services: 170. Services include: remedial math, remedial English, reading machines, remedial reading, tape recorders, note-taking services, oral tests, learning center, readers, extended time for tests, tutors, early syllabus, priority registration, priority seating, substitution of courses, texts on tape, typist/scribe, exams on tape or computer, other testing accomodations, waiver of foreign language degree requirement, waiver of math degree requirement, other. **Library:** Number of titles: 137,031; number of current serial subscriptions: 30,660. **Information technology resources:** Students are required to lease or own a computer. Number of campus computers available to all students: 5,700. School has a wireless network. Approximate number of users that can be accommodated: 4,000. Proportion of college-owned housing units wired for high-speed internet access: 100%. **Campus safety:** Security services offered: 24-hour foot-and-vehicle patrols, late-night transport/escort service, 24-hour emergency telephones, lighted pathways/sidewalks, student patrols, controlled dormitory access (key, security card, etc).

TRANSFER AND INTERNATIONAL STUDENTS

Transfer students: May apply for admission for the following academic terms: Fall, Spring. Applicants need a minimum number of credits to apply. For fall 2005: Transfer applications received: 452. Transfer applicants offered admission: 258. Transfer applicants enrolled: 150. **International students:** Number of foreign undergraduates: 323 (8% of student body). Number of countries represented: 77. Minimum TOEFL score required: 550 (paper); 213 (computer). Average TOEFL score: 596 (paper).

Berklee College of Music

- **Address:** 1140 Boylston Street, Boston, MA 02215
- **Website:** http://www.berklee.edu
- **Private**
- **Enrollment:** 4,037 full-time

KEY STATS

✔ **U.S News College Ranking:** Unranked Specialty School–Fine Arts
✔ **SAT or ACT Score (25th/75th percentile):** N/A
✔ **Tuition:** 2005-2006: $22,311
  Selectivity: Least selective   **Room/board:** $11,690
  Acceptance rate: N/A   **Average debt:** N/A
  Student/faculty ratio: N/A   **Proportion who borrowed:** N/A

UNDERGRADUATE STUDENT BODY STATS

2005-2006 enrollment: 4,037 full-time. Men: 74%; women: 26%. **Ethnic makeup:** African American: 6%; Asian American: 4%; Hispanic: 6%; White: 62%; International: 22%.

ADMISSIONS FACTS AND FIGURES

Phone: (800) 237-5533. **Email:** admissions@berklee.edu. **Website:** http://www.berklee.edu. **Application deadlines for fall 2007:** Regular decision: February 1. Early decision: Not offered. Early action: Send application by: December 1; Decision sent by: January 15. Admission can be deferred. **Application fee:** $75. Common application is not accepted. **Admissions requirements/recommendations:** High school units required (recommended): English: 4; Mathematics: 1; Science: 1; Social studies: 2; History: 6; Academic electives: 2. **Tests:** The college uses SAT or ACT scores in admissions decisions. Neither SAT nor ACT required. Campus visit: Recommended. Admissions interview: Recommended. Off-campus interview: Not available. **Factors that count in admissions decisions:** *Academic:* Secondary school record: Important. Class rank: Not considered. Letters of recommendation: Important. Standardized test scores: Important. Essay: Important. *Nonacademic:* Interview: Considered. Extracurricular activities: Important. Talent/ability: Important. Character/personal qualities: Considered. Alumni/ae relationship: Not considered. Geographical residence: Not considered. State residency: Not considered. Religious affiliation/commitment: Not considered. Minority status: Not considered. Volunteer work: Considered. Work experience: Considered.

ACADEMICS
Year founded: 1945. **Academic calendar:** Semester. **Degrees offered:** diploma, bachelor's. **Most popular majors:** Information not available. **Major fields of study:** visual and performing arts. **Areas of required coursework:** arts/fine arts, computer literacy. **Special academic programs:** cooperative (work-study plan) program, cross-registration, double major, English as a Second Language (ESL), internships, student-designed major. **Teacher certification offered in:** early childhood, elementary, middle/junior high, secondary. **Graduation rates:** Six-year: 44%.

COSTS AND FINANCIAL AID
Financial aid office: (617) 747-2274. **Expenses (2005-2006):** Tuition and fees 2005-2006: $22,311; room/board: $11,690. Estimated books and supplies: $834; transportation: $1,322. **Financial aid:** Priority filing date for institution's financial aid form: March 4.

CAMPUS LIFE AND EXTRACURRICULAR ACTIVITIES
Campus housing available: coed dorms. **Clubs and organizations:** Number of student organizations: 38. Activities include: choral groups, jazz band, music ensembles, musical theater, student government, student newspaper. Number of fraternities: 0.

SERVICES AND FACILITIES
Basic services: nonremedial tutoring, health insurance. **Counseling services:** career, personal, academic. **For learning-disabled students:** School does not offer a structured program with separate admission and additional fees. Services include: untimed tests, learning center, readers, extended time for tests, tutors. **Information technology resources:** Students are required to lease or own a computer. School has a wireless network. Proportion of college-owned housing units wired for high-speed internet access: 100%. **Campus safety:** Security services offered: 24-hour foot-and-vehicle patrols, late-night transport/escort service, 24-hour emergency telephones, controlled dormitory access (key, security card, etc).

TRANSFER AND INTERNATIONAL STUDENTS
Transfer students: May apply for admission for the following academic terms: Fall, Spring, Summer. Applicants do not need a minimum number of credits to apply. **International students:** Number of foreign undergraduates: 875 (22% of student body).

Boston Architectural College

- **Address:** 320 Newbury Street, Boston, MA 02115
- **Website:** http://www.the-bac.edu
- **Private**
- **Enrollment:** 344 full-time; 16 part-time

KEY STATS
✔ **U.S News College Ranking:** Unranked Specialty School–Fine Arts
✔ **SAT or ACT Score (25th/75th percentile):** N/A
✔ **Tuition:** 2006-2007: $9,060

Selectivity: Least selective	**Room/board:** N/A
Acceptance rate: 100%	**Average debt:** $23,784
Student/faculty ratio: 10/1	**Proportion who borrowed:** 82%

UNDERGRADUATE STUDENT BODY STATS
2005-2006 enrollment: 344 full-time; 16 part-time. Men: 61%; women: 39%. **Ethnic makeup:** African American: 2%; Asian American: 3%; Hispanic: 6%; White: 89%.

ADMISSIONS FACTS AND FIGURES
Phone: (617) 585-0123. **Email:** admissions@the-bac.edu. **Website:** http://www.the-bac.edu. **Application deadlines for fall 2007:** Regular decision: Rolling. Early decision: Not offered. Early action: Not offered. Admission can be deferred. **Application fee:** $50. Common application is accepted. **To apply online, go to:** https://www.applyweb.com/apply/thebac/menu.html. **Admissions requirements/recommendations:** High school units required (recommended): English: (4); Mathematics: (4); Science: (3); Foreign language: (3); Social studies: (1); History: (2); Total

units: (19). **Tests:** The college does not use SAT or ACT scores in admissions decisions. Neither SAT nor ACT required. **Campus visit:** Recommended. Admissions interview: Recommended. Off-campus interview: May be arranged. **Factors that count in admissions decisions:** *Academic:* Secondary school record: Not considered. Class rank: Not considered. Letters of recommendation: Not considered. Standardized test scores: Not considered. Essay: Not considered. *Nonacademic:* Interview: Not considered. Extracurricular activities: Not considered. Talent/ability: Not considered. Character/personal qualities: Not considered. Alumni/ae relationship: Not considered. Geographical residence: Not considered. State residency: Not considered. Religious affiliation/commitment: Not considered. Minority status: Not considered. Volunteer work: Not considered. Work experience: Not considered. **Other schools with the greatest overlap in applicants:** Harvard University; Northeastern University; Rhode Island School of Design; Suffolk University; Wentworth Institute of Technology. **Admissions statistics for the fall 2005 entering class:** Total applicants: 187. Total accepted: 187. Freshmen enrolled: 122; 41% were from out of state. Overall acceptance rate: 100%. **Size of waiting list:** 0 applicants; enrolled from waiting list: 0.

ACADEMICS
Year founded: 1889. **Academic calendar:** Semester. **Degrees offered:** certificate, bachelor's, post-bachelor's certificate, master's, first professional. **Most popular majors:** 59% architecture (B.Arch., B.A./B.S., M.Arch., M.A./M.S., Ph.D.), 8% landscape architecture (B.S., B.S.L.A., B.L.A., M.S.L.A., M.L.A., Ph.D.), 5% interior architecture. **Major fields of study:** architecture and related services. **Areas of required coursework:** arts/fine arts, humanities, computer literacy, mathematics, English (including composition), sciences (biological or physical), history, social science. **Special academic programs (% participation):** cross-registration (1%), distance learning (10%), independent study (2%), internships (0%), study abroad (1%). **Cooperative education programs:** art, computer science, technologies. **Faculty and instruction (2005-2006):** Total instructional faculty: 11 full-time, 307 part-time (66% men; 34% women; 10% minorities). Full-time faculty with Ph.D. or other terminal degree: 73%. Student/faculty ratio: 10/1. Classes of fewer than 20 students: 85%; of 20 to 49 students: 12%; of 50 or more students: 3%. **Advanced Placement and International Baccalaureate credit:** AP tests may be used for: Credit and/or placement. Scores accepted: 5. **Freshmen returning for sophomore year:** 61%. **Graduation rates:** Four-year: 14%; five-year: 36%; six-year: 28%.

COSTS AND FINANCIAL AID
Financial aid office: (617) 585-0125. **Expenses (2006-2007):** Tuition and fees 2006-2007: $9,060; room/board: N/A. **Financial aid:** Priority filing date for institution's financial aid form: April 15. Average financial aid package (proportion receiving): $3,770 (N/A). Among students who received need-based aid, the average percentage of need met: 46%. Among students who received aid based on merit, the average award (and the proportion receiving): $0 (N/A). The average athletic scholarship (and the proportion receiving): $0 (N/A). Average amount of debt of borrowers graduating in 2005: $23,784. Proportion who borrowed: 82%.

CAMPUS LIFE AND EXTRACURRICULAR ACTIVITIES
Students who live in college-owned, operated, or affiliated housing: 0%. **Student employment:** During the 2005-2006 academic year, 0% of undergraduates worked on campus. Activities include: student government. Number of fraternities: 0; sororities: 0.

SERVICES AND FACILITIES
Basic services: nonremedial tutoring, placement service, health insurance. **Remedial assistance:** writing, study skills, other. **Counseling services:** minority student, career, military, veteran student, academic, older student. **For learning-disabled students:** School does not offer a structured program with separate admission and additional fees. Total undergraduates in learning-disabled program or receiving services: 0. Services include: tape recorders, videotaped classes, untimed tests, note-taking services, oral tests, learning center, readers, extended time for tests, tutors, early syllabus, priority registration, priority seating, texts on tape, typist/scribe, exams on tape or computer, other testing accomodations. **Library:** Number of titles: 33,000; number of current serial subscriptions: 150. **Information technology resources:** Students are not required to lease or own a computer. Number of campus computers available to all students: 59. School does not have a wireless network. **Campus safety:** Security services offered: 24-hour foot-and-vehicle patrols, 24-hour emergency telephones, lighted pathways/sidewalks.

TRANSFER AND INTERNATIONAL STUDENTS

Transfer students: May apply for admission for the following academic terms: Fall, Spring. Applicants do not need a minimum number of credits to apply. For fall 2005: Transfer applications received: 123. Transfer applicants offered admission: 123. Transfer applicants enrolled: 73. **International students:** Number of foreign undergraduates: 0. Number of countries represented: 0. Minimum TOEFL score required: 550 (paper); 213 (computer). Average TOEFL score: 580 (paper).

Boston College

- **Address:** 140 Commonwealth Avenue, Chestnut Hill, MA 02467
- **Website:** http://www.bc.edu
- **Private; Religious affiliation:** Roman Catholic (Jesuit)
- **Enrollment:** 9,019 full-time

KEY STATS

✔ **U.S News College Ranking:** 34, National Universities
✔ **SAT Score (25th/75th percentile):** 1250-1420
✔ **Tuition:** 2006-2007: $33,506

Selectivity: Most selective	**Room/board:** $11,438
Acceptance rate: 31%	**Average debt:** $19,888
Student/faculty ratio: 13/1	**Proportion who borrowed:** 48%

UNDERGRADUATE STUDENT BODY STATS

2005-2006 enrollment: 9,019 full-time. Men: 48%; women: 52%. **Ethnic makeup:** African American: 6%; Asian American: 9%; Hispanic: 8%; White: 75%; International: 2%.

ADMISSIONS FACTS AND FIGURES

Phone: (617) 552-3100. **Email:** ugadmis@bc.edu. **Website:** http://www.bc.edu. **Application deadlines for fall 2007:** Regular decision: January 2; decision sent by April 15. Early decision: Not offered. Early action: Send application by: November 1; Decision sent by: December 25. Admission can be deferred. **Application fee:** $70. Common application is accepted. **To apply online, go to:** http://app.commonapp.org/. **Admissions requirements/recommendations:** High school units required (recommended): English: (4); Mathematics: (4); Science: (4); Foreign language: (4); Social studies: (4); Total units: (20). Tests: The college uses SAT or ACT scores in admissions decisions. Either SAT or ACT required. For admission to the fall 2007 entering class, the school will accept: ACT with writing. Campus visit: Recommended. Admissions interview: Neither required nor recommended. Off-campus interview: Not available. **Factors that count in admissions decisions:** *Academic:* Secondary school record: Very important. Class rank: Important. Letters of recommendation: Important. Standardized test scores: Important. Essay: Important. *Nonacademic:* Interview: Not considered. Extracurricular activities: Important. Talent/ability: Important. Character/personal qualities: Important. Alumni/ae relationship: Important. Geographical residence: Not considered. State residency: Not considered. Religious affiliation/commitment: Important. Minority status: Considered. Volunteer work: Important. Work experience: Considered. **Other schools with the greatest overlap in applicants:** Georgetown University; Harvard University; University of Notre Dame; University of Pennsylvania; Yale University. **Admissions statistics for the fall 2005 entering class:** Total applicants: 23,823. Total accepted: 7,302. Freshmen enrolled: 2,174; 72% were from out of state. Accepted through early-decision or early-action plans: 32%. Overall acceptance rate: 31%. Non-early acceptance rate: 25%. **Size of waiting list:** 5000 applicants; enrolled from waiting list: 225. **Credentials of fall 2005 freshmen:** 75% ranked in the top 10 percent of their high school class; 95% were in the top 25 percent, and 99% were in the top half. (Proportion submitting class standing: 45%.) **First-year students who submitted SAT scores:** 96%. Scores (25/75 percentile): Verbal: 610-700, Math: 640-720, Combined: 1250-1420. **First-year students submitting ACT scores:** 22%. Scores (25/75 percentile): English: N/A, Math: N/A, Composite: N/A.

ACADEMICS

Year founded: 1863. **Academic calendar:** Semester. **Degrees offered:** bachelor's, master's, post-master's certificate, first professional, doctorate. **Most popular majors:** 11% communication studies/speech communication and rhetoric, 10% finance, 8% English language and literature, 7% political science and government, 6% history. **Major fields of study:** area, ethnic, cultural, and gender studies; biological and biomedical sciences; business, management, marketing, and related support services; communication, journalism, and related programs; computer and information sciences and support services; education; English language and literature/letters; family and consumer sciences/human sciences; foreign languages, literatures, and linguistics; health professions and related clinical sciences; history; mathematics and statistics; philosophy and religious studies; physical sciences; psychology; social sciences; theology and religious vocations; visual and performing arts. **Areas of required coursework:** arts/fine arts, humanities, mathematics, English (including composition), philosophy, sciences (biological or physical), history, social science, other. **Pre-professional programs:** pre-law, pre-dentistry, pre-medicine, pre-veterinary science. **Special academic programs (% participation):** accelerated program (1%), cross-registration (4%), distance learning (1%), double major (29%), English as a Second Language (ESL) (1%), exchange student program (domestic) (1%), honors program (9%), independent study (23%), internships (3%), liberal arts/career combination (10%), student-designed major (1%), study abroad (38%), teacher certificate program (7%). **Teacher certification offered in:** early childhood, special education, elementary, secondary. **Reserve Officers Training Corps (ROTC):** Army ROTC: Offered at cooperating institution (Northeastern University); Navy ROTC: Offered at cooperating institution (Boston University); Air Force ROTC: Offered at cooperating institution (Boston University). **Faculty and instruction (2005-2006):** Total instructional faculty: 679 full-time, 542 part-time (7% minorities). Full-time faculty with Ph.D. or other terminal degree: 98%. Student/faculty ratio: 13/1. Classes of fewer than 20 students: 38%; of 20 to 49 students: 54%; of 50 or more students: 8%. **Advanced Placement and International Baccalaureate credit:** AP tests may be used for: Placement only. Scores accepted: 3, 4, 5. International Baccalaureate exams may be used for: Credit only. **Freshmen returning for sophomore year:** 95%. **Graduation rates:** Four-year: 88%; five-year: 90%; six-year: 91%. **Graduate study:** 28% of students pursue further study immediately upon graduation. Fields in which graduates pursue further study: Master of Business Administration (MBA), 1%; law, 24%; medicine, 8%; dentistry, 1%; education, 21%; arts and sciences, 28%; veterinary medicine, 1%.

COSTS AND FINANCIAL AID

Financial aid office: (617) 552-3320. **Expenses (2006-2007):** Tuition and fees 2006-2007: $33,506; room/board: $11,438. Estimated books and supplies: $650; transportation: $200; personal expenses: $1,000. **Financial aid:** Priority filing date for institution's financial aid form: February 1. In 2005-2006, 53% of undergraduates applied for financial aid. Of those, 40% were determined to have financial need; 100% had their need fully met. Average financial aid package (proportion receiving): $24,905 (40%). Average amount of gift aid, such as scholarships or grants (proportion receiving): $19,854 (36%). Average amount of self-help aid, such as work study or loans (proportion receiving): $6,821 (38%). Average need-based loan (excluding PLUS or other private loans): $4,987. Among students who received need-based aid, the average percentage of need met: 100%. Among students who received aid based on merit, the average award (and the proportion receiving): $11,233 (0%). The average athletic scholarship (and the proportion receiving): $30,459 (3%). Average amount of debt of borrowers graduating in 2005: $19,888. Proportion who borrowed: 48%.

CAMPUS LIFE AND EXTRACURRICULAR ACTIVITIES

Campus housing available (% using): coed dorms (98%), special housing for disabled students (2%). Students who live in college-owned, operated, or affiliated housing: 79%. **Student employment:** During the 2005-2006 academic year, 17% of undergraduates worked on campus. Average per-year earnings: $2,200. **Clubs and organizations:** Number of student organizations: 200. Activities include: choral groups, concert band, dance, drama/theater, jazz band, literary magazine, marching band, music ensembles, musical theater, pep band, radio station, student government, student newspaper, student film society, symphony orchestra, television station, yearbook. Number of fraternities: 0; sororities: 0. Average proportion of students who stay on campus on weekends: 90%. **Sports program (2005-2006):** Member of NCAA I. *Men's intercollegiate varsity sports:* alpine skiing, baseball, basketball, cross-country, fencing, football, golf, ice hockey, sailing, soccer, swimming and diving, tennis, track and field (indoor), track and field (outdoor). *Women's intercollegiate varsity sports:* alpine skiing, basketball, cross-country, fencing, field hockey, golf, ice hockey, lacrosse, sailing, soccer, softball, swimming and diving, tennis, track and field (indoor), track and field (outdoor), volleyball.

SERVICES AND FACILITIES

Basic services: nonremedial tutoring, women's center, placement service, day care, health service, health insurance. **Counseling services:** minority student, career, military, personal, veteran student, academic, older student, psychological, religious. **For learning-disabled students:** School does not offer a structured program with separate admission and additional fees. Total undergraduates in learning-disabled program or receiving services: 400. Services include: reading machines, tape recorders, note-taking services, learning center, readers, extended time for tests, tutors, priority registration, texts on tape, other testing accomodations. **Library:** Number of titles: 2,124,242; number of current serial subscriptions: 52,338. **Information technology resources:** Students are not required to lease or own a computer. Number of campus computers available to all students: 1,000. School has a wireless network. Approximate number of users that can be accommodated: 8,750. Proportion of college-owned housing units wired for high-speed internet access: 100%. **Campus safety:** Security services offered: 24-hour foot-and-vehicle patrols, late-night transport/escort service, 24-hour emergency telephones, lighted pathways/sidewalks, student patrols, controlled dormitory access (key, security card, etc).

TRANSFER AND INTERNATIONAL STUDENTS

Transfer students: May apply for admission for the following academic terms: Fall, Spring. Applicants need a minimum number of credits to apply. For fall 2005: Transfer applications received: 1,126. Transfer applicants offered admission: 148. Transfer applicants enrolled: 73. **International students:** Number of foreign undergraduates: 191 (2% of student body). Number of countries represented: 67. Minimum TOEFL score required: 600 (paper); 250 (computer).

Boston Conservatory

- **Address:** 8 The Fenway, Boston, MA 02215
- **Website:** http://www.bostonconservatory.edu
- **Private**
- **Enrollment:** N/A

KEY STATS

✔ **U.S News College Ranking:** Unranked Specialty School–Fine Arts
✔ **SAT or ACT Score (25th/75th percentile):** N/A
✔ **Tuition:** N/A

Selectivity: Least selective	**Room/board:** N/A
Acceptance rate: N/A	**Average debt:** N/A
Student/faculty ratio: N/A	**Proportion who borrowed:** N/A

Boston University

- **Address:** 1 Sherborn Street, Boston, MA 02215
- **Website:** http://www.bu.edu
- **Private**
- **Enrollment:** 17,384 full-time; 1,310 part-time

KEY STATS

✔ **U.S News College Ranking:** 57, National Universities
✔ **SAT Score (25th/75th percentile):** 1180-1370
✔ **Tuition:** 2006-2007: $33,792

Selectivity: More selective	**Room/board:** $10,480
Acceptance rate: 57%	**Average debt:** $21,196
Student/faculty ratio: 12/1	**Proportion who borrowed:** 57%

UNDERGRADUATE STUDENT BODY STATS

2005-2006 enrollment: 17,384 full-time; 1,310 part-time. Men: 42%; women: 58%. **Ethnic makeup:** African American: 3%; Asian American: 13%; Hispanic: 6%; White: 72%; International: 6%.

ADMISSIONS FACTS AND FIGURES

Phone: (617) 353-2300. **Email:** admissions@bu.edu. **Website:** http://www.bu.edu. **Application deadlines for fall 2007:** Regular decision: January 1. Early decision: Send application by: November 1; Decision sent by: December 15. Early action: Not offered. Admission can be deferred. **Application fee:** $75. Common application is accepted. **To apply online, go to:** http://www.bu.edu/admissions/apply/. **Admissions requirements/recommendations:** High school units required (recommended): English: 4 (4); Mathematics: 3 (4); Science: 3 (4); Foreign language: 2 (4); Social studies: 3 (4); History: 3 (4); Academic electives: 0 (0); Total units: 15 (20). Tests: The college uses SAT or ACT scores in admissions decisions. Either SAT or ACT required. For admission to the fall 2007 entering class, the school will accept: ACT with writing. Campus visit: Recommended. Admissions interview: Neither required nor recommended. Off-campus interview: May be arranged. **Factors that count in admissions decisions:** *Academic:* Secondary school record: Very important. Class rank: Important. Letters of recommendation: Important. Standardized test scores: Important. Essay: Important. *Nonacademic:* Interview: Considered. Extracurricular activities: Considered. Talent/ability: Not considered. Character/personal qualities: Considered. Alumni/ae relationship: Considered. Geographical residence: Considered. State residency: Considered. Religious affiliation/commitment: Not considered. Minority status: Considered. Volunteer work: Considered. Work experience: Considered. **Other schools with the greatest overlap in applicants:** Boston College; George Washington University; New York University; Northeastern University; Tufts University. **Admissions statistics for the fall 2005 entering class:** Total applicants: 31,431. Total accepted: 17,810. Freshmen enrolled: 4,212; 81% were from out of state. Accepted through early-decision or early-action plans: 9%. Overall acceptance rate: 57%. Early-decision acceptance rate: 55%. Non-early acceptance rate: 57%. **Size of waiting list:** 3551 applicants; enrolled from waiting list: 9. **Credentials of fall 2005 freshmen:** 58% ranked in the top 10 percent of their high school class; 87% were in the top 25 percent, and 99% were in the top half. (Proportion submitting class standing: 50%.) **Average high school grade point average:** 3.5. **First-year students who submitted SAT scores:** 96%. Scores (25/75 percentile): Verbal: 580-680, Math: 600-690, Combined: 1180-1370. **First-year students submitting ACT scores:** 25%. Scores (25/75 percentile): English: 26-31, Math: 25-30, Composite: 25-30.

ACADEMICS

Year founded: 1839. **Academic calendar:** Semester. **Degrees offered:** bachelor's, post-bachelor's certificate, master's, post-master's certificate, first professional, first professional certificate, doctorate. **Most popular majors:** 17% business, management, marketing, and related support services, 17% communication, journalism, and related programs, 17% social sciences, 8% engineering, 8% psychology. **Major fields of study:** area, ethnic, cultural, and gender studies; biological and biomedical sciences; business, management, marketing, and related support services; communication, journalism, and related programs; computer and information sciences and support services; education; engineering; engineering technologies/technicians; English language and literature/letters; foreign languages, literatures, and linguistics; health professions and related clinical sciences; history; mathematics and statistics; multi/interdisciplinary studies; natural resources and conservation; philosophy and religious studies; physical sciences; psychology; social sciences; theology and religious vocations; visual and performing arts. **Areas of required coursework:** humanities, computer literacy, mathematics, English (including composition), foreign languages, sciences (biological or physical), social science. **Pre-professional programs:** pre-law, pre-dentistry, pre-medicine. **Special academic programs (% participation):** accelerated program, cooperative (work-study plan) program, cross-registration, double major, dual enrollment, English as a Second Language (ESL), honors program, independent study, internships, liberal arts/career combination, student-designed major, study abroad (24%), teacher certificate program, other. **Teacher certification offered in:** early childhood, special education, elementary, middle/junior high, secondary, bilingual/bicultural. **Cooperative education programs:** engineering. **Reserve Officers Training Corps (ROTC):** Army ROTC: Offered on campus; Navy ROTC: Offered on campus; Air Force ROTC: Offered on campus. **Faculty and instruction (2005-2006):** Total instructional faculty: 1,454 full-time, 984 part-time (62% men; 38% women; 8% minorities). Full-time faculty with Ph.D. or other terminal degree: 86%. Student/faculty ratio: 12/1. Classes of fewer than 20 students: 51%; of 20 to 49 students: 40%; of 50 or more students: 10%. **Advanced Placement and International Baccalaureate credit:** AP tests may be used for: Credit and/or placement. Scores accepted: 3, 4, 5. International Baccalaureate exams may be used for: Credit and/or placement. **Freshmen returning for sophomore year:** 90%. **Graduation rates:** Four-year: 65%; five-year: 75%; six-year: 77%. **Graduate study:** 26% of students pursue further study immediately upon graduation. Fields in which graduates pursue further study: Master of Business Administration (MBA), 3%; law, 3%; medicine, 3%; arts and sciences, 17%.

COSTS AND FINANCIAL AID

Financial aid office: (617) 353-2965. **Expenses (2006-2007):** Tuition and fees 2006-2007: $33,792; room/board: $10,480. Estimated books and supplies: $792; transportation: $453; personal expenses: $1,183. **Financial aid:** Priority filing date for institution's financial aid form: February 15; deadline: February 15. In 2005-2006, 51% of undergraduates applied for financial aid. Of those, 46% were determined to have financial need; 49% had their need fully met. Average financial aid package (proportion receiving): $27,633 (46%). Average amount of gift aid, such as scholarships or grants (proportion receiving): $18,631 (42%). Average amount of self-help aid, such as work study or loans (proportion receiving): $5,818 (40%). Average need-based loan (excluding PLUS or other private loans): $4,835. Among students who received need-based aid, the average percentage of need met: 90%. Among students who received aid based on merit, the average award (and the proportion receiving): $16,606 (10%). The average athletic scholarship (and the proportion receiving): $33,322 (2%). Average amount of debt of borrowers graduating in 2005: $21,196. Proportion who borrowed: 57%.

CAMPUS LIFE AND EXTRACURRICULAR ACTIVITIES

Campus housing available: coed dorms, women's dorms, apartments for married students, apartment for single students, special housing for disabled students, cooperative housing, other housing options. Students who live in college-owned, operated, or affiliated housing: 66%. **Student employment:** During the 2005-2006 academic year, 18% of undergraduates worked on campus. Average per-year earnings: $1,500. **Clubs and organizations:** Number of student organizations: 400. Activities include: choral groups, concert band, dance, drama/theater, jazz band, literary magazine, marching band, music ensembles, musical theater, opera, pep band, radio station, student government, student newspaper, student film society, symphony orchestra, television station. Number of fraternities: 9; sororities: 9. Proportion of men in fraternities: 3%; of women in sororities: 5%. Average proportion of students who stay on campus on weekends: 80%. **Sports program (2005-2006):** Member of NCAA I. *Men's intercollegiate varsity sports:* basketball, cross-country, golf, ice hockey, soccer, swimming and diving, tennis, track and field (indoor), track and field (outdoor), wrestling. *Women's intercollegiate varsity sports:* basketball, cross-country, field hockey, golf, ice hockey, lacrosse, rowing, soccer, softball, swimming and diving, tennis, track and field (indoor), track and field (outdoor).

SERVICES AND FACILITIES

Basic services: nonremedial tutoring, placement service, day care, health service, health insurance, other. **Counseling services:** minority student, career, military, personal, academic, psychological, birth control, religious, other. **For learning-disabled students:** School does not offer a structured program with separate admission and additional fees. Total undergraduates in learning-disabled program or receiving services: 450. Services include: reading machines, tape recorders, note-taking services, oral tests, learning center, readers, extended time for tests, tutors, other testing accomodations, other. **Library:** Number of titles: 2,396,362; number of current serial subscriptions: 34,214. **Information technology resources:** Students are not required to lease or own a computer. Number of campus computers available to all students: 750. School has a wireless network. Approximate number of users that can be accommodated: 700. Proportion of college-owned housing units wired for high-speed internet access: 100%. **Campus safety:** Security services offered: 24-hour foot-and-vehicle patrols, late-night transport/escort service, 24-hour emergency telephones, lighted pathways/sidewalks, controlled dormitory access (key, security card, etc).

TRANSFER AND INTERNATIONAL STUDENTS

Transfer students: May apply for admission for the following academic terms: Fall, Spring. Applicants do not need a minimum number of credits to apply. For fall 2005: Transfer applications received: 1,986. Transfer applicants offered admission: 653. Transfer applicants enrolled: 236.
International students: Number of foreign undergraduates: 1025 (6% of student body). Number of countries represented: 104. Minimum TOEFL score required: 550 (paper); 215 (computer).

Brandeis University

- **Address:** 415 South Street, Waltham, MA 02454-9110
- **Website:** http://www.brandeis.edu
- **Private**
- **Enrollment:** 3,242 full-time; 25 part-time

KEY STATS

✔ **U.S News College Ranking:** 31, National Universities
✔ **SAT Score (25th/75th percentile):** 1270-1440
✔ **Tuition:** 2006-2007: $34,035

Selectivity: Most selective	**Room/board:** $9,463
Acceptance rate: 38%	**Average debt:** $21,437
Student/faculty ratio: 8/1	**Proportion who borrowed:** 61%

UNDERGRADUATE STUDENT BODY STATS

2005-2006 enrollment: 3,242 full-time; 25 part-time. Men: 44%; women: 56%. **Ethnic makeup:** African American: 3%; Asian American: 7%; Hispanic: 4%; White: 79%; International: 8%.

ADMISSIONS FACTS AND FIGURES

Phone: (781) 736-3500. **Email:** admissions@brandeis.edu. **Website:** http://www.brandeis.edu. **Application deadlines for fall 2007:** Regular decision: January 15; decision sent by April 1. Early decision: Send application by: November 15; Decision sent by: December 15. Early action: Not offered. Admission can be deferred. **Application fee:** $55. Common application is accepted. **To apply online, go to:** http://www.commonapp.org. **Admissions requirements/recommendations:** High school units required (recommended): English: (4); Mathematics: (3); Science: (1); Foreign language: (3); Social studies: (0); History: (1); Academic electives: (4); Total units: (16). Tests: The college uses SAT or ACT scores in admissions decisions. Either SAT or ACT required. For admission to the fall 2007 entering class, the school will accept: ACT with writing. Campus visit: Recommended. Admissions interview: Recommended. Off-campus interview: May be arranged. **Factors that count in admissions decisions:** *Academic:* Secondary school record: Very important. Class rank: Very important. Letters of recommendation: Important. Standardized test scores: Important. Essay: Important. *Nonacademic:* Interview: Considered. Extracurricular activities: Important. Talent/ability: Important. Character/personal qualities: Important. Alumni/ae relationship: Considered. Geographical residence: Considered. State residency: Considered. Religious affiliation/commitment: Not considered. Minority status: Considered. Volunteer work: Considered. Work experience: Considered. **Other schools with the greatest overlap in applicants:** Boston University; Brown University; Cornell University; New York University; Tufts University. **Admissions statistics for the fall 2005 entering class:** Total applicants: 7,343. Total accepted: 2,794. Freshmen enrolled: 739; 63% were from out of state. Accepted through early-decision or early-action plans: 22%. Overall acceptance rate: 38%. Early-decision acceptance rate: 52%. Non-early acceptance rate: 37%. **Size of waiting list:** 964 applicants; enrolled from waiting list: 74. **Credentials of fall 2005 freshmen:** 74% ranked in the top 10 percent of their high school class; 96% were in the top 25 percent, and 99% were in the top half. (Proportion submitting class standing: 86%.) **Average high school grade point average:** 3.9. **First-year students who submitted SAT scores:** 82%. Scores (25/75 percentile): Verbal: 630-720, Math: 640-720, Combined: 1270-1440. **First-year students submitting ACT scores:** 18%. Scores (25/75 percentile): English: 28-33, Math: 28-32, Composite: 28-33.

ACADEMICS

Year founded: 1948. **Academic calendar:** Semester. **Degrees offered:** bachelor's, post-bachelor's certificate, master's, doctorate. **Most popular majors:** 23% economics, 13% political science and government, 12% biology/biological sciences, 12% psychology, 8% sociology. **Major fields of study:** area, ethnic, cultural, and gender studies; biological and biomedical sciences; computer and information sciences and support services; English language and literature/letters; foreign languages, literatures, and linguistics; health professions and related clinical sciences; history; mathematics and statistics; multi/interdisciplinary studies; natural resources and conservation; philosophy and religious studies; physical sciences; psychology; social sciences; visual and performing arts. **Areas of required coursework:** humanities, English (including composition), foreign languages, sciences (biological or physical), social science, other. **Pre-professional programs:** pre-medicine. **Special academic programs (% participation):** cross-registration (4%), double major (34%), independent study (45%), internships (10%), student-designed major (1%), study abroad (21%), teacher certificate program (4%). **Teacher certification offered in:** elementary, secondary. **Reserve Officers Training Corps (ROTC):** Army ROTC: Offered at cooperating institution (Boston University); Air Force ROTC: Offered at cooperating institution (Boston University). **Faculty and instruction (2005-2006):** Total instructional faculty: 343 full-time, 130 part-time (58% men; 42% women; 10% minorities). Full-time faculty with Ph.D. or other terminal degree: 97%. Student/faculty ratio: 8/1. Classes of fewer than 20 students: 62%; of 20 to 49 students: 30%; of 50 or more students: 9%. **Advanced Placement and International Baccalaureate credit:** AP tests may be used for: Credit and/or placement. Scores accepted: 4, 5. International Baccalaureate exams may be used for: Credit and/or placement. **Freshmen returning for sophomore year:** 94%. **Graduation rates:** Four-year: 84%; five-year: 88%; six-year: 88%. **Graduate study:** 30% of students pursue further study immediately upon graduation; 19% within one year; 93% within five years. Fields in which graduates pursue further study: Master of Business Administration (MBA), 18%; law, 23%; medicine, 12%; dentistry, 1%; arts and sciences, 49%; veterinary medicine, 1%.

COSTS AND FINANCIAL AID

Financial aid office: (781) 736-3700. **Expenses (2006-2007):** Tuition and fees 2006-2007: $34,035; room/board: $9,463. Estimated books and supplies: $700 personal expenses: $1,000. **Financial aid:** Priority filing date for institution's financial aid form: January 15. In 2005-2006, 59% of undergraduates applied for financial aid. Of those, 47% were determined to have financial need; 29% had their need fully met. Average financial aid package (proportion receiving): $23,816 (47%). Average amount of gift aid, such as scholarships or grants (proportion receiving): $18,620 (45%). Average amount of self-help aid, such as work study or loans (proportion receiving): $6,812 (42%). Average need-based loan (excluding PLUS or other private loans): $5,744. Among students who received need-based aid, the average percentage of need met: 83%. Among students who received aid based on merit, the average award (and the proportion receiving): $12,952 (5%). The average athletic scholarship (and the proportion receiving): $0 (0%). Average amount of debt of borrowers graduating in 2005: $21,437. Proportion who borrowed: 61%.

CAMPUS LIFE AND EXTRACURRICULAR ACTIVITIES

Campus housing available (% using): coed dorms (95%), special housing for disabled students (5%). Students who live in college-owned, operated, or affiliated housing: 80%. **Student employment:** During the 2005-2006 academic year, 51% of undergraduates worked on campus. Average per-year earnings: $2,500. **Clubs and organizations:** Number of student organizations: 200. Activities include: choral groups, concert band, dance, drama/theater, jazz band, literary magazine, music ensembles, musical theater, radio station, student government, student newspaper, student film society, television station, yearbook. Number of fraternities: 0; sororities: 0. Average proportion of students who stay on campus on weekends: 80%. **Sports program (2005-2006):** Member of NCAA III. *Men's intercollegiate varsity sports:* baseball, basketball, cross-country, fencing, golf, sailing, soccer, swimming and diving, tennis, track and field (indoor), track and field (outdoor). *Women's intercollegiate varsity sports:* basketball, cross-country, fencing, sailing, soccer, softball, swimming and diving, tennis, track and field (indoor), track and field (outdoor), volleyball.

SERVICES AND FACILITIES

Basic services: women's center, placement service, health service, health insurance. **Counseling services:** minority student, career, personal, academic, older student, psychological, birth control, religious. **For learning-disabled students:** School does not offer a structured program with separate admission and additional fees. Total undergraduates in learning-disabled program or receiving services: 116. Services include: reading machines, tape recorders, note-taking services, extended time for tests, texts on tape, other testing accomodations, other. **Library:** Number of titles: 1,191,645; number of current serial subscriptions: 25,808. **Information technology resources:** Students are not required to lease or own a computer. Number of campus computers available to all students: 180. School has a wireless network. Approximate number of users that can be accommodated: 3,000. Proportion of college-owned housing units wired for high-speed internet access: 100%. **Campus safety:** Security services offered: 24-hour foot-and-vehicle patrols, late-night transport/escort service, 24-hour emergency telephones, lighted pathways/sidewalks, controlled dormitory access (key, security card, etc).

TRANSFER AND INTERNATIONAL STUDENTS

Transfer students: May apply for admission for the following academic terms: Fall. Applicants do not need a minimum number of credits to apply. For fall 2005: Transfer applications received: 307. Transfer applicants offered admission: 118. Transfer applicants enrolled: 52. **International students:** Number of foreign undergraduates: 245 (8% of student body). Minimum TOEFL score required: 600 (paper); 250 (computer). Average TOEFL score: 635 (paper).

Bridgewater State College

- **Address:** Boyden Hall, Bridgewater, MA 02325
- **Website:** http://www.bridgew.edu
- **Public**
- **Enrollment:** 6,435 full-time; 1,416 part-time

KEY STATS

✔ **U.S News College Ranking:** fourth tier, Universities–Master's (North)
✔ **SAT Score (25th/75th percentile):** 920-1120
✔ **Tuition:** 2006-2007: $5,854 in state, $11,994 out of state

Selectivity: Less selective	**Room/board:** $7,062
Acceptance rate: 80%	**Average debt:** $15,065
Student/faculty ratio: N/A	**Proportion who borrowed:** 31%

UNDERGRADUATE STUDENT BODY STATS

2005-2006 enrollment: 6,435 full-time; 1,416 part-time. Men: 40%; women: 60%. **Ethnic makeup:** African American: 4%; Asian American: 1%; Hispanic: 2%; White: 91%; International: 1%.

ADMISSIONS FACTS AND FIGURES

Phone: (508) 531-1237. **Email:** admission@bridgew.edu. **Website:** http://www.bridgew.edu. **Application deadlines for fall 2007:** Regular decision: February 15; decision sent by April 15. Early decision: Not offered. Early action: Send application by: November 15; Decision sent by: December 15. Admission can be deferred. **Application fee:** $25. Common application is accepted. To apply online, go to: http://www.bridgew.edu/admission/. **Admissions requirements/recommendations:** High school units required (recommended): English: 4; Mathematics: 3; Science: 3; Foreign language: 2; Social studies: 1; History: 1; Academic electives: 2; Total units: 16. Tests: The college uses SAT or ACT scores in admissions decisions. Either SAT or ACT required. For admission to the fall 2007 entering class, the school will accept: ACT with writing, ACT without writing. Campus visit: Neither required nor recommended. Admissions interview: Neither required nor recommended. Off-campus interview: Not available. **Factors that count in admissions decisions:** *Academic:* Secondary school record: Very important. Class rank: Considered. Letters of recommendation: Important. Standardized test scores: Considered. Essay: Considered. *Nonacademic:* Interview: Not considered. Extracurricular activities: Important. Talent/ability: Considered. Character/personal qualities: Considered. Alumni/ae relationship: Considered. Geographical residence: Not considered. State residency: Not considered. Religious affiliation/commitment: Not considered. Minority status: Considered. Volunteer work: Considered. Work experience: Considered. **Other schools with the greatest overlap in applicants:** Framingham State College; Northeastern University; University of Massachusetts–Amherst; University of Massachusetts–Dartmouth; Westfield State College. **Admissions statistics for the fall 2005 entering class:** Total applicants: 5,446. Total accepted: 4,369. Freshmen enrolled: 1,332; 5% were from out of state. Overall acceptance rate: 80%. Non-early acceptance rate: 80%. **Credentials of fall 2005 freshmen:** 6% ranked in the top 10 percent of their high school class; 30% were in the top 25 percent, and 69% were in the top half. (Proportion submitting class standing: 73%.) **Average high school grade point average:** 3.0. **First-year students who submitted SAT scores:** 96%. Scores (25/75 percentile): Verbal: 460-560; Math: 460-560, Combined: 920-1120. **First-year students submitting ACT scores:** 3%. Scores (25/75 percentile): English: N/A, Math: N/A, Composite: 19-23.

ACADEMICS

Year founded: 1840. **Academic calendar:** Semester. **Degrees offered:** certificate, bachelor's, post-bachelor's certificate, master's, post-master's certificate. **Most popular majors:** 15% psychology, 14% business/commerce, 12% education, 8% social sciences, 7% communication studies/speech communication and rhetoric. **Major fields of study:** architecture and related services; area, ethnic, cultural, and gender studies; biological and biomedical sciences; business, management, marketing, and related support services; communication, journalism, and related programs; computer and information sciences and support services; education; English language and literature/letters; foreign languages, literatures, and linguistics; health professions and related clinical sciences; history; legal professions and studies; mathematics and statistics; parks, recreation, leisure, and fitness studies; philosophy and religious studies; physical sciences; psychology; public administration and social service professions; science technologies/technicians; security and protective services; social sciences; transportation and materials moving; visual and performing arts. **Areas of required coursework:** arts/fine arts, humanities, mathematics, English (including composition), philosophy, foreign languages, sciences (biological or physical), history, social science, other. **Pre-professional programs:** pre-law, pre-medicine. **Special academic programs (% participation):** accelerated program, cross-registration, distance learning (23%), double major (13%), dual enrollment (2%), English as a Second Language (ESL) (.3%), exchange student program (domestic) (.3%), honors program (6%), independent study (2%), internships (3%), study abroad (3%), teacher certificate program (15%). **Teacher certification offered in:** early childhood, special education, elementary, middle/junior high, secondary. **Reserve Officers Training Corps (ROTC):** Army ROTC: Offered at cooperating institution (Stonehill College/Boston University); Air Force ROTC: Offered at cooperating institution (Boston University). **Faculty and instruction (2005-2006):** Total instructional faculty: N/A. Classes of fewer than 20 students: 40%; of 20 to 49 students: 58%; of 50 or more students: 1%. **Advanced Placement and International Baccalaureate credit:** AP tests may be used for: Credit only. Scores accepted: 3. International Baccalaureate exams may be used for: Credit only. **Freshmen returning for sophomore year:** 76%. **Graduation rates:** Four-year: 19%; five-year: 43%; six-year: 48%. **Graduate study:** 17% of students pursue further study within one year.

COSTS AND FINANCIAL AID

Financial aid office: (508) 531-1341. **Expenses (2006-2007):** Tuition and fees 2006-2007: $5,854 in state, $11,994 out of state; room/board: $7,062. Estimated books and supplies: $800; transportation: $800; personal expenses: $1,500. **Financial aid:** Priority filing date for institution's financial aid form: March 1. Average amount of debt of borrowers graduating in 2005: $15,065. Proportion who borrowed: 31%.

CAMPUS LIFE AND EXTRACURRICULAR ACTIVITIES

Campus housing available: coed dorms, women's dorms, apartment for single students. Students who live in college-owned, operated, or affiliated housing: 29%. **Student employment:** During the 2005-2006 academic year, 19% of undergraduates worked on campus. Average per-year earnings: $5,400. **Clubs and organizations:** Number of student organizations: 60. Activities include: choral groups, concert band, dance, drama/theater, jazz band, literary magazine, marching band, music ensembles, musical theater, radio station, student government, student newspaper, television station, yearbook. Number of fraternities: 3; sororities: 3. **Sports program (2005-2006):** Member of NCAA III. **Men's intercollegiate varsity sports:** baseball, basketball, cross-country, football, soccer, swimming and diving, tennis, track and field (indoor), track and field (outdoor), wrestling. **Women's intercollegiate varsity sports:** basketball, cross-country, field hockey, lacrosse, soccer, softball, swimming and diving, tennis, track and field (indoor), track and field (outdoor), volleyball.

SERVICES AND FACILITIES

Basic services: nonremedial tutoring, women's center, placement service, day care, health service, health insurance. **Remedial assistance:** math, writing, study skills. **Counseling services:** minority student, career, personal, academic, psychological, birth control, religious. **For learning-disabled students:** School does not offer a structured program with separate admission and additional fees. Total undergraduates in learning-disabled program or receiving services: 500. Services include: tape recorders, untimed tests, note-taking services, oral tests, learning center, readers, extended time for tests, tutors, priority seating, substitution of courses, texts on tape, exams on tape or computer, other testing accomodations, waiver of foreign language degree requirement, waiver of math degree requirement, other. **Library:** Number of titles: 291,544; number of current serial subscriptions: 3,218. **Information technology resources:** Students are required to lease or own a computer. Number of campus computers available to all students: 900. School has a wireless network. Approximate number of users that can be accommodated: 11,250. Proportion of college-owned housing units wired for high-speed internet access: 100%. **Campus safety:** Security services offered: 24-hour foot-and-vehicle patrols, late-night transport/escort service,

24-hour emergency telephones, lighted pathways/sidewalks, controlled dormitory access (key, security card, etc).

TRANSFER AND INTERNATIONAL STUDENTS

Transfer students: May apply for admission for the following academic terms: Fall, Spring. Applicants need a minimum number of credits to apply. For fall 2005: Transfer applications received: 1,254. Transfer applicants offered admission: 1,163. Transfer applicants enrolled: 704. **International students:** Number of foreign undergraduates: 94 (1% of student body). Minimum TOEFL score required: 500 (paper); 173 (computer). Average TOEFL score: 520 (paper).

Clark University

- **Address:** 950 Main Street, Worcester, MA 01610-1477
- **Website:** http://www.clarku.edu
- **Private**
- **Enrollment:** 2,097 full-time; 158 part-time

KEY STATS

✔ **U.S News College Ranking:** 81, National Universities
✔ **SAT Score (25th/75th percentile):** 1100-1310
✔ **Tuition:** 2006-2007: $31,465

Selectivity: More selective	**Room/board:** $5,900
Acceptance rate: 62%	**Average debt:** $18,990
Student/faculty ratio: 10/1	**Proportion who borrowed:** 88%

UNDERGRADUATE STUDENT BODY STATS

2005-2006 enrollment: 2,097 full-time; 158 part-time. Men: 40%; women: 60%. **Ethnic makeup:** African American: 2%; Asian American: 4%; Hispanic: 2%; White: 84%; International: 7%. **Religious preference:** Roman Catholic: 16%; Protestant: 19%; Jewish: 16%; Muslim: 1%; Hindu: 1%; Buddhist: 2%; No preference: 43%; Other: 2%.

ADMISSIONS FACTS AND FIGURES

Phone: (508) 793-7431. **Email:** admissions@clarku.edu. **Website:** http://www.clarku.edu. **Application deadlines for fall 2007:** Regular decision: January 15; decision sent by April 1. Early decision: Send application by: November 15; Decision sent by: December 15. Early action: Not offered. Admission can be deferred. **Application fee:** $50. Common application is accepted. **To apply online, go to:** http://www.clarku.edu/admissions/apply/index.cfm. **Admissions requirements/recommendations:** High school units required (recommended): English: (4); Mathematics: (3); Science: (3); Foreign language: (2); Social studies: (2); History: (2); Total units: (16). Tests: The college uses SAT or ACT scores in admissions decisions. Either SAT or ACT required. For admission to the fall 2007 entering class, the school will accept: ACT with writing, ACT without writing. Campus visit: Recommended. Admissions interview: Recommended. Off-campus interview: May be arranged. **Factors that count in admissions decisions:** **Academic:** Secondary school record: Very important. Class rank: Considered. Letters of recommendation: Very important. Standardized test scores: Very important. Essay: Important. **Nonacademic:** Interview: Considered. Extracurricular activities: Important. Talent/ability: Important. Character/personal qualities: Very important. Alumni/ae relationship: Considered. Geographical residence: Considered. State residency: Not considered. Religious affiliation/commitment: Not considered. Minority status: Considered. Volunteer work: Important. Work experience: Considered. **Other schools with the greatest overlap in applicants:** American University; Boston University; Brandeis University; George Washington University; University of Massachusetts–Amherst. **Admissions statistics for the fall 2005 entering class:** Total applicants: 4,463. Total accepted: 2,748. Freshmen enrolled: 560; 66% were from out of state. Accepted through early-decision or early-action plans: 13%. Overall acceptance rate: 62%. Early-decision acceptance rate: 82%. Non-early acceptance rate: 61%. **Size of waiting list:** 122 applicants; enrolled from waiting list: 8. **Credentials of fall 2005 freshmen:** 34% ranked in the top 10 percent of their high school class; 70% were in the top 25 percent, and 97% were in the top half. (Proportion submitting class standing: 52%.) **Average high school grade point average:** 3.4. **First-year students who submitted SAT scores:** 94%. Scores (25/75 percentile): Verbal: 560-660, Math: 540-650, Combined: 1100-1310. **First-year students submitting ACT scores:** 26%. Scores (25/75 percentile): English: 23-29, Math: 22-27, Composite: 24-28.

ACADEMICS

Year founded: 1887. **Academic calendar:** Semester. **Degrees offered:** bachelor's, post-bachelor's certificate, master's, post-master's certificate, doctorate. **Most popular majors:** 19% psychology, 12% economics, 9% biology, 7% history, 7% sociology. **Major fields of study:** area, ethnic, cultural, and gender studies; biological and biomedical sciences; business, management, marketing, and related support services; communication, journalism, and related programs; English language and literature/letters; foreign languages, literatures, and linguistics; history; mathematics and statistics; multi/interdisciplinary studies; natural resources and conservation; philosophy and religious studies; physical sciences; psychology; social sciences; visual and performing arts. **Areas of required coursework:** arts/fine arts, humanities, mathematics, English (including composition), philosophy, foreign languages, sciences (biological or physical), history, social science. **Pre-professional programs:** pre-law, pre-dentistry, pre-medicine, pre-veterinary science, pre-optometry. **Special academic programs (% participation):** cross-registration (3%), double major (14%), English as a Second Language (ESL), independent study (40%), internships (43%), liberal arts/career combination (16%), student-designed major (1%), study abroad (32%), teacher certificate program (5%), other. **Teacher certification offered in:** elementary, middle/junior high, secondary. **Reserve Officers Training Corps (ROTC):** Army ROTC: Offered at cooperating institution (Worcester Polytechnic Inst.); Navy ROTC: Offered at cooperating institution (College of the Holy Cross); Air Force ROTC: Offered at cooperating institution (Worcester Polytechnic Inst.). **Faculty and instruction (2005-2006):** Total instructional faculty: 167 full-time, 96 part-time (57% men; 43% women; 11% minorities). Full-time faculty with Ph.D. or other terminal degree: 98%. Student/faculty ratio: 10/1. Classes of fewer than 20 students: 61%; of 20 to 49 students: 34%; of 50 or more students: 4%. **Advanced Placement and International Baccalaureate credit:** AP tests may be used for: Placement only. Scores accepted: 4, 5. International Baccalaureate exams may be used for: Placement only. **Freshmen returning for sophomore year:** 86%. **Graduation rates:** Four-year: 63%; five-year: 69%; six-year: 70%. **Graduate study:** 36% of students pursue further study immediately upon graduation. Fields in which graduates pursue further study: Master of Business Administration (MBA), 20%; law, 8%; medicine, 4%; education, 12%; arts and sciences, 56%.

COSTS AND FINANCIAL AID

Financial aid office: (508) 793-7478. **Expenses (2006-2007):** Tuition and fees 2006-2007: $31,465; room/board: $5,900. Estimated books and supplies: $800; transportation: $250; personal expenses: $700. **Financial aid:** In 2005-2006, 73% of undergraduates applied for financial aid. Of those, 55% were determined to have financial need; 66% had their need fully met. Average financial aid package (proportion receiving): $21,898 (54%). Average amount of gift aid, such as scholarships or grants (proportion receiving): $17,645 (54%). Average amount of self-help aid, such as work study or loans (proportion receiving): $4,394 (45%). Average need-based loan (excluding PLUS or other private loans): $3,208. Among students who received need-based aid, the average percentage of need met: 93%. Among students who received aid based on merit, the average award (and the proportion receiving): $11,591 (26%). Average amount of debt of borrowers graduating in 2005: $18,990. Proportion who borrowed: 88%.

CAMPUS LIFE AND EXTRACURRICULAR ACTIVITIES

Campus housing available (% using): coed dorms (77%), women's dorms (9%), apartment for single students (10%), special housing for disabled students, other housing options (4%). Students who live in college-owned, operated, or affiliated housing: 77%. **Student employment:** During the 2005-2006 academic year, 45% of undergraduates worked on campus. Average per-year earnings: $1,800. **Clubs and organizations:** Number of student organizations: 85. Activities include: choral groups, concert band, dance, drama/theater, jazz band, literary magazine, marching band, music ensembles, musical theater, pep band, radio station, student government, student newspaper, student film society, symphony orchestra, television station, yearbook. Number of fraternities: 0; sororities: 0. Average proportion of students who stay on campus on weekends: 75%. **Sports program (2005-2006):** Member of NCAA III. **Men's intercollegiate varsity sports:** baseball, basketball, cross-country, lacrosse, soccer, swimming and diving, tennis. **Women's intercollegiate varsity sports:** basketball, cross-country, field hockey, rowing, soccer, softball, swimming and diving, tennis, volleyball.

SERVICES AND FACILITIES

Basic services: nonremedial tutoring, women's center, placement service, health service, health insurance. **Counseling services:** minority student, career, personal, academic, psychological, birth control. **For learning-dis-**

abled students: School does not offer a structured program with separate admission and additional fees. Total undergraduates in learning-disabled program or receiving services: 130. Services include: oral tests, readers, extended time for tests, texts on tape. **Library:** Number of titles: 605,421; number of current serial subscriptions: 1,303. **Information technology resources:** Students are not required to lease or own a computer. Number of campus computers available to all students: 280. School has a wireless network. Approximate number of users that can be accommodated: 10,000. Proportion of college-owned housing units wired for high-speed internet access: 100%. **Campus safety:** Security services offered: 24-hour foot-and-vehicle patrols, late-night transport/escort service, 24-hour emergency telephones, lighted pathways/sidewalks, student patrols, controlled dormitory access (key, security card, etc).

TRANSFER AND INTERNATIONAL STUDENTS

Transfer students: May apply for admission for the following academic terms: Fall, Spring. Applicants need a minimum number of credits to apply. For fall 2005: Transfer applications received: 226. Transfer applicants offered admission: 120. Transfer applicants enrolled: 39. **International students:** Number of foreign undergraduates: 157 (7% of student body). Number of countries represented: 58. Minimum TOEFL score required: 550 (paper); 230 (computer). Average TOEFL score: 605 (paper).

College of the Holy Cross

- **Address:** 1 College Street, Worcester, MA 01610
- **Website:** http://www.holycross.edu
- **Private; Religious affiliation:** Roman Catholic-Jesuit
- **Enrollment:** 2,788 full-time; 28 part-time

KEY STATS

✔ **U.S News College Ranking:** 32, Liberal Arts Colleges
✔ **SAT Score (25th/75th percentile):** 1200-1320
✔ **Tuition:** 2006-2007: $33,313

Selectivity: More selective	**Room/board:** $9,580
Acceptance rate: 48%	**Average debt:** $19,390
Student/faculty ratio: 11/1	**Proportion who borrowed:** 52%

UNDERGRADUATE STUDENT BODY STATS

2005-2006 enrollment: 2,788 full-time; 28 part-time. Men: 45%; women: 55%. **Ethnic makeup:** African American: 4%; Asian American: 4%; Hispanic: 5%; White: 85%; International: 1%. **Religious preference:** Roman Catholic: 77%; Protestant: 7%; Jewish: 1%; Buddhist: 1%; No preference: 8%; Christian: 6%.

ADMISSIONS FACTS AND FIGURES

Phone: (508) 793-2443. **Email:** admissions@holycross.edu. **Website:** http://www.holycross.edu. **Application deadlines for fall 2007:** Regular decision: January 15; decision sent by April 1. Early decision: Send application by: December 15; Decision sent by: January 15. Early action: Not offered. Admission can be deferred. **Application fee:** $50. Common application is accepted. **To apply online, go to:** http://www.applyweb.com/aw?hc. **Admissions requirements/recommendations:** High school units required (recommended): English: (4); Mathematics: (4); Science: (4); Foreign language: (3); Social studies: (2); History: (2); Academic electives: (1); Total units: (20). Tests: The college uses SAT or ACT scores in admissions decisions. Neither SAT nor ACT required. For admission to the fall 2007 entering class, the school will accept: ACT with writing, ACT without writing. Campus visit: Recommended. Admissions interview: Recommended. Off-campus interview: May be arranged. **Factors that count in admissions decisions:** *Academic:* Secondary school record: Very important. Class rank: Very important. Letters of recommendation: Important. Standardized test scores: Considered. Essay: Important. *Nonacademic:* Interview: Important. Extracurricular activities: Important. Talent/ability: Considered. Character/personal qualities: Important. Alumni/ae relationship: Important. Geographical residence: Considered. State residency: Not considered. Religious affiliation/commitment: Not considered. Minority status: Considered. Volunteer work: Considered. Work experience: Considered. **Other schools with the greatest overlap in applicants:** Boston College; Fairfield University; Georgetown University; Providence College; Villanova University. **Admissions statistics for the fall 2005 entering class:** Total applicants: 4,744. Total accepted: 2,270. Freshmen enrolled: 723; 62% were from out of state. Overall acceptance rate: 48%. Early-decision acceptance rate: 69%. Non-early acceptance rate: 46%. **Size of waiting list:** 713 applicants; enrolled from waiting list: 29. **Credentials of fall 2005 freshmen:** 66% ranked in the top 10 percent of their high school class; 93% were in the top 25 percent, and 100% were in the top half. (Proportion submitting class standing: 48%.) **First-year students who submitted SAT scores:** 93%. Scores (25/75 percentile): Verbal: 620-640, Math: 580-680, Combined: 1200-1320.

ACADEMICS

Year founded: 1843. **Academic calendar:** Semester. **Degrees offered:** bachelor's. **Most popular majors:** 34% social sciences, 11% English language and literature/letters, 11% history, 9% foreign languages, literatures, and linguistics, 9% psychology. **Major fields of study:** biological and biomedical sciences; business, management, marketing, and related support services; computer and information sciences and support services; English language and literature/letters; foreign languages, literatures, and linguistics; history; mathematics and statistics; philosophy and religious studies; physical sciences; psychology; social sciences; theology and religious vocations; visual and performing arts. **Areas of required coursework:** arts/fine arts, humanities, mathematics, English (including composition), philosophy, foreign languages, sciences (biological or physical), history, social science, other. **Pre-professional programs:** pre-dentistry, pre-medicine, pre-veterinary science. **Special academic programs (% participation):** accelerated program (0%), cross-registration (5%), double major (12%), exchange student program (domestic) (1%), honors program (5%), independent study (35%), internships (20%), student-designed major (2%), study abroad (22%), teacher certificate program (2%), other (13%). **Teacher certification offered in:** middle/junior high, secondary. **Reserve Officers Training Corps (ROTC):** Army ROTC: Offered at cooperating institution (Worcester Polytechnic Institute); Navy ROTC: Offered on campus; Air Force ROTC: Offered at cooperating institution (Worcester Polytechnic Institute). **Faculty and instruction (2005-2006):** Total instructional faculty: 240 full-time, 57 part-time (54% men; 46% women; 10% minorities). Full-time faculty with Ph.D. or other terminal degree: 92%. Student/faculty ratio: 11/1. Classes of fewer than 20 students: 51%; of 20 to 49 students: 48%; of 50 or more students: 2%. **Advanced Placement and International Baccalaureate credit:** AP tests may be used for: Credit and/or placement. Scores accepted: 4, 5. International Baccalaureate exams may be used for: Credit and/or placement. **Freshmen returning for sophomore year:** 96%. **Graduation rates:** Four-year: 89%; five-year: 91%; six-year: 91%. **Graduate study:** 24% of students pursue further study immediately upon graduation. Fields in which graduates pursue further study: law, 9%; medicine, 1%; dentistry, 1%; engineering, 1%; theology (or the seminary), 1%; education, 3%; arts and sciences, 8%.

COSTS AND FINANCIAL AID

Financial aid office: (508) 793-2266. **Expenses (2006-2007):** Tuition and fees 2006-2007: $33,313; room/board: $9,580. Estimated books and supplies: $700; transportation: $400; personal expenses: $900. **Financial aid:** Priority filing date for institution's financial aid form: February 1; deadline: February 1. In 2005-2006, 61% of undergraduates applied for financial aid. Of those, 54% were determined to have financial need; 99% had their need fully met. Average financial aid package (proportion receiving): $21,254 (53%). Average amount of gift aid, such as scholarships or grants (proportion receiving): $18,110 (44%). Average amount of self-help aid, such as work study or loans (proportion receiving): $5,760 (49%). Average need-based loan (excluding PLUS or other private loans): $4,198. Among students who received need-based aid, the average percentage of need met: 100%. Among students who received aid based on merit, the average award (and the proportion receiving): $15,517 (3%). The average athletic scholarship (and the proportion receiving): $39,999 (1%). Average amount of debt of borrowers graduating in 2005: $19,390. Proportion who borrowed: 52%.

CAMPUS LIFE AND EXTRACURRICULAR ACTIVITIES

Campus housing available: coed dorms, apartment for single students, special housing for disabled students. Students who live in college-owned, operated, or affiliated housing: 88%. **Student employment:** During the 2005-2006 academic year, 57% of undergraduates worked on campus. Average per-year earnings: $1,700. **Clubs and organizations:** Number of student organizations: 102. Activities include: choral groups, dance, drama/theater, jazz band, literary magazine, marching band, music ensembles, musical theater, pep band, radio station, student government, student newspaper, yearbook. Number of fraternities: 0; sororities: 0. Average proportion of students who stay on campus on weekends: 90%. **Sports program (2005-2006):** Member of NCAA I. **Men's intercollegiate varsity sports:** baseball, basketball, crew, cross-country, football, golf, ice hockey, lacrosse, soccer,

swimming and diving, tennis, track and field (indoor), track and field (outdoor). **Women's intercollegiate varsity sports:** basketball, cross-country, field hockey, golf, ice hockey, lacrosse, rowing, soccer, softball, swimming and diving, tennis, track and field (indoor), track and field (outdoor), volleyball.

SERVICES AND FACILITIES

Basic services: nonremedial tutoring, placement service, health service. **Counseling services:** minority student, career, personal, academic, psychological, religious. **For learning-disabled students:** School does not offer a structured program with separate admission and additional fees. Services include: learning center, extended time for tests. **Library:** Number of titles: 591,658; number of current serial subscriptions: 1,649. **Information technology resources:** Students are not required to lease or own a computer. Number of campus computers available to all students: 480. School has a wireless network. Proportion of college-owned housing units wired for high-speed internet access: 100%. **Campus safety:** Security services offered: 24-hour foot-and-vehicle patrols, late-night transport/escort service, 24-hour emergency telephones, lighted pathways/sidewalks, controlled dormitory access (key, security card, etc).

TRANSFER AND INTERNATIONAL STUDENTS

Transfer students: May apply for admission for the following academic terms: Fall, Spring. Applicants need a minimum number of credits to apply. For fall 2005: Transfer applications received: 94. Transfer applicants offered admission: 34. Transfer applicants enrolled: 16. **International students:** Number of foreign undergraduates: 28 (1% of student body). Number of countries represented: 15. Minimum TOEFL score required: 550 (paper); 213 (computer).

Curry College

- **Address:** 1071 Blue Hill Avenue, Milton, MA 02186
- **Website:** http://www.curry.edu
- **Private**
- **Enrollment:** 1,973 full-time; 752 part-time

KEY STATS

✔ **U.S News College Ranking:** third tier, Comp. Coll.–Bachelor's (North)
✔ **SAT Score (25th/75th percentile):** 921-1061
✔ **Tuition:** 2006-2007: $24,140

Selectivity: Less selective **Room/board:** $9,340
Acceptance rate: 69% **Average debt:** $25,051
Student/faculty ratio: 12/1 **Proportion who borrowed:** 55%

UNDERGRADUATE STUDENT BODY STATS

2005-2006 enrollment: 1,973 full-time; 752 part-time. Men: 42%; women: 58%. **Ethnic makeup:** African American: 8%; Asian American: 1%; Hispanic: 3%; White: 87%; International: 1%.

ADMISSIONS FACTS AND FIGURES

Phone: (800) 669-0686. **Email:** curryadm@curry.edu. **Website:** http://www.curry.edu. **Application deadlines for fall 2007:** Regular decision: Rolling; decision sent by May 1. Early decision: Send application by: December 1; Decision sent by: December 15. Early action: Not offered. Admission can be deferred. **Application fee:** $40. Common application is accepted. **Admissions requirements/recommendations:** High school units required (recommended): English: 4; Mathematics: 3; Science: 2; Foreign language: 2; Social studies: 2; History: 2; Total units: 16. Tests: The college uses SAT or ACT scores in admissions decisions. Neither SAT nor ACT required. For admission to the fall 2007 entering class, the school will accept: ACT with writing, ACT without writing. Campus visit: Recommended. Admissions interview: Recommended. Off-campus interview: May be arranged. **Factors that count in admissions decisions:** *Academic:* Secondary school record: Very important. Class rank: Considered. Letters of recommendation: Important. Standardized test scores: Important. Essay: Important. *Nonacademic:* Interview: Important. Extracurricular activities: Considered. Talent/ability: Considered. Character/personal qualities: Considered. Alumni/ae relationship: Considered. Geographical residence: Not considered. State residency: Not considered. Religious affiliation/commitment: Not considered. Minority status: Not considered. Volunteer work: Considered. Work experience: Not considered. **Other schools with the greatest overlap in applicants:** Bridgewater State College; Northeastern

University; Simmons College; Suffolk University; Westfield State College. **Admissions statistics for the fall 2005 entering class:** Total applicants: 3,006. Total accepted: 2,079. Freshmen enrolled: 600; 31% were from out of state. Accepted through early-decision or early-action plans: 4%. Overall acceptance rate: 69%. Early-decision acceptance rate: 29%. Non-early acceptance rate: 71%. **Credentials of fall 2005 freshmen:** 4% ranked in the top 10 percent of their high school class, and 57% were in the top half. (Proportion submitting class standing: 45%.) **Average high school grade point average:** 2.7. **First-year students who submitted SAT scores:** 75%. Scores (25/75 percentile): Verbal: 469-558, Math: 452-503, Combined: 921-1061.

ACADEMICS

Year founded: 1879. **Academic calendar:** Semester. **Degrees offered:** bachelor's, master's. **Most popular majors:** 24% criminal justice/safety studies, 23% nursing/registered nurse training (R.N., A.S.N., B.S.N., M.S.N.), 19% business administration and management, 11% communication studies/speech communication and rhetoric, 8% psychology. **Major fields of study:** biological and biomedical sciences; business, management, marketing, and related support services; communication, journalism, and related programs; computer and information sciences and support services; education; English language and literature/letters; health professions and related clinical sciences; liberal arts and sciences studies, and humanities; multi/interdisciplinary studies; natural resources and conservation; philosophy and religious studies; psychology; security and protective services; social sciences; visual and performing arts. **Areas of required coursework:** arts/fine arts, mathematics, English (including composition), philosophy, sciences (biological or physical), history, social science, other. **Special academic programs (% participation):** accelerated program (49.1%), cross-registration (0%), double major (5%), honors program (3.7%), independent study (12.5%), internships (15.7%), student-designed major (1%), study abroad (1%), teacher certificate program (2%). **Teacher certification offered in:** early childhood, special education, elementary. **Reserve Officers Training Corps (ROTC):** Army ROTC: Offered at cooperating institution (Stonehill College, Boston University). **Faculty and instruction (2005-2006):** Total instructional faculty: 102 full-time, 270 part-time (45% men; 55% women; 12% minorities). Full-time faculty with Ph.D. or other terminal degree: 52%. Student/faculty ratio: 12/1. Classes of fewer than 20 students: 59%; of 20 to 49 students: 41%; of 50 or more students: 1%. **Advanced Placement and International Baccalaureate credit:** AP tests may be used for: Credit and/or placement. Scores accepted: 3, 4, 5. International Baccalaureate exams may be used for: Credit only. **Freshmen returning for sophomore year:** 69%. **Graduation rates:** Four-year: 36%; five-year: 44%; six-year: 46%. **Graduate study:** 10% of students pursue further study immediately upon graduation; 6% within five years. Fields in which graduates pursue further study: Master of Business Administration (MBA), 40%; law, 5%; education, 15%; arts and sciences, 40%.

COSTS AND FINANCIAL AID

Financial aid office: (617) 333-2146. **Expenses (2006-2007):** Tuition and fees 2006-2007: $24,140; room/board: $9,340. Estimated books and supplies: $700; transportation: $1,000; personal expenses: $1,128. **Financial aid:** Priority filing date for institution's financial aid form: March 1. In 2005-2006, 68% of undergraduates applied for financial aid. Of those, 67% were determined to have financial need; 6% had their need fully met. Average financial aid package (proportion receiving): $14,733 (66%). Average amount of gift aid, such as scholarships or grants (proportion receiving): $9,925 (60%). Average amount of self-help aid, such as work study or loans (proportion receiving): $4,366 (64%). Average need-based loan (excluding PLUS or other private loans): $3,764. Among students who received need-based aid, the average percentage of need met: 68%. Among students who received aid based on merit, the average award (and the proportion receiving): $4,379 (1%). The average athletic scholarship (and the proportion receiving): $0 (0%). Average amount of debt of borrowers graduating in 2005: $25,051. Proportion who borrowed: 55%.

CAMPUS LIFE AND EXTRACURRICULAR ACTIVITIES

Campus housing available (% using): coed dorms (95%), women's dorms (3%), men's dorms (2%), special housing for disabled students. Students who live in college-owned, operated, or affiliated housing: 72%. **Student employment:** During the 2005-2006 academic year, 10% of undergraduates worked on campus. Average per-year earnings: $1,500. **Clubs and organizations:** Number of student organizations: 21. Activities include: choral groups, dance, drama/theater, literary magazine, musical theater, radio station, student government, student newspaper, student film society, television station, yearbook. Number of fraternities: 0; sororities: 0. Average proportion of students who stay on campus on weekends: 50%. **Sports pro-**

gram (2005-2006): Member of NCAA III. *Men's intercollegiate varsity sports:* baseball, basketball, football, ice hockey, lacrosse, soccer, tennis. *Women's intercollegiate varsity sports:* basketball, cross-country, lacrosse, soccer, softball, tennis.

SERVICES AND FACILITIES

Basic services: nonremedial tutoring. **Remedial assistance:** reading, math, writing, study skills. **Counseling services:** minority student, personal, older student, psychological. **For learning-disabled students:** School does not offer a structured program with separate admission and additional fees. Total undergraduates in learning-disabled program or receiving services: 359. Services include: remedial math, remedial English, reading machines, remedial reading, tape recorders, other special classes, diagnostic testing service, untimed tests, note-taking services, oral tests, learning center, readers, extended time for tests, tutors, texts on tape, other testing accomodations, other. **Library:** Number of titles: 92,589; number of current serial subscriptions: 555. **Information technology resources:** Students are not required to lease or own a computer. Number of campus computers available to all students: 190. School has a wireless network. Approximate number of users that can be accommodated: 1,000. Proportion of college-owned housing units wired for high-speed internet access: 100%. **Campus safety:** Security services offered: 24-hour foot-and-vehicle patrols, late-night transport/escort service, 24-hour emergency telephones, lighted pathways/sidewalks, student patrols, controlled dormitory access (key, security card, etc).

TRANSFER AND INTERNATIONAL STUDENTS

Transfer students: May apply for admission for the following academic terms: Fall, Spring. Applicants need a minimum number of credits to apply. For fall 2005: Transfer applications received: 431. Transfer applicants offered admission: 208. Transfer applicants enrolled: 108. **International students:** Number of foreign undergraduates: 22 (1% of student body). Number of countries represented: 18. Minimum TOEFL score required: 500 (paper); 173 (computer). Average TOEFL score: 500 (paper).

Eastern Nazarene College

- **Address:** 23 E. Elm Avenue, Quincy, MA 02170
- **Website:** http://www.enc.edu
- **Private; Religious affiliation:** Nazarene
- **Enrollment:** 1,065 full-time; 32 part-time

KEY STATS

✔ **U.S News College Ranking:** fourth tier, Universities–Master's (North)
✔ **SAT Score (25th/75th percentile):** 900-1190
✔ **Tuition:** N/A

Selectivity: Selective	**Room/board:** N/A
Acceptance rate: 56%	**Average debt:** N/A
Student/faculty ratio: 12/1	**Proportion who borrowed:** N/A

UNDERGRADUATE STUDENT BODY STATS

2005-2006 enrollment: 1,065 full-time; 32 part-time. Men: 39%; women: 61%. **Ethnic makeup:** African American: 13%; American-Indian: 1%; Asian American: 3%; Hispanic: 5%; White: 78%; International: 2%. **Religious preference:** Roman Catholic: 5%; Protestant: 30%; No preference: 9%; Nazarene: 55%; Other: 1%.

ADMISSIONS FACTS AND FIGURES

Phone: (617) 745-3732. **Email:** admissions@enc.edu. **Website:** http://www.enc.edu. **Application deadlines for fall 2007:** Regular decision: September 1. Early decision: Not offered. Early action: Not offered. Admission can be deferred. Common application is not accepted. **To apply online, go to:** http://www.enc.edu/main/admissions/application.htm. **Admissions requirements/recommendations:** High school units required (recommended): English: (4); Mathematics: (4); Science: (4); Foreign language: (4); Social studies: (2); History: (2); Academic electives: (0); Total units: (16). Tests: The college uses SAT or ACT scores in admissions decisions. Either SAT or ACT required. For admission to the fall 2007 entering class, the school will accept: ACT with writing, ACT without writing. Campus visit: Recommended. Admissions interview: Required. Off-campus interview: May be arranged. **Factors that count in admissions decisions:** *Academic:* Secondary school record: Very important. Class rank: Important. Letters of recommendation: Very important. Standardized test scores: Very important. Essay: Very important. **Nonacademic:** Interview: Very important. Extracurricular activities: Important. Talent/ability: Considered. Character/personal qualities: Very important. Alumni/ae relationship: Important. Geographical residence: Not considered. State residency: Not considered. Religious affiliation/commitment: Very important. Minority status: Not considered. Volunteer work: Considered. Work experience: Considered. **Other schools with the greatest overlap in applicants:** Eastern University; Gordon College; Northeastern University; University of Massachusetts–Boston. **Admissions statistics for the fall 2005 entering class:** Total applicants: 898. Total accepted: 503. Freshmen enrolled: 213; 49% were from out of state. Overall acceptance rate: 56%. **Average high school grade point average:** 3.2. **First-year students who submitted SAT scores:** 95%. Scores (25/75 percentile): Verbal: 450-600, Math: 450-590, Combined: 900-1190. **First-year students submitting ACT scores:** 14%. Scores (25/75 percentile): English: 19-25, Math: 18-25, Composite: 18-25.

ACADEMICS

Year founded: 1918. **Academic calendar:** 4-1-4. **Degrees offered:** certificate, associate, bachelor's, master's. **Most popular majors:** 31% business administration and management, 12% psychology, 8% communication and media studies, 6% education, 4% religion/religious studies. **Major fields of study:** biological and biomedical sciences; business, management, marketing, and related support services; communication, journalism, and related programs; computer and information sciences and support services; education; engineering; English language and literature/letters; health professions and related clinical sciences; history; liberal arts and sciences studies, and humanities; mathematics and statistics; multi/interdisciplinary studies; parks, recreation, leisure, and fitness studies; philosophy and religious studies; physical sciences; psychology; public administration and social service professions; security and protective services; social sciences; theology and religious vocations; visual and performing arts. **Areas of required coursework:** arts/fine arts, humanities, mathematics, English (including composition), philosophy, sciences (biological or physical), history, social science, other. **Pre-professional programs:** pre-law, pre-medicine, pre-theology, pre-pharmacy. **Special academic programs (% participation):** cooperative (work-study plan) program (2%), cross-registration (1%), double major (18.2%), honors program (9.3%), independent study (2%), internships (13.6%), liberal arts/career combination (8.7%), study abroad (4.2%), teacher certificate program (16.5%). **Teacher certification offered in:** early childhood, special education, elementary, middle/junior high, secondary. **Cooperative education programs:** health professions. **Reserve Officers Training Corps (ROTC):** Army ROTC: Offered at cooperating institution (Boston University); Air Force ROTC: Offered at cooperating institution (Boston University). **Faculty and instruction (2005-2006):** Total instructional faculty: 42 full-time, 5 part-time (66% men; 34% women; 4% minorities). Full-time faculty with Ph.D. or other terminal degree: 62%. Student/faculty ratio: 12/1. Classes of fewer than 20 students: 76%; of 20 to 49 students: 22%; of 50 or more students: 1%. **Advanced Placement and International Baccalaureate credit:** AP tests may be used for: Credit and/or placement. Scores accepted: 3, 4, 5. International Baccalaureate exams may be used for: Credit and/or placement. **Freshmen returning for sophomore year:** 72%. **Graduation rates:** Four-year: 38%; five-year: 40%; six-year: 44%. **Graduate study:** Fields in which graduates pursue further study: Master of Business Administration (MBA), 13%; law, 1%; medicine, 3%; engineering, 3%; theology (or the seminary), 32%; education, 23%; arts and sciences, 16%.

COSTS AND FINANCIAL AID

Financial aid office: (617) 745-3869.

CAMPUS LIFE AND EXTRACURRICULAR ACTIVITIES

Campus housing available (% using): women's dorms (48%), men's dorms (32%), apartments for married students (2%), special housing for disabled students (1%), other housing options (17%). Students who live in college-owned, operated, or affiliated housing: 78%. **Student employment:** During the 2005-2006 academic year, 55% of undergraduates worked on campus. Average per-year earnings: $4,500. **Clubs and organizations:** Number of student organizations: 26. Activities include: choral groups, concert band, drama/theater, jazz band, music ensembles, musical theater, radio station, student government, student newspaper, symphony orchestra, television station, yearbook. Number of fraternities: 0; sororities: 0. Average proportion of students who stay on campus on weekends: 70%. **Sports program (2005-2006):** Member of NCAA III. **Men's intercollegiate varsity sports:** baseball, basketball, cross-country, soccer, tennis. **Women's intercollegiate varsity sports:** basketball, cross-country, soccer, softball, tennis, volleyball.

SERVICES AND FACILITIES

Basic services: nonremedial tutoring, placement service, day care, health service, health insurance. **Remedial assistance:** reading, math, writing, study skills, other. **Counseling services:** minority student, career, personal, academic, older student, psychological, religious, other. **For learning-disabled students:** School does not offer a structured program with separate admission and additional fees. Total undergraduates in learning-disabled program or receiving services: 40. Services include: remedial math, remedial English, reading machines, remedial reading, tape recorders, diagnostic testing service, untimed tests, note-taking services, oral tests, learning center, readers, extended time for tests, tutors, priority seating, proofreading services, texts on tape, typist/scribe, exams on tape or computer, other testing accomodations, other. **Library:** Number of titles: 124,872; number of current serial subscriptions: 613. **Information technology resources:** Students are not required to lease or own a computer. Number of campus computers available to all students: 100. School has a wireless network. Approximate number of users that can be accommodated: 500. Proportion of college-owned housing units wired for high-speed internet access: 100%. **Campus safety:** Security services offered: 24-hour foot-and-vehicle patrols, late-night transport/escort service, 24-hour emergency telephones, controlled dormitory access (key, security card, etc).

TRANSFER AND INTERNATIONAL STUDENTS

Transfer students: May apply for admission for the following academic terms: Fall, Spring. Applicants need a minimum number of credits to apply. For fall 2005: Transfer applications received: 172. Transfer applicants offered admission: 76. Transfer applicants enrolled: 52. **International students:** Number of foreign undergraduates: 12 (2% of student body). Number of countries represented: 12. Minimum TOEFL score required: 500 (paper); 173 (computer).

Elms Coll. (Coll. of Our Lady of the Elms)

- **Address:** 291 Springfield Street, Chicopee, MA 01013
- **Website:** http://www.elms.edu
- **Private; Religious affiliation:** Roman Catholic
- **Enrollment:** N/A

KEY STATS

✔ **U.S News College Ranking:** fourth tier, Universities–Master's (North)
✔ **SAT Score (25th/75th percentile):** 870-1040
✔ **Tuition:** N/A

Selectivity: Less selective	Room/board: N/A
Acceptance rate: 87%	Average debt: N/A
Student/faculty ratio: N/A	Proportion who borrowed: N/A

Emerson College

- **Address:** 120 Boylston Street, Boston, MA 02116-4624
- **Website:** http://www.emerson.edu
- **Private**
- **Enrollment:** 3,092 full-time; 281 part-time

KEY STATS

✔ **U.S News College Ranking:** 15, Universities–Master's (North)
✔ **SAT Score (25th/75th percentile):** 1150-1320
✔ **Tuition:** 2006-2007: $25,834

Selectivity: More selective	Room/board: $10,870
Acceptance rate: 45%	Average debt: $16,222
Student/faculty ratio: 14/1	Proportion who borrowed: 55%

UNDERGRADUATE STUDENT BODY STATS

2005-2006 enrollment: 3,092 full-time; 281 part-time. Men: 43%; women: 57%. **Ethnic makeup:** African American: 2%; American-Indian: 1%; Asian American: 4%; Hispanic: 5%; White: 85%; International: 3%.

ADMISSIONS FACTS AND FIGURES

Phone: (617) 824-8600. **Email:** admission@emerson.edu. **Website:** http://www.emerson.edu. **Application deadlines for fall 2007:** Regular decision: January 5; decision sent by April 1. Early decision: Not offered. Early action: Send application by: November 1; Decision sent by: December 15. Admission can be deferred. **Application fee:** $60. Common application is not accepted. **To apply online, go to:** http://www.emerson.edu/undergraduate_admission. **Admissions requirements/recommendations:** High school units required (recommended): English: 4; Mathematics: 3; Science: 3; Foreign language: 3; Social studies: 3; Academic electives: (4); Total units: 16 (20). Tests: The college uses SAT or ACT scores in admissions decisions. Either SAT or ACT required. For admission to the fall 2007 entering class, the school will accept: ACT with writing. Campus visit: Recommended. Admissions interview: Neither required nor recommended. Off-campus interview: Not available. **Factors that count in admissions decisions:** *Academic:* Secondary school record: Important. Class rank: Important. Letters of recommendation: Important. Standardized test scores: Very important. Essay: Important. *Nonacademic:* Interview: Not considered. Extracurricular activities: Important. Talent/ability: Important. Character/personal qualities: Important. Alumni/ae relationship: Considered. Geographical residence: Considered. State residency: Not considered. Religious affiliation/commitment: Not considered. Minority status: Considered. Volunteer work: Considered. Work experience: Considered. **Other schools with the greatest overlap in applicants:** Boston University; Ithaca College; New York University; Northeastern University; Syracuse University. **Admissions statistics for the fall 2005 entering class:** Total applicants: 5,008. Total accepted: 2,278. Freshmen enrolled: 721; 78% were from out of state. Accepted through early-decision or early-action plans: 46%. Overall acceptance rate: 45%. Non-early acceptance rate: 44%. **Size of waiting list:** 1033 applicants; enrolled from waiting list: 0. **Credentials of fall 2005 freshmen:** 36% ranked in the top 10 percent of their high school class; 83% were in the top 25 percent, and 99% were in the top half. (Proportion submitting class standing: 54%.) **Average high school grade point average:** 3.6. **First-year students who submitted SAT scores:** 96%. Scores (25/75 percentile): Verbal: 590-670, Math: 560-650, Combined: 1150-1320. **First-year students submitting ACT scores:** 20%. Scores (25/75 percentile): English: 26-30, Math: 23-27, Composite: 25-29.

ACADEMICS

Year founded: 1880. **Academic calendar:** Semester. **Degrees offered:** bachelor's, master's, doctorate. **Most popular majors:** 18% cinematography and film/video production, 16% radio and television, 16% creative writing, 14% marketing/marketing management, 10% drama and dramatics/theater arts. **Major fields of study:** business, management, marketing, and related support services; communication, journalism, and related programs; English language and literature/letters; health professions and related clinical sciences; visual and performing arts. **Areas of required coursework:** arts/fine arts, humanities, mathematics, English (including composition), philosophy, foreign languages, sciences (biological or physical), history, social science. **Special academic programs (% participation):** cross-registration (6.7%), double major (3.6%), honors program (3.6%), independent study (17%), internships (58%), student-designed major (1%), study abroad (20.2%), teacher certificate program (1%). **Teacher certification offered in:** elementary, middle/junior high, secondary. **Faculty and instruction (2005-2006):** Total instructional faculty: 143 full-time, 238 part-time (56% men; 44% women; 8% minorities). Full-time faculty with Ph.D. or other terminal degree: 74%. Student/faculty ratio: 14/1. Classes of fewer than 20 students: 60%; of 20 to 49 students: 32%; of 50 or more students: 8%. **Advanced Placement and International Baccalaureate credit:** AP tests may be used for: Credit only. Scores accepted: 3, 4, 5. International Baccalaureate exams may be used for: Credit only. **Freshmen returning for sophomore year:** 86%. **Graduation rates:** Four-year: 66%; five-year: 69%; six-year: 69%. **Graduate study:** 13% of students pursue further study immediately upon graduation.

COSTS AND FINANCIAL AID

Financial aid office: (617) 824-8655. **Expenses (2006-2007):** Tuition and fees 2006-2007: $25,834; room/board: $10,870. Estimated books and supplies: $720; transportation: $567; personal expenses: $900. **Financial aid:** Priority filing date for institution's financial aid form: March 1. In 2005-2006, 64% of undergraduates applied for financial aid. Of those, 53% were determined to have financial need; 86% had their need fully met. Average financial aid package (proportion receiving): $13,823 (53%). Average amount of gift aid, such as scholarships or grants (proportion receiving): $11,514 (41%). Average amount of self-help aid, such as work study or loans (proportion receiving): $5,012 (52%). Average need-based loan (excluding PLUS or other private loans): $4,326. Among students who received need-based aid, the average percentage of need met: 67%. Among students who received aid based on merit, the average award (and the proportion receiving): $15,260 (16%). The average athletic scholarship (and the proportion receiving): $0 (0%). Average amount of debt of borrowers graduating in 2005: $16,222. Proportion who borrowed: 55%.

CAMPUS LIFE AND EXTRACURRICULAR ACTIVITIES

Campus housing available (% using): coed dorms (100%). Students who live in college-owned, operated, or affiliated housing: 42%. **Student employment:** During the 2005-2006 academic year, 25% of undergraduates worked on campus. Average per-year earnings: $1,400. **Clubs and organizations:** Number of student organizations: 66. Activities include: choral groups, dance, drama/theater, literary magazine, musical theater, radio station, student government, student newspaper, student film society, television station, yearbook. Number of fraternities: 4; sororities: 3. Proportion of men in fraternities: 3%; of women in sororities: 3%. Average proportion of students who stay on campus on weekends: 75%. **Sports program (2005-2006):** Member of NCAA III. *Men's intercollegiate varsity sports:* basketball, cross-country, lacrosse, soccer, tennis. *Women's intercollegiate varsity sports:* basketball, cross-country, lacrosse, soccer, softball, tennis, volleyball.

SERVICES AND FACILITIES

Basic services: health service. **Remedial assistance:** reading, math, writing, study skills. **Counseling services:** minority student, career, academic. **For learning-disabled students:** School does not offer a structured program with separate admission and additional fees. Total undergraduates in learning-disabled program or receiving services: 60. Services include: remedial math, remedial English, reading machines, remedial reading, tape recorders, note-taking services, oral tests, learning center, extended time for tests, tutors, texts on tape, other. **Library:** Number of titles: 173,513; number of current serial subscriptions: 642. **Information technology resources:** Students are not required to lease or own a computer. Number of campus computers available to all students: 458. School has a wireless network. Approximate number of users that can be accommodated: 1,000. Proportion of college-owned housing units wired for high-speed internet access: 100%. **Campus safety:** Security services offered: 24-hour foot-and-vehicle patrols, late-night transport/escort service, 24-hour emergency telephones, lighted pathways/sidewalks, controlled dormitory access (key, security card, etc).

TRANSFER AND INTERNATIONAL STUDENTS

Transfer students: May apply for admission for the following academic terms: Fall, Spring. Applicants do not need a minimum number of credits to apply. For fall 2005: Transfer applications received: 609. Transfer applicants offered admission: 321. Transfer applicants enrolled: 182. **International students:** Number of foreign undergraduates: 80 (3% of student body). Number of countries represented: 31. Minimum TOEFL score required: 550 (paper); 213 (computer). Average TOEFL score: 610 (paper).

Emmanuel College

- **Address:** 400 The Fenway, Boston, MA 02115
- **Website:** http://www.emmanuel.edu
- **Private; Religious affiliation:** Roman Catholic
- **Enrollment:** 1,503 full-time; 593 part-time

KEY STATS

✔ **U.S News College Ranking:** 51, Universities–Master's (North)
✔ **SAT Score (25th/75th percentile):** 960-1180
✔ **Tuition:** 2006-2007: $24,200

Selectivity: Selective	**Room/board:** $10,400
Acceptance rate: 61%	**Average debt:** $16,475
Student/faculty ratio: 16/1	**Proportion who borrowed:** 69%

UNDERGRADUATE STUDENT BODY STATS

2005-2006 enrollment: 1,503 full-time; 593 part-time. Men: 25%; women: 75%. **Ethnic makeup:** African American: 7%; Asian American: 4%; Hispanic: 4%; White: 83%; International: 3%.

ADMISSIONS FACTS AND FIGURES

Phone: (617) 735-9715. **Email:** enroll@emmanuel.edu. **Website:** http://www.emmanuel.edu. **Application deadlines for fall 2007:** Regular decision: March 1. Early decision: Send application by: November 1; Decision sent by: December 1. Early action: Not offered. Admission can be deferred. **Application fee:** $40. Common application is accepted. **Admissions requirements/recommendations:** High school units required (recommended): English: 4; Mathematics: 3; Science: 2; Foreign language: 2; Social studies: 2; Total units: 16. Tests: The college uses SAT or ACT scores in admissions decisions. Either SAT or ACT required. For admission to the fall 2007 entering class, the school will accept: ACT without writing. Campus visit: Recommended. Admissions interview: Recommended. Off-campus interview: Not available. **Factors that count in admissions decisions:** *Academic:* Secondary school record: Very important. Class rank: Considered. Letters of recommendation: Very important. Standardized test scores: Very important. Essay: Very important. *Nonacademic:* Interview: Not considered. Extracurricular activities: Considered. Talent/ability: Not considered. Character/personal qualities: Considered. Alumni/ae relationship: Considered. Geographical residence: Not considered. State residency: Not considered. Religious affiliation/commitment: Not considered. Minority status: Not considered. Volunteer work: Considered. Work experience: Not considered. **Other schools with the greatest overlap in applicants:** Boston University; Northeastern University; Stonehill College; Suffolk University; University of Massachusetts–Amherst. **Admissions statistics for the fall 2005 entering class:** Total applicants: 3,107. Total accepted: 1,881. Freshmen enrolled: 438; 37% were from out of state. Accepted through early-decision or early-action plans: 1%. Overall acceptance rate: 61%. Early-decision acceptance rate: 100%. Non-early acceptance rate: 61%. **Size of waiting list:** 0 applicants; enrolled from waiting list: 0. **Credentials of fall 2005 freshmen:** 15% ranked in the top 10 percent of their high school class; 41% were in the top 25 percent, and 78% were in the top half. (Proportion submitting class standing: 66%.) **Average high school grade point average:** 3.5. **First-year students who submitted SAT scores:** 99%. Scores (25/75 percentile): Verbal: 490-600, Math: 470-580, Combined: 960-1180. **First-year students submitting ACT scores:** 11%. Scores (25/75 percentile): English: N/A, Math: N/A, Composite: 20-25.

ACADEMICS

Year founded: 1919. **Academic calendar:** Semester. **Degrees offered:** bachelor's, master's, post-master's certificate. **Most popular majors:** 35% business, management, marketing, and related support services, 9% health professions and related clinical sciences, 8% education, 7% communication, journalism, and related programs, 7% psychology. **Major fields of study:** area, ethnic, cultural, and gender studies; biological and biomedical sciences; business, management, marketing, and related support services; communication, journalism, and related programs; education; English language and literature/letters; foreign languages, literatures, and linguistics; health professions and related clinical sciences; history; mathematics and statistics; multi/interdisciplinary studies; natural resources and conservation; philosophy and religious studies; physical sciences; psychology; social sciences; visual and performing arts. **Areas of required coursework:** arts/fine arts, humanities, computer literacy, mathematics, English (including composition), philosophy, foreign languages, sciences (biological or physical), history, social science, other. **Pre-professional programs:** pre-law, pre-dentistry, pre-medicine, pre-veterinary science. **Special academic programs (% participation):** accelerated program (31%), cross-registration (15%), double major (9%), exchange student program (domestic) (0%), honors program (13%), independent study (14%), internships (43%), student-designed major (2%), study abroad (3%), teacher certificate program (9%). **Teacher certification offered in:** elementary, secondary. **Reserve Officers Training Corps (ROTC):** Army ROTC: Offered at cooperating institution (Boston University). **Faculty and instruction (2005-2006):** Total instructional faculty: 67 full-time, 155 part-time (49% men; 51% women; 9% minorities). Full-time faculty with Ph.D. or other terminal degree: 85%. Student/faculty ratio: 16/1. Classes of fewer than 20 students: 63%; of 20 to 49 students: 38%; of 50 or more students: 0%. **Advanced Placement and International Baccalaureate credit:** AP tests may be used for: Credit only. Scores accepted: 3, 4, 5. International Baccalaureate exams may be used for: Credit only. **Freshmen returning for sophomore year:** 82%. **Graduation rates:** Four-year: 45%; five-year: 52%; six-year: 60%.

COSTS AND FINANCIAL AID

Financial aid office: (617) 735-9938. **Expenses (2006-2007):** Tuition and fees 2006-2007: $24,200; room/board: $10,400. Estimated books and supplies: $880; transportation: $270; personal expenses: $1,935. **Financial aid:** Priority filing date for institution's financial aid form: April 1. In 2005-2006, 92% of undergraduates applied for financial aid. Of those, 78% were determined to have financial need; 18% had their need fully met. Average financial aid package (proportion receiving): $16,201 (78%). Average

amount of gift aid, such as scholarships or grants (proportion receiving): $8,209 (61%). Average amount of self-help aid, such as work study or loans (proportion receiving): $5,128 (78%). Average need-based loan (excluding PLUS or other private loans): $4,368. Among students who received need-based aid, the average percentage of need met: 70%. Among students who received aid based on merit, the average award (and the proportion receiving): $9,202 (14%). The average athletic scholarship (and the proportion receiving): $0 (0%). Average amount of debt of borrowers graduating in 2005: $16,475. Proportion who borrowed: 69%.

CAMPUS LIFE AND EXTRACURRICULAR ACTIVITIES

Campus housing available (% using): coed dorms (100%). Students who live in college-owned, operated, or affiliated housing: 82%. **Student employment:** During the 2005-2006 academic year, 20% of undergraduates worked on campus. Average per-year earnings: $1,250. **Clubs and organizations:** Number of student organizations: 97. Activities include: choral groups, dance, drama/theater, literary magazine, musical theater, pep band, radio station, student government, student newspaper, symphony orchestra, yearbook. Number of fraternities: 0; sororities: 0. Average proportion of students who stay on campus on weekends: 90%. **Sports program (2005-2006):** Member of NCAA III. *Men's intercollegiate varsity sports:* basketball, cross-country, soccer, track and field (indoor), track and field (outdoor), volleyball. *Women's intercollegiate varsity sports:* basketball, cross-country, soccer, softball, tennis, track and field (indoor), track and field (outdoor), volleyball.

SERVICES AND FACILITIES

Basic services: nonremedial tutoring, placement service, health service. **Remedial assistance:** study skills. **Counseling services:** career, personal, academic, psychological, religious. **For learning-disabled students:** School does not offer a structured program with separate admission and additional fees. Total undergraduates in learning-disabled program or receiving services: 59. Services include: tape recorders, other special classes, note-taking services, oral tests, learning center, readers, extended time for tests, tutors, waiver of foreign language degree requirement, waiver of math degree requirement. **Library:** Number of titles: 97,907; number of current serial subscriptions: 396. **Information technology resources:** Students are not required to lease or own a computer. Number of campus computers available to all students: 190. School has a wireless network. Approximate number of users that can be accommodated: 800. Proportion of college-owned housing units wired for high-speed internet access: 100%. **Campus safety:** Security services offered: 24-hour foot-and-vehicle patrols, late-night transport/escort service, lighted pathways/sidewalks, controlled dormitory access (key, security card, etc).

TRANSFER AND INTERNATIONAL STUDENTS

Transfer students: May apply for admission for the following academic terms: Fall, Spring. Applicants do not need a minimum number of credits to apply. For fall 2005: Transfer applications received: 361. Transfer applicants offered admission: 110. Transfer applicants enrolled: 61. **International students:** Number of foreign undergraduates: 52 (3% of student body). Number of countries represented: 31. Minimum TOEFL score required: 550 (paper); 213 (computer). Average TOEFL score: 583 (paper).

Endicott College

- **Address:** 376 Hale Street, Beverly, MA 01915
- **Website:** http://www.endicott.edu
- **Private**
- **Enrollment:** 1,860 full-time; 178 part-time

KEY STATS

✔ **U.S News College Ranking:** 20, Comp. Coll.–Bachelor's (North)
✔ **SAT Score (25th/75th percentile):** 980-1160
✔ **Tuition:** 2005-2006: $19,336

Selectivity: Selective	**Room/board:** $9,766
Acceptance rate: 47%	**Average debt:** N/A
Student/faculty ratio: 18/1	**Proportion who borrowed:** N/A

UNDERGRADUATE STUDENT BODY STATS

2005-2006 enrollment: 1,860 full-time; 178 part-time. Men: 42%; women: 58%. **Ethnic makeup:** African American: 1%; Hispanic: 1%; White: 93%; International: 4%.

ADMISSIONS FACTS AND FIGURES

Phone: (978) 921-1000. **Email:** admissio@endicott.edu. **Website:** http://www.endicott.edu. **Application deadlines for fall 2007:** Regular decision: February 15. Early decision: Not offered. Early action: Not offered. Admission can be deferred. **Application fee:** $40. Common application is accepted. **Admissions requirements/recommendations:** High school units required (recommended): English: (16); Mathematics: (4); Science: (3); Foreign language: (0); Social studies: (2); History: (1); Academic electives: (4). Tests: The college uses SAT or ACT scores in admissions decisions. Either SAT or ACT required. For admission to the fall 2007 entering class, the school will accept: ACT without writing. Campus visit: Recommended. Admissions interview: Recommended. Off-campus interview: Not available. **Factors that count in admissions decisions:** *Academic:* Secondary school record: Very important. Class rank: Important. Letters of recommendation: Considered. Standardized test scores: Important. Essay: Important. *Nonacademic:* Interview: Considered. Extracurricular activities: Important. Talent/ability: Important. Character/personal qualities: Very important. Alumni/ae relationship: Important. Geographical residence: Important. State residency: Considered. Religious affiliation/commitment: Not considered. Minority status: Considered. Volunteer work: Important. Work experience: Important. **Other schools with the greatest overlap in applicants:** Merrimack College; Northeastern University; Salve Regina University; University of Massachusetts–Amherst; University of New Hampshire. **Admissions statistics for the fall 2005 entering class:** Total applicants: 3,081. Total accepted: 1,455. Freshmen enrolled: 502; 51% were from out of state. Overall acceptance rate: 47%. **Size of waiting list:** 407 applicants; enrolled from waiting list: 2. **Credentials of fall 2005 freshmen:** 11% ranked in the top 10 percent of their high school class; 39% were in the top 25 percent, and 89% were in the top half. (Proportion submitting class standing: 68%.) **First-year students who submitted SAT scores:** 96%. Scores (25/75 percentile): Verbal: 490-580, Math: 490-580, Combined: 980-1160. **First-year students submitting ACT scores:** 15%. Scores (25/75 percentile): English: N/A, Math: N/A, Composite: 20-23.

ACADEMICS

Year founded: 1939. **Academic calendar:** 4-1-4. **Degrees offered:** bachelor's, master's. **Most popular majors:** 33% business, management, marketing, and related support services, 16% visual and performing arts, 13% psychology, 11% parks, recreation, leisure, and fitness studies, 9% communication, journalism, and related programs. **Major fields of study:** business, management, marketing, and related support services; communication, journalism, and related programs; education; English language and literature/letters; health professions and related clinical sciences; liberal arts and sciences studies, and humanities; natural resources and conservation; parks, recreation, leisure, and fitness studies; psychology; security and protective services; social sciences; visual and performing arts. **Areas of required coursework:** humanities, mathematics, English (including composition), sciences (biological or physical), social science. **Special academic programs (% participation):** accelerated program, cross-registration, distance learning, honors program (7%), independent study, internships (100%), liberal arts/career combination, student-designed major, study abroad, teacher certificate program. **Teacher certification offered in:** early childhood, special education, elementary. **Reserve Officers Training Corps (ROTC):** Army ROTC: Offered at cooperating institution (MIT); Air Force ROTC: Offered at cooperating institution (U-Mass Lowell). **Faculty and instruction (2005-2006):** Total instructional faculty: 66 full-time, 84 part-time (44% men; 56% women; 3% minorities). Full-time faculty with Ph.D. or other terminal degree: 58%. Student/faculty ratio: 18/1. Classes of fewer than 20 students: 53%; of 20 to 49 students: 47%; of 50 or more students: 0%. **Advanced Placement and International Baccalaureate credit:** AP tests may be used for: Credit only. Scores accepted: 3, 4, 5. International Baccalaureate exams may be used for: Credit only. **Freshmen returning for sophomore year:** 81%. **Graduation rates:** Four-year: 48%; five-year: 55%; six-year: 52%. **Graduate study:** 14% of students pursue further study immediately upon graduation. Fields in which graduates pursue further study: Master of Business Administration (MBA), 14%; law, 7%; education, 57%.

COSTS AND FINANCIAL AID

Financial aid office: (978) 232-2070. **Expenses (2005-2006):** Tuition and fees 2005-2006: $19,336; room/board: $9,766. Estimated books and supplies: $600; transportation: $1,000; personal expenses: $1,000. **Financial aid:** Priority filing date for institution's financial aid form: March 15.

CAMPUS LIFE AND EXTRACURRICULAR ACTIVITIES

Campus housing available: coed dorms, women's dorms, apartment for single students, special housing for disabled students, special housing for international students, other housing options. Students who live in college-owned, operated, or affiliated housing: 86%. **Student employment:** During the 2005-2006 academic year, 19% of undergraduates worked on campus. Average per-year earnings: $1,500. **Clubs and organizations:** Number of student organizations: 24. Activities include: choral groups, dance, jazz band, literary magazine, radio station, student government, student newspaper, television station, yearbook. Number of fraternities: 0; sororities: 0. Average proportion of students who stay on campus on weekends: 68%. **Sports program (2005-2006):** Member of NCAA III. *Men's intercollegiate varsity sports:* baseball, basketball, cross-country, football, golf, lacrosse, soccer, tennis, volleyball. *Women's intercollegiate varsity sports:* basketball, cross-country, equestrian sports, field hockey, lacrosse, soccer, softball, tennis, volleyball.

SERVICES AND FACILITIES

Basic services: nonremedial tutoring, health service, health insurance. **Counseling services:** career, personal, academic, religious. **For learning-disabled students:** School does not offer a structured program with separate admission and additional fees. Services include: tape recorders, untimed tests, note-taking services, oral tests, learning center, readers, extended time for tests, tutors, priority seating, texts on tape. **Library:** Number of titles: 116,800; number of current serial subscriptions: 34,200. **Information technology resources:** Students are not required to lease or own a computer. Number of campus computers available to all students: 156. School has a wireless network. Approximate number of users that can be accommodated: 1,000. Proportion of college-owned housing units wired for high-speed internet access: 100%. **Campus safety:** Security services offered: 24-hour foot-and-vehicle patrols, late-night transport/escort service, 24-hour emergency telephones, lighted pathways/sidewalks, controlled dormitory access (key, security card, etc).

TRANSFER AND INTERNATIONAL STUDENTS

Transfer students: May apply for admission for the following academic terms: Fall, Spring. Applicants do not need a minimum number of credits to apply. For fall 2005: Transfer applications received: 204. Transfer applicants offered admission: 67. Transfer applicants enrolled: 43. **International students:** Number of foreign undergraduates: 61 (4% of student body). Minimum TOEFL score required: 550 (paper); 213 (computer). Average TOEFL score: 551 (paper).

Fitchburg State College

- **Address:** 160 Pearl Street, Fitchburg, MA 01420-2697
- **Website:** http://www.fsc.edu
- **Public**
- **Enrollment:** 2,950 full-time; 703 part-time

KEY STATS

✔ **U.S News College Ranking:** third tier, Universities–Master's (North)
✔ **SAT Score (25th/75th percentile):** 930-1120
✔ **Tuition:** 2006-2007: $5,542 in state, $11,622 out of state

Selectivity: Less selective	**Room/board:** $6,486
Acceptance rate: 67%	**Average debt:** $10,660
Student/faculty ratio: 16/1	**Proportion who borrowed:** 55%

UNDERGRADUATE STUDENT BODY STATS

2005-2006 enrollment: 2,950 full-time; 703 part-time. Men: 44%; women: 56%. **Ethnic makeup:** African American: 3%; Asian American: 2%; Hispanic: 3%; White: 90%; International: 1%.

ADMISSIONS FACTS AND FIGURES

Phone: (978) 665-3144. **Email:** admissions@fsc.edu. **Website:** http://www.fsc.edu. **Application deadlines for fall 2007:** Regular decision: Rolling. Early decision: Not offered. Early action: Not offered. Admission can be deferred. **Application fee:** $10. Common application is not accepted. **To apply online, go to:** http://www.fsc.edu/admissions/. **Admissions requirements/recommendations:** High school units required (recommended): English: 4; Mathematics: 3; Science: 3; Foreign language: 2; Social studies: 1; History: 1; Academic electives: 2; Total units: 16. Tests: The college uses SAT or ACT scores in admissions decisions. Either SAT or ACT required. For admission to the fall 2007 entering class, the school will accept: ACT with writing, ACT without writing. Campus visit: Recommended. Admissions interview: Neither required nor recommended. Off-campus interview: Not available. **Factors that count in admissions decisions:** *Academic:* Secondary school record: Very important. Class rank: Not considered. Letters of recommendation: Considered. Standardized test scores: Important. Essay: Important. *Nonacademic:* Interview: Not considered. Extracurricular activities: Considered. Talent/ability: Considered. Character/personal qualities: Not considered. Alumni/ae relationship: Considered. Geographical residence: Not considered. State residency: Not considered. Religious affiliation/commitment: Not considered. Minority status: Not considered. Volunteer work: Considered. Work experience: Considered. **Other schools with the greatest overlap in applicants:** Bridgewater State College; Framingham State College; University of Massachusetts–Lowell; Westfield State College; Worcester State College. **Admissions statistics for the fall 2005 entering class:** Total applicants: 3,070. Total accepted: 2,059. Freshmen enrolled: 607; 10% were from out of state. Overall acceptance rate: 67%. Size of waiting list: 10 applicants; enrolled from waiting list: 3. **Average high school grade point average:** 2.9. **First-year students who submitted SAT scores:** 99%. Scores (25/75 percentile): Verbal: 460-560, Math: 470-560, Combined: 930-1120. **First-year students submitting ACT scores:** 10%. Scores (25/75 percentile): English: N/A, Math: N/A, Composite: 18-23.

ACADEMICS

Year founded: 1894. **Academic calendar:** Semester. **Degrees offered:** certificate, bachelor's, post-bachelor's certificate, master's, post-master's certificate. **Most popular majors:** 18% business administration, management, and operations, 17% communication and media studies, 12% education, 9% nursing, 8% liberal arts and sciences studies, and humanities. **Major fields of study:** biological and biomedical sciences; business, management, marketing, and related support services; communication, journalism, and related programs; computer and information sciences and support services; education; engineering technologies/technicians; English language and literature/letters; health professions and related clinical sciences; history; liberal arts and sciences studies, and humanities; mathematics and statistics; parks, recreation, leisure, and fitness studies; psychology; public administration and social service professions; security and protective services; social sciences; visual and performing arts. **Areas of required coursework:** arts/fine arts, humanities, computer literacy, mathematics, English (including composition), philosophy, sciences (biological or physical), history, social science. **Special academic programs:** accelerated program, cross-registration, distance learning, double major, dual enrollment, honors program, independent study, internships, liberal arts/career combination, student-designed major, study abroad, teacher certificate program. **Teacher certification offered in:** early childhood, special education, elementary, vo-tech, middle/junior high, secondary. **Reserve Officers Training Corps (ROTC):** Army ROTC: Offered at cooperating institution (Worcester Polytech Institute). **Faculty and instruction (2005-2006):** Total instructional faculty: 166 full-time, 76 part-time (53% men; 47% women; 11% minorities). Full-time faculty with Ph.D. or other terminal degree: 90%. Student/faculty ratio: 16/1. Classes of fewer than 20 students: 52%; of 20 to 49 students: 48%. **Advanced Placement and International Baccalaureate credit:** AP tests may be used for: Credit and/or placement. Scores accepted: 3, 4, 5. **Freshmen returning for sophomore year:** 75%. **Graduation rates:** Four-year: 21%; five-year: 48%; six-year: 48%.

COSTS AND FINANCIAL AID

Financial aid office: (978) 665-3156. **Expenses (2006-2007):** Tuition and fees 2006-2007: $5,542 in state, $11,622 out of state; room/board: $6,486. Estimated books and supplies: $600; transportation: $350; personal expenses: $1,580. **Financial aid:** Priority filing date for institution's financial aid form: March 1. In 2005-2006, 84% of undergraduates applied for financial aid. Of those, 47% were determined to have financial need; 90% had their need fully met. Average financial aid package (proportion receiving): $6,565 (45%). Average amount of gift aid, such as scholarships or grants (proportion receiving): $3,308 (36%). Average amount of self-help aid, such as work study or loans (proportion receiving): $2,923 (42%). Average need-based loan (excluding PLUS or other private loans): $2,684. Among students who received need-based aid, the average percentage of need met: 93%. Among students who received aid based on merit, the average award (and the proportion receiving): $1,767 (1%). The average athletic scholarship (and the proportion receiving): $0 (0%). Average amount of debt of borrowers graduating in 2005: $10,660. Proportion who borrowed: 55%.

CAMPUS LIFE AND EXTRACURRICULAR ACTIVITIES

Campus housing available: coed dorms, special housing for disabled students, special housing for international students. Students who live in college-owned, operated, or affiliated housing: 43%. **Clubs and organizations:**

Number of student organizations: 57. Activities include: choral groups, concert band, dance, drama/theater, jazz band, literary magazine, radio station, student government, student newspaper, yearbook. Number of fraternities: 2; sororities: 3. Proportion of men in fraternities: 1%; of women in sororities: 2%. Average proportion of students who stay on campus on weekends: 35%. **Sports program (2005-2006):** Member of NCAA III. *Men's intercollegiate varsity sports:* baseball, basketball, cross-country, football, ice hockey, soccer, track and field (indoor), track and field (outdoor). *Women's intercollegiate varsity sports:* basketball, cross-country, field hockey, soccer, softball, track and field (indoor), track and field (outdoor).

SERVICES AND FACILITIES

Basic services: nonremedial tutoring, day care, health service, health insurance. **Remedial assistance:** reading, math, writing, study skills. **Counseling services:** career, personal, academic, psychological. **For learning-disabled students:** School does not offer a structured program with separate admission and additional fees. Services include: remedial math, remedial English, remedial reading, tape recorders, note-taking services, oral tests, extended time for tests, tutors, typist/scribe, exams on tape or computer, other testing accomodations. **Library:** Number of titles: 242,418; number of current serial subscriptions: 2,208. **Information technology resources:** Students are not required to lease or own a computer. Number of campus computers available to all students: 100. School has a wireless network. Approximate number of users that can be accommodated: 200. Proportion of college-owned housing units wired for high-speed internet access: 100%. **Campus safety:** Security services offered: 24-hour foot-and-vehicle patrols, late-night transport/escort service, 24-hour emergency telephones, lighted pathways/sidewalks, controlled dormitory access (key, security card, etc).

TRANSFER AND INTERNATIONAL STUDENTS

Transfer students: May apply for admission for the following academic terms: Fall, Spring. Applicants need a minimum number of credits to apply. For fall 2005: Transfer applications received: 789. Transfer applicants offered admission: 718. Transfer applicants enrolled: 392. **International students:** Number of foreign undergraduates: 24 (1% of student body). Minimum TOEFL score required: 550 (paper); 213 (computer).

Framingham State College

- **Address:** 100 State Street, PO Box 9101, Framingham, MA 01701-9101
- **Website:** http://www.framingham.edu
- **Public**
- **Enrollment:** 3,045 full-time; 727 part-time

KEY STATS

✔ **U.S News College Ranking:** fourth tier, Universities–Master's (North)
✔ **SAT Score (25th/75th percentile):** 960-1120
✔ **Tuition:** 2005-2006: $4,999 in state, $11,079 out of state

Selectivity: Selective	Room/board: $6,157
Acceptance rate: 64%	Average debt: $12,800
Student/faculty ratio: 15/1	Proportion who borrowed: 53%

UNDERGRADUATE STUDENT BODY STATS

2005-2006 enrollment: 3,045 full-time; 727 part-time. Men: 34%; women: 66%. **Ethnic makeup:** African American: 3%; Asian American: 3%; Hispanic: 3%; White: 89%; International: 1%.

ADMISSIONS FACTS AND FIGURES

Phone: (508) 626-4500. **Email:** admiss@frc.mass.edu. **Website:** http://www.framingham.edu. **Application deadlines for fall 2007:** Regular decision: May 1. Early decision: Not offered. Early action: Send application by: November 15; Decision sent by: December 15. Admission can be deferred. **Application fee:** $25. Common application is not accepted. **Admissions requirements/recommendations:** High school units required (recommended): English: 4 (4); Mathematics: 3 (4); Science: 3 (4); Foreign language: 2 (4); Social studies: 1 (1); History: 1 (2); Academic electives: 2 (2); Total units: 16 (20). Tests: The college uses SAT or ACT scores in admissions decisions. Either SAT or ACT required. For admission to the fall 2007 entering class, the school will accept: ACT with writing. Campus visit: Recommended. Admissions interview: Neither required nor recommended. Off-campus interview: Not available. **Factors that count in admissions decisions:** *Academic:* Secondary school record: Very important. Class rank:

Important. Letters of recommendation: Considered. Standardized test scores: Important. Essay: Considered. **Nonacademic:** Interview: Not considered. Extracurricular activities: Considered. Talent/ability: Considered. Character/personal qualities: Considered. Alumni/ae relationship: Considered. Geographical residence: Not considered. State residency: Considered. Religious affiliation/commitment: Not considered. Minority status: Not considered. Volunteer work: Considered. Work experience: Considered. **Other schools with the greatest overlap in applicants:** Bridgewater State College; University of Massachusetts–Amherst; University of Massachusetts–Dartmouth; University of Massachusetts–Lowell; Westfield State College. **Admissions statistics for the fall 2005 entering class:** Total applicants: 3,955. Total accepted: 2,518. Freshmen enrolled: 670; 8% were from out of state. Accepted through early-decision or early-action plans: 8%. Overall acceptance rate: 64%. Non-early acceptance rate: 63%. **Credentials of fall 2005 freshmen:** 8% ranked in the top 10 percent of their high school class; 31% were in the top 25 percent, and 74% were in the top half. (Proportion submitting class standing: 83%.) **Average high school grade point average:** 3.1. **First-year students who submitted SAT scores:** 99%. Scores (25/75 percentile): Verbal: 480-560, Math: 480-560, Combined: 960-1120.

ACADEMICS

Year founded: 1839. **Academic calendar:** Semester. **Degrees offered:** bachelor's, post-bachelor's certificate, master's. **Most popular majors:** 17% business, management, marketing, and related support services, 15% social sciences, 11% family and consumer sciences/human sciences, 11% psychology, 9% communication, journalism, and related programs. **Major fields of study:** agriculture, agriculture operations, and related sciences; biological and biomedical sciences; business, management, marketing, and related support services; communications technologies/technicians and support services; computer and information sciences and support services; education; English language and literature/letters; family and consumer sciences/human sciences; foreign languages, literatures, and linguistics; health professions and related clinical sciences; history; liberal arts and sciences studies, and humanities; mathematics and statistics; physical sciences; psychology; social sciences; visual and performing arts. **Areas of required coursework:** arts/fine arts, humanities, mathematics, English (including composition), foreign languages, sciences (biological or physical), history, social science. **Pre-professional programs:** pre-law, pre-dentistry, pre-medicine, pre-veterinary science. **Special academic programs:** cross-registration, distance learning, double major, honors program, independent study, internships, liberal arts/career combination, study abroad, teacher certificate program. **Teacher certification offered in:** early childhood, elementary, secondary. **Reserve Officers Training Corps (ROTC):** Army ROTC: Offered at cooperating institution (Boston College; WPI; Northeastern Univ.). **Faculty and instruction (2005-2006):** Total instructional faculty: 167 full-time, 67 part-time (46% men; 54% women; 8% minorities). Full-time faculty with Ph.D. or other terminal degree: 85%. Student/faculty ratio: 15/1. Classes of fewer than 20 students: 31%; of 20 to 49 students: 67%; of 50 or more students: 1%. **Advanced Placement and International Baccalaureate credit:** AP tests may be used for: Credit and/or placement. Scores accepted: 3, 4, 5. **Freshmen returning for sophomore year:** 72%. **Graduation rates:** Four-year: 23%; five-year: 38%; six-year: 42%. **Graduate study:** 15% of students pursue further study within one year.

COSTS AND FINANCIAL AID

Financial aid office: (508) 626-4534. **Expenses (2005-2006):** Tuition and fees 2005-2006: $4,999 in state, $11,079 out of state; room/board: $6,157. Estimated books and supplies: $700; transportation: $700; personal expenses: $1,200. **Financial aid:** Priority filing date for institution's financial aid form: March 1. In 2005-2006, 80% of undergraduates applied for financial aid. Of those, 56% were determined to have financial need; 71% had their need fully met. Average financial aid package (proportion receiving): $6,242 (56%). Average amount of gift aid, such as scholarships or grants (proportion receiving): $3,393 (45%). Average amount of self-help aid, such as work study or loans (proportion receiving): $2,201 (51%). Average need-based loan (excluding PLUS or other private loans): $2,052. Among students who received need-based aid, the average percentage of need met: 82%. Among students who received aid based on merit, the average award (and the proportion receiving): $1,923 (2%). The average athletic scholarship (and the proportion receiving): $0 (0%). Average amount of debt of borrowers graduating in 2005: $12,800. Proportion who borrowed: 53%.

CAMPUS LIFE AND EXTRACURRICULAR ACTIVITIES

Campus housing available (% using): coed dorms (75%), women's dorms (25%). Students who live in college-owned, operated, or affiliated housing:

49%. **Student employment:** During the 2005-2006 academic year, 10% of undergraduates worked on campus. Average per-year earnings: $982. **Clubs and organizations:** Number of student organizations: 50. Activities include: choral groups, dance, drama/theater, literary magazine, musical theater, radio station, student government, student newspaper, yearbook. Number of fraternities: 0; sororities: 0. Average proportion of students who stay on campus on weekends: 45%. **Sports program (2005-2006):** Member of NCAA III. **Men's intercollegiate varsity sports:** baseball, basketball, cross-country, football, ice hockey, soccer. **Women's intercollegiate varsity sports:** basketball, cross-country, field hockey, soccer, softball, volleyball.

SERVICES AND FACILITIES

Basic services: women's center, placement service, health service, health insurance. **Remedial assistance:** reading, math, writing, study skills. **Counseling services:** minority student, career, military, personal, veteran student, academic, older student, psychological, birth control, religious. **For learning-disabled students:** School does not offer a structured program with separate admission and additional fees. Services include: learning center, other. **Library:** Number of titles: 204,828; number of current serial subscriptions: 419. **Information technology resources:** Students are required to lease or own a computer. Number of campus computers available to all students: 200. School has a wireless network. Proportion of college-owned housing units wired for high-speed internet access: 100%. **Campus safety:** Security services offered: 24-hour foot-and-vehicle patrols, late-night transport/escort service, 24-hour emergency telephones, lighted pathways/sidewalks, controlled dormitory access (key, security card, etc).

TRANSFER AND INTERNATIONAL STUDENTS

Transfer students: May apply for admission for the following academic terms: Fall, Spring. Applicants need a minimum number of credits to apply. For fall 2005: Transfer applications received: 948. Transfer applicants offered admission: 604. Transfer applicants enrolled: 341. **International students:** Number of foreign undergraduates: 51 (1% of student body). Number of countries represented: 46. Minimum TOEFL score required: 550 (paper); 213 (computer). Average TOEFL score: 560 (paper).

Gordon College

- **Address:** 255 Grapevine Road, Wenham, MA 01984
- **Website:** http://www.gordon.edu
- **Private; Religious affiliation:** Protestant nondenominational
- **Enrollment:** 1,555 full-time; 34 part-time

KEY STATS

✔ **U.S News College Ranking:** third tier, Liberal Arts Colleges
✔ **SAT Score (25th/75th percentile):** 1090-1320
✔ **Tuition:** 2006-2007: $24,278

Selectivity: More selective	**Room/board:** $6,640
Acceptance rate: 84%	**Average debt:** $11,192
Student/faculty ratio: 14/1	**Proportion who borrowed:** 47%

UNDERGRADUATE STUDENT BODY STATS

2005-2006 enrollment: 1,555 full-time; 34 part-time. Men: 37%; women: 63%. **Ethnic makeup:** African American: 1%; Asian American: 2%; Hispanic: 3%; White: 91%; International: 2%.

ADMISSIONS FACTS AND FIGURES

Phone: (866) 464-6736. **Email:** admissions@gordon.edu. **Website:** http://www.gordon.edu. **Application deadlines for fall 2007:** Regular decision: Rolling. Early decision: Send application by: November 15; Decision sent by: December 15. Early action: Send application by: December 1; Decision sent by: January 1. Admission can be deferred. **Application fee:** $50. Common application is accepted. **To apply online, go to:** https://www.gordon.edu/Admissions/Application/NewApplicant.asp. **Admissions requirements/recommendations:** High school units required (recommended): English: 4; Mathematics: 2 (3); Science: 2 (3); Foreign language: 2 (4); Social studies: 2 (3); Academic electives: 5; Total units: 20 (25). Tests: The college uses SAT or ACT scores in admissions decisions. Either SAT or ACT required. For admission to the fall 2007 entering class, the school will accept: ACT with writing. Campus visit: Recommended. Admissions interview: Required. Off-campus interview: May be arranged. **Factors that count in admissions decisions:** *Academic:* Secondary school record: Very important. Class rank: Very important. Letters of recommendation: Very important. Standardized test scores: Very important. Essay: Very important. *Nonacademic:* Interview: Very important. Extracurricular activities: Very important. Talent/ability: Important. Character/personal qualities: Very important. Alumni/ae relationship: Considered. Geographical residence: Not considered. State residency: Not considered. Religious affiliation/commitment: Very important. Minority status: Considered. Volunteer work: Considered. Work experience: Considered. **Other schools with the greatest overlap in applicants:** Eastern Nazarene College; Grove City College; Houghton College; Messiah College; Wheaton College. **Admissions statistics for the fall 2005 entering class:** Total applicants: 1,098. Total accepted: 921. Freshmen enrolled: 414; 77% were from out of state. Accepted through early-decision or early-action plans: 66%. Overall acceptance rate: 84%. Early-decision acceptance rate: 89%. Non-early acceptance rate: 73%. **Credentials of fall 2005 freshmen:** 24% ranked in the top 10 percent of their high school class; 50% were in the top 25 percent, and 68% were in the top half. (Proportion submitting class standing: 74%.) **Average high school grade point average:** 3.6. **First-year students who submitted SAT scores:** 93%. Scores (25/75 percentile): Verbal: 550-670, Math: 540-650, Combined: 1090-1320. **First-year students submitting ACT scores:** 19%. Scores (25/75 percentile): English: N/A, Math: N/A, Composite: 23-29.

ACADEMICS

Year founded: 1889. **Academic calendar:** Semester. **Degrees offered:** bachelor's, master's. **Most popular majors:** 13% education, 12% English language and literature, 10% business/commerce, 10% social sciences, 8% psychology. **Major fields of study:** biological and biomedical sciences; business, management, marketing, and related support services; communication, journalism, and related programs; computer and information sciences and support services; education; English language and literature/letters; foreign languages, literatures, and linguistics; history; mathematics and statistics; multi/interdisciplinary studies; parks, recreation, leisure, and fitness studies; philosophy and religious studies; physical sciences; psychology; public administration and social service professions; social sciences; theology and religious vocations; visual and performing arts. **Areas of required coursework:** arts/fine arts, humanities, English (including composition), philosophy, foreign languages, sciences (biological or physical), history, social science, other. **Pre-professional programs:** pre-law, pre-medicine, pre-theology, pre-veterinary science. **Special academic programs:** cooperative (work-study plan) program, cross-registration, double major, exchange student program (domestic), honors program, independent study, internships, liberal arts/career combination, student-designed major, study abroad, teacher certificate program, other. **Teacher certification offered in:** early childhood, special education, elementary, middle/junior high, secondary, bilingual/bicultural. **Cooperative education programs:** engineering, health professions. **Reserve Officers Training Corps (ROTC):** Army ROTC: Offered at cooperating institution; Air Force ROTC: Offered at cooperating institution (University of Massachusetts at Lowell and Boston University). **Faculty and instruction (2005-2006):** Total instructional faculty: 93 full-time, 52 part-time (61% men; 39% women; 8% minorities). Full-time faculty with Ph.D. or other terminal degree: 86%. Student/faculty ratio: 14/1. Classes of fewer than 20 students: 65%; of 20 to 49 students: 29%; of 50 or more students: 6%. **Advanced Placement and International Baccalaureate credit:** AP tests may be used for: Credit only. Scores accepted: 4, 5. International Baccalaureate exams may be used for: Credit only. **Freshmen returning for sophomore year:** 87%. **Graduation rates:** Four-year: 54%; five-year: 71%; six-year: 74%. **Graduate study:** 20% of students pursue further study immediately upon graduation; 57% within five years. Fields in which graduates pursue further study: Master of Business Administration (MBA), 3%; law, 7%; medicine, 11%; theology (or the seminary), 7%.

COSTS AND FINANCIAL AID

Financial aid office: (978) 867-4246. **Expenses (2006-2007):** Tuition and fees 2006-2007: $24,278; room/board: $6,640. Estimated books and supplies: $800; transportation: $400; personal expenses: $1,000. **Financial aid:** Priority filing date for institution's financial aid form: March 1. In 2005-2006, 78% of undergraduates applied for financial aid. Of those, 67% were determined to have financial need; 18% had their need fully met. Average financial aid package (proportion receiving): $14,540 (67%). Average amount of gift aid, such as scholarships or grants (proportion receiving): $10,093 (65%). Average amount of self-help aid, such as work study or loans (proportion receiving): $5,398 (59%). Average need-based loan (excluding PLUS or other private loans): $4,473. Among students who received need-based aid, the average percentage of need met: 70%. Among students who received aid based on merit, the average award (and the proportion receiving): $12,383 (30%). The average athletic scholarship (and the proportion receiving): $0 (0%). Average amount of debt of borrowers graduating in 2005: $11,192. Proportion who borrowed: 47%.

CAMPUS LIFE AND EXTRACURRICULAR ACTIVITIES

Campus housing available (% using): coed dorms (77%), women's dorms (0%), men's dorms (3%), apartments for married students (0%), apartment for single students (20%). Students who live in college-owned, operated, or affiliated housing: 89%. **Student employment:** During the 2005-2006 academic year, 43% of undergraduates worked on campus. Average per-year earnings: $1,260. **Clubs and organizations:** Number of student organizations: 35. Activities include: choral groups, concert band, drama/theater, jazz band, literary magazine, music ensembles, musical theater, student government, student newspaper, symphony orchestra, yearbook. Number of fraternities: 0; sororities: 0. Average proportion of students who stay on campus on weekends: 70%. **Sports program (2005-2006):** Member of NCAA III. *Men's intercollegiate varsity sports:* baseball, basketball, cross-country, lacrosse, soccer, swimming and diving, tennis, track and field (indoor), track and field (outdoor). *Women's intercollegiate varsity sports:* basketball, cross-country, field hockey, lacrosse, soccer, softball, swimming and diving, tennis, track and field (indoor), track and field (outdoor), volleyball.

SERVICES AND FACILITIES

Basic services: placement service, health service, health insurance. **Remedial assistance:** reading, math, writing, study skills. **Counseling services:** minority student, career, personal, academic, psychological, religious. **For learning-disabled students:** School does not offer a structured program with separate admission and additional fees. Total undergraduates in learning-disabled program or receiving services: 120. Services include: learning center, tutors, other. **Library:** Number of titles: 148,295; number of current serial subscriptions: 533. **Information technology resources:** Students are not required to lease or own a computer. Number of campus computers available to all students: 180. School has a wireless network. Approximate number of users that can be accommodated: 360. Proportion of college-owned housing units wired for high-speed internet access: 100%. **Campus safety:** Security services offered: 24-hour foot-and-vehicle patrols, late-night transport/escort service, 24-hour emergency telephones, lighted pathways/sidewalks, controlled dormitory access (key, security card, etc).

TRANSFER AND INTERNATIONAL STUDENTS

Transfer students: May apply for admission for the following academic terms: Fall, Spring. Applicants do not need a minimum number of credits to apply. For fall 2005: Transfer applications received: 124. Transfer applicants offered admission: 91. Transfer applicants enrolled: 59. **International students:** Number of foreign undergraduates: 34 (2% of student body). Number of countries represented: 23. Minimum TOEFL score required: 550 (paper); 213 (computer). Average TOEFL score: 583 (paper).

Hampshire College

- **Address:** 893 West Street, Amherst, MA 01002
- **Website:** http://www.hampshire.edu
- **Private**
- **Enrollment:** 1,376 full-time

KEY STATS

✔ **U.S News College Ranking:** 91, Liberal Arts Colleges
✔ **SAT Score (25th/75th percentile):** 1160-1370
✔ **Tuition:** 2006-2007: $34,455

Selectivity: More selective	**Room/board:** $9,030
Acceptance rate: 64%	**Average debt:** $19,400
Student/faculty ratio: 12/1	**Proportion who borrowed:** 52%

UNDERGRADUATE STUDENT BODY STATS

2005-2006 enrollment: 1,376 full-time. Men: 41%; women: 59%. **Ethnic makeup:** African American: 3%; Asian American: 4%; Hispanic: 4%; White: 84%; International: 3%. **Religious preference:** Roman Catholic: 5%; Protestant: 10%; Jewish: 10%; No preference: 55%; Other: 20%.

ADMISSIONS FACTS AND FIGURES

Phone: (413) 559-5471. **Email:** admissions@hampshire.edu. **Website:** http://www.hampshire.edu. **Application deadlines for fall 2007:** Regular decision: January 15; decision sent by April 1. Early decision: Send application by: November 15; Decision sent by: December 15. Early action: Send application by: December 1; Decision sent by: February 1. Admission can be deferred. **Application fee:** $55. Common application is accepted. **Admissions requirements/recommendations:** High school units required (recommended): English: 4 (4); Mathematics: 4 (4); Science: 4 (4); Foreign language: 3 (3); Social studies: 2 (2); History: 2 (2); Total units: 19 (19). Tests: The college uses SAT or ACT scores in admissions decisions. Neither SAT nor ACT required. For admission to the fall 2007 entering class, the school will accept: ACT with writing, ACT without writing. Campus visit: Recommended. Admissions interview: Recommended. Off-campus interview: May be arranged. **Factors that count in admissions decisions:** *Academic:* Secondary school record: Important. Class rank: Considered. Letters of recommendation: Important. Standardized test scores: Considered. Essay: Very important. *Nonacademic:* Interview: Considered. Extracurricular activities: Important. Talent/ability: Important. Character/personal qualities: Very important. Alumni/ae relationship: Considered. Geographical residence: Not considered. State residency: Not considered. Religious affiliation/commitment: Not considered. Minority status: Considered. Volunteer work: Considered. Work experience: Considered. **Other schools with the greatest overlap in applicants:** Bard College; Oberlin College; Reed College; Sarah Lawrence College; University of California–Santa Cruz. **Admissions statistics for the fall 2005 entering class:** Total applicants: 2,243. Total accepted: 1,441. Freshmen enrolled: 399; 81% were from out of state. Accepted through early-decision or early-action plans: 13%. Overall acceptance rate: 64%. Early-decision acceptance rate: 77%. Non-early acceptance rate: 64%. **Size of waiting list:** 313 applicants; enrolled from waiting list: 0. **Credentials of fall 2005 freshmen:** 28% ranked in the top 10 percent of their high school class; 63% were in the top 25 percent, and 90% were in the top half. (Proportion submitting class standing: 41%.) **Average high school grade point average:** 3.4. **First-year students who submitted SAT scores:** 86%. Scores (25/75 percentile): Verbal: 600-710, Math: 560-660, Combined: 1160-1370. **First-year students submitting ACT scores:** 25%. Scores (25/75 percentile): English: N/A, Math: N/A, Composite: 24-30.

ACADEMICS

Year founded: 1965. **Academic calendar:** 4-1-4. **Degrees offered:** bachelor's. **Most popular majors:** 13% film/video and photographic arts, 10% English language and literature, 9% area, ethnic, cultural, and gender studies, 6% fine arts and art studies, 6% history. **Major fields of study:** agriculture, agriculture operations, and related sciences; architecture and related services; area, ethnic, cultural, and gender studies; biological and biomedical sciences; communication, journalism, and related programs; communications technologies/technicians and support services; computer and information sciences and support services; education; engineering technologies/technicians; English language and literature/letters; foreign languages, literatures, and linguistics; history; legal professions and studies; liberal arts and sciences studies, and humanities; mathematics and statistics; multi/interdisciplinary studies; natural resources and conservation; philosophy and religious studies; physical sciences; psychology; social sciences; visual and performing arts. **Areas of required coursework:** arts/fine arts, humanities, sciences (biological or physical), social science, other. **Special academic programs (% participation):** cross-registration (90%), independent study (80%), internships (53%), student-designed major (100%), study abroad (26%), teacher certificate program (0%). **Teacher certification offered in:** early childhood, elementary, middle/junior high, secondary. **Reserve Officers Training Corps (ROTC):** Army ROTC: Offered at cooperating institution (University of Massachusetts). **Faculty and instruction (2005-2006):** Total instructional faculty: 94 full-time, 43 part-time (49% men; 51% women; 15% minorities). Full-time faculty with Ph.D. or other terminal degree: 87%. Student/faculty ratio: 12/1. Classes of fewer than 20 students: 68%; of 20 to 49 students: 32%; of 50 or more students: 0%. **Advanced Placement and International Baccalaureate credit:** AP tests may be used for: Placement only. Scores accepted: 4, 5. International Baccalaureate exams may be used for: Placement only. **Freshmen returning for sophomore year:** 81%. **Graduation rates:** Four-year: 52%; five-year: 68%; six-year: 71%. **Graduate study:** 10% of students pursue further study immediately upon graduation. Fields in which graduates pursue further study: law, 15%; medicine, 10%; arts and sciences, 50%.

COSTS AND FINANCIAL AID

Financial aid office: (413) 559-5484. **Expenses (2006-2007):** Tuition and fees 2006-2007: $34,455; room/board: $9,030. Estimated books and supplies: $500; transportation: $150; personal expenses: $600. **Financial aid:** Priority filing date for institution's financial aid form: February 1; deadline: February 1. In 2005-2006, 59% of undergraduates applied for financial aid. Of those,

55% were determined to have financial need; 82% had their need fully met. Average financial aid package (proportion receiving): $27,080 (55%). Average amount of gift aid, such as scholarships or grants (proportion receiving): $20,600 (55%). Average amount of self-help aid, such as work study or loans (proportion receiving): $6,480 (54%). Average need-based loan (excluding PLUS or other private loans): $4,150. Among students who received need-based aid, the average percentage of need met: 97%. Among students who received aid based on merit, the average award (and the proportion receiving): $4,390 (10%). The average athletic scholarship (and the proportion receiving): $0 (0%). Average amount of debt of borrowers graduating in 2005: $19,400. Proportion who borrowed: 52%.

CAMPUS LIFE AND EXTRACURRICULAR ACTIVITIES

Campus housing available: coed dorms, women's dorms, men's dorms, apartment for single students, special housing for disabled students, special housing for international students, cooperative housing, other housing options. Students who live in college-owned, operated, or affiliated housing: 92%. **Student employment:** During the 2005-2006 academic year, 48% of undergraduates worked on campus. Average per-year earnings: $2,400. **Clubs and organizations:** Number of student organizations: 85. Activities include: choral groups, dance, drama/theater, jazz band, music ensembles, student government, student newspaper, student film society. Number of fraternities: 0; sororities: 0. Average proportion of students who stay on campus on weekends: 90%.

SERVICES AND FACILITIES

Basic services: women's center, day care, health service, health insurance. **Remedial assistance:** math, writing. **Counseling services:** minority student, career, personal, academic, psychological, birth control, religious. **For learning-disabled students:** School does not offer a structured program with separate admission and additional fees. Total undergraduates in learning-disabled program or receiving services: 71. Services include: reading machines, tape recorders, note-taking services, readers, extended time for tests. **Library:** Number of titles: 136,326; number of current serial subscriptions: 2,288. **Information technology resources:** Students are not required to lease or own a computer. Number of campus computers available to all students: 186. School has a wireless network. Proportion of college-owned housing units wired for high-speed internet access: 100%. **Campus safety:** Security services offered: 24-hour foot-and-vehicle patrols, late-night transport/escort service, 24-hour emergency telephones, lighted pathways/sidewalks, student patrols, controlled dormitory access (key, security card, etc).

TRANSFER AND INTERNATIONAL STUDENTS

Transfer students: May apply for admission for the following academic terms: Fall, Spring. Applicants need a minimum number of credits to apply. For fall 2005: Transfer applications received: 180. Transfer applicants offered admission: 67. Transfer applicants enrolled: 26. **International students:** Number of foreign undergraduates: 44 (3% of student body). Number of countries represented: 26. Minimum TOEFL score required: 577 (paper); 233 (computer).

Harvard University

- **Address:** Undergraduate Admissions Office, Byerly Hall, 8 Garden Street, Cambridge, MA 02138
- **Website:** http://www.college.harvard.edu
- **Private**
- **Enrollment:** 6,649 full-time

KEY STATS
✔ **U.S News College Ranking:** 2, National Universities
✔ **SAT Score (25th/75th percentile):** 1400-1580
✔ **Tuition:** 2006-2007: $33,709

Selectivity: Most selective	**Room/board:** $9,946
Acceptance rate: 9%	**Average debt:** $8,769
Student/faculty ratio: 7/1	**Proportion who borrowed:** 48%

UNDERGRADUATE STUDENT BODY STATS

2005-2006 enrollment: 6,649 full-time. Men: 51%; women: 49%. **Ethnic makeup:** African American: 8%; American-Indian: 1%; Asian American: 18%; Hispanic: 8%; White: 56%; International: 9%.

ADMISSIONS FACTS AND FIGURES

Phone: (617) 495-1551. **Email:** college@fas.harvard.edu. **Website:** http://www.college.harvard.edu. **Application deadlines for fall 2007:** Regular decision: January 1; decision sent by April 1. Early decision: Not offered. Early action: Send application by: November 1; Decision sent by: December 15. Admission can be deferred. **Application fee:** $65. Common application is accepted. **To apply online, go to:** http://www.admissions.college.harvard.edu/. **Admissions requirements/recommendations:** High school units required (recommended): English: (4); Mathematics: (4); Science: (4); Foreign language: (4); Social studies: (2); History: (3); Academic electives: (2); Total units: (25). Tests: The college uses SAT or ACT scores in admissions decisions. Either SAT or ACT required. For admission to the fall 2007 entering class, the school will accept: ACT with writing. Campus visit: Recommended. Admissions interview: Required. Off-campus interview: May be arranged. **Factors that count in admissions decisions:** *Academic:* Secondary school record: Very important. Class rank: Important. Letters of recommendation: Very important. Standardized test scores: Important. Essay: Very important. *Nonacademic:* Interview: Important. Extracurricular activities: Very important. Talent/ability: Very important. Character/personal qualities: Very important. Alumni/ae relationship: Considered. Geographical residence: Considered. State residency: Not considered. Religious affiliation/commitment: Not considered. Minority status: Considered. Volunteer work: Important. Work experience: Considered. **Admissions statistics for the fall 2005 entering class:** Total applicants: 22,796. Total accepted: 2,102. Freshmen enrolled: 1,640; 86% were from out of state. Accepted through early-decision or early-action plans: 50%. Overall acceptance rate: 9%. Non-early acceptance rate: 7%. **Size of waiting list:** N/A applicants; enrolled from waiting list: 23. **Credentials of fall 2005 freshmen:** 96% ranked in the top 10 percent of their high school class; 99% were in the top 25 percent, and 100% were in the top half. (Proportion submitting class standing: 84%.) **First-year students who submitted SAT scores:** 99%. Scores (25/75 percentile): Verbal: 700-790, Math: 700-790, Combined: 1400-1580. **First-year students submitting ACT scores:** 18%. Scores (25/75 percentile): English: 31-35, Math: 30-35, Composite: 30-34.

ACADEMICS

Year founded: 1636. **Academic calendar:** Semester. **Degrees offered:** certificate, bachelor's, post-bachelor's certificate, master's, post-master's certificate, first professional, first professional certificate, doctorate. **Most popular majors:** 16% economics, 11% political science and government, 7% psychology, 6% biology/biological sciences, 5% English language and literature. **Major fields of study:** area, ethnic, cultural, and gender studies; biological and biomedical sciences; computer and information sciences and support services; engineering; English language and literature/letters; foreign languages, literatures, and linguistics; history; liberal arts and sciences studies, and humanities; mathematics and statistics; natural resources and conservation; philosophy and religious studies; physical sciences; psychology; social sciences; visual and performing arts. **Areas of required coursework:** humanities, mathematics, English (including composition), foreign languages, sciences (biological or physical), history, social science. **Special academic programs (% participation):** accelerated program (4.6%), cross-registration (17.9%), double major (5%), honors program (60%), independent study (2.7%), student-designed major (.65%), study abroad (10%), teacher certificate program (.5%). **Teacher certification offered in:** middle/junior high, secondary. **Reserve Officers Training Corps (ROTC):** Army ROTC: Offered at cooperating institution (Massachusetts Institute of Technology); Navy ROTC: Offered at cooperating institution (Massachusetts Institute of Technology); Air Force ROTC: Offered at cooperating institution (Massachusetts Institute of Technology). **Faculty and instruction (2005-2006):** Total instructional faculty: 1,592 full-time, 443 part-time (68% men; 32% women; 12% minorities). Full-time faculty with Ph.D. or other terminal degree: 99%. Student/faculty ratio: 7/1. Classes of fewer than 20 students: 69%; of 20 to 49 students: 18%; of 50 or more students: 13%. **Advanced Placement and International Baccalaureate credit:** AP tests may be used for: Credit and/or placement. Scores accepted: 5. International Baccalaureate exams may be used for: Credit and/or placement. **Freshmen returning for sophomore year:** 97%. **Graduation rates:** Four-year: 87%; five-year: 95%; six-year: 98%.

COSTS AND FINANCIAL AID

Financial aid office: (617) 495-1581. **Expenses (2006-2007):** Tuition and fees 2006-2007: $33,709; room/board: $9,946. Estimated books and supplies: $1,000; transportation: $0; personal expenses: $1,795. **Financial aid:** Priority filing date for institution's financial aid form: February 1. In 2005-2006, 55% of undergraduates applied for financial aid. Of those, 50% were determined to have financial need; 100% had their need fully met. Average financial aid package (proportion receiving): $30,715 (50%). Average amount of gift aid, such as scholarships or grants (proportion receiving): $28,004 (49%). Average amount of self-help aid, such as work study or loans (proportion receiving): $3,369 (42%). Average need-based loan (excluding PLUS or other private loans): $3,439. Among students who received need-based aid, the average percentage of need met: 100%. Among students who received aid based on merit, the average award (and the proportion receiving): $0 (0%). The average athletic scholarship (and the proportion receiving): $0 (0%). Average amount of debt of borrowers graduating in 2005: $8,769. Proportion who borrowed: 48%.

CAMPUS LIFE AND EXTRACURRICULAR ACTIVITIES

Campus housing available: coed dorms, special housing for disabled students, cooperative housing. **Clubs and organizations:** Number of student organizations: 369. Activities include: choral groups, concert band, dance, drama/theater, jazz band, literary magazine, marching band, music ensembles, musical theater, opera, pep band, radio station, student government, student newspaper, student film society, symphony orchestra, television station, yearbook. **Sports program (2005-2006):** Member of NCAA I. *Men's intercollegiate varsity sports:* baseball, basketball, cross-country, fencing, football, golf, ice hockey, lacrosse, lightweight crew, sailing, soccer, squash, swimming and diving, tennis, track and field (indoor), track and field (outdoor), volleyball, water polo, wrestling, skiing, heavyweight crew. *Women's intercollegiate varsity sports:* basketball, cross-country, fencing, field hockey, golf, ice hockey, lacrosse, sailing, soccer, softball, squash, swimming and diving, tennis, track and field (indoor), track and field (outdoor), volleyball, water polo, skiing, heavyweight crew.

SERVICES AND FACILITIES

Basic services: placement service, health service, health insurance. **Counseling services:** career, personal, academic. **For learning-disabled students:** School does not offer a structured program with separate admission and additional fees. Services include: tape recorders, videotaped classes, untimed tests, note-taking services, readers, extended time for tests, early syllabus, other testing accomodations. **Information technology resources:** Students are not required to lease or own a computer. Number of campus computers available to all students: 242. School has a wireless network. **Campus safety:** Security services offered: 24-hour foot-and-vehicle patrols, late-night transport/escort service, 24-hour emergency telephones, lighted pathways/sidewalks, student patrols, controlled dormitory access (key, security card, etc).

TRANSFER AND INTERNATIONAL STUDENTS

Transfer students: May apply for admission for the following academic terms: Fall, Spring. Applicants need a minimum number of credits to apply. For fall 2005: Transfer applications received: 964. Transfer applicants offered admission: 85. Transfer applicants enrolled: 77. **International students:** Number of foreign undergraduates: 591 (9% of student body). Number of countries represented: 91.

Lasell College

- **Address:** 1844 Commonwealth Avenue, Newton, MA 02466
- **Website:** http://www.lasell.edu
- **Private**
- **Enrollment:** 1,194 full-time; 22 part-time

KEY STATS

✔ **U.S News College Ranking:** third tier, Comp. Coll.–Bachelor's (North)
✔ **SAT Score (25th/75th percentile):** 900-1050
✔ **Tuition:** 2006-2007: $20,900

Selectivity: Less selective	**Room/board:** $9,200
Acceptance rate: 67%	**Average debt:** $20,800
Student/faculty ratio: 14/1	**Proportion who borrowed:** 93%

UNDERGRADUATE STUDENT BODY STATS

2005-2006 enrollment: 1,194 full-time; 22 part-time. Men: 31%; women: 69%. **Ethnic makeup:** African American: 6%; Asian American: 3%; Hispanic: 6%; White: 82%; International: 3%.

ADMISSIONS FACTS AND FIGURES

Phone: (617) 243-2225. **Email:** info@lasell.edu. **Website:** http://www.lasell.edu. **Application deadlines for fall 2007:** Regular decision: September 1. Early decision: Not offered. Early action: Not offered. Admission can be deferred. **Application fee:** $40. Common application is accepted. **To apply online, go to:** http://www.lasell.edu/admission/application/. **Admissions requirements/recommendations:** High school units required (recommended): English: 4 (4); Mathematics: 3 (4); Science: 2 (3); Foreign language: 0 (2); Social studies: 2 (3); History: 2 (3); Academic electives: 2 (2); Total units: 15 (21). Tests: The college uses SAT or ACT scores in admissions decisions. Either SAT or ACT required. For admission to the fall 2007 entering class, the school will accept: ACT with writing. Campus visit: Recommended. Admissions interview: Recommended. Off-campus interview: May be arranged. **Factors that count in admissions decisions:** *Academic:* Secondary school record: Very important. Class rank: Important. Letters of recommendation: Important. Standardized test scores: Very important. Essay: Considered. *Nonacademic:* Interview: Important. Extracurricular activities: Important. Talent/ability: Important. Character/personal qualities: Important. Alumni/ae relationship: Considered. Geographical residence: Not considered. State residency: Not considered. Religious affiliation/commitment: Not considered. Minority status: Not considered. Volunteer work: Important. Work experience: Considered. **Other schools with the greatest overlap in applicants:** Curry College; Endicott College; Fashion Institute of Technology; Northeastern University; Suffolk University. **Admissions statistics for the fall 2005 entering class:** Total applicants: 2,652. Total accepted: 1,787. Freshmen enrolled: 375; 48% were from out of state. Overall acceptance rate: 67%. **Credentials of fall 2005 freshmen:** 5% ranked in the top 10 percent of their high school class; 30% were in the top 25 percent, and 70% were in the top half. (Proportion submitting class standing: 68%.) **Average high school grade point average:** 2.7. **First-year students who submitted SAT scores:** 90%. Scores (25/75 percentile): Verbal: 450-530, Math: 450-520, Combined: 900-1050. **First-year students submitting ACT scores:** 10%. Scores (25/75 percentile): English: N/A, Math: N/A, Composite: 20-21.

ACADEMICS

Year founded: 1851. **Academic calendar:** Semester. **Degrees offered:** bachelor's, post-bachelor's certificate, master's. **Most popular majors:** 14% fashion merchandising, 11% fashion/apparel design, 7% business administration and management, 6% accounting, 5% psychology. **Major fields of study:** biological and biomedical sciences; business, management, marketing, and related support services; communication, journalism, and related programs; computer and information sciences and support services; education; English language and literature/letters; family and consumer sciences/human sciences; health professions and related clinical sciences; history; legal professions and studies; liberal arts and sciences studies, and humanities; multi/interdisciplinary studies; parks, recreation, leisure, and fitness studies; psychology; public administration and social service professions; security and protective services; social sciences. **Areas of required coursework:** humanities, computer literacy, mathematics, English (including composition), sciences (biological or physical), history, social science. **Pre-professional programs:** pre-law, other. **Special academic programs (% participation):** double major (2%), English as a Second Language (ESL) (1%), honors program (17%), independent study (5%), internships (100%), liberal arts/career combination (100%), student-designed major (2%), study abroad (8%), teacher certificate program (10%). **Teacher certification offered in:** early childhood, elementary, secondary. **Faculty and instruction (2005-2006):** Total instructional faculty: 50 full-time, 120 part-time (42% men; 58% women; 5% minorities). Full-time faculty with Ph.D. or other terminal degree: 54%. Student/faculty ratio: 14/1. Classes of fewer than 20 students: 62%; of 20 to 49 students: 38%; of 50 or more students: 0%. **Advanced Placement and International Baccalaureate credit:** AP tests may be used for: Credit and/or placement. Scores accepted: 3, 4, 5. **Freshmen returning for sophomore year:** 66%. **Graduation rates:** Four-year: 35%; five-year: 44%; six-year: 58%. **Graduate study:** 22% of students pursue further study immediately upon graduation. Fields in which graduates pursue further study: Master of Business Administration (MBA), 19%; law, 7%; education, 37%; arts and sciences, 37%.

COSTS AND FINANCIAL AID

Financial aid office: (617) 243-2227. **Expenses (2006-2007):** Tuition and fees 2006-2007: $20,900; room/board: $9,200. Estimated books and supplies: $1,000; transportation: $500; personal expenses: $2,000. **Financial aid:** Priority filing date for institution's financial aid form: March 1. In 2005-2006, 99% of undergraduates applied for financial aid. Of those, 89% were determined to have financial need; 12% had their need fully met. Average financial aid package (proportion receiving): $14,900 (84%). Average amount of gift aid, such as scholarships or grants (proportion receiving): $12,200 (74%). Average amount of self-help aid, such as work study or loans (proportion receiving): $4,500 (74%). Average need-based loan (excluding PLUS or other private loans): $2,500. Among students who received need-based aid, the average percentage of need met: 67%. Among students who received aid based on merit, the average award (and the proportion receiving): $14,700 (13%). The average athletic scholarship (and the proportion receiving): $0 (0%). Average amount of debt of borrowers graduating in 2005: $20,800. Proportion who borrowed: 93%.

CAMPUS LIFE AND EXTRACURRICULAR ACTIVITIES

Campus housing available: coed dorms, women's dorms, apartment for single students, special housing for disabled students. Students who live in college-owned, operated, or affiliated housing: 80%. Average per-year earnings: $1,500. **Clubs and organizations:** Number of student organizations: 13. Activities include: choral groups, dance, drama/theater, jazz band, literary magazine, radio station, student government, student newspaper, yearbook. Number of fraternities: 0; sororities: 0. Average proportion of students who stay on campus on weekends: 40%. **Sports program (2005-2006):** Member of NCAA III. *Men's intercollegiate varsity sports:* basketball, cross-country, lacrosse, soccer, volleyball. *Women's intercollegiate varsity sports:* basketball, cross-country, field hockey, lacrosse, soccer, softball, volleyball.

SERVICES AND FACILITIES

Basic services: nonremedial tutoring, health service, health insurance. **Counseling services:** career, personal, academic, psychological, birth control. **For learning-disabled students:** School does not offer a structured program with separate admission and additional fees. Total undergraduates in learning-disabled program or receiving services: 22. Services include: remedial math, reading machines, remedial reading, tape recorders, untimed tests, note-taking services, oral tests, learning center, readers, extended time for tests, tutors, texts on tape, typist/scribe, other testing accomodations. **Library:** Number of titles: 56,000; number of current serial subscriptions: 479. **Information technology resources:** Students are not required to lease or own a computer. Number of campus computers available to all students: 150. School has a wireless network. Proportion of college-owned housing units wired for high-speed internet access: 100%. **Campus safety:** Security services offered: 24-hour foot-and-vehicle patrols, 24-hour emergency telephones, lighted pathways/sidewalks, controlled dormitory access (key, security card, etc).

TRANSFER AND INTERNATIONAL STUDENTS

Transfer students: May apply for admission for the following academic terms: Fall, Spring. Applicants do not need a minimum number of credits to apply. For fall 2005: Transfer applications received: 296. Transfer applicants offered admission: 146. Transfer applicants enrolled: 62. **International students:** Number of foreign undergraduates: 34 (3% of student body). Number of countries represented: 15. Minimum TOEFL score required: 525 (paper); 173 (computer).

Lesley University

- **Address:** 29 Everett Street, Cambridge, MA 02138
- **Website:** http://www.lesley.edu
- **Private**
- **Enrollment:** 1,023 full-time; 242 part-time

KEY STATS

- ✔ **U.S News College Ranking:** 38, Universities–Master's (North)
- ✔ **SAT Score (25th/75th percentile):** 940-1170
- ✔ **Tuition:** 2006-2007: $24,268

Selectivity: Selective	**Room/board:** $10,500
Acceptance rate: 72%	**Average debt:** $13,650
Student/faculty ratio: 11/1	**Proportion who borrowed:** 90%

UNDERGRADUATE STUDENT BODY STATS

2005-2006 enrollment: 1,023 full-time; 242 part-time. Men: 23%; women: 77%. **Ethnic makeup:** African American: 6%; Asian American: 5%; Hispanic: 5%; White: 80%; International: 3%.

ADMISSIONS FACTS AND FIGURES

Phone: (617) 349-8800. **Email:** lcadmissions@lesley.edu. **Website:** http://www.lesley.edu. **Application deadlines for fall 2007:** Regular decision: Rolling. Early decision: Not offered. Early action: Send application by: December 1; Decision sent by: January 1. Admission can be deferred. **Application fee:** $40. Common application is accepted. **To apply online, go to:** http://www.lesley.edu/lc/applying.html. **Admissions requirements/recommendations:** High school units required (recommended): English: 4 (4); Mathematics: 3 (4); Science: 3 (4); Foreign language: 1 (2); Social studies: 1 (2); History: 1 (2); Academic electives: 4 (0); Total units: 18 (20). Tests: The college uses SAT or ACT scores in admissions decisions. Either SAT or ACT required. For admission to the fall 2007 entering class, the school will accept: ACT with writing. Campus visit: Recommended. Admissions interview: Recommended. Off-campus interview: Not available. **Factors that count in admissions decisions:** *Academic:* Secondary school record: Very important. Class rank: Important. Letters of recommendation: Important. Standardized test scores: Important. Essay: Important. *Nonacademic:* Interview: Important. Extracurricular activities: Important. Talent/ability: Important. Character/personal qualities: Very important. Alumni/ae relationship: Considered. Geographical residence: Considered. State residency: Not considered. Religious affiliation/commitment: Not considered. Minority status: Considered. Volunteer work: Very important. Work experience: Considered. **Other schools with the greatest overlap in applicants:** Boston College; Emmanuel College; Northeastern University; Simmons College; Suffolk University. **Admissions statistics for the fall 2005 entering class:** Total applicants: 1,351. Total accepted: 967. Freshmen enrolled: 257; 51% were from out of state. Overall acceptance rate: 72%. Non-early acceptance rate: 72%. **Size of waiting list:** 18 applicants; enrolled from waiting list: 3. **Credentials of fall 2005 freshmen:** 23% ranked in the top 10 percent of their high school class; 50% were in the top 25 percent, and 78% were in the top half. (Proportion submitting class standing: 39%.) **Average high school grade point average:** 3.0. **First-year students who submitted SAT scores:** 94%. Scores (25/75 percentile): Verbal: 480-600, Math: 460-570, Combined: 940-1170. **First-year students submitting ACT scores:** 32%. Scores (25/75 percentile): English: 19-26, Math: 17-23, Composite: 19-25.

ACADEMICS

Year founded: 1909. **Academic calendar:** Semester. **Degrees offered:** certificate, diploma, associate, terminal-associate, bachelor's, post-bachelor's certificate, master's, post-master's certificate, doctorate. **Most popular majors:** 33% liberal arts and sciences studies, and humanities, 22% business, management, marketing, and related support services, 20% visual and performing arts, 12% education, 10% psychology. **Major fields of study:** area, ethnic, cultural, and gender studies; biological and biomedical sciences; communications technologies/technicians and support services; education; English language and literature/letters; family and consumer sciences/human sciences; health professions and related clinical sciences; liberal arts and sciences studies, and humanities; mathematics and statistics; natural resources and conservation; psychology; public administration and social service professions; visual and performing arts. **Areas of required coursework:** arts/fine arts, humanities, computer literacy, mathematics, English (including composition), philosophy, sciences (biological or physical), history, social science, other. **Special academic programs (% participation):** accelerated program (10%), cross-registration (50%), distance learning (5%), double major (60%), exchange student program (domestic) (5%), honors program (10%), independent study (35%), internships (100%), liberal arts/career combination (100%), student-designed major (7%), study abroad (10%), teacher certificate program (55%). **Teacher certification offered in:** early childhood, special education, elementary, middle/junior high, secondary. **Faculty and instruction (2005-2006):** Total instructional faculty: 53 full-time, 131 part-time (45% men; 55% women). Full-time faculty with Ph.D. or other terminal degree: 74%. Student/faculty ratio: 11/1. Classes of fewer than 20 students: 75%; of 20 to 49 students: 25%. **Advanced Placement and International Baccalaureate credit:** AP tests may be used for: Credit and/or placement. Scores accepted: 3, 4, 5. International Baccalaureate exams may be used for: Credit and/or placement. **Freshmen returning for sophomore year:** 77%. **Graduation rates:** Four-year: 32%; five-year: 47%; six-year: 60%. **Graduate study:** 32% of students pursue further study immediately upon graduation. Fields in which graduates pursue further study: law, 5%; education, 55%; arts and sciences, 40%.

COSTS AND FINANCIAL AID

Financial aid office: (617) 349-8581. **Expenses (2006-2007):** Tuition and fees 2006-2007: $24,268; room/board: $10,500. Estimated books and supplies: $1,137; transportation: $900; personal expenses: $900. **Financial aid:** Priority filing date for institution's financial aid form: March 1. In 2005-2006, 88% of undergraduates applied for financial aid. Of those, 71% were determined to have financial need; 26% had their need fully met. Average financial aid package (proportion receiving): $15,834 (71%). Average amount of gift aid, such as scholarships or grants (proportion receiving): $11,142 (67%). Average amount of self-help aid, such as work study or loans (proportion receiving): $5,941 (67%). Average need-based loan (excluding PLUS or other private loans): $4,183. Among students who received need-based aid, the average percentage of need met: 70%. Among students who received aid based on merit, the average award (and the proportion receiving): $6,056 (10%). The average athletic scholarship (and the proportion receiving): $0 (0%). Average amount of debt of borrowers graduating in 2005: $13,650. Proportion who borrowed: 90%.

CAMPUS LIFE AND EXTRACURRICULAR ACTIVITIES

Campus housing available (% using): coed dorms (60%), women's dorms (40%), other housing options. Students who live in college-owned, operated, or affiliated housing: 25%. **Student employment:** During the 2005-2006 academic year, 10% of undergraduates worked on campus. Average per-year earnings: $2,000. **Clubs and organizations:** Number of student organizations: 20. Activities include: choral groups, dance, drama/theater, literary magazine, music ensembles, musical theater, student government, student newspaper, yearbook. Number of fraternities: 0; sororities: 0. Average proportion of students who stay on campus on weekends: 80%. **Sports program (2005-2006):** Member of NCAA III. *Men's intercollegiate varsity sports:* basketball, volleyball. *Women's intercollegiate varsity sports:* basketball, rowing, soccer, softball, volleyball.

SERVICES AND FACILITIES

Basic services: nonremedial tutoring, placement service, health service, health insurance. **Remedial assistance:** math, writing, study skills. **Counseling services:** minority student, career, personal, veteran student, academic, older student, birth control, religious, other. **For learning-disabled students:** School does not offer a structured program with separate admission and additional fees. Services include: remedial math, reading machines, tape recorders, other special classes, untimed tests, note-taking services, oral tests, learning center, readers, extended time for tests, tutors, other. **Library:** Number of titles: 112,399; number of current serial subscriptions: 665. **Information technology resources:** Students are not required to lease or own a computer. Number of campus computers available to all students: 170. School has a wireless network. Approximate number of users that can be accommodated: 500. Proportion of college-owned housing units wired for high-speed internet access: 100%. **Campus safety:** Security services offered: 24-hour foot-and-vehicle patrols, late-night transport/escort service, 24-hour emergency telephones, lighted pathways/sidewalks, controlled dormitory access (key, security card, etc).

TRANSFER AND INTERNATIONAL STUDENTS

Transfer students: May apply for admission for the following academic terms: Fall, Spring. Applicants do not need a minimum number of credits to apply. For fall 2005: Transfer applications received: 313. Transfer applicants offered admission: 199. Transfer applicants enrolled: 94. **International students:** Number of foreign undergraduates: 33 (3% of student body). Number of countries represented: 27. Minimum TOEFL score required: 173 (computer).

Longy School of Music

- **Address:** 1 Follen Street, Cambridge, MA 02138
- **Website:** http://www.longy.edu
- **Private**
- **Enrollment:** 36 full-time; 11 part-time

KEY STATS

✔ **U.S News College Ranking:** Unranked Specialty School—Fine Arts
✔ **SAT or ACT Score (25th/75th percentile):** N/A
✔ **Tuition:** 2006-2007: $23,150

Selectivity: Least selective	Room/board: N/A
Acceptance rate: 88%	Average debt: $15,229
Student/faculty ratio: 5/1	Proportion who borrowed: 42%

UNDERGRADUATE STUDENT BODY STATS

2005-2006 enrollment: 36 full-time; 11 part-time. Men: 53%; women: 47%. **Ethnic makeup:** African American: 4%; Asian American: 6%; White: 62%; International: 28%.

ADMISSIONS FACTS AND FIGURES

Phone: (617) 876-0956. **Email:** music@longy.edu. **Website:** http://www.longy.edu. **Application deadlines for fall 2007:** Regular decision: July 1. Early decision: Not offered. Early action: Not offered. Admission can be deferred. **Application fee:** $90. Common application is not accepted. **Admissions requirements/recommendations:** Tests: The college does not use SAT or ACT scores in admissions decisions. Neither SAT nor ACT required. Campus visit: Recommended. Admissions interview: Recommended. Off-campus interview: Not available. **Factors that count in admissions decisions:** *Academic:* Secondary school record: Important. Class rank: Not considered. Letters of recommendation: Very important. Standardized test scores: Not considered. Essay: Very important. *Nonacademic:* Interview: Very important. Extracurricular activities: Very important. Talent/ability: Very important. Character/personal qualities: Very important. Alumni/ae relationship: Considered. Geographical residence: Not considered. State residency: Not considered. Religious affiliation/commitment: Not considered. Minority status: Not considered. Volunteer work: Considered. Work experience: Considered. **Other schools with the greatest overlap in applicants:** Boston Conservatory; Boston University; New England Conservatory of Music; New School University; San Francisco Conservatory of Music. **Admissions statistics for the fall 2005 entering class:** Total applicants: 26. Total accepted: 23. Freshmen enrolled: 9; 71% were from out of state. Overall acceptance rate: 88%. **Size of waiting list:** 0 applicants; enrolled from waiting list: 0.

ACADEMICS

Year founded: 1915. **Academic calendar:** Semester. **Degrees offered:** diploma, bachelor's, post-bachelor's certificate, master's. **Most popular majors:** 40% violin, viola, guitar, and other stringed instruments, 30% music theory and composition, 10% music performance, 10% piano and organ, 10% voice and opera. **Major fields of study:** visual and performing arts. **Areas of required coursework:** arts/fine arts. **Faculty and instruction (2005-2006):** Total instructional faculty: 0 full-time, 104 part-time (50% men; 50% women; 8% minorities). Student/faculty ratio: 5/1. Classes of fewer than 20 students: 92%; of 20 to 49 students: 6%; of 50 or more students: 2%. **Freshmen returning for sophomore year:** 57%. **Graduation rates:** Four-year: 57%; five-year: 71%; six-year: 54%. **Graduate study:** 50% of students pursue further study immediately upon graduation; 10% within one year; 30% within five years. Fields in which graduates pursue further study: education, 10%; arts and sciences, 90%.

COSTS AND FINANCIAL AID

Financial aid office: (617) 876-0956. **Expenses (2006-2007):** Tuition and fees 2006-2007: $23,150; room/board: N/A. **Financial aid:** Priority filing date for institution's financial aid form: February 24. In 2005-2006, 44% of undergraduates applied for financial aid. Of those, 39% were determined to have financial need; 14% had their need fully met. Average financial aid package (proportion receiving): $12,269 (39%). Average amount of gift aid, such as scholarships or grants (proportion receiving): $8,787 (39%). Average amount of self-help aid, such as work study or loans (proportion receiving): $4,063 (33%). Average need-based loan (excluding PLUS or other private loans): $4,063. Among students who received need-based aid, the average percentage of need met: 85%. Among students who received aid based on merit, the average award (and the proportion receiving): $8,187 (53%). The average athletic scholarship (and the proportion receiving): $0 (0%). Average amount of debt of borrowers graduating in 2005: $15,229. Proportion who borrowed: 42%.

CAMPUS LIFE AND EXTRACURRICULAR ACTIVITIES

Students who live in college-owned, operated, or affiliated housing: 0%. **Student employment:** During the 2005-2006 academic year, 36% of undergraduates worked on campus. Average per-year earnings: $1,800. Activities include: choral groups, dance, jazz band, music ensembles, opera, student government, symphony orchestra. Number of fraternities: 0; sororities: 0.

SERVICES AND FACILITIES

Basic services: health insurance. **Counseling services:** career, academic, psychological. **For learning-disabled students:** School does not offer a structured program with separate admission and additional fees. **Library:** Number of titles: 4,800; number of current serial subscriptions: 35. **Information technology resources:** Students are not required to lease or own a computer.

Number of campus computers available to all students: 6. School has a wireless network.

TRANSFER AND INTERNATIONAL STUDENTS

Transfer students: May apply for admission for the following academic terms: Fall, Spring. Applicants do not need a minimum number of credits to apply. For fall 2005: Transfer applications received: 26. Transfer applicants offered admission: 15. Transfer applicants enrolled: 6. **International students:** Number of foreign undergraduates: 13 (28% of student body). Number of countries represented: 9. Minimum TOEFL score required: 520 (paper); 190 (computer). Average TOEFL score: 538 (paper).

Massachusetts College of Art

■ **Address:** 621 Huntington Avenue, Boston, MA 02115
■ **Website:** http://www.massart.edu
■ **Public**
■ **Enrollment:** 1,379 full-time; 615 part-time

KEY STATS

✔ **U.S News College Ranking:** Unranked Specialty School–Fine Arts
✔ **SAT Score (25th/75th percentile):** 1000-1210
✔ **Tuition:** 2006-2007: $7,200 in state, $20,600 out of state
   Selectivity: Selective   **Room/board:** $11,090
   Acceptance rate: 61%   **Average debt:** N/A
   Student/faculty ratio: 13/1   **Proportion who borrowed:** N/A

UNDERGRADUATE STUDENT BODY STATS

2005-2006 enrollment: 1,379 full-time; 615 part-time. Men: 36%; women: 64%. **Ethnic makeup:** African American: 4%; American-Indian: 1%; Asian American: 5%; Hispanic: 5%; White: 81%; International: 3%.

ADMISSIONS FACTS AND FIGURES

Phone: (617) 879-7222. **Email:** admissions@massart.edu. **Website:** http://www.massart.edu. **Application deadlines for fall 2007:** Regular decision: February 15; decision sent by April 15. Early decision: Not offered. Early action: Send application by: December 1; Decision sent by: N/A. Admission can be deferred. **Application fee:** $30. Common application is not accepted. **Admissions requirements/recommendations:** High school units required (recommended): English: 4; Mathematics: 2; Science: 2; Foreign language: 2; Social studies: 2; History: 2; Academic electives: 2; Total units: 17. Tests: The college uses SAT or ACT scores in admissions decisions. Either SAT or ACT required. Campus visit: Recommended. Admissions interview: Recommended. Off-campus interview: Not available. **Factors that count in admissions decisions:** *Academic:* Secondary school record: Very important. Class rank: Considered. Letters of recommendation: Considered. Standardized test scores: Important. Essay: Very important. *Nonacademic:* Interview: Not considered. Extracurricular activities: Considered. Talent/ability: Very important. Character/personal qualities: Considered. Alumni/ae relationship: Not considered. Geographical residence: Not considered. State residency: Important. Religious affiliation/commitment: Not considered. Minority status: Considered. Volunteer work: Considered. Work experience: Considered. **Other schools with the greatest overlap in applicants:** Art Institute of Boston at Lesley University; Pratt Institute; Rhode Island School of Design; University of Massachusetts–Amherst; University of Massachusetts–Dartmouth. **Admissions statistics for the fall 2005 entering class:** Total applicants: 1,210. Total accepted: 735. Freshmen enrolled: 265; Overall acceptance rate: 61%. Non-early acceptance rate: 61%. **Size of waiting list:** 58 applicants; enrolled from waiting list: 22. **Credentials of fall 2005 freshmen:** 21% ranked in the top 10 percent of their high school class; 41% were in the top 25 percent, and 86% were in the top half. **Average high school grade point average:** 3.2. **First-year students who submitted SAT scores:** 100%. Scores (25/75 percentile): Verbal: 520-630, Math: 480-580, Combined: 1000-1210. **First-year students submitting ACT scores:** 4%. Scores (25/75 percentile): English: N/A, Math: N/A, Composite: N/A.

ACADEMICS

Year founded: 1873. **Academic calendar:** Semester. **Degrees offered:** bachelor's, post-bachelor's certificate, master's. **Most popular majors:** Information not available. **Major fields of study:** education; visual and performing arts. **Areas of required coursework:** arts/fine arts, humanities, mathematics,

English (including composition), sciences (biological or physical), history, social science. **Special academic programs (% participation):** cross-registration, double major (3%), exchange student program (domestic), independent study, internships, student-designed major, study abroad, teacher certificate program. **Teacher certification offered in:** early childhood, elementary, middle/junior high, secondary. **Faculty and instruction (2005-2006):** Total instructional faculty: 82 full-time, 123 part-time. Full-time faculty with Ph.D. or other terminal degree: 77%. Student/faculty ratio: 13/1. Classes of fewer than 20 students: 86%; of 20 to 49 students: 14%; of 50 or more students: 0%. **Advanced Placement and International Baccalaureate credit:** AP tests may be used for: Credit and/or placement. Scores accepted: 4, 5. **Freshmen returning for sophomore year:** 87%. **Graduation rates:** Four-year: 36%; five-year: 55%; six-year: 61%. **Graduate study:** 2% of students pursue further study within one year.

COSTS AND FINANCIAL AID

Financial aid office: (617) 879-7850. **Expenses (2006-2007):** Tuition and fees 2006-2007: $7,200 in state, $20,600 out of state; room/board: $11,090. Estimated books and supplies: $2,000 personal expenses: $1,350. **Financial aid:** Priority filing date for institution's financial aid form: March 15. In 2005-2006, 73% of undergraduates applied for financial aid. Of those, 57% were determined to have financial need; Average financial aid package (proportion receiving): $8,936 (57%). Average amount of gift aid, such as scholarships or grants (proportion receiving): $5,101 (37%). Average amount of self-help aid, such as work study or loans (proportion receiving): $4,229 (51%). Average need-based loan (excluding PLUS or other private loans): $3,988.

CAMPUS LIFE AND EXTRACURRICULAR ACTIVITIES

Campus housing available (% using): coed dorms (32%), apartment for single students (68%). Students who live in college-owned, operated, or affiliated housing: 26%. Activities include: student government, student newspaper, student film society.

SERVICES AND FACILITIES

Basic services: nonremedial tutoring, health service, health insurance. **Remedial assistance:** writing. **Counseling services:** career, personal, academic, psychological. **For learning-disabled students:** School does not offer a structured program with separate admission and additional fees. **Library:** Number of titles: 231,586; number of current serial subscriptions: 757. **Information technology resources:** Students are not required to lease or own a computer. Number of campus computers available to all students: 350. School has a wireless network. Proportion of college-owned housing units wired for high-speed internet access: 100%. **Campus safety:** Security services offered: 24-hour foot-and-vehicle patrols, late-night transport/escort service, 24-hour emergency telephones, lighted pathways/sidewalks, controlled dormitory access (key, security card, etc).

TRANSFER AND INTERNATIONAL STUDENTS

Transfer students: May apply for admission for the following academic terms: Fall, Spring. Applicants need a minimum number of credits to apply. For fall 2005: Transfer applications received: 492. Transfer applicants offered admission: 278. Transfer applicants enrolled: 176. **International students:** Number of foreign undergraduates: 54 (3% of student body). Number of countries represented: 30. Minimum TOEFL score required: 550 (paper); 200 (computer).

Massachusetts College of Liberal Arts

- Address: 375 Church Street, North Adams, MA 01247
- Website: http://www.mcla.edu
- Public
- Enrollment: 1,211 full-time; 224 part-time

KEY STATS

✔ **U.S News College Ranking:** fourth tier, Liberal Arts Colleges
✔ **SAT Score (25th/75th percentile):** 920-1150
✔ **Tuition:** 2006-2007: $6,326 in state, $15,271 out of state

Selectivity: Selective	Room/board: $6,542
Acceptance rate: 71%	Average debt: $16,478
Student/faculty ratio: 13/1	Proportion who borrowed: 64%

UNDERGRADUATE STUDENT BODY STATS

2005-2006 enrollment: 1,211 full-time; 224 part-time. Men: 39%; women: 61%. **Ethnic makeup:** African American: 3%; Asian American: 1%; Hispanic: 3%; White: 92%.

ADMISSIONS FACTS AND FIGURES

Phone: (413) 662-5410. **Email:** admissions@mcla.edu. **Website:** http://www.mcla.edu. **Application deadlines for fall 2007:** Regular decision: Rolling. Early decision: Not offered. Early action: Send application by: December 1; Decision sent by: December 15. Admission can be deferred. **Application fee:** $25. Common application is accepted. **Admissions requirements/recommendations:** High school units required (recommended): English: 4; Mathematics: 3; Science: 3; Foreign language: 2; Social studies: 2; History: 0; Academic electives: 2; Total units: 16. Tests: The college uses SAT or ACT scores in admissions decisions. Either SAT or ACT required. For admission to the fall 2007 entering class, the school will accept: ACT with writing, ACT without writing. Campus visit: Recommended. Admissions interview: Recommended. Off-campus interview: Not available. **Factors that count in admissions decisions:** *Academic:* Secondary school record: Very important. Class rank: Considered. Letters of recommendation: Considered. Standardized test scores: Important. Essay: Considered. *Nonacademic:* Interview: Considered. Extracurricular activities: Considered. Talent/ability: Considered. Character/personal qualities: Important. Alumni/ae relationship: Not considered. Geographical residence: Not considered. State residency: Not considered. Religious affiliation/commitment: Not considered. Minority status: Not considered. Volunteer work: Considered. Work experience: Considered. **Admissions statistics for the fall 2005 entering class:** Total applicants: 1,114. Total accepted: 794. Freshmen enrolled: 274; 24% were from out of state. Overall acceptance rate: 71%. Non-early acceptance rate: 71%. **Average high school grade point average:** 3.0. **First-year students who submitted SAT scores:** 95%. Scores (25/75 percentile): Verbal: 470-590, Math: 450-560, Combined: 920-1150. **First-year students submitting ACT scores:** 7%. Scores (25/75 percentile): English: N/A, Math: N/A, Composite: N/A.

ACADEMICS

Year founded: 1894. **Academic calendar:** Semester. **Degrees offered:** bachelor's, post-bachelor's certificate, master's, post-master's certificate. **Most popular majors:** 23% business, management, marketing, and related support services, 18% English language and literature/letters, 16% social sciences, 10% biological and biomedical sciences, 8% psychology. **Major fields of study:** biological and biomedical sciences; business, management, marketing, and related support services; computer and information sciences and support services; education; English language and literature/letters; history; mathematics and statistics; multi/interdisciplinary studies; natural resources and conservation; philosophy and religious studies; physical sciences; psychology; social sciences; visual and performing arts. **Areas of required coursework:** arts/fine arts, humanities, computer literacy, mathematics, English (including composition), philosophy, sciences (biological or physical), history, social science. **Pre-professional programs:** pre-law, pre-medicine. **Special academic programs (% participation):** cross-registration (1.3%), distance learning (0%), double major (4.2%), dual enrollment (0%), exchange student program (domestic) (.3%), honors program (11.1%), independent study (21.1%), internships (21.5%), liberal arts/career combination (.4%), student-designed major (3.8%), study abroad (2.8%), teacher certificate program (10.7%), weekend college (0%). **Teacher certification offered in:** early childhood, elementary, middle/junior high, secondary. **Faculty and instruction (2005-2006):** Total instructional faculty: 85 full-time, 48 part-time (56% men; 44% women; 4% minorities). Full-time faculty with Ph.D. or other terminal degree: 72%. Student/faculty ratio: 13/1. Classes of fewer than 20 students: 68%; of 20 to 49 students: 32%. **Advanced Placement and International Baccalaureate credit:** AP tests may be used for: Credit and/or placement. Scores accepted: 3. International Baccalaureate exams may be used for: Credit only. **Freshmen returning for sophomore year:** 73%. **Graduation rates:** Four-year: 35%; five-year: 46%; six-year: 47%.

COSTS AND FINANCIAL AID

Financial aid office: (413) 662-5219. **Expenses (2006-2007):** Tuition and fees 2006-2007: $6,326 in state, $15,271 out of state; room/board: $6,542. Estimated books and supplies: $800; transportation: $600; personal expenses: $1,669. **Financial aid:** Priority filing date for institution's financial aid form: March 1. In 2005-2006, 89% of undergraduates applied for financial aid. Of those, 66% were determined to have financial need; 32% had their need fully met. Average financial aid package (proportion receiving): $7,130 (65%). Average amount of gift aid, such as scholarships or grants (proportion receiving): $4,902 (49%). Average amount of self-help aid, such as work study or loans (proportion receiving): $4,116 (55%). Average need-based loan (excluding PLUS or other private loans): $3,241. Among students who received need-based aid, the average percentage of need met: 69%. Among students who received aid based on merit, the average award (and the proportion receiving): $4,135 (21%). Average amount of debt of borrowers graduating in 2005: $16,478. Proportion who borrowed: 64%.

CAMPUS LIFE AND EXTRACURRICULAR ACTIVITIES

Campus housing available: coed dorms, apartment for single students, special housing for disabled students. Students who live in college-owned, operated, or affiliated housing: 61%. **Student employment:** During the 2005-2006 academic year, 19% of undergraduates worked on campus. Average per-year earnings: $2,244. **Clubs and organizations:** Number of student organizations: 34. Activities include: choral groups, concert band, dance, drama/theater, jazz band, literary magazine, music ensembles, musical theater, radio station, student government, student newspaper, television station, yearbook. Number of fraternities: 2; sororities: 2. Proportion of men in fraternities: 1%; of women in sororities: 2%. Average proportion of students who stay on campus on weekends: 80%. **Sports program (2005-2006):** Member of NCAA III. *Men's intercollegiate varsity sports:* baseball, basketball, cross-country, golf, soccer. *Women's intercollegiate varsity sports:* basketball, soccer, softball, tennis, volleyball.

SERVICES AND FACILITIES

Basic services: nonremedial tutoring, women's center, placement service, health service, health insurance. **Remedial assistance:** reading, math, writing, study skills. **Counseling services:** minority student, career, personal, veteran student, academic, psychological, birth control. **For learning-disabled students:** School does not offer a structured program with separate admission and additional fees. Total undergraduates in learning-disabled program or receiving services: 95. Services include: remedial math, remedial English, reading machines, remedial reading, tape recorders, diagnostic testing service, untimed tests, note-taking services, oral tests, learning center, readers, extended time for tests, tutors, priority registration, priority seating, texts on tape, typist/scribe, exams on tape or computer. **Library:** Number of titles: 187,000; number of current serial subscriptions: 93. **Information technology resources:** Students are not required to lease or own a computer. Number of campus computers available to all students: 200. School has a wireless network. Proportion of college-owned housing units wired for high-speed internet access: 100%. **Campus safety:** Security services offered: 24-hour foot-and-vehicle patrols, late-night transport/escort service, 24-hour emergency telephones, lighted pathways/sidewalks, controlled dormitory access (key, security card, etc).

TRANSFER AND INTERNATIONAL STUDENTS

Transfer students: May apply for admission for the following academic terms: Fall, Spring. Applicants need a minimum number of credits to apply. For fall 2005: Transfer applications received: 349. Transfer applicants offered admission: 271. Transfer applicants enrolled: 176. **International students:** Number of foreign undergraduates: 1. Number of countries represented: 4. Minimum TOEFL score required: 550 (paper); 213 (computer).

Massachusetts Institute of Technology

- **Address:** 77 Massachusetts Avenue, Cambridge, MA 02139
- **Website:** http://web.mit.edu/
- **Private**
- **Enrollment:** 4,014 full-time; 52 part-time

KEY STATS

✔ **U.S News College Ranking:** 4, National Universities
✔ **SAT Score (25th/75th percentile):** 1430-1570
✔ **Tuition:** 2006-2007: $33,600

Selectivity: Most selective	**Room/board:** $9,950
Acceptance rate: 14%	**Average debt:** $19,748
Student/faculty ratio: 8/1	**Proportion who borrowed:** 50%

UNDERGRADUATE STUDENT BODY STATS

2005-2006 enrollment: 4,014 full-time; 52 part-time. Men: 57%; women: 43%. **Ethnic makeup:** African American: 6%; American-Indian: 2%; Asian American: 27%; Hispanic: 11%; White: 47%; International: 8%.

ADMISSIONS FACTS AND FIGURES

Phone: (617) 253-4791. **Email:** admissions@mit.edu. **Website:** http://web.mit.edu/. **Application deadlines for fall 2007:** Regular decision: January 1; decision sent by March 25. Early decision: Not offered. Early action: Send application by: November 1; Decision sent by: December 15. Admission can be deferred. **Application fee:** $65. Common application is not accepted. **To apply online, go to:** http://web.mit.edu/admissions. **Admissions requirements/recommendations:** High school units required (recommended): English: (4); Mathematics: (4); Science: (4); Foreign language: (2); Social studies: (2). Tests: The college uses SAT or ACT scores in admissions decisions. Either SAT or ACT required. For admission to the fall 2007 entering class, the school will accept: ACT with writing, ACT without writing. Campus visit: Neither required nor recommended. Admissions interview: Recommended. Off-campus interview: May be arranged. **Factors that count in admissions decisions:** *Academic:* Secondary school record: Important. Class rank: Important. Letters of recommendation: Important. Standardized test scores: Important. Essay: Considered. *Nonacademic:* Interview: Important. Extracurricular activities: Important. Talent/ability: Important. Character/personal qualities: Very important. Alumni/ae relationship: Considered. Geographical residence: Considered. State residency: Not considered. Religious affiliation/commitment: Not considered. Minority status: Considered. Volunteer work: Considered. Work experience: Considered. **Other schools with the greatest overlap in applicants:** California Institute of Technology; Harvard University; Princeton University; Stanford University; Yale University. **Admissions statistics for the fall 2005 entering class:** Total applicants: 10,440. Total accepted: 1,494. Freshmen enrolled: 996; 89% were from out of state. Accepted through early-decision or early-action plans: 29%. Overall acceptance rate: 14%. Non-early acceptance rate: 15%. **Size of waiting list:** 469 applicants; enrolled from waiting list: 0. **Credentials of fall 2005 freshmen:** 97% ranked in the top 10 percent of their high school class; 100% were in the top 25 percent, and 100% were in the top half. (Proportion submitting class standing: 56%.) **First-year students who submitted SAT scores:** 92%. Scores (25/75 percentile): Verbal: 690-770, Math: 740-800, Combined: 1430-1570. **First-year students submitting ACT scores:** 20%. Scores (25/75 percentile): English: N/A, Math: N/A, Composite: 31-34.

ACADEMICS

Year founded: 1861. **Academic calendar:** 4-1-4. **Degrees offered:** bachelor's, master's, doctorate. **Most popular majors:** 32% engineering, 17% computer science, 10% biology/biological sciences, 9% business, management, marketing, and related support services, 9% physical sciences. **Major fields of study:** architecture and related services; biological and biomedical sciences; business, management, marketing, and related support services; communication, journalism, and related programs; computer and information sciences and support services; engineering; English language and literature/letters; foreign languages, literatures, and linguistics; history; liberal arts and sciences studies, and humanities; mathematics and statistics; multi/interdisciplinary studies; philosophy and religious studies; physical sciences; psychology; social sciences; visual and performing arts. **Areas of required coursework:** arts/fine arts, humanities, mathematics, sciences (biological or physical), social science, other. **Pre-professional programs:** pre-law, pre-medicine. **Special academic programs (% participation):** cooperative (work-study plan) program (4%), cross-registration (13%), English as a Second Language (ESL) (5%), internships (11%), study abroad (6%), teacher certificate program (3%). **Teacher certification offered in:** middle/junior high, secondary. **Cooperative education programs:** computer science, engineering. **Reserve Officers Training Corps (ROTC):** Army ROTC: Offered on campus; Navy ROTC: Offered on campus; Air Force ROTC: Offered on campus. **Faculty and instruction (2005-2006):** Total instructional faculty: 1,177 full-time, 377 part-time (78% men; 22% women; 12% minorities). Full-time faculty with Ph.D. or other terminal degree: 94%. Student/faculty ratio: 8/1. Classes of fewer than 20 students: 68%; of 20 to 49 students: 21%; of 50 or more students: 11%. **Advanced Placement and International Baccalaureate credit:** AP tests may be used for: Credit and/or placement. Scores accepted: 4, 5. International Baccalaureate exams may be used for: Credit and/or placement. **Freshmen returning for sophomore year:** 98%. **Graduation rates:** Four-year: 82%; five-year: 92%; six-year: 94%. **Graduate study:** 47% of students pursue further study immediately upon graduation. Fields in which graduates pursue further study: law, 2%; medicine, 2%; engineering, 14%; arts and sciences, 27%.

COSTS AND FINANCIAL AID

Financial aid office: (617) 253-4971. **Expenses (2006-2007):** Tuition and fees 2006-2007: $33,600; room/board: $9,950. Estimated books and supplies: $1,100 personal expenses: $1,700. **Financial aid:** Priority filing date for institution's financial aid form: February 1; deadline: February 1. In 2005-2006, 72% of undergraduates applied for financial aid. Of those, 62% were determined to have financial need; 100% had their need fully met. Average financial aid package (proportion receiving): $29,831 (62%). Average amount of gift aid, such as scholarships or grants (proportion receiving): $26,013 (60%). Average amount of self-help aid, such as work study or loans (proportion receiving): $4,619 (56%). Average need-based loan (excluding PLUS or other private loans): $4,010. Among students who received need-based aid, the average percentage of need met: 100%. Among students who received aid based on merit, the average award (and the proportion receiving): $0 (0%). The average athletic scholarship (and the proportion receiving): $0 (0%). Average amount of debt of borrowers graduating in 2005: $19,748. Proportion who borrowed: 50%.

CAMPUS LIFE AND EXTRACURRICULAR ACTIVITIES

Campus housing available (% using): coed dorms (71%), women's dorms (6%), sorority housing (3%), fraternity housing (16%), apartments for married students (0%), apartment for single students (2%), special housing for disabled students, cooperative housing (1%), other housing options (1%). Students who live in college-owned, operated, or affiliated housing: 94%. **Student employment:** During the 2005-2006 academic year, 51% of undergraduates worked on campus. Average per-year earnings: $2,177. **Clubs and organizations:** Number of student organizations: 390. Activities include: choral groups, concert band, dance, drama/theater, jazz band, literary magazine, marching band, music ensembles, musical theater, radio station, student government, student newspaper, student film society, symphony orchestra, television station, yearbook. Number of fraternities: 28; sororities: 5. Proportion of men in fraternities: 55%; of women in sororities: 26%. **Sports program (2005-2006):** Member of NCAA III. *Men's intercollegiate varsity sports:* alpine skiing, baseball, basketball, crew, cross-country, fencing, football, golf, gymnastics, heavyweight crew, ice hockey, lacrosse, lightweight crew, riflery, sailing, soccer, squash, swimming and diving, tennis, track and field (indoor), track and field (outdoor), volleyball, water polo, wrestling. *Women's intercollegiate varsity sports:* alpine skiing, basketball, crew, cross-country, fencing, field hockey, gymnastics, ice hockey, lacrosse, lightweight crew, riflery, sailing, soccer, softball, swimming and diving, tennis, track and field (indoor), track and field (outdoor), volleyball, pistol.

SERVICES AND FACILITIES

Basic services: nonremedial tutoring, placement service, day care, health service, health insurance. **Counseling services:** minority student, career, personal, academic, psychological, religious, other. **For learning-disabled students:** School does not offer a structured program with separate admission and additional fees. Services include: reading machines, tape recorders, note-taking services, readers, extended time for tests, other. **Library:** Number of titles: 1,359,885; number of current serial subscriptions: 22,991. **Information technology resources:** Students are not required to lease or own a computer. Number of campus computers available to all students: 1,100. School has a wireless network. Approximate number of users that can be accommodated: 20,000. Proportion of college-owned housing units wired for high-speed internet access: 100%. **Campus safety:** Security services offered: 24-hour foot-and-vehicle patrols, late-night transport/escort service, 24-hour emergency telephones, lighted pathways/sidewalks, controlled dormitory access (key, security card, etc).

TRANSFER AND INTERNATIONAL STUDENTS

Transfer students: May apply for admission for the following academic terms: Fall, Spring. Applicants need a minimum number of credits to apply. For fall 2005: Transfer applications received: 231. Transfer applicants offered admission: 11. Transfer applicants enrolled: 9. **International students:** Number of foreign undergraduates: 306 (8% of student body). Number of countries represented: 84. Minimum TOEFL score required: 577 (paper); 233 (computer). Average TOEFL score: 639 (paper).

Merrimack College

- **Address:** 315 Turnpike Street, North Andover, MA 01845
- **Website:** http://www.merrimack.edu
- **Private; Religious affiliation:** Roman Catholic
- **Enrollment:** 1,950 full-time; 204 part-time

KEY STATS

✔ **U.S News College Ranking:** 9, Comp. Coll.–Bachelor's (North)
✔ **SAT Score (25th/75th percentile):** 1000-1150
✔ **Tuition:** 2005-2006: $23,450

Selectivity: Selective	**Room/board:** $9,730
Acceptance rate: 71%	**Average debt:** N/A
Student/faculty ratio: 12/1	**Proportion who borrowed:** N/A

UNDERGRADUATE STUDENT BODY STATS

2005-2006 enrollment: 1,950 full-time; 204 part-time. Men: 47%; women: 53%. **Ethnic makeup:** African American: 1%; Asian American: 1%; Hispanic: 2%; White: 95%; International: 1%.

ADMISSIONS FACTS AND FIGURES

Phone: (978) 837-5100. **Email:** Admission@Merrimack.edu. **Website:** http://www.merrimack.edu. **Application deadlines for fall 2007:** Regular decision: February 1; decision sent by April 1. Early decision: Not offered. Early action: Send application by: November 30; Decision sent by: December 15. Admission can be deferred. **Application fee:** $50. Common application is accepted. **Admissions requirements/recommendations:** High school units required (recommended): English: 4 (4); Mathematics: 3 (4); Science: 3 (4); Foreign language: 2 (3); Social studies: 1 (2); History: 1 (2); Academic electives: 3 (3); Total units: 17 (26). Tests: The college uses SAT or ACT scores in admissions decisions. Either SAT or ACT required. For admission to the fall 2007 entering class, the school will accept: ACT with writing. Campus visit: Recommended. Admissions interview: Recommended. Off-campus interview: May be arranged. **Factors that count in admissions decisions:** *Academic:* Secondary school record: Very important. Class rank: Important. Letters of recommendation: Important. Standardized test scores: Important. Essay: Very important. *Nonacademic:* Interview: Considered. Extracurricular activities: Considered. Talent/ability: Considered. Character/personal qualities: Important. Alumni/ae relationship: Considered. Geographical residence: Not considered. State residency: Not considered. Religious affiliation/commitment: Not considered. Minority status: Not considered. Volunteer work: Considered. Work experience: Considered. **Other schools with the greatest overlap in applicants:** Assumption College; Bentley College; Endicott College; St. Anselm College; Stonehill College. **Admissions statistics for the fall 2005 entering class:** Total applicants: 3,413. Total accepted: 2,436. Freshmen enrolled: 556; 26% were from out of state. Accepted through early-decision or early-action plans: 29%. Overall acceptance rate: 71%. Non-early acceptance rate: 72%. **Size of waiting list:** 406 applicants; enrolled from waiting list: 130. **Credentials of fall 2005 freshmen:** 19% ranked in the top 10 percent of their high school class; 47% were in the top 25 percent, and 85% were in the top half. (Proportion submitting class standing: 67%.) **Average high school grade point average:** 3.3. **First-year students who submitted SAT scores:** 97%. Scores (25/75 percentile): Verbal: 500-570, Math: 500-580, Combined: 1000-1150. **First-year students submitting ACT scores:** 2%. Scores (25/75 percentile): English: N/A, Math: N/A, Composite: 22-26.

ACADEMICS

Year founded: 1947. **Academic calendar:** Semester. **Degrees offered:** associate, bachelor's, master's. **Most popular majors:** 47% business, management, marketing, and related support services, 13% social sciences, 12% psychology, 5% communication, journalism, and related programs, 4% engineering. **Major fields of study:** biological and biomedical sciences; business, management, marketing, and related support services; communication, journalism, and related programs; computer and information sciences and support services; engineering; English language and literature/letters; foreign languages, literatures, and linguistics; health professions and related clinical sciences; history; liberal arts and sciences studies, and humanities; mathematics and statistics; natural resources and conservation; philosophy and religious studies; physical sciences; psychology; public administration and social service professions; social sciences; visual and performing arts. **Areas of required coursework:** humanities, mathematics, English (including composition), philosophy, sciences (biological or physical), history, social

science, other. **Pre-professional programs:** pre-dentistry, pre-medicine.
Special academic programs (% participation): cooperative (work-study plan) program (8%), cross-registration (2%), double major (5%), English as a Second Language (ESL) (1%), honors program (3%), independent study (4%), internships (10%), liberal arts/career combination (0%), student-designed major (0%), study abroad (8%), teacher certificate program (5%). **Teacher certification offered in:** elementary, middle/junior high, secondary. **Cooperative education programs:** business, computer science, engineering, health professions, humanities, natural science, other. **Reserve Officers Training Corps (ROTC):** Air Force ROTC: Offered at cooperating institution (University of Massachusetts-Lowell). **Faculty and instruction (2005-2006):** Total instructional faculty: 143 full-time, 80 part-time (57% men; 43% women; 8% minorities). Full-time faculty with Ph.D. or other terminal degree: 78%. Student/faculty ratio: 12/1. Classes of fewer than 20 students: 57%; of 20 to 49 students: 43%; of 50 or more students: 0%. **Advanced Placement and International Baccalaureate credit:** AP tests may be used for: Credit only. Scores accepted: 3, 4, 5. International Baccalaureate exams may be used for: Credit only. **Freshmen returning for sophomore year:** 81%. **Graduation rates:** Four-year: 54%; five-year: 70%; six-year: 65%. **Graduate study:** 14% of students pursue further study immediately upon graduation; 20% within one year. Fields in which graduates pursue further study: Master of Business Administration (MBA), 3%.

COSTS AND FINANCIAL AID
Financial aid office: (978) 837-5196. **Expenses (2005-2006):** Tuition and fees 2005-2006: $23,450; room/board: $9,730. Estimated books and supplies: $900; transportation: $575; personal expenses: $685.

CAMPUS LIFE AND EXTRACURRICULAR ACTIVITIES
Campus housing available (% using): coed dorms (83%), women's dorms (6%), men's dorms (4%), apartment for single students (5%), special housing for disabled students (1%), special housing for international students (1%). Students who live in college-owned, operated, or affiliated housing: 76%. **Student employment:** During the 2005-2006 academic year, 21% of undergraduates worked on campus. Average per-year earnings: $1,500. **Clubs and organizations:** Number of student organizations: 45. Activities include: dance, drama/theater, jazz band, musical theater, student government, student newspaper, television station, yearbook. Number of fraternities: 3; sororities: 3. Proportion of men in fraternities: 3%; of women in sororities: 5%. Average proportion of students who stay on campus on weekends: 83%. **Sports program (2005-2006):** Member of NCAA II. **Men's intercollegiate varsity sports:** baseball, basketball, cross-country, football, ice hockey, lacrosse, soccer, tennis. **Women's intercollegiate varsity sports:** basketball, cross-country, field hockey, lacrosse, soccer, softball, tennis, volleyball.

SERVICES AND FACILITIES
Basic services: nonremedial tutoring, health service, health insurance. **Remedial assistance:** math, writing, study skills. **Counseling services:** career, personal, academic, psychological. **For learning-disabled students:** School does not offer a structured program with separate admission and additional fees. Total undergraduates in learning-disabled program or receiving services: 117. Services include: tape recorders, note-taking services, oral tests, learning center, readers, extended time for tests, tutors, other. **Library:** Number of titles: 117,681; number of current serial subscriptions: 1,037. **Information technology resources:** Students are not required to lease or own a computer. Number of campus computers available to all students: 300. School has a wireless network. Approximate number of users that can be accommodated: 300. Proportion of college-owned housing units wired for high-speed internet access: 100%. **Campus safety:** Security services offered: 24-hour foot-and-vehicle patrols, late-night transport/escort service, 24-hour emergency telephones, lighted pathways/sidewalks, student patrols, controlled dormitory access (key, security card, etc.).

TRANSFER AND INTERNATIONAL STUDENTS
Transfer students: May apply for admission for the following academic terms: Fall, Spring. Applicants do not need a minimum number of credits to apply. For fall 2005: Transfer applications received: 196. Transfer applicants offered admission: 135. Transfer applicants enrolled: 63. **International students:** Number of foreign undergraduates: 24 (1% of student body). Number of countries represented: 17. Minimum TOEFL score required: 550 (paper); 230 (computer). Average TOEFL score: 600 (paper).

Montserrat College of Art

- **Address:** PO Box 26, 23 Essex Street, Beverly, MA 01915
- **Website:** http://www.montserrat.edu
- **Private**
- **Enrollment:** 279 full-time; 29 part-time

KEY STATS
✔ **U.S News College Ranking:** Unranked Specialty School–Fine Arts
✔ **SAT Score (25th/75th percentile):** 788-1231
✔ **Tuition:** 2006-2007: $21,300
  Selectivity: Less selective   **Room/board:** N/A
  Acceptance rate: 85%   **Average debt:** N/A
  Student/faculty ratio: 7/1   **Proportion who borrowed:** 84%

UNDERGRADUATE STUDENT BODY STATS
2005-2006 enrollment: 279 full-time; 29 part-time. Men: 38%; women: 62%. **Ethnic makeup:** African American: 1%; Asian American: 2%; Hispanic: 2%; White: 95%.

ADMISSIONS FACTS AND FIGURES
Phone: (978) 921-4242. **Email:** admiss@montserrat.edu. **Website:** http://www.montserrat.edu. **Application deadlines for fall 2007:** Regular decision: Rolling. Early decision: Not offered. Early action: Not offered. Admission can be deferred. **Application fee:** $40. Common application is not accepted. **Admissions requirements/recommendations:** High school units required (recommended): English: 4 (4); Social studies: 2 (2); History: 2 (2). Tests: The college uses SAT or ACT scores in admissions decisions. Neither SAT nor ACT required. For admission to the fall 2007 entering class, the school will accept: ACT with writing, ACT without writing. Campus visit: Recommended. Admissions interview: Recommended. Off-campus interview: May be arranged. **Factors that count in admissions decisions: Academic:** Secondary school record: Very important. Class rank: Considered. Letters of recommendation: Very important. Standardized test scores: Considered. Essay: Very important. **Nonacademic:** Interview: Very important. Extracurricular activities: Considered. Talent/ability: Very important. Character/personal qualities: Very important. Alumni/ae relationship: Not considered. Geographical residence: Not considered. State residency: Not considered. Religious affiliation/commitment: Not considered. Minority status: Not considered. Volunteer work: Considered. Work experience: Considered. **Other schools with the greatest overlap in applicants:** Art Institute of Boston at Lesley University; Maine College of Art; Massachusetts College of Art; Rhode Island School of Design. **Admissions statistics for the fall 2005 entering class:** Total applicants: 326. Total accepted: 276. Freshmen enrolled: 75; 55% were from out of state. Overall acceptance rate: 85%. **Average high school grade point average:** 2.8. **First-year students who submitted SAT scores:** 91%. Scores (25/75 percentile): Verbal: 416-642, Math: 372-589, Combined: 788-1231. **First-year students submitting ACT scores:** 6%. Scores (25/75 percentile): English: N/A, Math: N/A, Composite: 18-22.

ACADEMICS
Year founded: 1970. **Academic calendar:** Semester. **Degrees offered:** certificate, diploma, bachelor's. **Most popular majors:** 22% graphic design, 22% painting, 19% illustration. **Major fields of study:** visual and performing arts. **Areas of required coursework:** arts/fine arts, humanities, computer literacy, English (including composition), sciences (biological or physical), social science, other. **Special academic programs (% participation):** cross-registration (1%), dual enrollment, exchange student program (domestic) (0%), independent study (1%), internships (6%), student-designed major (0%), study abroad (0%), teacher certificate program (1%). **Teacher certification offered in:** early childhood, elementary, middle/junior high, secondary. **Reserve Officers Training Corps (ROTC):** Air Force ROTC: Offered at cooperating institution (Salem State College). **Faculty and instruction (2005-2006):** Total instructional faculty: 24 full-time, 39 part-time (46% men; 54% women; 2% minorities). Full-time faculty with Ph.D. or other terminal degree: 67%. Student/faculty ratio: 7/1. Classes of fewer than 20 students: 92%; of 20 to 49 students: 8%; of 50 or more students: 0%. **Advanced Placement and International Baccalaureate credit:** AP tests may be used for: Credit only. Scores accepted: 3, 4, 5. International Baccalaureate exams may be used for: Credit only. **Freshmen returning for sophomore year:** 64%. **Graduation rates:** Four-year: 43%; five-year: 52%; six-year: 51%.

COSTS AND FINANCIAL AID

Financial aid office: (978) 921-4242. **Expenses (2006-2007):** Tuition and fees 2006-2007: $21,300; room/board: N/A. Estimated books and supplies: $1,200; transportation: $1,500; personal expenses: $2,500. **Financial aid:** Priority filing date for institution's financial aid form: March 1; deadline: July 1. In 2005-2006, 94% of undergraduates applied for financial aid. Of those, 76% were determined to have financial need; Average financial aid package (proportion receiving): $9,947 (76%). Average amount of gift aid, such as scholarships or grants (proportion receiving): $4,548 (69%). Average amount of self-help aid, such as work study or loans (proportion receiving): $4,594 (76%). Average need-based loan (excluding PLUS or other private loans): $4,196. Proportion who borrowed: 84%.

CAMPUS LIFE AND EXTRACURRICULAR ACTIVITIES

Campus housing available (% using): apartment for single students (100%), special housing for disabled students. Students who live in college-owned, operated, or affiliated housing: 52%. **Student employment:** During the 2005-2006 academic year, 22% of undergraduates worked on campus. Average per-year earnings: $950. **Clubs and organizations:** Number of student organizations: 10. Activities include: literary magazine, student government. Number of fraternities: 0; sororities: 0. Average proportion of students who stay on campus on weekends: 45%.

SERVICES AND FACILITIES

Basic services: nonremedial tutoring, health insurance, other. **Remedial assistance:** writing, study skills. **Counseling services:** career, personal, academic, psychological. **For learning-disabled students:** School does not offer a structured program with separate admission and additional fees. Services include: reading machines, tape recorders, oral tests, learning center, extended time for tests, other. **Library:** Number of titles: 11,484; number of current serial subscriptions: 79. **Information technology resources:** Students are not required to lease or own a computer. Number of campus computers available to all students: 98. School has a wireless network. Approximate number of users that can be accommodated: 50. Proportion of college-owned housing units wired for high-speed internet access: 0%. **Campus safety:** Security services offered: controlled dormitory access (key, security card, etc).

TRANSFER AND INTERNATIONAL STUDENTS

Transfer students: May apply for admission for the following academic terms: Fall, Spring. Applicants do not need a minimum number of credits to apply. For fall 2005: Transfer applications received: 35. Transfer applicants offered admission: 34. Transfer applicants enrolled: 18. **International students:** Number of foreign undergraduates: 0. Number of countries represented: 1. Minimum TOEFL score required: 550 (paper); 213 (computer). Average TOEFL score: 580 (paper).

Mount Holyoke College

- **Address:** 50 College Street, South Hadley, MA 01075
- **Website:** http://www.mtholyoke.edu
- **Private**
- **Enrollment:** 2,052 full-time; 73 part-time

KEY STATS

- ✔ **U.S News College Ranking:** 24, Liberal Arts Colleges
- ✔ **SAT Score (25th/75th percentile):** 1230-1410
- ✔ **Tuition:** 2006-2007: $34,256

Selectivity: More selective	Room/board: $10,040
Acceptance rate: 52%	Average debt: $19,877
Student/faculty ratio: 10/1	Proportion who borrowed: 69%

UNDERGRADUATE STUDENT BODY STATS

2005-2006 enrollment: 2,052 full-time; 73 part-time. Men: 0%; women: 100%. **Ethnic makeup:** African American: 4%; American-Indian: 1%; Asian American: 12%; Hispanic: 5%; White: 63%; International: 14%.

ADMISSIONS FACTS AND FIGURES

Phone: (413) 538-2023. **Email:** admission@mtholyoke.edu. **Website:** http://www.mtholyoke.edu. **Application deadlines for fall 2007:** Regular decision: January 15; decision sent by April 1. Early decision: Send application by: November 15; Decision sent by: January 1. Early action: Not offered.

Admission can be deferred. **Application fee:** $60. Common application is accepted. **To apply online, go to:** http://www.mtholyoke.edu/adm/center/applications.shtml. **Admissions requirements/recommendations:** High school units required (recommended): English: (4); Mathematics: (3); Science: (3); Foreign language: (3); History: (3); Academic electives: (1). Tests: The college uses SAT or ACT scores in admissions decisions. Neither SAT nor ACT required. For admission to the fall 2007 entering class, the school will accept: ACT with writing, ACT without writing. Campus visit: Recommended. Admissions interview: Recommended. Off-campus interview: May be arranged. **Factors that count in admissions decisions:** *Academic:* Secondary school record: Very important. Class rank: Very important. Letters of recommendation: Very important. Standardized test scores: Considered. Essay: Very important. *Nonacademic:* Interview: Important. Extracurricular activities: Important. Talent/ability: Important. Character/personal qualities: Important. Alumni/ae relationship: Considered. Geographical residence: Considered. State residency: Not considered. Religious affiliation/commitment: Not considered. Minority status: Considered. Volunteer work: Important. Work experience: Important. **Other schools with the greatest overlap in applicants:** Brown University; Bryn Mawr College; Smith College; Tufts University; Wellesley College. **Admissions statistics for the fall 2005 entering class:** Total applicants: 2,924. Total accepted: 1,530. Freshmen enrolled: 504; 80% were from out of state. Accepted through early-decision or early-action plans: 26%. Overall acceptance rate: 52%. Early-decision acceptance rate: 54%. Non-early acceptance rate: 52%. **Size of waiting list:** 334 applicants; enrolled from waiting list: 0. **Credentials of fall 2005 freshmen:** 51% ranked in the top 10 percent of their high school class; 80% were in the top 25 percent, and 95% were in the top half. (Proportion submitting class standing: 47%.) **Average high school grade point average:** 3.6. **First-year students who submitted SAT scores:** 62%. Scores (25/75 percentile): Verbal: 620-720, Math: 610-690, Combined: 1230-1410. **First-year students submitting ACT scores:** 16%. Scores (25/75 percentile): English: 27-33, Math: 25-29, Composite: 27-30.

ACADEMICS

Year founded: 1837. **Academic calendar:** Semester. **Degrees offered:** certificate, bachelor's, post-bachelor's certificate, master's. **Most popular majors:** 11% psychology, 9% biology/biological sciences, 8% economics, 7% international relations and affairs, 6% English language and literature/letters. **Major fields of study:** architecture and related services; area, ethnic, cultural, and gender studies; biological and biomedical sciences; computer and information sciences and support services; education; English language and literature/letters; foreign languages, literatures, and linguistics; history; mathematics and statistics; multi/interdisciplinary studies; natural resources and conservation; philosophy and religious studies; physical sciences; psychology; social sciences; visual and performing arts. **Areas of required coursework:** humanities, foreign languages, sciences (biological or physical), social science, other. **Pre-professional programs:** pre-law, pre-dentistry, pre-medicine, pre-veterinary science. **Special academic programs (% participation):** cross-registration, double major (19%), exchange student program (domestic), independent study, internships, student-designed major (5%), study abroad, teacher certificate program (2%), other. **Teacher certification offered in:** early childhood, elementary, middle/junior high, secondary. **Reserve Officers Training Corps (ROTC):** Army ROTC: Offered at cooperating institution (University of Massachusetts Amherst); Air Force ROTC: Offered at cooperating institution (University of Massachusetts Amherst). **Faculty and instruction (2005-2006):** Total instructional faculty: 207 full-time, 34 part-time (47% men; 53% women; 26% minorities). Full-time faculty with Ph.D. or other terminal degree: 94%. Student/faculty ratio: 10/1. Classes of fewer than 20 students: 69%; of 20 to 49 students: 28%; of 50 or more students: 4%. **Advanced Placement and International Baccalaureate credit:** International Baccalaureate exams may be used for: Credit and/or placement. **Freshmen returning for sophomore year:** 93%. **Graduation rates:** Four-year: 74%; five-year: 78%; six-year: 80%. **Graduate study:** 20% of students pursue further study within one year; 39% within five years.

COSTS AND FINANCIAL AID

Financial aid office: (413) 538-2291. **Expenses (2006-2007):** Tuition and fees 2006-2007: $34,256; room/board: $10,040. Estimated books and supplies: $800 personal expenses: $800. **Financial aid:** Priority filing date for institution's financial aid form: January 15; deadline: February 1. In 2005-2006, 72% of undergraduates applied for financial aid. Of those, 63% were determined to have financial need; 100% had their need fully met. Average financial aid package (proportion receiving): $27,253 (63%). Average amount of gift aid, such as scholarships or grants (proportion receiving): $22,500 (60%). Average amount of self-help aid, such as work study or loans (proportion receiving): $5,949 (61%). Average need-based loan (excluding PLUS or other private loans): $4,470. Among students who received need-based aid, the average percentage of need met: 100%. Among students who received aid based on merit, the average award (and the proportion receiving): $11,981 (7%). The average athletic scholarship (and the proportion receiving): $0 (0%). Average amount of debt of borrowers graduating in 2005: $19,877. Proportion who borrowed: 69%.

CAMPUS LIFE AND EXTRACURRICULAR ACTIVITIES

Campus housing available (% using): women's dorms (99%), apartment for single students (1%), other housing options (0%). Students who live in college-owned, operated, or affiliated housing: 92%. **Student employment:** During the 2005-2006 academic year, 70% of undergraduates worked on campus. Average per-year earnings: $1,800. **Clubs and organizations:** Number of student organizations: 150. Activities include: choral groups, dance, drama/theater, jazz band, literary magazine, music ensembles, musical theater, radio station, student government, student newspaper, student film society, symphony orchestra, yearbook. Number of fraternities: 0; sororities: 0. Average proportion of students who stay on campus on weekends: 75%. **Sports program (2005-2006):** Member of NCAA III. *Women's intercollegiate varsity sports:* basketball, crew, cross-country, equestrian sports, field hockey, golf, lacrosse, soccer, squash, swimming and diving, tennis, track and field (indoor), track and field (outdoor), volleyball.

SERVICES AND FACILITIES

Basic services: nonremedial tutoring, women's center, day care, health service, health insurance. **Counseling services:** minority student, career, personal, academic, older student, psychological, birth control, religious. **For learning-disabled students:** School does not offer a structured program with separate admission and additional fees. Total undergraduates in learning-disabled program or receiving services: 125. Services include: other testing accommodations, tape recorders, diagnostic testing service, notetaking services, oral tests, readers, extended time for tests, tutors, priority seating, texts on tape, exams on tape or computer, other testing accomodations, other. **Library:** Number of titles: 721,223; number of current serial subscriptions: 3,805. **Information technology resources:** Students are not required to lease or own a computer. Number of campus computers available to all students: 561. School has a wireless network. Approximate number of users that can be accommodated: 3,000. Proportion of college-owned housing units wired for high-speed internet access: 100%. **Campus safety:** Security services offered: 24-hour foot-and-vehicle patrols, late-night transport/escort service, 24-hour emergency telephones, lighted pathways/sidewalks, student patrols, controlled dormitory access (key, security card, etc).

TRANSFER AND INTERNATIONAL STUDENTS

Transfer students: May apply for admission for the following academic terms: Fall, Spring. Applicants need a minimum number of credits to apply. For fall 2005: Transfer applications received: 207. Transfer applicants offered admission: 53. Transfer applicants enrolled: 25. **International students:** Number of foreign undergraduates: 291 (14% of student body). Number of countries represented: 67. Minimum TOEFL score required: 600 (paper); 250 (computer). Average TOEFL score: 638 (paper).

Mount Ida College

- **Address:** 777 Dedham Street, Newton, MA 02159
- **Website:** http://www.mountida.edu
- **Private**
- **Enrollment:** 1,210 full-time; 77 part-time

KEY STATS

✔ **U.S News College Ranking:** third tier, Comp. Coll.–Bachelor's (North)
✔ **SAT Score (25th/75th percentile):** 780-980
✔ **Tuition:** 2006-2007: $20,450

Selectivity: Less selective	**Room/board:** $10,225
Acceptance rate: 84%	**Average debt:** $18,328
Student/faculty ratio: N/A	**Proportion who borrowed:** 77%

UNDERGRADUATE STUDENT BODY STATS

2005-2006 enrollment: 1,210 full-time; 77 part-time. Men: 31%; women: 69%. **Ethnic makeup:** African American: 10%; Asian American: 2%; Hispanic: 6%; White: 75%; International: 6%.

ADMISSIONS FACTS AND FIGURES

Phone: (617) 928-4535. **Email:** admissions@mountida.edu. **Website:** http://www.mountida.edu. **Application deadlines for fall 2007:** Regular decision: August 15. Early decision: Not offered. Early action: Not offered. Admission can be deferred. **Application fee:** $35. Common application is not accepted. **Admissions requirements/recommendations:** High school units required (recommended): English: 4 (4); Mathematics: 3 (3); Science: 2 (3); Foreign language: 2 (2); Social studies: 2 (2); History: 2 (2); Academic electives: 0 (0). Tests: The college uses SAT or ACT scores in admissions decisions. Either SAT or ACT required. For admission to the fall 2007 entering class, the school will accept: ACT without writing. Campus visit: Recommended. Admissions interview: Recommended. Off-campus interview: May be arranged. **Factors that count in admissions decisions:** *Academic:* Secondary school record: Very important. Class rank: Considered. Letters of recommendation: Important. Standardized test scores: Important. Essay: Considered. *Nonacademic:* Interview: Considered. Extracurricular activities: Important. Talent/ability: Important. Character/personal qualities: Important. Alumni/ae relationship: Considered. Geographical residence: Not considered. State residency: Not considered. Religious affiliation/commitment: Not considered. Minority status: Not considered. Volunteer work: Important. Work experience: Important. **Other schools with the greatest overlap in applicants:** Becker College; Curry College; Endicott College; Lasell College; Newbury College. **Admissions statistics for the fall 2005 entering class:** Total applicants: 1,874. Total accepted: 1,579. Freshmen enrolled: 385; 45% were from out of state. Overall acceptance rate: 84%. **Average high school grade point average:** 2.5. **First-year students who submitted SAT scores:** 93%. Scores (25/75 percentile): Verbal: 390-490, Math: 390-490, Combined: 780-980. **First-year students submitting ACT scores:** 10%. Scores (25/75 percentile): English: N/A, Math: N/A, Composite: 16-21.

ACADEMICS

Year founded: 1899. **Academic calendar:** Semester. **Degrees offered:** certificate, associate, bachelor's. **Most popular majors:** Information not available. **Major fields of study:** biological and biomedical sciences; business, management, marketing, and related support services; education; English language and literature/letters; health professions and related clinical sciences; liberal arts and sciences studies, and humanities; psychology; public administration and social service professions. **Areas of required coursework:** humanities, computer literacy, mathematics, English (including composition), philosophy, sciences (biological or physical), history, social science, other. **Pre-professional programs:** pre-law, other. **Special academic programs (% participation):** accelerated program (.6%), distance learning (7%), double major (.6%), English as a Second Language (ESL) (4.5%), internships (87%), liberal arts/career combination (.5%), study abroad (.6%), teacher certificate program (1%), weekend college. **Teacher certification offered in:** early childhood. **Faculty and instruction (2005-2006):** Total instructional faculty: 60 full-time, 101 part-time (39% men; 61% women; 4% minorities). Full-time faculty with Ph.D. or other terminal degree: 62%. **Advanced Placement and International Baccalaureate credit:** AP tests may be used for: Credit only. Scores accepted: 3, 4, 5. International Baccalaureate exams may be used for: Credit only. **Freshmen returning for sophomore year:** 60%. **Graduation rates:** Six-year: 49%. **Graduate study:** 7% of students pursue further study immediately upon graduation; 8% within one year. Fields in which graduates pursue further study: Master of Business Administration (MBA), 7%; law, 21%; medicine, 7%; arts and sciences, 50%; veterinary medicine, 14%.

COSTS AND FINANCIAL AID

Financial aid office: (617) 928-4785. **Expenses (2006-2007):** Tuition and fees 2006-2007: $20,450; room/board: $10,225. Estimated books and supplies: $1,000; transportation: $700; personal expenses: $1,000. **Financial aid:** Priority filing date for institution's financial aid form: May 1. In 2005-2006, 86% of undergraduates applied for financial aid. Of those, 79% were determined to have financial need; 6% had their need fully met. Average financial aid package (proportion receiving): $11,436 (79%). Average amount of gift aid, such as scholarships or grants (proportion receiving): $8,240 (76%). Average amount of self-help aid, such as work study or loans (proportion receiving): $3,664 (74%). Average need-based loan (excluding PLUS or other private loans): $3,346. Among students who received need-based aid, the average percentage of need met: 51%. Among students who received aid based on merit, the average award (and the proportion receiving): $8,123 (20%). The average athletic scholarship (and the proportion receiving): $0 (0%). Average amount of debt of borrowers graduating in 2005: $18,328. Proportion who borrowed: 77%.

CAMPUS LIFE AND EXTRACURRICULAR ACTIVITIES

Campus housing available (% using): coed dorms (91%), women's dorms (8%), special housing for disabled students (1%). Students who live in college-owned, operated, or affiliated housing: 65%. **Student employment:** During the 2005-2006 academic year, 50% of undergraduates worked on campus. Average per-year earnings: $2,000. **Clubs and organizations:** Number of student organizations: 17. Activities include: choral groups, dance, drama/theater, literary magazine, radio station, student government, student newspaper, television station, yearbook. Number of fraternities: 0; sororities: 0. Average proportion of students who stay on campus on weekends: 25%. **Sports program (2005-2006):** Member of NCAA III. *Men's intercollegiate varsity sports:* basketball, football, lacrosse, soccer, volleyball. *Women's intercollegiate varsity sports:* basketball, cross-country, soccer, softball, volleyball.

SERVICES AND FACILITIES

Basic services: placement service, health service, health insurance. **Remedial assistance:** reading, math, writing, study skills. **Counseling services:** minority student, career, personal, academic, psychological, birth control, other. **For learning-disabled students:** School does not offer a structured program with separate admission and additional fees. Services include: reading machines, tape recorders, untimed tests, note-taking services, oral tests, learning center, extended time for tests, tutors, priority seating, texts on tape, other testing accomodations, other. **Library:** Number of titles: 80,656; number of current serial subscriptions: 315. **Information technology resources:** Students are not required to lease or own a computer. Number of campus computers available to all students: 122. School has a wireless network. Proportion of college-owned housing units wired for high-speed internet access: 100%. **Campus safety:** Security services offered: 24-hour foot-and-vehicle patrols, late-night transport/escort service, 24-hour emergency telephones, lighted pathways/sidewalks, student patrols, controlled dormitory access (key, security card, etc).

TRANSFER AND INTERNATIONAL STUDENTS

Transfer students: May apply for admission for the following academic terms: Fall, Spring. Applicants need a minimum number of credits to apply. **International students:** Number of foreign undergraduates: 81 (6% of student body). Minimum TOEFL score required: 450 (paper).

Newbury College

- **Address:** 129 Fischer Avenue, Brookline, MA 02445-5796
- **Website:** http://www.newbury.edu/
- **Private**
- **Enrollment:** N/A

KEY STATS
- ✔ **U.S News College Ranking:** fourth tier, Comp. Coll.–Bachelor's (North)
- ✔ **SAT or ACT Score (25th/75th percentile):** N/A
- ✔ **Tuition:** N/A

Selectivity: Less selective	**Room/board:** N/A
Acceptance rate: N/A	**Average debt:** N/A
Student/faculty ratio: N/A	**Proportion who borrowed:** N/A

New England Conservatory of Music

- **Address:** 290 Huntington Avenue, Boston, MA 02115
- **Website:** http://www.newenglandconservatory.edu
- **Private**
- **Enrollment:** 388 full-time; 24 part-time

KEY STATS
- ✔ **U.S News College Ranking:** Unranked Specialty School–Fine Arts
- ✔ **SAT or ACT Score (25th/75th percentile):** N/A
- ✔ **Tuition:** 2006-2007: $29,300

Selectivity: Least selective	**Room/board:** $11,089
Acceptance rate: 30%	**Average debt:** N/A
Student/faculty ratio: 4/1	**Proportion who borrowed:** N/A

UNDERGRADUATE STUDENT BODY STATS

2005-2006 enrollment: 388 full-time; 24 part-time. Men: 55%; women: 45%. **Ethnic makeup:** African American: 2%; American-Indian: 1%; Asian American: 9%; Hispanic: 5%; White: 66%; International: 17%.

ADMISSIONS FACTS AND FIGURES

Phone: (617) 585-1101. **Email:** admission@newenglandconservatory.edu. **Website:** http://www.newenglandconservatory.edu. **Application deadlines for fall 2007:** Regular decision: Rolling. Early decision: Not offered. Early action: Not offered. Admission can be deferred. **Application fee:** $100. Common application is not accepted. **To apply online, go to:** http://www.newenglandconservatory.edu/admission/colldownload.html. **Admissions requirements/recommendations:** Tests: The college uses SAT or ACT scores in admissions decisions. Either SAT or ACT required. For admission to the fall 2007 entering class, the school will accept: ACT with writing, ACT without writing. Campus visit: Neither required nor recommended. Admissions interview: Neither required nor recommended. Off-campus interview: Not available. **Factors that count in admissions decisions:** *Academic:* Secondary school record: Important. Class rank: Not considered. Letters of recommendation: Important. Standardized test scores: Considered. Essay: Considered. *Nonacademic:* Interview: Very important. Extracurricular activities: Not considered. Talent/ability: Very important. Character/personal qualities: Considered. Alumni/ae relationship: Not considered. Geographical residence: Not considered. State residency: Not considered. Religious affiliation/commitment: Not considered. Minority status: Not considered. Volunteer work: Not considered. Work experience: Not considered. **Other schools with the greatest overlap in applicants:** Juilliard School; Manhattan School of Music; Oberlin College; Rice University; University of Rochester. **Admissions statistics for the fall 2005 entering class:** Total applicants: 968. Total accepted: 292. Freshmen enrolled: 104; Overall acceptance rate: 30%. **Size of waiting list:** 337 applicants; enrolled from waiting list: 21.

ACADEMICS

Year founded: 1867. **Academic calendar:** Semester. **Degrees offered:** certificate, diploma, bachelor's, post-bachelor's certificate, master's, doctorate. **Most popular majors:** Information not available. **Major fields of study:** visual and performing arts. **Areas of required coursework:** arts/fine arts, humanities, English (including composition), history, other. **Special academic programs:** cross-registration, double major, dual enrollment, English as a Second Language (ESL), independent study, internships, study abroad. **Faculty and instruction (2005-2006):** Total instructional faculty: 83 full-time, 127 part-time (71% men; 29% women; 20% minorities). Full-time faculty with Ph.D. or other terminal degree: 27%. Student/faculty ratio: 4/1. Classes of fewer than 20 students: 78%; of 20 to 49 students: 22%; of 50 or more students: 0%. **Advanced Placement and International Baccalaureate credit:** AP tests may be used for: Credit and/or placement. Scores accepted: 3. **Freshmen returning for sophomore year:** 90%. **Graduation rates:** Four-year: 48%; five-year: 62%; six-year: 65%.

COSTS AND FINANCIAL AID

Financial aid office: (617) 585-1110. **Expenses (2006-2007):** Tuition and fees 2006-2007: $29,300; room/board: $11,089. Estimated books and supplies: $700; transportation: $316; personal expenses: $2,100. **Financial aid:** Priority filing date for institution's financial aid form: December 1; deadline: December 1.

CAMPUS LIFE AND EXTRACURRICULAR ACTIVITIES

Campus housing available (% using): coed dorms (100%). Students who live in college-owned, operated, or affiliated housing: 20%. **Student employment:** During the 2005-2006 academic year, 60% of undergraduates worked on campus. Average per-year earnings: $1,500. **Clubs and organizations:** Number of student organizations: 8. Activities include: choral groups, concert band, jazz band, music ensembles, musical theater, opera, student government, symphony orchestra. Number of fraternities: 1; sororities: 0. Proportion of men in fraternities: 15%; Average proportion of students who stay on campus on weekends: 95%.

SERVICES AND FACILITIES

Basic services: health insurance. **Remedial assistance:** writing, other. **Counseling services:** career, personal, academic, psychological. **For learning-disabled students:** School does not offer a structured program with separate admission and additional fees. **Library:** Number of titles: 82,964; number of current serial subscriptions: 295. **Information technology resources:** Students are not required to lease or own a computer. Number of campus computers available to all students: 52. School does not have a wireless network. Proportion of college-owned housing units wired for high-speed internet access: 0%. **Campus safety:** Security services offered: controlled dormitory access (key, security card, etc.).

TRANSFER AND INTERNATIONAL STUDENTS

Transfer students: May apply for admission for the following academic terms: Fall, Spring. Applicants need a minimum number of credits to apply. For fall 2005: Transfer applications received: 129. Transfer applicants offered admission: 32. Transfer applicants enrolled: 15. **International students:** Number of foreign undergraduates: 66 (17% of student body). Number of countries represented: 39. Minimum TOEFL score required: 550 (paper); 213 (computer).

Nichols College

- **Address:** Box 5000, Dudley, MA 01571
- **Website:** http://www.nichols.edu/
- **Private**
- **Enrollment:** 891 full-time; 354 part-time

KEY STATS

- ✔ **U.S News College Ranking:** Unranked Specialty School–Business
- ✔ **SAT Score (25th/75th percentile):** 800-990
- ✔ **Tuition:** 2006-2007: $23,900

Selectivity: Less selective	**Room/board:** $8,800
Acceptance rate: 87%	**Average debt:** $32,224
Student/faculty ratio: 20/1	**Proportion who borrowed:** 91%

UNDERGRADUATE STUDENT BODY STATS

2005-2006 enrollment: 891 full-time; 354 part-time. Men: 61%; women: 39%. **Ethnic makeup:** African American: 6%; Asian American: 2%; Hispanic: 4%; White: 87%.

ADMISSIONS FACTS AND FIGURES

Phone: (800) 470-3379. **Email:** admissions@nichols.edu. **Website:** http://www.nichols.edu/. **Application deadlines for fall 2007:** Regular decision: Rolling. Early decision: Not offered. Early action: Not offered. Admission can be deferred. **Application fee:** $25. Common application is accepted. **Admissions requirements/recommendations:** High school units required (recommended): English: 4; Mathematics: 2 (3); Science: 2 (3); Foreign language: (2); Social studies: 2 (3); History: 2 (2); Academic electives: (5). Tests: The college uses SAT or ACT scores in admissions decisions. Neither SAT nor ACT required. Campus visit: Recommended. Admissions interview: Recommended. Off-campus interview: Not available. **Factors that count in admissions decisions:** *Academic:* Secondary school record: Very important. Class rank: Considered. Letters of recommendation: Important. Standardized test scores: Considered. Essay: Important. *Nonacademic:* Interview: Considered. Extracurricular activities: Considered. Talent/ability: Not considered. Character/personal qualities: Very important. Alumni/ae relationship: Considered. Geographical residence: Not considered. State residency: Not considered. Religious affiliation/commitment: Not considered. Minority status: Not considered. Volunteer work: Considered. Work experience: Considered. **Other schools with the greatest overlap in applicants:** Bryant University; Curry College; Endicott College; Western New England College; Worcester State College. **Admissions statistics for the fall 2005 entering class:** Total applicants: 1,150. Total accepted: 999. Freshmen enrolled: 297; 37% were from out of state. Overall acceptance rate: 87%. **Credentials of fall 2005 freshmen:** 2% ranked in the top 10 percent of their high school class; 18% were in the top 25 percent, and 42% were in the top half. (Proportion submitting class standing: 54%.) **Average high school grade point average:** 2.4. **First-year students who submitted SAT scores:** 82%. Scores (25/75 percentile): Verbal: 400-480, Math: 400-510, Combined: 800-990.

ACADEMICS

Year founded: 1815. **Academic calendar:** Semester. **Degrees offered:** associate, bachelor's, master's. **Most popular majors:** 77% business, management, marketing, and related support services, 10% English language and literature/letters, 5% psychology, 3% English language and literature/letters, 2% security and protective services. **Major fields of study:** business, management, marketing, and related support services; education; English language and literature/letters; history; mathematics and statistics; parks, recreation, leisure, and fitness studies; psychology; security and protective services.

Areas of required coursework: arts/fine arts, humanities, computer literacy, mathematics, English (including composition), philosophy, sciences (biological or physical), history, social science, other. **Special academic programs:** accelerated program, distance learning, double major, external degree program, honors program, independent study, internships, study abroad, teacher certificate program. **Teacher certification offered in:** middle/junior high, secondary. **Reserve Officers Training Corps (ROTC):** Army ROTC: Offered at cooperating institution (Worcester Polytechnical Institute). **Faculty and instruction (2005-2006):** Total instructional faculty: 32 full-time, 167 part-time (77% men; 23% women). Full-time faculty with Ph.D. or other terminal degree: 50%. Student/faculty ratio: 20/1. Classes of fewer than 20 students: 57%; of 20 to 49 students: 42%; of 50 or more students: 1%. **Advanced Placement and International Baccalaureate credit:** AP tests may be used for: Credit only. Scores accepted: 3, 4, 5. International Baccalaureate exams may be used for: Credit only. **Freshmen returning for sophomore year:** 65%. **Graduation rates:** Four-year: 41%; five-year: 46%; six-year: 43%. **Graduate study:** 6% of students pursue further study immediately upon graduation; 4% within one year. Fields in which graduates pursue further study: Master of Business Administration (MBA), 90%; law, 5%; arts and sciences, 5%.

COSTS AND FINANCIAL AID

Financial aid office: (508) 213-2278. **Expenses (2006-2007):** Tuition and fees 2006-2007: $23,900; room/board: $8,800. Estimated books and supplies: $1,050; transportation: $500; personal expenses: $1,171. **Financial aid:** Priority filing date for institution's financial aid form: March 1; deadline: June 1. In 2005-2006, 89% of undergraduates applied for financial aid. Of those, 60% were determined to have financial need; 31% had their need fully met. Average financial aid package (proportion receiving): $16,228 (58%). Average amount of gift aid, such as scholarships or grants (proportion receiving): $9,940 (57%). Average amount of self-help aid, such as work study or loans (proportion receiving): $7,052 (54%). Average need-based loan (excluding PLUS or other private loans): $6,566. Among students who received need-based aid, the average percentage of need met: 74%. Among students who received aid based on merit, the average award (and the proportion receiving): $11,672 (17%). The average athletic scholarship (and the proportion receiving): $0 (0%). Average amount of debt of borrowers graduating in 2005: $32,224. Proportion who borrowed: 91%.

CAMPUS LIFE AND EXTRACURRICULAR ACTIVITIES

Campus housing available (% using): coed dorms (100%), special housing for disabled students (0%). Students who live in college-owned, operated, or affiliated housing: 80%. **Student employment:** During the 2005-2006 academic year, 5% of undergraduates worked on campus. Average per-year earnings: $1,800. **Clubs and organizations:** Number of student organizations: 26. Activities include: drama/theater, literary magazine, radio station, student government, student newspaper, yearbook. Number of fraternities: 0; sororities: 0. Average proportion of students who stay on campus on weekends: 60%. **Sports program (2005-2006):** Member of NCAA III. *Men's intercollegiate varsity sports:* baseball, basketball, football, golf, ice hockey, lacrosse, soccer, tennis. *Women's intercollegiate varsity sports:* basketball, field hockey, lacrosse, soccer, softball, tennis.

SERVICES AND FACILITIES

Basic services: nonremedial tutoring, placement service, health service, health insurance. **Remedial assistance:** reading, math, writing, study skills. **Counseling services:** minority student, career, military, personal, academic, older student, psychological, birth control, religious. **For learning-disabled students:** School does not offer a structured program with separate admission and additional fees. Total undergraduates in learning-disabled program or receiving services: 70. Services include: remedial math, reading machines, untimed tests, learning center, extended time for tests, tutors, exams on tape or computer. **Library:** Number of titles: 46,774; number of current serial subscriptions: 214. **Information technology resources:** Students are not required to lease or own a computer. Number of campus computers available to all students: 65. School has a wireless network. Approximate number of users that can be accommodated: 60. Proportion of college-owned housing units wired for high-speed internet access: 100%. **Campus safety:** Security services offered: 24-hour foot-and-vehicle patrols, late-night transport/escort service, 24-hour emergency telephones, lighted pathways/sidewalks, controlled dormitory access (key, security card, etc.).

TRANSFER AND INTERNATIONAL STUDENTS

Transfer students: May apply for admission for the following academic terms: Fall, Spring. Applicants do not need a minimum number of credits to apply. For fall 2005: Transfer applications received: 110. Transfer appli-

cants offered admission: 76. Transfer applicants enrolled: 43. **International students:** Number of foreign undergraduates: 2. Minimum TOEFL score required: 500 (paper); 173 (computer).

Northeastern University

- **Address:** 360 Huntington Avenue, Boston, MA 02115
- **Website:** http://www.northeastern.edu/
- **Private**
- **Enrollment:** 12,080 full-time

KEY STATS

✔ **U.S News College Ranking:** 98, National Universities
✔ **SAT Score (25th/75th percentile):** 1140-1320
✔ **Tuition:** 2006-2007: $30,309
Selectivity: More selective **Room/board:** $10,950
Acceptance rate: 47% **Average debt:** N/A
Student/faculty ratio: 16/1 **Proportion who borrowed:** N/A

UNDERGRADUATE STUDENT BODY STATS

2005-2006 enrollment: 12,080 full-time. Men: 48%; women: 52%. **Ethnic makeup:** African American: 6%; Asian American: 7%; Hispanic: 5%; White: 77%; International: 5%.

ADMISSIONS FACTS AND FIGURES

Phone: (617) 373-2200. **Email:** admissions@neu.edu. **Website:** http://www.northeastern.edu/. **Application deadlines for fall 2007:** Regular decision: January 15. Early decision: Not offered. Early action: Send application by: November 15; Decision sent by: December 31. Admission can be deferred. **Application fee:** $65. Common application is accepted. **To apply online, go to:** http://www.admissions.neu.edu/onlineapps.html. **Admissions requirements/recommendations:** High school units required (recommended): English: 4; Mathematics: 3 (4); Science: 3 (4); Foreign language: 2 (4); Social studies: 3; History: 2; Total units: 17. Tests: The college uses SAT or ACT scores in admissions decisions. Either SAT or ACT required. For admission to the fall 2007 entering class, the school will accept: ACT with writing. Campus visit: Recommended. Admissions interview: Neither required nor recommended. Off-campus interview: May be arranged. **Factors that count in admissions decisions:** *Academic:* Secondary school record: Very important. Class rank: Important. Letters of recommendation: Important. Standardized test scores: Important. Essay: Important. *Nonacademic:* Interview: Not considered. Extracurricular activities: Important. Talent/ability: Important. Character/personal qualities: Important. Alumni/ae relationship: Considered. Geographical residence: Considered. State residency: Considered. Religious affiliation/commitment: Not considered. Minority status: Considered. Volunteer work: Considered. Work experience: Considered. **Other schools with the greatest overlap in applicants:** Boston College; Boston University; New York University; University of Connecticut; University of Massachusetts–Amherst. **Admissions statistics for the fall 2005 entering class:** Total applicants: 25,467. Total accepted: 11,958. Freshmen enrolled: 2,831; 66% were from out of state. Overall acceptance rate: 47%. Non-early acceptance rate: 47%. **Size of waiting list:** 5406 applicants; enrolled from waiting list: 0. **Credentials of fall 2005 freshmen:** 36% ranked in the top 10 percent of their high school class; 73% were in the top 25 percent, and 94% were in the top half. (Proportion submitting class standing: 59%.) **First-year students who submitted SAT scores:** 94%. Scores (25/75 percentile): Verbal: 560-650, Math: 580-670, Combined: 1140-1320. **First-year students submitting ACT scores:** 16%. Scores (25/75 percentile): English: N/A, Math: N/A, Composite: 24-28.

ACADEMICS

Year founded: 1898. **Academic calendar:** Semester. **Degrees offered:** bachelor's, master's, post-master's certificate, first professional, doctorate. **Most popular majors:** 28% business, management, marketing, and related support services, 11% engineering, 8% health professions and related clinical sciences, 8% security and protective services, 7% communication, journalism, and related programs. **Major fields of study:** architecture and related services; area, ethnic, cultural, and gender studies; biological and biomedical sciences; business, management, marketing, and related support services; communication, journalism, and related programs; computer and information sciences and support services; education; engineering; engi-

neering technologies/technicians; English language and literature/letters; foreign languages, literatures, and linguistics; health professions and related clinical sciences; history; liberal arts and sciences studies, and humanities; mathematics and statistics; multi/interdisciplinary studies; natural resources and conservation; philosophy and religious studies; physical sciences; psychology; public administration and social service professions; security and protective services; social sciences; visual and performing arts. **Areas of required coursework:** English (including composition), other. **Pre-professional programs:** pre-law, pre-dentistry, pre-medicine, pre-veterinary science, pre-pharmacy. **Special academic programs:** accelerated program, cooperative (work-study plan) program, cross-registration, distance learning, double major, English as a Second Language (ESL), exchange student program (domestic), honors program, independent study, internships, liberal arts/career combination, student-designed major, study abroad, teacher certificate program. **Teacher certification offered in:** early childhood, special education, elementary, middle/junior high, secondary. **Cooperative education programs:** art, business, computer science, education, engineering, health professions, humanities, natural science, social/behavioral science, technologies, other. **Reserve Officers Training Corps (ROTC):** Army ROTC: Offered on campus; Navy ROTC: Offered at cooperating institution (Boston University); Air Force ROTC: Offered at cooperating institution (Boston University). **Faculty and instruction (2005-2006):** Total instructional faculty: 868 full-time, 360 part-time (58% men; 42% women; 13% minorities). Full-time faculty with Ph.D. or other terminal degree: 88%. Student/faculty ratio: 16/1. Classes of fewer than 20 students: 51%; of 20 to 49 students: 40%; of 50 or more students: 9%. **Advanced Placement and International Baccalaureate credit:** AP tests may be used for: Credit and/or placement. Scores accepted: 3, 4, 5. International Baccalaureate exams may be used for: Credit and/or placement. **Freshmen returning for sophomore year:** 88%. **Graduation rates:** Four-year: 0%; five-year: 54%; six-year: 61%. **Graduate study:** 19% of students pursue further study within one year.

COSTS AND FINANCIAL AID

Financial aid office: (617) 373-3190. **Expenses (2006-2007):** Tuition and fees 2006-2007: $30,309; room/board: $10,950. **Financial aid:** Priority filing date for institution's financial aid form: February 15. In 2005-2006, 72% of undergraduates applied for financial aid. Of those, 61% were determined to have financial need; 16% had their need fully met. Average financial aid package (proportion receiving): $16,085 (60%). Average amount of gift aid, such as scholarships or grants (proportion receiving): $11,629 (57%). Average amount of self-help aid, such as work study or loans (proportion receiving): $5,692 (53%). Average need-based loan (excluding PLUS or other private loans): $4,746. Among students who received need-based aid, the average percentage of need met: 61%. Among students who received aid based on merit, the average award (and the proportion receiving): $13,717 (20%). The average athletic scholarship (and the proportion receiving): $23,752 (2%).

CAMPUS LIFE AND EXTRACURRICULAR ACTIVITIES

Campus housing available: coed dorms, women's dorms, fraternity housing, apartment for single students, special housing for disabled students, special housing for international students, cooperative housing, other housing options. **Clubs and organizations:** Number of student organizations: 223. Activities include: choral groups, concert band, dance, drama/theater, jazz band, literary magazine, music ensembles, musical theater, pep band, radio station, student government, student newspaper, symphony orchestra, television station, yearbook. Number of fraternities: 9; sororities: 9. Proportion of men in fraternities: 4%; of women in sororities: 4%. **Sports program (2005-2006):** Member of NCAA I. *Men's intercollegiate varsity sports:* baseball, basketball, crew, cross-country, football, ice hockey, soccer, track and field (indoor), track and field (outdoor). *Women's intercollegiate varsity sports:* basketball, crew, cross-country, field hockey, ice hockey, soccer, swimming and diving, track and field (indoor), track and field (outdoor), volleyball.

SERVICES AND FACILITIES

Basic services: nonremedial tutoring, day care, health service, health insurance. **Remedial assistance:** reading, math, writing, study skills, other. **Counseling services:** minority student, career, personal, academic, older student, psychological, birth control, religious, other. **For learning-disabled students:** School does not offer a structured program with separate admission and additional fees. Total undergraduates in learning-disabled program or receiving services: 350. Services include: remedial math, remedial English, reading machines, tape recorders, videotaped classes, diagnostic testing service, note-taking services, oral tests, learning center, readers, extended time for tests, tutors, substitution of courses, texts on tape, other testing accomodations, other. **Library:** Number of titles: 987,658; number of current serial subscriptions: 7,397. **Information technology resources:** Students are not required to lease or own a computer. Number of campus computers available to all students: 1,993. School has a wireless network. Approximate number of users that can be accommodated: 4,200. Proportion of college-owned housing units wired for high-speed internet access: 100%. **Campus safety:** Security services offered: 24-hour foot-and-vehicle patrols, late-night transport/escort service, 24-hour emergency telephones, lighted pathways/sidewalks, student patrols, controlled dormitory access (key, security card, etc).

TRANSFER AND INTERNATIONAL STUDENTS

Transfer students: May apply for admission for the following academic terms: Fall, Spring. Applicants need a minimum number of credits to apply. For fall 2005: Transfer applications received: 2,411. Transfer applicants offered admission: 1,225. Transfer applicants enrolled: 584. **International students:** Number of foreign undergraduates: 597 (5% of student body). Number of countries represented: 94. Minimum TOEFL score required: 550 (paper); 213 (computer). Average TOEFL score: 570 (paper).

Pine Manor College

- ■ **Address:** 400 Heath Street, Chestnut Hill, MA 02467
- ■ **Website:** http://www.pmc.edu
- ■ **Private**
- ■ **Enrollment:** 448 full-time; 13 part-time

KEY STATS

✔ **U.S News College Ranking:** fourth tier, Liberal Arts Colleges
✔ **SAT Score (25th/75th percentile):** 720-950
✔ **Tuition:** 2006-2007: $16,600

Selectivity: Least selective	**Room/board:** $10,028
Acceptance rate: 73%	**Average debt:** $15,412
Student/faculty ratio: 13/1	**Proportion who borrowed:** 80%

UNDERGRADUATE STUDENT BODY STATS

2005-2006 enrollment: 448 full-time; 13 part-time. Men: 0%; women: 100%. **Ethnic makeup:** African American: 42%; American-Indian: 1%; Asian American: 5%; Hispanic: 12%; White: 31%; International: 9%.

ADMISSIONS FACTS AND FIGURES

Phone: (617) 731-7104. **Email:** admission@pmc.edu. **Website:** http://www.pmc.edu. **Application deadlines for fall 2007:** Regular decision: Rolling. Early decision: Not offered. Early action: Not offered. Admission can be deferred. **Application fee:** $25. Common application is accepted. **To apply online, go to:** http://www.pmc.edu/admissions/apply.html. **Admissions requirements/recommendations:** High school units required (recommended): English: (4); Mathematics: (3); Science: (3); Foreign language: (2); Social studies: (2). Tests: The college uses SAT or ACT scores in admissions decisions. Either SAT or ACT required. For admission to the fall 2007 entering class, the school will accept: ACT with writing, ACT without writing. Campus visit: Recommended. Admissions interview: Recommended. Off-campus interview: May be arranged. **Factors that count in admissions decisions:** *Academic:* Secondary school record: Very important. Class rank: Considered. Letters of recommendation: Very important. Standardized test scores: Very important. Essay: Very important. *Nonacademic:* Interview: Important. Extracurricular activities: Important. Talent/ability: Important. Character/personal qualities: Important. Alumni/ae relationship: Not considered. Geographical residence: Not considered. State residency: Not considered. Religious affiliation/commitment: Not considered. Minority status: Not considered. Volunteer work: Important. Work experience: Important. **Other schools with the greatest overlap in applicants:** Northeastern University; Regis College; Suffolk University; University of Massachusetts–Amherst; University of Massachusetts–Boston. **Admissions statistics for the fall 2005 entering class:** Total applicants: 496. Total accepted: 364. Freshmen enrolled: 138; 31% were from out of state. Overall acceptance rate: 73%. **Credentials of fall 2005 freshmen:** 8% ranked in the top 10 percent of their high school class; 23% were in the top 25 percent, and 58% were in the top half. (Proportion submitting class standing: 38%.) **Average high school grade point average:** 2.5. **First-year students who submitted SAT scores:** 91%. Scores (25/75 percentile): Verbal: 370-490, Math: 350-460, Combined: 720-950. **First-year**

students submitting ACT scores: 7%. Scores (25/75 percentile): English: 14-17, Math: 15-17, Composite: 16-18.

ACADEMICS

Year founded: 1911. **Academic calendar:** Semester. **Degrees offered:** associate, bachelor's. **Most popular majors:** 25% psychology, 20% business, management, marketing, and related support services; 11% social sciences, 10% visual and performing arts, 8% biological and biomedical sciences. **Major fields of study:** biological and biomedical sciences; business, management, marketing, and related support services; communication, journalism, and related programs; English language and literature/letters; history; liberal arts and sciences studies, and humanities; psychology; social sciences; visual and performing arts. **Areas of required coursework:** arts/fine arts, humanities, mathematics, English (including composition), sciences (biological or physical), history, social science, other. **Pre-professional programs:** pre-law, pre-dentistry, pre-medicine, pre-veterinary science. **Special academic programs (% participation):** cross-registration, double major, English as a Second Language (ESL), honors program, independent study, internships (100%), liberal arts/career combination, student-designed major, study abroad, teacher certificate program. **Teacher certification offered in:** early childhood, elementary, middle/junior high, secondary. **Faculty and instruction (2005-2006):** Total instructional faculty: 32 full-time, 32 part-time (25% men; 75% women; 11% minorities). Full-time faculty with Ph.D. or other terminal degree: 75%. Student/faculty ratio: 13/1. Classes of fewer than 20 students: 52%; of 20 to 49 students: 48%. **Advanced Placement and International Baccalaureate credit:** AP tests may be used for: Credit and/or placement. International Baccalaureate exams may be used for: Credit and/or placement. **Freshmen returning for sophomore year:** 64%. **Graduation rates:** Four-year: 30%; five-year: 36%; six-year: 39%. **Graduate study:** 5% of students pursue further study immediately upon graduation; 20% within one year; 70% within five years. Fields in which graduates pursue further study: Master of Business Administration (MBA), 10%; law, 20%; medicine, 5%; education, 30%; arts and sciences, 35%.

COSTS AND FINANCIAL AID

Financial aid office: (617) 731-7129. **Expenses (2006-2007):** Tuition and fees 2006-2007: $16,600; room/board: $10,028. Estimated books and supplies: $800; transportation: $800; personal expenses: $800. **Financial aid:** Priority filing date for institution's financial aid form: March 15. In 2005-2006, 83% of undergraduates applied for financial aid. Of those, 83% were determined to have financial need; 6% had their need fully met. Average financial aid package (proportion receiving): $14,984 (80%). Average amount of gift aid, such as scholarships or grants (proportion receiving): $11,556 (80%). Average amount of self-help aid, such as work study or loans (proportion receiving): $3,803 (73%). Average need-based loan (excluding PLUS or other private loans): $3,470. Among students who received need-based aid, the average percentage of need met: 73%. Among students who received aid based on merit, the average award (and the proportion receiving): $6,108 (3%). The average athletic scholarship (and the proportion receiving): $0 (0%). Average amount of debt of borrowers graduating in 2005: $15,412. Proportion who borrowed: 80%.

CAMPUS LIFE AND EXTRACURRICULAR ACTIVITIES

Campus housing available: women's dorms, special housing for disabled students. Students who live in college-owned, operated, or affiliated housing: 78%. **Student employment:** During the 2005-2006 academic year, 15% of undergraduates worked on campus. Average per-year earnings: $1,600. **Clubs and organizations:** Number of student organizations: 23. Activities include: choral groups, dance, drama/theater, literary magazine, radio station, student government, yearbook. Number of fraternities: 0; sororities: 0. Average proportion of students who stay on campus on weekends: 70%. **Sports program (2005-2006):** Member of NCAA III. *Women's intercollegiate varsity sports:* basketball, cross-country, lacrosse, soccer, softball, tennis, volleyball.

SERVICES AND FACILITIES

Basic services: nonremedial tutoring, health service, health insurance. **Remedial assistance:** reading, math, writing, study skills. **Counseling services:** minority student, career, personal, academic, psychological, birth control, religious. **For learning-disabled students:** School does not offer a structured program with separate admission and additional fees. Services include: untimed tests, note-taking services, oral tests, learning center, readers, extended time for tests, tutors, priority seating, texts on tape, other testing accomodations, waiver of foreign language degree requirement. **Library:** Number of titles: 65,632; number of current serial subscriptions: 272. **Information technology resources:** Students are not required to lease or own a computer. Number of campus computers available to all students: 108. School does not have a wireless network. Proportion of college-owned housing units wired for high-speed internet access: 100%. **Campus safety:** Security services offered: 24-hour foot-and-vehicle patrols, late-night transport/escort service, 24-hour emergency telephones, lighted pathways/sidewalks, controlled dormitory access (key, security card, etc).

TRANSFER AND INTERNATIONAL STUDENTS

Transfer students: May apply for admission for the following academic terms: Fall, Spring, Summer. Applicants need a minimum number of credits to apply. For fall 2005: Transfer applications received: 71. Transfer applicants offered admission: 42. Transfer applicants enrolled: 24. **International students:** Number of foreign undergraduates: 39 (9% of student body). Number of countries represented: 23. Minimum TOEFL score required: 450 (paper); 133 (computer). Average TOEFL score: 537 (paper).

Regis College

- **Address:** 235 Wellesley Street, Weston, MA 02493-1571
- **Website:** http://www.regiscollege.edu
- **Private; Religious affiliation:** Roman Catholic
- **Enrollment:** 621 full-time; 222 part-time

KEY STATS

✔ **U.S News College Ranking:** 51, Universities–Master's (North)
✔ **SAT Score (25th/75th percentile):** 830-1050
✔ **Tuition:** 2006-2007: $23,140

Selectivity: Selective	**Room/board:** $10,560
Acceptance rate: 76%	**Average debt:** $24,094
Student/faculty ratio: 13/1	**Proportion who borrowed:** 77%

UNDERGRADUATE STUDENT BODY STATS

2005-2006 enrollment: 621 full-time; 222 part-time. Men: 3%; women: 97%. **Ethnic makeup:** African American: 14%; Asian American: 7%; Hispanic: 10%; White: 69%; International: 1%. **Religious preference:** Protestant: 25%; Jewish: 1%; Muslim: 1%; Buddhist: 3%; No preference: 14%; Roman Catholic: 50%; Other: 6%.

ADMISSIONS FACTS AND FIGURES

Phone: (866) 438-7344. **Email:** admission@regiscollege.edu. **Website:** http://www.regiscollege.edu. **Application deadlines for fall 2007:** Regular decision: Rolling. Early decision: Not offered. Early action: Not offered. Admission can be deferred. **Application fee:** $40. Common application is accepted. **Admissions requirements/recommendations:** High school units required (recommended): English: 4; Mathematics: 3; Science: 2; Foreign language: 2; Social studies: 2; Academic electives: 3 (4); Total units: 16 (17). Tests: The college uses SAT or ACT scores in admissions decisions. Either SAT or ACT required. For admission to the fall 2007 entering class, the school will accept: ACT with writing, ACT without writing. Campus visit: Recommended. Admissions interview: Recommended. Off-campus interview: May be arranged. **Factors that count in admissions decisions:** *Academic:* Secondary school record: Very important. Class rank: Important. Letters of recommendation: Important. Standardized test scores: Important. Essay: Important. *Nonacademic:* Interview: Important. Extracurricular activities: Important. Talent/ability: Important. Character/personal qualities: Very important. Alumni/ae relationship: Considered. Geographical residence: Not considered. State residency: Not considered. Religious affiliation/commitment: Not considered. Minority status: Not considered. Volunteer work: Important. Work experience: Important. **Other schools with the greatest overlap in applicants:** Curry College; Simmons College; University of Massachusetts–Amherst; University of Massachusetts–Boston; University of Massachusetts–Dartmouth. **Admissions statistics for the fall 2005 entering class:** Total applicants: 908. Total accepted: 688. Freshmen enrolled: 161; 17% were from out of state. Overall acceptance rate: 76%. **Credentials of fall 2005 freshmen:** 20% ranked in the top 10 percent of their high school class; 58% were in the top 25 percent, and 83% were in the top half. (Proportion submitting class standing: 61%.) **Average high school grade point average:** 3.0. **First-year students who submitted SAT scores:** 96%. Scores (25/75 percentile): Verbal: 420-530, Math: 410-520, Combined: 830-1050. **First-year students submitting ACT scores:** 15%. Scores (25/75 percentile): English: 14-20, Math: 16-19, Composite: 16-20.

ACADEMICS

Year founded: 1927. **Academic calendar:** Semester. **Degrees offered:** associate, transfer-associate, bachelor's, master's, post-master's certificate. **Most popular majors:** 35% nursing/registered nurse training (R.N., A.S.N., B.S.N., M.S.N.), 11% business/commerce, 9% biology/biological sciences, 7% communication studies/speech communication and rhetoric, 6% history. **Major fields of study:** biological and biomedical sciences; business, management, marketing, and related support services; communication, journalism, and related programs; computer and information sciences and support services; education; English language and literature/letters; foreign languages, literatures, and linguistics; health professions and related clinical sciences; history; legal professions and studies; liberal arts and sciences studies, and humanities; multi/interdisciplinary studies; psychology; public administration and social service professions; social sciences; visual and performing arts. **Areas of required coursework:** humanities, mathematics, English (including composition), sciences (biological or physical), social science, other. **Pre-professional programs:** pre-law, pre-dentistry, pre-medicine, pre-veterinary science. **Special academic programs:** accelerated program, cross-registration, double major, exchange student program (domestic), honors program, independent study, internships, student-designed major, study abroad, teacher certificate program. **Teacher certification offered in:** special education, elementary, middle/junior high, secondary. **Reserve Officers Training Corps (ROTC):** Army ROTC: Offered at cooperating institution (Boston College). **Faculty and instruction (2005-2006):** Total instructional faculty: 55 full-time, 58 part-time (23% men; 77% women; 3% minorities). Full-time faculty with Ph.D. or other terminal degree: 78%. Student/faculty ratio: 13/1. Classes of fewer than 20 students: 66%; of 20 to 49 students: 34%; of 50 or more students: 0%. **Advanced Placement and International Baccalaureate credit:** AP tests may be used for: Credit and/or placement. Scores accepted: 3, 4, 5. International Baccalaureate exams may be used for: Credit and/or placement. **Freshmen returning for sophomore year:** 80%. **Graduation rates:** Four-year: 64%; five-year: 65%; six-year: 65%. **Graduate study:** 20% of students pursue further study within one year. Fields in which graduates pursue further study: Master of Business Administration (MBA), 1%; law, 1%; education, 4%; arts and sciences, 14%.

COSTS AND FINANCIAL AID

Financial aid office: (781) 768-7180. **Expenses (2006-2007):** Tuition and fees 2006-2007: $23,140; room/board: $10,560. Estimated books and supplies: $900; transportation: $300; personal expenses: $1,520. **Financial aid:** Priority filing date for institution's financial aid form: February 15. In 2005-2006, 87% of undergraduates applied for financial aid. Of those, 81% were determined to have financial need; 12% had their need fully met. Average financial aid package (proportion receiving): $20,003 (80%). Average amount of gift aid, such as scholarships or grants (proportion receiving): $10,410 (71%). Average amount of self-help aid, such as work study or loans (proportion receiving): $6,565 (79%). Average need-based loan (excluding PLUS or other private loans): $5,166. Among students who received need-based aid, the average percentage of need met: 62%. Among students who received aid based on merit, the average award (and the proportion receiving): $7,940 (10%). The average athletic scholarship (and the proportion receiving): $0 (0%). Average amount of debt of borrowers graduating in 2005: $24,094. Proportion who borrowed: 77%.

CAMPUS LIFE AND EXTRACURRICULAR ACTIVITIES

Campus housing available (% using): women's dorms (100%). Students who live in college-owned, operated, or affiliated housing: 47%. **Student employment:** During the 2005-2006 academic year, 20% of undergraduates worked on campus. Average per-year earnings: $1,500. **Clubs and organizations:** Number of student organizations: 29. Activities include: choral groups, dance, drama/theater, literary magazine, music ensembles, musical theater, radio station, student government, yearbook. Number of fraternities: 0; sororities: 0. Average proportion of students who stay on campus on weekends: 40%. **Sports program (2005-2006):** Member of NCAA III. *Women's intercollegiate varsity sports:* basketball, cross-country, field hockey, lacrosse, soccer, softball, swimming and diving, tennis, track and field (indoor), track and field (outdoor), volleyball.

SERVICES AND FACILITIES

Basic services: nonremedial tutoring, health service, other. **Remedial assistance:** math, writing, study skills. **Counseling services:** career, academic, older student, psychological, religious. **For learning-disabled students:** School does not offer a structured program with separate admission and additional fees. Total undergraduates in learning-disabled program or receiving services: 43. Services include: remedial math, tape recorders, note-taking services, oral tests, learning center, readers, extended time for tests, tutors, priority seating, texts on tape, exams on tape or computer, other testing accomodations, waiver of math degree requirement, other. **Library:** Number of titles: 141,574; number of current serial subscriptions: 787. **Information technology resources:** Students are not required to lease or own a computer. Number of campus computers available to all students: 179. School has a wireless network. Approximate number of users that can be accommodated: 30. Proportion of college-owned housing units wired for high-speed internet access: 100%. **Campus safety:** Security services offered: 24-hour foot-and-vehicle patrols, late-night transport/escort service, 24-hour emergency telephones, lighted pathways/sidewalks, controlled dormitory access (key, security card, etc).

TRANSFER AND INTERNATIONAL STUDENTS
Transfer students: May apply for admission for the following academic terms: Fall, Spring. Applicants do not need a minimum number of credits to apply. For fall 2005: Transfer applications received: 104. Transfer applicants offered admission: 54. Transfer applicants enrolled: 44. **International students:** Number of foreign undergraduates: 9 (1% of student body). Number of countries represented: 9. Minimum TOEFL score required: 550 (paper); 213 (computer).

Salem State College

- **Address:** 352 Lafayette Street, Salem, MA 01970
- **Website:** http://www.salemstate.edu
- **Public**
- **Enrollment:** 5,468 full-time; 1,828 part-time

KEY STATS
- ✔ **U.S News College Ranking:** fourth tier, Universities–Master's (North)
- ✔ **SAT Score (25th/75th percentile):** 840-1050
- ✔ **Tuition:** 2006-2007: $5,594 in state, $11,734 out of state

Selectivity: Less selective	**Room/board:** $7,557
Acceptance rate: 90%	**Average debt:** N/A
Student/faculty ratio: 17/1	**Proportion who borrowed:** N/A

UNDERGRADUATE STUDENT BODY STATS
2005-2006 enrollment: 5,468 full-time; 1,828 part-time. Men: 37%; women: 63%. **Ethnic makeup:** African American: 6%; Asian American: 3%; Hispanic: 5%; White: 81%; International: 4%.

ADMISSIONS FACTS AND FIGURES
Phone: (978) 542-6200. **Email:** admissions@salemstate.edu. **Website:** http://www.salemstate.edu. **Application deadlines for fall 2007:** Regular decision: Rolling. Early decision: Not offered. Early action: Not offered. Admission can be deferred. **Application fee:** $25. Common application is accepted. **Admissions requirements/recommendations:** High school units required (recommended): English: 4 (4); Mathematics: 3 (3); Science: 3 (3); Foreign language: 2 (2); Social studies: 2 (2); History: 1 (3); Academic electives: 2 (2); Total units: 16 (18). Tests: The college uses SAT or ACT scores in admissions decisions. Either SAT or ACT required. For admission to the fall 2007 entering class, the school will accept: ACT with writing, ACT without writing. Campus visit: Recommended. Admissions interview: Recommended. **Factors that count in admissions decisions:** *Academic:* Secondary school record: Very important. Class rank: Not considered. Letters of recommendation: Considered. Standardized test scores: Very important. Essay: Not considered. *Nonacademic:* Interview: Considered. Extracurricular activities: Considered. Talent/ability: Considered. Character/personal qualities: Considered. Alumni/ae relationship: Not considered. Geographical residence: Not considered. State residency: Not considered. Religious affiliation/commitment: Not considered. Minority status: Not considered. Volunteer work: Considered. Work experience: Not considered. **Other schools with the greatest overlap in applicants:** Bridgewater State College; Framingham State College; Merrimack College; Northeastern University; University of Massachusetts–Amherst. **Admissions statistics for the fall 2005 entering class:** Total applicants: 4,827. Total accepted: 4,324. Freshmen enrolled: 1,226; 3% were from out of state. Overall acceptance rate: 90%. **Average high school grade point average:** 2.8. **First-year students who submitted SAT scores:** 96%. Scores (25/75 percentile): Verbal: 420-530, Math: 420-520, Combined: 840-1050. **First-year students submitting ACT scores:** 2%. Scores (25/75 percentile): English: N/A, Math: N/A, Composite: 18-21.

ACADEMICS
Year founded: 1854. **Academic calendar:** Semester. **Degrees offered:** bachelor's, master's, post-master's certificate. **Most popular majors:** Information not available. **Major fields of study:** biological and biomedical sciences; business, management, marketing, and related support services; computer and information sciences and support services; education; English language and literature/letters; foreign languages, literatures, and linguistics; health professions and related clinical sciences; history; liberal arts and sciences studies, and humanities; mathematics and statistics; physical sciences; psychology; public administration and social service professions; security and protective services; social sciences; visual and performing arts. **Areas of required coursework:** humanities, computer literacy, mathematics, English (including composition), foreign languages, sciences (biological or physical), history, social science, other. **Special academic programs:** accelerated program, cross-registration, distance learning, double major, English as a Second Language (ESL), honors program, independent study, internships, student-designed major, study abroad, teacher certificate program. **Teacher certification offered in:** early childhood, special education, elementary, middle/junior high, secondary, bilingual/bicultural. **Reserve Officers Training Corps (ROTC):** Air Force ROTC: Offered at cooperating institution (U-Mass Lowell). **Faculty and instruction (2005-2006):** Total instructional faculty: 296 full-time, 372 part-time (46% men; 54% women; 5% minorities). Student/faculty ratio: 17/1. Classes of fewer than 20 students: 52%; of 20 to 49 students: 47%; of 50 or more students: 1%. **Advanced Placement and International Baccalaureate credit:** AP tests may be used for: Credit and/or placement. **Freshmen returning for sophomore year:** 74%. **Graduation rates:** Four-year: 15%; five-year: 35%; six-year: 38%.

COSTS AND FINANCIAL AID
Financial aid office: (978) 542-6139. **Expenses (2006-2007):** Tuition and fees 2006-2007: $5,594 in state, $11,734 out of state; room/board: $7,557. **Financial aid:** Priority filing date for institution's financial aid form: April 1.

CAMPUS LIFE AND EXTRACURRICULAR ACTIVITIES
Campus housing available: coed dorms, women's dorms, men's dorms, special housing for disabled students. Students who live in college-owned, operated, or affiliated housing: 22%. Activities include: choral groups, dance, drama/theater, jazz band, literary magazine, music ensembles, musical theater, radio station, student government, student newspaper, student film society, yearbook. Number of fraternities: 0; sororities: 0. **Sports program (2005-2006):** Member of NCAA III. *Men's intercollegiate varsity sports:* baseball, basketball, cross-country, golf, ice hockey, soccer, tennis, track and field (indoor), track and field (outdoor). *Women's intercollegiate varsity sports:* basketball, cross-country, field hockey, soccer, softball, swimming and diving, tennis, track and field (indoor), track and field (outdoor), volleyball.

SERVICES AND FACILITIES
Basic services: nonremedial tutoring, women's center, health service, health insurance. **Remedial assistance:** study skills. **Counseling services:** minority student, career, veteran student, academic, psychological. **For learning-disabled students:** School does not offer a structured program with separate admission and additional fees. Services include: reading machines, tape recorders, note-taking services, learning center, extended time for tests, tutors, priority registration, priority seating, texts on tape, exams on tape or computer, other testing accomodations. **Library:** Number of titles: 311,953; number of current serial subscriptions: 26,396. **Information technology resources:** Students are required to lease or own a computer. Number of campus computers available to all students: 426. School has a wireless network. **Campus safety:** Security services offered: 24-hour foot-and-vehicle patrols, late-night transport/escort service, 24-hour emergency telephones, lighted pathways/sidewalks, student patrols, controlled dormitory access (key, security card, etc).

TRANSFER AND INTERNATIONAL STUDENTS
Transfer students: May apply for admission for the following academic terms: Fall, Spring. Applicants need a minimum number of credits to apply. For fall 2005: Transfer applications received: 1,346. Transfer applicants offered admission: 1,247. Transfer applicants enrolled: 809. **International students:** Number of foreign undergraduates: 274 (4% of student body). Minimum TOEFL score required: 500 (paper); 173 (computer).

Simmons College

■ **Address:** 300 The Fenway, Boston, MA 02115
■ **Website:** http://www.simmons.edu
■ **Private**
■ **Enrollment:** 1,688 full-time; 277 part-time

KEY STATS
✔ **U.S News College Ranking:** 13, Universities–Master's (North)
✔ **SAT Score (25th/75th percentile):** 1010-1200
✔ **Tuition:** 2006-2007: $26,702

Selectivity: Selective   **Room/board:** $10,710
Acceptance rate: 64%   **Average debt:** $26,300
Student/faculty ratio: 12/1   **Proportion who borrowed:** 90%

UNDERGRADUATE STUDENT BODY STATS
2005-2006 enrollment: 1,688 full-time; 277 part-time. Men: 1%; women: 99%. **Ethnic makeup:** African American: 7%; Asian American: 8%; Hispanic: 3%; White: 80%; International: 2%.

ADMISSIONS FACTS AND FIGURES
Phone: (800) 345-8468. **Email:** ugadm@simmons.edu. **Website:** http://www.simmons.edu. **Application deadlines for fall 2007:** Regular decision: March 1; decision sent by April 15. Early decision: Not offered. Early action: Send application by: December 1; Decision sent by: January 20. Admission can be deferred. **Application fee:** $35. Common application is accepted. **Admissions requirements/recommendations:** High school units required (recommended): English: 4 (4); Mathematics: 3 (4); Science: 3 (3); Foreign language: 3 (4); Social studies: 3 (4); History: 3 (3); Total units: 19 (22). Tests: The college uses SAT or ACT scores in admissions decisions. Either SAT or ACT required. For admission to the fall 2007 entering class, the school will accept: ACT with writing, ACT without writing. Campus visit: Recommended. Admissions interview: Recommended. Off-campus interview: May be arranged. **Factors that count in admissions decisions:** *Academic:* Secondary school record: Very important. Class rank: Important. Letters of recommendation: Important. Standardized test scores: Important. Essay: Important. *Nonacademic:* Interview: Considered. Extracurricular activities: Considered. Talent/ability: Considered. Character/personal qualities: Important. Alumni/ae relationship: Not considered. Geographical residence: Not considered. State residency: Not considered. Religious affiliation/commitment: Not considered. Minority status: Not considered. Volunteer work: Considered. Work experience: Considered. **Other schools with the greatest overlap in applicants:** Boston College; Boston University; Mount Holyoke College; Northeastern University; University of Massachusetts–Amherst. **Admissions statistics for the fall 2005 entering class:** Total applicants: 2,303. Total accepted: 1,469. Freshmen enrolled: 413; 45% were from out of state. Accepted through early-decision or early-action plans: 54%. Overall acceptance rate: 64%. Non-early acceptance rate: 64%. **Size of waiting list:** 17 applicants; enrolled from waiting list: 1. **Credentials of fall 2005 freshmen:** 25% ranked in the top 10 percent of their high school class; 59% were in the top 25 percent, and 93% were in the top half. (Proportion submitting class standing: 62%.) **Average high school grade point average:** 3.2. **First-year students who submitted SAT scores:** 94%. Scores (25/75 percentile): Verbal: 510-610, Math: 500-590, Combined: 1010-1200. **First-year students submitting ACT scores:** 22%. Scores (25/75 percentile): English: 21-27, Math: 19-24, Composite: 20-25.

ACADEMICS
Year founded: 1899. **Academic calendar:** Semester. **Degrees offered:** diploma, bachelor's, post-bachelor's certificate, master's, post-master's certificate, doctorate. **Most popular majors:** 19% health professions and related clinical sciences, 18% social sciences, 10% psychology, 9% communication, journalism, and related programs, 8% visual and performing arts. **Major fields of study:** area, ethnic, cultural, and gender studies; biological and biomedical sciences; business, management, marketing, and related support services; communication, journalism, and related programs; computer and information sciences and support services; education; English language and literature/letters; foreign languages, literatures, and linguistics; health professions and related clinical sciences; history; mathematics and statistics; multi/interdisciplinary studies; natural resources and conservation; philosophy and religious studies; physical sciences; psychology; social sciences; visual and performing arts. **Areas of required coursework:** arts/fine arts, humanities, computer literacy, mathematics, English (including composi-

tion), philosophy, foreign languages, sciences (biological or physical), history, social science, other. **Pre-professional programs:** pre-law, pre-medicine, pre-pharmacy. **Special academic programs (% participation):** accelerated program (10%), cross-registration (25%), double major (30%), exchange student program (domestic) (10%), honors program (20%), independent study (100%), internships (70%), liberal arts/career combination (100%), student-designed major (2%), study abroad (30%), teacher certificate program (40%). **Teacher certification offered in:** early childhood, special education, elementary, middle/junior high, secondary. **Reserve Officers Training Corps (ROTC):** Army ROTC: Offered at cooperating institution (Northeastern University). **Faculty and instruction (2005-2006):** Total instructional faculty: 226 full-time, 446 part-time (16% men; 84% women; 8% minorities). Full-time faculty with Ph.D. or other terminal degree: 74%. Student/faculty ratio: 12/1. Classes of fewer than 20 students: 65%; of 20 to 49 students: 30%; of 50 or more students: 5%. **Advanced Placement and International Baccalaureate credit:** AP tests may be used for: Placement only. Scores accepted: 4, 5. International Baccalaureate exams may be used for: Credit and/or placement. **Freshmen returning for sophomore year:** 84%. **Graduation rates:** Four-year: 50%; five-year: 56%; six-year: 73%. **Graduate study:** 17% of students pursue further study immediately upon graduation; 23% within one year. Fields in which graduates pursue further study: law, 3%; medicine, 1%; dentistry, 1%; education, 6%; arts and sciences, 42%; veterinary medicine, 1%.

COSTS AND FINANCIAL AID
Financial aid office: (617) 521-2001. **Expenses (2006-2007):** Tuition and fees 2006-2007: $26,702; room/board: $10,710. Estimated books and supplies: $960; transportation: $700; personal expenses: $1,420. **Financial aid:** Priority filing date for institution's financial aid form: February 1; deadline: March 1. In 2005-2006, 80% of undergraduates applied for financial aid. Of those, 72% were determined to have financial need; 4% had their need fully met. Average financial aid package (proportion receiving): $15,085 (70%). Average amount of gift aid, such as scholarships or grants (proportion receiving): $10,829 (65%). Average amount of self-help aid, such as work study or loans (proportion receiving): $3,908 (61%). Average need-based loan (excluding PLUS or other private loans): $2,908. Among students who received need-based aid, the average percentage of need met: 58%. Among students who received aid based on merit, the average award (and the proportion receiving): $11,898 (2%). The average athletic scholarship (and the proportion receiving): $0 (0%). Average amount of debt of borrowers graduating in 2005: $26,300. Proportion who borrowed: 90%.

CAMPUS LIFE AND EXTRACURRICULAR ACTIVITIES
Campus housing available (% using): women's dorms (100%), other housing options. Students who live in college-owned, operated, or affiliated housing: 75%. **Student employment:** During the 2005-2006 academic year, 50% of undergraduates worked on campus. Average per-year earnings: $2,000. **Clubs and organizations:** Number of student organizations: 50. Activities include: choral groups, dance, drama/theater, literary magazine, student government, student newspaper, student film society, yearbook. Number of fraternities: 0; sororities: 0. Average proportion of students who stay on campus on weekends: 75%. **Sports program (2005-2006):** Member of NCAA III. *Women's intercollegiate varsity sports:* basketball, field hockey, rowing, soccer, softball, swimming and diving, tennis, volleyball.

SERVICES AND FACILITIES
Basic services: nonremedial tutoring, women's center, placement service, health service, health insurance. **Remedial assistance:** reading, math, writing, study skills, other. **Counseling services:** minority student, career, personal, academic, older student, psychological, birth control, religious. **For learning-disabled students:** School does not offer a structured program with separate admission and additional fees. Total undergraduates in learning-disabled program or receiving services: 107. Services include: remedial math, reading machines, tape recorders, untimed tests, note-taking services, oral tests, learning center, readers, extended time for tests, tutors, texts on tape, typist/scribe, exams on tape or computer, other testing accomodations, waiver of foreign language degree requirement. **Library:** Number of titles: 245,156; number of current serial subscriptions: 26,595. **Information technology resources:** Students are not required to lease or own a computer. Number of campus computers available to all students: 420. School has a wireless network. Approximate number of users that can be accommodated: 1,200. Proportion of college-owned housing units wired for high-speed internet access: 100%. **Campus safety:** Security services offered: 24-hour foot-and-vehicle patrols, late-night transport/escort service, 24-hour emergency telephones, lighted pathways/sidewalks, controlled dormitory access (key, security card, etc).

TRANSFER AND INTERNATIONAL STUDENTS

Transfer students: May apply for admission for the following academic terms: Fall, Spring. Applicants need a minimum number of credits to apply. For fall 2005: Transfer applications received: 238. Transfer applicants offered admission: 131. Transfer applicants enrolled: 75. **International students:** Number of foreign undergraduates: 35 (2% of student body). Minimum TOEFL score required: 560 (paper); 220 (computer). Average TOEFL score: 594 (paper).

Simon's Rock College of Bard

- **Address:** 84 Alford Road, Great Barrington, MA 01230
- **Website:** http://www.simons-rock.edu
- **Private**
- **Enrollment:** 372 full-time; 6 part-time

KEY STATS

✔ **U.S News College Ranking:** 2, Comp. Coll.–Bachelor's (North)
✔ **SAT Score (25th/75th percentile):** 1110-1390
✔ **Tuition:** 2006-2007: $35,384

Selectivity: Selective	**Room/board:** $9,260
Acceptance rate: 77%	**Average debt:** $12,383
Student/faculty ratio: 8/1	**Proportion who borrowed:** 80%

UNDERGRADUATE STUDENT BODY STATS

2005-2006 enrollment: 372 full-time; 6 part-time. Men: 44%; women: 56%. **Ethnic makeup:** African American: 6%; Asian American: 5%; Hispanic: 5%; White: 81%; International: 3%.

ADMISSIONS FACTS AND FIGURES

Phone: (413) 528-7312. **Email:** admit@simons-rock.edu. **Website:** http://www.simons-rock.edu. **Application deadlines for fall 2007:** Regular decision: May 31. Early decision: Not offered. Early action: Not offered. Admission can be deferred. **Application fee:** $50. Common application is not accepted. **Admissions requirements/recommendations:** High school units required (recommended): English: (2); Mathematics: (2); Science: (2); Foreign language: (2); Social studies: (2); History: (2); Academic electives: (0); Total units: (10). Tests: The college uses SAT or ACT scores in admissions decisions. Either SAT or ACT required. For admission to the fall 2007 entering class, the school will accept: ACT with writing, ACT without writing. Campus visit: Recommended. Admissions interview: Required. **Factors that count in admissions decisions:** *Academic:* Secondary school record: Important. Class rank: Considered. Letters of recommendation: Important. Standardized test scores: Considered. Essay: Very important. *Nonacademic:* Interview: Very important. Extracurricular activities: Important. Talent/ability: Very important. Character/personal qualities: Very important. Alumni/ae relationship: Considered. Geographical residence: Not considered. State residency: Not considered. Religious affiliation/commitment: Not considered. Minority status: Important. Volunteer work: Important. Work experience: Considered. **Admissions statistics for the fall 2005 entering class:** Total applicants: 263. Total accepted: 203. Freshmen enrolled: 145; 82% were from out of state. Overall acceptance rate: 77%. **Size of waiting list:** 0 applicants; enrolled from waiting list: 0. **Average high school grade point average:** 3.8. **First-year students who submitted SAT scores:** 50%. Scores (25/75 percentile): Verbal: 580-700, Math: 530-690, Combined: 1110-1390. **First-year students submitting ACT scores:** 10%. Scores (25/75 percentile): English: 21-30, Math: 20-27, Composite: 22-28.

ACADEMICS

Year founded: 1964. **Academic calendar:** Semester. **Degrees offered:** associate, terminal-associate, bachelor's. **Most popular majors:** 26% visual and performing arts, 14% English language and literature/letters, 13% social sciences, 11% foreign languages, literatures, and linguistics, 8% psychology. **Major fields of study:** area, ethnic, cultural, and gender studies; biological and biomedical sciences; English language and literature/letters; foreign languages, literatures, and linguistics; history; legal professions and studies; liberal arts and sciences studies, and humanities; multi/interdisciplinary studies; philosophy and religious studies; psychology; science technologies/technicians; social sciences; visual and performing arts. **Areas of required coursework:** arts/fine arts, humanities, mathematics, English (including composition), foreign languages, sciences (biological or physical), history, social science, other. **Special academic programs:** accelerated program, cooperative (work-study plan) program, cross-registration, dual enrollment, exchange student program (domestic), independent study, internships, student-designed major, study abroad. **Cooperative education programs:** engineering. **Faculty and instruction (2005-2006):** Total instructional faculty: 40 full-time, 27 part-time (66% men; 34% women; 9% minorities). Full-time faculty with Ph.D. or other terminal degree: 93%. Student/faculty ratio: 8/1. Classes of fewer than 20 students: 99%; of 20 to 49 students: 1%. **Graduation rates:** Four-year: 65%; five-year: 80%; six-year: 84%.

COSTS AND FINANCIAL AID

Financial aid office: (413) 528-7297. **Expenses (2006-2007):** Tuition and fees 2006-2007: $35,384; room/board: $9,260. Estimated books and supplies: $1,000; transportation: $1,000. **Financial aid:** Priority filing date for institution's financial aid form: April 15. In 2005-2006, 83% of undergraduates applied for financial aid. Of those, 65% were determined to have financial need; 8% had their need fully met. Average financial aid package (proportion receiving): $15,760 (65%). Average amount of gift aid, such as scholarships or grants (proportion receiving): $10,724 (39%). Average amount of self-help aid, such as work study or loans (proportion receiving): $3,937 (43%). Average need-based loan (excluding PLUS or other private loans): $4,441. Among students who received need-based aid, the average percentage of need met: 55%. Among students who received aid based on merit, the average award (and the proportion receiving): $22,250 (6%). The average athletic scholarship (and the proportion receiving): $0 (0%). Average amount of debt of borrowers graduating in 2005: $12,383. Proportion who borrowed: 80%.

CAMPUS LIFE AND EXTRACURRICULAR ACTIVITIES

Campus housing available: coed dorms, women's dorms, men's dorms, apartment for single students. Students who live in college-owned, operated, or affiliated housing: 82%. Activities include: choral groups, dance, drama/theater, jazz band, literary magazine, music ensembles, radio station, student government, student newspaper, student film society, yearbook. Number of fraternities: 0; sororities: 0.

SERVICES AND FACILITIES

Basic services: nonremedial tutoring, women's center, health service, health insurance. **Counseling services:** minority student, career, personal, academic, psychological. **For learning-disabled students:** School does not offer a structured program with separate admission and additional fees. Services include: reading machines, diagnostic testing service, note-taking services, oral tests, learning center, readers, extended time for tests, tutors, priority seating, proofreading services, exams on tape or computer, take home exams. **Information technology resources:** Students are required to lease or own a computer. School has a wireless network. **Campus safety:** Security services offered: late-night transport/escort service, 24-hour emergency telephones, lighted pathways/sidewalks, controlled dormitory access (key, security card, etc).

TRANSFER AND INTERNATIONAL STUDENTS

Transfer students: May apply for admission for the following academic terms: Fall. Applicants do not need a minimum number of credits to apply. For fall 2005: Transfer applications received: 4. Transfer applicants offered admission: 4. Transfer applicants enrolled: 4. **International students:** Number of foreign undergraduates: 10 (3% of student body).

Smith College

- **Address:** 7 College Lane, Northampton, MA 01063
- **Website:** http://www.smith.edu
- **Private**
- **Enrollment:** 2,612 full-time; 30 part-time

KEY STATS

✔ **U.S News College Ranking:** 19, Liberal Arts Colleges
✔ **SAT Score (25th/75th percentile):** 1150-1380
✔ **Tuition:** 2006-2007: $32,558

Selectivity: More selective	**Room/board:** $10,880
Acceptance rate: 48%	**Average debt:** $25,023
Student/faculty ratio: 9/1	**Proportion who borrowed:** 69%

UNDERGRADUATE STUDENT BODY STATS

2005-2006 enrollment: 2,612 full-time; 30 part-time. Men: 0%; women: 100%. **Ethnic makeup:** African American: 6%; American-Indian: 1%; Asian American: 11%; Hispanic: 6%; White: 69%; International: 7%. **Religious preference:** Roman Catholic: 18%; Protestant: 19%; Jewish: 8%; Muslim: 1%; Hindu: 1%; Buddhist: 3%; No preference: 41%; Unknown: 3%; Other: 4%.

ADMISSIONS FACTS AND FIGURES

Phone: (413) 585-2500. **Email:** admission@smith.edu. **Website:** http://www.smith.edu. **Application deadlines for fall 2007:** Regular decision: January 15. Early decision: Send application by: November 15; Decision sent by: December 15. Early action: Not offered. Admission can be deferred. **Application fee:** $60. Common application is accepted. **To apply online, go to:** http://www.smith.edu/admission. **Admissions requirements/recommendations:** High school units required (recommended): English: (4); Mathematics: (4); Science: (3); Foreign language: (3); History: (2); Total units: (15). Tests: The college uses SAT or ACT scores in admissions decisions. Either SAT or ACT required. For admission to the fall 2007 entering class, the school will accept: ACT with writing, ACT without writing. Campus visit: Recommended. Admissions interview: Recommended. Off-campus interview: May be arranged. **Factors that count in admissions decisions:** *Academic:* Secondary school record: Very important. Class rank: Important. Letters of recommendation: Very important. Standardized test scores: Important. Essay: Important. *Nonacademic:* Interview; Important. Extracurricular activities: Important. Talent/ability: Important. Character/personal qualities: Very important. Alumni/ae relationship: Considered. Geographical residence: Not considered. State residency: Not considered. Religious affiliation/commitment: Not considered. Minority status: Considered. Volunteer work: Considered. Work experience: Considered. **Other schools with the greatest overlap in applicants:** Barnard College; Brown University; Bryn Mawr College; Mount Holyoke College; Wellesley College. **Admissions statistics for the fall 2005 entering class:** Total applicants: 3,408. Total accepted: 1,649. Freshmen enrolled: 615; 82% were from out of state. Overall acceptance rate: 48%. Early-decision acceptance rate: 76%. Non-early acceptance rate: 47%. **Size of waiting list:** N/A applicants; enrolled from waiting list: 120. **Credentials of fall 2005 freshmen:** 61% ranked in the top 10 percent of their high school class; 90% were in the top 25 percent, and 98% were in the top half. (Proportion submitting class standing: 58%.) **Average high school grade point average:** 3.8. **First-year students who submitted SAT scores:** 91%. Scores (25/75 percentile): Verbal: 580-710, Math: 570-670, Combined: 1150-1380. **First-year students submitting ACT scores:** 27%. Scores (25/75 percentile): English: N/A, Math: N/A, Composite: 25-31.

ACADEMICS

Year founded: 1871. **Academic calendar:** Semester. **Degrees offered:** bachelor's, post-bachelor's certificate, master's, post-master's certificate, doctorate. **Most popular majors:** 16% social sciences, 14% history, 11% psychology, 10% visual and performing arts, 9% foreign languages, literatures, and linguistics. **Pre-professional programs:** pre-law, pre-dentistry, pre-medicine, pre-theology, pre-veterinary science, pre-optometry, pre-pharmacy. **Special academic programs (% participation):** accelerated program (5%), cross-registration (34%), double major (14%), exchange student program (domestic) (1%), honors program (7%), independent study (38%), internships, student-designed major (.4%), study abroad (42%), teacher certificate program. **Teacher certification offered in:** elementary, middle/junior high, secondary. **Reserve Officers Training Corps (ROTC):** Army ROTC: Offered at cooperating institution (UMass-Amherst); Air Force ROTC: Offered at cooperating institution (UMass-Amherst). **Faculty and instruction (2005-2006):** Total instructional faculty: 288 full-time, 28 part-time (48% men; 52% women; 13% minorities). Full-time faculty with Ph.D. or other terminal degree: 96%. Student/faculty ratio: 9/1. Classes of fewer than 20 students: 71%; of 20 to 49 students: 26%; of 50 or more students: 4%. **Advanced Placement and International Baccalaureate credit:** AP tests may be used for: Placement only. Scores accepted: 4, 5. International Baccalaureate exams may be used for: Credit and/or placement. **Freshmen returning for sophomore year:** 91%. **Graduation rates:** Four-year: 82%; five-year: 85%; six-year: 86%. **Graduate study:** 22% of students pursue further study immediately upon graduation; 31% within one year; 42% within five years.

COSTS AND FINANCIAL AID

Financial aid office: (413) 585-2530. **Expenses (2006-2007):** Tuition and fees 2006-2007: $32,558; room/board: $10,880. **Financial aid:** In 2005-2006, 70% of undergraduates applied for financial aid. Of those, 60% were determined to have financial need; 100% had their need fully met. Average financial aid package (proportion receiving): $29,776 (60%). Average amount of gift aid, such as scholarships or grants (proportion receiving): $23,426 (60%). Average amount of self-help aid, such as work study or loans (proportion receiving): $5,662 (60%). Average need-based loan (excluding PLUS or other private loans): $3,772. Among students who received need-based aid, the average percentage of need met: 100%. Among students who received aid based on merit, the average award (and the proportion receiving): $5,709 (6%). The average athletic scholarship (and the proportion receiving): $0 (0%). Average amount of debt of borrowers graduating in 2005: $25,023. Proportion who borrowed: 69%.

CAMPUS LIFE AND EXTRACURRICULAR ACTIVITIES

Campus housing available (% using): women's dorms (98%), cooperative housing (1%), other housing options (1%). Students who live in college-owned, operated, or affiliated housing: 90%. **Student employment:** During the 2005-2006 academic year, 52% of undergraduates worked on campus. Average per-year earnings: $2,300. **Clubs and organizations:** Number of student organizations: 129. Activities include: choral groups, concert band, dance, drama/theater, jazz band, literary magazine, music ensembles, musical theater, radio station, student government, student newspaper, television station, yearbook. Number of fraternities: 0; sororities: 0. Average proportion of students who stay on campus on weekends: 90%. **Sports program (2005-2006):** Member of NCAA III. *Women's intercollegiate varsity sports:* basketball, cross-country, equestrian sports, field hockey, lacrosse, rowing, skiing, soccer, softball, squash, swimming and diving, tennis, track and field (indoor), track and field (outdoor), volleyball.

SERVICES AND FACILITIES

Basic services: nonremedial tutoring, women's center, placement service, day care, health service, health insurance. **Counseling services:** minority student, career, personal, academic, older student, psychological, birth control, religious. **For learning-disabled students:** School does not offer a structured program with separate admission and additional fees. Total undergraduates in learning-disabled program or receiving services: 89. Services include: reading machines, tape recorders, untimed tests, note-taking services, learning center, readers, extended time for tests, tutors, texts on tape, other testing accomodations, other. **Library:** Number of titles: 1,396,174; number of current serial subscriptions: 8,741. **Information technology resources:** Students are not required to lease or own a computer. Number of campus computers available to all students: 604. School has a wireless network. Approximate number of users that can be accommodated: 600. Proportion of college-owned housing units wired for high-speed internet access: 100%. **Campus safety:** Security services offered: 24-hour foot-and-vehicle patrols, late-night transport/escort service, 24-hour emergency telephones, lighted pathways/sidewalks, student patrols, controlled dormitory access (key, security card, etc).

TRANSFER AND INTERNATIONAL STUDENTS

Transfer students: May apply for admission for the following academic terms: Fall, Spring. Applicants need a minimum number of credits to apply. For fall 2005: Transfer applications received: 241. Transfer applicants offered admission: 114. Transfer applicants enrolled: 64. **International students:** Number of foreign undergraduates: 178 (7% of student body). Number of countries represented: 60. Minimum TOEFL score required: 600 (paper); 250 (computer). Average TOEFL score: 613 (paper).

Springfield College

- **Address:** 263 Alden Street, Springfield, MA 01109
- **Website:** http://www.springfieldcollege.edu
- Private
- **Enrollment:** 3,027 full-time; 450 part-time

KEY STATS

✔ **U.S News College Ranking:** 56, Universities–Master's (North)
✔ **SAT Score (25th/75th percentile):** 930-1120
✔ **Tuition:** 2006-2007: $22,715

Selectivity: Selective	**Room/board:** $8,170
Acceptance rate: 69%	**Average debt:** $24,355
Student/faculty ratio: 13/1	**Proportion who borrowed:** 94%

UNDERGRADUATE STUDENT BODY STATS

2005-2006 enrollment: 3,027 full-time; 450 part-time. Men: 40%; women: 60%. **Ethnic makeup:** African American: 22%; Asian American: 1%; Hispanic: 8%; White: 68%.

ADMISSIONS FACTS AND FIGURES

Phone: (413) 748-3136. **Email:** admissions@spfldcol.edu. **Website:** http://www.springfieldcollege.edu. **Application deadlines for fall 2007:** Regular decision: April 1. Early decision: Send application by: December 1; Decision sent by: February 1. Early action: Not offered. Admission can be deferred. **Application fee:** $50. Common application is accepted. **Admissions requirements/recommendations:** High school units required (recommended): English: 4; Mathematics: 3 (4); Science: 3 (4); Foreign language: (3); Social studies: 2 (2); History: 1; Academic electives: 1; Total units: 16. Tests: The college uses SAT or ACT scores in admissions decisions. Either SAT or ACT required. For admission to the fall 2007 entering class, the school will accept: ACT with writing. Campus visit: Recommended. Admissions interview: Recommended. Off-campus interview: May be arranged. **Factors that count in admissions decisions:** *Academic:* Secondary school record: Very important. Class rank: Considered. Letters of recommendation: Very important. Standardized test scores: Important. Essay: Very important. *Nonacademic:* Interview: Considered. Extracurricular activities: Very important. Talent/ability: Considered. Character/personal qualities: Very important. Alumni/ae relationship: Considered. Geographical residence: Considered. State residency: Not considered. Religious affiliation/commitment: Not considered. Minority status: Considered. Volunteer work: Important. Work experience: Important. **Other schools with the greatest overlap in applicants:** Ithaca College; Northeastern University; Quinnipiac University; SUNY College–Cortland; Sacred Heart University. **Admissions statistics for the fall 2005 entering class:** Total applicants: 2,326. Total accepted: 1,610. Freshmen enrolled: 574; 69% were from out of state. Accepted through early-decision or early-action plans: 9%. Overall acceptance rate: 69%. Early-decision acceptance rate: 43%. Non-early acceptance rate: 71%. **Size of waiting list:** 42 applicants; enrolled from waiting list: 14. **Credentials of fall 2005 freshmen:** 13% ranked in the top 10 percent of their high school class; 35% were in the top 25 percent, and 72% were in the top half. (Proportion submitting class standing: 69%.) **First-year students who submitted SAT scores:** 99%. Scores (25/75 percentile): Verbal: 460-550, Math: 470-570, Combined: 930-1120.

ACADEMICS

Year founded: 1885. **Academic calendar:** Semester. **Degrees offered:** bachelor's, master's, post-master's certificate, doctorate. **Most popular majors:** 23% health professions and related clinical sciences, 18% education, 17% parks, recreation, leisure, and fitness studies, 13% business, management, marketing, and related support services, 11% psychology. **Major fields of study:** area, ethnic, cultural, and gender studies; biological and biomedical sciences; business, management, marketing, and related support services; communication, journalism, and related programs; computer and information sciences and support services; education; English language and literature/letters; health professions and related clinical sciences; liberal arts and sciences studies, and humanities; mathematics and statistics; multi/interdisciplinary studies; natural resources and conservation; parks, recreation, leisure, and fitness studies; physical sciences; psychology; public administration and social service professions; security and protective services; social sciences; visual and performing arts. **Areas of required coursework:** arts/fine arts, humanities, computer literacy, mathematics, English (including composition), philosophy, foreign languages, sciences (biological or physical), history, social science, other. **Special academic programs (% participation):** cross-registration (5.2%), double major (5%), English as a Second Language (ESL) (.2%), independent study (17.4%), internships (27%), study abroad (4.1%), teacher certificate program (18%). **Teacher certification offered in:** early childhood, special education, elementary, middle/junior high, secondary. **Reserve Officers Training Corps (ROTC):** Army ROTC: Offered at cooperating institution (Western New England College); Air Force ROTC: Offered at cooperating institution (Western New England College). **Faculty and instruction (2005-2006):** Total instructional faculty: 211 full-time, 410 part-time (47% men; 53% women; 27% minorities). Full-time faculty with Ph.D. or other terminal degree: 78%. Student/faculty ratio: 13/1. Classes of fewer than 20 students: 45%; of 20 to 49 students: 53%; of 50 or more students: 2%. **Advanced Placement and International Baccalaureate credit:** AP tests may be used for: Credit only. Scores accepted: 3, 4, 5. International Baccalaureate exams may be used for: Credit only. **Freshmen returning for sophomore year:** 82%. **Graduation rates:** Four-year: 46%; five-year: 62%; six-year: 66%. **Graduate study:** 26% of students pursue further study immediately upon graduation; 41% within one year; 89% within five years. Fields in which graduates pursue further study: Master of Business Administration (MBA), 1%; law, 1%; medicine, 1%; dentistry, 1%; education, 69%; arts and sciences, 27%.

COSTS AND FINANCIAL AID

Financial aid office: (413) 748-3108. **Expenses (2006-2007):** Tuition and fees 2006-2007: $22,715; room/board: $8,170. Estimated books and supplies: $900; transportation: $660; personal expenses: $1,200. **Financial aid:** Priority filing date for institution's financial aid form: March 15. In 2005-2006, 92% of undergraduates applied for financial aid. Of those, 78% were determined to have financial need; 15% had their need fully met. Average financial aid package (proportion receiving): $15,637 (78%). Average amount of gift aid, such as scholarships or grants (proportion receiving): $11,078 (77%). Average amount of self-help aid, such as work study or loans (proportion receiving): $5,217 (70%). Average need-based loan (excluding PLUS or other private loans): $3,999. Among students who received need-based aid, the average percentage of need met: 77%. Among students who received aid based on merit, the average award (and the proportion receiving): $13,898 (14%). The average athletic scholarship (and the proportion receiving): $0 (0%). Average amount of debt of borrowers graduating in 2005: $24,355. Proportion who borrowed: 94%.

CAMPUS LIFE AND EXTRACURRICULAR ACTIVITIES

Campus housing available (% using): coed dorms (59%), men's dorms (14%), apartment for single students (26%), special housing for disabled students (1%). Students who live in college-owned, operated, or affiliated housing: 87%. **Student employment:** During the 2005-2006 academic year, 11% of undergraduates worked on campus. Average per-year earnings: $1,600. **Clubs and organizations:** Number of student organizations: 60. Activities include: choral groups, dance, drama/theater, jazz band, literary magazine, music ensembles, radio station, student government, student newspaper, yearbook. Number of fraternities: 0; sororities: 0. Average proportion of students who stay on campus on weekends: 65%. **Sports program (2005-2006):** Member of NCAA III. *Men's intercollegiate varsity sports:* baseball, basketball, cross-country, football, golf, gymnastics, lacrosse, soccer, swimming and diving, tennis, track and field (indoor), track and field (outdoor), volleyball, wrestling. *Women's intercollegiate varsity sports:* basketball, cross-country, field hockey, gymnastics, lacrosse, soccer, softball, swimming and diving, tennis, track and field (indoor), track and field (outdoor), volleyball.

SERVICES AND FACILITIES

Basic services: nonremedial tutoring, women's center, placement service, day care, health service, health insurance. **Remedial assistance:** math, writing, study skills. **Counseling services:** minority student, career, personal, academic, psychological, birth control, religious. **For learning-disabled students:** School does not offer a structured program with separate admission and additional fees. Total undergraduates in learning-disabled program or receiving services: 144. Services include: remedial math, reading machines, tape recorders, untimed tests, note-taking services, readers, extended time for tests, tutors. **Library:** Number of titles: 197,316; number of current serial subscriptions: 1,155. **Information technology resources:** Students are not required to lease or own a computer. Number of campus computers available to all students: 275. School has a wireless network. Approximate number of users that can be accommodated: 400. Proportion of college-owned housing units wired for high-speed internet access: 100%. **Campus safety:** Security services offered: 24-hour foot-and-vehicle patrols, late-night transport/escort service, 24-hour emergency telephones, lighted pathways/sidewalks, student patrols, controlled dormitory access (key, security card, etc).

TRANSFER AND INTERNATIONAL STUDENTS

Transfer students: May apply for admission for the following academic terms: Fall, Spring. Applicants do not need a minimum number of credits to apply. For fall 2005: Transfer applications received: 228. Transfer applicants offered admission: 126. Transfer applicants enrolled: 91. **International students:** Number of foreign undergraduates: 5. Number of countries represented: 8. Minimum TOEFL score required: 525 (paper); 195 (computer). Average TOEFL score: 530 (paper).

Stonehill College

- **Address:** 320 Washington Street, Easton, MA 02357
- **Website:** http://www.stonehill.edu
- **Private; Religious affiliation:** Roman Catholic
- **Enrollment:** 2,260 full-time; 171 part-time

KEY STATS

✔ **U.S News College Ranking:** 1, Comp. Coll.–Bachelor's (North)
✔ **SAT Score (25th/75th percentile):** 1130-1280
✔ **Tuition:** 2006-2007: $25,610

Selectivity: More selective	**Room/board:** $11,040
Acceptance rate: 57%	**Average debt:** $19,712
Student/faculty ratio: 14/1	**Proportion who borrowed:** 75%

UNDERGRADUATE STUDENT BODY STATS

2005-2006 enrollment: 2,260 full-time; 171 part-time. Men: 40%; women: 60%. **Ethnic makeup:** African American: 3%; Asian American: 3%; Hispanic: 3%; White: 91%; International: 1%. **Religious preference:** Protestant: 10%; Jewish: 1%; No preference: 15%; Roman Catholic: 67%; Greek Orthodox: 1%; Other: 6%.

ADMISSIONS FACTS AND FIGURES

Phone: (508) 565-1373. **Email:** admissions@stonehill.edu. **Website:** http://www.stonehill.edu. **Application deadlines for fall 2007:** Regular decision: January 15; decision sent by April 1. Early decision: Send application by: November 1; Decision sent by: December 15. Early action: Not offered. Admission can be deferred. **Application fee:** $50. Common application is accepted. **To apply online, go to:** http://www.commonapp.org/. **Admissions requirements/recommendations:** High school units required (recommended): English: 4 (4); Mathematics: 3 (4); Science: 1 (3); Foreign language: 2 (3); History: 3 (3); Academic electives: 3 (3); Total units: 16 (20). Tests: The college uses SAT or ACT scores in admissions decisions. Either SAT or ACT required. For admission to the fall 2007 entering class, the school will accept: ACT with writing. Campus visit: Recommended. Admissions interview: Neither required nor recommended. Off-campus interview: May be arranged. **Factors that count in admissions decisions:** *Academic:* Secondary school record: Very important. Class rank: Very important. Letters of recommendation: Important. Standardized test scores: Very important. Essay: Important. *Nonacademic:* Interview: Not considered. Extracurricular activities: Important. Talent/ability: Important. Character/personal qualities: Important. Alumni/ae relationship: Considered. Geographical residence: Considered. State residency: Not considered. Religious affiliation/commitment: Not considered. Minority status: Considered. Volunteer work: Considered. Work experience: Considered. **Other schools with the greatest overlap in applicants:** Boston College; College of the Holy Cross; Fairfield University; Northeastern University; Providence College. **Admissions statistics for the fall 2005 entering class:** Total applicants: 4,848. Total accepted: 2,745. Freshmen enrolled: 619; 45% were from out of state. Overall acceptance rate: 57%. Early-decision acceptance rate: 66%. Non-early acceptance rate: 56%. **Size of waiting list:** 660 applicants; enrolled from waiting list: 183. **Credentials of fall 2005 freshmen:** 48% ranked in the top 10 percent of their high school class; 87% were in the top 25 percent, and 99% were in the top half. (Proportion submitting class standing: 65%.) **Average high school grade point average:** 3.6. **First-year students who submitted SAT scores:** 97%. Scores (25/75 percentile): Verbal: 560-640; Math: 570-640; Combined: 1130-1280. **First-year students submitting ACT scores:** 17%. Scores (25/75 percentile): English: N/A, Math: N/A, Composite: 23-27.

ACADEMICS

Year founded: 1948. **Academic calendar:** Semester. **Degrees offered:** certificate, bachelor's, master's. **Most popular majors:** 21% business, management, marketing, and related support services, 17% social sciences, 8% education, 7% English language and literature/letters, 6% biological and biomedical sciences. **Major fields of study:** area, ethnic, cultural, and gender studies; biological and biomedical sciences; business, management, marketing, and related support services; communication, journalism, and related programs; computer and information sciences and support services; education; engineering; English language and literature/letters; foreign languages, literatures, and linguistics; health professions and related clinical sciences; history; mathematics and statistics; multi/interdisciplinary studies; philosophy and religious studies; physical sciences; psychology; public

administration and social service professions; security and protective services; social sciences; visual and performing arts. **Areas of required coursework:** mathematics, English (including composition), philosophy, foreign languages, sciences (biological or physical), history, social science. **Pre-professional programs:** pre-law, pre-dentistry, pre-medicine, pre-theology. **Special academic programs (% participation):** cross-registration (2%), double major (17%), dual enrollment (4%), honors program (11%), independent study (15%), internships (53%), liberal arts/career combination, student-designed major (3%), study abroad (28%), teacher certificate program (12%). **Teacher certification offered in:** early childhood, elementary, secondary. **Reserve Officers Training Corps (ROTC):** Army ROTC: Offered on campus. **Faculty and instruction (2005-2006):** Total instructional faculty: 132 full-time, 121 part-time (62% men; 38% women; 8% minorities). Full-time faculty with Ph.D. or other terminal degree: 86%. Student/faculty ratio: 14/1. Classes of fewer than 20 students: 47%; of 20 to 49 students: 53%; of 50 or more students: 0%. **Advanced Placement and International Baccalaureate credit:** AP tests may be used for: Credit only. Scores accepted: 4, 5. International Baccalaureate exams may be used for: Credit only. **Freshmen returning for sophomore year:** 90%. **Graduation rates:** Four-year: 80%; five-year: 82%; six-year: 82%. **Graduate study:** 18% of students pursue further study immediately upon graduation; 29% within one year. Fields in which graduates pursue further study: Master of Business Administration (MBA), 1%; law, 12%; medicine, 1%; theology (or the seminary), 1%; education, 7%; arts and sciences, 48%.

COSTS AND FINANCIAL AID

Financial aid office: (508) 565-1088. **Expenses (2006-2007):** Tuition and fees 2006-2007: $25,610; room/board: $11,040. Estimated books and supplies: $1,200; transportation: $180; personal expenses: $932. **Financial aid:** Priority filing date for institution's financial aid form: February 1; deadline: February 1. In 2005-2006, 78% of undergraduates applied for financial aid. Of those, 64% were determined to have financial need; 22% had their need fully met. Average financial aid package (proportion receiving): $17,700 (61%). Average amount of gift aid, such as scholarships or grants (proportion receiving): $12,848 (61%). Average amount of self-help aid, such as work study or loans (proportion receiving): $6,019 (57%). Average need-based loan (excluding PLUS or other private loans): $5,287. Among students who received need-based aid, the average percentage of need met: 80%. Among students who received aid based on merit, the average award (and the proportion receiving): $11,571 (24%). The average athletic scholarship (and the proportion receiving): $10,270 (3%). Average amount of debt of borrowers graduating in 2005: $19,712. Proportion who borrowed: 75%.

CAMPUS LIFE AND EXTRACURRICULAR ACTIVITIES

Campus housing available (% using): coed dorms (92%), women's dorms (4%), special housing for disabled students, other housing options (4%). Students who live in college-owned, operated, or affiliated housing: 84%. **Student employment:** During the 2005-2006 academic year, 35% of undergraduates worked on campus. Average per-year earnings: $1,400. **Clubs and organizations:** Number of student organizations: 73. Activities include: choral groups, dance, drama/theater, literary magazine, music ensembles, musical theater, pep band, radio station, student government, student newspaper, student film society, yearbook. Number of fraternities: 0; sororities: 0. Average proportion of students who stay on campus on weekends: 83%. **Sports program (2005-2006):** Member of NCAA II. *Men's intercollegiate varsity sports:* baseball, basketball, cross-country, football, ice hockey, soccer, tennis, track and field (indoor), track and field (outdoor). *Women's intercollegiate varsity sports:* basketball, cross-country, equestrian sports, field hockey, lacrosse, soccer, softball, tennis, track and field (indoor), track and field (outdoor), volleyball.

SERVICES AND FACILITIES

Basic services: nonremedial tutoring, women's center, placement service, health service, health insurance. **Counseling services:** minority student, career, military, personal, academic, older student, psychological, religious. **For learning-disabled students:** School does not offer a structured program with separate admission and additional fees. Total undergraduates in learning-disabled program or receiving services: 15. Services include: reading machines, tape recorders, diagnostic testing service, note-taking services, special bookstore section, learning center, readers, extended time for tests, tutors, texts on tape, exams on tape or computer, waiver of foreign language degree requirement, other. **Library:** Number of titles: 225,300; number of current serial subscriptions: 2,416. **Information technology resources:** Students are not required to lease or own a computer. Number of campus computers available to all students: 300. School has a wireless network. Approximate number of users that can be accommodated: 500. Proportion

of college-owned housing units wired for high-speed internet access: 100%.
Campus safety: Security services offered: 24-hour foot-and-vehicle patrols, late-night transport/escort service, 24-hour emergency telephones, lighted pathways/sidewalks, controlled dormitory access (key, security card, etc).

TRANSFER AND INTERNATIONAL STUDENTS
Transfer students: May apply for admission for the following academic terms: Fall, Spring. Applicants do not need a minimum number of credits to apply. For fall 2005: Transfer applications received: 172. Transfer applicants offered admission: 86. Transfer applicants enrolled: 27. **International students:** Number of foreign undergraduates: 12 (1% of student body). Number of countries represented: 8. Minimum TOEFL score required: 550 (paper); 213 (computer).

Suffolk University

- **Address:** 8 Ashburton Place, Boston, MA 02108
- **Website:** http://www.suffolk.edu
- **Private**
- **Enrollment:** 4,075 full-time; 709 part-time

KEY STATS
✔ **U.S News College Ranking:** 51, Universities–Master's (North)
✔ **SAT Score (25th/75th percentile):** 920-1130
✔ **Tuition:** 2006-2007: $22,690

Selectivity: Less selective	**Room/board:** $12,756
Acceptance rate: 82%	**Average debt:** $19,012
Student/faculty ratio: 12/1	**Proportion who borrowed:** 61%

UNDERGRADUATE STUDENT BODY STATS
2005-2006 enrollment: 4,075 full-time; 709 part-time. Men: 41%; women: 59%. **Ethnic makeup:** African American: 3%; Asian American: 7%; Hispanic: 4%; White: 76%; International: 9%.

ADMISSIONS FACTS AND FIGURES
Phone: (617) 573-8460. **Email:** admission@suffolk.edu. **Website:** http://www.suffolk.edu. **Application deadlines for fall 2007:** Regular decision: March 1. Early decision: Not offered. Early action: Send application by: November 15; Decision sent by: December 15. Admission can be deferred. **Application fee:** $50. Common application is accepted. **To apply online, go to:** http://www.applyweb.com/apply/suffolk. **Admissions requirements/recommendations:** High school units required (recommended): English: 4 (4); Mathematics: 3 (4); Science: 2 (3); Foreign language: 2 (3); Social studies: (1); History: 1 (2); Academic electives: 4 (4); Total units: 17 (22). Tests: The college uses SAT or ACT scores in admissions decisions. Either SAT or ACT required. Campus visit: Recommended. Admissions interview: Neither required nor recommended. Off-campus interview: May be arranged. **Factors that count in admissions decisions:** *Academic:* Secondary school record: Very important. Class rank: Important. Letters of recommendation: Important. Standardized test scores: Important. Essay: Considered. *Nonacademic:* Interview: Considered. Extracurricular activities: Considered. Talent/ability: Considered. Character/personal qualities: Considered. Alumni/ae relationship: Considered. Geographical residence: Not considered. State residency: Not considered. Religious affiliation/commitment: Not considered. Minority status: Not considered. Volunteer work: Important. Work experience: Important. **Other schools with the greatest overlap in applicants:** Bentley College; Boston College; Boston University; Emerson College; Northeastern University. **Admissions statistics for the fall 2005 entering class:** Total applicants: 6,229. Total accepted: 5,132. Freshmen enrolled: 1,136; 39% were from out of state. Accepted through early-decision or early-action plans: 7%. Overall acceptance rate: 82%. Non-early acceptance rate: 83%. **Size of waiting list:** 223 applicants; enrolled from waiting list: 177. **Credentials of fall 2005 freshmen:** 10% ranked in the top 10 percent of their high school class; 25% were in the top 25 percent, and 69% were in the top half. (Proportion submitting class standing: 57%.) **Average high school grade point average:** 2.9. **First-year students who submitted SAT scores:** 93%. Scores (25/75 percentile): Verbal: 460-570, Math: 460-560, Combined: 920-1130. **First-year students submitting ACT scores:** 9%. Scores (25/75 percentile): English: N/A, Math: N/A, Composite: 19-24.

ACADEMICS
Year founded: 1906. **Academic calendar:** Semester. **Degrees offered:** certificate, diploma, associate, bachelor's, post-bachelor's certificate, master's, post-master's certificate, first professional, first professional certificate, doctorate. **Most popular majors:** 44% business, management, marketing, and related support services, 16% social sciences, 14% communication, journalism, and related programs, 6% psychology, 5% visual and performing arts. **Major fields of study:** area, ethnic, cultural, and gender studies; biological and biomedical sciences; business, management, marketing, and related support services; communication, journalism, and related programs; communications technologies/technicians and support services; computer and information sciences and support services; education; engineering; engineering technologies/technicians; English language and literature/letters; foreign languages, literatures, and linguistics; history; legal professions and studies; liberal arts and sciences studies, and humanities; mathematics and statistics; multi/interdisciplinary studies; natural resources and conservation; physical sciences; psychology; public administration and social service professions; security and protective services; social sciences; visual and performing arts. **Areas of required coursework:** humanities, computer literacy, mathematics, English (including composition), philosophy, foreign languages, sciences (biological or physical), social science. **Pre-professional programs:** pre-law, pre-medicine. **Special academic programs (% participation):** accelerated program, cooperative (work-study plan) program (30%), cross-registration, distance learning (2%), double major (3%), dual enrollment (1%), English as a Second Language (ESL), honors program (7%), independent study, internships (50%), liberal arts/career combination, study abroad (11%). **Cooperative education programs:** art, business, computer science, education, engineering, health professions, humanities, natural science, social/behavioral science, other. **Reserve Officers Training Corps (ROTC):** Army ROTC: Offered at cooperating institution (Northeastern University). **Faculty and instruction (2005-2006):** Total instructional faculty: 355 full-time, 524 part-time (60% men; 40% women; 9% minorities). Full-time faculty with Ph.D. or other terminal degree: 90%. Student/faculty ratio: 12/1. Classes of fewer than 20 students: 43%; of 20 to 49 students: 56%; of 50 or more students: 0%. **Advanced Placement and International Baccalaureate credit:** AP tests may be used for: Credit and/or placement. Scores accepted: 3, 4, 5. International Baccalaureate exams may be used for: Credit and/or placement. **Freshmen returning for sophomore year:** 74%. **Graduation rates:** Four-year: 36%; five-year: 47%; six-year: 51%. **Graduate study:** 36% of students pursue further study immediately upon graduation. Fields in which graduates pursue further study: Master of Business Administration (MBA), 20%; law, 18%; medicine, 1%; dentistry, 1%; theology (or the seminary), 1%; education, 11%; arts and sciences, 10%.

COSTS AND FINANCIAL AID
Financial aid office: (617) 573-8470. **Expenses (2006-2007):** Tuition and fees 2006-2007: $22,690; room/board: $12,756. Estimated books and supplies: $1,000; transportation: $150; personal expenses: $1,800. **Financial aid:** Priority filing date for institution's financial aid form: March 1; deadline: April 1. In 2005-2006, 69% of undergraduates applied for financial aid. Of those, 54% were determined to have financial need; 14% had their need fully met. Average financial aid package (proportion receiving): $13,162 (54%). Average amount of gift aid, such as scholarships or grants (proportion receiving): $6,828 (47%). Average amount of self-help aid, such as work study or loans (proportion receiving): $5,878 (52%). Average need-based loan (excluding PLUS or other private loans): $4,660. Among students who received need-based aid, the average percentage of need met: 65%. Among students who received aid based on merit, the average award (and the proportion receiving): $5,537 (9%). Average amount of debt of borrowers graduating in 2005: $19,012. Proportion who borrowed: 61%.

CAMPUS LIFE AND EXTRACURRICULAR ACTIVITIES
Campus housing available (% using): coed dorms (100%). Students who live in college-owned, operated, or affiliated housing: 18%. **Student employment:** During the 2005-2006 academic year, 30% of undergraduates worked on campus. Average per-year earnings: $1,500. **Clubs and organizations:** Number of student organizations: 75. Activities include: choral groups, dance, drama/theater, literary magazine, musical theater, radio station, student government, student newspaper, student film society, television station, yearbook. Number of fraternities: 1; sororities: 1. Proportion of men in fraternities: 1%; of women in sororities: 1%. Average proportion of students who stay on campus on weekends: 50%. **Sports program (2005-2006):** Member of NCAA III. *Men's intercollegiate varsity sports:* baseball, basketball, cross-country, golf, ice hockey, soccer, tennis. *Women's intercollegiate varsity sports:* basketball, cross-country, softball, tennis, volleyball.

SERVICES AND FACILITIES

Basic services: nonremedial tutoring, women's center, health service, health insurance. **Remedial assistance:** reading, math, writing, study skills. **Counseling services:** minority student, career, personal, academic, older student, psychological, birth control, religious. **For learning-disabled students:** School does not offer a structured program with separate admission and additional fees. Total undergraduates in learning-disabled program or receiving services: 180. Services include: remedial math, remedial English, reading machines, remedial reading, tape recorders, untimed tests, note-taking services, oral tests, learning center, readers, extended time for tests, tutors, priority registration, priority seating, texts on tape, other testing accomodations, other. **Library:** Number of titles: 122,681; number of current serial subscriptions: 974. **Information technology resources:** Students are not required to lease or own a computer. Number of campus computers available to all students: 600. School has a wireless network. Approximate number of users that can be accommodated: 1,160. Proportion of college-owned housing units wired for high-speed internet access: 100%. **Campus safety:** Security services offered: late-night transport/escort service, controlled dormitory access (key, security card, etc).

TRANSFER AND INTERNATIONAL STUDENTS

Transfer students: May apply for admission for the following academic terms: Fall, Spring, Summer. Applicants do not need a minimum number of credits to apply. For fall 2005: Transfer applications received: 999. Transfer applicants offered admission: 757. Transfer applicants enrolled: 335. **International students:** Number of foreign undergraduates: 420 (9% of student body). Number of countries represented: 102. Minimum TOEFL score required: 525 (paper); 197 (computer). Average TOEFL score: 502 (paper).

Tufts University

- **Address:** Medford, MA 02155
- **Website:** http://www.tufts.edu
- **Private**
- **Enrollment:** 4,971 full-time; 107 part-time

KEY STATS

- ✔ **U.S News College Ranking:** 27, National Universities
- ✔ **SAT Score (25th/75th percentile):** 1330-1480
- ✔ **Tuition:** 2006-2007: $34,730

Selectivity: Most selective	**Room/board:** $9,770
Acceptance rate: 28%	**Average debt:** $14,400
Student/faculty ratio: 7/1	**Proportion who borrowed:** 40%

UNDERGRADUATE STUDENT BODY STATS

2005-2006 enrollment: 4,971 full-time; 107 part-time. Men: 48%; women: 52%. **Ethnic makeup:** African American: 7%; Asian American: 13%; Hispanic: 7%; White: 67%; International: 6%.

ADMISSIONS FACTS AND FIGURES

Phone: (617) 627-3170. **Email:** admissions.inquiry@ase.tufts.edu. **Website:** http://www.tufts.edu. **Application deadlines for fall 2007:** Regular decision: January 1; decision sent by April 1. Early decision: Send application by: November 15; Decision sent by: December 15. Early action: Not offered. Admission can be deferred. **Application fee:** $70. Common application is accepted. **Admissions requirements/recommendations:** High school units required (recommended): English: (4); Mathematics: (3); Science: (2); Foreign language: (3); History: (2); Total units: (16). Tests: The college uses SAT or ACT scores in admissions decisions. Either SAT or ACT required. For admission to the fall 2007 entering class, the school will accept: ACT with writing. Campus visit: Recommended. Admissions interview: Neither required nor recommended. **Factors that count in admissions decisions:** *Academic:* Secondary school record: Very important. Class rank: Important. Letters of recommendation: Important. Standardized test scores: Important. Essay: Important. *Nonacademic:* Interview: Considered. Extracurricular activities: Important. Talent/ability: Important. Character/personal qualities: Important. Alumni/ae relationship: Considered. Geographical residence: Considered. State residency: Not considered. Religious affiliation/commitment: Not considered. Minority status: Considered. Volunteer work: Important. Work experience: Important. **Admissions statistics for the fall 2005 entering class:** Total applicants: 15,536. Total accepted: 4,398. Freshmen enrolled: 1,365; 78% were from out of state. Accepted through

early-decision or early-action plans: 33%. Overall acceptance rate: 28%. Early-decision acceptance rate: 36%. Non-early acceptance rate: 28%. **Credentials of fall 2005 freshmen:** 80% ranked in the top 10 percent of their high school class; 96% were in the top 25 percent, and 100% were in the top half. (Proportion submitting class standing: 66%.) **First-year students who submitted SAT scores:** 95%. Scores (25/75 percentile): Verbal: 660-740, Math: 670-740, Combined: 1330-1480. **First-year students submitting ACT scores:** 24%. Scores (25/75 percentile): English: N/A, Math: N/A, Composite: 28-32.

ACADEMICS

Year founded: 1852. **Academic calendar:** Semester. **Degrees offered:** bachelor's, master's, post-master's certificate, first professional, first professional certificate, doctorate. **Most popular majors:** 12% international relations and affairs, 10% economics, 9% English language and literature, 7% political science and government, 6% psychology. **Major fields of study:** area, ethnic, cultural, and gender studies; biological and biomedical sciences; computer and information sciences and support services; education; engineering; English language and literature/letters; foreign languages, literatures, and linguistics; history; liberal arts and sciences studies, and humanities; mathematics and statistics; multi/interdisciplinary studies; philosophy and religious studies; physical sciences; psychology; social sciences; visual and performing arts. **Areas of required coursework:** arts/fine arts, humanities, mathematics, English (including composition), foreign languages, sciences (biological or physical), social science. **Special academic programs:** cross-registration, double major, exchange student program (domestic), independent study, internships, liberal arts/career combination, student-designed major, study abroad, teacher certificate program, other. **Teacher certification offered in:** early childhood, special education, elementary, middle/junior high, secondary. **Reserve Officers Training Corps (ROTC):** Army ROTC: Offered at cooperating institution (MIT); Navy ROTC: Offered at cooperating institution (MIT); Air Force ROTC: Offered at cooperating institution (MIT). **Faculty and instruction (2005-2006):** Total instructional faculty: 765 full-time, 429 part-time (59% men; 41% women). Full-time faculty with Ph.D. or other terminal degree: 93%. Student/faculty ratio: 7/1. Classes of fewer than 20 students: 75%; of 20 to 49 students: 20%; of 50 or more students: 5%. **Advanced Placement and International Baccalaureate credit:** AP tests may be used for: Credit and/or placement. Scores accepted: 4, 5. International Baccalaureate exams may be used for: Credit and/or placement. **Freshmen returning for sophomore year:** 96%. **Graduation rates:** Four-year: 84%; five-year: 89%; six-year: 90%.

COSTS AND FINANCIAL AID

Financial aid office: (617) 627-2000. **Expenses (2006-2007):** Tuition and fees 2006-2007: $34,730; room/board: $9,770. Estimated books and supplies: $800; transportation: $200; personal expenses: $1,200. **Financial aid:** Priority filing date for institution's financial aid form: February 15; deadline: February 15. In 2005-2006, 45% of undergraduates applied for financial aid. Of those, 38% were determined to have financial need; 100% had their need fully met. Average financial aid package (proportion receiving): $25,749 (38%). Average amount of gift aid, such as scholarships or grants (proportion receiving): $22,465 (36%). Average amount of self-help aid, such as work study or loans (proportion receiving): $5,292 (36%). Average need-based loan (excluding PLUS or other private loans): $4,287. Among students who received need-based aid, the average percentage of need met: 100%. Among students who received aid based on merit, the average award (and the proportion receiving): $500 (2%). The average athletic scholarship (and the proportion receiving): $0 (0%). Average amount of debt of borrowers graduating in 2005: $14,400. Proportion who borrowed: 40%.

CAMPUS LIFE AND EXTRACURRICULAR ACTIVITIES

Campus housing available: coed dorms, women's dorms, sorority housing, fraternity housing, special housing for disabled students, cooperative housing, other housing options. Students who live in college-owned, operated, or affiliated housing: 75%. **Student employment:** During the 2005-2006 academic year, 20% of undergraduates worked on campus. Average per-year earnings: $2,000. **Clubs and organizations:** Number of student organizations: 170. Activities include: choral groups, concert band, dance, drama/theater, jazz band, literary magazine, marching band, music ensembles, musical theater, pep band, radio station, student government, student newspaper, student film society, symphony orchestra, television station, yearbook. Number of fraternities: 10; sororities: 3. Proportion of men in fraternities: 15%; of women in sororities: 4%. **Sports program (2005-2006):** Member of NCAA III. *Men's intercollegiate varsity sports:* baseball, basketball, cross-country, football, golf, ice hockey, lacrosse, soccer, swimming and diving, tennis, track and field (indoor), track and field (outdoor). *Women's* *intercollegiate varsity sports:* basketball, cross-country, fencing, field hockey, lacrosse, rowing, soccer, softball, squash, swimming and diving, tennis, track and field (indoor), track and field (outdoor), volleyball.

SERVICES AND FACILITIES

Basic services: nonremedial tutoring, women's center, placement service, day care, health service, health insurance. **Counseling services:** minority student, career, military, personal, veteran student, academic, older student, psychological, birth control, religious. **For learning-disabled students:** School does not offer a structured program with separate admission and additional fees. Services include: tape recorders, note-taking services, oral tests, learning center, readers, extended time for tests, tutors. **Library:** Number of titles: 1,686,211; number of current serial subscriptions: 4,341. **Information technology resources:** Students are not required to lease or own a computer. Number of campus computers available to all students: 500. School does not have a wireless network. Proportion of college-owned housing units wired for high-speed internet access: 100%. **Campus safety:** Security services offered: 24-hour foot-and-vehicle patrols, late-night transport/escort service, 24-hour emergency telephones, lighted pathways/sidewalks, controlled dormitory access (key, security card, etc).

TRANSFER AND INTERNATIONAL STUDENTS

Transfer students: May apply for admission for the following academic terms: Fall. Applicants do not need a minimum number of credits to apply. For fall 2005: Transfer applications received: 645. Transfer applicants offered admission: 90. Transfer applicants enrolled: 39. **International students:** Number of foreign undergraduates: 315 (6% of student body). Number of countries represented: 68. Average TOEFL score: 640 (paper).

University of Massachusetts—Amherst

■ **Address:** Whitmore, 181 President's Drive, Amherst, MA 01003-9313
■ **Website:** http://www.umass.edu
■ **Public**
■ **Enrollment:** 18,054 full-time; 1,340 part-time

KEY STATS

✔ **U.S News College Ranking:** 98, National Universities
✔ **SAT Score (25th/75th percentile):** 1030-1250
✔ **Tuition:** 2006-2007: $9,595 in state, $17,818 out of state

Selectivity: Selective	**Room/board:** $6,989
Acceptance rate: 80%	**Average debt:** $14,672
Student/faculty ratio: 17/1	**Proportion who borrowed:** 61%

UNDERGRADUATE STUDENT BODY STATS

2005-2006 enrollment: 18,054 full-time; 1,340 part-time. Men: 50%; women: 50%. **Ethnic makeup:** African American: 5%; Asian American: 7%; Hispanic: 3%; White: 83%; International: 1%. **Religious preference:** Roman Catholic: 18%; Protestant: 6%; Jewish: 4%; No preference: 69%; Other: 3%.

ADMISSIONS FACTS AND FIGURES

Phone: (413) 545-0222. **Website:** http://www.umass.edu. **Application deadlines for fall 2007:** Regular decision: January 15. Early decision: Not offered. Early action: Send application by: November 1; Decision sent by: December 15. Admission can be deferred. **Application fee:** $40. Common application is accepted. **To apply online, go to:** http://www.umass.edu/admissions/applying/. **Admissions requirements/recommendations:** High school units required (recommended): English: 4; Mathematics: 3; Science: 3; Foreign language: 2; Social studies: 2; Academic electives: 2; Total units: 16. Tests: The college uses SAT or ACT scores in admissions decisions. Either SAT or ACT required. For admission to the fall 2007 entering class, the school will accept: ACT without writing. Campus visit: Recommended. Admissions interview: Neither required nor recommended. Off-campus interview: Not available. **Factors that count in admissions decisions:** *Academic:* Secondary school record: Very important. Class rank: Important. Letters of recommendation: Considered. Standardized test scores: Important. Essay: Considered. *Nonacademic:* Interview: Not considered. Extracurricular activities: Considered. Talent/ability: Considered. Character/personal qualities: Considered. Alumni/ae relationship: Not considered. Geographical residence: Considered. State residency: Considered. Religious affiliation/commitment: Not considered. Minority status: Considered. Volunteer work: Considered. Work experience: Considered. **Other schools with the greatest**

overlap in applicants: Boston College; Boston University; Northeastern University; University of Connecticut; University of New Hampshire. **Admissions statistics for the fall 2005 entering class:** Total applicants: 20,205. Total accepted: 16,240. Freshmen enrolled: 4,427; 21% were from out of state. Overall acceptance rate: 80%. Non-early acceptance rate: 80%. **Size of waiting list:** 329 applicants; enrolled from waiting list: 86. **Credentials of fall 2005 freshmen:** 19% ranked in the top 10 percent of their high school class; 51% were in the top 25 percent, and 88% were in the top half. (Proportion submitting class standing: 58%.) **Average high school grade point average:** 3.4. **First-year students who submitted SAT scores:** 99%. Scores (25/75 percentile): Verbal: 510-620, Math: 520-630, Combined: 1030-1250.

ACADEMICS

Year founded: 1863. **Academic calendar:** Semester. **Degrees offered:** associate, bachelor's, master's, post-master's certificate, doctorate. **Most popular majors:** 14% business, management, marketing, and related support services, 13% social sciences, 7% communication, journalism, and related programs, 7% education, 6% psychology. **Major fields of study:** agriculture, agriculture operations, and related sciences; architecture and related services; area, ethnic, cultural, and gender studies; biological and biomedical sciences; business, management, marketing, and related support services; communication, journalism, and related programs; computer and information sciences and support services; education; engineering; English language and literature/letters; family and consumer sciences/human sciences; foreign languages, literatures, and linguistics; health professions and related clinical sciences; history; legal professions and studies; liberal arts and sciences studies, and humanities; mathematics and statistics; multi/interdisciplinary studies; natural resources and conservation; parks, recreation, leisure, and fitness studies; philosophy and religious studies; physical sciences; psychology; social sciences; visual and performing arts. **Areas of required coursework:** arts/fine arts, humanities, mathematics, English (including composition), foreign languages, sciences (biological or physical), history, social science, other. **Pre-professional programs:** pre-law, pre-dentistry, pre-medicine, pre-veterinary science. **Special academic programs (% participation):** accelerated program, cooperative (work-study plan) program, cross-registration, distance learning, double major, dual enrollment, English as a Second Language (ESL), exchange student program (domestic), honors program (11%), independent study, internships, liberal arts/career combination, student-designed major, study abroad (17%), teacher certificate program, other. **Teacher certification offered in:** early childhood, special education, elementary, middle/junior high, secondary, bilingual/bicultural. **Cooperative education programs:** agriculture, art, business, computer science, education, engineering, health professions, humanities, natural science, social/behavioral science. **Reserve Officers Training Corps (ROTC):** Army ROTC: Offered on campus; Air Force ROTC: Offered on campus. **Faculty and instruction (2005-2006):** Total instructional faculty: 1,148 full-time, 190 part-time (65% men; 35% women; 15% minorities). Full-time faculty with Ph.D. or other terminal degree: 93%. Student/faculty ratio: 17/1. Classes of fewer than 20 students: 41%; of 20 to 49 students: 42%; of 50 or more students: 17%. **Advanced Placement and International Baccalaureate credit:** AP tests may be used for: Credit and/or placement. Scores accepted: 4, 5. International Baccalaureate exams may be used for: Credit only. **Freshmen returning for sophomore year:** 84%. **Graduation rates:** Four-year: 46%; five-year: 62%; six-year: 66%. **Graduate study:** 22% of students pursue further study immediately upon graduation. Fields in which graduates pursue further study: Master of Business Administration (MBA), 10%; law, 9%; medicine, 8%.

COSTS AND FINANCIAL AID

Financial aid office: (413) 545-0801. **Expenses (2006-2007):** Tuition and fees 2006-2007: $9,595 in state, $17,818 out of state; room/board: $6,989. Estimated books and supplies: $1,000; transportation: $400; personal expenses: $1,000. **Financial aid:** Priority filing date for institution's financial aid form: March 1. In 2005-2006, 70% of undergraduates applied for financial aid. Of those, 52% were determined to have financial need; 26% had their need fully met. Average financial aid package (proportion receiving): $11,276 (51%). Average amount of gift aid, such as scholarships or grants (proportion receiving): $7,158 (39%). Average amount of self-help aid, such as work study or loans (proportion receiving): $4,805 (47%). Average need-based loan (excluding PLUS or other private loans): $4,007. Among students who received need-based aid, the average percentage of need met: 87%. Among students who received aid based on merit, the average award (and the proportion receiving): $4,796 (2%). The average athletic scholarship (and the proportion receiving): $13,369 (1%). Average amount of debt of borrowers graduating in 2005: $14,672. Proportion who borrowed: 61%.

CAMPUS LIFE AND EXTRACURRICULAR ACTIVITIES

Campus housing available (% using): coed dorms (91%), women's dorms (1%), men's dorms (1%), sorority housing (1%), fraternity housing (1%), apartments for married students (2%), apartment for single students (0%), special housing for disabled students (0%), special housing for international students (1%), other housing options (2%). Students who live in college-owned, operated, or affiliated housing: 62%. **Clubs and organizations:** Number of student organizations: 200. Activities include: choral groups, concert band, dance, drama/theater, jazz band, literary magazine, marching band, music ensembles, musical theater, opera, pep band, radio station, student government, student newspaper, student film society, symphony orchestra, television station, yearbook. Number of fraternities: 20; sororities: 13. Proportion of men in fraternities: 1%; of women in sororities: 1%. Average proportion of students who stay on campus on weekends: 50%. **Sports program (2005-2006):** Member of NCAA I. *Men's intercollegiate varsity sports:* alpine skiing, baseball, basketball, cross-country, football, ice hockey, lacrosse, skiing, soccer, swimming and diving, track and field (indoor), track and field (outdoor). *Women's intercollegiate varsity sports:* alpine skiing, basketball, crew, cross-country, field hockey, lacrosse, skiing, soccer, softball, swimming and diving, tennis, track and field (indoor), track and field (outdoor).

SERVICES AND FACILITIES

Basic services: nonremedial tutoring, women's center, placement service, day care, health service, health insurance. **Remedial assistance:** math, writing, study skills. **Counseling services:** minority student, career, personal, veteran student, academic, psychological, birth control. **For learning-disabled students:** School does not offer a structured program with separate admission and additional fees. Services include: reading machines, tape recorders, other special classes, untimed tests, note-taking services, oral tests, readers, extended time for tests, early syllabus, priority seating, texts on tape, exams on tape or computer, other testing accomodations, other. **Library:** Number of titles: 3,236,964; number of current serial subscriptions: 41,503.
Information technology resources: Students are not required to lease or own a computer. Number of campus computers available to all students: 450. School has a wireless network. Approximate number of users that can be accommodated: 1,000. Proportion of college-owned housing units wired for high-speed internet access: 95%. **Campus safety:** Security services offered: 24-hour foot-and-vehicle patrols, late-night transport/escort service, 24-hour emergency telephones, lighted pathways/sidewalks, student patrols, controlled dormitory access (key, security card, etc).

TRANSFER AND INTERNATIONAL STUDENTS

Transfer students: May apply for admission for the following academic terms: Fall, Spring. Applicants do not need a minimum number of credits to apply. For fall 2005: Transfer applications received: 2,863. Transfer applicants offered admission: 1,946. Transfer applicants enrolled: 1,067.
International students: Number of foreign undergraduates: 218 (1% of student body). Number of countries represented: 97. Minimum TOEFL score required: 550 (paper); 213 (computer).

University of Massachusetts–Boston

- **Address:** 100 Morrissey Boulevard, Boston, MA 02125-3393
- **Website:** http://www.umb.edu
- **Public**
- **Enrollment:** 5,768 full-time; 3,190 part-time

KEY STATS

✔ **U.S News College Ranking:** fourth tier, National Universities
✔ **SAT Score (25th/75th percentile):** 960-1180
✔ **Tuition:** 2006-2007: $8,546 in state, $16,590 out of state

Selectivity: Selective	**Room/board:** N/A
Acceptance rate: 60%	**Average debt:** $18,534
Student/faculty ratio: 14/1	**Proportion who borrowed:** N/A

UNDERGRADUATE STUDENT BODY STATS

2005-2006 enrollment: 5,768 full-time; 3,190 part-time. Men: 43%; women: 57%. **Ethnic makeup:** African American: 15%; American-Indian: 1%; Asian American: 12%; Hispanic: 7%; White: 62%; International: 4%.

ADMISSIONS FACTS AND FIGURES

Phone: (617) 287-6100. **Email:** undergrad@umb.edu. **Website:** http://www.umb.edu. **Application deadlines for fall 2007:** Regular decision: August 11. Early decision: Not offered. Early action: Not offered. Admission can be deferred. **Application fee:** $40. Common application is accepted. **To apply online, go to:** http://www.umb.edu/admissions/. **Admissions requirements/recommendations:** High school units required (recommended): English: 4; Mathematics: 3; Science: 3; Foreign language: 2; History: 2; Academic electives: 2; Total units: 16. Tests: The college uses SAT or ACT scores in admissions decisions. SAT required. For admission to the fall 2007 entering class, the school will accept: ACT with writing, ACT without writing. Campus visit: Neither required nor recommended. Admissions interview: Neither required nor recommended. Off-campus interview: Not available. **Factors that count in admissions decisions:** *Academic:* Secondary school record: Very important. Class rank: Not considered. Letters of recommendation: Important. Standardized test scores: Very important. Essay: Important. *Nonacademic:* Interview: Considered. Extracurricular activities: Considered. Talent/ability: Considered. Character/personal qualities: Very important. Alumni/ae relationship: Not considered. Geographical residence: Not considered. State residency: Not considered. Religious affiliation/commitment: Not considered. Minority status: Not considered. Volunteer work: Considered. Work experience: Considered. **Other schools with the greatest overlap in applicants:** Northeastern University; Salem State College; University of Massachusetts–Amherst; University of Massachusetts–Lowell. **Admissions statistics for the fall 2005 entering class:** Total applicants: 3,174. Total accepted: 1,920. Freshmen enrolled: 781; 6% were from out of state. Overall acceptance rate: 60%. **Size of waiting list:** 2 applicants; enrolled from waiting list: N/A. **Average high school grade point average:** 3.0. **First-year students who submitted SAT scores:** 88%. Scores (25/75 percentile): Verbal: 470-580, Math: 490-600, Combined: 960-1180.

ACADEMICS

Year founded: 1964. **Academic calendar:** Semester. **Degrees offered:** certificate, bachelor's, post-bachelor's certificate, master's, post-master's certificate, doctorate. **Most popular majors:** 24% business/commerce, 13% psychology, 8% English language and literature, 8% health services/allied health/health sciences, 6% political science and government. **Major fields of study:** area, ethnic, cultural, and gender studies; biological and biomedical sciences; business, management, marketing, and related support services; computer and information sciences and support services; education; engineering; English language and literature/letters; foreign languages, literatures, and linguistics; health professions and related clinical sciences; history; legal professions and studies; mathematics and statistics; multi/interdisciplinary studies; philosophy and religious studies; physical sciences; psychology; public administration and social service professions; security and protective services; social sciences; visual and performing arts. **Areas of required coursework:** arts/fine arts, humanities, computer literacy, mathematics, English (including composition), philosophy, foreign languages, sciences (biological or physical), history, social science. **Pre-professional programs:** pre-law, pre-medicine. **Special academic programs:** accelerated program, cooperative (work-study plan) program, cross-registration, distance learning, double major, dual enrollment, English as a Second Language (ESL), external degree program, honors program, independent study, internships, liberal arts/career combination, student-designed major, study abroad, teacher certificate program. **Teacher certification offered in:** early childhood, special education, elementary, middle/junior high, secondary, bilingual/bicultural. **Reserve Officers Training Corps (ROTC):** Army ROTC: Offered at cooperating institution (Boston University); Navy ROTC: Offered at cooperating institution (Boston University). **Faculty and instruction (2005-2006):** Total instructional faculty: 445 full-time, 368 part-time (49% men; 51% women; 18% minorities). Full-time faculty with Ph.D. or other terminal degree: 95%. Student/faculty ratio: 14/1. Classes of fewer than 20 students: 48%; of 20 to 49 students: 48%; of 50 or more students: 3%. **Advanced Placement and International Baccalaureate credit:** AP tests may be used for: Credit and/or placement. Scores accepted: 3, 4, 5. International Baccalaureate exams may be used for: Credit and/or placement. **Freshmen returning for sophomore year:** 71%. **Graduation rates:** Four-year: 15%; five-year: 31%; six-year: 35%.

COSTS AND FINANCIAL AID

Financial aid office: (617) 287-6300. **Expenses (2006-2007):** Tuition and fees 2006-2007: $8,546 in state, $16,590 out of state; room/board: N/A. **Financial aid:** Priority filing date for institution's financial aid form: March 1. Average amount of debt of borrowers graduating in 2005: $18,534.

CAMPUS LIFE AND EXTRACURRICULAR ACTIVITIES

Campus housing available: other housing options. Average per-year earnings: $3,000. **Clubs and organizations:** Number of student organizations: 70. Activities include: choral groups, concert band, dance, drama/theater, jazz band, literary magazine, music ensembles, radio station, student government, student newspaper, student film society, symphony orchestra, yearbook. Number of fraternities: 0; sororities: 0. **Sports program (2005-2006):** Member of NCAA III. *Men's intercollegiate varsity sports:* baseball, basketball, cross-country, ice hockey, lacrosse, soccer, tennis. *Women's intercollegiate varsity sports:* basketball, cross-country, ice hockey, soccer, softball, tennis, volleyball.

SERVICES AND FACILITIES

Basic services: nonremedial tutoring, women's center, placement service, day care, health service, health insurance. **Remedial assistance:** math, writing. **Counseling services:** career, personal, veteran student, academic, psychological. **For learning-disabled students:** School does not offer a structured program with separate admission and additional fees. Services include: reading machines, tape recorders, note-taking services, oral tests, readers, extended time for tests, other. **Library:** Number of titles: 584,016; number of current serial subscriptions: 25,575. **Information technology resources:** Students are not required to lease or own a computer. Number of campus computers available to all students: 300. School has a wireless network. **Campus safety:** Security services offered: 24-hour foot-and-vehicle patrols, late-night transport/escort service, 24-hour emergency telephones, lighted pathways/sidewalks.

TRANSFER AND INTERNATIONAL STUDENTS

Transfer students: May apply for admission for the following academic terms: Fall, Spring. Applicants do not need a minimum number of credits to apply. For fall 2005: Transfer applications received: 2,639. Transfer applicants offered admission: 2,089. Transfer applicants enrolled: 1,275. **International students:** Number of foreign undergraduates: 271 (4% of student body). Number of countries represented: 90. Minimum TOEFL score required: 550 (paper); 213 (computer).

University of Massachusetts–Dartmouth

- **Address:** 285 Old Westport Road, North Dartmouth, MA 02747-2300
- **Website:** http://www.umassd.edu
- **Public**
- **Enrollment:** 6,449 full-time; 1,070 part-time

KEY STATS

✔ **U.S News College Ranking:** 51, Universities–Master's (North)
✔ **SAT Score (25th/75th percentile):** 970-1160
✔ **Tuition:** 2006-2007: $8,309 in state, $14,991 out of state

Selectivity: Selective	**Room/board:** $8,574
Acceptance rate: 74%	**Average debt:** $16,214
Student/faculty ratio: 17/1	**Proportion who borrowed:** 65%

UNDERGRADUATE STUDENT BODY STATS

2005-2006 enrollment: 6,449 full-time; 1,070 part-time. Men: 49%; women: 51%. **Ethnic makeup:** African American: 6%; Asian American: 3%; Hispanic: 2%; White: 88%.

ADMISSIONS FACTS AND FIGURES

Phone: (508) 999-8605. **Email:** admissions@umassd.edu. **Website:** http://www.umassd.edu. **Application deadlines for fall 2007:** Regular decision: Rolling. Early decision: Send application by: November 15; Decision sent by: December 15. Early action: Not offered. Admission can be deferred. **Application fee:** $35. Common application is accepted. **To apply online, go to:** http://www.umassd.edu/admissions/applyonline.cfm. **Admissions requirements/recommendations:** High school units required (recommended): English: 4; Mathematics: 3; Science: 3; Foreign language: 2; Social studies: 1; History: 1; Academic electives: 2; Total units: 16. Tests: The college uses SAT or ACT scores in admissions decisions. Either SAT or ACT required. For admission to the fall 2007 entering class, the school will accept: ACT with writing, ACT without writing. Campus visit: Recommended. Admissions interview: Neither required nor recommended. **Factors that count in admissions decisions:** *Academic:* Secondary school record: Very important. Class rank: Considered. Letters of recommendation: Considered. Standardized

test scores: Very important. Essay: Considered. *Nonacademic:* Interview: Considered. Extracurricular activities: Considered. Talent/ability: Considered. Character/personal qualities: Considered. Alumni/ae relationship: Considered. Geographical residence: Not considered. State residency: Not considered. Religious affiliation/commitment: Not considered. Minority status: Not considered. Volunteer work: Considered. Work experience: Considered. **Other schools with the greatest overlap in applicants:** Bridgewater State College; Northeastern University; University of Connecticut; University of Massachusetts–Amherst; University of Rhode Island. **Admissions statistics for the fall 2005 entering class:** Total applicants: 6,432. Total accepted: 4,730. Freshmen enrolled: 1,545; 4% were from out of state. Accepted through early-decision or early-action plans: 3%. Overall acceptance rate: 74%. Early-decision acceptance rate: 79%. Non-early acceptance rate: 73%. **Credentials of fall 2005 freshmen:** 9% ranked in the top 10 percent of their high school class; 39% were in the top 25 percent, and 77% were in the top half. (Proportion submitting class standing: 64%.) **Average high school grade point average:** 3.0. First-year students who submitted SAT scores: 99%. Scores (25/75 percentile): Verbal: 480-570, Math: 490-590, Combined: 970-1160. **First-year students submitting ACT scores:** 6%. Scores (25/75 percentile): English: N/A, Math: N/A, Composite: 20-24.

ACADEMICS

Year founded: 1895. **Academic calendar:** Semester. **Degrees offered:** certificate, bachelor's, post-bachelor's certificate, master's, post-master's certificate, doctorate. **Most popular majors:** 28% business, management, marketing, and related support services, 12% social sciences, 11% visual and performing arts, 9% psychology, 8% engineering. **Major fields of study:** biological and biomedical sciences; business, management, marketing, and related support services; computer and information sciences and support services; education; engineering; English language and literature/letters; foreign languages, literatures, and linguistics; health professions and related clinical sciences; history; liberal arts and sciences studies, and humanities; mathematics and statistics; multi/interdisciplinary studies; philosophy and religious studies; physical sciences; psychology; social sciences; visual and performing arts. **Areas of required coursework:** arts/fine arts, humanities, computer literacy, mathematics, English (including composition), sciences (biological or physical), social science, other. **Pre-professional programs:** pre-law, pre-dentistry, pre-medicine, pre-veterinary science, pre-pharmacy. **Special academic programs (% participation):** cooperative (work-study plan) program (5%), cross-registration (1%), distance learning (3%), double major (2%), dual enrollment (1%), honors program (15%), independent study (10%), internships (35%), student-designed major (1%), study abroad (10%), teacher certificate program (5%). **Teacher certification offered in:** elementary, middle/junior high, secondary. **Cooperative education programs:** engineering. **Reserve Officers Training Corps (ROTC):** Army ROTC: Offered at cooperating institution (Providence College). **Faculty and instruction (2005-2006):** Total instructional faculty: 355 full-time, 216 part-time (59% men; 41% women; 13% minorities). Full-time faculty with Ph.D. or other terminal degree: 85%. Student/faculty ratio: 17/1. Classes of fewer than 20 students: 38%; of 20 to 49 students: 54%; of 50 or more students: 8%. **Advanced Placement and International Baccalaureate credit:** AP tests may be used for: Credit and/or placement. Scores accepted: 3, 4, 5. International Baccalaureate exams may be used for: Credit and/or placement. **Freshmen returning for sophomore year:** 77%. **Graduation rates:** Four-year: 28%; five-year: 47%; six-year: 51%.

COSTS AND FINANCIAL AID

Financial aid office: (508) 999-8632. **Expenses (2006-2007):** Tuition and fees 2006-2007: $8,309 in state, $14,991 out of state; room/board: $8,574. Estimated books and supplies: $800; transportation: $500; personal expenses: $1,390. **Financial aid:** Priority filing date for institution's financial aid form: March 1. In 2005-2006, 78% of undergraduates applied for financial aid. Of those, 62% were determined to have financial need; 64% had their need fully met. Average financial aid package (proportion receiving): $10,805 (60%). Average amount of gift aid, such as scholarships or grants (proportion receiving): $5,500 (51%). Average amount of self-help aid, such as work study or loans (proportion receiving): $6,676 (54%). Average need-based loan (excluding PLUS or other private loans): $6,375. Among students who received need-based aid, the average percentage of need met: 95%. Among students who received aid based on merit, the average award (and the proportion receiving): $2,500 (5%). Average amount of debt of borrowers graduating in 2005: $16,214. Proportion who borrowed: 65%.

CAMPUS LIFE AND EXTRACURRICULAR ACTIVITIES

Campus housing available (% using): coed dorms (52%), apartment for single students (47%), special housing for disabled students (1%). Students who live in college-owned, operated, or affiliated housing: 54%. **Student employment:** During the 2005-2006 academic year, 26% of undergraduates worked on campus. **Clubs and organizations:** Number of student organizations: 100. Activities include: choral groups, concert band, dance, drama/theater, jazz band, literary magazine, music ensembles, musical theater, pep band, radio station, student government, student newspaper, symphony orchestra, yearbook. Number of fraternities: 5; sororities: 3. Average proportion of students who stay on campus on weekends: 40%. **Sports program (2005-2006):** Member of NCAA III. *Men's intercollegiate varsity sports:* baseball, basketball, cross-country, football, golf, ice hockey, lacrosse, soccer, swimming and diving, tennis, track and field (indoor), track and field (outdoor). *Women's intercollegiate varsity sports:* basketball, cross-country, equestrian sports, field hockey, lacrosse, soccer, softball, swimming and diving, tennis, track and field (indoor), track and field (outdoor), volleyball.

SERVICES AND FACILITIES

Basic services: nonremedial tutoring, women's center, placement service, day care, health service, health insurance. **Remedial assistance:** reading, math, writing, study skills. **Counseling services:** minority student, career, military, personal, veteran student, academic, older student, psychological, birth control, religious, other. **For learning-disabled students:** School does not offer a structured program with separate admission and additional fees. Services include: remedial math, remedial English, reading machines, tape recorders, untimed tests, note-taking services, oral tests, learning center, readers, extended time for tests, tutors, texts on tape, other testing accommodations, waiver of foreign language degree requirement, other. **Library:** Number of titles: 461,523; number of current serial subscriptions: 2,741. **Information technology resources:** Students are not required to lease or own a computer. Number of campus computers available to all students: 650. School has a wireless network. Approximate number of users that can be accommodated: 500. Proportion of college-owned housing units wired for high-speed internet access: 100%. **Campus safety:** Security services offered: 24-hour foot-and-vehicle patrols, late-night transport/escort service, 24-hour emergency telephones, lighted pathways/sidewalks, controlled dormitory access (key, security card, etc).

TRANSFER AND INTERNATIONAL STUDENTS

Transfer students: May apply for admission for the following academic terms: Fall, Spring. Applicants do not need a minimum number of credits to apply. For fall 2005: Transfer applications received: 958. Transfer applicants offered admission: 791. Transfer applicants enrolled: 493.
International students: Number of foreign undergraduates: 32. Number of countries represented: 17. Minimum TOEFL score required: 550 (paper); 213 (computer). Average TOEFL score: 600 (paper).

University of Massachusetts–Lowell

- **Address:** 1 University Avenue, Lowell, MA 01854
- **Website:** http://www.uml.edu
- **Public**
- **Enrollment:** 5,695 full-time; 2,614 part-time

KEY STATS

✔ **U.S News College Ranking:** third tier, National Universities
✔ **SAT Score (25th/75th percentile):** 980-1200
✔ **Tuition:** 2006-2007: $8,444 in state, $15,557 out of state

Selectivity: Selective	**Room/board:** $6,520
Acceptance rate: 70%	**Average debt:** $14,833
Student/faculty ratio: 15/1	**Proportion who borrowed:** 57%

UNDERGRADUATE STUDENT BODY STATS

2005-2006 enrollment: 5,695 full-time; 2,614 part-time. Men: 60%; women: 40%. **Ethnic makeup:** African American: 4%; Asian American: 7%; Hispanic: 5%; White: 82%; International: 1%.

ADMISSIONS FACTS AND FIGURES

Phone: (978) 934-3931. **Email:** admissions@uml.edu. **Website:** http://www.uml.edu. **Application deadlines for fall 2007:** Regular decision: Rolling. Early decision: Not offered. Early action: Not offered. Admission can be deferred. **Application fee:** $20. Common application is not accepted.
Admissions requirements/recommendations: High school units required (recommended): English: 4; Mathematics: 3; Science: 3; Foreign language:

2; Social studies: 2; Academic electives: 2; Total units: 16. Tests: The college uses SAT or ACT scores in admissions decisions. Either SAT or ACT required. For admission to the fall 2007 entering class, the school will accept; ACT with writing, ACT without writing. Campus visit: Recommended. Admissions interview: Recommended. Off-campus interview: Not available. **Factors that count in admissions decisions:** *Academic:* Secondary school record: Very important. Class rank: Important. Letters of recommendation: Important. Standardized test scores: Very important. Essay: Important. *Nonacademic:* Interview: Considered. Extracurricular activities: Considered. Talent/ability: Considered. Character/personal qualities: Considered. Alumni/ae relationship: Not considered. Geographical residence: Not considered. State residency: Not considered. Religious affiliation/commitment: Not considered. Minority status: Not considered. Volunteer work: Considered. Work experience: Considered. **Other schools with the greatest overlap in applicants:** Northeastern University; University of Massachusetts–Amherst; University of Massachusetts–Boston; University of Massachusetts–Dartmouth; Wentworth Institute of Technology.
Admissions statistics for the fall 2005 entering class: Total applicants: 4,321. Total accepted: 3,013. Freshmen enrolled: 1,088; 8% were from out of state. Overall acceptance rate: 70%. **Credentials of fall 2005 freshmen:** 11% ranked in the top 10 percent of their high school class; 40% were in the top 25 percent, and 80% were in the top half. (Proportion submitting class standing: 99%.) **Average high school grade point average:** 3.1. **First-year students who submitted SAT scores:** 99%. Scores (25/75 percentile): Verbal: 480-590, Math: 500-610, Combined: 980-1200.

ACADEMICS

Year founded: 1894. **Academic calendar:** Semester. **Degrees offered:** certificate, associate, bachelor's, post-bachelor's certificate, master's, post-master's certificate, doctorate. **Most popular majors:** 19% business administration and management, 14% electrical and electronic engineering technologies/technicians, 12% computer science, 9% nursing/registered nurse training (R.N., A.S.N., B.S.N., M.S.N.), 8% criminal justice/law enforcement administration. **Major fields of study:** area, ethnic, cultural, and gender studies; biological and biomedical sciences; business, management, marketing, and related support services; computer and information sciences and support services; education; engineering; engineering technologies/technicians; English language and literature/letters; foreign languages, literatures, and linguistics; health professions and related clinical sciences; history; liberal arts and sciences studies, and humanities; mathematics and statistics; philosophy and religious studies; physical sciences; psychology; security and protective services; social sciences; visual and performing arts. **Areas of required coursework:** humanities, mathematics, English (including composition), foreign languages, sciences (biological or physical), history, social science. **Special academic programs:** accelerated program, cooperative (work-study plan) program, cross-registration, distance learning, double major, dual enrollment, honors program, internships, liberal arts/career combination, study abroad, teacher certificate program. **Teacher certification offered in:** elementary, middle/junior high, secondary. **Cooperative education programs:** engineering. **Reserve Officers Training Corps (ROTC):** Air Force ROTC: Offered on campus. **Faculty and instruction (2005-2006):** Total instructional faculty: 383 full-time, 240 part-time (62% men; 38% women; 13% minorities). Full-time faculty with Ph.D. or other terminal degree: 95%. Student/faculty ratio: 15/1. Classes of fewer than 20 students: 56%; of 20 to 49 students: 39%; of 50 or more students: 4%. **Advanced Placement and International Baccalaureate credit:** AP tests may be used for: Credit only. Scores accepted: 3, 4, 5. **Freshmen returning for sophomore year:** 74%. **Graduation rates:** Four-year: 25%; five-year: 44%; six-year: 46%.

COSTS AND FINANCIAL AID

Financial aid office: (978) 934-4226. **Expenses (2006-2007):** Tuition and fees 2006-2007: $8,444 in state, $15,557 out of state; room/board: $6,520. Estimated books and supplies: $600; transportation: $200; personal expenses: $862. **Financial aid:** Priority filing date for institution's financial aid form: March 1. In 2005-2006, 70% of undergraduates applied for financial aid. Of those, 49% were determined to have financial need; 68% had their need fully met. Average financial aid package (proportion receiving): $8,733 (48%). Average amount of gift aid, such as scholarships or grants (proportion receiving): $4,419 (42%). Average amount of self-help aid, such as work study or loans (proportion receiving): $5,199 (46%). Average need-based loan (excluding PLUS or other private loans): $4,270. Among students who received need-based aid, the average percentage of need met: 93%. Among students who received aid based on merit, the average award (and the proportion receiving): $3,843 (3%). The average athletic scholarship (and the proportion receiving): $7,628 (2%). Average amount of debt of borrowers graduating in 2005: $14,833. Proportion who borrowed: 57%.

CAMPUS LIFE AND EXTRACURRICULAR ACTIVITIES
Campus housing available (% using): coed dorms (88%), women's dorms (5%), men's dorms (5%), apartments for married students (1%), apartment for single students (1%), special housing for disabled students (0%). Students who live in college-owned, operated, or affiliated housing: 34%. **Student employment:** During the 2005-2006 academic year, 12% of undergraduates worked on campus. Average per-year earnings: $2,250. **Clubs and organizations:** Number of student organizations: 100. Activities include: choral groups, concert band, dance, drama/theater, jazz band, literary magazine, marching band, music ensembles, pep band, radio station, student government, student newspaper, student film society, symphony orchestra, yearbook. Number of fraternities: 0; sororities: 0. Average proportion of students who stay on campus on weekends: 60%. **Sports program (2005-2006):** Member of NCAA II. *Men's intercollegiate varsity sports:* baseball, basketball, cross-country, football, ice hockey, soccer, track and field (indoor), track and field (outdoor). *Women's intercollegiate varsity sports:* basketball, cross-country, field hockey, soccer, softball, tennis, track and field (indoor), track and field (outdoor), volleyball.

SERVICES AND FACILITIES
Basic services: nonremedial tutoring, women's center, placement service, health service, health insurance. **Remedial assistance:** reading, math, writing, study skills, other. **Counseling services:** minority student, career, military, personal, veteran student, academic, older student, psychological, birth control, religious. **For learning-disabled students:** School does not offer a structured program with separate admission and additional fees. Total undergraduates in learning-disabled program or receiving services: 202. Services include: tape recorders, untimed tests, note-taking services, oral tests, learning center, readers, extended time for tests, tutors, priority registration, priority seating, other testing accomodations. **Library:** Number of titles: 397,652; number of current serial subscriptions: 534. **Information technology resources:** Students are not required to lease or own a computer. Number of campus computers available to all students: 4,000. School has a wireless network. Approximate number of users that can be accommodated: 25. Proportion of college-owned housing units wired for high-speed internet access: 100%. **Campus safety:** Security services offered: 24-hour foot-and-vehicle patrols, late-night transport/escort service, 24-hour emergency telephones, lighted pathways/sidewalks, controlled dormitory access (key, security card, etc).

TRANSFER AND INTERNATIONAL STUDENTS
Transfer students: May apply for admission for the following academic terms: Fall, Spring. Applicants need a minimum number of credits to apply. For fall 2005: Transfer applications received: 1,381. Transfer applicants offered admission: 1,145. Transfer applicants enrolled: 717. **International students:** Number of foreign undergraduates: 74 (1% of student body). Minimum TOEFL score required: 550 (paper); 213 (computer). Average TOEFL score: 550 (paper).

Wellesley College

- **Address:** 106 Central Street, Wellesley, MA 02481-8203
- **Website:** http://www.wellesley.edu
- **Private**
- **Enrollment:** 2,216 full-time; 115 part-time

KEY STATS
- ✔ **U.S News College Ranking:** 4, Liberal Arts Colleges
- ✔ **SAT Score (25th/75th percentile):** 1310-1480
- ✔ **Tuition:** 2006-2007: $33,072

Selectivity: Most selective	**Room/board:** $10,216
Acceptance rate: 34%	**Average debt:** $11,821
Student/faculty ratio: 9/1	**Proportion who borrowed:** 51%

UNDERGRADUATE STUDENT BODY STATS
2005-2006 enrollment: 2,216 full-time; 115 part-time. Men: 2%; women: 98%. **Ethnic makeup:** African American: 6%; Asian American: 27%; Hispanic: 7%; White: 52%; International: 8%.

ADMISSIONS FACTS AND FIGURES
Phone: (781) 283-2270. **Email:** admission@wellesley.edu. **Website:** http://www.wellesley.edu. **Application deadlines for fall 2007:** Regular decision: January 15; decision sent by April 1. Early decision: Send application by: November 1; Decision sent by: December 15. Early action: Not offered. Admission can be deferred. **Application fee:** $50. Common application is accepted. **To apply online, go to:** https://www.applyweb.com/apply/wellesley/menu.html. **Admissions requirements/recommendations:** High school units required (recommended): English: (4); Mathematics: (4); Science: (3); Foreign language: (4); Social studies: (4); History: (4); Academic electives: (0). Tests: The college uses SAT or ACT scores in admissions decisions. Either SAT or ACT required. For admission to the fall 2007 entering class, the school will accept: ACT with writing. Campus visit: Recommended. Admissions interview: Recommended. Off-campus interview: May be arranged. **Factors that count in admissions decisions:** *Academic:* Secondary school record: Very important. Class rank: Important. Letters of recommendation: Very important. Standardized test scores: Very important. Essay: Very important. *Nonacademic:* Interview: Considered. Extracurricular activities: Important. Talent/ability: Considered. Character/personal qualities: Very important. Alumni/ae relationship: Considered. Geographical residence: Considered. State residency: Considered. Religious affiliation/commitment: Not considered. Minority status: Considered. Volunteer work: Considered. Work experience: Considered. **Other schools with the greatest overlap in applicants:** Barnard College; Brown University; Smith College; University of California–Berkeley; University of California–Los Angeles. **Admissions statistics for the fall 2005 entering class:** Total applicants: 4,347. Total accepted: 1,463. Freshmen enrolled: 605; 86% were from out of state. Accepted through early-decision or early-action plans: 19%. Overall acceptance rate: 34%. Early-decision acceptance rate: 47%. Non-early acceptance rate: 33%. **Size of waiting list:** 886 applicants; enrolled from waiting list: 45. **Credentials of fall 2005 freshmen:** 77% ranked in the top 10 percent of their high school class; 95% were in the top 25 percent, and 100% were in the top half. (Proportion submitting class standing: 53%.) **First-year students who submitted SAT scores:** 95%. Scores (25/75 percentile): Verbal: 660-750, Math: 650-730, Combined: 1310-1480. **First-year students submitting ACT scores:** 32%. Scores (25/75 percentile): English: N/A, Math: N/A, Composite: 28-31.

ACADEMICS
Year founded: 1870. **Academic calendar:** Semester. **Degrees offered:** bachelor's. **Most popular majors:** 15% psychology, 12% economics, 10% English language and literature, 10% political science and government, 8% international relations and affairs. **Major fields of study:** architecture and related services; area, ethnic, cultural, and gender studies; biological and biomedical sciences; computer and information sciences and support services; education; English language and literature/letters; foreign languages, literatures, and linguistics; history; mathematics and statistics; multi/interdisciplinary studies; natural resources and conservation; philosophy and religious studies; physical sciences; psychology; social sciences; visual and performing arts. **Areas of required coursework:** arts/fine arts, humanities, mathematics, English (including composition), philosophy, foreign languages, sciences (biological or physical), history, social science, other. **Special academic programs (% participation):** cross-registration (23%), double major (32%), exchange student program (domestic) (17%), honors program (19%), independent study (49%), internships (0%), student-designed major (2%), study abroad (43%), teacher certificate program. **Reserve Officers Training Corps (ROTC):** Army ROTC: Offered at cooperating institution (M.I.T); Air Force ROTC: Offered at cooperating institution (M.I.T.). **Faculty and instruction (2005-2006):** Total instructional faculty: 227 full-time, 102 part-time (43% men; 57% women; 19% minorities). Full-time faculty with Ph.D. or other terminal degree: 97%. Student/faculty ratio: 9/1. Classes of fewer than 20 students: 63%; of 20 to 49 students: 35%; of 50 or more students: 2%. **Advanced Placement and International Baccalaureate credit:** AP tests may be used for: Credit only. Scores accepted: 3, 4, 5. International Baccalaureate exams may be used for: Credit only. **Freshmen returning for sophomore year:** 95%. **Graduation rates:** Four-year: 88%; five-year: 92%; six-year: 93%. **Graduate study:** 23% of students pursue further study within one year; 68% within five years. Fields in which graduates pursue further study: Master of Business Administration (MBA), 11%; law, 15%; medicine, 8%; engineering, 2%; theology (or the seminary), 1%; education, 7%; arts and sciences, 38%.

COSTS AND FINANCIAL AID
Financial aid office: (781) 283-2360. **Expenses (2006-2007):** Tuition and fees 2006-2007: $33,072; room/board: $10,216. Estimated books and supplies: $1,000; transportation: $1,000. **Financial aid:** Priority filing date for institu-

tion's financial aid form: January 15. In 2005-2006, 69% of undergraduates applied for financial aid. Of those, 60% were determined to have financial need; 100% had their need fully met. Average financial aid package (proportion receiving): $27,907 (60%). Average amount of gift aid, such as scholarships or grants (proportion receiving): $25,283 (58%). Average amount of self-help aid, such as work study or loans (proportion receiving): $3,977 (54%). Average need-based loan (excluding PLUS or other private loans): $3,197. Among students who received need-based aid, the average percentage of need met: 100%. Average amount of debt of borrowers graduating in 2005: $11,821. Proportion who borrowed: 51%.

CAMPUS LIFE AND EXTRACURRICULAR ACTIVITIES

Campus housing available (% using): women's dorms (100%), apartment for single students, special housing for disabled students, cooperative housing. Students who live in college-owned, operated, or affiliated housing: 97%. **Student employment:** During the 2005-2006 academic year, 20% of undergraduates worked on campus. Average per-year earnings: $1,500. **Clubs and organizations:** Number of student organizations: 170. Activities include: choral groups, dance, drama/theater, jazz band, literary magazine, music ensembles, musical theater, radio station, student government, student newspaper, student film society, yearbook. Number of fraternities: 0; sororities: 0. **Sports program (2005-2006):** Member of NCAA III. *Women's intercollegiate varsity sports:* basketball, cross-country, fencing, field hockey, golf, lacrosse, rowing, soccer, softball, squash, swimming and diving, tennis, track and field (indoor), track and field (outdoor), volleyball.

SERVICES AND FACILITIES

Basic services: nonremedial tutoring, women's center, health service, health insurance. **Counseling services:** minority student, career, personal, academic, older student, psychological, birth control, religious. **For learning-disabled students:** School does not offer a structured program with separate admission and additional fees. Services include: tape recorders, note-taking services, learning center, extended time for tests. **Library:** Number of titles: 832,415; number of current serial subscriptions: 13,983. **Information technology resources:** Students are not required to lease or own a computer. Number of campus computers available to all students: 468. School has a wireless network. Approximate number of users that can be accommodated: 325. Proportion of college-owned housing units wired for high-speed internet access: 100%. **Campus safety:** Security services offered: 24-hour foot-and-vehicle patrols, late-night transport/escort service, 24-hour emergency telephones, lighted pathways/sidewalks, controlled dormitory access (key, security card, etc).

TRANSFER AND INTERNATIONAL STUDENTS

Transfer students: May apply for admission for the following academic terms: Fall, Spring. Applicants do not need a minimum number of credits to apply. For fall 2005: Transfer applications received: 123. Transfer applicants offered admission: 49. Transfer applicants enrolled: 28. **International students:** Number of foreign undergraduates: 182 (8% of student body). Number of countries represented: 65. Average TOEFL score: 629 (paper).

Wentworth Institute of Technology

- **Address:** 550 Huntington Avenue, Boston, MA 02115-5998
- **Website:** http://www.wit.edu
- **Private**
- **Enrollment:** 3,141 full-time; 495 part-time

KEY STATS

✔ **U.S News College Ranking:** Unranked Specialty School–Engineering
✔ **SAT Score:** 1073
✔ **Tuition:** 2005-2006: $18,500

Selectivity: Less selective	**Room/board:** $9,000
Acceptance rate: 60%	**Average debt:** N/A
Student/faculty ratio: N/A	**Proportion who borrowed:** N/A

UNDERGRADUATE STUDENT BODY STATS

2005-2006 enrollment: 3,141 full-time; 495 part-time. Men: 80%; women: 20%. **Ethnic makeup:** African American: 4%; Asian American: 5%; Hispanic: 3%; White: 85%; International: 3%.

ADMISSIONS FACTS AND FIGURES

Phone: (617) 989-4000. **Email:** admissions@wit.edu. **Website:** http://www.wit.edu. **Application deadlines for fall 2007:** Regular decision: February 15. Early decision: Not offered. Early action: Not offered. Admission can be deferred. **Application fee:** $30. Common application is accepted. **To apply online, go to:** http://www.wit.edu/prospective/admissions/overview.html. **Admissions requirements/recommendations:** High school units required (recommended): English: 4; Mathematics: 3 (4); Science: 1 (3); Total units: 8 (16). Tests: The college uses SAT or ACT scores in admissions decisions. Either SAT or ACT required. Campus visit: Recommended. Admissions interview: Neither required nor recommended. Off-campus interview: Not available. **Factors that count in admissions decisions: *Academic:*** Secondary school record: Very important. Class rank: Considered. Letters of recommendation: Important. Standardized test scores: Important. Essay: Important. ***Nonacademic:*** Interview: Considered. Extracurricular activities: Considered. Talent/ability: Not considered. Character/personal qualities: Not considered. Alumni/ae relationship: Considered. Geographical residence: Not considered. State residency: Not considered. Religious affiliation/commitment: Not considered. Minority status: Not considered. Volunteer work: Considered. Work experience: Considered. **Other schools with the greatest overlap in applicants:** Northeastern University; Rensselaer Polytechnic Institute; Rochester Institute of Technology; Roger Williams University; Worcester Polytechnic Institute. **Admissions statistics for the fall 2005 entering class:** Total applicants: 3,040. Total accepted: 1,825. Freshmen enrolled: 832; 45% were from out of state. Overall acceptance rate: 60%. **Size of waiting list:** 2 applicants; enrolled from waiting list: 0. **Credentials of fall 2005 freshmen:** 2% ranked in the top 10 percent of their high school class; 21% were in the top 25 percent. **First-year students who submitted SAT scores:** 97%. Scores (25/75 percentile): Verbal: N/A, Math: N/A, Combined: N/A. **First-year students submitting ACT scores:** 5%. Scores (25/75 percentile): English: N/A, Math: N/A, Composite: N/A.

ACADEMICS

Year founded: 1904. **Academic calendar:** Semester. **Degrees offered:** certificate, associate, bachelor's. **Most popular majors:** Information not available. **Major fields of study:** architecture and related services; business, management, marketing, and related support services; computer and information sciences and support services; construction trades; engineering; engineering technologies/technicians; visual and performing arts. **Special academic programs:** cooperative (work-study plan) program, cross-registration, internships, other. **Reserve Officers Training Corps (ROTC):** Army ROTC: Offered at cooperating institution (Northeastern University). **Faculty and instruction (2005-2006):** Total instructional faculty: N/A. Classes of fewer than 20 students: 36%; of 20 to 49 students: 62%; of 50 or more students: 2%. **Advanced Placement and International Baccalaureate credit:** AP tests may be used for: Credit only. Scores accepted: 3, 4, 5. International Baccalaureate exams may be used for: Credit only. **Freshmen returning for sophomore year:** 75%. **Graduation rates:** Six-year: 40%. **Graduate study:** 2% of students pursue further study immediately upon graduation.

COSTS AND FINANCIAL AID

Financial aid office: (617) 989-4020. **Expenses (2005-2006):** Tuition and fees 2005-2006: $18,500; room/board: $9,000. Estimated books and supplies: $1,000; transportation: $1,000; personal expenses: $2,500. **Financial aid:** Priority filing date for institution's financial aid form: March 1.

CAMPUS LIFE AND EXTRACURRICULAR ACTIVITIES

Campus housing available: coed dorms. Students who live in college-owned, operated, or affiliated housing: 41%. **Student employment:** During the 2005-2006 academic year, 19% of undergraduates worked on campus. Average per-year earnings: $1,083. **Clubs and organizations:** Number of student organizations: 43. Activities include: choral groups, drama/theater, literary magazine, music ensembles, musical theater, radio station, student government, student newspaper, student film society, yearbook. Number of fraternities: 0; sororities: 0. **Sports program (2005-2006):** Member of NCAA III. *Men's intercollegiate varsity sports:* baseball, basketball, golf, ice hockey, lacrosse, riflery, soccer, tennis, volleyball. *Women's intercollegiate varsity sports:* basketball, riflery, soccer, softball, tennis, volleyball.

SERVICES AND FACILITIES

Basic services: nonremedial tutoring, women's center, placement service, health service, health insurance. **Remedial assistance:** reading, math, writing, study skills. **Counseling services:** minority student, career, military, personal, veteran student, academic, older student, psychological, birth control, religious. **For learning-disabled students:** School does not offer a structured program with separate admission and additional fees. Services include: remedial math, remedial English, tape recorders, untimed tests, note-taking services, oral tests, learning center, readers, extended time for tests, tutors, other. **Information technology resources:** Students are not required to lease or own a computer. School has a wireless network. **Campus safety:** Security services offered: 24-hour foot-and-vehicle patrols, late-night transport/escort service, 24-hour emergency telephones, lighted pathways/sidewalks, controlled dormitory access (key, security card, etc).

TRANSFER AND INTERNATIONAL STUDENTS

Transfer students: May apply for admission for the following academic terms: Fall, Spring. Applicants do not need a minimum number of credits to apply. For fall 2005: Transfer applications received: 359. Transfer applicants offered admission: 235. Transfer applicants enrolled: 163. **International students:** Number of foreign undergraduates: 104 (3% of student body). Number of countries represented: 44. Minimum TOEFL score required: 525 (paper); 71 (computer).

Western New England College

- **Address:** 1215 Wilbraham Road, Springfield, MA 01119-2684
- **Website:** http://www.wnec.edu
- **Private**
- **Enrollment:** 2,363 full-time; 477 part-time

KEY STATS

✔ **U.S News College Ranking:** 51, Universities–Master's (North)
✔ **SAT Score (25th/75th percentile):** 960-1170
✔ **Tuition:** 2006-2007: $24,626

Selectivity: Selective	**Room/board:** $9,526
Acceptance rate: 75%	**Average debt:** N/A
Student/faculty ratio: 15/1	**Proportion who borrowed:** N/A

UNDERGRADUATE STUDENT BODY STATS

2005-2006 enrollment: 2,363 full-time; 477 part-time. Men: 62%; women: 38%. **Ethnic makeup:** African American: 4%; Asian American: 2%; Hispanic: 3%; White: 91%.

ADMISSIONS FACTS AND FIGURES

Phone: (413) 782-1321. **Email:** ugradmis@wnec.edu. **Website:** http://www.wnec.edu. **Application deadlines for fall 2007:** Regular decision: Rolling. Early decision: Not offered. Early action: Not offered. Admission can be deferred. **Application fee:** $50. Common application is accepted. **To apply online, go to:** http://www1.wnec.edu/admissions/. **Admissions requirements/recommendations:** High school units required (recommended): English: 4 (4); Mathematics: 2 (4); Science: 1 (2); Foreign language: 0 (2); Social studies: 1 (2); History: 1 (2); Total units: 10 (18). Tests: The college uses SAT or ACT scores in admissions decisions. Either SAT or ACT required. For admission to the fall 2007 entering class, the school will accept: ACT with writing, ACT without writing. Campus visit: Recommended. Admissions interview: Recommended. Off-campus interview: May be arranged. **Factors that count in admissions decisions:** *Academic:* Secondary school record: Considered. Class rank: Considered. Letters of recommendation: Very important. Standardized test scores: Very important. Essay: Considered. *Nonacademic:* Interview: Considered. Extracurricular activities: Considered. Talent/ability: Considered. Character/personal qualities: Considered. Alumni/ae relationship: Considered. Geographical residence: Not considered. State residency: Not considered. Religious affiliation/commitment: Not considered. Minority status: Considered. Volunteer work: Considered. Work experience: Considered. **Admissions statistics for the fall 2005 entering class:** Total applicants: 4,243. Total accepted: 3,193. Freshmen enrolled: 666; 67% were from out of state. Overall acceptance rate: 75%. **Credentials of fall 2005 freshmen:** 10% ranked in the top 10 percent of their high school class; 32% were in the top 25 percent, and 73% were in the top half. (Proportion submitting class standing: 60%.) Average high school grade point average: 3.1. **First-year students who submitted SAT scores:** 99%. Scores (25/75 percentile): Verbal: 480-570, Math: 480-600, Combined: 960-1170. **First-year students submitting ACT scores:** 9%. Scores (25/75 percentile): English: N/A, Math: N/A, Composite: 20-24.

ACADEMICS

Year founded: 1919. **Academic calendar:** Semester. **Degrees offered:** associate, bachelor's, master's, first professional. **Most popular majors:** 34% business, management, marketing, and related support services, 33% security and protective services, 8% psychology, 7% engineering, 3% communication studies/speech communication and rhetoric. **Major fields of study:** area, ethnic, cultural, and gender studies; biological and biomedical sciences; business, management, marketing, and related support services; communication, journalism, and related programs; computer and information sciences and support services; education; engineering; English language and literature/letters; history; liberal arts and sciences studies, and humanities; mathematics and statistics; multi/interdisciplinary studies; parks, recreation, leisure, and fitness studies; philosophy and religious studies; physical sciences; psychology; public administration and social service professions; security and protective services; social sciences. **Areas of required coursework:** arts/fine arts, humanities, computer literacy, mathematics, English (including composition), philosophy, sciences (biological or physical), history, social science. **Pre-professional programs:** pre-law, pre-dentistry, pre-medicine, other. **Special academic programs:** cross-registration, distance learning, double major, dual enrollment, honors program, independent study, internships, liberal arts/career combination, student-designed major, study abroad, teacher certificate program. **Teacher certification offered in:** elementary, secondary. **Cooperative education programs:** business, computer science, education, engineering, humanities, natural science, social/behavioral science. **Reserve Officers Training Corps (ROTC):** Army ROTC: Offered on campus; Air Force ROTC: Offered at cooperating institution (UMass Amherst). **Faculty and instruction (2005-2006):** Total instructional faculty: 164 full-time, 156 part-time (63% men; 37% women; 6% minorities). Full-time faculty with Ph.D. or other terminal degree: 91%. Student/faculty ratio: 15/1. Classes of fewer than 20 students: 50%; of 20 to 49 students: 50%; of 50 or more students: 0%. **Advanced Placement and International Baccalaureate credit:** AP tests may be used for: Credit and/or placement. Scores accepted: 3, 4, 5. **Freshmen returning for sophomore year:** 74%. **Graduation rates:** Four-year: 46%; five-year: 58%; six-year: 57%.

COSTS AND FINANCIAL AID

Financial aid office: (413) 796-2080. **Expenses (2006-2007):** Tuition and fees 2006-2007: $24,626; room/board: $9,526. Estimated books and supplies: $950; transportation: $430; personal expenses: $1,210. **Financial aid:** Priority filing date for institution's financial aid form: April 15. In 2005-2006, 91% of undergraduates applied for financial aid. Of those, 73% were determined to have financial need; 12% had their need fully met. Average financial aid package (proportion receiving): $13,646 (71%). Average amount of gift aid, such as scholarships or grants (proportion receiving): $8,462 (70%). Average amount of self-help aid, such as work study or loans (proportion receiving): $4,843 (65%). Average need-based loan (excluding PLUS or other private loans): $3,948. Among students who received need-based aid, the average percentage of need met: 68%. Among students who received aid based on merit, the average award (and the proportion receiving): $6,851 (9%). The average athletic scholarship (and the proportion receiving): $0 (0%).

CAMPUS LIFE AND EXTRACURRICULAR ACTIVITIES

Campus housing available: coed dorms, apartment for single students, special housing for disabled students. Students who live in college-owned, operated, or affiliated housing: 71%. **Clubs and organizations:** Number of student organizations: 60. Activities include: choral groups, concert band, dance, drama/theater, jazz band, literary magazine, music ensembles, pep band, radio station, student government, student newspaper, yearbook. Number of fraternities: 0; sororities: 0. Average proportion of students who stay on campus on weekends: 75%. **Sports program (2005-2006):** Member of NCAA III. **Men's intercollegiate varsity sports:** baseball, basketball, cross-country, football, golf, ice hockey, lacrosse, soccer, tennis, wrestling. **Women's intercollegiate varsity sports:** basketball, cross-country, field hockey, lacrosse, soccer, softball, swimming and diving, tennis, volleyball.

SERVICES AND FACILITIES

Basic services: nonremedial tutoring, health service, health insurance, other. **Counseling services:** minority student, career, military, personal, veteran student, academic, older student, psychological, birth control, religious. **For learning-disabled students:** School does not offer a structured program with separate admission and additional fees. Services include: remedial math, remedial English, reading machines, remedial reading, tape recorders, note-taking services, learning center, readers, extended time for tests, tutors, other. **Library:** Number of titles: 123,420; number of current serial subscriptions: 153. **Information technology resources:** Students are not required to lease or own a computer. Number of campus computers available to all students: 460. School has a wireless network. Proportion of college-owned housing units wired for high-speed internet access: 100%. **Campus safety:** Security services offered: 24-hour foot-and-vehicle patrols, late-night transport/escort service, 24-hour emergency telephones, lighted pathways/sidewalks, controlled dormitory access (key, security card, etc).

TRANSFER AND INTERNATIONAL STUDENTS

Transfer students: May apply for admission for the following academic terms: Fall, Spring. Applicants need a minimum number of credits to apply. For fall 2005: Transfer applications received: 291. Transfer applicants offered admission: 206. Transfer applicants enrolled: 108. **International students:** Number of foreign undergraduates: 7. Minimum TOEFL score required: 500 (paper); 173 (computer).

Westfield State College

- **Address:** Western Avenue, Westfield, MA 01086
- **Website:** http://www.wsc.mass.edu
- **Public**
- **Enrollment:** 4,112 full-time; 555 part-time

KEY STATS
✔ **U.S News College Ranking:** fourth tier, Universities–Master's (North)
✔ **SAT Score (25th/75th percentile):** 940-1110
✔ **Tuition:** 2006-2007: $5,657 in state, $11,737 out of state
   Selectivity: Less selective   **Room/board:** $6,470
   Acceptance rate: 74%   **Average debt:** N/A
   Student/faculty ratio: 18/1   **Proportion who borrowed:** N/A

UNDERGRADUATE STUDENT BODY STATS
2005-2006 enrollment: 4,112 full-time; 555 part-time. Men: 45%; women: 55%. **Ethnic makeup:** African American: 3%; Asian American: 1%; Hispanic: 3%; White: 92%.

ADMISSIONS FACTS AND FIGURES
Phone: (413) 572-5218. **Email:** admissions@wsc.ma.edu. **Website:** http://www.wsc.mass.edu. **Application deadlines for fall 2007:** Regular decision: March 1; decision sent by April 15. Early decision: Not offered. Early action: Not offered. Admission can be deferred. **Application fee:** $25. Common application is not accepted. **To apply online, go to:** https://infowise.wsc.ma.edu. **Admissions requirements/recommendations:** High school units required (recommended): English: 4; Mathematics: 3; Science: 3; Foreign language: 2; Social studies: 1; History: 1; Academic electives: 2; Total units: 16. Tests: The college uses SAT or ACT scores in admissions decisions. Either SAT or ACT required. For admission to the fall 2007 entering class, the school will accept: ACT with writing, ACT without writing. Campus visit: Recommended. Admissions interview: Neither required nor recommended. Off-campus interview: Not available. **Factors that count in admissions decisions:** *Academic:* Secondary school record: Very important. Class rank: Not considered. Letters of recommendation: Considered. Standardized test scores: Very important. Essay: Considered. *Nonacademic:* Interview: Not considered. Extracurricular activities: Important. Talent/ability: Important. Character/personal qualities: Considered. Alumni/ae relationship: Not considered. Geographical residence: Not considered. State residency: Not considered. Religious affiliation/commitment: Not considered. Minority status: Considered. Volunteer work: Considered. Work experience: Considered. **Admissions statistics for the fall 2005 entering class:** Total applicants: 4,248. Total accepted: 3,129. Freshmen enrolled: 1,183; 7% were from out of state. Overall acceptance rate: 74%. **Average high school grade point average:** 2.9. **First-year students who submitted SAT scores:** 89%. Scores (25/75 percentile): Verbal: 470-550, Math: 470-560, Combined: 940-1110. **First-year students submitting ACT scores:** 1%. Scores (25/75 percentile): English: N/A, Math: N/A, Composite: 20-24.

ACADEMICS
Year founded: 1838. **Academic calendar:** Semester. **Degrees offered:** bachelor's, post-bachelor's certificate, master's, post-master's certificate. **Most popular majors:** 16% security and protective services, 12% business, management, marketing, and related support services, 12% liberal arts and sciences studies, and humanities, 11% education, 11% psychology. **Major fields of study:** architecture and related services; area, ethnic, cultural, and gender

studies; biological and biomedical sciences; business, management, marketing, and related support services; communication, journalism, and related programs; computer and information sciences and support services; education; English language and literature/letters; foreign languages, literatures, and linguistics; history; liberal arts and sciences studies, and humanities; mathematics and statistics; multi/interdisciplinary studies; natural resources and conservation; parks, recreation, leisure, and fitness studies; philosophy and religious studies; physical sciences; psychology; public administration and social service professions; security and protective services; social sciences; visual and performing arts. **Areas of required coursework:** arts/fine arts, mathematics, English (including composition), sciences (biological or physical), social science, other. **Special academic programs:** cooperative (work-study plan) program, cross-registration, distance learning, double major, dual enrollment, exchange student program (domestic), honors program, independent study, internships, student-designed major, study abroad, teacher certificate program. **Teacher certification offered in:** early childhood, special education, elementary, middle/junior high, secondary. **Cooperative education programs:** art, business, computer science, education, humanities, natural science, social/behavioral science. **Reserve Officers Training Corps (ROTC):** Army ROTC: Offered at cooperating institution (Western New England College); Air Force ROTC: Offered at cooperating institution (Western New England College). **Faculty and instruction (2005-2006):** Total instructional faculty: 179 full-time, 165 part-time (53% men; 47% women; 8% minorities). Full-time faculty with Ph.D. or other terminal degree: 83%. Student/faculty ratio: 18/1. Classes of fewer than 20 students: 32%; of 20 to 49 students: 67%; of 50 or more students: 1%. **Advanced Placement and International Baccalaureate credit:** AP tests may be used for: Credit and/or placement. Scores accepted: 3, 4, 5. **Freshmen returning for sophomore year:** 77%. **Graduation rates:** Four-year: 38%; five-year: 51%; six-year: 55%.

COSTS AND FINANCIAL AID
Financial aid office: (413) 572-5218. **Expenses (2006-2007):** Tuition and fees 2006-2007: $5,657 in state, $11,737 out of state; room/board: $6,470. Estimated books and supplies: $800 personal expenses: $1,263. **Financial aid:** Priority filing date for institution's financial aid form: March 1.

CAMPUS LIFE AND EXTRACURRICULAR ACTIVITIES
Campus housing available: coed dorms, apartment for single students, special housing for disabled students, other housing options. Students who live in college-owned, operated, or affiliated housing: 58%. **Student employment:** During the 2005-2006 academic year, 9% of undergraduates worked on campus. Average per-year earnings: $2,650. **Clubs and organizations:** Number of student organizations: 55. Activities include: choral groups, concert band, drama/theater, jazz band, literary magazine, music ensembles, musical theater, pep band, radio station, student government, student newspaper, television station, yearbook. Number of fraternities: 0; sororities: 0. Average proportion of students who stay on campus on weekends: 33%. **Sports program (2005-2006):** Member of NCAA III. *Men's intercollegiate varsity sports:* baseball, basketball, cross-country, football, soccer, track and field (indoor), track and field (outdoor). *Women's intercollegiate varsity sports:* basketball, cross-country, field hockey, soccer, softball, swimming and diving, track and field (indoor), track and field (outdoor), volleyball.

SERVICES AND FACILITIES
Basic services: nonremedial tutoring, women's center, placement service, health service. **Counseling services:** career, personal, academic, psychological. **For learning-disabled students:** School does not offer a structured program with separate admission and additional fees. **Library:** Number of titles: 142,504; number of current serial subscriptions: 634. **Information technology resources:** Students are not required to lease or own a computer. Number of campus computers available to all students: 320. School has a wireless network. Approximate number of users that can be accommodated: 8,000. Proportion of college-owned housing units wired for high-speed internet access: 100%. **Campus safety:** Security services offered: 24-hour foot-and-vehicle patrols, late-night transport/escort service, 24-hour emergency telephones, lighted pathways/sidewalks, student patrols, controlled dormitory access (key, security card, etc).

TRANSFER AND INTERNATIONAL STUDENTS
Transfer students: May apply for admission for the following academic terms: Fall, Spring. Applicants need a minimum number of credits to apply. For fall 2005: Transfer applications received: 574. Transfer applicants offered admission: 503. Transfer applicants enrolled: 333. **International students:** Number of foreign undergraduates: 2. Minimum TOEFL score required: 550 (paper); 213 (computer).

Wheaton College

- **Address:** East Main Street, Norton, MA 02766
- **Website:** http://www.wheatoncollege.edu
- **Private**
- **Enrollment:** 1,559 full-time; 10 part-time

KEY STATS

✔ **U.S News College Ranking:** 55, Liberal Arts Colleges
✔ **SAT Score (25th/75th percentile):** 1140-1320
✔ **Tuition:** 2006-2007: $34,610

Selectivity: More selective	**Room/board:** $8,150
Acceptance rate: 44%	**Average debt:** $22,380
Student/faculty ratio: 12/1	**Proportion who borrowed:** 61%

UNDERGRADUATE STUDENT BODY STATS

2005-2006 enrollment: 1,559 full-time; 10 part-time. Men: 38%; women: 62%. **Ethnic makeup:** African American: 3%; Asian American: 3%; Hispanic: 4%; White: 87%; International: 3%.

ADMISSIONS FACTS AND FIGURES

Phone: (508) 286-8251. **Email:** admission@wheatoncollege.edu. **Website:** http://www.wheatoncollege.edu. **Application deadlines for fall 2007:** Regular decision: January 15; decision sent by April 1. Early decision: Send application by: November 15; Decision sent by: December 15. Early action: Not offered. Admission can be deferred. **Application fee:** $55. Common application is accepted. **To apply online, go to:** http://www.wheatoncollege.edu/Admission/applying.html. **Admissions requirements/recommendations:** High school units required (recommended): English: 4 (4); Mathematics: 4 (4); Science: 3 (3); Foreign language: 4 (4); Social studies: 2 (3); History: 2 (2); Total units: 16 (20). Tests: The college uses SAT or ACT scores in admissions decisions. Neither SAT nor ACT required. For admission to the fall 2007 entering class, the school will accept: ACT with writing, ACT without writing. Campus visit: Recommended. Admissions interview: Recommended. Off-campus interview: May be arranged. **Factors that count in admissions decisions:** *Academic:* Secondary school record: Very important. Class rank: Important. Letters of recommendation: Important. Standardized test scores: Considered. Essay: Very important. *Nonacademic:* Interview: Important. Extracurricular activities: Very important. Talent/ability: Very important. Character/personal qualities: Very important. Alumni/ae relationship: Important. Geographical residence: Considered. State residency: Considered. Religious affiliation/commitment: Not considered. Minority status: Considered. Volunteer work: Important. Work experience: Important. **Other schools with the greatest overlap in applicants:** Boston University; Clark University; Connecticut College; Mount Holyoke College; Skidmore College. **Admissions statistics for the fall 2005 entering class:** Total applicants: 3,697. Total accepted: 1,638. Freshmen enrolled: 467; 68% were from out of state. Accepted through early-decision or early-action plans: 39%. Overall acceptance rate: 44%. Early-decision acceptance rate: 83%. Non-early acceptance rate: 42%. **Size of waiting list:** 763 applicants; enrolled from waiting list: 20. **Credentials of fall 2005 freshmen:** 56% ranked in the top 10 percent of their high school class; 82% were in the top 25 percent, and 97% were in the top half. (Proportion submitting class standing: 42%.) **Average high school grade point average:** 3.5. First-year students who submitted SAT scores: 52%. Scores (25/75 percentile): Verbal: 570-670, Math: 570-650, Combined: 1140-1320. **First-year students submitting ACT scores:** 10%. Scores (25/75 percentile): English: N/A, Math: N/A, Composite: 26-30.

ACADEMICS

Year founded: 1834. **Academic calendar:** Semester. **Degrees offered:** bachelor's. **Most popular majors:** 16% English language and literature, 15% psychology, 10% economics, 8% history, 8% social sciences. **Major fields of study:** area, ethnic, cultural, and gender studies; biological and biomedical sciences; computer and information sciences and support services; English language and literature/letters; foreign languages, literatures, and linguistics; history; mathematics and statistics; multi/interdisciplinary studies; natural resources and conservation; philosophy and religious studies; physical sciences; psychology; social sciences; visual and performing arts. **Areas of required coursework:** arts/fine arts, humanities, mathematics, English (including composition), foreign languages, sciences (biological or physical), history, social science. **Pre-professional programs:** pre-law, pre-dentistry, pre-medicine, pre-veterinary science, pre-optometry. **Special academic programs**

(% participation): accelerated program (0%), cross-registration (2%), double major (14%), dual enrollment (0%), exchange student program (domestic) (2%), honors program (6%), independent study (50%), internships (80%), liberal arts/career combination (0%), student-designed major (2%), study abroad (25%), teacher certificate program (7%). **Teacher certification offered in:** early childhood, elementary, secondary. **Reserve Officers Training Corps (ROTC):** Army ROTC: Offered at cooperating institution (Stonehill College). **Faculty and instruction (2005-2006):** Total instructional faculty: 121 full-time, 40 part-time (50% men; 50% women). Full-time faculty with Ph.D. or other terminal degree: 98%. Student/faculty ratio: 12/1. Classes of fewer than 20 students: 60%; of 20 to 49 students: 36%; of 50 or more students: 4%. **Advanced Placement and International Baccalaureate credit:** AP tests may be used for: Credit and/or placement. Scores accepted: 4, 5. International Baccalaureate exams may be used for: Credit and/or placement. **Freshmen returning for sophomore year:** 87%. **Graduation rates:** Four-year: 70%; five-year: 75%; six-year: 75%. **Graduate study:** 22% of students pursue further study immediately upon graduation; 28% within one year; 55% within five years. Fields in which graduates pursue further study: Master of Business Administration (MBA), 3%; law, 9%; medicine, 4%; dentistry, 2%; engineering, 2%; theology (or the seminary), 3%; education, 21%; arts and sciences, 54%; veterinary medicine, 2%.

COSTS AND FINANCIAL AID

Financial aid office: (508) 286-8232. **Expenses (2006-2007):** Tuition and fees 2006-2007: $34,610; room/board: $8,150. Estimated books and supplies: $940; transportation: $300; personal expenses: $760. **Financial aid:** In 2005-2006, 54% of undergraduates applied for financial aid. Of those, 49% were determined to have financial need; 38% had their need fully met. Average financial aid package (proportion receiving): $23,155 (49%). Average amount of gift aid, such as scholarships or grants (proportion receiving): $18,303 (47%). Average amount of self-help aid, such as work study or loans (proportion receiving): $5,992 (47%). Average need-based loan (excluding PLUS or other private loans): $4,667. Among students who received need-based aid, the average percentage of need met: 94%. Among students who received aid based on merit, the average award (and the proportion receiving): $10,760 (12%). The average athletic scholarship (and the proportion receiving): $0 (0%). Average amount of debt of borrowers graduating in 2005: $22,380. Proportion who borrowed: 61%.

CAMPUS LIFE AND EXTRACURRICULAR ACTIVITIES

Campus housing available: coed dorms, women's dorms, men's dorms, other housing options. Students who live in college-owned, operated, or affiliated housing: 93%. **Student employment:** During the 2005-2006 academic year, 19% of undergraduates worked on campus. Average per-year earnings: $1,087. **Clubs and organizations:** Number of student organizations: 50. Activities include: choral groups, concert band, dance, drama/theater, jazz band, literary magazine, music ensembles, musical theater, pep band, radio station, student government, student newspaper, student film society, symphony orchestra, yearbook. Number of fraternities: 0; sororities: 0. Average proportion of students who stay on campus on weekends: 82%. **Sports program (2005-2006):** Member of NCAA III. *Men's intercollegiate varsity sports:* baseball, basketball, cross-country, lacrosse, soccer, swimming and diving, tennis, track and field (indoor), track and field (outdoor). *Women's intercollegiate varsity sports:* basketball, cross-country, field hockey, lacrosse, soccer, softball, swimming and diving, syncronized swimming, tennis, track and field (indoor), track and field (outdoor), volleyball.

SERVICES AND FACILITIES

Basic services: nonremedial tutoring, women's center, placement service, health service, health insurance, other. **Remedial assistance:** writing, study skills. **Counseling services:** minority student, career, personal, academic, psychological, birth control, religious. **For learning-disabled students:** School does not offer a structured program with separate admission and additional fees. Total undergraduates in learning-disabled program or receiving services: 145. Services include: reading machines, tape recorders, note-taking services, oral tests, learning center, readers, extended time for tests, other. **Library:** Number of titles: 371,675; number of current serial subscriptions: 7,691. **Information technology resources:** Students are not required to lease or own a computer. Number of campus computers available to all students: 285. School has a wireless network. Approximate number of users that can be accommodated: 500. Proportion of college-owned housing units wired for high-speed internet access: 100%. **Campus safety:** Security services offered: 24-hour foot-and-vehicle patrols, late-night transport/escort service, 24-hour emergency telephones, lighted pathways/sidewalks, controlled dormitory access (key, security card, etc).

TRANSFER AND INTERNATIONAL STUDENTS

Transfer students: May apply for admission for the following academic terms: Fall, Spring. Applicants do not need a minimum number of credits to apply. For fall 2005: Transfer applications received: 94. Transfer applicants offered admission: 17. Transfer applicants enrolled: 6. **International students:** Number of foreign undergraduates: 40 (3% of student body). Number of countries represented: 46. Minimum TOEFL score required: 550 (paper); 213 (computer). Average TOEFL score: 600 (paper).

Wheelock College

- ■ **Address:** 200 The Riverway, Boston, MA 02215
- ■ **Website:** http://www.wheelock.edu
- ■ **Private**
- ■ **Enrollment:** 635 full-time; 40 part-time

KEY STATS
- ✔ **U.S News College Ranking:** 68, Universities–Master's (North)
- ✔ **SAT Score (25th/75th percentile):** 880-1090
- ✔ **Tuition:** 2006-2007: $24,890

Selectivity: Less selective	**Room/board:** $9,910
Acceptance rate: 77%	**Average debt:** $17,525
Student/faculty ratio: 10/1	**Proportion who borrowed:** 95%

UNDERGRADUATE STUDENT BODY STATS

2005-2006 enrollment: 635 full-time; 40 part-time. Men: 5%; women: 95%. **Ethnic makeup:** African American: 7%; American-Indian: 1%; Asian American: 2%; Hispanic: 5%; White: 85%.

ADMISSIONS FACTS AND FIGURES

Phone: (617) 879-2206. **Email:** undergrad@wheelock.edu. **Website:** http://www.wheelock.edu. **Application deadlines for fall 2007:** Regular decision: Rolling. Early decision: Send application by: December 1; Decision sent by: January 1. Early action: Not offered. Admission can be deferred. **Application fee:** $35. Common application is accepted. **To apply online, go to:** http://www.wheelock.edu/admissions/. **Admissions requirements/recommendations:** High school units required (recommended): English: 4 (4); Mathematics: 3 (3); Science: 2 (3); Foreign language: 0 (2); Social studies: 2 (2); History: 0 (1); Academic electives: 0; Total units: 16 (20). Tests: The college uses SAT or ACT scores in admissions decisions. Either SAT or ACT required. For admission to the fall 2007 entering class, the school will accept: ACT without writing: Campus visit: Recommended. Admissions interview: Recommended. Off-campus interview: Not available. **Factors that count in admissions decisions:** *Academic:* Secondary school record: Very important. Class rank: Important. Letters of recommendation: Important. Standardized test scores: Important. Essay: Very important. *Nonacademic:* Interview: Considered. Extracurricular activities: Important. Talent/ability: Considered. Character/personal qualities: Important. Alumni/ae relationship: Considered. Geographical residence: Not considered. State residency: Not considered. Religious affiliation/commitment: Not considered. Minority status: Not considered. Volunteer work: Important. Work experience: Considered. **Other schools with the greatest overlap in applicants:** Bridgewater State College; Emmanuel College; Lesley University; Salem State College; University of Massachusetts–Amherst. **Admissions statistics for the fall 2005 entering class:** Total applicants: 703. Total accepted: 538. Freshmen enrolled: 181; 38% were from out of state. Accepted through early-decision or early-action plans: 20%. Overall acceptance rate: 77%. Early-decision acceptance rate: 100%. Non-early acceptance rate: 75%. **Credentials of fall 2005 freshmen:** 11% ranked in the top 10 percent of their high school class; 34% were in the top 25 percent, and 66% were in the top half. (Proportion submitting class standing: 67%.) **Average high school grade point average:** 3.0. **First-year students who submitted SAT scores:** 96%. Scores (25/75 percentile): Verbal: 450-560, Math: 430-530, Combined: 880-1090. **First-year students submitting ACT scores:** 7%. Scores (25/75 percentile): English: N/A, Math: N/A, Composite: 17-25.

ACADEMICS

Year founded: 1888. **Academic calendar:** Semester. **Degrees offered:** certificate, bachelor's, post-bachelor's certificate, master's, post-master's certificate. **Most popular majors:** 28% human development and family studies, 23% elementary education and teaching, 19% social work, 15% adult and continuing education and teaching, 8% visual and performing arts. **Major**

fields of study: area, ethnic, cultural, and gender studies; education; family and consumer sciences/human sciences; liberal arts and sciences studies, and humanities; public administration and social service professions; visual and performing arts. **Areas of required coursework:** arts/fine arts, humanities, mathematics, English (including composition), philosophy, sciences (biological or physical), history, social science, other. **Special academic programs (% participation):** cross-registration (7.8%), double major (58.44%), independent study (55.8%), internships (100%), liberal arts/career combination (57%), study abroad (5.2%), teacher certificate program (33.8%). **Teacher certification offered in:** early childhood, special education, elementary, bilingual/bicultural. **Faculty and instruction (2005-2006):** Total instructional faculty: 58 full-time, 86 part-time (20% men; 80% women; 27% minorities). Full-time faculty with Ph.D. or other terminal degree: 86%. Student/faculty ratio: 10/1. Classes of fewer than 20 students: 56%; of 20 to 49 students: 44%; of 50 or more students: 0%. **Advanced Placement and International Baccalaureate credit:** Scores accepted: 4, 5. International Baccalaureate exams may be used for: Credit and/or placement. **Freshmen returning for sophomore year:** 73%. **Graduation rates:** Four-year: 43%; five-year: 51%; six-year: 55%. **Graduate study:** 60% of students pursue further study immediately upon graduation. Fields in which graduates pursue further study: education, 80%; arts and sciences, 20%.

COSTS AND FINANCIAL AID

Financial aid office: (617) 879-2206. **Expenses (2006-2007):** Tuition and fees 2006-2007: $24,890; room/board: $9,910. Estimated books and supplies: $880 personal expenses: $990. **Financial aid:** Priority filing date for institution's financial aid form: February 15. In 2005-2006, 99% of undergraduates applied for financial aid. Of those, 91% were determined to have financial need; 2% had their need fully met. Average financial aid package (proportion receiving): $15,741 (91%). Average amount of gift aid, such as scholarships or grants (proportion receiving): $8,248 (91%). Average amount of self-help aid, such as work study or loans (proportion receiving): $5,218 (91%). Average need-based loan (excluding PLUS or other private loans): $4,483. Among students who received need-based aid, the average percentage of need met: 57%. Among students who received aid based on merit, the average award (and the proportion receiving): $12,106 (6%). The average athletic scholarship (and the proportion receiving): $0 (0%). Average amount of debt of borrowers graduating in 2005: $17,525. Proportion who borrowed: 95%.

CAMPUS LIFE AND EXTRACURRICULAR ACTIVITIES

Campus housing available (% using): coed dorms (30%), women's dorms (70%), special housing for disabled students. **Student employment:** During the 2005-2006 academic year, 30% of undergraduates worked on campus. Average per-year earnings: $8. **Clubs and organizations:** Number of student organizations: 26. Activities include: choral groups, dance, drama/theater, music ensembles, musical theater, student government, student newspaper, symphony orchestra. Number of fraternities: 0; sororities: 0. Average proportion of students who stay on campus on weekends: 60%. **Sports program (2005-2006):** Member of NCAA III. *Men's intercollegiate varsity sports:* basketball, field hockey, soccer, softball, swimming and diving. *Women's intercollegiate varsity sports:* basketball, field hockey, soccer, softball, swimming and diving.

SERVICES AND FACILITIES

Basic services: nonremedial tutoring. **Remedial assistance:** reading, math, writing, study skills. **Counseling services:** career, personal, academic, older student, psychological. **For learning-disabled students:** School does not offer a structured program with separate admission and additional fees. Services include: reading machines, tape recorders, note-taking services, oral tests, learning center, readers, extended time for tests, tutors, priority registration, priority seating, typist/scribe, exams on tape or computer, other testing accomodations. **Library:** Number of titles: 83,578; number of current serial subscriptions: 563. **Information technology resources:** Students are not required to lease or own a computer. Number of campus computers available to all students: 86. School has a wireless network. Approximate number of users that can be accommodated: 250. Proportion of college-owned housing units wired for high-speed internet access: 100%. **Campus safety:** Security services offered: 24-hour foot-and-vehicle patrols, late-night transport/escort service, 24-hour emergency telephones, lighted pathways/sidewalks, controlled dormitory access (key, security card, etc).

TRANSFER AND INTERNATIONAL STUDENTS

Transfer students: May apply for admission for the following academic terms: Fall, Spring. Applicants do not need a minimum number of credits to apply. For fall 2005: Transfer applications received: 118. Transfer appli-

cants offered admission: 81. Transfer applicants enrolled: 63. **International students:** Number of foreign undergraduates: 2. Number of countries represented: 5. Minimum TOEFL score required: 500 (paper); 173 (computer).

Williams College

- ■ **Address:** 988 Main Street, Williamstown, MA 01267
- ■ **Website:** http://www.williams.edu
- ■ **Private**
- ■ **Enrollment:** 1,984 full-time; 33 part-time

KEY STATS
✔ **U.S News College Ranking:** 1, Liberal Arts Colleges
✔ **SAT Score (25th/75th percentile):** 1340-1530
✔ **Tuition:** 2006-2007: $33,700

Selectivity: Most selective	**Room/board:** $8,950
Acceptance rate: 19%	**Average debt:** $10,900
Student/faculty ratio: 7/1	**Proportion who borrowed:** 39%

UNDERGRADUATE STUDENT BODY STATS
2005-2006 enrollment: 1,984 full-time; 33 part-time. Men: 49%; women: 51%. **Ethnic makeup:** African American: 9%; Asian American: 9%; Hispanic: 9%; White: 66%; International: 6%.

ADMISSIONS FACTS AND FIGURES
Phone: (413) 597-2211. **Email:** admission@williams.edu. **Website:** http://www.williams.edu. **Application deadlines for fall 2007:** Regular decision: January 1; decision sent by April 1. Early decision: Send application by: November 10; Decision sent by December 15. Early action: Not offered. Admission can be deferred. **Application fee:** $60. Common application is accepted. **To apply online, go to:** http://www.williams.edu/Admissions/applying/index.html. **Admissions requirements/recommendations:** High school units required (recommended): English: (4); Mathematics: (4); Science: (3); Foreign language: (4); Social studies: (3). Tests: The college uses SAT or ACT scores in admissions decisions. Either SAT or ACT required. For admission to the fall 2007 entering class, the school will accept: ACT with writing. Campus visit: Recommended. Admissions interview: Neither required nor recommended. Off-campus interview: May be arranged. **Factors that count in admissions decisions:** *Academic:* Secondary school record: Very important. Class rank: Important. Letters of recommendation: Very important. Standardized test scores: Very important. Essay: Very important. *Nonacademic:* Interview: Not considered. Extracurricular activities: Important. Talent/ability: Important. Character/personal qualities: Considered. Alumni/ae relationship: Considered. Geographical residence: Considered. State residency: Not considered. Religious affiliation/commitment: Not considered. Minority status: Considered. Volunteer work: Considered. Work experience: Considered. **Other schools with the greatest overlap in applicants:** Amherst College; Dartmouth College; Harvard University; Middlebury College; Yale University. **Admissions statistics for the fall 2005 entering class:** Total applicants: 5,822. Total accepted: 1,095. Freshmen enrolled: 536; 87% were from out of state. Accepted through early-decision or early-action plans: 39%. Overall acceptance rate: 19%. Early-decision acceptance rate: 39%. Non-early acceptance rate: 17%. **Size of waiting list:** 1123 applicants; enrolled from waiting list: 23. **Credentials of fall 2005 freshmen:** 88% ranked in the top 10 percent of their high school class; 98% were in the top 25 percent, and 99% were in the top half. (Proportion submitting class standing: 38%.) **First-year students who submitted SAT scores:** 99%. Scores (25/75 percentile): Verbal: 670-770, Math: 670-760, Combined: 1340-1530. **First-year students submitting ACT scores:** 19%. Scores (25/75 percentile): English: N/A, Math: N/A, Composite: 29-33.

ACADEMICS
Year founded: 1793. **Academic calendar:** 4-1-4. **Degrees offered:** bachelor's, master's. **Most popular majors:** 17% economics, 14% English language and literature, 13% art/art studies, 13% psychology, 12% history. **Major fields of study:** area, ethnic, cultural, and gender studies; biological and biomedical sciences; computer and information sciences and support services; English language and literature/letters; foreign languages, literatures, and linguistics; history; mathematics and statistics; philosophy and religious studies; physical sciences; psychology; social sciences; visual and performing arts. **Special academic programs (% participation):** accelerated program (1%), cross-registration (1%), double major (29%), honors program (24%), independent study (67%), internships (16%), student-designed major (1%), study abroad (50%). **Faculty and instruction (2005-2006):** Total instructional faculty: 257 full-time, 55 part-time (62% men; 38% women; 16% minorities). Full-time faculty with Ph.D. or other terminal degree: 98%. Student/faculty ratio: 7/1. Classes of fewer than 20 students: 72%; of 20 to 49 students: 24%; of 50 or more students: 4%. **Advanced Placement and International Baccalaureate credit:** AP tests may be used for: Credit and/or placement. International Baccalaureate exams may be used for: Credit and/or placement. **Freshmen returning for sophomore year:** 97%. **Graduation rates:** Four-year: 90%; five-year: 95%; six-year: 95%.

COSTS AND FINANCIAL AID
Financial aid office: (413) 597-4181. **Expenses (2006-2007):** Tuition and fees 2006-2007: $33,700; room/board: $8,950. Estimated books and supplies: $800; transportation: $500; personal expenses: $1,200. **Financial aid:** In 2005-2006, 51% of undergraduates applied for financial aid. Of those, 44% were determined to have financial need; 100% had their need fully met. Average financial aid package (proportion receiving): $30,309 (44%). Average amount of gift aid, such as scholarships or grants (proportion receiving): $27,189 (43%). Average amount of self-help aid, such as work study or loans (proportion receiving): $3,470 (44%). Average need-based loan (excluding PLUS or other private loans): $2,976. Among students who received need-based aid, the average percentage of need met: 100%. Among students who received aid based on merit, the average award (and the proportion receiving): $0 (0%). The average athletic scholarship (and the proportion receiving): $0 (0%). Average amount of debt of borrowers graduating in 2005: $10,900. Proportion who borrowed: 39%.

CAMPUS LIFE AND EXTRACURRICULAR ACTIVITIES
Campus housing available (% using): coed dorms (93%), cooperative housing (7%). Students who live in college-owned, operated, or affiliated housing: 95%. **Student employment:** During the 2005-2006 academic year, 63% of undergraduates worked on campus. Average per-year earnings: $1,700. **Clubs and organizations:** Number of student organizations: 136. Activities include: choral groups, dance, drama/theater, jazz band, literary magazine, music ensembles, musical theater, radio station, student government, student newspaper, student film society, symphony orchestra, yearbook. Number of fraternities: 0; sororities: 0. Average proportion of students who stay on campus on weekends: 100%. **Sports program (2005-2006):** Member of NCAA III. *Men's intercollegiate varsity sports:* baseball, basketball, cross-country, football, golf, ice hockey, lacrosse, skiing, soccer, swimming and diving, tennis, track and field (indoor), track and field (outdoor), wrestling. *Women's intercollegiate varsity sports:* basketball, cross-country, field hockey, golf, ice hockey, lacrosse, rowing, skiing, soccer, softball, squash, swimming and diving, tennis, track and field (indoor), track and field (outdoor), volleyball.

SERVICES AND FACILITIES
Basic services: health service. **Remedial assistance:** math, writing, other. **Counseling services:** career, personal, academic, psychological, religious. **For learning-disabled students:** School does not offer a structured program with separate admission and additional fees. Services include: tape recorders, note-taking services, extended time for tests, other. **Library:** Number of titles: 934,278; number of current serial subscriptions: 13,493. **Information technology resources:** Students are not required to lease or own a computer. Number of campus computers available to all students: 377. School has a wireless network. Approximate number of users that can be accommodated: 1,500. Proportion of college-owned housing units wired for high-speed internet access: 100%. **Campus safety:** Security services offered: 24-hour foot-and-vehicle patrols, late-night transport/escort service, 24-hour emergency telephones, lighted pathways/sidewalks, controlled dormitory access (key, security card, etc.).

TRANSFER AND INTERNATIONAL STUDENTS
Transfer students: May apply for admission for the following academic terms: Fall. Applicants do not need a minimum number of credits to apply. For fall 2005: Transfer applications received: 109. Transfer applicants offered admission: 10. Transfer applicants enrolled: 4. **International students:** Number of foreign undergraduates: 116 (6% of student body). Number of countries represented: 41.

Worcester Polytechnic Institute

- **Address:** 100 Institute Road, Worcester, MA 01609
- **Website:** http://www.wpi.edu
- **Private**
- **Enrollment:** 2,811 full-time; 42 part-time

KEY STATS
- ✔ **U.S News College Ranking:** 64, National Universities
- ✔ **SAT Score (25th/75th percentile):** 1180-1380
- ✔ **Tuition:** 2006-2007: $33,318

Selectivity: More selective	**Room/board:** $9,960
Acceptance rate: 85%	**Average debt:** $34,325
Student/faculty ratio: 13/1	**Proportion who borrowed:** 80%

UNDERGRADUATE STUDENT BODY STATS
2005-2006 enrollment: 2,811 full-time; 42 part-time. Men: 75%; women: 25%. **Ethnic makeup:** African American: 2%; Asian American: 6%; Hispanic: 4%; White: 83%; International: 5%.

ADMISSIONS FACTS AND FIGURES
Phone: (508) 831-5286. **Email:** admissions@wpi.edu. **Website:** http://www.wpi.edu. **Application deadlines for fall 2007:** Regular decision: February 1; decision sent by April 1. Early decision: Not offered. Early action: Send application by: January 1; Decision sent by: February 1. Admission can be deferred. **Application fee:** $60. Common application is accepted. **To apply online, go to:** http://www.admissions.wpi.edu/Admissions/application.html. **Admissions requirements/recommendations:** High school units required (recommended): English: 4; Mathematics: 4; Science: 2; Foreign language: (2); Social studies: (2); History: (1); Total units: 10. Tests: The college uses SAT or ACT scores in admissions decisions. Either SAT or ACT required. For admission to the fall 2007 entering class, the school will accept: ACT with writing, ACT without writing. Campus visit: Recommended. Admissions interview: Neither required nor recommended. Off-campus interview: May be arranged. **Factors that count in admissions decisions:** *Academic:* Secondary school record: Very important. Class rank: Important. Letters of recommendation: Important. Standardized test scores: Important. Essay: Important. *Nonacademic:* Interview: Considered. Extracurricular activities: Important. Talent/ability: Considered. Character/personal qualities: Important. Alumni/ae relationship: Considered. Geographical residence: Considered. State residency: Not considered. Religious affiliation/commitment: Not considered. Minority status: Considered. Volunteer work: Considered. Work experience: Considered. **Other schools with the greatest overlap in applicants:** Boston University; Massachusetts Institute of Technology; Northeastern University; Rensselaer Polytechnic Institute; University of Massachusetts–Amherst. **Admissions statistics for the fall 2005 entering class:** Total applicants: 3,314. Total accepted: 2,822. Freshmen enrolled: 735; 50% were from out of state. Accepted through early-decision or early-action plans: 36%. Overall acceptance rate: 85%. Non-early acceptance rate: 82%. **Size of waiting list:** 110 applicants; enrolled from waiting list: 14. **Credentials of fall 2005 freshmen:** 46% ranked in the top 10 percent of their high school class; 77% were in the top 25 percent, and 96% were in the top half. (Proportion submitting class standing: 65%.) **Average high school grade point average:** 3.6. **First-year students who submitted SAT scores:** 97%. Scores (25/75 percentile): Verbal: 560-670, Math: 620-710, Combined: 1180-1380. **First-year students submitting ACT scores:** 27%. Scores (25/75 percentile): English: N/A, Math: N/A, Composite: 24-29.

ACADEMICS
Year founded: 1865. **Academic calendar:** Quarter. **Degrees offered:** bachelor's, master's, doctorate. **Most popular majors:** 21% electrical, electronics, and communications engineering, 21% mechanical engineering, 16% computer and information sciences, 9% business administration and management, 7% biology/biological sciences. **Major fields of study:** biological and biomedical sciences; business, management, marketing, and related support services; computer and information sciences and support services; engineering; engineering technologies/technicians; English language and literature/letters; liberal arts and sciences studies, and humanities; mathematics and statistics; multi/interdisciplinary studies; physical sciences; social sciences. **Areas of required coursework:** humanities, mathematics, sciences (biological or physical), social science. **Pre-professional programs:** pre-law, pre-dentistry, pre-medicine, pre-veterinary science. **Special academic programs (% participation):** accelerated program (10%), cooperative (work-study plan) program (9%), cross-registration (5%), double major (4%), dual enrollment (2%), English as a Second Language (ESL) (.75%), honors program (100%), independent study (1.5%), liberal arts/career combination (2%), student-designed major, study abroad (47%), teacher certificate program (1.5%), other (71%). **Teacher certification offered in:** middle/junior high, secondary. **Cooperative education programs:** business, computer science, engineering, natural science, social/behavioral science. **Reserve Officers Training Corps (ROTC):** Army ROTC: Offered on campus; Navy ROTC: Offered at cooperating institution (College of the Holy Cross); Air Force ROTC: Offered on campus. **Faculty and instruction (2005-2006):** Total instructional faculty: 234 full-time, 85 part-time (79% men; 21% women; 14% minorities). Full-time faculty with Ph.D. or other terminal degree: 96%. Student/faculty ratio: 13/1. Classes of fewer than 20 students: 71%; of 20 to 49 students: 20%; of 50 or more students: 8%. **Advanced Placement and International Baccalaureate credit:** AP tests may be used for: Credit and/or placement. Scores accepted: 4, 5. International Baccalaureate exams may be used for: Credit and/or placement. **Freshmen returning for sophomore year:** 92%. **Graduation rates:** Four-year: 61%; five-year: 71%; six-year: 73%. **Graduate study:** 22% of students pursue further study immediately upon graduation. Fields in which graduates pursue further study: Master of Business Administration (MBA), 9%; law, 1%; medicine, 10%; engineering, 51%; arts and sciences, 35%; veterinary medicine, 2%.

COSTS AND FINANCIAL AID
Financial aid office: (508) 831-5469. **Expenses (2006-2007):** Tuition and fees 2006-2007: $33,318; room/board: $9,960. Estimated books and supplies: $1,000; transportation: $0; personal expenses: $1,200. **Financial aid:** Priority filing date for institution's financial aid form: February 1. In 2005-2006, 80% of undergraduates applied for financial aid. Of those, 71% were determined to have financial need; 23% had their need fully met. Average financial aid package (proportion receiving): $20,849 (70%). Average amount of gift aid, such as scholarships or grants (proportion receiving): $16,052 (68%). Average amount of self-help aid, such as work study or loans (proportion receiving): $6,516 (57%). Average need-based loan (excluding PLUS or other private loans): $6,245. Among students who received need-based aid, the average percentage of need met: 67%. Among students who received aid based on merit, the average award (and the proportion receiving): $18,228 (15%). The average athletic scholarship (and the proportion receiving): $0 (0%). Average amount of debt of borrowers graduating in 2005: $34,325. Proportion who borrowed: 80%.

CAMPUS LIFE AND EXTRACURRICULAR ACTIVITIES
Campus housing available (% using): coed dorms (62%), sorority housing (3%), fraternity housing (21%), apartment for single students (11%), special housing for disabled students (0%), special housing for international students (1%), other housing options (2%). Students who live in college-owned, operated, or affiliated housing: 58%. **Student employment:** During the 2005-2006 academic year, 23% of undergraduates worked on campus. Average per-year earnings: $4,160. **Clubs and organizations:** Number of student organizations: 153. Activities include: choral groups, concert band, dance, drama/theater, jazz band, literary magazine, marching band, music ensembles, musical theater, pep band, radio station, student government, student newspaper, student film society, symphony orchestra, yearbook. Number of fraternities: 11; sororities: 2. Proportion of men in fraternities: 29%; of women in sororities: 26%. Average proportion of students who stay on campus on weekends: 90%. **Sports program (2005-2006):** Member of NCAA III. *Men's intercollegiate varsity sports:* baseball, basketball, crew, cross-country, football, soccer, swimming and diving, track and field (indoor), track and field (outdoor), wrestling. *Women's intercollegiate varsity sports:* basketball, crew, cross-country, field hockey, soccer, softball, swimming and diving, track and field (indoor), track and field (outdoor), volleyball.

SERVICES AND FACILITIES
Basic services: nonremedial tutoring, women's center, placement service, health service, health insurance, other. **Counseling services:** minority student, career, military, personal, veteran student, academic, older student, psychological, birth control, religious, other. **For learning-disabled students:** School does not offer a structured program with separate admission and additional fees. Services include: reading machines, tape recorders, note-taking services, oral tests, learning center, readers, extended time for tests, tutors. **Library:** Number of titles: 268,718; number of current serial subscriptions: 23,591. **Information technology resources:** Students are not required to lease or own a computer. Number of campus computers available to all students: 707. School has a wireless network. Approximate number of users that can be accommodated: 4,000. Proportion of college-owned housing units wired for high-speed internet access: 100%. **Campus safety:** Security services offered: 24-hour foot-and-vehicle patrols, late-night transport/escort service, 24-hour emergency telephones, lighted pathways/sidewalks, controlled dormitory access (key, security card, etc).

TRANSFER AND INTERNATIONAL STUDENTS

Transfer students: May apply for admission for the following academic terms: Fall, Spring. Applicants do not need a minimum number of credits to apply. For fall 2005: Transfer applications received: 159. Transfer applicants offered admission: 86. Transfer applicants enrolled: 55. **International students:** Number of foreign undergraduates: 147 (5% of student body). Number of countries represented: 70. Minimum TOEFL score required: 550 (paper); 213 (computer). Average TOEFL score: 623 (paper).

Worcester State College

- **Address:** 486 Chandler Street, Worcester, MA 01602-2597
- **Website:** http://www.worcester.edu
- **Public**
- **Enrollment:** 3,242 full-time; 1,356 part-time

KEY STATS

✔ **U.S News College Ranking:** fourth tier, Universities–Master's (North)
✔ **SAT Score (25th/75th percentile):** 910-1103
✔ **Tuition:** 2005-2006: $5,079 in state, $11,159 out of state

Selectivity: Less selective	**Room/board:** $7,420
Acceptance rate: 59%	**Average debt:** N/A
Student/faculty ratio: 17/1	**Proportion who borrowed:** N/A

UNDERGRADUATE STUDENT BODY STATS

2005-2006 enrollment: 3,242 full-time; 1,356 part-time. Men: 40%; women: 60%. **Ethnic makeup:** African American: 4%; Asian American: 3%; Hispanic: 4%; White: 86%; International: 3%.

ADMISSIONS FACTS AND FIGURES

Phone: (508) 929-8758. **Email:** admissions@worcester.edu. **Website:** http://www.worcester.edu. **Application deadlines for fall 2007:** Regular decision: June 1. Early decision: Not offered. Early action: Not offered. Admission can be deferred. **Application fee:** $20. Common application is not accepted. **Admissions requirements/recommendations:** High school units required (recommended): English: 4; Mathematics: 3; Science: 3; Foreign language: 2; Social studies: 1; History: 1; Academic electives: 2; Total units: 18. Tests: The college uses SAT or ACT scores in admissions decisions. Either SAT or ACT required. For admission to the fall 2007 entering class, the school will accept: ACT with writing, ACT without writing. Campus visit: Recommended. Admissions interview: Neither required nor recommended. Off-campus interview: Not available. **Factors that count in admissions decisions:** *Academic:* Secondary school record: Very important. Class rank: Not considered. Letters of recommendation: Considered. Standardized test scores: Very important. Essay: Considered. *Nonacademic:* Interview: Considered. Extracurricular activities: Considered. Talent/ability: Considered. Character/personal qualities: Considered. Alumni/ae relationship: Considered. Geographical residence: Not considered. State residency: Not considered. Religious affiliation/commitment: Not considered. Minority status: Not considered. Volunteer work: Not considered. Work experience: Not considered. **Other schools with the greatest overlap in applicants:** Anna Maria College; Assumption College; Clark University; Fitchburg State College; Westfield State College. **Admissions statistics for the fall 2005 entering class:** Total applicants: 3,113. Total accepted: 1,841. Freshmen enrolled: 648; 4% were from out of state. Overall acceptance rate: 59%. **Credentials of fall 2005 freshmen:** 10% ranked in the top 10 percent of their high school class; 29% were in the top 25 percent. **Average high school grade point average:** 3.0. **First-year students who submitted SAT scores:** 94%. Scores (25/75 percentile): Verbal: 450-550, Math: 460-553, Combined: 910-1103. **First-year students submitting ACT scores:** 7%. Scores (25/75 percentile): English: N/A, Math: N/A, Composite: 17-22.

ACADEMICS

Year founded: 1874. **Academic calendar:** Semester. **Degrees offered:** certificate, bachelor's, post-bachelor's certificate, master's. **Most popular majors:** 23% psychology, 20% business administration and management, 8% education, 6% nursing/registered nurse training (R.N., A.S.N., B.S.N., M.S.N.), 5% radio and television broadcasting technology/technician. **Major fields of study:** biological and biomedical sciences; business, management, marketing, and related support services; communication, journalism, and related programs; computer and information sciences and support services; education; English language and literature/letters; foreign languages, literatures, and linguistics; health professions and related clinical sciences; history; mathematics and statistics; multi/interdisciplinary studies; physical sciences; psychology; security and protective services; social sciences. **Areas of required coursework:** arts/fine arts, humanities, mathematics, English (including composition), sciences (biological or physical), history, social science, other. **Pre-professional programs:** pre-law, pre-dentistry, pre-medicine, pre-veterinary science. **Special academic programs:** cooperative (work-study plan) program, cross-registration, distance learning, double major, dual enrollment, English as a Second Language (ESL), exchange student program (domestic), honors program, independent study, internships, liberal arts/career combination, study abroad, teacher certificate program, other. **Teacher certification offered in:** early childhood, elementary, middle/junior high, secondary. **Cooperative education programs:** other. **Reserve Officers Training Corps (ROTC):** Army ROTC: Offered at cooperating institution (Worcester Polytechnic Institute); Navy ROTC: Offered at cooperating institution (College of Holy Cross); Air Force ROTC: Offered at cooperating institution (College of Holy Cross). **Faculty and instruction (2005-2006):** Total instructional faculty: 167 full-time, 220 part-time (49% men; 51% women; 11% minorities). Full-time faculty with Ph.D. or other terminal degree: 76%. Student/faculty ratio: 17/1. Classes of fewer than 20 students: 51%; of 20 to 49 students: 49%; of 50 or more students: 0%. **Advanced Placement and International Baccalaureate credit:** AP tests may be used for: Credit and/or placement. Scores accepted: 3, 4, 5. International Baccalaureate exams may be used for: Credit only. **Freshmen returning for sophomore year:** 74%. **Graduation rates:** Four-year: 30%; five-year: 41%; six-year: 41%.

COSTS AND FINANCIAL AID

Financial aid office: (508) 929-8056. **Expenses (2005-2006):** Tuition and fees 2005-2006: $5,079 in state, $11,159 out of state; room/board: $7,420. Estimated books and supplies: $984; transportation: $500; personal expenses: $1,316. **Financial aid:** Priority filing date for institution's financial aid form: March 1.

CAMPUS LIFE AND EXTRACURRICULAR ACTIVITIES

Campus housing available: coed dorms, women's dorms, men's dorms, special housing for disabled students. Students who live in college-owned, operated, or affiliated housing: 30%. **Clubs and organizations:** Number of student organizations: 14. Activities include: choral groups, concert band, dance, drama/theater, jazz band, music ensembles, radio station, student government, student newspaper, television station, yearbook. Number of fraternities: 0; sororities: 0. Average proportion of students who stay on campus on weekends: 15%. **Sports program (2005-2006):** Member of NCAA III. *Men's intercollegiate varsity sports:* baseball, basketball, cross-country, football, golf, ice hockey, soccer, track and field (indoor), track and field (outdoor). *Women's intercollegiate varsity sports:* basketball, cross-country, field hockey, lacrosse, soccer, softball, tennis, track and field (indoor), track and field (outdoor), volleyball.

SERVICES AND FACILITIES

Basic services: nonremedial tutoring, women's center, placement service, health service, health insurance. **Remedial assistance:** math, other. **Counseling services:** minority student, career, military, personal, veteran student, academic, birth control, religious. **For learning-disabled students:** School does not offer a structured program with separate admission and additional fees. Total undergraduates in learning-disabled program or receiving services: 82. Services include: remedial math, remedial English, reading machines, remedial reading, tape recorders, untimed tests, note-taking services, oral tests, learning center, readers, extended time for tests, tutors, priority registration, priority seating, other. **Library:** Number of titles: 163,461; number of current serial subscriptions: 533. **Information technology resources:** Students are required to lease or own a computer. School has a wireless network. Proportion of college-owned housing units wired for high-speed internet access: 100%. **Campus safety:** Security services offered: 24-hour foot-and-vehicle patrols, late-night transport/escort service, 24-hour emergency telephones, lighted pathways/sidewalks, controlled dormitory access (key, security card, etc).

TRANSFER AND INTERNATIONAL STUDENTS

Transfer students: May apply for admission for the following academic terms: Fall, Winter, Spring, Summer. Applicants need a minimum number of credits to apply. For fall 2005: Transfer applications received: 1,276. Transfer applicants offered admission: 739. Transfer applicants enrolled: 541. **International students:** Number of foreign undergraduates: 115 (3% of student body). Number of countries represented: 30. Minimum TOEFL score required: 550 (paper); 213 (computer). Average TOEFL score: 538 (paper).

Michigan

Adrian College

- **Address:** 110 S. Madison Street, Adrian, MI 49221
- **Website:** http://www.adrian.edu
- **Private; Religious affiliation:** United Methodist
- **Enrollment:** 935 full-time; 37 part-time

KEY STATS
✔ **U.S News College Ranking:** fourth tier, Liberal Arts Colleges
✔ **ACT Score (25th/75th percentile):** 19-24
✔ **Tuition:** 2006-2007: $19,900

Selectivity: Selective	**Room/board:** $7,280
Acceptance rate: 78%	**Average debt:** $20,849
Student/faculty ratio: 15/1	**Proportion who borrowed:** 79%

UNDERGRADUATE STUDENT BODY STATS
2005-2006 enrollment: 935 full-time; 37 part-time. Men: 48%; women: 52%. **Ethnic makeup:** African American: 5%; Hispanic: 2%; White: 91%; International: 1%. **Religious preference:** Roman Catholic: 20%; Protestant: 28%; Unknown: 41%; United Methodist: 11%.

ADMISSIONS FACTS AND FIGURES
Phone: (800) 877-2246. **Email:** admissions@adrian.edu. **Website:** http://www.adrian.edu. **Application deadlines for fall 2007:** Regular decision: August 1. Early decision: Not offered. Early action: Not offered. Admission can be deferred. Common application is accepted. **Admissions requirements/recommendations:** High school units required (recommended): English: (4); Mathematics: (3); Science: (2); Foreign language: (2); Social studies: (1); History: (1); Academic electives: (2); Total units: (15). Tests: The college uses SAT or ACT scores in admissions decisions. Either SAT or ACT required. For admission to the fall 2007 entering class, the school will accept: ACT with writing, ACT without writing. Campus visit: Recommended. Admissions interview: Recommended. Off-campus interview: May be arranged. **Factors that count in admissions decisions:** *Academic:* Secondary school record: Very important. Class rank: Very important. Letters of recommendation: Not considered. Standardized test scores: Important. Essay: Not considered. *Nonacademic:* Interview: Considered. Extracurricular activities: Not considered. Talent/ability: Important. Character/personal qualities: Considered. Alumni/ae relationship: Considered. Geographical residence: Not considered. State residency: Not considered. Religious affiliation/commitment: Not considered. Minority status: Considered. Volunteer work: Not considered. Work experience: Not considered. **Other schools with the greatest overlap in applicants:** Albion College; Central Michigan University; Grand Valley State University; Michigan State University; Western Michigan University. **Admissions statistics for the fall 2005 entering class:** Total applicants: 1,116. Total accepted: 876. Freshmen enrolled: 267; 14% were from out of state. Overall acceptance rate: 78%. **Credentials of fall 2005 freshmen:** 11% ranked in the top 10 percent of their high school class; 40% were in the top 25 percent, and 77% were in the top half. (Proportion submitting class standing: 77%.) **Average high school grade point average:** 3.2. **First-year students submitting ACT scores:** 98%. Scores (25/75 percentile): English: 17-23, Math: 18-24, Composite: 19-24.

ACADEMICS
Year founded: 1859. **Academic calendar:** Semester. **Degrees offered:** associate, transfer-associate, bachelor's. **Most popular majors:** 22% visual and performing arts, 16% business, management, marketing, and related support services, 16% social sciences, 14% parks, recreation, leisure, and fitness studies, 9% biological and biomedical sciences. **Major fields of study:** area, ethnic, cultural, and gender studies; biological and biomedical sciences; business, management, marketing, and related support services; communication, journalism, and related programs; education; English language and literature/letters; family and consumer sciences/human sciences; foreign languages, literatures, and linguistics; health professions and related clinical sciences; history; mathematics and statistics; natural resources and conservation; parks, recreation, leisure, and fitness studies; philosophy and religious studies; physical sciences; psychology; public administration and social service professions; security and protective services; social sciences; visual and performing arts. **Areas of required coursework:** arts/fine arts, humanities, mathematics, English (including composition), philosophy, foreign languages, sciences (biological or physical), social science, other. **Pre-professional programs:** pre-law, pre-dentistry, pre-medicine, pre-theology, pre-veterinary science, pre-optometry, pre-pharmacy, other. **Special academic programs:** accelerated program, cooperative (work-study plan) program, double major, dual enrollment, English as a Second Language (ESL), honors program, independent study, internships, liberal arts/career combination, student-designed major, study abroad, teacher certificate program. **Teacher certification offered in:** elementary, middle/junior high, secondary, bilingual/bicultural. **Faculty and instruction (2005-2006):** Total instructional faculty: 64 full-time, 53 part-time (51% men; 49% women; 7% minorities). Full-time faculty with Ph.D. or other terminal degree: 67%. Student/faculty ratio: 15/1. Classes of fewer than 20 students: 83%; of 20 to 49 students: 17%; of 50 or more students: 0%. **Advanced Placement and International Baccalaureate credit:** AP tests may be used for: Credit and/or placement. Scores accepted: 4, 5. International Baccalaureate exams may be used for: Credit and/or placement. **Freshmen returning for sophomore year:** 64%. **Graduation rates:** Four-year: 30%; five-year: 47%; six-year: 49%. **Graduate study:** 45% of students pursue further study immediately upon graduation. Fields in which graduates pursue further study: law, 7%; theology (or the seminary), 5%; education, 11%.

COSTS AND FINANCIAL AID
Financial aid office: (517) 264-3107. **Expenses (2006-2007):** Tuition and fees 2006-2007: $19,900; room/board: $7,280. Estimated books and supplies: $570; transportation: $690; personal expenses: $852. **Financial aid:** Priority filing date for institution's financial aid form: March 1; deadline: March 1. In 2005-2006, 99% of undergraduates applied for financial aid. Of those, 78% were determined to have financial need; 69% had their need fully met. Average financial aid package (proportion receiving): $17,074 (78%). Average amount of gift aid, such as scholarships or grants (proportion receiving): $10,282 (78%). Average amount of self-help aid, such as work study or loans (proportion receiving): $5,598 (71%). Average need-based loan (excluding PLUS or other private loans): $4,235. Among students who received need-based aid, the average percentage of need met: 98%. Among students who received aid based on merit, the average award (and the proportion receiving): $8,059 (20%). The average athletic scholarship (and the proportion receiving): $0 (0%). Average amount of debt of borrowers graduating in 2005: $20,849. Proportion who borrowed: 79%.

CAMPUS LIFE AND EXTRACURRICULAR ACTIVITIES
Campus housing available (% using): coed dorms (89%), sorority housing (7%), fraternity housing (4%), special housing for disabled students. Students who live in college-owned, operated, or affiliated housing: 73%. **Student employment:** During the 2005-2006 academic year, 60% of undergraduates worked on campus. Average per-year earnings: $1,800. **Clubs and organizations:** Number of student organizations: 60. Activities include: choral groups, concert band, dance, drama/theater, jazz band, literary magazine, marching band, music ensembles, musical theater, pep band, radio station, student government, student newspaper, symphony orchestra. Number of fraternities: 4; sororities: 3. Proportion of men in fraternities: 18%; of women in sororities: 26%. Average proportion of students who stay on campus on weekends: 50%. **Sports program (2005-2006):** Member of NCAA III. *Men's intercollegiate varsity sports:* baseball, basketball, cross-country, football, golf, soccer, tennis, track and field (indoor), track and field (outdoor). *Women's intercollegiate varsity sports:* basketball, cross-country, golf, soccer, softball, tennis, track and field (indoor), track and field (outdoor), volleyball.

SERVICES AND FACILITIES
Basic services: nonremedial tutoring, health service, health insurance. **Remedial assistance:** reading, math, study skills. **Counseling services:** minority student, career, personal, veteran student, academic, older student,

psychological, birth control, religious. **For learning-disabled students:** School does not offer a structured program with separate admission and additional fees. Total undergraduates in learning-disabled program or receiving services: 36. Services include: remedial math, reading machines, remedial reading, tape recorders, other special classes, diagnostic testing service, untimed tests, note-taking services, oral tests, learning center, readers, extended time for tests, tutors, exams on tape or computer, other testing accomodations. **Library:** Number of titles: 149,778; number of current serial subscriptions: 625. **Information technology resources:** Students are not required to lease or own a computer. Number of campus computers available to all students: 120. School has a wireless network. Proportion of college-owned housing units wired for high-speed internet access: 100%. **Campus safety:** Security services offered: 24-hour foot-and-vehicle patrols, late-night transport/escort service, 24-hour emergency telephones, lighted pathways/sidewalks, controlled dormitory access (key, security card, etc.).

TRANSFER AND INTERNATIONAL STUDENTS
Transfer students: May apply for admission for the following academic terms: Fall, Spring. Applicants do not need a minimum number of credits to apply. For fall 2005: Transfer applications received: 138. Transfer applicants offered admission: 27. Transfer applicants enrolled: 43. **International students:** Number of foreign undergraduates: 10 (1% of student body). Minimum TOEFL score required: 500 (paper); 173 (computer).

Albion College

- **Address:** 611 E. Porter, Albion, MI 49224
- **Website:** http://www.albion.edu
- **Private; Religious affiliation:** Methodist
- **Enrollment:** 1,941 full-time; 38 part-time

KEY STATS
✔ **U.S News College Ranking:** 91, Liberal Arts Colleges
✔ **ACT Score (25th/75th percentile):** 22-27
✔ **Tuition:** 2006-2007: $26,122

Selectivity: More selective	**Room/board:** $7,406
Acceptance rate: 82%	**Average debt:** $23,010
Student/faculty ratio: 13/1	**Proportion who borrowed:** 63%

UNDERGRADUATE STUDENT BODY STATS
2005-2006 enrollment: 1,941 full-time; 38 part-time. Men: 44%; women: 56%. **Ethnic makeup:** African American: 4%; American-Indian: 1%; Asian American: 2%; Hispanic: 1%; White: 92%; International: 1%. **Religious preference:** Roman Catholic: 28%; Protestant: 19%; Jewish: 1%; No preference: 3%; Unknown: 32%; Methodist: 12%; Other: 5%.

ADMISSIONS FACTS AND FIGURES
Phone: (800) 858-6770. **Email:** admissions@albion.edu. **Website:** http://www.albion.edu. **Application deadlines for fall 2007:** Regular decision: March 1. Early decision: Not offered. Early action: Send application by: December 1; Decision sent by: January 1. Admission can be deferred. **Application fee:** $20. Common application is accepted. **To apply online, go to:** http://www.applyweb.com/apply/albion/. **Admissions requirements/recommendations:** High school units required (recommended): English: 4 (4); Mathematics: 3 (3); Science: 3 (3); Foreign language: 0 (3); Social studies: 3 (3); History: 1 (3); Academic electives: 0 (0); Total units: 15 (17). **Tests:** The college uses SAT or ACT scores in admissions decisions. Neither SAT nor ACT required. For admission to the fall 2007 entering class, the school will accept: ACT without writing. Campus visit: Required. Admissions interview: Required. Off-campus interview: May be arranged. **Factors that count in admissions decisions:** *Academic:* Secondary school record: Very important. Class rank: Considered. Letters of recommendation: Very important. Standardized test scores: Important. Essay: Important. *Nonacademic:* Interview: Very important. Extracurricular activities: Important. Talent/ability: Important. Character/personal qualities: Very important. Alumni/ae relationship: Considered. Geographical residence: Considered. State residency: Not considered. Religious affiliation/commitment: Not considered. Minority status: Considered. Volunteer work: Important. Work experience: Considered. **Other schools with the greatest overlap in applicants:** Hope College; Kalamazoo College; Michigan State University; University of Michigan–Ann Arbor; Western Michigan University. **Admissions statistics for the fall 2005 entering class:** Total applicants: 1,946. Total accepted: 1,593.

Freshmen enrolled: 574; 10% were from out of state. Accepted through early-decision or early-action plans: 68%. Overall acceptance rate: 82%. Non-early acceptance rate: 69%. **Credentials of fall 2005 freshmen:** 30% ranked in the top 10 percent of their high school class; 64% were in the top 25 percent, and 90% were in the top half. (Proportion submitting class standing: 70%.) **Average high school grade point average:** 3.6. **First-year students who submitted SAT scores:** 13%. Scores (25/75 percentile): Verbal: 520-645, Math: 540-670, Combined: 1060-1315. **First-year students submitting ACT scores:** 90%. Scores (25/75 percentile): English: 21-28, Math: 21-27, Composite: 22-27.

ACADEMICS
Year founded: 1835. **Academic calendar:** Semester. **Degrees offered:** bachelor's. **Most popular majors:** 20% social sciences, 11% psychology, 9% biological and biomedical sciences, 9% physical sciences, 9% visual and performing arts. **Major fields of study:** area, ethnic, cultural, and gender studies; biological and biomedical sciences; business, management, marketing, and related support services; communication, journalism, and related programs; computer and information sciences and support services; education; English language and literature/letters; foreign languages, literatures, and linguistics; health professions and related clinical sciences; history; liberal arts and sciences studies, and humanities; mathematics and statistics; multi/interdisciplinary studies; parks, recreation, leisure, and fitness studies; philosophy and religious studies; physical sciences; psychology; public administration and social service professions; social sciences; visual and performing arts. **Areas of required coursework:** arts/fine arts, humanities, sciences (biological or physical), social science. **Pre-professional programs:** pre-law, pre-dentistry, pre-medicine, pre-theology, pre-veterinary science, pre-optometry, pre-pharmacy. **Special academic programs (% participation):** double major (20%), dual enrollment (1%), honors program (19%), independent study (46%), internships (40%), liberal arts/career combination, student-designed major (1%), study abroad (25%), teacher certificate program (13%). **Teacher certification offered in:** elementary, secondary. **Reserve Officers Training Corps (ROTC):** Army ROTC: Offered at cooperating institution (Western Michigan University). **Faculty and instruction (2005-2006):** Total instructional faculty: 139 full-time, 36 part-time (59% men; 41% women; 9% minorities). Full-time faculty with Ph.D. or other terminal degree: 91%. Student/faculty ratio: 13/1. Classes of fewer than 20 students: 63%; of 20 to 49 students: 36%; of 50 or more students: 1%. **Advanced Placement and International Baccalaureate credit:** AP tests may be used for: Credit only. Scores accepted: 3, 4, 5. International Baccalaureate exams may be used for: Credit only. **Freshmen returning for sophomore year:** 85%. **Graduation rates:** Four-year: 67%; five-year: 72%; six-year: 72%. **Graduate study:** 38% of students pursue further study within one year. Fields in which graduates pursue further study: Master of Business Administration (MBA), 4%; law, 13%; medicine, 10%; dentistry, 3%; engineering, 1%; theology (or the seminary), 2%; education, 9%; arts and sciences, 55%; veterinary medicine, 2%.

COSTS AND FINANCIAL AID
Financial aid office: (517) 629-0440. **Expenses (2006-2007):** Tuition and fees 2006-2007: $26,122; room/board: $7,406. Estimated books and supplies: $700; transportation: $350; personal expenses: $350. **Financial aid:** Priority filing date for institution's financial aid form: March 1. In 2005-2006, 71% of undergraduates applied for financial aid. Of those, 60% were determined to have financial need; 59% had their need fully met. Average financial aid package (proportion receiving): $20,101 (60%). Average amount of gift aid, such as scholarships or grants (proportion receiving): $15,969 (60%). Average amount of self-help aid, such as work study or loans (proportion receiving): $5,146 (46%). Average need-based loan (excluding PLUS or other private loans): $4,444. Among students who received need-based aid, the average percentage of need met: 94%. Among students who received aid based on merit, the average award (and the proportion receiving): $11,250 (37%). Average amount of debt of borrowers graduating in 2005: $23,010. Proportion who borrowed: 63%.

CAMPUS LIFE AND EXTRACURRICULAR ACTIVITIES
Campus housing available (% using): coed dorms (69%), women's dorms (1%), fraternity housing (14%), apartments for married students (0%), apartment for single students (11%), special housing for disabled students (0%), cooperative housing (1%), other housing options (4%). Students who live in college-owned, operated, or affiliated housing: 88%. **Student employment:** During the 2005-2006 academic year, 43% of undergraduates worked on campus. Average per-year earnings: $827. **Clubs and organizations:** Number of student organizations: 110. Activities include: choral groups, concert band, dance, drama/theater, jazz band, literary magazine, marching band,

music ensembles, musical theater, pep band, radio station, student government, student newspaper, symphony orchestra, television station, yearbook. Number of fraternities: 6; sororities: 6. Proportion of men in fraternities: 32%; of women in sororities: 32%. Average proportion of students who stay on campus on weekends: 75%. **Sports program (2005-2006):** Member of NCAA III. *Men's intercollegiate varsity sports:* baseball, basketball, cross-country, football, golf, soccer, swimming and diving, tennis, track and field (indoor), track and field (outdoor). *Women's intercollegiate varsity sports:* basketball, cross-country, golf, soccer, softball, swimming and diving, tennis, track and field (indoor), track and field (outdoor), volleyball.

SERVICES AND FACILITIES

Basic services: nonremedial tutoring, women's center, placement service, health service. **Remedial assistance:** reading, math, writing, study skills. **Counseling services:** minority student, career, personal, academic, older student, psychological, birth control, religious. **For learning-disabled students:** School does not offer a structured program with separate admission and additional fees. Total undergraduates in learning-disabled program or receiving services: 118. Services include: reading machines, tape recorders, videotaped classes, untimed tests, note-taking services, oral tests, learning center, readers, extended time for tests, tutors, priority seating, texts on tape, exams on tape or computer, other testing accomodations, other. **Library:** Number of titles: 371,933; number of current serial subscriptions: 2,462. **Information technology resources:** Students are not required to lease or own a computer. Number of campus computers available to all students: 453. School has a wireless network. Approximate number of users that can be accommodated: 2,200. Proportion of college-owned housing units wired for high-speed internet access: 100%. **Campus safety:** Security services offered: 24-hour foot-and-vehicle patrols, late-night transport/escort service, 24-hour emergency telephones, lighted pathways/sidewalks, controlled dormitory access (key, security card, etc).

TRANSFER AND INTERNATIONAL STUDENTS

Transfer students: May apply for admission for the following academic terms: Fall, Spring. Applicants need a minimum number of credits to apply. For fall 2005: Transfer applications received: 93. Transfer applicants offered admission: 48. Transfer applicants enrolled: 24. **International students:** Number of foreign undergraduates: 15 (1% of student body). Minimum TOEFL score required: 550 (paper); 270 (computer).

Alma College

- **Address:** 614 W. Superior Street, Alma, MI 48801-1599
- **Website:** http://www.alma.edu
- **Private; Religious affiliation:** Presbyterian
- **Enrollment:** 1,242 full-time; 42 part-time

KEY STATS

✔ **U.S News College Ranking:** third tier, Liberal Arts Colleges
✔ **ACT Score (25th/75th percentile):** 21-27
✔ **Tuition:** 2006-2007: $22,380

Selectivity: More selective	**Room/board:** $7,774
Acceptance rate: 81%	**Average debt:** $18,947
Student/faculty ratio: 13/1	**Proportion who borrowed:** 87%

UNDERGRADUATE STUDENT BODY STATS

2005-2006 enrollment: 1,242 full-time; 42 part-time. Men: 41%; women: 59%. **Ethnic makeup:** African American: 2%; American-Indian: 1%; Asian American: 1%; Hispanic: 2%; White: 94%; International: 1%. **Religious preference:** Roman Catholic: 22%; Protestant: 24%; No preference: 1%; Unknown: 31%; Presbyterian: 9%; Other: 13%.

ADMISSIONS FACTS AND FIGURES

Phone: (800) 321-2562. **Email:** admissions@alma.edu. **Website:** http://www.alma.edu. **Application deadlines for fall 2007:** Regular decision: Rolling. Early decision: Not offered. Early action: Not offered. Admission can be deferred. **Application fee:** $25. Common application is accepted. **To apply online, go to:** http://www.alma.edu/admissions/apply. **Admissions requirements/recommendations:** High school units required (recommended): English: 4; Mathematics: 3; Science: 3; Foreign language: (2); Social studies: 3; Total units: 15. Tests: The college uses SAT or ACT scores in admissions decisions. Either SAT or ACT required. For admission to the

fall 2007 entering class, the school will accept: ACT with writing, ACT without writing, the new SAT, the old SAT. Campus visit: Recommended. Admissions interview: Recommended. Off-campus interview: Not available. **Factors that count in admissions decisions:** *Academic:* Secondary school record: Important. Class rank: Important. Letters of recommendation: Considered. Standardized test scores: Important. Essay: Considered. *Nonacademic:* Interview: Considered. Extracurricular activities: Considered. Talent/ability: Considered. Character/personal qualities: Considered. Alumni/ae relationship: Not considered. Geographical residence: Not considered. State residency: Not considered. Religious affiliation/commitment: Not considered. Minority status: Not considered. Volunteer work: Considered. Work experience: Considered. **Other schools with the greatest overlap in applicants:** Albion College; Central Michigan University; Grand Valley State University; Hope College; Michigan State University. **Admissions statistics for the fall 2005 entering class:** Total applicants: 1,471. Total accepted: 1,189. Freshmen enrolled: 336; 4% were from out of state. Overall acceptance rate: 81%. **Credentials of fall 2005 freshmen:** 32% ranked in the top 10 percent of their high school class; 62% were in the top 25 percent, and 89% were in the top half. (Proportion submitting class standing: 83%.) **Average high school grade point average:** 3.5. **First-year students who submitted SAT scores:** 13%. Scores (25/75 percentile): Verbal: 520-670, Math: 510-650, Combined: 1030-1320. **First-year students submitting ACT scores:** 93%. Scores (25/75 percentile): English: 20-27, Math: 20-27, Composite: 21-27.

ACADEMICS

Year founded: 1886. **Academic calendar:** Other. **Degrees offered:** bachelor's. **Most popular majors:** 16% business administration and management, 13% biology/biological sciences, 10% kinesiology and exercise science, 9% history, 7% education. **Major fields of study:** biological and biomedical sciences; business, management, marketing, and related support services; communication, journalism, and related programs; computer and information sciences and support services; education; English language and literature/letters; foreign languages, literatures, and linguistics; health professions and related clinical sciences; history; legal professions and studies; liberal arts and sciences studies, and humanities; mathematics and statistics; multi/interdisciplinary studies; parks, recreation, leisure, and fitness studies; philosophy and religious studies; physical sciences; psychology; social sciences; theology and religious vocations; visual and performing arts. **Areas of required coursework:** arts/fine arts, humanities, mathematics, English (including composition), philosophy, foreign languages, sciences (biological or physical), history, social science. **Pre-professional programs:** pre-law, pre-dentistry, pre-medicine, pre-theology, other. **Special academic programs (% participation):** double major (13.8%), dual enrollment (9.9%), exchange student program (domestic) (6.9%), honors program, independent study (40.5%), internships (22.4%), student-designed major (.4%), study abroad (12.9%), teacher certificate program (20.7%). **Teacher certification offered in:** early childhood, elementary, secondary. **Reserve Officers Training Corps (ROTC):** Army ROTC: Offered at cooperating institution (Central Michigan University). **Faculty and instruction (2005-2006):** Total instructional faculty: 82 full-time, 37 part-time (62% men; 38% women; 4% minorities). Full-time faculty with Ph.D. or other terminal degree: 88%. Student/faculty ratio: 13/1. Classes of fewer than 20 students: 59%; of 20 to 49 students: 39%; of 50 or more students: 2%. **Advanced Placement and International Baccalaureate credit:** AP tests may be used for: Credit only. Scores accepted: 3, 4, 5. International Baccalaureate exams may be used for: Credit only. **Freshmen returning for sophomore year:** 81%. **Graduation rates:** Four-year: 58%; five-year: 71%; six-year: 72%. **Graduate study:** 16% of students pursue further study immediately upon graduation; 31% within one year; 48% within five years. Fields in which graduates pursue further study: law, 9%; medicine, 9%; dentistry, 2%; engineering, 2%; arts and sciences, 12%.

COSTS AND FINANCIAL AID

Financial aid office: (989) 463-7347. **Expenses (2006-2007):** Tuition and fees 2006-2007: $22,380; room/board: $7,774. Estimated books and supplies: $700; transportation: $750; personal expenses: $700. **Financial aid:** Priority filing date for institution's financial aid form: March 1. In 2005-2006, 100% of undergraduates applied for financial aid. Of those, 76% were determined to have financial need; 27% had their need fully met. Average financial aid package (proportion receiving): $17,812 (75%). Average amount of gift aid, such as scholarships or grants (proportion receiving): $13,480 (75%). Average amount of self-help aid, such as work study or loans (proportion receiving): $5,324 (62%). Average need-based loan (excluding PLUS or other private loans): $5,228. Among students who received need-based aid, the average percentage of need met: 84%. Among students who received aid based on merit, the average award (and the proportion receiving): $12,840 (23%). The average athletic scholarship (and the proportion receiving): $0 (0%). Average amount of debt of borrowers graduating in 2005: $18,947. Proportion who borrowed: 87%.

CAMPUS LIFE AND EXTRACURRICULAR ACTIVITIES

Campus housing available (% using): coed dorms (70%), women's dorms (18%), sorority housing (4%), fraternity housing (4%), apartment for single students (1%), special housing for disabled students (1%), other housing options (2%). Students who live in college-owned, operated, or affiliated housing: 83%. **Student employment:** During the 2005-2006 academic year, 36% of undergraduates worked on campus. Average per-year earnings: $800. **Clubs and organizations:** Number of student organizations: 96. Activities include: choral groups, dance, drama/theater, jazz band, literary magazine, marching band, music ensembles, radio station, student government, student newspaper, symphony orchestra, yearbook. Number of fraternities: 5; sororities: 5. Proportion of men in fraternities: 17%; of women in sororities: 26%. Average proportion of students who stay on campus on weekends: 65%. **Sports program (2005-2006):** Member of NCAA III. *Men's intercollegiate varsity sports:* baseball, basketball, cross-country, football, golf, soccer, swimming and diving, tennis, track and field (outdoor). *Women's intercollegiate varsity sports:* basketball, cross-country, golf, soccer, softball, swimming and diving, tennis, track and field (outdoor), volleyball.

SERVICES AND FACILITIES

Basic services: nonremedial tutoring, health service. **Remedial assistance:** reading, math, writing, study skills. **Counseling services:** minority student, career, personal, academic, older student, birth control, religious. **For learning-disabled students:** School does not offer a structured program with separate admission and additional fees. Total undergraduates in learning-disabled program or receiving services: 100. Services include: reading machines, tape recorders, diagnostic testing service, untimed tests, note-taking services, oral tests, readers, extended time for tests, tutors, early syllabus, priority seating, texts on tape. **Library:** Number of titles: 266,554; number of current serial subscriptions: 1,583. **Information technology resources:** Students are not required to lease or own a computer. Number of campus computers available to all students: 274. School has a wireless network. Approximate number of users that can be accommodated: 2,000. Proportion of college-owned housing units wired for high-speed internet access: 100%. **Campus safety:** Security services offered: late-night transport/escort service, 24-hour emergency telephones, lighted pathways/sidewalks, controlled dormitory access (key, security card, etc).

TRANSFER AND INTERNATIONAL STUDENTS

Transfer students: May apply for admission for the following academic terms: Fall, Winter, Spring. Applicants do not need a minimum number of credits to apply. For fall 2005: Transfer applications received: 140. Transfer applicants offered admission: 56. Transfer applicants enrolled: 36. **International students:** Number of foreign undergraduates: 11 (1% of student body). Number of countries represented: 7. Minimum TOEFL score required: 525 (paper); 195 (computer).

Andrews University

- **Address:** Berrien Springs, MI 49104
- **Website:** http://www.andrews.edu
- **Private; Religious affiliation:** Seventh-day Adventist
- **Enrollment:** 1,489 full-time; 237 part-time

KEY STATS

✔ **U.S News College Ranking:** third tier, National Universities
✔ **ACT Score (25th/75th percentile):** 20-25
✔ **Tuition:** 2006-2007: $17,664

Selectivity: More selective	**Room/board:** $6,460
Acceptance rate: 40%	**Average debt:** $23,195
Student/faculty ratio: 11/1	**Proportion who borrowed:** 66%

UNDERGRADUATE STUDENT BODY STATS

2005-2006 enrollment: 1,489 full-time; 237 part-time. Men: 45%; women: 55%. **Ethnic makeup:** African American: 20%; Asian American: 8%; Hispanic: 11%; White: 48%; International: 12%.

ADMISSIONS FACTS AND FIGURES

Phone: (800) 253-2874. **Email:** enroll@andrews.edu. **Website:** http://www.andrews.edu. **Application deadlines for fall 2007:** Regular decision: Rolling. Early decision: Not offered. Early action: Not offered. Admission can be deferred. **Application fee:** $32. Common application is accepted. **Admissions requirements/recommendations:** High school units required (recommended): English: 3 (4); Mathematics: 2 (3); Science: 2 (2); Social studies: 1 (1); History: 2 (2); Total units: 13 (15). Tests: The college uses SAT or ACT scores in admissions decisions. Either SAT or ACT required. For admission to the fall 2007 entering class, the school will accept: ACT with writing, ACT without writing. Campus visit: Recommended. Admissions interview: Recommended. **Factors that count in admissions decisions:** *Academic:* Secondary school record: Very important. Class rank: Not considered. Letters of recommendation: Very important. Standardized test scores: Considered. Essay: Very important. *Nonacademic:* Interview: Considered. Extracurricular activities: Not considered. Talent/ability: Considered. Character/personal qualities: Very important. Alumni/ae relationship: Important. Geographical residence: Not considered. State residency: Not considered. Religious affiliation/commitment: Important. Minority status: Not considered. Volunteer work: Not considered. Work experience: Not considered. **Admissions statistics for the fall 2005 entering class:** Total applicants: 1,324. Total accepted: 527. Freshmen enrolled: 305; 63% were from out of state. Overall acceptance rate: 40%. **Credentials of fall 2005 freshmen:** 16% ranked in the top 10 percent of their high school class; 40% were in the top 25 percent, and 72% were in the top half. (Proportion submitting class standing: 64%.) **Average high school grade point average:** 3.4. **First-year students who submitted SAT scores:** 48%. Scores (25/75 percentile): Verbal: 470-610, Math: 460-590, Combined: 930-1200. **First-year students submitting ACT scores:** 71%. Scores (25/75 percentile): English: 20-27, Math: 18-25, Composite: 20-25.

ACADEMICS

Year founded: 1874. **Academic calendar:** Semester. **Degrees offered:** associate, bachelor's, master's, first professional, doctorate. **Most popular majors:** 15% health professions and related clinical sciences, 11% business, management, marketing, and related support services, 11% visual and performing arts, 7% biological and biomedical sciences, 7% foreign languages, literatures, and linguistics. **Major fields of study:** agriculture, agriculture operations, and related sciences; architecture and related services; biological and biomedical sciences; business, management, marketing, and related support services; communication, journalism, and related programs; computer and information sciences and support services; construction trades; education; engineering; engineering technologies/technicians; English language and literature/letters; family and consumer sciences/human sciences; foreign languages, literatures, and linguistics; health professions and related clinical sciences; liberal arts and sciences studies, and humanities; mathematics and statistics; mechanic and repair technologies/technicians; multi/interdisciplinary studies; natural resources and conservation; philosophy and religious studies; physical sciences; psychology; public administration and social service professions; social sciences; theology and religious vocations; visual and performing arts. **Areas of required coursework:** arts/fine arts, humanities, computer literacy, mathematics, English (including composition), sciences (biological or physical), history, social science. **Pre-professional programs:** pre-law, pre-dentistry, pre-medicine, pre-theology, pre-veterinary science, pre-optometry, pre-pharmacy. **Special academic programs:** accelerated program, cooperative (work-study plan) program, cross-registration, distance learning, double major, dual enrollment, English as a Second Language (ESL), honors program, internships, student-designed major, study abroad, teacher certificate program. **Teacher certification offered in:** elementary, secondary. **Cooperative education programs:** agriculture, art, business, computer science, education, engineering, health professions, natural science, technologies. **Faculty and instruction (2005-2006):** Total instructional faculty: 207 full-time, 61 part-time (66% men; 34% women; 25% minorities). Full-time faculty with Ph.D. or other terminal degree: 71%. Student/faculty ratio: 11/1. Classes of fewer than 20 students: 64%; of 20 to 49 students: 30%; of 50 or more students: 6%. **Advanced Placement and International Baccalaureate credit:** AP tests may be used for: Credit and/or placement. Scores accepted: 3, 4, 5. International Baccalaureate exams may be used for: Credit and/or placement. **Freshmen returning for sophomore year:** 79%. **Graduation rates:** Four-year: 28%; five-year: 43%; six-year: 50%.

COSTS AND FINANCIAL AID

Financial aid office: (269) 471-3334. **Expenses (2006-2007):** Tuition and fees 2006-2007: $17,664; room/board: $6,460. Estimated books and supplies: $1,000; transportation: $750; personal expenses: $600. **Financial aid:** Priority filing date for institution's financial aid form: March 15. In 2005-

2006, 99% of undergraduates applied for financial aid. Of those, 64% were determined to have financial need; 47% had their need fully met. Average financial aid package (proportion receiving): $21,103 (64%). Average amount of gift aid, such as scholarships or grants (proportion receiving): $7,105 (48%). Average amount of self-help aid, such as work study or loans (proportion receiving): $8,099 (57%). Average need-based loan (excluding PLUS or other private loans): $7,477. Among students who received need-based aid, the average percentage of need met: 98%. Among students who received aid based on merit, the average award (and the proportion receiving): $5,472 (33%). The average athletic scholarship (and the proportion receiving): $0 (0%). Average amount of debt of borrowers graduating in 2005: $23,195. Proportion who borrowed: 66%.

CAMPUS LIFE AND EXTRACURRICULAR ACTIVITIES

Campus housing available (% using): women's dorms (55%), men's dorms (38%), apartments for married students (2%). Students who live in college-owned, operated, or affiliated housing: 54%. **Student employment:** During the 2005-2006 academic year, 70% of undergraduates worked on campus. Average per-year earnings: $2,400. **Clubs and organizations:** Number of student organizations: 45. Activities include: choral groups, concert band, drama/theater, literary magazine, music ensembles, musical theater, radio station, student government, student newspaper, symphony orchestra, yearbook. Number of fraternities: 0; sororities: 0.

SERVICES AND FACILITIES

Basic services: nonremedial tutoring, placement service, day care, health service, health insurance. **Remedial assistance:** reading, math, writing, study skills, other. **Counseling services:** minority student, career, personal, veteran student, academic, older student, psychological, birth control, religious. **For learning-disabled students:** School does not offer a structured program with separate admission and additional fees. Total undergraduates in learning-disabled program or receiving services: 18. Services include: remedial math, remedial English, reading machines, remedial reading, tape recorders, videotaped classes, diagnostic testing service, untimed tests, note-taking services, oral tests, learning center, readers, extended time for tests, tutors, priority seating, proofreading services, texts on tape, typist/scribe, exams on tape or computer, other testing accomodations. **Library:** Number of titles: 755,462; number of current serial subscriptions: 13,693. **Information technology resources:** Students are not required to lease or own a computer. Number of campus computers available to all students: 130. School has a wireless network. Approximate number of users that can be accommodated: 2,000. Proportion of college-owned housing units wired for high-speed internet access: 100%. **Campus safety:** Security services offered: 24-hour foot-and-vehicle patrols, late-night transport/escort service, lighted pathways/sidewalks, student patrols, controlled dormitory access (key, security card, etc).

TRANSFER AND INTERNATIONAL STUDENTS

Transfer students: May apply for admission for the following academic terms: Fall, Winter, Spring, Summer. Applicants need a minimum number of credits to apply. For fall 2005: Transfer applications received: 381. Transfer applicants offered admission: 223. Transfer applicants enrolled: 131. **International students:** Number of foreign undergraduates: 192 (12% of student body). Minimum TOEFL score required: 550 (paper); 213 (computer).

Aquinas College

- **Address:** 1607 Robinson Road SE, Grand Rapids, MI 49506-1799
- **Website:** http://www.aquinas.edu
- **Private; Religious affiliation:** Roman Catholic
- **Enrollment:** 1,469 full-time; 313 part-time

KEY STATS

✔ **U.S News College Ranking:** 47, Universities–Master's (Midwest)
✔ **ACT Score (25th/75th percentile):** 19-25
✔ **Tuition:** 2006-2007: $19,000

Selectivity: Selective	**Room/board:** $6,174
Acceptance rate: 86%	**Average debt:** $14,645
Student/faculty ratio: 14/1	**Proportion who borrowed:** 65%

UNDERGRADUATE STUDENT BODY STATS

2005-2006 enrollment: 1,469 full-time; 313 part-time. Men: 35%; women:, 65%. **Ethnic makeup:** African American: 4%; Asian American: 2%; Hispanic: 4%; White: 89%. **Religious preference:** Protestant: 11%; No preference: 3%; Unknown: 27%; Roman Catholic: 52%; Agnostic, Atheist, Eastern Orthodox, Non-Denominational: 4%; Other: 3%.

ADMISSIONS FACTS AND FIGURES

Phone: (616) 732-4460. **Email:** admissions@aquinas.edu. **Website:** http://www.aquinas.edu. **Application deadlines for fall 2007:** Regular decision: Rolling. Early decision: Not offered. Early action: Not offered. Admission can be deferred. Common application is accepted. **To apply online, go to:** http://www.aquinas.edu/undergraduate/applying/applicat.htm. **Admissions requirements/recommendations:** High school units required (recommended): English: 4; Mathematics: 4; Science: 3; Social studies: 4; Total units: 15. Tests: The college uses SAT or ACT scores in admissions decisions. Either SAT or ACT required. For admission to the fall 2007 entering class, the school will accept: ACT with writing, ACT without writing. Campus visit: Recommended. Admissions interview: Neither required nor recommended. **Factors that count in admissions decisions:** *Academic:* Secondary school record: Very important. Class rank: Not considered. Letters of recommendation: Considered. Standardized test scores: Very important. Essay: Not considered. *Nonacademic:* Interview: Not considered. Extracurricular activities: Considered. Talent/ability: Considered. Character/personal qualities: Considered. Alumni/ae relationship: Not considered. Geographical residence: Not considered. State residency: Not considered. Religious affiliation/commitment: Not considered. Minority status: Not considered. Volunteer work: Considered. Work experience: Considered. **Other schools with the greatest overlap in applicants:** Central Michigan University; Grand Valley State University; Michigan State University; University of Michigan–Ann Arbor; Western Michigan University. **Admissions statistics for the fall 2005 entering class:** Total applicants: 1,646. Total accepted: 1,409. Freshmen enrolled: 363; 6% were from out of state. Overall acceptance rate: 86%. **Size of waiting list:** 0 applicants; enrolled from waiting list: 0. **Credentials of fall 2005 freshmen:** 17% ranked in the top 10 percent of their high school class; 41% were in the top 25 percent, and 77% were in the top half. (Proportion submitting class standing: 73%.) **Average high school grade point average:** 3.4. **First-year students submitting ACT scores:** 100%. Scores (25/75 percentile): English: 19-26, Math: 18-25, Composite: 19-25.

ACADEMICS

Year founded: 1886. **Academic calendar:** Semester. **Degrees offered:** associate, bachelor's, master's. **Most popular majors:** 22% education, 21% business, management, marketing, and related support services, 9% social sciences, 6% communication, journalism, and related programs, 6% psychology. **Major fields of study:** biological and biomedical sciences; business, management, marketing, and related support services; communication, journalism, and related programs; computer and information sciences and support services; education; English language and literature/letters; foreign languages, literatures, and linguistics; health professions and related clinical sciences; history; liberal arts and sciences studies, and humanities; mathematics and statistics; natural resources and conservation; parks, recreation, leisure, and fitness studies; philosophy and religious studies; physical sciences; psychology; public administration and social service professions; social sciences; theology and religious vocations; visual and performing arts. **Areas of required coursework:** arts/fine arts, humanities, computer literacy, mathematics, English (including composition), philosophy, foreign languages, sciences (biological or physical), history, social science. **Pre-professional programs:** pre-law, pre-dentistry, pre-medicine, pre-theology, pre-veterinary science, pre-optometry, pre-pharmacy, other. **Special academic programs (% participation):** distance learning (7.35%), double major (10.5%), dual enrollment (.78%), exchange student program (domestic) (1.8%), honors program (3.67%), independent study (39%), internships (23%), liberal arts/career combination (14%), student-designed major (.26%), study abroad (14.7%), teacher certificate program (41.7%). **Teacher certification offered in:** early childhood, special education, elementary, middle/junior high, secondary, bilingual/bicultural. **Faculty and instruction (2005-2006):** Total instructional faculty: 94 full-time, 105 part-time (51% men; 49% women; 7% minorities). Full-time faculty with Ph.D. or other terminal degree: 66%. Student/faculty ratio: 14/1. Classes of fewer than 20 students: 64%; of 20 to 49 students: 35%; of 50 or more students: 1%. **Advanced Placement and International Baccalaureate credit:** AP tests may be used for: Credit only. Scores accepted: 3, 4, 5. **Freshmen returning for sophomore year:** 76%. **Graduation rates:** Four-year: 27%; five-year: 44%; six-year: 51%. **Graduate study:** 15% of students pursue further study immediately upon graduation. Fields in which graduates pursue further study: Master of Business Administration (MBA), 23%; law, 15%; medicine, 23%; education, 23%; arts and sciences, 23%.

COSTS AND FINANCIAL AID
Financial aid office: (616) 632-2893. **Expenses (2006-2007):** Tuition and fees 2006-2007: $19,000; room/board: $6,174. Estimated books and supplies: $716; transportation: $692; personal expenses: $706. **Financial aid:** Priority filing date for institution's financial aid form: March 1. In 2005-2006, 84% of undergraduates applied for financial aid. Of those, 72% were determined to have financial need; 46% had their need fully met. Average financial aid package (proportion receiving): $14,380 (72%). Average amount of gift aid, such as scholarships or grants (proportion receiving): $11,245 (72%). Average amount of self-help aid, such as work study or loans (proportion receiving): $3,135 (72%). Average need-based loan (excluding PLUS or other private loans): $3,135. Among students who received need-based aid, the average percentage of need met: 87%. Among students who received aid based on merit, the average award (and the proportion receiving): $9,798 (28%). The average athletic scholarship (and the proportion receiving): $3,426 (4%). Average amount of debt of borrowers graduating in 2005: $14,645. Proportion who borrowed: 65%.

CAMPUS LIFE AND EXTRACURRICULAR ACTIVITIES
Campus housing available (% using): coed dorms (75%). Students who live in college-owned, operated, or affiliated housing: 75%. **Student employment:** During the 2005-2006 academic year, 21% of undergraduates worked on campus. Average per-year earnings: $3,016. **Clubs and organizations:** Number of student organizations: 46. Activities include: choral groups, dance, drama/theater, jazz band, literary magazine, music ensembles, radio station, student government, student newspaper. Number of fraternities: 0; sororities: 0. Average proportion of students who stay on campus on weekends: 35%. **Sports program (2005-2006):** Member of NAIA. *Men's intercollegiate varsity sports:* baseball, basketball, cross-country, golf, soccer, tennis, track and field (indoor), track and field (outdoor). *Women's intercollegiate varsity sports:* basketball, cross-country, golf, soccer, softball, tennis, track and field (indoor), track and field (outdoor), volleyball.

SERVICES AND FACILITIES
Basic services: nonremedial tutoring, women's center, placement service, day care, health service, health insurance. **Remedial assistance:** reading, math, writing, study skills. **Counseling services:** minority student, career, personal, veteran student, academic, older student, psychological, religious. **For learning-disabled students:** School does not offer a structured program with separate admission and additional fees. Total undergraduates in learning-disabled program or receiving services: 95. Services include: remedial math, remedial English, remedial reading, tape recorders, other special classes, untimed tests, note-taking services, oral tests, learning center, readers, extended time for tests, tutors, priority registration, texts on tape, exams on tape or computer, other testing accomodations, other. **Library:** Number of titles: 93,785; number of current serial subscriptions: 679. **Information technology resources:** Students are not required to lease or own a computer. Number of campus computers available to all students: 176. School has a wireless network. Approximate number of users that can be accommodated: 2,048. Proportion of college-owned housing units wired for high-speed internet access: 100%. **Campus safety:** Security services offered: 24-hour foot-and-vehicle patrols, late-night transport/escort service, 24-hour emergency telephones, lighted pathways/sidewalks, controlled dormitory access (key, security card, etc).

TRANSFER AND INTERNATIONAL STUDENTS
Transfer students: May apply for admission for the following academic terms: Fall, Spring, Summer. Applicants do not need a minimum number of credits to apply. For fall 2005: Transfer applications received: 365. Transfer applicants offered admission: 176. Transfer applicants enrolled: 75. **International students:** Number of foreign undergraduates: 8. Number of countries represented: 10. Minimum TOEFL score required: 550 (paper); 213 (computer).

Baker College of Flint

- **Address:** 1050 W. Bristol Road, Flint, MI 48507
- **Website:** http://www.baker.edu
- **Private**
- **Enrollment:** 3,457 full-time; 2,608 part-time

KEY STATS
- ✔ **U.S News College Ranking:** fourth tier, Comp. Coll.–Bachelor's (Midwest)
- ✔ **SAT or ACT Score (25th/75th percentile):** N/A
- ✔ **Tuition:** 2006-2007: $8,100

Selectivity: Less selective	**Room/board:** N/A
Acceptance rate: 100%	**Average debt:** N/A
Student/faculty ratio: N/A	**Proportion who borrowed:** N/A

UNDERGRADUATE STUDENT BODY STATS
2005-2006 enrollment: 3,457 full-time; 2,608 part-time. Men: 30%; women: 70%. **Ethnic makeup:** African American: 28%; Asian American: 1%; Hispanic: 2%; White: 69%.

ADMISSIONS FACTS AND FIGURES
Phone: (810) 766-4000. **Email:** troy.crowe@baker.edu. **Website:** http://www.baker.edu. **Application deadlines for fall 2007:** Regular decision: September 20. Early decision: Not offered. Early action: Not offered. Admission can be deferred. **Application fee:** $20. Common application is accepted. **Admissions requirements/recommendations:** Tests: The college does not use SAT or ACT scores in admissions decisions. Neither SAT nor ACT required. Campus visit: Recommended. Admissions interview: Recommended. Off-campus interview: May be arranged. **Factors that count in admissions decisions:** *Academic:* Class rank: Not considered. Letters of recommendation: Not considered. Standardized test scores: Not considered. Essay: Not considered. *Nonacademic:* Interview: Not considered. Extracurricular activities: Not considered. Talent/ability: Not considered. Character/personal qualities: Not considered. Alumni/ae relationship: Not considered. Geographical residence: Not considered. State residency: Not considered. Religious affiliation/commitment: Not considered. Minority status: Not considered. Volunteer work: Not considered. Work experience: Not considered. **Admissions statistics for the fall 2005 entering class:** Total applicants: 2,848. Total accepted: 2,848. 1% were from out of state. Overall acceptance rate: 100%.

ACADEMICS
Year founded: 1911. **Academic calendar:** Quarter. **Degrees offered:** certificate, diploma, associate, bachelor's, master's. **Most popular majors:** Information not available. **Major fields of study:** business, management, marketing, and related support services; engineering; engineering technologies/technicians; family and consumer sciences/human sciences; health professions and related clinical sciences; visual and performing arts. **Special academic programs:** accelerated program, cooperative (work-study plan) program, cross-registration, distance learning, double major, dual enrollment, honors program, independent study, internships, teacher certificate program. **Graduation rates:** Six-year: 25%.

COSTS AND FINANCIAL AID
Financial aid office: (810) 766-4202. **Expenses (2006-2007):** Tuition and fees 2006-2007: $8,100; room/board: N/A.

CAMPUS LIFE AND EXTRACURRICULAR ACTIVITIES
Campus housing available: coed dorms. Number of fraternities: 0; sororities: 0. Average proportion of students who stay on campus on weekends: 50%.

SERVICES AND FACILITIES
Basic services: placement service. **Counseling services:** career, personal, academic. **For learning-disabled students:** School does not offer a structured program with separate admission and additional fees. **Information technology resources:** Students are not required to lease or own a computer. School has a wireless network. Proportion of college-owned housing units wired for high-speed internet access: 100%. **Campus safety:** Security services offered: 24-hour foot-and-vehicle patrols, 24-hour emergency telephones, lighted pathways/sidewalks, controlled dormitory access (key, security card, etc).

TRANSFER AND INTERNATIONAL STUDENTS

Transfer students: May apply for admission for the following academic terms: Fall, Winter, Spring, Summer. Applicants do not need a minimum number of credits to apply. **International students:** Number of foreign undergraduates: 0. Minimum TOEFL score required: 500 (paper); 173 (computer).

Calvin College

- **Address:** 3201 Burton Street SE, Grand Rapids, MI 49546
- **Website:** http://www.calvin.edu
- **Private; Religious affiliation:** Christian Reformed
- **Enrollment:** 3,968 full-time; 157 part-time

KEY STATS

✔ **U.S News College Ranking:** 1, Comp. Coll.–Bachelor's (Midwest)
✔ **ACT Score (25th/75th percentile):** 23-28
✔ **Tuition:** 2006-2007: $20,470

Selectivity: More selective	**Room/board:** $7,040
Acceptance rate: 98%	**Average debt:** $19,400
Student/faculty ratio: 12/1	**Proportion who borrowed:** 67%

UNDERGRADUATE STUDENT BODY STATS

2005-2006 enrollment: 3,968 full-time; 157 part-time. Men: 46%; women: 54%. **Ethnic makeup:** African American: 1%; Asian American: 3%; Hispanic: 1%; White: 87%; International: 7%. **Religious preference:** Roman Catholic: 1%; Protestant: 50%; No preference: 1%; Christian Reformed: 48%.

ADMISSIONS FACTS AND FIGURES

Phone: (616) 526-6106. **Email:** admissions@calvin.edu. **Website:** http://www.calvin.edu. **Application deadlines for fall 2007:** Regular decision: August 15. Early decision: Not offered. Early action: Not offered. Admission can be deferred. **Application fee:** $35. Common application is accepted. **To apply online, go to:** http://www.calvin.edu/admin/admissions/apply.htm. **Admissions requirements/recommendations:** High school units required (recommended): English: 3 (4); Mathematics: 3 (3); Science: 2 (2); Foreign language: 0 (2); Social studies: 2 (3); Academic electives: 3 (3); Total units: 12 (17). Tests: The college uses SAT or ACT scores in admissions decisions. Either SAT or ACT required. For admission to the fall 2007 entering class, the school will accept: ACT with writing, ACT without writing. Campus visit: Recommended. Admissions interview: Recommended. Off-campus interview: May be arranged. **Factors that count in admissions decisions:** *Academic:* Secondary school record: Very important. Class rank: Considered. Letters of recommendation: Important. Standardized test scores: Very important. Essay: Important. *Nonacademic:* Interview: Not considered. Extracurricular activities: Important. Talent/ability: Not considered. Character/personal qualities: Important. Alumni/ae relationship: Not considered. Geographical residence: Not considered. State residency: Not considered. Religious affiliation/commitment: Very important. Minority status: Not considered. Volunteer work: Considered. Work experience: Considered. **Other schools with the greatest overlap in applicants:** Grand Valley State University; Hope College; Michigan State University; University of Michigan–Ann Arbor; Wheaton College. **Admissions statistics for the fall 2005 entering class:** Total applicants: 2,156. Total accepted: 2,104. Freshmen enrolled: 1,007; 43% were from out of state. Overall acceptance rate: 98%. **Credentials of fall 2005 freshmen:** 26% ranked in the top 10 percent of their high school class; 54% were in the top 25 percent, and 80% were in the top half. (Proportion submitting class standing: 83%.) **Average high school grade point average:** 3.6. **First-year students who submitted SAT scores:** 35%. Scores (25/75 percentile): Verbal: 540-663, Math: 550-670, Combined: 1090-1333. **First-year students submitting ACT scores:** 84%. Scores (25/75 percentile): English: 22-29, Math: 23-28, Composite: 23-28.

ACADEMICS

Year founded: 1876. **Academic calendar:** 4-1-4. **Degrees offered:** bachelor's, post-bachelor's certificate, master's. **Most popular majors:** 9% elementary education and teaching, 8% business administration and management, 7% English language and literature, 7% engineering, 7% nursing. **Major fields of study:** area, ethnic, cultural, and gender studies; biological and biomedical sciences; business, management, marketing, and related support services; communication, journalism, and related programs; computer and information sciences and support services; education; engineering; English language

and literature/letters; foreign languages, literatures, and linguistics; health professions and related clinical sciences; history; legal professions and studies; liberal arts and sciences studies, and humanities; mathematics and statistics; multi/interdisciplinary studies; natural resources and conservation; parks, recreation, leisure, and fitness studies; philosophy and religious studies; physical sciences; psychology; public administration and social service professions; social sciences; theology and religious vocations; visual and performing arts. **Areas of required coursework:** arts/fine arts, humanities, computer literacy, mathematics, English (including composition), philosophy, foreign languages, sciences (biological or physical), history, social science, other. **Pre-professional programs:** pre-law, pre-dentistry, pre-medicine, pre-theology, pre-veterinary science, pre-optometry, pre-pharmacy, other. **Special academic programs (% participation):** accelerated program, double major (10%), dual enrollment, English as a Second Language (ESL), honors program (15%), independent study (5%), internships (50%), student-designed major (3%), study abroad (50%), teacher certificate program (20%), other. **Teacher certification offered in:** early childhood, special education, elementary, middle/junior high, secondary, bilingual/bicultural. **Reserve Officers Training Corps (ROTC):** Army ROTC: Offered at cooperating institution (Western Michigan). **Faculty and instruction (2005-2006):** Total instructional faculty: 309 full-time, 89 part-time (62% men; 38% women; 7% minorities). Full-time faculty with Ph.D. or other terminal degree: 82%. Student/faculty ratio: 12/1. Classes of fewer than 20 students: 39%; of 20 to 49 students: 59%; of 50 or more students: 1%. **Advanced Placement and International Baccalaureate credit:** AP tests may be used for: Credit and/or placement. Scores accepted: 3, 4, 5. International Baccalaureate exams may be used for: Credit only. **Freshmen returning for sophomore year:** 87%. **Graduation rates:** Four-year: 54%; five-year: 70%; six-year: 74%. **Graduate study:** 19% of students pursue further study immediately upon graduation; 39% within one year. Fields in which graduates pursue further study: Master of Business Administration (MBA), 2%; law, 7%; medicine, 15%; engineering, 9%; theology (or the seminary), 8%; education, 6%; arts and sciences, 51%; veterinary medicine, 1%.

COSTS AND FINANCIAL AID

Financial aid office: (616) 526-6137. **Expenses (2006-2007):** Tuition and fees 2006-2007: $20,470; room/board: $7,040. Estimated books and supplies: $760; transportation: $760; personal expenses: $980. **Financial aid:** Priority filing date for institution's financial aid form: February 15. In 2005-2006, 75% of undergraduates applied for financial aid. Of those, 62% were determined to have financial need; 33% had their need fully met. Average financial aid package (proportion receiving): $13,000 (61%). Average amount of gift aid, such as scholarships or grants (proportion receiving): $8,300 (61%). Average amount of self-help aid, such as work study or loans (proportion receiving): $7,000 (51%). Average need-based loan (excluding PLUS or other private loans): $6,100. Among students who received need-based aid, the average percentage of need met: 80%. Among students who received aid based on merit, the average award (and the proportion receiving): $3,800 (29%). The average athletic scholarship (and the proportion receiving): $0 (0%). Average amount of debt of borrowers graduating in 2005: $19,400. Proportion who borrowed: 67%.

CAMPUS LIFE AND EXTRACURRICULAR ACTIVITIES

Campus housing available (% using): women's dorms (43%), men's dorms (37%), apartment for single students (20%), other housing options. Students who live in college-owned, operated, or affiliated housing: 58%. **Student employment:** During the 2005-2006 academic year, 40% of undergraduates worked on campus. Average per-year earnings: $1,800. **Clubs and organizations:** Number of student organizations: 59. Activities include: choral groups, concert band, dance, drama/theater, jazz band, literary magazine, music ensembles, musical theater, pep band, radio station, student government, student newspaper, student film society, symphony orchestra, yearbook. Number of fraternities: 0; sororities: 0. Average proportion of students who stay on campus on weekends: 80%. **Sports program (2005-2006):** Member of NCAA III. **Men's intercollegiate varsity sports:** baseball, basketball, cross-country, golf, soccer, swimming and diving, tennis, track and field (indoor), track and field (outdoor). **Women's intercollegiate varsity sports:** basketball, cross-country, golf, soccer, softball, swimming and diving, tennis, track and field (indoor), track and field (outdoor), volleyball.

SERVICES AND FACILITIES

Basic services: nonremedial tutoring, placement service, health service, health insurance. **Remedial assistance:** reading, math, writing, study skills. **Counseling services:** minority student, career, personal, academic, psychological, religious. **For learning-disabled students:** School does not offer a structured program with separate admission and additional fees. Total undergraduates in learning-disabled program or receiving services: 104. Services include: tape recorders, note-taking services, readers, extended time for tests, tutors, priority registration, texts on tape, other testing accomodations, other. **Library:** Number of titles: 824,806; number of current serial subscriptions: 15,000. **Information technology resources:** Students are not required to lease or own a computer. Number of campus computers available to all students: 900. School has a wireless network. Approximate number of users that can be accommodated: 5,000. Proportion of college-owned housing units wired for high-speed internet access: 100%. **Campus safety:** Security services offered: 24-hour foot-and-vehicle patrols, late-night transport/escort service, 24-hour emergency telephones, lighted pathways/sidewalks, controlled dormitory access (key, security card, etc).

TRANSFER AND INTERNATIONAL STUDENTS

Transfer students: May apply for admission for the following academic terms: Fall, Spring, Summer. Applicants do not need a minimum number of credits to apply. For fall 2005: Transfer applications received: 172. Transfer applicants offered admission: 165. Transfer applicants enrolled: 101. **International students:** Number of foreign undergraduates: 288 (7% of student body). Number of countries represented: 62. Minimum TOEFL score required: 550 (paper); 213 (computer).

Central Michigan University

■ **Address:** 105 Warriner Hall, Mount Pleasant, MI 48859
■ **Website:** http://www.cmich.edu
■ **Public**
■ **Enrollment:** 17,620 full-time; 2,377 part-time

KEY STATS
✔ **U.S News College Ranking:** fourth tier, National Universities
✔ **ACT Score (25th/75th percentile):** 19-24
✔ **Tuition:** 2005-2006: $5,868 in state, $13,632 out of state
   Selectivity: Selective   **Room/board:** $6,376
   Acceptance rate: 75%   **Average debt:** $16,537
   Student/faculty ratio: 22/1 **Proportion who borrowed:** 64%

UNDERGRADUATE STUDENT BODY STATS

2005-2006 enrollment: 17,620 full-time; 2,377 part-time. Men: 43%; women: 57%. **Ethnic makeup:** African American: 6%; American-Indian: 1%; Asian American: 1%; Hispanic: 2%; White: 89%; International: 1%.

ADMISSIONS FACTS AND FIGURES

Phone: (989) 774-3076. **Email:** cmuadmit@cmich.edu. **Website:** http://www.cmich.edu. **Application deadlines for fall 2007:** Regular decision: Rolling. Early decision: Not offered. Early action: Not offered. Admission can be deferred. **Application fee:** $35. Common application is accepted. **To apply online, go to:** http://www.cmich.edu/applications/default.htm. **Admissions requirements/recommendations:** High school units required (recommended): English: (4); Mathematics: (4); Science: (3); Foreign language: (2); Social studies: (2); History: (2); Academic electives: (0); Total units: (19). Tests: The college uses SAT or ACT scores in admissions decisions. ACT required. For admission to the fall 2007 entering class, the school will accept: ACT with writing, ACT without writing. Campus visit: Recommended. Admissions interview: Recommended. Off-campus interview: Not available. **Factors that count in admissions decisions:** *Academic:* Secondary school record: Very important. Class rank: Important. Letters of recommendation: Considered. Standardized test scores: Very important. Essay: Considered. *Nonacademic:* Interview: Considered. Extracurricular activities: Considered. Talent/ability: Considered. Character/personal qualities: Considered. Alumni/ae relationship: Considered. Geographical residence: Not considered. State residency: Not considered. Religious affiliation/commitment: Not considered. Minority status: Considered. Volunteer work: Considered. Work experience: Considered. **Other schools with the greatest overlap in applicants:** Grand Valley State University; Michigan State University; Western Michigan University. **Admissions statistics for the fall 2005 entering class:** Total applicants: 13,550. Total accepted: 10,198. Freshmen enrolled: 3,718; 2% were from out of state. Overall acceptance rate: 75%. **Size of waiting list:** 398 applicants; enrolled from waiting list: 287. **Credentials of fall 2005 freshmen:** 15% ranked in the top 10 percent of their high school class; 38% were in the top 25 percent, and 74% were in the top half. (Proportion submitting class standing: 92%.) **Average high**

school grade point average: 3.3. **First-year students who submitted SAT scores:** 4%. Scores (25/75 percentile): Verbal: 450-570, Math: 450-580, Combined: 900-1150. **First-year students submitting ACT scores:** 97%. Scores (25/75 percentile): English: 18-24, Math: 18-24, Composite: 19-24.

ACADEMICS

Year founded: 1892. **Academic calendar:** Semester. **Degrees offered:** bachelor's, post-bachelor's certificate, master's, post-master's certificate, doctorate. **Most popular majors:** 27% business, management, marketing, and related support services, 11% education, 8% social sciences, 6% health professions and related clinical sciences, 5% communication, journalism, and related programs. **Major fields of study:** architecture and related services; area, ethnic, cultural, and gender studies; biological and biomedical sciences; business, management, marketing, and related support services; communication, journalism, and related programs; computer and information sciences and support services; education; engineering; engineering technologies/technicians; English language and literature/letters; family and consumer sciences/human sciences; foreign languages, literatures, and linguistics; health professions and related clinical sciences; history; liberal arts and sciences studies, and humanities; mathematics and statistics; multi/interdisciplinary studies; natural resources and conservation; parks, recreation, leisure, and fitness studies; philosophy and religious studies; physical sciences; psychology; public administration and social service professions; social sciences; visual and performing arts. **Areas of required coursework:** arts/fine arts, humanities, mathematics, English (including composition), sciences (biological or physical), social science. **Pre-professional programs:** pre-law, pre-dentistry, pre-medicine, pre-veterinary science, pre-optometry, pre-pharmacy, other. **Special academic programs (% participation):** accelerated program, distance learning, double major (13%), dual enrollment, English as a Second Language (ESL), external degree program, honors program, independent study, internships (55%), student-designed major, study abroad, teacher certificate program (16%). **Teacher certification offered in:** early childhood, special education, elementary, vo-tech, middle/junior high, secondary, bilingual/bicultural. **Reserve Officers Training Corps (ROTC):** Army ROTC: Offered on campus. **Faculty and instruction (2005-2006):** Total instructional faculty: 704 full-time, 391 part-time (60% men; 40% women; 13% minorities). Full-time faculty with Ph.D. or other terminal degree: 82%. Student/faculty ratio: 22/1. Classes of fewer than 20 students: 31%; of 20 to 49 students: 58%; of 50 or more students: 11%. **Advanced Placement and International Baccalaureate credit:** AP tests may be used for: Credit and/or placement. Scores accepted: 3, 4, 5. International Baccalaureate exams may be used for: Credit and/or placement. **Freshmen returning for sophomore year:** 77%. **Graduation rates:** Four-year: 21%; five-year: 46%; six-year: 55%. **Graduate study:** 17% of students pursue further study immediately upon graduation.

COSTS AND FINANCIAL AID

Financial aid office: (989) 774-3674. **Expenses (2005-2006):** Tuition and fees 2005-2006: $5,868 in state, $13,632 out of state; room/board: $6,376. Estimated books and supplies: $750; transportation: $500; personal expenses: $1,240. **Financial aid:** Priority filing date for institution's financial aid form: March 21. In 2005-2006, 69% of undergraduates applied for financial aid. Of those, 52% were determined to have financial need; 71% had their need fully met. Average financial aid package (proportion receiving): $9,632 (51%). Average amount of gift aid, such as scholarships or grants (proportion receiving): $3,929 (40%). Average amount of self-help aid, such as work study or loans (proportion receiving): $5,603 (46%). Average need-based loan (excluding PLUS or other private loans): $5,129. Among students who received need-based aid, the average percentage of need met: 94%. Among students who received aid based on merit, the average award (and the proportion receiving): $3,096 (10%). The average athletic scholarship (and the proportion receiving): $10,731 (1%). Average amount of debt of borrowers graduating in 2005: $16,537. Proportion who borrowed: 64%.

CAMPUS LIFE AND EXTRACURRICULAR ACTIVITIES

Campus housing available (% using): coed dorms (90%), women's dorms (6%), men's dorms (3%), sorority housing (0%), fraternity housing (0%), apartments for married students (1%), apartment for single students (0%), special housing for disabled students (0%), other housing options. Students who live in college-owned, operated, or affiliated housing: 33%. **Student employment:** During the 2005-2006 academic year, 21% of undergraduates worked on campus. Average per-year earnings: $1,800. **Clubs and organizations:** Number of student organizations: 251. Activities include: choral groups, concert band, dance, drama/theater, jazz band, literary magazine, marching band, music ensembles, musical theater, pep band, radio station, student government, student newspaper, student film society, symphony orchestra, television station, yearbook. Number of fraternities: 14; sororities: 11. Proportion of men in fraternities: 6%; of women in sororities: 7%. Average proportion of students who stay on campus on weekends: 41%. **Sports program (2005-2006):** Member of NCAA I. *Men's intercollegiate varsity sports:* baseball, basketball, cross-country, football, track and field (indoor), track and field (outdoor), wrestling. *Women's intercollegiate varsity sports:* basketball, cross-country, field hockey, gymnastics, soccer, softball, track and field (indoor), track and field (outdoor), volleyball.

SERVICES AND FACILITIES

Basic services: nonremedial tutoring, women's center, placement service, day care, health service, health insurance. **Remedial assistance:** reading, math, writing, study skills. **Counseling services:** minority student, career, military, personal, veteran student, academic, psychological, birth control. **For learning-disabled students:** School does not offer a structured program with separate admission and additional fees. Total undergraduates in learning-disabled program or receiving services: 130. Services include: remedial math, remedial English, reading machines, tape recorders, untimed tests, note-taking services, oral tests, readers, extended time for tests, tutors, priority seating. **Library:** Number of titles: 1,012,774; number of current serial subscriptions: 3,330. **Information technology resources:** Students are not required to lease or own a computer. Number of campus computers available to all students: 3,000. School has a wireless network. Approximate number of users that can be accommodated: 400. Proportion of college-owned housing units wired for high-speed internet access: 100%. **Campus safety:** Security services offered: 24-hour foot-and-vehicle patrols, late-night transport/escort service, 24-hour emergency telephones, lighted pathways/sidewalks, student patrols, controlled dormitory access (key, security card, etc).

TRANSFER AND INTERNATIONAL STUDENTS

Transfer students: May apply for admission for the following academic terms: Fall, Winter, Spring, Summer. Applicants need a minimum number of credits to apply. For fall 2005: Transfer applications received: 2,748. Transfer applicants offered admission: 1,896. Transfer applicants enrolled: 1,107. **International students:** Number of foreign undergraduates: 123 (1% of student body). Number of countries represented: 39. Minimum TOEFL score required: 500 (paper); 173 (computer). Average TOEFL score: 575 (paper).

Cleary University

- **Address:** 3601 Plymouth Road, Ann Arbor, MI 48105
- **Website:** http://www.cleary.edu
- **Private**
- **Enrollment:** 396 full-time; 167 part-time

KEY STATS

✔ **U.S News College Ranking:** Unranked Specialty School–Business
✔ **SAT or ACT Score (25th/75th percentile):** N/A
✔ **Tuition:** 2006-2007: $14,535

Selectivity: Least selective	**Room/board:** N/A
Acceptance rate: 94%	**Average debt:** N/A
Student/faculty ratio: 10/1	**Proportion who borrowed:** 29%

UNDERGRADUATE STUDENT BODY STATS

2005-2006 enrollment: 396 full-time; 167 part-time. Men: 42%; women: 58%. **Ethnic makeup:** African American: 7%; American-Indian: 1%; Asian American: 1%; Hispanic: 1%; White: 89%.

ADMISSIONS FACTS AND FIGURES

Phone: (734) 332-4477. **Email:** admissions@cleary.edu. **Website:** http://www.cleary.edu. **Application deadlines for fall 2007:** Regular decision: August 15. Early decision: Not offered. Early action: Send application by: N/A; Decision sent by: N/A. Admission can be deferred. **Application fee:** $25. Common application is accepted. **To apply online, go to:** http://www.cleary.edu/main/futurestudent/. **Admissions requirements/recommendations:** High school units required (recommended): English: (4); Mathematics: (2); Science: (2); Foreign language: (0); Social studies: (2); History: (2); Academic electives: (12); Total units: (24). Tests: The college uses SAT or ACT scores in admissions decisions. Neither SAT nor ACT

required. For admission to the fall 2007 entering class, the school will accept: ACT with writing, ACT without writing. Campus visit: Recommended. Admissions interview: Recommended. Off-campus interview: May be arranged. **Factors that count in admissions decisions:** *Academic:* Secondary school record: Very important. Class rank: Considered. Letters of recommendation: Considered. Standardized test scores: Very important. Essay: Considered. *Nonacademic:* Interview: Important. Extracurricular activities: Not considered. Talent/ability: Not considered. Character/personal qualities: Not considered. Alumni/ae relationship: Not considered. Geographical residence: Not considered. State residency: Not considered. Religious affiliation/commitment: Not considered. Minority status: Not considered. Volunteer work: Not considered. Work experience: Not considered. **Other schools with the greatest overlap in applicants:** Baker University; Davenport University; Eastern Michigan University; Walsh College of Accountancy and Business Adm.. **Admissions statistics for the fall 2005 entering class:** Total applicants: 49. Total accepted: 46. Freshmen enrolled: 29; Overall acceptance rate: 94%. Non-early acceptance rate: 94%.

ACADEMICS

Year founded: 1883. **Academic calendar:** Quarter. **Degrees offered:** certificate, associate, bachelor's, post-bachelor's certificate, master's. **Most popular majors:** Information not available. **Major fields of study:** business, management, marketing, and related support services; computer and information sciences and support services. **Areas of required coursework:** humanities, computer literacy, mathematics, English (including composition), philosophy, other. **Special academic programs (% participation):** accelerated program (85%), cooperative (work-study plan) program (2%), distance learning (100%), dual enrollment (4%), independent study (1%), internships (1%). **Cooperative education programs:** business. **Faculty and instruction (2005-2006):** Total instructional faculty: 12 full-time, 94 part-time (56% men; 44% women; 18% minorities). Full-time faculty with Ph.D. or other terminal degree: 50%. Student/faculty ratio: 10/1. Classes of fewer than 20 students: 93%; of 20 to 49 students: 7%. **Advanced Placement and International Baccalaureate credit:** AP tests may be used for: Credit only. International Baccalaureate exams may be used for: Credit and/or placement. **Freshmen returning for sophomore year:** 79%. **Graduation rates:** Six-year: 12%.

COSTS AND FINANCIAL AID

Financial aid office: (800) 686-1883. **Expenses (2006-2007):** Tuition and fees 2006-2007: $14,535; room/board: N/A. **Financial aid:** Priority filing date for institution's financial aid form: July 1; deadline: July 1. In 2005-2006, 56% of undergraduates applied for financial aid. Of those, 52% were determined to have financial need; 2% had their need fully met. Average financial aid package (proportion receiving): $10,998 (52%). Average amount of gift aid, such as scholarships or grants (proportion receiving): $1,033 (37%). Average amount of self-help aid, such as work study or loans (proportion receiving): $1,365 (46%). Average need-based loan (excluding PLUS or other private loans): $1,380. Among students who received need-based aid, the average percentage of need met: 30%. Among students who received aid based on merit, the average award (and the proportion receiving): $2,727 (8%). The average athletic scholarship (and the proportion receiving): $0 (0%). Proportion who borrowed: 29%.

CAMPUS LIFE AND EXTRACURRICULAR ACTIVITIES

Student employment: During the 2005-2006 academic year, 2% of undergraduates worked on campus. **Clubs and organizations:** Number of student organizations: 5. Number of fraternities: 0; sororities: 0.

SERVICES AND FACILITIES

Basic services: nonremedial tutoring. **Remedial assistance:** math, writing, study skills. **Counseling services:** career, academic. **For learning-disabled students:** School does not offer a structured program with separate admission and additional fees. **Library:** Number of titles: 375; number of current serial subscriptions: 20. **Information technology resources:** Students are required to lease or own a computer. Number of campus computers available to all students: 68. School has a wireless network. **Campus safety:** Security services offered: lighted pathways/sidewalks, student patrols.

TRANSFER AND INTERNATIONAL STUDENTS

Transfer students: May apply for admission for the following academic terms: Fall, Winter, Spring. Applicants do not need a minimum number of credits to apply. For fall 2005: Transfer applications received: 169. Transfer applicants offered admission: 160. Transfer applicants enrolled: 125. **International students:** Number of foreign undergraduates: 0. Minimum TOEFL score required: 550 (paper); 213 (computer).

College for Creative Studies

- **Address:** 201 E. Kirby, Detroit, MI 48202
- **Website:** http://www.ccscad.edu
- **Private**
- **Enrollment:** 1,067 full-time; 224 part-time

KEY STATS

✔ **U.S News College Ranking:** Unranked Specialty School–Fine Arts

✔ **SAT or ACT Score (25th/75th percentile):** N/A

✔ **Tuition:** 2006-2007: $24,635

Selectivity: Least selective	**Room/board:** N/A
Acceptance rate: 60%	**Average debt:** $30,000
Student/faculty ratio: 9/1	**Proportion who borrowed:** 70%

UNDERGRADUATE STUDENT BODY STATS

2005-2006 enrollment: 1,067 full-time; 224 part-time. Men: 59%; women: 41%. **Ethnic makeup:** African American: 7%; Asian American: 5%; Hispanic: 4%; White: 79%; International: 5%.

ADMISSIONS FACTS AND FIGURES

Phone: (800) 952-2787. **Email:** admissions@ccscad.edu. **Website:** http://www.ccscad.edu. **Application deadlines for fall 2007:** Regular decision: August 1. Early decision: Not offered. Early action: Not offered. Admission can be deferred. Common application is not accepted. **Admissions requirements/recommendations:** High school units required (recommended): English: (4); Mathematics: (3); Science: (2); Foreign language: (2); Social studies: (2); Total units: (13). Tests: The college uses SAT or ACT scores in admissions decisions. Either SAT or ACT required. For admission to the fall 2007 entering class, the school will accept: ACT with writing, ACT without writing. Campus visit: Recommended. Admissions interview: Recommended. Off-campus interview: May be arranged. **Factors that count in admissions decisions:** *Academic:* Secondary school record: Not considered. Class rank: Not considered. Letters of recommendation: Not considered. Standardized test scores: Important. Essay: Not considered. *Nonacademic:* Interview: Not considered. Extracurricular activities: Not considered. Talent/ability: Very important. Character/personal qualities: Not considered. Alumni/ae relationship: Not considered. Geographical residence: Not considered. State residency: Not considered. Religious affiliation/commitment: Not considered. Minority status: Not considered. Volunteer work: Not considered. Work experience: Not considered. **Other schools with the greatest overlap in applicants:** Columbus College of Art and Design; Maryland Institute College of Art; Michigan State University; School of the Art Institute of Chicago; University of Michigan–Ann Arbor. **Admissions statistics for the fall 2005 entering class:** Total applicants: 598. Total accepted: 358. Freshmen enrolled: 207; 17% were from out of state. Overall acceptance rate: 60%. **Average high school grade point average:** 3.1. **First-year students who submitted SAT scores:** 16%. Scores (25/75 percentile): Verbal: N/A, Math: N/A, Combined: N/A. **First-year students submitting ACT scores:** 84%. Scores (25/75 percentile): English: N/A, Math: N/A, Composite: N/A.

ACADEMICS

Year founded: 1906. **Academic calendar:** Semester. **Degrees offered:** bachelor's. **Most popular majors:** Information not available. **Major fields of study:** visual and performing arts. **Areas of required coursework:** arts/fine arts, computer literacy, English (including composition), philosophy, sciences (biological or physical), history, social science. **Special academic programs:** cooperative (work-study plan) program, double major, dual enrollment, English as a Second Language (ESL), exchange student program (domestic), independent study, internships, study abroad, teacher certificate program. **Teacher certification offered in:** elementary, middle/junior high, secondary. **Faculty and instruction (2005-2006):** Total instructional faculty: 47 full-time, 180 part-time (66% men; 34% women). Full-time faculty with Ph.D. or other terminal degree: 57%. Student/faculty ratio: 9/1. **Advanced Placement and International Baccalaureate credit:** International Baccalaureate exams may be used for: Credit and/or placement. **Freshmen returning for sophomore year:** 78%. **Graduation rates:** Four-year: 30%; five-year: 48%; six-year: 55%.

COSTS AND FINANCIAL AID

Financial aid office: (313) 664-7495. **Expenses (2006-2007):** Tuition and fees 2006-2007: $24,635; room/board: N/A. Estimated books and supplies: $2,200; transportation: $1,500; personal expenses: $1,500. **Financial aid:** Priority filing date for institution's financial aid form: July 1. Average amount of debt of borrowers graduating in 2005: $30,000. Proportion who borrowed: 70%.

CAMPUS LIFE AND EXTRACURRICULAR ACTIVITIES

Campus housing available (% using): coed dorms (100%), apartment for single students. Students who live in college-owned, operated, or affiliated housing: 66%. **Student employment:** During the 2005-2006 academic year, 15% of undergraduates worked on campus. Average per-year earnings: $2,000. Activities include: student government.

SERVICES AND FACILITIES

Counseling services: minority student, career, personal, academic. **For learning-disabled students:** Services include: tape recorders, diagnostic testing service, untimed tests, note-taking services, oral tests, learning center, readers, tutors, other. **Library:** Number of titles: 36,131; number of current serial subscriptions: 205. **Information technology resources:** Students are not required to lease or own a computer. Number of campus computers available to all students: 400. School does not have a wireless network. Proportion of college-owned housing units wired for high-speed internet access: 100%. **Campus safety:** Security services offered: 24-hour foot-and-vehicle patrols, late-night transport/escort service, 24-hour emergency telephones, lighted pathways/sidewalks, controlled dormitory access (key, security card, etc).

TRANSFER AND INTERNATIONAL STUDENTS

Transfer students: May apply for admission for the following academic terms: Fall, Winter. Applicants do not need a minimum number of credits to apply. For fall 2005: Transfer applications received: 363. Transfer applicants offered admission: 212. Transfer applicants enrolled: 154. **International students:** Number of foreign undergraduates: 60 (5% of student body). Minimum TOEFL score required: 527 (paper); 213 (computer).

Concordia University

- **Address:** 4090 Geddes Road, Ann Arbor, MI 48105
- **Website:** http://www.cuaa.edu
- **Private; Religious affiliation:** Lutheran Church–Missouri Synod
- **Enrollment:** 506 full-time; 53 part-time

KEY STATS

✔ **U.S News College Ranking:** 44, Comp. Coll.–Bachelor's (Midwest)

✔ **ACT Score (25th/75th percentile):** 19-26

✔ **Tuition:** 2006-2007: $19,010

Selectivity: Selective	**Room/board:** $7,350
Acceptance rate: 82%	**Average debt:** $28,280
Student/faculty ratio: 9/1	**Proportion who borrowed:** 83%

UNDERGRADUATE STUDENT BODY STATS

2005-2006 enrollment: 506 full-time; 53 part-time. Men: 44%; women: 56%. **Ethnic makeup:** African American: 10%; American-Indian: 1%; Asian American: 1%; Hispanic: 2%; White: 84%; International: 1%. **Religious preference:** Roman Catholic: 8%; Protestant: 31%; No preference: 1%; Unknown: 6%; Lutheran Church–Missouri Synod: 51%; Other Lutheran: 2%; Other: 1%.

ADMISSIONS FACTS AND FIGURES

Phone: (800) 253-0680. **Email:** admissions@cuaa.edu. **Website:** http://www.cuaa.edu. **Application deadlines for fall 2007:** Regular decision: Rolling. Early decision: Not offered. Early action: Not offered. Admission can be deferred. **Application fee:** $25. Common application is not accepted. **To apply online, go to:** http://www.cuaa.edu/admissions/?d_id=196. **Admissions requirements/recommendations:** High school units required (recommended): English: (4); Mathematics: (3); Science: (2); Foreign language: (2); Social studies: (2); History: (0); Academic electives: (5); Total units: (20). Tests: The college uses SAT or ACT scores in admissions decisions. Either SAT or ACT required. For admission to the fall 2007 entering class, the school will accept: ACT with writing, ACT without writing. Campus visit: Recommended. Admissions interview: Neither required nor recommended. Off-campus interview: May be arranged. **Factors that count in admissions decisions:** *Academic:* Secondary school record: Very important. Class rank: Important. Letters of recommendation: Considered. Standardized test scores: Very important. Essay: Considered. *Nonacademic:* Interview: Considered. Extracurricular activities: Important. Talent/ability: Important. Character/personal qualities: Important. Alumni/ae relationship: Considered. Geographical residence: Not considered. State residency: Not considered. Religious affiliation/commitment: Important. Minority status: Not considered. Volunteer work: Considered. Work experience: Considered. **Other schools with the greatest overlap in applicants:** Central Michigan University; Eastern Michigan University; Madonna University; Oakland University; Western Michigan University. **Admissions statistics for the fall 2005 entering class:** Total applicants: 550. Total accepted: 451. Freshmen enrolled: 115; 24% were from out of state. Overall acceptance rate: 82%. **Average high school grade point average:** 3.3. **First-year students who submitted SAT scores:** 22%. Scores (25/75 percentile): Verbal: 460-625, Math: 510-640, Combined: 970-1265. **First-year students submitting ACT scores:** 90%. Scores (25/75 percentile): English: 18-27, Math: 18-25, Composite: 19-26.

ACADEMICS

Year founded: 1962. **Academic calendar:** Semester. **Degrees offered:** associate, bachelor's, post-bachelor's certificate, master's. **Most popular majors:** 26% curriculum and instruction, 16% business administration and management, 14% psychology, 13% criminal justice/law enforcement administration, 9% family systems. **Major fields of study:** biological and biomedical sciences; business, management, marketing, and related support services; communication, journalism, and related programs; computer and information sciences and support services; education; English language and literature/letters; family and consumer sciences/human sciences; foreign languages, literatures, and linguistics; health professions and related clinical sciences; history; legal professions and studies; mathematics and statistics; multi/interdisciplinary studies; parks, recreation, leisure, and fitness studies; philosophy and religious studies; physical sciences; psychology; security and protective services; social sciences; theology and religious vocations; visual and performing arts. **Areas of required coursework:** arts/fine arts, humanities, computer literacy, mathematics, English (including composition), foreign languages, sciences (biological or physical), history, social science, other. **Pre-professional programs:** pre-law, pre-dentistry, pre-medicine, pre-theology. **Special academic programs:** accelerated program, cooperative (work-study plan) program, double major, dual enrollment, independent study, internships, liberal arts/career combination, student-designed major, study abroad, teacher certificate program, weekend college. **Teacher certification offered in:** early childhood, elementary, secondary. **Cooperative education programs:** business, computer science. **Reserve Officers Training Corps (ROTC):** Army ROTC: Offered at cooperating institution (University of Michigan); Air Force ROTC: Offered at cooperating institution (University of Michigan). **Faculty and instruction (2005-2006):** Total instructional faculty: 36 full-time, 81 part-time (49% men; 51% women; 7% minorities). Full-time faculty with Ph.D. or other terminal degree: 56%. Student/faculty ratio: 9/1. Classes of fewer than 20 students: 80%; of 20 to 49 students: 18%; of 50 or more students: 1%. **Advanced Placement and International Baccalaureate credit:** AP tests may be used for: Credit and/or placement. Scores accepted: 3, 4, 5. International Baccalaureate exams may be used for: Credit and/or placement. **Freshmen returning for sophomore year:** 70%. **Graduation rates:** Four-year: 30%; five-year: 48%; six-year: 47%.

COSTS AND FINANCIAL AID

Financial aid office: (734) 995-7408. **Expenses (2006-2007):** Tuition and fees 2006-2007: $19,010; room/board: $7,350. Estimated books and supplies: $800; transportation: $250; personal expenses: $1,000. **Financial aid:** Priority filing date for institution's financial aid form: March 1. In 2005-2006, 95% of undergraduates applied for financial aid. Of those, 84% were determined to have financial need; 39% had their need fully met. Average financial aid package (proportion receiving): $14,959 (84%). Average amount of gift aid, such as scholarships or grants (proportion receiving): $10,784 (84%). Average amount of self-help aid, such as work study or loans (proportion receiving): $5,434 (66%). Average need-based loan (excluding PLUS or other private loans): $5,194. Among students who received need-based aid, the average percentage of need met: 87%. Among students who received aid based on merit, the average award (and the proportion receiving): $6,129 (14%). The average athletic scholarship (and the proportion receiving): $6,572 (11%). Average amount of debt of borrowers graduating in 2005: $28,280. Proportion who borrowed: 83%.

CAMPUS LIFE AND EXTRACURRICULAR ACTIVITIES

Campus housing available (% using): women's dorms (55%), men's dorms (44%), apartments for married students (1%). Students who live in college-owned, operated, or affiliated housing: 61%. **Student employment:** During the 2005-2006 academic year, 15% of undergraduates worked on campus. Average per-year earnings: $3,000. **Clubs and organizations:** Number of student organizations: 16. Activities include: choral groups, drama/theater, jazz band, music ensembles, musical theater, pep band, student government, student newspaper, yearbook. Number of fraternities: 0; sororities: 0. Average proportion of students who stay on campus on weekends: 60%. **Sports program (2005-2006):** Member of NAIA. *Men's intercollegiate varsity sports:* baseball, basketball, cross-country, gymnastics, soccer. *Women's intercollegiate varsity sports:* basketball, cross-country, golf, soccer, softball, volleyball.

SERVICES AND FACILITIES

Basic services: nonremedial tutoring, placement service, health service. **Remedial assistance:** writing, study skills. **Counseling services:** career, personal, academic, psychological, religious. **For learning-disabled students:** School does not offer a structured program with separate admission and additional fees. Total undergraduates in learning-disabled program or receiving services: 10. Services include: untimed tests, oral tests, learning center, extended time for tests, tutors, other testing accomodations, waiver of foreign language degree requirement. **Library:** Number of titles: 110,680; number of current serial subscriptions: 1,300. **Information technology resources:** Students are not required to lease or own a computer. Number of campus computers available to all students: 60. School has a wireless network. Approximate number of users that can be accommodated: 50. Proportion of college-owned housing units wired for high-speed internet access: 100%. **Campus safety:** Security services offered: 24-hour foot-and-vehicle patrols, late-night transport/escort service, lighted pathways/sidewalks, student patrols, controlled dormitory access (key, security card, etc).

TRANSFER AND INTERNATIONAL STUDENTS

Transfer students: May apply for admission for the following academic terms: Fall, Spring. Applicants need a minimum number of credits to apply. For fall 2005: Transfer applicants enrolled: 68. **International students:** Number of foreign undergraduates: 7 (1% of student body). Minimum TOEFL score required: 520 (paper); 190 (computer). Average TOEFL score: 530 (paper).

Cornerstone University

■ **Address:** 1001 E. Beltline NE, Grand Rapids, MI 49525
■ **Website:** http://www.cornerstone.edu
■ **Private; Religious affiliation:** Evangelical
■ **Enrollment:** 1,756 full-time; 418 part-time

KEY STATS

✔ **U.S News College Ranking:** fourth tier, Universities–Master's (Midwest)
✔ **ACT Score (25th/75th percentile):** 20-26
✔ **Tuition:** 2006-2007: $17,080

Selectivity: Selective	**Room/board:** $5,860
Acceptance rate: 76%	**Average debt:** $23,710
Student/faculty ratio: 14/1	**Proportion who borrowed:** 79%

UNDERGRADUATE STUDENT BODY STATS

2005-2006 enrollment: 1,756 full-time; 418 part-time. Men: 39%; women: 61%. **Ethnic makeup:** African American: 18%; Asian American: 1%; Hispanic: 3%; White: 77%; International: 1%. **Religious preference:** Roman Catholic: 2%; Protestant: 25%; No preference: 5%; Unknown: 3%; Evangelical: 65%.

ADMISSIONS FACTS AND FIGURES

Phone: (616) 222-1426. **Email:** admissions@cornerstone.edu. **Website:** http://www.cornerstone.edu. **Application deadlines for fall 2007:** Regular decision: September 15. Early decision: Not offered. Early action: Not offered. Admission can be deferred. **Application fee:** $25. Common application is not accepted. **Admissions requirements/recommendations:** High school units required (recommended): English: 4 (4); Mathematics: 3 (3); Science: 2 (2); Foreign language: 3 (3); Social studies: 3 (3); History: 2 (2); Academic electives: 4 (4); Total units: 22 (22). Tests: The college uses SAT or ACT scores in admissions decisions. Either SAT or ACT required. For admission to the fall 2007 entering class, the school will accept: ACT with writing, ACT without writing. Campus visit: Recommended. Admissions interview: Neither required nor recommended. Off-campus interview: May be arranged. **Factors that count in admissions decisions:** *Academic:* Secondary school record: Very important. Class rank: Important. Letters of recommendation: Very important. Standardized test scores: Very important. Essay: Very important. *Nonacademic:* Interview: Not considered. Extracurricular activities: Considered. Talent/ability: Important. Character/personal qualities: Very important. Alumni/ae relationship: Not considered. Geographical residence: Not considered. State residency: Not considered. Religious affiliation/commitment: Very important. Minority status: Not considered. Volunteer work: Not considered. Work experience: Not considered. **Other schools with the greatest overlap in applicants:** Calvin College; Cedarville University; Grand Valley State University; Spring Arbor University; Taylor University. **Admissions statistics for the fall 2005 entering class:** Total applicants: 1,122. Total accepted: 854. Freshmen enrolled: 417; 21% were from out of state. Overall acceptance rate: 76%. **Credentials of fall 2005 freshmen:** 15% ranked in the top 10 percent of their high school class; 39% were in the top 25 percent, and 73% were in the top half. (Proportion submitting class standing: 95%.) **Average high school grade point average:** 3.4. **First-year students who submitted SAT scores:** 8%. Scores (25/75 percentile): Verbal: 460-590, Math: 490-590, Combined: 950-1180. **First-year students submitting ACT scores:** 94%. Scores (25/75 percentile): English: N/A, Math: N/A, Composite: 20-26.

ACADEMICS

Year founded: 1941. **Academic calendar:** Semester. **Degrees offered:** diploma, associate, bachelor's, master's, first professional, first professional certificate. **Most popular majors:** 31% business, management, marketing, and related support services, 28% education, 6% biological and biomedical sciences, 6% philosophy and religious studies, 6% psychology. **Major fields of study:** biological and biomedical sciences; business, management, marketing, and related support services; communication, journalism, and related programs; computer and information sciences and support services; education; English language and literature/letters; family and consumer sciences/human sciences; foreign languages, literatures, and linguistics; health professions and related clinical sciences; history; legal professions and studies; multi/interdisciplinary studies; parks, recreation, leisure, and fitness studies; philosophy and religious studies; psychology; public administration and social service professions; social sciences; theology and religious vocations; visual and performing arts. **Areas of required coursework:** arts/fine arts, humanities, mathematics, English (including composition), philosophy, foreign languages, sciences (biological or physical), history, social science, other. **Pre-professional programs:** pre-law, pre-dentistry, pre-medicine, pre-theology, pre-veterinary science. **Special academic programs (% participation):** accelerated program (1%), distance learning (2%), double major (1%), dual enrollment (1%), English as a Second Language (ESL) (3%), honors program (1%), independent study (1%), internships (65%), liberal arts/career combination (65%), study abroad (2%), teacher certificate program (35%), weekend college (5%). **Teacher certification offered in:** early childhood, special education, elementary, middle/junior high, secondary. **Faculty and instruction (2005-2006):** Total instructional faculty: 76 full-time, 64 part-time (71% men; 29% women; 4% minorities). Full-time faculty with Ph.D. or other terminal degree: 49%. Student/faculty ratio: 14/1. Classes of fewer than 20 students: 54%; of 20 to 49 students: 44%; of 50 or more students: 2%. **Advanced Placement and International Baccalaureate credit:** AP tests may be used for: Credit and/or placement. Scores accepted: 3, 4, 5. International Baccalaureate exams may be used for: Credit and/or placement. **Freshmen returning for sophomore year:** 72%. **Graduation rates:** Four-year: 22%; five-year: 37%; six-year: 40%. **Graduate study:** 20% of students pursue further study immediately upon graduation; 25% within one year; 30% within five years. Fields in which graduates pursue further study: Master of Business Administration (MBA), 10%; law, 5%; medicine, 5%; theology (or the seminary), 40%; education, 20%; arts and sciences, 20%.

COSTS AND FINANCIAL AID

Financial aid office: (616) 222-1424. **Expenses (2006-2007):** Tuition and fees 2006-2007: $17,080; room/board: $5,860. Estimated books and supplies: $1,000; transportation: $1,202; personal expenses: $1,154. **Financial aid:** Priority filing date for institution's financial aid form: March 1; deadline: March 1. In 2005-2006, 97% of undergraduates applied for financial aid. Of those, 77% were determined to have financial need; 20% had their need fully met. Average financial aid package (proportion receiving): $13,320 (76%). Average amount of gift aid, such as scholarships or grants (proportion receiving): $6,656 (76%). Average amount of self-help aid, such as work study or loans (proportion receiving): $4,842 (69%). Average need-based loan (excluding PLUS or other private loans): $4,077. Among students who received need-based aid, the average percentage of need met:

85%. Among students who received aid based on merit, the average award (and the proportion receiving): $3,472 (16%). The average athletic scholarship (and the proportion receiving): $5,785 (11%). Average amount of debt of borrowers graduating in 2005: $23,710. Proportion who borrowed: 79%.

CAMPUS LIFE AND EXTRACURRICULAR ACTIVITIES

Campus housing available: women's dorms, men's dorms, apartments for married students, apartment for single students. Students who live in college-owned, operated, or affiliated housing: 57%. **Student employment:** During the 2005-2006 academic year, 25% of undergraduates worked on campus. Average per-year earnings: $3,000. Activities include: choral groups, concert band, dance, drama/theater, jazz band, literary magazine, music ensembles, musical theater, pep band, radio station, student government, student newspaper, student film society, symphony orchestra, yearbook. Number of fraternities: 0; sororities: 0. Average proportion of students who stay on campus on weekends: 30%. **Sports program (2005-2006):** Member of NAIA. *Men's intercollegiate varsity sports:* basketball, cross-country, golf, soccer, track and field (indoor), track and field (outdoor). *Women's intercollegiate varsity sports:* basketball, cross-country, soccer, softball, track and field (indoor), track and field (outdoor), volleyball.

SERVICES AND FACILITIES

Basic services: nonremedial tutoring, placement service, health service, health insurance. **Remedial assistance:** reading, math, writing, study skills. **Counseling services:** minority student, career, military, personal, academic, psychological, religious. **For learning-disabled students:** School does not offer a structured program with separate admission and additional fees. Total undergraduates in learning-disabled program or receiving services: 140. Services include: remedial math, remedial English, remedial reading, tape recorders, other special classes, videotaped classes, diagnostic testing service, untimed tests, note-taking services, oral tests, learning center, readers, extended time for tests, tutors, early syllabus, priority seating, proofreading services, texts on tape, typist/scribe, other testing accomodations. **Library:** Number of titles: 140,000; number of current serial subscriptions: 19,100. **Information technology resources:** Students are required to lease or own a computer. Number of campus computers available to all students: 1,200. School has a wireless network. Approximate number of users that can be accommodated: 1,200. Proportion of college-owned housing units wired for high-speed internet access: 100%. **Campus safety:** Security services offered: 24-hour foot-and-vehicle patrols, late-night transport/escort service, 24-hour emergency telephones, lighted pathways/sidewalks, student patrols, controlled dormitory access (key, security card, etc).

TRANSFER AND INTERNATIONAL STUDENTS

Transfer students: May apply for admission for the following academic terms: Fall, Spring, Summer. Applicants do not need a minimum number of credits to apply. For fall 2005: Transfer applications received: 317. Transfer applicants offered admission: 177. Transfer applicants enrolled: 107. **International students:** Number of foreign undergraduates: 11 (1% of student body). Number of countries represented: 14. Minimum TOEFL score required: 575 (paper); 235 (computer). Average TOEFL score: 580 (paper).

Davenport University

- **Address:** 415 E. Fulton Street, Grand Rapids, MI 49503
- **Website:** http://www.davenport.edu
- **Private**
- **Enrollment:** 3,104 full-time; 8,962 part-time

KEY STATS

✔ **U.S News College Ranking:** Unranked Specialty School–Business
✔ **SAT or ACT Score (25th/75th percentile):** N/A
✔ **Tuition:** 2006-2007: $8,880

Selectivity: Least selective	**Room/board:** N/A
Acceptance rate: 100%	**Average debt:** $8,439
Student/faculty ratio: N/A	**Proportion who borrowed:** 75%

UNDERGRADUATE STUDENT BODY STATS

2005-2006 enrollment: 3,104 full-time; 8,962 part-time. Men: 24%; women: 76%. **Ethnic makeup:** African American: 24%; Asian American: 1%; Hispanic: 4%; White: 71%.

ADMISSIONS FACTS AND FIGURES

Phone: (800) 455-2669. **Email:** Davenport.Admissions@davenport.edu. **Website:** http://www.davenport.edu. **Application deadlines for fall 2007:** Regular decision: Rolling. Early decision: Not offered. Early action: Not offered. Admission can be deferred. **Application fee:** $25. Common application is not accepted. **Admissions requirements/recommendations:** High school units required (recommended): English: 6; Mathematics: 6 (9); Social studies: 9. Tests: The college does not use SAT or ACT scores in admissions decisions. Neither SAT nor ACT required. Campus visit: Neither required nor recommended. Admissions interview: Neither required nor recommended. Off-campus interview: May be arranged. **Admissions statistics for the fall 2005 entering class:** Total applicants: 1,231. Total accepted: 1,231. Freshmen enrolled: 1,231; 1% were from out of state. Overall acceptance rate: 100%. **Average high school grade point average:** 2.5.

ACADEMICS

Year founded: 1866. **Academic calendar:** Semester. **Degrees offered:** diploma, associate, bachelor's, post-bachelor's certificate, master's. **Most popular majors:** Information not available. **Major fields of study:** agriculture, agriculture operations, and related sciences; business, management, marketing, and related support services; computer and information sciences and support services; health professions and related clinical sciences; legal professions and studies. **Areas of required coursework:** humanities, computer literacy, mathematics, English (including composition), sciences (biological or physical), social science. **Special academic programs:** accelerated program, distance learning, dual enrollment, English as a Second Language (ESL), independent study, internships, student-designed major, study abroad. **Cooperative education programs:** business. **Advanced Placement and International Baccalaureate credit:** International Baccalaureate exams may be used for: Credit only. **Freshmen returning for sophomore year:** 51%. **Graduation rates:** Six-year: 20%.

COSTS AND FINANCIAL AID

Financial aid office: (616) 451-3511. **Expenses (2006-2007):** Tuition and fees 2006-2007: $8,880; room/board: N/A. Estimated books and supplies: $1,000; transportation: $200; personal expenses: $2,526. **Financial aid:** Priority filing date for institution's financial aid form: March 15. Average amount of debt of borrowers graduating in 2005: $8,439. Proportion who borrowed: 75%.

CAMPUS LIFE AND EXTRACURRICULAR ACTIVITIES

Campus housing available: coed dorms. Students who live in college-owned, operated, or affiliated housing: 1%. Number of fraternities: 0; sororities: 0. Average proportion of students who stay on campus on weekends: 1%. **Sports program (2005-2006):** Member of NAIA. *Men's intercollegiate varsity sports:* basketball, golf, soccer. *Women's intercollegiate varsity sports:* basketball, soccer.

SERVICES AND FACILITIES

Basic services: nonremedial tutoring. **Remedial assistance:** reading, math, writing, study skills. **Counseling services:** career, personal, academic, older student. **For learning-disabled students:** Services include: remedial math, remedial English, reading machines, remedial reading, tape recorders, note-taking services, learning center, tutors, other. **Information technology resources:** Students are not required to lease or own a computer. **Campus safety:** Security services offered: late-night transport/escort service, lighted pathways/sidewalks, controlled dormitory access (key, security card, etc).

TRANSFER AND INTERNATIONAL STUDENTS

Transfer students: May apply for admission for the following academic terms: Fall, Winter, Spring, Summer. Applicants do not need a minimum number of credits to apply. For fall 2005: Transfer applications received: 2,599. Transfer applicants offered admission: 1,540. Transfer applicants enrolled: 1,537. **International students:** Number of foreign undergraduates: 17.

Eastern Michigan University

- **Address:** Ypsilanti, MI 48197
- **Website:** http://www.emich.edu/
- **Public**
- **Enrollment:** 12,998 full-time; 5,580 part-time

KEY STATS

✔ **U.S News College Ranking:** third tier, Universities–Master's (Midwest)
✔ **ACT Score (25th/75th percentile):** 18-24
✔ **Tuition:** 2005-2006: $6,541 in state, $17,896 out of state

Selectivity: Selective	**Room/board:** $6,356
Acceptance rate: 79%	**Average debt:** $21,397
Student/faculty ratio: 19/1	**Proportion who borrowed:** 58%

UNDERGRADUATE STUDENT BODY STATS

2005-2006 enrollment: 12,998 full-time; 5,580 part-time. Men: 40%; women: 60%. **Ethnic makeup:** African American: 18%; American-Indian: 1%; Asian American: 2%; Hispanic: 2%; White: 76%; International: 1%.

ADMISSIONS FACTS AND FIGURES

Phone: (734) 487-3060. **Email:** undergraduate.admissions@emich.edu. **Website:** http://www.emich.edu/. **Application deadlines for fall 2007:** Regular decision: Rolling. Early decision: Not offered. Early action: Not offered. Admission can be deferred. **Application fee:** $30. Common application is not accepted. **Admissions requirements/recommendations:** High school units required (recommended): English: (4); Mathematics: (3); Science: (2); Foreign language: (2); Social studies: (2); History: (1); Total units: (16). Tests: The college uses SAT or ACT scores in admissions decisions. Either SAT or ACT required. For admission to the fall 2007 entering class, the school will accept: ACT with writing, ACT without writing. Campus visit: Recommended. Admissions interview: Neither required nor recommended. Off-campus interview: Not available. **Factors that count in admissions decisions:** *Academic:* Secondary school record: Considered. Class rank: Not considered. Letters of recommendation: Considered. Standardized test scores: Very important. Essay: Not considered. *Nonacademic:* Interview: Considered. Extracurricular activities: Considered. Talent/ability: Considered. Character/personal qualities: Important. Alumni/ae relationship: Not considered. Geographical residence: Not considered. State residency: Not considered. Religious affiliation/commitment: Not considered. Minority status: Not considered. Volunteer work: Considered. Work experience: Not considered. **Other schools with the greatest overlap in applicants:** Central Michigan University; Grand Valley State University; Michigan State University; University of Michigan–Ann Arbor; Western Michigan University. **Admissions statistics for the fall 2005 entering class:** Total applicants: 10,151. Total accepted: 8,041. Freshmen enrolled: 2,386; 15% were from out of state. Overall acceptance rate: 79%. **Credentials of fall 2005 freshmen:** 12% ranked in the top 10 percent of their high school class; 35% were in the top 25 percent, and 68% were in the top half. (Proportion submitting class standing: 74%.) **Average high school grade point average:** 3.1. **First-year students who submitted SAT scores:** 15%. Scores (25/75 percentile): Verbal: 450-570, Math: 450-570, Combined: 900-1140. **First-year students submitting ACT scores:** 93%. Scores (25/75 percentile): English: 17-24, Math: 17-24, Composite: 18-24.

ACADEMICS

Year founded: 1849. **Academic calendar:** Semester. **Degrees offered:** bachelor's, post-bachelor's certificate, master's, post-master's certificate, doctorate. **Most popular majors:** 32% education, 18% business, management, marketing, and related support services, 7% social sciences, 6% health professions and related clinical sciences, 5% communication, journalism, and related programs. **Major fields of study:** architecture and related services; area, ethnic, cultural, and gender studies; biological and biomedical sciences; business, management, marketing, and related support services; communication, journalism, and related programs; communications technologies/technicians and support services; computer and information sciences and support services; education; engineering; engineering technologies/technicians; English language and literature/letters; family and consumer sciences/human sciences; foreign languages, literatures, and linguistics; health professions and related clinical sciences; history; legal professions and studies; mathematics and statistics; multi/interdisciplinary studies; parks, recreation, leisure, and fitness studies; philosophy and religious studies; physical sciences; psychology; public administration and social service professions; security and protective services; social sciences; transportation and materials moving; visual and performing arts. **Areas of required coursework:** arts/fine arts, humanities, computer literacy, mathematics, English (including composition), philosophy, sciences (biological or physical), history, social science, other. **Pre-professional programs:** pre-law, pre-dentistry, pre-medicine, pre-veterinary science, pre-optometry, pre-pharmacy, other. **Special academic programs:** accelerated program, cooperative (work-study plan) program, distance learning, double major, dual enrollment, English as a Second Language (ESL), honors program, independent study, internships, student-designed major, study abroad, teacher certificate program, weekend college. **Teacher certification offered in:** early childhood, special education, elementary, vo-tech, middle/junior high, secondary, bilingual/bicultural. **Cooperative education programs:** art, business, computer science, engineering, health professions, home economics, humanities, natural science, social/behavioral science, technologies. **Reserve Officers Training Corps (ROTC):** Army ROTC: Offered on campus; Navy ROTC: Offered at cooperating institution (University of Michigan-Ann Arbor); Air Force ROTC: Offered at cooperating institution (University of Michigan-Ann Arbor). **Faculty and instruction (2005-2006):** Total instructional faculty: 769 full-time, 427 part-time (49% men; 51% women; 15% minorities). Full-time faculty with Ph.D. or other terminal degree: 73%. Student/faculty ratio: 19/1. Classes of fewer than 20 students: 38%; of 20 to 49 students: 54%; of 50 or more students: 8%. **Advanced Placement and International Baccalaureate credit:** AP tests may be used for: Credit and/or placement. Scores accepted: 3, 4, 5. International Baccalaureate exams may be used for: Credit and/or placement. **Freshmen returning for sophomore year:** 72%. **Graduation rates:** Four-year: 11%; five-year: 29%; six-year: 39%. **Graduate study:** 14% of students pursue further study immediately upon graduation. Fields in which graduates pursue further study: Master of Business Administration (MBA), 6%; law, 1%; medicine, 2%; dentistry, 1%; engineering, 1%; theology (or the seminary), 1%; education, 20%; arts and sciences, 44%.

COSTS AND FINANCIAL AID

Financial aid office: (734) 487-0455. **Expenses (2005-2006):** Tuition and fees 2005-2006: $6,541 in state, $17,896 out of state; room/board: $6,356. Estimated books and supplies: $900; transportation: $800; personal expenses: $1,080. **Financial aid:** Priority filing date for institution's financial aid form: March 15. In 2005-2006, 64% of undergraduates applied for financial aid. Of those, 52% were determined to have financial need; 2% had their need fully met. Average financial aid package (proportion receiving): $6,472 (50%). Average amount of gift aid, such as scholarships or grants (proportion receiving): $3,146 (29%). Average amount of self-help aid, such as work study or loans (proportion receiving): $4,177 (42%). Average need-based loan (excluding PLUS or other private loans): $4,044. Among students who received need-based aid, the average percentage of need met: 60%. Among students who received aid based on merit, the average award (and the proportion receiving): $2,516 (8%). The average athletic scholarship (and the proportion receiving): $10,810 (3%). Average amount of debt of borrowers graduating in 2005: $21,397. Proportion who borrowed: 58%.

CAMPUS LIFE AND EXTRACURRICULAR ACTIVITIES

Campus housing available: coed dorms, sorority housing, apartments for married students, apartment for single students, special housing for disabled students, special housing for international students, other housing options. Students who live in college-owned, operated, or affiliated housing: 21%. **Student employment:** During the 2005-2006 academic year, 12% of undergraduates worked on campus. Average per-year earnings: $3,100. **Clubs and organizations:** Number of student organizations: 190. Activities include: choral groups, concert band, dance, drama/theater, jazz band, literary magazine, marching band, music ensembles, musical theater, pep band, radio station, student government, student newspaper, student film society, symphony orchestra, television station. Number of fraternities: 16; sororities: 13. Proportion of men in fraternities: 4%; of women in sororities: 4%. **Sports program (2005-2006):** Member of NCAA I. *Men's intercollegiate varsity sports:* baseball, basketball, cross-country, football, golf, swimming and diving, track and field (indoor), track and field (outdoor), wrestling. *Women's intercollegiate varsity sports:* basketball, cross-country, golf, gymnastics, soccer, softball, swimming and diving, tennis, track and field (indoor), track and field (outdoor), volleyball, rowing.

SERVICES AND FACILITIES

Basic services: nonremedial tutoring, women's center, placement service, day care, health service. **Remedial assistance:** math. **Counseling services:** minority student, career, military, personal, veteran student, academic, psy-

chological. **For learning-disabled students:** School does not offer a structured program with separate admission and additional fees. Services include: remedial math, reading machines, tape recorders, diagnostic testing service, note-taking services, learning center, readers, extended time for tests, tutors, priority registration, priority seating, texts on tape, other testing accomodations. **Library:** Number of titles: 939,650; number of current serial subscriptions: 12,940. **Information technology resources:** Students are not required to lease or own a computer. Number of campus computers available to all students: 1,500. School has a wireless network. Approximate number of users that can be accommodated: 1,300. Proportion of college-owned housing units wired for high-speed internet access: 100%. **Campus safety:** Security services offered: 24-hour foot-and-vehicle patrols, late-night transport/escort service, 24-hour emergency telephones, lighted pathways/sidewalks, student patrols, controlled dormitory access (key, security card, etc).

TRANSFER AND INTERNATIONAL STUDENTS

Transfer students: May apply for admission for the following academic terms: Fall, Winter, Spring, Summer. Applicants need a minimum number of credits to apply. For fall 2005: Transfer applications received: 3,299. Transfer applicants offered admission: 2,530. Transfer applicants enrolled: 1,694. **International students:** Number of foreign undergraduates: 236 (1% of student body). Number of countries represented: 56. Minimum TOEFL score required: 500 (paper); 173 (computer).

Ferris State University

- **Address:** 1201 South State Street CSS201, Big Rapids, MI 49307
- **Website:** http://www.ferris.edu
- **Public**
- **Enrollment:** 8,868 full-time; 2,569 part-time

KEY STATS

✔ **U.S News College Ranking:** third tier, Universities–Master's (Midwest)
✔ **ACT Score (25th/75th percentile):** 18-23
✔ **Tuition:** 2005-2006: $6,882 in state, $13,622 out of state
  Selectivity: Selective   **Room/board:** $6,816
  Acceptance rate: 47%   **Average debt:** $15,000
  Student/faculty ratio: 15/1   **Proportion who borrowed:** 85%

UNDERGRADUATE STUDENT BODY STATS

2005-2006 enrollment: 8,868 full-time; 2,569 part-time. Men: 53%; women: 47%. **Ethnic makeup:** African American: 6%; American-Indian: 1%; Asian American: 2%; Hispanic: 1%; White: 89%; International: 1%.

ADMISSIONS FACTS AND FIGURES

Phone: (231) 591-2100. **Email:** admissions@ferris.edu. **Website:** http://www.ferris.edu. **Application deadlines for fall 2007:** Regular decision: August 4. Early decision: Not offered. Early action: Not offered. Admission cannot be deferred. **Application fee:** $30. Common application is not accepted. **To apply online, go to:** http://www.ferris.edu/admissions/application/. **Admissions requirements/recommendations:** High school units required (recommended): English: 4 (4); Mathematics: 4 (4); Science: 4 (4); Foreign language: 3 (3); Social studies: 2 (4); History: 2 (0); Academic electives: 3 (0); Total units: 24 (22). Tests: The college uses SAT or ACT scores in admissions decisions. Either SAT or ACT required. For admission to the fall 2007 entering class, the school will accept: ACT with writing, ACT without writing. Campus visit: Recommended. Admissions interview: Neither required nor recommended. Off-campus interview: Not available. **Factors that count in admissions decisions:** *Academic:* Secondary school record: Considered. Class rank: Not considered. Letters of recommendation: Considered. Standardized test scores: Very important. Essay: Not considered. *Nonacademic:* Interview: Not considered. Extracurricular activities: Considered. Talent/ability: Not considered. Character/personal qualities: Important. Alumni/ae relationship: Considered. Geographical residence: Not considered. State residency: Not considered. Religious affiliation/commitment: Not considered. Minority status: Not considered. Volunteer work: Considered. Work experience: Not considered. **Other schools with the greatest overlap in applicants:** Central Michigan University; Grand Valley State University; Michigan State University; Northern Michigan University; University of Michigan–Flint. **Admissions statistics for the fall 2005 entering class:** Total applicants: 12,877. Total accepted: 6,021. Freshmen enrolled: 2,417; 1% were from out of state. Overall acceptance rate: 47%. **Average high**

school grade point average: 3.1. **First-year students submitting ACT scores:** 96%. Scores (25/75 percentile): English: 16-23, Math: 17-24, Composite: 18-23.

ACADEMICS

Year founded: 1884. **Academic calendar:** Semester. **Degrees offered:** certificate, associate, transfer-associate, terminal-associate, bachelor's, post-bachelor's certificate, master's, first professional. **Most popular majors:** 4% pharmacy (Pharm.D. [U.S.A.] Pharm.D., B.S./B.Pharm. [Canada]), 4% pre-pharmacy studies, 3% business administration and management, 3% criminal justice/police science, 3% elementary education and teaching. **Major fields of study:** biological and biomedical sciences; business, management, marketing, and related support services; communication, journalism, and related programs; communications technologies/technicians and support services; computer and information sciences and support services; education; engineering technologies/technicians; English language and literature/letters; family and consumer sciences/human sciences; health professions and related clinical sciences; history; mathematics and statistics; mechanic and repair technologies/technicians; parks, recreation, leisure, and fitness studies; physical sciences; precision production; psychology; public administration and social service professions; security and protective services; social sciences; visual and performing arts. **Areas of required coursework:** humanities, mathematics, English (including composition), sciences (biological or physical), social science, other. **Pre-professional programs:** pre-law, pre-dentistry, pre-medicine, pre-optometry, pre-pharmacy. **Special academic programs:** accelerated program, cooperative (work-study plan) program, cross-registration, distance learning, double major, dual enrollment, exchange student program (domestic), external degree program, honors program, independent study, internships, liberal arts/career combination, study abroad, teacher certificate program. **Teacher certification offered in:** elementary, vo-tech, secondary. **Cooperative education programs:** business, other. **Reserve Officers Training Corps (ROTC):** Army ROTC: Offered at cooperating institution (Central Michigan University). **Faculty and instruction (2005-2006):** Total instructional faculty: 545 full-time, 278 part-time (58% men; 42% women; 7% minorities). Full-time faculty with Ph.D. or other terminal degree: 51%. Student/faculty ratio: 15/1. Classes of fewer than 20 students: 50%; of 20 to 49 students: 47%; of 50 or more students: 3%. **Advanced Placement and International Baccalaureate credit:** AP tests may be used for: Credit only. Scores accepted: 3, 4, 5. **Freshmen returning for sophomore year:** 67%. **Graduation rates:** Four-year: 25%; five-year: 35%; six-year: 35%.

COSTS AND FINANCIAL AID

Financial aid office: (231) 591-2110. **Expenses (2005-2006):** Tuition and fees 2005-2006: $6,882 in state, $13,622 out of state; room/board: $6,816. Estimated books and supplies: $1,000; transportation: $1,214; personal expenses: $806. **Financial aid:** Priority filing date for institution's financial aid form: March 1. In 2005-2006, 95% of undergraduates applied for financial aid. Of those, 82% were determined to have financial need; 8% had their need fully met. Average financial aid package (proportion receiving): $8,000 (66%). Average amount of gift aid, such as scholarships or grants (proportion receiving): $3,500 (40%). Average amount of self-help aid, such as work study or loans (proportion receiving): $2,500 (57%). Average need-based loan (excluding PLUS or other private loans): $3,500. Among students who received need-based aid, the average percentage of need met: 75%. Among students who received aid based on merit, the average award (and the proportion receiving): $2,000 (4%). The average athletic scholarship (and the proportion receiving): $5,000 (19%). Average amount of debt of borrowers graduating in 2005: $15,000. Proportion who borrowed: 85%.

CAMPUS LIFE AND EXTRACURRICULAR ACTIVITIES

Campus housing available: coed dorms, apartments for married students, apartment for single students, special housing for disabled students, special housing for international students, other housing options. Students who live in college-owned, operated, or affiliated housing: 43%. **Student employment:** During the 2005-2006 academic year, 23% of undergraduates worked on campus. Average per-year earnings: $2,000. **Clubs and organizations:** Number of student organizations: 180. Activities include: choral groups, concert band, dance, drama/theater, jazz band, literary magazine, music ensembles, musical theater, pep band, radio station, student government, student newspaper, symphony orchestra, television station. Number of fraternities: 8; sororities: 6. Proportion of men in fraternities: 6%; of women in sororities: 2%. Average proportion of students who stay on campus on weekends: 50%. **Sports program (2005-2006):** Member of NCAA II. **Men's intercollegiate varsity sports:** basketball, cross-country, football, golf, ice hockey, tennis, track and field (indoor), track and field (outdoor). **Women's**

intercollegiate varsity sports: basketball, cross-country, golf, soccer, softball, tennis, track and field (indoor), track and field (outdoor), volleyball.

SERVICES AND FACILITIES

Basic services: nonremedial tutoring, placement service, day care, health service, health insurance, other. **Remedial assistance:** reading, math, writing, study skills. **Counseling services:** minority student, career, military, personal, veteran student, academic, psychological, birth control. **For learning-disabled students:** School does not offer a structured program with separate admission and additional fees. Services include: remedial math, remedial English, reading machines, remedial reading, tape recorders, other special classes, note-taking services, learning center, readers, extended time for tests, tutors, texts on tape. **Library:** Number of titles: 346,089; number of current serial subscriptions: 14,515. **Information technology resources:** Students are not required to lease or own a computer. Number of campus computers available to all students: 2,373. School has a wireless network. Proportion of college-owned housing units wired for high-speed internet access: 100%. **Campus safety:** Security services offered: 24-hour foot-and-vehicle patrols, late-night transport/escort service, 24-hour emergency telephones, lighted pathways/sidewalks, student patrols, controlled dormitory access (key, security card, etc.).

TRANSFER AND INTERNATIONAL STUDENTS

Transfer students: May apply for admission for the following academic terms: Fall, Winter, Summer. Applicants need a minimum number of credits to apply. For fall 2005: Transfer applications received: 4,199. Transfer applicants offered admission: 2,228. Transfer applicants enrolled: 1,381. **International students:** Number of foreign undergraduates: 152 (1% of student body). Number of countries represented: 46. Minimum TOEFL score required: 500 (paper); 173 (computer).

Grand Valley State University

- **Address:** 1 Campus Drive, Allendale, MI 49401
- **Website:** http://www.gvsu.edu
- **Public**
- **Enrollment:** 16,457 full-time; 2,446 part-time

KEY STATS

- ✔ **U.S News College Ranking:** 44, Universities–Master's (Midwest)
- ✔ **ACT Score (25th/75th percentile):** 21-26
- ✔ **Tuition:** 2005-2006: $6,220 in state, $12,510 out of state

Selectivity: More selective	**Room/board:** $6,360
Acceptance rate: 68%	**Average debt:** $16,606
Student/faculty ratio: 18/1	**Proportion who borrowed:** 73%

UNDERGRADUATE STUDENT BODY STATS

2005-2006 enrollment: 16,457 full-time; 2,446 part-time. Men: 39%; women: 61%. **Ethnic makeup:** African American: 5%; American-Indian: 1%; Asian American: 3%; Hispanic: 3%; White: 88%; International: 1%.

ADMISSIONS FACTS AND FIGURES

Phone: (800) 748-0246. **Email:** go2gvsu@gvsu.edu. **Website:** http://www.gvsu.edu. **Application deadlines for fall 2007:** Regular decision: May 1. Early decision: Not offered. Early action: Not offered. Admission cannot be deferred. **Application fee:** $30. Common application is accepted. **Admissions requirements/recommendations:** High school units required (recommended): English: (4); Mathematics: (4); Science: (4); Foreign language: (2); Social studies: (3); Total units: (20). Tests: The college uses SAT or ACT scores in admissions decisions. Either SAT or ACT required. For admission to the fall 2007 entering class, the school will accept: ACT with writing, ACT without writing. Campus visit: Recommended. Admissions interview: Recommended. Off-campus interview: May be arranged. **Factors that count in admissions decisions: Academic:** Secondary school record: Very important. Class rank: Important. Letters of recommendation: Considered. Standardized test scores: Very important. Essay: Important. **Nonacademic:** Interview: Considered. Extracurricular activities: Considered. Talent/ability: Considered. Character/personal qualities: Considered. Alumni/ae relationship: Considered. Geographical residence: Considered. State residency: Considered. Religious affiliation/commitment: Not considered. Minority status: Considered. Volunteer work: Considered. Work experience: Considered. **Other schools with the greatest overlap in applicants:** Central

Michigan University; Hope College; Michigan State University; Western Michigan University. **Admissions statistics for the fall 2005 entering class:** Total applicants: 13,255. Total accepted: 9,055. Freshmen enrolled: 3,412; 4% were from out of state. Overall acceptance rate: 68%. **Size of waiting list:** 364 applicants; enrolled from waiting list: 57. **Credentials of fall 2005 freshmen:** 22% ranked in the top 10 percent of their high school class; 55% were in the top 25 percent, and 91% were in the top half. (Proportion submitting class standing: 90%.) **First-year students who submitted SAT scores:** 2%. Scores (25/75 percentile): Verbal: N/A, Math: N/A, Combined: N/A. **First-year students submitting ACT scores:** 96%. Scores (25/75 percentile): English: 20-26, Math: 20-26, Composite: 21-26.

ACADEMICS

Year founded: 1960. **Academic calendar:** Semester. **Degrees offered:** bachelor's, post-bachelor's certificate, master's, post-master's certificate. **Most popular majors:** 19% business, management, marketing, and related support services, 14% health professions and related clinical sciences, 9% English language and literature/letters, 8% psychology, 8% social sciences. **Major fields of study:** architecture and related services; area, ethnic, cultural, and gender studies; biological and biomedical sciences; business, management, marketing, and related support services; communication, journalism, and related programs; computer and information sciences and support services; education; engineering; English language and literature/letters; foreign languages, literatures, and linguistics; health professions and related clinical sciences; history; legal professions and studies; liberal arts and sciences studies, and humanities; mathematics and statistics; multi/interdisciplinary studies; natural resources and conservation; parks, recreation, leisure, and fitness studies; philosophy and religious studies; physical sciences; psychology; public administration and social service professions; security and protective services; social sciences; visual and performing arts. **Areas of required coursework:** arts/fine arts, humanities, mathematics, English (including composition), philosophy, sciences (biological or physical), history, social science, other. **Pre-professional programs:** pre-law, pre-dentistry, pre-medicine, pre-veterinary science, pre-pharmacy. **Special academic programs:** cooperative (work-study plan) program, distance learning, double major, dual enrollment, honors program, independent study, internships, liberal arts/career combination, student-designed major, study abroad, teacher certificate program, other. **Teacher certification offered in:** early childhood, special education, elementary, middle/junior high, secondary. **Cooperative education programs:** education, engineering. **Faculty and instruction (2005-2006):** Total instructional faculty: 910 full-time, 460 part-time (52% men; 48% women; 10% minorities). Full-time faculty with Ph.D. or other terminal degree: 68%. Student/faculty ratio: 18/1. Classes of fewer than 20 students: 26%; of 20 to 49 students: 68%; of 50 or more students: 6%. **Advanced Placement and International Baccalaureate credit:** AP tests may be used for: Credit and/or placement. Scores accepted: 3, 4, 5. International Baccalaureate exams may be used for: Credit and/or placement. **Freshmen returning for sophomore year:** 80%. **Graduation rates:** Four-year: 20%; five-year: 46%; six-year: 50%.

COSTS AND FINANCIAL AID

Financial aid office: (616) 331-3234. **Expenses (2005-2006):** Tuition and fees 2005-2006: $6,220 in state, $12,510 out of state; room/board: $6,360. Estimated books and supplies: $800; transportation: $1,000; personal expenses: $940. **Financial aid:** Priority filing date for institution's financial aid form: February 15. In 2005-2006, 79% of undergraduates applied for financial aid. Of those, 55% were determined to have financial need; 85% had their need fully met. Average financial aid package (proportion receiving): $7,049 (55%). Average amount of gift aid, such as scholarships or grants (proportion receiving): $3,081 (34%). Average amount of self-help aid, such as work study or loans (proportion receiving): $3,640 (35%). Average need-based loan (excluding PLUS or other private loans): $3,419. Among students who received need-based aid, the average percentage of need met: 85%. Among students who received aid based on merit, the average award (and the proportion receiving): $2,078 (14%). The average athletic scholarship (and the proportion receiving): $6,110 (2%). Average amount of debt of borrowers graduating in 2005: $16,606. Proportion who borrowed: 73%.

CAMPUS LIFE AND EXTRACURRICULAR ACTIVITIES

Campus housing available: coed dorms, sorority housing, fraternity housing, apartments for married students, apartment for single students. Students who live in college-owned, operated, or affiliated housing: 29%. **Student employment:** During the 2005-2006 academic year, 16% of undergraduates worked on campus. Average per-year earnings: $1,900. **Clubs and organizations:** Number of student organizations: 163. Activities include: choral

groups, concert band, dance, drama/theater, jazz band, literary magazine, marching band, music ensembles, musical theater, pep band, radio station, student government, student newspaper, student film society, symphony orchestra, television station. Number of fraternities: 9; sororities: 8. Proportion of men in fraternities: 4%; of women in sororities: 3%. Average proportion of students who stay on campus on weekends: 50%. **Sports program (2005-2006):** Member of NCAA II. **Men's intercollegiate varsity sports:** baseball, basketball, cross-country, football, golf, swimming and diving, tennis, track and field (indoor), track and field (outdoor). **Women's intercollegiate varsity sports:** basketball, cross-country, golf, soccer, softball, swimming and diving, tennis, track and field (indoor), track and field (outdoor), volleyball.

SERVICES AND FACILITIES

Basic services: nonremedial tutoring, women's center, placement service, day care, health service, health insurance. **Remedial assistance:** math, writing. **Counseling services:** minority student, career, personal, academic, older student, psychological. **For learning-disabled students:** School does not offer a structured program with separate admission and additional fees. Services include: reading machines, tape recorders, videotaped classes, untimed tests, note-taking services, readers, extended time for tests, tutors. **Information technology resources:** Students are not required to lease or own a computer. Number of campus computers available to all students: 2,100. School has a wireless network. Proportion of college-owned housing units wired for high-speed internet access: 100%. **Campus safety:** Security services offered: 24-hour foot-and-vehicle patrols, late-night transport/escort service, 24-hour emergency telephones, lighted pathways/sidewalks, student patrols, controlled dormitory access (key, security card, etc).

TRANSFER AND INTERNATIONAL STUDENTS

Transfer students: May apply for admission for the following academic terms: Fall, Winter, Summer. Applicants need a minimum number of credits to apply. For fall 2005: Transfer applications received: 3,274. Transfer applicants offered admission: 2,103. Transfer applicants enrolled: 1,468. **International students:** Number of foreign undergraduates: 104 (1% of student body). Minimum TOEFL score required: 550 (paper); 213 (computer).

Hillsdale College

- **Address:** 33 E. College Street, Hillsdale, MI 49242
- **Website:** http://www.hillsdale.edu
- **Private**
- **Enrollment:** 1,262 full-time; 42 part-time

KEY STATS
✔ **U.S News College Ranking:** third tier, Liberal Arts Colleges
✔ **ACT Score (25th/75th percentile):** 24-29
✔ **Tuition:** 2006-2007: $18,160

Selectivity: More selective	**Room/board:** $7,130
Acceptance rate: 79%	**Average debt:** $17,000
Student/faculty ratio: 11/1	**Proportion who borrowed:** 65%

UNDERGRADUATE STUDENT BODY STATS

2005-2006 enrollment: 1,262 full-time; 42 part-time. Men: 48%; women: 52%. **Ethnic makeup:** White: 100%. **Religious preference:** Roman Catholic: 21%; Protestant: 45%; Jewish: 1%; No preference: 2%; Unknown: 31%.

ADMISSIONS FACTS AND FIGURES

Phone: (517) 607-2327. **Email:** admissions@hillsdale.edu. **Website:** http://www.hillsdale.edu. **Application deadlines for fall 2007:** Regular decision: February 15; decision sent by April 1. Early decision: Send application by: November 15; Decision sent by: December 1. Early action: Send application by: January 1; Decision sent by: January 20. Admission can be deferred. **Application fee:** $35. Common application is accepted. **To apply online, go to:** http://www.hillsdale.edu/admissions/application/apply.asp. **Admissions requirements/recommendations:** High school units required (recommended): English: 4 (4); Mathematics: 4 (4); Science: 3 (3); Foreign language: 2 (2); Social studies: 1 (1); History: 2 (2); Total units: 16 (16). Tests: The college uses SAT or ACT scores in admissions decisions. Either SAT or ACT required. For admission to the fall 2007 entering class, the school will accept: ACT with writing, ACT without writing. Campus visit: Recommended. Admissions interview: Recommended. Off-campus interview: May be arranged. **Factors that count in admissions decisions:** *Academic:* Secondary school record: Very important. Class rank: Important. Letters of recommendation: Important. Standardized test scores: Very important. Essay: Important. ***Nonacademic:*** Interview: Important. Extracurricular activities: Important. Talent/ability: Considered. Character/personal qualities: Very important. Alumni/ae relationship: Considered. Geographical residence: Considered. State residency: Not considered. Religious affiliation/commitment: Not considered. Minority status: Not considered. Volunteer work: Important. Work experience: Important. **Other schools with the greatest overlap in applicants:** Grove City College; Hope College; University of Michigan–Ann Arbor; University of Notre Dame; Wheaton College. **Admissions statistics for the fall 2005 entering class:** Total applicants: 1,093. Total accepted: 863. Freshmen enrolled: 368; 58% were from out of state. Overall acceptance rate: 79%. Non-early acceptance rate: 79%. **Credentials of fall 2005 freshmen:** 40% ranked in the top 10 percent of their high school class; 75% were in the top 25 percent, and 98% were in the top half. (Proportion submitting class standing: 57%.) **Average high school grade point average:** 3.7. **First-year students who submitted SAT scores:** 45%. Scores (25/75 percentile): Verbal: 580-720, Math: 540-670, Combined: 1120-1390. **First-year students submitting ACT scores:** 56%. Scores (25/75 percentile): English: 24-30, Math: 24-28, Composite: 24-29.

ACADEMICS

Year founded: 1844. **Academic calendar:** Semester. **Degrees offered:** bachelor's. **Most popular majors:** 25% social sciences, 23% business, management, marketing, and related support services, 14% biological and biomedical sciences, 8% English language and literature/letters, 7% education. **Major fields of study:** area, ethnic, cultural, and gender studies; biological and biomedical sciences; business, management, marketing, and related support services; communication, journalism, and related programs; education; English language and literature/letters; foreign languages, literatures, and linguistics; history; mathematics and statistics; multi/interdisciplinary studies; philosophy and religious studies; physical sciences; psychology; social sciences; visual and performing arts. **Areas of required coursework:** arts/fine arts, humanities, mathematics, English (including composition), sciences (biological or physical), history, social science, other. **Pre-professional programs:** pre-law, pre-dentistry, pre-medicine, pre-theology, pre-veterinary science, pre-optometry, pre-pharmacy. **Special academic programs (% participation):** double major (11%), dual enrollment (1%), honors program (12%), independent study (2%), internships (3%), study abroad (5%), teacher certificate program (15%). **Teacher certification offered in:** early childhood, elementary, secondary. **Faculty and instruction (2005-2006):** Total instructional faculty: 102 full-time, 43 part-time (70% men; 30% women). Full-time faculty with Ph.D. or other terminal degree: 89%. Student/faculty ratio: 11/1. Classes of fewer than 20 students: 74%; of 20 to 49 students: 25%; of 50 or more students: 1%. **Advanced Placement and International Baccalaureate credit:** AP tests may be used for: Credit and/or placement. Scores accepted: 3, 4, 5. International Baccalaureate exams may be used for: Credit and/or placement. **Freshmen returning for sophomore year:** 86%. **Graduation rates:** Four-year: 64%; five-year: 70%; six-year: 71%. **Graduate study:** 28% of students pursue further study immediately upon graduation; 10% within one year; 3% within five years. Fields in which graduates pursue further study: Master of Business Administration (MBA), 25%; law, 26%; medicine, 3%; dentistry, 2%; engineering, 1%; theology (or the seminary), 3%; education, 25%; arts and sciences, 16%; veterinary medicine, 1%.

COSTS AND FINANCIAL AID

Financial aid office: (517) 607-2350. **Expenses (2006-2007):** Tuition and fees 2006-2007: $18,160; room/board: $7,130. Estimated books and supplies: $800; transportation: $1,000; personal expenses: $1,000. **Financial aid:** Priority filing date for institution's financial aid form: February 15; deadline: April 1. In 2005-2006, 37% of undergraduates applied for financial aid. Of those, 32% were determined to have financial need; 63% had their need fully met. Average financial aid package (proportion receiving): $13,000 (32%). Average amount of gift aid, such as scholarships or grants (proportion receiving): $8,000 (32%). Average amount of self-help aid, such as work study or loans (proportion receiving): $6,200 (32%). Average need-based loan (excluding PLUS or other private loans): $5,130. Among students who received need-based aid, the average percentage of need met: 80%. Among students who received aid based on merit, the average award (and the proportion receiving): $6,750 (26%). The average athletic scholarship (and the proportion receiving): $9,500 (15%). Average amount of debt of borrowers graduating in 2005: $17,000. Proportion who borrowed: 65%.

CAMPUS LIFE AND EXTRACURRICULAR ACTIVITIES

Campus housing available (% using): women's dorms (43%), men's dorms (40%), sorority housing (9%), fraternity housing (7%), other housing options (1%). Students who live in college-owned, operated, or affiliated housing: 85%. **Student employment:** During the 2005-2006 academic year, 75% of undergraduates worked on campus. Average per-year earnings: $1,300. **Clubs and organizations:** Number of student organizations: 55. Activities include: choral groups, concert band, dance, drama/theater, jazz band, literary magazine, music ensembles, musical theater, pep band, student government, student newspaper, symphony orchestra, yearbook. Number of fraternities: 3; sororities: 3. Proportion of men in fraternities: 36%; of women in sororities: 46%. Average proportion of students who stay on campus on weekends: 87%. **Sports program (2005-2006):** Member of NCAA II. ***Men's intercollegiate varsity sports:*** baseball, basketball, cross-country, football, golf, soccer, swimming and diving, tennis, track and field (indoor), track and field (outdoor). ***Women's intercollegiate varsity sports:*** basketball, cross-country, soccer, softball, swimming and diving, tennis, track and field (indoor), track and field (outdoor), volleyball.

SERVICES AND FACILITIES

Basic services: nonremedial tutoring, placement service, health service. **Counseling services:** career, personal, academic, psychological, religious. **For learning-disabled students:** Services include: learning center, extended time for tests, tutors. **Library:** Number of titles: 240,000; number of current serial subscriptions: 1,700. **Information technology resources:** Students are not required to lease or own a computer. Number of campus computers available to all students: 260. School has a wireless network. Approximate number of users that can be accommodated: 50. Proportion of college-owned housing units wired for high-speed internet access: 100%. **Campus safety:** Security services offered: 24-hour foot-and-vehicle patrols, 24-hour emergency telephones, lighted pathways/sidewalks, controlled dormitory access (key, security card, etc).

TRANSFER AND INTERNATIONAL STUDENTS

Transfer students: May apply for admission for the following academic terms: Fall, Spring, Summer. Applicants do not need a minimum number of credits to apply. For fall 2005: Transfer applications received: 68. Transfer applicants offered admission: 47. Transfer applicants enrolled: 33. **International students:** Number of countries represented: 15. Minimum TOEFL score required: 550 (paper); 200 (computer). Average TOEFL score: 580 (paper).

Hope College

- **Address:** PO Box 9000, Holland, MI 49422-9000
- **Website:** http://www.hope.edu
- **Private; Religious affiliation:** Reformed Church
- **Enrollment:** 3,029 full-time; 112 part-time

KEY STATS

✔ **U.S News College Ranking:** 95, Liberal Arts Colleges
✔ **ACT Score (25th/75th percentile):** 23-29
✔ **Tuition:** 2006-2007: $22,570

Selectivity: More selective	**Room/board:** $6,982
Acceptance rate: 77%	**Average debt:** $20,812
Student/faculty ratio: 12/1	**Proportion who borrowed:** 62%

UNDERGRADUATE STUDENT BODY STATS

2005-2006 enrollment: 3,029 full-time; 112 part-time. Men: 39%; women: 61%. **Ethnic makeup:** African American: 2%; Asian American: 2%; Hispanic: 2%; White: 93%; International: 1%. **Religious preference:** Roman Catholic: 11%; Protestant: 50%; No preference: 1%; Unknown: 19%; Reformed Church: 19%.

ADMISSIONS FACTS AND FIGURES

Phone: (616) 395-7850. **Email:** admissions@hope.edu. **Website:** http://www.hope.edu. **Application deadlines for fall 2007:** Regular decision: Rolling. Early decision: Not offered. Early action: Not offered. Admission can be deferred. **Application fee:** $35. Common application is accepted. **To apply online, go to:** http://www.hope.edu/admissions/apply/application.html. **Admissions requirements/recommendations:** High school units required (recommended): English: 4 (4); Mathematics: 2 (3); Science: 1

(3); Foreign language: 2 (2); Social studies: 2 (2); History: 1 (1); Academic electives: 5 (3); Total units: 18 (20). Tests: The college uses SAT or ACT scores in admissions decisions. Either SAT or ACT required. Campus visit: Recommended. Admissions interview: Recommended. Off-campus interview: May be arranged. **Factors that count in admissions decisions:** *Academic:* Secondary school record: Very important. Class rank: Important. Letters of recommendation: Considered. Standardized test scores: Very important. Essay: Considered. *Nonacademic:* Interview: Considered. Extracurricular activities: Considered. Talent/ability: Considered. Character/personal qualities: Considered. Alumni/ae relationship: Considered. Geographical residence: Considered. State residency: Considered. Religious affiliation/commitment: Not considered. Minority status: Considered. Volunteer work: Considered. Work experience: Considered. **Other schools with the greatest overlap in applicants:** Calvin College; Grand Valley State University; Michigan State University; University of Michigan–Ann Arbor; Western Michigan University. **Admissions statistics for the fall 2005 entering class:** Total applicants: 2,674. Total accepted: 2,071. Freshmen enrolled: 760; 33% were from out of state. Overall acceptance rate: 77%. **Size of waiting list:** 331 applicants; enrolled from waiting list: 58. **Credentials of fall 2005 freshmen:** 34% ranked in the top 10 percent of their high school class; 61% were in the top 25 percent, and 95% were in the top half. (Proportion submitting class standing: 88%.) **Average high school grade point average:** 3.8. **First-year students who submitted SAT scores:** 30%. Scores (25/75 percentile): Verbal: 550-680, Math: 560-680, Combined: 1110-1360. **First-year students submitting ACT scores:** 93%. Scores (25/75 percentile): English: 22-30, Math: 23-29, Composite: 23-29.

ACADEMICS

Year founded: 1866. **Academic calendar:** Semester. **Degrees offered:** bachelor's. **Most popular majors:** 12% business administration and management, 11% psychology, 7% English/language arts teacher education, 7% political science and government, 6% English language and literature. **Major fields of study:** area, ethnic, cultural, and gender studies; biological and biomedical sciences; business, management, marketing, and related support services; communication, journalism, and related programs; computer and information sciences and support services; education; engineering; English language and literature/letters; foreign languages, literatures, and linguistics; health professions and related clinical sciences; history; liberal arts and sciences studies, and humanities; mathematics and statistics; multi/interdisciplinary studies; natural resources and conservation; parks, recreation, leisure, and fitness studies; philosophy and religious studies; physical sciences; psychology; public administration and social service professions; social sciences; visual and performing arts. **Areas of required coursework:** arts/fine arts, humanities, mathematics, English (including composition), philosophy, foreign languages, sciences (biological or physical), history, social science, other. **Pre-professional programs:** pre-law, pre-dentistry, pre-medicine, pre-theology, pre-veterinary science, pre-optometry, pre-pharmacy, other. **Special academic programs (% participation):** double major (18%), dual enrollment (1%), independent study (10%), internships (30%), student-designed major (1.5%), study abroad (25%), teacher certificate program (20%). **Teacher certification offered in:** special education, elementary, middle/junior high, secondary. **Faculty and instruction (2005-2006):** Total instructional faculty: 215 full-time, 101 part-time (55% men; 45% women; 10% minorities). Full-time faculty with Ph.D. or other terminal degree: 78%. Student/faculty ratio: 12/1. Classes of fewer than 20 students: 54%; of 20 to 49 students: 44%; of 50 or more students: 2%. **Advanced Placement and International Baccalaureate credit:** AP tests may be used for: Credit only. Scores accepted: 3, 4, 5. International Baccalaureate exams may be used for: Credit only. **Freshmen returning for sophomore year:** 87%. **Graduation rates:** Four-year: 64%; five-year: 74%; six-year: 74%. **Graduate study:** 25% of students pursue further study immediately upon graduation. Fields in which graduates pursue further study: Master of Business Administration (MBA), 5%; law, 5%; medicine, 11%; dentistry, 4%; engineering, 2%; theology (or the seminary), 5%; education, 13%; arts and sciences, 54%.

COSTS AND FINANCIAL AID

Financial aid office: (616) 395-7765. **Expenses (2006-2007):** Tuition and fees 2006-2007: $22,570; room/board: $6,982. Estimated books and supplies: $700; transportation: $282; personal expenses: $1,130. **Financial aid:** Priority filing date for institution's financial aid form: March 1. In 2005-2006, 73% of undergraduates applied for financial aid. Of those, 59% were determined to have financial need; 33% had their need fully met. Average financial aid package (proportion receiving): $18,272 (59%). Average amount of gift aid, such as scholarships or grants (proportion receiving): $12,828 (50%). Average amount of self-help aid, such as work study or loans (proportion

receiving): $5,444 (46%). Average need-based loan (excluding PLUS or other private loans): $4,680. Among students who received need-based aid, the average percentage of need met: 87%. Among students who received aid based on merit, the average award (and the proportion receiving): $6,880 (29%). The average athletic scholarship (and the proportion receiving): $0 (0%). Average amount of debt of borrowers graduating in 2005: $20,812. Proportion who borrowed: 62%.

CAMPUS LIFE AND EXTRACURRICULAR ACTIVITIES

Campus housing available (% using): coed dorms (42%), women's dorms (30%), men's dorms (10%), sorority housing (5%), fraternity housing (4%), apartments for married students (0%), apartment for single students (0%), special housing for disabled students (1%), cooperative housing (0%), other housing options (8%). Students who live in college-owned, operated, or affiliated housing: 68%. **Student employment:** During the 2005-2006 academic year, 23% of undergraduates worked on campus. Average per-year earnings: $2,000. **Clubs and organizations:** Number of student organizations: 57. Activities include: choral groups, concert band, dance, drama/theater, jazz band, literary magazine, music ensembles, musical theater, pep band, radio station, student government, student newspaper, student film society, symphony orchestra, television station, yearbook. Number of fraternities: 6; sororities: 7. Proportion of men in fraternities: 11%; of women in sororities: 13%. Average proportion of students who stay on campus on weekends: 85%. **Sports program (2005-2006):** Member of NCAA III. *Men's intercollegiate varsity sports:* baseball, basketball, cross-country, football, golf, soccer, swimming and diving, tennis, track and field (outdoor). *Women's intercollegiate varsity sports:* basketball, cross-country, golf, soccer, softball, swimming and diving, tennis, track and field (outdoor), volleyball.

SERVICES AND FACILITIES

Basic services: placement service, health service, health insurance. **Remedial assistance:** reading, math, writing, study skills. **Counseling services:** minority student, career, personal, veteran student, academic, older student, psychological, birth control, religious. **For learning-disabled students:** School does not offer a structured program with separate admission and additional fees. Services include: reading machines, tape recorders, untimed tests, note-taking services, oral tests, learning center, readers, extended time for tests, tutors, priority registration, texts on tape. **Library:** Number of titles: 364,771; number of current serial subscriptions: 2,955. **Information technology resources:** Students are not required to lease or own a computer. Number of campus computers available to all students: 300. School has a wireless network. Approximate number of users that can be accommodated: 17,500. Proportion of college-owned housing units wired for high-speed internet access: 100%. **Campus safety:** Security services offered: 24-hour foot-and-vehicle patrols, late-night transport/escort service, 24-hour emergency telephones, lighted pathways/sidewalks, controlled dormitory access (key, security card, etc).

TRANSFER AND INTERNATIONAL STUDENTS

Transfer students: May apply for admission for the following academic terms: Fall, Spring. Applicants do not need a minimum number of credits to apply. For fall 2005: Transfer applications received: 169. Transfer applicants offered admission: 110. Transfer applicants enrolled: 66. **International students:** Number of foreign undergraduates: 38 (1% of student body). Minimum TOEFL score required: 550 (paper); 213 (computer). Average TOEFL score: 620 (paper).

Kalamazoo College

- **Address:** 1200 Academy Street, Kalamazoo, MI 49006
- **Website:** http://www.kzoo.edu
- **Private**
- **Enrollment:** 1,263 full-time

KEY STATS

✔ **U.S News College Ranking:** 57, Liberal Arts Colleges
✔ **ACT Score (25th/75th percentile):** 26-31
✔ **Tuition:** 2006-2007: $27,054

Selectivity: More selective	**Room/board:** $6,915
Acceptance rate: 68%	**Average debt:** $24,022
Student/faculty ratio: 12/1	**Proportion who borrowed:** 55%

UNDERGRADUATE STUDENT BODY STATS

2005-2006 enrollment: 1,263 full-time. Men: 43%; women: 57%. **Ethnic makeup:** African American: 3%; Asian American: 5%; Hispanic: 2%; White: 90%.

ADMISSIONS FACTS AND FIGURES

Phone: (800) 253-3602. **Email:** admission@kzoo.edu. **Website:** http://www.kzoo.edu. **Application deadlines for fall 2007:** Regular decision: February 15; decision sent by April 1. Early decision: Send application by: November 15; Decision sent by: December 1. Early action: Send application by: December 1; Decision sent by: December 20. Admission can be deferred. **Application fee:** $35. Common application is accepted. **To apply online, go to:** http://www.kzoo.edu/admiss/admissions.html. **Admissions requirements/recommendations:** High school units required (recommended): English: (4); Mathematics: (3); Science: (3); Foreign language: (3); Social studies: (2); History: (2); Total units: 17. Tests: The college uses SAT or ACT scores in admissions decisions. Either SAT or ACT required. For admission to the fall 2007 entering class, the school will accept: ACT with writing. Campus visit: Recommended. Admissions interview: Recommended. Off-campus interview: May be arranged. **Factors that count in admissions decisions:** *Academic:* Secondary school record: Very important. Class rank: Important. Letters of recommendation: Important. Standardized test scores: Very important. Essay: Important. *Nonacademic:* Interview: Considered. Extracurricular activities: Very important. Talent/ability: Very important. Character/personal qualities: Important. Alumni/ae relationship: Considered. Geographical residence: Considered. State residency: Considered. Religious affiliation/commitment: Not considered. Minority status: Considered. Volunteer work: Important. Work experience: Important. **Other schools with the greatest overlap in applicants:** Beloit College; College of Wooster; Denison University; Michigan State University; University of Michigan–Ann Arbor. **Admissions statistics for the fall 2005 entering class:** Total applicants: 1,669. Total accepted: 1,133. Freshmen enrolled: 367; 28% were from out of state. Overall acceptance rate: 68%. Early-decision acceptance rate: 79%. Non-early acceptance rate: 68%. **Size of waiting list:** 31 applicants; enrolled from waiting list: 14. **Credentials of fall 2005 freshmen:** 43% ranked in the top 10 percent of their high school class; 77% were in the top 25 percent, and 99% were in the top half. (Proportion submitting class standing: 61%.) **Average high school grade point average:** 3.6. **First-year students who submitted SAT scores:** 62%. Scores (25/75 percentile): Verbal: 610-710, Math: 600-690, Combined: 1210-1400. **First-year students submitting ACT scores:** 87%. Scores (25/75 percentile): English: 26-31, Math: 25-29, Composite: 26-31.

ACADEMICS

Year founded: 1833. **Academic calendar:** Trimester. **Degrees offered:** bachelor's. **Most popular majors:** 16% economics, 14% biology, 13% psychology, 12% English language and literature, 9% chemistry. **Major fields of study:** area, ethnic, cultural, and gender studies; biological and biomedical sciences; computer and information sciences and support services; English language and literature/letters; foreign languages, literatures, and linguistics; health professions and related clinical sciences; history; liberal arts and sciences studies, and humanities; mathematics and statistics; multi/interdisciplinary studies; philosophy and religious studies; physical sciences; psychology; social sciences; visual and performing arts. **Areas of required coursework:** arts/fine arts, humanities, computer literacy, mathematics, English (including composition), philosophy, foreign languages, sciences (biological or physical), social science, other. **Pre-professional programs:** pre-law, pre-dentistry, pre-medicine, pre-veterinary science. **Special academic programs (% participation):** cross-registration, double major, dual enrollment, exchange student program (domestic), independent study, internships (65%), study abroad (83%), other. **Reserve Officers Training Corps (ROTC):** Army ROTC: Offered at cooperating institution (Western Michigan University). **Faculty and instruction (2005-2006):** Total instructional faculty: 100 full-time, 14 part-time (50% men; 50% women; 15% minorities). Full-time faculty with Ph.D. or other terminal degree: 85%. Student/faculty ratio: 12/1. Classes of fewer than 20 students: 68%; of 20 to 49 students: 32%; of 50 or more students: 0%. **Advanced Placement and International Baccalaureate credit:** AP tests may be used for: Credit only. Scores accepted: 4, 5. International Baccalaureate exams may be used for: Credit only. **Freshmen returning for sophomore year:** 87%. **Graduation rates:** Four-year: 73%; five-year: 78%; six-year: 80%. **Graduate study:** 30% of students pursue further study immediately upon graduation; 30% within one year; 50% within five years.

COSTS AND FINANCIAL AID

Financial aid office: (269) 337-7192. **Expenses (2006-2007):** Tuition and fees 2006-2007: $27,054; room/board: $6,915. Estimated books and supplies: $825; transportation: $345; personal expenses: $990. **Financial aid:** Priority filing date for institution's financial aid form: February 15. In 2005-2006, 66% of undergraduates applied for financial aid. Of those, 52% were determined to have financial need; 67% had their need fully met. Average financial aid package (proportion receiving): $25,005 (52%). Average amount of gift aid, such as scholarships or grants (proportion receiving): $9,367 (51%). Average amount of self-help aid, such as work study or loans (proportion receiving): N/A (51%). Average amount of debt of borrowers graduating in 2005: $24,022. Proportion who borrowed: 55%.

CAMPUS LIFE AND EXTRACURRICULAR ACTIVITIES

Campus housing available: coed dorms, special housing for disabled students, other housing options. Students who live in college-owned, operated, or affiliated housing: 74%. **Student employment:** During the 2005-2006 academic year, 20% of undergraduates worked on campus. Average per-year earnings: $900. **Clubs and organizations:** Number of student organizations: 50. Activities include: choral groups, concert band, dance, drama/theater, jazz band, literary magazine, music ensembles, musical theater, pep band, radio station, student government, student newspaper, symphony orchestra, yearbook. Number of fraternities: 0; sororities: 0. Average proportion of students who stay on campus on weekends: 75%. **Sports program (2005-2006):** Member of NCAA III. **Men's intercollegiate varsity sports:** baseball, basketball, cross-country, football, golf, soccer, swimming and diving, tennis. **Women's intercollegiate varsity sports:** basketball, cross-country, golf, soccer, softball, swimming and diving, tennis, volleyball.

SERVICES AND FACILITIES

Basic services: nonremedial tutoring, women's center, placement service, health service, health insurance. **Counseling services:** minority student, career, personal, academic, psychological, religious. **For learning-disabled students:** School does not offer a structured program with separate admission and additional fees. Services include: tape recorders, diagnostic testing service, learning center, extended time for tests. **Information technology resources:** Students are not required to lease or own a computer. Number of campus computers available to all students: 130. School has a wireless network. Proportion of college-owned housing units wired for high-speed internet access: 100%. **Campus safety:** Security services offered: 24-hour foot-and-vehicle patrols, late-night transport/escort service, 24-hour emergency telephones, lighted pathways/sidewalks, controlled dormitory access (key, security card, etc.).

TRANSFER AND INTERNATIONAL STUDENTS

Transfer students: May apply for admission for the following academic terms: Fall. Applicants do not need a minimum number of credits to apply. For fall 2005: Transfer applications received: 42. Transfer applicants offered admission: 11. Transfer applicants enrolled: 6. **International students:** Number of foreign undergraduates: 1. Number of countries represented: 1. Minimum TOEFL score required: 550 (paper); 213 (computer).

Kettering University

- **Address:** 1700 W. Third Avenue, Flint, MI 48504
- **Website:** http://www.kettering.edu
- **Private**
- **Enrollment:** 2,411 full-time

KEY STATS

✔ **U.S News College Ranking:** Unranked Specialty School–Engineering
✔ **ACT Score (25th/75th percentile):** 23-28
✔ **Tuition:** 2006-2007: $24,908

Selectivity: More selective	**Room/board:** $5,608
Acceptance rate: 73%	**Average debt:** $40,617
Student/faculty ratio: 11/1	**Proportion who borrowed:** 59%

UNDERGRADUATE STUDENT BODY STATS

2005-2006 enrollment: 2,411 full-time. Men: 85%; women: 15%. **Ethnic makeup:** African American: 5%; Asian American: 5%; Hispanic: 2%; White: 85%; International: 2%.

ADMISSIONS FACTS AND FIGURES

Phone: (800) 955-4464. **Email:** admissions@kettering.edu. **Website:** http://www.kettering.edu. **Application deadlines for fall 2007:** Regular decision: Rolling. Early decision: Not offered. Early action: Not offered. Admission can be deferred. **Application fee:** $35. Common application is not accepted. **To apply online, go to:** http://admissions.kettering.edu/. **Admissions requirements/recommendations:** High school units required (recommended): English: 3 (4); Mathematics: 4 (4); Science: 2 (4); Foreign language: (2); Social studies: (4); Academic electives: 5 (4); Total units: 16 (22). Tests: The college uses SAT or ACT scores in admissions decisions. Either SAT or ACT required. For admission to the fall 2007 entering class, the school will accept: ACT with writing, ACT without writing. Campus visit: Recommended. Admissions interview: Recommended. Off-campus interview: May be arranged. **Factors that count in admissions decisions:** *Academic:* Secondary school record: Very important. Class rank: Important. Letters of recommendation: Considered. Standardized test scores: Very important. Essay: Not considered. *Nonacademic:* Interview: Considered. Extracurricular activities: Considered. Talent/ability: Not considered. Character/personal qualities: Not considered. Alumni/ae relationship: Not considered. Geographical residence: Not considered. State residency: Not considered. Religious affiliation/commitment: Not considered. Minority status: Not considered. Volunteer work: Considered. Work experience: Considered. **Other schools with the greatest overlap in applicants:** Massachusetts Institute of Technology; Michigan State University; Michigan Technological University; Purdue University–West Lafayette; University of Michigan–Ann Arbor. **Admissions statistics for the fall 2005 entering class:** Total applicants: 2,127. Total accepted: 1,555. Freshmen enrolled: 495; 32% were from out of state. Overall acceptance rate: 73%. **Credentials of fall 2005 freshmen:** 31% ranked in the top 10 percent of their high school class; 62% were in the top 25 percent, and 91% were in the top half. (Proportion submitting class standing: 87%.) **Average high school grade point average:** 3.6. **First-year students who submitted SAT scores:** 27%. Scores (25/75 percentile): Verbal: 550-630, Math: 600-690, Combined: 1150-1320. **First-year students submitting ACT scores:** 73%. Scores (25/75 percentile): English: 21-27, Math: 25-29, Composite: 23-28.

ACADEMICS

Year founded: 1919. **Academic calendar:** Semester. **Degrees offered:** bachelor's, master's. **Most popular majors:** 85% engineering, 8% business, management, marketing, and related support services, 5% computer and information sciences and support services, 1% mathematics and statistics, 1% physical sciences. **Major fields of study:** business, management, marketing, and related support services; computer and information sciences and support services; engineering; mathematics and statistics; physical sciences. **Areas of required coursework:** humanities, mathematics, English (including composition), sciences (biological or physical), history, social science, other. **Special academic programs (% participation):** accelerated program, cooperative (work-study plan) program (100%), double major (10%), dual enrollment (5%), independent study, study abroad (20%). **Cooperative education programs:** business, computer science, engineering, natural science, other. **Faculty and instruction (2005-2006):** Total instructional faculty: 140 full-time, 17 part-time (80% men; 20% women; 20% minorities). Full-time faculty with Ph.D. or other terminal degree: 91%. Student/faculty ratio: 11/1. Classes of fewer than 20 students: 35%; of 20 to 49 students: 59%; of 50 or more students: 5%. **Advanced Placement and International Baccalaureate credit:** AP tests may be used for: Credit only. Scores accepted: 3, 4, 5. International Baccalaureate exams may be used for: Credit only. **Freshmen returning for sophomore year:** 85%. **Graduation rates:** Four-year: 3%; five-year: 49%; six-year: 61%. **Graduate study:** 5% of students pursue further study immediately upon graduation; 38% within one year; 62% within five years. Fields in which graduates pursue further study: Master of Business Administration (MBA), 40%; law, 1%; medicine, 1%; engineering, 35%.

COSTS AND FINANCIAL AID

Financial aid office: (810) 762-7859. **Expenses (2006-2007):** Tuition and fees 2006-2007: $24,908; room/board: $5,608. Estimated books and supplies: $1,034; transportation: $3,620; personal expenses: $2,924. **Financial aid:** Priority filing date for institution's financial aid form: February 14. In 2005-2006, 74% of undergraduates applied for financial aid. Of those, 68% were determined to have financial need; 11% had their need fully met. Average financial aid package (proportion receiving): $13,833 (68%). Average amount of gift aid, such as scholarships or grants (proportion receiving): $9,237 (61%). Average amount of self-help aid, such as work study or loans (proportion receiving): $5,027 (63%). Average need-based loan (excluding PLUS or other private loans): $3,974. Among students who received need-based aid, the average percentage of need met: 54%. Among students who received aid based on merit, the average award (and the proportion receiving): $6,945 (19%). The average athletic scholarship (and the proportion receiving): $0 (0%). Average amount of debt of borrowers graduating in 2005: $40,617. Proportion who borrowed: 59%.

CAMPUS LIFE AND EXTRACURRICULAR ACTIVITIES

Campus housing available (% using): coed dorms (24%), sorority housing (22%), fraternity housing (33%), apartment for single students (21%). Students who live in college-owned, operated, or affiliated housing: 48%. **Student employment:** During the 2005-2006 academic year, 6% of undergraduates worked on campus. Average per-year earnings: $1,050. **Clubs and organizations:** Number of student organizations: 52. Activities include: choral groups, drama/theater, jazz band, literary magazine, music ensembles, radio station, student government, student newspaper, yearbook. Number of fraternities: 11; sororities: 6. Proportion of men in fraternities: 40%; of women in sororities: 33%. Average proportion of students who stay on campus on weekends: 40%.

SERVICES AND FACILITIES

Basic services: nonremedial tutoring, women's center, placement service, health service, health insurance. **Remedial assistance:** study skills. **Counseling services:** minority student, career, personal, veteran student, academic, psychological, birth control, religious. **For learning-disabled students:** School does not offer a structured program with separate admission and additional fees. Services include: reading machines, tape recorders, diagnostic testing service, note-taking services, oral tests, readers, extended time for tests, tutors, priority registration, priority seating, texts on tape, other testing accomodations. **Library:** Number of titles: 128,500; number of current serial subscriptions: 1,200. **Information technology resources:** Students are not required to lease or own a computer. Number of campus computers available to all students: 450. School has a wireless network. Approximate number of users that can be accommodated: 3,000. Proportion of college-owned housing units wired for high-speed internet access: 100%. **Campus safety:** Security services offered: 24-hour foot-and-vehicle patrols, late-night transport/escort service, 24-hour emergency telephones, lighted pathways/sidewalks, controlled dormitory access (key, security card, etc).

TRANSFER AND INTERNATIONAL STUDENTS

Transfer students: May apply for admission for the following academic terms: Fall, Winter, Spring, Summer. Applicants do not need a minimum number of credits to apply. For fall 2005: Transfer applications received: 168. Transfer applicants offered admission: 84. Transfer applicants enrolled: 50. **International students:** Number of foreign undergraduates: 49 (2% of student body). Number of countries represented: 22. Minimum TOEFL score required: 550 (paper); 213 (computer). Average TOEFL score: 570 (paper).

Lake Superior State University

- **Address:** 650 W. Easterday Avenue, Sault Ste. Marie, MI 49783-1699
- **Website:** http://www.lssu.edu
- **Public**
- **Enrollment:** 2,267 full-time; 649 part-time

KEY STATS

✔ **U.S News College Ranking:** fourth tier, Universities–Master's (Midwest)
✔ **ACT Score (25th/75th percentile):** 18-24
✔ **Tuition:** 2005-2006: $6,306 in state, $12,294 out of state

Selectivity: Selective	**Room/board:** $6,536
Acceptance rate: 84%	**Average debt:** $19,825
Student/faculty ratio: 17/1	**Proportion who borrowed:** 63%

UNDERGRADUATE STUDENT BODY STATS

2005-2006 enrollment: 2,267 full-time; 649 part-time. Men: 48%; women: 52%. **Ethnic makeup:** African American: 1%; American-Indian: 10%; Asian American: 1%; Hispanic: 1%; White: 76%; International: 11%.

ADMISSIONS FACTS AND FIGURES

Phone: (906) 635-2231. **Email:** admissions@lssu.edu. **Website:** http://www.lssu.edu. **Application deadlines for fall 2007:** Regular decision: August 15. Early decision: Not offered. Early action: Not offered. Admission can be deferred. **Application fee:** $20. Common application is not accepted.

Admissions requirements/recommendations: High school units required (recommended): English: (4); Mathematics: (3); Science: (3); Foreign language: (2); Social studies: (2); History: (1); Academic electives: (0); Total units: (18). Tests: The college uses SAT or ACT scores in admissions decisions. ACT required. **Factors that count in admissions decisions:** *Academic:* Secondary school record: Very important. Class rank: Considered. Letters of recommendation: Considered. Standardized test scores: Very important. Essay: Not considered. *Nonacademic:* Interview: Considered. Extracurricular activities: Not considered. Talent/ability: Not considered. Character/personal qualities: Not considered. Alumni/ae relationship: Not considered. Geographical residence: Considered. State residency: Not considered. Religious affiliation/commitment: Not considered. Minority status: Not considered. Volunteer work: Not considered. Work experience: Not considered. **Other schools with the greatest overlap in applicants:** Ferris State University; Grand Valley State University; Northern Michigan University. **Admissions statistics for the fall 2005 entering class:** Total applicants: 1,523. Total accepted: 1,282. Freshmen enrolled: 487; 3% were from out of state. Overall acceptance rate: 84%. **Credentials of fall 2005 freshmen:** 10% ranked in the top 10 percent of their high school class; 30% were in the top 25 percent, and 64% were in the top half. (Proportion submitting class standing: 84%.) **Average high school grade point average:** 3.1. **First-year students submitting ACT scores:** 92%. Scores (25/75 percentile): English: 16-22, Math: 17-24, Composite: 18-24.

ACADEMICS

Year founded: 1946. **Academic calendar:** Semester. **Degrees offered:** certificate, associate, bachelor's, master's. **Most popular majors:** 19% business, management, marketing, and related support services, 19% security and protective services, 9% education, 7% health professions and related clinical sciences, 6% engineering. **Major fields of study:** biological and biomedical sciences; business, management, marketing, and related support services; communication, journalism, and related programs; computer and information sciences and support services; education; engineering; engineering technologies/technicians; English language and literature/letters; foreign languages, literatures, and linguistics; health professions and related clinical sciences; history; legal professions and studies; liberal arts and sciences studies, and humanities; mathematics and statistics; multi/interdisciplinary studies; natural resources and conservation; parks, recreation, leisure, and fitness studies; physical sciences; psychology; public administration and social service professions; security and protective services; social sciences; visual and performing arts. **Areas of required coursework:** humanities, computer literacy, mathematics, English (including composition), sciences (biological or physical), social science, other. **Special academic programs:** cooperative (work-study plan) program, cross-registration, distance learning, double major, honors program, independent study, internships, student-designed major, teacher certificate program, weekend college. **Faculty and instruction (2005-2006):** Total instructional faculty: 113 full-time, 89 part-time (54% men; 46% women). Full-time faculty with Ph.D. or other terminal degree: 61%. Student/faculty ratio: 17/1. Classes of fewer than 20 students: 40%; of 20 to 49 students: 50%; of 50 or more students: 10%. **Freshmen returning for sophomore year:** 65%. **Graduation rates:** Four-year: 21%; five-year: 34%; six-year: 40%.

COSTS AND FINANCIAL AID

Financial aid office: (906) 635-2678. **Expenses (2005-2006):** Tuition and fees 2005-2006: $6,306 in state, $12,294 out of state; room/board: $6,536. Estimated books and supplies: $785 personal expenses: $1,397. **Financial aid:** Priority filing date for institution's financial aid form: February 21. In 2005-2006, 86% of undergraduates applied for financial aid. Of those, 86% were determined to have financial need; 49% had their need fully met. Average financial aid package (proportion receiving): $8,157 (86%). Average amount of gift aid, such as scholarships or grants (proportion receiving): $3,407 (34%). Average amount of self-help aid, such as work study or loans (proportion receiving): $7,524 (66%). Average need-based loan (excluding PLUS or other private loans): $4,787. Among students who received need-based aid, the average percentage of need met: 75%. Among students who received aid based on merit, the average award (and the proportion receiving): $2,774 (7%). The average athletic scholarship (and the proportion receiving): $6,080 (6%). Average amount of debt of borrowers graduating in 2005: $19,825. Proportion who borrowed: 63%.

CAMPUS LIFE AND EXTRACURRICULAR ACTIVITIES

Campus housing available: coed dorms, women's dorms, men's dorms, sorority housing, fraternity housing, apartments for married students, apartment for single students, other housing options. Students who live in college-owned, operated, or affiliated housing: 29%. Activities include:

choral groups, concert band, drama/theater, jazz band, literary magazine, music ensembles, pep band, radio station, student government, student newspaper, symphony orchestra. **Sports program (2005-2006):** Member of NCAA II. *Men's intercollegiate varsity sports:* basketball, cross-country, golf, ice hockey, tennis, track and field (indoor), track and field (outdoor). *Women's intercollegiate varsity sports:* basketball, cross-country, softball, tennis, track and field (indoor), track and field (outdoor), volleyball.

TRANSFER AND INTERNATIONAL STUDENTS

Transfer students: May apply for admission for the following academic terms: Fall, Spring, Summer. Applicants do not need a minimum number of credits to apply. For fall 2005: Transfer applications received: 53. Transfer applicants offered admission: 458. Transfer applicants enrolled: 274. **International students:** Number of foreign undergraduates: 297 (11% of student body).

Lawrence Technological University

- **Address:** 21000 W. Ten Mile Road, Southfield, MI 48075
- **Website:** http://www.ltu.edu
- **Private**
- **Enrollment:** 1,604 full-time; 1,264 part-time

KEY STATS

✔ **U.S News College Ranking:** 47, Universities–Master's (Midwest)
✔ **ACT Score (25th/75th percentile):** 20-26
✔ **Tuition:** 2006-2007: $19,443

Selectivity: Selective	**Room/board:** $7,266
Acceptance rate: 76%	**Average debt:** $24,250
Student/faculty ratio: 12/1	**Proportion who borrowed:** 50%

UNDERGRADUATE STUDENT BODY STATS

2005-2006 enrollment: 1,604 full-time; 1,264 part-time. Men: 78%; women: 22%. **Ethnic makeup:** African American: 12%; Asian American: 3%; Hispanic: 2%; White: 80%; International: 2%.

ADMISSIONS FACTS AND FIGURES

Phone: (248) 204-3160. **Email:** admissions@ltu.edu. **Website:** http://www.ltu.edu. **Application deadlines for fall 2007:** Regular decision: Rolling. Early decision: Not offered. Early action: Not offered. Admission can be deferred. **Application fee:** $30. Common application is accepted. **To apply online, go to:** http://www.ltu.edu/futurestudents/apply.asp. **Admissions requirements/recommendations:** High school units required (recommended): English: 3 (4); Mathematics: 3 (4); Science: 2 (4); Social studies: 1 (1); History: 1 (1); Total units: 10 (14). Tests: The college uses SAT or ACT scores in admissions decisions. Either SAT or ACT required. For admission to the fall 2007 entering class, the school will accept ACT without writing. Campus visit: Recommended. Admissions interview: Neither required nor recommended. Off-campus interview: May be arranged. **Factors that count in admissions decisions:** *Academic:* Secondary school record: Very important. Class rank: Not considered. Letters of recommendation: Considered. Standardized test scores: Very important. Essay: Considered. *Nonacademic:* Interview: Considered. Extracurricular activities: Not considered. Talent/ability: Considered. Character/personal qualities: Considered. Alumni/ae relationship: Considered. Geographical residence: Not considered. State residency: Not considered. Religious affiliation/commitment: Not considered. Minority status: Not considered. Volunteer work: Not considered. Work experience: Not considered. **Other schools with the greatest overlap in applicants:** Kettering University; Michigan State University; Michigan Technological University; University of Michigan–Ann Arbor; Wayne State University. **Admissions statistics for the fall 2005 entering class:** Total applicants: 1,298. Total accepted: 990. Freshmen enrolled: 332; 2% were from out of state. Overall acceptance rate: 76%. **Credentials of fall 2005 freshmen:** 20% ranked in the top 10 percent of their high school class; 47% were in the top 25 percent, and 77% were in the top half. (Proportion submitting class standing: 68%.) **Average high school grade point average:** 3.2. **First-year students who submitted SAT scores:** 13%. Scores (25/75 percentile): Verbal: 430-630, Math: 490-630, Combined: 920-1260. **First-year students submitting ACT scores:** 89%. Scores (25/75 percentile): English: 17-25, Math: 21-27, Composite: 20-26.

ACADEMICS

Year founded: 1932. **Academic calendar:** Semester. **Degrees offered:** certificate, associate, bachelor's, master's, doctorate. **Most popular majors:** 24% architecture (B.Arch., B.A./B.S., M.Arch., M.A./M.S., Ph.D.), 20% mechanical engineering, 14% engineering technology, 10% electrical, electronics, and communications engineering, 8% computer science. **Major fields of study:** architecture and related services; biological and biomedical sciences; business, management, marketing, and related support services; communications technologies/technicians and support services; computer and information sciences and support services; engineering; engineering technologies/technicians; liberal arts and sciences studies, and humanities; mathematics and statistics; multi/interdisciplinary studies; physical sciences; psychology; visual and performing arts. **Areas of required coursework:** humanities, computer literacy, mathematics, English (including composition), sciences (biological or physical), history, social science. **Pre-professional programs:** pre-law, pre-dentistry, pre-medicine. **Special academic programs (% participation):** accelerated program (0%), cooperative (work-study plan) program (9.2%), distance learning (1.6%), double major (3.2%), dual enrollment (0%), English as a Second Language (ESL) (0%), independent study (17.2%), internships (6.4%), study abroad (5.1%). **Cooperative education programs:** business, computer science, engineering, natural science, technologies. **Reserve Officers Training Corps (ROTC):** Army ROTC: Offered at cooperating institution (University of Michigan-Ann Arbor); Navy ROTC: Offered at cooperating institution (University of Michigan-Ann Arbor); Air Force ROTC: Offered at cooperating institution (University of Michigan-Ann Arbor). **Faculty and instruction (2005-2006):** Total instructional faculty: 114 full-time, 261 part-time (77% men; 23% women; 11% minorities). Full-time faculty with Ph.D. or other terminal degree: 75%. Student/faculty ratio: 12/1. Classes of fewer than 20 students: 68%; of 20 to 49 students: 31%; of 50 or more students: 1%. **Advanced Placement and International Baccalaureate credit:** AP tests may be used for: Credit only. Scores accepted: 3, 4. International Baccalaureate exams may be used for: Credit only. **Freshmen returning for sophomore year:** 73%. **Graduation rates:** Four-year: 25%; five-year: 40%; six-year: 46%.

COSTS AND FINANCIAL AID

Financial aid office: (248) 204-2280. **Expenses (2006-2007):** Tuition and fees 2006-2007: $19,443; room/board: $7,266. Estimated books and supplies: $1,196; transportation: $1,614; personal expenses: $1,884. **Financial aid:** Priority filing date for institution's financial aid form: April 1. In 2005-2006, 73% of undergraduates applied for financial aid. Of those, 57% were determined to have financial need; 6% had their need fully met. Average financial aid package (proportion receiving): $10,157 (57%). Average amount of gift aid, such as scholarships or grants (proportion receiving): $6,783 (52%). Average amount of self-help aid, such as work study or loans (proportion receiving): $5,279 (53%). Average need-based loan (excluding PLUS or other private loans): $4,126. Among students who received need-based aid, the average percentage of need met: 80%. Among students who received aid based on merit, the average award (and the proportion receiving): $5,816 (18%). The average athletic scholarship (and the proportion receiving): $0 (0%). Average amount of debt of borrowers graduating in 2005: $24,250. Proportion who borrowed: 50%.

CAMPUS LIFE AND EXTRACURRICULAR ACTIVITIES

Campus housing available (% using): apartments for married students (1%), apartment for single students (98%), special housing for disabled students (1%). Students who live in college-owned, operated, or affiliated housing: 14%. **Student employment:** During the 2005-2006 academic year, 6% of undergraduates worked on campus. Average per-year earnings: $7,313. **Clubs and organizations:** Number of student organizations: 40. Activities include: literary magazine, music ensembles, student government, student newspaper. Number of fraternities: 6; sororities: 4. Proportion of men in fraternities: 5%; of women in sororities: 7%. Average proportion of students who stay on campus on weekends: 40%.

SERVICES AND FACILITIES

Basic services: placement service, health insurance. **Remedial assistance:** math, writing, study skills, other. **Counseling services:** minority student, career, personal, academic, psychological. **For learning-disabled students:** School does not offer a structured program with separate admission and additional fees. Total undergraduates in learning-disabled program or receiving services: 18. Services include: remedial math, remedial English, reading machines, tape recorders, untimed tests, note-taking services, oral tests, learning center, readers, extended time for tests, tutors, priority seating, texts on tape, other testing accomodations. **Library:** Number of titles: 84,411; number of current serial subscriptions: 1,070. **Information technol-**

ogy resources: Students are required to lease or own a computer. Number of campus computers available to all students: 3,050. School has a wireless network. Approximate number of users that can be accommodated: 3,500. Proportion of college-owned housing units wired for high-speed internet access: 100%. **Campus safety:** Security services offered: 24-hour foot-and-vehicle patrols, late-night transport/escort service, 24-hour emergency telephones, lighted pathways/sidewalks, controlled dormitory access (key, security card, etc).

TRANSFER AND INTERNATIONAL STUDENTS

Transfer students: May apply for admission for the following academic terms: Fall, Winter, Spring, Summer. Applicants need a minimum number of credits to apply. For fall 2005: Transfer applications received: 667. Transfer applicants offered admission: 457. Transfer applicants enrolled: 293. **International students:** Number of foreign undergraduates: 60 (2% of student body). Number of countries represented: 22. Minimum TOEFL score required: 550 (paper); 213 (computer). Average TOEFL score: 577 (paper).

Madonna University

- **Address:** 36600 Schoolcraft Road, Livonia, MI 48150
- **Website:** http://www.madonna.edu
- **Private; Religious affiliation:** Roman Catholic
- **Enrollment:** 1,676 full-time; 1,690 part-time

KEY STATS
- ✔ **U.S News College Ranking:** third tier, Universities–Master's (Midwest)
- ✔ **ACT Score (25th/75th percentile):** 22-26
- ✔ **Tuition:** 2006-2007: $10,960

Selectivity: Selective	**Room/board:** $5,946
Acceptance rate: 86%	**Average debt:** $19,252
Student/faculty ratio: 14/1	**Proportion who borrowed:** 40%

UNDERGRADUATE STUDENT BODY STATS

2005-2006 enrollment: 1,676 full-time; 1,690 part-time. Men: 25%; women: 75%. **Ethnic makeup:** African American: 14%; Asian American: 2%; Hispanic: 3%; White: 77%; International: 3%. **Religious preference:** Protestant: 21%; Jewish: 1%; Muslim: 1%; No preference: 2%; Unknown: 32%; Roman Catholic: 40%.

ADMISSIONS FACTS AND FIGURES

Phone: (734) 432-5339. **Website:** http://www.madonna.edu. **Application deadlines for fall 2007:** Regular decision: Rolling. Early decision: Not offered. Early action: Not offered. Admission can be deferred. **Application fee:** $25. Common application is accepted. **Admissions requirements/recommendations:** High school units required (recommended): English: 3 (4); Mathematics: 2 (3); Science: 3 (3); Foreign language: 0 (2); Social studies: 3 (3); History: 0 (3); Total units: 19 (19). Tests: The college uses SAT or ACT scores in admissions decisions. Either SAT or ACT required. For admission to the fall 2007 entering class, the school will accept: ACT with writing, ACT without writing. Campus visit: Recommended. Admissions interview: Recommended. Off-campus interview: May be arranged. **Factors that count in admissions decisions:** *Academic:* Secondary school record: Very important. Class rank: Considered. Letters of recommendation: Important. Standardized test scores: Important. Essay: Important. *Nonacademic:* Interview: Considered. Extracurricular activities: Considered. Talent/ability: Not considered. Character/personal qualities: Considered. Alumni/ae relationship: Not considered. Geographical residence: Not considered. State residency: Not considered. Religious affiliation/commitment: Not considered. Minority status: Not considered. Volunteer work: Considered. Work experience: Considered. **Admissions statistics for the fall 2005 entering class:** Total applicants: 573. Total accepted: 490. Freshmen enrolled: 200; 2% were from out of state. Overall acceptance rate: 86%. **Average high school grade point average:** 3.2. First-year students who submitted SAT scores: 3%. Scores (25/75 percentile): Verbal: N/A, Math: N/A, Combined: N/A. **First-year students submitting ACT scores:** 97%. Scores (25/75 percentile): English: 23-27, Math: 22-26, Composite: 22-26.

ACADEMICS

Year founded: 1947. **Academic calendar:** Semester. **Degrees offered:** certificate, associate, bachelor's, post-bachelor's certificate, master's, post-master's certificate. **Most popular majors:** 15% business, management, marketing, and related support services, 15% health professions and related clinical sciences, 10% security and protective services, 7% English language and literature/letters, 7% psychology. **Major fields of study:** area, ethnic, cultural, and gender studies; biological and biomedical sciences; business, management, marketing, and related support services; communication, journalism, and related programs; computer and information sciences and support services; education; engineering technologies/technicians; English language and literature/letters; family and consumer sciences/human sciences; foreign languages, literatures, and linguistics; health professions and related clinical sciences; history; legal professions and studies; liberal arts and sciences studies, and humanities; mathematics and statistics; multi/interdisciplinary studies; natural resources and conservation; philosophy and religious studies; physical sciences; psychology; public administration and social service professions; science technologies/technicians; security and protective services; social sciences; theology and religious vocations; visual and performing arts. **Areas of required coursework:** arts/fine arts, humanities, computer literacy, mathematics, English (including composition), sciences (biological or physical), history, social science. **Pre-professional programs:** other. **Special academic programs (% participation):** accelerated program (0%), cooperative (work-study plan) program (17%), cross-registration (0%), distance learning (57%), double major (1%), dual enrollment (0%), English as a Second Language (ESL) (2%), independent study (5%), internships (12%), study abroad (1%), teacher certificate program (23%). **Teacher certification offered in:** early childhood, special education, elementary, vo-tech, middle/junior high, secondary. **Cooperative education programs:** business, computer science, health professions, technologies. **Faculty and instruction (2005-2006):** Total instructional faculty: 108 full-time, 238 part-time (38% men; 62% women; 7% minorities). Full-time faculty with Ph.D. or other terminal degree: 53%. Student/faculty ratio: 14/1. Classes of fewer than 20 students: 62%; of 20 to 49 students: 36%; of 50 or more students: 1%. **Advanced Placement and International Baccalaureate credit:** AP tests may be used for: Credit only. Scores accepted: 3, 4, 5. **Freshmen returning for sophomore year:** 74%. **Graduation rates:** Four-year: 17%; five-year: 36%; six-year: 48%. **Graduate study:** 6% of students pursue further study immediately upon graduation. Fields in which graduates pursue further study: Master of Business Administration (MBA), 10%; education, 20%; arts and sciences, 16%.

COSTS AND FINANCIAL AID

Financial aid office: (734) 432-5662. **Expenses (2006-2007):** Tuition and fees 2006-2007: $10,960; room/board: $5,946. Estimated books and supplies: $888; transportation: $772; personal expenses: $968. **Financial aid:** Priority filing date for institution's financial aid form: February 21; deadline: April 1. In 2005-2006, 58% of undergraduates applied for financial aid. Of those, 47% were determined to have financial need; 9% had their need fully met. Average financial aid package (proportion receiving): $6,381 (47%). Average amount of gift aid, such as scholarships or grants (proportion receiving): $3,982 (41%). Average amount of self-help aid, such as work study or loans (proportion receiving): $3,434 (39%). Average need-based loan (excluding PLUS or other private loans): $3,348. Among students who received need-based aid, the average percentage of need met: 55%. Among students who received aid based on merit, the average award (and the proportion receiving): $6,426 (20%). The average athletic scholarship (and the proportion receiving): $2,347 (4%). Average amount of debt of borrowers graduating in 2005: $19,252. Proportion who borrowed: 40%.

CAMPUS LIFE AND EXTRACURRICULAR ACTIVITIES

Campus housing available (% using): women's dorms (68%), men's dorms (32%). Students who live in college-owned, operated, or affiliated housing: 4%. **Student employment:** During the 2005-2006 academic year, 17% of undergraduates worked on campus. Average per-year earnings: $2,270. **Clubs and organizations:** Number of student organizations: 16. Activities include: choral groups, music ensembles, radio station, student government, student newspaper, television station. Number of fraternities: 0; sororities: 0. Average proportion of students who stay on campus on weekends: 1%. **Sports program (2005-2006):** Member of NAIA. *Men's intercollegiate varsity sports:* baseball, basketball, golf, soccer. *Women's intercollegiate varsity sports:* basketball, golf, soccer, softball, volleyball.

SERVICES AND FACILITIES

Basic services: nonremedial tutoring, placement service, health insurance. **Remedial assistance:** reading, math, writing, study skills. **Counseling services:** minority student, career, personal, academic, older student, psychological, religious. **For learning-disabled students:** School does not offer a structured program with separate admission and additional fees. Total

undergraduates in learning-disabled program or receiving services: 42. Services include: remedial math, remedial English, reading machines, tape recorders, diagnostic testing service, note-taking services, oral tests, learning center, readers, extended time for tests, tutors, priority seating, texts on tape, other testing accomodations, other. **Library:** Number of titles: 110,000; number of current serial subscriptions: 11,273. **Information technology resources:** Students are not required to lease or own a computer. Number of campus computers available to all students: 146. School has a wireless network. Approximate number of users that can be accommodated: 200. Proportion of college-owned housing units wired for high-speed internet access: 100%. **Campus safety:** Security services offered: 24-hour foot-and-vehicle patrols, late-night transport/escort service, 24-hour emergency telephones, lighted pathways/sidewalks, student patrols, controlled dormitory access (key, security card, etc).

TRANSFER AND INTERNATIONAL STUDENTS

Transfer students: May apply for admission for the following academic terms: Fall, Winter, Spring, Summer. Applicants need a minimum number of credits to apply. For fall 2005: Transfer applications received: 1,118. Transfer applicants offered admission: 801. Transfer applicants enrolled: 600. **International students:** Number of foreign undergraduates: 102 (3% of student body). Number of countries represented: 37. Minimum TOEFL score required: 540 (paper); 207 (computer). Average TOEFL score: 550 (paper).

Marygrove College

- **Address:** 8425 W. McNichols Road, Detroit, MI 48221
- **Website:** http://www.marygrove.edu
- **Private; Religious affiliation:** Roman Catholic
- **Enrollment:** 398 full-time; 334 part-time

KEY STATS
✔ **U.S News College Ranking:** fourth tier, Universities–Master's (Midwest)
✔ **ACT Score (25th/75th percentile):** 16-20
✔ **Tuition:** 2006-2007: $13,880

Selectivity: Less selective	**Room/board:** $6,400
Acceptance rate: 42%	**Average debt:** N/A
Student/faculty ratio: 15/1	**Proportion who borrowed:** N/A

UNDERGRADUATE STUDENT BODY STATS

2005-2006 enrollment: 398 full-time; 334 part-time. Men: 23%; women: 77%. **Ethnic makeup:** African American: 64%; Hispanic: 1%; White: 32%; International: 3%.

ADMISSIONS FACTS AND FIGURES

Phone: (313) 927-1240. **Email:** info@marygrove.edu. **Website:** http://www.marygrove.edu. **Application deadlines for fall 2007:** Regular decision: August 1. Early decision: Not offered. Early action: Not offered. Admission can be deferred. **Application fee:** $25. Common application is not accepted. **Admissions requirements/recommendations:** High school units required (recommended): English: (4); Mathematics: (2); Science: (2); Foreign language: (2); Social studies: (2); Total units: (16). Tests: The college uses SAT or ACT scores in admissions decisions. Neither SAT nor ACT required. For admission to the fall 2007 entering class, the school will accept: ACT with writing, ACT without writing. Campus visit: Recommended. Admissions interview: Neither required nor recommended. Off-campus interview: May be arranged. **Factors that count in admissions decisions:** *Academic:* Secondary school record: Very important. Class rank: Not considered. Letters of recommendation: Important. Standardized test scores: Considered. Essay: Not considered. *Nonacademic:* Interview: Important. Extracurricular activities: Considered. Talent/ability: Considered. Character/personal qualities: Not considered. Alumni/ae relationship: Considered. Geographical residence: Not considered. State residency: Not considered. Religious affiliation/commitment: Not considered. Minority status: Not considered. Volunteer work: Not considered. Work experience: Not considered. **Other schools with the greatest overlap in applicants:** Madonna University; University of Detroit Mercy; Wayne State University. **Admissions statistics for the fall 2005 entering class:** Total applicants: 412. Total accepted: 173. Freshmen enrolled: 80; Overall acceptance rate: 42%. **Average high school grade point average:** 2.9. **First-year students submitting ACT**

scores: 70%. Scores (25/75 percentile): English: 14-20, Math: 15-18, Composite: 16-20.

ACADEMICS

Year founded: 1905. **Academic calendar:** Semester. **Degrees offered:** certificate, associate, bachelor's, post-bachelor's certificate, master's. **Most popular majors:** 21% social sciences, 11% business administration, management, and operations, 9% English language and literature, 9% education, 8% computer and information sciences. **Major fields of study:** biological and biomedical sciences; business, management, marketing, and related support services; computer and information sciences and support services; education; English language and literature/letters; family and consumer sciences/human sciences; health professions and related clinical sciences; history; mathematics and statistics; multi/interdisciplinary studies; philosophy and religious studies; physical sciences; psychology; public administration and social service professions; social sciences; theology and religious vocations; visual and performing arts. **Areas of required coursework:** arts/fine arts, humanities, computer literacy, mathematics, English (including composition), philosophy, foreign languages, sciences (biological or physical), history, social science, other. **Pre-professional programs:** pre-law, pre-dentistry, pre-medicine. **Special academic programs:** distance learning, double major, honors program, independent study, study abroad, teacher certificate program. **Teacher certification offered in:** early childhood, special education, elementary, middle/junior high, adult education, secondary. **Cooperative education programs:** business, education, health professions, social/behavioral science. **Faculty and instruction (2005-2006):** Total instructional faculty: 61 full-time, 6 part-time (37% men; 63% women; 27% minorities). Full-time faculty with Ph.D. or other terminal degree: 87%. Student/faculty ratio: 15/1. **Freshmen returning for sophomore year:** 63%. **Graduation rates:** Four-year: 5%; five-year: 10%; six-year: 23%.

COSTS AND FINANCIAL AID

Financial aid office: (313) 927-1692. **Expenses (2006-2007):** Tuition and fees 2006-2007: $13,880; room/board: $6,400.

CAMPUS LIFE AND EXTRACURRICULAR ACTIVITIES

Campus housing available (% using): coed dorms (100%). Students who live in college-owned, operated, or affiliated housing: 11%. **Clubs and organizations:** Number of student organizations: 12. Activities include: choral groups, music ensembles, student government. Number of fraternities: 0; sororities: 0. **Sports program (2005-2006):** *Men's intercollegiate varsity sports:* basketball. *Women's intercollegiate varsity sports:* basketball.

SERVICES AND FACILITIES

Basic services: nonremedial tutoring, placement service, day care, other. **Remedial assistance:** reading, math, writing, study skills. **Counseling services:** career, veteran student, academic, religious. **For learning-disabled students:** Services include: remedial math, remedial English, remedial reading, tutors. **Library:** Number of titles: 77,799; number of current serial subscriptions: 452. **Information technology resources:** Students are not required to lease or own a computer. Number of campus computers available to all students: 100. School does not have a wireless network. Proportion of college-owned housing units wired for high-speed internet access: 100%. **Campus safety:** Security services offered: 24-hour foot-and-vehicle patrols, 24-hour emergency telephones, lighted pathways/sidewalks.

TRANSFER AND INTERNATIONAL STUDENTS

Transfer students: May apply for admission for the following academic terms: Fall, Winter, Spring, Summer. Applicants do not need a minimum number of credits to apply. For fall 2005: Transfer applications received: 279. Transfer applicants offered admission: 156. Transfer applicants enrolled: 90. **International students:** Number of foreign undergraduates: 17 (3% of student body). Number of countries represented: 14. Minimum TOEFL score required: 520 (paper); 190 (computer).

Michigan State University

- **Address:** East Lansing, MI 48824
- **Website:** http://www.msu.edu/
- **Public**
- **Enrollment:** 32,200 full-time; 3,478 part-time

KEY STATS
✔ **U.S News College Ranking:** 70, National Universities
✔ **ACT Score (25th/75th percentile):** 22-27
✔ **Tuition:** 2005-2006: $8,312 in state, $20,010 out of state
Selectivity: More selective   **Room/board:** $5,788
Acceptance rate: 76%   **Average debt:** $22,147
Student/faculty ratio: 18/1   **Proportion who borrowed:** 56%

UNDERGRADUATE STUDENT BODY STATS

2005-2006 enrollment: 32,200 full-time; 3,478 part-time. Men: 46%; women: 54%. **Ethnic makeup:** African American: 9%; American-Indian: 1%; Asian American: 5%; Hispanic: 3%; White: 79%; International: 3%.

ADMISSIONS FACTS AND FIGURES

Phone: (517) 355-8332. **Email:** admis@msu.edu. **Website:** http://www.msu.edu/. **Application deadlines for fall 2007:** Regular decision: Rolling; decision sent by September 1. Early decision: Not offered. Early action: Not offered. Admission can be deferred. **Application fee:** $35. Common application is accepted. **To apply online, go to:** http://admissions.msu.edu/apply.asp. **Admissions requirements/recommendations:** High school units required (recommended): English: 4; Mathematics: 3; Science: 3; Foreign language: 2; Social studies: 1; History: 2; Total units: 14. Tests: The college uses SAT or ACT scores in admissions decisions. Either SAT or ACT required. For admission to the fall 2007 entering class, the school will accept: ACT with writing. Campus visit: Neither required nor recommended. Admissions interview: Neither required nor recommended. Off-campus interview: May be arranged. **Factors that count in admissions decisions:** *Academic:* Secondary school record: Very important. Class rank: Considered. Letters of recommendation: Considered. Standardized test scores: Very important. Essay: Considered. *Nonacademic:* Interview: Considered. Extracurricular activities: Considered. Talent/ability: Considered. Character/personal qualities: Considered. Alumni/ae relationship: Not considered. Geographical residence: Not considered. State residency: Not considered. Religious affiliation/commitment: Not considered. Minority status: Not considered. Volunteer work: Not considered. Work experience: Not considered. **Other schools with the greatest overlap in applicants:** Central Michigan University; Indiana University–Bloomington; University of Illinois–Urbana-Champaign; University of Michigan–Ann Arbor; Western Michigan University. **Admissions statistics for the fall 2005 entering class:** Total applicants: 21,844. Total accepted: 16,686. Freshmen enrolled: 7,485; 12% were from out of state. Overall acceptance rate: 76%. **Size of waiting list:** 945 applicants; enrolled from waiting list: 50. **Credentials of fall 2005 freshmen:** 26% ranked in the top 10 percent of their high school class; 64% were in the top 25 percent, and 94% were in the top half. (Proportion submitting class standing: 75%.) **Average high school grade point average:** 3.6. **First-year students who submitted SAT scores:** 25%. Scores (25/75 percentile): Verbal: 490-620, Math: 520-650, Combined: 1010-1270. **First-year students submitting ACT scores:** 94%. Scores (25/75 percentile): English: 21-27, Math: 21-27, Composite: 22-27.

ACADEMICS

Year founded: 1855. **Academic calendar:** Semester. **Degrees offered:** certificate, bachelor's, master's, post-master's certificate, first professional, doctorate. **Most popular majors:** 19% business, management, marketing, and related support services, 14% communication, journalism, and related programs, 10% social sciences, 7% engineering, 5% agriculture, agriculture operations, and related sciences. **Major fields of study:** agriculture, agriculture operations, and related sciences; architecture and related services; area, ethnic, cultural, and gender studies; biological and biomedical sciences; business, management, marketing, and related support services; communication, journalism, and related programs; computer and information sciences and support services; education; engineering; English language and literature/letters; family and consumer sciences/human sciences; foreign languages, literatures, and linguistics; health professions and related clinical sciences; history; legal professions and studies; liberal arts and sciences studies, and humanities; mathematics and statistics; multi/interdisciplinary studies; natural resources and conservation; parks, recreation, leisure, and fitness studies; philosophy and religious studies; physical sciences; psychology; public administration and social service professions; security and protective services; social sciences; visual and performing arts. **Areas of required coursework:** humanities, mathematics, English (including composition), sciences (biological or physical), social science. **Pre-professional programs:** pre-law, pre-medicine, pre-veterinary science. **Special academic programs (% participation):** accelerated program (4%), cooperative (work-study plan) program (1%), distance learning, double major (5%), dual enrollment, English as a Second Language (ESL), honors program (10%), independent study (61%), internships, liberal arts/career combination, student-designed major, study abroad (19%), teacher certificate program, weekend college. **Teacher certification offered in:** special education, elementary, middle/junior high, secondary. **Cooperative education programs:** engineering. **Reserve Officers Training Corps (ROTC):** Army ROTC: Offered on campus; Air Force ROTC: Offered on campus. **Faculty and instruction (2005-2006):** Total instructional faculty: 2,411 full-time, 351 part-time (63% men; 37% women; 18% minorities). Full-time faculty with Ph.D. or other terminal degree: 94%. Student/faculty ratio: 18/1. Classes of fewer than 20 students: 21%; of 20 to 49 students: 55%; of 50 or more students: 23%. **Advanced Placement and International Baccalaureate credit:** AP tests may be used for: Credit and/or placement. Scores accepted: 2. **Freshmen returning for sophomore year:** 90%. **Graduation rates:** Four-year: 41%; five-year: 70%; six-year: 74%. **Graduate study:** 20% of students pursue further study immediately upon graduation; 20% within one year. Fields in which graduates pursue further study: Master of Business Administration (MBA), 2%; law, 14%; medicine, 8%; dentistry, 1%; engineering, 10%; theology (or the seminary), 1%; education, 8%; arts and sciences, 55%; veterinary medicine, 1%.

COSTS AND FINANCIAL AID

Financial aid office: (517) 353-5940. **Expenses (2005-2006):** Tuition and fees 2005-2006: $8,312 in state, $20,010 out of state; room/board: $5,788. Estimated books and supplies: $854; transportation: $376; personal expenses: $1,150. **Financial aid:** In 2005-2006, 58% of undergraduates applied for financial aid. Of those, 40% were determined to have financial need; 27% had their need fully met. Average financial aid package (proportion receiving): $8,468 (40%). Average amount of gift aid, such as scholarships or grants (proportion receiving): $4,167 (25%). Average amount of self-help aid, such as work study or loans (proportion receiving): $4,277 (34%). Average need-based loan (excluding PLUS or other private loans): $3,861. Among students who received need-based aid, the average percentage of need met: 72%. Among students who received aid based on merit, the average award (and the proportion receiving): $3,824 (7%). The average athletic scholarship (and the proportion receiving): $13,952 (1%). Average amount of debt of borrowers graduating in 2005: $22,147. Proportion who borrowed: 56%.

CAMPUS LIFE AND EXTRACURRICULAR ACTIVITIES

Campus housing available: coed dorms, women's dorms, sorority housing, fraternity housing, apartments for married students, apartment for single students, other housing options. Students who live in college-owned, operated, or affiliated housing: 42%. **Clubs and organizations:** Number of student organizations: 500. Activities include: choral groups, concert band, dance, drama/theater, jazz band, marching band, music ensembles, musical theater, opera, pep band, radio station, student government, student newspaper, student film society, symphony orchestra, television station, yearbook. Number of fraternities: 32; sororities: 13. Average proportion of students who stay on campus on weekends: 50%. **Sports program (2005-2006):** Member of NCAA I. *Men's intercollegiate varsity sports:* baseball, basketball, cross-country, football, golf, ice hockey, soccer, swimming and diving, tennis, track and field (indoor), track and field (outdoor), wrestling. *Women's intercollegiate varsity sports:* basketball, cross-country, field hockey, golf, gymnastics, soccer, softball, swimming and diving, tennis, track and field (indoor), track and field (outdoor), volleyball, rowing.

SERVICES AND FACILITIES

Basic services: nonremedial tutoring, women's center, placement service, day care, health service, health insurance. **Remedial assistance:** reading, math, writing, study skills. **Counseling services:** minority student, career, military, personal, veteran student, academic, older student, psychological, birth control, religious. **For learning-disabled students:** School does not offer a structured program with separate admission and additional fees. Total undergraduates in learning-disabled program or receiving services: 412. Services include: remedial math, remedial English, diagnostic testing service, tutors, priority registration. **Library:** Number of titles: 4,830,861; number of current serial subscriptions: 37,832. **Information technology**

resources: Students are required to lease or own a computer. Number of campus computers available to all students: 2,200. School has a wireless network. Approximate number of users that can be accommodated: 8,000. Proportion of college-owned housing units wired for high-speed internet access: 99%. **Campus safety:** Security services offered: 24-hour emergency telephones, lighted pathways/sidewalks, controlled dormitory access (key, security card, etc).

TRANSFER AND INTERNATIONAL STUDENTS

Transfer students: May apply for admission for the following academic terms: Fall, Spring, Summer. Applicants do not need a minimum number of credits to apply. For fall 2005: Transfer applications received: 4,225. Transfer applicants offered admission: 2,020. Transfer applicants enrolled: 1,511. **International students:** Number of foreign undergraduates: 1051 (3% of student body). Number of countries represented: 92. Minimum TOEFL score required: 550 (paper); 213 (computer).

Michigan Technological University

- **Address:** 1400 Townsend Drive, Houghton, MI 49931
- **Website:** http://www.mtu.edu
- **Public**
- **Enrollment:** 5,159 full-time; 455 part-time

KEY STATS

✔ **U.S News College Ranking:** third tier, National Universities
✔ **ACT Score (25th/75th percentile):** 22-28
✔ **Tuition:** 2006-2007: $8,910 in state, $20,679 out of state

Selectivity: More selective	**Room/board:** $6,840
Acceptance rate: 85%	**Average debt:** $13,587
Student/faculty ratio: 11/1	**Proportion who borrowed:** 53%

UNDERGRADUATE STUDENT BODY STATS

2005-2006 enrollment: 5,159 full-time; 455 part-time. Men: 78%; women: 22%. **Ethnic makeup:** African American: 2%; American-Indian: 1%; Asian American: 1%; Hispanic: 1%; White: 91%; International: 4%.

ADMISSIONS FACTS AND FIGURES

Phone: (906) 487-2335. **Email:** mtu4u@mtu.edu. **Website:** http://www.mtu.edu. **Application deadlines for fall 2007:** Regular decision: Rolling. Early decision: Not offered. Early action: Not offered. Admission can be deferred. **Application fee:** $40. Common application is accepted. **To apply online, go to:** http://www.mtu.edu/apply/. **Admissions requirements/recommendations:** High school units required (recommended): English: 3 (4); Mathematics: 3 (4); Science: 2 (3); Foreign language: (2); Social studies: (3); History: (1); Academic electives: (1); Total units: 15. Tests: The college uses SAT or ACT scores in admissions decisions. Either SAT or ACT required. For admission to the fall 2007 entering class, the school will accept: ACT with writing, ACT without writing. Campus visit: Recommended. Admissions interview: Recommended. Off-campus interview: May be arranged. **Factors that count in admissions decisions:** *Academic:* Secondary school record: Very important. Class rank: Very important. Letters of recommendation: Considered. Standardized test scores: Very important. Essay: Considered. *Nonacademic:* Interview: Considered. Extracurricular activities: Considered. Talent/ability: Considered. Character/personal qualities: Considered. Alumni/ae relationship: Considered. Geographical residence: Not considered. State residency: Not considered. Religious affiliation/commitment: Not considered. Minority status: Not considered. Volunteer work: Considered. Work experience: Considered. **Other schools with the greatest overlap in applicants:** Michigan State University; University of Michigan–Ann Arbor; University of Minnesota–Twin Cities; University of Wisconsin–Madison; Western Michigan University. **Admissions statistics for the fall 2005 entering class:** Total applicants: 3,928. Total accepted: 3,326. Freshmen enrolled: 1,327; 27% were from out of state. Overall acceptance rate: 85%. **Credentials of fall 2005 freshmen:** 25% ranked in the top 10 percent of their high school class; 56% were in the top 25 percent, and 87% were in the top half. (Proportion submitting class standing: 93%.) **Average high school grade point average:** 3.5. **First-year students who submitted SAT scores:** 17%. Scores (25/75 percentile): Verbal: 530-660, Math: 580-700, Combined: 1110-1360. **First-year students submitting ACT scores:** 94%. Scores (25/75 percentile): English: 20-27, Math: 24-29, Composite: 22-28.

ACADEMICS

Year founded: 1885. **Academic calendar:** Semester. **Degrees offered:** certificate, associate, terminal-associate, bachelor's, post-bachelor's certificate, master's, doctorate. **Most popular majors:** 62% engineering, 10% business, management, marketing, and related support services, 6% engineering technologies/technicians, 5% computer and information sciences and support services, 4% biological and biomedical sciences. **Major fields of study:** biological and biomedical sciences; business, management, marketing, and related support services; communication, journalism, and related programs; communications technologies/technicians and support services; computer and information sciences and support services; engineering; engineering technologies/technicians; health professions and related clinical sciences; history; liberal arts and sciences studies, and humanities; mathematics and statistics; natural resources and conservation; parks, recreation, leisure, and fitness studies; physical sciences; psychology; social sciences; visual and performing arts. **Areas of required coursework:** humanities, computer literacy, mathematics, English (including composition), sciences (biological or physical), social science, other. **Pre-professional programs:** pre-law, pre-dentistry, pre-medicine, pre-veterinary science, pre-optometry, pre-pharmacy, other. **Special academic programs (% participation):** cooperative (work-study plan) program (18.8%), distance learning, double major (5.6%), dual enrollment, English as a Second Language (ESL), exchange student program (domestic), honors program, independent study (5.2%), internships (4.4%), study abroad (8.5%), teacher certificate program (2%), other. **Teacher certification offered in:** secondary. **Cooperative education programs:** agriculture, art, business, computer science, education, engineering, health professions, humanities, natural science, social/behavioral science, technologies, other. **Reserve Officers Training Corps (ROTC):** Army ROTC: Offered on campus; Air Force ROTC: Offered on campus. **Faculty and instruction (2005-2006):** Total instructional faculty: 343 full-time, 46 part-time (74% men; 26% women; 15% minorities). Full-time faculty with Ph.D. or other terminal degree: 88%. Student/faculty ratio: 11/1. Classes of fewer than 20 students: 43%; of 20 to 49 students: 45%; of 50 or more students: 12%. **Advanced Placement and International Baccalaureate credit:** AP tests may be used for: Credit and/or placement. Scores accepted: 3, 4, 5. International Baccalaureate exams may be used for: Credit and/or placement. **Freshmen returning for sophomore year:** 81%. **Graduation rates:** Four-year: 23%; five-year: 52%; six-year: 59%. **Graduate study:** 13% of students pursue further study immediately upon graduation; 17% within one year; 75% within five years. Fields in which graduates pursue further study: Master of Business Administration (MBA), 27%; engineering, 60%; arts and sciences, 13%.

COSTS AND FINANCIAL AID

Financial aid office: (906) 487-2622. **Expenses (2006-2007):** Tuition and fees 2006-2007: $8,910 in state, $20,679 out of state; room/board: $6,840. Estimated books and supplies: $1,000; transportation: $750; personal expenses: $1,013. **Financial aid:** Priority filing date for institution's financial aid form: February 18. In 2005-2006, 75% of undergraduates applied for financial aid. Of those, 53% were determined to have financial need; 36% had their need fully met. Average financial aid package (proportion receiving): $8,517 (52%). Average amount of gift aid, such as scholarships or grants (proportion receiving): $5,025 (45%). Average amount of self-help aid, such as work study or loans (proportion receiving): $11,113 (45%). Average need-based loan (excluding PLUS or other private loans): $4,394. Among students who received need-based aid, the average percentage of need met: 78%. Among students who received aid based on merit, the average award (and the proportion receiving): $3,300 (20%). The average athletic scholarship (and the proportion receiving): $10,243 (3%). Average amount of debt of borrowers graduating in 2005: $13,587. Proportion who borrowed: 53%.

CAMPUS LIFE AND EXTRACURRICULAR ACTIVITIES

Campus housing available (% using): coed dorms (80%), sorority housing (3%), fraternity housing (7%), apartments for married students (1%), apartment for single students (9%), special housing for disabled students, special housing for international students. Students who live in college-owned, operated, or affiliated housing: 43%. **Student employment:** During the 2005-2006 academic year, 25% of undergraduates worked on campus. Average per-year earnings: $6,430. **Clubs and organizations:** Number of student organizations: 200. Activities include: choral groups, concert band, dance, drama/theater, jazz band, literary magazine, music ensembles, musical theater, opera, pep band, radio station, student government, student newspaper, student film society, symphony orchestra. Number of fraternities: 15; sororities: 8. Proportion of men in fraternities: 9%; of women in sororities: 15%. **Sports program (2005-2006):** Member of NCAA II. *Men's intercollegiate varsity sports:* basketball, cross-country, football, ice hockey, tennis,

track and field (outdoor), skiing. *Women's intercollegiate varsity sports:* basketball, cross-country, tennis, track and field (outdoor), volleyball, skiing.

SERVICES AND FACILITIES

Basic services: nonremedial tutoring, placement service, day care, health service, health insurance, other. **Remedial assistance:** reading, math, writing, other. **Counseling services:** minority student, career, military, personal, veteran student, academic, older student, psychological, birth control, other. **For learning-disabled students:** School does not offer a structured program with separate admission and additional fees. Total undergraduates in learning-disabled program or receiving services: 30. Services include: reading machines, tape recorders, other special classes, untimed tests, note-taking services, oral tests, learning center, readers, extended time for tests, tutors. **Library:** Number of titles: 821,279; number of current serial subscriptions: 2,768. **Information technology resources:** Students are not required to lease or own a computer. Number of campus computers available to all students: 1,300. School has a wireless network. Approximate number of users that can be accommodated: 2,000. Proportion of college-owned housing units wired for high-speed internet access: 100%. **Campus safety:** Security services offered: 24-hour foot-and-vehicle patrols, late-night transport/escort service, 24-hour emergency telephones, lighted pathways/sidewalks, student patrols, controlled dormitory access (key, security card, etc).

TRANSFER AND INTERNATIONAL STUDENTS

Transfer students: May apply for admission for the following academic terms: Fall, Spring, Summer. Applicants do not need a minimum number of credits to apply. For fall 2005: Transfer applications received: 587. Transfer applicants offered admission: 337. Transfer applicants enrolled: 213. **International students:** Number of foreign undergraduates: 220 (4% of student body). Number of countries represented: 45. Minimum TOEFL score required: 500 (paper); 173 (computer). Average TOEFL score: 570 (paper).

Northern Michigan University

- **Address:** 1401 Presque Isle Avenue, Marquette, MI 49855
- **Website:** http://www.nmu.edu
- **Public**
- **Enrollment:** 7,841 full-time; 873 part-time

KEY STATS

✔ **U.S News College Ranking:** third tier, Universities–Master's (Midwest)
✔ **ACT Score (25th/75th percentile):** 20-25
✔ **Tuition:** 2005-2006: $5,958 in state, $10,232 out of state

Selectivity: Selective	Room/board: $6,482
Acceptance rate: 84%	Average debt: $16,842
Student/faculty ratio: 23/1	Proportion who borrowed: 67%

UNDERGRADUATE STUDENT BODY STATS

2005-2006 enrollment: 7,841 full-time; 873 part-time. Men: 47%; women: 53%. **Ethnic makeup:** African American: 2%; American-Indian: 2%; Asian American: 1%; Hispanic: 1%; White: 94%.

ADMISSIONS FACTS AND FIGURES

Phone: (906) 227-2650. **Email:** admiss@nmu.edu. **Website:** http://www.nmu.edu. **Application deadlines for fall 2007:** Regular decision: Rolling. Early decision: Not offered. Early action: Not offered. Admission can be deferred. **Application fee:** $30. Common application is accepted. **To apply online, go to:** http://www.nmu.edu/admissions1/admiss1.html. **Admissions requirements/recommendations:** High school units required (recommended): English: (4); Mathematics: (3); Science: (2); Foreign language: (3); Social studies: (2); History: (2); Total units: 12 (19). Tests: The college uses SAT or ACT scores in admissions decisions. Either SAT or ACT required. For admission to the fall 2007 entering class, the school will accept: ACT with writing, ACT without writing. Campus visit: Recommended. Admissions interview: Neither required nor recommended. Off-campus interview: May be arranged. **Factors that count in admissions decisions:** *Academic:* Secondary school record: Very important. Class rank: Considered. Letters of recommendation: Considered. Standardized test scores: Very important. Essay: Considered. *Nonacademic:* Interview: Considered. Extracurricular activities: Considered. Talent/ability: Considered. Character/personal qualities: Not considered. Alumni/ae relationship: Not considered. Geographical residence: Not considered. State residency: Not considered. Religious affiliation/commitment: Not considered. Minority status: Not considered. Volunteer work: Considered. Work experience: Considered. **Other schools with the greatest overlap in applicants:** Central Michigan University; Lake Superior State University; Michigan State University; Michigan Technological University; Western Michigan University. **Admissions statistics for the fall 2005 entering class:** Total applicants: 4,772. Total accepted: 3,995. Freshmen enrolled: 1,399; 26% were from out of state. Overall acceptance rate: 84%. **First-year students submitting ACT scores:** 99%. Scores (25/75 percentile): English: 19-25, Math: 19-25, Composite: 20-25.

ACADEMICS

Year founded: 1899. **Academic calendar:** Semester. **Degrees offered:** certificate, diploma, associate, bachelor's, post-bachelor's certificate, master's. **Most popular majors:** 17% education, 16% business, management, marketing, and related support services, 8% health professions and related clinical sciences, 8% social sciences, 7% visual and performing arts. **Major fields of study:** agriculture, agriculture operations, and related sciences; architecture and related services; biological and biomedical sciences; business, management, marketing, and related support services; communication, journalism, and related programs; computer and information sciences and support services; education; engineering technologies/technicians; English language and literature/letters; family and consumer sciences/human sciences; foreign languages, literatures, and linguistics; health professions and related clinical sciences; history; liberal arts and sciences studies, and humanities; mathematics and statistics; natural resources and conservation; parks, recreation, leisure, and fitness studies; philosophy and religious studies; physical sciences; psychology; public administration and social service professions; security and protective services; social sciences; visual and performing arts. **Areas of required coursework:** arts/fine arts, humanities, computer literacy, mathematics, English (including composition), sciences (biological or physical), social science, other. **Pre-professional programs:** pre-law, pre-dentistry, pre-medicine, pre-veterinary science, pre-optometry, pre-pharmacy. **Special academic programs:** distance learning, double major, dual enrollment, exchange student program (domestic), honors program, independent study, internships, liberal arts/career combination, student-designed major, study abroad, teacher certificate program, weekend college, other. **Teacher certification offered in:** special education, elementary, middle/junior high, secondary, bilingual/bicultural. **Reserve Officers Training Corps (ROTC):** Army ROTC: Offered on campus. **Faculty and instruction (2005-2006):** Total instructional faculty: 305 full-time, 125 part-time. Full-time faculty with Ph.D. or other terminal degree: 65%. Student/faculty ratio: 23/1. Classes of fewer than 20 students: 37%; of 20 to 49 students: 54%; of 50 or more students: 9%. **Advanced Placement and International Baccalaureate credit:** AP tests may be used for: Credit only. Scores accepted: 3, 4. International Baccalaureate exams may be used for: Credit only. **Freshmen returning for sophomore year:** 73%. **Graduation rates:** Four-year: 14%; five-year: 37%; six-year: 45%. **Graduate study:** 19% of students pursue further study immediately upon graduation. Fields in which graduates pursue further study: Master of Business Administration (MBA), 1%; law, 3%; medicine, 4%; dentistry, 1%; engineering, 1%; theology (or the seminary), 1%; education, 3%.

COSTS AND FINANCIAL AID

Financial aid office: (906) 227-2327. **Expenses (2005-2006):** Tuition and fees 2005-2006: $5,958 in state, $10,232 out of state; room/board: $6,482. Estimated books and supplies: $645; transportation: $688; personal expenses: $979. **Financial aid:** Priority filing date for institution's financial aid form: February 20. In 2005-2006, 91% of undergraduates applied for financial aid. Of those, 63% were determined to have financial need; 23% had their need fully met. Average financial aid package (proportion receiving): $6,935 (61%). Average amount of gift aid, such as scholarships or grants (proportion receiving): $3,504 (41%). Average amount of self-help aid, such as work study or loans (proportion receiving): $4,033 (48%). Average need-based loan (excluding PLUS or other private loans): $3,602. Among students who received need-based aid, the average percentage of need met: 71%. Among students who received aid based on merit, the average award (and the proportion receiving): $2,670 (10%). The average athletic scholarship (and the proportion receiving): $8,804 (2%). Average amount of debt of borrowers graduating in 2005: $16,842. Proportion who borrowed: 67%.

CAMPUS LIFE AND EXTRACURRICULAR ACTIVITIES

Campus housing available: coed dorms, apartments for married students, apartment for single students, special housing for disabled students. Students who live in college-owned, operated, or affiliated housing: 34%. Average per-year earnings: $3,500. **Clubs and organizations:** Number of student organizations: 201. Activities include: choral groups, concert band, dance, drama/theater, jazz band, literary magazine, marching band, music ensembles, musical theater, opera, pep band, radio station, student government, student newspaper, student film society, symphony orchestra, television station. Number of fraternities: 3; sororities: 2. Proportion of men in fraternities: 2%; of women in sororities: 2%. Average proportion of students who stay on campus on weekends: 75%. **Sports program (2005-2006):** Member of NCAA II. *Men's intercollegiate varsity sports:* basketball, football, golf, ice hockey, skiing. *Women's intercollegiate varsity sports:* basketball, cross-country, skiing, soccer, swimming and diving, track and field (indoor), track and field (outdoor), volleyball.

SERVICES AND FACILITIES

Basic services: nonremedial tutoring, placement service, health service. **Remedial assistance:** reading, math, writing, study skills. **Counseling services:** minority student, career, military, personal, veteran student, academic, older student, psychological, birth control, religious. **For learning-disabled students:** School does not offer a structured program with separate admission and additional fees. Services include: note-taking services, oral tests, learning center, readers, extended time for tests, tutors, texts on tape, typist/scribe, exams on tape or computer, other testing accomodations, other. **Library:** Number of titles: 615,406; number of current serial subscriptions: 4,573. **Information technology resources:** Students are required to lease or own a computer. Number of campus computers available to all students: 9,000. School has a wireless network. Proportion of college-owned housing units wired for high-speed internet access: 100%. **Campus safety:** Security services offered: 24-hour foot-and-vehicle patrols, late-night transport/escort service, 24-hour emergency telephones, lighted pathways/sidewalks, controlled dormitory access (key, security card, etc).

TRANSFER AND INTERNATIONAL STUDENTS

Transfer students: May apply for admission for the following academic terms: Fall, Winter, Summer. Applicants need a minimum number of credits to apply. For fall 2005: Transfer applications received: 1,127. Transfer applicants offered admission: 752. Transfer applicants enrolled: 514. **International students:** Number of foreign undergraduates: 33. Minimum TOEFL score required: 500 (paper); 173 (computer).

Northwood University

- **Address:** 4000 Whiting Drive, Midland, MI 48640
- **Website:** http://www.northwood.edu
- **Private**
- **Enrollment:** 2,587 full-time; 990 part-time

KEY STATS

✔ **U.S News College Ranking:** Unranked Specialty School–Business
✔ **ACT Score (25th/75th percentile):** 18-23
✔ **Tuition:** 2006-2007: $15,801

Selectivity: Selective	**Room/board:** $6,942
Acceptance rate: 85%	**Average debt:** $18,389
Student/faculty ratio: 34/1	**Proportion who borrowed:** 57%

UNDERGRADUATE STUDENT BODY STATS

2005-2006 enrollment: 2,587 full-time; 990 part-time. Men: 55%; women: 45%. **Ethnic makeup:** African American: 13%; Asian American: 2%; Hispanic: 2%; White: 74%; International: 9%.

ADMISSIONS FACTS AND FIGURES

Phone: (989) 837-4273. **Email:** admissions@northwood.edu. **Website:** http://www.northwood.edu. **Application deadlines for fall 2007:** Regular decision: Rolling. Early decision: Not offered. Early action: Not offered. Admission can be deferred. **Application fee:** $25. Common application is accepted. **To apply online, go to:** https://www.northwood.edu/forms/undergraduate/admission1.asp. **Admissions requirements/recommendations:** High school units required (recommended): English: (4); Mathematics: (3); Science: (2); Foreign language: (3); Social studies: (3); Total units: (16). Tests: The college uses SAT or ACT scores in admissions decisions. Either SAT or ACT required. For admission to the fall 2007 entering class, the school will accept: ACT with writing, ACT without writing. Campus visit: Recommended. Admissions interview: Recommended. Off-campus interview: May be arranged. **Factors that count in admissions decisions:**

Academic: Secondary school record: Very important. Class rank: Important. Letters of recommendation: Considered. Standardized test scores: Very important. Essay: Important. **Nonacademic:** Interview: Considered. Extracurricular activities: Considered. Talent/ability: Not considered. Character/personal qualities: Considered. Alumni/ae relationship: Considered. Geographical residence: Not considered. State residency: Not considered. Religious affiliation/commitment: Not considered. Minority status: Not considered. Volunteer work: Not considered. Work experience: Not considered. **Admissions statistics for the fall 2005 entering class:** Total applicants: 1,638. Total accepted: 1,391. Freshmen enrolled: 505; 15% were from out of state. Overall acceptance rate: 85%. **Credentials of fall 2005 freshmen:** 7% ranked in the top 10 percent of their high school class; 24% were in the top 25 percent, and 51% were in the top half. (Proportion submitting class standing: 47%.) Average high school grade point average: 3.0. First-year students who submitted SAT scores: 13%. Scores (25/75 percentile): Verbal: 420-523, Math: 440-533, Combined: 860-1056. First-year students submitting ACT scores: 93%. Scores (25/75 percentile): English: 16-22, Math: 17-23, Composite: 18-23.

ACADEMICS

Year founded: 1959. **Academic calendar:** Quarter. **Degrees offered:** associate, transfer-associate, terminal-associate, bachelor's, master's. **Most popular majors:** 22% marketing/marketing management, 14% vehicle and vehicle parts and accessories marketing operations, 13% business administration and management, 10% sport and fitness administration/management, 8% international business/trade/commerce. **Major fields of study:** business, management, marketing, and related support services; communication, journalism, and related programs; computer and information sciences and support services; parks, recreation, leisure, and fitness studies. **Areas of required coursework:** humanities, computer literacy, mathematics, English (including composition), philosophy, sciences (biological or physical), social science. **Special academic programs:** accelerated program, distance learning, double major, dual enrollment, English as a Second Language (ESL), external degree program, honors program, independent study, internships, study abroad, weekend college. **Cooperative education programs:** business. **Faculty and instruction (2005-2006):** Total instructional faculty: 52 full-time, 39 part-time (65% men; 35% women; 9% minorities). Full-time faculty with Ph.D. or other terminal degree: 37%. Student/faculty ratio: 34/1. Classes of fewer than 20 students: 34%; of 20 to 49 students: 62%; of 50 or more students: 4%. **Advanced Placement and International Baccalaureate credit:** AP tests may be used for: Credit and/or placement. Scores accepted: 3, 4, 5. International Baccalaureate exams may be used for: Credit and/or placement. **Freshmen returning for sophomore year:** 74%. **Graduation rates:** Four-year: 39%; five-year: 49%; six-year: 52%. **Graduate study:** 6% of students pursue further study immediately upon graduation. Fields in which graduates pursue further study: Master of Business Administration (MBA), 51%; law, 25%; education, 8%; arts and sciences, 16%.

COSTS AND FINANCIAL AID

Financial aid office: (989) 837-4230. **Expenses (2006-2007):** Tuition and fees 2006-2007: $15,801; room/board: $6,942. Estimated books and supplies: $1,356; transportation: $651; personal expenses: $1,485. **Financial aid:** In 2005-2006, 69% of undergraduates applied for financial aid. Of those, 58% were determined to have financial need; 27% had their need fully met. Average financial aid package (proportion receiving): $13,063 (58%). Average amount of gift aid, such as scholarships or grants (proportion receiving): $5,201 (51%). Average amount of self-help aid, such as work study or loans (proportion receiving): $3,973 (50%). Average need-based loan (excluding PLUS or other private loans): $3,590. Among students who received need-based aid, the average percentage of need met: 92%. Among students who received aid based on merit, the average award (and the proportion receiving): $4,884 (27%). The average athletic scholarship (and the proportion receiving): $9,818 (6%). Average amount of debt of borrowers graduating in 2005: $18,389. Proportion who borrowed: 57%.

CAMPUS LIFE AND EXTRACURRICULAR ACTIVITIES

Campus housing available (% using): women's dorms (22%), men's dorms (37%), apartment for single students (41%). Students who live in college-owned, operated, or affiliated housing: 40%. **Student employment:** During the 2005-2006 academic year, 12% of undergraduates worked on campus. Average per-year earnings: $1,500. **Clubs and organizations:** Number of student organizations: 34. Activities include: choral groups, dance, drama/theater, jazz band, student government, student newspaper, yearbook. Number of fraternities: 11; sororities: 5. Proportion of men in fraternities: 20%; of women in sororities: 15%. Average proportion of students who stay on campus on weekends: 40%. **Sports program (2005-2006):** Member of NCAA II.

Men's intercollegiate varsity sports: baseball, basketball, cross-country, football, golf, soccer, tennis, track and field (indoor), track and field (outdoor). **Women's intercollegiate varsity sports:** basketball, cross-country, golf, soccer, softball, tennis, track and field (indoor), track and field (outdoor), volleyball.

SERVICES AND FACILITIES

Basic services: nonremedial tutoring, placement service, health service. **Remedial assistance:** reading, math, writing, study skills. **Counseling services:** career, personal, academic, psychological. **For learning-disabled students:** School does not offer a structured program with separate admission and additional fees. Total undergraduates in learning-disabled program or receiving services: 79. Services include: remedial math, remedial English, reading machines, untimed tests, oral tests, learning center, extended time for tests, tutors, priority registration. **Library:** Number of titles: 40,006; number of current serial subscriptions: 334. **Information technology resources:** Students are not required to lease or own a computer. Number of campus computers available to all students: 215. School has a wireless network. Approximate number of users that can be accommodated: 5,000. Proportion of college-owned housing units wired for high-speed internet access: 100%. **Campus safety:** Security services offered: 24-hour foot-and-vehicle patrols, late-night transport/escort service, 24-hour emergency telephones, lighted pathways/sidewalks, student patrols, controlled dormitory access (key, security card, etc.).

TRANSFER AND INTERNATIONAL STUDENTS

Transfer students: May apply for admission for the following academic terms: Fall, Winter, Spring, Summer. Applicants do not need a minimum number of credits to apply. For fall 2005: Transfer applications received: 404. Transfer applicants offered admission: 348. Transfer applicants enrolled: 245. **International students:** Number of foreign undergraduates: 179 (9% of student body). Number of countries represented: 31. Minimum TOEFL score required: 500 (paper); 173 (computer). Average TOEFL score: 550 (paper).

Oakland University

- **Address:** Rochester, MI 48309-4401
- **Website:** http://www.oakland.edu
- **Public**
- **Enrollment:** 9,760 full-time; 3,688 part-time

KEY STATS

✔ **U.S News College Ranking:** fourth tier, National Universities
✔ **ACT Score (25th/75th percentile):** 19-24
✔ **Tuition:** N/A

Selectivity: Selective	**Room/board:** N/A
Acceptance rate: 82%	**Average debt:** N/A
Student/faculty ratio: 23/1	**Proportion who borrowed:** N/A

UNDERGRADUATE STUDENT BODY STATS

2005-2006 enrollment: 9,760 full-time; 3,688 part-time. Men: 38%; women: 62%. **Ethnic makeup:** African American: 9%; Asian American: 4%; Hispanic: 2%; White: 84%; International: 1%.

ADMISSIONS FACTS AND FIGURES

Phone: (248) 370-3360. **Email:** ouinfo@oakland.edu. **Website:** http://www.oakland.edu. **Application deadlines for fall 2007:** Regular decision: Rolling. Early decision: Not offered. Early action: Not offered. Admission can be deferred. **Application fee:** $40. Common application is not accepted. **To apply online, go to:** http://www.oakland.edu/admissions/index.html. **Admissions requirements/recommendations:** High school units required (recommended): English: 4; Mathematics: 3; Science: 3; Foreign language: (2); Social studies: 3. Tests: The college does not use SAT or ACT scores in admissions decisions. Neither SAT nor ACT required. For admission to the fall 2007 entering class, the school will accept: ACT with writing, ACT without writing. Campus visit: Recommended. Admissions interview: Neither required nor recommended. Off-campus interview: May be arranged. **Factors that count in admissions decisions:** *Academic:* Secondary school record: Very important. Class rank: Very important. Letters of recommendation: Important. Standardized test scores: Not considered. Essay: Considered. *Nonacademic:* Interview: Considered. Extracurricular activities: Important. Talent/ability: Important.

Character/personal qualities: Important. Alumni/ae relationship: Considered. Geographical residence: Not considered. State residency: Not considered. Religious affiliation/commitment: Not considered. Minority status: Not considered. Volunteer work: Important. Work experience: Considered. **Other schools with the greatest overlap in applicants:** Central Michigan University; Michigan State University; University of Michigan–Ann Arbor; Wayne State University; Western Michigan University. **Admissions statistics for the fall 2005 entering class:** Total applicants: 5,948. Total accepted: 4,890. Freshmen enrolled: 2,213; 1% were from out of state. Overall acceptance rate: 82%. **Credentials of fall 2005 freshmen:** 39% were in the top 25 percent, and 86% were in the top half. (Proportion submitting class standing: 80%.) **Average high school grade point average:** 3.2. **First-year students submitting ACT scores:** 91%. Scores (25/75 percentile): English: 18-24, Math: 18-24, Composite: 19-24.

ACADEMICS

Year founded: 1957. **Academic calendar:** Semester. **Degrees offered:** bachelor's, post-bachelor's certificate, master's, post-master's certificate, doctorate. **Most popular majors:** 22% business, management, marketing, and related support services, 15% education, 10% communication, journalism, and related programs, 8% health professions and related clinical sciences, 7% engineering. **Major fields of study:** area, ethnic, cultural, and gender studies; biological and biomedical sciences; business, management, marketing, and related support services; communication, journalism, and related programs; computer and information sciences and support services; education; engineering; English language and literature/letters; foreign languages, literatures, and linguistics; health professions and related clinical sciences; history; liberal arts and sciences studies, and humanities; mathematics and statistics; philosophy and religious studies; physical sciences; psychology; public administration and social service professions; social sciences; visual and performing arts. **Areas of required coursework:** arts/fine arts, humanities, computer literacy, mathematics, English (including composition), philosophy, foreign languages, sciences (biological or physical), history, social science, other. **Pre-professional programs:** pre-law, pre-dentistry, pre-medicine, pre-veterinary science, pre-optometry. **Special academic programs:** accelerated program, cooperative (work-study plan) program, distance learning, double major, English as a Second Language (ESL), honors program, independent study, internships, student-designed major, study abroad, teacher certificate program. **Teacher certification offered in:** early childhood, special education, elementary, secondary. **Cooperative education programs:** business, computer science, engineering. **Reserve Officers Training Corps (ROTC):** Air Force ROTC: Offered at cooperating institution (University of Michigan–Ann Arbor). **Faculty and instruction (2005-2006):** Total instructional faculty: 449 full-time, 441 part-time (52% men; 48% women; 18% minorities). Full-time faculty with Ph.D. or other terminal degree: 92%. Student/faculty ratio: 23/1. Classes of fewer than 20 students: 31%; of 20 to 49 students: 52%; of 50 or more students: 17%. **Advanced Placement and International Baccalaureate credit:** AP tests may be used for: Credit and/or placement. Scores accepted: 3, 4, 5. International Baccalaureate exams may be used for: Credit and/or placement. **Freshmen returning for sophomore year:** 72%. **Graduation rates:** Four-year: 13%; five-year: 36%; six-year: 45%. **Graduate study:** 19% of students pursue further study immediately upon graduation. Fields in which graduates pursue further study: Master of Business Administration (MBA), 16%; law, 6%; medicine, 4%; dentistry, 1%; engineering, 16%; education, 16%; arts and sciences, 16%; veterinary medicine, 1%.

COSTS AND FINANCIAL AID

Financial aid office: (248) 370-2550. **Financial aid:** Priority filing date for institution's financial aid form: February 15.

CAMPUS LIFE AND EXTRACURRICULAR ACTIVITIES

Campus housing available: coed dorms, sorority housing, apartments for married students, apartment for single students, special housing for disabled students, other housing options. Students who live in college-owned, operated, or affiliated housing: 13%. **Clubs and organizations:** Number of student organizations: 140. Activities include: choral groups, concert band, dance, drama/theater, jazz band, literary magazine, music ensembles, musical theater, pep band, radio station, student government, student newspaper, student film society, symphony orchestra, television station. Number of fraternities: 3; sororities: 7. Proportion of men in fraternities: 1%; of women in sororities: 1%. Average proportion of students who stay on campus on weekends: 20%. **Sports program (2005-2006):** Member of NCAA I. *Men's intercollegiate varsity sports:* baseball, basketball, cross-country, golf, soccer, swimming and diving, track and field (outdoor). *Women's intercollegiate*

varsity sports: basketball, cross-country, golf, soccer, softball, swimming and diving, tennis, track and field (outdoor), volleyball.

SERVICES AND FACILITIES

Basic services: nonremedial tutoring, placement service, day care, health service. **Remedial assistance:** reading, math, writing, study skills. **Counseling services:** minority student, career, personal, veteran student, academic, older student, psychological, birth control. **For learning-disabled students:** School does not offer a structured program with separate admission and additional fees. Total undergraduates in learning-disabled program or receiving services: 200. Services include: remedial math, remedial English, reading machines, tape recorders, videotaped classes, diagnostic testing service, note-taking services, learning center, readers, extended time for tests, tutors, priority registration, priority seating, texts on tape, other. **Library:** Number of titles: 893,335; number of current serial subscriptions: 11,896. **Information technology resources:** Students are not required to lease or own a computer. Number of campus computers available to all students: 713. School has a wireless network. **Campus safety:** Security services offered: 24-hour foot-and-vehicle patrols, late-night transport/escort service, 24-hour emergency telephones, lighted pathways/sidewalks, student patrols, controlled dormitory access (key, security card, etc).

TRANSFER AND INTERNATIONAL STUDENTS

Transfer students: May apply for admission for the following academic terms: Fall, Winter, Spring, Summer. Applicants need a minimum number of credits to apply. For fall 2005: Transfer applications received: 2,478. Transfer applicants offered admission: 1,823. Transfer applicants enrolled: 1,350. **International students:** Number of foreign undergraduates: 109 (1% of student body). Number of countries represented: 48. Minimum TOEFL score required: 550 (paper); 213 (computer). Average TOEFL score: 570 (paper).

Olivet College

- **Address:** 320 S. Main Street, Olivet, MI 49076
- **Website:** http://www.olivetcollege.edu
- **Private; Religious affiliation:** Congregational Christian Church/United Church of Christ
- **Enrollment:** 1,016 full-time; 65 part-time

KEY STATS
- ✔ **U.S News College Ranking:** fourth tier, Liberal Arts Colleges
- ✔ **ACT Score (25th/75th percentile):** 19-25
- ✔ **Tuition:** 2006-2007: $17,584

Selectivity: Selective	**Room/board:** $6,060
Acceptance rate: 53%	**Average debt:** $23,606
Student/faculty ratio: 20/1	**Proportion who borrowed:** 94%

UNDERGRADUATE STUDENT BODY STATS

2005-2006 enrollment: 1,016 full-time; 65 part-time. Men: 56%; women: 44%. **Ethnic makeup:** African American: 14%; American-Indian: 1%; Asian American: 1%; Hispanic: 2%; White: 79%; International: 3%.

ADMISSIONS FACTS AND FIGURES

Phone: (269) 749-7635. **Email:** admissions@olivetcollege.edu. **Website:** http://www.olivetcollege.edu. **Application deadlines for fall 2007:** Regular decision: August 19. Early decision: Not offered. Early action: Not offered. Admission can be deferred. **Application fee:** $25. Common application is not accepted. To apply online, go to: http://www.olivetcollege.edu/enrollment/admissions.htm. **Admissions requirements/recommendations:** High school units required (recommended): English: 3 (3); Mathematics: 3 (3); Science: 2 (2); Foreign language: 0 (0); Social studies: 2 (2); History: 2 (2); Academic electives: 0 (0); Total units: 13 (13). Tests: The college uses SAT or ACT scores in admissions decisions. Either SAT or ACT required. For admission to the fall 2007 entering class, the school will accept: ACT with writing, ACT without writing. Campus visit: Recommended. Admissions interview: Recommended. Off-campus interview: May be arranged. **Factors that count in admissions decisions:** *Academic:* Secondary school record: Important. Class rank: Considered. Letters of recommendation: Important. Standardized test scores: Considered. Essay: Not considered. *Nonacademic:* Interview: Important. Extracurricular activities: Very important. Talent/ability: Considered. Character/personal qualities: Important. Alumni/ae relationship: Considered. Geographical residence: Not considered. State residency: Not considered. Religious affiliation/commitment: Not considered. Minority status: Important. Volunteer work: Very important. Work experience: Important. **Other schools with the greatest overlap in applicants:** Albion College; Alma College; Calvin College; Hope College; Kalamazoo College. **Admissions statistics for the fall 2005 entering class:** Total applicants: 1,037. Total accepted: 546. Freshmen enrolled: 260; Overall acceptance rate: 53%. **Credentials of fall 2005 freshmen:** 16% ranked in the top 10 percent of their high school class; 22% were in the top 25 percent, and 84% were in the top half. (Proportion submitting class standing: 100%.) **Average high school grade point average:** 3.0. **First-year students who submitted SAT scores:** 2%. Scores (25/75 percentile): Verbal: 515-589, Math: 505-582, Combined: 1020-1171. **First-year students submitting ACT scores:** 98%. Scores (25/75 percentile): English: 18-24, Math: 18-22, Composite: 19-25.

ACADEMICS

Year founded: 1844. **Academic calendar:** Semester. **Degrees offered:** certificate, bachelor's, master's. **Most popular majors:** 15% business administration and management, 12% education, 11% health and physical education, 8% psychology, 8% social sciences. **Major fields of study:** biological and biomedical sciences; business, management, marketing, and related support services; communication, journalism, and related programs; computer and information sciences and support services; education; English language and literature/letters; history; liberal arts and sciences studies, and humanities; mathematics and statistics; multi/interdisciplinary studies; natural resources and conservation; parks, recreation, leisure, and fitness studies; physical sciences; psychology; security and protective services; social sciences; visual and performing arts. **Areas of required coursework:** arts/fine arts, humanities, mathematics, English (including composition), sciences (biological or physical), history. **Pre-professional programs:** pre-law, pre-dentistry, pre-medicine, pre-veterinary science. **Special academic programs (% participation):** cooperative (work-study plan) program (15%), double major (9%), dual enrollment (0%), honors program (0%), independent study (63%), internships (15%), student-designed major (2%), teacher certificate program (13%). **Teacher certification offered in:** elementary, secondary. **Cooperative education programs:** business, education, natural science, social/behavioral science. **Faculty and instruction (2005-2006):** Total instructional faculty: 33 full-time, 62 part-time (51% men; 49% women; 12% minorities). Full-time faculty with Ph.D. or other terminal degree: 64%. Student/faculty ratio: 20/1. Classes of fewer than 20 students: 52%; of 20 to 49 students: 46%; of 50 or more students: 2%. **Advanced Placement and International Baccalaureate credit:** AP tests may be used for: Credit and/or placement. International Baccalaureate exams may be used for: Credit and/or placement. **Freshmen returning for sophomore year:** 63%. **Graduation rates:** Four-year: 34%; five-year: 38%; six-year: 38%.

COSTS AND FINANCIAL AID

Financial aid office: (269) 749-7102. **Expenses (2006-2007):** Tuition and fees 2006-2007: $17,584; room/board: $6,060. Estimated books and supplies: $900; transportation: $776; personal expenses: $1,000. **Financial aid:** Priority filing date for institution's financial aid form: March 1. In 2005-2006, 89% of undergraduates applied for financial aid. Of those, 83% were determined to have financial need; 18% had their need fully met. Average financial aid package (proportion receiving): $14,121 (83%). Average amount of gift aid, such as scholarships or grants (proportion receiving): $9,990 (83%). Average amount of self-help aid, such as work study or loans (proportion receiving): $4,696 (73%). Average need-based loan (excluding PLUS or other private loans): $3,857. Among students who received need-based aid, the average percentage of need met: 75%. Among students who received aid based on merit, the average award (and the proportion receiving): $10,830 (12%). The average athletic scholarship (and the proportion receiving): $0 (0%). Average amount of debt of borrowers graduating in 2005: $23,606. Proportion who borrowed: 94%.

CAMPUS LIFE AND EXTRACURRICULAR ACTIVITIES

Campus housing available (% using): coed dorms (48%), women's dorms (18%), men's dorms (24%), sorority housing (2%), fraternity housing (5%), apartments for married students (1%), special housing for international students (1%), other housing options (1%). Students who live in college-owned, operated, or affiliated housing: 64%. **Student employment:** During the 2005-2006 academic year, 28% of undergraduates worked on campus. Average per-year earnings: $1,600. **Clubs and organizations:** Number of student organizations: 40. Activities include: choral groups, concert band, drama/theater, jazz band, literary magazine, marching band, music ensembles, musical theater, radio station, student government, student newspaper, yearbook. Number of fraternities: 6; sororities: 5. Proportion of

men in fraternities: 27%; of women in sororities: 17%. Average proportion of students who stay on campus on weekends: 25%. **Sports program (2005-2006):** Member of NCAA III. ***Men's intercollegiate varsity sports:*** baseball, basketball, cross-country, football, golf, soccer, swimming and diving, track and field (indoor), track and field (outdoor), wrestling. ***Women's intercollegiate varsity sports:*** basketball, cross-country, golf, soccer, softball, swimming and diving, tennis, track and field (indoor), track and field (outdoor), volleyball.

SERVICES AND FACILITIES

Basic services: nonremedial tutoring, women's center, placement service, health service, health insurance, other. **Remedial assistance:** reading, writing, other. **Counseling services:** minority student, career, personal, academic, older student, psychological, birth control, religious. **For learning-disabled students:** School does not offer a structured program with separate admission and additional fees. Total undergraduates in learning-disabled program or receiving services: 19. Services include: remedial English, tape recorders, untimed tests, note-taking services, oral tests, readers, extended time for tests, tutors, priority seating, other. **Library:** Number of titles: 111,418; number of current serial subscriptions: 450. **Information technology resources:** Students are not required to lease or own a computer. Number of campus computers available to all students: 105. School has a wireless network. Approximate number of users that can be accommodated: 1,536. Proportion of college-owned housing units wired for high-speed internet access: 100%. **Campus safety:** Security services offered: 24-hour foot-and-vehicle patrols, late-night transport/escort service, 24-hour emergency telephones, lighted pathways/sidewalks, student patrols, controlled dormitory access (key, security card, etc).

TRANSFER AND INTERNATIONAL STUDENTS

Transfer students: May apply for admission for the following academic terms: Fall, Spring, Summer. Applicants do not need a minimum number of credits to apply. For fall 2005: Transfer applicants enrolled: 86. **International students:** Number of foreign undergraduates: 26 (3% of student body). Number of countries represented: 16. Minimum TOEFL score required: 500 (paper); 200 (computer). Average TOEFL score: 570 (paper).

Rochester College

- **Address:** 800 W. Avon Road, Rochester Hills, MI 48307
- **Website:** http://www.rc.edu
- **Private; Religious affiliation:** Church of Christ
- **Enrollment:** 674 full-time; 375 part-time

KEY STATS

✔ **U.S News College Ranking:** third tier, Comp. Coll.–Bachelor's (Midwest)
✔ **ACT Score (25th/75th percentile):** 18-24
✔ **Tuition:** 2006-2007: $12,548

Selectivity: Selective	Room/board: $6,820
Acceptance rate: 87%	Average debt: N/A
Student/faculty ratio: 8/1	Proportion who borrowed: N/A

UNDERGRADUATE STUDENT BODY STATS

2005-2006 enrollment: 674 full-time; 375 part-time. Men: 39%; women: 61%. **Ethnic makeup:** African American: 18%; American-Indian: 1%; Asian American: 1%; Hispanic: 1%; White: 78%; International: 1%. **Religious preference:** Roman Catholic: 11%; Protestant: 57%; Church of Christ: 19%; Other: 13%.

ADMISSIONS FACTS AND FIGURES

Phone: (248) 218-2031. **Email:** admissions@rc.edu. **Website:** http://www.rc.edu. **Application deadlines for fall 2007:** Regular decision: Rolling. Early decision: Not offered. Early action: Not offered. Admission can be deferred. **Application fee:** $25. Common application is not accepted. **Admissions requirements/recommendations:** Tests: The college uses SAT or ACT scores in admissions decisions. Either SAT or ACT required. For admission to the fall 2007 entering class, the school will accept: ACT with writing, ACT without writing. Campus visit: Recommended. Admissions interview: Neither required nor recommended. Off-campus interview: Not available. **Factors that count in admissions decisions:** *Academic:* Secondary school record: Important. Class rank: Considered. Letters of recommendation: Considered. Standardized test scores: Very important. Essay:

Considered. *Nonacademic:* Interview: Very important. Extracurricular activities: Not considered. Talent/ability: Considered. Character/personal qualities: Important. Alumni/ae relationship: Not considered. Geographical residence: Not considered. State residency: Not considered. Religious affiliation/commitment: Not considered. Minority status: Not considered. Volunteer work: Not considered. Work experience: Not considered. **Other schools with the greatest overlap in applicants:** Harding University; Lipscomb University; Madonna University; Oakland University. **Admissions statistics for the fall 2005 entering class:** Total applicants: 351. Total accepted: 305. Freshmen enrolled: 137; 11% were from out of state. Overall acceptance rate: 87%. **Credentials of fall 2005 freshmen:** 11% ranked in the top 10 percent of their high school class; 28% were in the top 25 percent, and 55% were in the top half. (Proportion submitting class standing: 80%.) **Average high school grade point average:** 3.0. **First-year students who submitted SAT scores:** 9%. Scores (25/75 percentile): Verbal: 470-680, Math: 360-590, Combined: 830-1270. **First-year students submitting ACT scores:** 89%. Scores (25/75 percentile): English: 17-25, Math: 17-24, Composite: 18-24.

ACADEMICS

Year founded: 1959. **Academic calendar:** Semester. **Degrees offered:** associate, bachelor's, master's. **Most popular majors:** 17% business, management, marketing, and related support services, 17% early childhood education and teaching, 15% counseling psychology, 12% business administration and management, 6% computer/information technology services administration and management. **Major fields of study:** business, management, marketing, and related support services; communication, journalism, and related programs; education; English language and literature/letters; history; multi/interdisciplinary studies; psychology; theology and religious vocations; visual and performing arts. **Areas of required coursework:** arts/fine arts, humanities, mathematics, English (including composition), philosophy, sciences (biological or physical), history, social science. **Pre-professional programs:** pre-law, pre-medicine, pre-theology. **Special academic programs (% participation):** accelerated program (73%), cross-registration (10%), distance learning (60%), double major (0%), honors program (1%), independent study (2%), internships (19%), liberal arts/career combination (3%), student-designed major (1%), study abroad (4%), teacher certificate program (2%). **Teacher certification offered in:** elementary, middle/junior high, secondary. **Faculty and instruction (2005-2006):** Total instructional faculty: 37 full-time, 90 part-time (47% men; 53% women; 1% minorities). Full-time faculty with Ph.D. or other terminal degree: 41%. Student/faculty ratio: 8/1. Classes of fewer than 20 students: 80%; of 20 to 49 students: 19%; of 50 or more students: 1%. **Advanced Placement and International Baccalaureate credit:** AP tests may be used for: Credit only. Scores accepted: 3, 4, 5. International Baccalaureate exams may be used for: Credit only. **Freshmen returning for sophomore year:** 60%. **Graduation rates:** Four-year: 13%; five-year: 26%; six-year: 28%. **Graduate study:** 5% of students pursue further study immediately upon graduation; 10% within one year; 25% within five years. Fields in which graduates pursue further study: Master of Business Administration (MBA), 10%; law, 5%; theology (or the seminary), 60%; education, 10%; arts and sciences, 15%.

COSTS AND FINANCIAL AID

Financial aid office: (248) 218-2028. **Expenses (2006-2007):** Tuition and fees 2006-2007: $12,548; room/board: $6,820. Estimated books and supplies: $1,422; transportation: $690. **Financial aid:** Priority filing date for institution's financial aid form: April 1; deadline: July 1. In 2005-2006, 57% of undergraduates applied for financial aid. Of those, 49% were determined to have financial need; Average financial aid package (proportion receiving): $4,635 (49%). Average amount of gift aid, such as scholarships or grants (proportion receiving): $2,033 (36%). Average amount of self-help aid, such as work study or loans (proportion receiving): $1,885 (37%). Average need-based loan (excluding PLUS or other private loans): $1,716. Among students who received aid based on merit, the average award (and the proportion receiving): $2,234 (14%). The average athletic scholarship (and the proportion receiving): $1,142 (11%).

CAMPUS LIFE AND EXTRACURRICULAR ACTIVITIES

Campus housing available (% using): women's dorms (50%), men's dorms (45%), apartments for married students (4%), apartment for single students (1%). Students who live in college-owned, operated, or affiliated housing: 24%. **Student employment:** During the 2005-2006 academic year, 22% of undergraduates worked on campus. Average per-year earnings: $2,000. **Clubs and organizations:** Number of student organizations: 20. Activities include: choral groups, concert band, dance, drama/theater, jazz band, music ensembles, musical theater, opera, student government, student newspaper, yearbook. Number of fraternities: 3; sororities: 3. Proportion of

men in fraternities: 10%; of women in sororities: 10%. Average proportion of students who stay on campus on weekends: 40%. **Sports program (2005-2006):** Member of NAIA.

SERVICES AND FACILITIES

Basic services: nonremedial tutoring, health insurance. **Remedial assistance:** reading, math, writing, study skills. **Counseling services:** career, personal, academic, psychological, religious. **For learning-disabled students:** School does not offer a structured program with separate admission and additional fees. Total undergraduates in learning-disabled program or receiving services: 21. Services include: reading machines, tape recorders, untimed tests, note-taking services, oral tests, extended time for tests, tutors, priority seating, texts on tape. **Library:** Number of titles: 45,997; number of current serial subscriptions: 202. **Information technology resources:** Students are not required to lease or own a computer. Number of campus computers available to all students: 73. School has a wireless network. Approximate number of users that can be accommodated: 400. Proportion of college-owned housing units wired for high-speed internet access: 100%. **Campus safety:** Security services offered: 24-hour emergency telephones, lighted pathways/sidewalks, controlled dormitory access (key, security card, etc).

TRANSFER AND INTERNATIONAL STUDENTS

Transfer students: May apply for admission for the following academic terms: Fall, Spring. Applicants need a minimum number of credits to apply. For fall 2005: Transfer applications received: 80. Transfer applicants offered admission: 71. Transfer applicants enrolled: 48. **International students:** Number of foreign undergraduates: 14 (1% of student body). Number of countries represented: 8. Minimum TOEFL score required: 500 (paper); 173 (computer). Average TOEFL score: 520 (paper).

Saginaw Valley State University

- **Address:** 7400 Bay Road, University Center, MI 48710
- **Website:** http://www.svsu.edu
- **Public**
- **Enrollment:** 6,044 full-time; 1,885 part-time

KEY STATS

✔ **U.S News College Ranking:** fourth tier, Universities–Master's (Midwest)
✔ **ACT Score (25th/75th percentile):** 18-24
✔ **Tuition:** 2005-2006: $5,282 in state, $11,891 out of state

Selectivity: Selective	**Room/board:** $6,150
Acceptance rate: 89%	**Average debt:** N/A
Student/faculty ratio: 20/1	**Proportion who borrowed:** N/A

UNDERGRADUATE STUDENT BODY STATS

2005-2006 enrollment: 6,044 full-time; 1,885 part-time. Men: 40%; women: 60%. **Ethnic makeup:** African American: 7%; Asian American: 1%; Hispanic: 2%; White: 87%; International: 3%.

ADMISSIONS FACTS AND FIGURES

Phone: (989) 964-4200. **Email:** admissions@svsu.edu. **Website:** http://www.svsu.edu. **Application deadlines for fall 2007:** Regular decision: Rolling. Early decision: Not offered. Early action: Not offered. Admission can be deferred. **Application fee:** $25. Common application is not accepted. **To apply online, go to:** http://www.applyweb.com/aw?svsu. **Admissions requirements/recommendations:** High school units required (recommended): English: 4 (4); Mathematics: 3 (4); Science: 2 (4); Foreign language: (2); Social studies: 3 (4); Total units: 12 (19). Tests: The college uses SAT or ACT scores in admissions decisions. ACT required. For admission to the fall 2007 entering class, the school will accept: ACT with writing, ACT without writing. Campus visit: Recommended. Admissions interview: Neither required nor recommended. Off-campus interview: May be arranged. **Factors that count in admissions decisions:** *Academic:* Secondary school record: Very important. Class rank: Not considered. Letters of recommendation: Considered. Standardized test scores: Very important. Essay: Not considered. *Nonacademic:* Interview: Not considered. Extracurricular activities: Not considered. Talent/ability: Not considered. Character/personal qualities: Not considered. Alumni/ae relationship: Not considered. Geographical residence: Not considered. State residency: Not considered. Religious affiliation/commitment: Not considered. Minority status: Not considered. Volunteer work: Not considered. Work experience: Not considered.

Admissions statistics for the fall 2005 entering class: Total applicants: 3,796. Total accepted: 3,392. Freshmen enrolled: 1,267; 1% were from out of state. Overall acceptance rate: 89%. **Credentials of fall 2005 freshmen:** 18% ranked in the top 10 percent of their high school class; 43% were in the top 25 percent, and 74% were in the top half. (Proportion submitting class standing: 88%.) **Average high school grade point average:** 3.3. **First-year students submitting ACT scores:** 98%. Scores (25/75 percentile): English: 17-23, Math: 17-24, Composite: 18-24.

ACADEMICS
Year founded: 1963. **Academic calendar:** Semester. **Degrees offered:** bachelor's, master's, post-master's certificate. **Most popular majors:** 20% elementary education and teaching, 8% criminal justice/safety studies, 7% nursing/registered nurse training (R.N., A.S.N., B.S.N., M.S.N.), 6% social work, 5% business administration and management. **Major fields of study:** biological and biomedical sciences; business, management, marketing, and related support services; communication, journalism, and related programs; computer and information sciences and support services; education; engineering; engineering technologies/technicians; English language and literature/letters; foreign languages, literatures, and linguistics; health professions and related clinical sciences; history; mathematics and statistics; multi/interdisciplinary studies; parks, recreation, leisure, and fitness studies; physical sciences; psychology; public administration and social service professions; security and protective services; social sciences; visual and performing arts. **Areas of required coursework:** arts/fine arts, mathematics, English (including composition), philosophy, sciences (biological or physical), history, social science. **Pre-professional programs:** pre-law, pre-dentistry, pre-medicine, pre-theology, pre-veterinary science. **Special academic programs:** accelerated program, cooperative (work-study plan) program, double major, dual enrollment, English as a Second Language (ESL), honors program, independent study, internships, student-designed major, study abroad, teacher certificate program. **Teacher certification offered in:** early childhood, special education, elementary, middle/junior high, secondary, bilingual/bicultural. **Cooperative education programs:** art, business, computer science, education, engineering, health professions, natural science. **Faculty and instruction (2005-2006):** Total instructional faculty: 260 full-time, 300 part-time. Full-time faculty with Ph.D. or other terminal degree: 79%. **Student/faculty ratio:** 20/1. Classes of fewer than 20 students: 27%; of 20 to 49 students: 67%; of 50 or more students: 6%. **Advanced Placement and International Baccalaureate credit:** AP tests may be used for: Credit only. Scores accepted: 3, 4, 5. International Baccalaureate exams may be used for: Credit only. **Freshmen returning for sophomore year:** 67%. **Graduation rates:** Four-year: 8%; five-year: 27%; six-year: 34%. **Graduate study:** 23% of students pursue further study within one year.

COSTS AND FINANCIAL AID
Financial aid office: (989) 964-4103. **Expenses (2005-2006):** Tuition and fees 2005-2006: $5,282 in state, $11,891 out of state; room/board: $6,150. Estimated books and supplies: $800; transportation: $0; personal expenses: $880. **Financial aid:** Priority filing date for institution's financial aid form: February 14.

CAMPUS LIFE AND EXTRACURRICULAR ACTIVITIES
Campus housing available (% using): coed dorms (89%), apartment for single students (11%), special housing for disabled students. Students who live in college-owned, operated, or affiliated housing: 24%. **Student employment:** During the 2005-2006 academic year, 9% of undergraduates worked on campus. Average per-year earnings: $1,437. **Clubs and organizations:** Number of student organizations: 75. Activities include: choral groups, concert band, dance, drama/theater, jazz band, literary magazine, marching band, music ensembles, musical theater, pep band, student government, student newspaper. Number of fraternities: 4; sororities: 5. Average proportion of students who stay on campus on weekends: 30%. **Sports program (2005-2006):** Member of NCAA II. *Men's intercollegiate varsity sports:* baseball, basketball, bowling, cross-country, football, golf, soccer, track and field (indoor), track and field (outdoor). *Women's intercollegiate varsity sports:* basketball, cross-country, soccer, softball, tennis, track and field (indoor), track and field (outdoor), volleyball.

SERVICES AND FACILITIES
Basic services: nonremedial tutoring, placement service, health service. **Remedial assistance:** other. **Counseling services:** minority student, career, personal, veteran student, academic, psychological. **For learning-disabled students:** School does not offer a structured program with separate admission and additional fees. Services include: reading machines, tape recorders, oral tests, readers, extended time for tests, other. **Library:** Number of titles:

636,202; number of current serial subscriptions: 10,009. **Information technology resources:** Students are not required to lease or own a computer. Number of campus computers available to all students: 1,033. School has a wireless network. Proportion of college-owned housing units wired for high-speed internet access: 100%. **Campus safety:** Security services offered: late-night transport/escort service, 24-hour emergency telephones, lighted pathways/sidewalks, controlled dormitory access (key, security card, etc).

TRANSFER AND INTERNATIONAL STUDENTS
Transfer students: May apply for admission for the following academic terms: Fall, Winter, Spring, Summer. Applicants do not need a minimum number of credits to apply. For fall 2005: Transfer applications received: 1,092. Transfer applicants offered admission: 952. Transfer applicants enrolled: 631. **International students:** Number of foreign undergraduates: 207 (3% of student body). Number of countries represented: 41. Minimum TOEFL score required: 500 (paper); 173 (computer). Average TOEFL score: 503 (paper).

Siena Heights University

- Address: 1247 E. Siena Heights Drive, Adrian, MI 49221
- Website: http://www.sienahts.edu
- Private; Religious affiliation: Roman Catholic
- Enrollment: N/A

KEY STATS
✔ **U.S News College Ranking:** fourth tier, Universities–Master's (Midwest)
✔ **SAT or ACT Score (25th/75th percentile):** N/A
✔ **Tuition:** N/A
 Selectivity: Less selective   **Room/board:** N/A
 Acceptance rate: N/A   **Average debt:** N/A
 Student/faculty ratio: N/A   **Proportion who borrowed:** N/A

Spring Arbor University

- Address: 106 E. Main Street, Spring Arbor, MI 49283-9799
- Website: http://www.arbor.edu
- Private; Religious affiliation: Free Methodist
- Enrollment: 1,913 full-time; 697 part-time

KEY STATS
✔ **U.S News College Ranking:** 59, Universities–Master's (Midwest)
✔ **ACT Score (25th/75th percentile):** 19-25
✔ **Tuition:** 2006-2007: $17,386
 Selectivity: Selective   **Room/board:** $6,070
 Acceptance rate: 75%   **Average debt:** $11,989
 Student/faculty ratio: 15/1   **Proportion who borrowed:** 84%

UNDERGRADUATE STUDENT BODY STATS
2005-2006 enrollment: 1,913 full-time; 697 part-time. Men: 32%; women: 68%. **Ethnic makeup:** African American: 7%; Asian American: 1%; Hispanic: 2%; White: 88%; International: 1%. **Religious preference:** Roman Catholic: 4%; Protestant: 43%; Unknown: 18%; Free Methodist: 15%; Baptist: 12%; Other: 8%.

ADMISSIONS FACTS AND FIGURES
Phone: (800) 968-0011. **Email:** admissions@arbor.edu. **Website:** http://www.arbor.edu. **Application deadlines for fall 2007:** Regular decision: August 1. Early decision: Not offered. Early action: Not offered. Admission can be deferred. **Application fee:** $30. Common application is not accepted. **To apply online, go to:** http://mysau.arbor.edu/wps/portal/onlineapp. **Admissions requirements/recommendations:** High school units required (recommended): English: 4; Mathematics: 3; Science: 2; Foreign language: (2); Social studies: 1; History: 1; Total units: 12 (3). Tests: The college uses SAT or ACT scores in admissions decisions. Either SAT or ACT required. For admission to the fall 2007 entering class, the school will accept: ACT with writing, ACT without writing. Campus visit: Recommended. Admissions interview: Neither required nor recommended. Off-campus

interview: May be arranged. **Factors that count in admissions decisions:** *Academic:* Secondary school record: Very important. Class rank: Considered. Letters of recommendation: Considered. Standardized test scores: Very important. Essay: Considered. *Nonacademic:* Interview: Considered. Extracurricular activities: Considered. Talent/ability: Considered. Character/personal qualities: Very important. Alumni/ae relationship: Not considered. Geographical residence: Not considered. State residency: Not considered. Religious affiliation/commitment: Very important. Minority status: Considered. Volunteer work: Not considered. Work experience: Not considered. **Other schools with the greatest overlap in applicants:** Central Michigan University; Cornerstone University; Grand Valley State University; Michigan State University; Western Michigan University. **Admissions statistics for the fall 2005 entering class:** Total applicants: 1,313. Total accepted: 986. Freshmen enrolled: 318; 14% were from out of state. Overall acceptance rate: 75%. **Credentials of fall 2005 freshmen:** 20% ranked in the top 10 percent of their high school class; 46% were in the top 25 percent, and 75% were in the top half. (Proportion submitting class standing: 87%.) **Average high school grade point average:** 3.3. **First-year students who submitted SAT scores:** 15%. Scores (25/75 percentile): Verbal: 490-620, Math: 480-600, Combined: 970-1220. **First-year students submitting ACT scores:** 92%. Scores (25/75 percentile): English: 18-26, Math: 17-25, Composite: 19-25.

ACADEMICS

Year founded: 1873. **Academic calendar:** Semester. **Degrees offered:** associate, transfer-associate, bachelor's, post-bachelor's certificate, master's. **Most popular majors:** 35% business administration, management, and operations, 22% family systems, 11% elementary education and teaching, 5% English language and literature, 4% nursing/registered nurse training (R.N., A.S.N., B.S.N., M.S.N.). **Major fields of study:** biological and biomedical sciences; business, management, marketing, and related support services; communication, journalism, and related programs; computer and information sciences and support services; education; engineering; English language and literature/letters; family and consumer sciences/human sciences; foreign languages, literatures, and linguistics; health professions and related clinical sciences; history; mathematics and statistics; parks, recreation, leisure, and fitness studies; philosophy and religious studies; physical sciences; psychology; public administration and social service professions; social sciences; theology and religious vocations; visual and performing arts. **Areas of required coursework:** arts/fine arts, humanities, computer literacy, mathematics, English (including composition), philosophy, sciences (biological or physical), history, social science, other. **Pre-professional programs:** pre-law, pre-dentistry, pre-medicine, pre-veterinary science, other. **Special academic programs (% participation):** accelerated program (59.02%), cross-registration (2.65%), distance learning (30.24%), double major (1.33%), dual enrollment (.53%), English as a Second Language (ESL) (0%), honors program (0%), independent study (11.41%), internships (34.75%), student-designed major (.53%), study abroad (21.88%), teacher certificate program (19.63%), weekend college (42.44%). **Teacher certification offered in:** early childhood, special education, elementary, middle/junior high, secondary. **Reserve Officers Training Corps (ROTC):** Army ROTC: Offered at cooperating institution (Eastern Michigan University). **Faculty and instruction (2005-2006):** Total instructional faculty: 80 full-time, 58 part-time (58% men; 42% women; 4% minorities). Full-time faculty with Ph.D. or other terminal degree: 60%. Student/faculty ratio: 15/1. Classes of fewer than 20 students: 58%; of 20 to 49 students: 38%; of 50 or more students: 4%. **Advanced Placement and International Baccalaureate credit:** AP tests may be used for: Credit and/or placement. Scores accepted: 3. International Baccalaureate exams may be used for: Credit and/or placement. **Freshmen returning for sophomore year:** 79%. **Graduation rates:** Four-year: 36%; five-year: 52%; six-year: 58%. **Graduate study:** 20% of students pursue further study immediately upon graduation; 30% within one year; 40% within five years. Fields in which graduates pursue further study: Master of Business Administration (MBA), 15%; law, 5%; medicine, 5%; dentistry, 1%; engineering, 1%; theology (or the seminary), 30%; education, 30%; arts and sciences, 8%.

COSTS AND FINANCIAL AID

Financial aid office: (517) 750-6463. **Expenses (2006-2007):** Tuition and fees 2006-2007: $17,386; room/board: $6,070. Estimated books and supplies: $625; transportation: $672; personal expenses: $755. **Financial aid:** Priority filing date for institution's financial aid form: March 1. In 2005-2006, 88% of undergraduates applied for financial aid. Of those, 75% were determined to have financial need; 38% had their need fully met. Average financial aid package (proportion receiving): $14,116 (74%). Average amount of gift aid, such as scholarships or grants (proportion receiving): $7,820 (71%). Average amount of self-help aid, such as work study or loans (proportion receiving):

$4,518 (63%). Average need-based loan (excluding PLUS or other private loans): $4,424. Among students who received need-based aid, the average percentage of need met: 83%. Among students who received aid based on merit, the average award (and the proportion receiving): $2,785 (3%). The average athletic scholarship (and the proportion receiving): $3,023 (7%). Average amount of debt of borrowers graduating in 2005: $11,989. Proportion who borrowed: 84%.

CAMPUS LIFE AND EXTRACURRICULAR ACTIVITIES

Campus housing available (% using): women's dorms (43%), men's dorms (28%), apartments for married students (2%), apartment for single students (15%), special housing for disabled students (1%), other housing options (11%). Students who live in college-owned, operated, or affiliated housing: 64%. **Student employment:** During the 2005-2006 academic year, 35% of undergraduates worked on campus. Average per-year earnings: $1,000. **Clubs and organizations:** Number of student organizations: 40. Activities include: choral groups, concert band, drama/theater, jazz band, literary magazine, music ensembles, pep band, radio station, student government, student newspaper, student film society, symphony orchestra, television station, yearbook. Number of fraternities: 0; sororities: 0. Average proportion of students who stay on campus on weekends: 60%. **Sports program (2005-2006):** Member of NAIA. *Men's intercollegiate varsity sports:* baseball, basketball, cross-country, golf, soccer, tennis, track and field (indoor), track and field (outdoor). *Women's intercollegiate varsity sports:* basketball, cross-country, soccer, softball, tennis, track and field (indoor), track and field (outdoor), volleyball.

SERVICES AND FACILITIES

Basic services: nonremedial tutoring, health service. **Remedial assistance:** reading, math, writing, study skills. **Counseling services:** minority student, career, military, personal, veteran student, academic, psychological, birth control, religious. **For learning-disabled students:** School does not offer a structured program with separate admission and additional fees. Total undergraduates in learning-disabled program or receiving services: 13. Services include: remedial math, remedial English, reading machines, remedial reading, tape recorders, untimed tests, note-taking services, oral tests, learning center, readers, extended time for tests, tutors, proofreading services, exams on tape or computer, other testing accomodations. **Library:** Number of titles: 101,940; number of current serial subscriptions: 659. **Information technology resources:** Students are not required to lease or own a computer. Number of campus computers available to all students: 171. School has a wireless network. Approximate number of users that can be accommodated: 1,100. Proportion of college-owned housing units wired for high-speed internet access: 96%. **Campus safety:** Security services offered: late-night transport/escort service, 24-hour emergency telephones, lighted pathways/sidewalks, student patrols, controlled dormitory access (key, security card, etc).

TRANSFER AND INTERNATIONAL STUDENTS

Transfer students: May apply for admission for the following academic terms: Fall, Winter, Spring, Summer. Applicants need a minimum number of credits to apply. For fall 2005: Transfer applications received: 424. Transfer applicants offered admission: 236. Transfer applicants enrolled: 137. **International students:** Number of foreign undergraduates: 22 (1% of student body). Number of countries represented: 8. Minimum TOEFL score required: 525 (paper); 197 (computer).

University of Detroit Mercy

- **Address:** 4001 W. McNichols, Detroit, MI 48221-3038
- **Website:** http://www.udmercy.edu
- **Private; Religious affiliation:** Roman Catholic (Jesuit/Sisters of Mercy)
- **Enrollment:** 1,983 full-time; 1,255 part-time

KEY STATS

✔ **U.S News College Ranking:** 22, Universities–Master's (Midwest)
✔ **ACT Score (25th/75th percentile):** 20-26
✔ **Tuition:** 2006-2007: $23,970

Selectivity: More selective	**Room/board:** $7,622
Acceptance rate: 69%	**Average debt:** N/A
Student/faculty ratio: 13/1	**Proportion who borrowed:** N/A

UNDERGRADUATE STUDENT BODY STATS

2005-2006 enrollment: 1,983 full-time; 1,255 part-time. Men: 35%; women: 65%. **Ethnic makeup:** African American: 31%; American-Indian: 1%; Asian American: 3%; Hispanic: 3%; White: 60%; International: 3%. **Religious preference:** Roman Catholic: 31%; Protestant: 10%; Unknown: 28%.

ADMISSIONS FACTS AND FIGURES

Phone: (313) 993-1245. **Email:** admissions@udmercy.edu. **Website:** http://www.udmercy.edu. **Application deadlines for fall 2007:** Regular decision: Rolling. Early decision: Not offered. Early action: Not offered. Admission can be deferred. **Application fee:** $25. Common application is accepted. **To apply online, go to:** https://jackson.udmercy.edu/apply/apply.jsp. **Admissions requirements/recommendations:** High school units required (recommended): English: (4); Mathematics: (3); Science: (2); Foreign language: (2); Social studies: (2); History: (2); Academic electives: (2). Tests: The college uses SAT or ACT scores in admissions decisions. Either SAT or ACT required. For admission to the fall 2007 entering class, the school will accept: ACT with writing, ACT without writing. Campus visit: Recommended. Admissions interview: Neither required nor recommended. Off-campus interview: May be arranged. **Factors that count in admissions decisions:** *Academic:* Letters of recommendation: Considered. Essay: Considered. *Nonacademic:* Interview: Considered. Extracurricular activities: Considered. Talent/ability: Considered. Character/personal qualities: Considered. Alumni/ae relationship: Considered. Geographical residence: Considered. State residency: Considered. Religious affiliation/commitment: Considered. Minority status: Considered. Volunteer work: Considered. Work experience: Considered. **Admissions statistics for the fall 2005 entering class:** Total applicants: 2,339. Total accepted: 1,605. Freshmen enrolled: 502; Overall acceptance rate: 69%. **Credentials of fall 2005 freshmen:** 24% ranked in the top 10 percent of their high school class; 55% were in the top 25 percent, and 83% were in the top half. (Proportion submitting class standing: 47%.) **Average high school grade point average:** 3.3. **First-year students submitting ACT scores:** 95%. Scores (25/75 percentile): English: 18-25, Math: 18-26, Composite: 20-26.

ACADEMICS

Year founded: 1877. **Academic calendar:** Semester. **Degrees offered:** certificate, associate, terminal-associate, bachelor's, post-bachelor's certificate, master's, post-master's certificate, first professional, first professional certificate, doctorate. **Most popular majors:** 34% health professions and related clinical sciences, 14% business, management, marketing, and related support services, 8% engineering, 6% biological and biomedical sciences, 5% education. **Major fields of study:** architecture and related services; biological and biomedical sciences; business, management, marketing, and related support services; communication, journalism, and related programs; computer and information sciences and support services; education; engineering; English language and literature/letters; health professions and related clinical sciences; legal professions and studies; liberal arts and sciences studies, and humanities; mathematics and statistics; philosophy and religious studies; physical sciences; psychology; public administration and social service professions; security and protective services; social sciences; visual and performing arts. **Areas of required coursework:** humanities, computer literacy, mathematics, English (including composition), philosophy, sciences (biological or physical), social science, other. **Pre-professional programs:** pre-law, pre-dentistry, pre-medicine, other. **Special academic programs:** cooperative (work-study plan) program, distance learning, double major, English as a Second Language (ESL), honors program, independent study, internships, liberal arts/career combination, study abroad, teacher certificate program, weekend college. **Teacher certification offered in:** special education, elementary, middle/junior high, secondary. **Cooperative education programs:** business, computer science, engineering, health professions, humanities, natural science, social/behavioral science. **Faculty and instruction (2005-2006):** Total instructional faculty: 259 full-time, 365 part-time (56% men; 44% women; 15% minorities). Full-time faculty with Ph.D. or other terminal degree: 85%. Student/faculty ratio: 13/1. Classes of fewer than 20 students: 60%; of 20 to 49 students: 37%; of 50 or more students: 2%. **Freshmen returning for sophomore year:** 76%. **Graduation rates:** Four-year: 31%; five-year: 47%; six-year: 54%.

COSTS AND FINANCIAL AID

Financial aid office: (313) 993-3350. **Expenses (2006-2007):** Tuition and fees 2006-2007: $23,970; room/board: $7,622. Estimated books and supplies: $1,386; transportation: $946; personal expenses: $2,819. **Financial aid:** Priority filing date for institution's financial aid form: March 1. In 2005-2006, 85% of undergraduates applied for financial aid. Of those, 78% were determined to have financial need; 21% had their need fully met. Average financial aid package (proportion receiving): $23,871 (78%). Average amount of gift aid, such as scholarships or grants (proportion receiving): $18,567 (70%). Average amount of self-help aid, such as work study or loans (proportion receiving): $5,304 (73%). Average need-based loan (excluding PLUS or other private loans): $4,210. Among students who received need-based aid, the average percentage of need met: 80%. Among students who received aid based on merit, the average award (and the proportion receiving): $13,628 (6%). The average athletic scholarship (and the proportion receiving): $4,623 (1%).

CAMPUS LIFE AND EXTRACURRICULAR ACTIVITIES

Campus housing available: coed dorms, apartments for married students. **Clubs and organizations:** Number of student organizations: 50. Activities include: drama/theater, literary magazine, pep band, radio station, student government, student newspaper. **Sports program (2005-2006):** Member of NCAA I. *Men's intercollegiate varsity sports:* basketball, cross-country, fencing, golf, soccer, track and field (indoor), track and field (outdoor). *Women's intercollegiate varsity sports:* basketball, cross-country, fencing, golf, soccer, softball, tennis, track and field (indoor), track and field (outdoor).

SERVICES AND FACILITIES

Basic services: nonremedial tutoring, placement service, health service, health insurance. **Remedial assistance:** reading, math, writing, study skills. **Counseling services:** career, personal, veteran student, academic, psychological, religious. **Information technology resources:** Students are not required to lease or own a computer. Number of campus computers available to all students: 250. School has a wireless network. Proportion of college-owned housing units wired for high-speed internet access: 100%. **Campus safety:** Security services offered: lighted pathways/sidewalks.

TRANSFER AND INTERNATIONAL STUDENTS

Transfer students: May apply for admission for the following academic terms: Fall, Winter, Spring, Summer. Applicants do not need a minimum number of credits to apply. For fall 2005: Transfer applications received: 1,779. Transfer applicants offered admission: 742. Transfer applicants enrolled: 334. **International students:** Number of foreign undergraduates: 81 (3% of student body).

University of Michigan—Ann Arbor

- **Address:** Ann Arbor, MI 48109
- **Website:** http://www.umich.edu
- **Public**
- **Enrollment:** 24,446 full-time; 1,021 part-time

KEY STATS

✔ **U.S News College Ranking:** 24, National Universities
✔ **ACT Score (25th/75th percentile):** 26-31
✔ **Tuition:** 2006-2007: $9,988 in state, $30,179 out of state

Selectivity: Most selective	**Room/board:** $7,838
Acceptance rate: 57%	**Average debt:** $22,312
Student/faculty ratio: 15/1	**Proportion who borrowed:** 42%

UNDERGRADUATE STUDENT BODY STATS

2005-2006 enrollment: 24,446 full-time; 1,021 part-time. Men: 49%; women: 51%. **Ethnic makeup:** African American: 7%; American-Indian: 1%; Asian American: 12%; Hispanic: 5%; White: 70%; International: 5%.

ADMISSIONS FACTS AND FIGURES

Phone: (734) 764-7433. **Email:** ugadmiss@umich.edu. **Website:** http://www.umich.edu. **Application deadlines for fall 2007:** Regular decision: February 1. Early decision: Not offered. Early action: Not offered. Admission can be deferred. **Application fee:** $40. Common application is not accepted. **To apply online, go to:** http://www.admissions.umich.edu. **Admissions requirements/recommendations:** High school units required (recommended): English: 4 (4); Mathematics: 3 (4); Science: 2 (3); Foreign language: 2 (4); Social studies: 3; History: (2); Academic electives: (2); Total units: (18). Tests: The college uses SAT or ACT scores in admissions decisions. Either SAT or ACT required. For admission to the fall 2007 entering class, the school will accept: ACT with writing. Campus visit: Recommended. Admissions interview: Neither required nor recommended. **Factors that count in admissions decisions:** *Academic:* Secondary school record: Very important. Class rank: Considered. Letters of recommendation: Important. Standardized test scores: Important. Essay: Important. *Nonacademic:* Interview: Not considered. Extracurricular activities: Considered. Talent/ability: Important. Character/personal qualities: Important. Alumni/ae relationship: Considered. Geographical residence: Considered. State residency: Important. Religious affiliation/commitment: Not considered. Minority status: Important. Volunteer work: Considered. Work experience: Considered. **Other schools with the greatest overlap in applicants:** Cornell University; Michigan State University; Northwestern University; University of Pennsylvania; Washington University in St. Louis. **Admissions statistics for the fall 2005 entering class:** Total applicants: 23,882. Total accepted: 13,610. Freshmen enrolled: 6,113; 36% were from out of state. Overall acceptance rate: 57%. **Size of waiting list:** 6489 applicants; enrolled from waiting list: 0. **Credentials of fall 2005 freshmen:** 89% ranked in the top 10 percent of their high school class; 98% were in the top 25 percent, and 99% were in the top half. (Proportion submitting class standing: 96%.) **Average high school grade point average:** 3.7. **First-year students who submitted SAT scores:** 57%. Scores (25/75 percentile): Verbal: 590-690, Math: 630-730, Combined: 1220-1420. **First-year students submitting ACT scores:** 69%. Scores (25/75 percentile): English: 26-31, Math: 26-32, Composite: 26-31.

ACADEMICS

Year founded: 1817. **Academic calendar:** Trimester. **Degrees offered:** certificate, bachelor's, post-bachelor's certificate, master's, post-master's certificate, first professional, doctorate. **Most popular majors:** 17% engineering, 9% economics, 8% psychology, 7% political science and government, 6% English language and literature. **Major fields of study:** architecture and related services; area, ethnic, cultural, and gender studies; biological and biomedical sciences; business, management, marketing, and related support services; communication, journalism, and related programs; computer and information sciences and support services; education; engineering; English language and literature/letters; foreign languages, literatures, and linguistics; health professions and related clinical sciences; history; liberal arts and sciences studies, and humanities; mathematics and statistics; multi/interdisciplinary studies; natural resources and conservation; parks, recreation, leisure, and fitness studies; philosophy and religious studies; physical sciences; psychology; social sciences; visual and performing arts. **Areas of required coursework:** mathematics, English (including composition), foreign languages. **Special academic programs:** accelerated program, cooperative (work-study plan) program, cross-registration, distance learning, double major, dual enrollment, English as a Second Language (ESL), exchange student program (domestic), honors program, independent study, internships, liberal arts/career combination, student-designed major, study abroad, teacher certificate program. **Teacher certification offered in:** elementary, secondary. **Reserve Officers Training Corps (ROTC):** Army ROTC: Offered on campus; Navy ROTC: Offered on campus; Air Force ROTC: Offered on campus. **Faculty and instruction (2005-2006):** Total instructional faculty: 2,390 full-time, 597 part-time (62% men; 38% women; 21% minorities). Full-time faculty with Ph.D. or other terminal degree: 92%. Student/faculty ratio: 15/1. Classes of fewer than 20 students: 43%; of 20 to 49 students: 40%; of 50 or more students: 16%. **Advanced Placement and International Baccalaureate credit:** AP tests may be used for: Credit and/or placement. International Baccalaureate exams may be used for: Credit only. **Freshmen returning for sophomore year:** 96%. **Graduation rates:** Four-year: 70%; five-year: 85%; six-year: 86%.

COSTS AND FINANCIAL AID

Financial aid office: (734) 763-4119. **Expenses (2006-2007):** Tuition and fees 2006-2007: $9,988 in state, $30,179 out of state; room/board: $7,838. Estimated books and supplies: $1,002 personal expenses: $2,124. **Financial aid:** Priority filing date for institution's financial aid form: February 15; deadline: April 30. In 2005-2006, 53% of undergraduates applied for financial aid. Of those, 45% were determined to have financial need; 90% had their need fully met. Average financial aid package (proportion receiving): $10,234 (45%). Average amount of gift aid, such as scholarships or grants (proportion receiving): $7,035 (25%). Average amount of self-help aid, such as work study or loans (proportion receiving): $6,779 (45%). Average need-based loan (excluding PLUS or other private loans): $5,695. Among students who received need-based aid, the average percentage of need met: 90%. Among students who received aid based on merit, the average award (and the proportion receiving): $5,418 (25%). The average athletic scholarship (and the proportion receiving): $23,627 (2%). Average amount of debt of borrowers graduating in 2005: $22,312. Proportion who borrowed: 42%.

CAMPUS LIFE AND EXTRACURRICULAR ACTIVITIES

Campus housing available: coed dorms, women's dorms, sorority housing, fraternity housing, apartments for married students, apartment for single students, special housing for disabled students, cooperative housing, other housing options. Students who live in college-owned, operated, or affiliated housing: 37%. **Clubs and organizations:** Number of student organizations: 900. Activities include: choral groups, concert band, dance, drama/theater, jazz band, literary magazine, marching band, music ensembles, musical theater, opera, pep band, radio station, student government, student newspaper, student film society, symphony orchestra, television station, yearbook. Number of fraternities: 34; sororities: 25. Proportion of men in fraternities: 13%; of women in sororities: 16%. **Sports program (2005-2006):** Member of NCAA I. *Men's intercollegiate varsity sports:* baseball, basketball, cross-country, football, golf, gymnastics, ice hockey, soccer, swimming and diving, tennis, track and field (indoor), track and field (outdoor), wrestling. *Women's intercollegiate varsity sports:* basketball, crew, cross-country, field hockey, golf, gymnastics, rowing, soccer, softball, swimming and diving, tennis, track and field (indoor), track and field (outdoor), volleyball, water polo.

SERVICES AND FACILITIES

Basic services: nonremedial tutoring, women's center, placement service, day care, health service, health insurance. **Counseling services:** minority student, career, military, personal, academic, psychological. **For learning-disabled students:** School does not offer a structured program with separate admission and additional fees. Services include: reading machines, tape recorders, videotaped classes, diagnostic testing service, untimed tests, note-taking services, oral tests, extended time for tests, tutors. **Library:** Number of titles: 8,133,917; number of current serial subscriptions: 81,085. **Information technology resources:** Students are not required to lease or own a computer. Number of campus computers available to all students: 2,700. School has a wireless network. Proportion of college-owned housing units wired for high-speed internet access: 100%. **Campus safety:** Security services offered: 24-hour foot-and-vehicle patrols, late-night transport/escort service, 24-hour emergency telephones, lighted pathways/sidewalks, controlled dormitory access (key, security card, etc).

TRANSFER AND INTERNATIONAL STUDENTS

Transfer students: May apply for admission for the following academic terms: Fall, Winter, Spring, Summer. Applicants need a minimum number of credits to apply. For fall 2005: Transfer applications received: 2,898. Transfer applicants offered admission: 1,296. Transfer applicants enrolled: 909. **International students:** Number of foreign undergraduates: 1185 (5% of student body). Minimum TOEFL score required: 570 (paper); 230 (computer).

University of Michigan–Dearborn

- **Address:** 4901 Evergreen, Dearborn, MI 48128-1491
- **Website:** http://www.umd.umich.edu
- **Public**
- **Enrollment:** 4,031 full-time; 2,540 part-time

KEY STATS

✔ **U.S News College Ranking:** 27, Universities–Master's (Midwest)
✔ **ACT Score (25th/75th percentile):** 21-26
✔ **Tuition:** 2005-2006: $6,784 in state, $14,593 out of state

Selectivity: More selective	Room/board: N/A
Acceptance rate: 71%	Average debt: $20,509
Student/faculty ratio: 16/1	Proportion who borrowed: 51%

UNDERGRADUATE STUDENT BODY STATS

2005-2006 enrollment: 4,031 full-time; 2,540 part-time. Men: 47%; women: 53%. **Ethnic makeup:** African American: 9%; American-Indian: 1%; Asian American: 6%; Hispanic: 3%; White: 80%; International: 2%.

ADMISSIONS FACTS AND FIGURES

Phone: (313) 593-5100. **Email:** admissions@umd.umich.edu. **Website:** http://www.umd.umich.edu. **Application deadlines for fall 2007:** Regular decision: Rolling. Early decision: Not offered. Early action: Not offered. Admission can be deferred. **Application fee:** $30. Common application is not accepted. **Admissions requirements/recommendations:** High school units required (recommended): English: (4); Mathematics: (4); Science: (3); Foreign language: (3); Social studies: (4); History: (4); Total units: (24). Tests: The college uses SAT or ACT scores in admissions decisions. Either SAT or ACT required. For admission to the fall 2007 entering class, the school will accept: ACT with writing, ACT without writing. Campus visit: Recommended. Admissions interview: Neither required nor recommended. Off-campus interview: Not available. **Factors that count in admissions decisions:** *Academic:* Secondary school record: Not considered. Class rank: Considered. Letters of recommendation: Not considered. Standardized test scores: Very important. Essay: Considered. *Nonacademic:* Interview: Considered. Extracurricular activities: Not considered. Talent/ability: Not considered. Character/personal qualities: Not considered. Alumni/ae relationship: Not considered. Geographical residence: Not considered. State residency: Not considered. Religious affiliation/commitment: Not considered. Minority status: Not considered. Volunteer work: Not considered. Work experience: Not considered. **Other schools with the greatest overlap in applicants:** Eastern Michigan University; Michigan State University; Oakland University; University of Michigan–Ann Arbor; Wayne State University. **Admissions statistics for the fall 2005 entering class:** Total applicants: 2,605. Total accepted: 1,842. Freshmen enrolled: 840; 0% were from out of state. Overall acceptance rate: 71%. **Credentials of fall 2005 freshmen:** 27% ranked in the top 10 percent of their high school class; 58% were in the top 25 percent, and 89% were in the top half. (Proportion submitting class standing: 78%.) **Average high school grade point average:** 3.5. **First-year students who submitted SAT scores:** 12%. Scores (25/75 percentile): Verbal: 460-598, Math: 483-628, Combined: 943-1226. **First-year students submitting ACT scores:** 98%. Scores (25/75 percentile): English: 20-26, Math: 20-26, Composite: 21-26.

ACADEMICS

Year founded: 1959. **Academic calendar:** Semester. **Degrees offered:** bachelor's, post-bachelor's certificate, master's. **Most popular majors:** 23% business, management, marketing, and related support services, 16% engineering, 11% education, 9% social sciences, 8% psychology. **Major fields of study:** area, ethnic, cultural, and gender studies; biological and biomedical sciences; business, management, marketing, and related support services; communication, journalism, and related programs; computer and information sciences and support services; education; engineering; English language and literature/letters; foreign languages, literatures, and linguistics; health professions and related clinical sciences; history; liberal arts and sciences studies, and humanities; mathematics and statistics; multi/interdisciplinary studies; natural resources and conservation; philosophy and religious studies; physical sciences; psychology; security and protective services; social sciences; visual and performing arts. **Areas of required coursework:** humanities, mathematics, English (including composition), sciences (biological or physical), history, social science. **Pre-professional programs:** pre-law, pre-medicine. **Special academic programs:** accelerated program, cooperative (work-study plan) program, cross-registration, distance learning, double major, dual enrollment, honors program, independent study, internships, liberal arts/career combination, student-designed major, study abroad, teacher certificate program. **Teacher certification offered in:** early childhood, special education, elementary, middle/junior high, secondary. **Cooperative education programs:** art, business, computer science, education, engineering, health professions, humanities, natural science, social/behavioral science. **Reserve Officers Training Corps (ROTC):** Army ROTC: Offered at cooperating institution (University of Michigan-Ann Arbor); Navy ROTC: Offered at cooperating institution (University of Michigan-Ann Arbor); Air Force ROTC: Offered at cooperating institution (University of Michigan-Ann Arbor). **Faculty and instruction (2005-2006):** Total instructional faculty: 287 full-time, 225 part-time (65% men; 35% women; 19% minorities). Full-time faculty with Ph.D. or other terminal degree: 87%. Student/faculty ratio: 16/1. Classes of fewer than 20 students: 41%; of 20 to 49 students: 54%; of 50 or more students: 5%. **Freshmen returning for sophomore year:** 82%. **Graduation rates:** Four-year: 12%; five-year: 37%; six-year: 50%.

COSTS AND FINANCIAL AID

Financial aid office: (313) 593-5300. **Expenses (2005-2006):** Tuition and fees 2005-2006: $6,784 in state, $14,593 out of state; room/board: N/A. **Financial aid:** Priority filing date for institution's financial aid form: February 15. In 2005-2006, 59% of undergraduates applied for financial aid. Of those, 46% were determined to have financial need; 8% had their need fully met. Average financial aid package (proportion receiving): $4,847 (46%). Average amount of gift aid, such as scholarships or grants (proportion receiving): N/A (30%). Average amount of self-help aid, such as work study or loans (proportion receiving): N/A (45%). Among students who received need-based aid, the average percentage of need met: 43%. Among

students who received aid based on merit, the average award (and the proportion receiving): $2,921 (33%). The average athletic scholarship (and the proportion receiving): $1,562 (1%). Average amount of debt of borrowers graduating in 2005: $20,509. Proportion who borrowed: 51%.

CAMPUS LIFE AND EXTRACURRICULAR ACTIVITIES

Students who live in college-owned, operated, or affiliated housing: 0%. **Clubs and organizations:** Number of student organizations: 130. Activities include: drama/theater, literary magazine, radio station, student government, student newspaper, student film society, television station. Number of fraternities: 2; sororities: 4. Proportion of men in fraternities: 3%; of women in sororities: 3%. **Sports program (2005-2006):** Member of NAIA. *Men's intercollegiate varsity sports:* basketball. *Women's intercollegiate varsity sports:* basketball, volleyball.

SERVICES AND FACILITIES

Basic services: nonremedial tutoring, women's center, placement service, other. **Counseling services:** career, personal, academic, older student, psychological. **For learning-disabled students:** School does not offer a structured program with separate admission and additional fees. Total undergraduates in learning-disabled program or receiving services: 18. Services include: remedial math, remedial English, reading machines, tape recorders, note-taking services, oral tests, readers, extended time for tests, tutors, priority registration, priority seating, texts on tape. **Library:** Number of titles: 351,808; number of current serial subscriptions: 563. **Information technology resources:** Students are not required to lease or own a computer. Number of campus computers available to all students: 140. School has a wireless network. Approximate number of users that can be accommodated: 500. **Campus safety:** Security services offered: 24-hour foot-and-vehicle patrols, late-night transport/escort service, 24-hour emergency telephones, lighted pathways/sidewalks.

TRANSFER AND INTERNATIONAL STUDENTS

Transfer students: May apply for admission for the following academic terms: Fall, Winter, Summer. Applicants need a minimum number of credits to apply. For fall 2005: Transfer applications received: 1,468. Transfer applicants offered admission: 1,087. Transfer applicants enrolled: 658. **International students:** Number of foreign undergraduates: 103 (2% of student body). Number of countries represented: 34. Minimum TOEFL score required: 550 (paper); 213 (computer). Average TOEFL score: 570 (paper).

University of Michigan–Flint

- **Address:** 303 E. Kearsley, Flint, MI 48502-1950
- **Website:** http://www.umflint.edu
- **Public**
- **Enrollment:** 3,458 full-time; 2,213 part-time

KEY STATS

✔ **U.S News College Ranking:** third tier, Universities–Master's (Midwest)
✔ **ACT Score (25th/75th percentile):** 18-24
✔ **Tuition:** 2005-2006: $6,398 in state, $12,150 out of state

Selectivity: Selective	**Room/board:** N/A
Acceptance rate: 85%	**Average debt:** $21,888
Student/faculty ratio: 15/1	**Proportion who borrowed:** 66%

UNDERGRADUATE STUDENT BODY STATS

2005-2006 enrollment: 3,458 full-time; 2,213 part-time. Men: 37%; women: 63%. **Ethnic makeup:** African American: 11%; American-Indian: 1%; Asian American: 2%; Hispanic: 3%; White: 83%; International: 1%.

ADMISSIONS FACTS AND FIGURES

Phone: (810) 762-3300. **Email:** admissions@umflint.edu. **Website:** http://www.umflint.edu. **Application deadlines for fall 2007:** Regular decision: Rolling. Early decision: Not offered. Early action: Not offered. Admission can be deferred. **Application fee:** $30. Common application is accepted. **To apply online, go to:** http://www.umflint.edu/resources/offices/admissions/applicationforms.php. **Admissions requirements/recommendations:** High school units required (recommended): English: 4 (4); Mathematics: 3 (4); Science: 2 (4); Foreign language: 0 (2); Social studies: 3 (3); History: 0 (2); Academic electives: 0 (0); Total units: 12 (21). Tests: The college uses SAT or ACT scores in admissions decisions. Either SAT or

ACT required. For admission to the fall 2007 entering class, the school will accept: ACT with writing, ACT without writing. Campus visit: Neither required nor recommended. Admissions interview: Neither required nor recommended. Off-campus interview: Not available. **Factors that count in admissions decisions:** *Academic:* Secondary school record: Very important. Class rank: Considered. Letters of recommendation: Considered. Standardized test scores: Very important. Essay: Considered. *Nonacademic:* Interview: Considered. Extracurricular activities: Important. Talent/ability: Considered. Character/personal qualities: Not considered. Alumni/ae relationship: Considered. Geographical residence: Considered. State residency: Not considered. Religious affiliation/commitment: Not considered. Minority status: Not considered. Volunteer work: Not considered. Work experience: Not considered. **Other schools with the greatest overlap in applicants:** Grand Valley State University; Oakland University; Saginaw Valley State University; University of Michigan–Dearborn. **Admissions statistics for the fall 2005 entering class:** Total applicants: 1,651. Total accepted: 1,396. Freshmen enrolled: 579; 0% were from out of state. Overall acceptance rate: 85%. **Credentials of fall 2005 freshmen:** 16% ranked in the top 10 percent of their high school class; 42% were in the top 25 percent, and 75% were in the top half. (Proportion submitting class standing: 92%.) **Average high school grade point average:** 3.2. **First-year students who submitted SAT scores:** 4%. Scores (25/75 percentile): Verbal: 435-540, Math: 400-550, Combined: 835-1090. **First-year students submitting ACT scores:** 96%. Scores (25/75 percentile): English: 17-24, Math: 17-24, Composite: 18-24.

ACADEMICS

Year founded: 1956. **Academic calendar:** Semester. **Degrees offered:** bachelor's, master's, first professional. **Most popular majors:** 25% education, 16% business, management, marketing, and related support services, 16% health professions and related clinical sciences, 5% multi/interdisciplinary studies, 5% social sciences. **Major fields of study:** area, ethnic, cultural, and gender studies; biological and biomedical sciences; business, management, marketing, and related support services; communication, journalism, and related programs; computer and information sciences and support services; education; engineering; English language and literature/letters; foreign languages, literatures, and linguistics; health professions and related clinical sciences; history; liberal arts and sciences studies, and humanities; mathematics and statistics; natural resources and conservation; philosophy and religious studies; physical sciences; psychology; public administration and social service professions; security and protective services; social sciences; visual and performing arts. **Areas of required coursework:** arts/fine arts, humanities, mathematics, English (including composition), philosophy, foreign languages, sciences (biological or physical), history, social science. **Preprofessional programs:** pre-law, pre-dentistry, pre-medicine, pre-veterinary science, pre-pharmacy, other. **Special academic programs:** cooperative (work-study plan) program, distance learning, double major, dual enrollment, honors program, independent study, internships, student-designed major, study abroad, teacher certificate program. **Teacher certification offered in:** early childhood, elementary, secondary, bilingual/bicultural. **Cooperative education programs:** business, computer science, engineering, humanities, natural science, social/behavioral science. **Faculty and instruction (2005-2006):** Total instructional faculty: 213 full-time, 207 part-time (44% men; 56% women; 16% minorities). Full-time faculty with Ph.D. or other terminal degree: 75%. Student/faculty ratio: 15/1. Classes of fewer than 20 students: 36%; of 20 to 49 students: 59%; of 50 or more students: 5%. **Freshmen returning for sophomore year:** 74%. **Graduation rates:** Four-year: 10%; five-year: 27%; six-year: 38%.

COSTS AND FINANCIAL AID

Financial aid office: (810) 762-3444. **Expenses (2005-2006):** Tuition and fees 2005-2006: $6,398 in state, $12,150 out of state; room/board: N/A. **Financial aid:** Priority filing date for institution's financial aid form: March 1. Average amount of debt of borrowers graduating in 2005: $21,888. Proportion who borrowed: 66%.

CAMPUS LIFE AND EXTRACURRICULAR ACTIVITIES

Students who live in college-owned, operated, or affiliated housing: 0%. **Clubs and organizations:** Number of student organizations: 63. Activities include: choral groups, concert band, dance, drama/theater, jazz band, literary magazine, music ensembles, musical theater, student government, student newspaper, television station. Number of fraternities: 2; sororities: 4. Proportion of men in fraternities: 1%; of women in sororities: 1%.

SERVICES AND FACILITIES

Basic services: nonremedial tutoring, women's center, placement service, day care, health service. **Remedial assistance:** reading, math, writing, study skills. **Counseling services:** minority student, career, personal, academic, older student, psychological. **For learning-disabled students:** School does not offer a structured program with separate admission and additional fees. Services include: remedial math, remedial English, remedial reading, note-taking services, extended time for tests, tutors. **Library:** Number of titles: 220,011; number of current serial subscriptions: 35,765. **Information technology resources:** Students are not required to lease or own a computer. Number of campus computers available to all students: 155. School has a wireless network. **Campus safety:** Security services offered: 24-hour foot-and-vehicle patrols, late-night transport/escort service, 24-hour emergency telephones, lighted pathways/sidewalks, student patrols.

TRANSFER AND INTERNATIONAL STUDENTS

Transfer students: May apply for admission for the following academic terms: Fall, Winter, Spring, Summer. Applicants need a minimum number of credits to apply. For fall 2005: Transfer applications received: 1,313. Transfer applicants offered admission: 1,109. Transfer applicants enrolled: 694. **International students:** Number of foreign undergraduates: 41 (1% of student body). Minimum TOEFL score required: 550 (paper); 213 (computer).

Walsh Coll. of Accountancy and Bus. Adm.

- **Address:** PO Box 7006, Troy, MI 48007-7006
- **Website:** http://www.walshcollege.edu
- **Private**
- **Enrollment:** N/A

KEY STATS

✔ **U.S News College Ranking:** Unranked Specialty School–Business
✔ **SAT or ACT Score (25th/75th percentile):** N/A
✔ **Tuition:** 2006-2007: $11,610

Selectivity: Least selective	**Room/board:** N/A
Acceptance rate: N/A	**Average debt:** $10,306
Student/faculty ratio: N/A	**Proportion who borrowed:** 45%

Wayne State University

- **Address:** 656 W. Kirby, Detroit, MI 48202
- **Website:** http://www.wayne.edu/
- **Public**
- **Enrollment:** 11,924 full-time; 8,812 part-time

KEY STATS

✔ **U.S News College Ranking:** fourth tier, National Universities
✔ **ACT Score (25th/75th percentile):** 17-23
✔ **Tuition:** 2005-2006: $6,439 in state, $13,771 out of state

Selectivity: Selective	**Room/board:** $6,845
Acceptance rate: 60%	**Average debt:** $19,329
Student/faculty ratio: 16/1	**Proportion who borrowed:** 50%

UNDERGRADUATE STUDENT BODY STATS

2005-2006 enrollment: 11,924 full-time; 8,812 part-time. Men: 41%; women: 59%. **Ethnic makeup:** African American: 33%; Asian American: 5%; Hispanic: 3%; White: 54%; International: 4%.

ADMISSIONS FACTS AND FIGURES

Phone: (313) 577-3577. **Email:** admissions@wayne.edu. **Website:** http://www.wayne.edu/. **Application deadlines for fall 2007:** Regular decision: August 1. Early decision: Not offered. Early action: Not offered. Admission can be deferred. **Application fee:** $30. Common application is not accepted. **To apply online, go to:** http://www.admissions.wayne.edu/ugrad/appl/index.html. **Admissions requirements/recommendations:** High school units required (recommended): English: (4); Mathematics: (4); Science: (3); Foreign language: (2); Social studies: (3); Academic electives:

(2); Total units: (18). Tests: The college uses SAT or ACT scores in admissions decisions. Either SAT or ACT required. For admission to the fall 2007 entering class, the school will accept: ACT with writing, ACT without writing. Campus visit: Recommended. Admissions interview: Neither required nor recommended. Off-campus interview: May be arranged. **Factors that count in admissions decisions:** *Academic:* Secondary school record: Important. Class rank: Not considered. Letters of recommendation: Considered. Standardized test scores: Very important. Essay: Not considered. *Nonacademic:* Interview: Not considered. Extracurricular activities: Not considered. Talent/ability: Considered. Character/personal qualities: Not considered. Alumni/ae relationship: Not considered. Geographical residence: Not considered. State residency: Not considered. Religious affiliation/commitment: Not considered. Minority status: Not considered. Volunteer work: Not considered. Work experience: Not considered. **Other schools with the greatest overlap in applicants:** Central Michigan University; Eastern Michigan University; Michigan State University; Oakland University; University of Michigan–Ann Arbor. **Admissions statistics for the fall 2005 entering class:** Total applicants: 11,410. Total accepted: 6,854. Freshmen enrolled: 2,878; 1% were from out of state. Overall acceptance rate: 60%. **Credentials of fall 2005 freshmen:** 25% ranked in the top 10 percent of their high school class; 50% were in the top 25 percent, and 77% were in the top half. (Proportion submitting class standing: 57%.) **Average high school grade point average:** 3.0. **First-year students submitting ACT scores:** 82%. Scores (25/75 percentile): English: 15-23, Math: 16-23, Composite: 17-23.

ACADEMICS

Year founded: 1868. **Academic calendar:** Semester. **Degrees offered:** bachelor's, post-bachelor's certificate, master's, post-master's certificate, first professional, doctorate. **Most popular majors:** 8% elementary education and teaching, 7% psychology, 6% nursing/registered nurse training (R.N., A.S.N., B.S.N., M.S.N.), 5% biology/biological sciences, 4% art/art studies. **Major fields of study:** area, ethnic, cultural, and gender studies; biological and biomedical sciences; business, management, marketing, and related support services; communication, journalism, and related programs; computer and information sciences and support services; education; engineering; engineering technologies/technicians; English language and literature/letters; family and consumer sciences/human sciences; foreign languages, literatures, and linguistics; health professions and related clinical sciences; history; mathematics and statistics; multi/interdisciplinary studies; natural resources and conservation; personal and culinary services; philosophy and religious studies; physical sciences; psychology; public administration and social service professions; security and protective services; social sciences; visual and performing arts. **Areas of required coursework:** arts/fine arts, humanities, computer literacy, mathematics, English (including composition), foreign languages, sciences (biological or physical), history, social science. **Pre-professional programs:** pre-law, pre-dentistry, pre-medicine, pre-veterinary science, pre-optometry. **Special academic programs:** accelerated program, cooperative (work-study plan) program, cross-registration, distance learning, double major, dual enrollment, English as a Second Language (ESL), external degree program, honors program, independent study, internships, liberal arts/career combination, study abroad, teacher certificate program, weekend college. **Teacher certification offered in:** early childhood, special education, elementary, vo-tech, middle/junior high, secondary, bilingual/bicultural. **Cooperative education programs:** art, business, computer science, education, engineering, health professions, humanities, natural science, social/behavioral science, technologies. **Reserve Officers Training Corps (ROTC):** Air Force ROTC: Offered at cooperating institution (University of Michigan-Ann Arbor). **Faculty and instruction (2005-2006):** Total instructional faculty: 1,004 full-time, 913 part-time (55% men; 45% women; 25% minorities). Full-time faculty with Ph.D. or other terminal degree: 70%. Student/faculty ratio: 16/1. Classes of fewer than 20 students: 39%; of 20 to 49 students: 55%; of 50 or more students: 6%. **Advanced Placement and International Baccalaureate credit:** AP tests may be used for: Credit and/or placement. Scores accepted: 3, 4, 5. International Baccalaureate exams may be used for: Credit only. **Freshmen returning for sophomore year:** 75%. **Graduation rates:** Four-year: 7%; five-year: 25%; six-year: 33%.

COSTS AND FINANCIAL AID

Financial aid office: (313) 577-3378. **Expenses (2005-2006):** Tuition and fees 2005-2006: $6,439 in state, $13,771 out of state; room/board: $6,845. Estimated books and supplies: $835; transportation: $1,566; personal expenses: $1,939. **Financial aid:** Priority filing date for institution's financial aid form: March 1. In 2005-2006, 65% of undergraduates applied for financial aid. Of those, 55% were determined to have financial need; 7% had their

need fully met. Average financial aid package (proportion receiving): $6,958 (54%). Average amount of gift aid, such as scholarships or grants (proportion receiving): $3,484 (38%). Average amount of self-help aid, such as work study or loans (proportion receiving): $3,653 (47%). Average need-based loan (excluding PLUS or other private loans): $3,756. Among students who received need-based aid, the average percentage of need met: 64%. Among students who received aid based on merit, the average award (and the proportion receiving): $2,030 (2%). The average athletic scholarship (and the proportion receiving): $7,420 (2%). Average amount of debt of borrowers graduating in 2005: $19,329. Proportion who borrowed: 50%.

CAMPUS LIFE AND EXTRACURRICULAR ACTIVITIES

Campus housing available: coed dorms, fraternity housing, apartments for married students, apartment for single students, special housing for disabled students. Students who live in college-owned, operated, or affiliated housing: 8%. **Student employment:** During the 2005-2006 academic year, 8% of undergraduates worked on campus. Average per-year earnings: $8,098. **Clubs and organizations:** Number of student organizations: 189. Activities include: choral groups, concert band, dance, drama/theater, jazz band, literary magazine, music ensembles, musical theater, opera, pep band, student government, student newspaper, student film society, symphony orchestra, yearbook. Number of fraternities: 11; sororities: 12. Proportion of men in fraternities: 2%; of women in sororities: 2%. **Sports program (2005-2006):** Member of NCAA II. *Men's intercollegiate varsity sports:* baseball, basketball, cross-country, fencing, football, golf, ice hockey, swimming and diving, tennis. *Women's intercollegiate varsity sports:* basketball, cross-country, fencing, ice hockey, softball, swimming and diving, tennis, volleyball.

SERVICES AND FACILITIES

Basic services: nonremedial tutoring, placement service, day care, health service, health insurance. **Remedial assistance:** reading, math, writing, study skills, other. **Counseling services:** career, personal, veteran student, academic, older student, psychological, religious. **For learning-disabled students:** School does not offer a structured program with separate admission and additional fees. Services include: reading machines, tape recorders, diagnostic testing service, untimed tests, note-taking services, learning center, extended time for tests, tutors, texts on tape. **Library:** Number of titles: 3,383,826; number of current serial subscriptions: 22,606. **Information technology resources:** Students are not required to lease or own a computer. Number of campus computers available to all students: 1,800. School has a wireless network. Approximate number of users that can be accommodated: 3,500. Proportion of college-owned housing units wired for high-speed internet access: 100%. **Campus safety:** Security services offered: 24-hour foot-and-vehicle patrols, 24-hour emergency telephones, lighted pathways/sidewalks, controlled dormitory access (key, security card, etc).

TRANSFER AND INTERNATIONAL STUDENTS

Transfer students: May apply for admission for the following academic terms: Fall, Winter, Spring, Summer. Applicants need a minimum number of credits to apply. For fall 2005: Transfer applications received: 6,331. Transfer applicants offered admission: 3,789. Transfer applicants enrolled: 2,752. **International students:** Number of foreign undergraduates: 831 (4% of student body). Number of countries represented: 58. Minimum TOEFL score required: 550 (paper); 213 (computer).

Western Michigan University

- **Address:** 1903 W. Michigan Avenue, Kalamazoo, MI 49008
- **Website:** http://www.wmich.edu
- **Public**
- **Enrollment:** 18,760 full-time; 2,674 part-time

KEY STATS
✔ **U.S News College Ranking:** third tier, National Universities
✔ **ACT Score (25th/75th percentile):** 20-25
✔ **Tuition:** 2005-2006: $6,478 in state, $15,856 out of state

Selectivity: Selective	Room/board: $6,651
Acceptance rate: 85%	Average debt: $15,300
Student/faculty ratio: 20/1	Proportion who borrowed: 47%

UNDERGRADUATE STUDENT BODY STATS

2005-2006 enrollment: 18,760 full-time; 2,674 part-time. Men: 49%; women: 51%. **Ethnic makeup:** African American: 6%; Asian American: 2%; Hispanic: 2%; White: 88%; International: 2%. **Religious preference:** Roman Catholic: 15%; Protestant: 13%; Jewish: 1%; Unknown: 71%.

ADMISSIONS FACTS AND FIGURES

Phone: (269) 387-2000. **Email:** ask-wmu@wmich.edu. **Website:** http://www.wmich.edu. **Application deadlines for fall 2007:** Regular decision: August 1. Early decision: Not offered. Early action: Not offered. Admission can be deferred. **Application fee:** $35. Common application is not accepted. **Admissions requirements/recommendations:** High school units required (recommended): English: 4 (4); Mathematics: 3 (3); Science: 2 (2); Foreign language: 0 (2); Social studies: 2 (3); History: 1 (1); Academic electives: 2 (2); Total units: 15 (18). Tests: The college uses SAT or ACT scores in admissions decisions. Either SAT or ACT required. For admission to the fall 2007 entering class, the school will accept: ACT with writing, ACT without writing. Campus visit: Recommended. Admissions interview: Neither required nor recommended. Off-campus interview: Not available. **Factors that count in admissions decisions: *Academic:*** Secondary school record: Very important. Class rank: Not considered. Letters of recommendation: Considered. Standardized test scores: Important. Essay: Considered. ***Nonacademic:*** Interview: Considered. Extracurricular activities: Considered. Talent/ability: Important. Character/personal qualities: Considered. Alumni/ae relationship: Important. Geographical residence: Not considered. State residency: Not considered. Religious affiliation/commitment: Not considered. Minority status: Important. Volunteer work: Considered. Work experience: Considered. **Other schools with the greatest overlap in applicants:** Central Michigan University; Eastern Michigan University; Grand Valley State University; Michigan State University; University of Michigan–Ann Arbor. **Admissions statistics for the fall 2005 entering class:** Total applicants: 12,928. Total accepted: 11,045. Freshmen enrolled: 3,751; 8% were from out of state. Overall acceptance rate: 85%. **Credentials of fall 2005 freshmen:** 13% ranked in the top 10 percent of their high school class; 33% were in the top 25 percent, and 69% were in the top half. (Proportion submitting class standing: 80%.) **Average high school grade point average:** 3.4. **First-year students submitting ACT scores:** 96%. Scores (25/75 percentile): English: 19-25, Math: 19-25, Composite: 20-25.

ACADEMICS

Year founded: 1903. **Academic calendar:** Semester. **Degrees offered:** bachelor's, post-bachelor's certificate, master's, doctorate. **Most popular majors:** 24% business, management, marketing, and related support services; 20% education, 7% communication, journalism, and related programs, 5% social sciences, 4% health professions and related clinical services. **Major fields of study:** area, ethnic, cultural, and gender studies; biological and biomedical sciences; business, management, marketing, and related support services; communication, journalism, and related programs; computer and information sciences and support services; education; engineering; engineering technologies/technicians; English language and literature/letters; family and consumer sciences/human sciences; foreign languages, literatures, and linguistics; health professions and related clinical sciences; history; liberal arts and sciences studies, and humanities; mathematics and statistics; mechanic and repair technologies/technicians; multi/interdisciplinary studies; natural resources and conservation; parks, recreation, leisure, and fitness studies; philosophy and religious studies; physical sciences; psychology; public administration and social service professions; security and protective services; social sciences; transportation and materials moving; visual and performing arts. **Areas of required coursework:** arts/fine arts, humanities, mathematics, English (including composition), sciences (biological or physical), social science. **Pre-professional programs:** pre-law, pre-dentistry, pre-medicine. **Special academic programs:** accelerated program, cooperative (work-study plan) program, cross-registration, distance learning, double major, dual enrollment, English as a Second Language (ESL), exchange student program (domestic), honors program, independent study, internships, student-designed major, study abroad, teacher certificate program. **Teacher certification offered in:** early childhood, special education, elementary, middle/junior high, secondary. **Reserve Officers Training Corps (ROTC):** Army ROTC: Offered on campus. **Faculty and instruction (2005-2006):** Total instructional faculty: 922 full-time, 538 part-time (57% men; 43% women). Full-time faculty with Ph.D. or other terminal degree: 83%.

Student/faculty ratio: 20/1. Classes of fewer than 20 students: 38%; of 20 to 49 students: 49%; of 50 or more students: 13%. **Advanced Placement and International Baccalaureate credit:** AP tests may be used for: Credit and/or placement. Scores accepted: 3, 4, 5. **Freshmen returning for sophomore year:** 75%. **Graduation rates:** Four-year: 20%; five-year: 47%; six-year: 54%.

COSTS AND FINANCIAL AID

Financial aid office: (269) 387-6000. **Expenses (2005-2006):** Tuition and fees 2005-2006: $6,478 in state, $15,856 out of state; room/board: $6,651. Estimated books and supplies: $880; transportation: $700; personal expenses: $2,000. **Financial aid:** Priority filing date for institution's financial aid form: March 15. In 2005-2006, 61% of undergraduates applied for financial aid. Of those, 49% were determined to have financial need; 47% had their need fully met. Average financial aid package (proportion receiving): $8,000 (49%). Average amount of gift aid, such as scholarships or grants (proportion receiving): $4,200 (22%). Average amount of self-help aid, such as work study or loans (proportion receiving): $3,100 (43%). Average need-based loan (excluding PLUS or other private loans): $4,000. Among students who received need-based aid, the average percentage of need met: 69%. Among students who received aid based on merit, the average award (and the proportion receiving): $3,600 (11%). The average athletic scholarship (and the proportion receiving): $5,300 (3%). Average amount of debt of borrowers graduating in 2005: $15,300. Proportion who borrowed: 47%.

CAMPUS LIFE AND EXTRACURRICULAR ACTIVITIES

Campus housing available: coed dorms, women's dorms, men's dorms, sorority housing, fraternity housing, apartments for married students, apartment for single students, special housing for disabled students, special housing for international students, other housing options. Students who live in college-owned, operated, or affiliated housing: 24%. **Student employment:** During the 2005-2006 academic year, 19% of undergraduates worked on campus. Average per-year earnings: $4,290. **Clubs and organizations:** Number of student organizations: 275. Activities include: choral groups, concert band, dance, drama/theater, jazz band, literary magazine, marching band, music ensembles, musical theater, opera, pep band, radio station, student government, student newspaper, symphony orchestra, yearbook. Number of fraternities: 14; sororities: 12. Proportion of men in fraternities: 2%; of women in sororities: 3%. **Sports program (2005-2006):** Member of NCAA I. ***Men's intercollegiate varsity sports:*** baseball, basketball, cross-country, football, ice hockey, soccer, tennis. ***Women's intercollegiate varsity sports:*** basketball, cross-country, golf, gymnastics, soccer, softball, tennis, track and field (indoor), track and field (outdoor), volleyball.

SERVICES AND FACILITIES

Basic services: nonremedial tutoring, placement service, health service, other. **Remedial assistance:** reading, math, writing, study skills. **Counseling services:** minority student, career, personal, academic, psychological, birth control, religious. **For learning-disabled students:** School does not offer a structured program with separate admission and additional fees. Total undergraduates in learning-disabled program or receiving services: 128. Services include: remedial math, remedial English, reading machines, remedial reading, tape recorders, learning center, readers, extended time for tests, priority registration, priority seating, texts on tape, other testing accomodations, other. **Library:** Number of titles: 2,040,692; number of current serial subscriptions: 9,715. **Information technology resources:** Students are not required to lease or own a computer. Number of campus computers available to all students: 2,000. School has a wireless network. Approximate number of users that can be accommodated: 24,000. Proportion of college-owned housing units wired for high-speed internet access: 100%. **Campus safety:** Security services offered: 24-hour foot-and-vehicle patrols, late-night transport/escort service, 24-hour emergency telephones, lighted pathways/sidewalks, controlled dormitory access (key, security card, etc).

TRANSFER AND INTERNATIONAL STUDENTS

Transfer students: May apply for admission for the following academic terms: Fall, Winter, Spring, Summer. Applicants do not need a minimum number of credits to apply. For fall 2005: Transfer applications received: 3,106. Transfer applicants offered admission: 2,493. Transfer applicants enrolled: 1,599. **International students:** Number of foreign undergraduates: 502 (2% of student body). Number of countries represented: 85. Minimum TOEFL score required: 550 (paper).

Minnesota

Augsburg College

- **Address:** 2211 Riverside Avenue S, Minneapolis, MN 55454
- **Website:** http://www.augsburg.edu
- **Private; Religious affiliation:** Lutheran
- **Enrollment:** 2,242 full-time; 566 part-time

KEY STATS

✔ **U.S News College Ranking:** 23, Universities–Master's (Midwest)
✔ **ACT Score (25th/75th percentile):** 20-26
✔ **Tuition:** 2006-2007: $23,422

Selectivity: Selective	**Room/board:** $6,604
Acceptance rate: 76%	**Average debt:** $27,514
Student/faculty ratio: 14/1	**Proportion who borrowed:** 76%

UNDERGRADUATE STUDENT BODY STATS

2005-2006 enrollment: 2,242 full-time; 566 part-time. Men: 42%; women: 58%. **Ethnic makeup:** African American: 5%; American-Indian: 1%; Asian American: 3%; Hispanic: 2%; White: 87%; International: 2%. **Religious preference:** Roman Catholic: 16%; Protestant: 7%; Jewish: 1%; Muslim: 1%; No preference: 2%; Unknown: 36%; Lutheran: 35%; Other: 2%.

ADMISSIONS FACTS AND FIGURES

Phone: (612) 330-1001. **Email:** admissions@augsburg.edu. **Website:** http://www.augsburg.edu. **Application deadlines for fall 2007:** Regular decision: August 15. Early decision: Not offered. Early action: Not offered. Admission can be deferred. **Application fee:** $25. Common application is not accepted. **Admissions requirements/recommendations:** High school units required (recommended): English: 4; Mathematics: 3; Science: 3; Foreign language: 2; Social studies: 3; History: (4); Academic electives: (2); Total units: 15 (6). Tests: The college uses SAT or ACT scores in admissions decisions. Either SAT or ACT required. For admission to the fall 2007 entering class, the school will accept: ACT with writing, ACT without writing. Campus visit: Recommended. Admissions interview: Recommended. Off-campus interview: May be arranged. **Factors that count in admissions decisions:** *Academic:* Secondary school record: Important. Class rank: Important. Letters of recommendation: Important. Standardized test scores: Very important. Essay: Very important. *Nonacademic:* Interview: Considered. Extracurricular activities: Important. Talent/ability: Considered. Character/personal qualities: Important. Alumni/ae relationship: Considered. Geographical residence: Not considered. State residency: Not considered. Religious affiliation/commitment: Not considered. Minority status: Not considered. Volunteer work: Considered. Work experience: Considered. **Other schools with the greatest overlap in applicants:** Concordia College–Moorhead; Hamline University; University of Minnesota–Duluth; University of Minnesota–Twin Cities; University of St. Thomas. **Admissions statistics for the fall 2005 entering class:** Total applicants: 996. Total accepted: 758. Freshmen enrolled: 335; 15% were from out of state. Overall acceptance rate: 76%. **Credentials of fall 2005 freshmen:** 17% ranked in the top 10 percent of their high school class; 37% were in the top 25 percent, and 69% were in the top half. (Proportion submitting class standing: 82%.) **Average high school grade point average:** 3.2. **First-year students who submitted SAT scores:** 9%. Scores (25/75 percentile): Verbal: 490-610, Math: 485-605, Combined: 975-1215. **First-year students submitting ACT scores:** 82%. Scores (25/75 percentile): English: 19-24, Math: 18-25, Composite: 20-26.

ACADEMICS

Year founded: 1869. **Academic calendar:** Semester. **Degrees offered:** certificate, bachelor's, master's, post-master's certificate. **Most popular majors:** 32% business, management, marketing, and related support services, 13% education, 8% social sciences, 6% communication, journalism, and related programs, 6% health professions and related clinical sciences. **Major fields of study:** area, ethnic, cultural, and gender studies; biological and biomedical sciences; business, management, marketing, and related support services; communication, journalism, and related programs; computer and information sciences and support services; education; engineering; English language and literature/letters; foreign languages, literatures, and linguistics; health professions and related clinical sciences; history; liberal arts and sciences studies, and humanities; mathematics and statistics; philosophy and religious studies; physical sciences; psychology; public administration and social service professions; social sciences; theology and religious vocations; visual and performing arts. **Areas of required coursework:** arts/fine arts, humanities, mathematics, English (including composition), social science. **Pre-professional programs:** pre-dentistry, pre-medicine, pre-theology, pre-veterinary science, pre-pharmacy, other. **Special academic programs (% participation):** accelerated program, cooperative (work-study plan) program, cross-registration (23%), double major (12%), English as a Second Language (ESL) (1%), honors program (9%), independent study (11%), internships (34%), liberal arts/career combination (0%), student-designed major (1%), study abroad (18%), teacher certificate program (13%), weekend college (66%). **Teacher certification offered in:** special education, elementary, middle/junior high, secondary. **Reserve Officers Training Corps (ROTC):** Army ROTC: Offered at cooperating institution (The University of Minnesota); Navy ROTC: Offered at cooperating institution (The University of Minnesota); Air Force ROTC: Offered at cooperating institution (The University of St. Thomas). **Faculty and instruction (2005-2006):** Total instructional faculty: 163 full-time, 207 part-time (49% men; 51% women; 8% minorities). Full-time faculty with Ph.D. or other terminal degree: 83%. Student/faculty ratio: 14/1. Classes of fewer than 20 students: 61%; of 20 to 49 students: 39%; of 50 or more students: 1%. **Advanced Placement and International Baccalaureate credit:** AP tests may be used for: Credit and/or placement. Scores accepted: 3, 4, 5. International Baccalaureate exams may be used for: Credit and/or placement. **Freshmen returning for sophomore year:** 80%. **Graduation rates:** Four-year: 40%; five-year: 57%; six-year: 54%. **Graduate study:** 25% of students pursue further study within one year.

COSTS AND FINANCIAL AID

Financial aid office: (612) 330-1046. **Expenses (2006-2007):** Tuition and fees 2006-2007: $23,422; room/board: $6,604. Estimated books and supplies: $1,000 personal expenses: $1,735. **Financial aid:** Priority filing date for institution's financial aid form: April 15; deadline: August 1. In 2005-2006, 89% of undergraduates applied for financial aid. Of those, 78% were determined to have financial need; 19% had their need fully met. Average financial aid package (proportion receiving): $12,842 (78%). Average amount of gift aid, such as scholarships or grants (proportion receiving): $10,531 (69%). Average amount of self-help aid, such as work study or loans (proportion receiving): $8,208 (74%). Average need-based loan (excluding PLUS or other private loans): $6,122. Among students who received need-based aid, the average percentage of need met: 68%. Among students who received aid based on merit, the average award (and the proportion receiving): $7,740 (8%). Average amount of debt of borrowers graduating in 2005: $27,514. Proportion who borrowed: 76%.

CAMPUS LIFE AND EXTRACURRICULAR ACTIVITIES

Campus housing available (% using): coed dorms (100%), special housing for disabled students. Students who live in college-owned, operated, or affiliated housing: 44%. **Student employment:** During the 2005-2006 academic year, 37% of undergraduates worked on campus. Average per-year earnings: $1,858. **Clubs and organizations:** Number of student organizations: 40. Activities include: choral groups, concert band, drama/theater, jazz band, literary magazine, music ensembles, radio station, student government, student newspaper, symphony orchestra, yearbook. Number of fraternities: 0; sororities: 0. Average proportion of students who stay on campus on weekends: 62%. **Sports program (2005-2006):** Member of NCAA III. *Men's intercollegiate varsity sports:* baseball, basketball, cross-country, football, golf, ice hockey, soccer, track and field (indoor), track and field (outdoor), wrestling. *Women's intercollegiate varsity sports:* basketball, cross-country, golf, ice hockey, soccer, softball, swimming and diving, track and field (indoor), track and field (outdoor), volleyball.

SERVICES AND FACILITIES

Basic services: nonremedial tutoring, women's center, placement service, health insurance. **Remedial assistance:** study skills. **Counseling services:** minority student, career, personal, academic, psychological, religious. **For learning-disabled students:** School does not offer a structured program with separate admission and additional fees. Total undergraduates in learning-disabled program or receiving services: 168. Services include: reading machines, tape recorders, note-taking services, oral tests, learning center, readers, extended time for tests, tutors, texts on tape, other testing accomodations. **Information technology resources:** Students are not required to lease or own a computer. Number of campus computers available to all students: 260. School has a wireless network. Approximate number of users that can be accommodated: 3,000. Proportion of college-owned housing units wired for high-speed internet access: 100%. **Campus safety:** Security services offered: 24-hour foot-and-vehicle patrols, late-night transport/escort service, lighted pathways/sidewalks, student patrols, controlled dormitory access (key, security card, etc).

TRANSFER AND INTERNATIONAL STUDENTS

Transfer students: May apply for admission for the following academic terms: Fall, Winter, Spring. Applicants do not need a minimum number of credits to apply. For fall 2005: Transfer applications received: 620. Transfer applicants offered admission: 550. Transfer applicants enrolled: 337. **International students:** Number of foreign undergraduates: 58 (2% of student body). Number of countries represented: 20. Minimum TOEFL score required: 550 (paper); 213 (computer). Average TOEFL score: 550 (paper).

Bemidji State University

- **Address:** 1500 Birchmont Drive NE, Bemidji, MN 56601
- **Website:** http://www.bemidjistate.edu
- **Public**
- **Enrollment:** 3,231 full-time; 1,291 part-time

KEY STATS

✔ **U.S News College Ranking:** third tier, Universities–Master's (Midwest)
✔ **ACT Score:** 22
✔ **Tuition:** 2006-2007: $6,490 in state, $6,490 out of state

Selectivity: Selective	**Room/board:** $5,628
Acceptance rate: 85%	**Average debt:** $18,247
Student/faculty ratio: 19/1	**Proportion who borrowed:** 77%

UNDERGRADUATE STUDENT BODY STATS

2005-2006 enrollment: 3,231 full-time; 1,291 part-time. Men: 45%; women: 55%. **Ethnic makeup:** African American: 1%; American-Indian: 3%; White: 90%; International: 6%.

ADMISSIONS FACTS AND FIGURES

Phone: (218) 755-2040. **Email:** admissions@bemidjistate.edu. **Website:** http://www.bemidjistate.edu. **Application deadlines for fall 2007:** Regular decision: Rolling. Early decision: Not offered. Early action: Not offered. Admission can be deferred. **Application fee:** $20. Common application is accepted. **Admissions requirements/recommendations:** High school units required (recommended): English: 4 (4); Mathematics: 3 (3); Science: 3 (3); Foreign language: 2 (2); Social studies: 3 (3); History: 1 (1); Academic electives: 0 (1); Total units: 16 (16). Tests: The college uses SAT or ACT scores in admissions decisions. ACT required. Campus visit: Recommended. Admissions interview: Recommended. Off-campus interview: May be arranged. **Factors that count in admissions decisions:** *Academic:* Secondary school record: Very important. Class rank: Very important. Letters of recommendation: Important. Standardized test scores: Very important. Essay: Considered. *Nonacademic:* Interview: Not considered. Extracurricular activities: Important. Talent/ability: Important. Character/personal qualities: Not considered. Alumni/ae relationship: Not considered. Geographical residence: Not considered. State residency: Not considered. Religious affiliation/commitment: Not considered. Minority status: Not considered. Volunteer work: Not considered. Work experience: Not considered. **Other schools with the greatest overlap in applicants:** Minnesota State University–Moorhead; St. Cloud State University; University of Minnesota–Duluth; University of North Dakota. **Admissions statistics for the fall 2005 entering class:** Total applicants: 1,443. Total accepted: 1,223. Freshmen enrolled: 616; Overall acceptance rate: 85%. **Credentials of fall**

2005 freshmen: 10% ranked in the top 10 percent of their high school class; 50% were in the top 25 percent, and 90% were in the top half.

ACADEMICS

Year founded: 1919. **Academic calendar:** Semester. **Degrees offered:** associate, bachelor's, master's. **Most popular majors:** 30% education, 15% business, management, marketing, and related support services, 10% visual and performing arts, 8% engineering technologies/technicians, 5% health professions and related clinical sciences. **Major fields of study:** biological and biomedical sciences; business, management, marketing, and related support services; communication, journalism, and related programs; computer and information sciences and support services; education; engineering technologies/technicians; English language and literature/letters; foreign languages, literatures, and linguistics; health professions and related clinical sciences; history; liberal arts and sciences studies, and humanities; mathematics and statistics; natural resources and conservation; parks, recreation, leisure, and fitness studies; philosophy and religious studies; psychology; public administration and social service professions; security and protective services; social sciences; visual and performing arts. **Areas of required coursework:** arts/fine arts, computer literacy, mathematics, English (including composition), sciences (biological or physical), history, social science. **Pre-professional programs:** pre-law, pre-dentistry, pre-medicine, pre-veterinary science, pre-optometry, pre-pharmacy. **Special academic programs (% participation):** cross-registration, distance learning (8%), double major (3%), dual enrollment, English as a Second Language (ESL) (1%), exchange student program (domestic), external degree program, honors program (2%), independent study (5%), internships (5%), liberal arts/career combination (16%), study abroad (4%), teacher certificate program (28%). **Teacher certification offered in:** early childhood, special education, elementary, vo-tech, middle/junior high, secondary. **Cooperative education programs:** education, health professions, technologies. **Faculty and instruction (2005-2006):** Total instructional faculty: 226 full-time, 83 part-time (56% men; 44% women; 4% minorities). Full-time faculty with Ph.D. or other terminal degree: 82%. Student/faculty ratio: 19/1. Classes of fewer than 20 students: 51%; of 20 to 49 students: 44%; of 50 or more students: 4%. **Advanced Placement and International Baccalaureate credit:** AP tests may be used for: Credit only. International Baccalaureate exams may be used for: Credit and/or placement. **Freshmen returning for sophomore year:** 70%. **Graduation rates:** Four-year: 26%; five-year: 43%; six-year: 40%. **Graduate study:** 17% of students pursue further study immediately upon graduation. Fields in which graduates pursue further study: Master of Business Administration (MBA), 5%; law, 1%; medicine, 1%; dentistry, 1%; education, 17%; arts and sciences, 27%.

COSTS AND FINANCIAL AID

Financial aid office: (218) 755-4143. **Expenses (2006-2007):** Tuition and fees 2006-2007: $6,490 in state, $6,490 out of state; room/board: $5,628. Estimated books and supplies: $800; transportation: $848; personal expenses: $1,252. **Financial aid:** Priority filing date for institution's financial aid form: May 15. In 2005-2006, 75% of undergraduates applied for financial aid. Of those, 57% were determined to have financial need; 30% had their need fully met. Average financial aid package (proportion receiving): $7,414 (57%). Average amount of gift aid, such as scholarships or grants (proportion receiving): $4,132 (41%). Average amount of self-help aid, such as work study or loans (proportion receiving): $3,843 (47%). Average need-based loan (excluding PLUS or other private loans): $3,421. Among students who received need-based aid, the average percentage of need met: 78%. Among students who received aid based on merit, the average award (and the proportion receiving): $6,656 (17%). The average athletic scholarship (and the proportion receiving): $2,989 (5%). Average amount of debt of borrowers graduating in 2005: $18,247. Proportion who borrowed: 77%.

CAMPUS LIFE AND EXTRACURRICULAR ACTIVITIES

Campus housing available (% using): coed dorms (1%), women's dorms (25%), men's dorms (25%), fraternity housing, apartments for married students, apartment for single students, other housing options (49%). Students who live in college-owned, operated, or affiliated housing: 25%. **Student employment:** During the 2005-2006 academic year, 70% of undergraduates worked on campus. Average per-year earnings: $4,000. **Clubs and organizations:** Number of student organizations: 100. Activities include: choral groups, concert band, dance, drama/theater, jazz band, literary magazine, music ensembles, musical theater, opera, pep band, radio station, student government, student newspaper, student film society, symphony orchestra, television station. Number of fraternities: 2; sororities: 2. Average proportion of students who stay on campus on weekends: 30%. **Sports program (2005-2006):** Member of NCAA II. *Men's intercollegiate varsity sports:*

baseball, basketball, football, golf, ice hockey, track and field (indoor), track and field (outdoor). **Women's intercollegiate varsity sports:** basketball, cross-country, golf, ice hockey, soccer, softball, tennis, track and field (indoor), track and field (outdoor), volleyball.

SERVICES AND FACILITIES

Basic services: nonremedial tutoring, women's center, placement service, day care, health service, health insurance. **Remedial assistance:** reading, math, writing, study skills. **Counseling services:** minority student, career, personal, veteran student, academic, older student, psychological, birth control. **For learning-disabled students:** School does not offer a structured program with separate admission and additional fees. Total undergraduates in learning-disabled program or receiving services: 107. Services include: remedial math, remedial English, reading machines, remedial reading, tape recorders, diagnostic testing service, untimed tests, note-taking services, oral tests, learning center, readers, extended time for tests, tutors, early syllabus, priority registration, priority seating, texts on tape, exams on tape or computer, other testing accomodations. **Library:** Number of titles: 405,045; number of current serial subscriptions: 2,700. **Information technology resources:** Students are not required to lease or own a computer. Number of campus computers available to all students: 1,600. School has a wireless network. Approximate number of users that can be accommodated: 4,000. Proportion of college-owned housing units wired for high-speed internet access: 100%. **Campus safety:** Security services offered: 24-hour foot-and-vehicle patrols, late-night transport/escort service, 24-hour emergency telephones, lighted pathways/sidewalks, student patrols, controlled dormitory access (key, security card, etc).

TRANSFER AND INTERNATIONAL STUDENTS

Transfer students: May apply for admission for the following academic terms: Fall, Spring, Summer. Applicants do not need a minimum number of credits to apply. For fall 2005: Transfer applications received: 419. Transfer applicants offered admission: 409. Transfer applicants enrolled: 321. **International students:** Number of foreign undergraduates: 270 (6% of student body). Number of countries represented: 41. Minimum TOEFL score required: 550 (paper).

Bethel University

- **Address:** 3900 Bethel Drive, St. Paul, MN 55112
- **Website:** http://www.bethel.edu
- **Private; Religious affiliation:** Baptist General Conference
- **Enrollment:** 2,875 full-time; 322 part-time

KEY STATS

✔ **U.S News College Ranking:** 14, Universities–Master's (Midwest)
✔ **ACT Score (25th/75th percentile):** 22-28
✔ **Tuition:** 2006-2007: $22,700
  Selectivity: More selective **Room/board:** $7,140
  Acceptance rate: 87% **Average debt:** $25,325
  Student/faculty ratio: 14/1 **Proportion who borrowed:** 75%

UNDERGRADUATE STUDENT BODY STATS

2005-2006 enrollment: 2,875 full-time; 322 part-time. Men: 38%; women: 62%. **Ethnic makeup:** African American: 3%; Asian American: 2%; Hispanic: 2%; White: 92%. **Religious preference:** Roman Catholic: 3%; Protestant: 67%; Unknown: 6%; Baptist General Conference: 24%.

ADMISSIONS FACTS AND FIGURES

Phone: (800) 255-8706. **Email:** BUadmissions-cas@bethel.edu. **Website:** http://www.bethel.edu. **Application deadlines for fall 2007:** Regular decision: March 1; decision sent by January 15. Early decision: Not offered. Early action: Send application by: December 1; Decision sent by: January 15. Admission cannot be deferred. **Application fee:** $25. Common application is not accepted. **To apply online, go to:** https://www.applyweb.com/aw?bethel. **Admissions requirements/recommendations:** High school units required (recommended): English: (4); Mathematics: (3); Science: (3); Foreign language: (2); Social studies: (4); History: (3); Total units: (19). Tests: The college uses SAT or ACT scores in admissions decisions. Either SAT or ACT required. For admission to the fall 2007 entering class, the school will accept: ACT with writing, ACT without writing. Campus visit: Recommended. Admissions interview: Recommended. Off-campus inter-

view: Not available. **Factors that count in admissions decisions: Academic:** Secondary school record: Very important. Class rank: Very important. Letters of recommendation: Important. Standardized test scores: Very important. Essay: Important. **Nonacademic:** Interview: Important. Extracurricular activities: Considered. Talent/ability: Not considered. Character/personal qualities: Important. Alumni/ae relationship: Considered. Geographical residence: Not considered. State residency: Not considered. Religious affiliation/commitment: Important. Minority status: Considered. Volunteer work: Considered. Work experience: Not considered. **Other schools with the greatest overlap in applicants:** Gustavus Adolphus College; Northwestern College; St. Olaf College; University of Minnesota–Twin Cities; Wheaton College. **Admissions statistics for the fall 2005 entering class:** Total applicants: 1,636. Total accepted: 1,427. Freshmen enrolled: 731; 26% were from out of state. Overall acceptance rate: 87%. Non-early acceptance rate: 90%. **Size of waiting list:** 24 applicants; enrolled from waiting list: 24. **Credentials of fall 2005 freshmen:** 32% ranked in the top 10 percent of their high school class; 63% were in the top 25 percent, and 87% were in the top half. (Proportion submitting class standing: 83%.) **First-year students who submitted SAT scores:** 15%. Scores (25/75 percentile): Verbal: 520-670, Math: 520-630, Combined: 1040-1300. **First-year students submitting ACT scores:** 94%. Scores (25/75 percentile): English: 21-29, Math: 21-27, Composite: 22-28.

ACADEMICS

Year founded: 1871. **Academic calendar:** 4-1-4. **Degrees offered:** certificate, associate, bachelor's, post-bachelor's certificate, master's, post-master's certificate, first professional, doctorate. **Most popular majors:** 24% business, management, marketing, and related support services, 15% education, 14% health professions and related clinical sciences, 8% theology and religious vocations, 6% communication, journalism, and related programs. **Major fields of study:** biological and biomedical sciences; business, management, marketing, and related support services; communication, journalism, and related programs; computer and information sciences and support services; education; engineering; English language and literature/letters; foreign languages, literatures, and linguistics; health professions and related clinical sciences; history; mathematics and statistics; multi/interdisciplinary studies; natural resources and conservation; parks, recreation, leisure, and fitness studies; philosophy and religious studies; physical sciences; psychology; public administration and social service professions; social sciences; theology and religious vocations; visual and performing arts. **Areas of required coursework:** arts/fine arts, humanities, mathematics, English (including composition), sciences (biological or physical), history, social science. **Pre-professional programs:** pre-law, pre-dentistry, pre-medicine, pre-theology, pre-veterinary science, pre-optometry, pre-pharmacy. **Special academic programs (% participation):** accelerated program, distance learning, double major (8%), dual enrollment, exchange student program (domestic), external degree program, honors program (3%), independent study (16%), internships (28%), liberal arts/career combination, student-designed major (2%), study abroad (33%), teacher certificate program (18%), other. **Teacher certification offered in:** early childhood, elementary, middle/junior high, secondary. **Cooperative education programs:** business, education, engineering, health professions, natural science. **Reserve Officers Training Corps (ROTC):** Army ROTC: Offered at cooperating institution (University of Minnesota); Air Force ROTC: Offered at cooperating institution (University of St. Thomas). **Faculty and instruction (2005-2006):** Total instructional faculty: 175 full-time, 136 part-time (50% men; 50% women; 6% minorities). Full-time faculty with Ph.D. or other terminal degree: 74%. Student/faculty ratio: 14/1. Classes of fewer than 20 students: 50%; of 20 to 49 students: 46%; of 50 or more students: 4%. **Advanced Placement and International Baccalaureate credit:** AP tests may be used for: Credit only. Scores accepted: 3, 4, 5. International Baccalaureate exams may be used for: Credit only. **Freshmen returning for sophomore year:** 86%. **Graduation rates:** Four-year: 62%; five-year: 72%; six-year: 72%. **Graduate study:** 13% of students pursue further study immediately upon graduation. Fields in which graduates pursue further study: Master of Business Administration (MBA), 10%; law, 4%; theology (or the seminary), 13%; education, 21%; arts and sciences, 34%.

COSTS AND FINANCIAL AID

Financial aid office: (800) 255-8706. **Expenses (2006-2007):** Tuition and fees 2006-2007: $22,700; room/board: $7,140. Estimated books and supplies: $860; transportation: $0; personal expenses: $1,700. **Financial aid:** Priority filing date for institution's financial aid form: April 15. In 2005-2006, 79% of undergraduates applied for financial aid. Of those, 66% were determined to have financial need; 24% had their need fully met. Average financial aid package (proportion receiving): $14,918 (66%). Average amount of gift aid, such as scholarships or grants (proportion receiving): $8,846 (66%).

Average amount of self-help aid, such as work study or loans (proportion receiving): $6,112 (61%). Average need-based loan (excluding PLUS or other private loans): $4,368. Among students who received need-based aid, the average percentage of need met: 78%. Among students who received aid based on merit, the average award (and the proportion receiving): $3,545 (25%). The average athletic scholarship (and the proportion receiving): $0 (0%). Average amount of debt of borrowers graduating in 2005: $25,325. Proportion who borrowed: 75%.

CAMPUS LIFE AND EXTRACURRICULAR ACTIVITIES

Campus housing available: coed dorms, apartment for single students, special housing for disabled students. Students who live in college-owned, operated, or affiliated housing: 72%. **Student employment:** During the 2005-2006 academic year, 40% of undergraduates worked on campus. Average per-year earnings: $1,500. **Clubs and organizations:** Number of student organizations: 61. Activities include: choral groups, concert band, dance, drama/theater, jazz band, literary magazine, music ensembles, musical theater, pep band, radio station, student government, student newspaper, student film society, symphony orchestra, television station. Number of fraternities: 0; sororities: 0. Average proportion of students who stay on campus on weekends: 70%. **Sports program (2005-2006):** Member of NCAA III. *Men's intercollegiate varsity sports:* baseball, basketball, cross-country, football, golf, ice hockey, soccer, tennis, track and field (indoor), track and field (outdoor). *Women's intercollegiate varsity sports:* basketball, cross-country, ice hockey, soccer, softball, tennis, track and field (indoor), track and field (outdoor), volleyball.

SERVICES AND FACILITIES

Basic services: nonremedial tutoring, placement service, day care, health service. **Counseling services:** minority student, career, personal, academic, older student, psychological, religious. **For learning-disabled students:** School does not offer a structured program with separate admission and additional fees. Total undergraduates in learning-disabled program or receiving services: 64. Services include: remedial math, remedial English, remedial reading, tape recorders, learning center, tutors, early syllabus, priority seating. **Library:** Number of titles: 167,005; number of current serial subscriptions: 20,104. **Information technology resources:** Students are not required to lease or own a computer. Number of campus computers available to all students: 420. School has a wireless network. Approximate number of users that can be accommodated: 1,000. Proportion of college-owned housing units wired for high-speed internet access: 100%. **Campus safety:** Security services offered: 24-hour foot-and-vehicle patrols, late-night transport/escort service, lighted pathways/sidewalks, student patrols, controlled dormitory access (key, security card, etc).

TRANSFER AND INTERNATIONAL STUDENTS

Transfer students: May apply for admission for the following academic terms: Fall, Winter, Spring. Applicants do not need a minimum number of credits to apply. For fall 2005: Transfer applications received: 303. Transfer applicants offered admission: 237. Transfer applicants enrolled: 146. **International students:** Number of foreign undergraduates: 11. Minimum TOEFL score required: 525 (paper); 195 (computer).

Carleton College

- **Address:** 1 N. College Street, Northfield, MN 55057
- **Website:** http://www.carleton.edu
- **Private**
- **Enrollment:** 1,936 full-time; 23 part-time

KEY STATS

✔ **U.S News College Ranking:** 6, Liberal Arts Colleges
✔ **ACT Score (25th/75th percentile):** 1320-1500
✔ **Tuition:** 2006-2007: $34,272

Selectivity: Most selective	**Room/board:** $8,592
Acceptance rate: 29%	**Average debt:** $17,842
Student/faculty ratio: 9/1	**Proportion who borrowed:** 60%

UNDERGRADUATE STUDENT BODY STATS

2005-2006 enrollment: 1,936 full-time; 23 part-time. Men: 48%; women: 52%. **Ethnic makeup:** African American: 6%; American-Indian: 1%; Asian American: 10%; Hispanic: 5%; White: 73%; International: 6%. **Religious**

preference: Roman Catholic: 14%; Protestant: 29%; Jewish: 8%; Muslim: 1%; Hindu: 1%; Buddhist: 2%; No preference: 38%; Unitarian Universalist: 4%; Other: 3%.

ADMISSIONS FACTS AND FIGURES

Phone: (507) 646-4190. **Email:** admissions@acs.carleton.edu. **Website:** http://www.carleton.edu. **Application deadlines for fall 2007:** Regular decision: January 15; decision sent by April 15. Early decision: Send application by: November 15; Decision sent by: December 15. Early action: Not offered. Admission can be deferred. **Application fee:** $30. Common application is accepted. **To apply online, go to:** http://www.carleton.edu/admissions/application/. **Admissions requirements/recommendations:** High school units required (recommended): English: (4); Mathematics: (3); Science: (3); Foreign language: (3); Social studies: (3). Tests: The college uses SAT or ACT scores in admissions decisions. Either SAT or ACT required. For admission to the fall 2007 entering class, the school will accept: ACT with writing. Campus visit: Recommended. Admissions interview: Recommended. Off-campus interview: May be arranged. **Factors that count in admissions decisions:** *Academic:* Secondary school record: Very important. Class rank: Very important. Letters of recommendation: Important. Standardized test scores: Important. Essay: Important. *Nonacademic:* Interview: Considered. Extracurricular activities: Important. Talent/ability: Important. Character/personal qualities: Important. Alumni/ae relationship: Important. Geographical residence: Considered. State residency: Considered. Religious affiliation/commitment: Not considered. Minority status: Important. Volunteer work: Important. Work experience: Important. **Other schools with the greatest overlap in applicants:** Brown University; Harvard University; Macalester College; Williams College; Yale University. **Admissions statistics for the fall 2005 entering class:** Total applicants: 5,036. Total accepted: 1,471. Freshmen enrolled: 541; 73% were from out of state. Accepted through early-decision or early-action plans: 38%. Overall acceptance rate: 29%. Early-decision acceptance rate: 51%. Non-early acceptance rate: 27%. **Size of waiting list:** 1430 applicants; enrolled from waiting list: 0. **Credentials of fall 2005 freshmen:** 71% ranked in the top 10 percent of their high school class; 91% were in the top 25 percent, and 100% were in the top half. (Proportion submitting class standing: 61%.) **First-year students who submitted SAT scores:** 78%. Scores (25/75 percentile): Verbal: 660-760, Math: 660-740, Combined: 1320-1500. **First-year students submitting ACT scores:** 53%. Scores (25/75 percentile): English: N/A, Math: N/A, Composite: 27-32.

ACADEMICS

Year founded: 1866. **Academic calendar:** Trimester. **Degrees offered:** bachelor's. **Most popular majors:** 15% political science and government, 12% biology/biological sciences, 10% economics, 8% psychology, 7% English language and literature. **Major fields of study:** area, ethnic, cultural, and gender studies; biological and biomedical sciences; computer and information sciences and support services; English language and literature/letters; foreign languages, literatures, and linguistics; history; mathematics and statistics; philosophy and religious studies; physical sciences; psychology; social sciences; visual and performing arts. **Areas of required coursework:** arts/fine arts, humanities, mathematics, English (including composition), foreign languages, sciences (biological or physical), social science, other. **Pre-professional programs:** pre-law, pre-dentistry, pre-medicine, pre-theology, pre-veterinary science, pre-optometry, pre-pharmacy. **Special academic programs (% participation):** accelerated program (11.4%), cross-registration (2.4%), double major (5%), independent study (30.4%), internships (3.2%), student-designed major (3.6%), study abroad (66.4%), teacher certificate program (.8%). **Teacher certification offered in:** secondary. **Cooperative education programs:** education, engineering, other. **Faculty and instruction (2005-2006):** Total instructional faculty: 198 full-time, 18 part-time (58% men; 42% women; 21% minorities). Full-time faculty with Ph.D. or other terminal degree: 94%. Student/faculty ratio: 9/1. Classes of fewer than 20 students: 66%; of 20 to 49 students: 34%; of 50 or more students: 1%. **Advanced Placement and International Baccalaureate credit:** AP tests may be used for: Credit and/or placement. Scores accepted: 2, 3, 4, 5. International Baccalaureate exams may be used for: Credit and/or placement. **Freshmen returning for sophomore year:** 97%. **Graduation rates:** Four-year: 81%; five-year: 86%; six-year: 87%. **Graduate study:** 22% of students pursue further study immediately upon graduation; 75% within five years. Fields in which graduates pursue further study: Master of Business Administration (MBA), 6%; law, 11%; medicine, 8%; engineering, 3%; theology (or the seminary), 1%; education, 2%; arts and sciences, 45%.

COSTS AND FINANCIAL AID

Financial aid office: (507) 646-4138. **Expenses (2006-2007):** Tuition and fees 2006-2007: $34,272; room/board: $8,592. Estimated books and supplies: $603; transportation: $700; personal expenses: $603. **Financial aid:** Priority filing date for institution's financial aid form: February 15; deadline: February 15. In 2005-2006, 88% of undergraduates applied for financial aid. Of those, 60% were determined to have financial need; 100% had their need fully met. Average financial aid package (proportion receiving): $26,649 (60%). Average amount of gift aid, such as scholarships or grants (proportion receiving): $20,842 (58%). Average amount of self-help aid, such as work study or loans (proportion receiving): $6,217 (58%). Average need-based loan (excluding PLUS or other private loans): $3,691. Among students who received need-based aid, the average percentage of need met: 100%. Among students who received aid based on merit, the average award (and the proportion receiving): $4,876 (8%). The average athletic scholarship (and the proportion receiving): $0 (0%). Average amount of debt of borrowers graduating in 2005: $17,842. Proportion who borrowed: 60%.

CAMPUS LIFE AND EXTRACURRICULAR ACTIVITIES

Campus housing available (% using): coed dorms (90%), apartment for single students (7%), special housing for disabled students (1%), other housing options (2%). Students who live in college-owned, operated, or affiliated housing: 90%. **Student employment:** During the 2005-2006 academic year, 56% of undergraduates worked on campus. Average per-year earnings: $2,505. **Clubs and organizations:** Number of student organizations: 132. Activities include: choral groups, concert band, dance, drama/theater, jazz band, literary magazine, music ensembles, musical theater, radio station, student government, student newspaper, student film society, symphony orchestra, yearbook. Number of fraternities: 0; sororities: 0. Average proportion of students who stay on campus on weekends: 97%. **Sports program (2005-2006):** Member of NCAA III. *Men's intercollegiate varsity sports:* baseball, basketball, cross-country, football, golf, soccer, swimming and diving, tennis, track and field (indoor), track and field (outdoor). *Women's intercollegiate varsity sports:* basketball, cross-country, golf, soccer, softball, swimming and diving, syncronized swimming, tennis, track and field (indoor), track and field (outdoor), volleyball.

SERVICES AND FACILITIES

Basic services: nonremedial tutoring, women's center, placement service, health service, health insurance. **Counseling services:** minority student, career, personal, academic, psychological, birth control, religious, other. **For learning-disabled students:** School does not offer a structured program with separate admission and additional fees. Services include: reading machines, tape recorders, diagnostic testing service, note-taking services, learning center, extended time for tests, tutors, texts on tape, other testing accomodations. **Library:** Number of titles: 946,259; number of current serial subscriptions: 7,154. **Information technology resources:** Students are not required to lease or own a computer. Number of campus computers available to all students: 267. School has a wireless network. Approximate number of users that can be accommodated: 600. Proportion of college-owned housing units wired for high-speed internet access: 100%. **Campus safety:** Security services offered: 24-hour foot-and-vehicle patrols, late-night transport/escort service, 24-hour emergency telephones, lighted pathways/sidewalks, student patrols, controlled dormitory access (key, security card, etc).

TRANSFER AND INTERNATIONAL STUDENTS

Transfer students: May apply for admission for the following academic terms: Fall. Applicants need a minimum number of credits to apply. For fall 2005: Transfer applications received: 190. Transfer applicants offered admission: 8. Transfer applicants enrolled: 5. **International students:** Number of foreign undergraduates: 109 (6% of student body). Number of countries represented: 36. Minimum TOEFL score required: 600 (paper); 250 (computer).

College of St. Benedict

- **Address:** 37 S. College Avenue, St. Joseph, MN 56374
- **Website:** http://www.csbsju.edu
- **Private; Religious affiliation:** Roman Catholic (Benedictine)
- **Enrollment:** 1,993 full-time; 52 part-time

KEY STATS

✔ **U.S News College Ranking:** 95, Liberal Arts Colleges
✔ **ACT Score (25th/75th percentile):** 23-27
✔ **Tuition:** 2006-2007: $24,924

Selectivity: More selective	**Room/board:** $6,898
Acceptance rate: 86%	**Average debt:** $24,764
Student/faculty ratio: 13/1	**Proportion who borrowed:** 72%

UNDERGRADUATE STUDENT BODY STATS

2005-2006 enrollment: 1,993 full-time; 52 part-time. Men: 0%; women: 100%. **Ethnic makeup:** African American: 1%; Asian American: 3%; Hispanic: 1%; White: 92%; International: 4%. **Religious preference:** Protestant: 20%; No preference: 4%; Roman Catholic (Benedictine): 66%; Other Christian: 7%; Other: 3%.

ADMISSIONS FACTS AND FIGURES

Phone: (320) 363-2196. **Email:** admissions@csbsju.edu. **Website:** http://www.csbsju.edu. **Application deadlines for fall 2007:** Regular decision: Rolling. Early decision: Not offered. Early action: Not offered. Admission can be deferred. Common application is accepted. **To apply online, go to:** http://www.csbsju.edu/admission/. **Admissions requirements/recommendations:** High school units required (recommended): English: (4); Mathematics: (3); Science: (2); Foreign language: (2); Social studies: (2); History: (0); Academic electives: (4); Total units: (17). Tests: The college uses SAT or ACT scores in admissions decisions. Either SAT or ACT required. For admission to the fall 2007 entering class, the school will accept: ACT with writing, ACT without writing. Campus visit: Recommended. Admissions interview: Recommended. Off-campus interview: May be arranged. **Factors that count in admissions decisions:** *Academic:* Secondary school record: Very important. Class rank: Important. Letters of recommendation: Important. Standardized test scores: Very important. Essay: Very important. *Nonacademic:* Interview: Considered. Extracurricular activities: Important. Talent/ability: Considered. Character/personal qualities: Considered. Alumni/ae relationship: Considered. Geographical residence: Important. State residency: Not considered. Religious affiliation/commitment: Not considered. Minority status: Important. Volunteer work: Important. Work experience: Considered. **Other schools with the greatest overlap in applicants:** Gustavus Adolphus College; St. Cloud State University; University of Minnesota–Duluth; University of Minnesota–Twin Cities; University of St. Thomas. **Admissions statistics for the fall 2005 entering class:** Total applicants: 1,472. Total accepted: 1,267. Freshmen enrolled: 576; 13% were from out of state. Overall acceptance rate: 86%. **Size of waiting list:** 40 applicants; enrolled from waiting list: 15. **Credentials of fall 2005 freshmen:** 44% ranked in the top 10 percent of their high school class; 79% were in the top 25 percent, and 97% were in the top half. (Proportion submitting class standing: 85%.) **Average high school grade point average:** 3.7. **First-year students who submitted SAT scores:** 11%. Scores (25/75 percentile): Verbal: 520-630, Math: 520-640, Combined: 1040-1270. **First-year students submitting ACT scores:** 95%. Scores (25/75 percentile): English: 22-29, Math: 23-27, Composite: 23-27.

ACADEMICS

Year founded: 1887. **Academic calendar:** Semester. **Degrees offered:** bachelor's. **Most popular majors:** 11% psychology, 10% biology/biological sciences, 10% speech and rhetorical studies, 9% business administration and management, 8% elementary education and teaching. **Major fields of study:** biological and biomedical sciences; business, management, marketing, and related support services; computer and information sciences and support services; education; English language and literature/letters; foreign languages, literatures, and linguistics; health professions and related clinical sciences; history; liberal arts and sciences studies, and humanities; mathematics and statistics; multi/interdisciplinary studies; natural resources and conservation; philosophy and religious studies; physical sciences; psychology; public administration and social service professions; social sciences; theology and religious vocations; visual and performing arts. **Areas of required coursework:** arts/fine arts, humanities, mathematics, English (including composition), philosophy, foreign languages, sciences (biological or physical), history, social science. **Pre-professional programs:** pre-law, pre-dentistry, pre-medicine, pre-theology, pre-veterinary science, pre-optometry, pre-pharmacy, other. **Special academic programs (% participation):** accelerated program (5%), cross-registration (100%), double major (7%), dual enrollment (.5%), English as a Second Language (ESL) (.7%), honors program (14%), independent study (29%), internships (26%), liberal arts/career combination (1%), student-designed major (.6%), study abroad (58%), teacher certificate program (14%). **Teacher certification offered in:** elementary, middle/junior high, secondary. **Reserve Officers Training Corps (ROTC):** Army ROTC: Offered at cooperating institution (Saint John's University). **Faculty and instruction (2005-2006):** Total instructional faculty: 148 full-time, 22 part-time (44% men; 56% women; 7% minorities). Full-time faculty with Ph.D. or other terminal degree: 83%. Student/faculty ratio: 13/1. Classes of fewer than 20 students: 47%; of 20 to 49 students: 53%; of 50 or more students: 0%. **Advanced Placement and International Baccalaureate credit:** AP tests may be used for: Credit and/or placement. Scores accepted: 3, 4, 5. International Baccalaureate exams may be used for: Credit and/or placement. **Freshmen returning for sophomore year:** 89%. **Graduation rates:** Four-year: 71%; five-year: 77%; six-year: 77%. **Graduate study:** 16% of students pursue further study within one year. Fields in which graduates pursue further study: Master of Business Administration (MBA), 6%; law, 6%; medicine, 5%; theology (or the seminary), 1%; education, 13%; arts and sciences, 68%; veterinary medicine, 1%.

COSTS AND FINANCIAL AID
Financial aid office: (320) 363-5388. **Expenses (2006-2007):** Tuition and fees 2006-2007: $24,924; room/board: $6,898. Estimated books and supplies: $800; transportation: $200; personal expenses: $700. **Financial aid:** Priority filing date for institution's financial aid form: March 15. In 2005-2006, 76% of undergraduates applied for financial aid. Of those, 66% were determined to have financial need; 43% had their need fully met. Average financial aid package (proportion receiving): $19,044 (66%). Average amount of gift aid, such as scholarships or grants (proportion receiving): $12,290 (61%). Average amount of self-help aid, such as work study or loans (proportion receiving): $6,810 (60%). Average need-based loan (excluding PLUS or other private loans): $6,030. Among students who received need-based aid, the average percentage of need met: 91%. Among students who received aid based on merit, the average award (and the proportion receiving): $8,210 (29%). The average athletic scholarship (and the proportion receiving): $0 (0%). Average amount of debt of borrowers graduating in 2005: $24,764. Proportion who borrowed: 72%.

CAMPUS LIFE AND EXTRACURRICULAR ACTIVITIES
Campus housing available (% using): women's dorms (67%), apartment for single students (33%), special housing for disabled students. Students who live in college-owned, operated, or affiliated housing: 82%. **Student employment:** During the 2005-2006 academic year, 29% of undergraduates worked on campus. Average per-year earnings: $1,640. **Clubs and organizations:** Number of student organizations: 89. Activities include: choral groups, concert band, dance, drama/theater, jazz band, literary magazine, music ensembles, musical theater, opera, pep band, radio station, student government, student newspaper, symphony orchestra. Number of fraternities: 0; sororities: 0. **Sports program (2005-2006):** Member of NCAA III. *Women's intercollegiate varsity sports:* basketball, cross-country, golf, ice hockey, nordic skiing, soccer, softball, swimming and diving, tennis, track and field (indoor), track and field (outdoor), volleyball.

SERVICES AND FACILITIES
Basic services: nonremedial tutoring, women's center, placement service, health service, health insurance. **Remedial assistance:** study skills, other. **Counseling services:** minority student, career, personal, academic, psychological, religious. **For learning-disabled students:** School does not offer a structured program with separate admission and additional fees. Total undergraduates in learning-disabled program or receiving services: 25. Services include: reading machines, untimed tests, extended time for tests, tutors, priority registration, substitution of courses, other. **Library:** Number of titles: 673,477; number of current serial subscriptions: 1,440. **Information technology resources:** Students are not required to lease or own a computer. Number of campus computers available to all students: 604. School has a wireless network. Proportion of college-owned housing units wired for high-speed internet access: 100%. **Campus safety:** Security services offered: 24-hour foot-and-vehicle patrols, late-night transport/escort service, 24-hour emergency telephones, lighted pathways/sidewalks, student patrols, controlled dormitory access (key, security card, etc).

TRANSFER AND INTERNATIONAL STUDENTS
Transfer students: May apply for admission for the following academic terms: Fall, Spring. Applicants do not need a minimum number of credits to apply. For fall 2005: Transfer applications received: 65. Transfer applicants offered admission: 55. Transfer applicants enrolled: 42. **International students:** Number of foreign undergraduates: 73 (4% of student body). Number of countries represented: 37. Minimum TOEFL score required: 500 (paper); 173 (computer). Average TOEFL score: 530 (paper).

College of St. Catherine

- **Address:** 2004 Randolph Avenue, St. Paul, MN 55105
- **Website:** http://www.stkate.edu
- **Private; Religious affiliation:** Roman Catholic
- **Enrollment:** 2,362 full-time; 1,243 part-time

KEY STATS
✔ **U.S News College Ranking:** 13, Universities–Master's (Midwest)
✔ **ACT Score (25th/75th percentile):** 22-27
✔ **Tuition:** 2006-2007: $22,870

Selectivity: More selective	**Room/board:** $6,432
Acceptance rate: 78%	**Average debt:** $27,528
Student/faculty ratio: 11/1	**Proportion who borrowed:** 77%

UNDERGRADUATE STUDENT BODY STATS
2005-2006 enrollment: 2,362 full-time; 1,243 part-time. Men: 3%; women: 97%. **Ethnic makeup:** African American: 8%; Asian American: 7%; Hispanic: 3%; White: 80%; International: 2%. **Religious preference:** Protestant: 25%; Jewish: 1%; Muslim: 1%; Hindu: 1%; No preference: 2%; Unknown: 21%; Roman Catholic: 48%; Other: 1%.

ADMISSIONS FACTS AND FIGURES
Phone: (800) 945-4599. **Email:** admissions@stkate.edu. **Website:** http://www.stkate.edu. **Application deadlines for fall 2007:** Regular decision: Rolling. Early decision: Not offered. Early action: Not offered. Admission can be deferred. Common application is not accepted. **To apply online, go to:** http://www.stkate.edu/admissions/apply_home.html. **Admissions requirements/recommendations:** High school units required (recommended): English: (4); Mathematics: (3); Science: (2); Foreign language: (4); Social studies: (2); Total units: (15). **Tests:** The college uses SAT or ACT scores in admissions decisions. Either SAT or ACT required. For admission to the fall 2007 entering class, the school will accept: ACT with writing, ACT without writing. Campus visit: Recommended. Admissions interview: Recommended. Off-campus interview: May be arranged. **Factors that count in admissions decisions:** *Academic:* Secondary school record: Very important. Class rank: Important. Letters of recommendation: Important. Standardized test scores: Important. Essay: Important. *Nonacademic:* Interview: Considered. Extracurricular activities: Important. Talent/ability: Considered. Character/personal qualities: Considered. Alumni/ae relationship: Considered. Geographical residence: Not considered. State residency: Not considered. Religious affiliation/commitment: Not considered. Minority status: Considered. Volunteer work: Considered. Work experience: Considered. **Other schools with the greatest overlap in applicants:** College of St. Benedict; Hamline University; University of Minnesota–Twin Cities; University of St. Thomas. **Admissions statistics for the fall 2005 entering class:** Total applicants: 1,475. Total accepted: 1,157. Freshmen enrolled: 413; 15% were from out of state. Overall acceptance rate: 78%. **Credentials of fall 2005 freshmen:** 34% ranked in the top 10 percent of their high school class; 75% were in the top 25 percent, and 95% were in the top half. (Proportion submitting class standing: 83%.) **Average high school grade point average:** 3.6. **First-year students who submitted SAT scores:** 20%. Scores (25/75 percentile): Verbal: 518-660, Math: 495-650, Combined: 1013-1310. **First-year students submitting ACT scores:** 90%. Scores (25/75 percentile): English: 21-28, Math: 20-26, Composite: 22-27.

ACADEMICS
Year founded: 1905. **Academic calendar:** 4-1-4. **Degrees offered:** certificate, associate, bachelor's, post-bachelor's certificate, master's, post-master's certificate, doctorate. **Most popular majors:** 20% nursing/registered nurse training (R.N., A.S.N., B.S.N., M.S.N.), 9% elementary education and teaching, 8% business administration and management, 6% accounting, 6% social work. **Major fields of study:** area, ethnic, cultural, and gender studies;

biological and biomedical sciences; business, management, marketing, and related support services; communication, journalism, and related programs; computer and information sciences and support services; education; English language and literature/letters; family and consumer sciences/human sciences; foreign languages, literatures, and linguistics; health professions and related clinical sciences; history; mathematics and statistics; multi/interdisciplinary studies; parks, recreation, leisure, and fitness studies; philosophy and religious studies; physical sciences; psychology; public administration and social service professions; security and protective services; social sciences; theology and religious vocations; visual and performing arts. **Areas of required coursework:** arts/fine arts, computer literacy, mathematics, English (including composition), philosophy, foreign languages, sciences (biological or physical), history, social science, other. **Pre-professional programs:** pre-law, pre-dentistry, pre-medicine, pre-theology, pre-veterinary science, pre-optometry, pre-pharmacy, other. **Special academic programs (% participation):** cross-registration (1%), double major (7%), dual enrollment (2%), English as a Second Language (ESL) (1%), exchange student program (domestic) (0%), honors program (2%), independent study (18%), internships (42%), student-designed major (1%), study abroad (21%), weekend college (14%). **Teacher certification offered in:** early childhood, elementary, middle/junior high, secondary. **Cooperative education programs:** engineering. **Reserve Officers Training Corps (ROTC):** Air Force ROTC: Offered at cooperating institution (University of St. Thomas). **Faculty and instruction (2005-2006):** Total instructional faculty: 246 full-time, 237 part-time (21% men; 79% women; 6% minorities). Full-time faculty with Ph.D. or other terminal degree: 77%. Student/faculty ratio: 11/1. Classes of fewer than 20 students: 75%; of 20 to 49 students: 23%; of 50 or more students: 2%. **Advanced Placement and International Baccalaureate credit:** AP tests may be used for: Credit only. Scores accepted: 3, 4, 5. International Baccalaureate exams may be used for: Credit only. **Freshmen returning for sophomore year:** 80%. **Graduation rates:** Four-year: 40%; five-year: 55%; six-year: 59%. **Graduate study:** 21% of students pursue further study within one year; 25% within five years.

COSTS AND FINANCIAL AID
Financial aid office: (651) 690-6540. **Expenses (2006-2007):** Tuition and fees 2006-2007: $22,870; room/board: $6,432. Estimated books and supplies: $680; transportation: $150; personal expenses: $934. **Financial aid:** Priority filing date for institution's financial aid form: April 15. In 2005-2006, 83% of undergraduates applied for financial aid. Of those, 72% were determined to have financial need; 16% had their need fully met. Average financial aid package (proportion receiving): $22,474 (69%). Average amount of gift aid, such as scholarships or grants (proportion receiving): $7,248 (58%). Average amount of self-help aid, such as work study or loans (proportion receiving): $5,930 (60%). Average need-based loan (excluding PLUS or other private loans): $4,887. Among students who received need-based aid, the average percentage of need met: 76%. Among students who received aid based on merit, the average award (and the proportion receiving): $12,876 (16%). Average amount of debt of borrowers graduating in 2005: $27,528. Proportion who borrowed: 77%.

CAMPUS LIFE AND EXTRACURRICULAR ACTIVITIES
Campus housing available (% using): women's dorms (76%), apartment for single students (21%), other housing options (3%). Students who live in college-owned, operated, or affiliated housing: 37%. **Student employment:** During the 2005-2006 academic year, 34% of undergraduates worked on campus. Average per-year earnings: $2,158. **Clubs and organizations:** Number of student organizations: 40. Activities include: choral groups, concert band, dance, drama/theater, literary magazine, music ensembles, musical theater, student government, student newspaper, symphony orchestra. ; sororities: 1. Average proportion of students who stay on campus on weekends: 35%. **Sports program (2005-2006):** Member of NCAA III. *Women's intercollegiate varsity sports:* basketball, cross-country, ice hockey, soccer, softball, swimming and diving, tennis, track and field (indoor), track and field (outdoor), volleyball.

SERVICES AND FACILITIES
Basic services: nonremedial tutoring, women's center, placement service, day care, health service, health insurance. **Remedial assistance:** math, writing, study skills. **Counseling services:** minority student, career, personal, academic, psychological, religious. **For learning-disabled students:** School does not offer a structured program with separate admission and additional fees. Services include: remedial math, reading machines, tape recorders, diagnostic testing service, untimed tests, note-taking services, oral tests, learning center, readers, extended time for tests, tutors, other. **Library:** Number of titles: 252,107; number of current serial subscriptions: 14,526.

Information technology resources: Students are not required to lease or own a computer. Number of campus computers available to all students: 180. School has a wireless network. Proportion of college-owned housing units wired for high-speed internet access: 100%. **Campus safety:** Security services offered: 24-hour foot-and-vehicle patrols, 24-hour emergency telephones, lighted pathways/sidewalks, controlled dormitory access (key, security card, etc).

TRANSFER AND INTERNATIONAL STUDENTS
Transfer students: May apply for admission for the following academic terms: Fall, Winter, Spring, Summer. Applicants do not need a minimum number of credits to apply. For fall 2005: Transfer applications received: 1,790. Transfer applicants offered admission: 1,113. Transfer applicants enrolled: 723. **International students:** Number of foreign undergraduates: 64 (2% of student body). Number of countries represented: 26. Minimum TOEFL score required: 500 (paper); 173 (computer).

College of St. Scholastica

- **Address:** 1200 Kenwood Avenue, Duluth, MN 55811
- **Website:** http://www.css.edu
- **Private; Religious affiliation:** Roman Catholic
- **Enrollment:** 2,296 full-time; 317 part-time

KEY STATS
✔ **U.S News College Ranking:** 21, Universities–Master's (Midwest)
✔ **ACT Score (25th/75th percentile):** 21-26
✔ **Tuition:** 2006-2007: $23,574

Selectivity: More selective **Room/board:** $6,514
Acceptance rate: 87% **Average debt:** $29,942
Student/faculty ratio: 13/1 **Proportion who borrowed:** 84%

UNDERGRADUATE STUDENT BODY STATS
2005-2006 enrollment: 2,296 full-time; 317 part-time. Men: 30%; women: 70%. **Ethnic makeup:** African American: 1%; American-Indian: 1%; Asian American: 2%; Hispanic: 1%; White: 91%; International: 3%. **Religious preference:** Protestant: 24%; No preference: 10%; Unknown: 14%; Roman Catholic: 33%; Other: 8%.

ADMISSIONS FACTS AND FIGURES
Phone: (218) 723-6046. **Email:** admissions@css.edu. **Website:** http://www.css.edu. **Application deadlines for fall 2007:** Regular decision: Rolling. Early decision: Not offered. Early action: Not offered. Admission can be deferred. **Application fee:** $25. Common application is accepted. **To apply online, go to:** https://www.css.edu/app/admissions/new_apply.cfm. **Admissions requirements/recommendations:** High school units required (recommended): English: (4); Mathematics: (2); Science: (3); Foreign language: (3); Social studies: (3); History: (3). Tests: The college uses SAT or ACT scores in admissions decisions. Either SAT or ACT required. For admission to the fall 2007 entering class, the school will accept: ACT with writing, ACT without writing. Campus visit: Recommended. Admissions interview: Recommended. Off-campus interview: May be arranged. **Factors that count in admissions decisions:** *Academic:* Secondary school record: Not considered. Class rank: Important. Letters of recommendation: Considered. Standardized test scores: Very important. Essay: Considered. *Nonacademic:* Interview: Considered. Extracurricular activities: Considered. Talent/ability: Considered. Character/personal qualities: Considered. Alumni/ae relationship: Considered. Geographical residence: Considered. State residency: Considered. Religious affiliation/commitment: Considered. Minority status: Considered. Volunteer work: Considered. Work experience: Considered. **Other schools with the greatest overlap in applicants:** College of St. Benedict; Gustavus Adolphus College; University of Minnesota–Duluth; University of Minnesota–Twin Cities; University of St. Thomas. **Admissions statistics for the fall 2005 entering class:** Total applicants: 1,459. Total accepted: 1,268. Freshmen enrolled: 490; 10% were from out of state. Overall acceptance rate: 87%. **Credentials of fall 2005 freshmen:** 25% ranked in the top 10 percent of their high school class; 54% were in the top 25 percent, and 82% were in the top half. (Proportion submitting class standing: 87%.) **Average high school grade point average:** 3.5. **First-year students who submitted SAT scores:** 7%. Scores (25/75 percentile): Verbal: 490-600, Math: 520-620, Combined: 1010-1220. **First-year students submitting ACT**

scores: 94%. Scores (25/75 percentile): English: 20-26, Math: 20-26, Composite: 21-26.

ACADEMICS

Year founded: 1912. **Academic calendar:** Semester. **Degrees offered:** certificate, bachelor's, post-bachelor's certificate, master's, post-master's certificate, first professional. **Most popular majors:** 30% business, management, marketing, and related support services, 29% health professions and related clinical sciences, 9% computer and information sciences and support services, 7% social sciences, 6% biological and biomedical sciences. **Major fields of study:** biological and biomedical sciences; business, management, marketing, and related support services; communication, journalism, and related programs; computer and information sciences and support services; education; English language and literature/letters; health professions and related clinical sciences; history; liberal arts and sciences studies, and humanities; mathematics and statistics; multi/interdisciplinary studies; philosophy and religious studies; physical sciences; psychology; public administration and social service professions; social sciences; visual and performing arts. **Areas of required coursework:** arts/fine arts, mathematics, English (including composition), philosophy, foreign languages, sciences (biological or physical), history, social science, other. **Pre-professional programs:** pre-law, pre-dentistry, pre-medicine, pre-veterinary science, pre-optometry, pre-pharmacy, other. **Special academic programs (% participation):** accelerated program (35%), cross-registration, distance learning, double major (7%), dual enrollment, honors program, independent study, internships, liberal arts/career combination, student-designed major, study abroad, teacher certificate program. **Teacher certification offered in:** elementary, middle/junior high, secondary. **Reserve Officers Training Corps (ROTC):** Air Force ROTC: Offered at cooperating institution (University of Minnesota Duluth). **Faculty and instruction (2005-2006):** Total instructional faculty: 142 full-time, 110 part-time (35% men; 65% women; 5% minorities). Full-time faculty with Ph.D. or other terminal degree: 56%. Student/faculty ratio: 13/1. Classes of fewer than 20 students: 57%; of 20 to 49 students: 38%; of 50 or more students: 5%. **Advanced Placement and International Baccalaureate credit:** AP tests may be used for: Credit and/or placement. Scores accepted: 3, 4, 5. International Baccalaureate exams may be used for: Credit and/or placement. **Freshmen returning for sophomore year:** 82%. **Graduation rates:** Four-year: 50%; five-year: 61%; six-year: 62%. **Graduate study:** 29% of students pursue further study immediately upon graduation.

COSTS AND FINANCIAL AID

Financial aid office: (218) 723-6047. **Expenses (2006-2007):** Tuition and fees 2006-2007: $23,574; room/board: $6,514. Estimated books and supplies: $900; transportation: $602; personal expenses: $1,002. **Financial aid:** Priority filing date for institution's financial aid form: March 15. In 2005-2006, 86% of undergraduates applied for financial aid. Of those, 78% were determined to have financial need; 84% had their need fully met. Average financial aid package (proportion receiving): $17,059 (77%). Average amount of gift aid, such as scholarships or grants (proportion receiving): $5,618 (70%). Average amount of self-help aid, such as work study or loans (proportion receiving): $5,114 (58%). Average need-based loan (excluding PLUS or other private loans): $4,571. Among students who received need-based aid, the average percentage of need met: 84%. Among students who received aid based on merit, the average award (and the proportion receiving): $8,003 (17%). Average amount of debt of borrowers graduating in 2005: $29,942. Proportion who borrowed: 84%.

CAMPUS LIFE AND EXTRACURRICULAR ACTIVITIES

Campus housing available (% using): coed dorms (39%), apartment for single students (60%), special housing for disabled students (1%), other housing options (0%). Students who live in college-owned, operated, or affiliated housing: 51%. **Student employment:** During the 2005-2006 academic year, 37% of undergraduates worked on campus. Average per-year earnings: $762. **Clubs and organizations:** Number of student organizations: 64. Activities include: choral groups, concert band, dance, drama/theater, jazz band, literary magazine, music ensembles, pep band, student government, student newspaper, television station. Number of fraternities: 0; sororities: 0. Average proportion of students who stay on campus on weekends: 65%. **Sports program (2005-2006):** Member of NCAA III. *Men's intercollegiate varsity sports:* baseball, basketball, cross-country, ice hockey, soccer, tennis, track and field (indoor), track and field (outdoor). *Women's intercollegiate varsity sports:* basketball, cross-country, soccer, softball, tennis, track and field (indoor), track and field (outdoor), volleyball.

SERVICES AND FACILITIES

Basic services: nonremedial tutoring, placement service, health service, health insurance. **Remedial assistance:** study skills. **Counseling services:** minority student, career, personal, veteran student, academic, older student, psychological, religious. **For learning-disabled students:** School does not offer a structured program with separate admission and additional fees. Services include: reading machines, tape recorders, note-taking services, oral tests, readers, extended time for tests, tutors, priority registration, substitution of courses, texts on tape, typist/scribe, other testing accommodations, other. **Library:** Number of titles: 148,971; number of current serial subscriptions: 614. **Information technology resources:** Students are not required to lease or own a computer. Number of campus computers available to all students: 183. School has a wireless network. Approximate number of users that can be accommodated: 600. Proportion of college-owned housing units wired for high-speed internet access: 100%. **Campus safety:** Security services offered: 24-hour foot-and-vehicle patrols, late-night transport/escort service, 24-hour emergency telephones, lighted pathways/sidewalks, controlled dormitory access (key, security card, etc).

TRANSFER AND INTERNATIONAL STUDENTS

Transfer students: May apply for admission for the following academic terms: Fall, Spring, Summer. Applicants need a minimum number of credits to apply. For fall 2005: Transfer applications received: 465. Transfer applicants offered admission: 347. Transfer applicants enrolled: 186. **International students:** Number of foreign undergraduates: 69 (3% of student body). Number of countries represented: 28. Minimum TOEFL score required: 550 (paper); 213 (computer). Average TOEFL score: 608 (paper).

College of Visual Arts

- **Address:** 344 Summit Avenue, St. Paul, MN 55102
- **Website:** http://www.cva.edu
- **Private**
- **Enrollment:** 171 full-time; 19 part-time

KEY STATS

✔ **U.S News College Ranking:** Unranked Specialty School–Fine Arts
✔ **ACT Score (25th/75th percentile):** 18-23
✔ **Tuition:** 2006-2007: $19,939

Selectivity: Less selective	**Room/board:** N/A
Acceptance rate: 65%	**Average debt:** N/A
Student/faculty ratio: 16/1	**Proportion who borrowed:** 76%

UNDERGRADUATE STUDENT BODY STATS

2005-2006 enrollment: 171 full-time; 19 part-time. Men: 40%; women: 60%. **Ethnic makeup:** African American: 1%; American-Indian: 1%; Asian American: 1%; Hispanic: 1%; White: 95%.

ADMISSIONS FACTS AND FIGURES

Phone: (651) 224-3416. **Email:** admissions@cva.edu. **Website:** http://www.cva.edu. **Application deadlines for fall 2007:** Regular decision: Rolling. Early decision: Not offered. Early action: Not offered. Admission can be deferred. **Application fee:** $40. Common application is accepted. **To apply online, go to:** https://secure.factorof4.net/cva/application_form.htm. **Admissions requirements/recommendations:** High school units required (recommended): English: (4); Mathematics: (3); Science: (3); Foreign language: (2); Social studies: (3); History: (3). Tests: The college uses SAT or ACT scores in admissions decisions. Either SAT or ACT required. For admission to the fall 2007 entering class, the school will accept: ACT with writing, ACT without writing. Campus visit: Recommended. Admissions interview: Recommended. Off-campus interview: May be arranged. **Factors that count in admissions decisions:** *Academic:* Secondary school record: Important. Class rank: Considered. Letters of recommendation: Not considered. Standardized test scores: Considered. Essay: Considered. *Nonacademic:* Interview: Not considered. Extracurricular activities: Not considered. Talent/ability: Very important. Character/personal qualities: Considered. Alumni/ae relationship: Considered. Geographical residence: Considered. State residency: Not considered. Religious affiliation/commitment: Not considered. Minority status: Important. Volunteer work: Considered. Work experience: Considered. **Admissions statistics for the fall 2005 entering class:** Total applicants: 129. Total accepted: 84. Freshmen enrolled: 52; 2% were from out of state. Overall acceptance rate: 65%. **First-**

year students who submitted SAT scores: 5%. Scores (25/75 percentile): Verbal: N/A, Math: N/A, Combined: N/A. **First-year students submitting ACT scores:** 100%. Scores (25/75 percentile): English: 17-24, Math: 17-21, Composite: 18-23.

ACADEMICS

Year founded: 1924. **Academic calendar:** Semester. **Degrees offered:** bachelor's. **Most popular majors:** 33% graphic design, 29% fine/studio arts, 25% illustration, 13% photography. **Major fields of study:** visual and performing arts. **Areas of required coursework:** arts/fine arts, humanities, computer literacy, mathematics, English (including composition), sciences (biological or physical), history, social science. **Special academic programs (% participation):** honors program (0%), independent study (13%), internships (0%), study abroad (0%). **Faculty and instruction (2005-2006):** Total instructional faculty: 8 full-time, 75 part-time (58% men; 42% women; 0% minorities). Full-time faculty with Ph.D. or other terminal degree: 0%. Student/faculty ratio: 16/1. Classes of fewer than 20 students: 88%; of 20 to 49 students: 12%; of 50 or more students: 0%. **Advanced Placement and International Baccalaureate credit:** AP tests may be used for: Credit only. Scores accepted: 4, 5. **Freshmen returning for sophomore year:** 57%. **Graduation rates:** Four-year: 10%; five-year: 24%; six-year: 34%.

COSTS AND FINANCIAL AID

Financial aid office: (651) 224-3416. **Expenses (2006-2007):** Tuition and fees 2006-2007: $19,939; room/board: N/A. Estimated books and supplies: $2,222; transportation: $2,698; personal expenses: $3,084. **Financial aid:** Priority filing date for institution's financial aid form: April 1; deadline: June 1. In 2005-2006, 82% of undergraduates applied for financial aid. Of those, 75% were determined to have financial need; 3% had their need fully met. Average financial aid package (proportion receiving): $8,429 (75%). Average amount of gift aid, such as scholarships or grants (proportion receiving): $1,939 (62%). Average amount of self-help aid, such as work study or loans (proportion receiving): $4,840 (73%). Average need-based loan (excluding PLUS or other private loans): $4,336. Among students who received need-based aid, the average percentage of need met: 42%. Among students who received aid based on merit, the average award (and the proportion receiving): $1,991 (9%). The average athletic scholarship (and the proportion receiving): $0 (0%). Proportion who borrowed: 76%.

CAMPUS LIFE AND EXTRACURRICULAR ACTIVITIES

Activities include: student government.

SERVICES AND FACILITIES

Remedial assistance: reading, writing, study skills. **Counseling services:** minority student, career, academic, older student. **Library:** Number of titles: 7,096; number of current serial subscriptions: 40. **Information technology resources:** Students are not required to lease or own a computer. School does not have a wireless network. **Campus safety:** Security services offered: late-night transport/escort service.

TRANSFER AND INTERNATIONAL STUDENTS

Transfer students: May apply for admission for the following academic terms: Fall, Spring. Applicants do not need a minimum number of credits to apply. For fall 2005: Transfer applicants enrolled: 2. **International students:** Number of countries represented: 2. Minimum TOEFL score required: 500 (paper); 173 (computer).

Concordia College–Moorhead

- **Address:** 901 Eighth Street S, Moorhead, MN 56562
- **Website:** http://www.cord.edu
- **Private; Religious affiliation:** Lutheran
- **Enrollment:** 2,693 full-time; 66 part-time

KEY STATS

✔ **U.S News College Ranking:** third tier, Liberal Arts Colleges
✔ **ACT Score (25th/75th percentile):** 21-27
✔ **Tuition:** 2006-2007: $20,980

Selectivity: More selective	**Room/board:** $5,090
Acceptance rate: 83%	**Average debt:** $21,532
Student/faculty ratio: 15/1	**Proportion who borrowed:** 72%

UNDERGRADUATE STUDENT BODY STATS

2005-2006 enrollment: 2,693 full-time; 66 part-time. Men: 37%; women: 63%. **Ethnic makeup:** African American: 1%; Asian American: 2%; Hispanic: 1%; White: 92%; International: 4%. **Religious preference:** Roman Catholic: 15%; Protestant: 5%; No preference: 4%; Unknown: 9%; Lutheran: 52%; Baptist: 2%; Other: 13%.

ADMISSIONS FACTS AND FIGURES

Phone: (800) 699-9897. **Email:** admissions@cord.edu. **Website:** http://www.cord.edu. **Application deadlines for fall 2007:** Regular decision: Rolling. Early decision: Not offered. Early action: Not offered. Admission can be deferred. **Application fee:** $20. Common application is accepted. **To apply online, go to:** http://www.cord.edu/dept/admissions/application-form.html. **Admissions requirements/recommendations:** High school units required (recommended): English: (4); Mathematics: (3); Science: (3); Foreign language: (2); Social studies: (3); Academic electives: (2); Total units: 15 (17). Tests: The college uses SAT or ACT scores in admissions decisions. Either SAT or ACT required. For admission to the fall 2007 entering class, the school will accept: ACT with writing, ACT without writing. Campus visit: Recommended. Admissions interview: Recommended. **Factors that count in admissions decisions:** *Academic:* Secondary school record: Important. Class rank: Important. Letters of recommendation: Considered. Standardized test scores: Considered. Essay: Considered. *Nonacademic:* Interview: Considered. Extracurricular activities: Considered. Talent/ability: Considered. Character/personal qualities: Considered. Alumni/ae relationship: Considered. Geographical residence: Not considered. State residency: Not considered. Religious affiliation/commitment: Not considered. Minority status: Considered. Volunteer work: Considered. Work experience: Not considered. **Other schools with the greatest overlap in applicants:** Minnesota State University–Moorhead; North Dakota State University; University of Minnesota–Duluth; University of Minnesota–Twin Cities; University of North Dakota. **Admissions statistics for the fall 2005 entering class:** Total applicants: 2,645. Total accepted: 2,206. Freshmen enrolled: 773; 28% were from out of state. Overall acceptance rate: 83%. **Credentials of fall 2005 freshmen:** 30% ranked in the top 10 percent of their high school class; 59% were in the top 25 percent, and 86% were in the top half. (Proportion submitting class standing: 93%.) **First-year students who submitted SAT scores:** 11%. Scores (25/75 percentile): Verbal: 500-620, Math: 490-620, Combined: 990-1240. **First-year students submitting ACT scores:** 96%. Scores (25/75 percentile): English: 20-28, Math: 20-27, Composite: 21-27.

ACADEMICS

Year founded: 1891. **Academic calendar:** Semester. **Degrees offered:** bachelor's, master's. **Most popular majors:** 10% communication and media studies, 9% business administration, management, and operations, 8% biology, 6% psychology, 5% music. **Major fields of study:** biological and biomedical sciences; business, management, marketing, and related support services; communication, journalism, and related programs; computer and information sciences and support services; education; English language and literature/letters; family and consumer sciences/human sciences; foreign languages, literatures, and linguistics; health professions and related clinical sciences; history; mathematics and statistics; parks, recreation, leisure, and fitness studies; philosophy and religious studies; physical sciences; psychology; public administration and social service professions; social sciences; theology and religious vocations; visual and performing arts. **Areas of required coursework:** arts/fine arts, mathematics, English (including composition), philosophy, foreign languages, sciences (biological or physical), history, social science, other. **Pre-professional programs:** pre-law, pre-dentistry, pre-medicine, pre-veterinary science. **Special academic programs (% participation):** accelerated program (12.6%), cooperative (work-study plan) program (41%), cross-registration (17.9%), double major (29.8%), dual enrollment (1.8%), exchange student program (domestic) (1.4%), honors program (12.2%), independent study (27.8%), internships (21.4%), student-designed major (.3%), study abroad (13.1%), teacher certificate program (15.2%). **Teacher certification offered in:** elementary, middle/junior high, secondary. **Cooperative education programs:** art, business, computer science, education, health professions, natural science, social/behavioral science. **Reserve Officers Training Corps (ROTC):** Army ROTC: Offered at cooperating institution (North Dakota State University); Air Force ROTC: Offered at cooperating institution (North Dakota State University). **Faculty and instruction (2005-2006):** Total instructional faculty: 190 full-time, 62 part-time (52% men; 48% women; 6% minorities). Full-time faculty with Ph.D. or other terminal degree: 73%. Student/faculty ratio: 15/1. Classes of fewer than 20 students: 45%; of 20 to 49 students: 53%; of 50 or more students: 2%. **Advanced Placement and International Baccalaureate credit:** AP tests may be used for: Credit and/or placement. Scores accepted: 3, 4, 5.

International Baccalaureate exams may be used for: Credit only. **Freshmen returning for sophomore year:** 80%. **Graduation rates:** Four-year: 56%; five-year: 62%; six-year: 63%. **Graduate study:** 66% of students pursue further study immediately upon graduation. Fields in which graduates pursue further study: Master of Business Administration (MBA), 5%; law, 8%; medicine, 9%; dentistry, 1%; engineering, 3%; theology (or the seminary), 6%; education, 3%.

COSTS AND FINANCIAL AID

Financial aid office: (218) 299-3010. **Expenses (2006-2007):** Tuition and fees 2006-2007: $20,980; room/board: $5,090. Estimated books and supplies: $740; transportation: $350; personal expenses: $1,170. **Financial aid:** Priority filing date for institution's financial aid form: April 15. In 2005-2006, 81% of undergraduates applied for financial aid. Of those, 70% were determined to have financial need; 27% had their need fully met. Average financial aid package (proportion receiving): $14,468 (70%). Average amount of gift aid, such as scholarships or grants (proportion receiving): $9,349 (69%). Average amount of self-help aid, such as work study or loans (proportion receiving): $5,284 (65%). Average need-based loan (excluding PLUS or other private loans): $4,831. Among students who received need-based aid, the average percentage of need met: 92%. Among students who received aid based on merit, the average award (and the proportion receiving): $5,643 (27%). The average athletic scholarship (and the proportion receiving): $0 (0%). Average amount of debt of borrowers graduating in 2005: $21,532. Proportion who borrowed: 72%.

CAMPUS LIFE AND EXTRACURRICULAR ACTIVITIES

Campus housing available (% using): coed dorms (14%), women's dorms (42%), men's dorms (24%), apartment for single students (20%). Students who live in college-owned, operated, or affiliated housing: 65%. **Student employment:** During the 2005-2006 academic year, 40% of undergraduates worked on campus. Average per-year earnings: $1,600. **Clubs and organizations:** Number of student organizations: 96. Activities include: choral groups, concert band, dance, drama/theater, jazz band, literary magazine, music ensembles, musical theater, pep band, radio station, student government, student newspaper, symphony orchestra, television station, yearbook. Number of fraternities: 0; sororities: 1. of women in sororities: 1%. Average proportion of students who stay on campus on weekends: 75%. **Sports program (2005-2006):** Member of NCAA III. *Men's intercollegiate varsity sports:* baseball, basketball, cross-country, football, golf, ice hockey, soccer, tennis, track and field (indoor), track and field (outdoor), wrestling. *Women's intercollegiate varsity sports:* basketball, cross-country, golf, ice hockey, soccer, softball, swimming and diving, tennis, track and field (indoor), track and field (outdoor), volleyball.

SERVICES AND FACILITIES

Basic services: nonremedial tutoring, women's center, placement service, day care, health service, health insurance. **Remedial assistance:** study skills. **Counseling services:** minority student, career, personal, academic, older student, psychological, birth control, religious. **For learning-disabled students:** School does not offer a structured program with separate admission and additional fees. Total undergraduates in learning-disabled program or receiving services: 13. Services include: reading machines, tape recorders, note-taking services, learning center, readers, extended time for tests, tutors, priority registration, priority seating, texts on tape. **Library:** Number of titles: 322,622; number of current serial subscriptions: 3,397. **Information technology resources:** Students are not required to lease or own a computer. Number of campus computers available to all students: 381. School has a wireless network. Approximate number of users that can be accommodated: 400. Proportion of college-owned housing units wired for high-speed internet access: 100%. **Campus safety:** Security services offered: 24-hour foot-and-vehicle patrols, late-night transport/escort service, 24-hour emergency telephones, lighted pathways/sidewalks, controlled dormitory access (key, security card, etc).

TRANSFER AND INTERNATIONAL STUDENTS

Transfer students: May apply for admission for the following academic terms: Fall, Spring, Summer. Applicants do not need a minimum number of credits to apply. For fall 2005: Transfer applications received: 173. Transfer applicants offered admission: 101. Transfer applicants enrolled: 47. **International students:** Number of foreign undergraduates: 102 (4% of student body). Number of countries represented: 36. Minimum TOEFL score required: 533 (paper); 200 (computer). Average TOEFL score: 578 (paper).

Concordia University–St. Paul

- **Address:** 275 Syndicate Street N, St. Paul, MN 55104-5494
- **Website:** http://www.csp.edu
- **Private; Religious affiliation:** Lutheran Church-Missouri Synod
- **Enrollment:** 1,472 full-time; 264 part-time

KEY STATS

✔ **U.S News College Ranking:** 46, Comp. Coll.–Bachelor's (Midwest)
✔ **ACT Score (25th/75th percentile):** 18-25
✔ **Tuition:** 2006-2007: $22,378

Selectivity: Selective	**Room/board:** $6,596
Acceptance rate: 64%	**Average debt:** $20,715
Student/faculty ratio: 10/1	**Proportion who borrowed:** 68%

UNDERGRADUATE STUDENT BODY STATS

2005-2006 enrollment: 1,472 full-time; 264 part-time. Men: 39%; women: 61%. **Ethnic makeup:** African American: 7%; Asian American: 5%; Hispanic: 2%; White: 85%. **Religious preference:** Roman Catholic: 17%; Protestant: 25%; No preference: 2%; Unknown: 27%; Lutheran Church-Missouri Synod: 19%; Other: 10%.

ADMISSIONS FACTS AND FIGURES

Phone: (651) 641-8230. **Email:** admission@csp.edu. **Website:** http://www.csp.edu. **Application deadlines for fall 2007:** Regular decision: August 1. Early decision: Not offered. Early action: Not offered. Admission can be deferred. **Application fee:** $30. Common application is accepted. **Admissions requirements/recommendations:** High school units required (recommended): English: 4; Mathematics: 2; Science: 2; Foreign language: (1); Social studies: 1; History: 1; Total units: 15 (16). Tests: The college uses SAT or ACT scores in admissions decisions. ACT required. For admission to the fall 2007 entering class, the school will accept: ACT with writing, ACT without writing. Campus visit: Recommended. Admissions interview: Recommended. Off-campus interview: May be arranged. **Factors that count in admissions decisions:** *Academic:* Secondary school record: Very important. Class rank: Very important. Letters of recommendation: Very important. Standardized test scores: Very important. Essay: Considered. *Nonacademic:* Interview: Important. Extracurricular activities: Considered. Talent/ability: Important. Character/personal qualities: Important. Alumni/ae relationship: Considered. Geographical residence: Not considered. State residency: Not considered. Religious affiliation/commitment: Important. Minority status: Important. Volunteer work: Not considered. Work experience: Not considered. **Other schools with the greatest overlap in applicants:** Hamline University; St. Cloud State University; University of Minnesota–Duluth; University of Minnesota–Twin Cities; University of St. Thomas. **Admissions statistics for the fall 2005 entering class:** Total applicants: 651. Total accepted: 415. Freshmen enrolled: 165; 26% were from out of state. Overall acceptance rate: 64%. **Credentials of fall 2005 freshmen:** 16% ranked in the top 10 percent of their high school class; 33% were in the top 25 percent, and 61% were in the top half. (Proportion submitting class standing: 91%.) **Average high school grade point average:** 3.2. **First-year students who submitted SAT scores:** 7%. Scores (25/75 percentile): Verbal: 400-660, Math: 440-610, Combined: 840-1270. **First-year students submitting ACT scores:** 93%. Scores (25/75 percentile): English: 16-25, Math: 17-25, Composite: 18-25.

ACADEMICS

Year founded: 1893. **Academic calendar:** Semester. **Degrees offered:** certificate, associate, bachelor's, post-bachelor's certificate, master's. **Most popular majors:** 56% business, management, marketing, and related support services, 11% education, 6% family and consumer sciences/human sciences, 6% security and protective services, 4% theology and religious vocations. **Major fields of study:** biological and biomedical sciences; business, management, marketing, and related support services; communication, journalism, and related programs; education; English language and literature/letters; family and consumer sciences/human sciences; history; mathematics and statistics; multi/interdisciplinary studies; natural resources and conservation; parks, recreation, leisure, and fitness studies; physical sciences; psychology; public administration and social service professions; social sciences; theology and religious vocations; visual and performing arts. **Areas of required coursework:** arts/fine arts, humanities, mathematics, English (including composition), sciences (biological or physical), history, social science, other. **Pre-professional programs:** pre-law, pre-dentistry, pre-medicine, pre-theology, pre-veterinary science, pre-pharmacy. **Special academic programs (% participation):** accelerated program (69%), distance learning (17%), double major (3%), internships (12%), study abroad (2%), teacher certificate program (11%). **Teacher certification offered in:** early childhood, special education, elementary, middle/junior high, secondary, bilingual/bicultural. **Reserve Officers Training Corps (ROTC):** Army ROTC: Offered at cooperating institution (University of Minnesota); Navy ROTC: Offered at cooperating institution (University of Minnesota); Air Force ROTC: Offered at cooperating institution (University of St. Thomas). **Faculty and instruction (2005-2006):** Total instructional faculty: 84 full-time, 353 part-time (60% men; 40% women; 5% minorities). Full-time faculty with Ph.D. or other terminal degree: 64%. Student/faculty ratio: 10/1. Classes of fewer than 20 students: 81%; of 20 to 49 students: 19%; of 50 or more students: 0%. **Advanced Placement and International Baccalaureate credit:** AP tests may be used for: Credit and/or placement. Scores accepted: 3, 4, 5. International Baccalaureate exams may be used for: Credit and/or placement. **Freshmen returning for sophomore year:** 70%. **Graduation rates:** Four-year: 29%; five-year: 40%; six-year: 45%.

COSTS AND FINANCIAL AID

Financial aid office: (651) 603-6300. **Expenses (2006-2007):** Tuition and fees 2006-2007: $22,378; room/board: $6,596. Estimated books and supplies: $700; transportation: $900; personal expenses: $900. **Financial aid:** Priority filing date for institution's financial aid form: May 1. In 2005-2006, 78% of undergraduates applied for financial aid. Of those, 66% were determined to have financial need; 17% had their need fully met. Average financial aid package (proportion receiving): $11,847 (66%). Average amount of gift aid, such as scholarships or grants (proportion receiving): $9,760 (53%). Average amount of self-help aid, such as work study or loans (proportion receiving): $4,617 (58%). Average need-based loan (excluding PLUS or other private loans): $4,154. Among students who received need-based aid, the average percentage of need met: 65%. Among students who received aid based on merit, the average award (and the proportion receiving): $6,202 (6%). The average athletic scholarship (and the proportion receiving): $4,749 (3%). Average amount of debt of borrowers graduating in 2005: $20,715. Proportion who borrowed: 68%.

CAMPUS LIFE AND EXTRACURRICULAR ACTIVITIES

Campus housing available (% using): coed dorms (17%), women's dorms (40%), men's dorms (33%), apartments for married students (8%), other housing options (2%). Students who live in college-owned, operated, or affiliated housing: 25%. Activities include: choral groups, concert band, drama/theater, jazz band, music ensembles, musical theater, student government, student newspaper, television station. Number of fraternities: 0; sororities: 0. **Sports program (2005-2006):** Member of NCAA II. *Men's intercollegiate varsity sports:* baseball, basketball, cross-country, football, golf, track and field (indoor), track and field (outdoor). *Women's intercollegiate varsity sports:* basketball, cross-country, golf, soccer, softball, track and field (indoor), track and field (outdoor), volleyball.

SERVICES AND FACILITIES

Basic services: nonremedial tutoring, health service, health insurance. **Remedial assistance:** reading, math, writing, study skills. **Counseling services:** minority student, career, personal, academic, older student, psychological, religious. **For learning-disabled students:** School does not offer a structured program with separate admission and additional fees. Services include: remedial math, remedial English, reading machines, remedial reading, tape recorders, videotaped classes, untimed tests, note-taking services, oral tests, learning center, readers, extended time for tests, tutors. **Library:** Number of titles: 135,132; number of current serial subscriptions: 416. **Information technology resources:** Students are required to lease or own a computer. School has a wireless network. **Campus safety:** Security services offered: 24-hour foot-and-vehicle patrols, late-night transport/escort service, 24-hour emergency telephones, lighted pathways/sidewalks, student patrols, controlled dormitory access (key, security card, etc).

TRANSFER AND INTERNATIONAL STUDENTS

Transfer students: May apply for admission for the following academic terms: Fall, Spring, Summer. Applicants need a minimum number of credits to apply. For fall 2005: Transfer applications received: 214. Transfer applicants offered admission: 125. Transfer applicants enrolled: 83. **International students:** Number of foreign undergraduates: 6. Minimum TOEFL score required: 500 (paper); 173 (computer). Average TOEFL score: 530 (paper).

Crown College

■ **Address:** 8700 College View Drive, St. Bonifacius, MN 55375
■ **Website:** http://www.crown.edu
■ **Private; Religious affiliation:** Christian and Missionary Alliance
■ **Enrollment:** 843 full-time; 345 part-time

KEY STATS
✔ **U.S News College Ranking:** third tier, Comp. Coll.–Bachelor's (Midwest)
✔ **ACT Score (25th/75th percentile):** 19-24
✔ **Tuition:** 2006-2007: $17,054
   Selectivity: Selective   **Room/board:** $6,654
   Acceptance rate: 71%   **Average debt:** $22,672
   Student/faculty ratio: 22/1   **Proportion who borrowed:** 87%

UNDERGRADUATE STUDENT BODY STATS

2005-2006 enrollment: 843 full-time; 345 part-time. Men: 41%; women: 59%. **Ethnic makeup:** African American: 3%; American-Indian: 1%; Asian American: 6%; Hispanic: 2%; White: 88%.

ADMISSIONS FACTS AND FIGURES

Phone: (952) 446-4142. **Email:** info@crown.edu. **Website:** http://www.crown.edu. **Application deadlines for fall 2007:** Regular decision: Rolling. Early decision: Not offered. Early action: Not offered. Admission can be deferred. **Application fee:** $35. Common application is not accepted. **To apply online, go to:** http://www.crown.edu/admissions/application.htm. **Admissions requirements/recommendations:** High school units required (recommended): English: (4); Mathematics: (3); Science: (3); Foreign language: (2); Social studies: (3). Tests: The college uses SAT or ACT scores in admissions decisions. Either SAT or ACT required. For admission to the fall 2007 entering class, the school will accept: ACT with writing, ACT without writing. Campus visit: Recommended. Admissions interview: Recommended. Off-campus interview: May be arranged. **Factors that count in admissions decisions:** *Academic:* Secondary school record: Very important. Class rank: Important. Letters of recommendation: Very important. Standardized test scores: Very important. Essay: Very important. *Nonacademic:* Interview: Considered. Extracurricular activities: Considered. Talent/ability: Considered. Character/personal qualities: Important. Alumni/ae relationship: Not considered. Geographical residence: Not considered. State residency: Not considered. Religious affiliation/commitment: Very important. Minority status: Not considered. Volunteer work: Considered. Work experience: Considered. **Other schools with the greatest overlap in applicants:** North Central College; Northwestern College. **Admissions statistics for the fall 2005 entering class:** Total applicants: 435. Total accepted: 311. 29% were from out of state. Overall acceptance rate: 71%. **Credentials of fall 2005 freshmen:** 13% ranked in the top 10 percent of their high school class; 28% were in the top 25 percent, and 57% were in the top half. (Proportion submitting class standing: 70%.) **Average high school grade point average:** 3.2. **First-year students who submitted SAT scores:** 11%. Scores (25/75 percentile): Verbal: 485-620, Math: 480-600, Combined: 965-1220. **First-year students submitting ACT scores:** 86%. Scores (25/75 percentile): English: 18-25, Math: 17-24, Composite: 19-24.

ACADEMICS

Year founded: 1916. **Academic calendar:** Semester. **Degrees offered:** certificate, associate, bachelor's, master's. **Most popular majors:** 23% military technologies, 15% education, 11% business, management, marketing, and related support services, 4% biological and biomedical sciences, 4% psychology. **Major fields of study:** agriculture, agriculture operations, and related sciences; biological and biomedical sciences; computer and information sciences and support services; education; history; liberal arts and sciences studies, and humanities; psychology; theology and religious vocations. **Areas of required coursework:** humanities, computer literacy, English (including composition), sciences (biological or physical), history, other. **Pre-professional programs:** pre-law. **Special academic programs:** accelerated program, distance learning, double major, dual enrollment, English as a Second Language (ESL), honors program, independent study, internships, study abroad, teacher certificate program, weekend college, other. **Teacher certification offered in:** early childhood, elementary, middle/junior high, secondary. **Faculty and instruction (2005-2006):** Total instructional faculty: 39 full-time, 25 part-time (69% men; 31% women; 5% minorities). Full-time faculty with Ph.D. or other terminal degree: 56%. Student/faculty ratio: 22/1. Classes of fewer than 20 students: 69%; of 20 to 49 students:

31%. **Freshmen returning for sophomore year:** 71%. **Graduation rates:** Four-year: 32%; five-year: 46%; six-year: 50%.

COSTS AND FINANCIAL AID

Financial aid office: (952) 446-4177. **Expenses (2006-2007):** Tuition and fees 2006-2007: $17,054; room/board: $6,654. Estimated books and supplies: $1,400; transportation: $800; personal expenses: $2,120. **Financial aid:** Priority filing date for institution's financial aid form: April 1; deadline: August 1. In 2005-2006, 72% of undergraduates applied for financial aid. Of those, 63% were determined to have financial need; 8% had their need fully met. Average financial aid package (proportion receiving): $11,529 (63%). Average amount of gift aid, such as scholarships or grants (proportion receiving): $4,675 (47%). Average amount of self-help aid, such as work study or loans (proportion receiving): $4,889 (56%). Average need-based loan (excluding PLUS or other private loans): $4,075. Among students who received need-based aid, the average percentage of need met: 61%. Among students who received aid based on merit, the average award (and the proportion receiving): $2,606 (8%). Average amount of debt of borrowers graduating in 2005: $22,672. Proportion who borrowed: 87%.

CAMPUS LIFE AND EXTRACURRICULAR ACTIVITIES

Campus housing available (% using): women's dorms (45%), men's dorms (35%), apartments for married students (5%), apartment for single students (15%). Students who live in college-owned, operated, or affiliated housing: 72%. **Clubs and organizations:** Number of student organizations: 13. Activities include: choral groups, concert band, drama/theater, jazz band, music ensembles, musical theater, pep band, student government, student newspaper, yearbook. Number of fraternities: 0; sororities: 0. Average proportion of students who stay on campus on weekends: 30%. **Sports program (2005-2006):** Member of NAIA. *Men's intercollegiate varsity sports:* baseball, basketball, cross-country, football, golf, soccer. *Women's intercollegiate varsity sports:* basketball, cross-country, golf, soccer, softball, volleyball.

SERVICES AND FACILITIES

Basic services: nonremedial tutoring, placement service, health service, health insurance. **Remedial assistance:** reading, math, writing, study skills. **Counseling services:** career, personal, academic, psychological, religious. **For learning-disabled students:** School does not offer a structured program with separate admission and additional fees. Total undergraduates in learning-disabled program or receiving services: 6. Services include: remedial math, remedial English, remedial reading, tape recorders, untimed tests, note-taking services, oral tests, learning center, readers, extended time for tests, tutors, priority registration, priority seating, other testing accomodations, other. **Library:** Number of titles: 78,386; number of current serial subscriptions: 15,000. **Information technology resources:** Students are not required to lease or own a computer. Number of campus computers available to all students: 105. School has a wireless network. Proportion of college-owned housing units wired for high-speed internet access: 95%. **Campus safety:** Security services offered: late-night transport/escort service, 24-hour emergency telephones, lighted pathways/sidewalks, controlled dormitory access (key, security card, etc).

TRANSFER AND INTERNATIONAL STUDENTS

Transfer students: May apply for admission for the following academic terms: Fall, Spring, Summer. Applicants do not need a minimum number of credits to apply. For fall 2005: Transfer applications received: 435. Transfer applicants offered admission: 311. Transfer applicants enrolled: 170. **International students:** Number of foreign undergraduates: 2. Number of countries represented: 3. Minimum TOEFL score required: 450 (paper); 130 (computer).

Gustavus Adolphus College

- **Address:** 800 W. College Avenue, St. Peter, MN 56082
- **Website:** http://www.gac.edu
- **Private; Religious affiliation:** Lutheran
- **Enrollment:** 2,571 full-time; 49 part-time

KEY STATS

✔ **U.S News College Ranking:** 79, Liberal Arts Colleges
✔ **ACT Score (25th/75th percentile):** 23-28
✔ **Tuition:** 2006-2007: $26,440

Selectivity: More selective	**Room/board:** $6,400
Acceptance rate: 79%	**Average debt:** $19,500
Student/faculty ratio: 12/1	**Proportion who borrowed:** 68%

UNDERGRADUATE STUDENT BODY STATS

2005-2006 enrollment: 2,571 full-time; 49 part-time. Men: 43%; women: 57%. **Ethnic makeup:** African American: 1%; Asian American: 4%; Hispanic: 2%; White: 92%; International: 1%. **Religious preference:** Roman Catholic: 17%; Protestant: 18%; No preference: 3%; Unknown: 4%; Lutheran: 58%.

ADMISSIONS FACTS AND FIGURES

Phone: (507) 933-7676. **Email:** admission@gac.edu. **Website:** http://www.gac.edu. **Application deadlines for fall 2007:** Regular decision: April 1. Early decision: Not offered. Early action: Not offered. Admission can be deferred. **Application fee:** None. Common application is accepted. **To apply online, go to:** http://www.collegenet.com. **Admissions requirements/recommendations:** High school units required (recommended): English: 4 (4); Mathematics: 3 (4); Science: 2 (3); Foreign language: 2 (3); Social studies: 2 (2); History: 2 (2); Academic electives: 0 (2); Total units: 17 (22). Tests: The college uses SAT or ACT scores in admissions decisions. Either SAT or ACT required. For admission to the fall 2007 entering class, the school will accept: ACT with writing, ACT without writing. Campus visit: Recommended. Admissions interview: Recommended. Off-campus interview: Not available. **Factors that count in admissions decisions:** *Academic:* Secondary school record: Very important. Class rank: Important. Letters of recommendation: Important. Standardized test scores: Very important. Essay: Very important. *Nonacademic:* Interview: Important. Extracurricular activities: Important. Talent/ability: Important. Character/personal qualities: Important. Alumni/ae relationship: Considered. Geographical residence: Considered. State residency: Not considered. Religious affiliation/commitment: Important. Minority status: Considered. Volunteer work: Considered. Work experience: Considered. **Other schools with the greatest overlap in applicants:** Luther College; St. Olaf College; St. Thomas University; University of Minnesota–Twin Cities. **Admissions statistics for the fall 2005 entering class:** Total applicants: 2,689. Total accepted: 2,135. Freshmen enrolled: 705; 18% were from out of state. Overall acceptance rate: 79%. **Size of waiting list:** 0 applicants; enrolled from waiting list: 0. **Credentials of fall 2005 freshmen:** 41% ranked in the top 10 percent of their high school class; 71% were in the top 25 percent, and 95% were in the top half. (Proportion submitting class standing: 92%.) **Average high school grade point average:** 3.7. **First-year students who submitted SAT scores:** 21%. Scores (25/75 percentile): Verbal: 570-670, Math: 560-680, Combined: 1130-1350. **First-year students submitting ACT scores:** 99%. Scores (25/75 percentile): English: N/A, Math: N/A, Composite: 23-28.

ACADEMICS

Year founded: 1862. **Academic calendar:** 4-1-4. **Degrees offered:** bachelor's. **Most popular majors:** 23% business/corporate communications, 12% biology, 10% communication and media studies, 10% psychology, 6% English language and literature. **Major fields of study:** area, ethnic, cultural, and gender studies; biological and biomedical sciences; business, management, marketing, and related support services; communication, journalism, and related programs; computer and information sciences and support services; education; English language and literature/letters; foreign languages, literatures, and linguistics; health professions and related clinical sciences; history; mathematics and statistics; multi/interdisciplinary studies; natural resources and conservation; parks, recreation, leisure, and fitness studies; philosophy and religious studies; physical sciences; psychology; security and protective services; social sciences; visual and performing arts. **Areas of required coursework:** arts/fine arts, humanities, mathematics, English (including composition), sciences (biological or physical), social science, other. **Pre-professional programs:** pre-law, pre-dentistry, pre-medicine, pre-theology, pre-veterinary science, pre-optometry, pre-pharmacy, other. **Special academic programs (% participation):** double major (24%), honors program (5%), independent study (27%), internships (64%), liberal arts/career combination (5%), student-designed major (1%), study abroad (58%), teacher certificate program (11%). **Teacher certification offered in:** elementary, middle/junior high, secondary, bilingual/bicultural. **Reserve Officers Training Corps (ROTC):** Army ROTC: Offered at cooperating institution (Minnesota State University-Mankato). **Faculty and instruction (2005-2006):** Total instructional faculty: 187 full-time, 88 part-time (60% men; 40% women; 7% minorities). Full-time faculty with Ph.D. or other terminal degree: 89%. Student/faculty ratio: 12/1. Classes of fewer than 20 students: 57%; of 20 to 49 students: 41%; of 50 or more students: 2%. **Advanced Placement and International Baccalaureate credit:** AP tests may be used for: Credit and/or placement. Scores accepted: 4, 5. International Baccalaureate exams may be used for: Credit and/or placement. **Freshmen returning for sophomore year:** 89%. **Graduation rates:** Four-year: 79%; five-year: 81%; six-year: 81%. **Graduate study:** 32% of students pursue further study immediately upon graduation; 36% within one year.

COSTS AND FINANCIAL AID

Financial aid office: (507) 933-7527. **Expenses (2006-2007):** Tuition and fees 2006-2007: $26,440; room/board: $6,400. Estimated books and supplies: $800; transportation: $350; personal expenses: $680. **Financial aid:** Priority filing date for institution's financial aid form: February 15; deadline: April 15. In 2005-2006, 75% of undergraduates applied for financial aid. Of those, 62% were determined to have financial need; Average financial aid package (proportion receiving): $17,200 (61%). Average amount of gift aid, such as scholarships or grants (proportion receiving): $13,900 (61%). Average amount of self-help aid, such as work study or loans (proportion receiving): $5,300 (51%). Average need-based loan (excluding PLUS or other private loans): $4,350. Among students who received need-based aid, the average percentage of need met: 87%. Among students who received aid based on merit, the average award (and the proportion receiving): $5,750 (28%). The average athletic scholarship (and the proportion receiving): $0 (0%). Average amount of debt of borrowers graduating in 2005: $19,500. Proportion who borrowed: 68%.

CAMPUS LIFE AND EXTRACURRICULAR ACTIVITIES

Campus housing available (% using): coed dorms (97%), apartment for single students (3%). Students who live in college-owned, operated, or affiliated housing: 83%. **Student employment:** During the 2005-2006 academic year, 5% of undergraduates worked on campus. Average per-year earnings: $5,000. **Clubs and organizations:** Number of student organizations: 105. Activities include: choral groups, concert band, dance, drama/theater, jazz band, literary magazine, music ensembles, musical theater, pep band, radio station, student government, student newspaper, symphony orchestra, television station, yearbook. Number of fraternities: 7; sororities: 5. Proportion of men in fraternities: 20%; of women in sororities: 17%. Average proportion of students who stay on campus on weekends: 85%. **Sports program (2005-2006):** Member of NCAA III. *Men's intercollegiate varsity sports:* baseball, basketball, cross-country, football, golf, ice hockey, nordic skiing, soccer, swimming and diving, tennis, track and field (indoor), track and field (outdoor). *Women's intercollegiate varsity sports:* basketball, cross-country, golf, gymnastics, ice hockey, nordic skiing, soccer, softball, swimming and diving, tennis, track and field (indoor), track and field (outdoor), volleyball.

SERVICES AND FACILITIES

Basic services: women's center, placement service, health service, health insurance. **Counseling services:** minority student, career, personal, academic, psychological, birth control, religious. **For learning-disabled students:** Services include: reading machines, tape recorders, note-taking services, oral tests, learning center, readers, extended time for tests, tutors. **Library:** Number of titles: 546,697; number of current serial subscriptions: 2,075. **Information technology resources:** Students are not required to lease or own a computer. Number of campus computers available to all students: 450. School has a wireless network. Proportion of college-owned housing units wired for high-speed internet access: 100%. **Campus safety:** Security services offered: 24-hour foot-and-vehicle patrols, late-night transport/escort service, 24-hour emergency telephones, lighted pathways/sidewalks, student patrols, controlled dormitory access (key, security card, etc).

TRANSFER AND INTERNATIONAL STUDENTS

Transfer students: May apply for admission for the following academic terms: Fall, Spring. Applicants need a minimum number of credits to apply.

For fall 2005: Transfer applications received: 109. Transfer applicants offered admission: 74. Transfer applicants enrolled: 44. **International students:** Number of foreign undergraduates: 30 (1% of student body). Number of countries represented: 21. Minimum TOEFL score required: 550 (paper); 213 (computer). Average TOEFL score: 612 (paper).

Hamline University

- **Address:** 1536 Hewitt Avenue, St. Paul, MN 55104-1284
- **Website:** http://www.hamline.edu
- **Private; Religious affiliation:** Methodist
- **Enrollment:** 1,945 full-time; 101 part-time

KEY STATS

✔ **U.S News College Ranking:** 9, Universities–Master's (Midwest)
✔ **ACT Score (25th/75th percentile):** 21-27
✔ **Tuition:** 2006-2007: $24,351

Selectivity: More selective	**Room/board:** $7,280
Acceptance rate: 78%	**Average debt:** $23,311
Student/faculty ratio: 13/1	**Proportion who borrowed:** 81%

UNDERGRADUATE STUDENT BODY STATS

2005-2006 enrollment: 1,945 full-time; 101 part-time. Men: 39%; women: 61%. **Ethnic makeup:** African American: 3%; American-Indian: 1%; Asian American: 6%; Hispanic: 2%; White: 85%; International: 3%. **Religious preference:** Roman Catholic: 19%; Protestant: 33%; Jewish: 1%; Muslim: 1%; Buddhist: 1%; No preference: 25%; Unknown: 12%; Methodist: 7%; Other: 2%.

ADMISSIONS FACTS AND FIGURES

Phone: (651) 523-2207. **Email:** cla-admis@hamline.edu. **Website:** http://www.hamline.edu. **Application deadlines for fall 2007:** Regular decision: Rolling. Early decision: Not offered. Early action: Send application by: December 1; Decision sent by: December 15. Admission can be deferred. Common application is accepted. **To apply online, go to:** http://www.hamline.edu/cla/admission/applyonline.html. **Admissions requirements/recommendations:** High school units required (recommended): English: 0 (4); Mathematics: 0 (3); Science: 0 (3); Foreign language: 0 (2); Social studies: 0 (4); History: 0 (0); Academic electives: 0 (4); Total units: 0 (20). Tests: The college uses SAT or ACT scores in admissions decisions. Either SAT or ACT required. For admission to the fall 2007 entering class, the school will accept: ACT with writing, ACT without writing. Campus visit: Recommended. Admissions interview: Recommended. Off-campus interview: May be arranged. **Factors that count in admissions decisions:** *Academic:* Secondary school record: Very important. Class rank: Very important. Letters of recommendation: Important. Standardized test scores: Important. Essay: Important. *Nonacademic:* Interview: Important. Extracurricular activities: Important. Talent/ability: Important. Character/personal qualities: Considered. Alumni/ae relationship: Considered. Geographical residence: Not considered. State residency: Not considered. Religious affiliation/commitment: Not considered. Minority status: Considered. Volunteer work: Considered. Work experience: Considered. **Other schools with the greatest overlap in applicants:** Augsburg College; College of St. Benedict; Gustavus Adolphus College; University of Minnesota–Twin Cities; University of St. Thomas. **Admissions statistics for the fall 2005 entering class:** Total applicants: 1,806. Total accepted: 1,417. Freshmen enrolled: 461; 18% were from out of state. Accepted through early-decision or early-action plans: 47%. Overall acceptance rate: 78%. Non-early acceptance rate: 72%. **Size of waiting list:** 25 applicants; enrolled from waiting list: 10. **Credentials of fall 2005 freshmen:** 27% ranked in the top 10 percent of their high school class; 51% were in the top 25 percent, and 80% were in the top half. (Proportion submitting class standing: 92%.) **Average high school grade point average:** 3.5. **First-year students who submitted SAT scores:** 21%. Scores (25/75 percentile): Verbal: 560-670, Math: 530-643, Combined: 1090-1313. **First-year students submitting ACT scores:** 92%. Scores (25/75 percentile): English: 20-28, Math: 20-27, Composite: 21-27.

ACADEMICS

Year founded: 1854. **Academic calendar:** 4-1-4. **Degrees offered:** certificate, bachelor's, post-bachelor's certificate, master's, post-master's certificate, first professional, first professional certificate, doctorate. **Most popular majors:** 15% psychology, 12% political science and government, 8% business administration and management, 7% criminal justice/safety studies, 6% English language and literature. **Major fields of study:** area, ethnic, cultural, and gender studies; biological and biomedical sciences; business, management, marketing, and related support services; communication, journalism, and related programs; English language and literature/letters; foreign languages, literatures, and linguistics; history; legal professions and studies; mathematics and statistics; multi/interdisciplinary studies; natural resources and conservation; parks, recreation, leisure, and fitness studies; philosophy and religious studies; physical sciences; psychology; security and protective services; social sciences; visual and performing arts. **Areas of required coursework:** arts/fine arts, humanities, computer literacy, English (including composition), sciences (biological or physical), social science, other. **Pre-professional programs:** pre-law, pre-medicine, other. **Special academic programs (% participation):** cross-registration (24.5%), double major (29.1%), English as a Second Language (ESL) (1%), independent study (19.2%), internships (54%), student-designed major (2%), study abroad (2%), teacher certificate program (12%). **Teacher certification offered in:** special education, elementary, middle/junior high, adult education, secondary, bilingual/bicultural. **Reserve Officers Training Corps (ROTC):** Air Force ROTC: Offered at cooperating institution (University of Saint Thomas). **Faculty and instruction (2005-2006):** Total instructional faculty: 174 full-time, 326 part-time (45% men; 55% women). Full-time faculty with Ph.D. or other terminal degree: 77%. Student/faculty ratio: 13/1. Classes of fewer than 20 students: 51%; of 20 to 49 students: 43%; of 50 or more students: 6%. **Advanced Placement and International Baccalaureate credit:** AP tests may be used for: Credit and/or placement. Scores accepted: 3, 4, 5. International Baccalaureate exams may be used for: Credit and/or placement. **Freshmen returning for sophomore year:** 83%. **Graduation rates:** Four-year: 63%; five-year: 67%; six-year: 69%. **Graduate study:** 20% of students pursue further study immediately upon graduation; 5% within one year; 10% within five years. Fields in which graduates pursue further study: Master of Business Administration (MBA), 7%; law, 46%; medicine, 7%; engineering, 7%; education, 13%; arts and sciences, 20%.

COSTS AND FINANCIAL AID
Financial aid office: (651) 523-3000. **Expenses (2006-2007):** Tuition and fees 2006-2007: $24,351; room/board: $7,280. Estimated books and supplies: $1,200; transportation: $0; personal expenses: $0. **Financial aid:** Priority filing date for institution's financial aid form: March 1. In 2005-2006, 95% of undergraduates applied for financial aid. Of those, 75% were determined to have financial need; 48% had their need fully met. Average financial aid package (proportion receiving): $23,870 (75%). Average amount of gift aid, such as scholarships or grants (proportion receiving): $6,841 (65%). Average amount of self-help aid, such as work study or loans (proportion receiving): $5,527 (64%). Average need-based loan (excluding PLUS or other private loans): $3,718. Among students who received need-based aid, the average percentage of need met: 85%. Among students who received aid based on merit, the average award (and the proportion receiving): $8,755 (16%). The average athletic scholarship (and the proportion receiving): $0 (0%). Average amount of debt of borrowers graduating in 2005: $23,311. Proportion who borrowed: 81%.

CAMPUS LIFE AND EXTRACURRICULAR ACTIVITIES
Campus housing available (% using): coed dorms (89%), fraternity housing (0%), apartments for married students (0%), apartment for single students (10%), special housing for international students (0%), other housing options (1%). Students who live in college-owned, operated, or affiliated housing: 41%. **Student employment:** During the 2005-2006 academic year, 44% of undergraduates worked on campus. Average per-year earnings: $2,700. **Clubs and organizations:** Number of student organizations: 85. Activities include: choral groups, concert band, dance, drama/theater, jazz band, literary magazine, music ensembles, pep band, radio station, student government, student newspaper, symphony orchestra, television station, yearbook. Number of fraternities: 1; sororities: 2. Proportion of men in fraternities: 3%; Average proportion of students who stay on campus on weekends: 60%. **Sports program (2005-2006):** Member of NCAA III. *Men's intercollegiate varsity sports:* baseball, basketball, cross-country, football, ice hockey, soccer, swimming and diving, tennis, track and field (indoor), track and field (outdoor). *Women's intercollegiate varsity sports:* basketball, cross-country, gymnastics, ice hockey, soccer, softball, swimming and diving, tennis, track and field (indoor), track and field (outdoor), volleyball.

SERVICES AND FACILITIES
Basic services: nonremedial tutoring, women's center, placement service, health service, health insurance. **Remedial assistance:** math, writing, study skills. **Counseling services:** minority student, career, personal, academic,

psychological, religious. **For learning-disabled students:** School does not offer a structured program with separate admission and additional fees. Total undergraduates in learning-disabled program or receiving services: 42. Services include: reading machines, tape recorders, untimed tests, note-taking services, oral tests, learning center, readers, extended time for tests, tutors, priority registration, priority seating, texts on tape, other testing accommodations. **Library:** Number of titles: 282,278; number of current serial subscriptions: 3,651. **Information technology resources:** Students are not required to lease or own a computer. Number of campus computers available to all students: 200. School has a wireless network. Approximate number of users that can be accommodated: 400. Proportion of college-owned housing units wired for high-speed internet access: 90%. **Campus safety:** Security services offered: 24-hour foot-and-vehicle patrols, late-night transport/escort service, 24-hour emergency telephones, lighted pathways/sidewalks, student patrols, controlled dormitory access (key, security card, etc).

TRANSFER AND INTERNATIONAL STUDENTS
Transfer students: May apply for admission for the following academic terms: Fall, Winter, Spring, Summer. Applicants do not need a minimum number of credits to apply. For fall 2005: Transfer applications received: 421. Transfer applicants offered admission: 251. Transfer applicants enrolled: 124. **International students:** Number of foreign undergraduates: 59 (3% of student body). Number of countries represented: 28. Minimum TOEFL score required: 550 (paper); 213 (computer). Average TOEFL score: 565 (paper).

Macalester College

- **Address:** 1600 Grand Avenue, St. Paul, MN 55105
- **Website:** http://www.macalester.edu
- **Private; Religious affiliation:** Presbyterian (historic affiliation)
- **Enrollment:** 1,827 full-time; 42 part-time

KEY STATS
✔ **U.S News College Ranking:** 24, Liberal Arts Colleges
✔ **SAT Score (25th/75th percentile):** 1260-1450
✔ **Tuition:** 2006-2007: $31,038

Selectivity: Most selective	**Room/board:** $7,982
Acceptance rate: 44%	**Average debt:** $14,889
Student/faculty ratio: 11/1	**Proportion who borrowed:** 75%

UNDERGRADUATE STUDENT BODY STATS
2005-2006 enrollment: 1,827 full-time; 42 part-time. Men: 42%; women: 58%. **Ethnic makeup:** African American: 4%; American-Indian: 1%; Asian American: 7%; Hispanic: 4%; White: 72%; International: 12%.

ADMISSIONS FACTS AND FIGURES
Phone: (651) 696-6357. **Email:** admissions@macalester.edu. **Website:** http://www.macalester.edu. **Application deadlines for fall 2007:** Regular decision: January 15; decision sent by April 1. Early decision: Send application by November 15; Decision sent by: December 15. Early action: Not offered. Admission can be deferred. **Application fee:** $40. Common application is accepted. **To apply online, go to:** http://www.macalester.edu/admissions/applying.html. **Admissions requirements/recommendations:** High school units required (recommended): English: (4); Mathematics: (3); Science: (3); Foreign language: (3); History: (3); Total units: (19). Tests: The college uses SAT or ACT scores in admissions decisions. Either SAT or ACT required. For admission to the fall 2007 entering class, the school will accept: ACT with writing, ACT without writing. Campus visit: Recommended. Admissions interview: Recommended. Off-campus interview: May be arranged. **Factors that count in admissions decisions:** *Academic:* Secondary school record: Very important. Class rank: Considered. Letters of recommendation: Important. Standardized test scores: Important. Essay: Important. *Nonacademic:* Interview: Considered. Extracurricular activities: Important. Talent/ability: Considered. Character/personal qualities: Important. Alumni/ae relationship: Considered. Geographical residence: Not considered. State residency: Not considered. Religious affiliation/commitment: Not considered. Minority status: Considered. Volunteer work: Considered. Work experience: Considered. **Other schools with the greatest overlap in applicants:** Carleton College; Grinnell College; Oberlin College; University of Chicago; Vassar College. **Admissions statistics for the fall 2005 entering class:** Total applicants: 4,317.

Total accepted: 1,893. Freshmen enrolled: 491; 73% were from out of state. Accepted through early-decision or early-action plans: 22%. Overall acceptance rate: 44%. Early-decision acceptance rate: 47%. Non-early acceptance rate: 44%. **Size of waiting list:** 263 applicants; enrolled from waiting list: 18. **Credentials of fall 2005 freshmen:** 65% ranked in the top 10 percent of their high school class; 94% were in the top 25 percent, and 100% were in the top half. (Proportion submitting class standing: 62%.) **First-year students who submitted SAT scores:** 77%. Scores (25/75 percentile): Verbal: 630-740, Math: 630-710, Combined: 1260-1450. **First-year students submitting ACT scores:** 54%. Scores (25/75 percentile): English: 23-34, Math: 27-31, Composite: 28-32.

ACADEMICS

Year founded: 1874. **Academic calendar:** Semester. **Degrees offered:** bachelor's. **Most popular majors:** 10% economics, 8% psychology, 7% biology, 7% international/global studies, 6% English language and literature. **Major fields of study:** area, ethnic, cultural, and gender studies; biological and biomedical sciences; computer and information sciences and support services; English language and literature/letters; foreign languages, literatures, and linguistics; history; liberal arts and sciences studies, and humanities; mathematics and statistics; multi/interdisciplinary studies; natural resources and conservation; philosophy and religious studies; physical sciences; psychology; social sciences; visual and performing arts. **Areas of required coursework:** arts/fine arts, humanities, mathematics, foreign languages, sciences (biological or physical), social science, other. **Pre-professional programs:** pre-law, pre-medicine. **Special academic programs (% participation):** cross-registration (35%), double major (26%), honors program (14%), independent study (62%), internships (34%), student-designed major (1%), study abroad (52%). **Cooperative education programs:** engineering, other. **Reserve Officers Training Corps (ROTC):** Army ROTC: Offered at cooperating institution (University of Minnesota); Navy ROTC: Offered at cooperating institution (University of Minnesota); Air Force ROTC: Offered at cooperating institution (University of St. Thomas). **Faculty and instruction (2005-2006):** Total instructional faculty: 151 full-time, 72 part-time (52% men; 48% women; 18% minorities). Full-time faculty with Ph.D. or other terminal degree: 92%. Student/faculty ratio: 11/1. Classes of fewer than 20 students: 69%; of 20 to 49 students: 30%; of 50 or more students: 1%. **Advanced Placement and International Baccalaureate credit:** AP tests may be used for: Credit only. Scores accepted: 3, 4, 5. International Baccalaureate exams may be used for: Credit and/or placement. **Freshmen returning for sophomore year:** 93%. **Graduation rates:** Four-year: 79%; five-year: 84%; six-year: 85%. **Graduate study:** 18% of students pursue further study immediately upon graduation; 37% within one year. Fields in which graduates pursue further study: Master of Business Administration (MBA), 2%; law, 16%; medicine, 9%; engineering, 2%; education, 9%; arts and sciences, 61%.

COSTS AND FINANCIAL AID

Financial aid office: (651) 696-6214. **Expenses (2006-2007):** Tuition and fees 2006-2007: $31,038; room/board: $7,982. Estimated books and supplies: $850; transportation: $500; personal expenses: $780. **Financial aid:** Priority filing date for institution's financial aid form: February 8; deadline: April 15. In 2005-2006, 72% of undergraduates applied for financial aid. Of those, 69% were determined to have financial need; 100% had their need fully met. Average financial aid package (proportion receiving): $25,238 (69%). Average amount of gift aid, such as scholarships or grants (proportion receiving): $19,806 (69%). Average amount of self-help aid, such as work study or loans (proportion receiving): $5,452 (69%). Average need-based loan (excluding PLUS or other private loans): $3,627. Among students who received need-based aid, the average percentage of need met: 100%. Among students who received aid based on merit, the average award (and the proportion receiving): $4,686 (6%). The average athletic scholarship (and the proportion receiving): $0 (0%). Average amount of debt of borrowers graduating in 2005: $14,889. Proportion who borrowed: 75%.

CAMPUS LIFE AND EXTRACURRICULAR ACTIVITIES

Campus housing available (% using): coed dorms (89%), apartment for single students (3%), special housing for disabled students (1%), cooperative housing (2%), other housing options (5%). Students who live in college-owned, operated, or affiliated housing: 68%. **Student employment:** During the 2005-2006 academic year, 75% of undergraduates worked on campus. Average per-year earnings: $2,000. **Clubs and organizations:** Number of student organizations: 72. Activities include: choral groups, concert band, dance, drama/theater, jazz band, literary magazine, music ensembles, radio station, student government, student newspaper, symphony orchestra, yearbook. Number of fraternities: 0; sororities: 0. Average proportion of students who stay on campus on weekends: 93%. **Sports program (2005-2006):**

Member of NCAA III. **Men's intercollegiate varsity sports:** baseball, basketball, cross-country, football, golf, nordic skiing, soccer, swimming and diving, tennis, track and field (indoor), track and field (outdoor). **Women's intercollegiate varsity sports:** basketball, cross-country, golf, nordic skiing, soccer, softball, swimming and diving, tennis, track and field (indoor), track and field (outdoor), volleyball, water polo.

SERVICES AND FACILITIES

Basic services: nonremedial tutoring, women's center, placement service, health service, health insurance. **Remedial assistance:** reading, math, writing, study skills, other. **Counseling services:** minority student, career, personal, academic, psychological, birth control, religious, other. **For learning-disabled students:** School does not offer a structured program with separate admission and additional fees. Total undergraduates in learning-disabled program or receiving services: 29. Services include: reading machines, tape recorders, untimed tests, note-taking services, oral tests, learning center, readers, extended time for tests, tutors. **Library:** Number of titles: 455,554; number of current serial subscriptions: 2,647. **Information technology resources:** Students are not required to lease or own a computer. Number of campus computers available to all students: 400. School has a wireless network. Proportion of college-owned housing units wired for high-speed internet access: 100%. **Campus safety:** Security services offered: 24-hour foot-and-vehicle patrols, late-night transport/escort service, 24-hour emergency telephones, lighted pathways/sidewalks, controlled dormitory access (key, security card, etc).

TRANSFER AND INTERNATIONAL STUDENTS

Transfer students: May apply for admission for the following academic terms: Fall. Applicants do not need a minimum number of credits to apply. For fall 2005: Transfer applications received: 265. Transfer applicants offered admission: 58. Transfer applicants enrolled: 23. **International students:** Number of foreign undergraduates: 225 (12% of student body). Number of countries represented: 78. Minimum TOEFL score required: 573 (paper); 230 (computer). Average TOEFL score: 620 (paper).

Metropolitan State University

- **Address:** 700 E. Seventh Street, St. Paul, MN 55106
- **Website:** http://www.metrostate.edu
- **Public**
- **Enrollment:** N/A

KEY STATS
- ✔ **U.S News College Ranking:** fourth tier, Universities–Master's (Midwest)
- ✔ **SAT or ACT Score (25th/75th percentile):** N/A
- ✔ **Tuition:** 2006-2007: $5,334 in state, $10,164 out of state

Selectivity: Less selective	**Room/board:** N/A
Acceptance rate: N/A	**Average debt:** N/A
Student/faculty ratio: N/A	**Proportion who borrowed:** N/A

Minneapolis College of Art and Design

- **Address:** 2501 Stevens Avenue, Minneapolis, MN 55404
- **Website:** http://www.mcad.edu
- **Private**
- **Enrollment:** 622 full-time; 34 part-time

KEY STATS
- ✔ **U.S News College Ranking:** Unranked Specialty School–Fine Arts
- ✔ **ACT Score:** 23
- ✔ **Tuition:** 2006-2007: $26,110

Selectivity: Selective	**Room/board:** N/A
Acceptance rate: 77%	**Average debt:** $46,987
Student/faculty ratio: 15/1	**Proportion who borrowed:** 82%

UNDERGRADUATE STUDENT BODY STATS

2005-2006 enrollment: 622 full-time; 34 part-time. Men: 51%; women: 49%. **Ethnic makeup:** African American: 2%; American-Indian: 1%; Asian American: 3%; Hispanic: 3%; White: 91%.

ADMISSIONS FACTS AND FIGURES

Phone: (612) 874-3760. **Email:** admissions@mcad.edu. **Website:** http://www.mcad.edu. **Application deadlines for fall 2007:** Regular decision: Rolling. Early decision: Not offered. Early action: Not offered. Admission can be deferred. **Application fee:** $35. Common application is not accepted. **To apply online, go to:** http://www.mcad.edu/admissions. **Admissions requirements/recommendations:** High school units required (recommended): English: (4); Social studies: (4); History: (4); Total units: (16). Tests: The college uses SAT or ACT scores in admissions decisions. Either SAT or ACT required. For admission to the fall 2007 entering class, the school will accept: ACT with writing, ACT without writing. Campus visit: Recommended. Admissions interview: Recommended. Off-campus interview: May be arranged. **Factors that count in admissions decisions:** *Academic:* Secondary school record: Very important. Class rank: Not considered. Letters of recommendation: Important. Standardized test scores: Very important. Essay: Very important. *Nonacademic:* Interview: Considered. Extracurricular activities: Considered. Talent/ability: Very important. Character/personal qualities: Considered. Alumni/ae relationship: Not considered. Geographical residence: Not considered. State residency: Not considered. Religious affiliation/commitment: Not considered. Minority status: Not considered. Volunteer work: Considered. Work experience: Not considered. **Other schools with the greatest overlap in applicants:** College of Visual Arts; Kansas City Art Institute; Milwaukee Institute of Art and Design; School of the Art Institute of Chicago; University of Minnesota–Twin Cities. **Admissions statistics for the fall 2005 entering class:** Total applicants: 332. Total accepted: 254. Freshmen enrolled: 112; 40% were from out of state. Overall acceptance rate: 77%. **Size of waiting list:** 0 applicants; enrolled from waiting list: 0. **Average high school grade point average:** 3.3. **First-year students who submitted SAT scores:** 13%. Scores (25/75 percentile): Verbal: N/A, Math: N/A, Combined: N/A. **First-year students submitting ACT scores:** 87%. Scores (25/75 percentile): English: N/A, Math: N/A, Composite: N/A.

ACADEMICS

Year founded: 1886. **Academic calendar:** Semester. **Degrees offered:** bachelor's, post-bachelor's certificate, master's. **Most popular majors:** 35% graphic design, 27% film/video and photographic arts, 23% fine/studio arts, 13% commercial and advertising art, 2% visual and performing arts. **Major fields of study:** communications technologies/technicians and support services; visual and performing arts. **Areas of required coursework:** arts/fine arts, computer literacy. **Special academic programs (% participation):** cooperative (work-study plan) program (35%), distance learning (20%), double major (2%), exchange student program (domestic) (2%), internships (88%), study abroad (12%). **Faculty and instruction (2005-2006):** Total instructional faculty: 38 full-time, 73 part-time (57% men; 43% women; 6% minorities). Student/faculty ratio: 15/1. Classes of fewer than 20 students: 83%; of 20 to 49 students: 16%; of 50 or more students: 0%. **Advanced Placement and International Baccalaureate credit:** AP tests may be used for: Credit only. Scores accepted: 4, 5. **Freshmen returning for sophomore year:** 78%. **Graduation rates:** Four-year: 66%; five-year: 68%; six-year: 69%. **Graduate study:** 5% of students pursue further study immediately upon graduation; 10% within one year; 25% within five years. Fields in which graduates pursue further study: education, 25%; arts and sciences, 75%.

COSTS AND FINANCIAL AID

Financial aid office: (612) 874-3782. **Expenses (2006-2007):** Tuition and fees 2006-2007: $26,110; room/board: N/A. Estimated books and supplies: $2,300; transportation: $900; personal expenses: $500. **Financial aid:** Priority filing date for institution's financial aid form: March 15. In 2005-2006, 88% of undergraduates applied for financial aid. Of those, 78% were determined to have financial need; 11% had their need fully met. Average financial aid package (proportion receiving): $12,341 (78%). Average amount of gift aid, such as scholarships or grants (proportion receiving): $8,535 (74%). Average amount of self-help aid, such as work study or loans (proportion receiving): $4,422 (75%). Average need-based loan (excluding PLUS or other private loans): $3,933. Among students who received need-based aid, the average percentage of need met: 54%. Among students who received aid based on merit, the average award (and the proportion receiving): $12,725 (12%). The average athletic scholarship (and the proportion receiving): $0 (0%). Average amount of debt of borrowers graduating in 2005: $46,987. Proportion who borrowed: 82%.

CAMPUS LIFE AND EXTRACURRICULAR ACTIVITIES

Campus housing available (% using): apartment for single students (100%). Students who live in college-owned, operated, or affiliated housing: 42%. **Student employment:** During the 2005-2006 academic year, 15% of undergraduates worked on campus. Average per-year earnings: $1,150. **Clubs and organizations:** Number of student organizations: 10. Activities include: radio station, student government, student film society. Number of fraternities: 0; sororities: 0. Average proportion of students who stay on campus on weekends: 95%.

SERVICES AND FACILITIES

Basic services: nonremedial tutoring, health insurance. **Remedial assistance:** writing, study skills. **Counseling services:** career, personal, academic, psychological. **For learning-disabled students:** School does not offer a structured program with separate admission and additional fees. Total undergraduates in learning-disabled program or receiving services: 13. Services include: tape recorders, note-taking services, learning center, readers, extended time for tests, tutors. **Library:** Number of titles: 57,270; number of current serial subscriptions: 138. **Information technology resources:** Students are not required to lease or own a computer. Number of campus computers available to all students: 200. School has a wireless network. Approximate number of users that can be accommodated: 500. Proportion of college-owned housing units wired for high-speed internet access: 100%. **Campus safety:** Security services offered: 24-hour foot-and-vehicle patrols, late-night transport/escort service, lighted pathways/sidewalks, controlled dormitory access (key, security card, etc).

TRANSFER AND INTERNATIONAL STUDENTS

Transfer students: May apply for admission for the following academic terms: Fall, Spring. Applicants do not need a minimum number of credits to apply. For fall 2005: Transfer applications received: 130. Transfer applicants offered admission: 101. Transfer applicants enrolled: 64. **International students:** Number of countries represented: 5. Minimum TOEFL score required: 550 (paper); 213 (computer).

Minnesota State University–Mankato

- **Address:** 309 Wigley Administration Center, Mankato, MN 56001
- **Website:** http://www.mnsu.edu
- **Public**
- **Enrollment:** 11,336 full-time; 1,347 part-time

KEY STATS

✔ **U.S News College Ranking:** third tier, Universities–Master's (Midwest)
✔ **ACT Score (25th/75th percentile):** 19-24
✔ **Tuition:** 2006-2007: $5,846 in state, $11,674 out of state

Selectivity: Selective	**Room/board:** $5,083
Acceptance rate: 90%	**Average debt:** $16,500
Student/faculty ratio: 23/1	**Proportion who borrowed:** 75%

UNDERGRADUATE STUDENT BODY STATS

2005-2006 enrollment: 11,336 full-time; 1,347 part-time. Men: 47%; women: 53%. **Ethnic makeup:** African American: 2%; Asian American: 2%; Hispanic: 1%; White: 92%; International: 3%.

ADMISSIONS FACTS AND FIGURES

Phone: (507) 389-1822. **Email:** admissions@mnsu.edu. **Website:** http://www.mnsu.edu. **Application deadlines for fall 2007:** Regular decision: August 27. Early decision: Not offered. Early action: Not offered. Admission can be deferred. **Application fee:** $20. Common application is not accepted. **To apply online, go to:** http://www.mnsu.edu/admissions/freshman/application/application/. **Admissions requirements/recommendations:** High school units required (recommended): English: 4; Mathematics: 3; Science: 3; Foreign language: 2; Social studies: 2; History: 1; Total units: 16. Tests: The college uses SAT or ACT scores in admissions decisions. Neither SAT nor ACT required. For admission to the fall 2007 entering class, the school will accept: ACT with writing, ACT without writing. Campus visit: Recommended. Admissions interview: Neither required nor recommended. Off-campus interview: Not available. **Factors that count in admissions decisions:** *Academic:* Secondary school record: Very important. Class rank: Very important. Letters of recommendation: Considered. Standardized test scores: Very important. Essay: Not considered. *Nonacademic:* Interview: Not considered. Extracurricular activities: Not considered. Talent/ability: Not considered. Character/personal qualities: Not considered. Alumni/ae relationship: Not considered. Geographical residence: Not considered. State residency: Not considered. Religious affiliation/commitment: Not considered. Minority status: Not considered. Volunteer work: Not considered. Work experience: Not considered. **Other schools with the greatest overlap in applicants:** Minnesota State University–Moorhead; St. Cloud State University; University of Minnesota–Duluth; University of Minnesota–Twin Cities; Winona State University. **Admissions statistics for the fall 2005 entering class:** Total applicants: 5,605. Total accepted: 5,035. Freshmen enrolled: 2,257; 15% were from out of state. Overall acceptance rate: 90%. **Credentials of fall 2005 freshmen:** 8% ranked in the top 10 percent of their high school class; 27% were in the top 25 percent, and 70% were in the top half. (Proportion submitting class standing: 93%.) **First-year students submitting ACT scores:** 96%. Scores (25/75 percentile): English: 18-23, Math: 18-24, Composite: 19-24.

ACADEMICS

Year founded: 1867. **Academic calendar:** Semester. **Degrees offered:** certificate, associate, bachelor's, master's, post-master's certificate. **Most popular majors:** 9% elementary education and teaching, 7% business administration and management, 5% computer and information sciences, 5% nursing/registered nurse training (R.N., A.S.N., B.S.N., M.S.N.), 4% marketing/marketing management. **Major fields of study:** agriculture, agriculture operations, and related sciences; area, ethnic, cultural, and gender studies; biological and biomedical sciences; business, management, marketing, and related support services; communication, journalism, and related programs; computer and information sciences and support services; education; engineering; engineering technologies/technicians; English language and literature/letters; family and consumer sciences/human sciences; foreign languages, literatures, and linguistics; health professions and related clinical sciences; history; liberal arts and sciences studies, and humanities; mathematics and statistics; natural resources and conservation; parks, recreation, leisure, and fitness studies; philosophy and religious studies; physical sciences; psychology; public administration and social service professions; security and protective services; social sciences; transportation and materials moving; visual and performing arts. **Areas of required coursework:** arts/fine arts, humanities, mathematics, English (including composition), sciences (biological or physical), social science, other. **Pre-professional programs:** prelaw, pre-dentistry, pre-medicine, pre-theology, pre-veterinary science, pre-optometry, pre-pharmacy, other. **Special academic programs:** cross-registration, distance learning, double major, dual enrollment, English as a Second Language (ESL), exchange student program (domestic), honors program, independent study, internships, student-designed major, study abroad, teacher certificate program. **Teacher certification offered in:** early childhood, special education, elementary, middle/junior high, secondary, bilingual/bicultural. **Cooperative education programs:** business, computer science, education, engineering, health professions, home economics, humanities, natural science, social/behavioral science, technologies. **Reserve Officers Training Corps (ROTC):** Army ROTC: Offered on campus. **Faculty and instruction (2005-2006):** Total instructional faculty: 491 full-time, 226 part-time (55% men; 45% women; 5% minorities). Full-time faculty with Ph.D. or other terminal degree: 79%. Student/faculty ratio: 23/1. Classes of fewer than 20 students: 35%; of 20 to 49 students: 55%; of 50 or more students: 10%. **Advanced Placement and International Baccalaureate credit:** AP tests may be used for: Credit only. Scores accepted: 3, 4, 5. International Baccalaureate exams may be used for: Credit only. **Freshmen returning for sophomore year:** 78%. **Graduation rates:** Four-year: 18%; five-year: 42%; six-year: 49%. **Graduate study:** 10% of students pursue further study within one year.

COSTS AND FINANCIAL AID

Financial aid office: (507) 389-1866. **Expenses (2006-2007):** Tuition and fees 2006-2007: $5,846 in state, $11,674 out of state; room/board: $5,083. Estimated books and supplies: $820; transportation: $990; personal expenses: $1,532. **Financial aid:** Priority filing date for institution's financial aid form: March 15. In 2005-2006, 75% of undergraduates applied for financial aid. Of those, 50% were determined to have financial need; 45% had their need fully met. Average financial aid package (proportion receiving): $6,939 (50%). Average amount of gift aid, such as scholarships or grants (proportion receiving): $3,643 (31%). Average amount of self-help aid, such as work study or loans (proportion receiving): $4,279 (46%). Average need-based loan (excluding PLUS or other private loans): $3,989. Among students who received need-based aid, the average percentage of need met: 79%. Among students who received aid based on merit, the average award (and the proportion receiving): $1,801 (6%). The average athletic scholarship (and the proportion receiving): $5,163 (2%). Average amount of debt of borrowers graduating in 2005: $16,500. Proportion who borrowed: 75%.

CAMPUS LIFE AND EXTRACURRICULAR ACTIVITIES

Campus housing available (% using): coed dorms (100%). Students who live in college-owned, operated, or affiliated housing: 22%. **Student employment:** During the 2005-2006 academic year, 17% of undergraduates worked on campus. Average per-year earnings: $1,900. **Clubs and organizations:** Number of student organizations: 189. Activities include: choral groups, concert band, dance, drama/theater, jazz band, literary magazine, music ensembles, musical theater, pep band, radio station, student government, student newspaper, student film society, symphony orchestra. Number of fraternities: 7; sororities: 4. Proportion of men in fraternities: 3%; of women in sororities: 2%. Average proportion of students who stay on campus on weekends: 40%. **Sports program (2005-2006):** Member of NCAA II. *Men's intercollegiate varsity sports:* baseball, basketball, cross-country, football, golf, ice hockey, swimming and diving, tennis, track and field (indoor), track and field (outdoor), wrestling. *Women's intercollegiate varsity sports:* basketball, bowling, cross-country, golf, ice hockey, soccer, softball, swimming and diving, tennis, track and field (indoor), track and field (outdoor), volleyball.

SERVICES AND FACILITIES

Basic services: nonremedial tutoring, women's center, placement service, day care, health service, health insurance, other. **Remedial assistance:** reading, math, writing, study skills, other. **Counseling services:** minority student, career, personal, veteran student, academic, older student, psychological, birth control. **For learning-disabled students:** School does not offer a structured program with separate admission and additional fees. Total undergraduates in learning-disabled program or receiving services: 122. Services include: reading machines, tape recorders, note-taking services, oral tests, learning center, readers, extended time for tests, tutors, priority registration, priority seating, texts on tape. **Library:** Number of titles: 779,403; number of current serial subscriptions: 4,283. **Information technology resources:** Students are not required to lease or own a computer. Number of campus computers available to all students: 1,286. School has a wireless network. Approximate number of users that can be accommodated: 15,000. Proportion of college-owned housing units wired for high-speed internet access: 100%. **Campus safety:** Security services offered: 24-hour foot-and-vehicle patrols, late-night transport/escort service, 24-hour emergency telephones, lighted pathways/sidewalks, student patrols, controlled dormitory access (key, security card, etc.).

TRANSFER AND INTERNATIONAL STUDENTS

Transfer students: May apply for admission for the following academic terms: Fall, Spring, Summer. Applicants do not need a minimum number of credits to apply. For fall 2005: Transfer applications received: 1,918. Transfer applicants offered admission: 1,798. Transfer applicants enrolled: 1,097. **International students:** Number of foreign undergraduates: 336 (3% of student body). Number of countries represented: 59. Minimum TOEFL score required: 500 (paper); 173 (computer).

Minnesota State University–Moorhead

- **Address:** 1104 Seventh Avenue S, Moorhead, MN 56563
- **Website:** http://www.mnstate.edu
- **Public**
- **Enrollment:** 6,198 full-time; 1,044 part-time

KEY STATS

✔ **U.S News College Ranking:** third tier, Universities–Master's (Midwest)
✔ **ACT Score (25th/75th percentile):** 19-24
✔ **Tuition:** N/A

Selectivity: Selective	**Room/board:** N/A
Acceptance rate: 83%	**Average debt:** N/A
Student/faculty ratio: 20/1	**Proportion who borrowed:** N/A

UNDERGRADUATE STUDENT BODY STATS

2005-2006 enrollment: 6,198 full-time; 1,044 part-time. Men: 41%; women: 59%. **Ethnic makeup:** African American: 1%; American-Indian: 1%; Asian American: 1%; Hispanic: 1%; White: 93%; International: 3%.

ADMISSIONS FACTS AND FIGURES

Phone: (800) 593-7246. **Email:** dragon@mnstate.edu. **Website:** http://www.mnstate.edu. **Application deadlines for fall 2007:** Regular decision: August 1. Early decision: Not offered. Early action: Not offered. Admission can be deferred. **Application fee:** $20. Common application is not accepted. **To apply online, go to:** http://www.mnstate.edu/admissions/apply.cfm. **Admissions requirements/recommendations:** High school units required (recommended): English: 4; Mathematics: 3; Science: 3; Foreign language: 0; Social studies: 3; History: 0; Academic electives: 3; Total units: 16. Tests: The college uses SAT or ACT scores in admissions decisions. Either SAT or ACT required. For admission to the fall 2007 entering class, the school will accept: ACT with writing, ACT without writing. Campus visit: Recommended. Admissions interview: Neither required nor recommended. Off-campus interview: Not available. **Factors that count in admissions decisions: Academic:** Secondary school record: Very important. Class rank: Very important. Letters of recommendation: Not considered. Standardized test scores: Very important. Essay: Not considered. *Nonacademic:* Interview: Not considered. Extracurricular activities: Not considered. Talent/ability: Not considered. Character/personal qualities: Not considered. Alumni/ae relationship: Not considered. Geographical residence: Not considered. State residency: Not considered. Religious affiliation/commitment: Not considered. Minority status: Not considered. Volunteer work: Not considered. Work experience: Not considered. **Admissions statistics for the fall 2005 entering class:** Total applicants: 2,783. Total accepted: 2,317. Freshmen enrolled: 1,135; 38% were from out of state. Overall acceptance rate: 83%. **Credentials of fall 2005 freshmen:** 10% ranked in the top 10 percent of their high school class; 28% were in the top 25 percent, and 63% were in the top half. (Proportion submitting class standing: 93%.) **First-year students who submitted SAT scores:** 3%. Scores (25/75 percentile): Verbal: 480-580, Math: 465-535, Combined: 945-1115. **First-year students submitting ACT scores:** 94%. Scores (25/75 percentile): English: 18-24, Math: 18-24, Composite: 19-24.

ACADEMICS

Year founded: 1887. **Academic calendar:** Semester. **Degrees offered:** certificate, associate, transfer-associate, bachelor's, post-bachelor's certificate, master's, post-master's certificate. **Most popular majors:** 9% elementary education and teaching, 8% mass communication/media studies, 6% business administration and management, 4% biology/biological sciences, 4% criminal justice/safety studies. **Major fields of study:** area, ethnic, cultural, and gender studies; biological and biomedical sciences; business, management, marketing, and related support services; communication, journalism, and related programs; computer and information sciences and support services; education; engineering technologies/technicians; English language and literature/letters; foreign languages, literatures, and linguistics; health professions and related clinical sciences; history; legal professions and studies; mathematics and statistics; multi/interdisciplinary studies; parks, recreation, leisure, and fitness studies; philosophy and religious studies; physical sciences; psychology; public administration and social service professions; security and protective services; social sciences; visual and performing arts. **Areas of required coursework:** arts/fine arts, humanities, mathematics, English (including composition), sciences (biological or physical), social science, other. **Pre-professional programs:** pre-law, pre-dentistry, pre-medicine, pre-veterinary science, pre-optometry, pre-pharmacy, other. **Special academic programs:** cross-registration, distance learning, double major, dual enrollment, exchange student program (domestic), external degree program, honors program, independent study, internships, student-designed major, study abroad, teacher certificate program. **Teacher certification offered in:** early childhood, special education, elementary, vo-tech, middle/junior high, secondary. **Reserve Officers Training Corps (ROTC):** Army ROTC: Offered at cooperating institution (North Dakota State University); Air Force ROTC: Offered at cooperating institution (North Dakota State University). **Faculty and instruction (2005-2006):** Total instructional faculty: 270 full-time, 33 part-time (56% men; 44% women; 6% minorities). Full-time faculty with Ph.D. or other terminal degree: 85%. Student/faculty ratio: 20/1. Classes of fewer than 20 students: 36%; of 20 to 49 students: 57%; of 50 or more students: 6%. **Advanced Placement and International Baccalaureate credit:** AP tests may be used for: Credit only. Scores accepted: 3, 4, 5. International Baccalaureate exams may be used for: Credit and/or placement. **Freshmen returning for sophomore year:** 68%. **Graduation rates:** Four-year: 18%; five-year: 36%; six-year: 42%. **Graduate study:** 15% of students pursue further study within one year.

COSTS AND FINANCIAL AID

Financial aid office: (218) 477-2251. **Financial aid:** Priority filing date for institution's financial aid form: February 15.

CAMPUS LIFE AND EXTRACURRICULAR ACTIVITIES

Campus housing available: coed dorms, women's dorms, men's dorms, sorority housing, apartment for single students, special housing for disabled students. Students who live in college-owned, operated, or affiliated housing: 21%. **Student employment:** During the 2005-2006 academic year, 6% of undergraduates worked on campus. Average per-year earnings: $3,800. **Clubs and organizations:** Number of student organizations: 109. Activities include: choral groups, concert band, dance, drama/theater, jazz band, literary magazine, music ensembles, musical theater, radio station, student government, student newspaper, student film society, symphony orchestra. Number of fraternities: 1; sororities: 2. Proportion of men in fraternities: 3%; of women in sororities: 2%. Average proportion of students who stay on campus on weekends: 25%. **Sports program (2005-2006):** Member of NCAA II. *Men's intercollegiate varsity sports:* basketball, cross-country, football, track and field (indoor), track and field (outdoor), wrestling. *Women's intercollegiate varsity sports:* basketball, cross-country, golf, soccer, softball, swimming and diving, tennis, track and field (indoor), track and field (outdoor), volleyball.

SERVICES AND FACILITIES

Basic services: nonremedial tutoring, women's center, placement service, day care, health service, health insurance, other. **Remedial assistance:** math, study skills. **Counseling services:** minority student, career, personal, veteran student, academic, older student, psychological, birth control. **For learning-disabled students:** School does not offer a structured program with separate admission and additional fees. **Library:** Number of titles: 656,104; number of current serial subscriptions: 2,245. **Information technology resources:** Students are not required to lease or own a computer. Number of campus computers available to all students: 791. School has a wireless network. Approximate number of users that can be accommodated: 425. Proportion of college-owned housing units wired for high-speed internet access: 80%. **Campus safety:** Security services offered: 24-hour foot-and-vehicle patrols, late-night transport/escort service, 24-hour emergency telephones, lighted pathways/sidewalks, student patrols, controlled dormitory access (key, security card, etc).

TRANSFER AND INTERNATIONAL STUDENTS

Transfer students: May apply for admission for the following academic terms: Fall, Spring, Summer. Applicants need a minimum number of credits to apply. For fall 2005: Transfer applications received: 1,303. Transfer applicants offered admission: 1,059. Transfer applicants enrolled: 742. **International students:** Number of foreign undergraduates: 187 (3% of student body). Number of countries represented: 42. Minimum TOEFL score required: 500 (paper); 173 (computer).

Northwestern College

- **Address:** 3003 Snelling Avenue N, St. Paul, MN 55113-1598
- **Website:** http://www.nwc.edu
- **Private; Religious affiliation:** Christian nondenominational
- **Enrollment:** 1,726 full-time; 41 part-time

KEY STATS

✔ **U.S News College Ranking:** 25, Comp. Coll.–Bachelor's (Midwest)
✔ **ACT Score (25th/75th percentile):** 21-26
✔ **Tuition:** 2006-2007: $19,990

Selectivity: More selective	**Room/board:** $6,460
Acceptance rate: 98%	**Average debt:** $21,778
Student/faculty ratio: 16/1	**Proportion who borrowed:** 62%

UNDERGRADUATE STUDENT BODY STATS

2005-2006 enrollment: 1,726 full-time; 41 part-time. Men: 40%; women: 60%. **Ethnic makeup:** African American: 2%; Asian American: 4%; Hispanic: 2%; White: 91%; International: 1%. **Religious preference:** Roman Catholic: 2%; Protestant: 98%.

ADMISSIONS FACTS AND FIGURES

Phone: (800) 827-6827. **Email:** admissions@nwc.edu. **Website:** http://www.nwc.edu. **Application deadlines for fall 2007:** Regular decision: August 1. Early decision: Not offered. Early action: Not offered. Admission can be deferred. **Application fee:** $30. Common application is not accepted. **Admissions requirements/recommendations:** High school units required (recommended): English: (4); Mathematics: (3); Science: (3); Foreign language: (2); Social studies: (3); History: (0); Academic electives: (1); Total units: (16). Tests: The college uses SAT or ACT scores in admissions decisions. Either SAT or ACT required. For admission to the fall 2007 entering class, the school will accept: ACT with writing, ACT without writing. Campus visit: Recommended. Admissions interview: Recommended. Off-campus interview: May be arranged. **Factors that count in admissions decisions: Academic:** Secondary school record: Very important. Class rank: Very important. Letters of recommendation: Very important. Standardized test scores: Very important. Essay: Very important. **Nonacademic:** Interview: Important. Extracurricular activities: Important. Talent/ability: Important. Character/personal qualities: Very important. Alumni/ae relationship: Important. Geographical residence: Not considered. State residency: Not considered. Religious affiliation/commitment: Very important. Minority status: Not considered. Volunteer work: Important. Work experience: Important. **Other schools with the greatest overlap in applicants:** Bethel College; Crown College; North Central College; University of Minnesota–Duluth; University of Minnesota–Twin Cities. **Admissions statistics for the fall 2005 entering class:** Total applicants: 918. Total accepted: 904. Freshmen enrolled: 469; 33% were from out of state. Overall acceptance rate: 98%. **Size of waiting list:** 0 applicants; enrolled from waiting list: 0. **Credentials of fall 2005 freshmen:** 26% ranked in the top 10 percent of their high school class; 51% were in the top 25 percent, and 79% were in the top half. (Proportion submitting class standing: 79%.) **Average high school grade point average:** 3.5. **First-year students who submitted SAT scores:** 12%. Scores (25/75 percentile): Verbal: 500-660, Math: 510-620, Combined: 1010-1280. **First-year students submitting ACT scores:** 94%. Scores (25/75 percentile): English: 21-28, Math: 19-26, Composite: 21-26.

ACADEMICS

Year founded: 1902. **Academic calendar:** Semester. **Degrees offered:** certificate, associate, bachelor's, master's. **Most popular majors:** 10% elementary education and teaching, 10% psychology, 6% communication studies/speech communication and rhetoric, 5% business administration and management, 5% history. **Major fields of study:** biological and biomedical sciences; business, management, marketing, and related support services; communication, journalism, and related programs; education; English language and literature/letters; history; mathematics and statistics; multi/interdisciplinary studies; parks, recreation, leisure, and fitness studies; psychology; security and protective services; social sciences; theology and religious vocations; visual and performing arts. **Areas of required coursework:** arts/fine arts, humanities, computer literacy, mathematics, English (including composition), sciences (biological or physical), history, social science, other. **Pre-professional programs:** pre-medicine, pre-theology. **Special academic programs (% participation):** distance learning (60%), double major (82%), exchange student program (domestic) (3%), honors program (0%), independent study (14%), internships (69%), student-designed major (1%), study abroad (3%), teacher certificate program (20%). **Teacher certification offered in:** early childhood, elementary, middle/junior high, secondary. **Reserve Officers Training Corps (ROTC):** Army ROTC: Offered at cooperating institution (University of Minnesota (Twin Cities)); Air Force ROTC: Offered at cooperating institution (University of St. Thomas). **Faculty and instruction (2005-2006):** Total instructional faculty: 85 full-time, 80 part-time (61% men; 39% women; 8% minorities). Full-time faculty with Ph.D. or other terminal degree: 67%. Student/faculty ratio: 16/1. Classes of fewer than 20 students: 46%; of 20 to 49 students: 48%; of 50 or more students: 6%. **Advanced Placement and International Baccalaureate credit:** AP tests may be used for: Credit only. Scores accepted: 3, 4, 5. International Baccalaureate exams may be used for: Credit only. **Freshmen returning for sophomore year:** 78%. **Graduation rates:** Four-year: 42%; five-year: 56%; six-year: 57%. **Graduate study:** 8% of students pursue further study within one year. Fields in which graduates pursue further study: theology (or the seminary), 4%; arts and sciences, 3%.

COSTS AND FINANCIAL AID

Financial aid office: (651) 631-5212. **Expenses (2006-2007):** Tuition and fees 2006-2007: $19,990; room/board: $6,460. Estimated books and supplies: $600; transportation: $700; personal expenses: $1,900. **Financial aid:** Priority filing date for institution's financial aid form: March 1. In 2005-2006, 97% of undergraduates applied for financial aid. Of those, 82% were determined to have financial need; 11% had their need fully met. Average financial aid package (proportion receiving): $14,453 (82%). Average amount of gift aid, such as scholarships or grants (proportion receiving): $10,316 (82%). Average amount of self-help aid, such as work study or loans (proportion receiving): $4,937 (69%). Average need-based loan (excluding PLUS or other private loans): $4,372. Among students who received need-based aid, the average percentage of need met: 75%. Among students who received aid based on merit, the average award (and the proportion receiving): $5,089 (15%). The average athletic scholarship (and the proportion receiving): $0 (0%). Average amount of debt of borrowers graduating in 2005: $21,778. Proportion who borrowed: 62%.

CAMPUS LIFE AND EXTRACURRICULAR ACTIVITIES

Campus housing available (% using): coed dorms (72%), women's dorms (6%), apartment for single students (22%). Students who live in college-owned, operated, or affiliated housing: 63%. **Student employment:** During the 2005-2006 academic year, 12% of undergraduates worked on campus. Average per-year earnings: $2,500. **Clubs and organizations:** Number of student organizations: 19. Activities include: choral groups, concert band, drama/theater, jazz band, literary magazine, music ensembles, musical theater, opera, radio station, student government, student newspaper, symphony orchestra, yearbook. Number of fraternities: 0; sororities: 0. **Sports program (2005-2006):** Member of NAIA. **Men's intercollegiate varsity sports:** baseball, basketball, cross-country, football, golf, soccer, tennis, track and field (indoor), track and field (outdoor). **Women's intercollegiate varsity sports:** basketball, cross-country, soccer, softball, tennis, track and field (indoor), track and field (outdoor), volleyball.

SERVICES AND FACILITIES

Basic services: nonremedial tutoring, placement service, health service, health insurance. **Remedial assistance:** reading, math, writing, study skills. **Counseling services:** minority student, career, personal, academic, psychological, religious. **For learning-disabled students:** School does not offer a structured program with separate admission and additional fees. Total undergraduates in learning-disabled program or receiving services: 62. Services include: remedial math, remedial English, reading machines, remedial reading, tape recorders, other special classes, videotaped classes, untimed tests, note-taking services, oral tests, learning center, readers, extended time for tests, tutors, priority registration, priority seating, proofreading services, texts on tape, other testing accomodations, other. **Library:** Number of titles: 88,373; number of current serial subscriptions: 1,181. **Information technology resources:** Students are required to lease or own a computer. Number of campus computers available to all students: 100. School has a wireless network. Approximate number of users that can be accommodated: 900. Proportion of college-owned housing units wired for high-speed internet access: 100%. **Campus safety:** Security services offered: 24-hour foot-and-vehicle patrols, late-night transport/escort service, lighted pathways/sidewalks, controlled dormitory access (key, security card, etc).

TRANSFER AND INTERNATIONAL STUDENTS

Transfer students: May apply for admission for the following academic terms: Fall, Spring, Summer. Applicants do not need a minimum number of credits to apply. For fall 2005: Transfer applications received: 190. Transfer applicants offered admission: 188. Transfer applicants enrolled: 124. **International students:** Number of foreign undergraduates: 10 (1% of student body). Number of countries represented: 6. Minimum TOEFL score required: 530 (paper); 197 (computer).

Southwest Minnesota State University

- **Address:** 1501 State Street, Marshall, MN 56258
- **Website:** http://www.southwestmsu.edu
- **Public**
- **Enrollment:** 2,434 full-time; 3,171 part-time

KEY STATS

✔ **U.S News College Ranking:** third tier, Comp. Coll.–Bachelor's (Midwest)
✔ **ACT Score (25th/75th percentile):** 17-26
✔ **Tuition:** 2006-2007: $6,240 in state, $6,240 out of state

Selectivity: Selective	**Room/board:** $5,324
Acceptance rate: 43%	**Average debt:** $16,678
Student/faculty ratio: 23/1	**Proportion who borrowed:** 83%

UNDERGRADUATE STUDENT BODY STATS

2005-2006 enrollment: 2,434 full-time; 3,171 part-time. Men: 42%; women: 58%. **Ethnic makeup:** African American: 4%; American-Indian: 1%; Asian American: 1%; Hispanic: 2%; White: 85%; International: 8%.

ADMISSIONS FACTS AND FIGURES

Phone: (507) 537-6286. **Email:** shearerr@southwestmsu.edu. **Website:** http://www.southwestmsu.edu. **Application deadlines for fall 2007:** Regular decision: August 20. Early decision: Not offered. Early action: Not offered. Admission can be deferred. **Application fee:** $20. Common application is accepted. **To apply online, go to:** https://www.applyweb.com/aw?swsu/. **Admissions requirements/recommendations:** High school units required (recommended): English: 4 (4); Mathematics: 3 (3); Science: 3 (3); Foreign language: 2 (2); Social studies: 3 (3); Total units: 17 (17). Tests: The college uses SAT or ACT scores in admissions decisions. ACT required. For admission to the fall 2007 entering class, the school will accept: ACT with writing, ACT without writing. Campus visit: Required. Admissions interview: Required. Off-campus interview: May be arranged. **Factors that count in admissions decisions:** *Academic:* Secondary school record: Very important. Class rank: Very important. Letters of recommendation: Important. Standardized test scores: Very important. Essay: Considered. *Nonacademic:* Interview: Considered. Extracurricular activities: Considered. Talent/ability: Considered. Character/personal qualities: Considered. Alumni/ae relationship: Considered. Geographical residence: Considered. State residency: Considered. Religious affiliation/commitment: Not considered. Minority status: Considered. Volunteer work: Considered. Work experience: Considered. **Other schools with the greatest overlap in applicants:** Bemidji State University; Minnesota State University–Mankato; Minnesota State University–Moorhead; South Dakota State University; St. Cloud State University. **Admissions statistics for the fall 2005 entering class:** Total applicants: 1,507. Total accepted: 647. Freshmen enrolled: 590; Overall acceptance rate: 43%. **Credentials of fall 2005 freshmen:** 10% ranked in the top 10 percent of their high school class; 26% were in the top 25 percent, and 73% were in the top half. (Proportion submitting class standing: 96%.) **Average high school grade point average:** 3.5. **First-year students who submitted SAT scores:** 2%. Scores (25/75 percentile): Verbal: N/A, Math: N/A, Combined: N/A. **First-year students submitting ACT scores:** 82%. Scores (25/75 percentile): English: N/A, Math: N/A, Composite: 17-26.

ACADEMICS

Year founded: 1963. **Academic calendar:** Semester. **Degrees offered:** associate, bachelor's, master's. **Most popular majors:** 20% education, 18% business administration and management, 7% health and physical education, 4% accounting, 4% social work. **Major fields of study:** agriculture, agriculture operations, and related sciences; biological and biomedical sciences; business, management, marketing, and related support services; communication, journalism, and related programs; computer and information sciences and support services; education; English language and literature/letters; foreign languages, literatures, and linguistics; history; mathematics and statistics; multi/interdisciplinary studies; natural resources and conservation; parks, recreation, leisure, and fitness studies; philosophy and religious studies; physical sciences; psychology; public administration and social service professions; security and protective services; social sciences; visual and performing arts. **Areas of required coursework:** arts/fine arts, humanities, mathematics, English (including composition), foreign languages, sciences (biological or physical), history, social science, other. **Pre-professional programs:** pre-law, pre-dentistry, pre-medicine, pre-theology, pre-veterinary science, pre-optometry, pre-pharmacy, other. **Special academic programs:** accelerated program, cross-registration, distance learning, double major, dual enrollment, English as a Second Language (ESL), exchange student program (domestic), external degree program, honors program, independent study, internships, liberal arts/career combination, student-designed major, study abroad, teacher certificate program, weekend college, other. **Teacher certification offered in:** early childhood, special education, elementary, middle/junior high, adult education, secondary. **Cooperative education programs:** business. **Faculty and instruction (2005-2006):** Total instructional faculty: 116 full-time, 97 part-time (57% men; 43% women; 8% minorities). Full-time faculty with Ph.D. or other terminal degree: 75%. Student/faculty ratio: 23/1. Classes of fewer than 20 students: 44%; of 20 to 49 students: 54%; of 50 or more students: 3%. **Advanced Placement and International Baccalaureate credit:** AP tests may be used for: Credit only. Scores accepted: 3. International Baccalaureate exams may be used for: Credit and/or placement. **Freshmen returning for sophomore year:** 70%. **Graduation rates:** Four-year: 18%; five-year: 35%; six-year: 42%. **Graduate study:** 10% of students pursue further study immediately upon graduation. Fields in which graduates pursue further study: Master of Business Administration (MBA), 5%; law, 3%; medicine, 11%; education, 8%; arts and sciences, 73%.

COSTS AND FINANCIAL AID

Financial aid office: (507) 537-6281. **Expenses (2006-2007):** Tuition and fees 2006-2007: $6,240 in state, $6,240 out of state; room/board: $5,324. Estimated books and supplies: $1,000; transportation: $800; personal expenses: $1,600. **Financial aid:** Priority filing date for institution's financial aid form: March 1. In 2005-2006, 78% of undergraduates applied for financial aid. Of those, 61% were determined to have financial need; 29% had their need fully met. Average financial aid package (proportion receiving): $6,736 (60%). Average amount of gift aid, such as scholarships or grants (proportion receiving): $3,680 (42%). Average amount of self-help aid, such as work study or loans (proportion receiving): $3,745 (52%). Average need-based loan (excluding PLUS or other private loans): $3,432. Among students who received need-based aid, the average percentage of need met: 40%. Among students who received aid based on merit, the average award (and the proportion receiving): $1,798 (14%). The average athletic scholarship (and the proportion receiving): $2,275 (9%). Average amount of debt of borrowers graduating in 2005: $16,678. Proportion who borrowed: 83%.

CAMPUS LIFE AND EXTRACURRICULAR ACTIVITIES

Campus housing available (% using): coed dorms (47%), women's dorms (25%), men's dorms (23%), special housing for disabled students (5%). Students who live in college-owned, operated, or affiliated housing: 29%. **Student employment:** During the 2005-2006 academic year, 22% of undergraduates worked on campus. Average per-year earnings: $1,500. **Clubs and organizations:** Number of student organizations: 74. Activities include: choral groups, concert band, dance, drama/theater, jazz band, literary magazine, marching band, music ensembles, musical theater, pep band, radio station, student government, student newspaper, symphony orchestra, television station. Number of fraternities: 0; sororities: 0. Average proportion of students who stay on campus on weekends: 33%. **Sports program (2005-2006):** Member of NCAA II. *Men's intercollegiate varsity sports:* baseball, basketball, football, wrestling. *Women's intercollegiate varsity sports:* basketball, golf, soccer, softball, tennis, volleyball.

SERVICES AND FACILITIES

Basic services: women's center, placement service, day care, health service, health insurance. **Remedial assistance:** reading, math, writing, study skills. **Counseling services:** minority student, career, military, personal, veteran student, academic, psychological, birth control. **For learning-disabled students:** School does not offer a structured program with separate admission and additional fees. Total undergraduates in learning-disabled program or receiving services: 50. Services include: remedial math, remedial English, reading machines, other special classes, videotaped classes, diagnostic testing service, note-taking services, oral tests, learning center, extended time for tests, tutors, early syllabus, priority registration, priority seating, proofreading services, texts on tape, typist/scribe, exams on tape or computer, other testing accomodations, waiver of foreign language degree requirement. **Library:** Number of titles: 202,363; number of current serial subscriptions: 946. **Information technology resources:** Students are not required to lease or own a computer. Number of campus computers available to all students: 310. School has a wireless network. Approximate number of users that can be accommodated: 600. Proportion of college-owned housing units wired for high-speed internet access: 100%. **Campus safety:** Security services offered: 24-hour foot-and-vehicle patrols, late-night transport/escort service, 24-hour emergency telephones, lighted pathways/sidewalks, student patrols, controlled dormitory access (key, security card, etc).

TRANSFER AND INTERNATIONAL STUDENTS

Transfer students: May apply for admission for the following academic terms: Fall, Spring, Summer. Applicants need a minimum number of credits to apply. For fall 2005: Transfer applications received: 336. Transfer applicants offered admission: 305. Transfer applicants enrolled: 242. **International students:** Number of foreign undergraduates: 198 (8% of student body). Number of countries represented: 27. Minimum TOEFL score required: 500 (paper). Average TOEFL score: 566 (paper).

St. Cloud State University

- **Address:** 720 S. Fourth Avenue, St. Cloud, MN 56301
- **Website:** http://www.stcloudstate.edu
- **Public**
- **Enrollment:** 11,611 full-time; 2,875 part-time

KEY STATS

✔ **U.S News College Ranking:** third tier, Universities–Master's (Midwest)
✔ **ACT Score (25th/75th percentile):** 19-24
✔ **Tuition:** 2006-2007: $5,718 in state, $11,625 out of state

Selectivity: Selective	**Room/board:** N/A
Acceptance rate: 78%	**Average debt:** $20,431
Student/faculty ratio: 17/1	**Proportion who borrowed:** 52%

UNDERGRADUATE STUDENT BODY STATS

2005-2006 enrollment: 11,611 full-time; 2,875 part-time. Men: 45%; women: 55%. **Ethnic makeup:** African American: 2%; American-Indian: 1%; Asian American: 2%; Hispanic: 1%; White: 90%; International: 5%.

ADMISSIONS FACTS AND FIGURES

Phone: (320) 308-2244. **Email:** scsu4u@stcloudstate.edu. **Website:** http://www.stcloudstate.edu. **Application deadlines for fall 2007:** Regular decision: June 1. Early decision: Not offered. Early action: Not offered. Admission can be deferred. **Application fee:** $20. Common application is not accepted. **Admissions requirements/recommendations:** High school units required (recommended): English: 4; Mathematics: 3; Science: 3; Foreign language: 2; Social studies: 3; History: 1; Total units: 17. Tests: The college uses SAT or ACT scores in admissions decisions. Either SAT or ACT required. For admission to the fall 2007 entering class, the school will accept: ACT with writing, ACT without writing. Campus visit: Recommended. Admissions interview: Neither required nor recommended. Off-campus interview: Not available. **Factors that count in admissions decisions:** *Academic:* Secondary school record: Very important. Class rank: Very important. Letters of recommendation: Considered. Standardized test scores: Considered. Essay: Considered. *Nonacademic:* Interview: Not considered. Extracurricular activities: Considered. Talent/ability: Considered. Character/personal qualities: Not considered. Alumni/ae relationship: Not considered. Geographical residence: Not considered. State residency: Not considered. Religious affiliation/commitment: Not considered. Minority status: Not considered. Volunteer work: Not considered. Work experience: Not considered. **Admissions statistics for the fall 2005 entering class:** Total applicants: 5,912. Total accepted: 4,622. Freshmen enrolled: 2,152; 12% were from out of state. Overall acceptance rate: 78%. **Credentials of fall 2005 freshmen:** 7% ranked in the top 10 percent of their high school class; 29% were in the top 25 percent, and 76% were in the top half. (Proportion submitting class standing: 93%.) **First-year students submitting ACT scores:** 89%. Scores (25/75 percentile): English: 18-24, Math: 18-24, Composite: 19-24.

ACADEMICS

Year founded: 1869. **Academic calendar:** Semester. **Degrees offered:** associate, bachelor's, post-bachelor's certificate, master's, post-master's certificate. **Most popular majors:** 23% business, management, marketing, and related support services, 18% education, 9% social sciences, 5% liberal arts and sciences studies, and humanities, 5% psychology. **Major fields of study:** agriculture, agriculture operations, and related sciences; area, ethnic, cultural, and gender studies; biological and biomedical sciences; business, management, marketing, and related support services; computer and information sciences and support services; education; engineering; engineering technologies/technicians; English language and literature/letters; foreign languages, literatures, and linguistics; health professions and related clinical sciences; liberal arts and sciences studies, and humanities; mathematics and statistics; multi/interdisciplinary studies; natural resources and conservation; parks, recreation, leisure, and fitness studies; philosophy and religious studies; physical sciences; psychology; public administration and social service professions; security and protective services; social sciences; transportation and materials moving; visual and performing arts. **Areas of required coursework:** humanities, computer literacy, mathematics, English (including composition), philosophy, sciences (biological or physical), history, social science. **Pre-professional programs:** pre-law, pre-dentistry, pre-medicine, pre-veterinary science, pre-optometry, pre-pharmacy, other. **Special academic programs:** accelerated program, cooperative (work-study plan) program, cross-registration, distance learning, double major, dual enrollment, English as a Second Language (ESL), honors program, independent study, internships, student-designed major, study abroad, teacher certificate program. **Teacher certification offered in:** early childhood, special education, elementary, middle/junior high, secondary, bilingual/bicultural. **Reserve Officers Training Corps (ROTC):** Army ROTC: Offered on campus. **Faculty and instruction (2005-2006):** Total instructional faculty: 650 full-time, 211 part-time (56% men; 44% women; 15% minorities). Full-time faculty with Ph.D. or other terminal degree: 80%. Student/faculty ratio: 17/1. Classes of fewer than 20 students: 36%; of 20 to 49 students: 58%; of 50 or more students: 6%. **Advanced Placement and International Baccalaureate credit:** AP tests may be used for: Credit only. Scores accepted: 3, 4, 5. International Baccalaureate exams may be used for: Credit and/or placement. **Freshmen returning for sophomore year:** 71%. **Graduation rates:** Six-year: 42%. **Graduate study:** 16% of students pursue further study within one year.

COSTS AND FINANCIAL AID

Financial aid office: (320) 308-2047. **Expenses (2006-2007):** Tuition and fees 2006-2007: $5,718 in state, $11,625 out of state; room/board: N/A. **Financial aid:** In 2005-2006, 64% of undergraduates applied for financial aid. Of those, 45% were determined to have financial need; 60% had their need fully met. Average financial aid package (proportion receiving): $9,634 (45%). Average amount of gift aid, such as scholarships or grants (proportion receiving): $3,803 (34%). Average amount of self-help aid, such as work study or loans (proportion receiving): $4,852 (44%). Average need-based loan (excluding PLUS or other private loans): $4,187. Among students who received need-based aid, the average percentage of need met: 96%. Among students who received aid based on merit, the average award (and the proportion receiving): $1,812 (4%). The average athletic scholarship (and the proportion receiving): $3,951 (2%). Average amount of debt of borrowers graduating in 2005: $20,431. Proportion who borrowed: 52%.

CAMPUS LIFE AND EXTRACURRICULAR ACTIVITIES

Campus housing available (% using): coed dorms (86%), women's dorms (5%), men's dorms (6%), apartment for single students (3%), special housing for disabled students, special housing for international students. Students who live in college-owned, operated, or affiliated housing: 18%. **Clubs and organizations:** Number of student organizations: 230. Activities include: choral groups, concert band, dance, drama/theater, music ensembles, musical theater, opera, radio station, student government, student newspaper, symphony orchestra, television station. Number of fraternities: 5; sororities: 4. Average proportion of students who stay on campus on weekends: 21%. **Sports program (2005-2006):** Member of NCAA II. *Men's intercollegiate varsity sports:* baseball, basketball, cross-country, football, golf, ice hockey, swimming and diving, tennis, track and field (indoor), track and field (outdoor), wrestling. *Women's intercollegiate varsity sports:* basketball, cross-country, golf, ice hockey, nordic skiing, soccer, softball, swimming and diving, tennis, track and field (indoor), track and field (outdoor), volleyball.

SERVICES AND FACILITIES

Basic services: women's center, placement service, day care, health service, health insurance, other. **Remedial assistance:** reading, math, writing, study skills. **Counseling services:** minority student, career, military, personal, veteran student, academic, older student, psychological, birth control. **For learning-disabled students:** School does not offer a structured program with separate admission and additional fees. Total undergraduates in learning-disabled program or receiving services: 150. Services include: remedial math, remedial English, remedial reading, note-taking services, oral tests, learning center, readers, extended time for tests, other. **Library:** Number of titles: 909,613; number of current serial subscriptions: 13,546. **Information technology resources:** Students are not required to lease or own a computer. Number of campus computers available to all students: 1,429. School has a wireless network. Approximate number of users that can be accommodated: 4,680. Proportion of college-owned housing units wired for high-speed internet access: 100%. **Campus safety:** Security services offered: 24-hour foot-and-vehicle patrols, late-night transport/escort service, 24-hour emergency telephones, lighted pathways/sidewalks, student patrols, controlled dormitory access (key, security card, etc).

TRANSFER AND INTERNATIONAL STUDENTS

Transfer students: May apply for admission for the following academic terms: Fall, Spring, Summer. Applicants need a minimum number of credits to apply. For fall 2005: Transfer applications received: 1,883. Transfer applicants offered admission: 1,824. Transfer applicants enrolled: 1,238.

International students: Number of foreign undergraduates: 587 (5% of student body). Number of countries represented: 78. Minimum TOEFL score required: 500 (paper); 173 (computer).

St. John's University

- **Address:** PO Box 7155, Collegeville, MN 56321
- **Website:** http://www.csbsju.edu
- **Private; Religious affiliation:** Roman Catholic (Benedictine)
- **Enrollment:** 1,845 full-time; 30 part-time

KEY STATS

✔ **U.S News College Ranking:** 69, Liberal Arts Colleges
✔ **ACT Score (25th/75th percentile):** 23-28
✔ **Tuition:** 2006-2007: $24,924

Selectivity: More selective	**Room/board:** $6,496
Acceptance rate: 87%	**Average debt:** $24,663
Student/faculty ratio: 12/1	**Proportion who borrowed:** 63%

UNDERGRADUATE STUDENT BODY STATS

2005-2006 enrollment: 1,845 full-time; 30 part-time. Men: 100%; women: 0%. **Ethnic makeup:** African American: 1%; Asian American: 2%; Hispanic: 1%; White: 93%; International: 4%. **Religious preference:** Protestant: 21%; No preference: 8%; Roman Catholic (Benedictine): 63%; Christian: 5%; Other: 3%.

ADMISSIONS FACTS AND FIGURES

Phone: (320) 363-2196. **Email:** admissions@csbsju.edu. **Website:** http://www.csbsju.edu. **Application deadlines for fall 2007:** Regular decision: Rolling. Early decision: Not offered. Early action: Not offered. Admission can be deferred. Common application is accepted. **To apply online, go to:** http://www.csbsju.edu/admission/. **Admissions requirements/recommendations:** High school units required (recommended): English: (4); Mathematics: (3); Science: (2); Foreign language: (2); Social studies: (2); Academic electives: (4); Total units: (17). Tests: The college uses SAT or ACT scores in admissions decisions. Either SAT or ACT required. For admission to the fall 2007 entering class, the school will accept: ACT with writing, ACT without writing. Campus visit: Recommended. Admissions interview: Recommended. Off-campus interview: May be arranged. **Factors that count in admissions decisions:** *Academic:* Secondary school record: Very important. Class rank: Important. Letters of recommendation: Important. Standardized test scores: Very important. Essay: Very important. *Nonacademic:* Interview: Considered. Extracurricular activities: Important. Talent/ability: Considered. Character/personal qualities: Considered. Alumni/ae relationship: Considered. Geographical residence: Important. State residency: Not considered. Religious affiliation/commitment: Not considered. Minority status: Important. Volunteer work: Important. Work experience: Considered. **Other schools with the greatest overlap in applicants:** Gustavus Adolphus College; St. Olaf College; University of Minnesota–Duluth; University of Minnesota–Twin Cities; University of St. Thomas. **Admissions statistics for the fall 2005 entering class:** Total applicants: 1,167. Total accepted: 1,017. Freshmen enrolled: 447; 15% were from out of state. Overall acceptance rate: 87%. **Credentials of fall 2005 freshmen:** 22% ranked in the top 10 percent of their high school class; 51% were in the top 25 percent, and 91% were in the top half. (Proportion submitting class standing: 83%.) **Average high school grade point average:** 3.5. **First-year students who submitted SAT scores:** 19%, Scores (25/75 percentile): Verbal: 530-660, Math: 540-650, Combined: 1070-1310. **First-year students submitting ACT scores:** 92%. Scores (25/75 percentile): English: 21-27, Math: 23-28, Composite: 23-28.

ACADEMICS

Year founded: 1857. **Academic calendar:** Semester. **Degrees offered:** bachelor's, master's, first professional. **Most popular majors:** 16% business administration and management, 11% biology/biological sciences, 11% political science and government, 9% economics, 7% English language and literature. **Major fields of study:** biological and biomedical sciences; business, management, marketing, and related support services; computer and information sciences and support services; education; English language and literature/letters; foreign languages, literatures, and linguistics; health professions and related clinical sciences; history; liberal arts and sciences studies, and humanities; mathematics and statistics; multi/interdisciplinary

studies; natural resources and conservation; philosophy and religious studies; physical sciences; psychology; public administration and social service professions; social sciences; theology and religious vocations; visual and performing arts. **Areas of required coursework:** arts/fine arts, humanities, mathematics, English (including composition), philosophy, foreign languages, sciences (biological or physical), history, social science. **Pre-professional programs:** pre-law, pre-dentistry, pre-medicine, pre-theology, pre-veterinary science, pre-optometry, pre-pharmacy, other. **Special academic programs (% participation):** accelerated program (5%), cross-registration (100%), double major (7%), dual enrollment (.5%), English as a Second Language (ESL) (.3%), honors program (13%), independent study (28%), internships (16%), liberal arts/career combination (1%), student-designed major (2%), study abroad (45%), teacher certificate program (4%). **Teacher certification offered in:** elementary, middle/junior high, secondary. **Reserve Officers Training Corps (ROTC):** Army ROTC: Offered on campus. **Faculty and instruction (2005-2006):** Total instructional faculty: 147 full-time, 29 part-time (71% men; 29% women; 8% minorities). Full-time faculty with Ph.D. or other terminal degree: 88%. Student/faculty ratio: 12/1. Classes of fewer than 20 students: 47%; of 20 to 49 students: 53%; of 50 or more students: 0%. **Advanced Placement and International Baccalaureate credit:** AP tests may be used for: Credit and/or placement. Scores accepted: 3, 4, 5. International Baccalaureate exams may be used for: Credit and/or placement. **Freshmen returning for sophomore year:** 89%. **Graduation rates:** Four-year: 71%; five-year: 77%; six-year: 78%. **Graduate study:** 21% of students pursue further study within one year. Fields in which graduates pursue further study: Master of Business Administration (MBA), 11%; law, 19%; medicine, 11%; dentistry, 2%; theology (or the seminary), 5%; education, 3%; arts and sciences, 50%.

COSTS AND FINANCIAL AID

Financial aid office: (320) 363-3664. **Expenses (2006-2007):** Tuition and fees 2006-2007: $24,924; room/board: $6,496. Estimated books and supplies: $800; transportation: $200; personal expenses: $700. **Financial aid:** Priority filing date for institution's financial aid form: March 15. In 2005-2006, 69% of undergraduates applied for financial aid. Of those, 58% were determined to have financial need; 40% had their need fully met. Average financial aid package (proportion receiving): $17,573 (58%). Average amount of gift aid, such as scholarships or grants (proportion receiving): N/A (58%). Average amount of self-help aid, such as work study or loans (proportion receiving): N/A (53%). Among students who received need-based aid, the average percentage of need met: 87%. Among students who received aid based on merit, the average award (and the proportion receiving): $7,643 (35%). The average athletic scholarship (and the proportion receiving): $0 (0%). Average amount of debt of borrowers graduating in 2005: $24,663. Proportion who borrowed: 63%.

CAMPUS LIFE AND EXTRACURRICULAR ACTIVITIES

Campus housing available (% using): men's dorms (75%), apartment for single students (25%), special housing for disabled students. Students who live in college-owned, operated, or affiliated housing: 82%. **Student employment:** During the 2005-2006 academic year, 36% of undergraduates worked on campus. Average per-year earnings: $1,830. **Clubs and organizations:** Number of student organizations: 89. Activities include: choral groups, concert band, dance, drama/theater, jazz band, literary magazine, music ensembles, musical theater, opera, pep band, radio station, student government, student newspaper, symphony orchestra. Number of fraternities: 0; sororities: 0. **Sports program (2005-2006):** Member of NCAA III. *Men's intercollegiate varsity sports:* baseball, basketball, cross-country, football, golf, ice hockey, nordic skiing, soccer, swimming and diving, tennis, track and field (indoor), track and field (outdoor), wrestling.

SERVICES AND FACILITIES

Basic services: nonremedial tutoring, placement service, health service, health insurance. **Remedial assistance:** study skills, other. **Counseling services:** minority student, career, personal, academic, psychological, religious. **For learning-disabled students:** School does not offer a structured program with separate admission and additional fees. Total undergraduates in learning-disabled program or receiving services: 60. Services include: reading machines, untimed tests, extended time for tests, tutors, priority registration, substitution of courses, other. **Library:** Number of titles: 673,477; number of current serial subscriptions: 1,440. **Information technology resources:** Students are not required to lease or own a computer. Number of campus computers available to all students: 604. School has a wireless network. Proportion of college-owned housing units wired for high-speed internet access: 100%. **Campus safety:** Security services offered: 24-hour foot-and-vehicle patrols, late-night transport/escort service, 24-hour emergency telephones, lighted pathways/sidewalks, student patrols, controlled dormitory access (key, security card, etc).

TRANSFER AND INTERNATIONAL STUDENTS

Transfer students: May apply for admission for the following academic terms: Fall, Spring. Applicants do not need a minimum number of credits to apply. For fall 2005: Transfer applications received: 79. Transfer applicants offered admission: 73. Transfer applicants enrolled: 61. **International students:** Number of foreign undergraduates: 65 (4% of student body). Number of countries represented: 37. Minimum TOEFL score required: 500 (paper); 173 (computer). Average TOEFL score: 530 (paper).

St. Mary's University of Minnesota

■ **Address:** 700 Terrace Heights, Winona, MN 55987-1399
■ **Website:** http://www.smumn.edu
■ **Private; Religious affiliation:** Roman Catholic
■ **Enrollment:** 1,286 full-time; 394 part-time

KEY STATS

✔ **U.S News College Ranking:** 30, Universities–Master's (Midwest)
✔ **ACT Score (25th/75th percentile):** 19-25
✔ **Tuition:** 2006-2007: $19,641

Selectivity: Selective	**Room/board:** $5,900
Acceptance rate: 83%	**Average debt:** $26,633
Student/faculty ratio: 12/1	**Proportion who borrowed:** 73%

UNDERGRADUATE STUDENT BODY STATS

2005-2006 enrollment: 1,286 full-time; 394 part-time. Men: 47%; women: 53%. **Ethnic makeup:** African American: 4%; Asian American: 2%; Hispanic: 2%; White: 90%; International: 1%. **Religious preference:** Protestant: 18%; Muslim: 1%; No preference: 2%; Unknown: 3%; Roman Catholic: 51%; Other: 25%.

ADMISSIONS FACTS AND FIGURES

Phone: (507) 457-1700. **Email:** admissions@smumn.edu. **Website:** http://www.smumn.edu. **Application deadlines for fall 2007:** Regular decision: May 1; decision sent by May 1. Early decision: Not offered. Early action: Not offered. Admission can be deferred. **Application fee:** $25. Common application is accepted. **Admissions requirements/recommendations:** High school units required (recommended): English: 4; Mathematics: 3; Science: 3; Foreign language: 0 (2); Social studies: 2; History: 0; Academic electives: 6; Total units: 18. Tests: The college uses SAT or ACT scores in admissions decisions. Either SAT or ACT required. For admission to the fall 2007 entering class, the school will accept: ACT with writing, ACT without writing. Campus visit: Recommended. Admissions interview: Recommended. Off-campus interview: May be arranged. **Factors that count in admissions decisions:** *Academic:* Secondary school record: Very important. Class rank: Important. Letters of recommendation: Considered. Standardized test scores: Very important. Essay: Considered. *Nonacademic:* Interview: Important. Extracurricular activities: Considered. Talent/ability: Important. Character/personal qualities: Important. Alumni/ae relationship: Considered. Geographical residence: Not considered. State residency: Not considered. Religious affiliation/commitment: Not considered. Minority status: Not considered. Volunteer work: Considered. Work experience: Not considered. **Other schools with the greatest overlap in applicants:** Minnesota State University–Mankato; University of Minnesota–Twin Cities; University of St. Thomas; Winona State University. **Admissions statistics for the fall 2005 entering class:** Total applicants: 1,048. Total accepted: 873. Freshmen enrolled: 311; 35% were from out of state. Overall acceptance rate: 83%. **Credentials of fall 2005 freshmen:** 19% ranked in the top 10 percent of their high school class; 47% were in the top 25 percent, and 70% were in the top half. (Proportion submitting class standing: 81%.) **Average high school grade point average:** 3.2. **First-year students who submitted SAT scores:** 6%. Scores (25/75 percentile): Verbal: 520-630, Math: 500-645, Combined: 1020-1275. **First-year students submitting ACT scores:** 94%. Scores (25/75 percentile): English: 18-25, Math: 18-25, Composite: 19-25.

ACADEMICS

Year founded: 1912. **Academic calendar:** Semester. **Degrees offered:** certificate, diploma, bachelor's, post-bachelor's certificate, master's, post-master's certificate, doctorate. **Most popular majors:** 12% business/commerce, 9%

marketing/marketing management, 7% information science/studies, 5% business administration and management, 4% psychology. **Major fields of study:** biological and biomedical sciences; business, management, marketing, and related support services; communication, journalism, and related programs; computer and information sciences and support services; education; engineering; engineering technologies/technicians; English language and literature/letters; foreign languages, literatures, and linguistics; health professions and related clinical sciences; history; mathematics and statistics; multi/interdisciplinary studies; philosophy and religious studies; physical sciences; psychology; public administration and social service professions; security and protective services; social sciences; theology and religious vocations; visual and performing arts. **Areas of required coursework:** arts/fine arts, humanities, mathematics, English (including composition), philosophy, sciences (biological or physical), history, social science, other. **Pre-professional programs:** pre-law, pre-dentistry, pre-medicine, pre-theology, pre-veterinary science. **Special academic programs (% participation):** cross-registration (2%), double major (15%), dual enrollment (5%), English as a Second Language (ESL) (1%), honors program (22%), independent study (16%), internships (34%), student-designed major (1%), study abroad (25%), teacher certificate program (10%). **Teacher certification offered in:** early childhood, elementary, middle/junior high, secondary. **Cooperative education programs:** health professions, technologies. **Reserve Officers Training Corps (ROTC):** Army ROTC: Offered at cooperating institution (University of Wisconsin, LaCrosse). **Faculty and instruction (2005-2006):** Total instructional faculty: 101 full-time, 460 part-time (52% men; 48% women; 2% minorities). Full-time faculty with Ph.D. or other terminal degree: 80%. Student/faculty ratio: 12/1. Classes of fewer than 20 students: 56%; of 20 to 49 students: 44%; of 50 or more students: 0%. **Advanced Placement and International Baccalaureate credit:** AP tests may be used for: Credit only. Scores accepted: 3, 4, 5. International Baccalaureate exams may be used for: Credit only. **Freshmen returning for sophomore year:** 74%. **Graduation rates:** Four-year: 53%; five-year: 63%; six-year: 61%. **Graduate study:** 29% of students pursue further study immediately upon graduation. Fields in which graduates pursue further study: Master of Business Administration (MBA), 6%; law, 5%; medicine, 13%; theology (or the seminary), 13%; education, 27%; arts and sciences, 36%.

COSTS AND FINANCIAL AID

Financial aid office: (507) 457-1438. **Expenses (2006-2007):** Tuition and fees 2006-2007: $19,641; room/board: $5,900. Estimated books and supplies: $1,186; transportation: $275; personal expenses: $800. **Financial aid:** Priority filing date for institution's financial aid form: March 15. In 2005-2006, 88% of undergraduates applied for financial aid. Of those, 79% were determined to have financial need; 61% had their need fully met. Average financial aid package (proportion receiving): $14,833 (79%). Average amount of gift aid, such as scholarships or grants (proportion receiving): $7,900 (79%). Average amount of self-help aid, such as work study or loans (proportion receiving): $6,933 (79%). Average need-based loan (excluding PLUS or other private loans): $5,633. Among students who received need-based aid, the average percentage of need met: 89%. Average amount of debt of borrowers graduating in 2005: $26,633. Proportion who borrowed: 73%.

CAMPUS LIFE AND EXTRACURRICULAR ACTIVITIES

Campus housing available (% using): coed dorms (56%), women's dorms (10%), men's dorms (8%), apartment for single students (24%), special housing for disabled students (2%). Students who live in college-owned, operated, or affiliated housing: 82%. **Student employment:** During the 2005-2006 academic year, 20% of undergraduates worked on campus. Average per-year earnings: $927. **Clubs and organizations:** Number of student organizations: 85. Activities include: choral groups, concert band, dance, drama/theater, jazz band, literary magazine, music ensembles, musical theater, radio station, student government, student newspaper, yearbook. Number of fraternities: 0; sororities: 0. Proportion of men in fraternities: 6%; of women in sororities: 3%. Average proportion of students who stay on campus on weekends: 75%. **Sports program (2005-2006):** Member of NCAA III. *Men's intercollegiate varsity sports:* baseball, basketball, cross-country, golf, ice hockey, soccer, swimming and diving, tennis, track and field (indoor), track and field (outdoor). *Women's intercollegiate varsity sports:* basketball, cross-country, golf, ice hockey, soccer, softball, swimming and diving, tennis, track and field (indoor), track and field (outdoor), volleyball.

SERVICES AND FACILITIES

Basic services: nonremedial tutoring, health service. **Remedial assistance:** study skills. **Counseling services:** career, personal, academic, psychological, religious. **For learning-disabled students:** School does not offer a structured program with separate admission and additional fees. Total undergraduates in learning-disabled program or receiving services: 20. Services include: reading machines, tape recorders, untimed tests, note-taking services, oral tests, learning center, readers, extended time for tests, tutors, texts on tape, other testing accomodations. **Library:** Number of titles: 170,154; number of current serial subscriptions: 634. **Information technology resources:** Students are not required to lease or own a computer. Number of campus computers available to all students: 356. School has a wireless network. Approximate number of users that can be accommodated: 540. Proportion of college-owned housing units wired for high-speed internet access: 100%. **Campus safety:** Security services offered: 24-hour foot-and-vehicle patrols, late-night transport/escort service, 24-hour emergency telephones, lighted pathways/sidewalks, student patrols, controlled dormitory access (key, security card, etc).

TRANSFER AND INTERNATIONAL STUDENTS

Transfer students: May apply for admission for the following academic terms: Fall, Spring, Summer. Applicants need a minimum number of credits to apply. For fall 2005: Transfer applications received: 230. Transfer applicants offered admission: 161. Transfer applicants enrolled: 139. **International students:** Number of foreign undergraduates: 19 (1% of student body). Number of countries represented: 12. Minimum TOEFL score required: 520 (paper); 190 (computer). Average TOEFL score: 530 (paper).

St. Olaf College

- **Address:** 1520 St. Olaf Avenue, Northfield, MN 55057
- **Website:** http://www.stolaf.edu
- **Private; Religious affiliation:** Lutheran
- **Enrollment:** 3,005 full-time; 53 part-time

KEY STATS
✔ **U.S News College Ranking:** 55, Liberal Arts Colleges
✔ **ACT Score (25th/75th percentile):** 25-30
✔ **Tuition:** 2006-2007: $28,200

Selectivity: More selective	**Room/board:** $7,400
Acceptance rate: 73%	**Average debt:** $19,410
Student/faculty ratio: 13/1	**Proportion who borrowed:** 65%

UNDERGRADUATE STUDENT BODY STATS

2005-2006 enrollment: 3,005 full-time; 53 part-time. Men: 42%; women: 58%. **Ethnic makeup:** African American: 1%; Asian American: 5%; Hispanic: 1%; White: 92%; International: 1%. **Religious preference:** Roman Catholic: 13%; Protestant: 26%; No preference: 2%; Unknown: 17%; Lutheran: 41%; Other: 1%.

ADMISSIONS FACTS AND FIGURES

Phone: (507) 646-3025. **Email:** admissions@stolaf.edu. **Website:** http://www.stolaf.edu. **Application deadlines for fall 2007:** Regular decision: Rolling; decision sent by March 1. Early decision: Send application by: November 15; Decision sent by: December 6. Early action: Send application by: December 15; Decision sent by: February 1. Admission can be deferred. **Application fee:** $35. Common application is accepted. **To apply online, go to:** http://www.stolaf.edu/admissions/onlineapp/index.html. **Admissions requirements/recommendations:** High school units required (recommended): English: 4 (4); Mathematics: 2 (4); Science: 2 (4); Foreign language: 2 (4); Social studies: 1 (2); History: 1 (2); Academic electives: 2 (4); Total units: 14 (24). Tests: The college uses SAT or ACT scores in admissions decisions. Either SAT or ACT required. For admission to the fall 2007 entering class, the school will accept: ACT with writing, ACT without writing. Campus visit: Recommended. Admissions interview: Recommended. Off-campus interview: Not available. **Factors that count in admissions decisions:** *Academic:* Secondary school record: Very important. Class rank: Considered. Letters of recommendation: Important. Standardized test scores: Important. Essay: Very important. *Nonacademic:* Interview: Considered. Extracurricular activities: Important. Talent/ability: Important. Character/personal qualities: Important. Alumni/ae relationship: Considered. Geographical residence: Considered. State residency: Considered. Religious affiliation/commitment: Considered. Minority status: Considered. Volunteer work: Considered. Work experience: Considered. **Other schools with the greatest overlap in applicants:** Carleton College; Gustavus Adolphus College; Luther College; University of Minnesota–Twin

Cities; University of Wisconsin–Madison. **Admissions statistics for the fall 2005 entering class:** Total applicants: 2,991. Total accepted: 2,183. Freshmen enrolled: 764; 42% were from out of state. Accepted through early-decision or early-action plans: 81%. Overall acceptance rate: 73%. Early-decision acceptance rate: 97%. Non-early acceptance rate: 45%. **Size of waiting list:** 88 applicants; enrolled from waiting list: 17. **Credentials of fall 2005 freshmen:** 49% ranked in the top 10 percent of their high school class; 76% were in the top 25 percent, and 96% were in the top half. (Proportion submitting class standing: 79%.) **Average high school grade point average:** 3.6. **First-year students who submitted SAT scores:** 46%. Scores (25/75 percentile): Verbal: 590-700, Math: 580-690, Combined: 1170-1390. **First-year students submitting ACT scores:** 85%. Scores (25/75 percentile): English: 24-31, Math: 24-29, Composite: 25-30.

ACADEMICS

Year founded: 1874. **Academic calendar:** 4-1-4. **Degrees offered:** bachelor's. **Most popular majors:** 10% English language and literature, 9% psychology, 8% biology/biological sciences, 8% economics, 7% mathematics. **Major fields of study:** area, ethnic, cultural, and gender studies; biological and biomedical sciences; computer and information sciences and support services; education; English language and literature/letters; family and consumer sciences/human sciences; foreign languages, literatures, and linguistics; health professions and related clinical sciences; history; liberal arts and sciences studies, and humanities; mathematics and statistics; multi/interdisciplinary studies; natural resources and conservation; parks, recreation, leisure, and fitness studies; philosophy and religious studies; physical sciences; psychology; public administration and social service professions; social sciences; visual and performing arts. **Areas of required coursework:** arts/fine arts, humanities, mathematics, English (including composition), philosophy, foreign languages, sciences (biological or physical), history, social science, other. **Pre-professional programs:** pre-law, pre-dentistry, pre-medicine, pre-theology, pre-veterinary science, pre-pharmacy, other. **Special academic programs (% participation):** cross-registration (1%), double major (36%), dual enrollment (1%), independent study (44%), internships (15%), student-designed major (2%), study abroad (68%), teacher certificate program (8%). **Teacher certification offered in:** elementary, middle/junior high, secondary. **Faculty and instruction (2005-2006):** Total instructional faculty: 197 full-time, 135 part-time (55% men; 45% women; 5% minorities). Full-time faculty with Ph.D. or other terminal degree: 93%. Student/faculty ratio: 13/1. Classes of fewer than 20 students: 47%; of 20 to 49 students: 49%; of 50 or more students: 5%. **Advanced Placement and International Baccalaureate credit:** AP tests may be used for: Credit and/or placement. Scores accepted: 4, 5. International Baccalaureate exams may be used for: Credit and/or placement. **Freshmen returning for sophomore year:** 93%. **Graduation rates:** Four-year: 78%; five-year: 83%; six-year: 84%. **Graduate study:** 29% of students pursue further study immediately upon graduation; 60% within five years. Fields in which graduates pursue further study: Master of Business Administration (MBA), 5%; law, 17%; medicine, 20%; dentistry, 1%; engineering, 2%; theology (or the seminary), 10%; education, 7%; arts and sciences, 38%.

COSTS AND FINANCIAL AID

Financial aid office: (507) 646-3019. **Expenses (2006-2007):** Tuition and fees 2006-2007: $28,200; room/board: $7,400. Estimated books and supplies: $900; transportation: $650; personal expenses: $800. **Financial aid:** Priority filing date for institution's financial aid form: December 1; deadline: February 1. In 2005-2006, 69% of undergraduates applied for financial aid. Of those, 62% were determined to have financial need; 100% had their need fully met. Average financial aid package (proportion receiving): $21,869 (62%). Average amount of gift aid, such as scholarships or grants (proportion receiving): $14,973 (62%). Average amount of self-help aid, such as work study or loans (proportion receiving): $6,378 (62%). Average need-based loan (excluding PLUS or other private loans): $5,515. Among students who received need-based aid, the average percentage of need met: 100%. Among students who received aid based on merit, the average award (and the proportion receiving): $7,210 (17%). Average amount of debt of borrowers graduating in 2005: $19,410. Proportion who borrowed: 65%.

CAMPUS LIFE AND EXTRACURRICULAR ACTIVITIES

Campus housing available (% using): coed dorms (96%), other housing options (4%). Students who live in college-owned, operated, or affiliated housing: 96%. **Clubs and organizations:** Number of student organizations: 112. Activities include: choral groups, concert band, dance, drama/theater, jazz band, literary magazine, music ensembles, musical theater, opera, pep band, radio station, student government, student newspaper, student film society, symphony orchestra, television station, yearbook. Number of fraternities: 0; sororities: 0. Average proportion of students who stay on campus on weekends: 80%. **Sports program (2005-2006):** Member of NCAA III. ***Men's intercollegiate varsity sports:*** baseball, basketball, cross-country, football, golf, ice hockey, skiing, soccer, swimming and diving, tennis, track and field (indoor), track and field (outdoor), wrestling. ***Women's intercollegiate varsity sports:*** basketball, cross-country, golf, ice hockey, skiing, soccer, softball, swimming and diving, tennis, track and field (indoor), track and field (outdoor), volleyball.

SERVICES AND FACILITIES
Basic services: nonremedial tutoring, placement service, health service, health insurance, other. **Counseling services:** minority student, career, personal, academic, older student, psychological, birth control, religious. **For learning-disabled students:** School does not offer a structured program with separate admission and additional fees. Total undergraduates in learning-disabled program or receiving services: 29. Services include: tape recorders, note-taking services, oral tests, readers, extended time for tests, tutors, texts on tape, exams on tape or computer, other testing accomodations, other. **Library:** Number of titles: 707,351; number of current serial subscriptions: 2,538. **Information technology resources:** Students are not required to lease or own a computer. Number of campus computers available to all students: 804. School has a wireless network. Approximate number of users that can be accommodated: 1,080. Proportion of college-owned housing units wired for high-speed internet access: 100%. **Campus safety:** Security services offered: 24-hour foot-and-vehicle patrols, late-night transport/escort service, 24-hour emergency telephones, lighted pathways/sidewalks, controlled dormitory access (key, security card, etc).

TRANSFER AND INTERNATIONAL STUDENTS
Transfer students: May apply for admission for the following academic terms: Fall, Winter, Spring. Applicants do not need a minimum number of credits to apply. For fall 2005: Transfer applications received: 167. Transfer applicants offered admission: 67. Transfer applicants enrolled: 44. **International students:** Number of foreign undergraduates: 22 (1% of student body). Number of countries represented: 27. Minimum TOEFL score required: 550 (paper); 213 (computer). Average TOEFL score: 601 (paper).

University of Minnesota–Crookston

- **Address:** 2900 University Avenue, Crookston, MN 56716
- **Website:** http://www.umcrookston.edu
- **Public**
- **Enrollment:** 966 full-time; 1,168 part-time

KEY STATS
✔ **U.S News College Ranking:** third tier, Comp. Coll.–Bachelor's (Midwest)
✔ **ACT Score (25th/75th percentile):** 18-24
✔ **Tuition:** 2006-2007: $8,514 in state, $8,514 out of state

Selectivity: Selective	**Room/board:** $5,420
Acceptance rate: 92%	**Average debt:** $14,194
Student/faculty ratio: 19/1	**Proportion who borrowed:** 60%

UNDERGRADUATE STUDENT BODY STATS
2005-2006 enrollment: 966 full-time; 1,168 part-time. Men: 49%; women: 51%. **Ethnic makeup:** African American: 4%; American-Indian: 1%; Asian American: 1%; Hispanic: 2%; White: 89%; International: 3%.

ADMISSIONS FACTS AND FIGURES
Phone: (800) 232-6466. **Email:** info@mail.crk.umn.edu. **Website:** http://www.umcrookston.edu. **Application deadlines for fall 2007:** Regular decision: Rolling. Early decision: Not offered. Early action: Not offered. Admission can be deferred. **Application fee:** $30. Common application is accepted. **To apply online, go to:** http://admissions.umcrookston.edu/Apply/index.htm. **Admissions requirements/recommendations:** High school units required (recommended): English: (4); Mathematics: (3); Science: (3); Foreign language: (2); Social studies: (2). Tests: The college uses SAT or ACT scores in admissions decisions. ACT required. For admission to the fall 2007 entering class, the school will accept: ACT with writing, ACT without writing. Campus visit: Recommended. Admissions interview: Neither required nor recommended. Off-campus interview: May be arranged. **Factors that count in admissions decisions:** *Academic:* Secondary school record: Very important. Class rank: Very important. Letters of recommenda-

tion: Considered. Standardized test scores: Very important. Essay: Considered. *Nonacademic:* Extracurricular activities: Considered. Talent/ability: Important. Character/personal qualities: Considered. Alumni/ae relationship: Considered. Geographical residence: Not considered. State residency: Not considered. Religious affiliation/commitment: Not considered. Minority status: Not considered. Volunteer work: Considered. Work experience: Considered. **Other schools with the greatest overlap in applicants:** Bemidji State University; Minnesota State University–Moorhead; North Dakota State University; University of Minnesota–Twin Cities; University of North Dakota. **Admissions statistics for the fall 2005 entering class:** Total applicants: 408. Total accepted: 376. Freshmen enrolled: 198; 30% were from out of state. Overall acceptance rate: 92%. **Credentials of fall 2005 freshmen:** 12% ranked in the top 10 percent of their high school class; 32% were in the top 25 percent, and 66% were in the top half. (Proportion submitting class standing: 84%.) **Average high school grade point average:** 3.1. **First-year students who submitted SAT scores:** 5%. Scores (25/75 percentile): Verbal: 380-600, Math: 410-570, Combined: 790-1170. **First-year students submitting ACT scores:** 95%. Scores (25/75 percentile): English: 17-23, Math: 17-24, Composite: 18-24.

ACADEMICS
Year founded: 1966. **Academic calendar:** Semester. **Degrees offered:** certificate, associate, bachelor's. **Most popular majors:** 21% business administration and management, 16% natural resources/conservation, 12% management information systems, 6% kindergarten/preschool education and teaching, 5% plant sciences. **Major fields of study:** agriculture, agriculture operations, and related sciences; business, management, marketing, and related support services; communication, journalism, and related programs; education; engineering; engineering technologies/technicians; health professions and related clinical sciences; multi/interdisciplinary studies; natural resources and conservation; parks, recreation, leisure, and fitness studies; transportation and materials moving. **Areas of required coursework:** humanities, computer literacy, mathematics, English (including composition), sciences (biological or physical), social science, other. **Pre-professional programs:** pre-dentistry, pre-medicine, pre-veterinary science, pre-pharmacy. **Special academic programs (% participation):** cross-registration, distance learning, double major, English as a Second Language (ESL), external degree program, independent study, internships (85%), study abroad (5%), teacher certificate program. **Teacher certification offered in:** early childhood, secondary. **Reserve Officers Training Corps (ROTC):** Air Force ROTC: Offered at cooperating institution (University of North Dakota). **Faculty and instruction (2005-2006):** Total instructional faculty: 53 full-time, 51 part-time (65% men; 35% women; 5% minorities). Full-time faculty with Ph.D. or other terminal degree: 49%. Student/faculty ratio: 19/1. Classes of fewer than 20 students: 62%; of 20 to 49 students: 36%; of 50 or more students: 2%. **Advanced Placement and International Baccalaureate credit:** AP tests may be used for: Credit only. Scores accepted: 3, 4. International Baccalaureate exams may be used for: Credit only. **Freshmen returning for sophomore year:** 63%. **Graduation rates:** Four-year: 19%; five-year: 33%; six-year: 38%. **Graduate study:** 5% of students pursue further study immediately upon graduation; 6% within one year. Fields in which graduates pursue further study: Master of Business Administration (MBA), 1%; law, 1%; medicine, 1%; engineering, 1%; education, 1%; arts and sciences, 1%; veterinary medicine, 1%.

COSTS AND FINANCIAL AID
Financial aid office: (218) 281-8576. **Expenses (2006-2007):** Tuition and fees 2006-2007: $8,514 in state, $8,514 out of state; room/board: $5,420. Estimated books and supplies: $800; transportation: $1,000; personal expenses: $1,000. **Financial aid:** Priority filing date for institution's financial aid form: March 15. In 2005-2006, 80% of undergraduates applied for financial aid. Of those, 67% were determined to have financial need; 45% had their need fully met. Average financial aid package (proportion receiving): $10,303 (67%). Average amount of gift aid, such as scholarships or grants (proportion receiving): $5,365 (56%). Average amount of self-help aid, such as work study or loans (proportion receiving): $7,489 (62%). Average need-based loan (excluding PLUS or other private loans): $7,071. Among students who received need-based aid, the average percentage of need met: 82%. Among students who received aid based on merit, the average award (and the proportion receiving): $2,667 (9%). Average amount of debt of borrowers graduating in 2005: $14,194. Proportion who borrowed: 60%.

CAMPUS LIFE AND EXTRACURRICULAR ACTIVITIES
Campus housing available (% using): coed dorms (60%), apartment for single students (40%). Students who live in college-owned, operated, or affili-

ated housing: 34%. **Student employment:** During the 2005-2006 academic year, 7% of undergraduates worked on campus. Average per-year earnings: $1,700. **Clubs and organizations:** Number of student organizations: 38. Activities include: choral groups, drama/theater, music ensembles, pep band, student government. Number of fraternities: 1; sororities: 1. Proportion of men in fraternities: 3%; of women in sororities: 2%. Average proportion of students who stay on campus on weekends: 25%. **Sports program (2005-2006):** Member of NCAA II. *Men's intercollegiate varsity sports:* baseball, basketball, football, golf, ice hockey. *Women's intercollegiate varsity sports:* basketball, equestrian sports, golf, soccer, softball, tennis, volleyball.

SERVICES AND FACILITIES

Basic services: nonremedial tutoring, placement service, day care, health service, health insurance. **Remedial assistance:** math, writing, study skills. **Counseling services:** minority student, career, military, personal, veteran student, academic, older student, psychological, birth control, religious. **For learning-disabled students:** School does not offer a structured program with separate admission and additional fees. Total undergraduates in learning-disabled program or receiving services: 52. Services include: remedial math, remedial English, reading machines, tape recorders, untimed tests, note-taking services, oral tests, learning center, readers, extended time for tests, tutors, priority registration, priority seating, other testing accomodations, other. **Library:** Number of titles: 33,350; number of current serial subscriptions: 477. **Information technology resources:** Students are required to lease or own a computer. Number of campus computers available to all students: 20. School has a wireless network. Approximate number of users that can be accommodated: 1,250. Proportion of college-owned housing units wired for high-speed internet access: 100%. **Campus safety:** Security services offered: late-night transport/escort service, 24-hour emergency telephones, lighted pathways/sidewalks, controlled dormitory access (key, security card, etc).

TRANSFER AND INTERNATIONAL STUDENTS

Transfer students: May apply for admission for the following academic terms: Fall, Spring, Summer. Applicants need a minimum number of credits to apply. For fall 2005: Transfer applications received: 176. Transfer applicants offered admission: 163. Transfer applicants enrolled: 107. **International students:** Number of foreign undergraduates: 30 (3% of student body). Number of countries represented: 24. Minimum TOEFL score required: 500 (paper); 173 (computer). Average TOEFL score: 550 (paper).

University of Minnesota–Duluth

- **Address:** 1049 University Drive, Duluth, MN 55812-2496
- **Website:** http://www.d.umn.edu
- **Public**
- **Enrollment:** 8,583 full-time; 905 part-time

KEY STATS

✔ **U.S News College Ranking:** 40, Universities–Master's (Midwest)
✔ **ACT Score (25th/75th percentile):** 20-25
✔ **Tuition:** 2006-2007: $8,932 in state, $19,299 out of state
 Selectivity: Selective   **Room/board:** N/A
 Acceptance rate: 75%   **Average debt:** $20,221
 Student/faculty ratio: 21/1   **Proportion who borrowed:** 71%

UNDERGRADUATE STUDENT BODY STATS

2005-2006 enrollment: 8,583 full-time; 905 part-time. Men: 52%; women: 48%. **Ethnic makeup:** African American: 1%; American-Indian: 1%; Asian American: 3%; Hispanic: 1%; White: 93%; International: 1%.

ADMISSIONS FACTS AND FIGURES

Phone: (218) 726-7171. **Email:** umdadmis@d.umn.edu. **Website:** http://www.d.umn.edu. **Application deadlines for fall 2007:** Regular decision: August 1. Early decision: Not offered. Early action: Not offered. Admission can be deferred. **Application fee:** $35. Common application is not accepted. **To apply online, go to:** http://www.d.umn.edu/admissions/online.html. **Admissions requirements/recommendations:** High school units required (recommended): English: 4; Mathematics: 3; Science: 3; Foreign language: 2; Social studies: 2; Total units: 14. Tests: The college uses SAT or ACT scores in admissions decisions. Either SAT or ACT required. For admission to the fall 2007 entering class, the school will accept: ACT with writing.

Campus visit: Recommended. Admissions interview: Neither required nor recommended. Off-campus interview: Not available. **Factors that count in admissions decisions:** *Academic:* Secondary school record: Important. Class rank: Very important. Letters of recommendation: Considered. Standardized test scores: Very important. Essay: Considered. *Nonacademic:* Interview: Considered. Extracurricular activities: Considered. Talent/ability: Considered. Character/personal qualities: Considered. Alumni/ae relationship: Considered. Geographical residence: Not considered. State residency: Not considered. Religious affiliation/commitment: Not considered. Minority status: Considered. Volunteer work: Not considered. Work experience: Not considered. **Other schools with the greatest overlap in applicants:** Minnesota State University–Mankato; St. Cloud State University; University of Minnesota–Twin Cities; University of St. Thomas; Winona State University. **Admissions statistics for the fall 2005 entering class:** Total applicants: 6,989. Total accepted: 5,222. Freshmen enrolled: 2,164; 11% were from out of state. Overall acceptance rate: 75%. **Credentials of fall 2005 freshmen:** 14% ranked in the top 10 percent of their high school class; 39% were in the top 25 percent, and 82% were in the top half. (Proportion submitting class standing: 99%.) **First-year students who submitted SAT scores:** 4%. Scores (25/75 percentile): Verbal: 510-610, Math: 490-620, Combined: 1000-1230. **First-year students submitting ACT scores:** 99%. Scores (25/75 percentile): English: 19-25, Math: 19-26, Composite: 20-25.

ACADEMICS

Year founded: 1947. **Academic calendar:** Semester. **Degrees offered:** bachelor's, master's. **Most popular majors:** 19% business, management, marketing, and related support services; 17% education, 9% social sciences, 8% biological and biomedical sciences, 7% psychology. **Major fields of study:** area, ethnic, cultural, and gender studies; biological and biomedical sciences; business, management, marketing, and related support services; communication, journalism, and related programs; computer and information sciences and support services; education; engineering; English language and literature/letters; foreign languages, literatures, and linguistics; health professions and related clinical sciences; history; mathematics and statistics; multi/interdisciplinary studies; natural resources and conservation; parks, recreation, leisure, and fitness studies; philosophy and religious studies; physical sciences; psychology; social sciences; visual and performing arts. **Areas of required coursework:** arts/fine arts, humanities, computer literacy, mathematics, English (including composition), philosophy, foreign languages, sciences (biological or physical), history, social science. **Pre-professional programs:** pre-law, pre-dentistry, pre-medicine, pre-veterinary science, pre-optometry, pre-pharmacy, other. **Special academic programs:** cross-registration, distance learning, double major, honors program, independent study, internships, student-designed major, study abroad, teacher certificate program. **Teacher certification offered in:** early childhood, special education, elementary, middle/junior high, secondary. **Reserve Officers Training Corps (ROTC):** Air Force ROTC: Offered on campus. **Faculty and instruction (2005-2006):** Total instructional faculty: 373 full-time, 118 part-time (57% men; 43% women; 16% minorities). Full-time faculty with Ph.D. or other terminal degree: 76%. Student/faculty ratio: 21/1. Classes of fewer than 20 students: 43%; of 20 to 49 students: 47%; of 50 or more students: 10%. **Advanced Placement and International Baccalaureate credit:** AP tests may be used for: Credit and/or placement. Scores accepted: 3, 4, 5. International Baccalaureate exams may be used for: Credit and/or placement. **Freshmen returning for sophomore year:** 75%. **Graduation rates:** Four-year: 21%; five-year: 43%; six-year: 46%. **Graduate study:** 15% of students pursue further study immediately upon graduation.

COSTS AND FINANCIAL AID

Financial aid office: (218) 726-8000. **Expenses (2005-2006):** Tuition and fees 2005-2006: $8,944 in state, $20,051 out of state; room/board: N/A. Estimated books and supplies: $1,144; transportation: $1,012; personal expenses: $2,324. **Financial aid:** In 2005-2006, 75% of undergraduates applied for financial aid. Of those, 53% were determined to have financial need; 68% had their need fully met. Average financial aid package (proportion receiving): $8,149 (52%). Average amount of gift aid, such as scholarships or grants (proportion receiving): $5,758 (38%). Average amount of self-help aid, such as work study or loans (proportion receiving): $3,896 (46%). Average need-based loan (excluding PLUS or other private loans): $3,747. Among students who received need-based aid, the average percentage of need met: 66%. Among students who received aid based on merit, the average award (and the proportion receiving): $2,240 (10%). The average athletic scholarship (and the proportion receiving): $4,109 (2%). Average amount of debt of borrowers graduating in 2005: $20,221. Proportion who borrowed: 71%.

CAMPUS LIFE AND EXTRACURRICULAR ACTIVITIES

Campus housing available (% using): coed dorms (46%), women's dorms (4%), men's dorms (2%), apartment for single students (48%). Students who live in college-owned, operated, or affiliated housing: 33%. **Student employment:** During the 2005-2006 academic year, 18% of undergraduates worked on campus. Average per-year earnings: $2,721. **Clubs and organizations:** Number of student organizations: 114. Activities include: choral groups, concert band, dance, drama/theater, jazz band, music ensembles, musical theater, pep band, radio station, student government, student newspaper, symphony orchestra. Number of fraternities: 4; sororities: 3. Average proportion of students who stay on campus on weekends: 45%. **Sports program (2005-2006):** Member of NCAA II. **Men's intercollegiate varsity sports:** baseball, basketball, cross-country, football, ice hockey, track and field (indoor), track and field (outdoor). **Women's intercollegiate varsity sports:** basketball, cross-country, ice hockey, soccer, softball, tennis, track and field (indoor), track and field (outdoor), volleyball.

SERVICES AND FACILITIES

Basic services: nonremedial tutoring, women's center, placement service, day care, health service, health insurance. **Remedial assistance:** writing, study skills. **Counseling services:** minority student, career, personal, veteran student, academic, older student, psychological, birth control, religious. **For learning-disabled students:** School does not offer a structured program with separate admission and additional fees. Services include: remedial English, reading machines, tape recorders, diagnostic testing service, note-taking services, learning center, readers, extended time for tests, tutors. **Library:** Number of titles: 578,966; number of current serial subscriptions: 23,170. **Information technology resources:** Students are not required to lease or own a computer. Number of campus computers available to all students: 693. School has a wireless network. Approximate number of users that can be accommodated: 4,320. Proportion of college-owned housing units wired for high-speed internet access: 100%. **Campus safety:** Security services offered: 24-hour foot-and-vehicle patrols, 24-hour emergency telephones, lighted pathways/sidewalks, student patrols, controlled dormitory access (key, security card, etc).

TRANSFER AND INTERNATIONAL STUDENTS

Transfer students: May apply for admission for the following academic terms: Fall, Spring. Applicants need a minimum number of credits to apply. For fall 2005: Transfer applications received: 924. Transfer applicants offered admission: 676. Transfer applicants enrolled: 429. **International students:** Number of foreign undergraduates: 115 (1% of student body). Number of countries represented: 40. Minimum TOEFL score required: 550 (paper); 213 (computer). Average TOEFL score: 560 (paper).

University of Minnesota–Morris

- **Address:** 600 E. Fourth Street, Morris, MN 56267
- **Website:** http://www.morris.umn.edu
- **Public**
- **Enrollment:** 1,527 full-time; 151 part-time

KEY STATS

✔ **U.S News College Ranking:** third tier, Liberal Arts Colleges
✔ **ACT Score (25th/75th percentile):** 22-27
✔ **Tuition:** 2006-2007: $10,330 in state, $10,330 out of state

Selectivity: More selective	**Room/board:** $6,150
Acceptance rate: 82%	**Average debt:** $21,228
Student/faculty ratio: 11/1	**Proportion who borrowed:** 75%

UNDERGRADUATE STUDENT BODY STATS

2005-2006 enrollment: 1,527 full-time; 151 part-time. Men: 40%; women: 60%. **Ethnic makeup:** African American: 2%; American-Indian: 9%; Asian American: 3%; Hispanic: 1%; White: 83%; International: 1%.

ADMISSIONS FACTS AND FIGURES

Phone: (800) 992-8863. **Email:** admissions@morris.umn.edu. **Website:** http://www.morris.umn.edu. **Application deadlines for fall 2007:** Regular decision: March 15. Early decision: Not offered. Early action: Not offered. Admission can be deferred. **Application fee:** $35. Common application is accepted. **To apply online, go to:** http://www.morris.umn.edu/prospective/applynow/index.html. **Admissions requirements/recommendations:** High school units required (recommended): English: (4); Mathematics: (3); Science: (3); Foreign language: (2); Social studies: (4); History: (1); Total units: (17). Tests: The college uses SAT or ACT scores in admissions decisions. Either SAT or ACT required. For admission to the fall 2007 entering class, the school will accept: ACT with writing. Campus visit: Recommended. Admissions interview: Recommended. Off-campus interview: May be arranged. **Factors that count in admissions decisions:** **Academic:** Secondary school record: Very important. Class rank: Very important. Letters of recommendation: Important. Standardized test scores: Very important. Essay: Important. **Nonacademic:** Interview: Considered. Extracurricular activities: Important. Talent/ability: Important. Character/personal qualities: Important. Alumni/ae relationship: Considered. Geographical residence: Not considered. State residency: Not considered. Religious affiliation/commitment: Not considered. Minority status: Considered. Volunteer work: Important. Work experience: Important. **Other schools with the greatest overlap in applicants:** Macalester College; St. Olaf College; University of Minnesota–Twin Cities; University of Wisconsin–Madison. **Admissions statistics for the fall 2005 entering class:** Total applicants: 1,097. Total accepted: 901. Freshmen enrolled: 388; 14% were from out of state. Overall acceptance rate: 82%. **Credentials of fall 2005 freshmen:** 31% ranked in the top 10 percent of their high school class; 60% were in the top 25 percent, and 87% were in the top half. (Proportion submitting class standing: 87%.) **First-year students who submitted SAT scores:** 17%. Scores (25/75 percentile): Verbal: 570-680, Math: 565-680, Combined: 1135-1360. **First-year students submitting ACT scores:** 94%. Scores (25/75 percentile): English: 21-28, Math: 21-27, Composite: 22-27.

ACADEMICS

Year founded: 1959. **Academic calendar:** Semester. **Degrees offered:** bachelor's. **Most popular majors:** 9% English language and literature, 8% biology, 8% elementary education and teaching, 7% business administration and management, 7% human services. **Major fields of study:** agriculture, agriculture operations, and related sciences; area, ethnic, cultural, and gender studies; biological and biomedical sciences; business, management, marketing, and related support services; computer and information sciences and support services; education; English language and literature/letters; foreign languages, literatures, and linguistics; history; liberal arts and sciences studies, and humanities; mathematics and statistics; multi/interdisciplinary studies; philosophy and religious studies; physical sciences; psychology; public administration and social service professions; social sciences; visual and performing arts. **Areas of required coursework:** arts/fine arts, humanities, mathematics, English (including composition), philosophy, foreign languages, sciences (biological or physical), history, social science. **Pre-professional programs:** pre-law, pre-dentistry, pre-medicine, pre-veterinary science, pre-optometry, pre-pharmacy, other. **Special academic programs (% participation):** distance learning (2%), double major (21%), exchange student program (domestic) (1%), honors program (4%), independent study (15%), internships (25%), student-designed major (4%), study abroad (33%), teacher certificate program (16%). **Teacher certification offered in:** elementary, middle/junior high, secondary. **Faculty and instruction (2005-2006):** Total instructional faculty: 121 full-time, 55 part-time (53% men; 47% women; 13% minorities). Full-time faculty with Ph.D. or other terminal degree: 93%. Student/faculty ratio: 11/1. Classes of fewer than 20 students: 69%; of 20 to 49 students: 27%; of 50 or more students: 3%. **Advanced Placement and International Baccalaureate credit:** AP tests may be used for: Credit and/or placement. Scores accepted: 3, 4, 5. International Baccalaureate exams may be used for: Credit and/or placement. **Freshmen returning for sophomore year:** 84%. **Graduation rates:** Four-year: 40%; five-year: 56%; six-year: 59%. **Graduate study:** 28% of students pursue further study immediately upon graduation; 30% within one year; 30% within five years. Fields in which graduates pursue further study: Master of Business Administration (MBA), 3%; law, 11%; medicine, 4%; dentistry, 1%; engineering, 2%; education, 30%; arts and sciences, 40%; veterinary medicine, 2%.

COSTS AND FINANCIAL AID

Financial aid office: (320) 589-6035. **Expenses (2006-2007):** Tuition and fees 2006-2007: $10,330 in state, $10,330 out of state; room/board: $6,150. Estimated books and supplies: $900; transportation: $500. **Financial aid:** Priority filing date for institution's financial aid form: March 1. In 2005-2006, 83% of undergraduates applied for financial aid. Of those, 68% were determined to have financial need; 44% had their need fully met. Average financial aid package (proportion receiving): $12,660 (67%). Average amount of gift aid, such as scholarships or grants (proportion receiving): $5,885 (58%). Average amount of self-help aid, such as work study or loans (proportion receiving): $7,420 (61%). Average need-based loan (excluding PLUS or other private loans): $7,333. Among students who received need-based aid, the average percentage of need met: 82%. Among students who received aid based on merit, the average award (and the proportion receiving): $3,052 (20%). The average athletic scholarship (and the proportion receiving): $0 (0%). Average amount of debt of borrowers graduating in 2005: $21,228. Proportion who borrowed: 75%.

CAMPUS LIFE AND EXTRACURRICULAR ACTIVITIES

Campus housing available (% using): coed dorms (74%), apartment for single students (26%). Students who live in college-owned, operated, or affiliated housing: 45%. **Student employment:** During the 2005-2006 academic year, 45% of undergraduates worked on campus. Average per-year earnings: $1,200. **Clubs and organizations:** Number of student organizations: 114. Activities include: choral groups, concert band, dance, drama/theater, jazz band, literary magazine, music ensembles, musical theater, opera, pep band, radio station, student government, student newspaper, student film society, symphony orchestra, television station. Number of fraternities: 0; sororities: 0. Average proportion of students who stay on campus on weekends: 75%. **Sports program (2005-2006):** Member of NCAA II. *Men's intercollegiate varsity sports:* baseball, basketball, football, golf, tennis, track and field (indoor), track and field (outdoor), wrestling. *Women's intercollegiate varsity sports:* basketball, cross-country, golf, soccer, softball, swimming and diving, tennis, track and field (indoor), track and field (outdoor), volleyball.

SERVICES AND FACILITIES

Basic services: nonremedial tutoring, women's center, placement service, health service, health insurance. **Remedial assistance:** study skills. **Counseling services:** minority student, career, personal, academic, psychological, birth control. **For learning-disabled students:** School does not offer a structured program with separate admission and additional fees. Services include: reading machines, tape recorders, other special classes, videotaped classes, untimed tests, note-taking services, oral tests, learning center, readers, extended time for tests, tutors, priority registration, priority seating, texts on tape, typist/scribe, other testing accomodations. **Library:** Number of titles: 413,811; number of current serial subscriptions: 16,823. **Information technology resources:** Students are not required to lease or own a computer. Number of campus computers available to all students: 240. School has a wireless network. Approximate number of users that can be accommodated: 300. Proportion of college-owned housing units wired for high-speed internet access: 100%. **Campus safety:** Security services offered: 24-hour foot-and-vehicle patrols, late-night transport/escort service, 24-hour emergency telephones, lighted pathways/sidewalks, controlled dormitory access (key, security card, etc).

TRANSFER AND INTERNATIONAL STUDENTS

Transfer students: May apply for admission for the following academic terms: Fall, Winter, Spring. Applicants do not need a minimum number of credits to apply. For fall 2005: Transfer applications received: 109. Transfer applicants offered admission: 83. Transfer applicants enrolled: 62. **International students:** Number of foreign undergraduates: 17 (1% of student body). Number of countries represented: 11. Minimum TOEFL score required: 550 (paper); 213 (computer).

University of Minnesota–Twin Cities

■ **Address:** 100 Church Street SE, Minneapolis, MN 55455-0213
■ **Website:** http://www.umn.edu
■ **Public**
■ **Enrollment:** 26,957 full-time; 5,860 part-time

KEY STATS

✔ **U.S News College Ranking:** 67, National Universities
✔ **ACT Score (25th/75th percentile):** 23-28
✔ **Tuition:** 2006-2007: $9,432 in state, $21,062 out of state

Selectivity: More selective	**Room/board:** $6,824
Acceptance rate: 71%	**Average debt:** N/A
Student/faculty ratio: 15/1	**Proportion who borrowed:** N/A

UNDERGRADUATE STUDENT BODY STATS

2005-2006 enrollment: 26,957 full-time; 5,860 part-time. Men: 47%; women: 53%. **Ethnic makeup:** African American: 5%; American-Indian: 1%; Asian American: 9%; Hispanic: 2%; White: 82%; International: 2%.

ADMISSIONS FACTS AND FIGURES

Phone: (800) 752-1000. **Website:** http://www.umn.edu. **Application deadlines for fall 2007:** Regular decision: Rolling. Early decision: Not offered. Early action: Not offered. Admission can be deferred. **Application fee:** $45. Common application is not accepted. **To apply online, go to:** http://admissions.tc.umn.edu/. **Admissions requirements/recommendations:** High school units required (recommended): English: 4 (4); Mathematics: 3 (3); Science: 3 (3); Foreign language: 2 (2); Social studies: 3 (3); History: 1; Total units: 16 (16). Tests: The college uses SAT or ACT scores in admissions decisions. Either SAT or ACT required. For admission to the fall 2007 entering class, the school will accept: ACT with writing. Campus visit: Recommended. Admissions interview: Neither required nor recommended. Off-campus interview: Not available. **Factors that count in admissions decisions:** *Academic:* Secondary school record: Very important. Class rank: Very important. Letters of recommendation: Considered. Standardized test scores: Very important. Essay: Considered. *Nonacademic:* Interview: Not considered. Extracurricular activities: Considered. Talent/ability: Considered. Character/personal qualities: Considered. Alumni/ae relationship: Considered. Geographical residence: Considered. State residency: Considered. Religious affiliation/commitment: Not considered. Minority status: Considered. Volunteer work: Considered. Work experience: Considered. **Other schools with the greatest overlap in applicants:** Iowa State University; University of Michigan–Ann Arbor; University of Minnesota–Duluth; University of St. Thomas; University of Wisconsin–Madison. **Admissions statistics for the fall 2005 entering class:** Total applicants: 20,641. Total accepted: 14,708. Freshmen enrolled: 5,305; 33% were from out of state. Overall acceptance rate: 71%. **Credentials of fall 2005 freshmen:** 34% ranked in the top 10 percent of their high school class; 74% were in the top 25 percent, and 97% were in the top half. (Proportion submitting class standing: 89%.) **First-year students who submitted SAT scores:** 19%. Scores (25/75 percentile): Verbal: 540-660, Math: 570-690, Combined: 1110-1350. **First-year students submitting ACT scores:** 94%. Scores (25/75 percentile): English: 21-28, Math: 22-28, Composite: 23-28.

ACADEMICS

Year founded: 1851. **Academic calendar:** Semester. **Degrees offered:** certificate, diploma, bachelor's, post-bachelor's certificate, master's, post-master's certificate, first professional, first professional certificate, doctorate. **Most popular majors:** 12% social sciences, 11% engineering, 9% business, management, marketing, and related support services, 7% psychology, 6% English language and literature/letters. **Major fields of study:** agriculture, agriculture operations, and related sciences; architecture and related services; area, ethnic, cultural, and gender studies; biological and biomedical sciences; business, management, marketing, and related support services; communication, journalism, and related programs; computer and information sciences and support services; construction trades; education; engineering; English language and literature/letters; family and consumer sciences/human sciences; foreign languages, literatures, and linguistics; health professions and related clinical sciences; history; mathematics and statistics; multi/interdisciplinary studies; natural resources and conservation; parks, recreation, leisure, and fitness studies; personal and culinary services; philosophy and religious studies; physical sciences; psychology; social sciences; visual and performing arts. **Areas of required coursework:** arts/fine arts, humanities, mathematics, English (including composition), foreign languages, sciences (biological or physical), history, social science. **Pre-professional programs:** pre-law, pre-dentistry, pre-medicine, pre-veterinary science, pre-pharmacy, other. **Special academic programs:** accelerated program, cooperative (work-study plan) program, cross-registration, distance learning, double major, dual enrollment, English as a Second Language (ESL), exchange student program (domestic), external degree program, honors program, independent study, internships, liberal arts/career combination, student-designed major, study abroad, teacher certificate program. **Teacher certification offered in:** early childhood, special education, elementary, vo-tech, middle/junior high, adult education, secondary. **Cooperative education programs:** computer science, engineering. **Reserve Officers Training Corps (ROTC):** Army ROTC: Offered on campus; Navy ROTC: Offered on campus; Air Force ROTC: Offered on campus. **Faculty and instruction (2005-2006):** Total instructional faculty: 1,680 full-time, 253 part-time (70% men; 30% women; 12% minorities). Full-time faculty with Ph.D. or other terminal degree: 69%. Student/faculty ratio: 15/1. Classes of fewer than 20 students: 41%; of 20 to 49 students: 44%; of 50 or more students: 15%. **Advanced Placement and International Baccalaureate credit:** AP tests may be used for: Credit only. Scores accepted: 3, 4, 5. International Baccalaureate exams may be used for: Credit only. **Freshmen returning for sophomore year:** 86%. **Graduation rates:** Four-year: 32%; five-year: 56%; six-year: 61%.

COSTS AND FINANCIAL AID

Financial aid office: (612) 624-1111. **Expenses (2006-2007):** Tuition and fees 2006-2007: $9,432 in state, $21,062 out of state; room/board: $6,824. Estimated books and supplies: $900 personal expenses: $2,120. **Financial aid:** In 2005-2006, 67% of undergraduates applied for financial aid. Of those, 49% were determined to have financial need; 46% had their need fully met. Average financial aid package (proportion receiving): $11,007 (48%). Average amount of gift aid, such as scholarships or grants (proportion receiving): $6,663 (35%). Average amount of self-help aid, such as work study or loans (proportion receiving): $7,999 (43%). Average need-based loan (excluding PLUS or other private loans): $7,369. Among students who received need-based aid, the average percentage of need met: 83%. Among students who received aid based on merit, the average award (and the proportion receiving): $4,363 (11%).

CAMPUS LIFE AND EXTRACURRICULAR ACTIVITIES

Campus housing available (% using): coed dorms (68%), sorority housing, fraternity housing, apartments for married students (19%), apartment for single students (13%), special housing for disabled students, special housing for international students, cooperative housing, other housing options. Students who live in college-owned, operated, or affiliated housing: 22%. **Student employment:** During the 2005-2006 academic year, 18% of undergraduates worked on campus. **Clubs and organizations:** Number of student organizations: 680. Activities include: choral groups, concert band, dance, drama/theater, jazz band, literary magazine, marching band, music ensembles, musical theater, opera, pep band, radio station, student government, student newspaper, student film society, symphony orchestra, television station. Number of fraternities: 29; sororities: 15. Proportion of men in fraternities: 2%; of women in sororities: 2%. **Sports program (2005-2006):** Member of NCAA I. *Men's intercollegiate varsity sports:* baseball, basketball, cross-country, football, golf, gymnastics, ice hockey, swimming and diving, tennis, track and field (indoor), track and field (outdoor), wrestling. *Women's intercollegiate varsity sports:* basketball, cross-country, golf, gymnastics, ice hockey, rowing, soccer, softball, swimming and diving, tennis, track and field (indoor), track and field (outdoor), volleyball.

SERVICES AND FACILITIES

Basic services: nonremedial tutoring, women's center, placement service, day care, health service, health insurance. **Remedial assistance:** reading, math, writing, study skills. **Counseling services:** minority student, career, military, personal, veteran student, academic, older student, psychological, birth control. **For learning-disabled students:** School does not offer a structured program with separate admission and additional fees. Total undergraduates in learning-disabled program or receiving services: 214. Services include: reading machines, note-taking services, readers, extended time for tests, tutors, early syllabus, texts on tape, exams on tape or computer. **Library:** Number of titles: 6,374,293; number of current serial subscriptions: 35,801. **Information technology resources:** Students are not required to lease or own a computer. Number of campus computers available to all students: 20,000. School has a wireless network. Approximate number of users that can be accommodated: 20,000. Proportion of college-owned housing units wired for high-speed internet access: 100%. **Campus safety:** Security services offered: 24-hour foot-and-vehicle patrols, late-night transport/escort service, 24-hour emergency telephones, lighted pathways/sidewalks, student patrols, controlled dormitory access (key, security card, etc.).

TRANSFER AND INTERNATIONAL STUDENTS

Transfer students: May apply for admission for the following academic terms: Fall, Spring. Applicants need a minimum number of credits to apply. For fall 2005: Transfer applications received: 7,483. Transfer applicants offered admission: 2,904. Transfer applicants enrolled: 1,882. **International students:** Number of foreign undergraduates: 467 (2% of student body). Number of countries represented: 56. Minimum TOEFL score required: 550 (paper); 213 (computer).

University of St. Thomas

- **Address:** 2115 Summit Avenue, St. Paul, MN 55105-1096
- **Website:** http://www.stthomas.edu
- **Private; Religious affiliation:** Roman Catholic
- **Enrollment:** 5,142 full-time; 442 part-time

KEY STATS

✔ **U.S News College Ranking:** third tier, National Universities
✔ **ACT Score (25th/75th percentile):** 22-27
✔ **Tuition:** 2006-2007: $24,808

Selectivity: More selective	**Room/board:** $6,932
Acceptance rate: 91%	**Average debt:** $26,621
Student/faculty ratio: 12/1	**Proportion who borrowed:** 66%

UNDERGRADUATE STUDENT BODY STATS

2005-2006 enrollment: 5,142 full-time; 442 part-time. Men: 50%; women: 50%. **Ethnic makeup:** African American: 3%; American-Indian: 1%; Asian American: 5%; Hispanic: 2%; White: 89%; International: 1%. **Religious preference:** Protestant: 26%; No preference: 3%; Unknown: 11%; Roman Catholic: 53%; Other: 7%.

ADMISSIONS FACTS AND FIGURES

Phone: (651) 962-6150. **Email:** admissions@stthomas.edu. **Website:** http://www.stthomas.edu. **Application deadlines for fall 2007:** Regular decision: Rolling. Early decision: Not offered. Early action: Not offered. Admission can be deferred. Common application is not accepted. **To apply online, go to:** http://www.stthomas.edu/admissions/undergraduate/apply/. **Admissions requirements/recommendations:** High school units required (recommended): English: (4); Mathematics: 3 (4); Science: (2); Foreign language: (4); Social studies: (2); Total units: 3 (18). Tests: The college uses SAT or ACT scores in admissions decisions. Either SAT or ACT required. For admission to the fall 2007 entering class, the school will accept: ACT with writing, ACT without writing. Campus visit: Recommended. Admissions interview: Recommended. Off-campus interview: May be arranged. **Factors that count in admissions decisions:** *Academic:* Secondary school record: Very important. Class rank: Important. Letters of recommendation: Considered. Standardized test scores: Very important. Essay: Important. *Nonacademic:* Interview: Not considered. Extracurricular activities: Considered. Talent/ability: Considered. Character/personal qualities: Considered. Alumni/ae relationship: Considered. Geographical residence: Considered. State residency: Not considered. Religious affiliation/commitment: Not considered. Minority status: Considered. Volunteer work: Considered. Work experience: Not considered. **Other schools with the greatest overlap in applicants:** College of St. Benedict; St. John's University; University of Minnesota–Twin Cities; University of Wisconsin–Madison. **Admissions statistics for the fall 2005 entering class:** Total applicants: 4,189. Total accepted: 3,832. Freshmen enrolled: 1,326; 19% were from out of state. Overall acceptance rate: 91%. Size of waiting list: 0 applicants; enrolled from waiting list: 0. **Credentials of fall 2005 freshmen:** 23% ranked in the top 10 percent of their high school class; 56% were in the top 25 percent, and 89% were in the top half. (Proportion submitting class standing: 82%.) **Average high school grade point average:** 3.6. **First-year students who submitted SAT scores:** 15%. Scores (25/75 percentile): Verbal: 540-658, Math: 530-650, Combined: 1070-1308. **First-year students submitting ACT scores:** 97%. Scores (25/75 percentile): English: 21-28, Math: 22-27, Composite: 22-27.

ACADEMICS

Year founded: 1885. **Academic calendar:** 4-1-4. **Degrees offered:** certificate, bachelor's, post-bachelor's certificate, master's, post-master's certificate, first professional, doctorate. **Most popular majors:** 40% business, management, marketing, and related support services, 9% social sciences, 7% communication, journalism, and related programs, 6% philosophy and religious studies, 6% psychology. **Major fields of study:** area, ethnic, cultural, and gender studies; biological and biomedical sciences; business, management, marketing, and related support services; communication, journalism, and related programs; computer and information sciences and support services; education; engineering; English language and literature/letters; foreign languages, literatures, and linguistics; health professions and related clinical sciences; history; legal professions and studies; liberal arts and sciences studies, and humanities; mathematics and statistics; multi/interdisciplinary studies; natural resources and conservation; parks, recreation, leisure, and fitness studies; philosophy and religious studies; physical sciences; psychology; public administration and social service professions; social sciences; theology and religious vocations; visual and performing arts. **Areas of required coursework:** arts/fine arts, computer literacy, mathematics, English (including composition), philosophy, foreign languages, sciences (biological or physical), history, social science, other. **Pre-professional programs:** pre-law, pre-dentistry, pre-medicine, pre-veterinary science, pre-pharmacy, other. **Special academic programs:** cross-registration, double major, exchange student program (domestic), honors program, independent study, internships, student-designed major, study abroad, teacher certificate program. **Teacher certification offered in:** elementary, middle/junior high, secondary. **Reserve Officers Training Corps (ROTC):** Army ROTC: Offered at cooperating institution (University of Minnesota); Navy ROTC: Offered at cooperating institution (University of Minnesota); Air Force ROTC: Offered on campus. **Faculty and instruction (2005-2006):** Total instructional faculty: 384 full-time, 381 part-time (61% men; 39% women; 8% minorities). Full-time faculty with Ph.D. or other terminal degree: 87%. Student/faculty ratio: 12/1. Classes of fewer than 20 students: 35%; of 20 to 49 students: 62%; of 50 or more students: 2%. **Advanced Placement and International Baccalaureate credit:** AP tests may be used for: Placement only. Scores accepted: 3, 4, 5. International Baccalaureate exams may be used for: Credit and/or placement. **Freshmen returning for sophomore year:** 87%. **Graduation rates:** Four-year: 59%; five-year: 72%; six-year: 74%. **Graduate study:** 28% of students pursue further study within one year. Fields in which graduates pursue further study: Master of Business Administration (MBA), 6%; law, 15%; medicine, 22%; engineering, 2%; theology (or the seminary), 12%; education, 18%; arts and sciences, 27%.

COSTS AND FINANCIAL AID

Financial aid office: (651) 962-6550. **Expenses (2006-2007):** Tuition and fees 2006-2007: $24,808; room/board: $6,932. Estimated books and supplies: $950; transportation: $700; personal expenses: $1,450. **Financial aid:** Priority filing date for institution's financial aid form: April 1. In 2005-2006, 61% of undergraduates applied for financial aid. Of those, 46% were determined to have financial need; 49% had their need fully met. Average financial aid package (proportion receiving): $18,695 (46%). Average amount of gift aid, such as scholarships or grants (proportion receiving): $9,049 (44%). Average amount of self-help aid, such as work study or loans (proportion receiving): $6,618 (41%). Average need-based loan (excluding PLUS or other private loans): $4,408. Among students who received need-based aid, the average percentage of need met: 99%. Among students who received aid based on merit, the average award (and the proportion receiving): $7,920 (12%). The average athletic scholarship (and the proportion receiving): $0 (0%). Average amount of debt of borrowers graduating in 2005: $26,621. Proportion who borrowed: 66%.

CAMPUS LIFE AND EXTRACURRICULAR ACTIVITIES

Campus housing available: women's dorms, men's dorms, apartments for married students, apartment for single students, special housing for disabled students. Students who live in college-owned, operated, or affiliated housing: 44%. **Student employment:** During the 2005-2006 academic year, 39% of undergraduates worked on campus. Average per-year earnings: $2,812. **Clubs and organizations:** Number of student organizations: 84. Activities include: choral groups, concert band, dance, drama/theater, jazz band, literary magazine, music ensembles, pep band, student government, student newspaper, yearbook. Number of fraternities: 0; sororities: 0. Average proportion of students who stay on campus on weekends: 30%. **Sports program (2005-2006):** Member of NCAA III. *Men's intercollegiate varsity sports:* baseball, basketball, cross-country, football, golf, ice hockey, soccer, swimming and diving, tennis, track and field (indoor), track and field (outdoor). *Women's intercollegiate varsity sports:* basketball, cross-country, golf, ice hockey, soccer, softball, swimming and diving, tennis, track and field (indoor), track and field (outdoor), volleyball.

SERVICES AND FACILITIES

Basic services: nonremedial tutoring, women's center, placement service, day care, health service, health insurance. **Remedial assistance:** reading, math, writing, study skills. **Counseling services:** minority student, career, personal, veteran student, academic, older student, psychological, religious, other. **For learning-disabled students:** School does not offer a structured program with separate admission and additional fees. Total undergraduates in learning-disabled program or receiving services: 175. Services include: remedial math, reading machines, remedial reading, tape recorders, note-taking services, oral tests, learning center, readers, extended time for tests, tutors, early syllabus, priority registration, substitution of courses, texts on tape, typist/scribe, exams on tape or computer, other testing accomodations, other. **Library:** Number of titles: 527,841; number of current serial subscrip-

tions: 5,261. **Information technology resources:** Students are not required to lease or own a computer. Number of campus computers available to all students: 1,654. School has a wireless network. Proportion of college-owned housing units wired for high-speed internet access: 100%. **Campus safety:** Security services offered: 24-hour foot-and-vehicle patrols, late-night transport/escort service, 24-hour emergency telephones, lighted pathways/sidewalks, controlled dormitory access (key, security card, etc).

TRANSFER AND INTERNATIONAL STUDENTS

Transfer students: May apply for admission for the following academic terms: Fall, Spring, Summer. Applicants do not need a minimum number of credits to apply. For fall 2005: Transfer applications received: 587. Transfer applicants offered admission: 501. Transfer applicants enrolled: 319. **International students:** Number of foreign undergraduates: 53 (1% of student body). Minimum TOEFL score required: 550 (paper); 213 (computer). Average TOEFL score: 566 (paper).

Winona State University

- ■ **Address:** PO Box 5838, Winona, MN 55987-5838
- ■ **Website:** http://www.winona.edu
- ■ **Public**
- ■ **Enrollment:** 6,795 full-time; 652 part-time

KEY STATS

✔ **U.S News College Ranking:** 62, Universities–Master's (Midwest)
✔ **ACT Score (25th/75th percentile):** 20-24
✔ **Tuition:** 2006-2007: $6,120 in state, $10,420 out of state

Selectivity: Selective	**Room/board:** $6,300
Acceptance rate: 80%	**Average debt:** $16,588
Student/faculty ratio: 17/1	**Proportion who borrowed:** 66%

UNDERGRADUATE STUDENT BODY STATS

2005-2006 enrollment: 6,795 full-time; 652 part-time. Men: 38%; women: 62%. **Ethnic makeup:** African American: 1%; Asian American: 2%; Hispanic: 1%; White: 93%; International: 3%.

ADMISSIONS FACTS AND FIGURES

Phone: (507) 457-5100. **Email:** admissions@winona.edu. **Website:** http://www.winona.edu. **Application deadlines for fall 2007:** Early decision: Not offered. Early action: Send application by: N/A; Decision sent by: N/A. Admission can be deferred. **Application fee:** $20. Common application is accepted. **Admissions requirements/recommendations:** High school units required (recommended): English: 4; Mathematics: 3; Science: 3; Foreign language: 2; Social studies: 3; History: 1; Academic electives: 1; Total units: 19. Tests: The college uses SAT or ACT scores in admissions decisions. ACT required. For admission to the fall 2007 entering class, the school will accept: ACT with writing, ACT without writing. Campus visit: Recommended. Admissions interview: Neither required nor recommended. Off-campus interview: Not available. **Factors that count in admissions decisions:** *Academic:* Secondary school record: Very important. Class rank: Very important. Letters of recommendation: Not considered. Standardized test scores: Very important. Essay: Not considered. *Nonacademic:* Interview: Not considered. Extracurricular activities: Not considered. Talent/ability: Considered. Character/personal qualities: Not considered. Alumni/ae relationship: Considered. Geographical residence: Not considered. State residency: Not considered. Religious affiliation/commitment: Not considered. Minority status: Not considered. Volunteer work: Not considered. Work experience: Not considered. **Other schools with the greatest overlap in applicants:** University of Minnesota–Duluth; University of Minnesota–Twin Cities; University of Wisconsin–Eau Claire; University of Wisconsin–La Crosse; University of Wisconsin–Madison. **Admissions statistics for the fall 2005 entering class:** Total applicants: 5,356. Total accepted: 4,303. Freshmen enrolled: 1,720; 13% were from out of state. Overall acceptance rate: 80%. Non-early acceptance rate: 80%. **Size of waiting list:** 78 applicants; enrolled from waiting list: 34. **Credentials of fall 2005 freshmen:** 11% ranked in the top 10 percent of their high school class; 25% were in the top 25 percent, and 80% were in the top half. (Proportion submitting class standing: 94%.) **First-year students submitting ACT scores:** 98%. Scores (25/75 percentile): English: 19-24, Math: 19-25, Composite: 20-24.

ACADEMICS

Year founded: 1858. **Academic calendar:** Semester. **Degrees offered:** certificate, associate, bachelor's, master's, post-master's certificate. **Most popular majors:** 23% business, management, marketing, and related support services, 22% education, 9% health professions and related clinical sciences, 6% communication, journalism, and related programs, 5% parks, recreation, leisure, and fitness studies. **Major fields of study:** biological and biomedical sciences; business, management, marketing, and related support services; communication, journalism, and related programs; computer and information sciences and support services; education; engineering; English language and literature/letters; health professions and related clinical sciences; history; legal professions and studies; mathematics and statistics; multi/interdisciplinary studies; natural resources and conservation; parks, recreation, leisure, and fitness studies; public administration and social service professions; security and protective services; visual and performing arts. **Areas of required coursework:** arts/fine arts, humanities, computer literacy, mathematics, English (including composition), foreign languages, sciences (biological or physical), history, social science, other. **Pre-professional programs:** pre-law, pre-dentistry, pre-medicine, pre-veterinary science, pre-optometry, pre-pharmacy, other. **Special academic programs:** accelerated program, cooperative (work-study plan) program, cross-registration, distance learning, double major, English as a Second Language (ESL), honors program, independent study, internships, student-designed major, study abroad, teacher certificate program. **Teacher certification offered in:** early childhood, special education, elementary, middle/junior high, adult education, secondary. **Cooperative education programs:** art, business, computer science, education, engineering, health professions, humanities, natural science, social/behavioral science, technologies, other. **Reserve Officers Training Corps (ROTC):** Army ROTC: Offered at cooperating institution (Univ. of Wisconsin-La Crosse); Navy ROTC: Offered at cooperating institution (Univ. of Wisconsin-La Crosse); Air Force ROTC: Offered at cooperating institution (Univ. of Wisconsin-La Crosse). **Faculty and instruction (2005-2006):** Total instructional faculty: 342 full-time, 227 part-time (50% men; 50% women; 7% minorities). Full-time faculty with Ph.D. or other terminal degree: 75%. Student/faculty ratio: 17/1. Classes of fewer than 20 students: 43%; of 20 to 49 students: 51%; of 50 or more students: 6%. **Advanced Placement and International Baccalaureate credit:** AP tests may be used for: Credit and/or placement. Scores accepted: 4, 5. International Baccalaureate exams may be used for: Credit and/or placement. **Freshmen returning for sophomore year:** 75%. **Graduation rates:** Four-year: 23%; five-year: 48%; six-year: 52%. **Graduate study:** 12% of students pursue further study within one year.

COSTS AND FINANCIAL AID

Financial aid office: (507) 457-5090. **Expenses (2006-2007):** Tuition and fees 2006-2007: $6,120 in state, $10,420 out of state; room/board: $6,300. Estimated books and supplies: $1,080; transportation: $580; personal expenses: $1,000. Average amount of debt of borrowers graduating in 2005: $16,588. Proportion who borrowed: 66%.

CAMPUS LIFE AND EXTRACURRICULAR ACTIVITIES

Campus housing available: coed dorms, women's dorms, men's dorms, apartment for single students, special housing for disabled students, special housing for international students. Students who live in college-owned, operated, or affiliated housing: 34%. **Student employment:** During the 2005-2006 academic year, 36% of undergraduates worked on campus. Average per-year earnings: $3,780. **Clubs and organizations:** Number of student organizations: 156. Activities include: choral groups, concert band, dance, drama/theater, jazz band, literary magazine, music ensembles, musical theater, pep band, radio station, student government, student newspaper, student film society, symphony orchestra, television station. Number of fraternities: 6; sororities: 3. Average proportion of students who stay on campus on weekends: 65%. **Sports program (2005-2006):** Member of NCAA II. *Men's intercollegiate varsity sports:* baseball, basketball, bowling, cross-country, football, golf, tennis. *Women's intercollegiate varsity sports:* basketball, cross-country, golf, gymnastics, soccer, softball, tennis, track and field (indoor), track and field (outdoor), volleyball.

SERVICES AND FACILITIES

Basic services: nonremedial tutoring, women's center, placement service, day care, health service, health insurance. **Remedial assistance:** math, writing, study skills. **Counseling services:** minority student, career, military, personal, veteran student, academic, older student, psychological, birth control. **For learning-disabled students:** School does not offer a structured program with separate admission and additional fees. Services include: remedial math, remedial English, reading machines, note-taking services, oral tests, learning center, extended time for tests, tutors, priority registration, priority seating, texts on tape, other testing accomodations. **Library:** Number of titles: 325,611; number of current serial subscriptions: 7,362. **Information technology resources:** Students are required to lease or own a computer. Number of campus computers available to all students: 400. School has a wireless network. Approximate number of users that can be accommodated: 10,000. Proportion of college-owned housing units wired for high-speed internet access: 100%. **Campus safety:** Security services offered: 24-hour foot-and-vehicle patrols, late-night transport/escort service, 24-hour emergency telephones, lighted pathways/sidewalks, student patrols, controlled dormitory access (key, security card, etc).

TRANSFER AND INTERNATIONAL STUDENTS

Transfer students: May apply for admission for the following academic terms: Fall, Spring, Summer. Applicants need a minimum number of credits to apply. For fall 2005: Transfer applications received: 1,265. Transfer applicants offered admission: 1,015. Transfer applicants enrolled: 476. **International students:** Number of foreign undergraduates: 233 (3% of student body). Number of countries represented: 54. Minimum TOEFL score required: 500 (paper); 173 (computer). Average TOEFL score: 568 (paper).

Mississippi

Alcorn State University

- **Address:** 1000 ASU Drive #359, Alcorn State, MS 39096
- **Website:** http://www.alcorn.edu
- **Public**
- **Enrollment:** 2,676 full-time; 286 part-time

KEY STATS

✔ **U.S News College Ranking:** third tier, Universities–Master's (South)
✔ **ACT Score (25th/75th percentile):** 16-19
✔ **Tuition:** 2005-2006: $3,919 in state, $8,887 out of state

Selectivity: Less selective	**Room/board:** $4,272
Acceptance rate: 68%	**Average debt:** $17,000
Student/faculty ratio: 16/1	**Proportion who borrowed:** 73%

UNDERGRADUATE STUDENT BODY STATS

2005-2006 enrollment: 2,676 full-time; 286 part-time. Men: 37%; women: 63%. **Ethnic makeup:** African American: 92%; White: 6%; International: 2%.

ADMISSIONS FACTS AND FIGURES

Phone: (601) 877-6147. **Email:** ebarnes@lorman.alcorn.edu. **Website:** http://www.alcorn.edu. **Application deadlines for fall 2007:** Regular decision: Rolling. Early decision: Not offered. Early action: Not offered. Admission can be deferred. Common application is not accepted. **Admissions requirements/recommendations:** High school units required (recommended): English: 4; Mathematics: 3; Science: 3; Foreign language: (1); Social studies: 3; Academic electives: 2; Total units: 15. Tests: The college uses SAT or ACT scores in admissions decisions. Either SAT or ACT required. For admission to the fall 2007 entering class, the school will accept: ACT with writing, ACT without writing. Campus visit: Recommended. Admissions interview: Neither required nor recommended. Off-campus interview: May be arranged. **Factors that count in admissions decisions:** *Academic:* Secondary school record: Very important. Class rank: Very important. Letters of recommendation: Considered. Standardized test scores: Important. Essay: Not considered. *Nonacademic:* Interview: Considered. Extracurricular activities: Not considered. Talent/ability: Not considered. Character/personal qualities: Not considered. Alumni/ae relationship: Not considered. Geographical residence: Not considered. State residency: Not considered. Religious affiliation/commitment: Not considered. Minority status: Not considered. Volunteer work: Not considered. Work experience: Not considered. **Admissions statistics for the fall 2005 entering class:** Total applicants: 2,335. Total accepted: 1,581. Freshmen enrolled: 497; 26% were from out of state. Overall acceptance rate: 68%. **Credentials of fall 2005 freshmen:** 75% ranked in the top half of their high school class. (Proportion submitting class standing: 54%.) **Average high school grade point average:** 2.9. **First-year students who submitted SAT scores:** 8%. Scores (25/75 percentile): Verbal: 420-520, Math: 410-500, Combined: 830-1020. **First-year students submitting ACT scores:** 92%. Scores (25/75 percentile): English: 15-20, Math: 15-18, Composite: 16-19.

ACADEMICS

Year founded: 1871. **Academic calendar:** Semester. **Degrees offered:** associate, bachelor's, master's, post-master's certificate. **Most popular majors:** 21% liberal arts and sciences studies, and humanities, 11% health professions and related clinical sciences, 10% business, management, marketing, and related support services, 10% education. **Major fields of study:** agriculture, agriculture operations, and related sciences; biological and biomedical sciences; business, management, marketing, and related support services; communication, journalism, and related programs; computer and information sciences and support services; education; engineering technologies/technicians; English language and literature/letters; family and consumer sciences/human sciences; health professions and related clinical sciences; history; liberal arts and sciences studies, and humanities; mathematics and statistics; parks, recreation, leisure, and fitness studies;

physical sciences; psychology; security and protective services; social sciences; visual and performing arts. **Areas of required coursework:** arts/fine arts, humanities, mathematics, English (including composition), sciences (biological or physical), history, social science, other. **Pre-professional programs:** pre-law, pre-dentistry, pre-medicine, pre-veterinary science, pre-optometry, pre-pharmacy, other. **Special academic programs:** accelerated program, cooperative (work-study plan) program, distance learning, double major, honors program, independent study, internships, liberal arts/career combination, teacher certificate program. **Teacher certification offered in:** early childhood, special education, elementary, secondary. **Cooperative education programs:** agriculture, business, education, health professions, home economics, natural science, social/behavioral science, technologies, other. **Reserve Officers Training Corps (ROTC):** Army ROTC: Offered on campus. **Faculty and instruction (2005-2006):** Total instructional faculty: 175 full-time, 34 part-time (58% men; 42% women; 78% minorities). Full-time faculty with Ph.D. or other terminal degree: 64%. Student/faculty ratio: 16/1. Classes of fewer than 20 students: 51%; of 20 to 49 students: 42%; of 50 or more students: 6%. **Advanced Placement and International Baccalaureate credit:** AP tests may be used for: Credit and/or placement. **Freshmen returning for sophomore year:** 70%. **Graduation rates:** Four-year: 24%; five-year: 37%; six-year: 46%.

COSTS AND FINANCIAL AID

Financial aid office: (601) 877-6190. **Expenses (2005-2006):** Tuition and fees 2005-2006: $3,919 in state, $8,887 out of state; room/board: $4,272. Estimated books and supplies: $1,320; transportation: $2,200; personal expenses: $2,200. **Financial aid:** Priority filing date for institution's financial aid form: April 1. In 2005-2006, 100% of undergraduates applied for financial aid. Of those, 96% were determined to have financial need; 43% had their need fully met. Average financial aid package (proportion receiving): $9,500 (85%). Average amount of gift aid, such as scholarships or grants (proportion receiving): N/A (66%). Average amount of self-help aid, such as work study or loans (proportion receiving): N/A (60%). Among students who received need-based aid, the average percentage of need met: 74%. Among students who received aid based on merit, the average award (and the proportion receiving): $5,380 (18%). The average athletic scholarship (and the proportion receiving): $6,537 (10%). Average amount of debt of borrowers graduating in 2005: $17,000. Proportion who borrowed: 73%.

CAMPUS LIFE AND EXTRACURRICULAR ACTIVITIES

Campus housing available (% using): women's dorms (56%), men's dorms (44%). Students who live in college-owned, operated, or affiliated housing: 48%. Activities include: choral groups, concert band, dance, drama/theater, jazz band, marching band, music ensembles, radio station, student government, student newspaper, television station, yearbook. Number of fraternities: 4; sororities: 4. Proportion of men in fraternities: 7%; of women in sororities: 12%. **Sports program (2005-2006):** Member of NCAA I. *Men's intercollegiate varsity sports:* baseball, basketball, cross-country, football, golf, tennis, track and field (indoor), track and field (outdoor). *Women's intercollegiate varsity sports:* basketball, bowling, cross-country, golf, soccer, softball, tennis, track and field (indoor), track and field (outdoor), volleyball.

SERVICES AND FACILITIES

Basic services: placement service. **Remedial assistance:** reading, math, other. **Counseling services:** career, academic, psychological, other. **Library:** Number of titles: 220,393; number of current serial subscriptions: 1,046. **Information technology resources:** Students are not required to lease or own a computer. Number of campus computers available to all students: 1,000. School does not have a wireless network. Proportion of college-owned housing units wired for high-speed internet access: 100%. **Campus safety:** Security services offered: 24-hour foot-and-vehicle patrols, 24-hour emergency telephones, lighted pathways/sidewalks, controlled dormitory access (key, security card, etc).

TRANSFER AND INTERNATIONAL STUDENTS

Transfer students: May apply for admission for the following academic terms: Fall, Spring, Summer. Applicants need a minimum number of credits to apply. For fall 2005: Transfer applicants enrolled: 254. **International**

students: Number of foreign undergraduates: 54 (2% of student body). Minimum TOEFL score required: 525 (paper); 195 (computer).

Belhaven College

- **Address:** 1500 Peachtree Street, Jackson, MS 39202
- **Website:** http://www.belhaven.edu
- **Private; Religious affiliation:** Presbyterian
- **Enrollment:** 2,166 full-time; 72 part-time

KEY STATS
- ✔ **U.S News College Ranking:** 41, Comp. Coll.–Bachelor's (South)
- ✔ **ACT Score:** 23
- ✔ **Tuition:** 2005-2006: $14,100

Selectivity: Selective	**Room/board:** $5,430
Acceptance rate: 57%	**Average debt:** N/A
Student/faculty ratio: 21/1	**Proportion who borrowed:** N/A

UNDERGRADUATE STUDENT BODY STATS

2005-2006 enrollment: 2,166 full-time; 72 part-time. Men: 32%; women: 68%. **Ethnic makeup:** African American: 39%; American-Indian: 1%; Asian American: 1%; Hispanic: 3%; White: 56%; International: 1%. **Religious preference:** Roman Catholic: 4%; Protestant: 62%; Unknown: 17%; Presbyterian: 17%.

ADMISSIONS FACTS AND FIGURES

Phone: (601) 968-5940. **Email:** admissions@belhaven.edu. **Website:** http://www.belhaven.edu. **Application deadlines for fall 2007:** Regular decision: Rolling. Early decision: Not offered. Early action: Not offered. Admission can be deferred. **Application fee:** $25. Common application is not accepted. **Admissions requirements/recommendations:** High school units required (recommended): English: 4; Mathematics: 2; Science: 1; Foreign language: (2); History: 1; Academic electives: 8; Total units: 16. Tests: The college uses SAT or ACT scores in admissions decisions. Either SAT or ACT required. For admission to the fall 2007 entering class, the school will accept: ACT with writing, ACT without writing. Campus visit: Recommended. Admissions interview: Neither required nor recommended. Off-campus interview: May be arranged. **Factors that count in admissions decisions:** *Academic:* Secondary school record: Very important. Class rank: Considered. Letters of recommendation: Very important. Standardized test scores: Very important. Essay: Considered. *Nonacademic:* Interview: Not considered. Extracurricular activities: Not considered. Talent/ability: Not considered. Character/personal qualities: Not considered. Alumni/ae relationship: Not considered. Geographical residence: Not considered. State residency: Not considered. Religious affiliation/commitment: Not considered. Minority status: Not considered. Volunteer work: Not considered. Work experience: Not considered. **Admissions statistics for the fall 2005 entering class:** Total applicants: 734. Total accepted: 420. Freshmen enrolled: 202; 27% were from out of state. Overall acceptance rate: 57%. **Average high school grade point average:** 3.3. **First-year students who submitted SAT scores:** 44%. Scores (25/75 percentile): Verbal: N/A, Math: N/A, Combined: N/A. **First-year students submitting ACT scores:** 76%. Scores (25/75 percentile): English: N/A, Math: N/A, Composite: N/A.

ACADEMICS

Year founded: 1883. **Academic calendar:** Semester. **Degrees offered:** certificate, associate, bachelor's, master's. **Most popular majors:** 57% business administration and management, 6% elementary education and teaching, 6% psychology, 5% drama and dramatics/theater arts, 5% sport and fitness administration/management. **Major fields of study:** biological and biomedical sciences; business, management, marketing, and related support services; communication, journalism, and related programs; computer and information sciences and support services; education; English language and literature/letters; history; liberal arts and sciences studies, and humanities; mathematics and statistics; multi/interdisciplinary studies; parks, recreation, leisure, and fitness studies; philosophy and religious studies; physical sciences; psychology; social sciences; visual and performing arts. **Areas of required coursework:** arts/fine arts, mathematics, English (including composition), foreign languages, sciences (biological or physical), history, other. **Pre-professional programs:** pre-law, pre-dentistry, pre-medicine, pre-theology, pre-pharmacy, other. **Special academic programs (% participation):** accelerated program (46%), double major (.5%), dual enrollment, English as

a Second Language (ESL), honors program (5%), independent study (22), internships (12%), student-designed major, study abroad (0%), teacher certificate program (6%). **Teacher certification offered in:** early childhood, special education, elementary, middle/junior high, secondary. **Faculty and instruction (2005-2006):** Total instructional faculty: 70 full-time, 155 part-time (62% men; 38% women). Full-time faculty with Ph.D. or other terminal degree: 84%. Student/faculty ratio: 21/1. **Advanced Placement and International Baccalaureate credit:** AP tests may be used for: Credit only. Scores accepted: 3, 4, 5. International Baccalaureate exams may be used for: Credit only. **Freshmen returning for sophomore year:** 67%. **Graduation rates:** Four-year: 32%; five-year: 40%; six-year: 43%.

COSTS AND FINANCIAL AID

Financial aid office: (601) 968-5934. **Expenses (2005-2006):** Tuition and fees 2005-2006: $14,100; room/board: $5,430. Estimated books and supplies: $700; transportation: $600. **Financial aid:** Priority filing date for institution's financial aid form: March 1.

CAMPUS LIFE AND EXTRACURRICULAR ACTIVITIES

Campus housing available (% using): women's dorms (59%), men's dorms (40%), special housing for disabled students (1%). **Student employment:** During the 2005-2006 academic year, 6% of undergraduates worked on campus. Average per-year earnings: $1,545. **Clubs and organizations:** Number of student organizations: 21. Activities include: choral groups, dance, drama/theater, literary magazine, music ensembles, musical theater, pep band, student government, student newspaper, yearbook. Number of fraternities: 0; sororities: 0. Average proportion of students who stay on campus on weekends: 68%. **Sports program (2005-2006):** Member of NAIA. *Men's intercollegiate varsity sports:* baseball, basketball, cross-country, football, golf, soccer, tennis. *Women's intercollegiate varsity sports:* basketball, cross-country, soccer, softball, tennis, volleyball.

SERVICES AND FACILITIES

Basic services: nonremedial tutoring, health service. **Remedial assistance:** reading, math, writing, study skills. **Counseling services:** career, personal, academic, older student, psychological, religious. **For learning-disabled students:** School does not offer a structured program with separate admission and additional fees. Total undergraduates in learning-disabled program or receiving services: 7. Services include: remedial math, remedial English, remedial reading, tape recorders, untimed tests, extended time for tests, priority registration, priority seating, other. **Library:** Number of titles: 101,681; number of current serial subscriptions: 14,671. **Information technology resources:** Students are not required to lease or own a computer. Number of campus computers available to all students: 50. School has a wireless network. Approximate number of users that can be accommodated: 400. Proportion of college-owned housing units wired for high-speed internet access: 100%. **Campus safety:** Security services offered: 24-hour foot-and-vehicle patrols, late-night transport/escort service, 24-hour emergency telephones, lighted pathways/sidewalks, controlled dormitory access (key, security card, etc).

TRANSFER AND INTERNATIONAL STUDENTS

Transfer students: May apply for admission for the following academic terms: Fall, Winter, Spring, Summer. Applicants need a minimum number of credits to apply. For fall 2005: Transfer applications received: 300. Transfer applicants offered admission: 175. Transfer applicants enrolled: 106. **International students:** Number of foreign undergraduates: 19 (1% of student body). Number of countries represented: 21. Minimum TOEFL score required: 500 (paper); 173 (computer). Average TOEFL score: 550 (paper).

Mountain College

- Address: PO Box 160, Blue Mountain, MS 38610-0160
- Website: http://www.bmc.edu
- Private; Religious affiliation: Southern Baptist
- Enrollment: 283 full-time; 82 part-time

KEY STATS
✔ U.S News College Ranking: 41, Comp. Coll.—Bachelor's (South)
✔ ACT Score (25th/75th percentile): 17-23
✔ Tuition: 2006-2007: $7,490

Selectivity: Selective	Room/board: $3,766
Acceptance rate: 55%	Average debt: $11,484
Student/faculty ratio: 11/1	Proportion who borrowed: 83%

UNDERGRADUATE STUDENT BODY STATS
2005-2006 enrollment: 283 full-time; 82 part-time. Men: 23%; women: 77%. **Ethnic makeup:** African American: 14%; White: 86%. **Religious preference:** Roman Catholic: 1%; Protestant: 32%; No preference: 4%; Southern Baptist: 63%.

ADMISSIONS FACTS AND FIGURES
Phone: (662) 685-4161. **Email:** admissions@bmc.edu. **Website:** http://www.bmc.edu. **Application deadlines for fall 2007:** Regular decision: September 5. Early decision: Not offered. Early action: Not offered. Admission can be deferred. **Application fee:** $10. Common application is not accepted. **Admissions requirements/recommendations:** High school units required (recommended): English: 4 (4); Mathematics: 3 (3); Science: 3 (3); Foreign language: 2 (2); Social studies: 1 (3); History: 2; Total units: 15 (15). Tests: The college uses SAT or ACT scores in admissions decisions. Either SAT or ACT required. For admission to the fall 2007 entering class, the school will accept: ACT without writing. Campus visit: Recommended. Admissions interview: Recommended. Off-campus interview: May be arranged. **Factors that count in admissions decisions:** *Academic:* Secondary school record: Very important. Class rank: Very important. Letters of recommendation: Considered. Standardized test scores: Very important. Essay: Considered. *Nonacademic:* Interview: Considered. Extracurricular activities: Considered. Talent/ability: Considered. Character/personal qualities: Considered. Alumni/ae relationship: Considered. Geographical residence: Not considered. State residency: Not considered. Religious affiliation/commitment: Not considered. Minority status: Not considered. Volunteer work: Considered. Work experience: Considered. **Other schools with the greatest overlap in applicants:** Mississippi State University; University of Mississippi. **Admissions statistics for the fall 2005 entering class:** Total applicants: 170. Total accepted: 93. Freshmen enrolled: 45; 27% were from out of state. Overall acceptance rate: 55%. **Credentials of fall 2005 freshmen:** 25% ranked in the top 10 percent of their high school class; 43% were in the top 25 percent, and 72% were in the top half. (Proportion submitting class standing: 70%.) **Average high school grade point average:** 3.3. **First-year students who submitted SAT scores:** 4%. Scores (25/75 percentile): Verbal: N/A, Math: N/A, Combined: N/A. **First-year students submitting ACT scores:** 96%. Scores (25/75 percentile): English: 17-29, Math: 15-25, Composite: 17-23.

ACADEMICS
Year founded: 1873. **Academic calendar:** Semester. **Degrees offered:** bachelor's. **Most popular majors:** 49% education, 12% philosophy and religious studies, 10% social sciences, 6% psychology, 5% English language and literature/letters. **Major fields of study:** biological and biomedical sciences; business, management, marketing, and related support services; education; English language and literature/letters; foreign languages, literatures, and linguistics; health professions and related clinical sciences; history; mathematics and statistics; multi/interdisciplinary studies; parks, recreation, leisure, and fitness studies; psychology; social sciences; theology and religious vocations; visual and performing arts. **Areas of required coursework:** arts/fine arts, humanities, computer literacy, mathematics, English (including composition), sciences (biological or physical), history, social science, other. **Pre-professional programs:** pre-law, pre-dentistry, pre-medicine, pre-theology, pre-veterinary science, pre-optometry, pre-pharmacy. **Special academic programs (% participation):** double major (0%), honors program (0%), internships (2%), teacher certificate program (67%). **Teacher certification offered in:** special education, elementary, secondary. **Faculty and instruction (2005-2006):** Total instructional faculty: 24 full-time, 12 part-time (44% men; 56% women; 0% minorities). Full-time faculty with Ph.D. or other terminal degree: 50%. Student/faculty ratio: 11/1. Classes of fewer than 20 students: 75%; of 20 to 49 students: 24%; of 50 or more students: 1%. **Advanced Placement and International Baccalaureate credit:** AP tests may be used for: Placement only. Scores accepted: 3, 4, 5. **Freshmen returning for sophomore year:** 68%. **Graduation rates:** Four-year: 33%; five-year: 43%; six-year: 42%. **Graduate study:** 19% of students pursue further study immediately upon graduation. Fields in which graduates pursue further study: Master of Business Administration (MBA), 1%; theology (or the seminary), 8%; education, 6%; arts and sciences, 4%.

COSTS AND FINANCIAL AID
Financial aid office: (662) 685-4771. **Expenses (2006-2007):** Tuition and fees 2006-2007: $7,490; room/board: $3,766. Estimated books and supplies: $700 personal expenses: $2,428. **Financial aid:** Priority filing date for institution's financial aid form: March 31; deadline: July 15. In 2005-2006, 83% of undergraduates applied for financial aid. Of those, 72% were determined to have financial need; 54% had their need fully met. Average financial aid package (proportion receiving): $7,942 (72%). Average amount of gift aid, such as scholarships or grants (proportion receiving): $2,830 (49%). Average amount of self-help aid, such as work study or loans (proportion receiving): $3,980 (51%). Average need-based loan (excluding PLUS or other private loans): $3,592. Among students who received need-based aid, the average percentage of need met: 46%. Among students who received aid based on merit, the average award (and the proportion receiving): $4,041 (11%). The average athletic scholarship (and the proportion receiving): $10,241 (6%). Average amount of debt of borrowers graduating in 2005: $11,484. Proportion who borrowed: 83%.

CAMPUS LIFE AND EXTRACURRICULAR ACTIVITIES
Campus housing available (% using): women's dorms (80%), men's dorms (20%), special housing for disabled students (0%). Students who live in college-owned, operated, or affiliated housing: 34%. **Student employment:** During the 2005-2006 academic year, 0% of undergraduates worked on campus. Average per-year earnings: $0. **Clubs and organizations:** Number of student organizations: 28. Activities include: choral groups, drama/theater, literary magazine, music ensembles, musical theater, student government, yearbook. Number of fraternities: 0; sororities: 0. Average proportion of students who stay on campus on weekends: 15%. **Sports program (2005-2006):** Member of NAIA. *Women's intercollegiate varsity sports:* basketball, tennis.

SERVICES AND FACILITIES
Basic services: nonremedial tutoring, placement service, health service, health insurance. **Remedial assistance:** reading, math, writing, study skills. **Counseling services:** career, academic, psychological, religious. **For learning-disabled students:** School does not offer a structured program with separate admission and additional fees. Services include: remedial math, remedial English, remedial reading, tape recorders, untimed tests, note-taking services, oral tests, learning center, readers, extended time for tests, tutors, typist/scribe. **Library:** Number of titles: 57,245; number of current serial subscriptions: 185. **Information technology resources:** Students are not required to lease or own a computer. Number of campus computers available to all students: 59. School has a wireless network. Proportion of college-owned housing units wired for high-speed internet access: 97%. **Campus safety:** Security services offered: late-night transport/escort service, lighted pathways/sidewalks, controlled dormitory access (key, security card, etc).

TRANSFER AND INTERNATIONAL STUDENTS
Transfer students: May apply for admission for the following academic terms: Fall, Spring, Summer. Applicants need a minimum number of credits to apply. For fall 2005: Transfer applications received: 147. Transfer applicants offered admission: 83. Transfer applicants enrolled: 69. **International students:** Number of foreign undergraduates: 1. Number of countries represented: 1. Minimum TOEFL score required: 500 (paper); 173 (computer).

Delta State University

- **Address:** Highway 8 W, Cleveland, MS 38733
- **Website:** http://www.deltastate.edu
- **Public**
- **Enrollment:** 2,754 full-time; 504 part-time

KEY STATS

✔ **U.S News College Ranking:** third tier, Universities–Master's (South)
✔ **ACT Score (25th/75th percentile):** 16-21
✔ **Tuition:** 2005-2006: $4,252 in state, $9,192 out of state

Selectivity: Selective	Room/board: $3,947
Acceptance rate: 33%	Average debt: $18,200
Student/faculty ratio: 18/1	Proportion who borrowed: 75%

UNDERGRADUATE STUDENT BODY STATS

2005-2006 enrollment: 2,754 full-time; 504 part-time. Men: 40%; women: 60%. **Ethnic makeup:** African American: 39%; Asian American: 1%; Hispanic: 1%; White: 60%.

ADMISSIONS FACTS AND FIGURES

Phone: (662) 846-4018. **Email:** dheslep@deltastate.edu. **Website:** http://www.deltastate.edu. **Application deadlines for fall 2007:** Regular decision: August 1. Early decision: Not offered. Early action: Not offered. Admission can be deferred. **Application fee:** $15. Common application is not accepted. **Admissions requirements/recommendations:** High school units required (recommended): English: 4; Mathematics: 3; Science: 3; Foreign language: 1; Social studies: 3; Academic electives: 1; Total units: 16. Tests: The college uses SAT or ACT scores in admissions decisions. Either SAT or ACT required. For admission to the fall 2007 entering class, the school will accept: ACT with writing, ACT without writing. Campus visit: Recommended. Admissions interview: Neither required nor recommended. Off-campus interview: Not available. **Factors that count in admissions decisions:** *Academic:* Secondary school record: Very important. Class rank: Very important. Letters of recommendation: Considered. Standardized test scores: Very important. Essay: Not considered. *Nonacademic:* Interview: Considered. Extracurricular activities: Not considered. Talent/ability: Not considered. Character/personal qualities: Not considered. Geographical residence: Not considered. State residency: Not considered. Religious affiliation/commitment: Not considered. Minority status: Not considered. Volunteer work: Not considered. Work experience: Not considered. **Admissions statistics for the fall 2005 entering class:** Total applicants: 1,541. Total accepted: 502. Freshmen enrolled: 398; 14% were from out of state. Overall acceptance rate: 33%. **Credentials of fall 2005 freshmen:** 49% were in the top 25 percent, and 79% were in the top half. (Proportion submitting class standing: 82%.) **Average high school grade point average:** 3.0. **First-year students submitting ACT scores:** 99%. Scores (25/75 percentile): English: 15-22, Math: 15-20, Composite: 16-21.

ACADEMICS

Year founded: 1924. **Academic calendar:** Semester. **Degrees offered:** bachelor's, master's, post-master's certificate, doctorate. **Most popular majors:** 34% education, 29% business, management, marketing, and related support services, 6% health professions and related clinical sciences, 5% public administration and social service professions, 4% visual and performing arts. **Major fields of study:** biological and biomedical sciences; business, management, marketing, and related support services; communication, journalism, and related programs; education; English language and literature/letters; family and consumer sciences/human sciences; foreign languages, literatures, and linguistics; health professions and related clinical sciences; history; liberal arts and sciences studies, and humanities; mathematics and statistics; multi/interdisciplinary studies; physical sciences; psychology; public administration and social service professions; security and protective services; social sciences; transportation and materials moving; visual and performing arts. **Areas of required coursework:** arts/fine arts, computer literacy, mathematics, English (including composition), sciences (biological or physical), history, social science. **Special academic programs:** cooperative (work-study plan) program, distance learning, double major, dual enrollment, honors program, independent study, internships, teacher certificate program, weekend college. **Teacher certification offered in:** early childhood, special education, secondary. **Reserve Officers Training Corps (ROTC):** Army ROTC: Offered at cooperating institution (Ms Valley State University). **Faculty and instruction (2005-2006):** Total instructional faculty:

165 full-time, 109 part-time (51% men; 49% women; 11% minorities). Full-time faculty with Ph.D. or other terminal degree: 71%. Student/faculty ratio: 18/1. **Advanced Placement and International Baccalaureate credit:** AP tests may be used for: Credit only. Scores accepted: 3, 4, 5. **Freshmen returning for sophomore year:** 70%. **Graduation rates:** Four-year: 23%; five-year: 41%; six-year: 47%. **Graduate study:** 42% of students pursue further study immediately upon graduation.

COSTS AND FINANCIAL AID

Financial aid office: (662) 846-4670. **Expenses (2005-2006):** Tuition and fees 2005-2006: $4,252 in state, $9,192 out of state; room/board: $3,947. Estimated books and supplies: $700. **Financial aid:** Priority filing date for institution's financial aid form: March 1. In 2005-2006, 88% of undergraduates applied for financial aid. Of those, 80% were determined to have financial need; 70% had their need fully met. Average financial aid package (proportion receiving): $8,200 (80%). Average amount of gift aid, such as scholarships or grants (proportion receiving): $3,550 (62%). Average amount of self-help aid, such as work study or loans (proportion receiving): $1,600 (80%). Average need-based loan (excluding PLUS or other private loans): $4,280. Among students who received need-based aid, the average percentage of need met: 73%. Average amount of debt of borrowers graduating in 2005: $18,200. Proportion who borrowed: 75%.

CAMPUS LIFE AND EXTRACURRICULAR ACTIVITIES

Campus housing available: women's dorms, men's dorms, apartments for married students. Students who live in college-owned, operated, or affiliated housing: 33%. **Clubs and organizations:** Number of student organizations: 50. Activities include: choral groups, concert band, drama/theater, jazz band, literary magazine, marching band, music ensembles, musical theater, opera, student government, student newspaper, symphony orchestra, yearbook. Number of fraternities: 8; sororities: 6. **Sports program (2005-2006):** Member of NCAA II. *Men's intercollegiate varsity sports:* baseball, basketball, cheerleading, football, golf, soccer, swimming and diving, tennis. *Women's intercollegiate varsity sports:* basketball, cheerleading, cross-country, soccer, softball, swimming and diving, tennis.

SERVICES AND FACILITIES

Basic services: placement service, day care, health service, health insurance. **Remedial assistance:** reading, math, writing, study skills. **Counseling services:** career, personal, academic, birth control. **For learning-disabled students:** Services include: remedial math, remedial English, remedial reading, untimed tests. **Library:** Number of titles: 357,769; number of current serial subscriptions: 1,280. **Information technology resources:** Students are not required to lease or own a computer. Number of campus computers available to all students: 293. School does not have a wireless network. **Campus safety:** Security services offered: 24-hour foot-and-vehicle patrols, late-night transport/escort service, 24-hour emergency telephones, lighted pathways/sidewalks, controlled dormitory access (key, security card, etc).

TRANSFER AND INTERNATIONAL STUDENTS

Transfer students: May apply for admission for the following academic terms: Fall, Spring, Summer. Applicants need a minimum number of credits to apply. For fall 2005: Transfer applicants enrolled: 593. **International students:** Number of foreign undergraduates: 0. Number of countries represented: 17. Minimum TOEFL score required: 525 (paper); 196 (computer).

Jackson State University

- **Address:** 1400 J.R. Lynch Street, Jackson, MS 39217
- **Website:** http://www.jsums.edu
- **Public**
- **Enrollment:** 5,720 full-time; 940 part-time

KEY STATS

✔ **U.S News College Ranking:** fourth tier, National Universities
✔ **ACT Score (25th/75th percentile):** 16-20
✔ **Tuition:** 2005-2006: $3,964 in state, $8,872 out of state

Selectivity: Less selective	Room/board: $4,994
Acceptance rate: 39%	Average debt: N/A
Student/faculty ratio: 22/1	Proportion who borrowed: N/A

UNDERGRADUATE STUDENT BODY STATS

2005-2006 enrollment: 5,720 full-time; 940 part-time. Men: 37%; women: 63%. **Ethnic makeup:** African American: 96%; White: 2%; International: 1%.

ADMISSIONS FACTS AND FIGURES

Phone: (601) 979-2100. **Email:** admappl@ccaix.jsums.edu. **Website:** http://www.jsums.edu. **Application deadlines for fall 2007:** Regular decision: August 1. Early decision: Not offered. Early action: Not offered. Admission cannot be deferred. Common application is accepted. **Admissions requirements/recommendations:** High school units required (recommended): English: 4 (4); Mathematics: 3 (4); Science: 3 (4); Foreign language: 1 (2); Social studies: 1 (2); History: 2 (2); Academic electives: 1 (2); Total units: 16 (21). Tests: The college uses SAT or ACT scores in admissions decisions. Either SAT or ACT required. For admission to the fall 2007 entering class, the school will accept: ACT with writing, ACT without writing. Campus visit: Neither required nor recommended. Admissions interview: Neither required nor recommended. Off-campus interview: Not available. **Factors that count in admissions decisions: Academic:** Secondary school record: Very important. Class rank: Very important. Letters of recommendation: Not considered. Standardized test scores: Very important. Essay: Not considered. *Nonacademic:* Interview: Important. Extracurricular activities: Considered. Talent/ability: Important. Character/personal qualities: Important. Alumni/ae relationship: Important. Geographical residence: Not considered. State residency: Not considered. Religious affiliation/commitment: Not considered. Minority status: Not considered. Volunteer work: Not considered. Work experience: Not considered. **Admissions statistics for the fall 2005 entering class:** Total applicants: 11,448. Total accepted: 4,485. Freshmen enrolled: 1,159; Overall acceptance rate: 39%. **Credentials of fall 2005 freshmen:** 70% ranked in the top half of their high school class. **First-year students submitting ACT scores:** 85%. Scores (25/75 percentile): English: N/A, Math: N/A, Composite: 16-20.

ACADEMICS

Year founded: 1877. **Academic calendar:** Semester. **Degrees offered:** bachelor's, master's, doctorate. **Most popular majors:** 7% industrial technology/technician, 6% education, 5% biology/biological sciences, 4% business administration and management, 4% elementary education and teaching. **Major fields of study:** agriculture, agriculture operations, and related sciences; architecture and related services; area, ethnic, cultural, and gender studies; biological and biomedical sciences; business, management, marketing, and related support services; communications technologies/technicians and support services; computer and information sciences and support services; construction trades; education; engineering; engineering technologies/technicians; English language and literature/letters; family and consumer sciences/human sciences; foreign languages, literatures, and linguistics; health professions and related clinical sciences; legal professions and studies; liberal arts and sciences studies, and humanities; library science; mathematics and statistics; mechanic and repair technologies/technicians; military technologies; multi/interdisciplinary studies; natural resources and conservation; parks, recreation, leisure, and fitness studies; personal and culinary services; philosophy and religious studies; physical sciences; precision production; psychology; security and protective services; social sciences; theology and religious vocations; transportation and materials moving; visual and performing arts. **Areas of required coursework:** arts/fine arts, humanities, computer literacy, mathematics, English (including composition), philosophy, foreign languages, sciences (biological or physical), history, social science. **Special academic programs:** cooperative (work-study plan) program, distance learning, double major, dual enrollment, exchange student program (domestic), honors program, independent study, internships, study abroad, teacher certificate program. **Teacher certification offered in:** early childhood, special education, elementary, secondary. **Reserve Officers Training Corps (ROTC):** Army ROTC: Offered on campus. **Faculty and instruction (2005-2006):** Total instructional faculty: 354 full-time, 83 part-time (54% men; 46% women; 81% minorities). Full-time faculty with Ph.D. or other terminal degree: 75%. Student/faculty ratio: 22/1. **Freshmen returning for sophomore year:** 76%. **Graduation rates:** Six-year: 33%.

COSTS AND FINANCIAL AID

Financial aid office: (601) 979-2227. **Expenses (2005-2006):** Tuition and fees 2005-2006: $3,964 in state, $8,872 out of state; room/board: $4,994. Estimated books and supplies: $1,300; transportation: $1,450; personal expenses: $2,718. **Financial aid:** Priority filing date for institution's financial aid form: April 15; deadline: April 15.

CAMPUS LIFE AND EXTRACURRICULAR ACTIVITIES

Campus housing available (% using): women's dorms (58%), men's dorms (42%), other housing options. Students who live in college-owned, operated, or affiliated housing: 29%. Activities include: choral groups, jazz band, marching band, pep band, radio station, student government, student newspaper, television station, yearbook. Number of fraternities: 3; sororities: 4. Proportion of men in fraternities: 1%; of women in sororities: 3%. **Sports program (2005-2006):** Member of NCAA I. *Men's intercollegiate varsity sports:* baseball, basketball, cross-country, football, golf, tennis, track and field (indoor), track and field (outdoor). *Women's intercollegiate varsity sports:* basketball, bowling, cross-country, golf, soccer, softball, tennis, track and field (indoor), track and field (outdoor), volleyball.

SERVICES AND FACILITIES

Basic services: nonremedial tutoring, placement service, day care, health service, health insurance. **Remedial assistance:** reading, math, writing, study skills. **Counseling services:** career, military, academic, psychological, birth control. **For learning-disabled students:** School does not offer a structured program with separate admission and additional fees. Services include: remedial math, remedial English, reading machines, remedial reading, tape recorders, other special classes, diagnostic testing service, note-taking services, special bookstore section, oral tests, learning center, readers, extended time for tests, tutors. **Library:** Number of titles: 440,956; number of current serial subscriptions: 1,186. **Information technology resources:** Students are not required to lease or own a computer. Number of campus computers available to all students: 400. School has a wireless network. Proportion of college-owned housing units wired for high-speed internet access: 100%. **Campus safety:** Security services offered: 24-hour foot-and-vehicle patrols, 24-hour emergency telephones, lighted pathways/sidewalks, controlled dormitory access (key, security card, etc).

TRANSFER AND INTERNATIONAL STUDENTS

Transfer students: May apply for admission for the following academic terms: Fall, Spring, Summer. Applicants need a minimum number of credits to apply. **International students:** Number of foreign undergraduates: 72 (1% of student body). Minimum TOEFL score required: 525 (paper); 197 (computer). Average TOEFL score: 525 (paper).

Millsaps College

- **Address:** 1701 N. State Street, Jackson, MS 39210-0001
- **Website:** http://www.millsaps.edu
- **Private; Religious affiliation:** United Methodist
- **Enrollment:** 1,039 full-time; 46 part-time

KEY STATS

✔ **U.S News College Ranking:** 82, Liberal Arts Colleges
✔ **ACT Score (25th/75th percentile):** 23-30
✔ **Tuition:** 2006-2007: $22,032

Selectivity: More selective	**Room/board:** $7,956
Acceptance rate: 82%	**Average debt:** $22,285
Student/faculty ratio: 12/1	**Proportion who borrowed:** 63%

UNDERGRADUATE STUDENT BODY STATS

2005-2006 enrollment: 1,039 full-time; 46 part-time. Men: 51%; women: 49%. **Ethnic makeup:** African American: 12%; Asian American: 3%; Hispanic: 1%; White: 82%; International: 1%. **Religious preference:** Roman Catholic: 17%; Protestant: 33%; Jewish: 1%; Hindu: 1%; Unknown: 28%; United Methodist: 19%; Other: 1%.

ADMISSIONS FACTS AND FIGURES

Phone: (601) 974-1050. **Email:** admissions@millsaps.edu. **Website:** http://www.millsaps.edu. **Application deadlines for fall 2007:** Regular decision: June 1. Early decision: Not offered. Early action: Send application by: December 1; Decision sent by: December 15. Admission can be deferred. **Application fee:** $25. Common application is accepted. **To apply online, go to:** http://www.millsaps.edu/admiss/apply/appinstructions.shtml. **Admissions requirements/recommendations:** High school units required (recommended): English: 4 (4); Mathematics: 3 (4); Science: 3 (4); Foreign language: (2); Social studies: 2 (2); History: 2 (2); Academic electives: (2); Total units: 14 (20). Tests: The college uses SAT or ACT scores in admissions decisions. Either SAT or ACT required. For admission to the fall 2007 entering class, the school will accept: ACT with writing; ACT without writing. Campus visit: Recommended. Admissions interview: Recommended. Off-campus interview: May be arranged. **Factors that count in admissions decisions:** *Academic:* Secondary school record: Very important. Class rank: Important. Letters of recommendation: Important. Standardized test scores: Very important. Essay: Important. *Nonacademic:* Interview: Important. Extracurricular activities: Important. Talent/ability: Important. Character/personal qualities: Very important. Alumni/ae relationship: Not considered. Geographical residence: Not considered. State residency: Not considered. Religious affiliation/commitment: Not considered. Minority status: Not considered. Volunteer work: Important. Work experience: Considered. **Other schools with the greatest overlap in applicants:** Hendrix College; Louisiana State University–Baton Rouge; Loyola University New Orleans; Mississippi State University. **Admissions statistics for the fall 2005 entering class:** Total applicants: 1,008. Total accepted: 829. Freshmen enrolled: 258; 60% were from out of state. Accepted through early-decision or early-action plans: 50%. Overall acceptance rate: 82%. Non-early acceptance rate: 75%. **Credentials of fall 2005 freshmen:** 38% ranked in the top 10 percent of their high school class; 63% were in the top 25 percent, and 87% were in the top half. (Proportion submitting class standing: 68%.) **Average high school grade point average:** 3.6. **First-year students who submitted SAT scores:** 45%. Scores (25/75 percentile): Verbal: 538-683, Math: 540-650, Combined: 1078-1333. **First-year students submitting ACT scores:** 86%. Scores (25/75 percentile): English: 24-31, Math: 21-28, Composite: 23-30.

ACADEMICS

Year founded: 1890. **Academic calendar:** Semester. **Degrees offered:** bachelor's, master's. **Most popular majors:** 14% psychology, 13% business, management, marketing, and related support services, 8% biology, 7% English language and literature/letters, 7% sociology. **Major fields of study:** area, ethnic, cultural, and gender studies; biological and biomedical sciences; business, management, marketing, and related support services; computer and information sciences and support services; education; English language and literature/letters; foreign languages, literatures, and linguistics; history; mathematics and statistics; multi/interdisciplinary studies; philosophy and religious studies; physical sciences; psychology; social sciences; visual and performing arts. **Areas of required coursework:** arts/fine arts, humanities, mathematics, English (including composition), sciences (biological or physical), history, social science, other. **Pre-professional programs:** pre-law, pre-dentistry, pre-medicine, pre-theology, pre-veterinary science, pre-optometry, pre-pharmacy, other. **Special academic programs (% participation):** accelerated program (2%), double major (10%), honors program (24%), independent study (25%), internships (68%), liberal arts/career combination (4%), student-designed major (1%), study abroad (29%), teacher certificate program (8%). **Teacher certification offered in:** special education, elementary, middle/junior high, secondary. **Reserve Officers Training Corps (ROTC):** Army ROTC: Offered at cooperating institution (Jackson State University). **Faculty and instruction (2005-2006):** Total instructional faculty: 92 full-time, 5 part-time (56% men; 44% women; 7% minorities). Full-time faculty with Ph.D. or other terminal degree: 97%. Student/faculty ratio: 12/1. Classes of fewer than 20 students: 64%; of 20 to 49 students: 36%. **Advanced Placement and International Baccalaureate credit:** AP tests may be used for: Credit and/or placement. Scores accepted: 4, 5. International Baccalaureate exams may be used for: Credit and/or placement. **Freshmen returning for sophomore year:** 82%. **Graduation rates:** Four-year: 63%; five-year: 69%; six-year: 71%. **Graduate study:** 43% of students pursue further study immediately upon graduation; 56% within one year; 70% within five years. Fields in which graduates pursue further study: Master of Business Administration (MBA), 16%; law, 23%; medicine, 9%; dentistry, 3%; engineering, 1%; theology (or the seminary), 5%; education, 9%; arts and sciences, 38%; veterinary medicine, 1%.

COSTS AND FINANCIAL AID

Financial aid office: (601) 974-1220. **Expenses (2006-2007):** Tuition and fees 2006-2007: $22,032; room/board: $7,956. Estimated books and supplies: $1,000; transportation: $500; personal expenses: $1,000. **Financial aid:** Priority filing date for institution's financial aid form: March 1. In 2005-2006, 69% of undergraduates applied for financial aid. Of those, 57% were determined to have financial need; 26% had their need fully met. Average financial aid package (proportion receiving): $17,774 (57%). Average amount of gift aid, such as scholarships or grants (proportion receiving): $13,773 (57%). Average amount of self-help aid, such as work study or loans (proportion receiving): $5,157 (45%). Average need-based loan (excluding PLUS or other private loans): $4,241. Among students who received need-based aid, the average percentage of need met: 80%. Among students who received aid based on merit, the average award (and the proportion receiv-

ing): $13,310 (38%). The average athletic scholarship (and the proportion receiving): $0 (0%). Average amount of debt of borrowers graduating in 2005: $22,285. Proportion who borrowed: 63%.

CAMPUS LIFE AND EXTRACURRICULAR ACTIVITIES

Campus housing available (% using): coed dorms (78%), women's dorms (10%), fraternity housing (12%). Students who live in college-owned, operated, or affiliated housing: 81%. **Student employment:** During the 2005-2006 academic year, 30% of undergraduates worked on campus. Average per-year earnings: $1,548. **Clubs and organizations:** Number of student organizations: 85. Activities include: choral groups, dance, drama/theater, literary magazine, music ensembles, musical theater, student government, student newspaper, student film society, yearbook. Number of fraternities: 6; sororities: 6. Proportion of men in fraternities: 54%; of women in sororities: 52%. Average proportion of students who stay on campus on weekends: 75%. **Sports program (2005-2006):** Member of NCAA III. *Men's intercollegiate varsity sports:* baseball, basketball, cross-country, football, golf, soccer, tennis. *Women's intercollegiate varsity sports:* basketball, cross-country, golf, soccer, softball, tennis, volleyball.

SERVICES AND FACILITIES

Basic services: nonremedial tutoring, placement service, health service. **Counseling services:** minority student, career, personal, academic, older student, birth control, religious, other. **For learning-disabled students:** School does not offer a structured program with separate admission and additional fees. Total undergraduates in learning-disabled program or receiving services: 50. Services include: tape recorders, other special classes, untimed tests, note-taking services, oral tests, learning center, readers, extended time for tests, tutors, priority seating, other. **Library:** Number of titles: 193,040; number of current serial subscriptions: 874. **Information technology resources:** Students are not required to lease or own a computer. Number of campus computers available to all students: 135. School has a wireless network. Approximate number of users that can be accommodated: 1,500. Proportion of college-owned housing units wired for high-speed internet access: 100%. **Campus safety:** Security services offered: 24-hour foot-and-vehicle patrols, late-night transport/escort service, 24-hour emergency telephones, lighted pathways/sidewalks, student patrols, controlled dormitory access (key, security card, etc).

TRANSFER AND INTERNATIONAL STUDENTS

Transfer students: May apply for admission for the following academic terms: Fall, Spring. Applicants need a minimum number of credits to apply. For fall 2005: Transfer applications received: 144. Transfer applicants offered admission: 96. Transfer applicants enrolled: 45. **International students:** Number of foreign undergraduates: 7 (1% of student body). Number of countries represented: 7. Minimum TOEFL score required: 550 (paper); 220 (computer).

Mississippi College

- **Address:** MC Box 4001, Clinton, MS 39058
- **Website:** http://www.mc.edu
- **Private; Religious affiliation:** Southern Baptist
- **Enrollment:** 2,229 full-time; 324 part-time

KEY STATS

✔ **U.S News College Ranking:** 29, Universities–Master's (South)
✔ **ACT Score (25th/75th percentile):** 20-26
✔ **Tuition:** 2006-2007: $12,288

Selectivity: More selective	**Room/board:** N/A
Acceptance rate: 57%	**Average debt:** $19,484
Student/faculty ratio: 11/1	**Proportion who borrowed:** 61%

UNDERGRADUATE STUDENT BODY STATS

2005-2006 enrollment: 2,229 full-time; 324 part-time. Men: 41%; women: 59%. **Ethnic makeup:** African American: 21%; Asian American: 1%; White: 75%; International: 2%. **Religious preference:** Roman Catholic: 2%; Protestant: 16%; Unknown: 26%; Southern Baptist: 54%; Other: 2%.

ADMISSIONS FACTS AND FIGURES

Phone: (601) 925-3800. **Email:** enrollment-services@mc.edu. **Website:** http://www.mc.edu. **Application deadlines for fall 2007:** Regular decision:

August 15. Early decision: Send application by: December 1; Decision sent by: December 15. Early action: Not offered. Admission can be deferred. Common application is accepted. **To apply online, go to:** http://www.mc.edu/admissions. **Admissions requirements/recommendations:** High school units required (recommended): English: (4); Mathematics: (3); Science: (3); Foreign language: (1); Social studies: (3); Academic electives: (5); Total units: (22). Tests: The college uses SAT or ACT scores in admissions decisions. Either SAT or ACT required. For admission to the fall 2007 entering class, the school will accept: ACT with writing, ACT without writing. Campus visit: Recommended. Admissions interview: Neither required nor recommended. Off-campus interview: May be arranged. **Factors that count in admissions decisions:** *Academic:* Secondary school record: Important. Class rank: Considered. Letters of recommendation: Considered. Standardized test scores: Very important. Essay: Very important. *Nonacademic:* Interview: Considered. Extracurricular activities: Important. Talent/ability: Considered. Character/personal qualities: Important. Alumni/ae relationship: Considered. Geographical residence: Not considered. State residency: Not considered. Religious affiliation/commitment: Not considered. Minority status: Not considered. Volunteer work: Considered. Work experience: Considered. **Other schools with the greatest overlap in applicants:** Belhaven College; Millsaps College; Mississippi State University; University of Mississippi; University of Southern Mississippi. **Admissions statistics for the fall 2005 entering class:** Total applicants: 2,038. Total accepted: 1,164. Freshmen enrolled: 394; 36% were from out of state. Accepted through early-decision or early-action plans: 46%. Overall acceptance rate: 57%. Early-decision acceptance rate: 97%. Non-early acceptance rate: 53%. **Credentials of fall 2005 freshmen:** 27% ranked in the top 10 percent of their high school class; 56% were in the top 25 percent, and 80% were in the top half. (Proportion submitting class standing: 74%.) **Average high school grade point average:** 3.3. **First-year students who submitted SAT scores:** 12%. Scores (25/75 percentile): Verbal: 520-620, Math: 500-620, Combined: 1020-1240. **First-year students submitting ACT scores:** 79%. Scores (25/75 percentile): English: 20-27, Math: 17-25, Composite: 20-26.

ACADEMICS

Year founded: 1826. **Academic calendar:** Semester. **Degrees offered:** bachelor's, post-bachelor's certificate, master's, first professional. **Most popular majors:** 10% business administration and management, 9% nursing/registered nurse training (R.N., A.S.N., B.S.N., M.S.N.), 8% elementary education and teaching, 7% psychology, 6% health/medical preparatory programs. **Major fields of study:** biological and biomedical sciences; business, management, marketing, and related support services; communication, journalism, and related programs; computer and information sciences and support services; education; English language and literature/letters; foreign languages, literatures, and linguistics; health professions and related clinical sciences; history; legal professions and studies; mathematics and statistics; parks, recreation, leisure, and fitness studies; philosophy and religious studies; physical sciences; psychology; public administration and social service professions; security and protective services; social sciences; theology and religious vocations; visual and performing arts. **Areas of required coursework:** arts/fine arts, humanities, computer literacy, mathematics, English (including composition), philosophy, sciences (biological or physical), history, social science, other. **Pre-professional programs:** pre-law, pre-dentistry, pre-medicine, pre-theology, pre-veterinary science, pre-optometry, pre-pharmacy, other. **Special academic programs:** accelerated program, double major, dual enrollment, honors program, independent study, internships, study abroad, teacher certificate program. **Teacher certification offered in:** early childhood, special education, elementary, secondary. **Reserve Officers Training Corps (ROTC):** Army ROTC: Offered at cooperating institution (Jackson State University). **Faculty and instruction (2005-2006):** Total instructional faculty: 161 full-time, 147 part-time (54% men; 46% women; 5% minorities). Full-time faculty with Ph.D. or other terminal degree: 73%. Student/faculty ratio: 11/1. Classes of fewer than 20 students: 48%; of 20 to 49 students: 51%; of 50 or more students: 1%. **Advanced Placement and International Baccalaureate credit:** AP tests may be used for: Credit only. Scores accepted: 3, 4. International Baccalaureate exams may be used for: Credit only. **Freshmen returning for sophomore year:** 76%. **Graduation rates:** Four-year: 52%; five-year: 64%; six-year: 66%.

COSTS AND FINANCIAL AID

Financial aid office: (601) 925-3319. **Expenses (2006-2007):** Tuition and fees 2006-2007: $12,288; room/board: N/A. Estimated books and supplies: $900; transportation: $1,575; personal expenses: $1,575. **Financial aid:** Priority filing date for institution's financial aid form: March 1. In 2005-2006, 88% of undergraduates applied for financial aid. Of those, 55% were determined to have financial need; 34% had their need fully met. Average

financial aid package (proportion receiving): $14,145 (55%). Average amount of gift aid, such as scholarships or grants (proportion receiving): $8,291 (41%). Average amount of self-help aid, such as work study or loans (proportion receiving): $6,882 (40%). Average need-based loan (excluding PLUS or other private loans): $6,706. Among students who received need-based aid, the average percentage of need met: 70%. Among students who received aid based on merit, the average award (and the proportion receiving): $8,210 (44%). The average athletic scholarship (and the proportion receiving): $0 (0%). Average amount of debt of borrowers graduating in 2005: $19,484. Proportion who borrowed: 61%.

CAMPUS LIFE AND EXTRACURRICULAR ACTIVITIES

Campus housing available (% using): women's dorms (52%), men's dorms (48%), special housing for disabled students. Students who live in college-owned, operated, or affiliated housing: 61%. **Student employment:** During the 2005-2006 academic year, 20% of undergraduates worked on campus. Average per-year earnings: $2,100. **Clubs and organizations:** Number of student organizations: 63. Activities include: choral groups, concert band, drama/theater, jazz band, literary magazine, marching band, music ensembles, musical theater, opera, radio station, student government, student newspaper, yearbook. Number of fraternities: 5; sororities: 4. Proportion of men in fraternities: 3%; of women in sororities: 6%. Average proportion of students who stay on campus on weekends: 50%. **Sports program (2005-2006):** Member of NCAA III. *Men's intercollegiate varsity sports:* baseball, basketball, cross-country, football, golf, soccer, tennis, track and field (indoor), track and field (outdoor). *Women's intercollegiate varsity sports:* basketball, cross-country, golf, soccer, softball, tennis, track and field (indoor), track and field (outdoor), volleyball.

SERVICES AND FACILITIES

Basic services: placement service, health service. **Remedial assistance:** math, study skills, other. **Counseling services:** career, academic, psychological. **For learning-disabled students:** School does not offer a structured program with separate admission and additional fees. Total undergraduates in learning-disabled program or receiving services: 40. Services include: remedial math, remedial English, tape recorders, note-taking services, oral tests, readers, extended time for tests, tutors, other. **Library:** Number of titles: 249,961; number of current serial subscriptions: 889. **Information technology resources:** Students are not required to lease or own a computer. Number of campus computers available to all students: 345. School has a wireless network. Approximate number of users that can be accommodated: 1,850. Proportion of college-owned housing units wired for high-speed internet access: 99%. **Campus safety:** Security services offered: 24-hour foot-and-vehicle patrols, late-night transport/escort service, 24-hour emergency telephones, lighted pathways/sidewalks, controlled dormitory access (key, security card, etc).

TRANSFER AND INTERNATIONAL STUDENTS

Transfer students: May apply for admission for the following academic terms: Fall, Spring, Summer. Applicants need a minimum number of credits to apply. For fall 2005: Transfer applications received: 907. Transfer applicants offered admission: 478. Transfer applicants enrolled: 371. **International students:** Number of foreign undergraduates: 39 (2% of student body). Number of countries represented: 4. Minimum TOEFL score required: 500 (paper); 173 (computer). Average TOEFL score: 500 (paper).

Mississippi State University

- **Address:** PO Box 6334, Mississippi State, MS 39762
- **Website:** http://www.msstate.edu
- **Public**
- **Enrollment:** 11,098 full-time; 1,457 part-time

KEY STATS

✔ **U.S News College Ranking:** third tier, National Universities
✔ **ACT Score (25th/75th percentile):** 19-27
✔ **Tuition:** 2005-2006: $4,312 in state, $9,772 out of state

Selectivity: More selective	**Room/board:** $5,030
Acceptance rate: 69%	**Average debt:** $18,230
Student/faculty ratio: 14/1	**Proportion who borrowed:** 49%

UNDERGRADUATE STUDENT BODY STATS

2005-2006 enrollment: 11,098 full-time; 1,457 part-time. Men: 52%; women: 48%. **Religious preference:** Roman Catholic: 8%; Protestant: 64%; Unknown: 26%; Other: 2%.

ADMISSIONS FACTS AND FIGURES

Phone: (662) 325-2224. **Email:** admit@admissions.msstate.edu. **Website:** http://www.msstate.edu. **Application deadlines for fall 2007:** Regular decision: Rolling. Early decision: Not offered. Early action: Not offered. Admission cannot be deferred. **Application fee:** $25. Common application is not accepted. **To apply online, go to:** http://www.admissions.msstate.edu. **Admissions requirements/recommendations:** High school units required (recommended): English: 4 (4); Mathematics: 3 (4); Science: 3 (4); Foreign language: 1 (2); Social studies: 1 (2); History: 2 (2); Academic electives: 1 (2); Total units: 16 (21). Tests: The college uses SAT or ACT scores in admissions decisions. Either SAT or ACT required. For admission to the fall 2007 entering class, the school will accept: ACT with writing, ACT without writing. Campus visit: Recommended. Admissions interview: Neither required nor recommended. Off-campus interview: May be arranged. **Factors that count in admissions decisions:** *Academic:* Secondary school record: Considered. Class rank: Important. Letters of recommendation: Not considered. Standardized test scores: Very important. Essay: Not considered. *Nonacademic:* Interview: Not considered. Extracurricular activities: Not considered. Talent/ability: Considered. Character/personal qualities: Not considered. Alumni/ae relationship: Not considered. Geographical residence: Not considered. State residency: Not considered. Religious affiliation/commitment: Not considered. Minority status: Not considered. Volunteer work: Not considered. Work experience: Not considered. **Admissions statistics for the fall 2005 entering class:** Total applicants: 5,778. Total accepted: 3,982. Freshmen enrolled: 1,966; 23% were from out of state. Overall acceptance rate: 69%. **Credentials of fall 2005 freshmen:** 26% ranked in the top 10 percent of their high school class; 55% were in the top 25 percent, and 82% were in the top half. (Proportion submitting class standing: 70%.) **Average high school grade point average:** 3.2. **First-year students submitting ACT scores:** 100%. Scores (25/75 percentile): English: 20-29, Math: 18-26, Composite: 19-27.

ACADEMICS

Year founded: 1878. **Academic calendar:** Semester. **Degrees offered:** bachelor's, master's, post-master's certificate, first professional, doctorate. **Most popular majors:** 26% business, management, marketing, and related support services, 15% education, 12% engineering, 6% agriculture, agriculture operations, and related sciences, 5% psychology. **Major fields of study:** agriculture, agriculture operations, and related sciences; architecture and related services; biological and biomedical sciences; business, management, marketing, and related support services; communication, journalism, and related programs; computer and information sciences and support services; education; engineering; engineering technologies/technicians; English language and literature/letters; family and consumer sciences/human sciences; foreign languages, literatures, and linguistics; health professions and related clinical sciences; history; liberal arts and sciences studies, and humanities; mathematics and statistics; multi/interdisciplinary studies; natural resources and conservation; philosophy and religious studies; physical sciences; psychology; public administration and social service professions; social sciences; visual and performing arts. **Areas of required coursework:** arts/fine arts, humanities, computer literacy, mathematics, English (including composition), sciences (biological or physical), history, social science, other. **Pre-professional programs:** pre-law, pre-dentistry, pre-medicine, pre-theology, pre-veterinary science, pre-optometry, pre-pharmacy, other. **Special academic programs (% participation):** accelerated program, cooperative (work-study plan) program (11.7%), distance learning (3%), double major (3.4%), dual enrollment (0%), English as a Second Language (ESL), exchange student program (domestic), honors program (2.3%), independent study (2%), internships, liberal arts/career combination, student-designed major, study abroad, teacher certificate program, weekend college. **Teacher certification offered in:** early childhood, special education, elementary, vo-tech, middle/junior high, secondary. **Cooperative education programs:** agriculture, art, business, computer science, education, engineering, health professions, home economics, humanities, natural science, social/behavioral science, technologies, vocational arts, other. **Reserve Officers Training Corps (ROTC):** Army ROTC: Offered on campus; Air Force ROTC: Offered on campus. **Faculty and instruction (2005-2006):** Total instructional faculty: 846 full-time, 155 part-time (64% men; 36% women; 13% minorities). Full-time faculty with Ph.D. or other terminal degree: 79%. Student/faculty ratio: 14/1. Classes of fewer than 20 students: 40%; of 20 to 49 students: 49%; of 50 or more students: 11%. **Advanced Placement and International**

Baccalaureate credit: AP tests may be used for: Credit only. Scores accepted: 3, 4, 5. International Baccalaureate exams may be used for: Credit only. **Freshmen returning for sophomore year:** 81%. **Graduation rates:** Four-year: 25%; five-year: 49%; six-year: 56%.

COSTS AND FINANCIAL AID

Financial aid office: (662) 325-2450. **Expenses (2005-2006):** Tuition and fees 2005-2006: $4,312 in state, $9,772 out of state; room/board: $5,030. Estimated books and supplies: $900; transportation: $1,030; personal expenses: $1,828. **Financial aid:** Priority filing date for institution's financial aid form: April 1. In 2005-2006, 63% of undergraduates applied for financial aid. Of those, 53% were determined to have financial need; 35% had their need fully met. Average financial aid package (proportion receiving): $7,653 (51%). Average amount of gift aid, such as scholarships or grants (proportion receiving): $3,767 (46%). Average amount of self-help aid, such as work study or loans (proportion receiving): $3,817 (40%). Average need-based loan (excluding PLUS or other private loans): $3,419. Among students who received need-based aid, the average percentage of need met: 64%. Among students who received aid based on merit, the average award (and the proportion receiving): $2,519 (16%). The average athletic scholarship (and the proportion receiving): $6,851 (3%). Average amount of debt of borrowers graduating in 2005: $18,230. Proportion who borrowed: 49%.

CAMPUS LIFE AND EXTRACURRICULAR ACTIVITIES

Campus housing available: women's dorms, men's dorms, sorority housing, fraternity housing, apartments for married students, apartment for single students, special housing for disabled students, other housing options. Students who live in college-owned, operated, or affiliated housing: 30%. **Student employment:** During the 2005-2006 academic year, 17% of undergraduates worked on campus. Average per-year earnings: $6,273. **Clubs and organizations:** Number of student organizations: 306. Activities include: choral groups, concert band, dance, drama/theater, jazz band, literary magazine, marching band, music ensembles, musical theater, pep band, radio station, student government, student newspaper, symphony orchestra, television station, yearbook. Number of fraternities: 18; sororities: 11. Proportion of men in fraternities: 17%; of women in sororities: 18%. Average proportion of students who stay on campus on weekends: 15%. **Sports program (2005-2006):** Member of NCAA I. *Men's intercollegiate varsity sports:* baseball, basketball, cross-country, football, golf, tennis, track and field (outdoor). *Women's intercollegiate varsity sports:* basketball, cross-country, golf, soccer, softball, tennis, track and field (indoor), track and field (outdoor), volleyball.

SERVICES AND FACILITIES

Basic services: nonremedial tutoring, day care, health service. **Remedial assistance:** reading, math, writing, study skills, other. **Counseling services:** minority student, career, military, personal, veteran student, academic, older student, psychological, birth control, religious. **For learning-disabled students:** School does not offer a structured program with separate admission and additional fees. Total undergraduates in learning-disabled program or receiving services: 78. Services include: reading machines, tape recorders, note-taking services, oral tests, learning center, readers, extended time for tests, priority registration, priority seating, texts on tape. **Library:** Number of titles: 2,074,652; number of current serial subscriptions: 16,552. **Information technology resources:** Students are not required to lease or own a computer. Number of campus computers available to all students: 2,000. School has a wireless network. Approximate number of users that can be accommodated: 5,000. Proportion of college-owned housing units wired for high-speed internet access: 100%. **Campus safety:** Security services offered: 24-hour foot-and-vehicle patrols, late-night transport/escort service, 24-hour emergency telephones, lighted pathways/sidewalks, student patrols, controlled dormitory access (key, security card, etc).

TRANSFER AND INTERNATIONAL STUDENTS

Transfer students: May apply for admission for the following academic terms: Fall, Spring, Summer. Applicants do not need a minimum number of credits to apply. For fall 2005: Transfer applications received: 2,807. Transfer applicants offered admission: 1,868. Transfer applicants enrolled: 1,428. **International students:** Number of countries represented: 35. Minimum TOEFL score required: 525 (paper); 195 (computer).

Mississippi University for Women

- **Address:** 1100 College Street, Columbus, MS 39701
- **Website:** http://www.muw.edu
- **Public**
- **Enrollment:** 1,674 full-time; 450 part-time

KEY STATS

✔ **U.S News College Ranking:** 31, Universities–Master's (South)
✔ **ACT Score (25th/75th percentile):** 18-25
✔ **Tuition:** 2006-2007: $3,690 in state, $8,914 out of state
  Selectivity: More selective   **Room/board:** $4,260
  Acceptance rate: 59%   **Average debt:** $13,800
  Student/faculty ratio: 12/1   **Proportion who borrowed:** 71%

UNDERGRADUATE STUDENT BODY STATS

2005-2006 enrollment: 1,674 full-time; 450 part-time. Men: 16%; women: 84%. **Ethnic makeup:** African American: 32%; Asian American: 1%; Hispanic: 1%; White: 65%; International: 1%.

ADMISSIONS FACTS AND FIGURES

Phone: (662) 329-7106. **Email:** admissions@muw.edu. **Website:** http://www.muw.edu. **Application deadlines for fall 2007:** Regular decision: Rolling. Early decision: Not offered. Early action: Not offered. Admission cannot be deferred. Common application is accepted. **Admissions requirements/recommendations:** High school units required (recommended): English: 4; Mathematics: 3; Science: 3; Social studies: 3; Academic electives: 2. Tests: The college uses SAT or ACT scores in admissions decisions. Either SAT or ACT required. For admission to the fall 2007 entering class, the school will accept: ACT with writing, ACT without writing. Campus visit: Recommended. Admissions interview: Neither required nor recommended. Off-campus interview: Not available. **Factors that count in admissions decisions:** *Academic:* Secondary school record: Very important. Class rank: Important. Letters of recommendation: Not considered. Standardized test scores: Very important. Essay: Not considered. *Nonacademic:* Interview: Not considered. Extracurricular activities: Not considered. Talent/ability: Not considered. Character/personal qualities: Not considered. Alumni/ae relationship: Not considered. Geographical residence: Not considered. State residency: Not considered. Religious affiliation/commitment: Not considered. Minority status: Not considered. Volunteer work: Not considered. Work experience: Not considered. **Other schools with the greatest overlap in applicants:** Mississippi State University; University of Mississippi; University of Southern Mississippi. **Admissions statistics for the fall 2005 entering class:** Total applicants: 720. Total accepted: 426. Freshmen enrolled: 226; 16% were from out of state. Overall acceptance rate: 59%. **Credentials of fall 2005 freshmen:** 34% ranked in the top 10 percent of their high school class; 61% were in the top 25 percent, and 85% were in the top half. (Proportion submitting class standing: 81%.) **Average high school grade point average:** 3.3. **First-year students who submitted SAT scores:** 2%. Scores (25/75 percentile): Verbal: 420-500, Math: 430-620, Combined: 850-1120. **First-year students submitting ACT scores:** 97%. Scores (25/75 percentile): English: 19-26, Math: 17-23, Composite: 18-25.

ACADEMICS

Year founded: 1884. **Academic calendar:** Semester. **Degrees offered:** associate, bachelor's, master's, post-master's certificate. **Most popular majors:** 17% nursing/registered nurse training (R.N., A.S.N., B.S.N., M.S.N.), 13% elementary education and teaching, 12% business administration and management, 7% family systems, 6% communication studies/speech communication and rhetoric. **Major fields of study:** biological and biomedical sciences; business, management, marketing, and related support services; communication, journalism, and related programs; education; English language and literature/letters; family and consumer sciences/human sciences; foreign languages, literatures, and linguistics; health professions and related clinical sciences; history; legal professions and studies; mathematics and statistics; parks, recreation, leisure, and fitness studies; personal and culinary services; physical sciences; psychology; social sciences; visual and performing arts. **Areas of required coursework:** arts/fine arts, humanities, computer literacy, mathematics, English (including composition), philosophy, sciences (biological or physical), history, social science, other. **Pre-professional programs:** pre-law, pre-dentistry, pre-medicine, pre-theology, pre-veterinary science, pre-optometry, pre-pharmacy, other. **Special academic programs:** cross-registration, distance learning, double major, dual enroll-

ment, honors program, independent study, internships, study abroad, teacher certificate program. **Teacher certification offered in:** early childhood, special education, elementary, middle/junior high, secondary. **Reserve Officers Training Corps (ROTC):** Army ROTC: Offered at cooperating institution (Mississippi State University); Air Force ROTC: Offered at cooperating institution (Mississippi State University). **Faculty and instruction (2005-2006):** Total instructional faculty: 135 full-time, 69 part-time (35% men; 65% women; 8% minorities). Full-time faculty with Ph.D. or other terminal degree: 59%. Student/faculty ratio: 12/1. Classes of fewer than 20 students: 53%; of 20 to 49 students: 46%; of 50 or more students: 1%. **Advanced Placement and International Baccalaureate credit:** AP tests may be used for: Credit and/or placement. Scores accepted: 3, 4, 5. International Baccalaureate exams may be used for: Credit and/or placement. **Freshmen returning for sophomore year:** 69%. **Graduation rates:** Four-year: 30%; five-year: 39%; six-year: 43%.

COSTS AND FINANCIAL AID

Financial aid office: (662) 329-7114. **Expenses (2006-2007):** Tuition and fees 2006-2007: $3,690 in state, $8,914 out of state; room/board: $4,260. Estimated books and supplies: $800; transportation: $1,500; personal expenses: $1,000. **Financial aid:** Priority filing date for institution's financial aid form: March 1. In 2005-2006, 79% of undergraduates applied for financial aid. Of those, 68% were determined to have financial need; 64% had their need fully met. Average financial aid package (proportion receiving): $7,084 (67%). Average amount of gift aid, such as scholarships or grants (proportion receiving): $3,822 (50%). Average amount of self-help aid, such as work study or loans (proportion receiving): $4,358 (49%). Average need-based loan (excluding PLUS or other private loans): $4,322. Among students who received need-based aid, the average percentage of need met: 65%. Among students who received aid based on merit, the average award (and the proportion receiving): $4,626 (18%). The average athletic scholarship (and the proportion receiving): $7,092 (0%). Average amount of debt of borrowers graduating in 2005: $13,800. Proportion who borrowed: 71%.

CAMPUS LIFE AND EXTRACURRICULAR ACTIVITIES

Campus housing available (% using): women's dorms (64%), men's dorms (12%), special housing for disabled students (1%), other housing options (23%). Students who live in college-owned, operated, or affiliated housing: 28%. **Student employment:** During the 2005-2006 academic year, 20% of undergraduates worked on campus. Average per-year earnings: $3,200. **Clubs and organizations:** Number of student organizations: 96. Activities include: choral groups, dance, drama/theater, literary magazine, music ensembles, musical theater, radio station, student government, student newspaper. Number of fraternities: 2; sororities: 15. Proportion of men in fraternities: 9%; of women in sororities: 15%. Average proportion of students who stay on campus on weekends: 50%. **Sports program (2005-2006):** Member of NCAA II. *Women's intercollegiate varsity sports:* basketball, softball, tennis, volleyball.

SERVICES AND FACILITIES

Basic services: nonremedial tutoring, women's center, placement service, day care, health service, health insurance. **Remedial assistance:** reading, math, writing, study skills. **Counseling services:** minority student, career, military, personal, veteran student, academic, older student, psychological, birth control, religious. **For learning-disabled students:** School does not offer a structured program with separate admission and additional fees. Total undergraduates in learning-disabled program or receiving services: 5. Services include: remedial math, remedial English, remedial reading, tape recorders, note-taking services, oral tests, learning center, readers, extended time for tests, tutors, priority seating. **Library:** Number of titles: 12,601; number of current serial subscriptions: 11,535. **Information technology resources:** Students are not required to lease or own a computer. Number of campus computers available to all students: 800. School has a wireless network. Approximate number of users that can be accommodated: 3,500. Proportion of college-owned housing units wired for high-speed internet access: 100%. **Campus safety:** Security services offered: 24-hour foot-and-vehicle patrols, late-night transport/escort service, 24-hour emergency telephones, lighted pathways/sidewalks, student patrols, controlled dormitory access (key, security card, etc.).

TRANSFER AND INTERNATIONAL STUDENTS

Transfer students: May apply for admission for the following academic terms: Fall, Spring, Summer. Applicants need a minimum number of credits to apply. For fall 2005: Transfer applications received: 726. Transfer applicants offered admission: 465. Transfer applicants enrolled: 319. **International students:** Number of foreign undergraduates: 24 (1% of student body). Number of countries represented: 18. Minimum TOEFL score required: 525 (paper); 197 (computer).

Mississippi Valley State University

- **Address:** 14000 Highway 82 W, Itta Bena, MS 38941-1400
- **Website:** http://www.mvsu.edu
- **Public**
- **Enrollment:** 2,434 full-time; 314 part-time

KEY STATS

✔ **U.S News College Ranking:** third tier, Comp. Coll.–Bachelor's (South)
✔ **ACT Score (25th/75th percentile):** 15-18
✔ **Tuition:** 2005-2006: $3,832 in state, $8,840 out of state

Selectivity: Less selective	**Room/board:** $3,506
Acceptance rate: 25%	**Average debt:** N/A
Student/faculty ratio: 22/1	**Proportion who borrowed:** N/A

UNDERGRADUATE STUDENT BODY STATS

2005-2006 enrollment: 2,434 full-time; 314 part-time. Men: 31%; women: 69%. **Ethnic makeup:** African American: 94%; White: 6%.

ADMISSIONS FACTS AND FIGURES

Phone: (662) 254-3344. **Email:** admsn@mvsu.edu. **Website:** http://www.mvsu.edu. **Application deadlines for fall 2007:** Regular decision: August 1. Early decision: Not offered. Early action: Not offered. Admission can be deferred. Common application is not accepted. **Admissions requirements/recommendations:** High school units required (recommended): English: 4; Mathematics: 3; Science: 3; Foreign language: 1; Social studies: 3; History: 0; Academic electives: 2; Total units: 16 (18). Tests: The college uses SAT or ACT scores in admissions decisions. ACT required. For admission to the fall 2007 entering class, the school will accept: ACT with writing, ACT without writing. Admissions interview: Recommended. Off-campus interview: May be arranged. **Factors that count in admissions decisions:** *Academic:* Secondary school record: Very important. Class rank: Very important. Letters of recommendation: Considered. Standardized test scores: Very important. Essay: Not considered. *Nonacademic:* Interview: Considered. Extracurricular activities: Considered. Talent/ability: Considered. Character/personal qualities: Not considered. Alumni/ae relationship: Not considered. Geographical residence: Not considered. State residency: Very important. Religious affiliation/commitment: Not considered. Minority status: Not considered. Volunteer work: Not considered. Work experience: Not considered. **Admissions statistics for the fall 2005 entering class:** Total applicants: 4,832. Total accepted: 1,226. Freshmen enrolled: 407; 22% were from out of state. Overall acceptance rate: 25%. **Credentials of fall 2005 freshmen:** 10% ranked in the top 10 percent of their high school class; 23% were in the top 25 percent, and 75% were in the top half. **Average high school grade point average:** 2.7. **First-year students submitting ACT scores:** 83%. Scores (25/75 percentile): English: N/A, Math: N/A, Composite: 15-18.

ACADEMICS

Year founded: 1950. **Academic calendar:** Semester. **Degrees offered:** bachelor's, master's. **Most popular majors:** 14% kindergarten/preschool education and teaching, 14% social work, 9% business administration and management, 9% history, 8% physical education teaching and coaching. **Major fields of study:** biological and biomedical sciences; business, management, marketing, and related support services; communication, journalism, and related programs; computer and information sciences and support services; education; engineering technologies/technicians; English language and literature/letters; health professions and related clinical sciences; mathematics and statistics; physical sciences; public administration and social service professions; security and protective services; social sciences; visual and performing arts. **Areas of required coursework:** arts/fine arts, mathematics, English (including composition), sciences (biological or physical), history, social science. **Special academic programs:** cooperative (work-study plan) program, distance learning, honors program, independent study, internships, teacher certificate program. **Teacher certification offered in:** early childhood, special education, elementary, secondary. **Reserve Officers Training Corps (ROTC):** Army ROTC: Offered on campus. **Faculty and instruction (2005-2006):** Total instructional faculty: 117 full-time, 66 part-time (49% men; 51% women; 84% minorities). Full-time faculty with Ph.D. or other terminal degree: 61%. Student/faculty ratio: 22/1. Classes of fewer

than 20 students: 47%; of 20 to 49 students: 46%; of 50 or more students: 7%. **Freshmen returning for sophomore year:** 66%. **Graduation rates:** Four-year: 19%; five-year: 34%; six-year: 38%.

COSTS AND FINANCIAL AID

Financial aid office: (662) 254-3335. **Expenses (2005-2006):** Tuition and fees 2005-2006: $3,832 in state, $8,840 out of state; room/board: $3,506. Estimated books and supplies: $1,000.

CAMPUS LIFE AND EXTRACURRICULAR ACTIVITIES

Campus housing available: women's dorms, men's dorms, apartments for married students, apartment for single students. Students who live in college-owned, operated, or affiliated housing: 28%. **Clubs and organizations:** Number of student organizations: 44. Activities include: choral groups, concert band, dance, drama/theater, marching band, music ensembles, radio station, student government, student newspaper, yearbook. Number of fraternities: 5; sororities: 4. **Sports program (2005-2006):** Member of NCAA I. *Men's intercollegiate varsity sports:* baseball, basketball, cross-country, football, golf, tennis, track and field (indoor), track and field (outdoor). *Women's intercollegiate varsity sports:* basketball, bowling, cross-country, golf, soccer, softball, tennis, track and field (indoor), track and field (outdoor), volleyball.

SERVICES AND FACILITIES

Basic services: placement service, health service. **Remedial assistance:** reading, math, writing, study skills. **Counseling services:** career, personal. **Library:** Number of titles: 101,109; number of current serial subscriptions: 347. **Information technology resources:** Students are not required to lease or own a computer. Number of campus computers available to all students: 250. School does not have a wireless network. **Campus safety:** Security services offered: 24-hour emergency telephones, lighted pathways/sidewalks, controlled dormitory access (key, security card, etc).

TRANSFER AND INTERNATIONAL STUDENTS

Transfer students: May apply for admission for the following academic terms: Fall, Spring, Summer. Applicants need a minimum number of credits to apply. For fall 2005: Transfer applicants enrolled: 220. **International students:** Number of foreign undergraduates: 0. Minimum TOEFL score required: 525 (paper). Average TOEFL score: 560 (paper).

Rust College

- **Address:** 150 Rust Avenue, Holly Springs, MS 38635
- **Website:** http://www.rustcollege.edu
- **Private; Religious affiliation:** Methodist
- **Enrollment:** 816 full-time; 154 part-time

KEY STATS

✔ **U.S News College Ranking:** fourth tier, Comp. Coll.–Bachelor's (South)
✔ **ACT Score (25th/75th percentile):** 14-18
✔ **Tuition:** 2005-2006: $6,060

Selectivity: Less selective	**Room/board:** $2,600
Acceptance rate: 44%	**Average debt:** N/A
Student/faculty ratio: N/A	**Proportion who borrowed:** N/A

UNDERGRADUATE STUDENT BODY STATS

2005-2006 enrollment: 816 full-time; 154 part-time. Men: 39%; women: 61%. **Ethnic makeup:** African American: 92%; White: 1%; International: 7%. **Religious preference:** Roman Catholic: 2%; Protestant: 70%; Muslim: 1%; No preference: 27%.

ADMISSIONS FACTS AND FIGURES

Phone: (662) 252-8000. **Email:** admissions@rustcollege.edu. **Website:** http://www.rustcollege.edu. **Application deadlines for fall 2007:** Regular decision: Rolling; decision sent by August 15. Early decision: Not offered. Early action: Not offered. Admission can be deferred. **Application fee:** $10. Common application is not accepted. **Admissions requirements/recommendations:** High school units required (recommended): English: 4; Mathematics: 3; Science: 3; Foreign language: 0; Social studies: 3; Academic electives: 6; Total units: 19. Tests: The college uses SAT or ACT scores in admissions decisions. Neither SAT nor ACT required. Campus visit: Recommended. Admissions interview: Recommended. **Factors that count in admissions decisions:** *Academic:* Secondary school record: Important. Class rank: Important. Letters of recommendation: Very important. Standardized test scores: Important. Essay: Not considered. *Nonacademic:* Interview: Considered. Extracurricular activities: Considered. Talent/ability: Very important. Character/personal qualities: Important. Alumni/ae relationship: Not considered. Geographical residence: Not considered. State residency: Considered. Religious affiliation/commitment: Not considered. Minority status: Not considered. Volunteer work: Not considered. Work experience: Not considered. **Admissions statistics for the fall 2005 entering class:** Total applicants: 3,678. Total accepted: 1,613. Freshmen enrolled: 256; Overall acceptance rate: 44%.

ACADEMICS

Year founded: 1866. **Academic calendar:** Semester. **Degrees offered:** associate, bachelor's. **Most popular majors:** 19% computer science, 16% biology/biological sciences, 12% broadcast journalism, 12% business administration and management, 7% English language and literature/letters. **Major fields of study:** biological and biomedical sciences; business, management, marketing, and related support services; communication, journalism, and related programs; computer and information sciences and support services; education; English language and literature/letters; mathematics and statistics; physical sciences; public administration and social service professions; social sciences; visual and performing arts. **Areas of required coursework:** arts/fine arts, humanities, computer literacy, mathematics, English (including composition), philosophy, sciences (biological or physical), history, social science. **Special academic programs (% participation):** double major (0%), honors program (12%), independent study, internships (47%), liberal arts/career combination, study abroad (3%), teacher certificate program (3%). **Teacher certification offered in:** early childhood, elementary. **Faculty and instruction (2005-2006):** Total instructional faculty: 42 full-time, 3 part-time (62% men; 38% women; 80% minorities). Full-time faculty with Ph.D. or other terminal degree: 45%. **Advanced Placement and International Baccalaureate credit:** AP tests may be used for: Credit only. Scores accepted: 2, 3, 4, 5. International Baccalaureate exams may be used for: Credit only. **Freshmen returning for sophomore year:** 57%. **Graduation rates:** Four-year: 12%; five-year: 21%; six-year: 30%.

COSTS AND FINANCIAL AID

Financial aid office: (662) 252-8000. **Expenses (2005-2006):** Tuition and fees 2005-2006: $6,060; room/board: $2,600. Estimated books and supplies: $500. **Financial aid:** Priority filing date for institution's financial aid form: May 1.

CAMPUS LIFE AND EXTRACURRICULAR ACTIVITIES

Campus housing available (% using): women's dorms (64%), men's dorms (35%), apartments for married students (1%). **Student employment:** During the 2005-2006 academic year, 54% of undergraduates worked on campus. Average per-year earnings: $1,152. **Clubs and organizations:** Number of student organizations: 38. Activities include: choral groups, concert band, dance, drama/theater, marching band, music ensembles, pep band, radio station, student government, student newspaper, television station, yearbook. Number of fraternities: 4; sororities: 3. Average proportion of students who stay on campus on weekends: 50%. **Sports program (2005-2006):** Member of NCAA III. *Men's intercollegiate varsity sports:* baseball, basketball, cross-country, soccer, tennis, track and field (outdoor), volleyball. *Women's intercollegiate varsity sports:* basketball, cross-country, softball, tennis, track and field (outdoor), volleyball.

SERVICES AND FACILITIES

Basic services: day care, health service. **Remedial assistance:** reading, math, writing, study skills, other. **Counseling services:** minority student, career, academic, religious. **For learning-disabled students:** Services include: remedial math, remedial English, diagnostic testing service, tutors. **Information technology resources:** Students are not required to lease or own a computer. Number of campus computers available to all students: 220. School does not have a wireless network. **Campus safety:** Security services offered: 24-hour foot-and-vehicle patrols, late-night transport/escort service, 24-hour emergency telephones, lighted pathways/sidewalks, controlled dormitory access (key, security card, etc).

TRANSFER AND INTERNATIONAL STUDENTS

Transfer students: May apply for admission for the following academic terms: Fall, Spring, Summer. Applicants need a minimum number of credits to apply. **International students:** Number of foreign undergraduates: 47 (7% of student body). Minimum TOEFL score required: 540 (paper). Average TOEFL score: 570 (paper).

Tougaloo College

■ **Address:** 500 W. County Line Road, Tougaloo, MS 39174
■ **Website:** http://www.tougaloo.edu
■ **Private; Religious affiliation:** Christian Church (Disciples of Christ)
■ **Enrollment:** 894 full-time; 39 part-time

KEY STATS
✔ **U.S News College Ranking:** fourth tier, Liberal Arts Colleges
✔ **ACT Score:** 20
✔ **Tuition:** 2006-2007: $9,755

Selectivity: Selective	**Room/board:** $5,270
Acceptance rate: 20%	**Average debt:** $20,000
Student/faculty ratio: 11/1	**Proportion who borrowed:** 85%

UNDERGRADUATE STUDENT BODY STATS

2005-2006 enrollment: 894 full-time; 39 part-time. Men: 31%; women: 69%. **Ethnic makeup:** African American: 99%; International: 1%.

ADMISSIONS FACTS AND FIGURES

Phone: (601) 977-7764. **Email:** information@mail.tougaloo.edu. **Website:** http://www.tougaloo.edu. **Application deadlines for fall 2007:** Regular decision: Rolling. Early decision: Not offered. Early action: Send application by: November 1; Decision sent by: December 1. Admission can be deferred. **Application fee:** $25. Common application is accepted. **To apply online, go to:** http://www.tougaloo.edu/content/Admissions/application.pdf. **Admissions requirements/recommendations:** High school units required (recommended): English: 3 (4); Mathematics: 2 (4); Science: 2 (2); Foreign language: (2); Social studies: (2); History: 2; Academic electives: 5; Total units: 16 (14). Tests: The college uses SAT or ACT scores in admissions decisions. Either SAT or ACT required. For admission to the fall 2007 entering class, the school will accept: ACT with writing, ACT without writing. Campus visit: Recommended. Admissions interview: Recommended. Off-campus interview: May be arranged. **Factors that count in admissions decisions:** *Academic:* Secondary school record: Very important. Class rank: Very important. Letters of recommendation: Very important. Standardized test scores: Important. Essay: Not considered. *Nonacademic:* Interview: Important. Extracurricular activities: Very important. Talent/ability: Very important. Character/personal qualities: Very important. Alumni/ae relationship: Not considered. Geographical residence: Not considered. State residency: Not considered. Religious affiliation/commitment: Not considered. Minority status: Not considered. Volunteer work: Very important. Work experience: Important. **Other schools with the greatest overlap in applicants:** Alcorn State University; Dillard University; Jackson State University; Mississippi State University; Xavier University of Louisiana. **Admissions statistics for the fall 2005 entering class:** Total applicants: 5,502. Total accepted: 1,108. Freshmen enrolled: 208; 26% were from out of state. Overall acceptance rate: 20%. Non-early acceptance rate: 20%. **Credentials of fall 2005 freshmen:** 25% ranked in the top 10 percent of their high school class; 40% were in the top 25 percent, and 80% were in the top half. (Proportion submitting class standing: 90%.) **Average high school grade point average:** 3.1. **First-year students who submitted SAT scores:** 33%. Scores (25/75 percentile): Verbal: N/A, Math: N/A, Combined: N/A. **First-year students submitting ACT scores:** 67%. Scores (25/75 percentile): English: N/A, Math: N/A, Composite: N/A.

ACADEMICS

Year founded: 1869. **Academic calendar:** Semester. **Degrees offered:** associate, bachelor's. **Most popular majors:** 35% social sciences, 17% English language and literature/letters, 15% physical sciences, 14% education, 11% biological and biomedical sciences. **Major fields of study:** biological and biomedical sciences; business, management, marketing, and related support services; communication, journalism, and related programs; education; English language and literature/letters; history; legal professions and studies; liberal arts and sciences studies, and humanities; psychology; social sciences. **Areas of required coursework:** arts/fine arts, humanities, computer literacy, mathematics, English (including composition), philosophy, foreign languages, sciences (biological or physical), history, social science, other. **Pre-professional programs:** pre-law, pre-dentistry, pre-medicine, pre-veterinary science, pre-pharmacy. **Special academic programs (% participation):** double major, dual enrollment, exchange student program (domestic), honors program, independent study, internships (50%), liberal arts/career combination, study abroad, teacher certificate program. **Teacher certification offered in:** early childhood, special education, elementary, middle/junior high, secondary. **Cooperative education programs:** art, business, computer science, education, health professions, humanities, natural science, social/behavioral science. **Reserve Officers Training Corps (ROTC):** Army ROTC: Offered at cooperating institution (Jackson State University); Air Force ROTC: Offered at cooperating institution (Jackson State University). **Faculty and instruction (2005-2006):** Total instructional faculty: 80 full-time, 6 part-time (43% men; 57% women; 78% minorities). Full-time faculty with Ph.D. or other terminal degree: 56%. Student/faculty ratio: 11/1. **Advanced Placement and International Baccalaureate credit:** AP tests may be used for: Credit and/or placement. Scores accepted: 3, 4, 5. International Baccalaureate exams may be used for: Credit only. **Freshmen returning for sophomore year:** 77%. **Graduation rates:** Six-year: 48%. **Graduate study:** 66% of students pursue further study immediately upon graduation; 15% within one year; 10% within five years. Fields in which graduates pursue further study: Master of Business Administration (MBA), 15%; law, 20%; medicine, 15%; dentistry, 10%; engineering, 10%; education, 10%; arts and sciences, 20%.

COSTS AND FINANCIAL AID
Financial aid office: (601) 977-7769. **Expenses (2006-2007):** Tuition and fees 2006-2007: $9,755; room/board: $5,270. Estimated books and supplies: $1,300; transportation: $2,000; personal expenses: $2,600. **Financial aid:** Priority filing date for institution's financial aid form: January 15. In 2005-2006, 96% of undergraduates applied for financial aid. Of those, 75% were determined to have financial need; 22% had their need fully met. Average financial aid package (proportion receiving): $4,775 (75%). Average amount of gift aid, such as scholarships or grants (proportion receiving): $2,500 (23%). Average amount of self-help aid, such as work study or loans (proportion receiving): $3,800 (51%). Average need-based loan (excluding PLUS or other private loans): $5,000. Among students who received need-based aid, the average percentage of need met: 50%. Among students who received aid based on merit, the average award (and the proportion receiving): $5,000 (4%). The average athletic scholarship (and the proportion receiving): $7,107 (5%). Average amount of debt of borrowers graduating in 2005: $20,000. Proportion who borrowed: 85%.

CAMPUS LIFE AND EXTRACURRICULAR ACTIVITIES
Campus housing available (% using): women's dorms (55%), men's dorms (45%). Students who live in college-owned, operated, or affiliated housing: 65%. **Student employment:** During the 2005-2006 academic year, 10% of undergraduates worked on campus. Average per-year earnings: $3,000. **Clubs and organizations:** Number of student organizations: 52. Activities include: choral groups, dance, drama/theater, jazz band, literary magazine, music ensembles, musical theater, pep band, student government, student newspaper, student film society, yearbook. Number of fraternities: 4; sororities: 4. Proportion of men in fraternities: 20%; of women in sororities: 20%. Average proportion of students who stay on campus on weekends: 50%. **Sports program (2005-2006):** Member of NAIA. *Men's intercollegiate varsity sports:* basketball, cross-country, golf, tennis. *Women's intercollegiate varsity sports:* basketball, cross-country, tennis.

SERVICES AND FACILITIES
Basic services: nonremedial tutoring, placement service, health service, health insurance. **Remedial assistance:** reading, math, writing, study skills. **Counseling services:** minority student, career, military, personal, veteran student, academic, older student, psychological, religious. **For learning-disabled students:** School does not offer a structured program with separate admission and additional fees. Total undergraduates in learning-disabled program or receiving services: 5. Services include: remedial math, remedial English, remedial reading, note-taking services, oral tests, learning center, readers, extended time for tests, tutors, priority registration, priority seating, exams on tape or computer, other testing accomodations. **Library:** Number of titles: 190,258; number of current serial subscriptions: 221. **Information technology resources:** Students are not required to lease or own a computer. Number of campus computers available to all students: 200. School does not have a wireless network. Proportion of college-owned housing units wired for high-speed internet access: 75%. **Campus safety:** Security services offered: 24-hour foot-and-vehicle patrols, late-night transport/escort service, 24-hour emergency telephones, lighted pathways/sidewalks, student patrols, controlled dormitory access (key, security card, etc).

TRANSFER AND INTERNATIONAL STUDENTS
Transfer students: May apply for admission for the following academic terms: Fall, Spring. Applicants do not need a minimum number of credits to apply. For fall 2005: Transfer applications received: 49. Transfer applicants enrolled: 49. **International students:** Number of foreign undergradu-

ates: 6 (1% of student body). Minimum TOEFL score required: 500 (paper); 250 (computer). Average TOEFL score: 500 (paper).

University of Mississippi

- **Address:** PO Box 1848, University, MS 38677-1848
- **Website:** http://www.olemiss.edu
- **Public**
- **Enrollment:** 11,143 full-time; 1,054 part-time

KEY STATS
✔ **U.S News College Ranking:** third tier, National Universities
✔ **ACT Score (25th/75th percentile):** 20-26
✔ **Tuition:** 2006-2007: $4,602 in state, $10,566 out of state

Selectivity: Selective	**Room/board:** $6,952
Acceptance rate: 73%	**Average debt:** N/A
Student/faculty ratio: 19/1	**Proportion who borrowed:** N/A

UNDERGRADUATE STUDENT BODY STATS
2005-2006 enrollment: 11,143 full-time; 1,054 part-time. Men: 47%; women: 53%. **Ethnic makeup:** African American: 13%; Asian American: 1%; Hispanic: 1%; White: 84%; International: 1%.

ADMISSIONS FACTS AND FIGURES
Phone: (662) 915-7226. **Email:** admissions@olemiss.edu. **Website:** http://www.olemiss.edu. **Application deadlines for fall 2007:** Regular decision: July 20. Early decision: Not offered. Early action: Not offered. Admission cannot be deferred. **Application fee:** $25. Common application is not accepted. **Admissions requirements/recommendations:** High school units required (recommended): English: 4; Mathematics: 3 (4); Science: 3 (4); Foreign language: 1 (2); Social studies: 1 (2); History: 2; Academic electives: 1; Total units: 15. Tests: The college uses SAT or ACT scores in admissions decisions. Neither SAT nor ACT required. For admission to the fall 2007 entering class, the school will accept: ACT with writing, ACT without writing. Campus visit: Recommended. **Factors that count in admissions decisions:** *Academic:* Secondary school record: Very important. Class rank: Important. Letters of recommendation: Not considered. Standardized test scores: Important. Essay: Not considered. *Nonacademic:* Interview: Not considered. Extracurricular activities: Not considered. Talent/ability: Considered. Character/personal qualities: Not considered. Alumni/ae relationship: Considered. Geographical residence: Not considered. State residency: Considered. Religious affiliation/commitment: Not considered. Minority status: Not considered. Volunteer work: Not considered. Work experience: Not considered. **Admissions statistics for the fall 2005 entering class:** Total applicants: 6,763. Total accepted: 4,942. Freshmen enrolled: 2,192; Overall acceptance rate: 73%. **Credentials of fall 2005 freshmen:** 47% were in the top 25 percent, and 74% were in the top half. (Proportion submitting class standing: 63%.) **Average high school grade point average:** 3.3. **First-year students submitting ACT scores:** 79%. Scores (25/75 percentile): English: 20-28, Math: 18-25, Composite: 20-26.

ACADEMICS
Year founded: 1844. **Academic calendar:** Semester. **Degrees offered:** bachelor's, master's, first professional, doctorate. **Most popular majors:** 8% marketing/marketing management, 7% elementary education and teaching, 6% accounting, 5% family and consumer sciences/human sciences, 5% finance. **Major fields of study:** architecture and related services; area, ethnic, cultural, and gender studies; biological and biomedical sciences; business, management, marketing, and related support services; communication, journalism, and related programs; computer and information sciences and support services; education; engineering; English language and literature/letters; family and consumer sciences/human sciences; foreign languages, literatures, and linguistics; health professions and related clinical sciences; history; legal professions and studies; liberal arts and sciences studies, and humanities; mathematics and statistics; parks, recreation, leisure, and fitness studies; philosophy and religious studies; physical sciences; psychology; public administration and social service professions; security and protective services; social sciences; visual and performing arts. **Areas of required coursework:** arts/fine arts, humanities, mathematics, English (including composition), sciences (biological or physical), social science. **Pre-professional programs:** pre-law, pre-dentistry, pre-medicine, pre-veterinary science, pre-optometry, pre-pharmacy, other. **Special academic programs:** accelerated

program, cooperative (work-study plan) program, distance learning, double major, English as a Second Language (ESL), honors program, independent study, internships, study abroad, teacher certificate program. **Teacher certification offered in:** special education, elementary, secondary. **Cooperative education programs:** engineering. **Reserve Officers Training Corps (ROTC):** Army ROTC: Offered on campus; Navy ROTC: Offered on campus; Air Force ROTC: Offered on campus. **Faculty and instruction (2005-2006):** Total instructional faculty: 622 full-time, 224 part-time (59% men; 41% women). Student/faculty ratio: 19/1. Classes of fewer than 20 students: 44%; of 20 to 49 students: 41%; of 50 or more students: 15%. **Advanced Placement and International Baccalaureate credit:** Scores accepted: 3, 4, 5. **Freshmen returning for sophomore year:** 77%. **Graduation rates:** Four-year: 34%; five-year: 53%; six-year: 56%.

COSTS AND FINANCIAL AID

Financial aid office: (662) 915-7175. **Expenses (2006-2007):** Tuition and fees 2006-2007: $4,602 in state, $10,566 out of state; room/board: $6,952.

CAMPUS LIFE AND EXTRACURRICULAR ACTIVITIES

Campus housing available: women's dorms, men's dorms, sorority housing, fraternity housing, apartments for married students. **Clubs and organizations:** Number of student organizations: 200. Activities include: choral groups, concert band, dance, drama/theater, jazz band, literary magazine, marching band, music ensembles, musical theater, pep band, radio station, student government, student newspaper, symphony orchestra, television station, yearbook. Number of fraternities: 19; sororities: 13. Proportion of men in fraternities: 27%; of women in sororities: 33%. **Sports program (2005-2006):** Member of NCAA I. *Men's intercollegiate varsity sports:* baseball, basketball, cross-country, football, golf, tennis, track and field (indoor), track and field (outdoor). *Women's intercollegiate varsity sports:* basketball, cross-country, golf, riflery, soccer, softball, tennis, track and field (indoor), track and field (outdoor), volleyball.

SERVICES AND FACILITIES

Basic services: women's center, health service, health insurance. **Remedial assistance:** reading, math, writing, other. **Counseling services:** personal, academic, psychological. **For learning-disabled students:** School does not offer a structured program with separate admission and additional fees. **Information technology resources:** Students are not required to lease or own a computer. Number of campus computers available to all students: 700. School has a wireless network. Approximate number of users that can be accommodated: 1,000. Proportion of college-owned housing units wired for high-speed internet access: 100%. **Campus safety:** Security services offered: 24-hour foot-and-vehicle patrols, late-night transport/escort service, 24-hour emergency telephones, lighted pathways/sidewalks, controlled dormitory access (key, security card, etc).

TRANSFER AND INTERNATIONAL STUDENTS

Transfer students: May apply for admission for the following academic terms: Fall, Spring, Summer. Applicants need a minimum number of credits to apply. For fall 2005: Transfer applications received: 2,001. Transfer applicants offered admission: 1,486. Transfer applicants enrolled: 1,100. **International students:** Number of foreign undergraduates: 111 (1% of student body). Minimum TOEFL score required: 193 (computer). Average TOEFL score: 523 (paper).

University of Southern Mississippi

- **Address:** 118 College Drive, Hattiesburg, MS 39406-0001
- **Website:** http://www.usm.edu
- **Public**
- **Enrollment:** 10,727 full-time; 1,741 part-time

KEY STATS

✔ **U.S News College Ranking:** fourth tier, National Universities
✔ **ACT Score (25th/75th percentile):** 18-24
✔ **Tuition:** 2006-2007: $4,342 in state, $9,772 out of state

Selectivity: Selective	Room/board: $4,420
Acceptance rate: 61%	Average debt: $12,712
Student/faculty ratio: 18/1	Proportion who borrowed: 66%

2005-2006 enrollment: 10,727 full-time; 1,741 part-time. Men: 39%; women: 61%. **Ethnic makeup:** African American: 28%; Asian American: 1%; Hispanic: 1%; White: 69%; International: 1%.

ADMISSIONS FACTS AND FIGURES

Phone: (601) 266-5000. **Email:** admissions@usm.edu. **Website:** http://www.usm.edu. **Application deadlines for fall 2007:** Regular decision: August 25. Early decision: Not offered. Early action: Not offered. Admission can be deferred. Common application is accepted. **Admissions requirements/recommendations:** High school units required (recommended): English: 4 (4); Mathematics: 3 (3); Science: 3 (3); Foreign language: 0 (2); Social studies: 1 (1); History: 2 (2); Academic electives: 2 (2); Total units: 16 (18). Tests: The college uses SAT or ACT scores in admissions decisions. Either SAT or ACT required. For admission to the fall 2007 entering class, the school will accept: ACT without writing. Campus visit: Neither required nor recommended. Admissions interview: Neither required nor recommended. **Factors that count in admissions decisions:** *Academic:* Secondary school record: Very important. Class rank: Important. Letters of recommendation: Not considered. Standardized test scores: Very important. Essay: Not considered. *Nonacademic:* Interview: Important. Extracurricular activities: Not considered. Talent/ability: Considered. Character/personal qualities: Not considered. Alumni/ae relationship: Considered. Geographical residence: Not considered. State residency: Not considered. Religious affiliation/commitment: Not considered. Minority status: Not considered. Volunteer work: Not considered. Work experience: Not considered. **Other schools with the greatest overlap in applicants:** Mississippi State University; University of Mississippi. **Admissions statistics for the fall 2005 entering class:** Total applicants: 5,153. Total accepted: 3,151. Freshmen enrolled: 1,346; 25% were from out of state. Overall acceptance rate: 61%. **Credentials of fall 2005 freshmen:** 19% ranked in the top 10 percent of their high school class; 47% were in the top 25 percent, and 79% were in the top half. (Proportion submitting class standing: 79%.) **Average high school grade point average:** 3.1. **First-year students who submitted SAT scores:** 8%. Scores (25/75 percentile): Verbal: 460-575, Math: 480-565, Combined: 940-1140. **First-year students submitting ACT scores:** 82%. Scores (25/75 percentile): English: 19-25, Math: 17-22, Composite: 18-24.

ACADEMICS

Year founded: 1910. **Academic calendar:** Semester. **Degrees offered:** bachelor's, master's, post-master's certificate, doctorate. **Most popular majors:** 20% business administration and management, 11% elementary education and teaching, 10% nursing/registered nurse training (R.N., A.S.N., B.S.N., M.S.N.), 7% psychology, 6% parks, recreation, and leisure studies. **Major fields of study:** architecture and related services; area, ethnic, cultural, and gender studies; biological and biomedical sciences; business, management, marketing, and related support services; communication, journalism, and related programs; computer and information sciences and support services; education; engineering technologies/technicians; English language and literature/letters; family and consumer sciences/human sciences; foreign languages, literatures, and linguistics; health professions and related clinical sciences; history; legal professions and studies; library science; mathematics and statistics; parks, recreation, leisure, and fitness studies; philosophy and religious studies; physical sciences; psychology; public administration and social service professions; security and protective services; social sciences; visual and performing arts. **Areas of required coursework:** arts/fine arts, humanities, computer literacy, mathematics, English (including composition), sciences (biological or physical), history, social science. **Pre-professional programs:** pre-law, pre-dentistry, pre-medicine, pre-veterinary science, pre-optometry, pre-pharmacy, other. **Special academic programs (% participation):** cooperative (work-study plan) program (1%), distance learning (70%), double major (4.2%), dual enrollment (.8%), English as a Second Language (ESL) (0%), honors program (3.2%), independent study (5.5%), internships (44.3%), study abroad (7.8%), teacher certificate program (7%). **Teacher certification offered in:** early childhood, special education, elementary, vo-tech, middle/junior high, adult education, secondary, bilingual/bicultural. **Cooperative education programs:** computer science, engineering, other. **Reserve Officers Training Corps (ROTC):** Army ROTC: Offered on campus; Air Force ROTC: Offered on campus. **Faculty and instruction (2005-2006):** Total instructional faculty: 691 full-time, 133 part-time (55% men; 45% women; 11% minorities). Full-time faculty with Ph.D. or other terminal degree: 81%. Student/faculty ratio: 18/1. Classes of fewer than 20 students: 51%; of 20 to 49 students: 39%; of 50 or more students: 10%. **Advanced Placement and International Baccalaureate credit:** AP tests may be used for: Credit only. Scores accepted: 3, 4, 5. International Baccalaureate exams may be used for: Credit only. **Freshmen returning for**

sophomore year: 73%. **Graduation rates:** Four-year: 23%; five-year: 41%; six-year: 46%. **Graduate study:** 10% of students pursue further study immediately upon graduation; 15% within one year. Fields in which graduates pursue further study: Master of Business Administration (MBA), 20%; law, 12%; medicine, 10%; dentistry, 1%; engineering, 5%; theology (or the seminary), 1%; education, 16%; arts and sciences, 34%; veterinary medicine, 1%.

COSTS AND FINANCIAL AID

Financial aid office: (601) 266-4774. **Expenses (2006-2007):** Tuition and fees 2006-2007: $4,342 in state, $9,772 out of state; room/board: $4,420. Estimated books and supplies: $1,000; transportation: $1,000; personal expenses: $2,700. **Financial aid:** Priority filing date for institution's financial aid form: March 15. In 2005-2006, 79% of undergraduates applied for financial aid. Of those, 75% were determined to have financial need; 26% had their need fully met. Average financial aid package (proportion receiving): $7,504 (69%). Average amount of gift aid, such as scholarships or grants (proportion receiving): $3,601 (42%). Average amount of self-help aid, such as work study or loans (proportion receiving): $4,358 (50%). Average need-based loan (excluding PLUS or other private loans): $4,497. Among students who received need-based aid, the average percentage of need met: 85%. Among students who received aid based on merit, the average award (and the proportion receiving): $2,104 (7%). The average athletic scholarship (and the proportion receiving): $6,087 (3%). Average amount of debt of borrowers graduating in 2005: $12,712. Proportion who borrowed: 66%.

CAMPUS LIFE AND EXTRACURRICULAR ACTIVITIES

Campus housing available (% using): women's dorms (51%), men's dorms (29%), sorority housing (8%), fraternity housing (6%), apartments for married students (6%), special housing for disabled students (0%). Students who live in college-owned, operated, or affiliated housing: 24%. **Student employment:** During the 2005-2006 academic year, 9% of undergraduates worked on campus. Average per-year earnings: $3,000. **Clubs and organizations:** Number of student organizations: 248. Activities include: choral groups, concert band, dance, drama/theater, jazz band, literary magazine, marching band, music ensembles, musical theater, opera, pep band, radio station, student government, student newspaper, student film society, symphony orchestra, yearbook. Number of fraternities: 16; sororities: 12. Proportion of men in fraternities: 10%; of women in sororities: 11%. Average proportion of students who stay on campus on weekends: 10%. **Sports program (2005-2006):** Member of NCAA I. *Men's intercollegiate varsity sports:* baseball, basketball, football, golf, tennis, track and field (indoor), track and field (outdoor). *Women's intercollegiate varsity sports:* basketball, cross-country, golf, soccer, softball, tennis, track and field (indoor), track and field (outdoor), volleyball.

SERVICES AND FACILITIES

Basic services: nonremedial tutoring, placement service, day care, health service, health insurance. **Remedial assistance:** reading, math, writing, study skills. **Counseling services:** minority student, career, military, personal, veteran student, academic, older student, psychological, birth control. **For learning-disabled students:** School does not offer a structured program with separate admission and additional fees. Total undergraduates in learning-disabled program or receiving services: 72. Services include: remedial math, remedial English, reading machines, remedial reading, tape recorders, other special classes, videotaped classes, diagnostic testing service, untimed tests, note-taking services, special bookstore section, oral tests, learning center, readers, extended time for tests, tutors, priority seating, texts on tape, other testing accomodations, other. **Library:** Number of titles: 1,411,011; number of current serial subscriptions: 6,839. **Information technology resources:** Students are not required to lease or own a computer. Number of campus computers available to all students: 133. School has a wireless network. Approximate number of users that can be accommodated: 4,000. Proportion of college-owned housing units wired for high-speed internet access: 90%. **Campus safety:** Security services offered: 24-hour foot-and-vehicle patrols, late-night transport/escort service, 24-hour emergency telephones, lighted pathways/sidewalks, controlled dormitory access (key, security card, etc).

TRANSFER AND INTERNATIONAL STUDENTS

Transfer students: May apply for admission for the following academic terms: Fall, Spring, Summer. Applicants need a minimum number of credits to apply. For fall 2005: Transfer applications received: 4,179. Transfer applicants offered admission: 2,768. Transfer applicants enrolled: 1,634. **International students:** Number of foreign undergraduates: 103 (1% of student body). Number of countries represented: 65. Minimum TOEFL score required: 525 (paper); 197 (computer). Average TOEFL score: 525 (paper).

William Carey College

■ **Address:** 498 Tuscan Avenue, Hattiesburg, MS 39401-5499
■ **Website:** http://www.wmcarey.edu
■ **Private; Religious affiliation:** Baptist
■ **Enrollment:** 1,373 full-time; 183 part-time

KEY STATS

✔ **U.S News College Ranking:** fourth tier, Universities–Master's (South)
✔ **ACT Score (25th/75th percentile):** 19-25
✔ **Tuition:** 2006-2007: $8,715
　Selectivity: Selective 　**Room/board:** $3,615
　Acceptance rate: 88% 　**Average debt:** $16,000
　Student/faculty ratio: 15/1 　**Proportion who borrowed:** 85%

UNDERGRADUATE STUDENT BODY STATS

2005-2006 enrollment: 1,373 full-time; 183 part-time. Men: 29%; women: 71%. **Ethnic makeup:** African American: 26%; American-Indian: 1%; Asian American: 1%; Hispanic: 1%; White: 70%; International: 1%.

ADMISSIONS FACTS AND FIGURES

Phone: (601) 318-6103. **Email:** admissions@wmcarey.edu. **Website:** http://www.wmcarey.edu. **Application deadlines for fall 2007:** Regular decision: Rolling. Early decision: Not offered. Early action: Not offered. Admission can be deferred. **Application fee:** $20. Common application is not accepted. **Admissions requirements/recommendations:** High school units required (recommended): English: (8); Mathematics: (6); Science: (6); Social studies: (5). Tests: The college uses SAT or ACT scores in admissions decisions. Either SAT or ACT required. For admission to the fall 2007 entering class, the school will accept: ACT with writing, ACT without writing. Campus visit: Recommended. Admissions interview: Neither required nor recommended. Off-campus interview: Not available. **Factors that count in admissions decisions:** *Academic:* Secondary school record: Very important. Class rank: Considered. Letters of recommendation: Considered. Standardized test scores: Very important. Essay: Not considered. *Nonacademic:* Interview: Not considered. Extracurricular activities: Not considered. Talent/ability: Not considered. Character/personal qualities: Not considered. Alumni/ae relationship: Not considered. Geographical residence: Not considered. State residency: Not considered. Religious affiliation/commitment: Not considered. Minority status: Not considered. Volunteer work: Not considered. Work experience: Not considered. **Admissions statistics for the fall 2005 entering class:** Total applicants: 301. Total accepted: 264. Freshmen enrolled: 164; 21% were from out of state. Overall acceptance rate: 88%. **First-year students who submitted SAT scores:** 7%. Scores (25/75 percentile): Verbal: 370-600, Math: 470-600, Combined: 840-1200. **First-year students submitting ACT scores:** 93%. Scores (25/75 percentile): English: 19-27, Math: 17-23, Composite: 19-25.

ACADEMICS

Year founded: 1906. **Academic calendar:** Trimester. **Degrees offered:** bachelor's, master's. **Most popular majors:** 22% nursing/registered nurse training (R.N., A.S.N., B.S.N., M.S.N.), 16% psychology, 13% general studies, 12% elementary education and teaching, 11% business administration and management. **Major fields of study:** biological and biomedical sciences; communication, journalism, and related programs; education; English language and literature/letters; health professions and related clinical sciences; history; liberal arts and sciences studies, and humanities; mathematics and statistics; parks, recreation, leisure, and fitness studies; physical sciences; psychology; social sciences; theology and religious vocations; visual and performing arts. **Areas of required coursework:** arts/fine arts, humanities, computer literacy, mathematics, English (including composition), sciences (biological or physical), history, social science, other. **Pre-professional programs:** pre-law, pre-dentistry, pre-veterinary science, pre-pharmacy. **Special academic programs (% participation):** accelerated program (10%), cross-registration (20%), double major (1.6%), dual enrollment (0%), honors program (1.3%), independent study (33.8%), internships (19%), study abroad (0%), teacher certificate program (16.8%). **Teacher certification offered in:** elementary, secondary. **Reserve Officers Training Corps (ROTC):** Army ROTC: Offered at cooperating institution

(University of Southern Mississippi); Air Force ROTC: Offered at cooperating institution (University of Southern Mississippi). **Faculty and instruction (2005-2006):** Total instructional faculty: 96 full-time, 106 part-time (42% men; 58% women; 3% minorities). Full-time faculty with Ph.D. or other terminal degree: 66%. Student/faculty ratio: 15/1. Classes of fewer than 20 students: 48%; of 20 to 49 students: 52%; of 50 or more students: 1%. **Advanced Placement and International Baccalaureate credit:** AP tests may be used for: Credit and/or placement. Scores accepted: 3. International Baccalaureate exams may be used for: Credit and/or placement. **Freshmen returning for sophomore year:** 66%. **Graduation rates:** Four-year: 26%; five-year: 37%; six-year: 41%.

COSTS AND FINANCIAL AID

Financial aid office: (601) 318-6153. **Expenses (2006-2007):** Tuition and fees 2006-2007: $8,715; room/board: $3,615. Estimated books and supplies: $1,350; transportation: $1,602; personal expenses: $3,165. **Financial aid:** Priority filing date for institution's financial aid form: April 1. In 2005-2006, 98% of undergraduates applied for financial aid. Of those, 96% were determined to have financial need; 97% had their need fully met. Average financial aid package (proportion receiving): $12,000 (96%). Average amount of gift aid, such as scholarships or grants (proportion receiving): $6,000 (96%). Average amount of self-help aid, such as work study or loans (proportion receiving): $6,000 (94%). Average need-based loan (excluding PLUS or other private loans): $5,000. Among students who received need-based aid, the average percentage of need met: 85%. Among students who received aid based on merit, the average award (and the proportion receiving): $6,000 (11%). The average athletic scholarship (and the proportion receiving): $6,500 (2%). Average amount of debt of borrowers graduating in 2005: $16,000. Proportion who borrowed: 85%.

CAMPUS LIFE AND EXTRACURRICULAR ACTIVITIES

Campus housing available (% using): women's dorms (50%), men's dorms (37%), apartment for single students (13%). Students who live in college-owned, operated, or affiliated housing: 26%. **Student employment:** During the 2005-2006 academic year, 20% of undergraduates worked on campus. Average per-year earnings: $1,700. **Clubs and organizations:** Number of student organizations: 30. Activities include: choral groups, drama/theater, music ensembles, musical theater, student government, student newspaper, yearbook. Number of fraternities: 2; sororities: 2. Proportion of men in fraternities: 1%; of women in sororities: 1%. Average proportion of students who stay on campus on weekends: 25%. **Sports program (2005-2006):** Member of NAIA. *Men's intercollegiate varsity sports:* baseball, basketball, golf, soccer. *Women's intercollegiate varsity sports:* basketball, golf, soccer, softball.

SERVICES AND FACILITIES

Basic services: nonremedial tutoring, placement service, health insurance. **Remedial assistance:** math, writing, study skills. **Counseling services:** career, personal, academic. **For learning-disabled students:** School does not offer a structured program with separate admission and additional fees. Total undergraduates in learning-disabled program or receiving services: 13. Services include: remedial math, remedial English, reading machines, remedial reading, tape recorders, diagnostic testing service, untimed tests, note-taking services, oral tests, extended time for tests, tutors. **Library:** Number of titles: 97,998; number of current serial subscriptions: 772. **Information technology resources:** Students are not required to lease or own a computer. Number of campus computers available to all students: 199. School does not have a wireless network. Proportion of college-owned housing units wired for high-speed internet access: 100%. **Campus safety:** Security services offered: 24-hour foot-and-vehicle patrols, late-night transport/escort service, 24-hour emergency telephones, lighted pathways/sidewalks, controlled dormitory access (key, security card, etc).

TRANSFER AND INTERNATIONAL STUDENTS

Transfer students: May apply for admission for the following academic terms: Fall, Winter, Spring, Summer. Applicants need a minimum number of credits to apply. For fall 2005: Transfer applications received: 667. Transfer applicants offered admission: 629. Transfer applicants enrolled: 209. **International students:** Number of foreign undergraduates: 22 (1% of student body). Minimum TOEFL score required: 525 (paper); 195 (computer). Average TOEFL score: 525 (paper).

Missouri

Avila University

- **Address:** 11901 Wornall Road, Kansas City, MO 64145
- **Website:** http://www.Avila.edu
- **Private; Religious affiliation:** Roman Catholic
- **Enrollment:** 910 full-time; 304 part-time

KEY STATS

✔ **U.S News College Ranking:** third tier, Universities–Master's (Midwest)
✔ **ACT Score (25th/75th percentile):** 19-24
✔ **Tuition:** 2006-2007: $17,750

Selectivity: Selective	**Room/board:** $5,500
Acceptance rate: 61%	**Average debt:** $16,398
Student/faculty ratio: 13/1	**Proportion who borrowed:** 100%

UNDERGRADUATE STUDENT BODY STATS

2005-2006 enrollment: 910 full-time; 304 part-time. Men: 34%; women: 66%. **Ethnic makeup:** African American: 17%; American-Indian: 2%; Asian American: 2%; Hispanic: 6%; White: 68%; International: 5%. **Religious preference:** Roman Catholic: 25%; Protestant: 1%; Unknown: 13%; Other: 16%.

ADMISSIONS FACTS AND FIGURES

Phone: (816) 501-2400. **Email:** admissions@mail.avila.edu. **Website:** http://www.Avila.edu. **Application deadlines for fall 2007:** Regular decision: Rolling. Early decision: Not offered. Early action: Not offered. Admission can be deferred. **Application fee:** None. Common application is accepted. **Admissions requirements/recommendations:** High school units required (recommended): English: 4 (4); Mathematics: 3 (3); Science: 2 (2); Foreign language: 3 (3); Social studies: 3 (3); Total units: 16 (16). Tests: The college uses SAT or ACT scores in admissions decisions. Either SAT or ACT required. For admission to the fall 2007 entering class, the school will accept: ACT with writing, ACT without writing. Campus visit: Recommended. Admissions interview: Neither required nor recommended. Off-campus interview: May be arranged. **Factors that count in admissions decisions:** *Academic:* Secondary school record: Very important. Class rank: Considered. Letters of recommendation: Considered. Standardized test scores: Very important. Essay: Considered. *Nonacademic:* Interview: Considered. Extracurricular activities: Considered. Talent/ability: Considered. Character/personal qualities: Considered. Alumni/ae relationship: Not considered. Geographical residence: Not considered. State residency: Not considered. Religious affiliation/commitment: Not considered. Minority status: Not considered. Volunteer work: Not considered. Work experience: Not considered. **Other schools with the greatest overlap in applicants:** Central Missouri State University; Rockhurst University; University of Kansas; University of Missouri–Kansas City; William Jewell College. **Admissions statistics for the fall 2005 entering class:** Total applicants: 1,505. Total accepted: 912. Freshmen enrolled: 162; Overall acceptance rate: 61%. **Average high school grade point average:** 3.0. **First-year students who submitted SAT scores:** 6%. Scores (25/75 percentile): Verbal: 440-610, Math: 455-610, Combined: 895-1220. **First-year students submitting ACT scores:** 88%. Scores (25/75 percentile): English: 18-25, Math: 18-24, Composite: 19-24.

ACADEMICS

Year founded: 1916. **Academic calendar:** Semester. **Degrees offered:** certificate, associate, bachelor's, master's. **Most popular majors:** Information not available. **Major fields of study:** biological and biomedical sciences; business, management, marketing, and related support services; communication, journalism, and related programs; computer and information sciences and support services; education; English language and literature/letters; health professions and related clinical sciences; history; legal professions and studies; liberal arts and sciences studies, and humanities; mathematics and statistics; multi/interdisciplinary studies; parks, recreation, leisure, and fitness studies; philosophy and religious studies; physical sciences; psychology; public administration and social service professions; social sciences; visual and performing arts. **Areas of required coursework:** arts/fine arts, computer literacy, mathematics, English (including composition), philosophy, sciences (biological or physical), history, social science, other. **Pre-professional programs:** pre-law, pre-dentistry, pre-medicine, pre-veterinary science, pre-optometry, pre-pharmacy, other. **Special academic programs (% participation):** accelerated program (10%), cooperative (work-study plan) program (0%), cross-registration (27%), distance learning (19%), double major (2%), dual enrollment (0%), English as a Second Language (ESL) (4%), exchange student program (domestic) (0%), independent study (10%), internships (50%), liberal arts/career combination (100%), teacher certificate program (22%), weekend college (10%). **Teacher certification offered in:** special education, elementary, middle/junior high, secondary. **Cooperative education programs:** health professions. **Reserve Officers Training Corps (ROTC):** Army ROTC: Offered at cooperating institution (University of Missouri-Kansas City). **Faculty and instruction (2005-2006):** Total instructional faculty: 64 full-time, 135 part-time (43% men; 57% women; 5% minorities). Full-time faculty with Ph.D. or other terminal degree: 67%. Student/faculty ratio: 13/1. Classes of fewer than 20 students: 71%; of 20 to 49 students: 29%. **Advanced Placement and International Baccalaureate credit:** AP tests may be used for: Credit only. Scores accepted: 3, 4, 5. International Baccalaureate exams may be used for: Credit only. **Freshmen returning for sophomore year:** 72%. **Graduation rates:** Six-year: 38%. **Graduate study:** 18% of students pursue further study immediately upon graduation; 25% within one year; 40% within five years.

COSTS AND FINANCIAL AID

Financial aid office: (816) 501-3600. **Expenses (2006-2007):** Tuition and fees 2006-2007: $17,750; room/board: $5,500. Estimated books and supplies: $800; transportation: $600; personal expenses: $2,200. **Financial aid:** Priority filing date for institution's financial aid form: April 1. In 2005-2006, 87% of undergraduates applied for financial aid. Of those, 76% were determined to have financial need; 10% had their need fully met. Average financial aid package (proportion receiving): $11,751 (33%). Average amount of gift aid, such as scholarships or grants (proportion receiving): $7,465 (31%). Average amount of self-help aid, such as work study or loans (proportion receiving): $5,594 (27%). Average need-based loan (excluding PLUS or other private loans): $5,221. Among students who received need-based aid, the average percentage of need met: 25%. Among students who received aid based on merit, the average award (and the proportion receiving): $8,933 (13%). The average athletic scholarship (and the proportion receiving): $2,893 (1%). Average amount of debt of borrowers graduating in 2005: $16,398. Proportion who borrowed: 100%.

CAMPUS LIFE AND EXTRACURRICULAR ACTIVITIES

Campus housing available (% using): coed dorms (100%). **Student employment:** During the 2005-2006 academic year, 10% of undergraduates worked on campus. Average per-year earnings: $1,200. **Clubs and organizations:** Number of student organizations: 32. Activities include: choral groups, dance, drama/theater, literary magazine, musical theater, student government, student newspaper, student film society. Number of fraternities: 0; sororities: 0. **Sports program (2005-2006):** Member of NAIA. *Men's intercollegiate varsity sports:* baseball, basketball, football, soccer. *Women's intercollegiate varsity sports:* basketball, golf, soccer, softball, volleyball.

SERVICES AND FACILITIES

Basic services: nonremedial tutoring, health service, health insurance. **Remedial assistance:** reading, math, writing, study skills. **Counseling services:** career, personal, academic. **For learning-disabled students:** School does not offer a structured program with separate admission and additional fees. Services include: remedial math, remedial English, tape recorders, other special classes, note-taking services, oral tests, learning center, readers, extended time for tests, tutors, other. **Library:** Number of titles: 82,583; number of current serial subscriptions: 490. **Information technology resources:** Students are not required to lease or own a computer. Number of campus computers available to all students: 127. School does not have a wireless network. Proportion of college-owned housing units wired for high-speed internet access: 100%. **Campus safety:** Security services offered: late-night transport/escort service, 24-hour emergency telephones, lighted pathways/sidewalks, controlled dormitory access (key, security card, etc).

TRANSFER AND INTERNATIONAL STUDENTS

Transfer students: May apply for admission for the following academic terms: Fall, Winter, Spring, Summer. Applicants do not need a minimum number of credits to apply. For fall 2005: Transfer applications received: 537. Transfer applicants offered admission: 351. Transfer applicants enrolled: 205. **International students:** Number of foreign undergraduates: 14 (5% of student body). Minimum TOEFL score required: 500 (paper); 173 (computer).

Central Methodist University

- Address: 411 Central Methodist Square, Fayette, MO 65248
- Website: http://www.centralmethodist.edu
- Private; **Religious affiliation:** United Methodist Methodist
- Enrollment: 790 full-time; 28 part-time

KEY STATS

✔ **U.S News College Ranking:** third tier, Comp. Coll.–Bachelor's (Midwest)
✔ **ACT Score (25th/75th percentile):** 18-23
✔ **Tuition:** 2005-2006: $15,200

Selectivity: Selective	**Room/board:** $5,360
Acceptance rate: 68%	**Average debt:** N/A
Student/faculty ratio: 14/1	**Proportion who borrowed:** N/A

UNDERGRADUATE STUDENT BODY STATS

2005-2006 enrollment: 790 full-time; 28 part-time. Men: 50%; women: 50%. **Ethnic makeup:** African American: 7%; Hispanic: 2%; White: 89%; International: 2%. **Religious preference:** Roman Catholic: 14%; Protestant: 22%; Hindu: 1%; No preference: 32%; United Methodist Methodist: 17%; Baptist: 14%.

ADMISSIONS FACTS AND FIGURES

Phone: (660) 248-6251. **Email:** admissions@centralmethodist.edu. **Website:** http://www.centralmethodist.edu. **Application deadlines for fall 2007:** Regular decision: Rolling. Early decision: Not offered. Early action: Not offered. Admission can be deferred. **Application fee:** $20. Common application is accepted. **To apply online, go to:** http://www.centralmethodist.edu/forms/admit/fayette_addmap.html. **Admissions requirements/recommendations:** High school units required (recommended): English: (4); Mathematics: (3); Science: (2); Foreign language: (2); Social studies: (2); Total units: (20). Tests: The college uses SAT or ACT scores in admissions decisions. Either SAT or ACT required. For admission to the fall 2007 entering class, the school will accept: ACT with writing, ACT without writing. Campus visit: Recommended. Admissions interview: Recommended. Off-campus interview: May be arranged. **Factors that count in admissions decisions:** *Academic:* Secondary school record: Very important. Class rank: Very important. Letters of recommendation: Considered. Standardized test scores: Very important. Essay: Not considered. *Nonacademic:* Interview: Considered. Extracurricular activities: Very important. Talent/ability: Important. Character/personal qualities: Important. Alumni/ae relationship: Considered. Geographical residence: Considered. State residency: Considered. Religious affiliation/commitment: Important. Minority status: Important. Volunteer work: Important. Work experience: Important. **Other schools with the greatest overlap in applicants:** Central Missouri State University; Missouri State University; Missouri Valley College; Truman State University; University of Missouri–Columbia. **Admissions statistics for the fall 2005 entering class:** Total applicants: 1,335. Total accepted: 903. Freshmen enrolled: 224; 7% were from out of state. Overall acceptance rate: 68%. **Credentials of fall 2005 freshmen:** 10% ranked in the top 10 percent of their high school class; 31% were in the top 25 percent, and 65% were in the top half. (Proportion submitting class standing: 97%.) **Average high school grade point average:** 3.2. **First-year students who submitted SAT scores:** 2%. Scores (25/75 percentile): Verbal: N/A, Math: N/A, Combined: N/A. **First-year students submitting ACT scores:** 96%. Scores (25/75 percentile): English: 17-22, Math: 17-23, Composite: 18-23.

ACADEMICS

Year founded: 1854. **Academic calendar:** Semester. **Degrees offered:** associate, bachelor's. **Most popular majors:** 37% education, 17% business, man-

agement, marketing, and related support services, 11% health professions and related clinical sciences, 8% psychology, 5% biological and biomedical sciences. **Major fields of study:** biological and biomedical sciences; business, management, marketing, and related support services; communication, journalism, and related programs; computer and information sciences and support services; education; English language and literature/letters; foreign languages, literatures, and linguistics; health professions and related clinical sciences; history; mathematics and statistics; multi/interdisciplinary studies; natural resources and conservation; parks, recreation, leisure, and fitness studies; philosophy and religious studies; physical sciences; psychology; public administration and social service professions; security and protective services; social sciences; visual and performing arts. **Areas of required coursework:** humanities, computer literacy, mathematics, English (including composition), sciences (biological or physical), history, social science, other. **Pre-professional programs:** pre-law, pre-dentistry, pre-medicine, pre-veterinary science, pre-optometry, pre-pharmacy. **Special academic programs (% participation):** accelerated program, distance learning, double major (10%), dual enrollment, honors program (3%), independent study (5%), internships (15%), liberal arts/career combination, student-designed major (4%), study abroad (.5%), teacher certificate program (37%). **Teacher certification offered in:** early childhood, special education, elementary, middle/junior high, secondary. **Reserve Officers Training Corps (ROTC):** Army ROTC: Offered at cooperating institution (University of Missouri, Columbia); Air Force ROTC: Offered at cooperating institution (University of Missouri, Columbia). **Faculty and instruction (2005-2006):** Total instructional faculty: 51 full-time, 25 part-time (62% men; 38% women; 0% minorities). Full-time faculty with Ph.D. or other terminal degree: 69%. Student/faculty ratio: 14/1. Classes of fewer than 20 students: 68%; of 20 to 49 students: 30%; of 50 or more students: 2%. **Advanced Placement and International Baccalaureate credit:** AP tests may be used for: Credit only. Scores accepted: 3, 4, 5. International Baccalaureate exams may be used for: Credit and/or placement. **Freshmen returning for sophomore year:** 62%. **Graduation rates:** Four-year: 26%; five-year: 38%; six-year: 41%.

COSTS AND FINANCIAL AID

Financial aid office: (660) 248-6244. **Expenses (2005-2006):** Tuition and fees 2005-2006: $15,200; room/board: $5,360. Estimated books and supplies: $750 personal expenses: $3,000. **Financial aid:** Priority filing date for institution's financial aid form: March 15.

CAMPUS LIFE AND EXTRACURRICULAR ACTIVITIES

Campus housing available (% using): coed dorms (40%), women's dorms (28%), men's dorms (31%), apartments for married students (1%). Students who live in college-owned, operated, or affiliated housing: 65%. **Clubs and organizations:** Number of student organizations: 40. Activities include: choral groups, concert band, drama/theater, jazz band, literary magazine, marching band, music ensembles, musical theater, radio station, student government, student newspaper, symphony orchestra, television station, yearbook. Number of fraternities: 6; sororities: 4. Proportion of men in fraternities: 17%; of women in sororities: 20%. Average proportion of students who stay on campus on weekends: 30%. **Sports program (2005-2006):** Member of NAIA. *Men's intercollegiate varsity sports:* baseball, basketball, cross-country, football, golf, soccer, track and field (indoor), track and field (outdoor). *Women's intercollegiate varsity sports:* basketball, cross-country, golf, soccer, softball, track and field (indoor), track and field (outdoor), volleyball.

SERVICES AND FACILITIES

Basic services: nonremedial tutoring, placement service, health service, health insurance. **Remedial assistance:** math, writing, study skills, other. **Counseling services:** career, personal, academic, psychological, religious. **For learning-disabled students:** School does not offer a structured program with separate admission and additional fees. Services include: learning center, readers, extended time for tests, tutors. **Library:** Number of titles: 98,820; number of current serial subscriptions: 241. **Information technology resources:** Students are not required to lease or own a computer. Number of campus computers available to all students: 155. School has a wireless network. Proportion of college-owned housing units wired for high-speed internet access: 100%. **Campus safety:** Security services offered: 24-hour foot-and-vehicle patrols, late-night transport/escort service, 24-hour emergency telephones, lighted pathways/sidewalks, controlled dormitory access (key, security card, etc).

TRANSFER AND INTERNATIONAL STUDENTS

Transfer students: May apply for admission for the following academic terms: Fall, Spring, Summer. Applicants need a minimum number of credits to apply. For fall 2005: Transfer applications received: 283. Transfer applicants offered admission: 176. Transfer applicants enrolled: 84. **International students:** Number of foreign undergraduates: 14 (2% of student body). Number of countries represented: 6. Minimum TOEFL score required: 500 (paper); 173 (computer).

Central Missouri State University

- **Address:** Administration Building, Suite 304, Warrensburg, MO 64093
- **Website:** http://www.cmsu.edu
- **Public**
- **Enrollment:** 7,168 full-time; 1,649 part-time

KEY STATS

- ✔ **U.S News College Ranking:** third tier, Universities–Master's (Midwest)
- ✔ **ACT Score (25th/75th percentile):** 19-24
- ✔ **Tuition:** 2006-2007: $5,835 in state, $11,250 out of state

Selectivity: Selective	**Room/board:** $5,609
Acceptance rate: 85%	**Average debt:** $9,632
Student/faculty ratio: 16/1	**Proportion who borrowed:** 63%

UNDERGRADUATE STUDENT BODY STATS

2005-2006 enrollment: 7,168 full-time; 1,649 part-time. Men: 44%; women: 56%. **Ethnic makeup:** African American: 7%; American-Indian: 1%; Asian American: 1%; Hispanic: 2%; White: 88%; International: 2%.

ADMISSIONS FACTS AND FIGURES

Phone: (660) 543-4290. **Email:** admit@cmsu1.cmsu.edu. **Website:** http://www.cmsu.edu. **Application deadlines for fall 2007:** Regular decision: August 19. Early decision: Not offered. Early action: Not offered. Admission can be deferred. **Application fee:** $30. Common application is accepted. **To apply online, go to:** http://www.cmsu.edu/admit/online_app.htm. **Admissions requirements/recommendations:** High school units required (recommended): English: 4; Mathematics: 3; Science: 2; Foreign language: (2); Social studies: 3; Academic electives: 3; Total units: 16 (2). Tests: The college uses SAT or ACT scores in admissions decisions. Either SAT or ACT required. For admission to the fall 2007 entering class, the school will accept: ACT with writing, ACT without writing. Campus visit: Recommended. Admissions interview: Neither required nor recommended. Off-campus interview: May be arranged. **Factors that count in admissions decisions:** *Academic:* Secondary school record: Considered. Class rank: Very important. Letters of recommendation: Considered. Standardized test scores: Very important. Essay: Not considered. *Nonacademic:* Interview: Not considered. Extracurricular activities: Considered. Talent/ability: Considered. Character/personal qualities: Considered. Alumni/ae relationship: Considered. Geographical residence: Not considered. State residency: Not considered. Religious affiliation/commitment: Not considered. Minority status: Not considered. Volunteer work: Not considered. Work experience: Not considered. **Other schools with the greatest overlap in applicants:** Missouri State University; Missouri State University; Northwest Missouri State University; University of Missouri–Columbia; University of Missouri–Columbia; University of Missouri–Kansas City; University of Missouri–Kansas City. **Admissions statistics for the fall 2005 entering class:** Total applicants: 3,619. Total accepted: 3,066. Freshmen enrolled: 1,575; 4% were from out of state. Overall acceptance rate: 85%. **Credentials of fall 2005 freshmen:** 14% ranked in the top 10 percent of their high school class; 40% were in the top 25 percent, and 75% were in the top half. (Proportion submitting class standing: 91%.) **Average high school grade point average:** 3.3. **First-year students submitting ACT scores:** 93%. Scores (25/75 percentile): English: 18-24, Math: 17-24, Composite: 19-24.

ACADEMICS

Year founded: 1871. **Academic calendar:** Semester. **Degrees offered:** associate, bachelor's, post-bachelor's certificate, master's, post-master's certificate. **Most popular majors:** 9% curriculum and instruction, 5% criminal justice and corrections, 4% business administration, management, and operations, 4% computer and information sciences and support services, 4% graphic design. **Major fields of study:** agriculture, agriculture operations, and related sciences; architecture and related services; area, ethnic, cultural, and gender studies; biological and biomedical sciences; business, management, marketing, and related support services; communication, journalism, and related programs; communications technologies/technicians and support services; computer and information sciences and support services; education; engineering; engineering technologies/technicians; English language and literature/letters; family and consumer sciences/human sciences; foreign languages, literatures, and linguistics; health professions and related clinical sciences; history; liberal arts and sciences studies, and humanities; mathematics and statistics; parks, recreation, leisure, and fitness studies; psychology; public administration and social service professions; security and protective services; social sciences; transportation and materials moving; visual and performing arts. **Areas of required coursework:** arts/fine arts, humanities, computer literacy, mathematics, English (including composition), sciences (biological or physical), history, social science, other. **Pre-professional programs:** pre-law, pre-dentistry, pre-medicine, pre-veterinary science, pre-optometry, pre-pharmacy. **Special academic programs:** cooperative (work-study plan) program, cross-registration, distance learning, double major, dual enrollment, English as a Second Language (ESL), honors program, independent study, internships, student-designed major, study abroad, teacher certificate program, weekend college. **Teacher certification offered in:** early childhood, special education, elementary, vo-tech, middle/junior high, adult education, secondary, bilingual/bicultural. **Cooperative education programs:** education, technologies, other. **Reserve Officers Training Corps (ROTC):** Army ROTC: Offered on campus; Air Force ROTC: Offered at cooperating institution (University of Missouri-Columbia). **Faculty and instruction (2005-2006):** Total instructional faculty: 439 full-time, 236 part-time (55% men; 45% women; 9% minorities). Full-time faculty with Ph.D. or other terminal degree: 75%. Student/faculty ratio: 16/1. Classes of fewer than 20 students: 46%; of 20 to 49 students: 51%; of 50 or more students: 3%. **Advanced Placement and International Baccalaureate credit:** AP tests may be used for: Credit only. Scores accepted: 3. International Baccalaureate exams may be used for: Credit only. **Freshmen returning for sophomore year:** 71%. **Graduation rates:** Four-year: 20%; five-year: 42%; six-year: 49%. **Graduate study:** 17% of students pursue further study immediately upon graduation. Fields in which graduates pursue further study: Master of Business Administration (MBA), 5%; law, 2%; education, 36%; arts and sciences, 19%.

COSTS AND FINANCIAL AID

Financial aid office: (660) 543-4040. **Expenses (2006-2007):** Tuition and fees 2006-2007: $5,835 in state, $11,250 out of state; room/board: $5,609. Estimated transportation: $900. **Financial aid:** Priority filing date for institution's financial aid form: March 1. In 2005-2006, 90% of undergraduates applied for financial aid. Of those, 81% were determined to have financial need; 80% had their need fully met. Average financial aid package (proportion receiving): $8,450 (81%). Average amount of gift aid, such as scholarships or grants (proportion receiving): $3,375 (48%). Average amount of self-help aid, such as work study or loans (proportion receiving): $2,150 (60%). Average need-based loan (excluding PLUS or other private loans): $4,275. Among students who received need-based aid, the average percentage of need met: 88%. Among students who received aid based on merit, the average award (and the proportion receiving): $2,065 (4%). The average athletic scholarship (and the proportion receiving): $4,425 (4%). Average amount of debt of borrowers graduating in 2005: $9,632. Proportion who borrowed: 63%.

CAMPUS LIFE AND EXTRACURRICULAR ACTIVITIES

Campus housing available (% using): coed dorms (72%), women's dorms (2%), sorority housing (5%), fraternity housing (5%), apartments for married students (4%), apartment for single students (9%), special housing for disabled students (0%), special housing for international students (1%), other housing options (2%). Students who live in college-owned, operated, or affiliated housing: 32%. **Student employment:** During the 2005-2006 academic year, 18% of undergraduates worked on campus. Average per-year earnings: $1,187. **Clubs and organizations:** Number of student organizations: 180. Activities include: choral groups, concert band, dance, drama/theater, jazz band, literary magazine, marching band, music ensembles, musical theater, pep band, radio station, student government, student newspaper, student film society, symphony orchestra, television station. Number of fraternities: 12; sororities: 10. Proportion of men in fraternities: 15%; of women in sororities: 11%. Average proportion of students who stay on campus on weekends: 33%. **Sports program (2005-2006):** Member of NCAA II. *Men's intercollegiate varsity sports:* baseball, basketball, cross-country, football, golf, track and field (indoor), track and field (outdoor), wrestling. *Women's intercollegiate varsity sports:* basketball, bowling, cross-country, soccer, softball, track and field (indoor), track and field (outdoor), volleyball.

SERVICES AND FACILITIES

Basic services: nonremedial tutoring, women's center, placement service, day care, health service, health insurance. **Remedial assistance:** reading, math, writing, study skills. **Counseling services:** minority student, career, personal, academic, psychological, birth control, religious. **For learning-disabled students:** School does not offer a structured program with separate admission and additional fees. Total undergraduates in learning-disabled program or receiving services: 217. Services include: remedial math, remedial English, reading machines, remedial reading, tape recorders, other special classes, videotaped classes, note-taking services, special bookstore section, oral tests, learning center, readers, extended time for tests, tutors, early syllabus, priority registration, priority seating, proofreading services, texts on tape, typist/scribe, exams on tape or computer, other testing accomodations, waiver of foreign language degree requirement, waiver of math degree requirement, other. **Library:** Number of titles: 1,263,497; number of current serial subscriptions: 2,505. **Information technology resources:** Students are not required to lease or own a computer. Number of campus computers available to all students: 9,692. School has a wireless network. Approximate number of users that can be accommodated: 2,400. Proportion of college-owned housing units wired for high-speed internet access: 100%. **Campus safety:** Security services offered: 24-hour foot-and-vehicle patrols, late-night transport/escort service, 24-hour emergency telephones, lighted pathways/sidewalks, student patrols, controlled dormitory access (key, security card, etc).

TRANSFER AND INTERNATIONAL STUDENTS

Transfer students: May apply for admission for the following academic terms: Fall, Spring, Summer. Applicants need a minimum number of credits to apply. For fall 2005: Transfer applications received: 1,370. Transfer applicants offered admission: 1,130. Transfer applicants enrolled: 868. **International students:** Number of foreign undergraduates: 196 (2% of student body). Number of countries represented: 51. Minimum TOEFL score required: 500 (paper); 173 (computer). Average TOEFL score: 527 (paper).

College of the Ozarks

- **Address:** PO Box 17, Point Lookout, MO 65726
- **Website:** http://www.cofo.edu
- **Private; Religious affiliation:** Presbyterian
- **Enrollment:** 1,311 full-time; 22 part-time

KEY STATS

- ✔ **U.S News College Ranking:** 29, Comp. Coll.–Bachelor's (Midwest)
- ✔ **ACT Score (25th/75th percentile):** 20-24
- ✔ **Tuition:** 2006-2007: $280

Selectivity: Selective	**Room/board:** $4,100
Acceptance rate: 11%	**Average debt:** N/A
Student/faculty ratio: 16/1	**Proportion who borrowed:** N/A

UNDERGRADUATE STUDENT BODY STATS

2005-2006 enrollment: 1,311 full-time; 22 part-time. Men: 45%; women: 55%. **Ethnic makeup:** African American: 1%; American-Indian: 1%; Asian American: 1%; Hispanic: 1%; White: 95%; International: 2%. **Religious preference:** Roman Catholic: 4%; Protestant: 73%; Unknown: 20%; Other: 3%.

ADMISSIONS FACTS AND FIGURES

Phone: (800) 222-0525. **Email:** admiss4@cofo.edu. **Website:** http://www.cofo.edu. **Application deadlines for fall 2007:** Regular decision: August 20. Early decision: Not offered. Early action: Not offered. Admission cannot be deferred. **Application fee:** None. Common application is not accepted. **Admissions requirements/recommendations:** High school units required (recommended): English: (4); Mathematics: (3); Science: (2); Foreign language: (2); Social studies: (3); Academic electives: (1); Total units: (24). Tests: The college uses SAT or ACT scores in admissions decisions. ACT required. For admission to the fall 2007 entering class, the school will accept: ACT with writing, ACT without writing. Campus visit: Required. Admissions interview: Required. Off-campus interview: May be arranged. **Factors that count in admissions decisions:** *Academic:* Secondary school record: Very important. Class rank: Very important. Letters of recommendation: Important. Standardized test scores: Considered. Essay: Not considered. *Nonacademic:* Interview: Very important. Extracurricular activities: Important. Talent/ability: Important. Character/personal qualities: Very

important. Alumni/ae relationship: Considered. Geographical residence: Considered. State residency: Considered. Religious affiliation/commitment: Not considered. Minority status: Not considered. Volunteer work: Important. Work experience: Considered. **Other schools with the greatest overlap in applicants:** Missouri Southern State University; Missouri State University; Southwest Baptist University; University of Missouri–Columbia. **Admissions statistics for the fall 2005 entering class:** Total applicants: 2,666. Total accepted: 285. Freshmen enrolled: 242; 37% were from out of state. Overall acceptance rate: 11%. **Size of waiting list:** 340 applicants; enrolled from waiting list: 0. **Credentials of fall 2005 freshmen:** 13% ranked in the top 10 percent of their high school class; 39% were in the top 25 percent, and 85% were in the top half. (Proportion submitting class standing: 86%.) **Average high school grade point average:** 3.3. **First-year students submitting ACT scores:** 100%. Scores (25/75 percentile): English: 19-25, Math: 19-24, Composite: 20-24.

ACADEMICS

Year founded: 1906. **Academic calendar:** Semester. **Degrees offered:** bachelor's. **Most popular majors:** 18% business administration and management, 18% elementary education and teaching, 8% agricultural business and management, 6% criminal justice/police science, 6% public relations, advertising, and applied communication. **Major fields of study:** agriculture, agriculture operations, and related sciences; business, management, marketing, and related support services; communication, journalism, and related programs; communications technologies/technicians and support services; computer and information sciences and support services; education; English language and literature/letters; family and consumer sciences/human sciences; foreign languages, literatures, and linguistics; health professions and related clinical sciences; history; legal professions and studies; mathematics and statistics; mechanic and repair technologies/technicians; multi/interdisciplinary studies; parks, recreation, leisure, and fitness studies; philosophy and religious studies; physical sciences; psychology; public administration and social service professions; security and protective services; social sciences; theology and religious vocations; transportation and materials moving; visual and performing arts. **Areas of required coursework:** arts/fine arts, humanities, computer literacy, mathematics, English (including composition), philosophy, foreign languages, sciences (biological or physical), history, social science, other. **Pre-professional programs:** pre-law, pre-medicine, pre-veterinary science, pre-pharmacy. **Special academic programs (% participation):** cooperative (work-study plan) program (98%), double major (27%), dual enrollment (1%), English as a Second Language (ESL) (1%), exchange student program (domestic) (1%), independent study (1%), internships (25%), liberal arts/career combination, student-designed major (2%), study abroad (1%), teacher certificate program (24%). **Teacher certification offered in:** early childhood, elementary, vo-tech, middle/junior high, secondary. **Reserve Officers Training Corps (ROTC):** Army ROTC: Offered on campus. **Faculty and instruction (2005-2006):** Total instructional faculty: 72 full-time, 32 part-time (; 2% minorities). Full-time faculty with Ph.D. or other terminal degree: 57%. Student/faculty ratio: 16/1. Classes of fewer than 20 students: 55%; of 20 to 49 students: 43%; of 50 or more students: 2%. **Advanced Placement and International Baccalaureate credit:** AP tests may be used for: Placement only. International Baccalaureate exams may be used for: Credit and/or placement. **Freshmen returning for sophomore year:** 84%. **Graduation rates:** Six-year: 49%. **Graduate study:** 15% of students pursue further study immediately upon graduation; 23% within five years. Fields in which graduates pursue further study: Master of Business Administration (MBA), 16%; law, 2%; medicine, 2%; dentistry, 1%; engineering, 3%; theology (or the seminary), 12%; education, 49%; arts and sciences, 14%; veterinary medicine, 1%.

COSTS AND FINANCIAL AID

Financial aid office: (417) 334-6411. **Expenses (2006-2007):** Tuition and fees 2006-2007: $280; room/board: $4,100. Estimated books and supplies: $800; transportation: $2,000; personal expenses: $330. **Financial aid:** Priority filing date for institution's financial aid form: March 15. In 2005-2006, 97% of undergraduates applied for financial aid. Of those, 90% were determined to have financial need; 41% had their need fully met. Average financial aid package (proportion receiving): $14,849 (90%). Average amount of gift aid, such as scholarships or grants (proportion receiving): $12,519 (90%). Average amount of self-help aid, such as work study or loans (proportion receiving): $2,884 (68%). Among students who received need-based aid, the average percentage of need met: 86%. Among students who received aid based on merit, the average award (and the proportion receiving): $15,220 (9%). The average athletic scholarship (and the proportion receiving): $2,577 (3%).

CAMPUS LIFE AND EXTRACURRICULAR ACTIVITIES

Campus housing available (% using): women's dorms (54%), men's dorms (46%). Students who live in college-owned, operated, or affiliated housing: 84%. **Student employment:** During the 2005-2006 academic year, 100% of undergraduates worked on campus. Average per-year earnings: $2,900. **Clubs and organizations:** Number of student organizations: 46. Activities include: choral groups, concert band, drama/theater, jazz band, literary magazine, music ensembles, musical theater, pep band, radio station, student government, student newspaper, yearbook. Number of fraternities: 0; sororities: 0. Average proportion of students who stay on campus on weekends: 80%. **Sports program (2005-2006):** Member of NAIA. *Men's intercollegiate varsity sports:* baseball, basketball. *Women's intercollegiate varsity sports:* basketball, volleyball.

SERVICES AND FACILITIES

Basic services: nonremedial tutoring, placement service, health service, health insurance. **Remedial assistance:** study skills. **Counseling services:** career, personal, psychological, religious. **For learning-disabled students:** School does not offer a structured program with separate admission and additional fees. Total undergraduates in learning-disabled program or receiving services: 7. Services include: remedial reading, tape recorders, note-taking services, extended time for tests, tutors, texts on tape, other testing accomodations, other. **Library:** Number of titles: 120,109; number of current serial subscriptions: 453. **Information technology resources:** Students are not required to lease or own a computer. Number of campus computers available to all students: 160. School does not have a wireless network. Proportion of college-owned housing units wired for high-speed internet access: 100%. **Campus safety:** Security services offered: 24-hour foot-and-vehicle patrols, late-night transport/escort service, 24-hour emergency telephones, lighted pathways/sidewalks, student patrols, controlled dormitory access (key, security card, etc.).

TRANSFER AND INTERNATIONAL STUDENTS

Transfer students: May apply for admission for the following academic terms: Fall, Spring. Applicants do not need a minimum number of credits to apply. For fall 2005: Transfer applications received: 453. Transfer applicants offered admission: 80. Transfer applicants enrolled: 73. **International students:** Number of foreign undergraduates: 21 (2% of student body). Number of countries represented: 12. Minimum TOEFL score required: 550 (paper); 213 (computer). Average TOEFL score: 555 (paper).

Columbia College

- **Address:** 1001 Rogers Street, Columbia, MO 65216
- **Website:** http://www.ccis.edu
- **Private; Religious affiliation:** Christian Church (Disciples of Christ)
- **Enrollment:** 757 full-time; 252 part-time

KEY STATS

✔ **U.S News College Ranking:** 35, Comp. Coll.–Bachelor's (Midwest)
✔ **ACT Score (25th/75th percentile):** 19-25
✔ **Tuition:** 2006-2007: $12,414

Selectivity: Selective	**Room/board:** $5,164
Acceptance rate: 62%	**Average debt:** $14,879
Student/faculty ratio: 13/1	**Proportion who borrowed:** 65%

UNDERGRADUATE STUDENT BODY STATS

2005-2006 enrollment: 757 full-time; 252 part-time. Men: 39%; women: 61%. **Ethnic makeup:** African American: 5%; American-Indian: 1%; Asian American: 1%; Hispanic: 3%; White: 84%; International: 6%. **Religious preference:** Roman Catholic: 6%; Protestant: 1%; Unknown: 80%; Christian Church (Disciples of Christ): 2%; Other: 11%.

ADMISSIONS FACTS AND FIGURES

Phone: (573) 875-7352. **Email:** admissions@ccis.edu. **Website:** http://www.ccis.edu. **Application deadlines for fall 2007:** Regular decision: Rolling. Early decision: Not offered. Early action: Not offered. Admission can be deferred. **Application fee:** $25. Common application is accepted. **To apply online, go to:** http://www.ccis.edu/ApplyOnline/onlineapp-ug.asp. **Admissions requirements/recommendations:** High school units required (recommended): English: 4 (4); Mathematics: 3 (3); Science: 2 (2); Foreign language: 0 (0); Social studies: 2 (2); History: 0 (0); Academic electives: 0

(0); Total units: 11 (11). Tests: The college uses SAT or ACT scores in admissions decisions. Either SAT or ACT required. For admission to the fall 2007 entering class, the school will accept: ACT with writing, ACT without writing. Campus visit: Recommended. Admissions interview: Recommended. Off-campus interview: May be arranged. **Factors that count in admissions decisions:** *Academic:* Secondary school record: Important. Class rank: Very important. Letters of recommendation: Considered. Standardized test scores: Very important. Essay: Considered. *Nonacademic:* Interview: Considered. Extracurricular activities: Considered. Talent/ability: Considered. Character/personal qualities: Considered. Alumni/ae relationship: Considered. Geographical residence: Considered. State residency: Not considered. Religious affiliation/commitment: Considered. Minority status: Not considered. Volunteer work: Considered. Work experience: Not considered. **Other schools with the greatest overlap in applicants:** Central Methodist University; Truman State University; University of Missouri–Columbia; Webster University; William Woods University. **Admissions statistics for the fall 2005 entering class:** Total applicants: 819. Total accepted: 509. Freshmen enrolled: 192; 10% were from out of state. Overall acceptance rate: 62%. **Size of waiting list:** 0 applicants; enrolled from waiting list: 0. **Credentials of fall 2005 freshmen:** 14% ranked in the top 10 percent of their high school class; 35% were in the top 25 percent, and 68% were in the top half. (Proportion submitting class standing: 89%.) **Average high school grade point average:** 3.2. **First-year students who submitted SAT scores:** 4%. Scores (25/75 percentile): Verbal: 520-582, Math: 497-587, Combined: 1017-1169. **First-year students submitting ACT scores:** 90%. Scores (25/75 percentile): English: 19-25, Math: 18-26, Composite: 19-25.

ACADEMICS

Year founded: 1851. **Academic calendar:** Semester. **Degrees offered:** associate, transfer-associate, terminal-associate, bachelor's, master's. **Most popular majors:** 20% business/commerce, 16% business administration and management, 13% general studies, 12% criminal justice/law enforcement administration, 8% psychology. **Major fields of study:** biological and biomedical sciences; business, management, marketing, and related support services; computer and information sciences and support services; education; English language and literature/letters; history; liberal arts and sciences studies, and humanities; mathematics and statistics; multi/interdisciplinary studies; natural resources and conservation; physical sciences; psychology; public administration and social service professions; security and protective services; social sciences; visual and performing arts. **Areas of required coursework:** arts/fine arts, humanities, computer literacy, mathematics, English (including composition), sciences (biological or physical), history, social science, other. **Pre-professional programs:** pre-law, pre-dentistry, pre-medicine, pre-veterinary science. **Special academic programs (% participation):** accelerated program (25%), cooperative (work-study plan) program (27%), cross-registration (4%), distance learning (50%), double major (14%), dual enrollment (.01%), English as a Second Language (ESL) (5%), honors program (24%), independent study (3%), internships (15%), student-designed major (3%), study abroad (1%), teacher certificate program (21%). **Teacher certification offered in:** special education, elementary, middle/junior high, secondary. **Reserve Officers Training Corps (ROTC):** Army ROTC: Offered at cooperating institution (University of Missouri-Columbia); Navy ROTC: Offered at cooperating institution (University of Missouri-Columbia); Air Force ROTC: Offered at cooperating institution (University of Missouri-Columbia). **Faculty and instruction (2005-2006):** Total instructional faculty: 56 full-time, 116 part-time (55% men; 45% women; 9% minorities). Full-time faculty with Ph.D. or other terminal degree: 84%. Student/faculty ratio: 13/1. Classes of fewer than 20 students: 63%; of 20 to 49 students: 37%; of 50 or more students: 0%. **Advanced Placement and International Baccalaureate credit:** AP tests may be used for: Credit and/or placement. Scores accepted: 3. International Baccalaureate exams may be used for: Credit only. **Freshmen returning for sophomore year:** 63%. **Graduation rates:** Four-year: 29%; five-year: 35%; six-year: 42%.

COSTS AND FINANCIAL AID

Financial aid office: (573) 875-7390. **Expenses (2006-2007):** Tuition and fees 2006-2007: $12,414; room/board: $5,164. Estimated books and supplies: $700; transportation: $1,200; personal expenses: $1,200. **Financial aid:** Priority filing date for institution's financial aid form: March 1. In 2005-2006, 88% of undergraduates applied for financial aid. Of those, 60% were determined to have financial need; 31% had their need fully met. Average financial aid package (proportion receiving): $14,709 (59%). Average amount of gift aid, such as scholarships or grants (proportion receiving): $7,616 (35%). Average amount of self-help aid, such as work study or loans (proportion receiving): $3,640 (45%). Average need-based loan (excluding

PLUS or other private loans): $2,820. Among students who received need-based aid, the average percentage of need met: 83%. Among students who received aid based on merit, the average award (and the proportion receiving): $4,379 (19%). The average athletic scholarship (and the proportion receiving): $11,474 (9%). Average amount of debt of borrowers graduating in 2005: $14,879. Proportion who borrowed: 65%.

CAMPUS LIFE AND EXTRACURRICULAR ACTIVITIES
Campus housing available (% using): coed dorms (80%), women's dorms (20%), apartment for single students. Students who live in college-owned, operated, or affiliated housing: 35%. **Student employment:** During the 2005-2006 academic year, 8% of undergraduates worked on campus. Average per-year earnings: $1,880. **Clubs and organizations:** Number of student organizations: 28. Activities include: choral groups, drama/theater, literary magazine, student government, student newspaper. Number of fraternities: 0; sororities: 0. **Sports program (2005-2006):** Member of NAIA. *Men's intercollegiate varsity sports:* basketball, soccer. *Women's intercollegiate varsity sports:* basketball, softball, volleyball.

SERVICES AND FACILITIES
Basic services: nonremedial tutoring, health service. **Remedial assistance:** math, writing, study skills. **Counseling services:** career, personal, academic. **For learning-disabled students:** School does not offer a structured program with separate admission and additional fees. Total undergraduates in learning-disabled program or receiving services: 14. Services include: extended time for tests, tutors, other. **Library:** Number of titles: 63,289; number of current serial subscriptions: 15,660. **Information technology resources:** Students are not required to lease or own a computer. Number of campus computers available to all students: 90. School has a wireless network. Approximate number of users that can be accommodated: 300. Proportion of college-owned housing units wired for high-speed internet access: 100%. **Campus safety:** Security services offered: 24-hour foot-and-vehicle patrols, late-night transport/escort service, 24-hour emergency telephones, lighted pathways/sidewalks, controlled dormitory access (key, security card, etc).

TRANSFER AND INTERNATIONAL STUDENTS
Transfer students: May apply for admission for the following academic terms: Fall, Spring, Summer. Applicants need a minimum number of credits to apply. For fall 2005: Transfer applications received: 287. Transfer applicants offered admission: 269. Transfer applicants enrolled: 142. **International students:** Number of foreign undergraduates: 54 (6% of student body). Number of countries represented: 21. Minimum TOEFL score required: 500 (paper); 173 (computer). Average TOEFL score: 510 (paper).

Culver-Stockton College

■ **Address:** 1 College Hill, Canton, MO 63435
■ **Website:** http://www.culver.edu
■ **Private; Religious affiliation:** Christian Church (Disciples of Christ)
■ **Enrollment:** 766 full-time; 74 part-time

KEY STATS
✔ **U.S News College Ranking:** 52, Comp. Coll.–Bachelor's (Midwest)
✔ **ACT Score (25th/75th percentile):** 18-26
✔ **Tuition:** 2006-2007: $15,450

Selectivity: Selective	**Room/board:** $6,550
Acceptance rate: 76%	**Average debt:** $18,429
Student/faculty ratio: 13/1	**Proportion who borrowed:** 89%

UNDERGRADUATE STUDENT BODY STATS
2005-2006 enrollment: 766 full-time; 74 part-time. Men: 42%; women: 58%. **Ethnic makeup:** African American: 7%; Hispanic: 3%; White: 88%; International: 1%. **Religious preference:** Roman Catholic: 16%; Protestant: 56%; No preference: 21%; Christian Church (Disciples of Christ): 7%.

ADMISSIONS FACTS AND FIGURES
Phone: (800) 537-1883. **Email:** enrollment@culver.edu. **Website:** http://www.culver.edu. **Application deadlines for fall 2007:** Regular decision: Rolling. Early decision: Not offered. Early action: Not offered. Admission can be deferred. **Application fee:** $25. Common application is not accepted. **To apply online, go to:** http://www.culver.edu/enrollment/app/. **Admissions requirements/recommendations:** High school units required (recom-

mended): English: 0 (4); Mathematics: 0 (2); Science: 0 (2); Foreign language: 0 (0); Social studies: 0 (3); History: 0 (0); Academic electives: 0 (0); Total units: 15 (0). Tests: The college uses SAT or ACT scores in admissions decisions. Neither SAT nor ACT required. For admission to the fall 2007 entering class, the school will accept: ACT with writing, ACT without writing. Campus visit: Recommended. Admissions interview: Recommended. Off-campus interview: May be arranged. **Factors that count in admissions decisions:** *Academic:* Secondary school record: Very important. Class rank: Very important. Letters of recommendation: Considered. Standardized test scores: Very important. Essay: Considered. *Nonacademic:* Interview: Considered. Extracurricular activities: Considered. Talent/ability: Considered. Character/personal qualities: Considered. Alumni/ae relationship: Considered. Geographical residence: Not considered. State residency: Not considered. Religious affiliation/commitment: Considered. Minority status: Not considered. Volunteer work: Considered. Work experience: Considered. **Other schools with the greatest overlap in applicants:** Central Methodist University; Columbia College; Hannibal-LaGrange College; Quincy University; Truman State University. **Admissions statistics for the fall 2005 entering class:** Total applicants: 959. Total accepted: 727. Freshmen enrolled: 155; 51% were from out of state. Overall acceptance rate: 76%. **Credentials of fall 2005 freshmen:** 16% ranked in the top 10 percent of their high school class; 37% were in the top 25 percent, and 68% were in the top half. (Proportion submitting class standing: 98%.) **Average high school grade point average:** 3.3. **First-year students who submitted SAT scores:** 3%. Scores (25/75 percentile): Verbal: N/A, Math: N/A, Combined: N/A. **First-year students submitting ACT scores:** 96%. Scores (25/75 percentile): English: 18-25, Math: 17-24, Composite: 18-26.

ACADEMICS
Year founded: 1853. **Academic calendar:** Semester. **Degrees offered:** bachelor's. **Most popular majors:** 18% nursing/registered nurse training (R.N., A.S.N., B.S.N., M.S.N.), 14% business/commerce, 7% criminal justice/law enforcement administration, 6% elementary education and teaching, 5% psychology. **Major fields of study:** biological and biomedical sciences; business, management, marketing, and related support services; communication, journalism, and related programs; education; English language and literature/letters; health professions and related clinical sciences; history; mathematics and statistics; parks, recreation, leisure, and fitness studies; philosophy and religious studies; psychology; security and protective services; visual and performing arts. **Areas of required coursework:** arts/fine arts, humanities, computer literacy, mathematics, English (including composition), sciences (biological or physical), social science, other. **Pre-professional programs:** pre-law, pre-dentistry, pre-medicine, pre-theology, pre-veterinary science, pre-optometry, pre-pharmacy, other. **Special academic programs (% participation):** distance learning (0%), double major (8%), dual enrollment (2%), honors program (10%), independent study (14%), internships (35%), liberal arts/career combination (100%), student-designed major (3%), study abroad (4%), teacher certificate program (15%). **Teacher certification offered in:** early childhood, special education, elementary, middle/junior high, secondary. **Faculty and instruction (2005-2006):** Total instructional faculty: 44 full-time, 45 part-time (55% men; 45% women; 3% minorities). Full-time faculty with Ph.D. or other terminal degree: 68%. Student/faculty ratio: 13/1. Classes of fewer than 20 students: 62%; of 20 to 49 students: 36%; of 50 or more students: 2%. **Advanced Placement and International Baccalaureate credit:** AP tests may be used for: Credit and/or placement. Scores accepted: 3, 4, 5. International Baccalaureate exams may be used for: Credit only. **Freshmen returning for sophomore year:** 70%. **Graduation rates:** Four-year: 47%; five-year: 55%; six-year: 49%. **Graduate study:** 12% of students pursue further study immediately upon graduation. Fields in which graduates pursue further study: Master of Business Administration (MBA), 2%; law, 4%; theology (or the seminary), 1%; arts and sciences, 5%.

COSTS AND FINANCIAL AID
Financial aid office: (573) 288-6307. **Expenses (2006-2007):** Tuition and fees 2006-2007: $15,450; room/board: $6,550. Estimated books and supplies: $800; transportation: $2,000; personal expenses: $502. **Financial aid:** Priority filing date for institution's financial aid form: June 15. In 2005-2006, 100% of undergraduates applied for financial aid. Of those, 89% were determined to have financial need; 26% had their need fully met. Average financial aid package (proportion receiving): $11,986 (89%). Average amount of gift aid, such as scholarships or grants (proportion receiving): $8,650 (89%). Average amount of self-help aid, such as work study or loans (proportion receiving): $3,906 (76%). Average need-based loan (excluding PLUS or other private loans): $3,680. Among students who received need-based aid, the average percentage of need met: 75%. Among students who received aid based on merit, the average award (and the pro-

portion receiving): $12,103 (10%). The average athletic scholarship (and the proportion receiving): $3,052 (11%). Average amount of debt of borrowers graduating in 2005: $18,429. Proportion who borrowed: 89%.

CAMPUS LIFE AND EXTRACURRICULAR ACTIVITIES
Campus housing available (% using): coed dorms (25%), women's dorms (26%), men's dorms (21%), sorority housing (15%), fraternity housing (13%). Students who live in college-owned, operated, or affiliated housing: 68%. **Student employment:** During the 2005-2006 academic year, 51% of undergraduates worked on campus. Average per-year earnings: $1,500.
Clubs and organizations: Number of student organizations: 40. Activities include: choral groups, concert band, dance, drama/theater, jazz band, literary magazine, music ensembles, musical theater, opera, radio station, student government, student newspaper. Number of fraternities: 4; sororities: 3. Proportion of men in fraternities: 23%; of women in sororities: 27%. Average proportion of students who stay on campus on weekends: 50%.
Sports program (2005-2006): Member of NAIA. *Men's intercollegiate varsity sports:* baseball, basketball, football, golf, soccer. *Women's intercollegiate varsity sports:* basketball, golf, soccer, softball, volleyball.

SERVICES AND FACILITIES
Basic services: nonremedial tutoring, placement service. **Remedial assistance:** other. **Counseling services:** career, personal, veteran student, academic, psychological, religious. **For learning-disabled students:** School does not offer a structured program with separate admission and additional fees. Total undergraduates in learning-disabled program or receiving services: 5. Services include: tape recorders, videotaped classes, untimed tests, note-taking services, oral tests, learning center, readers, extended time for tests, tutors. **Library:** Number of titles: 165,402; number of current serial subscriptions: 193. **Information technology resources:** Students are not required to lease or own a computer. Number of campus computers available to all students: 102. School has a wireless network. Approximate number of users that can be accommodated: 500. Proportion of college-owned housing units wired for high-speed internet access: 100%. **Campus safety:** Security services offered: 24-hour foot-and-vehicle patrols, late-night transport/escort service, 24-hour emergency telephones, lighted pathways/sidewalks, controlled dormitory access (key, security card, etc).

TRANSFER AND INTERNATIONAL STUDENTS
Transfer students: May apply for admission for the following academic terms: Fall, Spring, Summer. Applicants do not need a minimum number of credits to apply. For fall 2005: Transfer applications received: 314. Transfer applicants offered admission: 218. Transfer applicants enrolled: 95. **International students:** Number of foreign undergraduates: 6 (1% of student body). Number of countries represented: 4. Minimum TOEFL score required: 500 (paper); 173 (computer).

Drury University

- **Address:** 900 N. Benton Avenue, Springfield, MO 65802
- **Website:** http://www.drury.edu
- **Private; Religious affiliation:** Christian Church (Disciples of Christ)/United Church of Christ
- **Enrollment:** 1,541 full-time; 39 part-time

KEY STATS
✔ **U.S News College Ranking:** 9, Universities–Master's (Midwest)
✔ **ACT Score (25th/75th percentile):** 23-28
✔ **Tuition:** 2006-2007: $15,512

Selectivity: More selective	**Room/board:** $5,790
Acceptance rate: 78%	**Average debt:** $17,585
Student/faculty ratio: 13/1	**Proportion who borrowed:** 42%

UNDERGRADUATE STUDENT BODY STATS
2005-2006 enrollment: 1,541 full-time; 39 part-time. Men: 44%; women: 56%. **Ethnic makeup:** African American: 1%; American-Indian: 1%; Asian American: 2%; Hispanic: 2%; White: 91%; International: 4%.

ADMISSIONS FACTS AND FIGURES
Phone: (417) 873-7205. **Email:** druryad@drury.edu. **Website:** http://www.drury.edu. **Application deadlines for fall 2007:** Regular decision: March 15. Early decision: Not offered. Early action: Not offered. Admission

can be deferred. **Application fee:** $25. Common application is not accepted. **To apply online, go to:** http://www.drury.edu/admission/freshmen. **Admissions requirements/recommendations:** High school units required (recommended): English: 4 (4); Mathematics: 3 (4); Science: 3 (3); Foreign language: 2 (2); Social studies: 3 (3); Total units: 12 (12). Tests: The college uses SAT or ACT scores in admissions decisions. Either SAT or ACT required. For admission to the fall 2007 entering class, the school will accept: ACT with writing, ACT without writing. Campus visit: Recommended. Admissions interview: Recommended. Off-campus interview: May be arranged. **Factors that count in admissions decisions:** *Academic:* Secondary school record: Considered. Class rank: Important. Letters of recommendation: Important. Standardized test scores: Very important. Essay: Important. *Nonacademic:* Interview: Considered. Extracurricular activities: Considered. Talent/ability: Considered. Character/personal qualities: Important. Alumni/ae relationship: Considered. Geographical residence: Considered. State residency: Not considered. Religious affiliation/commitment: Not considered. Minority status: Considered. Volunteer work: Considered. Work experience: Considered. **Other schools with the greatest overlap in applicants:** Missouri State University; Truman State University; University of Missouri–Columbia; Washington University in St. Louis. **Admissions statistics for the fall 2005 entering class:** Total applicants: 1,106. Total accepted: 858. Freshmen enrolled: 378; 22% were from out of state. Overall acceptance rate: 78%. **Credentials of fall 2005 freshmen:** 38% ranked in the top 10 percent of their high school class; 67% were in the top 25 percent, and 91% were in the top half. (Proportion submitting class standing: 91%.) **Average high school grade point average:** 3.7. **First-year students who submitted SAT scores:** 16%. Scores (25/75 percentile): Verbal: 530-640, Math: 523-650, Combined: 1053-1290. **First-year students submitting ACT scores:** 94%. Scores (25/75 percentile): English: 22-30, Math: 22-27, Composite: 23-28.

ACADEMICS
Year founded: 1873. **Academic calendar:** Semester. **Degrees offered:** bachelor's, master's. **Most popular majors:** 18% business, management, marketing, and related support services, 13% biological and biomedical sciences, 10% communication, journalism, and related programs, 8% psychology, 8% social sciences. **Major fields of study:** biological and biomedical sciences; business, management, marketing, and related support services; communication, journalism, and related programs; computer and information sciences and support services; education; English language and literature/letters; foreign languages, literatures, and linguistics; health professions and related clinical sciences; history; legal professions and studies; liberal arts and sciences studies, and humanities; mathematics and statistics; natural resources and conservation; parks, recreation, leisure, and fitness studies; philosophy and religious studies; physical sciences; psychology; security and protective services; social sciences; visual and performing arts. **Areas of required coursework:** arts/fine arts, humanities, computer literacy, mathematics, English (including composition), philosophy, foreign languages, sciences (biological or physical), history, social science, other. **Pre-professional programs:** pre-law, pre-dentistry, pre-medicine, pre-veterinary science, pre-optometry, pre-pharmacy, other. **Special academic programs (% participation):** accelerated program, cooperative (work-study plan) program (55%), distance learning (12%), double major (20%), dual enrollment, English as a Second Language (ESL), honors program (10%), independent study, internships (75%), liberal arts/career combination (100%), student-designed major, study abroad (40%), teacher certificate program (20%), other. **Teacher certification offered in:** early childhood, elementary, middle/junior high, secondary. **Cooperative education programs:** other. **Reserve Officers Training Corps (ROTC):** Army ROTC: Offered on campus. **Faculty and instruction (2005-2006):** Total instructional faculty: 123 full-time, 62 part-time (59% men; 41% women; 7% minorities). Full-time faculty with Ph.D. or other terminal degree: 89%. Student/faculty ratio: 13/1. Classes of fewer than 20 students: 62%; of 20 to 49 students: 37%; of 50 or more students: 1%. **Advanced Placement and International Baccalaureate credit:** AP tests may be used for: Credit and/or placement. Scores accepted: 3, 4, 5. International Baccalaureate exams may be used for: Credit and/or placement. **Freshmen returning for sophomore year:** 81%. **Graduation rates:** Four-year: 48%; five-year: 63%; six-year: 63%. **Graduate study:** 31% of students pursue further study within one year. Fields in which graduates pursue further study: Master of Business Administration (MBA), 15%; law, 8%; medicine, 15%; engineering, 2%; theology (or the seminary), 3%; education, 5%; arts and sciences, 52%.

COSTS AND FINANCIAL AID
Financial aid office: (417) 873-7312. **Expenses (2006-2007):** Tuition and fees 2006-2007: $15,512; room/board: $5,790. **Financial aid:** Priority filing date

for institution's financial aid form: March 15. In 2005-2006, 97% of undergraduates applied for financial aid. Of those, 89% were determined to have financial need; 92% had their need fully met. Average financial aid package (proportion receiving): $7,737 (89%). Average amount of gift aid, such as scholarships or grants (proportion receiving): $6,889 (88%). Average amount of self-help aid, such as work study or loans (proportion receiving): $5,868 (83%). Average need-based loan (excluding PLUS or other private loans): $5,549. Among students who received need-based aid, the average percentage of need met: 83%. Among students who received aid based on merit, the average award (and the proportion receiving): $2,979 (14%). The average athletic scholarship (and the proportion receiving): $6,989 (4%). Average amount of debt of borrowers graduating in 2005: $17,585. Proportion who borrowed: 42%.

CAMPUS LIFE AND EXTRACURRICULAR ACTIVITIES

Campus housing available (% using): coed dorms (20%), women's dorms (16%), men's dorms (7%), fraternity housing (11%), apartments for married students (4%), apartment for single students (37%), other housing options (4%). Students who live in college-owned, operated, or affiliated housing: 52%. **Student employment:** During the 2005-2006 academic year, 30% of undergraduates worked on campus. Average per-year earnings: $2,000. **Clubs and organizations:** Number of student organizations: 60. Activities include: choral groups, concert band, dance, drama/theater, jazz band, literary magazine, music ensembles, musical theater, opera, pep band, radio station, student government, student newspaper, student film society, symphony orchestra, television station. Number of fraternities: 4; sororities: 4. Proportion of men in fraternities: 32%; of women in sororities: 24%. Average proportion of students who stay on campus on weekends: 50%. **Sports program (2005-2006):** Member of NCAA II. *Men's intercollegiate varsity sports:* basketball, cross-country, golf, soccer, swimming and diving, tennis. *Women's intercollegiate varsity sports:* basketball, cross-country, golf, soccer, swimming and diving, tennis, volleyball.

SERVICES AND FACILITIES

Basic services: placement service, health service. **Remedial assistance:** math, writing, other. **Counseling services:** career, personal, academic, psychological, birth control, religious. **For learning-disabled students:** School does not offer a structured program with separate admission and additional fees. Total undergraduates in learning-disabled program or receiving services: 28. Services include: reading machines, tape recorders, other special classes, videotaped classes, untimed tests, note-taking services, oral tests, readers, extended time for tests, tutors, early syllabus, priority registration, priority seating, texts on tape, typist/scribe, exams on tape or computer, other testing accomodations, waiver of foreign language degree requirement, waiver of math degree requirement. **Information technology resources:** Students are not required to lease or own a computer. Number of campus computers available to all students: 365. School has a wireless network. Approximate number of users that can be accommodated: 2,000. Proportion of college-owned housing units wired for high-speed internet access: 100%. **Campus safety:** Security services offered: 24-hour foot-and-vehicle patrols, late-night transport/escort service, 24-hour emergency telephones, lighted pathways/sidewalks, controlled dormitory access (key, security card, etc.).

TRANSFER AND INTERNATIONAL STUDENTS

Transfer students: May apply for admission for the following academic terms: Fall, Winter, Spring, Summer. Applicants do not need a minimum number of credits to apply. For fall 2005: Transfer applications received: 204. Transfer applicants offered admission: 135. Transfer applicants enrolled: 95. **International students:** Number of foreign undergraduates: 56 (4% of student body). Number of countries represented: 45. Minimum TOEFL score required: 550 (paper); 197 (computer). Average TOEFL score: 573 (paper).

Evangel University

- **Address:** 1111 N. Glenstone, Springfield, MO 65802
- **Website:** http://www.evangel.edu
- **Private; Religious affiliation:** Assemblies of God
- **Enrollment:** 1,672 full-time; 63 part-time

KEY STATS

✔ **U.S News College Ranking:** third tier, Comp. Coll.–Bachelor's (Midwest)
✔ **ACT Score (25th/75th percentile):** 18-25
✔ **Tuition:** 2005-2006: $12,800

Selectivity: Selective	**Room/board:** $4,620
Acceptance rate: 81%	**Average debt:** N/A
Student/faculty ratio: 17/1	**Proportion who borrowed:** N/A

UNDERGRADUATE STUDENT BODY STATS

2005-2006 enrollment: 1,672 full-time; 63 part-time. Men: 42%; women: 58%. **Ethnic makeup:** African American: 4%; American-Indian: 1%; Asian American: 2%; Hispanic: 4%; White: 89%.

ADMISSIONS FACTS AND FIGURES

Phone: (800) 382-6435. **Email:** admissions@evangel.edu. **Website:** http://www.evangel.edu. **Application deadlines for fall 2007:** Regular decision: August 15. Early decision: Not offered. Early action: Not offered. Admission cannot be deferred. **Application fee:** $25. Common application is not accepted. **Admissions requirements/recommendations:** High school units required (recommended): English: 3 (3); Mathematics: 2 (2); Science: 3 (3); Foreign language: 0 (0); Social studies: 2 (2); History: 0 (0); Academic electives: 0 (0); Total units: 11 (11). Tests: The college uses SAT or ACT scores in admissions decisions. Either SAT or ACT required. For admission to the fall 2007 entering class, the school will accept: ACT with writing. Campus visit: Recommended. Admissions interview: Neither required nor recommended. **Factors that count in admissions decisions:** *Academic:* Secondary school record: Very important. Class rank: Important. Letters of recommendation: Not considered. Standardized test scores: Very important. Essay: Not considered. *Nonacademic:* Interview: Not considered. Extracurricular activities: Not considered. Talent/ability: Not considered. Character/personal qualities: Not considered. Alumni/ae relationship: Not considered. Geographical residence: Not considered. State residency: Not considered. Religious affiliation/commitment: Not considered. Minority status: Not considered. Volunteer work: Not considered. Work experience: Not considered. **Other schools with the greatest overlap in applicants:** College of the Ozarks; Drury University; Missouri State University; Southwest Baptist University. **Admissions statistics for the fall 2005 entering class:** Total applicants: 881. Total accepted: 713. Freshmen enrolled: 423; 73% were from out of state. Overall acceptance rate: 81%. **Credentials of fall 2005 freshmen:** 17% ranked in the top 10 percent of their high school class; 42% were in the top 25 percent, and 69% were in the top half. (Proportion submitting class standing: 91%.) **First-year students who submitted SAT scores:** 23%. Scores (25/75 percentile): Verbal: N/A, Math: N/A, Combined: N/A. **First-year students submitting ACT scores:** 73%. Scores (25/75 percentile): English: 17-25, Math: 17-24, Composite: 18-25.

ACADEMICS

Year founded: 1955. **Academic calendar:** Semester. **Degrees offered:** associate, bachelor's, master's. **Most popular majors:** 18% psychology, 17% business/commerce, 15% education, 12% communication studies/speech communication and rhetoric, 11% history. **Major fields of study:** biological and biomedical sciences; business, management, marketing, and related support services; communication, journalism, and related programs; computer and information sciences and support services; education; English language and literature/letters; foreign languages, literatures, and linguistics; health professions and related clinical sciences; history; mathematics and statistics; multi/interdisciplinary studies; parks, recreation, leisure, and fitness studies; philosophy and religious studies; physical sciences; psychology; social sciences; visual and performing arts. **Areas of required coursework:** arts/fine arts, humanities, computer literacy, mathematics, English (including composition), sciences (biological or physical), history, social science. **Pre-professional programs:** pre-law, pre-dentistry, pre-medicine, pre-theology, pre-veterinary science, pre-optometry, pre-pharmacy. **Special academic programs (% participation):** double major (10%), internships (50%). **Teacher certification offered in:** early childhood, special education, elementary, middle/junior high, secondary. **Cooperative education programs:** engineering. **Reserve Officers Training Corps (ROTC):** Army ROTC:

Offered on campus. **Faculty and instruction (2005-2006):** Total instructional faculty: 103 full-time, 60 part-time (69% men; 31% women; 3% minorities). Full-time faculty with Ph.D. or other terminal degree: 61%. Student/faculty ratio: 17/1. Classes of fewer than 20 students: 62%; of 20 to 49 students: 36%; of 50 or more students: 2%. **Advanced Placement and International Baccalaureate credit:** International Baccalaureate exams may be used for: Credit and/or placement. **Freshmen returning for sophomore year:** 65%. **Graduation rates:** Four-year: 41%; five-year: 42%; six-year: 44%.

COSTS AND FINANCIAL AID
Financial aid office: (417) 865-2815. **Expenses (2005-2006):** Tuition and fees 2005-2006: $12,800; room/board: $4,620. **Financial aid:** Priority filing date for institution's financial aid form: February 15.

CAMPUS LIFE AND EXTRACURRICULAR ACTIVITIES
Campus housing available: coed dorms, women's dorms, men's dorms, apartments for married students. Students who live in college-owned, operated, or affiliated housing: 71%. **Student employment:** During the 2005-2006 academic year, 23% of undergraduates worked on campus. Average per-year earnings: $1,600. **Clubs and organizations:** Number of student organizations: 40. Activities include: choral groups, concert band, drama/theater, jazz band, literary magazine, music ensembles, musical theater, pep band, radio station, student government, student newspaper, symphony orchestra, television station, yearbook. Number of fraternities: 0; sororities: 0. Average proportion of students who stay on campus on weekends: 80%. **Sports program (2005-2006):** Member of NAIA. *Men's intercollegiate varsity sports:* baseball, basketball, cross-country, football, golf, track and field (indoor), track and field (outdoor). *Women's intercollegiate varsity sports:* basketball, cross-country, golf, softball, tennis, track and field (indoor), track and field (outdoor), volleyball.

SERVICES AND FACILITIES
Basic services: nonremedial tutoring, placement service, health service. **Remedial assistance:** reading, math, writing, study skills. **Counseling services:** career, personal, veteran student, academic, religious. **For learning-disabled students:** School does not offer a structured program with separate admission and additional fees. Total undergraduates in learning-disabled program or receiving services: 17. Services include: remedial math, remedial English, remedial reading, tape recorders, diagnostic testing service, untimed tests, oral tests, learning center, readers, extended time for tests, tutors, other testing accomodations. **Library:** Number of titles: 91,867; number of current serial subscriptions: 1,063. **Information technology resources:** Students are not required to lease or own a computer. Number of campus computers available to all students: 392. School does not have a wireless network. Proportion of college-owned housing units wired for high-speed internet access: 100%. **Campus safety:** Security services offered: 24-hour foot-and-vehicle patrols, late-night transport/escort service, 24-hour emergency telephones, lighted pathways/sidewalks, student patrols, controlled dormitory access (key, security card, etc).

TRANSFER AND INTERNATIONAL STUDENTS
Transfer students: May apply for admission for the following academic terms: Fall, Spring, Summer. Applicants do not need a minimum number of credits to apply. For fall 2005: Transfer applications received: 262. Transfer applicants offered admission: 192. Transfer applicants enrolled: 143. **International students:** Number of foreign undergraduates: 5. Number of countries represented: 7. Minimum TOEFL score required: 490 (paper).

Fontbonne University

- **Address:** 6800 Wydown Boulevard, St. Louis, MO 63105
- **Website:** http://www.fontbonne.edu
- **Private; Religious affiliation:** Roman Catholic
- **Enrollment:** 1,547 full-time; 531 part-time

KEY STATS
✔ **U.S News College Ranking:** 65, Universities–Master's (Midwest)
✔ **ACT Score (25th/75th percentile):** 19-24
✔ **Tuition:** 2006-2007: $17,440

Selectivity: Selective	**Room/board:** $6,739
Acceptance rate: 74%	**Average debt:** $17,500
Student/faculty ratio: 12/1	**Proportion who borrowed:** 85%

UNDERGRADUATE STUDENT BODY STATS
2005-2006 enrollment: 1,547 full-time; 531 part-time. Men: 25%; women: 75%. **Ethnic makeup:** African American: 32%; Asian American: 1%; Hispanic: 1%; White: 65%.

ADMISSIONS FACTS AND FIGURES
Phone: (314) 889-1400. **Email:** admissions@fontbonne.edu. **Website:** http://www.fontbonne.edu. **Application deadlines for fall 2007:** Regular decision: Rolling. Early decision: Not offered. Early action: Not offered. Admission can be deferred. **Application fee:** $25. Common application is accepted. **Admissions requirements/recommendations:** High school units required (recommended): English: 4; Mathematics: 3; Science: 3; Social studies: 3; Academic electives: 3; Total units: 16. Tests: The college uses SAT or ACT scores in admissions decisions. Either SAT or ACT required. For admission to the fall 2007 entering class, the school will accept: ACT without writing. Campus visit: Recommended. Admissions interview: Recommended. Off-campus interview: May be arranged. **Factors that count in admissions decisions:** *Academic:* Secondary school record: Very important. Class rank: Very important. Letters of recommendation: Important. Standardized test scores: Very important. Essay: Important. *Nonacademic:* Interview: Considered. Extracurricular activities: Considered. Talent/ability: Considered. Character/personal qualities: Very important. Alumni/ae relationship: Important. Geographical residence: Not considered. State residency: Not considered. Religious affiliation/commitment: Not considered. Minority status: Considered. Volunteer work: Considered. Work experience: Considered. **Admissions statistics for the fall 2005 entering class:** Total applicants: 618. Total accepted: 456. Freshmen enrolled: 195; 11% were from out of state. Overall acceptance rate: 74%. **Credentials of fall 2005 freshmen:** 14% ranked in the top 10 percent of their high school class; 34% were in the top 25 percent, and 71% were in the top half. (Proportion submitting class standing: 79%.) **Average high school grade point average:** 3.2. **First-year students submitting ACT scores:** 91%. Scores (25/75 percentile): English: 19-26, Math: 17-24, Composite: 19-24.

ACADEMICS
Year founded: 1923. **Academic calendar:** Semester. **Degrees offered:** bachelor's, post-bachelor's certificate, master's. **Most popular majors:** 45% business administration and management, 8% special education and teaching, 6% organizational behavior studies, 5% communication studies/speech communication and rhetoric, 5% elementary education and teaching. **Major fields of study:** biological and biomedical sciences; business, management, marketing, and related support services; communication, journalism, and related programs; computer and information sciences and support services; education; English language and literature/letters; family and consumer sciences/human sciences; health professions and related clinical sciences; history; legal professions and studies; liberal arts and sciences studies, and humanities; mathematics and statistics; parks, recreation, leisure, and fitness studies; psychology; public administration and social service professions; visual and performing arts. **Areas of required coursework:** arts/fine arts, humanities, computer literacy, mathematics, English (including composition), philosophy, sciences (biological or physical), history, social science, other. **Pre-professional programs:** pre-law, pre-dentistry, pre-medicine, pre-veterinary science, pre-optometry, other. **Special academic programs (% participation):** accelerated program, cooperative (work-study plan) program, cross-registration, distance learning (18%), double major, dual enrollment, English as a Second Language (ESL), exchange student program (domestic), honors program, independent study, internships, liberal arts/career combination, student-designed major, study abroad, teacher certificate program. **Teacher certification offered in:** early childhood, special education, elementary, middle/junior high, secondary. **Reserve Officers Training Corps (ROTC):** Army ROTC: Offered at cooperating institution (Washington University); Air Force ROTC: Offered at cooperating institution (Washington University). **Faculty and instruction (2005-2006):** Total instructional faculty: 66 full-time, 239 part-time (33% men; 67% women; 10% minorities). Full-time faculty with Ph.D. or other terminal degree: 73%. Student/faculty ratio: 12/1. Classes of fewer than 20 students: 84%; of 20 to 49 students: 16%; of 50 or more students: 0%. **Advanced Placement and International Baccalaureate credit:** AP tests may be used for: Credit only. Scores accepted: 4, 5. **Freshmen returning for sophomore year:** 72%. **Graduation rates:** Four-year: 33%; five-year: 51%; six-year: 54%. **Graduate study:** 15% of students pursue further study within one year.

COSTS AND FINANCIAL AID
Financial aid office: (314) 889-1414. **Expenses (2006-2007):** Tuition and fees 2006-2007: $17,440; room/board: $6,739. Estimated books and supplies: $650; transportation: $950. **Financial aid:** Priority filing date for institution's

financial aid form: April 1. In 2005-2006, 95% of undergraduates applied for financial aid. Of those, 66% were determined to have financial need; 76% had their need fully met. Average financial aid package (proportion receiving): $14,500 (66%). Average amount of gift aid, such as scholarships or grants (proportion receiving): $5,200 (66%). Average amount of self-help aid, such as work study or loans (proportion receiving): $4,000 (66%). Average need-based loan (excluding PLUS or other private loans): $3,000. Among students who received need-based aid, the average percentage of need met: 46%. Among students who received aid based on merit, the average award (and the proportion receiving): $5,000 (40%). The average athletic scholarship (and the proportion receiving): $0 (0%). Average amount of debt of borrowers graduating in 2005: $17,500. Proportion who borrowed: 85%.

CAMPUS LIFE AND EXTRACURRICULAR ACTIVITIES

Campus housing available: coed dorms, apartment for single students, special housing for international students. Students who live in college-owned, operated, or affiliated housing: 19%. **Clubs and organizations:** Number of student organizations: 34. Activities include: dance, drama/theater, literary magazine, music ensembles, student government, student newspaper. Number of fraternities: 0; sororities: 0. Average proportion of students who stay on campus on weekends: 50%. **Sports program (2005-2006):** Member of NCAA III. *Men's intercollegiate varsity sports:* baseball, basketball, golf, soccer, tennis. *Women's intercollegiate varsity sports:* basketball, cross-country, soccer, softball, tennis, track and field (outdoor), volleyball.

SERVICES AND FACILITIES

Remedial assistance: reading, math, writing, study skills. **Counseling services:** career, personal, academic. **For learning-disabled students:** School does not offer a structured program with separate admission and additional fees. Services include: remedial math, remedial English, reading machines, remedial reading, tape recorders, other special classes, untimed tests, note-taking services, special bookstore section, oral tests, learning center, readers, extended time for tests, tutors. **Library:** Number of titles: 79,888; number of current serial subscriptions: 264. **Information technology resources:** Students are not required to lease or own a computer. Number of campus computers available to all students: 110. School has a wireless network. Proportion of college-owned housing units wired for high-speed internet access: 100%. **Campus safety:** Security services offered: late-night transport/escort service, 24-hour emergency telephones, lighted pathways/sidewalks, controlled dormitory access (key, security card, etc).

TRANSFER AND INTERNATIONAL STUDENTS

Transfer students: May apply for admission for the following academic terms: Fall, Spring, Summer. Applicants do not need a minimum number of credits to apply. For fall 2005: Transfer applications received: 368. Transfer applicants offered admission: 279. Transfer applicants enrolled: 177. **International students:** Number of foreign undergraduates: 8. Number of countries represented: 1. Minimum TOEFL score required: 500 (paper); 193 (computer). Average TOEFL score: 500 (paper).

Hannibal-LaGrange College

- **Address:** 2800 Palmyra Road, Hannibal, MO 63401
- **Website:** http://www.hlg.edu
- **Private; Religious affiliation:** Southern Baptist Convention
- **Enrollment:** 781 full-time; 275 part-time

KEY STATS

✔ **U.S News College Ranking:** fourth tier, Comp. Coll.–Bachelor's (Midwest)
✔ **ACT Score (25th/75th percentile):** 20-25
✔ **Tuition:** 2006-2007: $12,708

Selectivity: Selective	**Room/board:** $4,930
Acceptance rate: 96%	**Average debt:** $16,689
Student/faculty ratio: 12/1	**Proportion who borrowed:** N/A

UNDERGRADUATE STUDENT BODY STATS

2005-2006 enrollment: 781 full-time; 275 part-time. Men: 38%; women: 62%. **Ethnic makeup:** African American: 2%; Hispanic: 1%; White: 94%; International: 3%. **Religious preference:** Roman Catholic: 3%; Protestant: 9%; Southern Baptist Convention: 75%.

ADMISSIONS FACTS AND FIGURES

Phone: (800) 454-1119. **Email:** admissio@hlg.edu. **Website:** http://www.hlg.edu. **Application deadlines for fall 2007:** Regular decision: August 26. Early decision: Not offered. Early action: Not offered. Admission cannot be deferred. **Application fee:** $25. Common application is not accepted. **Admissions requirements/recommendations:** High school units required (recommended): English: (4); Mathematics: (3); Science: (3); History: (2). Tests: The college uses SAT or ACT scores in admissions decisions. Either SAT or ACT required. For admission to the fall 2007 entering class, the school will accept: ACT with writing, ACT without writing. Campus visit: Recommended. Admissions interview: Recommended. Off-campus interview: May be arranged. **Factors that count in admissions decisions:** *Academic:* Secondary school record: Important. Class rank: Considered. Letters of recommendation: Considered. Standardized test scores: Very important. Essay: Not considered. *Nonacademic:* Interview: Considered. Extracurricular activities: Considered. Talent/ability: Considered. Character/personal qualities: Important. Alumni/ae relationship: Considered. Geographical residence: Not considered. State residency: Not considered. Religious affiliation/commitment: Not considered. Minority status: Not considered. Volunteer work: Considered. Work experience: Not considered. **Other schools with the greatest overlap in applicants:** Culver-Stockton College; Missouri Baptist University; Quincy University; Southwest Baptist University; University of Missouri–Columbia. **Admissions statistics for the fall 2005 entering class:** Total applicants: 332. Total accepted: 318. Freshmen enrolled: 119; 25% were from out of state. Overall acceptance rate: 96%. **Credentials of fall 2005 freshmen:** 20% ranked in the top 10 percent of their high school class; 38% were in the top 25 percent, and 71% were in the top half. **First-year students who submitted SAT scores:** 2%. Scores (25/75 percentile): Verbal: 445-650, Math: 490-550, Combined: 935-1200. **First-year students submitting ACT scores:** 98%. Scores (25/75 percentile): English: 19-27, Math: 18-24, Composite: 20-25.

ACADEMICS

Year founded: 1858. **Academic calendar:** Semester. **Degrees offered:** certificate, associate, bachelor's. **Most popular majors:** 28% business administration and management, 11% social work, 8% elementary education and teaching. **Major fields of study:** agriculture, agriculture operations, and related sciences; biological and biomedical sciences; communication, journalism, and related programs; computer and information sciences and support services; education; English language and literature/letters; health professions and related clinical sciences; liberal arts and sciences studies, and humanities; mathematics and statistics; parks, recreation, leisure, and fitness studies; psychology; public administration and social service professions; security and protective services; theology and religious vocations; visual and performing arts. **Areas of required coursework:** arts/fine arts, humanities, mathematics, English (including composition), sciences (biological or physical), history, social science, other. **Pre-professional programs:** pre-law, pre-medicine, pre-theology, other. **Special academic programs (% participation):** accelerated program (17%), cooperative (work-study plan) program (4%), double major, dual enrollment, honors program (4%), independent study, internships (20%), teacher certificate program (17%), weekend college (16%). **Teacher certification offered in:** early childhood, elementary, middle/junior high, secondary. **Cooperative education programs:** engineering. **Faculty and instruction (2005-2006):** Total instructional faculty: 52 full-time, 29 part-time (48% men; 52% women; 2% minorities). Full-time faculty with Ph.D. or other terminal degree: 38%. Student/faculty ratio: 12/1. **Advanced Placement and International Baccalaureate credit:** AP tests may be used for: Credit only. Scores accepted: 3. **Freshmen returning for sophomore year:** 64%. **Graduation rates:** Six-year: 46%. **Graduate study:** 27% of students pursue further study immediately upon graduation.

COSTS AND FINANCIAL AID

Financial aid office: (573) 221-3675. **Expenses (2006-2007):** Tuition and fees 2006-2007: $12,708; room/board: $4,930. **Financial aid:** Priority filing date for institution's financial aid form: July 1. Of those, 74% were determined to have financial need; Average financial aid package (proportion receiving): N/A (74%). Average amount of gift aid, such as scholarships or grants (proportion receiving): N/A (72%). Average amount of self-help aid, such as work study or loans (proportion receiving): N/A (68%). The average athletic scholarship (and the proportion receiving): $2,500 (12%). Average amount of debt of borrowers graduating in 2005: $16,689.

CAMPUS LIFE AND EXTRACURRICULAR ACTIVITIES

Campus housing available (% using): women's dorms (56%), men's dorms (30%), apartment for single students (14%). Students who live in college-owned, operated, or affiliated housing: 45%. **Student employment:** During the 2005-2006 academic year, 12% of undergraduates worked on campus. Average per-year earnings: $1,100. **Clubs and organizations:** Number of student organizations: 20. Activities include: choral groups, concert band, drama/theater, jazz band, music ensembles, student government, student newspaper, yearbook. Number of fraternities: 0; sororities: 0. Average proportion of students who stay on campus on weekends: 65%. **Sports program (2005-2006):** Member of NAIA. *Men's intercollegiate varsity sports:* baseball, basketball, cross-country, golf, soccer. *Women's intercollegiate varsity sports:* basketball, cross-country, soccer, softball, volleyball.

SERVICES AND FACILITIES

Basic services: nonremedial tutoring, health insurance. **Remedial assistance:** math, writing. **Counseling services:** career, academic, religious. **For learning-disabled students:** School does not offer a structured program with separate admission and additional fees. Services include: untimed tests, note-taking services, oral tests, extended time for tests, tutors, priority seating. **Library:** Number of titles: 86,508; number of current serial subscriptions: 6,451. **Information technology resources:** Students are not required to lease or own a computer. Number of campus computers available to all students: 82. School does not have a wireless network. Proportion of college-owned housing units wired for high-speed internet access: 94%. **Campus safety:** Security services offered: late-night transport/escort service, 24-hour emergency telephones, lighted pathways/sidewalks, student patrols, controlled dormitory access (key, security card, etc.).

TRANSFER AND INTERNATIONAL STUDENTS

Transfer students: May apply for admission for the following academic terms: Fall, Spring, Summer. Applicants need a minimum number of credits to apply. **International students:** Number of foreign undergraduates: 28 (3% of student body). Number of countries represented: 7. Minimum TOEFL score required: 520 (paper); 190 (computer).

Kansas City Art Institute

- **Address:** 4415 Warwick Boulevard, Kansas City, MO 64111
- **Website:** http://www.kcai.edu
- **Private**
- **Enrollment:** 578 full-time; 12 part-time

KEY STATS

✔ **U.S News College Ranking:** Unranked Specialty School–Fine Arts
✔ **ACT Score (25th/75th percentile):** 20-24
✔ **Tuition:** 2006-2007: $24,000

Selectivity: Selective	**Room/board:** $7,500
Acceptance rate: 74%	**Average debt:** $24,000
Student/faculty ratio: 9/1	**Proportion who borrowed:** 90%

UNDERGRADUATE STUDENT BODY STATS

2005-2006 enrollment: 578 full-time; 12 part-time. Men: 44%; women: 56%. **Ethnic makeup:** African American: 4%; American-Indian: 1%; Asian American: 4%; Hispanic: 6%; White: 82%; International: 3%.

ADMISSIONS FACTS AND FIGURES

Phone: (800) 522-5224. **Email:** admiss@kcai.edu. **Website:** http://www.kcai.edu. **Application deadlines for fall 2007:** Early decision: Not offered. Early action: Not offered. Admission can be deferred. **Application fee:** $35. Common application is not accepted. **Admissions requirements/recommendations:** High school units required (recommended): English: (4); Mathematics: (3); Science: (3); Foreign language: (2); Social studies: (3); History: (1); Total units: (20). Tests: The college uses SAT or ACT scores in admissions decisions. Either SAT or ACT required. Campus visit: Recommended. Admissions interview: Required. Off-campus interview: May be arranged. **Factors that count in admissions decisions:** *Academic:* Secondary school record: Very important. Class rank: Considered. Letters of recommendation: Very important. Standardized test scores: Very important. Essay: Very important. *Nonacademic:* Interview: Important. Extracurricular activities: Considered. Talent/ability: Very important. Character/personal qualities: Important. Alumni/ae relationship: Considered. Geographical residence: Not considered. State residency: Not considered. Religious affiliation/commitment: Not considered. Minority status: Not considered. Volunteer work: Considered. Work experience: Considered. **Other schools with the greatest overlap in applicants:** Cooper Union; Maryland Institute

College of Art; Milwaukee Institute of Art and Design; Rhode Island School of Design; School of the Art Institute of Chicago. **Admissions statistics for the fall 2005 entering class:** Total applicants: 435. Total accepted: 321. Freshmen enrolled: 112; 70% were from out of state. Overall acceptance rate: 74%. **Credentials of fall 2005 freshmen:** 10% ranked in the top 10 percent of their high school class; 35% were in the top 25 percent, and 68% were in the top half. (Proportion submitting class standing: 72%.) **Average high school grade point average:** 3.3. **First-year students who submitted SAT scores:** 20%. Scores (25/75 percentile): Verbal: 490-630, Math: 460-590, Combined: 950-1220. **First-year students submitting ACT scores:** 58%. Scores (25/75 percentile): English: 19-26, Math: 18-23, Composite: 20-24.

ACADEMICS

Year founded: 1885. **Academic calendar:** Semester. **Degrees offered:** bachelor's. **Most popular majors:** 22% painting, 13% design and visual communications, 11% fiber, textile, and weaving arts, 10% sculpture. **Major fields of study:** visual and performing arts. **Areas of required coursework:** arts/fine arts, humanities, philosophy, sciences (biological or physical), history, social science. **Special academic programs (% participation):** double major (12%), dual enrollment (7%), exchange student program (domestic) (1%), independent study (30%), internships (47%), liberal arts/career combination (12%), study abroad (6%). **Faculty and instruction (2005-2006):** Total instructional faculty: 43 full-time, 36 part-time (56% men; 44% women; 1% minorities). Full-time faculty with Ph.D. or other terminal degree: 81%. Student/faculty ratio: 9/1. Classes of fewer than 20 students: 72%; of 20 to 49 students: 28%; of 50 or more students: 0%. **Advanced Placement and International Baccalaureate credit:** AP tests may be used for: Credit only. Scores accepted: 4, 5. **Freshmen returning for sophomore year:** 79%. **Graduation rates:** Four-year: 49%; five-year: 60%; six-year: 55%.

COSTS AND FINANCIAL AID

Financial aid office: (816) 802-3448. **Expenses (2006-2007):** Tuition and fees 2006-2007: $24,000; room/board: $7,500. Estimated books and supplies: $1,500; transportation: $1,500; personal expenses: $2,000. **Financial aid:** Priority filing date for institution's financial aid form: March 1; deadline: August 1. In 2005-2006, 89% of undergraduates applied for financial aid. Of those, 80% were determined to have financial need; 10% had their need fully met. Average financial aid package (proportion receiving): $15,107 (79%). Average amount of gift aid, such as scholarships or grants (proportion receiving): $10,432 (79%). Average amount of self-help aid, such as work study or loans (proportion receiving): $5,135 (72%). Average need-based loan (excluding PLUS or other private loans): $4,847. Among students who received need-based aid, the average percentage of need met: 59%. Among students who received aid based on merit, the average award (and the proportion receiving): $11,876 (20%). The average athletic scholarship (and the proportion receiving): $0 (0%). Average amount of debt of borrowers graduating in 2005: $24,000. Proportion who borrowed: 90%.

CAMPUS LIFE AND EXTRACURRICULAR ACTIVITIES

Campus housing available: coed dorms, women's dorms, men's dorms, apartments for married students, apartment for single students. Students who live in college-owned, operated, or affiliated housing: 25%. **Student employment:** During the 2005-2006 academic year, 32% of undergraduates worked on campus. Average per-year earnings: $1,000. **Clubs and organizations:** Number of student organizations: 6. Activities include: dance, student government, student film society. Number of fraternities: 0; sororities: 0. Average proportion of students who stay on campus on weekends: 75%.

SERVICES AND FACILITIES

Basic services: nonremedial tutoring, health insurance. **Remedial assistance:** reading, writing, study skills, other. **Counseling services:** personal, academic, psychological. **For learning-disabled students:** School does not offer a structured program with separate admission and additional fees. Total undergraduates in learning-disabled program or receiving services: 50. Services include: remedial English, remedial reading, tape recorders, untimed tests, note-taking services, oral tests, learning center, readers, extended time for tests, tutors, texts on tape, typist/scribe, exams on tape or computer, other testing accomodations. **Library:** Number of titles: 31,899; number of current serial subscriptions: 100. **Information technology resources:** Students are not required to lease or own a computer. Number of campus computers available to all students: 175. School has a wireless network. Proportion of college-owned housing units wired for high-speed internet access: 100%. **Campus safety:** Security services offered: 24-hour foot-and-vehicle patrols, late-night transport/escort service, 24-hour emergency telephones, lighted pathways/sidewalks, controlled dormitory access (key, security card, etc.).

TRANSFER AND INTERNATIONAL STUDENTS

Transfer students: May apply for admission for the following academic terms: Fall, Spring. Applicants need a minimum number of credits to apply. For fall 2005: Transfer applications received: 119. Transfer applicants offered admission: 93. Transfer applicants enrolled: 63. **International students:** Number of foreign undergraduates: 16 (3% of student body). Number of countries represented: 16. Minimum TOEFL score required: 550 (paper); 215 (computer).

Lincoln University

- **Address:** PO Box 29, Jefferson City, MO 65102-0029
- **Website:** http://www.lincolnu.edu
- **Public**
- **Enrollment:** 2,004 full-time; 446 part-time

KEY STATS

✔ **U.S News College Ranking:** fourth tier, Universities–Master's (Midwest)
✔ **ACT Score (25th/75th percentile):** 17
✔ **Tuition:** 2006-2007: $5,122 in state, $8,952 out of state

Selectivity: Least selective	**Room/board:** $3,790
Acceptance rate: 94%	**Average debt:** $16,471
Student/faculty ratio: 17/1	**Proportion who borrowed:** 63%

UNDERGRADUATE STUDENT BODY STATS

2005-2006 enrollment: 2,004 full-time; 446 part-time. Men: 42%; women: 58%. **Ethnic makeup:** African American: 48%; Hispanic: 1%; White: 45%; International: 5%.

ADMISSIONS FACTS AND FIGURES

Phone: (573) 681-5599. **Email:** enroll@lincolnu.edu. **Website:** http://www.lincolnu.edu. **Application deadlines for fall 2007:** Regular decision: August 1; decision sent by July 15. Early decision: Not offered. Early action: Not offered. Admission can be deferred. **Application fee:** $17. Common application is not accepted. **Admissions requirements/recommendations:** High school units required (recommended): English: (4); Mathematics: (3); Science: (2); Foreign language: (2); Social studies: (3); History: (1); Total units: (16). Tests: The college does not use SAT or ACT scores in admissions decisions. Neither SAT nor ACT required. Campus visit: Recommended. Admissions interview: Neither required nor recommended. Off-campus interview: May be arranged. **Factors that count in admissions decisions:** *Academic:* Secondary school record: Not considered. Class rank: Not considered. Letters of recommendation: Not considered. Standardized test scores: Not considered. Essay: Not considered. *Nonacademic:* Interview: Not considered. Extracurricular activities: Not considered. Talent/ability: Not considered. Character/personal qualities: Not considered. Alumni/ae relationship: Not considered. Geographical residence: Not considered. State residency: Not considered. Religious affiliation/commitment: Not considered. Minority status: Not considered. Volunteer work: Not considered. Work experience: Not considered. **Other schools with the greatest overlap in applicants:** Central Missouri State University; Missouri State University; Missouri State University; Missouri Western State University; Missouri Western State University; Southeast Missouri State University; Southeast Missouri State University; University of Missouri–Columbia; University of Missouri–Columbia. **Admissions statistics for the fall 2005 entering class:** Total applicants: 1,487. Total accepted: 1,405. Freshmen enrolled: 632; 19% were from out of state. Overall acceptance rate: 94%. **Credentials of fall 2005 freshmen:** 5% ranked in the top 10 percent of their high school class; 17% were in the top 25 percent, and 43% were in the top half. (Proportion submitting class standing: 87%.) **Average high school grade point average:** 2.6.

ACADEMICS

Year founded: 1866. **Academic calendar:** Semester. **Degrees offered:** associate, bachelor's, master's. **Most popular majors:** 18% business administration and management, 10% criminal justice/law enforcement administration, 10% information science/studies, 10% liberal arts and sciences/liberal studies, 7% elementary education and teaching. **Major fields of study:** agriculture, agriculture operations, and related sciences; biological and biomedical sciences; business, management, marketing, and related support services; communication, journalism, and related programs; computer and information sciences and support services; education; engineering technologies/technicians; English language and literature/letters; foreign languages, literatures, and linguistics; health professions and related clinical sciences; liberal arts and sciences studies, and humanities; mathematics and statistics; parks, recreation, leisure, and fitness studies; physical sciences; psychology; public administration and social service professions; security and protective services; social sciences; theology and religious vocations; visual and performing arts. **Areas of required coursework:** humanities, mathematics, English (including composition), sciences (biological or physical), history, social science, other. **Pre-professional programs:** pre-dentistry, pre-medicine, pre-veterinary science, pre-optometry, pre-pharmacy. **Special academic programs (% participation):** cooperative (work-study plan) program (1%), honors program (3%), internships (2%), teacher certificate program (8%). **Teacher certification offered in:** early childhood, special education, elementary, middle/junior high, secondary. **Cooperative education programs:** agriculture, social/behavioral science. **Reserve Officers Training Corps (ROTC):** Army ROTC: Offered on campus. **Faculty and instruction (2005-2006):** Total instructional faculty: 124. Full-time faculty with Ph.D. or other terminal degree: 62%. Student/faculty ratio: 17/1. Classes of fewer than 20 students: 56%; of 20 to 49 students: 42%; of 50 or more students: 1%. **Advanced Placement and International Baccalaureate credit:** AP tests may be used for: Credit and/or placement. Scores accepted: 3, 4, 5. **Freshmen returning for sophomore year:** 52%. **Graduation rates:** Four-year: 9%; five-year: 23%; six-year: 33%.

COSTS AND FINANCIAL AID

Financial aid office: (573) 681-6156. **Expenses (2006-2007):** Tuition and fees 2006-2007: $5,122 in state, $8,952 out of state; room/board: $3,790. Estimated books and supplies: $950; transportation: $500; personal expenses: $1,930. **Financial aid:** Priority filing date for institution's financial aid form: March 1. In 2005-2006, 80% of undergraduates applied for financial aid. Of those, 75% were determined to have financial need; 14% had their need fully met. Average financial aid package (proportion receiving): $8,000 (70%). Average amount of gift aid, such as scholarships or grants (proportion receiving): $3,000 (40%). Average amount of self-help aid, such as work study or loans (proportion receiving): $3,000 (45%). Average need-based loan (excluding PLUS or other private loans): $2,000. Among students who received need-based aid, the average percentage of need met: 35%. Among students who received aid based on merit, the average award (and the proportion receiving): $3,000 (11%). The average athletic scholarship (and the proportion receiving): $6,000 (5%). Average amount of debt of borrowers graduating in 2005: $16,471. Proportion who borrowed: 63%.

CAMPUS LIFE AND EXTRACURRICULAR ACTIVITIES

Campus housing available (% using): coed dorms (17%), women's dorms (43%), men's dorms (40%). Students who live in college-owned, operated, or affiliated housing: 34%. **Clubs and organizations:** Number of student organizations: 14. Activities include: choral groups, dance, jazz band, marching band, radio station, student government, student newspaper. Number of fraternities: 2; sororities: 3. Average proportion of students who stay on campus on weekends: 50%. **Sports program (2005-2006):** Member of NCAA II. *Men's intercollegiate varsity sports:* baseball, basketball, football, golf, track and field (indoor), track and field (outdoor). *Women's intercollegiate varsity sports:* basketball, cross-country, softball, tennis, track and field (indoor), track and field (outdoor).

SERVICES AND FACILITIES

Basic services: nonremedial tutoring, health service, health insurance. **Remedial assistance:** reading, math, writing, study skills. **Counseling services:** career, personal. **For learning-disabled students:** Services include: remedial math, remedial English, remedial reading, tape recorders, readers, tutors. **Library:** Number of titles: 182,369; number of current serial subscriptions: 837. **Information technology resources:** Students are not required to lease or own a computer. Number of campus computers available to all students: 375. Proportion of college-owned housing units wired for high-speed internet access: 100%. **Campus safety:** Security services offered: 24-hour foot-and-vehicle patrols, 24-hour emergency telephones, lighted pathways/sidewalks, controlled dormitory access (key, security card, etc).

TRANSFER AND INTERNATIONAL STUDENTS

Transfer students: May apply for admission for the following academic terms: Fall, Spring. Applicants do not need a minimum number of credits to apply. For fall 2005: Transfer applications received: 225. Transfer applicants offered admission: 222. Transfer applicants enrolled: 172. **International students:** Number of foreign undergraduates: 123 (5% of student body). Number of countries represented: 28. Minimum TOEFL score required: 500 (paper).

Lindenwood University

- **Address:** 209 S. Kingshighway, St. Charles, MO 63301-1695
- **Website:** http://www.lindenwood.edu
- **Private**
- **Enrollment:** 5,092 full-time; 646 part-time

KEY STATS

✔ **U.S News College Ranking:** fourth tier, Universities–Master's (Midwest)
✔ **ACT Score (25th/75th percentile):** 19-26
✔ **Tuition:** 2006-2007: $12,240

Selectivity: Selective	**Room/board:** $6,000
Acceptance rate: 43%	**Average debt:** N/A
Student/faculty ratio: 14/1	**Proportion who borrowed:** N/A

UNDERGRADUATE STUDENT BODY STATS

2005-2006 enrollment: 5,092 full-time; 646 part-time. Men: 43%; women: 57%. **Ethnic makeup:** African American: 12%; Asian American: 1%; Hispanic: 1%; White: 79%; International: 7%.

ADMISSIONS FACTS AND FIGURES

Phone: (636) 949-4949. **Email:** admissions@lindenwood.edu. **Website:** http://www.lindenwood.edu. **Application deadlines for fall 2007:** Regular decision: Rolling. Early decision: Not offered. Early action: Not offered. Admission can be deferred. **Application fee:** $30. Common application is not accepted. **Admissions requirements/recommendations:** High school units required (recommended): English: 4 (4); Mathematics: 3 (3); Science: 3 (3); Foreign language: 2 (2); Social studies: 3 (3); History: (0); Academic electives: (0); Total units: 16 (16). Tests: The college uses SAT or ACT scores in admissions decisions. Either SAT or ACT required. For admission to the fall 2007 entering class, the school will accept: ACT with writing, ACT without writing. Campus visit: Recommended. Admissions interview: Recommended. Off-campus interview: May be arranged. **Factors that count in admissions decisions:** *Academic:* Secondary school record: Very important. Class rank: Important. Letters of recommendation: Considered. Standardized test scores: Important. Essay: Considered. *Nonacademic:* Interview: Very important. Extracurricular activities: Important. Talent/ability: Very important. Character/personal qualities: Important. Alumni/ae relationship: Considered. Geographical residence: Not considered. State residency: Not considered. Religious affiliation/commitment: Not considered. Minority status: Not considered. Volunteer work: Considered. Work experience: Considered. **Admissions statistics for the fall 2005 entering class:** Total applicants: 2,906. Total accepted: 1,249. Freshmen enrolled: 821; 21% were from out of state. Overall acceptance rate: 43%. **Size of waiting list:** 0 applicants; enrolled from waiting list: 0. **Credentials of fall 2005 freshmen:** 14% ranked in the top 10 percent of their high school class; 39% were in the top 25 percent, and 75% were in the top half. (Proportion submitting class standing: 74%.) **Average high school grade point average:** 3.1. **First-year students who submitted SAT scores:** 4%. Scores (25/75 percentile): Verbal: N/A, Math: N/A, Combined: N/A. **First-year students submitting ACT scores:** 76%. Scores (25/75 percentile): English: 19-26, Math: 18-25, Composite: 19-26.

ACADEMICS

Year founded: 1827. **Academic calendar:** 4-1-4. **Degrees offered:** certificate, bachelor's, post-bachelor's certificate, master's, post-master's certificate, first professional. **Most popular majors:** 23% business/commerce, 7% elementary education and teaching, 6% criminology, 6% mass communication/media studies, 4% psychology. **Major fields of study:** agriculture, agriculture operations, and related sciences; area, ethnic, cultural, and gender studies; biological and biomedical sciences; business, management, marketing, and related support services; communication, journalism, and related programs; computer and information sciences and support services; education; English language and literature/letters; foreign languages, literatures, and linguistics; health professions and related clinical sciences; history; legal professions and studies; liberal arts and sciences studies, and humanities; mathematics and statistics; multi/interdisciplinary studies; parks, recreation, leisure, and fitness studies; personal and culinary services; philosophy and religious studies; physical sciences; psychology; public administration and social service professions; security and protective services; social sciences; theology and religious vocations; visual and performing arts. **Areas of required coursework:** arts/fine arts, humanities, mathematics, English (including composition), philosophy, foreign languages, sciences

(biological or physical); history, social science. **Pre-professional programs:** pre-law, pre-dentistry, pre-medicine, pre-veterinary science, pre-optometry, pre-pharmacy. **Special academic programs (% participation):** accelerated program (20%), cooperative (work-study plan) program (60%), cross-registration (35%), distance learning (1%), double major, dual enrollment (12%), exchange student program (domestic) (1%), external degree program, honors program (5%), independent study (90%), internships (50%), liberal arts/career combination (100%), student-designed major (5%), study abroad (2%), teacher certificate program (20%). **Teacher certification offered in:** early childhood, special education, elementary, middle/junior high, secondary. **Cooperative education programs:** business, computer science, education, engineering, health professions, humanities, natural science, social/behavioral science, technologies. **Reserve Officers Training Corps (ROTC):** Army ROTC: Offered on campus. **Faculty and instruction (2005-2006):** Total instructional faculty: 210 full-time, 321 part-time (56% men; 44% women; 8% minorities). Full-time faculty with Ph.D. or other terminal degree: 60%. Student/faculty ratio: 14/1. Classes of fewer than 20 students: 59%; of 20 to 49 students: 40%; of 50 or more students: 0%. **Advanced Placement and International Baccalaureate credit:** AP tests may be used for: Credit only. Scores accepted: 3, 4, 5. International Baccalaureate exams may be used for: Credit only. **Freshmen returning for sophomore year:** 68%. **Graduation rates:** Four-year: 27%; five-year: 42%; six-year: 45%. **Graduate study:** 24% of students pursue further study immediately upon graduation; 28% within one year; 35% within five years. Fields in which graduates pursue further study: Master of Business Administration (MBA), 34%; law, 2%; medicine, 2%; dentistry, 1%; engineering, 1%; theology (or the seminary), 1%; education, 56%; arts and sciences, 2%; veterinary medicine, 1%.

COSTS AND FINANCIAL AID

Financial aid office: (636) 949-4923. **Expenses (2006-2007):** Tuition and fees 2006-2007: $12,240; room/board: $6,000. Estimated books and supplies: $2,900; transportation: $3,000. **Financial aid:** Priority filing date for institution's financial aid form: March 15.

CAMPUS LIFE AND EXTRACURRICULAR ACTIVITIES

Campus housing available: women's dorms, men's dorms, sorority housing, fraternity housing, apartments for married students, apartment for single students, special housing for disabled students, other housing options. Students who live in college-owned, operated, or affiliated housing: 70%. **Student employment:** During the 2005-2006 academic year, 50% of undergraduates worked on campus. Average per-year earnings: $2,400. **Clubs and organizations:** Number of student organizations: 72. Activities include: choral groups, concert band, dance, drama/theater, jazz band, literary magazine, marching band, music ensembles, musical theater, radio station, student government, student newspaper, student film society, symphony orchestra, television station, yearbook. Number of fraternities: 2; sororities: 2. Proportion of men in fraternities: 2%; of women in sororities: 2%. Average proportion of students who stay on campus on weekends: 60%. **Sports program (2005-2006):** Member of NAIA. *Men's intercollegiate varsity sports:* baseball, basketball, bowling, cheerleading, cross-country, football, golf, ice hockey, riflery, soccer, swimming and diving, tennis, track and field (indoor), track and field (outdoor), volleyball, wrestling, roller hockey. *Women's intercollegiate varsity sports:* basketball, bowling, cheerleading, cross-country, field hockey, golf, ice hockey, riflery, soccer, softball, swimming and diving, tennis, track and field (indoor), track and field (outdoor), volleyball.

SERVICES AND FACILITIES

Basic services: nonremedial tutoring, placement service. **Remedial assistance:** reading, math, writing. **For learning-disabled students:** School does not offer a structured program with separate admission and additional fees. Total undergraduates in learning-disabled program or receiving services: 15. Services include: remedial math, remedial English, reading machines, remedial reading, untimed tests, note-taking services, oral tests, readers, extended time for tests, tutors, typist/scribe. **Library:** Number of titles: 170,920; number of current serial subscriptions: 598. **Information technology resources:** Students are not required to lease or own a computer. Number of campus computers available to all students: 177. School has a wireless network. Approximate number of users that can be accommodated: 180. Proportion of college-owned housing units wired for high-speed internet access: 70%. **Campus safety:** Security services offered: 24-hour foot-and-vehicle patrols, late-night transport/escort service, lighted pathways/sidewalks, controlled dormitory access (key, security card, etc).

TRANSFER AND INTERNATIONAL STUDENTS

Transfer students: May apply for admission for the following academic terms: Fall, Winter, Spring, Summer. Applicants need a minimum number of credits to apply. For fall 2005: Transfer applicants enrolled: 612. **International students:** Number of foreign undergraduates: 351 (7% of student body). Number of countries represented: 67. Minimum TOEFL score required: 500 (paper); 173 (computer).

Maryville University of St. Louis

- **Address:** 13550 Conway Road, St Louis, MO 63141-7299
- **Website:** http://www.maryville.edu
- **Private**
- **Enrollment:** 1,610 full-time; 1,049 part-time

KEY STATS

✔ **U.S News College Ranking:** 29, Universities–Master's (Midwest)
✔ **ACT Score (25th/75th percentile):** 21-27
✔ **Tuition:** 2006-2007: $18,120

Selectivity: More selective	**Room/board:** $7,720
Acceptance rate: 73%	**Average debt:** $26,310
Student/faculty ratio: 13/1	**Proportion who borrowed:** 60%

UNDERGRADUATE STUDENT BODY STATS

2005-2006 enrollment: 1,610 full-time; 1,049 part-time. Men: 26%; women: 74%. **Ethnic makeup:** African American: 6%; Asian American: 2%; Hispanic: 1%; White: 90%; International: 1%. **Religious preference:** Roman Catholic: 13%; Protestant: 6%; No preference: 78%; Baptist: 1%; Other: 2%.

ADMISSIONS FACTS AND FIGURES

Phone: (800) 627-9855. **Email:** admissions@maryville.edu. **Website:** http://www.maryville.edu. **Application deadlines for fall 2007:** Regular decision: August 15. Early decision: Not offered. Early action: Not offered. Admission can be deferred. **Application fee:** $25. Common application is accepted. **Admissions requirements/recommendations:** High school units required (recommended): English: 4; Mathematics: 3; Science: 2; Foreign language: (3); Social studies: 2; Academic electives: 8; Total units: 22. Tests: The college uses SAT or ACT scores in admissions decisions. Either SAT or ACT required. For admission to the fall 2007 entering class, the school will accept: ACT with writing, ACT without writing. Campus visit: Recommended. Admissions interview: Recommended. Off-campus interview: May be arranged. **Factors that count in admissions decisions:** *Academic:* Secondary school record: Considered. Class rank: Considered. Letters of recommendation: Considered. Standardized test scores: Very important. Essay: Not considered. *Nonacademic:* Interview: Very important. Extracurricular activities: Important. Talent/ability: Considered. Character/personal qualities: Considered. Alumni/ae relationship: Important. Geographical residence: Not considered. State residency: Not considered. Religious affiliation/commitment: Not considered. Minority status: Not considered. Volunteer work: Not considered. Work experience: Not considered. **Other schools with the greatest overlap in applicants:** St. Louis University; Truman State University; University of Missouri–Columbia; University of Missouri–St. Louis; Webster University. **Admissions statistics for the fall 2005 entering class:** Total applicants: 1,357. Total accepted: 984. Freshmen enrolled: 335; 27% were from out of state. Overall acceptance rate: 73%. **Credentials of fall 2005 freshmen:** 24% ranked in the top 10 percent of their high school class; 54% were in the top 25 percent, and 84% were in the top half. (Proportion submitting class standing: 93%.) **Average high school grade point average:** 3.5. **First-year students who submitted SAT scores:** 4%. Scores (25/75 percentile): Verbal: N/A, Math: N/A, Combined: N/A. **First-year students submitting ACT scores:** 99%. Scores (25/75 percentile): English: 21-27, Math: 19-26, Composite: 21-27.

ACADEMICS

Year founded: 1872. **Academic calendar:** Semester. **Degrees offered:** certificate, bachelor's, master's, doctorate. **Most popular majors:** 13% nursing/registered nurse training (R.N., A.S.N., B.S.N., M.S.N.), 11% business/commerce, 7% management information systems, 6% health/medical preparatory programs, 5% accounting. **Major fields of study:** biological and biomedical sciences; business, management, marketing, and related support services; communication, journalism, and related programs; computer and information sciences and support services; education; engi-

neering; English language and literature/letters; health professions and related clinical sciences; history; legal professions and studies; liberal arts and sciences studies, and humanities; mathematics and statistics; multi/interdisciplinary studies; natural resources and conservation; physical sciences; psychology; social sciences; visual and performing arts. **Areas of required coursework:** arts/fine arts, humanities, mathematics, English (including composition), sciences (biological or physical), history, social science, other. **Pre-professional programs:** pre-law, pre-dentistry, pre-medicine. **Special academic programs:** accelerated program, cooperative (work-study plan) program, cross-registration, distance learning, double major, dual enrollment, English as a Second Language (ESL), honors program, independent study, internships, liberal arts/career combination, student-designed major, study abroad, teacher certificate program, weekend college. **Teacher certification offered in:** early childhood, special education, elementary, middle/junior high, secondary. **Cooperative education programs:** art, business, computer science, education, health professions, humanities, natural science, social/behavioral science. **Reserve Officers Training Corps (ROTC):** Army ROTC: Offered at cooperating institution (Washington University). **Faculty and instruction (2005-2006):** Total instructional faculty: 99 full-time, 244 part-time (43% men; 57% women; 10% minorities). Full-time faculty with Ph.D. or other terminal degree: 90%. Student/faculty ratio: 13/1. Classes of fewer than 20 students: 62%; of 20 to 49 students: 38%; of 50 or more students: 0%. **Advanced Placement and International Baccalaureate credit:** AP tests may be used for: Credit only. Scores accepted: 3, 4, 5. International Baccalaureate exams may be used for: Credit only. **Freshmen returning for sophomore year:** 77%. **Graduation rates:** Four-year: 55%; five-year: 70%; six-year: 63%. **Graduate study:** 60% of students pursue further study immediately upon graduation; 20% within one year; 20% within five years. Fields in which graduates pursue further study: Master of Business Administration (MBA), 30%; law, 2%; medicine, 2%; education, 8%; arts and sciences, 25%.

COSTS AND FINANCIAL AID

Financial aid office: (314) 529-9360. **Expenses (2006-2007):** Tuition and fees 2006-2007: $18,120; room/board: $7,720. Estimated books and supplies: $1,180; transportation: $1,910; personal expenses: $1,570. **Financial aid:** Priority filing date for institution's financial aid form: March 1. In 2005-2006, 84% of undergraduates applied for financial aid. Of those, 72% were determined to have financial need; 13% had their need fully met. Average financial aid package (proportion receiving): $14,272 (72%). Average amount of gift aid, such as scholarships or grants (proportion receiving): $7,795 (70%). Average amount of self-help aid, such as work study or loans (proportion receiving): $4,100 (63%). Average need-based loan (excluding PLUS or other private loans): $3,833. Among students who received need-based aid, the average percentage of need met: 75%. Among students who received aid based on merit, the average award (and the proportion receiving): $4,639 (18%). The average athletic scholarship (and the proportion receiving): $0 (0%). Average amount of debt of borrowers graduating in 2005: $26,310. Proportion who borrowed: 60%.

CAMPUS LIFE AND EXTRACURRICULAR ACTIVITIES

Campus housing available (% using): coed dorms (63%), apartment for single students (37%). Students who live in college-owned, operated, or affiliated housing: 32%. **Student employment:** During the 2005-2006 academic year, 21% of undergraduates worked on campus. Average per-year earnings: $1,630. **Clubs and organizations:** Number of student organizations: 48. Activities include: choral groups, dance, drama/theater, jazz band, literary magazine, music ensembles, pep band, student government, student newspaper. Number of fraternities: 0; sororities: 0. Average proportion of students who stay on campus on weekends: 70%. **Sports program (2005-2006):** Member of NCAA III. *Men's intercollegiate varsity sports:* baseball, basketball, cheerleading, cross-country, golf, soccer, tennis, track and field (indoor), track and field (outdoor). *Women's intercollegiate varsity sports:* basketball, cheerleading, cross-country, golf, soccer, softball, tennis, track and field (indoor), track and field (outdoor), volleyball.

SERVICES AND FACILITIES

Basic services: nonremedial tutoring, placement service, health service. **Remedial assistance:** study skills, other. **Counseling services:** minority student, career, personal, veteran student, academic, older student, psychological, birth control, religious, other. **For learning-disabled students:** School does not offer a structured program with separate admission and additional fees. Total undergraduates in learning-disabled program or receiving services: 44. Services include: tape recorders, untimed tests, note-taking services, oral tests, learning center, readers, extended time for tests, tutors, priority seating, texts on tape. **Library:** Number of titles: 211,708; number of current serial subscriptions: 11,918. **Information technology resources:** Students are not required to lease or own a computer. Number of campus computers available to all students: 419. School has a wireless network. Approximate number of users that can be accommodated: 350. Proportion of college-owned housing units wired for high-speed internet access: 100%. **Campus safety:** Security services offered: 24-hour foot-and-vehicle patrols, late-night transport/escort service, 24-hour emergency telephones, lighted pathways/sidewalks, controlled dormitory access (key, security card, etc).

TRANSFER AND INTERNATIONAL STUDENTS

Transfer students: May apply for admission for the following academic terms: Fall, Spring, Summer. Applicants need a minimum number of credits to apply. For fall 2005: Transfer applications received: 966. Transfer applicants offered admission: 681. Transfer applicants enrolled: 437. **International students:** Number of foreign undergraduates: 23 (1% of student body). Number of countries represented: 19. Minimum TOEFL score required: 500 (paper); 173 (computer). Average TOEFL score: 540 (paper).

Missouri Baptist University

- **Address:** 1 College Park Drive, St. Louis, MO 63141
- **Website:** http://www.mobap.edu
- **Private; Religious affiliation:** Southern Baptist
- **Enrollment:** 1,202 full-time; 2,283 part-time

KEY STATS

✔ **U.S News College Ranking:** fourth tier, Comp. Coll.–Bachelor's (Midwest)
✔ **ACT Score (25th/75th percentile):** 17-23
✔ **Tuition:** 2006-2007: $14,664

Selectivity: Less selective	**Room/board:** $5,990
Acceptance rate: 52%	**Average debt:** $19,082
Student/faculty ratio: N/A	**Proportion who borrowed:** 65%

UNDERGRADUATE STUDENT BODY STATS

2005-2006 enrollment: 1,202 full-time; 2,283 part-time. Men: 41%; women: 59%. **Ethnic makeup:** African American: 11%; Hispanic: 2%; White: 82%; International: 4%.

ADMISSIONS FACTS AND FIGURES

Phone: (314) 434-2290. **Email:** admissions@mobap.edu. **Website:** http://www.mobap.edu. **Application deadlines for fall 2007:** Regular decision: Rolling. Early decision: Not offered. Early action: Not offered. **Application fee:** $25. Common application is not accepted. **To apply online, go to:** http://www.mobap.edu/admissions/index.asp. **Admissions requirements/recommendations:** Tests: The college uses SAT or ACT scores in admissions decisions. Neither SAT nor ACT required. **Factors that count in admissions decisions:** *Academic:* Secondary school record: Very important. Class rank: Very important. Letters of recommendation: Considered. Standardized test scores: Very important. Essay: Considered. *Nonacademic:* Interview: Considered. Extracurricular activities: Considered. Talent/ability: Not considered. Character/personal qualities: Considered. Alumni/ae relationship: Considered. Geographical residence: Not considered. State residency: Not considered. Religious affiliation/commitment: Not considered. Minority status: Not considered. Work experience: Not considered. **Admissions statistics for the fall 2005 entering class:** Total applicants: 551. Total accepted: 288. Freshmen enrolled: 223; Overall acceptance rate: 52%. **First-year students who submitted SAT scores:** 7%. Scores (25/75 percentile): Verbal: 390-490, Math: 415-510, Combined: 805-1000. **First-year students submitting ACT scores:** 76%. Scores (25/75 percentile): English: 15-23, Math: 16-23, Composite: 17-23.

ACADEMICS

Year founded: 1964. **Academic calendar:** Semester. **Degrees offered:** certificate, associate, terminal-associate, bachelor's, post-bachelor's certificate, master's. **Most popular majors:** Information not available. **Major fields of study:** business, management, marketing, and related support services; communication, journalism, and related programs; computer and information sciences and support services; education; English language and literature/letters; family and consumer sciences/human sciences; history; mathematics and statistics; multi/interdisciplinary studies; parks, recreation, leisure, and fitness studies; philosophy and religious studies; physical sciences; psychology; public administration and social service professions;

security and protective services; social sciences; theology and religious vocations; visual and performing arts. **Areas of required coursework:** arts/fine arts, humanities, computer literacy, mathematics, English (including composition), philosophy, foreign languages, sciences (biological or physical), social science. **Special academic programs:** accelerated program, double major, dual enrollment, independent study, internships, student-designed major, study abroad. **Teacher certification offered in:** early childhood, special education, elementary, middle/junior high, secondary. **Reserve Officers Training Corps (ROTC):** Army ROTC: Offered at cooperating institution (Washington University). **Freshmen returning for sophomore year:** 66%. **Graduation rates:** Four-year: 35%; five-year: 46%; six-year: 49%.

COSTS AND FINANCIAL AID

Financial aid office: (314) 392-2366. **Expenses (2006-2007):** Tuition and fees 2006-2007: $14,664; room/board: $5,990. Estimated books and supplies: $1,186 personal expenses: $1,915. **Financial aid:** Priority filing date for institution's financial aid form: April 1; deadline: November 15. In 2005-2006, 72% of undergraduates applied for financial aid. Of those, 72% were determined to have financial need; Average financial aid package (proportion receiving): $4,602 (72%). Average amount of gift aid, such as scholarships or grants (proportion receiving): $1,663 (15%). Average amount of self-help aid, such as work study or loans (proportion receiving): $6,056 (59%). Average need-based loan (excluding PLUS or other private loans): $5,946. Among students who received need-based aid, the average percentage of need met: 13%. Among students who received aid based on merit, the average award (and the proportion receiving): $3,480 (24%). The average athletic scholarship (and the proportion receiving): $5,615 (44%). Average amount of debt of borrowers graduating in 2005: $19,082. Proportion who borrowed: 65%.

CAMPUS LIFE AND EXTRACURRICULAR ACTIVITIES

Campus housing available: women's dorms, men's dorms, apartment for single students. Activities include: choral groups, concert band, drama/theater, jazz band, literary magazine, music ensembles, musical theater, radio station, student government. Number of fraternities: 0; sororities: 0. **Sports program (2005-2006):** Member of NAIA. *Men's intercollegiate varsity sports:* baseball, basketball, cross-country, golf, soccer, volleyball, wrestling. *Women's intercollegiate varsity sports:* basketball, cheerleading, cross-country, golf, soccer, softball, track and field (indoor), track and field (outdoor), volleyball.

SERVICES AND FACILITIES

Information technology resources: School has a wireless network. **Campus safety:** Security services offered: 24-hour foot-and-vehicle patrols, late-night transport/escort service, 24-hour emergency telephones, lighted pathways/sidewalks.

TRANSFER AND INTERNATIONAL STUDENTS

International students: Number of foreign undergraduates: 43 (4% of student body).

Missouri Southern State University

- **Address:** 3950 E. Newman Road, Joplin, MO 64801-1595
- **Website:** http://www.mssu.edu
- **Public**
- **Enrollment:** 3,849 full-time; 1,624 part-time

KEY STATS

✔ **U.S News College Ranking:** third tier, Comp. Coll.–Bachelor's (Midwest)
✔ **ACT Score (25th/75th percentile):** 19-24
✔ **Tuition:** 2006-2007: $4,096 in state, $7,996 out of state

Selectivity: Selective	**Room/board:** $4,480
Acceptance rate: 99%	**Average debt:** N/A
Student/faculty ratio: 18/1	**Proportion who borrowed:** N/A

UNDERGRADUATE STUDENT BODY STATS

2005-2006 enrollment: 3,849 full-time; 1,624 part-time. Men: 40%; women: 60%. **Ethnic makeup:** African American: 3%; American-Indian: 2%; Asian American: 1%; Hispanic: 2%; White: 90%; International: 2%.

ADMISSIONS FACTS AND FIGURES

Phone: (417) 625-9378. **Email:** admissions@mssu.edu. **Website:** http://www.mssu.edu. **Application deadlines for fall 2007:** Regular decision: Rolling. Early decision: Not offered. Early action: Not offered. Admission can be deferred. **Application fee:** $15. Common application is accepted. **Admissions requirements/recommendations:** High school units required (recommended): English: 4 (4); Mathematics: 3 (3); Science: 2 (2); Foreign language: 2 (2); Social studies: 3 (3); Academic electives: 3 (3); Total units: 16 (16). Tests: The college uses SAT or ACT scores in admissions decisions. Either SAT or ACT required. For admission to the fall 2007 entering class, the school will accept: ACT with writing, ACT without writing. Campus visit: Recommended. Admissions interview: Neither required nor recommended. Off-campus interview: Not available. **Factors that count in admissions decisions:** *Academic:* Secondary school record: Very important. Class rank: Very important. Letters of recommendation: Considered. Standardized test scores: Very important. Essay: Not considered. *Nonacademic:* Interview: Not considered. Extracurricular activities: Not considered. Talent/ability: Not considered. Character/personal qualities: Not considered. Alumni/ae relationship: Not considered. Geographical residence: Not considered. State residency: Not considered. Religious affiliation/commitment: Not considered. Minority status: Not considered. Volunteer work: Not considered. Work experience: Not considered. **Admissions statistics for the fall 2005 entering class:** Total applicants: 1,576. Total accepted: 1,560. Freshmen enrolled: 897; 17% were from out of state. Overall acceptance rate: 99%. **Credentials of fall 2005 freshmen:** 17% ranked in the top 10 percent of their high school class; 43% were in the top 25 percent, and 72% were in the top half. (Proportion submitting class standing: 94%.) **First-year students submitting ACT scores:** 86%. Scores (25/75 percentile): English: 18-25, Math: 17-24, Composite: 19-24.

ACADEMICS

Year founded: 1937. **Academic calendar:** Semester. **Degrees offered:** certificate, associate, bachelor's, master's. **Most popular majors:** 21% business, management, marketing, and related support services, 18% education, 12% health professions and related clinical sciences, 9% security and protective services, 7% liberal arts and sciences studies, and humanities. **Major fields of study:** biological and biomedical sciences; business, management, marketing, and related support services; communication, journalism, and related programs; computer and information sciences and support services; education; English language and literature/letters; foreign languages, literatures, and linguistics; health professions and related clinical sciences; history; mathematics and statistics; parks, recreation, leisure, and fitness studies; physical sciences; psychology; social sciences; visual and performing arts. **Areas of required coursework:** arts/fine arts, humanities, computer literacy, mathematics, English (including composition), foreign languages, sciences (biological or physical), history, social science, other. **Pre-professional programs:** pre-law, pre-dentistry, pre-medicine, pre-veterinary science, pre-optometry, pre-pharmacy, other. **Special academic programs:** accelerated program, cooperative (work-study plan) program, distance learning, double major, dual enrollment, English as a Second Language (ESL), exchange student program (domestic), honors program, independent study, internships, liberal arts/career combination, study abroad, teacher certificate program, weekend college. **Teacher certification offered in:** elementary, middle/junior high, secondary. **Cooperative education programs:** education, health professions, technologies. **Faculty and instruction (2005-2006):** Total instructional faculty: 206 full-time, 102 part-time (58% men; 42% women; 8% minorities). Full-time faculty with Ph.D. or other terminal degree: 64%. Student/faculty ratio: 18/1. Classes of fewer than 20 students: 47%; of 20 to 49 students: 51%; of 50 or more students: 2%. **Advanced Placement and International Baccalaureate credit:** AP tests may be used for: Credit only. Scores accepted: 3, 4, 5. International Baccalaureate exams may be used for: Credit and/or placement. **Freshmen returning for sophomore year:** 64%. **Graduation rates:** Four-year: 14%; five-year: 29%; six-year: 32%. **Graduate study:** 15% of students pursue further study immediately upon graduation.

COSTS AND FINANCIAL AID

Financial aid office: (417) 625-9325. **Expenses (2006-2007):** Tuition and fees 2006-2007: $4,096 in state, $7,996 out of state; room/board: $4,480. Estimated books and supplies: $600; transportation: $600; personal expenses: $1,500. **Financial aid:** Priority filing date for institution's financial aid form: February 15. In 2005-2006, 91% of undergraduates applied for financial aid. Of those, 79% were determined to have financial need; Average financial aid package (proportion receiving): $6,722 (79%). Average amount of gift aid, such as scholarships or grants (proportion receiving): $4,636 (66%). Average amount of self-help aid, such as work study or loans (proportion receiving): $2,139 (61%). Average need-based loan (excluding PLUS or other private loans): $3,249. Among students who received need-based aid, the average percentage of need met: 69%. Among students who received aid based on merit, the average award (and the proportion receiving): $2,560 (34%). The average athletic scholarship (and the proportion receiving): $4,334 (6%).

CAMPUS LIFE AND EXTRACURRICULAR ACTIVITIES

Campus housing available: coed dorms, women's dorms, men's dorms, apartment for single students, special housing for disabled students. Students who live in college-owned, operated, or affiliated housing: 12%. **Clubs and organizations:** Number of student organizations: 95. Activities include: choral groups, concert band, dance, drama/theater, jazz band, literary magazine, marching band, music ensembles, musical theater, pep band, radio station, student government, student newspaper, student film society, symphony orchestra, television station. Number of fraternities: 2; sororities: 2. Proportion of men in fraternities: 1%; of women in sororities: 1%. **Sports program (2005-2006):** Member of NCAA II. *Men's intercollegiate varsity sports:* baseball, basketball, cross-country, football, golf, soccer, track and field (indoor), track and field (outdoor). *Women's intercollegiate varsity sports:* basketball, cross-country, soccer, softball, tennis, track and field (indoor), track and field (outdoor), volleyball.

SERVICES AND FACILITIES

Basic services: nonremedial tutoring, placement service, day care, health service, health insurance. **Remedial assistance:** reading, math, writing, study skills. **Counseling services:** career, personal, veteran student, academic. **For learning-disabled students:** School does not offer a structured program with separate admission and additional fees. Total undergraduates in learning-disabled program or receiving services: 23. Services include: remedial math, remedial English, tape recorders, note-taking services, oral tests, learning center, readers, extended time for tests, tutors, priority registration, priority seating, texts on tape, other testing accomodations. **Library:** Number of titles: 234,291; number of current serial subscriptions: 533. **Information technology resources:** Students are not required to lease or own a computer. Number of campus computers available to all students: 499. School has a wireless network. Proportion of college-owned housing units wired for high-speed internet access: 100%. **Campus safety:** Security services offered: 24-hour foot-and-vehicle patrols, late-night transport/escort service, 24-hour emergency telephones, controlled dormitory access (key, security card, etc).

TRANSFER AND INTERNATIONAL STUDENTS

Transfer students: May apply for admission for the following academic terms: Fall, Spring, Summer. Applicants do not need a minimum number of credits to apply. For fall 2005: Transfer applications received: 936. Transfer applicants offered admission: 934. Transfer applicants enrolled: 536. **International students:** Number of foreign undergraduates: 85 (2% of student body). Number of countries represented: 34. Minimum TOEFL score required: 535 (paper); 200 (computer).

Missouri State University

- **Address:** 901 S. National Avenue, Springfield, MO 65897
- **Website:** http://www.missouristate.edu
- **Public**
- **Enrollment:** 12,630 full-time; 3,527 part-time

KEY STATS

✔ **U.S News College Ranking:** 59, Universities–Master's (Midwest)
✔ **ACT Score (25th/75th percentile):** 21-26
✔ **Tuition:** 2006-2007: $5,738 in state, $10,658 out of state

Selectivity: Selective	**Room/board:** $5,078
Acceptance rate: 77%	**Average debt:** $12,997
Student/faculty ratio: 18/1	**Proportion who borrowed:** 54%

UNDERGRADUATE STUDENT BODY STATS

2005-2006 enrollment: 12,630 full-time; 3,527 part-time. Men: 44%; women: 56%. **Ethnic makeup:** African American: 2%; American-Indian: 1%; Asian American: 1%; Hispanic: 1%; White: 92%; International: 2%.

ADMISSIONS FACTS AND FIGURES

Phone: (800) 492-7900. **Email:** smsuinfo@smsu.edu. **Website:** http://www.missouristate.edu. **Application deadlines for fall 2007:** Regular decision: July 20. Early decision: Not offered. Early action: Not offered. Admission cannot be deferred. **Application fee:** $30. Common application is not accepted. **To apply online, go to:** http://www.missouristate.edu/apply.asp. **Admissions requirements/recommendations:** High school units required (recommended): English: 4; Mathematics: 3; Science: 2; Social studies: 3; Academic electives: 3. Tests: The college uses SAT or ACT scores in admissions decisions. Either SAT or ACT required. For admission to the fall 2007 entering class, the school will accept: ACT with writing, ACT without writing. Campus visit: Recommended. Admissions interview: Neither required nor recommended. **Factors that count in admissions decisions:** *Academic:* Secondary school record: Not considered. Class rank: Very important. Letters of recommendation: Considered. Standardized test scores: Very important. Essay: Considered. *Nonacademic:* Interview: Considered. Extracurricular activities: Considered. Talent/ability: Considered. Character/personal qualities: Considered. Alumni/ae relationship: Not considered. Geographical residence: Not considered. State residency: Not considered. Religious affiliation/commitment: Not considered. Minority status: Considered. Volunteer work: Considered. Work experience: Considered. **Other schools with the greatest overlap in applicants:** Central Missouri State University; Drury University; Southeast Missouri State University; Truman State University; University of Missouri–Columbia. **Admissions statistics for the fall 2005 entering class:** Total applicants: 6,866. Total accepted: 5,257. Freshmen enrolled: 2,621; 7% were from out of state. Overall acceptance rate: 77%. **Credentials of fall 2005 freshmen:** 22% ranked in the top 10 percent of their high school class; 49% were in the top 25 percent, and 81% were in the top half. (Proportion submitting class standing: 92%.) **Average high school grade point average:** 3.6. **First-year students submitting ACT scores:** 96%. Scores (25/75 percentile): English: 20-27, Math: 19-26, Composite: 21-26.

ACADEMICS

Year founded: 1906. **Academic calendar:** Semester. **Degrees offered:** bachelor's, post-bachelor's certificate, master's, post-master's certificate, doctorate. **Most popular majors:** Information not available. **Major fields of study:** agriculture, agriculture operations, and related sciences; architecture and related services; biological and biomedical sciences; business, management, marketing, and related support services; communication, journalism, and related programs; computer and information sciences and support services; education; engineering; engineering technologies/technicians; English language and literature/letters; family and consumer sciences/human sciences; foreign languages, literatures, and linguistics; health professions and related clinical sciences; history; liberal arts and sciences studies, and humanities; mathematics and statistics; multi/interdisciplinary studies; natural resources and conservation; parks, recreation, leisure, and fitness studies; philosophy and religious studies; physical sciences; psychology; public administration and social service professions; science technologies/technicians; security and protective services; social sciences; visual and performing arts. **Areas of required coursework:** arts/fine arts, humanities, computer literacy, mathematics, English (including composition), sciences (biological or physical), history, social science. **Pre-professional programs:** pre-law, pre-dentistry, pre-medicine, pre-veterinary science, pre-optometry, pre-pharmacy. **Special academic programs:** accelerated program, cooperative (work-study plan) program, distance learning, double major, dual enrollment, English as a Second Language (ESL), exchange student program (domestic), honors program, independent study, internships, student-designed major, study abroad, teacher certificate program. **Teacher certification offered in:** early childhood, special education, elementary, middle/junior high, secondary. **Reserve Officers Training Corps (ROTC):** Army ROTC: Offered on campus. **Faculty and instruction (2005-2006):** Total instructional faculty: 728 full-time, 299 part-time (57% men; 43% women; 5% minorities). Full-time faculty with Ph.D. or other terminal degree: 78%. Student/faculty ratio: 18/1. Classes of fewer than 20 students: 41%; of 20 to 49 students: 51%; of 50 or more students: 8%. **Advanced Placement and International Baccalaureate credit:** AP tests may be used for: Credit and/or placement. Scores accepted: 3, 4, 5. International Baccalaureate exams may be used for: Credit only. **Freshmen returning for sophomore year:** 73%. **Graduation rates:** Four-year: 23%; five-year: 45%; six-year: 48%.

COSTS AND FINANCIAL AID

Financial aid office: (417) 836-5262. **Expenses (2006-2007):** Tuition and fees 2006-2007: $5,738 in state, $10,658 out of state; room/board: $5,078. **Financial aid:** Priority filing date for institution's financial aid form: March 30. In 2005-2006, 83% of undergraduates applied for financial aid. Of those, 61% were determined to have financial need; 22% had their need fully met. Average financial aid package (proportion receiving): $6,125 (60%). Average amount of gift aid, such as scholarships or grants (propor-

tion receiving): $4,308 (41%). Average amount of self-help aid, such as work study or loans (proportion receiving): $3,756 (50%). Average need-based loan (excluding PLUS or other private loans): $3,649. Among students who received need-based aid, the average percentage of need met: 61%. Among students who received aid based on merit, the average award (and the proportion receiving): $7,328 (33%). The average athletic scholarship (and the proportion receiving): $9,123 (2%). Average amount of debt of borrowers graduating in 2005: $12,997. Proportion who borrowed: 54%.

CAMPUS LIFE AND EXTRACURRICULAR ACTIVITIES

Campus housing available: coed dorms, sorority housing, fraternity housing, apartments for married students, apartment for single students, special housing for disabled students, special housing for international students, other housing options. Students who live in college-owned, operated, or affiliated housing: 24%. **Student employment:** During the 2005-2006 academic year, 16% of undergraduates worked on campus. **Clubs and organizations:** Number of student organizations: 300. Activities include: choral groups, concert band, dance, drama/theater, jazz band, literary magazine, marching band, music ensembles, musical theater, pep band, radio station, student government, student newspaper, student film society, symphony orchestra, television station. Number of fraternities: 14; sororities: 10. Average proportion of students who stay on campus on weekends: 50%. **Sports program (2005-2006):** Member of NCAA I. *Men's intercollegiate varsity sports:* baseball, basketball, cross-country, football, golf, soccer, swimming and diving, tennis, track and field (indoor), track and field (outdoor). *Women's intercollegiate varsity sports:* basketball, cross-country, field hockey, golf, soccer, softball, swimming and diving, tennis, track and field (indoor), track and field (outdoor), volleyball.

SERVICES AND FACILITIES

Basic services: placement service, health service, health insurance. **Counseling services:** minority student, career, personal, veteran student, academic, older student, psychological, birth control. **For learning-disabled students:** School does not offer a structured program with separate admission and additional fees. Services include: diagnostic testing service, untimed tests, note-taking services, oral tests, learning center, readers, extended time for tests, other. **Information technology resources:** Students are not required to lease or own a computer. Proportion of college-owned housing units wired for high-speed internet access: 100%. **Campus safety:** Security services offered: 24-hour foot-and-vehicle patrols, late-night transport/escort service, 24-hour emergency telephones, lighted pathways/sidewalks, controlled dormitory access (key, security card, etc).

TRANSFER AND INTERNATIONAL STUDENTS

Transfer students: May apply for admission for the following academic terms: Fall, Spring, Summer. Applicants need a minimum number of credits to apply. For fall 2005: Transfer applications received: 1,853. Transfer applicants offered admission: 1,533. Transfer applicants enrolled: 1,119. **International students:** Number of foreign undergraduates: 262 (2% of student body). Minimum TOEFL score required: 500 (paper); 173 (computer).

Missouri Valley College

- **Address:** 500 E. College, Marshall, MO 65340
- **Website:** http://www.moval.edu
- **Private; Religious affiliation:** Presbyterian
- **Enrollment:** N/A

KEY STATS
✔ **U.S News College Ranking:** fourth tier, Comp. Coll.–Bachelor's (Midwest)
✔ **SAT or ACT Score (25th/75th percentile):** N/A
✔ **Tuition:** 2006-2007: $14,750

Selectivity: Less selective	Room/board: $5,650
Acceptance rate: N/A	Average debt: $14,500
Student/faculty ratio: N/A	Proportion who borrowed: 80%

Missouri Western State University

- **Address:** 4525 Downs Drive, St. Joseph, MO 64507
- **Website:** http://www.mwsc.edu
- **Public**
- **Enrollment:** N/A

KEY STATS

✔ **U.S News College Ranking:** fourth tier, Comp. Coll.–Bachelor's (Midwest)
✔ **SAT or ACT Score (25th/75th percentile):** N/A
✔ **Tuition:** 2006-2007: $5,168 in state, $9,008 out of state

Selectivity: Less selective	**Room/board:** $5,904
Acceptance rate: N/A	**Average debt:** N/A
Student/faculty ratio: N/A	**Proportion who borrowed:** N/A

Northwest Missouri State University

- **Address:** 800 University Drive, Maryville, MO 64468
- **Website:** http://www.nwmissouri.edu
- **Public**
- **Enrollment:** N/A

KEY STATS

✔ **U.S News College Ranking:** fourth tier, Universities–Master's (Midwest)
✔ **SAT or ACT Score (25th/75th percentile):** N/A
✔ **Tuition:** 2006-2007: $6,030 in state, $10,416 out of state

Selectivity: Less selective	**Room/board:** $6,422
Acceptance rate: N/A	**Average debt:** N/A
Student/faculty ratio: N/A	**Proportion who borrowed:** N/A

Park University

- **Address:** 8700 N.W. River Park Drive, Parkville, MO 64152
- **Website:** http://www.park.edu
- **Private**
- **Enrollment:** 1,002 full-time; 11,686 part-time

KEY STATS

✔ **U.S News College Ranking:** fourth tier, Universities–Master's (Midwest)
✔ **ACT Score (25th/75th percentile):** 18-23
✔ **Tuition:** 2005-2006: $6,870

Selectivity: Less selective	**Room/board:** $5,180
Acceptance rate: 74%	**Average debt:** N/A
Student/faculty ratio: 14/1	**Proportion who borrowed:** N/A

UNDERGRADUATE STUDENT BODY STATS

2005-2006 enrollment: 1,002 full-time; 11,686 part-time. Men: 52%; women: 48%. **Ethnic makeup:** African American: 21%; American-Indian: 1%; Asian American: 3%; Hispanic: 16%; White: 57%; International: 2%.

ADMISSIONS FACTS AND FIGURES

Phone: (800) 745-7275. **Email:** admissions@mail.park.edu. **Website:** http://www.park.edu. **Application deadlines for fall 2007:** Regular decision: August 1. Early decision: Not offered. Early action: Not offered. **Application fee:** $25. Common application is not accepted. **Admissions requirements/recommendations:** High school units required (recommended): English: (3); Mathematics: (2); Science: (2); Foreign language: (2); Social studies: (3); History: (1); Academic electives: (6); Total units: (19). Tests: The college uses SAT or ACT scores in admissions decisions. ACT required. **Factors that count in admissions decisions:** *Academic:* Secondary school record: Very important. Class rank: Very important. Letters of recommendation: Considered. Standardized test scores: Very important. Essay: Considered. *Nonacademic:* Interview: Not considered. Extracurricular activities: Not considered. Talent/ability: Not considered. Character/personal qualities: Not considered. Alumni/ae relationship: Not considered.

Geographical residence: Not considered. State residency: Not considered. Religious affiliation/commitment: Not considered. Minority status: Not considered. Volunteer work: Not considered. Work experience: Not considered. **Admissions statistics for the fall 2005 entering class:** Total applicants: 352. Total accepted: 260. Freshmen enrolled: 142; Overall acceptance rate: 74%. **Credentials of fall 2005 freshmen:** 12% ranked in the top 10 percent of their high school class; 38% were in the top 25 percent, and 77% were in the top half. (Proportion submitting class standing: 75%.) **First-year students submitting ACT scores:** 70%. Scores (25/75 percentile): English: 16-24, Math: 16-22, Composite: 18-23.

ACADEMICS

Year founded: 1875. **Academic calendar:** Semester. **Degrees offered:** associate, bachelor's, master's. **Most popular majors:** 64% business, management, marketing, and related support services, 15% psychology, 7% public administration and social service professions, 5% computer and information sciences and support services, 2% education. **Major fields of study:** biological and biomedical sciences; business, management, marketing, and related support services; communication, journalism, and related programs; computer and information sciences and support services; education; engineering; English language and literature/letters; foreign languages, literatures, and linguistics; health professions and related clinical sciences; history; legal professions and studies; liberal arts and sciences studies, and humanities; multi/interdisciplinary studies; physical sciences; psychology; public administration and social service professions; security and protective services; social sciences; transportation and materials moving; visual and performing arts. **Areas of required coursework:** arts/fine arts, humanities, mathematics, English (including composition), foreign languages, sciences (biological or physical), social science. **Pre-professional programs:** pre-law. **Special academic programs:** accelerated program, distance learning, double major, English as a Second Language (ESL), honors program, independent study, student-designed major, study abroad, teacher certificate program, weekend college, other. **Teacher certification offered in:** early childhood, elementary, middle/junior high, secondary. **Reserve Officers Training Corps (ROTC):** Army ROTC: Offered on campus. **Faculty and instruction (2005-2006):** Total instructional faculty: 97 full-time, 745 part-time. Full-time faculty with Ph.D. or other terminal degree: 51%. Student/faculty ratio: 14/1. **Freshmen returning for sophomore year:** 69%. **Graduation rates:** Four-year: 21%; five-year: 39%; six-year: 42%.

COSTS AND FINANCIAL AID

Financial aid office: (816) 584-6190. **Expenses (2005-2006):** Tuition and fees 2005-2006: $6,870; room/board: $5,180. Estimated books and supplies: $1,200; transportation: $450; personal expenses: $1,745. **Financial aid:** Priority filing date for institution's financial aid form: April 1.

CAMPUS LIFE AND EXTRACURRICULAR ACTIVITIES

Campus housing available: coed dorms, apartments for married students, apartment for single students. **Clubs and organizations:** Number of student organizations: 36. Number of fratemiities: 0; sororities: 0. **Sports program (2005-2006):** Member of NAIA. *Men's intercollegiate varsity sports:* baseball, basketball, cross-country, soccer, track and field (indoor), track and field (outdoor). *Women's intercollegiate varsity sports:* basketball, cross-country, golf, soccer, softball, track and field (indoor), track and field (outdoor), volleyball.

SERVICES AND FACILITIES

Basic services: nonremedial tutoring, placement service, health service, health insurance. **Remedial assistance:** reading, math, writing, study skills. **Counseling services:** personal. **For learning-disabled students:** School does not offer a structured program with separate admission and additional fees. Total undergraduates in learning-disabled program or receiving services: 22. Services include: remedial math, remedial English, reading machines, remedial reading, tape recorders, other special classes, videotaped classes, untimed tests, note-taking services, oral tests, learning center, readers, extended time for tests, tutors, texts on tape, other testing accomodations. **Library:** Number of titles: 50,307; number of current serial subscriptions: 591. **Information technology resources:** Students are not required to lease or own a computer. Number of campus computers available to all students: 702. School does not have a wireless network. Proportion of college-owned housing units wired for high-speed internet access: 50%.

TRANSFER AND INTERNATIONAL STUDENTS

Transfer students: May apply for admission for the following academic terms: Fall, Winter, Spring, Summer. Applicants do not need a minimum number of credits to apply. **International students:** Number of foreign undergraduates: 215 (2% of student body). Minimum TOEFL score required: 500 (paper); 173 (computer).

Rockhurst University

- **Address:** 1100 Rockhurst Road, Kansas City, MO 64110-2561
- **Website:** http://www.rockhurst.edu
- **Private; Religious affiliation:** Roman Catholic (Jesuit)
- **Enrollment:** 1,261 full-time; 830 part-time

KEY STATS
✔ **U.S News College Ranking:** 14, Universities–Master's (Midwest)
✔ **ACT Score (25th/75th percentile):** 22-28
✔ **Tuition:** 2006-2007: $20,840
  Selectivity: More selective   **Room/board:** $6,000
  Acceptance rate: 74%   **Average debt:** $17,890
  Student/faculty ratio: 10/1   **Proportion who borrowed:** 72%

UNDERGRADUATE STUDENT BODY STATS
2005-2006 enrollment: 1,261 full-time; 830 part-time. Men: 42%; women: 58%. **Ethnic makeup:** African American: 7%; American-Indian: 1%; Asian American: 2%; Hispanic: 5%; White: 83%; International: 1%. **Religious preference:** Protestant: 20%; Roman Catholic (Jesuit): 64%; Other: 16%.

ADMISSIONS FACTS AND FIGURES
Phone: (816) 501-4100. **Email:** admissions@rockhurst.edu. **Website:** http://www.rockhurst.edu. **Application deadlines for fall 2007:** Regular decision: June 30. Early decision: Not offered. Early action: Send application by: July 1; Decision sent by: August 1. Admission can be deferred. **Application fee:** $25. Common application is accepted. **To apply online, go to:** http://www.rockhurst.edu/admission/ugrad/process/index.asp. **Admissions requirements/recommendations:** High school units required (recommended): English: 4 (4); Mathematics: 3 (3); Science: 3 (3); Academic electives: 4 (4); Total units: 16 (16). Tests: The college uses SAT or ACT scores in admissions decisions. Either SAT or ACT required. For admission to the fall 2007 entering class, the school will accept: ACT with writing, ACT without writing. Campus visit: Recommended. Admissions interview: Recommended. Off-campus interview: May be arranged. **Factors that count in admissions decisions:** *Academic:* Secondary school record: Important. Class rank: Important. Letters of recommendation: Important. Standardized test scores: Very important. Essay: Not considered. *Nonacademic:* Interview: Considered. Extracurricular activities: Considered. Talent/ability: Considered. Character/personal qualities: Important. Alumni/ae relationship: Considered. Geographical residence: Not considered. State residency: Not considered. Religious affiliation/commitment: Considered. Minority status: Not considered. Volunteer work: Considered. Work experience: Not considered. **Other schools with the greatest overlap in applicants:** Creighton University; St. Louis University; University of Kansas; University of Missouri–Columbia; University of Missouri–Kansas City. **Admissions statistics for the fall 2005 entering class:** Total applicants: 1,775. Total accepted: 1,314. Freshmen enrolled: 371; 62% were from out of state. Overall acceptance rate: 74%. Non-early acceptance rate: 74%. **Credentials of fall 2005 freshmen:** 31% ranked in the top 10 percent of their high school class; 65% were in the top 25 percent, and 87% were in the top half. (Proportion submitting class standing: 78%.) **Average high school grade point average:** 3.6. First-year students who submitted SAT scores: 14%. Scores (25/75 percentile): Verbal: 530-640, Math: 530-640, Combined: 1060-1280. **First-year students submitting ACT scores:** 95%. Scores (25/75 percentile): English: 22-29, Math: 21-27, Composite: 22-28.

ACADEMICS
Year founded: 1910. **Academic calendar:** Semester. **Degrees offered:** certificate, bachelor's, post-bachelor's certificate, master's, doctorate. **Most popular majors:** 31% business, management, marketing, and related support services, 19% health professions and related clinical sciences, 11% psychology, 9% social sciences, 4% biological and biomedical sciences. **Major fields of study:** biological and biomedical sciences; business, management, marketing, and related support services; communication, journalism, and related programs; computer and information sciences and support services; education; English language and literature/letters; foreign languages, literatures, and linguistics; health professions and related clinical sciences; history; mathematics and statistics; multi/interdisciplinary studies; philosophy and religious studies; physical sciences; psychology; public administration and social service professions; social sciences. **Areas of required coursework:** arts/fine arts, humanities, computer literacy, mathematics, English (including composition), philosophy, sciences (biological or physical), history, other. **Pre-professional programs:** pre-law, pre-dentistry, pre-medicine, pre-veterinary science, pre-optometry, pre-pharmacy, other. **Special academic programs (% participation):** accelerated program (25%), cooperative (work-study plan) program (9%), cross-registration (4%), distance learning, double major (5%), dual enrollment, exchange student program (domestic) (0%), honors program (1%), independent study (15%), internships (5%), study abroad (14%), teacher certificate program (4%). **Teacher certification offered in:** elementary, secondary. **Cooperative education programs:** art, business, computer science, education, health professions, humanities, natural science, social/behavioral science, technologies, other. **Reserve Officers Training Corps (ROTC):** Army ROTC: Offered at cooperating institution (University of MO at KC). **Faculty and instruction (2005-2006):** Total instructional faculty: 126 full-time, 89 part-time (58% men; 42% women; 3% minorities). Full-time faculty with Ph.D. or other terminal degree: 87%. Student/faculty ratio: 10/1. Classes of fewer than 20 students: 40%; of 20 to 49 students: 57%; of 50 or more students: 2%. **Advanced Placement and International Baccalaureate credit:** International Baccalaureate exams may be used for: Credit and/or placement. **Freshmen returning for sophomore year:** 82%. **Graduation rates:** Four-year: 50%; five-year: 59%; six-year: 65%. **Graduate study:** 27% of students pursue further study immediately upon graduation. Fields in which graduates pursue further study: Master of Business Administration (MBA), 22%; law, 11%; medicine, 12%; engineering, 1%; education, 4%; arts and sciences, 29%.

COSTS AND FINANCIAL AID
Financial aid office: (816) 501-4100. **Expenses (2006-2007):** Tuition and fees 2006-2007: $20,840; room/board: $6,000. Estimated books and supplies: $1,400; transportation: $1,029; personal expenses: $1,029. **Financial aid:** Priority filing date for institution's financial aid form: March 1; deadline: June 30. In 2005-2006, 97% of undergraduates applied for financial aid. Of those, 81% were determined to have financial need; 16% had their need fully met. Average financial aid package (proportion receiving): $19,719 (78%). Average amount of gift aid, such as scholarships or grants (proportion receiving): $5,869 (51%). Average amount of self-help aid, such as work study or loans (proportion receiving): $3,598 (43%). Average need-based loan (excluding PLUS or other private loans): $3,314. Among students who received need-based aid, the average percentage of need met: 97%. Among students who received aid based on merit, the average award (and the proportion receiving): $8,523 (10%). The average athletic scholarship (and the proportion receiving): $11,845 (11%). Average amount of debt of borrowers graduating in 2005: $17,890. Proportion who borrowed: 72%.

CAMPUS LIFE AND EXTRACURRICULAR ACTIVITIES
Campus housing available: coed dorms, women's dorms, men's dorms, apartment for single students, special housing for disabled students, other housing options. Students who live in college-owned, operated, or affiliated housing: 61%. **Student employment:** During the 2005-2006 academic year, 15% of undergraduates worked on campus. Average per-year earnings: $2,500. **Clubs and organizations:** Number of student organizations: 42. Activities include: choral groups, dance, drama/theater, literary magazine, musical theater, student government, student newspaper, yearbook. Number of fraternities: 4; sororities: 2. Proportion of men in fraternities: 34%; of women in sororities: 20%. Average proportion of students who stay on campus on weekends: 52%. **Sports program (2005-2006):** Member of NCAA II. *Men's intercollegiate varsity sports:* baseball, basketball, golf, soccer, tennis. *Women's intercollegiate varsity sports:* basketball, soccer, softball, tennis, volleyball.

SERVICES AND FACILITIES
Basic services: nonremedial tutoring, health service, health insurance. **Remedial assistance:** reading, math, writing, study skills. **Counseling services:** minority student, career, personal, veteran student, academic, older student, psychological, birth control, religious. **For learning-disabled students:** School does not offer a structured program with separate admission and additional fees. Services include: learning center, extended time for tests. **Library:** Number of titles: 316,200; number of current serial subscriptions: 850. **Information technology resources:** Students are not required to lease or own a computer. Number of campus computers available to all students: 500. School has a wireless network. Proportion of college-owned housing units wired for high-speed internet access: 100%. **Campus safety:** Security services offered: 24-hour foot-and-vehicle patrols, late-night trans-

port/escort service, 24-hour emergency telephones, lighted pathways/sidewalks, controlled dormitory access (key, security card, etc).

TRANSFER AND INTERNATIONAL STUDENTS
Transfer students: May apply for admission for the following academic terms: Fall, Spring, Summer. Applicants need a minimum number of credits to apply. For fall 2005: Transfer applications received: 490. Transfer applicants offered admission: 247. Transfer applicants enrolled: 120. **International students:** Number of foreign undergraduates: 17 (1% of student body). Number of countries represented: 17. Minimum TOEFL score required: 550 (paper); 213 (computer).

Southeast Missouri State University

- **Address:** 1 University Plaza, Cape Girardeau, MO 63701
- **Website:** http://www.semo.edu
- Public
- **Enrollment:** 6,796 full-time; 2,172 part-time

KEY STATS
✔ **U.S News College Ranking:** third tier, Universities–Master's (Midwest)
✔ **ACT Score (25th/75th percentile):** 19-24
✔ **Tuition:** 2006-2007: $5,145 in state, $9,000 out of state

Selectivity: Selective	**Room/board:** $5,321
Acceptance rate: 89%	**Average debt:** $16,006
Student/faculty ratio: 17/1	**Proportion who borrowed:** 63%

UNDERGRADUATE STUDENT BODY STATS
2005-2006 enrollment: 6,796 full-time; 2,172 part-time. Men: 41%; women: 59%. **Ethnic makeup:** African American: 9%; American-Indian: 1%; Hispanic: 1%; White: 87%; International: 2%.

ADMISSIONS FACTS AND FIGURES
Phone: (573) 651-2590. **Email:** admissions@semo.edu. **Website:** http://www.semo.edu. **Application deadlines for fall 2007:** Regular decision: Rolling. Early decision: Not offered. Early action: Not offered. Admission cannot be deferred. **Application fee:** $20. Common application is accepted. **To apply online, go to:** http://www.semo.edu/admissions/apply.htm. **Admissions requirements/recommendations:** High school units required (recommended): English: 4 (4); Mathematics: 3 (4); Science: 3 (4); Foreign language: 0 (2); Social studies: 2 (2); History: 1 (1); Academic electives: 3 (3); Total units: 17 (21). Tests: The college uses SAT or ACT scores in admissions decisions. Either SAT or ACT required. For admission to the fall 2007 entering class, the school will accept: ACT with writing, ACT without writing. Campus visit: Recommended. Admissions interview: Neither required nor recommended. Off-campus interview: May be arranged. **Factors that count in admissions decisions:** *Academic:* Secondary school record: Very important. Class rank: Considered. Letters of recommendation: Not considered. Standardized test scores: Very important. Essay: Not considered. *Nonacademic:* Interview: Not considered. Extracurricular activities: Not considered. Talent/ability: Not considered. Character/personal qualities: Not considered. Alumni/ae relationship: Not considered. Geographical residence: Not considered. State residency: Not considered. Religious affiliation/commitment: Not considered. Minority status: Not considered. Volunteer work: Not considered. Work experience: Not considered. **Other schools with the greatest overlap in applicants:** Missouri State University; Southern Illinois University–Carbondale; St. Louis University; Truman State University; University of Missouri–Columbia. **Admissions statistics for the fall 2005 entering class:** Total applicants: 4,060. Total accepted: 3,619. Freshmen enrolled: 1,679; 12% were from out of state. Overall acceptance rate: 89%. **Credentials of fall 2005 freshmen:** 13% ranked in the top 10 percent of their high school class; 35% were in the top 25 percent, and 65% were in the top half. (Proportion submitting class standing: 89%.) **Average high school grade point average:** 3.3. **First-year students submitting ACT scores:** 91%. Scores (25/75 percentile): English: 19-25, Math: 18-24, Composite: 19-24.

ACADEMICS
Year founded: 1873. **Academic calendar:** Semester. **Degrees offered:** certificate, associate, bachelor's, master's, post-master's certificate. **Most popular majors:** 9% elementary education and teaching, 8% general studies, 7% communication studies/speech communication and rhetoric, 6% business

administration and management, 5% marketing/marketing management. **Major fields of study:** agriculture, agriculture operations, and related sciences; biological and biomedical sciences; business, management, marketing, and related support services; communication, journalism, and related programs; computer and information sciences and support services; education; engineering; engineering technologies/technicians; English language and literature/letters; family and consumer sciences/human sciences; foreign languages, literatures, and linguistics; health professions and related clinical sciences; history; liberal arts and sciences studies, and humanities; mathematics and statistics; multi/interdisciplinary studies; natural resources and conservation; parks, recreation, leisure, and fitness studies; philosophy and religious studies; physical sciences; psychology; public administration and social service professions; security and protective services; social sciences; visual and performing arts. **Areas of required coursework:** arts/fine arts, humanities, mathematics, English (including composition), foreign languages, sciences (biological or physical), history. **Pre-professional programs:** pre-law, pre-dentistry, pre-medicine, pre-veterinary science, pre-optometry, pre-pharmacy, other. **Special academic programs (% participation):** accelerated program, distance learning (90.3%), double major (16.3%), dual enrollment (12.4%), English as a Second Language (ESL) (.1%), exchange student program (domestic), honors program (12.7%), independent study (22%), internships (31.8%), student-designed major (14%), study abroad (2.3%), teacher certificate program (28.2%), other (65.6%). **Teacher certification offered in:** early childhood, special education, elementary, middle/junior high, secondary. **Reserve Officers Training Corps (ROTC):** Air Force ROTC: Offered on campus. **Faculty and instruction (2005-2006):** Total instructional faculty: 400 full-time, 208 part-time (47% men; 53% women; 9% minorities). Full-time faculty with Ph.D. or other terminal degree: 80%. Student/faculty ratio: 17/1. Classes of fewer than 20 students: 40%; of 20 to 49 students: 59%; of 50 or more students: 1%. **Advanced Placement and International Baccalaureate credit:** International Baccalaureate exams may be used for: Credit only. **Freshmen returning for sophomore year:** 71%. **Graduation rates:** Four-year: 23%; five-year: 46%; six-year: 50%.

COSTS AND FINANCIAL AID
Financial aid office: (573) 651-2253. **Expenses (2006-2007):** Tuition and fees 2006-2007: $5,145 in state, $9,000 out of state; room/board: $5,321. Estimated books and supplies: $400; transportation: $993; personal expenses: $1,937. **Financial aid:** Priority filing date for institution's financial aid form: March 1. In 2005-2006, 71% of undergraduates applied for financial aid. Of those, 53% were determined to have financial need; 21% had their need fully met. Average financial aid package (proportion receiving): $6,531 (53%). Average amount of gift aid, such as scholarships or grants (proportion receiving): $4,224 (39%). Average amount of self-help aid, such as work study or loans (proportion receiving): $3,919 (42%). Average need-based loan (excluding PLUS or other private loans): $3,678. Among students who received need-based aid, the average percentage of need met: 65%. Among students who received aid based on merit, the average award (and the proportion receiving): $3,795 (13%). The average athletic scholarship (and the proportion receiving): $7,776 (2%). Average amount of debt of borrowers graduating in 2005: $16,006. Proportion who borrowed: 63%.

CAMPUS LIFE AND EXTRACURRICULAR ACTIVITIES
Campus housing available (% using): coed dorms (89%), sorority housing (5%), fraternity housing (3%), apartments for married students (1%), apartment for single students (1%), special housing for disabled students (1%). Students who live in college-owned, operated, or affiliated housing: 27%. **Student employment:** During the 2005-2006 academic year, 20% of undergraduates worked on campus. Average per-year earnings: $2,073. **Clubs and organizations:** Number of student organizations: 138. Activities include: choral groups, concert band, dance, drama/theater, jazz band, literary magazine, marching band, music ensembles, musical theater, opera, pep band, radio station, student government, student newspaper, symphony orchestra. Number of fraternities: 11; sororities: 8. Proportion of men in fraternities: 14%; of women in sororities: 10%. Average proportion of students who stay on campus on weekends: 70%. **Sports program (2005-2006):** Member of NCAA I. **Men's intercollegiate varsity sports:** baseball, basketball, cross-country, football, golf, track and field (indoor), track and field (outdoor). **Women's intercollegiate varsity sports:** basketball, cross-country, gymnastics, soccer, softball, tennis, track and field (indoor), track and field (outdoor), volleyball.

SERVICES AND FACILITIES
Basic services: nonremedial tutoring, placement service, day care, health service, health insurance. **Remedial assistance:** reading, math, writing, study skills. **Counseling services:** minority student, career, military, personal, vet-

eran student, academic, older student, psychological, religious. **For learning-disabled students:** School does not offer a structured program with separate admission and additional fees. Total undergraduates in learning-disabled program or receiving services: 100. Services include: remedial math, remedial English, reading machines, tape recorders, untimed tests, note-taking services, oral tests, learning center, readers, extended time for tests, tutors, texts on tape, other testing accomodations. **Library:** Number of titles: 430,314; number of current serial subscriptions: 29,407. **Information technology resources:** Students are not required to lease or own a computer. Number of campus computers available to all students: 1,022. School has a wireless network. Approximate number of users that can be accommodated: 700. Proportion of college-owned housing units wired for high-speed internet access: 100%. **Campus safety:** Security services offered: 24-hour foot-and-vehicle patrols, late-night transport/escort service, 24-hour emergency telephones, lighted pathways/sidewalks, controlled dormitory access (key, security card, etc).

TRANSFER AND INTERNATIONAL STUDENTS
Transfer students: May apply for admission for the following academic terms: Fall, Spring, Summer. Applicants need a minimum number of credits to apply. For fall 2005: Transfer applications received: 1,172. Transfer applicants offered admission: 1,153. Transfer applicants enrolled: 670. **International students:** Number of foreign undergraduates: 151 (2% of student body). Number of countries represented: 36. Minimum TOEFL score required: 500 (paper); 173 (computer).

Southwest Baptist University

■ **Address:** 1600 University Avenue, Bolivar, MO 65613
■ **Website:** http://www.sbuniv.edu
■ **Private; Religious affiliation:** Southern Baptist
■ **Enrollment:** 1,778 full-time; 923 part-time

KEY STATS
✔ **U.S News College Ranking:** third tier, Universities–Master's (Midwest)
✔ **ACT Score (25th/75th percentile):** 20-26
✔ **Tuition:** 2006-2007: $14,100

Selectivity: Selective	**Room/board:** $4,200
Acceptance rate: 85%	**Average debt:** $11,268
Student/faculty ratio: 15/1	**Proportion who borrowed:** 73%

UNDERGRADUATE STUDENT BODY STATS
2005-2006 enrollment: 1,778 full-time; 923 part-time. Men: 34%; women: 66%. **Ethnic makeup:** African American: 3%; American-Indian: 1%; Asian American: 1%; Hispanic: 1%; White: 94%; International: 1%. **Religious preference:** Roman Catholic: 1%; Protestant: 22%; Unknown: 10%; Southern Baptist: 67%.

ADMISSIONS FACTS AND FIGURES
Phone: (800) 526-5859. **Email:** admitme@sbuniv.edu. **Website:** http://www.sbuniv.edu. **Application deadlines for fall 2007:** Regular decision: Rolling. Early decision: Not offered. Early action: Not offered. Admission can be deferred. **Application fee:** $30. Common application is not accepted. **To apply online, go to:** https://www.applyweb.com/. **Admissions requirements/recommendations:** High school units required (recommended): English: (4); Mathematics: (3); Science: (2); Social studies: (2); History: (0); Academic electives: (0); Total units: (13). Tests: The college uses SAT or ACT scores in admissions decisions. Either SAT or ACT required. For admission to the fall 2007 entering class, the school will accept: ACT with writing, ACT without writing. Campus visit: Recommended. Admissions interview: Recommended. Off-campus interview: May be arranged. **Factors that count in admissions decisions:** *Academic:* Secondary school record: Important. Class rank: Very important. Letters of recommendation: Important. Standardized test scores: Very important. Essay: Important. *Nonacademic:* Interview: Considered. Extracurricular activities: Not considered. Talent/ability: Considered. Character/personal qualities: Considered. Alumni/ae relationship: Not considered. Geographical residence: Not considered. State residency: Not considered. Religious affiliation/commitment: Not considered. Minority status: Not considered. Volunteer work: Not considered. Work experience: Not considered. **Other schools with the greatest overlap in applicants:** Drury University; Missouri State University; Oklahoma Baptist University; Truman State University; University of Missouri–Columbia.

Admissions statistics for the fall 2005 entering class: Total applicants: 720. Total accepted: 614. Freshmen enrolled: 393; 31% were from out of state. Overall acceptance rate: 85%. **Credentials of fall 2005 freshmen:** 20% ranked in the top 10 percent of their high school class; 43% were in the top 25 percent, and 74% were in the top half. (Proportion submitting class standing: 89%.) **Average high school grade point average:** 3.4. **First-year students who submitted SAT scores:** 13%. Scores (25/75 percentile): Verbal: 460-600, Math: 470-590, Combined: 930-1190. **First-year students submitting ACT scores:** 92%. Scores (25/75 percentile): English: 20-28, Math: 18-26, Composite: 20-26.

ACADEMICS
Year founded: 1878. **Academic calendar:** Semester. **Degrees offered:** certificate, associate, bachelor's, master's, post-master's certificate, doctorate. **Most popular majors:** 20% education, 16% psychology, 11% business, management, marketing, and related support services, 10% theology and religious vocations, 7% health professions and related clinical sciences. **Major fields of study:** biological and biomedical sciences; business, management, marketing, and related support services; communication, journalism, and related programs; computer and information sciences and support services; education; engineering technologies/technicians; English language and literature/letters; foreign languages, literatures, and linguistics; health professions and related clinical sciences; history; mathematics and statistics; multi/interdisciplinary studies; parks, recreation, leisure, and fitness studies; physical sciences; psychology; public administration and social service professions; security and protective services; social sciences; theology and religious vocations; visual and performing arts. **Areas of required coursework:** arts/fine arts, humanities, computer literacy, mathematics, English (including composition), sciences (biological or physical), history, social science, other. **Pre-professional programs:** pre-law, pre-dentistry, pre-medicine, pre-veterinary science, pre-optometry, pre-pharmacy, other. **Special academic programs:** distance learning, double major, dual enrollment, honors program, independent study, internships, study abroad, teacher certificate program. **Teacher certification offered in:** early childhood, elementary, middle/junior high, secondary. **Reserve Officers Training Corps (ROTC):** Army ROTC: Offered at cooperating institution (Southwest Missouri State University). **Faculty and instruction (2005-2006):** Total instructional faculty: 105 full-time, 141 part-time (52% men; 48% women; 1% minorities). Full-time faculty with Ph.D. or other terminal degree: 64%. Student/faculty ratio: 15/1. Classes of fewer than 20 students: 63%; of 20 to 49 students: 35%; of 50 or more students: 2%. **Advanced Placement and International Baccalaureate credit:** AP tests may be used for: Credit only. Scores accepted: 3, 4, 5. International Baccalaureate exams may be used for: Credit and/or placement. **Freshmen returning for sophomore year:** 71%. **Graduation rates:** Four-year: 32%; five-year: 44%; six-year: 45%. **Graduate study:** 11% of students pursue further study immediately upon graduation; 50% within five years.

COSTS AND FINANCIAL AID
Financial aid office: (417) 328-1822. **Expenses (2006-2007):** Tuition and fees 2006-2007: $14,100; room/board: $4,200. Estimated books and supplies: $1,000; transportation: $1,000; personal expenses: $1,000. **Financial aid:** Priority filing date for institution's financial aid form: March 15. In 2005-2006, 82% of undergraduates applied for financial aid. Of those, 69% were determined to have financial need; 22% had their need fully met. Average financial aid package (proportion receiving): $10,651 (69%). Average amount of gift aid, such as scholarships or grants (proportion receiving): $3,534 (40%). Average amount of self-help aid, such as work study or loans (proportion receiving): $4,828 (55%). Average need-based loan (excluding PLUS or other private loans): $4,372. Among students who received need-based aid, the average percentage of need met: 68%. Among students who received aid based on merit, the average award (and the proportion receiving): $5,031 (23%). The average athletic scholarship (and the proportion receiving): $8,541 (11%). Average amount of debt of borrowers graduating in 2005: $11,268. Proportion who borrowed: 73%.

CAMPUS LIFE AND EXTRACURRICULAR ACTIVITIES
Campus housing available (% using): women's dorms (48%), men's dorms (37%), apartment for single students (12%), other housing options (3%). Students who live in college-owned, operated, or affiliated housing: 63%. **Student employment:** During the 2005-2006 academic year, 20% of undergraduates worked on campus. Average per-year earnings: $3,000. **Clubs and organizations:** Number of student organizations: 25. Activities include: choral groups, concert band, drama/theater, jazz band, music ensembles, musical theater, opera, pep band, student government, student newspaper, symphony orchestra, yearbook. Number of fraternities: 0; sororities: 0.

Average proportion of students who stay on campus on weekends: 74%. **Sports program (2005-2006):** Member of NCAA II. *Men's intercollegiate varsity sports:* baseball, basketball, cross-country, football, golf, tennis, track and field (indoor), track and field (outdoor). *Women's intercollegiate varsity sports:* basketball, cross-country, soccer, softball, tennis, track and field (indoor), track and field (outdoor), volleyball.

SERVICES AND FACILITIES

Basic services: nonremedial tutoring, placement service, health service, health insurance. **Remedial assistance:** reading, math, writing, study skills, other. **Counseling services:** career, personal, academic, psychological, religious. **For learning-disabled students:** School does not offer a structured program with separate admission and additional fees. Total undergraduates in learning-disabled program or receiving services: 49. Services include: remedial math, remedial English, tape recorders, videotaped classes, untimed tests, oral tests, learning center, readers, extended time for tests, tutors, priority seating, texts on tape, other testing accomodations. **Library:** Number of titles: 196,425; number of current serial subscriptions: 49,600. **Information technology resources:** Students are not required to lease or own a computer. Number of campus computers available to all students: 261. School has a wireless network. Approximate number of users that can be accommodated: 2,000. Proportion of college-owned housing units wired for high-speed internet access: 90%. **Campus safety:** Security services offered: 24-hour foot-and-vehicle patrols, 24-hour emergency telephones, lighted pathways/sidewalks, controlled dormitory access (key, security card, etc).

TRANSFER AND INTERNATIONAL STUDENTS

Transfer students: May apply for admission for the following academic terms: Fall, Winter, Spring, Summer. Applicants need a minimum number of credits to apply. For fall 2005: Transfer applications received: 224. Transfer applicants offered admission: 163. Transfer applicants enrolled: 138. **International students:** Number of foreign undergraduates: 16 (1% of student body). Number of countries represented: 16. Minimum TOEFL score required: 550 (paper); 213 (computer).

Stephens College

- **Address:** 1200 E. Broadway Box 2121, Columbia, MO 65215
- **Website:** http://www.stephens.edu
- **Private**
- **Enrollment:** 574 full-time; 180 part-time

KEY STATS

✔ **U.S News College Ranking:** fourth tier, Liberal Arts Colleges
✔ **ACT Score (25th/75th percentile):** 21-27
✔ **Tuition:** 2006-2007: $20,500

Selectivity: More selective	**Room/board:** $7,975
Acceptance rate: 64%	**Average debt:** $19,396
Student/faculty ratio: 12/1	**Proportion who borrowed:** 63%

UNDERGRADUATE STUDENT BODY STATS

2005-2006 enrollment: 574 full-time; 180 part-time. Men: 3%; women: 97%. **Ethnic makeup:** African American: 8%; American-Indian: 1%; Asian American: 2%; Hispanic: 3%; White: 86%; International: 1%.

ADMISSIONS FACTS AND FIGURES

Phone: (800) 876-7207. **Email:** apply@stephens.edu. **Website:** http://www.stephens.edu. **Application deadlines for fall 2007:** Regular decision: Rolling. Early decision: Not offered. Early action: Not offered. Admission can be deferred. **Application fee:** $25. Common application is accepted. **Admissions requirements/recommendations:** High school units required (recommended): English: 4 (4); Mathematics: 2 (3); Science: 2 (3); Foreign language: 2 (2); Social studies: 2 (3); History: (2). Tests: The college uses SAT or ACT scores in admissions decisions. Neither SAT nor ACT required. For admission to the fall 2007 entering class, the school will accept: ACT with writing, ACT without writing. Campus visit: Recommended. Admissions interview: Recommended. Off-campus interview: May be arranged. **Factors that count in admissions decisions:** *Academic:* Secondary school record: Very important. Class rank: Considered. Letters of recommendation: Very important. Standardized test scores: Very important. Essay: Very important. *Nonacademic:* Interview: Considered. Extracurricular activities: Considered. Talent/ability: Important.

Character/personal qualities: Considered. Alumni/ae relationship: Considered. Geographical residence: Not considered. State residency: Not considered. Religious affiliation/commitment: Not considered. Minority status: Not considered. Volunteer work: Considered. Work experience: Considered. **Admissions statistics for the fall 2005 entering class:** Total applicants: 642. Total accepted: 414. Freshmen enrolled: 207; 54% were from out of state. Overall acceptance rate: 64%. **Credentials of fall 2005 freshmen:** 19% ranked in the top 10 percent of their high school class; 59% were in the top 25 percent, and 90% were in the top half. (Proportion submitting class standing: 85%.) **Average high school grade point average:** 3.5. **First-year students who submitted SAT scores:** 20%. Scores (25/75 percentile): Verbal: 540-610, Math: 480-580, Combined: 1020-1190. **First-year students submitting ACT scores:** 80%. Scores (25/75 percentile): English: 22-27, Math: 19-25, Composite: 21-27.

ACADEMICS

Year founded: 1833. **Academic calendar:** Semester. **Degrees offered:** associate, bachelor's, post-bachelor's certificate, master's. **Most popular majors:** 22% drama and dramatics/theater arts, 13% fashion/apparel design, 7% health information/medical records administration/administrator, 6% fashion merchandising, 6% mass communication/media studies. **Major fields of study:** biological and biomedical sciences; business, management, marketing, and related support services; communication, journalism, and related programs; education; English language and literature/letters; family and consumer sciences/human sciences; health professions and related clinical sciences; legal professions and studies; liberal arts and sciences studies, and humanities; psychology; social sciences; visual and performing arts. **Areas of required coursework:** arts/fine arts, humanities, mathematics, English (including composition), philosophy, sciences (biological or physical), history, social science, other. **Pre-professional programs:** pre-law, pre-dentistry, pre-medicine, pre-veterinary science, pre-pharmacy. **Special academic programs (% participation):** cross-registration, distance learning, double major, dual enrollment, external degree program, internships (85%), student-designed major, study abroad, teacher certificate program. **Teacher certification offered in:** early childhood, elementary. **Reserve Officers Training Corps (ROTC):** Army ROTC: Offered at cooperating institution (University of Missouri-Columbia); Navy ROTC: Offered at cooperating institution (University of Missouri-Columbia); Air Force ROTC: Offered at cooperating institution (University of Missouri-Columbia). **Faculty and instruction (2005-2006):** Total instructional faculty: 41 full-time, 49 part-time (29% men; 71% women; 0% minorities). Full-time faculty with Ph.D. or other terminal degree: 51%. Student/faculty ratio: 12/1. Classes of fewer than 20 students: 75%; of 20 to 49 students: 24%; of 50 or more students: 1%. **Advanced Placement and International Baccalaureate credit:** AP tests may be used for: Credit and/or placement. Scores accepted: 3, 4, 5. International Baccalaureate exams may be used for: Credit only. **Freshmen returning for sophomore year:** 70%. **Graduation rates:** Four-year: 43%; five-year: 51%; six-year: 52%. **Graduate study:** 21% of students pursue further study immediately upon graduation. Fields in which graduates pursue further study: Master of Business Administration (MBA), 28%; law, 11%; education, 6%.

COSTS AND FINANCIAL AID

Financial aid office: (573) 876-7106. **Expenses (2006-2007):** Tuition and fees 2006-2007: $20,500; room/board: $7,975. Estimated books and supplies: $1,000; transportation: $965; personal expenses: $1,800. **Financial aid:** Priority filing date for institution's financial aid form: March 15. In 2005-2006, 83% of undergraduates applied for financial aid. Of those, 73% were determined to have financial need; 21% had their need fully met. Average financial aid package (proportion receiving): $16,894 (73%). Average amount of gift aid, such as scholarships or grants (proportion receiving): $6,533 (54%). Average amount of self-help aid, such as work study or loans (proportion receiving): $4,433 (58%). Average need-based loan (excluding PLUS or other private loans): $3,907. Among students who received need-based aid, the average percentage of need met: 83%. Among students who received aid based on merit, the average award (and the proportion receiving): $7,714 (21%). The average athletic scholarship (and the proportion receiving): $2,959 (9%). Average amount of debt of borrowers graduating in 2005: $19,396. Proportion who borrowed: 63%.

CAMPUS LIFE AND EXTRACURRICULAR ACTIVITIES

Campus housing available: women's dorms, men's dorms, apartment for single students. Students who live in college-owned, operated, or affiliated housing: 70%. **Student employment:** During the 2005-2006 academic year, 48% of undergraduates worked on campus. Average per-year earnings: $1,200. **Clubs and organizations:** Number of student organizations: 45. Activities include: choral groups, dance, drama/theater, literary magazine, musical theater, radio station, student government, student newspaper, television station, yearbook. Number of fraternities: 0; sororities: 2. of women in sororities: 8%. Average proportion of students who stay on campus on weekends: 85%. **Sports program (2005-2006):** Member of NCAA III. *Women's intercollegiate varsity sports:* basketball, soccer, swimming and diving, tennis, volleyball.

SERVICES AND FACILITIES

Basic services: nonremedial tutoring, women's center, health service. **Remedial assistance:** reading, math, writing, study skills. **Counseling services:** career, personal, academic, psychological, birth control. **For learning-disabled students:** School does not offer a structured program with separate admission and additional fees. Services include: oral tests, learning center, extended time for tests, priority seating, exams on tape or computer. **Information technology resources:** Students are not required to lease or own a computer. School has a wireless network. Approximate number of users that can be accommodated: 7,500. Proportion of college-owned housing units wired for high-speed internet access: 100%. **Campus safety:** Security services offered: 24-hour foot-and-vehicle patrols, late-night transport/escort service, 24-hour emergency telephones, lighted pathways/sidewalks, controlled dormitory access (key, security card, etc).

TRANSFER AND INTERNATIONAL STUDENTS

Transfer students: May apply for admission for the following academic terms: Fall, Spring. Applicants need a minimum number of credits to apply. For fall 2005: Transfer applications received: 116. Transfer applicants offered admission: 47. Transfer applicants enrolled: 47. **International students:** Number of foreign undergraduates: 5 (1% of student body). Number of countries represented: 2. Minimum TOEFL score required: 550 (paper); 213 (computer).

St. Louis University

- **Address:** 221 N. Grand Boulevard, St. Louis, MO 63103
- **Website:** http://www.slu.edu
- **Private; Religious affiliation:** Roman Catholic
- **Enrollment:** 6,817 full-time; 604 part-time

KEY STATS

- ✔ **U.S News College Ranking:** 77, National Universities
- ✔ **ACT Score (25th/75th percentile):** 24-29
- ✔ **Tuition:** 2006-2007: $26,448

Selectivity: More selective	**Room/board:** $8,230
Acceptance rate: 78%	**Average debt:** $24,552
Student/faculty ratio: 12/1	**Proportion who borrowed:** 67%

UNDERGRADUATE STUDENT BODY STATS

2005-2006 enrollment: 6,817 full-time; 604 part-time. Men: 43%; women: 57%. **Ethnic makeup:** African American: 8%; Asian American: 5%; Hispanic: 3%; White: 82%; International: 2%. **Religious preference:** Protestant: 21%; Jewish: 1%; Muslim: 1%; No preference: 8%; Unknown: 22%; Roman Catholic: 42%; Other: 5%.

ADMISSIONS FACTS AND FIGURES

Phone: (314) 977-2500. **Email:** admitme@slu.edu. **Website:** http://www.slu.edu. **Application deadlines for fall 2007:** Regular decision: August 1. Early decision: Not offered. Early action: Not offered. Admission can be deferred. Common application is accepted. **To apply online, go to:** http://www.slu.edu/admissions/app_forms.html. **Admissions requirements/recommendations:** High school units required (recommended): English: 4 (4); Mathematics: 4 (4); Science: 3 (3); Foreign language: 2 (2); Social studies: 3 (3); History: 0 (0); Academic electives: 3 (3); Total units: 20 (20). Tests: The college uses SAT or ACT scores in admissions decisions. Either SAT or ACT required. For admission to the fall 2007 entering class, the school will accept: ACT with writing, ACT without writing. Campus visit: Recommended. Admissions interview: Recommended. Off-campus interview: May be arranged. **Factors that count in admissions decisions:** *Academic:* Secondary school record: Important. Class rank: Not considered. Letters of recommendation: Very important. Standardized test scores: Very important. Essay: Important. *Nonacademic:* Interview: Considered. Extracurricular activities: Important. Talent/ability: Considered. Character/personal qualities: Considered. Alumni/ae relationship: Not con-

sidered. Geographical residence: Not considered. State residency: Not considered. Religious affiliation/commitment: Not considered. Minority status: Not considered. Volunteer work: Considered. Work experience: Considered. **Other schools with the greatest overlap in applicants:** Loyola University Chicago; Marquette University; Truman State University; University of Illinois–Urbana-Champaign; University of Missouri–Columbia. **Admissions statistics for the fall 2005 entering class:** Total applicants: 8,105. Total accepted: 6,310. Freshmen enrolled: 1,521; 62% were from out of state. Overall acceptance rate: 78%. **Credentials of fall 2005 freshmen:** 36% ranked in the top 10 percent of their high school class; 66% were in the top 25 percent, and 90% were in the top half. (Proportion submitting class standing: 68%.) **Average high school grade point average:** 3.7. **First-year students who submitted SAT scores:** 40%. Scores (25/75 percentile): Verbal: 550-650, Math: 550-670, Combined: 1100-1320. **First-year students submitting ACT scores:** 89%. Scores (25/75 percentile): English: 23-30, Math: 23-29, Composite: 24-29.

ACADEMICS

Year founded: 1818. **Academic calendar:** Semester. **Degrees offered:** certificate, bachelor's, post-bachelor's certificate, master's, post-master's certificate, first professional, doctorate. **Most popular majors:** 8% nursing/registered nurse training (R.N., A.S.N., B.S.N., M.S.N.), 8% psychology, 6% finance, 6% marketing/marketing management, 5% accounting. **Major fields of study:** area, ethnic, cultural, and gender studies; biological and biomedical sciences; business, management, marketing, and related support services; communication, journalism, and related programs; computer and information sciences and support services; education; engineering; engineering technologies/technicians; English language and literature/letters; family and consumer sciences/human sciences; foreign languages, literatures, and linguistics; health professions and related clinical sciences; history; liberal arts and sciences studies, and humanities; mathematics and statistics; multi/interdisciplinary studies; natural resources and conservation; parks, recreation, leisure, and fitness studies; philosophy and religious studies; physical sciences; psychology; public administration and social service professions; security and protective services; social sciences; theology and religious vocations; transportation and materials moving; visual and performing arts. **Areas of required coursework:** humanities, mathematics, English (including composition), philosophy, sciences (biological or physical), history, social science, other. **Pre-professional programs:** pre-law, pre-medicine, other. **Special academic programs:** accelerated program, cooperative (work-study plan) program, cross-registration, distance learning, double major, dual enrollment, English as a Second Language (ESL), honors program, independent study, internships, liberal arts/career combination, student-designed major, study abroad, teacher certificate program. **Teacher certification offered in:** early childhood, special education, elementary, middle/junior high, secondary. **Cooperative education programs:** business, engineering. **Reserve Officers Training Corps (ROTC):** Army ROTC: Offered at cooperating institution (Washington University); Air Force ROTC: Offered on campus. **Faculty and instruction (2005-2006):** Total instructional faculty: 616 full-time, 478 part-time (56% men; 44% women; 10% minorities). Full-time faculty with Ph.D. or other terminal degree: 92%. Student/faculty ratio: 12/1. Classes of fewer than 20 students: 48%; of 20 to 49 students: 46%; of 50 or more students: 6%. **Advanced Placement and International Baccalaureate credit:** AP tests may be used for: Credit and/or placement. Scores accepted: 3, 4, 5. International Baccalaureate exams may be used for: Credit and/or placement. **Freshmen returning for sophomore year:** 87%. **Graduation rates:** Four-year: 61%; five-year: 74%; six-year: 75%. **Graduate study:** 30% of students pursue further study immediately upon graduation. Fields in which graduates pursue further study: law, 7%; medicine, 7%.

COSTS AND FINANCIAL AID

Financial aid office: (314) 977-2350. **Expenses (2006-2007):** Tuition and fees 2006-2007: $26,448; room/board: $8,230. Estimated books and supplies: $1,040; transportation: $1,550; personal expenses: $1,050. **Financial aid:** Priority filing date for institution's financial aid form: March 1. In 2005-2006, 72% of undergraduates applied for financial aid. Of those, 60% were determined to have financial need; 19% had their need fully met. Average financial aid package (proportion receiving): $18,858 (60%). Average amount of gift aid, such as scholarships or grants (proportion receiving): $12,875 (57%). Average amount of self-help aid, such as work study or loans (proportion receiving): $4,815 (48%). Average need-based loan (excluding PLUS or other private loans): $4,192. Among students who received need-based aid, the average percentage of need met: 59%. Among students who received aid based on merit, the average award (and the proportion receiving): $9,455 (24%). The average athletic scholarship (and the proportion

receiving): $14,361 (3%). Average amount of debt of borrowers graduating in 2005: $24,552. Proportion who borrowed: 67%.

CAMPUS LIFE AND EXTRACURRICULAR ACTIVITIES

Campus housing available (% using): coed dorms (41%), women's dorms (7%), men's dorms (7%), sorority housing (4%), fraternity housing (2%), apartments for married students (0%), apartment for single students (39%). Students who live in college-owned, operated, or affiliated housing: 57%. **Student employment:** During the 2005-2006 academic year, 20% of undergraduates worked on campus. Average per-year earnings: $2,900. **Clubs and organizations:** Number of student organizations: 108. Activities include: choral groups, dance, drama/theater, jazz band, literary magazine, music ensembles, musical theater, pep band, radio station, student government, student newspaper, student film society, television station. Number of fraternities: 13; sororities: 6. Proportion of men in fraternities: 19%; of women in sororities: 15%. Average proportion of students who stay on campus on weekends: 80%. **Sports program (2005-2006):** Member of NCAA I. *Men's intercollegiate varsity sports:* baseball, basketball, cross-country, golf, soccer, swimming and diving, tennis, track and field (outdoor). *Women's intercollegiate varsity sports:* basketball, cross-country, field hockey, golf, soccer, softball, swimming and diving, tennis, track and field (outdoor), volleyball.

SERVICES AND FACILITIES

Basic services: nonremedial tutoring, placement service, health service. **Counseling services:** minority student, career, military, personal, academic, older student, psychological, religious. **For learning-disabled students:** School does not offer a structured program with separate admission and additional fees. Total undergraduates in learning-disabled program or receiving services: 60. Services include: tape recorders, other special classes, diagnostic testing service, note-taking services, extended time for tests, tutors, priority registration, priority seating, texts on tape, exams on tape or computer, other testing accomodations, other. **Library:** Number of titles: 1,893,063; number of current serial subscriptions: 20,127. **Information technology resources:** Students are not required to lease or own a computer. Number of campus computers available to all students: 1,350. School has a wireless network. Approximate number of users that can be accommodated: 9,000. Proportion of college-owned housing units wired for high-speed internet access: 100%. **Campus safety:** Security services offered: 24-hour foot-and-vehicle patrols, late-night transport/escort service, 24-hour emergency telephones, lighted pathways/sidewalks, controlled dormitory access (key, security card, etc.).

TRANSFER AND INTERNATIONAL STUDENTS

Transfer students: May apply for admission for the following academic terms: Fall, Spring, Summer. Applicants need a minimum number of credits to apply. For fall 2005: Transfer applications received: 1,690. Transfer applicants offered admission: 860. Transfer applicants enrolled: 432. **International students:** Number of foreign undergraduates: 130 (2% of student body). Number of countries represented: 55. Minimum TOEFL score required: 525 (paper); 194 (computer).

Truman State University

- **Address:** 100 E. Normal Street, Kirksville, MO 63501
- **Website:** http://www.truman.edu
- **Public**
- **Enrollment:** 5,460 full-time; 111 part-time

KEY STATS

✔ **U.S News College Ranking:** 8, Universities–Master's (Midwest)
✔ **ACT Score (25th/75th percentile):** 25-30
✔ **Tuition:** 2006-2007: $6,092 in state, $10,522 out of state

Selectivity: More selective	**Room/board:** $5,570
Acceptance rate: 82%	**Average debt:** $16,546
Student/faculty ratio: 15/1	**Proportion who borrowed:** 43%

UNDERGRADUATE STUDENT BODY STATS

2005-2006 enrollment: 5,460 full-time; 111 part-time. Men: 42%; women: 58%. **Ethnic makeup:** African American: 4%; Asian American: 2%; Hispanic: 2%; White: 88%; International: 3%. **Religious preference:** Roman Catholic: 29%; Protestant: 59%; Jewish: 1%; Buddhist: 1%; No preference: 17%; Eastern Orthodox: 0%; Other: 2%.

ADMISSIONS FACTS AND FIGURES

Phone: (660) 785-4114. **Email:** admissions@truman.edu. **Website:** http://www.truman.edu. **Application deadlines for fall 2007:** Regular decision: March 1. Early decision: Not offered. Early action: Send application by: November 15; Decision sent by: December 15. Admission can be deferred. **Application fee:** None. Common application is accepted. **To apply online, go to:** http://admissions.truman.edu/apply/index.asp. **Admissions requirements/recommendations:** High school units required (recommended): English: 4 (4); Mathematics: 3 (4); Science: 3 (3); Foreign language: 2 (2); Social studies: 3 (3); Total units: 16 (17). Tests: The college uses SAT or ACT scores in admissions decisions. Either SAT or ACT required. For admission to the fall 2007 entering class, the school will accept: ACT with writing, ACT without writing. Campus visit: Recommended. Admissions interview: Recommended. Off-campus interview: May be arranged. **Factors that count in admissions decisions:** *Academic:* Secondary school record: Very important. Class rank: Very important. Letters of recommendation: Not considered. Standardized test scores: Very important. Essay: Important. *Nonacademic:* Interview: Not considered. Extracurricular activities: Considered. Talent/ability: Considered. Character/personal qualities: Considered. Alumni/ae relationship: Considered. Geographical residence: Considered. State residency: Considered. Religious affiliation/commitment: Not considered. Minority status: Considered. Volunteer work: Considered. Work experience: Considered. **Other schools with the greatest overlap in applicants:** Missouri State University; St. Louis University; University of Illinois–Urbana-Champaign; University of Missouri–Columbia; Washington University in St. Louis. **Admissions statistics for the fall 2005 entering class:** Total applicants: 4,912. Total accepted: 4,035. Freshmen enrolled: 1,448; 24% were from out of state. Accepted through early-decision or early-action plans: 62%. Overall acceptance rate: 82%. **Credentials of fall 2005 freshmen:** 48% ranked in the top 10 percent of their high school class; 80% were in the top 25 percent, and 99% were in the top half. (Proportion submitting class standing: 97%.) **Average high school grade point average:** 3.8. **First-year students who submitted SAT scores:** 20%. Scores (25/75 percentile): Verbal: 570-670, Math: 560-660, Combined: 1130-1330. **First-year students submitting ACT scores:** 96%. Scores (25/75 percentile): English: 25-31, Math: 24-29, Composite: 25-30.

ACADEMICS

Year founded: 1867. **Academic calendar:** Semester. **Degrees offered:** bachelor's, master's. **Most popular majors:** 20% business administration and management, 10% biology, 9% psychology, 8% English language and literature, 8% parks, recreation, leisure, and fitness studies. **Major fields of study:** agriculture, agriculture operations, and related sciences; biological and biomedical sciences; business, management, marketing, and related support services; communication, journalism, and related programs; computer and information sciences and support services; English language and literature/letters; foreign languages, literatures, and linguistics; health professions and related clinical sciences; history; legal professions and studies; mathematics and statistics; multi/interdisciplinary studies; parks, recreation, leisure, and fitness studies; philosophy and religious studies; physical sciences; psychology; security and protective services; social sciences; visual and performing arts. **Areas of required coursework:** arts/fine arts, humanities, computer literacy, mathematics, English (including composition), foreign languages, sciences (biological or physical), history, social science. **Pre-professional programs:** pre-law, pre-dentistry, pre-medicine, pre-veterinary science, pre-optometry, pre-pharmacy, other. **Special academic programs (% participation):** double major (6%), dual enrollment, honors program (1%), internships, student-designed major (1%), study abroad (9%), teacher certificate program. **Teacher certification offered in:** early childhood, special education, elementary, middle/junior high, secondary. **Reserve Officers Training Corps (ROTC):** Army ROTC: Offered on campus. **Faculty and instruction (2005-2006):** Total instructional faculty: 353 full-time, 25 part-time (59% men; 41% women; 10% minorities). Full-time faculty with Ph.D. or other terminal degree: 83%. Student/faculty ratio: 15/1. Classes of fewer than 20 students: 33%; of 20 to 49 students: 65%; of 50 or more students: 2%. **Advanced Placement and International Baccalaureate credit:** AP tests may be used for: Credit and/or placement. Scores accepted: 3, 4, 5. International Baccalaureate exams may be used for: Credit and/or placement. **Freshmen returning for sophomore year:** 86%. **Graduation rates:** Four-year: 41%; five-year: 62%; six-year: 66%. **Graduate study:** 45% of students pursue further study immediately upon graduation. Fields in which graduates pursue further study: Master of Business Administration (MBA), 1%; law, 4%; medicine, 5%; dentistry, 1%; engineering, 1%; theology (or the seminary), 1%; education, 9%; arts and sciences, 11%; veterinary medicine, 1%.

COSTS AND FINANCIAL AID

Financial aid office: (660) 785-4130. **Expenses (2006-2007):** Tuition and fees 2006-2007: $6,092 in state, $10,522 out of state; room/board: $5,570. Estimated books and supplies: $900; transportation: $1,300; personal expenses: $2,500. **Financial aid:** Priority filing date for institution's financial aid form: April 1. In 2005-2006, 61% of undergraduates applied for financial aid. Of those, 42% were determined to have financial need; 62% had their need fully met. Average financial aid package (proportion receiving): $6,706 (42%). Average amount of gift aid, such as scholarships or grants (proportion receiving): $2,934 (17%). Average amount of self-help aid, such as work study or loans (proportion receiving): $3,497 (34%). Average need-based loan (excluding PLUS or other private loans): $4,039. Among students who received need-based aid, the average percentage of need met: 78%. Among students who received aid based on merit, the average award (and the proportion receiving): $4,002 (45%). The average athletic scholarship (and the proportion receiving): $3,679 (5%). Average amount of debt of borrowers graduating in 2005: $16,546. Proportion who borrowed: 43%.

CAMPUS LIFE AND EXTRACURRICULAR ACTIVITIES

Campus housing available (% using): coed dorms (80%), women's dorms (8%), sorority housing (3%), apartments for married students (1%), apartment for single students (7%), special housing for disabled students (1%). Students who live in college-owned, operated, or affiliated housing: 51%. **Student employment:** During the 2005-2006 academic year, 21% of undergraduates worked on campus. Average per-year earnings: $1,696. **Clubs and organizations:** Number of student organizations: 240. Activities include: choral groups, concert band, dance, drama/theater, jazz band, literary magazine, marching band, music ensembles, musical theater, pep band, radio station, student government, student newspaper, student film society, symphony orchestra, television station, yearbook. Number of fraternities: 18; sororities: 11. Proportion of men in fraternities: 31%; of women in sororities: 22%. Average proportion of students who stay on campus on weekends: 95%. **Sports program (2005-2006):** Member of NCAA II. *Men's intercollegiate varsity sports:* baseball, basketball, cross-country, football, golf, soccer, swimming and diving, tennis, track and field (indoor), track and field (outdoor), wrestling. *Women's intercollegiate varsity sports:* basketball, cross-country, golf, soccer, softball, swimming and diving, tennis, track and field (indoor), track and field (outdoor), volleyball.

SERVICES AND FACILITIES

Basic services: women's center, placement service, health service. **Counseling services:** minority student, career, academic, psychological, birth control, other. **For learning-disabled students:** School does not offer a structured program with separate admission and additional fees. Total undergraduates in learning-disabled program or receiving services: 72. Services include: reading machines, note-taking services, oral tests, readers, extended time for tests, tutors, priority registration, priority seating, other testing accomodations, other. **Library:** Number of titles: 460,116; number of current serial subscriptions: 3,396. **Information technology resources:** Students are not required to lease or own a computer. Number of campus computers available to all students: 857. School has a wireless network. Approximate number of users that can be accommodated: 600. Proportion of college-owned housing units wired for high-speed internet access: 100%. **Campus safety:** Security services offered: 24-hour foot-and-vehicle patrols, late-night transport/escort service, 24-hour emergency telephones, lighted pathways/sidewalks, student patrols, controlled dormitory access (key, security card, etc).

TRANSFER AND INTERNATIONAL STUDENTS

Transfer students: May apply for admission for the following academic terms: Fall, Spring, Summer. Applicants do not need a minimum number of credits to apply. For fall 2005: Transfer applications received: 317. Transfer applicants offered admission: 198. Transfer applicants enrolled: 113. **International students:** Number of foreign undergraduates: 184 (3% of student body). Number of countries represented: 46. Minimum TOEFL score required: 550 (paper); 231 (computer). Average TOEFL score: 587 (paper).

University of Missouri–Columbia

- **Address:** 305 Jesse Hall, Columbia, MO 65211
- **Website:** http://www.missouri.edu
- **Public**
- **Enrollment:** 19,979 full-time; 1,396 part-time

KEY STATS

✔ **U.S News College Ranking:** 88, National Universities
✔ **ACT Score (25th/75th percentile):** 23-28
✔ **Tuition:** 2006-2007: $7,858 in state, $16,983 out of state
Selectivity: More selective   **Room/board:** $6,540
Acceptance rate: 89%   **Average debt:** $17,907
Student/faculty ratio: 18/1   **Proportion who borrowed:** 50%

UNDERGRADUATE STUDENT BODY STATS

2005-2006 enrollment: 19,979 full-time; 1,396 part-time. Men: 48%; women: 52%. **Ethnic makeup:** African American: 6%; American-Indian: 1%; Asian American: 3%; Hispanic: 2%; White: 88%; International: 1%.

ADMISSIONS FACTS AND FIGURES

Phone: (573) 882-7786. **Email:** mu4u@missouri.edu. **Website:** http://www.missouri.edu. **Application deadlines for fall 2007:** Regular decision: Rolling. Early decision: Not offered. Early action: Not offered. Admission can be deferred. **Application fee:** $45. Common application is not accepted. **To apply online, go to:** http://admissions.missouri.edu/applying/index.php. **Admissions requirements/recommendations:** High school units required (recommended): English: 4; Mathematics: 4; Science: 3; Foreign language: 2; Social studies: 3; Total units: 17. Tests: The college uses SAT or ACT scores in admissions decisions. Either SAT or ACT required. For admission to the fall 2007 entering class, the school will accept: ACT with writing, ACT without writing. Campus visit: Recommended. Admissions interview: Neither required nor recommended. Off-campus interview: Not available. **Factors that count in admissions decisions:** *Academic:* Secondary school record: Important. Class rank: Very important. Letters of recommendation: Considered. Standardized test scores: Very important. Essay: Considered. *Nonacademic:* Interview: Not considered. Extracurricular activities: Not considered. Talent/ability: Considered. Character/personal qualities: Not considered. Alumni/ae relationship: Not considered. Geographical residence: Not considered. State residency: Not considered. Religious affiliation/commitment: Not considered. Minority status: Considered. Volunteer work: Considered. Work experience: Considered. **Admissions statistics for the fall 2005 entering class:** Total applicants: 11,524. Total accepted: 10,217. Freshmen enrolled: 4,718; Overall acceptance rate: 89%. **Credentials of fall 2005 freshmen:** 27% ranked in the top 10 percent of their high school class; 57% were in the top 25 percent, and 88% were in the top half. (Proportion submitting class standing: 87%.) **First-year students who submitted SAT scores:** 17%. Scores (25/75 percentile): Verbal: 540-660, Math: 540-650, Combined: 1080-1310. **First-year students submitting ACT scores:** 95%. Scores (25/75 percentile): English: 22-29, Math: 21-27, Composite: 23-28.

ACADEMICS

Year founded: 1839. **Academic calendar:** Semester. **Degrees offered:** bachelor's, master's, post-master's certificate, first professional, doctorate. **Most popular majors:** 18% business, management, marketing, and related support services, 12% communication, journalism, and related programs, 7% engineering, 7% health professions and related clinical sciences, 6% social sciences. **Major fields of study:** agriculture, agriculture operations, and related sciences; area, ethnic, cultural, and gender studies; biological and biomedical sciences; business, management, marketing, and related support services; communication, journalism, and related programs; computer and information sciences and support services; education; engineering; English language and literature/letters; family and consumer sciences/human sciences; foreign languages, literatures, and linguistics; health professions and related clinical sciences; history; liberal arts and sciences studies, and humanities; mathematics and statistics; multi/interdisciplinary studies; natural resources and conservation; parks, recreation, leisure, and fitness studies; philosophy and religious studies; physical sciences; psychology; public administration and social service professions; social sciences; visual and performing arts. **Areas of required coursework:** computer literacy, mathematics, English (including composition), sciences (biological or physical), history, other. **Pre-professional programs:** pre-law, pre-dentistry, pre-medicine, pre-veterinary science, pre-pharmacy, other.

Special academic programs: accelerated program, cooperative (work-study plan) program, distance learning, double major, dual enrollment, English as a Second Language (ESL), exchange student program (domestic), external degree program, honors program, independent study, internships, student-designed major, study abroad, teacher certificate program, other. **Teacher certification offered in:** early childhood, special education, elementary, vo-tech, middle/junior high, adult education, secondary, bilingual/bicultural. **Cooperative education programs:** agriculture, business, computer science, education, engineering, health professions, natural science, social/behavioral science, technologies, other. **Reserve Officers Training Corps (ROTC):** Army ROTC: Offered on campus; Navy ROTC: Offered on campus; Air Force ROTC: Offered on campus. **Faculty and instruction (2005-2006):** Total instructional faculty: 1,066 full-time, 83 part-time (66% men; 34% women; 17% minorities). Full-time faculty with Ph.D. or other terminal degree: 91%. Student/faculty ratio: 18/1. Classes of fewer than 20 students: 43%; of 20 to 49 students: 43%; of 50 or more students: 14%. **Advanced Placement and International Baccalaureate credit:** AP tests may be used for: Credit and/or placement. Scores accepted: 3, 4, 5. International Baccalaureate exams may be used for: Credit only. **Freshmen returning for sophomore year:** 84%. **Graduation rates:** Four-year: 44%; five-year: 66%; six-year: 68%. **Graduate study:** 22% of students pursue further study immediately upon graduation.

COSTS AND FINANCIAL AID

Financial aid office: (573) 882-7506. **Expenses (2006-2007):** Tuition and fees 2006-2007: $7,858 in state, $16,983 out of state; room/board: $6,540. Estimated books and supplies: $950; transportation: $1,386; personal expenses: $1,386. **Financial aid:** Priority filing date for institution's financial aid form: March 1. In 2005-2006, 63% of undergraduates applied for financial aid. Of those, 43% were determined to have financial need; 24% had their need fully met. Average financial aid package (proportion receiving): $10,676 (42%). Average amount of gift aid, such as scholarships or grants (proportion receiving): $5,404 (36%). Average amount of self-help aid, such as work study or loans (proportion receiving): $4,326 (35%). Average need-based loan (excluding PLUS or other private loans): $4,177. Among students who received need-based aid, the average percentage of need met: 85%. Among students who received aid based on merit, the average award (and the proportion receiving): $4,170 (23%). The average athletic scholarship (and the proportion receiving): $9,180 (4%). Average amount of debt of borrowers graduating in 2005: $17,907. Proportion who borrowed: 50%.

CAMPUS LIFE AND EXTRACURRICULAR ACTIVITIES

Campus housing available: coed dorms, women's dorms, men's dorms, sorority housing, fraternity housing, apartments for married students. Students who live in college-owned, operated, or affiliated housing: 38%. **Clubs and organizations:** Number of student organizations: 518. Activities include: choral groups, concert band, dance, drama/theater, jazz band, literary magazine, marching band, music ensembles, musical theater, opera, pep band, radio station, student government, student newspaper, student film society, symphony orchestra, television station, yearbook. Number of fraternities: 29; sororities: 13. Proportion of men in fraternities: 21%; of women in sororities: 24%. **Sports program (2005-2006):** Member of NCAA I. *Men's intercollegiate varsity sports:* baseball, basketball, cross-country, football, golf, swimming and diving, track and field (indoor), track and field (outdoor), wrestling. *Women's intercollegiate varsity sports:* basketball, cross-country, golf, gymnastics, soccer, softball, swimming and diving, tennis, track and field (indoor), track and field (outdoor), volleyball.

SERVICES AND FACILITIES

Basic services: nonremedial tutoring, women's center, placement service, day care, health service, health insurance. **Counseling services:** minority student, career, military, personal, veteran student, academic, older student, psychological, birth control, religious. **For learning-disabled students:** School does not offer a structured program with separate admission and additional fees. Services include: reading machines, tape recorders, diagnostic testing service, untimed tests, note-taking services, oral tests, learning center, readers, extended time for tests, tutors, other testing accomodations, other. **Library:** Number of titles: 4,902,180; number of current serial subscriptions: 33,487. **Information technology resources:** Students are not required to lease or own a computer. Number of campus computers available to all students: 1,615. School has a wireless network. Proportion of college-owned housing units wired for high-speed internet access: 95%. **Campus safety:** Security services offered: 24-hour foot-and-vehicle patrols, late-night transport/escort service, 24-hour emergency telephones, lighted pathways/sidewalks, student patrols, controlled dormitory access (key, security card, etc).

TRANSFER AND INTERNATIONAL STUDENTS

Transfer students: May apply for admission for the following academic terms: Fall, Winter, Spring, Summer. Applicants need a minimum number of credits to apply. For fall 2005: Transfer applications received: 1,888. Transfer applicants offered admission: 1,718. Transfer applicants enrolled: 1,208. **International students:** Number of foreign undergraduates: 242 (1% of student body). Number of countries represented: 53. Minimum TOEFL score required: 500 (paper); 173 (computer).

University of Missouri–Kansas City

- **Address:** 5100 Rockhill Road, Kansas City, MO 64110
- **Website:** http://www.umkc.edu
- **Public**
- **Enrollment:** 5,676 full-time; 3,815 part-time

KEY STATS

✔ **U.S News College Ranking:** third tier, National Universities
✔ **ACT Score (25th/75th percentile):** 21-27
✔ **Tuition:** 2006-2007: $7,591 in state, $17,857 out of state
  Selectivity: More selective **Room/board:** $6,823
  Acceptance rate: 75% **Average debt:** $16,387
  Student/faculty ratio: 11/1 **Proportion who borrowed:** 87%

UNDERGRADUATE STUDENT BODY STATS

2005-2006 enrollment: 5,676 full-time; 3,815 part-time. Men: 40%; women: 60%. **Ethnic makeup:** African American: 15%; American-Indian: 1%; Asian American: 6%; Hispanic: 4%; White: 72%; International: 3%.

ADMISSIONS FACTS AND FIGURES

Phone: (816) 235-1111. **Email:** admit@umkc.edu. **Website:** http://www.umkc.edu. **Application deadlines for fall 2007:** Regular decision: Rolling. Early decision: Not offered. Early action: Not offered. Admission can be deferred. **Application fee:** $35. Common application is not accepted. **To apply online, go to:** http://www.umkc.edu/admissions/decision.asp#. **Admissions requirements/recommendations:** High school units required (recommended): English: 4 (4); Mathematics: 4 (4); Science: 3 (3); Foreign language: 2 (2); Social studies: 3 (3); Total units: 17. Tests: The college uses SAT or ACT scores in admissions decisions. Either SAT or ACT required. For admission to the fall 2007 entering class, the school will accept: ACT with writing, ACT without writing. Campus visit: Recommended. Admissions interview: Neither required nor recommended. Off-campus interview: Not available. **Factors that count in admissions decisions:** *Academic:* Secondary school record: Very important. Class rank: Very important. Letters of recommendation: Considered. Standardized test scores: Very important. Essay: Considered. *Nonacademic:* Interview: Considered. Extracurricular activities: Considered. Talent/ability: Considered. Character/personal qualities: Considered. Alumni/ae relationship: Not considered. Geographical residence: Not considered. State residency: Not considered. Religious affiliation/commitment: Not considered. Minority status: Not considered. Volunteer work: Considered. Work experience: Considered. **Other schools with the greatest overlap in applicants:** Central Missouri State University; Missouri State University; Northwest Missouri State University; University of Kansas; University of Missouri–Columbia. **Admissions statistics for the fall 2005 entering class:** Total applicants: 3,018. Total accepted: 2,254. Freshmen enrolled: 1,028; 20% were from out of state. Overall acceptance rate: 75%. **Credentials of fall 2005 freshmen:** 30% ranked in the top 10 percent of their high school class; 55% were in the top 25 percent, and 84% were in the top half. (Proportion submitting class standing: 83%.) **Average high school grade point average:** 3.3. **First-year students who submitted SAT scores:** 6%. Scores (25/75 percentile): Verbal: N/A, Math: N/A, Combined: N/A. **First-year students submitting ACT scores:** 93%. Scores (25/75 percentile): English: 20-27, Math: 19-26, Composite: 21-27.

ACADEMICS

Year founded: 1929. **Academic calendar:** Semester. **Degrees offered:** bachelor's, master's, post-master's certificate, first professional, first professional certificate, doctorate. **Most popular majors:** 21% liberal arts and sciences studies, and humanities, 13% business, management, marketing, and related support services, 9% education, 7% health professions and related clinical sciences, 7% social sciences. **Major fields of study:** architecture and related services; area, ethnic, cultural, and gender studies; biological and biomedical sciences; business, management, marketing, and related support services; communication, journalism, and related programs; computer and information sciences and support services; education; engineering; English language and literature/letters; foreign languages, literatures, and linguistics; health professions and related clinical sciences; history; liberal arts and sciences studies, and humanities; mathematics and statistics; multi/interdisciplinary studies; natural resources and conservation; philosophy and religious studies; physical sciences; psychology; security and protective services; social sciences; visual and performing arts. **Areas of required coursework:** humanities, mathematics, English (including composition), foreign languages, sciences (biological or physical), history, social science. **Pre-professional programs:** pre-law, pre-dentistry, pre-medicine, pre-pharmacy, other. **Special academic programs:** accelerated program, cooperative (work-study plan) program, distance learning, double major, dual enrollment, English as a Second Language (ESL), honors program, independent study, internships, study abroad, teacher certificate program. **Teacher certification offered in:** early childhood, special education, elementary, middle/junior high, secondary, bilingual/bicultural. **Reserve Officers Training Corps (ROTC):** Army ROTC: Offered on campus; Air Force ROTC: Offered at cooperating institution (University of Missouri-Columbia). **Faculty and instruction (2005-2006):** Total instructional faculty: 641 full-time, 414 part-time (57% men; 43% women; 15% minorities). Full-time faculty with Ph.D. or other terminal degree: 75%. Student/faculty ratio: 11/1. Classes of fewer than 20 students: 53%; of 20 to 49 students: 41%; of 50 or more students: 7%. **Advanced Placement and International Baccalaureate credit:** AP tests may be used for: Credit and/or placement. Scores accepted: 3, 4, 5. International Baccalaureate exams may be used for: Credit and/or placement. **Freshmen returning for sophomore year:** 73%. **Graduation rates:** Four-year: 17%; five-year: 30%; six-year: 47%.

COSTS AND FINANCIAL AID

Financial aid office: (816) 235-1154. **Expenses (2006-2007):** Tuition and fees 2006-2007: $7,591 in state, $17,857 out of state; room/board: $6,823. Estimated books and supplies: $946 personal expenses: $4,700. **Financial aid:** Priority filing date for institution's financial aid form: March 1. In 2005-2006, 88% of undergraduates applied for financial aid. Of those, 64% were determined to have financial need; 44% had their need fully met. Average financial aid package (proportion receiving): $9,859 (64%). Average amount of gift aid, such as scholarships or grants (proportion receiving): $5,428 (41%). Average amount of self-help aid, such as work study or loans (proportion receiving): $6,708 (57%). Average need-based loan (excluding PLUS or other private loans): $6,311. Among students who received need-based aid, the average percentage of need met: 51%. Among students who received aid based on merit, the average award (and the proportion receiving): $4,223 (13%). The average athletic scholarship (and the proportion receiving): $11,534 (2%). Average amount of debt of borrowers graduating in 2005: $16,387. Proportion who borrowed: 87%.

CAMPUS LIFE AND EXTRACURRICULAR ACTIVITIES

Campus housing available: coed dorms, sorority housing, fraternity housing, other housing options. Students who live in college-owned, operated, or affiliated housing: 12%. **Student employment:** During the 2005-2006 academic year, 6% of undergraduates worked on campus. Average per-year earnings: $5,700. **Clubs and organizations:** Number of student organizations: 220. Activities include: choral groups, concert band, dance, drama/theater, jazz band, literary magazine, music ensembles, opera, radio station, student government, student newspaper, symphony orchestra. Number of fraternities: 5; sororities: 7. Proportion of men in fraternities: 4%; of women in sororities: 5%. Average proportion of students who stay on campus on weekends: 15%. **Sports program (2005-2006):** Member of NCAA I. *Men's intercollegiate varsity sports:* basketball, cheerleading, cross-country, golf, riflery, soccer, tennis, track and field (indoor), track and field (outdoor). *Women's intercollegiate varsity sports:* basketball, cross-country, golf, riflery, softball, tennis, track and field (indoor), track and field (outdoor).

SERVICES AND FACILITIES

Basic services: nonremedial tutoring, women's center, placement service, day care, health service, health insurance. **Remedial assistance:** reading, math, writing, study skills. **Counseling services:** minority student, career, personal, veteran student, academic, older student, psychological, birth control, religious. **For learning-disabled students:** School does not offer a structured program with separate admission and additional fees. Total undergraduates in learning-disabled program or receiving services: 65. Services include: reading machines, tape recorders, diagnostic testing service, note-taking services, learning center, readers, extended time for tests,

tutors, priority seating, texts on tape, other testing accomodations, other. **Library:** Number of titles: 1,312,025; number of current serial subscriptions: 25,915. **Information technology resources:** Students are not required to lease or own a computer. Number of campus computers available to all students: 278. School has a wireless network. Approximate number of users that can be accommodated: 3,500. Proportion of college-owned housing units wired for high-speed internet access: 100%. **Campus safety:** Security services offered: 24-hour foot-and-vehicle patrols, late-night transport/escort service, 24-hour emergency telephones, lighted pathways/sidewalks, controlled dormitory access (key, security card, etc).

TRANSFER AND INTERNATIONAL STUDENTS

Transfer students: May apply for admission for the following academic terms: Fall, Winter, Summer. Applicants need a minimum number of credits to apply. For fall 2005: Transfer applications received: 2,947. Transfer applicants offered admission: 2,075. Transfer applicants enrolled: 1,183. **International students:** Number of foreign undergraduates: 184 (3% of student body). Number of countries represented: 43. Minimum TOEFL score required: 500 (paper); 173 (computer). Average TOEFL score: 550 (paper).

University of Missouri–Rolla

- **Address:** 207 Parker Hall-1870 Miner Circle, Rolla, MO 65409-0910
- **Website:** http://www.umr.edu
- **Public**
- **Enrollment:** 3,893 full-time; 420 part-time

KEY STATS

✔ **U.S News College Ranking:** 112, National Universities
✔ **ACT Score (25th/75th percentile):** 24-30
✔ **Tuition:** 2006-2007: $7,889 in state, $18,155 out of state
  Selectivity: More selective   **Room/board:** $6,255
  Acceptance rate: 92%   **Average debt:** $20,233
  Student/faculty ratio: 14/1   **Proportion who borrowed:** 65%

UNDERGRADUATE STUDENT BODY STATS

2005-2006 enrollment: 3,893 full-time; 420 part-time. Men: 78%; women: 22%. **Ethnic makeup:** African American: 4%; Asian American: 2%; Hispanic: 2%; White: 89%; International: 2%.

ADMISSIONS FACTS AND FIGURES

Phone: (573) 341-4165. **Email:** admissions@umr.edu. **Website:** http://www.umr.edu. **Application deadlines for fall 2007:** Regular decision: July 1. Early decision: Not offered. Early action: Not offered. Admission can be deferred. **Application fee:** $35. Common application is accepted. **To apply online, go to:** http://www.umr.edu/?apply. **Admissions requirements/recommendations:** High school units required (recommended): English: 4; Mathematics: 4; Science: 3; Foreign language: 2; Social studies: 3; Total units: 17. Tests: The college uses SAT or ACT scores in admissions decisions. Either SAT or ACT required. For admission to the fall 2007 entering class, the school will accept: ACT with writing, ACT without writing. Campus visit: Recommended. Admissions interview: Neither required nor recommended. Off-campus interview: Not available. **Factors that count in admissions decisions:** *Academic:* Secondary school record: Very important. Class rank: Very important. Letters of recommendation: Considered. Standardized test scores: Very important. Essay: Considered. *Nonacademic:* Interview: Considered. Extracurricular activities: Considered. Talent/ability: Considered. Character/personal qualities: Considered. Alumni/ae relationship: Not considered. Geographical residence: Not considered. State residency: Not considered. Religious affiliation/commitment: Not considered. Minority status: Not considered. Volunteer work: Considered. Work experience: Considered. **Other schools with the greatest overlap in applicants:** Purdue University–West Lafayette; Truman State University; University of Illinois–Urbana-Champaign; University of Missouri–Columbia; Washington University in St. Louis. **Admissions statistics for the fall 2005 entering class:** Total applicants: 2,022. Total accepted: 1,852. Freshmen enrolled: 884; 21% were from out of state. Overall acceptance rate: 92%. **Credentials of fall 2005 freshmen:** 38% ranked in the top 10 percent of their high school class; 69% were in the top 25 percent, and 94% were in the top half. (Proportion submitting class standing: 90%.) **Average high school grade point average:** 3.6. **First-year students who submitted SAT scores:** 12%. Scores (25/75 percentile): Verbal: 550-660, Math: 600-690, Combined: 1150-1350. **First-year**

students submitting ACT scores: 93%. Scores (25/75 percentile): English: 23-29, Math: 25-30, Composite: 24-30.

ACADEMICS

Year founded: 1870. **Academic calendar:** Semester. **Degrees offered:** certificate, bachelor's, post-bachelor's certificate, master's, doctorate. **Most popular majors:** 67% engineering, 11% computer and information sciences and support services, 5% business, management, marketing, and related support services, 4% physical sciences, 3% psychology. **Major fields of study:** agriculture, agriculture operations, and related sciences; biological and biomedical sciences; business, management, marketing, and related support services; computer and information sciences and support services; education; engineering; English language and literature/letters; health professions and related clinical sciences; history; legal professions and studies; mathematics and statistics; philosophy and religious studies; physical sciences; psychology; social sciences. **Areas of required coursework:** humanities, computer literacy, mathematics, English (including composition), sciences (biological or physical), history, social science. **Pre-professional programs:** pre-law, pre-medicine. **Special academic programs (% participation):** accelerated program, cooperative (work-study plan) program (24%), distance learning (26.6%), double major (4.5%), dual enrollment (2.6%), English as a Second Language (ESL), honors program (2.7%), independent study (49%), internships (5%), student-designed major, study abroad (.6%), teacher certificate program (1.6%). **Teacher certification offered in:** middle/junior high, secondary. **Cooperative education programs:** business, computer science, engineering, humanities, natural science, social/behavioral science. **Reserve Officers Training Corps (ROTC):** Army ROTC: Offered on campus; Navy ROTC: Offered at cooperating institution; Air Force ROTC: Offered on campus. **Faculty and instruction (2005-2006):** Total instructional faculty: 319 full-time, 70 part-time (83% men; 17% women; 21% minorities). Full-time faculty with Ph.D. or other terminal degree: 90%. Student/faculty ratio: 14/1. Classes of fewer than 20 students: 41%; of 20 to 49 students: 50%; of 50 or more students: 9%. **Advanced Placement and International Baccalaureate credit:** AP tests may be used for: Credit only. Scores accepted: 3, 4, 5. International Baccalaureate exams may be used for: Credit only. **Freshmen returning for sophomore year:** 85%. **Graduation rates:** Four-year: 16%; five-year: 57%; six-year: 64%. **Graduate study:** 35% of students pursue further study immediately upon graduation.

COSTS AND FINANCIAL AID

Financial aid office: (573) 341-4282. **Expenses (2006-2007):** Tuition and fees 2006-2007: $7,889 in state, $18,155 out of state; room/board: $6,255. Estimated books and supplies: $875 personal expenses: $2,129. **Financial aid:** Priority filing date for institution's financial aid form: March 1. In 2005-2006, 67% of undergraduates applied for financial aid. Of those, 53% were determined to have financial need; 18% had their need fully met. Average financial aid package (proportion receiving): $10,513 (52%). Average amount of gift aid, such as scholarships or grants (proportion receiving): $6,106 (45%). Average amount of self-help aid, such as work study or loans (proportion receiving): $4,799 (41%). Average need-based loan (excluding PLUS or other private loans): $4,645. Among students who received need-based aid, the average percentage of need met: 78%. Among students who received aid based on merit, the average award (and the proportion receiving): $6,220 (29%). The average athletic scholarship (and the proportion receiving): $9,410 (3%). Average amount of debt of borrowers graduating in 2005: $20,233. Proportion who borrowed: 65%.

CAMPUS LIFE AND EXTRACURRICULAR ACTIVITIES

Campus housing available (% using): coed dorms (58%), women's dorms, men's dorms, sorority housing (10%), fraternity housing (25%), apartments for married students (2%), apartment for single students (2%), special housing for disabled students (1%), cooperative housing (1%), other housing options (1%). Students who live in college-owned, operated, or affiliated housing: 58%. **Student employment:** During the 2005-2006 academic year, 21% of undergraduates worked on campus. Average per-year earnings: $1,296. **Clubs and organizations:** Number of student organizations: 200. Activities include: choral groups, concert band, dance, drama/theater, jazz band, literary magazine, marching band, music ensembles, musical theater, pep band, radio station, student government, student newspaper, symphony orchestra, yearbook. Number of fraternities: 21; sororities: 4. Proportion of men in fraternities: 25%; of women in sororities: 24%. Average proportion of students who stay on campus on weekends: 50%. **Sports program (2005-2006):** Member of NCAA II. *Men's intercollegiate varsity sports:* baseball, basketball, cross-country, football, golf, soccer, swimming and diving, tennis, track and field (indoor), track and field (outdoor). *Women's intercolle-*

giate varsity sports: basketball, cross-country, soccer, softball, track and field (indoor), track and field (outdoor).

SERVICES AND FACILITIES

Basic services: nonremedial tutoring, placement service, health service, health insurance. **Counseling services:** minority student, career, personal, veteran student, academic, psychological, birth control, religious. **For learning-disabled students:** School does not offer a structured program with separate admission and additional fees. Services include: reading machines, tape recorders, note-taking services, oral tests, learning center, readers, extended time for tests, tutors. **Library:** Number of titles: 551,450; number of current serial subscriptions: 2,318. **Information technology resources:** Students are not required to lease or own a computer. Number of campus computers available to all students: 854. School has a wireless network. Approximate number of users that can be accommodated: 800. Proportion of college-owned housing units wired for high-speed internet access: 100%. **Campus safety:** Security services offered: 24-hour foot-and-vehicle patrols, late-night transport/escort service, 24-hour emergency telephones, lighted pathways/sidewalks, student patrols, controlled dormitory access (key, security card, etc).

TRANSFER AND INTERNATIONAL STUDENTS

Transfer students: May apply for admission for the following academic terms: Fall, Spring, Summer. Applicants need a minimum number of credits to apply. For fall 2005: Transfer applicants enrolled: 273. **International students:** Number of foreign undergraduates: 82 (2% of student body). Number of countries represented: 30. Minimum TOEFL score required: 550 (paper); 213 (computer). Average TOEFL score: 573 (paper).

University of Missouri—St. Louis

- **Address:** 1 University Boulevard, St. Louis, MO 63121-4400
- **Website:** http://www.umsl.edu
- **Public**
- **Enrollment:** 5,887 full-time; 6,732 part-time

KEY STATS

✔ **U.S News College Ranking:** fourth tier, National Universities
✔ **ACT Score (25th/75th percentile):** 21-26
✔ **Tuition:** 2006-2007: $7,948 in state, $18,214 out of state

Selectivity: More selective	**Room/board:** $7,178
Acceptance rate: 52%	**Average debt:** $19,435
Student/faculty ratio: 20/1	**Proportion who borrowed:** 56%

UNDERGRADUATE STUDENT BODY STATS

2005-2006 enrollment: 5,887 full-time; 6,732 part-time. Men: 39%; women: 61%. **Ethnic makeup:** African American: 17%; Asian American: 3%; Hispanic: 2%; White: 76%; International: 2%.

ADMISSIONS FACTS AND FIGURES

Phone: (314) 516-5451. **Email:** admissions@umsl.edu. **Website:** http://www.umsl.edu. **Application deadlines for fall 2007:** Regular decision: August 28. Early decision: Not offered. Early action: Not offered. Admission can be deferred. **Application fee:** $35. Common application is not accepted. **To apply online, go to:** http://www.umsl.edu/admission/apply/index.html. **Admissions requirements/recommendations:** High school units required (recommended): English: 4; Mathematics: 4; Science: 3; Foreign language: 2; Social studies: 3; Total units: 17. Tests: The college uses SAT or ACT scores in admissions decisions. Either SAT or ACT required. For admission to the fall 2007 entering class, the school will accept: ACT with writing, ACT without writing. Campus visit: Recommended. Admissions interview: Neither required nor recommended. Off-campus interview: Not available. **Factors that count in admissions decisions:** *Academic:* Secondary school record: Very important. Class rank: Very important. Letters of recommendation: Considered. Standardized test scores: Very important. Essay: Considered. *Nonacademic:* Interview: Not considered. Extracurricular activities: Not considered. Talent/ability: Not considered. Character/personal qualities: Not considered. Alumni/ae relationship: Not considered. Geographical residence: Not considered. State residency: Not considered. Religious affiliation/commitment: Not considered. Minority status: Not considered. Volunteer work: Not considered. Work experience: Not considered. **Other schools with the greatest overlap in applicants:** Lindenwood

University; Maryville University of St. Louis; St. Louis University; University of Missouri–Columbia; Webster University. **Admissions statistics for the fall 2005 entering class:** Total applicants: 2,207. Total accepted: 1,151. Freshmen enrolled: 532; 9% were from out of state. Overall acceptance rate: 52%. **Credentials of fall 2005 freshmen:** 21% ranked in the top 10 percent of their high school class; 50% were in the top 25 percent, and 83% were in the top half. (Proportion submitting class standing: 84%.) **First-year students who submitted SAT scores:** 10%. Scores (25/75 percentile): Verbal: 460-640, Math: 490-610, Combined: 950-1250. **First-year students submitting ACT scores:** 91%. Scores (25/75 percentile): English: 21-27, Math: 20-26, Composite: 21-26.

ACADEMICS

Year founded: 1963. **Academic calendar:** Semester. **Degrees offered:** bachelor's, post-bachelor's certificate, master's, first professional, doctorate. **Most popular majors:** 28% business, management, marketing, and related support services, 15% education, 11% social sciences, 8% communication, journalism, and related programs, 8% health professions and related clinical sciences. **Major fields of study:** biological and biomedical sciences; business, management, marketing, and related support services; communication, journalism, and related programs; computer and information sciences and support services; education; engineering; English language and literature/letters; foreign languages, literatures, and linguistics; health professions and related clinical sciences; history; liberal arts and sciences studies, and humanities; mathematics and statistics; multi/interdisciplinary studies; philosophy and religious studies; physical sciences; psychology; public administration and social service professions; social sciences; visual and performing arts. **Areas of required coursework:** humanities, mathematics, English (including composition), foreign languages, sciences (biological or physical), history, social science. **Pre-professional programs:** pre-law, pre-dentistry, pre-medicine, pre-veterinary science, pre-optometry, pre-pharmacy, other. **Special academic programs:** accelerated program, cooperative (work-study plan) program, cross-registration, distance learning, double major, dual enrollment, English as a Second Language (ESL), exchange student program (domestic), honors program, independent study, internships, student-designed major, study abroad, teacher certificate program, other. **Teacher certification offered in:** early childhood, special education, elementary, middle/junior high, secondary. **Cooperative education programs:** business, computer science, health professions. **Reserve Officers Training Corps (ROTC):** Army ROTC: Offered at cooperating institution (Washington University); Air Force ROTC: Offered at cooperating institution (St. Louis University). **Faculty and instruction (2005-2006):** Total instructional faculty: 371 full-time, 322 part-time (51% men; 49% women; 19% minorities). Full-time faculty with Ph.D. or other terminal degree: 81%. Student/faculty ratio: 20/1. Classes of fewer than 20 students: 43%; of 20 to 49 students: 48%; of 50 or more students: 9%. **Advanced Placement and International Baccalaureate credit:** AP tests may be used for: Credit and/or placement. Scores accepted: 3, 4, 5. International Baccalaureate exams may be used for: Credit only. **Freshmen returning for sophomore year:** 71%. **Graduation rates:** Four-year: 23%; five-year: 37%; six-year: 43%. **Graduate study:** 8% of students pursue further study immediately upon graduation; 15% within one year; 35% within five years. Fields in which graduates pursue further study: Master of Business Administration (MBA), 17%; law, 2%; education, 33%; arts and sciences, 36%.

COSTS AND FINANCIAL AID

Financial aid office: (314) 516-5526. **Expenses (2006-2007):** Tuition and fees 2006-2007: $7,948 in state, $18,214 out of state; room/board: $7,178. Estimated books and supplies: $880; transportation: $1,000; personal expenses: $5,000. **Financial aid:** Priority filing date for institution's financial aid form: April 1. In 2005-2006, 63% of undergraduates applied for financial aid. Of those, 54% were determined to have financial need; 8% had their need fully met. Average financial aid package (proportion receiving): $9,633 (53%). Average amount of gift aid, such as scholarships or grants (proportion receiving): $4,137 (33%). Average amount of self-help aid, such as work study or loans (proportion receiving): $4,506 (48%). Average need-based loan (excluding PLUS or other private loans): $4,371. Among students who received need-based aid, the average percentage of need met: 65%. Among students who received aid based on merit, the average award (and the proportion receiving): $4,701 (10%). The average athletic scholarship (and the proportion receiving): $9,103 (1%). Average amount of debt of borrowers graduating in 2005: $19,435. Proportion who borrowed: 56%.

CAMPUS LIFE AND EXTRACURRICULAR ACTIVITIES

Campus housing available (% using): coed dorms (28%), women's dorms, sorority housing (0%), fraternity housing (0%), apartments for married stu-

dents (0%), apartment for single students (72%), special housing for disabled students (0%), other housing options. Students who live in college-owned, operated, or affiliated housing: 8%. **Student employment:** During the 2005-2006 academic year, 8% of undergraduates worked on campus. Average per-year earnings: $8,000. **Clubs and organizations:** Number of student organizations: 110. Activities include: choral groups, dance, drama/theater, jazz band, literary magazine, music ensembles, musical theater, opera, pep band, radio station, student government, student newspaper, student film society. Number of fraternities: 3; sororities: 3. Proportion of men in fraternities: 1%; of women in sororities: 1%. Average proportion of students who stay on campus on weekends: 27%. **Sports program (2005-2006):** Member of NCAA II. **Men's intercollegiate varsity sports:** baseball, basketball, golf, soccer, tennis. **Women's intercollegiate varsity sports:** basketball, golf, soccer, softball, tennis, volleyball.

SERVICES AND FACILITIES

Basic services: nonremedial tutoring, women's center, placement service, day care, health service, health insurance. **Counseling services:** minority student, career, personal, veteran student, academic, older student, psychological, birth control. **For learning-disabled students:** School does not offer a structured program with separate admission and additional fees. Total undergraduates in learning-disabled program or receiving services: 96. Services include: remedial math, tape recorders, note-taking services, oral tests, readers, extended time for tests, priority seating, texts on tape, exams on tape or computer, other. **Library:** Number of titles: 1,130,095; number of current serial subscriptions: 8,785. **Information technology resources:** Students are not required to lease or own a computer. Number of campus computers available to all students: 1,150. School has a wireless network. Approximate number of users that can be accommodated: 1,500. Proportion of college-owned housing units wired for high-speed internet access: 100%. **Campus safety:** Security services offered: 24-hour foot-and-vehicle patrols, late-night transport/escort service, 24-hour emergency telephones, lighted pathways/sidewalks, controlled dormitory access (key, security card, etc).

TRANSFER AND INTERNATIONAL STUDENTS

Transfer students: May apply for admission for the following academic terms: Fall, Spring, Summer. Applicants need a minimum number of credits to apply. For fall 2005: Transfer applications received: 3,625. Transfer applicants offered admission: 2,814. Transfer applicants enrolled: 1,911. **International students:** Number of foreign undergraduates: 170 (2% of student body). Number of countries represented: 55. Minimum TOEFL score required: 500 (paper); 173 (computer). Average TOEFL score: 537 (paper).

Washington University in St. Louis

- **Address:** 1 Brookings Drive, St. Louis, MO 63130-4899
- **Website:** http://www.wustl.edu
- **Private**
- **Enrollment:** 6,169 full-time; 1,297 part-time

KEY STATS
✔ **U.S News College Ranking:** 12, National Universities
✔ **SAT Score (25th/75th percentile):** 1360-1520
✔ **Tuition:** 2006-2007: $33,788

Selectivity: Most selective	**Room/board:** $10,452
Acceptance rate: 19%	**Average debt:** N/A
Student/faculty ratio: 7/1	**Proportion who borrowed:** 43%

UNDERGRADUATE STUDENT BODY STATS
2005-2006 enrollment: 6,169 full-time; 1,297 part-time. Men: 48%; women: 52%. **Ethnic makeup:** African American: 9%; Asian American: 10%; Hispanic: 3%; White: 73%; International: 4%.

ADMISSIONS FACTS AND FIGURES
Phone: (800) 638-0700. **Email:** admissions@wustl.edu. **Website:** http://www.wustl.edu. **Application deadlines for fall 2007:** Regular decision: January 15; decision sent by April 1. Early decision: Send application by: November 15; Decision sent by: December 15. Early action: Not offered. Admission can be deferred. **Application fee:** $55. Common application is accepted. **To apply online, go to:** http://admissions.wustl.edu. **Admissions requirements/recommendations:** High school units required (recommended): English: (4); Mathematics: (4); Science: (4); Foreign language: (2);

Social studies: (4); History: (4); Total units: (20). Tests: The college uses SAT or ACT scores in admissions decisions. Either SAT or ACT required. For admission to the fall 2007 entering class, the school will accept: ACT with writing. Campus visit: Recommended. Admissions interview: Neither required nor recommended. Off-campus interview: May be arranged. **Factors that count in admissions decisions:** *Academic:* Secondary school record: Very important. Class rank: Very important. Letters of recommendation: Very important. Standardized test scores: Very important. Essay: Very important. *Nonacademic:* Interview: Considered. Extracurricular activities: Very important. Talent/ability: Very important. Character/personal qualities: Very important. Alumni/ae relationship: Considered. Geographical residence: Not considered. State residency: Not considered. Religious affiliation/commitment: Not considered. Minority status: Considered. Volunteer work: Very important. Work experience: Very important. **Other schools with the greatest overlap in applicants:** Duke University; Harvard University; Northwestern University; Stanford University; Yale University. **Admissions statistics for the fall 2005 entering class:** Total applicants: 21,515. Total accepted: 4,044. Freshmen enrolled: 1,388; 90% were from out of state. Overall acceptance rate: 19%. Non-early acceptance rate: 19%. **Size of waiting list:** N/A applicants; enrolled from waiting list: 144. **Credentials of fall 2005 freshmen:** 93% ranked in the top 10 percent of their high school class; 100% were in the top 25 percent, and 100% were in the top half. (Proportion submitting class standing: 59%.) **First-year students who submitted SAT scores:** 87%. Scores (25/75 percentile): Verbal: 670-750, Math: 690-770, Combined: 1360-1520. **First-year students submitting ACT scores:** 49%. Scores (25/75 percentile): English: 30-34, Math: 29-34, Composite: 30-33.

ACADEMICS

Year founded: 1853. **Academic calendar:** Semester. **Degrees offered:** certificate, bachelor's, post-bachelor's certificate, master's, first professional, doctorate. **Most popular majors:** 14% engineering, 12% psychology, 11% business, management, marketing, and related support services, 11% premedicine/pre-medical studies, 4% English language and literature/letters. **Major fields of study:** architecture and related services; area, ethnic, cultural, and gender studies; biological and biomedical sciences; business, management, marketing, and related support services; communication, journalism, and related programs; computer and information sciences and support services; education; engineering; English language and literature/letters; foreign languages, literatures, and linguistics; history; liberal arts and sciences studies, and humanities; mathematics and statistics; multi/interdisciplinary studies; natural resources and conservation; philosophy and religious studies; physical sciences; psychology; social sciences; visual and performing arts. **Areas of required coursework:** English (including composition), other. **Pre-professional programs:** pre-law, pre-dentistry, pre-medicine, pre-veterinary science. **Special academic programs:** accelerated program, cooperative (work-study plan) program, cross-registration, double major, dual enrollment, English as a Second Language (ESL), exchange student program (domestic), independent study, internships, liberal arts/career combination, student-designed major, study abroad, teacher certificate program, other. **Teacher certification offered in:** elementary, middle/junior high, secondary. **Cooperative education programs:** business, engineering. **Reserve Officers Training Corps (ROTC):** Army ROTC: Offered on campus; Air Force ROTC: Offered at cooperating institution (St. Louis University). **Faculty and instruction (2005-2006):** Total instructional faculty: 850 full-time, 231 part-time (66% men; 34% women). Full-time faculty with Ph.D. or other terminal degree: 99%. Student/faculty ratio: 7/1. Classes of fewer than 20 students: 73%; of 20 to 49 students: 19%; of 50 or more students: 9%. **Advanced Placement and International Baccalaureate credit:** AP tests may be used for: Credit and/or placement. Scores accepted: 4, 5. International Baccalaureate exams may be used for: Credit only. **Freshmen returning for sophomore year:** 97%. **Graduation rates:** Four-year: 82%; five-year: 90%; six-year: 91%. **Graduate study:** 29% of students pursue further study immediately upon graduation.

COSTS AND FINANCIAL AID

Financial aid office: (888) 547-6670. **Expenses (2006-2007):** Tuition and fees 2006-2007: $33,788; room/board: $10,452. Estimated books and supplies: $1,100 personal expenses: $1,770. **Financial aid:** In 2005-2006, 71% of undergraduates applied for financial aid. Of those, 44% were determined to have financial need; 99% had their need fully met. Average financial aid package (proportion receiving): $25,653 (43%). Average amount of gift aid, such as scholarships or grants (proportion receiving): $21,191 (42%). Average amount of self-help aid, such as work study or loans (proportion receiving): $6,647 (33%). Average need-based loan (excluding PLUS or other private loans): $5,884. Among students who received need-based aid,

the average percentage of need met: 100%. Among students who received aid based on merit, the average award (and the proportion receiving): $7,090 (13%). The average athletic scholarship (and the proportion receiving): $0 (0%). Proportion who borrowed: 43%.

CAMPUS LIFE AND EXTRACURRICULAR ACTIVITIES

Campus housing available: coed dorms, fraternity housing, apartments for married students, apartment for single students, other housing options. Students who live in college-owned, operated, or affiliated housing: 73%. **Student employment:** During the 2005-2006 academic year, 17% of undergraduates worked on campus. Average per-year earnings: $2,000. **Clubs and organizations:** Number of student organizations: 200. Activities include: choral groups, concert band, dance, drama/theater, jazz band, literary magazine, music ensembles, musical theater, opera, pep band, radio station, student government, student newspaper, student film society, symphony orchestra, television station, yearbook. Number of fraternities: 12; sororities: 6. Proportion of men in fraternities: 25%; of women in sororities: 25%. Average proportion of students who stay on campus on weekends: 97%. **Sports program (2005-2006):** Member of NCAA III. *Men's intercollegiate varsity sports:* baseball, basketball, cross-country, football, soccer, swimming and diving, tennis, track and field (indoor), track and field (outdoor). *Women's intercollegiate varsity sports:* basketball, cross-country, soccer, softball, swimming and diving, tennis, track and field (indoor), track and field (outdoor), volleyball.

SERVICES AND FACILITIES

Basic services: nonremedial tutoring, women's center, placement service, day care, health service, health insurance, other. **Remedial assistance:** study skills. **Counseling services:** minority student, career, personal, academic, older student, psychological, birth control, religious. **For learning-disabled students:** School does not offer a structured program with separate admission and additional fees. Services include: tape recorders, note-taking services, learning center, readers, extended time for tests, tutors, texts on tape, typist/scribe, other testing accomodations. **Library:** Number of titles: 3,694,504; number of current serial subscriptions: 44,806. **Information technology resources:** Students are not required to lease or own a computer. Number of campus computers available to all students: 2,500. School has a wireless network. Approximate number of users that can be accommodated: 4,500. Proportion of college-owned housing units wired for high-speed internet access: 90%. **Campus safety:** Security services offered: 24-hour foot-and-vehicle patrols, late-night transport/escort service, 24-hour emergency telephones, lighted pathways/sidewalks, student patrols, controlled dormitory access (key, security card, etc).

TRANSFER AND INTERNATIONAL STUDENTS

Transfer students: May apply for admission for the following academic terms: Fall, Spring. Applicants need a minimum number of credits to apply. For fall 2005: Transfer applications received: 840. Transfer applicants offered admission: 268. Transfer applicants enrolled: 147. **International students:** Number of foreign undergraduates: 279 (4% of student body). Number of countries represented: 64. Minimum TOEFL score required: 550 (paper); 213 (computer).

Webster University

- **Address:** 470 E. Lockwood Avenue, St. Louis, MO 63119
- **Website:** http://www.webster.edu
- **Private**
- **Enrollment:** 3,108 full-time; 1,466 part-time

KEY STATS

✔ **U.S News College Ranking:** 23, Universities–Master's (Midwest)
✔ **ACT Score (25th/75th percentile):** 21-27
✔ **Tuition:** 2006-2007: $18,240

Selectivity: More selective	**Room/board:** $8,022
Acceptance rate: 55%	**Average debt:** $18,690
Student/faculty ratio: 12/1	**Proportion who borrowed:** 50%

UNDERGRADUATE STUDENT BODY STATS

2005-2006 enrollment: 3,108 full-time; 1,466 part-time. Men: 41%; women: 59%. **Ethnic makeup:** African American: 10%; Asian American: 1%; Hispanic: 2%; White: 71%; International: 15%. **Religious preference:** Roman

Catholic: 24%; Protestant: 43%; Jewish: 1%; Muslim: 1%; Hindu: 1%; Buddhist: 1%; No preference: 29%.

ADMISSIONS FACTS AND FIGURES

Phone: (314) 968-6991. **Email:** admit@webster.edu. **Website:** http://www.webster.edu. **Application deadlines for fall 2007:** Regular decision: June 1. Early decision: Not offered. Early action: Not offered. Admission can be deferred. **Application fee:** $25. Common application is accepted. **Admissions requirements/recommendations:** High school units required (recommended): English: (4); Mathematics: (3); Science: (3); Foreign language: (2); Social studies: (3); Academic electives: (4); Total units: (19). **Tests:** The college uses SAT or ACT scores in admissions decisions. Either SAT or ACT required. For admission to the fall 2007 entering class, the school will accept: ACT with writing, ACT without writing. Campus visit: Recommended. Admissions interview: Recommended. Off-campus interview: May be arranged. **Factors that count in admissions decisions:** *Academic:* Secondary school record: Very important. Class rank: Important. Letters of recommendation: Important. Standardized test scores: Very important. Essay: Important. *Nonacademic:* Interview: Considered. Extracurricular activities: Considered. Talent/ability: Very important. Character/personal qualities: Important. Alumni/ae relationship: Not considered. Geographical residence: Considered. State residency: Not considered. Religious affiliation/commitment: Not considered. Minority status: Important. Volunteer work: Considered. Work experience: Not considered. **Other schools with the greatest overlap in applicants:** Southeast Missouri State University; Southern Illinois University–Edwardsville; St. Louis University; University of Missouri–Columbia; University of Missouri–St. Louis. **Admissions statistics for the fall 2005 entering class:** Total applicants: 1,468. Total accepted: 807. Freshmen enrolled: 481; 34% were from out of state. Overall acceptance rate: 55%. **Credentials of fall 2005 freshmen:** 23% ranked in the top 10 percent of their high school class; 48% were in the top 25 percent, and 83% were in the top half. (Proportion submitting class standing: 83%.) **Average high school grade point average:** 3.4. **First-year students who submitted SAT scores:** 17%. Scores (25/75 percentile): Verbal: 525-620, Math: 495-615, Combined: 1020-1235. **First-year students submitting ACT scores:** 84%. Scores (25/75 percentile): English: N/A, Math: N/A, Composite: 21-27.

ACADEMICS

Year founded: 1915. **Academic calendar:** Semester. **Degrees offered:** certificate, bachelor's, post-bachelor's certificate, master's, post-master's certificate, doctorate. **Most popular majors:** 34% business, management, marketing, and related support services, 13% communication, journalism, and related programs, 11% visual and performing arts, 9% computer and information sciences and support services, 6% social sciences. **Major fields of study:** biological and biomedical sciences; business, management, marketing, and related support services; communication, journalism, and related programs; computer and information sciences and support services; education; English language and literature/letters; foreign languages, literatures, and linguistics; health professions and related clinical sciences; history; legal professions and studies; mathematics and statistics; natural resources and conservation; philosophy and religious studies; psychology; social sciences; visual and performing arts. **Areas of required coursework:** arts/fine arts, humanities, mathematics, English (including composition), philosophy, sciences (biological or physical), history, social science, other. **Pre-professional programs:** pre-law, pre-dentistry, pre-medicine, pre-veterinary science, other. **Special academic programs (% participation):** accelerated program (18%), cooperative (work-study plan) program (34%), distance learning (5%), double major (5.5%), dual enrollment, English as a Second Language (ESL) (23.2%), independent study (3.3%), internships (21.6%), student-designed major, study abroad (38.7%), teacher certificate program (4.3%). **Teacher certification offered in:** early childhood, special education, elementary, middle/junior high, secondary. **Cooperative education programs:** computer science. **Reserve Officers Training Corps (ROTC):** Army ROTC: Offered at cooperating institution (Washington Univ., St. Louis Univ.); Air Force ROTC: Offered at cooperating institution (St. Louis Univ.). **Faculty and instruction (2005-2006):** Total instructional faculty: 169 full-time, 641 part-time (56% men; 44% women; 7% minorities). Full-time faculty with Ph.D. or other terminal degree: 79%. Student/faculty ratio: 12/1. Classes of fewer than 20 students: 86%; of 20 to 49 students: 14%; of 50 or more students: 0%. **Advanced Placement and International Baccalaureate credit:** AP tests may be used for: Credit only. Scores accepted: 3, 4, 5. International Baccalaureate exams may be used for: Credit only. **Freshmen returning for sophomore year:** 80%. **Graduation rates:** Four-year: 43%; five-year: 55%; six-year: 56%. **Graduate study:** 10% of students pursue further study within one year. Fields in which graduates pursue further study:

Master of Business Administration (MBA), 40%; law, 2%; medicine, 2%; engineering, 2%; education, 10%; arts and sciences, 44%.

COSTS AND FINANCIAL AID

Financial aid office: (314) 968-6992. **Expenses (2006-2007):** Tuition and fees 2006-2007: $18,240; room/board: $8,022. Estimated books and supplies: $1,000; transportation: $1,300. **Financial aid:** Priority filing date for institution's financial aid form: April 1. In 2005-2006, 80% of undergraduates applied for financial aid. Of those, 68% were determined to have financial need; Average financial aid package (proportion receiving): $17,299 (68%). Average amount of gift aid, such as scholarships or grants (proportion receiving): $4,900 (57%). Average amount of self-help aid, such as work study or loans (proportion receiving): $5,222 (61%). Average need-based loan (excluding PLUS or other private loans): $4,121. Among students who received aid based on merit, the average award (and the proportion receiving): $9,204 (22%). Average amount of debt of borrowers graduating in 2005: $18,690. Proportion who borrowed: 50%.

CAMPUS LIFE AND EXTRACURRICULAR ACTIVITIES

Campus housing available (% using): coed dorms (40%), apartment for single students (60%). Students who live in college-owned, operated, or affiliated housing: 6%. **Student employment:** During the 2005-2006 academic year, 22% of undergraduates worked on campus. Average per-year earnings: $1,943. **Clubs and organizations:** Number of student organizations: 72. Activities include: choral groups, dance, drama/theater, jazz band, literary magazine, music ensembles, musical theater, opera, radio station, student government, student newspaper, student film society, symphony orchestra, television station, yearbook. Number of fraternities: 0; sororities: 0. Average proportion of students who stay on campus on weekends: 60%. **Sports program (2005-2006):** Member of NCAA III. *Men's intercollegiate varsity sports:* baseball, basketball, golf, soccer, swimming and diving, tennis. *Women's intercollegiate varsity sports:* basketball, cross-country, soccer, softball, swimming and diving, tennis, volleyball.

SERVICES AND FACILITIES

Basic services: nonremedial tutoring. **Remedial assistance:** reading, math, writing, study skills. **Counseling services:** career, personal, academic. **For learning-disabled students:** School does not offer a structured program with separate admission and additional fees. Services include: remedial math, remedial English, reading machines, tape recorders, untimed tests, note-taking services, oral tests, learning center, readers, extended time for tests, tutors, priority seating, texts on tape. **Library:** Number of titles: 283,742; number of current serial subscriptions: 2,429. **Information technology resources:** Students are not required to lease or own a computer. Number of campus computers available to all students: 450. School has a wireless network. Proportion of college-owned housing units wired for high-speed internet access: 100%. **Campus safety:** Security services offered: 24-hour foot-and-vehicle patrols, late-night transport/escort service, 24-hour emergency telephones, lighted pathways/sidewalks, controlled dormitory access (key, security card, etc).

TRANSFER AND INTERNATIONAL STUDENTS

Transfer students: May apply for admission for the following academic terms: Fall, Spring, Summer. Applicants do not need a minimum number of credits to apply. For fall 2005: Transfer applications received: 757. Transfer applicants offered admission: 649. Transfer applicants enrolled: 507. **International students:** Number of foreign undergraduates: 665 (15% of student body). Number of countries represented: 35. Minimum TOEFL score required: 470 (paper); 150 (computer). Average TOEFL score: 510 (paper).

Westminster College

- **Address:** 501 Westminster Avenue, Fulton, MO 65251
- **Website:** http://www.westminster-mo.edu
- **Private; Religious affiliation:** Presbyterian
- **Enrollment:** 896 full-time; 22 part-time

KEY STATS

✔ **U.S News College Ranking:** third tier, Liberal Arts Colleges
✔ **ACT Score (25th/75th percentile):** 22-27
✔ **Tuition:** 2006-2007: $15,030

Selectivity: More selective	**Room/board:** $6,140
Acceptance rate: 79%	**Average debt:** $17,534
Student/faculty ratio: 14/1	**Proportion who borrowed:** 66%

UNDERGRADUATE STUDENT BODY STATS

2005-2006 enrollment: 896 full-time; 22 part-time. Men: 57%; women: 43%. **Ethnic makeup:** African American: 4%; American-Indian: 2%; Asian American: 1%; Hispanic: 2%; White: 81%; International: 9%. **Religious preference:** Roman Catholic: 24%; Protestant: 45%; Jewish: 1%; Muslim: 1%; Hindu: 1%; Buddhist: 1%; No preference: 12%; Unknown: 1%; Presbyterian: 11%; Other: 3%.

ADMISSIONS FACTS AND FIGURES

Phone: (800) 475-3361. **Email:** admissions@westminster-mo.edu. **Website:** http://www.westminster-mo.edu. **Application deadlines for fall 2007:** Regular decision: Rolling. Early decision: Not offered. Early action: Not offered. Admission can be deferred. Common application is accepted. **To apply online, go to:** http://www.westminster-mo.edu/application/index.asp. **Admissions requirements/recommendations:** High school units required (recommended): English: 4; Mathematics: 3; Science: 2; Foreign language: (2); Social studies: (2); Academic electives: (2); Total units: 16. Tests: The college uses SAT or ACT scores in admissions decisions. Either SAT or ACT required. For admission to the fall 2007 entering class, the school will accept: ACT with writing, ACT without writing. Campus visit: Recommended. Admissions interview: Recommended. Off-campus interview: May be arranged. **Factors that count in admissions decisions:** *Academic:* Secondary school record: Very important. Class rank: Important. Letters of recommendation: Important. Standardized test scores: Very important. Essay: Considered. *Nonacademic:* Interview: Considered. Extracurricular activities: Important. Talent/ability: Considered. Character/personal qualities: Very important. Alumni/ae relationship: Considered. Geographical residence: Not considered. State residency: Not considered. Religious affiliation/commitment: Not considered. Minority status: Not considered. Volunteer work: Important. Work experience: Considered. **Other schools with the greatest overlap in applicants:** Truman State University; University of Missouri–Columbia; William Jewell College. **Admissions statistics for the fall 2005 entering class:** Total applicants: 1,155. Total accepted: 908. Freshmen enrolled: 270; 32% were from out of state. Overall acceptance rate: 79%. **Credentials of fall 2005 freshmen:** 18% ranked in the top 10 percent of their high school class; 46% were in the top 25 percent, and 83% were in the top half. (Proportion submitting class standing: 76%.) **Average high school grade point average:** 3.5. **First-year students who submitted SAT scores:** 24%. Scores (25/75 percentile): Verbal: 530-620, Math: 490-630, Combined: 1020-1250. **First-year students submitting ACT scores:** 82%. Scores (25/75 percentile): English: 22-28, Math: 20-26, Composite: 22-27.

ACADEMICS

Year founded: 1851. **Academic calendar:** Semester. **Degrees offered:** bachelor's. **Most popular majors:** 26% business, management, marketing, and related support services; 13% social sciences, 11% education, 9% computer and information sciences and support services, 8% biological and biomedical sciences. **Major fields of study:** biological and biomedical sciences; business, management, marketing, and related support services; communication, journalism, and related programs; computer and information sciences and support services; education; English language and literature/letters; foreign languages, literatures, and linguistics; history; mathematics and statistics; natural resources and conservation; philosophy and religious studies; physical sciences; psychology; social sciences. **Areas of required coursework:** arts/fine arts, humanities, mathematics, English (including composition), philosophy, foreign languages, sciences (biological or physical), history, social science, other. **Pre-professional programs:** pre-

law, pre-dentistry, pre-medicine, pre-theology, pre-veterinary science, pre-optometry, pre-pharmacy. **Special academic programs (% participation):** cross-registration (2%), double major (23%), independent study (5%), internships (45%), student-designed major (9%), study abroad (3%), teacher certificate program (11%). **Teacher certification offered in:** early childhood, elementary, middle/junior high, secondary. **Reserve Officers Training Corps (ROTC):** Army ROTC: Offered at cooperating institution (University of Missouri, Columbia); Navy ROTC: Offered at cooperating institution (University of Missouri, Columbia); Air Force ROTC: Offered at cooperating institution (University of Missouri, Columbia). **Faculty and instruction (2005-2006):** Total instructional faculty: 58 full-time, 24 part-time (63% men; 37% women; 9% minorities). Full-time faculty with Ph.D. or other terminal degree: 72%. Student/faculty ratio: 14/1. Classes of fewer than 20 students: 54%; of 20 to 49 students: 46%; of 50 or more students: 0%. **Advanced Placement and International Baccalaureate credit:** AP tests may be used for: Credit and/or placement. Scores accepted: 4, 5. International Baccalaureate exams may be used for: Credit and/or placement. **Freshmen returning for sophomore year:** 74%. **Graduation rates:** Four-year: 47%; five-year: 60%; six-year: 61%. **Graduate study:** 17% of students pursue further study immediately upon graduation; 20% within one year; 30% within five years. Fields in which graduates pursue further study: Master of Business Administration (MBA), 20%; law, 15%; medicine, 4%; dentistry, 5%; engineering, 2%; theology (or the seminary), 3%; education, 20%; arts and sciences, 30%; veterinary medicine, 1%.

COSTS AND FINANCIAL AID

Financial aid office: (573) 592-5364. **Expenses (2006-2007):** Tuition and fees 2006-2007: $15,030; room/board: $6,140. Estimated books and supplies: $800; transportation: $0; personal expenses: $2,000. **Financial aid:** Priority filing date for institution's financial aid form: February 15; deadline: February 15. In 2005-2006, 70% of undergraduates applied for financial aid. Of those, 58% were determined to have financial need; 44% had their need fully met. Average financial aid package (proportion receiving): $16,226 (58%). Average amount of gift aid, such as scholarships or grants (proportion receiving): $11,001 (58%). Average amount of self-help aid, such as work study or loans (proportion receiving): $3,260 (57%). Average need-based loan (excluding PLUS or other private loans): $2,631. Among students who received need-based aid, the average percentage of need met: 89%. Among students who received aid based on merit, the average award (and the proportion receiving): $8,946 (41%). The average athletic scholarship (and the proportion receiving): $0 (0%). Average amount of debt of borrowers graduating in 2005: $17,534. Proportion who borrowed: 66%.

CAMPUS LIFE AND EXTRACURRICULAR ACTIVITIES

Campus housing available (% using): coed dorms (47%), women's dorms (6%), men's dorms (6%), fraternity housing (22%), apartment for single students (12%), special housing for disabled students, other housing options (7%). Students who live in college-owned, operated, or affiliated housing: 80%. **Student employment:** During the 2005-2006 academic year, 16% of undergraduates worked on campus. Average per-year earnings: $1,786. **Clubs and organizations:** Number of student organizations: 60. Activities include: choral groups, dance, drama/theater, jazz band, literary magazine, music ensembles, musical theater, student government, student newspaper, yearbook. Number of fraternities: 6; sororities: 2. Proportion of men in fraternities: 56%; of women in sororities: 38%. Average proportion of students who stay on campus on weekends: 60%. **Sports program (2005-2006):** Member of NCAA III. *Men's intercollegiate varsity sports:* baseball, basketball, football, golf, soccer, tennis. *Women's intercollegiate varsity sports:* basketball, golf, soccer, softball, tennis, volleyball.

SERVICES AND FACILITIES

Basic services: nonremedial tutoring, women's center, placement service, health service, health insurance. **Remedial assistance:** reading, math, writing, study skills. **Counseling services:** minority student, career, personal, academic, psychological, birth control. **For learning-disabled students:** School does not offer a structured program with separate admission and additional fees. Total undergraduates in learning-disabled program or receiving services: 44. Services include: remedial math, reading machines, tape recorders, other special classes, untimed tests, note-taking services, oral tests, learning center, readers, extended time for tests, tutors, texts on tape, other testing accomodations, other. **Library:** Number of titles: 97,177; number of current serial subscriptions: 332. **Information technology resources:** Students are not required to lease or own a computer. Number of campus computers available to all students: 215. School has a wireless network. Approximate number of users that can be accommodated: 100. Proportion of college-owned housing units wired for high-speed internet access: 95%. **Campus safety:** Security services offered: 24-hour foot-and-vehicle patrols, late-night transport/escort service, 24-hour emergency telephones, lighted pathways/sidewalks, controlled dormitory access (key, security card, etc).

TRANSFER AND INTERNATIONAL STUDENTS

Transfer students: May apply for admission for the following academic terms: Fall, Spring. Applicants do not need a minimum number of credits to apply. For fall 2005: Transfer applications received: 123. Transfer applicants offered admission: 75. Transfer applicants enrolled: 48. **International students:** Number of foreign undergraduates: 82 (9% of student body). Number of countries represented: 36. Minimum TOEFL score required: 550 (paper); 213 (computer). Average TOEFL score: 680 (paper).

William Jewell College

- **Address:** 500 College Hill, Liberty, MO 64068
- **Website:** http://www.jewell.edu
- **Private; Religious affiliation:** Baptist
- **Enrollment:** 1,285 full-time; 46 part-time

KEY STATS

✔ **U.S News College Ranking:** third tier, Liberal Arts Colleges
✔ **ACT Score (25th/75th percentile):** 23-28
✔ **Tuition:** 2006-2007: $20,150

Selectivity More selective	**Room/board:** $5,510
Acceptance rate: 64%	**Average debt:** $17,133
Student/faculty ratio: 13/1	**Proportion who borrowed:** 71%

UNDERGRADUATE STUDENT BODY STATS

2005-2006 enrollment: 1,285 full-time; 46 part-time. Men: 41%; women: 59%. **Ethnic makeup:** African American: 5%; American-Indian: 1%; Asian American: 1%; Hispanic: 3%; White: 91%. **Religious preference:** Roman Catholic: 12%; Protestant: 70%; No preference: 18%.

ADMISSIONS FACTS AND FIGURES

Phone: (888) 253-9355. **Email:** admission@william.jewell.edu. **Website:** http://www.jewell.edu. **Application deadlines for fall 2007:** Regular decision: August 1. Early decision: Not offered. Early action: Not offered. Admission can be deferred. **Application fee:** $25. Common application is accepted. **To apply online, go to:** http://www.jewell.edu/apply/. **Admissions requirements/recommendations:** High school units required (recommended): English: 4; Mathematics: 3 (1); Science: 3; Foreign language: 2 (1); Social studies: 3; Academic electives: (2); Total units: 15. Tests: The college uses SAT or ACT scores in admissions decisions. Either SAT or ACT required. For admission to the fall 2007 entering class, the school will accept: ACT without writing. Campus visit: Recommended. Admissions interview: Recommended. Off-campus interview: May be arranged. **Factors that count in admissions decisions:** *Academic:* Secondary school record: Very important. Class rank: Important. Letters of recommendation: Important. Standardized test scores: Important. Essay: Important. *Nonacademic:* Interview: Important. Extracurricular activities: Important. Talent/ability: Important. Character/personal qualities: Important. Alumni/ae relationship: Important. Geographical residence: Important. State residency: Considered. Religious affiliation/commitment: Considered. Minority status: Considered. Volunteer work: Considered. Work experience: Considered. **Other schools with the greatest overlap in applicants:** Nebraska Wesleyan University; St. Louis University; Truman State University; University of Missouri–Columbia; University of Missouri–Kansas City. **Admissions statistics for the fall 2005 entering class:** Total applicants: 1,681. Total accepted: 1,084. Freshmen enrolled: 304; 10% were from out of state. Overall acceptance rate: 64%. **Credentials of fall 2005 freshmen:** 30% ranked in the top 10 percent of their high school class; 60% were in the top 25 percent, and 83% were in the top half. (Proportion submitting class standing: 90%.) **Average high school grade point average:** 3.7. **First-year students who submitted SAT scores:** 17%. Scores (25/75 percentile): Verbal: 490-630, Math: 480-650, Combined: 970-1280. **First-year students submitting ACT scores:** 97%. Scores (25/75 percentile): English: 22-29, Math: 21-27, Composite: 23-28.

ACADEMICS

Year founded: 1849. **Academic calendar:** Semester. **Degrees offered:** bachelor's. **Most popular majors:** 25% business administration and management,

18% nursing/registered nurse training (R.N., A.S.N., B.S.N., M.S.N.), 9% psychology, 7% elementary education and teaching, 6% history. **Major fields of study:** area, ethnic, cultural, and gender studies; biological and biomedical sciences; business, management, marketing, and related support services; communication, journalism, and related programs; computer and information sciences and support services; education; English language and literature/letters; foreign languages, literatures, and linguistics; health professions and related clinical sciences; history; legal professions and studies; mathematics and statistics; multi/interdisciplinary studies; parks, recreation, leisure, and fitness studies; philosophy and religious studies; physical sciences; psychology; social sciences; theology and religious vocations; visual and performing arts. **Areas of required coursework:** arts/fine arts, humanities, mathematics, English (including composition), philosophy, foreign languages, sciences (biological or physical), history, social science. **Pre-professional programs:** pre-law, pre-medicine. **Special academic programs (% participation):** accelerated program (9.5%), double major (18.5%), dual enrollment (21%), honors program (4%), independent study (33%), internships (33%), student-designed major (1%), study abroad (17%), teacher certificate program (8%). **Teacher certification offered in:** elementary, secondary. **Cooperative education programs:** engineering. **Faculty and instruction (2005-2006):** Total instructional faculty: 76 full-time, 79 part-time (51% men; 49% women). Full-time faculty with Ph.D. or other terminal degree: 86%. Student/faculty ratio: 13/1. Classes of fewer than 20 students: 74%; of 20 to 49 students: 25%; of 50 or more students: 1%. **Advanced Placement and International Baccalaureate credit:** AP tests may be used for: Credit only. Scores accepted: 4. International Baccalaureate exams may be used for: Credit only. **Freshmen returning for sophomore year:** 86%. **Graduation rates:** Four-year: 54%; five-year: 63%; six-year: 64%. **Graduate study:** 24% of students pursue further study immediately upon graduation; 15% within one year. Fields in which graduates pursue further study: Master of Business Administration (MBA), 9%; law, 9%; medicine, 6%; engineering, 3%; theology (or the seminary), 6%; education, 32%; arts and sciences, 27%.

COSTS AND FINANCIAL AID

Financial aid office: (888) 253-9355. **Expenses (2006-2007):** Tuition and fees 2006-2007: $20,150; room/board: $5,510. Estimated books and supplies: $800; transportation: $1,200; personal expenses: $1,800. **Financial aid:** Priority filing date for institution's financial aid form: March 1. In 2005-2006, 80% of undergraduates applied for financial aid. Of those, 57% were determined to have financial need; Average financial aid package (proportion receiving): $15,288 (57%). Average amount of gift aid, such as scholarships or grants (proportion receiving): $11,260 (56%). Average amount of self-help aid, such as work study or loans (proportion receiving): $5,234 (50%). Average need-based loan (excluding PLUS or other private loans): $4,502. The average athletic scholarship (and the proportion receiving): $4,920 (13%). Average amount of debt of borrowers graduating in 2005: $17,133. Proportion who borrowed: 71%.

CAMPUS LIFE AND EXTRACURRICULAR ACTIVITIES

Campus housing available (% using): coed dorms (14%), women's dorms (38%), men's dorms (24%), sorority housing (14%), fraternity housing (11%), special housing for disabled students (0%). Students who live in college-owned, operated, or affiliated housing: 63%. **Student employment:** During the 2005-2006 academic year, 14% of undergraduates worked on campus. Average per-year earnings: $643. **Clubs and organizations:** Number of student organizations: 71. Activities include: choral groups, concert band, dance, drama/theater, jazz band, music ensembles, musical theater, opera, pep band, student government, student newspaper, symphony orchestra. Number of fraternities: 3; sororities: 4. Proportion of men in fraternities: 33%; of women in sororities: 31%. Average proportion of students who stay on campus on weekends: 50%. **Sports program (2005-2006):** Member of NAIA. *Men's intercollegiate varsity sports:* baseball, basketball, cheerleading, cross-country, football, golf, soccer, tennis, track and field (indoor), track and field (outdoor). *Women's intercollegiate varsity sports:* basketball, cheerleading, cross-country, golf, soccer, softball, tennis, track and field (indoor), track and field (outdoor), volleyball.

SERVICES AND FACILITIES

Basic services: nonremedial tutoring, placement service, health service. **Counseling services:** minority student, career, personal, academic, older student, psychological, religious. **For learning-disabled students:** School does not offer a structured program with separate admission and additional fees. Total undergraduates in learning-disabled program or receiving services: 9. Services include: tape recorders, untimed tests, note-taking services, extended time for tests, tutors, early syllabus, priority seating, proofreading services, exams on tape or computer, other testing accomodations. **Library:**

Number of titles: 237,798; number of current serial subscriptions: 595. **Information technology resources:** Students are not required to lease or own a computer. Number of campus computers available to all students: 120. School has a wireless network. Proportion of college-owned housing units wired for high-speed internet access: 100%. **Campus safety:** Security services offered: 24-hour foot-and-vehicle patrols, late-night transport/escort service, 24-hour emergency telephones, lighted pathways/sidewalks, controlled dormitory access (key, security card, etc).

TRANSFER AND INTERNATIONAL STUDENTS

Transfer students: May apply for admission for the following academic terms: Fall, Spring, Summer. Applicants need a minimum number of credits to apply. For fall 2005: Transfer applications received: 226. Transfer applicants offered admission: 122. Transfer applicants enrolled: 74. **International students:** Number of foreign undergraduates: 5. Number of countries represented: 10. Minimum TOEFL score required: 550 (paper); 213 (computer). Average TOEFL score: 600 (paper).

William Woods University

- **Address:** 1 University Avenue, Fulton, MO 65251
- **Website:** http://www.williamwoods.edu
- **Private; Religious affiliation:** Disciples of Christ
- **Enrollment:** 808 full-time; 365 part-time

KEY STATS

✔ **U.S News College Ranking:** third tier, Universities–Master's (Midwest)
✔ **ACT Score (25th/75th percentile):** 19-25
✔ **Tuition:** 2006-2007: $15,570

Selectivity: Selective	**Room/board:** $6,100
Acceptance rate: 68%	**Average debt:** $13,865
Student/faculty ratio: 13/1	**Proportion who borrowed:** 85%

UNDERGRADUATE STUDENT BODY STATS

2005-2006 enrollment: 808 full-time; 365 part-time. Men: 25%; women: 75%. **Ethnic makeup:** African American: 3%; American-Indian: 1%; Hispanic: 2%; White: 90%; International: 4%. **Religious preference:** Roman Catholic: 25%; Protestant: 2%; Jewish: 1%; Buddhist: 1%; No preference: 21%; Unknown: 2%; Disciples of Christ: 2%; Christian: 20%; Other: 26%.

ADMISSIONS FACTS AND FIGURES

Phone: (573) 592-4221. **Email:** admissions@williamwoods.edu. **Website:** http://www.williamwoods.edu. **Application deadlines for fall 2007:** Regular decision: August 15. Early decision: Not offered. Early action: Not offered. Admission can be deferred. **Application fee:** $25. Common application is not accepted. **To apply online, go to:** http://www.williamwoods.edu/ Info.asp?1895. **Admissions requirements/recommendations:** High school units required (recommended): English: 4 (4); Mathematics: 3 (3); Science: 3 (3); Foreign language: 2 (1); Social studies: 2 (3); History: 3 (2); Academic electives: (4); Total units: 16 (20). Tests: The college uses SAT or ACT scores in admissions decisions. Either SAT or ACT required. For admission to the fall 2007 entering class, the school will accept: ACT with writing, ACT without writing. Campus visit: Recommended. Admissions interview: Neither required nor recommended. Off-campus interview: Not available. **Factors that count in admissions decisions:** *Academic:* Secondary school record: Very important. Class rank: Very important. Letters of recommendation: Important. Standardized test scores: Important. Essay: Not considered. *Nonacademic:* Interview: Considered. Extracurricular activities: Important. Talent/ability: Not considered. Character/personal qualities: Important. Alumni/ae relationship: Not considered. Geographical residence: Not considered. State residency: Not considered. Religious affiliation/commitment: Not considered. Minority status: Not considered. Volunteer work: Not considered. Work experience: Not considered. **Other schools with the greatest overlap in applicants:** Columbia College; Culver-Stockton College; Stephens College; Westminster College; William Jewell College. **Admissions statistics for the fall 2005 entering class:** Total applicants: 792. Total accepted: 540. Freshmen enrolled: 253; 37% were from out of state. Overall acceptance rate: 68%. **Size of waiting list:** 0 applicants; enrolled from waiting list: 0. **Credentials of fall 2005 freshmen:** 15% ranked in the top 10 percent of their high school class; 40% were in the top 25 percent, and 77% were in the top half. (Proportion submitting class standing: 85%.) **Average high school grade point average:** 3.3. **First-year students who submitted SAT scores:** 19%.

Scores (25/75 percentile): Verbal: 455-575, Math: 420-470, Combined: 875-1045. **First-year students submitting ACT scores:** 86%. Scores (25/75 percentile): English: 18-25, Math: 18-24, Composite: 19-25.

ACADEMICS

Year founded: 1870. **Academic calendar:** Semester. **Degrees offered:** associate, bachelor's, master's, post-master's certificate. **Most popular majors:** 45% business administration and management, 12% computer and information sciences, 11% equestrian/equine studies, 8% education, 6% art/art studies. **Major fields of study:** agriculture, agriculture operations, and related sciences; biological and biomedical sciences; business, management, marketing, and related support services; communication, journalism, and related programs; computer and information sciences and support services; education; English language and literature/letters; foreign languages, literatures, and linguistics; health professions and related clinical sciences; history; legal professions and studies; mathematics and statistics; multi/interdisciplinary studies; parks, recreation, leisure, and fitness studies; psychology; public administration and social service professions; security and protective services; social sciences; visual and performing arts. **Areas of required coursework:** arts/fine arts, humanities, mathematics, English (including composition), sciences (biological or physical), history, social science. **Pre-professional programs:** pre-law, pre-medicine. **Special academic programs:** accelerated program, cross-registration, double major, dual enrollment, exchange student program (domestic), honors program, independent study, internships, liberal arts/career combination, student-designed major, study abroad, teacher certificate program. **Teacher certification offered in:** special education, elementary, middle/junior high, secondary. **Reserve Officers Training Corps (ROTC):** Army ROTC: Offered at cooperating institution (University of Missouri); Navy ROTC: Offered at cooperating institution (University of Missouri); Air Force ROTC: Offered at cooperating institution (University of Missouri). **Faculty and instruction (2005-2006):** Total instructional faculty: 52 full-time, 30 part-time (43% men; 57% women; 4% minorities). Full-time faculty with Ph.D. or other terminal degree: 44%. Student/faculty ratio: 13/1. Classes of fewer than 20 students: 81%; of 20 to 49 students: 19%; of 50 or more students: 0%. **Advanced Placement and International Baccalaureate credit:** AP tests may be used for: Credit only. Scores accepted: 3, 4, 5. International Baccalaureate exams may be used for: Credit only. **Freshmen returning for sophomore year:** 72%. **Graduation rates:** Four-year: 39%; five-year: 45%; six-year: 50%.

COSTS AND FINANCIAL AID

Financial aid office: (573) 592-4232. **Expenses (2006-2007):** Tuition and fees 2006-2007: $15,570; room/board: $6,100. Estimated books and supplies: $1,000; transportation: $1,750; personal expenses: $2,700. **Financial aid:** Priority filing date for institution's financial aid form: March 1. In 2005-2006, 91% of undergraduates applied for financial aid. Of those, 64% were determined to have financial need; 31% had their need fully met. Average financial aid package (proportion receiving): $12,617 (63%). Average amount of gift aid, such as scholarships or grants (proportion receiving): $9,235 (61%). Average amount of self-help aid, such as work study or loans (proportion receiving): $4,667 (49%). Average need-based loan (excluding PLUS or other private loans): $3,931. Among students who received need-based aid, the average percentage of need met: 79%. Among students who received aid based on merit, the average award (and the proportion receiving): $9,356 (34%). The average athletic scholarship (and the proportion receiving): $5,268 (3%). Average amount of debt of borrowers graduating in 2005: $13,865. Proportion who borrowed: 85%.

CAMPUS LIFE AND EXTRACURRICULAR ACTIVITIES

Campus housing available (% using): coed dorms (32%), women's dorms (23%), sorority housing (36%), fraternity housing (9%). Students who live in college-owned, operated, or affiliated housing: 52%. **Student employment:** During the 2005-2006 academic year, 25% of undergraduates worked on campus. Average per-year earnings: $845. **Clubs and organizations:** Number of student organizations: 47. Activities include: choral groups, dance, drama/theater, literary magazine, musical theater, radio station, student government, student newspaper. Number of fraternities: 2; sororities: 4. Proportion of men in fraternities: 22%; of women in sororities: 29%. Average proportion of students who stay on campus on weekends: 50%. **Sports program (2005-2006):** Member of NAIA. *Men's intercollegiate varsity sports:* baseball, cross-country, golf, soccer, track and field (indoor), track and field (outdoor). *Women's intercollegiate varsity sports:* basketball, cross-country, golf, soccer, softball, track and field (indoor), track and field (outdoor), volleyball.

SERVICES AND FACILITIES

Basic services: nonremedial tutoring, placement service, health service. **Remedial assistance:** math, writing. **Counseling services:** minority student, personal, academic, psychological, birth control, religious. **For learning-disabled students:** School does not offer a structured program with separate admission and additional fees. Total undergraduates in learning-disabled program or receiving services: 28. Services include: remedial math, remedial English, tape recorders, untimed tests, note-taking services, oral tests, readers, extended time for tests, tutors, texts on tape, other testing accomodations, other. **Library:** Number of titles: 134,338; number of current serial subscriptions: 15,796. **Information technology resources:** Students are not required to lease or own a computer. Number of campus computers available to all students: 225. School has a wireless network. Approximate number of users that can be accommodated: 250. Proportion of college-owned housing units wired for high-speed internet access: 100%. **Campus safety:** Security services offered: 24-hour foot-and-vehicle patrols, lighted pathways/sidewalks, controlled dormitory access (key, security card, etc).

TRANSFER AND INTERNATIONAL STUDENTS

Transfer students: May apply for admission for the following academic terms: Fall, Winter, Spring, Summer. Applicants need a minimum number of credits to apply. For fall 2005: Transfer applications received: 166. Transfer applicants offered admission: 158. Transfer applicants enrolled: 158. **International students:** Number of foreign undergraduates: 42 (4% of student body). Number of countries represented: 14. Minimum TOEFL score required: 525 (paper); 195 (computer). Average TOEFL score: 550 (paper).

Montana

Carroll College

- **Address:** 1601 N. Benton Avenue, Helena, MT 59625-0002
- **Website:** http://www.carroll.edu
- **Private; Religious affiliation:** Roman Catholic
- **Enrollment:** 1,245 full-time; 207 part-time

KEY STATS

✔ **U.S News College Ranking:** 2, Comp. Coll.–Bachelor's (West)
✔ **ACT Score (25th/75th percentile):** 21-26
✔ **Tuition:** 2006-2007: $18,410

Selectivity: Selective	**Room/board:** $6,350
Acceptance rate: 79%	**Average debt:** $25,659
Student/faculty ratio: 13/1	**Proportion who borrowed:** 75%

UNDERGRADUATE STUDENT BODY STATS

2005-2006 enrollment: 1,245 full-time; 207 part-time. Men: 43%; women: 57%. **Ethnic makeup:** American-Indian: 1%; Asian American: 1%; Hispanic: 1%; White: 96%; International: 1%. **Religious preference:** Roman Catholic: 39%; Protestant: 1%; Unknown: 43%; Roman Catholic: 1%; Lutheran: 6%; Other: 10%.

ADMISSIONS FACTS AND FIGURES

Phone: (406) 447-4384. **Email:** enroll@carroll.edu. **Website:** http://www.carroll.edu. **Application deadlines for fall 2007:** Regular decision: June 1. Early decision: Not offered. Early action: Not offered. Admission can be deferred. **Application fee:** $35. Common application is accepted. **Admissions requirements/recommendations:** High school units required (recommended): English: (4); Mathematics: (3); Science: (2); Foreign language: (2); Social studies: (1); History: (2); Academic electives: (2); Total units: (17). Tests: The college uses SAT or ACT scores in admissions decisions. Either SAT or ACT required. For admission to the fall 2007 entering class, the school will accept: ACT with writing, ACT without writing. Campus visit: Recommended. Admissions interview: Recommended. Off-campus interview: May be arranged. **Factors that count in admissions decisions:** *Academic:* Secondary school record: Very important. Class rank: Important. Letters of recommendation: Important. Standardized test scores: Very important. Essay: Important. *Nonacademic:* Interview: Considered. Extracurricular activities: Considered. Talent/ability: Considered. Character/personal qualities: Important. Alumni/ae relationship: Considered. Geographical residence: Not considered. State residency: Not considered. Religious affiliation/commitment: Considered. Minority status: Not considered. Volunteer work: Considered. Work experience: Considered. **Other schools with the greatest overlap in applicants:** Gonzaga University; Montana State University–Bozeman; Pacific Lutheran University; University of Montana; University of Portland. **Admissions statistics for the fall 2005 entering class:** Total applicants: 1,048. Total accepted: 827. Freshmen enrolled: 304; 45% were from out of state. Overall acceptance rate: 79%. **Credentials of fall 2005 freshmen:** 22% ranked in the top 10 percent of their high school class; 44% were in the top 25 percent, and 80% were in the top half. (Proportion submitting class standing: 87%.) **Average high school grade point average:** 3.4. **First-year students who submitted SAT scores:** 53%. Scores (25/75 percentile): Verbal: 480-590, Math: 480-600, Combined: 960-1190. **First-year students submitting ACT scores:** 70%. Scores (25/75 percentile): English: 20-25, Math: 20-26, Composite: 21-26.

ACADEMICS

Year founded: 1909. **Academic calendar:** Semester. **Degrees offered:** associate, bachelor's. **Most popular majors:** 21% business, management, marketing, and related support services, 14% education, 10% biological and biomedical sciences, 10% social sciences, 9% health professions and related clinical sciences. **Major fields of study:** biological and biomedical sciences; business, management, marketing, and related support services; communication, journalism, and related programs; computer and information sciences and support services; education; engineering; English language and literature/letters; foreign languages, literatures, and linguistics; health professions and related clinical sciences; history; legal professions and studies; mathematics and statistics; natural resources and conservation; parks, recreation, leisure, and fitness studies; philosophy and religious studies; physical sciences; psychology; public administration and social service professions; social sciences; theology and religious vocations; visual and performing arts. **Areas of required coursework:** arts/fine arts, humanities, mathematics, English (including composition), philosophy, sciences (biological or physical), history, social science, other. **Pre-professional programs:** pre-law, pre-dentistry, pre-medicine, pre-theology, pré-veterinary science, pre-optometry, pre-pharmacy, other. **Special academic programs (% participation):** accelerated program (2%), cooperative (work-study plan) program (35%), double major (15%), dual enrollment (5%), English as a Second Language (ESL) (2%), honors program (9%), independent study (20%), internships (35%), liberal arts/career combination, student-designed major (1%), study abroad (25%), teacher certificate program (16%). **Teacher certification offered in:** special education, elementary, middle/junior high, secondary, bilingual/bicultural. **Cooperative education programs:** business, computer science, engineering, natural science, social/behavioral science. **Reserve Officers Training Corps (ROTC):** Army ROTC: Offered on campus. **Faculty and instruction (2005-2006):** Total instructional faculty: 80 full-time, 54 part-time (60% men; 40% women; 2% minorities). Full-time faculty with Ph.D. or other terminal degree: 70%. Student/faculty ratio: 13/1. Classes of fewer than 20 students: 62%; of 20 to 49 students: 36%; of 50 or more students: 2%. **Advanced Placement and International Baccalaureate credit:** AP tests may be used for: Credit and/or placement. Scores accepted: 3, 4, 5. International Baccalaureate exams may be used for: Credit and/or placement. **Freshmen returning for sophomore year:** 79%. **Graduation rates:** Four-year: 42%; five-year: 59%; six-year: 61%. **Graduate study:** 22% of students pursue further study immediately upon graduation; 3% within one year; 1% within five years. Fields in which graduates pursue further study: Master of Business Administration (MBA), 35%; law, 10%; medicine, 30%; dentistry, 5%; engineering, 4%; theology (or the seminary), 2%; education, 10%; arts and sciences, 2%; veterinary medicine, 2%.

COSTS AND FINANCIAL AID

Financial aid office: (406) 447-5423. **Expenses (2006-2007):** Tuition and fees 2006-2007: $18,410; room/board: $6,350. Estimated books and supplies: $700; transportation: $1,200; personal expenses: $1,600. **Financial aid:** Priority filing date for institution's financial aid form: March 1. In 2005-2006, 99% of undergraduates applied for financial aid. Of those, 67% were determined to have financial need; 13% had their need fully met. Average financial aid package (proportion receiving): $15,113 (67%). Average amount of gift aid, such as scholarships or grants (proportion receiving): $9,053 (62%). Average amount of self-help aid, such as work study or loans (proportion receiving): $6,051 (41%). Average need-based loan (excluding PLUS or other private loans): $4,831. Among students who received need-based aid, the average percentage of need met: 80%. Among students who received aid based on merit, the average award (and the proportion receiving): $6,109 (32%). The average athletic scholarship (and the proportion receiving): $8,056 (7%). Average amount of debt of borrowers graduating in 2005: $25,659. Proportion who borrowed: 75%.

CAMPUS LIFE AND EXTRACURRICULAR ACTIVITIES

Campus housing available (% using): coed dorms (77%), apartment for single students (21%), other housing options (2%). Students who live in college-owned, operated, or affiliated housing: 53%. **Student employment:** During the 2005-2006 academic year, 10% of undergraduates worked on campus. Average per-year earnings: $1,587. **Clubs and organizations:** Number of student organizations: 37. Activities include: choral groups, dance, drama/theater, literary magazine, music ensembles, musical theater, pep band, radio station, student government, student newspaper, yearbook. Number of fraternities: 0; sororities: 0. Average proportion of students who stay on campus on weekends: 40%. **Sports program (2005-2006):** Member of NAIA. *Men's intercollegiate varsity sports:* basketball, football, golf. *Women's intercollegiate varsity sports:* basketball, golf, soccer, volleyball.

SERVICES AND FACILITIES

Basic services: nonremedial tutoring, placement service, health service. **Remedial assistance:** reading, math, writing, study skills. **Counseling services:** career, personal, academic, psychological, religious. **For learning-disabled students:** School does not offer a structured program with separate admission and additional fees. Total undergraduates in learning-disabled program or receiving services: 10. Services include: note-taking services, oral tests, learning center, readers, extended time for tests, tutors, other. **Library:** Number of titles: 111,000; number of current serial subscriptions: 300. **Information technology resources:** Students are not required to lease or own a computer. Number of campus computers available to all students: 180. School has a wireless network. Approximate number of users that can be accommodated: 450. Proportion of college-owned housing units wired for high-speed internet access: 100%. **Campus safety:** Security services offered: 24-hour foot-and-vehicle patrols, late-night transport/escort service, 24-hour emergency telephones, lighted pathways/sidewalks, controlled dormitory access (key, security card, etc).

TRANSFER AND INTERNATIONAL STUDENTS

Transfer students: May apply for admission for the following academic terms: Fall, Spring. Applicants need a minimum number of credits to apply. For fall 2005: Transfer applications received: 176. Transfer applicants offered admission: 114. Transfer applicants enrolled: 54. **International students:** Number of foreign undergraduates: 10 (1% of student body). Number of countries represented: 14. Minimum TOEFL score required: 550 (paper). Average TOEFL score: 585 (paper).

Montana State University–Billings

- **Address:** 1500 University Drive, Billings, MT 59101
- **Website:** http://www.msubillings.edu
- **Public**
- **Enrollment:** 3,170 full-time; 1,237 part-time

KEY STATS

✔ **U.S News College Ranking:** third tier, Universities–Master's (West)
✔ **ACT Score (25th/75th percentile):** 19-23
✔ **Tuition:** N/A

Selectivity: Selective	**Room/board:** N/A
Acceptance rate: 97%	**Average debt:** $15,719
Student/faculty ratio: 20/1	**Proportion who borrowed:** 68%

UNDERGRADUATE STUDENT BODY STATS

2005-2006 enrollment: 3,170 full-time; 1,237 part-time. Men: 36%; women: 64%. **Ethnic makeup:** African American: 1%; American-Indian: 5%; Asian American: 1%; Hispanic: 3%; White: 89%; International: 1%.

ADMISSIONS FACTS AND FIGURES

Phone: (406) 657-2158. **Email:** admissions@msubillings.edu. **Website:** http://www.msubillings.edu. **Application deadlines for fall 2007:** Regular decision: July 1. Early decision: Not offered. Early action: Not offered. Admission cannot be deferred. **Application fee:** $30. Common application is not accepted. **To apply online, go to:** http://www.msubillings.edu/admissions/apply.htm. **Admissions requirements/recommendations:** High school units required (recommended): English: 4 (4); Mathematics: 3 (3); Science: 2 (2); Social studies: 3 (3); Total units: 14 (14). Tests: The college uses SAT or ACT scores in admissions decisions. Either SAT or ACT required. For admission to the fall 2007 entering class, the school will accept: ACT with writing, ACT without writing. Campus visit: Recommended. Admissions interview: Neither required nor recommended. Off-campus interview: May be arranged. **Factors that count in admissions decisions:** *Academic:* Secondary school record: Very important. Class rank: Very important. Letters of recommendation: Not considered. Standardized test scores: Very important. Essay: Not considered. *Nonacademic:* Interview: Not considered. Extracurricular activities: Not considered. Talent/ability: Not considered. Character/personal qualities: Considered. Alumni/ae relationship: Not considered. Geographical residence: Not considered. State residency: Not considered. Religious affiliation/commitment: Not considered. Minority status: Not considered. Volunteer work: Not considered. Work experience: Not considered. **Other schools with the greatest overlap in applicants:** Montana State University–Bozeman; Montana State University–Northern; Montana Tech of the University of Montana; Rocky Mountain College; University of

Montana. **Admissions statistics for the fall 2005 entering class:** Total applicants: 1,546. Total accepted: 1,493. Freshmen enrolled: 977; 8% were from out of state. Overall acceptance rate: 97%. **Credentials of fall 2005 freshmen:** 10% ranked in the top 10 percent of their high school class; 30% were in the top 25 percent, and 66% were in the top half. (Proportion submitting class standing: 79%.) **Average high school grade point average:** 3.2. **First-year students who submitted SAT scores:** 18%. Scores (25/75 percentile): Verbal: 450-550, Math: 460-570, Combined: 910-1120. **First-year students submitting ACT scores:** 66%. Scores (25/75 percentile): English: 17-23, Math: 17-24, Composite: 19-23.

ACADEMICS

Year founded: 1927. **Academic calendar:** Semester. **Degrees offered:** certificate, associate, transfer-associate, terminal-associate, bachelor's, post-bachelor's certificate, master's. **Most popular majors:** 18% business/commerce, 18% liberal arts and sciences/liberal studies, 15% elementary education and teaching, 10% secondary education and teaching, 8% psychology. **Major fields of study:** biological and biomedical sciences; business, management, marketing, and related support services; communication, journalism, and related programs; education; English language and literature/letters; foreign languages, literatures, and linguistics; health professions and related clinical sciences; history; liberal arts and sciences studies, and humanities; mathematics and statistics; multi/interdisciplinary studies; natural resources and conservation; parks, recreation, leisure, and fitness studies; physical sciences; psychology; social sciences; visual and performing arts. **Areas of required coursework:** arts/fine arts, humanities, mathematics, English (including composition), sciences (biological or physical), history, social science, other. **Pre-professional programs:** pre-law, pre-medicine, pre-pharmacy. **Special academic programs (% participation):** accelerated program (2%), cooperative (work-study plan) program (33%), cross-registration (1%), distance learning (40%), double major (17%), dual enrollment (3%), English as a Second Language (ESL), external degree program (2%), honors program (1%), independent study (12%), internships (13%), study abroad (1%), teacher certificate program (4%), weekend college (1%), other (27%). **Teacher certification offered in:** early childhood, special education, elementary, middle/junior high, secondary. **Cooperative education programs:** art, business, computer science, education, health professions, humanities, natural science, social/behavioral science, technologies, vocational arts. **Faculty and instruction (2005-2006):** Total instructional faculty: 156 full-time, 101 part-time (54% men; 46% women; 2% minorities). Full-time faculty with Ph.D. or other terminal degree: 87%. Student/faculty ratio: 20/1. Classes of fewer than 20 students: 47%; of 20 to 49 students: 47%; of 50 or more students: 5%. **Advanced Placement and International Baccalaureate credit:** AP tests may be used for: Credit only. Scores accepted: 3. International Baccalaureate exams may be used for: Credit only. **Freshmen returning for sophomore year:** 56%. **Graduation rates:** Four-year: 12%; five-year: 21%; six-year: 27%. **Graduate study:** 10% of students pursue further study within one year. Fields in which graduates pursue further study: Master of Business Administration (MBA), 8%; education, 19%; arts and sciences, 73%.

COSTS AND FINANCIAL AID

Financial aid office: (406) 657-2188. **Financial aid:** Priority filing date for institution's financial aid form: March 1; deadline: July 1. In 2005-2006, 85% of undergraduates applied for financial aid. Of those, 70% were determined to have financial need; 20% had their need fully met. Average financial aid package (proportion receiving): $7,566 (67%). Average amount of gift aid, such as scholarships or grants (proportion receiving): $4,373 (51%). Average amount of self-help aid, such as work study or loans (proportion receiving): $3,434 (57%). Average need-based loan (excluding PLUS or other private loans): $3,250. Among students who received need-based aid, the average percentage of need met: 67%. Among students who received aid based on merit, the average award (and the proportion receiving): $9,025 (3%). The average athletic scholarship (and the proportion receiving): $4,926 (5%). Average amount of debt of borrowers graduating in 2005: $15,719. Proportion who borrowed: 68%.

CAMPUS LIFE AND EXTRACURRICULAR ACTIVITIES

Campus housing available (% using): coed dorms (95%), apartments for married students (5%). Students who live in college-owned, operated, or affiliated housing: 16%. **Student employment:** During the 2005-2006 academic year, 11% of undergraduates worked on campus. Average per-year earnings: $1,525. **Clubs and organizations:** Number of student organizations: 51. Activities include: choral groups, concert band, drama/theater, jazz band, literary magazine, music ensembles, pep band, radio station, student government, student newspaper, symphony orchestra. Number of fraternities: 0; sororities: 0. Average proportion of students who stay on campus on weekends: 50%. **Sports program (2005-2006):** Member of NCAA II. *Men's intercollegiate varsity sports:* baseball, basketball, cross-country, golf, soccer, tennis. *Women's intercollegiate varsity sports:* basketball, cross-country, golf, soccer, softball, tennis, volleyball.

SERVICES AND FACILITIES

Basic services: nonremedial tutoring, placement service, day care, health service, health insurance. **Remedial assistance:** reading, math, writing, study skills. **Counseling services:** minority student, career, military, personal, veteran student, academic, older student, psychological, birth control, religious. **For learning-disabled students:** School does not offer a structured program with separate admission and additional fees. Total undergraduates in learning-disabled program or receiving services: 54. Services include: remedial math, remedial English, reading machines, remedial reading, tape recorders, note-taking services, oral tests, learning center, readers, extended time for tests, tutors, priority registration, priority seating, texts on tape, other testing accomodations. **Library:** Number of titles: 294,562; number of current serial subscriptions: 790. **Information technology resources:** Students are not required to lease or own a computer. Number of campus computers available to all students: 850. School has a wireless network. Approximate number of users that can be accommodated: 60. Proportion of college-owned housing units wired for high-speed internet access: 98%. **Campus safety:** Security services offered: 24-hour foot-and-vehicle patrols, late-night transport/escort service, 24-hour emergency telephones, lighted pathways/sidewalks, controlled dormitory access (key, security card, etc).

TRANSFER AND INTERNATIONAL STUDENTS

Transfer students: May apply for admission for the following academic terms: Fall, Spring, Summer. Applicants need a minimum number of credits to apply. For fall 2005: Transfer applications received: 431. Transfer applicants offered admission: 431. Transfer applicants enrolled: 431. **International students:** Number of foreign undergraduates: 38 (1% of student body). Number of countries represented: 13. Minimum TOEFL score required: 500 (paper); 173 (computer). Average TOEFL score: 500 (paper).

Montana State University–Bozeman

■ **Address:** Bozeman, MT 59717
■ **Website:** http://www.montana.edu
■ **Public**
■ **Enrollment:** 9,285 full-time; 1,557 part-time

KEY STATS

✔ **U.S News College Ranking:** fourth tier, National Universities
✔ **ACT Score (25th/75th percentile):** 20-26
✔ **Tuition:** 2006-2007: $5,773 in state, $15,582 out of state

Selectivity: Selective	**Room/board:** $6,450
Acceptance rate: 74%	**Average debt:** $18,081
Student/faculty ratio: 16/1	**Proportion who borrowed:** 66%

UNDERGRADUATE STUDENT BODY STATS

2005-2006 enrollment: 9,285 full-time; 1,557 part-time. Men: 53%; women: 47%. **Ethnic makeup:** American-Indian: 2%; Asian American: 1%; Hispanic: 1%; White: 93%; International: 1%.

ADMISSIONS FACTS AND FIGURES

Phone: (406) 994-2452. **Email:** admissions@montana.edu. **Website:** http://www.montana.edu. **Application deadlines for fall 2007:** Regular decision: Rolling. Early decision: Not offered. Early action: Not offered. Admission can be deferred. **Application fee:** $30. Common application is not accepted. **To apply online, go to:** http://www.montana.edu/wwwcat/appopts.html. **Admissions requirements/recommendations:** High school units required (recommended): English: 4; Mathematics: 3; Science: 2; Social studies: 3; Total units: 14. Tests: The college uses SAT or ACT scores in admissions decisions. Either SAT or ACT required. For admission to the fall 2007 entering class, the school will accept: ACT with writing, ACT without writing. Campus visit: Recommended. Admissions interview: Recommended. Off-campus interview: May be arranged. **Factors that count in admissions decisions:** *Academic:* Secondary school record: Very important. Class rank: Very important. Standardized test scores: Very important. *Nonacademic:* Interview: Not considered. Extracurricular activities: Not considered.

Talent/ability: Not considered. Character/personal qualities: Not considered. Alumni/ae relationship: Not considered. Geographical residence: Not considered. State residency: Not considered. Religious affiliation/commitment: Not considered. Minority status: Not considered. Volunteer work: Not considered. Work experience: Not considered. **Other schools with the greatest overlap in applicants:** Carroll College; Montana State University–Billings; Montana Tech of the University of Montana; University of Montana. **Admissions statistics for the fall 2005 entering class:** Total applicants: 5,124. Total accepted: 3,784. Freshmen enrolled: 2,236; 34% were from out of state. Overall acceptance rate: 74%. **Credentials of fall 2005 freshmen:** 17% ranked in the top 10 percent of their high school class; 41% were in the top 25 percent, and 71% were in the top half. (Proportion submitting class standing: 77%.) **Average high school grade point average:** 3.3. **First-year students who submitted SAT scores:** 48%. Scores (25/75 percentile): Verbal: 490-610, Math: 500-630, Combined: 990-1240. **First-year students submitting ACT scores:** 74%. Scores (25/75 percentile): English: 19-26, Math: 20-26, Composite: 20-26.

ACADEMICS

Year founded: 1893. **Academic calendar:** Semester. **Degrees offered:** certificate, bachelor's, master's, post-master's certificate, doctorate. **Most popular majors:** 13% business, management, marketing, and related support services, 11% engineering, 10% visual and performing arts, 9% education, 8% health professions and related clinical sciences. **Major fields of study:** agriculture, agriculture operations, and related sciences; architecture and related services; biological and biomedical sciences; business, management, marketing, and related support services; computer and information sciences and support services; education; engineering; engineering technologies/technicians; English language and literature/letters; family and consumer sciences/human sciences; foreign languages, literatures, and linguistics; health professions and related clinical sciences; history; liberal arts and sciences studies, and humanities; mathematics and statistics; multi/interdisciplinary studies; natural resources and conservation; parks, recreation, leisure, and fitness studies; philosophy and religious studies; physical sciences; psychology; social sciences; visual and performing arts. **Areas of required coursework:** arts/fine arts, humanities, mathematics, English (including composition), sciences (biological or physical), social science. **Pre-professional programs:** pre-law, pre-dentistry, pre-medicine, pre-veterinary science, pre-optometry, other. **Special academic programs:** cross-registration, distance learning, double major, English as a Second Language (ESL), exchange student program (domestic), honors program, independent study, internships, student-designed major, study abroad, teacher certificate program. **Teacher certification offered in:** elementary, secondary. **Reserve Officers Training Corps (ROTC):** Army ROTC: Offered on campus; Air Force ROTC: Offered on campus. **Faculty and instruction (2005-2006):** Total instructional faculty: 553 full-time, 274 part-time (60% men; 40% women; 3% minorities). Full-time faculty with Ph.D. or other terminal degree: 82%. Student/faculty ratio: 16/1. Classes of fewer than 20 students: 42%; of 20 to 49 students: 44%; of 50 or more students: 14%. **Advanced Placement and International Baccalaureate credit:** AP tests may be used for: Credit and/or placement. Scores accepted: 3, 4, 5. International Baccalaureate exams may be used for: Credit only. **Freshmen returning for sophomore year:** 71%. **Graduation rates:** Four-year: 19%; five-year: 40%; six-year: 46%.

COSTS AND FINANCIAL AID

Financial aid office: (406) 994-2845. **Expenses (2006-2007):** Tuition and fees 2006-2007: $5,773 in state, $15,582 out of state; room/board: $6,450. Estimated books and supplies: $1,000; transportation: $2,670. **Financial aid:** Priority filing date for institution's financial aid form: March 1. Average amount of debt of borrowers graduating in 2005: $18,081. Proportion who borrowed: 66%.

CAMPUS LIFE AND EXTRACURRICULAR ACTIVITIES

Campus housing available (% using): coed dorms (13%), women's dorms (3%), men's dorms (2%), sorority housing, fraternity housing, apartments for married students, apartment for single students, other housing options (82%). Students who live in college-owned, operated, or affiliated housing: 25%. **Student employment:** During the 2005-2006 academic year, 20% of undergraduates worked on campus. Average per-year earnings: $3,500. **Clubs and organizations:** Number of student organizations: 140. Activities include: choral groups, concert band, dance, drama/theater, jazz band, literary magazine, marching band, music ensembles, musical theater, pep band, radio station, student government, student newspaper, student film society, television station. Number of fraternities: 9; sororities: 4. Proportion of men in fraternities: 3%; of women in sororities: 3%. **Sports program (2005-2006):**

Member of NCAA I. *Men's intercollegiate varsity sports:* basketball, cross-country, football, skiing, tennis, track and field (indoor), track and field (outdoor). *Women's intercollegiate varsity sports:* basketball, cross-country, golf, skiing, tennis, track and field (indoor), track and field (outdoor), volleyball.

SERVICES AND FACILITIES

Basic services: nonremedial tutoring, women's center, placement service, day care, health service, health insurance. **Remedial assistance:** reading, math, writing. **Counseling services:** minority student, career, military, personal, veteran student, academic, older student, psychological. **For learning-disabled students:** School does not offer a structured program with separate admission and additional fees. Total undergraduates in learning-disabled program or receiving services: 189. Services include: remedial math, remedial English, reading machines, remedial reading, tape recorders, note-taking services, oral tests, learning center, readers, extended time for tests, tutors, priority registration, priority seating, texts on tape, other testing accomodations, other. **Library:** Number of titles: 712,241; number of current serial subscriptions: 8,757. **Information technology resources:** Students are not required to lease or own a computer. Number of campus computers available to all students: 850. **Campus safety:** Security services offered: 24-hour foot-and-vehicle patrols, late-night transport/escort service, 24-hour emergency telephones, lighted pathways/sidewalks, controlled dormitory access (key, security card, etc).

TRANSFER AND INTERNATIONAL STUDENTS

Transfer students: May apply for admission for the following academic terms: Fall, Spring, Summer. Applicants need a minimum number of credits to apply. For fall 2005: Transfer applications received: 1,443. Transfer applicants offered admission: 1,139. Transfer applicants enrolled: 761. **International students:** Number of foreign undergraduates: 125 (1% of student body). Number of countries represented: 59. Minimum TOEFL score required: 525 (paper); 195 (computer). Average TOEFL score: 592 (paper).

Montana State University–Northern

- **Address:** PO Box 7751, Havre, MT 59501
- **Website:** http://www.msun.edu
- **Public**
- **Enrollment:** N/A

KEY STATS

✔ **U.S News College Ranking:** fourth tier, Universities–Master's (West)
✔ **SAT or ACT Score (25th/75th percentile):** N/A
✔ **Tuition:** 2006-2007: $4,840 in state, $13,400 out of state

Selectivity: Less selective	**Room/board:** $8,000
Acceptance rate: N/A	**Average debt:** N/A
Student/faculty ratio: N/A	**Proportion who borrowed:** N/A

Montana Tech of the Univ. of Montana

- **Address:** 1300 W. Park Street, Butte, MT 59701
- **Website:** http://www.mtech.edu
- **Public**
- **Enrollment:** 1,729 full-time; 413 part-time

KEY STATS

✔ **U.S News College Ranking:** Unranked Specialty School–Engineering
✔ **ACT Score (25th/75th percentile):** 21-27
✔ **Tuition:** 2006-2007: $13,610 in state, $22,074 out of state

Selectivity: Selective	**Room/board:** $5,594
Acceptance rate: 98%	**Average debt:** $19,000
Student/faculty ratio: N/A	**Proportion who borrowed:** 80%

UNDERGRADUATE STUDENT BODY STATS

2005-2006 enrollment: 1,729 full-time; 413 part-time. Men: 55%; women: 45%. **Ethnic makeup:** American-Indian: 1%; Asian American: 1%; Hispanic: 1%; White: 93%; International: 3%.

ADMISSIONS FACTS AND FIGURES

Phone: (406) 496-4178. **Email:** admissions@mtech.edu. **Website:** http://www.mtech.edu. **Application deadlines for fall 2007:** Regular decision: Rolling. Early decision: Send application by: N/A; Decision sent by: N/A. Early action: Not offered. Admission can be deferred. **Application fee:** $30. Common application is not accepted. **To apply online, go to:** http://www.applyweb.com/aw?mtech. **Admissions requirements/recommendations:** High school units required (recommended): English: 4 (0); Mathematics: 3 (3); Science: 2 (0); Foreign language: (2); Social studies: 3; History: 3; Total units: 14. Tests: The college uses SAT or ACT scores in admissions decisions. Either SAT or ACT required. For admission to the fall 2007 entering class, the school will accept: ACT with writing, ACT without writing. Campus visit: Recommended. Admissions interview: Neither required nor recommended. Off-campus interview: Not available. **Factors that count in admissions decisions:** *Academic:* Secondary school record: Not considered. Class rank: Considered. Letters of recommendation: Not considered. Standardized test scores: Considered. Essay: Not considered. *Nonacademic:* Interview: Not considered. Extracurricular activities: Not considered. Talent/ability: Not considered. Character/personal qualities: Not considered. Alumni/ae relationship: Not considered. Geographical residence: Not considered. State residency: Not considered. Religious affiliation/commitment: Not considered. Minority status: Not considered. Volunteer work: Not considered. Work experience: Not considered. **Other schools with the greatest overlap in applicants:** Colorado School of Mines; Michigan Technological University; Montana State University–Billings; University of Montana; University of Washington. **Admissions statistics for the fall 2005 entering class:** Total applicants: 414. Total accepted: 407. Freshmen enrolled: 397; 12% were from out of state. Overall acceptance rate: 98%. Non-early acceptance rate: 53%. **Credentials of fall 2005 freshmen:** 13% ranked in the top 10 percent of their high school class; 35% were in the top 25 percent, and 66% were in the top half. (Proportion submitting class standing: 77%.) **Average high school grade point average:** 3.2. **First-year students who submitted SAT scores:** 27%. Scores (25/75 percentile): Verbal: 470-600, Math: 490-630, Combined: 960-1230. **First-year students submitting ACT scores:** 52%. Scores (25/75 percentile): English: 17-24, Math: 18-26, Composite: 21-27.

ACADEMICS

Year founded: 1893. **Academic calendar:** Semester. **Degrees offered:** certificate, associate, transfer-associate, terminal-associate, bachelor's, post-bachelor's certificate, master's. **Most popular majors:** 19% engineering, 15% petroleum engineering, 13% nursing/registered nurse training (R.N., A.S.N., B.S.N., M.S.N.). **Major fields of study:** biological and biomedical sciences; business, management, marketing, and related support services; computer and information sciences and support services; engineering; English language and literature/letters; health professions and related clinical sciences; liberal arts and sciences studies, and humanities; mathematics and statistics; physical sciences. **Areas of required coursework:** humanities, mathematics, English (including composition), sciences (biological or physical). **Pre-professional programs:** pre-law, pre-dentistry, pre-medicine, pre-veterinary science, pre-optometry, pre-pharmacy. **Special academic programs (% participation):** cooperative (work-study plan) program (35%), distance learning, double major, dual enrollment, independent study, internships, teacher certificate program. **Teacher certification offered in:** secondary. **Reserve Officers Training Corps (ROTC):** Army ROTC: Offered on campus. **Faculty and instruction (2005-2006):** Total instructional faculty: N/A. Classes of fewer than 20 students: 62%; of 20 to 49 students: 32%; of 50 or more students: 5%. **Advanced Placement and International Baccalaureate credit:** AP tests may be used for: Placement only. Scores accepted: 3, 4, 5. International Baccalaureate exams may be used for: Credit and/or placement. **Freshmen returning for sophomore year:** 65%. **Graduation rates:** Four-year: 9%; five-year: 30%; six-year: 42%. **Graduate study:** 31% of students pursue further study within one year.

COSTS AND FINANCIAL AID

Financial aid office: (406) 496-4212. **Expenses (2006-2007):** Tuition and fees 2006-2007: $13,610 in state, $22,074 out of state; room/board: $5,594. **Financial aid:** Priority filing date for institution's financial aid form: March 1. In 2005-2006, 94% of undergraduates applied for financial aid. Of those, 88% were determined to have financial need; 57% had their need fully met. Average financial aid package (proportion receiving): $5,000 (69%). Average amount of gift aid, such as scholarships or grants (proportion receiving): $2,000 (63%). Average amount of self-help aid, such as work study or loans (proportion receiving): N/A (50%). Among students who received need-based aid, the average percentage of need met: 75%. Among students who received aid based on merit, the average award (and the proportion receiving): $2,000 (22%). The average athletic scholarship (and the proportion receiving): $2,500 (9%). Average amount of debt of borrowers graduating in 2005: $19,000. Proportion who borrowed: 80%.

CAMPUS LIFE AND EXTRACURRICULAR ACTIVITIES

Campus housing available: coed dorms, apartments for married students. Students who live in college-owned, operated, or affiliated housing: 28%. **Student employment:** During the 2005-2006 academic year, 20% of undergraduates worked on campus. Average per-year earnings: $2,000. **Clubs and organizations:** Number of student organizations: 53. Activities include: pep band, radio station, student government, student newspaper, yearbook. Number of fraternities: 0; sororities: 0. Average proportion of students who stay on campus on weekends: 65%. **Sports program (2005-2006):** Member of NAIA. *Men's intercollegiate varsity sports:* basketball, football, golf. *Women's intercollegiate varsity sports:* basketball, golf, volleyball.

SERVICES AND FACILITIES

Basic services: placement service, health service, health insurance. **Remedial assistance:** math. **Counseling services:** career, personal, veteran student, academic, older student. **For learning-disabled students:** School does not offer a structured program with separate admission and additional fees. Services include: remedial math, tape recorders, oral tests, learning center, extended time for tests, tutors. **Library:** Number of titles: 161,187; number of current serial subscriptions: 495. **Information technology resources:** Students are not required to lease or own a computer. Number of campus computers available to all students: 500. School has a wireless network. Approximate number of users that can be accommodated: 1,500. Proportion of college-owned housing units wired for high-speed internet access: 90%. **Campus safety:** Security services offered: 24-hour foot-and-vehicle patrols, late-night transport/escort service, 24-hour emergency telephones, lighted pathways/sidewalks, controlled dormitory access (key, security card, etc).

TRANSFER AND INTERNATIONAL STUDENTS

Transfer students: May apply for admission for the following academic terms: Fall, Spring, Summer. Applicants need a minimum number of credits to apply. For fall 2005: Transfer applications received: 211. Transfer applicants offered admission: 165. Transfer applicants enrolled: 122. **International students:** Number of foreign undergraduates: 73 (3% of student body). Number of countries represented: 14. Minimum TOEFL score required: 580 (paper); 177 (computer). Average TOEFL score: 586 (paper).

Rocky Mountain College

■ **Address:** 1511 Poly Drive, Billings, MT 59102
■ **Website:** http://www.rocky.edu
■ **Private; Religious affiliation:** United Methodist, United Church of Christ, Presbyterian (U.S.A.)
■ **Enrollment:** 895 full-time; 69 part-time

KEY STATS

✔ **U.S News College Ranking:** 9, Comp. Coll.–Bachelor's (West)
✔ **ACT Score (25th/75th percentile):** 19-25
✔ **Tuition:** 2006-2007: $16,389

Selectivity: Selective	**Room/board:** $6,624
Acceptance rate: 78%	**Average debt:** $18,653
Student/faculty ratio: 13/1	**Proportion who borrowed:** 75%

UNDERGRADUATE STUDENT BODY STATS

2005-2006 enrollment: 895 full-time; 69 part-time. Men: 46%; women: 54%. **Ethnic makeup:** African American: 1%; American-Indian: 7%; Asian American: 2%; Hispanic: 2%; White: 82%; International: 5%. **Religious preference:** Roman Catholic: 18%; Protestant: 9%; No preference: 30%; United Methodist, United Church of Christ, Presbyterian (U.S.A.): 11%; Lutheran: 10%; Other: 22%.

ADMISSIONS FACTS AND FIGURES

Phone: (406) 657-1026. **Email:** admissions@rocky.edu. **Website:** http://www.rocky.edu. **Application deadlines for fall 2007:** Regular decision: Rolling. Early decision: Not offered. Early action: Not offered. Admission can be deferred. **Application fee:** $25. Common application is accepted. **To apply online, go to:** http://admissions.rocky.edu/index.php?top-groupid=18&groupid=88. **Admissions requirements/recommendations:** High

school units required (recommended): English: 4; Mathematics: 2 (3); Science: 2; Foreign language: 1 (2); Social studies: 2; History: 2; Total units: 13. Tests: The college uses SAT or ACT scores in admissions decisions. Either SAT or ACT required. For admission to the fall 2007 entering class, the school will accept: ACT with writing, ACT without writing. Campus visit: Recommended. Admissions interview: Recommended. Off-campus interview: May be arranged. **Factors that count in admissions decisions:** *Academic:* Secondary school record: Very important. Class rank: Important. Letters of recommendation: Considered. Standardized test scores: Very important. Essay: Considered. *Nonacademic:* Interview: Considered. Extracurricular activities: Considered. Talent/ability: Considered. Character/personal qualities: Important. Alumni/ae relationship: Considered. Geographical residence: Not considered. State residency: Not considered. Religious affiliation/commitment: Not considered. Minority status: Not considered. Volunteer work: Considered. Work experience: Considered. **Other schools with the greatest overlap in applicants:** Carroll College; Montana State University–Billings; Montana State University–Bozeman; University of Montana. **Admissions statistics for the fall 2005 entering class:** Total applicants: 728. Total accepted: 565. Freshmen enrolled: 218; 44% were from out of state. Overall acceptance rate: 78%. **Credentials of fall 2005 freshmen:** 15% ranked in the top 10 percent of their high school class; 40% were in the top 25 percent, and 73% were in the top half. (Proportion submitting class standing: 85%.) **Average high school grade point average:** 3.3. **First-year students who submitted SAT scores:** 32%. Scores (25/75 percentile): Verbal: 450-580, Math: 460-590, Combined: 910-1170. **First-year students submitting ACT scores:** 83%. Scores (25/75 percentile): English: 18-25, Math: 18-25, Composite: 19-25.

ACADEMICS

Year founded: 1878. **Academic calendar:** Semester. **Degrees offered:** associate, bachelor's, master's. **Most popular majors:** 18% business administration and management, 11% elementary education and teaching, 10% physician assistant, 9% biology/biological sciences, 7% psychology. **Major fields of study:** agriculture, agriculture operations, and related sciences; biological and biomedical sciences; business, management, marketing, and related support services; communication, journalism, and related programs; computer and information sciences and support services; education; English language and literature/letters; health professions and related clinical sciences; history; mathematics and statistics; multi/interdisciplinary studies; natural resources and conservation; parks, recreation, leisure, and fitness studies; philosophy and religious studies; physical sciences; psychology; social sciences; transportation and materials moving; visual and performing arts. **Areas of required coursework:** arts/fine arts, humanities, mathematics, English (including composition), sciences (biological or physical), social science, other. **Pre-professional programs:** pre-medicine, pre-veterinary science, other. **Special academic programs:** double major, dual enrollment, honors program, independent study, internships, student-designed major, study abroad, teacher certificate program. **Teacher certification offered in:** elementary, secondary. **Faculty and instruction (2005-2006):** Total instructional faculty: 53 full-time, 60 part-time (56% men; 44% women; 4% minorities). Full-time faculty with Ph.D. or other terminal degree: 62%. Student/faculty ratio: 13/1. Classes of fewer than 20 students: 69%; of 20 to 49 students: 30%; of 50 or more students: 1%. **Advanced Placement and International Baccalaureate credit:** AP tests may be used for: Credit only. Scores accepted: 3, 4. International Baccalaureate exams may be used for: Credit and/or placement. **Freshmen returning for sophomore year:** 74%. **Graduation rates:** Four-year: 26%; five-year: 39%; six-year: 42%. **Graduate study:** 22% of students pursue further study within one year. Fields in which graduates pursue further study: Master of Business Administration (MBA), 9%; law, 9%; medicine, 5%; education, 9%; arts and sciences, 68%.

COSTS AND FINANCIAL AID

Financial aid office: (406) 657-1031. **Expenses (2006-2007):** Tuition and fees 2006-2007: $16,389; room/board: $6,624. Estimated books and supplies: $900; transportation: $1,000; personal expenses: $1,000. **Financial aid:** Priority filing date for institution's financial aid form: March 1. In 2005-2006, 85% of undergraduates applied for financial aid. Of those, 73% were determined to have financial need; 22% had their need fully met. Average financial aid package (proportion receiving): $13,378 (73%). Average amount of gift aid, such as scholarships or grants (proportion receiving): $8,525 (73%). Average amount of self-help aid, such as work study or loans (proportion receiving): $3,374 (55%). Average need-based loan (excluding PLUS or other private loans): $2,576. Among students who received need-based aid, the average percentage of need met: 71%. Among students who received aid based on merit, the average award (and the proportion receiving): $7,335 (10%). The average athletic scholarship (and the proportion

receiving): $4,116 (3%). Average amount of debt of borrowers graduating in 2005: $18,653. Proportion who borrowed: 75%.

CAMPUS LIFE AND EXTRACURRICULAR ACTIVITIES

Campus housing available (% using): coed dorms (18%), apartments for married students (6%), apartment for single students (2%), special housing for disabled students (0%), other housing options (74%). Students who live in college-owned, operated, or affiliated housing: 49%. **Student employment:** During the 2005-2006 academic year, 22% of undergraduates worked on campus. Average per-year earnings: $754. **Clubs and organizations:** Number of student organizations: 23. Activities include: choral groups, concert band, drama/theater, jazz band, literary magazine, music ensembles, pep band, student government, student newspaper, yearbook. Number of fraternities: 0; sororities: 0. Average proportion of students who stay on campus on weekends: 50%. **Sports program (2005-2006):** Member of NAIA. *Men's intercollegiate varsity sports:* basketball, football, golf. *Women's intercollegiate varsity sports:* basketball, golf, soccer, volleyball.

SERVICES AND FACILITIES

Basic services: nonremedial tutoring, placement service, day care, health service. **Remedial assistance:** reading, math, writing, study skills. **Counseling services:** minority student, career, personal, academic, psychological, religious. **For learning-disabled students:** School does not offer a structured program with separate admission and additional fees. Total undergraduates in learning-disabled program or receiving services: 35. Services include: remedial math, remedial English, remedial reading, tape recorders, other special classes, untimed tests, note-taking services, readers, extended time for tests, tutors, texts on tape, exams on tape or computer, other testing accomodations. **Library:** Number of titles: 45,321; number of current serial subscriptions: 304. **Information technology resources:** Students are not required to lease or own a computer. Number of campus computers available to all students: 104. School has a wireless network. Approximate number of users that can be accommodated: 50. Proportion of college-owned housing units wired for high-speed internet access: 100%. **Campus safety:** Security services offered: late-night transport/escort service, lighted pathways/sidewalks, student patrols, controlled dormitory access (key, security card, etc).

TRANSFER AND INTERNATIONAL STUDENTS

Transfer students: May apply for admission for the following academic terms: Fall, Spring, Summer. Applicants need a minimum number of credits to apply. For fall 2005: Transfer applications received: 209. Transfer applicants offered admission: 129. Transfer applicants enrolled: 96. **International students:** Number of foreign undergraduates: 50 (5% of student body). Number of countries represented: 13. Minimum TOEFL score required: 525 (paper); 197 (computer). Average TOEFL score: 540 (paper).

University of Great Falls

- **Address:** 1301 20th Street S, Great Falls, MT 59405
- **Website:** http://www.ugf.edu
- **Private; Religious affiliation:** Roman Catholic
- **Enrollment:** 485 full-time; 188 part-time

KEY STATS

✔ **U.S News College Ranking:** fourth tier, Universities–Master's (West)
✔ **ACT Score (25th/75th percentile):** 19-24
✔ **Tuition:** 2006-2007: $15,612

Selectivity: Less selective	Room/board: $5,780
Acceptance rate: 79%	Average debt: $26,450
Student/faculty ratio: 11/1	Proportion who borrowed: 83%

UNDERGRADUATE STUDENT BODY STATS

2005-2006 enrollment: 485 full-time; 188 part-time. Men: 36%; women: 64%. **Ethnic makeup:** African American: 3%; American-Indian: 4%; Asian American: 2%; Hispanic: 5%; White: 85%; International: 2%. **Religious preference:** Roman Catholic: 28%; Unknown: 72%.

ADMISSIONS FACTS AND FIGURES

Phone: (406) 791-5200. **Email:** enroll@ugf.edu. **Website:** http://www.ugf.edu. **Application deadlines for fall 2007:** Regular decision: August 31. Early decision: Not offered. Early action: Not offered. Admission can be deferred. **Application fee:** $35. Common application is accepted. **To**

apply online, go to: http://www.ugf.edu/apply/undergradApp.htm. **Admissions requirements/recommendations:** High school units required (recommended): English: 4 (4); Mathematics: 3 (3); Science: 3 (3); Foreign language: 0 (2); Social studies: 1 (2); History: 3 (3); Academic electives: 5 (3); Total units: 20 (22). Tests: The college uses SAT or ACT scores in admissions decisions. Neither SAT nor ACT required. For admission to the fall 2007 entering class, the school will accept: ACT with writing, ACT without writing. Campus visit: Recommended. Admissions interview: Recommended. Off-campus interview: May be arranged. **Factors that count in admissions decisions:** *Academic:* Secondary school record: Considered. Class rank: Considered. Letters of recommendation: Considered. Standardized test scores: Important. Essay: Important. *Nonacademic:* Interview: Very important. Extracurricular activities: Important. Talent/ability: Considered. Character/personal qualities: Very important. Alumni/ae relationship: Not considered. Geographical residence: Considered. State residency: Not considered. Religious affiliation/commitment: Important. Minority status: Considered. Volunteer work: Important. Work experience: Considered. **Other schools with the greatest overlap in applicants:** Carroll College; Montana State University–Bozeman; Montana State University–Northern; Montana Tech of the University of Montana; University of Montana. **Admissions statistics for the fall 2005 entering class:** Total applicants: 242. Total accepted: 192. Freshmen enrolled: 122; 33% were from out of state. Overall acceptance rate: 79%. **Average high school grade point average:** 3.0. **First-year students who submitted SAT scores:** 12%. Scores (25/75 percentile): Verbal: 410-540, Math: 380-520, Combined: 790-1060. **First-year students submitting ACT scores:** 29%. Scores (25/75 percentile): English: N/A, Math: N/A, Composite: 19-24.

ACADEMICS

Year founded: 1932. **Academic calendar:** Semester. **Degrees offered:** associate, terminal-associate, bachelor's, master's. **Most popular majors:** 24% elementary education and teaching, 21% psychology, 7% criminal justice/safety studies, 5% business administration and management, 5% legal assistant/paralegal. **Major fields of study:** biological and biomedical sciences; business, management, marketing, and related support services; computer and information sciences and support services; education; English language and literature/letters; history; legal professions and studies; mathematics and statistics; parks, recreation, leisure, and fitness studies; physical sciences; psychology; security and protective services; social sciences; theology and religious vocations; visual and performing arts. **Areas of required coursework:** arts/fine arts, humanities, computer literacy, mathematics, English (including composition), philosophy, foreign languages, sciences (biological or physical), history, social science, other. **Special academic programs (% participation):** cooperative (work-study plan) program (6%), distance learning (16%), double major (15%), dual enrollment (0%), independent study (10%), internships (15%), teacher certificate program (5%). **Teacher certification offered in:** special education, elementary, middle/junior high, secondary. **Cooperative education programs:** art, business, computer science, education, social/behavioral science. **Faculty and instruction (2005-2006):** Total instructional faculty: 33 full-time, 50 part-time (60% men; 40% women; 4% minorities). Full-time faculty with Ph.D. or other terminal degree: 61%. Student/faculty ratio: 11/1. Classes of fewer than 20 students: 84%; of 20 to 49 students: 16%; of 50 or more students: 0%. **Advanced Placement and International Baccalaureate credit:** AP tests may be used for: Credit only. Scores accepted: 5. International Baccalaureate exams may be used for: Credit and/or placement. **Freshmen returning for sophomore year:** 45%. **Graduation rates:** Six-year: 23%. **Graduate study:** 30% of students pursue further study immediately upon graduation. Fields in which graduates pursue further study: law, 5%; education, 10%.

COSTS AND FINANCIAL AID

Financial aid office: (406) 791-5235. **Expenses (2006-2007):** Tuition and fees 2006-2007: $15,612; room/board: $5,780. Estimated books and supplies: $1,100; transportation: $600; personal expenses: $1,000. **Financial aid:** Priority filing date for institution's financial aid form: March 1. In 2005-2006, 88% of undergraduates applied for financial aid. Of those, 84% were determined to have financial need; 4% had their need fully met. Average financial aid package (proportion receiving): $10,989 (83%). Average amount of gift aid, such as scholarships or grants (proportion receiving): $3,719 (53%). Average amount of self-help aid, such as work study or loans (proportion receiving): $4,581 (77%). Average need-based loan (excluding PLUS or other private loans): $4,024. Among students who received need-based aid, the average percentage of need met: 41%. Among students who received aid based on merit, the average award (and the proportion receiving): $3,933 (3%). The average athletic scholarship (and the proportion

receiving): $4,420 (28%). Average amount of debt of borrowers graduating in 2005: $26,450. Proportion who borrowed: 83%.

CAMPUS LIFE AND EXTRACURRICULAR ACTIVITIES

Campus housing available (% using): coed dorms (45%), apartments for married students (3%), apartment for single students (52%). Students who live in college-owned, operated, or affiliated housing: 35%. **Student employment:** During the 2005-2006 academic year, 15% of undergraduates worked on campus. Average per-year earnings: $2,000. **Clubs and organizations:** Number of student organizations: 14. Activities include: choral groups, concert band, drama/theater, jazz band, literary magazine, music ensembles, pep band, radio station, student government, student newspaper, symphony orchestra. Number of fraternities: 0; sororities: 0. Average proportion of students who stay on campus on weekends: 25%. **Sports program (2005-2006):** Member of NAIA. *Men's intercollegiate varsity sports:* basketball, gymnastics, wrestling. *Women's intercollegiate varsity sports:* basketball, golf, volleyball.

SERVICES AND FACILITIES

Basic services: nonremedial tutoring, placement service, health service, health insurance. **Remedial assistance:** reading, math, writing, study skills. **Counseling services:** minority student, career, personal, veteran student, academic, older student, psychological, religious. **For learning-disabled students:** School does not offer a structured program with separate admission and additional fees. Total undergraduates in learning-disabled program or receiving services: 36. Services include: remedial math, remedial English, reading machines, remedial reading, tape recorders, videotaped classes, diagnostic testing service, untimed tests, note-taking services, oral tests, learning center, readers, extended time for tests, tutors, texts on tape, other testing accomodations. **Library:** Number of titles: 109,264; number of current serial subscriptions: 279. **Information technology resources:** Students are not required to lease or own a computer. Number of campus computers available to all students: 73. School does not have a wireless network. Proportion of college-owned housing units wired for high-speed internet access: 75%. **Campus safety:** Security services offered: 24-hour foot-and-vehicle patrols, late-night transport/escort service, 24-hour emergency telephones, lighted pathways/sidewalks, controlled dormitory access (key, security card, etc).

TRANSFER AND INTERNATIONAL STUDENTS

Transfer students: May apply for admission for the following academic terms: Fall, Spring, Summer. Applicants need a minimum number of credits to apply. For fall 2005: Transfer applications received: 189. Transfer applicants offered admission: 162. Transfer applicants enrolled: 126. **International students:** Number of foreign undergraduates: 10 (2% of student body). Number of countries represented: 5. Minimum TOEFL score required: 500 (paper); 173 (computer).

University of Montana

- **Address:** 32 Campus Drive, Missoula, MT 59812
- **Website:** http://www.umt.edu
- **Public**
- **Enrollment:** 8,704 full-time; 1,524 part-time

KEY STATS

✔ **U.S News College Ranking:** third tier, National Universities
✔ **ACT Score (25th/75th percentile):** 20-25
✔ **Tuition:** 2006-2007: $5,174 in state, $14,979 out of state
  Selectivity: Selective   **Room/board:** $5,860
  Acceptance rate: 83%   **Average debt:** $16,929
  Student/faculty ratio: 20/1   **Proportion who borrowed:** 71%

UNDERGRADUATE STUDENT BODY STATS

2005-2006 enrollment: 8,704 full-time; 1,524 part-time. Men: 47%; women: 53%. **Ethnic makeup:** African American: 1%; American-Indian: 4%; Asian American: 1%; Hispanic: 1%; White: 92%; International: 1%.

ADMISSIONS FACTS AND FIGURES

Phone: (800) 462-8636. **Email:** admiss@umontana.edu. **Website:** http://www.umt.edu. **Application deadlines for fall 2007:** Regular decision: Rolling. Early decision: Not offered. Early action: Not offered. Admission

can be deferred. **Application fee:** $30. Common application is accepted. **To apply online, go to:** http://admissions.umt.edu/hottopics/academics/applying.htm. **Admissions requirements/recommendations:** High school units required (recommended): English: 4; Mathematics: 3; Science: 2; Foreign language: (2); Social studies: 2; History: 1; Academic electives: 2; Total units: 16. Tests: The college uses SAT or ACT scores in admissions decisions. Either SAT or ACT required. For admission to the fall 2007 entering class, the school will accept: ACT with writing, ACT without writing. Campus visit: Recommended. Admissions interview: Neither required nor recommended. **Factors that count in admissions decisions:** *Academic:* Secondary school record: Very important. Class rank: Very important. Letters of recommendation: Considered. Standardized test scores: Very important. Essay: Considered. *Nonacademic:* Interview: Not considered. Extracurricular activities: Important. Talent/ability: Important. Character/personal qualities: Not considered. Alumni/ae relationship: Not considered. Geographical residence: Not considered. State residency: Not considered. Religious affiliation/commitment: Not considered. Minority status: Not considered. Volunteer work: Not considered. Work experience: Not considered. **Other schools with the greatest overlap in applicants:** Colorado State University; Gonzaga University; Montana State University–Bozeman; University of Colorado–Boulder; University of Oregon. **Admissions statistics for the fall 2005 entering class:** Total applicants: 5,802. Total accepted: 4,827. Freshmen enrolled: 1,864; 38% were from out of state. Overall acceptance rate: 83%. **Credentials of fall 2005 freshmen:** 17% ranked in the top 10 percent of their high school class; 41% were in the top 25 percent, and 71% were in the top half. (Proportion submitting class standing: 81%.) **Average high school grade point average:** 3.2. **First-year students who submitted SAT scores:** 40%. Scores (25/75 percentile): Verbal: 508-585, Math: 486-578, Combined: 994-1163. **First-year students submitting ACT scores:** 58%. Scores (25/75 percentile): English: 19-25, Math: 19-25, Composite: 20-25.

ACADEMICS

Year founded: 1893. **Academic calendar:** Semester. **Degrees offered:** certificate, associate, terminal-associate, bachelor's, master's, post-master's certificate, first professional, doctorate. **Most popular majors:** 21% business, management, marketing, and related support services; 7% communication, journalism, and related programs; 7% education, 7% natural resources and conservation, 6% psychology. **Major fields of study:** area, ethnic, cultural, and gender studies; biological and biomedical sciences; business, management, marketing, and related support services; communication, journalism, and related programs; computer and information sciences and support services; education; English language and literature/letters; foreign languages, literatures, and linguistics; health professions and related clinical sciences; history; liberal arts and sciences studies, and humanities; mathematics and statistics; multi/interdisciplinary studies; natural resources and conservation; parks, recreation, leisure, and fitness studies; philosophy and religious studies; physical sciences; public administration and social service professions; social sciences; visual and performing arts. **Areas of required coursework:** arts/fine arts, mathematics, English (including composition), sciences (biological or physical), history, social science, other. **Pre-professional programs:** pre-law, pre-dentistry, pre-medicine, pre-veterinary science, pre-optometry, pre-pharmacy, other. **Special academic programs:** distance learning, double major, English as a Second Language (ESL), exchange student program (domestic), external degree program, honors program, independent study, internships, study abroad, teacher certificate program, other. **Teacher certification offered in:** early childhood, special education, elementary, middle/junior high, secondary, bilingual/bicultural. **Cooperative education programs:** art, business, computer science, education, health professions, humanities, natural science, social/behavioral science, technologies, other. **Reserve Officers Training Corps (ROTC):** Army ROTC: Offered on campus. **Faculty and instruction (2005-2006):** Total instructional faculty: 500 full-time, 147 part-time (61% men; 39% women; 8% minorities). Full-time faculty with Ph.D. or other terminal degree: 86%. Student/faculty ratio: 20/1. Classes of fewer than 20 students: 44%; of 20 to 49 students: 44%; of 50 or more students: 12%. **Advanced Placement and International Baccalaureate credit:** AP tests may be used for: Credit only. Scores accepted: 3, 4, 5. International Baccalaureate exams may be used for: Credit only. **Freshmen returning for sophomore year:** 70%. **Graduation rates:** Four-year: 20%; five-year: 37%; six-year: 44%. **Graduate study:** 21% of students pursue further study immediately upon graduation; 21% within one year.

COSTS AND FINANCIAL AID

Financial aid office: (406) 243-5373. **Expenses (2006-2007):** Tuition and fees 2006-2007: $5,174 in state, $14,979 out of state; room/board: $5,860. Estimated books and supplies: $850; transportation: $1,200; personal expenses: $2,262. **Financial aid:** Priority filing date for institution's financial aid form: February 15. In 2005-2006, 78% of undergraduates applied for financial aid. Of those, 57% were determined to have financial need; 12% had their need fully met. Average financial aid package (proportion receiving): $7,199 (56%). Average amount of gift aid, such as scholarships or grants (proportion receiving): $3,408 (40%). Average amount of self-help aid, such as work study or loans (proportion receiving): $4,094 (49%). Average need-based loan (excluding PLUS or other private loans): $3,386. Among students who received need-based aid, the average percentage of need met: 65%. Among students who received aid based on merit, the average award (and the proportion receiving): $4,770 (19%). The average athletic scholarship (and the proportion receiving): $4,225 (2%). Average amount of debt of borrowers graduating in 2005: $16,929. Proportion who borrowed: 71%.

CAMPUS LIFE AND EXTRACURRICULAR ACTIVITIES

Campus housing available (% using): coed dorms (70%), women's dorms (4%), men's dorms (3%), sorority housing, fraternity housing, apartments for married students (15%), apartment for single students (4%), special housing for disabled students (1%), special housing for international students (2%), other housing options (1%). Students who live in college-owned, operated, or affiliated housing: 24%. Average per-year earnings: $1,330. **Clubs and organizations:** Number of student organizations: 150. Activities include: choral groups, concert band, dance, drama/theater, jazz band, literary magazine, marching band, music ensembles, musical theater, opera, pep band, radio station, student government, student newspaper, symphony orchestra, television station. Number of fraternities: 6; sororities: 4. Proportion of men in fraternities: 6%; of women in sororities: 6%. Average proportion of students who stay on campus on weekends: 90%. **Sports program (2005-2006):** Member of NCAA I. *Men's intercollegiate varsity sports:* basketball, cross-country, football, tennis, track and field (indoor), track and field (outdoor). *Women's intercollegiate varsity sports:* basketball, cross-country, golf, soccer, tennis, track and field (indoor), track and field (outdoor), volleyball.

SERVICES AND FACILITIES

Basic services: nonremedial tutoring, women's center, placement service, day care, health service, health insurance. **Remedial assistance:** math, writing, study skills. **Counseling services:** minority student, career, military, personal, veteran student, academic, older student, psychological, birth control. **For learning-disabled students:** School does not offer a structured program with separate admission and additional fees. Total undergraduates in learning-disabled program or receiving services: 275. Services include: reading machines, tape recorders, note-taking services, oral tests, learning center, readers, extended time for tests, tutors, priority registration, priority seating, proofreading services, texts on tape, typist/scribe, exams on tape or computer, other testing accomodations. **Library:** Number of titles: 1,103,448; number of current serial subscriptions: 13,208. **Information technology resources:** Students are not required to lease or own a computer. Number of campus computers available to all students: 500. School has a wireless network. Approximate number of users that can be accommodated: 1,728. Proportion of college-owned housing units wired for high-speed internet access: 100%. **Campus safety:** Security services offered: 24-hour foot-and-vehicle patrols, late-night transport/escort service, 24-hour emergency telephones, lighted pathways/sidewalks, controlled dormitory access (key, security card, etc).

TRANSFER AND INTERNATIONAL STUDENTS

Transfer students: May apply for admission for the following academic terms: Fall, Spring, Summer. Applicants need a minimum number of credits to apply. For fall 2005: Transfer applications received: 1,761. Transfer applicants offered admission: 1,504. Transfer applicants enrolled: 812. **International students:** Number of foreign undergraduates: 147 (1% of student body). Number of countries represented: 60. Minimum TOEFL score required: 500 (paper); 173 (computer). Average TOEFL score: 525 (paper).

University of Montana–Western

- **Address:** 710 S. Atlantic, Dillon, MT 59725
- **Website:** http://www.umwestern.edu
- **Public**
- **Enrollment:** 941 full-time; 218 part-time

KEY STATS

✔ **U.S News College Ranking:** third tier, Comp. Coll.–Bachelor's (West)
✔ **ACT Score (25th/75th percentile):** 17-22
✔ **Tuition:** 2006-2007: $4,726 in state, $12,532 out of state
  Selectivity: Less selective   **Room/board:** $4,920
  Acceptance rate: 99%   **Average debt:** $22,682
  Student/faculty ratio: N/A   **Proportion who borrowed:** 86%

UNDERGRADUATE STUDENT BODY STATS

2005-2006 enrollment: 941 full-time; 218 part-time. Men: 41%; women: 59%. **Ethnic makeup:** African American: 1%; American-Indian: 4%; Asian American: 2%; Hispanic: 2%; White: 91%; International: 1%.

ADMISSIONS FACTS AND FIGURES

Phone: (406) 683-7331. **Email:** admissions@umwestern.edu. **Website:** http://www.umwestern.edu. **Application deadlines for fall 2007:** Regular decision: Rolling. Early decision: Not offered. Early action: Not offered. Admission can be deferred. **Application fee:** $30. Common application is not accepted. **Admissions requirements/recommendations:** High school units required (recommended): English: 4; Mathematics: 3; Science: 2; Social studies: 3; Academic electives: 4; Total units: 16. Tests: The college uses SAT or ACT scores in admissions decisions. Either SAT or ACT required. For admission to the fall 2007 entering class, the school will accept: ACT with writing, ACT without writing. Campus visit: Recommended. Admissions interview: Neither required nor recommended. Off-campus interview: Not available. **Factors that count in admissions decisions:** *Academic:* Secondary school record: Very important. Class rank: Very important. Letters of recommendation: Not considered. Standardized test scores: Very important. Essay: Not considered. *Nonacademic:* Interview: Not considered. Extracurricular activities: Considered. Talent/ability: Considered. Character/personal qualities: Not considered. Alumni/ae relationship: Considered. Geographical residence: Not considered. State residency: Considered. Religious affiliation/commitment: Not considered. Minority status: Considered. Volunteer work: Not considered. Work experience: Not considered. **Other schools with the greatest overlap in applicants:** Idaho State University; Montana State University–Bozeman; Montana Tech of the University of Montana; University of Montana. **Admissions statistics for the fall 2005 entering class:** Total applicants: 418. Total accepted: 413. Freshmen enrolled: 230; Overall acceptance rate: 99%. **Credentials of fall 2005 freshmen:** 4% ranked in the top 10 percent of their high school class; 17% were in the top 25 percent, and 48% were in the top half. (Proportion submitting class standing: 92%.) **Average high school grade point average:** 2.9. **First-year students who submitted SAT scores:** 20%. Scores (25/75 percentile): Verbal: 420-520, Math: 400-510, Combined: 820-1030. **First-year students submitting ACT scores:** 65%. Scores (25/75 percentile): English: 15-21, Math: 17-24, Composite: 17-22.

ACADEMICS

Year founded: 1893. **Academic calendar:** Semester. **Degrees offered:** associate, bachelor's. **Most popular majors:** Information not available. **Major fields of study:** education; liberal arts and sciences studies, and humanities; multi/interdisciplinary studies. **Areas of required coursework:** arts/fine arts, humanities, computer literacy, mathematics, English (including composition), philosophy, sciences (biological or physical), social science. **Pre-professional programs:** pre-law, pre-medicine, pre-veterinary science, pre-pharmacy. **Special academic programs (% participation):** cooperative (work-study plan) program (10%), double major (10%), dual enrollment (10%), honors program (5%), independent study (2%), internships (20%), study abroad (2%), teacher certificate program (65%). **Teacher certification offered in:** special education, elementary, middle/junior high, secondary. **Cooperative education programs:** business, social/behavioral science. **Freshmen returning for sophomore year:** 59%. **Graduation rates:** Four-year: 9%; five-year: 24%; six-year: 29%. **Graduate study:** 6% of students pursue further study immediately upon graduation.

COSTS AND FINANCIAL AID

Financial aid office: (406) 683-7511. **Expenses (2006-2007):** Tuition and fees 2006-2007: $4,726 in state, $12,532 out of state; room/board: $4,920. Estimated books and supplies: $800; transportation: $1,000; personal expenses: $190. **Financial aid:** Priority filing date for institution's financial aid form: March 1. In 2005-2006, 89% of undergraduates applied for financial aid. Of those, 73% were determined to have financial need; 2% had their need fully met. Average financial aid package (proportion receiving): $2,735 (73%). Average amount of gift aid, such as scholarships or grants (proportion receiving): $2,287 (58%). Average amount of self-help aid, such as work study or loans (proportion receiving): $2,448 (64%). Average need-based loan (excluding PLUS or other private loans): $3,687. Among students who received need-based aid, the average percentage of need met: 18%. Among students who received aid based on merit, the average award (and the proportion receiving): $3,037 (0%). The average athletic scholarship (and the proportion receiving): $2,436 (36%). Average amount of debt of borrowers graduating in 2005: $22,682. Proportion who borrowed: 86%.

CAMPUS LIFE AND EXTRACURRICULAR ACTIVITIES

Campus housing available (% using): coed dorms (48%), women's dorms (23%), men's dorms (24%), apartments for married students (5%), apartment for single students (0%), special housing for disabled students (0%). **Student employment:** During the 2005-2006 academic year, 10% of undergraduates worked on campus. Average per-year earnings: $2,000. **Clubs and organizations:** Number of student organizations: 22. Activities include: choral groups, drama/theater, music ensembles, pep band, radio station, student government, student newspaper, yearbook. Number of fraternities: 0; sororities: 0. Average proportion of students who stay on campus on weekends: 20%. **Sports program (2005-2006):** Member of NAIA. *Men's intercollegiate varsity sports:* basketball, equestrian Sports, football, golf, rodeo. *Women's intercollegiate varsity sports:* basketball, equestrian sports, golf, rodeo, volleyball, jv women's basketball.

SERVICES AND FACILITIES

Basic services: placement service, day care, health insurance. **Remedial assistance:** math, writing, study skills. **Counseling services:** career, personal, academic, psychological, birth control. **For learning-disabled students:** School does not offer a structured program with separate admission and additional fees. Total undergraduates in learning-disabled program or receiving services: 32. Services include: remedial math, reading machines, tape recorders, videotaped classes, untimed tests, note-taking services, oral tests, learning center, readers, extended time for tests, tutors, priority registration, texts on tape. **Library:** Number of titles: 57,467; number of current serial subscriptions: 472. **Information technology resources:** Students are not required to lease or own a computer. Number of campus computers available to all students: 200. School does not have a wireless network. Proportion of college-owned housing units wired for high-speed internet access: 100%. **Campus safety:** Security services offered: late-night transport/escort service, 24-hour emergency telephones, lighted pathways/sidewalks, controlled dormitory access (key, security card, etc).

TRANSFER AND INTERNATIONAL STUDENTS

Transfer students: May apply for admission for the following academic terms: Fall, Spring, Summer. Applicants need a minimum number of credits to apply. **International students:** Number of foreign undergraduates: 6 (1% of student body). Number of countries represented: 5. Minimum TOEFL score required: 500 (paper); 173 (computer).

Nebraska

Bellevue University

- **Address:** 1000 Galvin Road S, Bellevue, NE 68005
- **Website:** http://www.bellevue.edu
- **Private**
- **Enrollment:** 2,849 full-time; 1,598 part-time

KEY STATS

✔ **U.S News College Ranking:** fourth tier, Universities–Master's (Midwest)
✔ **SAT or ACT Score (25th/75th percentile):** N/A
✔ **Tuition:** 2006-2007: $5,345

Selectivity: Less selective	**Room/board:** N/A
Acceptance rate: 100%	**Average debt:** N/A
Student/faculty ratio: 22/1	**Proportion who borrowed:** N/A

UNDERGRADUATE STUDENT BODY STATS

2005-2006 enrollment: 2,849 full-time; 1,598 part-time. Men: 51%; women: 49%. **Ethnic makeup:** African American: 10%; American-Indian: 1%; Asian American: 2%; Hispanic: 6%; White: 75%; International: 6%.

ADMISSIONS FACTS AND FIGURES

Phone: (800) 756-7920. **Email:** info@bellevue.edu. **Website:** http://www.bellevue.edu. **Application deadlines for fall 2007:** Regular decision: Rolling. Early decision: Not offered. Early action: Not offered. Admission can be deferred. **Application fee:** $50. Common application is not accepted. **Admissions requirements/recommendations:** High school units required (recommended): English: (3); Mathematics: (3); Science: (3); Foreign language: (3); Social studies: (3); History: (3); Academic electives: (3). Tests: The college does not use SAT or ACT scores in admissions decisions. Neither SAT nor ACT required. Campus visit: Neither required nor recommended. Admissions interview: Neither required nor recommended. Off-campus interview: May be arranged. **Factors that count in admissions decisions:** *Academic:* Secondary school record: Not considered. Class rank: Not considered. Letters of recommendation: Not considered. Standardized test scores: Not considered. Essay: Not considered. *Nonacademic:* Interview: Not considered. Extracurricular activities: Not considered. Talent/ability: Not considered. Character/personal qualities: Not considered. Alumni/ae relationship: Not considered. Geographical residence: Not considered. State residency: Not considered. Religious affiliation/commitment: Not considered. Minority status: Not considered. Volunteer work: Not considered. Work experience: Not considered. **Other schools with the greatest overlap in applicants:** Nebraska Wesleyan University; University of Nebraska–Lincoln; University of Nebraska–Omaha. **Admissions statistics for the fall 2005 entering class:** Total applicants: 287. Total accepted: 287. Freshmen enrolled: 70; Overall acceptance rate: 100%.

ACADEMICS

Year founded: 1966. **Academic calendar:** Continuos. **Degrees offered:** certificate, bachelor's, master's. **Most popular majors:** 32% business/commerce, 18% business administration and management, 14% social sciences, 11% management information systems and services, 10% health and medical administrative services. **Major fields of study:** biological and biomedical sciences; business, management, marketing, and related support services; communication, journalism, and related programs; communications technologies/technicians and support services; computer and information sciences and support services; education; health professions and related clinical sciences; history; liberal arts and sciences studies, and humanities; psychology; public administration and social service professions; security and protective services; social sciences; visual and performing arts. **Areas of required coursework:** humanities, mathematics, English (including composition), philosophy, sciences (biological or physical), social science. **Special academic programs (% participation):** accelerated program (30%), distance learning (58%), double major (5%), dual enrollment (1%), English as a Second Language (ESL) (4%). **Faculty and instruction (2005-2006):** Total instructional faculty: 72 full-time, 402 part-time (60% men; 40% women;

5% minorities). Full-time faculty with Ph.D. or other terminal degree: 51%. Student/faculty ratio: 22/1. Classes of fewer than 20 students: 71%; of 20 to 49 students: 29%; of 50 or more students: 0%. **Advanced Placement and International Baccalaureate credit:** AP tests may be used for: Credit and/or placement. Scores accepted: 3. International Baccalaureate exams may be used for: Credit and/or placement. **Graduation rates:** Six-year: 27%.

COSTS AND FINANCIAL AID

Financial aid office: (402) 293-3763. **Expenses (2006-2007):** Tuition and fees 2006-2007: $5,345; room/board: N/A. **Financial aid:** In 2005-2006, 94% of undergraduates applied for financial aid. Of those, 94% were determined to have financial need; Average financial aid package (proportion receiving): $4,424 (94%). Average amount of gift aid, such as scholarships or grants (proportion receiving): $2,127 (38%). Average amount of self-help aid, such as work study or loans (proportion receiving): $4,072 (84%). Average need-based loan (excluding PLUS or other private loans): $4,085.

CAMPUS LIFE AND EXTRACURRICULAR ACTIVITIES

Campus housing available (% using): apartments for married students, apartment for single students (100%), special housing for international students, other housing options. **Student employment:** During the 2005-2006 academic year, 1% of undergraduates worked on campus. Average per-year earnings: $2,000. **Clubs and organizations:** Number of student organizations: 13. Activities include: literary magazine, student government. Number of fraternities: 0; sororities: 0. **Sports program (2005-2006):** Member of NAIA. *Men's intercollegiate varsity sports:* baseball, basketball, soccer. *Women's intercollegiate varsity sports:* soccer, softball, volleyball.

SERVICES AND FACILITIES

Basic services: nonremedial tutoring, health insurance. **Remedial assistance:** reading, math, writing, study skills, other. **Counseling services:** career, veteran student, academic, older student. **For learning-disabled students:** School does not offer a structured program with separate admission and additional fees. Total undergraduates in learning-disabled program or receiving services: 26. Services include: tape recorders, videotaped classes, note-taking services, oral tests, readers, extended time for tests, priority seating, texts on tape, exams on tape or computer, other testing accomodations, other. **Library:** Number of titles: 83,817; number of current serial subscriptions: 33,576. **Information technology resources:** Students are not required to lease or own a computer. Number of campus computers available to all students: 547. School has a wireless network. Approximate number of users that can be accommodated: 40. **Campus safety:** Security services offered: 24-hour emergency telephones, lighted pathways/sidewalks.

TRANSFER AND INTERNATIONAL STUDENTS

Transfer students: May apply for admission for the following academic terms: Fall, Winter, Spring, Summer. Applicants do not need a minimum number of credits to apply. For fall 2005: Transfer applications received: 262. Transfer applicants offered admission: 395. Transfer applicants enrolled: 548. **International students:** Number of foreign undergraduates: 245 (6% of student body). Minimum TOEFL score required: 500 (paper); 173 (computer).

Chadron State College

- **Address:** 1000 Main Street, Chadron, NE 69337
- **Website:** http://www.csc.edu
- **Public**
- **Enrollment:** 1,632 full-time; 520 part-time

KEY STATS

✔ **U.S News College Ranking:** fourth tier, Universities–Master's (Midwest)
✔ **ACT Score (25th/75th percentile):** 18-24
✔ **Tuition:** 2006-2007: $3,855 in state, $6,945 out of state

Selectivity: Selective	**Room/board:** $4,065
Acceptance rate: N/A	**Average debt:** N/A
Student/faculty ratio: 25/1	**Proportion who borrowed:** N/A

UNDERGRADUATE STUDENT BODY STATS

2005-2006 enrollment: 1,632 full-time; 520 part-time. Men: 43%; women: 57%. **Ethnic makeup:** African American: 1%; American-Indian: 2%; Asian American: 1%; Hispanic: 2%; White: 93%; International: 1%.

ADMISSIONS FACTS AND FIGURES

Phone: (308) 432-6263. **Email:** inquire@csc.edu. **Website:** http://www.csc.edu. **Application deadlines for fall 2007:** Regular decision: Rolling. Early decision: Not offered. Early action: Not offered. Admission cannot be deferred. **Application fee:** $15. Common application is not accepted. **Admissions requirements/recommendations:** High school units required (recommended): English: (4); Mathematics: (3); Science: (3); Social studies: (3); History: (1). Tests: The college uses SAT or ACT scores in admissions decisions. Neither SAT nor ACT required. For admission to the fall 2007 entering class, the school will accept: ACT with writing, ACT without writing. Campus visit: Neither required nor recommended. Admissions interview: Neither required nor recommended. Off-campus interview: Not available. **Factors that count in admissions decisions:** *Academic:* Secondary school record: Considered. Class rank: Considered. Letters of recommendation: Considered. Standardized test scores: Considered. Essay: Not considered. *Nonacademic:* Interview: Not considered. Extracurricular activities: Considered. Talent/ability: Considered. Character/personal qualities: Not considered. Alumni/ae relationship: Considered. Geographical residence: Considered. State residency: Considered. Religious affiliation/commitment: Not considered. Minority status: Considered. Volunteer work: Not considered. Work experience: Not considered. **Other schools with the greatest overlap in applicants:** University of Nebraska–Kearney; University of Nebraska–Lincoln; University of Wyoming. **Admissions statistics for the fall 2005 entering class:** Freshmen enrolled: 326; **Credentials of fall 2005 freshmen:** 13% ranked in the top 10 percent of their high school class; 28% were in the top 25 percent, and 58% were in the top half. (Proportion submitting class standing: 98%.) **Average high school grade point average:** 3.2. **First-year students who submitted SAT scores:** 2%. Scores (25/75 percentile): Verbal: N/A, Math: N/A, Combined: N/A. **First-year students submitting ACT scores:** 91%. Scores (25/75 percentile): English: N/A, Math: N/A, Composite: 18-24.

ACADEMICS

Year founded: 1911. **Academic calendar:** Semester. **Degrees offered:** bachelor's, master's, post-master's certificate. **Most popular majors:** 13% business administration and management, 13% elementary education and teaching, 8% biology/biological sciences, 5% security and loss prevention services, 3% psychology. **Major fields of study:** agriculture, agriculture operations, and related sciences; biological and biomedical sciences; business, management, marketing, and related support services; computer and information sciences and support services; education; engineering technologies/technicians; English language and literature/letters; family and consumer sciences/human sciences; foreign languages, literatures, and linguistics; health professions and related clinical sciences; history; liberal arts and sciences studies, and humanities; library science; mathematics and statistics; parks, recreation, leisure, and fitness studies; physical sciences; psychology; public administration and social service professions; security and protective services; social sciences; visual and performing arts. **Pre-professional programs:** pre-law, pre-dentistry, pre-medicine, pre-veterinary science, pre-optometry, pre-pharmacy. **Special academic programs:** accelerated program, cooperative (work-study plan) program, distance learning, double major, dual enrollment, honors program, independent study, internships, student-designed major, study abroad, teacher certificate program. **Teacher certifica-**

tion offered in: early childhood, special education, elementary, vo-tech, middle/junior high, secondary. **Faculty and instruction (2005-2006):** Total instructional faculty: 101 full-time, 9 part-time (65% men; 35% women; 5% minorities). Full-time faculty with Ph.D. or other terminal degree: 77%. Student/faculty ratio: 25/1. **Advanced Placement and International Baccalaureate credit:** AP tests may be used for: Credit and/or placement. **Freshmen returning for sophomore year:** 69%. **Graduation rates:** Four-year: 26%; five-year: 42%; six-year: 44%.

COSTS AND FINANCIAL AID

Financial aid office: (308) 432-6230. **Expenses (2006-2007):** Tuition and fees 2006-2007: $3,855 in state, $6,945 out of state; room/board: $4,065. **Financial aid:** Priority filing date for institution's financial aid form: June 1.

CAMPUS LIFE AND EXTRACURRICULAR ACTIVITIES

Campus housing available: coed dorms, women's dorms, men's dorms, apartments for married students, apartment for single students. Activities include: choral groups, concert band, dance, drama/theater, jazz band, literary magazine, music ensembles, musical theater, pep band, radio station, student government, student newspaper. Number of fraternities: 0; sororities: 0. **Sports program (2005-2006):** Member of NCAA II. *Men's intercollegiate varsity sports:* basketball, football, track and field (indoor), track and field (outdoor), wrestling. *Women's intercollegiate varsity sports:* basketball, golf, track and field (indoor), track and field (outdoor), volleyball.

SERVICES AND FACILITIES

Basic services: placement service, day care, health service, health insurance. **Remedial assistance:** reading, math, writing, study skills. **Counseling services:** minority student, career, personal, academic, older student, psychological. **For learning-disabled students:** Services include: remedial math, remedial English, remedial reading, untimed tests, oral tests, readers, tutors. **Information technology resources:** Students are not required to lease or own a computer. School does not have a wireless network. **Campus safety:** Security services offered: 24-hour foot-and-vehicle patrols, late-night transport/escort service, 24-hour emergency telephones, lighted pathways/sidewalks, controlled dormitory access (key, security card, etc).

TRANSFER AND INTERNATIONAL STUDENTS

Transfer students: May apply for admission for the following academic terms: Fall, Spring, Summer. Applicants do not need a minimum number of credits to apply. For fall 2005: Transfer applicants enrolled: 263. **International students:** Number of foreign undergraduates: 15 (1% of student body). Minimum TOEFL score required: 550 (paper); 213 (computer). Average TOEFL score: 570 (paper).

College of St. Mary

- **Address:** 1901 S. 72nd Street, Omaha, NE 68124-2377
- **Website:** http://www.csm.edu
- **Private; Religious affiliation:** Roman Catholic
- **Enrollment:** 641 full-time; 298 part-time

KEY STATS

✔ **U.S News College Ranking:** third tier, Comp. Coll.–Bachelor's (Midwest)
✔ **ACT Score (25th/75th percentile):** 18-23
✔ **Tuition:** 2006-2007: $19,120

Selectivity: Selective	**Room/board:** $6,070
Acceptance rate: 56%	**Average debt:** $18,047
Student/faculty ratio: 9/1	**Proportion who borrowed:** 91%

UNDERGRADUATE STUDENT BODY STATS

2005-2006 enrollment: 641 full-time; 298 part-time. Men: 0%; women: 100%. **Ethnic makeup:** African American: 7%; American-Indian: 1%; Asian American: 1%; Hispanic: 3%; White: 87%; International: 1%. **Religious preference:** Roman Catholic: 32%; Other: 68%.

ADMISSIONS FACTS AND FIGURES

Phone: (402) 399-2407. **Email:** enroll@csm.edu. **Website:** http://www.csm.edu. **Application deadlines for fall 2007:** Regular decision: Rolling. Early decision: Not offered. Early action: Not offered. Admission can be deferred. **Application fee:** $30. Common application is accepted. **Admissions requirements/recommendations:** High school units required (recommended): English: (4); Mathematics: (3); Science: (3); Foreign language: (1); Social studies: (2); History: (2). Tests: The college uses SAT or ACT scores in admissions decisions. Neither SAT nor ACT required. For admission to the fall 2007 entering class, the school will accept: ACT with writing, ACT without writing. Campus visit: Recommended. Admissions interview: Recommended. Off-campus interview: May be arranged. **Factors that count in admissions decisions:** *Academic:* Secondary school record: Very important. Class rank: Very important. Letters of recommendation: Considered. Standardized test scores: Very important. Essay: Important. *Nonacademic:* Interview: Considered. Extracurricular activities: Considered. Talent/ability: Considered. Character/personal qualities: Considered. Alumni/ae relationship: Not considered. Geographical residence: Not considered. State residency: Not considered. Religious affiliation/commitment: Not considered. Minority status: Not considered. Volunteer work: Considered. Work experience: Not considered. **Other schools with the greatest overlap in applicants:** Bellevue University; Creighton University; Nebraska Wesleyan University; University of Nebraska–Lincoln; University of Nebraska–Omaha. **Admissions statistics for the fall 2005 entering class:** Total applicants: 417. Total accepted: 233. 14% were from out of state. Overall acceptance rate: 56%. **Credentials of fall 2005 freshmen:** 11% ranked in the top 10 percent of their high school class; 46% were in the top 25 percent, and 75% were in the top half. (Proportion submitting class standing: 75%.) **Average high school grade point average:** 3.3. **First-year students submitting ACT scores:** 73%. Scores (25/75 percentile): English: 16-22, Math: 16-23, Composite: 18-23.

ACADEMICS

Year founded: 1923. **Academic calendar:** Semester. **Degrees offered:** certificate, associate, bachelor's, post-bachelor's certificate, master's. **Most popular majors:** 22% business/commerce, 21% nursing/registered nurse training (R.N., A.S.N., B.S.N., M.S.N.), 15% elementary education and teaching, 11% legal professions and studies, 6% computer and information sciences and support services. **Major fields of study:** biological and biomedical sciences; business, management, marketing, and related support services; education; English language and literature/letters; health professions and related clinical sciences; legal professions and studies; liberal arts and sciences studies, and humanities; mathematics and statistics; physical sciences; psychology; public administration and social service professions; visual and performing arts. **Areas of required coursework:** arts/fine arts, humanities, computer literacy, mathematics, English (including composition), philosophy, sciences (biological or physical), history, social science. **Pre-professional programs:** pre-law, pre-dentistry, pre-medicine, pre-veterinary science, pre-pharmacy. **Special academic programs (% participation):** accelerated program (7%), double major (1%), teacher certificate program (5%), weekend college (4%). **Teacher certification offered in:** early childhood, special education, elementary, middle/junior high, secondary. **Reserve Officers Training Corps (ROTC):** Army ROTC: Offered at cooperating institution (Creighton University); Air Force ROTC: Offered at cooperating institution (University of Nebraska at Omaha). **Faculty and instruction (2005-2006):** Total instructional faculty: 54 full-time, 115 part-time (25% men; 75% women; 4% minorities). Full-time faculty with Ph.D. or other terminal degree: 35%. Student/faculty ratio: 9/1. Classes of fewer than 20 students: 84%; of 20 to 49 students: 16%; of 50 or more students: 1%. **Advanced Placement and International Baccalaureate credit:** AP tests may be used for: Credit only. Scores accepted: 3, 4, 5. International Baccalaureate exams may be used for: Credit only. **Freshmen returning for sophomore year:** 69%. **Graduation rates:** Four-year: 39%; five-year: 46%; six-year: 48%. **Graduate study:** 35% of students pursue further study within one year; 28% within five years.

COSTS AND FINANCIAL AID

Financial aid office: (402) 399-2362. **Expenses (2006-2007):** Tuition and fees 2006-2007: $19,120; room/board: $6,070. Estimated books and supplies: $800; transportation: $2,475; personal expenses: $1,557. **Financial aid:** Priority filing date for institution's financial aid form: March 1; deadline: March 15. In 2005-2006, 77% of undergraduates applied for financial aid. Of those, 71% were determined to have financial need; 12% had their need fully met. Average financial aid package (proportion receiving): $10,127 (62%). Average amount of gift aid, such as scholarships or grants (proportion receiving): $7,014 (57%). Average amount of self-help aid, such as work study or loans (proportion receiving): $4,471 (51%). Average need-based loan (excluding PLUS or other private loans): $4,213. Among students who received need-based aid, the average percentage of need met: 51%. Among students who received aid based on merit, the average award (and the proportion receiving): $8,008 (15%). The average athletic scholarship (and the proportion receiving): $4,317 (2%). Average amount of debt of borrowers graduating in 2005: $18,047. Proportion who borrowed: 91%.

CAMPUS LIFE AND EXTRACURRICULAR ACTIVITIES

Campus housing available (% using): women's dorms (84%), other housing options (16%). Students who live in college-owned, operated, or affiliated housing: 15%. **Clubs and organizations:** Number of student organizations: 18. Activities include: choral groups, student government. Number of fraternities: 0; sororities: 0. Average proportion of students who stay on campus on weekends: 40%. **Sports program (2005-2006):** Member of NAIA. **Women's intercollegiate varsity sports:** basketball, cross-country, soccer, softball, volleyball.

SERVICES AND FACILITIES

Basic services: nonremedial tutoring, placement service, day care, health insurance. **Remedial assistance:** math, writing, study skills. **Counseling services:** minority student, career, personal, academic, older student, psychological, religious. **For learning-disabled students:** School does not offer a structured program with separate admission and additional fees. Total undergraduates in learning-disabled program or receiving services: 21. Services include: remedial math, remedial English, reading machines, tape recorders, diagnostic testing service, note-taking services, oral tests, learning center, readers, extended time for tests, tutors, texts on tape, exams on tape or computer, other testing accomodations. **Library:** Number of titles: 78,700; number of current serial subscriptions: 245. **Information technology resources:** Students are not required to lease or own a computer. Number of campus computers available to all students: 90. School has a wireless network. **Campus safety:** Security services offered: 24-hour foot-and-vehicle patrols, late-night transport/escort service, lighted pathways/sidewalks, controlled dormitory access (key, security card, etc).

TRANSFER AND INTERNATIONAL STUDENTS

Transfer students: May apply for admission for the following academic terms: Fall, Spring, Summer. Applicants need a minimum number of credits to apply. For fall 2005: Transfer applications received: 434. Transfer applicants offered admission: 226. Transfer applicants enrolled: 194. **International students:** Number of foreign undergraduates: 8 (1% of student body). Number of countries represented: 7. Minimum TOEFL score required: 550 (paper).

Concordia University

- **Address:** 800 N. Columbia, Seward, NE 68434
- **Website:** http://www.cune.edu
- **Private; Religious affiliation:** Missouri Synod Lutheran
- **Enrollment:** 1,091 full-time; 85 part-time

KEY STATS

✔ **U.S News College Ranking:** 37, Universities–Master's (Midwest)
✔ **ACT Score (25th/75th percentile):** 20-27
✔ **Tuition:** 2006-2007: $18,750

Selectivity: Selective	**Room/board:** $4,940
Acceptance rate: 88%	**Average debt:** $15,522
Student/faculty ratio: N/A	**Proportion who borrowed:** 86%

UNDERGRADUATE STUDENT BODY STATS

2005-2006 enrollment: 1,091 full-time; 85 part-time. Men: 45%; women: 55%. **Ethnic makeup:** African American: 1%; Hispanic: 2%; White: 95%; International: 1%. **Religious preference:** Roman Catholic: 6%; Protestant: 13%; No preference: 1%; Unknown: 4%; Missouri Synod Lutheran: 76%.

ADMISSIONS FACTS AND FIGURES

Phone: (800) 535-5494. **Email:** admiss@seward.cune.edu. **Website:** http://www.cune.edu. **Application deadlines for fall 2007:** Regular decision: August 1. Early decision: Not offered. Early action: Not offered. Admission cannot be deferred. **Application fee:** $25. Common application is not accepted. **Admissions requirements/recommendations:** High school units required (recommended): English: (4); Mathematics: (3); Science: (2); Foreign language: (2); Social studies: (3). Tests: The college uses SAT or ACT scores in admissions decisions. Either SAT or ACT required. For admission to the fall 2007 entering class, the school will accept: ACT with writing, ACT without writing. Campus visit: Recommended. Admissions interview: Recommended. Off-campus interview: May be arranged. **Factors that count in admissions decisions:** *Academic:* Secondary school record: Very important. Class rank: Important. Letters of recommendation: Considered. Standardized test scores: Very important. Essay: Not considered. *Nonacademic:* Interview: Not considered. Extracurricular activities: Not considered. Talent/ability: Not considered. Character/personal qualities: Not considered. Alumni/ae relationship: Not considered. Geographical residence: Not considered. State residency: Not considered. Religious affiliation/commitment: Not considered. Minority status: Not considered. Volunteer work: Not considered. Work experience: Not considered. **Other schools with the greatest overlap in applicants:** Doane College; Hastings College; Nebraska Wesleyan University; University of Nebraska–Kearney; University of Nebraska–Lincoln. **Admissions statistics for the fall 2005 entering class:** Total applicants: 784. Total accepted: 691. Freshmen enrolled: 291; 41% were from out of state. Overall acceptance rate: 88%. **Credentials of fall 2005 freshmen:** 22% ranked in the top 10 percent of their high school class; 44% were in the top 25 percent, and 73% were in the top half. (Proportion submitting class standing: 90%.) **Average high school grade point average:** 3.4. **First-year students who submitted SAT scores:** 25%. Scores (25/75 percentile): Verbal: 450-600, Math: 450-580, Combined: 900-1180. **First-year students submitting ACT scores:** 91%. Scores (25/75 percentile): English: N/A, Math: N/A, Composite: 20-27.

ACADEMICS

Year founded: 1894. **Academic calendar:** Semester. **Degrees offered:** bachelor's, master's. **Most popular majors:** 39% education, 18% business, management, marketing, and related support services, 11% theology and religious vocations, 6% biological and biomedical sciences, 6% visual and performing arts. **Major fields of study:** biological and biomedical sciences; business, management, marketing, and related support services; communication, journalism, and related programs; computer and information sciences and support services; education; English language and literature/letters; history; mathematics and statistics; multi/interdisciplinary studies; parks, recreation, leisure, and fitness studies; physical sciences; psychology; social sciences; theology and religious vocations; visual and performing arts. **Areas of required coursework:** arts/fine arts, humanities, mathematics, English (including composition), sciences (biological or physical), history, social science, other. **Pre-professional programs:** pre-law, pre-dentistry, pre-medicine, pre-theology, pre-veterinary science, pre-pharmacy. **Special academic programs (% participation):** accelerated program (10%), distance learning (4%), double major (21%), English as a Second Language (ESL) (1%), exchange student program (domestic) (5%), independent study (20%), internships (70%), study abroad (2%), teacher certificate program (40%). **Teacher certification offered in:** early childhood, special education, elementary, middle/junior high, secondary, bilingual/bicultural. **Reserve Officers Training Corps (ROTC):** Army ROTC: Offered at cooperating institution (University of Nebraska-Lincoln); Air Force ROTC: Offered at cooperating institution (University of Nebraska-Lincoln). **Faculty and instruction (2005-2006):** Total instructional faculty: 54 full-time, 85 part-time (55% men; 45% women; 1% minorities). Full-time faculty with Ph.D. or other terminal degree: 78%. Classes of fewer than 20 students: 54%; of 20 to 49 students: 46%; of 50 or more students: 0%. **Advanced Placement and International Baccalaureate credit:** AP tests may be used for: Credit and/or placement. Scores accepted: 3, 4, 5. International Baccalaureate exams may be used for: Credit and/or placement. **Freshmen returning for sophomore year:** 79%. **Graduation rates:** Four-year: 32%; five-year: 53%; six-year: 59%.

COSTS AND FINANCIAL AID

Financial aid office: (402) 643-7270. **Expenses (2006-2007):** Tuition and fees 2006-2007: $18,750; room/board: $4,940. Estimated books and supplies: $700; transportation: $900; personal expenses: $1,200. **Financial aid:** Priority filing date for institution's financial aid form: March 1; deadline: May 1. In 2005-2006, 91% of undergraduates applied for financial aid. Of those, 80% were determined to have financial need; 75% had their need fully met. Average financial aid package (proportion receiving): $15,019 (80%). Average amount of gift aid, such as scholarships or grants (proportion receiving): $4,471 (64%). Average amount of self-help aid, such as work study or loans (proportion receiving): $3,547 (35%). Average need-based loan (excluding PLUS or other private loans): $3,572. Among students who received need-based aid, the average percentage of need met: 91%. Among students who received aid based on merit, the average award (and the proportion receiving): $5,896 (20%). The average athletic scholarship (and the proportion receiving): $4,166 (32%). Average amount of debt of borrowers graduating in 2005: $15,522. Proportion who borrowed: 86%.

CAMPUS LIFE AND EXTRACURRICULAR ACTIVITIES

Campus housing available (% using): women's dorms (55%), men's dorms (43%), apartments for married students (1%), apartment for single students (1%), special housing for disabled students. Students who live in college-owned, operated, or affiliated housing: 70%. **Student employment:** During the 2005-2006 academic year, 50% of undergraduates worked on campus. Average per-year earnings: $753. **Clubs and organizations:** Number of student organizations: 35. Activities include: choral groups, concert band, drama/theater, jazz band, literary magazine, music ensembles, pep band, student government, student newspaper, yearbook. Number of fraternities: 0; sororities: 0. **Sports program (2005-2006):** Member of NAIA. *Men's intercollegiate varsity sports:* baseball, basketball, cross-country, football, golf, soccer, tennis, track and field (indoor), track and field (outdoor). *Women's intercollegiate varsity sports:* basketball, cross-country, golf, soccer, softball, tennis, track and field (indoor), track and field (outdoor), volleyball.

SERVICES AND FACILITIES

Basic services: nonremedial tutoring, placement service, health service, health insurance. **Remedial assistance:** writing, study skills, other. **Counseling services:** career, personal, academic, psychological, religious. **For learning-disabled students:** School does not offer a structured program with separate admission and additional fees. Total undergraduates in learning-disabled program or receiving services: 12. Services include: tape recorders, note-taking services, learning center, readers, extended time for tests, tutors, proofreading services, other testing accomodations, other. **Library:** Number of titles: 241,123; number of current serial subscriptions: 12,415. **Information technology resources:** Students are not required to lease or own a computer. Number of campus computers available to all students: 162. School does not have a wireless network. Proportion of college-owned housing units wired for high-speed internet access: 100%. **Campus safety:** Security services offered: 24-hour foot-and-vehicle patrols, 24-hour emergency telephones, lighted pathways/sidewalks, controlled dormitory access (key, security card, etc).

TRANSFER AND INTERNATIONAL STUDENTS

Transfer students: May apply for admission for the following academic terms: Fall, Spring. Applicants do not need a minimum number of credits to apply. For fall 2005: Transfer applications received: 111. Transfer applicants offered admission: 74. Transfer applicants enrolled: 51. **International students:** Number of foreign undergraduates: 8 (1% of student body). Number of countries represented: 4. Minimum TOEFL score required: 500 (paper); 173 (computer). Average TOEFL score: 500 (paper).

Creighton University

■ **Address:** 2500 California Plaza, Omaha, NE 68178
■ **Website:** http://www.creighton.edu
■ **Private; Religious affiliation:** Roman Catholic (Jesuit)
■ **Enrollment:** 3,731 full-time; 257 part-time

KEY STATS

✔ **U.S News College Ranking:** 1, Universities–Master's (Midwest)
✔ **ACT Score (25th/75th percentile):** 23-29
✔ **Tuition:** 2006-2007: $23,832

Selectivity: More selective	**Room/board:** $7,842
Acceptance rate: 87%	**Average debt:** $26,013
Student/faculty ratio: 12/1	**Proportion who borrowed:** 74%

UNDERGRADUATE STUDENT BODY STATS

2005-2006 enrollment: 3,731 full-time; 257 part-time. Men: 41%; women: 59%. **Ethnic makeup:** African American: 3%; American-Indian: 1%; Asian American: 7%; Hispanic: 4%; White: 84%; International: 1%.

ADMISSIONS FACTS AND FIGURES

Phone: (800) 282-5835. **Email:** admissions@creighton.edu. **Website:** http://www.creighton.edu. **Application deadlines for fall 2007:** Regular decision: August 1. Early decision: Not offered. Early action: Not offered. Admission can be deferred. **Application fee:** $40. Common application is accepted. **To apply online, go to:** http://admissions.creighton.edu/onlineapp.html. **Admissions requirements/recommendations:** High school units required (recommended): English: 4 (4); Mathematics: 3 (3); Science: 2 (2); Foreign language: 2 (2); Social studies: 1 (1); History: 1 (1); Academic electives: 3 (3); Total units: 16 (16). Tests: The college uses SAT or ACT scores in admissions decisions. Either SAT or ACT required. For admission to the fall 2007 entering class, the school will accept: ACT with writing, ACT without writing. Campus visit: Recommended. Admissions interview: Recommended. Off-campus interview: May be arranged. **Factors that count in admissions decisions:** *Academic:* Secondary school record: Very important. Class rank: Considered. Letters of recommendation: Considered. Standardized test scores: Important. Essay: Important. *Nonacademic:* Interview: Not considered. Extracurricular activities: Considered. Talent/ability: Considered. Character/personal qualities: Considered. Alumni/ae relationship: Not considered. Geographical residence: Not considered. State residency: Not considered. Religious affiliation/commitment: Not considered. Minority status: Considered. Volunteer work: Considered. Work experience: Not considered. **Other schools with the greatest overlap in applicants:** Drake University; Marquette University; St. Louis University; University of Nebraska–Lincoln; University of Notre Dame. **Admissions statistics for the fall 2005 entering class:** Total applicants: 3,435. Total accepted: 2,985. Freshmen enrolled: 971; 58% were from out of state. Overall acceptance rate: 87%. **Size of waiting list:** 85 applicants; enrolled from waiting list: 10. **Credentials of fall 2005 freshmen:** 40% ranked in the top 10 percent of their high school class; 73% were in the top 25 percent, and 95% were in the top half. (Proportion submitting class standing: 76%.) **Average high school grade point average:** 3.7. First-year students who submitted SAT scores: 39%. Scores (25/75 percentile): Verbal: 530-660, Math: 540-660, Combined: 1070-1320. **First-year students submitting ACT scores:** 91%. Scores (25/75 percentile): English: 23-29, Math: 23-28, Composite: 23-29.

ACADEMICS

Year founded: 1878. **Academic calendar:** Semester. **Degrees offered:** certificate, associate, bachelor's, post-bachelor's certificate, master's, post-master's certificate, first professional, doctorate. **Most popular majors:** 26% health professions and related clinical sciences, 21% business administration and management, 13% nursing, 6% communication, journalism, and related programs, 6% psychology. **Major fields of study:** area, ethnic, cultural, and gender studies; business, management, marketing, and related support services; communication, journalism, and related programs; education; English language and literature/letters; foreign languages, literatures, and linguistics; history; multi/interdisciplinary studies; philosophy and religious studies; psychology; social sciences; theology and religious vocations; visual and performing arts. **Areas of required coursework:** arts/fine arts, humanities, mathematics, English (including composition), philosophy, foreign languages, sciences (biological or physical), history, social science, other. **Pre-professional programs:** pre-law, pre-dentistry, pre-medicine, pre-theology, pre-veterinary science, pre-optometry, pre-pharmacy, other. **Special academic programs:** accelerated program, cross-registration, distance learning, double major, dual enrollment, English as a Second Language (ESL), honors program, independent study, internships, study abroad, teacher certificate program. **Teacher certification offered in:** special education, elementary, middle/junior high, secondary, bilingual/bicultural. **Reserve Officers Training Corps (ROTC):** Army ROTC: Offered on campus; Air Force ROTC: Offered at cooperating institution (University of Nebraska at Omaha). **Faculty and instruction (2005-2006):** Total instructional faculty: 475 full-time, 174 part-time (57% men; 43% women; 11% minorities). Full-time faculty with Ph.D. or other terminal degree: 85%. Student/faculty ratio: 12/1. Classes of fewer than 20 students: 46%; of 20 to 49 students: 49%; of 50 or more students: 4%. **Advanced Placement and International Baccalaureate credit:** AP tests may be used for: Credit and/or placement. Scores accepted: 3, 4, 5. International Baccalaureate exams may be used for: Credit and/or placement. **Freshmen returning for sophomore year:** 87%. **Graduation rates:** Four-year: 63%; five-year: 73%; six-year: 72%. **Graduate study:** 40% of students pursue further study immediately upon graduation; 55% within one year. Fields in which graduates pursue further study: Master of Business Administration (MBA), 9%; law, 10%; medicine, 22%; dentistry, 4%; education, 4%; arts and sciences, 51%.

COSTS AND FINANCIAL AID

Financial aid office: (402) 280-2731. **Expenses (2006-2007):** Tuition and fees 2006-2007: $23,832; room/board: $7,842. Estimated books and supplies: $1,000; transportation: $800; personal expenses: $1,400. **Financial aid:** Priority filing date for institution's financial aid form: April 1. In 2005-2006, 67% of undergraduates applied for financial aid. Of those, 55% were determined to have financial need; 52% had their need fully met. Average financial aid package (proportion receiving): $20,201 (55%). Average amount of gift aid, such as scholarships or grants (proportion receiving): $12,003 (50%). Average amount of self-help aid, such as work study or loans (proportion receiving): $7,606 (49%). Average need-based loan

(excluding PLUS or other private loans): $6,575. Among students who received need-based aid, the average percentage of need met: 86%. Among students who received aid based on merit, the average award (and the proportion receiving): $8,627 (34%). The average athletic scholarship (and the proportion receiving): $16,746 (4%). Average amount of debt of borrowers graduating in 2005: $26,013. Proportion who borrowed: 74%.

CAMPUS LIFE AND EXTRACURRICULAR ACTIVITIES

Campus housing available (% using): coed dorms (67%), women's dorms (8%), apartments for married students (4%), apartment for single students (21%), special housing for disabled students (0%). Students who live in college-owned, operated, or affiliated housing: 59%. **Student employment:** During the 2005-2006 academic year, 30% of undergraduates worked on campus. Average per-year earnings: $1,700. **Clubs and organizations:** Number of student organizations: 180. Activities include: choral groups, concert band, dance, drama/theater, jazz band, literary magazine, music ensembles, musical theater, pep band, student government, student newspaper, symphony orchestra, yearbook. Number of fraternities: 5; sororities: 5. Proportion of men in fraternities: 21%; of women in sororities: 28%. Average proportion of students who stay on campus on weekends: 80%. **Sports program (2005-2006):** Member of NCAA I. *Men's intercollegiate varsity sports:* baseball, basketball, cross-country, golf, soccer, tennis. *Women's intercollegiate varsity sports:* basketball, crew, cross-country, golf, soccer, softball, tennis, volleyball.

SERVICES AND FACILITIES

Basic services: nonremedial tutoring, women's center, placement service, day care, health service, health insurance. **Remedial assistance:** reading, math, writing, study skills. **Counseling services:** minority student, career, military, personal, veteran student, academic, older student, psychological, religious. **For learning-disabled students:** School does not offer a structured program with separate admission and additional fees. Total undergraduates in learning-disabled program or receiving services: 45. Services include: reading machines, tape recorders, diagnostic testing service, note-taking services, oral tests, readers, extended time for tests, tutors, priority registration, priority seating, proofreading services, substitution of courses, texts on tape, typist/scribe, exams on tape or computer, other testing accomodations, other. **Library:** Number of titles: 886,703; number of current serial subscriptions: 29,630. **Information technology resources:** Students are not required to lease or own a computer. Number of campus computers available to all students: 780. School has a wireless network. Proportion of college-owned housing units wired for high-speed internet access: 100%. **Campus safety:** Security services offered: 24-hour foot-and-vehicle patrols, late-night transport/escort service, 24-hour emergency telephones, lighted pathways/sidewalks, student patrols, controlled dormitory access (key, security card, etc).

TRANSFER AND INTERNATIONAL STUDENTS

Transfer students: May apply for admission for the following academic terms: Fall, Spring. Applicants need a minimum number of credits to apply. For fall 2005: Transfer applications received: 285. Transfer applicants offered admission: 166. Transfer applicants enrolled: 107. **International students:** Number of foreign undergraduates: 24 (1% of student body). Number of countries represented: 43. Minimum TOEFL score required: 550 (paper); 213 (computer). Average TOEFL score: 580 (paper).

Dana College

- **Address:** 2848 College Drive, Blair, NE 68008-1099
- **Website:** http://www.dana.edu
- **Private; Religious affiliation:** Lutheran
- **Enrollment:** 653 full-time; 23 part-time

KEY STATS

✔ **U.S News College Ranking:** third tier, Comp. Coll.–Bachelor's (Midwest)
✔ **ACT Score (25th/75th percentile):** 19-24
✔ **Tuition:** 2006-2007: $18,650

Selectivity: Selective	Room/board: $5,810
Acceptance rate: 76%	Average debt: $17,774
Student/faculty ratio: 12/1	Proportion who borrowed: 89%

UNDERGRADUATE STUDENT BODY STATS

2005-2006 enrollment: 653 full-time; 23 part-time. Men: 55%; women: 45%. **Ethnic makeup:** African American: 5%; American-Indian: 1%; Asian American: 1%; Hispanic: 3%; White: 90%; International: 1%. **Religious preference:** Roman Catholic: 21%; Protestant: 1%; Jewish: 1%; No preference: 5%; Unknown: 18%; Lutheran: 25%; Other: 29%.

ADMISSIONS FACTS AND FIGURES

Phone: (800) 444-3262. **Email:** admissions@dana.edu. **Website:** http://www.dana.edu. **Application deadlines for fall 2007:** Regular decision: August 1. Early decision: Not offered. Early action: Not offered. Admission can be deferred. Common application is not accepted. **Admissions requirements/recommendations:** High school units required (recommended): English: (4); Mathematics: (3); Science: (3); Foreign language: (2); Social studies: (4); Total units: (16). Tests: The college uses SAT or ACT scores in admissions decisions. Either SAT or ACT required. For admission to the fall 2007 entering class, the school will accept: ACT with writing, ACT without writing. Campus visit: Recommended. Admissions interview: Neither required nor recommended. Off-campus interview: Not available. **Factors that count in admissions decisions:** *Academic:* Secondary school record: Very important. Class rank: Considered. Letters of recommendation: Considered. Standardized test scores: Very important. Essay: Considered. *Nonacademic:* Interview: Considered. Extracurricular activities: Considered. Talent/ability: Not considered. Character/personal qualities: Considered. Alumni/ae relationship: Considered. Geographical residence: Not considered. State residency: Not considered. Religious affiliation/commitment: Not considered. Minority status: Not considered. Volunteer work: Considered. Work experience: Considered. **Other schools with the greatest overlap in applicants:** Midland Lutheran College; Morningside College; Nebraska Wesleyan University; University of Nebraska–Lincoln; University of Nebraska–Omaha. **Admissions statistics for the fall 2005 entering class:** Total applicants: 901. Total accepted: 686. Freshmen enrolled: 208; 40% were from out of state. Overall acceptance rate: 76%. **Credentials of fall 2005 freshmen:** 10% ranked in the top 10 percent of their high school class; 35% were in the top 25 percent, and 66% were in the top half. (Proportion submitting class standing: 92%.) **Average high school grade point average:** 3.3. **First-year students who submitted SAT scores:** 9%. Scores (25/75 percentile): Verbal: 420-540, Math: 430-520, Combined: 850-1060. **First-year students submitting ACT scores:** 96%. Scores (25/75 percentile): English: 18-24, Math: 18-24, Composite: 19-24.

ACADEMICS

Year founded: 1884. **Academic calendar:** 4-1-4. **Degrees offered:** bachelor's. **Most popular majors:** 29% education, 27% business, management, marketing, and related support services, 7% parks, recreation, leisure, and fitness studies, 6% biological and biomedical sciences, 5% psychology. **Major fields of study:** biological and biomedical sciences; business, management, marketing, and related support services; communication, journalism, and related programs; computer and information sciences and support services; education; English language and literature/letters; foreign languages, literatures, and linguistics; health professions and related clinical sciences; history; legal professions and studies; mathematics and statistics; natural resources and conservation; parks, recreation, leisure, and fitness studies; philosophy and religious studies; physical sciences; psychology; public administration and social service professions; security and protective services; visual and performing arts. **Areas of required coursework:** arts/fine arts, humanities, mathematics, English (including composition), foreign languages, sciences (biological or physical), history, social science, other. **Pre-professional programs:** pre-law, pre-dentistry, pre-medicine, pre-theology, pre-veterinary science, pre-optometry, pre-pharmacy, other. **Special academic programs:** cross-registration, double major, dual enrollment, English as a Second Language (ESL), honors program, independent study, internships, liberal arts/career combination, student-designed major, study abroad, teacher certificate program. **Teacher certification offered in:** special education, elementary, secondary. **Reserve Officers Training Corps (ROTC):** Army ROTC: Offered at cooperating institution (Creighton University); Navy ROTC: Offered at cooperating institution (University of Nebraska-Omaha). **Faculty and instruction (2005-2006):** Total instructional faculty: 42 full-time, 33 part-time (49% men; 51% women; 4% minorities). Full-time faculty with Ph.D. or other terminal degree: 69%. Student/faculty ratio: 12/1. Classes of fewer than 20 students: 67%; of 20 to 49 students: 31%; of 50 or more students: 2%. **Advanced Placement and International Baccalaureate credit:** International Baccalaureate exams may be used for: Credit and/or placement. **Freshmen returning for sophomore year:** 63%. **Graduation rates:** Four-year: 35%; five-year: 49%; six-year: 51%. **Graduate study:** 6% of students pursue further study immediately upon graduation; 1% within one year; 1% within five years. Fields in which graduates pursue further study: law, 1%; medicine, 2%; arts and sciences, 2%.

COSTS AND FINANCIAL AID

Financial aid office: (402) 426-7226. **Expenses (2006-2007):** Tuition and fees 2006-2007: $18,650; room/board: $5,810. Estimated books and supplies: $800; transportation: $500; personal expenses: $1,330. **Financial aid:** Priority filing date for institution's financial aid form: March 15. In 2005-2006, 94% of undergraduates applied for financial aid. Of those, 81% were determined to have financial need; 32% had their need fully met. Average financial aid package (proportion receiving): $15,665 (81%). Average amount of gift aid, such as scholarships or grants (proportion receiving): $4,321 (48%). Average amount of self-help aid, such as work study or loans (proportion receiving): $4,440 (65%). Average need-based loan (excluding PLUS or other private loans): $4,133. Among students who received need-based aid, the average percentage of need met: 88%. Among students who received aid based on merit, the average award (and the proportion receiving): $5,686 (13%). The average athletic scholarship (and the proportion receiving): $7,047 (60%). Average amount of debt of borrowers graduating in 2005: $17,774. Proportion who borrowed: 89%.

CAMPUS LIFE AND EXTRACURRICULAR ACTIVITIES

Campus housing available (% using): coed dorms (90%), women's dorms (9%), apartments for married students (1%). Students who live in college-owned, operated, or affiliated housing: 63%. **Student employment:** During the 2005-2006 academic year, 21% of undergraduates worked on campus. Average per-year earnings: $350. **Clubs and organizations:** Number of student organizations: 25. Activities include: choral groups, concert band, dance, drama/theater, jazz band, literary magazine, music ensembles, musical theater, pep band, student government, student newspaper, student film society, television station, yearbook. Number of fraternities: 0; sororities: 0. Average proportion of students who stay on campus on weekends: 68%. **Sports program (2005-2006):** Member of NAIA. *Men's intercollegiate varsity sports:* baseball, basketball, cross-country, football, soccer, track and field (indoor), track and field (outdoor), wrestling. *Women's intercollegiate varsity sports:* basketball, cross-country, golf, soccer, softball, track and field (indoor), track and field (outdoor), volleyball.

SERVICES AND FACILITIES

Basic services: placement service, health service, health insurance. **Remedial assistance:** study skills. **Counseling services:** career, personal, academic, religious. **For learning-disabled students:** School does not offer a structured program with separate admission and additional fees. Services include: remedial math, remedial English, reading machines, tape recorders, diagnostic testing service, untimed tests, note-taking services, learning center, readers, extended time for tests, tutors, other testing accomodations. **Library:** Number of titles: 158,752; number of current serial subscriptions: 14,200. **Information technology resources:** Students are not required to lease or own a computer. Number of campus computers available to all students: 110. School has a wireless network. Approximate number of users that can be accommodated: 1,000. Proportion of college-owned housing units wired for high-speed internet access: 100%. **Campus safety:** Security services offered: 24-hour foot-and-vehicle patrols, late-night transport/escort service, 24-hour emergency telephones, lighted pathways/sidewalks, student patrols, controlled dormitory access (key, security card, etc).

TRANSFER AND INTERNATIONAL STUDENTS

Transfer students: May apply for admission for the following academic terms: Fall, Winter, Spring, Summer. Applicants need a minimum number of credits to apply. For fall 2005: Transfer applications received: 118. Transfer applicants offered admission: 113. Transfer applicants enrolled: 59. **International students:** Number of foreign undergraduates: 4 (1% of student body). Number of countries represented: 2. Minimum TOEFL score required: 500 (paper); 173 (computer).

Doane College

- **Address:** 1014 Boswell Avenue, Crete, NE 68333
- **Website:** http://www.doane.edu
- **Private; Religious affiliation:** United Church of Christ
- **Enrollment:** 1,349 full-time; 247 part-time

KEY STATS

✔ **U.S News College Ranking:** 23, Universities–Master's (Midwest)
✔ **ACT Score (25th/75th percentile):** 20-27
✔ **Tuition:** 2006-2007: $18,770

Selectivity: Selective	**Room/board:** $5,150
Acceptance rate: 81%	**Average debt:** $14,915
Student/faculty ratio: 10/1	**Proportion who borrowed:** 79%

UNDERGRADUATE STUDENT BODY STATS

2005-2006 enrollment: 1,349 full-time; 247 part-time. Men: 51%; women: 49%. **Ethnic makeup:** African American: 2%; Asian American: 2%; Hispanic: 1%; White: 94%.

ADMISSIONS FACTS AND FIGURES

Phone: (402) 826-8222. **Email:** admissions@doane.edu. **Website:** http://www.doane.edu. **Application deadlines for fall 2007:** Regular decision: Rolling. Early decision: Not offered. Early action: Not offered. Admission can be deferred. **Application fee:** $20. Common application is accepted. **To apply online, go to:** http://www.doane.edu/apply. **Admissions requirements/recommendations:** High school units required (recommended): English: (4); Mathematics: (3); Science: (3); Foreign language: (2); Social studies: (3). Tests: The college uses SAT or ACT scores in admissions decisions. Either SAT or ACT required. For admission to the fall 2007 entering class, the school will accept: ACT with writing, ACT without writing. Campus visit: Recommended. Admissions interview: Neither required nor recommended. Off-campus interview: May be arranged. **Factors that count in admissions decisions:** *Academic:* Secondary school record: Very important. Class rank: Considered. Letters of recommendation: Important. Standardized test scores: Important. Essay: Important. *Nonacademic:* Interview: Not considered. Extracurricular activities: Considered. Talent/ability: Considered. Character/personal qualities: Important. Alumni/ae relationship: Not considered. Geographical residence: Not considered. State residency: Not considered. Religious affiliation/commitment: Not considered. Minority status: Not considered. Volunteer work: Considered. Work experience: Considered. **Other schools with the greatest overlap in applicants:** Hastings College; Nebraska Wesleyan University; University of Nebraska–Lincoln. **Admissions statistics for the fall 2005 entering class:** Total applicants: 1,127. Total accepted: 913. Freshmen enrolled: 262; 17% were from out of state. Overall acceptance rate: 81%. **Credentials of fall 2005 freshmen:** 12% ranked in the top 10 percent of their high school class; 51% were in the top 25 percent, and 78% were in the top half. (Proportion submitting class standing: 98%.) **Average high school grade point average:** 3.4. **First-year students who submitted SAT scores:** 10%. Scores (25/75 percentile): Verbal: 460-590, Math: 460-660, Combined: 920-1250. **First-year students submitting ACT scores:** 96%. Scores (25/75 percentile): English: 20-28, Math: 19-27, Composite: 20-27.

ACADEMICS

Year founded: 1872. **Academic calendar:** 4-1-4. **Degrees offered:** bachelor's, master's. **Most popular majors:** 27% social sciences, 21% education, 13% biological and biomedical sciences, 7% visual and performing arts, 5% psychology. **Major fields of study:** biological and biomedical sciences; communication, journalism, and related programs; computer and information sciences and support services; education; English language and literature/letters; foreign languages, literatures, and linguistics; history; mathematics and statistics; multi/interdisciplinary studies; parks, recreation, leisure, and fitness studies; philosophy and religious studies; physical sciences; psychology; public administration and social service professions; social sciences; visual and performing arts. **Areas of required coursework:** arts/fine arts, humanities, mathematics, English (including composition), philosophy, sciences (biological or physical), history, social science. **Pre-professional programs:** pre-law, pre-dentistry, pre-medicine, pre-theology, pre-veterinary science, pre-optometry, pre-pharmacy, other. **Special academic programs:** double major, dual enrollment, English as a Second Language (ESL), honors program, independent study, internships, liberal arts/career combination, student-designed major, study abroad, teacher certificate pro-

gram. **Teacher certification offered in:** early childhood, special education, elementary, middle/junior high, secondary. **Cooperative education programs:** engineering, health professions. **Reserve Officers Training Corps (ROTC):** Army ROTC: Offered at cooperating institution (University of Nebraska); Air Force ROTC: Offered at cooperating institution (University of Nebraska). **Faculty and instruction (2005-2006):** Total instructional faculty: 77 full-time, 63 part-time (; 4% minorities). Full-time faculty with Ph.D. or other terminal degree: 65%. Student/faculty ratio: 10/1. Classes of fewer than 20 students: 77%; of 20 to 49 students: 23%. **Advanced Placement and International Baccalaureate credit:** AP tests may be used for: Credit only. Scores accepted: 3, 4, 5. International Baccalaureate exams may be used for: Credit only. **Freshmen returning for sophomore year:** 78%. **Graduation rates:** Four-year: 62%; five-year: 66%; six-year: 64%.

COSTS AND FINANCIAL AID

Financial aid office: (402) 826-8260. **Expenses (2006-2007):** Tuition and fees 2006-2007: $18,770; room/board: $5,150. Estimated books and supplies: $800; transportation: $600; personal expenses: $1,030. **Financial aid:** Priority filing date for institution's financial aid form: March 1. In 2005-2006, 91% of undergraduates applied for financial aid. Of those, 78% were determined to have financial need; 59% had their need fully met. Average financial aid package (proportion receiving): $14,435 (78%). Average amount of gift aid, such as scholarships or grants (proportion receiving): $10,360 (77%). Average amount of self-help aid, such as work study or loans (proportion receiving): $4,521 (70%). Average need-based loan (excluding PLUS or other private loans): $4,207. Among students who received need-based aid, the average percentage of need met: 95%. Among students who received aid based on merit, the average award (and the proportion receiving): $9,358 (9%). The average athletic scholarship (and the proportion receiving): $0 (0%). Average amount of debt of borrowers graduating in 2005: $14,915. Proportion who borrowed: 79%.

CAMPUS LIFE AND EXTRACURRICULAR ACTIVITIES

Campus housing available: coed dorms, women's dorms, men's dorms. Students who live in college-owned, operated, or affiliated housing: 84%. **Student employment:** During the 2005-2006 academic year, 14% of undergraduates worked on campus. Average per-year earnings: $500. **Clubs and organizations:** Number of student organizations: 77. Activities include: choral groups, concert band, dance, drama/theater, jazz band, literary magazine, music ensembles, pep band, radio station, student government, student newspaper, television station, yearbook. Number of fraternities: 5; sororities: 4. Proportion of men in fraternities: 31%; of women in sororities: 28%. Average proportion of students who stay on campus on weekends: 80%. **Sports program (2005-2006):** Member of NAIA. *Men's intercollegiate varsity sports:* baseball, basketball, cross-country, football, golf, soccer, tennis, track and field (indoor), track and field (outdoor). *Women's intercollegiate varsity sports:* basketball, cross-country, golf, soccer, softball, tennis, track and field (indoor), track and field (outdoor), volleyball.

SERVICES AND FACILITIES

Basic services: nonremedial tutoring, placement service, health service. **Remedial assistance:** reading, math, writing, study skills. **Counseling services:** minority student, academic. **For learning-disabled students:** School does not offer a structured program with separate admission and additional fees. Services include: remedial math, tape recorders, note-taking services, learning center, extended time for tests, tutors, other. **Library:** Number of titles: 88,829; number of current serial subscriptions: 939. **Information technology resources:** Students are not required to lease or own a computer. Number of campus computers available to all students: 350. School has a wireless network. Approximate number of users that can be accommodated: 450. Proportion of college-owned housing units wired for high-speed internet access: 100%. **Campus safety:** Security services offered: 24-hour foot-and-vehicle patrols, lighted pathways/sidewalks.

TRANSFER AND INTERNATIONAL STUDENTS

Transfer students: May apply for admission for the following academic terms: Fall, Spring. Applicants need a minimum number of credits to apply. For fall 2005: Transfer applications received: 99. Transfer applicants offered admission: 52. Transfer applicants enrolled: 30. **International students:** Number of foreign undergraduates: 4. Minimum TOEFL score required: 525 (paper); 525 (computer).

Grace University

- **Address:** 1311 S. Ninth Street, Omaha, NE 68108-3629
- **Website:** http://www.graceuniversity.edu
- **Private; Religious affiliation:** Christian interdenominational
- **Enrollment:** N/A

KEY STATS

✔ **U.S News College Ranking:** third tier, Comp. Coll.–Bachelor's (Midwest)
✔ **ACT Score (25th/75th percentile):** 19-26
✔ **Tuition:** 2006-2007: $11,980

Selectivity: Selective	**Room/board:** $5,300
Acceptance rate: 39%	**Average debt:** $18,502
Student/faculty ratio: N/A	**Proportion who borrowed:** 98%

Hastings College

- **Address:** 710 N. Turner Avenue, Hastings, NE 68901-7621
- **Website:** http://www.hastings.edu
- **Private; Religious affiliation:** Presbyterian Church (USA)
- **Enrollment:** 1,121 full-time; 23 part-time

KEY STATS

✔ **U.S News College Ranking:** fourth tier, Liberal Arts Colleges
✔ **ACT Score (25th/75th percentile):** 20-26
✔ **Tuition:** 2005-2006: $17,268

Selectivity: Selective	**Room/board:** $4,950
Acceptance rate: 79%	**Average debt:** N/A
Student/faculty ratio: 12/1	**Proportion who borrowed:** N/A

UNDERGRADUATE STUDENT BODY STATS

2005-2006 enrollment: 1,121 full-time; 23 part-time. Men: 51%; women: 49%. **Ethnic makeup:** African American: 3%; Asian American: 1%; Hispanic: 2%; White: 94%; International: 1%. **Religious preference:** Roman Catholic: 22%; Protestant: 31%; Presbyterian Church (USA): 7%; Other: 40%.

ADMISSIONS FACTS AND FIGURES

Phone: (402) 461-7403. **Email:** mmolliconi@hastings.edu. **Website:** http://www.hastings.edu. **Application deadlines for fall 2007:** Regular decision: August 1. Early decision: Not offered. Early action: Not offered. Admission cannot be deferred. **Application fee:** $20. Common application is accepted. **Admissions requirements/recommendations:** High school units required (recommended): English: 3 (4); Mathematics: 3 (4); Science: 3 (4); Foreign language: 0 (2); Social studies: 4 (4); History: 3 (4); Academic electives: (0). Tests: The college uses SAT or ACT scores in admissions decisions. Either SAT or ACT required. For admission to the fall 2007 entering class, the school will accept: ACT with writing, ACT without writing. Campus visit: Recommended. Admissions interview: Neither required nor recommended. Off-campus interview: May be arranged. **Factors that count in admissions decisions:** *Academic:* Secondary school record: Very important. Class rank: Very important. Letters of recommendation: Very important. Standardized test scores: Very important. Essay: Considered. *Nonacademic:* Interview: Considered. Extracurricular activities: Important. Talent/ability: Important. Character/personal qualities: Important. Alumni/ae relationship: Considered. Geographical residence: Not considered. State residency: Not considered. Religious affiliation/commitment: Not considered. Minority status: Considered. Volunteer work: Not considered. Work experience: Not considered. **Other schools with the greatest overlap in applicants:** Doane College; Nebraska Wesleyan University. **Admissions statistics for the fall 2005 entering class:** Total applicants: 1,413. Total accepted: 1,115. Freshmen enrolled: 311; 20% were from out of state. Overall acceptance rate: 79%. **Credentials of fall 2005 freshmen:** 14% ranked in the top 10 percent of their high school class; 37% were in the top 25 percent, and 72% were in the top half. (Proportion submitting class standing: 100%.) **First-year students who submitted SAT scores:** 9%. Scores (25/75 percentile): Verbal: 460-600, Math: 490-590, Combined: 950-1190. **First-year students submitting ACT scores:** 91%. Scores (25/75 percentile): English: 20-26, Math: 20-26, Composite: 20-26.

ACADEMICS

Year founded: 1882. **Academic calendar:** 4-1-4. **Degrees offered:** bachelor's, master's. **Most popular majors:** 22% education, 17% business, management, marketing, and related support services, 12% psychology, 9% multi/interdisciplinary studies, 8% visual and performing arts. **Major fields of study:** biological and biomedical sciences; business, management, marketing, and related support services; communication, journalism, and related programs; communications technologies/technicians and support services; computer and information sciences and support services; education; English language and literature/letters; foreign languages, literatures, and linguistics; health professions and related clinical sciences; history; legal professions and studies; liberal arts and sciences studies, and humanities; mathematics and statistics; multi/interdisciplinary studies; parks, recreation, leisure, and fitness studies; philosophy and religious studies; physical sciences; psychology; security and protective services; social sciences; visual and performing arts. **Areas of required coursework:** arts/fine arts, humanities, computer literacy, mathematics, English (including composition), philosophy, foreign languages, sciences (biological or physical), history, social science, other. **Pre-professional programs:** pre-law, pre-dentistry, pre-medicine, pre-theology, pre-veterinary science, pre-optometry, pre-pharmacy, other. **Special academic programs (% participation):** double major (32.1%), exchange student program (domestic) (1%), independent study (38.9%), internships (19%), student-designed major (3.2%), study abroad (1.8%), teacher certificate program (33.5%). **Teacher certification offered in:** early childhood, special education, elementary, secondary. **Faculty and instruction (2005-2006):** Total instructional faculty: 79 full-time, 42 part-time (57% men; 43% women; 1% minorities). Full-time faculty with Ph.D. or other terminal degree: 71%. Student/faculty ratio: 12/1. Classes of fewer than 20 students: 66%; of 20 to 49 students: 33%; of 50 or more students: 1%. **Advanced Placement and International Baccalaureate credit:** AP tests may be used for: Credit and/or placement. Scores accepted: 3, 4, 5. International Baccalaureate exams may be used for: Credit and/or placement. **Freshmen returning for sophomore year:** 75%. **Graduation rates:** Four-year: 51%; five-year: 62%; six-year: 62%. **Graduate study:** 17% of students pursue further study immediately upon graduation. Fields in which graduates pursue further study: law, 2%; medicine, 1%.

COSTS AND FINANCIAL AID

Financial aid office: (402) 461-7391. **Expenses (2005-2006):** Tuition and fees 2005-2006: $17,268; room/board: $4,950. Estimated books and supplies: $680; transportation: $500; personal expenses: $2,172. **Financial aid:** Priority filing date for institution's financial aid form: May 1.

CAMPUS LIFE AND EXTRACURRICULAR ACTIVITIES

Campus housing available (% using): coed dorms (18%), women's dorms (24%), men's dorms (27%), apartment for single students (24%), other housing options (7%). Students who live in college-owned, operated, or affiliated housing: 75%. **Student employment:** During the 2005-2006 academic year, 45% of undergraduates worked on campus. Average per-year earnings: $500. **Clubs and organizations:** Number of student organizations: 75. Activities include: choral groups, concert band, drama/theater, jazz band, literary magazine, marching band, music ensembles, musical theater, pep band, radio station, student government, student newspaper, symphony orchestra, television station, yearbook. Number of fraternities: 4; sororities: 4. Proportion of men in fraternities: 16%; of women in sororities: 32%. Average proportion of students who stay on campus on weekends: 70%. **Sports program (2005-2006):** Member of NAIA. *Men's intercollegiate varsity sports:* baseball, basketball, cross-country, football, golf, soccer, tennis, track and field (indoor), track and field (outdoor). *Women's intercollegiate varsity sports:* basketball, cross-country, golf, soccer, softball, tennis, track and field (indoor), track and field (outdoor), volleyball.

SERVICES AND FACILITIES

Basic services: health service. **Counseling services:** minority student, career, personal, academic, psychological, birth control, religious. **For learning-disabled students:** School does not offer a structured program with separate admission and additional fees. Total undergraduates in learning-disabled program or receiving services: 46. Services include: untimed tests, note-taking services, oral tests, learning center, readers, extended time for tests, tutors, other testing accomodations. **Library:** Number of titles: 113,318; number of current serial subscriptions: 636. **Information technology resources:** Students are not required to lease or own a computer. Number of campus computers available to all students: 181. School has a wireless network. Approximate number of users that can be accommodated: 240. Proportion of college-owned housing units wired for high-speed internet access: 100%. **Campus safety:** Security services offered: 24-hour foot-and-vehicle patrols,

late-night transport/escort service, 24-hour emergency telephones, lighted pathways/sidewalks, controlled dormitory access (key, security card, etc).

TRANSFER AND INTERNATIONAL STUDENTS

Transfer students: May apply for admission for the following academic terms: Fall, Winter, Spring, Summer. Applicants need a minimum number of credits to apply. For fall 2005: Transfer applications received: 98. Transfer applicants offered admission: 78. Transfer applicants enrolled: 52. **International students:** Number of foreign undergraduates: 8 (1% of student body). Number of countries represented: 8. Minimum TOEFL score required: 600 (paper); 250 (computer).

Midland Lutheran College

- ■ **Address:** 900 N. Clarkson Street, Fremont, NE 68025
- ■ **Website:** http://www.mlc.edu
- ■ **Private; Religious affiliation:** Lutheran
- ■ **Enrollment:** 888 full-time; 21 part-time

KEY STATS

✔ **U.S News College Ranking:** third tier, Comp. Coll.–Bachelor's (Midwest)
✔ **ACT Score (25th/75th percentile):** 19-24
✔ **Tuition:** 2006-2007: $19,510

Selectivity: Selective	**Room/board:** $4,950
Acceptance rate: 86%	**Average debt:** $19,419
Student/faculty ratio: 8/1	**Proportion who borrowed:** 85%

UNDERGRADUATE STUDENT BODY STATS

2005-2006 enrollment: 888 full-time; 21 part-time. Men: 45%; women: 55%. **Ethnic makeup:** African American: 3%; Asian American: 1%; Hispanic: 2%; White: 94%. **Religious preference:** Roman Catholic: 24%; Protestant: 17%; No preference: 1%; Unknown: 10%; Lutheran: 40%; Other: 8%.

ADMISSIONS FACTS AND FIGURES

Phone: (402) 941-6501. **Email:** admissions@mlc.edu. **Website:** http://www.mlc.edu. **Application deadlines for fall 2007:** Regular decision: August 6. Early decision: Not offered. Early action: Not offered. Admission cannot be deferred. **Application fee:** $30. Common application is accepted. **Admissions requirements/recommendations:** High school units required (recommended): English: (3); Mathematics: (2); Science: (2); Foreign language: (2); Academic electives: (10); Total units: (17). Tests: The college uses SAT or ACT scores in admissions decisions. Either SAT or ACT required. For admission to the fall 2007 entering class, the school will accept: ACT with writing, ACT without writing. Campus visit: Recommended. **Factors that count in admissions decisions:** *Academic:* Secondary school record: Very important. Class rank: Very important. Letters of recommendation: Considered. Standardized test scores: Very important. Essay: Not considered. *Nonacademic:* Interview: Not considered. Extracurricular activities: Not considered. Talent/ability: Not considered. Character/personal qualities: Not considered. Alumni/ae relationship: Not considered. Geographical residence: Not considered. State residency: Not considered. Religious affiliation/commitment: Not considered. Minority status: Not considered. Volunteer work: Not considered. Work experience: Not considered. **Other schools with the greatest overlap in applicants:** Doane College; Nebraska Wesleyan University; University of Nebraska–Kearney; University of Nebraska–Lincoln; University of Nebraska–Omaha. **Admissions statistics for the fall 2005 entering class:** Total applicants: 898. Total accepted: 768. Freshmen enrolled: 249; 19% were from out of state. Overall acceptance rate: 86%. **Credentials of fall 2005 freshmen:** 10% ranked in the top 10 percent of their high school class; 37% were in the top 25 percent, and 70% were in the top half. (Proportion submitting class standing: 97%.) **Average high school grade point average:** 3.2. **First-year students who submitted SAT scores:** 9%. Scores (25/75 percentile): Verbal: N/A; Math: N/A; Combined: N/A. **First-year students submitting ACT scores:** 93%. Scores (25/75 percentile): English: N/A; Math: N/A; Composite: 19-24.

ACADEMICS

Year founded: 1883. **Academic calendar:** 4-1-4. **Degrees offered:** bachelor's. **Most popular majors:** 32% business, management, marketing, and related support services, 18% education, 17% health professions and related clinical sciences, 9% parks, recreation, leisure, and fitness studies, 8% biological and biomedical sciences. **Major fields of study:** biological and biomedical sciences; business, management, marketing, and related support services; communication, journalism, and related programs; computer and information sciences and support services; education; English language and literature/letters; foreign languages, literatures, and linguistics; health professions and related clinical sciences; history; mathematics and statistics; parks, recreation, leisure, and fitness studies; philosophy and religious studies; psychology; social sciences; theology and religious vocations; visual and performing arts. **Areas of required coursework:** arts/fine arts, humanities, computer literacy, mathematics, English (including composition), philosophy, foreign languages, sciences (biological or physical), history, social science. **Pre-professional programs:** pre-law, pre-dentistry, pre-medicine, pre-theology, pre-veterinary science, pre-optometry, pre-pharmacy, other. **Special academic programs (% participation):** cooperative (work-study plan) program (1%), cross-registration (1%), double major (20%), independent study (5%), internships (11%), liberal arts/career combination (70%), student-designed major (1%), study abroad (1%), teacher certificate program (1%). **Teacher certification offered in:** early childhood, elementary, secondary. **Faculty and instruction (2005-2006):** Total instructional faculty: 61 full-time, 34 part-time (48% men; 52% women; 2% minorities). Full-time faculty with Ph.D. or other terminal degree: 57%. Student/faculty ratio: 8/1. Classes of fewer than 20 students: 49%; of 20 to 49 students: 49%; of 50 or more students: 2%. **Advanced Placement and International Baccalaureate credit:** AP tests may be used for: Credit only. Scores accepted: 3, 4, 5. **Freshmen returning for sophomore year:** 70%. **Graduation rates:** Four-year: 35%; five-year: 39%; six-year: 46%. **Graduate study:** 15% of students pursue further study immediately upon graduation.

COSTS AND FINANCIAL AID

Financial aid office: (402) 941-6520. **Expenses (2006-2007):** Tuition and fees 2006-2007: $19,510; room/board: $4,950. Estimated books and supplies: $800; transportation: $80; personal expenses: $1,380. **Financial aid:** In 2005-2006, 96% of undergraduates applied for financial aid. Of those, 86% were determined to have financial need; 45% had their need fully met. Average financial aid package (proportion receiving): $16,271 (86%). Average amount of gift aid, such as scholarships or grants (proportion receiving): $9,884 (86%). Average amount of self-help aid, such as work study or loans (proportion receiving): $6,455 (75%). Average need-based loan (excluding PLUS or other private loans): $6,282. Among students who received need-based aid, the average percentage of need met: 91%. Among students who received aid based on merit, the average award (and the proportion receiving): $9,192 (14%). The average athletic scholarship (and the proportion receiving): $6,385 (8%). Average amount of debt of borrowers graduating in 2005: $19,419. Proportion who borrowed: 85%.

CAMPUS LIFE AND EXTRACURRICULAR ACTIVITIES

Campus housing available (% using): coed dorms (10%), women's dorms (51%), men's dorms (39%). Students who live in college-owned, operated, or affiliated housing: 63%. **Student employment:** During the 2005-2006 academic year, 35% of undergraduates worked on campus. Average per-year earnings: $1,000. **Clubs and organizations:** Number of student organizations: 36. Activities include: choral groups, concert band, drama/theater, jazz band, literary magazine, music ensembles, pep band, student government, student newspaper, television station. Number of fraternities: 3; sororities: 4. Average proportion of students who stay on campus on weekends: 40%. **Sports program (2005-2006):** Member of NAIA. *Men's intercollegiate varsity sports:* baseball, basketball, cross-country, football, golf, soccer, tennis, track and field (indoor), track and field (outdoor). *Women's intercollegiate varsity sports:* basketball, cross-country, golf, soccer, softball, tennis, track and field (indoor), track and field (outdoor), volleyball.

SERVICES AND FACILITIES

Basic services: nonremedial tutoring, placement service, health service, health insurance. **Remedial assistance:** reading, math, writing, study skills. **Counseling services:** career, personal, academic, older student, religious. **For learning-disabled students:** School does not offer a structured program with separate admission and additional fees. Services include: remedial math, remedial reading, tape recorders, videotaped classes, diagnostic testing service, note-taking services, oral tests, learning center, readers, extended time for tests, tutors, other. **Library:** Number of titles: 109,500; number of current serial subscriptions: 675. **Information technology resources:** Students are not required to lease or own a computer. Number of campus computers available to all students: 1,240. School has a wireless network. Proportion of college-owned housing units wired for high-speed internet access: 100%. **Campus safety:** Security services offered: 24-hour foot-and-vehicle patrols, 24-hour emergency telephones, lighted pathways/sidewalks, student patrols, controlled dormitory access (key, security card, etc).

TRANSFER AND INTERNATIONAL STUDENTS

Transfer students: May apply for admission for the following academic terms: Fall, Spring. Applicants do not need a minimum number of credits to apply. **International students:** Number of countries represented: 7. Minimum TOEFL score required: 500 (paper); 173 (computer).

Nebraska Wesleyan University

- **Address:** 5000 St. Paul Avenue, Lincoln, NE 68504-2794
- **Website:** http://www.nebrwesleyan.edu
- **Private; Religious affiliation:** United Methodist
- **Enrollment:** 1,606 full-time; 236 part-time

KEY STATS

✔ **U.S News College Ranking:** third tier, Liberal Arts Colleges
✔ **ACT Score (25th/75th percentile):** 21-26
✔ **Tuition:** 2006-2007: $19,302

Selectivity: More selective	**Room/board:** $5,165
Acceptance rate: 84%	**Average debt:** $17,100
Student/faculty ratio: 13/1	**Proportion who borrowed:** 70%

UNDERGRADUATE STUDENT BODY STATS

2005-2006 enrollment: 1,606 full-time; 236 part-time. Men: 43%; women: 57%. **Ethnic makeup:** African American: 1%; American-Indian: 1%; Asian American: 1%; Hispanic: 2%; White: 95%. **Religious preference:** Roman Catholic: 23%; Protestant: 38%; No preference: 10%; Unknown: 2%; United Methodist: 20%; Other: 2%.

ADMISSIONS FACTS AND FIGURES

Phone: (402) 465-2218. **Email:** admissions@nebrwesleyan.edu. **Website:** http://www.nebrwesleyan.edu. **Application deadlines for fall 2007:** Regular decision: August 15. Early decision: Send application by: November 15; Decision sent by: December 15. Early action: Not offered. Admission can be deferred. **Application fee:** $20. Common application is accepted. **To apply online, go to:** http://www.nebrwesleyan.edu/admissions/apply/index.php. **Admissions requirements/recommendations:** High school units required (recommended): English: (4); Mathematics: (3); Science: (3); Foreign language: (2); Social studies: (3). Tests: The college uses SAT or ACT scores in admissions decisions. Either SAT or ACT required. For admission to the fall 2007 entering class, the school will accept: ACT with writing, ACT without writing. Campus visit: Recommended. Admissions interview: Neither required nor recommended. Off-campus interview: Not available. **Factors that count in admissions decisions:** *Academic:* Secondary school record: Considered. Class rank: Very important. Letters of recommendation: Considered. Standardized test scores: Very important. Essay: Considered. *Nonacademic:* Interview: Considered. Extracurricular activities: Important. Talent/ability: Important. Character/personal qualities: Important. Alumni/ae relationship: Considered. Geographical residence: Considered. State residency: Not considered. Religious affiliation/commitment: Not considered. Minority status: Considered. Volunteer work: Considered. Work experience: Not considered. **Other schools with the greatest overlap in applicants:** Doane College; Hastings College; Midland Lutheran College; University of Nebraska–Lincoln; University of Nebraska–Omaha. **Admissions statistics for the fall 2005 entering class:** Total applicants: 1,508. Total accepted: 1,262. Freshmen enrolled: 406; 10% were from out of state. Accepted through early-decision or early-action plans: 28%. Overall acceptance rate: 84%. Early-decision acceptance rate: 96%. Non-early acceptance rate: 82%. **Credentials of fall 2005 freshmen:** 22% ranked in the top 10 percent of their high school class; 57% were in the top 25 percent, and 88% were in the top half. (Proportion submitting class standing: 93%.) **First-year students submitting ACT scores:** 99%. Scores (25/75 percentile): English: 20-27, Math: 20-26, Composite: 21-26.

ACADEMICS

Year founded: 1887. **Academic calendar:** Semester. **Degrees offered:** certificate, bachelor's, master's, post-master's certificate. **Most popular majors:** 17% business, management, marketing, and related support services, 14% education, 10% health professions and related clinical sciences, 10% parks, recreation, leisure, and fitness studies, 10% psychology. **Major fields of study:** area, ethnic, cultural, and gender studies; biological and biomedical sciences; business, management, marketing, and related support services; communication, journalism, and related programs; computer and informa-

tion sciences and support services; education; English language and literature/letters; foreign languages, literatures, and linguistics; health professions and related clinical sciences; history; mathematics and statistics; multi/interdisciplinary studies; parks, recreation, leisure, and fitness studies; philosophy and religious studies; physical sciences; psychology; public administration and social service professions; social sciences; visual and performing arts. **Areas of required coursework:** arts/fine arts, humanities, mathematics, English (including composition), philosophy, foreign languages, sciences (biological or physical), social science, other. **Pre-professional programs:** pre-law, pre-dentistry, pre-medicine, pre-theology, pre-veterinary science, pre-optometry, pre-pharmacy, other. **Special academic programs (% participation):** double major (13%), dual enrollment (4%), exchange student program (domestic), independent study (30%), internships (62%), liberal arts/career combination, study abroad (9%), teacher certificate program (15%). **Teacher certification offered in:** special education, elementary, middle/junior high, secondary. **Reserve Officers Training Corps (ROTC):** Army ROTC: Offered at cooperating institution (University of Nebraska Lincoln); Air Force ROTC: Offered at cooperating institution (University of Nebraska Lincoln). **Faculty and instruction (2005-2006):** Total instructional faculty: 102 full-time, 123 part-time (48% men; 52% women). Full-time faculty with Ph.D. or other terminal degree: 80%. Student/faculty ratio: 13/1. Classes of fewer than 20 students: 54%; of 20 to 49 students: 43%; of 50 or more students: 3%. **Advanced Placement and International Baccalaureate credit:** AP tests may be used for: Credit only. Scores accepted: 3, 4, 5. International Baccalaureate exams may be used for: Credit only. **Freshmen returning for sophomore year:** 81%. **Graduation rates:** Four-year: 55%; five-year: 66%; six-year: 69%.

COSTS AND FINANCIAL AID

Financial aid office: (402) 465-2212. **Expenses (2006-2007):** Tuition and fees 2006-2007: $19,302; room/board: $5,165. Estimated books and supplies: $1,200 personal expenses: $2,800. **Financial aid:** In 2005-2006, 81% of undergraduates applied for financial aid. Of those, 68% were determined to have financial need; 16% had their need fully met. Average financial aid package (proportion receiving): $12,858 (68%). Average amount of gift aid, such as scholarships or grants (proportion receiving): $8,532 (67%). Average amount of self-help aid, such as work study or loans (proportion receiving): $4,556 (59%). Average need-based loan (excluding PLUS or other private loans): $4,298. Among students who received need-based aid, the average percentage of need met: 69%. Among students who received aid based on merit, the average award (and the proportion receiving): $5,881 (23%). The average athletic scholarship (and the proportion receiving): $0 (0%). Average amount of debt of borrowers graduating in 2005: $17,100. Proportion who borrowed: 70%.

CAMPUS LIFE AND EXTRACURRICULAR ACTIVITIES

Campus housing available (% using): coed dorms (36%), women's dorms (11%), sorority housing (9%), fraternity housing (8%), apartment for single students (2%), other housing options (34%). Students who live in college-owned, operated, or affiliated housing: 63%. **Student employment:** During the 2005-2006 academic year, 25% of undergraduates worked on campus. Average per-year earnings: $1,100. **Clubs and organizations:** Number of student organizations: 84. Activities include: choral groups, concert band, drama/theater, jazz band, literary magazine, music ensembles, musical theater, opera, pep band, radio station, student government, student newspaper, yearbook. Number of fraternities: 4; sororities: 4. Proportion of men in fraternities: 24%; of women in sororities: 22%. Average proportion of students who stay on campus on weekends: 70%. **Sports program (2005-2006):** Member of NAIA. **Men's intercollegiate varsity sports:** baseball, basketball, cross-country, football, golf, soccer, tennis, track and field (indoor), track and field (outdoor). **Women's intercollegiate varsity sports:** basketball, cheerleading, cross-country, golf, soccer, softball, tennis, track and field (indoor), track and field (outdoor), volleyball.

SERVICES AND FACILITIES

Basic services: nonremedial tutoring, women's center, placement service, health service, health insurance. **Counseling services:** minority student, career, personal, academic, older student, psychological, birth control, religious. **For learning-disabled students:** School does not offer a structured program with separate admission and additional fees. Services include: tape recorders, videotaped classes, untimed tests, note-taking services, oral tests, readers, extended time for tests, tutors, other. **Library:** Number of titles: 207,278; number of current serial subscriptions: 708. **Information technology resources:** Students are not required to lease or own a computer. Number of campus computers available to all students: 360. School has a wireless network. Proportion of college-owned housing units wired for high-speed internet access: 100%. **Campus safety:** Security services offered: 24-hour foot-and-vehicle patrols, 24-hour emergency telephones, lighted pathways/sidewalks, controlled dormitory access (key, security card, etc).

TRANSFER AND INTERNATIONAL STUDENTS

Transfer students: May apply for admission for the following academic terms: Fall, Winter, Spring, Summer. Applicants do not need a minimum number of credits to apply. For fall 2005: Transfer applications received: 179. Transfer applicants offered admission: 133. Transfer applicants enrolled: 66. **International students:** Number of foreign undergraduates: 1. Minimum TOEFL score required: 525 (paper); 195 (computer).

Peru State College

- **Address:** Box 10, Peru, NE 68421-0010
- **Website:** http://www.peru.edu
- **Public**
- **Enrollment:** 1,017 full-time; 693 part-time

KEY STATS

✔ **U.S News College Ranking:** fourth tier, Universities–Master's (Midwest)
✔ **ACT Score:** 20
✔ **Tuition:** 2006-2007: $3,800 in state, $6,860 out of state

Selectivity: Selective	**Room/board:** $4,816
Acceptance rate: 58%	**Average debt:** N/A
Student/faculty ratio: 21/1	**Proportion who borrowed:** N/A

UNDERGRADUATE STUDENT BODY STATS

2005-2006 enrollment: 1,017 full-time; 693 part-time. Men: 46%; women: 54%. **Ethnic makeup:** African American: 4%; American-Indian: 1%; Asian American: 1%; Hispanic: 2%; White: 92%.

ADMISSIONS FACTS AND FIGURES

Phone: (402) 872-2221. **Email:** Admissions@oakmail.peru.edu. **Website:** http://www.peru.edu. **Application deadlines for fall 2007:** Regular decision: Rolling. Early decision: Not offered. Early action: Not offered. Admission cannot be deferred. **Application fee:** None. Common application is accepted. **To apply online, go to:** http://www.hpcnet.org/peru/admissionsoffice. **Admissions requirements/recommendations:** High school units required (recommended): English: (4); Mathematics: (3); Science: (2); Social studies: (3); Total units: (14). Tests: The college uses SAT or ACT scores in admissions decisions. Neither SAT nor ACT required. For admission to the fall 2007 entering class, the school will accept: ACT with writing, ACT without writing. Campus visit: Recommended. Admissions interview: Neither required nor recommended. Off-campus interview: Not available. **Factors that count in admissions decisions:** *Academic:* Secondary school record: Not considered. Class rank: Considered. Letters of recommendation: Not considered. Standardized test scores: Considered. Essay: Not considered. *Nonacademic:* Interview: Not considered. Extracurricular activities: Not considered. Talent/ability: Not considered. Character/personal qualities: Not considered. Alumni/ae relationship: Not considered. Geographical residence: Not considered. State residency: Not considered. Religious affiliation/commitment: Not considered. Minority status: Not considered. Volunteer work: Not considered. Work experience: Not considered. **Other schools with the greatest overlap in applicants:** Doane College; Northwest Missouri State University; University of Nebraska–Kearney; University of Nebraska–Lincoln; University of Nebraska–Omaha. **Admissions statistics for the fall 2005 entering class:** Total applicants: 740. Total accepted: 429. Freshmen enrolled: 213; 10% were from out of state. Overall acceptance rate: 58%. **Credentials of fall 2005 freshmen:** 10% ranked in the top 10 percent of their high school class; 20% were in the top 25 percent, and 45% were in the top half. (Proportion submitting class standing: 91%.) **Average high school grade point average:** 3.0. **First-year students submitting ACT scores:** 87%. Scores (25/75 percentile): English: N/A, Math: N/A, Composite: N/A.

ACADEMICS

Year founded: 1867. **Academic calendar:** Semester. **Degrees offered:** certificate, bachelor's, post-bachelor's certificate, master's. **Most popular majors:** 27% elementary education and teaching, 19% business administration, management, and operations, 18% business administration and management, 10% physical education teaching and coaching, 6% psychology. **Major**

fields of study: agriculture, agriculture operations, and related sciences; biological and biomedical sciences; business, management, marketing, and related support services; computer and information sciences and support services; education; English language and literature/letters; liberal arts and sciences studies, and humanities; mathematics and statistics; psychology; security and protective services. **Areas of required coursework:** arts/fine arts, humanities, computer literacy, mathematics, English (including composition), sciences (biological or physical), history, social science, other. **Pre-professional programs:** pre-law, pre-dentistry, pre-medicine, pre-veterinary science, pre-optometry, pre-pharmacy, other. **Special academic programs:** accelerated program, cooperative (work-study plan) program, cross-registration, distance learning, double major, dual enrollment, external degree program, honors program, independent study, internships, liberal arts/career combination, teacher certificate program. **Teacher certification offered in:** early childhood, special education, elementary, middle/junior high, secondary. **Cooperative education programs:** art, business, computer science, education, humanities, natural science, social/behavioral science, other. **Reserve Officers Training Corps (ROTC):** Army ROTC: Offered at cooperating institution (Creighton University); Air Force ROTC: Offered at cooperating institution (University of Nebraska at Omaha). **Faculty and instruction (2005-2006):** Total instructional faculty: 45 full-time, 73 part-time (; 1% minorities). Full-time faculty with Ph.D. or other terminal degree: 78%. Student/faculty ratio: 21/1. Classes of fewer than 20 students: 50%; of 20 to 49 students: 47%; of 50 or more students: 2%. **Advanced Placement and International Baccalaureate credit:** AP tests may be used for: Credit and/or placement. Scores accepted: 3. International Baccalaureate exams may be used for: Credit and/or placement. **Freshmen returning for sophomore year:** 61%. **Graduation rates:** Four-year: 34%; five-year: 38%; six-year: 37%. **Graduate study:** 14% of students pursue further study immediately upon graduation. Fields in which graduates pursue further study: Master of Business Administration (MBA), 21%; law, 7%; education, 71%.

COSTS AND FINANCIAL AID

Financial aid office: (402) 872-2228. **Expenses (2006-2007):** Tuition and fees 2006-2007: $3,800 in state, $6,860 out of state; room/board: $4,816. Estimated books and supplies: $700; transportation: $1,000; personal expenses: $1,000. **Financial aid:** Priority filing date for institution's financial aid form: March 1.

CAMPUS LIFE AND EXTRACURRICULAR ACTIVITIES

Campus housing available (% using): coed dorms (34%), women's dorms (20%), men's dorms (31%), apartments for married students (3%), apartment for single students, special housing for disabled students (1%), other housing options (11%). Students who live in college-owned, operated, or affiliated housing: 22%. **Student employment:** During the 2005-2006 academic year, 10% of undergraduates worked on campus. Average per-year earnings: $1,600. **Clubs and organizations:** Number of student organizations: 31. Activities include: choral groups, concert band, dance, drama/theater, jazz band, literary magazine, music ensembles, musical theater, pep band, radio station, student government, student newspaper, student film society, yearbook. Number of fraternities: 0; sororities: 0. Average proportion of students who stay on campus on weekends: 25%. **Sports program (2005-2006):** Member of NAIA. **Men's intercollegiate varsity sports:** baseball, basketball, football. **Women's intercollegiate varsity sports:** basketball, cross-country, golf, softball, volleyball.

SERVICES AND FACILITIES

Basic services: nonremedial tutoring, placement service, day care, health service, health insurance. **Remedial assistance:** study skills. **Counseling services:** minority student, career, veteran student, academic, older student, birth control. **For learning-disabled students:** School does not offer a structured program with separate admission and additional fees. Total undergraduates in learning-disabled program or receiving services: 20. Services include: tape recorders, videotaped classes, note-taking services, oral tests, learning center, readers, extended time for tests, tutors, priority seating, proofreading services, texts on tape, typist/scribe, other testing accomodations. **Library:** Number of titles: 108,879; number of current serial subscriptions: 246. **Information technology resources:** Students are not required to lease or own a computer. Number of campus computers available to all students: 163. School has a wireless network. Proportion of college-owned housing units wired for high-speed internet access: 100%. **Campus safety:** Security services offered: 24-hour foot-and-vehicle patrols, late-night transport/escort service, 24-hour emergency telephones, lighted pathways/sidewalks.

TRANSFER AND INTERNATIONAL STUDENTS

Transfer students: May apply for admission for the following academic terms: Fall, Spring, Summer. Applicants do not need a minimum number of credits to apply. For fall 2005: Transfer applications received: 450. Transfer applicants offered admission: 270. Transfer applicants enrolled: 223. **International students:** Number of foreign undergraduates: 4. Minimum TOEFL score required: 550 (paper); 230 (computer).

Union College

- Address: 3800 S. 48th Street, Lincoln, NE 68506
- Website: http://www.ucollege.edu
- Private; Religious affiliation: Seventh-day Adventist
- Enrollment: 757 full-time; 128 part-time

KEY STATS

✔ **U.S News College Ranking:** 46, Comp. Coll.–Bachelor's (Midwest)
✔ **ACT Score (25th/75th percentile):** 19-25
✔ **Tuition:** 2006-2007: $15,230

Selectivity: Selective	**Room/board:** $4,948
Acceptance rate: 43%	**Average debt:** $23,379
Student/faculty ratio: 13/1	**Proportion who borrowed:** 64%

UNDERGRADUATE STUDENT BODY STATS

2005-2006 enrollment: 757 full-time; 128 part-time. Men: 45%; women: 55%. **Ethnic makeup:** African American: 2%; American-Indian: 1%; Asian American: 2%; Hispanic: 6%; White: 79%; International: 10%.

ADMISSIONS FACTS AND FIGURES

Phone: (800) 228-4600. **Email:** ucenroll@ucollege.edu. **Website:** http://www.ucollege.edu. **Application deadlines for fall 2007:** Regular decision: Rolling. Early decision: Not offered. Early action: Not offered. Admission can be deferred. Common application is accepted. **Admissions requirements/recommendations:** High school units required (recommended): English: 3 (4); Mathematics: 2 (3); Science: 2 (3); Foreign language: (1); Social studies: 1; History: 1; Academic electives: 3; Total units: 20. Tests: The college uses SAT or ACT scores in admissions decisions. Either SAT or ACT required. For admission to the fall 2007 entering class, the school will accept: ACT with writing, ACT without writing. Campus visit: Recommended. Admissions interview: Recommended. Off-campus interview: May be arranged. **Factors that count in admissions decisions:** *Academic:* Secondary school record: Very important. Class rank: Important. Letters of recommendation: Very important. Standardized test scores: Very important. Essay: Considered. *Nonacademic:* Interview: Important. Extracurricular activities: Important. Talent/ability: Considered. Character/personal qualities: Very important. Alumni/ae relationship: Not considered. Geographical residence: Not considered. State residency: Not considered. Religious affiliation/commitment: Important. Minority status: Not considered. Volunteer work: Considered. Work experience: Not considered. **Other schools with the greatest overlap in applicants:** Andrews University; Pacific Union College; Southern Adventist University; Southwestern Adventist University; Walla Walla College. **Admissions statistics for the fall 2005 entering class:** Total applicants: 614. Total accepted: 264. Freshmen enrolled: 180; 83% were from out of state. Overall acceptance rate: 43%. **Credentials of fall 2005 freshmen:** 17% ranked in the top 10 percent of their high school class; 31% were in the top 25 percent, and 57% were in the top half. (Proportion submitting class standing: 57%.) **Average high school grade point average:** 3.4. **First-year students who submitted SAT scores:** 9%. Scores (25/75 percentile): Verbal: N/A, Math: N/A, Combined: N/A. **First-year students submitting ACT scores:** 88%. Scores (25/75 percentile): English: 18-26, Math: 17-24, Composite: 19-25.

ACADEMICS

Year founded: 1891. **Academic calendar:** Semester. **Degrees offered:** associate, bachelor's, master's. **Most popular majors:** 20% business, management, marketing, and related support services, 13% physician assistant, 11% elementary education and teaching, 11% nursing, 8% social work. **Major fields of study:** biological and biomedical sciences; business, management, marketing, and related support services; communication, journalism, and related programs; computer and information sciences and support services; education; English language and literature/letters; foreign languages, literatures, and linguistics; health professions and related clinical sciences; his-

tory; liberal arts and sciences studies, and humanities; mathematics and statistics; parks, recreation, leisure, and fitness studies; philosophy and religious studies; physical sciences; psychology; public administration and social service professions; social sciences; theology and religious vocations; visual and performing arts. **Areas of required coursework:** arts/fine arts, humanities, computer literacy, mathematics, English (including composition), sciences (biological or physical), history, social science, other. **Pre-professional programs:** pre-law, pre-dentistry, pre-medicine, pre-pharmacy, other. **Special academic programs (% participation):** double major (5%), dual enrollment (3%), English as a Second Language (ESL) (4%), honors program (5%), internships (58%), student-designed major (2%), study abroad (3%), teacher certificate program (11%). **Teacher certification offered in:** elementary, secondary. **Faculty and instruction (2005-2006):** Total instructional faculty: 54 full-time, 38 part-time (11% minorities). Full-time faculty with Ph.D. or other terminal degree: 41%. Student/faculty ratio: 13/1. Classes of fewer than 20 students: 70%; of 20 to 49 students: 27%; of 50 or more students: 3%. **Advanced Placement and International Baccalaureate credit:** AP tests may be used for: Credit and/or placement. Scores accepted: 4, 5. International Baccalaureate exams may be used for: Credit and/or placement. **Freshmen returning for sophomore year:** 71%. **Graduation rates:** Four-year: 27%; five-year: 51%; six-year: 52%. **Graduate study:** 11% of students pursue further study immediately upon graduation.

COSTS AND FINANCIAL AID

Financial aid office: (402) 486-2505. **Expenses (2006-2007):** Tuition and fees 2006-2007: $15,230; room/board: $4,948. Estimated books and supplies: $980; transportation: $1,480; personal expenses: $1,480. **Financial aid:** Priority filing date for institution's financial aid form: March 15. In 2005-2006, 61% of undergraduates applied for financial aid. Of those, 61% were determined to have financial need; 20% had their need fully met. Average financial aid package (proportion receiving): $8,376 (61%). Average amount of gift aid, such as scholarships or grants (proportion receiving): $5,334 (56%). Average amount of self-help aid, such as work study or loans (proportion receiving): $5,707 (47%). Average need-based loan (excluding PLUS or other private loans): $4,807. Among students who received need-based aid, the average percentage of need met: 44%. Average amount of debt of borrowers graduating in 2005: $23,379. Proportion who borrowed: 64%.

CAMPUS LIFE AND EXTRACURRICULAR ACTIVITIES

Campus housing available (% using): women's dorms (49%), men's dorms (40%), apartments for married students (2%), apartment for single students (9%). Students who live in college-owned, operated, or affiliated housing: 58%. **Student employment:** During the 2005-2006 academic year, 50% of undergraduates worked on campus. Average per-year earnings: $1,800. **Clubs and organizations:** Number of student organizations: 21. Activities include: choral groups, concert band, drama/theater, music ensembles, student government, student newspaper, symphony orchestra, yearbook. Number of fraternities: 0; sororities: 0. Average proportion of students who stay on campus on weekends: 45%.

SERVICES AND FACILITIES

Basic services: nonremedial tutoring, placement service, health service, health insurance. **Remedial assistance:** reading, math, writing, study skills. **Counseling services:** career, personal, academic, psychological, religious. **For learning-disabled students:** School does not offer a structured program with separate admission and additional fees. Total undergraduates in learning-disabled program or receiving services: 38. Services include: remedial math, remedial English, reading machines, tape recorders, videotaped classes, diagnostic testing service, untimed tests, note-taking services, oral tests, learning center, readers, extended time for tests, tutors, proofreading services, texts on tape, typist/scribe, exams on tape or computer, other testing accomodations, other. **Library:** Number of titles: 159,646; number of current serial subscriptions: 590. **Information technology resources:** Students are not required to lease or own a computer. Number of campus computers available to all students: 85. School has a wireless network. Approximate number of users that can be accommodated: 1,000. Proportion of college-owned housing units wired for high-speed internet access: 0%. **Campus safety:** Security services offered: 24-hour foot-and-vehicle patrols, late-night transport/escort service, 24-hour emergency telephones, lighted pathways/sidewalks, student patrols.

TRANSFER AND INTERNATIONAL STUDENTS

Transfer students: May apply for admission for the following academic terms: Fall, Spring. Applicants need a minimum number of credits to apply. For fall 2005: Transfer applications received: 179. Transfer applicants offered admission: 114. Transfer applicants enrolled: 78. **International stu-**

dents: Number of foreign undergraduates: 80 (10% of student body). Number of countries represented: 26. Minimum TOEFL score required: 550 (paper); 213 (computer).

University of Nebraska–Kearney

■ **Address:** 905 W. 25th Street, Kearney, NE 68849
■ **Website:** http://www.unk.edu
■ **Public**
■ **Enrollment:** 4,895 full-time; 486 part-time

KEY STATS

✔ **U.S News College Ranking:** 65, Universities–Master's (Midwest)
✔ **ACT Score (25th/75th percentile):** 20-25
✔ **Tuition:** 2006-2007: $4,764 in state, $8,838 out of state
  Selectivity: Selective   **Room/board:** $5,686
  Acceptance rate: 84%   **Average debt:** $16,175
  Student/faculty ratio: 17/1   **Proportion who borrowed:** 74%

UNDERGRADUATE STUDENT BODY STATS

2005-2006 enrollment: 4,895 full-time; 486 part-time. Men: 46%; women: 54%. **Ethnic makeup:** African American: 1%; Asian American: 1%; Hispanic: 3%; White: 88%; International: 7%.

ADMISSIONS FACTS AND FIGURES

Phone: (308) 865-8526. **Email:** admissionsug@unk.edu. **Website:** http://www.unk.edu. **Application deadlines for fall 2007:** Regular decision: Rolling. Early decision: Not offered. Early action: Not offered. Admission cannot be deferred. **Application fee:** $45. Common application is not accepted. **Admissions requirements/recommendations:** High school units required (recommended): English: 4; Mathematics: 3; Science: 3; Foreign language: 2; Social studies: 3; Academic electives: 1; Total units: 16. Tests: The college uses SAT or ACT scores in admissions decisions. Either SAT or ACT required. For admission to the fall 2007 entering class, the school will accept: ACT with writing, ACT without writing. Campus visit: Recommended. Admissions interview: Neither required nor recommended. Off-campus interview: May be arranged. **Factors that count in admissions decisions:** *Academic:* Secondary school record: Considered. Class rank: Very important. Letters of recommendation: Considered. Standardized test scores: Very important. Essay: Not considered. *Nonacademic:* Interview: Not considered. Extracurricular activities: Considered. Talent/ability: Considered. Character/personal qualities: Not considered. Alumni/ae relationship: Not considered. Geographical residence: Considered. State residency: Considered. Religious affiliation/commitment: Not considered. Minority status: Considered. Volunteer work: Not considered. Work experience: Not considered. **Other schools with the greatest overlap in applicants:** Doane College; Hastings College; University of Nebraska–Lincoln; University of Nebraska–Omaha; Wayne State College. **Admissions statistics for the fall 2005 entering class:** Total applicants: 2,443. Total accepted: 2,057. Freshmen enrolled: 1,062; 6% were from out of state. Overall acceptance rate: 84%. **Credentials of fall 2005 freshmen:** 13% ranked in the top 10 percent of their high school class; 37% were in the top 25 percent, and 72% were in the top half. (Proportion submitting class standing: 89%.) **Average high school grade point average:** 3.3. **First-year students who submitted SAT scores:** 1%. Scores (25/75 percentile): Verbal: 410-600, Math: 430-570, Combined: 840-1170. **First-year students submitting ACT scores:** 90%. Scores (25/75 percentile): English: 19-25, Math: 18-25, Composite: 20-25.

ACADEMICS

Year founded: 1903. **Academic calendar:** Semester. **Degrees offered:** bachelor's, master's, post-master's certificate. **Most popular majors:** 15% business administration and management, 15% elementary education and teaching, 10% operations management and supervision, 5% criminal justice/safety studies, 5% journalism. **Major fields of study:** agriculture, agriculture operations, and related sciences; biological and biomedical sciences; business, management, marketing, and related support services; communication, journalism, and related programs; computer and information sciences and support services; education; English language and literature/letters; family and consumer sciences/human sciences; foreign languages, literatures, and linguistics; health professions and related clinical sciences; history; liberal arts and sciences studies, and humanities; mathematics and statistics; parks, recreation, leisure, and fitness studies; philosophy and religious stud-

ies; physical sciences; psychology; public administration and social service professions; security and protective services; social sciences; transportation and materials moving; visual and performing arts. **Areas of required coursework:** humanities, mathematics, English (including composition), sciences (biological or physical), history, social science, other. **Pre-professional programs:** pre-law, pre-dentistry, pre-medicine, pre-veterinary science, pre-optometry, pre-pharmacy, other. **Special academic programs:** cooperative (work-study plan) program, distance learning, double major, dual enrollment, English as a Second Language (ESL), exchange student program (domestic), honors program, independent study, internships, study abroad, teacher certificate program. **Teacher certification offered in:** early childhood, special education, elementary, middle/junior high, secondary, bilingual/bicultural. **Cooperative education programs:** health professions. **Faculty and instruction (2005-2006):** Total instructional faculty: 306 full-time, 74 part-time (54% men; 46% women; 6% minorities). Full-time faculty with Ph.D. or other terminal degree: 73%. Student/faculty ratio: 17/1. Classes of fewer than 20 students: 34%; of 20 to 49 students: 59%; of 50 or more students: 7%. **Advanced Placement and International Baccalaureate credit:** International Baccalaureate exams may be used for: Credit and/or placement. **Freshmen returning for sophomore year:** 83%. **Graduation rates:** Four-year: 20%; five-year: 46%; six-year: 52%.

COSTS AND FINANCIAL AID

Financial aid office: (308) 865-8520. **Expenses (2006-2007):** Tuition and fees 2006-2007: $4,764 in state, $8,838 out of state; room/board: $5,686. Estimated books and supplies: $810; transportation: $632; personal expenses: $2,348. **Financial aid:** Priority filing date for institution's financial aid form: April 1. In 2005-2006, 73% of undergraduates applied for financial aid. Of those, 59% were determined to have financial need; 31% had their need fully met. Average financial aid package (proportion receiving): $7,227 (57%). Average amount of gift aid, such as scholarships or grants (proportion receiving): $3,176 (39%). Average amount of self-help aid, such as work study or loans (proportion receiving): $3,830 (48%). Average need-based loan (excluding PLUS or other private loans): $3,590. Among students who received need-based aid, the average percentage of need met: 79%. Among students who received aid based on merit, the average award (and the proportion receiving): $1,994 (30%). The average athletic scholarship (and the proportion receiving): $2,700 (5%). Average amount of debt of borrowers graduating in 2005: $16,175. Proportion who borrowed: 74%.

CAMPUS LIFE AND EXTRACURRICULAR ACTIVITIES

Campus housing available: coed dorms, women's dorms, men's dorms, sorority housing, fraternity housing, apartments for married students. Students who live in college-owned, operated, or affiliated housing: 35%. **Clubs and organizations:** Number of student organizations: 144. Activities include: choral groups, concert band, dance, drama/theater, jazz band, marching band, music ensembles, musical theater, opera, pep band, radio station, student government, student newspaper, symphony orchestra, television station. Number of fraternities: 7; sororities: 5. Proportion of men in fraternities: 10%; of women in sororities: 8%. **Sports program (2005-2006):** Member of NCAA II. **Men's intercollegiate varsity sports:** baseball, basketball, cheerleading, cross-country, football, golf, tennis, track and field (indoor), track and field (outdoor), wrestling. **Women's intercollegiate varsity sports:** basketball, cross-country, golf, softball, swimming and diving, tennis, track and field (indoor), track and field (outdoor), volleyball.

SERVICES AND FACILITIES

Basic services: nonremedial tutoring, placement service, day care, health service, health insurance. **Remedial assistance:** math, study skills. **Counseling services:** minority student, career, personal, veteran student, academic. **For learning-disabled students:** School does not offer a structured program with separate admission and additional fees. **Library:** Number of titles: 608,638; number of current serial subscriptions: 1,270. **Information technology resources:** Students are not required to lease or own a computer. Number of campus computers available to all students: 630. School has a wireless network. Approximate number of users that can be accommodated: 1,800. Proportion of college-owned housing units wired for high-speed internet access: 92%. **Campus safety:** Security services offered: 24-hour foot-and-vehicle patrols, 24-hour emergency telephones, lighted pathways/sidewalks, controlled dormitory access (key, security card, etc).

TRANSFER AND INTERNATIONAL STUDENTS

Transfer students: May apply for admission for the following academic terms: Fall, Spring, Summer. Applicants do not need a minimum number of credits to apply. For fall 2005: Transfer applications received: 549. Transfer applicants offered admission: 387. Transfer applicants enrolled:

361. International students: Number of foreign undergraduates: 367 (7% of student body). Number of countries represented: 41. Minimum TOEFL score required: 500 (paper); 173 (computer).

University of Nebraska–Lincoln

- **Address:** 14th and R Streets, Lincoln, NE 68588
- **Website:** http://www.unl.edu
- **Public**
- **Enrollment:** 15,768 full-time; 1,269 part-time

KEY STATS
✔ **U.S News College Ranking:** 98, National Universities
✔ **ACT Score (25th/75th percentile):** 22-28
✔ **Tuition:** 2006-2007: $5,972 in state, $15,506 out of state
  Selectivity: More selective **Room/board:** $5,978
  Acceptance rate: 75% **Average debt:** $16,909
  Student/faculty ratio: 19/1 **Proportion who borrowed:** 61%

UNDERGRADUATE STUDENT BODY STATS
2005-2006 enrollment: 15,768 full-time; 1,269 part-time. Men: 53%; women: 47%. **Ethnic makeup:** African American: 2%; American-Indian: 1%; Asian American: 3%; Hispanic: 3%; White: 89%; International: 3%.

ADMISSIONS FACTS AND FIGURES
Phone: (800) 742-8800. **Email:** Admissions@unl.edu. **Website:** http://www.unl.edu. **Application deadlines for fall 2007:** Regular decision: May 1. Early decision: Not offered. Early action: Not offered. Admission cannot be deferred. **Application fee:** $45. Common application is not accepted. **To apply online, go to:** http://nebraska.unl.edu/apply/. **Admissions requirements/recommendations:** High school units required (recommended): English: 4; Mathematics: 4; Science: 3; Foreign language: 2; Social studies: 3; History: (1); Total units: 16. Tests: The college uses SAT or ACT scores in admissions decisions. Either SAT or ACT required. For admission to the fall 2007 entering class, the school will accept: ACT with writing, ACT without writing. Campus visit: Recommended. Admissions interview: Recommended. Off-campus interview: Not available. **Factors that count in admissions decisions:** *Academic:* Secondary school record: Important. Class rank: Very important. Letters of recommendation: Considered. Standardized test scores: Very important. Essay: Not considered. *Nonacademic:* Interview: Not considered. Extracurricular activities: Not considered. Talent/ability: Considered. Character/personal qualities: Not considered. Alumni/ae relationship: Not considered. Geographical residence: Not considered. State residency: Not considered. Religious affiliation/commitment: Not considered. Minority status: Not considered. Volunteer work: Not considered. Work experience: Not considered. **Other schools with the greatest overlap in applicants:** Iowa State University; University of Kansas; University of Nebraska–Kearney; University of Nebraska–Omaha; Washington University in St. Louis. **Admissions statistics for the fall 2005 entering class:** Total applicants: 7,474. Total accepted: 5,633. Freshmen enrolled: 3,560; 22% were from out of state. Overall acceptance rate: 75%. **Credentials of fall 2005 freshmen:** 27% ranked in the top 10 percent of their high school class; 54% were in the top 25 percent, and 84% were in the top half. (Proportion submitting class standing: 93%.) **First-year students who submitted SAT scores:** 17%. Scores (25/75 percentile): Verbal: 530-660, Math: 540-670, Combined: 1070-1330. **First-year students submitting ACT scores:** 96%. Scores (25/75 percentile): English: 21-28, Math: 21-28, Composite: 22-28.

ACADEMICS
Year founded: 1869. **Academic calendar:** Semester. **Degrees offered:** associate, terminal-associate, bachelor's, post-bachelor's certificate, master's, post-master's certificate, first professional, doctorate. **Most popular majors:** 22% business, management, marketing, and related support services, 9% education, 9% engineering, 8% communication, journalism, and related programs, 7% agriculture, agriculture operations, and related sciences. **Major fields of study:** agriculture, agriculture operations, and related sciences; architecture and related services; area, ethnic, cultural, and gender studies; biological and biomedical sciences; business, management, marketing, and related support services; communication, journalism, and related programs; computer and information sciences and support services; education; engineering; engineering technologies/technicians; English language and literature/letters; family and consumer sciences/human sciences; foreign

languages, literatures, and linguistics; health professions and related clinical sciences; history; legal professions and studies; liberal arts and sciences studies, and humanities; mathematics and statistics; multi/interdisciplinary studies; natural resources and conservation; parks, recreation, leisure, and fitness studies; philosophy and religious studies; physical sciences; psychology; security and protective services; social sciences; visual and performing arts. **Areas of required coursework:** arts/fine arts, humanities, mathematics, English (including composition), foreign languages, sciences (biological or physical), history, social science, other. **Pre-professional programs:** pre-law, pre-dentistry, pre-medicine, pre-veterinary science, pre-optometry, pre-pharmacy, other. **Special academic programs:** accelerated program, cooperative (work-study plan) program, cross-registration, distance learning, double major, dual enrollment, English as a Second Language (ESL), exchange student program (domestic), honors program, independent study, internships, liberal arts/career combination, student-designed major, study abroad, teacher certificate program. **Teacher certification offered in:** early childhood, special education, elementary, vo-tech, middle/junior high, secondary, bilingual/bicultural. **Cooperative education programs:** computer science, engineering. **Reserve Officers Training Corps (ROTC):** Army ROTC: Offered on campus; Navy ROTC: Offered on campus; Air Force ROTC: Offered on campus. **Faculty and instruction (2005-2006):** Total instructional faculty: 1,047 full-time, 10 part-time (73% men; 27% women; 15% minorities). Full-time faculty with Ph.D. or other terminal degree: 97%. Student/faculty ratio: 19/1. Classes of fewer than 20 students: 37%; of 20 to 49 students: 49%; of 50 or more students: 14%. **Advanced Placement and International Baccalaureate credit:** AP tests may be used for: Credit only. Scores accepted: 3, 4, 5. International Baccalaureate exams may be used for: Credit only. **Freshmen returning for sophomore year:** 81%. **Graduation rates:** Four-year: 22%; five-year: 54%; six-year: 63%. **Graduate study:** 36% of students pursue further study immediately upon graduation.

COSTS AND FINANCIAL AID
Financial aid office: (402) 472-2030. **Expenses (2006-2007):** Tuition and fees 2006-2007: $5,972 in state, $15,506 out of state; room/board: $5,978. Estimated books and supplies: $824; transportation: $854; personal expenses: $2,008. **Financial aid:** Priority filing date for institution's financial aid form: April 1. In 2005-2006, 63% of undergraduates applied for financial aid. Of those, 47% were determined to have financial need; 27% had their need fully met. Average financial aid package (proportion receiving): $8,258 (46%). Average amount of gift aid, such as scholarships or grants (proportion receiving): $4,867 (36%). Average amount of self-help aid, such as work study or loans (proportion receiving): $4,274 (38%). Average need-based loan (excluding PLUS or other private loans): $4,011. Among students who received need-based aid, the average percentage of need met: 85%. Among students who received aid based on merit, the average award (and the proportion receiving): $4,999 (6%). The average athletic scholarship (and the proportion receiving): $8,589 (1%). Average amount of debt of borrowers graduating in 2005: $16,909. Proportion who borrowed: 61%.

CAMPUS LIFE AND EXTRACURRICULAR ACTIVITIES
Campus housing available (% using): coed dorms (56%), women's dorms (7%), sorority housing (17%), fraternity housing (11%), apartments for married students (1%), special housing for disabled students, special housing for international students, cooperative housing (1%). Students who live in college-owned, operated, or affiliated housing: 37%. Average per-year earnings: $3,120. **Clubs and organizations:** Number of student organizations: 380. Activities include: choral groups, concert band, dance, drama/theater, jazz band, literary magazine, marching band, music ensembles, musical theater, opera, pep band, radio station, student government, student newspaper, student film society, symphony orchestra, television station, yearbook. Number of fraternities: 28; sororities: 17. Proportion of men in fraternities: 14%; of women in sororities: 18%. **Sports program (2005-2006):** Member of NCAA I. *Men's intercollegiate varsity sports:* baseball, basketball, cross-country, football, golf, gymnastics, tennis, track and field (indoor), track and field (outdoor), wrestling. *Women's intercollegiate varsity sports:* basketball, bowling, cross-country, golf, gymnastics, riflery, soccer, softball, swimming and diving, tennis, track and field (indoor), track and field (outdoor), volleyball.

SERVICES AND FACILITIES
Basic services: nonremedial tutoring, women's center, placement service, day care, health service, health insurance. **Remedial assistance:** reading, math, writing, study skills. **Counseling services:** minority student, career, military, personal, veteran student, academic, older student, psychological, birth control. **For learning-disabled students:** School does not offer a structured program with separate admission and additional fees. Total under-

graduates in learning-disabled program or receiving services: 130. Services include: reading machines, tape recorders, note-taking services, oral tests, readers, extended time for tests, priority registration, priority seating, texts on tape, other testing accomodations. **Library:** Number of titles: 2,900,719; number of current serial subscriptions: 44,105. **Information technology resources:** Students are not required to lease or own a computer. Number of campus computers available to all students: 650. School has a wireless network. Approximate number of users that can be accommodated: 13,000. Proportion of college-owned housing units wired for high-speed internet access: 100%. **Campus safety:** Security services offered: 24-hour foot-and-vehicle patrols, late-night transport/escort service, 24-hour emergency telephones, lighted pathways/sidewalks, student patrols, controlled dormitory access (key, security card, etc).

TRANSFER AND INTERNATIONAL STUDENTS

Transfer students: May apply for admission for the following academic terms: Fall, Spring, Summer. Applicants need a minimum number of credits to apply. For fall 2005: Transfer applications received: 1,760. Transfer applicants offered admission: 1,267. Transfer applicants enrolled: 930. **International students:** Number of foreign undergraduates: 463 (3% of student body). Number of countries represented: 70. Minimum TOEFL score required: 525 (paper); 193 (computer). Average TOEFL score: 568 (paper).

University of Nebraska–Omaha

- **Address:** 6001 Dodge Street, Omaha, NE 68182
- **Website:** http://www.unomaha.edu
- **Public**
- **Enrollment:** 8,532 full-time; 2,797 part-time

KEY STATS

✔ **U.S News College Ranking:** 70, Universities–Master's (Midwest)
✔ **ACT Score (25th/75th percentile):** 20-25
✔ **Tuition:** 2006-2007: $5,118 in state, $13,646 out of state

Selectivity: Selective	**Room/board:** $6,630
Acceptance rate: 89%	**Average debt:** $16,900
Student/faculty ratio: 18/1	**Proportion who borrowed:** 48%

UNDERGRADUATE STUDENT BODY STATS

2005-2006 enrollment: 8,532 full-time; 2,797 part-time. Men: 47%; women: 53%. **Ethnic makeup:** African American: 6%; Asian American: 3%; Hispanic: 3%; White: 85%; International: 2%.

ADMISSIONS FACTS AND FIGURES

Phone: (402) 554-2393. **Email:** unoadm@unomaha.edu. **Website:** http://www.unomaha.edu. **Application deadlines for fall 2007:** Regular decision: August 1. Early decision: Not offered. Early action: Not offered. Admission cannot be deferred. **Application fee:** $45. Common application is not accepted. **To apply online, go to:** http://www.ses.unomaha.edu/admissions/. **Admissions requirements/recommendations:** High school units required (recommended): English: 4; Mathematics: 3; Science: 3; Foreign language: 2; Social studies: 1; History: 2; Academic electives: 1; Total units: 16. Tests: The college uses SAT or ACT scores in admissions decisions. Either SAT or ACT required. For admission to the fall 2007 entering class, the school will accept: ACT with writing, ACT without writing. Campus visit: Neither required nor recommended. Admissions interview: Neither required nor recommended. Off-campus interview: Not available. **Factors that count in admissions decisions:** *Academic:* Secondary school record: Very important. Class rank: Very important. Letters of recommendation: Not considered. Standardized test scores: Very important. Essay: Not considered. *Nonacademic:* Interview: Not considered. Extracurricular activities: Not considered. Talent/ability: Not considered. Character/personal qualities: Considered. Alumni/ae relationship: Not considered. Geographical residence: Not considered. State residency: Not considered. Religious affiliation/commitment: Not considered. Minority status: Not considered. Volunteer work: Not considered. Work experience: Not considered. **Other schools with the greatest overlap in applicants:** Bellevue University; Creighton University; University of Nebraska–Lincoln. **Admissions statistics for the fall 2005 entering class:** Total applicants: 3,732. Total accepted: 3,310. Freshmen enrolled: 1,758; 8% were from out of state. Overall acceptance rate: 89%. **Credentials of fall 2005 freshmen:** 13% ranked in the top 10 percent of their high school class; 35% were in the top 25 percent, and 68%

were in the top half. (Proportion submitting class standing: 92%.) **Average high school grade point average:** 3.3. **First-year students who submitted SAT scores:** 8%. Scores (25/75 percentile): Verbal: 490-620, Math: 490-600, Combined: 980-1220. **First-year students submitting ACT scores:** 95%. Scores (25/75 percentile): English: 19-26, Math: 18-25, Composite: 20-25.

ACADEMICS

Year founded: 1908. **Academic calendar:** Semester. **Degrees offered:** certificate, bachelor's, post-bachelor's certificate, master's, post-master's certificate, doctorate. **Most popular majors:** 31% business, management, marketing, and related support services, 13% education, 10% security and protective services, 6% communication, journalism, and related programs, 5% psychology. **Major fields of study:** area, ethnic, cultural, and gender studies; biological and biomedical sciences; business, management, marketing, and related support services; communication, journalism, and related programs; computer and information sciences and support services; education; engineering; English language and literature/letters; foreign languages, literatures, and linguistics; health professions and related clinical sciences; history; liberal arts and sciences studies, and humanities; library science; mathematics and statistics; multi/interdisciplinary studies; natural resources and conservation; parks, recreation, leisure, and fitness studies; philosophy and religious studies; physical sciences; psychology; public administration and social service professions; security and protective services; social sciences; transportation and materials moving; visual and performing arts. **Areas of required coursework:** arts/fine arts, humanities, mathematics, English (including composition), philosophy, sciences (biological or physical), history, social science, other. **Pre-professional programs:** pre-law, pre-dentistry, pre-medicine, pre-veterinary science, pre-optometry, pre-pharmacy, other. **Special academic programs (% participation):** cooperative (work-study plan) program (11%), cross-registration (.5%), distance learning, double major (2%), dual enrollment (2.5%), English as a Second Language (ESL), honors program (8%), independent study (20%), internships (22%), student-designed major (.05%), study abroad (9.2%), teacher certificate program (14.4%). **Teacher certification offered in:** early childhood, special education, elementary, middle/junior high, secondary. **Cooperative education programs:** agriculture, engineering, health professions, home economics. **Reserve Officers Training Corps (ROTC):** Army ROTC: Offered at cooperating institution (Creighton University); Air Force ROTC: Offered on campus. **Faculty and instruction (2005-2006):** Total instructional faculty: 482 full-time, 360 part-time (55% men; 45% women; 16% minorities). Full-time faculty with Ph.D. or other terminal degree: 85%. Student/faculty ratio: 18/1. Classes of fewer than 20 students: 35%; of 20 to 49 students: 51%; of 50 or more students: 13%. **Advanced Placement and International Baccalaureate credit:** AP tests may be used for: Credit only. Scores accepted: 3. International Baccalaureate exams may be used for: Credit and/or placement. **Freshmen returning for sophomore year:** 74%. **Graduation rates:** Four-year: 10%; five-year: 29%; six-year: 36%. **Graduate study:** 18% of students pursue further study immediately upon graduation.

COSTS AND FINANCIAL AID

Financial aid office: (402) 554-2327. **Expenses (2006-2007):** Tuition and fees 2006-2007: $5,118 in state, $13,646 out of state; room/board: $6,630. Estimated books and supplies: $750; transportation: $950; personal expenses: $1,940. **Financial aid:** Priority filing date for institution's financial aid form: March 1. In 2005-2006, 62% of undergraduates applied for financial aid. Of those, 44% were determined to have financial need; Average financial aid package (proportion receiving): N/A (44%). Average amount of gift aid, such as scholarships or grants (proportion receiving): N/A (33%). Average amount of self-help aid, such as work study or loans (proportion receiving): N/A (36%). Average amount of debt of borrowers graduating in 2005: $16,900. Proportion who borrowed: 48%.

CAMPUS LIFE AND EXTRACURRICULAR ACTIVITIES

Campus housing available (% using): coed dorms (100%). Students who live in college-owned, operated, or affiliated housing: 9%. **Student employment:** During the 2005-2006 academic year, 8% of undergraduates worked on campus. Average per-year earnings: $3,900. **Clubs and organizations:** Number of student organizations: 112. Activities include: choral groups, concert band, dance, drama/theater, jazz band, literary magazine, marching band, music ensembles, musical theater, opera, pep band, radio station, student government, student newspaper, student film society, symphony orchestra, television station. Number of fraternities: 7; sororities: 9. Proportion of men in fraternities: 2%; of women in sororities: 2%. Average proportion of students who stay on campus on weekends: 70%. **Sports program (2005-2006):** Member of NCAA II. *Men's intercollegiate varsity sports:* baseball, basketball, football, ice hockey, wrestling. *Women's intercollegiate* *varsity sports:* basketball, cross-country, golf, soccer, softball, swimming and diving, tennis, track and field (indoor), track and field (outdoor), volleyball.

SERVICES AND FACILITIES

Basic services: nonremedial tutoring, women's center, placement service, day care, health service, health insurance. **Counseling services:** minority student, career, personal, academic, older student, psychological, birth control. **For learning-disabled students:** School does not offer a structured program with separate admission and additional fees. Total undergraduates in learning-disabled program or receiving services: 50. Services include: reading machines, tape recorders, other special classes, videotaped classes, note-taking services, oral tests, readers, extended time for tests, tutors, priority registration, priority seating, texts on tape, other. **Library:** Number of titles: 1,060,106; number of current serial subscriptions: 2,796. **Information technology resources:** Students are not required to lease or own a computer. Number of campus computers available to all students: 2,200. School has a wireless network. Approximate number of users that can be accommodated: 3,500. Proportion of college-owned housing units wired for high-speed internet access: 100%. **Campus safety:** Security services offered: 24-hour foot-and-vehicle patrols, late-night transport/escort service, 24-hour emergency telephones, lighted pathways/sidewalks, controlled dormitory access (key, security card, etc).

TRANSFER AND INTERNATIONAL STUDENTS

Transfer students: May apply for admission for the following academic terms: Fall, Spring, Summer. Applicants need a minimum number of credits to apply. For fall 2005: Transfer applications received: 1,775. Transfer applicants offered admission: 1,553. Transfer applicants enrolled: 1,084. **International students:** Number of foreign undergraduates: 253 (2% of student body). Number of countries represented: 39. Minimum TOEFL score required: 487 (paper); 163 (computer).

Wayne State College

- **Address:** 1111 Main Street, Wayne, NE 68787
- **Website:** http://www.wsc.edu
- **Public**
- **Enrollment:** 2,483 full-time; 223 part-time

KEY STATS

✔ **U.S News College Ranking:** third tier, Universities–Master's (Midwest)
✔ **ACT Score (25th/75th percentile):** 18-25
✔ **Tuition:** 2006-2007: $4,013 in state, $7,088 out of state

Selectivity: Selective	**Room/board:** $4,470
Acceptance rate: 100%	**Average debt:** N/A
Student/faculty ratio: 18/1	**Proportion who borrowed:** N/A

UNDERGRADUATE STUDENT BODY STATS

2005-2006 enrollment: 2,483 full-time; 223 part-time. Men: 44%; women: 56%. **Ethnic makeup:** African American: 3%; American-Indian: 1%; Asian American: 1%; Hispanic: 2%; White: 93%; International: 1%.

ADMISSIONS FACTS AND FIGURES

Phone: (800) 228-9972. **Email:** admit1@wsc.edu. **Website:** http://www.wsc.edu. **Application deadlines for fall 2007:** Regular decision: Rolling. Early decision: Not offered. Early action: Not offered. Admission can be deferred. **Application fee:** $30. Common application is not accepted. **Admissions requirements/recommendations:** High school units required (recommended): English: (4); Mathematics: (3); Science: (2); Social studies: (3); Total units: (12). Tests: The college does not use SAT or ACT scores in admissions decisions. Neither SAT nor ACT required. Campus visit: Recommended. Admissions interview: Neither required nor recommended. Off-campus interview: May be arranged. **Factors that count in admissions decisions:** *Academic:* Secondary school record: Not considered. Class rank: Not considered. Letters of recommendation: Not considered. Standardized test scores: Not considered. Essay: Not considered. *Nonacademic:* Interview: Not considered. Extracurricular activities: Not considered. Talent/ability: Not considered. Character/personal qualities: Not considered. Alumni/ae relationship: Not considered. Geographical residence: Not considered. State residency: Not considered. Religious affiliation/commitment: Not considered. Minority status: Not considered. Volunteer work: Not considered. Work experience: Not considered. **Admissions statistics for the fall 2005 entering**

class: Total applicants: 1,202. Total accepted: 1,202. Freshmen enrolled: 593; 13% were from out of state. Overall acceptance rate: 100%. **Credentials of fall 2005 freshmen:** 13% ranked in the top 10 percent of their high school class; 33% were in the top 25 percent, and 64% were in the top half. (Proportion submitting class standing: 96%.) **Average high school grade point average:** 3.3. **First-year students submitting ACT scores:** 97%. Scores (25/75 percentile): English: 17-24, Math: 17-25, Composite: 18-25.

ACADEMICS

Year founded: 1909. **Academic calendar:** Semester. **Degrees offered:** bachelor's, master's, post-master's certificate. **Most popular majors:** 25% business, management, marketing, and related support services, 25% education, 9% psychology, 7% parks, recreation, leisure, and fitness studies, 5% security and protective services. **Major fields of study:** biological and biomedical sciences; business, management, marketing, and related support services; communication, journalism, and related programs; computer and information sciences and support services; education; engineering technologies/technicians; English language and literature/letters; family and consumer sciences/human sciences; foreign languages, literatures, and linguistics; health professions and related clinical sciences; history; mathematics and statistics; multi/interdisciplinary studies; parks, recreation, leisure, and fitness studies; physical sciences; psychology; security and protective services; social sciences; visual and performing arts. **Areas of required coursework:** arts/fine arts, humanities, computer literacy, mathematics, English (including composition), philosophy, sciences (biological or physical), history, social science, other. **Pre-professional programs:** pre-law, pre-dentistry, pre-medicine, pre-veterinary science, pre-optometry, pre-pharmacy, other. **Special academic programs:** cooperative (work-study plan) program, distance learning, double major, dual enrollment, honors program, independent study, internships, student-designed major, study abroad, teacher certificate program. **Teacher certification offered in:** early childhood, special education, elementary, vo-tech, middle/junior high, secondary, bilingual/bicultural. **Cooperative education programs:** agriculture, art, business, computer science, education, health professions, home economics, humanities, natural science, social/behavioral science, technologies. **Reserve Officers Training Corps (ROTC):** Army ROTC: Offered at cooperating institution (University of South Dakota). **Faculty and instruction (2005-2006):** Total instructional faculty: 126 full-time, 79 part-time (44% men; 56% women; 3% minorities). Full-time faculty with Ph.D. or other terminal degree: 75%. Student/faculty ratio: 18/1. Classes of fewer than 20 students: 43%; of 20 to 49 students: 55%; of 50 or more students: 1%. **Advanced Placement and International Baccalaureate credit:** AP tests may be used for: Credit and/or placement. Scores accepted: 3, 5. **Freshmen returning for sophomore year:** 68%. **Graduation rates:** Four-year: 23%; five-year: 39%; six-year: 45%.

COSTS AND FINANCIAL AID

Financial aid office: (402) 375-7230. **Expenses (2006-2007):** Tuition and fees 2006-2007: $4,013 in state, $7,088 out of state; room/board: $4,470. **Financial aid:** Priority filing date for institution's financial aid form: May 1. In 2005-2006, 82% of undergraduates applied for financial aid. Of those, 63% were determined to have financial need; 31% had their need fully met. Average financial aid package (proportion receiving): $3,264 (62%). Average amount of gift aid, such as scholarships or grants (proportion receiving): $1,574 (42%). Average amount of self-help aid, such as work study or loans (proportion receiving): $1,971 (52%). Average need-based loan (excluding PLUS or other private loans): $1,912. Among students who received need-based aid, the average percentage of need met: 37%.

CAMPUS LIFE AND EXTRACURRICULAR ACTIVITIES

Campus housing available: coed dorms, women's dorms. Students who live in college-owned, operated, or affiliated housing: 44%. **Clubs and organizations:** Number of student organizations: 95. Activities include: choral groups, concert band, dance, drama/theater, jazz band, literary magazine, marching band, music ensembles, musical theater, pep band, radio station, student government, student newspaper, television station. Number of fraternities: 2; sororities: 3. **Sports program (2005-2006):** Member of NCAA II. *Men's intercollegiate varsity sports:* baseball, basketball, cross-country, football, golf, track and field (indoor), track and field (outdoor). *Women's intercollegiate varsity sports:* basketball, cross-country, golf, soccer, softball, track and field (indoor), track and field (outdoor), volleyball.

SERVICES AND FACILITIES

Basic services: placement service, health service. **Counseling services:** minority student, career, personal, academic, psychological. **For learning-disabled students:** School does not offer a structured program with separate admission and additional fees. Services include: reading machines, tape recorders, diagnostic testing service, note-taking services, learning center, readers, extended time for tests, tutors, other testing accomodations, other. **Library:** Number of titles: 247,113; number of current serial subscriptions: 557. **Information technology resources:** Students are not required to lease or own a computer. Number of campus computers available to all students: 350. School has a wireless network. Approximate number of users that can be accommodated: 800. Proportion of college-owned housing units wired for high-speed internet access: 100%. **Campus safety:** Security services offered: 24-hour emergency telephones, lighted pathways/sidewalks, controlled dormitory access (key, security card, etc).

TRANSFER AND INTERNATIONAL STUDENTS
Transfer students: May apply for admission for the following academic terms: Fall, Spring, Summer. Applicants do not need a minimum number of credits to apply. For fall 2005: Transfer applications received: 289. Transfer applicants offered admission: 261. Transfer applicants enrolled: 187. **International students:** Number of foreign undergraduates: 22 (1% of student body). Minimum TOEFL score required: 550 (paper); 213 (computer).

York College

■ **Address:** 1125 E. Eighth Street, York, NE 68467
■ **Website:** http://www.york.edu
■ **Private; Religious affiliation:** Church of Christ
■ **Enrollment:** 412 full-time; 38 part-time

KEY STATS
✔ **U.S News College Ranking:** third tier, Comp. Coll.–Bachelor's (Midwest)
✔ **ACT Score (25th/75th percentile):** 17-27
✔ **Tuition:** 2006-2007: $13,500

Selectivity: Selective	**Room/board:** $4,300
Acceptance rate: 99%	**Average debt:** $22,581
Student/faculty ratio: 11/1	**Proportion who borrowed:** 89%

UNDERGRADUATE STUDENT BODY STATS
2005-2006 enrollment: 412 full-time; 38 part-time. Men: 49%; women: 51%. **Ethnic makeup:** African American: 5%; Asian American: 2%; Hispanic: 4%; White: 87%; International: 2%. **Religious preference:** Roman Catholic: 7%; Protestant: 19%; No preference: 3%; Unknown: 9%; Church of Christ: 62%.

ADMISSIONS FACTS AND FIGURES
Phone: (800) 950-9675. **Email:** enroll@york.edu. **Website:** http://www.york.edu. **Application deadlines for fall 2007:** Regular decision: August 31. Early decision: Not offered. Early action: Not offered. Admission can be deferred. **Application fee:** $20. Common application is not accepted. **Admissions requirements/recommendations:** High school units required (recommended): English: 3 (4); Mathematics: 2 (4); Science: 2 (4); Foreign language: (3); Social studies: 1 (4); History: 1 (4); Total units: 15 (21). Tests: The college uses SAT or ACT scores in admissions decisions. Either SAT or ACT required. For admission to the fall 2007 entering class, the school will accept: ACT with writing, ACT without writing. Campus visit: Recommended. Admissions interview: Neither required nor recommended. Off-campus interview: Not available. **Factors that count in admissions decisions:** *Academic:* Secondary school record: Very important. Class rank: Very important. Letters of recommendation: Very important. Standardized test scores: Very important. Essay: Considered. *Nonacademic:* Interview: Considered. Extracurricular activities: Not considered. Talent/ability: Not considered. Character/personal qualities: Considered. Alumni/ae relationship: Not considered. Geographical residence: Not considered. State residency: Not considered. Religious affiliation/commitment: Not considered. Minority status: Not considered. Volunteer work: Considered. Work experience: Considered. **Other schools with the greatest overlap in applicants:** Abilene Christian University; Harding University; Oklahoma Christian University; University of Nebraska–Kearney; University of Nebraska–Lincoln. **Admissions statistics for the fall 2005 entering class:** Total applicants: 206. Total accepted: 203. Freshmen enrolled: 119; 63% were from out of state. Overall acceptance rate: 99%. **Credentials of fall 2005 freshmen:** 12% ranked in the top 10 percent of their high school class; 26% were in the top 25 percent, and 56% were in the top half. (Proportion submitting class standing: 83%.) **Average high school grade point average:** 3.2. **First-year students who submitted SAT scores:** 10%. Scores (25/75 per-

centile): Verbal: 453-593, Math: 363-650, Combined: 816-1243. **First-year students submitting ACT scores:** 87%. Scores (25/75 percentile): English: 15-27, Math: 15-26, Composite: 17-27.

ACADEMICS
Year founded: 1890. **Academic calendar:** Semester. **Degrees offered:** associate, bachelor's. **Most popular majors:** 37% education, 16% business, management, marketing, and related support services, 11% biological and biomedical sciences, 8% communication, journalism, and related programs, 8% psychology. **Major fields of study:** biological and biomedical sciences; business, management, marketing, and related support services; education; English language and literature/letters; history; liberal arts and sciences studies, and humanities; psychology; theology and religious vocations; visual and performing arts. **Areas of required coursework:** arts/fine arts, humanities, mathematics, English (including composition), philosophy, sciences (biological or physical), history, social science. **Pre-professional programs:** pre-medicine, other. **Teacher certification offered in:** early childhood, special education, elementary, middle/junior high, secondary. **Reserve Officers Training Corps (ROTC):** Army ROTC: Offered at cooperating institution (University of Nebraska at Lincoln); Navy ROTC: Offered at cooperating institution (University of Nebraska at Lincoln); Air Force ROTC: Offered at cooperating institution (University of Nebraska at Lincoln). **Faculty and instruction (2005-2006):** Total instructional faculty: 35 full-time, 25 part-time (63% men; 37% women; 0% minorities). Full-time faculty with Ph.D. or other terminal degree: 43%. Student/faculty ratio: 11/1. Classes of fewer than 20 students: 77%; of 20 to 49 students: 22%; of 50 or more students: 1%. **Advanced Placement and International Baccalaureate credit:** AP tests may be used for: Credit only. Scores accepted: 3. International Baccalaureate exams may be used for: Credit only. **Freshmen returning for sophomore year:** 69%. **Graduation rates:** Four-year: 18%; five-year: 30%; six-year: 40%. **Graduate study:** 15% of students pursue further study immediately upon graduation; 11% within one year; 2% within five years. Fields in which graduates pursue further study: Master of Business Administration (MBA), 2%; medicine, 6%; education, 2%; arts and sciences, 9%.

COSTS AND FINANCIAL AID
Financial aid office: (402) 363-5624. **Expenses (2006-2007):** Tuition and fees 2006-2007: $13,500; room/board: $4,300. Estimated books and supplies: $1,000; transportation: $400; personal expenses: $1,170. **Financial aid:** Priority filing date for institution's financial aid form: April 1. In 2005-2006, 87% of undergraduates applied for financial aid. Of those, 79% were determined to have financial need; 18% had their need fully met. Average financial aid package (proportion receiving): $5,231 (79%). Average amount of gift aid, such as scholarships or grants (proportion receiving): N/A (74%). Average amount of self-help aid, such as work study or loans (proportion receiving): N/A (73%). Among students who received aid based on merit, the average award (and the proportion receiving): $0 (0%). The average athletic scholarship (and the proportion receiving): $4,595 (47%). Average amount of debt of borrowers graduating in 2005: $22,581. Proportion who borrowed: 89%.

CAMPUS LIFE AND EXTRACURRICULAR ACTIVITIES
Campus housing available (% using): women's dorms (48%), men's dorms (44%); apartments for married students (0%), apartment for single students (8%), cooperative housing (0%). Students who live in college-owned, operated, or affiliated housing: 60%. **Student employment:** During the 2005-2006 academic year, 0% of undergraduates worked on campus. Average per-year earnings: $0. **Clubs and organizations:** Number of student organizations: 23. Activities include: choral groups, drama/theater, music ensembles, student government, student newspaper, yearbook. Number of fraternities: 4; sororities: 4. Proportion of men in fraternities: 46%; of women in sororities: 64%. Average proportion of students who stay on campus on weekends: 85%. **Sports program (2005-2006):** Member of NAIA. *Men's intercollegiate varsity sports:* baseball, basketball, cross-country, golf, soccer, track and field (indoor), track and field (outdoor), wrestling. *Women's intercollegiate varsity sports:* basketball, cross-country, golf, soccer, softball, track and field (indoor), track and field (outdoor), volleyball.

SERVICES AND FACILITIES
Basic services: placement service. **Remedial assistance:** reading, math, writing, study skills. **Counseling services:** career, personal, academic, psychological, religious. **For learning-disabled students:** Total undergraduates in learning-disabled program or receiving services: 5. Services include: remedial math, remedial English, remedial reading, tape recorders, diagnostic testing service, untimed tests, note-taking services, oral tests, learning center, readers, extended time for tests, tutors, priority seating, texts on tape,

other testing accomodations. **Library:** Number of titles: 102,152; number of current serial subscriptions: 301. **Information technology resources:** Students are not required to lease or own a computer. Number of campus computers available to all students: 57. School does not have a wireless network. Proportion of college-owned housing units wired for high-speed internet access: 100%. **Campus safety:** Security services offered: lighted pathways/sidewalks, student patrols, controlled dormitory access (key, security card, etc).

TRANSFER AND INTERNATIONAL STUDENTS

Transfer students: May apply for admission for the following academic terms: Fall, Spring, Summer. Applicants do not need a minimum number of credits to apply. For fall 2005: Transfer applications received: 46. Transfer applicants offered admission: 42. Transfer applicants enrolled: 37.
International students: Number of foreign undergraduates: 9 (2% of student body). Number of countries represented: 14. Minimum TOEFL score required: 500 (paper); 173 (computer).

Nevada

Sierra Nevada College

- **Address:** 999 Tahoe Boulevard, Incline Village, NV 89451
- **Website:** http://www.sierranevada.edu
- **Private**
- **Enrollment:** 329 full-time; 56 part-time

KEY STATS
✔ **U.S News College Ranking:** third tier, Comp. Coll.–Bachelor's (West)
✔ **SAT Score (25th/75th percentile):** 820-1204
✔ **Tuition:** 2005-2006: $19,650

Selectivity: Less selective	**Room/board:** $7,450
Acceptance rate: 84%	**Average debt:** N/A
Student/faculty ratio: 11/1	**Proportion who borrowed:** N/A

UNDERGRADUATE STUDENT BODY STATS
2005-2006 enrollment: 329 full-time; 56 part-time. Men: 49%; women: 51%. **Ethnic makeup:** African American: 1%; American-Indian: 2%; Asian American: 2%; Hispanic: 3%; White: 92%; International: 1%.

ADMISSIONS FACTS AND FIGURES
Phone: (800) 332-8666. **Email:** admissions@sierranevada.edu. **Website:** http://www.sierranevada.edu. **Application deadlines for fall 2007:** Regular decision: Rolling. Early decision: Not offered. Early action: Not offered. Admission can be deferred. Common application is accepted. **Admissions requirements/recommendations:** High school units required (recommended): English: (4); Mathematics: (3); Science: (2); Foreign language: (2); Social studies: (2); History: (2). Tests: The college uses SAT or ACT scores in admissions decisions. Neither SAT nor ACT required. For admission to the fall 2007 entering class, the school will accept: ACT with writing, ACT without writing. Campus visit: Recommended. Admissions interview: Recommended. Off-campus interview: May not be arranged. **Factors that count in admissions decisions:** *Academic:* Secondary school record: Important. Class rank: Considered. Letters of recommendation: Important. Standardized test scores: Considered. Essay: Important. *Nonacademic:* Interview: Considered. Extracurricular activities: Considered. Talent/ability: Considered. Character/personal qualities: Considered. Alumni/ae relationship: Considered. Geographical residence: Not considered. State residency: Not considered. Religious affiliation/commitment: Considered. Minority status: Considered. Volunteer work: Considered. Work experience: Considered. **Other schools with the greatest overlap in applicants:** Evergreen State College; Prescott College; Sonoma State University; University of Nevada–Reno. **Admissions statistics for the fall 2005 entering class:** Total applicants: 82. Total accepted: 69. Freshmen enrolled: 69; 73% were from out of state. Overall acceptance rate: 84%. **First-year students who submitted SAT scores:** 71%. Scores (25/75 percentile): Verbal: 420-591, Math: 400-613, Combined: 820-1204. **First-year students submitting ACT scores:** 32%. Scores (25/75 percentile): English: 18-26, Math: 17-25, Composite: 20-25.

ACADEMICS
Year founded: 1969. **Academic calendar:** Semester. **Degrees offered:** bachelor's, post-bachelor's certificate, master's. **Most popular majors:** 28% business administration and management, 23% humanities/humanistic studies, 15% psychology, 12% fine and studio art. **Major fields of study:** biological and biomedical sciences; business, management, marketing, and related support services; computer and information sciences and support services; education; English language and literature/letters; liberal arts and sciences studies, and humanities; psychology; visual and performing arts. **Areas of required coursework:** arts/fine arts, humanities, computer literacy, mathematics, English (including composition), foreign languages, sciences (biological or physical), history, social science, other. **Pre-professional programs:** pre-medicine, pre-veterinary science, pre-pharmacy. **Special academic programs (% participation):** cooperative (work-study plan) program (65%), honors program (15%), independent study, internships (35%), study abroad (10%). **Teacher certification offered in:** special education, elementary, second-

ary. **Cooperative education programs:** health professions. **Reserve Officers Training Corps (ROTC):** Army ROTC: Offered at cooperating institution (Univ. of Nevada, Reno). **Faculty and instruction (2005-2006):** Total instructional faculty: 20 full-time, 51 part-time (45% men; 55% women; 3% minorities). Full-time faculty with Ph.D. or other terminal degree: 75%. Student/faculty ratio: 11/1. **Advanced Placement and International Baccalaureate credit:** AP tests may be used for: Credit only. Scores accepted: 3, 4, 5. International Baccalaureate exams may be used for: Credit only. **Freshmen returning for sophomore year:** 70%. **Graduation rates:** Four-year: 17%; five-year: 24%; six-year: 23%.

COSTS AND FINANCIAL AID
Financial aid office: (775) 831-1314. **Expenses (2005-2006):** Tuition and fees 2005-2006: $19,650; room/board: $7,450. Estimated books and supplies: $800; transportation: $500; personal expenses: $2,136. **Financial aid:** Priority filing date for institution's financial aid form: May 1; deadline: August 1.

CAMPUS LIFE AND EXTRACURRICULAR ACTIVITIES
Campus housing available: coed dorms. Students who live in college-owned, operated, or affiliated housing: 10%. **Student employment:** During the 2005-2006 academic year, 70% of undergraduates worked on campus. Average per-year earnings: $2,000. **Clubs and organizations:** Number of student organizations: 25. Activities include: choral groups, literary magazine, music ensembles, student government, student newspaper. Number of fraternities: 0; sororities: 0. Average proportion of students who stay on campus on weekends: 80%. **Sports program (2005-2006):** *Men's intercollegiate varsity sports:* skiing. *Women's intercollegiate varsity sports:* skiing.

SERVICES AND FACILITIES
Basic services: health insurance. **Remedial assistance:** math, writing, study skills. **Counseling services:** career, academic, psychological, birth control. **For learning-disabled students:** School does not offer a structured program with separate admission and additional fees. Services include: remedial math, remedial English, untimed tests, note-taking services, oral tests, tutors. **Information technology resources:** Students are required to lease or own a computer. Number of campus computers available to all students: 50. School has a wireless network. Proportion of college-owned housing units wired for high-speed internet access: 100%. **Campus safety:** Security services offered: late-night transport/escort service, lighted pathways/sidewalks, student patrols, controlled dormitory access (key, security card, etc).

TRANSFER AND INTERNATIONAL STUDENTS
Transfer students: May apply for admission for the following academic terms: Fall, Spring. Applicants do not need a minimum number of credits to apply. For fall 2005: Transfer applicants enrolled: 35. **International students:** Number of foreign undergraduates: 3 (1% of student body). Minimum TOEFL score required: 550 (paper); 172 (computer).

University of Nevada–Las Vegas

- **Address:** 4505 Maryland Parkway, Las Vegas, NV 89154
- **Website:** http://www.unlv.edu
- **Public**
- **Enrollment:** 15,788 full-time; 6,289 part-time

KEY STATS
✔ **U.S News College Ranking:** fourth tier, National Universities
✔ **SAT Score (25th/75th percentile):** 890-1130
✔ **Tuition:** 2006-2007: $3,510 in state, $13,420 out of state

Selectivity: Selective	**Room/board:** $10,220
Acceptance rate: 81%	**Average debt:** $17,394
Student/faculty ratio: 20/1	**Proportion who borrowed:** 40%

UNDERGRADUATE STUDENT BODY STATS

2005-2006 enrollment: 15,788 full-time; 6,289 part-time. Men: 44%; women: 56%. **Ethnic makeup:** African American: 8%; American-Indian: 1%; Asian American: 14%; Hispanic: 11%; White: 61%; International: 4%.

ADMISSIONS FACTS AND FIGURES

Phone: (702) 774-8658. **Email:** undergraduate.recruitment@unlv.edu. **Website:** http://www.unlv.edu. **Application deadlines for fall 2007:** Regular decision: February 1. Early decision: Not offered. Early action: Not offered. Admission can be deferred. **Application fee:** $60. Common application is not accepted. **To apply online, go to:** http://www.unlv.edu/main/admissions/applyOnline.html. **Admissions requirements/recommendations:** High school units required (recommended): English: 4; Mathematics: 3; Science: 3; Social studies: 3; Total units: 13. Tests: The college uses SAT or ACT scores in admissions decisions. Neither SAT nor ACT required. For admission to the fall 2007 entering class, the school will accept: ACT with writing, ACT without writing. Campus visit: Recommended. Admissions interview: Neither required nor recommended. Off-campus interview: Not available. **Factors that count in admissions decisions:** *Academic:* Secondary school record: Very important. Class rank: Not considered. Letters of recommendation: Considered. Standardized test scores: Very important. Essay: Considered. *Nonacademic:* Interview: Not considered. Extracurricular activities: Not considered. Talent/ability: Not considered. Character/personal qualities: Not considered. Alumni/ae relationship: Not considered. Geographical residence: Not considered. State residency: Not considered. Religious affiliation/commitment: Not considered. Minority status: Not considered. Volunteer work: Not considered. Work experience: Not considered. **Other schools with the greatest overlap in applicants:** Arizona State University; San Diego State University; University of California–Los Angeles; University of Nevada–Reno; University of Southern California. **Admissions statistics for the fall 2005 entering class:** Total applicants: 6,952. Total accepted: 5,663. Freshmen enrolled: 3,138; 25% were from out of state. Overall acceptance rate: 81%. **Credentials of fall 2005 freshmen:** 18% ranked in the top 10 percent of their high school class; 44% were in the top 25 percent, and 79% were in the top half. (Proportion submitting class standing: 84%.) **Average high school grade point average:** 3.2. **First-year students who submitted SAT scores:** 59%. Scores (25/75 percentile): Verbal: 440-560, Math: 450-570, Combined: 890-1130. **First-year students submitting ACT scores:** 38%. Scores (25/75 percentile): English: 17-23, Math: 17-24, Composite: 18-24.

ACADEMICS

Year founded: 1957. **Academic calendar:** Semester. **Degrees offered:** certificate, bachelor's, post-bachelor's certificate, master's, post-master's certificate, first professional, first professional certificate, doctorate. **Most popular majors:** 31% business, management, marketing, and related support services, 12% education, 7% communication, journalism, and related programs, 7% psychology, 6% visual and performing arts. **Major fields of study:** architecture and related services; area, ethnic, cultural, and gender studies; biological and biomedical sciences; business, management, marketing, and related support services; communication, journalism, and related programs; computer and information sciences and support services; education; engineering; engineering technologies/technicians; English language and literature/letters; foreign languages, literatures, and linguistics; health professions and related clinical sciences; history; legal professions and studies; liberal arts and sciences studies, and humanities; mathematics and statistics; multi/interdisciplinary studies; natural resources and conservation; parks, recreation, leisure, and fitness studies; personal and culinary services; philosophy and religious studies; physical sciences; psychology; public administration and social service professions; security and protective services; social sciences; visual and performing arts. **Areas of required coursework:** arts/fine arts, humanities, computer literacy, mathematics, English (including composition), sciences (biological or physical), history, social science. **Pre-professional programs:** pre-law, pre-dentistry, pre-medicine, pretheology, pre-veterinary science, pre-optometry, pre-pharmacy, other. **Special academic programs:** accelerated program, cooperative (work-study plan) program, cross-registration, distance learning, double major, dual enrollment, English as a Second Language (ESL), exchange student program (domestic), honors program, independent study, internships, student-designed major, study abroad, teacher certificate program. **Teacher certification offered in:** early childhood, special education, elementary, vo-tech, adult education, secondary. **Cooperative education programs:** business, education, engineering, health professions, other. **Reserve Officers Training Corps (ROTC):** Army ROTC: Offered on campus. **Faculty and instruction (2005-2006):** Total instructional faculty: 851 full-time, 683 part-time. Full-time faculty with Ph.D. or other terminal degree: 88%. Student/faculty ratio: 20/1. Classes of

fewer than 20 students: 29%; of 20 to 49 students: 57%; of 50 or more students: 14%. **Advanced Placement and International Baccalaureate credit:** AP tests may be used for: Credit and/or placement. Scores accepted: 3, 4, 5. International Baccalaureate exams may be used for: Credit and/or placement. **Freshmen returning for sophomore year:** 72%. **Graduation rates:** Four-year: 14%; five-year: 32%; six-year: 41%.

COSTS AND FINANCIAL AID

Financial aid office: (702) 895-3424. **Expenses (2006-2007):** Tuition and fees 2006-2007: $3,510 in state, $13,420 out of state; room/board: $10,220. Estimated books and supplies: $850; transportation: $700; personal expenses: $1,800. **Financial aid:** Priority filing date for institution's financial aid form: February 1. In 2005-2006, 77% of undergraduates applied for financial aid. Of those, 43% were determined to have financial need; 43% had their need fully met. Average financial aid package (proportion receiving): $6,416 (42%). Average amount of gift aid, such as scholarships or grants (proportion receiving): $3,117 (21%). Average amount of self-help aid, such as work study or loans (proportion receiving): $5,317 (20%). Average need-based loan (excluding PLUS or other private loans): $4,104. Among students who received need-based aid, the average percentage of need met: 70%. Among students who received aid based on merit, the average award (and the proportion receiving): $2,473 (22%). The average athletic scholarship (and the proportion receiving): $7,990 (3%). Average amount of debt of borrowers graduating in 2005: $17,394. Proportion who borrowed: 40%.

CAMPUS LIFE AND EXTRACURRICULAR ACTIVITIES

Campus housing available: coed dorms, special housing for international students. Students who live in college-owned, operated, or affiliated housing: 7%. **Student employment:** During the 2005-2006 academic year, 15% of undergraduates worked on campus. Average per-year earnings: $4,000. **Clubs and organizations:** Number of student organizations: 180. Activities include: choral groups, concert band, dance, drama/theater, jazz band, marching band, music ensembles, musical theater, opera, pep band, student government, student newspaper, student film society, symphony orchestra, television station. Number of fraternities: 18; sororities: 9. Proportion of men in fraternities: 5%; of women in sororities: 3%. Average proportion of students who stay on campus on weekends: 10%. **Sports program (2005-2006):** Member of NCAA I. *Men's intercollegiate varsity sports:* baseball, basketball, football, golf, soccer, swimming and diving, tennis. *Women's intercollegiate varsity sports:* basketball, cross-country, golf, soccer, softball, swimming and diving, tennis, track and field (indoor), track and field (outdoor), volleyball.

SERVICES AND FACILITIES

Basic services: nonremedial tutoring, women's center, placement service, day care, health service, health insurance. **Remedial assistance:** reading, math, writing, study skills. **Counseling services:** minority student, career, personal, veteran student, academic, older student, psychological, birth control, religious. **For learning-disabled students:** School does not offer a structured program with separate admission and additional fees. Total undergraduates in learning-disabled program or receiving services: 175. Services include: reading machines, tape recorders, diagnostic testing service, note-taking services, oral tests, learning center, readers, extended time for tests, priority registration, priority seating, substitution of courses, texts on tape, typist/scribe, exams on tape or computer, other testing accomodations, other. **Library:** Number of titles: 1,395,737; number of current serial subscriptions: 20,146. **Information technology resources:** Students are not required to lease or own a computer. Number of campus computers available to all students: 2,100. School has a wireless network. Approximate number of users that can be accommodated: 2,500. Proportion of college-owned housing units wired for high-speed internet access: 100%. **Campus safety:** Security services offered: 24-hour foot-and-vehicle patrols, late-night transport/escort service, 24-hour emergency telephones, lighted pathways/sidewalks, controlled dormitory access (key, security card, etc).

TRANSFER AND INTERNATIONAL STUDENTS

Transfer students: May apply for admission for the following academic terms: Fall, Spring, Summer. Applicants need a minimum number of credits to apply. For fall 2005: Transfer applications received: 4,339. Transfer applicants offered admission: 3,608. Transfer applicants enrolled: 2,029. **International students:** Number of foreign undergraduates: 813 (4% of student body). Number of countries represented: 62. Minimum TOEFL score required: 310 (paper); 40 (computer). Average TOEFL score: 382 (paper).

University of Nevada–Reno

- **Address:** Reno, NV 89557
- **Website:** http://www.unr.edu
- **Public**
- **Enrollment:** 10,257 full-time; 2,680 part-time

KEY STATS

✔ **U.S News College Ranking:** third tier, National Universities
✔ **SAT Score (25th/75th percentile):** 950-1170
✔ **Tuition:** 2006-2007: $3,576 in state, $13,487 out of state

Selectivity: Selective	**Room/board:** $7,599
Acceptance rate: 86%	**Average debt:** N/A
Student/faculty ratio: 20/1	**Proportion who borrowed:** N/A

UNDERGRADUATE STUDENT BODY STATS

2005-2006 enrollment: 10,257 full-time; 2,680 part-time. Men: 46%; women: 54%. **Ethnic makeup:** African American: 2%; American-Indian: 1%; Asian American: 7%; Hispanic: 7%; White: 81%; International: 2%.

ADMISSIONS FACTS AND FIGURES

Phone: (775) 784-4700. **Email:** asknevada@unr.edu. **Website:** http://www.unr.edu. **Application deadlines for fall 2007:** Regular decision: Rolling. Early decision: Not offered. Early action: Send application by: November 15; Decision sent by: N/A. Admission can be deferred. **Application fee:** $60. Common application is not accepted. **To apply online, go to:** http://www.ss.unr.edu/admissions. **Admissions requirements/recommendations:** High school units required (recommended): English: 4; Mathematics: 3; Science: 3; Foreign language: 0; Social studies: 3; History: 0; Academic electives: 0; Total units: 13. Tests: The college does not use SAT or ACT scores in admissions decisions. Neither SAT nor ACT required. Campus visit: Recommended. Admissions interview: Neither required nor recommended. Off-campus interview: Not available. **Factors that count in admissions decisions:** *Academic:* Secondary school record: Very important. Class rank: Not considered. Letters of recommendation: Not considered. Standardized test scores: Considered. Essay: Not considered. *Nonacademic:* Interview: Not considered. Extracurricular activities: Not considered. Talent/ability: Not considered. Character/personal qualities: Not considered. Alumni/ae relationship: Not considered. Geographical residence: Not considered. State residency: Not considered. Religious affiliation/commitment: Not considered. Minority status: Not considered. Volunteer work: Not considered. Work experience: Not considered. **Admissions statistics for the fall 2005 entering class:** Total applicants: 4,793. Total accepted: 4,138. Freshmen enrolled: 2,432; 17% were from out of state. Overall acceptance rate: 86%. Non-early acceptance rate: 86%. **Average high school grade point average:** 3.4. **First-year students who submitted SAT scores:** 70%. Scores (25/75 percentile): Verbal: 470-580, Math: 480-590, Combined: 950-1170. **First-year students submitting ACT scores:** 54%. Scores (25/75 percentile): English: 19-25, Math: 19-25, Composite: 20-25.

ACADEMICS

Year founded: 1864. **Academic calendar:** Semester. **Degrees offered:** bachelor's, post-bachelor's certificate, master's, post-master's certificate, first professional, doctorate. **Most popular majors:** 14% business, management, marketing, and related support services, 11% education, 9% health professions and related clinical sciences, 8% social sciences, 7% engineering. **Major fields of study:** agriculture, agriculture operations, and related sciences; area, ethnic, cultural, and gender studies; biological and biomedical sciences; business, management, marketing, and related support services; communication, journalism, and related programs; computer and information sciences and support services; education; engineering; engineering technologies/technicians; English language and literature/letters; family and consumer sciences/human sciences; foreign languages, literatures, and linguistics; health professions and related clinical sciences; history; liberal arts and sciences studies, and humanities; mathematics and statistics; natural resources and conservation; philosophy and religious studies; physical sciences; psychology; public administration and social service professions; social sciences; visual and performing arts. **Areas of required coursework:** arts/fine arts, humanities, mathematics, English (including composition), sciences (biological or physical), social science, other. **Pre-professional programs:** pre-law, pre-veterinary science, other. **Special academic programs:** distance learning, double major, dual enrollment, English as a Second Language (ESL), exchange student program (domestic), honors program,

independent study, internships, study abroad, teacher certificate program. **Teacher certification offered in:** early childhood, special education, elementary, middle/junior high, secondary, bilingual/bicultural. **Reserve Officers Training Corps (ROTC):** Army ROTC: Offered on campus. **Faculty and instruction (2005-2006):** Total instructional faculty: 489 full-time, 471 part-time (56% men; 44% women; 12% minorities). Full-time faculty with Ph.D. or other terminal degree: 82%. Student/faculty ratio: 20/1. Classes of fewer than 20 students: 37%; of 20 to 49 students: 51%; of 50 or more students: 12%. **Freshmen returning for sophomore year:** 75%. **Graduation rates:** Four-year: 16%; five-year: 43%; six-year: 52%. **Graduate study:** 35% of students pursue further study within one year. Fields in which graduates pursue further study: Master of Business Administration (MBA), 10%; law, 5%; medicine, 3%; dentistry, 1%; engineering, 7%; theology (or the seminary), 1%; education, 16%; arts and sciences, 21%; veterinary medicine, 1%.

COSTS AND FINANCIAL AID

Financial aid office: (775) 784-4666. **Expenses (2006-2007):** Tuition and fees 2006-2007: $3,576 in state, $13,487 out of state; room/board: $7,599. **Financial aid:** Priority filing date for institution's financial aid form: February 1.

CAMPUS LIFE AND EXTRACURRICULAR ACTIVITIES

Campus housing available (% using): coed dorms (76%), women's dorms (5%), men's dorms (4%), apartments for married students (2%), apartment for single students (13%), special housing for disabled students (0%). Students who live in college-owned, operated, or affiliated housing: 14%. **Student employment:** During the 2005-2006 academic year, 20% of undergraduates worked on campus. Average per-year earnings: $5,310. **Clubs and organizations:** Number of student organizations: 189. Activities include: choral groups, concert band, dance, drama/theater, jazz band, literary magazine, marching band, music ensembles, musical theater, opera, pep band, radio station, student government, student newspaper, yearbook. Number of fraternities: 9; sororities: 4. Proportion of men in fraternities: 7%; of women in sororities: 5%. Average proportion of students who stay on campus on weekends: 80%. **Sports program (2005-2006):** Member of NCAA I. *Men's intercollegiate varsity sports:* alpine skiing, baseball, basketball, football, golf, nordic skiing, riflery, tennis. *Women's intercollegiate varsity sports:* alpine skiing, basketball, cross-country, golf, nordic skiing, riflery, soccer, softball, swimming and diving, tennis, track and field (indoor), track and field (outdoor), volleyball.

SERVICES AND FACILITIES

Basic services: nonremedial tutoring, placement service, day care, health service, health insurance. **Remedial assistance:** reading, math, writing, study skills. **Counseling services:** minority student, career, military, personal, veteran student, academic, older student, psychological, birth control, religious. **For learning-disabled students:** School does not offer a structured program with separate admission and additional fees. Total undergraduates in learning-disabled program or receiving services: 357. Services include: remedial math, remedial English, reading machines, tape recorders, other special classes, diagnostic testing service, note-taking services, oral tests, learning center, readers, extended time for tests, tutors, priority seating, texts on tape. **Library:** Number of titles: 1,149,824; number of current serial subscriptions: 15,906. **Information technology resources:** Students are not required to lease or own a computer. Number of campus computers available to all students: 500. School has a wireless network. Approximate number of users that can be accommodated: 500. Proportion of college-owned housing units wired for high-speed internet access: 100%. **Campus safety:** Security services offered: 24-hour foot-and-vehicle patrols, late-night transport/escort service, 24-hour emergency telephones, lighted pathways/sidewalks, controlled dormitory access (key, security card, etc).

TRANSFER AND INTERNATIONAL STUDENTS

Transfer students: May apply for admission for the following academic terms: Fall, Spring, Summer. Applicants need a minimum number of credits to apply. For fall 2005: Transfer applications received: 1,964. Transfer applicants offered admission: 1,783. Transfer applicants enrolled: 1,058. **International students:** Number of foreign undergraduates: 272 (2% of student body). Number of countries represented: 279. Minimum TOEFL score required: 500 (paper); 173 (computer). Average TOEFL score: 523 (paper).

New Hampshire

Colby-Sawyer College

- **Address:** 541 Main Street, New London, NH 03257-7835
- **Website:** http://www.colby-sawyer.edu
- **Private**
- **Enrollment:** 954 full-time; 17 part-time

KEY STATS
- ✔ **U.S News College Ranking:** 11, Comp. Coll.–Bachelor's (North)
- ✔ **SAT Score (25th/75th percentile):** 920-1100
- ✔ **Tuition:** 2006-2007: $26,350

Selectivity: Less selective	**Room/board:** $9,900
Acceptance rate: 90%	**Average debt:** $18,175
Student/faculty ratio: 11/1	**Proportion who borrowed:** 79%

UNDERGRADUATE STUDENT BODY STATS
2005-2006 enrollment: 954 full-time; 17 part-time. Men: 36%; women: 64%. **Ethnic makeup:** African American: 1%; Asian American: 1%; White: 97%; International: 1%.

ADMISSIONS FACTS AND FIGURES
Phone: (800) 272-1015. **Email:** admissions@colby-sawyer.edu. **Website:** http://www.colby-sawyer.edu. **Application deadlines for fall 2007:** Regular decision: April 1. Early decision: Send application by: December 1; Decision sent by: December 15. Early action: Not offered. Admission can be deferred. **Application fee:** $45. Common application is accepted. **Admissions requirements/recommendations:** High school units required (recommended): English: 4; Mathematics: 3; Science: 2; Foreign language: 2; Social studies: 3; Total units: 15. Tests: The college uses SAT or ACT scores in admissions decisions. Either SAT or ACT required. For admission to the fall 2007 entering class, the school will accept ACT with writing. Campus visit: Recommended. Admissions interview: Recommended. Off-campus interview: May be arranged. **Factors that count in admissions decisions:** *Academic:* Secondary school record: Very important. Class rank: Considered. Letters of recommendation: Important. Standardized test scores: Important. Essay: Important. *Nonacademic:* Interview: Important. Extracurricular activities: Considered. Talent/ability: Considered. Character/personal qualities: Considered. Alumni/ae relationship: Considered. Geographical residence: Considered. State residency: Not considered. Religious affiliation/commitment: Not considered. Minority status: Not considered. Volunteer work: Considered. Work experience: Considered. **Other schools with the greatest overlap in applicants:** Plymouth State University; Salve Regina University; St. Anselm College; St. Michael's College; University of New Hampshire. **Admissions statistics for the fall 2005 entering class:** Total applicants: 1,474. Total accepted: 1,328. Freshmen enrolled: 282; 73% were from out of state. Overall acceptance rate: 90%. Non-early acceptance rate: 90%. **Average high school grade point average:** 2.9. **First-year students who submitted SAT scores:** 97%. Scores (25/75 percentile): Verbal: 460-550, Math: 460-550, Combined: 920-1100. **First-year students submitting ACT scores:** 16%. Scores (25/75 percentile): English: N/A, Math: N/A, Composite: 19-24.

ACADEMICS
Year founded: 1837. **Academic calendar:** Semester. **Degrees offered:** associate, transfer-associate, bachelor's. **Most popular majors:** 17% business administration and management, 9% psychology, 9% sport and fitness administration/management, 7% mass communication/media studies, 7% nursing/registered nurse training (R.N., A.S.N., B.S.N., M.S.N.). **Major fields of study:** biological and biomedical sciences; business, management, marketing, and related support services; communication, journalism, and related programs; education; English language and literature/letters; health professions and related clinical sciences; natural resources and conservation; parks, recreation, leisure, and fitness studies; psychology; social sciences; visual and performing arts. **Areas of required coursework:** arts/fine arts, humanities, computer literacy, mathematics, English (including composition), sciences (biological or physical), history, social science, other.

Special academic programs (% participation): accelerated program, cross-registration, double major, dual enrollment, English as a Second Language (ESL), exchange student program (domestic), honors program, independent study, internships (98%), study abroad, teacher certificate program (10%). **Teacher certification offered in:** early childhood, elementary, middle/junior high, secondary. **Reserve Officers Training Corps (ROTC):** Army ROTC: Offered at cooperating institution (University of New Hampshire); Air Force ROTC: Offered at cooperating institution (University of New Hampshire). **Faculty and instruction (2005-2006):** Total instructional faculty: 59 full-time, 65 part-time (42% men; 58% women; 2% minorities). Full-time faculty with Ph.D. or other terminal degree: 78%. Student/faculty ratio: 11/1. Classes of fewer than 20 students: 60%; of 20 to 49 students: 40%; of 50 or more students: 0%. **Advanced Placement and International Baccalaureate credit:** AP tests may be used for: Credit and/or placement. Scores accepted: 3, 4, 5. International Baccalaureate exams may be used for: Credit and/or placement. **Freshmen returning for sophomore year:** 78%. **Graduation rates:** Four-year: 48%; five-year: 58%; six-year: 55%.

COSTS AND FINANCIAL AID
Financial aid office: (603) 526-3717. **Expenses (2006-2007):** Tuition and fees 2006-2007: $26,350; room/board: $9,900. Estimated books and supplies: $750 personal expenses: $1,000. **Financial aid:** Priority filing date for institution's financial aid form: February 15. In 2005-2006, 83% of undergraduates applied for financial aid. Of those, 72% were determined to have financial need; 18% had their need fully met. Average financial aid package (proportion receiving): $16,430 (72%). Average amount of gift aid, such as scholarships or grants (proportion receiving): $11,994 (69%). Average amount of self-help aid, such as work study or loans (proportion receiving): $5,566 (69%). Average need-based loan (excluding PLUS or other private loans): $3,926. Among students who received need-based aid, the average percentage of need met: 71%. Among students who received aid based on merit, the average award (and the proportion receiving): $4,200 (10%). The average athletic scholarship (and the proportion receiving): $0 (0%). Average amount of debt of borrowers graduating in 2005: $18,175. Proportion who borrowed: 79%.

CAMPUS LIFE AND EXTRACURRICULAR ACTIVITIES
Campus housing available (% using): coed dorms (88%), women's dorms (7%), special housing for disabled students, other housing options (5%). Students who live in college-owned, operated, or affiliated housing: 90%. **Clubs and organizations:** Number of student organizations: 45. Activities include: choral groups, dance, drama/theater, literary magazine, musical theater, radio station, student government, student newspaper, yearbook. Number of fraternities: 0; sororities: 0. Average proportion of students who stay on campus on weekends: 70%. **Sports program (2005-2006):** Member of NCAA III. *Men's intercollegiate varsity sports:* alpine skiing, baseball, basketball, equestrian Sports, soccer, swimming and diving, tennis, track and field (outdoor). *Women's intercollegiate varsity sports:* alpine skiing, basketball, equestrian sports, lacrosse, soccer, swimming and diving, tennis, track and field (outdoor), volleyball.

SERVICES AND FACILITIES
Basic services: nonremedial tutoring, health service, health insurance. **Counseling services:** career, personal, academic, birth control. **For learning-disabled students:** School does not offer a structured program with separate admission and additional fees. Total undergraduates in learning-disabled program or receiving services: 92. Services include: tape recorders, learning center, extended time for tests, tutors. **Library:** Number of titles: 91,070; number of current serial subscriptions: 406. **Information technology resources:** Students are not required to lease or own a computer. Number of campus computers available to all students: 188. School has a wireless network. Approximate number of users that can be accommodated: 1,000. Proportion of college-owned housing units wired for high-speed internet access: 100%. **Campus safety:** Security services offered: 24-hour foot-and-vehicle patrols, late-night transport/escort service, 24-hour emergency telephones, lighted pathways/sidewalks, controlled dormitory access (key, security card, etc).

TRANSFER AND INTERNATIONAL STUDENTS

Transfer students: May apply for admission for the following academic terms: Fall, Spring. Applicants do not need a minimum number of credits to apply. For fall 2005: Transfer applications received: 31. Transfer applicants offered admission: 28. Transfer applicants enrolled: 19. **International students:** Number of foreign undergraduates: 9 (1% of student body). Number of countries represented: 6. Minimum TOEFL score required: 500 (paper); 173 (computer).

Daniel Webster College

- ■ **Address:** 20 University Drive, Nashua, NH 03063
- ■ **Website:** http://www.dwc.edu
- ■ **Private**
- ■ **Enrollment:** N/A

KEY STATS

- ✔ **U.S News College Ranking:** fourth tier, Comp. Coll.–Bachelor's (North)
- ✔ **SAT or ACT Score (25th/75th percentile):** N/A
- ✔ **Tuition:** N/A

Selectivity: Less selective	**Room/board:** N/A
Acceptance rate: N/A	**Average debt:** N/A
Student/faculty ratio: N/A	**Proportion who borrowed:** N/A

Dartmouth College

- ■ **Address:** 6016 McNutt Hall, Hanover, NH 03755
- ■ **Website:** http://www.dartmouth.edu
- ■ **Private**
- ■ **Enrollment:** 4,050 full-time; 60 part-time

KEY STATS

- ✔ **U.S News College Ranking:** 9, National Universities
- ✔ **SAT Score (25th/75th percentile):** 1350-1550
- ✔ **Tuition:** 2006-2007: $33,501

Selectivity: Most selective	**Room/board:** $9,840
Acceptance rate: 17%	**Average debt:** $19,305
Student/faculty ratio: 8/1	**Proportion who borrowed:** 48%

UNDERGRADUATE STUDENT BODY STATS

2005-2006 enrollment: 4,050 full-time; 60 part-time. Men: 50%; women: 50%. **Ethnic makeup:** African American: 7%; American-Indian: 3%; Asian American: 14%; Hispanic: 6%; White: 65%; International: 5%.

ADMISSIONS FACTS AND FIGURES

Phone: (603) 646-2875. **Email:** admissions.office@dartmouth.edu. **Website:** http://www.dartmouth.edu. **Application deadlines for fall 2007:** Regular decision: January 1; decision sent by April 1. Early decision: Send application by: November 1; Decision sent by: December 15. Early action: Not offered. Admission can be deferred. **Application fee:** $70. Common application is accepted. **To apply online, go to:** http://www.apply.embark.com/ugrad/dartmouth. **Admissions requirements/recommendations:** High school units required (recommended): English: (4); Mathematics: (4); Science: (3); Social studies: (3); History: (3); Total units: (17). Tests: The college uses SAT or ACT scores in admissions decisions. Either SAT or ACT required. For admission to the fall 2007 entering class, the school will accept: ACT with writing. Campus visit: Neither required nor recommended. Admissions interview: Neither required nor recommended. Off-campus interview: Not available. **Factors that count in admissions decisions:** *Academic:* Secondary school record: Very important. Class rank: Very important. Letters of recommendation: Very important. Standardized test scores: Very important. Essay: Very important. *Nonacademic:* Interview: Considered. Extracurricular activities: Very important. Talent/ability: Important. Character/personal qualities: Very important. Alumni/ae relationship: Considered. Geographical residence: Considered. State residency: Not considered. Religious affiliation/commitment: Not considered. Minority status: Considered. Volunteer work: Important. Work experience: Considered. **Other schools with the greatest overlap in applicants:** Brown University; Harvard

University; Princeton University; Stanford University; Yale University. **Admissions statistics for the fall 2005 entering class:** Total applicants: 12,756. Total accepted: 2,171. Freshmen enrolled: 1,074; 97% were from out of state. Overall acceptance rate: 17%. Non-early acceptance rate: 17%. **Size of waiting list:** 1200 applicants; enrolled from waiting list: 16. **Credentials of fall 2005 freshmen:** 87% ranked in the top 10 percent of their high school class; 98% were in the top 25 percent, and 100% were in the top half. (Proportion submitting class standing: 48%.) **First-year students who submitted SAT scores:** 89%. Scores (25/75 percentile): Verbal: 670-770, Math: 680-780, Combined: 1350-1550. **First-year students submitting ACT scores:** 11%. Scores (25/75 percentile): English: N/A, Math: N/A, Composite: 29-34.

ACADEMICS

Year founded: 1769. **Academic calendar:** Quarter. **Degrees offered:** bachelor's, post-bachelor's certificate, master's, first professional, doctorate. **Most popular majors:** 12% economics, 10% history, 10% political science and government, 8% psychology, 6% English language and literature. **Major fields of study:** area, ethnic, cultural, and gender studies; biological and biomedical sciences; computer and information sciences and support services; engineering; English language and literature/letters; foreign languages, literatures, and linguistics; history; liberal arts and sciences studies, and humanities; mathematics and statistics; multi/interdisciplinary studies; natural resources and conservation; philosophy and religious studies; physical sciences; psychology; social sciences; visual and performing arts. **Areas of required coursework:** arts/fine arts, humanities, mathematics, English (including composition), foreign languages, sciences (biological or physical), social science, other. **Special academic programs (% participation):** double major (18.3%), exchange student program (domestic) (2%), honors program (19.7%), independent study (33%), student-designed major (1%), study abroad (55%), teacher certificate program (1%). **Teacher certification offered in:** elementary, secondary. **Reserve Officers Training Corps (ROTC):** Army ROTC: Offered at cooperating institution (Norwich University). **Faculty and instruction (2005-2006):** Total instructional faculty: 493 full-time, 140 part-time (65% men; 35% women; 12% minorities). Full-time faculty with Ph.D. or other terminal degree: 94%. Student/faculty ratio: 8/1. Classes of fewer than 20 students: 64%; of 20 to 49 students: 27%; of 50 or more students: 10%. **Advanced Placement and International Baccalaureate credit:** AP tests may be used for: Credit and/or placement. Scores accepted: 4, 5. **Freshmen returning for sophomore year:** 97%. **Graduation rates:** Four-year: 84%; five-year: 91%; six-year: 93%. **Graduate study:** 22% of students pursue further study immediately upon graduation; 65% within five years. Fields in which graduates pursue further study: law, 14%; medicine, 9%; engineering, 4%; arts and sciences, 19%.

COSTS AND FINANCIAL AID

Financial aid office: (603) 646-2451. **Expenses (2006-2007):** Tuition and fees 2006-2007: $33,501; room/board: $9,840. Estimated books and supplies: $1,320; transportation: $700; personal expenses: $1,302. **Financial aid:** In 2005-2006, 62% of undergraduates applied for financial aid. Of those, 52% were determined to have financial need; 100% had their need fully met. Average financial aid package (proportion receiving): $30,019 (52%). Average amount of gift aid, such as scholarships or grants (proportion receiving): $25,720 (50%). Average amount of self-help aid, such as work study or loans (proportion receiving): $5,523 (50%). Average need-based loan (excluding PLUS or other private loans): $4,345. Among students who received need-based aid, the average percentage of need met: 100%. Among students who received aid based on merit, the average award (and the proportion receiving): $461 (0%). The average athletic scholarship (and the proportion receiving): $0 (0%). Average amount of debt of borrowers graduating in 2005: $19,305. Proportion who borrowed: 48%.

CAMPUS LIFE AND EXTRACURRICULAR ACTIVITIES

Campus housing available (% using): coed dorms (81%), sorority housing (3%), fraternity housing (8%), apartment for single students (5%), special housing for international students, cooperative housing, other housing options (3%). Students who live in college-owned, operated, or affiliated housing: 82%. **Student employment:** During the 2005-2006 academic year, 21% of undergraduates worked on campus. Average per-year earnings: $2,250. **Clubs and organizations:** Number of student organizations: 330. Activities include: choral groups, concert band, dance, drama/theater, jazz band, literary magazine, marching band, music ensembles, musical theater, opera, pep band, radio station, student government, student newspaper, student film society, symphony orchestra, television station, yearbook. Number of fraternities: 15; sororities: 9. Proportion of men in fraternities: 37%; of women in sororities: 37%. **Sports program (2005-2006):** Member of NCAA I. *Men's intercollegiate varsity sports:* alpine skiing, baseball, basketball, cross-country, football, golf, heavyweight crew, ice hockey, lacrosse, lightweight crew, nordic skiing, skiing, soccer, squash, swimming and diving, tennis, track and field (indoor), track and field (outdoor), co-ed sailing, co-ed equestrian. *Women's intercollegiate varsity sports:* alpine skiing, basketball, crew, cross-country, field hockey, golf, ice hockey, lacrosse, nordic skiing, sailing, soccer, softball, squash, swimming and diving, tennis, track and field (indoor), track and field (outdoor), volleyball, co-ed sailing, co-ed equestrian.

SERVICES AND FACILITIES
Basic services: nonremedial tutoring, women's center, placement service, health service, health insurance, other. **Counseling services:** minority student, career, personal, academic, psychological, birth control, religious. **For learning-disabled students:** School does not offer a structured program with separate admission and additional fees. Total undergraduates in learning-disabled program or receiving services: 160. Services include: reading machines, tape recorders, note-taking services, learning center, readers, extended time for tests, tutors, priority seating, texts on tape, other testing accomodations, other. **Library:** Number of titles: 2,474,288; number of current serial subscriptions: 52,575. **Information technology resources:** Students are required to lease or own a computer. Number of campus computers available to all students: 500. School has a wireless network. Approximate number of users that can be accommodated: 28,000. Proportion of college-owned housing units wired for high-speed internet access: 100%. **Campus safety:** Security services offered: 24-hour foot-and-vehicle patrols, late-night transport/escort service, 24-hour emergency telephones, lighted pathways/sidewalks, controlled dormitory access (key, security card, etc).

TRANSFER AND INTERNATIONAL STUDENTS
Transfer students: May apply for admission for the following academic terms: Fall. Applicants need a minimum number of credits to apply. For fall 2005: Transfer applications received: 312. Transfer applicants offered admission: 36. Transfer applicants enrolled: 16. **International students:** Number of foreign undergraduates: 206 (5% of student body). Number of countries represented: 43.

Franklin Pierce College

- **Address:** 20 College Road, Rindge, NH 03461
- **Website:** http://www.fpc.edu
- **Private**
- **Enrollment:** 1,596 full-time; 39 part-time

KEY STATS
✔ **U.S News College Ranking:** fourth tier, Liberal Arts Colleges
✔ **SAT Score (25th/75th percentile):** 870-1070
✔ **Tuition:** 2006-2007: $25,300

Selectivity: Less selective	**Room/board:** $8,200
Acceptance rate: 74%	**Average debt:** $28,036
Student/faculty ratio: 16/1	**Proportion who borrowed:** 80%

UNDERGRADUATE STUDENT BODY STATS
2005-2006 enrollment: 1,596 full-time; 39 part-time. Men: 51%; women: 49%. **Ethnic makeup:** African American: 4%; Asian American: 1%; Hispanic: 2%; White: 91%; International: 2%.

ADMISSIONS FACTS AND FIGURES
Phone: (800) 437-0048. **Email:** admissions@fpc.edu. **Website:** http://www.fpc.edu. **Application deadlines for fall 2007:** Regular decision: Rolling. Early decision: Not offered. Early action: Not offered. Admission can be deferred. Common application is accepted. **To apply online, go to:** http://www.fpc.edu/pages/Admission/apps/onlineap.html. **Admissions requirements/recommendations:** High school units required (recommended): English: 4; Mathematics: 3; Science: 2; Foreign language: 0; Social studies: 3; History: 0; Academic electives: 4; Total units: 16. Tests: The college uses SAT or ACT scores in admissions decisions. Either SAT or ACT required. For admission to the fall 2007 entering class, the school will accept: ACT with writing. Campus visit: Recommended. Admissions interview: Recommended. Off-campus interview: Not available. **Factors that count in admissions decisions:** *Academic:* Secondary school record: Important. Class rank: Considered. Letters of recommendation: Very important. Standardized test scores: Important. Essay: Important. ***Nonacademic:***

Interview: Considered. Extracurricular activities: Considered. Talent/ability: Considered. Character/personal qualities: Very important. Alumni/ae relationship: Not considered. Geographical residence: Not considered. State residency: Not considered. Religious affiliation/commitment: Not considered. Minority status: Not considered. Volunteer work: Considered. Work experience: Considered. **Other schools with the greatest overlap in applicants:** Keene State College; Plymouth State University; Roger Williams University; Southern New Hampshire University; University of New Hampshire. **Admissions statistics for the fall 2005 entering class:** Total applicants: 4,068. Total accepted: 3,021. Freshmen enrolled: 507; 83% were from out of state. Overall acceptance rate: 74%. **Size of waiting list:** 0 applicants; enrolled from waiting list: 0. **Credentials of fall 2005 freshmen:** 1% ranked in the top 10 percent of their high school class; 21% were in the top 25 percent, and 51% were in the top half. (Proportion submitting class standing: 58%.) **Average high school grade point average:** 2.8. **First-year students who submitted SAT scores:** 84%. Scores (25/75 percentile): Verbal: 440-540, Math: 430-530, Combined: 870-1070.

ACADEMICS
Year founded: 1962. **Academic calendar:** Semester. **Degrees offered:** bachelor's. **Most popular majors:** 17% visual and performing arts, 15% business, management, marketing, and related support services, 13% communication, journalism, and related programs, 8% English language and literature/letters, 6% security and protective services. **Major fields of study:** area, ethnic, cultural, and gender studies; biological and biomedical sciences; business, management, marketing, and related support services; communication, journalism, and related programs; computer and information sciences and support services; English language and literature/letters; history; liberal arts and sciences studies, and humanities; mathematics and statistics; natural resources and conservation; parks, recreation, leisure, and fitness studies; psychology; public administration and social service professions; security and protective services; social sciences; visual and performing arts. **Areas of required coursework:** arts/fine arts, humanities, mathematics, English (including composition), sciences (biological or physical), history, social science, other. **Pre-professional programs:** pre-law, pre-medicine, other. **Special academic programs:** distance learning, double major, dual enrollment, English as a Second Language (ESL), exchange student program (domestic), honors program, independent study, internships, student-designed major, study abroad, teacher certificate program, other. **Teacher certification offered in:** elementary, secondary. **Reserve Officers Training Corps (ROTC):** Army ROTC: Offered at cooperating institution (University of New Hampshire); Air Force ROTC: Offered at cooperating institution (University of New Hampshire). **Faculty and instruction (2005-2006):** Total instructional faculty: 74 full-time, 76 part-time (61% men; 39% women; 7% minorities). Full-time faculty with Ph.D. or other terminal degree: 74%. Student/faculty ratio: 16/1. Classes of fewer than 20 students: 65%; of 20 to 49 students: 33%; of 50 or more students: 2%. **Advanced Placement and International Baccalaureate credit:** AP tests may be used for: Credit only. Scores accepted: 3, 4, 5. International Baccalaureate exams may be used for: Credit and/or placement. **Freshmen returning for sophomore year:** 63%. **Graduation rates:** Four-year: 45%; five-year: 49%; six-year: 50%. **Graduate study:** 16% of students pursue further study immediately upon graduation; 19% within one year. Fields in which graduates pursue further study: Master of Business Administration (MBA), 33%; law, 3%; medicine, 1%; education, 33%; arts and sciences, 30%.

COSTS AND FINANCIAL AID
Financial aid office: (603) 899-4186. **Expenses (2006-2007):** Tuition and fees 2006-2007: $25,300; room/board: $8,200. Estimated books and supplies: $885; transportation: $550; personal expenses: $1,200. **Financial aid:** Priority filing date for institution's financial aid form: May 1. In 2005-2006, 82% of undergraduates applied for financial aid. Of those, 74% were determined to have financial need; 11% had their need fully met. Average financial aid package (proportion receiving): $16,346 (74%). Average amount of gift aid, such as scholarships or grants (proportion receiving): $11,888 (73%). Average amount of self-help aid, such as work study or loans (proportion receiving): $5,167 (67%). Average need-based loan (excluding PLUS or other private loans): $4,486. Among students who received need-based aid, the average percentage of need met: 67%. Among students who received aid based on merit, the average award (and the proportion receiving): $11,589 (19%). The average athletic scholarship (and the proportion receiving): $13,354 (3%). Average amount of debt of borrowers graduating in 2005: $28,036. Proportion who borrowed: 80%.

CAMPUS LIFE AND EXTRACURRICULAR ACTIVITIES

Campus housing available (% using): coed dorms (55%), apartment for single students (24%), special housing for disabled students (4%), other housing options (17%). Students who live in college-owned, operated, or affiliated housing: 85%. **Student employment:** During the 2005-2006 academic year, 50% of undergraduates worked on campus. Average per-year earnings: $1,500. **Clubs and organizations:** Number of student organizations: 35. Activities include: choral groups, dance, drama/theater, literary magazine, music ensembles, musical theater, radio station, student government, student newspaper, television station, yearbook. Number of fraternities: 0; sororities: 0. Average proportion of students who stay on campus on weekends: 75%. **Sports program (2005-2006):** Member of NCAA II. *Men's intercollegiate varsity sports:* baseball, basketball, cross-country, golf, ice hockey, lacrosse, soccer, tennis. *Women's intercollegiate varsity sports:* basketball, cross-country, field hockey, golf, lacrosse, soccer, softball, tennis, volleyball, rowing.

SERVICES AND FACILITIES

Basic services: nonremedial tutoring, health service, health insurance. **Remedial assistance:** math, writing. **Counseling services:** career, personal, academic, psychological. **For learning-disabled students:** School does not offer a structured program with separate admission and additional fees. Total undergraduates in learning-disabled program or receiving services: 88. Services include: remedial math, remedial English, untimed tests, note-taking services, oral tests, readers, extended time for tests, tutors, proofreading services. **Library:** Number of titles: 133,082; number of current serial subscriptions: 193. **Information technology resources:** Students are not required to lease or own a computer. Number of campus computers available to all students: 240. School has a wireless network. Approximate number of users that can be accommodated: 100. Proportion of college-owned housing units wired for high-speed internet access: 100%. **Campus safety:** Security services offered: 24-hour foot-and-vehicle patrols, late-night transport/escort service, 24-hour emergency telephones, lighted pathways/sidewalks, student patrols, controlled dormitory access (key, security card, etc).

TRANSFER AND INTERNATIONAL STUDENTS

Transfer students: May apply for admission for the following academic terms: Fall, Spring, Summer. Applicants do not need a minimum number of credits to apply. For fall 2005: Transfer applications received: 191. Transfer applicants offered admission: 103. Transfer applicants enrolled: 36. **International students:** Number of foreign undergraduates: 37 (2% of student body). Number of countries represented: 12. Minimum TOEFL score required: 500 (paper); 173 (computer).

Granite State College

- ■ **Address:** 8 Old Suncook Road, Concord, NH 03301
- ■ **Website:** http://www.granite.edu
- ■ **Public**
- ■ **Enrollment:** 491 full-time; 873 part-time

KEY STATS

- ✔ **U.S News College Ranking:** Unranked, Liberal Arts Colleges
- ✔ **SAT or ACT Score (25th/75th percentile):** N/A
- ✔ **Tuition:** 2006-2007: $5,187 in state, $5,691 out of state
  - **Selectivity:** N/A **Room/board:** N/A
  - **Acceptance rate:** N/A **Average debt:** $13,855
  - **Student/faculty ratio:** 20/1 **Proportion who borrowed:** N/A

UNDERGRADUATE STUDENT BODY STATS

2005-2006 enrollment: 491 full-time; 873 part-time. Men: 24%; women: 76%. **Ethnic makeup:** African American: 1%; American-Indian: 1%; Asian American: 1%; Hispanic: 1%; White: 97%.

ADMISSIONS FACTS AND FIGURES

Phone: (603) 513-1391. **Email:** ruth.nawn@granite.edu. **Website:** http://www.granite.edu. **Application deadlines for fall 2007:** Regular decision: Rolling. Early decision: Not offered. Early action: Not offered. **Application fee:** $45. Common application is not accepted. **To apply online, go to:** http://www.granite.edu/admission/apply.htm. **Admissions requirements/recommendations:** Tests: The college does not use SAT or ACT scores in admissions decisions. Neither SAT nor ACT required. Campus visit: Neither required nor recommended. Admissions interview: Required. Off-campus interview: May be arranged. **Factors that count in admissions decisions:** *Academic:* Secondary school record: Not considered. Class rank: Not considered. Letters of recommendation: Not considered. Standardized test scores: Not considered. Essay: Not considered. *Nonacademic:* Interview: Considered. Extracurricular activities: Not considered. Talent/ability: Not considered. Character/personal qualities: Not considered. Alumni/ae relationship: Not considered. Geographical residence: Not considered. State residency: Not considered. Religious affiliation/commitment: Not considered. Minority status: Not considered. Volunteer work: Not considered. Work experience: Not considered. **Other schools with the greatest overlap in applicants:** Daniel Webster College; Franklin Pierce College; Rivier College; Southern New Hampshire University. **Admissions statistics for the fall 2005 entering class:** Freshmen enrolled: 48; 8% were from out of state.

ACADEMICS

Year founded: 1972. **Academic calendar:** Trimester. **Degrees offered:** certificate, associate, transfer-associate, terminal-associate, bachelor's, post-bachelor's certificate. **Most popular majors:** 45% liberal arts and sciences/liberal studies, 26% behavioral sciences, 23% business administration and management, 3% computer programming, 3% criminal justice/safety studies. **Major fields of study:** business, management, marketing, and related support services; computer and information sciences and support services; education; liberal arts and sciences studies, and humanities; multi/interdisciplinary studies; security and protective services. **Areas of required coursework:** humanities, computer literacy, mathematics, English (including composition), sciences (biological or physical), social science. **Special academic programs:** cooperative (work-study plan) program, distance learning, double major, dual enrollment, honors program, independent study, internships, student-designed major, teacher certificate program, weekend college. **Teacher certification offered in:** special education. **Faculty and instruction (2005-2006):** Total instructional faculty: N/A full-time, 139 part-time (40% men; 60% women; 0% minorities). Student/faculty ratio: 20/1. Classes of fewer than 20 students: 91%; of 20 to 49 students: 9%. **Advanced Placement and International Baccalaureate credit:** AP tests may be used for: Credit and/or placement. Scores accepted: 3, 4, 5. International Baccalaureate exams may be used for: Credit and/or placement. **Freshmen returning for sophomore year:** 50%.

COSTS AND FINANCIAL AID

Financial aid office: (603) 228-3000. **Expenses (2006-2007):** Tuition and fees 2006-2007: $5,187 in state, $5,691 out of state; room/board: N/A. Estimated books and supplies: $900; transportation: $675; personal expenses: $1,800. Average amount of debt of borrowers graduating in 2005: $13,855.

CAMPUS LIFE AND EXTRACURRICULAR ACTIVITIES

Students who live in college-owned, operated, or affiliated housing: 0%. **Clubs and organizations:** Number of student organizations: 1. Number of fraternities: 330; sororities: 0.

SERVICES AND FACILITIES

Basic services: nonremedial tutoring. **Remedial assistance:** other. **Counseling services:** career, veteran student, academic, other. **For learning-disabled students:** School does not offer a structured program with separate admission and additional fees. **Library:** Number of titles: 0; number of current serial subscriptions: 21. **Information technology resources:** Students are not required to lease or own a computer. Number of campus computers available to all students: 162. School has a wireless network. Approximate number of users that can be accommodated: 100. **Campus safety:** Security services offered: lighted pathways/sidewalks.

TRANSFER AND INTERNATIONAL STUDENTS

Transfer students: May apply for admission for the following academic terms: Fall, Winter, Spring, Summer. Applicants need a minimum number of credits to apply. For fall 2005: Transfer applications received: 132. Transfer applicants offered admission: 132. Transfer applicants enrolled: 132. **International students:** Number of foreign undergraduates: 2. Minimum TOEFL score required: 500 (paper); 173 (computer).

Keene State College

- **Address:** 229 Main Street, Keene, NH 03435
- **Website:** http://www.keene.edu
- **Public**
- **Enrollment:** 4,170 full-time; 559 part-time

KEY STATS

✔ **U.S News College Ranking:** 83, Universities–Master's (North)
✔ **SAT Score (25th/75th percentile):** 900-1100
✔ **Tuition:** 2006-2007: $7,818 in state, $15,088 out of state

Selectivity: Less selective	**Room/board:** $7,027
Acceptance rate: 76%	**Average debt:** $20,065
Student/faculty ratio: 17/1	**Proportion who borrowed:** 74%

UNDERGRADUATE STUDENT BODY STATS

2005-2006 enrollment: 4,170 full-time; 559 part-time. Men: 44%; women: 56%. **Ethnic makeup:** Asian American: 1%; Hispanic: 1%; White: 97%; International: 1%.

ADMISSIONS FACTS AND FIGURES

Phone: (603) 358-2276. **Email:** admissions@keene.edu. **Website:** http://www.keene.edu. **Application deadlines for fall 2007:** Regular decision: April 1. Early decision: Not offered. Early action: Not offered. Admission can be deferred. **Application fee:** $35. Common application is not accepted. **To apply online, go to:** http://www.keene.edu/admissions/applying.cfm. **Admissions requirements/recommendations:** High school units required (recommended): English: 4; Mathematics: 3; Science: 3; Social studies: 2; Academic electives: 2; Total units: 14. Tests: The college uses SAT or ACT scores in admissions decisions. Either SAT or ACT required. For admission to the fall 2007 entering class, the school will accept: ACT without writing. Campus visit: Recommended. Admissions interview: Recommended. Off-campus interview: Not available. **Factors that count in admissions decisions:** *Academic:* Secondary school record: Very important. Class rank: Considered. Letters of recommendation: Important. Standardized test scores: Important. Essay: Important. *Nonacademic:* Interview: Important. Extracurricular activities: Considered. Talent/ability: Considered. Character/personal qualities: Considered. Alumni/ae relationship: Considered. Geographical residence: Not considered. State residency: Not considered. Religious affiliation/commitment: Not considered. Minority status: Considered. Volunteer work: Considered. Work experience: Considered. **Admissions statistics for the fall 2005 entering class:** Total applicants: 3,527. Total accepted: 2,693. Freshmen enrolled: 1,008; 53% were from out of state. Overall acceptance rate: 76%. **Credentials of fall 2005 freshmen:** 4% ranked in the top 10 percent of their high school class; 21% were in the top 25 percent, and 60% were in the top half. (Proportion submitting class standing: 79%.) **Average high school grade point average:** 2.9. **First-year students who submitted SAT scores:** 98%. Scores (25/75 percentile): Verbal: 450-550, Math: 450-550, Combined: 900-1100.

ACADEMICS

Year founded: 1909. **Academic calendar:** Semester. **Degrees offered:** certificate, diploma, associate, bachelor's, post-bachelor's certificate, master's, post-master's certificate. **Most popular majors:** 19% education, 14% psychology, 11% social sciences, 10% engineering technologies/technicians, 10% visual and performing arts. **Major fields of study:** architecture and related services; area, ethnic, cultural, and gender studies; biological and biomedical sciences; business, management, marketing, and related support services; communication, journalism, and related programs; computer and information sciences and support services; education; engineering technologies/technicians; English language and literature/letters; foreign languages, literatures, and linguistics; health professions and related clinical sciences; history; liberal arts and sciences studies, and humanities; mathematics and statistics; multi/interdisciplinary studies; natural resources and conservation; parks, recreation, leisure, and fitness studies; physical sciences; psychology; social sciences; visual and performing arts. **Areas of required coursework:** arts/fine arts, humanities, mathematics, English (including composition), sciences (biological or physical), history, social science, other. **Special academic programs:** cooperative (work-study plan) program, double major, English as a Second Language (ESL), exchange student program (domestic), honors program, independent study, internships, student-designed major, study abroad, teacher certificate program. **Teacher certification offered in:** early childhood, special education, elementary, middle/junior

high, secondary. **Cooperative education programs:** business, computer science, humanities, natural science, social/behavioral science, technologies, other. **Reserve Officers Training Corps (ROTC):** Air Force ROTC: Offered at cooperating institution (University of Massachusetts-Lowell). **Faculty and instruction (2005-2006):** Total instructional faculty: 187 full-time, 222 part-time. Student/faculty ratio: 17/1. Classes of fewer than 20 students: 59%; of 20 to 49 students: 37%; of 50 or more students: 4%. **Advanced Placement and International Baccalaureate credit:** AP tests may be used for: Credit and/or placement. Scores accepted: 3, 4, 5. **Freshmen returning for sophomore year:** 77%. **Graduation rates:** Four-year: 27%; five-year: 50%; six-year: 53%. **Graduate study:** 13% of students pursue further study immediately upon graduation.

COSTS AND FINANCIAL AID

Financial aid office: (603) 358-2280. **Expenses (2006-2007):** Tuition and fees 2006-2007: $7,818 in state, $15,088 out of state; room/board: $7,027. Estimated books and supplies: $600; transportation: $800; personal expenses: $750. **Financial aid:** Average amount of debt of borrowers graduating in 2005: $20,065. Proportion who borrowed: 74%.

CAMPUS LIFE AND EXTRACURRICULAR ACTIVITIES

Campus housing available (% using): coed dorms (78%), women's dorms (8%), apartments for married students (0%), apartment for single students (12%), special housing for disabled students, other housing options (2%). Students who live in college-owned, operated, or affiliated housing: 54%. **Student employment:** During the 2005-2006 academic year, 13% of undergraduates worked on campus. Average per-year earnings: $926. **Clubs and organizations:** Number of student organizations: 65. Activities include: choral groups, concert band, dance, drama/theater, jazz band, literary magazine, music ensembles, musical theater, radio station, student government, student newspaper, student film society, television station, yearbook. Number of fraternities: 2; sororities: 5. Proportion of men in fraternities: 3%; of women in sororities: 3%. Average proportion of students who stay on campus on weekends: 65%. **Sports program (2005-2006):** Member of NCAA III. *Men's intercollegiate varsity sports:* baseball, basketball, cross-country, lacrosse, soccer, swimming and diving, track and field (indoor), track and field (outdoor). *Women's intercollegiate varsity sports:* basketball, cross-country, field hockey, lacrosse, soccer, softball, swimming and diving, track and field (indoor), track and field (outdoor), volleyball.

SERVICES AND FACILITIES

Basic services: nonremedial tutoring, women's center, health service, health insurance. **Remedial assistance:** reading, math, writing, study skills. **Counseling services:** minority student, career, personal, veteran student, academic, older student, psychological, birth control, religious. **For learning-disabled students:** School does not offer a structured program with separate admission and additional fees. Services include: reading machines, tape recorders, untimed tests, note-taking services, oral tests, readers, extended time for tests, tutors. **Library:** Number of titles: 306,652; number of current serial subscriptions: 896. **Information technology resources:** Students are not required to lease or own a computer. Number of campus computers available to all students: 500. School has a wireless network. Approximate number of users that can be accommodated: 200. Proportion of college-owned housing units wired for high-speed internet access: 100%. **Campus safety:** Security services offered: 24-hour foot-and-vehicle patrols, late-night transport/escort service, 24-hour emergency telephones, lighted pathways/sidewalks, controlled dormitory access (key, security card, etc).

TRANSFER AND INTERNATIONAL STUDENTS

Transfer students: May apply for admission for the following academic terms: Fall, Spring. Applicants do not need a minimum number of credits to apply. For fall 2005: Transfer applications received: 455. Transfer applicants offered admission: 349. Transfer applicants enrolled: 219. **International students:** Number of foreign undergraduates: 37 (1% of student body). Number of countries represented: 5. Minimum TOEFL score required: 500 (paper); 173 (computer).

New England College

- **Address:** 7 Main Street, Henniker, NH 03242
- **Website:** http://www.nec.edu
- **Private**
- **Enrollment:** 972 full-time; 69 part-time

KEY STATS
✔ **U.S News College Ranking:** 34, Comp. Coll.–Bachelor's (North)
✔ **SAT Score (25th/75th percentile):** 790-990
✔ **Tuition:** 2006-2007: $24,136

Selectivity: Less selective	**Room/board:** $8,456
Acceptance rate: 83%	**Average debt:** $29,777
Student/faculty ratio: 11/1	**Proportion who borrowed:** 74%

UNDERGRADUATE STUDENT BODY STATS
2005-2006 enrollment: 972 full-time; 69 part-time. Men: 48%; women: 52%. **Ethnic makeup:** African American: 2%; Asian American: 2%; Hispanic: 2%; White: 90%; International: 3%.

ADMISSIONS FACTS AND FIGURES
Phone: (800) 521-7642. **Email:** admission@nec.edu. **Website:** http://www.nec.edu. **Application deadlines for fall 2007:** Regular decision: Rolling. Early decision: Not offered. Early action: Not offered. Admission can be deferred. **Application fee:** $30. Common application is accepted. **To apply online, go to:** http://www.nec.edu/admissions/admissions.html#apply. **Admissions requirements/recommendations:** High school units required (recommended): English: 4 (4); Mathematics: 2 (3); Science: 2 (3); Foreign language: 0 (2); Social studies: 2 (3); History: 0 (0); Academic electives: 0 (0); Total units: 12 (12). Tests: The college does not use SAT or ACT scores in admissions decisions. Neither SAT nor ACT required. Campus visit: Recommended. Admissions interview: Recommended. Off-campus interview: May be arranged. **Factors that count in admissions decisions:** *Academic:* Secondary school record: Very important. Class rank: Considered. Letters of recommendation: Very important. Standardized test scores: Considered. Essay: Very important. *Nonacademic:* Interview: Very important. Extracurricular activities: Very important. Talent/ability: Very important. Character/personal qualities: Important. Alumni/ae relationship: Considered. Geographical residence: Not considered. State residency: Not considered. Religious affiliation/commitment: Not considered. Minority status: Not considered. Volunteer work: Considered. Work experience: Considered. **Other schools with the greatest overlap in applicants:** Colby-Sawyer College; Franklin Pierce College; Keene State College; Plymouth State University; University of New Hampshire. **Admissions statistics for the fall 2005 entering class:** Total applicants: 1,817. Total accepted: 1,512. Freshmen enrolled: 356; 68% were from out of state. Overall acceptance rate: 83%. **Credentials of fall 2005 freshmen:** 9% ranked in the top 10 percent of their high school class; 29% were in the top 25 percent, and 68% were in the top half. (Proportion submitting class standing: 61%.) **Average high school grade point average:** 2.5. **First-year students who submitted SAT scores:** 77%. Scores (25/75 percentile): Verbal: 400-500; Math: 390-490, Combined: 790-990. **First-year students submitting ACT scores:** 5%. Scores (25/75 percentile): English: 15-23, Math: 15-21, Composite: 15-21.

ACADEMICS
Year founded: 1946. **Academic calendar:** Semester. **Degrees offered:** associate, bachelor's, master's. **Most popular majors:** 29% business administration and management, 13% psychology, 11% criminal justice/law enforcement administration, 11% sport and fitness administration/management, 7% visual and performing arts. **Major fields of study:** communication, journalism, and related programs; education; engineering; history; legal professions and studies; mathematics and statistics; natural resources and conservation; philosophy and religious studies; psychology; social sciences; visual and performing arts. **Areas of required coursework:** arts/fine arts, humanities, computer literacy, mathematics, English (including composition), sciences (biological or physical), social science, other. **Pre-professional programs:** pre-law, pre-medicine, other. **Special academic programs (% participation):** cross-registration (2%), distance learning (0%), double major (9%), English as a Second Language (ESL) (3%), honors program (15%), independent study (11%), internships (21%), student-designed major (1%), study abroad (7%), teacher certificate program (19%). **Teacher certification offered in:** special education, elementary, secondary. **Reserve Officers Training Corps (ROTC):** Army ROTC: Offered at cooperating institution

(University of New Hampshire); Air Force ROTC: Offered at cooperating institution (University of New Hampshire). **Faculty and instruction (2005-2006):** Total instructional faculty: 57 full-time, 95 part-time (50% men; 50% women; 2% minorities). Full-time faculty with Ph.D. or other terminal degree: 63%. Student/faculty ratio: 11/1. Classes of fewer than 20 students: 68%; of 20 to 49 students: 32%; of 50 or more students: 0%. **Advanced Placement and International Baccalaureate credit:** AP tests may be used for: Credit and/or placement. Scores accepted: 3, 4, 5. International Baccalaureate exams may be used for: Credit only. **Freshmen returning for sophomore year:** 65%. **Graduation rates:** Four-year: 36%; five-year: 44%; six-year: 48%. **Graduate study:** 15% of students pursue further study immediately upon graduation; 20% within one year. Fields in which graduates pursue further study: Master of Business Administration (MBA), 4%; law, 9%; medicine, 4%; education, 22%; arts and sciences, 30%.

COSTS AND FINANCIAL AID
Financial aid office: (603) 428-2414. **Expenses (2006-2007):** Tuition and fees 2006-2007: $24,136; room/board: $8,456. Estimated books and supplies: $800; transportation: $900; personal expenses: $1,150. **Financial aid:** Priority filing date for institution's financial aid form: February 15; deadline: May 1. In 2005-2006, 88% of undergraduates applied for financial aid. Of those, 74% were determined to have financial need; 32% had their need fully met. Average financial aid package (proportion receiving): $22,536 (74%). Average amount of gift aid, such as scholarships or grants (proportion receiving): $10,140 (73%). Average amount of self-help aid, such as work study or loans (proportion receiving): $9,830 (72%). Average need-based loan (excluding PLUS or other private loans): $8,430. Among students who received need-based aid, the average percentage of need met: 86%. Among students who received aid based on merit, the average award (and the proportion receiving): $8,282 (5%). The average athletic scholarship (and the proportion receiving): $0 (0%). Average amount of debt of borrowers graduating in 2005: $29,777. Proportion who borrowed: 74%.

CAMPUS LIFE AND EXTRACURRICULAR ACTIVITIES
Campus housing available (% using): coed dorms (100%), apartment for single students. Students who live in college-owned, operated, or affiliated housing: 68%. **Student employment:** During the 2005-2006 academic year, 5% of undergraduates worked on campus. Average per-year earnings: $3,000. **Clubs and organizations:** Number of student organizations: 28. Activities include: dance, drama/theater, literary magazine, music ensembles, radio station, student government, student newspaper, yearbook. Number of fraternities: 3; sororities: 2. Proportion of men in fraternities: 3%; of women in sororities: 4%. Average proportion of students who stay on campus on weekends: 80%. **Sports program (2005-2006):** Member of NCAA III. **Men's intercollegiate varsity sports:** baseball, basketball, cross-country, ice hockey, lacrosse, soccer. **Women's intercollegiate varsity sports:** basketball, cross-country, field hockey, ice hockey, lacrosse, soccer, softball.

SERVICES AND FACILITIES
Basic services: nonremedial tutoring, women's center, placement service, health service, health insurance. **Remedial assistance:** math, writing, study skills. **Counseling services:** career, personal, veteran student, academic, older student, psychological, birth control. **For learning-disabled students:** School does not offer a structured program with separate admission and additional fees. Total undergraduates in learning-disabled program or receiving services: 79. Services include: remedial math, tape recorders, untimed tests, note-taking services, oral tests, learning center, extended time for tests, tutors, other testing accomodations, waiver of math degree requirement. **Library:** Number of titles: 100,000; number of current serial subscriptions: 15,300. **Information technology resources:** Students are not required to lease or own a computer. Number of campus computers available to all students: 130. School has a wireless network. Approximate number of users that can be accommodated: 2,000. Proportion of college-owned housing units wired for high-speed internet access: 100%. **Campus safety:** Security services offered: 24-hour foot-and-vehicle patrols, late-night transport/escort service, 24-hour emergency telephones, lighted pathways/sidewalks, controlled dormitory access (key, security card, etc).

TRANSFER AND INTERNATIONAL STUDENTS
Transfer students: May apply for admission for the following academic terms: Fall, Spring, Summer. Applicants do not need a minimum number of credits to apply. For fall 2005: Transfer applications received: 148. Transfer applicants offered admission: 112. Transfer applicants enrolled: 62. **International students:** Number of foreign undergraduates: 34 (3% of student body). Number of countries represented: 16. Minimum TOEFL score required: 550 (paper); 213 (computer). Average TOEFL score: 496 (paper).

Plymouth State University

- **Address:** 17 High Street, Plymouth, NH 03264-1595
- **Website:** http://www.plymouth.edu
- **Public**
- **Enrollment:** 3,956 full-time; 236 part-time

KEY STATS

- ✔ **U.S News College Ranking:** fourth tier, Universities–Master's (North)
- ✔ **SAT Score (25th/75th percentile):** 860-1070
- ✔ **Tuition:** 2005-2006: $7,028 in state, $13,868 out of state
  - **Selectivity:** Less selective   **Room/board:** $6,780
  - **Acceptance rate:** 77%   **Average debt:** $23,088
  - **Student/faculty ratio:** 17/1   **Proportion who borrowed:** 73%

UNDERGRADUATE STUDENT BODY STATS

2005-2006 enrollment: 3,956 full-time; 236 part-time. Men: 51%; women: 49%. **Ethnic makeup:** African American: 1%; Asian American: 1%; Hispanic: 1%; White: 97%; International: 1%.

ADMISSIONS FACTS AND FIGURES

Phone: (603) 535-2237. **Email:** plymouthadmit@plymouth.edu. **Website:** http://www.plymouth.edu. **Application deadlines for fall 2007:** Regular decision: April 1. Early decision: Not offered. Early action: Not offered. Admission can be deferred. **Application fee:** $35. Common application is not accepted. **To apply online, go to:** http://www.plymouth.edu/admit/apply/. **Admissions requirements/recommendations:** High school units required (recommended): English: 4 (4); Mathematics: 3 (3); Science: 2 (3); Foreign language: 0 (2); Social studies: 2 (3); History: 1 (2); Academic electives: 0 (0); Total units: 13 (18). Tests: The college uses SAT or ACT scores in admissions decisions. Either SAT or ACT required. For admission to the fall 2007 entering class, the school will accept: ACT with writing. Campus visit: Recommended. Admissions interview: Neither required nor recommended. Off-campus interview: Not available. **Factors that count in admissions decisions:** *Academic:* Secondary school record: Very important. Class rank: Important. Letters of recommendation: Important. Standardized test scores: Important. Essay: Important. *Nonacademic:* Interview: Not considered. Extracurricular activities: Considered. Talent/ability: Important. Character/personal qualities: Important. Alumni/ae relationship: Considered. Geographical residence: Not considered. State residency: Not considered. Religious affiliation/commitment: Not considered. Minority status: Considered. Volunteer work: Considered. Work experience: Considered. **Other schools with the greatest overlap in applicants:** Bridgewater State College; Keene State College; Southern New Hampshire University; University of Massachusetts–Amherst; University of New Hampshire. **Admissions statistics for the fall 2005 entering class:** Total applicants: 3,655. Total accepted: 2,818. Freshmen enrolled: 1,003; 43% were from out of state. Overall acceptance rate: 77%. **Size of waiting list:** 0 applicants; enrolled from waiting list: 0. **Credentials of fall 2005 freshmen:** 4% ranked in the top 10 percent of their high school class; 16% were in the top 25 percent, and 52% were in the top half. (Proportion submitting class standing: 81%.) **Average high school grade point average:** 2.9. **First-year students who submitted SAT scores:** 98%. Scores (25/75 percentile): Verbal: 430-530, Math: 430-540, Combined: 860-1070. **First-year students submitting ACT scores:** 6%. Scores (25/75 percentile): English: N/A, Math: N/A, Composite: 17-20.

ACADEMICS

Year founded: 1871. **Academic calendar:** Semester. **Degrees offered:** bachelor's, post-bachelor's certificate, master's, post-master's certificate. **Most popular majors:** 21% education, 17% business, management, marketing, and related support services, 9% parks, recreation, leisure, and fitness studies, 9% visual and performing arts, 8% communication, journalism, and related programs. **Major fields of study:** architecture and related services; biological and biomedical sciences; business, management, marketing, and related support services; communication, journalism, and related programs; computer and information sciences and support services; education; English language and literature/letters; foreign languages, literatures, and linguistics; health professions and related clinical sciences; history; liberal arts and sciences studies, and humanities; mathematics and statistics; multi/interdisciplinary studies; parks, recreation, leisure, and fitness studies; philosophy and religious studies; physical sciences; psychology; public administration and social service professions; security and protective services; social sciences; visual and performing arts. **Areas of required course-**

work: arts/fine arts, humanities, computer literacy, mathematics, English (including composition), sciences (biological or physical), history, social science, other. **Special academic programs (% participation):** double major (1%), exchange student program (domestic) (1%), honors program (7%), independent study (11%), internships (44%), student-designed major (3%), study abroad (3%), teacher certificate program (17%). **Teacher certification offered in:** early childhood, special education, elementary, middle/junior high, secondary. **Reserve Officers Training Corps (ROTC):** Army ROTC: Offered at cooperating institution (University of New Hampshire); Air Force ROTC: Offered at cooperating institution (University of New Hampshire). **Faculty and instruction (2005-2006):** Total instructional faculty: 175 full-time, 277 part-time (51% men; 49% women; 3% minorities). Full-time faculty with Ph.D. or other terminal degree: 87%. Student/faculty ratio: 17/1. Classes of fewer than 20 students: 46%; of 20 to 49 students: 52%; of 50 or more students: 2%. **Advanced Placement and International Baccalaureate credit:** AP tests may be used for: Credit and/or placement. Scores accepted: 3, 4, 5. **Freshmen returning for sophomore year:** 75%. **Graduation rates:** Four-year: 28%; five-year: 44%; six-year: 46%. **Graduate study:** 11% of students pursue further study immediately upon graduation.

COSTS AND FINANCIAL AID

Financial aid office: (603) 535-2338. **Expenses (2005-2006):** Tuition and fees 2005-2006: $7,028 in state, $13,868 out of state; room/board: $6,780. Estimated books and supplies: $786; transportation: $538; personal expenses: $1,298. **Financial aid:** Priority filing date for institution's financial aid form: March 1. Average amount of debt of borrowers graduating in 2005: $23,088. Proportion who borrowed: 73%.

CAMPUS LIFE AND EXTRACURRICULAR ACTIVITIES

Campus housing available (% using): coed dorms (74%), sorority housing (1%), apartments for married students, apartment for single students (24%), special housing for disabled students (1%). Students who live in college-owned, operated, or affiliated housing: 53%. **Student employment:** During the 2005-2006 academic year, 16% of undergraduates worked on campus. Average per-year earnings: $855. **Clubs and organizations:** Number of student organizations: 107. Activities include: choral groups, concert band, dance, drama/theater, jazz band, literary magazine, music ensembles, musical theater, radio station, student government, student newspaper, student film society, yearbook. Number of fraternities: 2; sororities: 4. Proportion of men in fraternities: 1%; of women in sororities: 1%. Average proportion of students who stay on campus on weekends: 60%. **Sports program (2005-2006):** Member of NCAA III. *Men's intercollegiate varsity sports:* alpine skiing, baseball, basketball, football, ice hockey, lacrosse, soccer, wrestling. *Women's intercollegiate varsity sports:* alpine skiing, basketball, field hockey, lacrosse, soccer, softball, swimming and diving, tennis, volleyball.

SERVICES AND FACILITIES

Basic services: nonremedial tutoring, women's center, placement service, health service. **Counseling services:** minority student, career, military, personal, veteran student, academic, older student, psychological, birth control, religious. **For learning-disabled students:** School does not offer a structured program with separate admission and additional fees. Services include: untimed tests, note-taking services, oral tests, readers, extended time for tests, tutors, texts on tape. **Library:** Number of titles: 309,865; number of current serial subscriptions: 976. **Information technology resources:** Students are not required to lease or own a computer. Number of campus computers available to all students: 500. School has a wireless network. Approximate number of users that can be accommodated: 400. Proportion of college-owned housing units wired for high-speed internet access: 100%. **Campus safety:** Security services offered: 24-hour foot-and-vehicle patrols, late-night transport/escort service, 24-hour emergency telephones, lighted pathways/sidewalks, student patrols, controlled dormitory access (key, security card, etc).

TRANSFER AND INTERNATIONAL STUDENTS

Transfer students: May apply for admission for the following academic terms: Fall, Spring. Applicants do not need a minimum number of credits to apply. For fall 2005: Transfer applications received: 427. Transfer applicants offered admission: 313. Transfer applicants enrolled: 190. **International students:** Number of foreign undergraduates: 21 (1% of student body). Number of countries represented: 10. Minimum TOEFL score required: 520 (paper); 190 (computer). Average TOEFL score: 540 (paper).

Rivier College

- **Address:** 420 Main Street, Nashua, NH 03060
- **Website:** http://www.rivier.edu
- **Private; Religious affiliation:** Roman Catholic
- **Enrollment:** 845 full-time; 543 part-time

KEY STATS

✔ **U.S News College Ranking:** fourth tier, Universities–Master's (North)
✔ **SAT Score (25th/75th percentile):** 890-1050
✔ **Tuition:** 2006-2007: $21,920

Selectivity: Less selective	**Room/board:** $7,942
Acceptance rate: 59%	**Average debt:** N/A
Student/faculty ratio: 10/1	**Proportion who borrowed:** N/A

UNDERGRADUATE STUDENT BODY STATS

2005-2006 enrollment: 845 full-time; 543 part-time. Men: 21%; women: 79%. **Ethnic makeup:** African American: 2%; Asian American: 1%; Hispanic: 3%; White: 94%.

ADMISSIONS FACTS AND FIGURES

Phone: (603) 888-1311. **Email:** rivadmit@rivier.edu. **Website:** http://www.rivier.edu. **Application deadlines for fall 2007:** Regular decision: August 30. Early decision: Not offered. Early action: Not offered. Admission can be deferred. **Application fee:** $25. Common application is not accepted. **Admissions requirements/recommendations:** High school units required (recommended): English: 4; Mathematics: 3; Science: 1; Foreign language: 2; Social studies: 2; History: 1; Academic electives: 3; Total units: 16. Tests: The college uses SAT or ACT scores in admissions decisions. Either SAT or ACT required. Campus visit: Recommended. Admissions interview: Recommended. Off-campus interview: May be arranged. **Factors that count in admissions decisions:** *Academic:* Secondary school record: Very important. Class rank: Important. Letters of recommendation: Important. Standardized test scores: Very important. Essay: Important. *Nonacademic:* Interview: Considered. Extracurricular activities: Considered. Talent/ability: Considered. Character/personal qualities: Considered. Alumni/ae relationship: Considered. Geographical residence: Not considered. State residency: Not considered. Religious affiliation/commitment: Not considered. Minority status: Not considered. Volunteer work: Not considered. Work experience: Not considered. **Other schools with the greatest overlap in applicants:** Keene State College; Plymouth State University; Southern New Hampshire University; St. Anselm College; University of New Hampshire. **Admissions statistics for the fall 2005 entering class:** Total applicants: 1,388. Total accepted: 813. Freshmen enrolled: 305; 41% were from out of state. Overall acceptance rate: 59%. **Size of waiting list:** 21 applicants; enrolled from waiting list: 21. **Credentials of fall 2005 freshmen:** 15% ranked in the top 10 percent of their high school class; 40% were in the top 25 percent, and 75% were in the top half. (Proportion submitting class standing: 80%.) **Average high school grade point average:** 2.8. **First-year students who submitted SAT scores:** 99%. Scores (25/75 percentile): Verbal: 430-560, Math: 460-490, Combined: 890-1050. **First-year students submitting ACT scores:** 1%. Scores (25/75 percentile): English: N/A, Math: N/A, Composite: N/A.

ACADEMICS

Year founded: 1933. **Academic calendar:** Semester. **Degrees offered:** certificate, associate, bachelor's, post-bachelor's certificate, master's, post-master's certificate. **Most popular majors:** 18% education, 14% nursing, 6% business, management, marketing, and related support services, 5% psychology, 3% biology. **Major fields of study:** biological and biomedical sciences; business, management, marketing, and related support services; communication, journalism, and related programs; computer and information sciences and support services; education; English language and literature/letters; foreign languages, literatures, and linguistics; health professions and related clinical sciences; history; liberal arts and sciences studies, and humanities; mathematics and statistics; multi/interdisciplinary studies; psychology; security and protective services; social sciences; visual and performing arts. **Areas of required coursework:** arts/fine arts, humanities, mathematics, English (including composition), philosophy, foreign languages, sciences (biological or physical), history, social science. **Pre-professional programs:** pre-law, predentistry, pre-medicine, pre-veterinary science, other. **Special academic programs (% participation):** accelerated program (1%), double major (.5%), English as a Second Language (ESL) (1%), honors program (2%), independent study (7%), internships (7%), student-designed major (2%), teacher cer-

tificate program (22%). **Teacher certification offered in:** early childhood, special education, elementary, middle/junior high, secondary. **Reserve Officers Training Corps (ROTC):** Air Force ROTC: Offered at cooperating institution (Daniel Webster College). **Faculty and instruction (2005-2006):** Total instructional faculty: 71 full-time, 108 part-time (31% men; 69% women; 2% minorities). Full-time faculty with Ph.D. or other terminal degree: 69%. Student/faculty ratio: 10/1. Classes of fewer than 20 students: 61%; of 20 to 49 students: 38%; of 50 or more students: 0%. **Advanced Placement and International Baccalaureate credit:** AP tests may be used for: Credit only. **Freshmen returning for sophomore year:** 73%. **Graduation rates:** Four-year: 42%; five-year: 48%; six-year: 51%.

COSTS AND FINANCIAL AID

Financial aid office: (603) 897-8533. **Expenses (2006-2007):** Tuition and fees 2006-2007: $21,920; room/board: $7,942. **Financial aid:** Priority filing date for institution's financial aid form: February 1. In 2005-2006, 92% of undergraduates applied for financial aid. Of those, 82% were determined to have financial need; 36% had their need fully met. Average financial aid package (proportion receiving): $14,176 (82%). Average amount of gift aid, such as scholarships or grants (proportion receiving): $8,309 (79%). Average amount of self-help aid, such as work study or loans (proportion receiving): $6,769 (75%). Average need-based loan (excluding PLUS or other private loans): $6,309. Among students who received need-based aid, the average percentage of need met: 77%. Among students who received aid based on merit, the average award (and the proportion receiving): $11,230 (18%). The average athletic scholarship (and the proportion receiving): $0 (0%).

CAMPUS LIFE AND EXTRACURRICULAR ACTIVITIES

Campus housing available (% using): coed dorms (100%). Students who live in college-owned, operated, or affiliated housing: 32%. **Student employment:** During the 2005-2006 academic year, 28% of undergraduates worked on campus. Average per-year earnings: $650. **Clubs and organizations:** Number of student organizations: 40. Activities include: dance, drama/theater, music ensembles, student government, student newspaper, yearbook. Number of fraternities: 0; sororities: 0. Average proportion of students who stay on campus on weekends: 40%. **Sports program (2005-2006):** Member of NCAA III. *Men's intercollegiate varsity sports:* baseball, basketball, cross-country, soccer, volleyball. *Women's intercollegiate varsity sports:* basketball, cross-country, soccer, softball, volleyball.

SERVICES AND FACILITIES

Basic services: placement service, health service, health insurance. **Remedial assistance:** reading, math, writing, study skills. **Counseling services:** career, personal, academic, psychological, religious. **For learning-disabled students:** School does not offer a structured program with separate admission and additional fees. Total undergraduates in learning-disabled program or receiving services: 60. Services include: reading machines, tape recorders, untimed tests, note-taking services, oral tests, readers, extended time for tests, early syllabus, priority registration, priority seating, substitution of courses, texts on tape, typist/scribe, exams on tape or computer, other testing accomodations, waiver of foreign language degree requirement. **Library:** Number of titles: 99,879; number of current serial subscriptions: 478. **Information technology resources:** Students are not required to lease or own a computer. Number of campus computers available to all students: 100. School has a wireless network. Approximate number of users that can be accommodated: 500. Proportion of college-owned housing units wired for high-speed internet access: 100%. **Campus safety:** Security services offered: 24-hour foot-and-vehicle patrols, late-night transport/escort service, 24-hour emergency telephones, lighted pathways/sidewalks, controlled dormitory access (key, security card, etc).

TRANSFER AND INTERNATIONAL STUDENTS

Transfer students: May apply for admission for the following academic terms: Fall, Spring, Summer. Applicants do not need a minimum number of credits to apply. For fall 2005: Transfer applications received: 1,128. Transfer applicants offered admission: 790. Transfer applicants enrolled: 300. **International students:** Number of foreign undergraduates: 0. Minimum TOEFL score required: 500 (paper); 173 (computer).

Southern New Hampshire University

- **Address:** 2500 N. River Road, Manchester, NH 03106
- **Website:** http://www.snhu.edu
- **Private**
- **Enrollment:** 1,670 full-time; 44 part-time

KEY STATS

✔ **U.S News College Ranking:** Unranked Specialty School–Business
✔ **SAT Score (25th/75th percentile):** 910-1098
✔ **Tuition:** 2006-2007: $30,524

Selectivity: Less selective	Room/board: $8,480
Acceptance rate: 72%	Average debt: $21,138
Student/faculty ratio: 15/1	Proportion who borrowed: N/A

UNDERGRADUATE STUDENT BODY STATS

2005-2006 enrollment: 1,670 full-time; 44 part-time. Men: 45%; women: 55%. **Ethnic makeup:** African American: 1%; Asian American: 2%; Hispanic: 1%; White: 91%; International: 4%. **Religious preference:** Roman Catholic: 36%; Jewish: 2%; Buddhist: 1%; No preference: 25%; Baptist: 3%; Other: 33%.

ADMISSIONS FACTS AND FIGURES

Phone: (603) 645-9611. **Email:** admission@snhu.edu. **Website:** http://www.snhu.edu. **Application deadlines for fall 2007:** Regular decision: Rolling. Early decision: Not offered. Early action: Send application by: November 15; Decision sent by: December 15. Admission can be deferred. **Application fee:** $35. Common application is accepted. **To apply online, go to:** https://apply.embark.com/Ugrad/snh/17/. **Admissions requirements/recommendations:** High school units required (recommended): English: 4 (4); Mathematics: 2 (3); Science: 2 (3); Foreign language: 0 (2); Social studies: 2 (2); History: 1 (2); Academic electives: 2 (3); Total units: 14 (19). Tests: The college uses SAT or ACT scores in admissions decisions. SAT required. For admission to the fall 2007 entering class, the school will accept: ACT with writing. Campus visit: Recommended. Admissions interview: Recommended. Off-campus interview: May be arranged. **Factors that count in admissions decisions:** *Academic:* Secondary school record: Very important. Class rank: Considered. Letters of recommendation: Important. Standardized test scores: Important. Essay: Important. *Nonacademic:* Interview: Considered. Extracurricular activities: Important. Talent/ability: Considered. Character/personal qualities: Considered. Alumni/ae relationship: Considered. Geographical residence: Considered. State residency: Not considered. Religious affiliation/commitment: Not considered. Minority status: Not considered. Volunteer work: Considered. Work experience: Considered. **Other schools with the greatest overlap in applicants:** Endicott College; Franklin Pierce College; Johnson and Wales University; Merrimack College; University of New Hampshire. **Admissions statistics for the fall 2005 entering class:** Total applicants: 2,295. Total accepted: 1,644. Freshmen enrolled: 479; 61% were from out of state. Overall acceptance rate: 72%. Non-early acceptance rate: 72%. **Credentials of fall 2005 freshmen:** 6% ranked in the top 10 percent of their high school class; 26% were in the top 25 percent, and 64% were in the top half. (Proportion submitting class standing: 81%.) **Average high school grade point average:** 3.0. **First-year students who submitted SAT scores:** 99%. Scores (25/75 percentile): Verbal: 453-543, Math: 457-555, Combined: 910-1098.

ACADEMICS

Year founded: 1932. **Academic calendar:** Other. **Degrees offered:** certificate, associate, transfer-associate, bachelor's, post-bachelor's certificate, master's, doctorate. **Most popular majors:** 72% business, management, marketing, and related support services, 16% personal and culinary services, 3% psychology, 2% English language and literature/letters, 2% communication, journalism, and related programs. **Major fields of study:** business, management, marketing, and related support services; communication, journalism, and related programs; computer and information sciences and support services; education; English language and literature/letters; family and consumer sciences/human sciences; history; liberal arts and sciences studies, and humanities; natural resources and conservation; parks, recreation, leisure, and fitness studies; personal and culinary services; psychology; public administration and social service professions; social sciences; visual and performing arts. **Areas of required coursework:** arts/fine arts, humanities, computer literacy, mathematics, English (including composition), philosophy, sciences (biological or physical), history, social science. **Pre-professional programs:** pre-law, other. **Special academic programs:** accelerated program, cooperative (work-study plan) program, distance learning, double major, English as a Second Language (ESL), honors program, independent study, internships, study abroad, teacher certificate program, weekend college. **Teacher certification offered in:** early childhood, special education, elementary, middle/junior high, secondary. **Reserve Officers Training Corps (ROTC):** Army ROTC: Offered at cooperating institution (University of New Hampshire); Air Force ROTC: Offered at cooperating institution (University of New Hampshire). **Faculty and instruction (2005-2006):** Total instructional faculty: 126 full-time, 249 part-time (64% men; 36% women; 4% minorities). Full-time faculty with Ph.D. or other terminal degree: 63%. Student/faculty ratio: 15/1. Classes of fewer than 20 students: 50%; of 20 to 49 students: 50%. **Advanced Placement and International Baccalaureate credit:** AP tests may be used for: Credit and/or placement. Scores accepted: 3, 4, 5. International Baccalaureate exams may be used for: Placement only. **Freshmen returning for sophomore year:** 70%. **Graduation rates:** Four-year: 34%; five-year: 49%; six-year: 56%. **Graduate study:** 9% of students pursue further study within one year.

COSTS AND FINANCIAL AID

Financial aid office: (603) 645-9645. **Expenses (2006-2007):** Tuition and fees 2006-2007: $30,524; room/board: $8,480. Estimated books and supplies: $850. **Financial aid:** Priority filing date for institution's financial aid form: March 15. In 2005-2006, 80% of undergraduates applied for financial aid. Of those, 70% were determined to have financial need; 12% had their need fully met. Average financial aid package (proportion receiving): $14,063 (70%). Average amount of gift aid, such as scholarships or grants (proportion receiving): $9,105 (67%). Average amount of self-help aid, such as work study or loans (proportion receiving): $4,428 (65%). Average need-based loan (excluding PLUS or other private loans): $3,745. Among students who received need-based aid, the average percentage of need met: 70%. Among students who received aid based on merit, the average award (and the proportion receiving): $3,426 (17%). The average athletic scholarship (and the proportion receiving): $15,049 (4%). Average amount of debt of borrowers graduating in 2005: $21,138.

CAMPUS LIFE AND EXTRACURRICULAR ACTIVITIES

Campus housing available (% using): coed dorms (53%), women's dorms (1%), apartment for single students (44%), special housing for disabled students (0%), other housing options (2%). Students who live in college-owned, operated, or affiliated housing: 74%. **Student employment:** During the 2005-2006 academic year, 6% of undergraduates worked on campus. Average per-year earnings: $1,580. **Clubs and organizations:** Number of student organizations: 57. Activities include: choral groups, dance, drama/theater, literary magazine, musical theater, radio station, student government, student newspaper, yearbook. Number of fraternities: 3; sororities: 4. Proportion of men in fraternities: 4%; of women in sororities: 5%. Average proportion of students who stay on campus on weekends: 65%. **Sports program (2005-2006):** Member of NCAA II. *Men's intercollegiate varsity sports:* baseball, basketball, cross-country, golf, ice hockey, lacrosse, soccer, tennis. *Women's intercollegiate varsity sports:* basketball, cross-country, lacrosse, soccer, softball, tennis, volleyball.

SERVICES AND FACILITIES

Basic services: health service, health insurance. **Remedial assistance:** math, writing, study skills. **Counseling services:** minority student, career, personal, academic, older student, psychological, birth control. **For learning-disabled students:** School does not offer a structured program with separate admission and additional fees. Total undergraduates in learning-disabled program or receiving services: 75. Services include: reading machines, tape recorders, untimed tests, note-taking services, oral tests, learning center, readers, extended time for tests, tutors, priority registration, priority seating, texts on tape. **Library:** Number of titles: 89,620; number of current serial subscriptions: 31,866. **Information technology resources:** Students are not required to lease or own a computer. Number of campus computers available to all students: 447. School has a wireless network. Approximate number of users that can be accommodated: 1,000. Proportion of college-owned housing units wired for high-speed internet access: 100%. **Campus safety:** Security services offered: 24-hour foot-and-vehicle patrols, late-night transport/escort service, 24-hour emergency telephones, lighted pathways/sidewalks, student patrols, controlled dormitory access (key, security card, etc).

TRANSFER AND INTERNATIONAL STUDENTS

Transfer students: May apply for admission for the following academic terms: Fall, Spring. Applicants need a minimum number of credits to apply. For fall 2005: Transfer applications received: 353. Transfer applicants offered admission: 255. Transfer applicants enrolled: 142. **International students:** Number of foreign undergraduates: 73 (4% of student body). Number of countries represented: 65. Minimum TOEFL score required: 500 (paper); 173 (computer).

St. Anselm College

- **Address:** 100 St. Anselm Drive, Manchester, NH 03102-1310
- **Website:** http://www.anselm.edu
- **Private; Religious affiliation:** Roman Catholic (Benedictine)
- **Enrollment:** 1,937 full-time; 49 part-time

KEY STATS

✔ **U.S News College Ranking:** third tier, Liberal Arts Colleges
✔ **SAT Score (25th/75th percentile):** 1020-1200
✔ **Tuition:** 2006-2007: $26,120

Selectivity: Selective	**Room/board:** $9,620
Acceptance rate: 73%	**Average debt:** $22,246
Student/faculty ratio: 13/1	**Proportion who borrowed:** 72%

UNDERGRADUATE STUDENT BODY STATS

2005-2006 enrollment: 1,937 full-time; 49 part-time. Men: 42%; women: 58%. **Ethnic makeup:** African American: 1%; Asian American: 1%; Hispanic: 1%; White: 96%; International: 1%.

ADMISSIONS FACTS AND FIGURES

Phone: (603) 641-7500. **Email:** admission@anselm.edu. **Website:** http://www.anselm.edu. **Application deadlines for fall 2007:** Regular decision: Rolling. Early decision: Send application by: November 15; Decision sent by: December 15. Early action: Not offered. Admission can be deferred. **Application fee:** $55. Common application is accepted. **To apply online, go to:** http://www.anselm.edu/admission/applying/Application.htm. **Admissions requirements/recommendations:** High school units required (recommended): English: 4 (4); Mathematics: 3 (4); Science: 3 (4); Foreign language: 2 (4); Social studies: 2; History: 1 (2); Academic electives: 3; Total units: 18 (20). Tests: The college uses SAT or ACT scores in admissions decisions. Either SAT or ACT required. For admission to the fall 2007 entering class, the school will accept: ACT with writing, ACT without writing. Campus visit: Recommended. Admissions interview: Recommended. Off-campus interview: May be arranged. **Factors that count in admissions decisions:** *Academic:* Secondary school record: Very important. Class rank: Considered. Letters of recommendation: Very important. Standardized test scores: Very important. Essay: Very important. *Nonacademic:* Interview: Not considered. Extracurricular activities: Considered. Talent/ability: Considered. Character/personal qualities: Considered. Alumni/ae relationship: Considered. Geographical residence: Considered. State residency: Considered. Religious affiliation/commitment: Not considered. Minority status: Considered. Volunteer work: Considered. Work experience: Considered. **Other schools with the greatest overlap in applicants:** Boston College; Providence College; Stonehill College; University of Massachusetts–Amherst; University of New Hampshire. **Admissions statistics for the fall 2005 entering class:** Total applicants: 3,258. Total accepted: 2,366. Freshmen enrolled: 519; 80% were from out of state. Accepted through early-decision or early-action plans: 16%. Overall acceptance rate: 73%. Early-decision acceptance rate: 79%. Non-early acceptance rate: 72%. **Size of waiting list:** 363 applicants; enrolled from waiting list: 150. **Credentials of fall 2005 freshmen:** 15% ranked in the top 10 percent of their high school class; 45% were in the top 25 percent, and 83% were in the top half. (Proportion submitting class standing: 67%.) **Average high school grade point average:** 3.1. **First-year students who submitted SAT scores:** 98%. Scores (25/75 percentile): Verbal: 510-600; Math: 510-600, Combined: 1020-1200. **First-year students submitting ACT scores:** 17%. Scores (25/75 percentile): English: 21-25, Math: 20-27, Composite: 21-26.

ACADEMICS

Year founded: 1889. **Academic calendar:** Semester. **Degrees offered:** bachelor's. **Most popular majors:** 20% business/commerce, 10% criminal justice/safety studies, 9% nursing, 9% psychology, 8% sociology. **Major fields of study:** biological and biomedical sciences; business, management, marketing, and related support services; computer and information sciences and support services; engineering; English language and literature/letters; foreign languages, literatures, and linguistics; health professions and

related clinical sciences; history; liberal arts and sciences studies, and humanities; mathematics and statistics; multi/interdisciplinary studies; natural resources and conservation; philosophy and religious studies; physical sciences; psychology; social sciences; theology and religious vocations; visual and performing arts. **Areas of required coursework:** humanities, English (including composition), philosophy, foreign languages, sciences (biological or physical), other. **Pre-professional programs:** pre-law, pre-dentistry, pre-medicine, pre-theology, pre-veterinary science, pre-optometry, pre-pharmacy. **Special academic programs (% participation):** cross-registration (4%), dual enrollment (0%), exchange student program (domestic) (1%), honors program (10%), independent study (8%), internships (45%), liberal arts/career combination (1%), study abroad (6%), teacher certificate program (3%). **Teacher certification offered in:** secondary. **Reserve Officers Training Corps (ROTC):** Army ROTC: Offered at cooperating institution (University of New Hampshire); Air Force ROTC: Offered at cooperating institution (University of Massachusetts-Lowell). **Faculty and instruction (2005-2006):** Total instructional faculty: 131 full-time, 46 part-time (56% men; 44% women; 3% minorities). Full-time faculty with Ph.D. or other terminal degree: 92%. Student/faculty ratio: 13/1. Classes of fewer than 20 students: 52%; of 20 to 49 students: 44%; of 50 or more students: 4%. **Advanced Placement and International Baccalaureate credit:** AP tests may be used for: Credit and/or placement. Scores accepted: 3, 4, 5. International Baccalaureate exams may be used for: Credit and/or placement. **Freshmen returning for sophomore year:** 84%. **Graduation rates:** Four-year: 71%; five-year: 74%; six-year: 75%. **Graduate study:** Fields in which graduates pursue further study: Master of Business Administration (MBA), 11%; law, 18%; medicine, 1%; dentistry, 1%; education, 17%; arts and sciences, 15%; veterinary medicine, 1%.

COSTS AND FINANCIAL AID

Financial aid office: (603) 641-7110. **Expenses (2006-2007):** Tuition and fees 2006-2007: $26,120; room/board: $9,620. Estimated books and supplies: $1,000; transportation: $500; personal expenses: $1,000. **Financial aid:** Priority filing date for institution's financial aid form: March 15; deadline: March 15. In 2005-2006, 82% of undergraduates applied for financial aid. Of those, 71% were determined to have financial need; 22% had their need fully met. Average financial aid package (proportion receiving): $18,164 (71%). Average amount of gift aid, such as scholarships or grants (proportion receiving): $12,728 (70%). Average amount of self-help aid, such as work study or loans (proportion receiving): $6,138 (64%). Average need-based loan (excluding PLUS or other private loans): $5,218. Among students who received need-based aid, the average percentage of need met: 83%. Among students who received aid based on merit, the average award (and the proportion receiving): $13,306 (18%). The average athletic scholarship (and the proportion receiving): $30,218 (0%). Average amount of debt of borrowers graduating in 2005: $22,246. Proportion who borrowed: 72%.

CAMPUS LIFE AND EXTRACURRICULAR ACTIVITIES

Campus housing available (% using): coed dorms (0%), women's dorms (38%), men's dorms (27%), apartment for single students (29%), special housing for disabled students (1%), other housing options (5%). Students who live in college-owned, operated, or affiliated housing: 87%. **Student employment:** During the 2005-2006 academic year, 9% of undergraduates worked on campus. Average per-year earnings: $900. **Clubs and organizations:** Number of student organizations: 68. Activities include: choral groups, dance, drama/theater, jazz band, literary magazine, pep band, radio station, student government, student newspaper, student film society, television station, yearbook. Number of fraternities: 0; sororities: 0. Average proportion of students who stay on campus on weekends: 60%. **Sports program (2005-2006):** Member of NCAA II. *Men's intercollegiate varsity sports:* alpine skiing, baseball, basketball, cross-country, football, golf, ice hockey, lacrosse, soccer, tennis. *Women's intercollegiate varsity sports:* alpine skiing, basketball, cross-country, field hockey, golf, lacrosse, soccer, softball, tennis, volleyball.

SERVICES AND FACILITIES

Basic services: nonremedial tutoring, health service, health insurance. **Counseling services:** career, personal, academic, psychological, religious. **For learning-disabled students:** School does not offer a structured program with separate admission and additional fees. Total undergraduates in learning-disabled program or receiving services: 31. Services include: tape recorders, extended time for tests, tutors, priority seating, exams on tape or computer, other testing accomodations, other. **Library:** Number of titles: 232,000; number of current serial subscriptions: 1,500. **Information technology resources:** Students are not required to lease or own a computer. Number of campus computers available to all students: 145. School has a wireless network. Approximate number of users that can be accommodated: 200. Proportion of college-owned housing units wired for high-speed internet access: 100%. **Campus safety:** Security services offered: 24-hour foot-and-vehicle patrols, late-night transport/escort service, 24-hour emergency telephones, lighted pathways/sidewalks, controlled dormitory access (key, security card, etc).

TRANSFER AND INTERNATIONAL STUDENTS

Transfer students: May apply for admission for the following academic terms: Fall, Spring. Applicants do not need a minimum number of credits to apply. For fall 2005: Transfer applications received: 90. Transfer applicants offered admission: 46. Transfer applicants enrolled: 27. **International students:** Number of foreign undergraduates: 19 (1% of student body). Number of countries represented: 16. Minimum TOEFL score required: 550 (paper); 250 (computer).

University of New Hampshire

- **Address:** Thompson Hall, Durham, NH 03824
- **Website:** http://www.unh.edu
- **Public**
- **Enrollment:** 10,911 full-time; 618 part-time

KEY STATS

✔ **U.S News College Ranking:** 105, National Universities
✔ **SAT Score (25th/75th percentile):** 1030-1230
✔ **Tuition:** 2006-2007: $10,401 in state, $22,851 out of state
  Selectivity: Selective   **Room/board:** $7,584
  Acceptance rate: 72%   **Average debt:** $21,459
  Student/faculty ratio: 17/1   **Proportion who borrowed:** 68%

UNDERGRADUATE STUDENT BODY STATS

2005-2006 enrollment: 10,911 full-time; 618 part-time. Men: 44%; women: 56%. **Ethnic makeup:** African American: 1%; Asian American: 2%; Hispanic: 2%; White: 93%; International: 1%. **Religious preference:** Roman Catholic: 33%; Protestant: 22%; Jewish: 2%; No preference: 31%; Other: 12%.

ADMISSIONS FACTS AND FIGURES

Phone: (603) 862-1360. **Email:** admissions@unh.edu. **Website:** http://www.unh.edu. **Application deadlines for fall 2007:** Regular decision: February 1; decision sent by April 15. Early decision: Not offered. Early action: Send application by: December 1; Decision sent by: January 15. Admission can be deferred. **Application fee:** $45. Common application is accepted. **To apply online, go to:** http://www.unh.edu/admissions/apply.html. **Admissions requirements/recommendations:** High school units required (recommended): English: 4; Mathematics: 4; Science: 4; Foreign language: 3; Social studies: 3; Total units: 18. Tests: The college uses SAT or ACT scores in admissions decisions. Either SAT or ACT required. For admission to the fall 2007 entering class, the school will accept: ACT with writing. Campus visit: Recommended. Admissions interview: Neither required nor recommended. Off-campus interview: Not available. **Factors that count in admissions decisions:** *Academic:* Secondary school record: Very important. Class rank: Very important. Letters of recommendation: Important. Standardized test scores: Considered. Essay: Considered. *Nonacademic:* Interview: Not considered. Extracurricular activities: Considered. Talent/ability: Considered. Character/personal qualities: Considered. Alumni/ae relationship: Considered. Geographical residence: Considered. State residency: Considered. Religious affiliation/commitment: Not considered. Minority status: Considered. Volunteer work: Considered. Work experience: Considered. **Other schools with the greatest overlap in applicants:** Boston University; Northeastern University; University of Connecticut; University of Massachusetts–Amherst; University of Vermont. **Admissions statistics for the fall 2005 entering class:** Total applicants: 12,310. Total accepted: 8,804. Freshmen enrolled: 2,622; 46% were from out of state. Accepted through early-decision or early-action plans: 30%. Overall acceptance rate: 72%. Non-early acceptance rate: 77%. **Credentials of fall 2005 freshmen:** 20% ranked in the top 10 percent of their high school class; 61% were in the top 25 percent, and 97% were in the top half. (Proportion submitting class standing: 69%.) **First-year students who submitted SAT scores:** 100%. Scores (25/75 percentile): Verbal: 510-610, Math: 520-620, Combined: 1030-1230.

ACADEMICS

Year founded: 1866. **Academic calendar:** Semester. **Degrees offered:** certificate, associate, bachelor's, master's, post-master's certificate, doctorate. **Most popular majors:** 15% business administration, management, and operations, 8% psychology, 6% English language and literature, 5% communication and media studies, 5% political science and government. **Major fields of study:** agriculture, agriculture operations, and related sciences; architecture and related services; area, ethnic, cultural, and gender studies; biological and biomedical sciences; business, management, marketing, and related support services; communication, journalism, and related programs; computer and information sciences and support services; education; engineering; English language and literature/letters; family and consumer sciences/human sciences; foreign languages, literatures, and linguistics; health professions and related clinical sciences; history; liberal arts and sciences studies, and humanities; mathematics and statistics; multi/interdisciplinary studies; natural resources and conservation; parks, recreation, leisure, and fitness studies; personal and culinary services; philosophy and religious studies; physical sciences; psychology; public administration and social service professions; social sciences; visual and performing arts. **Areas of required coursework:** arts/fine arts, humanities, mathematics, English (including composition), philosophy, sciences (biological or physical), history, social science. **Pre-professional programs:** pre-law, pre-dentistry, pre-medicine, pre-veterinary science; pre-optometry, pre-pharmacy. **Special academic programs (% participation):** cross-registration, double major (5%), English as a Second Language (ESL) (.02%), exchange student program (domestic) (8%), honors program (7%), independent study (8%), internships, student-designed major, study abroad (17%), teacher certificate program (2%). **Teacher certification offered in:** early childhood, special education, elementary, vo-tech, middle/junior high, adult education, secondary, bilingual/bicultural. **Reserve Officers Training Corps (ROTC):** Army ROTC: Offered on campus; Air Force ROTC: Offered on campus. **Faculty and instruction (2005-2006):** Total instructional faculty: 694 full-time, 268 part-time (57% men; 43% women; 6% minorities). Full-time faculty with Ph.D. or other terminal degree: 84%. Student/faculty ratio: 17/1. Classes of fewer than 20 students: 46%; of 20 to 49 students: 40%; of 50 or more students: 15%. **Advanced Placement and International Baccalaureate credit:** AP tests may be used for: Credit and/or placement. Scores accepted: 4, 5. International Baccalaureate exams may be used for: Credit only. **Freshmen returning for sophomore year:** 85%. **Graduation rates:** Four-year: 53%; five-year: 70%; six-year: 73%.

COSTS AND FINANCIAL AID

Financial aid office: (603) 862-3600. **Expenses (2006-2007):** Tuition and fees 2006-2007: $10,401 in state, $22,851 out of state; room/board: $7,584. **Financial aid:** Priority filing date for institution's financial aid form: March 1. In 2005-2006, 72% of undergraduates applied for financial aid. Of those, 59% were determined to have financial need; 20% had their need fully met. Average financial aid package (proportion receiving): $14,888 (58%). Average amount of gift aid, such as scholarships or grants (proportion receiving): $2,293 (37%). Average amount of self-help aid, such as work study or loans (proportion receiving): $2,890 (55%). Average need-based loan (excluding PLUS or other private loans): $3,385. Among students who received need-based aid, the average percentage of need met: 78%. Among students who received aid based on merit, the average award (and the proportion receiving): $5,827 (24%). The average athletic scholarship (and the proportion receiving): $18,786 (2%). Average amount of debt of borrowers graduating in 2005: $21,459. Proportion who borrowed: 68%.

CAMPUS LIFE AND EXTRACURRICULAR ACTIVITIES

Campus housing available (% using): coed dorms (75%), women's dorms (2%), apartments for married students (2%), apartment for single students (19%), special housing for international students (2%). Students who live in college-owned, operated, or affiliated housing: 57%. **Student employment:** During the 2005-2006 academic year, 31% of undergraduates worked on campus. Average per-year earnings: $1,763. **Clubs and organizations:** Number of student organizations: 200. Activities include: choral groups, concert band, dance, drama/theater, jazz band, literary magazine, marching band, music ensembles, musical theater, pep band, radio station, student government, student newspaper, student film society, symphony orchestra, television station, yearbook. Number of fraternities: 8; sororities: 5. Proportion of men in fraternities: 4%; of women in sororities: 5%. Average proportion of students who stay on campus on weekends: 65%. **Sports program (2005-2006):** Member of NCAA I. *Men's intercollegiate varsity sports:* basketball, cross-country, football, ice hockey, skiing, soccer, swimming and diving, tennis, track and field (indoor), track and field (outdoor). *Women's intercollegiate varsity sports:* basketball, cross-country, field hockey, gymnastics, ice hockey, lacrosse, rowing, skiing, soccer, swimming and diving, tennis, track and field (indoor), track and field (outdoor), volleyball.

SERVICES AND FACILITIES

Basic services: nonremedial tutoring, women's center, placement service, day care, health service, health insurance, other. **Counseling services:** minority student, career, military, personal, veteran student, academic, older student, psychological, birth control, religious. **For learning-disabled students:** School does not offer a structured program with separate admission and additional fees. Total undergraduates in learning-disabled program or receiving services: 225. Services include: reading machines, note-taking services, oral tests, readers, extended time for tests, priority registration, priority seating, texts on tape, typist/scribe, other testing accomodations, other. **Library:** Number of titles: 1,795,812; number of current serial subscriptions: 33,924. **Information technology resources:** Students are not required to lease or own a computer. Number of campus computers available to all students: 345. School has a wireless network. Approximate number of users that can be accommodated: 15,000. Proportion of college-owned housing units wired for high-speed internet access: 100%. **Campus safety:** Security services offered: 24-hour foot-and-vehicle patrols, late-night transport/escort service, 24-hour emergency telephones, lighted pathways/sidewalks, student patrols, controlled dormitory access (key, security card, etc).

TRANSFER AND INTERNATIONAL STUDENTS

Transfer students: May apply for admission for the following academic terms: Fall, Spring. Applicants do not need a minimum number of credits to apply. For fall 2005: Transfer applications received: 1,125. Transfer applicants offered admission: 723. Transfer applicants enrolled: 439.
International students: Number of foreign undergraduates: 73 (1% of student body). Number of countries represented: 28. Minimum TOEFL score required: 550 (paper); 213 (computer).

New Jersey

Bloomfield College

- **Address:** 467 Franklin Street, Bloomfield, NJ 07003
- **Website:** http://www.bloomfield.edu
- **Private; Religious affiliation:** Presbyterian
- **Enrollment:** 1,721 full-time; 491 part-time

KEY STATS
- ✔ **U.S News College Ranking:** third tier, Comp. Coll.–Bachelor's (North)
- ✔ **SAT Score (25th/75th percentile):** 770-950
- ✔ **Tuition:** 2006-2007: $16,400

Selectivity: Less selective	**Room/board:** $8,100
Acceptance rate: 47%	**Average debt:** N/A
Student/faculty ratio: 14/1	**Proportion who borrowed:** N/A

UNDERGRADUATE STUDENT BODY STATS
2005-2006 enrollment: 1,721 full-time; 491 part-time. Men: 31%; women: 69%. **Ethnic makeup:** African American: 53%; Asian American: 4%; Hispanic: 18%; White: 23%; International: 2%.

ADMISSIONS FACTS AND FIGURES
Phone: (800) 848-4555. **Email:** admission@bloomfield.edu. **Website:** http://www.bloomfield.edu. **Application deadlines for fall 2007:** Regular decision: July 1. Early decision: Not offered. Early action: Send application by: N/A; Decision sent by: N/A. Admission can be deferred. **Application fee:** $35. Common application is accepted. **To apply online, go to:** http://www.bloomfield.edu/admissions/instructions.htm. **Admissions requirements/recommendations:** High school units required (recommended): Total units: 14. Tests: The college uses SAT or ACT scores in admissions decisions. Either SAT or ACT required. For admission to the fall 2007 entering class, the school will accept: ACT with writing, ACT without writing. Campus visit: Recommended. Admissions interview: Recommended. Off-campus interview: Not available. **Factors that count in admissions decisions:** *Academic:* Secondary school record: Very important. Class rank: Considered. Letters of recommendation: Very important. Standardized test scores: Very important. Essay: Very important. *Nonacademic:* Interview: Important. Extracurricular activities: Important. Talent/ability: Considered. Character/personal qualities: Considered. Alumni/ae relationship: Considered. Geographical residence: Not considered. State residency: Not considered. Religious affiliation/commitment: Not considered. Minority status: Not considered. Volunteer work: Important. Work experience: Considered. **Other schools with the greatest overlap in applicants:** Montclair State University; New Jersey City University; Rutgers–Newark; William Paterson University of New Jersey. **Admissions statistics for the fall 2005 entering class:** Total applicants: 2,531. Total accepted: 1,179. Freshmen enrolled: 413; 6% were from out of state. Overall acceptance rate: 47%. Non-early acceptance rate: 47%. **Credentials of fall 2005 freshmen:** 1% ranked in the top 10 percent of their high school class; 11% were in the top 25 percent, and 42% were in the top half. (Proportion submitting class standing: 67%.) **Average high school grade point average:** 2.7. **First-year students who submitted SAT scores:** 88%. Scores (25/75 percentile): Verbal: 380-470, Math: 390-480, Combined: 770-950.

ACADEMICS
Year founded: 1868. **Academic calendar:** Semester. **Degrees offered:** certificate, bachelor's, post-bachelor's certificate. **Most popular majors:** 28% business, management, marketing, and related support services, 16% social sciences, 14% psychology, 10% health professions and related clinical sciences, 9% visual and performing arts. **Major fields of study:** biological and biomedical sciences; business, management, marketing, and related support services; computer and information sciences and support services; education; English language and literature/letters; health professions and related clinical sciences; history; mathematics and statistics; philosophy and religious studies; physical sciences; psychology; social sciences; visual and performing arts. **Areas of required coursework:** arts/fine arts, humanities, computer literacy, mathematics, English (including composition), sciences (biological or physical), social science. **Pre-professional programs:** pre-medicine, other. **Special academic programs (% participation):** accelerated program (31%), cooperative (work-study plan) program (25%), distance learning, double major (1%), dual enrollment, English as a Second Language (ESL) (7%), honors program (1%), independent study (24%), internships (0%), liberal arts/career combination (0%), student-designed major (0%), study abroad (0%), teacher certificate program (6%), weekend college (31%). **Teacher certification offered in:** early childhood, special education, elementary, secondary. **Reserve Officers Training Corps (ROTC):** Army ROTC: Offered at cooperating institution (Seton Hall University). **Faculty and instruction (2005-2006):** Total instructional faculty: 62 full-time, 220 part-time (45% men; 55% women; 34% minorities). Full-time faculty with Ph.D. or other terminal degree: 77%. Student/faculty ratio: 14/1. Classes of fewer than 20 students: 77%; of 20 to 49 students: 23%; of 50 or more students: 1%. **Advanced Placement and International Baccalaureate credit:** AP tests may be used for: Credit and/or placement. Scores accepted: 3, 4, 5. **Freshmen returning for sophomore year:** 69%. **Graduation rates:** Four-year: 9%; five-year: 24%; six-year: 29%. **Graduate study:** 5% of students pursue further study immediately upon graduation; 62% within five years.

COSTS AND FINANCIAL AID
Financial aid office: (973) 748-9000. **Expenses (2006-2007):** Tuition and fees 2006-2007: $16,400; room/board: $8,100. Estimated books and supplies: $500; transportation: $300; personal expenses: $1,496. **Financial aid:** Priority filing date for institution's financial aid form: March 15; deadline: October 1. In 2005-2006, 95% of undergraduates applied for financial aid. Of those, 86% were determined to have financial need; 46% had their need fully met. Average financial aid package (proportion receiving): $15,061 (86%). Average amount of gift aid, such as scholarships or grants (proportion receiving): $10,205 (80%). Average amount of self-help aid, such as work study or loans (proportion receiving): $4,674 (74%). Average need-based loan (excluding PLUS or other private loans): $4,441. Among students who received need-based aid, the average percentage of need met: 64%. Among students who received aid based on merit, the average award (and the proportion receiving): $5,265 (3%). The average athletic scholarship (and the proportion receiving): $11,302 (2%).

CAMPUS LIFE AND EXTRACURRICULAR ACTIVITIES
Campus housing available (% using): coed dorms (49%), sorority housing (1%), fraternity housing (1%), apartment for single students, other housing options (48%). Students who live in college-owned, operated, or affiliated housing: 17%. **Student employment:** During the 2005-2006 academic year, 8% of undergraduates worked on campus. Average per-year earnings: $1,600. **Clubs and organizations:** Number of student organizations: 25. Activities include: choral groups, dance, drama/theater, literary magazine, radio station, student government, student film society, yearbook. Number of fraternities: 2; sororities: 3. Proportion of men in fraternities: 1%; of women in sororities: 1%. Average proportion of students who stay on campus on weekends: 30%. **Sports program (2005-2006):** Member of NCAA II. **Men's intercollegiate varsity sports:** baseball, basketball, cross-country, soccer, tennis. **Women's intercollegiate varsity sports:** basketball, cross-country, soccer, softball, volleyball.

SERVICES AND FACILITIES
Basic services: nonremedial tutoring, placement service, health service, health insurance. **Remedial assistance:** reading, math, writing, study skills. **Counseling services:** career, personal, veteran student, academic, older student, psychological, birth control, religious. **For learning-disabled students:** School does not offer a structured program with separate admission and additional fees. Total undergraduates in learning-disabled program or receiving services: 26. Services include: remedial math, remedial English, reading machines, remedial reading, tape recorders, other special classes, diagnostic testing service, note-taking services, learning center, readers, extended time for tests, tutors, priority seating, texts on tape, typist/scribe, exams on tape or computer. **Library:** Number of titles: 70,000; number of current serial subscriptions: 456. **Information technology resources:**

Students are not required to lease or own a computer. Number of campus computers available to all students: 191. School has a wireless network. Approximate number of users that can be accommodated: 100. Proportion of college-owned housing units wired for high-speed internet access: 100%. **Campus safety:** Security services offered: 24-hour foot-and-vehicle patrols, late-night transport/escort service, 24-hour emergency telephones, lighted pathways/sidewalks.

TRANSFER AND INTERNATIONAL STUDENTS

Transfer students: May apply for admission for the following academic terms: Fall, Spring, Summer. Applicants need a minimum number of credits to apply. For fall 2005: Transfer applications received: 1,060. Transfer applicants offered admission: 652. Transfer applicants enrolled: 261. **International students:** Number of foreign undergraduates: 38 (2% of student body). Number of countries represented: 7. Minimum TOEFL score required: 550 (paper); 213 (computer). Average TOEFL score: 583 (paper).

Caldwell College

- **Address:** 9 Ryerson Avenue, Caldwell, NJ 07006
- **Website:** http://www.caldwell.edu
- **Private; Religious affiliation:** Roman Catholic
- **Enrollment:** 1,059 full-time; 612 part-time

KEY STATS

✔ **U.S News College Ranking:** 22, Comp. Coll.–Bachelor's (North)
✔ **SAT Score (25th/75th percentile):** 850-1070
✔ **Tuition:** 2006-2007: $20,200

Selectivity: Less selective	**Room/board:** $8,000
Acceptance rate: 78%	**Average debt:** $17,548
Student/faculty ratio: 13/1	**Proportion who borrowed:** 74%

UNDERGRADUATE STUDENT BODY STATS

2005-2006 enrollment: 1,059 full-time; 612 part-time. Men: 32%; women: 68%. **Ethnic makeup:** African American: 16%; Asian American: 2%; Hispanic: 11%; White: 66%; International: 5%. **Religious preference:** Protestant: 25%; Jewish: 5%; Unknown: 3%; Roman Catholic: 67%.

ADMISSIONS FACTS AND FIGURES

Phone: (973) 618-3500. **Email:** admissions@caldwell.edu. **Website:** http://www.caldwell.edu. **Application deadlines for fall 2007:** Regular decision: Rolling. Early decision: Not offered. Early action: Send application by: January 1; Decision sent by: January 15. Admission can be deferred. **Application fee:** $40. Common application is accepted. **To apply online, go to:** http://www.collegeboard.org. **Admissions requirements/recommendations:** High school units required (recommended): English: 4; Mathematics: 2; Science: 2; Foreign language: 2; History: 1; Academic electives: 5; Total units: 16. Tests: The college uses SAT or ACT scores in admissions decisions. Either SAT or ACT required. For admission to the fall 2007 entering class, the school will accept: ACT with writing, ACT without writing. Campus visit: Recommended. Admissions interview: Recommended. Off-campus interview: May be arranged. **Factors that count in admissions decisions:** *Academic:* Secondary school record: Very important. Class rank: Important. Letters of recommendation: Important. Standardized test scores: Important. Essay: Considered. *Nonacademic:* Interview: Considered. Extracurricular activities: Very important. Talent/ability: Important. Character/personal qualities: Considered. Alumni/ae relationship: Considered. Geographical residence: Not considered. State residency: Not considered. Religious affiliation/commitment: Not considered. Minority status: Not considered. Volunteer work: Considered. Work experience: Considered. **Other schools with the greatest overlap in applicants:** Kean University; Montclair State University; Rutgers–New Brunswick; Seton Hall University; William Paterson University of New Jersey. **Admissions statistics for the fall 2005 entering class:** Total applicants: 1,234. Total accepted: 960. Freshmen enrolled: 298; 8% were from out of state. Overall acceptance rate: 78%. Non-early acceptance rate: 78%. **Credentials of fall 2005 freshmen:** 4% ranked in the top 10 percent of their high school class; 15% were in the top 25 percent, and 47% were in the top half. (Proportion submitting class standing: 53%.) **Average high school grade point average:** 3.1. **First-year students who submitted SAT scores:** 98%. Scores (25/75 percentile): Verbal: 430-530, Math: 420-540, Combined: 850-1070.

ACADEMICS

Year founded: 1939. **Academic calendar:** Semester. **Degrees offered:** certificate, bachelor's, post-bachelor's certificate, master's, post-master's certificate. **Most popular majors:** Information not available. **Major fields of study:** area, ethnic, cultural, and gender studies; biological and biomedical sciences; business, management, marketing, and related support services; communication, journalism, and related programs; computer and information sciences and support services; education; English language and literature/letters; foreign languages, literatures, and linguistics; history; mathematics and statistics; multi/interdisciplinary studies; physical sciences; psychology; security and protective services; social sciences; visual and performing arts. **Areas of required coursework:** arts/fine arts, humanities, computer literacy, mathematics, English (including composition), philosophy, foreign languages, sciences (biological or physical), history, social science, other. **Special academic programs (% participation):** accelerated program, cooperative (work-study plan) program (21%), distance learning, double major (23%), English as a Second Language (ESL), external degree program, honors program, independent study, internships (24%), liberal arts/career combination, student-designed major (0%), study abroad (11%), teacher certificate program (16%), weekend college. **Teacher certification offered in:** early childhood, special education, elementary, middle/junior high, secondary. **Cooperative education programs:** art, business, computer science, education, humanities, social/behavioral science. **Reserve Officers Training Corps (ROTC):** Army ROTC: Offered at cooperating institution (Seton Hall University). **Faculty and instruction (2005-2006):** Total instructional faculty: 77 full-time, 101 part-time (; 12% minorities). Full-time faculty with Ph.D. or other terminal degree: 87%. Student/faculty ratio: 13/1. **Advanced Placement and International Baccalaureate credit:** AP tests may be used for: Credit and/or placement. Scores accepted: 3, 4, 5. International Baccalaureate exams may be used for: Credit only. **Freshmen returning for sophomore year:** 70%. **Graduation rates:** Four-year: 35%; five-year: 45%; six-year: 51%. **Graduate study:** 20% of students pursue further study immediately upon graduation; 40% within one year; 50% within five years. Fields in which graduates pursue further study: Master of Business Administration (MBA), 20%; law, 3%; medicine, 2%; theology (or the seminary), 1%; education, 30%; arts and sciences, 10%.

COSTS AND FINANCIAL AID

Financial aid office: (973) 618-3221. **Expenses (2006-2007):** Tuition and fees 2006-2007: $20,200; room/board: $8,000. Estimated books and supplies: $950; transportation: $600; personal expenses: $1,000. **Financial aid:** Priority filing date for institution's financial aid form: April 1. In 2005-2006, 77% of undergraduates applied for financial aid. Of those, 44% were determined to have financial need; 71% had their need fully met. Average financial aid package (proportion receiving): N/A (44%). Average amount of gift aid, such as scholarships or grants (proportion receiving): N/A (35%). Average amount of self-help aid, such as work study or loans (proportion receiving): N/A (44%). Among students who received need-based aid, the average percentage of need met: 58%. Among students who received aid based on merit, the average award (and the proportion receiving): $5,703 (N/A). The average athletic scholarship (and the proportion receiving): $3,664 (11%). Average amount of debt of borrowers graduating in 2005: $17,548. Proportion who borrowed: 74%.

CAMPUS LIFE AND EXTRACURRICULAR ACTIVITIES

Campus housing available (% using): coed dorms (98%), other housing options (2%). Students who live in college-owned, operated, or affiliated housing: 24%. **Student employment:** During the 2005-2006 academic year, 13% of undergraduates worked on campus. Average per-year earnings: $1,000. **Clubs and organizations:** Number of student organizations: 34. Activities include: choral groups, drama/theater, jazz band, literary magazine, music ensembles, musical theater, student government, student newspaper, yearbook. Number of fraternities: 0; sororities: 0. Average proportion of students who stay on campus on weekends: 33%. **Sports program (2005-2006):** Member of NCAA II. *Men's intercollegiate varsity sports:* baseball, basketball, golf, soccer, tennis. *Women's intercollegiate varsity sports:* basketball, cross-country, soccer, softball, tennis.

SERVICES AND FACILITIES

Basic services: placement service, health service, other. **Remedial assistance:** reading, math, writing, study skills. **Counseling services:** minority student, personal, academic, older student, religious, other. **For learning-disabled students:** School does not offer a structured program with separate admission and additional fees. Services include: remedial math, remedial English, reading machines, remedial reading, tape recorders, other special classes, untimed tests, note-taking services, oral tests, learning center, readers, extended time for tests, tutors. **Library:** Number of titles: 144,698; number of current serial subscriptions: 327. **Information technology resources:** Students are not required to lease or own a computer. Number of campus computers available to all students: 234. School has a wireless network. Approximate number of users that can be accommodated: 50. Proportion of college-owned housing units wired for high-speed internet access: 100%. **Campus safety:** Security services offered: 24-hour foot-and-vehicle patrols, late-night transport/escort service, 24-hour emergency telephones, lighted pathways/sidewalks, controlled dormitory access (key, security card, etc).

TRANSFER AND INTERNATIONAL STUDENTS

Transfer students: May apply for admission for the following academic terms: Fall, Spring. Applicants need a minimum number of credits to apply. **International students:** Number of foreign undergraduates: 77 (5% of student body). Minimum TOEFL score required: 450 (paper); 133 (computer). Average TOEFL score: 550 (paper).

Centenary College

- **Address:** 400 Jefferson Street, Hackettstown, NJ 07840
- **Website:** http://www.centenarycollege.edu
- **Private; Religious affiliation:** United Methodist
- **Enrollment:** 1,614 full-time; 270 part-time

KEY STATS

✔ **U.S News College Ranking:** third tier, Comp. Coll.–Bachelor's (North)
✔ **SAT Score (25th/75th percentile):** 830-1040
✔ **Tuition:** 2006-2007: $21,230

Selectivity: Less selective	**Room/board:** $9,100
Acceptance rate: 87%	**Average debt:** $20,383
Student/faculty ratio: 15/1	**Proportion who borrowed:** 98%

UNDERGRADUATE STUDENT BODY STATS

2005-2006 enrollment: 1,614 full-time; 270 part-time. Men: 36%; women: 64%. **Ethnic makeup:** African American: 5%; Asian American: 2%; Hispanic: 4%; White: 86%; International: 2%.

ADMISSIONS FACTS AND FIGURES

Phone: (800) 236-8679. **Email:** admissions@centenarycollege.edu. **Website:** http://www.centenarycollege.edu. **Application deadlines for fall 2007:** Regular decision: August 15. Early decision: Not offered. Early action: Not offered. Admission can be deferred. **Application fee:** $30. Common application is accepted. **Admissions requirements/recommendations:** High school units required (recommended): English: 4 (4); Mathematics: 3 (4); Science: 2 (4); Foreign language: (2); Social studies: (4); Total units: 16 (20). Tests: The college uses SAT or ACT scores in admissions decisions. Either SAT or ACT required. Campus visit: Recommended. Admissions interview: Recommended. Off-campus interview: Not available. **Factors that count in admissions decisions: Academic:** Secondary school record: Very important. Class rank: Important. Letters of recommendation: Considered. Standardized test scores: Very important. Essay: Very important. *Nonacademic:* Interview: Important. Extracurricular activities: Considered. Talent/ability: Considered. Character/personal qualities: Important. Alumni/ae relationship: Considered. Geographical residence: Not considered. State residency: Not considered. Religious affiliation/commitment: Not considered. Minority status: Not considered. Volunteer work: Considered. Work experience: Not considered. **Other schools with the greatest overlap in applicants:** Caldwell College; Monmouth University; Montclair State University; Rutgers–New Brunswick; William Paterson University of New Jersey. **Admissions statistics for the fall 2005 entering class:** Total applicants: 652. Total accepted: 564. Freshmen enrolled: 266; 16% were from out of state. Overall acceptance rate: 87%. **Credentials of fall 2005 freshmen:** 3% ranked in the top 10 percent of their high school class; 18% were in the top 25 percent, and 55% were in the top half. (Proportion submitting class standing: 44%.) **Average high school grade point average:** 2.6. **First-year students who submitted SAT scores:** 93%. Scores (25/75 percentile): Verbal: 410-520, Math: 420-520, Combined: 830-1040. **First-year students submitting ACT scores:** 2%. Scores (25/75 percentile): English: N/A, Math: N/A, Composite: 16-17.

ACADEMICS

Year founded: 1867. **Academic calendar:** Semester. **Degrees offered:** associate, bachelor's, master's. **Most popular majors:** 54% business, management, marketing, and related support services, 13% social sciences, 10% agriculture, agriculture operations, and related sciences, 9% psychology, 8% English language and literature/letters. **Major fields of study:** agriculture, agriculture operations, and related sciences; business, management, marketing, and related support services; communication, journalism, and related programs; English language and literature/letters; history; liberal arts and sciences studies, and humanities; mathematics and statistics; psychology; security and protective services; social sciences; visual and performing arts. **Areas of required coursework:** arts/fine arts, humanities, mathematics, English (including composition), sciences (biological or physical), history, social science. **Special academic programs (% participation):** accelerated program (30%), double major (10%), English as a Second Language (ESL) (5%), exchange student program (domestic) (2%), honors program (6%), independent study (10%), internships (35%), liberal arts/career combination (100%), student-designed major (1%), study abroad (5%), teacher certificate program (14%). **Teacher certification offered in:** special education, elementary, middle/junior high, secondary. **Faculty and instruction (2005-2006):** Total instructional faculty: 62 full-time, 207 part-time (52% men; 48% women; 2% minorities). Full-time faculty with Ph.D. or other terminal degree: 77%. Student/faculty ratio: 15/1. Classes of fewer than 20 students: 60%; of 20 to 49 students: 40%; of 50 or more students: 0%. **Advanced Placement and International Baccalaureate credit:** AP tests may be used for: Credit only. Scores accepted: 3, 4, 5. International Baccalaureate exams may be used for: Credit only. **Freshmen returning for sophomore year:** 73%. **Graduation rates:** Six-year: 35%. **Graduate study:** 5% of students pursue further study immediately upon graduation; 7% within one year; 8% within five years.

COSTS AND FINANCIAL AID

Financial aid office: (908) 852-1400. **Expenses (2006-2007):** Tuition and fees 2006-2007: $21,230; room/board: $9,100. Estimated books and supplies: $750. **Financial aid:** Priority filing date for institution's financial aid form: April 15. In 2005-2006, 93% of undergraduates applied for financial aid. Of those, 79% were determined to have financial need; 15% had their need fully met. Average financial aid package (proportion receiving): $13,647 (78%). Average amount of gift aid, such as scholarships or grants (proportion receiving): $10,478 (71%). Average amount of self-help aid, such as work study or loans (proportion receiving): $4,515 (69%). Average need-based loan (excluding PLUS or other private loans): $4,269. Among students who received need-based aid, the average percentage of need met: 65%. Among students who received aid based on merit, the average award (and the proportion receiving): $13,205 (11%). The average athletic scholarship (and the proportion receiving): $0 (0%). Average amount of debt of borrowers graduating in 2005: $20,383. Proportion who borrowed: 98%.

CAMPUS LIFE AND EXTRACURRICULAR ACTIVITIES

Campus housing available (% using): coed dorms (75%), apartment for single students (25%). Students who live in college-owned, operated, or affiliated housing: 58%. **Clubs and organizations:** Number of student organizations: 22. Activities include: drama/theater, literary magazine, radio station, student government, student newspaper, television station, yearbook. Number of fraternities: 2; sororities: 3. Proportion of men in fraternities: 1%; of women in sororities: 1%. Average proportion of students who stay on campus on weekends: 74%. **Sports program (2005-2006):** Member of NCAA III. *Men's intercollegiate varsity sports:* baseball, basketball, cross-country, golf, lacrosse, soccer, wrestling. *Women's intercollegiate varsity sports:* basketball, cross-country, lacrosse, soccer, softball, volleyball.

SERVICES AND FACILITIES

Basic services: nonremedial tutoring, women's center, placement service, health service. **Remedial assistance:** reading, math, writing. **Counseling services:** career, personal, academic, psychological. **For learning-disabled students:** School does not offer a structured program with separate admission and additional fees. Total undergraduates in learning-disabled program or receiving services: 105. Services include: remedial math, remedial English, reading machines, remedial reading, tape recorders, untimed tests, note-taking services, oral tests, learning center, readers, extended time for tests, tutors. **Library:** Number of titles: 72,606; number of current serial subscriptions: 84. **Information technology resources:** Students are required to lease or own a computer. School has a wireless network. Approximate number of users that can be accommodated: 1,500. Proportion of college-owned housing units wired for high-speed internet access: 100%. **Campus safety:** Security services offered: late-night transport/escort service, 24-hour emergency telephones, lighted pathways/sidewalks, controlled dormitory access (key, security card, etc.).

TRANSFER AND INTERNATIONAL STUDENTS

Transfer students: May apply for admission for the following academic terms: Fall, Spring, Summer. Applicants do not need a minimum number of credits to apply. For fall 2005: Transfer applications received: 334. Transfer applicants offered admission: 320. Transfer applicants enrolled: 142. **International students:** Number of foreign undergraduates: 35 (2% of student body). Minimum TOEFL score required: 450 (paper); 133 (computer). Average TOEFL score: 480 (paper).

College of New Jersey

- **Address:** PO Box 7718, 2000 Pennington Road, Ewing, NJ 08628-0718
- **Website:** http://www.tcnj.edu
- **Public**
- **Enrollment:** 5,726 full-time; 169 part-time

KEY STATS

✔ **U.S News College Ranking:** 5, Universities–Master's (North)
✔ **SAT Score (25th/75th percentile):** 1170-1370
✔ **Tuition:** 2005-2006: $9,857 in state, $15,120 out of state
   Selectivity: More selective   **Room/board:** $8,807
   Acceptance rate: 45%   **Average debt:** $18,518
   Student/faculty ratio: 12/1   **Proportion who borrowed:** 54%

UNDERGRADUATE STUDENT BODY STATS

2005-2006 enrollment: 5,726 full-time; 169 part-time. Men: 42%; women: 58%. **Ethnic makeup:** African American: 6%; Asian American: 5%; Hispanic: 7%; White: 82%. **Religious preference:** Roman Catholic: 48%; Protestant: 17%; Jewish: 5%; Muslim: 1%; Hindu: 2%; Buddhist: 1%; No preference: 15%; Christian: 9%; Other: 2%.

ADMISSIONS FACTS AND FIGURES

Phone: (609) 771-2131. **Email:** admiss@vm.tcnj.edu. **Website:** http://www.tcnj.edu. **Application deadlines for fall 2007:** Regular decision: February 15. Early decision: Send application by: November 15; Decision sent by: December 15. Early action: Not offered. Admission cannot be deferred. **Application fee:** $50. Common application is accepted. **To apply online, go to:** http://www.tcnj.edu/~admiss/apply/. **Admissions requirements/recommendations:** High school units required (recommended): English: 4 (4); Mathematics: 3 (3); Science: 3 (3); Foreign language: 2 (3); Social studies: 2 (3); Total units: 18 (20). Tests: The college uses SAT or ACT scores in admissions decisions. Either SAT or ACT required. For admission to the fall 2007 entering class, the school will accept: ACT with writing, ACT without writing. Campus visit: Recommended. Admissions interview: Recommended. Off-campus interview: May be arranged. **Factors that count in admissions decisions: Academic:** Secondary school record: Very important. Class rank: Very important. Letters of recommendation: Important. Standardized test scores: Very important. Essay: Important. *Nonacademic:* Interview: Considered. Extracurricular activities: Important. Talent/ability: Very important. Character/personal qualities: Very important. Alumni/ae relationship: Considered. Geographical residence: Considered. State residency: Considered. Religious affiliation/commitment: Not considered. Minority status: Considered. Volunteer work: Important. Work experience: Considered. **Other schools with the greatest overlap in applicants:** Lehigh University; New York University; Rutgers–New Brunswick; University of Delaware; Villanova University. **Admissions statistics for the fall 2005 entering class:** Total applicants: 7,300. Total accepted: 3,289. Freshmen enrolled: 1,236; 5% were from out of state. Accepted through early-decision or early-action plans: 16%. Overall acceptance rate: 45%. Early-decision acceptance rate: 36%. Non-early acceptance rate: 46%. **Size of waiting list:** 502 applicants; enrolled from waiting list: 133. **Credentials of fall 2005 freshmen:** 68% ranked in the top 10 percent of their high school class; 94% were in the top 25 percent, and 99% were in the top half. (Proportion submitting class standing: 81%.) **First-year students who submitted SAT scores:** 98%. Scores (25/75 percentile): Verbal: 570-670, Math: 600-700, Combined: 1170-1370.

ACADEMICS

Year founded: 1855. **Academic calendar:** Semester. **Degrees offered:** bachelor's, post-bachelor's certificate, master's, post-master's certificate. **Most**

popular majors: 15% business administration and management, 9% psychology, 7% biology/biological sciences, 7% elementary education and teaching, 4% criminal justice/law enforcement administration. **Major fields of study:** area, ethnic, cultural, and gender studies; biological and biomedical sciences; business, management, marketing, and related support services; computer and information sciences and support services; education; engineering; English language and literature/letters; foreign languages, literatures, and linguistics; health professions and related clinical sciences; history; mathematics and statistics; philosophy and religious studies; physical sciences; psychology; security and protective services; social sciences; visual and performing arts. **Areas of required coursework:** arts/fine arts, humanities, mathematics, English (including composition), philosophy, sciences (biological or physical), history, social science, other. **Pre-professional programs:** pre-law, pre-dentistry, pre-medicine, pre-optometry. **Special academic programs (% participation):** double major (13%), exchange student program (domestic) (1%), honors program (10%), independent study (35%), internships (45%), study abroad (3%), teacher certificate program (17%). **Teacher certification offered in:** early childhood, special education, elementary, middle/junior high, secondary, bilingual/bicultural. **Reserve Officers Training Corps (ROTC):** Army ROTC: Offered at cooperating institution (Princeton University); Air Force ROTC: Offered at cooperating institution (Rutgers University). **Faculty and instruction (2005-2006):** Total instructional faculty: 341 full-time, 364 part-time (50% men; 50% women; 14% minorities). Full-time faculty with Ph.D. or other terminal degree: 86%. Student/faculty ratio: 12/1. Classes of fewer than 20 students: 47%; of 20 to 49 students: 53%; of 50 or more students: 1%. **Advanced Placement and International Baccalaureate credit:** AP tests may be used for: Credit only. Scores accepted: 4, 5. International Baccalaureate exams may be used for: Credit only. **Freshmen returning for sophomore year:** 95%. **Graduation rates:** Four-year: 60%; five-year: 79%; six-year: 82%. **Graduate study:** 23% of students pursue further study immediately upon graduation; 28% within one year; 35% within five years. Fields in which graduates pursue further study: Master of Business Administration (MBA), 4%; law, 11%; medicine, 11%; dentistry, 1%; engineering, 5%; theology (or the seminary), 1%; education, 25%; arts and sciences, 41%; veterinary medicine, 1%.

COSTS AND FINANCIAL AID

Financial aid office: (609) 771-2211. **Expenses (2005-2006):** Tuition and fees 2005-2006: $9,857 in state, $15,120 out of state; room/board: $8,807. Estimated books and supplies: $736; transportation: $528; personal expenses: $1,470. **Financial aid:** Priority filing date for institution's financial aid form: March 1; deadline: October 1. In 2005-2006, 69% of undergraduates applied for financial aid. Of those, 45% were determined to have financial need; 21% had their need fully met. Average financial aid package (proportion receiving): $9,317 (41%). Average amount of gift aid, such as scholarships or grants (proportion receiving): N/A (16%). Average amount of self-help aid, such as work study or loans (proportion receiving): N/A (31%). Among students who received need-based aid, the average percentage of need met: 58%. Among students who received aid based on merit, the average award (and the proportion receiving): $4,444 (22%). The average athletic scholarship (and the proportion receiving): $0 (0%). Average amount of debt of borrowers graduating in 2005: $18,518. Proportion who borrowed: 54%.

CAMPUS LIFE AND EXTRACURRICULAR ACTIVITIES

Campus housing available (% using): coed dorms (95%), apartment for single students, special housing for disabled students (1%), other housing options (4%). Students who live in college-owned, operated, or affiliated housing: 65%. **Student employment:** During the 2005-2006 academic year, 29% of undergraduates worked on campus. Average per-year earnings: $1,492. **Clubs and organizations:** Number of student organizations: 194. Activities include: choral groups, concert band, dance, drama/theater, jazz band, literary magazine, music ensembles, musical theater, opera, pep band, radio station, student government, student newspaper, symphony orchestra, yearbook. Number of fraternities: 7; sororities: 7. Proportion of men in fraternities: 12%; of women in sororities: 14%. Average proportion of students who stay on campus on weekends: 65%. **Sports program (2005-2006):** Member of NCAA III. *Men's intercollegiate varsity sports:* baseball, basketball, cross-country, football, golf, soccer, swimming and diving, tennis, track and field (indoor), track and field (outdoor), wrestling. *Women's intercollegiate varsity sports:* basketball, cross-country, field hockey, lacrosse, soccer, softball, swimming and diving, tennis, track and field (indoor), track and field (outdoor).

SERVICES AND FACILITIES

Basic services: nonremedial tutoring, women's center, placement service, day care, health service, health insurance. **Counseling services:** minority student, career, personal, veteran student, academic, psychological, religious. **For learning-disabled students:** School does not offer a structured program with separate admission and additional fees. Services include: tape recorders, note-taking services, readers, extended time for tests, other. **Library:** Number of titles: 552,556; number of current serial subscriptions: 25,503. **Information technology resources:** Students are not required to lease or own a computer. Number of campus computers available to all students: 886. School has a wireless network. Approximate number of users that can be accommodated: 1,000. Proportion of college-owned housing units wired for high-speed internet access: 100%. **Campus safety:** Security services offered: 24-hour foot-and-vehicle patrols, late-night transport/escort service, 24-hour emergency telephones, lighted pathways/sidewalks, student patrols, controlled dormitory access (key, security card, etc).

TRANSFER AND INTERNATIONAL STUDENTS

Transfer students: May apply for admission for the following academic terms: Fall, Spring. Applicants need a minimum number of credits to apply. For fall 2005: Transfer applications received: 1,035. Transfer applicants offered admission: 470. Transfer applicants enrolled: 259. **International students:** Number of foreign undergraduates: 5. Number of countries represented: 20. Minimum TOEFL score required: 550 (paper); 213 (computer).

College of St. Elizabeth

- ■ **Address:** 2 Convent Road, Morristown, NJ 07960-6989
- ■ **Website:** http://www.cse.edu
- ■ **Private; Religious affiliation:** Roman Catholic
- ■ **Enrollment:** 671 full-time; 534 part-time

KEY STATS

- ✔ **U.S News College Ranking:** 13, Comp. Coll.–Bachelor's (North)
- ✔ **SAT Score (25th/75th percentile):** 790-1060
- ✔ **Tuition:** 2006-2007: $21,050

Selectivity: Less selective	**Room/board:** $9,424
Acceptance rate: 79%	**Average debt:** $24,290
Student/faculty ratio: 11/1	**Proportion who borrowed:** 60%

UNDERGRADUATE STUDENT BODY STATS

2005-2006 enrollment: 671 full-time; 534 part-time. Men: 8%; women: 92%. **Ethnic makeup:** African American: 16%; Asian American: 6%; Hispanic: 15%; White: 59%; International: 4%. **Religious preference:** Roman Catholic: 46%; Protestant: 12%; Muslim: 1%; Hindu: 1%; Unknown: 39%.

ADMISSIONS FACTS AND FIGURES

Phone: (973) 290-4700. **Email:** apply@cse.edu. **Website:** http://www.cse.edu. **Application deadlines for fall 2007:** Regular decision: August 15. Early decision: Not offered. Early action: Not offered. Admission can be deferred. **Application fee:** $35. Common application is not accepted. **To apply online, go to:** http://www.applyweb.com/apply/cofse. **Admissions requirements/recommendations:** High school units required (recommended): English: 3 (4); Mathematics: 2 (3); Science: 1 (2); Foreign language: 2 (2); Social studies: 0 (0); History: 1 (3); Academic electives: 7 (7); Total units: 16 (23). Tests: The college uses SAT or ACT scores in admissions decisions. Either SAT or ACT required. For admission to the fall 2007 entering class, the school will accept: ACT with writing, ACT without writing. Campus visit: Recommended. Admissions interview: Recommended. Off-campus interview: May be arranged. **Factors that count in admissions decisions:** *Academic:* Secondary school record: Very important. Class rank: Very important. Letters of recommendation: Very important. Standardized test scores: Very important. Essay: Important. *Nonacademic:* Interview: Considered. Extracurricular activities: Considered. Talent/ability: Considered. Character/personal qualities: Important. Alumni/ae relationship: Considered. Geographical residence: Considered. State residency: Not considered. Religious affiliation/commitment: Not considered. Minority status: Not considered. Volunteer work: Considered. Work experience: Considered. **Other schools with the greatest overlap in applicants:** Kean University; Montclair State University; Ramapo College of New Jersey; Rutgers–New Brunswick; William Paterson University of New Jersey. **Admissions statistics for the fall 2005 entering class:** Total applicants: 422.

Total accepted: 335. Freshmen enrolled: 130; 2% were from out of state. Overall acceptance rate: 79%. **Size of waiting list:** 0 applicants; enrolled from waiting list: 0. **Credentials of fall 2005 freshmen:** 16% ranked in the top 10 percent of their high school class; 44% were in the top 25 percent, and 71% were in the top half. (Proportion submitting class standing: 83%.) **First-year students who submitted SAT scores:** 98%. Scores (25/75 percentile): Verbal: 400-530, Math: 390-530, Combined: 790-1060.

ACADEMICS

Year founded: 1899. **Academic calendar:** Semester. **Degrees offered:** certificate, bachelor's, post-bachelor's certificate, master's. **Most popular majors:** Information not available. **Major fields of study:** area, ethnic, cultural, and gender studies; biological and biomedical sciences; business, management, marketing, and related support services; communication, journalism, and related programs; computer and information sciences and support services; education; English language and literature/letters; foreign languages, literatures, and linguistics; health professions and related clinical sciences; history; mathematics and statistics; multi/interdisciplinary studies; philosophy and religious studies; physical sciences; psychology; social sciences; theology and religious vocations; visual and performing arts. **Areas of required coursework:** arts/fine arts, humanities, mathematics, English (including composition), philosophy, foreign languages, sciences (biological or physical), history, social science, other. **Pre-professional programs:** pre-law, pre-dentistry, pre-medicine, pre-veterinary science. **Special academic programs (% participation):** accelerated program (33%), cross-registration (4%), distance learning (4%), double major (19%), dual enrollment (0%), English as a Second Language (ESL) (3%), honors program (8%), independent study (18%), internships (13%), liberal arts/career combination (18%), student-designed major (1%), study abroad (1%), teacher certificate program (18%), weekend college (48%). **Teacher certification offered in:** early childhood, special education, elementary, middle/junior high, secondary. **Cooperative education programs:** health professions. **Faculty and instruction (2005-2006):** Total instructional faculty: 64 full-time, 114 part-time (36% men; 64% women; 9% minorities). Full-time faculty with Ph.D. or other terminal degree: 83%. Student/faculty ratio: 11/1. Classes of fewer than 20 students: 83%; of 20 to 49 students: 17%; of 50 or more students: 0%. **Advanced Placement and International Baccalaureate credit:** AP tests may be used for: Credit and/or placement. Scores accepted: 3, 4, 5. International Baccalaureate exams may be used for: Credit and/or placement. **Freshmen returning for sophomore year:** 83%. **Graduation rates:** Four-year: 49%; five-year: 54%; six-year: 62%.

COSTS AND FINANCIAL AID

Financial aid office: (973) 290-4445. **Expenses (2006-2007):** Tuition and fees 2006-2007: $21,050; room/board: $9,424. Estimated books and supplies: $1,100; transportation: $1,000; personal expenses: $1,250. **Financial aid:** Priority filing date for institution's financial aid form: March 1. In 2005-2006, 89% of undergraduates applied for financial aid. Of those, 77% were determined to have financial need; 19% had their need fully met. Average financial aid package (proportion receiving): $16,889 (75%). Average amount of gift aid, such as scholarships or grants (proportion receiving): $14,123 (69%). Average amount of self-help aid, such as work study or loans (proportion receiving): $4,456 (64%). Average need-based loan (excluding PLUS or other private loans): $3,883. Among students who received need-based aid, the average percentage of need met: 75%. Among students who received aid based on merit, the average award (and the proportion receiving): $13,073 (16%). The average athletic scholarship (and the proportion receiving): $0 (0%). Average amount of debt of borrowers graduating in 2005: $24,290. Proportion who borrowed: 60%.

CAMPUS LIFE AND EXTRACURRICULAR ACTIVITIES

Campus housing available (% using): women's dorms (100%). Students who live in college-owned, operated, or affiliated housing: 66%. **Student employment:** During the 2005-2006 academic year, 42% of undergraduates worked on campus. Average per-year earnings: $3,600. **Clubs and organizations:** Number of student organizations: 17. Activities include: choral groups, drama/theater, literary magazine, music ensembles, student government, student newspaper, yearbook. Number of fraternities: 0; sororities: 0. Average proportion of students who stay on campus on weekends: 30%. **Sports program (2005-2006):** Member of NCAA III. *Women's intercollegiate varsity sports:* basketball, equestrian sports, soccer, softball, swimming and diving, tennis, volleyball.

SERVICES AND FACILITIES

Basic services: nonremedial tutoring, health service, health insurance. **Remedial assistance:** math, writing, study skills. **Counseling services:** minority student, career, personal, academic, older student, psychological, religious. **For learning-disabled students:** School does not offer a structured program with separate admission and additional fees. Total undergraduates in learning-disabled program or receiving services: 38. Services include: remedial math, remedial English, remedial reading, tape recorders, untimed tests, oral tests, learning center, readers, extended time for tests, tutors, priority seating, proofreading services, texts on tape, exams on tape or computer, other testing accomodations. **Library:** Number of titles: 138,486; number of current serial subscriptions: 594. **Information technology resources:** Students are not required to lease or own a computer. Number of campus computers available to all students: 152. School does not have a wireless network. Approximate number of users that can be accommodated: 250. Proportion of college-owned housing units wired for high-speed internet access: 100%. **Campus safety:** Security services offered: 24-hour foot-and-vehicle patrols, late-night transport/escort service, 24-hour emergency telephones, lighted pathways/sidewalks, controlled dormitory access (key, security card, etc).

TRANSFER AND INTERNATIONAL STUDENTS

Transfer students: May apply for admission for the following academic terms: Fall, Spring, Summer. Applicants do not need a minimum number of credits to apply. For fall 2005: Transfer applications received: 66. Transfer applicants offered admission: 49. Transfer applicants enrolled: 33. **International students:** Number of foreign undergraduates: 39 (4% of student body). Number of countries represented: 26. Minimum TOEFL score required: 500 (paper); 173 (computer). Average TOEFL score: 505 (paper).

Drew University

- **Address:** 36 Madison Avenue, Madison, NJ 07940-1493
- **Website:** http://www.drew.edu
- **Private; Religious affiliation:** Methodist
- **Enrollment:** 1,561 full-time; 52 part-time

KEY STATS

✔ **U.S News College Ranking:** 69, Liberal Arts Colleges
✔ **SAT Score (25th/75th percentile):** 1090-1310
✔ **Tuition:** 2006-2007: $33,068

Selectivity: More selective	**Room/board:** $9,000
Acceptance rate: 77%	**Average debt:** $17,586
Student/faculty ratio: 12/1	**Proportion who borrowed:** 60%

UNDERGRADUATE STUDENT BODY STATS

2005-2006 enrollment: 1,561 full-time; 52 part-time. Men: 43%; women: 57%. **Ethnic makeup:** African American: 3%; Asian American: 6%; Hispanic: 6%; White: 84%; International: 1%.

ADMISSIONS FACTS AND FIGURES

Phone: (973) 408-3739. **Email:** cadm@drew.edu. **Website:** http://www.drew.edu. **Application deadlines for fall 2007:** Regular decision: February 15; decision sent by March 31. Early decision: Send application by: December 1; Decision sent by: December 24. Early action: Not offered. Admission can be deferred. **Application fee:** $50. Common application is accepted. **Admissions requirements/recommendations:** High school units required (recommended): English: (4); Mathematics: (3); Science: (2); Foreign language: (2); Social studies: (2); History: (2); Academic electives: (3); Total units: (18). Tests: The college uses SAT or ACT scores in admissions decisions. Neither SAT nor ACT required. For admission to the fall 2007 entering class, the school will accept: ACT without writing. Campus visit: Recommended. Admissions interview: Recommended. Off-campus interview: May be arranged. **Factors that count in admissions decisions:** *Academic:* Secondary school record: Very important. Class rank: Considered. Letters of recommendation: Important. Standardized test scores: Considered. Essay: Important. *Nonacademic:* Interview: Important. Extracurricular activities: Important. Talent/ability: Very important. Character/personal qualities: Considered. Alumni/ae relationship: Considered. Geographical residence: Considered. State residency: Not considered. Religious affiliation/commitment: Not considered. Minority status: Considered. Volunteer work: Considered. Work experience: Considered. **Other schools with the greatest overlap in applicants:** Boston University; College of New Jersey; Muhlenberg College; New York University; Rutgers–New Brunswick. **Admissions statistics for the fall 2005 entering**

class: Total applicants: 3,802. Total accepted: 2,941. Freshmen enrolled: 391; 46% were from out of state. Accepted through early-decision or early-action plans: 18%. Overall acceptance rate: 77%. Early-decision acceptance rate: 92%. Non-early acceptance rate: 77%. **Size of waiting list:** 405 applicants; enrolled from waiting list: 358. **Credentials of fall 2005 freshmen:** 36% ranked in the top 10 percent of their high school class; 66% were in the top 25 percent, and 90% were in the top half. (Proportion submitting class standing: 45%.) **Average high school grade point average:** 3.3. First-year students who submitted SAT scores: 99%. Scores (25/75 percentile): Verbal: 550-660, Math: 540-650, Combined: 1090-1310. **First-year students submitting ACT scores:** 12%. Scores (25/75 percentile): English: 22-29, Math: 22-27, Composite: 24-27.

ACADEMICS

Year founded: 1867. **Academic calendar:** Semester. **Degrees offered:** bachelor's, post-bachelor's certificate, master's, first professional, doctorate. **Most popular majors:** 14% political science and government, 11% psychology, 10% economics, 9% English language and literature, 8% sociology. **Major fields of study:** area, ethnic, cultural, and gender studies; biological and biomedical sciences; computer and information sciences and support services; English language and literature/letters; foreign languages, literatures, and linguistics; history; mathematics and statistics; multi/interdisciplinary studies; philosophy and religious studies; physical sciences; psychology; social sciences; visual and performing arts. **Areas of required coursework:** arts/fine arts, humanities, computer literacy, English (including composition), philosophy, foreign languages, sciences (biological or physical), history, social science. **Special academic programs (% participation):** accelerated program, cross-registration, double major (18%), exchange student program (domestic), honors program (7%), independent study, internships (47%), student-designed major, study abroad, teacher certificate program (3%), other. **Cooperative education programs:** other. **Faculty and instruction (2005-2006):** Total instructional faculty: 148 full-time, 85 part-time. Full-time faculty with Ph.D. or other terminal degree: 94%. Student/faculty ratio: 12/1. Classes of fewer than 20 students: 63%; of 20 to 49 students: 35%; of 50 or more students: 2%. **Advanced Placement and International Baccalaureate credit:** AP tests may be used for: Credit and/or placement. Scores accepted: 4, 5. International Baccalaureate exams may be used for: Credit and/or placement. **Freshmen returning for sophomore year:** 86%. **Graduation rates:** Four-year: 69%; five-year: 72%; six-year: 73%. **Graduate study:** 21% of students pursue further study immediately upon graduation. Fields in which graduates pursue further study: law, 21%; medicine, 5%; education, 19%; arts and sciences, 53%; veterinary medicine, 2%.

COSTS AND FINANCIAL AID

Financial aid office: (973) 408-3112. **Expenses (2006-2007):** Tuition and fees 2006-2007: $33,068; room/board: $9,000. Estimated books and supplies: $1,090 personal expenses: $2,438. **Financial aid:** In 2005-2006, 62% of undergraduates applied for financial aid. Of those, 49% were determined to have financial need; 33% had their need fully met. Average financial aid package (proportion receiving): $23,012 (48%). Average amount of gift aid, such as scholarships or grants (proportion receiving): $17,577 (47%). Average amount of self-help aid, such as work study or loans (proportion receiving): $5,642 (40%). Average need-based loan (excluding PLUS or other private loans): $4,843. Among students who received need-based aid, the average percentage of need met: 81%. Among students who received aid based on merit, the average award (and the proportion receiving): $12,232 (28%). Average amount of debt of borrowers graduating in 2005: $17,586. Proportion who borrowed: 60%.

CAMPUS LIFE AND EXTRACURRICULAR ACTIVITIES

Campus housing available: coed dorms, special housing for disabled students, other housing options. Students who live in college-owned, operated, or affiliated housing: 85%. **Student employment:** During the 2005-2006 academic year, 29% of undergraduates worked on campus. Average per-year earnings: $1,200. **Clubs and organizations:** Number of student organizations: 98. Activities include: choral groups, dance, drama/theater, literary magazine, music ensembles, radio station, student government, student newspaper, student film society, symphony orchestra, yearbook. Number of fraternities: 0; sororities: 0. Average proportion of students who stay on campus on weekends: 67%. **Sports program (2005-2006):** Member of NCAA III. **Men's intercollegiate varsity sports:** baseball, basketball, cross-country, fencing, lacrosse, soccer, swimming and diving, tennis. **Women's intercollegiate varsity sports:** basketball, cross-country, equestrian sports, fencing, field hockey, lacrosse, soccer, softball, swimming and diving, tennis.

SERVICES AND FACILITIES

Basic services: nonremedial tutoring, placement service, day care, health service, health insurance. **Remedial assistance:** math, writing, study skills. **Counseling services:** minority student, career, personal, academic, older student, psychological, birth control, religious. **For learning-disabled students:** School does not offer a structured program with separate admission and additional fees. Total undergraduates in learning-disabled program or receiving services: 47. Services include: tape recorders, note-taking services, extended time for tests, tutors, texts on tape. **Library:** Number of titles: 571,850; number of current serial subscriptions: 27,380. **Information technology resources:** Students are required to lease or own a computer. Number of campus computers available to all students: 155. School has a wireless network. Approximate number of users that can be accommodated: 600. Proportion of college-owned housing units wired for high-speed internet access: 100%. **Campus safety:** Security services offered: 24-hour foot-and-vehicle patrols, late-night transport/escort service, 24-hour emergency telephones, lighted pathways/sidewalks, controlled dormitory access (key, security card, etc).

TRANSFER AND INTERNATIONAL STUDENTS

Transfer students: May apply for admission for the following academic terms: Fall; Spring. Applicants need a minimum number of credits to apply. For fall 2005: Transfer applications received: 109. Transfer applicants offered admission: 63. Transfer applicants enrolled: 33. **International students:** Number of foreign undergraduates: 15 (1% of student body). Number of countries represented: 14. Minimum TOEFL score required: 550 (paper); 213 (computer).

Fairleigh Dickinson University

- **Address:** 1000 River Road, Teaneck, NJ 07666
- **Website:** http://www.fdu.edu
- **Private**
- **Enrollment:** 4,433 full-time; 3,898 part-time

KEY STATS

✔ **U.S News College Ranking:** 68, Universities–Master's (North)
✔ **SAT Score (25th/75th percentile):** 920-1120
✔ **Tuition:** 2006-2007: $23,144

Selectivity: Selective	**Room/board:** $9,438
Acceptance rate: 68%	**Average debt:** N/A
Student/faculty ratio: 16/1	**Proportion who borrowed:** N/A

UNDERGRADUATE STUDENT BODY STATS

2005-2006 enrollment: 4,433 full-time; 3,898 part-time. Men: 45%; women: 55%. **Ethnic makeup:** African American: 14%; Asian American: 5%; Hispanic: 12%; White: 64%; International: 5%.

ADMISSIONS FACTS AND FIGURES

Phone: (800) 338-8803. **Email:** globaleducation@fdu.edu. **Website:** http://www.fdu.edu. **Application deadlines for fall 2007:** Regular decision: Rolling. Early decision: Not offered. Early action: Not offered. Admission can be deferred. **Application fee:** $40. Common application is accepted. **Admissions requirements/recommendations:** High school units required (recommended): English: 4; Mathematics: 3; Science: 2; Foreign language: 2; History: 2; Academic electives: 4; Total units: 17. Tests: The college uses SAT or ACT scores in admissions decisions. Either SAT or ACT required. For admission to the fall 2007 entering class, the school will accept: ACT with writing, ACT without writing. Campus visit: Recommended. Admissions interview: Recommended. Off-campus interview: May be arranged. **Factors that count in admissions decisions:** *Academic:* Secondary school record: Very important. Class rank: Important. Letters of recommendation: Very important. Standardized test scores: Very important. Essay: Considered. *Nonacademic:* Interview: Important. Extracurricular activities: Considered. Talent/ability: Considered. Character/personal qualities: Important. Alumni/ae relationship: Considered. Geographical residence: Not considered. State residency: Not considered. Religious affiliation/commitment: Not considered. Minority status: Not considered. Volunteer work: Not considered. Work experience: Not considered. **Admissions statistics for the fall 2005 entering class:** Total applicants: 5,604. Total accepted: 3,822. Freshmen enrolled: 1,115; Overall acceptance rate: 68%. **Credentials of fall 2005 freshmen:** 10% ranked in the top 10 percent of their high school class;

30% were in the top 25 percent, and 67% were in the top half. (Proportion submitting class standing: 60%.) **First-year students who submitted SAT scores:** 89%. Scores (25/75 percentile): Verbal: 460-560, Math: 460-560, Combined: 920-1120.

ACADEMICS

Year founded: 1942. **Academic calendar:** Semester. **Degrees offered:** certificate, associate, terminal-associate, bachelor's, post-bachelor's certificate, master's, post-master's certificate, doctorate. **Most popular majors:** 24% general studies, 10% psychology, 7% business administration and management, 6% business/managerial economics, 5% marketing/marketing management. **Major fields of study:** biological and biomedical sciences; business, management, marketing, and related support services; communication, journalism, and related programs; computer and information sciences and support services; engineering; engineering technologies/technicians; English language and literature/letters; foreign languages, literatures, and linguistics; health professions and related clinical sciences; history; liberal arts and sciences studies, and humanities; mathematics and statistics; multi/interdisciplinary studies; natural resources and conservation; philosophy and religious studies; physical sciences; psychology; security and protective services; social sciences; visual and performing arts. **Areas of required coursework:** arts/fine arts, humanities, computer literacy, mathematics, English (including composition), philosophy, foreign languages, sciences (biological or physical), history, social science, other. **Pre-professional programs:** pre-law, pre-dentistry, pre-medicine, pre-veterinary science, pre-optometry, pre-pharmacy. **Special academic programs:** accelerated program, cooperative (work-study plan) program, distance learning, double major, English as a Second Language (ESL), external degree program, honors program, independent study, internships, liberal arts/career combination, student-designed major, study abroad, teacher certificate program, weekend college. **Teacher certification offered in:** special education, elementary, bilingual/bicultural. **Reserve Officers Training Corps (ROTC):** Army ROTC: Offered at cooperating institution (Seton Hall University). **Faculty and instruction (2005-2006):** Total instructional faculty: 290 full-time, 575 part-time. Full-time faculty with Ph.D. or other terminal degree: 77%. Student/faculty ratio: 16/1. Classes of fewer than 20 students: 64%; of 20 to 49 students: 34%; of 50 or more students: 2%. **Advanced Placement and International Baccalaureate credit:** AP tests may be used for: Credit only. Scores accepted: 3, 4, 5. International Baccalaureate exams may be used for: Credit only. **Freshmen returning for sophomore year:** 74%. **Graduation rates:** Four-year: 30%; five-year: 46%; six-year: 48%.

COSTS AND FINANCIAL AID

Financial aid office: (201) 692-2823. **Expenses (2006-2007):** Tuition and fees 2006-2007: $23,144; room/board: $9,438. Estimated books and supplies: $874; transportation: $1,304; personal expenses: $2,548. **Financial aid:** Priority filing date for institution's financial aid form: February 15; deadline: February 15.

CAMPUS LIFE AND EXTRACURRICULAR ACTIVITIES

Campus housing available: coed dorms, apartment for single students, special housing for disabled students, other housing options. Activities include: dance, drama/theater, literary magazine, pep band, radio station, student government, student newspaper, student film society, television station, yearbook. Average proportion of students who stay on campus on weekends: 40%. **Sports program (2005-2006):** Member of NCAA III. *Men's intercollegiate varsity sports:* baseball, basketball, cross-country, football, golf, lacrosse, soccer, swimming and diving, tennis. *Women's intercollegiate varsity sports:* basketball, cross-country, field hockey, lacrosse, soccer, softball, swimming and diving, tennis, volleyball.

SERVICES AND FACILITIES

For learning-disabled students: School does not offer a structured program with separate admission and additional fees. Services include: remedial math, remedial English, reading machines, remedial reading, tape recorders, other special classes, diagnostic testing service, oral tests, learning center, extended time for tests, tutors, other. **Information technology resources:** Students are not required to lease or own a computer. Number of campus computers available to all students: 400. School has a wireless network. **Campus safety:** Security services offered: 24-hour foot-and-vehicle patrols, late-night transport/escort service, 24-hour emergency telephones, lighted pathways/sidewalks.

TRANSFER AND INTERNATIONAL STUDENTS

Transfer students: May apply for admission for the following academic terms: Fall, Winter, Spring, Summer. Applicants need a minimum number of credits to apply. For fall 2005: Transfer applications received: 1,582. Transfer applicants offered admission: 1,170. Transfer applicants enrolled: 559. **International students:** Number of foreign undergraduates: 281 (5% of student body). Number of countries represented: 65. Minimum TOEFL score required: 550 (paper); 213 (computer). Average TOEFL score: 589 (paper).

Felician College

- ■ **Address:** 262 S. Main Street, Lodi, NJ 07644
- ■ **Website:** http://www.felician.edu
- ■ **Private; Religious affiliation:** Roman Catholic
- ■ **Enrollment:** 1,157 full-time; 393 part-time

KEY STATS

✔ **U.S News College Ranking:** fourth tier, Comp. Coll.–Bachelor's (North)
✔ **SAT Score (25th/75th percentile):** 815-1010
✔ **Tuition:** 2006-2007: $18,200

Selectivity: Less selective	**Room/board:** $7,950
Acceptance rate: 87%	**Average debt:** $19,500
Student/faculty ratio: N/A	**Proportion who borrowed:** N/A

UNDERGRADUATE STUDENT BODY STATS

2005-2006 enrollment: 1,157 full-time; 393 part-time. Men: 24%; women: 76%. **Ethnic makeup:** African American: 12%; Asian American: 7%; Hispanic: 17%; White: 63%.

ADMISSIONS FACTS AND FIGURES

Phone: (201) 559-6131. **Email:** admissions@inet.felician.edu. **Website:** http://www.felician.edu. **Application deadlines for fall 2007:** Regular decision: Rolling. Early decision: Not offered. Early action: Not offered. Admission cannot be deferred. **Application fee:** $30. Common application is accepted. **Admissions requirements/recommendations:** High school units required (recommended): English: (4); Mathematics: (2); Science: (2); Social studies: (2); Academic electives: (3); Total units: (13). Tests: The college uses SAT or ACT scores in admissions decisions. SAT required. Campus visit: Neither required nor recommended. Admissions interview: Neither required nor recommended. Off-campus interview: Not available. **Factors that count in admissions decisions:** *Academic:* Secondary school record: Very important. Class rank: Considered. Letters of recommendation: Considered. Standardized test scores: Very important. Essay: Considered. *Nonacademic:* Interview: Considered. Extracurricular activities: Considered. Talent/ability: Not considered. Character/personal qualities: Considered. Alumni/ae relationship: Considered. Geographical residence: Not considered. State residency: Not considered. Religious affiliation/commitment: Not considered. Minority status: Not considered. Volunteer work: Considered. Work experience: Considered. **Other schools with the greatest overlap in applicants:** College of New Jersey; Fairleigh Dickinson University. **Admissions statistics for the fall 2005 entering class:** Total applicants: 1,250. Total accepted: 1,090. Freshmen enrolled: 262; Overall acceptance rate: 87%. **First-year students who submitted SAT scores:** 80%. Scores (25/75 percentile): Verbal: 410-500; Math: 405-510, Combined: 815-1010.

ACADEMICS

Year founded: 1942. **Academic calendar:** Semester. **Degrees offered:** associate, bachelor's, master's. **Most popular majors:** Information not available. **Major fields of study:** biological and biomedical sciences; business, management, marketing, and related support services; computer and information sciences and support services; education; English language and literature/letters; health professions and related clinical sciences; history; liberal arts and sciences studies, and humanities; mathematics and statistics; psychology; theology and religious vocations; visual and performing arts. **Areas of required coursework:** arts/fine arts, humanities, computer literacy, mathematics, English (including composition), philosophy, sciences (biological or physical), history, social science. **Special academic programs:** accelerated program, cooperative (work-study plan) program, cross-registration, distance learning, double major, dual enrollment, English as a Second Language (ESL), honors program, independent study, internships, liberal arts/career combination, student-designed major, study abroad, teacher certificate program, weekend college. **Teacher certification offered in:** special education, elementary. **Freshmen returning for sophomore year:** 64%. **Graduation rates:** Four-year: 18%; five-year: 36%; six-year: 32%.

COSTS AND FINANCIAL AID

Financial aid office: (201) 559-6010. **Expenses (2006-2007):** Tuition and fees 2006-2007: $18,200; room/board: $7,950. Estimated books and supplies: $2,100; transportation: $2,100; personal expenses: $1,575. **Financial aid:** In 2005-2006, 85% of undergraduates applied for financial aid. Of those, 76% were determined to have financial need; 13% had their need fully met. Average financial aid package (proportion receiving): $13,161 (76%). Average amount of gift aid, such as scholarships or grants (proportion receiving): $6,000 (50%). Average amount of self-help aid, such as work study or loans (proportion receiving): $4,500 (51%). Average need-based loan (excluding PLUS or other private loans): $4,300. Among students who received need-based aid, the average percentage of need met: 85%. Among students who received aid based on merit, the average award (and the proportion receiving): $9,962 (8%). The average athletic scholarship (and the proportion receiving): $5,550 (15%). Average amount of debt of borrowers graduating in 2005: $19,500.

CAMPUS LIFE AND EXTRACURRICULAR ACTIVITIES

Campus housing available: coed dorms, women's dorms, men's dorms, special housing for disabled students. **Clubs and organizations:** Number of student organizations: 23. Activities include: choral groups, drama/theater, literary magazine, student government. Number of fraternities: 1; sororities: 2. **Sports program (2005-2006):** Member of NCAA II. *Men's intercollegiate varsity sports:* baseball, basketball, cross-country, golf, soccer. *Women's intercollegiate varsity sports:* basketball, cross-country, soccer, softball, volleyball.

SERVICES AND FACILITIES

Basic services: health service, health insurance. **Counseling services:** personal, academic, religious. **For learning-disabled students:** School does not offer a structured program with separate admission and additional fees. Services include: extended time for tests. **Library:** Number of titles: 101,040; number of current serial subscriptions: 563. **Information technology resources:** Students are not required to lease or own a computer. Proportion of college-owned housing units wired for high-speed internet access: 100%. **Campus safety:** Security services offered: 24-hour foot-and-vehicle patrols, 24-hour emergency telephones, lighted pathways/sidewalks, controlled dormitory access (key, security card, etc).

TRANSFER AND INTERNATIONAL STUDENTS

Transfer students: May apply for admission for the following academic terms: Fall, Spring, Summer. Applicants do not need a minimum number of credits to apply.

Georgian Court University

- ■ **Address:** 900 Lakewood Avenue, Lakewood, NJ 08701-2697
- ■ **Website:** http://www.georgian.edu
- ■ **Private; Religious affiliation:** Roman Catholic
- ■ **Enrollment:** 1,345 full-time; 654 part-time

KEY STATS

✔ **U.S News College Ranking:** third tier, Universities–Master's (North)
✔ **SAT Score (25th/75th percentile):** 830-1050
✔ **Tuition:** 2006-2007: $20,332

Selectivity: Less selective	**Room/board:** $7,800
Acceptance rate: 75%	**Average debt:** $33,036
Student/faculty ratio: 12/1	**Proportion who borrowed:** 75%

UNDERGRADUATE STUDENT BODY STATS

2005-2006 enrollment: 1,345 full-time; 654 part-time. Men: 9%; women: 91%. **Ethnic makeup:** African American: 6%; Asian American: 2%; Hispanic: 6%; White: 85%; International: 1%. **Religious preference:** Protestant: 9%; Jewish: 1%; No preference: 2%; Unknown: 42%; Roman Catholic: 41%; Other: 5%.

ADMISSIONS FACTS AND FIGURES

Phone: (732) 364-2200. **Email:** admissions@georgian.edu. **Website:** http://www.georgian.edu. **Application deadlines for fall 2007:** Regular decision: August 1. Early decision: Not offered. Early action: Send application by: November 15; Decision sent by: December 30. Admission cannot be deferred. **Application fee:** $40. Common application is not accepted. **To apply online, go to:** http://registrar.georgian.edu/IQWeb/Secure/

Guest/Onlineapp.asp. **Admissions requirements/recommendations:** High school units required (recommended): English: 4; Mathematics: 2; Science: 1; Foreign language: 2; History: 1; Academic electives: 6; Total units: 16. Tests: The college uses SAT or ACT scores in admissions decisions. Either SAT or ACT required. For admission to the fall 2007 entering class, the school will accept: ACT with writing, ACT without writing. Campus visit: Recommended. Admissions interview: Recommended. Off-campus interview: May be arranged. **Factors that count in admissions decisions:** *Academic:* Secondary school record: Very important. Class rank: Considered. Letters of recommendation: Considered. Standardized test scores: Important. Essay: Considered. *Nonacademic:* Interview: Considered. Extracurricular activities: Considered. Talent/ability: Considered. Character/personal qualities: Considered. Alumni/ae relationship: Considered. Geographical residence: Not considered. State residency: Not considered. Religious affiliation/commitment: Not considered. Minority status: Not considered. Volunteer work: Considered. Work experience: Considered. **Other schools with the greatest overlap in applicants:** College of New Jersey; Monmouth University; Richard Stockton College of New Jersey; Rowan University; Rutgers–New Brunswick. **Admissions statistics for the fall 2005 entering class:** Total applicants: 532. Total accepted: 397. Freshmen enrolled: 188; Overall acceptance rate: 75%. Non-early acceptance rate: 75%. **Credentials of fall 2005 freshmen:** 11% ranked in the top 10 percent of their high school class; 42% were in the top 25 percent, and 63% were in the top half. (Proportion submitting class standing: 72%.) **Average high school grade point average:** 3.2. **First-year students who submitted SAT scores:** 100%. Scores (25/75 percentile): Verbal: 420-530, Math: 410-520, Combined: 830-1050.

ACADEMICS

Year founded: 1908. **Academic calendar:** Semester. **Degrees offered:** certificate, bachelor's, post-bachelor's certificate, master's, post-master's certificate. **Most popular majors:** 20% elementary education and teaching, 15% psychology, 11% special education and teaching, 8% business administration and management, 8% humanities/humanistic studies. **Major fields of study:** biological and biomedical sciences; business, management, marketing, and related support services; computer and information sciences and support services; education; English language and literature/letters; foreign languages, literatures, and linguistics; health professions and related clinical sciences; history; liberal arts and sciences studies, and humanities; mathematics and statistics; multi/interdisciplinary studies; philosophy and religious studies; physical sciences; psychology; public administration and social service professions; security and protective services; social sciences; visual and performing arts. **Areas of required coursework:** arts/fine arts, humanities, English (including composition), philosophy, foreign languages, sciences (biological or physical), social science, other. **Special academic programs:** accelerated program, distance learning, double major, dual enrollment, English as a Second Language (ESL), honors program, independent study, internships, liberal arts/career combination, study abroad, teacher certificate program. **Teacher certification offered in:** early childhood, special education, elementary, middle/junior high, secondary, bilingual/bicultural. **Faculty and instruction (2005-2006):** Total instructional faculty: 110 full-time, 188 part-time (46% men; 54% women; 7% minorities). Full-time faculty with Ph.D. or other terminal degree: 85%. Student/faculty ratio: 12/1. Classes of fewer than 20 students: 73%; of 20 to 49 students: 27%. **Advanced Placement and International Baccalaureate credit:** AP tests may be used for: Credit and/or placement. Scores accepted: 3, 4, 5. **Freshmen returning for sophomore year:** 78%. **Graduation rates:** Four-year: 29%; five-year: 44%; six-year: 56%.

COSTS AND FINANCIAL AID

Financial aid office: (732) 364-2200. **Expenses (2006-2007):** Tuition and fees 2006-2007: $20,332; room/board: $7,800. Estimated books and supplies: $1,250; transportation: $1,500; personal expenses: $2,400. **Financial aid:** Average financial aid package (proportion receiving): $15,700 (92%). Average amount of gift aid, such as scholarships or grants (proportion receiving): $9,651 (74%). Average amount of self-help aid, such as work study or loans (proportion receiving): $8,512 (73%). Average need-based loan (excluding PLUS or other private loans): $8,446. Among students who received need-based aid, the average percentage of need met: 83%. Among students who received aid based on merit, the average award (and the proportion receiving): $5,562 (8%). Average amount of debt of borrowers graduating in 2005: $33,036. Proportion who borrowed: 75%.

CAMPUS LIFE AND EXTRACURRICULAR ACTIVITIES

Campus housing available (% using): women's dorms (100%). **Student employment:** During the 2005-2006 academic year, 14% of undergraduates

worked on campus. Average per-year earnings: $1,306. **Clubs and organizations:** Number of student organizations: 43. Activities include: choral groups, concert band, jazz band, literary magazine, music ensembles, student government, student newspaper, yearbook. Number of fraternities: 0; sororities: 0. Average proportion of students who stay on campus on weekends: 10%. **Sports program (2005-2006):** Member of NCAA II. *Women's intercollegiate varsity sports:* basketball, cross-country, soccer, softball, tennis, volleyball.

SERVICES AND FACILITIES

Basic services: nonremedial tutoring, placement service, health service, health insurance. **Remedial assistance:** reading, math, writing, study skills. **Counseling services:** career, personal, veteran student, academic, religious. **For learning-disabled students:** School does not offer a structured program with separate admission and additional fees. Services include: remedial math, remedial English, remedial reading, tape recorders, diagnostic testing service, untimed tests, note-taking services, oral tests, learning center, readers, tutors, other testing accomodations. **Library:** Number of titles: 145,413; number of current serial subscriptions: 1,123. **Information technology resources:** Students are not required to lease or own a computer. Number of campus computers available to all students: 172. School has a wireless network. Proportion of college-owned housing units wired for high-speed internet access: 100%. **Campus safety:** Security services offered: 24-hour foot-and-vehicle patrols, late-night transport/escort service, 24-hour emergency telephones, lighted pathways/sidewalks, controlled dormitory access (key, security card, etc.).

TRANSFER AND INTERNATIONAL STUDENTS

Transfer students: May apply for admission for the following academic terms: Fall, Spring. Applicants need a minimum number of credits to apply. For fall 2005: Transfer applications received: 593. Transfer applicants offered admission: 428. Transfer applicants enrolled: 279. **International students:** Number of foreign undergraduates: 10 (1% of student body). Number of countries represented: 11. Minimum TOEFL score required: 550 (paper); 213 (computer).

Kean University

- **Address:** PO Box 411, Union, NJ 07083
- **Website:** http://www.kean.edu
- **Public**
- **Enrollment:** 7,591 full-time; 2,444 part-time

KEY STATS
✔ **U.S News College Ranking:** third tier, Universities–Master's (North)
✔ **SAT Score (25th/75th percentile):** 860-1040
✔ **Tuition:** 2006-2007: $8,036 in state, $10,863 out of state

Selectivity: Less selective	**Room/board:** $8,880
Acceptance rate: 71%	**Average debt:** $13,128
Student/faculty ratio: 15/1	**Proportion who borrowed:** 40%

UNDERGRADUATE STUDENT BODY STATS

2005-2006 enrollment: 7,591 full-time; 2,444 part-time. Men: 36%; women: 64%. **Ethnic makeup:** African American: 21%; Asian American: 6%; Hispanic: 20%; White: 50%; International: 2%.

ADMISSIONS FACTS AND FIGURES

Phone: (908) 737-7100. **Email:** admitme@kean.edu. **Website:** http://www.kean.edu. **Application deadlines for fall 2007:** Regular decision: May 31. Early decision: Not offered. Early action: Not offered. Admission cannot be deferred. **Application fee:** $50. Common application is not accepted. **Admissions requirements/recommendations:** High school units required (recommended): English: 4; Mathematics: 3 (4); Science: 2; Foreign language: (2); Social studies: (2); History: 2; Academic electives: 5; Total units: 16. Tests: The college uses SAT or ACT scores in admissions decisions. Either SAT or ACT required. For admission to the fall 2007 entering class, the school will accept: ACT with writing, ACT without writing. Campus visit: Recommended. Admissions interview: Recommended. Off-campus interview: Not available. **Factors that count in admissions decisions:** *Academic:* Secondary school record: Very important. Class rank: Considered. Letters of recommendation: Considered. Standardized test scores: Important. Essay: Considered. *Nonacademic:* Interview: Considered.

Extracurricular activities: Considered. Talent/ability: Considered. Character/personal qualities: Considered. Alumni/ae relationship: Considered. Geographical residence: Not considered. State residency: Not considered. Religious affiliation/commitment: Not considered. Minority status: Not considered. Volunteer work: Considered. Work experience: Considered. **Other schools with the greatest overlap in applicants:** Montclair State University; New Jersey City University; Rutgers–New Brunswick; Seton Hall University; William Paterson University of New Jersey. **Admissions statistics for the fall 2005 entering class:** Total applicants: 4,289. Total accepted: 3,039. Freshmen enrolled: 1,432; 2% were from out of state. Overall acceptance rate: 71%. **Credentials of fall 2005 freshmen:** 7% ranked in the top 10 percent of their high school class; 22% were in the top 25 percent, and 57% were in the top half. (Proportion submitting class standing: 55%.) **Average high school grade point average:** 2.9. **First-year students who submitted SAT scores:** 87%. Scores (25/75 percentile): Verbal: 430-510; Math: 430-530; Combined: 860-1040.

ACADEMICS

Year founded: 1855. **Academic calendar:** Semester. **Degrees offered:** bachelor's, post-bachelor's certificate, master's, post-master's certificate. **Most popular majors:** 10% business administration and management, 8% psychology, 7% elementary education and teaching, 6% accounting, 6% kindergarten/preschool education and teaching. **Major fields of study:** biological and biomedical sciences; business, management, marketing, and related support services; communication, journalism, and related programs; communications technologies/technicians and support services; computer and information sciences and support services; education; engineering technologies/technicians; English language and literature/letters; foreign languages, literatures, and linguistics; health professions and related clinical sciences; history; liberal arts and sciences studies, and humanities; mathematics and statistics; parks, recreation, leisure, and fitness studies; philosophy and religious studies; physical sciences; psychology; public administration and social service professions; science technologies/technicians; security and protective services; social sciences; visual and performing arts. **Areas of required coursework:** arts/fine arts, humanities, computer literacy, mathematics, English (including composition), sciences (biological or physical), history, social science, other. **Pre-professional programs:** other. **Special academic programs:** accelerated program, cooperative (work-study plan) program, cross-registration, distance learning, double major, dual enrollment, English as a Second Language (ESL), honors program, independent study, internships, liberal arts/career combination, study abroad, teacher certificate program, weekend college. **Teacher certification offered in:** early childhood, special education, elementary, middle/junior high, secondary, bilingual/bicultural. **Cooperative education programs:** art, business, computer science, education, health professions, humanities, natural science, social/behavioral science, technologies. **Reserve Officers Training Corps (ROTC):** Army ROTC: Offered at cooperating institution (Seton Hall University); Air Force ROTC: Offered at cooperating institution (NJ Inst. of Technology). **Faculty and instruction (2005-2006):** Total instructional faculty: 382 full-time, 778 part-time (52% men; 48% women; 24% minorities). Full-time faculty with Ph.D. or other terminal degree: 87%. Student/faculty ratio: 15/1. Classes of fewer than 20 students: 45%; of 20 to 49 students: 55%; of 50 or more students: 0%. **Advanced Placement and International Baccalaureate credit:** AP tests may be used for: Credit only. Scores accepted: 3, 4, 5. International Baccalaureate exams may be used for: Credit only. **Freshmen returning for sophomore year:** 76%. **Graduation rates:** Four-year: 16%; five-year: 38%; six-year: 45%.

COSTS AND FINANCIAL AID

Financial aid office: (908) 737-3190. **Expenses (2006-2007):** Tuition and fees 2006-2007: $8,036 in state, $10,863 out of state; room/board: $8,880. **Financial aid:** Priority filing date for institution's financial aid form: March 15. In 2005-2006, 77% of undergraduates applied for financial aid. Of those, 56% were determined to have financial need; 16% had their need fully met. Average financial aid package (proportion receiving): $7,929 (53%). Average amount of gift aid, such as scholarships or grants (proportion receiving): $5,705 (52%). Average amount of self-help aid, such as work study or loans (proportion receiving): $4,048 (51%). Average need-based loan (excluding PLUS or other private loans): $3,848. Among students who received need-based aid, the average percentage of need met: 54%. Among students who received aid based on merit, the average award (and the proportion receiving): $2,184 (2%). Average amount of debt of borrowers graduating in 2005: $13,128. Proportion who borrowed: 40%.

CAMPUS LIFE AND EXTRACURRICULAR ACTIVITIES

Campus housing available (% using): coed dorms (18%), apartment for single students (1%), special housing for disabled students (2%), other housing options (79%). Students who live in college-owned, operated, or affiliated housing: 14%. **Student employment:** During the 2005-2006 academic year, 8% of undergraduates worked on campus. Average per-year earnings: $3,360. **Clubs and organizations:** Number of student organizations: 147. Activities include: choral groups, dance, drama/theater, jazz band, literary magazine, music ensembles, musical theater, radio station, student government, student newspaper, television station, yearbook. Number of fraternities: 13; sororities: 17. Average proportion of students who stay on campus on weekends: 10%. **Sports program (2005-2006):** Member of NCAA III. **Men's intercollegiate varsity sports:** baseball, basketball, cross-country, football, lacrosse, soccer, track and field (indoor), track and field (outdoor). **Women's intercollegiate varsity sports:** basketball, cross-country, field hockey, lacrosse, soccer, softball, swimming and diving, tennis, track and field (indoor), track and field (outdoor), volleyball.

SERVICES AND FACILITIES

Basic services: nonremedial tutoring, placement service, day care, health service, health insurance. **Remedial assistance:** reading, math, writing, study skills. **Counseling services:** minority student, career, personal, veteran student, academic, older student, psychological, birth control. **For learning-disabled students:** School does not offer a structured program with separate admission and additional fees. Total undergraduates in learning-disabled program or receiving services: 160. Services include: remedial math, remedial English, reading machines, remedial reading, tape recorders, other special classes, videotaped classes, diagnostic testing service, untimed tests, note-taking services, oral tests, learning center, readers, extended time for tests, tutors, priority registration, priority seating, proofreading services, texts on tape, typist/scribe, exams on tape or computer, take home exams, other testing accomodations. **Library:** Number of titles: 276,550; number of current serial subscriptions: 25,000. **Information technology resources:** Students are not required to lease or own a computer. Number of campus computers available to all students: 1,650. School has a wireless network. Approximate number of users that can be accommodated: 200. Proportion of college-owned housing units wired for high-speed internet access: 100%. **Campus safety:** Security services offered: 24-hour foot-and-vehicle patrols, late-night transport/escort service, 24-hour emergency telephones, lighted pathways/sidewalks, student patrols, controlled dormitory access (key, security card, etc).

TRANSFER AND INTERNATIONAL STUDENTS

Transfer students: May apply for admission for the following academic terms: Fall, Spring, Summer. Applicants need a minimum number of credits to apply. For fall 2005: Transfer applications received: 1,548. Transfer applicants offered admission: 1,411. Transfer applicants enrolled: 992. **International students:** Number of foreign undergraduates: 217 (2% of student body). Number of countries represented: 65.

Monmouth University

- **Address:** 400 Cedar Avenue, West Long Branch, NJ 07764-1898
- **Website:** http://www.monmouth.edu
- **Private**
- **Enrollment:** 4,116 full-time; 439 part-time

KEY STATS

✔ **U.S News College Ranking:** 62, Universities–Master's (North)
✔ **SAT Score (25th/75th percentile):** 990-1160
✔ **Tuition:** 2006-2007: $21,868

Selectivity: Selective	**Room/board:** $8,472
Acceptance rate: 69%	**Average debt:** $27,800
Student/faculty ratio: 15/1	**Proportion who borrowed:** 72%

UNDERGRADUATE STUDENT BODY STATS

2005-2006 enrollment: 4,116 full-time; 439 part-time. Men: 42%; women: 58%. **Ethnic makeup:** African American: 4%; Asian American: 2%; Hispanic: 4%; White: 89%.

ADMISSIONS FACTS AND FIGURES

Phone: (800) 543-9671. **Email:** admission@monmouth.edu. **Website:** http://www.monmouth.edu. **Application deadlines for fall 2007:** Regular decision: March 1; decision sent by April 1. Early decision: Send application by: December 1; Decision sent by: January 1. Early action: Send application by: December 15; Decision sent by: January 15. Admission can be deferred. **Application fee:** $35. Common application is accepted. **To apply online, go to:** http://www.monmouth.edu/~admissn/app1.html. **Admissions requirements/recommendations:** High school units required (recommended): English: 4; Mathematics: 3; Science: 2; Foreign language: (2); Social studies: (2); History: 2; Academic electives: 5; Total units: 16. Tests: The college uses SAT or ACT scores in admissions decisions. Either SAT or ACT required. For admission to the fall 2007 entering class, the school will accept: ACT with writing. Campus visit: Recommended. Admissions interview: Neither required nor recommended. Off-campus interview: Not available. **Factors that count in admissions decisions:** *Academic:* Secondary school record: Very important. Class rank: Considered. Letters of recommendation: Considered. Standardized test scores: Very important. Essay: Considered. *Nonacademic:* Interview: Considered. Extracurricular activities: Very important. Talent/ability: Not considered. Character/personal qualities: Considered. Alumni/ae relationship: Considered. Geographical residence: Not considered. State residency: Not considered. Religious affiliation/commitment: Not considered. Minority status: Not considered. Volunteer work: Very important. Work experience: Very important. **Other schools with the greatest overlap in applicants:** College of New Jersey; Montclair State University; Rider University; Rowan University; Rutgers–New Brunswick. **Admissions statistics for the fall 2005 entering class:** Total applicants: 5,089. Total accepted: 3,504. Freshmen enrolled: 943; 12% were from out of state. Accepted through early-decision or early-action plans: 60%. Overall acceptance rate: 69%. Early-decision acceptance rate: 59%. Non-early acceptance rate: 65%. **Size of waiting list:** 760 applicants; enrolled from waiting list: 22. **Credentials of fall 2005 freshmen:** 11% ranked in the top 10 percent of their high school class; 33% were in the top 25 percent, and 72% were in the top half. (Proportion submitting class standing: 65%.) **Average high school grade point average:** 3.1. **First-year students who submitted SAT scores:** 98%. Scores (25/75 percentile): Verbal: 490-570, Math: 500-590, Combined: 990-1160. **First-year students submitting ACT scores:** 2%. Scores (25/75 percentile): English: N/A, Math: N/A, Composite: 20-26.

ACADEMICS

Year founded: 1933. **Academic calendar:** Semester. **Degrees offered:** certificate, associate, bachelor's, post-bachelor's certificate, master's, post-master's certificate. **Most popular majors:** 29% business, management, marketing, and related support services, 18% education, 17% communication, journalism, and related programs, 7% psychology, 6% visual and performing arts. **Major fields of study:** biological and biomedical sciences; business, management, marketing, and related support services; communication, journalism, and related programs; computer and information sciences and support services; education; engineering; English language and literature/letters; foreign languages, literatures, and linguistics; health professions and related clinical sciences; history; mathematics and statistics; physical sciences; psychology; public administration and social service professions; security and protective services; social sciences; visual and performing arts. **Areas of required coursework:** arts/fine arts, humanities, computer literacy, mathematics, English (including composition), sciences (biological or physical), history, social science, other. **Pre-professional programs:** pre-law, pre-dentistry, pre-medicine, pre-veterinary science, pre-pharmacy. **Special academic programs (% participation):** cooperative (work-study plan) program (6%), distance learning (11%), double major (15%), honors program (11%), independent study (25%), internships (57%), study abroad (4%), teacher certificate program (18%). **Teacher certification offered in:** special education, elementary, middle/junior high, secondary. **Reserve Officers Training Corps (ROTC):** Air Force ROTC: Offered at cooperating institution (Rutgers, The State University of New Jersey, New Brunswick). **Faculty and instruction (2005-2006):** Total instructional faculty: 254 full-time, 267 part-time (50% men; 50% women; 10% minorities). Full-time faculty with Ph.D. or other terminal degree: 74%. Student/faculty ratio: 15/1. Classes of fewer than 20 students: 42%; of 20 to 49 students: 58%; of 50 or more students: 0%. **Advanced Placement and International Baccalaureate credit:** AP tests may be used for: Credit and/or placement. Scores accepted: 3, 4, 5. International Baccalaureate exams may be used for: Credit and/or placement. **Freshmen returning for sophomore year:** 75%. **Graduation rates:** Four-year: 33%; five-year: 52%; six-year: 53%.

COSTS AND FINANCIAL AID

Financial aid office: (732) 571-3463. **Expenses (2006-2007):** Tuition and fees 2006-2007: $21,868; room/board: $8,472. Estimated books and supplies: $900; transportation: $538; personal expenses: $1,920. **Financial aid:** Priority filing date for institution's financial aid form: March 1; deadline: June 30. In 2005-2006, 79% of undergraduates applied for financial aid. Of those, 64% were determined to have financial need; 6% had their need fully met. Average financial aid package (proportion receiving): $13,765 (64%). Average amount of gift aid, such as scholarships or grants (proportion receiving): $7,959 (27%). Average amount of self-help aid, such as work study or loans (proportion receiving): $5,009 (54%). Average need-based loan (excluding PLUS or other private loans): $4,413. Among students who received need-based aid, the average percentage of need met: 65%. Among students who received aid based on merit, the average award (and the proportion receiving): $4,955 (29%). The average athletic scholarship (and the proportion receiving): $12,678 (2%). Average amount of debt of borrowers graduating in 2005: $27,800. Proportion who borrowed: 72%.

CAMPUS LIFE AND EXTRACURRICULAR ACTIVITIES

Campus housing available (% using): coed dorms (83%), apartment for single students (15%), other housing options (2%). Students who live in college-owned, operated, or affiliated housing: 42%. **Student employment:** During the 2005-2006 academic year, 8% of undergraduates worked on campus. Average per-year earnings: $1,549. **Clubs and organizations:** Number of student organizations: 65. Activities include: choral groups, concert band, dance, drama/theater, jazz band, literary magazine, music ensembles, musical theater, pep band, radio station, student government, student newspaper, television station, yearbook. Number of fraternities: 8; sororities: 6. Proportion of men in fraternities: 8%; of women in sororities: 9%. **Sports program (2005-2006):** Member of NCAA I. *Men's intercollegiate varsity sports:* baseball, basketball, cross-country, football, golf, soccer, tennis, track and field (indoor), track and field (outdoor). *Women's intercollegiate varsity sports:* basketball, cross-country, field hockey, golf, lacrosse, soccer, softball, tennis, track and field (indoor), track and field (outdoor).

SERVICES AND FACILITIES

Basic services: nonremedial tutoring, women's center, placement service, health service, health insurance. **Remedial assistance:** reading, math, writing, study skills. **Counseling services:** minority student, career, personal, veteran student, academic, older student, psychological, birth control, religious, other. **For learning-disabled students:** School does not offer a structured program with separate admission and additional fees. Total undergraduates in learning-disabled program or receiving services: 211. Services include: remedial math, remedial English, reading machines, remedial reading, tape recorders, note-taking services, readers, extended time for tests, tutors, priority registration, priority seating, texts on tape, other testing accomodations, other. **Library:** Number of titles: 248,000; number of current serial subscriptions: 22,500. **Information technology resources:** Students are not required to lease or own a computer. Number of campus computers available to all students: 700. School has a wireless network. Approximate number of users that can be accommodated: 3,000. Proportion of college-owned housing units wired for high-speed internet access: 86%. **Campus safety:** Security services offered: 24-hour foot-and-vehicle patrols, late-night transport/escort service, 24-hour emergency telephones, lighted pathways/sidewalks, controlled dormitory access (key, security card, etc).

TRANSFER AND INTERNATIONAL STUDENTS

Transfer students: May apply for admission for the following academic terms: Fall, Spring, Summer. Applicants need a minimum number of credits to apply. For fall 2005: Transfer applications received: 1,070. Transfer applicants offered admission: 667. Transfer applicants enrolled: 351. **International students:** Number of foreign undergraduates: 14. Number of countries represented: 10. Minimum TOEFL score required: 525 (paper); 213 (computer). Average TOEFL score: 586 (paper).

Montclair State University

- **Address:** 1 Normal Avenue, Montclair, NJ 07043
- **Website:** http://www.montclair.edu
- **Public**
- **Enrollment:** 9,909 full-time; 2,265 part-time

KEY STATS

✔ **U.S News College Ranking:** 46, Universities–Master's (North)
✔ **SAT Score (25th/75th percentile):** 960-1130
✔ **Tuition:** 2005-2006: $7,709 in state, $12,156 out of state

Selectivity: Selective
Room/board: N/A
Acceptance rate: 54%
Average debt: $16,654
Student/faculty ratio: 17/1
Proportion who borrowed: 53%

UNDERGRADUATE STUDENT BODY STATS

2005-2006 enrollment: 9,909 full-time; 2,265 part-time. Men: 39%; women: 61%. **Ethnic makeup:** African American: 10%; Asian American: 6%; Hispanic: 17%; White: 63%; International: 3%. **Religious preference:** Roman Catholic: 44%; Protestant: 17%; Jewish: 3%; Muslim: 4%; Hindu: 2%; No preference: 17%; Other: 10%.

ADMISSIONS FACTS AND FIGURES

Phone: (973) 655-4444. **Email:** undergraduate.admissions@montclair.edu. **Website:** http://www.montclair.edu. **Application deadlines for fall 2007:** Regular decision: March 1; decision sent by October 1. Early decision: Not offered. Early action: Not offered. Admission can be deferred. **Application fee:** $55. Common application is not accepted. **To apply online, go to:** http://www.montclair.edu/admissions/apply.html. **Admissions requirements/recommendations:** High school units required (recommended): English: 4; Mathematics: 3; Science: 2; Foreign language: 2; Social studies: 2; Academic electives: 3; Total units: 16. Tests: The college uses SAT or ACT scores in admissions decisions. SAT required. For admission to the fall 2007 entering class, the school will accept: ACT with writing. Campus visit: Recommended. Admissions interview: Neither required nor recommended. Off-campus interview: Not available. **Factors that count in admissions decisions:** *Academic:* Secondary school record: Very important. Class rank: Important. Letters of recommendation: Considered. Standardized test scores: Important. Essay: Not considered. *Nonacademic:* Interview: Considered. Extracurricular activities: Considered. Talent/ability: Considered. Character/personal qualities: Not considered. Alumni/ae relationship: Not considered. Geographical residence: Not considered. State residency: Considered. Religious affiliation/commitment: Not considered. Minority status: Considered. Volunteer work: Considered. Work experience: Not considered. **Other schools with the greatest overlap in applicants:** College of New Jersey; Ramapo College of New Jersey; Rowan University; Rutgers–New Brunswick; William Paterson University of New Jersey. **Admissions statistics for the fall 2005 entering class:** Total applicants: 8,877. Total accepted: 4,783. Freshmen enrolled: 1,944; 2% were from out of state. Overall acceptance rate: 54%. **Credentials of fall 2005 freshmen:** 19% ranked in the top 10 percent of their high school class; 45% were in the top 25 percent, and 83% were in the top half. (Proportion submitting class standing: 75%.) **Average high school grade point average:** 3.2. **First-year students who submitted SAT scores:** 96%. Scores (25/75 percentile): Verbal: 470-560, Math: 490-570, Combined: 960-1130.

ACADEMICS

Year founded: 1908. **Academic calendar:** Semester. **Degrees offered:** certificate, bachelor's, post-bachelor's certificate, master's, doctorate. **Most popular majors:** 22% business administration and management, 12% family and consumer sciences/human sciences, 10% psychology, 7% social sciences, 7% visual and performing arts. **Major fields of study:** area, ethnic, cultural, and gender studies; biological and biomedical sciences; business, management, marketing, and related support services; communication, journalism, and related programs; computer and information sciences and support services; education; English language and literature/letters; family and consumer sciences/human sciences; foreign languages, literatures, and linguistics; health professions and related clinical sciences; history; legal professions and studies; liberal arts and sciences studies, and humanities; mathematics and statistics; multi/interdisciplinary studies; philosophy and religious studies; physical sciences; psychology; social sciences; visual and performing arts. **Areas of required coursework:** arts/fine arts, humanities, mathematics, English (including composition), philosophy, foreign languages, sciences (biological or physical), history, social science. **Pre-professional programs:** pre-law, pre-medicine, pre-pharmacy. **Special academic programs:** cooperative (work-study plan) program, double major, English as a Second Language (ESL), honors program, independent study, internships, study abroad, teacher certificate program. **Teacher certification offered in:** early childhood, special education, elementary, middle/junior high, secondary. **Cooperative education programs:** business, education, social/behavioral science. **Faculty and instruction (2005-2006):** Total instructional faculty: 474 full-time, 694 part-time (50% men; 50% women; 16% minorities). Full-time faculty with Ph.D. or other terminal degree: 95%. Student/faculty ratio: 17/1. Classes of fewer than 20 students: 25%; of 20 to 49 students: 73%; of 50 or more students: 2%. **Advanced Placement and International Baccalaureate credit:** AP tests may be used for: Credit only. Scores accepted: 3, 4, 5. **Freshmen returning for sophomore year:** 83%. **Graduation rates:** Four-year: 23%; five-year: 50%; six-year: 57%. **Graduate study:** 17% of students pursue further study within one year. Fields in which graduates pursue further study: Master of Business Administration (MBA), 10%; law, 9%; medicine, 7%; dentistry, 1%; engineering, 1%; education, 25%; arts and sciences, 46%; veterinary medicine, 1%.

COSTS AND FINANCIAL AID

Financial aid office: (973) 655-4461. **Expenses (2005-2006):** Tuition and fees 2005-2006: $7,709 in state, $12,156 out of state; room/board: N/A. Estimated books and supplies: $1,000; transportation: $1,094; personal expenses: $2,356. **Financial aid:** Priority filing date for institution's financial aid form: March 1. In 2005-2006, 61% of undergraduates applied for financial aid. Of those, 49% were determined to have financial need; 34% had their need fully met. Average financial aid package (proportion receiving): $7,826 (47%). Average amount of gift aid, such as scholarships or grants (proportion receiving): $2,849 (27%). Average amount of self-help aid, such as work study or loans (proportion receiving): $4,212 (39%). Average need-based loan (excluding PLUS or other private loans): $4,078. Among students who received need-based aid, the average percentage of need met: 54%. Among students who received aid based on merit, the average award (and the proportion receiving): $4,789 (4%). The average athletic scholarship (and the proportion receiving): $0 (0%). Average amount of debt of borrowers graduating in 2005: $16,654. Proportion who borrowed: 53%.

CAMPUS LIFE AND EXTRACURRICULAR ACTIVITIES

Campus housing available (% using): coed dorms (54%), women's dorms (3%), apartment for single students (34%), special housing for disabled students (1%), special housing for international students (1%), other housing options (7%). Students who live in college-owned, operated, or affiliated housing: 27%. **Clubs and organizations:** Number of student organizations: 57. Activities include: dance, drama/theater, literary magazine, musical theater, radio station, student government, student newspaper, yearbook. Number of fraternities: 14; sororities: 17. Proportion of men in fraternities: 1%; of women in sororities: 1%. Average proportion of students who stay on campus on weekends: 35%. **Sports program (2005-2006):** Member of NCAA III. **Men's intercollegiate varsity sports:** baseball, basketball, cross-country, football, golf, lacrosse, soccer, track and field (indoor), track and field (outdoor), wrestling. **Women's intercollegiate varsity sports:** basketball, cross-country, field hockey, golf, lacrosse, soccer, softball, tennis, track and field (indoor), track and field (outdoor), volleyball.

SERVICES AND FACILITIES

Basic services: women's center, placement service, day care, health service, health insurance. **Remedial assistance:** reading, math, writing, other. **Counseling services:** minority student, personal, academic, older student, psychological. **For learning-disabled students:** School does not offer a structured program with separate admission and additional fees. Total undergraduates in learning-disabled program or receiving services: 250. Services include: remedial math, remedial English, reading machines, remedial reading, tape recorders, untimed tests, note-taking services, oral tests, learning center, readers, extended time for tests, tutors, early syllabus, priority registration, priority seating, proofreading services, substitution of courses, texts on tape, typist/scribe, exams on tape or computer, other testing accommodations, waiver of foreign language degree requirement, other. **Library:** Number of titles: 476,696; number of current serial subscriptions: 3,031. **Information technology resources:** Students are not required to lease or own a computer. Number of campus computers available to all students: 650. School has a wireless network. Approximate number of users that can be accommodated: 8,296. Proportion of college-owned housing units wired for high-speed internet access: 100%. **Campus safety:** Security services offered: 24-hour emergency telephones, lighted pathways/sidewalks, controlled dormitory access (key, security card, etc).

TRANSFER AND INTERNATIONAL STUDENTS

Transfer students: May apply for admission for the following academic terms: Fall, Spring. Applicants need a minimum number of credits to apply. For fall 2005: Transfer applications received: 2,878. Transfer applicants offered admission: 1,824. Transfer applicants enrolled: 1,110. **International students:** Number of foreign undergraduates: 406 (3% of student body). Number of countries represented: 92. Minimum TOEFL score required: 550 (paper); 213 (computer).

New Jersey City University

- **Address:** 2039 Kennedy Boulevard, Jersey City, NJ 07305
- **Website:** http://www.njcu.edu/
- **Public**
- **Enrollment:** 4,192 full-time; 1,812 part-time

KEY STATS
✔ **U.S News College Ranking:** fourth tier, Universities–Master's (North)
✔ **SAT Score (25th/75th percentile):** 810-1000
✔ **Tuition:** 2005-2006: $7,040 in state, $12,080 out of state

Selectivity: Less selective	**Room/board:** $7,306
Acceptance rate: 54%	**Average debt:** N/A
Student/faculty ratio: N/A	**Proportion who borrowed:** N/A

UNDERGRADUATE STUDENT BODY STATS

2005-2006 enrollment: 4,192 full-time; 1,812 part-time. Men: 37%; women: 63%. **Ethnic makeup:** African American: 20%; Asian American: 8%; Hispanic: 33%; White: 38%; International: 1%.

ADMISSIONS FACTS AND FIGURES

Phone: (888) 441-6528. **Email:** admissions@njcu.edu. **Website:** http://www.njcu.edu/. **Application deadlines for fall 2007:** Regular decision: April 1. Early decision: Not offered. Early action: Not offered. Admission can be deferred. **Application fee:** $35. Common application is not accepted. **Admissions requirements/recommendations:** High school units required (recommended): English: 4 (4); Mathematics: 4 (4); Science: 4 (4); Foreign language: 0 (2); Social studies: 4 (4); Total units: 16 (18). Tests: The college uses SAT or ACT scores in admissions decisions. SAT required. Campus visit: Recommended. Admissions interview: Recommended. Off-campus interview: May be arranged. **Factors that count in admissions decisions:** *Academic:* Secondary school record: Very important. Class rank: Very important. Letters of recommendation: Important. Standardized test scores: Very important. Essay: Important. *Nonacademic:* Interview: Considered. Extracurricular activities: Considered. Talent/ability: Important. Character/personal qualities: Considered. Alumni/ae relationship: Considered. Geographical residence: Not considered. State residency: Not considered. Religious affiliation/commitment: Not considered. Minority status: Not considered. Volunteer work: Considered. Work experience: Considered. **Admissions statistics for the fall 2005 entering class:** Total applicants: 2,719. Total accepted: 1,467. Freshmen enrolled: 690; Overall acceptance rate: 54%. **Credentials of fall 2005 freshmen:** 10% ranked in the top 10 percent of their high school class; 23% were in the top 25 percent, and 66% were in the top half. (Proportion submitting class standing: 61%.) **First-year students who submitted SAT scores:** 91%. Scores (25/75 percentile): Verbal: 400-500, Math: 410-500, Combined: 810-1000.

ACADEMICS

Year founded: 1927. **Academic calendar:** Semester. **Degrees offered:** diploma, bachelor's, post-bachelor's certificate, master's. **Most popular majors:** Information not available. **Major fields of study:** biological and biomedical sciences; business, management, marketing, and related support services; communication, journalism, and related programs; computer and information sciences and support services; education; English language and literature/letters; family and consumer sciences/human sciences; foreign languages, literatures, and linguistics; health professions and related clinical sciences; history; mathematics and statistics; philosophy and religious studies; physical sciences; psychology; security and protective services; social sciences; visual and performing arts. **Areas of required coursework:** humanities, computer literacy, mathematics, English (including composition), sciences (biological or physical), history, social science. **Special academic programs:** cooperative (work-study plan) program, distance learning, dual enrollment, English as a Second Language (ESL), honors program,

independent study, internships, study abroad, teacher certificate program, weekend college. **Teacher certification offered in:** early childhood, special education, elementary, secondary. **Cooperative education programs:** art, business, computer science, education, health professions, humanities, natural science, social/behavioral science, technologies. **Advanced Placement and International Baccalaureate credit:** AP tests may be used for: Credit only. Scores accepted: 3, 4, 5. **Freshmen returning for sophomore year:** 74%. **Graduation rates:** Four-year: 9%; five-year: 26%; six-year: 36%.

COSTS AND FINANCIAL AID

Financial aid office: (201) 200-3173. **Expenses (2005-2006):** Tuition and fees 2005-2006: $7,040 in state, $12,080 out of state; room/board: $7,306. Estimated books and supplies: $1,600; transportation: $3,200; personal expenses: $3,800. **Financial aid:** Priority filing date for institution's financial aid form: April 15. In 2005-2006, 82% of undergraduates applied for financial aid. Of those, 76% were determined to have financial need; 11% had their need fully met. Average financial aid package (proportion receiving): $7,628 (73%). Average amount of gift aid, such as scholarships or grants (proportion receiving): $6,049 (54%). Average amount of self-help aid, such as work study or loans (proportion receiving): $3,889 (48%). Average need-based loan (excluding PLUS or other private loans): $3,765. Among students who received need-based aid, the average percentage of need met: 65%. Among students who received aid based on merit, the average award (and the proportion receiving): $3,672 (1%). The average athletic scholarship (and the proportion receiving): $0 (0%).

CAMPUS LIFE AND EXTRACURRICULAR ACTIVITIES

Campus housing available: coed dorms. Activities include: choral groups, concert band, drama/theater, jazz band, music ensembles, musical theater, opera, radio station, student government, student newspaper, student film society, symphony orchestra, yearbook. **Sports program (2005-2006):** Member of NCAA III. *Men's intercollegiate varsity sports:* baseball, basketball, cross-country, soccer, track and field (indoor), track and field (outdoor), volleyball. *Women's intercollegiate varsity sports:* basketball, bowling, cross-country, soccer, softball, track and field (indoor), track and field (outdoor), volleyball.

SERVICES AND FACILITIES

Remedial assistance: reading, math, writing. **For learning-disabled students:** School offers a structured program with separate admission and additional fees. **Library:** Number of titles: 253,846; number of current serial subscriptions: 929. **Information technology resources:** Students are not required to lease or own a computer. School does not have a wireless network. **Campus safety:** Security services offered: late-night transport/escort service, lighted pathways/sidewalks.

TRANSFER AND INTERNATIONAL STUDENTS

Transfer students: May apply for admission for the following academic terms: Fall, Spring. Applicants do not need a minimum number of credits to apply. **International students:** Number of foreign undergraduates: 62 (1% of student body). Minimum TOEFL score required: 500 (paper); 173 (computer).

New Jersey Institute of Technology

- **Address:** University Heights, Newark, NJ 07102-1982
- **Website:** http://www.njit.edu
- **Public**
- **Enrollment:** 4,082 full-time; 1,181 part-time

KEY STATS
✔ **U.S News College Ranking:** 124, National Universities
✔ **SAT Score (25th/75th percentile):** 1010-1240
✔ **Tuition:** 2005-2006: $9,822 in state, $16,026 out of state

Selectivity: Selective	**Room/board:** $8,572
Acceptance rate: 71%	**Average debt:** $16,000
Student/faculty ratio: 13/1	**Proportion who borrowed:** 45%

UNDERGRADUATE STUDENT BODY STATS

2005-2006 enrollment: 4,082 full-time; 1,181 part-time. Men: 81%; women: 19%. **Ethnic makeup:** African American: 11%; Asian American: 21%; Hispanic: 13%; White: 49%; International: 6%.

ADMISSIONS FACTS AND FIGURES

Phone: (973) 596-3300. **Email:** admissions@njit.edu. **Website:** http://www.njit.edu. **Application deadlines for fall 2007:** Regular decision: July 1. Early decision: Not offered. Early action: Not offered. Admission can be deferred. **Application fee:** $50. Common application is accepted. **To apply online, go to:** http://xena.njit.edu/cgi-bin/admn.exe. **Admissions requirements/recommendations:** High school units required (recommended): English: 4; Mathematics: 4; Science: 2; Total units: 16. Tests: The college uses SAT or ACT scores in admissions decisions. Either SAT or ACT required. For admission to the fall 2007 entering class, the school will accept: ACT with writing, ACT without writing. Campus visit: Recommended. Admissions interview: Neither required nor recommended. Off-campus interview: May be arranged. **Factors that count in admissions decisions:** *Academic:* Secondary school record: Very important. Class rank: Very important. Letters of recommendation: Considered. Standardized test scores: Very important. Essay: Considered. *Nonacademic:* Interview: Considered. Extracurricular activities: Considered. Talent/ability: Considered. Character/personal qualities: Considered. Alumni/ae relationship: Considered. Geographical residence: Considered. State residency: Considered. Religious affiliation/commitment: Not considered. Minority status: Not considered. Volunteer work: Not considered. Work experience: Considered. **Other schools with the greatest overlap in applicants:** Drexel University; Rowan University; Rutgers–New Brunswick; Rutgers–Newark; Stevens Institute of Technology. **Admissions statistics for the fall 2005 entering class:** Total applicants: 2,562. Total accepted: 1,831. Freshmen enrolled: 762; 9% were from out of state. Overall acceptance rate: 71%. **Size of waiting list:** 50 applicants; enrolled from waiting list: 25. **Credentials of fall 2005 freshmen:** 24% ranked in the top 10 percent of their high school class; 50% were in the top 25 percent, and 79% were in the top half. (Proportion submitting class standing: 66%.) **First-year students who submitted SAT scores:** 100%. Scores (25/75 percentile): Verbal: 470-590, Math: 540-650, Combined: 1010-1240.

ACADEMICS

Year founded: 1881. **Academic calendar:** Semester. **Degrees offered:** bachelor's, post-bachelor's certificate, master's, doctorate. **Most popular majors:** 16% computer and information sciences, 14% engineering technology, 10% information technology, 9% business administration and management, 9% computer engineering. **Major fields of study:** architecture and related services; biological and biomedical sciences; business, management, marketing, and related support services; computer and information sciences and support services; engineering; engineering technologies/technicians; English language and literature/letters; history; mathematics and statistics; multi/interdisciplinary studies; natural resources and conservation; physical sciences. **Areas of required coursework:** humanities, computer literacy, mathematics, English (including composition), sciences (biological or physical), history, social science, other. **Pre-professional programs:** pre-law, pre-dentistry, pre-medicine, pre-veterinary science, pre-optometry, pre-pharmacy. **Special academic programs (% participation):** accelerated program (8%), cooperative (work-study plan) program (15%), cross-registration (5%), distance learning (10%), double major (5%), dual enrollment (1%), English as a Second Language (ESL) (10%), honors program (15%), independent study (5%), internships (1%), liberal arts/career combination (1%), study abroad (1%), teacher certificate program (0%), weekend college (5%). **Teacher certification offered in:** elementary, middle/junior high, secondary. **Cooperative education programs:** business, computer science, education, engineering, natural science, social/behavioral science, technologies. **Reserve Officers Training Corps (ROTC):** Army ROTC: Offered on campus; Air Force ROTC: Offered on campus. **Faculty and instruction (2005-2006):** Total instructional faculty: 416 full-time, 238 part-time (85% men; 15% women; 17% minorities). Full-time faculty with Ph.D. or other terminal degree: 100%. Student/faculty ratio: 13/1. Classes of fewer than 20 students: 51%; of 20 to 49 students: 47%; of 50 or more students: 2%. **Advanced Placement and International Baccalaureate credit:** AP tests may be used for: Credit only. Scores accepted: 3, 4, 5. International Baccalaureate exams may be used for: Credit only. **Freshmen returning for sophomore year:** 82%. **Graduation rates:** Four-year: 18%; five-year: 46%; six-year: 56%. **Graduate study:** 15% of students pursue further study immediately upon graduation; 30% within one year; 60% within five years.

COSTS AND FINANCIAL AID

Financial aid office: (973) 596-3479. **Expenses (2005-2006):** Tuition and fees 2005-2006: $9,822 in state, $16,026 out of state; room/board: $8,572. Estimated books and supplies: $1,200; transportation: $500; personal expenses: $1,100. **Financial aid:** Priority filing date for institution's financial aid form: March 15; deadline: May 15. In 2005-2006, 76% of undergraduates applied for financial aid. Of those, 57% were determined to have financial need; 25% had their need fully met. Average financial aid package (proportion receiving): $13,200 (57%). Average amount of gift aid, such as scholarships or grants (proportion receiving): N/A (42%). Average amount of self-help aid, such as work study or loans (proportion receiving): N/A (34%). Among students who received need-based aid, the average percentage of need met: 81%. Among students who received aid based on merit, the average award (and the proportion receiving): $7,964 (13%). The average athletic scholarship (and the proportion receiving): $9,403 (2%). Average amount of debt of borrowers graduating in 2005: $16,000. Proportion who borrowed: 45%.

CAMPUS LIFE AND EXTRACURRICULAR ACTIVITIES

Campus housing available (% using): coed dorms (100%). Students who live in college-owned, operated, or affiliated housing: 27%. **Student employment:** During the 2005-2006 academic year, 25% of undergraduates worked on campus. Average per-year earnings: $3,000. **Clubs and organizations:** Number of student organizations: 72. Activities include: dance, drama/theater, literary magazine, radio station, student government, student newspaper, yearbook. Number of fraternities: 19; sororities: 8. Proportion of men in fraternities: 7%; of women in sororities: 5%. Average proportion of students who stay on campus on weekends: 30%. **Sports program (2005-2006):** Member of NCAA II. *Men's intercollegiate varsity sports:* baseball, basketball, cross-country, fencing, soccer, swimming and diving, tennis, volleyball. *Women's intercollegiate varsity sports:* basketball, cross-country, fencing, soccer, swimming and diving, tennis, volleyball.

SERVICES AND FACILITIES

Basic services: nonremedial tutoring, women's center, placement service, day care, health service, health insurance. **Remedial assistance:** reading, math, writing, study skills. **Counseling services:** minority student, career, military, personal, veteran student, academic, older student, psychological, birth control. **For learning-disabled students:** School does not offer a structured program with separate admission and additional fees. Services include: remedial math, remedial English, reading machines, remedial reading, tape recorders, note-taking services, oral tests, readers, extended time for tests. **Library:** Number of titles: 209,000; number of current serial subscriptions: 13,693. **Information technology resources:** Students are required to lease or own a computer. Number of campus computers available to all students: 1,938. School has a wireless network. Approximate number of users that can be accommodated: 1,500. Proportion of college-owned housing units wired for high-speed internet access: 100%. **Campus safety:** Security services offered: 24-hour foot-and-vehicle patrols, late-night transport/escort service, 24-hour emergency telephones, lighted pathways/sidewalks, controlled dormitory access (key, security card, etc).

TRANSFER AND INTERNATIONAL STUDENTS

Transfer students: May apply for admission for the following academic terms: Fall, Spring. Applicants do not need a minimum number of credits to apply. For fall 2005: Transfer applications received: 997. Transfer applicants offered admission: 645. Transfer applicants enrolled: 420. **International students:** Number of foreign undergraduates: 301 (6% of student body). Number of countries represented: 72. Minimum TOEFL score required: 550 (paper); 213 (computer). Average TOEFL score: 580 (paper).

Princeton University

- **Address:** Princeton, NJ 08544
- **Website:** http://www.princeton.edu
- **Private**
- **Enrollment:** 4,719 full-time; 187 part-time

KEY STATS

✔ **U.S News College Ranking:** 1, National Universities
✔ **SAT Score (25th/75th percentile):** 1380-1560
✔ **Tuition:** 2006-2007: $33,000

Selectivity: Most selective	**Room/board:** $9,200
Acceptance rate: 11%	**Average debt:** $4,370
Student/faculty ratio: 5/1	**Proportion who borrowed:** 26%

UNDERGRADUATE STUDENT BODY STATS

2005-2006 enrollment: 4,719 full-time; 187 part-time. Men: 54%; women: 46%. **Ethnic makeup:** African American: 9%; American-Indian: 1%; Asian American: 13%; Hispanic: 7%; White: 62%; International: 9%.

ADMISSIONS FACTS AND FIGURES

Phone: (609) 258-3060. **Website:** http://www.princeton.edu. **Application deadlines for fall 2007:** Regular decision: January 1; decision sent by April 14. Early decision: Send application by: November 1; Decision sent by: December 15. Early action: Not offered. Admission can be deferred. **Application fee:** $65. Common application is accepted. **To apply online, go to:** http://www.princeton.edu/pr/admissions/u/appl. **Admissions requirements/recommendations:** High school units required (recommended): English: (4); Mathematics: (4); Science: (3); Foreign language: (4); Social studies: (2); History: (2). Tests: The college uses SAT or ACT scores in admissions decisions. Either SAT or ACT required. For admission to the fall 2007 entering class, the school will accept: ACT with writing, ACT without writing. Campus visit: Recommended. Admissions interview: Recommended. Off-campus interview: May be arranged. **Factors that count in admissions decisions:** *Academic:* Secondary school record: Very important. Class rank: Very important. Letters of recommendation: Very important. Standardized test scores: Very important. Essay: Very important. *Nonacademic:* Interview: Considered. Extracurricular activities: Very important. Talent/ability: Very important. Character/personal qualities: Very important. Alumni/ae relationship: Considered. State residency: Not considered. Religious affiliation/commitment: Not considered. Minority status: Considered. Volunteer work: Important. Work experience: Important. **Other schools with the greatest overlap in applicants:** Columbia University; Harvard University; Stanford University; University of Pennsylvania; Yale University. **Admissions statistics for the fall 2005 entering class:** Total applicants: 16,510. Total accepted: 1,807. Freshmen enrolled: 1,229; 84% were from out of state. Overall acceptance rate: 11%. Early-decision acceptance rate: 29%. Non-early acceptance rate: 8%. **Size of waiting list:** 1207 applicants; enrolled from waiting list: 0. **Credentials of fall 2005 freshmen:** 94% ranked in the top 10 percent of their high school class; 99% were in the top 25 percent, and 100% were in the top half. (Proportion submitting class standing: 40%.) **Average high school grade point average:** 3.8. **First-year students who submitted SAT scores:** 100%. Scores (25/75 percentile): Verbal: 690-770, Math: 690-790, Combined: 1380-1560.

ACADEMICS

Year founded: 1746. **Academic calendar:** Semester. **Degrees offered:** bachelor's, master's, doctorate. **Most popular majors:** 12% political science and government, 11% history, 9% economics, 7% public policy analysis, 6% English language and literature. **Major fields of study:** architecture and related services; area, ethnic, cultural, and gender studies; biological and biomedical sciences; business, management, marketing, and related support services; engineering; English language and literature/letters; foreign languages, literatures, and linguistics; history; mathematics and statistics; multi/interdisciplinary studies; philosophy and religious studies; physical sciences; psychology; public administration and social service professions; social sciences; visual and performing arts. **Areas of required coursework:** humanities, mathematics, English (including composition), philosophy, foreign languages, sciences (biological or physical), history, social science. **Pre-professional programs:** pre-medicine. **Special academic programs:** cross-registration, independent study, student-designed major, study abroad, teacher certificate program. **Teacher certification offered in:** elementary, secondary. **Reserve Officers Training Corps (ROTC):** Army ROTC: Offered on campus; Air Force ROTC: Offered at cooperating institution (Rutgers University). **Faculty and instruction (2005-2006):** Total instructional faculty: 809 full-time, 251 part-time (71% men; 29% women; 16% minorities). Full-time faculty with Ph.D. or other terminal degree: 94%. Student/faculty ratio: 5/1. Classes of fewer than 20 students: 74%; of 20 to 49 students: 16%; of 50 or more students: 10%. **Advanced Placement and International Baccalaureate credit:** AP tests may be used for: Credit and/or placement. Scores accepted: 4, 5. **Freshmen returning for sophomore year:** 98%. **Graduation rates:** Four-year: 90%; five-year: 96%; six-year: 97%.

COSTS AND FINANCIAL AID

Financial aid office: (609) 258-3330. **Expenses (2006-2007):** Tuition and fees 2006-2007: $33,000; room/board: $9,200. Estimated books and supplies: $1,090 personal expenses: $2,210. **Financial aid:** Priority filing date for institution's financial aid form: February 1. In 2005-2006, 54% of undergraduates applied for financial aid. Of those, 51% were determined to have financial need; 100% had their need fully met. Average financial aid package (proportion receiving): $28,368 (51%). Average amount of gift aid, such

as scholarships or grants (proportion receiving): $26,468 (51%). Average amount of self-help aid, such as work study or loans (proportion receiving): $2,985 (36%). Average need-based loan (excluding PLUS or other private loans): $0. Among students who received need-based aid, the average percentage of need met: 100%. Average amount of debt of borrowers graduating in 2005: $4,370. Proportion who borrowed: 26%.

CAMPUS LIFE AND EXTRACURRICULAR ACTIVITIES

Campus housing available: coed dorms, women's dorms, men's dorms, special housing for disabled students. Students who live in college-owned, operated, or affiliated housing: 98%. **Student employment:** During the 2005-2006 academic year, 45% of undergraduates worked on campus. Average per-year earnings: $1,220. **Clubs and organizations:** Number of student organizations: 227. Activities include: choral groups, concert band, dance, drama/theater, jazz band, literary magazine, marching band, music ensembles, musical theater, opera, pep band, radio station, student government, student newspaper, student film society, symphony orchestra, yearbook. Number of fraternities: 0; sororities: 0. **Sports program (2005-2006):** Member of NCAA I. *Men's intercollegiate varsity sports:* baseball, basketball, cross-country, fencing, football, golf, ice hockey, lacrosse, soccer, swimming and diving, tennis, track and field (indoor), track and field (outdoor), volleyball, water polo, wrestling. *Women's intercollegiate varsity sports:* basketball, cross-country, fencing, field hockey, golf, ice hockey, lacrosse, rowing, soccer, softball, squash, swimming and diving, tennis, track and field (indoor), track and field (outdoor), volleyball, water polo.

SERVICES AND FACILITIES

Basic services: women's center, health service, health insurance. **Counseling services:** minority student, career, personal, academic, psychological, birth control, religious. **For learning-disabled students:** School does not offer a structured program with separate admission and additional fees. Total undergraduates in learning-disabled program or receiving services: 65. Services include: tutors. **Library:** Number of titles: 6,253,193; number of current serial subscriptions: 44,634. **Information technology resources:** Students are not required to lease or own a computer. Number of campus computers available to all students: 550. School has a wireless network. Approximate number of users that can be accommodated: 7,200. Proportion of college-owned housing units wired for high-speed internet access: 95%. **Campus safety:** Security services offered: 24-hour foot-and-vehicle patrols, late-night transport/escort service, 24-hour emergency telephones, lighted pathways/sidewalks, controlled dormitory access (key, security card, etc).

TRANSFER AND INTERNATIONAL STUDENTS

International students: Number of foreign undergraduates: 403 (9% of student body).

Ramapo College of New Jersey

- **Address:** 505 Ramapo Valley Road, Mahwah, NJ 07430-1680
- **Website:** http://www.ramapo.edu
- **Public**
- **Enrollment:** 4,254 full-time; 979 part-time

KEY STATS

- ✔ **U.S News College Ranking:** 8, Comp. Coll.–Bachelor's (North)
- ✔ **SAT Score (25th/75th percentile):** 1090-1260
- ✔ **Tuition:** 2005-2006: $8,791 in state, $13,708 out of state

Selectivity: More selective	**Room/board:** $9,116
Acceptance rate: 41%	**Average debt:** $15,937
Student/faculty ratio: 16/1	**Proportion who borrowed:** 37%

UNDERGRADUATE STUDENT BODY STATS

2005-2006 enrollment: 4,254 full-time; 979 part-time. Men: 40%; women: 60%. **Ethnic makeup:** African American: 7%; Asian American: 4%; Hispanic: 8%; White: 78%; International: 3%.

ADMISSIONS FACTS AND FIGURES

Phone: (201) 684-7300. **Email:** admissions@ramapo.edu. **Website:** http://www.ramapo.edu. **Application deadlines for fall 2007:** Regular decision: March 1. Early decision: Not offered. Early action: Send application by: November 15; Decision sent by: December 15. Admission can be deferred.

Application fee: $55. Common application is not accepted. **To apply online,** go to: https://apply.embark.com/ugrad/ramapo/. **Admissions requirements/recommendations:** High school units required (recommended): English: 4; Mathematics: 3; Science: 3; Foreign language: 2; Social studies: 3; History: o; Academic electives: 3; Total units: 18. **Tests:** The college uses SAT or ACT scores in admissions decisions. SAT required. For admission to the fall 2007 entering class, the school will accept: ACT with writing. Campus visit: Recommended. Admissions interview: Recommended. Off-campus interview: May be arranged. **Factors that count in admissions decisions:** *Academic:* Secondary school record: Very important. Class rank: Very important. Letters of recommendation: Important. Standardized test scores: Very important. Essay: Important. *Nonacademic:* Interview: Not considered. Extracurricular activities: Important. Talent/ability: Important. Character/personal qualities: Important. Alumni/ae relationship: Considered. Geographical residence: Considered. State residency: Considered. Religious affiliation/commitment: Not considered. Minority status: Not considered. Volunteer work: Considered. Work experience: Considered. **Other schools with the greatest overlap in applicants:** College of New Jersey; Montclair State University; Richard Stockton College of New Jersey; Rowan University; Rutgers–New Brunswick. **Admissions statistics for the fall 2005 entering class:** Total applicants: 4,507. Total accepted: 1,860. Freshmen enrolled: 748; 3% were from out of state. Overall acceptance rate: 41%. Non-early acceptance rate: 41%. **Size of waiting list:** 299 applicants; enrolled from waiting list: 31. **Credentials of fall 2005 freshmen:** 31% ranked in the top 10 percent of their high school class; 80% were in the top 25 percent, and 99% were in the top half. (Proportion submitting class standing: 70%.) **Average high school grade point average:** 3.5. **First-year students who submitted SAT scores:** 100%. Scores (25/75 percentile): Verbal: 540-620, Math: 550-640, Combined: 1090-1260.

ACADEMICS

Year founded: 1969. **Academic calendar:** Semester. **Degrees offered:** certificate, bachelor's, master's. **Most popular majors:** 14% communication studies/speech communication and rhetoric, 14% psychology, 12% business administration and management, 6% comparative literature, 6% nursing science (M.S., Ph.D.). **Major fields of study:** area, ethnic, cultural, and gender studies; biological and biomedical sciences; business, management, marketing, and related support services; communication, journalism, and related programs; computer and information sciences and support services; foreign languages, literatures, and linguistics; health professions and related clinical sciences; history; legal professions and studies; liberal arts and sciences studies, and humanities; mathematics and statistics; multi/interdisciplinary studies; natural resources and conservation; physical sciences; psychology; public administration and social service professions; social sciences; visual and performing arts. **Areas of required coursework:** humanities, computer literacy, mathematics, English (including composition), sciences (biological or physical), history, social science. **Pre-professional programs:** pre-law, pre-dentistry, pre-medicine, pre-optometry, other. **Special academic programs:** accelerated program, cooperative (work-study plan) program, double major, dual enrollment, English as a Second Language (ESL), exchange student program (domestic), external degree program, honors program, independent study, internships, liberal arts/career combination, student-designed major, study abroad, teacher certificate program. **Teacher certification offered in:** elementary, secondary. **Cooperative education programs:** art, business, computer science, education, health professions, humanities, natural science, social/behavioral science, vocational arts. **Reserve Officers Training Corps (ROTC):** Air Force ROTC: Offered at cooperating institution (New Jersey Institute of Technology). **Faculty and instruction (2005-2006):** Total instructional faculty: 187 full-time, 246 part-time. Full-time faculty with Ph.D. or other terminal degree: 91%. Student/faculty ratio: 16/1. Classes of fewer than 20 students: 38%; of 20 to 49 students: 62%; of 50 or more students: 0%. **Advanced Placement and International Baccalaureate credit:** AP tests may be used for: Credit only. Scores accepted: 2, 3, 4, 5. International Baccalaureate exams may be used for: Credit only. **Freshmen returning for sophomore year:** 87%. **Graduation rates:** Four-year: 39%; five-year: 55%; six-year: 57%.

COSTS AND FINANCIAL AID

Financial aid office: (201) 684-7549. **Expenses (2005-2006):** Tuition and fees 2005-2006: $8,791 in state, $13,708 out of state; room/board: $9,116. Estimated books and supplies: $1,000; transportation: $250; personal expenses: $1,300. **Financial aid:** Priority filing date for institution's financial aid form: March 1. In 2005-2006, 70% of undergraduates applied for financial aid. Of those, 48% were determined to have financial need; 16% had their need fully met. Average financial aid package (proportion receiving): $9,765 (47%). Average amount of gift aid, such as scholarships or grants (proportion receiving): $6,856 (24%). Average amount of self-help aid, such as work study or loans (proportion receiving): $3,984 (39%). Average need-based loan (excluding PLUS or other private loans): $3,860. Among students who received need-based aid, the average percentage of need met: 77%. Among students who received aid based on merit, the average award (and the proportion receiving): $7,914 (13%). The average athletic scholarship (and the proportion receiving): $0 (0%). Average amount of debt of borrowers graduating in 2005: $15,937. Proportion who borrowed: 37%.

CAMPUS LIFE AND EXTRACURRICULAR ACTIVITIES

Campus housing available (% using): coed dorms (58%), apartment for single students (42%). Students who live in college-owned, operated, or affiliated housing: 52%. **Student employment:** During the 2005-2006 academic year, 12% of undergraduates worked on campus. Average per-year earnings: $3,150. **Clubs and organizations:** Number of student organizations: 92. Activities include: choral groups, dance, drama/theater, literary magazine, music ensembles, musical theater, radio station, student government, student newspaper, student film society, television station, yearbook. Number of fraternities: 10; sororities: 7. Proportion of men in fraternities: 5%; of women in sororities: 6%. **Sports program (2005-2006):** Member of NCAA III. *Men's intercollegiate varsity sports:* baseball, basketball, cross-country, soccer, tennis, track and field (indoor), track and field (outdoor), volleyball. *Women's intercollegiate varsity sports:* basketball, cross-country, field hockey, soccer, softball, tennis, track and field (indoor), track and field (outdoor), volleyball.

SERVICES AND FACILITIES

Basic services: nonremedial tutoring, women's center, placement service, health service, health insurance, other. **Remedial assistance:** reading, math, writing, study skills. **Counseling services:** minority student, career, personal, veteran student, academic, older student, psychological, birth control. **For learning-disabled students:** School does not offer a structured program with separate admission and additional fees. Total undergraduates in learning-disabled program or receiving services: 140. Services include: remedial math, remedial English, reading machines, remedial reading, tape recorders, other special classes, note-taking services, learning center, extended time for tests, tutors, priority seating, texts on tape, other testing accomodations. **Library:** Number of titles: 162,399; number of current serial subscriptions: 558. **Information technology resources:** Students are not required to lease or own a computer. Number of campus computers available to all students: 605. School has a wireless network. Approximate number of users that can be accommodated: 1,000. Proportion of college-owned housing units wired for high-speed internet access: 100%. **Campus safety:** Security services offered: 24-hour foot-and-vehicle patrols, late-night transport/escort service, 24-hour emergency telephones, lighted pathways/sidewalks, student patrols, controlled dormitory access (key, security card, etc).

TRANSFER AND INTERNATIONAL STUDENTS

Transfer students: May apply for admission for the following academic terms: Fall, Spring. Applicants do not need a minimum number of credits to apply. For fall 2005: Transfer applications received: 1,205. Transfer applicants offered admission: 838. Transfer applicants enrolled: 496. **International students:** Number of foreign undergraduates: 140 (3% of student body). Number of countries represented: 53. Minimum TOEFL score required: 550 (paper); 213 (computer). Average TOEFL score: 580 (paper).

Richard Stockton College of New Jersey

- **Address:** PO Box 195, Pomona, NJ 08240-0195
- **Website:** http://www.stockton.edu
- **Public**
- **Enrollment:** 5,650 full-time; 920 part-time

KEY STATS

✔ **U.S News College Ranking:** third tier, Liberal Arts Colleges
✔ **SAT Score (25th/75th percentile):** 1030-1200
✔ **Tuition:** 2006-2007: $8,492 in state, $11,932 out of state

Selectivity: Selective	Room/board: $8,565
Acceptance rate: 52%	Average debt: $15,875
Student/faculty ratio: 19/1	Proportion who borrowed: 64%

UNDERGRADUATE STUDENT BODY STATS

2005-2006 enrollment: 5,650 full-time; 920 part-time. Men: 42%; women: 58%. **Ethnic makeup:** African American: 8%; Asian American: 4%; Hispanic: 6%; White: 82%.

ADMISSIONS FACTS AND FIGURES

Phone: (609) 652-4261. **Email:** admissions@stockton.edu. **Website:** http://www.stockton.edu. **Application deadlines for fall 2007:** Regular decision: May 1. Early decision: Not offered. Early action: Not offered. Admission cannot be deferred. **Application fee:** $50. Common application is accepted. **To apply online, go to:** https://apply.embark.com/ugrad/stockton/59/. **Admissions requirements/recommendations:** High school units required (recommended): English: 4 (4); Mathematics: 3 (3); Science: 2 (2); Foreign language: 0 (0); Social studies: 2 (2); History: 0 (0); Academic electives: 5 (5); Total units: 16 (16). Tests: The college uses SAT or ACT scores in admissions decisions. Either SAT or ACT required. For admission to the fall 2007 entering class, the school will accept: ACT with writing, ACT without writing. Campus visit: Recommended. Admissions interview: Neither required nor recommended. Off-campus interview: Not available. **Factors that count in admissions decisions:** *Academic:* Secondary school record: Very important. Class rank: Very important. Letters of recommendation: Considered. Standardized test scores: Very important. Essay: Considered. *Nonacademic:* Interview: Not considered. Extracurricular activities: Important. Talent/ability: Considered. Character/personal qualities: Considered. Alumni/ae relationship: Considered. Geographical residence: Not considered. State residency: Not considered. Religious affiliation/commitment: Not considered. Minority status: Considered. Volunteer work: Considered. Work experience: Considered. **Other schools with the greatest overlap in applicants:** College of New Jersey; Rowan University; Rutgers–New Brunswick; Temple University; University of Delaware. **Admissions statistics for the fall 2005 entering class:** Total applicants: 3,448. Total accepted: 1,777. Freshmen enrolled: 812; 3% were from out of state. Overall acceptance rate: 52%. **Size of waiting list:** 375 applicants; enrolled from waiting list: 0. **Credentials of fall 2005 freshmen:** 20% ranked in the top 10 percent of their high school class; 47% were in the top 25 percent, and 91% were in the top half. (Proportion submitting class standing: 78%.) **Average high school grade point average:** 3.0. **First-year students who submitted SAT scores:** 94%. Scores (25/75 percentile): Verbal: 510-590, Math: 520-610, Combined: 1030-1200. **First-year students submitting ACT scores:** 4%. Scores (25/75 percentile): English: 20-25, Math: 21-27, Composite: 21-26.

ACADEMICS

Year founded: 1969. **Academic calendar:** Semester. **Degrees offered:** certificate, bachelor's, master's. **Most popular majors:** 17% business administration and management, 12% psychology, 11% teacher education, 10% criminology, 6% biology/biological sciences. **Major fields of study:** biological and biomedical sciences; business, management, marketing, and related support services; communication, journalism, and related programs; computer and information sciences and support services; education; English language and literature/letters; foreign languages, literatures, and linguistics; health professions and related clinical sciences; history; liberal arts and sciences studies, and humanities; mathematics and statistics; natural resources and conservation; philosophy and religious studies; physical sciences; psychology; public administration and social service professions; social sciences; visual and performing arts. **Areas of required coursework:** arts/fine arts, humanities, mathematics, English (including composition), sciences (biological or physical), history, social science, other. **Pre-professional programs:** pre-law, pre-dentistry, pre-medicine, pre-veterinary science, pre-pharmacy. **Special academic programs (% participation):** cross-registration, distance learning (18%), double major (5%), dual enrollment, honors program, independent study (50%), internships (25%), liberal arts/career combination (5%), student-designed major (1%), study abroad (1%), teacher certificate program (7%). **Teacher certification offered in:** elementary, middle/junior high, secondary. **Faculty and instruction (2005-2006):** Total instructional faculty: 242 full-time, 209 part-time (; 15% minorities). Full-time faculty with Ph.D. or other terminal degree: 95%. Student/faculty ratio: 19/1. **Advanced Placement and International Baccalaureate credit:** AP tests may be used for: Credit only. Scores accepted: 3, 4, 5. International Baccalaureate exams may be used for: Credit only. **Freshmen returning for sophomore year:** 83%. **Graduation rates:** Four-year: 36%; five-year: 58%; six-year: 62%. **Graduate study:** 20% of students pursue further study immediately upon graduation; 44% within one year; 50% within five years. Fields in which graduates pursue further study: Master of Business Administration (MBA), 6%; law, 3%; medicine, 3%; engineering, 3%; education, 34%; arts and sciences, 16%.

COSTS AND FINANCIAL AID

Financial aid office: (609) 652-4201. **Expenses (2006-2007):** Tuition and fees 2006-2007: $8,492 in state, $11,932 out of state; room/board: $8,565. Estimated books and supplies: $1,100; transportation: $1,025; personal expenses: $1,200. **Financial aid:** Priority filing date for institution's financial aid form: March 1. In 2005-2006, 70% of undergraduates applied for financial aid. Of those, 54% were determined to have financial need; 50% had their need fully met. Average financial aid package (proportion receiving): $11,022 (52%). Average amount of gift aid, such as scholarships or grants (proportion receiving): $5,937 (29%). Average amount of self-help aid, such as work study or loans (proportion receiving): $4,154 (43%). Average need-based loan (excluding PLUS or other private loans): $3,980. Among students who received need-based aid, the average percentage of need met: 59%. Among students who received aid based on merit, the average award (and the proportion receiving): $2,523 (6%). The average athletic scholarship (and the proportion receiving): $0 (0%). Average amount of debt of borrowers graduating in 2005: $15,875. Proportion who borrowed: 64%.

CAMPUS LIFE AND EXTRACURRICULAR ACTIVITIES

Campus housing available (% using): coed dorms (98%), special housing for disabled students (2%). Students who live in college-owned, operated, or affiliated housing: 32%. **Student employment:** During the 2005-2006 academic year, 5% of undergraduates worked on campus. **Clubs and organizations:** Number of student organizations: 86. Activities include: choral groups, concert band, dance, drama/theater, literary magazine, music ensembles, musical theater, pep band, radio station, student government, student newspaper, television station, yearbook. Number of fraternities: 8; sororities: 11. Proportion of men in fraternities: 5%; of women in sororities: 5%. Average proportion of students who stay on campus on weekends: 45%. **Sports program (2005-2006):** Member of NCAA III. *Men's intercollegiate varsity sports:* baseball, basketball, cross-country, lacrosse, soccer, track and field (indoor), track and field (outdoor). *Women's intercollegiate varsity sports:* basketball, cross-country, field hockey, soccer, softball, tennis, track and field (indoor), track and field (outdoor), volleyball, rowing.

SERVICES AND FACILITIES

Basic services: nonremedial tutoring, day care, health service, health insurance, other. **Remedial assistance:** reading, math, writing, study skills. **Counseling services:** minority student, career, personal, veteran student, academic, older student, psychological, birth control. **For learning-disabled students:** School does not offer a structured program with separate admission and additional fees. Total undergraduates in learning-disabled program or receiving services: 240. Services include: reading machines, tape recorders, note-taking services, oral tests, readers, extended time for tests, priority registration, priority seating, texts on tape, other testing accomodations, other. **Library:** Number of titles: 264,027; number of current serial subscriptions: 20,394. **Information technology resources:** Students are not required to lease or own a computer. Number of campus computers available to all students: 1,375. School has a wireless network. Approximate number of users that can be accommodated: 500. Proportion of college-owned housing units wired for high-speed internet access: 100%. **Campus safety:** Security services offered: 24-hour foot-and-vehicle patrols, late-night transport/escort service, 24-hour emergency telephones, lighted pathways/sidewalks, controlled dormitory access (key, security card, etc).

TRANSFER AND INTERNATIONAL STUDENTS

Transfer students: May apply for admission for the following academic terms: Fall, Spring. Applicants do not need a minimum number of credits to apply. For fall 2005: Transfer applications received: 1,921. Transfer applicants offered admission: 1,358. Transfer applicants enrolled: 950. **International students:** Number of foreign undergraduates: 29. Number of countries represented: 21. Minimum TOEFL score required: 550 (paper); 213 (computer). Average TOEFL score: 550 (paper).

Rider University

- **Address:** 2083 Lawrenceville Road, Lawrenceville, NJ 08648-3099
- **Website:** http://www.rider.edu
- **Private**
- **Enrollment:** 3,611 full-time; 764 part-time

KEY STATS

✔ **U.S News College Ranking:** 31, Universities–Master's (North)
✔ **SAT Score (25th/75th percentile):** 950-1150
✔ **Tuition:** 2006-2007: $24,790

Selectivity: Selective   **Room/board:** $9,280
Acceptance rate: 81%   **Average debt:** $28,636
Student/faculty ratio: 13/1   **Proportion who borrowed:** 72%

UNDERGRADUATE STUDENT BODY STATS

2005-2006 enrollment: 3,611 full-time; 764 part-time. Men: 41%; women: 59%. **Ethnic makeup:** African American: 9%; Asian American: 3%; Hispanic: 5%; White: 81%; International: 2%.

ADMISSIONS FACTS AND FIGURES

Phone: (609) 896-5042. **Email:** admissions@rider.edu. **Website:** http://www.rider.edu. **Application deadlines for fall 2007:** Regular decision: Rolling. Early decision: Not offered. Early action: Send application by: November 15; Decision sent by: December 15. Admission can be deferred. **Application fee:** $45. Common application is accepted. **To apply online, go to:** http://www.rider.edu/160_932.htm. **Admissions requirements/recommendations:** High school units required (recommended): English: 4; Mathematics: 3 (4); Science: (3); Foreign language: (2); Social studies: (2); History: (2); Total units: 16. Tests: The college uses SAT or ACT scores in admissions decisions. Either SAT or ACT required. For admission to the fall 2007 entering class, the school will accept: ACT without writing. Campus visit: Recommended. Admissions interview: Neither required nor recommended. Off-campus interview: Not available. **Factors that count in admissions decisions: *Academic:*** Secondary school record: Very important. Class rank: Considered. Letters of recommendation: Very important. Standardized test scores: Very important. Essay: Very important. ***Nonacademic:*** Interview: Considered. Extracurricular activities: Considered. Talent/ability: Not considered. Character/personal qualities: Considered. Alumni/ae relationship: Considered. Geographical residence: Considered. State residency: Considered. Religious affiliation/commitment: Not considered. Minority status: Not considered. Volunteer work: Considered. Work experience: Considered. **Other schools with the greatest overlap in applicants:** College of New Jersey; Monmouth University; Rowan University; Rutgers–New Brunswick; University of Delaware. **Admissions statistics for the fall 2005 entering class:** Total applicants: 4,463. Total accepted: 3,629. Freshmen enrolled: 948; 28% were from out of state. Overall acceptance rate: 81%. Non-early acceptance rate: 81%. **Credentials of fall 2005 freshmen:** 10% ranked in the top 10 percent of their high school class; 34% were in the top 25 percent, and 69% were in the top half. (Proportion submitting class standing: 59%.) **Average high school grade point average:** 3.2. **First-year students who submitted SAT scores:** 98%. Scores (25/75 percentile): Verbal: 470-570, Math: 480-580, Combined: 950-1150. **First-year students submitting ACT scores:** 1%. Scores (25/75 percentile): English: N/A, Math: N/A, Composite: 20-24.

ACADEMICS

Year founded: 1865. **Academic calendar:** Semester. **Degrees offered:** certificate, associate, transfer-associate, bachelor's, master's, post-master's certificate. **Most popular majors:** 14% elementary education and teaching, 12% speech and rhetorical studies, 7% finance, 7% marketing/marketing management, 7% psychology. **Major fields of study:** area, ethnic, cultural, and gender studies; biological and biomedical sciences; business, management, marketing, and related support services; communication, journalism, and related programs; computer and information sciences and support services; education; English language and literature/letters; foreign languages, literatures, and linguistics; history; liberal arts and sciences studies, and humanities; mathematics and statistics; natural resources and conservation; philosophy and religious studies; physical sciences; psychology; social sciences; theology and religious vocations; visual and performing arts. **Areas of required coursework:** humanities, mathematics, English (including composition), sciences (biological or physical), history, social science. **Pre-professional programs:** pre-law, pre-dentistry, pre-medicine, pre-veterinary science.

Special academic programs (% participation): cross-registration, double major (23%), English as a Second Language (ESL) (3.2%), honors program (7.6%), independent study (24.4%), internships (24.4%), study abroad (1.4%), teacher certificate program (18%), weekend college (10.7%). **Teacher certification offered in:** early childhood, special education, elementary, middle/junior high, secondary, bilingual/bicultural. **Reserve Officers Training Corps (ROTC):** Army ROTC: Offered at cooperating institution (Princeton University). **Faculty and instruction (2005-2006):** Total instructional faculty: 234 full-time, 267 part-time (51% men; 49% women; 13% minorities). Full-time faculty with Ph.D. or other terminal degree: 96%. Student/faculty ratio: 13/1. Classes of fewer than 20 students: 47%; of 20 to 49 students: 51%; of 50 or more students: 2%. **Advanced Placement and International Baccalaureate credit:** AP tests may be used for: Credit only. Scores accepted: 3, 4, 5. **Freshmen returning for sophomore year:** 79%. **Graduation rates:** Four-year: 42%; five-year: 55%; six-year: 61%. **Graduate study:** 16% of students pursue further study within one year. Fields in which graduates pursue further study: Master of Business Administration (MBA), 34%; law, 6%; medicine, 8%; education, 14%; arts and sciences, 33%.

COSTS AND FINANCIAL AID

Financial aid office: (609) 896-5360. **Expenses (2006-2007):** Tuition and fees 2006-2007: $24,790; room/board: $9,280. Estimated books and supplies: $1,000; transportation: $2,000; personal expenses: $1,049. **Financial aid:** Priority filing date for institution's financial aid form: March 1; deadline: June 1. In 2005-2006, 78% of undergraduates applied for financial aid. Of those, 67% were determined to have financial need; 16% had their need fully met. Average financial aid package (proportion receiving): $17,454 (67%). Average amount of gift aid, such as scholarships or grants (proportion receiving): $11,825 (64%). Average amount of self-help aid, such as work study or loans (proportion receiving): $6,691 (51%). Average need-based loan (excluding PLUS or other private loans): $3,937. Among students who received need-based aid, the average percentage of need met: 70%. Among students who received aid based on merit, the average award (and the proportion receiving): $8,239 (16%). The average athletic scholarship (and the proportion receiving): $11,092 (7%). Average amount of debt of borrowers graduating in 2005: $28,636. Proportion who borrowed: 72%.

CAMPUS LIFE AND EXTRACURRICULAR ACTIVITIES

Campus housing available (% using): coed dorms (80%), women's dorms (5%), sorority housing (8%), fraternity housing (6%), apartment for single students (1%), other housing options. Students who live in college-owned, operated, or affiliated housing: 46%. **Student employment:** During the 2005-2006 academic year, 50% of undergraduates worked on campus. **Clubs and organizations:** Number of student organizations: 110. Activities include: choral groups, concert band, dance, drama/theater, jazz band, literary magazine, music ensembles, musical theater, opera, pep band, radio station, student government, student newspaper, student film society, symphony orchestra, television station, yearbook. Number of fraternities: 6; sororities: 6. Proportion of men in fraternities: 17%; of women in sororities: 16%. Average proportion of students who stay on campus on weekends: 56%. **Sports program (2005-2006):** Member of NCAA I. ***Men's intercollegiate varsity sports:*** baseball, basketball, cross-country, golf, soccer, swimming and diving, tennis, track and field (indoor), track and field (outdoor), wrestling. ***Women's intercollegiate varsity sports:*** basketball, cross-country, field hockey, soccer, softball, swimming and diving, tennis, track and field (indoor), track and field (outdoor), volleyball.

SERVICES AND FACILITIES

Basic services: nonremedial tutoring, women's center, placement service, health service. **Remedial assistance:** reading, math, writing, study skills. **Counseling services:** minority student, career, personal, veteran student, academic, older student, psychological, birth control, religious. **For learning-disabled students:** School does not offer a structured program with separate admission and additional fees. Total undergraduates in learning-disabled program or receiving services: 154. Services include: remedial math, reading machines, remedial reading, tape recorders, other special classes, diagnostic testing service, note-taking services, oral tests, learning center, readers, extended time for tests, tutors, priority registration, priority seating, substitution of courses, texts on tape, typist/scribe, other testing accomodations, other. **Library:** Number of titles: 446,772; number of current serial subscriptions: 25,647. **Information technology resources:** Students are not required to lease or own a computer. Number of campus computers available to all students: 520. School has a wireless network. Approximate number of users that can be accommodated: 150. Proportion of college-owned housing units wired for high-speed internet access: 100%. **Campus safety:** Security services offered: 24-hour foot-and-vehicle patrols, late-night transport/escort service, 24-hour emergency telephones, lighted pathways/sidewalks, student patrols, controlled dormitory access (key, security card, etc).

TRANSFER AND INTERNATIONAL STUDENTS

Transfer students: May apply for admission for the following academic terms: Fall, Spring. Applicants do not need a minimum number of credits to apply. For fall 2005: Transfer applications received: 433. Transfer applicants offered admission: 297. Transfer applicants enrolled: 204.
International students: Number of foreign undergraduates: 80 (2% of student body). Number of countries represented: 11. Minimum TOEFL score required: 550 (paper); 213 (computer).

Rowan University

■ **Address:** 201 Mullica Hill Road, Glassboro, NJ 08028
■ **Website:** http://www.rowan.edu
■ **Public**
■ **Enrollment:** 7,283 full-time; 1,201 part-time

KEY STATS

✔ **U.S News College Ranking:** 29, Universities–Master's (North)
✔ **SAT Score (25th/75th percentile):** 1020-1220
✔ **Tuition:** 2006-2007: $9,330 in state, $16,128 out of state
   Selectivity: Selective   **Room/board:** $8,742
   Acceptance rate: 47%   **Average debt:** $9,575
   Student/faculty ratio: 14/1   **Proportion who borrowed:** 97%

UNDERGRADUATE STUDENT BODY STATS

2005-2006 enrollment: 7,283 full-time; 1,201 part-time. Men: 45%; women: 55%. **Ethnic makeup:** African American: 9%; Asian American: 3%; Hispanic: 7%; White: 81%. **Religious preference:** Roman Catholic: 44%; Protestant: 20%; Jewish: 3%; Muslim: 1%; Buddhist: 1%; No preference: 15%; Unknown: 5%; Eastern Orthodox and other Christian: 9%; Other: 2%.

ADMISSIONS FACTS AND FIGURES

Phone: (856) 256-4200. **Email:** admissions@rowan.edu. **Website:** http://www.rowan.edu. **Application deadlines for fall 2007:** Regular decision: March 15; decision sent by April 15. Early decision: Not offered. Early action: Not offered. Admission can be deferred. **Application fee:** $50. Common application is not accepted. **Admissions requirements/recommendations:** High school units required (recommended): English: 4 (4); Mathematics: 3 (4); Science: 2 (3); Foreign language: (2); Social studies: 2 (2); History: (2); Academic electives: 5 (5); Total units: 16 (16). Tests: The college uses SAT or ACT scores in admissions decisions. Either SAT or ACT required. For admission to the fall 2007 entering class, the school will accept: ACT with writing, ACT without writing. Campus visit: Neither required nor recommended. Admissions interview: Neither required nor recommended. Off-campus interview: Not available. **Factors that count in admissions decisions:** *Academic:* Secondary school record: Very important. Class rank: Very important. Letters of recommendation: Important. Standardized test scores: Very important. Essay: Not considered. *Nonacademic:* Interview: Not considered. Extracurricular activities: Considered. Talent/ability: Important. Character/personal qualities: Considered. Alumni/ae relationship: Not considered. Geographical residence: Not considered. State residency: Not considered. Religious affiliation/commitment: Not considered. Minority status: Considered. Volunteer work: Considered. Work experience: Considered. **Other schools with the greatest overlap in applicants:** College of New Jersey; Drexel University; Rider University; Rutgers–New Brunswick; University of Delaware. **Admissions statistics for the fall 2005 entering class:** Total applicants: 7,303. Total accepted: 3,396. Freshmen enrolled: 1,247; 3% were from out of state. Overall acceptance rate: 47%. **Size of waiting list:** 130 applicants; enrolled from waiting list: 50. **Credentials of fall 2005 freshmen:** 18% ranked in the top 10 percent of their high school class; 52% were in the top 25 percent, and 89% were in the top half. (Proportion submitting class standing: 100%.) **Average high school grade point average:** 3.0. **First-year students who submitted SAT scores:** 99%. Scores (25/75 percentile): Verbal: 510-600, Math: 510-620, Combined: 1020-1220.

ACADEMICS

Year founded: 1923. **Academic calendar:** Semester. **Degrees offered:** bachelor's, master's, doctorate. **Most popular majors:** 21% education, 15% business, management, marketing, and related support services, 15%

communication, journalism, and related programs, 8% security and protective services, 7% social sciences. **Major fields of study:** biological and biomedical sciences; business, management, marketing, and related support services; communication, journalism, and related programs; communications technologies/technicians and support services; computer and information sciences and support services; education; engineering; English language and literature/letters; foreign languages, literatures, and linguistics; health professions and related clinical sciences; history; liberal arts and sciences studies, and humanities; library science; mathematics and statistics; natural resources and conservation; physical sciences; psychology; security and protective services; social sciences; visual and performing arts. **Areas of required coursework:** arts/fine arts, humanities, computer literacy, mathematics, English (including composition), sciences (biological or physical), social science, other. **Pre-professional programs:** pre-law, pre-dentistry, pre-medicine, pre-veterinary science, pre-optometry, pre-pharmacy, other. **Special academic programs:** accelerated program, cooperative (work-study plan) program, double major, English as a Second Language (ESL), honors program, independent study, internships, study abroad, teacher certificate program. **Teacher certification offered in:** early childhood, special education, elementary, middle/junior high, adult education, secondary, bilingual/bicultural. **Cooperative education programs:** business, education, engineering. **Reserve Officers Training Corps (ROTC):** Army ROTC: Offered at cooperating institution (Drexel University). **Faculty and instruction (2005-2006):** Total instructional faculty: 441 full-time, 451 part-time (57% men; 43% women; 14% minorities). Full-time faculty with Ph.D. or other terminal degree: 79%. Student/faculty ratio: 14/1. Classes of fewer than 20 students: 46%; of 20 to 49 students: 54%; of 50 or more students: 0%. **Advanced Placement and International Baccalaureate credit:** AP tests may be used for: Credit and/or placement. Scores accepted: 3, 4, 5. **Freshmen returning for sophomore year:** 85%. **Graduation rates:** Four-year: 36%; five-year: 59%; six-year: 62%. **Graduate study:** 20% of students pursue further study immediately upon graduation; 22% within one year. Fields in which graduates pursue further study: Master of Business Administration (MBA), 22%; law, 4%; medicine, 5%; engineering, 7%; education, 25%; arts and sciences, 37%.

COSTS AND FINANCIAL AID

Financial aid office: (856) 256-4250. **Expenses (2005-2006):** Tuition and fees 2005-2006: $8,607 in state, $14,901 out of state; room/board: $8,242. Estimated books and supplies: $800; transportation: $800; personal expenses: $1,000. **Financial aid:** Priority filing date for institution's financial aid form: March 15. In 2005-2006, 85% of undergraduates applied for financial aid. Of those, 83% were determined to have financial need; 38% had their need fully met. Average financial aid package (proportion receiving): $6,214 (83%). Average amount of gift aid, such as scholarships or grants (proportion receiving): $5,547 (48%). Average amount of self-help aid, such as work study or loans (proportion receiving): $3,913 (52%). Average need-based loan (excluding PLUS or other private loans): $3,476. Among students who received need-based aid, the average percentage of need met: 67%. Among students who received aid based on merit, the average award (and the proportion receiving): $2,933 (0%). The average athletic scholarship (and the proportion receiving): $0 (0%). Average amount of debt of borrowers graduating in 2005: $9,575. Proportion who borrowed: 97%.

CAMPUS LIFE AND EXTRACURRICULAR ACTIVITIES

Campus housing available (% using): coed dorms (52%), apartment for single students (19%), special housing for disabled students (10%), special housing for international students (3%), other housing options (16%). Students who live in college-owned, operated, or affiliated housing: 34%. **Student employment:** During the 2005-2006 academic year, 0% of undergraduates worked on campus. **Clubs and organizations:** Number of student organizations: 76. Activities include: choral groups, concert band, dance, drama/theater, jazz band, literary magazine, music ensembles, musical theater, opera, pep band, radio station, student government, student newspaper, student film society, television station, yearbook. Number of fraternities: 14; sororities: 11. Proportion of men in fraternities: 12%; of women in sororities: 8%. Average proportion of students who stay on campus on weekends: 75%. **Sports program (2005-2006):** Member of NCAA III. *Men's intercollegiate varsity sports:* baseball, basketball, cross-country, football, soccer, swimming and diving, track and field (indoor), track and field (outdoor). *Women's intercollegiate varsity sports:* basketball, cross-country, field hockey, lacrosse, soccer, softball, swimming and diving, track and field (indoor), track and field (outdoor).

SERVICES AND FACILITIES

Basic services: nonremedial tutoring, health service, health insurance. **Remedial assistance:** reading, math, writing, study skills. **Counseling services:** minority student, career, personal, veteran student, academic, psychological. **For learning-disabled students:** School does not offer a structured program with separate admission and additional fees. Total undergraduates in learning-disabled program or receiving services: 356. Services include: remedial math, remedial English, reading machines, remedial reading, tape recorders, untimed tests, oral tests, learning center, readers, extended time for tests, tutors, priority registration, priority seating, texts on tape, other testing accomodations, other. **Library:** Number of titles: 412,069; number of current serial subscriptions: 12,500. **Information technology resources:** Students are not required to lease or own a computer. Number of campus computers available to all students: 1,215. School has a wireless network. Approximate number of users that can be accommodated: 1,640. Proportion of college-owned housing units wired for high-speed internet access: 100%. **Campus safety:** Security services offered: 24-hour foot-and-vehicle patrols, late-night transport/escort service, 24-hour emergency telephones, lighted pathways/sidewalks, student patrols, controlled dormitory access (key, security card, etc).

TRANSFER AND INTERNATIONAL STUDENTS

Transfer students: May apply for admission for the following academic terms: Fall, Spring. Applicants need a minimum number of credits to apply. For fall 2005: Transfer applications received: 1,860. Transfer applicants offered admission: 1,212. Transfer applicants enrolled: 819. **International students:** Number of foreign undergraduates: 0. Number of countries represented: 32. Minimum TOEFL score required: 550 (paper); 213 (computer). Average TOEFL score: 550 (paper).

Rutgers–Camden

- **Address:** 406 Penn Street, Camden, NJ 08102
- **Website:** http://www.rutgers.edu/
- **Public**
- **Enrollment:** 2,949 full-time; 897 part-time

KEY STATS

✔ **U.S News College Ranking:** 31, Universities–Master's (North)
✔ **SAT Score (25th/75th percentile):** 1020-1210
✔ **Tuition:** 2005-2006: $9,028 in state, $16,626 out of state

Selectivity: More selective	**Room/board:** $8,088
Acceptance rate: 53%	**Average debt:** $17,378
Student/faculty ratio: 11/1	**Proportion who borrowed:** 69%

UNDERGRADUATE STUDENT BODY STATS

2005-2006 enrollment: 2,949 full-time; 897 part-time. Men: 42%; women: 58%. **Ethnic makeup:** African American: 15%; Asian American: 8%; Hispanic: 6%; White: 69%; International: 1%.

ADMISSIONS FACTS AND FIGURES

Phone: (856) 225-6104. **Email:** camden@ugadm.rutgers.edu. **Website:** http://www.rutgers.edu/. **Application deadlines for fall 2007:** Regular decision: Rolling; decision sent by February 28. Early decision: Not offered. Early action: Not offered. Admission cannot be deferred. **Application fee:** $50. Common application is not accepted. **To apply online, go to:** http://admissions.rutgers.edu. **Admissions requirements/recommendations:** High school units required (recommended): English: 4; Mathematics: 3 (4); Science: 2; Foreign language: 2; Academic electives: 5; Total units: 16. Tests: The college uses SAT or ACT scores in admissions decisions. Either SAT or ACT required. For admission to the fall 2007 entering class, the school will accept: ACT with writing. Campus visit: Recommended. Admissions interview: Neither required nor recommended. Off-campus interview: Not available. **Factors that count in admissions decisions:** *Academic:* Secondary school record: Very important. Class rank: Very important. Letters of recommendation: Considered. Standardized test scores: Very important. Essay: Considered. *Nonacademic:* Interview: Not considered. Extracurricular activities: Considered. Talent/ability: Not considered. Character/personal qualities: Not considered. Alumni/ae relationship: Not considered. Geographical residence: Considered. Religious affiliation/commitment: Not considered. Minority status: Considered. Volunteer work: Considered. Work experience: Considered. **Other schools with the greatest overlap in applicants:** College of

New Jersey; Montclair State University; New York University; Pennsylvania State University–University Park; Rowan University. **Admissions statistics for the fall 2005 entering class:** Total applicants: 6,153. Total accepted: 3,284. Freshmen enrolled: 353; 9% were from out of state. Overall acceptance rate: 53%. **Size of waiting list:** N/A applicants; enrolled from waiting list: 0. **Credentials of fall 2005 freshmen:** 27% ranked in the top 10 percent of their high school class; 64% were in the top 25 percent, and 96% were in the top half. (Proportion submitting class standing: 88%.) **First-year students who submitted SAT scores:** 99%. Scores (25/75 percentile): Verbal: 510-600, Math: 510-610, Combined: 1020-1210. **First-year students submitting ACT scores:** 1%. Scores (25/75 percentile): English: N/A, Math: N/A, Composite: N/A.

ACADEMICS

Year founded: 1927. **Academic calendar:** Semester. **Degrees offered:** bachelor's, master's, first professional. **Most popular majors:** 27% business, management, marketing, and related support services, 16% science technologies/technicians, 13% social sciences, 7% security and protective services, 6% English language and literature/letters. **Major fields of study:** area, ethnic, cultural, and gender studies; biological and biomedical sciences; business, management, marketing, and related support services; computer and information sciences and support services; English language and literature/letters; foreign languages, literatures, and linguistics; health professions and related clinical sciences; history; liberal arts and sciences studies, and humanities; mathematics and statistics; multi/interdisciplinary studies; natural resources and conservation; philosophy and religious studies; physical sciences; psychology; public administration and social service professions; security and protective services; social sciences; visual and performing arts. **Areas of required coursework:** arts/fine arts, humanities, mathematics, English (including composition), foreign languages, sciences (biological or physical), history, social science. **Special academic programs:** accelerated program, cooperative (work-study plan) program, cross-registration, distance learning, double major, dual enrollment, English as a Second Language (ESL), honors program, liberal arts/career combination, student-designed major, study abroad, teacher certificate program, other. **Reserve Officers Training Corps (ROTC):** Army ROTC: Offered at cooperating institution (University of Pennsylvania); Air Force ROTC: Offered at cooperating institution (University of Pennsylvania). **Faculty and instruction (2005-2006):** Total instructional faculty: 229 full-time, 172 part-time (61% men; 39% women; 16% minorities). Full-time faculty with Ph.D. or other terminal degree: 99%. Student/faculty ratio: 11/1. Classes of fewer than 20 students: 43%; of 20 to 49 students: 49%; of 50 or more students: 8%. **Advanced Placement and International Baccalaureate credit:** AP tests may be used for: Credit only. **Freshmen returning for sophomore year:** 83%. **Graduation rates:** Four-year: 26%; five-year: 52%; six-year: 59%.

COSTS AND FINANCIAL AID

Financial aid office: (856) 225-6039. **Expenses (2005-2006):** Tuition and fees 2005-2006: $9,028 in state, $16,626 out of state; room/board: $8,088. Estimated books and supplies: $815; transportation: $555; personal expenses: $1,756. **Financial aid:** Priority filing date for institution's financial aid form: March 15. In 2005-2006, 78% of undergraduates applied for financial aid. Of those, 62% were determined to have financial need; 43% had their need fully met. Average financial aid package (proportion receiving): $10,112 (62%). Average amount of gift aid, such as scholarships or grants (proportion receiving): $7,063 (43%). Average amount of self-help aid, such as work study or loans (proportion receiving): $4,287 (51%). Average need-based loan (excluding PLUS or other private loans): $4,023. Among students who received need-based aid, the average percentage of need met: 74%. Among students who received aid based on merit, the average award (and the proportion receiving): $4,624 (6%). The average athletic scholarship (and the proportion receiving): $6,624 (6%). Average amount of debt of borrowers graduating in 2005: $17,378. Proportion who borrowed: 69%.

CAMPUS LIFE AND EXTRACURRICULAR ACTIVITIES

Campus housing available: coed dorms, apartment for single students, special housing for disabled students. Students who live in college-owned, operated, or affiliated housing: 39%. **Student employment:** During the 2005-2006 academic year, 8% of undergraduates worked on campus. Average per-year earnings: $2,450. **Clubs and organizations:** Number of student organizations: 70. Activities include: drama/theater, literary magazine, radio station, student government, student newspaper, yearbook. Number of fraternities: 2; sororities: 5. **Sports program (2005-2006):** Member of NCAA III. *Men's intercollegiate varsity sports:* baseball, basketball, cross-country, golf, soccer, track and field (indoor), track and field (outdoor). *Women's* *intercollegiate varsity sports:* basketball, cross-country, rowing, soccer, softball, track and field (indoor), track and field (outdoor), volleyball.

SERVICES AND FACILITIES

Basic services: nonremedial tutoring, women's center, placement service, health service, health insurance. **Remedial assistance:** reading, math, writing, study skills. **Counseling services:** minority student, career, personal, academic, psychological. **For learning-disabled students:** Services include: remedial math, remedial English, remedial reading, extended time for tests. **Library:** Number of titles: 707,310; number of current serial subscriptions: 5,642. **Information technology resources:** Students are not required to lease or own a computer. Number of campus computers available to all students: 215. **Campus safety:** Security services offered: 24-hour foot-and-vehicle patrols, late-night transport/escort service, 24-hour emergency telephones, lighted pathways/sidewalks, student patrols, controlled dormitory access (key, security card, etc).

TRANSFER AND INTERNATIONAL STUDENTS

Transfer students: May apply for admission for the following academic terms: Fall, Spring. Applicants need a minimum number of credits to apply. For fall 2005: Transfer applications received: 2,124. Transfer applicants offered admission: 1,152. Transfer applicants enrolled: 417. **International students:** Number of foreign undergraduates: 26 (1% of student body). Number of countries represented: 32. Minimum TOEFL score required: 550 (paper); 213 (computer).

Rutgers–Newark

- **Address:** 249 University Avenue, Newark, NJ 07102-1896
- **Website:** http://rutgers-newark.rutgers.edu
- **Public**
- **Enrollment:** 4,911 full-time; 1,602 part-time

KEY STATS

✔ **U.S News College Ranking:** third tier, National Universities
✔ **SAT Score (25th/75th percentile):** 1020-1230
✔ **Tuition:** 2005-2006: $8,812 in state, $16,410 out of state

Selectivity: More selective	**Room/board:** $8,984
Acceptance rate: 47%	**Average debt:** $16,553
Student/faculty ratio: 11/1	**Proportion who borrowed:** 85%

UNDERGRADUATE STUDENT BODY STATS

2005-2006 enrollment: 4,911 full-time; 1,602 part-time. Men: 43%; women: 57%. **Ethnic makeup:** African American: 21%; Asian American: 23%; Hispanic: 18%; White: 35%; International: 2%.

ADMISSIONS FACTS AND FIGURES

Phone: (973) 353-5205. **Email:** admissions@asb-ugadm.rutgers.edu. **Website:** http://rutgers-newark.rutgers.edu. **Application deadlines for fall 2007:** Regular decision: Rolling; decision sent by February 28. Early decision: Not offered. Early action: Not offered. **Application fee:** $50. Common application is not accepted. **To apply online, go to:** http://admissions.rutgers.edu/. **Admissions requirements/recommendations:** High school units required (recommended): English: 4; Mathematics: 3 (4); Science: 2; Foreign language: 2; Academic electives: 5; Total units: 16. Tests: The college uses SAT or ACT scores in admissions decisions. Either SAT or ACT required. For admission to the fall 2007 entering class, the school will accept: ACT with writing. Campus visit: Recommended. Admissions interview: Neither required nor recommended. Off-campus interview: Not available. **Factors that count in admissions decisions:** *Academic:* Secondary school record: Very important. Class rank: Very important. Letters of recommendation: Considered. Standardized test scores: Very important. Essay: Considered. *Nonacademic:* Interview: Not considered. Extracurricular activities: Considered. Talent/ability: Not considered. Character/personal qualities: Not considered. Alumni/ae relationship: Not considered. Geographical residence: Considered. State residency: Considered. Religious affiliation/commitment: Not considered. Minority status: Considered. Volunteer work: Considered. Work experience: Considered. **Other schools with the greatest overlap in applicants:** College of New Jersey; Montclair State University; New York University; Pennsylvania State University–University Park; Rowan University. **Admissions statistics for the fall 2005 entering class:** Total applicants: 9,927. Total accepted: 4,653. Freshmen enrolled: 704; 6% were

from out of state. Overall acceptance rate: 47%. **Credentials of fall 2005 freshmen:** 35% ranked in the top 10 percent of their high school class; 70% were in the top 25 percent, and 100% were in the top half. (Proportion submitting class standing: 76%.) **First-year students who submitted SAT scores:** 99%. Scores (25/75 percentile): Verbal: 500-590, Math: 520-640, Combined: 1020-1230. **First-year students submitting ACT scores:** 1%. Scores (25/75 percentile): English: N/A, Math: N/A, Composite: N/A.

ACADEMICS

Year founded: 1946. **Academic calendar:** Semester. **Degrees offered:** bachelor's, master's, first professional, doctorate. **Most popular majors:** 28% business, management, marketing, and related support services, 11% health professions and related clinical sciences, 9% computer and information sciences and support services, 9% psychology, 9% security and protective services. **Major fields of study:** area, ethnic, cultural, and gender studies; biological and biomedical sciences; business, management, marketing, and related support services; communication, journalism, and related programs; computer and information sciences and support services; engineering; English language and literature/letters; foreign languages, literatures, and linguistics; health professions and related clinical sciences; history; mathematics and statistics; multi/interdisciplinary studies; natural resources and conservation; philosophy and religious studies; physical sciences; psychology; public administration and social service professions; security and protective services; social sciences; visual and performing arts. **Areas of required coursework:** arts/fine arts, humanities, computer literacy, mathematics, sciences (biological or physical), social science. **Pre-professional programs:** pre-law, pre-dentistry, pre-medicine. **Special academic programs:** accelerated program, cross-registration, distance learning, double major, dual enrollment, English as a Second Language (ESL), honors program, independent study, internships, liberal arts/career combination, student-designed major, study abroad, teacher certificate program, weekend college, other. **Reserve Officers Training Corps (ROTC):** Army ROTC: Offered at cooperating institution (Rutgers-New Brunswick); Air Force ROTC: Offered at cooperating institution (Rutgers-New Brunswick). **Faculty and instruction (2005-2006):** Total instructional faculty: 422 full-time, 231 part-time (60% men; 40% women; 15% minorities). Full-time faculty with Ph.D. or other terminal degree: 95%. Student/faculty ratio: 11/1. Classes of fewer than 20 students: 40%; of 20 to 49 students: 48%; of 50 or more students: 12%. **Freshmen returning for sophomore year:** 86%. **Graduation rates:** Four-year: 22%; five-year: 47%; six-year: 57%.

COSTS AND FINANCIAL AID

Financial aid office: (973) 353-5151. **Expenses (2005-2006):** Tuition and fees 2005-2006: $8,812 in state, $16,410 out of state; room/board: $8,984. Estimated books and supplies: $815; transportation: $555; personal expenses: $1,756. **Financial aid:** Priority filing date for institution's financial aid form: March 15. In 2005-2006, 75% of undergraduates applied for financial aid. Of those, 65% were determined to have financial need; 28% had their need fully met. Average financial aid package (proportion receiving): $10,138 (64%). Average amount of gift aid, such as scholarships or grants (proportion receiving): $7,362 (50%). Average amount of self-help aid, such as work study or loans (proportion receiving): $4,245 (48%). Average need-based loan (excluding PLUS or other private loans): $4,151. Among students who received need-based aid, the average percentage of need met: 72%. Among students who received aid based on merit, the average award (and the proportion receiving): $5,087 (5%). The average athletic scholarship (and the proportion receiving): $5,144 (5%). Average amount of debt of borrowers graduating in 2005: $16,553. Proportion who borrowed: 85%.

CAMPUS LIFE AND EXTRACURRICULAR ACTIVITIES

Campus housing available: coed dorms, sorority housing, fraternity housing, apartment for single students, special housing for disabled students. Students who live in college-owned, operated, or affiliated housing: 15%. **Student employment:** During the 2005-2006 academic year, 13% of undergraduates worked on campus. Average per-year earnings: $1,600. **Clubs and organizations:** Number of student organizations: 85. Activities include: choral groups, drama/theater, literary magazine, radio station, student government, student newspaper. Number of fraternities: 9; sororities: 9. **Sports program (2005-2006):** Member of NCAA III. *Men's intercollegiate varsity sports:* baseball, basketball, soccer, tennis, volleyball. *Women's intercollegiate varsity sports:* basketball, soccer, softball, tennis, volleyball.

SERVICES AND FACILITIES

Basic services: women's center, placement service, day care, health service, health insurance. **Remedial assistance:** reading, math, writing. **Counseling**

services: minority student, career, military, personal, academic, older student, psychological, birth control. **For learning-disabled students:** Services include: remedial math, remedial English, remedial reading, learning center, extended time for tests. **Library:** Number of titles: 1,042,941; number of current serial subscriptions: 6,380. **Information technology resources:** Students are not required to lease or own a computer. Number of campus computers available to all students: 494. School has a wireless network. **Campus safety:** Security services offered: 24-hour foot-and-vehicle patrols, late-night transport/escort service, 24-hour emergency telephones, lighted pathways/sidewalks, student patrols, controlled dormitory access (key, security card, etc).

TRANSFER AND INTERNATIONAL STUDENTS

Transfer students: May apply for admission for the following academic terms: Fall, Spring. Applicants need a minimum number of credits to apply. For fall 2005: Transfer applications received: 3,349. Transfer applicants offered admission: 1,280. Transfer applicants enrolled: 464. **International students:** Number of foreign undergraduates: 134 (2% of student body). Number of countries represented: 75. Minimum TOEFL score required: 550 (paper); 213 (computer).

Rutgers–New Brunswick

- **Address:** 65 Davidson Road, Room 202, Piscataway, NJ 08854-8097
- **Website:** http://www.rutgers.edu
- **Public**
- **Enrollment:** 24,361 full-time; 2,352 part-time

KEY STATS
✔ **U.S News College Ranking:** 60, National Universities
✔ **SAT Score (25th/75th percentile):** 1110-1320
✔ **Tuition:** 2005-2006: $9,221 in state, $16,819 out of state
  Selectivity: More selective **Room/board:** $8,838
  Acceptance rate: 61% **Average debt:** $15,362
  Student/faculty ratio: 14/1 **Proportion who borrowed:** 63%

UNDERGRADUATE STUDENT BODY STATS

2005-2006 enrollment: 24,361 full-time; 2,352 part-time. Men: 49%; women: 51%. **Ethnic makeup:** African American: 9%; Asian American: 23%; Hispanic: 8%; White: 58%; International: 2%.

ADMISSIONS FACTS AND FIGURES

Phone: (732) 932-4636. **Email:** admissions@asb-ugadm.rutgers.edu. **Website:** http://www.rutgers.edu. **Application deadlines for fall 2007:** Regular decision: Rolling; decision sent by February 28. Early decision: Not offered. Early action: Not offered. Admission cannot be deferred. **Application fee:** $50. Common application is not accepted. **To apply online, go to:** http://admissions.rutgers.edu. **Admissions requirements/recommendations:** High school units required (recommended): English: 4; Mathematics: 3 (4); Science: 2; Foreign language: 2 (2); Academic electives: 5; Total units: 16. Tests: The college uses SAT or ACT scores in admissions decisions. Either SAT or ACT required. For admission to the fall 2007 entering class, the school will accept: ACT with writing. Campus visit: Recommended. Admissions interview: Neither required nor recommended. Off-campus interview: Not available. **Factors that count in admissions decisions:** *Academic:* Secondary school record: Very important. Class rank: Very important. Letters of recommendation: Considered. Standardized test scores: Very important. Essay: Considered. *Nonacademic:* Interview: Considered. Extracurricular activities: Considered. Character/personal qualities: Not considered. Alumni/ae relationship: Not considered. Geographical residence: Considered. State residency: Considered. Religious affiliation/commitment: Not considered. Minority status: Considered. Volunteer work: Considered. Work experience: Considered. **Other schools with the greatest overlap in applicants:** College of New Jersey; Montclair State University; New York University; Pennsylvania State University–University Park; Rowan University. **Admissions statistics for the fall 2005 entering class:** Total applicants: 25,462. Total accepted: 15,437. Freshmen enrolled: 5,245; 10% were from out of state. Overall acceptance rate: 61%. **Credentials of fall 2005 freshmen:** 36% ranked in the top 10 percent of their high school class; 78% were in the top 25 percent, and 99% were in the top half. (Proportion submitting class standing: 70%.) **First-year students who submitted SAT scores:** 99%. Scores (25/75 percentile): Verbal: 540-640, Math: 570-680,

Combined: 1110-1320. **First-year students submitting ACT scores:** 1%. Scores (25/75 percentile): English: N/A, Math: N/A, Composite: N/A.

ACADEMICS

Year founded: 1766. **Academic calendar:** Semester. **Degrees offered:** bachelor's, master's, first professional, doctorate. **Most popular majors:** 20% social sciences, 10% psychology, 8% biological and biomedical sciences, 8% communication, journalism, and related programs, 7% engineering. **Major fields of study:** agriculture, agriculture operations, and related sciences; architecture and related services; area, ethnic, cultural, and gender studies; biological and biomedical sciences; business, management, marketing, and related support services; communication, journalism, and related programs; computer and information sciences and support services; education; engineering; English language and literature/letters; foreign languages, literatures, and linguistics; health professions and related clinical sciences; history; mathematics and statistics; multi/interdisciplinary studies; natural resources and conservation; philosophy and religious studies; physical sciences; psychology; public administration and social service professions; security and protective services; social sciences; visual and performing arts. **Areas of required coursework:** arts/fine arts, humanities, mathematics, English (including composition), sciences (biological or physical), social science. **Pre-professional programs:** pre-law, pre-dentistry, pre-medicine, pre-veterinary science. **Special academic programs:** accelerated program, cooperative (work-study plan) program, cross-registration, distance learning, double major, dual enrollment, English as a Second Language (ESL), honors program, independent study, liberal arts/career combination, student-designed major, study abroad, teacher certificate program. **Teacher certification offered in:** early childhood, special education, elementary, bilingual/bicultural. **Cooperative education programs:** agriculture, art, business, computer science, health professions, natural science, technologies. **Reserve Officers Training Corps (ROTC):** Army ROTC: Offered on campus; Air Force ROTC: Offered on campus. **Faculty and instruction (2005-2006):** Total instructional faculty: 1,535 full-time, 689 part-time (64% men; 36% women; 16% minorities). Full-time faculty with Ph.D. or other terminal degree: 99%. Student/faculty ratio: 14/1. Classes of fewer than 20 students: 42%; of 20 to 49 students: 39%; of 50 or more students: 19%. **Freshmen returning for sophomore year:** 89%. **Graduation rates:** Four-year: 42%; five-year: 63%; six-year: 71%.

COSTS AND FINANCIAL AID

Financial aid office: (732) 932-7057. **Expenses (2005-2006):** Tuition and fees 2005-2006: $9,221 in state, $16,819 out of state; room/board: $8,838. Estimated books and supplies: $815; transportation: $555; personal expenses: $1,756. **Financial aid:** Priority filing date for institution's financial aid form: March 15. In 2005-2006, 66% of undergraduates applied for financial aid. Of those, 51% were determined to have financial need; 39% had their need fully met. Average financial aid package (proportion receiving): $11,569 (50%). Average amount of gift aid, such as scholarships or grants (proportion receiving): $8,034 (33%). Average amount of self-help aid, such as work study or loans (proportion receiving): $4,557 (44%). Average need-based loan (excluding PLUS or other private loans): $4,170. Among students who received need-based aid, the average percentage of need met: 72%. Among students who received aid based on merit, the average award (and the proportion receiving): $5,311 (10%). The average athletic scholarship (and the proportion receiving): $6,016 (11%). Average amount of debt of borrowers graduating in 2005: $15,362. Proportion who borrowed: 63%.

CAMPUS LIFE AND EXTRACURRICULAR ACTIVITIES

Campus housing available: coed dorms, women's dorms, men's dorms, sorority housing, fraternity housing, apartments for married students, apartment for single students, cooperative housing, other housing options. Students who live in college-owned, operated, or affiliated housing: 49%. **Student employment:** During the 2005-2006 academic year, 26% of undergraduates worked on campus. Average per-year earnings: $1,600. **Clubs and organizations:** Number of student organizations: 350. Activities include: choral groups, concert band, dance, drama/theater, jazz band, literary magazine, marching band, music ensembles, opera, pep band, radio station, student government, student newspaper, student film society, symphony orchestra, television station, yearbook. Number of fraternities: 27; sororities: 17. **Sports program (2005-2006):** Member of NCAA I. *Men's intercollegiate varsity sports:* baseball, basketball, cross-country, fencing, football, golf, heavyweight crew, lacrosse, lightweight crew, soccer, swimming and diving, tennis, track and field (indoor), track and field (outdoor), wrestling. *Women's intercollegiate varsity sports:* basketball, crew, cross-country, fencing, field hockey, golf, gymnastics, lacrosse, soccer, softball, swimming and diving, tennis, track and field (indoor), track and field (outdoor), volleyball.

SERVICES AND FACILITIES

Basic services: women's center, placement service, health service, health insurance. **Remedial assistance:** reading, math, writing. **Counseling services:** minority student, career, academic. **For learning-disabled students:** Services include: remedial math, remedial English, remedial reading, extended time for tests. **Library:** Number of titles: 4,929,696; number of current serial subscriptions: 14,626. **Information technology resources:** Students are not required to lease or own a computer. Number of campus computers available to all students: 1,400. **Campus safety:** Security services offered: 24-hour foot-and-vehicle patrols, late-night transport/escort service, 24-hour emergency telephones, lighted pathways/sidewalks, student patrols, controlled dormitory access (key, security card, etc).

TRANSFER AND INTERNATIONAL STUDENTS

Transfer students: May apply for admission for the following academic terms: Fall, Spring. Applicants need a minimum number of credits to apply. For fall 2005: Transfer applications received: 5,971. Transfer applicants offered admission: 2,179. Transfer applicants enrolled: 1,028. **International students:** Number of foreign undergraduates: 477 (2% of student body). Number of countries represented: 114. Minimum TOEFL score required: 550 (paper); 213 (computer).

Seton Hall University

- **Address:** 400 S. Orange Avenue, South Orange, NJ 07079
- **Website:** http://www.shu.edu
- **Private; Religious affiliation:** Roman Catholic
- **Enrollment:** 4,801 full-time; 534 part-time

KEY STATS

- ✔ **U.S News College Ranking:** third tier, National Universities
- ✔ **SAT Score (25th/75th percentile):** 1010-1220
- ✔ **Tuition:** 2006-2007: $24,720

Selectivity: Selective	**Room/board:** $10,466
Acceptance rate: 84%	**Average debt:** N/A
Student/faculty ratio: 14/1	**Proportion who borrowed:** 66%

UNDERGRADUATE STUDENT BODY STATS

2005-2006 enrollment: 4,801 full-time; 534 part-time. Men: 46%; women: 54%. **Ethnic makeup:** African American: 11%; Asian American: 7%; Hispanic: 9%; White: 71%; International: 1%. **Religious preference:** Jewish: 1%; Unknown: 17%; Roman Catholic: 57%; Baptist: 4%; Other: 21%.

ADMISSIONS FACTS AND FIGURES

Phone: (973) 761-9332. **Email:** thehall@shu.edu. **Website:** http://www.shu.edu. **Application deadlines for fall 2007:** Regular decision: Rolling. Early decision: Not offered. Early action: Not offered. Admission can be deferred. **Application fee:** $55. Common application is accepted. **To apply online, go to:** http://admissions.shu.edu/Applying.htm. **Admissions requirements/recommendations:** High school units required (recommended): English: 4; Mathematics: 3; Science: 1; Foreign language: 2; Social studies: 2; History: 0; Academic electives: 4; Total units: 16. Tests: The college uses SAT or ACT scores in admissions decisions. Either SAT or ACT required. For admission to the fall 2007 entering class, the school will accept: ACT with writing. Campus visit: Recommended. Admissions interview: Recommended. Off-campus interview: Not available. **Factors that count in admissions decisions:** *Academic:* Secondary school record: Very important. Class rank: Considered. Letters of recommendation: Very important. Standardized test scores: Very important. Essay: Very important. *Nonacademic:* Interview: Considered. Extracurricular activities: Important. Talent/ability: Considered. Character/personal qualities: Considered. Alumni/ae relationship: Not considered. Geographical residence: Not considered. State residency: Not considered. Religious affiliation/commitment: Not considered. Minority status: Not considered. Volunteer work: Important. Work experience: Important. **Other schools with the greatest overlap in applicants:** Quinnipiac University; Rutgers–New Brunswick; Sacred Heart University; St. Peter's College; Villanova University. **Admissions statistics for the fall 2005 entering class:** Total applicants: 4,982. Total accepted: 4,160. Freshmen enrolled: 1,120; 30% were from out of

state. Overall acceptance rate: 84%. **Size of waiting list:** 899 applicants; enrolled from waiting list: 633. **Credentials of fall 2005 freshmen:** 25% ranked in the top 10 percent of their high school class; 51% were in the top 25 percent, and 84% were in the top half. (Proportion submitting class standing: 58%.) **Average high school grade point average:** 3.3. **First-year students who submitted SAT scores:** 99%. Scores (25/75 percentile): Verbal: 500-610, Math: 510-610, Combined: 1010-1220.

ACADEMICS

Year founded: 1856. **Academic calendar:** Semester. **Degrees offered:** bachelor's, master's, post-master's certificate, first professional, doctorate. **Most popular majors:** 21% business, management, marketing, and related support services, 16% health professions and related clinical sciences, 13% communication, journalism, and related programs, 8% social sciences, 7% education. **Major fields of study:** area, ethnic, cultural, and gender studies; biological and biomedical sciences; business, management, marketing, and related support services; communication, journalism, and related programs; computer and information sciences and support services; education; English language and literature/letters; foreign languages, literatures, and linguistics; health professions and related clinical sciences; history; liberal arts and sciences studies, and humanities; mathematics and statistics; parks, recreation, leisure, and fitness studies; philosophy and religious studies; physical sciences; psychology; public administration and social service professions; security and protective services; social sciences; theology and religious vocations; visual and performing arts. **Areas of required coursework:** humanities, mathematics, English (including composition), philosophy, foreign languages, sciences (biological or physical), social science. **Pre-professional programs:** pre-law, pre-dentistry, pre-medicine, pre-theology. **Special academic programs (% participation):** accelerated program (4%), cooperative (work-study plan) program, cross-registration, distance learning (2%), double major (4%), dual enrollment, English as a Second Language (ESL), honors program (2%), independent study, internships, liberal arts/career combination (5%), study abroad (3%), teacher certificate program (9%). **Teacher certification offered in:** special education, elementary, middle/junior high, secondary. **Cooperative education programs:** art, business, computer science, education, health professions, humanities, natural science, social/behavioral science. **Reserve Officers Training Corps (ROTC):** Army ROTC: Offered on campus. **Faculty and instruction (2005-2006):** Total instructional faculty: 441 full-time, 485 part-time (55% men; 45% women; 14% minorities). Full-time faculty with Ph.D. or other terminal degree: 90%. Student/faculty ratio: 14/1. Classes of fewer than 20 students: 50%; of 20 to 49 students: 49%; of 50 or more students: 2%. **Advanced Placement and International Baccalaureate credit:** AP tests may be used for: Credit and/or placement. Scores accepted: 4, 5. International Baccalaureate exams may be used for: Credit and/or placement. **Freshmen returning for sophomore year:** 81%. **Graduation rates:** Four-year: 41%; five-year: 54%; six-year: 56%. **Graduate study:** 25% of students pursue further study immediately upon graduation; 30% within one year.

COSTS AND FINANCIAL AID

Financial aid office: (973) 761-9350. **Expenses (2006-2007):** Tuition and fees 2006-2007: $24,720; room/board: $10,466. Estimated books and supplies: $1,300; transportation: $1,400; personal expenses: $1,800. **Financial aid:** Priority filing date for institution's financial aid form: February 15. In 2005-2006, 72% of undergraduates applied for financial aid. Of those, 61% were determined to have financial need; 22% had their need fully met. Average financial aid package (proportion receiving): $15,660 (61%). Average amount of gift aid, such as scholarships or grants (proportion receiving): $4,757 (38%). Average amount of self-help aid, such as work study or loans (proportion receiving): $3,888 (45%). Average need-based loan (excluding PLUS or other private loans): $3,622. Among students who received need-based aid, the average percentage of need met: 66%. Among students who received aid based on merit, the average award (and the proportion receiving): $11,959 (17%). The average athletic scholarship (and the proportion receiving): $22,210 (4%). Proportion who borrowed: 66%.

CAMPUS LIFE AND EXTRACURRICULAR ACTIVITIES

Campus housing available (% using): coed dorms (89%), apartment for single students (11%), special housing for disabled students. Students who live in college-owned, operated, or affiliated housing: 43%. **Student employment:** During the 2005-2006 academic year, 22% of undergraduates worked on campus. Average per-year earnings: $1,500. **Clubs and organizations:** Number of student organizations: 109. Activities include: choral groups, dance, drama/theater, literary magazine, music ensembles, musical theater, pep band, radio station, student government, student newspaper, student film society, television station. Number of fraternities: 12; sororities: 13.

Proportion of men in fraternities: 5%; of women in sororities: 3%. Average proportion of students who stay on campus on weekends: 63%. **Sports program (2005-2006):** Member of NCAA I. **Men's intercollegiate varsity sports:** baseball, basketball, cross-country, golf, soccer, swimming and diving, track and field (indoor), track and field (outdoor). **Women's intercollegiate varsity sports:** basketball, cross-country, soccer, softball, swimming and diving, tennis, track and field (indoor), track and field (outdoor), volleyball.

SERVICES AND FACILITIES

Basic services: nonremedial tutoring, health service, health insurance. **Remedial assistance:** reading, math, writing, study skills. **Counseling services:** career, personal, academic, psychological, religious. **For learning-disabled students:** School does not offer a structured program with separate admission and additional fees. Total undergraduates in learning-disabled program or receiving services: 372. Services include: remedial math, reading machines, remedial reading, tape recorders, diagnostic testing service, untimed tests, note-taking services, special bookstore section, oral tests, learning center, readers, extended time for tests, tutors, priority registration, priority seating, substitution of courses, texts on tape, exams on tape or computer, waiver of foreign language degree requirement, waiver of math degree requirement, other. **Library:** Number of titles: 538,000; number of current serial subscriptions: 1,305. **Information technology resources:** Students are required to lease or own a computer. Number of campus computers available to all students: 5,000. School has a wireless network. Approximate number of users that can be accommodated: 5,000. Proportion of college-owned housing units wired for high-speed internet access: 100%. **Campus safety:** Security services offered: 24-hour foot-and-vehicle patrols, late-night transport/escort service, 24-hour emergency telephones, lighted pathways/sidewalks, controlled dormitory access (key, security card, etc).

TRANSFER AND INTERNATIONAL STUDENTS

Transfer students: May apply for admission for the following academic terms: Fall, Spring. Applicants do not need a minimum number of credits to apply. For fall 2005: Transfer applications received: 763. Transfer applicants offered admission: 615. Transfer applicants enrolled: 275. **International students:** Number of foreign undergraduates: 50 (1% of student body). Number of countries represented: 54. Minimum TOEFL score required: 550 (paper); 213 (computer).

Stevens Institute of Technology

- **Address:** Castle Point on Hudson, Hoboken, NJ 07030
- **Website:** http://www.stevens.edu
- **Private**
- **Enrollment:** 1,788 full-time; 1 part-time

KEY STATS

- ✔ **U.S News College Ranking:** 77, National Universities
- ✔ **SAT Score (25th/75th percentile):** 1180-1370
- ✔ **Tuition:** 2006-2007: $32,995

Selectivity: More selective	Room/board: $10,000
Acceptance rate: 47%	Average debt: $14,700
Student/faculty ratio: 8/1	Proportion who borrowed: 68%

UNDERGRADUATE STUDENT BODY STATS

2005-2006 enrollment: 1,788 full-time; 1 part-time. Men: 75%; women: 25%. **Ethnic makeup:** African American: 5%; Asian American: 13%; Hispanic: 9%; White: 68%; International: 5%.

ADMISSIONS FACTS AND FIGURES

Phone: (201) 216-5194. **Email:** admissions@stevens.edu. **Website:** http://www.stevens.edu. **Application deadlines for fall 2007:** Regular decision: February 15; decision sent by March 15. Early decision: Send application by: November 15; Decision sent by: December 15. Early action: Not offered. Admission can be deferred. **Application fee:** $55. Common application is accepted. **To apply online, go to:** https://apply.embark.com/ugrad/stevens/14/. **Admissions requirements/recommendations:** High school units required (recommended): English: 4 (4); Mathematics: 4 (4); Science: 3 (4); Foreign language: (2); Social studies: (2); History: (2); Academic electives: (4); Total units: 14 (26). Tests: The college uses SAT or ACT scores in admissions decisions. Either SAT or ACT required. For admission to the fall 2007 entering class, the school will accept: ACT with writing, ACT without writing. Campus visit: Recommended. Admissions interview: Required. Off-campus interview: May be arranged. **Factors that count in admissions decisions:** *Academic:* Secondary school record: Very important. Class rank: Important. Letters of recommendation: Very important. Standardized test scores: Very important. Essay: Very important. *Nonacademic:* Interview: Very important. Extracurricular activities: Very important. Talent/ability: Important. Character/personal qualities: Very important. Alumni/ae relationship: Considered. Geographical residence: Not considered. State residency: Not considered. Religious affiliation/commitment: Not considered. Minority status: Not considered. Volunteer work: Very important. Work experience: Very important. **Other schools with the greatest overlap in applicants:** Carnegie Mellon University; Columbia University; Massachusetts Institute of Technology; Rensselaer Polytechnic Institute; Rutgers–New Brunswick. **Admissions statistics for the fall 2005 entering class:** Total applicants: 2,418. Total accepted: 1,131. Freshmen enrolled: 484; 39% were from out of state. Accepted through early-decision or early-action plans: 32%. Overall acceptance rate: 47%. Early-decision acceptance rate: 70%. Non-early acceptance rate: 44%. **Size of waiting list:** 269 applicants; enrolled from waiting list: 27. **Credentials of fall 2005 freshmen:** 49% ranked in the top 10 percent of their high school class; 81% were in the top 25 percent, and 96% were in the top half. (Proportion submitting class standing: 62%.) **Average high school grade point average:** 3.7. **First-year students who submitted SAT scores:** 95%. Scores (25/75 percentile): Verbal: 560-660, Math: 620-710, Combined: 1180-1370. **First-year students submitting ACT scores:** 10%. Scores (25/75 percentile): English: N/A, Math: N/A, Composite: 24-28.

ACADEMICS

Year founded: 1870. **Academic calendar:** Semester. **Degrees offered:** certificate, bachelor's, post-bachelor's certificate, master's, doctorate. **Most popular majors:** 66% engineering, 18% computer and information sciences and support services, 10% business, management, marketing, and related support services, 4% biological and biomedical sciences, 2% liberal arts and sciences studies, and humanities. **Major fields of study:** biological and biomedical sciences; business, management, marketing, and related support services; computer and information sciences and support services; engineering; engineering technologies/technicians; liberal arts and sciences studies, and humanities; mathematics and statistics; multi/interdisciplinary studies; physical sciences; social sciences; visual and performing arts. **Areas of required coursework:** humanities, computer literacy, mathematics, English (including composition), philosophy, sciences (biological or physical), history, social science, other. **Pre-professional programs:** pre-law, pre-dentistry, pre-medicine. **Special academic programs (% participation):** accelerated program (1%), cooperative (work-study plan) program (35%), cross-registration (5%), distance learning (0%), double major (16%), dual enrollment (5%), honors program (12%), independent study (4%), internships (45%), study abroad (5%). **Cooperative education programs:** computer science, engineering, natural science. **Reserve Officers Training Corps (ROTC):** Army ROTC: Offered at cooperating institution (Seton Hall University); Air Force ROTC: Offered at cooperating institution (New Jersey Institute of Technology). **Faculty and instruction (2005-2006):** Total instructional faculty: 210 full-time, 124 part-time. Full-time faculty with Ph.D. or other terminal degree: 91%. Student/faculty ratio: 8/1. Classes of fewer than 20 students: 45%; of 20 to 49 students: 49%; of 50 or more students: 7%. **Advanced Placement and International Baccalaureate credit:** AP tests may be used for: Credit and/or placement. Scores accepted: 4, 5. International Baccalaureate exams may be used for: Credit and/or placement. **Freshmen returning for sophomore year:** 89%. **Graduation rates:** Four-year: 31%; five-year: 66%; six-year: 72%. **Graduate study:** 12% of students pursue further study immediately upon graduation. Fields in which graduates pursue further study: Master of Business Administration (MBA), 14%; law, 5%; medicine, 17%; engineering, 36%; arts and sciences, 28%.

COSTS AND FINANCIAL AID

Financial aid office: (201) 216-5555. **Expenses (2006-2007):** Tuition and fees 2006-2007: $32,995; room/board: $10,000. Estimated books and supplies: $900 personal expenses: $750. **Financial aid:** Priority filing date for institution's financial aid form: February 15. In 2005-2006, 92% of undergraduates applied for financial aid. Of those, 80% were determined to have financial need; 17% had their need fully met. Average financial aid package (proportion receiving): $21,139 (68%). Average amount of gift aid, such as scholarships or grants (proportion receiving): $12,406 (54%). Average amount of self-help aid, such as work study or loans (proportion receiving): $4,823 (56%). Average need-based loan (excluding PLUS or other private loans): $4,158. Among students who received need-based aid, the average percentage of need met: 80%. Among students who received aid based on merit, the average award (and the proportion receiving): $10,977 (17%). The average athletic scholarship (and the proportion receiving): $0 (0%). Average amount of debt of borrowers graduating in 2005: $14,700. Proportion who borrowed: 68%.

CAMPUS LIFE AND EXTRACURRICULAR ACTIVITIES

Campus housing available (% using): coed dorms (71%), women's dorms (1%), sorority housing (3%), fraternity housing (13%), apartment for single students (12%), special housing for disabled students (0%). Students who live in college-owned, operated, or affiliated housing: 75%. **Student employment:** During the 2005-2006 academic year, 10% of undergraduates worked on campus. Average per-year earnings: $500. **Clubs and organizations:** Number of student organizations: 85. Activities include: choral groups, concert band, dance, drama/theater, jazz band, literary magazine, music ensembles, musical theater, pep band, radio station, student government, student newspaper, student film society, television station, yearbook. Number of fraternities: 10; sororities: 5. Proportion of men in fraternities: 34%; of women in sororities: 31%. Average proportion of students who stay on campus on weekends: 70%. **Sports program (2005-2006):** Member of NCAA III. *Men's intercollegiate varsity sports:* baseball, basketball, cross-country, fencing, lacrosse, soccer, swimming and diving, tennis, track and field (indoor), track and field (outdoor), volleyball, wrestling. *Women's intercollegiate varsity sports:* basketball, cross-country, equestrian sports, fencing, field hockey, lacrosse, soccer, swimming and diving, tennis, track and field (indoor), track and field (outdoor), volleyball.

SERVICES AND FACILITIES

Basic services: nonremedial tutoring, women's center, placement service, health service, health insurance. **Counseling services:** career, personal, academic, psychological. **For learning-disabled students:** School does not offer a structured program with separate admission and additional fees. Total undergraduates in learning-disabled program or receiving services: 15. Services include: untimed tests, oral tests, extended time for tests, tutors. **Library:** Number of titles: 114,736; number of current serial subscriptions: 8,314. **Information technology resources:** Students are not required to lease or own a computer. Number of campus computers available to all students: 2,000. School has a wireless network. Approximate number of users that can be accommodated: 3,000. Proportion of college-owned housing units wired for high-speed internet access: 99%. **Campus safety:** Security services offered: 24-hour foot-and-vehicle patrols, late-night transport/escort service, 24-hour emergency telephones, lighted pathways/sidewalks, controlled dormitory access (key, security card, etc).

TRANSFER AND INTERNATIONAL STUDENTS

Transfer students: May apply for admission for the following academic terms: Fall, Spring. Applicants need a minimum number of credits to apply. For fall 2005: Transfer applications received: 123. Transfer applicants offered admission: 56. Transfer applicants enrolled: 34. **International students:** Number of foreign undergraduates: 84 (5% of student body). Number of countries represented: 28. Minimum TOEFL score required: 550 (paper); 213 (computer).

St. Peter's College

- **Address:** 2641 Kennedy Boulevard, Jersey City, NJ 07306-5997
- **Website:** http://www.spc.edu
- **Private; Religious affiliation:** Jesuit Catholic
- **Enrollment:** 1,815 full-time; 411 part-time

KEY STATS

✔ **U.S News College Ranking:** third tier, Universities–Master's (North)
✔ **SAT Score (25th/75th percentile):** 860-1050
✔ **Tuition:** 2006-2007: $22,650

Selectivity: Less selective	**Room/board:** $9,260
Acceptance rate: 69%	**Average debt:** N/A
Student/faculty ratio: 13/1	**Proportion who borrowed:** N/A

UNDERGRADUATE STUDENT BODY STATS

2005-2006 enrollment: 1,815 full-time; 411 part-time. Men: 46%; women: 54%. **Ethnic makeup:** African American: 22%; Asian American: 7%; Hispanic: 24%; White: 44%; International: 3%. **Religious preference:** Roman Catholic: 60%; Protestant: 5%; Muslim: 2%; No preference: 10%; Hindu and Buddhist: 1%; Other: 22%.

ADMISSIONS FACTS AND FIGURES

Phone: (201) 915-9213. **Email:** admissions@spc.edu. **Website:** http://www.spc.edu. **Application deadlines for fall 2007:** Regular decision: August 15. Early decision: Not offered. Early action: Not offered. Admission can be deferred. Common application is accepted. **Admissions requirements/recommendations:** High school units required (recommended): English: 4 (4); Mathematics: 3 (4); Science: 2 (3); Foreign language: 3 (3); Social studies: 3 (3); History: 3 (3); Academic electives: 3 (3); Total units: 22 (24). Tests: The college uses SAT or ACT scores in admissions decisions. Either SAT or ACT required. For admission to the fall 2007 entering class, the school will accept: ACT with writing, ACT without writing. Campus visit: Recommended. Admissions interview: Recommended. Off-campus interview: May be arranged. **Factors that count in admissions decisions:** *Academic:* Secondary school record: Very important. Class rank: Important. Letters of recommendation: Important. Standardized test scores: Very important. Essay: Very important. *Nonacademic:* Interview: Considered. Extracurricular activities: Important. Talent/ability: Considered. Character/personal qualities: Considered. Alumni/ae relationship: Considered. Geographical residence: Considered. State residency: Considered. Religious affiliation/commitment: Not considered. Minority status: Not considered. Volunteer work: Considered. Work experience: Considered. **Admissions statistics for the fall 2005 entering class:** Total applicants: 2,863. Total accepted: 1,966. Freshmen enrolled: 491; 19% were from out of state. Overall acceptance rate: 69%. **Size of waiting list:** 100 applicants; enrolled from waiting list: 40. **Credentials of fall 2005 freshmen:** 13% ranked in the top 10 percent of their high school class; 37% were in the top 25 percent. **Average high school grade point average:** 3.1. **First-year students who submitted SAT scores:** 98%. Scores (25/75 percentile): Verbal: 420-520, Math: 440-530, Combined: 860-1050. **First-year students submitting ACT scores:** 7%. Scores (25/75 percentile): English: N/A, Math: N/A, Composite: 15-24.

ACADEMICS

Year founded: 1872. **Academic calendar:** Semester. **Degrees offered:** certificate, associate, bachelor's, master's. **Most popular majors:** 16% business administration and management, 9% elementary education and teaching, 9% marketing/marketing management, 7% accounting, 7% criminal justice/safety studies. **Major fields of study:** area, ethnic, cultural, and gender studies; biological and biomedical sciences; business, management, marketing, and related support services; communication, journalism, and related programs; computer and information sciences and support services; education; English language and literature/letters; foreign languages, literatures, and linguistics; health professions and related clinical sciences; history; liberal arts and sciences studies, and humanities; mathematics and statistics; multi/interdisciplinary studies; philosophy and religious studies; physical sciences; psychology; public administration and social service professions; security and protective services; social sciences; visual and performing arts. **Areas of required coursework:** arts/fine arts, humanities, computer literacy, mathematics, English (including composition), philosophy, foreign languages, sciences (biological or physical), history, social science, other. **Preprofessional programs:** pre-law, pre-dentistry, pre-medicine, pre-theology, pre-pharmacy. **Special academic programs:** cooperative (work-study plan) program, distance learning, double major, English as a Second Language (ESL), honors program, independent study, internships, student-designed major, study abroad, teacher certificate program. **Teacher certification offered in:** elementary, secondary. **Cooperative education programs:** art, business, computer science, education, humanities, natural science, social/behavioral science, other. **Reserve Officers Training Corps (ROTC):** Army ROTC: Offered at cooperating institution (Seton Hall University); Air Force ROTC: Offered at cooperating institution (New Jersey Institute of Technology (NJIT)). **Faculty and instruction (2005-2006):** Total instructional faculty: 104 full-time, 207 part-time (65% men; 35% women); 18% minorities). Full-time faculty with Ph.D. or other terminal degree: 82%. Student/faculty ratio: 13/1. Classes of fewer than 20 students: 67%; of 20 to 49 students: 33%; of 50 or more students: 0%. **Advanced Placement and International Baccalaureate credit:** AP tests may be used for: Credit and/or placement. Scores accepted: 3, 4, 5. International Baccalaureate exams may be used for: Credit only. **Freshmen returning for sophomore year:** 72%. **Graduation rates:** Four-year: 34%; five-year: 46%; six-year: 46%.

COSTS AND FINANCIAL AID

Financial aid office: (201) 915-4929. **Expenses (2006-2007):** Tuition and fees 2006-2007: $22,650; room/board: $9,260. Estimated books and supplies:

$700; transportation: $1,050; personal expenses: $600. **Financial aid:** In 2005-2006, 99% of undergraduates applied for financial aid. Of those, 65% were determined to have financial need; 13% had their need fully met. Average financial aid package (proportion receiving): $17,370 (64%). Average amount of gift aid, such as scholarships or grants (proportion receiving): $8,033 (59%). Average amount of self-help aid, such as work study or loans (proportion receiving): $3,425 (45%). Average need-based loan (excluding PLUS or other private loans): $3,397. Among students who received need-based aid, the average percentage of need met: 75%. Among students who received aid based on merit, the average award (and the proportion receiving): $11,437 (14%). The average athletic scholarship (and the proportion receiving): $14,645 (6%).

CAMPUS LIFE AND EXTRACURRICULAR ACTIVITIES

Campus housing available (% using): coed dorms (94%), other housing options (6%). Students who live in college-owned, operated, or affiliated housing: 44%. **Student employment:** During the 2005-2006 academic year, 20% of undergraduates worked on campus. Average per-year earnings: $2,000. **Clubs and organizations:** Number of student organizations: 24. Activities include: choral groups, drama/theater, literary magazine, radio station, student government, student newspaper, yearbook. Number of fraternities: 0; sororities: 0. Average proportion of students who stay on campus on weekends: 40%. **Sports program (2005-2006):** Member of NCAA I. *Men's intercollegiate varsity sports:* baseball, basketball, cross-country, football, golf, soccer, swimming and diving, tennis, track and field (indoor), track and field (outdoor). *Women's intercollegiate varsity sports:* basketball, bowling, cross-country, soccer, softball, swimming and diving, tennis, track and field (indoor), track and field (outdoor), volleyball.

SERVICES AND FACILITIES

Basic services: nonremedial tutoring, placement service, health service, health insurance. **Remedial assistance:** reading, math, writing, study skills. **Counseling services:** minority student, career, personal, veteran student, academic, older student, psychological, birth control, religious. **For learning-disabled students:** School does not offer a structured program with separate admission and additional fees. Total undergraduates in learning-disabled program or receiving services: 36. Services include: remedial math, remedial English, reading machines, remedial reading, tape recorders, diagnostic testing service, untimed tests, note-taking services, oral tests, learning center, readers, extended time for tests, tutors, priority registration, priority seating, other testing accomodations. **Library:** Number of titles: 250,000; number of current serial subscriptions: 1,594. **Information technology resources:** Students are not required to lease or own a computer. Number of campus computers available to all students: 325. School has a wireless network. Approximate number of users that can be accommodated: 1,800. Proportion of college-owned housing units wired for high-speed internet access: 90%. **Campus safety:** Security services offered: 24-hour foot-and-vehicle patrols, late-night transport/escort service, 24-hour emergency telephones, lighted pathways/sidewalks, controlled dormitory access (key, security card, etc).

TRANSFER AND INTERNATIONAL STUDENTS

Transfer students: May apply for admission for the following academic terms: Fall, Winter, Spring, Summer. Applicants need a minimum number of credits to apply. For fall 2005: Transfer applications received: 152. Transfer applicants offered admission: 99. Transfer applicants enrolled: 43. **International students:** Number of foreign undergraduates: 57 (3% of student body). Number of countries represented: 15. Minimum TOEFL score required: 520 (paper); 190 (computer).

Thomas Edison State College

- **Address:** 101 W. State Street, Trenton, NJ 08608-1176
- **Website:** http://www.tesc.edu
- **Public**
- **Enrollment:** N/A; 10,904 part-time

KEY STATS

✔ **U.S News College Ranking:** Unranked, Universities–Master's (North)
✔ **SAT or ACT Score (25th/75th percentile):** N/A
✔ **Tuition:** 2005-2006: $3,780 in state, $5,400 out of state

Selectivity: N/A	Room/board: N/A
Acceptance rate: N/A	Average debt: N/A
Student/faculty ratio: N/A	Proportion who borrowed: N/A

UNDERGRADUATE STUDENT BODY STATS

2005-2006 enrollment: N/A full-time; 10,904 part-time. Men: 56%; women: 44%. **Ethnic makeup:** African American: 12%; American-Indian: 1%; Asian American: 2%; Hispanic: 6%; White: 77%; International: 2%.

ADMISSIONS FACTS AND FIGURES

Phone: (888) 442-8372. **Email:** admissions@tesc.edu. **Website:** http://www.tesc.edu. **Application deadlines for fall 2007:** Regular decision: Rolling. Early decision: Not offered. Early action: Not offered. Admission cannot be deferred. **Application fee:** $75. Common application is not accepted. **To apply online, go to:** https://ssl.tesc.edu/public/f_colreg2.html. **Admissions requirements/recommendations:** Tests: The college does not use SAT or ACT scores in admissions decisions. Neither SAT nor ACT required.

ACADEMICS

Year founded: 1972. **Academic calendar:** Continuos. **Degrees offered:** certificate, associate, bachelor's, post-bachelor's certificate, master's. **Most popular majors:** 27% liberal arts and sciences/liberal studies, 15% nuclear engineering technology/technician, 5% business administration and management, 5% humanities/humanistic studies, 5% psychology. **Major fields of study:** agriculture, agriculture operations, and related sciences; biological and biomedical sciences; business, management, marketing, and related support services; communication, journalism, and related programs; computer and information sciences and support services; engineering technologies/technicians; English language and literature/letters; family and consumer sciences/human sciences; foreign languages, literatures, and linguistics; health professions and related clinical sciences; history; legal professions and studies; liberal arts and sciences studies, and humanities; mathematics and statistics; mechanic and repair technologies/technicians; multi/interdisciplinary studies; natural resources and conservation; parks, recreation, leisure, and fitness studies; philosophy and religious studies; psychology; public administration and social service professions; security and protective services; social sciences; transportation and materials moving; visual and performing arts. **Areas of required coursework:** humanities, mathematics, English (including composition), sciences (biological or physical), social science. **Special academic programs:** distance learning, external degree program, independent study, other. **Advanced Placement and International Baccalaureate credit:** AP tests may be used for: Credit only. Scores accepted: 3, 4, 5. International Baccalaureate exams may be used for: Credit only.

COSTS AND FINANCIAL AID

Financial aid office: (609) 633-9658. **Expenses (2005-2006):** Tuition and fees 2005-2006: $3,780 in state, $5,400 out of state; room/board: N/A.

SERVICES AND FACILITIES

Counseling services: military, veteran student, academic, older student, other. **For learning-disabled students:** School does not offer a structured program with separate admission and additional fees. Total undergraduates in learning-disabled program or receiving services: 8. Services include: extended time for tests, substitution of courses, texts on tape, exams on tape or computer, other testing accomodations, other. **Information technology resources:** Students are not required to lease or own a computer. School has a wireless network.

TRANSFER AND INTERNATIONAL STUDENTS

Transfer students: May apply for admission for the following academic terms: Fall, Winter, Spring, Summer. Applicants do not need a minimum number of credits to apply. **International students:** Number of foreign undergraduates: 232 (2% of student body). Number of countries represented: 76. Minimum TOEFL score required: 500 (paper); 173 (computer).

William Paterson University of New Jersey

- **Address:** 300 Pompton Road, Wayne, NJ 07470
- **Website:** http://ww2.wpunj.edu/
- **Public**
- **Enrollment:** 7,472 full-time; 1,638 part-time

KEY STATS
✔ **U.S News College Ranking:** third tier, Universities–Master's (North)
✔ **SAT Score (25th/75th percentile):** 900-1090
✔ **Tuition:** 2005-2006: $8,740 in state, $13,856 out of state

Selectivity: Selective	**Room/board:** $9,070
Acceptance rate: 67%	**Average debt:** $11,483
Student/faculty ratio: 15/1	**Proportion who borrowed:** 50%

UNDERGRADUATE STUDENT BODY STATS
2005-2006 enrollment: 7,472 full-time; 1,638 part-time. Men: 42%; women: 58%. **Ethnic makeup:** African American: 13%; Asian American: 6%; Hispanic: 17%; White: 63%; International: 1%. **Religious preference:** Roman Catholic: 41%; Protestant: 13%; Jewish: 3%; Muslim: 4%; Hindu: 1%; Buddhist: 1%; No preference: 13%; Unknown: 4%; Other: 7%.

ADMISSIONS FACTS AND FIGURES
Phone: (973) 720-2125. **Email:** admissions@wpunj.edu. **Website:** http://ww2.wpunj.edu/. **Application deadlines for fall 2007:** Regular decision: May 1. Early decision: Not offered. Early action: Not offered. Admission can be deferred. **Application fee:** $50. Common application is accepted. **To apply online, go to:** http://ww2.wpunj.edu/admissn/apply_now.cfm. **Admissions requirements/recommendations:** High school units required (recommended): English: 4; Mathematics: 3; Science: 2; Social studies: 2; Total units: 16. Tests: The college uses SAT or ACT scores in admissions decisions. Either SAT or ACT required. For admission to the fall 2007 entering class, the school will accept: ACT with writing, ACT without writing. Campus visit: Recommended. Admissions interview: Neither required nor recommended. Off-campus interview: May be arranged. **Factors that count in admissions decisions:** *Academic:* Secondary school record: Very important. Class rank: Very important. Letters of recommendation: Considered. Standardized test scores: Very important. Essay: Considered. *Nonacademic:* Interview: Considered. Extracurricular activities: Considered. Talent/ability: Considered. Character/personal qualities: Considered. Alumni/ae relationship: Considered. Geographical residence: Considered. State residency: Not considered. Religious affiliation/commitment: Not considered. Volunteer work: Considered. Work experience: Not considered. **Other schools with the greatest overlap in applicants:** Kean University; Montclair State University; Ramapo College of New Jersey; Rutgers–New Brunswick. **Admissions statistics for the fall 2005 entering class:** Total applicants: 5,380. Total accepted: 3,592. Freshmen enrolled: 1,421; 2% were from out of state. Overall acceptance rate: 67%. **Size of waiting list:** 80 applicants; enrolled from waiting list: 60. **Credentials of fall 2005 freshmen:** 12% ranked in the top 10 percent of their high school class; 30% were in the top 25 percent, and 68% were in the top half. (Proportion submitting class standing: 69%.) **First-year students who submitted SAT scores:** 98%. Scores (25/75 percentile): Verbal: 450-540, Math: 450-550, Combined: 900-1090.

ACADEMICS
Year founded: 1855. **Academic calendar:** Semester. **Degrees offered:** bachelor's, post-bachelor's certificate, master's, post-master's certificate. **Most popular majors:** 17% business, management, marketing, and related support services, 17% social sciences, 15% communication, journalism, and related programs, 11% psychology, 9% education. **Major fields of study:** area, ethnic, cultural, and gender studies; biological and biomedical sciences; business, management, marketing, and related support services; communication, journalism, and related programs; computer and information sciences and support services; education; English language and literature/letters; foreign languages, literatures, and linguistics; health professions and related clinical sciences; history; mathematics and statistics; natural resources and conservation; philosophy and religious studies;

physical sciences; psychology; social sciences; visual and performing arts. **Areas of required coursework:** arts/fine arts, humanities, mathematics, English (including composition), philosophy, foreign languages, sciences (biological or physical), history, social science, other. **Pre-professional programs:** pre-law, pre-dentistry, pre-medicine, pre-veterinary science. **Special academic programs (% participation):** accelerated program, cross-registration, distance learning, double major (2%), dual enrollment, English as a Second Language (ESL), exchange student program (domestic), honors program, independent study, internships, study abroad, teacher certificate program (22%), other. **Teacher certification offered in:** early childhood, special education, elementary, middle/junior high, secondary, bilingual/bicultural. **Reserve Officers Training Corps (ROTC):** Air Force ROTC: Offered at cooperating institution (New Jersey Institute of Technology). **Faculty and instruction (2005-2006):** Total instructional faculty: 372 full-time, 699 part-time (54% men; 46% women; 21% minorities). Full-time faculty with Ph.D. or other terminal degree: 90%. Student/faculty ratio: 15/1. Classes of fewer than 20 students: 44%; of 20 to 49 students: 55%; of 50 or more students: 1%. **Advanced Placement and International Baccalaureate credit:** AP tests may be used for: Credit only. Scores accepted: 3, 4, 5. **Freshmen returning for sophomore year:** 77%. **Graduation rates:** Four-year: 15%; five-year: 41%; six-year: 48%. **Graduate study:** 23% of students pursue further study within one year. Fields in which graduates pursue further study: law, 3%; medicine, 3%; education, 28%.

COSTS AND FINANCIAL AID
Financial aid office: (973) 720-2202. **Expenses (2005-2006):** Tuition and fees 2005-2006: $8,740 in state, $13,856 out of state; room/board: $9,070. Estimated books and supplies: $906; transportation: $1,040; personal expenses: $1,545. **Financial aid:** Priority filing date for institution's financial aid form: April 1; deadline: April 1. In 2005-2006, 67% of undergraduates applied for financial aid. Of those, 53% were determined to have financial need; 24% had their need fully met. Average financial aid package (proportion receiving): $10,130 (50%). Average amount of gift aid, such as scholarships or grants (proportion receiving): $5,955 (28%). Average amount of self-help aid, such as work study or loans (proportion receiving): $3,900 (40%). Average need-based loan (excluding PLUS or other private loans): $3,800. Among students who received need-based aid, the average percentage of need met: 83%. Among students who received aid based on merit, the average award (and the proportion receiving): $4,694 (1%). The average athletic scholarship (and the proportion receiving): $0 (0%). Average amount of debt of borrowers graduating in 2005: $11,483. Proportion who borrowed: 50%.

CAMPUS LIFE AND EXTRACURRICULAR ACTIVITIES
Campus housing available (% using): coed dorms (60%), apartment for single students (2%), special housing for disabled students (4%), other housing options (34%). Students who live in college-owned, operated, or affiliated housing: 24%. **Student employment:** During the 2005-2006 academic year, 3% of undergraduates worked on campus. **Clubs and organizations:** Number of student organizations: 83. Activities include: choral groups, concert band, dance, drama/theater, jazz band, literary magazine, music ensembles, musical theater, opera, pep band, radio station, student government, student newspaper, student film society, symphony orchestra, television station, yearbook. Number of fraternities: 6; sororities: 110. Proportion of men in fraternities: 1%; of women in sororities: 2%. Average proportion of students who stay on campus on weekends: 55%. **Sports program (2005-2006):** Member of NCAA III. *Men's intercollegiate varsity sports:* baseball, basketball, cross-country, football, soccer, swimming and diving, track and field (indoor), track and field (outdoor). *Women's intercollegiate varsity sports:* basketball, cross-country, field hockey, soccer, softball, swimming and diving, tennis, track and field (indoor), track and field (outdoor), volleyball.

SERVICES AND FACILITIES
Basic services: nonremedial tutoring, women's center, placement service, day care, health service, health insurance. **Remedial assistance:** reading, math, writing, study skills. **Counseling services:** minority student, career, personal, veteran student, academic, older student, psychological, birth control, religious. **For learning-disabled students:** School does not offer a structured program with separate admission and additional fees. Total undergraduates in learning-disabled program or receiving services: 203. Services include: remedial math, remedial English, reading machines, remedial reading, tape recorders, note-taking services, oral tests, readers, extended time for tests, tutors, texts on tape, other testing accomodations, other. **Library:** Number of titles: 372,437; number of current serial sub-

scriptions: 22,000. **Information technology resources:** Students are not required to lease or own a computer. Number of campus computers available to all students: 900. School has a wireless network. Proportion of college-owned housing units wired for high-speed internet access: 100%. **Campus safety:** Security services offered: 24-hour foot-and-vehicle patrols, late-night transport/escort service, 24-hour emergency telephones, lighted pathways/sidewalks, student patrols, controlled dormitory access (key, security card, etc).

TRANSFER AND INTERNATIONAL STUDENTS

Transfer students: May apply for admission for the following academic terms: Fall, Spring. Applicants need a minimum number of credits to apply. For fall 2005: Transfer applications received: 2,488. Transfer applicants offered admission: 1,326. Transfer applicants enrolled: 758. **International students:** Number of foreign undergraduates: 131 (1% of student body). Number of countries represented: 50. Minimum TOEFL score required: 550 (paper); 213 (computer).

New Mexico

College of Santa Fe

- **Address:** 1600 St. Michael's Drive, Santa Fe, NM 87505
- **Website:** http://www.csf.edu
- **Private**
- **Enrollment:** 640 full-time; 702 part-time

KEY STATS
- ✔ **U.S News College Ranking:** 29, Universities–Master's (West)
- ✔ **SAT Score (25th/75th percentile):** 990-1200
- ✔ **Tuition:** 2006-2007: $24,444

Selectivity: Selective	**Room/board:** $7,292
Acceptance rate: 73%	**Average debt:** $17,540
Student/faculty ratio: 7/1	**Proportion who borrowed:** 63%

UNDERGRADUATE STUDENT BODY STATS
2005-2006 enrollment: 640 full-time; 702 part-time. Men: 42%; women: 58%. **Ethnic makeup:** African American: 3%; American-Indian: 3%; Asian American: 1%; Hispanic: 26%; White: 65%; International: 1%. **Religious preference:** Roman Catholic: 2%; Protestant: 1%; No preference: 97%.

ADMISSIONS FACTS AND FIGURES
Phone: (505) 473-6133. **Email:** admissions@csf.edu. **Website:** http://www.csf.edu. **Application deadlines for fall 2007:** Regular decision: Rolling. Early decision: Not offered. Early action: Not offered. Admission can be deferred. **Application fee:** $35. Common application is accepted. **Admissions requirements/recommendations:** High school units required (recommended): English: 4 (4); Mathematics: 2 (3); Science: 2 (3); Foreign language: 0 (2); Social studies: 2 (2); History: 0 (2); Academic electives: 6 (4); Total units: 18 (22). Tests: The college uses SAT or ACT scores in admissions decisions. Either SAT or ACT required. For admission to the fall 2007 entering class, the school will accept: ACT with writing. Campus visit: Recommended. Admissions interview: Required. Off-campus interview: May be arranged. **Factors that count in admissions decisions: *Academic:*** Secondary school record: Very important. Class rank: Important. Letters of recommendation: Important. Standardized test scores: Important. Essay: Important. ***Nonacademic:*** Interview: Very important. Extracurricular activities: Important. Talent/ability: Very important. Character/personal qualities: Very important. Alumni/ae relationship: Considered. Geographical residence: Not considered. State residency: Not considered. Religious affiliation/commitment: Not considered. Minority status: Not considered. Volunteer work: Important. Work experience: Considered. **Admissions statistics for the fall 2005 entering class:** Total applicants: 598. Total accepted: 437. Freshmen enrolled: 129; 82% were from out of state. Overall acceptance rate: 73%. **Credentials of fall 2005 freshmen:** 9% ranked in the top 10 percent of their high school class; 30% were in the top 25 percent, and 65% were in the top half. (Proportion submitting class standing: 61%.) **Average high school grade point average:** 3.2. **First-year students who submitted SAT scores:** 73%. Scores (25/75 percentile): Verbal: 520-630, Math: 470-570, Combined: 990-1200. **First-year students submitting ACT scores:** 35%. Scores (25/75 percentile): English: 18-27, Math: 16-24, Composite: 18-25.

ACADEMICS
Year founded: 1874. **Academic calendar:** Semester. **Degrees offered:** associate, terminal-associate, bachelor's, master's. **Most popular majors:** 18% art/art studies, 17% film/cinema studies, 11% psychology, 10% drama and dramatics/theater arts, 8% creative writing. **Major fields of study:** area, ethnic, cultural, and gender studies; biological and biomedical sciences; business, management, marketing, and related support services; communication, journalism, and related programs; computer and information sciences and support services; education; English language and literature/letters; health professions and related clinical sciences; liberal arts and sciences studies, and humanities; multi/interdisciplinary studies; natural resources and conservation; philosophy and religious studies; psychology; public administration and social service professions; security and protective services; social sciences; visual and performing arts. **Areas of required coursework:** arts/fine arts, humanities, mathematics, English (including composition), philosophy, sciences (biological or physical), social science. **Pre-professional programs:** pre-law, pre-theology. **Special academic programs:** accelerated program, cooperative (work-study plan) program, double major, dual enrollment, exchange student program (domestic), independent study, internships, student-designed major, study abroad, teacher certificate program. **Teacher certification offered in:** elementary, middle/junior high, secondary, bilingual/bicultural. **Cooperative education programs:** art, business, other. **Reserve Officers Training Corps (ROTC):** Air Force ROTC: Offered at cooperating institution (University of New Mexico). **Faculty and instruction (2005-2006):** Total instructional faculty: 76 full-time, 199 part-time (57% men; 43% women; 12% minorities). Full-time faculty with Ph.D. or other terminal degree: 80%. Student/faculty ratio: 7/1. Classes of fewer than 20 students: 88%; of 20 to 49 students: 12%; of 50 or more students: 0%. **Advanced Placement and International Baccalaureate credit:** AP tests may be used for: Credit and/or placement. Scores accepted: 3, 4, 5. **Freshmen returning for sophomore year:** 70%. **Graduation rates:** Four-year: 21%; five-year: 36%; six-year: 40%. **Graduate study:** 21% of students pursue further study immediately upon graduation.

COSTS AND FINANCIAL AID
Financial aid office: (505) 473-6454. **Expenses (2006-2007):** Tuition and fees 2006-2007: $24,444; room/board: $7,292. Estimated books and supplies: $840; transportation: $618; personal expenses: $1,226. **Financial aid:** Priority filing date for institution's financial aid form: March 15. In 2005-2006, 76% of undergraduates applied for financial aid. Of those, 67% were determined to have financial need; 12% had their need fully met. Average financial aid package (proportion receiving): $18,934 (67%). Average amount of gift aid, such as scholarships or grants (proportion receiving): $10,083 (60%). Average amount of self-help aid, such as work study or loans (proportion receiving): $5,857 (62%). Average need-based loan (excluding PLUS or other private loans): $4,700. Among students who received need-based aid, the average percentage of need met: 77%. Among students who received aid based on merit, the average award (and the proportion receiving): $4,011 (15%). The average athletic scholarship (and the proportion receiving): $20,037 (1%). Average amount of debt of borrowers graduating in 2005: $17,540. Proportion who borrowed: 63%.

CAMPUS LIFE AND EXTRACURRICULAR ACTIVITIES
Campus housing available: coed dorms, women's dorms, men's dorms, apartment for single students, special housing for disabled students. Students who live in college-owned, operated, or affiliated housing: 62%. **Student employment:** During the 2005-2006 academic year, 40% of undergraduates worked on campus. Average per-year earnings: $2,000. **Clubs and organizations:** Number of student organizations: 18. Activities include: choral groups, dance, drama/theater, literary magazine, music ensembles, musical theater, student government, student newspaper, television station, yearbook. Number of fraternities: 0; sororities: 0. Average proportion of students who stay on campus on weekends: 75%. **Sports program (2005-2006):** Member of NAIA. ***Men's intercollegiate varsity sports:*** tennis. ***Women's intercollegiate varsity sports:*** tennis.

SERVICES AND FACILITIES
Basic services: nonremedial tutoring, placement service, health service, health insurance. **Remedial assistance:** study skills. **Counseling services:** career, personal, veteran student, academic, older student, psychological, birth control, religious. **For learning-disabled students:** School does not offer a structured program with separate admission and additional fees. Services include: reading machines, tape recorders, other special classes, videotaped classes, untimed tests, note-taking services, oral tests, learning center, readers, extended time for tests, tutors. **Information technology resources:** Students are not required to lease or own a computer. Number of campus computers available to all students: 74. School has a wireless network. Proportion of college-owned housing units wired for high-speed internet access: 100%. **Campus safety:** Security services offered: 24-hour foot-and-vehicle patrols, late-night transport/escort service, lighted pathways/sidewalks, controlled dormitory access (key, security card, etc).

Transfer students: May apply for admission for the following academic terms: Fall, Spring, Summer. Applicants need a minimum number of credits to apply. For fall 2005: Transfer applications received: 147. Transfer applicants offered admission: 101. Transfer applicants enrolled: 57. **International students:** Number of foreign undergraduates: 8 (1% of student body). Number of countries represented: 8. Minimum TOEFL score required: 550 (paper); 213 (computer).

College of the Southwest

- **Address:** 6610 Lovington Highway, Hobbs, NM 88240
- **Website:** http://www.csw.edu
- **Private**
- **Enrollment:** 392 full-time; 136 part-time

KEY STATS

✔ **U.S News College Ranking:** fourth tier, Universities–Master's (West)
✔ **ACT Score (25th/75th percentile):** 15-20
✔ **Tuition:** 2006-2007: $8,425

Selectivity: Less selective	**Room/board:** $5,400
Acceptance rate: 50%	**Average debt:** $17,420
Student/faculty ratio: 11/1	**Proportion who borrowed:** 66%

UNDERGRADUATE STUDENT BODY STATS

2005-2006 enrollment: 392 full-time; 136 part-time. Men: 39%; women: 61%. **Ethnic makeup:** African American: 4%; American-Indian: 8%; Asian American: 4%; Hispanic: 37%; White: 42%; International: 6%.

ADMISSIONS FACTS AND FIGURES

Phone: (505) 392-6563. **Email:** Admissions@csw.edu. **Website:** http://www.csw.edu. **Application deadlines for fall 2007:** Regular decision: Rolling. Early decision: Not offered. Early action: Not offered. Admission can be deferred. **Application fee:** $25. Common application is not accepted. **Admissions requirements/recommendations:** Tests: The college uses SAT or ACT scores in admissions decisions. Either SAT or ACT required. For admission to the fall 2007 entering class, the school will accept: ACT with writing, ACT without writing. Campus visit: Recommended. Admissions interview: Recommended. Off-campus interview: May be arranged. **Factors that count in admissions decisions:** *Academic:* Secondary school record: Very important. Class rank: Very important. Letters of recommendation: Considered. Standardized test scores: Very important. Essay: Not considered. *Nonacademic:* Interview: Important. Extracurricular activities: Important. Talent/ability: Very important. Character/personal qualities: Important. Alumni/ae relationship: Not considered. Geographical residence: Not considered. State residency: Not considered. Religious affiliation/commitment: Not considered. Minority status: Not considered. Volunteer work: Not considered. Work experience: Not considered. **Other schools with the greatest overlap in applicants:** Eastern New Mexico University; New Mexico State University; Texas Tech University. **Admissions statistics for the fall 2005 entering class:** Total applicants: 2,015. Total accepted: 998. Freshmen enrolled: 240; 50% were from out of state. Overall acceptance rate: 50%. **Credentials of fall 2005 freshmen:** 14% ranked in the top 10 percent of their high school class; 45% were in the top 25 percent, and 81% were in the top half. (Proportion submitting class standing: 96%.) **Average high school grade point average:** 3.2. **First-year students who submitted SAT scores:** 44%. Scores (25/75 percentile): Verbal: 370-500, Math: 370-540, Combined: 740-1040. **First-year students submitting ACT scores:** 56%. Scores (25/75 percentile): English: 12-20, Math: 15-20, Composite: 15-20.

ACADEMICS

Year founded: 1962. **Academic calendar:** Semester. **Degrees offered:** bachelor's, master's. **Most popular majors:** 47% education, 20% psychology, 18% criminal justice/law enforcement administration, 16% business/commerce, 6% English language and literature. **Major fields of study:** biological and biomedical sciences; business, management, marketing, and related support services; computer and information sciences and support services; education; English language and literature/letters; history; liberal arts and sciences studies, and humanities; mathematics and statistics; psychology; public administration and social service professions; security and protective services; social sciences; visual and performing arts. **Areas of required**

coursework: arts/fine arts, humanities, computer literacy, mathematics, English (including composition), sciences (biological or physical), history, social science, other. **Special academic programs (% participation):** distance learning (19%), double major (1%), internships (75%), teacher certificate program (35%). **Teacher certification offered in:** early childhood, special education, elementary, middle/junior high, secondary, bilingual/bicultural. **Cooperative education programs:** other. **Faculty and instruction (2005-2006):** Total instructional faculty: 27 full-time, 47 part-time (50% men; 50% women; 7% minorities). Full-time faculty with Ph.D. or other terminal degree: 63%. Student/faculty ratio: 11/1. Classes of fewer than 20 students: 86%; of 20 to 49 students: 14%; of 50 or more students: 0%. **Advanced Placement and International Baccalaureate credit:** AP tests may be used for: Credit only. Scores accepted: 3, 4, 5. International Baccalaureate exams may be used for: Credit only. **Freshmen returning for sophomore year:** 58%. **Graduation rates:** Four-year: 11%; five-year: 30%; six-year: 34%.

COSTS AND FINANCIAL AID

Financial aid office: (505) 392-6561. **Expenses (2006-2007):** Tuition and fees 2006-2007: $8,425; room/board: $5,400. Estimated books and supplies: $1,200; transportation: $1,200; personal expenses: $1,000. **Financial aid:** Priority filing date for institution's financial aid form: April 1; deadline: August 1. In 2005-2006, 98% of undergraduates applied for financial aid. Of those, 83% were determined to have financial need; 38% had their need fully met. Average financial aid package (proportion receiving): $8,437 (81%). Average amount of gift aid, such as scholarships or grants (proportion receiving): $4,104 (60%). Average amount of self-help aid, such as work study or loans (proportion receiving): $2,091 (12%). Average need-based loan (excluding PLUS or other private loans): $3,768. Among students who received need-based aid, the average percentage of need met: 62%. Among students who received aid based on merit, the average award (and the proportion receiving): $3,402 (16%). The average athletic scholarship (and the proportion receiving): $4,368 (21%). Average amount of debt of borrowers graduating in 2005: $17,420. Proportion who borrowed: 66%.

CAMPUS LIFE AND EXTRACURRICULAR ACTIVITIES

Campus housing available (% using): coed dorms (76%), women's dorms, apartment for single students (24%), special housing for disabled students. Students who live in college-owned, operated, or affiliated housing: 31%. **Student employment:** During the 2005-2006 academic year, 13% of undergraduates worked on campus. Average per-year earnings: $1,164. Activities include: drama/theater, literary magazine, musical theater, student government. Number of fraternities: 0; sororities: 0. Average proportion of students who stay on campus on weekends: 30%. **Sports program (2005-2006):** Member of NAIA. *Men's intercollegiate varsity sports:* baseball, cross-country, golf, soccer, track and field (indoor), track and field (outdoor). *Women's intercollegiate varsity sports:* cross-country, golf, soccer, softball, track and field (indoor), track and field (outdoor), volleyball.

SERVICES AND FACILITIES

Basic services: placement service. **Remedial assistance:** math, writing, study skills, other. **Counseling services:** personal, academic, psychological. **For learning-disabled students:** School does not offer a structured program with separate admission and additional fees. Total undergraduates in learning-disabled program or receiving services: 15. Services include: remedial math, remedial English, tape recorders, diagnostic testing service, untimed tests, note-taking services, oral tests, learning center, readers, extended time for tests, tutors, priority seating, texts on tape, other testing accomodations. **Library:** Number of titles: 76,217; number of current serial subscriptions: 287. **Information technology resources:** Students are not required to lease or own a computer. Number of campus computers available to all students: 80. School does not have a wireless network. Proportion of college-owned housing units wired for high-speed internet access: 100%. **Campus safety:** Security services offered: late-night transport/escort service, controlled dormitory access (key, security card, etc).

TRANSFER AND INTERNATIONAL STUDENTS

Transfer students: May apply for admission for the following academic terms: Fall, Winter, Spring, Summer. Applicants need a minimum number of credits to apply. For fall 2005: Transfer applications received: 176. Transfer applicants offered admission: 122. Transfer applicants enrolled: 83. **International students:** Number of foreign undergraduates: 8 (6% of student body). Number of countries represented: 27. Minimum TOEFL score required: 550 (paper); 213 (computer).

Eastern New Mexico University

- **Address:** Station 2, Portales, NM 88130
- **Website:** http://www.enmu.edu
- **Public**
- **Enrollment:** 2,510 full-time; 781 part-time

KEY STATS

✔ **U.S News College Ranking:** third tier, Universities–Master's (West)
✔ **ACT Score (25th/75th percentile):** 16-22
✔ **Tuition:** 2006-2007: $2,964 in state, $8,520 out of state

Selectivity: Less selective	**Room/board:** $4,568
Acceptance rate: 65%	**Average debt:** $10,772
Student/faculty ratio: 17/1	**Proportion who borrowed:** N/A

UNDERGRADUATE STUDENT BODY STATS

2005-2006 enrollment: 2,510 full-time; 781 part-time. Men: 44%; women: 56%. **Ethnic makeup:** African American: 7%; American-Indian: 3%; Asian American: 1%; Hispanic: 30%; White: 58%; International: 1%.

ADMISSIONS FACTS AND FIGURES

Phone: (505) 562-2178. **Email:** admissions.office@enmu.edu. **Website:** http://www.enmu.edu. **Application deadlines for fall 2007:** Regular decision: Rolling. Early decision: Not offered. Early action: Not offered. Admission can be deferred. Common application is not accepted. **To apply online, go to:** http://www.enmu.edu/admissions/apply/application.html. **Admissions requirements/recommendations:** High school units required (recommended): English: (4); Mathematics: (3); Science: (4); Foreign language: (1); Social studies: (2); Total units: (14). Tests: The college uses SAT or ACT scores in admissions decisions. Either SAT or ACT required. For admission to the fall 2007 entering class, the school will accept: ACT with writing, ACT without writing. Campus visit: Neither required nor recommended. Admissions interview: Neither required nor recommended. **Factors that count in admissions decisions:** *Academic:* Secondary school record: Very important. Class rank: Not considered. Letters of recommendation: Considered. Standardized test scores: Very important. Essay: Not considered. *Nonacademic:* Interview: Considered. Extracurricular activities: Considered. Talent/ability: Considered. Character/personal qualities: Not considered. Alumni/ae relationship: Not considered. Geographical residence: Not considered. State residency: Not considered. Religious affiliation/commitment: Not considered. Minority status: Not considered. Volunteer work: Not considered. Work experience: Not considered. **Admissions statistics for the fall 2005 entering class:** Total applicants: 1,804. Total accepted: 1,167. Freshmen enrolled: 567; 23% were from out of state. Overall acceptance rate: 65%. **Credentials of fall 2005 freshmen:** 12% ranked in the top 10 percent of their high school class; 34% were in the top 25 percent, and 67% were in the top half. (Proportion submitting class standing: 82%.) **Average high school grade point average:** 3.2. **First-year students who submitted SAT scores:** 9%. Scores (25/75 percentile): Verbal: 390-540, Math: 380-550, Combined: 770-1090. **First-year students submitting ACT scores:** 92%. Scores (25/75 percentile): English: 15-21, Math: 16-20, Composite: 16-22.

ACADEMICS

Year founded: 1934. **Academic calendar:** Semester. **Degrees offered:** associate, transfer-associate, bachelor's, master's. **Most popular majors:** 22% education, 17% business, management, marketing, and related support services, 11% liberal arts and sciences studies, and humanities, 6% visual and performing arts. **Major fields of study:** agriculture, agriculture operations, and related sciences; biological and biomedical sciences; business, management, marketing, and related support services; communication, journalism, and related programs; computer and information sciences and support services; education; engineering technologies/technicians; English language and literature/letters; family and consumer sciences/human sciences; foreign languages, literatures, and linguistics; health professions and related clinical sciences; history; liberal arts and sciences studies, and humanities; mathematics and statistics; multi/interdisciplinary studies; natural resources and conservation; parks, recreation, leisure, and fitness studies; philosophy and religious studies; physical sciences; psychology; public administration and social service professions; security and protective services; social sciences; visual and performing arts. **Areas of required coursework:** arts/fine arts, humanities, mathematics, English (including composition), sciences (biological or physical), social science, other. **Pre-professional programs:** pre-dentistry, pre-medicine, pre-veterinary science, pre-pharmacy. **Special academic programs:** accelerated program, cooperative (work-study plan) program, distance learning, double major, dual enrollment, exchange student program (domestic), honors program, independent study, internships, student-designed major, study abroad, teacher certificate program. **Teacher certification offered in:** early childhood, special education, elementary, vo-tech, secondary, bilingual/bicultural. **Cooperative education programs:** other. **Faculty and instruction (2005-2006):** Total instructional faculty: 149 full-time, 114 part-time (53% men; 47% women; 11% minorities). Full-time faculty with Ph.D. or other terminal degree: 78%. Student/faculty ratio: 17/1. Classes of fewer than 20 students: 52%; of 20 to 49 students: 43%; of 50 or more students: 5%. **Advanced Placement and International Baccalaureate credit:** AP tests may be used for: Credit only. Scores accepted: 3, 4, 5. **Freshmen returning for sophomore year:** 59%. **Graduation rates:** Four-year: 10%; five-year: 27%; six-year: 32%.

COSTS AND FINANCIAL AID

Financial aid office: (800) 367-3668. **Expenses (2006-2007):** Tuition and fees 2006-2007: $2,964 in state, $8,520 out of state; room/board: $4,568. **Financial aid:** In 2005-2006, 67% of undergraduates applied for financial aid. Of those, 67% were determined to have financial need; 82% had their need fully met. Average financial aid package (proportion receiving): $7,598 (67%). Average amount of gift aid, such as scholarships or grants (proportion receiving): $3,202 (59%). Average amount of self-help aid, such as work study or loans (proportion receiving): $4,139 (51%). Average need-based loan (excluding PLUS or other private loans): $4,215. Among students who received need-based aid, the average percentage of need met: 49%. Among students who received aid based on merit, the average award (and the proportion receiving): $3,140 (3%). The average athletic scholarship (and the proportion receiving): $2,359 (9%). Average amount of debt of borrowers graduating in 2005: $10,772.

CAMPUS LIFE AND EXTRACURRICULAR ACTIVITIES

Campus housing available: coed dorms, women's dorms, sorority housing, fraternity housing, apartments for married students, apartment for single students, special housing for disabled students. Students who live in college-owned, operated, or affiliated housing: 27%. **Clubs and organizations:** Number of student organizations: 56. Activities include: choral groups, concert band, dance, drama/theater, jazz band, literary magazine, marching band, music ensembles, musical theater, pep band, radio station, student government, student newspaper, student film society, symphony orchestra, television station, yearbook. Number of fraternities: 6; sororities: 2. **Sports program (2005-2006):** Member of NCAA II. *Men's intercollegiate varsity sports:* baseball, basketball, cross-country, football, soccer, track and field (outdoor). *Women's intercollegiate varsity sports:* basketball, cross-country, soccer, softball, tennis, track and field (outdoor), volleyball.

SERVICES AND FACILITIES

Remedial assistance: reading, math, writing. **Counseling services:** career, personal, academic, psychological, birth control. **For learning-disabled students:** School does not offer a structured program with separate admission and additional fees. Total undergraduates in learning-disabled program or receiving services: 40. Services include: tape recorders, videotaped classes, note-taking services, oral tests, readers, extended time for tests, tutors, proofreading services, substitution of courses, texts on tape, typist/scribe, other testing accomodations, other. **Library:** Number of titles: 764,560; number of current serial subscriptions: 17,200. **Information technology resources:** Students are not required to lease or own a computer. Number of campus computers available to all students: 482. School does not have a wireless network. **Campus safety:** Security services offered: 24-hour foot-and-vehicle patrols, late-night transport/escort service, 24-hour emergency telephones, lighted pathways/sidewalks, student patrols.

TRANSFER AND INTERNATIONAL STUDENTS

Transfer students: May apply for admission for the following academic terms: Fall, Spring, Summer. Applicants do not need a minimum number of credits to apply. For fall 2005: Transfer applications received: 1,141. Transfer applicants offered admission: 484. Transfer applicants enrolled: 310. **International students:** Number of foreign undergraduates: 29 (1% of student body). Number of countries represented: 16. Minimum TOEFL score required: 500 (paper).

New Mexico Highlands University

- **Address:** Box 9000, Las Vegas, NM 87701
- **Website:** http://www.nmhu.edu
- **Public**
- **Enrollment:** 1,292 full-time; 599 part-time

KEY STATS

- ✔ **U.S News College Ranking:** fourth tier, Universities–Master's (West)
- ✔ **ACT Score (25th/75th percentile):** 16-20
- ✔ **Tuition:** 2005-2006: $2,304 in state, $10,176 out of state

Selectivity: Less selective	**Room/board:** $3,456
Acceptance rate: 78%	**Average debt:** N/A
Student/faculty ratio: 22/1	**Proportion who borrowed:** N/A

UNDERGRADUATE STUDENT BODY STATS

2005-2006 enrollment: 1,292 full-time; 599 part-time. Men: 38%; women: 62%. **Ethnic makeup:** African American: 5%; American-Indian: 8%; Asian American: 1%; Hispanic: 60%; White: 25%.

ADMISSIONS FACTS AND FIGURES

Phone: (505) 454-3439. **Email:** admissions@nmhu.edu. **Website:** http://www.nmhu.edu. **Application deadlines for fall 2007:** Regular decision: Rolling. Early decision: Not offered. Early action: Not offered. Admission can be deferred. **Application fee:** $15. Common application is accepted. **Admissions requirements/recommendations:** Tests: The college uses SAT or ACT scores in admissions decisions. ACT required. Campus visit: Recommended. Admissions interview: Recommended. Off-campus interview: May be arranged. **Other schools with the greatest overlap in applicants:** Adams State College; Eastern New Mexico University; Fort Lewis College; New Mexico State University; University of New Mexico. **Admissions statistics for the fall 2005 entering class:** Total applicants: 1,774. Total accepted: 1,382. Freshmen enrolled: 237; 7% were from out of state. Overall acceptance rate: 78%. **Size of waiting list:** 0 applicants; enrolled from waiting list: 0. **Credentials of fall 2005 freshmen:** 12% ranked in the top 10 percent of their high school class; 32% were in the top 25 percent, and 54% were in the top half. (Proportion submitting class standing: 85%.) **Average high school grade point average:** 3.0. **First-year students who submitted SAT scores:** 7%. Scores (25/75 percentile): Verbal: 370-480, Math: 380-480, Combined: 750-960. **First-year students submitting ACT scores:** 76%. Scores (25/75 percentile): English: 14-28, Math: 14-28, Composite: 16-20.

ACADEMICS

Year founded: 1893. **Academic calendar:** Semester. **Degrees offered:** bachelor's, master's. **Most popular majors:** 28% education, 27% clinical/medical social work, 20% business, management, marketing, and related support services, 4% political science and government, 2% psychology. **Major fields of study:** biological and biomedical sciences; business, management, marketing, and related support services; communication, journalism, and related programs; computer and information sciences and support services; education; engineering; English language and literature/letters; family and consumer sciences/human sciences; foreign languages, literatures, and linguistics; health professions and related clinical sciences; history; mathematics and statistics; natural resources and conservation; parks, recreation, leisure, and fitness studies; physical sciences; psychology; security and protective services; social sciences; visual and performing arts. **Areas of required coursework:** arts/fine arts, humanities, computer literacy, mathematics, English (including composition), sciences (biological or physical), history, social science. **Pre-professional programs:** pre-law, pre-medicine. **Special academic programs:** cooperative (work-study plan) program, distance learning, double major, English as a Second Language (ESL), independent study, internships, study abroad, teacher certificate program. **Teacher certification offered in:** early childhood, special education, elementary, secondary, bilingual/bicultural. **Faculty and instruction (2005-2006):** Total instructional faculty: 77 full-time, 26 part-time (56% men; 44% women; 33% minorities). Student/faculty ratio: 22/1. Classes of fewer than 20 students: 74%; of 20 to 49 students: 25%; of 50 or more students: 1%. **Advanced Placement and International Baccalaureate credit:** AP tests may be used for: Credit and/or placement. Scores accepted: 3, 4, 5. **Freshmen returning for sophomore year:** 51%. **Graduation rates:** Six-year: 21%.

COSTS AND FINANCIAL AID

Financial aid office: (505) 454-3430. **Expenses (2005-2006):** Tuition and fees 2005-2006: $2,304 in state, $10,176 out of state; room/board: $3,456. Estimated books and supplies: $758; transportation: $2,110; personal expenses: $1,616. **Financial aid:** Priority filing date for institution's financial aid form: March 1.

CAMPUS LIFE AND EXTRACURRICULAR ACTIVITIES

Campus housing available (% using): coed dorms (43%), women's dorms (12%), men's dorms (30%), apartments for married students (15%). **Clubs and organizations:** Number of student organizations: 31. Activities include: choral groups, drama/theater, music ensembles, pep band, student government, student newspaper. Number of fraternities: 0; sororities: 0. Average proportion of students who stay on campus on weekends: 30%. **Sports program (2005-2006):** Member of NCAA II. *Men's intercollegiate varsity sports:* baseball, basketball, cross-country, football, wrestling. *Women's intercollegiate varsity sports:* basketball, cross-country, soccer, softball, track and field (outdoor), volleyball.

SERVICES AND FACILITIES

Basic services: nonremedial tutoring, placement service, day care, health service. **Remedial assistance:** reading, math, writing, study skills. **Counseling services:** minority student, career, academic, psychological. **For learning-disabled students:** School does not offer a structured program with separate admission and additional fees. Services include: remedial math, remedial English, reading machines, remedial reading, tape recorders, other special classes, videotaped classes, diagnostic testing service, untimed tests, note-taking services, oral tests, learning center, readers, extended time for tests, tutors. **Library:** Number of titles: 431,037; number of current serial subscriptions: 519. **Information technology resources:** Students are not required to lease or own a computer. Number of campus computers available to all students: 350. School has a wireless network. Proportion of college-owned housing units wired for high-speed internet access: 99%. **Campus safety:** Security services offered: 24-hour foot-and-vehicle patrols, lighted pathways/sidewalks, controlled dormitory access (key, security card, etc).

TRANSFER AND INTERNATIONAL STUDENTS

Transfer students: May apply for admission for the following academic terms: Fall, Spring, Summer. Applicants need a minimum number of credits to apply. For fall 2005: Transfer applications received: 444. Transfer applicants offered admission: 401. Transfer applicants enrolled: 390. **International students:** Number of foreign undergraduates: 6. Number of countries represented: 7. Minimum TOEFL score required: 540 (paper); 207 (computer).

New Mexico Institute of Mining and Tech.

- **Address:** 801 Leroy Place, Socorro, NM 87801
- **Website:** http://www.nmt.edu
- **Public**
- **Enrollment:** 1,125 full-time; 263 part-time

KEY STATS

- ✔ **U.S News College Ranking:** third tier, National Universities
- ✔ **ACT Score (25th/75th percentile):** 24-29
- ✔ **Tuition:** 2005-2006: $3,644 in state, $10,463 out of state

Selectivity: More selective	**Room/board:** $4,866
Acceptance rate: 81%	**Average debt:** $7,292
Student/faculty ratio: 11/1	**Proportion who borrowed:** 58%

UNDERGRADUATE STUDENT BODY STATS

2005-2006 enrollment: 1,125 full-time; 263 part-time. Men: 68%; women: 32%. **Ethnic makeup:** African American: 1%; American-Indian: 3%; Asian American: 3%; Hispanic: 20%; White: 70%; International: 3%.

ADMISSIONS FACTS AND FIGURES

Phone: (505) 835-5424. **Email:** admission@admin.nmt.edu. **Website:** http://www.nmt.edu. **Application deadlines for fall 2007:** Regular decision: August 1. Early decision: Not offered. Early action: Not offered. Admission can be deferred. **Application fee:** $15. Common application is not accepted. **To apply online, go to:** http://www.nmt.edu/mainpage/admission/app-form/homepage.html. **Admissions requirements/recommendations:** High school units required (recommended): English: 4 (4); Mathematics: 3 (4); Science: 2 (4); Foreign language: 0 (2); Social studies: 2 (3); History: 1 (1); Academic electives: 3 (0); Total units: 15 (18). Tests: The college uses SAT or ACT scores in admissions decisions. Either SAT or ACT required. For admission to the fall 2007 entering class, the school will accept: ACT with writing, ACT without writing. Campus visit: Recommended. Admissions interview: Neither required nor recommended. Off-campus interview: Not available. **Factors that count in admissions decisions:** *Academic:* Secondary school record: Very important. Class rank: Considered. Letters of recommendation: Not considered. Standardized test scores: Very important. Essay: Not considered. *Nonacademic:* Interview: Not considered. Extracurricular activities: Considered. Talent/ability: Considered. Character/personal qualities: Not considered. Alumni/ae relationship: Not considered. Geographical residence: Not considered. State residency: Not considered. Religious affiliation/commitment: Not considered. Minority status: Not considered. Volunteer work: Not considered. Work experience: Not considered. **Other schools with the greatest overlap in applicants:** Colorado School of Mines; Massachusetts Institute of Technology; New Mexico State University; Texas Tech University; University of New Mexico. **Admissions statistics for the fall 2005 entering class:** Total applicants: 428. Total accepted: 346. Freshmen enrolled: 281; 15% were from out of state. Overall acceptance rate: 81%. **Credentials of fall 2005 freshmen:** 41% ranked in the top 10 percent of their high school class; 71% were in the top 25 percent, and 88% were in the top half. (Proportion submitting class standing: 80%.) **Average high school grade point average:** 3.6. **First-year students who submitted SAT scores:** 46%. Scores (25/75 percentile): Verbal: 560-670, Math: 570-680, Combined: 1130-1350. **First-year students submitting ACT scores:** 85%. Scores (25/75 percentile): English: 23-29, Math: 24-29, Composite: 24-29.

ACADEMICS

Year founded: 1889. **Academic calendar:** Semester. **Degrees offered:** associate, terminal-associate, bachelor's, master's, doctorate. **Most popular majors:** 16% electrical, electronics, and communications engineering, 10% computer science, 10% mathematics, 10% physics, 9% chemical engineering. **Major fields of study:** biological and biomedical sciences; business, management, marketing, and related support services; computer and information sciences and support services; engineering; English language and literature/letters; liberal arts and sciences studies, and humanities; mathematics and statistics; physical sciences; psychology. **Areas of required coursework:** humanities, computer literacy, mathematics, English (including composition), sciences (biological or physical), social science. **Pre-professional programs:** pre-dentistry, pre-medicine, pre-veterinary science, pre-pharmacy. **Special academic programs:** accelerated program, cooperative (work-study plan) program, distance learning, double major, dual enrollment, exchange student program (domestic), independent study, internships, student-designed major, study abroad, teacher certificate program. **Teacher certification offered in:** secondary. **Faculty and instruction (2005-2006):** Total instructional faculty: 125 full-time, 22 part-time (78% men; 22% women; 16% minorities). Full-time faculty with Ph.D. or other terminal degree: 99%. Student/faculty ratio: 11/1. Classes of fewer than 20 students: 58%; of 20 to 49 students: 37%; of 50 or more students: 5%. **Advanced Placement and International Baccalaureate credit:** AP tests may be used for: Credit and/or placement. Scores accepted: 3, 4, 5. **Freshmen returning for sophomore year:** 74%. **Graduation rates:** Four-year: 16%; five-year: 36%; six-year: 43%.

COSTS AND FINANCIAL AID

Financial aid office: (505) 835-5333. **Expenses (2005-2006):** Tuition and fees 2005-2006: $3,644 in state, $10,463 out of state; room/board: $4,866. Estimated books and supplies: $880; transportation: $1,100; personal expenses: $2,980. **Financial aid:** Priority filing date for institution's financial aid form: March 1. In 2005-2006, 87% of undergraduates applied for financial aid. Of those, 40% were determined to have financial need; 56% had their need fully met. Average financial aid package (proportion receiving): $8,040 (39%). Average amount of gift aid, such as scholarships or grants (proportion receiving): $4,186 (25%). Average amount of self-help aid, such as work study or loans (proportion receiving): $4,165 (25%). Average need-based loan (excluding PLUS or other private loans): $4,202. Among students who received need-based aid, the average percentage of need met: 93%. Among students who received aid based on merit, the average award (and the proportion receiving): $4,851 (35%). The average athletic scholarship (and the proportion receiving): $0 (0%). Average amount of debt of borrowers graduating in 2005: $7,292. Proportion who borrowed: 58%.

CAMPUS LIFE AND EXTRACURRICULAR ACTIVITIES

Campus housing available: coed dorms, women's dorms, men's dorms, apartments for married students, apartment for single students. Students who live in college-owned, operated, or affiliated housing: 59%. **Clubs and organizations:** Number of student organizations: 65. Activities include: choral groups, concert band, dance, drama/theater, jazz band, music ensembles, musical theater, radio station, student government, student newspaper. Number of fraternities: 0; sororities: 0.

SERVICES AND FACILITIES

Basic services: nonremedial tutoring, placement service, day care, health service, health insurance. **Remedial assistance:** study skills. **Counseling services:** career, personal, academic. **For learning-disabled students:** School does not offer a structured program with separate admission and additional fees. Services include: tape recorders, untimed tests, note-taking services, oral tests, readers, extended time for tests, tutors. **Library:** Number of titles: 321,829; number of current serial subscriptions: 884. **Information technology resources:** Students are not required to lease or own a computer. Number of campus computers available to all students: 200. School does not have a wireless network. **Campus safety:** Security services offered: 24-hour foot-and-vehicle patrols.

TRANSFER AND INTERNATIONAL STUDENTS

Transfer students: May apply for admission for the following academic terms: Fall, Spring, Summer. Applicants need a minimum number of credits to apply. For fall 2005: Transfer applications received: 77. Transfer applicants offered admission: 66. Transfer applicants enrolled: 66. **International students:** Number of foreign undergraduates: 33 (3% of student body). Number of countries represented: 28. Minimum TOEFL score required: 540 (paper); 207 (computer).

New Mexico State University

- **Address:** Box 30001, MSC 3004, Las Cruces, NM 88003-8001
- **Website:** http://www.nmsu.edu
- **Public**
- **Enrollment:** 10,238 full-time; 2,418 part-time

KEY STATS

✔ **U.S News College Ranking:** fourth tier, National Universities
✔ **ACT Score (25th/75th percentile):** 18-23
✔ **Tuition:** 2006-2007: $3,918 in state, $13,206 out of state

Selectivity: Selective	Room/board: $5,576
Acceptance rate: 81%	Average debt: N/A
Student/faculty ratio: N/A	Proportion who borrowed: N/A

UNDERGRADUATE STUDENT BODY STATS

2005-2006 enrollment: 10,238 full-time; 2,418 part-time. Men: 44%; women: 56%. **Ethnic makeup:** African American: 3%; American-Indian: 3%; Asian American: 1%; Hispanic: 45%; White: 47%; International: 1%.

ADMISSIONS FACTS AND FIGURES

Phone: (505) 646-3121. **Email:** admissions@nmsu.edu. **Website:** http://www.nmsu.edu. **Application deadlines for fall 2007:** Regular decision: August 28. Early decision: Not offered. Early action: Not offered. Admission can be deferred. **Application fee:** $15. Common application is not accepted. **To apply online, go to:** http://www.nmsu.edu/~admission/admit-form.html. **Admissions requirements/recommendations:** High school units required (recommended): English: 4; Mathematics: 3; Science: 2; Foreign language: 1; Total units: 10. Tests: The college uses SAT or ACT scores in admissions decisions. Either SAT or ACT required. Campus visit: Recommended. Admissions interview: Neither required nor recommended. **Factors that count in admissions decisions:** *Academic:* Secondary school record: Very important. Class rank: Not considered. Letters of recommendation: Not considered. Standardized test scores: Very important. Essay: Not considered. *Nonacademic:* Interview: Not considered. Extracurricular activities: Not considered. Talent/ability: Not considered. Character/personal qualities: Not considered. Alumni/ae relationship: Not considered. Geographical residence: Not considered. State residency: Not considered. Religious affiliation/commitment: Not considered. Minority status: Not considered. Volunteer work: Not considered. Work experience: Not considered. **Admissions statistics for the fall 2005 entering class:** Total applicants: 5,522.

Total accepted: 4,482. Freshmen enrolled: 2,019; 16% were from out of state. Overall acceptance rate: 81%. **Credentials of fall 2005 freshmen:** 20% ranked in the top 10 percent of their high school class; 49% were in the top 25 percent, and 82% were in the top half. (Proportion submitting class standing: 88%.) **Average high school grade point average:** 3.4. **First-year students who submitted SAT scores:** 13%. Scores (25/75 percentile): Verbal: N/A, Math: N/A, Combined: N/A. **First-year students submitting ACT scores:** 86%. Scores (25/75 percentile): English: 17-24, Math: 17-23, Composite: 18-23.

ACADEMICS

Year founded: 1888. **Academic calendar:** Semester. **Degrees offered:** associate, bachelor's, master's, post-master's certificate, doctorate. **Most popular majors:** 6% elementary education and teaching, 5% criminal justice/safety studies, 4% engineering technology, 4% marketing/marketing management, 3% foreign languages and literatures. **Major fields of study:** agriculture, agriculture operations, and related sciences; architecture and related services; biological and biomedical sciences; business, management, marketing, and related support services; communication, journalism, and related programs; computer and information sciences and support services; education; engineering; engineering technologies/technicians; English language and literature/letters; family and consumer sciences/human sciences; foreign languages, literatures, and linguistics; health professions and related clinical sciences; history; liberal arts and sciences studies, and humanities; mathematics and statistics; natural resources and conservation; parks, recreation, leisure, and fitness studies; philosophy and religious studies; physical sciences; psychology; public administration and social service professions; security and protective services; social sciences; visual and performing arts. **Areas of required coursework:** arts/fine arts, humanities, computer literacy, mathematics, English (including composition), philosophy, sciences (biological or physical), history, social science. **Pre-professional programs:** pre-law, pre-medicine, pre-veterinary science, other. **Special academic programs:** accelerated program, cooperative (work-study plan) program, cross-registration, distance learning, double major, dual enrollment, English as a Second Language (ESL), exchange student program (domestic), external degree program, honors program, independent study, internships, student-designed major, study abroad, teacher certificate program, weekend college. **Teacher certification offered in:** early childhood, special education, elementary, vo-tech, middle/junior high, adult education, secondary, bilingual/bicultural. **Cooperative education programs:** agriculture, business, computer science, education, engineering, home economics, natural science, technologies. **Reserve Officers Training Corps (ROTC):** Army ROTC: Offered on campus; Air Force ROTC: Offered on campus. **Faculty and instruction (2005-2006):** Total instructional faculty: 657 full-time, 247 part-time (59% men; 41% women; 14% minorities). Full-time faculty with Ph.D. or other terminal degree: 84%. Classes of fewer than 20 students: 45%; of 20 to 49 students: 43%; of 50 or more students: 12%. **Freshmen returning for sophomore year:** 72%. **Graduation rates:** Four-year: 12%; five-year: 33%; six-year: 42%.

COSTS AND FINANCIAL AID

Financial aid office: (505) 646-4105. **Expenses (2006-2007):** Tuition and fees 2006-2007: $3,918 in state, $13,206 out of state; room/board: $5,576. **Financial aid:** Priority filing date for institution's financial aid form: March 1. In 2005-2006, 68% of undergraduates applied for financial aid. Of those, 60% were determined to have financial need; 15% had their need fully met. Average financial aid package (proportion receiving): $8,728 (57%). Average amount of gift aid, such as scholarships or grants (proportion receiving): $5,947 (52%). Average amount of self-help aid, such as work study or loans (proportion receiving): $4,333 (38%). Average need-based loan (excluding PLUS or other private loans): $4,189. Among students who received need-based aid, the average percentage of need met: 65%. Among students who received aid based on merit, the average award (and the proportion receiving): $3,066 (20%). The average athletic scholarship (and the proportion receiving): $10,672 (1%).

CAMPUS LIFE AND EXTRACURRICULAR ACTIVITIES

Campus housing available: coed dorms, women's dorms, men's dorms, sorority housing, fraternity housing, apartments for married students, apartment for single students, special housing for disabled students. Students who live in college-owned, operated, or affiliated housing: 17%. **Student employment:** During the 2005-2006 academic year, 30% of undergraduates worked on campus. Average per-year earnings: $3,000. **Clubs and organizations:** Number of student organizations: 253. Activities include: choral groups, concert band, dance, drama/theater, jazz band, literary magazine, marching band, music ensembles, musical theater, opera, pep band,

radio station, student government, student newspaper, symphony orchestra, television station. Number of fraternities: 12; sororities: 6. Average proportion of students who stay on campus on weekends: 79%. **Sports program (2005-2006):** Member of NCAA I. **Men's intercollegiate varsity sports:** baseball, basketball, cross-country, football, golf, tennis. **Women's intercollegiate varsity sports:** basketball, cross-country, equestrian sports, golf, softball, swimming and diving, tennis, track and field (indoor), track and field (outdoor), volleyball.

SERVICES AND FACILITIES

Basic services: nonremedial tutoring, women's center, placement service, health service, health insurance. **Counseling services:** minority student, career, personal, veteran student, academic, older student, psychological, birth control. **For learning-disabled students:** School does not offer a structured program with separate admission and additional fees. Services include: tape recorders, diagnostic testing service, untimed tests, note-taking services, oral tests, learning center, readers, extended time for tests, tutors. **Library:** Number of titles: 1,642,678; number of current serial subscriptions: 5,975. **Information technology resources:** Students are not required to lease or own a computer. Number of campus computers available to all students: 563. School has a wireless network. Approximate number of users that can be accommodated: 3,000. Proportion of college-owned housing units wired for high-speed internet access: 100%. **Campus safety:** Security services offered: 24-hour foot-and-vehicle patrols, late-night transport/escort service, 24-hour emergency telephones, lighted pathways/sidewalks, controlled dormitory access (key, security card, etc).

TRANSFER AND INTERNATIONAL STUDENTS

Transfer students: May apply for admission for the following academic terms: Fall, Spring, Summer. Applicants need a minimum number of credits to apply. For fall 2005: Transfer applications received: 1,139. Transfer applicants offered admission: 1,059. Transfer applicants enrolled: 684. **International students:** Number of foreign undergraduates: 91 (1% of student body). Number of countries represented: 42. Minimum TOEFL score required: 500 (paper); 173 (computer).

St. John's College

- **Address:** 1160 Camino Cruz Blanca, Santa Fe, NM 87505
- **Website:** http://www.sjcsf.edu
- **Private**
- **Enrollment:** N/A

KEY STATS

✔ **U.S News College Ranking:** third tier, Liberal Arts Colleges
✔ **SAT or ACT Score (25th/75th percentile):** N/A
✔ **Tuition:** 2006-2007: $34,506

Selectivity: Selective	**Room/board:** $8,270
Acceptance rate: N/A	**Average debt:** N/A
Student/faculty ratio: N/A	**Proportion who borrowed:** N/A

University of New Mexico

- **Address:** 1 University of New Mexico, Albuquerque, NM 87131-0001
- **Website:** http://www.unm.edu
- **Public**
- **Enrollment:** 14,839 full-time; 3,886 part-time

KEY STATS

✔ **U.S News College Ranking:** third tier, National Universities
✔ **ACT Score (25th/75th percentile):** 19-24
✔ **Tuition:** 2006-2007: $4,361 in state, $14,258 out of state

Selectivity: Selective	**Room/board:** $6,590
Acceptance rate: 74%	**Average debt:** N/A
Student/faculty ratio: 20/1	**Proportion who borrowed:** N/A

UNDERGRADUATE STUDENT BODY STATS

2005-2006 enrollment: 14,839 full-time; 3,886 part-time. Men: 42%; women: 58%. **Ethnic makeup:** African American: 3%; American-Indian: 6%; Asian American: 3%; Hispanic: 35%; White: 52%; International: 1%.

ADMISSIONS FACTS AND FIGURES

Phone: (505) 277-2446. **Email:** apply@unm.edu. **Website:** http://www.unm.edu. **Application deadlines for fall 2007:** Regular decision: June 15. Early decision: Not offered. Early action: Send application by: N/A; Decision sent by: N/A. Admission can be deferred. **Application fee:** $20. Common application is not accepted. **To apply online, go to:** http://www.unm.edu/preview/na_online.htm. **Admissions requirements/recommendations:** High school units required (recommended): English: 4; Mathematics: 3; Science: 2; Foreign language: 2; Social studies: 1; History: 1; Total units: 13. Tests: The college uses SAT or ACT scores in admissions decisions. Either SAT or ACT required. For admission to the fall 2007 entering class, the school will accept: ACT without writing. Campus visit: Recommended. Admissions interview: Neither required nor recommended. Off-campus interview: Not available. **Factors that count in admissions decisions:** *Academic:* Secondary school record: Very important. Class rank: Important. Letters of recommendation: Considered. Standardized test scores: Important. Essay: Considered. *Nonacademic:* Interview: Not considered. Extracurricular activities: Considered. Talent/ability: Not considered. Character/personal qualities: Considered. Alumni/ae relationship: Not considered. Geographical residence: Not considered. State residency: Not considered. Religious affiliation/commitment: Not considered. Minority status: Not considered. Volunteer work: Considered. Work experience: Considered. **Other schools with the greatest overlap in applicants:** Arizona State University; New Mexico Institute of Mining and Technology; New Mexico State University. **Admissions statistics for the fall 2005 entering class:** Total applicants: 7,134. Total accepted: 5,254. Freshmen enrolled: 3,095; 9% were from out of state. Overall acceptance rate: 74%. Non-early acceptance rate: 74%. **Credentials of fall 2005 freshmen:** 21% ranked in the top 10 percent of their high school class; 48% were in the top 25 percent, and 78% were in the top half. (Proportion submitting class standing: 88%.) **Average high school grade point average:** 3.3. **First-year students who submitted SAT scores:** 24%. Scores (25/75 percentile): Verbal: 480-600, Math: 470-600, Combined: 950-1200. **First-year students submitting ACT scores:** 91%. Scores (25/75 percentile): English: 18-25, Math: 17-24, Composite: 19-24.

ACADEMICS

Year founded: 1889. **Academic calendar:** Semester. **Degrees offered:** associate, bachelor's, master's, post-master's certificate, first professional, doctorate. **Most popular majors:** 15% business, management, marketing, and related support services, 12% education, 9% health professions and related clinical sciences, 8% liberal arts and sciences studies, and humanities, 7% social sciences. **Major fields of study:** architecture and related services; area, ethnic, cultural, and gender studies; biological and biomedical sciences; business, management, marketing, and related support services; communication, journalism, and related programs; computer and information sciences and support services; education; engineering; English language and literature/letters; family and consumer sciences/human sciences; foreign languages, literatures, and linguistics; health professions and related clinical sciences; history; liberal arts and sciences studies, and humanities; mathematics and statistics; natural resources and conservation; philosophy and religious studies; physical sciences; psychology; public administration and social service professions; security and protective services; social sciences; visual and performing arts. **Areas of required coursework:** arts/fine arts, humanities, mathematics, English (including composition), foreign languages, sciences (biological or physical), social science. **Special academic programs:** accelerated program, cooperative (work-study plan) program, distance learning, double major, dual enrollment, English as a Second Language (ESL), exchange student program (domestic), honors program, independent study, internships, student-designed major, study abroad, teacher certificate program, weekend college. **Teacher certification offered in:** early childhood, special education, elementary, adult education, secondary, bilingual/bicultural. **Cooperative education programs:** business, engineering, other. **Reserve Officers Training Corps (ROTC):** Army ROTC: Offered on campus; Navy ROTC: Offered on campus; Air Force ROTC: Offered on campus. **Faculty and instruction (2005-2006):** Total instructional faculty: 885 full-time, 526 part-time (55% men; 45% women; 20% minorities). Full-time faculty with Ph.D. or other terminal degree: 86%. Student/faculty ratio: 20/1. Classes of fewer than 20 students: 40%; of 20 to 49 students: 47%; of 50 or more students: 14%. **Advanced Placement and International Baccalaureate credit:** AP tests may be used for: Credit and/or placement.

Scores accepted: 3, 4, 5. International Baccalaureate exams may be used for: Credit and/or placement. **Freshmen returning for sophomore year:** 76%. **Graduation rates:** Six-year: 41%.

COSTS AND FINANCIAL AID

Financial aid office: (505) 277-3012. **Expenses (2006-2007):** Tuition and fees 2006-2007: $4,361 in state, $14,258 out of state; room/board: $6,590. **Financial aid:** Priority filing date for institution's financial aid form: March 1.

CAMPUS LIFE AND EXTRACURRICULAR ACTIVITIES

Campus housing available (% using): coed dorms (40%), sorority housing (7%), fraternity housing (5%), apartments for married students (3%), apartment for single students (30%), special housing for disabled students, special housing for international students (1%), other housing options (14%). Students who live in college-owned, operated, or affiliated housing: 11%. **Clubs and organizations:** Number of student organizations: 402. Activities include: choral groups, concert band, dance, drama/theater, jazz band, literary magazine, marching band, music ensembles, musical theater, opera, pep band, radio station, student government, student newspaper, student film society, symphony orchestra, television station. Number of fraternities: 10; sororities: 9. Proportion of men in fraternities: 3%; of women in sororities: 4%. **Sports program (2005-2006):** Member of NCAA I. *Men's intercollegiate varsity sports:* alpine skiing, baseball, basketball, cross-country, football, golf, nordic skiing, soccer, tennis, track and field (indoor), track and field (outdoor). *Women's intercollegiate varsity sports:* alpine skiing, basketball, cross-country, golf, nordic skiing, soccer, softball, swimming and diving, tennis, track and field (indoor), track and field (outdoor), volleyball.

SERVICES AND FACILITIES

Basic services: nonremedial tutoring, women's center, placement service, day care, health service, health insurance. **Remedial assistance:** reading, math, writing. **Counseling services:** minority student, career, personal, veteran student, academic, psychological. **For learning-disabled students:** School does not offer a structured program with separate admission and additional fees. Services include: remedial math, remedial English, reading machines, remedial reading, tape recorders, videotaped classes, untimed tests, note-taking services, learning center, readers, extended time for tests, tutors, substitution of courses, texts on tape, typist/scribe, exams on tape or computer, other testing accomodations, other. **Library:** Number of titles: 3,276,743; number of current serial subscriptions: 13,337. **Information technology resources:** Students are not required to lease or own a computer. Number of campus computers available to all students: 459. School has a wireless network. Approximate number of users that can be accommodated: 3,900. Proportion of college-owned housing units wired for high-speed internet access: 100%. **Campus safety:** Security services offered: 24-hour foot-and-vehicle patrols, late-night transport/escort service, 24-hour emergency telephones, lighted pathways/sidewalks, student patrols, controlled dormitory access (key, security card, etc).

TRANSFER AND INTERNATIONAL STUDENTS

Transfer students: May apply for admission for the following academic terms: Fall, Spring, Summer. Applicants need a minimum number of credits to apply. For fall 2005: Transfer applications received: 2,006. Transfer applicants offered admission: 1,556. Transfer applicants enrolled: 1,048. **International students:** Number of foreign undergraduates: 127 (1% of student body). Number of countries represented: 86. Minimum TOEFL score required: 520 (paper); 190 (computer).

Western New Mexico University

- **Address:** Box 680, Silver City, NM 88062
- **Website:** http://www.wnmu.edu
- **Public**
- **Enrollment:** 1,412 full-time; 831 part-time

KEY STATS

✔ **U.S News College Ranking:** fourth tier, Universities—Master's (West)
✔ **ACT Score (25th/75th percentile):** 16-21
✔ **Tuition:** 2006-2007: $2,915 in state, $11,231 out of state

Selectivity: Less selective	**Room/board:** $4,590
Acceptance rate: 100%	**Average debt:** N/A
Student/faculty ratio: 12/1	**Proportion who borrowed:** N/A

UNDERGRADUATE STUDENT BODY STATS

2005-2006 enrollment: 1,412 full-time; 831 part-time. Men: 36%; women: 64%. **Ethnic makeup:** African American: 3%; American-Indian: 3%; Hispanic: 48%; White: 44%; International: 1%.

ADMISSIONS FACTS AND FIGURES

Phone: (505) 538-6106. **Email:** admstudnt@iron.wnmu.edu. **Website:** http://www.wnmu.edu. **Application deadlines for fall 2007:** Regular decision: August 1. Early decision: Not offered. Early action: Not offered. Admission cannot be deferred. **Application fee:** None. Common application is not accepted. **To apply online, go to:** http://www.wnmu.edu/onlineapps.htm. **Admissions requirements/recommendations:** High school units required (recommended): English: 4 (4); Mathematics: 3 (3); Science: 2 (2); Foreign language: 0; Social studies: 2 (2); History: 1 (1); Academic electives: 0; Total units: 12 (12). Tests: The college does not use SAT or ACT scores in admissions decisions. Neither SAT nor ACT required. For admission to the fall 2007 entering class, the school will accept: ACT with writing, ACT without writing. Campus visit: Recommended. Admissions interview: Neither required nor recommended. Off-campus interview: May be arranged. **Factors that count in admissions decisions:** *Academic:* Secondary school record: Not considered. Class rank: Not considered. Letters of recommendation: Not considered. Standardized test scores: Considered. Essay: Not considered. *Nonacademic:* Interview: Not considered. Extracurricular activities: Not considered. Talent/ability: Not considered. Character/personal qualities: Not considered. Alumni/ae relationship: Not considered. Geographical residence: Not considered. State residency: Not considered. Religious affiliation/commitment: Not considered. Minority status: Not considered. Volunteer work: Not considered. Work experience: Not considered. **Admissions statistics for the fall 2005 entering class:** Total applicants: 1,755. Total accepted: 1,755. Freshmen enrolled: 309; 13% were from out of state. Overall acceptance rate: 100%. **Size of waiting list:** 0 applicants; enrolled from waiting list: 0. **Credentials of fall 2005 freshmen:** 10% ranked in the top 10 percent of their high school class; 26% were in the top 25 percent; and 56% were in the top half. (Proportion submitting class standing: 70%.)

ACADEMICS

Year founded: 1893. **Academic calendar:** Semester. **Degrees offered:** certificate, associate, bachelor's, master's. **Most popular majors:** Information not available. **Major fields of study:** biological and biomedical sciences; business, management, marketing, and related support services; computer and information sciences and support services; education; English language and literature/letters; foreign languages, literatures, and linguistics; health professions and related clinical sciences; history; liberal arts and sciences studies, and humanities; mathematics and statistics; natural resources and conservation; parks, recreation, leisure, and fitness studies; physical sciences; psychology; public administration and social service professions; security and protective services; social sciences; visual and performing arts. **Areas of required coursework:** arts/fine arts, humanities, computer literacy, mathematics, English (including composition), sciences (biological or physical), history, social science. **Special academic programs:** cooperative (work-study plan) program, distance learning, double major, dual enrollment, honors program, independent study, internships, teacher certificate program. **Teacher certification offered in:** early childhood, special education, elementary, vo-tech, secondary, bilingual/bicultural. **Cooperative education programs:** art, business, computer science, social/behavioral science, technologies, vocational arts. **Faculty and instruction (2005-2006):** Total instructional faculty: 114 full-time, 150 part-time (; 16% minorities). Full-time faculty with Ph.D. or other terminal degree: 91%. Student/faculty ratio: 12/1. Classes of fewer than 20 students: 80%; of 20 to 49 students: 20%; of 50 or more students: 1%. **Advanced Placement and International Baccalaureate credit:** AP tests may be used for: Credit and/or placement. Scores accepted: 4, 5. **Freshmen returning for sophomore year:** 54%. **Graduation rates:** Four-year: 3%; five-year: 11%; six-year: 19%.

COSTS AND FINANCIAL AID

Financial aid office: (505) 538-6173. **Expenses (2006-2007):** Tuition and fees 2006-2007: $2,915 in state, $11,231 out of state; room/board: $4,590. **Financial aid:** Priority filing date for institution's financial aid form: April 1.

CAMPUS LIFE AND EXTRACURRICULAR ACTIVITIES

Campus housing available: coed dorms, women's dorms, men's dorms, apartments for married students, apartment for single students. **Student employment:** During the 2005-2006 academic year, 15% of undergraduates worked on campus. Average per-year earnings: $3,000. Activities include: choral groups, concert band, dance, drama/theater, jazz band, marching band, music ensembles, pep band, student government, student newspaper. Number of fraternities: 0; sororities: 0. Average proportion of students who stay on campus on weekends: 25%. **Sports program (2005-2006):** Member of NCAA II. *Men's intercollegiate varsity sports:* basketball, cross-country, football, golf, tennis. *Women's intercollegiate varsity sports:* basketball, cross-country, golf, softball, tennis, volleyball.

SERVICES AND FACILITIES

Basic services: nonremedial tutoring, placement service, day care, health service, health insurance. **Remedial assistance:** reading, math, writing. **Counseling services:** career, personal, academic, birth control. **For learning-disabled students:** School does not offer a structured program with separate admission and additional fees. Total undergraduates in learning-disabled program or receiving services: 50. Services include: remedial math, remedial English, remedial reading, tape recorders, note-taking services, oral tests, learning center, readers, extended time for tests, tutors. **Library:** Number of titles: 210,103; number of current serial subscriptions: 763. **Information technology resources:** Students are not required to lease or own a computer. Number of campus computers available to all students: 125. School does not have a wireless network. Proportion of college-owned housing units wired for high-speed internet access: 100%. **Campus safety:** Security services offered: 24-hour emergency telephones, lighted pathways/sidewalks, controlled dormitory access (key, security card, etc).

TRANSFER AND INTERNATIONAL STUDENTS

Transfer students: May apply for admission for the following academic terms: Fall, Spring, Summer. Applicants do not need a minimum number of credits to apply. For fall 2005: Transfer applicants enrolled: 141. **International students:** Number of foreign undergraduates: 26 (1% of student body). Number of countries represented: 5. Minimum TOEFL score required: 550 (paper); 213 (computer).

New York

Adelphi University

- **Address:** 1 South Avenue, Garden City, NY 11530
- **Website:** http://www.adelphi.edu
- **Private**
- **Enrollment:** 3,961 full-time; 797 part-time

KEY STATS
✔ **U.S News College Ranking:** third tier, National Universities
✔ **SAT Score (25th/75th percentile):** 1000-1220
✔ **Tuition:** 2006-2007: $20,900

Selectivity: Selective	**Room/board:** $9,550
Acceptance rate: 68%	**Average debt:** $22,000
Student/faculty ratio: 11/1	**Proportion who borrowed:** 81%

UNDERGRADUATE STUDENT BODY STATS
2005-2006 enrollment: 3,961 full-time; 797 part-time. Men: 28%; women: 72%. **Ethnic makeup:** African American: 13%; Asian American: 5%; Hispanic: 8%; White: 70%; International: 3%. **Religious preference:** Roman Catholic: 55%; Protestant: 16%; Jewish: 8%; Muslim: 2%; Hindu: 1%; Buddhist: 1%; No preference: 12%; None: 1%; Other: 4%.

ADMISSIONS FACTS AND FIGURES
Phone: (800) 233-5744. **Email:** admissions@adelphi.edu. **Website:** http://www.adelphi.edu. **Application deadlines for fall 2007:** Regular decision: Rolling. Early decision: Not offered. Early action: Send application by: December 1; Decision sent by: December 31. Admission can be deferred. **Application fee:** $35. Common application is accepted. **To apply online, go to:** http://www.adelphi.edu/prepare/admis. **Admissions requirements/recommendations:** High school units required (recommended): English: 4 (4); Mathematics: 3 (3); Science: 3 (3); Foreign language: 2 (2); Total units: 16 (16). Tests: The college uses SAT or ACT scores in admissions decisions. Either SAT or ACT required. For admission to the fall 2007 entering class, the school will accept: ACT with writing. Campus visit: Recommended. Admissions interview: Recommended. Off-campus interview: Not available. **Factors that count in admissions decisions:** *Academic:* Secondary school record: Very important. Class rank: Important. Letters of recommendation: Considered. Standardized test scores: Important. Essay: Important. *Nonacademic:* Interview: Considered. Extracurricular activities: Important. Talent/ability: Important. Character/personal qualities: Important. Alumni/ae relationship: Considered. Geographical residence: Not considered. State residency: Not considered. Religious affiliation/commitment: Not considered. Minority status: Not considered. Volunteer work: Important. Work experience: Considered. **Other schools with the greatest overlap in applicants:** Fordham University; Hofstra University; Long Island University–C.W. Post Campus; SUNY–Stony Brook; St. John's University. **Admissions statistics for the fall 2005 entering class:** Total applicants: 5,197. Total accepted: 3,545. Freshmen enrolled: 770; 13% were from out of state. Accepted through early-decision or early-action plans: 13%. Overall acceptance rate: 68%. Non-early acceptance rate: 76%. **Credentials of fall 2005 freshmen:** 23% ranked in the top 10 percent of their high school class; 58% were in the top 25 percent, and 88% were in the top half. (Proportion submitting class standing: 46%.) **Average high school grade point average:** 3.2. **First-year students who submitted SAT scores:** 73%. Scores (25/75 percentile): Verbal: 490-600, Math: 510-620, Combined: 1000-1220. **First-year students submitting ACT scores:** 8%. Scores (25/75 percentile): English: 19-26, Math: 20-26, Composite: 21-25.

ACADEMICS
Year founded: 1896. **Academic calendar:** Semester. **Degrees offered:** associate, transfer-associate, bachelor's, post-bachelor's certificate, master's, post-master's certificate, first professional certificate, doctorate. **Most popular majors:** 16% business, management, marketing, and related support services, 14% nursing/registered nurse training (R.N., A.S.N., B.S.N., M.S.N.), 8% psychology, 7% social sciences, 5% communication and media studies.

Major fields of study: area, ethnic, cultural, and gender studies; biological and biomedical sciences; business, management, marketing, and related support services; communication, journalism, and related programs; computer and information sciences and support services; education; English language and literature/letters; foreign languages, literatures, and linguistics; health professions and related clinical sciences; history; liberal arts and sciences studies, and humanities; mathematics and statistics; multi/interdisciplinary studies; natural resources and conservation; philosophy and religious studies; physical sciences; psychology; public administration and social service professions; security and protective services; social sciences; visual and performing arts. **Areas of required coursework:** arts/fine arts, humanities, English (including composition), sciences (biological or physical), social science, other. **Pre-professional programs:** pre-law, pre-dentistry, pre-medicine, pre-veterinary science, pre-optometry, other. **Special academic programs (% participation):** accelerated program (15%), distance learning, double major (1.5%), dual enrollment, English as a Second Language (ESL), honors program (6.3%), independent study (4.4%), internships, liberal arts/career combination, student-designed major, study abroad (1%), teacher certificate program (15%), weekend college, other. **Teacher certification offered in:** early childhood, special education, elementary, middle/junior high, secondary, bilingual/bicultural. **Reserve Officers Training Corps (ROTC):** Army ROTC: Offered at cooperating institution (Hofstra University); Air Force ROTC: Offered at cooperating institution (New York Institute of Technology). **Faculty and instruction (2005-2006):** Total instructional faculty: 257 full-time, 600 part-time (43% men; 57% women; 13% minorities). Full-time faculty with Ph.D. or other terminal degree: 90%. Student/faculty ratio: 11/1. Classes of fewer than 20 students: 41%; of 20 to 49 students: 56%; of 50 or more students: 3%. **Advanced Placement and International Baccalaureate credit:** AP tests may be used for: Credit and/or placement. Scores accepted: 3, 4, 5. International Baccalaureate exams may be used for: Credit only. **Freshmen returning for sophomore year:** 80%. **Graduation rates:** Four-year: 44%; five-year: 53%; six-year: 54%. **Graduate study:** 40% of students pursue further study immediately upon graduation; 46% within one year.

COSTS AND FINANCIAL AID
Financial aid office: (516) 877-3365. **Expenses (2006-2007):** Tuition and fees 2006-2007: $20,900; room/board: $9,550. Estimated books and supplies: $1,000; transportation: $1,100; personal expenses: $1,200. **Financial aid:** Priority filing date for institution's financial aid form: March 1. In 2005-2006, 76% of undergraduates applied for financial aid. Of those, 66% were determined to have financial need; 1% had their need fully met. Average financial aid package (proportion receiving): $14,750 (66%). Average amount of gift aid, such as scholarships or grants (proportion receiving): $4,850 (59%). Average amount of self-help aid, such as work study or loans (proportion receiving): $4,620 (60%). Average need-based loan (excluding PLUS or other private loans): $4,090. Among students who received need-based aid, the average percentage of need met: 32%. Among students who received aid based on merit, the average award (and the proportion receiving): $8,000 (18%). The average athletic scholarship (and the proportion receiving): $9,850 (2%). Average amount of debt of borrowers graduating in 2005: $22,000. Proportion who borrowed: 81%.

CAMPUS LIFE AND EXTRACURRICULAR ACTIVITIES
Campus housing available (% using): coed dorms (74%), special housing for disabled students (3%), other housing options (23%). Students who live in college-owned, operated, or affiliated housing: 23%. **Student employment:** During the 2005-2006 academic year, 16% of undergraduates worked on campus. Average per-year earnings: $1,676. **Clubs and organizations:** Number of student organizations: 79. Activities include: choral groups, concert band, dance, drama/theater, jazz band, literary magazine, music ensembles, radio station, student government, student newspaper, student film society, symphony orchestra, yearbook. Number of fraternities: 1; sororities: 5. Proportion of men in fraternities: 6%; of women in sororities: 4%. Average proportion of students who stay on campus on weekends: 45%. **Sports program (2005-2006):** Member of NCAA II. *Men's intercollegiate varsity sports:* baseball, basketball, cross-country, golf, lacrosse, soccer, swimming and diving, tennis, track and field (indoor), track and field (outdoor).

Women's intercollegiate varsity sports: basketball, cross-country, lacrosse, soccer, softball, swimming and diving, tennis, track and field (indoor), track and field (outdoor), volleyball.

SERVICES AND FACILITIES

Basic services: nonremedial tutoring, placement service, day care, health service. **Remedial assistance:** reading, math, writing, study skills. **Counseling services:** minority student, career, personal, veteran student, academic, older student, psychological, birth control, religious. **For learning-disabled students:** School does not offer a structured program with separate admission and additional fees. Total undergraduates in learning-disabled program or receiving services: 134. Services include: reading machines, tape recorders, diagnostic testing service, note-taking services, oral tests, learning center, readers, extended time for tests, tutors, priority registration, other testing accomodations, other. **Library:** Number of titles: 656,815; number of current serial subscriptions: 34,336. **Information technology resources:** Students are not required to lease or own a computer. Number of campus computers available to all students: 665. School has a wireless network. Approximate number of users that can be accommodated: 1,190. Proportion of college-owned housing units wired for high-speed internet access: 100%. **Campus safety:** Security services offered: 24-hour foot-and-vehicle patrols, late-night transport/escort service, 24-hour emergency telephones, lighted pathways/sidewalks, student patrols, controlled dormitory access (key, security card, etc).

TRANSFER AND INTERNATIONAL STUDENTS

Transfer students: May apply for admission for the following academic terms: Fall, Spring. Applicants do not need a minimum number of credits to apply. For fall 2005: Transfer applications received: 2,256. Transfer applicants offered admission: 1,148. Transfer applicants enrolled: 695. **International students:** Number of foreign undergraduates: 163 (3% of student body). Number of countries represented: 37. Minimum TOEFL score required: 550 (paper); 213 (computer). Average TOEFL score: 595 (paper).

Alfred University

- **Address:** 1 Saxon Drive, Alfred, NY 14802-1205
- **Website:** http://www.alfred.edu
- **Private**
- **Enrollment:** 1,863 full-time; 98 part-time

KEY STATS

✔ **U.S News College Ranking:** 15, Universities–Master's (North)
✔ **SAT Score (25th/75th percentile):** 1020-1230
✔ **Tuition:** 2006-2007: $22,100

Selectivity: Selective	**Room/board:** $10,040
Acceptance rate: 77%	**Average debt:** $21,250
Student/faculty ratio: 12/1	**Proportion who borrowed:** 85%

UNDERGRADUATE STUDENT BODY STATS

2005-2006 enrollment: 1,863 full-time; 98 part-time. Men: 50%; women: 50%. **Ethnic makeup:** African American: 5%; Asian American: 2%; Hispanic: 3%; White: 88%; International: 2%.

ADMISSIONS FACTS AND FIGURES

Phone: (800) 541-9229. **Email:** admissions@alfred.edu. **Website:** http://www.alfred.edu. **Application deadlines for fall 2007:** Regular decision: Rolling. Early decision: Send application by: December 1; Decision sent by: December 15. Early action: Not offered. Admission can be deferred. **Application fee:** $40. Common application is accepted. **To apply online, go to:** http://www.applyweb.com/aw?alfred. **Admissions requirements/recommendations:** High school units required (recommended): English: 4; Mathematics: 2; Science: 2; Social studies: 2; Total units: 16. Tests: The college uses SAT or ACT scores in admissions decisions. Either SAT or ACT required. For admission to the fall 2007 entering class, the school will accept: ACT with writing, ACT without writing. Campus visit: Recommended. Admissions interview: Recommended. Off-campus interview: May be arranged. **Factors that count in admissions decisions:** *Academic:* Secondary school record: Very important. Class rank: Very important. Letters of recommendation: Important. Standardized test scores: Important. Essay: Important. *Nonacademic:* Interview: Considered. Extracurricular activities: Very important. Talent/ability: Considered.

Character/personal qualities: Very important. Alumni/ae relationship: Not considered. Geographical residence: Not considered. State residency: Not considered. Religious affiliation/commitment: Not considered. Minority status: Considered. Volunteer work: Important. Work experience: Important. **Other schools with the greatest overlap in applicants:** Clarkson University; Ithaca College; Rochester Institute of Technology; SUNY College of Arts and Sciences–Geneseo; SUNY College–Brockport. **Admissions statistics for the fall 2005 entering class:** Total applicants: 2,134. Total accepted: 1,640. Freshmen enrolled: 429; 30% were from out of state. Accepted through early-decision or early-action plans: 8%. Overall acceptance rate: 77%. Early-decision acceptance rate: 69%. Non-early acceptance rate: 77%. **Credentials of fall 2005 freshmen:** 19% ranked in the top 10 percent of their high school class; 48% were in the top 25 percent, and 83% were in the top half. (Proportion submitting class standing: 72%.) **Average high school grade point average:** 3.1. **First-year students who submitted SAT scores:** 87%. Scores (25/75 percentile): Verbal: 500-620, Math: 520-610, Combined: 1020-1230. **First-year students submitting ACT scores:** 24%. Scores (25/75 percentile): English: N/A, Math: N/A, Composite: 22-27.

ACADEMICS

Year founded: 1836. **Academic calendar:** Semester. **Degrees offered:** bachelor's, master's, post-master's certificate, doctorate. **Most popular majors:** 26% fine and studio art, 13% business, management, marketing, and related support services, 13% engineering, 7% psychology, 6% education. **Major fields of study:** area, ethnic, cultural, and gender studies; biological and biomedical sciences; business, management, marketing, and related support services; communication, journalism, and related programs; education; engineering; English language and literature/letters; foreign languages, literatures, and linguistics; health professions and related clinical sciences; history; liberal arts and sciences studies, and humanities; mathematics and statistics; multi/interdisciplinary studies; natural resources and conservation; philosophy and religious studies; physical sciences; psychology; public administration and social service professions; security and protective services; social sciences; visual and performing arts. **Areas of required coursework:** arts/fine arts, mathematics, English (including composition), philosophy, foreign languages, sciences (biological or physical), history, social science, other. **Pre-professional programs:** pre-law, pre-dentistry, pre-medicine, pre-veterinary science. **Special academic programs:** cooperative (work-study plan) program, cross-registration, double major, English as a Second Language (ESL), exchange student program (domestic), honors program, independent study, internships, liberal arts/career combination, student-designed major, study abroad, teacher certificate program. **Teacher certification offered in:** early childhood, elementary, middle/junior high. **Cooperative education programs:** engineering. **Reserve Officers Training Corps (ROTC):** Army ROTC: Offered at cooperating institution (St. Bonaventure University). **Faculty and instruction (2005-2006):** Total instructional faculty: 165 full-time, 40 part-time (61% men; 39% women). Full-time faculty with Ph.D. or other terminal degree: 91%. Student/faculty ratio: 12/1. Classes of fewer than 20 students: 64%; of 20 to 49 students: 33%; of 50 or more students: 2%. **Advanced Placement and International Baccalaureate credit:** AP tests may be used for: Credit only. Scores accepted: 3, 4, 5. International Baccalaureate exams may be used for: Credit only. **Freshmen returning for sophomore year:** 80%. **Graduation rates:** Four-year: 44%; five-year: 61%; six-year: 66%. **Graduate study:** 28% of students pursue further study within one year.

COSTS AND FINANCIAL AID

Financial aid office: (607) 871-2159. **Expenses (2006-2007):** Tuition and fees 2006-2007: $22,100; room/board: $10,040. Estimated books and supplies: $850; transportation: $350; personal expenses: $850. **Financial aid:** In 2005-2006, 91% of undergraduates applied for financial aid. Of those, 84% were determined to have financial need; 20% had their need fully met. Average financial aid package (proportion receiving): $21,663 (84%). Average amount of gift aid, such as scholarships or grants (proportion receiving): $15,798 (83%). Average amount of self-help aid, such as work study or loans (proportion receiving): $6,242 (74%). Average need-based loan (excluding PLUS or other private loans): $5,113. Among students who received need-based aid, the average percentage of need met: 88%. Among students who received aid based on merit, the average award (and the proportion receiving): $10,171 (7%). The average athletic scholarship (and the proportion receiving): $0 (0%). Average amount of debt of borrowers graduating in 2005: $21,250. Proportion who borrowed: 85%.

CAMPUS LIFE AND EXTRACURRICULAR ACTIVITIES

Campus housing available: coed dorms, apartment for single students, other housing options. Students who live in college-owned, operated, or affiliated housing: 67%. **Student employment:** During the 2005-2006 academic year, 50% of undergraduates worked on campus. Average per-year earnings: $1,100. **Clubs and organizations:** Number of student organizations: 95. Activities include: choral groups, concert band, dance, drama/theater, jazz band, literary magazine, music ensembles, musical theater, pep band, radio station, student government, student newspaper, student film society, television station, yearbook. Number of fraternities: 0; sororities: 0. Average proportion of students who stay on campus on weekends: 85%. **Sports program (2005-2006):** Member of NCAA III. *Men's intercollegiate varsity sports:* basketball, cross-country, football, lacrosse, soccer, swimming and diving, tennis, track and field (indoor), track and field (outdoor). *Women's intercollegiate varsity sports:* basketball, cross-country, lacrosse, soccer, softball, swimming and diving, tennis, track and field (indoor), track and field (outdoor), volleyball.

SERVICES AND FACILITIES

Basic services: nonremedial tutoring, women's center, placement service, health service, health insurance. **Remedial assistance:** study skills. **Counseling services:** minority student, career, personal, academic, psychological, birth control, other. **For learning-disabled students:** School does not offer a structured program with separate admission and additional fees. Total undergraduates in learning-disabled program or receiving services: 115. Services include: tape recorders, diagnostic testing service, untimed tests, note-taking services, oral tests, readers, extended time for tests, tutors, other testing accomodations, other. **Library:** Number of titles: 305,658; number of current serial subscriptions: 1,458. **Information technology resources:** Students are not required to lease or own a computer. Number of campus computers available to all students: 450. School has a wireless network. Approximate number of users that can be accommodated: 600. Proportion of college-owned housing units wired for high-speed internet access: 100%. **Campus safety:** Security services offered: late-night transport/escort service, 24-hour emergency telephones, lighted pathways/sidewalks, student patrols, controlled dormitory access (key, security card, etc).

TRANSFER AND INTERNATIONAL STUDENTS

Transfer students: May apply for admission for the following academic terms: Fall, Spring. Applicants do not need a minimum number of credits to apply. For fall 2005: Transfer applications received: 229. Transfer applicants offered admission: 131. Transfer applicants enrolled: 84. **International students:** Number of foreign undergraduates: 32 (2% of student body). Number of countries represented: 15.

Bard College

- **Address:** PO Box 5000, Annandale on Hudson, NY 12504
- **Website:** http://www.bard.edu
- **Private**
- **Enrollment:** 1,521 full-time; 64 part-time

KEY STATS

✔ **U.S News College Ranking:** 36, Liberal Arts Colleges
✔ **SAT Score (25th/75th percentile):** 1240-1440
✔ **Tuition:** 2006-2007: $34,782

Selectivity: Most selective	**Room/board:** $9,850
Acceptance rate: 32%	**Average debt:** $18,345
Student/faculty ratio: 9/1	**Proportion who borrowed:** 71%

UNDERGRADUATE STUDENT BODY STATS

2005-2006 enrollment: 1,521 full-time; 64 part-time. Men: 43%; women: 57%. **Ethnic makeup:** African American: 2%; Asian American: 4%; Hispanic: 4%; White: 82%; International: 8%.

ADMISSIONS FACTS AND FIGURES

Phone: (845) 758-7472. **Email:** admission@bard.edu. **Website:** http://www.bard.edu. **Application deadlines for fall 2007:** Regular decision: January 15; decision sent by April 1. Early decision: Not offered. Early action: Send application by: November 1; Decision sent by: January 1. Admission can be deferred. **Application fee:** $50. Common application is accepted. **Admissions requirements/recommendations:** High school units required (recommended): English: (4); Mathematics: (4); Science: (4); Foreign language: (4); Social studies: (4); History: (4); Total units: (24). Tests: The college uses SAT or ACT scores in admissions decisions. Neither SAT nor

ACT required. For admission to the fall 2007 entering class, the school will accept: ACT with writing, ACT without writing. Campus visit: Recommended. Admissions interview: Neither required nor recommended. Off-campus interview: May be arranged. **Factors that count in admissions decisions:** *Academic:* Secondary school record: Very important. Class rank: Considered. Letters of recommendation: Very important. Standardized test scores: Considered. Essay: Very important. *Nonacademic:* Interview: Considered. Extracurricular activities: Very important. Talent/ability: Very important. Character/personal qualities: Very important. Alumni/ae relationship: Considered. Geographical residence: Considered. State residency: Considered. Religious affiliation/commitment: Considered. Minority status: Considered. Volunteer work: Important. Work experience: Important. **Other schools with the greatest overlap in applicants:** New York University; Oberlin College; Reed College; Vassar College; Wesleyan University. **Admissions statistics for the fall 2005 entering class:** Total applicants: 4,142. Total accepted: 1,325. Freshmen enrolled: 515; 72% were from out of state. Overall acceptance rate: 32%. Non-early acceptance rate: 32%. **Size of waiting list:** 311 applicants; enrolled from waiting list: 0. **Credentials of fall 2005 freshmen:** 63% ranked in the top 10 percent of their high school class; 85% were in the top 25 percent, and 99% were in the top half. (Proportion submitting class standing: 50%.) **Average high school grade point average:** 3.5. **First-year students who submitted SAT scores:** 59%. Scores (25/75 percentile): Verbal: 650-750, Math: 590-690, Combined: 1240-1440.

ACADEMICS

Year founded: 1860. **Academic calendar:** Semester. **Degrees offered:** associate, bachelor's, master's, doctorate. **Most popular majors:** 38% visual and performing arts, 15% English language and literature/letters, 15% social sciences, 6% psychology, 5% foreign languages, literatures, and linguistics. **Major fields of study:** English language and literature/letters; liberal arts and sciences studies, and humanities; multi/interdisciplinary studies; social sciences; visual and performing arts. **Areas of required coursework:** arts/fine arts, humanities, mathematics, English (including composition), philosophy, sciences (biological or physical), history, social science, other. **Pre-professional programs:** pre-medicine. **Special academic programs (% participation):** cross-registration (1%), double major (3%), independent study (12%), internships (10%), student-designed major (3%), study abroad (42%), other. **Teacher certification offered in:** secondary. **Faculty and instruction (2005-2006):** Total instructional faculty: 130 full-time, 100 part-time (53% men; 47% women; 17% minorities). Full-time faculty with Ph.D. or other terminal degree: 95%. Student/faculty ratio: 9/1. Classes of fewer than 20 students: 75%; of 20 to 49 students: 25%; of 50 or more students: 0%. **Advanced Placement and International Baccalaureate credit:** AP tests may be used for: Credit only. Scores accepted: 5. International Baccalaureate exams may be used for: Credit only. **Freshmen returning for sophomore year:** 88%. **Graduation rates:** Four-year: 60%; five-year: 70%; six-year: 72%.

COSTS AND FINANCIAL AID

Financial aid office: (845) 758-7525. **Expenses (2006-2007):** Tuition and fees 2006-2007: $34,782; room/board: $9,850. Estimated books and supplies: $850; transportation: $550; personal expenses: $600. **Financial aid:** Priority filing date for institution's financial aid form: February 1; deadline: February 15. In 2005-2006, 69% of undergraduates applied for financial aid. Of those, 59% were determined to have financial need; 54% had their need fully met. Average financial aid package (proportion receiving): $25,107 (59%). Average amount of gift aid, such as scholarships or grants (proportion receiving): N/A (52%). Average amount of self-help aid, such as work study or loans (proportion receiving): N/A (44%). Among students who received need-based aid, the average percentage of need met: 89%. Among students who received aid based on merit, the average award (and the proportion receiving): $10,750 (4%). The average athletic scholarship (and the proportion receiving): $0 (0%). Average amount of debt of borrowers graduating in 2005: $18,345. Proportion who borrowed: 71%.

CAMPUS LIFE AND EXTRACURRICULAR ACTIVITIES

Campus housing available (% using): coed dorms (93%), women's dorms (6%), cooperative housing (1%). Students who live in college-owned, operated, or affiliated housing: 77%. **Student employment:** During the 2005-2006 academic year, 45% of undergraduates worked on campus. Average per-year earnings: $1,650. **Clubs and organizations:** Number of student organizations: 115. Activities include: choral groups, concert band, dance, drama/theater, jazz band, literary magazine, music ensembles, musical theater, opera, radio station, student government, student newspaper, student film society, symphony orchestra. Number of fraternities: 0; sororities: 0. Average proportion of students who stay on campus on weekends: 75%. **Sports program (2005-2006):** Member of NCAA III. *Men's intercollegiate* *varsity sports:* basketball, cross-country, soccer, tennis, volleyball. *Women's intercollegiate varsity sports:* basketball, cross-country, soccer, tennis, volleyball.

SERVICES AND FACILITIES

Basic services: nonremedial tutoring, placement service, health service, health insurance. **Remedial assistance:** study skills. **Counseling services:** minority student, career, personal, academic, older student, psychological, birth control, religious. **For learning-disabled students:** School does not offer a structured program with separate admission and additional fees. Total undergraduates in learning-disabled program or receiving services: 67. Services include: reading machines, tape recorders, untimed tests, oral tests, learning center, extended time for tests, tutors, texts on tape. **Library:** Number of titles: 286,000; number of current serial subscriptions: 13,000. **Information technology resources:** Students are not required to lease or own a computer. Number of campus computers available to all students: 400. School has a wireless network. Approximate number of users that can be accommodated: 500. Proportion of college-owned housing units wired for high-speed internet access: 100%. **Campus safety:** Security services offered: 24-hour foot-and-vehicle patrols, late-night transport/escort service, 24-hour emergency telephones, lighted pathways/sidewalks, student patrols, controlled dormitory access (key, security card, etc).

TRANSFER AND INTERNATIONAL STUDENTS

Transfer students: May apply for admission for the following academic terms: Fall, Spring. Applicants do not need a minimum number of credits to apply. For fall 2005: Transfer applications received: 154. Transfer applicants offered admission: 36. Transfer applicants enrolled: 15. **International students:** Number of foreign undergraduates: 120 (8% of student body). Number of countries represented: 46. Minimum TOEFL score required: 600 (paper); 250 (computer). Average TOEFL score: 620 (paper).

Barnard College

- ■ **Address:** 3009 Broadway, New York, NY 10027
- ■ **Website:** http://www.barnard.edu
- ■ **Private**
- ■ **Enrollment:** 2,296 full-time; 60 part-time

KEY STATS

✔ **U.S News College Ranking:** 26, Liberal Arts Colleges
✔ **SAT Score (25th/75th percentile):** 1290-1450
✔ **Tuition:** 2006-2007: $33,078

Selectivity: Most selective	**Room/board:** $11,392
Acceptance rate: 27%	**Average debt:** $19,496
Student/faculty ratio: 10/1	**Proportion who borrowed:** 45%

UNDERGRADUATE STUDENT BODY STATS

2005-2006 enrollment: 2,296 full-time; 60 part-time. Men: 0%; women: 100%. **Ethnic makeup:** African American: 5%; Asian American: 17%; Hispanic: 7%; White: 67%; International: 3%.

ADMISSIONS FACTS AND FIGURES

Phone: (212) 854-2014. **Email:** admissions@barnard.edu. **Website:** http://www.barnard.edu. **Application deadlines for fall 2007:** Regular decision: January 1; decision sent by April 1. Early decision: Send application by: November 15; Decision sent by: December 15. Early action: Not offered. Admission can be deferred. **Application fee:** $45. Common application is accepted. **Admissions requirements/recommendations:** High school units required (recommended): English: (4); Mathematics: (3); Science: (3); Foreign language; (3); History: (3); Total units: (16). Tests: The college uses SAT or ACT scores in admissions decisions. Either SAT or ACT required. For admission to the fall 2007 entering class, the school will accept: ACT without writing. Campus visit: Recommended. Admissions interview: Recommended. Off-campus interview: May be arranged. **Factors that count in admissions decisions:** *Academic:* Secondary school record: Very important. Class rank: Important. Letters of recommendation: Very important. Standardized test scores: Very important. Essay: Very important. *Nonacademic:* Interview: Considered. Extracurricular activities: Important. Talent/ability: Important. Character/personal qualities: Considered. Alumni/ae relationship: Considered. Geographical residence: Considered. State residency: Considered. Religious affiliation/commitment: Not consid-

ered. Minority status: Considered. Volunteer work: Important. Work experience: Considered. **Other schools with the greatest overlap in applicants:** Brown University; Columbia University; New York University; Yale University. **Admissions statistics for the fall 2005 entering class:** Total applicants: 4,431. Total accepted: 1,216. Freshmen enrolled: 571; 67% were from out of state. Accepted through early-decision or early-action plans: 30%. Overall acceptance rate: 27%. Early-decision acceptance rate: 41%. Non-early acceptance rate: 26%. **Size of waiting list:** 1046 applicants; enrolled from waiting list: 11. **Credentials of fall 2005 freshmen:** 83% ranked in the top 10 percent of their high school class; 99% were in the top 25 percent, and 100% were in the top half. (Proportion submitting class standing: 54%.) **Average high school grade point average:** 3.9. **First-year students who submitted SAT scores:** 86%. Scores (25/75 percentile): Verbal: 650-740, Math: 640-710, Combined: 1290-1450. **First-year students submitting ACT scores:** 14%. Scores (25/75 percentile): English: N/A, Math: N/A, Composite: 27-30.

ACADEMICS

Year founded: 1889. **Academic calendar:** Semester. **Degrees offered:** bachelor's. **Most popular majors:** 13% English language and literature, 13% psychology, 11% economics, 10% political science and government, 7% art history, criticism, and conservation. **Major fields of study:** architecture and related services; area, ethnic, cultural, and gender studies; biological and biomedical sciences; computer and information sciences and support services; engineering; English language and literature/letters; foreign languages, literatures, and linguistics; history; mathematics and statistics; multi/interdisciplinary studies; natural resources and conservation; philosophy and religious studies; physical sciences; psychology; social sciences; visual and performing arts. **Areas of required coursework:** arts/fine arts, humanities, mathematics, English (including composition), philosophy, foreign languages, sciences (biological or physical), history, social science, other. **Pre-professional programs:** pre-law, pre-dentistry, pre-medicine, other. **Special academic programs (% participation):** accelerated program (10%), cross-registration (100%), double major (6%), dual enrollment (2%), exchange student program (domestic) (2%), independent study (21%), internships (66%), student-designed major (2%), study abroad (30%), teacher certificate program (3%). **Teacher certification offered in:** early childhood, elementary, middle/junior high, secondary. **Faculty and instruction (2005-2006):** Total instructional faculty: 193 full-time, 126 part-time (36% men; 64% women; 11% minorities). Full-time faculty with Ph.D. or other terminal degree: 94%. Student/faculty ratio: 10/1. Classes of fewer than 20 students: 67%; of 20 to 49 students: 25%; of 50 or more students: 8%. **Advanced Placement and International Baccalaureate credit:** AP tests may be used for: Credit and/or placement. Scores accepted: 4, 5. International Baccalaureate exams may be used for: Credit and/or placement. **Freshmen returning for sophomore year:** 94%. **Graduation rates:** Four-year: 82%; five-year: 87%; six-year: 89%. **Graduate study:** 20% of students pursue further study immediately upon graduation. Fields in which graduates pursue further study: Master of Business Administration (MBA), 1%; law, 7%; medicine, 5%; education, 3%; arts and sciences, 6%.

COSTS AND FINANCIAL AID

Financial aid office: (212) 854-2154. **Expenses (2006-2007):** Tuition and fees 2006-2007: $33,078; room/board: $11,392. Estimated books and supplies: $1,080; transportation: $0; personal expenses: $1,288. **Financial aid:** In 2005-2006, 48% of undergraduates applied for financial aid. Of those, 42% were determined to have financial need; 100% had their need fully met. Average financial aid package (proportion receiving): $28,790 (42%). Average amount of gift aid, such as scholarships or grants (proportion receiving): $24,611 (40%). Average amount of self-help aid, such as work study or loans (proportion receiving): $5,256 (42%). Average need-based loan (excluding PLUS or other private loans): $3,693. Among students who received need-based aid, the average percentage of need met: 100%. Among students who received aid based on merit, the average award (and the proportion receiving): $0 (0%). The average athletic scholarship (and the proportion receiving): $0 (0%). Average amount of debt of borrowers graduating in 2005: $19,496. Proportion who borrowed: 45%.

CAMPUS LIFE AND EXTRACURRICULAR ACTIVITIES

Campus housing available (% using): coed dorms (6%), women's dorms (60%), apartment for single students (34%), special housing for disabled students. Students who live in college-owned, operated, or affiliated housing: 89%. **Student employment:** During the 2005-2006 academic year, 39% of undergraduates worked on campus. Average per-year earnings: $3,300. **Clubs and organizations:** Number of student organizations: 100. Activities include: choral groups, concert band, dance, drama/theater, literary magazine, marching band, music ensembles, musical theater, opera, pep band, radio station, student government, student newspaper, student film society, symphony orchestra, television station, yearbook. Number of fraternities: 0; sororities: 0. Average proportion of students who stay on campus on weekends: 71%. **Sports program (2005-2006):** Member of NCAA I. *Women's intercollegiate varsity sports:* archery, basketball, cross-country, fencing, field hockey, golf, lacrosse, rowing, soccer, softball, swimming and diving, tennis, track and field (indoor), track and field (outdoor), volleyball.

SERVICES AND FACILITIES

Basic services: nonremedial tutoring, women's center, health service, health insurance. **Counseling services:** career, personal, academic, psychological. **For learning-disabled students:** School does not offer a structured program with separate admission and additional fees. Services include: reading machines, tape recorders, diagnostic testing service, note-taking services, readers, extended time for tests, tutors, other. **Library:** Number of titles: 207,656; number of current serial subscriptions: 456. **Information technology resources:** Students are not required to lease or own a computer. Number of campus computers available to all students: 208. School has a wireless network. Approximate number of users that can be accommodated: 253. Proportion of college-owned housing units wired for high-speed internet access: 100%. **Campus safety:** Security services offered: 24-hour foot-and-vehicle patrols, late-night transport/escort service, lighted pathways/sidewalks, controlled dormitory access (key, security card, etc).

TRANSFER AND INTERNATIONAL STUDENTS

Transfer students: May apply for admission for the following academic terms: Fall, Spring. Applicants need a minimum number of credits to apply. For fall 2005: Transfer applications received: 402. Transfer applicants offered admission: 128. Transfer applicants enrolled: 68. **International students:** Number of foreign undergraduates: 73 (3% of student body). Number of countries represented: 36. Minimum TOEFL score required: 600 (paper); 250 (computer). Average TOEFL score: 634 (paper).

Boricua College

- **Address:** 3755 Broadway, New York, NY 10032
- **Website:** http://www.boricuacollege.edu/
- **Private**
- **Enrollment:** N/A

KEY STATS

✔ **U.S News College Ranking:** fourth tier, Comp. Coll.–Bachelor's (North)
✔ **SAT or ACT Score (25th/75th percentile):** N/A
✔ **Tuition:** N/A

Selectivity: Less selective	**Room/board:** N/A
Acceptance rate: N/A	**Average debt:** N/A
Student/faculty ratio: N/A	**Proportion who borrowed:** N/A

Canisius College

- **Address:** 2001 Main Street, Buffalo, NY 14208-1098
- **Website:** http://www.canisius.edu
- **Private; Religious affiliation:** Roman Catholic
- **Enrollment:** 3,310 full-time; 281 part-time

KEY STATS

✔ **U.S News College Ranking:** 29, Universities–Master's (North)
✔ **SAT Score (25th/75th percentile):** 1010-1210
✔ **Tuition:** 2006-2007: $24,937

Selectivity: Selective	**Room/board:** $9,480
Acceptance rate: 72%	**Average debt:** $21,801
Student/faculty ratio: 13/1	**Proportion who borrowed:** 72%

UNDERGRADUATE STUDENT BODY STATS

2005-2006 enrollment: 3,310 full-time; 281 part-time. Men: 43%; women: 57%. **Ethnic makeup:** African American: 6%; Asian American: 2%; Hispanic: 2%; White: 87%; International: 3%.

ADMISSIONS FACTS AND FIGURES

Phone: (800) 843-1517. **Email:** admissions@canisius.edu. **Website:** http://www.canisius.edu. **Application deadlines for fall 2007:** Regular decision: May 1. Early decision: Not offered. Early action: Not offered. Admission can be deferred. **Application fee:** $40. Common application is accepted. **To apply online, go to:** http://www.canisius.edu/canhp/departments/admissions/index.html. **Admissions requirements/recommendations:** High school units required (recommended): English: 4 (4); Mathematics: 3 (4); Science: 2 (4); Foreign language: 3 (4); Social studies: 1 (1); History: 3 (3); Academic electives: 0 (0); Total units: 16 (20). Tests: The college uses SAT or ACT scores in admissions decisions. Either SAT or ACT required. For admission to the fall 2007 entering class, the school will accept: ACT with writing, ACT without writing. Campus visit: Recommended. Admissions interview: Recommended. Off-campus interview: May be arranged. **Factors that count in admissions decisions:** *Academic:* Secondary school record: Very important. Class rank: Considered. Letters of recommendation: Important. Standardized test scores: Important. Essay: Important. *Nonacademic:* Interview: Important. Extracurricular activities: Important. Talent/ability: Important. Character/personal qualities: Important. Alumni/ae relationship: Considered. Geographical residence: Not considered. State residency: Not considered. Religious affiliation/commitment: Not considered. Minority status: Not considered. Volunteer work: Important. Work experience: Important. **Other schools with the greatest overlap in applicants:** Niagara University; SUNY College of Arts and Sciences–Geneseo; SUNY–Fredonia; St. Bonaventure University; University at Buffalo–SUNY. **Admissions statistics for the fall 2005 entering class:** Total applicants: 4,114. Total accepted: 2,962. Freshmen enrolled: 775; 10% were from out of state. Overall acceptance rate: 72%. **Credentials of fall 2005 freshmen:** 22% ranked in the top 10 percent of their high school class; 51% were in the top 25 percent, and 82% were in the top half. (Proportion submitting class standing: 75%.) **Average high school grade point average:** 3.5. **First-year students who submitted SAT scores:** 97%. Scores (25/75 percentile): Verbal: 500-600, Math: 510-610, Combined: 1010-1210. **First-year students submitting ACT scores:** 35%. Scores (25/75 percentile): English: N/A, Math: N/A, Composite: 21-26.

ACADEMICS

Year founded: 1870. **Academic calendar:** Semester. **Degrees offered:** bachelor's, master's. **Most popular majors:** 9% psychology, 7% business administration and management, 7% communication and media studies, 5% digital communication and media/multimedia, 5% secondary education and teaching. **Major fields of study:** area, ethnic, cultural, and gender studies; biological and biomedical sciences; business, management, marketing, and related support services; communication, journalism, and related programs; computer and information sciences and support services; education; English language and literature/letters; foreign languages, literatures, and linguistics; health professions and related clinical sciences; history; liberal arts and sciences studies, and humanities; mathematics and statistics; natural resources and conservation; philosophy and religious studies; physical sciences; psychology; security and protective services; social sciences; visual and performing arts. **Areas of required coursework:** arts/fine arts, humanities, mathematics, English (including composition), philosophy, foreign languages, sciences (biological or physical), history, social science. **Pre-professional programs:** pre-law, pre-dentistry, pre-medicine, pre-veterinary science, pre-optometry, pre-pharmacy. **Special academic programs (% participation):** cross-registration, distance learning, double major (8%), dual enrollment (3%), English as a Second Language (ESL), exchange student program (domestic), honors program, independent study, internships, study abroad, teacher certificate program. **Teacher certification offered in:** early childhood, special education, elementary, middle/junior high, secondary. **Reserve Officers Training Corps (ROTC):** Army ROTC: Offered on campus. **Faculty and instruction (2005-2006):** Total instructional faculty: 193 full-time, 332 part-time. Full-time faculty with Ph.D. or other terminal degree: 93%. Student/faculty ratio: 13/1. Classes of fewer than 20 students: 47%; of 20 to 49 students: 52%; of 50 or more students: 1%. **Advanced Placement and International Baccalaureate credit:** AP tests may be used for: Credit only. Scores accepted: 3, 4, 5. International Baccalaureate exams may be used for: Credit only. **Freshmen returning for sophomore year:** 83%. **Graduation rates:** Four-year: 51%; five-year: 66%; six-year: 67%. **Graduate study:** 24% of students pursue further study immediately upon graduation. Fields in which graduates pursue further study: Master of Business Administration (MBA), 12%; law, 6%; medicine, 15%; education, 44%; arts and sciences, 23%.

COSTS AND FINANCIAL AID

Financial aid office: (716) 888-2300. **Expenses (2006-2007):** Tuition and fees 2006-2007: $24,937; room/board: $9,480. Estimated books and supplies:

$700; transportation: $430; personal expenses: $700. **Financial aid:** Priority filing date for institution's financial aid form: February 15. In 2005-2006, 84% of undergrads applied for financial aid. Of those, 76% were determined to have financial need; 29% had their need fully met. Average financial aid package (proportion receiving): $18,883 (75%). Average amount of gift aid, such as scholarships or grants (proportion receiving): $13,101 (75%). Average amount of self-help aid, such as work study or loans (proportion receiving): $4,882 (58%). Average need-based loan (excluding PLUS or other private loans): $4,039. Among students who received need-based aid, the average percentage of need met: 79%. Among students who received aid based on merit, the average award (and the proportion receiving): $9,761 (19%). The average athletic scholarship (and the proportion receiving): $16,313 (3%). Average amount of debt of borrowers graduating in 2005: $21,801. Proportion who borrowed: 72%.

CAMPUS LIFE AND EXTRACURRICULAR ACTIVITIES

Campus housing available (% using): coed dorms (48%), women's dorms (1%), apartment for single students (49%), special housing for disabled students (1%), special housing for international students (1%). Students who live in college-owned, operated, or affiliated housing: 42%. **Student employment:** During the 2005-2006 academic year, 25% of undergraduates worked on campus. Average per-year earnings: $3,600. **Clubs and organizations:** Number of student organizations: 100. Activities include: choral groups, concert band, dance, drama/theater, jazz band, literary magazine, music ensembles, musical theater, pep band, radio station, student government, student newspaper, student film society, television station, yearbook. Number of fraternities: 1; sororities: 1. Proportion of men in fraternities: 1%; of women in sororities: 1%. Average proportion of students who stay on campus on weekends: 85%. **Sports program (2005-2006):** Member of NCAA I. *Men's intercollegiate varsity sports:* baseball, basketball, cross-country, golf, ice hockey, lacrosse, soccer, swimming and diving. *Women's intercollegiate varsity sports:* basketball, cross-country, lacrosse, soccer, softball, swimming and diving, syncronized swimming, volleyball.

SERVICES AND FACILITIES

Basic services: nonremedial tutoring, placement service, health service, health insurance. **Remedial assistance:** reading, math, writing, study skills. **Counseling services:** minority student, career, military, personal, veteran student, academic, older student, psychological, religious. **For learning-disabled students:** School does not offer a structured program with separate admission and additional fees. Total undergraduates in learning-disabled program or receiving services: 89. Services include: remedial math, remedial English, remedial reading, tape recorders, note-taking services, readers, extended time for tests, tutors, priority seating, substitution of courses, texts on tape, typist/scribe, exams on tape or computer, waiver of foreign language degree requirement, waiver of math degree requirement. **Library:** Number of titles: 341,156; number of current serial subscriptions: 1,183. **Information technology resources:** Students are not required to lease or own a computer. Number of campus computers available to all students: 325. School has a wireless network. Approximate number of users that can be accommodated: 5,000. Proportion of college-owned housing units wired for high-speed internet access: 99%. **Campus safety:** Security services offered: 24-hour foot-and-vehicle patrols, late-night transport/escort service, 24-hour emergency telephones, lighted pathways/sidewalks, controlled dormitory access (key, security card, etc).

TRANSFER AND INTERNATIONAL STUDENTS

Transfer students: May apply for admission for the following academic terms: Fall, Spring, Summer. Applicants need a minimum number of credits to apply. For fall 2005: Transfer applications received: 619. Transfer applicants offered admission: 364. Transfer applicants enrolled: 191. **International students:** Number of foreign undergraduates: 93 (3% of student body). Number of countries represented: 25. Minimum TOEFL score required: 500 (paper); 173 (computer).

Cazenovia College

- **Address:** 22 Sullivan Street, Cazenovia, NY 13035-1804
- **Website:** http://www.cazenovia.edu
- **Private**
- **Enrollment:** 812 full-time; 215 part-time

KEY STATS

✔ **U.S News College Ranking:** 34, Comp. Colleges–Bachelor's (North)
✔ **SAT Score (25th/75th percentile):** 880-1100
✔ **Tuition:** 2006-2007: $20,180

Selectivity: Less selective	**Room/board:** $8,445
Acceptance rate: 82%	**Average debt:** $27,321
Student/faculty ratio: 11/1	**Proportion who borrowed:** 85%

UNDERGRADUATE STUDENT BODY STATS

2005-2006 enrollment: 812 full-time; 215 part-time. Men: 21%; women: 79%. **Ethnic makeup:** African American: 4%; American-Indian: 1%; Asian American: 1%; Hispanic: 2%; White: 91%.

ADMISSIONS FACTS AND FIGURES

Phone: (800) 654-3210. **Email:** admission@cazenovia.edu. **Website:** http://www.cazenovia.edu. **Application deadlines for fall 2007:** Regular decision: August 15. Early decision: Not offered. Early action: Not offered. Admission can be deferred. **Application fee:** $30. Common application is accepted. **To apply online, go to:** http://www.cazenovia.edu/apply-online. **Admissions requirements/recommendations:** High school units required (recommended): English: 4 (4); Mathematics: 2 (2); Science: 2 (2); Foreign language: 0 (2); Social studies: 4 (4); History: 0 (0); Total units: 12 (12). Tests: The college uses SAT or ACT scores in admissions decisions. Neither SAT nor ACT required. For admission to the fall 2007 entering class, the school will accept: ACT with writing, ACT without writing. Campus visit: Recommended. Admissions interview: Recommended. Off-campus interview: May be arranged. **Factors that count in admissions decisions:** *Academic:* Secondary school record: Very important. Class rank: Very important. Letters of recommendation: Important. Standardized test scores: Important. Essay: Considered. *Nonacademic:* Interview: Considered. Extracurricular activities: Important. Talent/ability: Important. Character/personal qualities: Important. Alumni/ae relationship: Considered. Geographical residence: Not considered. State residency: Not considered. Religious affiliation/commitment: Not considered. Minority status: Considered. Volunteer work: Important. Work experience: Important. **Other schools with the greatest overlap in applicants:** College of St. Rose; Elmira College; Ithaca College; Le Moyne College; Utica College. **Admissions statistics for the fall 2005 entering class:** Total applicants: 1,286. Total accepted: 1,059. Freshmen enrolled: 285; 24% were from out of state. Overall acceptance rate: 82%. **Credentials of fall 2005 freshmen:** 9% ranked in the top 10 percent of their high school class; 29% were in the top 25 percent, and 67% were in the top half. (Proportion submitting class standing: 82%.) **Average high school grade point average:** 3.2. **First-year students who submitted SAT scores:** 93%. Scores (25/75 percentile): Verbal: 440-560, Math: 440-540, Combined: 880-1100. **First-year students submitting ACT scores:** 31%. Scores (25/75 percentile): English: N/A, Math: N/A, Composite: 18-23.

ACADEMICS

Year founded: 1824. **Academic calendar:** Semester. **Degrees offered:** certificate, associate, bachelor's. **Most popular majors:** 34% visual and performing arts, 30% business, management, marketing, and related support services, 11% public administration and social service professions, 8% liberal arts and sciences studies, and humanities, 7% psychology. **Major fields of study:** business, management, marketing, and related support services; communication, journalism, and related programs; education; English language and literature/letters; liberal arts and sciences studies, and humanities; natural resources and conservation; psychology; public administration and social service professions; social sciences; visual and performing arts. **Areas of required coursework:** arts/fine arts, humanities, computer literacy, mathematics, English (including composition), philosophy, sciences (biological or physical), social science. **Pre-professional programs:** pre-law. **Special academic programs (% participation):** honors program (3%), independent study (5%), internships (95%), study abroad (2%), teacher certificate program (3%). **Teacher certification offered in:** early childhood, special education. **Reserve Officers Training Corps (ROTC):** Army ROTC: Offered at cooperating institution (Syracuse University); Air Force ROTC: Offered at cooperating institution (Syracuse University). **Faculty and instruction (2005-2006):** Total instructional faculty: 49 full-time, 88 part-time. Full-time faculty with Ph.D. or other terminal degree: 69%. Student/faculty ratio: 11/1. Classes of fewer than 20 students: 86%; of 20 to 49 students: 14%. **Advanced Placement and International Baccalaureate credit:** AP tests may be used for: Credit and/or placement. Scores accepted: 3, 4, 5. International Baccalaureate exams may be used for: Credit and/or placement. **Freshmen returning for sophomore year:** 65%. **Graduation rates:** Four-year: 42%; five-year: 47%; six-year: 39%. **Graduate study:** 7% of students pursue further study immediately upon graduation.

COSTS AND FINANCIAL AID

Financial aid office: (315) 655-7887. **Expenses (2006-2007):** Tuition and fees 2006-2007: $20,180; room/board: $8,445. Estimated books and supplies: $900. **Financial aid:** Priority filing date for institution's financial aid form: March 15. In 2005-2006, 89% of undergraduates applied for financial aid. Of those, 81% were determined to have financial need; 18% had their need fully met. Average financial aid package (proportion receiving): $13,500 (81%). Average amount of gift aid, such as scholarships or grants (proportion receiving): $8,000 (60%). Average amount of self-help aid, such as work study or loans (proportion receiving): $4,250 (60%). Average need-based loan (excluding PLUS or other private loans): $3,063. Among students who received need-based aid, the average percentage of need met: 70%. Among students who received aid based on merit, the average award (and the proportion receiving): $5,000 (7%). The average athletic scholarship (and the proportion receiving): $0 (0%). Average amount of debt of borrowers graduating in 2005: $27,321. Proportion who borrowed: 85%.

CAMPUS LIFE AND EXTRACURRICULAR ACTIVITIES

Campus housing available (% using): coed dorms (70%), women's dorms (25%), other housing options (5%). Students who live in college-owned, operated, or affiliated housing: 83%. **Student employment:** During the 2005-2006 academic year, 3% of undergraduates worked on campus. Average per-year earnings: $1,700. **Clubs and organizations:** Number of student organizations: 46. Activities include: choral groups, dance, drama/theater, jazz band, literary magazine, musical theater, radio station, student government, student newspaper, student film society, television station, yearbook. Number of fraternities: 0; sororities: 0. Average proportion of students who stay on campus on weekends: 60%. **Sports program (2005-2006):** Member of NCAA III. *Men's intercollegiate varsity sports:* baseball, basketball, cheerleading, crew, cross-country, equestrian Sports, golf, lacrosse, soccer. *Women's intercollegiate varsity sports:* basketball, cheerleading, crew, cross-country, equestrian sports, lacrosse, rowing, soccer, softball, volleyball.

SERVICES AND FACILITIES

Basic services: nonremedial tutoring, placement service, health service, health insurance. **Remedial assistance:** reading, math, writing, study skills. **Counseling services:** minority student, career, personal, academic, older student, psychological, birth control, religious, other. **For learning-disabled students:** School does not offer a structured program with separate admission and additional fees. Total undergraduates in learning-disabled program or receiving services: 102. Services include: remedial math, remedial reading, tape recorders, oral tests, learning center, readers, extended time for tests, tutors, priority registration, other testing accomodations. **Library:** Number of titles: 94,064; number of current serial subscriptions: 430. **Information technology resources:** Students are not required to lease or own a computer. Number of campus computers available to all students: 217. School has a wireless network. Proportion of college-owned housing units wired for high-speed internet access: 100%. **Campus safety:** Security services offered: 24-hour foot-and-vehicle patrols, late-night transport/escort service, 24-hour emergency telephones, lighted pathways/sidewalks, controlled dormitory access (key, security card, etc).

TRANSFER AND INTERNATIONAL STUDENTS

Transfer students: May apply for admission for the following academic terms: Fall, Spring. Applicants do not need a minimum number of credits to apply. For fall 2005: Transfer applications received: 178. Transfer applicants offered admission: 109. Transfer applicants enrolled: 46. **International students:** Number of foreign undergraduates: 1. Number of countries represented: 2. Minimum TOEFL score required: 550 (paper); 213 (computer).

Clarkson University

- **Address:** Box 5605, Potsdam, NY 13699
- **Website:** http://www.clarkson.edu
- **Private**
- **Enrollment:** 2,633 full-time; 15 part-time

KEY STATS

✔ **U.S News College Ranking:** third tier, National Universities
✔ **SAT Score (25th/75th percentile):** 1100-1290
✔ **Tuition:** 2006-2007: $27,090
Selectivity: More selective   **Room/board:** $9,648
Acceptance rate: 86%   **Average debt:** $19,942
Student/faculty ratio: 17/1   **Proportion who borrowed:** 81%

UNDERGRADUATE STUDENT BODY STATS

2005-2006 enrollment: 2,633 full-time; 15 part-time. Men: 75%; women: 25%. **Ethnic makeup:** African American: 2%; Asian American: 2%; Hispanic: 2%; White: 92%; International: 2%. **Religious preference:** Roman Catholic: 35%; Protestant: 5%; Jewish: 1%; Muslim: 1%; Hindu: 1%; Buddhist: 1%; No preference: 40%; Other: 10%.

ADMISSIONS FACTS AND FIGURES

Phone: (800) 527-6577. **Email:** admission@clarkson.edu. **Website:** http://www.clarkson.edu. **Application deadlines for fall 2007:** Regular decision: March 15. Early decision: Send application by: December 1; Decision sent by: December 30. Early action: Not offered. Admission can be deferred. **Application fee:** $50. Common application is accepted. **Admissions requirements/recommendations:** High school units required (recommended): English: 4; Mathematics: 3 (4); Science: 2 (3); Total units: 16. Tests: The college uses SAT or ACT scores in admissions decisions. Either SAT or ACT required. For admission to the fall 2007 entering class, the school will accept: ACT with writing, ACT without writing. Campus visit: Recommended. Admissions interview: Recommended. Off-campus interview: May be arranged. **Factors that count in admissions decisions:** *Academic:* Secondary school record: Very important. Class rank: Important. Letters of recommendation: Important. Standardized test scores: Important. Essay: Considered. *Nonacademic:* Interview: Very important. Extracurricular activities: Important. Talent/ability: Considered. Character/personal qualities: Considered. Alumni/ae relationship: Considered. Geographical residence: Not considered. State residency: Not considered. Religious affiliation/commitment: Not considered. Minority status: Not considered. Volunteer work: Important. Work experience: Considered. **Other schools with the greatest overlap in applicants:** Cornell University; Rensselaer Polytechnic Institute; Rochester Institute of Technology; Syracuse University; Worcester Polytechnic Institute. **Admissions statistics for the fall 2005 entering class:** Total applicants: 2,405. Total accepted: 2,073. Freshmen enrolled: 630; 27% were from out of state. Accepted through early-decision or early-action plans: 20%. Overall acceptance rate: 86%. Early-decision acceptance rate: 90%. Non-early acceptance rate: 86%. **Size of waiting list:** 16 applicants; enrolled from waiting list: 1. **Credentials of fall 2005 freshmen:** 33% ranked in the top 10 percent of their high school class; 69% were in the top 25 percent, and 94% were in the top half. (Proportion submitting class standing: 76%.) **Average high school grade point average:** 3.5. **First-year students who submitted SAT scores:** 98%. Scores (25/75 percentile): Verbal: 520-620, Math: 580-670, Combined: 1100-1290. **First-year students submitting ACT scores:** 30%. Scores (25/75 percentile): English: N/A, Math: N/A, Composite: 22-28.

ACADEMICS

Year founded: 1896. **Academic calendar:** Semester. **Degrees offered:** bachelor's, master's, first professional, doctorate. **Most popular majors:** 47% engineering, 19% business administration and management, 12% multi/interdisciplinary studies, 6% biology/biological sciences. **Major fields of study:** biological and biomedical sciences; business, management, marketing, and related support services; communication, journalism, and related programs; computer and information sciences and support services; engineering; history; liberal arts and sciences studies, and humanities; mathematics and statistics; multi/interdisciplinary studies; physical sciences; psychology; social sciences. **Areas of required coursework:** humanities, computer literacy, mathematics, sciences (biological or physical), social science, other. **Pre-professional programs:** pre-law, pre-dentistry, pre-medicine, pre-veterinary science, other. **Special academic programs (% participa-**

tion): accelerated program, cooperative (work-study plan) program (10%), cross-registration (9%), double major (5%), dual enrollment (3%), English as a Second Language (ESL) (.1%), honors program (3%), independent study (4%), internships (.3%), liberal arts/career combination, student-designed major (.1%), study abroad (6%). **Reserve Officers Training Corps (ROTC):** Army ROTC: Offered on campus; Air Force ROTC: Offered on campus. **Faculty and instruction (2005-2006):** Total instructional faculty: 170 full-time, 22 part-time (77% men; 23% women; 11% minorities). Full-time faculty with Ph.D. or other terminal degree: 92%. Student/faculty ratio: 17/1. Classes of fewer than 20 students: 32%; of 20 to 49 students: 43%; of 50 or more students: 25%. **Advanced Placement and International Baccalaureate credit:** AP tests may be used for: Credit and/or placement. Scores accepted: 4, 5. International Baccalaureate exams may be used for: Credit only. **Freshmen returning for sophomore year:** 87%. **Graduation rates:** Four-year: 62%; five-year: 74%; six-year: 75%. **Graduate study:** 21% of students pursue further study immediately upon graduation; 27% within one year. Fields in which graduates pursue further study: Master of Business Administration (MBA), 15%; law, 5%; medicine, 3%; dentistry, 1%; engineering, 27%; education, 3%; arts and sciences, 32%.

COSTS AND FINANCIAL AID

Financial aid office: (315) 268-6479. **Expenses (2006-2007):** Tuition and fees 2006-2007: $27,090; room/board: $9,648. Estimated books and supplies: $1,100 personal expenses: $1,962. **Financial aid:** Priority filing date for institution's financial aid form: March 1. In 2005-2006, 89% of undergraduates applied for financial aid. Of those, 80% were determined to have financial need; Average financial aid package (proportion receiving): $18,723 (75%). Average amount of gift aid, such as scholarships or grants (proportion receiving): $11,200 (65%). Average amount of self-help aid, such as work study or loans (proportion receiving): $4,777 (72%). Average need-based loan (excluding PLUS or other private loans): $4,294. Among students who received need-based aid, the average percentage of need met: 87%. Among students who received aid based on merit, the average award (and the proportion receiving): $7,873 (8%). The average athletic scholarship (and the proportion receiving): $30,320 (1%). Average amount of debt of borrowers graduating in 2005: $19,942. Proportion who borrowed: 81%.

CAMPUS LIFE AND EXTRACURRICULAR ACTIVITIES

Campus housing available (% using): coed dorms (58%), women's dorms, men's dorms (7%), sorority housing (1%), fraternity housing (5%), apartments for married students (1%), apartment for single students (28%), special housing for disabled students. Students who live in college-owned, operated, or affiliated housing: 79%. **Student employment:** During the 2005-2006 academic year, 35% of undergraduates worked on campus. Average per-year earnings: $1,500. **Clubs and organizations:** Number of student organizations: 45. Activities include: choral groups, drama/theater, jazz band, literary magazine, musical theater, pep band, radio station, student government, student newspaper, symphony orchestra, television station, yearbook. Number of fraternities: 10; sororities: 2. Proportion of men in fraternities: 15%; of women in sororities: 13%. Average proportion of students who stay on campus on weekends: 90%. **Sports program (2005-2006):** Member of NCAA III. *Men's intercollegiate varsity sports:* alpine skiing, baseball, basketball, cross-country, golf, ice hockey, lacrosse, nordic skiing, skiing, soccer, swimming and diving, tennis. *Women's intercollegiate varsity sports:* alpine skiing, basketball, cross-country, ice hockey, lacrosse, nordic skiing, skiing, soccer, swimming and diving, tennis, volleyball.

SERVICES AND FACILITIES

Basic services: placement service, health service, health insurance, other. **Remedial assistance:** writing, study skills. **Counseling services:** minority student, career, veteran student, other. **For learning-disabled students:** School does not offer a structured program with separate admission and additional fees. Total undergraduates in learning-disabled program or receiving services: 44. Services include: reading machines, tape recorders, videotaped classes, untimed tests, note-taking services, oral tests, learning center, readers, extended time for tests, tutors, early syllabus, priority registration, priority seating, texts on tape, exams on tape or computer, other testing accomodations. **Library:** Number of titles: 298,044; number of current serial subscriptions: 2,124. **Information technology resources:** Students are required to lease or own a computer. Number of campus computers available to all students: 400. School has a wireless network. Approximate number of users that can be accommodated: 2,000. Proportion of college-owned housing units wired for high-speed internet access: 100%. **Campus safety:** Security services offered: 24-hour foot-and-vehicle patrols, late-night transport/escort service, 24-hour emergency telephones, lighted pathways/sidewalks, controlled dormitory access (key, security card, etc).

TRANSFER AND INTERNATIONAL STUDENTS

Transfer students: May apply for admission for the following academic terms: Fall, Spring. Applicants need a minimum number of credits to apply. For fall 2005: Transfer applications received: 216. Transfer applicants offered admission: 143. Transfer applicants enrolled: 78. **International students:** Number of foreign undergraduates: 60 (2% of student body). Number of countries represented: 17. Minimum TOEFL score required: 550 (paper); 213 (computer).

Colgate University

- **Address:** 13 Oak Drive, Hamilton, NY 13346
- **Website:** http://www.colgate.edu
- **Private**
- **Enrollment:** 2,747 full-time; 24 part-time

KEY STATS

✔ **U.S News College Ranking:** 16, Liberal Arts Colleges
✔ **SAT Score (25th/75th percentile):** 1280-1430
✔ **Tuition:** 2006-2007: $35,030

Selectivity: Most selective	**Room/board:** $8,530
Acceptance rate: 27%	**Average debt:** $13,452
Student/faculty ratio: 10/1	**Proportion who borrowed:** 38%

UNDERGRADUATE STUDENT BODY STATS

2005-2006 enrollment: 2,747 full-time; 24 part-time. Men: 49%; women: 51%. **Ethnic makeup:** African American: 4%; American-Indian: 1%; Asian American: 6%; Hispanic: 4%; White: 80%; International: 5%. **Religious preference:** Roman Catholic: 22%; Protestant: 20%; Jewish: 11%; Hindu: 1%; Buddhist: 1%; No preference: 34%; Unknown: 10%.

ADMISSIONS FACTS AND FIGURES

Phone: (315) 228-7401. **Email:** admission@mail.colgate.edu. **Website:** http://www.colgate.edu. **Application deadlines for fall 2007:** Regular decision: January 15; decision sent by April 1. Early decision: Send application by: November 15; Decision sent by: December 15. Early action: Not offered. Admission can be deferred. **Application fee:** $55. Common application is accepted. **Admissions requirements/recommendations:** High school units required (recommended): English: 4 (4); Mathematics: 3 (4); Science: 3 (4); Foreign language: 3 (4); Social studies: 2 (2); History: 1 (3); Academic electives: 0 (0); Total units: 16 (20). Tests: The college uses SAT or ACT scores in admissions decisions. Either SAT or ACT required. For admission to the fall 2007 entering class, the school will accept: ACT with writing, ACT without writing. Campus visit: Recommended. Admissions interview: Neither required nor recommended. Off-campus interview: May be arranged. **Factors that count in admissions decisions:** *Academic:* Secondary school record: Very important. Class rank: Very important. Letters of recommendation: Important. Standardized test scores: Important. Essay: Important. *Nonacademic:* Interview: Not considered. Extracurricular activities: Important. Talent/ability: Important. Character/personal qualities: Important. Alumni/ae relationship: Considered. Geographical residence: Considered. State residency: Not considered. Religious affiliation/commitment: Not considered. Minority status: Considered. Volunteer work: Considered. Work experience: Considered. **Other schools with the greatest overlap in applicants:** Boston College; Bowdoin College; Cornell University; Dartmouth College; Middlebury College. **Admissions statistics for the fall 2005 entering class:** Total applicants: 8,008. Total accepted: 2,168. Freshmen enrolled: 729; 71% were from out of state. Accepted through early-decision or early-action plans: 42%. Overall acceptance rate: 27%. Early-decision acceptance rate: 49%. Non-early acceptance rate: 25%. **Size of waiting list:** 1159 applicants; enrolled from waiting list: 34. **Credentials of fall 2005 freshmen:** 68% ranked in the top 10 percent of their high school class; 90% were in the top 25 percent, and 100% were in the top half. (Proportion submitting class standing: 35%.) **Average high school grade point average:** 3.6. **First-year students who submitted SAT scores:** 86%. Scores (25/75 percentile): Verbal: 630-710, Math: 650-720, Combined: 1280-1430. **First-year students submitting ACT scores:** 14%. Scores (25/75 percentile): English: 29-34, Math: 27-32, Composite: 29-32.

ACADEMICS

Year founded: 1819. **Academic calendar:** Semester. **Degrees offered:** bachelor's, master's. **Most popular majors:** 17% political science and government,

12% English language and literature, 9% economics, 7% history, 6% psychology. **Major fields of study:** area, ethnic, cultural, and gender studies; biological and biomedical sciences; computer and information sciences and support services; education; English language and literature/letters; foreign languages, literatures, and linguistics; history; liberal arts and sciences studies, and humanities; mathematics and statistics; multi/interdisciplinary studies; natural resources and conservation; philosophy and religious studies; physical sciences; psychology; social sciences; visual and performing arts. **Areas of required coursework:** humanities, sciences (biological or physical), social science, other. **Special academic programs (% participation):** double major (20.4%), honors program (23.5%), independent study (36.2%), internships (8%), student-designed major (.9%), study abroad (71%), teacher certificate program (.9%). **Teacher certification offered in:** elementary, secondary. **Faculty and instruction (2005-2006):** Total instructional faculty: 267 full-time, 52 part-time (57% men; 43% women; 18% minorities). Full-time faculty with Ph.D. or other terminal degree: 95%. Student/faculty ratio: 10/1. Classes of fewer than 20 students: 64%; of 20 to 49 students: 34%; of 50 or more students: 2%. **Advanced Placement and International Baccalaureate credit:** AP tests may be used for: Credit and/or placement. Scores accepted: 3, 4, 5. International Baccalaureate exams may be used for: Credit and/or placement. **Freshmen returning for sophomore year:** 94%. **Graduation rates:** Four-year: 88%; five-year: 90%; six-year: 91%. **Graduate study:** 19% of students pursue further study immediately upon graduation; 45% within five years. Fields in which graduates pursue further study: Master of Business Administration (MBA), 20%; law, 26%; medicine, 11%; dentistry, 3%; engineering, 2%; theology (or the seminary), 2%; education, 10%; arts and sciences, 23%; veterinary medicine, 3%.

COSTS AND FINANCIAL AID
Financial aid office: (315) 228-7431. **Expenses (2006-2007):** Tuition and fees 2006-2007: $35,030; room/board: $8,530. Estimated books and supplies: $880; transportation: $100; personal expenses: $860. **Financial aid:** Priority filing date for institution's financial aid form: January 15; deadline: January 15. In 2005-2006, 46% of undergraduates applied for financial aid. Of those, 44% were determined to have financial need; 100% had their need fully met. Average financial aid package (proportion receiving): $27,795 (44%). Average amount of gift aid, such as scholarships or grants (proportion receiving): $25,396 (39%). Average amount of self-help aid, such as work study or loans (proportion receiving): $5,338 (35%). Average need-based loan (excluding PLUS or other private loans): $4,350. Among students who received need-based aid, the average percentage of need met: 100%. Among students who received aid based on merit, the average award (and the proportion receiving): $0 (0%). The average athletic scholarship (and the proportion receiving): $29,865 (3%). Average amount of debt of borrowers graduating in 2005: $13,452. Proportion who borrowed: 38%.

CAMPUS LIFE AND EXTRACURRICULAR ACTIVITIES
Campus housing available (% using): coed dorms (55%), sorority housing (3%), fraternity housing (6%), apartment for single students (28%), cooperative housing (8%). Students who live in college-owned, operated, or affiliated housing: 83%. **Student employment:** During the 2005-2006 academic year, 23% of undergraduates worked on campus. Average per-year earnings: $1,850. **Clubs and organizations:** Number of student organizations: 122. Activities include: choral groups, concert band, dance, drama/theater, jazz band, literary magazine, marching band, music ensembles, musical theater, pep band, radio station, student government, student newspaper, student film society, symphony orchestra, television station, yearbook. Number of fraternities: 6; sororities: 4. Proportion of men in fraternities: 28%; of women in sororities: 32%. Average proportion of students who stay on campus on weekends: 95%. **Sports program (2005-2006):** Member of NCAA I. **Men's intercollegiate varsity sports:** basketball, crew, cross-country, football, golf, ice hockey, lacrosse, soccer, swimming and diving, track and field (indoor), track and field (outdoor). **Women's intercollegiate varsity sports:** basketball, crew, cross-country, field hockey, ice hockey, lacrosse, soccer, softball, swimming and diving, tennis, track and field (indoor), track and field (outdoor), volleyball.

SERVICES AND FACILITIES
Basic services: nonremedial tutoring, women's center, placement service, health service, health insurance. **Counseling services:** minority student, career, personal, academic, psychological, birth control, religious. **For learning-disabled students:** School does not offer a structured program with separate admission and additional fees. Total undergraduates in learning-disabled program or receiving services: 175. **Library:** Number of titles: 777,368; number of current serial subscriptions: 3,714. **Information technology resources:** Students are not required to lease or own a computer.

Number of campus computers available to all students: 727. School has a wireless network. Approximate number of users that can be accommodated: 2,500. Proportion of college-owned housing units wired for high-speed internet access: 100%. **Campus safety:** Security services offered: 24-hour foot-and-vehicle patrols, late-night transport/escort service, 24-hour emergency telephones, lighted pathways/sidewalks, student patrols, controlled dormitory access (key, security card, etc).

TRANSFER AND INTERNATIONAL STUDENTS
Transfer students: May apply for admission for the following academic terms: Fall, Spring. Applicants do not need a minimum number of credits to apply. For fall 2005: Transfer applications received: 199. Transfer applicants offered admission: 31. Transfer applicants enrolled: 17. **International students:** Number of foreign undergraduates: 137 (5% of student body). Number of countries represented: 36. Minimum TOEFL score required: 600 (paper); 250 (computer). Average TOEFL score: 619 (paper).

College of Mount St. Vincent

- **Address:** 6301 Riverdale Avenue, Riverdale, NY 10471
- **Website:** http://www.mountsaintvincent.edu
- **Private; Religious affiliation:** Roman Catholic
- **Enrollment:** 1,249 full-time; 278 part-time

KEY STATS
✔ **U.S News College Ranking:** third tier, Universities–Master's (North)
✔ **SAT Score (25th/75th percentile):** 910-1080
✔ **Tuition:** 2006-2007: $21,550

Selectivity: Less selective	**Room/board:** $8,500
Acceptance rate: 69%	**Average debt:** $17,000
Student/faculty ratio: 12/1	**Proportion who borrowed:** 80%

UNDERGRADUATE STUDENT BODY STATS
2005-2006 enrollment: 1,249 full-time; 278 part-time. Men: 26%; women: 74%. **Ethnic makeup:** African American: 12%; Asian American: 11%; Hispanic: 29%; White: 48%. **Religious preference:** Protestant: 2%; Jewish: 1%; No preference: 1%; Roman Catholic: 80%; Other: 1%.

ADMISSIONS FACTS AND FIGURES
Phone: (718) 405-3267. **Email:** admissions.office@mountsaintvincent.edu. **Website:** http://www.mountsaintvincent.edu. **Application deadlines for fall 2007:** Regular decision: Rolling. Early decision: Not offered. Early action: Send application by: November 1; Decision sent by: December 1. Admission can be deferred. **Application fee:** $35. Common application is accepted. **Admissions requirements/recommendations:** High school units required (recommended): English: 4 (4); Mathematics: 2 (3); Science: 2 (3); Foreign language: 2 (3); Social studies: 3 (4); History: 0 (0); Academic electives: 3 (3); Total units: 16 (20). Tests: The college uses SAT or ACT scores in admissions decisions. Either SAT or ACT required. Campus visit: Recommended. Admissions interview: Recommended. Off-campus interview: May be arranged. **Factors that count in admissions decisions:** *Academic:* Secondary school record: Very important. Class rank: Considered. Letters of recommendation: Very important. Standardized test scores: Very important. Essay: Important. *Nonacademic:* Interview: Important. Extracurricular activities: Important. Talent/ability: Not considered. Character/personal qualities: Very important. Alumni/ae relationship: Considered. Geographical residence: Not considered. State residency: Not considered. Religious affiliation/commitment: Not considered. Minority status: Not considered. Volunteer work: Considered. Work experience: Considered. **Other schools with the greatest overlap in applicants:** Fordham University; Iona College; Manhattan College; St. John's University. **Admissions statistics for the fall 2005 entering class:** Total applicants: 1,907. Total accepted: 1,309. Freshmen enrolled: 345; 16% were from out of state. Accepted through early-decision or early-action plans: 7%. Overall acceptance rate: 69%. Non-early acceptance rate: 68%. **Credentials of fall 2005 freshmen:** 12% ranked in the top 10 percent of their high school class; 40% were in the top 25 percent, and 69% were in the top half. (Proportion submitting class standing: 63%.) **Average high school grade point average:** 2.9. **First-year students who submitted SAT scores:** 100%. Scores (25/75 percentile): Verbal: 460-550, Math: 450-530, Combined: 910-1080.

ACADEMICS

Year founded: 1847. **Academic calendar:** Semester. **Degrees offered:** certificate, associate, bachelor's, master's, post-master's certificate. **Most popular majors:** 24% nursing/registered nurse training (R.N., A.S.N., B.S.N., M.S.N.), 17% business/commerce, 12% communication studies/speech communication and rhetoric, 11% psychology, 8% liberal arts and sciences/liberal studies. **Major fields of study:** biological and biomedical sciences; business, management, marketing, and related support services; communication, journalism, and related programs; computer and information sciences and support services; education; English language and literature/letters; foreign languages, literatures, and linguistics; health professions and related clinical sciences; history; liberal arts and sciences studies, and humanities; mathematics and statistics; philosophy and religious studies; physical sciences; psychology; social sciences. **Areas of required coursework:** arts/fine arts, humanities, computer literacy, mathematics, English (including composition), philosophy, foreign languages, sciences (biological or physical), history, social science, other. **Pre-professional programs:** pre-law, pre-dentistry, pre-medicine, pre-veterinary science, other. **Special academic programs (% participation):** cross-registration (49%), double major (1.4%), honors program (20.5%), independent study (25%), internships (35%), study abroad (4.8%), teacher certificate program (7.6%). **Teacher certification offered in:** early childhood, special education, elementary, middle/junior high, secondary. **Reserve Officers Training Corps (ROTC):** Air Force ROTC: Offered at cooperating institution (Manhattan College). **Faculty and instruction (2005-2006):** Total instructional faculty: 74 full-time, 84 part-time (46% men; 54% women; 12% minorities). Full-time faculty with Ph.D. or other terminal degree: 86%. Student/faculty ratio: 12/1. Classes of fewer than 20 students: 43%; of 20 to 49 students: 57%; of 50 or more students: 0%. **Advanced Placement and International Baccalaureate credit:** AP tests may be used for: Credit and/or placement. Scores accepted: 3, 4, 5. International Baccalaureate exams may be used for: Credit and/or placement. **Freshmen returning for sophomore year:** 78%. **Graduation rates:** Four-year: 35%; five-year: 44%; six-year: 57%. **Graduate study:** 10% of students pursue further study immediately upon graduation; 20% within one year; 35% within five years. Fields in which graduates pursue further study: Master of Business Administration (MBA), 7%; law, 2%; medicine, 2%; education, 14%; arts and sciences, 10%.

COSTS AND FINANCIAL AID

Financial aid office: (718) 405-3290. **Expenses (2006-2007):** Tuition and fees 2006-2007: $21,550; room/board: $8,500. Estimated books and supplies: $850; transportation: $200; personal expenses: $900. **Financial aid:** Priority filing date for institution's financial aid form: February 15. In 2005-2006, 90% of undergraduates applied for financial aid. Of those, 78% were determined to have financial need; Average financial aid package (proportion receiving): $17,000 (78%). Average amount of gift aid, such as scholarships or grants (proportion receiving): $7,600 (78%). Average amount of self-help aid, such as work study or loans (proportion receiving): $5,200 (78%). Average need-based loan (excluding PLUS or other private loans): $4,100. Among students who received need-based aid, the average percentage of need met: 74%. Among students who received aid based on merit, the average award (and the proportion receiving): $0 (N/A). The average athletic scholarship (and the proportion receiving): $0 (0%). Average amount of debt of borrowers graduating in 2005: $17,000. Proportion who borrowed: 80%.

CAMPUS LIFE AND EXTRACURRICULAR ACTIVITIES

Campus housing available (% using): coed dorms (62%), women's dorms (35%), special housing for disabled students (0%), other housing options (3%). Students who live in college-owned, operated, or affiliated housing: 49%. **Student employment:** During the 2005-2006 academic year, 5% of undergraduates worked on campus. Average per-year earnings: $800. **Clubs and organizations:** Number of student organizations: 36. Activities include: choral groups, dance, drama/theater, literary magazine, musical theater, radio station, student government, student newspaper, television station, yearbook. Number of fraternities: 0; sororities: 0. Average proportion of students who stay on campus on weekends: 55%. **Sports program (2005-2006):** Member of NCAA III. *Men's intercollegiate varsity sports:* baseball, basketball, cross-country, lacrosse, soccer, tennis, volleyball. *Women's intercollegiate varsity sports:* basketball, cross-country, lacrosse, soccer, softball, swimming and diving, tennis, track and field (outdoor), volleyball.

SERVICES AND FACILITIES

Basic services: nonremedial tutoring, health service. **Remedial assistance:** reading, math, writing, study skills. **Counseling services:** career, personal, academic, psychological, religious. **For learning-disabled students:** School does not offer a structured program with separate admission and additional fees. Total undergraduates in learning-disabled program or receiving services: 9. Services include: remedial math, remedial reading, untimed tests, note-taking services, learning center, readers, extended time for tests, tutors, substitution of courses, texts on tape, exams on tape or computer, other testing accomodations, waiver of foreign language degree requirement. **Library:** Number of titles: 106,669; number of current serial subscriptions: 12,284. **Information technology resources:** Students are not required to lease or own a computer. Number of campus computers available to all students: 218. School has a wireless network. Approximate number of users that can be accommodated: 2,000. Proportion of college-owned housing units wired for high-speed internet access: 100%. **Campus safety:** Security services offered: 24-hour foot-and-vehicle patrols, late-night transport/escort service, 24-hour emergency telephones, lighted pathways/sidewalks, controlled dormitory access (key, security card, etc).

TRANSFER AND INTERNATIONAL STUDENTS

Transfer students: May apply for admission for the following academic terms: Fall, Spring. Applicants do not need a minimum number of credits to apply. For fall 2005: Transfer applications received: 561. Transfer applicants offered admission: 205. Transfer applicants enrolled: 68. **International students:** Number of foreign undergraduates: 2. Number of countries represented: 5. Minimum TOEFL score required: 550 (paper); 213 (computer).

College of New Rochelle

- **Address:** Castle Place, New Rochelle, NY 10805-2338
- **Website:** http://www.cnr.edu
- **Private**
- **Enrollment:** N/A

KEY STATS

✔ **U.S News College Ranking:** fourth tier, Universities–Master's (North)
✔ **SAT or ACT Score (25th/75th percentile):** N/A
✔ **Tuition:** 2005-2006: $20,600

Selectivity: Less selective	**Room/board:** $7,800
Acceptance rate: N/A	**Average debt:** N/A
Student/faculty ratio: N/A	**Proportion who borrowed:** N/A

College of St. Rose

- **Address:** 432 Western Avenue, Albany, NY 12203-1490
- **Website:** http://www.strose.edu
- **Private; Religious affiliation:** Roman Catholic
- **Enrollment:** 2,795 full-time; 283 part-time

KEY STATS

✔ **U.S News College Ranking:** 68, Universities–Master's (North)
✔ **SAT Score (25th/75th percentile):** 970-1160
✔ **Tuition:** 2006-2007: $19,268

Selectivity: Selective	**Room/board:** $8,116
Acceptance rate: 71%	**Average debt:** $19,459
Student/faculty ratio: 15/1	**Proportion who borrowed:** 82%

UNDERGRADUATE STUDENT BODY STATS

2005-2006 enrollment: 2,795 full-time; 283 part-time. Men: 27%; women: 73%. **Ethnic makeup:** African American: 2%; Asian American: 1%; Hispanic: 3%; White: 93%.

ADMISSIONS FACTS AND FIGURES

Phone: (518) 454-5150. **Email:** admit@mail.strose.edu. **Website:** http://www.strose.edu. **Application deadlines for fall 2007:** Regular decision: February 1. Early decision: Not offered. Early action: Send application by: December 1; Decision sent by: October 1. Admission can be deferred. **Application fee:** $35. Common application is accepted. **Admissions requirements/recommendations:** High school units required (recommended): English: 4 (4); Mathematics: 3 (4); Science: 3 (4); Foreign language: 3 (4); Social studies: 4 (4); History: 4 (4); Academic electives: 0 (4); Total units: 45 (58). Tests: The college uses SAT or ACT scores in admissions decisions.

Either SAT or ACT required. For admission to the fall 2007 entering class, the school will accept: ACT with writing, ACT without writing. Campus visit: Recommended. Admissions interview: Recommended. Off-campus interview: May be arranged. **Factors that count in admissions decisions:** *Academic:* Secondary school record: Very important. Class rank: Considered. Letters of recommendation: Important. Standardized test scores: Important. Essay: Considered. *Nonacademic:* Interview: Important. Extracurricular activities: Very important. Talent/ability: Very important. Character/personal qualities: Important. Alumni/ae relationship: Considered. Geographical residence: Important. State residency: Considered. Religious affiliation/commitment: Not considered. Minority status: Considered. Volunteer work: Important. Work experience: Considered. **Other schools with the greatest overlap in applicants:** SUNY College–Cortland; SUNY College–Oneonta; SUNY–Albany; SUNY–Oswego; Siena College. **Admissions statistics for the fall 2005 entering class:** Total applicants: 3,134. Total accepted: 2,219. Freshmen enrolled: 598; 11% were from out of state. Overall acceptance rate: 71%. Non-early acceptance rate: 71%. **Credentials of fall 2005 freshmen:** 12% ranked in the top 10 percent of their high school class; 39% were in the top 25 percent, and 77% were in the top half. (Proportion submitting class standing: 88%.) **First-year students who submitted SAT scores:** 89%. Scores (25/75 percentile): Verbal: 490-580, Math: 480-580, Combined: 970-1160. **First-year students submitting ACT scores:** 11%. Scores (25/75 percentile): English: N/A, Math: N/A, Composite: 21-25.

ACADEMICS

Year founded: 1920. **Academic calendar:** Semester. **Degrees offered:** bachelor's, post-bachelor's certificate, master's, post-master's certificate. **Most popular majors:** 48% education, 10% business, management, marketing, and related support services, 9% communications technologies/technicians and support services, 8% visual and performing arts, 3% psychology. **Major fields of study:** agriculture, agriculture operations, and related sciences; area, ethnic, cultural, and gender studies; biological and biomedical sciences; business, management, marketing, and related support services; communications technologies/technicians and support services; computer and information sciences and support services; education; English language and literature/letters; foreign languages, literatures, and linguistics; health professions and related clinical sciences; history; liberal arts and sciences studies, and humanities; mathematics and statistics; natural resources and conservation; philosophy and religious studies; physical sciences; psychology; public administration and social service professions; security and protective services; social sciences; visual and performing arts. **Areas of required coursework:** arts/fine arts, humanities, computer literacy, mathematics, English (including composition), philosophy, foreign languages, sciences (biological or physical), history, social science, other. **Pre-professional programs:** pre-law, pre-dentistry, pre-medicine, pre-veterinary science. **Special academic programs (% participation):** accelerated program (2%), cross-registration, double major, independent study, internships, student-designed major (3%), study abroad, teacher certificate program. **Teacher certification offered in:** early childhood, special education, elementary, middle/junior high, secondary, bilingual/bicultural. **Reserve Officers Training Corps (ROTC):** Army ROTC: Offered at cooperating institution (Siena College); Navy ROTC: Offered at cooperating institution (RPI); Air Force ROTC: Offered at cooperating institution (University at Albany, State University of New York (SUNY)). **Faculty and instruction (2005-2006):** Total instructional faculty: 175 full-time, 306 part-time (41% men; 59% women; 8% minorities). Full-time faculty with Ph.D. or other terminal degree: 77%. Student/faculty ratio: 15/1. Classes of fewer than 20 students: 55%; of 20 to 49 students: 45%; of 50 or more students: 0%. **Advanced Placement and International Baccalaureate credit:** AP tests may be used for: Placement only. Scores accepted: 3, 4. International Baccalaureate exams may be used for: Credit and/or placement. **Freshmen returning for sophomore year:** 84%. **Graduation rates:** Four-year: 51%; five-year: 64%; six-year: 65%. **Graduate study:** 66% of students pursue further study within one year. Fields in which graduates pursue further study: Master of Business Administration (MBA), 4%; education, 74%; arts and sciences, 9%.

COSTS AND FINANCIAL AID

Financial aid office: (518) 458-5424. **Expenses (2006-2007):** Tuition and fees 2006-2007: $19,268; room/board: $8,116. Estimated books and supplies: $1,200; transportation: $500; personal expenses: $1,500. **Financial aid:** Priority filing date for institution's financial aid form: March 1; deadline: March 1. In 2005-2006, 94% of undergraduates applied for financial aid. Of those, 78% were determined to have financial need; 4% had their need fully met. Average financial aid package (proportion receiving): $7,486 (78%). Average amount of gift aid, such as scholarships or grants (proportion receiving): $3,377 (74%). Average amount of self-help aid, such as work

study or loans (proportion receiving): $2,657 (75%). Average need-based loan (excluding PLUS or other private loans): $1,987. Among students who received need-based aid, the average percentage of need met: 41%. Among students who received aid based on merit, the average award (and the proportion receiving): $2,203 (11%). The average athletic scholarship (and the proportion receiving): $6,392 (1%). Average amount of debt of borrowers graduating in 2005: $19,459. Proportion who borrowed: 82%.

CAMPUS LIFE AND EXTRACURRICULAR ACTIVITIES

Campus housing available: coed dorms, women's dorms, men's dorms, apartment for single students, special housing for disabled students. Students who live in college-owned, operated, or affiliated housing: 38%. **Student employment:** During the 2005-2006 academic year, 0% of undergraduates worked on campus. Activities include: choral groups, concert band, dance, drama/theater, jazz band, literary magazine, music ensembles, radio station, student government, student newspaper, television station, yearbook. Number of fraternities: 0; sororities: 0. Average proportion of students who stay on campus on weekends: 50%. **Sports program (2005-2006):** Member of NCAA II. **Men's intercollegiate varsity sports:** baseball, basketball, cross-country, golf, soccer, swimming and diving. **Women's intercollegiate varsity sports:** basketball, cross-country, soccer, softball, swimming and diving, tennis, volleyball.

SERVICES AND FACILITIES

Basic services: nonremedial tutoring, placement service, day care, health service, other. **Remedial assistance:** reading, math, writing, study skills. **Counseling services:** minority student, career, military, personal, veteran student, academic, older student, psychological, birth control, religious, other. **For learning-disabled students:** School does not offer a structured program with separate admission and additional fees. Total undergraduates in learning-disabled program or receiving services: 50. Services include: remedial math, remedial English, reading machines, note-taking services, oral tests, learning center, extended time for tests, tutors, priority seating, texts on tape, other testing accomodations. **Library:** Number of titles: 222,251; number of current serial subscriptions: 687. **Information technology resources:** Students are not required to lease or own a computer. Number of campus computers available to all students: 486. School has a wireless network. Approximate number of users that can be accommodated: 300. Proportion of college-owned housing units wired for high-speed internet access: 95%. **Campus safety:** Security services offered: 24-hour foot-and-vehicle patrols, late-night transport/escort service, 24-hour emergency telephones, lighted pathways/sidewalks, student patrols, controlled dormitory access (key, security card, etc).

TRANSFER AND INTERNATIONAL STUDENTS

Transfer students: May apply for admission for the following academic terms: Fall, Spring, Summer. Applicants do not need a minimum number of credits to apply. For fall 2005: Transfer applications received: 818. Transfer applicants offered admission: 531. Transfer applicants enrolled: 299. **International students:** Number of foreign undergraduates: 2. Minimum TOEFL score required: 500 (paper); 173 (computer).

Columbia University

- **Address:** 2960 Broadway, New York, NY 10027
- **Website:** http://www.columbia.edu
- **Private**
- **Enrollment:** 6,435 full-time; 884 part-time

KEY STATS

✔ **U.S News College Ranking:** 9, National Universities
✔ **SAT Score (25th/75th percentile):** 1340-1540
✔ **Tuition:** 2006-2007: $35,166

Selectivity: Most selective	**Room/board:** $9,648
Acceptance rate: 13%	**Average debt:** $16,541
Student/faculty ratio: 7/1	**Proportion who borrowed:** 47%

UNDERGRADUATE STUDENT BODY STATS

2005-2006 enrollment: 6,435 full-time; 884 part-time. Men: 52%; women: 48%. **Ethnic makeup:** African American: 7%; Asian American: 16%; Hispanic: 8%; White: 61%; International: 7%.

ADMISSIONS FACTS AND FIGURES

Phone: (212) 854-2522. **Email:** ugrad-admiss@columbia.edu. **Website:** http://www.columbia.edu. **Application deadlines for fall 2007:** Regular decision: January 2; decision sent by April 1. Early decision: Send application by: November 1; Decision sent by: December 15. Early action: Not offered. Admission can be deferred. **Application fee:** $65. Common application is not accepted. **To apply online, go to:** http://www.columbia.edu/cu/admissions/ugrad/. **Admissions requirements/recommendations:** High school units required (recommended): English: 4 (4); Mathematics: 4 (4); Science: 4 (4); Foreign language: 4 (4); Social studies: (4); History: 4 (4); Academic electives: 3 (3). Tests: The college uses SAT or ACT scores in admissions decisions. Either SAT or ACT required. For admission to the fall 2007 entering class, the school will accept: ACT with writing. Campus visit: Neither required nor recommended. Admissions interview: Neither required nor recommended. Off-campus interview: May not be arranged. **Factors that count in admissions decisions:** *Academic:* Secondary school record: Very important. Class rank: Very important. Letters of recommendation: Very important. Standardized test scores: Very important. Essay: Very important. *Nonacademic:* Interview: Considered. Extracurricular activities: Important. Talent/ability: Important. Character/personal qualities: Very important. Alumni/ae relationship: Considered. Geographical residence: Considered. State residency: Not considered. Religious affiliation/commitment: Not considered. Minority status: Considered. Volunteer work: Considered. Work experience: Not considered. **Admissions statistics for the fall 2005 entering class:** Total applicants: 18,119. Total accepted: 2,318. Freshmen enrolled: 1,339; 77% were from out of state. Overall acceptance rate: 13%. Early-decision acceptance rate: 39%. Non-early acceptance rate: 10%. **Credentials of fall 2005 freshmen:** 92% ranked in the top 10 percent of their high school class; 99% were in the top 25 percent, and 100% were in the top half. (Proportion submitting class standing: 55%.) **Average high school grade point average:** 3.9. **First-year students who submitted SAT scores:** 94%. Scores (25/75 percentile): Verbal: 670-760, Math: 670-780, Combined: 1340-1540. **First-year students submitting ACT scores:** 15%. Scores (25/75 percentile): English: 28-34, Math: 27-33, Composite: 28-33.

ACADEMICS

Year founded: 1754. **Academic calendar:** Semester. **Degrees offered:** certificate, bachelor's, post-bachelor's certificate, master's, first professional, first professional certificate, doctorate. **Most popular majors:** 22% social sciences, 18% engineering, 8% English language and literature/letters, 7% visual and performing arts, 6% history. **Major fields of study:** architecture and related services; area, ethnic, cultural, and gender studies; biological and biomedical sciences; computer and information sciences and support services; education; engineering; engineering technologies/technicians; English language and literature/letters; foreign languages, literatures, and linguistics; history; mathematics and statistics; multi/interdisciplinary studies; natural resources and conservation; philosophy and religious studies; physical sciences; psychology; social sciences; visual and performing arts. **Areas of required coursework:** humanities, English (including composition), philosophy, foreign languages, sciences (biological or physical), other. **Pre-professional programs:** pre-medicine. **Special academic programs:** cross-registration, double major, dual enrollment, honors program, independent study, internships, liberal arts/career combination, study abroad, teacher certificate program, other. **Reserve Officers Training Corps (ROTC):** Army ROTC: Offered at cooperating institution (Fordham University); Air Force ROTC: Offered at cooperating institution (Manhattan College). **Faculty and instruction (2005-2006):** Total instructional faculty: 1,296 full-time, 373 part-time (68% men; 32% women; 21% minorities). Full-time faculty with Ph.D. or other terminal degree: 100%. Student/faculty ratio: 7/1. Classes of fewer than 20 students: 72%; of 20 to 49 students: 20%; of 50 or more students: 8%. **Advanced Placement and International Baccalaureate credit:** AP tests may be used for: Credit and/or placement. Scores accepted: 4, 5. Freshmen returning for sophomore year: 98%. **Graduation rates:** Four-year: 92%; five-year: 94%; six-year: 94%.

COSTS AND FINANCIAL AID

Financial aid office: (212) 854-3711. **Expenses (2006-2007):** Tuition and fees 2006-2007: $35,166; room/board: $9,648. **Financial aid:** In 2005-2006, 52% of undergraduates applied for financial aid. Of those, 48% were determined to have financial need; 100% had their need fully met. Average financial aid package (proportion receiving): $28,138 (48%). Average amount of gift aid, such as scholarships or grants (proportion receiving): $23,874 (45%). Average amount of self-help aid, such as work study or loans (proportion receiving): $6,018 (43%). Average need-based loan (excluding PLUS or other private loans): $4,803. Among students who received need-based aid, the average percentage of need met: 100%. Average amount of debt of borrowers graduating in 2005: $16,541. Proportion who borrowed: 47%.

CAMPUS LIFE AND EXTRACURRICULAR ACTIVITIES

Campus housing available (% using): coed dorms (83%), sorority housing (1%), fraternity housing (4%), apartment for single students (6%), special housing for disabled students (5%), other housing options (1%). Students who live in college-owned, operated, or affiliated housing: 94%. **Clubs and organizations:** Number of student organizations: 150. Activities include: choral groups, concert band, dance, drama/theater, jazz band, literary magazine, marching band, music ensembles, musical theater, opera, pep band, radio station, student government, student newspaper, student film society, symphony orchestra, television station, yearbook. Number of fraternities: 14; sororities: 11. Proportion of men in fraternities: 15%; of women in sororities: 9%. Average proportion of students who stay on campus on weekends: 95%. **Sports program (2005-2006):** Member of NCAA I. *Men's intercollegiate varsity sports:* baseball, basketball, cross-country, fencing, football, golf, soccer, swimming and diving, tennis, track and field (indoor), track and field (outdoor), wrestling. *Women's intercollegiate varsity sports:* archery, basketball, cross-country, fencing, field hockey, golf, lacrosse, soccer, softball, swimming and diving, tennis, track and field (indoor), track and field (outdoor), volleyball, rowing.

SERVICES AND FACILITIES

Basic services: nonremedial tutoring, placement service, health service, health insurance. **For learning-disabled students:** School does not offer a structured program with separate admission and additional fees. Total undergraduates in learning-disabled program or receiving services: 125. Services include: reading machines, tape recorders, note-taking services, special bookstore section, learning center, readers, extended time for tests, early syllabus, priority registration, priority seating, substitution of courses, texts on tape, typist/scribe, exams on tape or computer, other testing accomodations, waiver of foreign language degree requirement, other. **Library:** Number of titles: 8,792,821; number of current serial subscriptions: 65,650. **Information technology resources:** Students are not required to lease or own a computer. School has a wireless network. Approximate number of users that can be accommodated: 20,000. Proportion of college-owned housing units wired for high-speed internet access: 100%. **Campus safety:** Security services offered: 24-hour foot-and-vehicle patrols, late-night transport/escort service, 24-hour emergency telephones, lighted pathways/sidewalks, controlled dormitory access (key, security card, etc).

TRANSFER AND INTERNATIONAL STUDENTS

Transfer students: May apply for admission for the following academic terms: Fall. Applicants need a minimum number of credits to apply. For fall 2005: Transfer applications received: 1,179. Transfer applicants offered admission: 122. Transfer applicants enrolled: 70. **International students:** Number of foreign undergraduates: 542 (7% of student body). Minimum TOEFL score required: 600 (paper); 250 (computer).

Concordia College

- **Address:** 171 White Plains Road, Bronxville, NY 10708
- **Website:** http://www.concordia-ny.edu
- **Private; Religious affiliation:** Lutheran
- **Enrollment:** 592 full-time; 57 part-time

KEY STATS

✔ **U.S News College Ranking:** 31, Comp. Colleges–Bachelor's (North)
✔ **SAT Score (25th/75th percentile):** 870-1070
✔ **Tuition:** 2006-2007: $20,800

Selectivity: Less selective	**Room/board:** $8,200
Acceptance rate: 76%	**Average debt:** $18,265
Student/faculty ratio: 15/1	**Proportion who borrowed:** 75%

UNDERGRADUATE STUDENT BODY STATS

2005-2006 enrollment: 592 full-time; 57 part-time. Men: 43%; women: 57%. **Ethnic makeup:** African American: 10%; Asian American: 2%; Hispanic: 7%; White: 73%; International: 8%. **Religious preference:** Roman Catholic: 34%; Protestant: 13%; Jewish: 1%; Muslim: 1%; Buddhist: 1%; No preference: 8%; Unknown: 15%; Lutheran: 25%; Other: 2%.

ADMISSIONS FACTS AND FIGURES

Phone: (800) 937-2655. **Email:** admission@concordia-ny.edu. **Website:** http://www.concordia-ny.edu. **Application deadlines for fall 2007:** Regular decision: August 15. Early decision: Not offered. Early action: Send application by: November 15; Decision sent by: December 1. Admission can be deferred. **Application fee:** $40. Common application is accepted. **To apply online, go to:** http://www.commonapp.org. **Admissions requirements/recommendations:** High school units required (recommended): English: (4); Mathematics: (3); Science: (2); Foreign language: (2); Social studies: (2); History: (2); Total units: (17). Tests: The college uses SAT or ACT scores in admissions decisions. Either SAT or ACT required. For admission to the fall 2007 entering class, the school will accept: ACT with writing, ACT without writing. Campus visit: Recommended. Admissions interview: Recommended. Off-campus interview: May be arranged. **Factors that count in admissions decisions:** *Academic:* Secondary school record: Very important. Class rank: Very important. Letters of recommendation: Important. Standardized test scores: Important. Essay: Important. *Nonacademic:* Interview: Considered. Extracurricular activities: Important. Talent/ability: Considered. Character/personal qualities: Very important. Alumni/ae relationship: Important. Geographical residence: Not considered. State residency: Not considered. Religious affiliation/commitment: Considered. Minority status: Not considered. Volunteer work: Very important. Work experience: Considered. **Other schools with the greatest overlap in applicants:** Fordham University; Hofstra University; Iona College; Manhattanville College; Pace University. **Admissions statistics for the fall 2005 entering class:** Total applicants: 692. Total accepted: 523. Freshmen enrolled: 175; 68% were from out of state. Accepted through early-decision or early-action plans: 5%. Overall acceptance rate: 76%. Non-early acceptance rate: 76%. **Credentials of fall 2005 freshmen:** 11% ranked in the top 10 percent of their high school class; 34% were in the top 25 percent, and 68% were in the top half. (Proportion submitting class standing: 25%.) **Average high school grade point average:** 2.8. **First-year students who submitted SAT scores:** 92%. Scores (25/75 percentile): Verbal: 440-540, Math: 430-530, Combined: 870-1070. **First-year students submitting ACT scores:** 8%. Scores (25/75 percentile): English: 17-22, Math: 16-20, Composite: 18-21.

ACADEMICS

Year founded: 1881. **Academic calendar:** Semester. **Degrees offered:** diploma, associate, bachelor's. **Most popular majors:** 24% business administration and management, 20% social sciences, 16% liberal arts and sciences/liberal studies, 8% foreign languages and literatures, 4% elementary education and teaching. **Major fields of study:** area, ethnic, cultural, and gender studies; biological and biomedical sciences; business, management, marketing, and related support services; education; English language and literature/letters; history; liberal arts and sciences studies, and humanities; mathematics and statistics; philosophy and religious studies; public administration and social service professions; social sciences; theology and religious vocations; visual and performing arts. **Areas of required coursework:** arts/fine arts, humanities, mathematics, English (including composition), philosophy, sciences (biological or physical), history, social science, other. **Pre-professional programs:** pre-law, pre-medicine, pre-theology. **Special academic programs (% participation):** accelerated program (20%), distance learning (3%), double major (1%), English as a Second Language (ESL) (3%), exchange student program (domestic) (1%), honors program (5%), independent study (9%), internships (11%), liberal arts/career combination, student-designed major (4%), study abroad (2%), teacher certificate program (17%). **Teacher certification offered in:** early childhood, elementary, middle/junior high. **Cooperative education programs:** health professions. **Faculty and instruction (2005-2006):** Total instructional faculty: 26 full-time, 44 part-time (57% men; 43% women; 17% minorities). Full-time faculty with Ph.D. or other terminal degree: 77%. Student/faculty ratio: 15/1. Classes of fewer than 20 students: 62%; of 20 to 49 students: 38%. **Advanced Placement and International Baccalaureate credit:** AP tests may be used for: Credit and/or placement. Scores accepted: 3. International Baccalaureate exams may be used for: Credit and/or placement. **Freshmen returning for sophomore year:** 76%. **Graduation rates:** Four-year: 37%; five-year: 43%; six-year: 44%.

COSTS AND FINANCIAL AID

Financial aid office: (914) 337-9300. **Expenses (2006-2007):** Tuition and fees 2006-2007: $20,800; room/board: $8,200. Estimated books and supplies: $900; transportation: $500; personal expenses: $1,600. **Financial aid:** Priority filing date for institution's financial aid form: February 15; deadline: May 31. In 2005-2006, 79% of undergraduates applied for financial aid. Of those, 68% were determined to have financial need; 20% had their need fully met. Average financial aid package (proportion receiving): $20,690 (68%). Average amount of gift aid, such as scholarships or grants (propor-

tion receiving): $9,700 (66%). Average amount of self-help aid, such as work study or loans (proportion receiving): $3,800 (53%). Average need-based loan (excluding PLUS or other private loans): $3,630. Among students who received need-based aid, the average percentage of need met: 70%. Among students who received aid based on merit, the average award (and the proportion receiving): $5,895 (12%). The average athletic scholarship (and the proportion receiving): $8,605 (6%). Average amount of debt of borrowers graduating in 2005: $18,265. Proportion who borrowed: 75%.

CAMPUS LIFE AND EXTRACURRICULAR ACTIVITIES

Campus housing available (% using): coed dorms (6%), women's dorms (53%), men's dorms (41%). Students who live in college-owned, operated, or affiliated housing: 64%. **Student employment:** During the 2005-2006 academic year, 35% of undergraduates worked on campus. Average per-year earnings: $1,300. **Clubs and organizations:** Number of student organizations: 24. Activities include: choral groups, dance, drama/theater, literary magazine, music ensembles, musical theater, student government, yearbook. Number of fraternities: 2; sororities: 1. Proportion of men in fraternities: 12%; of women in sororities: 6%. Average proportion of students who stay on campus on weekends: 70%. **Sports program (2005-2006):** Member of NCAA II. *Men's intercollegiate varsity sports:* baseball, basketball, cross-country, soccer, tennis. *Women's intercollegiate varsity sports:* basketball, cross-country, soccer, softball, tennis, volleyball.

SERVICES AND FACILITIES

Basic services: nonremedial tutoring, placement service, health service, health insurance, other. **Remedial assistance:** math, writing. **Counseling services:** career, personal, academic, older student, psychological, religious. **For learning-disabled students:** School does not offer a structured program with separate admission and additional fees. Total undergraduates in learning-disabled program or receiving services: 56. Services include: remedial math, remedial English, remedial reading, diagnostic testing service, untimed tests, note-taking services, oral tests, learning center, readers, extended time for tests, tutors, proofreading services, other testing accomodations, other. **Library:** Number of titles: 73,423; number of current serial subscriptions: 391. **Information technology resources:** Students are not required to lease or own a computer. Number of campus computers available to all students: 60. School has a wireless network. Approximate number of users that can be accommodated: 75. Proportion of college-owned housing units wired for high-speed internet access: 100%. **Campus safety:** Security services offered: 24-hour foot-and-vehicle patrols, late-night transport/escort service, 24-hour emergency telephones, lighted pathways/sidewalks, controlled dormitory access (key, security card, etc).

TRANSFER AND INTERNATIONAL STUDENTS

Transfer students: May apply for admission for the following academic terms: Fall, Spring. Applicants need a minimum number of credits to apply. For fall 2005: Transfer applications received: 88. Transfer applicants offered admission: 40. Transfer applicants enrolled: 21. **International students:** Number of foreign undergraduates: 53 (8% of student body). Number of countries represented: 34. Minimum TOEFL score required: 550 (paper); 213 (computer). Average TOEFL score: 555 (paper).

Cooper Union

■ **Address:** 30 Cooper Square, New York, NY 10003
■ **Website:** http://www.cooper.edu
■ **Private**
■ **Enrollment:** 949 full-time; 6 part-time

KEY STATS

✔ **U.S News College Ranking:** Unranked Specialty School–Engineering
✔ **SAT Score (25th/75th percentile):** 1210-1450
✔ **Tuition:** 2006-2007: $31,500

Selectivity: Most selective	**Room/board:** $9,360
Acceptance rate: 13%	**Average debt:** $11,617
Student/faculty ratio: 9/1	**Proportion who borrowed:** 32%

UNDERGRADUATE STUDENT BODY STATS

2005-2006 enrollment: 949 full-time; 6 part-time. Men: 64%; women: 36%. **Ethnic makeup:** African American: 5%; Asian American: 20%; Hispanic: 9%; White: 54%; International: 12%.

ADMISSIONS FACTS AND FIGURES

Phone: (212) 353-4120. **Email:** admissions@cooper.edu. **Website:** http://www.cooper.edu. **Application deadlines for fall 2007:** Regular decision: January 1; decision sent by April 1. Early decision: Send application by: December 1; Decision sent by: December 22. Early action: Not offered. Admission can be deferred. **Application fee:** $50. Common application is not accepted. **Admissions requirements/recommendations:** High school units required (recommended): English: 4 (4); Mathematics: 4 (4); Science: 2 (3); Foreign language: 0 (0); Social studies: 2 (4); History: 0 (0); Academic electives: 8 (10); Total units: 16 (18). Tests: The college uses SAT or ACT scores in admissions decisions. Either SAT or ACT required. For admission to the fall 2007 entering class, the school will accept: ACT without writing. Campus visit: Recommended. Admissions interview: Neither required nor recommended. Off-campus interview: Not available. **Factors that count in admissions decisions:** *Academic:* Secondary school record: Very important. Class rank: Not considered. Letters of recommendation: Considered. Standardized test scores: Very important. Essay: Important. *Nonacademic:* Interview: Considered. Extracurricular activities: Important. Talent/ability: Very important. Character/personal qualities: Considered. Alumni/ae relationship: Not considered. Geographical residence: Not considered. State residency: Not considered. Religious affiliation/commitment: Not considered. Minority status: Considered. Volunteer work: Considered. Work experience: Considered. **Other schools with the greatest overlap in applicants:** Carnegie Mellon University; Columbia University; Cornell University; New York University; SUNY–Binghamton. **Admissions statistics for the fall 2005 entering class:** Total applicants: 2,301. Total accepted: 308. Freshmen enrolled: 228; 40% were from out of state. Accepted through early-decision or early-action plans: 25%. Overall acceptance rate: 13%. Early-decision acceptance rate: 13%. Non-early acceptance rate: 13%. **Size of waiting list:** 45 applicants; enrolled from waiting list: 2. **Credentials of fall 2005 freshmen:** 85% ranked in the top 10 percent of their high school class; 98% were in the top 25 percent, and 98% were in the top half. (Proportion submitting class standing: 60%.) **Average high school grade point average:** 3.5. **First-year students who submitted SAT scores:** 99%. Scores (25/75 percentile): Verbal: 610-690, Math: 600-760, Combined: 1210-1450. **First-year students submitting ACT scores:** 1%. Scores (25/75 percentile): English: N/A, Math: N/A, Composite: N/A.

ACADEMICS

Year founded: 1859. **Academic calendar:** Semester. **Degrees offered:** certificate, bachelor's, master's. **Most popular majors:** 29% fine/studio arts, 15% electrical, electronics, and communications engineering, 14% architecture (B.Arch., B.A./B.S., M.Arch., M.A./M.S., Ph.D.), 12% mechanical engineering. **Major fields of study:** architecture and related services; engineering; visual and performing arts. **Areas of required coursework:** humanities, computer literacy, mathematics, sciences (biological or physical), history, social science. **Special academic programs (% participation):** cross-registration (15%), English as a Second Language (ESL) (2%), exchange student program (domestic) (5%), honors program (100%), independent study (20%), internships (75%), liberal arts/career combination (100%), study abroad (20%). **Faculty and instruction (2005-2006):** Total instructional faculty: 52 full-time, 167 part-time (73% men; 27% women). Full-time faculty with Ph.D. or other terminal degree: 77%. Student/faculty ratio: 9/1. Classes of fewer than 20 students: 67%; of 20 to 49 students: 33%. **Advanced Placement and International Baccalaureate credit:** AP tests may be used for: Credit and/or placement. Scores accepted: 4, 5. **Freshmen returning for sophomore year:** 94%. **Graduation rates:** Four-year: 66%; five-year: 79%; six-year: 77%. **Graduate study:** 51% of students pursue further study immediately upon graduation; 56% within one year; 62% within five years. Fields in which graduates pursue further study: Master of Business Administration (MBA), 10%; law, 7%; medicine, 1%; dentistry, 1%; engineering, 80%; veterinary medicine, 1%.

COSTS AND FINANCIAL AID

Financial aid office: (212) 353-4113. **Expenses (2006-2007):** Tuition and fees 2006-2007: $31,500; room/board: $9,360. Estimated books and supplies: $1,400; transportation: $700; personal expenses: $1,575. **Financial aid:** Priority filing date for institution's financial aid form: May 1; deadline: May 1. In 2005-2006, 36% of undergraduates applied for financial aid. Of those, 32% were determined to have financial need; 94% had their need fully met. Average financial aid package (proportion receiving): $6,340 (32%). Average amount of gift aid, such as scholarships or grants (proportion receiving): $3,268 (27%). Average amount of self-help aid, such as work study or loans (proportion receiving): $2,950 (26%). Average need-based loan (excluding PLUS or other private loans): $3,400. Among students who received need-based aid, the average percentage of need met: 90%. Among students who received aid based on merit, the average award (and the proportion receiving): $27,500 (100%). The average athletic scholarship (and the proportion receiving): $0 (0%). Average amount of debt of borrowers graduating in 2005: $11,617. Proportion who borrowed: 32%.

CAMPUS LIFE AND EXTRACURRICULAR ACTIVITIES

Campus housing available (% using): coed dorms (100%). Students who live in college-owned, operated, or affiliated housing: 20%. **Student employment:** During the 2005-2006 academic year, 70% of undergraduates worked on campus. Average per-year earnings: $989. **Clubs and organizations:** Number of student organizations: 85. Activities include: choral groups, dance, drama/theater, literary magazine, music ensembles, student government, student newspaper, student film society, yearbook. Number of fraternities: 2; sororities: 1. Proportion of men in fraternities: 10%; of women in sororities: 5%. Average proportion of students who stay on campus on weekends: 25%.

SERVICES AND FACILITIES

Basic services: nonremedial tutoring, placement service, health insurance. **Remedial assistance:** writing. **Counseling services:** career, personal, academic, psychological. **For learning-disabled students:** School does not offer a structured program with separate admission and additional fees. Total undergraduates in learning-disabled program or receiving services: 8. Services include: tape recorders, untimed tests, readers, extended time for tests, tutors, texts on tape, other testing accomodations. **Library:** Number of titles: 103,289; number of current serial subscriptions: 286. **Information technology resources:** Students are not required to lease or own a computer. Number of campus computers available to all students: 350. School does not have a wireless network. Proportion of college-owned housing units wired for high-speed internet access: 100%. **Campus safety:** Security services offered: controlled dormitory access (key, security card, etc).

TRANSFER AND INTERNATIONAL STUDENTS

Transfer students: May apply for admission for the following academic terms: Fall. Applicants need a minimum number of credits to apply. For fall 2005: Transfer applications received: 501. Transfer applicants offered admission: 49. Transfer applicants enrolled: 42. **International students:** Number of foreign undergraduates: 112 (12% of student body). Minimum TOEFL score required: 600 (paper); 250 (computer). Average TOEFL score: 630 (paper).

Cornell University

- **Address:** 349 Pine Tree Road, Ithaca, NY 14853
- **Website:** http://admissions.cornell.edu
- **Private**
- **Enrollment:** 13,515 full-time

KEY STATS

✔ **U.S News College Ranking:** 12, National Universities
✔ **SAT Score (25th/75th percentile):** 1290-1480
✔ **Tuition:** 2006-2007: $32,981

Selectivity: Most selective	**Room/board:** $10,726
Acceptance rate: 27%	**Average debt:** $23,450
Student/faculty ratio: 10/1	**Proportion who borrowed:** 54%

UNDERGRADUATE STUDENT BODY STATS

2005-2006 enrollment: 13,515 full-time. Men: 50%; women: 50%. **Ethnic makeup:** African American: 5%; Asian American: 16%; Hispanic: 5%; White: 66%; International: 8%.

ADMISSIONS FACTS AND FIGURES

Phone: (607) 255-5241. **Email:** admissions@cornell.edu. **Website:** http://admissions.cornell.edu. **Application deadlines for fall 2007:** Regular decision: January 1. Early decision: Send application by: November 1; Decision sent by: N/A. Early action: Not offered. Admission can be deferred. **Application fee:** $65. Common application is accepted. **To apply online, go to:** http://app.commonapp.org. **Admissions requirements/recommendations:** High school units required (recommended): English: 4; Mathematics: 3; Science: (3); Foreign language: (3); Social studies: (3); History: (3); Total units: 16. Tests: The college uses SAT or ACT scores in admissions decisions. Either SAT or ACT required. For admission to the fall 2007 entering class, the school will accept: ACT with writing. Campus visit: Recommended. Admissions interview: Neither required nor recommended. Off-campus interview: May be arranged. **Factors that count in admissions decisions:** *Academic:* Secondary school record: Very important. Class rank: Important. Letters of recommendation: Very important. Standardized test scores: Very important. Essay: Very important. *Nonacademic:* Interview: Considered. Extracurricular activities: Very important. Talent/ability: Very important. Character/personal qualities: Considered. Alumni/ae relationship: Considered. Geographical residence: Considered. State residency: Considered. Religious affiliation/commitment: Not considered. Minority status: Considered. Volunteer work: Considered. Work experience: Considered. **Admissions statistics for the fall 2005 entering class:** Total applicants: 24,452. Total accepted: 6,621. Freshmen enrolled: 3,108; 64% were from out of state. Overall acceptance rate: 27%. Early-decision acceptance rate: 42%. Non-early acceptance rate: 25%. **Size of waiting list:** 2643 applicants; enrolled from waiting list: 209. **Credentials of fall 2005 freshmen:** 81% ranked in the top 10 percent of their high school class; 96% were in the top 25 percent, and 99% were in the top half. (Proportion submitting class standing: 51%.) **First-year students who submitted SAT scores:** 98%. Scores (25/75 percentile): Verbal: 630-720, Math: 660-760, Combined: 1290-1480. **First-year students submitting ACT scores:** 18%. Scores (25/75 percentile): English: 26-33, Math: 27-33, Composite: 28-32.

ACADEMICS

Year founded: 1865. **Academic calendar:** Semester. **Degrees offered:** bachelor's, master's, first professional, doctorate. **Most popular majors:** 18% engineering, 12% agriculture, agriculture operations, and related sciences, 12% social sciences, 11% biological and biomedical sciences, 11% business, management, marketing, and related support services. **Major fields of study:** agriculture, agriculture operations, and related sciences; architecture and related services; area, ethnic, cultural, and gender studies; biological and biomedical sciences; business, management, marketing, and related support services; communication, journalism, and related programs; computer and information sciences and support services; education; engineering; English language and literature/letters; family and consumer sciences/human sciences; foreign languages, literatures, and linguistics; health professions and related clinical sciences; history; liberal arts and sciences studies, and humanities; mathematics and statistics; multi/interdisciplinary studies; natural resources and conservation; philosophy and religious studies; physical sciences; psychology; public administration and social service professions; social sciences; visual and performing arts. **Areas of required coursework:** English (including composition), social science. **Preprofessional programs:** pre-law, pre-medicine, pre-veterinary science. **Special academic programs:** accelerated program, cooperative (work-study plan) program, cross-registration, distance learning, double major, English as a Second Language (ESL), exchange student program (domestic), honors program, independent study, internships, liberal arts/career combination, student-designed major, study abroad, teacher certificate program, other. **Teacher certification offered in:** adult education, secondary. **Cooperative education programs:** agriculture, engineering. **Reserve Officers Training Corps (ROTC):** Army ROTC: Offered on campus; Navy ROTC: Offered on campus; Air Force ROTC: Offered on campus. **Faculty and instruction (2005-2006):** Total instructional faculty: 1,447 full-time, 74 part-time (75% men; 25% women; 13% minorities). Full-time faculty with Ph.D. or other terminal degree: 99%. Student/faculty ratio: 10/1. Classes of fewer than 20 students: 61%; of 20 to 49 students: 23%; of 50 or more students: 15%. **Advanced Placement and International Baccalaureate credit:** AP tests may be used for: Credit and/or placement. Scores accepted: 4, 5. International Baccalaureate exams may be used for: Credit and/or placement. **Freshmen returning for sophomore year:** 96%. **Graduation rates:** Four-year: 84%; five-year: 91%; six-year: 92%. **Graduate study:** 33% of students pursue further study immediately upon graduation. Fields in which graduates pursue further study: Master of Business Administration (MBA), 3%; law, 19%; medicine, 16%; engineering, 17%; arts and sciences, 3%; veterinary medicine, 5%.

COSTS AND FINANCIAL AID

Financial aid office: (607) 255-5145. **Expenses (2006-2007):** Tuition and fees 2006-2007: $32,981; room/board: $10,726. Estimated books and supplies: $680 personal expenses: $1,380. **Financial aid:** In 2005-2006, 51% of undergraduates applied for financial aid. Of those, 46% were determined to have financial need; 100% had their need fully met. Average financial aid package (proportion receiving): $29,500 (46%). Average amount of gift aid, such as scholarships or grants (proportion receiving): $22,000 (43%). Average amount of self-help aid, such as work study or loans (proportion receiving): $9,200 (43%). Average need-based loan (excluding PLUS or other private loans): $7,400. Among students who received need-based aid, the average

percentage of need met: 100%. Average amount of debt of borrowers graduating in 2005: $23,450. Proportion who borrowed: 54%.

CAMPUS LIFE AND EXTRACURRICULAR ACTIVITIES

Campus housing available (% using): coed dorms (64%), women's dorms (6%), men's dorms (0%), sorority housing (5%), fraternity housing (11%), apartments for married students (5%), apartment for single students (6%), special housing for disabled students (0%), special housing for international students (1%), cooperative housing (2%), other housing options (0%). Students who live in college-owned, operated, or affiliated housing: 54%. **Student employment:** During the 2005-2006 academic year, 51% of undergraduates worked on campus. Average per-year earnings: $1,800. **Clubs and organizations:** Number of student organizations: 864. Activities include: choral groups, concert band, dance, drama/theater, jazz band, literary magazine, marching band, music ensembles, musical theater, pep band, radio station, student government, student newspaper, student film society, symphony orchestra, yearbook. Number of fraternities: 49; sororities: 22. Proportion of men in fraternities: 28%; of women in sororities: 22%. Average proportion of students who stay on campus on weekends: 90%. **Sports program (2005-2006):** Member of NCAA I. *Men's intercollegiate varsity sports:* baseball, basketball, cross-country, football, golf, ice hockey, lacrosse, soccer, swimming and diving, tennis, track and field (indoor), track and field (outdoor), wrestling. *Women's intercollegiate varsity sports:* basketball, cross-country, equestrian sports, fencing, field hockey, gymnastics, ice hockey, lacrosse, soccer, softball, squash, swimming and diving, tennis, track and field (indoor), track and field (outdoor), volleyball, rowing.

SERVICES AND FACILITIES

Basic services: nonremedial tutoring, women's center, placement service, health service, health insurance. **Remedial assistance:** reading, math, writing, study skills, other. **Counseling services:** minority student, career, military, personal, veteran student, academic, older student, psychological, birth control, religious. **For learning-disabled students:** School does not offer a structured program with separate admission and additional fees. Total undergraduates in learning-disabled program or receiving services: 265. Services include: reading machines, note-taking services, learning center, readers, extended time for tests, other. **Library:** Number of titles: 7,403,263; number of current serial subscriptions: 80,633. **Information technology resources:** Students are not required to lease or own a computer. Number of campus computers available to all students: 3,000. School has a wireless network. Approximate number of users that can be accommodated: 35,000. Proportion of college-owned housing units wired for high-speed internet access: 95%. **Campus safety:** Security services offered: 24-hour foot-and-vehicle patrols, late-night transport/escort service, 24-hour emergency telephones, lighted pathways/sidewalks, student patrols, controlled dormitory access (key, security card, etc).

TRANSFER AND INTERNATIONAL STUDENTS

Transfer students: May apply for admission for the following academic terms: Fall, Spring. Applicants need a minimum number of credits to apply. For fall 2005: Transfer applications received: 2,011. Transfer applicants offered admission: 702. Transfer applicants enrolled: 481. **International students:** Number of foreign undergraduates: 1014 (8% of student body). Number of countries represented: 128. Minimum TOEFL score required: 600 (paper); 250 (computer). Average TOEFL score: 618 (paper).

CUNY–Baruch College

- **Address:** 1 Bernard Baruch Way, New York, NY 10010
- **Website:** http://www.baruch.cuny.edu
- **Public**
- **Enrollment:** 9,753 full-time; 3,091 part-time

KEY STATS

✔ **U.S News College Ranking:** 40, Universities–Master's (North)
✔ **SAT Score (25th/75th percentile):** 990-1200
✔ **Tuition:** 2006-2007: $4,300 in state, $11,100 out of state

Selectivity: More selective	**Room/board:** N/A
Acceptance rate: 33%	**Average debt:** $10,900
Student/faculty ratio: 19/1	**Proportion who borrowed:** 21%

UNDERGRADUATE STUDENT BODY STATS

2005-2006 enrollment: 9,753 full-time; 3,091 part-time. Men: 45%; women: 55%. **Ethnic makeup:** African American: 13%; Asian American: 28%; Hispanic: 17%; White: 31%; International: 11%.

ADMISSIONS FACTS AND FIGURES

Phone: (646) 312-1400. **Email:** admissions@baruch.cuny.edu. **Website:** http://www.baruch.cuny.edu. **Application deadlines for fall 2007:** Regular decision: February 1; decision sent by May 15. Early decision: Send application by: December 13; Decision sent by: January 7. Early action: Not offered. Admission can be deferred. **Application fee:** $65. Common application is not accepted. **To apply online, go to:** http://www.applyto.uapc.cuny.edu/. **Admissions requirements/recommendations:** High school units required (recommended): English: 4 (0); Mathematics: 3 (4); Science: 2 (0); Foreign language: 2 (3); Social studies: 4 (0); History: 0 (0); Academic electives: 0 (1); Total units: 16 (0). Tests: The college uses SAT or ACT scores in admissions decisions. Either SAT or ACT required. For admission to the fall 2007 entering class, the school will accept: ACT without writing. Campus visit: Neither required nor recommended. Admissions interview: Neither required nor recommended. Off-campus interview: Not available. **Factors that count in admissions decisions:** *Academic:* Secondary school record: Very important. Class rank: Considered. Letters of recommendation: Important. Standardized test scores: Very important. Essay: Important. *Nonacademic:* Interview: Considered. Extracurricular activities: Considered. Talent/ability: Considered. Character/personal qualities: Considered. Alumni/ae relationship: Considered. Geographical residence: Not considered. State residency: Not considered. Religious affiliation/commitment: Not considered. Minority status: Not considered. Volunteer work: Not considered. Work experience: Considered. **Other schools with the greatest overlap in applicants:** Albany State University; CUNY–Hunter College; CUNY–Queens College; Fordham University; New York University. **Admissions statistics for the fall 2005 entering class:** Total applicants: 14,917. Total accepted: 4,962. Freshmen enrolled: 1,641; 3% were from out of state. Overall acceptance rate: 33%. Early-decision acceptance rate: 25%. Non-early acceptance rate: 33%. **Credentials of fall 2005 freshmen:** 28% ranked in the top 10 percent of their high school class; 59% were in the top 25 percent, and 87% were in the top half. (Proportion submitting class standing: 99%.) **Average high school grade point average:** 3.0. **First-year students who submitted SAT scores:** 94%. Scores (25/75 percentile): Verbal: 460-570, Math: 530-630, Combined: 990-1200.

ACADEMICS

Year founded: 1919. **Academic calendar:** Semester. **Degrees offered:** certificate, bachelor's, post-bachelor's certificate, master's, post-master's certificate. **Most popular majors:** 24% accounting, 20% finance, 6% marketing/marketing management, 5% business administration and management, 4% computer and information sciences. **Major fields of study:** biological and biomedical sciences; business, management, marketing, and related support services; communication, journalism, and related programs; computer and information sciences and support services; engineering; English language and literature/letters; foreign languages, literatures, and linguistics; history; liberal arts and sciences studies, and humanities; mathematics and statistics; multi/interdisciplinary studies; philosophy and religious studies; psychology; public administration and social service professions; social sciences; visual and performing arts. **Areas of required coursework:** arts/fine arts, humanities, computer literacy, mathematics, English (including composition), philosophy, foreign languages, sciences (biological or physical), history, social science, other. **Pre-professional programs:** pre-law, pre-dentistry, pre-medicine, pre-veterinary science. **Special academic programs (% participation):** accelerated program (1%), cross-registration (1%), distance learning (0%), double major (1%), English as a Second Language (ESL) (2%), exchange student program (domestic) (1%), honors program (3%), independent study (4%), internships (50%), student-designed major (3%), study abroad (5%). **Cooperative education programs:** business. **Reserve Officers Training Corps (ROTC):** Army ROTC: Offered at cooperating institution (Fordham University). **Faculty and instruction (2005-2006):** Total instructional faculty: 473 full-time, 452 part-time (64% men; 36% women; 25% minorities). Full-time faculty with Ph.D. or other terminal degree: 92%. Student/faculty ratio: 19/1. Classes of fewer than 20 students: 28%; of 20 to 49 students: 60%; of 50 or more students: 12%. **Advanced Placement and International Baccalaureate credit:** AP tests may be used for: Credit and/or placement. Scores accepted: 4, 5. International Baccalaureate exams may be used for: Credit only. **Freshmen returning for sophomore year:** 88%. **Graduation rates:** Four-year: 28%; five-year: 53%; six-year: 51%. **Graduate study:** 5% of students pursue further study within one year.

COSTS AND FINANCIAL AID

Financial aid office: (646) 312-1360. **Expenses (2006-2007):** Tuition and fees 2006-2007: $4,300 in state, $11,100 out of state; room/board: N/A. **Financial aid:** Priority filing date for institution's financial aid form: March 15; deadline: April 30. In 2005-2006, 84% of undergraduates applied for financial aid. Of those, 82% were determined to have financial need; Average financial aid package (proportion receiving): $4,800 (82%). Among students who received need-based aid, the average percentage of need met: 63%. Among students who received aid based on merit, the average award (and the proportion receiving): $1,800 (7%). The average athletic scholarship (and the proportion receiving): $3,000 (9%). Average amount of debt of borrowers graduating in 2005: $10,900. Proportion who borrowed: 21%.

CAMPUS LIFE AND EXTRACURRICULAR ACTIVITIES

Students who live in college-owned, operated, or affiliated housing: 0%. **Student employment:** During the 2005-2006 academic year, 6% of undergraduates worked on campus. Average per-year earnings: $2,500. **Clubs and organizations:** Number of student organizations: 165. Activities include: choral groups, dance, drama/theater, literary magazine, musical theater, radio station, student government, student newspaper, yearbook. Number of fraternities: 4; sororities: 4. Proportion of men in fraternities: 10%; of women in sororities: 10%. Average proportion of students who stay on campus on weekends: 3%. **Sports program (2005-2006):** Member of NCAA III. **Men's intercollegiate varsity sports:** baseball, basketball, cheerleading, soccer, swimming and diving, tennis, volleyball. **Women's intercollegiate varsity sports:** basketball, cheerleading, cross-country, softball, swimming and diving, tennis, volleyball.

SERVICES AND FACILITIES

Basic services: nonremedial tutoring, placement service, day care, health service. **Remedial assistance:** other. **Counseling services:** career, personal, academic, psychological. **For learning-disabled students:** School does not offer a structured program with separate admission and additional fees. Services include: reading machines, tape recorders, videotaped classes, note-taking services, special bookstore section, oral tests, readers, extended time for tests, tutors, early syllabus, priority registration, priority seating, substitution of courses, texts on tape, typist/scribe, exams on tape or computer, waiver of foreign language degree requirement, other. **Library:** Number of titles: 456,132; number of current serial subscriptions: 4,548. **Information technology resources:** Students are not required to lease or own a computer. Number of campus computers available to all students: 1,300. School has a wireless network. **Campus safety:** Security services offered: 24-hour foot-and-vehicle patrols, 24-hour emergency telephones, lighted pathways/sidewalks.

TRANSFER AND INTERNATIONAL STUDENTS

Transfer students: May apply for admission for the following academic terms: Fall, Spring. Applicants do not need a minimum number of credits to apply. For fall 2005: Transfer applications received: 5,705. Transfer applicants offered admission: 1,977. Transfer applicants enrolled: 1,282. **International students:** Number of foreign undergraduates: 1366 (11% of student body). Number of countries represented: 108. Minimum TOEFL score required: 620 (paper); 260 (computer). Average TOEFL score: 650 (paper).

CUNY–Brooklyn College

- **Address:** 2900 Bedford Avenue, Brooklyn, NY 11210
- **Website:** http://www.brooklyn.cuny.edu
- **Public**
- **Enrollment:** 8,109 full-time; 3,255 part-time

KEY STATS

✔ **U.S News College Ranking:** 79, Universities–Master's (North)
✔ **SAT Score (25th/75th percentile):** 940-1160
✔ **Tuition:** 2006-2007: $4,377 in state, $9,017 out of state

Selectivity: Selective	**Room/board:** N/A
Acceptance rate: 46%	**Average debt:** $14,000
Student/faculty ratio: 15/1	**Proportion who borrowed:** 30%

UNDERGRADUATE STUDENT BODY STATS

2005-2006 enrollment: 8,109 full-time; 3,255 part-time. Men: 40%; women: 60%. **Ethnic makeup:** African American: 28%; Asian American: 11%; Hispanic: 12%; White: 41%; International: 7%.

ADMISSIONS FACTS AND FIGURES

Phone: (718) 951-5001. **Email:** adminqry@brooklyn.cuny.edu. **Website:** http://www.brooklyn.cuny.edu. **Application deadlines for fall 2007:** Early decision: Not offered. Early action: Not offered. Admission can be deferred. **Application fee:** $65. Common application is not accepted. **To apply online, go to:** http://www.applyto.uapc.cuny.edu/. **Admissions requirements/recommendations:** High school units required (recommended): English: 4 (4); Mathematics: 3 (3); Science: 3 (3); Foreign language: 3 (3); Social studies: 4 (4); Academic electives: 4 (4); Total units: 21 (21). Tests: The college uses SAT or ACT scores in admissions decisions. SAT required. Campus visit: Recommended. Admissions interview: Recommended. Off-campus interview: Not available. **Factors that count in admissions decisions:** *Academic:* Secondary school record: Very important. Class rank: Not considered. Letters of recommendation: Considered. Standardized test scores: Very important. Essay: Not considered. *Nonacademic:* Interview: Not considered. Extracurricular activities: Not considered. Talent/ability: Not considered. Character/personal qualities: Not considered. Alumni/ae relationship: Not considered. Geographical residence: Not considered. State residency: Not considered. Religious affiliation/commitment: Not considered. Minority status: Not considered. Volunteer work: Not considered. Work experience: Not considered. **Other schools with the greatest overlap in applicants:** CUNY–Baruch College; CUNY–Hunter College; SUNY–Albany; SUNY–Stony Brook; University at Buffalo–SUNY. **Admissions statistics for the fall 2005 entering class:** Total applicants: 13,494. Total accepted: 6,273. Freshmen enrolled: 1,413; 2% were from out of state. Overall acceptance rate: 46%. **Credentials of fall 2005 freshmen:** 13% ranked in the top 10 percent of their high school class; 43% were in the top 25 percent, and 78% were in the top half. (Proportion submitting class standing: 54%.) **Average high school grade point average:** 2.8. **First-year students who submitted SAT scores:** 94%. Scores (25/75 percentile): Verbal: 450-570, Math: 490-590, Combined: 940-1160.

ACADEMICS

Year founded: 1930. **Academic calendar:** Semester. **Degrees offered:** certificate, bachelor's, post-bachelor's certificate, master's, post-master's certificate. **Most popular majors:** 30% business, management, marketing, and related support services, 13% psychology, 10% social sciences, 8% education, 7% computer and information sciences and support services. **Major fields of study:** area, ethnic, cultural, and gender studies; biological and biomedical sciences; business, management, marketing, and related support services; communication, journalism, and related programs; communications technologies/technicians and support services; computer and information sciences and support services; education; English language and literature/letters; foreign languages, literatures, and linguistics; health professions and related clinical sciences; history; liberal arts and sciences studies, and humanities; mathematics and statistics; multi/interdisciplinary studies; natural resources and conservation; parks, recreation, leisure, and fitness studies; philosophy and religious studies; physical sciences; psychology; public administration and social service professions; social sciences; visual and performing arts. **Areas of required coursework:** arts/fine arts, humanities, computer literacy, mathematics, English (including composition), philosophy, foreign languages, sciences (biological or physical), history, social science, other. **Pre-professional programs:** pre-law, pre-medicine. **Special academic programs:** accelerated program, cooperative (work-study plan) program, cross-registration, distance learning, double major, dual enrollment, English as a Second Language (ESL), exchange student program (domestic), honors program, independent study, internships, study abroad, teacher certificate program, weekend college. **Teacher certification offered in:** early childhood, special education, elementary, middle/junior high, secondary, bilingual/bicultural. **Faculty and instruction (2005-2006):** Total instructional faculty: 510 full-time, 586 part-time (56% men; 44% women; 21% minorities). Full-time faculty with Ph.D. or other terminal degree: 90%. Student/faculty ratio: 15/1. Classes of fewer than 20 students: 41%; of 20 to 49 students: 55%; of 50 or more students: 4%. **Advanced Placement and International Baccalaureate credit:** AP tests may be used for: Credit only. Scores accepted: 3, 4, 5. International Baccalaureate exams may be used for: Credit only. **Freshmen returning for sophomore year:** 81%. **Graduation rates:** Four-year: 17%; five-year: 33%; six-year: 40%.

COSTS AND FINANCIAL AID

Financial aid office: (718) 951-5045. **Expenses (2006-2007):** Tuition and fees 2006-2007: $4,377 in state, $9,017 out of state; room/board: N/A. Estimated books and supplies: $850; transportation: $900; personal expenses: $2,100. **Financial aid:** Priority filing date for institution's financial aid form: April 1. In 2005-2006, 83% of undergraduates applied for financial aid. Of those, 81% were determined to have financial need; 96% had their need fully met. Average financial aid package (proportion receiving): $5,450 (78%). Average amount of gift aid, such as scholarships or grants (proportion receiving): $3,300 (68%). Average amount of self-help aid, such as work study or loans (proportion receiving): $2,200 (72%). Average need-based loan (excluding PLUS or other private loans): $2,850. Among students who received need-based aid, the average percentage of need met: 99%. Among students who received aid based on merit, the average award (and the proportion receiving): $4,000 (37%). The average athletic scholarship (and the proportion receiving): $0 (0%). Average amount of debt of borrowers graduating in 2005: $14,000. Proportion who borrowed: 30%.

CAMPUS LIFE AND EXTRACURRICULAR ACTIVITIES

Students who live in college-owned, operated, or affiliated housing: 0%. Average per-year earnings: $8. **Clubs and organizations:** Number of student organizations: 150. Activities include: choral groups, concert band, dance, drama/theater, jazz band, literary magazine, music ensembles, radio station, student government, student newspaper, student film society, symphony orchestra, television station, yearbook. Number of fraternities: 5; sororities: 7. Proportion of men in fraternities: 2%; of women in sororities: 2%. **Sports program (2005-2006):** Member of NCAA III. ***Men's intercollegiate varsity sports:*** basketball, cross-country, soccer, swimming and diving, tennis, track and field (indoor), volleyball. ***Women's intercollegiate varsity sports:*** basketball, cross-country, softball, tennis, track and field (indoor), volleyball.

SERVICES AND FACILITIES

Basic services: nonremedial tutoring, women's center, day care, health service, health insurance. **Counseling services:** minority student, career, military, personal, veteran student, academic, older student, psychological, birth control, religious. **For learning-disabled students:** School does not offer a structured program with separate admission and additional fees. Total undergraduates in learning-disabled program or receiving services: 74. Services include: reading machines, tape recorders, note-taking services, learning center, readers, extended time for tests, early syllabus, priority registration, texts on tape, exams on tape or computer. **Library:** Number of titles: 1,335,666; number of current serial subscriptions: 28,447. **Information technology resources:** Students are not required to lease or own a computer. Number of campus computers available to all students: 1,200. School has a wireless network. Proportion of college-owned housing units wired for high-speed internet access: 0%. **Campus safety:** Security services offered: 24-hour foot-and-vehicle patrols, late-night transport/escort service, 24-hour emergency telephones, lighted pathways/sidewalks.

TRANSFER AND INTERNATIONAL STUDENTS

Transfer students: May apply for admission for the following academic terms: Fall, Spring, Summer. Applicants need a minimum number of credits to apply. For fall 2005: Transfer applicants enrolled: 1,521. **International students:** Number of foreign undergraduates: 788 (7% of student body). Number of countries represented: 86. Minimum TOEFL score required: 500 (paper); 173 (computer).

CUNY–City College

- **Address:** 160 Convent Avenue, New York, NY 10031
- **Website:** http://www.ccny.cuny.edu
- **Public**
- **Enrollment:** 6,740 full-time; 2,754 part-time

KEY STATS

✔ **U.S News College Ranking:** 68, Universities–Master's (North)
✔ **SAT Score (25th/75th percentile):** 880-1170
✔ **Tuition:** 2006-2007: $4,157 in state, $10,957 out of state

Selectivity: Selective	Room/board: N/A
Acceptance rate: 43%	Average debt: $16,800
Student/faculty ratio: 11/1	Proportion who borrowed: 35%

UNDERGRADUATE STUDENT BODY STATS

2005-2006 enrollment: 6,740 full-time; 2,754 part-time. Men: 51%; women: 49%. **Ethnic makeup:** African American: 24%; Asian American: 18%; Hispanic: 34%; White: 11%; International: 12%.

ADMISSIONS FACTS AND FIGURES

Phone: (212) 650-6977. **Email:** admissions@ccny.cuny.edu. **Website:** http://www.ccny.cuny.edu. **Application deadlines for fall 2007:** Regular decision: Rolling. Early decision: Not offered. Early action: Not offered. Admission cannot be deferred. **Application fee:** $40. Common application is not accepted. **To apply online, go to:** http://www.applyto.uapc.cuny.edu/. **Admissions requirements/recommendations:** High school units required (recommended): English: 4 (4); Mathematics: 3 (3); Science: 2 (2); Foreign language: 3 (3); Social studies: 4 (4); Academic electives: 1 (1); Total units: 19 (19). Tests: The college uses SAT or ACT scores in admissions decisions. SAT required. Campus visit: Neither required nor recommended. Admissions interview: Neither required nor recommended. Off-campus interview: Not available. **Factors that count in admissions decisions:** *Academic:* Secondary school record: Very important. Class rank: Not considered. Letters of recommendation: Not considered. Standardized test scores: Very important. Essay: Not considered. *Nonacademic:* Interview: Not considered. Extracurricular activities: Not considered. Talent/ability: Not considered. Character/personal qualities: Not considered. Alumni/ae relationship: Not considered. Geographical residence: Not considered. State residency: Not considered. Religious affiliation/commitment: Not considered. Minority status: Not considered. Volunteer work: Not considered. Work experience: Not considered. **Other schools with the greatest overlap in applicants:** City University; Long Island University–Brooklyn; SUNY–Stony Brook; St. John's University. **Admissions statistics for the fall 2005 entering class:** Total applicants: 12,327. Total accepted: 5,343. Freshmen enrolled: 1,326; 13% were from out of state. Overall acceptance rate: 43%. **Credentials of fall 2005 freshmen:** 27% ranked in the top 10 percent of their high school class; 31% were in the top 25 percent, and 86% were in the top half. (Proportion submitting class standing: 49%.) **Average high school grade point average:** 2.7. **First-year students who submitted SAT scores:** 96%. Scores (25/75 percentile): Verbal: 420-560, Math: 460-610, Combined: 880-1170.

ACADEMICS

Year founded: 1847. **Academic calendar:** Semester. **Degrees offered:** bachelor's, post-bachelor's certificate, master's, post-master's certificate. **Most popular majors:** 17% social sciences, 14% multi/interdisciplinary studies, 11% education, 11% engineering, 11% physical sciences. **Major fields of study:** architecture and related services; area, ethnic, cultural, and gender studies; biological and biomedical sciences; business, management, marketing, and related support services; communication, journalism, and related programs; computer and information sciences and support services; education; engineering; English language and literature/letters; foreign languages, literatures, and linguistics; health professions and related clinical sciences; history; liberal arts and sciences studies, and humanities; mathematics and statistics; philosophy and religious studies; physical sciences; psychology; social sciences; visual and performing arts. **Areas of required coursework:** arts/fine arts, humanities, computer literacy, mathematics, English (including composition), philosophy, foreign languages, sciences (biological or physical), history, social science. **Pre-professional programs:** pre-law, pre-dentistry, pre-medicine. **Special academic programs:** cooperative (work-study plan) program, double major, English as a Second Language (ESL), honors program, independent study, internships, study abroad, teacher certificate program. **Teacher certification offered in:** early childhood, special education, elementary, middle/junior high, secondary, bilingual/bicultural. **Cooperative education programs:** art, engineering. **Faculty and instruction (2005-2006):** Total instructional faculty: 521 full-time; 597 part-time (59% men; 41% women; 30% minorities). Full-time faculty with Ph.D. or other terminal degree: 88%. Student/faculty ratio: 11/1. Classes of fewer than 20 students: 43%; of 20 to 49 students: 56%; of 50 or more students: 0%. **Advanced Placement and International Baccalaureate credit:** AP tests may be used for: Credit only. Scores accepted: 4, 5. International Baccalaureate exams may be used for: Credit only. **Freshmen returning for sophomore year:** 79%. **Graduation rates:** Four-year: 6%; five-year: 31%; six-year: 33%. **Graduate study:** 19% of students pursue further study immediately upon graduation. Fields in which graduates pursue further study: medicine, 1%; arts and sciences, 19%.

COSTS AND FINANCIAL AID

Financial aid office: (212) 650-5819. **Expenses (2006-2007):** Tuition and fees 2006-2007: $4,157 in state, $10,957 out of state; room/board: N/A. Estimated books and supplies: $1,000; transportation: $1,000; personal expenses: $0. **Financial aid:** Priority filing date for institution's financial aid form: April 1. In 2005-2006, 85% of undergraduates applied for financial aid. Of those, 81% were determined to have financial need; 52% had their need fully met. Average financial aid package (proportion receiving): $7,100 (77%). Average amount of gift aid, such as scholarships or grants (proportion receiving): $5,271 (73%). Average amount of self-help aid, such as work study or loans (proportion receiving): $5,800 (42%). Average need-based loan (excluding PLUS or other private loans): $3,200. Among students who received need-based aid, the average percentage of need met: 70%. Among students who received aid based on merit, the average award (and the proportion receiving): $2,200 (14%). The average athletic scholarship (and the proportion receiving): $0 (0%). Average amount of debt of borrowers graduating in 2005: $16,800. Proportion who borrowed: 35%.

CAMPUS LIFE AND EXTRACURRICULAR ACTIVITIES

Students who live in college-owned, operated, or affiliated housing: 0%. **Student employment:** During the 2005-2006 academic year, 9% of undergraduates worked on campus. Average per-year earnings: $1,000. **Clubs and organizations:** Number of student organizations: 100. Activities include: choral groups, dance, drama/theater, jazz band, music ensembles, radio station, student government, student newspaper, student film society, television station, yearbook. Number of fraternities: 3; sororities: 2. **Sports program (2005-2006):** Member of NCAA III. **Men's intercollegiate varsity sports:** baseball, basketball, soccer, tennis, track and field (indoor), track and field (outdoor), volleyball. **Women's intercollegiate varsity sports:** basketball, fencing, soccer, tennis, track and field (indoor), track and field (outdoor), volleyball.

SERVICES AND FACILITIES

Basic services: nonremedial tutoring, placement service, day care, health service. **Remedial assistance:** reading, math, writing, study skills. **Counseling services:** minority student, career, personal, academic, psychological, birth control. **For learning-disabled students:** School does not offer a structured program with separate admission and additional fees. Total undergraduates in learning-disabled program or receiving services: 56. Services include: reading machines, tape recorders, note-taking services, oral tests, learning center, readers, extended time for tests, tutors. **Library:** Number of titles: 1,448,648; number of current serial subscriptions: 31,602. **Information technology resources:** Students are not required to lease or own a computer. Number of campus computers available to all students: 1,160. School has a wireless network. Approximate number of users that can be accommodated: 2,000. **Campus safety:** Security services offered: 24-hour foot-and-vehicle patrols, late-night transport/escort service, 24-hour emergency telephones, lighted pathways/sidewalks.

TRANSFER AND INTERNATIONAL STUDENTS

Transfer students: May apply for admission for the following academic terms: Fall, Spring, Summer. Applicants do not need a minimum number of credits to apply. For fall 2005: Transfer applications received: 1,441. Transfer applicants offered admission: 1,344. Transfer applicants enrolled: 1,141. **International students:** Number of foreign undergraduates: 1144 (12% of student body). Minimum TOEFL score required: 500 (paper); 173 (computer). Average TOEFL score: 558 (paper).

CUNY–College of Staten Island

- **Address:** 2800 Victory Boulevard, Staten Island, NY 10314
- **Website:** http://www.csi.cuny.edu
- **Public**
- **Enrollment:** 7,293 full-time; 3,627 part-time

KEY STATS

✔ **U.S News College Ranking:** fourth tier, Universities–Master's (North)
✔ **SAT Score (25th/75th percentile):** 945-1125
✔ **Tuition:** 2005-2006: $4,328 in state, $8,968 out of state

Selectivity: Less selective	**Room/board:** N/A
Acceptance rate: 99%	**Average debt:** N/A
Student/faculty ratio: 18/1	**Proportion who borrowed:** N/A

UNDERGRADUATE STUDENT BODY STATS

2005-2006 enrollment: 7,293 full-time; 3,627 part-time. Men: 40%; women: 60%. **Ethnic makeup:** African American: 11%; Asian American: 8%; Hispanic: 12%; White: 63%; International: 5%.

ADMISSIONS FACTS AND FIGURES

Phone: (718) 982-2010. **Email:** admissions@mail.csi.cuny.edu. **Website:** http://www.csi.cuny.edu. **Application deadlines for fall 2007:** Regular decision: Rolling; decision sent by December 15. Early decision: Not offered. Early action: Not offered. Admission can be deferred. **Application fee:** $65. Common application is not accepted. **Admissions requirements/recommendations:** High school units required (recommended): English: 4 (4); Mathematics: 3 (3); Science: 2 (2); Foreign language: 2 (2); Social studies: 4 (4); Total units: 16 (16). Tests: The college uses SAT or ACT scores in admissions decisions. Neither SAT nor ACT required. For admission to the fall 2007 entering class, the school will accept: ACT with writing, ACT without writing. Campus visit: Recommended. Admissions interview: Neither required nor recommended. Off-campus interview: Not available. **Factors that count in admissions decisions:** *Academic:* Secondary school record: Very important. Class rank: Not considered. Letters of recommendation: Not considered. Standardized test scores: Important. Essay: Not considered. *Nonacademic:* Interview: Not considered. Extracurricular activities: Not considered. Talent/ability: Not considered. Character/personal qualities: Not considered. Alumni/ae relationship: Not considered. Geographical residence: Not considered. State residency: Not considered. Religious affiliation/commitment: Not considered. Minority status: Not considered. Volunteer work: Not considered. Work experience: Not considered. **Other schools with the greatest overlap in applicants:** CUNY–Baruch College; CUNY–Brooklyn College; CUNY–Hunter College; St. John's College; Wagner College. **Admissions statistics for the fall 2005 entering class:** Total applicants: 7,393. Total accepted: 7,333. Freshmen enrolled: 2,198; 1% were from out of state. Overall acceptance rate: 99%. **Average high school grade point average:** 3.0. **First-year students who submitted SAT scores:** 100%. Scores (25/75 percentile): Verbal: 460-560, Math: 485-565, Combined: 945-1125.

ACADEMICS

Year founded: 1955. **Academic calendar:** Semester. **Degrees offered:** associate, bachelor's, master's, post-master's certificate. **Most popular majors:** 27% business, management, marketing, and related support services, 11% social sciences, 10% psychology, 9% computer and information sciences and support services, 9% liberal arts and sciences studies, and humanities. **Major fields of study:** area, ethnic, cultural, and gender studies; biological and biomedical sciences; business, management, marketing, and related support services; communication, journalism, and related programs; computer and information sciences and support services; education; engineering; English language and literature/letters; foreign languages, literatures, and linguistics; health professions and related clinical sciences; history; liberal arts and sciences studies, and humanities; mathematics and statistics; philosophy and religious studies; physical sciences; psychology; public administration and social service professions; social sciences; visual and performing arts. **Areas of required coursework:** arts/fine arts, mathematics, English (including composition), foreign languages, sciences (biological or physical), history, social science. **Pre-professional programs:** pre-dentistry, pre-medicine, pre-optometry. **Special academic programs:** cooperative (work-study plan) program, cross-registration, distance learning, double major, English as a Second Language (ESL), honors program, independent study, internships, student-designed major, study abroad, teacher certificate program, weekend college. **Teacher certification offered in:** early childhood, elementary, secondary, bilingual/bicultural. **Faculty and instruction (2005-2006):** Total instructional faculty: 330 full-time, 512 part-time (53% men; 47% women; 16% minorities). Full-time faculty with Ph.D. or other terminal degree: 87%. Student/faculty ratio: 18/1. Classes of fewer than 20 students: 30%; of 20 to 49 students: 68%; of 50 or more students: 3%. **Advanced Placement and International Baccalaureate credit:** AP tests may be used for: Credit and/or placement. Scores accepted: 3, 4, 5. International Baccalaureate exams may be used for: Credit and/or placement. **Freshmen returning for sophomore year:** 83%. **Graduation rates:** Four-year: 20%; five-year: 45%; six-year: 42%.

COSTS AND FINANCIAL AID

Financial aid office: (718) 982-2030. **Expenses (2005-2006):** Tuition and fees 2005-2006: $4,328 in state, $8,968 out of state; room/board: N/A. **Financial aid:** Priority filing date for institution's financial aid form: March 31. In 2005-2006, 72% of undergraduates applied for financial aid. Of those, 54% were determined to have financial need; 6% had their need fully met. Average financial aid package (proportion receiving): $6,101 (52%). Average amount of gift aid, such as scholarships or grants (proportion receiving): $4,991 (50%). Average amount of self-help aid, such as work study or loans (proportion receiving): $2,173 (22%). Average need-based loan (excluding PLUS or other private loans): $3,366. Among students who received need-based aid, the average percentage of need met: 58%. Among students who received aid based on merit, the average award (and the proportion receiving): $2,682 (5%).

CAMPUS LIFE AND EXTRACURRICULAR ACTIVITIES

Students who live in college-owned, operated, or affiliated housing: 0%. **Clubs and organizations:** Number of student organizations: 38. Activities include: choral groups, dance, drama/theater, jazz band, literary magazine, radio station, student government, student newspaper, student film society, yearbook. Number of fraternities: 0; sororities: 0. **Sports program (2005-2006):** Member of NCAA III. *Men's intercollegiate varsity sports:* baseball, basketball, soccer, swimming and diving, tennis. *Women's intercollegiate varsity sports:* basketball, soccer, softball, swimming and diving, tennis, volleyball.

SERVICES AND FACILITIES

Basic services: nonremedial tutoring, women's center, placement service, day care, health service, health insurance. **Remedial assistance:** reading, math, writing. **Counseling services:** minority student, career, personal, veteran student, academic, older student, psychological, birth control, religious. **For learning-disabled students:** School does not offer a structured program with separate admission and additional fees. Total undergraduates in learning-disabled program or receiving services: 112. Services include: remedial math, remedial English, reading machines, remedial reading, tape recorders, note-taking services, oral tests, readers, extended time for tests, tutors, priority registration, texts on tape. **Library:** Number of titles: 229,345; number of current serial subscriptions: 820. **Information technology resources:** Students are not required to lease or own a computer. Number of campus computers available to all students: 1,254. School has a wireless network. Approximate number of users that can be accommodated: 2,500. Proportion of college-owned housing units wired for high-speed internet access: 100%. **Campus safety:** Security services offered: 24-hour foot-and-vehicle patrols, late-night transport/escort service, 24-hour emergency telephones, lighted pathways/sidewalks.

TRANSFER AND INTERNATIONAL STUDENTS

Transfer students: May apply for admission for the following academic terms: Fall, Spring, Summer. Applicants do not need a minimum number of credits to apply. For fall 2005: Transfer applications received: 1,113. Transfer applicants offered admission: 1,063. Transfer applicants enrolled: 610. **International students:** Number of foreign undergraduates: 523 (5% of student body). Number of countries represented: 76. Minimum TOEFL score required: 550 (paper); 213 (computer). Average TOEFL score: 550 (paper).

CUNY–Hunter College

- **Address:** 695 Park Avenue, New York, NY 10021
- **Website:** http://www.hunter.cuny.edu
- **Public**
- **Enrollment:** 10,406 full-time; 5,225 part-time

KEY STATS

✔ **U.S News College Ranking:** 62, Universities–Master's (North)
✔ **SAT Score (25th/75th percentile):** 980-1170
✔ **Tuition:** 2006-2007: $4,349 in state, $8,989 out of state

Selectivity: Selective	Room/board: N/A
Acceptance rate: 35%	Average debt: $8,780
Student/faculty ratio: 14/1	Proportion who borrowed: 38%

UNDERGRADUATE STUDENT BODY STATS

2005-2006 enrollment: 10,406 full-time; 5,225 part-time. Men: 32%; women: 68%. **Ethnic makeup:** African American: 14%; Asian American: 17%; Hispanic: 20%; White: 42%; International: 7%.

ADMISSIONS FACTS AND FIGURES

Phone: (212) 772-4490. **Email:** admissions@hunter.cuny.edu. **Website:** http://www.hunter.cuny.edu. **Application deadlines for fall 2007:** Regular decision: March 15. Early decision: Not offered. Early action: Not offered. Admission can be deferred. **Application fee:** $65. Common application is not accepted. **Admissions requirements/recommendations:** High school units required (recommended): English: 2 (4); Mathematics: 2 (3); Science: 1 (2); Foreign language: (2); Social studies: (4); Total units: (16). Tests: The college uses SAT or ACT scores in admissions decisions. Either SAT or ACT required. For admission to the fall 2007 entering class, the school will accept: ACT with writing, ACT without writing. Campus visit: Recommended. Admissions interview: Neither required nor recommended. **Factors that count in admissions decisions:** *Academic:* Secondary school record: Very important. Class rank: Not considered. Letters of recommendation: Not considered. Standardized test scores: Very important. Essay: Not considered. *Nonacademic:* Interview: Not considered. Extracurricular activities: Not considered. Talent/ability: Not considered. Character/personal qualities: Not considered. Alumni/ae relationship: Not considered. Geographical residence: Not considered. State residency: Not considered. Religious affiliation/commitment: Not considered. Minority status: Not considered. Volunteer work: Not considered. Work experience: Not considered. **Other schools with the greatest overlap in applicants:** Fordham University; New York University; SUNY–Binghamton; SUNY–Stony Brook. **Admissions statistics for the fall 2005 entering class:** Total applicants: 20,985. Total accepted: 7,443. Freshmen enrolled: 1,837; 4% were from out of state. Overall acceptance rate: 35%. **Credentials of fall 2005 freshmen:** 21% ranked in the top 10 percent of their high school class; 48% were in the top 25 percent, and 78% were in the top half. (Proportion submitting class standing: 85%.) **Average high school grade point average:** 3.0. **First-year students who submitted SAT scores:** 97%. Scores (25/75 percentile): Verbal: 480-580, Math: 500-590, Combined: 980-1170.

ACADEMICS

Year founded: 1870. **Academic calendar:** Semester. **Degrees offered:** bachelor's, master's, post-master's certificate. **Most popular majors:** 24% social sciences, 15% English language and literature/letters, 11% psychology, 9% visual and performing arts, 7% communication, journalism, and related programs. **Major fields of study:** area, ethnic, cultural, and gender studies; biological and biomedical sciences; business, management, marketing, and related support services; communication, journalism, and related programs; computer and information sciences and support services; education; English language and literature/letters; family and consumer sciences/human sciences; foreign languages, literatures, and linguistics; health professions and related clinical sciences; history; liberal arts and sciences studies, and humanities; mathematics and statistics; multi/interdisciplinary studies; philosophy and religious studies; physical sciences; psychology; social sciences; visual and performing arts. **Areas of required coursework:** arts/fine arts, humanities, mathematics, English (including composition), foreign languages, sciences (biological or physical), history, social science, other. **Pre-professional programs:** pre-law, pre-dentistry, pre-medicine, pre-veterinary science, pre-optometry, pre-pharmacy, other. **Special academic programs:** accelerated program, cross-registration, distance learning, double major, dual enrollment, English as a Second Language (ESL), exchange student program (domestic), honors program, independent study, internships, liberal arts/career combination, student-designed major, study abroad, teacher certificate program, other. **Teacher certification offered in:** early childhood, special education, elementary, middle/junior high, secondary, bilingual/bicultural. **Faculty and instruction (2005-2006):** Total instructional faculty: 633 full-time, 802 part-time (46% men; 54% women; 22% minorities). Full-time faculty with Ph.D. or other terminal degree: 87%. Student/faculty ratio: 14/1. Classes of fewer than 20 students: 36%; of 20 to 49 students: 56%; of 50 or more students: 8%. **Advanced Placement and International Baccalaureate credit:** AP tests may be used for: Credit and/or placement. Scores accepted: 4, 5. **Freshmen returning for sophomore year:** 80%. **Graduation rates:** Four-year: 10%; five-year: 29%; six-year: 36%.

COSTS AND FINANCIAL AID

Financial aid office: (212) 772-4820. **Expenses (2006-2007):** Tuition and fees 2006-2007: $4,349 in state, $8,989 out of state; room/board: N/A. Estimated books and supplies: $832; transportation: $816; personal expenses: $3,481. **Financial aid:** Priority filing date for institution's financial aid form: May 1. In 2005-2006, 70% of undergraduates applied for financial aid. Of those, 64% were determined to have financial need; 68% had their need fully met. Average financial aid package (proportion receiving): $5,383 (59%). Average amount of gift aid, such as scholarships or grants

(proportion receiving): $4,575 (53%). Average amount of self-help aid, such as work study or loans (proportion receiving): $4,594 (17%). Average need-based loan (excluding PLUS or other private loans): $3,691. Among students who received need-based aid, the average percentage of need met: 80%. Among students who received aid based on merit, the average award (and the proportion receiving): $5,805 (1%). Average amount of debt of borrowers graduating in 2005: $8,780. Proportion who borrowed: 38%.

CAMPUS LIFE AND EXTRACURRICULAR ACTIVITIES

Campus housing available (% using): coed dorms (3%), other housing options (97%). Students who live in college-owned, operated, or affiliated housing: 2%. **Clubs and organizations:** Number of student organizations: 150. Activities include: choral groups, dance, drama/theater, literary magazine, radio station, student government, student newspaper, student film society, symphony orchestra, television station, yearbook. Number of fraternities: 2; sororities: 2. **Sports program (2005-2006):** Member of NCAA III. **Men's intercollegiate varsity sports:** basketball, cross-country, fencing, soccer, tennis, track and field (indoor), track and field (outdoor), volleyball, wrestling. **Women's intercollegiate varsity sports:** basketball, cross-country, fencing, softball, swimming and diving, tennis, track and field (indoor), track and field (outdoor), volleyball.

SERVICES AND FACILITIES

Basic services: nonremedial tutoring, women's center, placement service, day care, health service. **Counseling services:** career, personal, academic, psychological, religious. **For learning-disabled students:** School does not offer a structured program with separate admission and additional fees. Total undergraduates in learning-disabled program or receiving services: 320. Services include: reading machines, tape recorders, diagnostic testing service, untimed tests, note-taking services, learning center, readers, extended time for tests, tutors, priority registration, priority seating, texts on tape, typist/scribe, exams on tape or computer, other testing accommodations, other. **Library:** Number of titles: 790,000; number of current serial subscriptions: 2,850. **Information technology resources:** Students are not required to lease or own a computer. Number of campus computers available to all students: 1,092. School has a wireless network. Proportion of college-owned housing units wired for high-speed internet access: 100%. **Campus safety:** Security services offered: 24-hour foot-and-vehicle patrols, late-night transport/escort service, 24-hour emergency telephones, lighted pathways/sidewalks, controlled dormitory access (key, security card, etc).

TRANSFER AND INTERNATIONAL STUDENTS

Transfer students: May apply for admission for the following academic terms: Fall, Spring. Applicants do not need a minimum number of credits to apply. For fall 2005: Transfer applications received: 4,964. Transfer applicants offered admission: 2,469. Transfer applicants enrolled: 1,490. **International students:** Number of foreign undergraduates: 1038 (7% of student body). Minimum TOEFL score required: 500 (paper); 173 (computer).

CUNY–Lehman College

- **Address:** 250 Bedford Park Boulevard W, Bronx, NY 10468
- **Website:** http://www.lehman.cuny.edu
- **Public**
- **Enrollment:** 5,119 full-time; 3,323 part-time

KEY STATS

✔ **U.S News College Ranking:** third tier, Universities–Master's (North)
✔ **SAT Score (25th/75th percentile):** 810-1000
✔ **Tuition:** 2006-2007: $4,290 in state, $8,930 out of state

Selectivity: Less selective	**Room/board:** N/A
Acceptance rate: 34%	**Average debt:** $11,000
Student/faculty ratio: 14/1	**Proportion who borrowed:** 32%

UNDERGRADUATE STUDENT BODY STATS

2005-2006 enrollment: 5,119 full-time; 3,323 part-time. Men: 28%; women: 72%. **Ethnic makeup:** African American: 34%; Asian American: 4%; Hispanic: 47%; White: 10%; International: 5%. **Religious preference:** Roman Catholic: 45%; Protestant: 10%; Muslim: 3%; Hindu: 2%; Buddhist: 1%; No preference: 14%; Other: 25%.

ADMISSIONS FACTS AND FIGURES

Phone: (718) 960-8131. **Email:** enroll@lehman.cuny.edu. **Website:** http://www.lehman.cuny.edu. **Application deadlines for fall 2007:** Regular decision: August 15. Early decision: Not offered. Early action: Not offered. Admission can be deferred. **Application fee:** $65. Common application is not accepted. **Admissions requirements/recommendations:** High school units required (recommended): English: 4 (4); Mathematics: 2 (3); Science: 2 (3); Foreign language: 2 (2); Social studies: 1 (2); History: 2 (2); Total units: 14 (16). Tests: The college uses SAT or ACT scores in admissions decisions. Either SAT or ACT required. Campus visit: Recommended. Admissions interview: Neither required nor recommended. Off-campus interview: Not available. **Factors that count in admissions decisions:** *Academic:* Secondary school record: Very important. Class rank: Not considered. Letters of recommendation: Considered. Standardized test scores: Very important. Essay: Considered. *Nonacademic:* Interview: Considered. Extracurricular activities: Considered. Talent/ability: Considered. Character/personal qualities: Considered. Alumni/ae relationship: Not considered. Geographical residence: Not considered. State residency: Not considered. Religious affiliation/commitment: Not considered. Minority status: Not considered. Volunteer work: Not considered. Work experience: Not considered. **Other schools with the greatest overlap in applicants:** CUNY–Baruch College; CUNY–City College; CUNY–Hunter College; New York University; Pace University. **Admissions statistics for the fall 2005 entering class:** Total applicants: 10,450. Total accepted: 3,537. Freshmen enrolled: 804; 1% were from out of state. Overall acceptance rate: 34%. **Credentials of fall 2005 freshmen:** 18% ranked in the top 10 percent of their high school class; 36% were in the top 25 percent. **Average high school grade point average:** 2.7. **First-year students who submitted SAT scores:** 85%. Scores (25/75 percentile): Verbal: 400-500, Math: 410-500, Combined: 810-1000.

ACADEMICS

Year founded: 1968. **Academic calendar:** Semester. **Degrees offered:** bachelor's, master's, post-master's certificate. **Most popular majors:** 11% social work, 10% sociology, 8% nursing, 8% psychology, 7% accounting and related services. **Major fields of study:** area, ethnic, cultural, and gender studies; biological and biomedical sciences; business, management, marketing, and related support services; communication, journalism, and related programs; computer and information sciences and support services; education; English language and literature/letters; family and consumer sciences/human sciences; foreign languages, literatures, and linguistics; health professions and related clinical sciences; history; mathematics and statistics; philosophy and religious studies; physical sciences; psychology; public administration and social service professions; social sciences; visual and performing arts. **Areas of required coursework:** arts/fine arts, humanities, computer literacy, mathematics, English (including composition), philosophy, foreign languages, sciences (biological or physical), history, social science, other. **Pre-professional programs:** pre-law, pre-medicine. **Special academic programs (% participation):** accelerated program (2%), cross-registration (5%), distance learning (7%), double major (2%), dual enrollment (10%), English as a Second Language (ESL) (1%), honors program (1%), independent study (3%), internships (10%), student-designed major (4%), study abroad (1%), teacher certificate program (3%), weekend college (20%). **Teacher certification offered in:** early childhood, special education, elementary, middle/junior high, secondary, bilingual/bicultural. **Reserve Officers Training Corps (ROTC):** Army ROTC: Offered at cooperating institution (Fordham University). **Faculty and instruction (2005-2006):** Total instructional faculty: 330 full-time, 484 part-time (46% men; 54% women; 38% minorities). Full-time faculty with Ph.D. or other terminal degree: 77%. Student/faculty ratio: 14/1. Classes of fewer than 20 students: 51%; of 20 to 49 students: 49%; of 50 or more students: 0%. **Advanced Placement and International Baccalaureate credit:** AP tests may be used for: Credit and/or placement. Scores accepted: 3, 4, 5. International Baccalaureate exams may be used for: Credit only. **Freshmen returning for sophomore year:** 73%. **Graduation rates:** Four-year: 7%; five-year: 25%; six-year: 33%.

COSTS AND FINANCIAL AID

Financial aid office: (718) 960-8545. **Expenses (2006-2007):** Tuition and fees 2006-2007: $4,290 in state, $8,930 out of state; room/board: N/A. **Financial aid:** In 2005-2006, 84% of undergraduates applied for financial aid. Of those, 83% were determined to have financial need; 3% had their need fully met. Average financial aid package (proportion receiving): $3,537 (83%). Average amount of gift aid, such as scholarships or grants (proportion receiving): $1,361 (77%). Average amount of self-help aid, such as work study or loans (proportion receiving): $1,157 (35%). Average need-based loan (excluding PLUS or other private loans): $1,559. Among students who received need-based aid, the average percentage of need met: 61%. Among students who received aid based on merit, the average award (and the proportion receiving): $1,400 (2%). The average athletic scholarship (and the proportion receiving): $0 (0%). Average amount of debt of borrowers graduating in 2005: $11,000. Proportion who borrowed: 32%.

CAMPUS LIFE AND EXTRACURRICULAR ACTIVITIES

Campus housing available: other housing options. Students who live in college-owned, operated, or affiliated housing: 0%. **Student employment:** During the 2005-2006 academic year, 2% of undergraduates worked on campus. Average per-year earnings: $3,680. **Clubs and organizations:** Number of student organizations: 36. Activities include: choral groups, concert band, dance, drama/theater, jazz band, literary magazine, music ensembles, musical theater, opera, radio station, student government, student newspaper, student film society, symphony orchestra, television station, yearbook. Number of fraternities: 2; sororities: 2. Proportion of men in fraternities: 2%; of women in sororities: 1%. **Sports program (2005-2006):** Member of NCAA III. *Men's intercollegiate varsity sports:* baseball, basketball, cross-country, swimming and diving, tennis, track and field (indoor), track and field (outdoor), volleyball. *Women's intercollegiate varsity sports:* basketball, cross-country, softball, swimming and diving, tennis, track and field (indoor), track and field (outdoor), volleyball.

SERVICES AND FACILITIES

Basic services: nonremedial tutoring, day care, health service. **Counseling services:** career, personal, veteran student, academic, psychological, birth control. **For learning-disabled students:** School does not offer a structured program with separate admission and additional fees. Services include: tape recorders, untimed tests, note-taking services, learning center, extended time for tests, tutors, texts on tape, other testing accomodations. **Library:** Number of titles: 571,002; number of current serial subscriptions: 4,950. **Information technology resources:** Students are not required to lease or own a computer. Number of campus computers available to all students: 1,200. School has a wireless network. Approximate number of users that can be accommodated: 1,240. Proportion of college-owned housing units wired for high-speed internet access: 100%. **Campus safety:** Security services offered: 24-hour foot-and-vehicle patrols, late-night transport/escort service, 24-hour emergency telephones, lighted pathways/sidewalks.

TRANSFER AND INTERNATIONAL STUDENTS

Transfer students: May apply for admission for the following academic terms: Fall, Spring. Applicants do not need a minimum number of credits to apply. **International students:** Number of foreign undergraduates: 395 (5% of student body). Number of countries represented: 70. Minimum TOEFL score required: 500 (paper); 173 (computer). Average TOEFL score: 520 (paper).

CUNY–Medgar Evers College

- **Address:** 1650 Bedford Avenue, Brooklyn, NY 11225
- **Website:** http://www.mec.cuny.edu
- **Public**
- **Enrollment:** 3,134 full-time; 2,078 part-time

KEY STATS

✔ **U.S News College Ranking:** fourth tier, Comp. Coll.–Bachelor's (North)
✔ **SAT Score (25th/75th percentile):** 680-870
✔ **Tuition:** 2005-2006: $4,252 in state, $8,892 out of state

Selectivity: Least selective	**Room/board:** N/A
Acceptance rate: 96%	**Average debt:** N/A
Student/faculty ratio: 15/1	**Proportion who borrowed:** N/A

UNDERGRADUATE STUDENT BODY STATS

2005-2006 enrollment: 3,134 full-time; 2,078 part-time. Men: 23%; women: 77%. **Ethnic makeup:** African American: 88%; Asian American: 1%; Hispanic: 4%; White: 3%; International: 4%.

ADMISSIONS FACTS AND FIGURES

Phone: (718) 270-6024. **Email:** enroll@mec.cuny.edu. **Website:** http://www.mec.cuny.edu. **Application deadlines for fall 2007:** Regular decision: August 23. Early decision: Not offered. Early action: Not offered. Admission can be deferred. **Application fee:** $65. Common application is accepted. **Admissions requirements/recommendations:** High school units required (recommended): English: (4); Mathematics: (3); Science: (2); History: (2); Academic electives: (4); Total units: (15). Tests: The college uses SAT or ACT scores in admissions decisions. Neither SAT nor ACT required. Campus visit: Recommended. Admissions interview: Neither required nor recommended. Off-campus interview: Not available. **Factors that count in admissions decisions:** *Academic:* Secondary school record: Important. Class rank: Not considered. Letters of recommendation: Not considered. Standardized test scores: Considered. Essay: Not considered. *Nonacademic:* Interview: Not considered. Extracurricular activities: Considered. Talent/ability: Not considered. Character/personal qualities: Not considered. Alumni/ae relationship: Not considered. Geographical residence: Not considered. State residency: Considered. Religious affiliation/commitment: Not considered. Minority status: Not considered. Volunteer work: Not considered. Work experience: Not considered. **Admissions statistics for the fall 2005 entering class:** Total applicants: 4,069. Total accepted: 3,918. Freshmen enrolled: 787; 0% were from out of state. Overall acceptance rate: 96%. **Credentials of fall 2005 freshmen:** 24% were in the top 25 percent, and 45% were in the top half. (Proportion submitting class standing: 26%.) **Average high school grade point average:** 1.7. **First-year students who submitted SAT scores:** 31%. Scores (25/75 percentile): Verbal: 340-440, Math: 340-430, Combined: 680-870. **First-year students submitting ACT scores:** 31%. Scores (25/75 percentile): English: N/A, Math: N/A, Composite: N/A.

ACADEMICS

Year founded: 1969. **Academic calendar:** Semester. **Degrees offered:** certificate, associate, bachelor's. **Most popular majors:** 24% business administration, management, and operations, 19% psychology, 14% accounting, 8% biology, 7% liberal arts and sciences/liberal studies. **Major fields of study:** biological and biomedical sciences; business, management, marketing, and related support services; education; English language and literature/letters; health professions and related clinical sciences; mathematics and statistics; natural resources and conservation; psychology; public administration and social service professions. **Areas of required coursework:** arts/fine arts, humanities, computer literacy, mathematics, English (including composition), foreign languages, history. **Special academic programs:** cooperative (work-study plan) program, distance learning, double major, English as a Second Language (ESL), honors program, independent study, internships, teacher certificate program, weekend college. **Teacher certification offered in:** early childhood, special education, elementary, middle/junior high. **Cooperative education programs:** art, business, computer science, education, health professions, natural science, social/behavioral science. **Faculty and instruction (2005-2006):** Total instructional faculty: 161 full-time, 192 part-time (46% men; 54% women; 88% minorities). Student/faculty ratio: 15/1. Classes of fewer than 20 students: 28%; of 20 to 49 students: 72%; of 50 or more students: 0%. **Advanced Placement and International Baccalaureate credit:** International Baccalaureate exams may be used for: Credit and/or placement. **Freshmen returning for sophomore year:** 58%. **Graduation rates:** Four-year: 5%; five-year: 11%; six-year: 15%.

COSTS AND FINANCIAL AID

Financial aid office: (718) 270-6038. **Expenses (2005-2006):** Tuition and fees 2005-2006: $4,252 in state, $8,892 out of state; room/board: N/A. Estimated books and supplies: $500; transportation: $600; personal expenses: $232. **Financial aid:** Priority filing date for institution's financial aid form: April 1. Average financial aid package (proportion receiving): N/A (76%). Average amount of gift aid, such as scholarships or grants (proportion receiving): N/A (71%). Average amount of self-help aid, such as work study or loans (proportion receiving): N/A (5%).

CAMPUS LIFE AND EXTRACURRICULAR ACTIVITIES

Students who live in college-owned, operated, or affiliated housing: 0%. **Clubs and organizations:** Number of student organizations: 30. Activities include: choral groups, dance, radio station, student government, student newspaper, television station, yearbook. Number of fraternities: 2; sororities: 2. **Sports program (2005-2006):** Member of NCAA III. *Men's intercollegiate varsity sports:* basketball, cross-country, soccer, track and field (indoor), track and field (outdoor), volleyball. *Women's intercollegiate varsity sports:* basketball, cross-country, soccer, softball, tennis, track and field (indoor), track and field (outdoor), volleyball.

SERVICES AND FACILITIES

Basic services: nonremedial tutoring, women's center, placement service, day care, health service. **Remedial assistance:** reading, math, writing, study skills. **Counseling services:** personal, academic. **For learning-disabled stu-**

dents: School does not offer a structured program with separate admission and additional fees. **Library:** Number of titles: 111,000; number of current serial subscriptions: 420. **Information technology resources:** Students are not required to lease or own a computer. Number of campus computers available to all students: 2,175. School has a wireless network. **Campus safety:** Security services offered: 24-hour foot-and-vehicle patrols.

TRANSFER AND INTERNATIONAL STUDENTS

Transfer students: May apply for admission for the following academic terms: Fall, Spring, Summer. Applicants need a minimum number of credits to apply. For fall 2005: Transfer applications received: 794. Transfer applicants offered admission: 794. Transfer applicants enrolled: 488. **International students:** Number of foreign undergraduates: 172 (4% of student body). Minimum TOEFL score required: 475 (paper). Average TOEFL score: 480 (paper).

CUNY–New York City Coll. of Technology

- **Address:** 300 Jay Street, Brooklyn, NY 11201
- **Website:** http://www.citytech.cuny.edu
- **Public**
- **Enrollment:** 7,106 full-time; 5,333 part-time

KEY STATS

✔ **U.S News College Ranking:** fourth tier, Comp. Coll.–Bachelor's (North)
✔ **SAT Score (25th/75th percentile):** 720-930
✔ **Tuition:** 2006-2007: $4,538 in state, $9,178 out of state

Selectivity: Least selective	**Room/board:** N/A
Acceptance rate: 88%	**Average debt:** N/A
Student/faculty ratio: 17/1	**Proportion who borrowed:** N/A

UNDERGRADUATE STUDENT BODY STATS

2005-2006 enrollment: 7,106 full-time; 5,333 part-time. Men: 50%; women: 50%. **Ethnic makeup:** African American: 39%; Asian American: 12%; Hispanic: 25%; White: 12%; International: 11%.

ADMISSIONS FACTS AND FIGURES

Phone: (718) 260-5500. **Email:** admissions@citytech.cuny.edu. **Website:** http://www.citytech.cuny.edu. **Application deadlines for fall 2007:** Regular decision: March 14. Early decision: Not offered. Early action: Not offered. Send application by: N/A; Decision sent by: N/A. Admission can be deferred. **Application fee:** $65. Common application is not accepted. **To apply online, go to:** http://www.applyto.uapc.cuny.edu. **Admissions requirements/recommendations:** High school units required (recommended): English: 4 (4); Mathematics: 2 (3); Science: 2 (2); Foreign language: 1 (2); Social studies: 2 (4); History: 0 (0); Academic electives: 1 (1); Total units: 14 (16). Tests: The college uses SAT or ACT scores in admissions decisions. Neither SAT nor ACT required. Campus visit: Neither required nor recommended. Admissions interview: Neither required nor recommended. Off-campus interview: Not available. **Factors that count in admissions decisions:** *Academic:* Secondary school record: Important. Class rank: Considered. Letters of recommendation: Considered. Standardized test scores: Considered. Essay: Not considered. *Nonacademic:* Interview: Not considered. Extracurricular activities: Not considered. Talent/ability: Not considered. Character/personal qualities: Not considered. Alumni/ae relationship: Not considered. Geographical residence: Not considered. State residency: Not considered. Religious affiliation/commitment: Not considered. Minority status: Not considered. Volunteer work: Not considered. Work experience: Not considered. **Other schools with the greatest overlap in applicants:** CUNY–Baruch College; CUNY–Brooklyn College; CUNY–City College; CUNY–Hunter College; CUNY–Lehman College. **Admissions statistics for the fall 2005 entering class:** Total applicants: 10,736. Total accepted: 9,428. Freshmen enrolled: 2,499; 0% were from out of state. Overall acceptance rate: 88%. Non-early acceptance rate: 88%. **Credentials of fall 2005 freshmen:** 6% ranked in the top 10 percent of their high school class; 19% were in the top 25 percent, and 46% were in the top half. (Proportion submitting class standing: 81%.) **Average high school grade point average:** 1.9. **First-year students who submitted SAT scores:** 60%. Scores (25/75 percentile): Verbal: 350-450, Math: 370-480, Combined: 720-930.

ACADEMICS

Year founded: 1946. **Academic calendar:** Semester. **Degrees offered:** certificate, associate, bachelor's. **Most popular majors:** 36% information science/studies, 14% community organization and advocacy, 13% hospitality administration/management, 12% design and visual communications, 8% legal administrative assistant/secretary. **Major fields of study:** architecture and related services; business, management, marketing, and related support services; computer and information sciences and support services; education; engineering technologies/technicians; family and consumer sciences/human sciences; health professions and related clinical sciences; legal professions and studies; mathematics and statistics; public administration and social service professions; visual and performing arts. **Areas of required coursework:** humanities, computer literacy, mathematics, English (including composition), philosophy, sciences (biological or physical), social science. **Special academic programs (% participation):** distance learning (1%), dual enrollment (3%), English as a Second Language (ESL) (35%), honors program (2%), independent study (1%), internships (3%), student-designed major (1%), study abroad (1%), teacher certificate program (4%). **Teacher certification offered in:** vo-tech, secondary. **Cooperative education programs:** art, business, computer science, education, engineering, health professions, technologies. **Faculty and instruction (2005-2006):** Total instructional faculty: 307 full-time, 645 part-time (59% men; 41% women; 32% minorities). Full-time faculty with Ph.D. or other terminal degree: 70%. Student/faculty ratio: 17/1. Classes of fewer than 20 students: 37%; of 20 to 49 students: 63%; of 50 or more students: 0%. **Advanced Placement and International Baccalaureate credit:** AP tests may be used for: Credit only. Scores accepted: 3, 4, 5. International Baccalaureate exams may be used for: Credit and/or placement. **Freshmen returning for sophomore year:** 75%. **Graduation rates:** Four-year: 6%; five-year: 6%; six-year: 11%.

COSTS AND FINANCIAL AID

Financial aid office: (718) 260-5700. **Expenses (2006-2007):** Tuition and fees 2006-2007: $4,538 in state, $9,178 out of state; room/board: N/A. **Financial aid:** In 2005-2006, 90% of undergraduates applied for financial aid. Of those, 84% were determined to have financial need; 66% had their need fully met. Average financial aid package (proportion receiving): $6,384 (80%). Average amount of gift aid, such as scholarships or grants (proportion receiving): $5,708 (77%). Average amount of self-help aid, such as work study or loans (proportion receiving): $3,240 (32%). Average need-based loan (excluding PLUS or other private loans): $5,402. Among students who received need-based aid, the average percentage of need met: 70%.

CAMPUS LIFE AND EXTRACURRICULAR ACTIVITIES

Student employment: During the 2005-2006 academic year, 2% of undergraduates worked on campus. Average per-year earnings: $10,000. **Clubs and organizations:** Number of student organizations: 27. Activities include: drama/theater, musical theater, student government, student newspaper. Number of fraternities: 0; sororities: 0. **Sports program (2005-2006):** Member of NCAA III. *Men's intercollegiate varsity sports:* basketball, cross-country, soccer, tennis, volleyball. *Women's intercollegiate varsity sports:* basketball, cross-country, softball, tennis, volleyball.

SERVICES AND FACILITIES

Basic services: nonremedial tutoring, placement service, day care, health service, health insurance. **Remedial assistance:** reading, math, writing, study skills. **Counseling services:** minority student, career, personal, veteran student, academic, older student, psychological, birth control. **For learning-disabled students:** School does not offer a structured program with separate admission and additional fees. Total undergraduates in learning-disabled program or receiving services: 461. Services include: remedial math, remedial English, reading machines, remedial reading, tape recorders, other special classes, diagnostic testing service, note-taking services, oral tests, learning center, readers, extended time for tests, tutors. **Library:** Number of titles: 183,000; number of current serial subscriptions: 23,000. **Information technology resources:** Students are not required to lease or own a computer. Number of campus computers available to all students: 395. School has a wireless network. **Campus safety:** Security services offered: 24-hour foot-and-vehicle patrols, late-night transport/escort service, 24-hour emergency telephones.

TRANSFER AND INTERNATIONAL STUDENTS

Transfer students: May apply for admission for the following academic terms: Fall, Spring, Summer. Applicants do not need a minimum number of credits to apply. For fall 2005: Transfer applicants enrolled: 848. **International students:** Number of foreign undergraduates: 1250 (11% of student body). Number of countries represented: 130.

CUNY–Queens College

- **Address:** 65-30 Kissena Boulevard, Flushing, NY 11367
- **Website:** http://www.qc.edu/
- **Public**
- **Enrollment:** 8,816 full-time; 4,202 part-time

KEY STATS

✔ **U.S News College Ranking:** 62, Universities–Master's (North)
✔ **SAT Score (25th/75th percentile):** 920-1130
✔ **Tuition:** 2006-2007: $4,376 in state, $11,176 out of state
   Selectivity: Selective   **Room/board:** N/A
   Acceptance rate: 43%   **Average debt:** $12,000
   Student/faculty ratio: 16/1   **Proportion who borrowed:** 40%

UNDERGRADUATE STUDENT BODY STATS

2005-2006 enrollment: 8,816 full-time; 4,202 part-time. Men: 38%; women: 62%. **Ethnic makeup:** African American: 9%; Asian American: 18%; Hispanic: 17%; White: 48%; International: 8%.

ADMISSIONS FACTS AND FIGURES

Phone: (718) 997-5600. **Email:** applyto@uapc.cuny.edu. **Website:** http://www.qc.edu/. **Application deadlines for fall 2007:** Regular decision: Rolling. Early decision: Not offered. Early action: Not offered. Admission can be deferred. **Application fee:** $65. Common application is not accepted. **To apply online, go to:** http://www.qc.edu/applying.htm. **Admissions requirements/recommendations:** High school units required (recommended): English: 4 (4); Mathematics: 3 (3); Science: 2 (3); Foreign language: 3 (3); Social studies: 4 (4); Total units: 16 (17). Tests: The college uses SAT or ACT scores in admissions decisions. Either SAT or ACT required. For admission to the fall 2007 entering class, the school will accept: ACT with writing, ACT without writing. Campus visit: Recommended. Admissions interview: Neither required nor recommended. Off-campus interview: Not available. **Factors that count in admissions decisions:** *Academic:* Secondary school record: Very important. Class rank: Not considered. Letters of recommendation: Not considered. Standardized test scores: Very important. Essay: Not considered. *Nonacademic:* Interview: Not considered. Extracurricular activities: Not considered. Talent/ability: Not considered. Character/personal qualities: Not considered. Alumni/ae relationship: Not considered. Geographical residence: Not considered. State residency: Not considered. Religious affiliation/commitment: Not considered. Minority status: Not considered. Volunteer work: Not considered. Work experience: Not considered. **Other schools with the greatest overlap in applicants:** Fordham University; Hofstra University; New York University; SUNY–Stony Brook; St. John's University. **Admissions statistics for the fall 2005 entering class:** Total applicants: 12,023. Total accepted: 5,217. Freshmen enrolled: 1,509; 1% were from out of state. Overall acceptance rate: 43%. **Credentials of fall 2005 freshmen:** 18% ranked in the top 10 percent of their high school class; 34% were in the top 25 percent, and 92% were in the top half. (Proportion submitting class standing: 70%.) **Average high school grade point average:** 3.2. **First-year students who submitted SAT scores:** 99%. Scores (25/75 percentile): Verbal: 440-550, Math: 480-580, Combined: 920-1130.

ACADEMICS

Year founded: 1937. **Academic calendar:** Semester. **Degrees offered:** bachelor's, post-bachelor's certificate, master's, post-master's certificate. **Most popular majors:** 15% accounting, 13% psychology, 10% sociology, 7% English language and literature, 7% computer and information sciences. **Major fields of study:** area, ethnic, cultural, and gender studies; biological and biomedical sciences; business, management, marketing, and related support services; communication, journalism, and related programs; computer and information sciences and support services; education; English language and literature/letters; family and consumer sciences/human sciences; foreign languages, literatures, and linguistics; health professions and related clinical sciences; history; mathematics and statistics; multi/interdisciplinary studies; natural resources and conservation; parks, recreation, leisure, and fitness studies; philosophy and religious studies; physical sciences; psychology; social sciences; visual and performing arts. **Areas of required coursework:** humanities, mathematics, English (including composition), foreign languages, sciences (biological or physical), history, social science, other. **Preprofessional programs:** pre-law, pre-dentistry, pre-medicine. **Special academic programs (% participation):** accelerated program (1%), cooperative (work-study plan) program (5%), cross-registration (2%), distance learning

(0%), double major (15%), English as a Second Language (ESL) (3%), honors program (1%), independent study (13%), internships (15%), liberal arts/career combination (8%), student-designed major (1%), study abroad (1%), teacher certificate program (7%), weekend college (1%). **Teacher certification offered in:** early childhood, special education, elementary, middle/junior high, secondary, bilingual/bicultural. **Cooperative education programs:** art, business, computer science, education, humanities, natural science, social/behavioral science, other. **Reserve Officers Training Corps (ROTC):** Army ROTC: Offered at cooperating institution (St. John's University); Navy ROTC: Offered at cooperating institution (St. John's University). **Faculty and instruction (2005-2006):** Total instructional faculty: 577 full-time, 683 part-time (54% men; 46% women; 17% minorities). Full-time faculty with Ph.D. or other terminal degree: 85%. Student/faculty ratio: 16/1. Classes of fewer than 20 students: 39%; of 20 to 49 students: 53%; of 50 or more students: 8%. **Advanced Placement and International Baccalaureate credit:** AP tests may be used for: Credit only. Scores accepted: 2, 3. **Freshmen returning for sophomore year:** 86%. **Graduation rates:** Four-year: 23%; five-year: 45%; six-year: 50%. **Graduate study:** 25% of students pursue further study within one year. Fields in which graduates pursue further study: Master of Business Administration (MBA), 3%; law, 11%; medicine, 4%; dentistry, 1%; engineering, 1%; theology (or the seminary), 1%; education, 37%; arts and sciences, 30%; veterinary medicine, 1%.

COSTS AND FINANCIAL AID
Financial aid office: (718) 997-5101. **Expenses (2006-2007):** Tuition and fees 2006-2007: $4,376 in state, $11,176 out of state; room/board: N/A. **Financial aid:** Priority filing date for institution's financial aid form: February 1. In 2005-2006, 89% of undergraduates applied for financial aid. Of those, 75% were determined to have financial need; 51% had their need fully met. Average financial aid package (proportion receiving): $8,400 (61%). Average amount of gift aid, such as scholarships or grants (proportion receiving): $5,000 (44%). Average amount of self-help aid, such as work study or loans (proportion receiving): $4,500 (31%). Average need-based loan (excluding PLUS or other private loans): $6,000. Among students who received need-based aid, the average percentage of need met: 95%. Among students who received aid based on merit, the average award (and the proportion receiving): $1,609 (3%). The average athletic scholarship (and the proportion receiving): $5,008 (1%). Average amount of debt of borrowers graduating in 2005: $12,000. Proportion who borrowed: 40%.

CAMPUS LIFE AND EXTRACURRICULAR ACTIVITIES
Students who live in college-owned, operated, or affiliated housing: 0%. **Student employment:** During the 2005-2006 academic year, 15% of undergraduates worked on campus. Average per-year earnings: $4,100. **Clubs and organizations:** Number of student organizations: 140. Activities include: choral groups, concert band, dance, drama/theater, jazz band, literary magazine, music ensembles, musical theater, radio station, student government, student newspaper, student film society, symphony orchestra, television station, yearbook. Number of fraternities: 2; sororities: 3. Proportion of men in fraternities: 1%; of women in sororities: 1%. Average proportion of students who stay on campus on weekends: 5%. **Sports program (2005-2006):** Member of NCAA II. **Men's intercollegiate varsity sports:** baseball, basketball, golf, swimming and diving, tennis, volleyball, water polo. **Women's intercollegiate varsity sports:** basketball, fencing, soccer, softball, swimming and diving, tennis, volleyball, water polo.

SERVICES AND FACILITIES
Basic services: nonremedial tutoring, women's center, day care, health service. **Counseling services:** minority student, career, personal, veteran student, academic, psychological, birth control, religious. **For learning-disabled students:** School does not offer a structured program with separate admission and additional fees. Total undergraduates in learning-disabled program or receiving services: 150. Services include: remedial math, remedial English, reading machines, remedial reading, tape recorders, other special classes, note-taking services, oral tests, learning center, readers, extended time for tests, tutors, priority registration, substitution of courses, texts on tape, other. **Library:** Number of titles: 1,020,503; number of current serial subscriptions: 5,220. **Information technology resources:** Students are not required to lease or own a computer. Number of campus computers available to all students: 1,500. School has a wireless network. Approximate number of users that can be accommodated: 1,000. **Campus safety:** Security services offered: 24-hour foot-and-vehicle patrols, late-night transport/escort service, 24-hour emergency telephones, lighted pathways/sidewalks.

TRANSFER AND INTERNATIONAL STUDENTS
Transfer students: May apply for admission for the following academic terms: Fall, Spring. Applicants do not need a minimum number of credits to apply. For fall 2005: Transfer applications received: 4,664. Transfer applicants offered admission: 2,736. Transfer applicants enrolled: 1,812. **International students:** Number of foreign undergraduates: 983 (8% of student body). Number of countries represented: 111. Minimum TOEFL score required: 500 (paper); 175 (computer). Average TOEFL score: 550 (paper).

CUNY—York College

- **Address:** 94-20 Guy R. Brewer Boulevard, Jamaica, NY 11451
- **Website:** http://www.york.cuny.edu
- **Public**
- **Enrollment:** 3,879 full-time; 2,021 part-time

KEY STATS
✔ **U.S News College Ranking:** fourth tier, Comp. Coll.–Bachelor's (North)
✔ **SAT Score (25th/75th percentile):** 725-930
✔ **Tuition:** 2006-2007: $4,080 in state, $10,880 out of state

Selectivity: Less selective	**Room/board:** N/A
Acceptance rate: 46%	**Average debt:** N/A
Student/faculty ratio: 17/1	**Proportion who borrowed:** N/A

UNDERGRADUATE STUDENT BODY STATS
2005-2006 enrollment: 3,879 full-time; 2,021 part-time. Men: 32%; women: 68%. **Ethnic makeup:** African American: 48%; Asian American: 10%; Hispanic: 15%; White: 26%.

ADMISSIONS FACTS AND FIGURES
Phone: (718) 262-2165. **Email:** admissions@york.cuny.edu. **Website:** http://www.york.cuny.edu. **Application deadlines for fall 2007:** Regular decision: Rolling. Early decision: Not offered. Early action: Not offered. Admission can be deferred. **Application fee:** $65. Common application is not accepted. **To apply online, go to:** https://portal.cuny.edu/cms/id/cuny/documents/informationpage/006373.htm. **Admissions requirements/recommendations:** High school units required (recommended): English: 4; Mathematics: 3; Science: 2; Foreign language: 2; Social studies: 2; Academic electives: 0; Total units: 16. Tests: The college uses SAT or ACT scores in admissions decisions. Neither SAT nor ACT required. For admission to the fall 2007 entering class, the school will accept: ACT without writing. Campus visit: Neither required nor recommended. Admissions interview: Neither required nor recommended. Off-campus interview: Not available. **Factors that count in admissions decisions:** *Academic:* Secondary school record: Very important. Class rank: Not considered. Letters of recommendation: Not considered. Standardized test scores: Very important. Essay: Not considered. *Nonacademic:* Interview: Not considered. Extracurricular activities: Not considered. Talent/ability: Not considered. Character/personal qualities: Not considered. Alumni/ae relationship: Not considered. Geographical residence: Not considered. State residency: Not considered. Religious affiliation/commitment: Not considered. Minority status: Not considered. Volunteer work: Not considered. Work experience: Not considered. **Other schools with the greatest overlap in applicants:** CUNY–Baruch College; CUNY–Brooklyn College; CUNY–Hunter College; CUNY–Lehman College; CUNY–Queens College. **Admissions statistics for the fall 2005 entering class:** Total applicants: 6,945. Total accepted: 3,204. Freshmen enrolled: 781; 13% were from out of state. Overall acceptance rate: 46%. **First-year students who submitted SAT scores:** 62%. Scores (25/75 percentile): Verbal: 355-460, Math: 370-470, Combined: 725-930.

ACADEMICS
Year founded: 1966. **Academic calendar:** Semester. **Degrees offered:** bachelor's. **Most popular majors:** 29% business administration and management, 14% psychology, 10% operations research, 9% health professions and related clinical sciences, 9% physical education teaching and coaching. **Major fields of study:** area, ethnic, cultural, and gender studies; biological and biomedical sciences; business, management, marketing, and related support services; education; English language and literature/letters; foreign languages, literatures, and linguistics; health professions and related clinical sciences; history; liberal arts and sciences studies, and humanities; mathematics and statistics; multi/interdisciplinary studies; natural resources and conservation; parks, recreation, leisure, and fitness studies; philosophy and

religious studies; physical sciences; psychology; public administration and social service professions; social sciences; visual and performing arts. **Areas of required coursework:** arts/fine arts, mathematics, English (including composition), philosophy, foreign languages, sciences (biological or physical), history, social science. **Pre-professional programs:** pre-dentistry, pre-medicine, other. **Special academic programs:** cooperative (work-study plan) program, double major, dual enrollment, English as a Second Language (ESL), honors program, independent study, internships, study abroad, teacher certificate program. **Teacher certification offered in:** early childhood, elementary, middle/junior high, secondary, bilingual/bicultural. **Cooperative education programs:** art, business, computer science, education, health professions, natural science, social/behavioral science, technologies. **Faculty and instruction (2005-2006):** Total instructional faculty: 180 full-time, 290 part-time (55% men; 45% women; 49% minorities). Student/faculty ratio: 17/1. **Advanced Placement and International Baccalaureate credit:** International Baccalaureate exams may be used for: Credit only. **Freshmen returning for sophomore year:** 77%. **Graduation rates:** Four-year: 5%; five-year: 19%; six-year: 27%.

COSTS AND FINANCIAL AID

Financial aid office: (718) 262-2230. **Expenses (2006-2007):** Tuition and fees 2006-2007: $4,080 in state, $10,880 out of state; room/board: N/A. **Financial aid:** Priority filing date for institution's financial aid form: May 1. In 2005-2006, 78% of undergraduates applied for financial aid. Of those, 72% were determined to have financial need; 3% had their need fully met. Average financial aid package (proportion receiving): $3,482 (69%). Average amount of gift aid, such as scholarships or grants (proportion receiving): $2,976 (67%). Average amount of self-help aid, such as work study or loans (proportion receiving): $5,077 (10%). Average need-based loan (excluding PLUS or other private loans): $3,623. Among students who received need-based aid, the average percentage of need met: 30%.

CAMPUS LIFE AND EXTRACURRICULAR ACTIVITIES

Average per-year earnings: $11,383. **Clubs and organizations:** Number of student organizations: 49. Activities include: dance, drama/theater, jazz band, literary magazine, musical theater, student government, student newspaper, student film society, television station, yearbook. Number of fraternities: 0; sororities: 0. **Sports program (2005-2006):** Member of NCAA III. *Men's intercollegiate varsity sports:* basketball, cross-country, soccer, swimming and diving, tennis, track and field (indoor), track and field (outdoor), volleyball. *Women's intercollegiate varsity sports:* basketball, cross-country, softball, swimming and diving, track and field (indoor), track and field (outdoor), volleyball.

SERVICES AND FACILITIES

Basic services: nonremedial tutoring, placement service, day care, health service. **Remedial assistance:** reading, math, writing. **Counseling services:** career, academic, psychological. **For learning-disabled students:** School does not offer a structured program with separate admission and additional fees. Services include: reading machines, tape recorders, videotaped classes, note-taking services, oral tests, readers, extended time for tests, tutors, typist/scribe, other testing accomodations, other. **Library:** Number of titles: 76,087; number of current serial subscriptions: 1,451. **Information technology resources:** Students are not required to lease or own a computer. Number of campus computers available to all students: 700. School has a wireless network. Approximate number of users that can be accommodated: 2,000. **Campus safety:** Security services offered: 24-hour foot-and-vehicle patrols, 24-hour emergency telephones, lighted pathways/sidewalks.

TRANSFER AND INTERNATIONAL STUDENTS

Transfer students: May apply for admission for the following academic terms: Fall, Spring. Applicants do not need a minimum number of credits to apply. For fall 2005: Transfer applicants offered admission: 1,299. Transfer applicants enrolled: 727. **International students:** Number of countries represented: 37. Minimum TOEFL score required: 470 (paper).

Daemen College

- **Address:** 4380 Main Street, Amherst, NY 14226-3592
- **Website:** http://www.daemen.edu
- **Private**
- **Enrollment:** 1,271 full-time; 332 part-time

KEY STATS

✔ **U.S News College Ranking:** third tier, Comp. Colleges–Bachelor's (North)
✔ **SAT Score (25th/75th percentile):** 970-1130
✔ **Tuition:** 2006-2007: $17,690

Selectivity: Selective	**Room/board:** $8,190
Acceptance rate: 79%	**Average debt:** $13,323
Student/faculty ratio: 13/1	**Proportion who borrowed:** 78%

UNDERGRADUATE STUDENT BODY STATS

2005-2006 enrollment: 1,271 full-time; 332 part-time. Men: 23%; women: 77%. **Ethnic makeup:** African American: 15%; American-Indian: 1%; Asian American: 1%; Hispanic: 2%; White: 79%; International: 1%. **Religious preference:** Roman Catholic: 46%; Protestant: 19%; No preference: 1%; Unknown: 17%; Other: 17%.

ADMISSIONS FACTS AND FIGURES

Phone: (800) 462-7652. **Email:** admissions@daemen.edu. **Website:** http://www.daemen.edu. **Application deadlines for fall 2007:** Regular decision: Rolling. Early decision: Not offered. Early action: Send application by: August 30; Decision sent by: September 1. Admission can be deferred. **Application fee:** $25. Common application is accepted. **Admissions requirements/recommendations:** High school units required (recommended): English: (4); Mathematics: (4); Science: (4); Social studies: (4); Total units: (16). Tests: The college uses SAT or ACT scores in admissions decisions. Either SAT or ACT required. For admission to the fall 2007 entering class, the school will accept: ACT with writing, ACT without writing. Campus visit: Recommended. Admissions interview: Recommended. Off-campus interview: May be arranged. **Factors that count in admissions decisions:** *Academic:* Secondary school record: Important. Class rank: Important. Letters of recommendation: Important. Standardized test scores: Very important. Essay: Important. *Nonacademic:* Interview: Important. Extracurricular activities: Considered. Talent/ability: Important. Character/personal qualities: Considered. Alumni/ae relationship: Considered. Geographical residence: Not considered. State residency: Not considered. Religious affiliation/commitment: Not considered. Minority status: Not considered. Volunteer work: Considered. Work experience: Considered. **Other schools with the greatest overlap in applicants:** Canisius College; Niagara University; SUNY–Buffalo State College; University at Buffalo–SUNY. **Admissions statistics for the fall 2005 entering class:** Total applicants: 1,609. Total accepted: 1,276. Freshmen enrolled: 366; 3% were from out of state. Accepted through early-decision or early-action plans: 2%. Overall acceptance rate: 79%. Non-early acceptance rate: 79%. **Size of waiting list:** 269 applicants; enrolled from waiting list: 71. **Credentials of fall 2005 freshmen:** 19% ranked in the top 10 percent of their high school class; 52% were in the top 25 percent, and 83% were in the top half. (Proportion submitting class standing: 69%.) **Average high school grade point average:** 3.6. **First-year students who submitted SAT scores:** 93%. Scores (25/75 percentile): Verbal: 480-560, Math: 490-570, Combined: 970-1130. **First-year students submitting ACT scores:** 36%. Scores (25/75 percentile): English: N/A, Math: N/A, Composite: 19-24.

ACADEMICS

Year founded: 1947. **Academic calendar:** Semester. **Degrees offered:** certificate, bachelor's, master's, post-master's certificate, first professional. **Most popular majors:** 27% nursing/registered nurse training (R.N., A.S.N., B.S.N., M.S.N.), 15% natural sciences, 14% elementary education and teaching, 11% business administration and management, 10% visual and performing arts. **Major fields of study:** biological and biomedical sciences; business, management, marketing, and related support services; education; English language and literature/letters; foreign languages, literatures, and linguistics; health professions and related clinical sciences; history; mathematics and statistics; multi/interdisciplinary studies; philosophy and religious studies; psychology; public administration and social service professions; social sciences; visual and performing arts. **Areas of required coursework:** computer literacy, English (including composition), other. **Pre-professional programs:** pre-law, other. **Special academic programs (% partici-**

pation): accelerated program (.4%), cross-registration, double major, dual enrollment, honors program, independent study (3.9%), internships, student-designed major, study abroad, teacher certificate program (19%), weekend college. **Teacher certification offered in:** early childhood, special education, elementary. **Reserve Officers Training Corps (ROTC):** Army ROTC: Offered at cooperating institution (Canisius College). **Faculty and instruction (2005-2006):** Total instructional faculty: 83 full-time, 177 part-time (40% men; 60% women; 5% minorities). Full-time faculty with Ph.D. or other terminal degree: 71%. Student/faculty ratio: 13/1. Classes of fewer than 20 students: 70%; of 20 to 49 students: 30%; of 50 or more students: 0%. **Advanced Placement and International Baccalaureate credit:** AP tests may be used for: Credit only. Scores accepted: 3, 4, 5. International Baccalaureate exams may be used for: Credit only. **Freshmen returning for sophomore year:** 71%. **Graduation rates:** Four-year: 26%; five-year: 39%; six-year: 40%. **Graduate study:** 28% of students pursue further study within one year. Fields in which graduates pursue further study: education, 40%; arts and sciences, 7%.

COSTS AND FINANCIAL AID

Financial aid office: (716) 839-8254. **Expenses (2006-2007):** Tuition and fees 2006-2007: $17,690; room/board: $8,190. **Financial aid:** Priority filing date for institution's financial aid form: February 15. In 2005-2006, 86% of undergraduates applied for financial aid. Of those, 86% were determined to have financial need; 30% had their need fully met. Average financial aid package (proportion receiving): $14,419 (85%). Average amount of gift aid, such as scholarships or grants (proportion receiving): $6,951 (78%). Average amount of self-help aid, such as work study or loans (proportion receiving): $4,774 (74%). Average need-based loan (excluding PLUS or other private loans): $4,054. Among students who received need-based aid, the average percentage of need met: 87%. Among students who received aid based on merit, the average award (and the proportion receiving): $5,369 (16%). The average athletic scholarship (and the proportion receiving): $7,379 (2%). Average amount of debt of borrowers graduating in 2005: $13,323. Proportion who borrowed: 78%.

CAMPUS LIFE AND EXTRACURRICULAR ACTIVITIES

Campus housing available (% using): coed dorms (33%), special housing for disabled students (0%), other housing options (67%). Students who live in college-owned, operated, or affiliated housing: 42%. **Student employment:** During the 2005-2006 academic year, 6% of undergraduates worked on campus. Average per-year earnings: $1,234. **Clubs and organizations:** Number of student organizations: 43. Activities include: choral groups, dance, drama/theater, literary magazine, student government, student newspaper, yearbook. Number of fraternities: 1; sororities: 4. Proportion of men in fraternities: 6%; of women in sororities: 4%. Average proportion of students who stay on campus on weekends: 62%. **Sports program (2005-2006):** Member of NAIA. **Men's intercollegiate varsity sports:** basketball, cross-country, golf, soccer. **Women's intercollegiate varsity sports:** basketball, cross-country, soccer, volleyball.

SERVICES AND FACILITIES

Basic services: nonremedial tutoring, health insurance. **Remedial assistance:** reading, math, writing, study skills. **Counseling services:** career, veteran student, academic, psychological, religious. **For learning-disabled students:** School does not offer a structured program with separate admission and additional fees. Total undergraduates in learning-disabled program or receiving services: 43. Services include: remedial math, remedial English, remedial reading, tape recorders, note-taking services, oral tests, learning center, readers, extended time for tests, tutors, priority registration, priority seating, texts on tape, other. **Library:** Number of titles: 139,641; number of current serial subscriptions: 881. **Information technology resources:** Students are not required to lease or own a computer. Number of campus computers available to all students: 68. School has a wireless network. Approximate number of users that can be accommodated: 250. Proportion of college-owned housing units wired for high-speed internet access: 100%. **Campus safety:** Security services offered: 24-hour foot-and-vehicle patrols, late-night transport/escort service, 24-hour emergency telephones, lighted pathways/sidewalks, controlled dormitory access (key, security card, etc).

TRANSFER AND INTERNATIONAL STUDENTS

Transfer students: May apply for admission for the following academic terms: Fall, Spring, Summer. Applicants do not need a minimum number of credits to apply. For fall 2005: Transfer applications received: 461. Transfer applicants offered admission: 305. Transfer applicants enrolled: 152. **International students:** Number of foreign undergraduates: 10 (1% of

student body). Number of countries represented: 10. Minimum TOEFL score required: 500 (paper); 173 (computer). Average TOEFL score: 570 (paper).

Dominican College of Blauvelt

- **Address:** 470 Western Highway, Orangeburg, NY 10962-1210
- **Website:** http://www.dc.edu
- **Private; Religious affiliation:** Roman Catholic
- **Enrollment:** 1,071 full-time; 338 part-time

KEY STATS
✔ **U.S News College Ranking:** third tier, Comp. Colleges–Bachelor's (North)
✔ **SAT Score (25th/75th percentile):** 800-992
✔ **Tuition:** 2006-2007: $18,610

Selectivity: Less selective	**Room/board:** $8,890
Acceptance rate: 83%	**Average debt:** $28,601
Student/faculty ratio: 14/1	**Proportion who borrowed:** 73%

UNDERGRADUATE STUDENT BODY STATS

2005-2006 enrollment: 1,071 full-time; 338 part-time. Men: 33%; women: 67%. **Ethnic makeup:** African American: 18%; Asian American: 7%; Hispanic: 15%; White: 60%.

ADMISSIONS FACTS AND FIGURES

Phone: (845) 359-3533. **Email:** admissions@dc.edu. **Website:** http://www.dc.edu. **Application deadlines for fall 2007:** Regular decision: Rolling. Early decision: Not offered. Early action: Not offered. Admission can be deferred. **Application fee:** $35. Common application is accepted. **Admissions requirements/recommendations:** High school units required (recommended): English: (6); Mathematics: (6); Science: (3); Foreign language: (3); Total units: (16). Tests: The college uses SAT or ACT scores in admissions decisions. Either SAT or ACT required. For admission to the fall 2007 entering class, the school will accept: ACT with writing. Campus visit: Recommended. Admissions interview: Recommended. Off-campus interview: Not available. **Factors that count in admissions decisions:** *Academic:* Secondary school record: Important. Class rank: Not considered. Letters of recommendation: Not considered. Standardized test scores: Important. Essay: Considered. *Nonacademic:* Interview: Considered. Extracurricular activities: Considered. Talent/ability: Considered. Character/personal qualities: Not considered. Alumni/ae relationship: Not considered. Geographical residence: Not considered. State residency: Not considered. Religious affiliation/commitment: Not considered. Minority status: Not considered. Volunteer work: Considered. Work experience: Not considered. **Other schools with the greatest overlap in applicants:** College of New Rochelle; Iona College; Ramapo College of New Jersey; St. Thomas Aquinas College. **Admissions statistics for the fall 2005 entering class:** Total applicants: 1,228. Total accepted: 1,014. Freshmen enrolled: 290; 27% were from out of state. Overall acceptance rate: 83%. **Average high school grade point average:** 2.7. **First-year students who submitted SAT scores:** 96%. Scores (25/75 percentile): Verbal: 406-492, Math: 400-500, Combined: 800-992. **First-year students submitting ACT scores:** 1%. Scores (25/75 percentile): English: N/A, Math: N/A, Composite: N/A.

ACADEMICS

Year founded: 1952. **Academic calendar:** Semester. **Degrees offered:** certificate, associate, bachelor's, master's, doctorate. **Most popular majors:** 31% business administration and management, 24% health professions and related clinical sciences, 9% education, 8% computer and information sciences, 5% humanities/humanistic studies. **Major fields of study:** biological and biomedical sciences; business, management, marketing, and related support services; computer and information sciences and support services; education; English language and literature/letters; foreign languages, literatures, and linguistics; health professions and related clinical sciences; history; legal professions and studies; liberal arts and sciences studies, and humanities; mathematics and statistics; psychology; public administration and social service professions; social sciences. **Areas of required coursework:** humanities, computer literacy, mathematics, English (including composition), philosophy, foreign languages, sciences (biological or physical), history, social science, other. **Pre-professional programs:** pre-law, pre-medicine, other. **Special academic programs (% participation):** accelerated program (12%), distance learning, dual enrollment (27%), honors program (1%), independent study (26%), internships (1%), teacher certificate program (18%), weekend college (24%). **Teacher certification offered in:** special education, elementary, secondary. **Faculty and instruction (2005-2006):** Total instructional faculty: 51 full-time, 112 part-time (39% men; 61% women; 7% minorities). Full-time faculty with Ph.D. or other terminal degree: 47%. Student/faculty ratio: 14/1. Classes of fewer than 20 students: 56%; of 20 to 49 students: 44%. **Advanced Placement and International Baccalaureate credit:** AP tests may be used for: Credit only. Scores accepted: 3. International Baccalaureate exams may be used for: Credit only. **Freshmen returning for sophomore year:** 66%. **Graduation rates:** Four-year: 37%; five-year: 50%; six-year: 57%.

COSTS AND FINANCIAL AID

Financial aid office: (845) 359-7800. **Expenses (2006-2007):** Tuition and fees 2006-2007: $18,610; room/board: $8,890. Estimated books and supplies: $1,200; transportation: $700; personal expenses: $1,200. **Financial aid:** Priority filing date for institution's financial aid form: February 15. In 2005-2006, 88% of undergraduates applied for financial aid. Of those, 78% were determined to have financial need; 14% had their need fully met. Average financial aid package (proportion receiving): $12,808 (77%). Average amount of gift aid, such as scholarships or grants (proportion receiving): $9,682 (74%). Average amount of self-help aid, such as work study or loans (proportion receiving): $4,447 (61%). Average need-based loan (excluding PLUS or other private loans): $3,788. Among students who received need-based aid, the average percentage of need met: 62%. Among students who received aid based on merit, the average award (and the proportion receiving): $10,959 (12%). The average athletic scholarship (and the proportion receiving): $19,001 (1%). Average amount of debt of borrowers graduating in 2005: $28,601. Proportion who borrowed: 73%.

CAMPUS LIFE AND EXTRACURRICULAR ACTIVITIES

Campus housing available (% using): coed dorms (93%), other housing options (7%). Students who live in college-owned, operated, or affiliated housing: 32%. **Student employment:** During the 2005-2006 academic year, 25% of undergraduates worked on campus. Average per-year earnings: $2,000. **Clubs and organizations:** Number of student organizations: 17. Activities include: choral groups, dance, drama/theater, literary magazine, musical theater, student government, student newspaper, yearbook. Number of fraternities: 0; sororities: 0. **Sports program (2005-2006):** Member of NCAA II. *Men's intercollegiate varsity sports:* baseball, basketball, cross-country, golf, lacrosse, soccer. *Women's intercollegiate varsity sports:* basketball, cross-country, soccer, softball, volleyball.

SERVICES AND FACILITIES

Basic services: nonremedial tutoring, placement service, health service. **Remedial assistance:** reading, math, writing, study skills. **Counseling services:** career, personal, academic, psychological, religious. **For learning-disabled students:** School does not offer a structured program with separate admission and additional fees. Services include: remedial math, remedial English, reading machines, remedial reading, diagnostic testing service, note-taking services, learning center, tutors. **Information technology resources:** Students are not required to lease or own a computer. Number of campus computers available to all students: 85. School does not have a wireless network. Proportion of college-owned housing units wired for high-speed internet access: 100%. **Campus safety:** Security services offered: 24-hour foot-and-vehicle patrols, late-night transport/escort service, controlled dormitory access (key, security card, etc).

TRANSFER AND INTERNATIONAL STUDENTS

Transfer students: May apply for admission for the following academic terms: Fall, Spring, Summer. Applicants do not need a minimum number of credits to apply. For fall 2005: Transfer applications received: 270. Transfer applicants offered admission: 206. Transfer applicants enrolled: 95. **International students:** Number of foreign undergraduates: 0. Number of countries represented: 0. Minimum TOEFL score required: 550 (paper); 213 (computer).

Dowling College

■ **Address:** Idle Hour Boulevard, Oakdale Long Island, NY 11769
■ **Website:** http://www.dowling.edu
■ **Private**
■ **Enrollment:** 2,298 full-time; 1,329 part-time

KEY STATS
✔ **U.S News College Ranking:** fourth tier, Universities–Master's (North)
✔ **SAT Score (25th/75th percentile):** 820-1040
✔ **Tuition:** 2006-2007: $13,800

Selectivity: Less selective	**Room/board:** N/A
Acceptance rate: 87%	**Average debt:** $18,920
Student/faculty ratio: 17/1	**Proportion who borrowed:** 81%

UNDERGRADUATE STUDENT BODY STATS

2005-2006 enrollment: 2,298 full-time; 1,329 part-time. Men: 39%; women: 61%. **Ethnic makeup:** African American: 9%; Asian American: 2%; Hispanic: 9%; White: 76%; International: 4%.

ADMISSIONS FACTS AND FIGURES

Phone: (631) 244-3030. **Email:** admissions@dowling.edu. **Website:** http://www.dowling.edu. **Application deadlines for fall 2007:** Regular decision: Rolling. Early decision: Not offered. Early action: Not offered. Admission cannot be deferred. **Application fee:** $25. Common application is accepted. **Admissions requirements/recommendations:** High school units required (recommended): English: 4 (4); Mathematics: 3 (3); Science: 2 (2); Social studies: 3 (3); Total units: 16 (16). Tests: The college uses SAT or ACT scores in admissions decisions. Neither SAT nor ACT required. Campus visit: Recommended. Admissions interview: Recommended. **Factors that count in admissions decisions:** *Academic:* Secondary school record: Very important. Class rank: Considered. Letters of recommendation: Considered. Standardized test scores: Considered. Essay: Considered. *Nonacademic:* Interview: Not considered. Extracurricular activities: Considered. Talent/ability: Considered. Character/personal qualities: Considered. Alumni/ae relationship: Considered. Geographical residence: Not considered. State residency: Not considered. Religious affiliation/commitment: Not considered. Minority status: Not considered. Volunteer work: Not considered. Work experience: Not considered. **Other schools with the greatest overlap in applicants:** Adelphi University; Hofstra University; Long Island University–C.W. Post Campus; SUNY–Stony Brook; St. Joseph's College New York–Brooklyn. **Admissions statistics for the fall 2005 entering class:** Total applicants: 2,399. Total accepted: 2,082. Freshmen enrolled: 465; 5% were from out of state. Overall acceptance rate: 87%. **Credentials of fall 2005 freshmen:** 6% ranked in the top 10 percent of their high school class; 19% were in the top 25 percent, and 50% were in the top half. (Proportion submitting class standing: 88%.) **Average high school grade point average:** 2.8. **First-year students who submitted SAT scores:** 60%. Scores (25/75 percentile): Verbal: 410-520, Math: 410-520, Combined: 820-1040.

ACADEMICS

Year founded: 1955. **Academic calendar:** Semester. **Degrees offered:** bachelor's, post-bachelor's certificate, master's, post-master's certificate, doctorate. **Most popular majors:** 32% business, management, marketing, and related support services, 18% education, 10% liberal arts and sciences studies, and humanities, 8% social sciences, 6% computer and information sciences and support services. **Major fields of study:** biological and biomedical sciences; business, management, marketing, and related support services; communication, journalism, and related programs; computer and information sciences and support services; education; engineering; English language and literature/letters; foreign languages, literatures, and linguistics; health professions and related clinical sciences; history; liberal arts and sciences studies, and humanities; mathematics and statistics; multi/interdisciplinary studies; philosophy and religious studies; psychology; social sciences; transportation and materials moving; visual and performing arts. **Areas of required coursework:** arts/fine arts, humanities, mathematics, English (including composition), philosophy, sciences (biological or physical), history, social science. **Pre-professional programs:** pre-law, pre-dentistry, pre-medicine, pre-veterinary science. **Special academic programs:** accelerated program, double major, English as a Second Language (ESL), honors program, independent study, internships, liberal arts/career combination, student-designed major, teacher certificate program, weekend college. **Teacher certification offered in:** special education, elementary, secondary. **Cooperative**

education programs: art, business, computer science, engineering, natural science, social/behavioral science, other. **Reserve Officers Training Corps (ROTC):** Air Force ROTC: Offered at cooperating institution (Manhattan College). **Faculty and instruction (2005-2006):** Total instructional faculty: 124 full-time, 376 part-time (57% men; 43% women; 8% minorities). Full-time faculty with Ph.D. or other terminal degree: 90%. Student/faculty ratio: 17/1. Classes of fewer than 20 students: 66%; of 20 to 49 students: 34%; of 50 or more students: 0%. **Advanced Placement and International Baccalaureate credit:** AP tests may be used for: Placement only. **Freshmen returning for sophomore year:** 67%. **Graduation rates:** Four-year: 17%; five-year: 31%; six-year: 40%. **Graduate study:** 25% of students pursue further study immediately upon graduation. Fields in which graduates pursue further study: Master of Business Administration (MBA), 15%; law, 1%; medicine, 1%; education, 30%; arts and sciences, 48%.

COSTS AND FINANCIAL AID

Financial aid office: (631) 244-3303. **Expenses (2006-2007):** Tuition and fees 2006-2007: $13,800; room/board: N/A. Estimated books and supplies: $1,000; transportation: $1,350; personal expenses: $1,066. **Financial aid:** Priority filing date for institution's financial aid form: April 30. In 2005-2006, 78% of undergraduates applied for financial aid. Of those, 66% were determined to have financial need; 18% had their need fully met. Average financial aid package (proportion receiving): $13,385 (65%). Average amount of gift aid, such as scholarships or grants (proportion receiving): $2,804 (65%). Average amount of self-help aid, such as work study or loans (proportion receiving): $3,232 (57%). Average need-based loan (excluding PLUS or other private loans): $3,691. Among students who received need-based aid, the average percentage of need met: 87%. Among students who received aid based on merit, the average award (and the proportion receiving): $3,690 (14%). The average athletic scholarship (and the proportion receiving): $11,738 (3%). Average amount of debt of borrowers graduating in 2005: $18,920. Proportion who borrowed: 81%.

CAMPUS LIFE AND EXTRACURRICULAR ACTIVITIES

Campus housing available (% using): coed dorms (100%). Students who live in college-owned, operated, or affiliated housing: 17%. **Student employment:** During the 2005-2006 academic year, 0% of undergraduates worked on campus. Average per-year earnings: $0. **Clubs and organizations:** Number of student organizations: 40. Activities include: choral groups, drama/theater, jazz band, literary magazine, music ensembles, musical theater, student government, student newspaper, symphony orchestra, yearbook. Number of fraternities: 1; sororities: 0. Average proportion of students who stay on campus on weekends: 50%. **Sports program (2005-2006):** Member of NCAA II. *Men's intercollegiate varsity sports:* baseball, basketball, golf, lacrosse, soccer, tennis. *Women's intercollegiate varsity sports:* basketball, cross-country, rowing, soccer, softball, tennis, volleyball.

SERVICES AND FACILITIES

Basic services: nonremedial tutoring, health service, health insurance. **Remedial assistance:** math, writing, study skills. **Counseling services:** minority student, career, personal, veteran student, academic, older student, psychological, religious. **For learning-disabled students:** School does not offer a structured program with separate admission and additional fees. Total undergraduates in learning-disabled program or receiving services: 139. Services include: remedial math, remedial English, tape recorders, untimed tests, note-taking services, readers, extended time for tests, tutors, priority registration, priority seating, texts on tape, other testing accomodations. **Library:** Number of titles: 232,380; number of current serial subscriptions: 961. **Information technology resources:** Students are not required to lease or own a computer. Number of campus computers available to all students: 210. School has a wireless network. Proportion of college-owned housing units wired for high-speed internet access: 100%. **Campus safety:** Security services offered: 24-hour foot-and-vehicle patrols, late-night transport/escort service, lighted pathways/sidewalks, controlled dormitory access (key, security card, etc).

TRANSFER AND INTERNATIONAL STUDENTS

Transfer students: May apply for admission for the following academic terms: Fall, Winter, Spring, Summer. Applicants need a minimum number of credits to apply. For fall 2005: Transfer applications received: 995. Transfer applicants offered admission: 670. Transfer applicants enrolled: 410. **International students:** Number of foreign undergraduates: 135 (4% of student body). Number of countries represented: 44. Minimum TOEFL score required: 500 (paper).

Elmira College

- Address: 1 Park Place, Elmira, NY 14901
- Website: http://www.elmira.edu
- Private
- Enrollment: 1,175 full-time; 309 part-time

KEY STATS

✔ **U.S News College Ranking:** 5, Comp. Colleges–Bachelor's (North)
✔ **SAT Score (25th/75th percentile):** 1030-1250
✔ **Tuition:** 2006-2007: $30,050
  Selectivity: More selective   **Room/board:** $9,100
  Acceptance rate: 64%   **Average debt:** $25,347
  Student/faculty ratio: 12/1   **Proportion who borrowed:** 69%

UNDERGRADUATE STUDENT BODY STATS

2005-2006 enrollment: 1,175 full-time; 309 part-time. Men: 29%; women: 71%. **Ethnic makeup:** African American: 2%; Asian American: 1%; Hispanic: 1%; White: 92%; International: 4%. **Religious preference:** Roman Catholic: 39%; Protestant: 30%; Jewish: 1%; Buddhist: 1%; Unknown: 29%.

ADMISSIONS FACTS AND FIGURES

Phone: (607) 735-1724. **Email:** admissions@elmira.edu. **Website:** http://www.elmira.edu. **Application deadlines for fall 2007:** Regular decision: March 1. Early decision: Send application by: November 15; Decision sent by: December 15. Early action: Not offered. Admission can be deferred. **Application fee:** $50. Common application is accepted. **Admissions requirements/recommendations:** High school units required (recommended): English: 4; Mathematics: 3; Science: 3; Foreign language: (2); Social studies: 3; History: 1; Academic electives: 2; Total units: 16. Tests: The college uses SAT or ACT scores in admissions decisions. Either SAT or ACT required. For admission to the fall 2007 entering class, the school will accept: ACT with writing, ACT without writing. Campus visit: Recommended. Admissions interview: Recommended. Off-campus interview: May be arranged. **Factors that count in admissions decisions:** *Academic:* Secondary school record: Very important. Class rank: Very important. Letters of recommendation: Important. Standardized test scores: Important. Essay: Important. *Nonacademic:* Interview: Important. Extracurricular activities: Important. Talent/ability: Considered. Character/personal qualities: Very important. Alumni/ae relationship: Considered. Geographical residence: Considered. State residency: Not considered. Religious affiliation/commitment: Not considered. Minority status: Considered. Volunteer work: Considered. Work experience: Considered. **Other schools with the greatest overlap in applicants:** Hobart and William Smith Colleges; Ithaca College; Quinnipiac University; St. Lawrence University; Syracuse University. **Admissions statistics for the fall 2005 entering class:** Total applicants: 1,966. Total accepted: 1,266. Freshmen enrolled: 323; 52% were from out of state. Accepted through early-decision or early-action plans: 20%. Overall acceptance rate: 64%. Early-decision acceptance rate: 61%. Non-early acceptance rate: 65%. **Size of waiting list:** 73 applicants; enrolled from waiting list: 9. **Credentials of fall 2005 freshmen:** 28% ranked in the top 10 percent of their high school class; 70% were in the top 25 percent, and 100% were in the top half. (Proportion submitting class standing: 73%.) **Average high school grade point average:** 3.5. **First-year students who submitted SAT scores:** 96%. Scores (25/75 percentile): Verbal: 520-630, Math: 510-620, Combined: 1030-1250. **First-year students submitting ACT scores:** 27%. Scores (25/75 percentile): English: 21-28, Math: 23-28, Composite: 23-27.

ACADEMICS

Year founded: 1855. **Academic calendar:** Other. **Degrees offered:** associate, bachelor's, master's. **Most popular majors:** 24% business administration and management, 10% elementary education and teaching, 8% psychology, 7% nursing/registered nurse training (R.N., A.S.N., B.S.N., M.S.N.), 5% English literature (British and Commonwealth). **Major fields of study:** area, ethnic, cultural, and gender studies; biological and biomedical sciences; business, management, marketing, and related support services; computer and information sciences and support services; education; English language and literature/letters; foreign languages, literatures, and linguistics; health professions and related clinical sciences; history; liberal arts and sciences studies, and humanities; mathematics and statistics; multi/interdisciplinary studies; philosophy and religious studies; physical sciences; psychology; public administration and social service professions; security and protective services; social sciences; visual and performing arts. **Areas of required**

coursework: arts/fine arts, humanities, mathematics, English (including composition), sciences (biological or physical), history, social science, other. **Pre-professional programs:** pre-law, pre-dentistry, pre-medicine, pre-veterinary science, pre-optometry, pre-pharmacy. **Special academic programs (% participation):** accelerated program (1%), distance learning (1%), double major (20%), English as a Second Language (ESL) (1%), exchange student program (domestic) (1%), honors program (2%), independent study (12%), internships (100%), liberal arts/career combination (1%), student-designed major (8%), study abroad (36%), teacher certificate program (10%). **Teacher certification offered in:** early childhood, elementary, middle/junior high, secondary. **Reserve Officers Training Corps (ROTC):** Army ROTC: Offered on campus; Air Force ROTC: Offered at cooperating institution (Cornell University). **Faculty and instruction (2005-2006):** Total instructional faculty: 82 full-time, 17 part-time (58% men; 42% women; 6% minorities). Full-time faculty with Ph.D. or other terminal degree: 100%. Student/faculty ratio: 12/1. Classes of fewer than 20 students: 77%; of 20 to 49 students: 23%; of 50 or more students: 0%. **Advanced Placement and International Baccalaureate credit:** AP tests may be used for: Credit and/or placement. Scores accepted: 3, 4, 5. International Baccalaureate exams may be used for: Credit and/or placement. **Freshmen returning for sophomore year:** 78%. **Graduation rates:** Four-year: 59%; five-year: 62%; six-year: 60%. **Graduate study:** 40% of students pursue further study immediately upon graduation; 67% within one year; 85% within five years. Fields in which graduates pursue further study: Master of Business Administration (MBA), 4%; law, 4%; medicine, 2%; theology (or the seminary), 2%; education, 46%; arts and sciences, 12%.

COSTS AND FINANCIAL AID
Financial aid office: (607) 735-1728. **Expenses (2006-2007):** Tuition and fees 2006-2007: $30,050; room/board: $9,100. Estimated books and supplies: $450; transportation: $550. **Financial aid:** Priority filing date for institution's financial aid form: February 1. In 2005-2006, 85% of undergraduates applied for financial aid. Of those, 78% were determined to have financial need; 16% had their need fully met. Average financial aid package (proportion receiving): $21,435 (78%). Average amount of gift aid, such as scholarships or grants (proportion receiving): $16,130 (78%). Average amount of self-help aid, such as work study or loans (proportion receiving): $6,415 (65%). Average need-based loan (excluding PLUS or other private loans): $5,795. Among students who received need-based aid, the average percentage of need met: 80%. Among students who received aid based on merit, the average award (and the proportion receiving): $15,717 (18%). The average athletic scholarship (and the proportion receiving): $0 (0%). Average amount of debt of borrowers graduating in 2005: $25,347. Proportion who borrowed: 69%.

CAMPUS LIFE AND EXTRACURRICULAR ACTIVITIES
Campus housing available (% using): coed dorms (71%), women's dorms (22%), apartment for single students (7%). Students who live in college-owned, operated, or affiliated housing: 92%. **Student employment:** During the 2005-2006 academic year, 23% of undergraduates worked on campus. Average per-year earnings: $1,800. **Clubs and organizations:** Number of student organizations: 91. Activities include: choral groups, concert band, dance, drama/theater, literary magazine, music ensembles, musical theater, pep band, radio station, student government, student newspaper, yearbook. Number of fraternities: 0; sororities: 0. Average proportion of students who stay on campus on weekends: 90%. **Sports program (2005-2006):** Member of NCAA III. *Men's intercollegiate varsity sports:* basketball, golf, ice hockey, lacrosse, soccer, tennis. *Women's intercollegiate varsity sports:* basketball, cheerleading, field hockey, golf, ice hockey, lacrosse, soccer, softball, tennis, volleyball.

SERVICES AND FACILITIES
Basic services: nonremedial tutoring, placement service, health service, health insurance, other. **Remedial assistance:** math, writing, other. **Counseling services:** career, personal, academic, psychological, birth control, religious. **For learning-disabled students:** School does not offer a structured program with separate admission and additional fees. Total undergraduates in learning-disabled program or receiving services: 59. Services include: reading machines, tape recorders, diagnostic testing service, untimed tests, note-taking services, oral tests, readers, extended time for tests, tutors, texts on tape, exams on tape or computer, other testing accomodations, other. **Library:** Number of titles: 391,038; number of current serial subscriptions: 859. **Information technology resources:** Students are not required to lease or own a computer. Number of campus computers available to all students: 115. School does not have a wireless network. Proportion of college-owned housing units wired for high-speed internet access: 98%. **Campus safety:**

Security services offered: 24-hour foot-and-vehicle patrols, late-night transport/escort service, 24-hour emergency telephones, lighted pathways/sidewalks, controlled dormitory access (key, security card, etc).

TRANSFER AND INTERNATIONAL STUDENTS
Transfer students: May apply for admission for the following academic terms: Fall, Winter, Spring. Applicants need a minimum number of credits to apply. For fall 2005: Transfer applications received: 138. Transfer applicants offered admission: 91. Transfer applicants enrolled: 55. **International students:** Number of foreign undergraduates: 49 (4% of student body). Number of countries represented: 23. Minimum TOEFL score required: 500 (paper); 173 (computer). Average TOEFL score: 530 (paper).

Excelsior College

- **Address:** 7 Columbia Circle, Albany, NY 12203
- **Website:** http://www.excelsior.edu
- **Private**
- **Enrollment:** N/A; 27,844 part-time

KEY STATS
✔ **U.S News College Ranking:** Unranked, Liberal Arts Colleges
✔ **SAT or ACT Score (25th/75th percentile):** N/A
✔ **Tuition:** N/A

Selectivity: N/A	**Room/board:** N/A
Acceptance rate: N/A	**Average debt:** N/A
Student/faculty ratio: N/A	**Proportion who borrowed:** N/A

UNDERGRADUATE STUDENT BODY STATS
2005-2006 enrollment: N/A full-time; 27,844 part-time. Men: 44%; women: 56%. **Ethnic makeup:** African American: 16%; American-Indian: 1%; Asian American: 7%; Hispanic: 6%; White: 69%; International: 1%.

ADMISSIONS FACTS AND FIGURES
Phone: (518) 464-8500. **Email:** admissions@excelsior.edu. **Website:** http://www.excelsior.edu. **Application deadlines for fall 2007:** Regular decision: Rolling. Early decision: Not offered. Early action: Not offered. Admission cannot be deferred. **Application fee:** $65. Common application is not accepted. **Admissions requirements/recommendations:** Tests: The college does not use SAT or ACT scores in admissions decisions. Neither SAT nor ACT required. Campus visit: Neither required nor recommended. Admissions interview: Neither required nor recommended. Off-campus interview: Not available. **Factors that count in admissions decisions:** *Academic:* Secondary school record: Not considered. Class rank: Not considered. Letters of recommendation: Not considered. Standardized test scores: Not considered. Essay: Not considered. *Nonacademic:* Interview: Not considered. Extracurricular activities: Not considered. Talent/ability: Not considered. Character/personal qualities: Not considered. Alumni/ae relationship: Not considered. Geographical residence: Not considered. State residency: Not considered. Religious affiliation/commitment: Not considered. Minority status: Not considered. Volunteer work: Not considered. Work experience: Not considered.

ACADEMICS
Year founded: 1970. **Academic calendar:** Continuos. **Degrees offered:** certificate, associate, transfer-associate, terminal-associate, bachelor's, post-bachelor's certificate, master's. **Most popular majors:** Information not available. **Major fields of study:** area, ethnic, cultural, and gender studies; biological and biomedical sciences; business, management, marketing, and related support services; communication, journalism, and related programs; computer and information sciences and support services; engineering technologies/technicians; English language and literature/letters; foreign languages, literatures, and linguistics; health professions and related clinical sciences; history; liberal arts and sciences studies, and humanities; mathematics and statistics; philosophy and religious studies; physical sciences; psychology; security and protective services; social sciences; visual and performing arts. **Areas of required coursework:** computer literacy, mathematics, English (including composition). **Special academic programs:** accelerated program, distance learning, external degree program, honors program, independent study. **Faculty and instruction (2005-2006):** Total instructional faculty: N/A. Classes of fewer than 20 students: 91%; of 20 to 49 students: 9%.

COSTS AND FINANCIAL AID

Financial aid office: (518) 464-8500.

CAMPUS LIFE AND EXTRACURRICULAR ACTIVITIES

Number of fraternities: 0; sororities: 0.

SERVICES AND FACILITIES

Basic services: nonremedial tutoring. **Counseling services:** career, military, academic. **For learning-disabled students:** School does not offer a structured program with separate admission and additional fees. **Information technology resources:** Students are not required to lease or own a computer.

TRANSFER AND INTERNATIONAL STUDENTS

Transfer students: May apply for admission for the following academic terms: Fall, Winter, Spring, Summer. Applicants do not need a minimum number of credits to apply. For fall 2005: Transfer applicants enrolled: 10,714. **International students:** Number of foreign undergraduates: 303 (1% of student body). Number of countries represented: 58.

Fashion Institute of Technology

- **Address:** Seventh Avenue at 27th Street, New York, NY 10001-5992
- **Website:** http://www.fitnyc.edu
- **Public**
- **Enrollment:** 6,661 full-time; 3,538 part-time

KEY STATS

✔ **U.S News College Ranking:** Unranked, Comp. Coll.–Bachelor's (North)
✔ **SAT or ACT Score (25th/75th percentile):** N/A
✔ **Tuition:** 2006-2007: $4,770 in state, $11,030 out of state

Selectivity: N/A	Room/board: $9,426
Acceptance rate: 42%	Average debt: $12,869
Student/faculty ratio: 17/1	Proportion who borrowed: 39%

UNDERGRADUATE STUDENT BODY STATS

2005-2006 enrollment: 6,661 full-time; 3,538 part-time. Men: 16%; women: 84%. **Ethnic makeup:** African American: 7%; Asian American: 10%; Hispanic: 10%; White: 63%; International: 10%.

ADMISSIONS FACTS AND FIGURES

Phone: (212) 217-7675. **Email:** fitinfo@fitsuny.edu. **Website:** http://www.fitnyc.edu. **Application deadlines for fall 2007:** Regular decision: Rolling. Early decision: Not offered. Early action: Send application by: November 15; Decision sent by: January 31. Admission can be deferred. **Application fee:** $40. Common application is not accepted. **Admissions requirements/recommendations:** Tests: The college does not use SAT or ACT scores in admissions decisions. Neither SAT nor ACT required. Campus visit: Recommended. Admissions interview: Neither required nor recommended. Off-campus interview: Not available. **Factors that count in admissions decisions:** *Academic:* Secondary school record: Very important. Class rank: Very important. Letters of recommendation: Not considered. Standardized test scores: Not considered. Essay: Very important. *Nonacademic:* Interview: Not considered. Extracurricular activities: Considered. Talent/ability: Very important. Character/personal qualities: Considered. Alumni/ae relationship: Not considered. Geographical residence: Not considered. State residency: Not considered. Religious affiliation/commitment: Not considered. Minority status: Not considered. Volunteer work: Not considered. Work experience: Not considered. **Other schools with the greatest overlap in applicants:** New School University; Pratt Institute; SUNY College–Oneonta. **Admissions statistics for the fall 2005 entering class:** Total applicants: 3,498. Total accepted: 1,475. Freshmen enrolled: 1,026; 39% were from out of state. Overall acceptance rate: 42%. Non-early acceptance rate: 42%. **Credentials of fall 2005 freshmen:** 13% ranked in the top 10 percent of their high school class; 45% were in the top 25 percent, and 82% were in the top half. (Proportion submitting class standing: 44%.) **Average high school grade point average:** 3.1.

ACADEMICS

Year founded: 1944. **Academic calendar:** Semester. **Degrees offered:** certificate, associate, bachelor's, master's. **Most popular majors:** 19% fashion merchandising, 10% fashion/apparel design, 7% advertising, 4% commercial and advertising art, 3% illustration. **Major fields of study:** business, management, marketing, and related support services; communication, journalism,

and related programs; family and consumer sciences/human sciences; visual and performing arts. **Areas of required coursework:** arts/fine arts, humanities, mathematics, English (including composition), foreign languages, sciences (biological or physical), history, social science. **Special academic programs (% participation):** distance learning (23%), English as a Second Language (ESL) (9%), honors program (4%), independent study (1%), internships (73%), study abroad (8%). **Faculty and instruction (2005-2006):** Total instructional faculty: 210 full-time, 748 part-time (50% men; 50% women; 15% minorities). Student/faculty ratio: 17/1. Classes of fewer than 20 students: 34%; of 20 to 49 students: 66%; of 50 or more students: 0%. **Advanced Placement and International Baccalaureate credit:** AP tests may be used for: Credit and/or placement. Scores accepted: 3. International Baccalaureate exams may be used for: Credit and/or placement. **Freshmen returning for sophomore year:** 82%. **Graduation rates:** Four-year: 63%; five-year: 66%; six-year: 52%.

COSTS AND FINANCIAL AID

Financial aid office: (212) 217-7439. **Expenses (2006-2007):** Tuition and fees 2006-2007: $4,770 in state, $11,030 out of state; room/board: $9,426. Estimated books and supplies: $1,600; transportation: $600; personal expenses: $1,500. **Financial aid:** Priority filing date for institution's financial aid form: February 15. In 2005-2006, 62% of undergraduates applied for financial aid. Of those, 40% were determined to have financial need; 17% had their need fully met. Average financial aid package (proportion receiving): $7,555 (39%). Average amount of gift aid, such as scholarships or grants (proportion receiving): $4,138 (29%). Average amount of self-help aid, such as work study or loans (proportion receiving): $4,062 (28%). Average need-based loan (excluding PLUS or other private loans): $3,664. Among students who received need-based aid, the average percentage of need met: 71%. Among students who received aid based on merit, the average award (and the proportion receiving): $2,208 (1%). The average athletic scholarship (and the proportion receiving): $0 (0%). Average amount of debt of borrowers graduating in 2005: $12,869. Proportion who borrowed: 39%.

CAMPUS LIFE AND EXTRACURRICULAR ACTIVITIES

Campus housing available (% using): coed dorms (25%), women's dorms (24%), apartment for single students (51%). Students who live in college-owned, operated, or affiliated housing: 17%. **Clubs and organizations:** Number of student organizations: 73. Activities include: choral groups, dance, drama/theater, literary magazine, music ensembles, musical theater, radio station, student government, student newspaper, television station, yearbook. Number of fraternities: 0; sororities: 0. Average proportion of students who stay on campus on weekends: 75%. **Sports program (2005-2006):** *Men's intercollegiate varsity sports:* basketball, bowling, cross-country, tennis, table tennis. *Women's intercollegiate varsity sports:* basketball, bowling, cross-country, tennis, volleyball, table tennis.

SERVICES AND FACILITIES

Basic services: nonremedial tutoring, placement service, health service, health insurance. **Remedial assistance:** reading, math, study skills. **Counseling services:** other. **For learning-disabled students:** School does not offer a structured program with separate admission and additional fees. Total undergraduates in learning-disabled program or receiving services: 0. Services include: remedial math, remedial English, reading machines, remedial reading, tape recorders, note-taking services, oral tests, learning center, readers, extended time for tests, tutors, early syllabus, priority registration, priority seating, proofreading services, substitution of courses, texts on tape, typist/scribe, exams on tape or computer, other testing accomodations, other. **Library:** Number of titles: 161,873; number of current serial subscriptions: 467. **Information technology resources:** Students are not required to lease or own a computer. Number of campus computers available to all students: 1,500. School has a wireless network. Approximate number of users that can be accommodated: 1,000. Proportion of college-owned housing units wired for high-speed internet access: 100%. **Campus safety:** Security services offered: 24-hour foot-and-vehicle patrols, late-night transport/escort service, lighted pathways/sidewalks, controlled dormitory access (key, security card, etc).

TRANSFER AND INTERNATIONAL STUDENTS

Transfer students: May apply for admission for the following academic terms: Fall, Spring. Applicants do not need a minimum number of credits to apply. **International students:** Number of foreign undergraduates: 757 (10% of student body). Number of countries represented: 60. Minimum TOEFL score required: 550 (paper); 213 (computer).

Fordham University

- **Address:** 113 W. 60th Street, New York, NY 10023
- **Website:** http://www.fordham.edu
- **Private; Religious affiliation:** Roman Catholic
- **Enrollment:** 6,887 full-time; 641 part-time

KEY STATS

✔ **U.S News College Ranking:** 70, National Universities
✔ **SAT Score (25th/75th percentile):** 1120-1310
✔ **Tuition:** 2006-2007: $30,445

Selectivity: More selective	**Room/board:** $11,630
Acceptance rate: 50%	**Average debt:** $16,976
Student/faculty ratio: 12/1	**Proportion who borrowed:** 61%

UNDERGRADUATE STUDENT BODY STATS

2005-2006 enrollment: 6,887 full-time; 641 part-time. Men: 41%; women: 59%. **Ethnic makeup:** African American: 5%; Asian American: 6%; Hispanic: 12%; White: 75%; International: 1%. **Religious preference:** Protestant: 10%; Jewish: 2%; Muslim: 2%; Hindu: 1%; Buddhist: 1%; Unknown: 12%; Roman Catholic: 63%; Greek Orthodox: 3%; Other: 6%.

ADMISSIONS FACTS AND FIGURES

Phone: (800) 367-3426. **Email:** enroll@fordham.edu. **Website:** http://www.fordham.edu. **Application deadlines for fall 2007:** Regular decision: January 15; decision sent by April 1. Early decision: Not offered. Early action: Send application by: November 1; Decision sent by: December 25. Admission can be deferred. **Application fee:** $50. Common application is accepted. **To apply online, go to:** http://www.fordham.edu/admiss/admiss.htm. **Admissions requirements/recommendations:** High school units required (recommended): English: 4 (4); Mathematics: 3 (4); Science: 3 (4); Foreign language: 2 (3); Social studies: 2 (2); History: 2 (2); Academic electives: 6 (6); Total units: 22 (25). Tests: The college uses SAT or ACT scores in admissions decisions. Either SAT or ACT required. For admission to the fall 2007 entering class, the school will accept: ACT with writing, ACT without writing. Campus visit: Recommended. Admissions interview: Recommended. Off-campus interview: May be arranged. **Factors that count in admissions decisions:** *Academic:* Secondary school record: Very important. Class rank: Very important. Letters of recommendation: Important. Standardized test scores: Very important. Essay: Important. *Nonacademic:* Interview: Considered. Extracurricular activities: Important. Talent/ability: Important. Character/personal qualities: Important. Alumni/ae relationship: Considered. Geographical residence: Not considered. State residency: Not considered. Religious affiliation/commitment: Not considered. Minority status: Considered. Volunteer work: Considered. Work experience: Considered. **Other schools with the greatest overlap in applicants:** Boston College; Boston University; New York University; St. John's University; Villanova University. **Admissions statistics for the fall 2005 entering class:** Total applicants: 15,225. Total accepted: 7,606. Freshmen enrolled: 1,755; 48% were from out of state. Accepted through early-decision or early-action plans: 19%. Overall acceptance rate: 50%. Non-early acceptance rate: 50%. **Size of waiting list:** 2117 applicants; enrolled from waiting list: 431. **Credentials of fall 2005 freshmen:** 39% ranked in the top 10 percent of their high school class; 75% were in the top 25 percent, and 96% were in the top half. (Proportion submitting class standing: 45%.) **Average high school grade point average:** 3.7. **First-year students who submitted SAT scores:** 95%. Scores (25/75 percentile): Verbal: 560-660, Math: 560-650, Combined: 1120-1310. **First-year students submitting ACT scores:** 17%. Scores (25/75 percentile): English: N/A, Math: N/A, Composite: 24-28.

ACADEMICS

Year founded: 1841. **Academic calendar:** Semester. **Degrees offered:** bachelor's, master's, post-master's certificate, first professional, doctorate. **Most popular majors:** 16% business administration and management, 14% communication studies/speech communication and rhetoric, 8% accounting, 7% English language and literature, 6% psychology. **Major fields of study:** area, ethnic, cultural, and gender studies; biological and biomedical sciences; business, management, marketing, and related support services; communication, journalism, and related programs; computer and information sciences and support services; education; engineering; English language and literature/letters; foreign languages, literatures, and linguistics; history; liberal arts and sciences studies, and humanities; mathematics and

statistics; multi/interdisciplinary studies; philosophy and religious studies; physical sciences; psychology; public administration and social service professions; social sciences; visual and performing arts. **Areas of required coursework:** arts/fine arts, humanities, mathematics, English (including composition), philosophy,.foreign languages, sciences (biological or physical), history, social science, other. **Pre-professional programs:** pre-law, pre-dentistry, pre-medicine, pre-theology, pre-veterinary science, pre-pharmacy. **Special academic programs (% participation):** double major (10.8%), English as a Second Language (ESL), exchange student program (domestic), honors program (2%), independent study, internships (75%), student-designed major (1.3%), study abroad (2.5%), teacher certificate program, other. **Teacher certification offered in:** early childhood, elementary, middle/junior high, secondary. **Reserve Officers Training Corps (ROTC):** Army ROTC: Offered on campus; Navy ROTC: Offered at cooperating institution (SUNY Maritime College); Air Force ROTC: Offered at cooperating institution (Manhattan College). **Faculty and instruction (2005-2006):** Total instructional faculty: 654 full-time, 639 part-time (57% men; 43% women; 15% minorities). Full-time faculty with Ph.D. or other terminal degree: 94%. Student/faculty ratio: 12/1. Classes of fewer than 20 students: 51%; of 20 to 49 students: 48%; of 50 or more students: 1%. **Advanced Placement and International Baccalaureate credit:** AP tests may be used for: Credit and/or placement. Scores accepted: 3, 4, 5. International Baccalaureate exams may be used for: Credit and/or placement. **Freshmen returning for sophomore year:** 90%. **Graduation rates:** Four-year: 72%; five-year: 77%; six-year: 78%. **Graduate study:** 20% of students pursue further study immediately upon graduation. Fields in which graduates pursue further study: Master of Business Administration (MBA), 9%; law, 21%; medicine, 10%; education, 27%; arts and sciences, 24%.

COSTS AND FINANCIAL AID

Financial aid office: (718) 817-3800. **Expenses (2006-2007):** Tuition and fees 2006-2007: $30,445; room/board: $11,630. Estimated books and supplies: $800; transportation: $740; personal expenses: $1,445. **Financial aid:** Priority filing date for institution's financial aid form: February 1; deadline: February 1. In 2005-2006, 76% of undergraduates applied for financial aid. Of those, 65% were determined to have financial need; 24% had their need fully met. Average financial aid package (proportion receiving): $20,104 (65%). Average amount of gift aid, such as scholarships or grants (proportion receiving): $14,953 (62%). Average amount of self-help aid, such as work study or loans (proportion receiving): $5,254 (52%). Average need-based loan (excluding PLUS or other private loans): $4,386. Among students who received need-based aid, the average percentage of need met: 75%. Among students who received aid based on merit, the average award (and the proportion receiving): $7,806 (12%). The average athletic scholarship (and the proportion receiving): $15,270 (2%). Average amount of debt of borrowers graduating in 2005: $16,976. Proportion who borrowed: 61%.

CAMPUS LIFE AND EXTRACURRICULAR ACTIVITIES

Campus housing available (% using): coed dorms (38%), apartment for single students (41%), other housing options (21%). Students who live in college-owned, operated, or affiliated housing: 58%. **Student employment:** During the 2005-2006 academic year, 8% of undergraduates worked on campus. Average per-year earnings: $3,000. **Clubs and organizations:** Number of student organizations: 133. Activities include: choral groups, concert band, dance, drama/theater, jazz band, literary magazine, music ensembles, musical theater, pep band, radio station, student government, student newspaper, student film society, symphony orchestra, television station, yearbook. Number of fraternities: 0; sororities: 0. Average proportion of students who stay on campus on weekends: 80%. **Sports program (2005-2006):** Member of NCAA I. *Men's intercollegiate varsity sports:* baseball, basketball, cross-country, football, golf, soccer, squash, swimming and diving, tennis, track and field (indoor), track and field (outdoor), water polo. *Women's intercollegiate varsity sports:* basketball, crew, cross-country, rowing, soccer, softball, swimming and diving, tennis, track and field (indoor), track and field (outdoor), volleyball.

SERVICES AND FACILITIES

Basic services: nonremedial tutoring, placement service, health service, other. **Remedial assistance:** study skills. **Counseling services:** minority student, career, personal, academic, psychological, religious. **For learning-disabled students:** School does not offer a structured program with separate admission and additional fees. Total undergraduates in learning-disabled program or receiving services: 68. Services include: tape recorders, note-taking services, readers, extended time for tests, tutors, texts on tape, typist/scribe, exams on tape or computer, other. **Library:** Number of titles: 2,113,225; number of current serial subscriptions: 49,929. **Information tech-**

nology resources: Students are not required to lease or own a computer. Number of campus computers available to all students: 1,400. School has a wireless network. Approximate number of users that can be accommodated: 15,000. Proportion of college-owned housing units wired for high-speed internet access: 100%. **Campus safety:** Security services offered: 24-hour foot-and-vehicle patrols, late-night transport/escort service, 24-hour emergency telephones, lighted pathways/sidewalks, controlled dormitory access (key, security card, etc).

TRANSFER AND INTERNATIONAL STUDENTS

Transfer students: May apply for admission for the following academic terms: Fall, Spring. Applicants do not need a minimum number of credits to apply. For fall 2005: Transfer applications received: 1,092. Transfer applicants offered admission: 533. Transfer applicants enrolled: 267. **International students:** Number of foreign undergraduates: 95 (1% of student body). Number of countries represented: 53. Minimum TOEFL score required: 575 (paper); 231 (computer). Average TOEFL score: 587 (paper).

Hamilton College

- **Address:** 198 College Hill Road, Clinton, NY 13323
- **Website:** http://www.hamilton.edu
- **Private**
- **Enrollment:** 1,800 full-time; 12 part-time

KEY STATS

✔ **U.S News College Ranking:** 17, Liberal Arts Colleges
✔ **SAT Score (25th/75th percentile):** 1270-1440
✔ **Tuition:** 2006-2007: $34,980

Selectivity: Most selective	Room/board: $8,910
Acceptance rate: 36%	Average debt: N/A
Student/faculty ratio: 10/1	Proportion who borrowed: N/A

UNDERGRADUATE STUDENT BODY STATS

2005-2006 enrollment: 1,800 full-time; 12 part-time. Men: 50%; women: 50%. **Ethnic makeup:** African American: 4%; American-Indian: 1%; Asian American: 6%; Hispanic: 4%; White: 80%; International: 5%. **Religious preference:** Roman Catholic: 28%; Protestant: 23%; Jewish: 11%; Muslim: 1%; Buddhist: 1%; No preference: 26%.

ADMISSIONS FACTS AND FIGURES

Phone: (315) 859-4421. **Email:** admission@hamilton.edu. **Website:** http://www.hamilton.edu. **Application deadlines for fall 2007:** Regular decision: January 1; decision sent by April 1. Early decision: Send application by: November 15; Decision sent by: January 1. Early action: Not offered. Admission can be deferred. **Application fee:** $50. Common application is accepted. **To apply online, go to:** http://www.hamilton.edu/admission/ApplicationProcess/Application.html. **Admissions requirements/recommendations:** High school units required (recommended): English: (4); Mathematics: (3); Science: (3); Foreign language: (3); Social studies: (3); Total units: (16). Tests: The college uses SAT or ACT scores in admissions decisions. Neither SAT nor ACT required. For admission to the fall 2007 entering class, the school will accept: ACT with writing, ACT without writing. Campus visit: Recommended. Admissions interview: Neither required nor recommended. Off-campus interview: May be arranged. **Factors that count in admissions decisions:** *Academic:* Secondary school record: Very important. Class rank: Very important. Letters of recommendation: Important. Standardized test scores: Important. Essay: Important. *Nonacademic:* Interview: Important. Extracurricular activities: Important. Talent/ability: Considered. Character/personal qualities: Important. Alumni/ae relationship: Considered. Geographical residence: Considered. State residency: Not considered. Religious affiliation/commitment: Not considered. Minority status: Considered. Volunteer work: Considered. Work experience: Considered. **Other schools with the greatest overlap in applicants:** Bates College; Bowdoin College; Colby College; Colgate University; Middlebury College. **Admissions statistics for the fall 2005 entering class:** Total applicants: 4,189. Total accepted: 1,502. Freshmen enrolled: 498; 65% were from out of state. Accepted through early-decision or early-action plans: 49%. Overall acceptance rate: 36%. Early-decision acceptance rate: 55%. Non-early acceptance rate: 33%. **Size of waiting list:** 680 applicants; enrolled from waiting list: 0. **Credentials of fall 2005 freshmen:** 70% ranked in the top 10 percent of their high school class; 91% were in the top 25 percent, and 99% were in the top

half. (Proportion submitting class standing: 49%.) **First-year students who submitted SAT scores:** 61%. Scores (25/75 percentile): Verbal: 630-720, Math: 640-720, Combined: 1270-1440. **First-year students submitting ACT scores:** 8%. Scores (25/75 percentile): English: N/A, Math: N/A, Composite: N/A.

ACADEMICS

Year founded: 1812. **Academic calendar:** Semester. **Degrees offered:** bachelor's. **Most popular majors:** 35% social sciences, 10% foreign languages, literatures, and linguistics, 9% English language and literature/letters, 8% visual and performing arts, 6% physical sciences. **Major fields of study:** area, ethnic, cultural, and gender studies; biological and biomedical sciences; communication, journalism, and related programs; communications technologies/technicians and support services; computer and information sciences and support services; English language and literature/letters; foreign languages, literatures, and linguistics; history; mathematics and statistics; multi/interdisciplinary studies; philosophy and religious studies; physical sciences; psychology; science technologies/technicians; social sciences; theology and religious vocations; visual and performing arts. **Pre-professional programs:** pre-law, pre-medicine. **Special academic programs:** accelerated program, cross-registration, double major, English as a Second Language (ESL), independent study, internships, student-designed major, study abroad, other. **Reserve Officers Training Corps (ROTC):** Army ROTC: Offered at cooperating institution (Syracuse University); Air Force ROTC: Offered at cooperating institution (Syracuse University). **Faculty and instruction (2005-2006):** Total instructional faculty: 173 full-time, 32 part-time (60% men; 40% women; 14% minorities). Full-time faculty with Ph.D. or other terminal degree: 95%. Student/faculty ratio: 10/1. Classes of fewer than 20 students: 75%; of 20 to 49 students: 25%; of 50 or more students: 0%. **Advanced Placement and International Baccalaureate credit:** International Baccalaureate exams may be used for: Credit only. **Freshmen returning for sophomore year:** 93%. **Graduation rates:** Four-year: 82%; five-year: 88%; six-year: 88%. **Graduate study:** 18% of students pursue further study immediately upon graduation.

COSTS AND FINANCIAL AID

Financial aid office: (315) 859-4434. **Expenses (2006-2007):** Tuition and fees 2006-2007: $34,980; room/board: $8,910. Estimated books and supplies: $500 personal expenses: $1,000. **Financial aid:** Priority filing date for institution's financial aid form: January 1; deadline: January 1. In 2005-2006, 65% of undergraduates applied for financial aid. Of those, 52% were determined to have financial need; 100% had their need fully met. Average financial aid package (proportion receiving): $27,035 (52%). Average amount of gift aid, such as scholarships or grants (proportion receiving): $21,045 (51%). Average amount of self-help aid, such as work study or loans (proportion receiving): $5,506 (50%). Average need-based loan (excluding PLUS or other private loans): $3,996. Among students who received need-based aid, the average percentage of need met: 100%. Among students who received aid based on merit, the average award (and the proportion receiving): $9,148 (5%). The average athletic scholarship (and the proportion receiving): $0 (0%).

CAMPUS LIFE AND EXTRACURRICULAR ACTIVITIES

Campus housing available: coed dorms, apartments for married students, apartment for single students, special housing for disabled students. Students who live in college-owned, operated, or affiliated housing: 98%. **Student employment:** During the 2005-2006 academic year, 33% of undergraduates worked on campus. Average per-year earnings: $1,000. **Clubs and organizations:** Number of student organizations: 78. Activities include: choral groups, concert band, dance, drama/theater, jazz band, literary magazine, music ensembles, musical theater, pep band, radio station, student government, student newspaper, student film society, symphony orchestra, television station. Number of fraternities: 9; sororities: 6. Proportion of men in fraternities: 29%; of women in sororities: 19%. Average proportion of students who stay on campus on weekends: 90%. **Sports program (2005-2006):** Member of NCAA III. *Men's intercollegiate varsity sports:* baseball, basketball, cross-country, football, golf, ice hockey, lacrosse, soccer, swimming and diving, tennis, track and field (indoor), track and field (outdoor). *Women's intercollegiate varsity sports:* basketball, cross-country, field hockey, ice hockey, lacrosse, rowing, soccer, softball, squash, swimming and diving, tennis, track and field (indoor), track and field (outdoor), volleyball.

SERVICES AND FACILITIES

Basic services: women's center, placement service, day care, health service. **Counseling services:** minority student, career, personal, academic, psychological, birth control, religious. **For learning-disabled students:** School does not offer a structured program with separate admission and additional fees. Services include: untimed tests, oral tests, learning center, readers, extended time for tests, tutors. **Information technology resources:** Students are not required to lease or own a computer. Number of campus computers available to all students: 522. School has a wireless network. Approximate number of users that can be accommodated: 500. Proportion of college-owned housing units wired for high-speed internet access: 100%. **Campus safety:** Security services offered: 24-hour foot-and-vehicle patrols, late-night transport/escort service, 24-hour emergency telephones, lighted pathways/sidewalks, controlled dormitory access (key, security card, etc).

TRANSFER AND INTERNATIONAL STUDENTS

Transfer students: May apply for admission for the following academic terms: Fall, Spring. Applicants do not need a minimum number of credits to apply. For fall 2005: Transfer applications received: 78. Transfer applicants offered admission: 28. Transfer applicants enrolled: 13. **International students:** Number of foreign undergraduates: 95 (5% of student body). Number of countries represented: 40. Minimum TOEFL score required: 600 (paper); 250 (computer). Average TOEFL score: 632 (paper).

Hartwick College

- **Address:** 1 Hartwick Drive, Oneonta, NY 13820-4020
- **Website:** http://www.hartwick.edu
- **Private**
- **Enrollment:** 1,405 full-time; 58 part-time

KEY STATS

✔ **U.S News College Ranking:** third tier, Liberal Arts Colleges
✔ **SAT Score (25th/75th percentile):** 1030-1240
✔ **Tuition:** 2006-2007: $28,030

Selectivity: Selective	**Room/board:** $7,910
Acceptance rate: 87%	**Average debt:** N/A
Student/faculty ratio: 11/1	**Proportion who borrowed:** N/A

UNDERGRADUATE STUDENT BODY STATS

2005-2006 enrollment: 1,405 full-time; 58 part-time. Men: 44%; women: 56%. **Ethnic makeup:** African American: 5%; American-Indian: 1%; Asian American: 1%; Hispanic: 4%; White: 85%; International: 4%. **Religious preference:** Roman Catholic: 30%; Protestant: 33%; Jewish: 4%; Hindu: 1%; Buddhist: 2%; No preference: 26%; Other: 4%.

ADMISSIONS FACTS AND FIGURES

Phone: (607) 431-4150. **Email:** admissions@hartwick.edu. **Website:** http://www.hartwick.edu. **Application deadlines for fall 2007:** Regular decision: February 15; decision sent by March 7. Early decision: Send application by: January 15; Decision sent by: January 31. Early action: Not offered. Admission can be deferred. **Application fee:** $35. Common application is accepted. **Admissions requirements/recommendations:** High school units required (recommended): English: (4); Mathematics: (3); Science: (3); Foreign language: (3); Social studies: (2); History: (2); Total units: (19). Tests: The college uses SAT or ACT scores in admissions decisions. Neither SAT nor ACT required. For admission to the fall 2007 entering class, the school will accept: ACT with writing, ACT without writing. Campus visit: Recommended. Admissions interview: Recommended. Off-campus interview: May be arranged. **Factors that count in admissions decisions:** *Academic:* Secondary school record: Very important. Class rank: Very important. Letters of recommendation: Important. Standardized test scores: Considered. Essay: Important. *Nonacademic:* Interview: Considered. Extracurricular activities: Important. Talent/ability: Considered. Character/personal qualities: Considered. Alumni/ae relationship: Considered. Geographical residence: Considered. State residency: Considered. Religious affiliation/commitment: Not considered. Minority status: Considered. Volunteer work: Considered. Work experience: Considered. **Other schools with the greatest overlap in applicants:** Hobart and William Smith Colleges; Ithaca College; SUNY College–Oneonta; Siena College; University of Vermont. **Admissions statistics for the fall 2005 entering class:** Total applicants: 2,211. Total accepted: 1,928. Freshmen enrolled: 409; 39% were from out of state. Accepted through early-decision or early-action plans: 17%. Overall acceptance rate: 87%. Early-decision acceptance rate: 90%. Non-early acceptance rate: 87%. **Size of waiting list:** 128 applicants; enrolled from waiting list: 51. **Credentials of fall 2005 freshmen:** 16%

ranked in the top 10 percent of their high school class, and 80% were in the top half. (Proportion submitting class standing: 68%.) **First-year students who submitted SAT scores:** 64%. Scores (25/75 percentile): Verbal: 520-620, Math: 510-620, Combined: 1030-1240.

ACADEMICS

Year founded: 1797. **Academic calendar:** Semester. **Degrees offered:** bachelor's. **Most popular majors:** 22% social sciences, 18% business/commerce, 12% visual and performing arts, 11% psychology, 7% biology/biological sciences. **Major fields of study:** biological and biomedical sciences; business, management, marketing, and related support services; computer and information sciences and support services; education; English language and literature/letters; foreign languages, literatures, and linguistics; health professions and related clinical sciences; history; mathematics and statistics; multi/interdisciplinary studies; philosophy and religious studies; physical sciences; psychology; social sciences; visual and performing arts. **Areas of required coursework:** arts/fine arts, humanities, mathematics, English (including composition), foreign languages, sciences (biological or physical), history, social science, other. **Pre-professional programs:** pre-law, pre-dentistry, pre-medicine, pre-veterinary science, pre-optometry, pre-pharmacy. **Special academic programs (% participation):** accelerated program (0%), double major (1%), exchange student program (domestic), honors program (8%), independent study (.18%), internships (50%), liberal arts/career combination, student-designed major (.01%), study abroad (80%), teacher certificate program (.04%). **Teacher certification offered in:** early childhood, elementary, middle/junior high, secondary. **Reserve Officers Training Corps (ROTC):** Army ROTC: Offered at cooperating institution (Rensselaer Polytechnic Institute); Air Force ROTC: Offered at cooperating institution (Siena College). **Faculty and instruction (2005-2006):** Total instructional faculty: 108 full-time, 61 part-time (59% men; 41% women; 4% minorities). Full-time faculty with Ph.D. or other terminal degree: 94%. Student/faculty ratio: 11/1. Classes of fewer than 20 students: 64%; of 20 to 49 students: 36%; of 50 or more students: 0%. **Advanced Placement and International Baccalaureate credit:** AP tests may be used for: Placement only. International Baccalaureate exams may be used for: Placement only. **Freshmen returning for sophomore year:** 77%. **Graduation rates:** Four-year: 49%; five-year: 54%; six-year: 55%. **Graduate study:** 24% of students pursue further study within one year.

COSTS AND FINANCIAL AID

Financial aid office: (607) 431-4130. **Expenses (2006-2007):** Tuition and fees 2006-2007: $28,030; room/board: $7,910. Estimated books and supplies: $1,000; transportation: $300; personal expenses: $400. **Financial aid:** Priority filing date for institution's financial aid form: February 15; deadline: May 1. In 2005-2006, 81% of undergraduates applied for financial aid. Of those, 74% were determined to have financial need; 15% had their need fully met. Average financial aid package (proportion receiving): $20,494 (74%). Average amount of gift aid, such as scholarships or grants (proportion receiving): N/A (73%). Average amount of self-help aid, such as work study or loans (proportion receiving): N/A (65%). Among students who received need-based aid, the average percentage of need met: 80%. Among students who received aid based on merit, the average award (and the proportion receiving): $10,835 (22%). The average athletic scholarship (and the proportion receiving): $22,477 (1%).

CAMPUS LIFE AND EXTRACURRICULAR ACTIVITIES

Campus housing available (% using): coed dorms (74%), sorority housing (4%), fraternity housing (3%), apartment for single students (7%), other housing options (3%). Students who live in college-owned, operated, or affiliated housing: 80%. **Student employment:** During the 2005-2006 academic year, 15% of undergraduates worked on campus. Average per-year earnings: $1,400. **Clubs and organizations:** Number of student organizations: 70. Activities include: choral groups, concert band, dance, drama/theater, jazz band, literary magazine, music ensembles, musical theater, radio station, student government, student newspaper, television station, yearbook. Number of fraternities: 4; sororities: 3. Proportion of men in fraternities: 9%; of women in sororities: 12%. Average proportion of students who stay on campus on weekends: 70%. **Sports program (2005-2006):** Member of NCAA III. **Men's intercollegiate varsity sports:** baseball, basketball, cross-country, football, golf, lacrosse, soccer, swimming and diving, tennis, track and field (indoor), track and field (outdoor). **Women's intercollegiate varsity sports:** basketball, cross-country, equestrian sports, field hockey, lacrosse, soccer, softball, swimming and diving, tennis, track and field (indoor), track and field (outdoor), volleyball, water polo.

SERVICES AND FACILITIES

Basic services: nonremedial tutoring, women's center, placement service, health service, health insurance. **Counseling services:** career, personal, academic, psychological, birth control, religious. **For learning-disabled students:** School does not offer a structured program with separate admission and additional fees. Total undergraduates in learning-disabled program or receiving services: 114. Services include: tape recorders, note-taking services, learning center, readers, extended time for tests, tutors. **Library:** Number of titles: 348,699; number of current serial subscriptions: 1,400. **Information technology resources:** Students are required to lease or own a computer. Number of campus computers available to all students: 2,000. School has a wireless network. Approximate number of users that can be accommodated: 800. Proportion of college-owned housing units wired for high-speed internet access: 100%. **Campus safety:** Security services offered: 24-hour foot-and-vehicle patrols, late-night transport/escort service, 24-hour emergency telephones, lighted pathways/sidewalks, controlled dormitory access (key, security card, etc).

TRANSFER AND INTERNATIONAL STUDENTS

Transfer students: May apply for admission for the following academic terms: Fall, Winter, Spring. Applicants do not need a minimum number of credits to apply. For fall 2005: Transfer applications received: 84. Transfer applicants offered admission: 79. Transfer applicants enrolled: 37. **International students:** Number of foreign undergraduates: 58 (4% of student body). Number of countries represented: 28. Minimum TOEFL score required: 550 (paper).

Hilbert College

- **Address:** 5200 S. Park Avenue, Hamburg, NY 14075-1597
- **Website:** http://www.hilbert.edu/
- **Private; Religious affiliation:** Roman Catholic (Franciscan)
- **Enrollment:** 738 full-time; 371 part-time

KEY STATS
- ✔ **U.S News College Ranking:** fourth tier, Comp. Coll.–Bachelor's (North)
- ✔ **SAT Score (25th/75th percentile):** 830-1040
- ✔ **Tuition:** 2006-2007: $15,700

Selectivity: Less selective	**Room/board:** $5,900
Acceptance rate: 99%	**Average debt:** $21,496
Student/faculty ratio: 11/1	**Proportion who borrowed:** 91%

UNDERGRADUATE STUDENT BODY STATS

2005-2006 enrollment: 738 full-time; 371 part-time. Men: 37%; women: 63%. **Ethnic makeup:** African American: 3%; American-Indian: 1%; Asian American: 1%; Hispanic: 2%; White: 93%.

ADMISSIONS FACTS AND FIGURES

Phone: (716) 649-7900. **Email:** admissions@hilbert.edu. **Website:** http://www.hilbert.edu/. **Application deadlines for fall 2007:** Regular decision: September 1. Early decision: Not offered. Early action: Not offered. Admission can be deferred. **Application fee:** $20. Common application is not accepted. **Admissions requirements/recommendations:** High school units required (recommended): English: 4 (4); Mathematics: 2 (3); Science: 2 (3); Foreign language: 0 (1); Social studies: 2 (3); History: 2 (0); Academic electives: 4 (0); Total units: 18 (19). Tests: The college uses SAT or ACT scores in admissions decisions. Neither SAT nor ACT required. For admission to the fall 2007 entering class, the school will accept: ACT with writing, ACT without writing. Campus visit: Recommended. Admissions interview: Neither required nor recommended. Off-campus interview: May be arranged. **Factors that count in admissions decisions:** *Academic:* Secondary school record: Very important. Class rank: Considered. Letters of recommendation: Important. Standardized test scores: Considered. Essay: Considered. *Nonacademic:* Interview: Considered. Extracurricular activities: Considered. Talent/ability: Considered. Character/personal qualities: Considered. Alumni/ae relationship: Not considered. Geographical residence: Not considered. State residency: Not considered. Religious affiliation/commitment: Not considered. Minority status: Not considered. Volunteer work: Considered. Work experience: Considered. **Other schools with the greatest overlap in applicants:** Canisius College; Medaille College; SUNY–Buffalo State College; St. Bonaventure University; University at Buffalo–SUNY. **Admissions statistics for the fall 2005 entering class:** Total

applicants: 421. Total accepted: 418. Freshmen enrolled: 166; 2% were from out of state. Overall acceptance rate: 99%. **Credentials of fall 2005 freshmen:** 4% ranked in the top 10 percent of their high school class; 14% were in the top 25 percent, and 45% were in the top half. (Proportion submitting class standing: 84%.) **Average high school grade point average:** 2.7. **First-year students who submitted SAT scores:** 61%. Scores (25/75 percentile): Verbal: 410-510, Math: 420-530, Combined: 830-1040. **First-year students submitting ACT scores:** 19%. Scores (25/75 percentile): English: N/A, Math: N/A, Composite: 18-23.

ACADEMICS

Year founded: 1957. **Academic calendar:** Semester. **Degrees offered:** associate, bachelor's. **Most popular majors:** 30% criminal justice/safety studies, 17% criminal justice/police science, 16% business administration and management, 8% legal assistant/paralegal, 7% human services. **Major fields of study:** business, management, marketing, and related support services; communication, journalism, and related programs; English language and literature/letters; health professions and related clinical sciences; legal professions and studies; liberal arts and sciences studies, and humanities; psychology; security and protective services. **Areas of required coursework:** arts/fine arts, humanities, computer literacy, mathematics, English (including composition), sciences (biological or physical), social science. **Pre-professional programs:** pre-law. **Special academic programs (% participation):** cross-registration (1%), honors program (5%), independent study (3%), internships (67%), study abroad (1%). **Reserve Officers Training Corps (ROTC):** Army ROTC: Offered at cooperating institution (Canisius College). **Faculty and instruction (2005-2006):** Total instructional faculty: 46 full-time, 68 part-time (63% men; 37% women; 4% minorities). Full-time faculty with Ph.D. or other terminal degree: 37%. Student/faculty ratio: 11/1. Classes of fewer than 20 students: 69%; of 20 to 49 students: 31%; of 50 or more students: 0%. **Advanced Placement and International Baccalaureate credit:** International Baccalaureate exams may be used for: Credit only. **Freshmen returning for sophomore year:** 76%. **Graduation rates:** Four-year: 31%; five-year: 46%; six-year: 38%. **Graduate study:** 17% of students pursue further study immediately upon graduation; 21% within one year; 10% within five years. Fields in which graduates pursue further study: Master of Business Administration (MBA), 3%; law, 5%; education, 2%; arts and sciences, 7%.

COSTS AND FINANCIAL AID

Financial aid office: (716) 649-7900. **Expenses (2006-2007):** Tuition and fees 2006-2007: $15,700; room/board: $5,900. Estimated books and supplies: $700; transportation: $700; personal expenses: $930. **Financial aid:** Priority filing date for institution's financial aid form: April 1. In 2005-2006, 99% of undergraduates applied for financial aid. Of those, 87% were determined to have financial need; 29% had their need fully met. Average financial aid package (proportion receiving): $10,127 (87%). Average amount of gift aid, such as scholarships or grants (proportion receiving): $6,265 (85%). Average amount of self-help aid, such as work study or loans (proportion receiving): $4,456 (77%). Average need-based loan (excluding PLUS or other private loans): $4,303. Among students who received need-based aid, the average percentage of need met: 77%. Among students who received aid based on merit, the average award (and the proportion receiving): $9,671 (12%). The average athletic scholarship (and the proportion receiving): $0 (0%). Average amount of debt of borrowers graduating in 2005: $21,496. Proportion who borrowed: 91%.

CAMPUS LIFE AND EXTRACURRICULAR ACTIVITIES

Campus housing available (% using): coed dorms (75%), apartment for single students (25%). Students who live in college-owned, operated, or affiliated housing: 11%. **Clubs and organizations:** Number of student organizations: 20. Activities include: drama/theater, literary magazine, student government, student newspaper. Number of fraternities: 0; sororities: 0. Average proportion of students who stay on campus on weekends: 5%. **Sports program (2005-2006):** Member of NCAA III. *Men's intercollegiate varsity sports:* baseball, basketball, cross-country, golf, soccer, volleyball. *Women's intercollegiate varsity sports:* basketball, cross-country, golf, soccer, softball, volleyball.

SERVICES AND FACILITIES

Basic services: placement service, health insurance. **Remedial assistance:** math, writing. **Counseling services:** minority student, career, personal, veteran student, academic, older student, religious. **For learning-disabled students:** School does not offer a structured program with separate admission and additional fees. Total undergraduates in learning-disabled program or receiving services: 36. Services include: remedial math, remedial English, tape recorders, note-taking services, oral tests, readers, extended time for tests, tutors. **Library:** Number of titles: 42,991; number of current serial subscriptions: 13,201. **Information technology resources:** Students are not required to lease or own a computer. Number of campus computers available to all students: 189. School has a wireless network. Approximate number of users that can be accommodated: 250. Proportion of college-owned housing units wired for high-speed internet access: 100%. **Campus safety:** Security services offered: 24-hour foot-and-vehicle patrols, late-night transport/escort service, 24-hour emergency telephones, lighted pathways/sidewalks, controlled dormitory access (key, security card, etc.).

TRANSFER AND INTERNATIONAL STUDENTS

Transfer students: May apply for admission for the following academic terms: Fall, Spring, Summer. Applicants do not need a minimum number of credits to apply. **International students:** Number of foreign undergraduates: 2. Minimum TOEFL score required: 500 (paper); 173 (computer).

Hobart and William Smith Colleges

- **Address:** 337 Pulteney Street, Geneva, NY 14456
- **Website:** http://www.hws.edu
- **Private**
- **Enrollment:** 1,865 full-time; 3 part-time

KEY STATS

✔ **U.S News College Ranking:** 67, Liberal Arts Colleges
✔ **SAT Score (25th/75th percentile):** 1090-1280
✔ **Tuition:** 2006-2007: $34,688
  Selectivity: More selective   **Room/board:** $8,828
  Acceptance rate: 65%   **Average debt:** $21,454
  Student/faculty ratio: 11/1   **Proportion who borrowed:** 65%

UNDERGRADUATE STUDENT BODY STATS

2005-2006 enrollment: 1,865 full-time; 3 part-time. Men: 46%; women: 54%. **Ethnic makeup:** African American: 4%; Asian American: 2%; Hispanic: 4%; White: 89%; International: 2%. **Religious preference:** Roman Catholic: 31%; Protestant: 30%; Jewish: 7%; Muslim: 1%; Hindu: 1%; Buddhist: 1%; No preference: 25%.

ADMISSIONS FACTS AND FIGURES

Phone: (315) 781-3622. **Email:** admissions@hws.edu. **Website:** http://www.hws.edu. **Application deadlines for fall 2007:** Regular decision: February 1; decision sent by April 1. Early decision: Send application by: November 15; Decision sent by: December 15. Early action: Not offered. Admission can be deferred. **Application fee:** $45. Common application is accepted. **Admissions requirements/recommendations:** High school units required (recommended): English: 4; Mathematics: 3; Science: 3; Foreign language: 2 (3); Social studies: 2; History: 2; Academic electives: 2 (4); Total units: 20. Tests: The college uses SAT or ACT scores in admissions decisions. Neither SAT nor ACT required. For admission to the fall 2007 entering class, the school will accept: ACT with writing, ACT without writing. Campus visit: Recommended. Admissions interview: Recommended. Off-campus interview: May be arranged. **Factors that count in admissions decisions: Academic:** Secondary school record: Very important. Class rank: Important. Letters of recommendation: Important. Standardized test scores: Important. Essay: Very important. **Nonacademic:** Interview: Considered. Extracurricular activities: Important. Talent/ability: Considered. Character/personal qualities: Important. Alumni/ae relationship: Considered. Geographical residence: Considered. State residency: Not considered. Religious affiliation/commitment: Not considered. Minority status: Considered. Volunteer work: Important. Work experience: Important. **Other schools with the greatest overlap in applicants:** Hamilton College; Skidmore College; St. Lawrence University; Union College; University of Vermont. **Admissions statistics for the fall 2005 entering class:** Total applicants: 3,410. Total accepted: 2,209. Freshmen enrolled: 545; 44% were from out of state. Accepted through early-decision or early-action plans: 29%. Overall acceptance rate: 65%. Early-decision acceptance rate: 78%. Non-early acceptance rate: 64%. **Size of waiting list:** 340 applicants; enrolled from waiting list: 27. **Credentials of fall 2005 freshmen:** 33% ranked in the top 10 percent of their high school class; 67% were in the top 25 percent, and 95% were in the top half. (Proportion submitting class standing: 44%.) **Average high school grade point average:** 3.2. **First-year students who submitted SAT scores:** 89%. Scores (25/75 percentile): Verbal: 540-640, Math: 550-640, Combined:

1090-1280. **First-year students submitting ACT scores:** 25%. Scores (25/75 percentile): English: N/A, Math: N/A, Composite: 23-28.

ACADEMICS

Year founded: 1822. **Academic calendar:** Semester. **Degrees offered:** bachelor's, master's. **Most popular majors:** 11% English language and literature, 10% history, 9% economics, 8% psychology, 6% public policy analysis. **Major fields of study:** architecture and related services; area, ethnic, cultural, and gender studies; biological and biomedical sciences; communication, journalism, and related programs; computer and information sciences and support services; English language and literature/letters; foreign languages, literatures, and linguistics; history; liberal arts and sciences studies, and humanities; mathematics and statistics; natural resources and conservation; philosophy and religious studies; physical sciences; psychology; public administration and social service professions; social sciences; visual and performing arts. **Areas of required coursework:** arts/fine arts, humanities, mathematics, sciences (biological or physical), social science, other. **Pre-professional programs:** pre-law, pre-dentistry, pre-medicine, pre-veterinary science, pre-optometry. **Special academic programs (% participation):** double major (15%), English as a Second Language (ESL) (1%), honors program (6%), independent study (50%), internships (18.5%), student-designed major (4%), study abroad (39%), teacher certificate program (8.3%). **Teacher certification offered in:** special education, elementary, secondary. **Faculty and instruction (2005-2006):** Total instructional faculty: 159 full-time, 14 part-time (62% men; 38% women; 14% minorities). Full-time faculty with Ph.D. or other terminal degree: 94%. Student/faculty ratio: 11/1. Classes of fewer than 20 students: 66%; of 20 to 49 students: 34%; of 50 or more students: 1%. **Advanced Placement and International Baccalaureate credit:** AP tests may be used for: Placement only. Scores accepted: 4, 5. International Baccalaureate exams may be used for: Credit only. **Freshmen returning for sophomore year:** 85%. **Graduation rates:** Four-year: 61%; five-year: 69%; six-year: 71%. **Graduate study:** 17% of students pursue further study immediately upon graduation; 29% within one year. Fields in which graduates pursue further study: Master of Business Administration (MBA), 1%; law, 3%; medicine, 1%; dentistry, 1%; engineering, 1%; theology (or the seminary), 1%; education, 6%; arts and sciences, 8%; veterinary medicine, 1%.

COSTS AND FINANCIAL AID

Financial aid office: (315) 781-3315. **Expenses (2006-2007):** Tuition and fees 2006-2007: $34,688; room/board: $8,828. Estimated books and supplies: $850; transportation: $210; personal expenses: $600. **Financial aid:** Priority filing date for institution's financial aid form: February 15; deadline: March 15. In 2005-2006, 72% of undergraduates applied for financial aid. Of those, 61% were determined to have financial need; 77% had their need fully met. Average financial aid package (proportion receiving): $24,303 (61%). Average amount of gift aid, such as scholarships or grants (proportion receiving): $20,480 (60%). Average amount of self-help aid, such as work study or loans (proportion receiving): $4,657 (53%). Average need-based loan (excluding PLUS or other private loans): $3,630. Among students who received need-based aid, the average percentage of need met: 88%. Among students who received aid based on merit, the average award (and the proportion receiving): $11,062 (16%). The average athletic scholarship (and the proportion receiving): $0 (0%). Average amount of debt of borrowers graduating in 2005: $21,454. Proportion who borrowed: 65%.

CAMPUS LIFE AND EXTRACURRICULAR ACTIVITIES

Campus housing available (% using): coed dorms (35%), women's dorms (10%), men's dorms (10%), fraternity housing (5%), apartment for single students (9%), cooperative housing (7%), other housing options (24%). Students who live in college-owned, operated, or affiliated housing: 83%. **Student employment:** During the 2005-2006 academic year, 51% of undergraduates worked on campus. Average per-year earnings: $1,800. **Clubs and organizations:** Number of student organizations: 60. Activities include: choral groups, dance, drama/theater, jazz band, literary magazine, music ensembles, radio station, student government, student newspaper, student film society, yearbook. Number of fraternities: 5; sororities: 0. Proportion of men in fraternities: 7%; Average proportion of students who stay on campus on weekends: 90%. **Sports program (2005-2006):** Member of NCAA III. **Men's intercollegiate varsity sports:** basketball, cross-country, football, golf, ice hockey, lacrosse, soccer, tennis. **Women's intercollegiate varsity sports:** basketball, cross-country, field hockey, lacrosse, rowing, soccer, squash, swimming and diving, tennis.

SERVICES AND FACILITIES

Basic services: nonremedial tutoring, women's center, placement service, health service, health insurance. **Remedial assistance:** math, writing, study skills. **Counseling services:** minority student, career, personal, academic, psychological, birth control, religious. **For learning-disabled students:** School does not offer a structured program with separate admission and additional fees. Total undergraduates in learning-disabled program or receiving services: 98. Services include: remedial math, remedial English, reading machines, remedial reading, tape recorders, untimed tests, note-taking services, oral tests, learning center, readers, extended time for tests, tutors, priority seating, texts on tape, typist/scribe, exams on tape or computer, other testing accomodations. **Library:** Number of titles: 387,650; number of current serial subscriptions: 3,574. **Information technology resources:** Students are not required to lease or own a computer. Number of campus computers available to all students: 300. School has a wireless network. Approximate number of users that can be accommodated: 50,000. Proportion of college-owned housing units wired for high-speed internet access: 100%. **Campus safety:** Security services offered: 24-hour foot-and-vehicle patrols, late-night transport/escort service, 24-hour emergency telephones, lighted pathways/sidewalks, controlled dormitory access (key, security card, etc).

TRANSFER AND INTERNATIONAL STUDENTS

Transfer students: May apply for admission for the following academic terms: Fall, Spring. Applicants need a minimum number of credits to apply. For fall 2005: Transfer applications received: 93. Transfer applicants offered admission: 43. Transfer applicants enrolled: 27. **International students:** Number of foreign undergraduates: 31 (2% of student body). Number of countries represented: 18. Minimum TOEFL score required: 550 (paper); 220 (computer). Average TOEFL score: 600 (paper).

Hofstra University

- **Address:** 100 Hofstra University, Hempstead, NY 11549
- **Website:** http://www.hofstra.edu
- **Private**
- **Enrollment:** 8,031 full-time; 853 part-time

KEY STATS

✔ **U.S News College Ranking:** third tier, National Universities
✔ **SAT Score (25th/75th percentile):** 1060-1240
✔ **Tuition:** 2006-2007: $23,230

Selectivity: More selective	**Room/board:** $9,800
Acceptance rate: 62%	**Average debt:** $20,500
Student/faculty ratio: 14/1	**Proportion who borrowed:** 61%

UNDERGRADUATE STUDENT BODY STATS

2005-2006 enrollment: 8,031 full-time; 853 part-time. Men: 47%; women: 53%. **Ethnic makeup:** African American: 9%; Asian American: 5%; Hispanic: 8%; White: 76%; International: 2%.

ADMISSIONS FACTS AND FIGURES

Phone: (516) 463-6700. **Email:** admitme@hofstra.edu. **Website:** http://www.hofstra.edu. **Application deadlines for fall 2007:** Regular decision: Rolling. Early decision: Not offered. Early action: Send application by: November 15; Decision sent by: December 15. Admission can be deferred. **Application fee:** $50. Common application is accepted. **To apply online, go to:** http://www.hofstra.edu/application. **Admissions requirements/recommendations:** High school units required (recommended): English: 4; Mathematics: 3 (4); Science: 3 (4); Foreign language: 2 (3); Social studies: 3 (4); Total units: 16. Tests: The college uses SAT or ACT scores in admissions decisions. Neither SAT nor ACT required. For admission to the fall 2007 entering class, the school will accept: ACT with writing. Campus visit: Recommended. Admissions interview: Recommended. Off-campus interview: May be arranged. **Factors that count in admissions decisions:** *Academic:* Secondary school record: Very important. Class rank: Very important. Letters of recommendation: Very important. Standardized test scores: Very important. Essay: Very important. *Nonacademic:* Interview: Important. Extracurricular activities: Important. Talent/ability: Important. Character/personal qualities: Important. Alumni/ae relationship: Considered. Geographical residence: Considered. State residency: Not considered. Religious affiliation/commitment: Not considered. Minority status: Considered. Volunteer work: Considered. Work experience: Considered. **Other schools with the greatest overlap in applicants:** Boston University; Fordham University; New York University; SUNY–Binghamton; SUNY–Stony Brook. **Admissions statistics for the fall 2005 entering class:**

Total applicants: 15,981. Total accepted: 9,953. Freshmen enrolled: 1,774; 46% were from out of state. Accepted through early-decision or early-action plans: 27%. Overall acceptance rate: 62%. Non-early acceptance rate: 70%. **Size of waiting list:** 1649 applicants; enrolled from waiting list: 227. **Credentials of fall 2005 freshmen:** 24% ranked in the top 10 percent of their high school class; 47% were in the top 25 percent, and 77% were in the top half. (Proportion submitting class standing: 51%.) **Average high school grade point average:** 3.2. **First-year students who submitted SAT scores:** 72%. Scores (25/75 percentile): Verbal: 520-620, Math: 540-620, Combined: 1060-1240. **First-year students submitting ACT scores:** 15%. Scores (25/75 percentile): English: N/A, Math: N/A, Composite: 21-26.

ACADEMICS

Year founded: 1935. **Academic calendar:** 4-1-4. **Degrees offered:** certificate, bachelor's, post-bachelor's certificate, master's, post-master's certificate, first professional, doctorate. **Most popular majors:** 12% psychology, 9% marketing/marketing management, 7% business administration and management, 6% accounting, 6% finance. **Major fields of study:** area, ethnic, cultural, and gender studies; biological and biomedical sciences; business, management, marketing, and related support services; communication, journalism, and related programs; computer and information sciences and support services; education; engineering; English language and literature/letters; foreign languages, literatures, and linguistics; health professions and related clinical sciences; history; legal professions and studies; liberal arts and sciences studies, and humanities; mathematics and statistics; multi/interdisciplinary studies; natural resources and conservation; philosophy and religious studies; physical sciences; psychology; social sciences; visual and performing arts. **Areas of required coursework:** humanities, mathematics, English (including composition), foreign languages, sciences (biological or physical), social science. **Pre-professional programs:** pre-law, pre-dentistry, pre-medicine, pre-veterinary science, pre-optometry, other. **Special academic programs:** accelerated program, cross-registration, double major, dual enrollment, English as a Second Language (ESL), external degree program, honors program, independent study, internships, liberal arts/career combination, student-designed major, study abroad, teacher certificate program, weekend college. **Teacher certification offered in:** early childhood, special education, elementary, middle/junior high, secondary, bilingual/bicultural. **Reserve Officers Training Corps (ROTC):** Army ROTC: Offered on campus. **Faculty and instruction (2005-2006):** Total instructional faculty: 527 full-time, 719 part-time (54% men; 46% women; 11% minorities). Full-time faculty with Ph.D. or other terminal degree: 91%. Student/faculty ratio: 14/1. Classes of fewer than 20 students: 45%; of 20 to 49 students: 51%; of 50 or more students: 3%. **Advanced Placement and International Baccalaureate credit:** AP tests may be used for: Credit and/or placement. Scores accepted: 3, 4, 5. International Baccalaureate exams may be used for: Credit only. **Freshmen returning for sophomore year:** 75%. **Graduation rates:** Four-year: 36%; five-year: 52%; six-year: 55%. **Graduate study:** 26% of students pursue further study within one year; 38% within five years. Fields in which graduates pursue further study: Master of Business Administration (MBA), 12%; law, 9%; medicine, 4%; education, 50%.

COSTS AND FINANCIAL AID

Financial aid office: (516) 463-6680. **Expenses (2006-2007):** Tuition and fees 2006-2007: $23,230; room/board: $9,800. Estimated books and supplies: $1,000; transportation: $1,516; personal expenses: $1,150. **Financial aid:** Priority filing date for institution's financial aid form: February 15. In 2005-2006, 72% of undergraduates applied for financial aid. Of those, 59% were determined to have financial need; 16% had their need fully met. Average financial aid package (proportion receiving): $12,750 (59%). Average amount of gift aid, such as scholarships or grants (proportion receiving): $8,475 (51%). Average amount of self-help aid, such as work study or loans (proportion receiving): $4,925 (49%). Average need-based loan (excluding PLUS or other private loans): $4,400. Among students who received need-based aid, the average percentage of need met: 52%. Among students who received aid based on merit, the average award (and the proportion receiving): $8,050 (14%). The average athletic scholarship (and the proportion receiving): $23,750 (2%). Average amount of debt of borrowers graduating in 2005: $20,500. Proportion who borrowed: 61%.

CAMPUS LIFE AND EXTRACURRICULAR ACTIVITIES

Campus housing available: coed dorms, women's dorms, apartments for married students, apartment for single students, special housing for disabled students, special housing for international students, other housing options. Students who live in college-owned, operated, or affiliated housing: 45%. **Student employment:** During the 2005-2006 academic year, 40% of undergraduates worked on campus. Average per-year earnings: $2,500.

Clubs and organizations: Number of student organizations: 150. Activities include: choral groups, concert band, dance, drama/theater, jazz band, literary magazine, music ensembles, musical theater, opera, pep band, radio station, student government, student newspaper, student film society, symphony orchestra, television station, yearbook. Number of fraternities: 17; sororities: 13. Proportion of men in fraternities: 6%; of women in sororities: 7%. **Sports program (2005-2006):** Member of NCAA I. *Men's intercollegiate varsity sports:* baseball, basketball, cross-country, football, golf, lacrosse, soccer, tennis, wrestling. *Women's intercollegiate varsity sports:* basketball, cross-country, field hockey, golf, lacrosse, soccer, softball, tennis, volleyball.

SERVICES AND FACILITIES

Basic services: nonremedial tutoring, placement service, day care, health service, health insurance. **Counseling services:** minority student, career, military, personal, veteran student, academic, older student, psychological, religious. **For learning-disabled students:** School does not offer a structured program with separate admission and additional fees. Total undergraduates in learning-disabled program or receiving services: 81. Services include: reading machines, extended time for tests, texts on tape, other testing accomodations, other. **Library:** Number of titles: 1,200,000; number of current serial subscriptions: 9,070. **Information technology resources:** Students are not required to lease or own a computer. Number of campus computers available to all students: 1,598. School has a wireless network. Approximate number of users that can be accommodated: 4,500. Proportion of college-owned housing units wired for high-speed internet access: 100%. **Campus safety:** Security services offered: 24-hour foot-and-vehicle patrols, late-night transport/escort service, 24-hour emergency telephones, lighted pathways/sidewalks, student patrols, controlled dormitory access (key, security card, etc).

TRANSFER AND INTERNATIONAL STUDENTS

Transfer students: May apply for admission for the following academic terms: Fall, Spring. Applicants do not need a minimum number of credits to apply. For fall 2005: Transfer applications received: 2,195. Transfer applicants offered admission: 1,554. Transfer applicants enrolled: 702.
International students: Number of foreign undergraduates: 136 (2% of student body). Number of countries represented: 48. Minimum TOEFL score required: 550 (paper); 213 (computer).

Houghton College

- **Address:** 1 Willard Avenue, Houghton, NY 14744
- **Website:** http://www.houghton.edu
- **Private; Religious affiliation:** Wesleyan Church
- **Enrollment:** 1,337 full-time; 61 part-time

KEY STATS

✔ **U.S News College Ranking:** third tier, Liberal Arts Colleges
✔ **SAT Score (25th/75th percentile):** 1050-1290
✔ **Tuition:** 2006-2007: $20,400

Selectivity: More selective	**Room/board:** $6,680
Acceptance rate: 90%	**Average debt:** $16,028
Student/faculty ratio: 13/1	**Proportion who borrowed:** 71%

UNDERGRADUATE STUDENT BODY STATS

2005-2006 enrollment: 1,337 full-time; 61 part-time. Men: 34%; women: 66%. **Ethnic makeup:** African American: 3%; Asian American: 1%; Hispanic: 1%; White: 92%; International: 3%. **Religious preference:** Roman Catholic: 5%; Protestant: 73%; No preference: 4%; Unknown: 3%; Wesleyan Church: 15%.

ADMISSIONS FACTS AND FIGURES

Phone: (800) 777-2556. **Email:** admission@houghton.edu. **Website:** http://www.houghton.edu. **Application deadlines for fall 2007:** Regular decision: Rolling. Early decision: Not offered. Early action: Not offered. Admission can be deferred. **Application fee:** $40. Common application is not accepted. **Admissions requirements/recommendations:** High school units required (recommended): English: (4); Mathematics: (3); Science: (2); Foreign language: (2); Social studies: (1); History: (2); Total units: (16). Tests: The college uses SAT or ACT scores in admissions decisions. Either SAT or ACT required. Campus visit: Recommended. Admissions interview: Recommended. Off-campus interview: Not available. **Factors that count in**

admissions decisions: *Academic:* Secondary school record: Very important. Class rank: Very important. Letters of recommendation: Important. Standardized test scores: Important. Essay: Important. ***Nonacademic:*** Interview: Considered. Extracurricular activities: Considered. Talent/ability: Considered. Character/personal qualities: Very important. Alumni/ae relationship: Considered. Geographical residence: Not considered. State residency: Not considered. Religious affiliation/commitment: Very important. Minority status: Considered. Volunteer work: Considered. Work experience: Considered. **Other schools with the greatest overlap in applicants:** Gordon College; Grove City College; Messiah College; Roberts Wesleyan College. **Admissions statistics for the fall 2005 entering class:** Total applicants: 1,009. Total accepted: 908. Freshmen enrolled: 323; 41% were from out of state. Overall acceptance rate: 90%. **Credentials of fall 2005 freshmen:** 32% ranked in the top 10 percent of their high school class; 68% were in the top 25 percent, and 91% were in the top half. (Proportion submitting class standing: 70%.) **Average high school grade point average:** 3.5. **First-year students who submitted SAT scores:** 92%. Scores (25/75 percentile): Verbal: 530-660, Math: 520-630, Combined: 1050-1290. **First-year students submitting ACT scores:** 30%. Scores (25/75 percentile): English: N/A, Math: N/A, Composite: 24-28.

ACADEMICS

Year founded: 1883. **Academic calendar:** Semester. **Degrees offered:** associate, bachelor's, master's. **Most popular majors:** 27% business, management, marketing, and related support services, 15% education, 8% English language and literature/letters, 7% psychology, 7% theology and religious vocations. **Major fields of study:** area, ethnic, cultural, and gender studies; biological and biomedical sciences; business, management, marketing, and related support services; communication, journalism, and related programs; computer and information sciences and support services; education; English language and literature/letters; foreign languages, literatures, and linguistics; history; liberal arts and sciences studies, and humanities; mathematics and statistics; multi/interdisciplinary studies; parks, recreation, leisure, and fitness studies; philosophy and religious studies; physical sciences; psychology; social sciences; theology and religious vocations; visual and performing arts. **Areas of required coursework:** arts/fine arts, humanities, mathematics, English (including composition), philosophy, foreign languages, sciences (biological or physical), history, social science, other.
Pre-professional programs: pre-law, pre-dentistry, pre-medicine, pre-theology, pre-veterinary science, pre-optometry, pre-pharmacy. **Special academic programs (% participation):** cross-registration (3%), double major (24%), exchange student program (domestic) (3%), honors program (8%), independent study (23%), internships (38%), liberal arts/career combination (45%), study abroad (41%), teacher certificate program (23%). **Teacher certification offered in:** special education, elementary, secondary. **Reserve Officers Training Corps (ROTC):** Army ROTC: Offered at cooperating institution (St. Bonaventure University). **Faculty and instruction (2005-2006):** Total instructional faculty: 88 full-time, 15 part-time (70% men; 30% women; 8% minorities). Full-time faculty with Ph.D. or other terminal degree: 77%. Student/faculty ratio: 13/1. Classes of fewer than 20 students: 64%; of 20 to 49 students: 34%; of 50 or more students: 2%. **Advanced Placement and International Baccalaureate credit:** AP tests may be used for: Credit only. Scores accepted: 4, 5. International Baccalaureate exams may be used for: Credit only. **Freshmen returning for sophomore year:** 84%. **Graduation rates:** Four-year: 56%; five-year: 65%; six-year: 65%. **Graduate study:** 33% of students pursue further study immediately upon graduation; 12% within one year; 26% within five years. Fields in which graduates pursue further study: Master of Business Administration (MBA), 2%; law, 1%; medicine, 3%; education, 81%.

COSTS AND FINANCIAL AID

Financial aid office: (585) 567-9328. **Expenses (2006-2007):** Tuition and fees 2006-2007: $20,400; room/board: $6,680. Estimated books and supplies: $800; transportation: $500; personal expenses: $2,000. **Financial aid:** Priority filing date for institution's financial aid form: March 1. In 2005-2006, 83% of undergraduates applied for financial aid. Of those, 76% were determined to have financial need; 29% had their need fully met. Average financial aid package (proportion receiving): $14,861 (76%). Average amount of gift aid, such as scholarships or grants (proportion receiving): $9,422 (66%). Average amount of self-help aid, such as work study or loans (proportion receiving): $5,439 (63%). Average need-based loan (excluding PLUS or other private loans): $3,691. Among students who received need-based aid, the average percentage of need met: 72%. Among students who received aid based on merit, the average award (and the proportion receiving): $10,810 (5%). The average athletic scholarship (and the proportion

receiving): $5,900 (0%). Average amount of debt of borrowers graduating in 2005: $16,028. Proportion who borrowed: 71%.

CAMPUS LIFE AND EXTRACURRICULAR ACTIVITIES

Campus housing available (% using): women's dorms (65%), men's dorms (34%), apartments for married students, apartment for single students (1%), special housing for disabled students, special housing for international students. Students who live in college-owned, operated, or affiliated housing: 82%. **Student employment:** During the 2005-2006 academic year, 47% of undergraduates worked on campus. Average per-year earnings: $2,000. **Clubs and organizations:** Number of student organizations: 40. Activities include: choral groups, concert band, drama/theater, jazz band, literary magazine, music ensembles, musical theater, opera, student government, student newspaper, symphony orchestra, yearbook. Number of fraternities: 0; sororities: 0. Average proportion of students who stay on campus on weekends: 67%. **Sports program (2005-2006):** Member of NAIA. *Men's intercollegiate varsity sports:* basketball, cross-country, soccer, track and field (indoor), track and field (outdoor). *Women's intercollegiate varsity sports:* basketball, cross-country, field hockey, soccer, track and field (indoor), track and field (outdoor), volleyball.

SERVICES AND FACILITIES

Basic services: placement service, health service. **Counseling services:** career, academic, psychological, religious. **For learning-disabled students:** School does not offer a structured program with separate admission and additional fees. Total undergraduates in learning-disabled program or receiving services: 33. Services include: reading machines, tape recorders, videotaped classes, diagnostic testing service, oral tests, extended time for tests, tutors, priority seating, texts on tape. **Library:** Number of titles: 245,177; number of current serial subscriptions: 4,090. **Information technology resources:** Students are required to lease or own a computer. Number of campus computers available to all students: 96. School has a wireless network. Approximate number of users that can be accommodated: 850. Proportion of college-owned housing units wired for high-speed internet access: 100%. **Campus safety:** Security services offered: 24-hour foot-and-vehicle patrols, 24-hour emergency telephones, lighted pathways/sidewalks, controlled dormitory access (key, security card, etc).

TRANSFER AND INTERNATIONAL STUDENTS

Transfer students: May apply for admission for the following academic terms: Fall, Spring, Summer. Applicants need a minimum number of credits to apply. For fall 2005: Transfer applications received: 152. Transfer applicants offered admission: 116. Transfer applicants enrolled: 57. **International students:** Number of foreign undergraduates: 35 (3% of student body). Number of countries represented: 21. Minimum TOEFL score required: 550 (paper); 213 (computer). Average TOEFL score: 600 (paper).

Iona College

- **Address:** 715 North Avenue, New Rochelle, NY 10801
- **Website:** http://www.iona.edu/info
- **Private; Religious affiliation:** Roman Catholic
- **Enrollment:** 3,122 full-time; 243 part-time

KEY STATS

✔ **U.S News College Ranking:** 40, Universities–Master's (North)
✔ **SAT Score (25th/75th percentile):** 1030-1220
✔ **Tuition:** 2006-2007: $23,218

Selectivity: Selective	**Room/board:** $9,998
Acceptance rate: 67%	**Average debt:** $21,495
Student/faculty ratio: 15/1	**Proportion who borrowed:** 70%

UNDERGRADUATE STUDENT BODY STATS

2005-2006 enrollment: 3,122 full-time; 243 part-time. Men: 46%; women: 54%. **Ethnic makeup:** African American: 7%; Asian American: 2%; Hispanic: 11%; White: 77%; International: 2%.

ADMISSIONS FACTS AND FIGURES

Phone: (914) 633-2502. **Email:** admissions@iona.edu. **Website:** http://www.iona.edu/info. **Application deadlines for fall 2007:** Regular decision: February 15; decision sent by March 20. **Early decision:** Not offered. Early action: Send application by December 1; Decision sent by: December

21. Admission can be deferred. **Application fee:** $50. Common application is accepted. **Admissions requirements/recommendations:** High school units required (recommended): English: 4 (4); Mathematics: 3 (4); Science: 2 (3); Foreign language: 2 (2); Social studies: 1 (1); History: 1 (2); Academic electives: 1 (2); Total units: 16 (20). Tests: The college uses SAT or ACT scores in admissions decisions. Either SAT or ACT required. For admission to the fall 2007 entering class, the school will accept: ACT with writing, ACT without writing. Campus visit: Recommended. Admissions interview: Recommended. Off-campus interview: Not available. **Factors that count in admissions decisions:** *Academic:* Secondary school record: Very important. Class rank: Important. Letters of recommendation: Considered. Standardized test scores: Important. Essay: Important. *Nonacademic:* Interview: Important. Extracurricular activities: Considered. Talent/ability: Considered. Character/personal qualities: Important. Alumni/ae relationship: Considered. Geographical residence: Considered. State residency: Not considered. Religious affiliation/commitment: Not considered. Minority status: Not considered. Volunteer work: Considered. Work experience: Considered. **Other schools with the greatest overlap in applicants:** Fordham University; Hofstra University; Manhattan College; Marist College; St. John's University. **Admissions statistics for the fall 2005 entering class:** Total applicants: 4,802. Total accepted: 3,217. Freshmen enrolled: 779; 25% were from out of state. Accepted through early-decision or early-action plans: 28%. Overall acceptance rate: 67%. Non-early acceptance rate: 66%. **Size of waiting list:** 179 applicants; enrolled from waiting list: 78. **Credentials of fall 2005 freshmen:** 29% ranked in the top 10 percent of their high school class; 51% were in the top 25 percent, and 94% were in the top half. (Proportion submitting class standing: 43%.) **Average high school grade point average:** 3.4. **First-year students who submitted SAT scores:** 95%. Scores (25/75 percentile): Verbal: 510-610, Math: 520-610, Combined: 1030-1220. **First-year students submitting ACT scores:** 5%. Scores (25/75 percentile): English: N/A, Math: N/A, Composite: N/A.

ACADEMICS

Year founded: 1940. **Academic calendar:** Semester. **Degrees offered:** certificate, bachelor's, post-bachelor's certificate, master's, post-master's certificate. **Most popular majors:** 38% business, management, marketing, and related support services, 13% communication, journalism, and related programs, 10% education, 9% criminal justice/law enforcement administration, 9% psychology. **Major fields of study:** biological and biomedical sciences; business, management, marketing, and related support services; communication, journalism, and related programs; computer and information sciences and support services; education; English language and literature/letters; foreign languages, literatures, and linguistics; health professions and related clinical sciences; history; liberal arts and sciences studies, and humanities; mathematics and statistics; multi/interdisciplinary studies; philosophy and religious studies; physical sciences; psychology; public administration and social service professions; security and protective services; social sciences; visual and performing arts. **Areas of required coursework:** arts/fine arts, humanities, computer literacy, mathematics, English (including composition), philosophy, foreign languages, sciences (biological or physical), history, social science, other. **Pre-professional programs:** pre-law, pre-dentistry, pre-medicine, pre-veterinary science, pre-optometry, pre-pharmacy, other. **Special academic programs:** accelerated program, distance learning, double major, honors program, independent study, internships, study abroad, teacher certificate program, weekend college. **Teacher certification offered in:** early childhood, elementary, secondary. **Reserve Officers Training Corps (ROTC):** Army ROTC: Offered at cooperating institution (Fordham University); Air Force ROTC: Offered at cooperating institution (Manhattan College). **Faculty and instruction (2005-2006):** Total instructional faculty: 176 full-time, 197 part-time (62% men; 38% women; 9% minorities). Full-time faculty with Ph.D. or other terminal degree: 91%. Student/faculty ratio: 15/1. Classes of fewer than 20 students: 43%; of 20 to 49 students: 57%. **Advanced Placement and International Baccalaureate credit:** AP tests may be used for: Placement only. Scores accepted: 3, 4, 5. International Baccalaureate exams may be used for: Placement only. **Freshmen returning for sophomore year:** 78%. **Graduation rates:** Four-year: 42%; five-year: 54%; six-year: 54%. **Graduate study:** 49% of students pursue further study immediately upon graduation; 18% within one year. Fields in which graduates pursue further study: Master of Business Administration (MBA), 38%; law, 8%; medicine, 4%; education, 30%; arts and sciences, 20%.

COSTS AND FINANCIAL AID

Financial aid office: (914) 633-2497. **Expenses (2006-2007):** Tuition and fees 2006-2007: $23,218; room/board: $9,998. Estimated books and supplies: $1,400; transportation: $600; personal expenses: $1,700. **Financial aid:**

Priority filing date for institution's financial aid form: March 15; deadline: April 15. In 2005-2006, 95% of undergraduates applied for financial aid. Of those, 75% were determined to have financial need; 21% had their need fully met. Average financial aid package (proportion receiving): $13,384 (75%). Average amount of gift aid, such as scholarships or grants (proportion receiving): $3,258 (27%). Average amount of self-help aid, such as work study or loans (proportion receiving): $3,707 (57%). Average need-based loan (excluding PLUS or other private loans): $2,794. Among students who received need-based aid, the average percentage of need met: 23%. Among students who received aid based on merit, the average award (and the proportion receiving): $9,753 (18%). The average athletic scholarship (and the proportion receiving): $9,403 (7%). Average amount of debt of borrowers graduating in 2005: $21,495. Proportion who borrowed: 70%.

CAMPUS LIFE AND EXTRACURRICULAR ACTIVITIES

Campus housing available (% using): coed dorms (80%), apartment for single students (18%), special housing for disabled students (2%). Students who live in college-owned, operated, or affiliated housing: 29%. **Student employment:** During the 2005-2006 academic year, 8% of undergraduates worked on campus. Average per-year earnings: $1,100. **Clubs and organizations:** Number of student organizations: 47. Activities include: choral groups, dance, drama/theater, literary magazine, musical theater, pep band, radio station, student government, student newspaper, student film society, television station, yearbook. Number of fraternities: 4; sororities: 6. Proportion of men in fraternities: 1%; of women in sororities: 1%. Average proportion of students who stay on campus on weekends: 65%. **Sports program (2005-2006):** Member of NCAA I. *Men's intercollegiate varsity sports:* baseball, basketball, cross-country, football, golf, ice hockey, soccer, swimming and diving, tennis, track and field (indoor), track and field (outdoor), water polo. *Women's intercollegiate varsity sports:* basketball, cross-country, soccer, softball, swimming and diving, tennis, track and field (indoor), track and field (outdoor), volleyball, water polo, rowing.

SERVICES AND FACILITIES

Basic services: nonremedial tutoring, placement service, health service, health insurance. **Remedial assistance:** reading, math, writing, study skills. **Counseling services:** career, personal, academic, psychological. **For learning-disabled students:** School does not offer a structured program with separate admission and additional fees. Total undergraduates in learning-disabled program or receiving services: 71. Services include: reading machines, tape recorders, untimed tests, note-taking services, oral tests, learning center, readers, extended time for tests, tutors. **Library:** Number of titles: 271,371; number of current serial subscriptions: 763. **Information technology resources:** Students are not required to lease or own a computer. Number of campus computers available to all students: 2,000. School has a wireless network. Approximate number of users that can be accommodated: 10,000. Proportion of college-owned housing units wired for high-speed internet access: 100%. **Campus safety:** Security services offered: 24-hour foot-and-vehicle patrols, late-night transport/escort service, 24-hour emergency telephones, lighted pathways/sidewalks, student patrols, controlled dormitory access (key, security card, etc).

TRANSFER AND INTERNATIONAL STUDENTS

Transfer students: May apply for admission for the following academic terms: Fall, Spring. Applicants need a minimum number of credits to apply. For fall 2005: Transfer applications received: 336. Transfer applicants offered admission: 226. Transfer applicants enrolled: 134. **International students:** Number of foreign undergraduates: 64 (2% of student body). Number of countries represented: 42. Minimum TOEFL score required: 550 (paper); 213 (computer). Average TOEFL score: 561 (paper).

Ithaca College

- **Address:** 100 Job Hall, Ithaca, NY 14850-7020
- **Website:** http://www.ithaca.edu
- **Private**
- **Enrollment:** 5,961 full-time; 137 part-time

KEY STATS

✔ **U.S News College Ranking:** 7, Universities–Master's (North)
✔ **SAT Score (25th/75th percentile):** 1080-1280
✔ **Tuition:** 2006-2007: $26,832

Selectivity: More selective	**Room/board:** $10,317
Acceptance rate: 76%	**Average debt:** N/A
Student/faculty ratio: 12/1	**Proportion who borrowed:** N/A

UNDERGRADUATE STUDENT BODY STATS

2005-2006 enrollment: 5,961 full-time; 137 part-time. Men: 44%; women: 56%. **Ethnic makeup:** African American: 3%; Asian American: 3%; Hispanic: 3%; White: 88%; International: 3%.

ADMISSIONS FACTS AND FIGURES

Phone: (800) 429-4274. **Email:** admission@ithaca.edu. **Website:** http://www.ithaca.edu. **Application deadlines for fall 2007:** Regular decision: February 1; decision sent by April 15. Early decision: Send application by: November 1; Decision sent by: December 15. Early action: Not offered. Admission can be deferred. **Application fee:** $55. Common application is accepted. **To apply online, go to:** http://www.ithaca.edu/admission/. **Admissions requirements/recommendations:** High school units required (recommended): English: 4; Mathematics: 3; Science: 3; Foreign language: 2; Social studies: 3; Academic electives: 1; Total units: 16. Tests: The college uses SAT or ACT scores in admissions decisions. Either SAT or ACT required. For admission to the fall 2007 entering class, the school will accept: ACT with writing. Campus visit: Recommended. Admissions interview: Recommended. Off-campus interview: Not available. **Factors that count in admissions decisions:** *Academic:* Secondary school record: Very important. Class rank: Important. Letters of recommendation: Important. Standardized test scores: Very important. Essay: Important. *Nonacademic:* Interview: Important. Extracurricular activities: Important. Talent/ability: Important. Character/personal qualities: Important. Alumni/ae relationship: Considered. Geographical residence: Not considered. State residency: Not considered. Religious affiliation/commitment: Not considered. Minority status: Not considered. Volunteer work: Considered. Work experience: Considered. **Other schools with the greatest overlap in applicants:** Boston University; New York University; Northeastern University; Pennsylvania State University–University Park; Syracuse University. **Admissions statistics for the fall 2005 entering class:** Total applicants: 10,421. Total accepted: 7,869. Freshmen enrolled: 1,680; 57% were from out of state. Accepted through early-decision or early-action plans: 6%. Overall acceptance rate: 76%. Early-decision acceptance rate: 74%. Non-early acceptance rate: 76%. **Credentials of fall 2005 freshmen:** 29% ranked in the top 10 percent of their high school class; 64% were in the top 25 percent, and 94% were in the top half. (Proportion submitting class standing: 63%.) **First-year students who submitted SAT scores:** 98%. Scores (25/75 percentile): Verbal: 540-640, Math: 540-640, Combined: 1080-1280. **First-year students submitting ACT scores:** 23%. Scores (25/75 percentile): English: N/A, Math: N/A, Composite: N/A.

ACADEMICS

Year founded: 1892. **Academic calendar:** Semester. **Degrees offered:** certificate, bachelor's, master's, doctorate. **Most popular majors:** 10% business administration and management, 10% radio and television, 6% rehabilitation and therapeutic professions, 5% film/video and photographic arts, 5% music. **Major fields of study:** area, ethnic, cultural, and gender studies; biological and biomedical sciences; business, management, marketing, and related support services; communication, journalism, and related programs; communications technologies/technicians and support services; computer and information sciences and support services; education; English language and literature/letters; foreign languages, literatures, and linguistics; health professions and related clinical sciences; history; legal professions and studies; liberal arts and sciences studies, and humanities; mathematics and statistics; multi/interdisciplinary studies; natural resources and conservation; parks, recreation, leisure, and fitness studies; philosophy and religious studies; physical sciences; psychology; social sciences; visual and performing arts. **Pre-professional programs:** pre-law, pre-dentistry, pre-medicine, pre-veterinary science, pre-optometry, other. **Special academic programs:** accelerated program, cross-registration, distance learning, double major, dual enrollment, honors program, independent study, internships, liberal arts/career combination, student-designed major, study abroad, teacher certificate program, other. **Teacher certification offered in:** special education, elementary, middle/junior high, secondary. **Reserve Officers Training Corps (ROTC):** Army ROTC: Offered at cooperating institution (Cornell University); Air Force ROTC: Offered at cooperating institution (Cornell University). **Faculty and instruction (2005-2006):** Total instructional faculty: 442 full-time, 214 part-time (52% men; 48% women; 8% minorities). Full-time faculty with Ph.D. or other terminal degree: 92%. Student/faculty ratio: 12/1. Classes of fewer than 20 students: 66%; of 20 to 49 students: 32%; of 50 or more students: 3%. **Advanced Placement and International Baccalaureate credit:** International Baccalaureate exams may be used for: Credit only. **Freshmen returning for sophomore year:** 87%. **Graduation rates:** Four-year: 64%; five-year: 72%; six-year: 74%. **Graduate study:** 40% of students pursue further study within one year. Fields in which graduates pursue further study: Master of Business Administration (MBA), 3%; law, 7%; medicine, 3%; education, 11%; arts and sciences, 76%.

COSTS AND FINANCIAL AID

Financial aid office: (607) 274-3131. **Expenses (2006-2007):** Tuition and fees 2006-2007: $26,832; room/board: $10,317. Estimated books and supplies: $1,005; transportation: $0; personal expenses: $1,354. **Financial aid:** Priority filing date for institution's financial aid form: February 1. In 2005-2006, 77% of undergraduates applied for financial aid. Of those, 70% were determined to have financial need; 45% had their need fully met. Average financial aid package (proportion receiving): $21,810 (70%). Average amount of gift aid, such as scholarships or grants (proportion receiving): $13,967 (65%). Average amount of self-help aid, such as work study or loans (proportion receiving): $7,534 (63%). Average need-based loan (excluding PLUS or other private loans): $6,091. Among students who received need-based aid, the average percentage of need met: 87%. Among students who received aid based on merit, the average award (and the proportion receiving): $9,582 (10%).

CAMPUS LIFE AND EXTRACURRICULAR ACTIVITIES

Campus housing available: coed dorms, women's dorms, sorority housing, fraternity housing, apartment for single students, special housing for disabled students, special housing for international students, other housing options. Students who live in college-owned, operated, or affiliated housing: 70%. **Student employment:** During the 2005-2006 academic year, 53% of undergraduates worked on campus. Average per-year earnings: $2,200. **Clubs and organizations:** Number of student organizations: 170. Activities include: choral groups, concert band, dance, drama/theater, jazz band, literary magazine, music ensembles, musical theater, opera, pep band, radio station, student government, student newspaper, student film society, symphony orchestra, television station, yearbook. Number of fraternities: 0; sororities: 1. Proportion of men in fraternities: 1%; of women in sororities: 1%. Average proportion of students who stay on campus on weekends: 95%. **Sports program (2005-2006):** Member of NCAA III. **Men's intercollegiate varsity sports:** baseball, basketball, cross-country, football, lacrosse, soccer, swimming and diving, tennis, track and field (indoor), track and field (outdoor), wrestling. **Women's intercollegiate varsity sports:** basketball, cross-country, field hockey, gymnastics, lacrosse, rowing, soccer, swimming and diving, tennis, track and field (indoor), track and field (outdoor), volleyball.

SERVICES AND FACILITIES

Basic services: health service, health insurance. **Counseling services:** minority student, career, military, personal, veteran student, academic, older student, psychological, birth control, religious. **For learning-disabled students:** School does not offer a structured program with separate admission and additional fees. Total undergraduates in learning-disabled program or receiving services: 315. Services include: reading machines, tape recorders, untimed tests, note-taking services, oral tests, readers, extended time for tests, priority seating, texts on tape, typist/scribe, exams on tape or computer, other testing accomodations, waiver of foreign language degree requirement, other. **Library:** Number of titles: 386,000; number of current serial subscriptions: 2,500. **Information technology resources:** Students are not required to lease or own a computer. Number of campus computers available to all students: 640. School has a wireless network. Proportion of college-owned housing units wired for high-speed internet access: 100%. **Campus safety:** Security services offered: 24-hour foot-and-vehicle patrols, late-night transport/escort service, 24-hour emergency telephones, lighted pathways/sidewalks, student patrols, controlled dormitory access (key, security card, etc).

TRANSFER AND INTERNATIONAL STUDENTS

Transfer students: May apply for admission for the following academic terms: Fall, Spring. Applicants do not need a minimum number of credits to apply. For fall 2005: Transfer applications received: 641. Transfer applicants offered admission: 379. Transfer applicants enrolled: 171. **International students:** Number of foreign undergraduates: 178 (3% of student body). Number of countries represented: 47. Minimum TOEFL score required: 550 (paper); 213 (computer).

Juilliard School

- **Address:** 60 Lincoln Center Plaza, New York, NY 10023-6588
- **Website:** http://www.juilliard.edu
- **Private**
- **Enrollment:** 478 full-time

KEY STATS

✔ **U.S News College Ranking:** Unranked Specialty School–Fine Arts
✔ **SAT or ACT Score (25th/75th percentile):** N/A
✔ **Tuition:** 2006-2007: $25,610

Selectivity: Least selective	**Room/board:** $10,095
Acceptance rate: 5%	**Average debt:** $23,831
Student/faculty ratio: N/A	**Proportion who borrowed:** 66%

UNDERGRADUATE STUDENT BODY STATS

2005-2006 enrollment: 478 full-time. Men: 52%; women: 48%. **Ethnic makeup:** African American: 12%; Asian American: 13%; Hispanic: 4%; White: 50%; International: 20%.

ADMISSIONS FACTS AND FIGURES

Phone: (212) 799-5000. **Email:** admissions@juilliard.edu. **Website:** http://www.juilliard.edu. **Application deadlines for fall 2007:** Regular decision: December 1; decision sent by April 1. Early decision: Not offered. Early action: Not offered. Admission cannot be deferred. **Application fee:** $100. Common application is not accepted. **Admissions requirements/recommendations:** Tests: The college does not use SAT or ACT scores in admissions decisions. Neither SAT nor ACT required. Campus visit: Recommended. Admissions interview: Required. **Factors that count in admissions decisions:** **Academic:** Secondary school record: Not considered. Class rank: Not considered. Letters of recommendation: Considered. Standardized test scores: Not considered. Essay: Considered. **Nonacademic:** Interview: Very important. Extracurricular activities: Not considered. Talent/ability: Very important. Character/personal qualities: Not considered. Alumni/ae relationship: Not considered. Geographical residence: Not considered. State residency: Not considered. Religious affiliation/commitment: Not considered. Minority status: Not considered. Volunteer work: Not considered. Work experience: Not considered. **Admissions statistics for the fall 2005 entering class:** Total applicants: 2,523. Total accepted: 136. Freshmen enrolled: 96; Overall acceptance rate: 5%. **Size of waiting list:** 48 applicants; enrolled from waiting list: 7.

ACADEMICS

Year founded: 1905. **Academic calendar:** Semester. **Degrees offered:** diploma, bachelor's, post-bachelor's certificate, master's, post-master's certificate, doctorate. **Most popular majors:** 72% music, 14% dance, 13% drama/theater arts and stagecraft. **Major fields of study:** visual and performing arts. **Areas of required coursework:** arts/fine arts, humanities, foreign languages, history, other. **Special academic programs:** accelerated program, cooperative (work-study plan) program, cross-registration, double major, honors program, study abroad. **Faculty and instruction (2005-2006):** Total instructional faculty: 114 full-time, 152 part-time (67% men; 33% women; 11% minorities). Classes of fewer than 20 students: 92%; of 20 to 49 students: 7%; of 50 or more students: 0%. **Freshmen returning for sophomore year:** 93%. **Graduation rates:** Four-year: 73%; five-year: 80%; six-year: 81%.

COSTS AND FINANCIAL AID

Financial aid office: (212) 799-5000. **Expenses (2006-2007):** Tuition and fees 2006-2007: $25,610; room/board: $10,095. Estimated books and supplies: $700; transportation: $850; personal expenses: $3,020. **Financial aid:** Priority filing date for institution's financial aid form: March 1. In 2005-

2006, 92% of undergraduates applied for financial aid. Of those, 77% were determined to have financial need; 19% had their need fully met. Average financial aid package (proportion receiving): $23,527 (77%). Average amount of gift aid, such as scholarships or grants (proportion receiving): $18,438 (76%). Average amount of self-help aid, such as work study or loans (proportion receiving): $6,082 (77%). Average need-based loan (excluding PLUS or other private loans): $4,940. Among students who received need-based aid, the average percentage of need met: 81%. Among students who received aid based on merit, the average award (and the proportion receiving): $10,961 (4%). The average athletic scholarship (and the proportion receiving): $0 (0%). Average amount of debt of borrowers graduating in 2005: $23,831. Proportion who borrowed: 66%.

CAMPUS LIFE AND EXTRACURRICULAR ACTIVITIES
Campus housing available: coed dorms, other housing options. **Student employment:** During the 2005-2006 academic year, 67% of undergraduates worked on campus. **Clubs and organizations:** Number of student organizations: 15. Activities include: choral groups, dance, drama/theater, jazz band, music ensembles, opera, student newspaper, symphony orchestra. Number of fraternities: 0; sororities: 0.

SERVICES AND FACILITIES
Basic services: health service, health insurance. **Remedial assistance:** writing. **Counseling services:** career, academic. **Library:** Number of titles: 95,519; number of current serial subscriptions: 230. **Information technology resources:** Students are not required to lease or own a computer. Number of campus computers available to all students: 70. School has a wireless network. Proportion of college-owned housing units wired for high-speed internet access: 100%. **Campus safety:** Security services offered: 24-hour foot-and-vehicle patrols, lighted pathways/sidewalks, controlled dormitory access (key, security card, etc).

TRANSFER AND INTERNATIONAL STUDENTS
Transfer students: May apply for admission for the following academic terms: Fall. Applicants do not need a minimum number of credits to apply. For fall 2005: Transfer applications received: 319. Transfer applicants offered admission: 17. Transfer applicants enrolled: 17. **International students:** Number of foreign undergraduates: 97 (20% of student body). Number of countries represented: 29. Minimum TOEFL score required: 200 (computer).

Keuka College

- **Address:** 141 Central Avenue, Keuka Park, NY 14478
- **Website:** http://www.keuka.edu
- **Private; Religious affiliation:** American Baptist
- **Enrollment:** 1,115 full-time; 153 part-time

KEY STATS
✔ **U.S News College Ranking:** 22, Comp. Colleges–Bachelor's (North)
✔ **SAT Score (25th/75th percentile):** 860-1070
✔ **Tuition:** 2006-2007: $19,120

Selectivity: Less selective	**Room/board:** $8,210
Acceptance rate: 81%	**Average debt:** $13,041
Student/faculty ratio: 14/1	**Proportion who borrowed:** 86%

UNDERGRADUATE STUDENT BODY STATS
2005-2006 enrollment: 1,115 full-time; 153 part-time. Men: 29%; women: 71%. **Ethnic makeup:** African American: 6%; American-Indian: 1%; Asian American: 1%; Hispanic: 2%; White: 90%.

ADMISSIONS FACTS AND FIGURES
Phone: (315) 279-5254. **Email:** admissions@mail.keuka.edu. **Website:** http://www.keuka.edu. **Application deadlines for fall 2007:** Regular decision: Rolling. Early decision: Not offered. Early action: Not offered. Admission can be deferred. **Application fee:** $30. Common application is not accepted. **Admissions requirements/recommendations:** High school units required (recommended): English: 4 (4); Mathematics: 3 (3); Science: 3 (3); Foreign language: 3 (3); Social studies: 3 (3); History: 2 (2); Total units: 18 (18). Tests: The college uses SAT or ACT scores in admissions decisions. Either SAT or ACT required. Campus visit: Recommended. Admissions interview: Recommended. Off-campus interview: May be arranged. **Factors that count**

in admissions decisions: *Academic:* Secondary school record: Very important. Class rank: Important. Letters of recommendation: Important. Standardized test scores: Important. Essay: Important. *Nonacademic:* Interview: Considered. Extracurricular activities: Important. Talent/ability: Considered. Character/personal qualities: Important. Alumni/ae relationship: Considered. Geographical residence: Not considered. State residency: Not considered. Religious affiliation/commitment: Not considered. Minority status: Not considered. Volunteer work: Considered. Work experience: Considered. **Other schools with the greatest overlap in applicants:** Elmira College; Nazareth College of Rochester; SUNY College of Arts and Sciences–Geneseo; St. Bonaventure University; St. John Fisher College. **Admissions statistics for the fall 2005 entering class:** Total applicants: 818. Total accepted: 659. Freshmen enrolled: 268; 9% were from out of state. Overall acceptance rate: 81%. **Credentials of fall 2005 freshmen:** 9% ranked in the top 10 percent of their high school class; 27% were in the top 25 percent, and 61% were in the top half. (Proportion submitting class standing: 87%.) **Average high school grade point average:** 2.9. **First-year students who submitted SAT scores:** 93%. Scores (25/75 percentile): Verbal: 420-530, Math: 440-540, Combined: 860-1070. **First-year students submitting ACT scores:** 39%. Scores (25/75 percentile): English: N/A, Math: N/A, Composite: 18-22.

ACADEMICS
Year founded: 1890. **Academic calendar:** 4-1-4. **Degrees offered:** bachelor's, master's. **Most popular majors:** 25% health professions and related clinical sciences, 21% business, management, marketing, and related support services, 18% education, 10% social sciences, 8% public administration and social service professions. **Major fields of study:** biological and biomedical sciences; business, management, marketing, and related support services; communication, journalism, and related programs; education; English language and literature/letters; foreign languages, literatures, and linguistics; health professions and related clinical sciences; liberal arts and sciences studies, and humanities; mathematics and statistics; physical sciences; psychology; public administration and social service professions; security and protective services; social sciences. **Areas of required coursework:** arts/fine arts, humanities, computer literacy, mathematics, English (including composition), philosophy, sciences (biological or physical), history, social science, other. **Pre-professional programs:** pre-law, pre-dentistry, pre-medicine, pre-veterinary science. **Special academic programs (% participation):** accelerated program, cooperative (work-study plan) program, cross-registration, double major, dual enrollment, independent study, internships (100%), student-designed major, study abroad, teacher certificate program (30%). **Teacher certification offered in:** early childhood, special education, elementary, middle/junior high, secondary. **Faculty and instruction (2005-2006):** Total instructional faculty: 57 full-time, 43 part-time (43% men; 57% women; 3% minorities). Full-time faculty with Ph.D. or other terminal degree: 88%. Student/faculty ratio: 14/1. Classes of fewer than 20 students: 55%; of 20 to 49 students: 43%; of 50 or more students: 2%. **Advanced Placement and International Baccalaureate credit:** AP tests may be used for: Credit only. Scores accepted: 3. International Baccalaureate exams may be used for: Credit only. **Freshmen returning for sophomore year:** 72%. **Graduation rates:** Four-year: 34%; five-year: 48%; six-year: 51%. **Graduate study:** 26% of students pursue further study within one year; 77% within five years. Fields in which graduates pursue further study: Master of Business Administration (MBA), 3%; education, 30%; arts and sciences, 5%.

COSTS AND FINANCIAL AID
Financial aid office: (315) 279-5232. **Expenses (2006-2007):** Tuition and fees 2006-2007: $19,120; room/board: $8,210. **Financial aid:** In 2005-2006, 99% of undergraduates applied for financial aid. Of those, 92% were determined to have financial need; 30% had their need fully met. Average financial aid package (proportion receiving): $16,103 (92%). Average amount of gift aid, such as scholarships or grants (proportion receiving): $10,578 (89%). Average amount of self-help aid, such as work study or loans (proportion receiving): $6,540 (82%). Average need-based loan (excluding PLUS or other private loans): $6,004. Among students who received need-based aid, the average percentage of need met: 80%. Among students who received aid based on merit, the average award (and the proportion receiving): $16,406 (8%). The average athletic scholarship (and the proportion receiving): $0 (0%). Average amount of debt of borrowers graduating in 2005: $13,041. Proportion who borrowed: 86%.

CAMPUS LIFE AND EXTRACURRICULAR ACTIVITIES
Campus housing available: coed dorms, women's dorms, special housing for disabled students, cooperative housing, other housing options. Students who live in college-owned, operated, or affiliated housing: 67%. **Student**

employment: During the 2005-2006 academic year, 25% of undergraduates worked on campus. Average per-year earnings: $6. **Clubs and organizations:** Number of student organizations: 33. Activities include: choral groups, concert band, dance, drama/theater, literary magazine, musical theater, radio station, student government, student newspaper, student film society, yearbook. Number of fraternities: 0; sororities: 0. Average proportion of students who stay on campus on weekends: 45%. **Sports program (2005-2006):** Member of NCAA III. *Men's intercollegiate varsity sports:* baseball, basketball, cross-country, golf, lacrosse, soccer, tennis. *Women's intercollegiate varsity sports:* basketball, cross-country, golf, lacrosse, soccer, softball, syncronized swimming, tennis, volleyball.

SERVICES AND FACILITIES

Basic services: health service, health insurance. **Remedial assistance:** math, writing, study skills, other. **Counseling services:** minority student, career, personal, veteran student, academic. **For learning-disabled students:** School does not offer a structured program with separate admission and additional fees. Total undergraduates in learning-disabled program or receiving services: 73. Services include: remedial math, remedial English, reading machines, remedial reading, tape recorders, note-taking services, learning center, readers, extended time for tests, tutors, texts on tape, typist/scribe. **Library:** Number of titles: 117,192; number of current serial subscriptions: 384. **Information technology resources:** Students are not required to lease or own a computer. Number of campus computers available to all students: 323. School has a wireless network. Proportion of college-owned housing units wired for high-speed internet access: 100%. **Campus safety:** Security services offered: 24-hour foot-and-vehicle patrols, late-night transport/escort service, 24-hour emergency telephones, lighted pathways/sidewalks, student patrols, controlled dormitory access (key, security card, etc).

TRANSFER AND INTERNATIONAL STUDENTS

Transfer students: May apply for admission for the following academic terms: Fall, Spring. Applicants do not need a minimum number of credits to apply. For fall 2005: Transfer applications received: 172. Transfer applicants offered admission: 111. Transfer applicants enrolled: 67. **International students:** Number of foreign undergraduates: 1. Minimum TOEFL score required: 500 (paper); 300 (computer). Average TOEFL score: 520 (paper).

Le Moyne College

- **Address:** 1419 Salt Springs Road, Syracuse, NY 13214-1301
- **Website:** http://www.lemoyne.edu
- **Private; Religious affiliation:** Roman Catholic (Jesuit)
- **Enrollment:** 2,318 full-time; 471 part-time

KEY STATS
✔ **U.S.News College Ranking:** 20, Universities–Master's (North)
✔ **SAT Score (25th/75th percentile):** 1010-1210
✔ **Tuition:** 2006-2007: $22,580

Selectivity: Selective	**Room/board:** $8,620
Acceptance rate: 72%	**Average debt:** $19,137
Student/faculty ratio: 13/1	**Proportion who borrowed:** 87%

UNDERGRADUATE STUDENT BODY STATS

2005-2006 enrollment: 2,318 full-time; 471 part-time. Men: 37%; women: 63%. **Ethnic makeup:** African American: 5%; American-Indian: 1%; Asian American: 2%; Hispanic: 4%; White: 88%; International: 1%. **Religious preference:** Protestant: 6%; No preference: 1%; Unknown: 50%; Roman Catholic (Jesuit): 40%.

ADMISSIONS FACTS AND FIGURES

Phone: (315) 445-4300. **Email:** admission@lemoyne.edu. **Website:** http://www.lemoyne.edu. **Application deadlines for fall 2007:** Regular decision: Rolling. Early decision: Send application by: December 1; Decision sent by: December 15. Early action: Not offered. Admission can be deferred. **Application fee:** $35. Common application is accepted. **Admissions requirements/recommendations:** High school units required (recommended): English: 4; Mathematics: 3 (4); Science: 3 (4); Foreign language: 3; Social studies: 4; Total units: 17. Tests: The college uses SAT or ACT scores in admissions decisions. Either SAT or ACT required. For admission to the fall 2007 entering class, the school will accept: ACT with writing, ACT without writing. Campus visit: Recommended. Admissions interview:

Recommended. Off-campus interview: Not available. **Factors that count in admissions decisions:** *Academic:* Secondary school record: Very important. Class rank: Important. Letters of recommendation: Important. Standardized test scores: Important. Essay: Important. *Nonacademic:* Interview: Important. Extracurricular activities: Important. Talent/ability: Important. Character/personal qualities: Considered. Alumni/ae relationship: Considered. Geographical residence: Considered. State residency: Considered. Religious affiliation/commitment: Not considered. Minority status: Not considered. Volunteer work: Considered. Work experience: Important. **Other schools with the greatest overlap in applicants:** SUNY College of Arts and Sciences–Geneseo; SUNY College–Cortland; SUNY–Oswego; St. John Fisher College; Syracuse University. **Admissions statistics for the fall 2005 entering class:** Total applicants: 2,946. Total accepted: 2,133. Freshmen enrolled: 520; 8% were from out of state. Accepted through early-decision or early-action plans: 8%. Overall acceptance rate: 72%. Early-decision acceptance rate: 92%. Non-early acceptance rate: 72%. **Size of waiting list:** 91 applicants; enrolled from waiting list: 23. **Credentials of fall 2005 freshmen:** 23% ranked in the top 10 percent of their high school class; 52% were in the top 25 percent, and 82% were in the top half. (Proportion submitting class standing: 73%.) **Average high school grade point average:** 3.4. **First-year students who submitted SAT scores:** 84%. Scores (25/75 percentile): Verbal: 500-600, Math: 510-610, Combined: 1010-1210. **First-year students submitting ACT scores:** 36%. Scores (25/75 percentile): English: 20-25, Math: 21-26, Composite: 21-26.

ACADEMICS

Year founded: 1946. **Academic calendar:** Semester. **Degrees offered:** bachelor's, post-bachelor's certificate, master's, post-master's certificate. **Most popular majors:** 23% business administration and management, 17% psychology, 10% English language and literature, 9% biology/biological sciences, 8% accounting. **Major fields of study:** biological and biomedical sciences; business, management, marketing, and related support services; communication, journalism, and related programs; English language and literature/letters; foreign languages, literatures, and linguistics; health professions and related clinical sciences; history; mathematics and statistics; multi/interdisciplinary studies; philosophy and religious studies; physical sciences; psychology; social sciences; visual and performing arts. **Areas of required coursework:** humanities, mathematics, English (including composition), philosophy, foreign languages, sciences (biological or physical), history, social science, other. **Pre-professional programs:** pre-law, pre-dentistry, pre-medicine, pre-veterinary science, pre-optometry, other. **Special academic programs (% participation):** accelerated program, double major (3%), dual enrollment, honors program (3.7%), independent study (18.7%), internships (28%), study abroad (6.3%), teacher certificate program (16.6%). **Teacher certification offered in:** special education, elementary, middle/junior high, secondary, bilingual/bicultural. **Reserve Officers Training Corps (ROTC):** Army ROTC: Offered at cooperating institution (Syracuse University); Air Force ROTC: Offered at cooperating institution (Syracuse University). **Faculty and instruction (2005-2006):** Total instructional faculty: 154 full-time, 170 part-time (59% men; 41% women; 10% minorities). Full-time faculty with Ph.D. or other terminal degree: 92%. Student/faculty ratio: 13/1. Classes of fewer than 20 students: 37%; of 20 to 49 students: 62%; of 50 or more students: 1%. **Advanced Placement and International Baccalaureate credit:** AP tests may be used for: Credit and/or placement. Scores accepted: 3, 4, 5. International Baccalaureate exams may be used for: Credit only. **Freshmen returning for sophomore year:** 86%. **Graduation rates:** Four-year: 60%; five-year: 69%; six-year: 73%. **Graduate study:** 29% of students pursue further study within one year. Fields in which graduates pursue further study: Master of Business Administration (MBA), 1%; law, 2%; medicine, 3%; education, 8%; arts and sciences, 15%.

COSTS AND FINANCIAL AID

Financial aid office: (315) 445-4400. **Expenses (2006-2007):** Tuition and fees 2006-2007: $22,580; room/board: $8,620. Estimated books and supplies: $700; transportation: $700; personal expenses: $1,400. **Financial aid:** Priority filing date for institution's financial aid form: February 1. In 2005-2006, 90% of undergraduates applied for financial aid. Of those, 80% were determined to have financial need; 28% had their need fully met. Average financial aid package (proportion receiving): $16,821 (80%). Average amount of gift aid, such as scholarships or grants (proportion receiving): $12,945 (79%). Average amount of self-help aid, such as work study or loans (proportion receiving): $4,756 (68%). Average need-based loan (excluding PLUS or other private loans): $4,423. Among students who received need-based aid, the average percentage of need met: 78%. Among students who received aid based on merit, the average award (and the proportion receiving): $9,415 (10%). The average athletic scholarship (and the

proportion receiving): $7,437 (7%). Average amount of debt of borrowers graduating in 2005: $19,137. Proportion who borrowed: 87%.

CAMPUS LIFE AND EXTRACURRICULAR ACTIVITIES

Campus housing available (% using): coed dorms (49%), women's dorms (11%), men's dorms (10%), apartment for single students (21%), special housing for disabled students, other housing options (9%). Students who live in college-owned, operated, or affiliated housing: 60%. **Student employment:** During the 2005-2006 academic year, 26% of undergraduates worked on campus. Average per-year earnings: $760. **Clubs and organizations:** Number of student organizations: 70. Activities include: choral groups, concert band, dance, drama/theater, jazz band, literary magazine, music ensembles, musical theater, pep band, radio station, student government, student newspaper, yearbook. Number of fraternities: 0; sororities: 0. Average proportion of students who stay on campus on weekends: 85%.
Sports program (2005-2006): Member of NCAA II. *Men's intercollegiate varsity sports:* baseball, basketball, cross-country, golf, lacrosse, soccer, swimming and diving, tennis. *Women's intercollegiate varsity sports:* basketball, cross-country, lacrosse, soccer, softball, swimming and diving, tennis, volleyball.

SERVICES AND FACILITIES

Basic services: nonremedial tutoring, placement service, health service. **Remedial assistance:** math, writing, study skills, other. **Counseling services:** minority student, career, personal, academic, older student, psychological, religious. **For learning-disabled students:** School does not offer a structured program with separate admission and additional fees. Total undergraduates in learning-disabled program or receiving services: 115. Services include: remedial math, remedial English, reading machines, tape recorders, note-taking services, learning center, extended time for tests, tutors, texts on tape, exams on tape or computer, other. **Library:** Number of titles: 261,330; number of current serial subscriptions: 35,429. **Information technology resources:** Students are not required to lease or own a computer. Number of campus computers available to all students: 325. School has a wireless network. Approximate number of users that can be accommodated: 800. Proportion of college-owned housing units wired for high-speed internet access: 100%. **Campus safety:** Security services offered: 24-hour foot-and-vehicle patrols, late-night transport/escort service, 24-hour emergency telephones, lighted pathways/sidewalks, controlled dormitory access (key, security card, etc).

TRANSFER AND INTERNATIONAL STUDENTS

Transfer students: May apply for admission for the following academic terms: Fall, Spring. Applicants do not need a minimum number of credits to apply. For fall 2005: Transfer applications received: 364. Transfer applicants offered admission: 256. Transfer applicants enrolled: 188.
International students: Number of foreign undergraduates: 19 (1% of student body). Number of countries represented: 12. Minimum TOEFL score required: 550 (paper); 213 (computer).

Long Island University—Brooklyn

■ **Address:** 1 University Plaza, Brooklyn, NY 11201
■ **Website:** http://www.brooklyn.liu.edu
■ **Private**
■ **Enrollment:** 4,412 full-time; 919 part-time

KEY STATS

✔ **U.S News College Ranking:** fourth tier, Universities–Master's (North)
✔ **SAT Score (25th/75th percentile):** 810-1080
✔ **Tuition:** 2006-2007: $23,010

Selectivity: Less selective	**Room/board:** $8,910
Acceptance rate: 62%	**Average debt:** $32,200
Student/faculty ratio: N/A	**Proportion who borrowed:** 97%

UNDERGRADUATE STUDENT BODY STATS

2005-2006 enrollment: 4,412 full-time; 919 part-time. Men: 28%; women: 72%. **Ethnic makeup:** African American: 40%; Asian American: 15%; Hispanic: 12%; White: 31%; International: 2%.

ADMISSIONS FACTS AND FIGURES

Phone: (718) 488-1011. **Email:** admissions@brooklyn.liu.edu. **Website:** http://www.brooklyn.liu.edu. **Application deadlines for fall 2007:** Regular decision: September 1. Early decision: Not offered. Early action: Not offered. Admission cannot be deferred. **Application fee:** $30. Common application is accepted. **To apply online, go to:** http://apply.brooklyn.liu.edu/undergradapply/. **Admissions requirements/recommendations:** High school units required (recommended): English: 4 (4); Mathematics: 2 (2); Science: 3 (3); Foreign language: 2 (2); Social studies: 3 (2); Academic electives: 128 (3); Total units: 17 (16). Tests: The college uses SAT or ACT scores in admissions decisions. Neither SAT nor ACT required. For admission to the fall 2007 entering class, the school will accept ACT with writing, ACT without writing. Campus visit: Recommended. Admissions interview: Recommended. Off-campus interview: Not available. **Factors that count in admissions decisions:** *Academic:* Secondary school record: Very important. Class rank: Considered. Letters of recommendation: Considered. Standardized test scores: Important. Essay: Considered. *Nonacademic:* Interview: Considered. Extracurricular activities: Considered. Talent/ability: Considered. Character/personal qualities: Considered. Alumni/ae relationship: Considered. Geographical residence: Not considered. State residency: Not considered. Religious affiliation/commitment: Not considered. Minority status: Not considered. Volunteer work: Considered. Work experience: Considered. **Admissions statistics for the fall 2005 entering class:** Total applicants: 4,985. Total accepted: 3,079. Freshmen enrolled: 1,028; Overall acceptance rate: 62%. **Average high school grade point average:** 3.0. **First-year students who submitted SAT scores:** 61%. Scores (25/75 percentile): Verbal: 400-520, Math: 410-560, Combined: 810-1080.

ACADEMICS

Year founded: 1926. **Academic calendar:** Semester. **Degrees offered:** certificate, associate, bachelor's, post-bachelor's certificate, master's, first professional, doctorate. **Most popular majors:** 17% nursing/registered nurse training (R.N., A.S.N., B.S.N., M.S.N.), 10% psychology, 8% business administration and management, 7% sociology, 6% physician assistant. **Major fields of study:** business, management, marketing, and related support services; communication, journalism, and related programs; education; foreign languages, literatures, and linguistics; health professions and related clinical sciences; history; multi/interdisciplinary studies; philosophy and religious studies; public administration and social service professions; social sciences; visual and performing arts. **Areas of required coursework:** humanities, computer literacy, mathematics, English (including composition), philosophy, sciences (biological or physical), history, social science. **Pre-professional programs:** pre-law, pre-medicine, pre-pharmacy, other. **Special academic programs:** accelerated program, cooperative (work-study plan) program, double major, English as a Second Language (ESL), honors program, independent study, internships, student-designed major, teacher certificate program. **Teacher certification offered in:** early childhood, special education, elementary, middle/junior high, secondary, bilingual/bicultural. **Cooperative education programs:** art, business, computer science, education, health professions, humanities, natural science, social/behavioral science, technologies. **Faculty and instruction (2005-2006):** Total instructional faculty: N/A. Classes of fewer than 20 students: 62%; of 20 to 49 students: 36%; of 50 or more students: 3%. **Advanced Placement and International Baccalaureate credit:** AP tests may be used for: Credit and/or placement. International Baccalaureate exams may be used for: Credit and/or placement. **Freshmen returning for sophomore year:** 53%. **Graduation rates:** Four-year: 4%; five-year: 13%; six-year: 21%. **Graduate study:** 22% of students pursue further study immediately upon graduation; 42% within one year; 36% within five years. Fields in which graduates pursue further study: law, 10%; arts and sciences, 40%.

COSTS AND FINANCIAL AID

Financial aid office: (718) 488-1037. **Expenses (2006-2007):** Tuition and fees 2006-2007: $23,010; room/board: $8,910. Estimated books and supplies: $1,750. **Financial aid:** In 2005-2006, 92% of undergraduates applied for financial aid. Of those, 86% were determined to have financial need; 45% had their need fully met. Average financial aid package (proportion receiving): $12,399 (84%). Average amount of gift-aid, such as scholarships or grants (proportion receiving): $8,744 (81%). Average amount of self-help aid, such as work study or loans (proportion receiving): $4,388 (77%). Average need-based loan (excluding PLUS or other private loans): $4,300. Among students who received need-based aid, the average percentage of need met: 45%. Among students who received aid based on merit, the average award (and the proportion receiving): $19,604 (4%). The average athletic scholarship (and the proportion receiving): $18,713 (2%). Average amount of debt of borrowers graduating in 2005: $32,200. Proportion who borrowed: 97%.

CAMPUS LIFE AND EXTRACURRICULAR ACTIVITIES

Campus housing available (% using): coed dorms (98%), special housing for disabled students (2%). Students who live in college-owned, operated, or affiliated housing: 0%. **Student employment:** During the 2005-2006 academic year, 3% of undergraduates worked on campus. Average per-year earnings: $5,000. **Clubs and organizations:** Number of student organizations: 60. Activities include: choral groups, dance, drama/theater, jazz band, literary magazine, music ensembles, radio station, student government, student newspaper, television station, yearbook. Number of fraternities: 5; sororities: 4. Proportion of men in fraternities: 1%; of women in sororities: 1%. Average proportion of students who stay on campus on weekends: 60%. **Sports program (2005-2006):** Member of NCAA I. *Men's intercollegiate varsity sports:* baseball, basketball, cross-country, golf, soccer, track and field (indoor), track and field (outdoor). *Women's intercollegiate varsity sports:* basketball, cross-country, golf, lacrosse, soccer, softball, tennis, track and field (indoor), track and field (outdoor), volleyball.

SERVICES AND FACILITIES

Basic services: placement service, health service, health insurance. **Remedial assistance:** reading, math, writing, study skills. **Counseling services:** minority student, career, academic, psychological, religious. **For learning-disabled students:** School does not offer a structured program with separate admission and additional fees. Total undergraduates in learning-disabled program or receiving services: 51. Services include: remedial math, remedial English, reading machines, remedial reading, tape recorders, other special classes, untimed tests, learning center, readers, extended time for tests, tutors, priority seating, texts on tape, other testing accomodations, other. **Library:** Number of titles: 276,089; number of current serial subscriptions: 1,402. **Information technology resources:** Students are not required to lease or own a computer. Number of campus computers available to all students: 700. School has a wireless network. Approximate number of users that can be accommodated: 6,000. Proportion of college-owned housing units wired for high-speed internet access: 100%. **Campus safety:** Security services offered: 24-hour foot-and-vehicle patrols, 24-hour emergency telephones, lighted pathways/sidewalks, controlled dormitory access (key, security card, etc).

TRANSFER AND INTERNATIONAL STUDENTS

Transfer students: May apply for admission for the following academic terms: Fall, Spring, Summer. Applicants do not need a minimum number of credits to apply. For fall 2005: Transfer applications received: 4,597. Transfer applicants offered admission: 1,103. Transfer applicants enrolled: 625. **International students:** Number of foreign undergraduates: 100 (2% of student body). Minimum TOEFL score required: 500 (paper); 173 (computer).

Long Island University–C.W. Post Campus

- **Address:** 720 Northern Boulevard, Brookville, NY 11548-1300
- **Website:** http://www.liu.edu
- **Private**
- **Enrollment:** 4,476 full-time; 693 part-time

KEY STATS

✔ **U.S News College Ranking:** fourth tier, Universities–Master's (North)
✔ **SAT Score (25th/75th percentile):** 890-1090
✔ **Tuition:** 2005-2006: $23,230

Selectivity: Less selective	**Room/board:** $8,700
Acceptance rate: 77%	**Average debt:** N/A
Student/faculty ratio: 10/1	**Proportion who borrowed:** N/A

UNDERGRADUATE STUDENT BODY STATS

2005-2006 enrollment: 4,476 full-time; 693 part-time. Men: 39%; women: 61%. **Ethnic makeup:** African American: 10%; Asian American: 3%; Hispanic: 8%; White: 75%; International: 3%.

ADMISSIONS FACTS AND FIGURES

Phone: (516) 299-2900. **Email:** enroll@cwpost.liu.edu. **Website:** http://www.liu.edu. **Application deadlines for fall 2007:** Regular decision: Rolling. Early decision: Not offered. Early action: Not offered. Admission can be deferred. **Application fee:** $30. Common application is accepted. **To apply online, go to:** http://www.liu.edu/cwpost. **Admissions requirements/recommendations:** High school units required (recommended): English: (4); Mathematics: (3); Science: (3); Foreign language: (2); Social studies: (4); History: (0); Academic electives: (0); Total units: (16). Tests: The college uses SAT or ACT scores in admissions decisions. SAT required. For admission to the fall 2007 entering class, the school will accept: ACT with writing, ACT without writing. Campus visit: Recommended. Admissions interview: Recommended. Off-campus interview: May be arranged. **Factors that count in admissions decisions:** *Academic:* Secondary school record: Considered. Class rank: Considered. Letters of recommendation: Considered. Standardized test scores: Considered. Essay: Considered. *Nonacademic:* Interview: Considered. Extracurricular activities: Considered. Talent/ability: Considered. Character/personal qualities: Not considered. Alumni/ae relationship: Not considered. Geographical residence: Not considered. State residency: Not considered. Religious affiliation/commitment: Not considered. Minority status: Not considered. Volunteer work: Considered. Work experience: Considered. **Other schools with the greatest overlap in applicants:** Adelphi University; Hofstra University; Molloy College; SUNY–Stony Brook; St. John's University. **Admissions statistics for the fall 2005 entering class:** Total applicants: 5,345. Total accepted: 4,102. Freshmen enrolled: 1,006; 13% were from out of state. Overall acceptance rate: 77%. **Credentials of fall 2005 freshmen:** 5% ranked in the top 10 percent of their high school class; 18% were in the top 25 percent, and 62% were in the top half. (Proportion submitting class standing: 34%.) **Average high school grade point average:** 2.9. **First-year students who submitted SAT scores:** 98%. Scores (25/75 percentile): Verbal: 450-540, Math: 440-550, Combined: 890-1090. **First-year students submitting ACT scores:** 12%. Scores (25/75 percentile): English: 15-22, Math: 17-24, Composite: 17-23.

ACADEMICS

Year founded: 1954. **Academic calendar:** Semester. **Degrees offered:** certificate, diploma, bachelor's, post-bachelor's certificate, master's, post-master's certificate, doctorate. **Most popular majors:** 10% elementary education and teaching, 9% criminal justice/safety studies, 7% psychology, 6% business administration and management, 5% accounting. **Major fields of study:** biological and biomedical sciences; business, management, marketing, and related support services; communication, journalism, and related programs; communications technologies/technicians and support services; computer and information sciences and support services; education; English language and literature/letters; foreign languages, literatures, and linguistics; health professions and related clinical sciences; history; liberal arts and sciences studies, and humanities; mathematics and statistics; philosophy and religious studies; physical sciences; psychology; public administration and social service professions; security and protective services; social sciences; visual and performing arts. **Areas of required coursework:** arts/fine arts, humanities, mathematics, English (including composition), philosophy, foreign languages, sciences (biological or physical), history, social science. **Special academic programs:** accelerated program, cooperative (work-study plan) program, cross-registration, double major, dual enrollment, English as a Second Language (ESL), exchange student program (domestic), honors program, independent study, internships, student-designed major, study abroad, teacher certificate program, weekend college. **Teacher certification offered in:** early childhood, special education, elementary, middle/junior high, secondary, bilingual/bicultural. **Cooperative education programs:** art, business, computer science, education, engineering, health professions, humanities, natural science, social/behavioral science, technologies. **Reserve Officers Training Corps (ROTC):** Army ROTC: Offered at cooperating institution (Hofstra University); Air Force ROTC: Offered at cooperating institution (Manhattan College). **Faculty and instruction (2005-2006):** Total instructional faculty: 358 full-time, 604 part-time (54% men; 46% women; 10% minorities). Student/faculty ratio: 10/1. **Advanced Placement and International Baccalaureate credit:** AP tests may be used for: Credit only. Scores accepted: 3, 4, 5. International Baccalaureate exams may be used for: Credit only. **Freshmen returning for sophomore year:** 70%. **Graduation rates:** Four-year: 24%; five-year: 39%; six-year: 39%.

COSTS AND FINANCIAL AID

Financial aid office: (516) 299-2338. **Expenses (2005-2006):** Tuition and fees 2005-2006: $23,230; room/board: $8,700. Estimated books and supplies: $625; transportation: $600; personal expenses: $1,400. **Financial aid:** Priority filing date for institution's financial aid form: March 1; deadline: March 1.

CAMPUS LIFE AND EXTRACURRICULAR ACTIVITIES

Campus housing available: coed dorms, women's dorms. Students who live in college-owned, operated, or affiliated housing: 42%. **Clubs and organizations:** Number of student organizations: 90. Activities include: choral groups, concert band, dance, drama/theater, jazz band, literary magazine, music ensembles, musical theater, pep band, radio station, student government, student newspaper, television station, yearbook. Number of fraternities: 5; sororities: 9. **Sports program (2005-2006):** Member of NCAA II. **Men's intercollegiate varsity sports:** baseball, basketball, cross-country, football, lacrosse, soccer, track and field (indoor), track and field (outdoor). **Women's intercollegiate varsity sports:** basketball, cross-country, field hockey, lacrosse, soccer, softball, swimming and diving, tennis, track and field (indoor), track and field (outdoor), volleyball.

SERVICES AND FACILITIES

Basic services: nonremedial tutoring, women's center, placement service, day care, health service, health insurance. **Remedial assistance:** reading, math, writing, study skills. **Counseling services:** minority student, career, personal, veteran student, academic, older student, psychological, birth control, religious. **For learning-disabled students:** School does not offer a structured program with separate admission and additional fees. Services include: reading machines, tape recorders, diagnostic testing service, untimed tests, note-taking services, readers, extended time for tests, tutors. **Information technology resources:** Students are not required to lease or own a computer. School has a wireless network. Proportion of college-owned housing units wired for high-speed internet access: 100%. **Campus safety:** Security services offered: 24-hour foot-and-vehicle patrols, late-night transport/escort service, 24-hour emergency telephones, lighted pathways/sidewalks, student patrols, controlled dormitory access (key, security card, etc).

TRANSFER AND INTERNATIONAL STUDENTS

Transfer students: May apply for admission for the following academic terms: Fall, Spring, Summer. Applicants need a minimum number of credits to apply. For fall 2005: Transfer applications received: 1,431. Transfer applicants offered admission: 1,069. Transfer applicants enrolled: 538. **International students:** Number of foreign undergraduates: 171 (3% of student body). Minimum TOEFL score required: 527 (paper); 197 (computer). Average TOEFL score: 567 (paper).

Manhattan College

- **Address:** Manhattan College Parkway, Riverdale, NY 10471
- **Website:** http://www.manhattan.edu
- **Private; Religious affiliation:** Roman Catholic
- **Enrollment:** 2,879 full-time; 147 part-time

KEY STATS

- ✔ **U.S News College Ranking:** 23, Universities–Master's (North)
- ✔ **SAT Score (25th/75th percentile):** 1030-1220
- ✔ **Tuition:** 2006-2007: $22,560

Selectivity: Selective	**Room/board:** $9,000
Acceptance rate: 57%	**Average debt:** N/A
Student/faculty ratio: 12/1	**Proportion who borrowed:** N/A

UNDERGRADUATE STUDENT BODY STATS

2005-2006 enrollment: 2,879 full-time; 147 part-time. Men: 54%; women: 46%. **Ethnic makeup:** African American: 2%; Asian American: 2%; Hispanic: 7%; White: 88%; International: 1%. **Religious preference:** Roman Catholic: 73%; Protestant: 20%; Jewish: 1%; Muslim: 2%; Hindu: 1%; Unknown: 3%.

ADMISSIONS FACTS AND FIGURES

Phone: (718) 862-7200. **Email:** admit@manhattan.edu. **Website:** http://www.manhattan.edu. **Application deadlines for fall 2007:** Regular decision: April 15. Early decision: Send application by: N/A; Decision sent by: N/A. Early action: Not offered. Admission can be deferred. **Application fee:** $50. Common application is accepted. **Admissions requirements/recommendations:** High school units required (recommended): English: 4 (4); Mathematics: 3 (4); Science: 2 (3); Foreign language: 2 (3); Social studies: 3 (3); History: 3 (3); Academic electives: 2 (2); Total units: 16 (16). Tests: The college uses SAT or ACT scores in admissions decisions. Either SAT or ACT required. For admission to the fall 2007 entering class, the school will accept: ACT with writing. Campus visit: Recommended. Admissions interview: Recommended. Off-campus interview: Not available. **Factors that count in admissions decisions:** *Academic:* Secondary school record: Very important. Class rank: Very important. Letters of recommendation: Very important. Standardized test scores: Very important. Essay: Very important. *Nonacademic:* Interview: Considered. Extracurricular activities: Important. Talent/ability: Important. Character/personal qualities: Important. Alumni/ae relationship: Considered. Geographical residence: Not considered. State residency: Not considered. Religious affiliation/commitment: Not considered. Minority status: Not considered. Volunteer work: Important. Work experience: Important. **Other schools with the greatest overlap in applicants:** Fordham University; Hofstra University; Iona College; Pace University; St. John's University. **Admissions statistics for the fall 2005 entering class:** Total applicants: 4,712. Total accepted: 2,708. Freshmen enrolled: 701; Overall acceptance rate: 57%. Non-early acceptance rate: 57%. **Size of waiting list:** 170 applicants; enrolled from waiting list: 9. **Average high school grade point average:** 3.3. **First-year students who submitted SAT scores:** 95%. Scores (25/75 percentile): Verbal: 510-600, Math: 520-620, Combined: 1030-1220. **First-year students submitting ACT scores:** 5%. Scores (25/75 percentile): English: N/A, Math: N/A, Composite: N/A.

ACADEMICS

Year founded: 1853. **Academic calendar:** Semester. **Degrees offered:** certificate, bachelor's, master's, post-master's certificate. **Most popular majors:** Information not available. **Major fields of study:** biological and biomedical sciences; business, management, marketing, and related support services; communication, journalism, and related programs; computer and information sciences and support services; education; engineering; English language and literature/letters; foreign languages, literatures, and linguistics; history; liberal arts and sciences studies, and humanities; mathematics and statistics; multi/interdisciplinary studies; philosophy and religious studies; physical sciences; psychology; social sciences. **Areas of required coursework:** arts/fine arts, humanities, computer literacy, mathematics, English (including composition), philosophy, foreign languages, sciences (biological or physical), history, social science. **Pre-professional programs:** pre-law, pre-dentistry, pre-medicine, pre-theology, pre-optometry, other. **Special academic programs (% participation):** cross-registration (35%), double major (30%), honors program (6%), independent study (30%), internships (40%), liberal arts/career combination (30%), study abroad (15%), teacher certificate program (20%). **Teacher certification offered in:** early childhood, special education, elementary, middle/junior high, secondary. **Cooperative education programs:** art, business, computer science, education, engineering, health professions, humanities, natural science, social/behavioral science, technologies. **Reserve Officers Training Corps (ROTC):** Army ROTC: Offered at cooperating institution (Fordham University); Air Force ROTC: Offered on campus. **Faculty and instruction (2005-2006):** Total instructional faculty: 172 full-time, 210 part-time (59% men; 41% women; 7% minorities). Full-time faculty with Ph.D. or other terminal degree: 97%. Student/faculty ratio: 12/1. Classes of fewer than 20 students: 49%; of 20 to 49 students: 51%. **Advanced Placement and International Baccalaureate credit:** AP tests may be used for: Credit and/or placement. Scores accepted: 3, 4, 5. International Baccalaureate exams may be used for: Credit and/or placement. **Freshmen returning for sophomore year:** 83%. **Graduation rates:** Four-year: 59%; five-year: 67%; six-year: 67%. **Graduate study:** 6% of students pursue further study immediately upon graduation; 10% within one year; 12% within five years. Fields in which graduates pursue further study: Master of Business Administration (MBA), 15%; law, 6%; medicine, 6%; dentistry, 5%; engineering, 15%; theology (or the seminary), 1%; education, 20%; arts and sciences, 5%.

COSTS AND FINANCIAL AID

Financial aid office: (718) 862-7100. **Expenses (2006-2007):** Tuition and fees 2006-2007: $22,560; room/board: $9,000. Estimated books and supplies: $1,000; transportation: $700; personal expenses: $1,000. **Financial aid:** Priority filing date for institution's financial aid form: April 1. In 2005-2006, 78% of undergraduates applied for financial aid. Of those, 63% were determined to have financial need; 14% had their need fully met. Average financial aid package (proportion receiving): $13,606 (61%). Average amount of gift aid, such as scholarships or grants (proportion receiving): N/A (59%). Average amount of self-help aid, such as work study or loans (proportion receiving): $4,046 (53%). Average need-based loan (excluding PLUS or other private loans): $3,984. Among students who received need-based aid, the average percentage of need met: 64%. Among students who received aid based on merit, the average award (and the proportion receiving): $7,052 (16%). The average athletic scholarship (and the proportion receiving): $11,398 (8%).

CAMPUS LIFE AND EXTRACURRICULAR ACTIVITIES

Campus housing available (% using): coed dorms (97%), women's dorms (2%), men's dorms (1%), special housing for disabled students (0%). **Student employment:** During the 2005-2006 academic year, 26% of undergraduates worked on campus. Average per-year earnings: $1,375. **Clubs and organizations:** Number of student organizations: 57. Activities include: choral groups, concert band, dance, drama/theater, jazz band, literary magazine, marching band, music ensembles, musical theater, radio station, student government, student newspaper, television station, yearbook. Number of fraternities: 2; sororities: 2. Proportion of men in fraternities: 2%; of women in sororities: 2%. Average proportion of students who stay on campus on weekends: 70%. **Sports program (2005-2006):** Member of NCAA I. *Men's intercollegiate varsity sports:* baseball, basketball, cross-country, golf, lacrosse, soccer, tennis, track and field (indoor), track and field (outdoor). *Women's intercollegiate varsity sports:* basketball, cross-country, lacrosse, soccer, softball, swimming and diving, tennis, track and field (indoor), track and field (outdoor), volleyball.

SERVICES AND FACILITIES

Basic services: nonremedial tutoring, placement service, health service, health insurance. **Counseling services:** minority student, career, military, personal, veteran student, academic, older student, psychological, religious. **For learning-disabled students:** School does not offer a structured program with separate admission and additional fees. Total undergraduates in learning-disabled program or receiving services: 150. **Library:** Number of titles: 274,550; number of current serial subscriptions: 1,533. **Information technology resources:** Students are not required to lease or own a computer. Number of campus computers available to all students: 480. School has a wireless network. Approximate number of users that can be accommodated: 2,048. Proportion of college-owned housing units wired for high-speed internet access: 100%. **Campus safety:** Security services offered: 24-hour foot-and-vehicle patrols, late-night transport/escort service, 24-hour emergency telephones, lighted pathways/sidewalks, controlled dormitory access (key, security card, etc.).

TRANSFER AND INTERNATIONAL STUDENTS

Transfer students: May apply for admission for the following academic terms: Fall, Spring, Summer. Applicants do not need a minimum number of credits to apply. For fall 2005: Transfer applications received: 489. Transfer applicants offered admission: 288. Transfer applicants enrolled: 140. **International students:** Number of foreign undergraduates: 20 (1% of student body). Minimum TOEFL score required: 520 (paper); 200 (computer). Average TOEFL score: 540 (paper).

Manhattan School of Music

- **Address:** 120 Claremont Avenue, New York, NY 10027
- **Website:** http://www.msmnyc.edu
- **Private**
- **Enrollment:** 408 full-time; 8 part-time

KEY STATS

✔ **U.S News College Ranking:** Unranked Specialty School–Fine Arts
✔ **SAT or ACT Score (25th/75th percentile):** N/A
✔ **Tuition:** 2006-2007: $27,860

Selectivity: Least selective	**Room/board:** $12,800
Acceptance rate: N/A	**Average debt:** $12,531
Student/faculty ratio: 5/1	**Proportion who borrowed:** 59%

UNDERGRADUATE STUDENT BODY STATS

2005-2006 enrollment: 408 full-time; 8 part-time. Men: 51%; women: 49%. **Ethnic makeup:** African American: 3%; Asian American: 7%; Hispanic: 4%; White: 65%; International: 21%.

ADMISSIONS FACTS AND FIGURES

Phone: (212) 749-2802. **Email:** admission@msmnyc.edu. **Website:** http://www.msmnyc.edu. **Application deadlines for fall 2007:** Regular decision: December 1; decision sent by April 1. Early decision: Not offered. Early action: Not offered. Admission can be deferred. **Application fee:** $100. Common application is not accepted. **To apply online, go to:** http://www.unifiedapps.org. **Admissions requirements/recommendations:** High school units required (recommended): English: 4 (4); Mathematics: 3 (3); Science: 3

(3); Foreign language: 4 (4); Social studies: 4 (4); History: 4 (4). Tests: The college uses SAT or ACT scores in admissions decisions. Neither SAT nor ACT required. For admission to the fall 2007 entering class, the school will accept: ACT with writing, ACT without writing. Campus visit: Recommended. Admissions interview: Neither required nor recommended. Off-campus interview: Not available. **Factors that count in admissions decisions:** *Academic:* Secondary school record: Very important. Class rank: Considered. Letters of recommendation: Very important. Standardized test scores: Considered. Essay: Very important. *Nonacademic:* Interview: Not considered. Extracurricular activities: Important. Talent/ability: Very important. Character/personal qualities: Very important. Alumni/ae relationship: Considered. Geographical residence: Not considered. State residency: Not considered. Religious affiliation/commitment: Not considered. Minority status: Considered. Volunteer work: Considered. Work experience: Considered. **Other schools with the greatest overlap in applicants:** Juilliard School; New England Conservatory of Music; Oberlin College. **Admissions statistics for the fall 2005 entering class:** Total applicants: 863. Freshmen enrolled: 98; 68% were from out of state. **Size of waiting list:** 7 applicants; enrolled from waiting list: 1.

ACADEMICS

Year founded: 1917. **Academic calendar:** Semester. **Degrees offered:** diploma, bachelor's, master's, post-master's certificate, doctorate. **Most popular majors:** 100% music. **Major fields of study: Areas of required coursework:** humanities, English (including composition), philosophy, history, social science, other. **Special academic programs (% participation):** cross-registration (3%), distance learning (1%), English as a Second Language (ESL) (20%), study abroad (1%). **Faculty and instruction (2005-2006):** Total instructional faculty: 75 full-time, 305 part-time (58% men; 42% women; 16% minorities). Full-time faculty with Ph.D. or other terminal degree: 25%. Student/faculty ratio: 5/1. Classes of fewer than 20 students: 89%; of 20 to 49 students: 5%; of 50 or more students: 6%. **Freshmen returning for sophomore year:** 82%. **Graduation rates:** Four-year: 57%; five-year: 58%; six-year: 58%. **Graduate study:** 56% of students pursue further study immediately upon graduation. Fields in which graduates pursue further study: education, 1%; arts and sciences, 99%.

COSTS AND FINANCIAL AID

Financial aid office: (212) 749-2802. **Expenses (2006-2007):** Tuition and fees 2006-2007: $27,860; room/board: $12,800. Estimated books and supplies: $1,000; transportation: $1,600; personal expenses: $3,000. **Financial aid:** Priority filing date for institution's financial aid form: March 1; deadline: March 1. In 2005-2006, 93% of undergraduates applied for financial aid. Of those, 93% were determined to have financial need; 5% had their need fully met. Average financial aid package (proportion receiving): $12,200 (93%). Average amount of gift aid, such as scholarships or grants (proportion receiving): $10,701 (77%). Average amount of self-help aid, such as work study or loans (proportion receiving): $5,137 (58%). Average need-based loan (excluding PLUS or other private loans): $4,387. Among students who received need-based aid, the average percentage of need met: 36%. Among students who received aid based on merit, the average award (and the proportion receiving): $8,416 (6%). The average athletic scholarship (and the proportion receiving): $0 (0%). Average amount of debt of borrowers graduating in 2005: $12,531. Proportion who borrowed: 59%.

CAMPUS LIFE AND EXTRACURRICULAR ACTIVITIES

Campus housing available (% using): coed dorms (40%), other housing options (60%). Students who live in college-owned, operated, or affiliated housing: 58%. **Student employment:** During the 2005-2006 academic year, 10% of undergraduates worked on campus. Average per-year earnings: $1,200. **Clubs and organizations:** Number of student organizations: 10. Activities include: choral groups, concert band, drama/theater, jazz band, music ensembles, musical theater, opera, student government, symphony orchestra. Number of fraternities: 0; sororities: 0. Average proportion of students who stay on campus on weekends: 80%.

SERVICES AND FACILITIES

Basic services: nonremedial tutoring, placement service, other. **Remedial assistance:** study skills, other. **Counseling services:** career, academic, other. **For learning-disabled students:** School does not offer a structured program with separate admission and additional fees. Total undergraduates in learning-disabled program or receiving services: 0. Services include: tutors, other. **Information technology resources:** Students are not required to lease or own a computer. Number of campus computers available to all students: 14. School has a wireless network. Approximate number of users that can be accommodated: 50. Proportion of college-owned housing units wired for high-speed internet access: 100%. **Campus safety:** Security services offered: lighted pathways/sidewalks, controlled dormitory access (key, security card, etc).

TRANSFER AND INTERNATIONAL STUDENTS

Transfer students: May apply for admission for the following academic terms: Fall. Applicants need a minimum number of credits to apply. For fall 2005: Transfer applications received: 202. Transfer applicants offered admission: 58. Transfer applicants enrolled: 29. **International students:** Number of foreign undergraduates: 87 (21% of student body). Minimum TOEFL score required: 550 (paper); 213 (computer). Average TOEFL score: 550 (paper).

Manhattanville College

- Address: 2900 Purchase Street, Purchase, NY 10577
- Website: http://www.mville.edu
- Private
- Enrollment: 1,652 full-time; 130 part-time

KEY STATS

✔ **U.S News College Ranking:** 46, Universities–Master's (North)
✔ **SAT Score (25th/75th percentile):** 980-1220
✔ **Tuition:** 2006-2007: $28,000

Selectivity: Selective	**Room/board:** $11,550
Acceptance rate: 60%	**Average debt:** $20,198
Student/faculty ratio: 13/1	**Proportion who borrowed:** 68%

UNDERGRADUATE STUDENT BODY STATS

2005-2006 enrollment: 1,652 full-time; 130 part-time. Men: 31%; women: 69%. **Ethnic makeup:** African American: 6%; American-Indian: 1%; Asian American: 3%; Hispanic: 15%; White: 68%; International: 8%.

ADMISSIONS FACTS AND FIGURES

Phone: (800) 328-4553. **Email:** admissions@mville.edu. **Website:** http://www.mville.edu. **Application deadlines for fall 2007:** Regular decision: March 1. Early decision: Send application by: December 1; Decision sent by: December 31. Early action: Not offered. Admission can be deferred. **Application fee:** $55. Common application is accepted. **To apply online, go to:** http://www.mville.edu/admissions/index.html. **Admissions requirements/recommendations:** High school units required (recommended): English: 4; Mathematics: 3; Science: 2; Social studies: 2; Academic electives: 5; Total units: 16. Tests: The college uses SAT or ACT scores in admissions decisions. Either SAT or ACT required. Campus visit: Recommended. Admissions interview: Recommended. Off-campus interview: May be arranged. **Factors that count in admissions decisions:** *Academic:* Secondary school record: Very important. Class rank: Not considered. Letters of recommendation: Important. Standardized test scores: Very important. Essay: Important. *Nonacademic:* Interview: Important. Extracurricular activities: Important. Talent/ability: Considered. Character/personal qualities: Considered. Alumni/ae relationship: Considered. Geographical residence: Considered. State residency: Not considered. Religious affiliation/commitment: Not considered. Minority status: Not considered. Volunteer work: Considered. Work experience: Considered. **Other schools with the greatest overlap in applicants:** Fordham University; Manhattan College; New York University; Pace University; SUNY–Purchase College. **Admissions statistics for the fall 2005 entering class:** Total applicants: 3,184. Total accepted: 1,900. Freshmen enrolled: 515; 40% were from out of state. Accepted through early-decision or early-action plans: 10%. Overall acceptance rate: 60%. Early-decision acceptance rate: 54%. Non-early acceptance rate: 60%. **Size of waiting list:** 105 applicants; enrolled from waiting list: 0. **Credentials of fall 2005 freshmen:** 21% ranked in the top 10 percent of their high school class; 47% were in the top 25 percent, and 80% were in the top half. (Proportion submitting class standing: 75%.) **Average high school grade point average:** 3.0. First-year students who submitted SAT scores: 96%. Scores (25/75 percentile): Verbal: 490-610, Math: 490-610, Combined: 980-1220. **First-year students submitting ACT scores:** 15%. Scores (25/75 percentile): English: N/A, Math: N/A, Composite: 22-26.

ACADEMICS

Year founded: 1841. **Academic calendar:** Semester. **Degrees offered:** certificate, bachelor's, master's. **Most popular majors:** 18% psychology, 14% business administration, management, and operations, 10% art/art studies, 10% education, 8% political science and government. **Major fields of study:** area, ethnic, cultural, and gender studies; biological and biomedical sciences; business, management, marketing, and related support services; computer and information sciences and support services; education; English language and literature/letters; foreign languages, literatures, and linguistics; history; liberal arts and sciences studies, and humanities; mathematics and statistics; philosophy and religious studies; physical sciences; psychology; social sciences; visual and performing arts. **Areas of required coursework:** arts/fine arts, humanities, computer literacy, mathematics, English (including composition), philosophy, foreign languages, sciences (biological or physical), history, social science, other. **Pre-professional programs:** pre-law, pre-medicine. **Special academic programs (% participation):** accelerated program (5%), cross-registration (1%), distance learning (0%), double major (17%), exchange student program (domestic) (1%), honors program (5%), independent study (50%), internships (25%), student-designed major (6%), study abroad (8%), teacher certificate program (8%), weekend college. **Teacher certification offered in:** early childhood, special education, elementary, middle/junior high, secondary, bilingual/bicultural. **Faculty and instruction (2005-2006):** Total instructional faculty: 90 full-time, 115 part-time (45% men; 55% women; 17% minorities). Full-time faculty with Ph.D. or other terminal degree: 96%. Student/faculty ratio: 13/1. Classes of fewer than 20 students: 72%; of 20 to 49 students: 27%; of 50 or more students: 1%. **Advanced Placement and International Baccalaureate credit:** AP tests may be used for: Credit and/or placement. Scores accepted: 4, 5. International Baccalaureate exams may be used for: Credit and/or placement. **Freshmen returning for sophomore year:** 77%. **Graduation rates:** Four-year: 51%; five-year: 57%; six-year: 57%. **Graduate study:** 18% of students pursue further study immediately upon graduation; 17% within one year. Fields in which graduates pursue further study: Master of Business Administration (MBA), 6%; law, 6%; medicine, 2%; dentistry, 2%; education, 57%; arts and sciences, 6%.

COSTS AND FINANCIAL AID

Financial aid office: (914) 323-5357. **Expenses (2006-2007):** Tuition and fees 2006-2007: $28,000; room/board: $11,550. Estimated books and supplies: $800 personal expenses: $800. **Financial aid:** Priority filing date for institution's financial aid form: March 1; deadline: March 1. In 2005-2006, 71% of undergraduates applied for financial aid. Of those, 63% were determined to have financial need; 19% had their need fully met. Average financial aid package (proportion receiving): $21,904 (63%). Average amount of gift aid, such as scholarships or grants (proportion receiving): $10,024 (55%). Average amount of self-help aid, such as work study or loans (proportion receiving): $4,346 (55%). Average need-based loan (excluding PLUS or other private loans): $3,997. Among students who received need-based aid, the average percentage of need met: 79%. Among students who received aid based on merit, the average award (and the proportion receiving): $8,496 (28%). The average athletic scholarship (and the proportion receiving): $0 (0%). Average amount of debt of borrowers graduating in 2005: $20,198. Proportion who borrowed: 68%.

CAMPUS LIFE AND EXTRACURRICULAR ACTIVITIES

Campus housing available (% using): coed dorms (100%). Students who live in college-owned, operated, or affiliated housing: 78%. **Student employment:** During the 2005-2006 academic year, 25% of undergraduates worked on campus. Average per-year earnings: $1,250. **Clubs and organizations:** Number of student organizations: 57. Activities include: choral groups, concert band, dance, drama/theater, jazz band, literary magazine, music ensembles, musical theater, opera, pep band, radio station, student government, student newspaper, student film society, symphony orchestra, television station, yearbook. Number of fraternities: 0; sororities: 0. Average proportion of students who stay on campus on weekends: 70%. **Sports program (2005-2006):** Member of NCAA III. *Men's intercollegiate varsity sports:* baseball, basketball, golf, ice hockey, lacrosse, soccer, tennis. *Women's intercollegiate varsity sports:* basketball, field hockey, ice hockey, lacrosse, soccer, softball, tennis.

SERVICES AND FACILITIES

Basic services: nonremedial tutoring, placement service, health service, health insurance. **Remedial assistance:** reading, math, writing, study skills. **Counseling services:** minority student, career, personal, academic, psychological, birth control, religious. **For learning-disabled students:** School does not offer a structured program with separate admission and additional fees. Total undergraduates in learning-disabled program or receiving services: 132. Services include: remedial math, remedial English, reading machines, tape recorders, untimed tests, oral tests, learning center, readers, extended time for tests, tutors, texts on tape, exams on tape or computer. **Library:** Number of titles: 243,122; number of current serial subscriptions: 18,930. **Information technology resources:** Students are not required to lease or own a computer. Number of campus computers available to all students: 175. School has a wireless network. Approximate number of users that can be accommodated: 490. Proportion of college-owned housing units wired for high-speed internet access: 100%. **Campus safety:** Security services offered: 24-hour foot-and-vehicle patrols, late-night transport/escort service, 24-hour emergency telephones, lighted pathways/sidewalks, controlled dormitory access (key, security card, etc).

TRANSFER AND INTERNATIONAL STUDENTS

Transfer students: May apply for admission for the following academic terms: Fall, Spring. Applicants do not need a minimum number of credits to apply. For fall 2005: Transfer applicants enrolled: 82. **International students:** Number of foreign undergraduates: 136 (8% of student body). Number of countries represented: 47. Minimum TOEFL score required: 550 (paper); 217 (computer). Average TOEFL score: 595 (paper).

Marist College

- **Address:** 3399 North Road, Poughkeepsie, NY 12601
- **Website:** http://www.marist.edu
- **Private**
- **Enrollment:** 4,413 full-time; 483 part-time

KEY STATS
✔ **U.S News College Ranking:** 15, Universities–Master's (North)
✔ **SAT Score (25th/75th percentile):** 1090-1260
✔ **Tuition:** 2006-2007: $22,576

Selectivity: More selective	**Room/board:** $9,790
Acceptance rate: 50%	**Average debt:** $20,419
Student/faculty ratio: 15/1	**Proportion who borrowed:** 54%

UNDERGRADUATE STUDENT BODY STATS

2005-2006 enrollment: 4,413 full-time; 483 part-time. Men: 43%; women: 57%. **Ethnic makeup:** African American: 3%; Asian American: 2%; Hispanic: 6%; White: 88%.

ADMISSIONS FACTS AND FIGURES

Phone: (845) 575-3226. **Email:** admissions@marist.edu. **Website:** http://www.marist.edu. **Application deadlines for fall 2007:** Regular decision: February 15; decision sent by March 15. Early decision: Send application by: November 15; Decision sent by: December 15. Early action: Send application by: December 1; Decision sent by: January 15. Admission can be deferred. **Application fee:** $40. Common application is accepted. **To apply online, go to:** http://www.marist.edu/admissions/freshmen/apply.html. **Admissions requirements/recommendations:** High school units required (recommended): English: 4; Mathematics: 3 (4); Science: 3 (4); Foreign language: 2 (3); Social studies: 2; History: 1; Academic electives: 2; Total units: 17. Tests: The college uses SAT or ACT scores in admissions decisions. Either SAT or ACT required. For admission to the fall 2007 entering class, the school will accept: ACT with writing. Campus visit: Recommended. Admissions interview: Neither required nor recommended. Off-campus interview: Not available. **Factors that count in admissions decisions:** *Academic:* Secondary school record: Very important. Class rank: Considered. Letters of recommendation: Important. Standardized test scores: Very important. Essay: Very important. *Nonacademic:* Interview: Not considered. Extracurricular activities: Important. Talent/ability: Important. Character/personal qualities: Important. Alumni/ae relationship: Considered. Geographical residence: Important. State residency: Important. Religious affiliation/commitment: Not considered. Minority status: Considered. Volunteer work: Important. Work experience: Important. **Other schools with the greatest overlap in applicants:** Fairfield University; Fordham University; Providence College; SUNY–Binghamton; University of Connecticut. **Admissions statistics for the fall 2005 entering class:** Total applicants: 7,077. Total accepted: 3,513. Freshmen enrolled: 1,017; 48% were from out of state. Accepted through early-decision or early-action plans: 42%. Overall acceptance rate: 50%. Non-early acceptance rate: 41%. **Size of waiting list:** 500 applicants; enrolled from waiting list: 60. **Credentials of fall 2005 freshmen:** 29% ranked in the top 10 percent of their high school class; 70% were in the top 25 percent, and 97% were in the top half. (Proportion submitting class standing: 56%.)

Average high school grade point average: 3.4. **First-year students who submitted SAT scores:** 91%. Scores (25/75 percentile): Verbal: 540-620, Math: 550-640, Combined: 1090-1260. **First-year students submitting ACT scores:** 12%. Scores (25/75 percentile): English: N/A, Math: N/A, Composite: 24-28.

ACADEMICS

Year founded: 1929. **Academic calendar:** Semester. **Degrees offered:** certificate, bachelor's, post-bachelor's certificate, master's. **Most popular majors:** 24% business/commerce, 22% communication and media studies, 11% education, 11% liberal arts and sciences studies, and humanities, 5% criminal justice and corrections. **Major fields of study:** area, ethnic, cultural, and gender studies; biological and biomedical sciences; business, management, marketing, and related support services; communication, journalism, and related programs; computer and information sciences and support services; education; English language and literature/letters; foreign languages, literatures, and linguistics; health professions and related clinical sciences; history; liberal arts and sciences studies, and humanities; mathematics and statistics; natural resources and conservation; philosophy and religious studies; physical sciences; psychology; public administration and social service professions; security and protective services; social sciences; visual and performing arts. **Areas of required coursework:** arts/fine arts, computer literacy, mathematics, English (including composition), philosophy, sciences (biological or physical), history, social science, other. **Pre-professional programs:** pre-law, pre-medicine, pre-veterinary science. **Special academic programs:** accelerated program, cooperative (work-study plan) program, cross-registration, distance learning, double major, dual enrollment, honors program, independent study, internships, student-designed major, study abroad, teacher certificate program, weekend college. **Teacher certification offered in:** early childhood, special education, secondary. **Reserve Officers Training Corps (ROTC):** Army ROTC: Offered on campus. **Faculty and instruction (2005-2006):** Total instructional faculty: 201 full-time, 395 part-time (56% men; 44% women; 10% minorities). Full-time faculty with Ph.D. or other terminal degree: 83%. Student/faculty ratio: 15/1. Classes of fewer than 20 students: 48%; of 20 to 49 students: 52%; of 50 or more students: 0%. **Advanced Placement and International Baccalaureate credit:** AP tests may be used for: Credit only. Scores accepted: 3, 4, 5. International Baccalaureate exams may be used for: Credit only. **Freshmen returning for sophomore year:** 89%. **Graduation rates:** Four-year: 68%; five-year: 76%; six-year: 75%. **Graduate study:** 26% of students pursue further study within one year. Fields in which graduates pursue further study: Master of Business Administration (MBA), 3%; law, 2%; medicine, 1%; education, 9%; arts and sciences, 11%.

COSTS AND FINANCIAL AID

Financial aid office: (845) 575-3230. **Expenses (2006-2007):** Tuition and fees 2006-2007: $22,576; room/board: $9,790. Estimated books and supplies: $1,200; transportation: $1,500; personal expenses: $115. **Financial aid:** Priority filing date for institution's financial aid form: February 15; deadline: May 1. In 2005-2006, 78% of undergraduates applied for financial aid. Of those, 62% were determined to have financial need; 18% had their need fully met. Average financial aid package (proportion receiving): $13,439 (61%). Average amount of gift aid, such as scholarships or grants (proportion receiving): $9,099 (58%). Average amount of self-help aid, such as work study or loans (proportion receiving): $5,452 (50%). Average need-based loan (excluding PLUS or other private loans): $4,741. Among students who received need-based aid, the average percentage of need met: 68%. Among students who received aid based on merit, the average award (and the proportion receiving): $5,837 (18%). The average athletic scholarship (and the proportion receiving): $9,794 (6%). Average amount of debt of borrowers graduating in 2005: $20,419. Proportion who borrowed: 54%.

CAMPUS LIFE AND EXTRACURRICULAR ACTIVITIES

Campus housing available (% using): coed dorms (55%), apartment for single students (44%), special housing for disabled students (1%), other housing options. Students who live in college-owned, operated, or affiliated housing: 72%. **Student employment:** During the 2005-2006 academic year, 27% of undergraduates worked on campus. Average per-year earnings: $1,300. **Clubs and organizations:** Number of student organizations: 76. Activities include: choral groups, concert band, dance, drama/theater, jazz band, literary magazine, marching band, music ensembles, musical theater, pep band, radio station, student government, student newspaper, student film society, television station, yearbook. Number of fraternities: 3; sororities: 4. Proportion of men in fraternities: 1%; of women in sororities: 3%. Average proportion of students who stay on campus on weekends: 80%. **Sports program (2005-2006):** Member of NCAA I. *Men's intercollegiate varsity sports:* baseball, basketball, cross-country, football, lacrosse, soccer, swimming and diving, tennis, track and field (indoor), track and field (outdoor). **Women's intercollegiate varsity sports:** basketball, cross-country, lacrosse, soccer, softball, swimming and diving, tennis, track and field (indoor), track and field (outdoor), volleyball, water polo, rowing.

SERVICES AND FACILITIES
Basic services: nonremedial tutoring, placement service, health service. **Remedial assistance:** reading, math, writing, study skills. **Counseling services:** career, personal, academic, older student, psychological, religious. **For learning-disabled students:** School does not offer a structured program with separate admission and additional fees. Total undergraduates in learning-disabled program or receiving services: 74. Services include: reading machines, tape recorders, note-taking services, oral tests, readers, extended time for tests, tutors, texts on tape, other testing accomodations, other. **Library:** Number of titles: 186,569; number of current serial subscriptions: 21,401. **Information technology resources:** Students are not required to lease or own a computer. Number of campus computers available to all students: 700. School has a wireless network. Approximate number of users that can be accommodated: 750. Proportion of college-owned housing units wired for high-speed internet access: 100%. **Campus safety:** Security services offered: 24-hour foot-and-vehicle patrols, late-night transport/escort service, 24-hour emergency telephones, lighted pathways/sidewalks, controlled dormitory access (key, security card, etc).

TRANSFER AND INTERNATIONAL STUDENTS
Transfer students: May apply for admission for the following academic terms: Fall, Spring. Applicants need a minimum number of credits to apply. For fall 2005: Transfer applications received: 442. Transfer applicants offered admission: 344. Transfer applicants enrolled: 185. **International students:** Number of foreign undergraduates: 13. Number of countries represented: 14. Minimum TOEFL score required: 560 (paper); 220 (computer). Average TOEFL score: 585 (paper).

Marymount Manhattan College

- **Address:** 221 E. 71st Street, New York, NY 10021
- **Website:** http://www.mmm.edu/
- **Private**
- **Enrollment:** 1,603 full-time; 404 part-time

KEY STATS
✔ **U.S News College Ranking:** fourth tier, Liberal Arts Colleges
✔ **SAT Score (25th/75th percentile):** 953-1200
✔ **Tuition:** 2006-2007: $19,638

Selectivity: Selective	**Room/board:** $10,890
Acceptance rate: 77%	**Average debt:** $29,706
Student/faculty ratio: 11/1	**Proportion who borrowed:** 80%

UNDERGRADUATE STUDENT BODY STATS
2005-2006 enrollment: 1,603 full-time; 404 part-time. Men: 23%; women: 77%. **Ethnic makeup:** African American: 12%; Asian American: 5%; Hispanic: 11%; White: 69%; International: 2%.

ADMISSIONS FACTS AND FIGURES
Phone: (212) 517-0430. **Email:** admissions@mmm.edu. **Website:** http://www.mmm.edu/. **Application deadlines for fall 2007:** Regular decision: Rolling. Early decision: Not offered. Early action: Not offered. Admission can be deferred. **Application fee:** $60. Common application is accepted. **To apply online, go to:** http://www.embark.com. **Admissions requirements/recommendations:** High school units required (recommended): English: 4; Mathematics: 3; Science: 1 (3); Foreign language: (3); Social studies: 3; Academic electives: 4; Total units: 16. Tests: The college uses SAT or ACT scores in admissions decisions. Neither SAT nor ACT required. For admission to the fall 2007 entering class, the school will accept: ACT with writing, ACT without writing. Campus visit: Recommended. Admissions interview: Recommended. Off-campus interview: May be arranged. **Factors that count in admissions decisions:** *Academic:* Secondary school record: Very important. Class rank: Considered. Letters of recommendation: Important. Standardized test scores: Important. Essay: Considered. *Nonacademic:* Interview: Important. Extracurricular activities: Important. Talent/ability: Important. Character/personal qualities: Important. Alumni/ae relationship: Considered. Geographical residence:

Not considered. State residency: Not considered. Religious affiliation/commitment: Not considered. Minority status: Not considered. Volunteer work: Considered. Work experience: Considered. **Other schools with the greatest overlap in applicants:** Fordham University; Hofstra University; New York University; Pace University; SUNY–Purchase College. **Admissions statistics for the fall 2005 entering class:** Total applicants: 2,033. Total accepted: 1,567. Freshmen enrolled: 448; 83% were from out of state. Overall acceptance rate: 77%. **Average high school grade point average:** 3.1. **First-year students who submitted SAT scores:** 89%. Scores (25/75 percentile): Verbal: 490-600, Math: 463-600, Combined: 953-1200. **First-year students submitting ACT scores:** 7%. Scores (25/75 percentile): English: N/A, Math: N/A, Composite: 20-25.

ACADEMICS
Year founded: 1936. **Academic calendar:** Semester. **Degrees offered:** certificate, associate, bachelor's. **Most popular majors:** 33% visual and performing arts, 26% communication, journalism, and related programs, 11% business, management, marketing, and related support services, 9% psychology, 9% social sciences. **Major fields of study:** agriculture, agriculture operations, and related sciences; biological and biomedical sciences; business, management, marketing, and related support services; communication, journalism, and related programs; English language and literature/letters; health professions and related clinical sciences; history; liberal arts and sciences studies, and humanities; psychology; social sciences; visual and performing arts. **Areas of required coursework:** arts/fine arts, humanities, mathematics, English (including composition), sciences (biological or physical), social science, other. **Pre-professional programs:** pre-law, pre-medicine. **Special academic programs (% participation):** accelerated program (11%), cross-registration (2%), distance learning (12%), double major (16%), dual enrollment (5%), English as a Second Language (ESL) (5%), exchange student program (domestic) (1%), honors program (13%), independent study (22%), internships (27%), study abroad (1%), teacher certificate program (12%). **Teacher certification offered in:** early childhood, special education, elementary, middle/junior high, secondary, bilingual/bicultural. **Faculty and instruction (2005-2006):** Total instructional faculty: 85 full-time, 230 part-time (41% men; 59% women; 14% minorities). Full-time faculty with Ph.D. or other terminal degree: 86%. Student/faculty ratio: 11/1. Classes of fewer than 20 students: 74%; of 20 to 49 students: 26%. **Advanced Placement and International Baccalaureate credit:** AP tests may be used for: Credit only. Scores accepted: 3, 4, 5. International Baccalaureate exams may be used for: Credit only. **Freshmen returning for sophomore year:** 69%. **Graduation rates:** Four-year: 28%; five-year: 40%; six-year: 42%. **Graduate study:** 31% of students pursue further study immediately upon graduation; 40% within one year; 46% within five years. Fields in which graduates pursue further study: Master of Business Administration (MBA), 22%; law, 16%; medicine, 5%; dentistry, 1%; education, 19%; arts and sciences, 37%.

COSTS AND FINANCIAL AID
Financial aid office: (212) 517-0480. **Expenses (2006-2007):** Tuition and fees 2006-2007: $19,638; room/board: $10,890. Estimated books and supplies: $1,000; transportation: $600; personal expenses: $1,500. **Financial aid:** Priority filing date for institution's financial aid form: March 15. Of those, 63% were determined to have financial need; 13% had their need fully met. Average financial aid package (proportion receiving): $11,386 (63%). Average amount of gift aid, such as scholarships or grants (proportion receiving): $4,222 (63%). Average amount of self-help aid, such as work study or loans (proportion receiving): $4,111 (56%). Average need-based loan (excluding PLUS or other private loans): $3,711. Among students who received need-based aid, the average percentage of need met: 46%. Among students who received aid based on merit, the average award (and the proportion receiving): $4,122 (12%). The average athletic scholarship (and the proportion receiving): $0 (0%). Average amount of debt of borrowers graduating in 2005: $29,706. Proportion who borrowed: 80%.

CAMPUS LIFE AND EXTRACURRICULAR ACTIVITIES
Campus housing available (% using): coed dorms (100%). Students who live in college-owned, operated, or affiliated housing: 41%. **Student employment:** During the 2005-2006 academic year, 17% of undergraduates worked on campus. Average per-year earnings: $1,500. **Clubs and organizations:** Number of student organizations: 22. Activities include: dance, drama/theater, literary magazine, musical theater, radio station, student government, student newspaper, student film society, television station, yearbook. Number of fraternities: 0; sororities: 0. Average proportion of students who stay on campus on weekends: 25%.

SERVICES AND FACILITIES

Basic services: nonremedial tutoring, placement service, health service, health insurance. **Remedial assistance:** reading, math, writing, study skills. **Counseling services:** minority student, career, personal, academic, older student, psychological. **For learning-disabled students:** School does not offer a structured program with separate admission and additional fees. Total undergraduates in learning-disabled program or receiving services: 30. Services include: remedial math, remedial English, remedial reading, tape recorders, diagnostic testing service, extended time for tests, tutors. **Library:** Number of titles: 70,000; number of current serial subscriptions: 21,000. **Information technology resources:** Students are not required to lease or own a computer. Number of campus computers available to all students: 205. School has a wireless network. Approximate number of users that can be accommodated: 300. Proportion of college-owned housing units wired for high-speed internet access: 85%. **Campus safety:** Security services offered: controlled dormitory access (key, security card, etc.).

TRANSFER AND INTERNATIONAL STUDENTS

Transfer students: May apply for admission for the following academic terms: Fall, Winter, Spring, Summer. Applicants need a minimum number of credits to apply. For fall 2005: Transfer applications received: 429. Transfer applicants offered admission: 309. Transfer applicants enrolled: 144. **International students:** Number of foreign undergraduates: 45 (2% of student body). Number of countries represented: 37. Minimum TOEFL score required: 550 (paper); 213 (computer). Average TOEFL score: 573 (paper).

Medaille College

- **Address:** 18 Agassiz Circle, Buffalo, NY 14214
- **Website:** http://www.medaille.edu
- **Private**
- **Enrollment:** 1,580 full-time; 197 part-time

KEY STATS

✔ **U.S News College Ranking:** fourth tier, Comp. Coll.–Bachelor's (North)
✔ **SAT Score (25th/75th percentile):** 960-1100
✔ **Tuition:** 2006-2007: $15,780

Selectivity: Selective	**Room/board:** $8,024
Acceptance rate: 73%	**Average debt:** $19,000
Student/faculty ratio: 17/1	**Proportion who borrowed:** 85%

UNDERGRADUATE STUDENT BODY STATS

2005-2006 enrollment: 1,580 full-time; 197 part-time. Men: 35%; women: 65%. **Ethnic makeup:** African American: 14%; Hispanic: 2%; White: 83%.

ADMISSIONS FACTS AND FIGURES

Phone: (716) 884-3281. **Email:** sdesing@medaille.edu. **Website:** http://www.medaille.edu. **Application deadlines for fall 2007:** Regular decision: Rolling; decision sent by September 1. Early decision: Not offered. Early action: Not offered. Admission can be deferred. **Application fee:** $35. Common application is accepted. **Admissions requirements/recommendations:** High school units required (recommended): English: 4 (4); Mathematics: 2 (3); Science: 2 (3); Foreign language: (2); Social studies: 4 (4); History: (2); Total units: 12 (20). Tests: The college uses SAT or ACT scores in admissions decisions. Either SAT or ACT required. For admission to the fall 2007 entering class, the school will accept: ACT with writing, ACT without writing. Campus visit: Recommended. Admissions interview: Required. Off-campus interview: May be arranged. **Factors that count in admissions decisions:** *Academic:* Secondary school record: Very important. Class rank: Considered. Letters of recommendation: Important. Standardized test scores: Very important. Essay: Important. *Nonacademic:* Interview: Very important. Extracurricular activities: Important. Talent/ability: Considered. Character/personal qualities: Considered. Alumni/ae relationship: Considered. Geographical residence: Not considered. State residency: Not considered. Religious affiliation/commitment: Not considered. Minority status: Not considered. Volunteer work: Considered. Work experience: Considered. **Other schools with the greatest overlap in applicants:** Canisius College; Daemen College; Hilbert College; SUNY–Buffalo State College; University at Buffalo–SUNY. **Admissions statistics for the fall 2005 entering class:** Total applicants: 978. Total accepted: 716. Freshmen enrolled: 218; 3% were from out of state. Overall acceptance rate: 73%.

Credentials of fall 2005 freshmen: 12% ranked in the top 10 percent of their high school class; 33% were in the top 25 percent, and 55% were in the top half. (Proportion submitting class standing: 82%.) **Average high school grade point average:** 3.2. **First-year students who submitted SAT scores:** 99%. Scores (25/75 percentile): Verbal: 490-560, Math: 470-540, Combined: 960-1100. **First-year students submitting ACT scores:** 1%. Scores (25/75 percentile): English: N/A, Math: N/A, Composite: 17-21.

ACADEMICS

Year founded: 1937. **Academic calendar:** Semester. **Degrees offered:** certificate, associate, bachelor's, master's. **Most popular majors:** 51% business administration and management, 11% education, 9% liberal arts and sciences/liberal studies, 8% criminal justice/police science, 4% sport and fitness administration/management. **Major fields of study:** biological and biomedical sciences; business, management, marketing, and related support services; communication, journalism, and related programs; computer and information sciences and support services; education; English language and literature/letters; health professions and related clinical sciences; liberal arts and sciences studies, and humanities; parks, recreation, leisure, and fitness studies; psychology; public administration and social service professions; security and protective services; social sciences; visual and performing arts. **Areas of required coursework:** arts/fine arts, humanities, computer literacy, mathematics, English (including composition), sciences (biological or physical), history, social science. **Pre-professional programs:** pre-law, pre-medicine, pre-veterinary science. **Special academic programs (% participation):** accelerated program (27%), double major (0%), dual enrollment (0%), honors program (5%), independent study (1%), internships (70%), teacher certificate program (45%), weekend college (3%). **Teacher certification offered in:** elementary, middle/junior high. **Reserve Officers Training Corps (ROTC):** Army ROTC: Offered at cooperating institution (Canisius College). **Faculty and instruction (2005-2006):** Total instructional faculty: 91 full-time, 221 part-time (51% men; 49% women; 7% minorities). Full-time faculty with Ph.D. or other terminal degree: 63%. Student/faculty ratio: 17/1. Classes of fewer than 20 students: 77%; of 20 to 49 students: 23%; of 50 or more students: 0%. **Advanced Placement and International Baccalaureate credit:** AP tests may be used for: Credit only. Scores accepted: 3, 4, 5. International Baccalaureate exams may be used for: Credit only. **Freshmen returning for sophomore year:** 70%. **Graduation rates:** Four-year: 28%; five-year: 39%; six-year: 24%. **Graduate study:** 15% of students pursue further study immediately upon graduation; 22% within one year; 25% within five years. Fields in which graduates pursue further study: Master of Business Administration (MBA), 25%; law, 2%; education, 68%; arts and sciences, 5%.

COSTS AND FINANCIAL AID

Financial aid office: (716) 880-2256. **Expenses (2006-2007):** Tuition and fees 2006-2007: $15,780; room/board: $8,024. Estimated books and supplies: $1,100; transportation: $2,000; personal expenses: $1,100. **Financial aid:** Priority filing date for institution's financial aid form: April 1. In 2005-2006, 81% of undergraduates applied for financial aid. Of those, 66% were determined to have financial need; 5% had their need fully met. Average financial aid package (proportion receiving): $18,094 (66%). Average amount of gift aid, such as scholarships or grants (proportion receiving): $8,187 (64%). Average amount of self-help aid, such as work study or loans (proportion receiving): $4,937 (66%). Average need-based loan (excluding PLUS or other private loans): $3,437. Among students who received need-based aid, the average percentage of need met: 65%. Among students who received aid based on merit, the average award (and the proportion receiving): $10,156 (19%). The average athletic scholarship (and the proportion receiving): $0 (0%). Average amount of debt of borrowers graduating in 2005: $19,000. Proportion who borrowed: 85%.

CAMPUS LIFE AND EXTRACURRICULAR ACTIVITIES

Campus housing available (% using): coed dorms (100%). Students who live in college-owned, operated, or affiliated housing: 23%. **Student employment:** During the 2005-2006 academic year, 2% of undergraduates worked on campus. Average per-year earnings: $1,800. **Clubs and organizations:** Number of student organizations: 15. Activities include: drama/theater, literary magazine, musical theater, radio station, student government, student newspaper, student film society, television station, yearbook. Number of fraternities: 0; sororities: 0. Average proportion of students who stay on campus on weekends: 25%. **Sports program (2005-2006):** Member of NCAA III. *Men's intercollegiate varsity sports:* baseball, basketball, golf, lacrosse, soccer, volleyball. *Women's intercollegiate varsity sports:* basketball, cross-country, golf, lacrosse, soccer, softball, volleyball.

SERVICES AND FACILITIES

Basic services: nonremedial tutoring, placement service, health service. **Remedial assistance:** reading, math, writing, study skills. **Counseling services:** career, personal, academic. **For learning-disabled students:** School does not offer a structured program with separate admission and additional fees. Total undergraduates in learning-disabled program or receiving services: 54. Services include: remedial math, remedial English, reading machines, remedial reading, tape recorders, videotaped classes, untimed tests, note-taking services, learning center, readers, extended time for tests, tutors, texts on tape, other. **Library:** Number of titles: 61,026; number of current serial subscriptions: 270. **Information technology resources:** Students are not required to lease or own a computer. Number of campus computers available to all students: 120. School does not have a wireless network. Proportion of college-owned housing units wired for high-speed internet access: 100%. **Campus safety:** Security services offered: 24-hour foot-and-vehicle patrols, late-night transport/escort service, 24-hour emergency telephones, lighted pathways/sidewalks, controlled dormitory access (key, security card, etc).

TRANSFER AND INTERNATIONAL STUDENTS

Transfer students: May apply for admission for the following academic terms: Fall, Spring, Summer. Applicants do not need a minimum number of credits to apply. For fall 2005: Transfer applications received: 117. Transfer applicants offered admission: 110. Transfer applicants enrolled: 100. **International students:** Number of foreign undergraduates: 5. Number of countries represented: 1. Minimum TOEFL score required: 550 (paper); 213 (computer). Average TOEFL score: 560 (paper).

Mercy College

- **Address:** 555 Broadway, Dobbs Ferry, NY 10522
- **Website:** http://www.mercy.edu
- **Private**
- **Enrollment:** 3,694 full-time; 1,942 part-time

KEY STATS

✔ **U.S News College Ranking:** fourth tier, Universities—Master's (North)
✔ **SAT or ACT Score (25th/75th percentile):** N/A
✔ **Tuition:** 2005-2006: $11,792

Selectivity: Less selective	**Room/board:** N/A
Acceptance rate: 42%	**Average debt:** N/A
Student/faculty ratio: 12/1	**Proportion who borrowed:** N/A

UNDERGRADUATE STUDENT BODY STATS

2005-2006 enrollment: 3,694 full-time; 1,942 part-time. Men: 29%; women: 71%. **Ethnic makeup:** African American: 31%; Asian American: 3%; Hispanic: 34%; White: 30%; International: 2%.

ADMISSIONS FACTS AND FIGURES

Phone: (914) 378-3487. **Email:** admissions@mercy.edu. **Website:** http://www.mercy.edu. **Application deadlines for fall 2007:** Regular decision: Rolling. Early decision: Not offered. Early action: Not offered. Admission can be deferred. **Application fee:** $37. Common application is accepted. **Admissions requirements/recommendations:** High school units required (recommended): English: 4 (4); Mathematics: 4 (4); Science: 3 (3); Foreign language: 3 (2); Social studies: 2 (2); History: 3 (3); Academic electives: 3 (0); Total units: 21. Tests: The college uses SAT or ACT scores in admissions decisions. Neither SAT nor ACT required. Campus visit: Neither required nor recommended. Admissions interview: Required. Off-campus interview: May be arranged. **Factors that count in admissions decisions:** *Academic:* Secondary school record: Considered. Class rank: Not considered. Letters of recommendation: Considered. Standardized test scores: Considered. Essay: Considered. *Nonacademic:* Interview: Very important. Extracurricular activities: Considered. Talent/ability: Considered. Character/personal qualities: Considered. Alumni/ae relationship: Not considered. Geographical residence: Not considered. State residency: Not considered. Religious affiliation/commitment: Not considered. Minority status: Not considered. Volunteer work: Considered. Work experience: Considered. **Other schools with the greatest overlap in applicants:** Iona College. **Admissions statistics for the fall 2005 entering class:** Total applicants: 2,110. Total accepted: 888. Freshmen enrolled: 605; 4% were from out of state. Overall acceptance rate: 42%.

ACADEMICS

Year founded: 1950. **Academic calendar:** Semester. **Degrees offered:** certificate, associate, bachelor's, master's, post-master's certificate. **Most popular majors:** 25% social sciences, 21% business, management, marketing, and related support services, 15% health professions and related clinical sciences, 14% psychology, 5% computer and information sciences and support services. **Major fields of study:** biological and biomedical sciences; business, management, marketing, and related support services; foreign languages, literatures, and linguistics; history; legal professions and studies; mathematics and statistics; multi/interdisciplinary studies; philosophy and religious studies; psychology; public administration and social service professions; security and protective services. **Areas of required coursework:** arts/fine arts, humanities, computer literacy, mathematics, English (including composition), philosophy, foreign languages, sciences (biological or physical), history, social science. **Pre-professional programs:** pre-law, pre-dentistry, pre-medicine, pre-veterinary science, pre-optometry, pre-pharmacy. **Special academic programs (% participation):** accelerated program, cooperative (work-study plan) program, cross-registration, distance learning (15%), double major, English as a Second Language (ESL), honors program, independent study, internships, study abroad, teacher certificate program, weekend college, other. **Teacher certification offered in:** early childhood, special education, elementary, secondary, bilingual/bicultural. **Cooperative education programs:** business, education, health professions, natural science, social/behavioral science, technologies. **Faculty and instruction (2005-2006):** Total instructional faculty: 175 full-time, 655 part-time. Full-time faculty with Ph.D. or other terminal degree: 65%. Student/faculty ratio: 12/1. **Advanced Placement and International Baccalaureate credit:** AP tests may be used for: Credit and/or placement. International Baccalaureate exams may be used for: Credit only. **Freshmen returning for sophomore year:** 59%. **Graduation rates:** Four-year: 9%; five-year: 16%; six-year: 20%. **Graduate study:** Fields in which graduates pursue further study: Master of Business Administration (MBA), 10%; education, 50%; arts and sciences, 35%; veterinary medicine, 5%.

COSTS AND FINANCIAL AID

Financial aid office: (914) 378-3421. **Expenses (2005-2006):** Tuition and fees 2005-2006: $11,792; room/board: N/A. **Financial aid:** Priority filing date for institution's financial aid form: May 1.

CAMPUS LIFE AND EXTRACURRICULAR ACTIVITIES

Campus housing available (% using): coed dorms (100%). Students who live in college-owned, operated, or affiliated housing: 3%. **Student employment:** During the 2005-2006 academic year, 40% of undergraduates worked on campus. Average per-year earnings: $13,000. **Clubs and organizations:** Number of student organizations: 16. Activities include: dance, radio station, student government, student newspaper, television station. Number of fraternities: 0; sororities: 0. Average proportion of students who stay on campus on weekends: 35%. **Sports program (2005-2006):** Member of NCAA II. *Men's intercollegiate varsity sports:* baseball, basketball, cross-country, golf, soccer, tennis, track and field (indoor), track and field (outdoor). *Women's intercollegiate varsity sports:* basketball, cross-country, soccer, softball, track and field (indoor), track and field (outdoor), volleyball.

SERVICES AND FACILITIES

Basic services: placement service, health service, health insurance. **Remedial assistance:** reading, math, writing. **Counseling services:** career, personal, academic, psychological. **For learning-disabled students:** School offers a structured program with separate admission and additional fees. Total undergraduates in learning-disabled program or receiving services: 44. Services include: remedial math, remedial English, reading machines, remedial reading, tape recorders, videotaped classes, note-taking services, oral tests, learning center, readers, extended time for tests, tutors, texts on tape. **Information technology resources:** Students are not required to lease or own a computer. Number of campus computers available to all students: 420. School has a wireless network. **Campus safety:** Security services offered: 24-hour foot-and-vehicle patrols, lighted pathways/sidewalks, controlled dormitory access (key, security card, etc).

TRANSFER AND INTERNATIONAL STUDENTS

Transfer students: May apply for admission for the following academic terms: Fall, Spring, Summer. Applicants need a minimum number of credits to apply. For fall 2005: Transfer applications received: 2,081. Transfer applicants offered admission: 1,430. Transfer applicants enrolled: 862. **International students:** Number of foreign undergraduates: 88 (2% of student body). Number of countries represented: 36. Minimum TOEFL score required: 500 (paper); 173 (computer). Average TOEFL score: 500 (paper).

Molloy College

- **Address:** 1000 Hempstead Avenue, PO Box 5002, Rockville Centre, NY 11571
- **Website:** http://www.molloy.edu
- **Private; Religious affiliation:** Roman Catholic
- **Enrollment:** 1,872 full-time; 856 part-time

KEY STATS

- ✔ **U.S News College Ranking:** 79, Universities–Master's (North)
- ✔ **SAT Score (25th/75th percentile):** 915-1155
- ✔ **Tuition:** 2005-2006: $16,560

Selectivity: Selective	**Room/board:** N/A
Acceptance rate: 60%	**Average debt:** $23,000
Student/faculty ratio: 11/1	**Proportion who borrowed:** 70%

UNDERGRADUATE STUDENT BODY STATS

2005-2006 enrollment: 1,872 full-time; 856 part-time. Men: 22%; women: 78%. **Ethnic makeup:** African American: 20%; Asian American: 6%; Hispanic: 8%; White: 66%. **Religious preference:** Protestant: 7%; Jewish: 3%; No preference: 8%; Unknown: 4%; Roman Catholic: 63%.

ADMISSIONS FACTS AND FIGURES

Phone: (888) 466-5569. **Email:** admissions@molloy.edu. **Website:** http://www.molloy.edu. **Application deadlines for fall 2007:** Regular decision: Rolling. Early decision: Not offered. Early action: Send application by: November 15; Decision sent by: December 1. Admission can be deferred. **Application fee:** $30. Common application is accepted. **Admissions requirements/recommendations:** High school units required (recommended): English: 4; Mathematics: 3; Science: 3; Foreign language: 3; Social studies: 4. Tests: The college uses SAT or ACT scores in admissions decisions. Either SAT or ACT required. For admission to the fall 2007 entering class, the school will accept: ACT with writing, ACT without writing. Campus visit: Recommended. Admissions interview: Recommended. Off-campus interview: Not available. **Factors that count in admissions decisions:** *Academic:* Secondary school record: Very important. Class rank: Important. Letters of recommendation: Considered. Standardized test scores: Very important. Essay: Considered. *Nonacademic:* Interview: Considered. Extracurricular activities: Considered. Talent/ability: Considered. Character/personal qualities: Not considered. Alumni/ae relationship: Considered. Geographical residence: Not considered. State residency: Not considered. Religious affiliation/commitment: Not considered. Minority status: Not considered. Volunteer work: Considered. Work experience: Considered. **Admissions statistics for the fall 2005 entering class:** Total applicants: 1,093. Total accepted: 660. Freshmen enrolled: 294; Overall acceptance rate: 60%. Non-early acceptance rate: 60%. **Credentials of fall 2005 freshmen:** 15% ranked in the top 10 percent of their high school class; 68% were in the top 25 percent, and 88% were in the top half. (Proportion submitting class standing: 61%.) **First-year students who submitted SAT scores:** 94%. Scores (25/75 percentile): Verbal: 450-565, Math: 465-590, Combined: 915-1155. **First-year students submitting ACT scores:** 4%. Scores (25/75 percentile): English: N/A, Math: N/A, Composite: N/A.

ACADEMICS

Year founded: 1955. **Academic calendar:** Semester. **Degrees offered:** associate, bachelor's, master's. **Most popular majors:** 30% health professions and related clinical sciences, 19% education, 10% business, management, marketing, and related support services, 6% public administration and social service professions, 5% visual and performing arts. **Major fields of study:** biological and biomedical sciences; business, management, marketing, and related support services; communication, journalism, and related programs; computer and information sciences and support services; education; English language and literature/letters; foreign languages, literatures, and linguistics; health professions and related clinical sciences; history; liberal arts and sciences studies, and humanities; mathematics and statistics; multi/interdisciplinary studies; philosophy and religious studies; psychology; public administration and social service professions; security and protective services; social sciences; visual and performing arts. **Areas of required coursework:** arts/fine arts, humanities, mathematics, English (including composition), philosophy, foreign languages, sciences (biological or physical), history, social science. **Pre-professional programs:** pre-law, pre-dentistry, pre-medicine, pre-veterinary science, pre-optometry. **Special academic programs:** accelerated program, cross-registration, distance learning, double major, English as a Second Language (ESL), honors program, independent study, internships, study abroad, teacher certificate program. **Teacher certification offered in:** special education, elementary, middle/junior high, secondary. **Reserve Officers Training Corps (ROTC):** Army ROTC: Offered at cooperating institution (St. John's University; Hofstra University); Navy ROTC: Offered at cooperating institution (SUNY Maritime (Nursing majors only)); Air Force ROTC: Offered at cooperating institution (New York Institute of Technology). **Faculty and instruction (2005-2006):** Total instructional faculty: 147 full-time, 283 part-time (35% men; 65% women; 9% minorities). Full-time faculty with Ph.D. or other terminal degree: 61%. Student/faculty ratio: 11/1. Classes of fewer than 20 students: 69%; of 20 to 49 students: 31%; of 50 or more students: 0%. **Advanced Placement and International Baccalaureate credit:** AP tests may be used for: Credit only. Scores accepted: 3. International Baccalaureate exams may be used for: Credit only. **Freshmen returning for sophomore year:** 82%. **Graduation rates:** Four-year: 44%; five-year: 58%; six-year: 61%. **Graduate study:** 19% of students pursue further study within one year.

COSTS AND FINANCIAL AID

Financial aid office: (516) 256-2217. **Expenses (2005-2006):** Tuition and fees 2005-2006: $16,560; room/board: N/A. **Financial aid:** Priority filing date for institution's financial aid form: May 1; deadline: May 1. In 2005-2006, 100% of undergraduates applied for financial aid. Of those, 81% were determined to have financial need; 18% had their need fully met. Average financial aid package (proportion receiving): $10,122 (81%). Average amount of gift aid, such as scholarships or grants (proportion receiving): $6,189 (74%). Average amount of self-help aid, such as work study or loans (proportion receiving): $5,162 (70%). Average need-based loan (excluding PLUS or other private loans): $4,797. Among students who received need-based aid, the average percentage of need met: 60%. Among students who received aid based on merit, the average award (and the proportion receiving): $10,788 (18%). The average athletic scholarship (and the proportion receiving): $6,258 (5%). Average amount of debt of borrowers graduating in 2005: $23,000. Proportion who borrowed: 70%.

CAMPUS LIFE AND EXTRACURRICULAR ACTIVITIES

Students who live in college-owned, operated, or affiliated housing: 0%. **Student employment:** During the 2005-2006 academic year, 2% of undergraduates worked on campus. Average per-year earnings: $8,000. **Clubs and organizations:** Number of student organizations: 22. Activities include: choral groups, drama/theater, jazz band, literary magazine, music ensembles, musical theater, student government, student newspaper, yearbook. Number of fraternities: 0; sororities: 0. **Sports program (2005-2006):** Member of NCAA II. *Men's intercollegiate varsity sports:* baseball, basketball, cross-country, lacrosse, soccer, track and field (indoor), track and field (outdoor). *Women's intercollegiate varsity sports:* basketball, cross-country, equestrian sports, soccer, softball, tennis, track and field (indoor), track and field (outdoor), volleyball.

SERVICES AND FACILITIES

Basic services: nonremedial tutoring, women's center, placement service, health service, health insurance. **Remedial assistance:** reading, math, writing, study skills. **Counseling services:** minority student, career, older student. **For learning-disabled students:** School does not offer a structured program with separate admission and additional fees. Total undergraduates in learning-disabled program or receiving services: 41. Services include: remedial math, remedial English, reading machines, remedial reading, tape recorders, note-taking services, extended time for tests, tutors, texts on tape, typist/scribe, other. **Library:** Number of titles: 120,000; number of current serial subscriptions: 715. **Information technology resources:** Students are not required to lease or own a computer. Number of campus computers available to all students: 326. School has a wireless network. Approximate number of users that can be accommodated: 480. **Campus safety:** Security services offered: 24-hour foot-and-vehicle patrols, late-night transport/escort service, 24-hour emergency telephones, lighted pathways/sidewalks.

TRANSFER AND INTERNATIONAL STUDENTS

Transfer students: May apply for admission for the following academic terms: Fall, Spring. Applicants do not need a minimum number of credits to apply. For fall 2005: Transfer applications received: 1,270. Transfer applicants offered admission: 731. Transfer applicants enrolled: 479. **International students:** Number of foreign undergraduates: 5. Number of countries represented: 5. Minimum TOEFL score required: 500 (paper); 175 (computer).

Mount St. Mary College

- **Address:** 330 Powell Avenue, Newburgh, NY 12550
- **Website:** http://www.msmc.edu
- **Private**
- **Enrollment:** 1,615 full-time; 424 part-time

KEY STATS

✔ **U.S News College Ranking:** third tier, Universities–Master's (North)
✔ **SAT Score (25th/75th percentile):** 910-1100
✔ **Tuition:** 2006-2007: $18,290

Selectivity: Less selective	**Room/board:** $9,640
Acceptance rate: 79%	**Average debt:** $20,000
Student/faculty ratio: 17/1	**Proportion who borrowed:** 70%

UNDERGRADUATE STUDENT BODY STATS

2005-2006 enrollment: 1,615 full-time; 424 part-time. Men: 27%; women: 73%. **Ethnic makeup:** African American: 11%; Asian American: 3%; Hispanic: 9%; White: 78%. **Religious preference:** Roman Catholic: 57%; Protestant: 2%; Jewish: 1%; No preference: 10%; Unknown: 12%; Christian, Baptist, Methodist: 11%; Other: 7%.

ADMISSIONS FACTS AND FIGURES

Phone: (845) 569-3248. **Email:** mtstmary@msmc.edu. **Website:** http://www.msmc.edu. **Application deadlines for fall 2007:** Regular decision: Rolling. Early decision: Not offered. Early action: Not offered. Admission can be deferred. **Application fee:** $35. Common application is accepted. **Admissions requirements/recommendations:** High school units required (recommended): English: 4 (4); Mathematics: 3 (3); Science: 3 (3); Foreign language: 3 (3); Social studies: 4 (4); Academic electives: 4 (4); Total units: 21 (21). Tests: The college uses SAT or ACT scores in admissions decisions. Either SAT or ACT required. For admission to the fall 2007 entering class, the school will accept: ACT with writing. Campus visit: Recommended. Admissions interview: Recommended. Off-campus interview: May be arranged. **Factors that count in admissions decisions:** *Academic:* Secondary school record: Very important. Class rank: Very important. Letters of recommendation: Considered. Standardized test scores: Very important. Essay: Considered. *Nonacademic:* Interview: Important. Extracurricular activities: Considered. Talent/ability: Considered. Character/personal qualities: Considered. Alumni/ae relationship: Considered. Geographical residence: Not considered. State residency: Not considered. Religious affiliation/commitment: Not considered. Minority status: Not considered. Volunteer work: Considered. Work experience: Considered. **Other schools with the greatest overlap in applicants:** College of St. Rose; Marist College; SUNY College of Arts and Sciences–New Paltz; SUNY College–Cortland; SUNY College–Oneonta. **Admissions statistics for the fall 2005 entering class:** Total applicants: 1,625. Total accepted: 1,285. Freshmen enrolled: 360; 21% were from out of state. Overall acceptance rate: 79%. **Credentials of fall 2005 freshmen:** 8% ranked in the top 10 percent of their high school class; 27% were in the top 25 percent, and 66% were in the top half. (Proportion submitting class standing: 72%.) **Average high school grade point average:** 3.0. **First-year students who submitted SAT scores:** 91%. Scores (25/75 percentile): Verbal: 450-550, Math: 460-550, Combined: 910-1100. **First-year students submitting ACT scores:** 15%. Scores (25/75 percentile): English: N/A, Math: N/A, Composite: 18-22.

ACADEMICS

Year founded: 1959. **Academic calendar:** Semester. **Degrees offered:** certificate, bachelor's, master's. **Most popular majors:** 21% business, management, marketing, and related support services, 19% education, 14% English language and literature/letters, 12% history, 11% health professions and related clinical sciences. **Major fields of study:** biological and biomedical sciences; business, management, marketing, and related support services; communication, journalism, and related programs; computer and information sciences and support services; education; English language and literature/letters; foreign languages, literatures, and linguistics; health professions and related clinical sciences; history; mathematics and statistics; multi/interdisciplinary studies; physical sciences; psychology; public administration and social service professions; social sciences. **Areas of required coursework:** arts/fine arts, humanities, computer literacy, mathematics, English (including composition), philosophy, sciences (biological or physical), history, social science. **Pre-professional programs:** pre-law, pre-dentistry, pre-medicine, pre-veterinary science. **Special academic programs (% partici-**

pation): accelerated program (26%), cooperative (work-study plan) program (22%), cross-registration (3%), distance learning (10%), double major (5%), dual enrollment (0%), honors program (6%), independent study (9%), internships (19%), liberal arts/career combination (40%), student-designed major (2%), study abroad (3%), teacher certificate program (17%). **Teacher certification offered in:** early childhood, special education, elementary, middle/junior high, secondary. **Cooperative education programs:** business, computer science, education, health professions, humanities, natural science, social/behavioral science, technologies. **Faculty and instruction (2005-2006):** Total instructional faculty: 71 full-time, 150 part-time (46% men; 54% women; 7% minorities). Full-time faculty with Ph.D. or other terminal degree: 82%. Student/faculty ratio: 17/1. Classes of fewer than 20 students: 45%; of 20 to 49 students: 54%; of 50 or more students: 1%. **Advanced Placement and International Baccalaureate credit:** AP tests may be used for: Credit and/or placement. Scores accepted: 4, 5. International Baccalaureate exams may be used for: Credit and/or placement. **Freshmen returning for sophomore year:** 73%. **Graduation rates:** Four-year: 49%; five-year: 57%; six-year: 55%. **Graduate study:** 30% of students pursue further study within one year; 54% within five years. Fields in which graduates pursue further study: Master of Business Administration (MBA), 14%; law, 1%; education, 30%; arts and sciences, 55%.

COSTS AND FINANCIAL AID

Financial aid office: (845) 569-3298. **Expenses (2006-2007):** Tuition and fees 2006-2007: $18,290; room/board: $9,640. Estimated books and supplies: $900; transportation: $1,300; personal expenses: $800. **Financial aid:** Priority filing date for institution's financial aid form: February 15. In 2005-2006, 75% of undergraduates applied for financial aid. Of those, 63% were determined to have financial need; 18% had their need fully met. Average financial aid package (proportion receiving): $10,170 (62%). Average amount of gift aid, such as scholarships or grants (proportion receiving): $6,522 (54%). Average amount of self-help aid, such as work study or loans (proportion receiving): $4,917 (58%). Average need-based loan (excluding PLUS or other private loans): $4,461. Among students who received need-based aid, the average percentage of need met: 56%. Among students who received aid based on merit, the average award (and the proportion receiving): $10,249 (15%). The average athletic scholarship (and the proportion receiving): $0 (0%). Average amount of debt of borrowers graduating in 2005: $20,000. Proportion who borrowed: 70%.

CAMPUS LIFE AND EXTRACURRICULAR ACTIVITIES

Campus housing available (% using): coed dorms (13%), women's dorms (62%), men's dorms (25%), special housing for disabled students. Students who live in college-owned, operated, or affiliated housing: 38%. **Student employment:** During the 2005-2006 academic year, 15% of undergraduates worked on campus. Average per-year earnings: $775. **Clubs and organizations:** Number of student organizations: 24. Activities include: choral groups, concert band, dance, drama/theater, literary magazine, music ensembles, musical theater, radio station, student government, student newspaper, student film society, yearbook. Number of fraternities: 0; sororities: 0. Average proportion of students who stay on campus on weekends: 69%. **Sports program (2005-2006):** Member of NCAA III. *Men's intercollegiate varsity sports:* baseball, basketball, soccer, swimming and diving, tennis. *Women's intercollegiate varsity sports:* basketball, soccer, softball, swimming and diving, tennis, volleyball.

SERVICES AND FACILITIES

Basic services: nonremedial tutoring, placement service, health service, health insurance. **Remedial assistance:** reading, math, writing, study skills. **Counseling services:** career, personal, academic, older student, psychological, religious. **For learning-disabled students:** School does not offer a structured program with separate admission and additional fees. Total undergraduates in learning-disabled program or receiving services: 87. Services include: remedial math, remedial English, remedial reading, tape recorders, other special classes, note-taking services, oral tests, learning center, readers, extended time for tests, tutors, priority registration, priority seating, texts on tape, other testing accomodations. **Library:** Number of titles: 114,814; number of current serial subscriptions: 880. **Information technology resources:** Students are not required to lease or own a computer. Number of campus computers available to all students: 325. School has a wireless network. Approximate number of users that can be accommodated: 2,000. Proportion of college-owned housing units wired for high-speed internet access: 100%. **Campus safety:** Security services offered: 24-hour foot-and-vehicle patrols, late-night transport/escort service, 24-hour emergency telephones, lighted pathways/sidewalks, controlled dormitory access (key, security card, etc.).

TRANSFER AND INTERNATIONAL STUDENTS

Transfer students: May apply for admission for the following academic terms: Fall, Spring. Applicants need a minimum number of credits to apply. For fall 2005: Transfer applications received: 300. Transfer applicants offered admission: 248. Transfer applicants enrolled: 194. **International students:** Number of foreign undergraduates: 0. Number of countries represented: 1. Minimum TOEFL score required: 500 (paper); 200 (computer). Average TOEFL score: 533 (paper).

Nazareth College of Rochester

- **Address:** 4245 East Avenue, Rochester, NY 14618-3790
- **Website:** http://www.naz.edu
- **Private**
- **Enrollment:** 1,864 full-time; 193 part-time

KEY STATS

✔ **U.S News College Ranking:** 25, Universities–Master's (North)
✔ **SAT Score (25th/75th percentile):** 1050-1250
✔ **Tuition:** 2006-2007: $21,616

Selectivity: More selective	**Room/board:** $8,920
Acceptance rate: 79%	**Average debt:** $19,785
Student/faculty ratio: 13/1	**Proportion who borrowed:** 82%

UNDERGRADUATE STUDENT BODY STATS

2005-2006 enrollment: 1,864 full-time; 193 part-time. Men: 24%; women: 76%. **Ethnic makeup:** African American: 5%; Asian American: 2%; Hispanic: 2%; White: 90%.

ADMISSIONS FACTS AND FIGURES

Phone: (585) 389-2860. **Email:** admissions@naz.edu. **Website:** http://www.naz.edu. **Application deadlines for fall 2007:** Regular decision: February 15. Early decision: Send application by: November 15; Decision sent by: December 15. Early action: Send application by: December 15; Decision sent by: January 15. Admission can be deferred. **Application fee:** $40. Common application is accepted. **To apply online, go to:** http://admissions.naz.edu/howtoapply.asp. **Admissions requirements/recommendations:** High school units required (recommended): English: 4 (4); Mathematics: 3 (4); Science: 3 (4); Foreign language: 3 (4); Social studies: 3 (4); Total units: 16 (20). Tests: The college uses SAT or ACT scores in admissions decisions. Either SAT or ACT required. For admission to the fall 2007 entering class, the school will accept: ACT with writing, ACT without writing. Campus visit: Recommended. Admissions interview: Recommended. Off-campus interview: May be arranged. **Factors that count in admissions decisions:** *Academic:* Secondary school record: Very important. Class rank: Very important. Letters of recommendation: Very important. Standardized test scores: Very important. Essay: Very important. *Nonacademic:* Interview: Important. Extracurricular activities: Considered. Talent/ability: Considered. Character/personal qualities: Considered. Alumni/ae relationship: Considered. Geographical residence: Considered. State residency: Considered. Religious affiliation/commitment: Not considered. Minority status: Considered. Volunteer work: Considered. Work experience: Considered. **Other schools with the greatest overlap in applicants:** Ithaca College; Le Moyne College; SUNY College of Arts and Sciences–Geneseo; SUNY–Fredonia; St. John Fisher College. **Admissions statistics for the fall 2005 entering class:** Total applicants: 1,972. Total accepted: 1,561. Freshmen enrolled: 453; 6% were from out of state. Accepted through early-decision or early-action plans: 43%. Overall acceptance rate: 79%. Early-decision acceptance rate: 67%. Non-early acceptance rate: 78%. **Size of waiting list:** 84 applicants; enrolled from waiting list: 26. **Credentials of fall 2005 freshmen:** 29% ranked in the top 10 percent of their high school class; 66% were in the top 25 percent, and 92% were in the top half. (Proportion submitting class standing: 87%.) **Average high school grade point average:** 3.4. **First-year students who submitted SAT scores:** 100%. Scores (25/75 percentile): Verbal: 520-630, Math: 530-620, Combined: 1050-1250. **First-year students submitting ACT scores:** 40%. Scores (25/75 percentile): English: N/A, Math: N/A, Composite: 22-28.

ACADEMICS

Year founded: 1924. **Academic calendar:** Semester. **Degrees offered:** bachelor's, master's, doctorate. **Most popular majors:** 17% health professions and related clinical sciences, 14% psychology, 11% English language and litera-

ture/letters, 11% business, management, marketing, and related support services, 8% education. **Major fields of study:** area, ethnic, cultural, and gender studies; biological and biomedical sciences; business, management, marketing, and related support services; communication, journalism, and related programs; computer and information sciences and support services; education; English language and literature/letters; foreign languages, literatures, and linguistics; health professions and related clinical sciences; history; mathematics and statistics; multi/interdisciplinary studies; philosophy and religious studies; physical sciences; psychology; public administration and social service professions; social sciences; visual and performing arts. **Areas of required coursework:** arts/fine arts, humanities, computer literacy, mathematics, English (including composition), philosophy, foreign languages, sciences (biological or physical), history, social science. **Pre-professional programs:** pre-law, pre-dentistry, pre-medicine, pre-veterinary science. **Special academic programs (% participation):** cross-registration (3.4%), double major (5.1%), exchange student program (domestic) (0%), honors program (1.7%), independent study (7.1%), internships (73.3%), study abroad (9.4%), teacher certificate program (32.6%). **Teacher certification offered in:** special education, elementary, middle/junior high, secondary. **Reserve Officers Training Corps (ROTC):** Army ROTC: Offered at cooperating institution (Rochester Institute of Technology); Air Force ROTC: Offered at cooperating institution (Rochester Institute of Technology). **Faculty and instruction (2005-2006):** Total instructional faculty: 135 full-time, 167 part-time (37% men; 63% women; 9% minorities). Full-time faculty with Ph.D. or other terminal degree: 93%. Student/faculty ratio: 13/1. Classes of fewer than 20 students: 58%; of 20 to 49 students: 42%; of 50 or more students: 0%. **Advanced Placement and International Baccalaureate credit:** AP tests may be used for: Credit only. Scores accepted: 3, 4, 5. International Baccalaureate exams may be used for: Credit only. **Freshmen returning for sophomore year:** 84%. **Graduation rates:** Four-year: 62%; five-year: 73%; six-year: 73%. **Graduate study:** 15% of students pursue further study immediately upon graduation; 56% within one year; 62% within five years. Fields in which graduates pursue further study: Master of Business Administration (MBA), 2%; law, 2%; medicine, 1%; education, 39%; arts and sciences, 7%.

COSTS AND FINANCIAL AID

Financial aid office: (585) 389-2310. **Expenses (2006-2007):** Tuition and fees 2006-2007: $21,616; room/board: $8,920. Estimated books and supplies: $800; transportation: $200; personal expenses: $1,100. **Financial aid:** Priority filing date for institution's financial aid form: February 15; deadline: May 1. In 2005-2006, 90% of undergraduates applied for financial aid. Of those, 78% were determined to have financial need; 17% had their need fully met. Average financial aid package (proportion receiving): $15,551 (78%). Average amount of gift aid, such as scholarships or grants (proportion receiving): $10,299 (78%). Average amount of self-help aid, such as work study or loans (proportion receiving): $5,441 (66%). Average need-based loan (excluding PLUS or other private loans): $4,719. Among students who received need-based aid, the average percentage of need met: 76%. Among students who received aid based on merit, the average award (and the proportion receiving): $7,811 (18%). Average amount of debt of borrowers graduating in 2005: $19,785. Proportion who borrowed: 82%.

CAMPUS LIFE AND EXTRACURRICULAR ACTIVITIES

Campus housing available (% using): coed dorms (62%), women's dorms (7%), apartment for single students (16%), special housing for disabled students (0%), other housing options (15%). Students who live in college-owned, operated, or affiliated housing: 59%. **Student employment:** During the 2005-2006 academic year, 14% of undergraduates worked on campus. Average per-year earnings: $108. **Clubs and organizations:** Number of student organizations: 51. Activities include: choral groups, concert band, dance, drama/theater, jazz band, literary magazine, music ensembles, musical theater, opera, radio station, student government, student newspaper, yearbook. Number of fraternities: 0; sororities: 0. Average proportion of students who stay on campus on weekends: 85%. **Sports program (2005-2006):** Member of NCAA III. *Men's intercollegiate varsity sports:* basketball, cross-country, golf, lacrosse, soccer, swimming and diving, tennis, track and field (indoor), track and field (outdoor), volleyball. *Women's intercollegiate varsity sports:* basketball, cross-country, equestrian sports, field hockey, golf, lacrosse, soccer, swimming and diving, tennis, track and field (indoor), track and field (outdoor), volleyball.

SERVICES AND FACILITIES

Basic services: nonremedial tutoring, placement service, day care, health service, health insurance. **Remedial assistance:** math, writing. **Counseling services:** minority student, career, personal, academic, older student, psychological, birth control, religious. **For learning-disabled students:** School does not offer a structured program with separate admission and additional fees. Total undergraduates in learning-disabled program or receiving services: 93. Services include: reading machines, tape recorders, untimed tests, note-taking services, oral tests, readers, extended time for tests, tutors, texts on tape, other. **Library:** Number of titles: 251,506; number of current serial subscriptions: 1,760. **Information technology resources:** Students are not required to lease or own a computer. Number of campus computers available to all students: 190. School has a wireless network. Approximate number of users that can be accommodated: 300. Proportion of college-owned housing units wired for high-speed internet access: 100%. **Campus safety:** Security services offered: 24-hour foot-and-vehicle patrols, late-night transport/escort service, 24-hour emergency telephones, lighted pathways/sidewalks, student patrols, controlled dormitory access (key, security card, etc).

TRANSFER AND INTERNATIONAL STUDENTS
Transfer students: May apply for admission for the following academic terms: Fall, Spring, Summer. Applicants need a minimum number of credits to apply. **International students:** Number of foreign undergraduates: 10 (1% of student body). Number of countries represented: 2. Minimum TOEFL score required: 550 (paper); 213 (computer). Average TOEFL score: 600 (paper).

New School University

- **Address:** 66 W. 12th Street, New York, NY 10011
- **Website:** http://www.newschool.edu
- **Private**
- **Enrollment:** 4,628 full-time; 754 part-time

KEY STATS
✔ **U.S News College Ranking:** third tier, National Universities
✔ **SAT Score (25th/75th percentile):** 1000-1250
✔ **Tuition:** 2006-2007: $29,210

Selectivity: Selective	**Room/board:** $11,750
Acceptance rate: 51%	**Average debt:** $19,071
Student/faculty ratio: 8/1	**Proportion who borrowed:** 61%

UNDERGRADUATE STUDENT BODY STATS
2005-2006 enrollment: 4,628 full-time; 754 part-time. Men: 30%; women: 70%. **Ethnic makeup:** African American: 5%; Asian American: 11%; Hispanic: 6%; White: 56%; International: 22%.

ADMISSIONS FACTS AND FIGURES
Phone: (877) 528-3321. **Email:** studentinfo@newschool.edu. **Website:** http://www.newschool.edu. **Application deadlines for fall 2007:** Regular decision: February 1; decision sent by April 1. Early decision: Send application by: November 15; Decision sent by: December 15. Early action: Not offered. Admission can be deferred. **Application fee:** $40. Common application is accepted. **Admissions requirements/recommendations:** High school units required (recommended): English: 4; Mathematics: (3); Science: (3); Foreign language: (2); Social studies: (3); History: (2); Total units: 16 (18). Tests: The college uses SAT or ACT scores in admissions decisions. Neither SAT nor ACT required. Campus visit: Recommended. Admissions interview: Recommended. Off-campus interview: May be arranged. **Factors that count in admissions decisions:** *Academic:* Secondary school record: Very important. Class rank: Considered. Letters of recommendation: Very important. Standardized test scores: Important. Essay: Very important. *Nonacademic:* Interview: Important. Extracurricular activities: Considered. Talent/ability: Important. Character/personal qualities: Important. Alumni/ae relationship: Considered. Geographical residence: Considered. State residency: Not considered. Religious affiliation/commitment: Not considered. Minority status: Considered. Volunteer work: Important. Work experience: Considered. **Admissions statistics for the fall 2005 entering class:** Total applicants: 3,951. Total accepted: 2,023. Freshmen enrolled: 803; Overall acceptance rate: 51%. Non-early acceptance rate: 51%. **Size of waiting list:** 183 applicants; enrolled from waiting list: 36. **Credentials of fall 2005 freshmen:** 17% ranked in the top 10 percent of their high school class; 48% were in the top 25 percent, and 82% were in the top half. (Proportion submitting class standing: 33%.) **Average high school grade point average:** 3.2. **First-year students who submitted SAT scores:** 68%. Scores (25/75 percentile): Verbal: 500-630, Math: 500-620, Combined: 1000-1250.

ACADEMICS
Year founded: 1919. **Academic calendar:** Semester. **Degrees offered:** certificate, diploma, associate, bachelor's, post-bachelor's certificate, master's, doctorate. **Most popular majors:** 51% visual and performing arts, 35% liberal arts and sciences studies, and humanities, 10% business, management, marketing, and related support services, 3% physical sciences. **Major fields of study:** architecture and related services; liberal arts and sciences studies, and humanities; visual and performing arts. **Areas of required coursework:** arts/fine arts, computer literacy, English (including composition), social science. **Special academic programs:** accelerated program, cooperative (work-study plan) program, cross-registration, distance learning, dual enrollment, English as a Second Language (ESL), exchange student program (domestic), independent study, internships, liberal arts/career combination, student-designed major, study abroad, teacher certificate program. **Faculty and instruction (2005-2006):** Total instructional faculty: 653 full-time, 1,967 part-time (60% men; 40% women; 16% minorities). Student/faculty ratio: 8/1. Classes of fewer than 20 students: 89%; of 20 to 49 students: 11%; of 50 or more students: 1%. **Advanced Placement and International Baccalaureate credit:** AP tests may be used for: Credit and/or placement. Scores accepted: 4, 5. International Baccalaureate exams may be used for: Credit and/or placement. **Freshmen returning for sophomore year:** 81%. **Graduation rates:** Four-year: 44%; five-year: 57%; six-year: 59%.

COSTS AND FINANCIAL AID
Financial aid office: (212) 229-8930. **Expenses (2006-2007):** Tuition and fees 2006-2007: $29,210; room/board: $11,750. Estimated books and supplies: $1,055; transportation: $630; personal expenses: $1,550. **Financial aid:** Priority filing date for institution's financial aid form: March 1. In 2005-2006, 55% of undergraduates applied for financial aid. Of those, 38% were determined to have financial need; 13% had their need fully met. Average financial aid package (proportion receiving): $14,338 (38%). Average amount of gift aid, such as scholarships or grants (proportion receiving): $10,012 (35%). Average amount of self-help aid, such as work study or loans (proportion receiving): $4,617 (32%). Average need-based loan (excluding PLUS or other private loans): $4,889. Among students who received need-based aid, the average percentage of need met: 81%. Among students who received aid based on merit, the average award (and the proportion receiving): $4,157 (15%). The average athletic scholarship (and the proportion receiving): $0 (0%). Average amount of debt of borrowers graduating in 2005: $19,071. Proportion who borrowed: 61%.

CAMPUS LIFE AND EXTRACURRICULAR ACTIVITIES
Campus housing available (% using): coed dorms (100%), special housing for disabled students (0%). Activities include: choral groups, concert band, dance, drama/theater, jazz band, literary magazine, music ensembles, musical theater, opera, student government, student newspaper, student film society, symphony orchestra. Number of fraternities: 0; sororities: 0. Average proportion of students who stay on campus on weekends: 95%.

SERVICES AND FACILITIES
Basic services: health service, health insurance. **Remedial assistance:** writing. **Counseling services:** career, personal, academic, psychological, birth control. **For learning-disabled students:** School does not offer a structured program with separate admission and additional fees. Total undergraduates in learning-disabled program or receiving services: 67. Services include: tape recorders, note-taking services, readers, extended time for tests, early syllabus, priority registration, priority seating, texts on tape, exams on tape or computer, other testing accomodations, other. **Library:** Number of titles: 111,250; number of current serial subscriptions: 561. **Information technology resources:** Students are not required to lease or own a computer. Number of campus computers available to all students: 997. School has a wireless network. Proportion of college-owned housing units wired for high-speed internet access: 90%. **Campus safety:** Security services offered: 24-hour emergency telephones, lighted pathways/sidewalks, controlled dormitory access (key, security card, etc).

TRANSFER AND INTERNATIONAL STUDENTS
Transfer students: May apply for admission for the following academic terms: Fall, Spring, Summer. Applicants need a minimum number of credits to apply. For fall 2005: Transfer applications received: 2,943. Transfer applicants offered admission: 1,891. Transfer applicants enrolled: 1,128. **International students:** Number of foreign undergraduates: 1180 (22% of student body). Number of countries represented: 105. Minimum TOEFL score required: 560 (paper); 213 (computer).

New York Institute of Technology

- **Address:** PO Box 8000, Old Westbury, NY 11568-8000
- **Website:** http://www.nyit.edu
- **Private**
- **Enrollment:** 4,686 full-time; 1,536 part-time

KEY STATS

- ✔ **U.S News College Ranking:** 77, Universities–Master's (North)
- ✔ **SAT Score (25th/75th percentile):** 1030-1240
- ✔ **Tuition:** 2006-2007: $20,358

Selectivity: Selective	**Room/board:** $9,226
Acceptance rate: 75%	**Average debt:** $20,725
Student/faculty ratio: 15/1	**Proportion who borrowed:** 61%

UNDERGRADUATE STUDENT BODY STATS

2005-2006 enrollment: 4,686 full-time; 1,536 part-time. Men: 61%; women: 39%. **Ethnic makeup:** African American: 11%; Asian American: 10%; Hispanic: 10%; White: 64%; International: 6%.

ADMISSIONS FACTS AND FIGURES

Phone: (516) 686-7520. **Email:** admissions@nyit.edu. **Website:** http://www.nyit.edu. **Application deadlines for fall 2007:** Regular decision: Rolling. Early decision: Not offered. Early action: Not offered. Admission can be deferred. **Application fee:** $50. Common application is accepted. **Admissions requirements/recommendations:** High school units required (recommended): English: 4 (4); Mathematics: 2 (3); Science: 2 (2); Social studies: 2 (2); Academic electives: 7 (7); Total units: 17 (17). Tests: The college uses SAT or ACT scores in admissions decisions. Either SAT or ACT required. For admission to the fall 2007 entering class, the school will accept: ACT without writing. Campus visit: Recommended. Admissions interview: Recommended. Off-campus interview: Not available. **Factors that count in admissions decisions:** *Academic:* Secondary school record: Very important. Class rank: Considered. Letters of recommendation: Considered. Standardized test scores: Important. Essay: Important. *Nonacademic:* Interview: Important. Extracurricular activities: Considered. Talent/ability: Considered. Character/personal qualities: Considered. Alumni/ae relationship: Not considered. Geographical residence: Not considered. State residency: Not considered. Religious affiliation/commitment: Not considered. Minority status: Not considered. Volunteer work: Considered. Work experience: Considered. **Admissions statistics for the fall 2005 entering class:** Total applicants: 3,743. Total accepted: 2,813. Freshmen enrolled: 990; 11% were from out of state. Overall acceptance rate: 75%. **Credentials of fall 2005 freshmen:** 20% ranked in the top 10 percent of their high school class; 49% were in the top 25 percent, and 77% were in the top half. (Proportion submitting class standing: 39%.) **Average high school grade point average:** 3.2. **First-year students who submitted SAT scores:** 84%. Scores (25/75 percentile): Verbal: 490-600, Math: 540-640, Combined: 1030-1240. **First-year students submitting ACT scores:** 7%. Scores (25/75 percentile): English: N/A, Math: N/A, Composite: 20-27.

ACADEMICS

Year founded: 1955. **Academic calendar:** Semester. **Degrees offered:** certificate, associate, bachelor's, post-bachelor's certificate, master's, post-master's certificate, first professional, doctorate. **Most popular majors:** 25% business, management, marketing, and related support services, 12% visual and performing arts, 11% architecture and related services, 11% communication, journalism, and related programs, 9% computer and information sciences and support services. **Major fields of study:** architecture and related services; biological and biomedical sciences; business, management, marketing, and related support services; communication, journalism, and related programs; computer and information sciences and support services; education; engineering; engineering technologies/technicians; English language and literature/letters; health professions and related clinical sciences; multi/interdisciplinary studies; physical sciences; psychology; security and protective services; social sciences; visual and performing arts. **Areas of required coursework:** humanities, computer literacy, mathematics, English (including composition), philosophy, sciences (biological or physical), history, social science, other. **Pre-professional programs:** pre-law, pre-medicine. **Special academic programs:** accelerated program, cooperative (work-study plan) program, cross-registration, distance learning, double major, dual enrollment, English as a Second Language (ESL), honors program, independent study, internships, liberal arts/career combination, study abroad,

teacher certificate program, weekend college, other. **Teacher certification offered in:** early childhood, elementary, vo-tech, middle/junior high, secondary. **Reserve Officers Training Corps (ROTC):** Army ROTC: Offered on campus; Air Force ROTC: Offered on campus. **Faculty and instruction (2005-2006):** Total instructional faculty: 279 full-time, 570 part-time (64% men; 36% women; 14% minorities). Student/faculty ratio: 15/1. Classes of fewer than 20 students: 68%; of 20 to 49 students: 31%; of 50 or more students: 1%. **Advanced Placement and International Baccalaureate credit:** AP tests may be used for: Credit and/or placement. Scores accepted: 3, 4, 5. International Baccalaureate exams may be used for: Credit and/or placement. **Freshmen returning for sophomore year:** 71%. **Graduation rates:** Four-year: 18%; five-year: 35%; six-year: 41%. **Graduate study:** 15% of students pursue further study immediately upon graduation; 13% within one year; 13% within five years. Fields in which graduates pursue further study: Master of Business Administration (MBA), 17%; law, 3%; medicine, 7%; engineering, 22%; education, 14%; arts and sciences, 14%.

COSTS AND FINANCIAL AID

Financial aid office: (516) 686-7680. **Expenses (2006-2007):** Tuition and fees 2006-2007: $20,358; room/board: $9,226. Estimated books and supplies: $1,200; transportation: $1,300; personal expenses: $2,550. **Financial aid:** Priority filing date for institution's financial aid form: March 1. In 2005-2006, 83% of undergraduates applied for financial aid. Of those, 75% were determined to have financial need; 23% had their need fully met. Average financial aid package (proportion receiving): $13,616 (74%). Average amount of gift aid, such as scholarships or grants (proportion receiving): $5,089 (65%). Average amount of self-help aid, such as work study or loans (proportion receiving): $4,004 (60%). Average need-based loan (excluding PLUS or other private loans): $3,857. Among students who received need-based aid, the average percentage of need met: 79%. Among students who received aid based on merit, the average award (and the proportion receiving): $7,268 (13%). The average athletic scholarship (and the proportion receiving): $13,637 (1%). Average amount of debt of borrowers graduating in 2005: $20,725. Proportion who borrowed: 61%.

CAMPUS LIFE AND EXTRACURRICULAR ACTIVITIES

Campus housing available (% using): coed dorms (100%), special housing for disabled students. Students who live in college-owned, operated, or affiliated housing: 4%. **Student employment:** During the 2005-2006 academic year, 10% of undergraduates worked on campus. Average per-year earnings: $2,500. **Clubs and organizations:** Number of student organizations: 100. Activities include: choral groups, dance, drama/theater, literary magazine, musical theater, radio station, student government, student newspaper, student film society, television station, yearbook. Number of fraternities: 5; sororities: 3. Proportion of men in fraternities: 1%; of women in sororities: 1%. Average proportion of students who stay on campus on weekends: 44%. **Sports program (2005-2006):** Member of NCAA II. *Men's intercollegiate varsity sports:* baseball, basketball, cross-country, lacrosse, soccer, track and field (indoor), track and field (outdoor). *Women's intercollegiate varsity sports:* basketball, cross-country, soccer, softball, track and field (indoor), track and field (outdoor), volleyball.

SERVICES AND FACILITIES

Basic services: nonremedial tutoring, placement service, health service, health insurance. **Remedial assistance:** reading, math, writing, study skills. **Counseling services:** minority student, career, personal, veteran student, academic, psychological. **For learning-disabled students:** School does not offer a structured program with separate admission and additional fees. Total undergraduates in learning-disabled program or receiving services: 125. Services include: remedial math, remedial English, remedial reading, tape recorders, untimed tests, note-taking services, oral tests, learning center, readers, tutors, early syllabus, exams on tape or computer. **Library:** Number of titles: 185,471; number of current serial subscriptions: 2,259. **Information technology resources:** Students are required to lease or own a computer. Number of campus computers available to all students: 740. School has a wireless network. Approximate number of users that can be accommodated: 600. Proportion of college-owned housing units wired for high-speed internet access: 100%. **Campus safety:** Security services offered: 24-hour foot-and-vehicle patrols, late-night transport/escort service, 24-hour emergency telephones, lighted pathways/sidewalks, controlled dormitory access (key, security card, etc).

TRANSFER AND INTERNATIONAL STUDENTS

Transfer students: May apply for admission for the following academic terms: Fall, Spring, Summer. Applicants need a minimum number of credits to apply. For fall 2005: Transfer applications received: 1,600. Transfer

applicants offered admission: 1,122. Transfer applicants enrolled: 568.
International students: Number of foreign undergraduates: 300 (6% of student body). Number of countries represented: 75. Minimum TOEFL score required: 550 (paper); 213 (computer). Average TOEFL score: 560 (paper).

New York University

- **Address:** 70 Washington Square S, New York, NY 10012
- **Website:** http://www.nyu.edu
- **Private**
- **Enrollment:** 18,981 full-time; 1,585 part-time

KEY STATS
✔ **U.S News College Ranking:** 34, National Universities
✔ **SAT Score (25th/75th percentile):** 1240-1420
✔ **Tuition:** 2006-2007: $33,420
   Selectivity: Most selective   **Room/board:** $11,780
   Acceptance rate: 37%   **Average debt:** $29,480
   Student/faculty ratio: 11/1   **Proportion who borrowed:** 61%

UNDERGRADUATE STUDENT BODY STATS
2005-2006 enrollment: 18,981 full-time; 1,585 part-time. Men: 39%; women: 61%. **Ethnic makeup:** African American: 5%; Asian American: 17%; Hispanic: 8%; White: 66%; International: 4%.

ADMISSIONS FACTS AND FIGURES
Phone: (212) 998-4500. **Email:** admissions@nyu.edu. **Website:** http://www.nyu.edu. **Application deadlines for fall 2007:** Regular decision: January 15; decision sent by April 1. Early decision: Send application by: November 1; Decision sent by: December 15. Early action: Not offered. Admission can be deferred. **Application fee:** $65. Common application is accepted. **To apply online, go to:** http://admissions.nyu.edu/appprocess/. **Admissions requirements/recommendations:** High school units required (recommended): English: 4; Mathematics: 3 (4); Science: 3; Foreign language: 2 (3); History: 4; Total units: 18. Tests: The college uses SAT or ACT scores in admissions decisions. Either SAT or ACT required. For admission to the fall 2007 entering class, the school will accept: ACT with writing. Campus visit: Recommended. Admissions interview: Neither required nor recommended. Off-campus interview: Not available. **Factors that count in admissions decisions: Academic:** Secondary school record: Very important. Class rank: Important. Letters of recommendation: Very important. Standardized test scores: Very important. Essay: Very important. *Nonacademic:* Interview: Not considered. Extracurricular activities: Important. Talent/ability: Important. Character/personal qualities: Important. Alumni/ae relationship: Important. Geographical residence: Important. State residency: Not considered. Religious affiliation/commitment: Not considered. Minority status: Important. Volunteer work: Important. Work experience: Considered. **Other schools with the greatest overlap in applicants:** Boston University; Columbia University; Harvard University; University of Pennsylvania; Yale University. **Admissions statistics for the fall 2005 entering class:** Total applicants: 34,509. Total accepted: 12,662. Freshmen enrolled: 4,676; 65% were from out of state. Accepted through early-decision or early-action plans: 33%. Overall acceptance rate: 37%. Early-decision acceptance rate: 47%. Non-early acceptance rate: 36%. **Size of waiting list:** 1608 applicants; enrolled from waiting list: 41. **Credentials of fall 2005 freshmen:** 68% ranked in the top 10 percent of their high school class; 95% were in the top 25 percent, and 100% were in the top half. (Proportion submitting class standing: 43%.) **Average high school grade point average:** 3.6. First-year students who submitted SAT scores: 93%. Scores (25/75 percentile): Verbal: 620-710, Math: 620-710, Combined: 1240-1420. **First-year students submitting ACT scores:** 7%. Scores (25/75 percentile): English: N/A, Math: N/A, Composite: 27-31.

ACADEMICS
Year founded: 1831. **Academic calendar:** Semester. **Degrees offered:** certificate, diploma, associate, transfer-associate, terminal-associate, bachelor's, post-bachelor's certificate, master's, post-master's certificate, first professional, first professional certificate, doctorate. **Most popular majors:** 8% drama and dramatics/theater arts, 7% finance, 7% liberal arts and sciences/liberal studies, 5% cinematography and film/video production, 5% economics. **Major fields of study:** area, ethnic, cultural, and gender studies; biological and biomedical sciences; business, management, marketing, and related support services; communication, journalism, and related programs; communications technologies/technicians and support services; computer and information sciences and support services; education; English language and literature/letters; family and consumer sciences/human sciences; foreign languages, literatures, and linguistics; health professions and related clinical sciences; history; legal professions and studies; liberal arts and sciences studies, and humanities; mathematics and statistics; multi/interdisciplinary studies; parks, recreation, leisure, and fitness studies; philosophy and religious studies; physical sciences; psychology; public administration and social service professions; social sciences; visual and performing arts. **Areas of required coursework:** arts/fine arts, humanities, mathematics, English (including composition), foreign languages, sciences (biological or physical), history, social science, other. **Pre-professional programs:** pre-law, pre-dentistry, pre-medicine, pre-veterinary science, pre-optometry. **Special academic programs:** accelerated program, cross-registration, distance learning, double major, English as a Second Language (ESL), exchange student program (domestic), honors program, independent study, internships, liberal arts/career combination, student-designed major, study abroad, teacher certificate program, weekend college, other. **Teacher certification offered in:** early childhood, special education, elementary, secondary. **Faculty and instruction (2005-2006):** Total instructional faculty: 1,952 full-time, 2,121 part-time (57% men; 43% women). Full-time faculty with Ph.D. or other terminal degree: 90%. Student/faculty ratio: 11/1. Classes of fewer than 20 students: 60%; of 20 to 49 students: 28%; of 50 or more students: 12%. **Advanced Placement and International Baccalaureate credit:** AP tests may be used for: Credit and/or placement. Scores accepted: 4, 5. International Baccalaureate exams may be used for: Credit and/or placement. **Freshmen returning for sophomore year:** 92%. **Graduation rates:** Four-year: 74%; five-year: 81%; six-year: 83%. **Graduate study:** 22% of students pursue further study immediately upon graduation; 25% within one year; 92% within five years. Fields in which graduates pursue further study: Master of Business Administration (MBA), 1%; law, 10%; medicine, 7%; dentistry, 1%; education, 5%; arts and sciences, 4%.

COSTS AND FINANCIAL AID
Financial aid office: (212) 998-4444. **Expenses (2006-2007):** Tuition and fees 2006-2007: $33,420; room/board: $11,780. **Financial aid:** In 2005-2006, 64% of undergraduates applied for financial aid. Of those, 54% were determined to have financial need; Average financial aid package (proportion receiving): $18,652 (54%). Average amount of gift aid, such as scholarships or grants (proportion receiving): $12,592 (51%). Average amount of self-help aid, such as work study or loans (proportion receiving): $6,635 (49%). Average need-based loan (excluding PLUS or other private loans): $5,070. Among students who received need-based aid, the average percentage of need met: 64%. Among students who received aid based on merit, the average award (and the proportion receiving): $6,925 (10%). The average athletic scholarship (and the proportion receiving): $0 (0%). Average amount of debt of borrowers graduating in 2005: $29,480. Proportion who borrowed: 61%.

CAMPUS LIFE AND EXTRACURRICULAR ACTIVITIES
Campus housing available: coed dorms, sorority housing, fraternity housing, apartment for single students, special housing for disabled students, other housing options. Students who live in college-owned, operated, or affiliated housing: 54%. **Student employment:** During the 2005-2006 academic year, 17% of undergraduates worked on campus. Average per-year earnings: $4,000. **Clubs and organizations:** Number of student organizations: 386. Activities include: choral groups, concert band, dance, drama/theater, jazz band, literary magazine, music ensembles, musical theater, opera, radio station, student government, student newspaper, student film society, symphony orchestra, television station, yearbook. Number of fraternities: 13; sororities: 13. Proportion of men in fraternities: 4%; of women in sororities: 2%. **Sports program (2005-2006):** Member of NCAA III. *Men's intercollegiate varsity sports:* basketball, cross-country, fencing, golf, soccer, swimming and diving, tennis, track and field (indoor), track and field (outdoor), volleyball, wrestling. *Women's intercollegiate varsity sports:* basketball, cheerleading, cross-country, fencing, soccer, swimming and diving, tennis, track and field (indoor), track and field (outdoor), volleyball.

SERVICES AND FACILITIES
Basic services: nonremedial tutoring, women's center, placement service, health service, health insurance. **Counseling services:** minority student, career, personal, academic, older student, psychological, birth control, religious. **For learning-disabled students:** School does not offer a structured program with separate admission and additional fees. Total undergraduates in learning-disabled program or receiving services: 324. Services include: read-

ing machines, tape recorders, note-taking services, learning center, readers, extended time for tests, tutors, other testing accomodations. **Library:** Number of titles: 5,390,289; number of current serial subscriptions: 54,024. **Information technology resources:** Students are not required to lease or own a computer. Number of campus computers available to all students: 4,500. School has a wireless network. Approximate number of users that can be accommodated: 12,000. Proportion of college-owned housing units wired for high-speed internet access: 100%. **Campus safety:** Security services offered: 24-hour foot-and-vehicle patrols, late-night transport/escort service, 24-hour emergency telephones, lighted pathways/sidewalks, student patrols, controlled dormitory access (key, security card, etc).

TRANSFER AND INTERNATIONAL STUDENTS
Transfer students: May apply for admission for the following academic terms: Fall, Spring, Summer. Applicants do not need a minimum number of credits to apply. For fall 2005: Transfer applications received: 4,412. Transfer applicants offered admission: 1,245. Transfer applicants enrolled: 695. **International students:** Number of foreign undergraduates: 820 (4% of student body). Number of countries represented: 91. Minimum TOEFL score required: 600 (paper); 250 (computer).

Niagara University

- **Address:** Niagara University, NY 14109
- **Website:** http://www.niagara.edu
- **Private; Religious affiliation:** Roman Catholic (Vincentian)
- **Enrollment:** 2,816 full-time; 126 part-time

KEY STATS
✔ **U.S News College Ranking:** 56, Universities–Master's (North)
✔ **SAT Score (25th/75th percentile):** 960-1130
✔ **Tuition:** 2006-2007: $21,240

Selectivity: Selective	**Room/board:** $8,850
Acceptance rate: 79%	**Average debt:** $17,163
Student/faculty ratio: 16/1	**Proportion who borrowed:** 80%

UNDERGRADUATE STUDENT BODY STATS
2005-2006 enrollment: 2,816 full-time; 126 part-time. Men: 39%; women: 61%. **Ethnic makeup:** African American: 4%; American-Indian: 1%; Asian American: 1%; Hispanic: 1%; White: 88%; International: 5%. **Religious preference:** Roman Catholic: 47%; Protestant: 15%; No preference: 8%; Unknown: 21%.

ADMISSIONS FACTS AND FIGURES
Phone: (716) 286-8700. **Email:** admissions@niagara.edu. **Website:** http://www.niagara.edu. **Application deadlines for fall 2007:** Regular decision: August 1. Early decision: Not offered. Early action: Send application by: December 10; Decision sent by: December 10. Admission can be deferred. **Application fee:** $30. Common application is not accepted. **Admissions requirements/recommendations:** High school units required (recommended): English: 4; Mathematics: 2; Science: 2; Foreign language: 2; Social studies: 2; Academic electives: 4; Total units: 16. Tests: The college uses SAT or ACT scores in admissions decisions. Either SAT or ACT required. For admission to the fall 2007 entering class, the school will accept: ACT with writing, ACT without writing. Campus visit: Recommended. Admissions interview: Recommended. Off-campus interview: May be arranged. **Factors that count in admissions decisions:** *Academic:* Secondary school record: Very important. Class rank: Important. Letters of recommendation: Important. Standardized test scores: Important. Essay: Considered. *Nonacademic:* Interview: Important. Extracurricular activities: Considered. Talent/ability: Considered. Character/personal qualities: Considered. Alumni/ae relationship: Considered. Geographical residence: Not considered. State residency: Not considered. Religious affiliation/commitment: Not considered. Minority status: Not considered. Volunteer work: Considered. Work experience: Considered. **Other schools with the greatest overlap in applicants:** Canisius College; SUNY College of Arts and Sciences–Geneseo; SUNY–Fredonia; St. John Fisher College; University at Buffalo–SUNY. **Admissions statistics for the fall 2005 entering class:** Total applicants: 3,246. Total accepted: 2,555. Freshmen enrolled: 735; 8% were from out of state. Overall acceptance rate: 79%. **Credentials of fall 2005 freshmen:** 14% ranked in the top 10 percent of their high school class; 40% were in the top 25 percent, and 78% were in the top half. (Proportion

submitting class standing: 78%.) **Average high school grade point average:** 3.3. **First-year students who submitted SAT scores:** 96%. Scores (25/75 percentile): Verbal: 480-560, Math: 480-570, Combined: 960-1130. **First-year students submitting ACT scores:** 30%. Scores (25/75 percentile): English: 19-25, Math: 19-26, Composite: 20-25.

ACADEMICS
Year founded: 1856. **Academic calendar:** Semester. **Degrees offered:** certificate, associate, bachelor's, post-bachelor's certificate, master's, post-master's certificate. **Most popular majors:** 33% business/commerce, 23% education, 8% security and protective services, 7% psychology, 5% visual and performing arts. **Major fields of study:** biological and biomedical sciences; business, management, marketing, and related support services; communication, journalism, and related programs; computer and information sciences and support services; education; English language and literature/letters; foreign languages, literatures, and linguistics; history; mathematics and statistics; philosophy and religious studies; physical sciences; psychology; security and protective services; social sciences; transportation and materials moving; visual and performing arts. **Areas of required coursework:** humanities, mathematics, English (including composition), philosophy, sciences (biological or physical), history, social science, other. **Pre-professional programs:** pre-law, pre-dentistry, pre-medicine, pre-theology, pre-veterinary science, pre-pharmacy. **Special academic programs (% participation):** cooperative (work-study plan) program (5%), cross-registration (1%), double major (4%), English as a Second Language (ESL), honors program (8%), independent study (5%), internships (4%), liberal arts/career combination (2%), study abroad (18%), teacher certificate program (20%). **Teacher certification offered in:** early childhood, special education, elementary, middle/junior high, secondary. **Cooperative education programs:** business, computer science, social/behavioral science, other. **Reserve Officers Training Corps (ROTC):** Army ROTC: Offered on campus. **Faculty and instruction (2005-2006):** Total instructional faculty: 136 full-time, 197 part-time. Full-time faculty with Ph.D. or other terminal degree: 96%. Student/faculty ratio: 16/1. Classes of fewer than 20 students: 42%; of 20 to 49 students: 58%. **Advanced Placement and International Baccalaureate credit:** AP tests may be used for: Credit only. Scores accepted: 3, 4, 5. International Baccalaureate exams may be used for: Credit only. **Freshmen returning for sophomore year:** 79%. **Graduation rates:** Four-year: 55%; five-year: 62%; six-year: 59%. **Graduate study:** 32% of students pursue further study immediately upon graduation. Fields in which graduates pursue further study: Master of Business Administration (MBA), 19%; law, 5%; medicine, 2%; dentistry, 1%; education, 37%; arts and sciences, 63%.

COSTS AND FINANCIAL AID
Financial aid office: (716) 286-8686. **Expenses (2006-2007):** Tuition and fees 2006-2007: $21,240; room/board: $8,850. Estimated books and supplies: $900; transportation: $700; personal expenses: $750. **Financial aid:** Priority filing date for institution's financial aid form: February 15. In 2005-2006, 86% of undergraduates applied for financial aid. Of those, 75% were determined to have financial need; 41% had their need fully met. Average financial aid package (proportion receiving): $16,821 (75%). Average amount of gift aid, such as scholarships or grants (proportion receiving): $9,334 (72%). Average amount of self-help aid, such as work study or loans (proportion receiving): $5,033 (58%). Average need-based loan (excluding PLUS or other private loans): $4,422. Among students who received need-based aid, the average percentage of need met: 83%. Among students who received aid based on merit, the average award (and the proportion receiving): $8,173 (19%). The average athletic scholarship (and the proportion receiving): $17,165 (5%). Average amount of debt of borrowers graduating in 2005: $17,163. Proportion who borrowed: 80%.

CAMPUS LIFE AND EXTRACURRICULAR ACTIVITIES
Campus housing available (% using): coed dorms (97%), apartment for single students (3%). Students who live in college-owned, operated, or affiliated housing: 53%. **Student employment:** During the 2005-2006 academic year, 17% of undergraduates worked on campus. Average per-year earnings: $1,800. **Clubs and organizations:** Number of student organizations: 60. Activities include: choral groups, dance, drama/theater, pep band, radio station, student government, student newspaper, television station, yearbook. Number of fraternities: 1; sororities: 2. Proportion of men in fraternities: 3%; of women in sororities: 4%. Average proportion of students who stay on campus on weekends: 54%. **Sports program (2005-2006):** Member of NCAA I. *Men's intercollegiate varsity sports:* baseball, basketball, cross-country, golf, ice hockey, soccer, swimming and diving, tennis. *Women's intercollegiate varsity sports:* basketball, cross-country, ice hockey, lacrosse, soccer, softball, swimming and diving, tennis, volleyball.

SERVICES AND FACILITIES

Basic services: nonremedial tutoring, placement service, health service, health insurance. **Remedial assistance:** reading, math, writing, study skills. **Counseling services:** minority student, career, personal, veteran student, academic, psychological, religious. **For learning-disabled students:** School does not offer a structured program with separate admission and additional fees. Total undergraduates in learning-disabled program or receiving services: 91. Services include: remedial math, remedial English, reading machines, remedial reading, tape recorders, note-taking services, learning center, extended time for tests, tutors, other testing accomodations. **Library:** Number of titles: 282,702; number of current serial subscriptions: 9,000. **Information technology resources:** Students are not required to lease or own a computer. Number of campus computers available to all students: 150. School has a wireless network. Approximate number of users that can be accommodated: 300. Proportion of college-owned housing units wired for high-speed internet access: 100%. **Campus safety:** Security services offered: 24-hour foot-and-vehicle patrols, late-night transport/escort service, 24-hour emergency telephones, lighted pathways/sidewalks, controlled dormitory access (key, security card, etc).

TRANSFER AND INTERNATIONAL STUDENTS

Transfer students: May apply for admission for the following academic terms: Fall, Spring, Summer. Applicants do not need a minimum number of credits to apply. For fall 2005: Transfer applications received: 450. Transfer applicants offered admission: 287. Transfer applicants enrolled: 172. **International students:** Number of foreign undergraduates: 141 (5% of student body). Minimum TOEFL score required: 550 (paper); 213 (computer). Average TOEFL score: 575 (paper).

Nyack College

- **Address:** 1 South Boulevard, Nyack, NY 10960-3698
- **Website:** http://www.nyack.edu
- **Private; Religious affiliation:** Christian and Missionary Alliance
- **Enrollment:** 1,703 full-time; 327 part-time

KEY STATS

✔ **U.S News College Ranking:** fourth tier, Universities–Master's (North)
✔ **SAT Score (25th/75th percentile):** 820-1070
✔ **Tuition:** 2006-2007: $16,200

Selectivity: Less selective	**Room/board:** $7,600
Acceptance rate: 93%	**Average debt:** N/A
Student/faculty ratio: 11/1	**Proportion who borrowed:** N/A

UNDERGRADUATE STUDENT BODY STATS

2005-2006 enrollment: 1,703 full-time; 327 part-time. Men: 39%; women: 61%. **Ethnic makeup:** African American: 35%; Asian American: 6%; Hispanic: 20%; White: 34%; International: 5%. **Religious preference:** Roman Catholic: 4%; Protestant: 82%; Unknown: 5%; Christian and Missionary Alliance: 9%.

ADMISSIONS FACTS AND FIGURES

Phone: (800) 336-9225. **Email:** admissions@nyack.edu. **Website:** http://www.nyack.edu. **Application deadlines for fall 2007:** Regular decision: Rolling. Early decision: Not offered. Early action: Not offered. Admission can be deferred. **Application fee:** $25. Common application is not accepted. **Admissions requirements/recommendations:** High school units required (recommended): English: 0 (4); Mathematics: 0 (3); Science: 0 (3); Foreign language: 0 (2); Social studies: 0 (3); History: 0 (3); Academic electives: 0 (4); Total units: 16 (0). Tests: The college uses SAT or ACT scores in admissions decisions. Neither SAT nor ACT required. For admission to the fall 2007 entering class, the school will accept: ACT with writing, ACT without writing. Campus visit: Recommended. Admissions interview: Recommended. Off-campus interview: May be arranged. **Factors that count in admissions decisions:** *Academic:* Secondary school record: Very important. Class rank: Very important. Letters of recommendation: Very important. Standardized test scores: Very important. Essay: Important. *Nonacademic:* Interview: Very important. Extracurricular activities: Important. Talent/ability: Considered. Character/personal qualities: Important. Alumni/ae relationship: Not considered. Geographical residence: Not considered. State residency: Not considered. Religious affiliation/commitment: Very important. Minority status: Not considered.

Volunteer work: Considered. Work experience: Considered. **Admissions statistics for the fall 2005 entering class:** Total applicants: 519. Total accepted: 483. Freshmen enrolled: 270; Overall acceptance rate: 93%. **Credentials of fall 2005 freshmen:** 9% ranked in the top 10 percent of their high school class; 24% were in the top 25 percent, and 55% were in the top half. (Proportion submitting class standing: 53%.) **Average high school grade point average:** 2.7. **First-year students who submitted SAT scores:** 74%. Scores (25/75 percentile): Verbal: 410-540, Math: 410-530, Combined: 820-1070. **First-year students submitting ACT scores:** 10%. Scores (25/75 percentile): English: N/A, Math: N/A, Composite: 17-23.

ACADEMICS

Year founded: 1882. **Academic calendar:** Semester. **Degrees offered:** associate, transfer-associate, terminal-associate, bachelor's, master's, first professional. **Most popular majors:** 51% business administration and management, 13% liberal arts and sciences/liberal studies, 8% psychology, 4% elementary education and teaching, 3% social work. **Major fields of study:** business, management, marketing, and related support services; communication, journalism, and related programs; computer and information sciences and support services; education; English language and literature/letters; history; liberal arts and sciences studies, and humanities; mathematics and statistics; multi/interdisciplinary studies; philosophy and religious studies; psychology; public administration and social service professions; social sciences; theology and religious vocations; visual and performing arts. **Areas of required coursework:** arts/fine arts, humanities, mathematics, English (including composition), philosophy, foreign languages, sciences (biological or physical), history, social science, other. **Pre-professional programs:** pre-law. **Special academic programs:** accelerated program, distance learning, double major, English as a Second Language (ESL), honors program, independent study, internships, liberal arts/career combination, study abroad, teacher certificate program. **Teacher certification offered in:** early childhood, elementary, middle/junior high, secondary. **Faculty and instruction (2005-2006):** Total instructional faculty: 102 full-time, 159 part-time (61% men; 39% women; 39% minorities). Full-time faculty with Ph.D. or other terminal degree: 57%. Student/faculty ratio: 11/1. Classes of fewer than 20 students: 76%; of 20 to 49 students: 24%; of 50 or more students: 1%. **Advanced Placement and International Baccalaureate credit:** AP tests may be used for: Credit and/or placement. Scores accepted: 3, 4, 5. International Baccalaureate exams may be used for: Credit and/or placement. **Freshmen returning for sophomore year:** 65%. **Graduation rates:** Four-year: 33%; five-year: 42%; six-year: 40%.

COSTS AND FINANCIAL AID

Financial aid office: (845) 358-1710. **Expenses (2006-2007):** Tuition and fees 2006-2007: $16,200; room/board: $7,600. Estimated books and supplies: $750; transportation: $1,200; personal expenses: $2,000. **Financial aid:** In 2005-2006, 89% of undergraduates applied for financial aid. Of those, 84% were determined to have financial need; 19% had their need fully met. Average financial aid package (proportion receiving): $14,124 (84%). Average amount of gift aid, such as scholarships or grants (proportion receiving): $8,851 (82%). Average amount of self-help aid, such as work study or loans (proportion receiving): $5,774 (78%). Average need-based loan (excluding PLUS or other private loans): $5,070. Among students who received need-based aid, the average percentage of need met: 65%. Among students who received aid based on merit, the average award (and the proportion receiving): $7,089 (14%). The average athletic scholarship (and the proportion receiving): $8,444 (3%).

CAMPUS LIFE AND EXTRACURRICULAR ACTIVITIES

Campus housing available (% using): women's dorms (61%), men's dorms (38%), apartments for married students (1%), apartment for single students (0%). Students who live in college-owned, operated, or affiliated housing: 38%. **Clubs and organizations:** Number of student organizations: 25. Activities include: choral groups, drama/theater, literary magazine, music ensembles, musical theater, radio station, student government, student newspaper, symphony orchestra, yearbook. Number of fraternities: 0; sororities: 0. Average proportion of students who stay on campus on weekends: 75%. **Sports program (2005-2006):** Member of NAIA. *Men's intercollegiate varsity sports:* baseball, basketball, cross-country, golf, soccer. *Women's intercollegiate varsity sports:* basketball, cross-country, soccer, softball, volleyball.

SERVICES AND FACILITIES

Basic services: nonremedial tutoring, placement service, health service, health insurance. **Remedial assistance:** reading, math, writing, study skills, other. **Counseling services:** career, personal, academic, psychological, religious. **For learning-disabled students:** School does not offer a structured program with separate admission and additional fees. Services include: remedial math, remedial English, remedial reading, tape recorders, other special classes, untimed tests, note-taking services, oral tests, learning center, readers, extended time for tests, tutors, other. **Library:** Number of titles: 142,741; number of current serial subscriptions: 903. **Information technology resources:** Students are not required to lease or own a computer. Number of campus computers available to all students: 180. School has a wireless network. Proportion of college-owned housing units wired for high-speed internet access: 100%. **Campus safety:** Security services offered: 24-hour foot-and-vehicle patrols, late-night transport/escort service, lighted pathways/sidewalks.

TRANSFER AND INTERNATIONAL STUDENTS

Transfer students: May apply for admission for the following academic terms: Fall, Spring, Summer. Applicants do not need a minimum number of credits to apply. For fall 2005: Transfer applications received: 261. Transfer applicants offered admission: 243. Transfer applicants enrolled: 132. **International students:** Number of foreign undergraduates: 94 (5% of student body). Minimum TOEFL score required: 550 (paper); 220 (computer).

Pace University

- **Address:** 1 Pace Plaza, New York, NY 10038
- **Website:** http://www.pace.edu
- **Private**
- **Enrollment:** 6,879 full-time; 2,049 part-time

KEY STATS

✔ **U.S News College Ranking:** third tier, National Universities
✔ **SAT Score (25th/75th percentile):** 977-1177
✔ **Tuition:** 2006-2007: $30,086

Selectivity: Selective	**Room/board:** $9,570
Acceptance rate: 73%	**Average debt:** $29,060
Student/faculty ratio: 14/1	**Proportion who borrowed:** 67%

UNDERGRADUATE STUDENT BODY STATS

2005-2006 enrollment: 6,879 full-time; 2,049 part-time. Men: 39%; women: 61%. **Ethnic makeup:** African American: 10%; Asian American: 11%; Hispanic: 12%; White: 63%; International: 4%.

ADMISSIONS FACTS AND FIGURES

Phone: (212) 346-1323. **Email:** infoctr@pace.edu. **Website:** http://www.pace.edu. **Application deadlines for fall 2007:** Regular decision: March 1. Early decision: Not offered. Early action: Send application by: November 30; Decision sent by: December 31. Admission can be deferred. **Application fee:** $45. Common application is accepted. **To apply online, go to:** http://apply.pace.edu. **Admissions requirements/recommendations:** High school units required (recommended): English: 4 (4); Mathematics: 3 (4); Science: 2 (2); Foreign language: 2 (3); Social studies: 1 (2); History: 2 (2); Academic electives: 2 (3); Total units: 16 (20). Tests: The college uses SAT or ACT scores in admissions decisions. Either SAT or ACT required. For admission to the fall 2007 entering class, the school will accept: ACT with writing, ACT without writing. Campus visit: Recommended. Admissions interview: Recommended. Off-campus interview: May be arranged. **Factors that count in admissions decisions:** *Academic:* Secondary school record: Very important. Class rank: Important. Letters of recommendation: Considered. Standardized test scores: Very important. Essay: Considered. *Nonacademic:* Interview: Not considered. Extracurricular activities: Considered. Talent/ability: Considered. Character/personal qualities: Considered. Alumni/ae relationship: Considered. Geographical residence: Not considered. State residency: Not considered. Religious affiliation/commitment: Not considered. Minority status: Not considered. Volunteer work: Considered. Work experience: Considered. **Other schools with the greatest overlap in applicants:** CUNY–Baruch College; CUNY–Hunter College; Fordham University; New York University; St. John's University. **Admissions statistics for the fall 2005 entering class:** Total applicants: 9,015. Total accepted: 6,541. Freshmen enrolled: 1,501; 37% were from out of state. Accepted through early-decision or early-action plans: 8%. Overall acceptance rate: 73%. Non-early acceptance rate: 72%. **Credentials of fall 2005 freshmen:** 19% ranked in the top 10 percent of their high school class; 42% were in the top 25 percent, and 82% were in the top half. (Proportion submitting class standing: 50%.) **Average**

high school grade point average: 3.2. **First-year students who submitted SAT scores:** 95%. Scores (25/75 percentile): Verbal: 485-579, Math: 492-598, Combined: 977-1177. **First-year students submitting ACT scores:** 2%. Scores (25/75 percentile): English: N/A, Math: N/A, Composite: 20-26.

ACADEMICS

Year founded: 1906. **Academic calendar:** Semester. **Degrees offered:** certificate, diploma, associate, bachelor's, post-bachelor's certificate, master's, post-master's certificate, first professional, first professional certificate, doctorate. **Most popular majors:** 44% business, management, marketing, and related support services, 14% computer and information sciences and support services, 8% communication, journalism, and related programs, 7% health professions and related clinical sciences, 6% psychology. **Major fields of study:** area, ethnic, cultural, and gender studies; biological and biomedical sciences; business, management, marketing, and related support services; communication, journalism, and related programs; computer and information sciences and support services; education; English language and literature/letters; foreign languages, literatures, and linguistics; health professions and related clinical sciences; history; liberal arts and sciences studies, and humanities; mathematics and statistics; multi/interdisciplinary studies; natural resources and conservation; philosophy and religious studies; physical sciences; psychology; public administration and social service professions; security and protective services; social sciences; visual and performing arts. **Areas of required coursework:** arts/fine arts, humanities, computer literacy, mathematics, English (including composition), philosophy, sciences (biological or physical), social science, other. **Pre-professional programs:** pre-law, pre-dentistry, pre-medicine, pre-veterinary science, other. **Special academic programs (% participation):** accelerated program (2%), cooperative (work-study plan) program (43%), distance learning (21%), dual enrollment (2%), English as a Second Language (ESL) (5%), honors program (8%), independent study (24%), internships (43%), study abroad (5%), teacher certificate program (4%). **Teacher certification offered in:** early childhood, elementary, middle/junior high, secondary. **Cooperative education programs:** business, computer science, education, health professions, social/behavioral science. **Reserve Officers Training Corps (ROTC):** Army ROTC: Offered at cooperating institution (St. John's University). **Faculty and instruction (2005-2006):** Total instructional faculty: 478 full-time, 760 part-time (53% men; 47% women; 16% minorities). Full-time faculty with Ph.D. or other terminal degree: 88%. Student/faculty ratio: 14/1. Classes of fewer than 20 students: 49%; of 20 to 49 students: 50%; of 50 or more students: 1%. **Advanced Placement and International Baccalaureate credit:** AP tests may be used for: Credit and/or placement. Scores accepted: 3, 4, 5. **Freshmen returning for sophomore year:** 77%. **Graduation rates:** Four-year: 40%; five-year: 54%; six-year: 56%. **Graduate study:** 12% of students pursue further study immediately upon graduation. Fields in which graduates pursue further study: Master of Business Administration (MBA), 19%; law, 2%; medicine, 2%; engineering, 2%; education, 30%; arts and sciences, 26%.

COSTS AND FINANCIAL AID

Financial aid office: (212) 346-1300. **Expenses (2006-2007):** Tuition and fees 2006-2007: $30,086; room/board: $9,570. Estimated books and supplies: $800; transportation: $600; personal expenses: $1,350. **Financial aid:** Priority filing date for institution's financial aid form: February 15. In 2005-2006, 77% of undergraduates applied for financial aid. Of those, 70% were determined to have financial need; 43% had their need fully met. Average financial aid package (proportion receiving): $15,062 (70%). Average amount of gift aid, such as scholarships or grants (proportion receiving): $11,094 (63%). Average amount of self-help aid, such as work study or loans (proportion receiving): $4,880 (59%). Average need-based loan (excluding PLUS or other private loans): $4,271. Among students who received need-based aid, the average percentage of need met: 51%. Among students who received aid based on merit, the average award (and the proportion receiving): $7,742 (5%). The average athletic scholarship (and the proportion receiving): $10,527 (0%). Average amount of debt of borrowers graduating in 2005: $29,060. Proportion who borrowed: 67%.

CAMPUS LIFE AND EXTRACURRICULAR ACTIVITIES

Campus housing available (% using): coed dorms (84%), apartment for single students (16%), other housing options. Students who live in college-owned, operated, or affiliated housing: 29%. **Student employment:** During the 2005-2006 academic year, 10% of undergraduates worked on campus. Average per-year earnings: $1,694. **Clubs and organizations:** Number of student organizations: 108. Activities include: choral groups, dance, drama/theater, literary magazine, musical theater, radio station, student government, student newspaper, student film society, television station, yearbook. Number of fraternities: 8; sororities: 10. Proportion of men in fraternities: 5%; of women in sororities: 5%. Average proportion of students who stay on campus on weekends: 50%. **Sports program (2005-2006):** Member of NCAA II. *Men's intercollegiate varsity sports:* baseball, basketball, cheerleading, cross-country, football, golf, lacrosse, swimming and diving, tennis, track and field (outdoor). *Women's intercollegiate varsity sports:* basketball, cheerleading, cross-country, equestrian sports, golf, soccer, softball, tennis, track and field (indoor), track and field (outdoor), volleyball.

SERVICES AND FACILITIES

Basic services: nonremedial tutoring, placement service, health service. **Remedial assistance:** math, writing. **Counseling services:** minority student, career, academic, psychological, other. **For learning-disabled students:** School does not offer a structured program with separate admission and additional fees. Total undergraduates in learning-disabled program or receiving services: 300. Services include: remedial math, remedial English, remedial reading, tape recorders, untimed tests, note-taking services, oral tests, learning center, readers, extended time for tests, tutors, priority registration, substitution of courses, texts on tape, typist/scribe, exams on tape or computer, take home exams, other testing accomodations, waiver of foreign language degree requirement, waiver of math degree requirement, other. **Library:** Number of titles: 824,488; number of current serial subscriptions: 4,269. **Information technology resources:** Students are not required to lease or own a computer. Number of campus computers available to all students: 508. School has a wireless network. Approximate number of users that can be accommodated: 1,000. Proportion of college-owned housing units wired for high-speed internet access: 100%. **Campus safety:** Security services offered: 24-hour foot-and-vehicle patrols, late-night transport/escort service, 24-hour emergency telephones, lighted pathways/sidewalks, controlled dormitory access (key, security card, etc).

TRANSFER AND INTERNATIONAL STUDENTS

Transfer students: May apply for admission for the following academic terms: Fall, Spring, Summer. Applicants need a minimum number of credits to apply. For fall 2005: Transfer applications received: 2,256. Transfer applicants offered admission: 1,435. Transfer applicants enrolled: 752. **International students:** Number of foreign undergraduates: 330 (4% of student body). Number of countries represented: 38. Minimum TOEFL score required: 550 (paper); 213 (computer). Average TOEFL score: 567 (paper).

Polytechnic University

- **Address:** 6 Metrotech Center, Brooklyn, NY 11201
- **Website:** http://www.poly.edu/
- **Private**
- **Enrollment:** 1,451 full-time; 68 part-time

KEY STATS

✔ **U.S News College Ranking:** third tier, National Universities
✔ **SAT Score (25th/75th percentile):** 1070-1290
✔ **Tuition:** 2006-2007: $29,789

Selectivity: More selective	**Room/board:** $8,500
Acceptance rate: 69%	**Average debt:** $22,125
Student/faculty ratio: 13/1	**Proportion who borrowed:** 78%

UNDERGRADUATE STUDENT BODY STATS

2005-2006 enrollment: 1,451 full-time; 68 part-time. Men: 82%; women: 18%. **Ethnic makeup:** African American: 12%; Asian American: 32%; Hispanic: 11%; White: 37%; International: 8%.

ADMISSIONS FACTS AND FIGURES

Phone: (718) 260-3100. **Email:** uadmit@poly.edu. **Website:** http://www.poly.edu/. **Application deadlines for fall 2007:** Regular decision: Rolling. Early decision: Not offered. Early action: Not offered. Admission can be deferred. **Application fee:** $60. Common application is accepted. **To apply online, go to:** http://www.poly.edu/admissions/undergrad/apply/applyonline.php. **Admissions requirements/recommendations:** High school units required (recommended): English: 4; Mathematics: 4; Science: 4; Foreign language: (2); Social studies: 0; Academic electives: 0; Total units: 12 (0). Tests: The college uses SAT or ACT scores in admissions decisions. Either SAT or ACT required. Campus visit: Recommended. Admissions interview: Recommended. Off-campus interview: May be arranged. **Factors that count in admissions decisions:** *Academic:* Secondary

school record: Very important. Class rank: Important. Letters of recommendation: Considered. Standardized test scores: Very important. Essay: Considered. *Nonacademic:* Interview: Considered. Extracurricular activities: Considered. Talent/ability: Not considered. Character/personal qualities: Considered. Alumni/ae relationship: Considered. Geographical residence: Not considered. State residency: Not considered. Religious affiliation/commitment: Not considered. Minority status: Not considered. Volunteer work: Considered. Work experience: Considered. **Other schools with the greatest overlap in applicants:** Cooper Union; Manhattan College; Rensselaer Polytechnic Institute; Rochester Institute of Technology; Stevens Institute of Technology. **Admissions statistics for the fall 2005 entering class:** Total applicants: 1,240. Total accepted: 860. Freshmen enrolled: 304; 7% were from out of state. Overall acceptance rate: 69%. **Size of waiting list:** 0 applicants; enrolled from waiting list: 0. **Credentials of fall 2005 freshmen:** 44% ranked in the top 10 percent of their high school class; 71% were in the top 25 percent, and 94% were in the top half. (Proportion submitting class standing: 25%.) **Average high school grade point average:** 3.2. **First-year students who submitted SAT scores:** 97%. Scores (25/75 percentile): Verbal: 500-610, Math: 570-680, Combined: 1070-1290.

ACADEMICS

Year founded: 1854. **Academic calendar:** Semester. **Degrees offered:** certificate, bachelor's, master's, doctorate. **Most popular majors:** 26% computer science, 21% computer engineering, 13% mechanical engineering, 11% electrical, electronics, and communications engineering, 9% business, management, marketing, and related support services. **Major fields of study:** biological and biomedical sciences; business, management, marketing, and related support services; communication, journalism, and related programs; computer and information sciences and support services; engineering; history; liberal arts and sciences studies, and humanities; mathematics and statistics; physical sciences. **Areas of required coursework:** humanities, computer literacy, mathematics, English (including composition), sciences (biological or physical), history, social science. **Pre-professional programs:** pre-medicine. **Special academic programs (% participation):** cooperative (work-study plan) program (52.1%), distance learning (5%), double major (2.5%), honors program (7.6%), internships (31%). **Cooperative education programs:** computer science, engineering. **Reserve Officers Training Corps (ROTC):** Army ROTC: Offered at cooperating institution (Fordham University); Air Force ROTC: Offered at cooperating institution (Fordham University). **Faculty and instruction (2005-2006):** Total instructional faculty: 128 full-time, 145 part-time (83% men; 17% women; 19% minorities). Full-time faculty with Ph.D. or other terminal degree: 91%. Student/faculty ratio: 13/1. Classes of fewer than 20 students: 40%; of 20 to 49 students: 50%; of 50 or more students: 9%. **Advanced Placement and International Baccalaureate credit:** AP tests may be used for: Credit and/or placement. Scores accepted: 4, 5. International Baccalaureate exams may be used for: Credit only. **Freshmen returning for sophomore year:** 82%. **Graduation rates:** Four-year: 32%; five-year: 43%; six-year: 46%. **Graduate study:** 19% of students pursue further study immediately upon graduation. Fields in which graduates pursue further study: Master of Business Administration (MBA), 1%; medicine, 1%; engineering, 15%; education, 1%.

COSTS AND FINANCIAL AID

Financial aid office: (718) 260-3300. **Expenses (2006-2007):** Tuition and fees 2006-2007: $29,789; room/board: $8,500. Estimated books and supplies: $1,000; transportation: $1,390; personal expenses: $1,575. **Financial aid:** Priority filing date for institution's financial aid form: January 31. In 2005-2006, 96% of undergraduates applied for financial aid. Of those, 82% were determined to have financial need; 56% had their need fully met. Average financial aid package (proportion receiving): $21,955 (82%). Average amount of gift aid, such as scholarships or grants (proportion receiving): $7,511 (75%). Average amount of self-help aid, such as work study or loans (proportion receiving): $5,268 (63%). Average need-based loan (excluding PLUS or other private loans): $4,928. Among students who received need-based aid, the average percentage of need met: 91%. Among students who received aid based on merit, the average award (and the proportion receiving): $16,578 (13%). The average athletic scholarship (and the proportion receiving): $0 (0%). Average amount of debt of borrowers graduating in 2005: $22,125. Proportion who borrowed: 78%.

CAMPUS LIFE AND EXTRACURRICULAR ACTIVITIES

Campus housing available (% using): coed dorms (100%). Students who live in college-owned, operated, or affiliated housing: 15%. **Student employment:** During the 2005-2006 academic year, 15% of undergraduates worked on campus. **Clubs and organizations:** Number of student organizations: 50.

Activities include: drama/theater, literary magazine, radio station, student government, student newspaper, student film society, yearbook. Number of fraternities: 3; sororities: 1. Proportion of men in fraternities: 3%; of women in sororities: 4%. Average proportion of students who stay on campus on weekends: 13%. **Sports program (2005-2006):** Member of NCAA III. *Men's intercollegiate varsity sports:* baseball, basketball, cross-country, soccer, tennis, track and field (indoor), track and field (outdoor), volleyball, judo. *Women's intercollegiate varsity sports:* basketball, cross-country, soccer, softball, tennis, track and field (indoor), track and field (outdoor), volleyball, judo.

SERVICES AND FACILITIES

Basic services: nonremedial tutoring, placement service. **Remedial assistance:** reading, math, writing, study skills. **Counseling services:** career, personal, academic, psychological. **For learning-disabled students:** School does not offer a structured program with separate admission and additional fees. Total undergraduates in learning-disabled program or receiving services: 6. Services include: untimed tests, note-taking services, learning center, extended time for tests, tutors, other testing accomodations. **Library:** Number of titles: 145,000; number of current serial subscriptions: 6,040. **Information technology resources:** Students are required to lease or own a computer. Number of campus computers available to all students: 1,330. School has a wireless network. Approximate number of users that can be accommodated: 5,000. Proportion of college-owned housing units wired for high-speed internet access: 100%. **Campus safety:** Security services offered: 24-hour emergency telephones, lighted pathways/sidewalks, controlled dormitory access (key, security card, etc).

TRANSFER AND INTERNATIONAL STUDENTS

Transfer students: May apply for admission for the following academic terms: Fall, Spring. Applicants do not need a minimum number of credits to apply. For fall 2005: Transfer applications received: 250. Transfer applicants offered admission: 162. Transfer applicants enrolled: 81. **International students:** Number of foreign undergraduates: 115 (8% of student body). Number of countries represented: 42. Average TOEFL score: 550 (paper).

Pratt Institute

- **Address:** 200 Willoughby Avenue, Brooklyn, NY 11205
- **Website:** http://www.pratt.edu
- **Private**
- **Enrollment:** 2,898 full-time; 146 part-time

KEY STATS

✔ **U.S News College Ranking:** Unranked Specialty School–Fine Arts
✔ **SAT Score (25th/75th percentile):** 905-1330
✔ **Tuition:** 2006-2007: $29,230

Selectivity: Selective	**Room/board:** $8,752
Acceptance rate: 52%	**Average debt:** N/A
Student/faculty ratio: 11/1	**Proportion who borrowed:** N/A

UNDERGRADUATE STUDENT BODY STATS

2005-2006 enrollment: 2,898 full-time; 146 part-time. Men: 40%; women: 60%. **Ethnic makeup:** African American: 8%; Asian American: 12%; Hispanic: 9%; White: 62%; International: 10%.

ADMISSIONS FACTS AND FIGURES

Phone: (718) 636-3514. **Email:** admissions@pratt.edu. **Website:** http://www.pratt.edu. **Application deadlines for fall 2007:** Regular decision: February 1. Early decision: Not offered. Early action: Send application by: November 15; Decision sent by: January 15. Admission can be deferred. **Application fee:** $40. Common application is accepted. **To apply online, go to:** http://www.pratt.edu/admiss/apply. **Admissions requirements/recommendations:** High school units required (recommended): English: (4); Mathematics: (3); Science: (2); Social studies: (1); Total units: (16). Tests: The college uses SAT or ACT scores in admissions decisions. Either SAT or ACT required. For admission to the fall 2007 entering class, the school will accept: ACT with writing, ACT without writing. Campus visit: Recommended. Admissions interview: Recommended. Off-campus interview: May be arranged. **Factors that count in admissions decisions:** *Academic:* Secondary school record: Very important. Class rank: Not considered. Letters of recommendation: Considered. Standardized test scores:

Important. Essay: Considered. *Nonacademic:* Interview: Important. Extracurricular activities: Considered. Talent/ability: Very important. Character/personal qualities: Important. Alumni/ae relationship: Very important. Geographical residence: Important. State residency: Not considered. Religious affiliation/commitment: Not considered. Minority status: Not considered. Volunteer work: Not considered. Work experience: Considered. **Admissions statistics for the fall 2005 entering class:** Total applicants: 3,794. Total accepted: 1,962. Freshmen enrolled: 625; Overall acceptance rate: 52%. Non-early acceptance rate: 52%. **Size of waiting list:** 172 applicants; enrolled from waiting list: 15. **Average high school grade point average:** 3.4. **First-year students who submitted SAT scores:** 89%. Scores (25/75 percentile): Verbal: 450-670, Math: 455-660, Combined: 905-1330. **First-year students submitting ACT scores:** 11%. Scores (25/75 percentile): English: N/A, Math: N/A, Composite: 21-27.

ACADEMICS

Year founded: 1887. **Academic calendar:** Semester. **Degrees offered:** associate, transfer-associate, terminal-associate, bachelor's, master's, post-master's certificate. **Most popular majors:** 16% graphic design, 14% architecture (B.Arch., B.A./B.S., M.Arch., M.A./M.S., Ph.D.), 8% illustration, 8% painting, 6% photography. **Major fields of study:** Areas of required coursework: arts/fine arts, humanities, computer literacy, English (including composition), philosophy, sciences (biological or physical), history, social science. **Special academic programs (% participation):** English as a Second Language (ESL) (16%), exchange student program (domestic) (.1%), independent study (1.1%), internships (2.5%), teacher certificate program (2.5%). **Teacher certification offered in:** special education, elementary, middle/junior high, secondary. **Faculty and instruction (2005-2006):** Total instructional faculty: 113 full-time, 776 part-time (60% men; 40% women; 14% minorities). Full-time faculty with Ph.D. or other terminal degree: 46%. Student/faculty ratio: 11/1. Classes of fewer than 20 students: 83%; of 20 to 49 students: 17%; of 50 or more students: 0%. **Advanced Placement and International Baccalaureate credit:** AP tests may be used for: Credit only. Scores accepted: 4, 5. International Baccalaureate exams may be used for: Credit only. **Freshmen returning for sophomore year:** 86%. **Graduation rates:** Six-year: 55%. **Graduate study:** 3% of students pursue further study immediately upon graduation.

COSTS AND FINANCIAL AID

Financial aid office: (718) 636-3599. **Expenses (2006-2007):** Tuition and fees 2006-2007: $29,230; room/board: $8,752. Estimated books and supplies: $3,000; transportation: $900; personal expenses: $650. **Financial aid:** Priority filing date for institution's financial aid form: February 1. In 2005-2006, 76% of undergraduates applied for financial aid. Of those, 67% were determined to have financial need; Average financial aid package (proportion receiving): $14,972 (67%). Average amount of gift aid, such as scholarships or grants (proportion receiving): $8,716 (62%). Average amount of self-help aid, such as work study or loans (proportion receiving): $7,251 (63%). Average need-based loan (excluding PLUS or other private loans): $4,419. Among students who received need-based aid, the average percentage of need met: 58%. Among students who received aid based on merit, the average award (and the proportion receiving): $9,463 (10%). The average athletic scholarship (and the proportion receiving): $0 (0%).

CAMPUS LIFE AND EXTRACURRICULAR ACTIVITIES

Campus housing available (% using): coed dorms (97%), apartment for single students (3%). **Student employment:** During the 2005-2006 academic year, 31% of undergraduates worked on campus. Average per-year earnings: $2,170. **Clubs and organizations:** Number of student organizations: 49. Activities include: literary magazine, music ensembles, radio station, student government, student newspaper, student film society, television station, yearbook. Number of fraternities: 2; sororities: 2. Average proportion of students who stay on campus on weekends: 80%. **Sports program (2005-2006):** Member of NCAA III. *Men's intercollegiate varsity sports:* basketball, cross-country, soccer, tennis, volleyball. *Women's intercollegiate varsity sports:* basketball, cross-country, soccer, tennis, volleyball.

SERVICES AND FACILITIES

Basic services: health service, health insurance. **Remedial assistance:** reading, math, writing, study skills. **Counseling services:** minority student, career, personal, veteran student, academic, psychological, birth control, religious. **For learning-disabled students:** School does not offer a structured program with separate admission and additional fees. Total undergraduates in learning-disabled program or receiving services: 252. Services include: tape recorders, diagnostic testing service, note-taking services, learning center, extended time for tests, tutors, early syllabus, priority seating, texts on tape, other testing accomodations. **Library:** Number of titles: 169,914; number of current serial subscriptions: 730. **Information technology resources:** Students are not required to lease or own a computer. Number of campus computers available to all students: 500. School has a wireless network. Proportion of college-owned housing units wired for high-speed internet access: 100%. **Campus safety:** Security services offered: 24-hour foot-and-vehicle patrols, 24-hour emergency telephones, lighted pathways/sidewalks, controlled dormitory access (key, security card, etc).

TRANSFER AND INTERNATIONAL STUDENTS

Transfer students: May apply for admission for the following academic terms: Fall, Spring. Applicants need a minimum number of credits to apply. **International students:** Number of foreign undergraduates: 296 (10% of student body). Number of countries represented: 43. Minimum TOEFL score required: 530 (paper); 197 (computer). Average TOEFL score: 550 (paper).

Rensselaer Polytechnic Institute

- **Address:** 110 Eighth Street, Troy, NY 12180-3590
- **Website:** http://www.rpi.edu
- **Private**
- **Enrollment:** 4,926 full-time; 25 part-time

KEY STATS

✔ **U.S News College Ranking:** 42, National Universities
✔ **SAT Score (25th/75th percentile):** 1220-1420
✔ **Tuition:** 2006-2007: $33,500

Selectivity: More selective	**Room/board:** $9,939
Acceptance rate: 78%	**Average debt:** $27,235
Student/faculty ratio: 14/1	**Proportion who borrowed:** 75%

UNDERGRADUATE STUDENT BODY STATS

2005-2006 enrollment: 4,926 full-time; 25 part-time. Men: 76%; women: 24%. **Ethnic makeup:** African American: 4%; Asian American: 11%; Hispanic: 5%; White: 75%; International: 3%.

ADMISSIONS FACTS AND FIGURES

Phone: (518) 276-6216. **Email:** admissions@rpi.edu. **Website:** http://www.rpi.edu. **Application deadlines for fall 2007:** Regular decision: January 1; decision sent by March 20. Early decision: Send application by: November 15; Decision sent by: December 31. Early action: Not offered. Admission can be deferred. **Application fee:** $70. Common application is accepted. **To apply online, go to:** http://admissions.rpi.edu. **Admissions requirements/recommendations:** High school units required (recommended): English: 4; Mathematics: 4; Science: 3 (4); Social studies: 2 (3); Total units: 15. Tests: The college uses SAT or ACT scores in admissions decisions. Either SAT or ACT required. For admission to the fall 2007 entering class, the school will accept: ACT with writing. Campus visit: Recommended. Admissions interview: Neither required nor recommended. Off-campus interview: Not available. **Factors that count in admissions decisions:** *Academic:* Secondary school record: Very important. Class rank: Very important. Letters of recommendation: Important. Standardized test scores: Very important. Essay: Important. *Nonacademic:* Interview: Not considered. Extracurricular activities: Important. Talent/ability: Considered. Character/personal qualities: Important. Alumni/ae relationship: Considered. Geographical residence: Considered. State residency: Not considered. Religious affiliation/commitment: Not considered. Minority status: Considered. Volunteer work: Considered. Work experience: Considered. **Other schools with the greatest overlap in applicants:** Carnegie Mellon University; Cornell University; Massachusetts Institute of Technology; University of Rochester; Worcester Polytechnic Institute. **Admissions statistics for the fall 2005 entering class:** Total applicants: 5,574. Total accepted: 4,340. Freshmen enrolled: 1,240; 58% were from out of state. Overall acceptance rate: 78%. Early-decision acceptance rate: 85%. Non-early acceptance rate: 78%. **Size of waiting list:** 67 applicants; enrolled from waiting list: 21. **Credentials of fall 2005 freshmen:** 61% ranked in the top 10 percent of their high school class; 95% were in the top 25 percent, and 99% were in the top half. (Proportion submitting class standing: 70%.) **First-year students who submitted SAT scores:** 85%. Scores (25/75 percentile): Verbal: 580-690, Math: 640-730, Combined: 1220-1420. **First-year students submitting ACT scores:** 15%. Scores (25/75 percentile): English: N/A, Math: N/A, Composite: 24-28.

ACADEMICS

Year founded: 1824. **Academic calendar:** Semester. **Degrees offered:** bachelor's, master's, doctorate. **Most popular majors:** 50% engineering, 19% computer and information sciences and support services, 9% business, management, marketing, and related support services, 5% communication, journalism, and related programs, 4% architecture and related services. **Major fields of study:** architecture and related services; biological and biomedical sciences; business, management, marketing, and related support services; communication, journalism, and related programs; computer and information sciences and support services; engineering; health professions and related clinical sciences; legal professions and studies; mathematics and statistics; philosophy and religious studies; physical sciences; psychology; social sciences; visual and performing arts. **Areas of required coursework:** humanities, computer literacy, mathematics, English (including composition), sciences (biological or physical), social science. **Pre-professional programs:** pre-law, pre-medicine. **Special academic programs (% participation):** accelerated program (2%), cooperative (work-study plan) program (10%), cross-registration (2%), distance learning, double major (20%), dual enrollment, exchange student program (domestic), honors program, independent study, internships (48%), liberal arts/career combination, student-designed major, study abroad (6%). **Cooperative education programs:** art, business, computer science, engineering, humanities, natural science, social/behavioral science, technologies, other. **Reserve Officers Training Corps (ROTC):** Army ROTC: Offered on campus; Navy ROTC: Offered on campus; Air Force ROTC: Offered on campus. **Faculty and instruction (2005-2006):** Total instructional faculty: 400 full-time, 81 part-time (80% men; 20% women; 21% minorities). Full-time faculty with Ph.D. or other terminal degree: 98%. Student/faculty ratio: 14/1. Classes of fewer than 20 students: 43%; of 20 to 49 students: 48%; of 50 or more students: 10%. **Advanced Placement and International Baccalaureate credit:** AP tests may be used for: Credit and/or placement. Scores accepted: 4, 5. International Baccalaureate exams may be used for: Credit and/or placement. **Freshmen returning for sophomore year:** 92%. **Graduation rates:** Four-year: 61%; five-year: 80%; six-year: 81%. **Graduate study:** 27% of students pursue further study immediately upon graduation. Fields in which graduates pursue further study: Master of Business Administration (MBA), 22%; law, 6%; medicine, 14%; engineering, 41%; education, 6%.

COSTS AND FINANCIAL AID

Financial aid office: (518) 276-6813. **Expenses (2006-2007):** Tuition and fees 2006-2007: $33,500; room/board: $9,939. Estimated books and supplies: $1,770. **Financial aid:** Priority filing date for institution's financial aid form: February 15. In 2005-2006, 78% of undergraduates applied for financial aid. Of those, 70% were determined to have financial need; 61% had their need fully met. Average financial aid package (proportion receiving): $26,072 (70%). Average amount of gift aid, such as scholarships or grants (proportion receiving): $19,500 (70%). Average amount of self-help aid, such as work study or loans (proportion receiving): $8,500 (44%). Average need-based loan (excluding PLUS or other private loans): $7,000. Among students who received need-based aid, the average percentage of need met: 81%. Among students who received aid based on merit, the average award (and the proportion receiving): $15,800 (19%). Average amount of debt of borrowers graduating in 2005: $27,235. Proportion who borrowed: 75%.

CAMPUS LIFE AND EXTRACURRICULAR ACTIVITIES

Campus housing available (% using): coed dorms (77%), sorority housing (1%), fraternity housing (1%), apartments for married students (2%), apartment for single students (18%), special housing for disabled students (0%), other housing options (1%). Students who live in college-owned, operated, or affiliated housing: 56%. **Student employment:** During the 2005-2006 academic year, 33% of undergraduates worked on campus. Average per-year earnings: $1,600. **Clubs and organizations:** Number of student organizations: 160. Activities include: choral groups, concert band, dance, drama/theater, jazz band, literary magazine, music ensembles, musical theater, pep band, radio station, student government, student newspaper, student film society, symphony orchestra, television station, yearbook. Number of fraternities: 32; sororities: 5. Proportion of men in fraternities: 39%; of women in sororities: 18%. Average proportion of students who stay on campus on weekends: 85%. **Sports program (2005-2006):** Member of NCAA III. *Men's intercollegiate varsity sports:* baseball, basketball, cross-country, football, golf, ice hockey, lacrosse, soccer, swimming and diving, tennis, track and field (indoor), track and field (outdoor). *Women's intercollegiate varsity sports:* basketball, cross-country, field hockey, ice hockey, lacrosse, soccer, softball, swimming and diving, tennis, track and field (indoor), track and field (outdoor).

SERVICES AND FACILITIES

Basic services: nonremedial tutoring, women's center, placement service, day care, health service, health insurance. **Remedial assistance:** math, writing, study skills. **Counseling services:** minority student, career, military, personal, veteran student, academic, older student, psychological, birth control, religious. **For learning-disabled students:** School does not offer a structured program with separate admission and additional fees. Total undergraduates in learning-disabled program or receiving services: 103. Services include: reading machines, tape recorders, note-taking services, learning center, extended time for tests, tutors, texts on tape, other testing accomodations. **Library:** Number of titles: 494,428; number of current serial subscriptions: 43,733. **Information technology resources:** Students are required to lease or own a computer. Number of campus computers available to all students: 5,162. School has a wireless network. Approximate number of users that can be accommodated: 4,625. Proportion of college-owned housing units wired for high-speed internet access: 100%. **Campus safety:** Security services offered: 24-hour foot-and-vehicle patrols, late-night transport/escort service, 24-hour emergency telephones, lighted pathways/sidewalks, controlled dormitory access (key, security card, etc).

TRANSFER AND INTERNATIONAL STUDENTS

Transfer students: May apply for admission for the following academic terms: Fall, Spring, Summer. Applicants need a minimum number of credits to apply. For fall 2005: Transfer applications received: 278. Transfer applicants offered admission: 167. Transfer applicants enrolled: 109. **International students:** Number of foreign undergraduates: 164 (3% of student body). Number of countries represented: 29. Minimum TOEFL score required: 570 (paper); 230 (computer). Average TOEFL score: 618 (paper).

Roberts Wesleyan College

- **Address:** 2301 Westside Drive, Rochester, NY 14624-1997
- **Website:** http://www.roberts.edu
- **Private; Religious affiliation:** Free Methodist
- **Enrollment:** 1,265 full-time; 143 part-time

KEY STATS

✔ **U.S News College Ranking:** 68, Universities–Master's (North)
✔ **SAT Score (25th/75th percentile):** 980-1210
✔ **Tuition:** 2005-2006: $19,054

Selectivity: Selective	**Room/board:** $7,054
Acceptance rate: 86%	**Average debt:** N/A
Student/faculty ratio: 13/1	**Proportion who borrowed:** N/A

UNDERGRADUATE STUDENT BODY STATS

2005-2006 enrollment: 1,265 full-time; 143 part-time. Men: 31%; women: 69%. **Ethnic makeup:** African American: 6%; Asian American: 1%; Hispanic: 2%; White: 87%; International: 3%. **Religious preference:** Roman Catholic: 13%; Protestant: 59%; No preference: 16%; Free Methodist: 12%.

ADMISSIONS FACTS AND FIGURES

Phone: (585) 594-6400. **Email:** admissions@roberts.edu. **Website:** http://www.roberts.edu. **Application deadlines for fall 2007:** Regular decision: Rolling. Early decision: Not offered. Early action: Not offered. Admission can be deferred. **Application fee:** $35. Common application is not accepted. **To apply online, go to:** http://www.roberts.edu/prospective%20students/apply/index.htm. **Admissions requirements/recommendations:** High school units required (recommended): English: 4; Mathematics: 3; Science: 3; Foreign language: (3); Social studies: 3; Total units: 13 (3). Tests: The college uses SAT or ACT scores in admissions decisions. Either SAT or ACT required. For admission to the fall 2007 entering class, the school will accept: ACT without writing. Campus visit: Recommended. Admissions interview: Recommended. Off-campus interview: May be arranged. **Factors that count in admissions decisions:** *Academic:* Secondary school record: Important. Class rank: Important. Letters of recommendation: Very important. Standardized test scores: Very important. Essay: Very important. *Nonacademic:* Interview: Considered. Extracurricular activities: Considered. Talent/ability: Considered. Character/personal qualities: Very important. Alumni/ae relationship: Considered. Geographical residence: Not considered. State residency: Not considered. Religious affiliation/commitment: Important. Minority status: Not considered. Volunteer work: Considered. Work experience: Considered. **Other schools with the greatest overlap in**

applicants: Houghton College; Messiah College; Nazareth College of Rochester; SUNY College–Brockport; St. John Fisher College. **Admissions statistics for the fall 2005 entering class:** Total applicants: 614. Total accepted: 526. Freshmen enrolled: 228; 15% were from out of state. Overall acceptance rate: 86%. **Credentials of fall 2005 freshmen:** 23% ranked in the top 10 percent of their high school class; 50% were in the top 25 percent, and 81% were in the top half. (Proportion submitting class standing: 75%.) **Average high school grade point average:** 3.3. **First-year students who submitted SAT scores:** 98%. Scores (25/75 percentile): Verbal: 490-610, Math: 490-600, Combined: 980-1210. **First-year students submitting ACT scores:** 34%. Scores (25/75 percentile): English: 18-25, Math: 18-25, Composite: 19-26.

ACADEMICS

Year founded: 1866. **Academic calendar:** Semester. **Degrees offered:** certificate, associate, bachelor's, master's. **Most popular majors:** 27% business, management, marketing, and related support services, 23% education, 14% health professions and related clinical sciences, 6% psychology, 5% visual and performing arts. **Major fields of study:** biological and biomedical sciences; business, management, marketing, and related support services; communication, journalism, and related programs; computer and information sciences and support services; education; English language and literature/letters; health professions and related clinical sciences; history; liberal arts and sciences studies, and humanities; mathematics and statistics; philosophy and religious studies; physical sciences; psychology; public administration and social service professions; security and protective services; social sciences; theology and religious vocations; visual and performing arts. **Areas of required coursework:** arts/fine arts, humanities, mathematics, English (including composition), philosophy, foreign languages, sciences (biological or physical), history, social science, other. **Pre-professional programs:** pre-law, pre-dentistry, pre-medicine, pre-veterinary science, pre-pharmacy, other. **Special academic programs:** accelerated program, cooperative (work-study plan) program, cross-registration, distance learning, double major, English as a Second Language (ESL), honors program, independent study, internships, study abroad, teacher certificate program. **Teacher certification offered in:** special education, elementary, middle/junior high, secondary. **Reserve Officers Training Corps (ROTC):** Army ROTC: Offered at cooperating institution (Rochester Institute of Technology); Air Force ROTC: Offered at cooperating institution (Rochester Institute of Technology). **Faculty and instruction (2005-2006):** Total instructional faculty: 98 full-time, 19 part-time (55% men; 45% women; 8% minorities). Full-time faculty with Ph.D. or other terminal degree: 62%. Student/faculty ratio: 13/1. Classes of fewer than 20 students: 69%; of 20 to 49 students: 30%; of 50 or more students: 1%. **Advanced Placement and International Baccalaureate credit:** AP tests may be used for: Credit only. Scores accepted: 3, 4, 5. International Baccalaureate exams may be used for: Credit only. **Freshmen returning for sophomore year:** 81%. **Graduation rates:** Four-year: 51%; five-year: 57%; six-year: 58%. **Graduate study:** 22% of students pursue further study immediately upon graduation; 40% within one year.

COSTS AND FINANCIAL AID

Financial aid office: (585) 594-6150. **Expenses (2005-2006):** Tuition and fees 2005-2006: $19,054; room/board: $7,054. Estimated books and supplies: $700; transportation: $730. **Financial aid:** Priority filing date for institution's financial aid form: March 15.

CAMPUS LIFE AND EXTRACURRICULAR ACTIVITIES

Campus housing available (% using): coed dorms (20%), women's dorms (40%), men's dorms (25%), apartments for married students (5%), apartment for single students (5%), special housing for disabled students (5%). Students who live in college-owned, operated, or affiliated housing: 50%. **Student employment:** During the 2005-2006 academic year, 10% of undergraduates worked on campus. Average per-year earnings: $2,000. Activities include: choral groups, concert band, dance, drama/theater, jazz band, music ensembles, musical theater, opera, radio station, student government, student newspaper, symphony orchestra, yearbook. Number of fraternities: 0; sororities: 0. Average proportion of students who stay on campus on weekends: 60%. **Sports program (2005-2006):** Member of NAIA. *Men's intercollegiate varsity sports:* baseball, cross-country, golf, soccer, tennis, track and field (indoor), track and field (outdoor). *Women's intercollegiate varsity sports:* basketball, cross-country, soccer, tennis, track and field (indoor), track and field (outdoor), volleyball.

SERVICES AND FACILITIES

Basic services: nonremedial tutoring, placement service, health service, health insurance. **Remedial assistance:** reading, math, writing, study skills.

Counseling services: minority student, career, personal, veteran student, academic, older student, psychological, religious. **For learning-disabled students:** School does not offer a structured program with separate admission and additional fees. Services include: remedial math, remedial English, reading machines, remedial reading, tape recorders, videotaped classes, untimed tests, note-taking services, oral tests, learning center, readers, extended time for tests, tutors. **Library:** Number of titles: 126,100; number of current serial subscriptions: 1,118. **Information technology resources:** Students are not required to lease or own a computer. Number of campus computers available to all students: 116. School has a wireless network. Approximate number of users that can be accommodated: 200. Proportion of college-owned housing units wired for high-speed internet access: 70%. **Campus safety:** Security services offered: 24-hour foot-and-vehicle patrols, late-night transport/escort service, 24-hour emergency telephones, lighted pathways/sidewalks, student patrols, controlled dormitory access (key, security card, etc).

TRANSFER AND INTERNATIONAL STUDENTS

Transfer students: May apply for admission for the following academic terms: Fall, Spring, Summer. Applicants need a minimum number of credits to apply. For fall 2005: Transfer applications received: 295. Transfer applicants offered admission: 207. Transfer applicants enrolled: 122. **International students:** Number of foreign undergraduates: 34 (3% of student body). Number of countries represented: 12. Minimum TOEFL score required: 550 (paper); 213 (computer).

Rochester Institute of Technology

- **Address:** 1 Lomb Memorial Drive, Rochester, NY 14623
- **Website:** http://www.rit.edu
- **Private**
- **Enrollment:** 11,440 full-time; 1,493 part-time

KEY STATS
- ✔ **U.S News College Ranking:** 7, Universities–Master's (North)
- ✔ **SAT Score (25th/75th percentile):** 1110-1310
- ✔ **Tuition:** 2005-2006: $22,977

Selectivity: More selective	**Room/board:** $8,451
Acceptance rate: 69%	**Average debt:** N/A
Student/faculty ratio: 13/1	**Proportion who borrowed:** N/A

UNDERGRADUATE STUDENT BODY STATS

2005-2006 enrollment: 11,440 full-time; 1,493 part-time. Men: 69%; women: 31%. **Ethnic makeup:** African American: 4%; Asian American: 6%; Hispanic: 3%; White: 75%; International: 11%.

ADMISSIONS FACTS AND FIGURES

Phone: (585) 475-6631. **Email:** admissions@rit.edu. **Website:** http://www.rit.edu. **Application deadlines for fall 2007:** Regular decision: Rolling. Early decision: Send application by: December 1; Decision sent by: January 15. Early action: Not offered. Admission can be deferred. **Application fee:** $50. Common application is accepted. **To apply online, go to:** http://www.rit.edu/~960www/application/undergraduate/. **Admissions requirements/recommendations:** High school units required (recommended): English: 4 (4); Mathematics: 2 (3); Science: 2 (3); Foreign language: 0 (3); Social studies: 4 (4); Academic electives: 10 (5); Total units: 22 (22). Tests: The college uses SAT or ACT scores in admissions decisions. Either SAT or ACT required. For admission to the fall 2007 entering class, the school will accept: ACT with writing, ACT without writing. Campus visit: Recommended. Admissions interview: Recommended. Off-campus interview: May be arranged. **Factors that count in admissions decisions:** *Academic:* Secondary school record: Very important. Class rank: Important. Letters of recommendation: Considered. Standardized test scores: Important. Essay: Considered. *Nonacademic:* Interview: Considered. Extracurricular activities: Considered. Talent/ability: Considered. Character/personal qualities: Considered. Alumni/ae relationship: Considered. Geographical residence: Considered. State residency: Not considered. Religious affiliation/commitment: Not considered. Minority status: Considered. Volunteer work: Considered. Work experience: Considered. **Other schools with the greatest overlap in applicants:** Clarkson University; Cornell University; Rensselaer Polytechnic Institute; Syracuse University; University at Buffalo–SUNY. **Admissions statistics for the fall 2005 entering class:** Total applicants: 9,384. Total accepted: 6,519. Freshmen enrolled: 2,217; 50% were from out of state. Accepted through early-decision or early-action plans: 26%. Overall acceptance rate: 69%. Early-decision acceptance rate: 73%. Non-early acceptance rate: 69%. **Size of waiting list:** 150 applicants; enrolled from waiting list: 25. **Credentials of fall 2005 freshmen:** 28% ranked in the top 10 percent of their high school class; 59% were in the top 25 percent, and 90% were in the top half. (Proportion submitting class standing: 74%.) **Average high school grade point average:** 3.7. **First-year students who submitted SAT scores:** 86%. Scores (25/75 percentile): Verbal: 540-640, Math: 570-670, Combined: 1110-1310. **First-year students submitting ACT scores:** 25%. Scores (25/75 percentile): English: N/A, Math: N/A, Composite: 24-28.

ACADEMICS

Year founded: 1829. **Academic calendar:** Quarter. **Degrees offered:** certificate, diploma, associate, bachelor's, post-bachelor's certificate, master's, doctorate. **Most popular majors:** 20% computer and information sciences and support services, 19% visual and performing arts, 14% business, management, marketing, and related support services, 13% engineering, 10% engineering technologies/technicians. **Major fields of study:** biological and biomedical sciences; business, management, marketing, and related support services; communication, journalism, and related programs; communications technologies/technicians and support services; computer and information sciences and support services; engineering; engineering technologies/technicians; family and consumer sciences/human sciences; foreign languages, literatures, and linguistics; health professions and related clinical sciences; legal professions and studies; mathematics and statistics; multi/interdisciplinary studies; natural resources and conservation; physical sciences; precision production; psychology; public administration and social service professions; security and protective services; social sciences; visual and performing arts. **Areas of required coursework:** arts/fine arts, humanities, computer literacy, mathematics, English (including composition), sciences (biological or physical), social science, other. **Pre-professional programs:** pre-law, pre-dentistry, pre-medicine, pre-veterinary science, pre-optometry. **Special academic programs (% participation):** accelerated program, cooperative (work-study plan) program (70%), cross-registration, distance learning, double major, English as a Second Language (ESL), exchange student program (domestic), honors program, independent study, internships, liberal arts/career combination, student-designed major, study abroad, weekend college. **Cooperative education programs:** business, computer science, engineering, natural science, social/behavioral science, technologies, other. **Reserve Officers Training Corps (ROTC):** Army ROTC: Offered on campus; Navy ROTC: Offered at cooperating institution (University of Rochester); Air Force ROTC: Offered on campus. **Faculty and instruction (2005-2006):** Total instructional faculty: 798 full-time, 406 part-time. Full-time faculty with Ph.D. or other terminal degree: 85%. Student/faculty ratio: 13/1. Classes of fewer than 20 students: 44%; of 20 to 49 students: 50%; of 50 or more students: 7%. **Advanced Placement and International Baccalaureate credit:** AP tests may be used for: Credit and/or placement. Scores accepted: 3, 4, 5. International Baccalaureate exams may be used for: Credit and/or placement. **Freshmen returning for sophomore year:** 89%. **Graduation rates:** Six-year: 59%. **Graduate study:** 10% of students pursue further study within one year.

COSTS AND FINANCIAL AID

Financial aid office: (585) 475-2186. **Expenses (2005-2006):** Tuition and fees 2005-2006: $22,977; room/board: $8,451. Estimated books and supplies: $900; transportation: $300; personal expenses: $725. **Financial aid:** Priority filing date for institution's financial aid form: March 1.

CAMPUS LIFE AND EXTRACURRICULAR ACTIVITIES

Campus housing available: coed dorms, sorority housing, fraternity housing, apartments for married students, apartment for single students, special housing for disabled students, special housing for international students, other housing options. Students who live in college-owned, operated, or affiliated housing: 60%. **Student employment:** During the 2005-2006 academic year, 25% of undergraduates worked on campus. Average per-year earnings: $2,000. **Clubs and organizations:** Number of student organizations: 195. Activities include: choral groups, concert band, dance, drama/theater, jazz band, literary magazine, music ensembles, musical theater, radio station, student government, student newspaper, student film society, yearbook. Number of fraternities: 17; sororities: 8. Proportion of men in fraternities: 5%; of women in sororities: 5%. **Sports program (2005-2006):** Member of NCAA III. *Men's intercollegiate varsity sports:* baseball, basketball, crew, cross-country, ice hockey, lacrosse, lightweight crew, soccer, swimming and diving, tennis, track and field (indoor), track and field (outdoor), wrestling. **Women's intercollegiate varsity sports:** basketball, crew, cross-country, ice hockey, lacrosse, lightweight crew, rowing, soccer, softball, swimming and diving, tennis, track and field (indoor), track and field (outdoor), volleyball.

SERVICES AND FACILITIES

Basic services: nonremedial tutoring, women's center, placement service, day care, health service, health insurance, other. **Remedial assistance:** math, writing, study skills. **Counseling services:** minority student, career, personal, veteran student, academic, psychological, birth control, religious. **For learning-disabled students:** School does not offer a structured program with separate admission and additional fees. Services include: reading machines, tape recorders, other special classes, diagnostic testing service, note-taking services, oral tests, learning center, readers, extended time for tests, tutors, priority registration, substitution of courses, texts on tape, typist/scribe, other testing accomodations. **Library:** Number of titles: 407,141; number of current serial subscriptions: 2,519. **Information technology resources:** Students are not required to lease or own a computer. Number of campus computers available to all students: 3,530. School has a wireless network. Approximate number of users that can be accommodated: 1,500. Proportion of college-owned housing units wired for high-speed internet access: 95%. **Campus safety:** Security services offered: 24-hour foot-and-vehicle patrols, late-night transport/escort service, 24-hour emergency telephones, lighted pathways/sidewalks, controlled dormitory access (key, security card, etc).

TRANSFER AND INTERNATIONAL STUDENTS

Transfer students: May apply for admission for the following academic terms: Fall, Winter, Spring, Summer. Applicants do not need a minimum number of credits to apply. For fall 2005: Transfer applications received: 2,176. Transfer applicants offered admission: 1,195. Transfer applicants enrolled: 776. **International students:** Number of foreign undergraduates: 1370 (11% of student body). Number of countries represented: 71. Minimum TOEFL score required: 525 (paper); 195 (computer). Average TOEFL score: 600 (paper).

Russell Sage College

- **Address:** 45 Ferry Street, Troy, NY 12180-4115
- **Website:** http://www.sage.edu/rsc/index.php
- **Private**
- **Enrollment:** 759 full-time; 79 part-time

KEY STATS

✔ **U.S News College Ranking:** 5, Comp. Colleges–Bachelor's (North)
✔ **SAT Score (25th/75th percentile):** 970-1210
✔ **Tuition:** 2006-2007: $24,720

Selectivity: Selective	**Room/board:** $8,370
Acceptance rate: 81%	**Average debt:** $21,000
Student/faculty ratio: 11/1	**Proportion who borrowed:** 90%

UNDERGRADUATE STUDENT BODY STATS

2005-2006 enrollment: 759 full-time; 79 part-time. Men: 0%; women: 100%. **Ethnic makeup:** African American: 4%; Asian American: 2%; Hispanic: 3%; White: 90%.

ADMISSIONS FACTS AND FIGURES

Phone: (888) 837-9724. **Email:** rscadm@sage.edu. **Website:** http://www.sage.edu/rsc/index.php. **Application deadlines for fall 2007:** Regular decision: August 1. Early decision: Send application by: December 1; Decision sent by: December 15. Early action: Not offered. Admission can be deferred. **Application fee:** $30. Common application is accepted. **Admissions requirements/recommendations:** High school units required (recommended): English: 4; Mathematics: 3; Science: 3; Foreign language: 2 (3); Social studies: 4; Total units: 16. Tests: The college uses SAT or ACT scores in admissions decisions. Either SAT or ACT required. For admission to the fall 2007 entering class, the school will accept: ACT with writing, ACT without writing. Campus visit: Recommended. Admissions interview: Recommended. Off-campus interview: Not available. **Factors that count in admissions decisions:** *Academic:* Secondary school record: Very important. Class rank: Very important. Letters of recommendation: Important. Standardized test scores: Very important. Essay: Important. *Nonacademic:* Interview: Important. Extracurricular activities: Important. Talent/ability:

Important. Character/personal qualities: Important. Alumni/ae relationship: Considered. Geographical residence: Not considered. State residency: Not considered. Religious affiliation/commitment: Not considered. Minority status: Not considered. Volunteer work: Important. Work experience: Considered. **Other schools with the greatest overlap in applicants:** College of St. Rose; SUNY College of Arts and Sciences–Geneseo; Siena College; Union College; Wells College. **Admissions statistics for the fall 2005 entering class:** Total applicants: 394. Total accepted: 321. Freshmen enrolled: 117; 13% were from out of state. Accepted through early-decision or early-action plans: 14%. Overall acceptance rate: 81%. Early-decision acceptance rate: 89%. Non-early acceptance rate: 81%. **Credentials of fall 2005 freshmen:** 30% ranked in the top 10 percent of their high school class; 67% were in the top 25 percent, and 95% were in the top half. (Proportion submitting class standing: 92%.) **Average high school grade point average:** 3.0. **First-year students who submitted SAT scores:** 76%. Scores (25/75 percentile): Verbal: 490-620, Math: 480-590, Combined: 970-1210. **First-year students submitting ACT scores:** 16%. Scores (25/75 percentile): English: N/A, Math: N/A, Composite: 21-25.

ACADEMICS

Year founded: 1916. **Academic calendar:** Semester. **Degrees offered:** bachelor's. **Most popular majors:** 24% education, 16% health professions and related clinical sciences, 11% biological and biomedical sciences, 10% psychology, 6% visual and performing arts. **Major fields of study:** area, ethnic, cultural, and gender studies; biological and biomedical sciences; business, management, marketing, and related support services; communication, journalism, and related programs; education; English language and literature/letters; foreign languages, literatures, and linguistics; health professions and related clinical sciences; history; mathematics and statistics; multi/interdisciplinary studies; natural resources and conservation; physical sciences; psychology; social sciences; visual and performing arts. **Areas of required coursework:** arts/fine arts, humanities, computer literacy, mathematics, English (including composition), foreign languages, sciences (biological or physical), history, social science, other. **Pre-professional programs:** pre-law, pre-dentistry, pre-medicine, pre-veterinary science. **Special academic programs (% participation):** accelerated program (28%), cross-registration (2%), distance learning (2%), double major (7%), dual enrollment (1%), honors program (30%), independent study (100%), internships (70%), liberal arts/career combination (28%), student-designed major (5%), study abroad (2%), teacher certificate program (22%). **Teacher certification offered in:** elementary, middle/junior high. **Cooperative education programs:** engineering, health professions. **Reserve Officers Training Corps (ROTC):** Army ROTC: Offered at cooperating institution (Siena College/R.P.I); Air Force ROTC: Offered at cooperating institution (R.P.I). **Faculty and instruction (2005-2006):** Total instructional faculty: 61 full-time, 38 part-time (31% men; 69% women; 4% minorities). Full-time faculty with Ph.D. or other terminal degree: 87%. Student/faculty ratio: 11/1. Classes of fewer than 20 students: 58%; of 20 to 49 students: 42%; of 50 or more students: 0%. **Advanced Placement and International Baccalaureate credit:** AP tests may be used for: Credit and/or placement. Scores accepted: 3, 4, 5. International Baccalaureate exams may be used for: Credit and/or placement. **Freshmen returning for sophomore year:** 81%. **Graduation rates:** Four-year: 46%; five-year: 59%; six-year: 67%. **Graduate study:** 51% of students pursue further study immediately upon graduation. Fields in which graduates pursue further study: Master of Business Administration (MBA), 7%; law, 1%; education, 31%; veterinary medicine, 1%.

COSTS AND FINANCIAL AID

Financial aid office: (518) 244-2215. **Expenses (2006-2007):** Tuition and fees 2006-2007: $24,720; room/board: $8,370. Estimated books and supplies: $900; transportation: $600; personal expenses: $1,200. **Financial aid:** Priority filing date for institution's financial aid form: March 1. In 2005-2006, 97% of undergraduates applied for financial aid. Of those, 86% were determined to have financial need; Average financial aid package (proportion receiving): $24,647 (86%). Average amount of gift aid, such as scholarships or grants (proportion receiving): $5,635 (68%). Average amount of self-help aid, such as work study or loans (proportion receiving): $1,500 (85%). Average need-based loan (excluding PLUS or other private loans): $3,371. Among students who received aid based on merit, the average award (and the proportion receiving): $10,701 (5%). The average athletic scholarship (and the proportion receiving): $0 (0%). Average amount of debt of borrowers graduating in 2005: $21,000. Proportion who borrowed: 90%.

CAMPUS LIFE AND EXTRACURRICULAR ACTIVITIES

Campus housing available (% using): women's dorms (45%), special housing for international students (0%), other housing options (55%). Students who live in college-owned, operated, or affiliated housing: 46%. **Student employment:** During the 2005-2006 academic year, 14% of undergraduates worked on campus. Average per-year earnings: $1,400. **Clubs and organizations:** Number of student organizations: 40. Activities include: choral groups, dance, drama/theater, literary magazine, music ensembles, musical theater, student government, student newspaper, yearbook. Number of fraternities: 0; sororities: 0. Average proportion of students who stay on campus on weekends: 50%. **Sports program (2005-2006):** Member of NCAA III. **Women's intercollegiate varsity sports:** basketball, soccer, softball, tennis, volleyball.

SERVICES AND FACILITIES

Basic services: nonremedial tutoring, women's center, placement service, health service, health insurance. **Remedial assistance:** reading, math, writing, study skills. **Counseling services:** minority student, career, personal, academic, older student, psychological, birth control, religious. **For learning-disabled students:** School does not offer a structured program with separate admission and additional fees. Total undergraduates in learning-disabled program or receiving services: 21. Services include: reading machines, tape recorders, untimed tests, note-taking services, oral tests, learning center, readers, extended time for tests, tutors, texts on tape, typist/scribe, exams on tape or computer, other testing accomodations. **Library:** Number of titles: 341,098; number of current serial subscriptions: 37,599. **Information technology resources:** Students are not required to lease or own a computer. Number of campus computers available to all students: 154. School has a wireless network. Approximate number of users that can be accommodated: 300. Proportion of college-owned housing units wired for high-speed internet access: 100%. **Campus safety:** Security services offered: 24-hour foot-and-vehicle patrols, late-night transport/escort service, 24-hour emergency telephones, lighted pathways/sidewalks, controlled dormitory access (key, security card, etc).

TRANSFER AND INTERNATIONAL STUDENTS

Transfer students: May apply for admission for the following academic terms: Fall, Spring. Applicants need a minimum number of credits to apply. For fall 2005: Transfer applications received: 251. Transfer applicants offered admission: 181. Transfer applicants enrolled: 119. **International students:** Number of foreign undergraduates: 2. Number of countries represented: 2. Minimum TOEFL score required: 550 (paper); 213 (computer).

Sarah Lawrence College

- **Address:** 1 Mead Way, Bronxville, NY 10708-5999
- **Website:** http://www.sarahlawrence.edu
- **Private**
- **Enrollment:** 1,266 full-time; 73 part-time

KEY STATS

✔ **U.S News College Ranking:** 45, Liberal Arts Colleges
✔ **ACT Score (25th/75th percentile):** 25-30
✔ **Tuition:** 2006-2007: $36,088

Selectivity: More selective	**Room/board:** $12,152
Acceptance rate: 45%	**Average debt:** $13,607
Student/faculty ratio: 6/1	**Proportion who borrowed:** 63%

UNDERGRADUATE STUDENT BODY STATS

2005-2006 enrollment: 1,266 full-time; 73 part-time. Men: 26%; women: 74%. **Ethnic makeup:** African American: 5%; American-Indian: 1%; Asian American: 4%; Hispanic: 4%; White: 83%; International: 2%.

ADMISSIONS FACTS AND FIGURES

Phone: (914) 395-2510. **Email:** slcadmit@sarahlawrence.edu. **Website:** http://www.sarahlawrence.edu. **Application deadlines for fall 2007:** Regular decision: January 1; decision sent by April 1. Early decision: Send application by: November 15; Decision sent by: December 15. Early action: Not offered. Admission can be deferred. **Application fee:** $60. Common application is accepted. **To apply online, go to:** http://www.slc.edu/index.php?pageID=1437. **Admissions requirements/recommendations:** High school units required (recommended): English: 4; Mathematics: 2 (4); Science: 2 (4); Foreign language: 2 (4); Social studies: (4); History: 2 (4); Total units: 12 (20). Tests: The college does not use SAT or ACT scores in admissions decisions. Neither SAT nor ACT required. Campus visit:

Recommended. Admissions interview: Recommended. Off-campus interview: May be arranged. **Factors that count in admissions decisions:** *Academic:* Secondary school record: Very important. Class rank: Considered. Letters of recommendation: Very important. Standardized test scores: Not considered. Essay: Very important. *Nonacademic:* Interview: Considered. Extracurricular activities: Important. Talent/ability: Important. Character/personal qualities: Important. Alumni/ae relationship: Considered. Geographical residence: Considered. State residency: Considered. Religious affiliation/commitment: Not considered. Minority status: Considered. Volunteer work: Considered. Work experience: Considered. **Other schools with the greatest overlap in applicants:** Bard College; Barnard College; Hampshire College; New York University; Oberlin College. **Admissions statistics for the fall 2005 entering class:** Total applicants: 2,634. Total accepted: 1,174. Freshmen enrolled: 376; 82% were from out of state. Accepted through early-decision or early-action plans: 29%. Overall acceptance rate: 45%. Early-decision acceptance rate: 54%. Non-early acceptance rate: 44%. **Size of waiting list:** 500 applicants; enrolled from waiting list: 0. **Credentials of fall 2005 freshmen:** 33% ranked in the top 10 percent of their high school class; 72% were in the top 25 percent, and 95% were in the top half. (Proportion submitting class standing: 34%.) **Average high school grade point average:** 3.6.

ACADEMICS

Year founded: 1926. **Academic calendar:** Semester. **Degrees offered:** certificate, bachelor's, master's. **Most popular majors:** Information not available. **Major fields of study:** liberal arts and sciences studies, and humanities. **Preprofessional programs:** pre-medicine. **Special academic programs (% participation):** double major, exchange student program (domestic) (15%), independent study (100%), internships (25%), student-designed major (100%), study abroad (41%), teacher certificate program. **Teacher certification offered in:** early childhood, elementary. **Faculty and instruction (2005-2006):** Total instructional faculty: 188 full-time, 34 part-time (51% men; 49% women; 24% minorities). Student/faculty ratio: 6/1. Classes of fewer than 20 students: 93%; of 20 to 49 students: 6%; of 50 or more students: 1%. **Advanced Placement and International Baccalaureate credit:** AP tests may be used for: Credit only. Scores accepted: 4, 5. International Baccalaureate exams may be used for: Credit only. **Freshmen returning for sophomore year:** 91%. **Graduation rates:** Four-year: 65%; five-year: 72%; six-year: 74%. **Graduate study:** 10% of students pursue further study immediately upon graduation; 10% within one year; 70% within five years. Fields in which graduates pursue further study: Master of Business Administration (MBA), 15%; law, 10%; medicine, 10%; education, 25%; arts and sciences, 25%.

COSTS AND FINANCIAL AID

Financial aid office: (914) 395-2570. **Expenses (2006-2007):** Tuition and fees 2006-2007: $36,088; room/board: $12,152. **Financial aid:** Priority filing date for institution's financial aid form: February 1; deadline: February 1. In 2005-2006, 57% of undergraduates applied for financial aid. Of those, 50% were determined to have financial need; 80% had their need fully met. Average financial aid package (proportion receiving): $28,671 (50%). Average amount of gift aid, such as scholarships or grants (proportion receiving): $21,981 (47%). Average amount of self-help aid, such as work study or loans (proportion receiving): $4,731 (46%). Average need-based loan (excluding PLUS or other private loans): $3,045. Among students who received need-based aid, the average percentage of need met: 90%. Among students who received aid based on merit, the average award (and the proportion receiving): $5,139 (6%). The average athletic scholarship (and the proportion receiving): $0 (0%). Average amount of debt of borrowers graduating in 2005: $13,607. Proportion who borrowed: 63%.

CAMPUS LIFE AND EXTRACURRICULAR ACTIVITIES

Campus housing available (% using): coed dorms (36%), women's dorms (1%), men's dorms (1%), apartment for single students (21%), cooperative housing (41%), other housing options (0%). Students who live in college-owned, operated, or affiliated housing: 84%. **Student employment:** During the 2005-2006 academic year, 19% of undergraduates worked on campus. Average per-year earnings: $995. **Clubs and organizations:** Number of student organizations: 32. Activities include: choral groups, dance, drama/theater, jazz band, literary magazine, music ensembles, musical theater, radio station, student government, student newspaper, student film society, symphony orchestra, yearbook. Number of fraternities: 0; sororities: 0. Average proportion of students who stay on campus on weekends: 90%. **Sports program (2005-2006): Men's intercollegiate varsity sports:** basketball, crew, equestrian Sports, tennis. **Women's intercollegiate varsity sports:** crew, equestrian sports, softball, swimming and diving, tennis, volleyball.

SERVICES AND FACILITIES

Basic services: nonremedial tutoring, health service, health insurance. **Counseling services:** minority student, career, personal, academic, older student, psychological, birth control. **For learning-disabled students:** School does not offer a structured program with separate admission and additional fees. Services include: tape recorders, note-taking services, readers, extended time for tests, texts on tape. **Library:** Number of titles: 282,676; number of current serial subscriptions: 916. **Information technology resources:** Students are not required to lease or own a computer. Number of campus computers available to all students: 150. School has a wireless network. Approximate number of users that can be accommodated: 243. Proportion of college-owned housing units wired for high-speed internet access: 100%. **Campus safety:** Security services offered: 24-hour foot-and-vehicle patrols, late-night transport/escort service, 24-hour emergency telephones, lighted pathways/sidewalks, controlled dormitory access (key, security card, etc).

TRANSFER AND INTERNATIONAL STUDENTS

Transfer students: May apply for admission for the following academic terms: Fall, Spring. Applicants need a minimum number of credits to apply. For fall 2005: Transfer applications received: 229. Transfer applicants offered admission: 57. Transfer applicants enrolled: 26. **International students:** Number of foreign undergraduates: 27 (2% of student body). Minimum TOEFL score required: 600 (paper); 250 (computer). Average TOEFL score: 650 (paper).

Siena College

- **Address:** 515 Loudon Road, Loudonville, NY 12211
- **Website:** http://www.siena.edu
- **Private; Religious affiliation:** Roman Catholic
- **Enrollment:** 3,056 full-time; 280 part-time

KEY STATS

✔ **U.S News College Ranking:** third tier, Liberal Arts Colleges
✔ **SAT Score (25th/75th percentile):** 1020-1220
✔ **Tuition:** 2006-2007: $21,525

Selectivity: Selective	**Room/board:** $8,475
Acceptance rate: 61%	**Average debt:** $17,415
Student/faculty ratio: 14/1	**Proportion who borrowed:** 73%

UNDERGRADUATE STUDENT BODY STATS

2005-2006 enrollment: 3,056 full-time; 280 part-time. Men: 43%; women: 57%. **Ethnic makeup:** African American: 2%; Asian American: 3%; Hispanic: 4%; White: 90%; International: 1%.

ADMISSIONS FACTS AND FIGURES

Phone: (888) 287-4362. **Email:** admit@siena.edu. **Website:** http://www.siena.edu. **Application deadlines for fall 2007:** Regular decision: March 1; decision sent by March 15. Early decision: Send application by: December 1; Decision sent by: December 15. Early action: Send application by: December 1; Decision sent by: January 1. Admission can be deferred. **Application fee:** $50. Common application is accepted. **Admissions requirements/recommendations:** High school units required (recommended): English: 4 (4); Mathematics: 3 (4); Science: 3 (4); Foreign language: 0 (3); Social studies: 1 (1); History: 2 (3); Academic electives: 0 (0); Total units: 13 (19). Tests: The college uses SAT or ACT scores in admissions decisions. Either SAT or ACT required. For admission to the fall 2007 entering class, the school will accept: ACT with writing. Campus visit: Recommended. Admissions interview: Recommended. Off-campus interview: May be arranged. **Factors that count in admissions decisions:** *Academic:* Secondary school record: Very important. Class rank: Considered. Letters of recommendation: Important. Standardized test scores: Important. Essay: Considered. *Nonacademic:* Interview: Considered. Extracurricular activities: Considered. Talent/ability: Considered. Character/personal qualities: Considered. Alumni/ae relationship: Considered. Geographical residence: Not considered. State residency: Not considered. Religious affiliation/commitment: Not considered. Minority status: Considered. Volunteer work: Considered. Work experience: Considered. **Other schools with the greatest overlap in applicants:** Marist College; Quinnipiac University; SUNY College of Arts and Sciences–Geneseo; SUNY–Albany; SUNY–Binghamton. **Admissions statistics for the fall 2005 entering class:** Total applicants: 4,326. Total accepted: 2,620. Freshmen enrolled: 763; 17% were from out of state.

Accepted through early-decision or early-action plans: 65%. Overall acceptance rate: 61%. Early-decision acceptance rate: 61%. Non-early acceptance rate: 47%. **Size of waiting list:** 388 applicants; enrolled from waiting list: 53. **Credentials of fall 2005 freshmen:** 22% ranked in the top 10 percent of their high school class; 58% were in the top 25 percent, and 92% were in the top half. (Proportion submitting class standing: 75%.) **Average high school grade point average:** 3.5. **First-year students who submitted SAT scores:** 93%. Scores (25/75 percentile): Verbal: 500-600, Math: 520-620, Combined: 1020-1220. **First-year students submitting ACT scores:** 7%. Scores (25/75 percentile): English: N/A, Math: N/A, Composite: 24-27.

ACADEMICS

Year founded: 1937. **Academic calendar:** Semester. **Degrees offered:** certificate, bachelor's. **Most popular majors:** 46% marketing/marketing management, 10% psychology, 9% biological and biomedical sciences, 8% English language and literature, 8% social sciences. **Major fields of study:** area, ethnic, cultural, and gender studies; biological and biomedical sciences; business, management, marketing, and related support services; computer and information sciences and support services; English language and literature/letters; foreign languages, literatures, and linguistics; history; mathematics and statistics; philosophy and religious studies; physical sciences; psychology; public administration and social service professions; social sciences; visual and performing arts. **Areas of required coursework:** arts/fine arts, humanities, mathematics, English (including composition), philosophy, sciences (biological or physical), history, social science, other. **Pre-professional programs:** pre-law, pre-dentistry, pre-medicine, pre-veterinary science, pre-optometry, other. **Special academic programs:** accelerated program, cross-registration, double major, English as a Second Language (ESL), honors program, independent study, internships, liberal arts/career combination, study abroad, teacher certificate program, other. **Teacher certification offered in:** secondary. **Cooperative education programs:** business, computer science, engineering, health professions, natural science, social/behavioral science, other. **Reserve Officers Training Corps (ROTC):** Army ROTC: Offered on campus; Air Force ROTC: Offered at cooperating institution (Rensselaer Polytechnic Institute). **Faculty and instruction (2005-2006):** Total instructional faculty: 180 full-time, 132 part-time (63% men; 38% women; 11% minorities). Full-time faculty with Ph.D. or other terminal degree: 91%. Student/faculty ratio: 14/1. Classes of fewer than 20 students: 38%; of 20 to 49 students: 62%; of 50 or more students: 0%. **Advanced Placement and International Baccalaureate credit:** International Baccalaureate exams may be used for: Credit only. **Freshmen returning for sophomore year:** 88%. **Graduation rates:** Four-year: 73%; five-year: 78%; six-year: 80%. **Graduate study:** 19% of students pursue further study within one year. Fields in which graduates pursue further study: Master of Business Administration (MBA), 2%; law, 18%; medicine, 13%; theology (or the seminary), 2%; education, 29%; arts and sciences, 36%.

COSTS AND FINANCIAL AID

Financial aid office: (518) 783-2427. **Expenses (2006-2007):** Tuition and fees 2006-2007: $21,525; room/board: $8,475. Estimated books and supplies: $900; transportation: $588; personal expenses: $882. **Financial aid:** Priority filing date for institution's financial aid form: February 15. In 2005-2006, 81% of undergraduates applied for financial aid. Of those, 68% were determined to have financial need; 18% had their need fully met. Average financial aid package (proportion receiving): $14,486 (68%). Average amount of gift aid, such as scholarships or grants (proportion receiving): $10,784 (66%). Average amount of self-help aid, such as work study or loans (proportion receiving): $4,287 (53%). Average need-based loan (excluding PLUS or other private loans): $4,282. Among students who received need-based aid, the average percentage of need met: 78%. Among students who received aid based on merit, the average award (and the proportion receiving): $6,485 (13%). The average athletic scholarship (and the proportion receiving): $12,301 (8%). Average amount of debt of borrowers graduating in 2005: $17,415. Proportion who borrowed: 73%.

CAMPUS LIFE AND EXTRACURRICULAR ACTIVITIES

Campus housing available (% using): coed dorms (72%), other housing options (28%). Students who live in college-owned, operated, or affiliated housing: 79%. **Student employment:** During the 2005-2006 academic year, 20% of undergraduates worked on campus. Average per-year earnings: $1,778. **Clubs and organizations:** Number of student organizations: 68. Activities include: dance, drama/theater, literary magazine, musical theater, radio station, student government, student newspaper, television station, yearbook. Number of fraternities: 0; sororities: 0. **Sports program (2005-2006):** Member of NCAA I. *Men's intercollegiate varsity sports:* baseball, basketball, cross-country, football, golf, lacrosse, soccer, tennis. *Women's* *intercollegiate varsity sports:* basketball, cross-country, field hockey, golf, lacrosse, soccer, softball, swimming and diving, tennis, volleyball, water polo.

SERVICES AND FACILITIES

Basic services: nonremedial tutoring, women's center, placement service, health service, other. **Counseling services:** minority student, career, military, personal, academic, older student, psychological, religious, other. **For learning-disabled students:** School does not offer a structured program with separate admission and additional fees. Total undergraduates in learning-disabled program or receiving services: 96. Services include: reading machines, tape recorders, note-taking services, oral tests, readers, extended time for tests, tutors, early syllabus, priority registration, priority seating, texts on tape, exams on tape or computer. **Library:** Number of titles: 331,442; number of current serial subscriptions: 919. **Information technology resources:** Students are not required to lease or own a computer. Number of campus computers available to all students: 456. School has a wireless network. Approximate number of users that can be accommodated: 200. Proportion of college-owned housing units wired for high-speed internet access: 100%. **Campus safety:** Security services offered: 24-hour foot-and-vehicle patrols, late-night transport/escort service, 24-hour emergency telephones, lighted pathways/sidewalks, controlled dormitory access (key, security card, etc).

TRANSFER AND INTERNATIONAL STUDENTS

Transfer students: May apply for admission for the following academic terms: Fall, Spring, Summer. Applicants do not need a minimum number of credits to apply. For fall 2005: Transfer applications received: 336. Transfer applicants offered admission: 275. Transfer applicants enrolled: 164. **International students:** Number of foreign undergraduates: 27 (1% of student body). Number of countries represented: 14. Minimum TOEFL score required: 550 (paper); 213 (computer).

Skidmore College

- **Address:** 815 N. Broadway, Saratoga Springs, NY 12866
- **Website:** http://www.skidmore.edu
- **Private**
- **Enrollment:** 2,524 full-time; 249 part-time

KEY STATS

✔ **U.S News College Ranking:** 48, Liberal Arts Colleges
✔ **SAT Score (25th/75th percentile):** 1160-1330
✔ **Tuition:** 2006-2007: $34,694

Selectivity: More selective	**Room/board:** N/A
Acceptance rate: 44%	**Average debt:** $15,857
Student/faculty ratio: 9/1	**Proportion who borrowed:** 48%

UNDERGRADUATE STUDENT BODY STATS

2005-2006 enrollment: 2,524 full-time; 249 part-time. Men: 39%; women: 61%. **Ethnic makeup:** African American: 3%; American-Indian: 1%; Asian American: 6%; Hispanic: 4%; White: 86%; International: 1%.

ADMISSIONS FACTS AND FIGURES

Phone: (518) 580-5570. **Email:** admissions@skidmore.edu. **Website:** http://www.skidmore.edu. **Application deadlines for fall 2007:** Regular decision: January 15; decision sent by April 1. Early decision: Send application by: November 15; Decision sent by: December 15. Early action: Not offered. Admission can be deferred. **Application fee:** $60. Common application is accepted. **To apply online, go to:** http://www.skidmore.edu/admissions/inquire/apply.htm. **Admissions requirements/recommendations:** High school units required (recommended): English: (4); Mathematics: (4); Science: (4); Foreign language: (4); Social studies: (4). Tests: The college uses SAT or ACT scores in admissions decisions. Either SAT or ACT required. For admission to the fall 2007 entering class, the school will accept: ACT with writing, ACT without writing. Campus visit: Recommended. Admissions interview: Recommended. Off-campus interview: May be arranged. **Factors that count in admissions decisions:** *Academic:* Secondary school record: Very important. Class rank: Important. Letters of recommendation: Important. Standardized test scores: Considered. Essay: Important. *Nonacademic:* Interview: Considered. Extracurricular activities: Important. Talent/ability: Important.

Character/personal qualities: Important. Alumni/ae relationship: Considered. Geographical residence: Considered. State residency: Not considered. Religious affiliation/commitment: Not considered. Minority status: Considered. Volunteer work: Important. Work experience: Important. **Other schools with the greatest overlap in applicants:** Connecticut College; Hamilton College; Tufts University; Vassar College; Wesleyan University. **Admissions statistics for the fall 2005 entering class:** Total applicants: 6,055. Total accepted: 2,642. Freshmen enrolled: 694; 71% were from out of state. Accepted through early-decision or early-action plans: 37%. Overall acceptance rate: 44%. Early-decision acceptance rate: 66%. Non-early acceptance rate: 42%. **Size of waiting list:** 1273 applicants; enrolled from waiting list: 19. **Credentials of fall 2005 freshmen:** 46% ranked in the top 10 percent of their high school class; 78% were in the top 25 percent, and 96% were in the top half. (Proportion submitting class standing: 34%.) **Average high school grade point average:** 3.3. **First-year students who submitted SAT scores:** 97%. Scores (25/75 percentile): Verbal: 580-670, Math: 580-660, Combined: 1160-1330. **First-year students submitting ACT scores:** 17%. Scores (25/75 percentile): English: N/A, Math: N/A, Composite: 25-28.

ACADEMICS

Year founded: 1903. **Academic calendar:** Semester. **Degrees offered:** bachelor's, master's. **Most popular majors:** 19% visual and performing arts, 15% social sciences, 12% business, management, marketing, and related support services, 10% English language and literature/letters, 8% psychology. **Major fields of study:** area, ethnic, cultural, and gender studies; biological and biomedical sciences; business, management, marketing, and related support services; computer and information sciences and support services; education; English language and literature/letters; foreign languages, literatures, and linguistics; history; liberal arts and sciences studies, and humanities; mathematics and statistics; natural resources and conservation; parks, recreation, leisure, and fitness studies; philosophy and religious studies; physical sciences; psychology; public administration and social service professions; social sciences; visual and performing arts. **Areas of required coursework:** arts/fine arts, humanities, mathematics, English (including composition), foreign languages, sciences (biological or physical), social science, other. **Pre-professional programs:** pre-law, pre-dentistry, pre-medicine, pre-veterinary science. **Special academic programs (% participation):** accelerated program (1%), cross-registration (1%), double major (18%), dual enrollment (1%), external degree program (7%), honors program (7%), independent study (47%), internships (25%), liberal arts/career combination (31%), student-designed major (1%), study abroad (45%), teacher certificate program (3%). **Teacher certification offered in:** elementary. **Reserve Officers Training Corps (ROTC):** Army ROTC: Offered at cooperating institution (RPI, Siena); Air Force ROTC: Offered at cooperating institution (RPI). **Faculty and instruction (2005-2006):** Total instructional faculty: 228 full-time, 93 part-time (46% men; 54% women; 12% minorities). Full-time faculty with Ph.D. or other terminal degree: 82%. Student/faculty ratio: 9/1. Classes of fewer than 20 students: 67%; of 20 to 49 students: 32%; of 50 or more students: 1%. **Advanced Placement and International Baccalaureate credit:** AP tests may be used for: Credit and/or placement. Scores accepted: 4, 5. International Baccalaureate exams may be used for: Credit and/or placement. **Freshmen returning for sophomore year:** 92%. **Graduation rates:** Four-year: 73%; five-year: 78%; six-year: 78%. **Graduate study:** 20% of students pursue further study immediately upon graduation; 55% within five years.

COSTS AND FINANCIAL AID

Financial aid office: (518) 580-5750. **Expenses (2006-2007):** Tuition and fees 2006-2007: $34,694; room/board: N/A. Estimated books and supplies: $1,000; transportation: $250; personal expenses: $1,000. **Financial aid:** In 2005-2006, 47% of undergraduates applied for financial aid. Of those, 41% were determined to have financial need; 91% had their need fully met. Average financial aid package (proportion receiving): $28,452 (41%). Average amount of gift aid, such as scholarships or grants (proportion receiving): $22,928 (41%). Average amount of self-help aid, such as work study or loans (proportion receiving): $5,524 (41%). Average need-based loan (excluding PLUS or other private loans): $3,818. Among students who received need-based aid, the average percentage of need met: 94%. Among students who received aid based on merit, the average award (and the proportion receiving): $10,000 (0%). The average athletic scholarship (and the proportion receiving): $0 (0%). Average amount of debt of borrowers graduating in 2005: $15,857. Proportion who borrowed: 48%.

CAMPUS LIFE AND EXTRACURRICULAR ACTIVITIES

Campus housing available: coed dorms, women's dorms, men's dorms, apartment for single students, special housing for disabled students, special housing for international students, other housing options. Students who live in college-owned, operated, or affiliated housing: 74%. **Student employment:** During the 2005-2006 academic year, 55% of undergraduates worked on campus. Average per-year earnings: $900. **Clubs and organizations:** Number of student organizations: 80. Activities include: choral groups, concert band, dance, drama/theater, jazz band, literary magazine, music ensembles, musical theater, opera, radio station, student government, student newspaper, student film society, symphony orchestra, television station, yearbook. Number of fraternities: 0; sororities: 0. **Sports program (2005-2006):** Member of NCAA III. *Men's intercollegiate varsity sports:* baseball, basketball, golf, ice hockey, lacrosse, soccer, swimming and diving, tennis. *Women's intercollegiate varsity sports:* basketball, equestrian sports, field hockey, lacrosse, rowing, soccer, softball, swimming and diving, tennis, volleyball.

SERVICES AND FACILITIES

Basic services: nonremedial tutoring, day care, health service, health insurance. **Remedial assistance:** other. **Counseling services:** career, personal, academic, psychological, birth control, religious. **For learning-disabled students:** School does not offer a structured program with separate admission and additional fees. Services include: reading machines, tape recorders, note-taking services, readers, extended time for tests, tutors, early syllabus, priority registration, priority seating, texts on tape, typist/scribe, other testing accomodations. **Library:** Number of titles: 420,650; number of current serial subscriptions: 936. **Information technology resources:** Students are not required to lease or own a computer. Number of campus computers available to all students: 400. School has a wireless network. Proportion of college-owned housing units wired for high-speed internet access: 100%. **Campus safety:** Security services offered: 24-hour foot-and-vehicle patrols, late-night transport/escort service, 24-hour emergency telephones, lighted pathways/sidewalks, controlled dormitory access (key, security card, etc).

TRANSFER AND INTERNATIONAL STUDENTS

Transfer students: May apply for admission for the following academic terms: Fall, Spring. Applicants do not need a minimum number of credits to apply. For fall 2005: Transfer applications received: 182. Transfer applicants offered admission: 61. Transfer applicants enrolled: 28. **International students:** Number of foreign undergraduates: 24 (1% of student body). Number of countries represented: 28. Minimum TOEFL score required: 590 (paper); 243 (computer).

St. Bonaventure University

- **Address:** Route 417, St. Bonaventure, NY 14778
- **Website:** http://www.sbu.edu
- **Private; Religious affiliation:** Roman Catholic
- **Enrollment:** 2,026 full-time; 115 part-time

KEY STATS

✔ **U.S News College Ranking:** 31, Universities–Master's (North)
✔ **SAT Score (25th/75th percentile):** 950-1140
✔ **Tuition:** 2006-2007: $22,515

Selectivity: Selective	Room/board: $7,760
Acceptance rate: 86%	Average debt: $16,900
Student/faculty ratio: 14/1	Proportion who borrowed: 72%

UNDERGRADUATE STUDENT BODY STATS

2005-2006 enrollment: 2,026 full-time; 115 part-time. Men: 51%; women: 49%. **Ethnic makeup:** African American: 3%; Asian American: 1%; Hispanic: 2%; White: 93%; International: 2%. **Religious preference:** Roman Catholic: 66%; Protestant: 15%; No preference: 9%; Unknown: 5%; Other: 5%.

ADMISSIONS FACTS AND FIGURES

Phone: (800) 462-5050. **Email:** admissions@sbu.edu. **Website:** http://www.sbu.edu. **Application deadlines for fall 2007:** Regular decision: June 15. Early decision: Not offered. Early action: Not offered. Admission can be deferred. **Application fee:** $30. Common application is accepted. **To apply online, go to:** http://www.sbu.edu/admissions/admissions_app.vep. **Admissions requirements/recommendations:** High school units required (recommended): English: 4 (4); Mathematics: 3 (3); Science: 3 (3); Foreign language: 2 (2); Social studies: 4 (4); Total units: (19). Tests: The college uses SAT or ACT scores in admissions decisions. Either SAT or ACT

required. For admission to the fall 2007 entering class, the school will accept: ACT without writing. Campus visit: Recommended. Admissions interview: Recommended. Off-campus interview: May be arranged. **Factors that count in admissions decisions: *Academic:*** Secondary school record: Very important. Class rank: Considered. Letters of recommendation: Very important. Standardized test scores: Important. Essay: Important. ***Nonacademic:*** Interview: Very important. Extracurricular activities: Important. Talent/ability: Important. Character/personal qualities: Very important. Alumni/ae relationship: Considered. Geographical residence: Not considered. State residency: Not considered. Religious affiliation/commitment: Not considered. Minority status: Not considered. Volunteer work: Important. Work experience: Considered. **Other schools with the greatest overlap in applicants:** Canisius College; Niagara University; SUNY–Buffalo State College; SUNY–Fredonia; St. John Fisher College. **Admissions statistics for the fall 2005 entering class:** Total applicants: 1,730. Total accepted: 1,490. Freshmen enrolled: 478; 26% were from out of state. Overall acceptance rate: 86%. **Credentials of fall 2005 freshmen:** 11% ranked in the top 10 percent of their high school class; 31% were in the top 25 percent, and 68% were in the top half. (Proportion submitting class standing: 73%.) **Average high school grade point average:** 3.0. **First-year students who submitted SAT scores:** 97%. Scores (25/75 percentile): Verbal: 480-570, Math: 470-570, Combined: 950-1140. **First-year students submitting ACT scores:** 34%. Scores (25/75 percentile): English: 18-23, Math: 18-23, Composite: 19-24.

ACADEMICS

Year founded: 1858. **Academic calendar:** Semester. **Degrees offered:** bachelor's, post-bachelor's certificate, master's, post-master's certificate. **Most popular majors:** 29% business, management, marketing, and related support services, 18% communication, journalism, and related programs, 15% social sciences, 14% education, 6% psychology. **Major fields of study:** area, ethnic, cultural, and gender studies; biological and biomedical sciences; business, management, marketing, and related support services; communication, journalism, and related programs; computer and information sciences and support services; education; English language and literature/letters; foreign languages, literatures, and linguistics; history; legal professions and studies; mathematics and statistics; natural resources and conservation; philosophy and religious studies; physical sciences; psychology; social sciences; theology and religious vocations; visual and performing arts. **Areas of required coursework:** arts/fine arts, humanities, computer literacy, mathematics, English (including composition), philosophy, foreign languages, sciences (biological or physical), history, social science. **Pre-professional programs:** pre-law, pre-dentistry, pre-medicine, pre-veterinary science, pre-optometry, pre-pharmacy. **Special academic programs (% participation):** cross-registration (3%), double major (11%), dual enrollment, honors program (12%), independent study (4%), internships (61%), student-designed major (1%), study abroad (26%), teacher certificate program (18%). **Teacher certification offered in:** special education, elementary. **Reserve Officers Training Corps (ROTC):** Army ROTC: Offered on campus. **Faculty and instruction (2005-2006):** Total instructional faculty: 153 full-time, 54 part-time (64% men; 36% women; 6% minorities). Full-time faculty with Ph.D. or other terminal degree: 80%. Student/faculty ratio: 14/1. Classes of fewer than 20 students: 57%; of 20 to 49 students: 43%; of 50 or more students: 0%. **Advanced Placement and International Baccalaureate credit:** AP tests may be used for: Credit and/or placement. Scores accepted: 3, 4, 5. International Baccalaureate exams may be used for: Placement only. **Freshmen returning for sophomore year:** 81%. **Graduation rates:** Four-year: 59%; five-year: 67%; six-year: 69%. **Graduate study:** 37% of students pursue further study immediately upon graduation. Fields in which graduates pursue further study: Master of Business Administration (MBA), 10%; law, 4%; medicine, 2%; engineering, 1%; theology (or the seminary), 1%; education, 53%; arts and sciences, 19%.

COSTS AND FINANCIAL AID

Financial aid office: (716) 375-2528. **Expenses (2006-2007):** Tuition and fees 2006-2007: $22,515; room/board: $7,760. Estimated books and supplies: $700; transportation: $400; personal expenses: $650. **Financial aid:** Priority filing date for institution's financial aid form: February 1. In 2005-2006, 84% of undergraduates applied for financial aid. Of those, 72% were determined to have financial need; 33% had their need fully met. Average financial aid package (proportion receiving): $16,944 (71%). Average amount of gift aid, such as scholarships or grants (proportion receiving): $11,762 (71%). Average amount of self-help aid, such as work study or loans (proportion receiving): $5,197 (59%). Average need-based loan (excluding PLUS or other private loans): $4,555. Among students who received need-based aid, the average percentage of need met: 82%. Among students who received aid based on merit, the average award (and the proportion receiv-

ing): $6,868 (16%). The average athletic scholarship (and the proportion receiving): $19,220 (4%). Average amount of debt of borrowers graduating in 2005: $16,900. Proportion who borrowed: 72%.

CAMPUS LIFE AND EXTRACURRICULAR ACTIVITIES

Campus housing available: coed dorms, women's dorms, men's dorms, apartment for single students, special housing for disabled students. Students who live in college-owned, operated, or affiliated housing: 75%. **Student employment:** During the 2005-2006 academic year, 36% of undergraduates worked on campus. Average per-year earnings: $1,500. **Clubs and organizations:** Number of student organizations: 60. Activities include: choral groups, concert band, dance, drama/theater, jazz band, literary magazine, music ensembles, musical theater, pep band, radio station, student government, student newspaper, television station, yearbook. Number of fraternities: 0; sororities: 0. Average proportion of students who stay on campus on weekends: 90%. **Sports program (2005-2006):** Member of NCAA I. *Men's intercollegiate varsity sports:* baseball, basketball, cross-country, golf, soccer, swimming and diving, tennis. *Women's intercollegiate varsity sports:* basketball, cross-country, lacrosse, soccer, softball, swimming and diving, tennis.

SERVICES AND FACILITIES

Basic services: nonremedial tutoring, placement service, health service, health insurance. **Remedial assistance:** reading, math, writing, study skills. **Counseling services:** career, personal, academic, psychological, religious. **For learning-disabled students:** School does not offer a structured program with separate admission and additional fees. Services include: tape recorders, untimed tests, note-taking services, learning center, readers, extended time for tests, tutors. **Library:** Number of titles: 241,000; number of current serial subscriptions: 1,500. **Information technology resources:** Students are not required to lease or own a computer. Number of campus computers available to all students: 460. School has a wireless network. Proportion of college-owned housing units wired for high-speed internet access: 100%. **Campus safety:** Security services offered: 24-hour foot-and-vehicle patrols, late-night transport/escort service, 24-hour emergency telephones, lighted pathways/sidewalks, controlled dormitory access (key, security card, etc).

TRANSFER AND INTERNATIONAL STUDENTS

Transfer students: May apply for admission for the following academic terms: Fall, Spring. Applicants need a minimum number of credits to apply. For fall 2005: Transfer applications received: 142. Transfer applicants offered admission: 95. Transfer applicants enrolled: 63. **International students:** Number of foreign undergraduates: 36 (2% of student body). Minimum TOEFL score required: 550 (paper); 213 (computer). Average TOEFL score: 561 (paper).

St. Francis College

- ■ **Address:** 180 Remsen Street, Brooklyn Heights, NY 11201
- ■ **Website:** http://www.stfranciscollege.edu
- ■ **Private; Religious affiliation:** Roman Catholic
- ■ **Enrollment:** 2,019 full-time; 317 part-time

KEY STATS

✔ **U.S News College Ranking:** 27, Comp. Colleges–Bachelor's (North)
✔ **SAT Score (25th/75th percentile):** 820-1070
✔ **Tuition:** 2006-2007: $14,020

Selectivity: Less selective	**Room/board:** N/A
Acceptance rate: 92%	**Average debt:** N/A
Student/faculty ratio: 18/1	**Proportion who borrowed:** 33%

UNDERGRADUATE STUDENT BODY STATS

2005-2006 enrollment: 2,019 full-time; 317 part-time. Men: 46%; women: 54%. **Ethnic makeup:** African American: 20%; Asian American: 2%; Hispanic: 16%; White: 54%; International: 9%. **Religious preference:** Roman Catholic: 61%; Jewish: 2%; Muslim: 3%; Buddhist: 1%; No preference: 8%; Other Christian: 8%; Other: 17%.

ADMISSIONS FACTS AND FIGURES

Phone: (718) 489-5200. **Email:** admissions@stfranciscollege.edu. **Website:** http://www.stfranciscollege.edu. **Application deadlines for fall 2007:** Regular decision: Rolling. Early decision: Not offered. Early action: Not offered.

Admission can be deferred. **Application fee:** $35. Common application is not accepted. **Admissions requirements/recommendations:** High school units required (recommended): English: 4; Mathematics: 2; Science: 2; Foreign language: 2; Social studies: 4; Academic electives: 2; Total units: 19. Tests: The college uses SAT or ACT scores in admissions decisions. SAT required. Campus visit: Recommended. Admissions interview: Recommended. Off-campus interview: Not available. **Factors that count in admissions decisions:** *Academic:* Secondary school record: Considered. Class rank: Important. Letters of recommendation: Important. Standardized test scores: Very important. Essay: Considered. *Nonacademic:* Interview: Important. Extracurricular activities: Considered. Talent/ability: Important. Character/personal qualities: Important. Alumni/ae relationship: Important. Geographical residence: Not considered. State residency: Not considered. Religious affiliation/commitment: Not considered. Minority status: Not considered. Volunteer work: Considered. Work experience: Not considered. **Other schools with the greatest overlap in applicants:** CUNY–Baruch College; Fordham University; Pace University; St. John's University; St. Joseph's College New York–Brooklyn. **Admissions statistics for the fall 2005 entering class:** Total applicants: 1,566. Total accepted: 1,438. Freshmen enrolled: 505; 0% were from out of state. Overall acceptance rate: 92%. **Average high school grade point average:** 3.3. **First-year students who submitted SAT scores:** 95%. Scores (25/75 percentile): Verbal: 410-530, Math: 410-540, Combined: 820-1070.

ACADEMICS

Year founded: 1884. **Academic calendar:** Semester. **Degrees offered:** associate, bachelor's, master's. **Most popular majors:** 21% business, management, marketing, and related support services, 13% liberal arts and sciences studies, and humanities, 9% communication, journalism, and related programs, 9% computer and information sciences and support services, 9% psychology. **Major fields of study:** area, ethnic, cultural, and gender studies; biological and biomedical sciences; business, management, marketing, and related support services; communication, journalism, and related programs; computer and information sciences and support services; education; English language and literature/letters; foreign languages, literatures, and linguistics; health professions and related clinical sciences; history; liberal arts and sciences studies, and humanities; mathematics and statistics; philosophy and religious studies; physical sciences; psychology; security and protective services; social sciences. **Areas of required coursework:** arts/fine arts, humanities, English (including composition), philosophy, history, social science, other. **Pre-professional programs:** pre-law, pre-dentistry, pre-medicine, other. **Special academic programs (% participation):** accelerated program, cooperative (work-study plan) program, cross-registration, double major, dual enrollment, English as a Second Language (ESL), exchange student program (domestic), honors program, independent study, internships, student-designed major (10%), study abroad, teacher certificate program (2%). **Teacher certification offered in:** early childhood, elementary, middle/junior high, secondary. **Cooperative education programs:** computer science, health professions. **Reserve Officers Training Corps (ROTC):** Army ROTC: Offered at cooperating institution (Polytechnic University); Air Force ROTC: Offered at cooperating institution (Manhattan College). **Faculty and instruction (2005-2006):** Total instructional faculty: 71 full-time, 143 part-time (62% men; 38% women; 15% minorities). Full-time faculty with Ph.D. or other terminal degree: 79%. Student/faculty ratio: 18/1. Classes of fewer than 20 students: 50%; of 20 to 49 students: 49%; of 50 or more students: 1%. **Advanced Placement and International Baccalaureate credit:** AP tests may be used for: Placement only. Scores accepted: 3, 4, 5. International Baccalaureate exams may be used for: Credit and/or placement. **Freshmen returning for sophomore year:** 75%. **Graduation rates:** Four-year: 35%; five-year: 52%; six-year: 54%.

COSTS AND FINANCIAL AID

Financial aid office: (718) 489-5255. **Expenses (2006-2007):** Tuition and fees 2006-2007: $14,020; room/board: N/A. **Financial aid:** Priority filing date for institution's financial aid form: February 15. In 2005-2006, 86% of undergraduates applied for financial aid. Of those, 64% were determined to have financial need; 31% had their need fully met. Average financial aid package (proportion receiving): $4,622 (64%). Average amount of gift aid, such as scholarships or grants (proportion receiving): $3,683 (55%). Average amount of self-help aid, such as work study or loans (proportion receiving): $2,000 (40%). Average need-based loan (excluding PLUS or other private loans): $1,825. Among students who received need-based aid, the average percentage of need met: 67%. Among students who received aid based on merit, the average award (and the proportion receiving): $3,867 (11%). The average athletic scholarship (and the proportion receiving): $3,553 (6%). Proportion who borrowed: 33%.

CAMPUS LIFE AND EXTRACURRICULAR ACTIVITIES

Student employment: During the 2005-2006 academic year, 13% of under-graduates worked on campus. Average per-year earnings: $2,200. **Clubs and organizations:** Number of student organizations: 35. Activities include: choral groups, dance, drama/theater, literary magazine, student government, student newspaper, yearbook. Number of fraternities: 1; sororities: 2. **Sports program (2005-2006):** Member of NCAA I. *Men's intercollegiate varsity sports:* baseball, basketball, cross-country, soccer, swimming and diving, tennis, track and field (indoor), track and field (outdoor), water polo. *Women's intercollegiate varsity sports:* basketball, cross-country, softball, swimming and diving, tennis, track and field (indoor), track and field (outdoor), volleyball, water polo.

SERVICES AND FACILITIES

Basic services: nonremedial tutoring, placement service, health service, health insurance. **Remedial assistance:** reading, math, writing, study skills. **Counseling services:** minority student, career, military, personal, veteran student, academic, older student, psychological, birth control, religious. **For learning-disabled students:** School does not offer a structured program with separate admission and additional fees. Total undergraduates in learning-disabled program or receiving services: 19. Services include: remedial math, remedial English, remedial reading, note-taking services, readers, other. **Library:** Number of titles: 120,000; number of current serial subscriptions: 400. **Information technology resources:** Students are not required to lease or own a computer. Number of campus computers available to all students: 138. School has a wireless network. Approximate number of users that can be accommodated: 1,000.

TRANSFER AND INTERNATIONAL STUDENTS

Transfer students: May apply for admission for the following academic terms: Fall, Winter, Spring, Summer. Applicants do not need a minimum number of credits to apply. For fall 2005: Transfer applications received: 320. Transfer applicants offered admission: 261. Transfer applicants enrolled: 190. **International students:** Number of foreign undergraduates: 200 (9% of student body). Number of countries represented: 53. Minimum TOEFL score required: 500 (paper).

St. John Fisher College

- **Address:** 3690 East Avenue, Rochester, NY 14618
- **Website:** http://www.sjfc.edu
- **Private; Religious affiliation:** In the Catholic tradition
- **Enrollment:** 2,448 full-time; 248 part-time

KEY STATS

✔ **U.S News College Ranking:** 68, Universities–Master's (North)
✔ **SAT Score (25th/75th percentile):** 990-1180
✔ **Tuition:** 2006-2007: $20,710

Selectivity: Selective	**Room/board:** $8,880
Acceptance rate: 65%	**Average debt:** $25,833
Student/faculty ratio: 15/1	**Proportion who borrowed:** 85%

UNDERGRADUATE STUDENT BODY STATS

2005-2006 enrollment: 2,448 full-time; 248 part-time. Men: 42%; women: 58%. **Ethnic makeup:** African American: 3%; Asian American: 2%; Hispanic: 3%; White: 91%. **Religious preference:** Roman Catholic: 60%; Protestant: 26%; Muslim: 1%; No preference: 10%; Eastern Orthodox: 1%; Other: 2%.

ADMISSIONS FACTS AND FIGURES

Phone: (585) 385-8064. **Email:** admissions@sjfc.edu. **Website:** http://www.sjfc.edu. **Application deadlines for fall 2007:** Regular decision: Rolling. Early decision: Send application by: December 1; Decision sent by: December 15. Early action: Not offered. Admission can be deferred. **Application fee:** $30. Common application is accepted. **To apply online, go to:** http://www.applyweb.com/apply/stjfc. **Admissions requirements/recommendations:** High school units required (recommended): English: (4); Mathematics: (3); Science: (3); Foreign language: (3); Social studies: (4); Total units: 16. Tests: The college uses SAT or ACT scores in admissions decisions. Either SAT or ACT required. For admission to the fall 2007 entering class, the school will accept: ACT with writing, ACT without writing.

Campus visit: Recommended. Admissions interview: Recommended. Off-campus interview: May be arranged. **Factors that count in admissions decisions:** *Academic:* Secondary school record: Very important. Class rank: Very important. Letters of recommendation: Very important. Standardized test scores: Important. Essay: Considered. *Nonacademic:* Interview: Important. Extracurricular activities: Important. Talent/ability: Important. Character/personal qualities: Very important. Alumni/ae relationship: Very important. Geographical residence: Considered. State residency: Considered. Religious affiliation/commitment: Not considered. Minority status: Important. Volunteer work: Important. Work experience: Important. **Other schools with the greatest overlap in applicants:** Canisius College; Nazareth College of Rochester; Niagara University; SUNY College of Arts and Sciences–Geneseo; SUNY College–Brockport. **Admissions statistics for the fall 2005 entering class:** Total applicants: 2,753. Total accepted: 1,795. Freshmen enrolled: 553; 2% were from out of state. Accepted through early-decision or early-action plans: 6%. Overall acceptance rate: 65%. Early-decision acceptance rate: 51%. Non-early acceptance rate: 66%. **Credentials of fall 2005 freshmen:** 15% ranked in the top 10 percent of their high school class; 53% were in the top 25 percent, and 91% were in the top half. (Proportion submitting class standing: 85%.) **Average high school grade point average:** 3.3. **First-year students who submitted SAT scores:** 67%. Scores (25/75 percentile): Verbal: 490-580, Math: 500-600, Combined: 990-1180. **First-year students submitting ACT scores:** 33%. Scores (25/75 percentile): English: 19-25, Math: 20-26, Composite: 21-25.

ACADEMICS

Year founded: 1948. **Academic calendar:** Semester. **Degrees offered:** bachelor's, post-bachelor's certificate, master's, post-master's certificate, doctorate. **Most popular majors:** 24% education, 23% business, management, marketing, and related support services, 11% communication, journalism, and related programs, 8% psychology, 6% social sciences. **Major fields of study:** area, ethnic, cultural, and gender studies; biological and biomedical sciences; business, management, marketing, and related support services; communication, journalism, and related programs; computer and information sciences and support services; education; English language and literature/letters; foreign languages, literatures, and linguistics; health professions and related clinical sciences; history; liberal arts and sciences studies, and humanities; mathematics and statistics; parks, recreation, leisure, and fitness studies; philosophy and religious studies; physical sciences; psychology; social sciences. **Areas of required coursework:** humanities, mathematics, English (including composition), philosophy, sciences (biological or physical), social science. **Pre-professional programs:** pre-law, pre-dentistry, pre-medicine, pre-veterinary science, pre-optometry, pre-pharmacy, other. **Special academic programs (% participation):** cross-registration (.6%), double major (19.6%), honors program (5%), independent study (7%), internships (20.1%), liberal arts/career combination (2.6%), student-designed major (1.5%), study abroad (5.8%), teacher certificate program (14.9%). **Teacher certification offered in:** early childhood, special education, elementary, middle/junior high, secondary. **Cooperative education programs:** engineering, natural science, other. **Reserve Officers Training Corps (ROTC):** Army ROTC: Offered at cooperating institution (Rochester Institute Of Technology); Air Force ROTC: Offered at cooperating institution (Rochester Institute of Technology). **Faculty and instruction (2005-2006):** Total instructional faculty: 152 full-time, 153 part-time (51% men; 49% women; 7% minorities). Full-time faculty with Ph.D. or other terminal degree: 82%. Student/faculty ratio: 15/1. Classes of fewer than 20 students: 45%; of 20 to 49 students: 53%; of 50 or more students: 2%. **Advanced Placement and International Baccalaureate credit:** AP tests may be used for: Credit only. Scores accepted: 3, 4, 5. International Baccalaureate exams may be used for: Credit only. **Freshmen returning for sophomore year:** 84%. **Graduation rates:** Four-year: 53%; five-year: 61%; six-year: 62%. **Graduate study:** 36% of students pursue further study within one year. Fields in which graduates pursue further study: Master of Business Administration (MBA), 7%; law, 2%; education, 50%; arts and sciences, 6%.

COSTS AND FINANCIAL AID

Financial aid office: (585) 385-8042. **Expenses (2006-2007):** Tuition and fees 2006-2007: $20,710; room/board: $8,880. Estimated books and supplies: $900; transportation: $200; personal expenses: $600. **Financial aid:** Priority filing date for institution's financial aid form: February 15. In 2005-2006, 92% of undergraduates applied for financial aid. Of those, 81% were determined to have financial need; 55% had their need fully met. Average financial aid package (proportion receiving): $15,727 (81%). Average amount of gift aid, such as scholarships or grants (proportion receiving): $10,103 (80%). Average amount of self-help aid, such as work study or loans (proportion receiving): $7,311 (70%). Average need-based loan (excluding PLUS or other private loans): $6,542. Among students who received need-based aid, the average percentage of need met: 79%. Among students who received aid based on merit, the average award (and the proportion receiving): $5,251 (16%). The average athletic scholarship (and the proportion receiving): $0 (0%). Average amount of debt of borrowers graduating in 2005: $25,833. Proportion who borrowed: 85%.

CAMPUS LIFE AND EXTRACURRICULAR ACTIVITIES

Campus housing available (% using): coed dorms (96%), women's dorms (4%). Students who live in college-owned, operated, or affiliated housing: 54%. **Student employment:** During the 2005-2006 academic year, 13% of undergraduates worked on campus. Average per-year earnings: $600. **Clubs and organizations:** Number of student organizations: 55. Activities include: choral groups, dance, drama/theater, literary magazine, musical theater, pep band, student government, student newspaper, television station, yearbook. Number of fraternities: 0; sororities: 0. Average proportion of students who stay on campus on weekends: 50%. **Sports program (2005-2006):** Member of NCAA III. *Men's intercollegiate varsity sports:* baseball, basketball, football, golf, lacrosse, soccer, tennis. *Women's intercollegiate varsity sports:* basketball, lacrosse, soccer, softball, tennis, volleyball.

SERVICES AND FACILITIES

Basic services: nonremedial tutoring, day care, health service, health insurance, other. **Remedial assistance:** math, writing. **Counseling services:** minority student, career, personal, academic, psychological, birth control, religious, other. **For learning-disabled students:** School does not offer a structured program with separate admission and additional fees. Total undergraduates in learning-disabled program or receiving services: 88. Services include: remedial English, tape recorders, note-taking services, readers, extended time for tests, tutors, texts on tape, other. **Library:** Number of titles: 185,390; number of current serial subscriptions: 9,000. **Information technology resources:** Students are not required to lease or own a computer. Number of campus computers available to all students: 348. School has a wireless network. Approximate number of users that can be accommodated: 800. Proportion of college-owned housing units wired for high-speed internet access: 100%. **Campus safety:** Security services offered: 24-hour foot-and-vehicle patrols, late-night transport/escort service, 24-hour emergency telephones, lighted pathways/sidewalks, controlled dormitory access (key, security card, etc).

TRANSFER AND INTERNATIONAL STUDENTS

Transfer students: May apply for admission for the following academic terms: Fall, Spring, Summer. Applicants need a minimum number of credits to apply. For fall 2005: Transfer applications received: 782. Transfer applicants offered admission: 485. Transfer applicants enrolled: 240. **International students:** Number of foreign undergraduates: 0. Number of countries represented: 9. Minimum TOEFL score required: 550 (paper); 213 (computer).

St. John's University

- **Address:** 8000 Utopia Parkway, Queens, NY 11439
- **Website:** http://new.stjohns.edu/
- **Private; Religious affiliation:** Roman Catholic
- **Enrollment:** 11,855 full-time; 3,237 part-time

KEY STATS

✔ **U.S News College Ranking:** third tier, National Universities
✔ **SAT Score (25th/75th percentile):** 940-1180
✔ **Tuition:** 2006-2007: $24,970

Selectivity: Selective	**Room/board:** $11,470
Acceptance rate: 63%	**Average debt:** $21,122
Student/faculty ratio: 18/1	**Proportion who borrowed:** 69%

UNDERGRADUATE STUDENT BODY STATS

2005-2006 enrollment: 11,855 full-time; 3,237 part-time. Men: 42%; women: 58%. **Ethnic makeup:** African American: 17%; Asian American: 16%; Hispanic: 15%; White: 49%; International: 3%. **Religious preference:** Protestant: 10%; Jewish: 3%; Muslim: 3%; Hindu: 3%; Buddhist: 1%; No preference: 6%; Unknown: 10%; Roman Catholic: 53%; Other: 4%.

ADMISSIONS FACTS AND FIGURES

Phone: (718) 990-2000. **Email:** admissions@stjohns.edu. **Website:** http://new.stjohns.edu/. **Application deadlines for fall 2007:** Regular decision: Rolling. Early decision: Not offered. Early action: Not offered. Admission can be deferred. **Application fee:** $30. Common application is accepted. **Admissions requirements/recommendations:** High school units required (recommended): English: 4; Mathematics: (3); Science: (2); Foreign language: (2); History: (2); Academic electives: (1); Total units: 16. Tests: The college uses SAT or ACT scores in admissions decisions. Either SAT or ACT required. For admission to the fall 2007 entering class, the school will accept: ACT with writing, ACT without writing. Campus visit: Recommended. Admissions interview: Recommended. Off-campus interview: May be arranged. **Factors that count in admissions decisions:** *Academic:* Secondary school record: Important. Class rank: Important. Letters of recommendation: Important. Standardized test scores: Important. Essay: Considered. *Nonacademic:* Interview: Considered. Extracurricular activities: Considered. Talent/ability: Considered. Character/personal qualities: Considered. Alumni/ae relationship: Not considered. Geographical residence: Not considered. State residency: Not considered. Religious affiliation/commitment: Not considered. Minority status: Not considered. Volunteer work: Not considered. Work experience: Considered. **Other schools with the greatest overlap in applicants:** Fordham University; Hofstra University; New York University; SUNY–Binghamton; SUNY–Stony Brook. **Admissions statistics for the fall 2005 entering class:** Total applicants: 20,669. Total accepted: 12,980. Freshmen enrolled: 3,159; 21% were from out of state. Overall acceptance rate: 63%. **Credentials of fall 2005 freshmen:** 18% ranked in the top 10 percent of their high school class; 43% were in the top 25 percent, and 76% were in the top half. (Proportion submitting class standing: 29%.) **Average high school grade point average:** 3.1. **First-year students who submitted SAT scores:** 98%. Scores (25/75 percentile): Verbal: 470-580, Math: 470-600, Combined: 940-1180. **First-year students submitting ACT scores:** 9%. Scores (25/75 percentile): English: N/A, Math: N/A, Composite: N/A.

ACADEMICS

Year founded: 1870. **Academic calendar:** Semester. **Degrees offered:** certificate, diploma, associate, transfer-associate, terminal-associate, bachelor's, post-bachelor's certificate, master's, post-master's certificate, first professional, doctorate. **Most popular majors:** 9% communication studies/speech communication and rhetoric, 8% computer and information sciences, 8% criminal justice/law enforcement administration, 8% finance, 6% business administration and management. **Major fields of study:** area, ethnic, cultural, and gender studies; biological and biomedical sciences; business, management, marketing, and related support services; communication, journalism, and related programs; communications technologies/technicians and support services; computer and information sciences and support services; education; engineering technologies/technicians; English language and literature/letters; foreign languages, literatures, and linguistics; health professions and related clinical sciences; history; legal professions and studies; liberal arts and sciences studies, and humanities; mathematics and statistics; natural resources and conservation; parks, recreation, leisure, and fitness studies; personal and culinary services; philosophy and religious studies; physical sciences; psychology; public administration and social service professions; security and protective services; social sciences; theology and religious vocations; visual and performing arts. **Areas of required coursework:** arts/fine arts, mathematics, English (including composition), philosophy, foreign languages, sciences (biological or physical), history, social science, other. **Pre-professional programs:** pre-law, pre-dentistry, pre-medicine, pre-theology, pre-optometry, pre-pharmacy. **Special academic programs:** accelerated program, cross-registration, distance learning, double major, dual enrollment, English as a Second Language (ESL), honors program, independent study, internships, liberal arts/career combination, study abroad, teacher certificate program, weekend college, other. **Teacher certification offered in:** early childhood, special education, elementary, middle/junior high, secondary, bilingual/bicultural. **Reserve Officers Training Corps (ROTC):** Army ROTC: Offered on campus. **Faculty and instruction (2005-2006):** Total instructional faculty: 599 full-time, 829 part-time (62% men; 38% women; 17% minorities). Full-time faculty with Ph.D. or other terminal degree: 91%. Student/faculty ratio: 18/1. Classes of fewer than 20 students: 35%; of 20 to 49 students: 58%; of 50 or more students: 8%. **Advanced Placement and International Baccalaureate credit:** AP tests may be used for: Credit and/or placement. Scores accepted: 3, 4, 5. **Freshmen returning for sophomore year:** 80%. **Graduation rates:** Four-year: 40%; five-year: 56%; six-year: 64%. **Graduate study:** 20% of students pursue further study immediately upon graduation. Fields in which graduates pursue further study: Master of Business Administration (MBA), 20%; law,

10%; medicine, 6%; dentistry, 3%; theology (or the seminary), 2%; education, 24%; arts and sciences, 34%.

COSTS AND FINANCIAL AID
Financial aid office: (718) 990-2000. **Expenses (2006-2007):** Tuition and fees 2006-2007: $24,970; room/board: $11,470. Estimated books and supplies: $1,000; transportation: $1,100; personal expenses: $2,700. **Financial aid:** Priority filing date for institution's financial aid form: February 1. In 2005-2006, 88% of undergraduates applied for financial aid. Of those, 81% were determined to have financial need; 12% had their need fully met. Average financial aid package (proportion receiving): $15,807 (81%). Average amount of gift aid, such as scholarships or grants (proportion receiving): $7,255 (71%). Average amount of self-help aid, such as work study or loans (proportion receiving): $4,576 (64%). Average need-based loan (excluding PLUS or other private loans): $4,268. Among students who received need-based aid, the average percentage of need met: 65%. Among students who received aid based on merit, the average award (and the proportion receiving): $8,180 (3%). The average athletic scholarship (and the proportion receiving): $19,282 (2%). Average amount of debt of borrowers graduating in 2005: $21,122. Proportion who borrowed: 69%.

CAMPUS LIFE AND EXTRACURRICULAR ACTIVITIES
Campus housing available (% using): coed dorms (92%), apartment for single students (8%). Students who live in college-owned, operated, or affiliated housing: 18%. **Student employment:** During the 2005-2006 academic year, 5% of undergraduates worked on campus. Average per-year earnings: $8,000. **Clubs and organizations:** Number of student organizations: 180. Activities include: choral groups, dance, drama/theater, jazz band, literary magazine, musical theater, pep band, radio station, student government, student newspaper, student film society, television station, yearbook. Number of fraternities: 23; sororities: 23. Proportion of men in fraternities: 8%; of women in sororities: 7%. Average proportion of students who stay on campus on weekends: 45%. **Sports program (2005-2006):** Member of NCAA I. *Men's intercollegiate varsity sports:* baseball, basketball, cross-country, fencing, football, golf, soccer, swimming and diving, tennis, track and field (indoor), track and field (outdoor). *Women's intercollegiate varsity sports:* basketball, cross-country, fencing, golf, soccer, softball, swimming and diving, tennis, track and field (indoor), track and field (outdoor), volleyball.

SERVICES AND FACILITIES
Basic services: nonremedial tutoring, health service, health insurance. **Remedial assistance:** reading, math, writing, other. **Counseling services:** career, personal, veteran student, academic, psychological, religious. **For learning-disabled students:** School does not offer a structured program with separate admission and additional fees. Total undergraduates in learning-disabled program or receiving services: 36. Services include: tape recorders, diagnostic testing service, untimed tests, oral tests, readers, extended time for tests, tutors. **Library:** Number of titles: 937,351; number of current serial subscriptions: 19,006. **Information technology resources:** Students are required to lease or own a computer. Number of campus computers available to all students: 11,640. School has a wireless network. Approximate number of users that can be accommodated: 15,000. Proportion of college-owned housing units wired for high-speed internet access: 100%. **Campus safety:** Security services offered: 24-hour foot-and-vehicle patrols, late-night transport/escort service, 24-hour emergency telephones, lighted pathways/sidewalks, controlled dormitory access (key, security card, etc).

TRANSFER AND INTERNATIONAL STUDENTS
Transfer students: May apply for admission for the following academic terms: Fall, Spring, Summer. Applicants do not need a minimum number of credits to apply. For fall 2005: Transfer applications received: 3,317. Transfer applicants offered admission: 1,219. Transfer applicants enrolled: 569. **International students:** Number of foreign undergraduates: 403 (3% of student body). Number of countries represented: 103. Minimum TOEFL score required: 500 (paper); 173 (computer). Average TOEFL score: 562 (paper).

St. Joseph's College New York–Brooklyn

- **Address:** 245 Clinton Avenue, Brooklyn, NY 11205-3688
- **Website:** http://www.sjcny.edu
- **Private**
- **Enrollment:** 3,637 full-time; 1,346 part-time

KEY STATS
✔ **U.S News College Ranking:** 20, Comp. Colleges–Bachelor's (North)
✔ **SAT Score (25th/75th percentile):** 960-1140
✔ **Tuition:** 2006-2007: $13,680

Selectivity: Selective	**Room/board:** N/A
Acceptance rate: 84%	**Average debt:** $16,638
Student/faculty ratio: 15/1	**Proportion who borrowed:** 66%

UNDERGRADUATE STUDENT BODY STATS
2005-2006 enrollment: 3,637 full-time; 1,346 part-time. Men: 25%; women: 75%. **Ethnic makeup:** African American: 11%; Asian American: 2%; Hispanic: 7%; White: 79%.

ADMISSIONS FACTS AND FIGURES
Phone: (718) 636-6868. **Email:** brooklynas@sjcny.edu. **Website:** http://www.sjcny.edu. **Application deadlines for fall 2007:** Regular decision: August 31. Early decision: Not offered. Early action: Not offered. Admission can be deferred. **Application fee:** $25. Common application is not accepted. **Admissions requirements/recommendations:** High school units required (recommended): English: 4; Mathematics: 3; Science: 2; Foreign language: 2; Social studies: 4; History: 1; Academic electives: 3; Total units: 20. Tests: The college uses SAT or ACT scores in admissions decisions. Either SAT or ACT required. For admission to the fall 2007 entering class, the school will accept: ACT with writing. Campus visit: Recommended. Admissions interview: Recommended. Off-campus interview: May be arranged. **Factors that count in admissions decisions:** *Academic:* Secondary school record: Very important. Class rank: Important. Letters of recommendation: Important. Standardized test scores: Very important. Essay: Important. *Nonacademic:* Interview: Considered. Extracurricular activities: Considered. Talent/ability: Considered. Character/personal qualities: Important. Alumni/ae relationship: Considered. Geographical residence: Not considered. State residency: Not considered. Religious affiliation/commitment: Not considered. Minority status: Not considered. Volunteer work: Not considered. Work experience: Considered. **Other schools with the greatest overlap in applicants:** CUNY–Brooklyn College; CUNY–Hunter College; Hofstra University; Long Island University–C.W. Post Campus; St. John's University. **Admissions statistics for the fall 2005 entering class:** Total applicants: 1,926. Total accepted: 1,614. Freshmen enrolled: 632; 1% were from out of state. Overall acceptance rate: 84%. **Credentials of fall 2005 freshmen:** 17% ranked in the top 10 percent of their high school class; 49% were in the top 25 percent, and 85% were in the top half. (Proportion submitting class standing: 54%.) **Average high school grade point average:** 3.2. **First-year students who submitted SAT scores:** 94%. Scores (25/75 percentile): Verbal: 470-560, Math: 490-580, Combined: 960-1140. **First-year students submitting ACT scores:** 4%. Scores (25/75 percentile): English: 20-26, Math: 21-26, Composite: 21-26.

ACADEMICS
Year founded: 1916. **Academic calendar:** Semester. **Degrees offered:** certificate, bachelor's, master's. **Most popular majors:** 39% education, 19% business, management, marketing, and related support services, 15% health professions and related clinical sciences, 6% psychology, 5% social sciences. **Major fields of study:** biological and biomedical sciences; business, management, marketing, and related support services; computer and information sciences and support services; education; English language and literature/letters; family and consumer sciences/human sciences; foreign languages, literatures, and linguistics; health professions and related clinical sciences; history; liberal arts and sciences studies, and humanities; mathematics and statistics; parks, recreation, leisure, and fitness studies; physical sciences; psychology; social sciences. **Areas of required coursework:** arts/fine arts, humanities, mathematics, English (including composition), philosophy, foreign languages, sciences (biological or physical), history, social science, other. **Pre-professional programs:** pre-law, pre-dentistry, pre-medicine, pre-veterinary science, pre-optometry, pre-pharmacy. **Special academic programs (% participation):** accelerated program (.5%), distance learning (15%), double major (2%), honors program (1%), internships (10%), liberal arts/career combination (90%), study abroad (5%), teacher certificate pro-

gram (45%), weekend college (10%). **Teacher certification offered in:** early childhood, special education, elementary, middle/junior high, secondary. **Faculty and instruction (2005-2006):** Total instructional faculty: 148 full-time, 365 part-time (48% men; 52% women; 14% minorities). Full-time faculty with Ph.D. or other terminal degree: 65%. Student/faculty ratio: 15/1. Classes of fewer than 20 students: 60%; of 20 to 49 students: 40%; of 50 or more students: 0%. **Advanced Placement and International Baccalaureate credit:** AP tests may be used for: Credit and/or placement. Scores accepted: 3, 4, 5. **Freshmen returning for sophomore year:** 83%. **Graduation rates:** Four-year: 63%; five-year: 64%; six-year: 69%. **Graduate study:** 0% of students pursue further study immediately upon graduation; 52% within one year; 15% within five years. Fields in which graduates pursue further study: Master of Business Administration (MBA), 2%; law, 1%; medicine, 1%; education, 62%; arts and sciences, 33%.

COSTS AND FINANCIAL AID

Financial aid office: (718) 636-6808. **Expenses (2006-2007):** Tuition and fees 2006-2007: $13,680; room/board: N/A. **Financial aid:** Priority filing date for institution's financial aid form: February 25. In 2005-2006, 84% of undergraduates applied for financial aid. Of those, 75% were determined to have financial need; 79% had their need fully met. Average financial aid package (proportion receiving): $6,560 (75%). Average amount of gift aid, such as scholarships or grants (proportion receiving): $4,079 (75%). Average amount of self-help aid, such as work study or loans (proportion receiving): $3,965 (42%). Average need-based loan (excluding PLUS or other private loans): $2,372. Among students who received need-based aid, the average percentage of need met: 43%. Among students who received aid based on merit, the average award (and the proportion receiving): $5,410 (19%). The average athletic scholarship (and the proportion receiving): $0 (0%). Average amount of debt of borrowers graduating in 2005: $16,638. Proportion who borrowed: 66%.

CAMPUS LIFE AND EXTRACURRICULAR ACTIVITIES

Campus housing available (% using): other housing options (100%). Students who live in college-owned, operated, or affiliated housing: 0%. **Student employment:** During the 2005-2006 academic year, 1% of undergraduates worked on campus. Average per-year earnings: $1,500. **Clubs and organizations:** Number of student organizations: 56. Activities include: choral groups, dance, drama/theater, jazz band, literary magazine, music ensembles, musical theater, student government, student newspaper, yearbook. Number of fraternities: 2; sororities: 3. **Sports program (2005-2006):** Member of NCAA III. **Men's intercollegiate varsity sports:** baseball, basketball, cross-country, equestrian Sports, golf, soccer, tennis, track and field (indoor), track and field (outdoor). **Women's intercollegiate varsity sports:** basketball, cross-country, equestrian sports, soccer, softball, swimming and diving, tennis, track and field (indoor), track and field (outdoor), volleyball.

SERVICES AND FACILITIES

Basic services: nonremedial tutoring, placement service. **Remedial assistance:** math, writing. **Counseling services:** career, personal, academic, religious, other. **For learning-disabled students:** School does not offer a structured program with separate admission and additional fees. Total undergraduates in learning-disabled program or receiving services: 31. Services include: note-taking services, learning center, extended time for tests, tutors, priority seating, texts on tape, typist/scribe, exams on tape or computer, other testing accomodations. **Library:** Number of titles: 224,073; number of current serial subscriptions: 1,039. **Information technology resources:** Students are not required to lease or own a computer. Number of campus computers available to all students: 490. School has a wireless network. Approximate number of users that can be accommodated: 110. Proportion of college-owned housing units wired for high-speed internet access: 0%. **Campus safety:** Security services offered: late-night transport/escort service, lighted pathways/sidewalks.

TRANSFER AND INTERNATIONAL STUDENTS

Transfer students: May apply for admission for the following academic terms: Fall, Spring. Applicants do not need a minimum number of credits to apply. For fall 2005: Transfer applications received: 1,064. Transfer applicants offered admission: 885. Transfer applicants enrolled: 637. **International students:** Number of foreign undergraduates: 13. Number of countries represented: 14. Minimum TOEFL score required: 550 (paper); 213 (computer). Average TOEFL score: 550 (paper).

St. Lawrence University

■ **Address:** 23 Romoda Drive, Canton, NY 13617
■ **Website:** http://www.stlawu.edu
■ **Private**
■ **Enrollment:** 2,111 full-time; 20 part-time

KEY STATS

✔ **U.S News College Ranking:** 57, Liberal Arts Colleges
✔ **SAT Score (25th/75th percentile):** 1050-1250
✔ **Tuition:** 2006-2007: $33,910
   Selectivity: More selective **Room/board:** $8,630
   Acceptance rate: 59% **Average debt:** $27,222
   Student/faculty ratio: 11/1 **Proportion who borrowed:** 74%

UNDERGRADUATE STUDENT BODY STATS

2005-2006 enrollment: 2,111 full-time; 20 part-time. Men: 48%; women: 52%. **Ethnic makeup:** African American: 2%; American-Indian: 1%; Asian American: 2%; Hispanic: 2%; White: 88%; International: 5%.

ADMISSIONS FACTS AND FIGURES

Phone: (315) 229-5261. **Email:** admissions@stlawu.edu. **Website:** http://www.stlawu.edu. **Application deadlines for fall 2007:** Regular decision: February 15; decision sent by March 15. Early decision: Send application by: November 15; Decision sent by: December 15. Early action: Not offered. Admission can be deferred. **Application fee:** $60. Common application is accepted. **To apply online, go to:** http://web.stlawu.edu/admis/online_app.html. **Admissions requirements/recommendations:** High school units required (recommended): English: (4); Mathematics: (4); Science: (4); Foreign language: (4); Social studies: (2); History: (2); Total units: (20). Tests: The college uses SAT or ACT scores in admissions decisions. Neither SAT nor ACT required. For admission to the fall 2007 entering class, the school will accept: ACT with writing, ACT without writing. Campus visit: Recommended. Admissions interview: Recommended. Off-campus interview: May be arranged. **Factors that count in admissions decisions:** *Academic:* Secondary school record: Important. Class rank: Important. Letters of recommendation: Very important. Standardized test scores: Considered. Essay: Very important. *Nonacademic:* Interview: Important. Extracurricular activities: Important. Talent/ability: Considered. Character/personal qualities: Very important. Alumni/ae relationship: Considered. Geographical residence: Considered. State residency: Not considered. Religious affiliation/commitment: Not considered. Minority status: Important. Volunteer work: Considered. Work experience: Considered. **Other schools with the greatest overlap in applicants:** Colby College; Hamilton College; Hobart and William Smith Colleges; Ithaca College; University of Vermont. **Admissions statistics for the fall 2005 entering class:** Total applicants: 2,989. Total accepted: 1,770. Freshmen enrolled: 537; 50% were from out of state. Accepted through early-decision or early-action plans: 28%. Overall acceptance rate: 59%. Early-decision acceptance rate: 80%. Non-early acceptance rate: 58%. **Size of waiting list:** 227 applicants; enrolled from waiting list: 43. **Credentials of fall 2005 freshmen:** 38% ranked in the top 10 percent of their high school class; 71% were in the top 25 percent, and 96% were in the top half. (Proportion submitting class standing: 55%.) **Average high school grade point average:** 3.4. **First-year students who submitted SAT scores:** 100%. Scores (25/75 percentile): Verbal: 520-620, Math: 530-630, Combined: 1050-1250.

ACADEMICS

Year founded: 1856. **Academic calendar:** Semester. **Degrees offered:** bachelor's, master's, post-master's certificate. **Most popular majors:** 30% social sciences, 12% English language and literature/letters, 12% psychology, 8% history, 8% visual and performing arts. **Major fields of study:** area, ethnic, cultural, and gender studies; biological and biomedical sciences; computer and information sciences and support services; English language and literature/letters; foreign languages, literatures, and linguistics; history; liberal arts and sciences studies, and humanities; mathematics and statistics; multi/interdisciplinary studies; natural resources and conservation; philosophy and religious studies; physical sciences; psychology; social sciences; visual and performing arts. **Areas of required coursework:** arts/fine arts, humanities, sciences (biological or physical), social science, other. **Pre-professional programs:** pre-law, pre-dentistry, pre-medicine, pre-veterinary science. **Special academic programs (% participation):** cross-registration, double major (25%), exchange student program (domestic), independent study (49%), internships (28%), student-designed major, study abroad (50%), teacher certificate program (6%). **Teacher certification offered in:** middle/junior high, secondary. **Cooperative education programs:** engineering. **Reserve Officers Training Corps (ROTC):** Army ROTC: Offered at cooperating institution (Clarkson University); Air Force ROTC: Offered at cooperating institution (Clarkson University). **Faculty and instruction (2005-2006):** Total instructional faculty: 167 full-time, 23 part-time (52% men; 48% women; 17% minorities). Full-time faculty with Ph.D. or other terminal degree: 99%. Student/faculty ratio: 11/1. Classes of fewer than 20 students: 66%; of 20 to 49 students: 34%; of 50 or more students: 1%. **Advanced Placement and International Baccalaureate credit:** AP tests may be used for: Credit and/or placement. Scores accepted: 4, 5. International Baccalaureate exams may be used for: Credit and/or placement. **Freshmen returning for sophomore year:** 88%. **Graduation rates:** Four-year: 71%; five-year: 75%; six-year: 75%. **Graduate study:** 25% of students pursue further study immediately upon graduation. Fields in which graduates pursue further study: Master of Business Administration (MBA), 8%; law, 10%; medicine, 15%; education, 30%; arts and sciences, 17%.

COSTS AND FINANCIAL AID

Financial aid office: (315) 229-5265. **Expenses (2006-2007):** Tuition and fees 2006-2007: $33,910; room/board: $8,630. Estimated books and supplies: $650; transportation: $300. **Financial aid:** Priority filing date for institution's financial aid form: February 15; deadline: February 15. In 2005-2006, 81% of undergraduates applied for financial aid. Of those, 73% were determined to have financial need; 59% had their need fully met. Average financial aid package (proportion receiving): $30,445 (66%). Average amount of gift aid, such as scholarships or grants (proportion receiving): $16,983 (64%). Average amount of self-help aid, such as work study or loans (proportion receiving): $5,450 (56%). Average need-based loan (excluding PLUS or other private loans): $4,427. Among students who received need-based aid, the average percentage of need met: 92%. Among students who received aid based on merit, the average award (and the proportion receiving): $13,726 (14%). The average athletic scholarship (and the proportion receiving): $37,408 (2%). Average amount of debt of borrowers graduating in 2005: $27,222. Proportion who borrowed: 74%.

CAMPUS LIFE AND EXTRACURRICULAR ACTIVITIES

Campus housing available (% using): coed dorms (75%), sorority housing (6%), fraternity housing (5%), apartment for single students (6%), special housing for disabled students, special housing for international students, other housing options (8%). Students who live in college-owned, operated, or affiliated housing: 99%. **Student employment:** During the 2005-2006 academic year, 38% of undergraduates worked on campus. Average per-year earnings: $1,110. **Clubs and organizations:** Number of student organizations: 125. Activities include: choral groups, dance, drama/theater, jazz band, literary magazine, music ensembles, radio station, student government, student newspaper, student film society, television station, yearbook. Number of fraternities: 2; sororities: 4. Proportion of men in fraternities: 8%; of women in sororities: 21%. Average proportion of students who stay on campus on weekends: 90%. **Sports program (2005-2006):** Member of NCAA III. *Men's intercollegiate varsity sports:* alpine skiing, baseball, basketball, crew, cross-country, equestrian Sports, football, golf, ice hockey, lacrosse, nordic skiing, soccer, squash, swimming and diving, tennis, track and field (indoor), track and field (outdoor). *Women's intercollegiate varsity sports:* alpine skiing, basketball, crew, cross-country, equestrian sports, field hockey, golf, ice hockey, lacrosse, nordic skiing, soccer, softball, squash, swimming and diving, tennis, track and field (indoor), track and field (outdoor), volleyball.

SERVICES AND FACILITIES

Basic services: nonremedial tutoring, women's center, health service, health insurance. **Counseling services:** career, personal, academic, psychological, birth control, religious. **For learning-disabled students:** School does not offer a structured program with separate admission and additional fees. Total undergraduates in learning-disabled program or receiving services: 230. Services include: reading machines, tape recorders, untimed tests, note-taking services, readers, extended time for tests, tutors, priority registration, priority seating, texts on tape, typist/scribe, exams on tape or computer, other testing accomodations, other. **Library:** Number of titles: 985,948; number of current serial subscriptions: 16,775. **Information technology resources:** Students are not required to lease or own a computer. Number of campus computers available to all students: 325. School has a wireless network. Proportion of college-owned housing units wired for high-speed internet access: 100%. **Campus safety:** Security services offered: 24-hour foot-and-vehicle patrols, late-night transport/escort service, 24-hour emer-

gency telephones, lighted pathways/sidewalks, student patrols, controlled dormitory access (key, security card, etc).

TRANSFER AND INTERNATIONAL STUDENTS

Transfer students: May apply for admission for the following academic terms: Fall, Spring. Applicants do not need a minimum number of credits to apply. For fall 2005: Transfer applications received: 104. Transfer applicants offered admission: 41. Transfer applicants enrolled: 17. **International students:** Number of foreign undergraduates: 96 (5% of student body). Number of countries represented: 17. Minimum TOEFL score required: 600 (paper); 250 (computer). Average TOEFL score: 653 (paper).

St. Thomas Aquinas College

- **Address:** 125 Route 340, Sparkill, NY 10976
- **Website:** http://www.stac.edu
- **Private**
- **Enrollment:** 1,328 full-time; 658 part-time

KEY STATS

✔ **U.S News College Ranking:** fourth tier, Universities–Master's (North)
✔ **SAT Score (25th/75th percentile):** 840-1040
✔ **Tuition:** 2006-2007: $17,600

Selectivity: Less selective	**Room/board:** $9,120
Acceptance rate: 76%	**Average debt:** $12,000
Student/faculty ratio: 15/1	**Proportion who borrowed:** 67%

UNDERGRADUATE STUDENT BODY STATS

2005-2006 enrollment: 1,328 full-time; 658 part-time. Men: 45%; women: 55%. **Ethnic makeup:** African American: 5%; Asian American: 2%; Hispanic: 16%; White: 75%; International: 1%.

ADMISSIONS FACTS AND FIGURES

Phone: (845) 398-4100. **Email:** admissions@stac.edu. **Website:** http://www.stac.edu. **Application deadlines for fall 2007:** Regular decision: Rolling. Early decision: Send application by: December 15; Decision sent by: N/A. Early action: Not offered. Admission can be deferred. **Application fee:** $30. Common application is accepted. **To apply online, go to:** http://apply-web.com/aw?stac. **Admissions requirements/recommendations:** High school units required (recommended): English: 4 (4); Mathematics: 3 (3); Science: 3 (3); Foreign language: 3 (3); Social studies: 4 (4); History: 1 (1); Total units: 20 (20). Tests: The college uses SAT or ACT scores in admissions decisions. Either SAT or ACT required. For admission to the fall 2007 entering class, the school will accept: ACT without writing. Campus visit: Recommended. Admissions interview: Recommended. Off-campus interview: May be arranged. **Factors that count in admissions decisions:** *Academic:* Secondary school record: Very important. Class rank: Considered. Letters of recommendation: Important. Standardized test scores: Important. Essay: Important. *Nonacademic:* Interview: Important. Extracurricular activities: Important. Talent/ability: Important. Character/personal qualities: Important. Alumni/ae relationship: Considered. Geographical residence: Not considered. State residency: Not considered. Religious affiliation/commitment: Not considered. Minority status: Not considered. Volunteer work: Considered. Work experience: Considered. **Admissions statistics for the fall 2005 entering class:** Total applicants: 1,243. Total accepted: 945. Freshmen enrolled: 328; 31% were from out of state. Overall acceptance rate: 76%. Non-early acceptance rate: 76%. **Credentials of fall 2005 freshmen:** 5% ranked in the top 10 percent of their high school class; 35% were in the top 25 percent, and 55% were in the top half. **Average high school grade point average:** 2.7. **First-year students who submitted SAT scores:** 98%. Scores (25/75 percentile): Verbal: 420-520, Math: 420-520, Combined: 840-1040. **First-year students submitting ACT scores:** 11%. Scores (25/75 percentile): English: N/A, Math: N/A, Composite: 17-23.

ACADEMICS

Year founded: 1952. **Academic calendar:** Semester. **Degrees offered:** certificate, associate, bachelor's, master's, post-master's certificate. **Most popular majors:** 20% business, management, marketing, and related support services, 19% social sciences, 11% education, 11% parks, recreation, leisure, and fitness studies, 9% communication, journalism, and related programs. **Major fields of study:** biological and biomedical sciences; business, management, marketing, and related support services; communication, journalism, and related programs; computer and information sciences and support services; education; English language and literature/letters; foreign languages, literatures, and linguistics; history; liberal arts and sciences studies, and humanities; multi/interdisciplinary studies; parks, recreation, leisure, and fitness studies; philosophy and religious studies; psychology; security and protective services; social sciences; visual and performing arts. **Areas of required coursework:** arts/fine arts, humanities, computer literacy, mathematics, English (including composition), philosophy, foreign languages, sciences (biological or physical), history, social science. **Pre-professional programs:** pre-law, pre-dentistry, pre-medicine, pre-pharmacy, other. **Special academic programs:** accelerated program, cross-registration, double major, dual enrollment, exchange student program (domestic), honors program, independent study, internships, liberal arts/career combination, study abroad, teacher certificate program, other. **Teacher certification offered in:** early childhood, special education, elementary, middle/junior high, secondary. **Cooperative education programs:** engineering, health professions. **Reserve Officers Training Corps (ROTC):** Air Force ROTC: Offered at cooperating institution (Manhattan College). **Faculty and instruction (2005-2006):** Total instructional faculty: 61 full-time, 78 part-time (55% men; 45% women; 10% minorities). Full-time faculty with Ph.D. or other terminal degree: 84%. Student/faculty ratio: 15/1. Classes of fewer than 20 students: 48%; of 20 to 49 students: 52%; of 50 or more students: 1%. **Advanced Placement and International Baccalaureate credit:** AP tests may be used for: Credit and/or placement. Scores accepted: 3, 4, 5. **Freshmen returning for sophomore year:** 70%. **Graduation rates:** Four-year: 34%; five-year: 49%; six-year: 51%.

COSTS AND FINANCIAL AID

Financial aid office: (845) 398-4097. **Expenses (2006-2007):** Tuition and fees 2006-2007: $17,600; room/board: $9,120. Estimated books and supplies: $750; transportation: $1,000; personal expenses: $1,000. **Financial aid:** Priority filing date for institution's financial aid form: February 15. In 2005-2006, 85% of undergraduates applied for financial aid. Of those, 62% were determined to have financial need; 19% had their need fully met. Average financial aid package (proportion receiving): $10,258 (61%). Average amount of gift aid, such as scholarships or grants (proportion receiving): $7,947 (57%). Average amount of self-help aid, such as work study or loans (proportion receiving): $4,008 (46%). Average need-based loan (excluding PLUS or other private loans): $3,808. Among students who received need-based aid, the average percentage of need met: 64%. Among students who received aid based on merit, the average award (and the proportion receiving): $5,412 (14%). The average athletic scholarship (and the proportion receiving): $5,949 (3%). Average amount of debt of borrowers graduating in 2005: $12,000. Proportion who borrowed: 67%.

CAMPUS LIFE AND EXTRACURRICULAR ACTIVITIES

Campus housing available (% using): women's dorms (60%), men's dorms (40%). Students who live in college-owned, operated, or affiliated housing: 42%. **Student employment:** During the 2005-2006 academic year, 10% of undergraduates worked on campus. Average per-year earnings: $1,500. **Clubs and organizations:** Number of student organizations: 27. Activities include: choral groups, dance, drama/theater, literary magazine, musical theater, opera, radio station, student government, student newspaper, yearbook. Number of fraternities: 0; sororities: 0. Average proportion of students who stay on campus on weekends: 35%. **Sports program (2005-2006):** Member of NCAA II. *Men's intercollegiate varsity sports:* baseball, basketball, cross-country, golf, soccer, tennis, track and field (indoor), track and field (outdoor). *Women's intercollegiate varsity sports:* basketball, cross-country, golf, lacrosse, soccer, softball, tennis, track and field (indoor), track and field (outdoor), volleyball.

SERVICES AND FACILITIES

Basic services: nonremedial tutoring, placement service, health service, health insurance. **Remedial assistance:** reading, math, writing, study skills. **Counseling services:** career, personal, academic, psychological. **For learning-disabled students:** School does not offer a structured program with separate admission and additional fees. Total undergraduates in learning-disabled program or receiving services: 70. Services include: remedial math, remedial English, reading machines, tape recorders, other special classes, note-taking services, oral tests, learning center, readers, extended time for tests, tutors, priority registration, priority seating, proofreading services, substitution of courses, texts on tape, other testing accomodations, waiver of foreign language degree requirement. **Library:** Number of titles: 102,968; number of current serial subscriptions: 515. **Information technology resources:** Students are not required to lease or own a computer. Number of campus computers available to all students: 200. School has a wireless network.

Proportion of college-owned housing units wired for high-speed internet access: 100%. **Campus safety:** Security services offered: 24-hour foot-and-vehicle patrols, late-night transport/escort service, 24-hour emergency telephones, lighted pathways/sidewalks, controlled dormitory access (key, security card, etc).

TRANSFER AND INTERNATIONAL STUDENTS

Transfer students: May apply for admission for the following academic terms: Fall, Spring. Applicants need a minimum number of credits to apply. For fall 2005: Transfer applications received: 195. Transfer applicants offered admission: 169. Transfer applicants enrolled: 105. **International students:** Number of foreign undergraduates: 19 (1% of student body). Number of countries represented: 12. Minimum TOEFL score required: 530 (paper); 173 (computer).

SUNY–Albany

- Address: 1400 Washington Avenue, Albany, NY 12222
- Website: http://www.albany.edu
- Public
- Enrollment: 11,211 full-time; 802 part-time

KEY STATS

✔ **U.S News College Ranking:** third tier, National Universities
✔ **SAT Score (25th/75th percentile):** 1020-1200
✔ **Tuition:** 2006-2007: $4,350 in state, $10,610 out of state

Selectivity: Selective	**Room/board:** $8,604
Acceptance rate: 63%	**Average debt:** $14,392
Student/faculty ratio: 19/1	**Proportion who borrowed:** 74%

UNDERGRADUATE STUDENT BODY STATS

2005-2006 enrollment: 11,211 full-time; 802 part-time. Men: 50%; women: 50%. **Ethnic makeup:** African American: 8%; Asian American: 6%; Hispanic: 7%; White: 77%; International: 2%.

ADMISSIONS FACTS AND FIGURES

Phone: (518) 442-5435. **Email:** ugadmissions@albany.edu. **Website:** http://www.albany.edu. **Application deadlines for fall 2007:** Regular decision: March 1. Early decision: Not offered. Early action: Send application by: November 15; Decision sent by: January 1. Admission can be deferred. **Application fee:** $40. Common application is accepted. **To apply online, go to:** http://www.applyweb.com/apply/suny31ud/. **Admissions requirements/recommendations:** High school units required (recommended): English: 4; Mathematics: 2 (4); Science: 2 (3); Foreign language: 1 (3); Social studies: 3; History: 2; Academic electives: 4; Total units: 18. Tests: The college uses SAT or ACT scores in admissions decisions. Either SAT or ACT required. For admission to the fall 2007 entering class, the school will accept: ACT with writing. Campus visit: Recommended. **Admissions statistics for the fall 2005 entering class:** Total applicants: 16,725. Total accepted: 10,461. Freshmen enrolled: 2,560; 8% were from out of state. Accepted through early-decision or early-action plans: 26%. Overall acceptance rate: 63%. Non-early acceptance rate: 57%. **Size of waiting list:** 304 applicants; enrolled from waiting list: 0. **Credentials of fall 2005 freshmen:** 14% ranked in the top 10 percent of their high school class; 46% were in the top 25 percent, and 87% were in the top half. (Proportion submitting class standing: 69%.) **Average high school grade point average:** 3.3. **First-year students who submitted SAT scores:** 98%. Scores (25/75 percentile): Verbal: 500-590, Math: 520-610, Combined: 1020-1200.

ACADEMICS

Year founded: 1844. **Academic calendar:** Semester. **Degrees offered:** bachelor's, post-bachelor's certificate, master's, post-master's certificate, doctorate. **Most popular majors:** 24% social sciences, 14% business, management, marketing, and related support services, 14% psychology, 9% English language and literature/letters, 9% communication, journalism, and related programs. **Major fields of study:** architecture and related services; area, ethnic, cultural, and gender studies; biological and biomedical sciences; business, management, marketing, and related support services; communication, journalism, and related programs; computer and information sciences and support services; education; English language and literature/letters; foreign languages, literatures, and linguistics; history; mathematics and statistics; multi/interdisciplinary studies; natural resources and conservation; philosophy and religious studies; physical sciences; psychology; public administration and social service professions; security and protective services; social sciences; visual and performing arts. **Areas of required coursework:** arts/fine arts, humanities, computer literacy, mathematics, foreign languages, sciences (biological or physical), history, social science, other. **Pre-professional programs:** pre-law, pre-dentistry, pre-medicine, pre-optometry. **Special academic programs:** accelerated program, cross-registration, distance learning, double major, dual enrollment, English as a Second Language (ESL), honors program, independent study, internships, liberal arts/career combination, student-designed major, study abroad, teacher certificate program, other. **Teacher certification offered in:** secondary. **Reserve Officers Training Corps (ROTC):** Army ROTC: Offered on campus; Air Force ROTC: Offered at cooperating institution (Rensselaer Polytechnic Institute). **Faculty and instruction (2005-2006):** Total instructional faculty: 631 full-time, 530 part-time (60% men; 40% women; 13% minorities). Full-time faculty with Ph.D. or other terminal degree: 98%. Student/faculty ratio: 19/1. Classes of fewer than 20 students: 25%; of 20 to 49 students: 50%; of 50 or more students: 25%. **Advanced Placement and International Baccalaureate credit:** AP tests may be used for: Credit and/or placement. Scores accepted: 3. International Baccalaureate exams may be used for: Credit and/or placement. **Freshmen returning for sophomore year:** 84%. **Graduation rates:** Four-year: 50%; five-year: 60%; six-year: 62%. **Graduate study:** 45% of students pursue further study immediately upon graduation.

COSTS AND FINANCIAL AID

Financial aid office: (518) 442-5757. **Expenses (2006-2007):** Tuition and fees 2006-2007: $4,350 in state, $10,610 out of state; room/board: $8,604. Estimated books and supplies: $1,000 personal expenses: $1,706. **Financial aid:** In 2005-2006, 76% of undergraduates applied for financial aid. Of those, 55% were determined to have financial need; 17% had their need fully met. Average financial aid package (proportion receiving): $8,258 (54%). Average amount of gift aid, such as scholarships or grants (proportion receiving): $4,673 (51%). Average amount of self-help aid, such as work study or loans (proportion receiving): $4,500 (46%). Average need-based loan (excluding PLUS or other private loans): $4,154. Among students who received need-based aid, the average percentage of need met: 73%. Among students who received aid based on merit, the average award (and the proportion receiving): $3,073 (7%). The average athletic scholarship (and the proportion receiving): $11,473 (1%). Average amount of debt of borrowers graduating in 2005: $14,392. Proportion who borrowed: 74%.

CAMPUS LIFE AND EXTRACURRICULAR ACTIVITIES

Campus housing available: coed dorms, women's dorms, men's dorms, apartments for married students, apartment for single students, special housing for international students, other housing options. Students who live in college-owned, operated, or affiliated housing: 61%. **Clubs and organizations:** Number of student organizations: 160. Activities include: choral groups, concert band, dance, drama/theater, jazz band, literary magazine, music ensembles, musical theater, pep band, radio station, student government, student newspaper, symphony orchestra, yearbook. Number of fraternities: 11; sororities: 18. Proportion of men in fraternities: 2%; of women in sororities: 5%. **Sports program (2005-2006):** Member of NCAA I. *Men's intercollegiate varsity sports:* baseball, basketball, cross-country, football, lacrosse, soccer, track and field (indoor), track and field (outdoor). *Women's intercollegiate varsity sports:* basketball, cross-country, field hockey, golf, lacrosse, soccer, softball, tennis, track and field (indoor), track and field (outdoor), volleyball.

SERVICES AND FACILITIES

Basic services: nonremedial tutoring, placement service, day care, health service, health insurance, other. **Remedial assistance:** reading, math, writing, study skills, other. **Counseling services:** minority student, career, personal, academic, psychological, birth control, religious, other. **For learning-disabled students:** School does not offer a structured program with separate admission and additional fees. Total undergraduates in learning-disabled program or receiving services: 260. **Library:** Number of titles: 2,064,576; number of current serial subscriptions: 38,859. **Information technology resources:** Students are not required to lease or own a computer. Number of campus computers available to all students: 500. School has a wireless network. Approximate number of users that can be accommodated: 2,100. Proportion of college-owned housing units wired for high-speed internet access: 100%. **Campus safety:** Security services offered: 24-hour foot-and-vehicle patrols, late-night transport/escort service, 24-hour emergency telephones, lighted pathways/sidewalks, student patrols, controlled dormitory access (key, security card, etc).

TRANSFER AND INTERNATIONAL STUDENTS

Transfer students: May apply for admission for the following academic terms: Fall, Spring, Summer. Applicants need a minimum number of credits to apply. For fall 2005: Transfer applications received: 4,576. Transfer applicants offered admission: 2,327. Transfer applicants enrolled: 1,419. **International students:** Number of foreign undergraduates: 211 (2% of student body). Number of countries represented: 203. Minimum TOEFL score required: 550 (paper); 213 (computer).

SUNY–Binghamton

- **Address:** PO Box 6000, Binghamton, NY 13902-6000
- **Website:** http://www.binghamton.edu
- **Public**
- **Enrollment:** 10,734 full-time; 440 part-time

KEY STATS

✔ **U.S News College Ranking:** 86, National Universities
✔ **SAT Score (25th/75th percentile):** 1160-1350
✔ **Tuition:** 2006-2007: $5,910 in state, $12,170 out of state
  Selectivity: More selective   **Room/board:** $8,588
  Acceptance rate: 43%   **Average debt:** $14,734
  Student/faculty ratio: 21/1   **Proportion who borrowed:** 60%

UNDERGRADUATE STUDENT BODY STATS

2005-2006 enrollment: 10,734 full-time; 440 part-time. Men: 52%; women: 48%. **Ethnic makeup:** African American: 5%; Asian American: 15%; Hispanic: 6%; White: 68%; International: 7%. **Religious preference:** Roman Catholic: 29%; Protestant: 19%; Jewish: 22%; Muslim: 1%; Hindu: 1%; Buddhist: 2%; No preference: 24%; Other: 2%.

ADMISSIONS FACTS AND FIGURES

Phone: (607) 777-2171. **Email:** admit@binghamton.edu. **Website:** http://www.binghamton.edu. **Application deadlines for fall 2007:** Regular decision: Rolling. Early decision: Not offered. Early action: Send application by: November 15; Decision sent by: December 22. Admission can be deferred. **Application fee:** $40. Common application is accepted. **To apply online, go to:** http://infostu.suny.edu. **Admissions requirements/recommendations:** High school units required (recommended): English: 4; Mathematics: 3 (4); Science: 2 (4); Foreign language: 3 (3); Social studies: 2; History: (3); Total units: 16. Tests: The college uses SAT or ACT scores in admissions decisions. Either SAT or ACT required. For admission to the fall 2007 entering class, the school will accept: ACT with writing. Campus visit: Recommended. Admissions interview: Neither required nor recommended. Off-campus interview: Not available. **Factors that count in admissions decisions:** *Academic:* Secondary school record: Very important. Class rank: Important. Letters of recommendation: Considered. Standardized test scores: Very important. Essay: Important. *Nonacademic:* Interview: Not considered. Extracurricular activities: Important. Talent/ability: Considered. Character/personal qualities: Considered. Alumni/ae relationship: Considered. Geographical residence: Considered. State residency: Considered. Religious affiliation/commitment: Not considered. Minority status: Considered. Volunteer work: Considered. Work experience: Considered. **Other schools with the greatest overlap in applicants:** Boston University; Cornell University; New York University; SUNY–Stony Brook; Syracuse University. **Admissions statistics for the fall 2005 entering class:** Total applicants: 21,658. Total accepted: 9,285. Freshmen enrolled: 2,215; 9% were from out of state. Accepted through early-decision or early-action plans: 32%. Overall acceptance rate: 43%. Non-early acceptance rate: 40%. **Size of waiting list:** 2711 applicants; enrolled from waiting list: 9. **Credentials of fall 2005 freshmen:** 47% ranked in the top 10 percent of their high school class; 87% were in the top 25 percent, and 99% were in the top half. (Proportion submitting class standing: 29%.) **Average high school grade point average:** 3.7. **First-year students who submitted SAT scores:** 91%. Scores (25/75 percentile): Verbal: 560-660, Math: 600-690, Combined: 1160-1350. **First-year students submitting ACT scores:** 11%. Scores (25/75 percentile): English: N/A, Math: N/A, Composite: 25-29.

ACADEMICS

Year founded: 1946. **Academic calendar:** Semester. **Degrees offered:** bachelor's, master's, post-master's certificate, doctorate. **Most popular majors:** 10% English language and literature, 10% business administration and management, 8% economics, 8% psychology, 7% biology/biological sciences. **Major fields of study:** area, ethnic, cultural, and gender studies; biological and biomedical sciences; business, management, marketing, and related support services; computer and information sciences and support services; engineering; English language and literature/letters; foreign languages, literatures, and linguistics; health professions and related clinical sciences; history; mathematics and statistics; multi/interdisciplinary studies; natural resources and conservation; philosophy and religious studies; physical sciences; psychology; social sciences; visual and performing arts. **Areas of required coursework:** arts/fine arts, humanities, mathematics, English (including composition), sciences (biological or physical), social science, other. **Pre-professional programs:** pre-law, pre-dentistry, pre-medicine, pre-veterinary science, pre-optometry. **Special academic programs (% participation):** accelerated program, distance learning, double major (9%), dual enrollment, English as a Second Language (ESL), exchange student program (domestic), honors program, independent study, internships (33%), liberal arts/career combination, student-designed major, study abroad (18%), teacher certificate program. **Teacher certification offered in:** special education, elementary, middle/junior high, secondary. **Reserve Officers Training Corps (ROTC):** Army ROTC: Offered at cooperating institution (Cornell); Air Force ROTC: Offered at cooperating institution (Cornell University). **Faculty and instruction (2005-2006):** Total instructional faculty: 537 full-time, 232 part-time (60% men; 40% women; 19% minorities). Full-time faculty with Ph.D. or other terminal degree: 93%. Student/faculty ratio: 21/1. Classes of fewer than 20 students: 41%; of 20 to 49 students: 45%; of 50 or more students: 15%. **Advanced Placement and International Baccalaureate credit:** AP tests may be used for: Credit and/or placement. Scores accepted: 3, 4, 5. International Baccalaureate exams may be used for: Credit and/or placement. **Freshmen returning for sophomore year:** 91%. **Graduation rates:** Four-year: 67%; five-year: 78%; six-year: 79%. **Graduate study:** 38% of students pursue further study immediately upon graduation. Fields in which graduates pursue further study: Master of Business Administration (MBA), 5%; law, 18%; medicine, 24%; dentistry, 1%; engineering, 3%; theology (or the seminary), 1%; arts and sciences, 25%.

COSTS AND FINANCIAL AID

Financial aid office: (607) 777-2428. **Expenses (2006-2007):** Tuition and fees 2006-2007: $5,910 in state, $12,170 out of state; room/board: $8,588. Estimated books and supplies: $800; transportation: $260. **Financial aid:** Priority filing date for institution's financial aid form: March 1. In 2005-2006, 67% of undergraduates applied for financial aid. Of those, 46% were determined to have financial need; 76% had their need fully met. Average financial aid package (proportion receiving): $11,516 (46%). Average amount of gift aid, such as scholarships or grants (proportion receiving): $4,788 (42%). Average amount of self-help aid, such as work study or loans (proportion receiving): $4,792 (43%). Average need-based loan (excluding PLUS or other private loans): $4,345. Among students who received need-based aid, the average percentage of need met: 80%. Among students who received aid based on merit, the average award (and the proportion receiving): $4,162 (3%). The average athletic scholarship (and the proportion receiving): $9,737 (2%). Average amount of debt of borrowers graduating in 2005: $14,734. Proportion who borrowed: 60%.

CAMPUS LIFE AND EXTRACURRICULAR ACTIVITIES

Campus housing available (% using): coed dorms (64%), apartments for married students (1%), apartment for single students (16%), special housing for disabled students (3%), other housing options (15%). Students who live in college-owned, operated, or affiliated housing: 58%. **Student employment:** During the 2005-2006 academic year, 13% of undergraduates worked on campus. Average per-year earnings: $1,200. **Clubs and organizations:** Number of student organizations: 204. Activities include: choral groups, concert band, dance, drama/theater, jazz band, literary magazine, music ensembles, musical theater, opera, pep band, radio station, student government, student newspaper, student film society, symphony orchestra, television station, yearbook. Number of fraternities: 20; sororities: 12. Proportion of men in fraternities: 8%; of women in sororities: 9%. Average proportion of students who stay on campus on weekends: 80%. **Sports program (2005-2006):** Member of NCAA I. *Men's intercollegiate varsity sports:* baseball, basketball, cross-country, golf, lacrosse, soccer, swimming and diving, tennis, track and field (indoor), track and field (outdoor), wrestling. *Women's intercollegiate varsity sports:* basketball, cross-country, lacrosse, soccer, softball, swimming and diving, tennis, track and field (indoor), track and field (outdoor), volleyball.

SERVICES AND FACILITIES

Basic services: nonremedial tutoring, women's center, placement service, day care, health service, health insurance. **Counseling services:** minority student, career, military, personal, veteran student, academic, older student, psychological, birth control, religious. **For learning-disabled students:** School does not offer a structured program with separate admission and additional fees. Total undergraduates in learning-disabled program or receiving services: 164. Services include: reading machines, other special classes, note-taking services, readers, extended time for tests, tutors, texts on tape, other testing accomodations, other. **Library:** Number of titles: 2,282,284; number of current serial subscriptions: 36,431. **Information technology resources:** Students are not required to lease or own a computer. Number of campus computers available to all students: 7,600. School has a wireless network. Approximate number of users that can be accommodated: 1,500. Proportion of college-owned housing units wired for high-speed internet access: 100%. **Campus safety:** Security services offered: 24-hour foot-and-vehicle patrols, late-night transport/escort service, 24-hour emergency telephones, lighted pathways/sidewalks, student patrols, controlled dormitory access (key, security card, etc).

TRANSFER AND INTERNATIONAL STUDENTS

Transfer students: May apply for admission for the following academic terms: Fall, Spring. Applicants do not need a minimum number of credits to apply. For fall 2005: Transfer applications received: 3,381. Transfer applicants offered admission: 1,579. Transfer applicants enrolled: 803. **International students:** Number of foreign undergraduates: 742 (7% of student body). Number of countries represented: 65. Minimum TOEFL score required: 550 (paper); 213 (computer).

SUNY—Buffalo State College

- **Address:** 1300 Elmwood Avenue, Buffalo, NY 14222
- **Website:** http://www.buffalostate.edu
- **Public**
- **Enrollment:** 7,818 full-time; 1,192 part-time

KEY STATS

✔ **U.S News College Ranking:** third tier, Universities–Master's (North)
✔ **SAT Score (25th/75th percentile):** 910-1080
✔ **Tuition:** 2006-2007: $5,285 in state, $11,545 out of state

Selectivity: Less selective	**Room/board:** $7,500
Acceptance rate: 44%	**Average debt:** $17,657
Student/faculty ratio: 16/1	**Proportion who borrowed:** 69%

UNDERGRADUATE STUDENT BODY STATS

2005-2006 enrollment: 7,818 full-time; 1,192 part-time. Men: 41%; women: 59%. **Ethnic makeup:** African American: 13%; Asian American: 2%; Hispanic: 4%; White: 81%.

ADMISSIONS FACTS AND FIGURES

Phone: (716) 878-4017. **Email:** admissio@buffalostate.edu. **Website:** http://www.buffalostate.edu. **Application deadlines for fall 2007:** Regular decision: Rolling. Early decision: Send application by: November 15; Decision sent by: December 15. Early action: Not offered. Admission can be deferred. **Application fee:** $40. Common application is not accepted. **To apply online, go to:** http://www.buffalostate.edu/admissions/applying/. **Admissions requirements/recommendations:** High school units required (recommended): English: (4); Mathematics: 2 (3); Science: 2 (3); Foreign language: (3); Academic electives: (4); Total units: (17). Tests: The college uses SAT or ACT scores in admissions decisions. SAT required. For admission to the fall 2007 entering class, the school will accept: ACT with writing, ACT without writing. Campus visit: Recommended. Admissions interview: Neither required nor recommended. Off-campus interview: May not be arranged. **Factors that count in admissions decisions:** *Academic:* Secondary school record: Very important. Class rank: Important. Letters of recommendation: Considered. Standardized test scores: Very important. Essay: Considered. *Nonacademic:* Interview: Considered. Extracurricular activities: Considered. Talent/ability: Considered. Character/personal qualities: Considered. Alumni/ae relationship: Not considered. Geographical residence: Not considered. State residency: Not considered. Religious affiliation/commitment: Not considered. Minority status: Not considered. Volunteer work: Considered. Work experience: Considered. **Other schools**

with the greatest overlap in applicants: SUNY College–Brockport; SUNY–Fredonia; University at Buffalo–SUNY. **Admissions statistics for the fall 2005 entering class:** Total applicants: 8,563. Total accepted: 3,736. Freshmen enrolled: 1,250; 1% were from out of state. Accepted through early-decision or early-action plans: 2%. Overall acceptance rate: 44%. Early-decision acceptance rate: 68%. Non-early acceptance rate: 44%. **Credentials of fall 2005 freshmen:** 6% ranked in the top 10 percent of their high school class; 25% were in the top 25 percent, and 73% were in the top half. (Proportion submitting class standing: 83%.) **Average high school grade point average:** 3.3. **First-year students who submitted SAT scores:** 89%. Scores (25/75 percentile): Verbal: 450-540, Math: 460-540, Combined: 910-1080. **First-year students submitting ACT scores:** 12%. Scores (25/75 percentile): English: N/A, Math: N/A, Composite: 19-23.

ACADEMICS

Year founded: 1871. **Academic calendar:** Semester. **Degrees offered:** bachelor's, master's, post-master's certificate. **Most popular majors:** 26% education, 10% visual and performing arts, 8% communication, journalism, and related programs, 7% business, management, marketing, and related support services, 7% social sciences. **Major fields of study:** biological and biomedical sciences; business, management, marketing, and related support services; communication, journalism, and related programs; computer and information sciences and support services; education; engineering technologies/technicians; English language and literature/letters; family and consumer sciences/human sciences; foreign languages, literatures, and linguistics; health professions and related clinical sciences; history; liberal arts and sciences studies, and humanities; mathematics and statistics; multi/interdisciplinary studies; philosophy and religious studies; physical sciences; psychology; public administration and social service professions; security and protective services; social sciences; visual and performing arts. **Areas of required coursework:** arts/fine arts, humanities, computer literacy, mathematics, English (including composition), philosophy, foreign languages, sciences (biological or physical), history, social science. **Pre-professional programs:** pre-law, pre-medicine, other. **Special academic programs (% participation):** cooperative (work-study plan) program (.3%), cross-registration (.5%), distance learning (.6%), double major (2%), dual enrollment (.2%), English as a Second Language (ESL) (.2%), exchange student program (domestic) (.3%), honors program (1%), independent study (1%), internships (5%), liberal arts/career combination, student-designed major (2%), study abroad (.6%), teacher certificate program (1%). **Teacher certification offered in:** early childhood, special education, elementary, vo-tech, middle/junior high, adult education, secondary, bilingual/bicultural. **Reserve Officers Training Corps (ROTC):** Army ROTC: Offered at cooperating institution (Canisius College). **Faculty and instruction (2005-2006):** Total instructional faculty: 399 full-time, 360 part-time (56% men; 44% women; 13% minorities). Full-time faculty with Ph.D. or other terminal degree: 78%. Student/faculty ratio: 16/1. Classes of fewer than 20 students: 53%; of 20 to 49 students: 39%; of 50 or more students: 8%. **Advanced Placement and International Baccalaureate credit:** AP tests may be used for: Credit only. Scores accepted: 3, 4, 5. International Baccalaureate exams may be used for: Credit only. **Freshmen returning for sophomore year:** 75%. **Graduation rates:** Four-year: 15%; five-year: 33%; six-year: 40%. **Graduate study:** 39% of students pursue further study immediately upon graduation; 44% within one year; 55% within five years. Fields in which graduates pursue further study: Master of Business Administration (MBA), 3%; law, 2%; education, 20%; arts and sciences, 12%.

COSTS AND FINANCIAL AID

Financial aid office: (716) 878-4901. **Expenses (2006-2007):** Tuition and fees 2006-2007: $5,285 in state, $11,545 out of state; room/board: $7,500. Estimated books and supplies: $900; transportation: $1,100; personal expenses: $1,000. **Financial aid:** Priority filing date for institution's financial aid form: March 15; deadline: May 1. In 2005-2006, 84% of undergraduates applied for financial aid. Of those, 73% were determined to have financial need; 64% had their need fully met. Average financial aid package (proportion receiving): $7,870 (73%). Average amount of gift aid, such as scholarships or grants (proportion receiving): $4,057 (66%). Average amount of self-help aid, such as work study or loans (proportion receiving): $4,044 (52%). Average need-based loan (excluding PLUS or other private loans): $3,889. Among students who received need-based aid, the average percentage of need met: 87%. Among students who received aid based on merit, the average award (and the proportion receiving): $3,212 (0%). The average athletic scholarship (and the proportion receiving): $0 (0%). Average amount of debt of borrowers graduating in 2005: $17,657. Proportion who borrowed: 69%.

CAMPUS LIFE AND EXTRACURRICULAR ACTIVITIES

Campus housing available (% using): coed dorms (80%), other housing options (20%). Students who live in college-owned, operated, or affiliated housing: 22%. **Student employment:** During the 2005-2006 academic year, 3% of undergraduates worked on campus. Average per-year earnings: $2,500. **Clubs and organizations:** Number of student organizations: 48. Activities include: choral groups, concert band, dance, drama/theater, jazz band, literary magazine, music ensembles, radio station, student government, student newspaper, student film society, yearbook. Number of fraternities: 11; sororities: 8. Proportion of men in fraternities: 1%; of women in sororities: 1%. Average proportion of students who stay on campus on weekends: 55%. **Sports program (2005-2006):** Member of NCAA III. *Men's intercollegiate varsity sports:* basketball, cross-country, football, ice hockey, soccer, swimming and diving, track and field (indoor), track and field (outdoor). *Women's intercollegiate varsity sports:* basketball, cross-country, ice hockey, lacrosse, soccer, softball, swimming and diving, track and field (indoor), track and field (outdoor), volleyball.

SERVICES AND FACILITIES

Basic services: women's center, day care, health service, health insurance. **Remedial assistance:** other. **Counseling services:** minority student, career, personal, veteran student, academic, older student, psychological, birth control, other. **For learning-disabled students:** School does not offer a structured program with separate admission and additional fees. Total undergraduates in learning-disabled program or receiving services: 285. Services include: remedial math, remedial English, reading machines, tape recorders, note-taking services, oral tests, learning center, readers, extended time for tests, tutors. **Library:** Number of titles: 667,314; number of current serial subscriptions: 1,070. **Information technology resources:** Students are not required to lease or own a computer. Number of campus computers available to all students: 1,050. School has a wireless network. Approximate number of users that can be accommodated: 125. Proportion of college-owned housing units wired for high-speed internet access: 100%. **Campus safety:** Security services offered: 24-hour foot-and-vehicle patrols, late-night transport/escort service, 24-hour emergency telephones, lighted pathways/sidewalks, student patrols, controlled dormitory access (key, security card, etc).

TRANSFER AND INTERNATIONAL STUDENTS

Transfer students: May apply for admission for the following academic terms: Fall, Spring, Summer. Applicants need a minimum number of credits to apply. For fall 2005: Transfer applications received: 2,642. Transfer applicants offered admission: 1,420. Transfer applicants enrolled: 983. **International students:** Number of foreign undergraduates: 36. Number of countries represented: 16. Minimum TOEFL score required: 500 (paper); 173 (computer).

SUNY College–Brockport

- **Address:** 350 New Campus Drive, Brockport, NY 14420
- **Website:** http://www.brockport.edu
- **Public**
- **Enrollment:** 6,178 full-time; 787 part-time

KEY STATS

✔ **U.S News College Ranking:** 79, Universities–Master's (North)
✔ **SAT Score (25th/75th percentile):** 980-1170
✔ **Tuition:** 2006-2007: $5,356 in state, $11,306 out of state

Selectivity: Selective	Room/board: $7,830
Acceptance rate: 46%	Average debt: $19,556
Student/faculty ratio: 19/1	Proportion who borrowed: 80%

UNDERGRADUATE STUDENT BODY STATS

2005-2006 enrollment: 6,178 full-time; 787 part-time. Men: 43%; women: 57%. **Ethnic makeup:** African American: 5%; Asian American: 1%; Hispanic: 3%; White: 90%; International: 1%.

ADMISSIONS FACTS AND FIGURES

Phone: (585) 395-2751. **Email:** admit@brockport.edu. **Website:** http://www.brockport.edu. **Application deadlines for fall 2007:** Regular decision: Rolling. Early decision: Not offered. Early action: Not offered. Admission can be deferred. **Application fee:** $40. Common application is not accepted. **To apply online, go to:** http://www.suny.edu/student/oas.

Admissions requirements/recommendations: High school units required (recommended): English: 4; Mathematics: 3; Science: 3; Foreign language: (3); Social studies: 4; Academic electives: 4; Total units: 18. Tests: The college uses SAT or ACT scores in admissions decisions. Either SAT or ACT required. For admission to the fall 2007 entering class, the school will accept: ACT without writing. Campus visit: Recommended. Admissions interview: Recommended. Off-campus interview: Not available. **Factors that count in admissions decisions:** *Academic:* Secondary school record: Very important. Class rank: Very important. Letters of recommendation: Important. Standardized test scores: Very important. Essay: Important. *Nonacademic:* Interview: Considered. Extracurricular activities: Important. Talent/ability: Important. Character/personal qualities: Considered. Alumni/ae relationship: Not considered. Geographical residence: Not considered. State residency: Not considered. Religious affiliation/commitment: Not considered. Minority status: Not considered. Volunteer work: Considered. Work experience: Considered. **Other schools with the greatest overlap in applicants:** SUNY College of Arts and Sciences–Geneseo; SUNY College–Cortland; SUNY–Fredonia; SUNY–Oswego; University at Buffalo–SUNY. **Admissions statistics for the fall 2005 entering class:** Total applicants: 7,816. Total accepted: 3,625. Freshmen enrolled: 988; 2% were from out of state. Overall acceptance rate: 46%. **Credentials of fall 2005 freshmen:** 17% ranked in the top 10 percent of their high school class; 49% were in the top 25 percent, and 89% were in the top half. (Proportion submitting class standing: 85%.) **Average high school grade point average:** 3.4. **First-year students who submitted SAT scores:** 97%. Scores (25/75 percentile): Verbal: 500-600, Math: 480-570, Combined: 980-1170. **First-year students submitting ACT scores:** 32%. Scores (25/75 percentile): English: 19-24, Math: 20-25, Composite: 20-25.

ACADEMICS

Year founded: 1867. **Academic calendar:** Semester. **Degrees offered:** bachelor's, master's, post-master's certificate. **Most popular majors:** 14% business administration and management, 12% physical education teaching and coaching, 10% health professions and related clinical sciences, 10% psychology, 8% security and protective services. **Major fields of study:** area, ethnic, cultural, and gender studies; biological and biomedical sciences; business, management, marketing, and related support services; communication, journalism, and related programs; computer and information sciences and support services; education; English language and literature/letters; foreign languages, literatures, and linguistics; health professions and related clinical sciences; history; mathematics and statistics; natural resources and conservation; parks, recreation, leisure, and fitness studies; philosophy and religious studies; physical sciences; psychology; public administration and social service professions; security and protective services; social sciences; visual and performing arts. **Areas of required coursework:** arts/fine arts, humanities, computer literacy, mathematics, English (including composition), foreign languages, sciences (biological or physical), history, social science, other. **Pre-professional programs:** pre-law, pre-dentistry, pre-medicine, pre-veterinary science, pre-optometry. **Special academic programs:** accelerated program, cross-registration, distance learning, double major, dual enrollment, honors program, independent study, internships, student-designed major, study abroad, teacher certificate program. **Teacher certification offered in:** early childhood, elementary, secondary, bilingual/bicultural. **Reserve Officers Training Corps (ROTC):** Army ROTC: Offered on campus; Navy ROTC: Offered at cooperating institution (University of Rochester); Air Force ROTC: Offered at cooperating institution (Rochester Institute of Technology). **Faculty and instruction (2005-2006):** Total instructional faculty: 321 full-time, 294 part-time (51% men; 49% women; 12% minorities). Full-time faculty with Ph.D. or other terminal degree: 78%. Student/faculty ratio: 19/1. Classes of fewer than 20 students: 46%; of 20 to 49 students: 51%; of 50 or more students: 3%. **Advanced Placement and International Baccalaureate credit:** AP tests may be used for: Credit and/or placement. Scores accepted: 3, 4, 5. International Baccalaureate exams may be used for: Credit only. **Freshmen returning for sophomore year:** 80%. **Graduation rates:** Four-year: 29%; five-year: 50%; six-year: 52%. **Graduate study:** 23% of students pursue further study within one year. Fields in which graduates pursue further study: Master of Business Administration (MBA), 3%; law, 2%; medicine, 5%; theology (or the seminary), 1%; education, 50%; arts and sciences, 37%; veterinary medicine, 1%.

COSTS AND FINANCIAL AID

Financial aid office: (585) 395-2501. **Expenses (2006-2007):** Tuition and fees 2006-2007: $5,356 in state, $11,306 out of state; room/board: $7,830. Estimated books and supplies: $1,000; transportation: $130; personal expenses: $2,104. **Financial aid:** Priority filing date for institution's financial aid form: March 15. In 2005-2006, 87% of undergraduates applied for

financial aid. Of those, 67% were determined to have financial need; 32% had their need fully met. Average financial aid package (proportion receiving): $8,501 (66%). Average amount of gift aid, such as scholarships or grants (proportion receiving): $3,643 (61%). Average amount of self-help aid, such as work study or loans (proportion receiving): $4,892 (57%). Average need-based loan (excluding PLUS or other private loans): $4,571. Among students who received need-based aid, the average percentage of need met: 80%. Among students who received aid based on merit, the average award (and the proportion receiving): $3,901 (3%). Average amount of debt of borrowers graduating in 2005: $19,556. Proportion who borrowed: 80%.

CAMPUS LIFE AND EXTRACURRICULAR ACTIVITIES

Campus housing available: coed dorms, special housing for disabled students, special housing for international students, other housing options. Students who live in college-owned, operated, or affiliated housing: 37%. **Student employment:** During the 2005-2006 academic year, 28% of undergraduates worked on campus. Average per-year earnings: $1,401. **Clubs and organizations:** Number of student organizations: 70. Activities include: choral groups, dance, drama/theater, literary magazine, music ensembles, radio station, student government, student newspaper, television station. Number of fraternities: 6; sororities: 4. Proportion of men in fraternities: 1%; of women in sororities: 2%. Average proportion of students who stay on campus on weekends: 45%. **Sports program (2005-2006):** Member of NCAA III. *Men's intercollegiate varsity sports:* baseball, basketball, cross-country, football, ice hockey, lacrosse, soccer, swimming and diving, track and field (indoor), track and field (outdoor), wrestling. *Women's intercollegiate varsity sports:* basketball, cross-country, field hockey, gymnastics, lacrosse, soccer, softball, swimming and diving, tennis, track and field (indoor), track and field (outdoor), volleyball.

SERVICES AND FACILITIES

Basic services: nonremedial tutoring, women's center, placement service, day care, health service, health insurance, other. **Remedial assistance:** reading, math, writing, study skills. **Counseling services:** minority student, career, military, personal, veteran student, academic, older student, psychological, birth control, religious, other. **For learning-disabled students:** School does not offer a structured program with separate admission and additional fees. Total undergraduates in learning-disabled program or receiving services: 150. Services include: remedial math, remedial English, reading machines, tape recorders, note-taking services, learning center, extended time for tests, tutors, priority registration, priority seating, texts on tape, exams on tape or computer, other testing accomodations. **Library:** Number of titles: 725,650; number of current serial subscriptions: 1,960. **Information technology resources:** Students are not required to lease or own a computer. Number of campus computers available to all students: 750. School has a wireless network. Approximate number of users that can be accommodated: 3,000. Proportion of college-owned housing units wired for high-speed internet access: 100%. **Campus safety:** Security services offered: 24-hour foot-and-vehicle patrols, late-night transport/escort service, 24-hour emergency telephones, lighted pathways/sidewalks, student patrols, controlled dormitory access (key, security card, etc).

TRANSFER AND INTERNATIONAL STUDENTS

Transfer students: May apply for admission for the following academic terms: Fall, Spring. Applicants do not need a minimum number of credits to apply. For fall 2005: Transfer applications received: 2,966. Transfer applicants offered admission: 1,738. Transfer applicants enrolled: 973. **International students:** Number of foreign undergraduates: 75 (1% of student body). Number of countries represented: 21. Minimum TOEFL score required: 530 (paper); 197 (computer). Average TOEFL score: 620 (paper).

SUNY College—Cortland

- **Address:** PO Box 2000, Cortland, NY 13045
- **Website:** http://www.cortland.edu
- **Public**
- **Enrollment:** 5,731 full-time; 256 part-time

KEY STATS

✔ **U.S News College Ranking:** third tier, Universities–Master's (North)
✔ **SAT Score (25th/75th percentile):** 985-1135
✔ **Tuition:** 2006-2007: $4,350 in state, $10,610 out of state

Selectivity: Selective	**Room/board:** N/A
Acceptance rate: 48%	**Average debt:** N/A
Student/faculty ratio: 16/1	**Proportion who borrowed:** N/A

UNDERGRADUATE STUDENT BODY STATS

2005-2006 enrollment: 5,731 full-time; 256 part-time. Men: 43%; women: 57%. **Ethnic makeup:** African American: 3%; American-Indian: 1%; Asian American: 1%; Hispanic: 4%; White: 91%; International: 1%.

ADMISSIONS FACTS AND FIGURES

Phone: (607) 753-4711. **Email:** admissions@cortland.edu. **Website:** http://www.cortland.edu. **Application deadlines for fall 2007:** Regular decision: Rolling. Early decision: Send application by: November 15; Decision sent by: December 15. Early action: Not offered. Admission can be deferred. **Application fee:** $40. Common application is not accepted. **To apply online, go to:** http://www.cortland.edu/admissions/apply.html. **Admissions requirements/recommendations:** High school units required (recommended): English: 4; Mathematics: 3 (4); Science: 3 (4); Foreign language: 3 (4); Social studies: 4; Total units: 20 (23). Tests: The college uses SAT or ACT scores in admissions decisions. Either SAT or ACT required. For admission to the fall 2007 entering class, the school will accept: ACT without writing. Campus visit: Recommended. Admissions interview: Recommended. Off-campus interview: Not available. **Factors that count in admissions decisions:** *Academic:* Secondary school record: Very important. Class rank: Considered. Letters of recommendation: Important. Standardized test scores: Very important. Essay: Important. *Nonacademic:* Interview: Considered. Extracurricular activities: Important. Talent/ability: Important. Character/personal qualities: Not considered. Alumni/ae relationship: Considered. Geographical residence: Considered. State residency: Considered. Religious affiliation/commitment: Not considered. Minority status: Considered. Volunteer work: Considered. Work experience: Considered. **Admissions statistics for the fall 2005 entering class:** Total applicants: 9,751. Total accepted: 4,725. Freshmen enrolled: 1,110; 0% were from out of state. Overall acceptance rate: 48%. Non-early acceptance rate: 48%. **Credentials of fall 2005 freshmen:** 6% ranked in the top 10 percent of their high school class; 40% were in the top 25 percent, and 87% were in the top half. (Proportion submitting class standing: 50%.) **Average high school grade point average:** 3.3. **First-year students who submitted SAT scores:** 98%. Scores (25/75 percentile): Verbal: 500-580, Math: 485-555, Combined: 985-1135.

ACADEMICS

Year founded: 1868. **Academic calendar:** Semester. **Degrees offered:** bachelor's, master's, post-master's certificate. **Most popular majors:** 15% physical education teaching and coaching, 6% communication studies/speech communication and rhetoric, 6% reading teacher education, 4% health professions and related clinical sciences, 4% kindergarten/preschool education and teaching. **Major fields of study: Areas of required coursework:** humanities, computer literacy, mathematics, English (including composition), foreign languages, sciences (biological or physical), history, social science. **Special academic programs:** cooperative (work-study plan) program, cross-registration, distance learning, double major, dual enrollment, exchange student program (domestic), honors program, independent study, internships, liberal arts/career combination, student-designed major, study abroad, teacher certificate program. **Reserve Officers Training Corps (ROTC):** Army ROTC: Offered at cooperating institution (Cornell University); Air Force ROTC: Offered at cooperating institution (Cornell University). **Faculty and instruction (2005-2006):** Total instructional faculty: 334 full-time, 221 part-time (50% men; 50% women; 9% minorities). Full-time faculty with Ph.D. or other terminal degree: 65%. Student/faculty ratio: 16/1. Classes of fewer than 20 students: 42%; of 20 to 49 students: 52%; of 50 or more students: 6%. **Advanced Placement and International Baccalaureate credit:** AP

tests may be used for: Credit only. **Freshmen returning for sophomore year:** 79%. **Graduation rates:** Four-year: 37%; five-year: 56%; six-year: 55%.

COSTS AND FINANCIAL AID

Financial aid office: (607) 753-4717. **Expenses (2006-2007):** Tuition and fees 2006-2007: $4,350 in state, $10,610 out of state; room/board: N/A. Estimated books and supplies: $800; transportation: $800; personal expenses: $1,320. **Financial aid:** In 2005-2006, 84% of undergraduates applied for financial aid. Of those, 65% were determined to have financial need; 20% had their need fully met. Average financial aid package (proportion receiving): $9,372 (63%). Average amount of gift aid, such as scholarships or grants (proportion receiving): $3,550 (56%). Average amount of self-help aid, such as work study or loans (proportion receiving): $3,363 (56%). Average need-based loan (excluding PLUS or other private loans): $3,784. Among students who received need-based aid, the average percentage of need met: 75%. Among students who received aid based on merit, the average award (and the proportion receiving): $6,724 (16%). The average athletic scholarship (and the proportion receiving): $0 (0%).

CAMPUS LIFE AND EXTRACURRICULAR ACTIVITIES

Campus housing available: coed dorms, sorority housing, fraternity housing, apartment for single students, special housing for international students. **Clubs and organizations:** Number of student organizations: 100. Activities include: choral groups, concert band, dance, drama/theater, jazz band, literary magazine, music ensembles, musical theater, radio station, student government, student newspaper, student film society, symphony orchestra, television station, yearbook. Number of fraternities: 2; sororities: 5. **Sports program (2005-2006):** Member of NCAA III. *Men's intercollegiate varsity sports:* baseball, basketball, cross-country, football, ice hockey, lacrosse, soccer, swimming and diving, track and field (indoor), track and field (outdoor), wrestling. *Women's intercollegiate varsity sports:* basketball, cross-country, field hockey, golf, gymnastics, ice hockey, lacrosse, soccer, softball, swimming and diving, tennis, track and field (indoor), track and field (outdoor), volleyball.

SERVICES AND FACILITIES

Basic services: nonremedial tutoring, placement service, day care, health service. **Counseling services:** minority student, career, military, personal, veteran student, academic, older student, psychological, birth control, religious. **For learning-disabled students:** School does not offer a structured program with separate admission and additional fees. Services include: reading machines, tape recorders, untimed tests, note-taking services, oral tests, learning center, readers, extended time for tests. **Information technology resources:** Students are not required to lease or own a computer. Number of campus computers available to all students: 649. School has a wireless network. **Campus safety:** Security services offered: 24-hour foot-and-vehicle patrols, late-night transport/escort service, 24-hour emergency telephones, lighted pathways/sidewalks, controlled dormitory access (key, security card, etc.).

TRANSFER AND INTERNATIONAL STUDENTS

Transfer students: May apply for admission for the following academic terms: Fall, Spring. Applicants do not need a minimum number of credits to apply. For fall 2005: Transfer applications received: 2,548. Transfer applicants offered admission: 1,060. Transfer applicants enrolled: 563. **International students:** Number of foreign undergraduates: 34 (1% of student body). Minimum TOEFL score required: 550 (paper); 218 (computer).

SUNY Coll. of Arts and Sciences—Geneseo

- **Address:** 1 College Circle, Geneseo, NY 14454-1401
- **Website:** http://www.geneseo.edu
- **Public**
- **Enrollment:** 5,174 full-time; 132 part-time

KEY STATS

✔ **U.S News College Ranking:** 14, Universities–Master's (North)
✔ **SAT Score (25th/75th percentile):** 1200-1340
✔ **Tuition:** 2006-2007: $5,525 in state, $11,785 out of state

Selectivity: More selective	**Room/board:** $8,128
Acceptance rate: 49%	**Average debt:** $16,000
Student/faculty ratio: 19/1	**Proportion who borrowed:** 75%

UNDERGRADUATE STUDENT BODY STATS

2005-2006 enrollment: 5,174 full-time; 132 part-time. Men: 41%; women: 59%. **Ethnic makeup:** African American: 2%; Asian American: 5%; Hispanic: 3%; White: 87%; International: 3%. **Religious preference:** Roman Catholic: 46%; Protestant: 21%; Jewish: 3%; No preference: 24%; Other: 6%.

ADMISSIONS FACTS AND FIGURES

Phone: (585) 245-5571. **Email:** admissions@geneseo.edu. **Website:** http://www.geneseo.edu. **Application deadlines for fall 2007:** Regular decision: January 15. Early decision: Send application by: November 15; Decision sent by: December 15. Early action: Not offered. Admission can be deferred. **Application fee:** $40. Common application is not accepted. **Admissions requirements/recommendations:** High school units required (recommended): English: (4); Mathematics: (4); Science: (4); Foreign language: (4); Social studies: (4); Total units: (20). Tests: The college uses SAT or ACT scores in admissions decisions. Either SAT or ACT required. For admission to the fall 2007 entering class, the school will accept: ACT with writing, ACT without writing. Campus visit: Recommended. Admissions interview: Neither required nor recommended. Off-campus interview: Not available. **Factors that count in admissions decisions:** *Academic:* Secondary school record: Very important. Class rank: Very important. Letters of recommendation: Important. Standardized test scores: Very important. Essay: Important. *Nonacademic:* Interview: Not considered. Extracurricular activities: Important. Talent/ability: Important. Character/personal qualities: Considered. Alumni/ae relationship: Not considered. Geographical residence: Not considered. State residency: Not considered. Religious affiliation/commitment: Not considered. Minority status: Important. Volunteer work: Considered. Work experience: Not considered. **Other schools with the greatest overlap in applicants:** Cornell University; Hamilton College; SUNY–Binghamton; University of Rochester. **Admissions statistics for the fall 2005 entering class:** Total applicants: 8,861. Total accepted: 4,317. Freshmen enrolled: 1,029; 1% were from out of state. Accepted through early-decision or early-action plans: 16%. Overall acceptance rate: 49%. Early-decision acceptance rate: 59%. Non-early acceptance rate: 48%. **Size of waiting list:** 957 applicants; enrolled from waiting list: 14. **Credentials of fall 2005 freshmen:** 51% ranked in the top 10 percent of their high school class; 89% were in the top 25 percent, and 99% were in the top half. (Proportion submitting class standing: 72%.) **Average high school grade point average:** 3.8. **First-year students who submitted SAT scores:** 84%. Scores (25/75 percentile): Verbal: 600-670, Math: 600-670, Combined: 1200-1340. **First-year students submitting ACT scores:** 17%. Scores (25/75 percentile): English: N/A, Math: N/A, Composite: 26-29.

ACADEMICS

Year founded: 1871. **Academic calendar:** Semester. **Degrees offered:** bachelor's, master's. **Most popular majors:** 20% education, 18% social sciences, 13% business, management, marketing, and related support services, 9% psychology, 8% biological and biomedical sciences. **Major fields of study:** area, ethnic, cultural, and gender studies; biological and biomedical sciences; business, management, marketing, and related support services; communication, journalism, and related programs; computer and information sciences and support services; education; English language and literature/letters; foreign languages, literatures, and linguistics; health professions and related clinical sciences; history; mathematics and statistics; multi/interdisciplinary studies; philosophy and religious studies; physical sciences; psychology; social sciences; visual and performing arts. **Areas of required coursework:** arts/fine arts, humanities, mathematics, English (including composition), foreign languages, sciences (biological or physical), history, social science, other. **Pre-professional programs:** pre-law, pre-dentistry, pre-medicine, pre-theology, pre-optometry. **Special academic programs:** cross-registration, double major, honors program, independent study, internships, study abroad, teacher certificate program. **Teacher certification offered in:** early childhood, special education, elementary, secondary. **Reserve Officers Training Corps (ROTC):** Army ROTC: Offered at cooperating institution (Rochester Institute of Technology); Air Force ROTC: Offered at cooperating institution (Rochester Institute of Technology). **Faculty and instruction (2005-2006):** Total instructional faculty: 242 full-time, 88 part-time (59% men; 41% women; 11% minorities). Full-time faculty with Ph.D. or other terminal degree: 87%. Student/faculty ratio: 19/1. Classes of fewer than 20 students: 22%; of 20 to 49 students: 68%; of 50 or more students: 9%. **Advanced Placement and International Baccalaureate credit:** AP tests may be used for: Credit only. Scores accepted: 3, 4, 5. International Baccalaureate exams may be used for: Credit only. **Freshmen returning for sophomore year:** 91%. **Graduation rates:** Four-year: 64%; five-year: 78%; six-year: 79%. **Graduate study:** 39% of students pursue further study immedi-

ately upon graduation. Fields in which graduates pursue further study: Master of Business Administration (MBA), 2%; law, 4%; medicine, 5%; engineering, 1%; education, 24%; arts and sciences, 17%; veterinary medicine, 1%.

COSTS AND FINANCIAL AID

Financial aid office: (585) 245-5731. **Expenses (2006-2007):** Tuition and fees 2006-2007: $5,525 in state, $11,785 out of state; room/board: $8,128. Estimated books and supplies: $800; transportation: $750; personal expenses: $750. **Financial aid:** Priority filing date for institution's financial aid form: February 15; deadline: February 15. In 2005-2006, 75% of undergraduates applied for financial aid. Of those, 47% were determined to have financial need; 85% had their need fully met. Average financial aid package (proportion receiving): $9,339 (47%). Average amount of gift aid, such as scholarships or grants (proportion receiving): $2,717 (39%). Average amount of self-help aid, such as work study or loans (proportion receiving): $6,884 (39%). Average need-based loan (excluding PLUS or other private loans): $5,424. Among students who received need-based aid, the average percentage of need met: 85%. Among students who received aid based on merit, the average award (and the proportion receiving): $1,900 (9%). The average athletic scholarship (and the proportion receiving): $0 (0%). Average amount of debt of borrowers graduating in 2005: $16,000. Proportion who borrowed: 75%.

CAMPUS LIFE AND EXTRACURRICULAR ACTIVITIES

Campus housing available (% using): coed dorms (93%), other housing options (7%). Students who live in college-owned, operated, or affiliated housing: 56%. **Student employment:** During the 2005-2006 academic year, 24% of undergraduates worked on campus. Average per-year earnings: $2,000. **Clubs and organizations:** Number of student organizations: 166. Activities include: choral groups, dance, drama/theater, jazz band, literary magazine, music ensembles, musical theater, radio station, student government, student newspaper, symphony orchestra, television station, yearbook. Number of fraternities: 10; sororities: 13. Proportion of men in fraternities: 10%; of women in sororities: 12%. **Sports program (2005-2006):** Member of NCAA III. *Men's intercollegiate varsity sports:* basketball, cross-country, ice hockey, lacrosse, soccer, swimming and diving, track and field (indoor), track and field (outdoor). *Women's intercollegiate varsity sports:* basketball, cross-country, equestrian sports, figure skating, lacrosse, soccer, softball, swimming and diving, tennis, track and field (indoor), track and field (outdoor), volleyball.

SERVICES AND FACILITIES

Basic services: placement service, health service, health insurance. **Remedial assistance:** writing, study skills, other. **Counseling services:** minority student, career, military, personal, veteran student, academic, older student, psychological, birth control, religious. **For learning-disabled students:** School does not offer a structured program with separate admission and additional fees. Total undergraduates in learning-disabled program or receiving services: 82. Services include: reading machines, note-taking services, readers, extended time for tests, priority registration, priority seating, other testing accomodations, other. **Library:** Number of titles: 664,850; number of current serial subscriptions: 18,773. **Information technology resources:** Students are not required to lease or own a computer. Number of campus computers available to all students: 1,000. School has a wireless network. Approximate number of users that can be accommodated: 1,800. Proportion of college-owned housing units wired for high-speed internet access: 100%. **Campus safety:** Security services offered: 24-hour foot-and-vehicle patrols, late-night transport/escort service, 24-hour emergency telephones, lighted pathways/sidewalks, student patrols, controlled dormitory access (key, security card, etc).

TRANSFER AND INTERNATIONAL STUDENTS

Transfer students: May apply for admission for the following academic terms: Fall, Spring. Applicants need a minimum number of credits to apply. For fall 2005: Transfer applications received: 1,529. Transfer applicants offered admission: 642. Transfer applicants enrolled: 304. **International students:** Number of foreign undergraduates: 154 (3% of student body). Number of countries represented: 34. Minimum TOEFL score required: 527 (paper); 197 (computer). Average TOEFL score: 545 (paper).

SUNY College of Arts and Sci.–New Paltz

- **Address:** 75 S. Manheim Boulevard, Suite 9, New Paltz, NY 12561-2443
- **Website:** http://www.newpaltz.edu
- **Public**
- **Enrollment:** 5,715 full-time; 706 part-time

KEY STATS

✔ **U.S News College Ranking:** 44, Universities–Master's (North)
✔ **SAT Score (25th/75th percentile):** 1040-1205
✔ **Tuition:** 2006-2007: $5,360 in state, $11,620 out of state

Selectivity: Selective	**Room/board:** $7,230
Acceptance rate: 44%	**Average debt:** $18,900
Student/faculty ratio: 16/1	**Proportion who borrowed:** 75%

UNDERGRADUATE STUDENT BODY STATS

2005-2006 enrollment: 5,715 full-time; 706 part-time. Men: 33%; women: 67%. **Ethnic makeup:** African American: 6%; Asian American: 3%; Hispanic: 10%; White: 78%; International: 3%.

ADMISSIONS FACTS AND FIGURES

Phone: (888) 639-7589. **Email:** admissions@newpaltz.edu. **Website:** http://www.newpaltz.edu. **Application deadlines for fall 2007:** Regular decision: April 1. Early decision: Not offered. Early action: Send application by: November 15; Decision sent by: January 1. Admission can be deferred. **Application fee:** $40. Common application is not accepted. **To apply online, go to:** http://www.newpaltz.edu/admissions/apply.html. **Admissions requirements/recommendations:** High school units required (recommended): English: 4 (4); Mathematics: 3 (4); Science: 3 (4); Foreign language: 2 (4); Social studies: 3 (4). Tests: The college uses SAT or ACT scores in admissions decisions. Either SAT or ACT required. For admission to the fall 2007 entering class, the school will accept: ACT with writing, ACT without writing. Campus visit: Recommended. Admissions interview: Neither required nor recommended. Off-campus interview: Not available. **Factors that count in admissions decisions:** *Academic:* Secondary school record: Very important. Class rank: Considered. Letters of recommendation: Considered. Standardized test scores: Very important. Essay: Considered. *Nonacademic:* Interview: Not considered. Extracurricular activities: Considered. Talent/ability: Considered. Character/personal qualities: Not considered. Alumni/ae relationship: Not considered. Geographical residence: Not considered. State residency: Not considered. Religious affiliation/commitment: Not considered. Minority status: Not considered. Volunteer work: Considered. Work experience: Considered. **Other schools with the greatest overlap in applicants:** New York University; SUNY College–Oneonta; SUNY–Albany; SUNY–Binghamton; SUNY–Stony Brook. **Admissions statistics for the fall 2005 entering class:** Total applicants: 11,358. Total accepted: 5,024. Freshmen enrolled: 1,050; 3% were from out of state. Accepted through early-decision or early-action plans: 27%. Overall acceptance rate: 44%. Non-early acceptance rate: 42%. **Size of waiting list:** 343 applicants; enrolled from waiting list: 0. **Credentials of fall 2005 freshmen:** 15% ranked in the top 10 percent of their high school class; 56% were in the top 25 percent, and 94% were in the top half. (Proportion submitting class standing: 43%.) **Average high school grade point average:** 3.3. **First-year students who submitted SAT scores:** 99%. Scores (25/75 percentile): Verbal: 520-600, Math: 520-605, Combined: 1040-1205.

ACADEMICS

Year founded: 1828. **Academic calendar:** Semester. **Degrees offered:** bachelor's, master's, post-master's certificate. **Most popular majors:** 20% education, 14% business, management, marketing, and related support services, 11% English language and literature/letters, 11% visual and performing arts, 10% social sciences. **Major fields of study:** area, ethnic, cultural, and gender studies; biological and biomedical sciences; business, management, marketing, and related support services; communication, journalism, and related programs; communications technologies/technicians and support services; computer and information sciences and support services; education; engineering; engineering technologies/technicians; English language and literature/letters; foreign languages, literatures, and linguistics; health professions and related clinical sciences; liberal arts and sciences studies, and humanities; mathematics and statistics; natural resources and conservation; philosophy and religious studies; physical sciences; psychology; science technologies/technicians; social sciences; theology and religious vocations; visual and performing arts. **Areas of required coursework:**

arts/fine arts, humanities, computer literacy, mathematics, English (including composition), philosophy, foreign languages, sciences (biological or physical), history, social science. **Pre-professional programs:** pre-law, pre-dentistry, pre-medicine, pre-veterinary science, pre-optometry. **Special academic programs:** cooperative (work-study plan) program, cross-registration, distance learning, double major, English as a Second Language (ESL), exchange student program (domestic), honors program, independent study, internships, liberal arts/career combination, student-designed major, study abroad, teacher certificate program. **Teacher certification offered in:** early childhood, special education, elementary, secondary, bilingual/bicultural. **Faculty and instruction (2005-2006):** Total instructional faculty: 294 full-time, 412 part-time (48% men; 52% women; 13% minorities). Student/faculty ratio: 16/1. Classes of fewer than 20 students: 46%; of 20 to 49 students: 50%; of 50 or more students: 4%. **Advanced Placement and International Baccalaureate credit:** AP tests may be used for: Credit and/or placement. Scores accepted: 3, 4, 5. International Baccalaureate exams may be used for: Credit and/or placement. **Freshmen returning for sophomore year:** 84%. **Graduation rates:** Four-year: 35%; five-year: 59%; six-year: 57%.

COSTS AND FINANCIAL AID

Financial aid office: (845) 257-3250. **Expenses (2006-2007):** Tuition and fees 2006-2007: $5,360 in state, $11,620 out of state; room/board: $7,230. Estimated books and supplies: $1,100; transportation: $800; personal expenses: $205. **Financial aid:** Priority filing date for institution's financial aid form: March 15. In 2005-2006, 77% of undergraduates applied for financial aid. Of those, 54% were determined to have financial need; 23% had their need fully met. Average financial aid package (proportion receiving): $2,367 (53%). Average amount of gift aid, such as scholarships or grants (proportion receiving): $2,130 (46%). Average amount of self-help aid, such as work study or loans (proportion receiving): $2,512 (46%). Average need-based loan (excluding PLUS or other private loans): $940. Among students who received need-based aid, the average percentage of need met: 67%. Among students who received aid based on merit, the average award (and the proportion receiving): $1,744 (3%). The average athletic scholarship (and the proportion receiving): $0 (0%). Average amount of debt of borrowers graduating in 2005: $18,900. Proportion who borrowed: 75%.

CAMPUS LIFE AND EXTRACURRICULAR ACTIVITIES

Campus housing available: coed dorms, special housing for disabled students, special housing for international students. Students who live in college-owned, operated, or affiliated housing: 48%. **Student employment:** During the 2005-2006 academic year, 12% of undergraduates worked on campus. Average per-year earnings: $950. **Clubs and organizations:** Number of student organizations: 115. Activities include: choral groups, concert band, dance, drama/theater, jazz band, music ensembles, musical theater, radio station, student government, student newspaper, symphony orchestra, television station, yearbook. Number of fraternities: 10; sororities: 12. Proportion of men in fraternities: 3%; of women in sororities: 2%. Average proportion of students who stay on campus on weekends: 75%. **Sports program (2005-2006):** Member of NCAA III. *Men's intercollegiate varsity sports:* baseball, basketball, cross-country, soccer, swimming and diving, tennis, track and field (indoor), track and field (outdoor), volleyball. *Women's intercollegiate varsity sports:* basketball, cross-country, field hockey, soccer, softball, swimming and diving, tennis, track and field (indoor), track and field (outdoor), volleyball.

SERVICES AND FACILITIES

Basic services: nonremedial tutoring, placement service, day care, health service, health insurance. **Counseling services:** minority student, career, personal, veteran student, psychological, birth control, religious. **For learning-disabled students:** School does not offer a structured program with separate admission and additional fees. Total undergraduates in learning-disabled program or receiving services: 135. Services include: reading machines, remedial reading, tape recorders, note-taking services, oral tests, learning center, readers, extended time for tests, tutors, priority seating, substitution of courses, texts on tape, typist/scribe. **Information technology resources:** Students are not required to lease or own a computer. Number of campus computers available to all students: 950. School has a wireless network. Proportion of college-owned housing units wired for high-speed internet access: 100%. **Campus safety:** Security services offered: 24-hour foot-and-vehicle patrols, late-night transport/escort service, 24-hour emergency telephones, lighted pathways/sidewalks, controlled dormitory access (key, security card, etc).

TRANSFER AND INTERNATIONAL STUDENTS

Transfer students: May apply for admission for the following academic terms: Fall, Spring. Applicants need a minimum number of credits to apply. For fall 2005: Transfer applications received: 2,651. Transfer applicants offered admission: 1,255. Transfer applicants enrolled: 726. **International students:** Number of foreign undergraduates: 164 (3% of student body). Minimum TOEFL score required: 550 (paper); 213 (computer). Average TOEFL score: 550 (paper).

SUNY College of A&T–Cobleskill

- **Address:** Cobleskill, NY 12043
- **Website:** http://www.cobleskill.edu
- **Public**
- **Enrollment:** 2,363 full-time; 115 part-time

KEY STATS
- ✔ **U.S News College Ranking:** fourth tier, Comp. Coll.–Bachelor's (North)
- ✔ **SAT Score (25th/75th percentile):** 800-1020
- ✔ **Tuition:** 2006-2007: $6,111 in state, $12,371 out of state

Selectivity: Less selective	**Room/board:** $8,220
Acceptance rate: 71%	**Average debt:** $6,300
Student/faculty ratio: 20/1	**Proportion who borrowed:** 77%

UNDERGRADUATE STUDENT BODY STATS

2005-2006 enrollment: 2,363 full-time; 115 part-time. Men: 54%; women: 46%. **Ethnic makeup:** African American: 6%; Asian American: 1%; Hispanic: 4%; White: 86%; International: 3%.

ADMISSIONS FACTS AND FIGURES

Phone: (518) 255-5525. **Email:** admissionsoffice@cobleskill.edu. **Website:** http://www.cobleskill.edu. **Application deadlines for fall 2007:** Regular decision: Rolling. Early decision: Not offered. Early action: Not offered. Admission can be deferred. **Application fee:** $40. Common application is not accepted. **To apply online, go to:** http://www.suny.edu/student. **Admissions requirements/recommendations:** High school units required (recommended): English: 4 (4); Mathematics: 1 (3); Science: 1 (3); Social studies: (3); Academic electives: 12 (4). Tests: The college uses SAT or ACT scores in admissions decisions. Neither SAT nor ACT required. For admission to the fall 2007 entering class, the school will accept: ACT with writing, ACT without writing. Campus visit: Recommended. Admissions interview: Neither required nor recommended. Off-campus interview: May be arranged. **Factors that count in admissions decisions:** *Academic:* Secondary school record: Very important. Class rank: Considered. Letters of recommendation: Considered. Standardized test scores: Considered. Essay: Not considered. *Nonacademic:* Interview: Not considered. Extracurricular activities: Considered. Talent/ability: Considered. Character/personal qualities: Considered. Alumni/ae relationship: Not considered. Geographical residence: Not considered. State residency: Not considered. Religious affiliation/commitment: Not considered. Minority status: Not considered. Volunteer work: Considered. Work experience: Considered. **Admissions statistics for the fall 2005 entering class:** Total applicants: 3,394. Total accepted: 2,419. Freshmen enrolled: 914; 9% were from out of state. Overall acceptance rate: 71%. **Credentials of fall 2005 freshmen:** 5% ranked in the top 10 percent of their high school class; 23% were in the top 25 percent, and 62% were in the top half. (Proportion submitting class standing: 79%.) **First-year students who submitted SAT scores:** 64%. Scores (25/75 percentile): Verbal: 400-510, Math: 400-510, Combined: 800-1020.

ACADEMICS

Year founded: 1911. **Academic calendar:** Semester. **Degrees offered:** certificate, associate, transfer-associate, terminal-associate, bachelor's. **Most popular majors:** 13% liberal arts and sciences/liberal studies, 11% plant sciences, 9% agricultural animal breeding, 9% child care and support services management, 5% computer and information sciences and support services. **Major fields of study:** agriculture, agriculture operations, and related sciences; business, management, marketing, and related support services; computer and information sciences and support services; family and consumer sciences/human sciences. **Areas of required coursework:** arts/fine arts, humanities, mathematics, English (including composition), foreign languages, sciences (biological or physical), history, social science. **Pre-professional programs:** pre-veterinary science. **Special academic programs:** dis-

tance learning, honors program, internships, study abroad, weekend college. **Faculty and instruction (2005-2006):** Total instructional faculty: 109 full-time, 44 part-time (64% men; 36% women; 8% minorities). Full-time faculty with Ph.D. or other terminal degree: 39%. Student/faculty ratio: 20/1. Classes of fewer than 20 students: 53%; of 20 to 49 students: 42%; of 50 or more students: 5%. **Freshmen returning for sophomore year:** 57%. **Graduation rates:** Six-year: 31%.

COSTS AND FINANCIAL AID

Financial aid office: (518) 255-5623. **Expenses (2006-2007):** Tuition and fees 2006-2007: $6,111 in state, $12,371 out of state; room/board: $8,220. **Financial aid:** Priority filing date for institution's financial aid form: February 15; deadline: March 15. In 2005-2006, 77% of undergraduates applied for financial aid. Of those, 64% were determined to have financial need; 4% had their need fully met. Average financial aid package (proportion receiving): $6,976 (64%). Average amount of gift aid, such as scholarships or grants (proportion receiving): $4,467 (58%). Average amount of self-help aid, such as work study or loans (proportion receiving): $3,316 (54%). Average need-based loan (excluding PLUS or other private loans): $3,190. Among students who received need-based aid, the average percentage of need met: 61%. Average amount of debt of borrowers graduating in 2005: $6,300. Proportion who borrowed: 77%.

CAMPUS LIFE AND EXTRACURRICULAR ACTIVITIES

Campus housing available (% using): coed dorms (79%), women's dorms (10%), men's dorms (10%), other housing options (1%). Students who live in college-owned, operated, or affiliated housing: 64%. **Student employment:** During the 2005-2006 academic year, 13% of undergraduates worked on campus. Average per-year earnings: $1,787. Activities include: choral groups, concert band, dance, jazz band, musical theater, student government, yearbook. Number of fraternities: 0; sororities: 0. Average proportion of students who stay on campus on weekends: 50%. **Sports program (2005-2006):** *Men's intercollegiate varsity sports:* baseball, basketball, cross-country, golf, lacrosse, soccer, swimming and diving, tennis, track and field (indoor), track and field (outdoor). *Women's intercollegiate varsity sports:* basketball, cross-country, golf, soccer, softball, swimming and diving, tennis, track and field (indoor), track and field (outdoor), volleyball.

SERVICES AND FACILITIES

Basic services: placement service, day care, health service, health insurance. **Remedial assistance:** reading, math, writing, study skills. **Counseling services:** minority student, career, personal, academic, older student, psychological, birth control. **For learning-disabled students:** School does not offer a structured program with separate admission and additional fees. Total undergraduates in learning-disabled program or receiving services: 379. Services include: remedial math, remedial English, reading machines, learning center, tutors. **Library:** Number of titles: 72,129; number of current serial subscriptions: 300. **Information technology resources:** Students are not required to lease or own a computer. School has a wireless network. Proportion of college-owned housing units wired for high-speed internet access: 100%. **Campus safety:** Security services offered: 24-hour foot-and-vehicle patrols, late-night transport/escort service, 24-hour emergency telephones, lighted pathways/sidewalks, controlled dormitory access (key, security card, etc).

TRANSFER AND INTERNATIONAL STUDENTS

Transfer students: May apply for admission for the following academic terms: Fall, Spring, Summer. Applicants do not need a minimum number of credits to apply. For fall 2005: Transfer applications received: 351. Transfer applicants offered admission: 279. Transfer applicants enrolled: 177. **International students:** Number of foreign undergraduates: 65 (3% of student body). Number of countries represented: 9. Minimum TOEFL score required: 500 (paper); 173 (computer).

SUNY College of Environ. Sci. and Forestry

- **Address:** 1 Forestry Drive, Syracuse, NY 13210
- **Website:** http://www.esf.edu
- **Public**
- **Enrollment:** 1,339 full-time; 200 part-time

KEY STATS

✔ **U.S News College Ranking:** 98, National Universities
✔ **SAT Score (25th/75th percentile):** 1040-1220
✔ **Tuition:** 2006-2007: $5,069 in state, $11,329 out of state
  Selectivity: More selective   **Room/board:** $10,600
  Acceptance rate: 57%   **Average debt:** $25,000
  Student/faculty ratio: 13/1   **Proportion who borrowed:** 92%

UNDERGRADUATE STUDENT BODY STATS

2005-2006 enrollment: 1,339 full-time; 200 part-time. Men: 62%; women: 38%. **Ethnic makeup:** African American: 1%; American-Indian: 1%; Asian American: 2%; Hispanic: 3%; White: 92%; International: 1%.

ADMISSIONS FACTS AND FIGURES

Phone: (315) 470-6600. **Email:** esfinfo@esf.edu. **Website:** http://www.esf.edu. **Application deadlines for fall 2007:** Regular decision: Rolling. Early decision: Not offered. Early action: Send application by: December 1; Decision sent by: January 1. Admission can be deferred. **Application fee:** $40. Common application is not accepted. **To apply online, go to:** http://www.esf.edu/admissions/undergrad/apply.htm. **Admissions requirements/recommendations:** High school units required (recommended): English: 4 (0); Mathematics: 3 (4); Science: 3 (4); Foreign language: 0 (3); Social studies: 3 (0); History: 1; Total units: 14 (11). Tests: The college uses SAT or ACT scores in admissions decisions. Either SAT or ACT required. For admission to the fall 2007 entering class, the school will accept: ACT with writing, ACT without writing. Campus visit: Recommended. Admissions interview: Recommended. Off-campus interview: May be arranged. **Factors that count in admissions decisions:** *Academic:* Secondary school record: Very important. Class rank: Not considered. Letters of recommendation: Important. Standardized test scores: Important. Essay: Very important. *Nonacademic:* Interview: Important. Extracurricular activities: Important. Talent/ability: Important. Character/personal qualities: Important. Alumni/ae relationship: Considered. Geographical residence: Considered. State residency: Not considered. Religious affiliation/commitment: Not considered. Minority status: Not considered. Volunteer work: Important. Work experience: Important. **Other schools with the greatest overlap in applicants:** Cornell University; Rochester Institute of Technology; SUNY–Binghamton; University of Maine–Orono; University of Vermont. **Admissions statistics for the fall 2005 entering class:** Total applicants: 1,056. Total accepted: 605. Freshmen enrolled: 260; 10% were from out of state. Accepted through early-decision or early-action plans: 32%. Overall acceptance rate: 57%. Non-early acceptance rate: 52%. **Size of waiting list:** 33 applicants; enrolled from waiting list: 12. **Credentials of fall 2005 freshmen:** 24% ranked in the top 10 percent of their high school class; 54% were in the top 25 percent, and 94% were in the top half. (Proportion submitting class standing: 73%.) **Average high school grade point average:** 3.6. **First-year students who submitted SAT scores:** 98%. Scores (25/75 percentile): Verbal: 520-610; Math: 520-610, Combined: 1040-1220. **First-year students submitting ACT scores:** 21%. Scores (25/75 percentile): English: N/A, Math: N/A, Composite: 22-26.

ACADEMICS

Year founded: 1911. **Academic calendar:** Semester. **Degrees offered:** associate, bachelor's, master's, doctorate. **Most popular majors:** 39% environmental biology, 23% environmental studies, 12% forestry, 7% landscape architecture (B.S., B.S.L.A., B.L.A., M.S.L.A., M.L.A., Ph.D.), 6% engineering. **Major fields of study:** architecture and related services; biological and biomedical sciences; engineering; natural resources and conservation; physical sciences. **Areas of required coursework:** arts/fine arts, humanities, mathematics, English (including composition), sciences (biological or physical), history, social science. **Pre-professional programs:** pre-law, pre-medicine, pre-veterinary science. **Special academic programs (% participation):** accelerated program (8%), cooperative (work-study plan) program (10%), cross-registration (100%), double major (10%), dual enrollment (5%), English as a Second Language (ESL) (1%), honors program (12%), independent study (60%), internships (35%), study abroad (35%), teacher certificate program.

Teacher certification offered in: secondary. **Cooperative education programs:** engineering. **Reserve Officers Training Corps (ROTC):** Army ROTC: Offered at cooperating institution (Syracuse University); Air Force ROTC: Offered at cooperating institution (Syracuse University). **Faculty and instruction (2005-2006):** Total instructional faculty: 130 full-time, 30 part-time (73% men; 27% women; 11% minorities). Full-time faculty with Ph.D. or other terminal degree: 95%. Student/faculty ratio: 13/1. Classes of fewer than 20 students: 77%; of 20 to 49 students: 16%; of 50 or more students: 7%. **Advanced Placement and International Baccalaureate credit:** AP tests may be used for: Credit only. Scores accepted: 3, 4, 5. International Baccalaureate exams may be used for: Credit only. **Freshmen returning for sophomore year:** 84%. **Graduation rates:** Four-year: 44%; five-year: 62%; six-year: 63%. **Graduate study:** 22% of students pursue further study immediately upon graduation; 26% within one year; 35% within five years. Fields in which graduates pursue further study: law, 5%; medicine, 5%; dentistry, 5%; engineering, 20%; education, 25%; arts and sciences, 35%; veterinary medicine, 5%.

COSTS AND FINANCIAL AID

Financial aid office: (315) 470-6706. **Expenses (2006-2007):** Tuition and fees 2006-2007: $5,069 in state, $11,329 out of state; room/board: $10,600. Estimated books and supplies: $1,050; transportation: $450; personal expenses: $550. **Financial aid:** Priority filing date for institution's financial aid form: March 1. In 2005-2006, 92% of undergraduates applied for financial aid. Of those, 82% were determined to have financial need; 90% had their need fully met. Average financial aid package (proportion receiving): $12,450 (75%). Average amount of gift aid, such as scholarships or grants (proportion receiving): $6,500 (74%). Average amount of self-help aid, such as work study or loans (proportion receiving): $6,950 (75%). Average need-based loan (excluding PLUS or other private loans): $6,400. Among students who received need-based aid, the average percentage of need met: 100%. Among students who received aid based on merit, the average award (and the proportion receiving): $2,000 (2%). The average athletic scholarship (and the proportion receiving): $0 (0%). Average amount of debt of borrowers graduating in 2005: $25,000. Proportion who borrowed: 92%.

CAMPUS LIFE AND EXTRACURRICULAR ACTIVITIES

Campus housing available: coed dorms, sorority housing, fraternity housing, apartments for married students, apartment for single students, special housing for disabled students, special housing for international students, other housing options. **Clubs and organizations:** Number of student organizations: 200. Activities include: choral groups, concert band, dance, drama/theater, jazz band, literary magazine, marching band, music ensembles, pep band, radio station, student government, student newspaper, student film society, symphony orchestra, television station, yearbook. Number of fraternities: 27; sororities: 20. Average proportion of students who stay on campus on weekends: 40%.

SERVICES AND FACILITIES

Basic services: nonremedial tutoring, placement service, day care, health service, health insurance. **Remedial assistance:** writing, study skills. **Counseling services:** minority student, career, military, personal, veteran student, academic, older student, psychological, birth control, religious. **For learning-disabled students:** School does not offer a structured program with separate admission and additional fees. Total undergraduates in learning-disabled program or receiving services: 61. Services include: diagnostic testing service, note-taking services, oral tests, extended time for tests, tutors, priority seating, other testing accomodations, other. **Library:** Number of titles: 138,518; number of current serial subscriptions: 2,022. **Information technology resources:** Students are not required to lease or own a computer. Number of campus computers available to all students: 120. School does not have a wireless network. Proportion of college-owned housing units wired for high-speed internet access: 100%. **Campus safety:** Security services offered: 24-hour foot-and-vehicle patrols, late-night transport/escort service, 24-hour emergency telephones, lighted pathways/sidewalks, controlled dormitory access (key, security card, etc).

TRANSFER AND INTERNATIONAL STUDENTS

Transfer students: May apply for admission for the following academic terms: Fall, Spring. Applicants do not need a minimum number of credits to apply. For fall 2005: Transfer applications received: 479. Transfer applicants offered admission: 345. Transfer applicants enrolled: 196.
International students: Number of foreign undergraduates: 14 (1% of student body). Minimum TOEFL score required: 550 (paper); 213 (computer).

SUNY College–Old Westbury

- **Address:** PO Box 210, Old Westbury, NY 11568
- **Website:** http://www.oldwestbury.edu
- **Public**
- **Enrollment:** 2,717 full-time; 656 part-time

KEY STATS

✔ **U.S News College Ranking:** third tier, Comp. Colleges–Bachelor's (North)
✔ **SAT Score (25th/75th percentile):** 890-1050
✔ **Tuition:** 2006-2007: $5,076 in state, $11,336 out of state

Selectivity: Less selective	**Room/board:** $8,083
Acceptance rate: 59%	**Average debt:** $14,532
Student/faculty ratio: 17/1	**Proportion who borrowed:** 52%

UNDERGRADUATE STUDENT BODY STATS

2005-2006 enrollment: 2,717 full-time; 656 part-time. Men: 39%; women: 61%. **Ethnic makeup:** African American: 28%; Asian American: 7%; Hispanic: 16%; White: 47%; International: 2%.

ADMISSIONS FACTS AND FIGURES

Phone: (516) 876-3073. **Email:** enroll@oldwestbury.edu. **Website:** http://www.oldwestbury.edu. **Application deadlines for fall 2007:** Regular decision: Rolling. Early decision: Send application by: N/A; Decision sent by: N/A. Early action: Not offered. Admission can be deferred. **Application fee:** $40. Common application is accepted. **To apply online, go to:** http://www.suny.edu/Student/Apply/Apply.cfm. **Admissions requirements/recommendations:** High school units required (recommended): English: 4 (4); Mathematics: 3 (3); Science: 3 (3); Foreign language: 2 (3); Social studies: 2 (2); History: 2 (2); Academic electives: 3 (2); Total units: 22 (22). Tests: The college uses SAT or ACT scores in admissions decisions. Either SAT or ACT required. For admission to the fall 2007 entering class, the school will accept: ACT with writing. Campus visit: Recommended. Admissions interview: Neither required nor recommended. Off-campus interview: Not available. **Factors that count in admissions decisions:** *Academic:* Secondary school record: Important. Class rank: Not considered. Letters of recommendation: Important. Standardized test scores: Important. Essay: Important. *Nonacademic:* Interview: Considered. Extracurricular activities: Considered. Talent/ability: Considered. Character/personal qualities: Considered. Alumni/ae relationship: Not considered. Geographical residence: Not considered. State residency: Not considered. Religious affiliation/commitment: Not considered. Minority status: Not considered. Volunteer work: Considered. Work experience: Considered. **Other schools with the greatest overlap in applicants:** Hofstra University; SUNY College of Arts and Sciences–New Paltz; SUNY–Farmingdale; SUNY–Stony Brook; St. John's University. **Admissions statistics for the fall 2005 entering class:** Total applicants: 3,267. Total accepted: 1,941. Freshmen enrolled: 404; 1% were from out of state. Overall acceptance rate: 59%. Non-early acceptance rate: 59%. **Credentials of fall 2005 freshmen:** 4% ranked in the top 10 percent of their high school class; 30% were in the top 25 percent, and 60% were in the top half. (Proportion submitting class standing: 66%.) **Average high school grade point average:** 2.6. **First-year students who submitted SAT scores:** 99%. Scores (25/75 percentile): Verbal: 440-520, Math: 450-530, Combined: 890-1050.

ACADEMICS

Year founded: 1965. **Academic calendar:** Semester. **Degrees offered:** certificate, bachelor's, master's. **Most popular majors:** 12% business administration and management, 11% accounting, 10% psychology, 8% elementary education and teaching, 8% information science/studies. **Major fields of study:** area, ethnic, cultural, and gender studies; biological and biomedical sciences; business, management, marketing, and related support services; communication, journalism, and related programs; computer and information sciences and support services; education; English language and literature/letters; foreign languages, literatures, and linguistics; liberal arts and sciences studies, and humanities; mathematics and statistics; philosophy and religious studies; physical sciences; psychology; social sciences; visual and performing arts. **Areas of required coursework:** arts/fine arts, humanities, computer literacy, mathematics, English (including composition), philosophy, foreign languages, sciences (biological or physical), history, social science. **Pre-professional programs:** pre-law, pre-medicine. **Special academic programs:** cross-registration, distance learning, double major, English as a Second Language (ESL), exchange student program (domestic), honors program, independent study, internships, liberal arts/career combination, study abroad, teacher certificate program, other. **Teacher certification offered in:** early childhood, special education, elementary, middle/junior high, secondary, bilingual/bicultural. **Reserve Officers Training Corps (ROTC):** Army ROTC: Offered at cooperating institution (Hofstra University); Air Force ROTC: Offered at cooperating institution (Manhattan College). **Faculty and instruction (2005-2006):** Total instructional faculty: 129 full-time, 124 part-time (49% men; 51% women; 29% minorities). Full-time faculty with Ph.D. or other terminal degree: 77%. Student/faculty ratio: 17/1. Classes of fewer than 20 students: 35%; of 20 to 49 students: 65%. **Advanced Placement and International Baccalaureate credit:** AP tests may be used for: Credit only. Scores accepted: 3, 4, 5. International Baccalaureate exams may be used for: Credit only. **Freshmen returning for sophomore year:** 74%. **Graduation rates:** Four-year: 20%; five-year: 26%; six-year: 23%. **Graduate study:** 52% of students pursue further study immediately upon graduation; 21% within one year; 26% within five years. Fields in which graduates pursue further study: Master of Business Administration (MBA), 32%; law, 7%; medicine, 5%; engineering, 1%; theology (or the seminary), 2%; education, 27%; arts and sciences, 11%.

COSTS AND FINANCIAL AID

Financial aid office: (516) 876-3222. **Expenses (2006-2007):** Tuition and fees 2006-2007: $5,076 in state, $11,336 out of state; room/board: $8,083. Estimated books and supplies: $800; transportation: $1,675; personal expenses: $1,210. **Financial aid:** Priority filing date for institution's financial aid form: April 14; deadline: May 11. In 2005-2006, 75% of undergraduates applied for financial aid. Of those, 75% were determined to have financial need; 100% had their need fully met. Average financial aid package (proportion receiving): $6,283 (75%). Average amount of gift aid, such as scholarships or grants (proportion receiving): $4,677 (62%). Average amount of self-help aid, such as work study or loans (proportion receiving): $2,441 (44%). Average need-based loan (excluding PLUS or other private loans): $2,341. Among students who received need-based aid, the average percentage of need met: 45%. Among students who received aid based on merit, the average award (and the proportion receiving): $0 (0%). The average athletic scholarship (and the proportion receiving): $0 (0%). Average amount of debt of borrowers graduating in 2005: $14,532. Proportion who borrowed: 52%.

CAMPUS LIFE AND EXTRACURRICULAR ACTIVITIES

Campus housing available (% using): coed dorms (100%). Students who live in college-owned, operated, or affiliated housing: 25%. **Student employment:** During the 2005-2006 academic year, 14% of undergraduates worked on campus. Average per-year earnings: $900. **Clubs and organizations:** Number of student organizations: 60. Activities include: choral groups, dance, drama/theater, radio station, student government, student newspaper, student film society, yearbook. Number of fraternities: 7; sororities: 6. Proportion of men in fraternities: 2%; of women in sororities: 2%. Average proportion of students who stay on campus on weekends: 38%. **Sports program (2005-2006):** Member of NCAA III. *Men's intercollegiate varsity sports:* baseball, basketball, cross-country, lacrosse, soccer, track and field (indoor), track and field (outdoor). *Women's intercollegiate varsity sports:* basketball, cross-country, soccer, softball, track and field (indoor), track and field (outdoor), volleyball.

SERVICES AND FACILITIES

Basic services: women's center, placement service, day care, health service, health insurance. **Remedial assistance:** reading, math, writing, study skills. **Counseling services:** minority student, career, personal, veteran student, academic, older student, psychological. **For learning-disabled students:** School does not offer a structured program with separate admission and additional fees. Total undergraduates in learning-disabled program or receiving services: 60. Services include: remedial math, remedial English, reading machines, tape recorders, untimed tests, note-taking services, oral tests, learning center, readers, extended time for tests, tutors, priority seating, texts on tape, other testing accomodations. **Library:** Number of titles: 208,446; number of current serial subscriptions: 432. **Information technology resources:** Students are not required to lease or own a computer. Number of campus computers available to all students: 350. School has a wireless network. Approximate number of users that can be accommodated: 900. Proportion of college-owned housing units wired for high-speed internet access: 75%. **Campus safety:** Security services offered: 24-hour foot-and-vehicle patrols, 24-hour emergency telephones, lighted pathways/sidewalks, student patrols, controlled dormitory access (key, security card, etc).

TRANSFER AND INTERNATIONAL STUDENTS

Transfer students: May apply for admission for the following academic terms: Fall, Spring. Applicants need a minimum number of credits to apply. For fall 2005: Transfer applications received: 1,178. Transfer applicants offered admission: 1,095. Transfer applicants enrolled: 596. **International students:** Number of foreign undergraduates: 56 (2% of student body). Number of countries represented: 26. Minimum TOEFL score required: 500 (paper); 175 (computer).

SUNY College—Oneonta

- **Address:** Ravine Parkway, Oneonta, NY 13820
- **Website:** http://www.oneonta.edu
- **Public**
- **Enrollment:** 5,488 full-time; 161 part-time

KEY STATS

✔ **U.S News College Ranking:** 83, Universities–Master's (North)
✔ **SAT Score (25th/75th percentile):** 1030-1190
✔ **Tuition:** 2006-2007: $5,347 in state, $11,607 out of state

Selectivity: Selective	**Room/board:** $7,696
Acceptance rate: 45%	**Average debt:** $16,900
Student/faculty ratio: 17/1	**Proportion who borrowed:** 68%

UNDERGRADUATE STUDENT BODY STATS

2005-2006 enrollment: 5,488 full-time; 161 part-time. Men: 43%; women: 57%. **Ethnic makeup:** African American: 3%; Asian American: 2%; Hispanic: 5%; White: 89%; International: 1%.

ADMISSIONS FACTS AND FIGURES

Phone: (607) 436-2524. **Email:** admissions@oneonta.edu. **Website:** http://www.oneonta.edu. **Application deadlines for fall 2007:** Regular decision: January 15. Early decision: Not offered. Early action: Send application by: November 15; Decision sent by: December 15. Admission can be deferred. **Application fee:** $40. Common application is not accepted. **To apply online, go to:** http://www.suny.edu/Student/Apply/Apply.cfm. **Admissions requirements/recommendations:** High school units required (recommended): English: 4 (4); Mathematics: 2 (3); Science: 2 (3); Foreign language: 2 (3); Social studies: 3 (3); History: 0 (0); Academic electives: 0 (0); Total units: 16 (16). Tests: The college uses SAT or ACT scores in admissions decisions. Either SAT or ACT required. For admission to the fall 2007 entering class, the school will accept: ACT with writing, ACT without writing. Campus visit: Recommended. Admissions interview: Recommended. Off-campus interview: May be arranged. **Factors that count in admissions decisions:** *Academic:* Secondary school record: Very important. Class rank: Considered. Letters of recommendation: Considered. Standardized test scores: Important. Essay: Important. *Nonacademic:* Interview: Important. Extracurricular activities: Important. Talent/ability: Important. Character/personal qualities: Important. Alumni/ae relationship: Considered. Geographical residence: Not considered. State residency: Not considered. Religious affiliation/commitment: Not considered. Minority status: Considered. Volunteer work: Important. Work experience: Considered. **Other schools with the greatest overlap in applicants:** SUNY College of Arts and Sciences–New Paltz; SUNY College–Cortland; SUNY–Albany; SUNY–Oswego; SUNY–Plattsburgh. **Admissions statistics for the fall 2005 entering class:** Total applicants: 10,900. Total accepted: 4,950. Freshmen enrolled: 1,145; 2% were from out of state. Accepted through early-decision or early-action plans: 33%. Overall acceptance rate: 45%. Non-early acceptance rate: 42%. **Size of waiting list:** 224 applicants; enrolled from waiting list: 5. **Credentials of fall 2005 freshmen:** 11% ranked in the top 10 percent of their high school class; 48% were in the top 25 percent, and 94% were in the top half. (Proportion submitting class standing: 44%.) **Average high school grade point average:** 3.4. **First-year students who submitted SAT scores:** 97%. Scores (25/75 percentile): Verbal: 510-590, Math: 520-600, Combined: 1030-1190. **First-year students submitting ACT scores:** 19%. Scores (25/75 percentile): English: N/A, Math: N/A, Composite: 22-25.

ACADEMICS

Year founded: 1889. **Academic calendar:** Semester. **Degrees offered:** bachelor's, post-bachelor's certificate, master's, post-master's certificate. **Most popular majors:** 25% education, 18% visual and performing arts, 11% com-munication, journalism, and related programs, 8% business, management, marketing, and related support services, 8% family and consumer sciences/human sciences. **Major fields of study:** area, ethnic, cultural, and gender studies; biological and biomedical sciences; business, management, marketing, and related support services; communication, journalism, and related programs; computer and information sciences and support services; education; English language and literature/letters; family and consumer sciences/human sciences; foreign languages, literatures, and linguistics; health professions and related clinical sciences; history; legal professions and studies; mathematics and statistics; multi/interdisciplinary studies; natural resources and conservation; philosophy and religious studies; physical sciences; psychology; security and protective services; social sciences; visual and performing arts. **Areas of required coursework:** arts/fine arts, humanities, computer literacy, mathematics, English (including composition), foreign languages, sciences (biological or physical), history, social science. **Pre-professional programs:** pre-law, pre-dentistry, pre-medicine, pre-veterinary science. **Special academic programs:** cross-registration, distance learning, double major, English as a Second Language (ESL), honors program, independent study, internships, study abroad, teacher certificate program, other. **Teacher certification offered in:** early childhood, elementary, middle/junior high, secondary. **Faculty and instruction (2005-2006):** Total instructional faculty: 252 full-time, 215 part-time (54% men; 46% women; 14% minorities). Full-time faculty with Ph.D. or other terminal degree: 82%. Student/faculty ratio: 17/1. Classes of fewer than 20 students: 42%; of 20 to 49 students: 53%; of 50 or more students: 5%. **Advanced Placement and International Baccalaureate credit:** AP tests may be used for: Credit and/or placement. Scores accepted: 3, 4, 5. International Baccalaureate exams may be used for: Credit and/or placement. **Freshmen returning for sophomore year:** 77%. **Graduation rates:** Four-year: 37%; five-year: 51%; six-year: 48%. **Graduate study:** 45% of students pursue further study within one year.

COSTS AND FINANCIAL AID

Financial aid office: (607) 436-2532. **Expenses (2006-2007):** Tuition and fees 2006-2007: $5,347 in state, $11,607 out of state; room/board: $7,696. Estimated books and supplies: $900; transportation: $1,000; personal expenses: $1,070. **Financial aid:** Priority filing date for institution's financial aid form: March 1. In 2005-2006, 79% of undergraduates applied for financial aid. Of those, 59% were determined to have financial need; 17% had their need fully met. Average financial aid package (proportion receiving): $9,244 (57%). Average amount of gift aid, such as scholarships or grants (proportion receiving): $3,666 (50%). Average amount of self-help aid, such as work study or loans (proportion receiving): $4,496 (48%). Average need-based loan (excluding PLUS or other private loans): $4,406. Among students who received need-based aid, the average percentage of need met: 64%. Among students who received aid based on merit, the average award (and the proportion receiving): $4,893 (20%). The average athletic scholarship (and the proportion receiving): $7,346 (0%). Average amount of debt of borrowers graduating in 2005: $16,900. Proportion who borrowed: 68%.

CAMPUS LIFE AND EXTRACURRICULAR ACTIVITIES

Campus housing available (% using): coed dorms (100%). Students who live in college-owned, operated, or affiliated housing: 58%. **Student employment:** During the 2005-2006 academic year, 14% of undergraduates worked on campus. Average per-year earnings: $1,200. **Clubs and organizations:** Number of student organizations: 70. Activities include: choral groups, concert band, dance, drama/theater, jazz band, literary magazine, music ensembles, musical theater, opera, radio station, student government, student newspaper, student film society, symphony orchestra, television station, yearbook. Number of fraternities: 3; sororities: 4. Proportion of men in fraternities: 2%; of women in sororities: 5%. Average proportion of students who stay on campus on weekends: 60%. **Sports program (2005-2006):** Member of NCAA III. *Men's intercollegiate varsity sports:* baseball, basketball, cross-country, lacrosse, soccer, swimming and diving, tennis, track and field (indoor), track and field (outdoor), wrestling. *Women's intercollegiate varsity sports:* basketball, cross-country, field hockey, lacrosse, soccer, softball, swimming and diving, tennis, track and field (indoor), track and field (outdoor), volleyball.

SERVICES AND FACILITIES

Basic services: nonremedial tutoring, women's center, placement service, day care, health service, health insurance. **Remedial assistance:** reading, math, writing, study skills. **Counseling services:** minority student, career, personal, academic, older student, psychological, birth control. **For learning-disabled students:** School does not offer a structured program with separate admission and additional fees. Total undergraduates in learning-disabled program or receiving services: 227. Services include: remedial math, remedial English, reading machines, remedial reading, tape recorders, videotaped classes, untimed tests, note-taking services, oral tests, learning center, readers, extended time for tests, tutors, texts on tape. **Library:** Number of titles: 556,445; number of current serial subscriptions: 19,391. **Information technology resources:** Students are not required to lease or own a computer. Number of campus computers available to all students: 760. School has a wireless network. Approximate number of users that can be accommodated: 2,000. Proportion of college-owned housing units wired for high-speed internet access: 100%. **Campus safety:** Security services offered: 24-hour foot-and-vehicle patrols, late-night transport/escort service, 24-hour emergency telephones, lighted pathways/sidewalks, controlled dormitory access (key, security card, etc.).

TRANSFER AND INTERNATIONAL STUDENTS

Transfer students: May apply for admission for the following academic terms: Fall, Spring. Applicants do not need a minimum number of credits to apply. For fall 2005: Transfer applications received: 2,017. Transfer applicants offered admission: 937. Transfer applicants enrolled: 500.
International students: Number of foreign undergraduates: 77 (1% of student body). Number of countries represented: 20. Minimum TOEFL score required: 500 (paper); 173 (computer). Average TOEFL score: 525 (paper).

SUNY College–Potsdam

- **Address:** 44 Pierrepont Avenue, Potsdam, NY 13676
- **Website:** http://www.potsdam.edu
- **Public**
- **Enrollment:** 3,465 full-time; 154 part-time

KEY STATS

✔ **U.S News College Ranking:** third tier, Universities–Master's (North)
✔ **SAT Score (25th/75th percentile):** 960-1170
✔ **Tuition:** 2005-2006: $5,289 in state, $11,549 out of state

Selectivity: Selective	Room/board: $7,670
Acceptance rate: 73%	Average debt: $16,117
Student/faculty ratio: 14/1	Proportion who borrowed: 82%

UNDERGRADUATE STUDENT BODY STATS

2005-2006 enrollment: 3,465 full-time; 154 part-time. Men: 42%; women: 58%. **Ethnic makeup:** African American: 2%; American-Indian: 2%; Asian American: 1%; Hispanic: 2%; White: 89%; International: 3%.

ADMISSIONS FACTS AND FIGURES

Phone: (315) 267-2180. **Email:** admissions@potsdam.edu. **Website:** http://www.potsdam.edu. **Application deadlines for fall 2007:** Regular decision: Rolling. Early decision: Not offered. Early action: Not offered. Admission can be deferred. **Application fee:** $40. Common application is not accepted. **To apply online, go to:** http://www.suny.edu/student. **Admissions requirements/recommendations:** High school units required (recommended): English: 4 (4); Mathematics: 2 (4); Science: 2 (4); Foreign language: 3 (4); Social studies: 4 (4); Total units: 16 (21). Tests: The college uses SAT or ACT scores in admissions decisions. Either SAT or ACT required. For admission to the fall 2007 entering class, the school will accept: ACT with writing, ACT without writing. Campus visit: Recommended. Admissions interview: Recommended. Off-campus interview: Not available. **Factors that count in admissions decisions:** *Academic:* Secondary school record: Very important. Class rank: Important. Letters of recommendation: Considered. Standardized test scores: Very important. Essay: Considered. *Nonacademic:* Interview: Considered. Extracurricular activities: Considered. Talent/ability: Important. Character/personal qualities: Considered. Alumni/ae relationship: Considered. Geographical residence: Not considered. State residency: Not considered. Religious affiliation/commitment: Not considered. Minority status: Not considered. Volunteer work: Considered. Work experience: Considered. **Other schools with the greatest overlap in applicants:** Ithaca College; SUNY–Fredonia; SUNY–Oswego; SUNY–Plattsburgh; St. Lawrence University. **Admissions statistics for the fall 2005 entering class:** Total applicants: 3,423. Total accepted: 2,512. Freshmen enrolled: 739; 3% were from out of state. Overall acceptance rate: 73%. **Size of waiting list:** 64 applicants; enrolled from waiting list: 27. **Credentials of fall 2005 freshmen:** 12% ranked in the top 10 percent of their high school class; 36% were in the top 25 percent, and 76%

were in the top half. (Proportion submitting class standing: 61%.) **Average high school grade point average:** 3.2. **First-year students who submitted SAT scores:** 95%. Scores (25/75 percentile): Verbal: 480-590, Math: 480-580, Combined: 960-1170. **First-year students submitting ACT scores:** 27%. Scores (25/75 percentile): English: N/A, Math: N/A, Composite: 20-26.

ACADEMICS

Year founded: 1816. **Academic calendar:** Semester. **Degrees offered:** bachelor's, master's. **Most popular majors:** 12% education, 11% music teacher education, 9% psychology, 8% English language and literature, 8% business administration and management. **Major fields of study:** biological and biomedical sciences; business, management, marketing, and related support services; computer and information sciences and support services; education; English language and literature/letters; foreign languages, literatures, and linguistics; health professions and related clinical sciences; liberal arts and sciences studies, and humanities; mathematics and statistics; multi/interdisciplinary studies; philosophy and religious studies; physical sciences; psychology; security and protective services; social sciences; visual and performing arts. **Areas of required coursework:** arts/fine arts, humanities, mathematics, English (including composition), philosophy, foreign languages, sciences (biological or physical), history, social science, other. **Pre-professional programs:** pre-law, pre-dentistry, pre-medicine, pre-veterinary science, pre-optometry, pre-pharmacy, other. **Special academic programs:** cross-registration, distance learning, double major, dual enrollment, exchange student program (domestic), honors program, independent study, internships, liberal arts/career combination, student-designed major, study abroad, teacher certificate program, other. **Teacher certification offered in:** early childhood, special education, elementary, middle/junior high, secondary. **Reserve Officers Training Corps (ROTC):** Army ROTC: Offered at cooperating institution (Clarkson University); Air Force ROTC: Offered at cooperating institution (Clarkson University). **Faculty and instruction (2005-2006):** Total instructional faculty: 249 full-time, 120 part-time (54% men; 46% women; 8% minorities). Full-time faculty with Ph.D. or other terminal degree: 88%. Student/faculty ratio: 14/1. Classes of fewer than 20 students: 59%; of 20 to 49 students: 39%; of 50 or more students: 2%. **Advanced Placement and International Baccalaureate credit:** AP tests may be used for: Credit and/or placement. Scores accepted: 3, 4, 5. International Baccalaureate exams may be used for: Credit and/or placement. **Freshmen returning for sophomore year:** 75%. **Graduation rates:** Four-year: 26%; five-year: 43%; six-year: 45%. **Graduate study:** 34% of students pursue further study within one year. Fields in which graduates pursue further study: Master of Business Administration (MBA), 6%; law, 4%; medicine, 5%; education, 57%; arts and sciences, 28%.

COSTS AND FINANCIAL AID

Financial aid office: (315) 267-2162. **Expenses (2005-2006):** Tuition and fees 2005-2006: $5,289 in state, $11,549 out of state; room/board: $7,670. Estimated books and supplies: $1,000; transportation: $800; personal expenses: $1,300. **Financial aid:** Priority filing date for institution's financial aid form: March 1; deadline: May 1. In 2005-2006, 85% of undergraduates applied for financial aid. Of those, 67% were determined to have financial need; 77% had their need fully met. Average financial aid package (proportion receiving): $11,771 (66%). Average amount of gift aid, such as scholarships or grants (proportion receiving): $4,518 (61%). Average amount of self-help aid, such as work study or loans (proportion receiving): $4,325 (56%). Average need-based loan (excluding PLUS or other private loans): $4,175. Among students who received need-based aid, the average percentage of need met: 78%. Among students who received aid based on merit, the average award (and the proportion receiving): $3,637 (11%). The average athletic scholarship (and the proportion receiving): $0 (0%). Average amount of debt of borrowers graduating in 2005: $16,117. Proportion who borrowed: 82%.

CAMPUS LIFE AND EXTRACURRICULAR ACTIVITIES

Campus housing available: coed dorms, women's dorms, apartment for single students, special housing for disabled students, special housing for international students, other housing options. Students who live in college-owned, operated, or affiliated housing: 54%. **Clubs and organizations:** Number of student organizations: 100. Activities include: choral groups, concert band, dance, drama/theater, jazz band, literary magazine, music ensembles, musical theater, opera, radio station, student government, student newspaper, symphony orchestra, yearbook. Number of fraternities: 6; sororities: 8. Proportion of men in fraternities: 2%; of women in sororities: 3%. Average proportion of students who stay on campus on weekends: 65%. **Sports program (2005-2006):** Member of NCAA III. *Men's intercollegiate varsity sports:* basketball, cross-country, golf, ice hockey, lacrosse, soccer, swimming and diving. *Women's intercollegiate varsity sports:* basketball, cross-country, equestrian sports, lacrosse, soccer, softball, swimming and diving, tennis, volleyball.

SERVICES AND FACILITIES

Basic services: nonremedial tutoring, women's center, placement service, day care, health service, health insurance. **Counseling services:** minority student, career, military, personal, veteran student, academic, older student, psychological, birth control. **For learning-disabled students:** School does not offer a structured program with separate admission and additional fees. Total undergraduates in learning-disabled program or receiving services: 116. Services include: reading machines, tape recorders, other special classes, note-taking services, oral tests, learning center, readers, extended time for tests, tutors, other. **Library:** Number of titles: 469,969; number of current serial subscriptions: 881. **Information technology resources:** Students are not required to lease or own a computer. Number of campus computers available to all students: 515. School has a wireless network. Approximate number of users that can be accommodated: 3,000. Proportion of college-owned housing units wired for high-speed internet access: 100%. **Campus safety:** Security services offered: 24-hour foot-and-vehicle patrols, late-night transport/escort service, 24-hour emergency telephones, lighted pathways/sidewalks, student patrols, controlled dormitory access (key, security card, etc).

TRANSFER AND INTERNATIONAL STUDENTS

Transfer students: May apply for admission for the following academic terms: Fall, Spring, Summer. Applicants need a minimum number of credits to apply. For fall 2005: Transfer applications received: 878. Transfer applicants offered admission: 593. Transfer applicants enrolled: 363. **International students:** Number of foreign undergraduates: 114 (3% of student body). Number of countries represented: 23. Minimum TOEFL score required: 550 (paper); 213 (computer). Average TOEFL score: 608 (paper).

SUNY–Empire State College

- **Address:** 1 Union Avenue, Saratoga Springs, NY 12866
- **Website:** http://www.esc.edu
- **Public**
- **Enrollment:** 3,189 full-time; 6,333 part-time

KEY STATS

✔ **U.S News College Ranking:** Unranked, Universities–Master's (North)
✔ **SAT or ACT Score (25th/75th percentile):** N/A
✔ **Tuition:** 2005-2006: $4,453 in state, $10,713 out of state

Selectivity: N/A	Room/board: $0
Acceptance rate: N/A	Average debt: N/A
Student/faculty ratio: 12/1	Proportion who borrowed: N/A

UNDERGRADUATE STUDENT BODY STATS

2005-2006 enrollment: 3,189 full-time; 6,333 part-time. Men: 41%; women: 59%. **Ethnic makeup:** African American: 12%; American-Indian: 1%; Asian American: 1%; Hispanic: 6%; White: 71%; International: 8%.

ADMISSIONS FACTS AND FIGURES

Phone: (518) 587-2100. **Email:** admissions@esc.edu. **Website:** http://www.esc.edu. **Application deadlines for fall 2007:** Regular decision: Rolling. Early decision: Not offered. Early action: Not offered. Admission can be deferred. Common application is not accepted. **To apply online, go to:** http://www.esc.edu/apply. **Admissions requirements/recommendations:** Tests: The college does not use SAT or ACT scores in admissions decisions. Neither SAT nor ACT required. Campus visit: Neither required nor recommended. Admissions interview: Neither required nor recommended. Off-campus interview: Not available. **Factors that count in admissions decisions:** *Academic:* Secondary school record: Not considered. Class rank: Not considered. Letters of recommendation: Not considered. Standardized test scores: Not considered. Essay: Very important. *Nonacademic:* Interview: Not considered. Extracurricular activities: Not considered. Talent/ability: Not considered. Character/personal qualities: Not considered. Alumni/ae relationship: Not considered. Geographical residence: Not considered. State residency: Not considered. Religious affiliation/commitment: Not considered. Minority status: Not considered. Volunteer work: Not considered. Work experience: Not considered. **Other schools with the greatest overlap in applicants:**

Excelsior College; Thomas Edison State College; Union Institute and University. **Admissions statistics for the fall 2005 entering class:** Freshmen enrolled: 463; 3% were from out of state.

ACADEMICS

Year founded: 1971. **Academic calendar:** Other. **Degrees offered:** associate, bachelor's, master's. **Most popular majors:** 47% business, management, marketing, and related support services, 16% public administration and social service professions, 10% multi/interdisciplinary studies, 5% English language and literature/letters, 5% physical sciences. **Major fields of study:** business, management, marketing, and related support services; education; English language and literature/letters; history; multi/interdisciplinary studies; physical sciences; psychology; public administration and social service professions; social sciences; visual and performing arts. **Areas of required coursework:** arts/fine arts, humanities, computer literacy, mathematics, English (including composition), philosophy, foreign languages, sciences (biological or physical), history, social science, other. **Special academic programs:** cross-registration, distance learning, double major, external degree program, independent study, student-designed major, other. **Faculty and instruction (2005-2006):** Total instructional faculty: 154 full-time, 921 part-time (48% men; 52% women; 11% minorities). Full-time faculty with Ph.D. or other terminal degree: 95%. Student/faculty ratio: 12/1. **Graduation rates:** Six-year: 16%.

COSTS AND FINANCIAL AID

Financial aid office: (518) 587-2100. **Expenses (2005-2006):** Tuition and fees 2005-2006: $4,453 in state, $10,713 out of state; room/board: $0. Estimated books and supplies: $1,400; transportation: $600; personal expenses: $3,800. **Financial aid:** Priority filing date for institution's financial aid form: April 1.

CAMPUS LIFE AND EXTRACURRICULAR ACTIVITIES

Students who live in college-owned, operated, or affiliated housing: 0%. Number of fraternities: 0; sororities: 0.

SERVICES AND FACILITIES

Counseling services: academic. **For learning-disabled students:** School does not offer a structured program with separate admission and additional fees. **Information technology resources:** Students are not required to lease or own a computer.

TRANSFER AND INTERNATIONAL STUDENTS

Transfer students: May apply for admission for the following academic terms: Fall, Winter, Spring, Summer. Applicants do not need a minimum number of credits to apply. For fall 2005: Transfer applicants enrolled: 2,436. **International students:** Number of foreign undergraduates: 663 (8% of student body). Number of countries represented: 12. Minimum TOEFL score required: 550 (paper); 213 (computer).

SUNY–Farmingdale

- **Address:** 2350 Broadhollow Road, Farmingdale, NY 11735-1021
- **Website:** http://www.farmingdale.edu
- **Public**
- **Enrollment:** 4,020 full-time; 2,441 part-time

KEY STATS

✔ **U.S News College Ranking:** third tier, Comp. Colleges–Bachelor's (North)
✔ **SAT Score (25th/75th percentile):** 889-1087
✔ **Tuition:** 2006-2007: $5,297 in state, $11,557 out of state

Selectivity: Less selective	Room/board: $11,168
Acceptance rate: 61%	Average debt: N/A
Student/faculty ratio: 19/1	Proportion who borrowed: N/A

UNDERGRADUATE STUDENT BODY STATS

2005-2006 enrollment: 4,020 full-time; 2,441 part-time. Men: 58%; women: 42%. **Ethnic makeup:** African American: 13%; Asian American: 5%; Hispanic: 9%; White: 72%; International: 1%.

ADMISSIONS FACTS AND FIGURES

Phone: (631) 420-2200. **Email:** admissions@farmingdale.edu. **Website:** http://www.farmingdale.edu. **Application deadlines for fall 2007:** Regular decision: Rolling. Early decision: Not offered. Early action: Not offered. Admission cannot be deferred. **Application fee:** $40. Common application is not accepted. **To apply online, go to:** https://www.applyweb.com/aw?suny95ud. **Admissions requirements/recommendations:** High school units required (recommended): English: 3 (4); Mathematics: 2 (3); Science: 1 (2); Total units: 7 (10). Tests: The college uses SAT or ACT scores in admissions decisions. SAT required. For admission to the fall 2007 entering class, the school will accept: ACT with writing. Campus visit: Recommended. Admissions interview: Required. Off-campus interview: Not available. **Factors that count in admissions decisions:** *Academic:* Secondary school record: Important. Class rank: Important. Letters of recommendation: Important. Standardized test scores: Important. Essay: Important. *Nonacademic:* Interview: Important. Extracurricular activities: Important. Talent/ability: Important. Character/personal qualities: Considered. Alumni/ae relationship: Considered. Geographical residence: Not considered. State residency: Not considered. Religious affiliation/commitment: Not considered. Minority status: Not considered. Volunteer work: Considered. Work experience: Considered. **Other schools with the greatest overlap in applicants:** CUNY–New York City College of Technology; Hofstra University; Long Island University–C.W. Post Campus; SUNY College–Old Westbury; SUNY–Stony Brook. **Admissions statistics for the fall 2005 entering class:** Total applicants: 4,115. Total accepted: 2,517. Freshmen enrolled: 1,053; 1% were from out of state. Overall acceptance rate: 61%. **Credentials of fall 2005 freshmen:** 2% ranked in the top 10 percent of their high school class; 11% were in the top 25 percent, and 53% were in the top half. (Proportion submitting class standing: 58%.) **Average high school grade point average:** 2.7. **First-year students who submitted SAT scores:** 70%. Scores (25/75 percentile): Verbal: 430-537, Math: 459-550, Combined: 889-1087.

ACADEMICS

Year founded: 1912. **Academic calendar:** Semester. **Degrees offered:** certificate, associate, bachelor's. **Most popular majors:** 33% business, management, marketing, and related support services, 14% computer and information sciences and support services, 14% engineering technologies/technicians, 13% communication, journalism, and related programs, 9% security and protective services. **Major fields of study:** agriculture, agriculture operations, and related sciences; biological and biomedical sciences; business, management, marketing, and related support services; computer and information sciences and support services; engineering technologies/technicians; English language and literature/letters; health professions and related clinical sciences; mathematics and statistics; multi/interdisciplinary studies; psychology; security and protective services; social sciences; transportation and materials moving; visual and performing arts. **Areas of required coursework:** humanities, computer literacy, mathematics, English (including composition), foreign languages, sciences (biological or physical), history, social science. **Special academic programs:** distance learning, English as a Second Language (ESL), honors program, independent study, internships, study abroad. **Reserve Officers Training Corps (ROTC):** Army ROTC: Offered at cooperating institution; Air Force ROTC: Offered at cooperating institution. **Faculty and instruction (2005-2006):** Total instructional faculty: 153 full-time, 306 part-time (56% men; 44% women; 11% minorities). Full-time faculty with Ph.D. or other terminal degree: 56%. Student/faculty ratio: 19/1. Classes of fewer than 20 students: 31%; of 20 to 49 students: 68%; of 50 or more students: 1%. **Advanced Placement and International Baccalaureate credit:** AP tests may be used for: Credit and/or placement. Scores accepted: 3, 4, 5. **Freshmen returning for sophomore year:** 70%. **Graduation rates:** Four-year: 13%; five-year: 21%; six-year: 22%. **Graduate study:** 50% of students pursue further study within one year.

COSTS AND FINANCIAL AID

Financial aid office: (631) 420-2328. **Expenses (2006-2007):** Tuition and fees 2006-2007: $5,297 in state, $11,557 out of state; room/board: $11,168. Estimated books and supplies: $1,108; transportation: $582; personal expenses: $845. **Financial aid:** Priority filing date for institution's financial aid form: April 4.

CAMPUS LIFE AND EXTRACURRICULAR ACTIVITIES

Campus housing available (% using): coed dorms (100%). Students who live in college-owned, operated, or affiliated housing: 9%. Activities include: drama/theater, literary magazine, radio station, student government, student newspaper, yearbook. Average proportion of students who stay on campus on weekends: 5%. **Sports program (2005-2006):** Member of NCAA III. *Men's intercollegiate varsity sports:* baseball, basketball, cross-country, golf, lacrosse, soccer, track and field (indoor), track and field (outdoor). *Women's*

intercollegiate varsity sports: basketball, cross-country, soccer, softball, track and field (indoor), track and field (outdoor), volleyball.

SERVICES AND FACILITIES

Basic services: nonremedial tutoring, placement service, day care, health service, health insurance. **Remedial assistance:** reading, math, writing, study skills. **Counseling services:** minority student, career, personal, academic, older student, psychological, birth control. **For learning-disabled students:** School does not offer a structured program with separate admission and additional fees. Services include: other testing accommodations, reading machines, tape recorders, diagnostic testing service, untimed tests, learning center, readers, extended time for tests, tutors. **Library:** Number of titles: 125,000; number of current serial subscriptions: 800. **Information technology resources:** Students are not required to lease or own a computer. Number of campus computers available to all students: 950. School has a wireless network. Proportion of college-owned housing units wired for high-speed internet access: 90%. **Campus safety:** Security services offered: 24-hour foot-and-vehicle patrols, 24-hour emergency telephones, lighted pathways/sidewalks, controlled dormitory access (key, security card, etc).

TRANSFER AND INTERNATIONAL STUDENTS

Transfer students: May apply for admission for the following academic terms: Fall, Spring. Applicants do not need a minimum number of credits to apply. For fall 2005: Transfer applications received: 1,440. Transfer applicants offered admission: 970. Transfer applicants enrolled: 575. **International students:** Number of foreign undergraduates: 44 (1% of student body). Minimum TOEFL score required: 500 (paper); 173 (computer).

SUNY–Fredonia

- **Address:** Fredonia, NY 14063-1136
- **Website:** http://www.fredonia.edu
- **Public**
- **Enrollment:** 4,839 full-time; 204 part-time

KEY STATS

✔ **U.S News College Ranking:** 56, Universities–Master's (North)
✔ **SAT Score (25th/75th percentile):** 1040-1200
✔ **Tuition:** 2006-2007: $5,482 in state, $11,742 out of state
   Selectivity: Selective   **Room/board:** $7,930
   Acceptance rate: 55%   **Average debt:** $12,500
   Student/faculty ratio: 16/1   **Proportion who borrowed:** 81%

UNDERGRADUATE STUDENT BODY STATS

2005-2006 enrollment: 4,839 full-time; 204 part-time. Men: 42%; women: 58%. **Ethnic makeup:** African American: 2%; American-Indian: 1%; Asian American: 2%; Hispanic: 3%; White: 93%.

ADMISSIONS FACTS AND FIGURES

Phone: (800) 252-1212. **Email:** admissionsinq@fredonia.edu. **Website:** http://www.fredonia.edu. **Application deadlines for fall 2007:** Regular decision: Rolling. Early decision: Send application by: November 15; Decision sent by: December 15. Early action: Not offered. Admission can be deferred. **Application fee:** $40. Common application is not accepted. **To apply online, go to:** http://www.fredonia.edu/admissions/applying.html. **Admissions requirements/recommendations:** High school units required (recommended): English: 4; Mathematics: 3 (4); Science: 3 (4); Foreign language: (4); Social studies: 4; Academic electives: 2; Total units: 18 (16). Tests: The college uses SAT or ACT scores in admissions decisions. Either SAT or ACT required. For admission to the fall 2007 entering class, the school will accept: ACT with writing, ACT without writing. Campus visit: Recommended. Admissions interview: Neither required nor recommended. Off-campus interview: Not available. **Factors that count in admissions decisions:** *Academic:* Secondary school record: Very important. Class rank: Considered. Letters of recommendation: Considered. Standardized test scores: Important. Essay: Considered. *Nonacademic:* Interview: Not considered. Extracurricular activities: Considered. Talent/ability: Considered. Character/personal qualities: Considered. Alumni/ae relationship: Considered. Geographical residence: Not considered. State residency: Not considered. Religious affiliation/commitment: Not considered. Minority status: Considered. Volunteer work: Considered. Work experience: Considered. **Other schools with the greatest overlap in applicants:** SUNY College of Arts and Sciences–Geneseo; SUNY College–Brockport; St. Bonaventure University; University at Buffalo–SUNY. **Admissions statistics for the fall 2005 entering class:** Total applicants: 5,902. Total accepted: 3,275. Freshmen enrolled: 1,037; 1% were from out of state. Accepted through early-decision or early-action plans: 4%. Overall acceptance rate: 55%. Early-decision acceptance rate: 60%. Non-early acceptance rate: 55%. **Credentials of fall 2005 freshmen:** 17% ranked in the top 10 percent of their high school class; 45% were in the top 25 percent, and 88% were in the top half. (Proportion submitting class standing: 88%.) **Average high school grade point average:** 3.5. **First-year students who submitted SAT scores:** 87%. Scores (25/75 percentile): Verbal: 520-600, Math: 520-600, Combined: 1040-1200. **First-year students submitting ACT scores:** 16%. Scores (25/75 percentile): English: N/A, Math: N/A, Composite: 22-26.

ACADEMICS

Year founded: 1826. **Academic calendar:** Semester. **Degrees offered:** bachelor's, master's, post-master's certificate. **Most popular majors:** 34% elementary education and teaching, 12% business administration and management, 11% communication studies/speech communication and rhetoric, 7% music teacher education, 3% reading teacher education. **Major fields of study:** biological and biomedical sciences; business, management, marketing, and related support services; communication, journalism, and related programs; communications technologies/technicians and support services; computer and information sciences and support services; education; foreign languages, literatures, and linguistics; health professions and related clinical sciences; liberal arts and sciences studies, and humanities; mathematics and statistics; philosophy and religious studies; physical sciences; psychology; public administration and social service professions; social sciences; visual and performing arts. **Areas of required coursework:** arts/fine arts, humanities, computer literacy, mathematics, English (including composition), foreign languages, sciences (biological or physical), history, social science, other. **Special academic programs:** cooperative (work-study plan) program, cross-registration, distance learning, double major, dual enrollment, English as a Second Language (ESL), honors program, independent study, internships, liberal arts/career combination, student-designed major, study abroad, teacher certificate program. **Teacher certification offered in:** early childhood, elementary, middle/junior high, secondary, bilingual/bicultural. **Cooperative education programs:** agriculture, engineering. **Reserve Officers Training Corps (ROTC):** Army ROTC: Offered at cooperating institution (St. Bonaventure University). **Faculty and instruction (2005-2006):** Total instructional faculty: 245 full-time, 160 part-time (55% men; 45% women; 9% minorities). Full-time faculty with Ph.D. or other terminal degree: 83%. Student/faculty ratio: 16/1. Classes of fewer than 20 students: 51%; of 20 to 49 students: 42%; of 50 or more students: 7%. **Advanced Placement and International Baccalaureate credit:** AP tests may be used for: Credit and/or placement. Scores accepted: 3, 4, 5. International Baccalaureate exams may be used for: Credit and/or placement. **Freshmen returning for sophomore year:** 85%. **Graduation rates:** Four-year: 49%; five-year: 61%; six-year: 62%. **Graduate study:** 37% of students pursue further study within one year.

COSTS AND FINANCIAL AID

Financial aid office: (716) 673-3253. **Expenses (2006-2007):** Tuition and fees 2006-2007: $5,482 in state, $11,742 out of state; room/board: $7,930. Estimated books and supplies: $1,000; transportation: $950; personal expenses: $638. **Financial aid:** Priority filing date for institution's financial aid form: February 1. In 2005-2006, 87% of undergraduates applied for financial aid. Of those, 63% were determined to have financial need; 29% had their need fully met. Average financial aid package (proportion receiving): $7,690 (62%). Average amount of gift aid, such as scholarships or grants (proportion receiving): $2,990 (55%). Average amount of self-help aid, such as work study or loans (proportion receiving): $3,859 (55%). Average need-based loan (excluding PLUS or other private loans): $3,744. Among students who received need-based aid, the average percentage of need met: 79%. Among students who received aid based on merit, the average award (and the proportion receiving): $1,605 (6%). The average athletic scholarship (and the proportion receiving): $1,704 (17%). Average amount of debt of borrowers graduating in 2005: $12,500. Proportion who borrowed: 81%.

CAMPUS LIFE AND EXTRACURRICULAR ACTIVITIES

Campus housing available (% using): coed dorms (58%), women's dorms (23%), men's dorms (15%), apartment for single students (4%). Students who live in college-owned, operated, or affiliated housing: 48%. **Student employment:** During the 2005-2006 academic year, 15% of undergraduates worked on campus. Average per-year earnings: $2,200. **Clubs and organiza-**

tions: Number of student organizations: 49. Activities include: choral groups, concert band, dance, drama/theater, jazz band, literary magazine, marching band, music ensembles, musical theater, opera, pep band, radio station, student government, student newspaper, symphony orchestra, television station. Number of fraternities: 4; sororities: 3. Proportion of men in fraternities: 5%; of women in sororities: 4%. Average proportion of students who stay on campus on weekends: 45%. **Sports program (2005-2006):** Member of NCAA III. **Men's intercollegiate varsity sports:** baseball, basketball, cross-country, ice hockey, soccer, swimming and diving, tennis, track and field (indoor), track and field (outdoor). **Women's intercollegiate varsity sports:** basketball, cheerleading, cross-country, lacrosse, soccer, softball, swimming and diving, tennis, track and field (indoor), track and field (outdoor), volleyball.

SERVICES AND FACILITIES

Basic services: nonremedial tutoring, women's center, placement service, day care, health service, health insurance. **Counseling services:** minority student, career, military, personal, veteran student, academic, older student, psychological, birth control, religious. **For learning-disabled students:** School does not offer a structured program with separate admission and additional fees. Total undergraduates in learning-disabled program or receiving services: 44. Services include: learning center, extended time for tests, tutors, other. **Library:** Number of titles: 14,121; number of current serial subscriptions: 4. **Information technology resources:** Students are not required to lease or own a computer. Number of campus computers available to all students: 486. School has a wireless network. Approximate number of users that can be accommodated: 450. Proportion of college-owned housing units wired for high-speed internet access: 100%. **Campus safety:** Security services offered: 24-hour foot-and-vehicle patrols, late-night transport/escort service, 24-hour emergency telephones, lighted pathways/sidewalks, student patrols, controlled dormitory access (key, security card, etc).

TRANSFER AND INTERNATIONAL STUDENTS

Transfer students: May apply for admission for the following academic terms: Fall, Winter, Spring, Summer. Applicants do not need a minimum number of credits to apply. For fall 2005: Transfer applications received: 1,421. Transfer applicants offered admission: 767. Transfer applicants enrolled: 459. **International students:** Number of foreign undergraduates: 9. Number of countries represented: 20. Minimum TOEFL score required: 500 (paper); 173 (computer). Average TOEFL score: 510 (paper).

SUNY–Oswego

- **Address:** 7060 State Route 104, Oswego, NY 13126
- **Website:** http://www.oswego.edu
- **Public**
- **Enrollment:** 6,620 full-time; 518 part-time

KEY STATS

✔ **U.S News College Ranking:** third tier, Universities–Master's (North)
✔ **SAT Score (25th/75th percentile):** 1040-1190
✔ **Tuition:** 2005-2006: $5,222 in state, $11,482 out of state

Selectivity: Selective	**Room/board:** $8,340
Acceptance rate: 56%	**Average debt:** N/A
Student/faculty ratio: 18/1	**Proportion who borrowed:** N/A

UNDERGRADUATE STUDENT BODY STATS

2005-2006 enrollment: 6,620 full-time; 518 part-time. Men: 46%; women: 54%. **Ethnic makeup:** African American: 4%; American-Indian: 1%; Asian American: 2%; Hispanic: 4%; White: 89%; International: 1%.

ADMISSIONS FACTS AND FIGURES

Phone: (315) 312-2250. **Email:** admiss@oswego.edu. **Website:** http://www.oswego.edu. **Application deadlines for fall 2007:** Regular decision: Rolling. Early decision: Send application by: November 15; Decision sent by: December 15. Early action: Not offered. Admission can be deferred. **Application fee:** $40. Common application is not accepted. **To apply online, go to:** http://infostu.suny.edu/. **Admissions requirements/recommendations:** High school units required (recommended): English: 4 (4); Mathematics: 3 (4); Science: 3 (4); Foreign language: 2 (4); Social studies: 4 (4); Total units: 18 (20). Tests: The college uses SAT or ACT scores in admissions decisions. Either SAT or ACT required. For admission to the fall 2007 entering class, the school will accept: ACT with writing, ACT without writing. Campus visit: Recommended. Admissions interview: Recommended. Off-campus interview: Not available. **Factors that count in admissions decisions:** *Academic:* Secondary school record: Very important. Class rank: Considered. Letters of recommendation: Considered. Standardized test scores: Very important. Essay: Considered. *Nonacademic:* Interview: Considered. Extracurricular activities: Considered. Talent/ability: Considered. Character/personal qualities: Considered. Alumni/ae relationship: Considered. Geographical residence: Considered. State residency: Considered. Religious affiliation/commitment: Not considered. Minority status: Considered. Volunteer work: Considered. Work experience: Considered. **Other schools with the greatest overlap in applicants:** Ithaca College; SUNY College of Arts and Sciences–Geneseo; SUNY College–Cortland; SUNY College–Oneonta; SUNY–Binghamton. **Admissions statistics for the fall 2005 entering class:** Total applicants: 7,565. Total accepted: 4,228. Freshmen enrolled: 1,354; 2% were from out of state. Overall acceptance rate: 56%. Early-decision acceptance rate: 66%. Non-early acceptance rate: 56%. **Credentials of fall 2005 freshmen:** 10% ranked in the top 10 percent of their high school class; 50% were in the top 25 percent, and 90% were in the top half. (Proportion submitting class standing: 81%.) **Average high school grade point average:** 3.3. **First-year students who submitted SAT scores:** 97%. Scores (25/75 percentile): Verbal: 510-600, Math: 530-590, Combined: 1040-1190. **First-year students submitting ACT scores:** 22%. Scores (25/75 percentile): English: N/A, Math: N/A, Composite: 21-25.

ACADEMICS

Year founded: 1861. **Academic calendar:** Semester. **Degrees offered:** certificate, bachelor's, master's, post-master's certificate. **Most popular majors:** 24% education, 19% business, management, marketing, and related support services, 11% communication, journalism, and related programs, 10% psychology, 6% security and protective services. **Major fields of study:** business, management, marketing, and related support services; education; English language and literature/letters; history; mathematics and statistics; multi/interdisciplinary studies; physical sciences; psychology; public administration and social service professions; social sciences; visual and performing arts. **Areas of required coursework:** arts/fine arts, humanities, computer literacy, mathematics, English (including composition), foreign languages, sciences (biological or physical), history, social science, other. **Pre-professional programs:** pre-law, pre-dentistry, pre-medicine, pre-veterinary science, pre-optometry. **Special academic programs (% participation):** cross-registration, distance learning (10%), double major, dual enrollment, English as a Second Language (ESL), exchange student program (domestic), honors program (4%), independent study (30%), internships (20%), liberal arts/career combination, study abroad, teacher certificate program (30%). **Teacher certification offered in:** early childhood, special education, elementary, vo-tech, middle/junior high, secondary, bilingual/bicultural. **Cooperative education programs:** agriculture, art, business, computer science, education, engineering, health professions. **Reserve Officers Training Corps (ROTC):** Army ROTC: Offered at cooperating institution (Syracuse University). **Faculty and instruction (2005-2006):** Total instructional faculty: 317 full-time, 194 part-time (57% men; 43% women; 8% minorities). Full-time faculty with Ph.D. or other terminal degree: 83%. Student/faculty ratio: 18/1. Classes of fewer than 20 students: 39%; of 20 to 49 students: 50%; of 50 or more students: 11%. **Advanced Placement and International Baccalaureate credit:** AP tests may be used for: Credit and/or placement. Scores accepted: 3. International Baccalaureate exams may be used for: Credit and/or placement. **Freshmen returning for sophomore year:** 77%. **Graduation rates:** Four-year: 33%; five-year: 51%; six-year: 55%. **Graduate study:** 18% of students pursue further study immediately upon graduation; 30% within one year. Fields in which graduates pursue further study: Master of Business Administration (MBA), 5%; law, 4%; medicine, 1%; dentistry, 1%; engineering, 1%; theology (or the seminary), 1%; education, 57%; arts and sciences, 30%.

COSTS AND FINANCIAL AID

Financial aid office: (315) 312-2248. **Expenses (2005-2006):** Tuition and fees 2005-2006: $5,222 in state, $11,482 out of state; room/board: $8,340. Estimated books and supplies: $800; transportation: $600; personal expenses: $800. **Financial aid:** Priority filing date for institution's financial aid form: April 1. In 2005-2006, 86% of undergraduates applied for financial aid. Of those, 67% were determined to have financial need; 31% had their need fully met. Average financial aid package (proportion receiving): $8,622 (66%). Average amount of gift aid, such as scholarships or grants (proportion receiving): $3,836 (61%). Average amount of self-help aid, such as work study or loans (proportion receiving): $4,936 (59%). Average need-based loan (excluding PLUS or other private loans): $4,720. Among stu-

dents who received need-based aid, the average percentage of need met: 84%. Among students who received aid based on merit, the average award (and the proportion receiving): $5,746 (16%).

CAMPUS LIFE AND EXTRACURRICULAR ACTIVITIES

Campus housing available (% using): coed dorms (100%), other housing options. Students who live in college-owned, operated, or affiliated housing: 56%. **Student employment:** During the 2005-2006 academic year, 34% of undergraduates worked on campus. Average per-year earnings: $1,236. **Clubs and organizations:** Number of student organizations: 130. Activities include: choral groups, concert band, dance, drama/theater, jazz band, literary magazine, music ensembles, musical theater, opera, pep band, radio station, student government, student newspaper, symphony orchestra, television station, yearbook. Number of fraternities: 12; sororities: 9. Proportion of men in fraternities: 7%; of women in sororities: 6%. Average proportion of students who stay on campus on weekends: 70%. **Sports program (2005-2006):** Member of NCAA III. *Men's intercollegiate varsity sports:* baseball, basketball, cross-country, golf, ice hockey, lacrosse, soccer, swimming and diving, tennis, track and field (indoor), track and field (outdoor), wrestling. *Women's intercollegiate varsity sports:* basketball, cross-country, field hockey, lacrosse, soccer, softball, swimming and diving, tennis, track and field (indoor), track and field (outdoor), volleyball.

SERVICES AND FACILITIES

Basic services: nonremedial tutoring, women's center, placement service, day care, health service, health insurance. **Remedial assistance:** reading, math, writing, study skills. **Counseling services:** career, personal, veteran student, academic, older student. **For learning-disabled students:** School does not offer a structured program with separate admission and additional fees. Total undergraduates in learning-disabled program or receiving services: 354. Services include: reading machines, tape recorders, note-taking services, readers, extended time for tests, tutors, priority registration, priority seating, texts on tape, other testing accomodations. **Library:** Number of titles: 475,220; number of current serial subscriptions: 3,401. **Information technology resources:** Students are not required to lease or own a computer. Number of campus computers available to all students: 300. School has a wireless network. Approximate number of users that can be accommodated: 5,000. Proportion of college-owned housing units wired for high-speed internet access: 100%. **Campus safety:** Security services offered: 24-hour foot-and-vehicle patrols, 24-hour emergency telephones, lighted pathways/sidewalks, controlled dormitory access (key, security card, etc).

TRANSFER AND INTERNATIONAL STUDENTS

Transfer students: May apply for admission for the following academic terms: Fall, Spring. Applicants need a minimum number of credits to apply. For fall 2005: Transfer applications received: 2,210. Transfer applicants offered admission: 1,218. Transfer applicants enrolled: 735. **International students:** Number of foreign undergraduates: 68 (1% of student body). Number of countries represented: 22. Minimum TOEFL score required: 550 (paper); 213 (computer). Average TOEFL score: 550 (paper).

SUNY–Plattsburgh

- **Address:** 101 Broad Street, Plattsburgh, NY 12901-2697
- **Website:** http://www.plattsburgh.edu
- **Public**
- **Enrollment:** 5,024 full-time; 370 part-time

KEY STATS

✔ **U.S News College Ranking:** third tier, Universities–Master's (North)
✔ **SAT Score (25th/75th percentile):** 940-1120
✔ **Tuition:** 2006-2007: $5,329 in state, $11,589 out of state

Selectivity: Selective	Room/board: $7,580
Acceptance rate: 62%	Average debt: $17,424
Student/faculty ratio: 17/1	Proportion who borrowed: 75%

UNDERGRADUATE STUDENT BODY STATS

2005-2006 enrollment: 5,024 full-time; 370 part-time. Men: 42%; women: 58%. **Ethnic makeup:** African American: 5%; Asian American: 2%; Hispanic: 4%; White: 83%; International: 6%.

ADMISSIONS FACTS AND FIGURES

Phone: (888) 673-0012. **Email:** admissions@plattsburgh.edu. **Website:** http://www.plattsburgh.edu. **Application deadlines for fall 2007:** Regular decision: August 1. Early decision: Send application by: November 15; Decision sent by: December 15. Early action: Not offered. Admission can be deferred. **Application fee:** $40. Common application is not accepted. **To apply online, go to:** http://www.plattsburgh.edu/admissions/apply.php. **Admissions requirements/recommendations:** High school units required (recommended): English: 4 (4); Mathematics: 3 (4); Science: 3 (4); Foreign language: 3 (3); Social studies: 3 (3); History: 1 (1); Academic electives: 1 (2); Total units: 18 (21). Tests: The college uses SAT or ACT scores in admissions decisions. Either SAT or ACT required. For admission to the fall 2007 entering class, the school will accept: ACT with writing, ACT without writing. Campus visit: Recommended. Admissions interview: Recommended. Off-campus interview: May be arranged. **Factors that count in admissions decisions:** *Academic:* Secondary school record: Very important. Class rank: Important. Letters of recommendation: Important. Standardized test scores: Very important. Essay: Important. *Nonacademic:* Interview: Very important. Extracurricular activities: Important. Talent/ability: Important. Character/personal qualities: Important. Alumni/ae relationship: Not considered. Geographical residence: Considered. State residency: Considered. Religious affiliation/commitment: Not considered. Minority status: Important. Volunteer work: Considered. Work experience: Considered. **Other schools with the greatest overlap in applicants:** SUNY College of Arts and Sciences–New Paltz; SUNY College–Oneonta; SUNY College–Potsdam; SUNY–Albany; SUNY–Oswego. **Admissions statistics for the fall 2005 entering class:** Total applicants: 5,321. Total accepted: 3,278. Freshmen enrolled: 1,040; 7% were from out of state. Overall acceptance rate: 62%. Non-early acceptance rate: 62%. **Size of waiting list:** 169 applicants; enrolled from waiting list: 22. **Credentials of fall 2005 freshmen:** 9% ranked in the top 10 percent of their high school class; 33% were in the top 25 percent, and 78% were in the top half. (Proportion submitting class standing: 67%.) **Average high school grade point average:** 3.0. First-year students who submitted SAT scores: 96%. Scores (25/75 percentile): Verbal: 470-560; Math: 470-560, Combined: 940-1120. **First-year students submitting ACT scores:** 19%. Scores (25/75 percentile): English: 18-23, Math: 18-24, Composite: 20-24.

ACADEMICS

Year founded: 1889. **Academic calendar:** Semester. **Degrees offered:** certificate, bachelor's, master's, post-master's certificate. **Most popular majors:** 19% business, management, marketing, and related support services, 18% education, 9% social sciences, 8% communication, journalism, and related programs, 7% psychology. **Major fields of study:** area, ethnic, cultural, and gender studies; biological and biomedical sciences; business, management, marketing, and related support services; communication, journalism, and related programs; computer and information sciences and support services; education; English language and literature/letters; family and consumer sciences/human sciences; foreign languages, literatures, and linguistics; health professions and related clinical sciences; history; liberal arts and sciences studies, and humanities; mathematics and statistics; natural resources and conservation; philosophy and religious studies; physical sciences; psychology; public administration and social service professions; security and protective services; social sciences; visual and performing arts. **Areas of required coursework:** arts/fine arts, humanities, computer literacy, mathematics, English (including composition), foreign languages, sciences (biological or physical), history, social science. **Pre-professional programs:** pre-law, pre-dentistry, pre-medicine, pre-veterinary science, pre-optometry. **Special academic programs (% participation):** cooperative (work-study plan) program, cross-registration (.01%), distance learning (.5%), double major (2.2%), dual enrollment, English as a Second Language (ESL) (.05%), exchange student program (domestic) (.03%), honors program (.75%), independent study (7%), internships (2%), liberal arts/career combination (5%), student-designed major (.5%), study abroad (1%), teacher certificate program (19%). **Teacher certification offered in:** early childhood, special education, elementary, middle/junior high, secondary. **Cooperative education programs:** business, computer science, humanities, technologies. **Faculty and instruction (2005-2006):** Total instructional faculty: 252 full-time, 203 part-time (54% men; 46% women; 9% minorities). Full-time faculty with Ph.D. or other terminal degree: 81%. Student/faculty ratio: 17/1. Classes of fewer than 20 students: 42%; of 20 to 49 students: 52%; of 50 or more students: 6%. **Advanced Placement and International Baccalaureate credit:** AP tests may be used for: Credit and/or placement. Scores accepted: 3, 4, 5. International Baccalaureate exams may be used for: Credit and/or placement. **Freshmen returning for sophomore year:** 77%. **Graduation rates:** Four-year: 32%; five-year: 51%; six-year: 57%. **Graduate study:** 10% of students pursue further study immediately upon graduation; 16% within one year;

25% within five years. Fields in which graduates pursue further study: Master of Business Administration (MBA), 1%; law, 1%; education, 60%; arts and sciences, 20%.

COSTS AND FINANCIAL AID

Financial aid office: (518) 564-4061. **Expenses (2006-2007):** Tuition and fees 2006-2007: $5,329 in state, $11,589 out of state; room/board: $7,580. Estimated books and supplies: $950; transportation: $550; personal expenses: $1,336. **Financial aid:** Priority filing date for institution's financial aid form: March 1. In 2005-2006, 80% of undergraduates applied for financial aid. Of those, 60% were determined to have financial need; 31% had their need fully met. Average financial aid package (proportion receiving): $9,524 (59%). Average amount of gift aid, such as scholarships or grants (proportion receiving): $4,262 (53%). Average amount of self-help aid, such as work study or loans (proportion receiving): $6,343 (54%). Average need-based loan (excluding PLUS or other private loans): $6,130. Among students who received need-based aid, the average percentage of need met: 90%. Among students who received aid based on merit, the average award (and the proportion receiving): $5,221 (27%). The average athletic scholarship (and the proportion receiving): $0 (0%). Average amount of debt of borrowers graduating in 2005: $17,424. Proportion who borrowed: 75%.

CAMPUS LIFE AND EXTRACURRICULAR ACTIVITIES

Campus housing available (% using): coed dorms (92%), other housing options (8%). Students who live in college-owned, operated, or affiliated housing: 47%. **Student employment:** During the 2005-2006 academic year, 19% of undergraduates worked on campus. Average per-year earnings: $1,600. **Clubs and organizations:** Number of student organizations: 84. Activities include: choral groups, concert band, dance, drama/theater, jazz band, literary magazine, music ensembles, musical theater, radio station, student government, student newspaper, student film society, symphony orchestra, television station. Number of fraternities: 7; sororities: 7. Proportion of men in fraternities: 7%; of women in sororities: 5%. Average proportion of students who stay on campus on weekends: 80%. **Sports program (2005-2006):** Member of NCAA III. *Men's intercollegiate varsity sports:* baseball, basketball, cross-country, golf, ice hockey, lacrosse, soccer, swimming and diving, track and field (indoor), track and field (outdoor). *Women's intercollegiate varsity sports:* basketball, cross-country, golf, ice hockey, soccer, softball, swimming and diving, tennis, track and field (indoor), track and field (outdoor), volleyball.

SERVICES AND FACILITIES

Basic services: nonremedial tutoring, women's center, placement service, health service, health insurance. **Remedial assistance:** reading, math, writing, study skills. **Counseling services:** minority student, career, military, personal, veteran student, academic, older student, psychological, birth control, religious. **For learning-disabled students:** School does not offer a structured program with separate admission and additional fees. Total undergraduates in learning-disabled program or receiving services: 250. Services include: reading machines, tape recorders, other special classes, diagnostic testing service, untimed tests, note-taking services, oral tests, learning center, readers, extended time for tests, tutors, proofreading services, substitution of courses, texts on tape, exams on tape or computer, waiver of foreign language degree requirement. **Library:** Number of titles: 683,581; number of current serial subscriptions: 1,461. **Information technology resources:** Students are not required to lease or own a computer. Number of campus computers available to all students: 450. School has a wireless network. Approximate number of users that can be accommodated: 300. Proportion of college-owned housing units wired for high-speed internet access: 100%. **Campus safety:** Security services offered: 24-hour foot-and-vehicle patrols, late-night transport/escort service, 24-hour emergency telephones, lighted pathways/sidewalks, controlled dormitory access (key, security card, etc).

TRANSFER AND INTERNATIONAL STUDENTS

Transfer students: May apply for admission for the following academic terms: Fall, Spring. Applicants need a minimum number of credits to apply. For fall 2005: Transfer applications received: 1,642. Transfer applicants offered admission: 1,020. Transfer applicants enrolled: 591. **International students:** Number of foreign undergraduates: 304 (6% of student body). Number of countries represented: 52. Minimum TOEFL score required: 450 (paper); 133 (computer). Average TOEFL score: 534 (paper).

SUNY–Purchase College

- **Address:** 735 Anderson Hill Road, Purchase, NY 10577
- **Website:** http://www.purchase.edu
- **Public**
- **Enrollment:** 3,231 full-time; 457 part-time

KEY STATS
- ✔ **U.S News College Ranking:** third tier, Universities–Master's (North)
- ✔ **SAT Score (25th/75th percentile):** 990-1200
- ✔ **Tuition:** 2006-2007: $5,529 in state, $11,789 out of state

Selectivity: Selective	**Room/board:** $9,168
Acceptance rate: 31%	**Average debt:** $15,307
Student/faculty ratio: 17/1	**Proportion who borrowed:** 66%

UNDERGRADUATE STUDENT BODY STATS
2005-2006 enrollment: 3,231 full-time; 457 part-time. Men: 45%; women: 55%. **Ethnic makeup:** African American: 8%; Asian American: 4%; Hispanic: 10%; White: 76%; International: 1%.

ADMISSIONS FACTS AND FIGURES
Phone: (914) 251-6300. **Email:** admissn@purchase.edu. **Website:** http://www.purchase.edu. **Application deadlines for fall 2007:** Regular decision: June 1; decision sent by May 1. Early decision: Send application by: November 1; Decision sent by: December 5. Early action: Not offered. Admission can be deferred. **Application fee:** $40. Common application is not accepted. **To apply online, go to:** http://www.purchase.edu/admissions/adm_applyonline.asp. **Admissions requirements/recommendations:** High school units required (recommended): English: (4); Mathematics: (4); Science: (3); Foreign language: (3); Social studies: (4); History: (0); Academic electives: (2); Total units: (20). Tests: The college uses SAT or ACT scores in admissions decisions. Either SAT or ACT required. Campus visit: Recommended. Admissions interview: Recommended. Off-campus interview: May be arranged. **Factors that count in admissions decisions: Academic:** Secondary school record: Very important. Class rank: Not considered. Letters of recommendation: Important. Standardized test scores: Very important. Essay: Very important. *Nonacademic:* Interview: Considered. Extracurricular activities: Considered. Talent/ability: Considered. Character/personal qualities: Not considered. Alumni/ae relationship: Not considered. Geographical residence: Not considered. State residency: Not considered. Religious affiliation/commitment: Not considered. Minority status: Not considered. Volunteer work: Not considered. Work experience: Not considered. **Other schools with the greatest overlap in applicants:** New York University; SUNY College of Arts and Sciences–New Paltz; SUNY–Albany; SUNY–Binghamton; SUNY–Stony Brook. **Admissions statistics for the fall 2005 entering class:** Total applicants: 6,946. Total accepted: 2,142. Freshmen enrolled: 718; 21% were from out of state. Overall acceptance rate: 31%. Early-decision acceptance rate: 73%. Non-early acceptance rate: 31%. **Credentials of fall 2005 freshmen:** 9% ranked in the top 10 percent of their high school class; 29% were in the top 25 percent, and 71% were in the top half. (Proportion submitting class standing: 31%.) **Average high school grade point average:** 3.0. **First-year students who submitted SAT scores:** 95%. Scores (25/75 percentile): Verbal: 510-620, Math: 480-580, Combined: 990-1200. **First-year students submitting ACT scores:** 14%. Scores (25/75 percentile): English: 20-26, Math: 17-23, Composite: 20-25.

ACADEMICS
Year founded: 1967. **Academic calendar:** Semester. **Degrees offered:** certificate, bachelor's, master's, post-master's certificate. **Most popular majors:** 37% visual and performing arts, 30% liberal arts and sciences studies, and humanities, 19% social sciences, 4% English language and literature/letters, 4% psychology. **Major fields of study:** area, ethnic, cultural, and gender studies; biological and biomedical sciences; communication, journalism, and related programs; English language and literature/letters; foreign languages, literatures, and linguistics; history; mathematics and statistics; multi/interdisciplinary studies; philosophy and religious studies; physical sciences; psychology; social sciences; visual and performing arts. **Areas of required coursework:** humanities, mathematics, English (including composition), foreign languages, sciences (biological or physical), history, social science, other. **Special academic programs:** cross-registration, distance learning, double major, English as a Second Language (ESL), independent study, internships, liberal arts/career combination,

student-designed major, study abroad. **Faculty and instruction (2005-2006):** Total instructional faculty: 143 full-time, 197 part-time (55% men; 45% women; 11% minorities). Full-time faculty with Ph.D. or other terminal degree: 50%. Student/faculty ratio: 17/1. Classes of fewer than 20 students: 51%; of 20 to 49 students: 43%; of 50 or more students: 6%. **Freshmen returning for sophomore year:** 74%. **Graduation rates:** Four-year: 32%; five-year: 44%; six-year: 43%.

COSTS AND FINANCIAL AID
Financial aid office: (914) 251-6350. **Expenses (2006-2007):** Tuition and fees 2006-2007: $5,529 in state, $11,789 out of state; room/board: $9,168. Estimated books and supplies: $1,500; transportation: $500; personal expenses: $700. **Financial aid:** Priority filing date for institution's financial aid form: February 15. In 2005-2006, 72% of undergraduates applied for financial aid. Of those, 54% were determined to have financial need; 18% had their need fully met. Average financial aid package (proportion receiving): $7,804 (53%). Average amount of gift aid, such as scholarships or grants (proportion receiving): $4,757 (39%). Average amount of self-help aid, such as work study or loans (proportion receiving): $4,417 (52%). Average need-based loan (excluding PLUS or other private loans): $4,214. Among students who received need-based aid, the average percentage of need met: 60%. Among students who received aid based on merit, the average award (and the proportion receiving): $14,771 (17%). The average athletic scholarship (and the proportion receiving): $0 (0%). Average amount of debt of borrowers graduating in 2005: $15,307. Proportion who borrowed: 66%.

CAMPUS LIFE AND EXTRACURRICULAR ACTIVITIES
Campus housing available: coed dorms, apartment for single students, special housing for disabled students, special housing for international students. Students who live in college-owned, operated, or affiliated housing: 67%. **Clubs and organizations:** Number of student organizations: 30. Activities include: choral groups, dance, drama/theater, jazz band, radio station, student government, student newspaper, student film society, television station. Number of fraternities: 0; sororities: 0. Average proportion of students who stay on campus on weekends: 70%. **Sports program (2005-2006):** Member of NCAA III. *Men's intercollegiate varsity sports:* baseball, basketball, cross-country, soccer, tennis, volleyball. *Women's intercollegiate varsity sports:* basketball, cross-country, soccer, softball, tennis, volleyball.

SERVICES AND FACILITIES
Basic services: day care, health service, health insurance. **Remedial assistance:** reading, math, writing, study skills. **Counseling services:** career, psychological. **Library:** Number of titles: 279,003; number of current serial subscriptions: 2,838. **Information technology resources:** Students are not required to lease or own a computer. Number of campus computers available to all students: 400. School has a wireless network. Proportion of college-owned housing units wired for high-speed internet access: 100%. **Campus safety:** Security services offered: 24-hour foot-and-vehicle patrols, 24-hour emergency telephones, lighted pathways/sidewalks, controlled dormitory access (key, security card, etc).

TRANSFER AND INTERNATIONAL STUDENTS
Transfer students: May apply for admission for the following academic terms: Fall, Spring. Applicants do not need a minimum number of credits to apply. For fall 2005: Transfer applications received: 1,565. Transfer applicants offered admission: 646. Transfer applicants enrolled: 373. **International students:** Number of foreign undergraduates: 50 (1% of student body). Number of countries represented: 35. Minimum TOEFL score required: 550 (paper); 213 (computer).

SUNY–Stony Brook

■ **Address:** Administration Building, Stony Brook, NY 11794
■ **Website:** http://www.stonybrook.edu
■ **Public**
■ **Enrollment:** 13,180 full-time; 1,107 part-time

KEY STATS
✔ **U.S News College Ranking:** 98, National Universities
✔ **SAT Score (25th/75th percentile):** 1080-1280
✔ **Tuition:** 2006-2007: $5,574 in state, $11,834 out of state
Selectivity: More selective   **Room/board:** $8,424
Acceptance rate: 51%   **Average debt:** $11,473
Student/faculty ratio: 17/1   **Proportion who borrowed:** 64%

UNDERGRADUATE STUDENT BODY STATS
2005-2006 enrollment: 13,180 full-time; 1,107 part-time. Men: 50%; women: 50%. **Ethnic makeup:** African American: 10%; Asian American: 22%; Hispanic: 9%; White: 54%; International: 5%.

ADMISSIONS FACTS AND FIGURES
Phone: (631) 632-6868. **Email:** enroll@stonybrook.edu. **Website:** http://www.stonybrook.edu. **Application deadlines for fall 2007:** Regular decision: Rolling. Early decision: Not offered. Early action: Send application by: November 15; Decision sent by: January 1. Admission can be deferred. **Application fee:** $40. Common application is not accepted. **To apply online, go to:** http://www.suny.edu/student/apply_online.cfm. **Admissions requirements/recommendations:** High school units required (recommended): English: 4 (4); Mathematics: 3 (4); Science: 3 (4); Foreign language: 2 (3); Social studies: 4 (4); Total units: 16 (19). Tests: The college uses SAT or ACT scores in admissions decisions. Either SAT or ACT required. For admission to the fall 2007 entering class, the school will accept: ACT with writing. Campus visit: Recommended. Admissions interview: Recommended. Off-campus interview: Not available. **Factors that count in admissions decisions:** *Academic:* Secondary school record: Very important. Class rank: Important. Letters of recommendation: Considered. Standardized test scores: Very important. Essay: Considered. *Nonacademic:* Interview: Considered. Extracurricular activities: Considered. Talent/ability: Considered. Character/personal qualities: Considered. Alumni/ae relationship: Considered. Geographical residence: Not considered. State residency: Not considered. Religious affiliation/commitment: Not considered. Minority status: Not considered. Volunteer work: Considered. Work experience: Not considered. **Other schools with the greatest overlap in applicants:** Boston University; Cornell University; New York University; SUNY–Albany; SUNY–Binghamton. **Admissions statistics for the fall 2005 entering class:** Total applicants: 18,206. Total accepted: 9,198. Freshmen enrolled: 2,508; 6% were from out of state. Accepted through early-decision or early-action plans: 23%. Overall acceptance rate: 51%. Non-early acceptance rate: 47%. **Credentials of fall 2005 freshmen:** 34% ranked in the top 10 percent of their high school class; 69% were in the top 25 percent, and 97% were in the top half. (Proportion submitting class standing: 43%.) **Average high school grade point average:** 3.6. **First-year students who submitted SAT scores:** 91%. Scores (25/75 percentile): Verbal: 520-620, Math: 560-660, Combined: 1080-1280.

ACADEMICS
Year founded: 1957. **Academic calendar:** Semester. **Degrees offered:** bachelor's, post-bachelor's certificate, master's, post-master's certificate, first professional, first professional certificate, doctorate. **Most popular majors:** 12% psychology, 9% business administration and management, 9% health professions and related clinical sciences, 8% computer and information sciences, 6% biology/biological sciences. **Major fields of study:** area, ethnic, cultural, and gender studies; biological and biomedical sciences; business, management, marketing, and related support services; computer and information sciences and support services; engineering; English language and literature/letters; foreign languages, literatures, and linguistics; health professions and related clinical sciences; history; liberal arts and sciences studies, and humanities; mathematics and statistics; multi/interdisciplinary studies; natural resources and conservation; philosophy and religious studies; physical sciences; psychology; public administration and social service professions; social sciences; visual and performing arts. **Areas of required coursework:** arts/fine arts, humanities, mathematics, English (including composition), philosophy, foreign languages, sciences (biological or physi-

cal), history, social science. **Pre-professional programs:** pre-law, pre-dentistry, pre-medicine. **Special academic programs:** cross-registration, distance learning, double major, dual enrollment, English as a Second Language (ESL), exchange student program (domestic), honors program, independent study, internships, student-designed major, study abroad, teacher certificate program, other. **Teacher certification offered in:** middle/junior high, secondary. **Reserve Officers Training Corps (ROTC):** Army ROTC: Offered at cooperating institution (Hofstra); Air Force ROTC: Offered at cooperating institution (New York Institute of Technology). **Faculty and instruction (2005-2006):** Total instructional faculty: 922 full-time, 454 part-time (63% men; 37% women; 16% minorities). Full-time faculty with Ph.D. or other terminal degree: 97%. Student/faculty ratio: 17/1. Classes of fewer than 20 students: 36%; of 20 to 49 students: 41%; of 50 or more students: 22%. **Advanced Placement and International Baccalaureate credit:** AP tests may be used for: Credit only. Scores accepted: 3. International Baccalaureate exams may be used for: Credit only. **Freshmen returning for sophomore year:** 87%. **Graduation rates:** Four-year: 38%; five-year: 55%; six-year: 59%. **Graduate study:** 34% of students pursue further study within one year.

COSTS AND FINANCIAL AID
Financial aid office: (631) 632-6840. **Expenses (2006-2007):** Tuition and fees 2006-2007: $5,574 in state, $11,834 out of state; room/board: $8,424. Estimated books and supplies: $900; transportation: $500; personal expenses: $1,292. **Financial aid:** Priority filing date for institution's financial aid form: March 1. In 2005-2006, 72% of undergraduates applied for financial aid. Of those, 57% were determined to have financial need; 16% had their need fully met. Average financial aid package (proportion receiving): $8,444 (55%). Average amount of gift aid, such as scholarships or grants (proportion receiving): $5,375 (51%). Average amount of self-help aid, such as work study or loans (proportion receiving): $5,102 (45%). Average need-based loan (excluding PLUS or other private loans): $4,074. Among students who received need-based aid, the average percentage of need met: 68%. Among students who received aid based on merit, the average award (and the proportion receiving): $3,247 (5%). The average athletic scholarship (and the proportion receiving): $9,656 (2%). Average amount of debt of borrowers graduating in 2005: $11,473. Proportion who borrowed: 64%.

CAMPUS LIFE AND EXTRACURRICULAR ACTIVITIES
Campus housing available: coed dorms, apartments for married students, apartment for single students, special housing for disabled students, other housing options. Students who live in college-owned, operated, or affiliated housing: 53%. **Student employment:** During the 2005-2006 academic year, 12% of undergraduates worked on campus. Average per-year earnings: $1,533. **Clubs and organizations:** Number of student organizations: 240. Activities include: choral groups, concert band, dance, drama/theater, jazz band, literary magazine, music ensembles, musical theater, opera, pep band, radio station, student government, student newspaper, student film society, symphony orchestra, yearbook. Number of fraternities: 18; sororities: 15. Proportion of men in fraternities: 1%; of women in sororities: 1%. Average proportion of students who stay on campus on weekends: 50%. **Sports program (2005-2006):** Member of NCAA I. *Men's intercollegiate varsity sports:* baseball, basketball, cross-country, football, lacrosse, soccer, softball, swimming and diving, tennis, track and field (indoor), track and field (outdoor). *Women's intercollegiate varsity sports:* basketball, cross-country, lacrosse, soccer, softball, swimming and diving, tennis, track and field (indoor), track and field (outdoor), volleyball.

SERVICES AND FACILITIES
Basic services: nonremedial tutoring, women's center, placement service, day care, health service, health insurance, other. **Remedial assistance:** other. **Counseling services:** minority student, career, military, personal, veteran student, academic, older student, psychological, birth control, religious. **For learning-disabled students:** School does not offer a structured program with separate admission and additional fees. Services include: reading machines, tape recorders, note-taking services, readers, extended time for tests, priority registration, priority seating, texts on tape, other testing accomodations. **Library:** Number of titles: 2,192,704; number of current serial subscriptions: 29,091. **Information technology resources:** Students are not required to lease or own a computer. Number of campus computers available to all students: 2,300. School does not have a wireless network. Proportion of college-owned housing units wired for high-speed internet access: 95%. **Campus safety:** Security services offered: 24-hour foot-and-vehicle patrols, late-night transport/escort service, 24-hour emergency telephones, lighted pathways/sidewalks, controlled dormitory access (key, security card, etc).

TRANSFER AND INTERNATIONAL STUDENTS

Transfer students: May apply for admission for the following academic terms: Fall, Spring. Applicants do not need a minimum number of credits to apply. For fall 2005: Transfer applications received: 4,581. Transfer applicants offered admission: 2,781. Transfer applicants enrolled: 1,760. **International students:** Number of foreign undergraduates: 669 (5% of student body). Number of countries represented: 72. Minimum TOEFL score required: 550 (paper); 213 (computer).

Syracuse University

- **Address:** 200 Crouse-Hinds Hall, Syracuse, NY 13244
- **Website:** http://www.syracuse.edu
- **Private**
- **Enrollment:** 12,128 full-time; 777 part-time

KEY STATS
✔ **U.S News College Ranking:** 52, National Universities
✔ **SAT Score (25th/75th percentile):** 1110-1320
✔ **Tuition:** 2006-2007: $29,965

Selectivity: More selective	**Room/board:** $10,420
Acceptance rate: 65%	**Average debt:** $19,200
Student/faculty ratio: 13/1	**Proportion who borrowed:** N/A

UNDERGRADUATE STUDENT BODY STATS

2005-2006 enrollment: 12,128 full-time; 777 part-time. Men: 43%; women: 57%. **Ethnic makeup:** African American: 6%; Asian American: 6%; Hispanic: 5%; White: 80%; International: 3%. **Religious preference:** Roman Catholic: 28%; Jewish: 14%; Other: 58%.

ADMISSIONS FACTS AND FIGURES

Phone: (315) 443-3611. **Email:** orange@syr.edu. **Website:** http://www.syracuse.edu. **Application deadlines for fall 2007:** Regular decision: January 1. Early decision: Send application by: November 15; Decision sent by: December 15. Early action: Not offered. Admission can be deferred. **Application fee:** $60. Common application is accepted. **To apply online, go to:** http://admissions.syracuse.edu. **Admissions requirements/recommendations:** High school units required (recommended): English: 4 (4); Mathematics: 3 (3); Science: 3 (3); Foreign language: 2 (3); Social studies: 3 (3); Academic electives: 5 (5); Total units: 20 (21). Tests: The college uses SAT or ACT scores in admissions decisions. Either SAT or ACT required. For admission to the fall 2007 entering class, the school will accept: ACT with writing. Campus visit: Recommended. Admissions interview: Recommended. Off-campus interview: May be arranged. **Factors that count in admissions decisions:** *Academic:* Secondary school record: Very important. Class rank: Very important. Letters of recommendation: Important. Standardized test scores: Very important. Essay: Very important. *Nonacademic:* Interview: Very important. Extracurricular activities: Important. Talent/ability: Very important. Character/personal qualities: Very important. Alumni/ae relationship: Considered. Geographical residence: Not considered. State residency: Not considered. Religious affiliation/commitment: Not considered. Minority status: Considered. Volunteer work: Considered. Work experience: Considered. **Other schools with the greatest overlap in applicants:** Boston University; Cornell University; New York University; Pennsylvania State University–University Park; University of Maryland–College Park. **Admissions statistics for the fall 2005 entering class:** Total applicants: 16,260. Total accepted: 10,514. Freshmen enrolled: 3,248; 58% were from out of state. Accepted through early-decision or early-action plans: 16%. Overall acceptance rate: 65%. Early-decision acceptance rate: 76%. Non-early acceptance rate: 64%. **Size of waiting list:** 1224 applicants; enrolled from waiting list: 0. **Credentials of fall 2005 freshmen:** 44% ranked in the top 10 percent of their high school class; 80% were in the top 25 percent, and 98% were in the top half. (Proportion submitting class standing: 50%.) **Average high school grade point average:** 3.6. **First-year students who submitted SAT scores:** 96%. Scores (25/75 percentile): Verbal: 540-650, Math: 570-670, Combined: 1110-1320. **First-year students submitting ACT scores:** 25%. Scores (25/75 percentile): English: N/A, Math: N/A, Composite: N/A.

ACADEMICS

Year founded: 1870. **Academic calendar:** Semester. **Degrees offered:** bachelor's, master's, post-master's certificate, first professional, doctorate. **Most**

popular majors: 18% business, management, marketing, and related support services, 15% visual and performing arts, 11% social sciences, 7% psychology, 6% communication, journalism, and related programs. **Major fields of study:** architecture and related services; area, ethnic, cultural, and gender studies; biological and biomedical sciences; business, management, marketing, and related support services; communication, journalism, and related programs; communications technologies/technicians and support services; computer and information sciences and support services; education; engineering; English language and literature/letters; family and consumer sciences/human sciences; foreign languages, literatures, and linguistics; health professions and related clinical sciences; history; legal professions and studies; liberal arts and sciences studies, and humanities; mathematics and statistics; multi/interdisciplinary studies; parks, recreation, leisure, and fitness studies; philosophy and religious studies; physical sciences; psychology; public administration and social service professions; security and protective services; social sciences; transportation and materials moving; visual and performing arts. **Areas of required coursework:** humanities, mathematics, English (including composition), sciences (biological or physical), social science, other. **Pre-professional programs:** pre-law, pre-dentistry, pre-medicine, pre-veterinary science, pre-optometry. **Special academic programs (% participation):** accelerated program, cooperative (work-study plan) program, distance learning, double major (5%), dual enrollment (20%), English as a Second Language (ESL), external degree program, honors program (8%), independent study, internships (50%), liberal arts/career combination (50%), student-designed major, study abroad (40%), teacher certificate program (5%), other. **Teacher certification offered in:** early childhood, special education, elementary, middle/junior high, secondary. **Cooperative education programs:** education, engineering, other. **Reserve Officers Training Corps (ROTC):** Army ROTC: Offered on campus; Air Force ROTC: Offered on campus. **Faculty and instruction (2005-2006):** Total instructional faculty: 865 full-time, 526 part-time (59% men; 41% women; 14% minorities). Full-time faculty with Ph.D. or other terminal degree: 88%. Student/faculty ratio: 13/1. Classes of fewer than 20 students: 64%; of 20 to 49 students: 28%; of 50 or more students: 8%. **Advanced Placement and International Baccalaureate credit:** AP tests may be used for: Credit only. Scores accepted: 3, 4, 5. International Baccalaureate exams may be used for: Credit and/or placement. **Freshmen returning for sophomore year:** 92%. **Graduation rates:** Four-year: 68%; five-year: 77%; six-year: 79%. **Graduate study:** 18% of students pursue further study immediately upon graduation. Fields in which graduates pursue further study: Master of Business Administration (MBA), 2%; law, 17%; medicine, 12%; education, 13%; arts and sciences, 10%.

COSTS AND FINANCIAL AID

Financial aid office: (315) 443-1513. **Expenses (2006-2007):** Tuition and fees 2006-2007: $29,965; room/board: $10,420. Estimated books and supplies: $1,235; transportation: $637; personal expenses: $1,010. **Financial aid:** In 2005-2006, 66% of undergraduates applied for financial aid. Of those, 58% were determined to have financial need; 65% had their need fully met. Average financial aid package (proportion receiving): $20,716 (58%). Average amount of gift aid, such as scholarships or grants (proportion receiving): $15,020 (52%). Average amount of self-help aid, such as work study or loans (proportion receiving): $6,540 (50%). Average need-based loan (excluding PLUS or other private loans): $5,300. Among students who received need-based aid, the average percentage of need met: 80%. Among students who received aid based on merit, the average award (and the proportion receiving): $8,840 (16%). The average athletic scholarship (and the proportion receiving): $30,090 (3%). Average amount of debt of borrowers graduating in 2005: $19,200.

CAMPUS LIFE AND EXTRACURRICULAR ACTIVITIES

Campus housing available (% using): coed dorms (66%), sorority housing (5%), fraternity housing (3%), apartments for married students (1%), apartment for single students (18%), special housing for disabled students (1%), special housing for international students (1%), other housing options (5%). Students who live in college-owned, operated, or affiliated housing: 75%. **Student employment:** During the 2005-2006 academic year, 20% of undergraduates worked on campus. Average per-year earnings: $1,000. **Clubs and organizations:** Number of student organizations: 270. Activities include: choral groups, concert band, dance, drama/theater, jazz band, literary magazine, marching band, music ensembles, musical theater, opera, pep band, radio station, student government, student newspaper, student film society, symphony orchestra, television station, yearbook. Number of fraternities: 27; sororities: 17. Proportion of men in fraternities: 18%; of women in sororities: 21%. Average proportion of students who stay on campus on weekends: 85%. **Sports program (2005-2006):** Member of NCAA I. *Men's*

intercollegiate varsity sports: basketball, crew, cross-country, football, lacrosse, soccer, swimming and diving, track and field (indoor), track and field (outdoor). **Women's intercollegiate varsity sports:** basketball, crew, cross-country, field hockey, lacrosse, soccer, softball, swimming and diving, tennis, track and field (indoor), track and field (outdoor), volleyball.

SERVICES AND FACILITIES

Basic services: nonremedial tutoring, women's center, placement service, day care, health service, health insurance. **Counseling services:** minority student, career, personal, academic, psychological, religious. **For learning-disabled students:** School does not offer a structured program with separate admission and additional fees. Services include: reading machines, tape recorders, diagnostic testing service, note-taking services, oral tests, learning center, readers, extended time for tests, tutors, texts on tape, other testing accomodations, other. **Library:** Number of titles: 3,487,551; number of current serial subscriptions: 20,637. **Information technology resources:** Students are not required to lease or own a computer. Number of campus computers available to all students: 1,700. School has a wireless network. Approximate number of users that can be accommodated: 15,000. Proportion of college-owned housing units wired for high-speed internet access: 100%. **Campus safety:** Security services offered: 24-hour foot-and-vehicle patrols, late-night transport/escort service, 24-hour emergency telephones, lighted pathways/sidewalks, student patrols, controlled dormitory access (key, security card, etc).

TRANSFER AND INTERNATIONAL STUDENTS

Transfer students: May apply for admission for the following academic terms: Fall, Spring. Applicants need a minimum number of credits to apply. For fall 2005: Transfer applications received: 862. Transfer applicants offered admission: 463. Transfer applicants enrolled: 218. **International students:** Number of foreign undergraduates: 343 (3% of student body). Number of countries represented: 64. Minimum TOEFL score required: 550 (paper); 213 (computer).

Touro College

■ **Address:** 27-33 W. 23rd Street, New York, NY 10001
■ **Website:** http://www.touro.edu/
■ **Private**
■ **Enrollment:** 9,357 full-time; 2,823 part-time

KEY STATS
✔ **U.S News College Ranking:** third tier, Universities–Master's (North)
✔ **SAT Score (25th/75th percentile):** 1040-1270
✔ **Tuition:** 2006-2007: $11,100
  Selectivity: More selective **Room/board:** $8,497
  Acceptance rate: 72% **Average debt:** N/A
  Student/faculty ratio: 11/1 **Proportion who borrowed:** N/A

UNDERGRADUATE STUDENT BODY STATS

2005-2006 enrollment: 9,357 full-time; 2,823 part-time. Men: 38%; women: 62%. **Ethnic makeup:** African American: 18%; Asian American: 4%; Hispanic: 11%; White: 67%.

ADMISSIONS FACTS AND FIGURES

Phone: (718) 252-7800. **Email:** lasadmit@adminm.touro.edu. **Website:** http://www.touro.edu/. **Application deadlines for fall 2007:** Regular decision: Rolling. Early decision: Not offered. Early action: Not offered. Admission can be deferred. **Application fee:** $50. Common application is not accepted. **Admissions requirements/recommendations:** High school units required (recommended): English: 4 (4); Mathematics: 2 (2); Science: 2 (2); Foreign language: 2 (2); Social studies: 0 (0); History: 2 (2); Academic electives: 4 (4); Total units: 16 (16). Tests: The college uses SAT or ACT scores in admissions decisions. Neither SAT nor ACT required. For admission to the fall 2007 entering class, the school will accept: ACT with writing, ACT without writing. Campus visit: Recommended. Admissions interview: Recommended. Off-campus interview: May be arranged. **Factors that count in admissions decisions:** *Academic:* Secondary school record: Very important. Class rank: Considered. Letters of recommendation: Considered. Standardized test scores: Very important. Essay: Important. *Nonacademic:* Interview: Important. Extracurricular activities: Considered. Talent/ability: Considered. Character/personal qualities: Considered. Alumni/ae relation-

ship: Considered. Geographical residence: Not considered. State residency: Not considered. Religious affiliation/commitment: Very important. Minority status: Not considered. Volunteer work: Considered. Work experience: Considered. **Admissions statistics for the fall 2005 entering class:** Total applicants: 1,698. Total accepted: 1,219. Freshmen enrolled: 913; Overall acceptance rate: 72%. **Credentials of fall 2005 freshmen:** 70% ranked in the top 10 percent of their high school class; 90% were in the top 25 percent, and 94% were in the top half. (Proportion submitting class standing: 90%.) **Average high school grade point average:** 3.2. First-year students who submitted SAT scores: 63%. Scores (25/75 percentile): Verbal: 520-640, Math: 520-630, Combined: 1040-1270. **First-year students submitting ACT scores:** 1%. Scores (25/75 percentile): English: N/A; Math: N/A, Composite: 22-25.

ACADEMICS

Year founded: 1971. **Academic calendar:** Semester. **Degrees offered:** certificate, associate, bachelor's, master's, first professional, doctorate. **Most popular majors:** 32% business administration and management, 18% liberal arts and sciences/liberal studies, 12% psychology, 8% human services, 8% physician assistant. **Major fields of study:** biological and biomedical sciences; business, management, marketing, and related support services; communications technologies/technicians and support services; computer and information sciences and support services; education; English language and literature/letters; foreign languages, literatures, and linguistics; health professions and related clinical sciences; history; liberal arts and sciences studies, and humanities; mathematics and statistics; multi/interdisciplinary studies; philosophy and religious studies; physical sciences; psychology; public administration and social service professions; social sciences. **Areas of required coursework:** humanities, computer literacy, mathematics, English (including composition), sciences (biological or physical). **Pre-professional programs:** pre-law, pre-dentistry, pre-medicine. **Special academic programs (% participation):** accelerated program (5%), cross-registration (1%), distance learning (10%), double major (1%), honors program (8%), independent study (38%), internships (4%), liberal arts/career combination (85%), study abroad (25%), teacher certificate program (6%). **Teacher certification offered in:** early childhood, special education, elementary, middle/junior high, secondary, bilingual/bicultural. **Faculty and instruction (2005-2006):** Total instructional faculty: 481 full-time, 881 part-time (50% men; 50% women; 12% minorities). Full-time faculty with Ph.D. or other terminal degree: 72%. Student/faculty ratio: 11/1. Classes of fewer than 20 students: 80%; of 20 to 49 students: 20%; of 50 or more students: 0%. **Advanced Placement and International Baccalaureate credit:** AP tests may be used for: Credit and/or placement. Scores accepted: 4, 5. **Freshmen returning for sophomore year:** 80%. **Graduation rates:** Four-year: 44%; five-year: 55%; six-year: 50%.

COSTS AND FINANCIAL AID

Financial aid office: (718) 252-7800. **Expenses (2006-2007):** Tuition and fees 2006-2007: $11,100; room/board: $8,497. Estimated books and supplies: $842; transportation: $647; personal expenses: $2,002. **Financial aid:** Priority filing date for institution's financial aid form: May 15; deadline: August 15. In 2005-2006, 93% of undergraduates applied for financial aid. Of those, 84% were determined to have financial need; Average financial aid package (proportion receiving): $11,675 (84%). Average amount of gift aid, such as scholarships or grants (proportion receiving): $4,000 (84%). Average amount of self-help aid, such as work study or loans (proportion receiving): $450 (73%). Average need-based loan (excluding PLUS or other private loans): $2,625. Among students who received need-based aid, the average percentage of need met: 75%. Among students who received aid based on merit, the average award (and the proportion receiving): $2,000 (16%). The average athletic scholarship (and the proportion receiving): $0 (0%).

CAMPUS LIFE AND EXTRACURRICULAR ACTIVITIES

Campus housing available (% using): women's dorms (1%), men's dorms (1%). Activities include: student government. Number of fraternities: 0; sororities: 0. Average proportion of students who stay on campus on weekends: 1%.

SERVICES AND FACILITIES

Basic services: nonremedial tutoring. **Remedial assistance:** reading, math, writing. **For learning-disabled students:** Services include: remedial math, remedial English, remedial reading. **Library:** Number of titles: 373,300; number of current serial subscriptions: 550. **Information technology resources:** Students are not required to lease or own a computer. Number of campus computers available to all students: 700. School does not have a wireless network. Proportion of college-owned housing units wired for high-speed internet access: 0%. **Campus safety:** Security services offered: 24-hour foot-and-vehicle patrols.

TRANSFER AND INTERNATIONAL STUDENTS
Transfer students: May apply for admission for the following academic terms: Fall, Spring, Summer. Applicants need a minimum number of credits to apply. For fall 2005: Transfer applications received: 1,020. Transfer applicants offered admission: 781. Transfer applicants enrolled: 651. **International students:** Number of foreign undergraduates: 4. Minimum TOEFL score required: 500 (paper); 173 (computer).

Union College

- **Address:** 807 Union Street, Schenectady, NY 12308
- **Website:** http://www.union.edu
- **Private**
- **Enrollment:** 2,209 full-time; 43 part-time

KEY STATS
✔ **U.S News College Ranking:** 39, Liberal Arts Colleges
✔ **SAT Score (25th/75th percentile):** 1160-1350
✔ **Tuition:** N/A

Selectivity: More selective	**Room/board:** N/A
Acceptance rate: 47%	**Average debt:** $15,132
Student/faculty ratio: 11/1	**Proportion who borrowed:** 53%

UNDERGRADUATE STUDENT BODY STATS
2005-2006 enrollment: 2,209 full-time; 43 part-time. Men: 55%; women: 45%. **Ethnic makeup:** African American: 3%; Asian American: 6%; Hispanic: 5%; White: 85%; International: 2%.

ADMISSIONS FACTS AND FIGURES
Phone: (888) 843-6688. **Email:** admissions@union.edu. **Website:** http://www.union.edu. **Application deadlines for fall 2007:** Regular decision: January 15; decision sent by April 1. Early decision: Send application by: November 15; Decision sent by: December 15. Early action: Not offered. Admission can be deferred. **Application fee:** $50. Common application is accepted. **To apply online, go to:** http://www.union.edu/Admissions/Applying/Applications.php. **Admissions requirements/recommendations:** High school units required (recommended): English: 4 (4); Mathematics: 3 (4); Science: 2 (4); Foreign language: 2 (4); Social studies: 1 (2); History: 1 (2); Total units: 16 (24). Tests: The college uses SAT or ACT scores in admissions decisions. Either SAT or ACT required. For admission to the fall 2007 entering class, the school will accept: ACT with writing, ACT without writing. Campus visit: Recommended. Admissions interview: Recommended. Off-campus interview: May be arranged. **Factors that count in admissions decisions:** *Academic:* Secondary school record: Very important. Class rank: Important. Letters of recommendation: Important. Standardized test scores: Considered. Essay: Considered. *Nonacademic:* Interview: Considered. Extracurricular activities: Important. Talent/ability: Important. Character/personal qualities: Important. Alumni/ae relationship: Considered. Geographical residence: Considered. State residency: Considered. Religious affiliation/commitment: Not considered. Minority status: Considered. Volunteer work: Considered. Work experience: Considered. **Other schools with the greatest overlap in applicants:** Colgate University; Hamilton College; Lafayette College; Skidmore College; University of Rochester. **Admissions statistics for the fall 2005 entering class:** Total applicants: 4,230. Total accepted: 1,997. Freshmen enrolled: 581; 58% were from out of state. Accepted through early-decision or early-action plans: 34%. Overall acceptance rate: 47%. Early-decision acceptance rate: 73%. Non-early acceptance rate: 45%. **Size of waiting list:** 759 applicants; enrolled from waiting list: 26. **Credentials of fall 2005 freshmen:** 62% ranked in the top 10 percent of their high school class; 87% were in the top 25 percent, and 98% were in the top half. (Proportion submitting class standing: 46%.) **Average high school grade point average:** 3.5. **First-year students who submitted SAT scores:** 96%. Scores (25/75 percentile): Verbal: 570-660, Math: 590-690, Combined: 1160-1350. **First-year students submitting ACT scores:** 23%. Scores (25/75 percentile): English: N/A, Math: N/A, Composite: 25-29.

ACADEMICS
Year founded: 1795. **Academic calendar:** Trimester. **Degrees offered:** bachelor's. **Most popular majors:** 11% economics, 10% political science and government, 10% psychology, 6% English language and literature, 6% mechanical engineering. **Major fields of study:** area, ethnic, cultural, and gender studies; biological and biomedical sciences; computer and information sciences and support services; engineering; English language and literature/letters; foreign languages, literatures, and linguistics; history; liberal arts and sciences studies, and humanities; mathematics and statistics; multi/interdisciplinary studies; philosophy and religious studies; physical sciences; psychology; social sciences; visual and performing arts. **Areas of required coursework:** humanities, mathematics, English (including composition), sciences (biological or physical), social science, other. **Pre-professional programs:** other. **Special academic programs (% participation):** accelerated program (4%), cross-registration, double major (7%), dual enrollment, honors program (9%), independent study (31%), internships (13%), liberal arts/career combination (1%), student-designed major (2%), study abroad (63%), teacher certificate program. **Teacher certification offered in:** secondary. **Cooperative education programs:** engineering. **Reserve Officers Training Corps (ROTC):** Army ROTC: Offered at cooperating institution (Siena College); Navy ROTC: Offered at cooperating institution (Rensselaer Polytechnic Institute); Air Force ROTC: Offered at cooperating institution (Rensselaer Polytechnic Institute). **Faculty and instruction (2005-2006):** Total instructional faculty: 182 full-time, 27 part-time (61% men; 39% women; 11% minorities). Full-time faculty with Ph.D. or other terminal degree: 96%. Student/faculty ratio: 11/1. Classes of fewer than 20 students: 69%; of 20 to 49 students: 30%; of 50 or more students: 2%. **Advanced Placement and International Baccalaureate credit:** AP tests may be used for: Credit and/or placement. Scores accepted: 4, 5. International Baccalaureate exams may be used for: Credit and/or placement. **Freshmen returning for sophomore year:** 93%. **Graduation rates:** Four-year: 80%; five-year: 83%; six-year: 84%. **Graduate study:** 30% of students pursue further study within one year. Fields in which graduates pursue further study: Master of Business Administration (MBA), 9%; law, 15%; medicine, 20%; dentistry, 1%; engineering, 7%; education, 11%; arts and sciences, 36%; veterinary medicine, 1%.

COSTS AND FINANCIAL AID
Financial aid office: (518) 388-6123. **Financial aid:** Priority filing date for institution's financial aid form: February 1; deadline: February 1. In 2005-2006, 58% of undergraduates applied for financial aid. Of those, 50% were determined to have financial need; 96% had their need fully met. Average financial aid package (proportion receiving): $27,359 (50%). Average amount of gift aid, such as scholarships or grants (proportion receiving): $22,736 (49%). Average amount of self-help aid, such as work study or loans (proportion receiving): $4,983 (48%). Average need-based loan (excluding PLUS or other private loans): $3,856. Among students who received need-based aid, the average percentage of need met: 97%. Among students who received aid based on merit, the average award (and the proportion receiving): $11,824 (13%). The average athletic scholarship (and the proportion receiving): $0 (0%). Average amount of debt of borrowers graduating in 2005: $15,132. Proportion who borrowed: 53%.

CAMPUS LIFE AND EXTRACURRICULAR ACTIVITIES
Campus housing available (% using): coed dorms (59%), sorority housing (6%), fraternity housing (8%), apartment for single students (7%), other housing options (20%). Students who live in college-owned, operated, or affiliated housing: 87%. **Student employment:** During the 2005-2006 academic year, 16% of undergraduates worked on campus. Average per-year earnings: $1,295. **Clubs and organizations:** Number of student organizations: 100. Activities include: choral groups, concert band, dance, drama/theater, jazz band, literary magazine, music ensembles, radio station, student government, student newspaper, student film society, symphony orchestra, yearbook. Number of fraternities: 9; sororities: 4. Proportion of men in fraternities: 24%; of women in sororities: 30%. Average proportion of students who stay on campus on weekends: 80%. **Sports program (2005-2006):** Member of NCAA III. *Men's intercollegiate varsity sports:* baseball, basketball, cross-country, football, ice hockey, lacrosse, soccer, swimming and diving, tennis, track and field (indoor), track and field (outdoor). *Women's intercollegiate varsity sports:* basketball, cross-country, field hockey, ice hockey, lacrosse, rowing, soccer, softball, swimming and diving, tennis, track and field (indoor), track and field (outdoor), volleyball.

SERVICES AND FACILITIES

Basic services: nonremedial tutoring, women's center, health service, other. **Counseling services:** career, personal, academic, psychological, religious. **For learning-disabled students:** School does not offer a structured program with separate admission and additional fees. Total undergraduates in learning-disabled program or receiving services: 26. Services include: reading machines, tape recorders, note-taking services, readers, extended time for tests, texts on tape, other testing accomodations, other. **Library:** Number of titles: 594,245; number of current serial subscriptions: 4,356. **Information technology resources:** Students are not required to lease or own a computer. Number of campus computers available to all students: 531. School has a wireless network. Approximate number of users that can be accommodated: 600. Proportion of college-owned housing units wired for high-speed internet access: 100%. **Campus safety:** Security services offered: 24-hour foot-and-vehicle patrols, late-night transport/escort service, 24-hour emergency telephones, lighted pathways/sidewalks, controlled dormitory access (key, security card, etc).

TRANSFER AND INTERNATIONAL STUDENTS

Transfer students: May apply for admission for the following academic terms: Fall, Winter, Spring. Applicants need a minimum number of credits to apply. For fall 2005: Transfer applications received: 84. Transfer applicants offered admission: 25. Transfer applicants enrolled: 22. **International students:** Number of foreign undergraduates: 40 (2% of student body). Number of countries represented: 16. Minimum TOEFL score required: 600 (paper); 250 (computer).

United States Merchant Marine Academy

- **Address:** 300 Steamboat Road, Kings Point, NY 11024
- **Website:** http://www.usmma.edu
- **Public**
- **Enrollment:** 1,021 full-time

KEY STATS

- ✔ **U.S News College Ranking:** Unranked Specialty School–Military Academies
- ✔ **SAT Score (25th/75th percentile):** 1160-1360
- ✔ **Tuition:** N/A

Selectivity: More selective	**Room/board:** $0
Acceptance rate: 24%	**Average debt:** $9,423
Student/faculty ratio: 11/1	**Proportion who borrowed:** N/A

UNDERGRADUATE STUDENT BODY STATS

2005-2006 enrollment: 1,021 full-time. Men: 87%; women: 13%.

ADMISSIONS FACTS AND FIGURES

Phone: (516) 773-5391. **Email:** admissions@usmma.edu. **Website:** http://www.usmma.edu. **Application deadlines for fall 2007:** Regular decision: March 1. Early decision: Send application by: November 1; Decision sent by: December 31. Early action: Not offered. Admission cannot be deferred. **Application fee:** None. Common application is not accepted. **Admissions requirements/recommendations:** High school units required (recommended): English: 4; Mathematics: 3 (4); Science: 3 (4); Foreign language: (2); Social studies: (4); Academic electives: 8; Total units: 18. Tests: The college uses SAT or ACT scores in admissions decisions. Either SAT or ACT required. For admission to the fall 2007 entering class, the school will accept: ACT with writing, ACT without writing. Campus visit: Recommended. Admissions interview: Recommended. Off-campus interview: May be arranged. **Factors that count in admissions decisions:** *Academic:* Secondary school record: Very important. Class rank: Important. Letters of recommendation: Important. Standardized test scores: Very important. Essay: Important. *Nonacademic:* Interview: Considered. Extracurricular activities: Important. Talent/ability: Important. Character/personal qualities: Very important. Alumni/ae relationship: Not considered. Geographical residence: Not considered. State residency: Considered. Religious affiliation/commitment: Not considered. Minority status: Considered. Volunteer work: Considered. Work experience: Considered. **Other schools with the greatest overlap in applicants:** United States Coast Guard Academy; United States Naval Academy. **Admissions statistics for the fall 2005 entering class:** Total applicants: 1,647. Total accepted: 397. Freshmen enrolled: 285; Overall acceptance rate: 24%. Non-early

acceptance rate: 24%. **Size of waiting list:** 283 applicants; enrolled from waiting list: 3. **Credentials of fall 2005 freshmen:** 18% ranked in the top 10 percent of their high school class; 46% were in the top 25 percent, and 88% were in the top half. (Proportion submitting class standing: 100%.) **First-year students who submitted SAT scores:** 82%. Scores (25/75 percentile): Verbal: 570-690, Math: 590-670, Combined: 1160-1360. **First-year students submitting ACT scores:** 22%. Scores (25/75 percentile): English: 24-27, Math: 28-31, Composite: 25-31.

ACADEMICS

Year founded: 1943. **Academic calendar:** Trimester. **Degrees offered:** bachelor's. **Most popular majors:** Information not available. **Major fields of study:** engineering; transportation and materials moving. **Areas of required coursework:** humanities, computer literacy, mathematics, English (including composition), sciences (biological or physical), history. **Special academic programs (% participation):** cooperative (work-study plan) program (100%), independent study (10%), internships (100%). **Cooperative education programs:** other. **Reserve Officers Training Corps (ROTC):** Navy ROTC: Offered on campus. **Faculty and instruction (2005-2006):** Total instructional faculty: 85 (88% men; 12% women; 8% minorities). Full-time faculty with Ph.D. or other terminal degree: 41%. Student/faculty ratio: 11/1. Classes of fewer than 20 students: 46%; of 20 to 49 students: 52%; of 50 or more students: 2%. **Advanced Placement and International Baccalaureate credit:** AP tests may be used for: Placement only. Scores accepted: 4, 5. **Freshmen returning for sophomore year:** 92%. **Graduation rates:** Six-year: 76%.

COSTS AND FINANCIAL AID

Financial aid office: (516) 773-5295. **Financial aid:** Average amount of debt of borrowers graduating in 2005: $9,423.

CAMPUS LIFE AND EXTRACURRICULAR ACTIVITIES

Campus housing available (% using): coed dorms (100%). **Student employment:** During the 2005-2006 academic year, 5% of undergraduates worked on campus. Average per-year earnings: $500. **Clubs and organizations:** Number of student organizations: 27. Activities include: choral groups, concert band, drama/theater, marching band, pep band, student government, student newspaper, yearbook. Number of fraternities: 0; sororities: 0. Average proportion of students who stay on campus on weekends: 60%. **Sports program (2005-2006):** Member of NCAA III. *Men's intercollegiate varsity sports:* baseball, basketball, cross-country, football, golf, lacrosse, riflery, soccer, swimming and diving, tennis, track and field (indoor), track and field (outdoor), wrestling. *Women's intercollegiate varsity sports:* basketball, cross-country, rowing, softball, swimming and diving, track and field (indoor), track and field (outdoor), volleyball.

SERVICES AND FACILITIES

Basic services: placement service, health service. **Remedial assistance:** math, writing, study skills. **Counseling services:** career, military, personal, academic, psychological. **Information technology resources:** Students are required to lease or own a computer. School has a wireless network. Approximate number of users that can be accommodated: 1,000. Proportion of college-owned housing units wired for high-speed internet access: 100%. **Campus safety:** Security services offered: 24-hour foot-and-vehicle patrols, 24-hour emergency telephones, lighted pathways/sidewalks.

TRANSFER AND INTERNATIONAL STUDENTS

Transfer students: May apply for admission for the following academic terms: Fall. Applicants do not need a minimum number of credits to apply. **International students:** Number of countries represented: 2. Minimum TOEFL score required: 550 (paper); 213 (computer). Average TOEFL score: 560 (paper).

United States Military Academy

- **Address:** 600 Thayer Road, West Point, NY 10996-2101
- **Website:** http://www.usma.edu
- **Public**
- **Enrollment:** 4,231 full-time

KEY STATS

✔ **U.S News College Ranking:** Unranked Specialty School–Military Academies

✔ **SAT Score (25th/75th percentile):** 1170-1360

✔ **Tuition:** N/A

Selectivity: More selective	**Room/board:** N/A
Acceptance rate: 14%	**Average debt:** N/A
Student/faculty ratio: 7/1	**Proportion who borrowed:** N/A

UNDERGRADUATE STUDENT BODY STATS

2005-2006 enrollment: 4,231 full-time. Men: 85%; women: 15%. **Ethnic makeup:** African American: 6%; American-Indian: 1%; Asian American: 7%; Hispanic: 7%; White: 78%; International: 1%.

ADMISSIONS FACTS AND FIGURES

Phone: (845) 938-4041. **Email:** admissions@usma.edu. **Website:** http://www.usma.edu. **Application deadlines for fall 2007:** Regular decision: March 21; decision sent by May 1. Early decision: Not offered. Early action: Not offered. Common application is not accepted. **Admissions requirements/recommendations:** High school units required (recommended): English: 4 (4); Mathematics: 4 (4); Science: 2 (2); Foreign language: 2 (2); History: 2 (1); Total units: (14). Tests: The college uses SAT or ACT scores in admissions decisions. Either SAT or ACT required. For admission to the fall 2007 entering class, the school will accept: ACT with writing. Campus visit: Recommended. Admissions interview: Recommended. Off-campus interview: May be arranged. **Factors that count in admissions decisions:** *Academic:* Secondary school record: Very important. Class rank: Very important. Letters of recommendation: Very important. Standardized test scores: Very important. Essay: Not considered. *Nonacademic:* Extracurricular activities: Very important. Talent/ability: Important. Character/personal qualities: Very important. Alumni/ae relationship: Considered. Geographical residence: Very important. State residency: Very important. Religious affiliation/commitment: Not considered. Minority status: Considered. Volunteer work: Very important. Work experience: Considered. **Other schools with the greatest overlap in applicants:** United States Air Force Academy; United States Naval Academy. **Admissions statistics for the fall 2005 entering class:** Total applicants: 10,778. Total accepted: 1,548. Freshmen enrolled: 1,199; 92% were from out of state. Overall acceptance rate: 14%. **Credentials of fall 2005 freshmen:** 48% ranked in the top 10 percent of their high school class; 77% were in the top 25 percent, and 95% were in the top half. (Proportion submitting class standing: 100%.) **Average high school grade point average:** 3.8. **First-year students who submitted SAT scores:** 64%. Scores (25/75 percentile): Verbal: 570-670, Math: 600-690, Combined: 1170-1360. **First-year students submitting ACT scores:** 36%. Scores (25/75 percentile): English: 25-30, Math: 26-31, Composite: 26-31.

ACADEMICS

Year founded: 1802. **Academic calendar:** Semester. **Degrees offered:** bachelor's. **Most popular majors:** 13% political science and government, 7% foreign languages and literatures, 7% history, 7% mechanical engineering/mechanical technology/technician, 6% systems engineering. **Major fields of study:** computer and information sciences and support services; engineering; foreign languages, literatures, and linguistics; history; legal professions and studies; mathematics and statistics. **Areas of required coursework:** arts/fine arts, humanities, computer literacy, mathematics, English (including composition), philosophy, foreign languages, sciences (biological or physical), history, social science, other. **Pre-professional programs:** other. **Special academic programs (% participation):** accelerated program, double major (2%), exchange student program (domestic), honors program. **Faculty and instruction (2005-2006):** Total instructional faculty: 595. Full-time faculty with Ph.D. or other terminal degree: 47%. Student/faculty ratio: 7/1. Classes of fewer than 20 students: 96%; of 20 to 49 students: 4%; of 50 or more students: 0%. **Freshmen returning for sophomore year:** 92%. **Graduation rates:** Four-year: 76%; five-year: 80%; six-year: 82%. **Graduate study:** Fields in which graduates pursue further study: medicine, 2%.

COSTS AND FINANCIAL AID

Financial aid office: (845) 938-4262.

CAMPUS LIFE AND EXTRACURRICULAR ACTIVITIES

Campus housing available (% using): coed dorms (100%). Students who live in college-owned, operated, or affiliated housing: 100%. **Student employment:** During the 2005-2006 academic year, 0% of undergraduates worked on campus. Average per-year earnings: $0. **Clubs and organizations:** Number of student organizations: 116. Activities include: choral groups, dance, drama/theater, jazz band, literary magazine, music ensembles, pep band, radio station, student government, student newspaper, television station, yearbook. Number of fraternities: 0; sororities: 0. Average proportion of students who stay on campus on weekends: 90%. **Sports program (2005-2006):** Member of NCAA I. *Men's intercollegiate varsity sports:* baseball, basketball, cross-country, football, golf, gymnastics, ice hockey, lacrosse, lightweight football, riflery, soccer, swimming and diving, tennis, track and field (indoor), wrestling. *Women's intercollegiate varsity sports:* basketball, cross-country, soccer, softball, swimming and diving, tennis, track and field (indoor), track and field (outdoor), volleyball.

SERVICES AND FACILITIES

Basic services: nonremedial tutoring, health service. **Remedial assistance:** reading, math, writing, study skills. **Counseling services:** military, academic, psychological, religious. **Library:** Number of titles: 468,651; number of current serial subscriptions: 1,100. **Information technology resources:** Students are required to lease or own a computer. Number of campus computers available to all students: 5,135. School has a wireless network. Proportion of college-owned housing units wired for high-speed internet access: 100%. **Campus safety:** Security services offered: 24-hour foot-and-vehicle patrols, late-night transport/escort service, 24-hour emergency telephones, lighted pathways/sidewalks, controlled dormitory access (key, security card, etc).

TRANSFER AND INTERNATIONAL STUDENTS

International students: Number of foreign undergraduates: 54 (1% of student body). Number of countries represented: 31.

University at Buffalo–SUNY

- **Address:** 3435 Main Street, Buffalo, NY 14214
- **Website:** http://www.buffalo.edu
- **Public**
- **Enrollment:** 16,911 full-time; 1,254 part-time

KEY STATS

✔ **U.S News College Ranking:** 120, National Universities

✔ **SAT Score (25th/75th percentile):** 1050-1240

✔ **Tuition:** 2006-2007: $6,068 in state, $12,328 out of state

Selectivity: More selective	**Room/board:** $7,526
Acceptance rate: 57%	**Average debt:** $17,834
Student/faculty ratio: 15/1	**Proportion who borrowed:** 70%

UNDERGRADUATE STUDENT BODY STATS

2005-2006 enrollment: 16,911 full-time; 1,254 part-time. Men: 54%; women: 46%. **Ethnic makeup:** African American: 7%; Asian American: 9%; Hispanic: 4%; White: 73%; International: 7%. **Religious preference:** Roman Catholic: 33%; Protestant: 26%; Jewish: 9%; Muslim: 1%; Hindu: 1%; Buddhist: 1%; No preference: 26%.

ADMISSIONS FACTS AND FIGURES

Phone: (716) 645-6900. **Email:** ub-admissions@buffalo.edu. **Website:** http://www.buffalo.edu. **Application deadlines for fall 2007:** Regular decision: Rolling. Early decision: Send application by: November 1; Decision sent by: December 15. Early action: Not offered. Admission cannot be deferred. **Application fee:** $40. Common application is not accepted. **To apply online, go to:** http://www.admissions.buffalo.edu/apply/. **Admissions requirements/recommendations:** High school units required (recommended): English: (4); Mathematics: (3); Science: (3); Foreign language: (3); Social studies: (4); Total units: (17). Tests: The college uses SAT or ACT scores in admissions decisions. Either SAT or ACT required. For admission to the fall 2007 entering class, the school will accept: ACT with writing. Campus visit: Recommended. Admissions interview: Neither required nor recommended. Off-campus interview: Not available. **Factors that count in**

admissions decisions: *Academic:* Secondary school record: Very important. Class rank: Important. Letters of recommendation: Considered. Standardized test scores: Very important. Essay: Considered. *Nonacademic:* Interview: Not considered. Extracurricular activities: Considered. Talent/ability: Considered. Character/personal qualities: Considered. Alumni/ae relationship: Not considered. Geographical residence: Considered. State residency: Not considered. Religious affiliation/commitment: Not considered. Minority status: Considered. Volunteer work: Considered. Work experience: Considered. **Other schools with the greatest overlap in applicants:** Cornell University; New York University; SUNY–Albany; SUNY–Binghamton; SUNY–Stony Brook. **Admissions statistics for the fall 2005 entering class:** Total applicants: 18,391. Total accepted: 10,466. Freshmen enrolled: 3,230; 6% were from out of state. Accepted through early-decision or early-action plans: 9%. Overall acceptance rate: 57%. Early-decision acceptance rate: 62%. Non-early acceptance rate: 57%. **Size of waiting list:** 785 applicants; enrolled from waiting list: 372. **Credentials of fall 2005 freshmen:** 24% ranked in the top 10 percent of their high school class; 59% were in the top 25 percent, and 93% were in the top half. (Proportion submitting class standing: 64%.) **Average high school grade point average:** 3.1. **First-year students who submitted SAT scores:** 95%. Scores (25/75 percentile): Verbal: 510-600, Math: 540-640, Combined: 1050-1240. **First-year students submitting ACT scores:** 21%. Scores (25/75 percentile): English: N/A, Math: N/A, Composite: 23-28.

ACADEMICS
Year founded: 1846. **Academic calendar:** Semester. **Degrees offered:** certificate, bachelor's, post-bachelor's certificate, master's, post-master's certificate, first professional, first professional certificate, doctorate. **Most popular majors:** 19% business, management, marketing, and related support services, 11% engineering, 10% communication, journalism, and related programs, 10% psychology, 9% social sciences. **Major fields of study:** architecture and related services; area, ethnic, cultural, and gender studies; biological and biomedical sciences; business, management, marketing, and related support services; communication, journalism, and related programs; computer and information sciences and support services; engineering; English language and literature/letters; foreign languages, literatures, and linguistics; health professions and related clinical sciences; history; liberal arts and sciences studies, and humanities; mathematics and statistics; multi/interdisciplinary studies; parks, recreation, leisure, and fitness studies; philosophy and religious studies; physical sciences; psychology; social sciences; visual and performing arts. **Areas of required coursework:** arts/fine arts, humanities, computer literacy, mathematics, English (including composition), foreign languages, sciences (biological or physical), history, social science, other. **Pre-professional programs:** pre-law, pre-dentistry, pre-medicine, pre-veterinary science, pre-optometry, pre-pharmacy, other. **Special academic programs (% participation):** accelerated program, cooperative (work-study plan) program (28.3%), cross-registration (12.8%), distance learning (12.5%), double major (7.3%), dual enrollment (.2%), English as a Second Language (ESL) (6.8%), exchange student program (domestic), honors program (7%), independent study (45%), internships (43.7%), liberal arts/career combination, student-designed major (.1%), study abroad (5.1%), other (.2%). **Cooperative education programs:** art, business, computer science, engineering, health professions, humanities, natural science, social/behavioral science, technologies, other. **Reserve Officers Training Corps (ROTC):** Army ROTC: Offered at cooperating institution (Canisius College). **Faculty and instruction (2005-2006):** Total instructional faculty: 1,159 full-time, 589 part-time (64% men; 36% women; 18% minorities). Full-time faculty with Ph.D. or other terminal degree: 97%. Student/faculty ratio: 15/1. Classes of fewer than 20 students: 37%; of 20 to 49 students: 43%; of 50 or more students: 20%. **Advanced Placement and International Baccalaureate credit:** AP tests may be used for: Credit only. Scores accepted: 3, 4, 5. International Baccalaureate exams may be used for: Credit only. **Freshmen returning for sophomore year:** 86%. **Graduation rates:** Four-year: 35%; five-year: 53%; six-year: 59%. **Graduate study:** 35% of students pursue further study within one year. Fields in which graduates pursue further study: Master of Business Administration (MBA), 10%; law, 8%; medicine, 5%; dentistry, 1%; engineering, 12%; education, 20%; arts and sciences, 22%.

COSTS AND FINANCIAL AID
Financial aid office: (866) 838-7257. **Expenses (2006-2007):** Tuition and fees 2006-2007: $6,068 in state, $12,328 out of state; room/board: $7,526. Estimated books and supplies: $893; transportation: $572; personal expenses: $834. **Financial aid:** Priority filing date for institution's financial aid form: March 1. In 2005-2006, 70% of undergraduates applied for financial aid. Of those, 52% were determined to have financial need; 48% had

their need fully met. Average financial aid package (proportion receiving): $6,890 (50%). Average amount of gift aid, such as scholarships or grants (proportion receiving): $3,237 (30%). Average amount of self-help aid, such as work study or loans (proportion receiving): $3,744 (49%). Average need-based loan (excluding PLUS or other private loans): $3,246. Among students who received need-based aid, the average percentage of need met: 70%. Among students who received aid based on merit, the average award (and the proportion receiving): $2,780 (11%). The average athletic scholarship (and the proportion receiving): $9,747 (1%). Average amount of debt of borrowers graduating in 2005: $17,834. Proportion who borrowed: 70%.

CAMPUS LIFE AND EXTRACURRICULAR ACTIVITIES
Campus housing available (% using): coed dorms (78%), apartment for single students (21%), special housing for disabled students (1%), special housing for international students, other housing options. Students who live in college-owned, operated, or affiliated housing: 38%. **Clubs and organizations:** Number of student organizations: 300. Activities include: choral groups, concert band, dance, drama/theater, jazz band, literary magazine, marching band, music ensembles, musical theater, pep band, radio station, student government, student newspaper, student film society, symphony orchestra, television station. Number of fraternities: 25; sororities: 22. Proportion of men in fraternities: 3%; of women in sororities: 4%. **Sports program (2005-2006):** Member of NCAA I. *Men's intercollegiate varsity sports:* baseball, basketball, cross-country, football, soccer, swimming and diving, tennis, track and field (indoor), track and field (outdoor), wrestling. *Women's intercollegiate varsity sports:* basketball, crew, cross-country, soccer, softball, swimming and diving, tennis, track and field (indoor), track and field (outdoor), volleyball.

SERVICES AND FACILITIES
Basic services: nonremedial tutoring, women's center, placement service, day care, health service, health insurance. **Remedial assistance:** reading, math, writing, study skills, other. **Counseling services:** minority student, career, personal, veteran student, academic, older student, psychological, birth control, religious. **For learning-disabled students:** School does not offer a structured program with separate admission and additional fees. Total undergraduates in learning-disabled program or receiving services: 175. Services include: remedial math, remedial English, reading machines, remedial reading, tape recorders, other special classes, note-taking services, oral tests, learning center, readers, extended time for tests, tutors, substitution of courses, texts on tape, waiver of foreign language degree requirement, other. **Library:** Number of titles: 3,390,583; number of current serial subscriptions: 34,965. **Information technology resources:** Students are not required to lease or own a computer. Number of campus computers available to all students: 2,475. School has a wireless network. Approximate number of users that can be accommodated: 9,420. Proportion of college-owned housing units wired for high-speed internet access: 100%. **Campus safety:** Security services offered: 24-hour foot-and-vehicle patrols, late-night transport/escort service, 24-hour emergency telephones, lighted pathways/sidewalks, student patrols, controlled dormitory access (key, security card, etc).

TRANSFER AND INTERNATIONAL STUDENTS
Transfer students: May apply for admission for the following academic terms: Fall, Spring. Applicants need a minimum number of credits to apply. For fall 2005: Transfer applications received: 5,068. Transfer applicants offered admission: 3,158. Transfer applicants enrolled: 1,628. **International students:** Number of foreign undergraduates: 1250 (7% of student body). Number of countries represented: 80. Minimum TOEFL score required: 550 (paper); 213 (computer). Average TOEFL score: 587 (paper).

University of Rochester

- **Address:** Wilson Boulevard, Rochester, NY 14627
- **Website:** http://www.rochester.edu
- **Private**
- **Enrollment:** 4,435 full-time; 261 part-time

KEY STATS
✔ **U.S News College Ranking:** 34, National Universities
✔ **SAT Score (25th/75th percentile):** 1250-1420
✔ **Tuition:** 2006-2007: $33,426

Selectivity: Most selective	**Room/board:** $10,192
Acceptance rate: 48%	**Average debt:** $26,100
Student/faculty ratio: 9/1	**Proportion who borrowed:** 56%

UNDERGRADUATE STUDENT BODY STATS
2005-2006 enrollment: 4,435 full-time; 261 part-time. Men: 50%; women: 50%. **Ethnic makeup:** African American: 5%; Asian American: 10%; Hispanic: 4%; White: 76%; International: 4%.

ADMISSIONS FACTS AND FIGURES
Phone: (585) 275-3221. **Email:** admit@admissions.rochester.edu. **Website:** http://www.rochester.edu. **Application deadlines for fall 2007:** Regular decision: January 15. Early decision: Send application by: November 1; Decision sent by: December 15. Early action: Not offered. Admission can be deferred. **Application fee:** $50. Common application is accepted. **To apply online, go to:** http://www.rochester.edu/admissions. **Admissions requirements/recommendations:** High school units required (recommended): Total units: (32). Tests: The college uses SAT or ACT scores in admissions decisions. Either SAT or ACT required. For admission to the fall 2007 entering class, the school will accept: ACT with writing, ACT without writing. Campus visit: Recommended. Admissions interview: Recommended. Off-campus interview: May be arranged. **Factors that count in admissions decisions:** *Academic:* Secondary school record: Very important. Class rank: Important. Letters of recommendation: Important. Standardized test scores: Considered. Essay: Important. *Nonacademic:* Interview: Very important. Extracurricular activities: Considered. Talent/ability: Important. Character/personal qualities: Very important. Alumni/ae relationship: Considered. Geographical residence: Not considered. State residency: Not considered. Religious affiliation/commitment: Not considered. Minority status: Important. Volunteer work: Considered. Work experience: Considered. **Other schools with the greatest overlap in applicants:** Boston College; Boston University; Brown University; Carnegie Mellon University; Cornell University. **Admissions statistics for the fall 2005 entering class:** Total applicants: 11,293. Total accepted: 5,380. Freshmen enrolled: 997; 53% were from out of state. Accepted through early-decision or early-action plans: 23%. Overall acceptance rate: 48%. Early-decision acceptance rate: 47%. Non-early acceptance rate: 48%. **Size of waiting list:** 1091 applicants; enrolled from waiting list: 29. **Credentials of fall 2005 freshmen:** 76% ranked in the top 10 percent of their high school class; 93% were in the top 25 percent, and 98% were in the top half. (Proportion submitting class standing: 45%.) **First-year students who submitted SAT scores:** 95%. Scores (25/75 percentile): Verbal: 610-710, Math: 640-710, Combined: 1250-1420. **First-year students submitting ACT scores:** 35%. Scores (25/75 percentile): English: N/A, Math: N/A, Composite: 26-30.

ACADEMICS
Year founded: 1850. **Academic calendar:** Semester. **Degrees offered:** certificate, bachelor's, post-bachelor's certificate, master's, post-master's certificate, first professional, first professional certificate, doctorate. **Most popular majors:** 22% social sciences, 12% psychology, 10% biology/biological sciences, 9% music performance, 8% engineering. **Major fields of study:** area, ethnic, cultural, and gender studies; biological and biomedical sciences; computer and information sciences and support services; education; engineering; English language and literature/letters; foreign languages, literatures, and linguistics; health professions and related clinical sciences; history; liberal arts and sciences studies, and humanities; mathematics and statistics; natural resources and conservation; philosophy and religious studies; physical sciences; psychology; social sciences; visual and performing arts. **Areas of required coursework:** humanities, sciences (biological or physical), social science, other. **Special academic programs (% participation):** cross-registration (.5%), double major (22%), dual enrollment (2%), English as a Second Language (ESL) (.2%), honors program (12%), independent

study (31%), internships (16%), liberal arts/career combination (4%), student-designed major (1%), study abroad (23%), teacher certificate program (.5%), other (4%). **Teacher certification offered in:** early childhood, special education, elementary, middle/junior high, secondary. **Cooperative education programs:** engineering. **Reserve Officers Training Corps (ROTC):** Navy ROTC: Offered on campus; Air Force ROTC: Offered at cooperating institution (Rochester Institute of Technology). **Faculty and instruction (2005-2006):** Total instructional faculty: 505 full-time, 263 part-time (65% men; 35% women; 9% minorities). Full-time faculty with Ph.D. or other terminal degree: 88%. Student/faculty ratio: 9/1. Classes of fewer than 20 students: 63%; of 20 to 49 students: 28%; of 50 or more students: 10%. **Advanced Placement and International Baccalaureate credit:** AP tests may be used for: Credit and/or placement. Scores accepted: 4, 5. International Baccalaureate exams may be used for: Credit and/or placement. **Freshmen returning for sophomore year:** 94%. **Graduation rates:** Four-year: 68%; five-year: 77%; six-year: 80%. **Graduate study:** 40% of students pursue further study immediately upon graduation; 10% within one year. Fields in which graduates pursue further study: law, 5%; medicine, 6%.

COSTS AND FINANCIAL AID
Financial aid office: (585) 275-3226. **Expenses (2006-2007):** Tuition and fees 2006-2007: $33,426; room/board: $10,192. Estimated books and supplies: $785; transportation: $320; personal expenses: $1,100. **Financial aid:** Priority filing date for institution's financial aid form: February 1. In 2005-2006, 68% of undergraduates applied for financial aid. Of those, 56% were determined to have financial need; 41% had their need fully met. Average financial aid package (proportion receiving): $24,474 (56%). Average amount of gift aid, such as scholarships or grants (proportion receiving): $19,585 (56%). Average amount of self-help aid, such as work study or loans (proportion receiving): $6,017 (47%). Average need-based loan (excluding PLUS or other private loans): $5,076. Among students who received need-based aid, the average percentage of need met: 87%. Among students who received aid based on merit, the average award (and the proportion receiving): $8,773 (33%). The average athletic scholarship (and the proportion receiving): $0 (0%). Average amount of debt of borrowers graduating in 2005: $26,100. Proportion who borrowed: 56%.

CAMPUS LIFE AND EXTRACURRICULAR ACTIVITIES
Campus housing available (% using): coed dorms (75%), sorority housing (4%), fraternity housing (7%), apartment for single students (10%), special housing for disabled students (1%), other housing options (3%). Students who live in college-owned, operated, or affiliated housing: 85%. **Student employment:** During the 2005-2006 academic year, 49% of undergraduates worked on campus. Average per-year earnings: $2,500. **Clubs and organizations:** Number of student organizations: 210. Activities include: choral groups, concert band, dance, drama/theater, jazz band, literary magazine, music ensembles, musical theater, opera, pep band, radio station, student government, student newspaper, student film society, symphony orchestra, yearbook. Number of fraternities: 18; sororities: 13. Proportion of men in fraternities: 3%; of women in sororities: 2%. Average proportion of students who stay on campus on weekends: 90%. **Sports program (2005-2006):** Member of NCAA III. *Men's intercollegiate varsity sports:* baseball, basketball, cross-country, football, golf, soccer, squash, swimming and diving, tennis, track and field (indoor), track and field (outdoor). *Women's intercollegiate varsity sports:* basketball, cross-country, field hockey, lacrosse, soccer, softball, swimming and diving, tennis, track and field (indoor), track and field (outdoor), volleyball.

SERVICES AND FACILITIES
Basic services: nonremedial tutoring, health service, health insurance. **Remedial assistance:** study skills. **Counseling services:** minority student, career, academic, psychological, religious. **For learning-disabled students:** School does not offer a structured program with separate admission and additional fees. Services include: reading machines, note-taking services, oral tests, learning center, readers, extended time for tests, tutors, early syllabus, priority registration, priority seating, typist/scribe, exams on tape or computer, other testing accomodations, other. **Information technology resources:** Students are not required to lease or own a computer. Number of campus computers available to all students: 300. School has a wireless network. Approximate number of users that can be accommodated: 300. Proportion of college-owned housing units wired for high-speed internet access: 100%. **Campus safety:** Security services offered: 24-hour foot-and-vehicle patrols, late-night transport/escort service, 24-hour emergency telephones, lighted pathways/sidewalks, student patrols, controlled dormitory access (key, security card, etc).

TRANSFER AND INTERNATIONAL STUDENTS

Transfer students: May apply for admission for the following academic terms: Fall, Spring. Applicants do not need a minimum number of credits to apply. For fall 2005: Transfer applications received: 549. Transfer applicants offered admission: 137. Transfer applicants enrolled: 78. **International students:** Number of foreign undergraduates: 180 (4% of student body). Number of countries represented: 32. Minimum TOEFL score required: 550 (paper); 213 (computer). Average TOEFL score: 610 (paper).

Utica College

- **Address:** 1600 Burrstone Road, Utica, NY 13502
- **Website:** http://www.utica.edu
- **Private**
- **Enrollment:** 2,030 full-time; 383 part-time

KEY STATS
- ✔ **U.S News College Ranking:** 15, Comp. Colleges–Bachelor's (North)
- ✔ **SAT Score (25th/75th percentile):** 870-1080
- ✔ **Tuition:** 2006-2007: $23,440

Selectivity: Less selective	**Room/board:** $9,510
Acceptance rate: 79%	**Average debt:** $25,565
Student/faculty ratio: 17/1	**Proportion who borrowed:** 89%

UNDERGRADUATE STUDENT BODY STATS

2005-2006 enrollment: 2,030 full-time; 383 part-time. Men: 41%; women: 59%. **Ethnic makeup:** African American: 9%; American-Indian: 1%; Asian American: 2%; Hispanic: 3%; White: 84%; International: 1%.

ADMISSIONS FACTS AND FIGURES

Phone: (315) 792-3006. **Email:** admiss@utica.edu. **Website:** http://www.utica.edu. **Application deadlines for fall 2007:** Regular decision: Rolling. Early decision: Not offered. Early action: Not offered. Admission can be deferred. **Application fee:** $40. Common application is accepted. **To apply online, go to:** https://apply.embark.com/ugrad/utica/65/. **Admissions requirements/recommendations:** High school units required (recommended): English: 4; Mathematics: 3; Science: 3; Foreign language: 2; Social studies: 3; Academic electives: 1; Total units: 16. Tests: The college uses SAT or ACT scores in admissions decisions. Neither SAT nor ACT required. For admission to the fall 2007 entering class, the school will accept: ACT with writing, ACT without writing. Campus visit: Recommended. Admissions interview: Recommended. Off-campus interview: May be arranged. **Factors that count in admissions decisions:** *Academic:* Secondary school record: Very important. Class rank: Considered. Letters of recommendation: Important. Standardized test scores: Considered. Essay: Important. *Nonacademic:* Interview: Important. Extracurricular activities: Important. Talent/ability: Important. Character/personal qualities: Important. Alumni/ae relationship: Considered. Geographical residence: Not considered. State residency: Not considered. Religious affiliation/commitment: Not considered. Minority status: Not considered. Volunteer work: Important. Work experience: Important. **Other schools with the greatest overlap in applicants:** Ithaca College; Le Moyne College; Nazareth College of Rochester; SUNY–Oswego; St. John Fisher College. **Admissions statistics for the fall 2005 entering class:** Total applicants: 2,497. Total accepted: 1,977. Freshmen enrolled: 470; 15% were from out of state. Overall acceptance rate: 79%. **Size of waiting list:** 88 applicants; enrolled from waiting list: 11. **Credentials of fall 2005 freshmen:** 8% ranked in the top 10 percent of their high school class; 28% were in the top 25 percent, and 66% were in the top half. (Proportion submitting class standing: 73%.) **Average high school grade point average:** 3.0. **First-year students who submitted SAT scores:** 81%. Scores (25/75 percentile): Verbal: 430-530, Math: 440-550, Combined: 870-1080. **First-year students submitting ACT scores:** 16%. Scores (25/75 percentile): English: 17-23, Math: 18-24, Composite: 19-24.

ACADEMICS

Year founded: 1946. **Academic calendar:** Semester. **Degrees offered:** bachelor's, post-bachelor's certificate, master's, first professional. **Most popular majors:** 16% business, management, marketing, and related support services, 15% health professions and related clinical sciences, 13% security and protective services, 12% psychology, 9% education. **Major fields of study:** biological and biomedical sciences; business, management, marketing, and related support services; communication, journalism, and related programs;

computer and information sciences and support services; English language and literature/letters; health professions and related clinical sciences; history; liberal arts and sciences studies, and humanities; mathematics and statistics; philosophy and religious studies; physical sciences; psychology; security and protective services; social sciences. **Areas of required coursework:** arts/fine arts, humanities, mathematics, English (including composition), philosophy, foreign languages, sciences (biological or physical), history, social science. **Pre-professional programs:** pre-law, pre-dentistry, pre-medicine, pre-veterinary science, pre-optometry, other. **Special academic programs (% participation):** accelerated program (1%), cooperative (work-study plan) program (1%), cross-registration (1%), distance learning (2%), double major (1%), dual enrollment (1%), exchange student program (domestic) (1%), honors program (2%), independent study (1%), internships (3%), liberal arts/career combination (1%), study abroad (1%), teacher certificate program (14%), weekend college (1%). **Teacher certification offered in:** early childhood, special education, elementary, middle/junior high, secondary. **Cooperative education programs:** art, business, computer science, education, health professions, humanities, natural science, social/behavioral science, technologies. **Reserve Officers Training Corps (ROTC):** Army ROTC: Offered on campus; Air Force ROTC: Offered at cooperating institution (Syracuse University). **Faculty and instruction (2005-2006):** Total instructional faculty: 119 full-time, 167 part-time (52% men; 48% women; 3% minorities). Full-time faculty with Ph.D. or other terminal degree: 92%. Student/faculty ratio: 17/1. Classes of fewer than 20 students: 66%; of 20 to 49 students: 34%; of 50 or more students: 0%. **Advanced Placement and International Baccalaureate credit:** AP tests may be used for: Credit and/or placement. Scores accepted: 3, 4, 5. International Baccalaureate exams may be used for: Credit and/or placement. **Freshmen returning for sophomore year:** 70%. **Graduation rates:** Four-year: 40%; five-year: 55%; six-year: 57%. **Graduate study:** Fields in which graduates pursue further study: law, 1%; medicine, 2%.

COSTS AND FINANCIAL AID

Financial aid office: (315) 792-3179. **Expenses (2006-2007):** Tuition and fees 2006-2007: $23,440; room/board: $9,510. Estimated books and supplies: $870; transportation: $630; personal expenses: $730. **Financial aid:** Priority filing date for institution's financial aid form: February 15. In 2005-2006, 97% of undergraduates applied for financial aid. Of those, 90% were determined to have financial need; 11% had their need fully met. Average financial aid package (proportion receiving): $18,190 (90%). Average amount of gift aid, such as scholarships or grants (proportion receiving): $7,451 (90%). Average amount of self-help aid, such as work study or loans (proportion receiving): $4,781 (87%). Average need-based loan (excluding PLUS or other private loans): $3,956. Among students who received need-based aid, the average percentage of need met: 73%. Among students who received aid based on merit, the average award (and the proportion receiving): $6,004 (7%). The average athletic scholarship (and the proportion receiving): $0 (0%). Average amount of debt of borrowers graduating in 2005: $25,565. Proportion who borrowed: 89%.

CAMPUS LIFE AND EXTRACURRICULAR ACTIVITIES

Campus housing available (% using): coed dorms (61%), apartment for single students (8%), special housing for disabled students (1%), other housing options (30%). Students who live in college-owned, operated, or affiliated housing: 42%. **Student employment:** During the 2005-2006 academic year, 16% of undergraduates worked on campus. Average per-year earnings: $1,309. **Clubs and organizations:** Number of student organizations: 80. Activities include: choral groups, concert band, dance, drama/theater, literary magazine, radio station, student government, student newspaper, student film society, yearbook. Number of fraternities: 4; sororities: 4. Proportion of men in fraternities: 1%; of women in sororities: 1%. Average proportion of students who stay on campus on weekends: 65%. **Sports program (2005-2006):** Member of NCAA III. *Men's intercollegiate varsity sports:* baseball, basketball, field hockey, football, golf, ice hockey, lacrosse, soccer, swimming and diving, tennis. *Women's intercollegiate varsity sports:* basketball, ice hockey, lacrosse, soccer, softball, swimming and diving, tennis, volleyball, water polo.

SERVICES AND FACILITIES

Basic services: women's center, placement service, health service, health insurance. **Remedial assistance:** math, writing, study skills. **Counseling services:** minority student, career, military, personal, veteran student, academic, older student, birth control, religious. **For learning-disabled students:** School does not offer a structured program with separate admission and additional fees. Services include: tutors, other. **Library:** Number of titles: 184,425; number of current serial subscriptions: 1,242. **Information technology resources:**

Students are not required to lease or own a computer. Number of campus computers available to all students: 146. School has a wireless network. Approximate number of users that can be accommodated: 500. Proportion of college-owned housing units wired for high-speed internet access: 100%. **Campus safety:** Security services offered: 24-hour foot-and-vehicle patrols, late-night transport/escort service, 24-hour emergency telephones, lighted pathways/sidewalks, controlled dormitory access (key, security card, etc).

TRANSFER AND INTERNATIONAL STUDENTS

Transfer students: May apply for admission for the following academic terms: Fall, Spring, Summer. Applicants need a minimum number of credits to apply. For fall 2005: Transfer applications received: 510. Transfer applicants offered admission: 389. Transfer applicants enrolled: 227.
International students: Number of foreign undergraduates: 31 (1% of student body). Number of countries represented: 15. Minimum TOEFL score required: 525 (paper); 195 (computer). Average TOEFL score: 590 (paper).

Vassar College

- **Address:** 124 Raymond Avenue, Poughkeepsie, NY 12604
- **Website:** http://www.vassar.edu
- **Private**
- **Enrollment:** 2,326 full-time; 52 part-time

KEY STATS
- ✔ **U.S News College Ranking:** 12, Liberal Arts Colleges
- ✔ **SAT Score (25th/75th percentile):** 1340-1450
- ✔ **Tuition:** 2006-2007: $36,030

Selectivity: Most selective	**Room/board:** $8,130
Acceptance rate: 29%	**Average debt:** $19,038
Student/faculty ratio: 9/1	**Proportion who borrowed:** 56%

UNDERGRADUATE STUDENT BODY STATS
2005-2006 enrollment: 2,326 full-time; 52 part-time. Men: 41%; women: 59%. **Ethnic makeup:** African American: 5%; Asian American: 9%; Hispanic: 6%; White: 75%; International: 5%.

ADMISSIONS FACTS AND FIGURES
Phone: (845) 437-7300. **Email:** admission@vassar.edu. **Website:** http://www.vassar.edu. **Application deadlines for fall 2007:** Regular decision: January 1; decision sent by April 1. Early decision: Send application by: November 15; Decision sent by: December 15. Early action: Not offered. Admission can be deferred. **Application fee:** $60. Common application is accepted. **Admissions requirements/recommendations:** High school units required (recommended): English: (4); Mathematics: (4); Science: (4); Foreign language: (4); Social studies: (2); History: (2); Total units: (20). Tests: The college uses SAT or ACT scores in admissions decisions. Either SAT or ACT required. For admission to the fall 2007 entering class, the school will accept: ACT without writing, the new SAT. Campus visit: Recommended. Admissions interview: Neither required nor recommended. Off-campus interview: May be arranged. **Factors that count in admissions decisions:** *Academic:* Secondary school record: Very important. Class rank: Important. Letters of recommendation: Important. Standardized test scores: Important. Essay: Important. *Nonacademic:* Interview: Considered. Extracurricular activities: Considered. Talent/ability: Considered. Character/personal qualities: Important. Alumni/ae relationship: Important. Geographical residence: Considered. State residency: Not considered. Religious affiliation/commitment: Not considered. Minority status: Considered. Volunteer work: Considered. Work experience: Considered. **Other schools with the greatest overlap in applicants:** Brown University; Columbia University; Wellesley College; Wesleyan University. **Admissions statistics for the fall 2005 entering class:** Total applicants: 6,314. Total accepted: 1,803. Freshmen enrolled: 650; 78% were from out of state. Accepted through early-decision or early-action plans: 38%. Overall acceptance rate: 29%. Early-decision acceptance rate: 42%. Non-early acceptance rate: 27%. **Size of waiting list:** 961 applicants; enrolled from waiting list: 36. **Credentials of fall 2005 freshmen:** 67% ranked in the top 10 percent of their high school class; 94% were in the top 25 percent, and 100% were in the top half. (Proportion submitting class standing: 68%.) **Average high school grade point average:** 3.7. **First-year students who submitted SAT scores:** 93%. Scores (25/75 percentile): Verbal: 680-730, Math: 660-720, Combined:

1340-1450. **First-year students submitting ACT scores:** 22%. Scores (25/75 percentile): English: N/A, Math: N/A, Composite: 28-32.

ACADEMICS
Year founded: 1861. **Academic calendar:** Semester. **Degrees offered:** bachelor's, master's. **Most popular majors:** 27% social sciences, 15% visual and performing arts, 11% English language and literature/letters, 9% psychology, 8% multi/interdisciplinary studies. **Major fields of study:** area, ethnic, cultural, and gender studies; biological and biomedical sciences; computer and information sciences and support services; education; English language and literature/letters; foreign languages, literatures, and linguistics; history; liberal arts and sciences studies, and humanities; mathematics and statistics; multi/interdisciplinary studies; natural resources and conservation; philosophy and religious studies; physical sciences; psychology; social sciences; visual and performing arts. **Areas of required coursework:** foreign languages, other. **Pre-professional programs:** pre-law, pre-dentistry, pre-medicine, pre-veterinary science. **Special academic programs (% participation):** cross-registration (1%), double major (11%), exchange student program (domestic) (4%), independent study (48%), internships (54%), student-designed major (1%), study abroad (33%). **Teacher certification offered in:** elementary, secondary. **Faculty and instruction (2005-2006):** Total instructional faculty: 277 full-time, 29 part-time (52% men; 48% women; 15% minorities). Full-time faculty with Ph.D. or other terminal degree: 92%. Student/faculty ratio: 9/1. Classes of fewer than 20 students: 68%; of 20 to 49 students: 31%; of 50 or more students: 1%. **Advanced Placement and International Baccalaureate credit:** AP tests may be used for: Credit and/or placement. Scores accepted: 4, 5. International Baccalaureate exams may be used for: Credit and/or placement. **Freshmen returning for sophomore year:** 95%. **Graduation rates:** Four-year: 86%; five-year: 91%; six-year: 91%. **Graduate study:** 22% of students pursue further study immediately upon graduation; 65% within five years. Fields in which graduates pursue further study: Master of Business Administration (MBA), 10%; law, 17%; medicine, 13%; dentistry, 1%; engineering, 1%; theology (or the seminary), 1%; education, 6%; arts and sciences, 57%; veterinary medicine, 1%.

COSTS AND FINANCIAL AID
Financial aid office: (845) 437-5320. **Expenses (2006-2007):** Tuition and fees 2006-2007: $36,030; room/board: $8,130. Estimated books and supplies: $860; transportation: $400; personal expenses: $1,050. **Financial aid:** Priority filing date for institution's financial aid form: February 1; deadline: February 1. In 2005-2006, 64% of undergraduates applied for financial aid. Of those, 54% were determined to have financial need; 100% had their need fully met. Average financial aid package (proportion receiving): $27,982 (54%). Average amount of gift aid, such as scholarships or grants (proportion receiving): $22,754 (53%). Average amount of self-help aid, such as work study or loans (proportion receiving): $5,228 (54%). Average need-based loan (excluding PLUS or other private loans): $3,378. Among students who received need-based aid, the average percentage of need met: 100%. Among students who received aid based on merit, the average award (and the proportion receiving): $0 (0%). The average athletic scholarship (and the proportion receiving): $0 (0%). Average amount of debt of borrowers graduating in 2005: $19,038. Proportion who borrowed: 56%.

CAMPUS LIFE AND EXTRACURRICULAR ACTIVITIES
Campus housing available (% using): coed dorms (69%), women's dorms (6%), apartments for married students (0%), apartment for single students (24%), cooperative housing (1%). Students who live in college-owned, operated, or affiliated housing: 95%. **Student employment:** During the 2005-2006 academic year, 71% of undergraduates worked on campus. Average per-year earnings: $1,140. **Clubs and organizations:** Number of student organizations: 105. Activities include: choral groups, concert band, dance, drama/theater, jazz band, literary magazine, music ensembles, musical theater, opera, radio station, student government, student newspaper, student film society, symphony orchestra, television station, yearbook. Number of fraternities: 0; sororities: 0. Average proportion of students who stay on campus on weekends: 85%. **Sports program (2005-2006):** Member of NCAA III. **Men's intercollegiate varsity sports:** baseball, basketball, cross-country, fencing, lacrosse, soccer, swimming and diving, tennis, volleyball. **Women's intercollegiate varsity sports:** basketball, cross-country, fencing, golf, lacrosse, rowing, soccer, squash, swimming and diving, tennis, volleyball.

SERVICES AND FACILITIES
Basic services: nonremedial tutoring, women's center, placement service, health service, health insurance. **Remedial assistance:** reading, math, writing, study skills. **Counseling services:** minority student, career, personal, veteran student, academic, older student, psychological, birth control,

religious. **For learning-disabled students:** School does not offer a structured program with separate admission and additional fees. Total undergraduates in learning-disabled program or receiving services: 68. Services include: reading machines, tape recorders, note-taking services, learning center, readers, extended time for tests, early syllabus, priority registration, priority seating, substitution of courses, texts on tape, typist/scribe, exams on tape or computer, other testing accomodations. **Library:** Number of titles: 888,745; number of current serial subscriptions: 6,566. **Information technology resources:** Students are not required to lease or own a computer. Number of campus computers available to all students: 350. School has a wireless network. Approximate number of users that can be accommodated: 1,200. Proportion of college-owned housing units wired for high-speed internet access: 100%. **Campus safety:** Security services offered: 24-hour foot-and-vehicle patrols, late-night transport/escort service, 24-hour emergency telephones, lighted pathways/sidewalks, student patrols, controlled dormitory access (key, security card, etc).

TRANSFER AND INTERNATIONAL STUDENTS

Transfer students: May apply for admission for the following academic terms: Fall, Spring. Applicants do not need a minimum number of credits to apply. For fall 2005: Transfer applications received: 178. Transfer applicants offered admission: 35. Transfer applicants enrolled: 14. **International students:** Number of foreign undergraduates: 118 (5% of student body). Number of countries represented: 58. Minimum TOEFL score required: 600 (paper); 250 (computer). Average TOEFL score: 640 (paper).

Vaughn College of Aeronautics and Tech.

- **Address:** 86-01 23rd Avenue, Flushing, NY 11369
- **Website:** http://www.vaughn.edu
- **Private**
- **Enrollment:** 842 full-time; 279 part-time

KEY STATS

✔ **U.S News College Ranking:** Unranked Specialty School–Engineering
✔ **SAT Score (25th/75th percentile):** 960-1150
✔ **Tuition:** 2006-2007: $13,960

Selectivity: Less selective	**Room/board:** N/A
Acceptance rate: 95%	**Average debt:** N/A
Student/faculty ratio: N/A	**Proportion who borrowed:** N/A

UNDERGRADUATE STUDENT BODY STATS

2005-2006 enrollment: 842 full-time; 279 part-time. Men: 88%; women: 12%. **Ethnic makeup:** African American: 19%; Asian American: 11%; Hispanic: 35%; White: 31%; International: 4%.

ADMISSIONS FACTS AND FIGURES

Phone: (718) 429-6600. **Email:** admitme@vaughn.edu. **Website:** http://www.vaughn.edu. **Application deadlines for fall 2007:** Regular decision: Rolling. Early decision: Not offered. Early action: Not offered. Admission can be deferred. **Application fee:** $45. Common application is accepted. **Admissions requirements/recommendations:** High school units required (recommended): English: 4 (4); Mathematics: 3 (3); Science: 3 (3); Foreign language: 2 (3); Social studies: 2 (3); History: 1 (1); Academic electives: 0 (0); Total units: 18 (20). Tests: The college uses SAT or ACT scores in admissions decisions. SAT required. For admission to the fall 2007 entering class, the school will accept: ACT with writing. Campus visit: Recommended. Admissions interview: Recommended. Off-campus interview: May be arranged. **Factors that count in admissions decisions:** *Academic:* Secondary school record: Very important. Class rank: Not considered. Letters of recommendation: Important. Standardized test scores: Considered. Essay: Considered. *Nonacademic:* Interview: Considered. Extracurricular activities: Considered. Talent/ability: Considered. Character/personal qualities: Considered. Alumni/ae relationship: Not considered. Geographical residence: Not considered. State residency: Not considered. Religious affiliation/commitment: Not considered. Minority status: Not considered. Volunteer work: Considered. Work experience: Considered. **Admissions statistics for the fall 2005 entering class:** Total applicants: 328. Total accepted: 311. Freshmen enrolled: 24; Overall acceptance rate: 95%. **First-year students who submitted SAT scores:** 88%. Scores (25/75 percentile): Verbal: 470-560, Math: 490-590, Combined: 960-1150.

ACADEMICS

Year founded: 1932. **Academic calendar:** Semester. **Degrees offered:** certificate, associate, bachelor's. **Most popular majors:** Information not available. **Major fields of study: Special academic programs:** cooperative (work-study plan) program, distance learning, independent study, internships. **Reserve Officers Training Corps (ROTC):** Army ROTC: Offered at cooperating institution (Hofstra University/St.John's University); Air Force ROTC: Offered at cooperating institution (Manhattan College). **Faculty and instruction (2005-2006):** Total instructional faculty: 43 full-time, 70 part-time (81% men; 19% women; 34% minorities). Full-time faculty with Ph.D. or other terminal degree: 26%. Classes of fewer than 20 students: 69%; of 20 to 49 students: 31%. **Advanced Placement and International Baccalaureate credit:** International Baccalaureate exams may be used for: Credit and/or placement. **Freshmen returning for sophomore year:** 60%. **Graduation rates:** Six-year: 37%. **Graduate study:** 5% of students pursue further study immediately upon graduation.

COSTS AND FINANCIAL AID

Financial aid office: (718) 429-6600. **Expenses (2006-2007):** Tuition and fees 2006-2007: $13,960; room/board: N/A. **Financial aid:** In 2005-2006, 95% of undergraduates applied for financial aid. Of those, 92% were determined to have financial need; Average financial aid package (proportion receiving): $4,900 (92%). Average amount of gift aid, such as scholarships or grants (proportion receiving): $1,000 (92%). Average amount of self-help aid, such as work study or loans (proportion receiving): $3,250 (92%). Average need-based loan (excluding PLUS or other private loans): $1,750. Among students who received need-based aid, the average percentage of need met: 80%. Among students who received aid based on merit, the average award (and the proportion receiving): $500 (2%). The average athletic scholarship (and the proportion receiving): $0 (0%).

CAMPUS LIFE AND EXTRACURRICULAR ACTIVITIES

Student employment: During the 2005-2006 academic year, 10% of undergraduates worked on campus. Average per-year earnings: $5,000. **Clubs and organizations:** Number of student organizations: 11. Activities include: student government, student newspaper, yearbook. Number of fraternities: 0; sororities: 0.

SERVICES AND FACILITIES

Basic services: nonremedial tutoring, placement service. **Remedial assistance:** reading, math, writing, study skills. **Counseling services:** minority student, career, personal, academic. **For learning-disabled students:** Services include: remedial math, remedial English, remedial reading, untimed tests, learning center, extended time for tests, tutors. **Information technology resources:** Students are not required to lease or own a computer. School has a wireless network.

TRANSFER AND INTERNATIONAL STUDENTS

Transfer students: May apply for admission for the following academic terms: Fall, Spring, Summer. Applicants do not need a minimum number of credits to apply. For fall 2005: Transfer applications received: 152. Transfer applicants offered admission: 138. Transfer applicants enrolled: 96. **International students:** Number of foreign undergraduates: 46 (4% of student body). Number of countries represented: 6. Minimum TOEFL score required: 500 (paper); 173 (computer). Average TOEFL score: 500 (paper).

Wagner College

- **Address:** 1 Campus Road, Staten Island, NY 10301
- **Website:** http://www.wagner.edu
- **Private; Religious affiliation:** Lutheran
- **Enrollment:** 1,892 full-time; 70 part-time

KEY STATS

✔ **U.S. News College Ranking:** 25, Universities–Master's (North)
✔ **SAT Score (25th/75th percentile):** 1060-1270
✔ **Tuition:** 2006-2007: $27,300

Selectivity: More selective	**Room/board:** $8,400
Acceptance rate: 61%	**Average debt:** $28,864
Student/faculty ratio: 14/1	**Proportion who borrowed:** 81%

UNDERGRADUATE STUDENT BODY STATS

2005-2006 enrollment: 1,892 full-time; 70 part-time. Men: 37%; women: 63%. **Ethnic makeup:** African American: 5%; Asian American: 2%; Hispanic: 5%; White: 87%; International: 1%. **Religious preference:** Roman Catholic: 34%; Protestant: 8%; Jewish: 2%; Muslim: 1%; Unknown: 53%; Lutheran: 2%.

ADMISSIONS FACTS AND FIGURES

Phone: (718) 390-3411. **Email:** admissions@wagner.edu. **Website:** http://www.wagner.edu. **Application deadlines for fall 2007:** Regular decision: March 1. Early decision: Send application by: January 1; Decision sent by: February 1. Early action: Not offered. Admission can be deferred. **Application fee:** $50. Common application is accepted. **Admissions requirements/recommendations:** High school units required (recommended): English: 4; Mathematics: 3; Science: 2; Foreign language: 2; Social studies: 1; History: 3; Academic electives: 6; Total units: 21. Tests: The college uses SAT or ACT scores in admissions decisions. Either SAT or ACT required. For admission to the fall 2007 entering class, the school will accept: ACT with writing, ACT without writing. Campus visit: Recommended. Admissions interview: Recommended. Off-campus interview: May be arranged. **Factors that count in admissions decisions:** *Academic:* Secondary school record: Very important. Class rank: Very important. Letters of recommendation: Important. Standardized test scores: Very important. Essay: Important. *Nonacademic:* Interview: Important. Extracurricular activities: Important. Talent/ability: Considered. Character/personal qualities: Considered. Alumni/ae relationship: Not considered. Geographical residence: Not considered. State residency: Not considered. Religious affiliation/commitment: Not considered. Minority status: Not considered. Volunteer work: Considered. Work experience: Considered. **Other schools with the greatest overlap in applicants:** Drew University; Fairfield University; Fordham University; Marist College; University of Scranton. **Admissions statistics for the fall 2005 entering class:** Total applicants: 2,858. Total accepted: 1,751. Freshmen enrolled: 579; 65% were from out of state. Accepted through early-decision or early-action plans: 16%. Overall acceptance rate: 61%. Early-decision acceptance rate: 61%. Non-early acceptance rate: 61%. **Size of waiting list:** 112 applicants; enrolled from waiting list: 3. **Credentials of fall 2005 freshmen:** 17% ranked in the top 10 percent of their high school class; 64% were in the top 25 percent, and 92% were in the top half. (Proportion submitting class standing: 64%.) **Average high school grade point average:** 3.5. **First-year students who submitted SAT scores:** 88%. Scores (25/75 percentile): Verbal: 530-630, Math: 530-640, Combined: 1060-1270. **First-year students submitting ACT scores:** 12%. Scores (25/75 percentile): English: 22-26, Math: 24-28, Composite: 23-27.

ACADEMICS

Year founded: 1883. **Academic calendar:** Semester. **Degrees offered:** bachelor's, master's, post-master's certificate. **Most popular majors:** 25% business, management, marketing, and related support services; 19% visual and performing arts, 14% health professions and related clinical sciences; 11% psychology, 11% social sciences. **Major fields of study:** biological and biomedical sciences; business, management, marketing, and related support services; computer and information sciences and support services; education; English language and literature/letters; foreign languages, literatures, and linguistics; health professions and related clinical sciences; history; mathematics and statistics; multi/interdisciplinary studies; philosophy and religious studies; physical sciences; psychology; public administration and social service professions; social sciences; visual and performing arts. **Areas of required coursework:** arts/fine arts, humanities, computer literacy, mathematics, English (including composition), philosophy, sciences (biological or physical), history, social science, other. **Pre-professional programs:** pre-law, pre-dentistry, pre-medicine, pre-veterinary science, pre-optometry, other. **Special academic programs (% participation):** double major (9%), exchange student program (domestic) (8%), honors program (10%), internships (100%), study abroad (20%), teacher certificate program (10%). **Teacher certification offered in:** special education, elementary. **Reserve Officers Training Corps (ROTC):** Army ROTC: Offered at cooperating institution (St. John's University). **Faculty and instruction (2005-2006):** Total instructional faculty: 96 full-time, 130 part-time (50% men; 50% women; 9% minorities). Full-time faculty with Ph.D. or other terminal degree: 93%. Student/faculty ratio: 14/1. Classes of fewer than 20 students: 59%; of 20 to 49 students: 40%; of 50 or more students: 0%. **Advanced Placement and International Baccalaureate credit:** AP tests may be used for: Credit and/or placement. Scores accepted: 4, 5. International Baccalaureate exams may be used for: Credit and/or placement. **Freshmen returning for sophomore year:** 88%. **Graduation rates:** Four-year: 64%; five-year: 68%; six-year: 66%.

COSTS AND FINANCIAL AID

Financial aid office: (718) 390-3183. **Expenses (2006-2007):** Tuition and fees 2006-2007: $27,300; room/board: $8,400. Estimated books and supplies: $701; transportation: $701; personal expenses: $1,219. **Financial aid:** Priority filing date for institution's financial aid form: February 15. In 2005-2006, 66% of undergraduates applied for financial aid. Of those, 52% were determined to have financial need; 27% had their need fully met. Average financial aid package (proportion receiving): $15,642 (52%). Average amount of gift aid, such as scholarships or grants (proportion receiving): $11,957 (50%). Average amount of self-help aid, such as work study or loans (proportion receiving): $5,042 (40%). Average need-based loan (excluding PLUS or other private loans): $4,511. Among students who received need-based aid, the average percentage of need met: 73%. Among students who received aid based on merit, the average award (and the proportion receiving): $8,286 (34%). The average athletic scholarship (and the proportion receiving): $18,317 (7%). Average amount of debt of borrowers graduating in 2005: $28,864. Proportion who borrowed: 81%.

CAMPUS LIFE AND EXTRACURRICULAR ACTIVITIES

Campus housing available (% using): coed dorms (74%), sorority housing (10%), fraternity housing (8%), other housing options (8%). Students who live in college-owned, operated, or affiliated housing: 75%. **Student employment:** During the 2005-2006 academic year, 33% of undergraduates worked on campus. Average per-year earnings: $1,200. **Clubs and organizations:** Number of student organizations: 65. Activities include: choral groups, concert band, dance, drama/theater, jazz band, literary magazine, music ensembles, musical theater, pep band, radio station, student government, student newspaper, yearbook. Number of fraternities: 5; sororities: 4. Proportion of men in fraternities: 11%; of women in sororities: 9%. Average proportion of students who stay on campus on weekends: 70%. **Sports program (2005-2006):** Member of NCAA I. *Men's intercollegiate varsity sports:* baseball, basketball, cross-country, football, golf, lacrosse, tennis, track and field (indoor), track and field (outdoor), wrestling. *Women's intercollegiate varsity sports:* basketball, cross-country, golf, lacrosse, soccer, softball, swimming and diving, tennis, track and field (indoor), track and field (outdoor), volleyball, water polo.

SERVICES AND FACILITIES

Basic services: nonremedial tutoring, placement service, health service, health insurance. **Remedial assistance:** math, writing. **Counseling services:** career, personal, academic, psychological, birth control, religious. **For learning-disabled students:** School does not offer a structured program with separate admission and additional fees. Total undergraduates in learning-disabled program or receiving services: 106. Services include: tape recorders, untimed tests, learning center, extended time for tests, tutors, priority registration, priority seating, other testing accomodations. **Library:** Number of titles: 141,462; number of current serial subscriptions: 538. **Information technology resources:** Students are not required to lease or own a computer. Number of campus computers available to all students: 260. School has a wireless network. Approximate number of users that can be accommodated: 1,020. Proportion of college-owned housing units wired for high-speed internet access: 100%. **Campus safety:** Security services offered: 24-hour foot-and-vehicle patrols, late-night transport/escort service, 24-hour emergency telephones, lighted pathways/sidewalks, controlled dormitory access (key, security card, etc.).

TRANSFER AND INTERNATIONAL STUDENTS

Transfer students: May apply for admission for the following academic terms: Fall, Spring. Applicants do not need a minimum number of credits to apply. For fall 2005: Transfer applications received: 189. Transfer applicants offered admission: 37. Transfer applicants enrolled: 21. **International students:** Number of foreign undergraduates: 13 (1% of student body). Number of countries represented: 7. Minimum TOEFL score required: 550 (paper); 217 (computer). Average TOEFL score: 580 (paper).

Webb Institute

- **Address:** 298 Crescent Beach Road, Glen Cove, NY 11542-1398
- **Website:** http://www.webb-institute.edu
- **Private**
- **Enrollment:** 80 full-time

KEY STATS

- ✔ **U.S News College Ranking:** Unranked Specialty School–Engineering
- ✔ **SAT Score (25th/75th percentile):** 1380-1450
- ✔ **Tuition:** 2006-2007: $0

Selectivity: Most selective	**Room/board:** $8,340
Acceptance rate: 30%	**Average debt:** $11,612
Student/faculty ratio: 8/1	**Proportion who borrowed:** 17%

UNDERGRADUATE STUDENT BODY STATS

2005-2006 enrollment: 80 full-time. Men: 80%; women: 20%. **Ethnic makeup:** African American: 1%; Asian American: 3%; Hispanic: 1%; White: 95%.

ADMISSIONS FACTS AND FIGURES

Phone: (516) 671-2213. **Email:** admissions@webb-institute.edu. **Website:** http://www.webb-institute.edu. **Application deadlines for fall 2007:** Regular decision: February 15. Early decision: Send application by: October 15; Decision sent by: December 15. Early action: Not offered. Admission cannot be deferred. **Application fee:** $25. Common application is not accepted. **Admissions requirements/recommendations:** High school units required (recommended): English: 4; Mathematics: 4; Science: 2; Foreign language: 0; Social studies: 2; History: 0; Academic electives: 4; Total units: 16. Tests: The college uses SAT or ACT scores in admissions decisions. SAT required. Campus visit: Recommended. Admissions interview: Required. Off-campus interview: Not available. **Factors that count in admissions decisions:** *Academic:* Secondary school record: Very important. Class rank: Very important. Letters of recommendation: Important. Standardized test scores: Very important. Essay: Not considered. *Nonacademic:* Interview: Very important. Extracurricular activities: Important. Talent/ability: Considered. Character/personal qualities: Very important. Alumni/ae relationship: Not considered. Geographical residence: Not considered. State residency: Not considered. Religious affiliation/commitment: Not considered. Minority status: Considered. Volunteer work: Considered. Work experience: Considered. **Other schools with the greatest overlap in applicants:** Cornell University; Massachusetts Institute of Technology; Rensselaer Polytechnic Institute; United States Naval Academy; University of Michigan–Ann Arbor. **Admissions statistics for the fall 2005 entering class:** Total applicants: 103. Total accepted: 31. Freshmen enrolled: 20; 95% were from out of state. Accepted through early-decision or early-action plans: 65%. Overall acceptance rate: 30%. Early-decision acceptance rate: 38%. Non-early acceptance rate: 26%. **Credentials of fall 2005 freshmen:** 70% ranked in the top 10 percent of their high school class; 100% were in the top 25 percent, and 100% were in the top half. (Proportion submitting class standing: 68%.) **Average high school grade point average:** 3.9. **First-year students who submitted SAT scores:** 100%. Scores (25/75 percentile): Verbal: 660-700, Math: 720-750, Combined: 1380-1450.

ACADEMICS

Year founded: 1889. **Academic calendar:** Semester. **Degrees offered:** bachelor's. **Most popular majors:** 100% naval architecture and marine engineering. **Major fields of study:** engineering. **Areas of required coursework:** humanities, computer literacy, mathematics, English (including composition), philosophy, sciences (biological or physical), history, social science. **Special academic programs (% participation):** double major (100%), internships (100%). **Faculty and instruction (2005-2006):** Total instructional faculty: 8 full-time, 7 part-time (100% men; 0% women; 0% minorities). Full-time faculty with Ph.D. or other terminal degree: 50%. Student/faculty ratio: 8/1. Classes of fewer than 20 students: 20%; of 20 to 49 students: 80%. **Freshmen returning for sophomore year:** 88%. **Graduation rates:** Four-year: 65%; five-year: 65%; six-year: 67%. **Graduate study:** 25% of students pursue further study immediately upon graduation; 25% within five years. Fields in which graduates pursue further study: Master of Business Administration (MBA), 5%; engineering, 90%; education, 5%.

COSTS AND FINANCIAL AID

Financial aid office: (516) 671-2213. **Expenses (2006-2007):** Tuition and fees 2006-2007: $0; room/board: $8,340. Estimated books and supplies: $600; transportation: $2,000; personal expenses: $600. **Financial aid:** Priority filing date for institution's financial aid form: July 1; deadline: August 1. In 2005-2006, 20% of undergraduates applied for financial aid. Of those, 11% were determined to have financial need; 44% had their need fully met. Average financial aid package (proportion receiving): $2,797 (11%). Average amount of gift aid, such as scholarships or grants (proportion receiving): $2,225 (3%). Average amount of self-help aid, such as work study or loans (proportion receiving): $2,769 (10%). Average need-based loan (excluding PLUS or other private loans): $2,769. Among students who received need-based aid, the average percentage of need met: 85%. Among students who received aid based on merit, the average award (and the proportion receiving): $1,160 (8%). The average athletic scholarship (and the proportion receiving): $0 (0%). Average amount of debt of borrowers graduating in 2005: $11,612. Proportion who borrowed: 17%.

CAMPUS LIFE AND EXTRACURRICULAR ACTIVITIES

Campus housing available (% using): women's dorms (20%), men's dorms (80%). Students who live in college-owned, operated, or affiliated housing: 100%. Activities include: choral groups, drama/theater, student government, student newspaper, yearbook. Number of fraternities: 0; sororities: 0. Average proportion of students who stay on campus on weekends: 60%. **Sports program (2005-2006):** *Men's intercollegiate varsity sports:* basketball, cross-country, sailing, soccer, tennis, track and field (outdoor), volleyball.

SERVICES AND FACILITIES

Remedial assistance: study skills. **Counseling services:** personal, academic, psychological. **Library:** Number of titles: 53,319; number of current serial subscriptions: 270. **Information technology resources:** Students are not required to lease or own a computer. Number of campus computers available to all students: 90. School has a wireless network. Approximate number of users that can be accommodated: 90. Proportion of college-owned housing units wired for high-speed internet access: 100%. **Campus safety:** Security services offered: 24-hour foot-and-vehicle patrols, 24-hour emergency telephones, lighted pathways/sidewalks, controlled dormitory access (key, security card, etc).

TRANSFER AND INTERNATIONAL STUDENTS

Transfer students: May apply for admission for the following academic terms: Fall. Applicants do not need a minimum number of credits to apply. For fall 2005: Transfer applications received: 7. Transfer applicants offered admission: 2. Transfer applicants enrolled: 2. **International students:** Number of foreign undergraduates: 0.

Wells College

- **Address:** 170 Main Street, Aurora, NY 13026
- **Website:** http://www.wells.edu
- **Private**
- **Enrollment:** 405 full-time; 12 part-time

KEY STATS

- ✔ **U.S News College Ranking:** third tier, Liberal Arts Colleges
- ✔ **SAT Score (25th/75th percentile):** 1000-1210
- ✔ **Tuition:** 2006-2007: $16,780

Selectivity: More selective	**Room/board:** $7,800
Acceptance rate: 65%	**Average debt:** $17,125
Student/faculty ratio: 8/1	**Proportion who borrowed:** 91%

UNDERGRADUATE STUDENT BODY STATS

2005-2006 enrollment: 405 full-time; 12 part-time. Men: 9%; women: 91%. **Ethnic makeup:** African American: 7%; Asian American: 3%; Hispanic: 4%; White: 83%; International: 2%.

ADMISSIONS FACTS AND FIGURES

Phone: (800) 952-9355. **Email:** admissions@wells.edu. **Website:** http://www.wells.edu. **Application deadlines for fall 2007:** Regular decision: March 1; decision sent by April 1. Early decision: Send application by: December 15; Decision sent by: January 15. Early action: Send application by: December 15; Decision sent by: February 1. Admission can be deferred.

Application fee: $40. Common application is accepted. To apply online, go to: http://www.commonapp.org. Admissions requirements/recommendations: High school units required (recommended): English: 4 (4); Mathematics: 3 (4); Science: 2 (3); Foreign language: o (2); Social studies: 1 (2); History: 2 (3); Academic electives: 2 (3); Total units: 16 (23). Tests: The college uses SAT or ACT scores in admissions decisions. Either SAT or ACT required. For admission to the fall 2007 entering class, the school will accept: ACT with writing, ACT without writing. Campus visit: Recommended. Admissions interview: Recommended. Off-campus interview: May be arranged. **Factors that count in admissions decisions:** *Academic:* Secondary school record: Very important. Class rank: Considered. Letters of recommendation: Very important. Standardized test scores: Very important. Essay: Important. *Nonacademic:* Interview: Important. Extracurricular activities: Very important. Talent/ability: Considered. Character/personal qualities: Considered. Alumni/ae relationship: Considered. Geographical residence: Not considered. State residency: Not considered. Religious affiliation/commitment: Not considered. Minority status: Not considered. Volunteer work: Considered. Work experience: Considered. **Other schools with the greatest overlap in applicants:** Elmira College; Hobart and William Smith Colleges; Le Moyne College; Mount Holyoke College; Smith College. **Admissions statistics for the fall 2005 entering class:** Total applicants: 1,036. Total accepted: 673. Freshmen enrolled: 130; 41% were from out of state. Accepted through early-decision or early-action plans: 38%. Overall acceptance rate: 65%. Early-decision acceptance rate: 80%. Non-early acceptance rate: 61%. **Credentials of fall 2005 freshmen:** 25% ranked in the top 10 percent of their high school class; 64% were in the top 25 percent, and 93% were in the top half. (Proportion submitting class standing: 58%.) **Average high school grade point average:** 3.5. **First-year students who submitted SAT scores:** 93%. Scores (25/75 percentile): Verbal: 520-630, Math: 480-580, Combined: 1000-1210. **First-year students submitting ACT scores:** 27%. Scores (25/75 percentile): English: N/A, Math: N/A, Composite: 20-26.

ACADEMICS

Year founded: 1868. **Academic calendar:** Semester. **Degrees offered:** bachelor's. **Most popular majors:** 24% social sciences, 17% psychology, 15% biological and biomedical sciences, 12% visual and performing arts, 10% English language and literature/letters. **Major fields of study: Areas of required coursework:** arts/fine arts, humanities, mathematics, foreign languages, sciences (biological or physical), social science. **Pre-professional programs:** pre-law, pre-dentistry, pre-medicine, pre-veterinary science, pre-pharmacy, other. **Special academic programs (% participation):** accelerated program (3%), cross-registration (25%), double major (3%), English as a Second Language (ESL) (.005%), independent study (50%), internships (90%), student-designed major (3%), study abroad (30%), teacher certificate program (12%). **Teacher certification offered in:** elementary, secondary. **Reserve Officers Training Corps (ROTC):** Air Force ROTC: Offered at cooperating institution (Cornell University). **Faculty and instruction (2005-2006):** Total instructional faculty: 49 full-time, 20 part-time (42% men; 58% women; 20% minorities). Full-time faculty with Ph.D. or other terminal degree: 94%. Student/faculty ratio: 8/1. Classes of fewer than 20 students: 82%; of 20 to 49 students: 18%; of 50 or more students: 0%. **Advanced Placement and International Baccalaureate credit:** AP tests may be used for: Credit and/or placement. Scores accepted: 4, 5. International Baccalaureate exams may be used for: Credit and/or placement. **Freshmen returning for sophomore year:** 76%. **Graduation rates:** Four-year: 54%; five-year: 57%; six-year: 57%. **Graduate study:** 20% of students pursue further study immediately upon graduation; 2% within one year; 5% within five years. Fields in which graduates pursue further study: Master of Business Administration (MBA), 1%; law, 4%; medicine, 2%; dentistry, 1%; theology (or the seminary), 1%; education, 8%; arts and sciences, 46%; veterinary medicine, 1%.

COSTS AND FINANCIAL AID

Financial aid office: (315) 364-3289. **Expenses (2006-2007):** Tuition and fees 2006-2007: $16,780; room/board: $7,800. Estimated books and supplies: $700; transportation: $0; personal expenses: $700. **Financial aid:** Priority filing date for institution's financial aid form: February 15. In 2005-2006, 87% of undergraduates applied for financial aid. Of those, 74% were determined to have financial need; 25% had their need fully met. Average financial aid package (proportion receiving): $17,290 (74%). Average amount of gift aid, such as scholarships or grants (proportion receiving): $11,668 (74%). Average amount of self-help aid, such as work study or loans (proportion receiving): $5,643 (74%). Average need-based loan (excluding PLUS or other private loans): $4,737. Among students who received need-based aid, the average percentage of need met: 92%. Among students who received aid based on merit, the average award (and the proportion receiv-

ing): $4,960 (14%). The average athletic scholarship (and the proportion receiving): $0 (0%). Average amount of debt of borrowers graduating in 2005: $17,125. Proportion who borrowed: 91%.

CAMPUS LIFE AND EXTRACURRICULAR ACTIVITIES

Campus housing available (% using): coed dorms (30%), women's dorms (70%). Students who live in college-owned, operated, or affiliated housing: 80%. **Student employment:** During the 2005-2006 academic year, 74% of undergraduates worked on campus. Average per-year earnings: $1,400. **Clubs and organizations:** Number of student organizations: 48. Activities include: choral groups, dance, drama/theater, jazz band, literary magazine, music ensembles, student government, student newspaper, yearbook.. Number of fraternities: 0; sororities: 0. Average proportion of students who stay on campus on weekends: 80%. **Sports program (2005-2006):** Member of NCAA III. *Men's intercollegiate varsity sports:* cross-country. *Women's intercollegiate varsity sports:* cross-country, field hockey, lacrosse, soccer, softball, swimming and diving, tennis.

SERVICES AND FACILITIES

Basic services: nonremedial tutoring, women's center, health service, health insurance. **Remedial assistance:** math, writing, study skills. **Counseling services:** minority student, career, personal, academic, older student, psychological, birth control, religious. **For learning-disabled students:** School does not offer a structured program with separate admission and additional fees. Total undergraduates in learning-disabled program or receiving services: 20. Services include: tape recorders, note-taking services, oral tests, extended time for tests, tutors, other. **Library:** Number of titles: 209,869; number of current serial subscriptions: 787. **Information technology resources:** Students are not required to lease or own a computer. Number of campus computers available to all students: 103. School does not have a wireless network. Proportion of college-owned housing units wired for high-speed internet access: 100%. **Campus safety:** Security services offered: 24-hour foot-and-vehicle patrols, late-night transport/escort service, 24-hour emergency telephones, lighted pathways/sidewalks, student patrols, controlled dormitory access (key, security card, etc).

TRANSFER AND INTERNATIONAL STUDENTS

Transfer students: May apply for admission for the following academic terms: Fall, Spring. Applicants need a minimum number of credits to apply. For fall 2005: Transfer applications received: 80. Transfer applicants offered admission: 56. Transfer applicants enrolled: 32. **International students:** Number of foreign undergraduates: 8 (2% of student body). Number of countries represented: 8. Minimum TOEFL score required: 550 (paper); 213 (computer). Average TOEFL score: 553 (paper).

Yeshiva University

- **Address:** 500 W. 185th Street, New York, NY 10033
- **Website:** http://www.yu.edu
- **Private**
- **Enrollment:** 2,840 full-time; 91 part-time

KEY STATS

✔ **U.S News College Ranking:** 44, National Universities
✔ **SAT Score (25th/75th percentile):** 1110-1350
✔ **Tuition:** 2006-2007: $28,700

Selectivity: More selective	**Room/board:** $8,670
Acceptance rate: 78%	**Average debt:** $18,628
Student/faculty ratio: 11/1	**Proportion who borrowed:** 49%

UNDERGRADUATE STUDENT BODY STATS

2005-2006 enrollment: 2,840 full-time; 91 part-time. Men: 54%; women: 46%. **Ethnic makeup:** White: 100%. **Religious preference:** Jewish: 100%.

ADMISSIONS FACTS AND FIGURES

Phone: (212) 960-5277. **Email:** yuadmit@ymail.yu.edu. **Website:** http://www.yu.edu. **Application deadlines for fall 2007:** Regular decision: February 15. Early decision: Not offered. Early action: Not offered. Admission can be deferred. **Application fee:** $50. Common application is not accepted. **Admissions requirements/recommendations:** High school units required (recommended): English: 4; Mathematics: 4; Science: 4; Foreign language: 4; Social studies: 2; History: 2; Academic electives: 0;

Total units: 20. Tests: The college uses SAT or ACT scores in admissions decisions. Neither SAT nor ACT required. For admission to the fall 2007 entering class, the school will accept: ACT with writing, ACT without writing. Campus visit: Recommended. Admissions interview: Required. Off-campus interview: May be arranged. **Factors that count in admissions decisions: *Academic:*** Secondary school record: Very important. Class rank: Important. Letters of recommendation: Considered. Standardized test scores: Very important. Essay: Very important. ***Nonacademic:*** Interview: Very important. Extracurricular activities: Considered. Talent/ability: Considered. Character/personal qualities: Very important. Alumni/ae relationship: Not considered. Geographical residence: Not considered. State residency: Not considered. Religious affiliation/commitment: Not considered. Minority status: Not considered. Volunteer work: Considered. Work experience: Not considered. **Other schools with the greatest overlap in applicants:** Barnard College; Brandeis University; CUNY–Queens College; Rutgers–New Brunswick; University of Pennsylvania. **Admissions statistics for the fall 2005 entering class:** Total applicants: 1,875. Total accepted: 1,467. Freshmen enrolled: 1,005; 63% were from out of state. Overall acceptance rate: 78%. **Credentials of fall 2005 freshmen:** 40% ranked in the top 10 percent of their high school class; 55% were in the top 25 percent, and 95% were in the top half. (Proportion submitting class standing: 87%.) **Average high school grade point average:** 3.3. **First-year students who submitted SAT scores:** 84%. Scores (25/75 percentile): Verbal: 550-670, Math: 560-680, Combined: 1110-1350. **First-year students submitting ACT scores:** 7%. Scores (25/75 percentile): English: N/A, Math: N/A, Composite: 23-29.

ACADEMICS

Year founded: 1886. **Academic calendar:** Semester. **Degrees offered:** associate, bachelor's, master's, post-master's certificate, first professional, doctorate. **Most popular majors:** 21% business administration and management, 14% psychology, 12% biology/biological sciences, 9% accounting, 7% English language and literature. **Major fields of study:** business, management, marketing, and related support services; communication, journalism, and related programs; computer and information sciences and support services; education; engineering; English language and literature/letters; foreign languages, literatures, and linguistics; health professions and related clinical sciences; history; mathematics and statistics; philosophy and religious studies; physical sciences; psychology; social sciences; visual and performing arts. **Areas of required coursework:** humanities, computer literacy, mathematics, English (including composition), foreign languages, sciences (biological or physical), social science. **Pre-professional programs:** pre-law, pre-dentistry, pre-medicine, other. **Special academic programs (% participation):** cross-registration (4%), double major (6%), dual enrollment (.7%), English as a Second Language (ESL) (1.6%), honors program (4%), independent study (2.4%), internships (15.3%), student-designed major (7.8%), study abroad (90%), teacher certificate program (3.8%). **Teacher certification offered in:** early childhood, elementary. **Faculty and instruction (2005-2006):** Total instructional faculty: 857 full-time, 375 part-time (63% men; 37% women; 16% minorities). Full-time faculty with Ph.D. or other terminal degree: 95%. Student/faculty ratio: 11/1. Classes of fewer than 20 students: 72%; of 20 to 49 students: 27%; of 50 or more students: 0%. **Advanced Placement and International Baccalaureate credit:** AP tests may be used for: Credit and/or placement. Scores accepted: 3, 4, 5. International Baccalaureate exams may be used for: Credit and/or placement. **Freshmen returning for sophomore year:** 87%. **Graduation rates:** Four-year: 57%; five-year: 74%; six-year: 82%.

COSTS AND FINANCIAL AID

Financial aid office: (212) 960-5399. **Expenses (2006-2007):** Tuition and fees 2006-2007: $28,700; room/board: $8,670. Estimated books and supplies: $1,100; transportation: $1,125; personal expenses: $3,009. **Financial aid:** Priority filing date for institution's financial aid form: February 15. In 2005-2006, 58% of undergraduates applied for financial aid. Of those, 47% were determined to have financial need; 28% had their need fully met. Average financial aid package (proportion receiving): $20,434 (46%). Average amount of gift aid, such as scholarships or grants (proportion receiving): $16,512 (43%). Average amount of self-help aid, such as work study or loans (proportion receiving): $6,090 (32%). Average need-based loan (excluding PLUS or other private loans): $6,002. Among students who received need-based aid, the average percentage of need met: 74%. Among students who received aid based on merit, the average award (and the proportion receiving): $9,029 (9%). The average athletic scholarship (and the proportion receiving): $0 (0%). Average amount of debt of borrowers graduating in 2005: $18,628. Proportion who borrowed: 49%.

CAMPUS LIFE AND EXTRACURRICULAR ACTIVITIES

Campus housing available (% using): women's dorms (42%), men's dorms (47%), apartments for married students (2%), apartment for single students (9%). Students who live in college-owned, operated, or affiliated housing: 90%. **Student employment:** During the 2005-2006 academic year, 5% of undergraduates worked on campus. Average per-year earnings: $2,500. **Clubs and organizations:** Number of student organizations: 100. Activities include: choral groups, concert band, dance, drama/theater, jazz band, literary magazine, music ensembles, musical theater, radio station, student government, student newspaper, student film society, yearbook. Number of fraternities: 0; sororities: 0. Average proportion of students who stay on campus on weekends: 15%. **Sports program (2005-2006):** Member of NCAA III. ***Men's intercollegiate varsity sports:*** basketball, cross-country, fencing, golf, soccer, tennis, volleyball, wrestling.

SERVICES AND FACILITIES

Basic services: nonremedial tutoring, placement service, health service, health insurance. **Remedial assistance:** reading, math, writing. **Counseling services:** career, personal, academic, psychological, religious. **For learning-disabled students:** School does not offer a structured program with separate admission and additional fees. Total undergraduates in learning-disabled program or receiving services: 53. Services include: remedial English, tape recorders, untimed tests, oral tests, extended time for tests, priority seating, other testing accomodations, waiver of foreign language degree requirement. **Library:** Number of titles: 1,102,632; number of current serial subscriptions: 41,040. **Information technology resources:** Students are not required to lease or own a computer. Number of campus computers available to all students: 800. School has a wireless network. Approximate number of users that can be accommodated: 2,100. Proportion of college-owned housing units wired for high-speed internet access: 100%. **Campus safety:** Security services offered: 24-hour foot-and-vehicle patrols, late-night transport/escort service, 24-hour emergency telephones, lighted pathways/sidewalks, controlled dormitory access (key, security card, etc).

TRANSFER AND INTERNATIONAL STUDENTS

Transfer students: May apply for admission for the following academic terms: Fall, Spring. Applicants do not need a minimum number of credits to apply. For fall 2005: Transfer applications received: 31. Transfer applicants offered admission: 23. Transfer applicants enrolled: 12. **International students:** Number of foreign undergraduates: 0. Number of countries represented: 17. Minimum TOEFL score required: 500 (paper); 173 (computer). Average TOEFL score: 585 (paper).

North Carolina

Appalachian State University

- **Address:** Boone, NC 28608
- **Website:** http://www.appstate.edu
- **Public**
- **Enrollment:** 12,043 full-time; 943 part-time

KEY STATS

✔ **U.S News College Ranking:** 12, Universities–Master's (South)
✔ **SAT Score (25th/75th percentile):** 1040-1220
✔ **Tuition:** 2006-2007: $3,917 in state, $13,659 out of state

Selectivity: Selective	Room/board: $5,650
Acceptance rate: 69%	Average debt: $15,433
Student/faculty ratio: 17/1	Proportion who borrowed: 50%

UNDERGRADUATE STUDENT BODY STATS

2005-2006 enrollment: 12,043 full-time; 943 part-time. Men: 50%; women: 50%. **Ethnic makeup:** African American: 3%; Asian American: 1%; Hispanic: 2%; White: 93%.

ADMISSIONS FACTS AND FIGURES

Phone: (828) 262-2120. **Email:** admissions@appstate.edu. **Website:** http://www.appstate.edu. **Application deadlines for fall 2007:** Regular decision: Rolling. Early decision: Not offered. Early action: Not offered. Admission can be deferred. **Application fee:** $45. Common application is not accepted. **To apply online, go to:** http://www.appstate.edu/www_docs/admissions/application.html. **Admissions requirements/recommendations:** High school units required (recommended): English: 4; Mathematics: 4; Science: 3; Foreign language: 2 (2); Social studies: 1; History: 1; Total units: 13 (2). Tests: The college uses SAT or ACT scores in admissions decisions. Either SAT or ACT required. For admission to the fall 2007 entering class, the school will accept: ACT with writing. Campus visit: Recommended. Admissions interview: Neither required nor recommended. Off-campus interview: Not available. **Factors that count in admissions decisions:** *Academic:* Secondary school record: Very important. Class rank: Very important. Letters of recommendation: Considered. Standardized test scores: Very important. Essay: Considered. *Nonacademic:* Interview: Considered. Extracurricular activities: Considered. Talent/ability: Considered. Character/personal qualities: Considered. Alumni/ae relationship: Considered. Geographical residence: Not considered. State residency: Considered. Religious affiliation/commitment: Not considered. Minority status: Not considered. Volunteer work: Considered. Work experience: Considered. **Other schools with the greatest overlap in applicants:** East Carolina University; North Carolina State University–Raleigh; University of North Carolina–Chapel Hill; University of North Carolina–Charlotte; University of North Carolina–Wilmington. **Admissions statistics for the fall 2005 entering class:** Total applicants: 9,923. Total accepted: 6,832. Freshmen enrolled: 2,543; 11% were from out of state. Overall acceptance rate: 69%. **Size of waiting list:** 1341 applicants; enrolled from waiting list: 1341. **Credentials of fall 2005 freshmen:** 16% ranked in the top 10 percent of their high school class; 50% were in the top 25 percent, and 89% were in the top half. (Proportion submitting class standing: 90%.) **Average high school grade point average:** 3.7. **First-year students who submitted SAT scores:** 100%. Scores (25/75 percentile): Verbal: 510-610, Math: 530-610, Combined: 1040-1220. **First-year students submitting ACT scores:** 19%. Scores (25/75 percentile): English: 19-25, Math: 20-25, Composite: 20-25.

ACADEMICS

Year founded: 1899. **Academic calendar:** Semester. **Degrees offered:** certificate, bachelor's, post-bachelor's certificate, master's, post-master's certificate, doctorate. **Most popular majors:** 8% elementary education and teaching, 6% psychology, 5% business administration and management, 5% management information systems, 4% marketing/marketing management. **Major fields of study:** architecture and related services; biological and biomedical sciences; business, management, marketing, and related support services; communication, journalism, and related programs; computer and information sciences and support services; education; engineering technologies/technicians; English language and literature/letters; family and consumer sciences/human sciences; foreign languages, literatures, and linguistics; health professions and related clinical sciences; history; liberal arts and sciences studies, and humanities; mathematics and statistics; parks, recreation, leisure, and fitness studies; philosophy and religious studies; physical sciences; psychology; public administration and social service professions; security and protective services; social sciences; visual and performing arts. **Areas of required coursework:** arts/fine arts, humanities, computer literacy, mathematics, English (including composition), sciences (biological or physical), history, social science. **Pre-professional programs:** pre-law, pre-dentistry, pre-medicine, pre-theology, pre-pharmacy, other. **Special academic programs:** distance learning, double major, dual enrollment, English as a Second Language (ESL), honors program, independent study, internships, liberal arts/career combination, student-designed major, study abroad, teacher certificate program. **Teacher certification offered in:** early childhood, special education, elementary, vo-tech, middle/junior high, secondary, bilingual/bicultural. **Reserve Officers Training Corps (ROTC):** Army ROTC: Offered on campus. **Faculty and instruction (2005-2006):** Total instructional faculty: 703 full-time, 295 part-time (55% men; 45% women; 7% minorities). Full-time faculty with Ph.D. or other terminal degree: 98%. Student/faculty ratio: 17/1. Classes of fewer than 20 students: 41%; of 20 to 49 students: 51%; of 50 or more students: 7%. **Advanced Placement and International Baccalaureate credit:** AP tests may be used for: Credit and/or placement. Scores accepted: 3, 4, 5. International Baccalaureate exams may be used for: Credit and/or placement. **Freshmen returning for sophomore year:** 84%. **Graduation rates:** Four-year: 35%; five-year: 60%; six-year: 62%. **Graduate study:** 20% of students pursue further study within one year.

COSTS AND FINANCIAL AID

Financial aid office: (828) 262-2190. **Expenses (2006-2007):** Tuition and fees 2006-2007: $3,917 in state, $13,659 out of state; room/board: $5,650. Estimated books and supplies: $600; transportation: $1,100; personal expenses: $1,200. **Financial aid:** Priority filing date for institution's financial aid form: March 15. In 2005-2006, 59% of undergraduates applied for financial aid. Of those, 34% were determined to have financial need; 38% had their need fully met. Average financial aid package (proportion receiving): $6,383 (32%). Average amount of gift aid, such as scholarships or grants (proportion receiving): $4,286 (27%). Average amount of self-help aid, such as work study or loans (proportion receiving): $3,521 (25%). Average need-based loan (excluding PLUS or other private loans): $3,399. Among students who received need-based aid, the average percentage of need met: 77%. Among students who received aid based on merit, the average award (and the proportion receiving): $2,875 (6%). The average athletic scholarship (and the proportion receiving): $7,107 (2%). Average amount of debt of borrowers graduating in 2005: $15,433. Proportion who borrowed: 50%.

CAMPUS LIFE AND EXTRACURRICULAR ACTIVITIES

Campus housing available (% using): coed dorms (83%), women's dorms (8%), men's dorms (7%), sorority housing, apartments for married students, special housing for disabled students, special housing for international students, other housing options (2%). Students who live in college-owned, operated, or affiliated housing: 38%. **Student employment:** During the 2005-2006 academic year, 15% of undergraduates worked on campus. Average per-year earnings: $3,500. **Clubs and organizations:** Number of student organizations: 274. Activities include: choral groups, concert band, dance, drama/theater, jazz band, literary magazine, marching band, music ensembles, musical theater, opera, pep band, radio station, student government, student newspaper, student film society, symphony orchestra, television station, yearbook. Number of fraternities: 15; sororities: 9. Proportion of men in fraternities: 8%; of women in sororities: 9%. Average proportion of students who stay on campus on weekends: 60%. **Sports program (2005-2006):** Member of NCAA I. *Men's intercollegiate varsity sports:* baseball, basketball, cross-country, football, golf, soccer, tennis, track and field (indoor), track and field (outdoor), wrestling. *Women's inter-*

collegiate varsity sports: basketball, cross-country, field hockey, golf, soccer, softball, tennis, track and field (indoor), track and field (outdoor), volleyball.

SERVICES AND FACILITIES

Basic services: nonremedial tutoring, women's center, placement service, day care, health service, health insurance. **Remedial assistance:** reading, math, writing, study skills. **Counseling services:** minority student, career, military, personal, veteran student, academic, older student, psychological, birth control. **For learning-disabled students:** School does not offer a structured program with separate admission and additional fees. Total undergraduates in learning-disabled program or receiving services: 399. Services include: remedial math, remedial English, reading machines, tape recorders, other special classes, diagnostic testing service, untimed tests, note-taking services, oral tests, learning center, readers, extended time for tests, tutors, priority registration, priority seating, texts on tape, other testing accomodations. **Library:** Number of titles: 917,360; number of current serial subscriptions: 5,543. **Information technology resources:** Students are not required to lease or own a computer. Number of campus computers available to all students: 1,557. School has a wireless network. Approximate number of users that can be accommodated: 1,500. Proportion of college-owned housing units wired for high-speed internet access: 100%. **Campus safety:** Security services offered: 24-hour foot-and-vehicle patrols, late-night transport/escort service, 24-hour emergency telephones, lighted pathways/sidewalks, controlled dormitory access (key, security card, etc).

TRANSFER AND INTERNATIONAL STUDENTS

Transfer students: May apply for admission for the following academic terms: Fall, Spring, Summer. Applicants need a minimum number of credits to apply. For fall 2005: Transfer applications received: 1,483. Transfer applicants offered admission: 1,237. Transfer applicants enrolled: 813. **International students:** Number of foreign undergraduates: 29. Minimum TOEFL score required: 500 (paper); 173 (computer).

Barton College

- **Address:** 704-A College Street, PO Box 5000, Wilson, NC 27893
- **Website:** http://www.barton.edu
- **Private; Religious affiliation:** Christian Church (Disciples of Christ)
- **Enrollment:** 917 full-time; 272 part-time

KEY STATS

✔ **U.S News College Ranking:** 53, Comp. Colleges–Bachelor's (South)
✔ **SAT Score (25th/75th percentile):** 820-1160
✔ **Tuition:** 2005-2006: $16,670

Selectivity: Less selective	**Room/board:** $5,880
Acceptance rate: 70%	**Average debt:** N/A
Student/faculty ratio: 11/1	**Proportion who borrowed:** N/A

UNDERGRADUATE STUDENT BODY STATS

2005-2006 enrollment: 917 full-time; 272 part-time. Men: 27%; women: 73%. **Ethnic makeup:** African American: 23%; Asian American: 1%; Hispanic: 2%; White: 72%; International: 2%. **Religious preference:** Roman Catholic: 8%; Protestant: 62%; No preference: 2%; Unknown: 25%; Christian Church (Disciples of Christ): 3%.

ADMISSIONS FACTS AND FIGURES

Phone: (800) 345-4973. **Email:** enroll@barton.edu. **Website:** http://www.barton.edu. **Application deadlines for fall 2007:** Regular decision: Rolling. Early decision: Not offered. Early action: Not offered. Admission cannot be deferred. **Application fee:** $25. Common application is not accepted. **To apply online, go to:** http://www.barton.edu/admissions/default.htm. **Admissions requirements/recommendations:** High school units required (recommended): English: 4; Mathematics: 3 (4); Science: 2; Foreign language: (2); Academic electives: 1; Total units: 13. Tests: The college uses SAT or ACT scores in admissions decisions. Either SAT or ACT required. For admission to the fall 2007 entering class, the school will accept: ACT with writing, ACT without writing. Campus visit: Recommended. Admissions interview: Recommended. Off-campus interview: May be arranged. **Factors that count in admissions decisions:** *Academic:* Secondary school record: Very important. Class rank: Important. Letters of recommendation: Considered. Standardized test scores: Very important. Essay: Not considered. *Nonacademic:* Interview:

Important. Extracurricular activities: Considered. Talent/ability: Considered. Character/personal qualities: Considered. Alumni/ae relationship: Considered. Geographical residence: Not considered. State residency: Not considered. Religious affiliation/commitment: Not considered. Minority status: Not considered. Volunteer work: Considered. Work experience: Considered. **Other schools with the greatest overlap in applicants:** Appalachian State University; Campbell University; East Carolina University; North Carolina State University–Raleigh; University of North Carolina–Wilmington. **Admissions statistics for the fall 2005 entering class:** Total applicants: 1,295. Total accepted: 908. Freshmen enrolled: 247; 27% were from out of state. Overall acceptance rate: 70%. **Credentials of fall 2005 freshmen:** 13% ranked in the top 10 percent of their high school class; 34% were in the top 25 percent, and 61% were in the top half. (Proportion submitting class standing: 86%.) **Average high school grade point average:** 3.1. First-year students who submitted SAT scores: 100%. Scores (25/75 percentile): Verbal: 400-570, Math: 420-590, Combined: 820-1160.

ACADEMICS

Year founded: 1902. **Academic calendar:** 4-1-4. **Degrees offered:** bachelor's, post-bachelor's certificate. **Most popular majors:** 28% business, management, marketing, and related support services, 15% health professions and related clinical sciences, 14% education, 8% public administration and social service professions, 6% biological and biomedical sciences. **Major fields of study:** biological and biomedical sciences; business, management, marketing, and related support services; communication, journalism, and related programs; computer and information sciences and support services; education; English language and literature/letters; foreign languages, literatures, and linguistics; health professions and related clinical sciences; history; liberal arts and sciences studies, and humanities; mathematics and statistics; multi/interdisciplinary studies; natural resources and conservation; parks, recreation, leisure, and fitness studies; philosophy and religious studies; physical sciences; psychology; public administration and social service professions; security and protective services; social sciences; visual and performing arts. **Areas of required coursework:** arts/fine arts, humanities, computer literacy, mathematics, English (including composition), sciences (biological or physical), history, social science, other. **Pre-professional programs:** pre-law, pre-dentistry, pre-medicine, pre-veterinary science, pre-optometry, pre-pharmacy, other. **Special academic programs (% participation):** cooperative (work-study plan) program, double major (15%), English as a Second Language (ESL), honors program, independent study (26%), internships (64%), study abroad (0%), teacher certificate program (12%), weekend college (21%). **Teacher certification offered in:** special education, elementary, middle/junior high, secondary. **Cooperative education programs:** natural science. **Faculty and instruction (2005-2006):** Total instructional faculty: 79 full-time, 32 part-time (47% men; 53% women; 9% minorities). Full-time faculty with Ph.D. or other terminal degree: 58%. Student/faculty ratio: 11/1. Classes of fewer than 20 students: 61%; of 20 to 49 students: 38%; of 50 or more students: 1%. **Advanced Placement and International Baccalaureate credit:** AP tests may be used for: Credit only. Scores accepted: 3, 4, 5. International Baccalaureate exams may be used for: Credit only. **Freshmen returning for sophomore year:** 64%. **Graduation rates:** Four-year: 29%; five-year: 40%; six-year: 44%. **Graduate study:** 13% of students pursue further study immediately upon graduation. Fields in which graduates pursue further study: Master of Business Administration (MBA), 29%; education, 19%; arts and sciences, 24%.

COSTS AND FINANCIAL AID

Financial aid office: (252) 399-6323. **Expenses (2005-2006):** Tuition and fees 2005-2006: $16,670; room/board: $5,880.

CAMPUS LIFE AND EXTRACURRICULAR ACTIVITIES

Campus housing available (% using): coed dorms (60%), women's dorms (27%), sorority housing (6%), fraternity housing, apartment for single students (7%), special housing for disabled students. Students who live in college-owned, operated, or affiliated housing: 51%. **Student employment:** During the 2005-2006 academic year, 5% of undergraduates worked on campus. Average per-year earnings: $2,500. **Clubs and organizations:** Number of student organizations: 39. Activities include: choral groups, drama/theater, literary magazine, musical theater, student government, student newspaper, symphony orchestra, television station. Number of fraternities: 4; sororities: 3. Proportion of men in fraternities: 14%; of women in sororities: 12%. Average proportion of students who stay on campus on weekends: 38%. **Sports program (2005-2006):** Member of NCAA II. *Men's intercollegiate varsity sports:* baseball, basketball, cross-country, golf, soccer, tennis. *Women's intercollegiate varsity sports:* basketball, cross-country, soccer, softball, tennis, volleyball.

SERVICES AND FACILITIES

Basic services: nonremedial tutoring, placement service, health service, health insurance. **Remedial assistance:** math, writing. **Counseling services:** career, personal, academic, birth control, religious. **For learning-disabled students:** School does not offer a structured program with separate admission and additional fees. Total undergraduates in learning-disabled program or receiving services: 31. Services include: remedial math, remedial English, reading machines, tape recorders, note-taking services, oral tests, learning center, readers, extended time for tests, tutors, priority seating, proofreading services, texts on tape, exams on tape or computer, other testing accomodations. **Library:** Number of titles: 176,095; number of current serial subscriptions: 14,901. **Information technology resources:** Students are not required to lease or own a computer. Number of campus computers available to all students: 210. School does not have a wireless network. Approximate number of users that can be accommodated: 50. Proportion of college-owned housing units wired for high-speed internet access: 100%. **Campus safety:** Security services offered: 24-hour foot-and-vehicle patrols, late-night transport/escort service, 24-hour emergency telephones, lighted pathways/sidewalks, controlled dormitory access (key, security card, etc).

TRANSFER AND INTERNATIONAL STUDENTS

Transfer students: May apply for admission for the following academic terms: Fall, Winter, Spring, Summer. Applicants do not need a minimum number of credits to apply. For fall 2005: Transfer applications received: 392. Transfer applicants offered admission: 229. Transfer applicants enrolled: 97. **International students:** Number of foreign undergraduates: 22 (2% of student body). Number of countries represented: 16. Minimum TOEFL score required: 525 (paper); 195 (computer).

Belmont Abbey College

- **Address:** 100 Belmont-Mount Holly Road, Belmont, NC 28012
- **Website:** http://www.belmontabbeycollege.edu
- **Private; Religious affiliation:** Roman Catholic
- **Enrollment:** 798 full-time; 89 part-time

KEY STATS

✔ **U.S News College Ranking:** 33, Comp. Colleges–Bachelor's (South)
✔ **SAT Score (25th/75th percentile):** 920-1130
✔ **Tuition:** 2006-2007: $17,728

Selectivity: Less selective	**Room/board:** $9,200
Acceptance rate: 76%	**Average debt:** $18,950
Student/faculty ratio: 14/1	**Proportion who borrowed:** 80%

UNDERGRADUATE STUDENT BODY STATS

2005-2006 enrollment: 798 full-time; 89 part-time. Men: 44%; women: 56%. **Ethnic makeup:** African American: 12%; Asian American: 1%; Hispanic: 4%; White: 77%; International: 6%. **Religious preference:** Protestant: 46%; No preference: 4%; Roman Catholic: 50%.

ADMISSIONS FACTS AND FIGURES

Phone: (704) 825-6665. **Email:** admissions@bac.edu. **Website:** http://www.belmontabbeycollege.edu. **Application deadlines for fall 2007:** Regular decision: August 1. Early decision: Not offered. Early action: Not offered. Admission can be deferred. **Application fee:** $35. Common application is not accepted. **Admissions requirements/recommendations:** High school units required (recommended): English: 4 (0); Mathematics: 3 (4); Science: 2 (0); Foreign language: 2 (3); Social studies: 2 (6); History: 0 (0); Academic electives: 3 (0); Total units: 16 (0). Tests: The college uses SAT or ACT scores in admissions decisions. Either SAT or ACT required. For admission to the fall 2007 entering class, the school will accept: ACT with writing, ACT without writing. Campus visit: Recommended. Admissions interview: Recommended. Off-campus interview: May be arranged. **Factors that count in admissions decisions:** *Academic:* Secondary school record: Very important. Class rank: Important. Letters of recommendation: Considered. Standardized test scores: Very important. Essay: Considered. *Nonacademic:* Interview: Important. Extracurricular activities: Considered. Talent/ability: Considered. Character/personal qualities: Important. Alumni/ae relationship: Not considered. Geographical residence: Not considered. State residency: Not considered. Religious affiliation/commitment: Not considered. Minority status: Not considered. Volunteer work: Considered. Work experience: Considered. **Other schools with the greatest overlap in applicants:**

Appalachian State University; East Carolina University; Lenoir-Rhyne College; University of North Carolina–Charlotte; University of North Carolina–Greensboro. **Admissions statistics for the fall 2005 entering class:** Total applicants: 901. Total accepted: 681. Freshmen enrolled: 227; 59% were from out of state. Overall acceptance rate: 76%. **Credentials of fall 2005 freshmen:** 4% ranked in the top 10 percent of their high school class; 13% were in the top 25 percent, and 43% were in the top half. (Proportion submitting class standing: 31%.) **Average high school grade point average:** 3.0. **First-year students who submitted SAT scores:** 84%. Scores (25/75 percentile): Verbal: 460-570, Math: 460-560, Combined: 920-1130. **First-year students submitting ACT scores:** 22%. Scores (25/75 percentile): English: 18-23, Math: 18-24, Composite: 18-23.

ACADEMICS

Year founded: 1876. **Academic calendar:** Semester. **Degrees offered:** bachelor's. **Most popular majors:** 40% business administration and management, 19% education, 6% psychology, 5% biology/biological sciences. **Major fields of study:** biological and biomedical sciences; business, management, marketing, and related support services; computer and information sciences and support services; education; English language and literature/letters; history; liberal arts and sciences studies, and humanities; philosophy and religious studies; psychology; social sciences; theology and religious vocations. **Areas of required coursework:** arts/fine arts, humanities, computer literacy, mathematics, English (including composition), philosophy, sciences (biological or physical), history, social science, other. **Pre-professional programs:** pre-law, pre-dentistry, pre-medicine, pre-theology, pre-veterinary science, pre-optometry, pre-pharmacy. **Special academic programs (% participation):** accelerated program (2%), cooperative (work-study plan) program (10%), double major (5%), dual enrollment (0%), honors program (2%), independent study (5%), internships (40%), study abroad (0%), teacher certificate program (10%). **Teacher certification offered in:** elementary. **Reserve Officers Training Corps (ROTC):** Army ROTC: Offered at cooperating institution (University of North Carolina–Charlotte); Navy ROTC: Offered at cooperating institution (University of North Carolina–Charlotte); Air Force ROTC: Offered at cooperating institution (University of North Carolina–Charlotte). **Faculty and instruction (2005-2006):** Total instructional faculty: 49 full-time, 37 part-time (56% men; 44% women; 2% minorities). Full-time faculty with Ph.D. or other terminal degree: 73%. Student/faculty ratio: 14/1. Classes of fewer than 20 students: 70%; of 20 to 49 students: 29%; of 50 or more students: 0%. **Advanced Placement and International Baccalaureate credit:** AP tests may be used for: Credit only. Scores accepted: 3, 4, 5. International Baccalaureate exams may be used for: Credit only. **Freshmen returning for sophomore year:** 60%. **Graduation rates:** Four-year: 29%; five-year: 41%; six-year: 44%. **Graduate study:** 24% of students pursue further study immediately upon graduation; 42% within one year; 77% within five years. Fields in which graduates pursue further study: Master of Business Administration (MBA), 26%; law, 10%; medicine, 3%; dentistry, 2%; theology (or the seminary), 4%; education, 21%; arts and sciences, 18%.

COSTS AND FINANCIAL AID

Financial aid office: (704) 825-6718. **Expenses (2006-2007):** Tuition and fees 2006-2007: $17,728; room/board: $9,200. Estimated books and supplies: $1,000; transportation: $2,300; personal expenses: $1,800. **Financial aid:** Priority filing date for institution's financial aid form: April 1. In 2005-2006, 80% of undergraduates applied for financial aid. Of those, 72% were determined to have financial need; 16% had their need fully met. Average financial aid package (proportion receiving): $12,113 (70%). Average amount of gift aid, such as scholarships or grants (proportion receiving): $9,029 (69%). Average amount of self-help aid, such as work study or loans (proportion receiving): $3,698 (60%). Average need-based loan (excluding PLUS or other private loans): $3,398. Among students who received need-based aid, the average percentage of need met: 57%. Among students who received aid based on merit, the average award (and the proportion receiving): $11,895 (28%). The average athletic scholarship (and the proportion receiving): $7,189 (8%). Average amount of debt of borrowers graduating in 2005: $18,950. Proportion who borrowed: 80%.

CAMPUS LIFE AND EXTRACURRICULAR ACTIVITIES

Campus housing available (% using): coed dorms (100%). Students who live in college-owned, operated, or affiliated housing: 55%. **Student employment:** During the 2005-2006 academic year, 25% of undergraduates worked on campus. Average per-year earnings: $2,500. **Clubs and organizations:** Number of student organizations: 29. Activities include: choral groups, drama/theater, literary magazine, musical theater, student government, student newspaper. Number of fraternities: 2; sororities: 4. Proportion of men in fraternities: 20%; of women in sororities: 20%. Average proportion of students who stay on campus on weekends: 70%. **Sports program (2005-2006):** Member of NCAA II. *Men's intercollegiate varsity sports:* baseball, basketball, cross-country, golf, lacrosse, soccer, tennis, wrestling. *Women's intercollegiate varsity sports:* basketball, cross-country, golf, lacrosse, soccer, softball, tennis, volleyball.

SERVICES AND FACILITIES
Basic services: nonremedial tutoring. **Counseling services:** career, academic, psychological, religious. **For learning-disabled students:** School does not offer a structured program with separate admission and additional fees. Total undergraduates in learning-disabled program or receiving services: 37. Services include: learning center, extended time for tests, tutors, priority registration, other testing accomodations, other. **Library:** Number of titles: 117,340; number of current serial subscriptions: 366. **Information technology resources:** Students are not required to lease or own a computer. Number of campus computers available to all students: 63. School does not have a wireless network. Approximate number of users that can be accommodated: 6,400. Proportion of college-owned housing units wired for high-speed internet access: 100%. **Campus safety:** Security services offered: 24-hour foot-and-vehicle patrols, 24-hour emergency telephones, lighted pathways/sidewalks, controlled dormitory access (key, security card, etc).

TRANSFER AND INTERNATIONAL STUDENTS
Transfer students: May apply for admission for the following academic terms: Fall, Spring. Applicants need a minimum number of credits to apply. For fall 2005: Transfer applications received: 239. Transfer applicants offered admission: 153. Transfer applicants enrolled: 81. **International students:** Number of foreign undergraduates: 53 (6% of student body). Number of countries represented: 20. Minimum TOEFL score required: 500 (paper); 173 (computer). Average TOEFL score: 620 (paper).

Bennett College

- **Address:** 900 E. Washington Street, Greensboro, NC 27401
- **Website:** http://www.bennett.edu
- **Private; Religious affiliation:** United Methodist
- **Enrollment:** 566 full-time; 6 part-time

KEY STATS
- ✔ **U.S News College Ranking:** fourth tier, Liberal Arts Colleges
- ✔ **SAT Score (25th/75th percentile):** 720-890
- ✔ **Tuition:** 2006-2007: $14,150

Selectivity: Least selective	**Room/board:** $6,258
Acceptance rate: 57%	**Average debt:** $15,539
Student/faculty ratio: 10/1	**Proportion who borrowed:** 96%

UNDERGRADUATE STUDENT BODY STATS
2005-2006 enrollment: 566 full-time; 6 part-time. Men: 0%; women: 100%. **Ethnic makeup:** African American: 95%; Hispanic: 2%; White: 1%; International: 1%.

ADMISSIONS FACTS AND FIGURES
Phone: (336) 370-8624. **Email:** admiss@bennett.edu. **Website:** http://www.bennett.edu. **Application deadlines for fall 2007:** Regular decision: Rolling. Early decision: Not offered. Early action: Not offered. Admission can be deferred. **Application fee:** $30. Common application is accepted. **To apply online, go to:** http://www.ncmentor.org/applications/nc_independents_common_app/apply.html?application_id=1556. **Admissions requirements/recommendations:** High school units required (recommended): English: 4 (4); Mathematics: 3 (3); Science: 2 (2); Foreign language: 2 (2); Social studies: 2 (2); History: 0 (0); Academic electives: 5 (5); Total units: 17 (17). Tests: The college uses SAT or ACT scores in admissions decisions. Either SAT or ACT required. For admission to the fall 2007 entering class, the school will accept: ACT with writing, ACT without writing. Campus visit: Recommended. Admissions interview: Neither required nor recommended. Off-campus interview: Not available. **Factors that count in admissions decisions:** *Academic:* Secondary school record: Very important. Class rank: Important. Letters of recommendation: Very important. Standardized test scores: Important. Essay: Very important. *Nonacademic:* Interview: Not considered. Extracurricular activities: Considered. Talent/ability: Considered. Character/personal qualities: Important. Alumni/ae relationship: Important. Geographical residence: Not considered. State

residency: Not considered. Religious affiliation/commitment: Not considered. Minority status: Not considered. Volunteer work: Important. Work experience: Considered. **Other schools with the greatest overlap in applicants:** Greensboro College; Guilford College; North Carolina A&T State University; North Carolina Central University; University of North Carolina–Greensboro. **Admissions statistics for the fall 2005 entering class:** Total applicants: 1,010. Total accepted: 577. Freshmen enrolled: 239; 75% were from out of state. Overall acceptance rate: 57%. **Credentials of fall 2005 freshmen:** 5% ranked in the top 10 percent of their high school class; 14% were in the top 25 percent, and 37% were in the top half. (Proportion submitting class standing: 66%.) **Average high school grade point average:** 2.5. **First-year students who submitted SAT scores:** 80%. Scores (25/75 percentile): Verbal: 360-460, Math: 360-430, Combined: 720-890. **First-year students submitting ACT scores:** 36%. Scores (25/75 percentile): English: 13-14, Math: 18-17, Composite: 13-18.

ACADEMICS
Year founded: 1873. **Academic calendar:** Semester. **Degrees offered:** bachelor's. **Most popular majors:** 25% biology/biological sciences, 13% mass communication/media studies, 12% psychology, 9% English language and literature, 7% multi/interdisciplinary studies. **Major fields of study:** biological and biomedical sciences; business, management, marketing, and related support services; communication, journalism, and related programs; computer and information sciences and support services; education; English language and literature/letters; health professions and related clinical sciences; mathematics and statistics; multi/interdisciplinary studies; psychology; public administration and social service professions; social sciences. **Areas of required coursework:** computer literacy, mathematics, English (including composition), foreign languages, sciences (biological or physical). **Special academic programs (% participation):** cooperative (work-study plan) program (10%), cross-registration (2%), internships, teacher certificate program. **Teacher certification offered in:** special education, elementary, middle/junior high, secondary. **Cooperative education programs:** engineering. **Reserve Officers Training Corps (ROTC):** Army ROTC: Offered at cooperating institution (North Carolina State A&T). **Faculty and instruction (2005-2006):** Total instructional faculty: 49 full-time, 17 part-time (39% men; 61% women; 71% minorities). Full-time faculty with Ph.D. or other terminal degree: 71%. Student/faculty ratio: 10/1. Classes of fewer than 20 students: 73%; of 20 to 49 students: 27%. **Advanced Placement and International Baccalaureate credit:** AP tests may be used for: Credit only. Scores accepted: 4, 5. International Baccalaureate exams may be used for: Credit and/or placement. **Freshmen returning for sophomore year:** 70%. **Graduation rates:** Four-year: 22%; five-year: 30%; six-year: 37%. **Graduate study:** 16% of students pursue further study immediately upon graduation; 32% within one year; 50% within five years.

COSTS AND FINANCIAL AID
Financial aid office: (336) 517-2205. **Expenses (2006-2007):** Tuition and fees 2006-2007: $14,150; room/board: $6,258. Estimated books and supplies: $1,200; transportation: $2,500; personal expenses: $3,000. **Financial aid:** Priority filing date for institution's financial aid form: March 15. In 2005-2006, 93% of undergraduates applied for financial aid. Of those, 86% were determined to have financial need; 4% had their need fully met. Average financial aid package (proportion receiving): $9,036 (85%). Average amount of gift aid, such as scholarships or grants (proportion receiving): $6,827 (73%). Average amount of self-help aid, such as work study or loans (proportion receiving): $3,469 (78%). Average need-based loan (excluding PLUS or other private loans): $3,183. Among students who received need-based aid, the average percentage of need met: 42%. Among students who received aid based on merit, the average award (and the proportion receiving): $14,393 (9%). The average athletic scholarship (and the proportion receiving): $0 (0%). Average amount of debt of borrowers graduating in 2005: $15,539. Proportion who borrowed: 96%.

CAMPUS LIFE AND EXTRACURRICULAR ACTIVITIES
Campus housing available (% using): women's dorms (100%). Students who live in college-owned, operated, or affiliated housing: 77%. **Clubs and organizations:** Number of student organizations: 50. Activities include: choral groups, dance, drama/theater, music ensembles, student government, student newspaper, yearbook. Number of fraternities: 0; sororities: 3. Average proportion of students who stay on campus on weekends: 45%. **Sports program (2005-2006):** Member of NCAA III. *Women's intercollegiate varsity sports:* basketball.

SERVICES AND FACILITIES

Basic services: nonremedial tutoring, women's center, placement service, day care, health service. **Remedial assistance:** reading, math, writing, study skills. **Counseling services:** career, personal, academic, psychological, birth control, religious. **For learning-disabled students:** Services include: remedial math, remedial English, reading machines, remedial reading, tape recorders, oral tests, learning center, extended time for tests, tutors, priority registration, priority seating, texts on tape, other testing accomodations. **Library:** Number of titles: 125,649; number of current serial subscriptions: 617. **Information technology resources:** Students are not required to lease or own a computer. Number of campus computers available to all students: 130. School does not have a wireless network. **Campus safety:** Security services offered: 24-hour foot-and-vehicle patrols, late-night transport/escort service, 24-hour emergency telephones, lighted pathways/sidewalks.

TRANSFER AND INTERNATIONAL STUDENTS

Transfer students: May apply for admission for the following academic terms: Fall, Spring. Applicants need a minimum number of credits to apply. For fall 2005: Transfer applications received: 50. Transfer applicants offered admission: 29. Transfer applicants enrolled: 22. **International students:** Number of foreign undergraduates: 8 (1% of student body). Number of countries represented: 5.

Brevard College

- **Address:** 400 N. Broad Street, Brevard, NC 28712
- **Website:** http://www.brevard.edu
- **Private; Religious affiliation:** Methodist
- **Enrollment:** 572 full-time; 25 part-time

KEY STATS

- ✔ **U.S News College Ranking:** 46, Comp. Colleges–Bachelor's (South)
- ✔ **SAT Score (25th/75th percentile):** 789-1245
- ✔ **Tuition:** 2006-2007: $17,820

Selectivity: Less selective	**Room/board:** $6,150
Acceptance rate: 74%	**Average debt:** $19,293
Student/faculty ratio: 9/1	**Proportion who borrowed:** 63%

UNDERGRADUATE STUDENT BODY STATS

2005-2006 enrollment: 572 full-time; 25 part-time. Men: 53%; women: 47%. **Ethnic makeup:** African American: 4%; American-Indian: 1%; Hispanic: 3%; White: 89%; International: 3%. **Religious preference:** Roman Catholic: 6%; Protestant: 29%; Jewish: 1%; No preference: 48%; Methodist: 14%; Other: 1%.

ADMISSIONS FACTS AND FIGURES

Phone: (828) 884-8300. **Email:** admissions@brevard.edu. **Website:** http://www.brevard.edu. **Application deadlines for fall 2007:** Regular decision: Rolling. Early decision: Not offered. Early action: Not offered. Admission can be deferred. **Application fee:** $30. Common application is accepted. **To apply online, go to:** http://brevard.edu/admissions/apply.asp. **Admissions requirements/recommendations:** High school units required (recommended): English: 4 (4); Mathematics: 3 (3); Science: 3 (3); Foreign language: 2 (2); Social studies: 4 (4); History: 1 (1); Academic electives: 4 (4); Total units: 22 (22). Tests: The college uses SAT or ACT scores in admissions decisions. Either SAT or ACT required. For admission to the fall 2007 entering class, the school will accept: ACT without writing. Campus visit: Recommended. Admissions interview: Recommended. Off-campus interview: May be arranged. **Factors that count in admissions decisions:** *Academic:* Secondary school record: Very important. Class rank: Important. Letters of recommendation: Considered. Standardized test scores: Important. Essay: Important. *Nonacademic:* Interview: Important. Extracurricular activities: Important. Talent/ability: Important. Character/personal qualities: Important. Alumni/ae relationship: Considered. Geographical residence: Not considered. State residency: Not considered. Religious affiliation/commitment: Considered. Minority status: Not considered. Volunteer work: Important. Work experience: Considered. **Other schools with the greatest overlap in applicants:** Appalachian State University; Lenoir-Rhyne College; Mars Hill College; University of North Carolina–Asheville; Warren Wilson College. **Admissions statistics for the fall 2005 entering class:** Total applicants: 590. Total accepted: 435. Freshmen enrolled: 148; 55% were from out of state. Overall acceptance rate: 74%.

Credentials of fall 2005 freshmen: 7% ranked in the top 10 percent of their high school class; 23% were in the top 25 percent, and 54% were in the top half. (Proportion submitting class standing: 59%.) **Average high school grade point average:** 3.1. **First-year students who submitted SAT scores:** 82%. Scores (25/75 percentile): Verbal: 392-627, Math: 397-618, Combined: 789-1245. **First-year students submitting ACT scores:** 32%. Scores (25/75 percentile): English: 14-26, Math: 15-24, Composite: 15-25.

ACADEMICS

Year founded: 1853. **Academic calendar:** Semester. **Degrees offered:** bachelor's. **Most popular majors:** 27% visual and performing arts, 20% parks, recreation, and leisure studies, 14% business administration and management, 9% environmental studies, 9% multi/interdisciplinary studies. **Major fields of study:** biological and biomedical sciences; business, management, marketing, and related support services; education; English language and literature/letters; health professions and related clinical sciences; history; legal professions and studies; mathematics and statistics; multi/interdisciplinary studies; natural resources and conservation; parks, recreation, leisure, and fitness studies; philosophy and religious studies; psychology; visual and performing arts. **Areas of required coursework:** arts/fine arts, humanities, computer literacy, mathematics, English (including composition), philosophy, foreign languages, sciences (biological or physical), history, social science, other. **Pre-professional programs:** pre-law, pre-dentistry, pre-medicine, pre-theology, pre-veterinary science, pre-pharmacy. **Special academic programs (% participation):** double major (2%), dual enrollment (4%), honors program (6%), independent study (80%), internships (85%), student-designed major (12%), study abroad (41%). **Teacher certification offered in:** elementary, middle/junior high, secondary. **Faculty and instruction (2005-2006):** Total instructional faculty: 56 full-time, 28 part-time (58% men; 42% women; 0% minorities). Full-time faculty with Ph.D. or other terminal degree: 61%. Student/faculty ratio: 9/1. Classes of fewer than 20 students: 82%; of 20 to 49 students: 18%; of 50 or more students: 0%. **Advanced Placement and International Baccalaureate credit:** AP tests may be used for: Credit only. Scores accepted: 3, 4, 5. International Baccalaureate exams may be used for: Credit only. **Freshmen returning for sophomore year:** 60%. **Graduation rates:** Four-year: 21%; five-year: 30%; six-year: 22%.

COSTS AND FINANCIAL AID

Financial aid office: (828) 884-8287. **Expenses (2006-2007):** Tuition and fees 2006-2007: $17,820; room/board: $6,150. Estimated books and supplies: $1,000; transportation: $1,000; personal expenses: $1,000. **Financial aid:** Priority filing date for institution's financial aid form: April 15. In 2005-2006, 73% of undergraduates applied for financial aid. Of those, 63% were determined to have financial need; 29% had their need fully met. Average financial aid package (proportion receiving): $15,245 (62%). Average amount of gift aid, such as scholarships or grants (proportion receiving): $10,172 (62%). Average amount of self-help aid, such as work study or loans (proportion receiving): $4,030 (55%). Average need-based loan (excluding PLUS or other private loans): $3,829. Among students who received need-based aid, the average percentage of need met: 82%. Among students who received aid based on merit, the average award (and the proportion receiving): $6,015 (16%). The average athletic scholarship (and the proportion receiving): $4,278 (11%). Average amount of debt of borrowers graduating in 2005: $19,293. Proportion who borrowed: 63%.

CAMPUS LIFE AND EXTRACURRICULAR ACTIVITIES

Campus housing available (% using): coed dorms (66%), women's dorms (16%), men's dorms (17%). Students who live in college-owned, operated, or affiliated housing: 71%. **Clubs and organizations:** Number of student organizations: 21. Activities include: choral groups, concert band, dance, drama/theater, jazz band, literary magazine, music ensembles, musical theater, opera, pep band, student government, student newspaper, yearbook. Number of fraternities: 0; sororities: 0. Average proportion of students who stay on campus on weekends: 50%. **Sports program (2005-2006):** Member of NAIA. *Men's intercollegiate varsity sports:* baseball, basketball, cheerleading, cross-country, golf, soccer, tennis, track and field (indoor), track and field (outdoor). *Women's intercollegiate varsity sports:* basketball, cheerleading, cross-country, soccer, softball, tennis, track and field (indoor), track and field (outdoor), volleyball.

SERVICES AND FACILITIES

Basic services: nonremedial tutoring, health service, health insurance. **Remedial assistance:** reading, math, writing, study skills. **Counseling services:** minority student, career, personal, veteran student, academic, psychological, birth control, religious. **For learning-disabled students:** School does not offer a structured program with separate admission and additional fees.

Total undergraduates in learning-disabled program or receiving services: 54. Services include: remedial math, other testing accommodations, reading machines, remedial reading, tape recorders, untimed tests, note-taking services, oral tests, learning center, readers, extended time for tests, tutors, priority registration, priority seating, substitution of courses, texts on tape, typist/scribe, exams on tape or computer, take home exams, other testing accomodations, other. **Library:** Number of titles: 57,996; number of current serial subscriptions: 20,455. **Information technology resources:** Students are not required to lease or own a computer. Number of campus computers available to all students: 78. School does not have a wireless network. Proportion of college-owned housing units wired for high-speed internet access: 100%. **Campus safety:** Security services offered: 24-hour foot-and-vehicle patrols, late-night transport/escort service, 24-hour emergency telephones, controlled dormitory access (key, security card, etc).

TRANSFER AND INTERNATIONAL STUDENTS
Transfer students: May apply for admission for the following academic terms: Fall, Spring, Summer. Applicants do not need a minimum number of credits to apply. For fall 2005: Transfer applications received: 145. Transfer applicants offered admission: 110. Transfer applicants enrolled: 62. **International students:** Number of foreign undergraduates: 16 (3% of student body). Number of countries represented: 9. Minimum TOEFL score required: 500 (paper); 203 (computer). Average TOEFL score: 550 (paper).

Campbell University

- **Address:** PO Box 546, Buies Creek, NC 27506
- **Website:** http://www.campbell.edu
- **Private; Religious affiliation:** Baptist
- **Enrollment:** 2,566 full-time; 126 part-time

KEY STATS
- ✔ **U.S News College Ranking:** 44, Universities–Master's (South)
- ✔ **SAT Score (25th/75th percentile):** 1005-1250
- ✔ **Tuition:** 2006-2007: $17,116

Selectivity: More selective	**Room/board:** $5,780
Acceptance rate: 61%	**Average debt:** $14,200
Student/faculty ratio: 12/1	**Proportion who borrowed:** 65%

UNDERGRADUATE STUDENT BODY STATS
2005-2006 enrollment: 2,566 full-time; 126 part-time. Men: 44%; women: 56%. **Religious preference:** Roman Catholic: 7%; Protestant: 1%; Hindu: 1%; No preference: 16%; Baptist: 40%; Christian: 12%; Other: 23%.

ADMISSIONS FACTS AND FIGURES
Phone: (910) 893-1320. **Email:** adm@mailcenter.campbell.edu. **Website:** http://www.campbell.edu. **Application deadlines for fall 2007:** Regular decision: September 1. Early decision: Not offered. Early action: Not offered. Admission can be deferred. **Application fee:** $35. Common application is accepted. **Admissions requirements/recommendations:** High school units required (recommended): English: 4; Mathematics: 3; Science: 2; Foreign language: 2; Social studies: 2; Total units: 13. Tests: The college uses SAT or ACT scores in admissions decisions. Either SAT or ACT required. For admission to the fall 2007 entering class, the school will accept: ACT with writing. Campus visit: Recommended. Admissions interview: Recommended. Off-campus interview: Not available. **Factors that count in admissions decisions:** *Academic:* Secondary school record: Very important. Class rank: Important. Letters of recommendation: Considered. Standardized test scores: Very important. Essay: Considered. *Nonacademic:* Interview: Important. Extracurricular activities: Considered. Talent/ability: Considered. Character/personal qualities: Important. Alumni/ae relationship: Considered. Geographical residence: Not considered. State residency: Not considered. Religious affiliation/commitment: Not considered. Minority status: Not considered. Volunteer work: Considered. Work experience: Considered. **Other schools with the greatest overlap in applicants:** Appalachian State University; East Carolina University; North Carolina State University–Raleigh; University of North Carolina–Chapel Hill; Wake Forest University. **Admissions statistics for the fall 2005 entering class:** Total applicants: 2,804. Total accepted: 1,709. Freshmen enrolled: 730; Overall acceptance rate: 61%. **Credentials of fall 2005 freshmen:** 37% ranked in the top 10 percent of their high school class; 78% were in the top 25 percent, and 89% were in the top half. (Proportion submitting class standing: 94%.) **Average**

high school grade point average: 3.6. **First-year students who submitted SAT scores:** 91%. Scores (25/75 percentile): Verbal: 510-620, Math: 495-630, Combined: 1005-1250. **First-year students submitting ACT scores:** 9%. Scores (25/75 percentile): English: N/A, Math: N/A, Composite: N/A.

ACADEMICS
Year founded: 1887. **Academic calendar:** Semester. **Degrees offered:** associate, bachelor's, master's, first professional, doctorate. **Most popular majors:** Information not available. **Major fields of study:** biological and biomedical sciences; business, management, marketing, and related support services; communication, journalism, and related programs; computer and information sciences and support services; education; English language and literature/letters; family and consumer sciences/human sciences; foreign languages, literatures, and linguistics; health professions and related clinical sciences; legal professions and studies; mathematics and statistics; parks, recreation, leisure, and fitness studies; philosophy and religious studies; psychology; public administration and social service professions; security and protective services; social sciences; theology and religious vocations; visual and performing arts. **Areas of required coursework:** arts/fine arts, humanities, computer literacy, mathematics, English (including composition), foreign languages, sciences (biological or physical), history, social science. **Pre-professional programs:** pre-law, pre-dentistry, pre-medicine, pre-veterinary science, pre-pharmacy, other. **Special academic programs:** accelerated program, cooperative (work-study plan) program, distance learning, double major, dual enrollment, honors program, independent study, internships, liberal arts/career combination, study abroad, teacher certificate program. **Teacher certification offered in:** elementary, middle/junior high, secondary. **Cooperative education programs:** education. **Reserve Officers Training Corps (ROTC):** Army ROTC: Offered on campus. **Faculty and instruction (2005-2006):** Total instructional faculty: 188 full-time, 148 part-time (53% men; 47% women; 4% minorities). Full-time faculty with Ph.D. or other terminal degree: 89%. Student/faculty ratio: 12/1. Classes of fewer than 20 students: 57%; of 20 to 49 students: 33%; of 50 or more students: 11%. **Advanced Placement and International Baccalaureate credit:** AP tests may be used for: Credit and/or placement. Scores accepted: 3, 4, 5. International Baccalaureate exams may be used for: Credit and/or placement. **Freshmen returning for sophomore year:** 79%. **Graduation rates:** Six-year: 50%.

COSTS AND FINANCIAL AID
Financial aid office: (910) 893-1310. **Expenses (2006-2007):** Tuition and fees 2006-2007: $17,116; room/board: $5,780. Estimated books and supplies: $1,100; transportation: $990; personal expenses: $3,314. **Financial aid:** Priority filing date for institution's financial aid form: March 15. In 2005-2006, 67% of undergraduates applied for financial aid. Of those, 57% were determined to have financial need; 20% had their need fully met. Average financial aid package (proportion receiving): $12,204 (57%). Average amount of gift aid, such as scholarships or grants (proportion receiving): $4,083 (39%). Average amount of self-help aid, such as work study or loans (proportion receiving): $4,769 (47%). Average need-based loan (excluding PLUS or other private loans): $4,382. Among students who received need-based aid, the average percentage of need met: 100%. Among students who received aid based on merit, the average award (and the proportion receiving): $6,134 (14%). The average athletic scholarship (and the proportion receiving): $12,475 (2%). Average amount of debt of borrowers graduating in 2005: $14,200. Proportion who borrowed: 65%.

CAMPUS LIFE AND EXTRACURRICULAR ACTIVITIES
Campus housing available: women's dorms, men's dorms, apartments for married students, apartment for single students, special housing for disabled students. **Student employment:** During the 2005-2006 academic year, 15% of undergraduates worked on campus. Average per-year earnings: $1,200. **Clubs and organizations:** Number of student organizations: 50. Activities include: choral groups, concert band, drama/theater, jazz band, literary magazine, music ensembles, musical theater, pep band, radio station, student government, student newspaper, yearbook. Number of fraternities: 0; sororities: 0. Average proportion of students who stay on campus on weekends: 80%. **Sports program (2005-2006):** Member of NCAA I. *Men's intercollegiate varsity sports:* baseball, basketball, cross-country, golf, soccer, tennis, track and field (indoor), track and field (outdoor), wrestling. *Women's intercollegiate varsity sports:* basketball, cross-country, golf, soccer, softball, swimming and diving, tennis, track and field (indoor), track and field (outdoor), volleyball.

SERVICES AND FACILITIES

Basic services: nonremedial tutoring, placement service, health service. **Remedial assistance:** study skills, other. **Counseling services:** career, personal, veteran student, academic, older student, psychological, religious. **For learning-disabled students:** School does not offer a structured program with separate admission and additional fees. Total undergraduates in learning-disabled program or receiving services: 46. Services include: remedial math, remedial English, tape recorders, untimed tests, note-taking services, oral tests, readers, extended time for tests, tutors, early syllabus, priority seating, proofreading services, texts on tape, typist/scribe, exams on tape or computer, other testing accomodations, waiver of foreign language degree requirement. **Library:** Number of titles: 268,000; number of current serial subscriptions: 12,645. **Information technology resources:** Students are not required to lease or own a computer. Number of campus computers available to all students: 250. School has a wireless network. Proportion of college-owned housing units wired for high-speed internet access: 85%. **Campus safety:** Security services offered: 24-hour foot-and-vehicle patrols, late-night transport/escort service, lighted pathways/sidewalks, controlled dormitory access (key, security card, etc).

TRANSFER AND INTERNATIONAL STUDENTS

Transfer students: May apply for admission for the following academic terms: Fall, Spring, Summer. Applicants do not need a minimum number of credits to apply. **International students:** Minimum TOEFL score required: 500 (paper); 173 (computer). Average TOEFL score: 557 (paper).

Catawba College

- **Address:** 2300 W. Innes Street, Salisbury, NC 28144
- **Website:** http://www.catawba.edu
- **Private; Religious affiliation:** United Church of Christ
- **Enrollment:** 1,222 full-time; 34 part-time

KEY STATS

✔ **U.S News College Ranking:** 23, Comp. Colleges–Bachelor's (South)
✔ **SAT Score (25th/75th percentile):** 940-1130
✔ **Tuition:** 2006-2007: $19,690

Selectivity: Selective	**Room/board:** $6,570
Acceptance rate: 68%	**Average debt:** $18,731
Student/faculty ratio: 15/1	**Proportion who borrowed:** 78%

UNDERGRADUATE STUDENT BODY STATS

2005-2006 enrollment: 1,222 full-time; 34 part-time. Men: 48%; women: 52%. **Ethnic makeup:** African American: 16%; American-Indian: 1%; Asian American: 1%; Hispanic: 1%; White: 80%; International: 2%. **Religious preference:** Roman Catholic: 16%; Protestant: 65%; Jewish: 1%; No preference: 14%; United Church of Christ: 4%.

ADMISSIONS FACTS AND FIGURES

Phone: (800) 228-2922. **Email:** admission@catawba.edu. **Website:** http://www.catawba.edu. **Application deadlines for fall 2007:** Regular decision: Rolling. Early decision: Not offered. Early action: Not offered. Admission can be deferred. **Application fee:** $25. Common application is accepted. **To apply online, go to:** http://www.applyweb.com/aw?catawba. **Admissions requirements/recommendations:** High school units required (recommended): English: 4 (4); Mathematics: 2 (3); Science: 2 (3); Foreign language: (2); Social studies: 2 (2); Academic electives: (2); Total units: 16. **Tests:** The college uses SAT or ACT scores in admissions decisions. Either SAT or ACT required. For admission to the fall 2007 entering class, the school will accept: ACT with writing. Campus visit: Recommended. Admissions interview: Recommended. Off-campus interview: May be arranged. **Factors that count in admissions decisions:** *Academic:* Secondary school record: Important. Class rank: Very important. Letters of recommendation: Important. Standardized test scores: Very important. Essay: Very important. *Nonacademic:* Interview: Important. Extracurricular activities: Important. Talent/ability: Important. Character/personal qualities: Important. Alumni/ae relationship: Not considered. Geographical residence: Not considered. State residency: Not considered. Religious affiliation/commitment: Not considered. Minority status: Not considered. Volunteer work: Considered. Work experience: Considered. **Other schools with the greatest overlap in applicants:** Appalachian State University; Elon University; North Carolina State University–Raleigh; University of North Carolina–Charlotte; University of North Carolina–Greensboro. **Admissions statistics for the fall 2005 entering class:** Total applicants: 724. Total accepted: 492. Freshmen enrolled: 223; 45% were from out of state. Overall acceptance rate: 68%. **Credentials of fall 2005 freshmen:** 16% ranked in the top 10 percent of their high school class; 39% were in the top 25 percent, and 75% were in the top half. (Proportion submitting class standing: 78%.) **Average high school grade point average:** 3.3. **First-year students who submitted SAT scores:** 87%. Scores (25/75 percentile): Verbal: 460-560; Math: 480-570, Combined: 940-1130. **First-year students submitting ACT scores:** 15%. Scores (25/75 percentile): English: 17-25, Math: 18-26, Composite: 19-25.

ACADEMICS

Year founded: 1851. **Academic calendar:** Semester. **Degrees offered:** bachelor's, master's. **Most popular majors:** 40% business administration, management, and operations, 18% computer and information sciences, 8% teacher education and professional development, 6% communication, journalism, and related programs, 5% social sciences. **Major fields of study:** biological and biomedical sciences; business, management, marketing, and related support services; communication, journalism, and related programs; computer and information sciences and support services; education; English language and literature/letters; foreign languages, literatures, and linguistics; health professions and related clinical sciences; history; legal professions and studies; mathematics and statistics; natural resources and conservation; parks, recreation, leisure, and fitness studies; philosophy and religious studies; physical sciences; psychology; social sciences; visual and performing arts. **Areas of required coursework:** arts/fine arts, humanities, computer literacy, mathematics, English (including composition), foreign languages, sciences (biological or physical), social science. **Pre-professional programs:** pre-law, pre-medicine. **Special academic programs:** cross-registration, double major, honors program, independent study, internships, liberal arts/career combination, student-designed major, study abroad, teacher certificate program. **Teacher certification offered in:** elementary, middle/junior high, secondary. **Reserve Officers Training Corps (ROTC):** Army ROTC: Offered at cooperating institution (UNC Charlotte). **Faculty and instruction (2005-2006):** Total instructional faculty: 72 full-time, 26 part-time (58% men; 42% women; 2% minorities). Full-time faculty with Ph.D. or other terminal degree: 83%. Student/faculty ratio: 15/1. Classes of fewer than 20 students: 66%; of 20 to 49 students: 34%; of 50 or more students: 0%. **Advanced Placement and International Baccalaureate credit:** AP tests may be used for: Credit only. Scores accepted: 3, 4, 5. International Baccalaureate exams may be used for: Credit only. **Freshmen returning for sophomore year:** 68%. **Graduation rates:** Four-year: 32%; five-year: 43%; six-year: 43%.

COSTS AND FINANCIAL AID

Financial aid office: (704) 637-4416. **Expenses (2006-2007):** Tuition and fees 2006-2007: $19,690; room/board: $6,570. Estimated books and supplies: $800; transportation: $1,200; personal expenses: $1,200. **Financial aid:** Priority filing date for institution's financial aid form: March 15. In 2005-2006, 86% of undergraduates applied for financial aid. Of those, 68% were determined to have financial need; 32% had their need fully met. Average financial aid package (proportion receiving): $14,174 (68%). Average amount of gift aid, such as scholarships or grants (proportion receiving): $4,256 (45%). Average amount of self-help aid, such as work study or loans (proportion receiving): $4,619 (51%). Average need-based loan (excluding PLUS or other private loans): $4,431. Among students who received need-based aid, the average percentage of need met: 81%. Among students who received aid based on merit, the average award (and the proportion receiving): $6,628 (10%). The average athletic scholarship (and the proportion receiving): $5,456 (22%). Average amount of debt of borrowers graduating in 2005: $18,731. Proportion who borrowed: 78%.

CAMPUS LIFE AND EXTRACURRICULAR ACTIVITIES

Campus housing available (% using): coed dorms (47%), women's dorms (16%), men's dorms (37%). Students who live in college-owned, operated, or affiliated housing: 48%. Average per-year earnings: $3,000. Activities include: choral groups, concert band, dance, drama/theater, jazz band, literary magazine, music ensembles, musical theater, pep band, student government, student newspaper, symphony orchestra, yearbook. Number of fraternities: 0; sororities: 0. Average proportion of students who stay on campus on weekends: 70%. **Sports program (2005-2006):** Member of NCAA II. *Men's intercollegiate varsity sports:* baseball, basketball, cross-country, football, golf, lacrosse, soccer, tennis. *Women's intercollegiate varsity sports:* basketball, cross-country, field hockey, golf, soccer, softball, swimming and diving, tennis, volleyball.

SERVICES AND FACILITIES

Basic services: nonremedial tutoring, placement service, health service, health insurance. **Counseling services:** career, personal, academic, older student, psychological, birth control, religious. **For learning-disabled students:** School does not offer a structured program with separate admission and additional fees. Services include: untimed tests, tutors, other testing accomodations. **Library:** Number of titles: 181,245; number of current serial subscriptions: 594. **Information technology resources:** Students are not required to lease or own a computer. Number of campus computers available to all students: 170. School has a wireless network. Proportion of college-owned housing units wired for high-speed internet access: 96%. **Campus safety:** Security services offered: 24-hour foot-and-vehicle patrols, late-night transport/escort service, 24-hour emergency telephones, lighted pathways/sidewalks, controlled dormitory access (key, security card, etc).

TRANSFER AND INTERNATIONAL STUDENTS

Transfer students: May apply for admission for the following academic terms: Fall, Spring, Summer. Applicants do not need a minimum number of credits to apply. For fall 2005: Transfer applications received: 157. Transfer applicants offered admission: 121. Transfer applicants enrolled: 97. **International students:** Number of foreign undergraduates: 19 (2% of student body). Number of countries represented: 22. Minimum TOEFL score required: 525 (paper); 197 (computer).

Chowan College

- **Address:** 200 Jones Drive, Murfreesboro, NC 27855
- **Website:** http://www.chowan.edu
- **Private; Religious affiliation:** Baptist
- **Enrollment:** 760 full-time; 36 part-time

KEY STATS

✔ **U.S News College Ranking:** fourth tier, Comp. Coll.–Bachelor's (South)
✔ **SAT Score (25th/75th percentile):** 760-980
✔ **Tuition:** 2006-2007: $15,950

Selectivity: Less selective	**Room/board:** $6,800
Acceptance rate: 58%	**Average debt:** $23,370
Student/faculty ratio: 14/1	**Proportion who borrowed:** 80%

UNDERGRADUATE STUDENT BODY STATS

2005-2006 enrollment: 760 full-time; 36 part-time. Men: 55%; women: 45%. **Ethnic makeup:** African American: 37%; American-Indian: 1%; Asian American: 1%; Hispanic: 3%; White: 57%; International: 1%. **Religious preference:** Roman Catholic: 1%; Protestant: 41%; No preference: 3%; Unknown: 9%; Baptist: 46%.

ADMISSIONS FACTS AND FIGURES

Phone: (252) 398-1236. **Email:** admission@chowan.edu. **Website:** http://www.chowan.edu. **Application deadlines for fall 2007:** Regular decision: Rolling. Early decision: Not offered. Early action: Not offered. Admission can be deferred. **Application fee:** $20. Common application is not accepted. **To apply online, go to:** http://www.chowan.edu/admis/appli_secure.htm. **Admissions requirements/recommendations:** High school units required (recommended): English: (4); Mathematics: (3); Science: (2); Social studies: (3); Academic electives: (8). Tests: The college uses SAT or ACT scores in admissions decisions. Either SAT or ACT required. For admission to the fall 2007 entering class, the school will accept: ACT with writing, ACT without writing. Campus visit: Recommended. Admissions interview: Recommended. Off-campus interview: May be arranged. **Factors that count in admissions decisions:** *Academic:* Secondary school record: Very important. Class rank: Considered. Letters of recommendation: Considered. Standardized test scores: Very important. Essay: Considered. *Nonacademic:* Interview: Considered. Extracurricular activities: Important. Talent/ability: Important. Character/personal qualities: Considered. Alumni/ae relationship: Considered. Geographical residence: Considered. State residency: Not considered. Religious affiliation/commitment: Not considered. Minority status: Not considered. Volunteer work: Considered. Work experience: Considered. **Other schools with the greatest overlap in applicants:** Campbell University; Mars Hill College; Meredith College; North Carolina Wesleyan College; Virginia Wesleyan College. **Admissions statistics for the fall 2005 entering class:** Total applicants: 2,270. Total accepted: 1,320. Freshmen enrolled: 286; 50% were from out of state. Overall acceptance rate: 58%.

Credentials of fall 2005 freshmen: 4% ranked in the top 10 percent of their high school class; 18% were in the top 25 percent, and 34% were in the top half. (Proportion submitting class standing: 74%.) **Average high school grade point average:** 2.6. **First-year students who submitted SAT scores:** 90%. Scores (25/75 percentile): Verbal: 370-490, Math: 390-490, Combined: 760-980. **First-year students submitting ACT scores:** 25%. Scores (25/75 percentile): English: N/A, Math: N/A, Composite: 15-19.

ACADEMICS

Year founded: 1848. **Academic calendar:** Semester. **Degrees offered:** associate, bachelor's, post-bachelor's certificate. **Most popular majors:** 13% education, 12% biology, 12% business administration and management, 12% graphic communications, 9% physical education teaching and coaching. **Major fields of study:** biological and biomedical sciences; business, management, marketing, and related support services; communications technologies/technicians and support services; education; English language and literature/letters; history; liberal arts and sciences studies, and humanities; mathematics and statistics; multi/interdisciplinary studies; parks, recreation, leisure, and fitness studies; philosophy and religious studies; physical sciences; psychology; security and protective services; visual and performing arts. **Areas of required coursework:** arts/fine arts, humanities, computer literacy, mathematics, English (including composition), foreign languages, sciences (biological or physical), history, social science. **Pre-professional programs:** pre-law, pre-medicine, pre-veterinary science. **Special academic programs:** distance learning, double major, honors program, independent study, internships, liberal arts/career combination, student-designed major, study abroad, teacher certificate program. **Teacher certification offered in:** early childhood, elementary, middle/junior high, secondary. **Faculty and instruction (2005-2006):** Total instructional faculty: 46 full-time, 20 part-time (55% men; 45% women; 9% minorities). Full-time faculty with Ph.D. or other terminal degree: 52%. Student/faculty ratio: 14/1. Classes of fewer than 20 students: 64%; of 20 to 49 students: 36%; of 50 or more students: 0%. **Advanced Placement and International Baccalaureate credit:** AP tests may be used for: Credit and/or placement. Scores accepted: 4, 5. **Freshmen returning for sophomore year:** 49%. **Graduation rates:** Four-year: 19%; five-year: 28%; six-year: 23%.

COSTS AND FINANCIAL AID

Financial aid office: (252) 398-1229. **Expenses (2006-2007):** Tuition and fees 2006-2007: $15,950; room/board: $6,800. Estimated books and supplies: $864; transportation: $536; personal expenses: $1,000. **Financial aid:** Priority filing date for institution's financial aid form: May 1; deadline: August 1. In 2005-2006, 95% of undergraduates applied for financial aid. Of those, 87% were determined to have financial need; 12% had their need fully met. Average financial aid package (proportion receiving): $12,504 (87%). Average amount of gift aid, such as scholarships or grants (proportion receiving): $9,526 (85%). Average amount of self-help aid, such as work study or loans (proportion receiving): $3,868 (76%). Average need-based loan (excluding PLUS or other private loans): $3,560. Among students who received need-based aid, the average percentage of need met: 69%. Among students who received aid based on merit, the average award (and the proportion receiving): $11,297 (9%). The average athletic scholarship (and the proportion receiving): $2,500 (2%). Average amount of debt of borrowers graduating in 2005: $23,370. Proportion who borrowed: 80%.

CAMPUS LIFE AND EXTRACURRICULAR ACTIVITIES

Campus housing available (% using): women's dorms (60%), men's dorms (40%), special housing for disabled students. Students who live in college-owned, operated, or affiliated housing: 85%. **Student employment:** During the 2005-2006 academic year, 5% of undergraduates worked on campus. Activities include: choral groups, concert band, drama/theater, jazz band, literary magazine, music ensembles, pep band, student government, yearbook. Number of fraternities: 3; sororities: 2. Proportion of men in fraternities: 5%; of women in sororities: 5%. Average proportion of students who stay on campus on weekends: 50%. **Sports program (2005-2006):** Member of NCAA III. *Men's intercollegiate varsity sports:* baseball, basketball, football, golf, soccer, tennis. *Women's intercollegiate varsity sports:* basketball, cross-country, soccer, softball, volleyball.

SERVICES AND FACILITIES

Basic services: nonremedial tutoring, placement service, health service. **Remedial assistance:** reading, math, study skills. **Counseling services:** career, academic, religious. **For learning-disabled students:** School does not offer a structured program with separate admission and additional fees. Services include: remedial math, remedial English, tape recorders, untimed tests, oral tests, learning center, extended time for tests, take home exams. **Information technology resources:** Students are not required to lease or own a computer. Number of campus computers available to all students: 350. School does not have a wireless network. Proportion of college-owned housing units wired for high-speed internet access: 100%. **Campus safety:** Security services offered: late-night transport/escort service, controlled dormitory access (key, security card, etc).

TRANSFER AND INTERNATIONAL STUDENTS

Transfer students: May apply for admission for the following academic terms: Fall, Spring, Summer. Applicants need a minimum number of credits to apply. **International students:** Number of foreign undergraduates: 9 (1% of student body). Minimum TOEFL score required: 450 (paper).

Davidson College

- ■ **Address:** 209 Ridge Road, Davidson, NC 28035
- ■ **Website:** http://www.davidson.edu
- ■ **Private; Religious affiliation:** Presbyterian (U.S.A.)
- ■ **Enrollment:** 1,683 full-time

KEY STATS

- ✔ **U.S News College Ranking:** 10, Liberal Arts Colleges
- ✔ **SAT Score (25th/75th percentile):** 1280-1440
- ✔ **Tuition:** 2006-2007: $30,194

Selectivity: Most selective	**Room/board:** $8,590
Acceptance rate: 27%	**Average debt:** $22,954
Student/faculty ratio: 10/1	**Proportion who borrowed:** 34%

UNDERGRADUATE STUDENT BODY STATS

2005-2006 enrollment: 1,683 full-time. Men: 50%; women: 50%. **Ethnic makeup:** African American: 6%; Asian American: 2%; Hispanic: 4%; White: 84%; International: 3%.

ADMISSIONS FACTS AND FIGURES

Phone: (800) 768-0380. **Email:** admission@davidson.edu. **Website:** http://www.davidson.edu. **Application deadlines for fall 2007:** Regular decision: January 2; decision sent by April 1. Early decision: Send application by: November 15; Decision sent by: December 15. Early action: Not offered. Admission can be deferred. **Application fee:** $50. Common application is accepted. **Admissions requirements/recommendations:** High school units required (recommended): English: 4; Mathematics: 3 (4); Science: 2 (4); Foreign language: 2 (4); Total units: 16. Tests: The college uses SAT or ACT scores in admissions decisions. Either SAT or ACT required. For admission to the fall 2007 entering class, the school will accept: ACT with writing, ACT without writing. Campus visit: Recommended. Admissions interview: Recommended. Off-campus interview: May be arranged. **Factors that count in admissions decisions:** *Academic:* Secondary school record: Very important. Class rank: Considered. Letters of recommendation: Very important. Standardized test scores: Considered. Essay: Important. *Nonacademic:* Interview: Not considered. Extracurricular activities: Important. Talent/ability: Important. Character/personal qualities: Very important. Alumni/ae relationship: Not considered. Geographical residence: Not considered. State residency: Not considered. Religious affiliation/commitment: Not considered. Minority status: Considered. Volunteer work: Very important. Work experience: Considered. **Other schools with the greatest overlap in applicants:** Dartmouth College; Duke University; University of North Carolina–Chapel Hill; University of Virginia; Wake Forest University. **Admissions statistics for the fall 2005 entering class:** Total applicants: 4,258. Total accepted: 1,146. Freshmen enrolled: 460; 84% were from out of state. Accepted through early-decision or early-action plans: 46%. Overall acceptance rate: 27%. Early-decision acceptance rate: 49%. Non-early acceptance rate: 24%. **Credentials of fall 2005 freshmen:** 77% ranked in the top 10 percent of their high school class; 97% were in the top 25 percent, and 100% were in the top half. (Proportion submitting class standing: 40%.) **Average high school grade point average:** 3.9. **First-year students who submitted SAT scores:** 94%. Scores (25/75 percentile): Verbal: 640-730, Math: 640-710, Combined: 1280-1440. **First-year students submitting ACT scores:** 38%. Scores (25/75 percentile): English: N/A, Math: N/A, Composite: 28-31.

ACADEMICS

Year founded: 1837. **Academic calendar:** Semester. **Degrees offered:** bachelor's. **Most popular majors:** 13% history, 12% biology/biological sciences, 11% English language and literature, 11% political science and government, 11% psychology. **Major fields of study:** biological and biomedical sciences; English language and literature/letters; foreign languages, literatures, and linguistics; history; mathematics and statistics; multi/interdisciplinary studies; philosophy and religious studies; physical sciences; psychology; social sciences; visual and performing arts. **Areas of required coursework:** arts/fine arts, mathematics, English (including composition), philosophy, foreign languages, sciences (biological or physical), history, social science, other. **Pre-professional programs:** pre-law, pre-medicine, pre-theology. **Special academic programs:** cross-registration, double major, exchange student program (domestic), honors program, independent study, student-designed major, study abroad, teacher certificate program. **Teacher certification offered in:** secondary. **Reserve Officers Training Corps (ROTC):** Army ROTC: Offered on campus; Air Force ROTC: Offered at cooperating institution (University of North Carolina–Charlotte). **Faculty and instruction (2005-2006):** Total instructional faculty: 159 full-time, 8 part-time (66% men; 34% women; 14% minorities). Full-time faculty with Ph.D. or other terminal degree: 99%. Student/faculty ratio: 10/1. Classes of fewer than 20 students: 64%; of 20 to 49 students: 36%; of 50 or more students: 0%. **Advanced Placement and International Baccalaureate credit:** AP tests may be used for: Credit only. Scores accepted: 4, 5. International Baccalaureate exams may be used for: Credit only. **Freshmen returning for sophomore year:** 96%. **Graduation rates:** Four-year: 84%; five-year: 86%; six-year: 87%. **Graduate study:** 24% of students pursue further study immediately upon graduation. Fields in which graduates pursue further study: Master of Business Administration (MBA), 4%; law, 20%; medicine, 18%; theology (or the seminary), 5%; education, 3%; arts and sciences, 19%; veterinary medicine, 2%.

COSTS AND FINANCIAL AID

Financial aid office: (704) 894-2232. **Expenses (2006-2007):** Tuition and fees 2006-2007: $30,194; room/board: $8,590. Estimated books and supplies: $1,000; transportation: $350; personal expenses: $1,175. **Financial aid:** In 2005-2006, 42% of undergraduates applied for financial aid. Of those, 35% were determined to have financial need; 100% had their need fully met. Average financial aid package (proportion receiving): $18,024 (35%). Average amount of gift aid, such as scholarships or grants (proportion receiving): $15,766 (32%). Average amount of self-help aid, such as work study or loans (proportion receiving): $4,069 (28%). Average need-based loan (excluding PLUS or other private loans): $3,926. Among students who received need-based aid, the average percentage of need met: 100%. Among students who received aid based on merit, the average award (and the proportion receiving): $8,824 (22%). The average athletic scholarship (and the proportion receiving): $12,194 (11%). Average amount of debt of borrowers graduating in 2005: $22,954. Proportion who borrowed: 34%.

CAMPUS LIFE AND EXTRACURRICULAR ACTIVITIES

Campus housing available: coed dorms, apartment for single students, special housing for disabled students. Students who live in college-owned, operated, or affiliated housing: 91%. **Clubs and organizations:** Number of student organizations: 185. Activities include: choral groups, concert band, dance, drama/theater, jazz band, music ensembles, musical theater, pep band, radio station, student government, student newspaper, symphony orchestra, yearbook. Number of fraternities: 7; sororities: 0. Proportion of men in fraternities: 40%; **Sports program (2005-2006):** Member of NCAA I. *Men's intercollegiate varsity sports:* baseball, basketball, cross-country, football, golf, soccer, swimming and diving, tennis, track and field (indoor), track and field (outdoor), wrestling. *Women's intercollegiate varsity sports:* basketball, cross-country, field hockey, lacrosse, soccer, swimming and diving, tennis, track and field (indoor), track and field (outdoor), volleyball.

SERVICES AND FACILITIES

Basic services: nonremedial tutoring, health service, health insurance. **Remedial assistance:** study skills. **Counseling services:** minority student, career, personal, academic, psychological, religious. **For learning-disabled students:** School does not offer a structured program with separate admission and additional fees. Services include: tape recorders, diagnostic testing service, note-taking services, oral tests, readers, extended time for tests, tutors, other testing accomodations. **Library:** Number of titles: 617,005; number of current serial subscriptions: 4,546. **Information technology resources:** Students are not required to lease or own a computer. Number of campus computers available to all students: 142. School has a wireless network. Proportion of college-owned housing units wired for high-speed internet access: 100%. **Campus safety:** Security services offered: 24-hour foot-and-vehicle patrols, late-night transport/escort service, 24-hour emergency telephones, lighted pathways/sidewalks, controlled dormitory access (key, security card, etc).

TRANSFER AND INTERNATIONAL STUDENTS

Transfer students: May apply for admission for the following academic terms: Fall, Spring. Applicants need a minimum number of credits to apply. For fall 2005: Transfer applications received: 51. Transfer applicants offered admission: 16. Transfer applicants enrolled: 5. **International students:** Number of foreign undergraduates: 58 (3% of student body). Number of countries represented: 29. Minimum TOEFL score required: 600 (paper); 250 (computer).

Duke University

- **Address:** 2138 Campus Drive, Box 90586, Durham, NC 27708
- **Website:** http://www.duke.edu/
- **Private; Religious affiliation:** Methodist
- **Enrollment:** 6,470 full-time; 64 part-time

KEY STATS

✔ **U.S News College Ranking:** 8, National Universities
✔ **SAT Score (25th/75th percentile):** 1360-1540
✔ **Tuition:** 2006-2007: $33,963
   Selectivity: Most selective   **Room/board:** $9,152
   Acceptance rate: 24%   **Average debt:** $24,391
   Student/faculty ratio: 8/1   **Proportion who borrowed:** 46%

UNDERGRADUATE STUDENT BODY STATS

2005-2006 enrollment: 6,470 full-time; 64 part-time. Men: 52%; women: 48%. **Ethnic makeup:** African American: 11%; Asian American: 14%; Hispanic: 7%; White: 63%; International: 5%. **Religious preference:** Roman Catholic: 21%; Protestant: 33%; Jewish: 12%; Muslim: 1%; Hindu: 3%; Buddhist: 2%; No preference: 19%; Methodist: 6%; Other: 3%.

ADMISSIONS FACTS AND FIGURES

Phone: (919) 684-3214. **Website:** http://www.duke.edu/. **Application deadlines for fall 2007:** Regular decision: January 2; decision sent by April 1. Early decision: Send application by: November 1; Decision sent by: December 15. Early action: Not offered. Admission can be deferred. **Application fee:** $75. Common application is accepted. **To apply online, go to:** http://www.admissions.duke.edu/jump/applying/apply.asp. **Admissions requirements/recommendations:** High school units required (recommended): English: 4; Mathematics: 4; Science: 4; Foreign language: 4; Social studies: 4. Tests: The college uses SAT or ACT scores in admissions decisions. Either SAT or ACT required. For admission to the fall 2007 entering class, the school will accept: ACT with writing. Campus visit: Recommended. Admissions interview: Recommended. Off-campus interview: May be arranged. **Factors that count in admissions decisions:** *Academic:* Secondary school record: Very important. Class rank: Considered. Letters of recommendation: Very important. Standardized test scores: Very important. Essay: Very important. *Nonacademic:* Interview: Considered. Extracurricular activities: Very important. Talent/ability: Very important. Character/personal qualities: Important. Alumni/ae relationship: Considered. Geographical residence: Considered. State residency: Considered. Religious affiliation/commitment: Not considered. Minority status: Considered. Volunteer work: Considered. Work experience: Considered. **Other schools with the greatest overlap in applicants:** Cornell University; Northwestern University; University of North Carolina–Chapel Hill; University of Virginia; Washington University in St. Louis. **Admissions statistics for the fall 2005 entering class:** Total applicants: 16,820. Total accepted: 3,992. Freshmen enrolled: 1,724; 87% were from out of state. Accepted through early-decision or early-action plans: 27%. Overall acceptance rate: 24%. Early-decision acceptance rate: 32%. Non-early acceptance rate: 23%. **Size of waiting list:** N/A applicants; enrolled from waiting list: 23. **Credentials of fall 2005 freshmen:** 88% ranked in the top 10 percent of their high school class; 97% were in the top 25 percent, and 99% were in the top half. (Proportion submitting class standing: 52%.) **First-year students who submitted SAT scores:** 96%. Scores (25/75 percentile): Verbal: 670-760, Math: 690-780, Combined: 1360-1540. **First-year students submitting ACT scores:** 33%. Scores (25/75 percentile): English: N/A, Math: N/A, Composite: 29-33.

ACADEMICS

Year founded: 1838. **Academic calendar:** Semester. **Degrees offered:** bachelor's, post-bachelor's certificate, master's, first professional, doctorate. **Most popular majors:** 12% economics, 10% psychology, 9% biology, 9% political science and government, 8% public policy analysis. **Major fields of study:** area, ethnic, cultural, and gender studies; biological and biomedical sciences; computer and information sciences and support services; engineering; English language and literature/letters; foreign languages, literatures, and linguistics; history; mathematics and statistics; multi/interdisciplinary studies; natural resources and conservation; philosophy and religious studies; physical sciences; psychology; public administration and social service professions; social sciences; visual and performing arts. **Areas of required coursework:** arts/fine arts, humanities, foreign languages, sciences (biological or physical), history, social science. **Pre-professional programs:** pre-law, pre-medicine. **Special academic programs:** double major, honors program, independent study, internships, liberal arts/career combination, student-designed major, study abroad, teacher certificate program. **Teacher certification offered in:** early childhood, elementary, middle/junior high, **Reserve Officers Training Corps (ROTC):** Army ROTC: Offered on campus; Navy ROTC: Offered on campus; Air Force ROTC: Offered on campus. **Faculty and instruction (2005-2006):** Total instructional faculty: 964 full-time, 90 part-time (71% men; 29% women; 14% minorities). Full-time faculty with Ph.D. or other terminal degree: 97%. Student/faculty ratio: 8/1. Classes of fewer than 20 students: 71%; of 20 to 49 students: 24%; of 50 or more students: 5%. **Advanced Placement and International Baccalaureate credit:** AP tests may be used for: Placement only. International Baccalaureate exams may be used for: Credit and/or placement. **Freshmen returning for sophomore year:** 97%. **Graduation rates:** Four-year: 87%; five-year: 93%; six-year: 93%. **Graduate study:** 25% of students pursue further study immediately upon graduation. Fields in which graduates pursue further study: law, 16%; medicine, 10%; arts and sciences, 14%.

COSTS AND FINANCIAL AID

Financial aid office: (919) 684-6225. **Expenses (2006-2007):** Tuition and fees 2006-2007: $33,963; room/board: $9,152. Estimated books and supplies: $1,000; transportation: $410; personal expenses: $1,505. **Financial aid:** In 2005-2006, 44% of undergraduates applied for financial aid. Of those, 40% were determined to have financial need; 100% had their need fully met. Average financial aid package (proportion receiving): $29,878 (40%). Average amount of gift aid, such as scholarships or grants (proportion receiving): $23,928 (38%). Average amount of self-help aid, such as work study or loans (proportion receiving): $5,787 (36%). Average need-based loan (excluding PLUS or other private loans): $4,270. Among students who received need-based aid, the average percentage of need met: 100%. Among students who received aid based on merit, the average award (and the proportion receiving): $24,016 (4%). The average athletic scholarship (and the proportion receiving): $29,402 (4%). Average amount of debt of borrowers graduating in 2005: $24,391. Proportion who borrowed: 46%.

CAMPUS LIFE AND EXTRACURRICULAR ACTIVITIES

Campus housing available (% using): coed dorms (80%), apartment for single students (20%). Students who live in college-owned, operated, or affiliated housing: 83%. Activities include: choral groups, concert band, dance, drama/theater, jazz band, literary magazine, marching band, music ensembles, musical theater, opera, pep band, radio station, student government, student newspaper, student film society, symphony orchestra, television station, yearbook. Number of fraternities: 15; sororities: 10. Proportion of men in fraternities: 27%; of women in sororities: 42%. Average proportion of students who stay on campus on weekends: 90%. **Sports program (2005-2006):** Member of NCAA I. *Men's intercollegiate varsity sports:* baseball, basketball, cross-country, fencing, football, golf, lacrosse, soccer, swimming and diving, tennis, track and field (indoor), track and field (outdoor), wrestling. *Women's intercollegiate varsity sports:* basketball, crew, cross-country, fencing, field hockey, golf, lacrosse, soccer, swimming and diving, tennis, track and field (indoor), track and field (outdoor), volleyball.

SERVICES AND FACILITIES

Basic services: women's center, placement service, health service, health insurance. **Counseling services:** minority student, career, personal, academic, psychological. **For learning-disabled students:** School does not offer a structured program with separate admission and additional fees. Services include: tape recorders, oral tests, extended time for tests, tutors, other testing accomodations. **Library:** Number of titles: 5,496,408; number of current serial subscriptions: 36,995. **Information technology resources:** Students are not required to lease or own a computer. Number of campus computers available to all students: 350. School has a wireless network. Proportion of college-owned housing units wired for high-speed internet access: 100%. **Campus safety:** Security services offered: 24-hour foot-and-vehicle patrols, late-night transport/escort service, 24-hour emergency telephones, lighted pathways/sidewalks, student patrols, controlled dormitory access (key, security card, etc).

TRANSFER AND INTERNATIONAL STUDENTS

Transfer students: May apply for admission for the following academic terms: Fall, Spring. Applicants need a minimum number of credits to apply. For fall 2005: Transfer applications received: 460. Transfer applicants offered admission: 28. Transfer applicants enrolled: 21. **International students:** Number of foreign undergraduates: 329 (5% of student body). Number of countries represented: 45.

East Carolina University

■ **Address:** East Fifth Street, Greenville, NC 27858-4353
■ **Website:** http://www.ecu.edu
■ **Public**
■ **Enrollment:** 15,832 full-time; 1,896 part-time

KEY STATS

✔ **U.S News College Ranking:** third tier, National Universities
✔ **SAT Score (25th/75th percentile):** 940-1130
✔ **Tuition:** 2005-2006: $3,454 in state, $13,668 out of state
  Selectivity: Selective   **Room/board:** N/A
  Acceptance rate: 74%   **Average debt:** $19,614
  Student/faculty ratio: 15/1   **Proportion who borrowed:** 79%

UNDERGRADUATE STUDENT BODY STATS

2005-2006 enrollment: 15,832 full-time; 1,896 part-time. Men: 40%; women: 60%. **Ethnic makeup:** African American: 15%; American-Indian: 1%; Asian American: 2%; Hispanic: 2%; White: 79%.

ADMISSIONS FACTS AND FIGURES

Phone: (252) 328-6640. **Email:** admis@mail.ecu.edu. **Website:** http://www.ecu.edu. **Application deadlines for fall 2007:** Early decision: Not offered. Early action: Not offered. Admission can be deferred. **Application fee:** $50. Common application is not accepted. **To apply online, go to:** http://www.ecu.edu/admissions/appl.html. **Admissions requirements/recommendations:** High school units required (recommended): English: 4; Mathematics: 4; Science: 3; Foreign language: 2; Social studies: 2; Academic electives: 4; Total units: 20. Tests: The college uses SAT or ACT scores in admissions decisions. Either SAT or ACT required. For admission to the fall 2007 entering class, the school will accept: ACT with writing. Campus visit: Recommended. Admissions interview: Neither required nor recommended. Off-campus interview: Not available. **Factors that count in admissions decisions:** *Academic:* Secondary school record: Very important. Class rank: Very important. Letters of recommendation: Considered. Standardized test scores: Very important. Essay: Not considered. *Nonacademic:* Interview: Not considered. Extracurricular activities: Considered. Talent/ability: Considered. Character/personal qualities: Considered. Alumni/ae relationship: Considered. Geographical residence: Considered. State residency: Considered. Religious affiliation/commitment: Not considered. Minority status: Not considered. Volunteer work: Not considered. Work experience: Not considered. **Admissions statistics for the fall 2005 entering class:** Total applicants: 11,628. Total accepted: 8,567. Freshmen enrolled: 3,273; 16% were from out of state. Overall acceptance rate: 74%. **Credentials of fall 2005 freshmen:** 14% ranked in the top 10 percent of their high school class; 42% were in the top 25 percent, and 79% were in the top half. (Proportion submitting class standing: 89%.) **Average high school grade point average:** 3.2. **First-year students who submitted SAT scores:** 93%. Scores (25/75 percentile): Verbal: 460-560, Math: 480-570, Combined: 940-1130. **First-year students submitting ACT scores:** 17%. Scores (25/75 percentile): English: 17-22, Math: 18-23, Composite: 18-22.

ACADEMICS

Year founded: 1907. **Academic calendar:** Semester. **Degrees offered:** bachelor's, master's, post-master's certificate, first professional, doctorate. **Most popular majors:** 7% nursing/registered nurse training (R.N., A.S.N., B.S.N., M.S.N.), 6% elementary education and teaching, 5% broadcast journalism, 4% business administration and management, 4% psychology. **Major fields**

of study: architecture and related services; area, ethnic, cultural, and gender studies; biological and biomedical sciences; business, management, marketing, and related support services; communication, journalism, and related programs; computer and information sciences and support services; education; engineering; engineering technologies/technicians; English language and literature/letters; family and consumer sciences/human sciences; foreign languages, literatures, and linguistics; health professions and related clinical sciences; history; liberal arts and sciences studies, and humanities; mathematics and statistics; parks, recreation, leisure, and fitness studies; philosophy and religious studies; physical sciences; psychology; public administration and social service professions; security and protective services; social sciences; visual and performing arts. **Areas of required coursework:** arts/fine arts, humanities, mathematics, English (including composition), sciences (biological or physical), social science, other. **Pre-professional programs:** pre-law, pre-dentistry, pre-medicine, pre-theology, pre-veterinary science, pre-optometry, pre-pharmacy. **Special academic programs:** accelerated program, cooperative (work-study plan) program, distance learning, double major, dual enrollment, English as a Second Language (ESL), exchange student program (domestic), honors program, independent study, internships, student-designed major, study abroad, teacher certificate program. **Teacher certification offered in:** early childhood, special education, elementary, vo-tech, middle/junior high, secondary, bilingual/bicultural. **Cooperative education programs:** other. **Reserve Officers Training Corps (ROTC):** Army ROTC: Offered on campus; Air Force ROTC: Offered on campus. **Faculty and instruction (2005-2006):** Total instructional faculty: 1,096 full-time, 196 part-time (63% men; 37% women; 8% minorities). Full-time faculty with Ph.D. or other terminal degree: 85%. Student/faculty ratio: 15/1. Classes of fewer than 20 students: 43%; of 20 to 49 students: 46%; of 50 or more students: 11%. **Advanced Placement and International Baccalaureate credit:** AP tests may be used for: Credit only. Scores accepted: 3, 4, 5. International Baccalaureate exams may be used for: Credit only. **Freshmen returning for sophomore year:** 77%. **Graduation rates:** Four-year: 25%; five-year: 48%; six-year: 54%.

COSTS AND FINANCIAL AID

Financial aid office: (252) 328-6610. **Expenses (2005-2006):** Tuition and fees 2005-2006: $3,454 in state, $13,668 out of state; room/board: N/A. Estimated books and supplies: $800 personal expenses: $2,482. **Financial aid:** Priority filing date for institution's financial aid form: April 15. In 2005-2006, 48% of undergraduates applied for financial aid. Of those, 32% were determined to have financial need; 17% had their need fully met. Average financial aid package (proportion receiving): $6,085 (32%). Average amount of gift aid, such as scholarships or grants (proportion receiving): $3,974 (21%). Average amount of self-help aid, such as work study or loans (proportion receiving): $3,771 (29%). Average need-based loan (excluding PLUS or other private loans): $3,597. Among students who received need-based aid, the average percentage of need met: 65%. Among students who received aid based on merit, the average award (and the proportion receiving): $2,593 (4%). The average athletic scholarship (and the proportion receiving): $11,108 (0%). Average amount of debt of borrowers graduating in 2005: $19,614. Proportion who borrowed: 79%.

CAMPUS LIFE AND EXTRACURRICULAR ACTIVITIES

Campus housing available (% using): coed dorms (66%), women's dorms (20%), men's dorms (9%), sorority housing (3%), fraternity housing (2%). Students who live in college-owned, operated, or affiliated housing: 27%. **Clubs and organizations:** Number of student organizations: 314. Activities include: choral groups, concert band, dance, drama/theater, jazz band, literary magazine, marching band, music ensembles, musical theater, opera, pep band, radio station, student government, student newspaper, student film society, symphony orchestra. Number of fraternities: 22; sororities: 13. **Sports program (2005-2006):** Member of NCAA I. *Men's intercollegiate varsity sports:* baseball, basketball, cross-country, football, golf, soccer, swimming and diving, tennis, track and field (indoor), track and field (outdoor). *Women's intercollegiate varsity sports:* basketball, cross-country, golf, soccer, softball, swimming and diving, tennis, track and field (indoor), track and field (outdoor), volleyball.

SERVICES AND FACILITIES

Basic services: nonremedial tutoring, placement service, health service. **Remedial assistance:** reading, math. **Counseling services:** minority student, career, military, personal, veteran student, academic, older student, psychological, birth control, religious, other. **For learning-disabled students:** School does not offer a structured program with separate admission and additional fees. Total undergraduates in learning-disabled program or receiving services: 302. Services include: remedial math, remedial English, reading machines, remedial reading, tape recorders, videotaped classes, note-taking services, readers, extended time for tests, tutors. **Library:** Number of titles: 1,248,086; number of current serial subscriptions: 13,779. **Information technology resources:** Students are not required to lease or own a computer. Number of campus computers available to all students: 2,315. School has a wireless network. Proportion of college-owned housing units wired for high-speed internet access: 100%. **Campus safety:** Security services offered: 24-hour foot-and-vehicle patrols, late-night transport/escort service, 24-hour emergency telephones, lighted pathways/sidewalks, student patrols, controlled dormitory access (key, security card, etc).

TRANSFER AND INTERNATIONAL STUDENTS

Transfer students: May apply for admission for the following academic terms: Fall, Spring, Summer. Applicants need a minimum number of credits to apply. For fall 2005: Transfer applications received: 2,524. Transfer applicants offered admission: 2,127. Transfer applicants enrolled: 1,412. **International students:** Number of foreign undergraduates: 63. Minimum TOEFL score required: 550 (paper); 213 (computer).

Elizabeth City State University

- **Address:** 1704 Weeksville Road, Elizabeth City, NC 27909
- **Website:** http://www.ecsu.edu
- **Public**
- **Enrollment:** 2,283 full-time; 321 part-time

KEY STATS

✔ **U.S News College Ranking:** 41, Comp. Colleges–Bachelor's (South)
✔ **SAT Score (25th/75th percentile):** 750-920
✔ **Tuition:** 2005-2006: $3,242 in state, $11,581 out of state

Selectivity: Least selective	**Room/board:** $4,710
Acceptance rate: 80%	**Average debt:** N/A
Student/faculty ratio: 15/1	**Proportion who borrowed:** N/A

UNDERGRADUATE STUDENT BODY STATS

2005-2006 enrollment: 2,283 full-time; 321 part-time. Men: 38%; women: 62%. **Ethnic makeup:** African American: 78%; Asian American: 1%; White: 21%.

ADMISSIONS FACTS AND FIGURES

Phone: (252) 335-3305. **Email:** admissions@mail.ecsu.edu. **Website:** http://www.ecsu.edu. **Application deadlines for fall 2007:** Regular decision: August 1. Early decision: Not offered. Early action: Not offered. Admission can be deferred. **Application fee:** $30. Common application is not accepted. **Admissions requirements/recommendations:** High school units required (recommended): English: 4; Mathematics: 3; Science: 3; Foreign language: (2); Social studies: 1; History: 1; Academic electives: 8; Total units: 20 (2). Tests: The college uses SAT or ACT scores in admissions decisions. Either SAT or ACT required. For admission to the fall 2007 entering class, the school will accept: ACT with writing, ACT without writing. Campus visit: Recommended. Admissions interview: Recommended. Off-campus interview: Not available. **Factors that count in admissions decisions:** *Academic:* Secondary school record: Very important. Class rank: Considered. Letters of recommendation: Important. Standardized test scores: Very important. Essay: Not considered. *Nonacademic:* Interview: Not considered. Extracurricular activities: Considered. Talent/ability: Important. Character/personal qualities: Important. Alumni/ae relationship: Important. Geographical residence: Very important. State residency: Important. Religious affiliation/commitment: Not considered. Minority status: Not considered. Volunteer work: Not considered. Work experience: Not considered. **Admissions statistics for the fall 2005 entering class:** Total applicants: 1,675. Total accepted: 1,342. Freshmen enrolled: 560; 15% were from out of state. Overall acceptance rate: 80%. **Credentials of fall 2005 freshmen:** 6% ranked in the top 10 percent of their high school class; 20% were in the top 25 percent, and 53% were in the top half. (Proportion submitting class standing: 92%.) **Average high school grade point average:** 2.8. **First-year students who submitted SAT scores:** 92%. Scores (25/75 percentile): Verbal: 370-460, Math: 380-460, Combined: 750-920. **First-year students submitting ACT scores:** 19%. Scores (25/75 percentile): English: 13-17, Math: 15-18, Composite: 14-18.

ACADEMICS

Year founded: 1891. **Academic calendar:** Semester. **Degrees offered:** bachelor's, post-bachelor's certificate, master's. **Most popular majors:** 19% business administration and management, 13% criminal justice/safety studies, 8% sociology, 7% biology/biological sciences, 6% computer science. **Major fields of study:** biological and biomedical sciences; business, management, marketing, and related support services; communication, journalism, and related programs; computer and information sciences and support services; education; engineering technologies/technicians; English language and literature/letters; history; mathematics and statistics; physical sciences; psychology; public administration and social service professions; security and protective services; social sciences; transportation and materials moving; visual and performing arts. **Areas of required coursework:** arts/fine arts, computer literacy, mathematics, English (including composition), sciences (biological or physical), history. **Pre-professional programs:** pre-law, pre-dentistry, pre-medicine, pre-pharmacy. **Special academic programs:** distance learning, double major, honors program, independent study, internships, study abroad, teacher certificate program, weekend college (37%), other. **Teacher certification offered in:** special education, elementary, middle/junior high, secondary. **Cooperative education programs:** education, technologies. **Reserve Officers Training Corps (ROTC):** Army ROTC: Offered on campus. **Faculty and instruction (2005-2006):** Total instructional faculty: 128 full-time, 97 part-time (56% men; 44% women; 40% minorities). Full-time faculty with Ph.D. or other terminal degree: 70%. Student/faculty ratio: 15/1. Classes of fewer than 20 students: 60%; of 20 to 49 students: 38%; of 50 or more students: 3%. **Advanced Placement and International Baccalaureate credit:** AP tests may be used for: Credit and/or placement. Scores accepted: 3, 4, 5. International Baccalaureate exams may be used for: Credit and/or placement. **Freshmen returning for sophomore year:** 75%. **Graduation rates:** Four-year: 27%; five-year: 46%; six-year: 49%. **Graduate study:** 17% of students pursue further study immediately upon graduation; 8% within one year; 1% within five years. Fields in which graduates pursue further study: Master of Business Administration (MBA), 5%; law, 2%; medicine, 1%; dentistry, 2%; education, 15%.

COSTS AND FINANCIAL AID

Financial aid office: (252) 335-3282. **Expenses (2005-2006):** Tuition and fees 2005-2006: $3,242 in state, $11,581 out of state; room/board: $4,710. Estimated books and supplies: $600; transportation: $500; personal expenses: $400. **Financial aid:** Priority filing date for institution's financial aid form: March 15; deadline: June 1.

CAMPUS LIFE AND EXTRACURRICULAR ACTIVITIES

Campus housing available (% using): coed dorms (63%), women's dorms (22%), men's dorms (15%). Students who live in college-owned, operated, or affiliated housing: 50%. **Clubs and organizations:** Number of student organizations: 32. Activities include: choral groups, concert band, dance, drama/theater, jazz band, literary magazine, marching band, music ensembles, pep band, radio station, student government, student newspaper, television station, yearbook. Number of fraternities: 5; sororities: 4. Proportion of men in fraternities: 8%; of women in sororities: 8%. Average proportion of students who stay on campus on weekends: 40%. **Sports program (2005-2006):** Member of NCAA II. **Men's intercollegiate varsity sports:** baseball, basketball, cross-country, football, golf. **Women's intercollegiate varsity sports:** basketball, bowling, cheerleading, cross-country, softball, tennis, volleyball.

SERVICES AND FACILITIES

Basic services: nonremedial tutoring, women's center, placement service, health service, health insurance. **Remedial assistance:** reading, math, writing, other. **Counseling services:** minority student, career, personal, veteran student, academic, older student, religious. **For learning-disabled students:** School does not offer a structured program with separate admission and additional fees. Total undergraduates in learning-disabled program or receiving services: 32. Services include: remedial math, remedial English, remedial reading, tape recorders, untimed tests, note-taking services, learning center, extended time for tests, tutors, early syllabus, priority seating, texts on tape, other. **Library:** Number of titles: 193,880; number of current serial subscriptions: 1,790. **Information technology resources:** Students are not required to lease or own a computer. Number of campus computers available to all students: 500. School has a wireless network. Approximate number of users that can be accommodated: 3,600. Proportion of college-owned housing units wired for high-speed internet access: 100%. **Campus safety:** Security services offered: 24-hour foot-and-vehicle patrols, 24-hour emergency telephones, lighted pathways/sidewalks, controlled dormitory access (key, security card, etc).

TRANSFER AND INTERNATIONAL STUDENTS

Transfer students: May apply for admission for the following academic terms: Fall, Spring, Summer. Applicants need a minimum number of credits to apply. For fall 2005: Transfer applications received: 265. Transfer applicants offered admission: 256. Transfer applicants enrolled: 169. **International students:** Number of foreign undergraduates: 0. Number of countries represented: 1. Minimum TOEFL score required: 550 (paper).

Elon University

- **Address:** 2700 Campus Box, Elon, NC 27244
- **Website:** http://www.elon.edu
- **Private; Religious affiliation:** United Church of Christ
- **Enrollment:** 4,607 full-time; 95 part-time

KEY STATS

✔ **U.S News College Ranking:** 3, Universities–Master's (South)
✔ **SAT Score (25th/75th percentile):** 1130-1290
✔ **Tuition:** 2006-2007: $20,441

Selectivity: More selective **Room/board:** $6,850
Acceptance rate: 41% **Average debt:** $21,687
Student/faculty ratio: 15/1 **Proportion who borrowed:** 45%

UNDERGRADUATE STUDENT BODY STATS

2005-2006 enrollment: 4,607 full-time; 95 part-time. Men: 39%; women: 61%. **Ethnic makeup:** African American: 7%; Asian American: 1%; Hispanic: 1%; White: 89%; International: 2%. **Religious preference:** Roman Catholic: 25%; Protestant: 37%; Jewish: 2%; No preference: 25%; United Church of Christ: 2%; Other: 9%.

ADMISSIONS FACTS AND FIGURES

Phone: (800) 334-8448. **Email:** admissions@elon.edu. **Website:** http://www.elon.edu. **Application deadlines for fall 2007:** Regular decision: January 10; decision sent by March 15. Early decision: Send application by: November 1; Decision sent by: December 1. Early action: Send application by: November 10; Decision sent by: December 20. Admission can be deferred. **Application fee:** $40. Common application is not accepted. **To apply online, go to:** http://www.elon.edu/admissions/application.asp. **Admissions requirements/recommendations:** High school units required (recommended): English: 4; Mathematics: 3 (4); Science: 3; Foreign language: 2 (3); Social studies: 2; History: 1. Tests: The college uses SAT or ACT scores in admissions decisions. Either SAT or ACT required. For admission to the fall 2007 entering class, the school will accept: ACT with writing. Campus visit: Recommended. Admissions interview: Neither required nor recommended. Off-campus interview: Not available. **Factors that count in admissions decisions:** *Academic:* Secondary school record: Very important. Class rank: Considered. Letters of recommendation: Important. Standardized test scores: Very important. Essay: Important. *Nonacademic:* Interview: Not considered. Extracurricular activities: Important. Talent/ability: Important. Character/personal qualities: Very important. Alumni/ae relationship: Important. Geographical residence: Not considered. State residency: Considered. Religious affiliation/commitment: Not considered. Minority status: Considered. Volunteer work: Considered. Work experience: Considered. **Other schools with the greatest overlap in applicants:** Furman University; James Madison University; North Carolina State University–Raleigh; University of North Carolina–Chapel Hill; Wake Forest University. **Admissions statistics for the fall 2005 entering class:** Total applicants: 9,065. Total accepted: 3,743. Freshmen enrolled: 1,237; 73% were from out of state. Accepted through early-decision or early-action plans: 66%. Overall acceptance rate: 41%. Early-decision acceptance rate: 65%. Non-early acceptance rate: 34%. **Size of waiting list:** 2251 applicants; enrolled from waiting list: 24. **Credentials of fall 2005 freshmen:** 32% ranked in the top 10 percent of their high school class; 67% were in the top 25 percent, and 93% were in the top half. (Proportion submitting class standing: 65%.) **Average high school grade point average:** 3.7. **First-year students who submitted SAT scores:** 100%. Scores (25/75 percentile): Verbal: 560-640, Math: 570-650, Combined: 1130-1290. **First-year students submitting ACT scores:** 28%. Scores (25/75 percentile): English: N/A, Math: N/A, Composite: 24-28.

ACADEMICS

Year founded: 1889. **Academic calendar:** 4-1-4. **Degrees offered:** bachelor's, master's, first professional, doctorate. **Most popular majors:** 21%

business/commerce, 20% communication and media studies, 10% education, 7% human services, 6% psychology. **Major fields of study:** biological and biomedical sciences; business, management, marketing, and related support services; communication, journalism, and related programs; computer and information sciences and support services; education; engineering; English language and literature/letters; foreign languages, literatures, and linguistics; health professions and related clinical sciences; history; mathematics and statistics; multi/interdisciplinary studies; natural resources and conservation; parks, recreation, leisure, and fitness studies; philosophy and religious studies; physical sciences; psychology; public administration and social service professions; social sciences; visual and performing arts. **Areas of required coursework:** humanities, mathematics, English (including composition), foreign languages, sciences (biological or physical), social science. **Pre-professional programs:** pre-law, pre-dentistry, pre-medicine, pre-theology, other. **Special academic programs (% participation):** accelerated program (6%), cross-registration (1%), distance learning (4%), double major (10%), dual enrollment (1%), English as a Second Language (ESL) (1%), exchange student program (domestic) (1%), honors program (13%), independent study (15%), internships (78%), liberal arts/career combination (2%), student-designed major (1%), study abroad (64%), teacher certificate program (9%). **Teacher certification offered in:** special education, elementary, middle/junior high, secondary. **Cooperative education programs:** art, business, computer science, education, engineering, health professions, humanities, natural science, social/behavioral science, technologies. **Reserve Officers Training Corps (ROTC):** Army ROTC: Offered at cooperating institution (North Carolina A&T University); Air Force ROTC: Offered at cooperating institution (North Carolina A&T University). **Faculty and instruction (2005-2006):** Total instructional faculty: 279 full-time, 91 part-time (54% men; 46% women; 9% minorities). Full-time faculty with Ph.D. or other terminal degree: 83%. Student/faculty ratio: 15/1. Classes of fewer than 20 students: 46%; of 20 to 49 students: 54%; of 50 or more students: 0%. **Advanced Placement and International Baccalaureate credit:** AP tests may be used for: Credit only. Scores accepted: 4, 5. International Baccalaureate exams may be used for: Credit only. **Freshmen returning for sophomore year:** 87%. **Graduation rates:** Four-year: 69%; five-year: 76%; six-year: 72%. **Graduate study:** 14% of students pursue further study immediately upon graduation; 15% within one year; 30% within five years.

COSTS AND FINANCIAL AID

Financial aid office: (336) 278-7640. **Expenses (2006-2007):** Tuition and fees 2006-2007: $20,441; room/board: $6,850. Estimated books and supplies: $900; transportation: $1,000; personal expenses: $1,500. **Financial aid:** Priority filing date for institution's financial aid form: February 15. In 2005-2006, 47% of undergraduates applied for financial aid. Of those, 34% were determined to have financial need; Average financial aid package (proportion receiving): $12,161 (34%). Average amount of gift aid, such as scholarships or grants (proportion receiving): $6,799 (30%). Average amount of self-help aid, such as work study or loans (proportion receiving): $5,362 (27%). Average need-based loan (excluding PLUS or other private loans): $3,771. Among students who received need-based aid, the average percentage of need met: 67%. Among students who received aid based on merit, the average award (and the proportion receiving): $4,119 (21%). The average athletic scholarship (and the proportion receiving): $13,941 (6%). Average amount of debt of borrowers graduating in 2005: $21,687. Proportion who borrowed: 45%.

CAMPUS LIFE AND EXTRACURRICULAR ACTIVITIES

Campus housing available (% using): coed dorms (65%), women's dorms (12%), men's dorms (4%), sorority housing (2%), fraternity housing (2%), apartment for single students (14%), special housing for international students (1%). Students who live in college-owned, operated, or affiliated housing: 57%. **Student employment:** During the 2005-2006 academic year, 20% of undergraduates worked on campus. Average per-year earnings: $2,500. **Clubs and organizations:** Number of student organizations: 140. Activities include: choral groups, concert band, dance, drama/theater, jazz band, literary magazine, marching band, music ensembles, musical theater, pep band, radio station, student government, student newspaper, student film society, symphony orchestra, television station, yearbook. Number of fraternities: 10; sororities: 11. Proportion of men in fraternities: 26%; of women in sororities: 43%. Average proportion of students who stay on campus on weekends: 70%. **Sports program (2005-2006):** Member of NCAA I. *Men's intercollegiate varsity sports:* baseball, basketball, cheerleading, cross-country, football, golf, soccer, tennis. *Women's intercollegiate varsity sports:* basketball, cheerleading, cross-country, golf, soccer, softball, tennis, track and field (indoor), track and field (outdoor), volleyball.

SERVICES AND FACILITIES

Basic services: nonremedial tutoring, placement service, health service. **Remedial assistance:** reading, math, writing. **Counseling services:** minority student, career, personal, veteran student, academic, older student, psychological, birth control, religious, other. **For learning-disabled students:** School does not offer a structured program with separate admission and additional fees. Total undergraduates in learning-disabled program or receiving services: 200. Services include: remedial English, remedial reading, note-taking services, extended time for tests, other. **Library:** Number of titles: 250,119; number of current serial subscriptions: 4,955. **Information technology resources:** Students are not required to lease or own a computer. Number of campus computers available to all students: 580. School has a wireless network. Approximate number of users that can be accommodated: 6,000. Proportion of college-owned housing units wired for high-speed internet access: 100%. **Campus safety:** Security services offered: 24-hour foot-and-vehicle patrols, late-night transport/escort service, 24-hour emergency telephones, lighted pathways/sidewalks, controlled dormitory access (key, security card, etc).

TRANSFER AND INTERNATIONAL STUDENTS

Transfer students: May apply for admission for the following academic terms: Fall, Spring. Applicants do not need a minimum number of credits to apply. For fall 2005: Transfer applications received: 298. Transfer applicants offered admission: 169. Transfer applicants enrolled: 79. **International students:** Number of foreign undergraduates: 79 (2% of student body). Number of countries represented: 40. Minimum TOEFL score required: 550 (paper); 213 (computer). Average TOEFL score: 635 (paper).

Fayetteville State University

- **Address:** 1200 Murchison Road, Fayetteville, NC 28301
- **Website:** http://www.uncfsu.edu
- **Public**
- **Enrollment:** 4,119 full-time; 910 part-time

KEY STATS

✔ **U.S News College Ranking:** fourth tier, Universities–Master's (South)
✔ **SAT Score (25th/75th percentile):** 740-930
✔ **Tuition:** 2006-2007: $3,205 in state, $12,941 out of state

Selectivity: Least selective	**Room/board:** $4,570
Acceptance rate: 80%	**Average debt:** $12,700
Student/faculty ratio: 22/1	**Proportion who borrowed:** 85%

UNDERGRADUATE STUDENT BODY STATS

2005-2006 enrollment: 4,119 full-time; 910 part-time. Men: 33%; women: 67%. **Ethnic makeup:** African American: 77%; American-Indian: 1%; Asian American: 1%; Hispanic: 4%; White: 17%.

ADMISSIONS FACTS AND FIGURES

Phone: (910) 672-1371. **Email:** admissions@uncfsu.edu. **Website:** http://www.uncfsu.edu. **Application deadlines for fall 2007:** Regular decision: August 25. Early decision: Not offered. Early action: Not offered. Admission can be deferred. **Application fee:** $25. Common application is not accepted. **Admissions requirements/recommendations:** High school units required (recommended): English: 4 (4); Mathematics: 3 (4); Science: 3 (3); Foreign language: 2 (2); Social studies: 2 (2); History: 2 (2); Academic electives: 6 (4); Total units: 21 (21). Tests: The college uses SAT or ACT scores in admissions decisions. Either SAT or ACT required. For admission to the fall 2007 entering class, the school will accept: ACT with writing, ACT without writing. Campus visit: Recommended. Admissions interview: Recommended. Off-campus interview: May be arranged. **Factors that count in admissions decisions:** *Academic:* Secondary school record: Very important. Class rank: Important. Letters of recommendation: Considered. Standardized test scores: Very important. Essay: Considered. *Nonacademic:* Interview: Considered. Extracurricular activities: Considered. Talent/ability: Important. Character/personal qualities: Important. Alumni/ae relationship: Not considered. Geographical residence: Not considered. State residency: Considered. Religious affiliation/commitment: Not considered. Minority status: Not considered. Volunteer work: Not considered. Work experience: Considered. **Other schools with the greatest overlap in applicants:** North Carolina A&T State University; North Carolina Central University; University of North Carolina–Pembroke; Winston-Salem State

University. **Admissions statistics for the fall 2005 entering class:** Total applicants: 2,318. Total accepted: 1,853. Freshmen enrolled: 848; 11% were from out of state. Overall acceptance rate: 80%. **Size of waiting list:** 0 applicants; enrolled from waiting list: 0. **Credentials of fall 2005 freshmen:** 2% ranked in the top 10 percent of their high school class; 13% were in the top 25 percent, and 48% were in the top half. (Proportion submitting class standing: 92%.) **Average high school grade point average:** 2.7. **First-year students who submitted SAT scores:** 100%. Scores (25/75 percentile): Verbal: 370-460, Math: 370-470, Combined: 740-930.

ACADEMICS

Year founded: 1867. **Academic calendar:** Semester. **Degrees offered:** bachelor's, master's, doctorate. **Most popular majors:** 17% business administration and management, 14% criminal justice/safety studies, 11% psychology, 11% sociology, 8% history. **Major fields of study:** biological and biomedical sciences; business, management, marketing, and related support services; computer and information sciences and support services; education; English language and literature/letters; foreign languages, literatures, and linguistics; history; mathematics and statistics; physical sciences; psychology; security and protective services; social sciences; visual and performing arts. **Areas of required coursework:** arts/fine arts, humanities, computer literacy, mathematics, English (including composition), philosophy, sciences (biological or physical), history, social science. **Pre-professional programs:** pre-dentistry, pre-medicine, pre-veterinary science, pre-pharmacy. **Special academic programs (% participation):** cooperative (work-study plan) program, distance learning, double major (1%), dual enrollment, honors program, independent study, internships, study abroad, teacher certificate program, weekend college, other. **Teacher certification offered in:** early childhood, special education, elementary, middle/junior high, secondary. **Cooperative education programs:** business, natural science, social/behavioral science. **Reserve Officers Training Corps (ROTC):** Army ROTC: Offered on campus; Air Force ROTC: Offered on campus. **Faculty and instruction (2005-2006):** Total instructional faculty: 200 full-time, 74 part-time (60% men; 40% women; 67% minorities). Full-time faculty with Ph.D. or other terminal degree: 91%. Student/faculty ratio: 22/1. Classes of fewer than 20 students: 38%; of 20 to 49 students: 61%; of 50 or more students: 0%. **Advanced Placement and International Baccalaureate credit:** AP tests may be used for: Credit and/or placement. Scores accepted: 3, 4, 5. **Freshmen returning for sophomore year:** 74%. **Graduation rates:** Four-year: 24%; five-year: 39%; six-year: 38%.

COSTS AND FINANCIAL AID

Financial aid office: (910) 672-1325. **Expenses (2006-2007):** Tuition and fees 2006-2007: $3,205 in state, $12,941 out of state; room/board: $4,570. Estimated books and supplies: $1,700. **Financial aid:** Priority filing date for institution's financial aid form: March 1; deadline: March 1. In 2005-2006, 96% of undergraduates applied for financial aid. Of those, 84% were determined to have financial need; 11% had their need fully met. Average financial aid package (proportion receiving): $8,063 (77%). Average amount of gift aid, such as scholarships or grants (proportion receiving): $3,460 (71%). Average amount of self-help aid, such as work study or loans (proportion receiving): $1,100 (12%). Average need-based loan (excluding PLUS or other private loans): $4,700. Among students who received need-based aid, the average percentage of need met: 86%. Among students who received aid based on merit, the average award (and the proportion receiving): $4,125 (7%). The average athletic scholarship (and the proportion receiving): $4,825 (2%). Average amount of debt of borrowers graduating in 2005: $12,700. Proportion who borrowed: 85%.

CAMPUS LIFE AND EXTRACURRICULAR ACTIVITIES

Campus housing available (% using): coed dorms (57%), women's dorms (43%). Students who live in college-owned, operated, or affiliated housing: 26%. **Student employment:** During the 2005-2006 academic year, 10% of undergraduates worked on campus. Average per-year earnings: $1,500. **Clubs and organizations:** Number of student organizations: 100. Activities include: choral groups, concert band, drama/theater, jazz band, marching band, music ensembles, pep band, radio station, student government, student newspaper, yearbook. Number of fraternities: 4; sororities: 2. Proportion of men in fraternities: 4%; of women in sororities: 2%. Average proportion of students who stay on campus on weekends: 60%. **Sports program (2005-2006):** Member of NCAA II. *Men's intercollegiate varsity sports:* basketball, cross-country, football, golf. *Women's intercollegiate varsity sports:* basketball, bowling, cross-country, softball, tennis, volleyball.

SERVICES AND FACILITIES

Basic services: nonremedial tutoring, placement service, day care, health service, health insurance. **Remedial assistance:** math, writing. **Counseling services:** career, military, personal, veteran student, academic. **For learning-disabled students:** School does not offer a structured program with separate admission and additional fees. **Library:** Number of titles: 333,079; number of current serial subscriptions: 2,723. **Information technology resources:** Students are not required to lease or own a computer. Number of campus computers available to all students: 325. School has a wireless network. Proportion of college-owned housing units wired for high-speed internet access: 100%. **Campus safety:** Security services offered: 24-hour foot-and-vehicle patrols, late-night transport/escort service, 24-hour emergency telephones, lighted pathways/sidewalks, student patrols, controlled dormitory access (key, security card, etc).

TRANSFER AND INTERNATIONAL STUDENTS

Transfer students: May apply for admission for the following academic terms: Fall, Winter, Spring, Summer. Applicants do not need a minimum number of credits to apply. For fall 2005: Transfer applications received: 872. Transfer applicants offered admission: 867. Transfer applicants enrolled: 699. **International students:** Number of foreign undergraduates: 1. Minimum TOEFL score required: 550 (paper); 213 (computer).

Gardner-Webb University

■ **Address:** PO Box 997, Boiling Springs, NC 28017
■ **Website:** http://www.gardner-webb.edu
■ **Private; Religious affiliation:** Baptist
■ **Enrollment:** 2,140 full-time; 434 part-time

KEY STATS

✔ **U.S News College Ranking:** 61, Universities–Master's (South)
✔ **SAT Score (25th/75th percentile):** 890-1140
✔ **Tuition:** 2006-2007: $17,210

Selectivity: Selective	**Room/board:** $5,740
Acceptance rate: 70%	**Average debt:** $7,014
Student/faculty ratio: 15/1	**Proportion who borrowed:** 53%

UNDERGRADUATE STUDENT BODY STATS

2005-2006 enrollment: 2,140 full-time; 434 part-time. Men: 35%; women: 65%. **Ethnic makeup:** African American: 14%; American-Indian: 1%; Asian American: 1%; Hispanic: 1%; White: 84%. **Religious preference:** Roman Catholic: 5%; Unknown: 11%; Baptist: 51%; Other: 33%.

ADMISSIONS FACTS AND FIGURES

Phone: (800) 253-6472. **Email:** admissions@gardner-webb.edu. **Website:** http://www.gardner-webb.edu. **Application deadlines for fall 2007:** Regular decision: Rolling. Early decision: Not offered. Early action: Not offered. Admission can be deferred. **Application fee:** $25. Common application is accepted. **Admissions requirements/recommendations:** High school units required (recommended): English: (4); Mathematics: (3); Science: (2); Foreign language: (2); Social studies: (2); History: (2); Academic electives: (2); Total units: (18). Tests: The college uses SAT or ACT scores in admissions decisions. Neither SAT nor ACT required. Campus visit: Recommended. Admissions interview: Recommended. Off-campus interview: May be arranged. **Factors that count in admissions decisions:** *Academic:* Secondary school record: Very important. Class rank: Very important. Letters of recommendation: Important. Standardized test scores: Very important. Essay: Important. *Nonacademic:* Interview: Considered. Extracurricular activities: Important. Talent/ability: Important. Character/personal qualities: Very important. Alumni/ae relationship: Considered. Geographical residence: Considered. State residency: Not considered. Religious affiliation/commitment: Considered. Minority status: Not considered. Volunteer work: Considered. Work experience: Not considered. **Other schools with the greatest overlap in applicants:** Appalachian State University; Campbell University; Elon University; University of North Carolina–Chapel Hill; University of North Carolina–Charlotte. **Admissions statistics for the fall 2005 entering class:** Total applicants: 2,073. Total accepted: 1,460. Freshmen enrolled: 438; 38% were from out of state. Overall acceptance rate: 70%. **Credentials of fall 2005 freshmen:** 18% ranked in the top 10 percent of their high school class; 44% were in the top 25 percent, and 74% were in the top half. (Proportion submitting class standing:

75%.) **Average high school grade point average:** 3.5. **First-year students who submitted SAT scores:** 85%. Scores (25/75 percentile): Verbal: 450-570, Math: 440-570, Combined: 890-1140. **First-year students submitting ACT scores:** 26%. Scores (25/75 percentile): English: N/A, Math: N/A, Composite: 19-23.

ACADEMICS

Year founded: 1905. **Academic calendar:** Semester. **Degrees offered:** associate, bachelor's, master's, first professional, doctorate. **Most popular majors:** 36% business, management, marketing, and related support services, 21% social sciences, 5% health professions and related clinical sciences, 5% parks, recreation, leisure, and fitness studies, 5% philosophy and religious studies. **Major fields of study:** biological and biomedical sciences; business, management, marketing, and related support services; communication, journalism, and related programs; computer and information sciences and support services; education; English language and literature/letters; foreign languages, literatures, and linguistics; health professions and related clinical sciences; history; mathematics and statistics; parks, recreation, leisure, and fitness studies; philosophy and religious studies; physical sciences; psychology; social sciences; visual and performing arts. **Areas of required coursework:** arts/fine arts, humanities, computer literacy, mathematics, English (including composition), foreign languages, sciences (biological or physical), history, social science. **Special academic programs (% participation):** distance learning (40%), double major (2%), English as a Second Language (ESL) (1%), honors program (2%), independent study (7%), internships (12%), study abroad (3%), teacher certificate program (5%). **Teacher certification offered in:** early childhood, elementary, middle/junior high, secondary. **Reserve Officers Training Corps (ROTC):** Army ROTC: Offered on campus. **Faculty and instruction (2005-2006):** Total instructional faculty: 133 full-time, 209 part-time. Full-time faculty with Ph.D. or other terminal degree: 78%. Student/faculty ratio: 15/1. Classes of fewer than 20 students: 62%; of 20 to 49 students: 38%; of 50 or more students: 0%. **Advanced Placement and International Baccalaureate credit:** AP tests may be used for: Credit only. International Baccalaureate exams may be used for: Credit only. **Freshmen returning for sophomore year:** 68%. **Graduation rates:** Four-year: 35%; five-year: 45%; six-year: 48%.

COSTS AND FINANCIAL AID

Financial aid office: (704) 406-4243. **Expenses (2006-2007):** Tuition and fees 2006-2007: $17,210; room/board: $5,740. Estimated books and supplies: $1,000 personal expenses: $650. **Financial aid:** Priority filing date for institution's financial aid form: March 15; deadline: June 30. In 2005-2006, 85% of undergraduates applied for financial aid. Of those, 74% were determined to have financial need; 22% had their need fully met. Average financial aid package (proportion receiving): $9,305 (74%). Average amount of gift aid, such as scholarships or grants (proportion receiving): $2,326 (66%). Average amount of self-help aid, such as work study or loans (proportion receiving): $3,355 (65%). Average need-based loan (excluding PLUS or other private loans): $3,624. Among students who received need-based aid, the average percentage of need met: 67%. Among students who received aid based on merit, the average award (and the proportion receiving): $4,291 (11%). The average athletic scholarship (and the proportion receiving): $8,305 (8%). Average amount of debt of borrowers graduating in 2005: $7,014. Proportion who borrowed: 53%.

CAMPUS LIFE AND EXTRACURRICULAR ACTIVITIES

Campus housing available (% using): women's dorms (43%), men's dorms (28%), apartment for single students (29%). Students who live in college-owned, operated, or affiliated housing: 42%. **Student employment:** During the 2005-2006 academic year, 7% of undergraduates worked on campus. Average per-year earnings: $1,114. **Clubs and organizations:** Number of student organizations: 60. Activities include: choral groups, concert band, dance, drama/theater, jazz band, literary magazine, music ensembles, musical theater, opera, pep band, radio station, student government, student newspaper, student film society, symphony orchestra, television station, yearbook. Number of fraternities: 0; sororities: 0. Average proportion of students who stay on campus on weekends: 60%. **Sports program (2005-2006):** Member of NCAA I. *Men's intercollegiate varsity sports:* baseball, basketball, cross-country, football, golf, soccer, tennis, track and field (indoor), track and field (outdoor), wrestling. *Women's intercollegiate varsity sports:* basketball, cross-country, golf, soccer, softball, swimming and diving, tennis, track and field (indoor), track and field (outdoor), volleyball.

SERVICES AND FACILITIES

Basic services: nonremedial tutoring, placement service, health insurance. **Remedial assistance:** reading, math, writing. **Counseling services:** career, personal, academic, psychological, religious. **For learning-disabled students:** School does not offer a structured program with separate admission and additional fees. Total undergraduates in learning-disabled program or receiving services: 70. Services include: remedial math, other testing accommodations, remedial English, reading machines, remedial reading, tape recorders, note-taking services, special bookstore section, oral tests, readers, extended time for tests, tutors, priority registration, priority seating, texts on tape, other testing accomodations, other. **Library:** Number of titles: 230,531; number of current serial subscriptions: 11,143. **Information technology resources:** Students are not required to lease or own a computer. Number of campus computers available to all students: 200. School has a wireless network. Approximate number of users that can be accommodated: 2,960. Proportion of college-owned housing units wired for high-speed internet access: 100%. **Campus safety:** Security services offered: 24-hour foot-and-vehicle patrols, late-night transport/escort service, 24-hour emergency telephones, lighted pathways/sidewalks, student patrols, controlled dormitory access (key, security card, etc).

TRANSFER AND INTERNATIONAL STUDENTS

Transfer students: May apply for admission for the following academic terms: Fall, Spring, Summer. Applicants need a minimum number of credits to apply. For fall 2005: Transfer applications received: 1,335. Transfer applicants offered admission: 1,217. Transfer applicants enrolled: 467. **International students:** Number of foreign undergraduates: 0. Number of countries represented: 21. Minimum TOEFL score required: 500 (paper); 173 (computer). Average TOEFL score: 545 (paper).

Greensboro College

- **Address:** 815 W. Market Street, Greensboro, NC 27401-1875
- **Website:** http://www.gborocollege.edu
- **Private; Religious affiliation:** Methodist
- **Enrollment:** 884 full-time; 248 part-time

KEY STATS
✔ **U.S News College Ranking:** fourth tier, Liberal Arts Colleges
✔ **SAT Score (25th/75th percentile):** 860-1070
✔ **Tuition:** 2005-2006: $18,120

Selectivity: Less selective	**Room/board:** $6,920
Acceptance rate: 69%	**Average debt:** N/A
Student/faculty ratio: 14/1	**Proportion who borrowed:** N/A

UNDERGRADUATE STUDENT BODY STATS
2005-2006 enrollment: 884 full-time; 248 part-time. Men: 45%; women: 55%. **Ethnic makeup:** African American: 19%; Asian American: 1%; White: 79%. **Religious preference:** Roman Catholic: 11%; Protestant: 44%; No preference: 19%; Unknown: 8%; Methodist: 18%.

ADMISSIONS FACTS AND FIGURES
Phone: (336) 272-7102. **Email:** admissions@gborocollege.edu. **Website:** http://www.gborocollege.edu. **Application deadlines for fall 2007:** Regular decision: Rolling. Early decision: Not offered. Early action: Send application by: December 15; Decision sent by: January 15. Admission can be deferred. **Application fee:** $35. Common application is accepted. **Admissions requirements/recommendations:** High school units required (recommended): English: 0 (4); Mathematics: 0 (3); Science: 0 (2); Foreign language: 0 (2); Social studies: 0 (0); History: 0 (2); Academic electives: 0 (0); Total units: 0 (0). Tests: The college uses SAT or ACT scores in admissions decisions. Either SAT or ACT required. For admission to the fall 2007 entering class, the school will accept: ACT with writing, ACT without writing. Campus visit: Recommended. Admissions interview: Recommended. Off-campus interview: May be arranged. **Factors that count in admissions decisions:** *Academic:* Secondary school record: Very important. Class rank: Very important. Letters of recommendation: Important. Standardized test scores: Important. Essay: Very important. *Nonacademic:* Interview: Important. Extracurricular activities: Very important. Talent/ability: Important. Character/personal qualities: Important. Alumni/ae relationship: Important. Geographical residence: Not considered. State residency: Not considered. Religious affiliation/commitment: Considered. Minority status: Not considered. Volunteer work: Considered. Work experience: Considered. **Other schools with the greatest overlap in applicants:** Appalachian State University; East Carolina University; Elon University; University of North

Carolina–Greensboro; University of North Carolina–Wilmington. **Admissions statistics for the fall 2005 entering class:** Total applicants: 1,112. Total accepted: 764. Freshmen enrolled: 217; 38% were from out of state. Overall acceptance rate: 69%. Non-early acceptance rate: 69%. **Credentials of fall 2005 freshmen:** 9% ranked in the top 10 percent of their high school class; 23% were in the top 25 percent, and 53% were in the top half. (Proportion submitting class standing: 80%.) **Average high school grade point average:** 3.1. **First-year students who submitted SAT scores:** 85%. Scores (25/75 percentile): Verbal: 420-510, Math: 440-560, Combined: 860-1070. **First-year students submitting ACT scores:** 24%. Scores (25/75 percentile): English: N/A, Math: N/A, Composite: 16-22.

ACADEMICS
Year founded: 1838. **Academic calendar:** Semester. **Degrees offered:** certificate, bachelor's, post-bachelor's certificate, master's. **Most popular majors:** 12% business administration and management, 7% sociology, 6% biology, 6% psychology, 5% political science and government. **Major fields of study:** biological and biomedical sciences; business, management, marketing, and related support services; education; English language and literature/letters; foreign languages, literatures, and linguistics; health professions and related clinical sciences; history; mathematics and statistics; multi/interdisciplinary studies; parks, recreation, leisure, and fitness studies; philosophy and religious studies; physical sciences; psychology; social sciences; visual and performing arts. **Areas of required coursework:** arts/fine arts, humanities, computer literacy, mathematics, English (including composition), foreign languages, sciences (biological or physical), history, social science, other. **Pre-professional programs:** pre-law, pre-dentistry, pre-medicine, pre-theology, pre-veterinary science. **Special academic programs:** accelerated program, cross-registration, double major, dual enrollment, English as a Second Language (ESL), honors program, independent study, internships, liberal arts/career combination, student-designed major, study abroad, teacher certificate program, weekend college, other. **Teacher certification offered in:** early childhood, special education, elementary, middle/junior high, secondary, bilingual/bicultural. **Cooperative education programs:** art, business, computer science, education, health professions, humanities, natural science, social/behavioral science, technologies. **Reserve Officers Training Corps (ROTC):** Army ROTC: Offered at cooperating institution (N.C. A&T University); Air Force ROTC: Offered at cooperating institution (N.C. A&T University). **Faculty and instruction (2005-2006):** Total instructional faculty: 63 full-time, 68 part-time (50% men; 50% women; 14% minorities). Full-time faculty with Ph.D. or other terminal degree: 81%. Student/faculty ratio: 14/1. Classes of fewer than 20 students: 81%; of 20 to 49 students: 19%; of 50 or more students: 0%. **Advanced Placement and International Baccalaureate credit:** AP tests may be used for: Placement only. Scores accepted: 3, 4, 5. International Baccalaureate exams may be used for: Credit and/or placement. **Freshmen returning for sophomore year:** 67%. **Graduation rates:** Four-year: 26%; five-year: 44%; six-year: 46%. **Graduate study:** 12% of students pursue further study within one year. Fields in which graduates pursue further study: theology (or the seminary), 2%; education, 1%; arts and sciences, 5%.

COSTS AND FINANCIAL AID
Financial aid office: (336) 272-7102. **Expenses (2005-2006):** Tuition and fees 2005-2006: $18,120; room/board: $6,920. Estimated books and supplies: $900; transportation: $300; personal expenses: $900. **Financial aid:** Priority filing date for institution's financial aid form: April 15.

CAMPUS LIFE AND EXTRACURRICULAR ACTIVITIES
Campus housing available (% using): coed dorms (51%), women's dorms (28%), men's dorms (19%), apartment for single students (2%), other housing options (0%). Students who live in college-owned, operated, or affiliated housing: 51%. **Student employment:** During the 2005-2006 academic year, 22% of undergraduates worked on campus. Average per-year earnings: $1,100. **Clubs and organizations:** Number of student organizations: 49. Activities include: choral groups, dance, drama/theater, jazz band, literary magazine, marching band, music ensembles, musical theater, opera, pep band, student government, student newspaper, yearbook. Number of fraternities: 3; sororities: 3. Average proportion of students who stay on campus on weekends: 65%. **Sports program (2005-2006):** Member of NCAA III. *Men's intercollegiate varsity sports:* baseball, basketball, cheerleading, cross-country, football, golf, lacrosse, soccer, tennis. *Women's intercollegiate varsity sports:* basketball, cheerleading, cross-country, lacrosse, soccer, softball, swimming and diving, tennis, volleyball.

SERVICES AND FACILITIES

Basic services: nonremedial tutoring, placement service, health service. **Remedial assistance:** math, writing, study skills, other. **Counseling services:** minority student, career, personal, academic, older student, psychological, birth control, religious. **For learning-disabled students:** School does not offer a structured program with separate admission and additional fees. Total undergraduates in learning-disabled program or receiving services: 175. Services include: remedial math, remedial English, reading machines, remedial reading, tape recorders, other special classes, diagnostic testing service, untimed tests, note-taking services, oral tests, learning center, readers, extended time for tests, tutors, priority seating, substitution of courses, texts on tape, typist/scribe, exams on tape or computer, other testing accomodations, other. **Library:** Number of titles: 110,596; number of current serial subscriptions: 251. **Information technology resources:** Students are not required to lease or own a computer. Number of campus computers available to all students: 150. School has a wireless network. Approximate number of users that can be accommodated: 100. Proportion of college-owned housing units wired for high-speed internet access: 100%. **Campus safety:** Security services offered: 24-hour foot-and-vehicle patrols, late-night transport/escort service, lighted pathways/sidewalks, controlled dormitory access (key, security card, etc.).

TRANSFER AND INTERNATIONAL STUDENTS

Transfer students: May apply for admission for the following academic terms: Fall, Spring, Summer. Applicants do not need a minimum number of credits to apply. For fall 2005: Transfer applications received: 243. Transfer applicants offered admission: 138. Transfer applicants enrolled: 87. **International students:** Number of foreign undergraduates: 1. Number of countries represented: 12. Minimum TOEFL score required: 550 (paper); 213 (computer).

Guilford College

- **Address:** 5800 W. Friendly Avenue, Greensboro, NC 27410
- **Website:** http://www.guilford.edu
- **Private; Religious affiliation:** Quaker
- **Enrollment:** 2,251 full-time; 431 part-time

KEY STATS

- ✔ **U.S News College Ranking:** fourth tier, Liberal Arts Colleges
- ✔ **SAT Score (25th/75th percentile):** 1020-1260
- ✔ **Tuition:** 2006-2007: $23,020

Selectivity: Selective	**Room/board:** $6,690
Acceptance rate: 63%	**Average debt:** $20,150
Student/faculty ratio: 17/1	**Proportion who borrowed:** 61%

UNDERGRADUATE STUDENT BODY STATS

2005-2006 enrollment: 2,251 full-time; 431 part-time. Men: 38%; women: 62%. **Ethnic makeup:** African American: 23%; American-Indian: 1%; Asian American: 1%; Hispanic: 2%; White: 72%; International: 1%. **Religious preference:** Roman Catholic: 6%; Protestant: 1%; Jewish: 2%; No preference: 43%; Quaker: 5%; Baptist: 12%; Other: 31%.

ADMISSIONS FACTS AND FIGURES

Phone: (800) 992-7759. **Email:** admission@guilford.edu. **Website:** http://www.guilford.edu. **Application deadlines for fall 2007:** Regular decision: February 1. Early decision: Not offered. Early action: Send application by: January 15; Decision sent by: February 15. Admission can be deferred. **Application fee:** $25. Common application is accepted. **Admissions requirements/recommendations:** High school units required (recommended): English: 4 (4); Mathematics: 3 (3); Science: 2 (3); Foreign language: 2 (2); Social studies: 2 (1); History: 1 (1); Academic electives: 2 (2); Total units: 18 (20). Tests: The college uses SAT or ACT scores in admissions decisions. Either SAT or ACT required. For admission to the fall 2007 entering class, the school will accept: ACT without writing. Campus visit: Recommended. Admissions interview: Recommended. Off-campus interview: May be arranged. **Factors that count in admissions decisions:** *Academic:* Secondary school record: Very important. Class rank: Important. Letters of recommendation: Important. Standardized test scores: Important. Essay: Important. *Nonacademic:* Interview: Considered. Extracurricular activities: Considered. Talent/ability: Considered. Character/personal qualities: Important. Alumni/ae relationship: Considered. Geographical residence: Considered.

State residency: Considered. Religious affiliation/commitment: Considered. Minority status: Considered. Volunteer work: Important. Work experience: Considered. **Other schools with the greatest overlap in applicants:** Appalachian State University; Elon University; Greensboro College; University of North Carolina–Chapel Hill; University of North Carolina–Greensboro. **Admissions statistics for the fall 2005 entering class:** Total applicants: 2,492. Total accepted: 1,564. Freshmen enrolled: 412; 59% were from out of state. Overall acceptance rate: 63%. Non-early acceptance rate: 63%. **Size of waiting list:** 115 applicants; enrolled from waiting list: 0. **Credentials of fall 2005 freshmen:** 14% ranked in the top 10 percent of their high school class; 44% were in the top 25 percent, and 78% were in the top half. (Proportion submitting class standing: 51%.) **Average high school grade point average:** 3.1. **First-year students who submitted SAT scores:** 92%. Scores (25/75 percentile): Verbal: 520-640, Math: 500-620, Combined: 1020-1260. **First-year students submitting ACT scores:** 16%. Scores (25/75 percentile): English: N/A, Math: N/A, Composite: 20-25.

ACADEMICS

Year founded: 1837. **Academic calendar:** Semester. **Degrees offered:** certificate, bachelor's. **Most popular majors:** 0% biology/biological sciences, 0% business, management, marketing, and related support services, 0% psychology, 0% security and protective services, 0% social sciences. **Major fields of study:** area, ethnic, cultural, and gender studies; biological and biomedical sciences; business, management, marketing, and related support services; computer and information sciences and support services; education; English language and literature/letters; foreign languages, literatures, and linguistics; health professions and related clinical sciences; history; mathematics and statistics; multi/interdisciplinary studies; natural resources and conservation; parks, recreation, leisure, and fitness studies; philosophy and religious studies; physical sciences; psychology; security and protective services; social sciences; visual and performing arts. **Areas of required coursework:** arts/fine arts, humanities, mathematics, English (including composition), philosophy, foreign languages, sciences (biological or physical), history, social science, other. **Special academic programs (% participation):** accelerated program (0%), cross-registration (5%), double major (30%), English as a Second Language (ESL) (0%), honors program (3%), independent study (88%), internships (31%), liberal arts/career combination (0%), student-designed major (0%), study abroad (24%), teacher certificate program (3%), weekend college (0%). **Teacher certification offered in:** elementary, secondary. **Faculty and instruction (2005-2006):** Total instructional faculty: 124 full-time, 78 part-time (54% men; 46% women; 12% minorities). Full-time faculty with Ph.D. or other terminal degree: 74%. Student/faculty ratio: 17/1. Classes of fewer than 20 students: 55%; of 20 to 49 students: 45%; of 50 or more students: 0%. **Advanced Placement and International Baccalaureate credit:** AP tests may be used for: Credit and/or placement. Scores accepted: 3, 4, 5. International Baccalaureate exams may be used for: Credit and/or placement. **Freshmen returning for sophomore year:** 74%. **Graduation rates:** Four-year: 44%; five-year: 55%; six-year: 55%. **Graduate study:** 24% of students pursue further study within one year. Fields in which graduates pursue further study: Master of Business Administration (MBA), 10%; law, 18%; medicine, 4%; engineering, 2%; theology (or the seminary), 8%; education, 12%; arts and sciences, 32%; veterinary medicine, 2%.

COSTS AND FINANCIAL AID

Financial aid office: (336) 316-2165. **Expenses (2006-2007):** Tuition and fees 2006-2007: $23,020; room/board: $6,690. Estimated books and supplies: $800; transportation: $600; personal expenses: $1,000. **Financial aid:** Priority filing date for institution's financial aid form: March 1. In 2005-2006, 53% of undergraduates applied for financial aid. Of those, 46% were determined to have financial need; 18% had their need fully met. Average financial aid package (proportion receiving): $11,661 (46%). Average amount of gift aid, such as scholarships or grants (proportion receiving): $8,325 (44%). Average amount of self-help aid, such as work study or loans (proportion receiving): $4,251 (42%). Average need-based loan (excluding PLUS or other private loans): $4,145. Among students who received need-based aid, the average percentage of need met: 67%. Among students who received aid based on merit, the average award (and the proportion receiving): $7,006 (18%). The average athletic scholarship (and the proportion receiving): $0 (0%). Average amount of debt of borrowers graduating in 2005: $20,150. Proportion who borrowed: 61%.

CAMPUS LIFE AND EXTRACURRICULAR ACTIVITIES

Campus housing available (% using): coed dorms (56%), women's dorms (11%), men's dorms (4%), apartment for single students (24%), special housing for international students (1%), other housing options (4%).

Students who live in college-owned, operated, or affiliated housing: 75%. **Student employment:** During the 2005-2006 academic year, 34% of undergraduates worked on campus. Average per-year earnings: $596. **Clubs and organizations:** Number of student organizations: 33. Activities include: choral groups, dance, drama/theater, jazz band, literary magazine, music ensembles, musical theater, radio station, student government, student newspaper, student film society, yearbook. Number of fraternities: 0; sororities: 0. Average proportion of students who stay on campus on weekends: 80%. **Sports program (2005-2006):** Member of NCAA III. *Men's intercollegiate varsity sports:* baseball, basketball, cross-country, football, golf, lacrosse, soccer, tennis. *Women's intercollegiate varsity sports:* basketball, cross-country, lacrosse, soccer, softball, swimming and diving, tennis, volleyball.

SERVICES AND FACILITIES

Basic services: nonremedial tutoring, women's center, placement service, day care, health service, health insurance. **Remedial assistance:** reading, math, writing, study skills, other. **Counseling services:** minority student, career, personal, veteran student, academic, older student, psychological, birth control, religious, other. **For learning-disabled students:** School does not offer a structured program with separate admission and additional fees. Total undergraduates in learning-disabled program or receiving services: 300. Services include: reading machines, tape recorders, other special classes, untimed tests, note-taking services, oral tests, learning center, readers, extended time for tests, tutors, texts on tape, other testing accomodations, waiver of foreign language degree requirement, waiver of math degree requirement. **Library:** Number of titles: 213,159; number of current serial subscriptions: 7,267. **Information technology resources:** Students are not required to lease or own a computer. Number of campus computers available to all students: 275. School has a wireless network. Proportion of college-owned housing units wired for high-speed internet access: 25%. **Campus safety:** Security services offered: 24-hour foot-and-vehicle patrols, late-night transport/escort service, 24-hour emergency telephones, lighted pathways/sidewalks, controlled dormitory access (key, security card, etc).

TRANSFER AND INTERNATIONAL STUDENTS

Transfer students: May apply for admission for the following academic terms: Fall, Spring. Applicants need a minimum number of credits to apply. For fall 2005: Transfer applications received: 235. Transfer applicants offered admission: 92. Transfer applicants enrolled: 57. **International students:** Number of foreign undergraduates: 23 (1% of student body). Number of countries represented: 15. Minimum TOEFL score required: 550 (paper); 213 (computer).

High Point University

- **Address:** 833 Montlieu Avenue, High Point, NC 27262-3598
- **Website:** http://www.highpoint.edu
- **Private; Religious affiliation:** United Methodist
- **Enrollment:** 2,325 full-time; 199 part-time

KEY STATS

✔ **U.S News College Ranking:** 15, Comp. Colleges–Bachelor's (South)
✔ **SAT Score (25th/75th percentile):** 920-1130
✔ **Tuition:** 2006-2007: $18,130

Selectivity: Less selective	**Room/board:** $7,590
Acceptance rate: 67%	**Average debt:** $20,125
Student/faculty ratio: 15/1	**Proportion who borrowed:** 83%

UNDERGRADUATE STUDENT BODY STATS

2005-2006 enrollment: 2,325 full-time; 199 part-time. Men: 37%; women: 63%. **Ethnic makeup:** African American: 23%; Asian American: 1%; Hispanic: 2%; White: 70%; International: 3%.

ADMISSIONS FACTS AND FIGURES

Phone: (800) 345-6993. **Email:** admiss@highpoint.edu. **Website:** http://www.highpoint.edu. **Application deadlines for fall 2007:** Regular decision: August 15. Early decision: Not offered. Early action: Not offered. Admission can be deferred. **Application fee:** $25. Common application is accepted. **To apply online, go to:** http://www.highpoint.edu/admissions. **Admissions requirements/recommendations:** High school units required (recommended): English: 4; Mathematics: 3; Science: 2; Foreign language:

2; Social studies: 2; History: 2; Academic electives: 1; Total units: 14. Tests: The college uses SAT or ACT scores in admissions decisions. Either SAT or ACT required. For admission to the fall 2007 entering class, the school will accept: ACT with writing, ACT without writing. **Campus visit:** Recommended. Admissions interview: Recommended. Off-campus interview: Not available. **Factors that count in admissions decisions:** *Academic:* Secondary school record: Very important. Class rank: Important. Letters of recommendation: Considered. Standardized test scores: Very important. Essay: Considered. *Nonacademic:* Interview: Considered. Extracurricular activities: Considered. Talent/ability: Considered. Character/personal qualities: Important. Alumni/ae relationship: Not considered. Geographical residence: Not considered. State residency: Not considered. Religious affiliation/commitment: Not considered. Minority status: Not considered. Volunteer work: Considered. Work experience: Considered. **Other schools with the greatest overlap in applicants:** Appalachian State University; Elon University; North Carolina State University–Raleigh; University of North Carolina–Chapel Hill; University of North Carolina–Greensboro. **Admissions statistics for the fall 2005 entering class:** Total applicants: 2,243. Total accepted: 1,512. Freshmen enrolled: 454; 61% were from out of state. Overall acceptance rate: 67%. **Credentials of fall 2005 freshmen:** 14% ranked in the top 10 percent of their high school class; 37% were in the top 25 percent, and 71% were in the top half. (Proportion submitting class standing: 67%.) **Average high school grade point average:** 3.1. **First-year students who submitted SAT scores:** 86%. Scores (25/75 percentile): Verbal: 460-570, Math: 460-560, Combined: 920-1130. **First-year students submitting ACT scores:** 20%. Scores (25/75 percentile): English: N/A, Math: N/A, Composite: 19-24.

ACADEMICS

Year founded: 1924. **Academic calendar:** Semester. **Degrees offered:** bachelor's, master's. **Most popular majors:** 28% business/commerce, 9% computer and information sciences, 7% human services, 6% psychology, 5% accounting. **Major fields of study:** area, ethnic, cultural, and gender studies; biological and biomedical sciences; business, management, marketing, and related support services; communication, journalism, and related programs; computer and information sciences and support services; education; English language and literature/letters; foreign languages, literatures, and linguistics; health professions and related clinical sciences; history; mathematics and statistics; multi/interdisciplinary studies; natural resources and conservation; parks, recreation, leisure, and fitness studies; philosophy and religious studies; physical sciences; psychology; public administration and social service professions; security and protective services; social sciences; visual and performing arts. **Areas of required coursework:** arts/fine arts, humanities, mathematics, English (including composition), philosophy, foreign languages, sciences (biological or physical), history, social science, other. **Pre-professional programs:** pre-law, pre-dentistry, pre-medicine, pre-pharmacy, other. **Special academic programs (% participation):** cross-registration (1.4%), distance learning (.6%), double major (4.6%), English as a Second Language (ESL), honors program (7.2%), independent study (17.8%), internships (9.2%), student-designed major (.2%), study abroad (1.7%), teacher certificate program (5.7%). **Teacher certification offered in:** special education, elementary, middle/junior high, secondary. **Cooperative education programs:** health professions, other. **Reserve Officers Training Corps (ROTC):** Army ROTC: Offered at cooperating institution (North Carolina A&T); Air Force ROTC: Offered at cooperating institution (North Carolina A&T). **Faculty and instruction (2005-2006):** Total instructional faculty: 122 full-time, 105 part-time (62% men; 38% women; 4% minorities). Full-time faculty with Ph.D. or other terminal degree: 76%. Student/faculty ratio: 15/1. Classes of fewer than 20 students: 76%; of 20 to 49 students: 23%; of 50 or more students: 0%. **Advanced Placement and International Baccalaureate credit:** AP tests may be used for: Credit and/or placement. Scores accepted: 3, 4, 5. International Baccalaureate exams may be used for: Credit and/or placement. **Freshmen returning for sophomore year:** 77%. **Graduation rates:** Four-year: 35%; five-year: 35%; six-year: 50%.

COSTS AND FINANCIAL AID

Financial aid office: (336) 841-9128. **Expenses (2006-2007):** Tuition and fees 2006-2007: $18,130; room/board: $7,590. Estimated books and supplies: $1,200; transportation: $600; personal expenses: $1,800. **Financial aid:** Priority filing date for institution's financial aid form: March 1. In 2005-2006, 84% of undergraduates applied for financial aid. Of those, 68% were determined to have financial need; 3% had their need fully met. Average financial aid package (proportion receiving): $14,750 (68%). Average amount of gift aid, such as scholarships or grants (proportion receiving): $5,500 (68%). Average amount of self-help aid, such as work study or loans (proportion receiving): $5,900 (68%). Average need-based loan (excluding

PLUS or other private loans): $5,500. Among students who received need-based aid, the average percentage of need met: 72%. Among students who received aid based on merit, the average award (and the proportion receiving): $7,000 (13%). The average athletic scholarship (and the proportion receiving): $11,704 (7%). Average amount of debt of borrowers graduating in 2005: $20,125. Proportion who borrowed: 83%.

CAMPUS LIFE AND EXTRACURRICULAR ACTIVITIES

Campus housing available (% using): coed dorms (12%), women's dorms (32%), men's dorms (21%), sorority housing (8%), fraternity housing (6%), apartment for single students (21%). Students who live in college-owned, operated, or affiliated housing: 75%. **Student employment:** During the 2005-2006 academic year, 15% of undergraduates worked on campus. Average per-year earnings: $1,500. **Clubs and organizations:** Number of student organizations: 96. Activities include: choral groups, concert band, drama/theater, literary magazine, music ensembles, musical theater, pep band, radio station, student government, student newspaper, television station, yearbook. Number of fraternities: 5; sororities: 4. Proportion of men in fraternities: 20%; of women in sororities: 31%. Average proportion of students who stay on campus on weekends: 80%. **Sports program (2005-2006):** Member of NCAA III. *Men's intercollegiate varsity sports:* baseball, basketball, cross-country, golf, soccer, tennis, track and field (indoor), track and field (outdoor). *Women's intercollegiate varsity sports:* basketball, cross-country, golf, soccer, tennis, track and field (indoor), track and field (outdoor), volleyball.

SERVICES AND FACILITIES

Basic services: nonremedial tutoring, placement service, health service, health insurance. **Remedial assistance:** reading, math, writing, study skills. **Counseling services:** minority student, career, military, personal, veteran student, academic, older student, psychological, birth control, religious. **For learning-disabled students:** School does not offer a structured program with separate admission and additional fees. Total undergraduates in learning-disabled program or receiving services: 94. Services include: remedial math, remedial English, reading machines, remedial reading, tape recorders, note-taking services, oral tests, learning center, readers, extended time for tests, tutors, priority registration, priority seating, texts on tape, other testing accomodations. **Library:** Number of titles: 169,039; number of current serial subscriptions: 12,761. **Information technology resources:** Students are not required to lease or own a computer. Number of campus computers available to all students: 325. School has a wireless network. Approximate number of users that can be accommodated: 300. Proportion of college-owned housing units wired for high-speed internet access: 100%. **Campus safety:** Security services offered: 24-hour foot-and-vehicle patrols, late-night transport/escort service, 24-hour emergency telephones, lighted pathways/sidewalks, student patrols, controlled dormitory access (key, security card, etc).

TRANSFER AND INTERNATIONAL STUDENTS

Transfer students: May apply for admission for the following academic terms: Fall, Spring, Summer. Applicants need a minimum number of credits to apply. For fall 2005: Transfer applications received: 487. Transfer applicants offered admission: 341. Transfer applicants enrolled: 229. **International students:** Number of foreign undergraduates: 80 (3% of student body). Minimum TOEFL score required: 500 (paper); 173 (computer).

Johnson C. Smith University

- **Address:** 100 Beatties Ford Road, Charlotte, NC 28216
- **Website:** http://www.jcsu.edu
- **Private**
- **Enrollment:** 1,340 full-time; 64 part-time

KEY STATS

✔ **U.S News College Ranking:** 30, Comp. Colleges–Bachelor's (South)
✔ **SAT Score (25th/75th percentile):** 826-1002
✔ **Tuition:** 2006-2007: $15,004

Selectivity: Selective	**Room/board:** $5,840
Acceptance rate: 37%	**Average debt:** $25,000
Student/faculty ratio: 14/1	**Proportion who borrowed:** 90%

UNDERGRADUATE STUDENT BODY STATS

2005-2006 enrollment: 1,340 full-time; 64 part-time. Men: 40%; women: 60%. **Ethnic makeup:** African American: 100%.

ADMISSIONS FACTS AND FIGURES

Phone: (704) 378-1010. **Email:** admissions@jcsu.edu. **Website:** http://www.jcsu.edu. **Application deadlines for fall 2007:** Regular decision: Rolling. Early decision: Not offered. Early action: Not offered. Admission can be deferred. **Application fee:** $25. Common application is not accepted. **Admissions requirements/recommendations:** High school units required (recommended): English: 4; Mathematics: 2; Science: 1; Social studies: 2; Academic electives: 7; Total units: 16. Tests: The college uses SAT or ACT scores in admissions decisions. Either SAT or ACT required. Campus visit: Recommended. Admissions interview: Recommended. Off-campus interview: May be arranged. **Factors that count in admissions decisions:** *Academic:* Secondary school record: Very important. Class rank: Important. Letters of recommendation: Considered. Standardized test scores: Very important. Essay: Considered. *Nonacademic:* Interview: Important. Extracurricular activities: Not considered. Talent/ability: Considered. Character/personal qualities: Not considered. Alumni/ae relationship: Not considered. Geographical residence: Not considered. State residency: Not considered. Religious affiliation/commitment: Not considered. Minority status: Not considered. Volunteer work: Not considered. Work experience: Not considered. **Other schools with the greatest overlap in applicants:** Clark Atlanta University; Hampton University; Howard University; North Carolina A&T State University; North Carolina Central University. **Admissions statistics for the fall 2005 entering class:** Total applicants: 4,231. Total accepted: 1,549. Freshmen enrolled: 444; 73% were from out of state. Overall acceptance rate: 37%. **Credentials of fall 2005 freshmen:** 42% ranked in the top 10 percent of their high school class; 89% were in the top 25 percent, and 92% were in the top half. (Proportion submitting class standing: 100%.) **Average high school grade point average:** 2.8. **First-year students who submitted SAT scores:** 82%. Scores (25/75 percentile): Verbal: 412-504, Math: 414-498, Combined: 826-1002. **First-year students submitting ACT scores:** 18%. Scores (25/75 percentile): English: 20-21, Math: 17-19, Composite: 17-20.

ACADEMICS

Year founded: 1867. **Academic calendar:** Semester. **Degrees offered:** bachelor's. **Most popular majors:** 16% business administration and management, 14% computer and information sciences, 13% mass communication/media studies, 9% liberal arts and sciences/liberal studies, 8% criminology. **Major fields of study:** biological and biomedical sciences; business, management, marketing, and related support services; communication, journalism, and related programs; computer and information sciences and support services; education; engineering; English language and literature/letters; foreign languages, literatures, and linguistics; history; liberal arts and sciences studies, and humanities; mathematics and statistics; multi/interdisciplinary studies; parks, recreation, leisure, and fitness studies; physical sciences; psychology; public administration and social service professions; social sciences; visual and performing arts. **Areas of required coursework:** arts/fine arts, humanities, computer literacy, mathematics, English (including composition), philosophy, foreign languages, sciences (biological or physical), history, social science. **Pre-professional programs:** pre-law, pre-medicine, pre-pharmacy, other. **Special academic programs (% participation):** accelerated program (14%), cooperative (work-study plan) program (25%), cross-registration (2%), double major (1%), exchange student program (domestic) (4%), honors program (10%), independent study (8%), internships, liberal arts/career combination (10%), study abroad (5%), teacher certificate program (9%). **Teacher certification offered in:** elementary, secondary. **Cooperative education programs:** business, computer science, education, engineering, humanities, natural science, social/behavioral science. **Reserve Officers Training Corps (ROTC):** Army ROTC: Offered at cooperating institution (University of North Carolina at Charlotte); Air Force ROTC: Offered at cooperating institution (University of North Carolina at Charlotte). **Faculty and instruction (2005-2006):** Total instructional faculty: 90 full-time, 31 part-time (57% men; 43% women; 70% minorities). Full-time faculty with Ph.D. or other terminal degree: 69%. Student/faculty ratio: 14/1. Classes of fewer than 20 students: 62%; of 20 to 49 students: 38%. **Advanced Placement and International Baccalaureate credit:** International Baccalaureate exams may be used for: Credit and/or placement. **Freshmen returning for sophomore year:** 63%. **Graduation rates:** Four-year: 23%; five-year: 30%; six-year: 40%. **Graduate study:** 24% of students pursue further study within one year. Fields in which graduates pursue further study: Master of Business Administration (MBA), 15%; law, 11%; medicine, 3%; engineering, 5%; arts and sciences, 66%.

COSTS AND FINANCIAL AID

Financial aid office: (704) 378-1035. **Expenses (2006-2007):** Tuition and fees 2006-2007: $15,004; room/board: $5,840. Estimated books and supplies: $1,080; transportation: $1,300; personal expenses: $2,594. **Financial aid:** Priority filing date for institution's financial aid form: March 15; deadline: June 30. In 2005-2006, 89% of undergraduates applied for financial aid. Of those, 86% were determined to have financial need; 4% had their need fully met. Average financial aid package (proportion receiving): $9,725 (85%). Average amount of gift aid, such as scholarships or grants (proportion receiving): $3,000 (71%). Average amount of self-help aid, such as work study or loans (proportion receiving): $2,000 (32%). Average need-based loan (excluding PLUS or other private loans): $5,500. Among students who received need-based aid, the average percentage of need met: 60%. Among students who received aid based on merit, the average award (and the proportion receiving): $2,717 (8%). The average athletic scholarship (and the proportion receiving): $6,231 (9%). Average amount of debt of borrowers graduating in 2005: $25,000. Proportion who borrowed: 90%.

CAMPUS LIFE AND EXTRACURRICULAR ACTIVITIES

Campus housing available (% using): coed dorms (22%), women's dorms (44%), men's dorms (34%). Students who live in college-owned, operated, or affiliated housing: 70%. **Student employment:** During the 2005-2006 academic year, 10% of undergraduates worked on campus. Average per-year earnings: $5,000. **Clubs and organizations:** Number of student organizations: 67. Activities include: choral groups, concert band, dance, jazz band, marching band, music ensembles, pep band, student government, student newspaper, yearbook. Number of fraternities: 5; sororities: 5. Proportion of men in fraternities: 17%; of women in sororities: 11%. Average proportion of students who stay on campus on weekends: 70%. **Sports program (2005-2006):** Member of NCAA II. *Men's intercollegiate varsity sports:* basketball, cross-country, football, golf, tennis, track and field (outdoor). *Women's intercollegiate varsity sports:* basketball, bowling, cross-country, golf, softball, tennis, track and field (outdoor), volleyball.

SERVICES AND FACILITIES

Basic services: placement service, health service, health insurance. **Remedial assistance:** reading, math, writing, study skills, other. **Counseling services:** minority student, career, personal, academic, older student, psychological, religious. **For learning-disabled students:** School does not offer a structured program with separate admission and additional fees. Total undergraduates in learning-disabled program or receiving services: 40. Services include: reading machines, tape recorders, untimed tests, note-taking services, oral tests, learning center, readers, extended time for tests, tutors, priority registration, priority seating, proofreading services, exams on tape or computer, other testing accomodations. **Library:** Number of titles: 97,302; number of current serial subscriptions: 291. **Information technology resources:** Students are required to lease or own a computer. Number of campus computers available to all students: 1,650. School has a wireless network. Approximate number of users that can be accommodated: 5,000. Proportion of college-owned housing units wired for high-speed internet access: 100%. **Campus safety:** Security services offered: 24-hour foot-and-vehicle patrols, 24-hour emergency telephones, lighted pathways/sidewalks, controlled dormitory access (key, security card, etc).

TRANSFER AND INTERNATIONAL STUDENTS

Transfer students: May apply for admission for the following academic terms: Fall, Spring, Summer. Applicants need a minimum number of credits to apply. For fall 2005: Transfer applications received: 184. Transfer applicants offered admission: 61. Transfer applicants enrolled: 35. **International students:** Number of foreign undergraduates: 4. Number of countries represented: 4. Minimum TOEFL score required: 600 (paper).

Lees-McRae College

- **Address:** PO Box 128, Banner Elk, NC 28604
- **Website:** http://www.lmc.edu
- **Private; Religious affiliation:** Presbyterian
- **Enrollment:** 866 full-time; 16 part-time

KEY STATS

✔ **U.S News College Ranking:** fourth tier, Liberal Arts Colleges
✔ **SAT Score (25th/75th percentile):** 900-1110
✔ **Tuition:** 2006-2007: $18,000

Selectivity: Less selective	**Room/board:** $6,000
Acceptance rate: 74%	**Average debt:** $9,565
Student/faculty ratio: 16/1	**Proportion who borrowed:** 49%

UNDERGRADUATE STUDENT BODY STATS

2005-2006 enrollment: 866 full-time; 16 part-time. Men: 44%; women: 56%. **Ethnic makeup:** African American: 3%; American-Indian: 1%; Asian American: 1%; Hispanic: 2%; White: 88%; International: 4%. **Religious preference:** Roman Catholic: 7%; Protestant: 41%; Jewish: 1%; No preference: 51%.

ADMISSIONS FACTS AND FIGURES

Phone: (828) 898-8723. **Email:** admissions@lmc.edu. **Website:** http://www.lmc.edu. **Application deadlines for fall 2007:** Regular decision: July 1. Early decision: Not offered. Early action: Not offered. Admission can be deferred. **Application fee:** $25. Common application is accepted. **Admissions requirements/recommendations:** High school units required (recommended): English: 4; Mathematics: 3; Science: 2; Foreign language: (2); Social studies: (2); History: 1; Academic electives: 5; Total units: 18. Tests: The college uses SAT or ACT scores in admissions decisions. Either SAT or ACT required. For admission to the fall 2007 entering class, the school will accept: ACT with writing, ACT without writing. Campus visit: Recommended. Admissions interview: Recommended. Off-campus interview: May be arranged. **Factors that count in admissions decisions:** *Academic:* Secondary school record: Very important. Class rank: Considered. Letters of recommendation: Considered. Standardized test scores: Very important. Essay: Considered. *Nonacademic:* Interview: Considered. Extracurricular activities: Considered. Talent/ability: Considered. Character/personal qualities: Considered. Alumni/ae relationship: Not considered. Geographical residence: Not considered. State residency: Not considered. Religious affiliation/commitment: Not considered. Minority status: Not considered. Volunteer work: Not considered. Work experience: Not considered. **Admissions statistics for the fall 2005 entering class:** Total applicants: 1,003. Total accepted: 743. Freshmen enrolled: 224; 25% were from out of state. Overall acceptance rate: 74%. **Credentials of fall 2005 freshmen:** 8% ranked in the top 10 percent of their high school class; 24% were in the top 25 percent, and 58% were in the top half. (Proportion submitting class standing: 74%.) **Average high school grade point average:** 3.1. **First-year students who submitted SAT scores:** 85%. Scores (25/75 percentile): Verbal: 450-560, Math: 450-550, Combined: 900-1110. **First-year students submitting ACT scores:** 20%. Scores (25/75 percentile): English: 19-24, Math: 18-24, Composite: 19-24.

ACADEMICS

Year founded: 1900. **Academic calendar:** Semester. **Degrees offered:** bachelor's. **Most popular majors:** 38% education, 20% biological and biomedical sciences, 12% business, management, marketing, and related support services. **Major fields of study:** biological and biomedical sciences; business, management, marketing, and related support services; communication, journalism, and related programs; education; English language and literature/letters; health professions and related clinical sciences; history; multi/interdisciplinary studies; natural resources and conservation; philosophy and religious studies; psychology; social sciences; visual and performing arts. **Areas of required coursework:** arts/fine arts, humanities, computer literacy, mathematics, English (including composition), philosophy, sciences (biological or physical), history, social science, other. **Pre-professional programs:** pre-medicine, pre-veterinary science. **Special academic programs (% participation):** double major (5%), English as a Second Language (ESL) (1%), honors program (5%), independent study (5%), internships (5%), student-designed major (1%), study abroad (5%), teacher certificate program (15%). **Teacher certification offered in:** elementary. **Faculty and instruction (2005-2006):** Total instructional faculty: 55. Full-time faculty with Ph.D. or other terminal degree: 65%. Student/faculty ratio: 16/1. Classes of fewer than 20 students: 77%; of 20 to 49 students: 23%; of 50 or more students: 0%. **Advanced Placement and International Baccalaureate credit:** AP tests may be used for: Credit only. Scores accepted: 3, 4, 5. International Baccalaureate exams may be used for: Credit only. **Freshmen returning for sophomore year:** 59%. **Graduation rates:** Four-year: 20%; five-year: 26%; six-year: 28%.

COSTS AND FINANCIAL AID

Financial aid office: (828) 898-8793. **Expenses (2006-2007):** Tuition and fees 2006-2007: $18,000; room/board: $6,000. Estimated books and supplies: $800; transportation: $250; personal expenses: $2,500. **Financial aid:** Priority filing date for institution's financial aid form: March 15; deadline: March 15. In 2005-2006, 75% of undergraduates applied for financial aid. Of those, 65% were determined to have financial need; 97% had their need fully met. Average financial aid package (proportion receiving): $10,174 (65%). Average amount of gift aid, such as scholarships or grants (proportion receiving): $4,976 (65%). Average amount of self-help aid, such as work study or loans (proportion receiving): $2,108 (64%). Average need-based loan (excluding PLUS or other private loans): $3,705. Among students who received need-based aid, the average percentage of need met: 90%. Among students who received aid based on merit, the average award (and the proportion receiving): $4,800 (42%). The average athletic scholarship (and the proportion receiving): $3,750 (94%). Average amount of debt of borrowers graduating in 2005: $9,565. Proportion who borrowed: 49%.

CAMPUS LIFE AND EXTRACURRICULAR ACTIVITIES

Campus housing available (% using): coed dorms (33%), women's dorms (34%), men's dorms (32%), apartments for married students (1%), special housing for disabled students (0%). Students who live in college-owned, operated, or affiliated housing: 75%. **Student employment:** During the 2005-2006 academic year, 42% of undergraduates worked on campus. Average per-year earnings: $1,400. **Clubs and organizations:** Number of student organizations: 25. Activities include: choral groups, dance, drama/theater, music ensembles, musical theater, pep band, student government, yearbook. Number of fraternities: 0; sororities: 0. Average proportion of students who stay on campus on weekends: 60%. **Sports program (2005-2006):** Member of NCAA II. *Men's intercollegiate varsity sports:* basketball, cross-country, golf, lacrosse, soccer, tennis, track and field (indoor), track and field (outdoor), volleyball. *Women's intercollegiate varsity sports:* basketball, cross-country, lacrosse, soccer, softball, tennis, track and field (indoor), track and field (outdoor), volleyball.

SERVICES AND FACILITIES

Basic services: nonremedial tutoring, placement service, health service, health insurance. **Remedial assistance:** reading, math, writing, study skills. **Counseling services:** career, personal, academic, older student, psychological, birth control, religious. **For learning-disabled students:** School does not offer a structured program with separate admission and additional fees. Services include: remedial math, remedial English, reading machines, remedial reading, other special classes, untimed tests, note-taking services, oral tests, learning center, readers, extended time for tests, tutors. **Library:** Number of titles: 111,167; number of current serial subscriptions: 11,575. **Information technology resources:** Students are not required to lease or own a computer. Number of campus computers available to all students: 90. School has a wireless network. Approximate number of users that can be accommodated: 2,000. Proportion of college-owned housing units wired for high-speed internet access: 100%. **Campus safety:** Security services offered: 24-hour foot-and-vehicle patrols, late-night transport/escort service, lighted pathways/sidewalks, controlled dormitory access (key, security card, etc).

TRANSFER AND INTERNATIONAL STUDENTS

Transfer students: May apply for admission for the following academic terms: Fall, Spring, Summer. Applicants do not need a minimum number of credits to apply. For fall 2005: Transfer applications received: 102. Transfer applicants offered admission: 80. Transfer applicants enrolled: 59. **International students:** Number of foreign undergraduates: 37 (4% of student body). Number of countries represented: 12. Minimum TOEFL score required: 500 (paper); 173 (computer). Average TOEFL score: 550 (paper).

Lenoir-Rhyne College

- **Address:** PO Box 7163, Hickory, NC 28603-7163
- **Website:** http://www.lrc.edu
- **Private; Religious affiliation:** Lutheran
- **Enrollment:** 1,305 full-time; 121 part-time

KEY STATS

✔ **U.S News College Ranking:** 11, Comp. Colleges–Bachelor's (South)
✔ **SAT Score (25th/75th percentile):** 930-1160
✔ **Tuition:** 2006-2007: $20,180
   Selectivity: Selective   **Room/board:** $7,130
   Acceptance rate: 83%   **Average debt:** $24,951
   Student/faculty ratio: 13/1   **Proportion who borrowed:** 92%

UNDERGRADUATE STUDENT BODY STATS

2005-2006 enrollment: 1,305 full-time; 121 part-time. Men: 37%; women: 63%. **Ethnic makeup:** African American: 8%; Asian American: 2%; Hispanic: 1%; White: 87%. **Religious preference:** Roman Catholic: 5%; Protestant: 44%; No preference: 2%; Unknown: 27%; Lutheran: 18%; Mormon: 0%; Other: 4%.

ADMISSIONS FACTS AND FIGURES

Phone: (828) 328-7300. **Email:** admission@lrc.edu. **Website:** http://www.lrc.edu. **Application deadlines for fall 2007:** Regular decision: August 15. Early decision: Not offered. Early action: Not offered. Admission can be deferred. **Application fee:** $35. Common application is not accepted. **Admissions requirements/recommendations:** High school units required (recommended): English: 4; Mathematics: 3; Science: 1; Foreign language: 2; History: 1; Total units: 12. Tests: The college uses SAT or ACT scores in admissions decisions. Either SAT or ACT required. For admission to the fall 2007 entering class, the school will accept ACT without writing. Campus visit: Recommended. Admissions interview: Recommended. Off-campus interview: May be arranged. **Factors that count in admissions decisions:** *Academic:* Secondary school record: Very important. Class rank: Important. Letters of recommendation: Considered. Standardized test scores: Very important. Essay: Considered. *Nonacademic:* Interview: Important. Extracurricular activities: Considered. Talent/ability: Considered. Character/personal qualities: Considered. Alumni/ae relationship: Not considered. Geographical residence: Not considered. State residency: Not considered. Religious affiliation/commitment: Not considered. Minority status: Not considered. Volunteer work: Considered. Work experience: Not considered. **Other schools with the greatest overlap in applicants:** Appalachian State University; Gardner-Webb University; University of North Carolina–Chapel Hill; University of North Carolina–Charlotte; University of North Carolina–Greensboro. **Admissions statistics for the fall 2005 entering class:** Total applicants: 1,693. Total accepted: 1,408. Freshmen enrolled: 330; 30% were from out of state. Overall acceptance rate: 83%. **Credentials of fall 2005 freshmen:** 18% ranked in the top 10 percent of their high school class; 46% were in the top 25 percent, and 81% were in the top half. (Proportion submitting class standing: 85%.) **Average high school grade point average:** 3.5. **First-year students who submitted SAT scores:** 89%. Scores (25/75 percentile): Verbal: 460-570; Math: 470-590; Combined: 930-1160. **First-year students submitting ACT scores:** 19%. Scores (25/75 percentile): English: 18-23, Math: 17-24, Composite: 17-23.

ACADEMICS

Year founded: 1891. **Academic calendar:** Semester. **Degrees offered:** bachelor's, master's. **Most popular majors:** 23% business, management, marketing, and related support services, 18% education, 10% health professions and related clinical sciences, 7% psychology, 6% social sciences. **Major fields of study:** biological and biomedical sciences; business, management, marketing, and related support services; communication, journalism, and related programs; computer and information sciences and support services; education; English language and literature/letters; foreign languages, literatures, and linguistics; health professions and related clinical sciences; history; liberal arts and sciences studies, and humanities; mathematics and statistics; natural resources and conservation; parks, recreation, leisure, and fitness studies; philosophy and religious studies; physical sciences; psychology; public administration and social service professions; social sciences; theology and religious vocations; visual and performing arts. **Areas of required coursework:** arts/fine arts, humanities, computer literacy, mathematics, English (including composition), philosophy, foreign languages, sciences (biological or physical), history, social science, other. **Pre-professional programs:** pre-law, pre-medicine. **Special academic programs:** accelerated program, cooperative (work-study plan) program, cross-registration, distance learning, double major, English as a Second Language (ESL), honors program, independent study, internships, liberal arts/career combination, student-designed major, study abroad, teacher certificate program. **Teacher certification offered in:** early childhood, special education, elementary, middle/junior high, secondary, bilingual/bicultural. **Reserve Officers Training Corps (ROTC):** Army ROTC: Offered at cooperating institution (Davidson College). **Faculty and instruction (2005-2006):** Total instructional faculty: 88 full-time, 78 part-time (49% men; 51% women; 5% minorities). Full-time faculty with Ph.D. or other terminal degree: 75%. Student/faculty ratio: 13/1. Classes of fewer than 20 students: 62%; of 20 to 49 students: 37%; of 50 or more students: 1%. **Advanced Placement and International Baccalaureate credit:** AP tests may be used for: Credit and/or placement. Scores accepted: 3, 4, 5. International Baccalaureate exams may be used for: Credit and/or placement. **Freshmen returning for sophomore year:** 71%. **Graduation rates:** Four-year: 41%; five-year: 49%; six-year: 51%.

COSTS AND FINANCIAL AID

Financial aid office: (828) 328-7304. **Expenses (2006-2007):** Tuition and fees 2006-2007: $20,180; room/board: $7,130. Estimated books and supplies: $1,000; transportation: $1,000; personal expenses: $1,500. **Financial aid:** Priority filing date for institution's financial aid form: March 1; deadline: September 1. In 2005-2006, 97% of undergraduates applied for financial aid. Of those, 79% were determined to have financial need; 24% had their need fully met. Average financial aid package (proportion receiving): $14,779 (79%). Average amount of gift aid, such as scholarships or grants (proportion receiving): $12,076 (79%). Average amount of self-help aid, such as work study or loans (proportion receiving): $4,311 (55%). Average need-based loan (excluding PLUS or other private loans): $4,237. Among students who received need-based aid, the average percentage of need met: 72%. Among students who received aid based on merit, the average award (and the proportion receiving): $6,362 (18%). The average athletic scholarship (and the proportion receiving): $5,816 (4%). Average amount of debt of borrowers graduating in 2005: $24,951. Proportion who borrowed: 92%.

CAMPUS LIFE AND EXTRACURRICULAR ACTIVITIES

Campus housing available (% using): coed dorms (99%), fraternity housing (1%), special housing for disabled students (0%). Students who live in college-owned, operated, or affiliated housing: 58%. **Student employment:** During the 2005-2006 academic year, 27% of undergraduates worked on campus. Average per-year earnings: $750. **Clubs and organizations:** Number of student organizations: 60. Activities include: choral groups, concert band, dance, drama/theater, jazz band, literary magazine, music ensembles, musical theater, pep band, radio station, student government, student newspaper, symphony orchestra, television station, yearbook. Number of fraternities: 3; sororities: 4. Proportion of men in fraternities: 23%; of women in sororities: 27%. Average proportion of students who stay on campus on weekends: 30%. **Sports program (2005-2006):** Member of NCAA II. *Men's intercollegiate varsity sports:* baseball, basketball, cross-country, football, golf, soccer, track and field (outdoor). *Women's intercollegiate varsity sports:* basketball, cross-country, golf, soccer, softball, swimming and diving, tennis, track and field (outdoor), volleyball.

SERVICES AND FACILITIES

Basic services: nonremedial tutoring, placement service, health service, health insurance. **Remedial assistance:** reading, math, writing, study skills. **Counseling services:** minority student, career, personal, academic, psychological, religious. **For learning-disabled students:** School does not offer a structured program with separate admission and additional fees. Total undergraduates in learning-disabled program or receiving services: 32. Services include: remedial math, remedial English, reading machines, tape recorders, note-taking services, oral tests, readers, extended time for tests, tutors, priority seating, substitution of courses, typist/scribe, exams on tape or computer, other testing accomodations, waiver of foreign language degree requirement. **Library:** Number of titles: 154,243; number of current serial subscriptions: 986. **Information technology resources:** Students are not required to lease or own a computer. Number of campus computers available to all students: 149. School has a wireless network. Approximate number of users that can be accommodated: 500. Proportion of college-owned housing units wired for high-speed internet access: 100%. **Campus safety:** Security services offered: 24-hour foot-and-vehicle patrols, late-night transport/escort service, 24-hour emergency telephones, lighted pathways/sidewalks, controlled dormitory access (key, security card, etc.).

TRANSFER AND INTERNATIONAL STUDENTS

Transfer students: May apply for admission for the following academic terms: Fall, Spring, Summer. Applicants need a minimum number of credits to apply. For fall 2005: Transfer applications received: 330. Transfer applicants offered admission: 215. Transfer applicants enrolled: 110. **International students:** Number of foreign undergraduates: 6. Number of countries represented: 4. Minimum TOEFL score required: 500 (paper); 173 (computer). Average TOEFL score: 500 (paper).

Livingstone College

- ■ **Address:** 701 W. Monroe Street, Salisbury, NC 28144
- ■ **Website:** http://www.livingstone.edu/
- ■ **Private; Religious affiliation:** African Methodist Episcopal Zion
- ■ **Enrollment:** 863 full-time; 32 part-time

KEY STATS

✔ **U.S News College Ranking:** fourth tier, Comp. Coll.–Bachelor's (South)
✔ **SAT Score (25th/75th percentile):** 628-830
✔ **Tuition:** 2006-2007: $12,174

Selectivity: Less selective	**Room/board:** $5,641
Acceptance rate: 93%	**Average debt:** $10,500
Student/faculty ratio: 15/1	**Proportion who borrowed:** 92%

UNDERGRADUATE STUDENT BODY STATS

2005-2006 enrollment: 863 full-time; 32 part-time. Men: 55%; women: 45%. **Ethnic makeup:** African American: 92%; Hispanic: 1%; White: 4%; International: 2%. **Religious preference:** Roman Catholic: 1%; Protestant: 1%; Unknown: 38%; African Methodist Episcopal Zion: 15%; Other: 44%.

ADMISSIONS FACTS AND FIGURES

Phone: (704) 216-6001. **Email:** admissions@livingstone.edu. **Website:** http://www.livingstone.edu/. **Application deadlines for fall 2007:** Regular decision: Rolling. Early decision: Not offered. Early action: Not offered. Admission can be deferred. **Application fee:** $25. Common application is accepted. **Admissions requirements/recommendations:** High school units required (recommended): English: 4; Mathematics: 3; Science: 2; Foreign language: 2; Social studies: 2; History: 1. Tests: The college uses SAT or ACT scores in admissions decisions. Neither SAT nor ACT required. For admission to the fall 2007 entering class, the school will accept: ACT with writing, ACT without writing. Campus visit: Recommended. Admissions interview: Neither required nor recommended. Off-campus interview: Not available. **Factors that count in admissions decisions:** *Academic:* Secondary school record: Considered. Class rank: Considered. Letters of recommendation: Important. Standardized test scores: Considered. Essay: Considered. *Nonacademic:* Interview: Considered. Extracurricular activities: Considered. Talent/ability: Considered. Character/personal qualities: Considered. Alumni/ae relationship: Considered. Geographical residence: Considered. State residency: Considered. Religious affiliation/commitment: Not considered. Minority status: Not considered. Volunteer work: Considered. Work experience: Considered. **Other schools with the greatest overlap in applicants:** Catawba College; Johnson C. Smith University; North Carolina A&T State University; St. Augustine's College; University of North Carolina–Charlotte. **Admissions statistics for the fall 2005 entering class:** Total applicants: 1,526. Total accepted: 1,419. Freshmen enrolled: 191; 48% were from out of state. Overall acceptance rate: 93%. **Credentials of fall 2005 freshmen:** 22% ranked in the top 10 percent of their high school class; 47% were in the top 25 percent. **First-year students who submitted SAT scores:** 72%. Scores (25/75 percentile): Verbal: 310-410, Math: 318-420, Combined: 628-830. **First-year students submitting ACT scores:** 27%. Scores (25/75 percentile): English: 9-16, Math: 14-16, Composite: 12-17.

ACADEMICS

Year founded: 1879. **Academic calendar:** Semester. **Degrees offered:** bachelor's. **Most popular majors:** 22% business administration and management, 14% criminal justice/safety studies, 11% computer and information sciences, 8% psychology, 8% sociology. **Major fields of study:** biological and biomedical sciences; business, management, marketing, and related support services; computer and information sciences and support services; education; engineering; English language and literature/letters; history; mathematics and statistics; parks, recreation, leisure, and fitness studies; psychology; public administration and social service professions; security and protective services; social sciences; theology and religious vocations; visual and performing arts. **Areas of required coursework:** arts/fine arts, humanities, computer literacy, mathematics, English (including composition), philosophy, foreign languages, sciences (biological or physical), history, social science, other. **Pre-professional programs:** pre-law, pre-theology. **Special academic programs:** accelerated program, cross-registration, double major, dual enrollment, independent study, internships, teacher certificate program, weekend college, other. **Teacher certification offered in:** elementary, middle/junior high, secondary. **Cooperative education programs:** education, engineering, other. **Reserve Officers Training Corps (ROTC):** Army ROTC: Offered at cooperating institution (University of North Carolina–Charlotte). **Faculty and instruction (2005-2006):** Total instructional faculty: 54 full-time, 19 part-time (60% men; 40% women). Full-time faculty with Ph.D. or other terminal degree: 50%. Student/faculty ratio: 15/1. Classes of fewer than 20 students: 62%; of 20 to 49 students: 34%; of 50 or more students: 4%. **Advanced Placement and International Baccalaureate credit:** AP tests may be used for: Placement only. **Freshmen returning for sophomore year:** 64%. **Graduation rates:** Four-year: 8%; five-year: 28%; six-year: 30%. **Graduate study:** 30% of students pursue further study immediately upon graduation; 35% within one year; 30% within five years.

COSTS AND FINANCIAL AID
Financial aid office: (704) 216-6069. **Expenses (2006-2007):** Tuition and fees 2006-2007: $12,174; room/board: $5,641. Estimated books and supplies: $1,100; transportation: $800; personal expenses: $3,000. **Financial aid:** Priority filing date for institution's financial aid form: March 15; deadline: May 1. In 2005-2006, 96% of undergraduates applied for financial aid. Of those, 92% were determined to have financial need; 10% had their need fully met. Average financial aid package (proportion receiving): $10,531 (92%). Average amount of gift aid, such as scholarships or grants (proportion receiving): $7,412 (90%). Average amount of self-help aid, such as work study or loans (proportion receiving): $3,711 (82%). Average need-based loan (excluding PLUS or other private loans): $3,479. Among students who received need-based aid, the average percentage of need met: 57%. Among students who received aid based on merit, the average award (and the proportion receiving): $7,986 (8%). The average athletic scholarship (and the proportion receiving): $5,479 (23%). Average amount of debt of borrowers graduating in 2005: $10,500. Proportion who borrowed: 92%.

CAMPUS LIFE AND EXTRACURRICULAR ACTIVITIES
Campus housing available (% using): women's dorms (42%), men's dorms (52%), apartments for married students (1%), apartment for single students (2%), special housing for disabled students (1%), special housing for international students (2%). Students who live in college-owned, operated, or affiliated housing: 59%. **Student employment:** During the 2005-2006 academic year, 10% of undergraduates worked on campus. Average per-year earnings: $1,000. **Clubs and organizations:** Number of student organizations: 16. Activities include: choral groups, concert band, dance, drama/theater, jazz band, marching band, music ensembles, musical theater, pep band, radio station, student government, student film society, yearbook. Number of fraternities: 4; sororities: 4. Proportion of men in fraternities: 2%; of women in sororities: 2%. Average proportion of students who stay on campus on weekends: 40%. **Sports program (2005-2006):** Member of NCAA II. **Men's intercollegiate varsity sports:** basketball, cross-country, football, track and field (indoor), track and field (outdoor). **Women's intercollegiate varsity sports:** basketball, bowling, cross-country, softball, tennis, track and field (indoor), track and field (outdoor), volleyball.

SERVICES AND FACILITIES
Basic services: nonremedial tutoring, placement service, health service, health insurance. **Remedial assistance:** reading, math, writing, study skills, other. **Counseling services:** minority student, career, personal, academic, older student, psychological, religious. **For learning-disabled students:** School does not offer a structured program with separate admission and additional fees. Total undergraduates in learning-disabled program or receiving services: 24. Services include: remedial math, remedial English, remedial reading, tape recorders, videotaped classes, diagnostic testing service, untimed tests, oral tests, learning center, readers, extended time for tests, tutors, other. **Library:** Number of titles: 80,000; number of current serial subscriptions: 0. **Information technology resources:** Students are not required to lease or own a computer. Number of campus computers available to all students: 200. School has a wireless network. Approximate number of users that can be accommodated: 50. Proportion of college-owned housing units wired for high-speed internet access: 100%. **Campus safety:** Security services offered: 24-hour foot-and-vehicle patrols, 24-hour emergency telephones, lighted pathways/sidewalks, controlled dormitory access (key, security card, etc).

TRANSFER AND INTERNATIONAL STUDENTS
Transfer students: May apply for admission for the following academic terms: Fall, Spring. Applicants do not need a minimum number of credits to apply. For fall 2005: Transfer applications received: 231. Transfer applicants offered admission: 209. Transfer applicants enrolled: 51. **International students:** Number of foreign undergraduates: 21 (2% of student body). Minimum TOEFL score required: 500 (paper); 213 (computer). Average TOEFL score: 500 (paper).

Mars Hill College

- **Address:** 100 Athletic Street, Mars Hill, NC 28754
- **Website:** http://www.mhc.edu
- **Private; Religious affiliation:** Baptist
- **Enrollment:** 1,201 full-time; 107 part-time

KEY STATS
✔ **U.S News College Ranking:** 38, Comp. Colleges–Bachelor's (South)
✔ **SAT Score (25th/75th percentile):** 910-1130
✔ **Tuition:** 2006-2007: $17,950

Selectivity: Selective	**Room/board:** $6,206
Acceptance rate: 61%	**Average debt:** $22,250
Student/faculty ratio: 13/1	**Proportion who borrowed:** 50%

UNDERGRADUATE STUDENT BODY STATS
2005-2006 enrollment: 1,201 full-time; 107 part-time. Men: 40%; women: 60%. **Ethnic makeup:** African American: 12%; Asian American: 1%; Hispanic: 2%; White: 83%; International: 2%. **Religious preference:** Roman Catholic: 6%; Protestant: 21%; Unknown: 29%; Baptist: 44%.

ADMISSIONS FACTS AND FIGURES
Phone: (800) 543-1514. **Email:** admissions@mhc.edu. **Website:** http://www.mhc.edu. **Application deadlines for fall 2007:** Regular decision: Rolling. Early decision: Not offered. Early action: Not offered. **Application fee:** $25. Common application is not accepted. **To apply online, go to:** http://www.mhc.edu/admissions/online.html. **Admissions requirements/recommendations:** High school units required (recommended): English: (4); Mathematics: (3); Science: (2); Foreign language: (2); History: (2); Academic electives: (4); Total units: (18). Tests: The college uses SAT or ACT scores in admissions decisions. Either SAT or ACT required. For admission to the fall 2007 entering class, the school will accept: ACT with writing, ACT without writing. Campus visit: Recommended. Admissions interview: Neither required nor recommended. **Factors that count in admissions decisions:** *Academic:* Secondary school record: Very important. Class rank: Very important. Letters of recommendation: Considered. Standardized test scores: Very important. Essay: Considered. *Nonacademic:* Interview: Considered. Extracurricular activities: Important. Talent/ability: Very important. Character/personal qualities: Important. Alumni/ae relationship: Considered. Geographical residence: Not considered. State residency: Considered. Religious affiliation/commitment: Considered. Minority status: Not considered. Volunteer work: Considered. Work experience: Considered. **Other schools with the greatest overlap in applicants:** Appalachian State University; Gardner-Webb University; University of North Carolina–Asheville; University of North Carolina–Chapel Hill; Western Carolina University. **Admissions statistics for the fall 2005 entering class:** Total applicants: 2,074. Total accepted: 1,268. Freshmen enrolled: 286; 38% were from out of state. Overall acceptance rate: 61%. **Credentials of fall 2005 freshmen:** 12% ranked in the top 10 percent of their high school class; 33% were in the top 25 percent, and 69% were in the top half. (Proportion submitting class standing: 92%.) **First-year students who submitted SAT scores:** 85%. Scores (25/75 percentile): Verbal: 450-560, Math: 460-570, Combined: 910-1130.

ACADEMICS
Year founded: 1856. **Academic calendar:** Semester. **Degrees offered:** bachelor's. **Most popular majors:** 20% elementary education and teaching, 17% business administration and management, 6% history, 6% psychology, 6% social work. **Major fields of study:** biological and biomedical sciences; business, management, marketing, and related support services; computer and

information sciences and support services; education; English language and literature/letters; family and consumer sciences/human sciences; foreign languages, literatures, and linguistics; health professions and related clinical sciences; history; mathematics and statistics; parks, recreation, leisure, and fitness studies; philosophy and religious studies; physical sciences; psychology; public administration and social service professions; social sciences; visual and performing arts. **Areas of required coursework:** arts/fine arts, humanities, computer literacy, mathematics, English (including composition), sciences (biological or physical), social science. **Pre-professional programs:** pre-law, pre-medicine. **Special academic programs:** cooperative (work-study plan) program, cross-registration, distance learning, double major, dual enrollment, English as a Second Language (ESL), independent study, internships, student-designed major, study abroad, teacher certificate program. **Teacher certification offered in:** special education, elementary, middle/junior high, secondary, bilingual/bicultural. **Cooperative education programs:** art, business, computer science, education, health professions, humanities, natural science, social/behavioral science. **Faculty and instruction (2005-2006):** Total instructional faculty: 74 full-time, 75 part-time. Full-time faculty with Ph.D. or other terminal degree: 57%. Student/faculty ratio: 13/1. Classes of fewer than 20 students: 69%; of 20 to 49 students: 31%. **Advanced Placement and International Baccalaureate credit:** AP tests may be used for: Credit and/or placement. Scores accepted: 3. International Baccalaureate exams may be used for: Credit and/or placement. **Freshmen returning for sophomore year:** 68%. **Graduation rates:** Four-year: 32%; five-year: 40%; six-year: 41%.

COSTS AND FINANCIAL AID

Financial aid office: (828) 689-1103. **Expenses (2006-2007):** Tuition and fees 2006-2007: $17,950; room/board: $6,206. Estimated books and supplies: $1,100; transportation: $1,000; personal expenses: $900. **Financial aid:** Priority filing date for institution's financial aid form: April 15. In 2005-2006, 100% of undergraduates applied for financial aid. Of those, 50% were determined to have financial need; 23% had their need fully met. Average financial aid package (proportion receiving): $13,339 (46%). Average amount of gift aid, such as scholarships or grants (proportion receiving): $10,547 (46%). Average amount of self-help aid, such as work study or loans (proportion receiving): $3,857 (35%). Average need-based loan (excluding PLUS or other private loans): $3,567. Among students who received need-based aid, the average percentage of need met: 72%. Among students who received aid based on merit, the average award (and the proportion receiving): $12,346 (5%). The average athletic scholarship (and the proportion receiving): $3,959 (4%). Average amount of debt of borrowers graduating in 2005: $22,250. Proportion who borrowed: 50%.

CAMPUS LIFE AND EXTRACURRICULAR ACTIVITIES

Campus housing available (% using): women's dorms (42%), men's dorms (42%), apartment for single students (16%). Students who live in college-owned, operated, or affiliated housing: 58%. **Student employment:** During the 2005-2006 academic year, 17% of undergraduates worked on campus. Average per-year earnings: $1,150. Activities include: choral groups, concert band, dance, drama/theater, jazz band, literary magazine, marching band, music ensembles, musical theater, student government, student newspaper, yearbook. Number of fraternities: 6; sororities: 5. **Sports program (2005-2006):** Member of NCAA II. *Men's intercollegiate varsity sports:* baseball, basketball, cross-country, football, golf, lacrosse, soccer, tennis, track and field (outdoor). *Women's intercollegiate varsity sports:* basketball, cheerleading, cross-country, golf, soccer, softball, swimming and diving, tennis, track and field (outdoor), volleyball.

SERVICES AND FACILITIES

Basic services: nonremedial tutoring, placement service, health service. **Remedial assistance:** reading, math, writing, study skills. **Counseling services:** career, personal, academic, religious. **For learning-disabled students:** School offers a structured program with separate admission and additional fees. Services include: remedial math, remedial English, remedial reading, tape recorders, diagnostic testing service, oral tests, readers, extended time for tests, tutors. **Library:** Number of titles: 84,801; number of current serial subscriptions: 10,718. **Information technology resources:** Students are not required to lease or own a computer. Number of campus computers available to all students: 212. **Campus safety:** Security services offered: 24-hour foot-and-vehicle patrols, late-night transport/escort service, 24-hour emergency telephones, lighted pathways/sidewalks, controlled dormitory access (key, security card, etc.).

TRANSFER AND INTERNATIONAL STUDENTS

Transfer students: May apply for admission for the following academic terms: Fall, Spring, Summer. Applicants need a minimum number of credits to apply. For fall 2005: Transfer applications received: 261. Transfer applicants offered admission: 154. Transfer applicants enrolled: 114. **International students:** Number of foreign undergraduates: 19 (2% of student body). Minimum TOEFL score required: 500 (paper); 176 (computer).

Meredith College

- **Address:** 3800 Hillsborough Street, Raleigh, NC 27607-5298
- **Website:** http://www.meredith.edu
- **Private**
- **Enrollment:** 1,645 full-time; 370 part-time

KEY STATS

✔ **U.S News College Ranking:** 15, Universities–Master's (South)
✔ **SAT Score (25th/75th percentile):** 940-1130
✔ **Tuition:** 2006-2007: $21,200

Selectivity: Selective	**Room/board:** $5,940
Acceptance rate: 95%	**Average debt:** $21,266
Student/faculty ratio: 11/1	**Proportion who borrowed:** 79%

UNDERGRADUATE STUDENT BODY STATS

2005-2006 enrollment: 1,645 full-time; 370 part-time. Men: 1%; women: 99%. **Ethnic makeup:** African American: 11%; Asian American: 2%; Hispanic: 2%; White: 84%; International: 1%.

ADMISSIONS FACTS AND FIGURES

Phone: (919) 760-8581. **Email:** admissions@meredith.edu. **Website:** http://www.meredith.edu. **Application deadlines for fall 2007:** Regular decision: Rolling. Early decision: Send application by: October 15; Decision sent by: November 1. Early action: Not offered. Admission can be deferred. **Application fee:** $40. Common application is accepted. **To apply online, go to:** http://www.ncmentor.org/applications/ nc_independents_common_app/apply.html?application_id=1510. **Admissions requirements/recommendations:** High school units required (recommended): English: 4; Mathematics: 3; Science: 3; Foreign language: 2; Academic electives: 1; Total units: 16. Tests: The college uses SAT or ACT scores in admissions decisions. Either SAT or ACT required. For admission to the fall 2007 entering class, the school will accept: ACT without writing. Campus visit: Recommended. Admissions interview: Recommended. Off-campus interview: May be arranged. **Factors that count in admissions decisions:** *Academic:* Secondary school record: Very important. Class rank: Very important. Letters of recommendation: Important. Standardized test scores: Important. Essay: Considered. *Nonacademic:* Interview: Considered. Extracurricular activities: Considered. Talent/ability: Considered. Character/personal qualities: Important. Alumni/ae relationship: Considered. Geographical residence: Not considered. State residency: Not considered. Religious affiliation/commitment: Not considered. Minority status: Not considered. Volunteer work: Considered. Work experience: Considered. **Other schools with the greatest overlap in applicants:** Appalachian State University; East Carolina University; Elon University; North Carolina State University–Raleigh; University of North Carolina–Chapel Hill. **Admissions statistics for the fall 2005 entering class:** Total applicants: 1,132. Total accepted: 1,073. Freshmen enrolled: 451; 12% were from out of state. Accepted through early-decision or early-action plans: 12%. Overall acceptance rate: 95%. Early-decision acceptance rate: 60%. Non-early acceptance rate: 98%. **Credentials of fall 2005 freshmen:** 19% ranked in the top 10 percent of their high school class; 47% were in the top 25 percent, and 78% were in the top half. (Proportion submitting class standing: 87%.) **Average high school grade point average:** 3.2. **First-year students who submitted SAT scores:** 97%. Scores (25/75 percentile): Verbal: 470-570, Math: 470-560, Combined: 940-1130. **First-year students submitting ACT scores:** 22%. Scores (25/75 percentile): English: 20-24, Math: 17-20, Composite: 20-23.

ACADEMICS

Year founded: 1891. **Academic calendar:** Semester. **Degrees offered:** bachelor's, post-bachelor's certificate, master's. **Most popular majors:** 12% psychology, 7% interior design, 6% health/medical preparatory programs, 5% accounting, 4% business administration and management. **Major fields of

study: area, ethnic, cultural, and gender studies; biological and biomedical sciences; business, management, marketing, and related support services; communication, journalism, and related programs; computer and information sciences and support services; education; English language and literature/letters; family and consumer sciences/human sciences; foreign languages, literatures, and linguistics; health professions and related clinical sciences; history; mathematics and statistics; multi/interdisciplinary studies; natural resources and conservation; parks, recreation, leisure, and fitness studies; philosophy and religious studies; physical sciences; psychology; public administration and social service professions; social sciences; visual and performing arts. **Areas of required coursework:** arts/fine arts, humanities, computer literacy, mathematics, English (including composition), foreign languages, sciences (biological or physical), history, social science, other. **Pre-professional programs:** pre-law, pre-dentistry, pre-medicine, pre-veterinary science, pre-pharmacy, other. **Special academic programs (% participation):** accelerated program (4.3%), cooperative (work-study plan) program (2.4%), cross-registration (9.3%), double major (7.4%), dual enrollment (0%), honors program (9.3%), independent study (11.2%), internships (38.8%), student-designed major (0%), study abroad (13.8%), teacher certificate program (14.3%), other (4.3%). **Teacher certification offered in:** early childhood, elementary, middle/junior high, secondary. **Cooperative education programs:** art, business, computer science, home economics, humanities, natural science, social/behavioral science, other. **Reserve Officers Training Corps (ROTC):** Army ROTC: Offered at cooperating institution (North Carolina State University); Air Force ROTC: Offered at cooperating institution (North Carolina State University). **Faculty and instruction (2005-2006):** Total instructional faculty: 128 full-time, 122 part-time (32% men; 68% women; 6% minorities). Full-time faculty with Ph.D. or other terminal degree: 89%. Student/faculty ratio: 11/1. Classes of fewer than 20 students: 71%; of 20 to 49 students: 29%; of 50 or more students: 1%. **Advanced Placement and International Baccalaureate credit:** AP tests may be used for: Credit only. Scores accepted: 3, 4, 5. International Baccalaureate exams may be used for: Credit only. **Freshmen returning for sophomore year:** 76%. **Graduation rates:** Four-year: 57%; five-year: 66%; six-year: 68%. **Graduate study:** 17% of students pursue further study immediately upon graduation; 21% within one year. Fields in which graduates pursue further study: medicine, 3%; dentistry, 3%; theology (or the seminary), 1%; education, 3%; arts and sciences, 60%.

COSTS AND FINANCIAL AID

Financial aid office: (919) 760-8565. **Expenses (2006-2007):** Tuition and fees 2006-2007: $21,200; room/board: $5,940. Estimated books and supplies: $750; transportation: $400; personal expenses: $1,250. **Financial aid:** Priority filing date for institution's financial aid form: February 15. In 2005-2006, 79% of undergraduates applied for financial aid. Of those, 68% were determined to have financial need; 12% had their need fully met. Average financial aid package (proportion receiving): $14,059 (68%). Average amount of gift aid, such as scholarships or grants (proportion receiving): $10,948 (67%). Average amount of self-help aid, such as work study or loans (proportion receiving): $4,432 (61%). Average need-based loan (excluding PLUS or other private loans): $3,858. Among students who received need-based aid, the average percentage of need met: 70%. Among students who received aid based on merit, the average award (and the proportion receiving): $5,089 (12%). The average athletic scholarship (and the proportion receiving): $0 (0%). Average amount of debt of borrowers graduating in 2005: $21,266. Proportion who borrowed: 79%.

CAMPUS LIFE AND EXTRACURRICULAR ACTIVITIES

Campus housing available (% using): women's dorms (100%). Students who live in college-owned, operated, or affiliated housing: 48%. **Student employment:** During the 2005-2006 academic year, 18% of undergraduates worked on campus. Average per-year earnings: $1,300. **Clubs and organizations:** Number of student organizations: 91. Activities include: choral groups, concert band, dance, drama/theater, literary magazine, music ensembles, musical theater, student government, student newspaper, yearbook. Number of fraternities: 0; sororities: 0. Average proportion of students who stay on campus on weekends: 55%. **Sports program (2005-2006):** Member of NCAA III. *Women's intercollegiate varsity sports:* basketball, soccer, softball, tennis, volleyball.

SERVICES AND FACILITIES

Basic services: nonremedial tutoring, health service, health insurance. **Remedial assistance:** math, writing, study skills. **Counseling services:** minority student, career, personal, veteran student, academic, older student, psychological, birth control, religious, other. **For learning-disabled students:** School does not offer a structured program with separate admission and

additional fees. Services include: remedial math, remedial English, reading machines, tape recorders, note-taking services, oral tests, learning center, readers, extended time for tests, tutors, priority registration, priority seating, substitution of courses, texts on tape, typist/scribe, exams on tape or computer, other testing accomodations, other. **Library:** Number of titles: 186,100; number of current serial subscriptions: 669. **Information technology resources:** Students are not required to lease or own a computer. Number of campus computers available to all students: 73. School has a wireless network. Proportion of college-owned housing units wired for high-speed internet access: 100%. **Campus safety:** Security services offered: 24-hour foot-and-vehicle patrols, late-night transport/escort service, 24-hour emergency telephones, lighted pathways/sidewalks, controlled dormitory access (key, security card, etc).

TRANSFER AND INTERNATIONAL STUDENTS

Transfer students: May apply for admission for the following academic terms: Fall, Spring. Applicants do not need a minimum number of credits to apply. For fall 2005: Transfer applications received: 185. Transfer applicants offered admission: 180. Transfer applicants enrolled: 103. **International students:** Number of foreign undergraduates: 14 (1% of student body). Number of countries represented: 12. Minimum TOEFL score required: 500 (paper); 173 (computer).

Methodist College

- **Address:** 5400 Ramsey Street, Fayetteville, NC 28311-1498
- **Website:** http://www.methodist.edu
- **Private; Religious affiliation:** United Methodist
- **Enrollment:** 1,672 full-time; 389 part-time

KEY STATS

✔ **U.S News College Ranking:** third tier, Comp. Colleges–Bachelor's (South)
✔ **SAT Score (25th/75th percentile):** 890-1110
✔ **Tuition:** 2006-2007: $19,080
   Selectivity: Less selective **Room/board:** $7,170
   Acceptance rate: 78% **Average debt:** $19,989
   Student/faculty ratio: 13/1 **Proportion who borrowed:** 75%

UNDERGRADUATE STUDENT BODY STATS

2005-2006 enrollment: 1,672 full-time; 389 part-time. Men: 54%; women: 46%. **Ethnic makeup:** African American: 20%; American-Indian: 1%; Asian American: 2%; Hispanic: 6%; White: 68%; International: 3%. **Religious preference:** Roman Catholic: 9%; Protestant: 42%; Jewish: 1%; No preference: 35%; United Methodist: 13%.

ADMISSIONS FACTS AND FIGURES

Phone: (910) 630-7027. **Email:** admissions@methodist.edu. **Website:** http://www.methodist.edu. **Application deadlines for fall 2007:** Regular decision: Rolling. Early decision: Not offered. Early action: Not offered. Admission can be deferred. **Application fee:** $25. Common application is accepted. **To apply online, go to:** http://www.methodist.edu/Admissions/application.shtml. **Admissions requirements/recommendations:** High school units required (recommended): English: 4 (4); Mathematics: 3 (4); Science: 3 (3); Foreign language: 0 (2); Social studies: 1 (1); History: 2 (3); Academic electives: 4 (4); Total units: 16 (20). Tests: The college uses SAT or ACT scores in admissions decisions. Either SAT or ACT required. For admission to the fall 2007 entering class, the school will accept: ACT with writing, ACT without writing. Campus visit: Recommended. Admissions interview: Recommended. Off-campus interview: Not available. **Factors that count in admissions decisions: Academic:** Secondary school record: Very important. Class rank: Considered. Letters of recommendation: Considered. Standardized test scores: Important. Essay: Considered. *Nonacademic:* Interview: Considered. Extracurricular activities: Considered. Talent/ability: Considered. Character/personal qualities: Considered. Alumni/ae relationship: Considered. Geographical residence: Not considered. State residency: Not considered. Religious affiliation/commitment: Not considered. Minority status: Not considered. Volunteer work: Considered. Work experience: Considered. **Other schools with the greatest overlap in applicants:** Campbell University; Coastal Carolina University; East Carolina University; North Carolina State University–Raleigh; University of North Carolina–Wilmington. **Admissions statistics for the fall 2005 entering class:** Total applicants: 1,897. Total accepted: 1,482. Freshmen enrolled: 439; 51%

were from out of state. Overall acceptance rate: 78%. **Size of waiting list:** 0 applicants; enrolled from waiting list: 0. **Credentials of fall 2005 freshmen:** 10% ranked in the top 10 percent of their high school class; 34% were in the top 25 percent, and 70% were in the top half. (Proportion submitting class standing: 81%.) **Average high school grade point average:** 3.2. **First-year students who submitted SAT scores:** 72%. Scores (25/75 percentile): Verbal: 440-550, Math: 450-560, Combined: 890-1110. **First-year students submitting ACT scores:** 28%. Scores (25/75 percentile): English: 17-22, Math: 17-23, Composite: 18-22.

ACADEMICS

Year founded: 1956. **Academic calendar:** Semester. **Degrees offered:** associate, bachelor's, master's. **Most popular majors:** 49% business, management, marketing, and related support services, 9% parks, recreation, leisure, and fitness studies, 8% social sciences, 6% biological and biomedical sciences, 3% security and protective services. **Major fields of study:** biological and biomedical sciences; business, management, marketing, and related support services; communication, journalism, and related programs; computer and information sciences and support services; education; English language and literature/letters; foreign languages, literatures, and linguistics; health professions and related clinical sciences; history; mathematics and statistics; parks, recreation, leisure, and fitness studies; philosophy and religious studies; physical sciences; psychology; public administration and social service professions; security and protective services; social sciences; visual and performing arts. **Areas of required coursework:** arts/fine arts, humanities, computer literacy, mathematics, English (including composition), foreign languages, sciences (biological or physical), history, social science, other. **Pre-professional programs:** pre-law, pre-dentistry, pre-medicine, pre-theology, pre-veterinary science, pre-pharmacy, other. **Special academic programs:** distance learning, double major, dual enrollment, English as a Second Language (ESL), honors program, independent study, internships, liberal arts/career combination, study abroad, teacher certificate program, weekend college. **Teacher certification offered in:** special education, elementary, middle/junior high, secondary, bilingual/bicultural. **Reserve Officers Training Corps (ROTC):** Army ROTC: Offered on campus; Air Force ROTC: Offered at cooperating institution (Fayetteville State University). **Faculty and instruction (2005-2006):** Total instructional faculty: 119 full-time, 90 part-time (57% men; 43% women; 14% minorities). Full-time faculty with Ph.D. or other terminal degree: 65%. Student/faculty ratio: 13/1. Classes of fewer than 20 students: 74%; of 20 to 49 students: 25%; of 50 or more students: 1%. **Advanced Placement and International Baccalaureate credit:** AP tests may be used for: Credit only. Scores accepted: 3, 4, 5. International Baccalaureate exams may be used for: Credit only. **Freshmen returning for sophomore year:** 66%. **Graduation rates:** Four-year: 22%; five-year: 30%; six-year: 32%.

COSTS AND FINANCIAL AID

Financial aid office: (910) 630-7193. **Expenses (2006-2007):** Tuition and fees 2006-2007: $19,080; room/board: $7,170. Estimated books and supplies: $800. **Financial aid:** Priority filing date for institution's financial aid form: May 1. In 2005-2006, 84% of undergraduates applied for financial aid. Of those, 74% were determined to have financial need; 59% had their need fully met. Average financial aid package (proportion receiving): $15,822 (74%). Average amount of gift aid, such as scholarships or grants (proportion receiving): $6,679 (73%). Average amount of self-help aid, such as work study or loans (proportion receiving): $4,204 (68%). Average need-based loan (excluding PLUS or other private loans): $3,505. Among students who received need-based aid, the average percentage of need met: 73%. Among students who received aid based on merit, the average award (and the proportion receiving): $5,929 (9%). The average athletic scholarship (and the proportion receiving): $0 (0%). Average amount of debt of borrowers graduating in 2005: $19,989. Proportion who borrowed: 75%.

CAMPUS LIFE AND EXTRACURRICULAR ACTIVITIES

Campus housing available (% using): coed dorms (20%), women's dorms (20%), men's dorms (30%), apartment for single students (30%). Students who live in college-owned, operated, or affiliated housing: 65%. **Clubs and organizations:** Number of student organizations: 76. Activities include: choral groups, concert band, dance, drama/theater, jazz band, literary magazine, music ensembles, musical theater, pep band, student government, student newspaper, symphony orchestra, yearbook. Number of fraternities: 2; sororities: 2. Average proportion of students who stay on campus on weekends: 70%. **Sports program (2005-2006):** Member of NCAA III. *Men's intercollegiate varsity sports:* baseball, basketball, cross-country, football, golf, soccer, tennis, track and field (indoor), track and field (outdoor). *Women's*

intercollegiate varsity sports: basketball, cross-country, golf, lacrosse, soccer, softball, tennis, track and field (indoor), track and field (outdoor), volleyball.

SERVICES AND FACILITIES

Basic services: nonremedial tutoring, women's center, placement service, health service, health insurance, other. **Counseling services:** career, military, personal, veteran student, academic, psychological, religious. **For learning-disabled students:** School does not offer a structured program with separate admission and additional fees. Services include: remedial math, other testing accommodations, remedial English, tape recorders, videotaped classes, untimed tests, note-taking services, oral tests, learning center, readers, extended time for tests, tutors. **Library:** Number of titles: 124,500; number of current serial subscriptions: 571. **Information technology resources:** Students are not required to lease or own a computer. Number of campus computers available to all students: 200. School has a wireless network. Proportion of college-owned housing units wired for high-speed internet access: 100%. **Campus safety:** Security services offered: 24-hour foot-and-vehicle patrols, late-night transport/escort service, 24-hour emergency telephones, lighted pathways/sidewalks, controlled dormitory access (key, security card, etc).

TRANSFER AND INTERNATIONAL STUDENTS

Transfer students: May apply for admission for the following academic terms: Fall, Spring, Summer. Applicants need a minimum number of credits to apply. For fall 2005: Transfer applications received: 350. Transfer applicants offered admission: 325. Transfer applicants enrolled: 208. **International students:** Number of foreign undergraduates: 63 (3% of student body). Number of countries represented: 31. Minimum TOEFL score required: 500 (paper); 173 (computer).

Montreat College

- **Address:** PO Box 1267, Montreat, NC 28757-1267
- **Website:** http://www.montreat.edu
- **Private; Religious affiliation:** Presbyterian (U.S.A.)
- **Enrollment:** 979 full-time; 11 part-time

KEY STATS

✔ **U.S News College Ranking:** Unranked Specialty School–Business
✔ **SAT Score (25th/75th percentile):** 880-1090
✔ **Tuition:** 2005-2006: $15,560

Selectivity: Less selective	**Room/board:** $5,008
Acceptance rate: 40%	**Average debt:** N/A
Student/faculty ratio: 19/1	**Proportion who borrowed:** N/A

UNDERGRADUATE STUDENT BODY STATS

2005-2006 enrollment: 979 full-time; 11 part-time. Men: 38%; women: 62%. **Ethnic makeup:** African American: 22%; American-Indian: 10%; Asian American: 1%; Hispanic: 2%; White: 65%; International: 1%. **Religious preference:** Roman Catholic: 4%; Protestant: 18%; No preference: 6%; Unknown: 14%; Presbyterian (U.S.A.): 12%; Southern Baptist: 38%; Other: 8%.

ADMISSIONS FACTS AND FIGURES

Phone: (800) 622-6968. **Email:** admissions@montreat.edu. **Website:** http://www.montreat.edu. **Application deadlines for fall 2007:** Regular decision: August 11. Early decision: Not offered. Early action: Not offered. Admission can be deferred. **Application fee:** $15. Common application is accepted. **Admissions requirements/recommendations:** High school units required (recommended): English: 4; Mathematics: 3; Science: 3; Foreign language: 1; Social studies: 3; History: 0; Academic electives: 0; Total units: 14. Tests: The college uses SAT or ACT scores in admissions decisions. Either SAT or ACT required. For admission to the fall 2007 entering class, the school will accept: ACT with writing, ACT without writing. Campus visit: Recommended. Admissions interview: Recommended. Off-campus interview: May be arranged. **Factors that count in admissions decisions:** *Academic:* Secondary school record: Important. Class rank: Important. Letters of recommendation: Very important. Standardized test scores: Important. Essay: Very important. *Nonacademic:* Interview: Considered. Extracurricular activities: Considered. Talent/ability: Considered. Character/personal qualities: Important. Alumni/ae relationship: Considered. Geographical residence: Not considered. State residency: Not considered. **Religious affiliation/commitment:** Not considered. **Minority status:** Not considered. **Volunteer work:** Important. **Work experience:** Considered. **Other schools with the greatest overlap in applicants:** Brevard College; Gardner-Webb University; Lees-McRae College; Lenoir-Rhyne College; Mars Hill College. **Admissions statistics for the fall 2005 entering class:** Total applicants: 378. Total accepted: 150. Freshmen enrolled: 141; 23% were from out of state. Overall acceptance rate: 40%. **Credentials of fall 2005 freshmen:** 7% ranked in the top 10 percent of their high school class; 25% were in the top 25 percent, and 56% were in the top half. (Proportion submitting class standing: 72%.) **Average high school grade point average:** 3.1. **First-year students who submitted SAT scores:** 77%. Scores (25/75 percentile): Verbal: 440-550, Math: 440-540, Combined: 880-1090. **First-year students submitting ACT scores:** 25%. Scores (25/75 percentile): English: N/A, Math: N/A, Composite: 18-26.

ACADEMICS

Year founded: 1916. **Academic calendar:** Semester. **Degrees offered:** associate, bachelor's, master's. **Most popular majors:** 64% business, management, marketing, and related support services, 9% parks, recreation, leisure, and fitness studies, 5% philosophy and religious studies, 4% education, 2% public administration and social service professions. **Major fields of study:** area, ethnic, cultural, and gender studies; biological and biomedical sciences; business, management, marketing, and related support services; computer and information sciences and support services; education; English language and literature/letters; history; natural resources and conservation; parks, recreation, leisure, and fitness studies; public administration and social service professions; theology and religious vocations; visual and performing arts. **Areas of required coursework:** arts/fine arts, humanities, computer literacy, mathematics, English (including composition), philosophy, sciences (biological or physical), history, social science, other. **Pre-professional programs:** pre-medicine, pre-veterinary science. **Special academic programs:** accelerated program, double major, dual enrollment, independent study, internships, student-designed major, study abroad, teacher certificate program. **Teacher certification offered in:** elementary. **Faculty and instruction (2005-2006):** Total instructional faculty: 32 full-time, 59 part-time (70% men; 30% women; 4% minorities). Full-time faculty with Ph.D. or other terminal degree: 75%. Student/faculty ratio: 19/1. Classes of fewer than 20 students: 89%; of 20 to 49 students: 11%; of 50 or more students: 0%. **Advanced Placement and International Baccalaureate credit:** AP tests may be used for: Credit only. Scores accepted: 3, 4, 5. **Freshmen returning for sophomore year:** 58%. **Graduation rates:** Four-year: 30%; five-year: 38%; six-year: 41%.

COSTS AND FINANCIAL AID

Financial aid office: (800) 545-4656. **Expenses (2005-2006):** Tuition and fees 2005-2006: $15,560; room/board: $5,008. Estimated books and supplies: $900; transportation: $1,082; personal expenses: $1,752. **Financial aid:** Priority filing date for institution's financial aid form: March 15.

CAMPUS LIFE AND EXTRACURRICULAR ACTIVITIES

Campus housing available (% using): women's dorms (52%), men's dorms (45%). Students who live in college-owned, operated, or affiliated housing: 70%. **Student employment:** During the 2005-2006 academic year, 3% of undergraduates worked on campus. Average per-year earnings: $1,700. **Clubs and organizations:** Number of student organizations: 4. Activities include: choral groups, drama/theater, literary magazine, music ensembles, musical theater, student government, student newspaper. Number of fraternities: 0; sororities: 0. Average proportion of students who stay on campus on weekends: 50%. **Sports program (2005-2006):** Member of NAIA. *Men's intercollegiate varsity sports:* baseball, basketball, cross-country, golf, soccer, tennis. *Women's intercollegiate varsity sports:* basketball, cross-country, soccer, softball, tennis, volleyball.

SERVICES AND FACILITIES

Basic services: nonremedial tutoring, health service, health insurance. **Remedial assistance:** other. **Counseling services:** career, personal, academic, psychological, religious. **For learning-disabled students:** School does not offer a structured program with separate admission and additional fees. Total undergraduates in learning-disabled program or receiving services: 0. **Library:** Number of titles: 82,552; number of current serial subscriptions: 808. **Information technology resources:** Students are not required to lease or own a computer. Number of campus computers available to all students: 60. School has a wireless network. Approximate number of users that can be accommodated: 325. Proportion of college-owned housing units wired for high-speed internet access: 100%. **Campus safety:** Security services offered:

24-hour emergency telephones, lighted pathways/sidewalks, controlled dormitory access (key, security card, etc).

TRANSFER AND INTERNATIONAL STUDENTS

Transfer students: May apply for admission for the following academic terms: Fall, Spring. Applicants need a minimum number of credits to apply. For fall 2005: Transfer applicants enrolled: 41. **International students:** Number of foreign undergraduates: 8 (1% of student body). Minimum TOEFL score required: 500 (paper); 173 (computer).

Mount Olive College

- **Address:** 634 Henderson Street, Mount Olive, NC 28365
- **Website:** http://www.moc.edu/index.cfm
- **Private; Religious affiliation:** Original Free Will Baptist
- **Enrollment:** 1,946 full-time; 884 part-time

KEY STATS
✔ **U.S News College Ranking:** fourth tier, Comp. Coll.–Bachelor's (South)
✔ **SAT Score (25th/75th percentile):** 830-1050
✔ **Tuition:** 2006-2007: $12,620

Selectivity: Less selective	**Room/board:** $4,952
Acceptance rate: 72%	**Average debt:** $8,901
Student/faculty ratio: 17/1	**Proportion who borrowed:** 57%

UNDERGRADUATE STUDENT BODY STATS

2005-2006 enrollment: 1,946 full-time; 884 part-time. Men: 40%; women: 60%.

ADMISSIONS FACTS AND FIGURES

Phone: (919) 658-2502. **Email:** admissions@moc.edu. **Website:** http://www.moc.edu/index.cfm. **Application deadlines for fall 2007:** Regular decision: Rolling. Early decision: Not offered. Early action: Not offered. Admission can be deferred. **Application fee:** $20. Common application is accepted. **Admissions requirements/recommendations:** High school units required (recommended): English: 4; Mathematics: 3; Science: 3; Foreign language: 0; Social studies: 3; Academic electives: 3; Total units: 17. Tests: The college uses SAT or ACT scores in admissions decisions. Either SAT or ACT required. For admission to the fall 2007 entering class, the school will accept: ACT with writing, ACT without writing. Campus visit: Recommended. Admissions interview: Recommended. Off-campus interview: May be arranged. **Factors that count in admissions decisions:** *Academic:* Secondary school record: Very important. Class rank: Important. Letters of recommendation: Considered. Standardized test scores: Important. Essay: Not considered. *Nonacademic:* Interview: Important. Extracurricular activities: Important. Talent/ability: Important. Character/personal qualities: Very important. Alumni/ae relationship: Considered. Geographical residence: Considered. State residency: Not considered. Religious affiliation/commitment: Not considered. Minority status: Not considered. Volunteer work: Considered. Work experience: Not considered. **Admissions statistics for the fall 2005 entering class:** Total applicants: 807. Total accepted: 577. Freshmen enrolled: 314; 11% were from out of state. Overall acceptance rate: 72%. **Credentials of fall 2005 freshmen:** 9% ranked in the top 10 percent of their high school class; 36% were in the top 25 percent, and 69% were in the top half. (Proportion submitting class standing: 90%.) **Average high school grade point average:** 3.2. **First-year students who submitted SAT scores:** 41%. Scores (25/75 percentile): Verbal: 410-510, Math: 420-540, Combined: 830-1050. **First-year students submitting ACT scores:** 25%. Scores (25/75 percentile): English: N/A, Math: N/A, Composite: 15-20.

ACADEMICS

Year founded: 1951. **Academic calendar:** Semester. **Degrees offered:** associate, transfer-associate, terminal-associate, bachelor's. **Most popular majors:** 60% business, management, marketing, and related support services, 15% security and protective services, 6% psychology, 4% computer and information sciences and support services, 4% education. **Major fields of study:** biological and biomedical sciences; business, management, marketing, and related support services; computer and information sciences and support services; education; English language and literature/letters; health professions and related clinical sciences; history; mathematics and statistics; parks, recreation, leisure, and fitness studies; philosophy and religious studies; psychol-

ogy; security and protective services; theology and religious vocations; visual and performing arts. **Areas of required coursework:** arts/fine arts, humanities, computer literacy, mathematics, English (including composition), philosophy, sciences (biological or physical), history, social science.
Pre-professional programs: pre-law, pre-medicine, pre-theology, pre-veterinary science, pre-pharmacy. **Special academic programs:** accelerated program, cooperative (work-study plan) program, distance learning, double major, dual enrollment, external degree program, honors program, independent study, internships, liberal arts/career combination, teacher certificate program. **Teacher certification offered in:** early childhood, middle/junior high, secondary. **Cooperative education programs:** business, computer science, education. **Faculty and instruction (2005-2006):** Total instructional faculty: 73 full-time, 168 part-time (63% men; 37% women; 15% minorities). Full-time faculty with Ph.D. or other terminal degree: 79%. Student/faculty ratio: 17/1. Classes of fewer than 20 students: 77%; of 20 to 49 students: 23%; of 50 or more students: 0%. **Advanced Placement and International Baccalaureate credit:** AP tests may be used for: Credit only. International Baccalaureate exams may be used for: Credit and/or placement. **Freshmen returning for sophomore year:** 72%. **Graduation rates:** Four-year: 17%; five-year: 23%; six-year: 28%.

COSTS AND FINANCIAL AID
Financial aid office: (919) 658-2502. **Expenses (2006-2007):** Tuition and fees 2006-2007: $12,620; room/board: $4,952. Estimated books and supplies: $1,054; transportation: $738; personal expenses: $1,578. **Financial aid:** Priority filing date for institution's financial aid form: March 1. In 2005-2006, 71% of undergraduates applied for financial aid. Of those, 52% were determined to have financial need; 18% had their need fully met. Average financial aid package (proportion receiving): $7,091 (49%). Average amount of gift aid, such as scholarships or grants (proportion receiving): $4,983 (49%). Average amount of self-help aid, such as work study or loans (proportion receiving): $2,636 (40%). Average need-based loan (excluding PLUS or other private loans): $2,577. Among students who received need-based aid, the average percentage of need met: 67%. Among students who received aid based on merit, the average award (and the proportion receiving): $3,919 (12%). The average athletic scholarship (and the proportion receiving): $3,891 (3%). Average amount of debt of borrowers graduating in 2005: $8,901. Proportion who borrowed: 57%.

CAMPUS LIFE AND EXTRACURRICULAR ACTIVITIES
Campus housing available: women's dorms, men's dorms, apartment for single students. Students who live in college-owned, operated, or affiliated housing: 10%. **Student employment:** During the 2005-2006 academic year, 18% of undergraduates worked on campus. Average per-year earnings: $800. **Clubs and organizations:** Number of student organizations: 34. Activities include: choral groups, concert band, literary magazine, music ensembles, musical theater, pep band, student government, student newspaper, symphony orchestra, yearbook. Number of fraternities: 2; sororities: 0. Average proportion of students who stay on campus on weekends: 40%. **Sports program (2005-2006):** Member of NCAA II. *Men's intercollegiate varsity sports:* baseball, basketball, cross-country, golf, soccer, tennis, volleyball. *Women's intercollegiate varsity sports:* basketball, cross-country, golf, soccer, softball, tennis, volleyball.

SERVICES AND FACILITIES
Basic services: nonremedial tutoring, placement service, health service. **Remedial assistance:** reading, math, writing, study skills. **Counseling services:** career, military, personal, veteran student, academic, older student, psychological, religious. **For learning-disabled students:** Services include: learning center, tutors. **Information technology resources:** Students are not required to lease or own a computer. Number of campus computers available to all students: 50. **Campus safety:** Security services offered: lighted pathways/sidewalks, controlled dormitory access (key, security card, etc).

TRANSFER AND INTERNATIONAL STUDENTS
Transfer students: May apply for admission for the following academic terms: Fall, Spring, Summer. Applicants need a minimum number of credits to apply. For fall 2005: Transfer applications received: 436. Transfer applicants offered admission: 379. Transfer applicants enrolled: 298. **International students:** Minimum TOEFL score required: 500 (paper); 173 (computer).

North Carolina A&T State University

- **Address:** 1601 E. Market Street, Greensboro, NC 27411
- **Website:** http://www.ncat.edu
- **Public**
- **Enrollment:** 8,856 full-time; 879 part-time

KEY STATS
✔ **U.S News College Ranking:** third tier, Universities–Master's (South)
✔ **SAT or ACT Score (25th/75th percentile):** N/A
✔ **Tuition:** 2006-2007: $3,872 in state, $13,314 out of state

Selectivity: Less selective	**Room/board:** $6,631
Acceptance rate: 46%	**Average debt:** N/A
Student/faculty ratio: N/A	**Proportion who borrowed:** N/A

UNDERGRADUATE STUDENT BODY STATS
2005-2006 enrollment: 8,856 full-time; 879 part-time. Men: 47%; women: 53%. **Ethnic makeup:** African American: 93%; Asian American: 1%; Hispanic: 1%; White: 5%.

ADMISSIONS FACTS AND FIGURES
Phone: (336) 334-7946. **Email:** uadmit@ncat.edu. **Website:** http://www.ncat.edu. **Application deadlines for fall 2007:** Regular decision: Rolling. Early decision: Not offered. Early action: Not offered. Admission can be deferred. **Application fee:** $45. Common application is accepted. **To apply online, go to:** http://www.ncat.edu/admissions.html. **Admissions requirements/recommendations:** High school units required (recommended): English: 4; Mathematics: 4; Science: 3; Foreign language: 2; Social studies: 1; History: 1; Academic electives: 2; Total units: 17. Tests: The college uses SAT or ACT scores in admissions decisions. Either SAT or ACT required. For admission to the fall 2007 entering class, the school will accept: ACT with writing. Campus visit: Recommended. Admissions interview: Neither required nor recommended. **Factors that count in admissions decisions:** *Academic:* Secondary school record: Important. Class rank: Important. Letters of recommendation: Considered. Standardized test scores: Important. Essay: Considered. *Nonacademic:* Interview: Not considered. Extracurricular activities: Considered. Talent/ability: Considered. Character/personal qualities: Considered. Alumni/ae relationship: Considered. Geographical residence: Considered. State residency: Considered. Religious affiliation/commitment: Not considered. Minority status: Considered. Volunteer work: Considered. Work experience: Considered. **Admissions statistics for the fall 2005 entering class:** Total applicants: 11,963. Total accepted: 5,461. Freshmen enrolled: 3,437; 30% were from out of state. Overall acceptance rate: 46%. **Credentials of fall 2005 freshmen:** 1% ranked in the top 10 percent of their high school class; 11% were in the top 25 percent, and 48% were in the top half. (Proportion submitting class standing: 17%.) **Average high school grade point average:** 2.9.

ACADEMICS
Year founded: 1891. **Academic calendar:** Semester. **Degrees offered:** bachelor's, master's, doctorate. **Most popular majors:** 16% engineering, 15% business, management, marketing, and related support services, 7% health professions and related clinical sciences, 6% agriculture, agriculture operations, and related sciences, 6% communication, journalism, and related programs. **Major fields of study:** agriculture, agriculture operations, and related sciences; architecture and related services; biological and biomedical sciences; business, management, marketing, and related support services; communication, journalism, and related programs; computer and information sciences and support services; education; engineering; engineering technologies/technicians; English language and literature/letters; family and consumer sciences/human sciences; foreign languages, literatures, and linguistics; health professions and related clinical sciences; history; mathematics and statistics; parks, recreation, leisure, and fitness studies; physical sciences; psychology; public administration and social service professions; social sciences; visual and performing arts. **Areas of required coursework:** arts/fine arts, humanities, computer literacy, mathematics, English (including composition), foreign languages, sciences (biological or physical), history, social science. **Special academic programs:** cooperative (work-study plan) program, cross-registration, distance learning, double major, dual enrollment, external degree program, honors program, independent study, internships, liberal arts/career combination, study abroad, teacher certificate program, weekend college. **Reserve Officers Training Corps (ROTC):** Army ROTC: Offered on campus; Air Force ROTC: Offered on campus. **Advanced**

Placement and International Baccalaureate credit: AP tests may be used for: Credit and/or placement. **Graduation rates:** Four-year: 22%; five-year: 36%; six-year: 41%.

COSTS AND FINANCIAL AID
Financial aid office: (336) 334-7973. **Expenses (2006-2007):** Tuition and fees 2006-2007: $3,872 in state, $13,314 out of state; room/board: $6,631. Estimated books and supplies: $1,000; transportation: $1,200; personal expenses: $1,500. **Financial aid:** Priority filing date for institution's financial aid form: March 15. In 2005-2006, 86% of undergraduates applied for financial aid. Of those, 75% were determined to have financial need; 7% had their need fully met. Average financial aid package (proportion receiving): $5,898 (72%). Average amount of gift aid, such as scholarships or grants (proportion receiving): $4,028 (54%). Average amount of self-help aid, such as work study or loans (proportion receiving): $3,520 (60%). Average need-based loan (excluding PLUS or other private loans): $7,202. Among students who received need-based aid, the average percentage of need met: 50%. Among students who received aid based on merit, the average award (and the proportion receiving): $4,466 (3%). The average athletic scholarship (and the proportion receiving): $3,592 (22%).

CAMPUS LIFE AND EXTRACURRICULAR ACTIVITIES
Campus housing available: women's dorms, men's dorms, apartment for single students, other housing options. Activities include: choral groups, concert band, dance, drama/theater, jazz band, marching band, music ensembles, pep band, radio station, student government, student newspaper, symphony orchestra, television station, yearbook. Number of fraternities: 5; sororities: 4. **Sports program (2005-2006):** Member of NCAA I. *Men's intercollegiate varsity sports:* baseball, basketball, cross-country, football, tennis, track and field (indoor), track and field (outdoor). *Women's intercollegiate varsity sports:* basketball, bowling, cross-country, softball, swimming and diving, tennis, track and field (indoor), track and field (outdoor), volleyball.

SERVICES AND FACILITIES
Information technology resources: Students are not required to lease or own a computer.

TRANSFER AND INTERNATIONAL STUDENTS
Transfer students: May apply for admission for the following academic terms: Fall, Spring. Applicants need a minimum number of credits to apply. For fall 2005: Transfer applications received: 1,117. Transfer applicants offered admission: 1,000. Transfer applicants enrolled: 504. **International students:** Number of foreign undergraduates: 42.

North Carolina Central University

■ **Address:** 1801 Fayetteville Street, Durham, NC 27707
■ **Website:** http://www.nccu.edu
■ **Public**
■ **Enrollment:** 5,005 full-time; 1,348 part-time

KEY STATS
✔ **U.S News College Ranking:** third tier, Universities–Master's (South)
✔ **SAT Score (25th/75th percentile):** 750-960
✔ **Tuition:** 2006-2007: $3,396 in state, $13,140 out of state
Selectivity: Least selective   **Room/board:** $4,756
Acceptance rate: 77%   **Average debt:** $15,000
Student/faculty ratio: 16/1   **Proportion who borrowed:** N/A

UNDERGRADUATE STUDENT BODY STATS
2005-2006 enrollment: 5,005 full-time; 1,348 part-time. Men: 34%; women: 66%. **Ethnic makeup:** African American: 90%; Asian American: 1%; Hispanic: 1%; White: 8%.

ADMISSIONS FACTS AND FIGURES
Phone: (919) 530-6298. **Email:** admissions@nccu.edu. **Website:** http://www.nccu.edu. **Application deadlines for fall 2007:** Regular decision: August 6. Early decision: Not offered. Early action: Not offered. Admission can be deferred. **Application fee:** $30. Common application is accepted. **Admissions requirements/recommendations:** High school units required (recommended): English: 4; Mathematics: 4; Science: 3; Foreign language:

2; Social studies: 2; History: 1; Academic electives: 3; Total units: 20. Tests: The college uses SAT or ACT scores in admissions decisions. Either SAT or ACT required. For admission to the fall 2007 entering class, the school will accept: ACT with writing, ACT without writing. Campus visit: Recommended. Admissions interview: Recommended. Off-campus interview: May not be arranged. **Factors that count in admissions decisions:** *Academic:* Secondary school record: Very important. Class rank: Important. Letters of recommendation: Considered. Standardized test scores: Important. Essay: Considered. *Nonacademic:* Interview: Considered. Extracurricular activities: Considered. Talent/ability: Considered. Character/personal qualities: Considered. Alumni/ae relationship: Considered. Geographical residence: Considered. State residency: Considered. Religious affiliation/commitment: Not considered. Minority status: Not considered. Volunteer work: Not considered. Work experience: Not considered. **Other schools with the greatest overlap in applicants:** Fayetteville State University; North Carolina A&T State University; Shaw University; St. Augustine's College; Winston-Salem State University. **Admissions statistics for the fall 2005 entering class:** Total applicants: 3,321. Total accepted: 2,545. Freshmen enrolled: 1,226; 16% were from out of state. Overall acceptance rate: 77%. **Credentials of fall 2005 freshmen:** 5% ranked in the top 10 percent of their high school class; 16% were in the top 25 percent, and 51% were in the top half. (Proportion submitting class standing: 86%.) **Average high school grade point average:** 2.7. **First-year students who submitted SAT scores:** 85%. Scores (25/75 percentile): Verbal: 370-480, Math: 380-480, Combined: 750-960. **First-year students submitting ACT scores:** 20%. Scores (25/75 percentile): English: 13-19, Math: 15-19, Composite: 15-19.

ACADEMICS
Year founded: 1910. **Academic calendar:** Semester. **Degrees offered:** bachelor's, master's, first professional. **Most popular majors:** 14% business administration and management, 10% criminal justice/safety studies, 8% political science and government, 7% family and consumer sciences/human sciences, 7% psychology. **Major fields of study:** biological and biomedical sciences; business, management, marketing, and related support services; communication, journalism, and related programs; computer and information sciences and support services; education; English language and literature/letters; family and consumer sciences/human sciences; foreign languages, literatures, and linguistics; health professions and related clinical sciences; history; legal professions and studies; mathematics and statistics; natural resources and conservation; parks, recreation, leisure, and fitness studies; physical sciences; psychology; public administration and social service professions; security and protective services; social sciences; visual and performing arts. **Areas of required coursework:** arts/fine arts, humanities, computer literacy, mathematics, English (including composition), foreign languages, sciences (biological or physical), history, social science. **Special academic programs:** distance learning, double major, English as a Second Language (ESL), exchange student program (domestic), honors program, independent study, internships, study abroad, teacher certificate program, weekend college. **Teacher certification offered in:** early childhood, special education, elementary, middle/junior high, secondary. **Reserve Officers Training Corps (ROTC):** Army ROTC: Offered at cooperating institution (Duke University); Air Force ROTC: Offered at cooperating institution (Duke University). **Faculty and instruction (2005-2006):** Total instructional faculty: 325 full-time, 235 part-time (46% men; 54% women; 70% minorities). Full-time faculty with Ph.D. or other terminal degree: 73%. Student/faculty ratio: 16/1. Classes of fewer than 20 students: 36%; of 20 to 49 students: 57%; of 50 or more students: 6%. **Advanced Placement and International Baccalaureate credit:** AP tests may be used for: Credit and/or placement. International Baccalaureate exams may be used for: Credit and/or placement. **Freshmen returning for sophomore year:** 79%. **Graduation rates:** Four-year: 23%; five-year: 38%; six-year: 49%.

COSTS AND FINANCIAL AID
Financial aid office: (919) 530-6180. **Expenses (2006-2007):** Tuition and fees 2006-2007: $3,396 in state, $13,140 out of state; room/board: $4,756. Estimated books and supplies: $1,500; transportation: $600; personal expenses: $1,575. **Financial aid:** Priority filing date for institution's financial aid form: March 1. In 2005-2006, 80% of undergraduates applied for financial aid. Of those, 80% were determined to have financial need; 61% had their need fully met. Average financial aid package (proportion receiving): $8,196 (80%). Average amount of gift aid, such as scholarships or grants (proportion receiving): $1,818 (67%). Average amount of self-help aid, such as work study or loans (proportion receiving): $2,964 (73%). Average need-based loan (excluding PLUS or other private loans): $3,205. Among students who received need-based aid, the average percentage of need met:

74%. Among students who received aid based on merit, the average award (and the proportion receiving): $3,748 (1%). The average athletic scholarship (and the proportion receiving): $6,109 (1%). Average amount of debt of borrowers graduating in 2005: $15,000.

CAMPUS LIFE AND EXTRACURRICULAR ACTIVITIES
Campus housing available (% using): coed dorms (65%), women's dorms (24%), men's dorms (11%), other housing options. Students who live in college-owned, operated, or affiliated housing: 42%. **Clubs and organizations:** Number of student organizations: 83. Activities include: choral groups, concert band, dance, drama/theater, jazz band, literary magazine, marching band, music ensembles, pep band, radio station, student government, student newspaper, yearbook. Number of fraternities: 5; sororities: 4. **Sports program (2005-2006):** Member of NCAA II. *Men's intercollegiate varsity sports:* basketball, cross-country, football, golf, tennis, track and field (indoor), track and field (outdoor). *Women's intercollegiate varsity sports:* basketball, bowling, cross-country, softball, tennis, track and field (indoor), track and field (outdoor), volleyball.

SERVICES AND FACILITIES
Basic services: nonremedial tutoring, placement service, health service, health insurance. **Remedial assistance:** reading, math, writing, study skills. **Counseling services:** minority student, career, personal, veteran student, academic, older student, psychological, birth control, religious. **For learning-disabled students:** School does not offer a structured program with separate admission and additional fees. Total undergraduates in learning-disabled program or receiving services: 110. Services include: reading machines, tape recorders, untimed tests, note-taking services, oral tests, learning center, readers, extended time for tests, tutors, early syllabus, priority registration, priority seating, proofreading services, substitution of courses, texts on tape, typist/scribe, exams on tape or computer, take home exams, other testing accomodations, waiver of foreign language degree requirement, waiver of math degree requirement. **Library:** Number of titles: 1,199; number of current serial subscriptions: 28. **Information technology resources:** Students are not required to lease or own a computer. Number of campus computers available to all students: 800. School has a wireless network. Approximate number of users that can be accommodated: 1,000. Proportion of college-owned housing units wired for high-speed internet access: 100%. **Campus safety:** Security services offered: 24-hour foot-and-vehicle patrols, late-night transport/escort service, 24-hour emergency telephones, lighted pathways/sidewalks, controlled dormitory access (key, security card, etc).

TRANSFER AND INTERNATIONAL STUDENTS
Transfer students: May apply for admission for the following academic terms: Fall, Spring, Summer. Applicants need a minimum number of credits to apply. For fall 2005: Transfer applications received: 701. Transfer applicants offered admission: 593. Transfer applicants enrolled: 383. **International students:** Number of foreign undergraduates: 32 (1% of student body). Number of countries represented: 14.

North Carolina School of the Arts

- **Address:** 1533 S. Main Street, Winston-Salem, NC 27127-2189
- **Website:** http://www.ncarts.edu
- **Public**
- **Enrollment:** 723 full-time

KEY STATS
✔ **U.S News College Ranking:** Unranked Specialty School–Fine Arts
✔ **SAT or ACT Score (25th/75th percentile):** N/A
✔ **Tuition:** 2006-2007: $2,755 in state, $14,035 out of state
   Selectivity: Least selective   **Room/board:** $5,956
   Acceptance rate: 42%   **Average debt:** $19,196
   Student/faculty ratio: 8/1   **Proportion who borrowed:** 69%

UNDERGRADUATE STUDENT BODY STATS
2005-2006 enrollment: 723 full-time. Men: 61%; women: 39%.

ADMISSIONS FACTS AND FIGURES
Phone: (336) 770-3291. **Email:** admissions@ncarts.edu. **Website:** http://www.ncarts.edu. **Application deadlines for fall 2007:** Regular decision: March 1. Early decision: Not offered. Early action: Not offered. Admission can be deferred. **Application fee:** $50. Common application is not accepted. **Admissions requirements/recommendations:** High school units required (recommended): English: 4; Mathematics: 3; Science: 3; Foreign language: (2); Social studies: 2; History: 1; Academic electives: 4; Total units: 20. Tests: The college does not use SAT or ACT scores in admissions decisions. Neither SAT nor ACT required. Campus visit: Recommended. Admissions interview: Required. Off-campus interview: May be arranged. **Factors that count in admissions decisions:** *Academic:* Secondary school record: Very important. Class rank: Not considered. Letters of recommendation: Very important. Standardized test scores: Important. Essay: Not considered. *Nonacademic:* Interview: Very important. Extracurricular activities: Considered. Talent/ability: Very important. Character/personal qualities: Considered. Alumni/ae relationship: Not considered. Geographical residence: Not considered. State residency: Not considered. Religious affiliation/commitment: Not considered. Minority status: Considered. Volunteer work: Not considered. Work experience: Considered. **Other schools with the greatest overlap in applicants:** Boston University; Juilliard School; SUNY–Purchase College. **Admissions statistics for the fall 2005 entering class:** Total applicants: 750. Total accepted: 312. Overall acceptance rate: 42%. **Size of waiting list:** 24 applicants; enrolled from waiting list: 5.

ACADEMICS
Year founded: 1963. **Academic calendar:** Trimester. **Degrees offered:** diploma, bachelor's, master's, post-master's certificate. **Most popular majors:** Information not available. **Major fields of study:** visual and performing arts. **Areas of required coursework:** arts/fine arts, humanities, mathematics, English (including composition), sciences (biological or physical), social science. **Special academic programs:** cooperative (work-study plan) program, English as a Second Language (ESL), independent study, internships. **Faculty and instruction (2005-2006):** Total instructional faculty: 110. Full-time faculty with Ph.D. or other terminal degree: 37%. Student/faculty ratio: 8/1. **Advanced Placement and International Baccalaureate credit:** AP tests may be used for: Credit only. International Baccalaureate exams may be used for: Credit only. **Freshmen returning for sophomore year:** 75%. **Graduation rates:** Six-year: 48%.

COSTS AND FINANCIAL AID
Financial aid office: (336) 770-3297. **Expenses (2006-2007):** Tuition and fees 2006-2007: $2,755 in state, $14,035 out of state; room/board: $5,956. **Financial aid:** Priority filing date for institution's financial aid form: March 1. In 2005-2006, 75% of undergraduates applied for financial aid. Of those, 60% were determined to have financial need; 12% had their need fully met. Average financial aid package (proportion receiving): $11,542 (60%). Average amount of gift aid, such as scholarships or grants (proportion receiving): $5,087 (57%). Average amount of self-help aid, such as work study or loans (proportion receiving): $4,039 (55%). Average need-based loan (excluding PLUS or other private loans): $4,028. Among students who received need-based aid, the average percentage of need met: 80%. Among students who received aid based on merit, the average award (and the proportion receiving): $2,345 (17%). The average athletic scholarship (and the proportion receiving): $0 (0%). Average amount of debt of borrowers graduating in 2005: $19,196. Proportion who borrowed: 69%.

CAMPUS LIFE AND EXTRACURRICULAR ACTIVITIES
Campus housing available: coed dorms, women's dorms, men's dorms, apartment for single students, special housing for disabled students. **Student employment:** During the 2005-2006 academic year, 15% of undergraduates worked on campus. Average per-year earnings: $750. Activities include: choral groups, dance, drama/theater, music ensembles, musical theater, opera, student government, symphony orchestra. Number of fraternities: 0; sororities: 0.

SERVICES AND FACILITIES
Basic services: health service. **Counseling services:** career, personal, academic, psychological. **For learning-disabled students:** School does not offer a structured program with separate admission and additional fees. **Library:** Number of titles: 105,000; number of current serial subscriptions: 470. **Information technology resources:** Students are not required to lease or own a computer. Number of campus computers available to all students: 60. School has a wireless network. Proportion of college-owned housing units wired for high-speed internet access: 100%. **Campus safety:** Security services offered: 24-hour foot-and-vehicle patrols, late-night transport/escort service, 24-hour emergency telephones, lighted pathways/sidewalks, controlled dormitory access (key, security card, etc).

TRANSFER AND INTERNATIONAL STUDENTS

Transfer students: May apply for admission for the following academic terms: Fall. Applicants do not need a minimum number of credits to apply. For fall 2005: Transfer applications received: 160. Transfer applicants offered admission: 84. Transfer applicants enrolled: 58. **International students:** Average TOEFL score: 550 (paper).

North Carolina State University–Raleigh

- **Address:** Box 7001, Raleigh, NC 27695
- **Website:** http://www.ncsu.edu
- **Public**
- **Enrollment:** 19,226 full-time; 3,541 part-time

KEY STATS
- ✔ **U.S News College Ranking:** 81, National Universities
- ✔ **SAT Score (25th/75th percentile):** 1090-1280
- ✔ **Tuition:** 2006-2007: $4,784 in state, $16,982 out of state
  - **Selectivity:** More selective
  - **Acceptance rate:** 66%
  - **Student/faculty ratio:** 16/1
  - **Room/board:** $7,040
  - **Average debt:** $14,505
  - **Proportion who borrowed:** 52%

UNDERGRADUATE STUDENT BODY STATS

2005-2006 enrollment: 19,226 full-time; 3,541 part-time. Men: 57%; women: 43%. **Ethnic makeup:** African American: 10%; American-Indian: 1%; Asian American: 5%; Hispanic: 2%; White: 81%; International: 1%.

ADMISSIONS FACTS AND FIGURES

Phone: (919) 515-2434. **Email:** undergrad_admissions@ncsu.edu. **Website:** http://www.ncsu.edu. **Application deadlines for fall 2007:** Regular decision: February 1. Early decision: Not offered. Early action: Send application by: November 1; Decision sent by: January 15. Admission can be deferred. **Application fee:** $60. Common application is not accepted. **To apply online, go to:** http://www.ncsu.edu/uga. **Admissions requirements/recommendations:** High school units required (recommended): English: 4 (4); Mathematics: 4 (4); Science: 3 (4); Foreign language: 2 (2); Social studies: 1 (1); History: 1 (1); Academic electives: 1 (4); Total units: 16 (20). Tests: The college uses SAT or ACT scores in admissions decisions. Either SAT or ACT required. For admission to the fall 2007 entering class, the school will accept: ACT with writing. Campus visit: Recommended. Admissions interview: Neither required nor recommended. Off-campus interview: Not available. **Factors that count in admissions decisions:** *Academic:* Secondary school record: Very important. Class rank: Very important. Letters of recommendation: Considered. Standardized test scores: Very important. Essay: Considered. *Nonacademic:* Interview: Not considered. Extracurricular activities: Considered. Talent/ability: Considered. Character/personal qualities: Considered. Alumni/ae relationship: Considered. Geographical residence: Considered. State residency: Considered. Religious affiliation/commitment: Not considered. Minority status: Considered. Volunteer work: Considered. Work experience: Considered. **Other schools with the greatest overlap in applicants:** East Carolina University; University of North Carolina–Chapel Hill; University of North Carolina–Charlotte; Virginia Tech; Wake Forest University. **Admissions statistics for the fall 2005 entering class:** Total applicants: 13,610. Total accepted: 9,039. Freshmen enrolled: 4,253; 9% were from out of state. Accepted through early-decision or early-action plans: 77%. Overall acceptance rate: 66%. Non-early acceptance rate: 94%. **Size of waiting list:** 758 applicants; enrolled from waiting list: 130. **Credentials of fall 2005 freshmen:** 36% ranked in the top 10 percent of their high school class; 78% were in the top 25 percent, and 98% were in the top half. (Proportion submitting class standing: 88%.) **Average high school grade point average:** 4.0. **First-year students who submitted SAT scores:** 94%. Scores (25/75 percentile): Verbal: 530-620, Math: 560-660, Combined: 1090-1280. **First-year students submitting ACT scores:** 6%. Scores (25/75 percentile): English: 21-28, Math: 24-29, Composite: 23-27.

ACADEMICS

Year founded: 1887. **Academic calendar:** Semester. **Degrees offered:** certificate, associate, bachelor's, post-bachelor's certificate, master's, first professional, first professional certificate, doctorate. **Most popular majors:** 24% engineering, 14% business, management, marketing, and related support services, 10% biological and biomedical sciences, 7% communication, journalism, and related programs, 7% social sciences. **Major fields of study:** agriculture, agriculture operations, and related sciences; architecture and related services; biological and biomedical sciences; business, management, marketing, and related support services; communication, journalism, and related programs; computer and information sciences and support services; education; engineering; engineering technologies/technicians; English language and literature/letters; foreign languages, literatures, and linguistics; history; liberal arts and sciences studies, and humanities; mathematics and statistics; multi/interdisciplinary studies; natural resources and conservation; parks, recreation, leisure, and fitness studies; philosophy and religious studies; physical sciences; psychology; public administration and social service professions; social sciences; visual and performing arts. **Areas of required coursework:** arts/fine arts, humanities, computer literacy, mathematics, English (including composition), foreign languages, sciences (biological or physical), history, social science. **Pre-professional programs:** pre-law, pre-dentistry, pre-medicine, pre-veterinary science. **Special academic programs (% participation):** accelerated program, cooperative (work-study plan) program (6%), cross-registration, distance learning (27%), double major (12%), dual enrollment, exchange student program (domestic) (1%), honors program (20%), independent study, internships, liberal arts/career combination, student-designed major, study abroad (12%), teacher certificate program (4%). **Teacher certification offered in:** vo-tech, middle/junior high, secondary. **Cooperative education programs:** agriculture, computer science, engineering, humanities, natural science, social/behavioral science. **Reserve Officers Training Corps (ROTC):** Army ROTC: Offered on campus; Navy ROTC: Offered on campus; Air Force ROTC: Offered on campus. **Faculty and instruction (2005-2006):** Total instructional faculty: 1,671 full-time, 193 part-time (71% men; 29% women; 15% minorities). Full-time faculty with Ph.D. or other terminal degree: 91%. Student/faculty ratio: 16/1. Classes of fewer than 20 students: 31%; of 20 to 49 students: 54%; of 50 or more students: 15%. **Advanced Placement and International Baccalaureate credit:** AP tests may be used for: Credit and/or placement. Scores accepted: 3, 4, 5. International Baccalaureate exams may be used for: Credit and/or placement. **Freshmen returning for sophomore year:** 90%. **Graduation rates:** Four-year: 36%; five-year: 65%; six-year: 71%. **Graduate study:** 41% of students pursue further study within five years. Fields in which graduates pursue further study: Master of Business Administration (MBA), 9%; law, 5%; medicine, 4%; dentistry, 1%; engineering, 21%; theology (or the seminary), 2%; education, 7%; arts and sciences, 49%; veterinary medicine, 3%.

COSTS AND FINANCIAL AID

Financial aid office: (919) 515-2421. **Expenses (2006-2007):** Tuition and fees 2006-2007: $4,784 in state, $16,982 out of state; room/board: $7,040. Estimated books and supplies: $900; transportation: $500; personal expenses: $1,230. **Financial aid:** Priority filing date for institution's financial aid form: March 1. In 2005-2006, 55% of undergraduates applied for financial aid. Of those, 39% were determined to have financial need; 44% had their need fully met. Average financial aid package (proportion receiving): $8,403 (38%). Average amount of gift aid, such as scholarships or grants (proportion receiving): $5,917 (37%). Average amount of self-help aid, such as work study or loans (proportion receiving): $3,392 (30%). Average need-based loan (excluding PLUS or other private loans): $3,066. Among students who received need-based aid, the average percentage of need met: 81%. Among students who received aid based on merit, the average award (and the proportion receiving): $7,344 (23%). The average athletic scholarship (and the proportion receiving): $13,785 (1%). Average amount of debt of borrowers graduating in 2005: $14,505. Proportion who borrowed: 52%.

CAMPUS LIFE AND EXTRACURRICULAR ACTIVITIES

Campus housing available (% using): coed dorms (84%), women's dorms, men's dorms, sorority housing (2%), fraternity housing (2%), apartments for married students, apartment for single students (12%), special housing for disabled students, special housing for international students. Students who live in college-owned, operated, or affiliated housing: 34%. **Student employment:** During the 2005-2006 academic year, 12% of undergraduates worked on campus. Average per-year earnings: $1,900. **Clubs and organizations:** Number of student organizations: 353. Activities include: choral groups, concert band, dance, drama/theater, jazz band, literary magazine, marching band, music ensembles, musical theater, pep band, radio station, student government, student newspaper, student film society, symphony orchestra, yearbook. Number of fraternities: 25; sororities: 15. Proportion of men in fraternities: 9%; of women in sororities: 10%. Average proportion of students who stay on campus on weekends: 60%. **Sports program (2005-2006):** Member of NCAA I. *Men's intercollegiate varsity sports:* baseball, basketball, cheerleading, cross-country, football, golf, riflery, soccer, swimming and diving, tennis, track and field (indoor), track and field (outdoor), wrestling. **Women's intercollegiate varsity sports:** basketball, cheerleading, cross-country, golf, gymnastics, riflery, soccer, softball, swimming and diving, tennis, track and field (indoor), track and field (outdoor), volleyball.

SERVICES AND FACILITIES

Basic services: nonremedial tutoring, women's center, placement service, health service. **Remedial assistance:** math. **Counseling services:** minority student, career, military, personal, veteran student, academic, older student, psychological, birth control, religious. **For learning-disabled students:** School does not offer a structured program with separate admission and additional fees. Total undergraduates in learning-disabled program or receiving services: 209. Services include: reading machines, tape recorders, note-taking services, readers, extended time for tests, priority registration, priority seating, substitution of courses, texts on tape, typist/scribe, exams on tape or computer. **Library:** Number of titles: 3,359,489; number of current serial subscriptions: 57,486. **Information technology resources:** Students are not required to lease or own a computer. Number of campus computers available to all students: 2,845. School has a wireless network. Approximate number of users that can be accommodated: 8,750. Proportion of college-owned housing units wired for high-speed internet access: 100%. **Campus safety:** Security services offered: 24-hour foot-and-vehicle patrols, late-night transport/escort service, 24-hour emergency telephones, lighted pathways/sidewalks, student patrols, controlled dormitory access (key, security card, etc).

TRANSFER AND INTERNATIONAL STUDENTS

Transfer students: May apply for admission for the following academic terms: Fall, Spring, Summer. Applicants need a minimum number of credits to apply. For fall 2005: Transfer applications received: 3,478. Transfer applicants offered admission: 1,305. Transfer applicants enrolled: 1,027. **International students:** Number of foreign undergraduates: 210 (1% of student body). Number of countries represented: 52. Minimum TOEFL score required: 550 (paper); 213 (computer). Average TOEFL score: 689 (paper).

North Carolina Wesleyan College

- **Address:** 3400 N. Wesleyan Boulevard, Rocky Mount, NC 27804
- **Website:** http://www.ncwc.edu
- **Private; Religious affiliation:** Methodist
- **Enrollment:** 995 full-time; 757 part-time

KEY STATS

✔ **U.S News College Ranking:** third tier, Comp. Colleges–Bachelor's (South)
✔ **SAT Score (25th/75th percentile):** 855-1111
✔ **Tuition:** 2006-2007: $17,600

Selectivity: Less selective	**Room/board:** $6,870
Acceptance rate: 81%	**Average debt:** $17,125
Student/faculty ratio: 17/1	**Proportion who borrowed:** 88%

UNDERGRADUATE STUDENT BODY STATS

2005-2006 enrollment: 995 full-time; 757 part-time. Men: 45%; women: 55%. **Ethnic makeup:** African American: 45%; American-Indian: 1%; Asian American: 1%; Hispanic: 3%; White: 50%; International: 1%. **Religious preference:** Roman Catholic: 5%; Protestant: 42%; No preference: 53%.

ADMISSIONS FACTS AND FIGURES

Phone: (800) 488-6292. **Email:** adm@ncwc.edu. **Website:** http://www.ncwc.edu. **Application deadlines for fall 2007:** Regular decision: July 30. Early decision: Not offered. Early action: Not offered. Admission can be deferred. **Application fee:** $25. Common application is accepted. **To apply online, go to:** http://www.ncwc.edu/Admission/day_apply_inst.htm. **Admissions requirements/recommendations:** High school units required (recommended): English: 4 (4); Mathematics: 3 (3); Foreign language: 2 (2); Social studies: 2 (2). Tests: The college uses SAT or ACT scores in admissions decisions. Neither SAT nor ACT required. For admission to the fall 2007 entering class, the school will accept: ACT with writing. Campus visit: Neither required nor recommended. Admissions interview: Neither required nor recommended. Off-campus interview: May be arranged. **Factors that count in admissions decisions:** *Academic:* Secondary school record: Very important. Class rank: Important. Letters of recommendation: Important. Standardized test scores: Important. Essay: Considered. *Nonacademic:* Interview: Important. Extracurricular activities: Important.

Talent/ability: Considered. Character/personal qualities: Important. Alumni/ae relationship: Considered. Geographical residence: Not considered. State residency: Not considered. Religious affiliation/commitment: Not considered. Minority status: Not considered. Volunteer work: Considered. Work experience: Not considered. **Other schools with the greatest overlap in applicants:** Barton College; Campbell University; East Carolina University; Elon University; North Carolina Central University. **Admissions statistics for the fall 2005 entering class:** Total applicants: 1,169. Total accepted: 951. Freshmen enrolled: 288; 35% were from out of state. Overall acceptance rate: 81%. **Credentials of fall 2005 freshmen:** 14% ranked in the top 10 percent of their high school class; 32% were in the top 25 percent, and 89% were in the top half. (Proportion submitting class standing: 53%.) **First-year students who submitted SAT scores:** 88%. Scores (25/75 percentile): Verbal: 425-555, Math: 430-556, Combined: 855-1111.

ACADEMICS

Year founded: 1956. **Academic calendar:** Semester. **Degrees offered:** certificate, bachelor's. **Most popular majors:** 51% business, management, marketing, and related support services, 18% security and protective services, 13% computer and information sciences and support services, 7% psychology, 3% social sciences. **Major fields of study:** biological and biomedical sciences; business, management, marketing, and related support services; computer and information sciences and support services; education; English language and literature/letters; history; legal professions and studies; mathematics and statistics; multi/interdisciplinary studies; natural resources and conservation; parks, recreation, leisure, and fitness studies; philosophy and religious studies; physical sciences; psychology; security and protective services; social sciences; theology and religious vocations; visual and performing arts. **Areas of required coursework:** humanities, computer literacy, mathematics, English (including composition), sciences (biological or physical), history, social science, other. **Pre-professional programs:** pre-medicine. **Special academic programs (% participation):** accelerated program, cooperative (work-study plan) program, cross-registration, distance learning, double major, dual enrollment, honors program (2%), independent study, internships (2%), liberal arts/career combination, teacher certificate program (5%), weekend college. **Teacher certification offered in:** early childhood, middle/junior high. **Faculty and instruction (2005-2006):** Total instructional faculty: 53 full-time, 100 part-time (64% men; 36% women). Full-time faculty with Ph.D. or other terminal degree: 77%. Student/faculty ratio: 17/1. Classes of fewer than 20 students: 72%; of 20 to 49 students: 28%; of 50 or more students: 0%. **Freshmen returning for sophomore year:** 60%. **Graduation rates:** Four-year: 22%; five-year: 37%; six-year: 36%. **Graduate study:** 4% of students pursue further study immediately upon graduation; 7% within one year; 14% within five years.

COSTS AND FINANCIAL AID

Financial aid office: (252) 985-5200. **Expenses (2006-2007):** Tuition and fees 2006-2007: $17,600; room/board: $6,870. Estimated books and supplies: $1,000; transportation: $1,000; personal expenses: $1,200. **Financial aid:** Priority filing date for institution's financial aid form: March 15. In 2005-2006, 94% of undergraduates applied for financial aid. Of those, 84% were determined to have financial need; Average financial aid package (proportion receiving): $17,598 (84%). Average amount of gift aid, such as scholarships or grants (proportion receiving): $12,018 (84%). Average amount of self-help aid, such as work study or loans (proportion receiving): $5,580 (84%). Average need-based loan (excluding PLUS or other private loans): $4,590. Among students who received need-based aid, the average percentage of need met: 88%. Among students who received aid based on merit, the average award (and the proportion receiving): $6,983 (6%). The average athletic scholarship (and the proportion receiving): $0 (0%). Average amount of debt of borrowers graduating in 2005: $17,125. Proportion who borrowed: 88%.

CAMPUS LIFE AND EXTRACURRICULAR ACTIVITIES

Campus housing available (% using): coed dorms (61%), women's dorms (20%), men's dorms (19%), special housing for disabled students. Students who live in college-owned, operated, or affiliated housing: 32%. **Student employment:** During the 2005-2006 academic year, 25% of undergraduates worked on campus. Average per-year earnings: $500. **Clubs and organizations:** Number of student organizations: 34. Activities include: choral groups, drama/theater, literary magazine, music ensembles, student government, student newspaper, yearbook. Number of fraternities: 4; sororities: 3. Proportion of men in fraternities: 1%; Average proportion of students who stay on campus on weekends: 50%. **Sports program (2005-2006):** Member of NCAA III. **Men's intercollegiate varsity sports:** baseball, basketball, football, golf, soccer, tennis. **Women's intercollegiate varsity sports:** basketball, lacrosse, soccer, softball, tennis, volleyball.

SERVICES AND FACILITIES

Basic services: nonremedial tutoring, placement service, health service. **Remedial assistance:** reading, math, writing, study skills. **Counseling services:** minority student, career, personal, veteran student, academic, older student, psychological, religious. **For learning-disabled students:** School does not offer a structured program with separate admission and additional fees. Services include: remedial math, remedial English, remedial reading, tape recorders, other special classes, diagnostic testing service, untimed tests, note-taking services, special bookstore section, oral tests, learning center, readers, extended time for tests, tutors, priority registration, priority seating, texts on tape, other testing accomodations. **Library:** Number of titles: 93,293; number of current serial subscriptions: 475. **Information technology resources:** Students are not required to lease or own a computer. Number of campus computers available to all students: 100. School does not have a wireless network. Proportion of college-owned housing units wired for high-speed internet access: 100%. **Campus safety:** Security services offered: 24-hour foot-and-vehicle patrols, late-night transport/escort service, 24-hour emergency telephones, lighted pathways/sidewalks, student patrols, controlled dormitory access (key, security card, etc.).

TRANSFER AND INTERNATIONAL STUDENTS

Transfer students: May apply for admission for the following academic terms: Fall, Spring, Summer. Applicants need a minimum number of credits to apply. For fall 2005: Transfer applications received: 201. Transfer applicants offered admission: 127. Transfer applicants enrolled: 71. **International students:** Number of foreign undergraduates: 9 (1% of student body). Number of countries represented: 4. Minimum TOEFL score required: 500 (paper); 150 (computer). Average TOEFL score: 500 (paper).

Peace College

- **Address:** 15 E. Peace Street, Raleigh, NC 27604-1194
- **Website:** http://www.peace.edu
- **Private; Religious affiliation:** Presbyterian (U.S.A.)
- **Enrollment:** 647 full-time; 21 part-time

KEY STATS

✔ **U.S News College Ranking:** 35, Comp. Colleges–Bachelor's (South)
✔ **SAT Score (25th/75th percentile):** 860-1040
✔ **Tuition:** 2005-2006: $18,906

Selectivity: Less selective	**Room/board:** $6,918
Acceptance rate: 78%	**Average debt:** N/A
Student/faculty ratio: 13/1	**Proportion who borrowed:** N/A

UNDERGRADUATE STUDENT BODY STATS

2005-2006 enrollment: 647 full-time; 21 part-time. Men: 0%; women: 100%. **Ethnic makeup:** African American: 15%; Asian American: 2%; Hispanic: 3%; White: 78%; International: 1%. **Religious preference:** Roman Catholic: 10%; Protestant: 51%; No preference: 1%; Unknown: 24%; Presbyterian (U.S.A.): 10%; Other: 4%.

ADMISSIONS FACTS AND FIGURES

Phone: (800) 732-2347. **Email:** admissions@peace.edu. **Website:** http://www.peace.edu. **Application deadlines for fall 2007:** Regular decision: August 1. Early decision: Not offered. Early action: Not offered. Admission can be deferred. **Application fee:** $25. Common application is accepted. **Admissions requirements/recommendations:** High school units required (recommended): English: 4 (4); Mathematics: 3 (3); Science: 3 (4); Foreign language: 2 (2); Social studies: 1 (2); History: 2 (2). Tests: The college uses SAT or ACT scores in admissions decisions. Either SAT or ACT required. For admission to the fall 2007 entering class, the school will accept: ACT with writing, ACT without writing. Campus visit: Recommended. Admissions interview: Recommended. Off-campus interview: May be arranged. **Factors that count in admissions decisions:** *Academic:* Secondary school record: Very important, Class rank: Considered. Letters of recommendation: Considered. Standardized test scores: Very important. Essay: Considered. *Nonacademic:* Interview: Considered. Extracurricular activities: Important. Talent/ability: Important. Character/personal qualities: Very important. Alumni/ae relationship: Considered. Geographical residence:

Considered. State residency: Considered. Religious affiliation/commitment: Not considered. Minority status: Not considered. Volunteer work: Important. Work experience: Considered. **Other schools with the greatest overlap in applicants:** East Carolina University; Meredith College; North Carolina State University–Raleigh; University of North Carolina–Chapel Hill; University of North Carolina–Wilmington. **Admissions statistics for the fall 2005 entering class:** Total applicants: 787. Total accepted: 614. Freshmen enrolled: 179; 14% were from out of state. Overall acceptance rate: 78%. **Credentials of fall 2005 freshmen:** 10% ranked in the top 10 percent of their high school class; 20% were in the top 25 percent, and 52% were in the top half. (Proportion submitting class standing: 60%.) **Average high school grade point average:** 2.9. **First-year students who submitted SAT scores:** 96%. Scores (25/75 percentile): Verbal: 430-530, Math: 430-510, Combined: 860-1040. **First-year students submitting ACT scores:** 4%. Scores (25/75 percentile): English: 14-19, Math: 14-19, Composite: 15-18.

ACADEMICS

Year founded: 1857. **Academic calendar:** Semester. **Degrees offered:** bachelor's. **Most popular majors:** 15% business administration and management, 13% communication studies/speech communication and rhetoric, 13% psychology, 12% biology/biological sciences, 9% liberal arts and sciences/liberal studies. **Major fields of study:** biological and biomedical sciences; business, management, marketing, and related support services; communication, journalism, and related programs; English language and literature/letters; foreign languages, literatures, and linguistics; liberal arts and sciences studies, and humanities; psychology; social sciences; visual and performing arts. **Areas of required coursework:** arts/fine arts, humanities, computer literacy, mathematics, English (including composition), philosophy, foreign languages, sciences (biological or physical), history, social science, other. **Pre-professional programs:** pre-law, pre-dentistry, pre-medicine, pre-veterinary science, pre-optometry, pre-pharmacy. **Special academic programs (% participation):** cross-registration (10%), double major (8%), dual enrollment, honors program (15%), independent study (1%), internships (100%), study abroad (17%). **Reserve Officers Training Corps (ROTC):** Army ROTC: Offered at cooperating institution (North Carolina State University); Navy ROTC: Offered at cooperating institution (North Carolina State University); Air Force ROTC: Offered at cooperating institution (North Carolina State University). **Faculty and instruction (2005-2006):** Total instructional faculty: 42 full-time, 29 part-time (42% men; 58% women; 8% minorities). Full-time faculty with Ph.D. or other terminal degree: 79%. Student/faculty ratio: 13/1. Classes of fewer than 20 students: 69%; of 20 to 49 students: 29%; of 50 or more students: 2%. **Advanced Placement and International Baccalaureate credit:** AP tests may be used for: Credit and/or placement. Scores accepted: 3. **Freshmen returning for sophomore year:** 66%. **Graduation rates:** Four-year: 39%; five-year: 44%; six-year: 43%. **Graduate study:** 8% of students pursue further study immediately upon graduation; 9% within one year; 15% within five years. Fields in which graduates pursue further study: Master of Business Administration (MBA), 2%; law, 12%; medicine, 2%; education, 36%; arts and sciences, 43%; veterinary medicine, 5%.

COSTS AND FINANCIAL AID

Financial aid office: (919) 508-2249. **Expenses (2005-2006):** Tuition and fees 2005-2006: $18,906; room/board: $6,918. Estimated books and supplies: $1,000; transportation: $600; personal expenses: $2,200.

CAMPUS LIFE AND EXTRACURRICULAR ACTIVITIES

Campus housing available (% using): women's dorms (100%). Students who live in college-owned, operated, or affiliated housing: 60%. **Student employment:** During the 2005-2006 academic year, 51% of undergraduates worked on campus. Average per-year earnings: $2,000. **Clubs and organizations:** Number of student organizations: 30. Activities include: choral groups, dance, drama/theater, literary magazine, musical theater, student government, student newspaper, symphony orchestra, yearbook. Number of fraternities: 0; sororities: 0. Average proportion of students who stay on campus on weekends: 35%. **Sports program (2005-2006):** Member of NCAA III. **Women's intercollegiate varsity sports:** basketball, cross-country, soccer, softball, tennis, volleyball.

SERVICES AND FACILITIES

Basic services: nonremedial tutoring, placement service, health service. **Remedial assistance:** reading, math, writing, study skills. **Counseling services:** minority student, career, personal, academic, birth control, religious. **For learning-disabled students:** School does not offer a structured program with separate admission and additional fees. Total undergraduates in learning-disabled program or receiving services: 72. Services include: remedial math, remedial English, reading machines, tape recorders, untimed tests, learning center, extended time for tests, tutors, priority seating, other testing accomodations. **Library:** Number of titles: 51,483; number of current serial subscriptions: 4,198. **Information technology resources:** Students are not required to lease or own a computer. Number of campus computers available to all students: 167. School has a wireless network. Approximate number of users that can be accommodated: 500. Proportion of college-owned housing units wired for high-speed internet access: 100%. **Campus safety:** Security services offered: 24-hour foot-and-vehicle patrols, late-night transport/escort service, 24-hour emergency telephones, lighted pathways/sidewalks, controlled dormitory access (key, security card, etc).

TRANSFER AND INTERNATIONAL STUDENTS

Transfer students: May apply for admission for the following academic terms: Fall, Spring. Applicants need a minimum number of credits to apply. For fall 2005: Transfer applications received: 111. Transfer applicants offered admission: 75. Transfer applicants enrolled: 31. **International students:** Number of foreign undergraduates: 4 (1% of student body). Number of countries represented: 4. Minimum TOEFL score required: 550 (paper); 213 (computer). Average TOEFL score: 560 (paper).

Pfeiffer University

- **Address:** PO Box 960, Misenheimer, NC 28109
- **Website:** http://www.pfeiffer.edu
- **Private; Religious affiliation:** Methodist
- **Enrollment:** 1,055 full-time; 147 part-time

KEY STATS
✔ **U.S News College Ranking:** third tier, Universities–Master's (South)
✔ **SAT Score (25th/75th percentile):** 900-1090
✔ **Tuition** 2006-2007: $16,450

Selectivity: Less selective	**Room/board:** $6,650
Acceptance rate: 73%	**Average debt:** N/A
Student/faculty ratio: 13/1	**Proportion who borrowed:** N/A

UNDERGRADUATE STUDENT BODY STATS

2005-2006 enrollment: 1,055 full-time; 147 part-time. Men: 41%; women: 59%. **Ethnic makeup:** African American: 22%; American-Indian: 1%; Asian American: 1%; Hispanic: 2%; White: 71%; International: 3%. **Religious preference:** Roman Catholic: 8%; Protestant: 41%; No preference: 10%; Unknown: 9%; Methodist: 24%; Other: 8%.

ADMISSIONS FACTS AND FIGURES

Phone: (800) 338-2060. **Email:** admissions@pfeiffer.edu. **Website:** http://www.pfeiffer.edu. **Application deadlines for fall 2007:** Regular decision: Rolling. Early decision: Not offered. Early action: Not offered. Admission cannot be deferred. **Application fee:** $25. Common application is not accepted. **Admissions requirements/recommendations:** High school units required (recommended): English: 4; Mathematics: 3; Science: 2; Foreign language: (2); Social studies: 2; History: 2; Total units: 12. Tests: The college uses SAT or ACT scores in admissions decisions. Either SAT or ACT required. For admission to the fall 2007 entering class, the school will accept: ACT with writing, ACT without writing. Campus visit: Recommended. Admissions interview: Recommended. Off-campus interview: May be arranged. **Factors that count in admissions decisions:** *Academic:* Secondary school record: Very important. Class rank: Considered. Letters of recommendation: Important. Standardized test scores: Very important. Essay: Considered. *Nonacademic:* Interview: Considered. Extracurricular activities: Important. Talent/ability: Important. Character/personal qualities: Very important. Alumni/ae relationship: Considered. Geographical residence: Not considered. State residency: Not considered. Religious affiliation/commitment: Considered. Minority status: Not considered. Volunteer work: Very important. Work experience: Considered. **Other schools with the greatest overlap in applicants:** Appalachian State University; East Carolina University; North Carolina State University–Raleigh; University of North Carolina–Charlotte; University of North Carolina–Greensboro. **Admissions statistics for the fall 2005 entering class:** Total applicants: 634. Total accepted: 462. Freshmen enrolled: 200; 27% were from out of state. Overall acceptance rate: 73%. **Credentials of fall 2005 freshmen:** 13% ranked in the top 10 percent of their high school class; 34% were in the top 25 percent, and 64% were in the top half. **Average high**

school grade point average: 3.3. **First-year students who submitted SAT scores:** 93%. Scores (25/75 percentile): Verbal: 440-540, Math: 460-550, Combined: 900-1090. **First-year students submitting ACT scores:** 21%. Scores (25/75 percentile): English: N/A, Math: N/A, Composite: 18-22.

ACADEMICS

Year founded: 1885. **Academic calendar:** Semester. **Degrees offered:** bachelor's, post-bachelor's certificate, master's. **Most popular majors:** 43% business, management, marketing, and related support services, 16% security and protective services, 11% education, 4% biological and biomedical sciences, 4% health professions and related clinical sciences. **Major fields of study:** area, ethnic, cultural, and gender studies; biological and biomedical sciences; business, management, marketing, and related support services; communication, journalism, and related programs; computer and information sciences and support services; education; engineering; English language and literature/letters; health professions and related clinical sciences; history; legal professions and studies; liberal arts and sciences studies, and humanities; mathematics and statistics; multi/interdisciplinary studies; natural resources and conservation; parks, recreation, leisure, and fitness studies; philosophy and religious studies; physical sciences; psychology; public administration and social service professions; security and protective services; social sciences; theology and religious vocations; visual and performing arts. **Areas of required coursework:** arts/fine arts, humanities, computer literacy, mathematics, English (including composition), philosophy, sciences (biological or physical), history, social science, other. **Pre-professional programs:** pre-law, pre-medicine, pre-theology. **Special academic programs:** accelerated program, cooperative (work-study plan) program, distance learning, double major, dual enrollment, honors program, independent study, internships, liberal arts/career combination, study abroad, teacher certificate program. **Teacher certification offered in:** special education, elementary, secondary. **Cooperative education programs:** art, business, computer science, education, engineering, humanities, natural science, social/behavioral science, technologies. **Reserve Officers Training Corps (ROTC):** Army ROTC: Offered at cooperating institution (Davidson College). **Faculty and instruction (2005-2006):** Total instructional faculty: 65 full-time, 78 part-time (68% men; 32% women). Full-time faculty with Ph.D. or other terminal degree: 71%. Student/faculty ratio: 13/1. Classes of fewer than 20 students: 70%; of 20 to 49 students: 30%; of 50 or more students: 0%. **Advanced Placement and International Baccalaureate credit:** AP tests may be used for: Credit only. Scores accepted: 3. International Baccalaureate exams may be used for: Credit and/or placement. **Freshmen returning for sophomore year:** 70%. **Graduation rates:** Four-year: 36%; five-year: 49%; six-year: 39%.

COSTS AND FINANCIAL AID

Financial aid office: (800) 338-2060. **Expenses (2006-2007):** Tuition and fees 2006-2007: $16,450; room/board: $6,650. Estimated books and supplies: $1,100. **Financial aid:** Priority filing date for institution's financial aid form: April 15.

CAMPUS LIFE AND EXTRACURRICULAR ACTIVITIES

Campus housing available (% using): coed dorms (54%), women's dorms (20%), men's dorms (26%). Students who live in college-owned, operated, or affiliated housing: 61%. **Student employment:** During the 2005-2006 academic year, 23% of undergraduates worked on campus. Clubs **and organizations:** Number of student organizations: 30. Activities include: choral groups, concert band, drama/theater, jazz band, literary magazine, music ensembles, musical theater, pep band, student government, student newspaper, yearbook. Number of fraternities: 0; sororities: 0. Average proportion of students who stay on campus on weekends: 75%. **Sports program (2005-2006):** Member of NCAA II. *Men's intercollegiate varsity sports:* baseball, basketball, cross-country, golf, lacrosse, soccer, tennis, track and field (indoor), track and field (outdoor). *Women's intercollegiate varsity sports:* basketball, cross-country, golf, lacrosse, soccer, softball, swimming and diving, tennis, track and field (indoor), track and field (outdoor), volleyball.

SERVICES AND FACILITIES

Basic services: women's center, health service, health insurance. **Remedial assistance:** reading, math, writing, study skills. **Counseling services:** minority student, career, military, personal, veteran student, academic, older student, psychological, birth control, religious. **For learning-disabled students:** School does not offer a structured program with separate admission and additional fees. Total undergraduates in learning-disabled program or receiving services: 15. Services include: remedial math, reading machines, tape recorders, other special classes, note-taking services, oral tests, learning center, readers, extended time for tests, tutors. **Library:** Number of titles: 123,919; number of current serial subscriptions: 396. **Information technol-**

ogy resources: Students are not required to lease or own a computer. Number of campus computers available to all students: 100. School has a wireless network. Approximate number of users that can be accommodated: 200. Proportion of college-owned housing units wired for high-speed internet access: 100%. **Campus safety:** Security services offered: 24-hour foot-and-vehicle patrols, late-night transport/escort service, 24-hour emergency telephones, lighted pathways/sidewalks, controlled dormitory access (key, security card, etc).

TRANSFER AND INTERNATIONAL STUDENTS

Transfer students: May apply for admission for the following academic terms: Fall, Spring, Summer. Applicants do not need a minimum number of credits to apply. For fall 2005: Transfer applications received: 228. Transfer applicants enrolled: 106. **International students:** Number of foreign undergraduates: 38 (3% of student body). Number of countries represented: 18. Minimum TOEFL score required: 500 (paper); 173 (computer). Average TOEFL score: 550 (paper).

Queens University of Charlotte

- **Address:** 1900 Selwyn Avenue, Charlotte, NC 28274
- **Website:** http://www.queens.edu
- **Private; Religious affiliation:** Presbyterian
- **Enrollment:** 1,016 full-time; 607 part-time

KEY STATS
- ✔ **U.S News College Ranking:** 37, Universities–Master's (South)
- ✔ **SAT Score (25th/75th percentile):** 970-1130
- ✔ **Tuition:** 2006-2007: $19,450

Selectivity: Selective	**Room/board:** $6,980
Acceptance rate: 67%	**Average debt:** $16,270
Student/faculty ratio: 15/1	**Proportion who borrowed:** 86%

UNDERGRADUATE STUDENT BODY STATS

2005-2006 enrollment: 1,016 full-time; 607 part-time. Men: 23%; women: 77%. **Ethnic makeup:** African American: 17%; American-Indian: 1%; Asian American: 2%; Hispanic: 4%; White: 72%; International: 5%. **Religious preference:** Roman Catholic: 16%; Protestant: 29%; Jewish: 1%; Muslim: 1%; Hindu: 1%; Unknown: 30%; Presbyterian: 10%; Christian: 8%; Other: 4%.

ADMISSIONS FACTS AND FIGURES

Phone: (800) 849-0202. **Email:** admissions@queens.edu. **Website:** http://www.queens.edu. **Application deadlines for fall 2007:** Regular decision: Rolling. Early decision: Not offered. Early action: Not offered. Admission can be deferred. **Application fee:** $40. Common application is accepted. **Admissions requirements/recommendations:** High school units required (recommended): English: (4); Mathematics: (3); Science: (2); Foreign language: (2); Social studies: (2). Tests: The college uses SAT or ACT scores in admissions decisions. Either SAT or ACT required. For admission to the fall 2007 entering class, the school will accept: ACT with writing. Campus visit: Recommended. Admissions interview: Recommended. Off-campus interview: May be arranged. **Factors that count in admissions decisions:** *Academic:* Secondary school record: Very important. Class rank: Important. Letters of recommendation: Considered. Standardized test scores: Very important. Essay: Considered. *Nonacademic:* Interview: Important. Extracurricular activities: Very important. Talent/ability: Considered. Character/personal qualities: Very important. Alumni/ae relationship: Considered. Geographical residence: Not considered. State residency: Not considered. Religious affiliation/commitment: Not considered. Minority status: Not considered. Volunteer work: Important. Work experience: Considered. **Other schools with the greatest overlap in applicants:** Appalachian State University; Elon University; North Carolina State University–Raleigh; University of North Carolina–Chapel Hill; University of North Carolina–Charlotte. **Admissions statistics for the fall 2005 entering class:** Total applicants: 1,019. Total accepted: 678. Freshmen enrolled: 242; 52% were from out of state. Overall acceptance rate: 67%. **Credentials of fall 2005 freshmen:** 16% ranked in the top 10 percent of their high school class; 45% were in the top 25 percent, and 80% were in the top half. (Proportion submitting class standing: 57%.) **Average high school grade point average:** 3.4. **First-year students who submitted SAT scores:** 93%. Scores (25/75 percentile): Verbal: 480-570, Math: 490-560, Combined: 970-1130. **First-year

students submitting ACT scores: 30%. Scores (25/75 percentile): English: 19-25, Math: 18-24, Composite: 19-24.

ACADEMICS

Year founded: 1857. **Academic calendar:** Semester. **Degrees offered:** associate, bachelor's, post-bachelor's certificate, master's. **Most popular majors:** 33% business, management, marketing, and related support services, 15% communication, journalism, and related programs, 10% health professions and related clinical sciences, 8% psychology, 6% social sciences. **Major fields of study:** area, ethnic, cultural, and gender studies; biological and biomedical sciences; business, management, marketing, and related support services; communication, journalism, and related programs; computer and information sciences and support services; education; English language and literature/letters; foreign languages, literatures, and linguistics; health professions and related clinical sciences; mathematics and statistics; philosophy and religious studies; psychology; social sciences; visual and performing arts. **Areas of required coursework:** humanities, mathematics, English (including composition), foreign languages, sciences (biological or physical), history, social science, other. **Pre-professional programs:** pre-law, pre-dentistry, pre-medicine, pre-veterinary science, pre-optometry, pre-pharmacy. **Special academic programs (% participation):** cross-registration (1%), double major (5%), dual enrollment (1%), honors program (5%), independent study (5%), internships (100%), liberal arts/career combination (98%), student-designed major, study abroad (90%), teacher certificate program (12%), weekend college. **Teacher certification offered in:** elementary, secondary. **Reserve Officers Training Corps (ROTC):** Army ROTC: Offered at cooperating institution (University of North Carolina); Air Force ROTC: Offered at cooperating institution (University of North Carolina). **Faculty and instruction (2005-2006):** Total instructional faculty: 68 full-time, 43 part-time (39% men; 61% women; 5% minorities). Full-time faculty with Ph.D. or other terminal degree: 78%. Student/faculty ratio: 15/1. Classes of fewer than 20 students: 63%; of 20 to 49 students: 38%. **Advanced Placement and International Baccalaureate credit:** AP tests may be used for: Credit and/or placement. Scores accepted: 3, 4, 5. International Baccalaureate exams may be used for: Credit and/or placement. **Freshmen returning for sophomore year:** 75%. **Graduation rates:** Four-year: 54%; five-year: 62%; six-year: 60%. **Graduate study:** 10% of students pursue further study immediately upon graduation; 20% within one year; 30% within five years.

COSTS AND FINANCIAL AID

Financial aid office: (704) 337-2225. **Expenses (2006-2007):** Tuition and fees 2006-2007: $19,450; room/board: $6,980. Estimated books and supplies: $800; transportation: $750; personal expenses: $900. **Financial aid:** Priority filing date for institution's financial aid form: March 1. In 2005-2006, 71% of undergraduates applied for financial aid. Of those, 58% were determined to have financial need; 27% had their need fully met. Average financial aid package (proportion receiving): $13,121 (58%). Average amount of gift aid, such as scholarships or grants (proportion receiving): $10,304 (57%). Average amount of self-help aid, such as work study or loans (proportion receiving): $3,585 (49%). Average need-based loan (excluding PLUS or other private loans): $3,243. Among students who received need-based aid, the average percentage of need met: 73%. Among students who received aid based on merit, the average award (and the proportion receiving): $10,079 (39%). The average athletic scholarship (and the proportion receiving): $5,368 (9%). Average amount of debt of borrowers graduating in 2005: $16,270. Proportion who borrowed: 86%.

CAMPUS LIFE AND EXTRACURRICULAR ACTIVITIES

Campus housing available (% using): coed dorms (99%), special housing for disabled students (1%). Students who live in college-owned, operated, or affiliated housing: 70%. **Student employment:** During the 2005-2006 academic year, 13% of undergraduates worked on campus. Average per-year earnings: $2,000. **Clubs and organizations:** Number of student organizations: 33. Activities include: choral groups, dance, drama/theater, literary magazine, music ensembles, musical theater, pep band, student government, student newspaper, yearbook. Number of fraternities: 1; sororities: 4. Proportion of men in fraternities: 30%; of women in sororities: 30%. Average proportion of students who stay on campus on weekends: 70%. **Sports program (2005-2006):** Member of NCAA II. *Men's intercollegiate varsity sports:* basketball, cross-country, golf, lacrosse, soccer, tennis, track and field (outdoor). *Women's intercollegiate varsity sports:* basketball, cross-country, golf, lacrosse, soccer, softball, tennis, track and field (outdoor), volleyball.

SERVICES AND FACILITIES

Basic services: nonremedial tutoring, placement service, health service, health insurance. **Remedial assistance:** reading, math, writing, study skills, other. **Counseling services:** minority student, career, personal, academic, older student, psychological, birth control, religious. **For learning-disabled students:** School does not offer a structured program with separate admission and additional fees. Services include: reading machines, tape recorders, other special classes, untimed tests, note-taking services, oral tests, learning center, readers, extended time for tests, tutors, priority seating, texts on tape, other testing accomodations, other. **Library:** Number of titles: 144,480; number of current serial subscriptions: 287. **Information technology resources:** Students are not required to lease or own a computer. Number of campus computers available to all students: 104. School has a wireless network. Approximate number of users that can be accommodated: 75. Proportion of college-owned housing units wired for high-speed internet access: 100%. **Campus safety:** Security services offered: 24-hour foot-and-vehicle patrols, late-night transport/escort service, 24-hour emergency telephones, lighted pathways/sidewalks, controlled dormitory access (key, security card, etc).

TRANSFER AND INTERNATIONAL STUDENTS

Transfer students: May apply for admission for the following academic terms: Fall, Spring, Summer. Applicants do not need a minimum number of credits to apply. For fall 2005: Transfer applications received: 231. Transfer applicants offered admission: 79. Transfer applicants enrolled: 45. **International students:** Number of foreign undergraduates: 71 (5% of student body). Number of countries represented: 57. Minimum TOEFL score required: 550 (paper); 213 (computer).

Salem College

- **Address:** PO Box 10548, Winston-Salem, NC 27108
- **Website:** http://www.salem.edu
- **Private; Religious affiliation:** Moravian
- **Enrollment:** 702 full-time; 166 part-time

KEY STATS
- ✔ **U.S News College Ranking:** third tier, Liberal Arts Colleges
- ✔ **SAT Score (25th/75th percentile):** 980-1250
- ✔ **Tuition:** 2006-2007: $18,164

Selectivity: Selective	**Room/board:** $9,551
Acceptance rate: 69%	**Average debt:** $17,125
Student/faculty ratio: 12/1	**Proportion who borrowed:** 70%

UNDERGRADUATE STUDENT BODY STATS

2005-2006 enrollment: 702 full-time; 166 part-time. Men: 2%; women: 98%. **Ethnic makeup:** African American: 19%; Asian American: 1%; Hispanic: 3%; White: 68%; International: 8%.

ADMISSIONS FACTS AND FIGURES

Phone: (336) 721-2621. **Email:** admissions@salem.edu. **Website:** http://www.salem.edu. **Application deadlines for fall 2007:** Regular decision: Rolling. Early decision: Not offered. Early action: Not offered. Admission can be deferred. **Application fee:** $30. Common application is accepted. **Admissions requirements/recommendations:** High school units required (recommended): English: 4 (0); Mathematics: 3 (0); Science: 3 (0); Foreign language: 2 (0); Social studies: 2 (0); History: 0 (0); Academic electives: 0 (0); Total units: 16 (0). Tests: The college uses SAT or ACT scores in admissions decisions. Either SAT or ACT required. For admission to the fall 2007 entering class, the school will accept: ACT with writing, ACT without writing. Campus visit: Recommended. Admissions interview: Recommended. Off-campus interview: May be arranged. **Factors that count in admissions decisions:** *Academic:* Secondary school record: Very important. Class rank: Considered. Letters of recommendation: Important. Standardized test scores: Important. Essay: Important. *Nonacademic:* Interview: Important. Extracurricular activities: Important. Talent/ability: Considered. Character/personal qualities: Considered. Alumni/ae relationship: Considered. Geographical residence: Not considered. State residency: Not considered. Religious affiliation/commitment: Not considered. Minority status: Considered. Volunteer work: Considered. Work experience: Considered. **Other schools with the greatest overlap in applicants:** Elon University; Meredith College; University of North Carolina–Chapel Hill; University of North Carolina–Greensboro; Wake Forest University. **Admissions statistics for the fall 2005 entering class:** Total applicants: 387. Total accepted: 267. Freshmen enrolled: 131; 49% were from out of state. Overall acceptance

rate: 69%. **Credentials of fall 2005 freshmen:** 33% ranked in the top 10 percent of their high school class; 58% were in the top 25 percent, and 88% were in the top half. (Proportion submitting class standing: 64%.) **Average high school grade point average:** 3.7. **First-year students who submitted SAT scores:** 79%. Scores (25/75 percentile): Verbal: 500-630, Math: 480-620, Combined: 980-1250. **First-year students submitting ACT scores:** 13%. Scores (25/75 percentile): English: 18-27, Math: 18-23, Composite: 21-26.

ACADEMICS

Year founded: 1772. **Academic calendar:** 4-1-4. **Degrees offered:** bachelor's, master's. **Most popular majors:** 14% social sciences, 12% communication, journalism, and related programs, 11% English language and literature/letters, 11% business, management, marketing, and related support services, 10% visual and performing arts. **Major fields of study:** area, ethnic, cultural, and gender studies; biological and biomedical sciences; business, management, marketing, and related support services; communication, journalism, and related programs; English language and literature/letters; foreign languages, literatures, and linguistics; history; mathematics and statistics; philosophy and religious studies; physical sciences; psychology; social sciences; visual and performing arts. **Areas of required coursework:** arts/fine arts, mathematics, English (including composition), foreign languages, sciences (biological or physical), history, social science. **Pre-professional programs:** pre-law, pre-medicine. **Special academic programs (% participation):** cross-registration (17%), double major (18%), dual enrollment (10%), honors program (10%), independent study (66%), internships (100%), liberal arts/career combination (7%), student-designed major (1%), study abroad (11%), teacher certificate program (5%). **Teacher certification offered in:** early childhood, special education, elementary, middle/junior high, secondary, bilingual/bicultural. **Faculty and instruction (2005-2006):** Total instructional faculty: 57 full-time, 34 part-time (45% men; 55% women; 11% minorities). Full-time faculty with Ph.D. or other terminal degree: 88%. Student/faculty ratio: 12/1. Classes of fewer than 20 students: 84%; of 20 to 49 students: 16%; of 50 or more students: 0%. **Advanced Placement and International Baccalaureate credit:** AP tests may be used for: Credit and/or placement. Scores accepted: 3, 4, 5. International Baccalaureate exams may be used for: Credit and/or placement. **Freshmen returning for sophomore year:** 77%. **Graduation rates:** Four-year: 41%; five-year: 48%; six-year: 50%. **Graduate study:** 18% of students pursue further study immediately upon graduation; 2% within one year. Fields in which graduates pursue further study: Master of Business Administration (MBA), 5%; law, 5%; medicine, 5%; theology (or the seminary), 5%; education, 5%; arts and sciences, 75%.

COSTS AND FINANCIAL AID

Financial aid office: (336) 721-2808. **Expenses (2006-2007):** Tuition and fees 2006-2007: $18,164; room/board: $9,551. Estimated books and supplies: $900; transportation: $2,550; personal expenses: $550. **Financial aid:** Priority filing date for institution's financial aid form: March 15. In 2005-2006, 93% of undergraduates applied for financial aid. Of those, 73% were determined to have financial need; 100% had their need fully met. Average financial aid package (proportion receiving): $13,986 (73%). Average amount of gift aid, such as scholarships or grants (proportion receiving): N/A (57%). Average amount of self-help aid, such as work study or loans (proportion receiving): N/A (73%). Among students who received need-based aid, the average percentage of need met: 100%. Among students who received aid based on merit, the average award (and the proportion receiving): $13,732 (7%). Average amount of debt of borrowers graduating in 2005: $17,125. Proportion who borrowed: 70%.

CAMPUS LIFE AND EXTRACURRICULAR ACTIVITIES

Campus housing available (% using): women's dorms (94%), apartment for single students (6%). Students who live in college-owned, operated, or affiliated housing: 86%. **Clubs and organizations:** Number of student organizations: 26. Activities include: choral groups, dance, drama/theater, literary magazine, marching band, music ensembles, musical theater, student government, student newspaper, yearbook. Number of fraternities: 0; sororities: 0. Average proportion of students who stay on campus on weekends: 50%.

SERVICES AND FACILITIES

Basic services: nonremedial tutoring, health service. **Remedial assistance:** writing, study skills. **Counseling services:** career, personal, academic, older student, psychological, religious. **For learning-disabled students:** School does not offer a structured program with separate admission and additional fees. Services include: tape recorders, note-taking services, extended time for tests, tutors. **Library:** Number of titles: 135,000; number of current serial subscriptions: 694. **Information technology resources:** Students are not required to lease or own a computer. Number of campus computers available to all students: 56. School has a wireless network. Approximate number of users that can be accommodated: 200. Proportion of college-owned housing units wired for high-speed internet access: 100%. **Campus safety:** Security services offered: 24-hour foot-and-vehicle patrols, late-night transport/escort service, 24-hour emergency telephones, lighted pathways/sidewalks, controlled dormitory access (key, security card, etc).

TRANSFER AND INTERNATIONAL STUDENTS

Transfer students: May apply for admission for the following academic terms: Fall, Winter, Spring, Summer. Applicants need a minimum number of credits to apply. For fall 2005: Transfer applications received: 66. Transfer applicants offered admission: 34. Transfer applicants enrolled: 24. **International students:** Number of foreign undergraduates: 67 (8% of student body). Minimum TOEFL score required: 550 (paper); 213 (computer).

Shaw University

- **Address:** 118 E. South Street, Raleigh, NC 27601
- **Website:** http://www.shawuniversity.edu
- **Private; Religious affiliation:** Baptist
- **Enrollment:** 2,283 full-time; 282 part-time

KEY STATS

- ✔ **U.S News College Ranking:** fourth tier, Comp. Coll.–Bachelor's (South)
- ✔ **SAT Score (25th/75th percentile):** 650-860
- ✔ **Tuition:** 2006-2007: $9,850

Selectivity: Least selective	**Room/board:** $6,410
Acceptance rate: 65%	**Average debt:** N/A
Student/faculty ratio: 15/1	**Proportion who borrowed:** N/A

UNDERGRADUATE STUDENT BODY STATS

2005-2006 enrollment: 2,283 full-time; 282 part-time. Men: 37%; women: 63%. **Ethnic makeup:** African American: 89%; White: 9%; International: 1%.

ADMISSIONS FACTS AND FIGURES

Phone: (800) 214-6683. **Email:** admission@shawu.edu. **Website:** http://www.shawuniversity.edu. **Application deadlines for fall 2007:** Regular decision: July 30. Early decision: Not offered. Early action: Not offered. Admission can be deferred. **Application fee:** $25. Common application is accepted. **Admissions requirements/recommendations:** High school units required (recommended): English: 3; Mathematics: 2; Science: 2; Foreign language: 0; Social studies: 2; History: 0; Academic electives: 9; Total units: 18. Tests: The college uses SAT or ACT scores in admissions decisions. Either SAT or ACT required. For admission to the fall 2007 entering class, the school will accept: ACT with writing, ACT without writing. Campus visit: Recommended. Admissions interview: Recommended. Off-campus interview: May be arranged. **Factors that count in admissions decisions:** *Academic:* Secondary school record: Not considered. Class rank: Important. Letters of recommendation: Very important. Standardized test scores: Very important. Essay: Important. *Nonacademic:* Interview: Considered. Extracurricular activities: Important. Talent/ability: Important. Character/personal qualities: Important. Alumni/ae relationship: Considered. Geographical residence: Important. State residency: Important. Religious affiliation/commitment: Not considered. Minority status: Not considered. Volunteer work: Considered. Work experience: Considered. **Other schools with the greatest overlap in applicants:** Johnson C. Smith University; Livingstone College; North Carolina Central University; University of North Carolina–Greensboro; Virginia Union University. **Admissions statistics for the fall 2005 entering class:** Total applicants: 4,226. Total accepted: 2,728. Freshmen enrolled: 601; 54% were from out of state. Overall acceptance rate: 65%. **Credentials of fall 2005 freshmen:** 1% ranked in the top 10 percent of their high school class; 8% were in the top 25 percent, and 31% were in the top half. (Proportion submitting class standing: 57%.) **Average high school grade point average:** 2.4. **First-year students who submitted SAT scores:** 60%. Scores (25/75 percentile): Verbal: 330-430, Math: 320-430, Combined: 650-860. **First-year students submitting ACT scores:** 20%. Scores (25/75 percentile): English: N/A, Math: N/A, Composite: 12-16.

ACADEMICS

Year founded: 1865. **Academic calendar:** Semester. **Degrees offered:** associate, bachelor's, master's, first professional. **Most popular majors:** 32% business, management, marketing, and related support services, 13% security and protective services, 10% psychology, 9% public administration and social service professions, 6% social sciences. **Major fields of study:** biological and biomedical sciences; business, management, marketing, and related support services; communication, journalism, and related programs; computer and information sciences and support services; education; English language and literature/letters; foreign languages, literatures, and linguistics; health professions and related clinical sciences; liberal arts and sciences studies, and humanities; mathematics and statistics; natural resources and conservation; parks, recreation, leisure, and fitness studies; philosophy and religious studies; physical sciences; psychology; public administration and social service professions; security and protective services; social sciences; visual and performing arts. **Areas of required coursework:** humanities, computer literacy, mathematics, English (including composition), sciences (biological or physical), social science. **Pre-professional programs:** pre-pharmacy. **Special academic programs:** accelerated program, cross-registration, distance learning, double major, dual enrollment, honors program, independent study, internships, student-designed major, study abroad, teacher certificate program, weekend college. **Teacher certification offered in:** early childhood, special education, elementary, secondary. **Reserve Officers Training Corps (ROTC):** Army ROTC: Offered at cooperating institution (Saint Augustine's College); Air Force ROTC: Offered at cooperating institution (North Carolina State University). **Faculty and instruction (2005-2006):** Total instructional faculty: 111 full-time, 179 part-time (63% men; 37% women; 83% minorities). Full-time faculty with Ph.D. or other terminal degree: 65%. Student/faculty ratio: 15/1. Classes of fewer than 20 students: 71%; of 20 to 49 students: 26%; of 50 or more students: 3%. **Advanced Placement and International Baccalaureate credit:** AP tests may be used for: Credit only. **Freshmen returning for sophomore year:** 67%. **Graduation rates:** Four-year: 15%; five-year: 26%; six-year: 29%.

COSTS AND FINANCIAL AID

Financial aid office: (919) 546-8240. **Expenses (2006-2007):** Tuition and fees 2006-2007: $9,850; room/board: $6,410. **Financial aid:** Priority filing date for institution's financial aid form: March 1; deadline: June 1.

CAMPUS LIFE AND EXTRACURRICULAR ACTIVITIES

Campus housing available (% using): women's dorms (49%), men's dorms (51%). Students who live in college-owned, operated, or affiliated housing: 38%. Average per-year earnings: $12,000. Activities include: choral groups, concert band, dance, drama/theater, jazz band, marching band, music ensembles, musical theater, pep band, radio station, student government, student newspaper, yearbook. Number of fraternities: 4; sororities: 4. Proportion of men in fraternities: 4%; of women in sororities: 5%. Average proportion of students who stay on campus on weekends: 40%. **Sports program (2005-2006):** Member of NCAA II. *Men's intercollegiate varsity sports:* baseball, basketball, cross-country, football, golf, tennis, track and field (indoor), track and field (outdoor). *Women's intercollegiate varsity sports:* basketball, bowling, cross-country, softball, tennis, track and field (indoor), track and field (outdoor), volleyball.

SERVICES AND FACILITIES

Basic services: nonremedial tutoring, placement service, health service, health insurance. **Counseling services:** minority student, career, military, personal, veteran student, academic, older student, psychological, birth control, religious. **For learning-disabled students:** School does not offer a structured program with separate admission and additional fees. Total undergraduates in learning-disabled program or receiving services: 50. Services include: tape recorders, diagnostic testing service, untimed tests, note-taking services, oral tests, extended time for tests, tutors, priority seating, texts on tape. **Library:** Number of titles: 155,623; number of current serial subscriptions: 32,584. **Information technology resources:** Students are not required to lease or own a computer. Number of campus computers available to all students: 350. School has a wireless network. Proportion of college-owned housing units wired for high-speed internet access: 100%. **Campus safety:** Security services offered: 24-hour foot-and-vehicle patrols, late-night transport/escort service, 24-hour emergency telephones, lighted pathways/sidewalks, controlled dormitory access (key, security card, etc).

TRANSFER AND INTERNATIONAL STUDENTS

Transfer students: May apply for admission for the following academic terms: Fall, Spring, Summer. Applicants need a minimum number of credits to apply. For fall 2005: Transfer applications received: 445. Transfer

applicants offered admission: 267. Transfer applicants enrolled: 181.
International students: Number of foreign undergraduates: 37 (1% of student body). Number of countries represented: 11.

St. Andrews Presbyterian College

- **Address:** 1700 Dogwood Mile, Laurinburg, NC 28352
- **Website:** http://www.sapc.edu
- **Private; Religious affiliation:** Presbyterian
- **Enrollment:** 706 full-time; 75 part-time

KEY STATS

✔ **U.S News College Ranking:** fourth tier, Liberal Arts Colleges
✔ **SAT Score (25th/75th percentile):** 920-1160
✔ **Tuition:** 2006-2007: $17,162

Selectivity: Selective	**Room/board:** $7,540
Acceptance rate: 76%	**Average debt:** $9,329
Student/faculty ratio: 13/1	**Proportion who borrowed:** 55%

UNDERGRADUATE STUDENT BODY STATS

2005-2006 enrollment: 706 full-time; 75 part-time. Men: 38%; women: 62%. **Ethnic makeup:** African American: 10%; American-Indian: 1%; Hispanic: 3%; White: 82%; International: 4%.

ADMISSIONS FACTS AND FIGURES

Phone: (800) 763-0198. **Email:** admission@sapc.edu. **Website:** http://www.sapc.edu. **Application deadlines for fall 2007:** Regular decision: Rolling. Early decision: Not offered. Early action: Not offered. Admission can be deferred. **Application fee:** $30. Common application is accepted. **To apply online, go to:** http://www.applyweb.com/aw?andrews. **Admissions requirements/recommendations:** High school units required (recommended): English: (4); Mathematics: (3); Science: (2); Foreign language: (2); History: (2); Total units: 11. Tests: The college uses SAT or ACT scores in admissions decisions. Either SAT or ACT required. For admission to the fall 2007 entering class, the school will accept: ACT with writing. Campus visit: Recommended. Admissions interview: Recommended. Off-campus interview: Not available. **Factors that count in admissions decisions:** *Academic:* Secondary school record: Very important. Class rank: Very important. Letters of recommendation: Not considered. Standardized test scores: Important. Essay: Not considered. *Nonacademic:* Interview: Considered. Extracurricular activities: Considered. Talent/ability: Considered. Character/personal qualities: Considered. Alumni/ae relationship: Not considered. Geographical residence: Not considered. State residency: Not considered. Religious affiliation/commitment: Not considered. Minority status: Not considered. Volunteer work: Considered. Work experience: Considered. **Admissions statistics for the fall 2005 entering class:** Total applicants: 859. Total accepted: 656. Freshmen enrolled: 191; 63% were from out of state. Overall acceptance rate: 76%. **Average high school grade point average:** 3.0. **First-year students who submitted SAT scores:** 90%. Scores (25/75 percentile): Verbal: 460-590, Math: 460-570, Combined: 920-1160. **First-year students submitting ACT scores:** 30%. Scores (25/75 percentile): English: 18-22, Math: 17-24, Composite: 18-23.

ACADEMICS

Year founded: 1896. **Academic calendar:** Semester. **Degrees offered:** bachelor's. **Most popular majors:** 25% business administration and management, 15% education, 11% social sciences, 7% liberal arts and sciences/liberal studies, 7% psychology. **Major fields of study:** area, ethnic, cultural, and gender studies; biological and biomedical sciences; business, management, marketing, and related support services; communication, journalism, and related programs; education; English language and literature/letters; health professions and related clinical sciences; history; liberal arts and sciences studies, and humanities; mathematics and statistics; multi/interdisciplinary studies; philosophy and religious studies; physical sciences; psychology; security and protective services; social sciences; visual and performing arts. **Areas of required coursework:** arts/fine arts, humanities, computer literacy, mathematics, English (including composition), foreign languages, sciences (biological or physical), history, social science. **Pre-professional programs:** pre-law, pre-medicine, pre-veterinary science. **Special academic programs (% participation):** double major (5%), honors program (2%), internships (80%), student-designed major, study abroad, teacher certificate program, weekend college. **Teacher certification offered in:** elementary. **Faculty and instruction**

(2005-2006): Total instructional faculty: 43 full-time, 36 part-time (58% men; 42% women; 3% minorities). Full-time faculty with Ph.D. or other terminal degree: 79%. Student/faculty ratio: 13/1. Classes of fewer than 20 students: 75%; of 20 to 49 students: 24%; of 50 or more students: 1%. **Advanced Placement and International Baccalaureate credit:** AP tests may be used for: Credit only. Scores accepted: 3, 4, 5. International Baccalaureate exams may be used for: Credit only. **Freshmen returning for sophomore year:** 67%. **Graduation rates:** Four-year: 37%; five-year: 43%; six-year: 44%. **Graduate study:** 26% of students pursue further study immediately upon graduation; 63% within one year. Fields in which graduates pursue further study: Master of Business Administration (MBA), 10%; law, 2%; medicine, 1%; theology (or the seminary), 10%; education, 10%; arts and sciences, 70%.

COSTS AND FINANCIAL AID

Financial aid office: (910) 277-5560. **Expenses (2006-2007):** Tuition and fees 2006-2007: $17,162; room/board: $7,540. Estimated books and supplies: $1,000; transportation: $2,000; personal expenses: $1,798. **Financial aid:** In 2005-2006, 75% of undergraduates applied for financial aid. Of those, 60% were determined to have financial need; 25% had their need fully met. Average financial aid package (proportion receiving): $12,198 (59%). Average amount of gift aid, such as scholarships or grants (proportion receiving): $8,928 (59%). Average amount of self-help aid, such as work study or loans (proportion receiving): $4,172 (47%). Average need-based loan (excluding PLUS or other private loans): $3,401. Among students who received need-based aid, the average percentage of need met: 73%. Among students who received aid based on merit, the average award (and the proportion receiving): $8,776 (39%). The average athletic scholarship (and the proportion receiving): $3,208 (16%). Average amount of debt of borrowers graduating in 2005: $9,329. Proportion who borrowed: 55%.

CAMPUS LIFE AND EXTRACURRICULAR ACTIVITIES

Campus housing available: coed dorms, women's dorms, men's dorms. Students who live in college-owned, operated, or affiliated housing: 85%. **Student employment:** During the 2005-2006 academic year, 33% of undergraduates worked on campus. Average per-year earnings: $1,800. **Clubs and organizations:** Number of student organizations: 28. Activities include: choral groups, dance, drama/theater, literary magazine, music ensembles, student government, student newspaper, yearbook. Number of fraternities: 0; sororities: 0. Average proportion of students who stay on campus on weekends: 75%. **Sports program (2005-2006):** Member of NCAA II. *Men's intercollegiate varsity sports:* baseball, basketball, cross-country, golf, lacrosse, soccer, tennis, track and field (indoor), track and field (outdoor). *Women's intercollegiate varsity sports:* basketball, cross-country, golf, lacrosse, soccer, softball, tennis, track and field (outdoor), volleyball.

SERVICES AND FACILITIES

Basic services: health insurance. **Remedial assistance:** math. **Counseling services:** career, personal, academic, psychological, religious. **For learning-disabled students:** School does not offer a structured program with separate admission and additional fees. Total undergraduates in learning-disabled program or receiving services: 38. Services include: reading machines, tape recorders, untimed tests, note-taking services, learning center, extended time for tests, priority seating, texts on tape, exams on tape or computer, other testing accomodations, other. **Library:** Number of titles: 109,308; number of current serial subscriptions: 21,813. **Information technology resources:** Students are not required to lease or own a computer. Number of campus computers available to all students: 90. School has a wireless network. Approximate number of users that can be accommodated: 22. Proportion of college-owned housing units wired for high-speed internet access: 100%. **Campus safety:** Security services offered: 24-hour foot-and-vehicle patrols, lighted pathways/sidewalks, controlled dormitory access (key, security card, etc).

TRANSFER AND INTERNATIONAL STUDENTS

Transfer students: May apply for admission for the following academic terms: Fall, Spring. Applicants do not need a minimum number of credits to apply. For fall 2005: Transfer applications received: 187. Transfer applicants offered admission: 134. Transfer applicants enrolled: 86. **International students:** Number of foreign undergraduates: 31 (4% of student body). Number of countries represented: 14. Minimum TOEFL score required: 550 (paper); 213 (computer). Average TOEFL score: 597 (paper).

St. Augustine's College

- **Address:** 1315 Oakwood Avenue, Raleigh, NC 27610-2298
- **Website:** http://www.st-aug.edu
- **Private; Religious affiliation:** Episcopal
- **Enrollment:** 1,122 full-time; 41 part-time

KEY STATS

✔ **U.S News College Ranking:** fourth tier, Liberal Arts Colleges
✔ **SAT Score (25th/75th percentile):** 800-890
✔ **Tuition:** 2006-2007: $12,456

Selectivity: Less selective	**Room/board:** $6,372
Acceptance rate: 49%	**Average debt:** $28,602
Student/faculty ratio: 13/1	**Proportion who borrowed:** 72%

UNDERGRADUATE STUDENT BODY STATS

2005-2006 enrollment: 1,122 full-time; 41 part-time. Men: 50%; women: 50%. **Ethnic makeup:** African American: 94%; Hispanic: 1%; International: 5%. **Religious preference:** Roman Catholic: 1%; Protestant: 98%; Episcopal: 1%.

ADMISSIONS FACTS AND FIGURES

Phone: (919) 516-4016. **Email:** admissions@es.st-aug.edu. **Website:** http://www.st-aug.edu. **Application deadlines for fall 2007:** Regular decision: July 1. Early decision: Not offered. Early action: Not offered. Admission can be deferred. **Application fee:** $25. Common application is not accepted. **Admissions requirements/recommendations:** High school units required (recommended): English: 4; Mathematics: 2; Science: 2; Social studies: 2; Academic electives: 10; Total units: 20 (2). Tests: The college uses SAT or ACT scores in admissions decisions. Either SAT or ACT required. For admission to the fall 2007 entering class, the school will accept: ACT with writing, ACT without writing. Campus visit: Recommended. Admissions interview: Neither required nor recommended. Off-campus interview: May be arranged. **Factors that count in admissions decisions:** *Academic:* Secondary school record: Very important. Class rank: Considered. Letters of recommendation: Important. Standardized test scores: Important. Essay: Considered. *Nonacademic:* Interview: Considered. Extracurricular activities: Considered. Talent/ability: Important. Character/personal qualities: Important. Alumni/ae relationship: Considered. Geographical residence: Considered. State residency: Considered. Religious affiliation/commitment: Considered. Minority status: Important. Volunteer work: Considered. Work experience: Considered. **Other schools with the greatest overlap in applicants:** North Carolina A&T State University; North Carolina Central University; North Carolina State University–Raleigh; Shaw University; Winston-Salem State University. **Admissions statistics for the fall 2005 entering class:** Total applicants: 1,979. Total accepted: 975. Freshmen enrolled: 262; 63% were from out of state. Overall acceptance rate: 49%. **Credentials of fall 2005 freshmen:** 12% ranked in the top 10 percent of their high school class; 58% were in the top 25 percent, and 83% were in the top half. (Proportion submitting class standing: 52%.) **Average high school grade point average:** 2.4. **First-year students who submitted SAT scores:** 58%. Scores (25/75 percentile): Verbal: 400-450, Math: 400-440, Combined: 800-890. **First-year students submitting ACT scores:** 42%. Scores (25/75 percentile): English: N/A, Math: N/A, Composite: 15-17.

ACADEMICS

Year founded: 1867. **Academic calendar:** Semester. **Degrees offered:** bachelor's. **Most popular majors:** 13% health and physical education, 13% organizational behavior studies, 9% business administration and management, 9% communication studies/speech communication and rhetoric, 8% computer and information sciences. **Major fields of study:** biological and biomedical sciences; communication, journalism, and related programs; computer and information sciences and support services; education; English language and literature/letters; legal professions and studies; mathematics and statistics; parks, recreation, leisure, and fitness studies; physical sciences; psychology; security and protective services; social sciences; visual and performing arts. **Areas of required coursework:** arts/fine arts, humanities, computer literacy, mathematics, English (including composition), philosophy, foreign languages, sciences (biological or physical), history, social science, other. **Pre-professional programs:** pre-law, pre-medicine. **Special academic programs (% participation):** accelerated program (1%), cooperative (work-study plan) program (1%), cross-registration (1%), double major (1%), honors program (1%), independent study (2%), internships (3%), study abroad (1%), teacher certificate program (1%), weekend college (4%). **Teacher certification offered in:** early childhood, special education, elementary, middle/junior high, secondary. **Cooperative education programs:** art, business, computer science, education, health professions, humanities, natural science, social/behavioral science, technologies. **Reserve Officers Training Corps (ROTC):** Army ROTC: Offered on campus; Air Force ROTC: Offered at cooperating institution (North Carolina State University). **Faculty and instruction (2005-2006):** Total instructional faculty: 73 full-time, 39 part-time (53% men; 47% women; 58% minorities). Full-time faculty with Ph.D. or other terminal degree: 64%. Student/faculty ratio: 13/1. Classes of fewer than 20 students: 65%; of 20 to 49 students: 35%; of 50 or more students: 0%. **Advanced Placement and International Baccalaureate credit:** AP tests may be used for: Credit and/or placement. Scores accepted: 3, 4, 5. International Baccalaureate exams may be used for: Credit and/or placement. **Freshmen returning for sophomore year:** 61%. **Graduation rates:** Four-year: 18%; five-year: 35%; six-year: 40%. **Graduate study:** 20% of students pursue further study immediately upon graduation; 25% within one year; 30% within five years. Fields in which graduates pursue further study: Master of Business Administration (MBA), 25%; law, 5%; medicine, 2%; theology (or the seminary), 5%; arts and sciences, 1%.

COSTS AND FINANCIAL AID

Financial aid office: (919) 516-4131. **Expenses (2006-2007):** Tuition and fees 2006-2007: $12,456; room/board: $6,372. Estimated books and supplies: $1,000; transportation: $1,200; personal expenses: $2,040. **Financial aid:** Priority filing date for institution's financial aid form: April 15. In 2005-2006, 73% of undergraduates applied for financial aid. Of those, 73% were determined to have financial need; 7% had their need fully met. Average financial aid package (proportion receiving): $11,688 (73%). Average amount of gift aid, such as scholarships or grants (proportion receiving): $9,164 (42%). Average amount of self-help aid, such as work study or loans (proportion receiving): $1,902 (31%). Average need-based loan (excluding PLUS or other private loans): $1,131. Among students who received need-based aid, the average percentage of need met: 7%. Among students who received aid based on merit, the average award (and the proportion receiving): $6,816 (32%). The average athletic scholarship (and the proportion receiving): $6,145 (17%). Average amount of debt of borrowers graduating in 2005: $28,602. Proportion who borrowed: 72%.

CAMPUS LIFE AND EXTRACURRICULAR ACTIVITIES

Campus housing available (% using): women's dorms (50%), men's dorms (50%). Students who live in college-owned, operated, or affiliated housing: 61%. **Student employment:** During the 2005-2006 academic year, 46% of undergraduates worked on campus. Average per-year earnings: $2,024. **Clubs and organizations:** Number of student organizations: 56. Activities include: choral groups, concert band, dance, drama/theater, jazz band, literary magazine, music ensembles, pep band, radio station, student government, student newspaper, student film society, television station, yearbook. Number of fraternities: 4; sororities: 4. Proportion of men in fraternities: 3%; of women in sororities: 3%. Average proportion of students who stay on campus on weekends: 80%. **Sports program (2005-2006):** Member of NCAA II. *Men's intercollegiate varsity sports:* baseball, basketball, cross-country, football, golf, tennis, track and field (indoor), track and field (outdoor). *Women's intercollegiate varsity sports:* basketball, bowling, cross-country, softball, tennis, track and field (indoor), track and field (outdoor), volleyball.

SERVICES AND FACILITIES

Basic services: nonremedial tutoring, placement service, health service, health insurance. **Remedial assistance:** reading, math, writing, study skills. **Counseling services:** minority student, career, military, personal, veteran student, academic, older student, psychological, birth control, religious. **For learning-disabled students:** School does not offer a structured program with separate admission and additional fees. Total undergraduates in learning-disabled program or receiving services: 5. Services include: remedial math, remedial English, remedial reading, diagnostic testing service, untimed tests, learning center, extended time for tests, tutors. **Library:** Number of titles: 100,346; number of current serial subscriptions: 174. **Information technology resources:** Students are not required to lease or own a computer. Number of campus computers available to all students: 250. School does not have a wireless network. Proportion of college-owned housing units wired for high-speed internet access: 100%. **Campus safety:** Security services offered: 24-hour foot-and-vehicle patrols, 24-hour emergency telephones, lighted pathways/sidewalks, controlled dormitory access (key, security card, etc).

TRANSFER AND INTERNATIONAL STUDENTS

Transfer students: May apply for admission for the following academic terms: Fall, Spring, Summer. Applicants need a minimum number of credits to apply. For fall 2005: Transfer applications received: 101. Transfer applicants offered admission: 64. Transfer applicants enrolled: 32. **International students:** Number of foreign undergraduates: 52 (5% of student body). Number of countries represented: 21. Minimum TOEFL score required: 500 (paper); 180 (computer).

University of North Carolina–Asheville

- **Address:** 1 University Heights, Asheville, NC 28804
- **Website:** http://www.unca.edu
- **Public**
- **Enrollment:** 2,820 full-time; 656 part-time

KEY STATS

- ✔ **U.S News College Ranking:** third tier, Liberal Arts Colleges
- ✔ **SAT Score (25th/75th percentile):** 1080-1300
- ✔ **Tuition:** 2006-2007: $3,882 in state, $14,007 out of state

Selectivity: More selective	**Room/board:** $5,880
Acceptance rate: 63%	**Average debt:** $15,309
Student/faculty ratio: 13/1	**Proportion who borrowed:** 51%

UNDERGRADUATE STUDENT BODY STATS

2005-2006 enrollment: 2,820 full-time; 656 part-time. Men: 42%; women: 58%. **Ethnic makeup:** African American: 2%; Asian American: 2%; Hispanic: 2%; White: 93%; International: 1%.

ADMISSIONS FACTS AND FIGURES

Phone: (828) 251-6481. **Email:** admissions@unca.edu. **Website:** http://www.unca.edu. **Application deadlines for fall 2007:** Regular decision: February 16; decision sent by March 23. Early decision: Not offered. Early action: Send application by: November 10; Decision sent by: December 18. Admission can be deferred. **Application fee:** $50. Common application is not accepted. **To apply online, go to:** http://www.unca.edu/admissions. **Admissions requirements/recommendations:** High school units required (recommended): English: 4; Mathematics: 4; Science: 3; Foreign language: 2; Social studies: 1; History: 1; Academic electives: (4); Total units: 15. Tests: The college uses SAT or ACT scores in admissions decisions. Either SAT or ACT required. For admission to the fall 2007 entering class, the school will accept: ACT with writing. Campus visit: Recommended. Admissions interview: Recommended. Off-campus interview: Not available. **Factors that count in admissions decisions:** *Academic:* Secondary school record: Very important. Class rank: Very important. Letters of recommendation: Considered. Standardized test scores: Important. Essay: Considered. *Nonacademic:* Interview: Considered. Extracurricular activities: Considered. Talent/ability: Considered. Character/personal qualities: Not considered. Alumni/ae relationship: Considered. Geographical residence: Considered. State residency: Considered. Religious affiliation/commitment: Not considered. Minority status: Considered. Volunteer work: Considered. Work experience: Considered. **Other schools with the greatest overlap in applicants:** Appalachian State University; North Carolina State University–Raleigh; University of North Carolina–Chapel Hill; University of North Carolina–Greensboro; University of North Carolina–Wilmington. **Admissions statistics for the fall 2005 entering class:** Total applicants: 2,362. Total accepted: 1,482. Freshmen enrolled: 472; 16% were from out of state. Overall acceptance rate: 63%. Non-early acceptance rate: 63%. **Credentials of fall 2005 freshmen:** 25% ranked in the top 10 percent of their high school class; 68% were in the top 25 percent, and 98% were in the top half. (Proportion submitting class standing: 83%.) **Average high school grade point average:** 3.8. **First-year students who submitted SAT scores:** 96%. Scores (25/75 percentile): Verbal: 540-660, Math: 540-640, Combined: 1080-1300. **First-year students submitting ACT scores:** 21%. Scores (25/75 percentile): English: 21-28, Math: 21-26, Composite: 22-27.

ACADEMICS

Year founded: 1927. **Academic calendar:** Semester. **Degrees offered:** certificate, bachelor's, post-bachelor's certificate, master's. **Most popular majors:** 13% psychology, 11% business administration and management, 9% English language and literature, 8% mass communication/media studies, 7% environmental studies. **Major fields of study:** area, ethnic, cultural, and

gender studies; biological and biomedical sciences; business, management, marketing, and related support services; communication, journalism, and related programs; computer and information sciences and support services; engineering; English language and literature/letters; foreign languages, literatures, and linguistics; health professions and related clinical sciences; history; liberal arts and sciences studies, and humanities; mathematics and statistics; natural resources and conservation; philosophy and religious studies; physical sciences; psychology; social sciences; visual and performing arts. **Areas of required coursework:** arts/fine arts, humanities, mathematics, English (including composition), foreign languages, sciences (biological or physical), social science, other. **Pre-professional programs:** pre-law, pre-dentistry, pre-medicine, pre-veterinary science, pre-pharmacy. **Special academic programs (% participation):** cross-registration, distance learning, double major (4.2%), dual enrollment, exchange student program (domestic), honors program (10.1%), independent study, internships, liberal arts/career combination, student-designed major, study abroad (13.2%), teacher certificate program (7%). **Teacher certification offered in:** elementary, middle/junior high, secondary. **Faculty and instruction (2005-2006):** Total instructional faculty: 199 full-time, 110 part-time (56% men; 44% women; 7% minorities). Full-time faculty with Ph.D. or other terminal degree: 84%. Student/faculty ratio: 13/1. Classes of fewer than 20 students: 52%; of 20 to 49 students: 47%; of 50 or more students: 1%. **Advanced Placement and International Baccalaureate credit:** AP tests may be used for: Credit and/or placement. Scores accepted: 3, 4, 5. International Baccalaureate exams may be used for: Credit and/or placement. **Freshmen returning for sophomore year:** 78%. **Graduation rates:** Four-year: 28%; five-year: 51%; six-year: 54%. **Graduate study:** 21% of students pursue further study within one year.

COSTS AND FINANCIAL AID

Financial aid office: (828) 251-6535. **Expenses (2006-2007):** Tuition and fees 2006-2007: $3,882 in state, $14,007 out of state; room/board: $5,880. Estimated books and supplies: $850; transportation: $1,500; personal expenses: $1,541. **Financial aid:** Priority filing date for institution's financial aid form: March 1. In 2005-2006, 66% of undergraduates applied for financial aid. Of those, 43% were determined to have financial need; 39% had their need fully met. Average financial aid package (proportion receiving): $8,152 (42%). Average amount of gift aid, such as scholarships or grants (proportion receiving): $3,400 (39%). Average amount of self-help aid, such as work study or loans (proportion receiving): $3,929 (32%). Average need-based loan (excluding PLUS or other private loans): $3,855. Among students who received need-based aid, the average percentage of need met: 78%. Among students who received aid based on merit, the average award (and the proportion receiving): $3,389 (9%). The average athletic scholarship (and the proportion receiving): $6,190 (3%). Average amount of debt of borrowers graduating in 2005: $15,309. Proportion who borrowed: 51%.

CAMPUS LIFE AND EXTRACURRICULAR ACTIVITIES

Campus housing available: coed dorms, women's dorms, men's dorms, special housing for disabled students, other housing options. Students who live in college-owned, operated, or affiliated housing: 34%. **Student employment:** During the 2005-2006 academic year, 24% of undergraduates worked on campus. Average per-year earnings: $1,500. **Clubs and organizations:** Number of student organizations: 80. Activities include: choral groups, concert band, dance, drama/theater, jazz band, literary magazine, music ensembles, musical theater, pep band, radio station, student government, student newspaper. Number of fraternities: 3; sororities: 2. Proportion of men in fraternities: 3%; of women in sororities: 2%. Average proportion of students who stay on campus on weekends: 65%. **Sports program (2005-2006):** Member of NCAA I. *Men's intercollegiate varsity sports:* baseball, basketball, cross-country, soccer, tennis, track and field (indoor), track and field (outdoor). *Women's intercollegiate varsity sports:* basketball, cross-country, soccer, tennis, track and field (indoor), track and field (outdoor), volleyball.

SERVICES AND FACILITIES

Basic services: nonremedial tutoring, women's center, placement service, health service, health insurance. **Counseling services:** minority student, career, personal, veteran student, academic, older student, psychological, birth control. **For learning-disabled students:** School does not offer a structured program with separate admission and additional fees. Total undergraduates in learning-disabled program or receiving services: 100. Services include: reading machines, tape recorders, note-taking services, oral tests, readers, extended time for tests, tutors, other. **Library:** Number of titles: 262,283; number of current serial subscriptions: 4,810. **Information technology resources:** Students are not required to lease or own a computer. Number of campus computers available to all students: 390. School has a wireless network. Proportion of college-owned housing units wired for high-speed internet access: 100%. **Campus safety:** Security services offered: 24-hour foot-and-vehicle patrols, late-night transport/escort service, 24-hour emergency telephones, lighted pathways/sidewalks, controlled dormitory access (key, security card, etc).

TRANSFER AND INTERNATIONAL STUDENTS

Transfer students: May apply for admission for the following academic terms: Fall, Spring. Applicants need a minimum number of credits to apply. For fall 2005: Transfer applications received: 465. Transfer applicants offered admission: 389. Transfer applicants enrolled: 227. **International students:** Number of foreign undergraduates: 28 (1% of student body). Number of countries represented: 21. Minimum TOEFL score required: 550 (paper); 213 (computer). Average TOEFL score: 593 (paper).

University of North Carolina–Chapel Hill

- ■ **Address:** South Building, CB #9100, Chapel Hill, NC 27599
- ■ **Website:** http://www.unc.edu
- ■ **Public**
- ■ **Enrollment:** 15,911 full-time; 853 part-time

KEY STATS

- ✔ **U.S News College Ranking:** 27, National Universities
- ✔ **SAT Score (25th/75th percentile):** 1210-1390
- ✔ **Tuition:** 2005-2006: $4,613 in state, $18,411 out of state
- **Selectivity:** Most selective   **Room/board:** $6,516
- **Acceptance rate:** 37%   **Average debt:** $13,801
- **Student/faculty ratio:** 14/1   **Proportion who borrowed:** 34%

UNDERGRADUATE STUDENT BODY STATS

2005-2006 enrollment: 15,911 full-time; 853 part-time. Men: 42%; women: 58%. **Ethnic makeup:** African American: 11%; American-Indian: 1%; Asian American: 6%; Hispanic: 3%; White: 77%; International: 1%.

ADMISSIONS FACTS AND FIGURES

Phone: (919) 966-3621. **Email:** uadm@email.unc.edu. **Website:** http://www.unc.edu. **Application deadlines for fall 2007:** Regular decision: January 15. Early decision: Not offered. Early action: Send application by: November 1; Decision sent by: January 31. Admission can be deferred. **Application fee:** $70. Common application is not accepted. **To apply online, go to:** http://www.admissions.unc.edu/. **Admissions requirements/recommendations:** High school units required (recommended): English: 4 (4); Mathematics: 3 (4); Science: 3 (4); Foreign language: 2 (4); Social studies: 2 (3); Academic electives: 2. Tests: The college uses SAT or ACT scores in admissions decisions. Either SAT or ACT required. For admission to the fall 2007 entering class, the school will accept: ACT with writing. Campus visit: Recommended. Admissions interview: Neither required nor recommended. Off-campus interview: Not available. **Factors that count in admissions decisions:** *Academic:* Secondary school record: Very important. Class rank: Very important. Letters of recommendation: Very important. Standardized test scores: Very important. Essay: Very important. *Nonacademic:* Interview: Not considered. Extracurricular activities: Very important. Talent/ability: Very important. Character/personal qualities: Very important. Alumni/ae relationship: Important. Geographical residence: Not considered. State residency: Very important. Religious affiliation/commitment: Not considered. Minority status: Important. Volunteer work: Important. Work experience: Important. **Other schools with the greatest overlap in applicants:** Duke University; Harvard University; North Carolina State University–Raleigh; University of Virginia; Wake Forest University. **Admissions statistics for the fall 2005 entering class:** Total applicants: 18,414. Total accepted: 6,736. Freshmen enrolled: 3,751; 17% were from out of state. Accepted through early-decision or early-action plans: 73%. Overall acceptance rate: 37%. Non-early acceptance rate: 27%. **Size of waiting list:** 1689 applicants; enrolled from waiting list: 7. **Credentials of fall 2005 freshmen:** 74% ranked in the top 10 percent of their high school class; 95% were in the top 25 percent, and 99% were in the top half. (Proportion submitting class standing: 79%.) **Average high school grade point average:** 4.0. **First-year students who submitted SAT scores:** 99%. Scores (25/75 percentile): Verbal: 600-690, Math: 610-700, Combined: 1210-1390. **First-year students submitting ACT scores:** 22%. Scores (25/75 percentile): English: 24-31, Math: 25-31, Composite: 25-31.

ACADEMICS

Year founded: 1789. **Academic calendar:** Semester. **Degrees offered:** certificate, bachelor's, post-bachelor's certificate, master's, post-master's certificate, first professional, first professional certificate, doctorate. **Most popular majors:** 17% communication, journalism, and related programs, 14% social sciences, 11% business, management, marketing, and related support services, 10% psychology, 9% biological and biomedical sciences. **Major fields of study:** area, ethnic, cultural, and gender studies; biological and biomedical sciences; business, management, marketing, and related support services; communication, journalism, and related programs; computer and information sciences and support services; education; English language and literature/letters; family and consumer sciences/human sciences; foreign languages, literatures, and linguistics; health professions and related clinical sciences; history; liberal arts and sciences studies, and humanities; mathematics and statistics; multi/interdisciplinary studies; natural resources and conservation; parks, recreation, leisure, and fitness studies; philosophy and religious studies; physical sciences; psychology; public administration and social service professions; social sciences; visual and performing arts. **Areas of required coursework:** arts/fine arts, humanities, mathematics, English (including composition), philosophy, foreign languages, sciences (biological or physical), history, social science, other. **Pre-professional programs:** predentistry, pre-medicine. **Special academic programs (% participation):** cross-registration (1.49%), distance learning (19.25%), double major (22.83%), dual enrollment, honors program (5.77%), independent study (16.1%), internships, student-designed major (.28%), study abroad (23.26%), teacher certificate program. **Teacher certification offered in:** early childhood, special education, elementary, middle/junior high, secondary, bilingual/bicultural. **Reserve Officers Training Corps (ROTC):** Army ROTC: Offered on campus; Navy ROTC: Offered on campus; Air Force ROTC: Offered on campus. **Faculty and instruction (2005-2006):** Total instructional faculty: 1,382 full-time, 115 part-time (62% men; 38% women; 16% minorities). Full-time faculty with Ph.D. or other terminal degree: 90%. Student/faculty ratio: 14/1. Classes of fewer than 20 students: 50%; of 20 to 49 students: 39%; of 50 or more students: 11%. **Advanced Placement and International Baccalaureate credit:** AP tests may be used for: Credit and/or placement. Scores accepted: 3, 4, 5. International Baccalaureate exams may be used for: Credit and/or placement. **Freshmen returning for sophomore year:** 96%. **Graduation rates:** Four-year: 71%; five-year: 82%; six-year: 84%. **Graduate study:** 31% of students pursue further study immediately upon graduation. Fields in which graduates pursue further study: Master of Business Administration (MBA), 1%; law, 17%; medicine, 8%; dentistry, 3%; theology (or the seminary), 2%; education, 5%; arts and sciences, 22%.

COSTS AND FINANCIAL AID

Financial aid office: (919) 962-8396. **Expenses (2005-2006):** Tuition and fees 2005-2006: $4,613 in state, $18,411 out of state; room/board: $6,516. Estimated books and supplies: $900; transportation: $522; personal expenses: $1,200. **Financial aid:** Priority filing date for institution's financial aid form: March 1. In 2005-2006, 64% of undergraduates applied for financial aid. Of those, 33% were determined to have financial need; 75% had their need fully met. Average financial aid package (proportion receiving): $10,051 (32%). Average amount of gift aid, such as scholarships or grants (proportion receiving): $7,547 (32%). Average amount of self-help aid, such as work study or loans (proportion receiving): $3,799 (18%). Average need-based loan (excluding PLUS or other private loans): $3,919. Among students who received need-based aid, the average percentage of need met: 100%. Among students who received aid based on merit, the average award (and the proportion receiving): $5,425 (15%). The average athletic scholarship (and the proportion receiving): $12,932 (2%). Average amount of debt of borrowers graduating in 2005: $13,801. Proportion who borrowed: 34%.

CAMPUS LIFE AND EXTRACURRICULAR ACTIVITIES

Campus housing available: coed dorms, women's dorms, men's dorms, sorority housing, fraternity housing, apartments for married students, apartment for single students, special housing for disabled students, special housing for international students, other housing options. Students who live in college-owned, operated, or affiliated housing: 42%. **Student employment:** During the 2005-2006 academic year, 29% of undergraduates worked on campus. Clubs **and organizations:** Number of student organizations: 625. Activities include: choral groups, concert band, dance, drama/theater, jazz band, literary magazine, marching band, music ensembles, musical theater, pep band, radio station, student government, student newspaper, student film society, symphony orchestra, television station, yearbook. Number of fraternities: 33; sororities: 19. Proportion of men in fraternities: 11%; of women in sororities: 12%. **Sports program (2005-2006):** Member of NCAA I. *Men's intercollegiate varsity sports:* baseball, basketball, cheerleading, cross-country, fencing, football, golf, lacrosse, soccer, swimming and diving, tennis, track and field (indoor), track and field (outdoor), wrestling. **Women's intercollegiate varsity sports:** basketball, crew, cross-country, fencing, field hockey, golf, gymnastics, lacrosse, rowing, soccer, softball, swimming and diving, tennis, track and field (indoor), track and field (outdoor), volleyball.

SERVICES AND FACILITIES

Basic services: nonremedial tutoring, women's center, placement service, day care, health service, health insurance. **Remedial assistance:** math, writing, study skills. **Counseling services:** minority student, career, military, personal, veteran student, academic, older student, psychological, birth control, religious, other. **For learning-disabled students:** School does not offer a structured program with separate admission and additional fees. Services include: reading machines, tape recorders, note-taking services, learning center, readers, extended time for tests, other. **Library:** Number of titles: 5,710,686; number of current serial subscriptions: 53,444. **Information technology resources:** Students are required to lease or own a computer. Number of campus computers available to all students: 840. School has a wireless network. Approximate number of users that can be accommodated: 18,030. Proportion of college-owned housing units wired for high-speed internet access: 100%. **Campus safety:** Security services offered: 24-hour foot-and-vehicle patrols, late-night transport/escort service, 24-hour emergency telephones, lighted pathways/sidewalks, student patrols, controlled dormitory access (key, security card, etc).

TRANSFER AND INTERNATIONAL STUDENTS

Transfer students: May apply for admission for the following academic terms: Fall, Summer. Applicants need a minimum number of credits to apply. For fall 2005: Transfer applications received: 2,744. Transfer applicants offered admission: 1,246. Transfer applicants enrolled: 827. **International students:** Number of foreign undergraduates: 219 (1% of student body). Number of countries represented: 107. Minimum TOEFL score required: 600 (paper); 250 (computer). Average TOEFL score: 630 (paper).

University of North Carolina–Charlotte

- **Address:** 9201 University City Boulevard, Charlotte, NC 28223-0001
- **Website:** http://www.uncc.edu/
- **Public**
- **Enrollment:** 13,640 full-time; 2,915 part-time

KEY STATS

✔ **U.S News College Ranking:** 31, Universities–Master's (South)
✔ **SAT Score (25th/75th percentile):** 980-1160
✔ **Tuition:** 2005-2006: $3,480 in state, $13,900 out of state

Selectivity: Selective	**Room/board:** N/A
Acceptance rate: 78%	**Average debt:** $18,407
Student/faculty ratio: 15/1	**Proportion who borrowed:** 56%

UNDERGRADUATE STUDENT BODY STATS

2005-2006 enrollment: 13,640 full-time; 2,915 part-time. Men: 47%; women: 53%. **Ethnic makeup:** African American: 15%; Asian American: 5%; Hispanic: 3%; White: 75%; International: 1%.

ADMISSIONS FACTS AND FIGURES

Phone: (704) 687-2213. **Email:** unccadm@email.uncc.edu. **Website:** http://www.uncc.edu/. **Application deadlines for fall 2007:** Regular decision: July 1. Early decision: Not offered. Early action: Send application by: October 15; Decision sent by: December 15. Admission cannot be deferred. **Application fee:** $50. Common application is accepted. **To apply online, go to:** http://www.admissions.uncc.edu/. **Admissions requirements/recommendations:** High school units required (recommended): English: 4; Mathematics: 3; Science: 3; Foreign language: 2; Social studies: 2; History: (1); Academic electives: 2; Total units: 16. Tests: The college uses SAT or ACT scores in admissions decisions. Either SAT or ACT required. For admission to the fall 2007 entering class, the school will accept: ACT with writing. Campus visit: Recommended. Admissions interview: Neither required nor recommended. Off-campus interview: Not available. **Factors that count in admissions decisions:** *Academic:* Secondary school record: Very important. Class rank: Not considered. Letters of recommendation: Considered. Standardized test scores: Very important. Essay: Not consid-

ered. *Nonacademic:* Interview: Not considered. Extracurricular activities: Considered. Talent/ability: Considered. Character/personal qualities: Considered. Alumni/ae relationship: Not considered. Geographical residence: Considered. State residency: Considered. Religious affiliation/commitment: Not considered. Minority status: Not considered. Volunteer work: Considered. Work experience: Considered. **Other schools with the greatest overlap in applicants:** Appalachian State University; North Carolina State University–Raleigh; University of North Carolina–Chapel Hill; University of North Carolina–Greensboro; University of North Carolina–Wilmington. **Admissions statistics for the fall 2005 entering class:** Total applicants: 8,665. Total accepted: 6,738. Freshmen enrolled: 2,890; 11% were from out of state. Accepted through early-decision or early-action plans: 21%. Overall acceptance rate: 78%. Non-early acceptance rate: 92%. **Credentials of fall 2005 freshmen:** 11% ranked in the top 10 percent of their high school class; 37% were in the top 25 percent, and 93% were in the top half. (Proportion submitting class standing: 98%.) **Average high school grade point average:** 3.5. **First-year students who submitted SAT scores:** 99%. Scores (25/75 percentile): Verbal: 480-570, Math: 500-590, Combined: 980-1160. **First-year students submitting ACT scores:** 15%. Scores (25/75 percentile): English: 18-23, Math: 18-24, Composite: 19-23.

ACADEMICS

Year founded: 1946. **Academic calendar:** Semester. **Degrees offered:** certificate, bachelor's, post-bachelor's certificate, master's, post-master's certificate, doctorate. **Most popular majors:** 8% psychology, 6% finance, 5% business administration and management, 5% communication studies/speech communication and rhetoric, 5% elementary education and teaching. **Major fields of study:** architecture and related services; area, ethnic, cultural, and gender studies; biological and biomedical sciences; business, management, marketing, and related support services; communication, journalism, and related programs; computer and information sciences and support services; education; engineering; engineering technologies/technicians; English language and literature/letters; family and consumer sciences/human sciences; foreign languages, literatures, and linguistics; health professions and related clinical sciences; history; mathematics and statistics; parks, recreation, leisure, and fitness studies; philosophy and religious studies; physical sciences; psychology; public administration and social service professions; security and protective services; social sciences; visual and performing arts. **Areas of required coursework:** arts/fine arts, humanities, computer literacy, mathematics, English (including composition), philosophy, foreign languages, sciences (biological or physical), history, social science. **Pre-professional programs:** pre-law, pre-dentistry, pre-medicine, pre-veterinary science, pre-optometry, pre-pharmacy, other. **Special academic programs (% participation):** cooperative (work-study plan) program (1.5%), distance learning (.25%), double major (5.49%), dual enrollment (.5%), English as a Second Language (ESL) (1.4%), honors program (1%), independent study (10%), internships (1.8%), study abroad (5.3%), teacher certificate program (8.2%), weekend college (.3%). **Teacher certification offered in:** special education, elementary, middle/junior high, secondary. **Cooperative education programs:** art, business, computer science, education, engineering, health professions, humanities, natural science, social/behavioral science, technologies. **Reserve Officers Training Corps (ROTC):** Army ROTC: Offered on campus; Air Force ROTC: Offered on campus. **Faculty and instruction (2005-2006):** Total instructional faculty: 858 full-time, 386 part-time (55% men; 45% women; 13% minorities). Full-time faculty with Ph.D. or other terminal degree: 86%. Student/faculty ratio: 15/1. Classes of fewer than 20 students: 36%; of 20 to 49 students: 49%; of 50 or more students: 15%. **Advanced Placement and International Baccalaureate credit:** AP tests may be used for: Credit only. Scores accepted: 3, 4, 5. International Baccalaureate exams may be used for: Credit only. **Freshmen returning for sophomore year:** 77%. **Graduation rates:** Four-year: 24%; five-year: 43%; six-year: 48%. **Graduate study:** 16% of students pursue further study within one year. Fields in which graduates pursue further study: Master of Business Administration (MBA), 20%; law, 3%; medicine, 4%; engineering, 14%; theology (or the seminary), 3%; education, 10%; arts and sciences, 24%.

COSTS AND FINANCIAL AID

Financial aid office: (704) 687-2461. **Expenses (2005-2006):** Tuition and fees 2005-2006: $3,480 in state, $13,900 out of state; room/board: N/A. Estimated books and supplies: $1,000; transportation: $1,150; personal expenses: $1,520. **Financial aid:** Priority filing date for institution's financial aid form: April 1. In 2005-2006, 62% of undergraduates applied for financial aid. Of those, 47% were determined to have financial need; 30% had their need fully met. Average financial aid package (proportion receiving): $8,730 (45%). Average amount of gift aid, such as scholarships or grants (proportion receiving): $4,215 (37%). Average amount of self-help aid, such as work study or loans (proportion receiving): $3,927 (38%). Average need-based loan (excluding PLUS or other private loans): $3,829. Among students who received need-based aid, the average percentage of need met: 63%. Among students who received aid based on merit, the average award (and the proportion receiving): $6,310 (16%). The average athletic scholarship (and the proportion receiving): $6,399 (1%). Average amount of debt of borrowers graduating in 2005: $18,407. Proportion who borrowed: 56%.

CAMPUS LIFE AND EXTRACURRICULAR ACTIVITIES

Campus housing available (% using): coed dorms (56%), women's dorms (2%), sorority housing (2%), apartment for single students (34%), special housing for disabled students (2%), special housing for international students (2%), other housing options (2%). Students who live in college-owned, operated, or affiliated housing: 26%. Student employment: During the 2005-2006 academic year, 7% of undergraduates worked on campus. Average per-year earnings: $3,000. Clubs and organizations: Number of student organizations: 200. Activities include: choral groups, concert band, dance, drama/theater, jazz band, literary magazine, music ensembles, musical theater, opera, pep band, student government, student newspaper, student film society, yearbook. Number of fraternities: 14; sororities: 10. Proportion of men in fraternities: 1%; of women in sororities: 1%. Average proportion of students who stay on campus on weekends: 70%. Sports program (2005-2006): Member of NCAA I. Men's intercollegiate varsity sports: baseball, basketball, cross-country, golf, soccer, tennis, track and field (indoor), track and field (outdoor). Women's intercollegiate varsity sports: basketball, cross-country, soccer, softball, tennis, track and field (indoor), track and field (outdoor), volleyball.

SERVICES AND FACILITIES

Basic services: nonremedial tutoring, women's center, placement service, health service, health insurance. Remedial assistance: math, writing, study skills. Counseling services: minority student, career, military, personal, veteran student, academic, older student, psychological, birth control. For learning-disabled students: School does not offer a structured program with separate admission and additional fees. Total undergraduates in learning-disabled program or receiving services: 85. Services include: remedial math, reading machines, tape recorders, untimed tests, note-taking services, oral tests, learning center, extended time for tests, tutors. Library: Number of titles: 942,816; number of current serial subscriptions: 10,599. Information technology resources: Students are not required to lease or own a computer. Number of campus computers available to all students: 1,300. School has a wireless network. Approximate number of users that can be accommodated: 1,500. Proportion of college-owned housing units wired for high-speed internet access: 100%. Campus safety: Security services offered: 24-hour foot-and-vehicle patrols, late-night transport/escort service, 24-hour emergency telephones, lighted pathways/sidewalks, controlled dormitory access (key, security card, etc).

TRANSFER AND INTERNATIONAL STUDENTS

Transfer students: May apply for admission for the following academic terms: Fall, Spring, Summer. Applicants need a minimum number of credits to apply. For fall 2005: Transfer applications received: 3,217. Transfer applicants offered admission: 2,808. Transfer applicants enrolled: 1,919. International students: Number of foreign undergraduates: 204 (1% of student body). Number of countries represented: 80. Minimum TOEFL score required: 507 (paper); 180 (computer). Average TOEFL score: 530 (paper).

University of North Carolina–Greensboro

- Address: 1000 Spring Garden Street, Greensboro, NC 27402
- Website: http://www.uncg.edu/
- Public
- Enrollment: 10,584 full-time; 1,707 part-time

KEY STATS
✔ U.S News College Ranking: third tier, National Universities
✔ SAT Score (25th/75th percentile): 940-1160
✔ Tuition: 2006-2007: $3,813 in state, $15,081 out of state

Selectivity: Selective	Room/board: $5,706
Acceptance rate: 60%	Average debt: $13,661
Student/faculty ratio: 16/1	Proportion who borrowed: 60%

UNDERGRADUATE STUDENT BODY STATS

2005-2006 enrollment: 10,584 full-time; 1,707 part-time. Men: 32%; women: 68%. Ethnic makeup: African American: 20%; Asian American: 3%; Hispanic: 2%; White: 74%; International: 1%.

ADMISSIONS FACTS AND FIGURES

Phone: (336) 334-5243. Email: undergrad_admissions@uncg.edu. Website: http://www.uncg.edu/. Application deadlines for fall 2007: Regular decision: August 1. Early decision: Not offered. Early action: Not offered. Admission can be deferred. Application fee: $45. Common application is accepted. Admissions requirements/recommendations: High school units required (recommended): English: 4; Mathematics: 3; Science: 3; Foreign language: 2; Social studies: 1; History: 1; Academic electives: 1; Total units: 16. Tests: The college uses SAT or ACT scores in admissions decisions. Either SAT or ACT required. For admission to the fall 2007 entering class, the school will accept: ACT with writing. Campus visit: Neither required nor recommended. Admissions interview: Neither required nor recommended. Off-campus interview: Not available. Factors that count in admissions decisions: Academic: Secondary school record: Very important. Class rank: Not considered. Letters of recommendation: Considered. Standardized test scores: Important. Essay: Not considered. Nonacademic: Interview: Not considered. Extracurricular activities: Not considered. Talent/ability: Not considered. Character/personal qualities: Not considered. Alumni/ae relationship: Not considered. Geographical residence: Not considered. State residency: Not considered. Religious affiliation/commitment: Not considered. Minority status: Not considered. Volunteer work: Not considered. Work experience: Not considered. Admissions statistics for the fall 2005 entering class: Total applicants: 8,987. Total accepted: 5,370. Freshmen enrolled: 2,424; 9% were from out of state. Overall acceptance rate: 60%. Credentials of fall 2005 freshmen: 14% ranked in the top 10 percent of their high school class; 45% were in the top 25 percent, and 84% were in the top half. (Proportion submitting class standing: 91%.) Average high school grade point average: 3.5. First-year students who submitted SAT scores: 97%. Scores (25/75 percentile): Verbal: 470-580, Math: 470-580, Combined: 940-1160.

ACADEMICS

Year founded: 1891. Academic calendar: Semester. Degrees offered: bachelor's, post-bachelor's certificate, master's, post-master's certificate, doctorate. Most popular majors: 20% business, management, marketing, and related support services, 11% visual and performing arts, 10% education, 10% health professions and related clinical sciences, 10% social sciences. Major fields of study: area, ethnic, cultural, and gender studies; biological and biomedical sciences; business, management, marketing, and related support services; communication, journalism, and related programs; computer and information sciences and support services; education; English language and literature/letters; family and consumer sciences/human sciences; foreign languages, literatures, and linguistics; health professions and related clinical sciences; history; liberal arts and sciences studies, and humanities; mathematics and statistics; multi/interdisciplinary studies; parks, recreation, leisure, and fitness studies; philosophy and religious studies; physical sciences; psychology; public administration and social service professions; social sciences; visual and performing arts. Areas of required coursework: arts/fine arts, humanities, mathematics, English (including composition), philosophy, foreign languages, sciences (biological or physical), history, social science. Pre-professional programs: pre-law, pre-dentistry, pre-medicine, pre-veterinary science. Special academic programs: accelerated program, cross-registration, distance learning, double major, dual enrollment, honors program, independent study, internships, study abroad, teacher certificate program, other. Teacher certification offered in: early childhood, special education, elementary, middle/junior high, secondary. Reserve Officers Training Corps (ROTC): Army ROTC: Offered at cooperating institution (NCAT); Air Force ROTC: Offered at cooperating institution (NCAT). Faculty and instruction (2005-2006): Total instructional faculty: 746 full-time, 243 part-time (46% men; 54% women; 11% minorities). Full-time faculty with Ph.D. or other terminal degree: 81%. Student/faculty ratio: 16/1. Classes of fewer than 20 students: 42%; of 20 to 49 students: 47%; of 50 or more students: 11%. Advanced Placement and International Baccalaureate credit: International Baccalaureate exams may be used for: Credit only. Freshmen returning for sophomore year: 76%. Graduation rates: Four-year: 38%; five-year: 49%; six-year: 51%.

COSTS AND FINANCIAL AID

Financial aid office: (336) 334-5702. Expenses (2006-2007): Tuition and fees 2006-2007: $3,813 in state, $15,081 out of state; room/board: $5,706. Estimated books and supplies: $1,510; transportation: $230; personal expenses: $1,406. Financial aid: Priority filing date for institution's financial aid form: March 1. In 2005-2006, 68% of undergraduates applied for financial aid. Of those, 67% were determined to have financial need; 22% had their need fully met. Average financial aid package (proportion receiving): $7,008 (65%). Average amount of gift aid, such as scholarships or grants (proportion receiving): $3,814 (31%). Average amount of self-help aid, such as work study or loans (proportion receiving): $3,752 (42%). Average need-based loan (excluding PLUS or other private loans): $3,654. Among students who received need-based aid, the average percentage of need met: 60%. Among students who received aid based on merit, the average award (and the proportion receiving): $3,909 (5%). The average athletic scholarship (and the proportion receiving): $8,930 (2%). Average amount of debt of borrowers graduating in 2005: $13,661. Proportion who borrowed: 60%.

CAMPUS LIFE AND EXTRACURRICULAR ACTIVITIES
Campus housing available (% using): coed dorms (85%), women's dorms (7%), apartment for single students (7%), special housing for international students (1%). Students who live in college-owned, operated, or affiliated housing: 32%. **Student employment:** During the 2005-2006 academic year, 3% of undergraduates worked on campus. Average per-year earnings: $1,817. Activities include: choral groups, concert band, dance, drama/theater, jazz band, literary magazine, music ensembles, musical theater, opera, pep band, radio station, student government, student newspaper, student film society, symphony orchestra. **Sports program (2005-2006):** Member of NCAA I. *Men's intercollegiate varsity sports:* baseball, basketball, cross-country, golf, soccer, tennis, track and field (outdoor), wrestling. *Women's intercollegiate varsity sports:* basketball, cross-country, golf, soccer, softball, tennis, track and field (outdoor), volleyball.

SERVICES AND FACILITIES
Basic services: nonremedial tutoring, placement service, day care, health service, health insurance. **Remedial assistance:** reading, math, writing, study skills. **Counseling services:** minority student, career, personal, academic, psychological. **For learning-disabled students:** School does not offer a structured program with separate admission and additional fees. Total undergraduates in learning-disabled program or receiving services: 243. Services include: tape recorders, diagnostic testing service, note-taking services, oral tests, learning center, readers, extended time for tests, tutors. **Library:** Number of titles: 3,400,000; number of current serial subscriptions: 4,648. **Information technology resources:** Students are not required to lease or own a computer. Number of campus computers available to all students: 500. School has a wireless network. Proportion of college-owned housing units wired for high-speed internet access: 100%. **Campus safety:** Security services offered: 24-hour foot-and-vehicle patrols, late-night transport/escort service, 24-hour emergency telephones, lighted pathways/sidewalks, controlled dormitory access (key, security card, etc).

TRANSFER AND INTERNATIONAL STUDENTS
Transfer students: May apply for admission for the following academic terms: Fall, Spring, Summer. Applicants need a minimum number of credits to apply. For fall 2005: Transfer applications received: 2,971. Transfer applicants offered admission: 1,736. Transfer applicants enrolled: 1,212. **International students:** Number of foreign undergraduates: 87 (1% of student body). Number of countries represented: 20. Minimum TOEFL score required: 550 (paper); 213 (computer).

University of North Carolina–Pembroke

- **Address:** PO Box 1510, Pembroke, NC 28372
- **Website:** http://www.uncp.edu
- **Public**
- **Enrollment:** 3,702 full-time; 1,261 part-time

KEY STATS
✔ **U.S News College Ranking:** third tier, Universities–Master's (South)
✔ **SAT Score (25th/75th percentile):** 850-1030
✔ **Tuition:** 2006-2007: $3,322 in state, $12,582 out of state
  Selectivity: Less selective   **Room/board:** $5,200
  Acceptance rate: 86%   **Average debt:** $14,766
  Student/faculty ratio: 16/1   **Proportion who borrowed:** 70%

UNDERGRADUATE STUDENT BODY STATS
2005-2006 enrollment: 3,702 full-time; 1,261 part-time. Men: 35%; women: 65%. **Ethnic makeup:** African American: 24%; American-Indian: 22%; Asian American: 2%; Hispanic: 3%; White: 48%; International: 1%.

ADMISSIONS FACTS AND FIGURES
Phone: (910) 521-6262. **Email:** admissions@papa.uncp.edu. **Website:** http://www.uncp.edu. **Application deadlines for fall 2007:** Regular decision: Rolling. Early decision: Not offered. Early action: Not offered. Admission can be deferred. **Application fee:** $40. Common application is accepted. **Admissions requirements/recommendations:** High school units required (recommended): English: 4; Mathematics: 3; Science: 3; Foreign language: 2; Social studies: 1; History: 1; Total units: 14. Tests: The college uses SAT or ACT scores in admissions decisions. ACT required. For admission to the fall 2007 entering class, the school will accept: ACT with writing. Campus visit: Recommended. Admissions interview: Recommended. Off-campus interview: May be arranged. **Factors that count in admissions decisions:** *Academic:* Secondary school record: Very important. Class rank: Very important. Letters of recommendation: Considered. Standardized test scores: Very important. Essay: Considered. *Nonacademic:* Interview: Considered. Extracurricular activities: Not considered. Talent/ability: Considered. Character/personal qualities: Considered. Alumni/ae relationship: Not considered. Geographical residence: Not considered. State residency: Not considered. Religious affiliation/commitment: Not considered. Minority status: Not considered. Volunteer work: Not considered. Work experience: Not considered. **Admissions statistics for the fall 2005 entering class:** Total applicants: 2,374. Total accepted: 2,036. Freshmen enrolled: 984; 1% were from out of state. Overall acceptance rate: 86%. **Credentials of fall 2005 freshmen:** 9% ranked in the top 10 percent of their high school class; 30% were in the top 25 percent, and 64% were in the top half. (Proportion submitting class standing: 88%.) **Average high school grade point average:** 3.1. **First-year students who submitted SAT scores:** 94%. Scores (25/75 percentile): Verbal: 420-510, Math: 430-520, Combined: 850-1030. **First-year students submitting ACT scores:** 10%. Scores (25/75 percentile): English: 14-19, Math: 16-21, Composite: 16-20.

ACADEMICS
Year founded: 1887. **Academic calendar:** Semester. **Degrees offered:** bachelor's, master's. **Most popular majors:** 17% education, 15% business administration and management, 13% sociology, 8% biology/biological sciences, 7% parks, recreation, and leisure facilities management. **Major fields of study:** area, ethnic, cultural, and gender studies; biological and biomedical sciences; business, management, marketing, and related support services; communication, journalism, and related programs; computer and information sciences and support services; education; English language and literature/letters; foreign languages, literatures, and linguistics; health professions and related clinical sciences; history; mathematics and statistics; natural resources and conservation; parks, recreation, leisure, and fitness studies; philosophy and religious studies; physical sciences; psychology; public administration and social service professions; security and protective services; social sciences; visual and performing arts. **Areas of required coursework:** arts/fine arts, humanities, computer literacy, mathematics, English (including composition), philosophy, sciences (biological or physical), history, social science, other. **Special academic programs:** accelerated program, cooperative (work-study plan) program, cross-registration, distance learning, double major, dual enrollment, English as a Second Language (ESL), exchange student program (domestic), honors program, independent study, internships, study abroad, teacher certificate program. **Teacher certification offered in:** early childhood, special education, elementary, middle/junior high, secondary. **Reserve Officers Training Corps (ROTC):** Army ROTC: Offered on campus; Air Force ROTC: Offered on campus. **Faculty and instruction (2005-2006):** Total instructional faculty: 238 full-time, 128 part-time (57% men; 43% women; 18% minorities). Full-time faculty with Ph.D. or other terminal degree: 69%. Student/faculty ratio: 16/1. Classes of fewer than 20 students: 45%; of 20 to 49 students: 52%; of 50 or more students: 3%. **Freshmen returning for sophomore year:** 70%. **Graduation rates:** Four-year: 20%; five-year: 32%; six-year: 37%. **Graduate study:** Fields in which graduates pursue further study: arts and sciences, 91%.

COSTS AND FINANCIAL AID
Financial aid office: (910) 521-6255. **Expenses (2006-2007):** Tuition and fees 2006-2007: $3,322 in state, $12,582 out of state; room/board: $5,200. Estimated books and supplies: $1,000; transportation: $1,800; personal expenses: $1,472. **Financial aid:** Priority filing date for institution's financial aid form: March 15. In 2005-2006, 84% of undergraduates applied for

financial aid. Of those, 77% were determined to have financial need; 11% had their need fully met. Average financial aid package (proportion receiving): $6,446 (70%). Average amount of gift aid, such as scholarships or grants (proportion receiving): $4,136 (61%). Average amount of self-help aid, such as work study or loans (proportion receiving): $3,440 (57%). Average need-based loan (excluding PLUS or other private loans): $3,357. Among students who received need-based aid, the average percentage of need met: 62%. Among students who received aid based on merit, the average award (and the proportion receiving): $1,208 (4%). The average athletic scholarship (and the proportion receiving): $0 (0%). Average amount of debt of borrowers graduating in 2005: $14,766. Proportion who borrowed: 70%.

CAMPUS LIFE AND EXTRACURRICULAR ACTIVITIES

Campus housing available (% using): coed dorms (21%), women's dorms (28%), men's dorms (23%), other housing options (28%). Students who live in college-owned, operated, or affiliated housing: 28%. **Clubs and organizations:** Number of student organizations: 75. Activities include: choral groups, concert band, dance, drama/theater, jazz band, literary magazine, marching band, music ensembles, musical theater, pep band, student government, student newspaper, student film society, television station, yearbook. Number of fraternities: 10; sororities: 8. **Sports program (2005-2006):** Member of NCAA II. *Men's intercollegiate varsity sports:* baseball, basketball, cross-country, golf, soccer, track and field (outdoor), wrestling. *Women's intercollegiate varsity sports:* basketball, cross-country, soccer, softball, tennis, track and field (outdoor), volleyball.

SERVICES AND FACILITIES

Basic services: nonremedial tutoring, placement service, health service, health insurance. **Remedial assistance:** reading, math, writing, study skills. **Counseling services:** career, personal, veteran student. **For learning-disabled students:** School does not offer a structured program with separate admission and additional fees. Total undergraduates in learning-disabled program or receiving services: 414. Services include: remedial math, remedial English, reading machines, remedial reading, tape recorders, note-taking services, oral tests, readers, extended time for tests, tutors, early syllabus, priority registration, priority seating, texts on tape, exams on tape or computer, other testing accomodations. **Information technology resources:** Students are not required to lease or own a computer. Number of campus computers available to all students: 400. School has a wireless network. Proportion of college-owned housing units wired for high-speed internet access: 100%. **Campus safety:** Security services offered: 24-hour foot-and-vehicle patrols, 24-hour emergency telephones, lighted pathways/sidewalks, controlled dormitory access (key, security card, etc.).

TRANSFER AND INTERNATIONAL STUDENTS

Transfer students: May apply for admission for the following academic terms: Fall, Spring, Summer. Applicants need a minimum number of credits to apply. For fall 2005: Transfer applications received: 597. Transfer applicants offered admission: 539. Transfer applicants enrolled: 497. **International students:** Number of foreign undergraduates: 33 (1% of student body). Minimum TOEFL score required: 500 (paper); 173 (computer).

University of North Carolina–Wilmington

- **Address:** 601 S. College Road, Wilmington, NC 28403-5963
- **Website:** http://www.uncw.edu
- **Public**
- **Enrollment:** 9,591 full-time; 990 part-time

KEY STATS

✔ **U.S News College Ranking:** 20, Universities–Master's (South)
✔ **SAT Score (25th/75th percentile):** 1060-1210
✔ **Tuition:** 2005-2006: $3,695 in state, $13,630 out of state

Selectivity: More selective	**Room/board:** $6,412
Acceptance rate: 61%	**Average debt:** $15,620
Student/faculty ratio: 18/1	**Proportion who borrowed:** 52%

UNDERGRADUATE STUDENT BODY STATS

2005-2006 enrollment: 9,591 full-time; 990 part-time. Men: 41%; women: 59%. **Ethnic makeup:** African American: 5%; American-Indian: 1%; Asian American: 2%; Hispanic: 2%; White: 90%.

ADMISSIONS FACTS AND FIGURES

Phone: (910) 962-3243. **Email:** admissions@uncw.edu. **Website:** http://www.uncw.edu. **Application deadlines for fall 2007:** Regular decision: February 1; decision sent by January 15. Early decision: Not offered. Early action: Send application by: November 1; Decision sent by: January 20. Admission cannot be deferred. **Application fee:** $45. Common application is accepted. **To apply online, go to:** http://www.uncw.edu/admissions. **Admissions requirements/recommendations:** High school units required (recommended): English: 4; Mathematics: 3; Science: 3; Foreign language: 2; Social studies: 2; History: 1; Academic electives: 5. Tests: The college uses SAT or ACT scores in admissions decisions. Either SAT or ACT required. For admission to the fall 2007 entering class, the school will accept: ACT with writing. Campus visit: Recommended. Admissions interview: Neither required nor recommended. Off-campus interview: Not available. **Factors that count in admissions decisions:** *Academic:* Secondary school record: Very important. Class rank: Important. Letters of recommendation: Important. Standardized test scores: Very important. Essay: Important. *Nonacademic:* Interview: Not considered. Extracurricular activities: Considered. Talent/ability: Considered. Character/personal qualities: Considered. Alumni/ae relationship: Considered. Geographical residence: Considered. State residency: Very important. Religious affiliation/commitment: Not considered. Minority status: Considered. Volunteer work: Considered. Work experience: Considered. **Other schools with the greatest overlap in applicants:** Appalachian State University; East Carolina University; North Carolina State University–Raleigh. **Admissions statistics for the fall 2005 entering class:** Total applicants: 8,820. Total accepted: 5,377. Freshmen enrolled: 1,943; 16% were from out of state. Overall acceptance rate: 61%. Non-early acceptance rate: 61%. **Size of waiting list:** 1000 applicants; enrolled from waiting list: 103. **Credentials of fall 2005 freshmen:** 21% ranked in the top 10 percent of their high school class; 60% were in the top 25 percent, and 93% were in the top half. (Proportion submitting class standing: 85%.) **Average high school grade point average:** 3.6. **First-year students who submitted SAT scores:** 97%. Scores (25/75 percentile): Verbal: 520-600, Math: 540-610, Combined: 1060-1210. **First-year students submitting ACT scores:** 17%. Scores (25/75 percentile): English: 20-24, Math: 20-25, Composite: 21-25.

ACADEMICS

Year founded: 1947. **Academic calendar:** Semester. **Degrees offered:** bachelor's, master's, doctorate. **Most popular majors:** 8% elementary education and teaching, 7% marketing/marketing management, 7% psychology, 7% speech and rhetorical studies, 6% English language and literature. **Major fields of study:** biological and biomedical sciences; business, management, marketing, and related support services; computer and information sciences and support services; education; English language and literature/letters; foreign languages, literatures, and linguistics; health professions and related clinical sciences; history; mathematics and statistics; natural resources and conservation; parks, recreation, leisure, and fitness studies; philosophy and religious studies; physical sciences; psychology; public administration and social service professions; security and protective services; social sciences; visual and performing arts. **Areas of required coursework:** arts/fine arts, humanities, mathematics, English (including composition), philosophy, foreign languages, sciences (biological or physical), history, social science. **Preprofessional programs:** pre-law, pre-dentistry, pre-medicine, pre-veterinary science, pre-optometry, pre-pharmacy, other. **Special academic programs:** accelerated program, cooperative (work-study plan) program, distance learning, double major, exchange student program (domestic), honors program, independent study, internships, study abroad, teacher certificate program, other. **Teacher certification offered in:** early childhood, special education, elementary, middle/junior high, secondary. **Faculty and instruction (2005-2006):** Total instructional faculty: 491 full-time, 285 part-time (56% men; 44% women; 10% minorities). Full-time faculty with Ph.D. or other terminal degree: 87%. Student/faculty ratio: 18/1. Classes of fewer than 20 students: 27%; of 20 to 49 students: 65%; of 50 or more students: 8%. **Advanced Placement and International Baccalaureate credit:** AP tests may be used for: Credit and/or placement. Scores accepted: 3, 4, 5. International Baccalaureate exams may be used for: Credit only. **Freshmen returning for sophomore year:** 85%. **Graduation rates:** Four-year: 41%; five-year: 61%; six-year: 61%. **Graduate study:** 26% of students pursue further study immediately upon graduation; 14% within one year.

COSTS AND FINANCIAL AID

Financial aid office: (910) 962-3177. **Expenses (2005-2006):** Tuition and fees 2005-2006: $3,695 in state, $13,630 out of state; room/board: $6,412. Estimated books and supplies: $1,000; transportation: $1,300; personal expenses: $700. **Financial aid:** Priority filing date for institution's financial aid form: April 1. In 2005-2006, 57% of undergraduates applied for financial aid. Of those, 36% were determined to have financial need; 64% had their need fully met. Average financial aid package (proportion receiving): $6,526 (36%). Average amount of gift aid, such as scholarships or grants (proportion receiving): $3,554 (30%). Average amount of self-help aid, such as work study or loans (proportion receiving): $4,190 (31%). Average need-based loan (excluding PLUS or other private loans): $4,006. Among students who received need-based aid, the average percentage of need met: 87%. Among students who received aid based on merit, the average award (and the proportion receiving): $1,625 (2%). The average athletic scholarship (and the proportion receiving): $6,457 (2%). Average amount of debt of borrowers graduating in 2005: $15,620. Proportion who borrowed: 52%.

CAMPUS LIFE AND EXTRACURRICULAR ACTIVITIES

Campus housing available (% using): coed dorms (51%), women's dorms (8%), apartment for single students (33%), special housing for international students (4%), other housing options (4%). Students who live in college-owned, operated, or affiliated housing: 22%. **Clubs and organizations:** Number of student organizations: 167. Activities include: choral groups, concert band, dance, drama/theater, jazz band, literary magazine, music ensembles, musical theater, opera, pep band, radio station, student government, student newspaper, student film society, symphony orchestra, television station. Number of fraternities: 12; sororities: 12. Proportion of men in fraternities: 7%; of women in sororities: 8%. Average proportion of students who stay on campus on weekends: 75%. **Sports program (2005-2006):** Member of NCAA I. *Men's intercollegiate varsity sports:* baseball, basketball, cross-country, golf, soccer, swimming and diving, tennis, track and field (indoor), track and field (outdoor). *Women's intercollegiate varsity sports:* basketball, cross-country, golf, soccer, softball, swimming and diving, tennis, track and field (indoor), track and field (outdoor), volleyball.

SERVICES AND FACILITIES

Basic services: nonremedial tutoring, placement service, health service. **Remedial assistance:** reading, math, writing. **Counseling services:** minority student, career, personal, veteran student, academic, older student, psychological. **For learning-disabled students:** School does not offer a structured program with separate admission and additional fees. Total undergraduates in learning-disabled program or receiving services: 180. Services include: reading machines, tape recorders, note-taking services, oral tests, learning center, readers, extended time for tests, tutors, priority registration, texts on tape, other testing accomodations, other. **Library:** Number of titles: 984,080; number of current serial subscriptions: 3,668. **Information technology resources:** Students are not required to lease or own a computer. Number of campus computers available to all students: 1,149. School has a wireless network. Approximate number of users that can be accommodated: 3,690. Proportion of college-owned housing units wired for high-speed internet access: 100%. **Campus safety:** Security services offered: 24-hour foot-and-vehicle patrols, late-night transport/escort service, 24-hour emergency telephones, lighted pathways/sidewalks, controlled dormitory access (key, security card, etc).

TRANSFER AND INTERNATIONAL STUDENTS

Transfer students: May apply for admission for the following academic terms: Fall, Spring, Summer. Applicants need a minimum number of credits to apply. For fall 2005: Transfer applications received: 2,346. Transfer applicants offered admission: 1,887. Transfer applicants enrolled: 1,228. **International students:** Number of foreign undergraduates: 51 (1% of student body). Number of countries represented: 37. Minimum TOEFL score required: 550 (paper); 213 (computer). Average TOEFL score: 381 (paper).

Wake Forest University

■ **Address:** Box 7305, Reynolda Station, Winston-Salem, NC 27109
■ **Website:** http://www.wfu.edu
■ **Private**
■ **Enrollment:** 4,138 full-time; 125 part-time

KEY STATS

✔ **U.S News College Ranking:** 30, National Universities
✔ **SAT Score (25th/75th percentile):** 1260-1410
✔ **Tuition:** 2006-2007: $32,140
  Selectivity: Most selective   **Room/board:** N/A
  Acceptance rate: 39%   **Average debt:** $22,831
  Student/faculty ratio: 10/1   **Proportion who borrowed:** 39%

UNDERGRADUATE STUDENT BODY STATS

2005-2006 enrollment: 4,138 full-time; 125 part-time. Men: 49%; women: 51%. **Ethnic makeup:** African American: 7%; Asian American: 4%; Hispanic: 2%; White: 86%; International: 1%. **Religious preference:** Roman Catholic: 24%; Protestant: 59%; Jewish: 2%; Hindu: 1%; No preference: 5%; Other: 9%.

ADMISSIONS FACTS AND FIGURES

Phone: (336) 758-5201. **Email:** admissions@wfu.edu. **Website:** http://www.wfu.edu. **Application deadlines for fall 2007:** Regular decision: January 15; decision sent by April 1. Early decision: Send application by: November 15; Decision sent by: N/A. Early action: Not offered. Admission can be deferred. **Application fee:** $40. Common application is accepted. **To apply online, go to:** http://www.wfu.edu/admissions/online-app/introduction.html. **Admissions requirements/recommendations:** High school units required (recommended): English: 4 (4); Mathematics: 3 (4); Science: 1 (4); Foreign language: 2 (4); Social studies: 2 (4); Total units: 16 (20). Tests: The college uses SAT or ACT scores in admissions decisions. Either SAT or ACT required. For admission to the fall 2007 entering class, the school will accept: ACT with writing. Campus visit: Recommended. Admissions interview: Neither required nor recommended. Off-campus interview: Not available. **Factors that count in admissions decisions:** *Academic:* Secondary school record: Very important. Class rank: Very important. Letters of recommendation: Important. Standardized test scores: Very important. Essay: Very important. *Nonacademic:* Interview: Considered. Extracurricular activities: Important. Talent/ability: Important. Character/personal qualities: Very important. Alumni/ae relationship: Considered. Geographical residence: Considered. State residency: Considered. Religious affiliation/commitment: Considered. Minority status: Considered. Volunteer work: Considered. Work experience: Not considered. **Other schools with the greatest overlap in applicants:** Duke University; Emory University; University of North Carolina–Chapel Hill; University of Richmond; Vanderbilt University. **Admissions statistics for the fall 2005 entering class:** Total applicants: 7,484. Total accepted: 2,882. Freshmen enrolled: 1,120; 72% were from out of state. Accepted through early-decision or early-action plans: 32%. Overall acceptance rate: 39%. Early-decision acceptance rate: 53%. Non-early acceptance rate: 37%. **Credentials of fall 2005 freshmen:** 61% ranked in the top 10 percent of their high school class; 94% were in the top 25 percent, and 98% were in the top half. (Proportion submitting class standing: 62%.) **First-year students who submitted SAT scores:** 99%. Scores (25/75 percentile): Verbal: 620-700, Math: 640-710, Combined: 1260-1410.

ACADEMICS

Year founded: 1834. **Academic calendar:** Semester. **Degrees offered:** bachelor's, master's, first professional, doctorate. **Most popular majors:** 12% business/commerce, 11% social sciences, 10% communication studies/speech communication and rhetoric, 8% biology/biological sciences, 8% psychology. **Major fields of study:** biological and biomedical sciences; business, management, marketing, and related support services; communication, journalism, and related programs; computer and information sciences and support services; education; engineering; English language and literature/letters; foreign languages, literatures, and linguistics; history; mathematics and statistics; natural resources and conservation; parks, recreation, leisure, and fitness studies; philosophy and religious studies; physical sciences; psychology; social sciences; visual and performing arts. **Areas of required coursework:** arts/fine arts, humanities, computer literacy, mathematics, English (including composition), philosophy, foreign languages, sciences (biological or physical), history, social science, other. **Pre-professional**

programs: pre-law, pre-medicine. **Special academic programs (% participation):** cross-registration, double major (13.2%), dual enrollment, honors program, independent study, internships, study abroad, teacher certificate program. **Teacher certification offered in:** elementary, middle/junior high, secondary. **Cooperative education programs:** engineering, health professions. **Reserve Officers Training Corps (ROTC):** Army ROTC: Offered on campus. **Faculty and instruction (2005-2006):** Total instructional faculty: 450 full-time, 98 part-time (62% men; 38% women; 11% minorities). Full-time faculty with Ph.D. or other terminal degree: 90%. Student/faculty ratio: 10/1. Classes of fewer than 20 students: 54%; of 20 to 49 students: 44%; of 50 or more students: 3%. **Advanced Placement and International Baccalaureate credit:** AP tests may be used for: Credit only. **Freshmen returning for sophomore year:** 94%. **Graduation rates:** Four-year: 78%; five-year: 88%; six-year: 88%. **Graduate study:** 31% of students pursue further study within one year. Fields in which graduates pursue further study: law, 7%; medicine, 5%; arts and sciences, 15%.

COSTS AND FINANCIAL AID

Financial aid office: (336) 758-5154. **Expenses (2006-2007):** Tuition and fees 2006-2007: $32,140; room/board: N/A. Estimated books and supplies: $850; transportation: $640; personal expenses: $1,320. **Financial aid:** Priority filing date for institution's financial aid form: February 1; deadline: March 1. In 2005-2006, 44% of undergraduates applied for financial aid. Of those, 36% were determined to have financial need; 32% had their need fully met. Average financial aid package (proportion receiving): $22,581 (35%). Average amount of gift aid, such as scholarships or grants (proportion receiving): $16,797 (33%). Average amount of self-help aid, such as work study or loans (proportion receiving): $8,127 (29%). Average need-based loan (excluding PLUS or other private loans): $6,643. Among students who received need-based aid, the average percentage of need met: 87%. Among students who received aid based on merit, the average award (and the proportion receiving): $10,520 (29%). The average athletic scholarship (and the proportion receiving): $24,030 (5%). Average amount of debt of borrowers graduating in 2005: $22,831. Proportion who borrowed: 39%.

CAMPUS LIFE AND EXTRACURRICULAR ACTIVITIES

Campus housing available (% using): coed dorms (71%), sorority housing (8%), fraternity housing (7%), apartment for single students (10%), special housing for disabled students (1%), other housing options (3%). Students who live in college-owned, operated, or affiliated housing: 71%. **Student employment:** During the 2005-2006 academic year, 45% of undergraduates worked on campus. Average per-year earnings: $1,100. **Clubs and organizations:** Number of student organizations: 155. Activities include: choral groups, concert band, dance, drama/theater, jazz band, literary magazine, marching band, music ensembles, pep band, radio station, student government, student newspaper, student film society, symphony orchestra, television station, yearbook. Number of fraternities: 13; sororities: 10. Proportion of men in fraternities: 33%; of women in sororities: 53%. Average proportion of students who stay on campus on weekends: 70%. **Sports program (2005-2006):** Member of NCAA I. *Men's intercollegiate varsity sports:* baseball, basketball, cheerleading, cross-country, football, golf, soccer, tennis, track and field (indoor), track and field (outdoor). *Women's intercollegiate varsity sports:* basketball, cheerleading, cross-country, field hockey, golf, soccer, tennis, track and field (indoor), track and field (outdoor), volleyball.

SERVICES AND FACILITIES

Basic services: nonremedial tutoring, other. **Remedial assistance:** study skills. **Counseling services:** minority student, career, military, personal, academic, older student, psychological, birth control, religious. **For learning-disabled students:** School does not offer a structured program with separate admission and additional fees. Total undergraduates in learning-disabled program or receiving services: 145. Services include: learning center, extended time for tests, tutors, other. **Library:** Number of titles: 1,788,033; number of current serial subscriptions: 32,566. **Information technology resources:** Students are required to lease or own a computer. Number of campus computers available to all students: 4,405. School has a wireless network. Approximate number of users that can be accommodated: 20,000. Proportion of college-owned housing units wired for high-speed internet access: 100%. **Campus safety:** Security services offered: 24-hour foot-and-vehicle patrols, late-night transport/escort service, 24-hour emergency telephones, lighted pathways/sidewalks, controlled dormitory access (key, security card, etc).

TRANSFER AND INTERNATIONAL STUDENTS

Transfer students: May apply for admission for the following academic terms: Fall, Spring. Applicants do not need a minimum number of credits

to apply. For fall 2005: Transfer applications received: 263. Transfer applicants offered admission: 95. Transfer applicants enrolled: 51. **International students:** Number of foreign undergraduates: 38 (1% of student body). Number of countries represented: 26. Minimum TOEFL score required: 600 (paper); 250 (computer).

Warren Wilson College

■ **Address:** PO Box 9000, Asheville, NC 28815
■ **Website:** http://www.warren-wilson.edu
■ **Private; Religious affiliation:** Presbyterian
■ **Enrollment:** 820 full-time; 12 part-time

KEY STATS

✔ **U.S News College Ranking:** 37, Universities–Master's (South)
✔ **SAT Score (25th/75th percentile):** 1060-1290
✔ **Tuition:** 2006-2007: $20,126

Selectivity: Selective	**Room/board:** $6,000
Acceptance rate: 77%	**Average debt:** $16,211
Student/faculty ratio: 11/1	**Proportion who borrowed:** 59%

UNDERGRADUATE STUDENT BODY STATS

2005-2006 enrollment: 820 full-time; 12 part-time. Men: 40%; women: 60%. **Ethnic makeup:** African American: 1%; Asian American: 1%; Hispanic: 2%; White: 93%; International: 3%.

ADMISSIONS FACTS AND FIGURES

Phone: (800) 934-3536. **Email:** admit@warren-wilson.edu. **Website:** http://www.warren-wilson.edu. **Application deadlines for fall 2007:** Regular decision: February 28; decision sent by March 31. Early decision: Send application by: November 15; Decision sent by: December 1. Early action: Not offered. Admission can be deferred. Common application is accepted. **Admissions requirements/recommendations:** High school units required (recommended): English: 4; Mathematics: 3; Science: 2; Foreign language: (2); History: 3. Tests: The college uses SAT or ACT scores in admissions decisions. Either SAT or ACT required. Campus visit: Recommended. Admissions interview: Recommended. Off-campus interview: May be arranged. **Factors that count in admissions decisions:** *Academic:* Secondary school record: Very important. Class rank: Very important. Letters of recommendation: Important. Standardized test scores: Important. Essay: Very important. *Nonacademic:* Interview: Important. Extracurricular activities: Important. Talent/ability: Important. Character/personal qualities: Important. Alumni/ae relationship: Not considered. Geographical residence: Not considered. State residency: Not considered. Religious affiliation/commitment: Not considered. Minority status: Not considered. Volunteer work: Very important. Work experience: Very important. **Other schools with the greatest overlap in applicants:** Appalachian State University; Earlham College; Guilford College; Hampshire College. **Admissions statistics for the fall 2005 entering class:** Total applicants: 857. Total accepted: 664. Freshmen enrolled: 245; 87% were from out of state. Overall acceptance rate: 77%. Non-early acceptance rate: 77%. **Credentials of fall 2005 freshmen:** 13% ranked in the top 10 percent of their high school class; 35% were in the top 25 percent, and 79% were in the top half. (Proportion submitting class standing: 70%.) **Average high school grade point average:** 3.4. **First-year students who submitted SAT scores:** 87%. Scores (25/75 percentile): Verbal: 550-670, Math: 510-620, Combined: 1060-1290. **First-year students submitting ACT scores:** 24%. Scores (25/75 percentile): English: N/A, Math: N/A, Composite: 24-24.

ACADEMICS

Year founded: 1894. **Academic calendar:** Semester. **Degrees offered:** bachelor's, master's. **Most popular majors:** Information not available. **Major fields of study:** Areas of required coursework: arts/fine arts, mathematics, English (including composition), philosophy, sciences (biological or physical), history, social science, other. **Pre-professional programs:** pre-law, pre-medicine, pre-veterinary science. **Special academic programs (% participation):** cooperative (work-study plan) program (100%), cross-registration (1%), double major (7%), English as a Second Language (ESL) (1%), honors program (2%), independent study (50%), internships (30%), student-designed major (5%), study abroad (70%), teacher certificate program (8%). **Teacher certification offered in:** elementary, secondary. **Cooperative education programs:** engineering, other. **Faculty and instruction (2005-2006):** Total instructional faculty: 62 full-time, 13 part-time (51% men; 49% women; 8% minorities). Full-time faculty with Ph.D. or other terminal degree: 92%. Student/faculty ratio: 11/1. Classes of fewer than 20 students: 87%; of 20 to 49 students: 13%; of 50 or more students: 0%. **Advanced Placement and International Baccalaureate credit:** AP tests may be used for: Credit only. Scores accepted: 3, 4, 5. International Baccalaureate exams may be used for: Credit only. **Freshmen returning for sophomore year:** 59%. **Graduation rates:** Four-year: 37%; five-year: 48%; six-year: 45%. **Graduate study:** 17% of students pursue further study immediately upon graduation.

COSTS AND FINANCIAL AID

Financial aid office: (828) 771-2082. **Expenses (2006-2007):** Tuition and fees 2006-2007: $20,126; room/board: $6,000. Estimated books and supplies: $830; transportation: $1,172; personal expenses: $1,172. **Financial aid:** Priority filing date for institution's financial aid form: April 1. In 2005-2006, 69% of undergraduates applied for financial aid. Of those, 57% were determined to have financial need; 17% had their need fully met. Average financial aid package (proportion receiving): $11,365 (57%). Average amount of gift aid, such as scholarships or grants (proportion receiving): $8,908 (49%). Average amount of self-help aid, such as work study or loans (proportion receiving): $5,084 (55%). Average need-based loan (excluding PLUS or other private loans): $3,419. Among students who received need-based aid, the average percentage of need met: 75%. Among students who received aid based on merit, the average award (and the proportion receiving): $2,203 (11%). The average athletic scholarship (and the proportion receiving): $0 (0%). Average amount of debt of borrowers graduating in 2005: $16,211. Proportion who borrowed: 59%.

CAMPUS LIFE AND EXTRACURRICULAR ACTIVITIES

Campus housing available (% using): coed dorms (83%), women's dorms (13%), men's dorms (4%). Students who live in college-owned, operated, or affiliated housing: 88%. **Student employment:** During the 2005-2006 academic year, 100% of undergraduates worked on campus. Average per-year earnings: $2,472. **Clubs and organizations:** Number of student organizations: 21. Activities include: choral groups, dance, drama/theater, jazz band, literary magazine, music ensembles, musical theater, student government, student newspaper, student film society, yearbook. Number of fraternities: 0; sororities: 0. Average proportion of students who stay on campus on weekends: 90%.

SERVICES AND FACILITIES

Basic services: health service, other. **Remedial assistance:** study skills. **Counseling services:** career, personal, academic, religious. **For learning-disabled students:** School does not offer a structured program with separate admission and additional fees. Total undergraduates in learning-disabled program or receiving services: 30. Services include: untimed tests, note-taking services, oral tests, learning center, extended time for tests, tutors. **Library:** Number of titles: 107,747; number of current serial subscriptions: 817. **Information technology resources:** Students are not required to lease or own a computer. Number of campus computers available to all students: 92. School has a wireless network. Approximate number of users that can be accommodated: 256. Proportion of college-owned housing units wired for high-speed internet access: 100%. **Campus safety:** Security services offered: 24-hour foot-and-vehicle patrols, late-night transport/escort service, 24-hour emergency telephones, lighted pathways/sidewalks, student patrols, controlled dormitory access (key, security card, etc.).

TRANSFER AND INTERNATIONAL STUDENTS

Transfer students: May apply for admission for the following academic terms: Fall, Spring. Applicants do not need a minimum number of credits to apply. For fall 2005: Transfer applications received: 193. Transfer applicants offered admission: 126. Transfer applicants enrolled: 68. **International students:** Number of foreign undergraduates: 23 (3% of student body). Minimum TOEFL score required: 550 (paper); 213 (computer).

Western Carolina University

- **Address:** Cullowhee, NC 28723
- **Website:** http://www.wcu.edu
- **Public**
- **Enrollment:** 6,015 full-time; 965 part-time

KEY STATS

✔ **U.S News College Ranking:** 52, Universities–Master's (South)
✔ **SAT Score (25th/75th percentile):** 930-1110
✔ **Tuition:** 2006-2007: $3,900 in state, $13,483 out of state
  Selectivity: Less selective   **Room/board:** $5,210
  Acceptance rate: 75%   **Average debt:** $17,782
  Student/faculty ratio: 14/1   **Proportion who borrowed:** 49%

UNDERGRADUATE STUDENT BODY STATS

2005-2006 enrollment: 6,015 full-time; 965 part-time. Men: 48%; women: 52%. **Ethnic makeup:** African American: 5%; American-Indian: 2%; Asian American: 1%; Hispanic: 1%; White: 88%; International: 3%.

ADMISSIONS FACTS AND FIGURES

Phone: (828) 227-7317. **Email:** admiss@email.wcu.edu. **Website:** http://www.wcu.edu. **Application deadlines for fall 2007:** Regular decision: August 1. Early decision: Not offered. Early action: Not offered. Admission cannot be deferred. **Application fee:** $40. Common application is not accepted. **To apply online, go to:** http://admissions.wcu.edu/apply.html. **Admissions requirements/recommendations:** High school units required (recommended): English: 4 (4); Mathematics: 3 (3); Science: 3 (3); Foreign language: 2 (2); Social studies: 2 (2); History: 1 (1); Academic electives: 5 (7); Total units: 20 (24). Tests: The college uses SAT or ACT scores in admissions decisions. Either SAT or ACT required. For admission to the fall 2007 entering class, the school will accept: ACT with writing. Campus visit: Recommended. Admissions interview: Neither required nor recommended. Off-campus interview: Not available. **Factors that count in admissions decisions:** *Academic:* Secondary school record: Very important. Class rank: Important. Letters of recommendation: Considered. Standardized test scores: Very important. Essay: Considered. *Nonacademic:* Interview: Considered. Extracurricular activities: Important. Talent/ability: Very important. Character/personal qualities: Very important. Alumni/ae relationship: Not considered. Geographical residence: Not considered. State residency: Important. Religious affiliation/commitment: Not considered. Minority status: Not considered. Volunteer work: Important. Work experience: Important. **Other schools with the greatest overlap in applicants:** Appalachian State University; Campbell University; University of North Carolina–Asheville; University of North Carolina–Charlotte; University of North Carolina–Greensboro. **Admissions statistics for the fall 2005 entering class:** Total applicants: 4,964. Total accepted: 3,705. Freshmen enrolled: 1,557; 7% were from out of state. Overall acceptance rate: 75%. **Size of waiting list:** 16 applicants; enrolled from waiting list: 4. **Credentials of fall 2005 freshmen:** 8% ranked in the top 10 percent of their high school class; 27% were in the top 25 percent, and 61% were in the top half. (Proportion submitting class standing: 95%.) **Average high school grade point average:** 3.3. **First-year students who submitted SAT scores:** 95%. Scores (25/75 percentile): Verbal: 460-550, Math: 470-560, Combined: 930-1110. **First-year students submitting ACT scores:** 17%. Scores (25/75 percentile): English: 16-21, Math: 17-22, Composite: 18-22.

ACADEMICS

Year founded: 1889. **Academic calendar:** Semester. **Degrees offered:** bachelor's, master's, post-master's certificate, doctorate. **Most popular majors:** 24% business, management, marketing, and related support services, 15% education, 11% health professions and related clinical sciences, 8% security and protective services, 5% engineering technologies/technicians. **Major fields of study:** biological and biomedical sciences; business, management, marketing, and related support services; communication, journalism, and related programs; computer and information sciences and support services; education; engineering technologies/technicians; English language and literature/letters; foreign languages, literatures, and linguistics; health professions and related clinical sciences; history; liberal arts and sciences studies, and humanities; mathematics and statistics; natural resources and conservation; parks, recreation, leisure, and fitness studies; philosophy and religious studies; physical sciences; psychology; public administration and social service professions; security and protective services; social sciences; visual and performing arts. **Areas of required coursework:** arts/fine arts, humanities, computer literacy, mathematics, English (including composition), sciences (biological or physical), history, social science, other. **Pre-professional programs:** pre-law, pre-dentistry, pre-medicine, pre-veterinary science, pre-optometry, pre-pharmacy, other. **Special academic programs (% participation):** accelerated program, cooperative (work-study plan) program, distance learning, double major (5%), dual enrollment, English as a Second Language (ESL), exchange student program (domestic), honors program, independent study, internships, student-designed major, study abroad, teacher certificate program (22%). **Teacher certification offered in:** early childhood, special education, elementary, middle/junior high, secondary. **Cooperative education programs:** art, business, computer science, education, engineering, health professions, home economics, humanities, natural science, social/behavioral science, technologies. **Faculty and instruction (2005-2006):** Total instructional faculty: 433 full-time, 211 part-time (53% men; 47% women; 4% minorities). Full-time faculty with Ph.D. or other terminal degree: 76%. Student/faculty ratio: 14/1. Classes of fewer than 20 students: 35%; of 20 to 49 students: 64%; of 50 or more students: 1%. **Advanced Placement and International Baccalaureate credit:** AP tests may be used for: Credit only. Scores accepted: 3, 4. **Freshmen returning for sophomore year:** 71%. **Graduation rates:** Four-year: 23%; five-year: 43%; six-year: 47%. **Graduate study:** 16% of students pursue further study immediately upon graduation; 25% within one year. Fields in which graduates pursue further study: Master of Business Administration (MBA), 9%; law, 2%; engineering, 2%; education, 30%; arts and sciences, 32%.

COSTS AND FINANCIAL AID

Financial aid office: (828) 227-7290. **Expenses (2006-2007):** Tuition and fees 2006-2007: $3,900 in state, $13,483 out of state; room/board: $5,210. Estimated books and supplies: $567; transportation: $862; personal expenses: $1,228. **Financial aid:** Priority filing date for institution's financial aid form: March 31. In 2005-2006, 70% of undergraduates applied for financial aid. Of those, 48% were determined to have financial need; 41% had their need fully met. Average financial aid package (proportion receiving): $6,574 (47%). Average amount of gift aid, such as scholarships or grants (proportion receiving): $3,416 (46%). Average amount of self-help aid, such as work study or loans (proportion receiving): $3,541 (37%). Average need-based loan (excluding PLUS or other private loans): $3,386. Among students who received need-based aid, the average percentage of need met: 79%. Among students who received aid based on merit, the average award (and the proportion receiving): $2,487 (12%). The average athletic scholarship (and the proportion receiving): $2,830 (8%). Average amount of debt of borrowers graduating in 2005: $17,782. Proportion who borrowed: 49%.

CAMPUS LIFE AND EXTRACURRICULAR ACTIVITIES

Campus housing available (% using): coed dorms (65%), women's dorms (10%), men's dorms (18%), sorority housing (3%), fraternity housing (3%), apartments for married students (1%). Students who live in college-owned, operated, or affiliated housing: 42%. **Student employment:** During the 2005-2006 academic year, 22% of undergraduates worked on campus. Average per-year earnings: $2,038. **Clubs and organizations:** Number of student organizations: 91. Activities include: choral groups, concert band, dance, drama/theater, jazz band, literary magazine, marching band, music ensembles, musical theater, pep band, radio station, student government, student newspaper, student film society, television station, yearbook. Number of fraternities: 11; sororities: 9. Proportion of men in fraternities: 7%; of women in sororities: 8%. Average proportion of students who stay on campus on weekends: 65%. **Sports program (2005-2006):** Member of NCAA I. **Men's intercollegiate varsity sports:** baseball, basketball, cross-country, football, golf, track and field (indoor), track and field (outdoor). **Women's intercollegiate varsity sports:** basketball, cross-country, golf, soccer, tennis, track and field (indoor), track and field (outdoor), volleyball.

SERVICES AND FACILITIES

Basic services: nonremedial tutoring, women's center, placement service, day care, health service, health insurance. **Remedial assistance:** math, writing, study skills. **Counseling services:** minority student, career, personal, veteran student, academic, psychological, birth control. **For learning-disabled students:** School does not offer a structured program with separate admission and additional fees. Total undergraduates in learning-disabled program or receiving services: 75. Services include: reading machines, tape recorders, note-taking services, oral tests, learning center, readers, extended time for tests, tutors, priority registration, priority seating, texts on tape, other testing accomodations. **Library:** Number of titles: 701,832; number of current serial subscriptions: 1,838. **Information technology resources:** Students are required to lease or own a computer. Number of campus computers available to all students: 809. School has a wireless network. Approximate number of users that can be accommodated: 14,000. Proportion of college-owned housing units wired for high-speed internet access: 100%. **Campus safety:** Security services offered: 24-hour foot-and-vehicle patrols, late-night transport/escort service, 24-hour emergency telephones, lighted pathways/sidewalks, student patrols, controlled dormitory access (key, security card, etc).

TRANSFER AND INTERNATIONAL STUDENTS

Transfer students: May apply for admission for the following academic terms: Fall, Spring, Summer. Applicants do not need a minimum number of credits to apply. For fall 2005: Transfer applications received: 1,448. Transfer applicants offered admission: 1,098. Transfer applicants enrolled: 728. **International students:** Number of foreign undergraduates: 197 (3% of student body). Number of countries represented: 36. Minimum TOEFL score required: 550 (paper); 213 (computer). Average TOEFL score: 461 (paper).

Wingate University

- **Address:** PO Box 159, Wingate, NC 28174
- **Website:** http://www.wingate.edu
- **Private; Religious affiliation:** Baptist
- **Enrollment:** 1,311 full-time; 30 part-time

KEY STATS

✔ **U.S News College Ranking:** 19, Comp. Colleges–Bachelor's (South)
✔ **SAT Score (25th/75th percentile):** 910-1140
✔ **Tuition:** 2006-2007: $17,650

Selectivity: Less selective	**Room/board:** $6,750
Acceptance rate: 84%	**Average debt:** $18,759
Student/faculty ratio: 14/1	**Proportion who borrowed:** 70%

UNDERGRADUATE STUDENT BODY STATS

2005-2006 enrollment: 1,311 full-time; 30 part-time. Men: 48%; women: 52%. **Ethnic makeup:** African American: 11%; American-Indian: 1%; Asian American: 1%; Hispanic: 1%; White: 84%; International: 3%. **Religious preference:** Roman Catholic: 13%; Protestant: 30%; No preference: 18%; Unknown: 1%; Baptist: 32%; Other: 5%.

ADMISSIONS FACTS AND FIGURES

Phone: (800) 755-5550. **Email:** admit@wingate.edu. **Website:** http://www.wingate.edu. **Application deadlines for fall 2007:** Regular decision: Rolling. Early decision: Not offered. Early action: Not offered. Admission can be deferred. **Application fee:** $30. Common application is not accepted. **To apply online, go to:** http://www.ncmentor.org/applications/nc_independents_common_long/apply/wingate.html. **Admissions requirements/recommendations:** High school units required (recommended): English: 4 (4); Mathematics: 3 (3); Science: 2 (2); Foreign language: 2 (2); Social studies: 2 (2); Total units: 14 (13). Tests: The college uses SAT or ACT scores in admissions decisions. Either SAT or ACT required. For admission to the fall 2007 entering class, the school will accept: ACT with writing, ACT without writing. Campus visit: Recommended. Admissions interview: Recommended. Off-campus interview: May be arranged. **Factors that count in admissions decisions:** *Academic:* Secondary school record: Very important. Class rank: Very important. Letters of recommendation: Important. Standardized test scores: Very important. Essay: Important. *Nonacademic:* Interview: Not considered. Extracurricular activities: Considered. Talent/ability: Considered. Character/personal qualities: Considered. Alumni/ae relationship: Not considered. Geographical residence: Not considered. State residency: Not considered. Religious affiliation/commitment: Not considered. Minority status: Not considered. Volunteer work: Not considered. Work experience: Not considered. **Other schools with the greatest overlap in applicants:** Campbell University; Elon University; Gardner-Webb University; High Point University; University of North Carolina–Charlotte. **Admissions statistics for the fall 2005 entering class:** Total applicants: 1,247. Total accepted: 1,050. Freshmen enrolled: 371; 45% were from out of state. Overall acceptance rate: 84%. **Credentials of fall 2005 freshmen:** 19% ranked in the top 10 percent of their high school class; 41% were in the top 25 percent, and 72% were in the top half. (Proportion submitting class standing: 75%.) **Average high school grade point average:**

3.3. First-year students who submitted SAT scores: 90%. Scores (25/75 percentile): Verbal: 450-560, Math: 460-580, Combined: 910-1140. **First-year students submitting ACT scores:** 9%. Scores (25/75 percentile): English: N/A, Math: N/A, Composite: 18-24.

ACADEMICS

Year founded: 1896. **Academic calendar:** Semester. **Degrees offered:** bachelor's, master's, first professional. **Most popular majors:** 21% business, management, marketing, and related support services, 12% communication, journalism, and related programs, 11% education, 11% parks, recreation, leisure, and fitness studies, 9% biological and biomedical sciences. **Major fields of study:** biological and biomedical sciences; business, management, marketing, and related support services; communication, journalism, and related programs; computer and information sciences and support services; education; English language and literature/letters; foreign languages, literatures, and linguistics; health professions and related clinical sciences; liberal arts and sciences studies, and humanities; mathematics and statistics; multi/interdisciplinary studies; parks, recreation, leisure, and fitness studies; philosophy and religious studies; physical sciences; psychology; public administration and social service professions; social sciences; visual and performing arts. **Areas of required coursework:** arts/fine arts, humanities, computer literacy, mathematics, English (including composition), philosophy, foreign languages, sciences (biological or physical), history, social science. **Pre-professional programs:** pre-law, pre-dentistry, pre-medicine, pre-veterinary science, pre-pharmacy. **Special academic programs:** cross-registration, double major, dual enrollment, honors program, independent study, internships, study abroad, teacher certificate program (6%). **Teacher certification offered in:** early childhood, elementary, middle/junior high. **Reserve Officers Training Corps (ROTC):** Army ROTC: Offered at cooperating institution (University of North Carolina–Charlotte); Air Force ROTC: Offered at cooperating institution (University of North Carolina–Charlotte). **Faculty and instruction (2005-2006):** Total instructional faculty: 99 full-time, 53 part-time (61% men; 39% women; 7% minorities). Full-time faculty with Ph.D. or other terminal degree: 94%. Student/faculty ratio: 14/1. Classes of fewer than 20 students: 50%; of 20 to 49 students: 50%; of 50 or more students: 1%. **Advanced Placement and International Baccalaureate credit:** AP tests may be used for: Credit and/or placement. Scores accepted: 3, 4, 5. International Baccalaureate exams may be used for: Credit only. **Freshmen returning for sophomore year:** 71%. **Graduation rates:** Four-year: 34%; five-year: 50%; six-year: 48%. **Graduate study:** 15% of students pursue further study immediately upon graduation; 20% within one year; 25% within five years. Fields in which graduates pursue further study: Master of Business Administration (MBA), 5%; law, 1%; medicine, 1%; theology (or the seminary), 5%; education, 5%; arts and sciences, 5%.

COSTS AND FINANCIAL AID

Financial aid office: (704) 233-8209. **Expenses (2006-2007):** Tuition and fees 2006-2007: $17,650; room/board: $6,750. Estimated books and supplies: $1,000; transportation: $650; personal expenses: $950. **Financial aid:** Priority filing date for institution's financial aid form: May 1. In 2005-2006, 75% of undergraduates applied for financial aid. Of those, 63% were determined to have financial need; 26% had their need fully met. Average financial aid package (proportion receiving): $12,528 (63%). Average amount of gift aid, such as scholarships or grants (proportion receiving): $2,971 (51%). Average amount of self-help aid, such as work study or loans (proportion receiving): $2,187 (45%). Average need-based loan (excluding PLUS or other private loans): $3,966. Among students who received need-based aid, the average percentage of need met: 76%. Among students who received aid based on merit, the average award (and the proportion receiving): $4,955 (29%). The average athletic scholarship (and the proportion receiving): $6,528 (9%). Average amount of debt of borrowers graduating in 2005: $18,759. Proportion who borrowed: 70%.

CAMPUS LIFE AND EXTRACURRICULAR ACTIVITIES

Campus housing available (% using): women's dorms (21%), men's dorms (22%), fraternity housing, apartments for married students, apartment for single students (57%). Students who live in college-owned, operated, or affiliated housing: 81%. **Student employment:** During the 2005-2006 academic year, 25% of undergraduates worked on campus. Average per-year earnings: $700. **Clubs and organizations:** Number of student organizations: 57. Activities include: choral groups, drama/theater, jazz band, literary magazine, music ensembles, pep band, student government, student newspaper, television station, yearbook. Number of fraternities: 4; sororities: 4. Proportion of men in fraternities: 9%; of women in sororities: 10%. Average proportion of students who stay on campus on weekends: 60%. **Sports program (2005-2006):** Member of NCAA II. *Men's intercollegiate var-*

sity sports: baseball, basketball, cheerleading, cross-country, football, golf, lacrosse, soccer, tennis. *Women's intercollegiate varsity sports:* basketball, cross-country, golf, soccer, softball, swimming and diving, tennis, volleyball.

SERVICES AND FACILITIES

Basic services: nonremedial tutoring, health service. **Counseling services:** minority student, career, academic, psychological, religious. **For learning-disabled students:** School does not offer a structured program with separate admission and additional fees. Total undergraduates in learning-disabled program or receiving services: 84. **Library:** Number of titles: 107,718; number of current serial subscriptions: 142. **Information technology resources:** Students are not required to lease or own a computer. Number of campus computers available to all students: 118. School has a wireless network. Approximate number of users that can be accommodated: 180. Proportion of college-owned housing units wired for high-speed internet access: 100%. **Campus safety:** Security services offered: 24-hour foot-and-vehicle patrols, 24-hour emergency telephones, lighted pathways/sidewalks, controlled dormitory access (key, security card, etc).

TRANSFER AND INTERNATIONAL STUDENTS

Transfer students: May apply for admission for the following academic terms: Fall, Spring, Summer. Applicants need a minimum number of credits to apply. For fall 2005: Transfer applications received: 168. Transfer applicants offered admission: 111. Transfer applicants enrolled: 62. **International students:** Number of foreign undergraduates: 40 (3% of student body). Number of countries represented: 14. Minimum TOEFL score required: 550 (paper); 213 (computer).

Winston-Salem State University

- **Address:** 601 Martin Luther King Jr. Drive, Winston-Salem, NC 27110
- **Website:** http://www.wssu.edu
- **Public**
- **Enrollment:** 4,631 full-time; 633 part-time

KEY STATS

✔ **U.S News College Ranking:** 35, Comp. Colleges–Bachelor's (South)
✔ **SAT Score (25th/75th percentile):** 810-970
✔ **Tuition:** 2006-2007: $3,108 in state, $11,748 out of state

Selectivity: Less selective	**Room/board:** $5,476
Acceptance rate: 79%	**Average debt:** $10,200
Student/faculty ratio: 18/1	**Proportion who borrowed:** 80%

UNDERGRADUATE STUDENT BODY STATS

2005-2006 enrollment: 4,631 full-time; 633 part-time. Men: 30%; women: 70%. **Ethnic makeup:** African American: 85%; Asian American: 1%; Hispanic: 1%; White: 13%.

ADMISSIONS FACTS AND FIGURES

Phone: (336) 750-2070. **Email:** admissions@wssu.edu. **Website:** http://www.wssu.edu. **Application deadlines for fall 2007:** Regular decision: July 15. Early decision: Not offered. Early action: Not offered. Admission can be deferred. **Application fee:** $30. Common application is accepted. **To apply online, go to:** http://www.wssu.edu/admiss.asp. **Admissions requirements/recommendations:** High school units required (recommended): English: 4; Mathematics: 4; Science: 3; Foreign language: 2; Social studies: 1; History: 1; Total units: 12 (14). Tests: The college uses SAT or ACT scores in admissions decisions. Either SAT or ACT required. For admission to the fall 2007 entering class, the school will accept: ACT with writing. Campus visit: Neither required nor recommended. Admissions interview: Neither required nor recommended. Off-campus interview: Not available. **Factors that count in admissions decisions:** *Academic:* Secondary school record: Very important. Class rank: Important. Letters of recommendation: Considered. Standardized test scores: Very important. Essay: Considered. *Nonacademic:* Interview: Considered. Extracurricular activities: Important. Talent/ability: Considered. Character/personal qualities: Considered. Alumni/ae relationship: Not considered. Geographical residence: Not considered. State residency: Not considered. Religious affiliation/commitment: Not considered. Minority status: Not considered. Volunteer work: Not considered. Work experience: Not considered. **Admissions statistics for the fall 2005 entering class:** Total applicants: 2,889. Total accepted: 2,286. Freshmen enrolled: 1,083; 10% were from out of state. Overall acceptance rate: 79%. **Credentials of fall 2005 freshmen:** 4% ranked in the top 10 percent of their high school class; 19% were in the top 25 percent, and 52% were in the top half. (Proportion submitting class standing: 90%.) **Average high school grade point average:** 2.8. **First-year students who submitted SAT scores:** 78%. Scores (25/75 percentile): Verbal: 400-480, Math: 410-490, Combined: 810-970. **First-year students submitting ACT scores:** 13%. Scores (25/75 percentile): English: N/A, Math: N/A, Composite: N/A.

ACADEMICS
Year founded: 1892. **Academic calendar:** Semester. **Degrees offered:** bachelor's, post-bachelor's certificate, master's. **Most popular majors:** 44% health professions and related clinical sciences, 11% business, management, marketing, and related support services, 7% computer and information sciences and support services, 7% social sciences, 5% psychology. **Major fields of study:** biological and biomedical sciences; business, management, marketing, and related support services; communication, journalism, and related programs; computer and information sciences and support services; education; English language and literature/letters; foreign languages, literatures, and linguistics; health professions and related clinical sciences; history; liberal arts and sciences studies, and humanities; mathematics and statistics; multi/interdisciplinary studies; parks, recreation, leisure, and fitness studies; public administration and social service professions; security and protective services; social sciences; visual and performing arts. **Areas of required coursework:** arts/fine arts, humanities, computer literacy, mathematics, English (including composition), sciences (biological or physical), history, social science. **Pre-professional programs:** pre-dentistry, pre-medicine, pre-pharmacy. **Special academic programs (% participation):** accelerated program (5%), cooperative (work-study plan) program, distance learning (6%), double major (1%), dual enrollment, English as a Second Language (ESL), honors program, independent study, internships, study abroad, teacher certificate program (1%), weekend college. **Teacher certification offered in:** early childhood, special education, elementary, middle/junior high, secondary. **Cooperative education programs:** business. **Reserve Officers Training Corps (ROTC):** Army ROTC: Offered on campus. **Faculty and instruction (2005-2006):** Total instructional faculty: 234 full-time, 153 part-time (45% men; 55% women; 61% minorities). Full-time faculty with Ph.D. or other terminal degree: 68%. Student/faculty ratio: 18/1. Classes of fewer than 20 students: 44%; of 20 to 49 students: 54%; of 50 or more students: 2%. **Advanced Placement and International Baccalaureate credit:** AP tests may be used for: Credit and/or placement. Scores accepted: 3, 4, 5. **Freshmen returning for sophomore year:** 77%. **Graduation rates:** Four-year: 22%; five-year: 43%; six-year: 52%. **Graduate study:** 10% of students pursue further study immediately upon graduation; 15% within one year. Fields in which graduates pursue further study: Master of Business Administration (MBA), 1%; education, 1%; arts and sciences, 1%.

COSTS AND FINANCIAL AID
Financial aid office: (336) 750-3280. **Expenses (2006-2007):** Tuition and fees 2006-2007: $3,108 in state, $11,748 out of state; room/board: $5,476. Estimated books and supplies: $1,000 personal expenses: $2,500. **Financial aid:** Priority filing date for institution's financial aid form: April 1; deadline: May 1. In 2005-2006, 91% of undergraduates applied for financial aid. Of those, 89% were determined to have financial need; 4% had their need fully met. Average financial aid package (proportion receiving): $3,477 (86%). Average amount of gift aid, such as scholarships or grants (proportion receiving): $2,666 (82%). Average amount of self-help aid, such as work study or loans (proportion receiving): $3,663 (78%). Average need-based loan (excluding PLUS or other private loans): $3,501. Among students who received need-based aid, the average percentage of need met: 82%. Among students who received aid based on merit, the average award (and the proportion receiving): $4,099 (2%). The average athletic scholarship (and the proportion receiving): $2,304 (5%). Average amount of debt of borrowers graduating in 2005: $10,200. Proportion who borrowed: 80%.

CAMPUS LIFE AND EXTRACURRICULAR ACTIVITIES
Campus housing available (% using): coed dorms (34%), women's dorms (34%), men's dorms (32%). Students who live in college-owned, operated, or affiliated housing: 32%. **Student employment:** During the 2005-2006 academic year, 8% of undergraduates worked on campus. Clubs **and organizations:** Number of student organizations: 33. Activities include: choral groups, concert band, drama/theater, jazz band, marching band, music ensembles, pep band, radio station, student government, student newspaper, yearbook. Number of fraternities: 4; sororities: 4. Proportion of men in fraternities: 5%; of women in sororities: 5%. Average proportion of students who stay on campus on weekends: 40%. **Sports program (2005-2006):** Member of NCAA II. *Men's intercollegiate varsity sports:* basketball, cross-country, football, golf, tennis, track and field (outdoor). *Women's intercollegiate varsity sports:* basketball, bowling, cross-country, softball, tennis, track and field (outdoor), volleyball.

SERVICES AND FACILITIES
Basic services: nonremedial tutoring, health service, health insurance. **Remedial assistance:** reading, math, writing, study skills. **Counseling services:** career, military, personal, academic, psychological, birth control. **For learning-disabled students:** School does not offer a structured program with separate admission and additional fees. Services include: remedial math, remedial English, reading machines, remedial reading, tape recorders, untimed tests, note-taking services, oral tests, learning center, readers, extended time for tests, tutors. **Information technology resources:** Students are not required to lease or own a computer. Number of campus computers available to all students: 500. School has a wireless network. Approximate number of users that can be accommodated: 5,000. Proportion of college-owned housing units wired for high-speed internet access: 100%. **Campus safety:** Security services offered: 24-hour foot-and-vehicle patrols, late-night transport/escort service, 24-hour emergency telephones, lighted pathways/sidewalks, controlled dormitory access (key, security card, etc).

TRANSFER AND INTERNATIONAL STUDENTS
Transfer students: May apply for admission for the following academic terms: Fall, Spring, Summer. Applicants do not need a minimum number of credits to apply. For fall 2005: Transfer applications received: 708. Transfer applicants offered admission: 708. Transfer applicants enrolled: 452. **International students:** Number of foreign undergraduates: 0. Minimum TOEFL score required: 550 (paper).

North Dakota

Dickinson State University

- **Address:** 291 Campus Drive, Dickinson, ND 58601
- **Website:** http://www.dickinsonstate.com
- **Public**
- **Enrollment:** 1,755 full-time; 761 part-time

KEY STATS

✔ **U.S News College Ranking:** fourth tier, Comp. Coll.–Bachelor's (Midwest)
✔ **ACT Score (25th/75th percentile):** 21
✔ **Tuition:** 2006-2007: $4,471 in state, $10,560 out of state

Selectivity: Selective	**Room/board:** $3,882
Acceptance rate: 95%	**Average debt:** N/A
Student/faculty ratio: 17/1	**Proportion who borrowed:** N/A

UNDERGRADUATE STUDENT BODY STATS

2005-2006 enrollment: 1,755 full-time; 761 part-time. Men: 42%; women: 58%. **Ethnic makeup:** African American: 2%; American-Indian: 2%; Asian American: 1%; Hispanic: 2%; White: 89%; International: 6%. **Religious preference:** Roman Catholic: 50%; Protestant: 40%; Unknown: 10%.

ADMISSIONS FACTS AND FIGURES

Phone: (701) 483-2175. **Email:** dsu.hawks@dsu.nodak.edu. **Website:** http://www.dickinsonstate.com. **Application deadlines for fall 2007:** Regular decision: Rolling. Early decision: Not offered. Early action: Not offered. Admission can be deferred. **Application fee:** $35. Common application is not accepted. **Admissions requirements/recommendations:** High school units required (recommended): English: (4); Mathematics: (3); Science: (3); Social studies: (3); Total units: (13). Tests: The college uses SAT or ACT scores in admissions decisions. ACT required. For admission to the fall 2007 entering class, the school will accept: ACT with writing. Campus visit: Recommended. Admissions interview: Recommended. Off-campus interview: May be arranged. **Factors that count in admissions decisions:** *Academic:* Secondary school record: Important. Class rank: Considered. Letters of recommendation: Not considered. Standardized test scores: Very important. Essay: Considered. *Nonacademic:* Interview: Not considered. Extracurricular activities: Not considered. Talent/ability: Not considered. Character/personal qualities: Not considered. Alumni/ae relationship: Not considered. Geographical residence: Not considered. State residency: Not considered. Religious affiliation/commitment: Not considered. Minority status: Not considered. Volunteer work: Not considered. Work experience: Not considered. **Other schools with the greatest overlap in applicants:** Black Hills State University; Dakota State University; Mayville State University; Minot State University; Montana State University–Billings. **Admissions statistics for the fall 2005 entering class:** Total applicants: 586. Total accepted: 555. Freshmen enrolled: 376; Overall acceptance rate: 95%. **First-year students submitting ACT scores:** 77%. Scores (25/75 percentile): English: N/A, Math: N/A, Composite: N/A.

ACADEMICS

Year founded: 1918. **Academic calendar:** Semester. **Degrees offered:** certificate, associate, bachelor's. **Most popular majors:** 25% business, management, marketing, and related support services, 22% education, 15% liberal arts and sciences studies, and humanities, 7% agriculture, agriculture operations, and related sciences, 6% health professions and related clinical sciences. **Major fields of study:** agriculture, agriculture operations, and related sciences; biological and biomedical sciences; business, management, marketing, and related support services; communication, journalism, and related programs; computer and information sciences and support services; education; English language and literature/letters; foreign languages, literatures, and linguistics; health professions and related clinical sciences; history; liberal arts and sciences studies, and humanities; mathematics and statistics; multi/interdisciplinary studies; physical sciences; psychology; social sciences; visual and performing arts. **Areas of required coursework:** arts/fine arts, humanities, computer literacy, mathematics, English (includ-

ing composition), sciences (biological or physical), history, social science, other. **Pre-professional programs:** pre-law, pre-dentistry, pre-medicine, pre-veterinary science, pre-optometry, pre-pharmacy. **Special academic programs (% participation):** accelerated program (10%), cooperative (work-study plan) program (20%), cross-registration (10%), distance learning (40%), double major, dual enrollment, honors program (5%), independent study (40%), internships, liberal arts/career combination (40%), student-designed major, study abroad (5%), teacher certificate program (30%), other. **Teacher certification offered in:** early childhood, elementary, vo-tech, middle/junior high, secondary. **Cooperative education programs:** agriculture, business, computer science, health professions, natural science, social/behavioral science. **Faculty and instruction (2005-2006):** Total instructional faculty: 90 full-time, 86 part-time (47% men; 53% women; 3% minorities). Full-time faculty with Ph.D. or other terminal degree: 51%. Student/faculty ratio: 17/1. Classes of fewer than 20 students: 55%; of 20 to 49 students: 42%; of 50 or more students: 3%. **Freshmen returning for sophomore year:** 66%. **Graduation rates:** Four-year: 12%; five-year: 25%; six-year: 25%. **Graduate study:** 14% of students pursue further study immediately upon graduation; 3% within one year. Fields in which graduates pursue further study: Master of Business Administration (MBA), 20%; law, 2%; medicine, 1%; dentistry, 2%; education, 6%; arts and sciences, 30%.

COSTS AND FINANCIAL AID

Financial aid office: (701) 483-2371. **Expenses (2006-2007):** Tuition and fees 2006-2007: $4,471 in state, $10,560 out of state; room/board: $3,882. Estimated books and supplies: $800; transportation: $1,485; personal expenses: $1,485. **Financial aid:** Priority filing date for institution's financial aid form: March 15.

CAMPUS LIFE AND EXTRACURRICULAR ACTIVITIES

Campus housing available (% using): coed dorms (29%), women's dorms (26%), men's dorms (18%), apartments for married students (1%), apartment for single students (25%), other housing options (1%). Students who live in college-owned, operated, or affiliated housing: 22%. **Student employment:** During the 2005-2006 academic year, 9% of undergraduates worked on campus. Average per-year earnings: $1,500. **Clubs and organizations:** Number of student organizations: 46. Activities include: choral groups, concert band, dance, drama/theater, jazz band, literary magazine, marching band, music ensembles, musical theater, pep band, student government, student newspaper, student film society. Number of fraternities: 0; sororities: 0. Average proportion of students who stay on campus on weekends: 40%. **Sports program (2005-2006):** Member of NAIA. *Men's intercollegiate varsity sports:* baseball, basketball, cross-country, football, golf, track and field (indoor), track and field (outdoor), wrestling. *Women's intercollegiate varsity sports:* basketball, cross-country, golf, softball, track and field (indoor), track and field (outdoor), volleyball.

SERVICES AND FACILITIES

Basic services: nonremedial tutoring, placement service, health service, health insurance. **Remedial assistance:** math, writing, study skills, other. **Counseling services:** minority student, career, military, personal, veteran student, academic, older student. **For learning-disabled students:** School does not offer a structured program with separate admission and additional fees. Total undergraduates in learning-disabled program or receiving services: 76. Services include: remedial math, remedial English, tape recorders, untimed tests, note-taking services, oral tests, learning center, readers, extended time for tests, tutors, early syllabus, priority registration, priority seating, proofreading services, texts on tape, typist/scribe, exams on tape or computer, other testing accomodations, other. **Library:** Number of titles: 162,751; number of current serial subscriptions: 18,000. **Information technology resources:** Students are not required to lease or own a computer. Number of campus computers available to all students: 200. School has a wireless network. Approximate number of users that can be accommodated: 300. Proportion of college-owned housing units wired for high-speed internet access: 100%. **Campus safety:** Security services offered: 24-hour foot-and-vehicle patrols, lighted pathways/sidewalks, controlled dormitory access (key, security card, etc).

TRANSFER AND INTERNATIONAL STUDENTS

Transfer students: May apply for admission for the following academic terms: Fall, Spring, Summer. Applicants need a minimum number of credits to apply. For fall 2005: Transfer applications received: 344. Transfer applicants offered admission: 324. Transfer applicants enrolled: 254. **International students:** Number of foreign undergraduates: 143 (6% of student body). Number of countries represented: 28. Minimum TOEFL score required: 525 (paper); 195 (computer). Average TOEFL score: 540 (paper).

Jamestown College

- **Address:** 6086 College Lane, Jamestown, ND 58405
- **Website:** http://www.jc.edu
- **Private; Religious affiliation:** Presbyterian
- **Enrollment:** 960 full-time; 66 part-time

KEY STATS

- ✔ **U.S News College Ranking:** third tier, Comp. Col.–Bachelor's (Midwest)
- ✔ **ACT Score (25th/75th percentile):** 19-25
- ✔ **Tuition:** 2006-2007: $10,550

Selectivity: Selective	**Room/board:** $4,340
Acceptance rate: 88%	**Average debt:** $21,131
Student/faculty ratio: 15/1	**Proportion who borrowed:** 95%

UNDERGRADUATE STUDENT BODY STATS

2005-2006 enrollment: 960 full-time; 66 part-time. Men: 44%; women: 56%. **Ethnic makeup:** African American: 1%; American-Indian: 1%; Asian American: 1%; Hispanic: 1%; White: 92%; International: 4%. **Religious preference:** Roman Catholic: 22%; Protestant: 54%; Unknown: 20%; Presbyterian: 4%.

ADMISSIONS FACTS AND FIGURES

Phone: (701) 252-3467. **Email:** admissions@jc.edu. **Website:** http://www.jc.edu. **Application deadlines for fall 2007:** Regular decision: Rolling. Early decision: Not offered. Early action: Not offered. Admission can be deferred. **Application fee:** $20. Common application is accepted. **Admissions requirements/recommendations:** High school units required (recommended): English: 4 (4); Mathematics: 3 (3); Science: 4 (4); Foreign language: 2 (2); Social studies: 3 (3). Tests: The college uses SAT or ACT scores in admissions decisions. Either SAT or ACT required. For admission to the fall 2007 entering class, the school will accept: ACT without writing. Campus visit: Recommended. Admissions interview: Neither required nor recommended. Off-campus interview: May be arranged. **Factors that count in admissions decisions:** *Academic:* Secondary school record: Very important. Class rank: Considered. Letters of recommendation: Considered. Standardized test scores: Very important. Essay: Not considered. *Nonacademic:* Interview: Considered. Extracurricular activities: Considered. Talent/ability: Considered. Character/personal qualities: Considered. Alumni/ae relationship: Considered. Geographical residence: Not considered. State residency: Not considered. Religious affiliation/commitment: Not considered. Minority status: Not considered. Volunteer work: Considered. Work experience: Considered. **Other schools with the greatest overlap in applicants:** Concordia College–Moorhead; Minnesota State University–Moorhead; North Dakota State University; University of Mary; University of North Dakota. **Admissions statistics for the fall 2005 entering class:** Total applicants: 1,026. Total accepted: 903. Freshmen enrolled: 286; 52% were from out of state. Overall acceptance rate: 88%. **Credentials of fall 2005 freshmen:** 16% ranked in the top 10 percent of their high school class; 40% were in the top 25 percent, and 69% were in the top half. (Proportion submitting class standing: 85%.) **Average high school grade point average:** 3.3. **First-year students who submitted SAT scores:** 8%. Scores (25/75 percentile): Verbal: N/A, Math: N/A, Combined: N/A. **First-year students submitting ACT scores:** 92%. Scores (25/75 percentile): English: N/A, Math: N/A, Composite: 19-25.

ACADEMICS

Year founded: 1884. **Academic calendar:** Semester. **Degrees offered:** bachelor's. **Most popular majors:** 15% business administration and management, 13% elementary education and teaching, 13% nursing, 7% biology, 6% history. **Major fields of study:** biological and biomedical sciences; business, management, marketing, and related support services; communication, journalism, and related programs; computer and information sciences and

support services; education; English language and literature/letters; foreign languages, literatures, and linguistics; health professions and related clinical sciences; history; mathematics and statistics; philosophy and religious studies; physical sciences; psychology; security and protective services; social sciences; visual and performing arts. **Areas of required coursework:** arts/fine arts, humanities, computer literacy, mathematics, English (including composition), philosophy, foreign languages, sciences (biological or physical), history, social science. **Pre-professional programs:** pre-dentistry, pre-medicine, pre-veterinary science, pre-optometry, pre-pharmacy. **Special academic programs (% participation):** cooperative (work-study plan) program (6%), double major (19%), dual enrollment (0%), honors program (1%), independent study (5%), internships (19%), student-designed major (0%), teacher certificate program (19%). **Teacher certification offered in:** early childhood, elementary, middle/junior high, secondary. **Cooperative education programs:** art, business, computer science, education, humanities, natural science. **Faculty and instruction (2005-2006):** Total instructional faculty: 56 full-time, 20 part-time (51% men; 49% women; 4% minorities). Full-time faculty with Ph.D. or other terminal degree: 50%. Student/faculty ratio: 15/1. Classes of fewer than 20 students: 51%; of 20 to 49 students: 47%; of 50 or more students: 2%. **Advanced Placement and International Baccalaureate credit:** International Baccalaureate exams may be used for: Credit and/or placement. **Freshmen returning for sophomore year:** 71%. **Graduation rates:** Four-year: 34%; five-year: 42%; six-year: 52%. **Graduate study:** 15% of students pursue further study immediately upon graduation. Fields in which graduates pursue further study: Master of Business Administration (MBA), 1%; law, 1%; medicine, 3%; dentistry, 1%; engineering, 1%; theology (or the seminary), 1%; education, 1%; arts and sciences, 2%.

COSTS AND FINANCIAL AID

Financial aid office: (701) 252-3467. **Expenses (2006-2007):** Tuition and fees 2006-2007: $10,550; room/board: $4,340. Estimated books and supplies: $1,000; transportation: $1,500; personal expenses: $1,300. **Financial aid:** In 2005-2006, 100% of undergraduates applied for financial aid. Of those, 81% were determined to have financial need; 20% had their need fully met. Average financial aid package (proportion receiving): $8,094 (81%). Average amount of gift aid, such as scholarships or grants (proportion receiving): $4,844 (81%). Average amount of self-help aid, such as work study or loans (proportion receiving): $4,153 (64%). Average need-based loan (excluding PLUS or other private loans): $3,848. Among students who received need-based aid, the average percentage of need met: 65%. Among students who received aid based on merit, the average award (and the proportion receiving): $7,821 (19%). The average athletic scholarship (and the proportion receiving): $1,547 (11%). Average amount of debt of borrowers graduating in 2005: $21,131. Proportion who borrowed: 95%.

CAMPUS LIFE AND EXTRACURRICULAR ACTIVITIES

Campus housing available (% using): coed dorms (100%). Students who live in college-owned, operated, or affiliated housing: 61%. **Clubs and organizations:** Number of student organizations: 33. Activities include: choral groups, concert band, dance, drama/theater, jazz band, music ensembles, musical theater, pep band, student government, student newspaper, yearbook. Number of fraternities: 0; sororities: 0. Average proportion of students who stay on campus on weekends: 60%. **Sports program (2005-2006):** Member of NAIA. *Men's intercollegiate varsity sports:* baseball, basketball, cross-country, football, golf, track and field (indoor), track and field (outdoor), wrestling. *Women's intercollegiate varsity sports:* basketball, cross-country, golf, soccer, softball, track and field (indoor), track and field (outdoor), volleyball.

SERVICES AND FACILITIES

Basic services: nonremedial tutoring. **Remedial assistance:** writing, study skills. **Counseling services:** career, personal, academic, psychological, religious. **For learning-disabled students:** School does not offer a structured program with separate admission and additional fees. Total undergraduates in learning-disabled program or receiving services: 5. Services include: remedial math, untimed tests, note-taking services, oral tests, learning-center, readers, extended time for tests, tutors. **Library:** Number of titles: 111,731; number of current serial subscriptions: 624. **Information technology resources:** Students are not required to lease or own a computer. Number of campus computers available to all students: 430. School has a wireless network. Approximate number of users that can be accommodated: 1,000. Proportion of college-owned housing units wired for high-speed internet access: 100%. **Campus safety:** Security services offered: late-night transport/escort service, lighted pathways/sidewalks, controlled dormitory access (key, security card, etc).

Transfer students: May apply for admission for the following academic terms: Fall, Spring, Summer. Applicants do not need a minimum number of credits to apply. For fall 2005: Transfer applications received: 146. Transfer applicants offered admission: 139. Transfer applicants enrolled: 57. **International students:** Number of foreign undergraduates: 36 (4% of student body). Number of countries represented: 9. Minimum TOEFL score required: 525 (paper); 197 (computer).

Mayville State University

- **Address:** 330 Third Street NE, Mayville, ND 58257
- **Website:** http://www.mayvillestate.edu
- **Public**
- **Enrollment:** 625 full-time; 287 part-time

KEY STATS
✔ **U.S News College Ranking:** fourth tier, Comp. Coll.–Bachelor's (Midwest)
✔ **ACT Score (25th/75th percentile):** 17-22
✔ **Tuition:** 2006-2007: $5,257 in state, $11,291 out of state

Selectivity: Less selective	**Room/board:** $3,884
Acceptance rate: 68%	**Average debt:** N/A
Student/faculty ratio: 15/1	**Proportion who borrowed:** N/A

UNDERGRADUATE STUDENT BODY STATS
2005-2006 enrollment: 625 full-time; 287 part-time. Men: 46%; women: 54%. **Ethnic makeup:** African American: 3%; American-Indian: 3%; Hispanic: 2%; White: 86%; International: 6%.

ADMISSIONS FACTS AND FIGURES
Phone: (701) 788-5222. **Email:** admit@mayvillestate.edu. **Website:** http://www.mayvillestate.edu. **Application deadlines for fall 2007:** Regular decision: Rolling. Early decision: Not offered. Early action: Not offered. Admission can be deferred. **Application fee:** $35. Common application is not accepted. **Admissions requirements/recommendations:** High school units required (recommended): English: 4; Mathematics: 3; Science: 3; Foreign language: (2); Social studies: 3; Total units: 17. Tests: The college uses SAT or ACT scores in admissions decisions. Either SAT or ACT required. For admission to the fall 2007 entering class, the school will accept: ACT with writing, ACT without writing. Campus visit: Neither required nor recommended. Admissions interview: Neither required nor recommended. Off-campus interview: May be arranged. **Factors that count in admissions decisions:** *Academic:* Secondary school record: Not considered. Class rank: Not considered. Letters of recommendation: Not considered. Standardized test scores: Important. Essay: Not considered. *Nonacademic:* Interview: Considered. Extracurricular activities: Not considered. Talent/ability: Not considered. Character/personal qualities: Considered. Alumni/ae relationship: Not considered. Geographical residence: Not considered. State residency: Not considered. Religious affiliation/commitment: Not considered. Minority status: Not considered. Volunteer work: Not considered. Work experience: Not considered. **Other schools with the greatest overlap in applicants:** Minnesota State University–Moorhead; North Dakota State University; University of Minnesota–Crookston; University of North Dakota; Valley City State University. **Admissions statistics for the fall 2005 entering class:** Total applicants: 307. Total accepted: 208. Freshmen enrolled: 145; 35% were from out of state. Overall acceptance rate: 68%. **Credentials of fall 2005 freshmen:** 35% were in the top 25 percent, and 64% were in the top half. (Proportion submitting class standing: 81%.) **Average high school grade point average:** 2.9. **First-year students submitting ACT scores:** 81%. Scores (25/75 percentile): English: 15-21, Math: 17-22, Composite: 17-22.

ACADEMICS
Year founded: 1889. **Academic calendar:** Semester. **Degrees offered:** associate, bachelor's. **Most popular majors:** 29% elementary education and teaching, 23% business administration and management, 9% computer and information sciences, 7% health and physical education, 6% child care provider/assistant. **Major fields of study:** biological and biomedical sciences; business, management, marketing, and related support services; computer and information sciences and support services; education; English language and literature/letters; family and consumer sciences/human sciences; liberal arts and sciences studies, and humanities; mathematics and statistics; parks, recreation, leisure, and fitness studies; physical sciences; psychology; social sciences. **Areas of required coursework:** arts/fine arts, humanities, computer literacy, mathematics, English (including composition), sciences (biological or physical), history, social science, other. **Pre-professional programs:** pre-law, pre-dentistry, pre-medicine, pre-veterinary science, pre-optometry, pre-pharmacy, other. **Special academic programs:** accelerated program, cooperative (work-study plan) program, distance learning, double major, dual enrollment, honors program, internships, student-designed major, teacher certificate program. **Teacher certification offered in:** early childhood, elementary, middle/junior high, secondary. **Cooperative education programs:** business, computer science, education, natural science, social/behavioral science. **Reserve Officers Training Corps (ROTC):** Air Force ROTC: Offered at cooperating institution (North Dakota State University). **Faculty and instruction (2005-2006):** Total instructional faculty: 37 full-time, 37 part-time (54% men; 46% women; 4% minorities). Full-time faculty with Ph.D. or other terminal degree: 51%. Student/faculty ratio: 15/1. Classes of fewer than 20 students: 59%; of 20 to 49 students: 41%; of 50 or more students: 0%. **Advanced Placement and International Baccalaureate credit:** AP tests may be used for: Credit only. Scores accepted: 3, 4, 5. **Freshmen returning for sophomore year:** 57%. **Graduation rates:** Four-year: 31%; five-year: 40%; six-year: 38%. **Graduate study:** 6% of students pursue further study immediately upon graduation; 6% within one year. Fields in which graduates pursue further study: Master of Business Administration (MBA), 1%; medicine, 1%; education, 2%; arts and sciences, 2%.

COSTS AND FINANCIAL AID
Financial aid office: (701) 788-4767. **Expenses (2006-2007):** Tuition and fees 2006-2007: $5,257 in state, $11,291 out of state; room/board: $3,884. **Financial aid:** Priority filing date for institution's financial aid form: March 15. In 2005-2006, 80% of undergraduates applied for financial aid. Of those, 60% were determined to have financial need; 56% had their need fully met. Average financial aid package (proportion receiving): $7,420 (60%). Average amount of gift aid, such as scholarships or grants (proportion receiving): $3,433 (34%). Average amount of self-help aid, such as work study or loans (proportion receiving): $3,667 (14%). Average need-based loan (excluding PLUS or other private loans): $4,374. Among students who received need-based aid, the average percentage of need met: 86%. Among students who received aid based on merit, the average award (and the proportion receiving): N/A (2%).

CAMPUS LIFE AND EXTRACURRICULAR ACTIVITIES
Campus housing available (% using): coed dorms (13%), women's dorms (41%), men's dorms (43%), apartments for married students, apartment for single students (3%). Students who live in college-owned, operated, or affiliated housing: 30%. **Student employment:** During the 2005-2006 academic year, 40% of undergraduates worked on campus. Average per-year earnings: $1,200. **Clubs and organizations:** Number of student organizations: 18. Activities include: choral groups, drama/theater, literary magazine, music ensembles, musical theater, pep band, student government, student newspaper, student film society. Number of fraternities: 0; sororities: 0. Average proportion of students who stay on campus on weekends: 25%. **Sports program (2005-2006):** Member of NAIA. *Men's intercollegiate varsity sports:* baseball, basketball, football, soccer. *Women's intercollegiate varsity sports:* basketball, soccer, softball, volleyball.

SERVICES AND FACILITIES
Basic services: nonremedial tutoring, placement service, day care, health service, health insurance. **Remedial assistance:** math, writing, study skills. **Counseling services:** career, personal, veteran student, academic. **For learning-disabled students:** School does not offer a structured program with separate admission and additional fees. Total undergraduates in learning-disabled program or receiving services: 27. Services include: remedial math, remedial English, tape recorders, untimed tests, note-taking services, oral tests, learning center, readers, extended time for tests, tutors, texts on tape. **Library:** Number of titles: 93,685; number of current serial subscriptions: 424. **Information technology resources:** Students are required to lease or own a computer. Number of campus computers available to all students: 750. School has a wireless network. Proportion of college-owned housing units wired for high-speed internet access: 100%. **Campus safety:** Security services offered: lighted pathways/sidewalks, controlled dormitory access (key, security card, etc).

TRANSFER AND INTERNATIONAL STUDENTS
Transfer students: May apply for admission for the following academic terms: Fall, Spring, Summer. Applicants do not need a minimum number of credits to apply. For fall 2005: Transfer applications received: 202. Transfer applicants offered admission: 185. Transfer applicants enrolled:

143. **International students:** Number of foreign undergraduates: 55 (6% of student body). Number of countries represented: 12. Minimum TOEFL score required: 525 (paper); 195 (computer).

Minot State University

- ■ **Address:** 500 University Avenue W, Minot, ND 58707
- ■ **Website:** http://www.minotstateu.edu
- ■ **Public**
- ■ **Enrollment:** 2,473 full-time; 1,074 part-time

KEY STATS

✔ **U.S News College Ranking:** fourth tier, Universities–Master's (Midwest)
✔ **ACT Score (25th/75th percentile):** 21
✔ **Tuition:** 2006-2007: $4,492 in state, $10,818 out of state
  Selectivity: Less selective   **Room/board:** $5,294
  Acceptance rate: 92%   **Average debt:** $15,900
  Student/faculty ratio: 15/1   **Proportion who borrowed:** 97%

UNDERGRADUATE STUDENT BODY STATS

2005-2006 enrollment: 2,473 full-time; 1,074 part-time. Men: 37%; women: 63%. **Ethnic makeup:** African American: 2%; American-Indian: 3%; Asian American: 1%; Hispanic: 2%; White: 85%; International: 6%.

ADMISSIONS FACTS AND FIGURES

Phone: (701) 858-3350. **Email:** askmsu@minotstateu.edu. **Website:** http://www.minotstateu.edu. **Application deadlines for fall 2007:** Regular decision: Rolling. Early decision: Not offered. Early action: Not offered. Admission can be deferred. **Application fee:** $35. Common application is not accepted. **To apply online, go to:** http://www.rdb.und.nodak.edu/www_ea/plsql/ea_home. **Admissions requirements/recommendations:** High school units required (recommended): English: 4; Mathematics: 3; Science: 3; Social studies: 3; Total units: 13. **Tests:** The college uses SAT or ACT scores in admissions decisions. Either SAT or ACT required. For admission to the fall 2007 entering class, the school will accept: ACT with writing. Campus visit: Recommended. Admissions interview: Neither required nor recommended. Off-campus interview: May be arranged. **Factors that count in admissions decisions:** *Academic:* Secondary school record: Very important. Class rank: Considered. Letters of recommendation: Considered. Standardized test scores: Very important. Essay: Not considered. *Nonacademic:* Interview: Considered. Extracurricular activities: Considered. Talent/ability: Considered. Character/personal qualities: Considered. Alumni/ae relationship: Considered. Geographical residence: Considered. State residency: Considered. Religious affiliation/commitment: Not considered. Minority status: Considered. Volunteer work: Considered. Work experience: Considered. **Other schools with the greatest overlap in applicants:** North Dakota State University; University of North Dakota. **Admissions statistics for the fall 2005 entering class:** Total applicants: 671. Total accepted: 616. Freshmen enrolled: 471; Overall acceptance rate: 92%. **Size of waiting list:** N/A applicants; enrolled from waiting list: 0.

ACADEMICS

Year founded: 1913. **Academic calendar:** Semester. **Degrees offered:** certificate, bachelor's, post-bachelor's certificate, master's. **Most popular majors:** 13% elementary education and teaching, 10% nursing/registered nurse training (R.N., A.S.N., B.S.N., M.S.N.), 9% business administration and management, 9% criminal justice/safety studies, 5% accounting. **Major fields of study:** biological and biomedical sciences; business, management, marketing, and related support services; communication, journalism, and related programs; communications technologies/technicians and support services; computer and information sciences and support services; education; English language and literature/letters; foreign languages, literatures, and linguistics; health professions and related clinical sciences; history; liberal arts and sciences studies, and humanities; parks, recreation, leisure, and fitness studies; physical sciences; psychology; public administration and social service professions; security and protective services; social sciences; visual and performing arts. **Areas of required coursework:** humanities, mathematics, English (including composition), sciences (biological or physical), history, social science, other. **Pre-professional programs:** pre-law, pre-dentistry, pre-medicine, pre-veterinary science, pre-optometry, pre-pharmacy. **Special academic programs (% participation):** distance learning, double major (10%), dual enrollment, honors program (1%), independ-

ent study (5%), internships (53%), student-designed major (5%), study abroad (3%), teacher certificate program (19%). **Teacher certification offered in:** early childhood, special education, elementary, middle/junior high, secondary. **Cooperative education programs:** business, education, health professions. **Faculty and instruction (2005-2006):** Total instructional faculty: 172 full-time, 101 part-time (48% men; 52% women). Student/faculty ratio: 15/1. Classes of fewer than 20 students: 62%; of 20 to 49 students: 35%; of 50 or more students: 3%. **Advanced Placement and International Baccalaureate credit:** International Baccalaureate exams may be used for: Credit and/or placement. **Freshmen returning for sophomore year:** 61%. **Graduation rates:** Four-year: 10%; five-year: 24%; six-year: 32%. **Graduate study:** 17% of students pursue further study within one year. Fields in which graduates pursue further study: law, 2%; medicine, 2%; theology (or the seminary), 1%; education, 8%; arts and sciences, 64%; veterinary medicine, 1%.

COSTS AND FINANCIAL AID

Financial aid office: (701) 858-3375. **Expenses (2006-2007):** Tuition and fees 2006-2007: $4,492 in state, $10,818 out of state; room/board: $5,294. Estimated books and supplies: $800 personal expenses: $2,900. **Financial aid:** Priority filing date for institution's financial aid form: March 15. In 2005-2006, 91% of undergraduates applied for financial aid. Of those, 81% were determined to have financial need; 97% had their need fully met. Average financial aid package (proportion receiving): $6,658 (81%). Average amount of gift aid, such as scholarships or grants (proportion receiving): $1,812 (64%). Average amount of self-help aid, such as work study or loans (proportion receiving): $2,927 (64%). Average need-based loan (excluding PLUS or other private loans): $2,836. Among students who received need-based aid, the average percentage of need met: 97%. Among students who received aid based on merit, the average award (and the proportion receiving): $620 (10%). The average athletic scholarship (and the proportion receiving): $1,172 (3%). Average amount of debt of borrowers graduating in 2005: $15,900. Proportion who borrowed: 97%.

CAMPUS LIFE AND EXTRACURRICULAR ACTIVITIES

Campus housing available: coed dorms, women's dorms, men's dorms, apartments for married students, apartment for single students, special housing for disabled students. **Student employment:** During the 2005-2006 academic year, 6% of undergraduates worked on campus. Average per-year earnings: $2,000. **Clubs and organizations:** Number of student organizations: 53. Activities include: choral groups, concert band, dance, drama/theater, jazz band, literary magazine, marching band, music ensembles, musical theater, opera, pep band, radio station, student government, student newspaper, symphony orchestra, television station. Number of fraternities: 0; sororities: 0. Average proportion of students who stay on campus on weekends: 10%. **Sports program (2005-2006):** Member of NAIA. *Men's intercollegiate varsity sports:* baseball, basketball, cross-country, football, golf, track and field (indoor), track and field (outdoor). *Women's intercollegiate varsity sports:* basketball, cross-country, golf, softball, track and field (indoor), track and field (outdoor), volleyball.

SERVICES AND FACILITIES

Basic services: nonremedial tutoring, women's center, placement service, health service, health insurance. **Remedial assistance:** math, writing, study skills, other. **Counseling services:** minority student, career, personal, veteran student, academic, older student, psychological, birth control, religious. **For learning-disabled students:** School does not offer a structured program with separate admission and additional fees. Total undergraduates in learning-disabled program or receiving services: 28. Services include: remedial math, reading machines, tape recorders, videotaped classes, untimed tests, note-taking services, oral tests, learning center, readers, extended time for tests, tutors, priority registration, priority seating. **Library:** Number of titles: 428,407; number of current serial subscriptions: 668. **Information technology resources:** Students are not required to lease or own a computer. Number of campus computers available to all students: 700. School has a wireless network. Approximate number of users that can be accommodated: 800. Proportion of college-owned housing units wired for high-speed internet access: 95%. **Campus safety:** Security services offered: 24-hour emergency telephones, lighted pathways/sidewalks, controlled dormitory access (key, security card, etc).

TRANSFER AND INTERNATIONAL STUDENTS

Transfer students: May apply for admission for the following academic terms: Fall, Spring, Summer. Applicants need a minimum number of credits to apply. **International students:** Number of foreign undergraduates: 230 (6% of student body). Number of countries represented: 22. Minimum

TOEFL score required: 525 (paper); 195 (computer). Average TOEFL score: 593 (paper).

North Dakota State University

- **Address:** 1301 12th Avenue N, Fargo, ND 58105-5454
- **Website:** http://www.ndsu.edu
- **Public**
- **Enrollment:** 9,410 full-time; 1,086 part-time

KEY STATS

✔ **U.S News College Ranking:** third tier, National Universities
✔ **ACT Score (25th/75th percentile):** 20-26
✔ **Tuition:** 2006-2007: $5,710 in state, $13,682 out of state
- **Selectivity:** Selective
- **Room/board:** $5,132
- **Acceptance rate:** 84%
- **Average debt:** $20,568
- **Student/faculty ratio:** 19/1
- **Proportion who borrowed:** 70%

UNDERGRADUATE STUDENT BODY STATS

2005-2006 enrollment: 9,410 full-time; 1,086 part-time. Men: 55%; women: 45%. **Ethnic makeup:** African American: 2%; American-Indian: 1%; Asian American: 1%; Hispanic: 1%; White: 94%; International: 1%.

ADMISSIONS FACTS AND FIGURES

Phone: (701) 231-8643. **Email:** NDSU.Admission@ndsu.edu. **Website:** http://www.ndsu.edu. **Application deadlines for fall 2007:** Regular decision: August 15. Early decision: Not offered. Early action: Not offered. Admission can be deferred. **Application fee:** $35. Common application is not accepted. **To apply online, go to:** http://www.ndsu.edu/prospective_students/apply-now/. **Admissions requirements/recommendations:** High school units required (recommended): English: 4 (4); Mathematics: 3 (3); Science: 3 (3); Foreign language: 0•(0); Social studies: 3 (3); History: 0; Academic electives: 0; Total units: 13 (13). Tests: The college uses SAT or ACT scores in admissions decisions. Either SAT or ACT required. For admission to the fall 2007 entering class, the school will accept: ACT with writing, ACT without writing. Campus visit: Recommended. Admissions interview: Recommended. Off-campus interview: May be arranged. **Factors that count in admissions decisions:** *Academic:* Secondary school record: Very important. Class rank: Considered. Letters of recommendation: Considered. Standardized test scores: Very important. Essay: Not considered. *Nonacademic:* Interview: Not considered. Extracurricular activities: Not considered. Talent/ability: Not considered. Character/personal qualities: Not considered. Alumni/ae relationship: Not considered. Geographical residence: Not considered. State residency: Not considered. Religious affiliation/commitment: Not considered. Minority status: Not considered. Volunteer work: Not considered. Work experience: Not considered. **Other schools with the greatest overlap in applicants:** Bemidji State University; South Dakota State University; St. Cloud State University; University of Minnesota–Twin Cities; University of North Dakota. **Admissions statistics for the fall 2005 entering class:** Total applicants: 4,007. Total accepted: 3,346. Freshmen enrolled: 2,021; 52% were from out of state. Overall acceptance rate: 84%. **Credentials of fall 2005 freshmen:** 18% ranked in the top 10 percent of their high school class; 43% were in the top 25 percent, and 75% were in the top half. (Proportion submitting class standing: 86%.) **Average high school grade point average:** 3.4. **First-year students who submitted SAT scores:** 3%. Scores (25/75 percentile): Verbal: N/A, Math: N/A, Combined: N/A. **First-year students submitting ACT scores:** 96%. Scores (25/75 percentile): English: 19-25, Math: 20-26, Composite: 20-26.

ACADEMICS

Year founded: 1890. **Academic calendar:** Semester. **Degrees offered:** certificate, bachelor's, master's, post-master's certificate, first professional, doctorate. **Most popular majors:** 7% business administration and management, 6% civil engineering, 5% mechanical engineering, 5% pharmacy, pharmaceutical sciences, and administration, 4% electrical, electronics, and communications engineering. **Major fields of study:** agriculture, agriculture operations, and related sciences; architecture and related services; area, ethnic, cultural, and gender studies; biological and biomedical sciences; business, management, marketing, and related support services; communication, journalism, and related programs; computer and information sciences and support services; education; engineering; English language and literature/letters; family and consumer sciences/human sciences;

foreign languages, literatures, and linguistics; health professions and related clinical sciences; history; liberal arts and sciences studies, and humanities; mathematics and statistics; multi/interdisciplinary studies; natural resources and conservation; parks, recreation, leisure, and fitness studies; philosophy and religious studies; physical sciences; psychology; security and protective services; social sciences; visual and performing arts. **Areas of required coursework:** arts/fine arts, humanities, computer literacy, mathematics, English (including composition), sciences (biological or physical), social science, other. **Pre-professional programs:** pre-law, pre-dentistry, pre-medicine, pre-veterinary science, pre-optometry, pre-pharmacy, other. **Special academic programs:** cooperative (work-study plan) program, cross-registration, distance learning, double major, dual enrollment, English as a Second Language (ESL), honors program, independent study, internships, student-designed major, study abroad, teacher certificate program, other. **Teacher certification offered in:** secondary. **Cooperative education programs:** agriculture, art, business, computer science, education, engineering, health professions, home economics, humanities, natural science, social/behavioral science, technologies. **Reserve Officers Training Corps (ROTC):** Army ROTC: Offered on campus; Air Force ROTC: Offered on campus. **Faculty and instruction (2005-2006):** Total instructional faculty: 525 full-time, 91 part-time (70% men; 30% women; 0% minorities). Full-time faculty with Ph.D. or other terminal degree: 84%. Student/faculty ratio: 19/1. Classes of fewer than 20 students: 38%; of 20 to 49 students: 47%; of 50 or more students: 15%. **Advanced Placement and International Baccalaureate credit:** AP tests may be used for: Credit and/or placement. Scores accepted: 3, 4, 5. International Baccalaureate exams may be used for: Credit and/or placement. **Freshmen returning for sophomore year:** 76%. **Graduation rates:** Four-year: 19%; five-year: 46%; six-year: 55%. **Graduate study:** 23% of students pursue further study immediately upon graduation; 23% within one year. Fields in which graduates pursue further study: Master of Business Administration (MBA), 2%; law, 3%; medicine, 2%; engineering, 5%; education, 1%; veterinary medicine, 1%.

COSTS AND FINANCIAL AID

Financial aid office: (800) 726-3188. **Expenses (2006-2007):** Tuition and fees 2006-2007: $5,710 in state, $13,682 out of state; room/board: $5,132. Estimated books and supplies: $750; transportation: $921; personal expenses: $1,939. **Financial aid:** Priority filing date for institution's financial aid form: March 15. In 2005-2006, 76% of undergraduates applied for financial aid. Of those, 59% were determined to have financial need; 28% had their need fully met. Average financial aid package (proportion receiving): $4,884 (59%). Average amount of gift aid, such as scholarships or grants (proportion receiving): $3,130 (39%). Average amount of self-help aid, such as work study or loans (proportion receiving): $4,245 (49%). Average need-based loan (excluding PLUS or other private loans): $4,128. Among students who received need-based aid, the average percentage of need met: 67%. Among students who received aid based on merit, the average award (and the proportion receiving): $1,506 (8%). The average athletic scholarship (and the proportion receiving): $4,682 (1%). Average amount of debt of borrowers graduating in 2005: $20,568. Proportion who borrowed: 70%.

CAMPUS LIFE AND EXTRACURRICULAR ACTIVITIES

Campus housing available (% using): coed dorms (38%), women's dorms (26%), men's dorms (20%), apartments for married students (6%), apartment for single students (10%), other housing options. Students who live in college-owned, operated, or affiliated housing: 30%. **Student employment:** During the 2005-2006 academic year, 19% of undergraduates worked on campus. Average per-year earnings: $3,625. **Clubs and organizations:** Number of student organizations: 226. Activities include: choral groups, concert band, drama/theater, jazz band, literary magazine, marching band, music ensembles, musical theater, pep band, radio station, student government, student newspaper. Number of fraternities: 11; sororities: 4. Proportion of men in fraternities: 2%; of women in sororities: 1%. Average proportion of students who stay on campus on weekends: 68%. **Sports program (2005-2006):** Member of NCAA II. *Men's intercollegiate varsity sports:* baseball, basketball, cross-country, football, golf, track and field (indoor), track and field (outdoor), wrestling. *Women's intercollegiate varsity sports:* basketball, cross-country, golf, soccer, softball, track and field (indoor), track and field (outdoor), volleyball.

SERVICES AND FACILITIES

Basic services: nonremedial tutoring, placement service, day care, health service, health insurance. **Remedial assistance:** reading, math, writing, study skills. **Counseling services:** minority student, career, military, personal, veteran student, academic, older student, psychological, religious. **For learning-**

disabled students: School does not offer a structured program with separate admission and additional fees. Total undergraduates in learning-disabled program or receiving services: 90. Services include: remedial math, remedial English, remedial reading, tutors. **Library:** Number of titles: 510,000; number of current serial subscriptions: 18,000. **Information technology resources:** Students are not required to lease or own a computer. Number of campus computers available to all students: 500. School has a wireless network. Approximate number of users that can be accommodated: 1,600. Proportion of college-owned housing units wired for high-speed internet access: 90%. **Campus safety:** Security services offered: late-night transport/escort service, 24-hour emergency telephones, lighted pathways/sidewalks, controlled dormitory access (key, security card, etc).

TRANSFER AND INTERNATIONAL STUDENTS

Transfer students: May apply for admission for the following academic terms: Fall, Spring, Summer. Applicants do not need a minimum number of credits to apply. For fall 2005: Transfer applications received: 1,352. Transfer applicants offered admission: 986. Transfer applicants enrolled: 719. **International students:** Number of foreign undergraduates: 138 (1% of student body). Number of countries represented: 41. Minimum TOEFL score required: 525 (paper); 193 (computer).

University of Mary

- **Address:** 7500 University Drive, Bismarck, ND 58504
- **Website:** http://www.umary.edu
- **Private; Religious affiliation:** Roman Catholic
- **Enrollment:** 2,044 full-time; 153 part-time

KEY STATS
✔ **U.S News College Ranking:** fourth tier, Universities–Master's (Midwest)
✔ **ACT Score (25th/75th percentile):** 20-25
✔ **Tuition:** 2006-2007: $11,374

Selectivity: Selective	**Room/board:** $4,310
Acceptance rate: 86%	**Average debt:** N/A
Student/faculty ratio: 16/1	**Proportion who borrowed:** N/A

UNDERGRADUATE STUDENT BODY STATS

2005-2006 enrollment: 2,044 full-time; 153 part-time. Men: 39%; women: 61%. **Ethnic makeup:** African American: 2%; American-Indian: 4%; Asian American: 1%; Hispanic: 2%; White: 90%; International: 1%. **Religious preference:** Protestant: 34%; No preference: 4%; Unknown: 4%; Roman Catholic: 47%; Other: 11%.

ADMISSIONS FACTS AND FIGURES

Phone: (701) 355-8030. **Email:** marauder@umary.edu. **Website:** http://www.umary.edu. **Application deadlines for fall 2007:** Regular decision: August 23. Early decision: Not offered. Early action: Not offered. Admission can be deferred. **Application fee:** $15. Common application is accepted. **Admissions requirements/recommendations:** High school units required (recommended): English: (4); Mathematics: (3); Science: (3); Social studies: (4); Total units: (14). Tests: The college uses SAT or ACT scores in admissions decisions. Either SAT or ACT required. For admission to the fall 2007 entering class, the school will accept: ACT with writing, ACT without writing. Campus visit: Recommended. Admissions interview: Recommended. Off-campus interview: May be arranged. **Factors that count in admissions decisions:** *Academic:* Secondary school record: Very important. Class rank: Important. Letters of recommendation: Very important. Standardized test scores: Very important. Essay: Not considered. *Nonacademic:* Interview: Considered. Extracurricular activities: Considered. Talent/ability: Important. Character/personal qualities: Important. Alumni/ae relationship: Important. Geographical residence: Not considered. State residency: Not considered. Religious affiliation/commitment: Not considered. Minority status: Not considered. Volunteer work: Considered. Work experience: Considered. **Other schools with the greatest overlap in applicants:** Dickinson State University; Jamestown College; North Dakota State University; University of North Dakota. **Admissions statistics for the fall 2005 entering class:** Total applicants: 1,040. Total accepted: 897. Freshmen enrolled: 392; 45% were from out of state. Overall acceptance rate: 86%. **Credentials of fall 2005 freshmen:** 16% ranked in the top 10 percent of their high school class; 44% were in the top 25 percent, and 80% were in the top half. (Proportion submitting class standing: 94%.) **Average high school grade point average:**

3.3. First-year students who submitted SAT scores: 9%. Scores (25/75 percentile): Verbal: N/A, Math: N/A, Combined: N/A. **First-year students submitting ACT scores:** 91%. Scores (25/75 percentile): English: 19-25, Math: 19-25, Composite: 20-25.

ACADEMICS

Year founded: 1959. **Academic calendar:** Semester. **Degrees offered:** associate, bachelor's, master's, doctorate. **Most popular majors:** 39% business, management, marketing, and related support services, 20% education, 16% health professions and related clinical sciences, 7% liberal arts and sciences studies, and humanities, 5% computer and information sciences and support services. **Major fields of study:** biological and biomedical sciences; business, management, marketing, and related support services; communication, journalism, and related programs; computer and information sciences and support services; education; English language and literature/letters; health professions and related clinical sciences; history; liberal arts and sciences studies, and humanities; mathematics and statistics; parks, recreation, leisure, and fitness studies; philosophy and religious studies; psychology; public administration and social service professions; security and protective services; social sciences; theology and religious vocations; visual and performing arts. **Areas of required coursework:** arts/fine arts, humanities, computer literacy, mathematics, English (including composition), philosophy, sciences (biological or physical), social science, other. **Pre-professional programs:** pre-law, pre-dentistry, pre-medicine, pre-theology, pre-veterinary science, pre-optometry, pre-pharmacy, other. **Special academic programs (% participation):** accelerated program (23%), cooperative (work-study plan) program (5%), distance learning (2%), double major (10%), independent study (30%), internships (30%), liberal arts/career combination (100%), study abroad (1%), teacher certificate program (11%). **Teacher certification offered in:** early childhood, special education, elementary, middle/junior high, secondary. **Cooperative education programs:** business, computer science, education, health professions, natural science, social/behavioral science. **Faculty and instruction (2005-2006):** Total instructional faculty: 100 full-time, 249 part-time (55% men; 45% women; 5% minorities). Full-time faculty with Ph.D. or other terminal degree: 36%. Student/faculty ratio: 16/1. Classes of fewer than 20 students: 63%; of 20 to 49 students: 31%; of 50 or more students: 7%. **Advanced Placement and International Baccalaureate credit:** AP tests may be used for: Credit and/or placement. Scores accepted: 3, 4, 5. International Baccalaureate exams may be used for: Credit only. **Freshmen returning for sophomore year:** 71%. **Graduation rates:** Four-year: 42%; five-year: 55%; six-year: 51%. **Graduate study:** 14% of students pursue further study immediately upon graduation; 25% within one year; 30% within five years. Fields in which graduates pursue further study: Master of Business Administration (MBA), 50%; law, 5%; medicine, 5%; dentistry, 5%; engineering, 1%; theology (or the seminary), 1%; education, 20%; arts and sciences, 12%; veterinary medicine, 1%.

COSTS AND FINANCIAL AID

Financial aid office: (701) 355-8079. **Expenses (2006-2007):** Tuition and fees 2006-2007: $11,374; room/board: $4,310. Estimated books and supplies: $800 personal expenses: $2,250.

CAMPUS LIFE AND EXTRACURRICULAR ACTIVITIES

Campus housing available (% using): women's dorms (44%), men's dorms (32%), apartment for single students (24%), special housing for disabled students. Students who live in college-owned, operated, or affiliated housing: 35%. **Student employment:** During the 2005-2006 academic year, 3% of undergraduates worked on campus. Average per-year earnings: $900. **Clubs and organizations:** Number of student organizations: 21. Activities include: choral groups, concert band, drama/theater, jazz band, literary magazine, music ensembles, musical theater, pep band, radio station, student government, student newspaper, yearbook. Number of fraternities: 0; sororities: 0. Average proportion of students who stay on campus on weekends: 60%. **Sports program (2005-2006):** Member of NAIA. *Men's intercollegiate varsity sports:* baseball, basketball, cross-country, football, golf, soccer, tennis, track and field (indoor), track and field (outdoor), wrestling. *Women's intercollegiate varsity sports:* basketball, cross-country, golf, soccer, softball, tennis, track and field (indoor), track and field (outdoor), volleyball.

SERVICES AND FACILITIES

Basic services: nonremedial tutoring, placement service, health service. **Remedial assistance:** reading, math, writing, study skills. **Counseling services:** minority student, career, personal, veteran student, academic, older student, psychological, birth control, religious. **For learning-disabled students:** School does not offer a structured program with separate admission and additional fees. Total undergraduates in learning-disabled program or receiving services: 17. Services include: remedial math, remedial English, reading machines, remedial reading, tape recorders, other special classes, untimed tests, note-taking services, oral tests, learning center, readers, extended time for tests, tutors, proofreading services, texts on tape, exams on tape or computer, other testing accomodations, other. **Library:** Number of titles: 63,370; number of current serial subscriptions: 475. **Information technology resources:** Students are not required to lease or own a computer. Number of campus computers available to all students: 235. School does not have a wireless network. Proportion of college-owned housing units wired for high-speed internet access: 100%. **Campus safety:** Security services offered: 24-hour foot-and-vehicle patrols, lighted pathways/sidewalks, controlled dormitory access (key, security card, etc).

TRANSFER AND INTERNATIONAL STUDENTS

Transfer students: May apply for admission for the following academic terms: Fall, Spring, Summer. Applicants do not need a minimum number of credits to apply. For fall 2005: Transfer applications received: 498. Transfer applicants offered admission: 408. Transfer applicants enrolled: 203. **International students:** Number of foreign undergraduates: 25 (1% of student body). Number of countries represented: 21. Minimum TOEFL score required: 500 (paper); 175 (computer).

University of North Dakota

- **Address:** University Station, Grand Forks, ND 58202
- **Website:** http://www.und.edu
- **Public**
- **Enrollment:** 9,364 full-time; 1,134 part-time

KEY STATS
✔ **U.S News College Ranking:** third tier, National Universities
✔ **ACT Score (25th/75th percentile):** 21-26
✔ **Tuition:** 2006-2007: $5,792 in state, $13,786 out of state
  Selectivity: Selective   **Room/board:** $5,596
  Acceptance rate: 73%   **Average debt:** $31,086
  Student/faculty ratio: 18/1   **Proportion who borrowed:** 71%

UNDERGRADUATE STUDENT BODY STATS

2005-2006 enrollment: 9,364 full-time; 1,134 part-time. Men: 54%; women: 46%. **Ethnic makeup:** African American: 1%; American-Indian: 3%; Asian American: 1%; Hispanic: 1%; White: 94%. **Religious preference:** Roman Catholic: 33%; Protestant: 47%; Jewish: 1%; No preference: 9%; Unknown: 1%; None: 9%.

ADMISSIONS FACTS AND FIGURES

Phone: (800) 225-5863. **Email:** enrollment_services@mail.und.nodak.edu. **Website:** http://www.und.edu. **Application deadlines for fall 2007:** Regular decision: July 1. Early decision: Not offered. Early action: Not offered. Admission can be deferred. **Application fee:** $35. Common application is not accepted. **To apply online, go to:** http://www.und.edu/enroll/apply.html. **Admissions requirements/recommendations:** High school units required (recommended): English: 4; Mathematics: 3; Science: 3; Foreign language: (1); Social studies: 3; Total units: 13 (1). Tests: The college uses SAT or ACT scores in admissions decisions. Either SAT or ACT required. For admission to the fall 2007 entering class, the school will accept: ACT with writing, ACT without writing. Campus visit: Recommended. Admissions interview: Recommended. Off-campus interview: May be arranged. **Factors that count in admissions decisions: *Academic:*** Secondary school record: Considered. Class rank: Considered. Letters of recommendation: Considered. Standardized test scores: Very important. Essay: Not considered. *Nonacademic:* Interview: Not considered. Extracurricular activities: Not considered. Talent/ability: Not considered. Character/personal qualities: Not considered. Alumni/ae relationship: Not considered. Geographical residence: Not considered. State residency: Not considered. Religious affiliation/commitment: Not considered. Minority status: Not considered. Volunteer work: Not considered. Work experience: Not considered. **Other schools with the greatest overlap in applicants:** Minnesota State University–Moorhead; North Dakota State University; St. Cloud State University; University of Minnesota–Duluth; University of Minnesota–Twin Cities. **Admissions statistics for the fall 2005 entering class:** Total applicants: 3,749. Total accepted: 2,725. Freshmen enrolled: 1,884; 54% were from out of state. Overall acceptance rate: 73%. **Credentials of fall 2005 freshmen:** 16%

ranked in the top 10 percent of their high school class; 41% were in the top 25 percent, and 76% were in the top half. (Proportion submitting class standing: 80%.) **Average high school grade point average:** 3.4. **First-year students submitting ACT scores:** 91%. Scores (25/75 percentile): English: 20-25, Math: 20-26, Composite: 21-26.

ACADEMICS

Year founded: 1883. **Academic calendar:** Semester. **Degrees offered:** certificate, diploma, bachelor's, master's, post-master's certificate, first professional, doctorate. **Most popular majors:** 11% aeronautics/aviation/aerospace science and technology, 5% business/commerce, 5% communication studies/speech communication and rhetoric, 5% elementary education and teaching, 5% nursing/registered nurse training (R.N., A.S.N., B.S.N., M.S.N.). **Major fields of study:** area, ethnic, cultural, and gender studies; biological and biomedical sciences; business, management, marketing, and related support services; communication, journalism, and related programs; computer and information sciences and support services; education; engineering; engineering technologies/technicians; English language and literature/letters; foreign languages, literatures, and linguistics; health professions and related clinical sciences; history; liberal arts and sciences studies, and humanities; mathematics and statistics; multi/interdisciplinary studies; parks, recreation, leisure, and fitness studies; philosophy and religious studies; physical sciences; psychology; public administration and social service professions; security and protective services; social sciences; transportation and materials moving; visual and performing arts. **Areas of required coursework:** arts/fine arts, humanities, English (including composition), sciences (biological or physical), social science. **Pre-professional programs:** pre-law, pre-dentistry, pre-medicine, pre-veterinary science, pre-optometry. **Special academic programs:** accelerated program, cooperative (work-study plan) program, cross-registration, distance learning, double major, dual enrollment, English as a Second Language (ESL), exchange student program (domestic), external degree program, honors program, independent study, internships, liberal arts/career combination, student-designed major, study abroad, teacher certificate program, weekend college. **Teacher certification offered in:** early childhood, special education, elementary, middle/junior high, secondary, bilingual/bicultural. **Cooperative education programs:** art, business, computer science, education, engineering, health professions, home economics, humanities, natural science, social/behavioral science, technologies, vocational arts, other. **Reserve Officers Training Corps (ROTC):** Army ROTC: Offered on campus; Air Force ROTC: Offered on campus. **Faculty and instruction (2005-2006):** Total instructional faculty: 668 full-time, 157 part-time (63% men; 37% women; 13% minorities). Full-time faculty with Ph.D. or other terminal degree: 75%. Student/faculty ratio: 18/1. Classes of fewer than 20 students: 36%; of 20 to 49 students: 54%; of 50 or more students: 10%. **Advanced Placement and International Baccalaureate credit:** AP tests may be used for: Credit only. Scores accepted: 3, 4. International Baccalaureate exams may be used for: Credit only. **Freshmen returning for sophomore year:** 77%. **Graduation rates:** Four-year: 23%; five-year: 49%; six-year: 56%. **Graduate study:** 21% of students pursue further study immediately upon graduation; 28% within one year. Fields in which graduates pursue further study: Master of Business Administration (MBA), 8%; law, 11%; medicine, 18%; dentistry, 4%; engineering, 10%; theology (or the seminary), 2%; education, 16%; arts and sciences, 29%; veterinary medicine, 2%.

COSTS AND FINANCIAL AID

Financial aid office: (701) 777-3121. **Expenses (2006-2007):** Tuition and fees 2006-2007: $5,792 in state, $13,786 out of state; room/board: $5,596. Estimated books and supplies: $800 personal expenses: $2,970. **Financial aid:** Priority filing date for institution's financial aid form: March 15. In 2005-2006, 79% of undergraduates applied for financial aid. Of those, 55% were determined to have financial need; 43% had their need fully met. Average financial aid package (proportion receiving): $8,807 (54%). Average amount of gift aid, such as scholarships or grants (proportion receiving): $3,129 (24%). Average amount of self-help aid, such as work study or loans (proportion receiving): $5,621 (50%). Average need-based loan (excluding PLUS or other private loans): $4,345. Among students who received need-based aid, the average percentage of need met: 86%. Among students who received aid based on merit, the average award (and the proportion receiving): $2,941 (4%). The average athletic scholarship (and the proportion receiving): $4,421 (4%). Average amount of debt of borrowers graduating in 2005: $31,086. Proportion who borrowed: 71%.

CAMPUS LIFE AND EXTRACURRICULAR ACTIVITIES

Campus housing available (% using): coed dorms (9%), women's dorms (8%), men's dorms (9%), sorority housing (2%), fraternity housing (2%), apartments for married students (1%), apartment for single students (5%), special housing for disabled students (1%), other housing options (63%). Students who live in college-owned, operated, or affiliated housing: 29%. **Student employment:** During the 2005-2006 academic year, 22% of undergraduates worked on campus. Average per-year earnings: $4,017. **Clubs and organizations:** Number of student organizations: 230. Activities include: choral groups, concert band, dance, drama/theater, jazz band, literary magazine, marching band, music ensembles, musical theater, pep band, radio station, student government, student newspaper, student film society, symphony orchestra, television station. Number of fraternities: 13; sororities: 7. Proportion of men in fraternities: 10%; of women in sororities: 8%. Average proportion of students who stay on campus on weekends: 16%. **Sports program (2005-2006):** Member of NCAA II. *Men's intercollegiate varsity sports:* baseball, basketball, cross-country, football, golf, ice hockey, swimming and diving, track and field (indoor), track and field (outdoor). *Women's intercollegiate varsity sports:* basketball, cross-country, golf, ice hockey, soccer, softball, swimming and diving, tennis, track and field (indoor), track and field (outdoor), volleyball.

SERVICES AND FACILITIES

Basic services: nonremedial tutoring, women's center, placement service, day care, health service, health insurance, other. **Remedial assistance:** study skills, other. **Counseling services:** minority student, career, military, personal, veteran student, academic, older student, psychological, birth control, other. **For learning-disabled students:** School does not offer a structured program with separate admission and additional fees. **Library:** Number of titles: 1,410,209; number of current serial subscriptions: 15,763. **Information technology resources:** Students are not required to lease or own a computer. Number of campus computers available to all students: 1,100. School has a wireless network. Approximate number of users that can be accommodated: 2,100. Proportion of college-owned housing units wired for high-speed internet access: 100%. **Campus safety:** Security services offered: 24-hour foot-and-vehicle patrols, late-night transport/escort service, 24-hour emergency telephones, lighted pathways/sidewalks, student patrols, controlled dormitory access (key, security card, etc).

TRANSFER AND INTERNATIONAL STUDENTS

Transfer students: May apply for admission for the following academic terms: Fall, Spring, Summer. Applicants do not need a minimum number of credits to apply. For fall 2005: Transfer applications received: 1,311. Transfer applicants offered admission: 1,003. Transfer applicants enrolled: 689. **International students:** Number of countries represented: 32. Minimum TOEFL score required: 525 (paper); 195 (computer). Average TOEFL score: 560 (paper).

Valley City State University

- **Address:** 101 College Street SW, Valley City, ND 58072
- **Website:** http://www.vcsu.edu
- **Public**
- **Enrollment:** 783 full-time; 230 part-time

KEY STATS

✔ **U.S News College Ranking:** third tier, Comp. Coll.–Bachelor's (Midwest)
✔ **ACT Score (25th/75th percentile):** 18-23
✔ **Tuition:** 2006-2007: $5,308 in state, $11,576 out of state

Selectivity: Less selective	**Room/board:** $4,918
Acceptance rate: 94%	**Average debt:** $18,394
Student/faculty ratio: 13/1	**Proportion who borrowed:** 60%

UNDERGRADUATE STUDENT BODY STATS

2005-2006 enrollment: 783 full-time; 230 part-time. Men: 47%; women: 53%. **Ethnic makeup:** African American: 2%; American-Indian: 2%; Hispanic: 1%; White: 89%; International: 5%.

ADMISSIONS FACTS AND FIGURES

Phone: (701) 845-7101. **Email:** enrollment.services@vcsu.edu. **Website:** http://www.vcsu.edu. **Application deadlines for fall 2007:** Regular decision: Rolling. Early decision: Not offered. Early action: Not offered. Admission can be deferred. **Application fee:** $35. Common application is not accepted. **To apply online, go to:** http://www.vcsu.edu/enrollmentservices/. **Admissions requirements/recommendations:** High school units required

(recommended): English: 4; Mathematics: 3; Science: 3; Foreign language: (2); Social studies: 3; Total units: 13 (2). Tests: The college uses SAT or ACT scores in admissions decisions. Either SAT or ACT required. For admission to the fall 2007 entering class, the school will accept: ACT with writing, ACT without writing. Campus visit: Recommended. Admissions interview: Neither required nor recommended. Off-campus interview: Not available. **Factors that count in admissions decisions:** *Academic:* Secondary school record: Very important. Class rank: Considered. Letters of recommendation: Not considered. Standardized test scores: Considered. Essay: Not considered. *Nonacademic:* Interview: Not considered. Extracurricular activities: Not considered. Talent/ability: Not considered. Character/personal qualities: Not considered. Alumni/ae relationship: Not considered. Geographical residence: Not considered. State residency: Not considered. Religious affiliation/commitment: Not considered. Minority status: Not considered. Volunteer work: Not considered. Work experience: Not considered. **Other schools with the greatest overlap in applicants:** Jamestown College; Minnesota State University–Moorhead; North Dakota State University; University of North Dakota. **Admissions statistics for the fall 2005 entering class:** Total applicants: 256. Total accepted: 240. Freshmen enrolled: 176; 40% were from out of state. Overall acceptance rate: 94%. **Credentials of fall 2005 freshmen:** 6% ranked in the top 10 percent of their high school class; 22% were in the top 25 percent, and 53% were in the top half. (Proportion submitting class standing: 97%.) **Average high school grade point average:** 3.0. **First-year students who submitted SAT scores:** 11%. Scores (25/75 percentile): Verbal: 450-580, Math: 450-570, Combined: 900-1150. **First-year students submitting ACT scores:** 88%. Scores (25/75 percentile): English: 16-22, Math: 17-23, Composite: 18-23.

ACADEMICS

Year founded: 1890. **Academic calendar:** Semester. **Degrees offered:** bachelor's, master's. **Most popular majors:** 34% elementary education and teaching, 17% secondary education and teaching, 15% business administration and management, 5% biology/biological sciences, 5% psychology. **Major fields of study:** biological and biomedical sciences; business, management, marketing, and related support services; communication, journalism, and related programs; computer and information sciences and support services; education; English language and literature/letters; foreign languages, literatures, and linguistics; health professions and related clinical sciences; history; mathematics and statistics; multi/interdisciplinary studies; natural resources and conservation; parks, recreation, leisure, and fitness studies; physical sciences; psychology; social sciences; visual and performing arts. **Areas of required coursework:** arts/fine arts, humanities, computer literacy, mathematics, English (including composition), sciences (biological or physical), social science. **Pre-professional programs:** pre-law, pre-dentistry, pre-medicine, pre-optometry, pre-pharmacy. **Special academic programs (% participation):** distance learning, double major, independent study, internships (10%), student-designed major (3.6%), study abroad (1%), teacher certificate program (50%). **Teacher certification offered in:** elementary, vo-tech, middle/junior high, secondary, bilingual/bicultural. **Faculty and instruction (2005-2006):** Total instructional faculty: 58 full-time, 32 part-time (52% men; 48% women; 1% minorities). Full-time faculty with Ph.D. or other terminal degree: 40%. Student/faculty ratio: 13/1. Classes of fewer than 20 students: 74%; of 20 to 49 students: 25%; of 50 or more students: 1%. **Advanced Placement and International Baccalaureate credit:** AP tests may be used for: Credit only. Scores accepted: 3, 4. **Freshmen returning for sophomore year:** 69%. **Graduation rates:** Four-year: 21%; five-year: 35%; six-year: 46%. **Graduate study:** 3% of students pursue further study immediately upon graduation; 5% within one year.

COSTS AND FINANCIAL AID

Financial aid office: (701) 845-7412. **Expenses (2006-2007):** Tuition and fees 2006-2007: $5,308 in state, $11,576 out of state; room/board: $4,918. Estimated books and supplies: $700; transportation: $1,050; personal expenses: $1,824. **Financial aid:** Priority filing date for institution's financial aid form: March 15. In 2005-2006, 82% of undergraduates applied for financial aid. Of those, 64% were determined to have financial need; 25% had their need fully met. Average financial aid package (proportion receiving): $6,299 (63%). Average amount of gift aid, such as scholarships or grants (proportion receiving): $3,028 (36%). Average amount of self-help aid, such as work study or loans (proportion receiving): $3,885 (57%). Average need-based loan (excluding PLUS or other private loans): $3,686. Among students who received need-based aid, the average percentage of need met: 75%. Among students who received aid based on merit, the average award (and the proportion receiving): $1,626 (13%). The average athletic scholarship (and the proportion receiving): $998 (5%). Average amount of

debt of borrowers graduating in 2005: $18,394. Proportion who borrowed: 60%.

CAMPUS LIFE AND EXTRACURRICULAR ACTIVITIES
Campus housing available (% using): coed dorms (38%), women's dorms (33%), men's dorms (19%), apartments for married students (7%). Students who live in college-owned, operated, or affiliated housing: 35%. **Student employment:** During the 2005-2006 academic year, 24% of undergraduates worked on campus. Average per-year earnings: $875. **Clubs and organizations:** Number of student organizations: 28. Activities include: choral groups, concert band, drama/theater, jazz band, literary magazine, music ensembles, musical theater, pep band, student government, student newspaper, yearbook. Number of fraternities: 1; sororities: 1. Proportion of men in fraternities: 1%; of women in sororities: 1%. Average proportion of students who stay on campus on weekends: 20%. **Sports program (2005-2006):** Member of NAIA. *Men's intercollegiate varsity sports:* baseball, basketball, football. *Women's intercollegiate varsity sports:* basketball, softball, volleyball.

SERVICES AND FACILITIES
Basic services: nonremedial tutoring, placement service, health service, health insurance. **Remedial assistance:** writing, other. **Counseling services:** minority student, career, military, personal, veteran student, academic, older student, psychological, birth control. **For learning-disabled students:** School does not offer a structured program with separate admission and additional fees. Total undergraduates in learning-disabled program or receiving services: 20. Services include: remedial math, remedial English, tape recorders, untimed tests, note-taking services, oral tests, readers, extended time for tests, tutors, priority seating. **Library:** Number of titles: 94,000; number of current serial subscriptions: 7,500. **Information technology resources:** Students are required to lease or own a computer. Number of campus computers available to all students: 980. School has a wireless network. Approximate number of users that can be accommodated: 725. Proportion of college-owned housing units wired for high-speed internet access: 100%. **Campus safety:** Security services offered: 24-hour foot-and-vehicle patrols, lighted pathways/sidewalks, student patrols, controlled dormitory access (key, security card, etc).

TRANSFER AND INTERNATIONAL STUDENTS
Transfer students: May apply for admission for the following academic terms: Fall, Spring, Summer. Applicants need a minimum number of credits to apply. For fall 2005: Transfer applications received: 106. Transfer applicants offered admission: 90. Transfer applicants enrolled: 73. **International students:** Number of foreign undergraduates: 54 (5% of student body). Number of countries represented: 9. Minimum TOEFL score required: 525 (paper); 195 (computer).

Ohio

Antioch College

- **Address:** 795 Livermore Street, Yellow Springs, OH 45387
- **Website:** http://www.antioch-college.edu
- **Private**
- **Enrollment:** 460 full-time; 4 part-time

KEY STATS

✔ **U.S News College Ranking:** third tier, Liberal Arts Colleges
✔ **SAT Score (25th/75th percentile):** 1120-1340
✔ **Tuition:** 2006-2007: $27,212

Selectivity: Selective	**Room/board:** $7,004
Acceptance rate: 51%	**Average debt:** $17,125
Student/faculty ratio: 11/1	**Proportion who borrowed:** 97%

UNDERGRADUATE STUDENT BODY STATS

2005-2006 enrollment: 460 full-time; 4 part-time. Men: 43%; women: 57%. **Ethnic makeup:** African American: 4%; American-Indian: 1%; Asian American: 1%; Hispanic: 3%; White: 91%.

ADMISSIONS FACTS AND FIGURES

Phone: (800) 543-9436. **Email:** admissions@antioch-college.edu. **Website:** http://www.antioch-college.edu. **Application deadlines for fall 2007:** Regular decision: Rolling. Early decision: Not offered. Early action: Send application by: November 1; Decision sent by: December 15. Admission can be deferred. Common application is accepted. **Admissions requirements/recommendations:** High school units required (recommended): English: 4; Mathematics: (4); Science: (4); Foreign language: (4); Social studies: (4); History: (4); Academic electives: (2); Total units: (29). Tests: The college uses SAT or ACT scores in admissions decisions. Neither SAT nor ACT required. For admission to the fall 2007 entering class, the school will accept: ACT with writing, ACT without writing. Campus visit: Recommended. Admissions interview: Recommended. Off-campus interview: May be arranged. **Factors that count in admissions decisions:** *Academic:* Secondary school record: Very important. Class rank: Not considered. Letters of recommendation: Very important. Standardized test scores: Considered. Essay: Very important. *Nonacademic:* Interview: Considered. Extracurricular activities: Important. Talent/ability: Very important. Character/personal qualities: Very important. Alumni/ae relationship: Not considered. Geographical residence: Not considered. State residency: Not considered. Religious affiliation/commitment: Not considered. Minority status: Not considered. Volunteer work: Important. Work experience: Important. **Admissions statistics for the fall 2005 entering class:** Total applicants: 368. Total accepted: 187. Freshmen enrolled: 53; 61% were from out of state. Overall acceptance rate: 51%. Non-early acceptance rate: 51%. **Credentials of fall 2005 freshmen:** 13% ranked in the top 10 percent of their high school class; 39% were in the top 25 percent, and 70% were in the top half. (Proportion submitting class standing: 51%.) **Average high school grade point average:** 3.2. **First-year students who submitted SAT scores:** 49%. Scores (25/75 percentile): Verbal: 600-710, Math: 520-630, Combined: 1120-1340. **First-year students submitting ACT scores:** 21%. Scores (25/75 percentile): English: N/A, Math: N/A, Composite: N/A.

ACADEMICS

Year founded: 1852. **Academic calendar:** Trimester. **Degrees offered:** bachelor's. **Most popular majors:** 33% area, ethnic, cultural, and gender studies, 28% multi/interdisciplinary studies, 13% liberal arts and sciences studies, and humanities, 7% natural resources and conservation, 7% philosophy and religious studies. **Major fields of study:** area, ethnic, cultural, and gender studies; biological and biomedical sciences; business, management, marketing, and related support services; communication, journalism, and related programs; education; English language and literature/letters; foreign languages, literatures, and linguistics; liberal arts and sciences studies, and humanities; multi/interdisciplinary studies; natural resources and conservation; philosophy and religious studies; physical sciences; social sciences;

visual and performing arts. **Areas of required coursework:** arts/fine arts, humanities, mathematics, English (including composition), philosophy, foreign languages, sciences (biological or physical), history, social science, other. **Pre-professional programs:** pre-law, pre-medicine, pre-veterinary science. **Special academic programs (% participation):** accelerated program, cooperative (work-study plan) program (100%), cross-registration (3%), double major (3%), dual enrollment (2%), exchange student program (domestic) (7%), independent study, internships, student-designed major (10%), study abroad (45%), teacher certificate program. **Teacher certification offered in:** early childhood, special education, elementary, vo-tech, middle/junior high, secondary. **Cooperative education programs:** agriculture, art, business, computer science, education, engineering, health professions, home economics, humanities, natural science, social/behavioral science, technologies, vocational arts. **Faculty and instruction (2005-2006):** Total instructional faculty: 51 full-time, 17 part-time (47% men; 53% women; 7% minorities). Full-time faculty with Ph.D. or other terminal degree: 65%. Student/faculty ratio: 11/1. Classes of fewer than 20 students: 91%; of 20 to 49 students: 9%. **Freshmen returning for sophomore year:** 65%. **Graduation rates:** Four-year: 32%; five-year: 48%; six-year: 50%.

COSTS AND FINANCIAL AID

Financial aid office: (937) 769-1100. **Expenses (2006-2007):** Tuition and fees 2006-2007: $27,212; room/board: $7,004. **Financial aid:** Priority filing date for institution's financial aid form: February 1. In 2005-2006, 81% of undergraduates applied for financial aid. Of those, 77% were determined to have financial need; 100% had their need fully met. Average financial aid package (proportion receiving): $22,853 (N/A). Average amount of gift aid, such as scholarships or grants (proportion receiving): $13,719 (70%). Average amount of self-help aid, such as work study or loans (proportion receiving): $6,888 (73%). Average need-based loan (excluding PLUS or other private loans): $4,910. Among students who received need-based aid, the average percentage of need met: 100%. Among students who received aid based on merit, the average award (and the proportion receiving): $9,571 (4%). Average amount of debt of borrowers graduating in 2005: $17,125. Proportion who borrowed: 97%.

CAMPUS LIFE AND EXTRACURRICULAR ACTIVITIES

Campus housing available: coed dorms, special housing for disabled students, special housing for international students, other housing options. Students who live in college-owned, operated, or affiliated housing: 95%. Activities include: choral groups, dance, drama/theater, literary magazine, music ensembles, radio station, student government, student newspaper. Average proportion of students who stay on campus on weekends: 95%.

SERVICES AND FACILITIES

Basic services: nonremedial tutoring, women's center, placement service, health service, health insurance. **Remedial assistance:** reading, math, writing, study skills. **Counseling services:** minority student, personal, veteran student, academic, older student, psychological, birth control. **For learning-disabled students:** School does not offer a structured program with separate admission and additional fees. Total undergraduates in learning-disabled program or receiving services: 50. Services include: remedial math, remedial English, reading machines, remedial reading, tape recorders, note-taking services, oral tests, learning center, readers, extended time for tests, tutors, early syllabus, priority seating, proofreading services, texts on tape, typist/scribe, exams on tape or computer, take home exams, other testing accomodations, other. **Information technology resources:** Students are not required to lease or own a computer. Number of campus computers available to all students: 68. School has a wireless network. **Campus safety:** Security services offered: 24-hour foot-and-vehicle patrols, late-night transport/escort service, 24-hour emergency telephones, lighted pathways/sidewalks, controlled dormitory access (key, security card, etc).

TRANSFER AND INTERNATIONAL STUDENTS

Transfer students: May apply for admission for the following academic terms: Fall, Spring. Applicants do not need a minimum number of credits to apply. For fall 2005: Transfer applications received: 47. Transfer applicants offered admission: 24. Transfer applicants enrolled: 10. **International**

students: Number of foreign undergraduates: 1. Number of countries represented: 0. Minimum TOEFL score required: 570 (paper). Average TOEFL score: 570 (paper).

Art Academy of Cincinnati

- **Address:** 1125 St. Gregory Street, Cincinnati, OH 45202
- **Website:** http://www.artacademy.edu
- **Private**
- **Enrollment:** N/A

KEY STATS
- ✔ **U.S News College Ranking:** Unranked Specialty School–Fine Arts
- ✔ **ACT Score (25th/75th percentile):** 18-25
- ✔ **Tuition:** 2006-2007: $19,600

Selectivity: Selective	**Room/board:** N/A
Acceptance rate: 67%	**Average debt:** $20,026
Student/faculty ratio: N/A	**Proportion who borrowed:** 68%

Ashland University

- **Address:** 401 College Avenue, Ashland, OH 44805
- **Website:** http://www.ashland.edu
- **Private; Religious affiliation:** Brethren Church
- **Enrollment:** 2,511 full-time; 280 part-time

KEY STATS
- ✔ **U.S News College Ranking:** 53, Universities–Master's (Midwest)
- ✔ **ACT Score (25th/75th percentile):** 20-25
- ✔ **Tuition:** 2006-2007: $21,430

Selectivity: Selective	**Room/board:** $7,791
Acceptance rate: 91%	**Average debt:** $18,250
Student/faculty ratio: 13/1	**Proportion who borrowed:** 75%

UNDERGRADUATE STUDENT BODY STATS
2005-2006 enrollment: 2,511 full-time; 280 part-time. Men: 41%; women: 59%. **Ethnic makeup:** African American: 8%; Hispanic: 2%; White: 88%; International: 1%. **Religious preference:** Roman Catholic: 11%; Protestant: 16%; No preference: 4%; Unknown: 61%; Brethren Church: 2%; Methodist: 5%; Other: 1%.

ADMISSIONS FACTS AND FIGURES
Phone: (419) 289-5052. **Email:** enrollme@ashland.edu. **Website:** http://www.ashland.edu. **Application deadlines for fall 2007:** Regular decision: Rolling. Early decision: Not offered. Early action: Not offered. Admission can be deferred. Common application is accepted. **To apply online, go to:** http://www.exploreashland.com/forms.html. **Admissions requirements/recommendations:** High school units required (recommended): English: 3 (4); Mathematics: 2 (3); Science: 2 (3); Foreign language: 0 (2); Social studies: 2 (3); History: 1 (1); Total units: 14 (18). Tests: The college uses SAT or ACT scores in admissions decisions. Either SAT or ACT required. For admission to the fall 2007 entering class, the school will accept: ACT with writing, ACT without writing. Campus visit: Recommended. Admissions interview: Recommended. Off-campus interview: Not available. **Factors that count in admissions decisions:** *Academic:* Secondary school record: Very important. Class rank: Important. Letters of recommendation: Important. Standardized test scores: Important. Essay: Important. *Nonacademic:* Interview: Important. Extracurricular activities: Considered. Talent/ability: Considered. Character/personal qualities: Considered. Alumni/ae relationship: Considered. Geographical residence: Considered. State residency: Not considered. Religious affiliation/commitment: Not considered. Minority status: Not considered. Volunteer work: Considered. Work experience: Considered. **Other schools with the greatest overlap in applicants:** Bowling Green State University; Kent State University; Ohio State University–Columbus; Ohio University; University of Akron. **Admissions statistics for the fall 2005 entering class:** Total applicants: 1,950. Total accepted: 1,780. Freshmen enrolled: 550; 8% were from out of state. Overall acceptance rate: 91%. **Credentials of fall 2005 freshmen:** 17% ranked in the top 10 percent of their high school class; 43% were in the top 25 per-

cent, and 71% were in the top half. (Proportion submitting class standing: 92%.) **Average high school grade point average:** 3.4. **First-year students who submitted SAT scores:** 32%. Scores (25/75 percentile): Verbal: 470-590, Math: 470-590, Combined: 940-1180. **First-year students submitting ACT scores:** 99%. Scores (25/75 percentile): English: 19-26, Math: 19-25, Composite: 20-25.

ACADEMICS
Year founded: 1878. **Academic calendar:** Semester. **Degrees offered:** certificate, associate, bachelor's, master's, first professional, doctorate. **Most popular majors:** 36% education, 19% business, management, marketing, and related support services, 7% social sciences, 6% communications technologies/technicians and support services, 6% health professions and related clinical sciences. **Major fields of study:** biological and biomedical sciences; business, management, marketing, and related support services; communication, journalism, and related programs; communications technologies/technicians and support services; education; English language and literature/letters; family and consumer sciences/human sciences; foreign languages, literatures, and linguistics; history; mathematics and statistics; parks, recreation, leisure, and fitness studies; philosophy and religious studies; physical sciences; psychology; public administration and social service professions; security and protective services; social sciences; visual and performing arts. **Areas of required coursework:** arts/fine arts, humanities, mathematics, English (including composition), philosophy, sciences (biological or physical), history, social science. **Pre-professional programs:** pre-law, pre-dentistry, pre-medicine, pre-theology, pre-veterinary science, pre-optometry, pre-pharmacy, other. **Special academic programs:** cooperative (work-study plan) program, double major, English as a Second Language (ESL), honors program, independent study, internships, student-designed major, study abroad, teacher certificate program, weekend college. **Teacher certification offered in:** early childhood, special education, elementary, vo-tech, middle/junior high, secondary. **Faculty and instruction (2005-2006):** Total instructional faculty: 232 full-time, 353 part-time (53% men; 47% women; 5% minorities). Full-time faculty with Ph.D. or other terminal degree: 86%. Student/faculty ratio: 13/1. Classes of fewer than 20 students: 59%; of 20 to 49 students: 41%; of 50 or more students: 0%. **Advanced Placement and International Baccalaureate credit:** AP tests may be used for: Credit and/or placement. Scores accepted: 3. **Freshmen returning for sophomore year:** 73%. **Graduation rates:** Four-year: 47%; five-year: 56%; six-year: 56%. **Graduate study:** 13% of students pursue further study immediately upon graduation; 12% within five years. Fields in which graduates pursue further study: Master of Business Administration (MBA), 2%; law, 1%; medicine, 1%; theology (or the seminary), 1%; education, 1%; arts and sciences, 6%.

COSTS AND FINANCIAL AID
Financial aid office: (419) 289-5002. **Expenses (2006-2007):** Tuition and fees 2006-2007: $21,430; room/board: $7,791. Estimated books and supplies: $800; transportation: $755; personal expenses: $2,614. **Financial aid:** Priority filing date for institution's financial aid form: March 15; deadline: March 15. In 2005-2006, 100% of undergraduates applied for financial aid. Of those, 78% were determined to have financial need; Average financial aid package (proportion receiving): $17,116 (78%). Average amount of gift aid, such as scholarships or grants (proportion receiving): $11,409 (78%). Average amount of self-help aid, such as work study or loans (proportion receiving): $5,636 (68%). Average need-based loan (excluding PLUS or other private loans): $4,183. Among students who received need-based aid, the average percentage of need met: 90%. Among students who received aid based on merit, the average award (and the proportion receiving): $6,206 (16%). The average athletic scholarship (and the proportion receiving): $11,526 (3%). Average amount of debt of borrowers graduating in 2005: $18,250. Proportion who borrowed: 75%.

CAMPUS LIFE AND EXTRACURRICULAR ACTIVITIES
Campus housing available (% using): coed dorms (32%), women's dorms (36%), men's dorms (18%), fraternity housing (6%), apartment for single students (8%). Students who live in college-owned, operated, or affiliated housing: 78%. **Student employment:** During the 2005-2006 academic year, 25% of undergraduates worked on campus. Average per-year earnings: $1,500. **Clubs and organizations:** Number of student organizations: 96. Activities include: choral groups, concert band, dance, drama/theater, jazz band, literary magazine, marching band, music ensembles, musical theater, pep band, radio station, student government, student newspaper, symphony orchestra, television station, yearbook. Number of fraternities: 3; sororities: 5. Proportion of men in fraternities: 7%; of women in sororities: 13%. Average proportion of students who stay on campus on weekends: 50%. **Sports program (2005-2006):** Member of NCAA II. *Men's intercollegiate var-*

sity sports: baseball, basketball, cross-country, football, golf, soccer, swimming and diving, track and field (indoor), track and field (outdoor), wrestling. **Women's intercollegiate varsity sports:** basketball, cross-country, golf, soccer, softball, swimming and diving, tennis, track and field (indoor), track and field (outdoor), volleyball.

SERVICES AND FACILITIES

Basic services: nonremedial tutoring, placement service, health service, health insurance. **Remedial assistance:** writing, study skills. **Counseling services:** minority student, career, personal, academic, psychological, religious. **For learning-disabled students:** School does not offer a structured program with separate admission and additional fees. Total undergraduates in learning-disabled program or receiving services: 138. Services include: remedial English, reading machines, tape recorders, untimed tests, note-taking services, oral tests, learning center, readers, extended time for tests, tutors, priority registration, texts on tape. **Library:** Number of titles: 305,288; number of current serial subscriptions: 504. **Information technology resources:** Students are not required to lease or own a computer. Number of campus computers available to all students: 1,000. School has a wireless network. Approximate number of users that can be accommodated: 1,200. Proportion of college-owned housing units wired for high-speed internet access: 95%. **Campus safety:** Security services offered: 24-hour foot-and-vehicle patrols, late-night transport/escort service, 24-hour emergency telephones, lighted pathways/sidewalks, controlled dormitory access (key, security card, etc).

TRANSFER AND INTERNATIONAL STUDENTS

Transfer students: May apply for admission for the following academic terms: Fall, Spring, Summer. Applicants need a minimum number of credits to apply. For fall 2005: Transfer applications received: 239. Transfer applicants offered admission: 155. Transfer applicants enrolled: 92. **International students:** Number of foreign undergraduates: 37 (1% of student body). Number of countries represented: 13. Minimum TOEFL score required: 500 (paper); 173 (computer). Average TOEFL score: 527 (paper).

Baldwin-Wallace College

- **Address:** 275 Eastland Road, Berea, OH 44017
- **Website:** http://www.bw.edu
- **Private; Religious affiliation:** Methodist
- **Enrollment:** 2,994 full-time; 687 part-time

KEY STATS

✔ **U.S News College Ranking:** 11, Universities–Master's (Midwest)
✔ **ACT Score (25th/75th percentile):** 21-26
✔ **Tuition:** 2006-2007: $21,236

Selectivity: More selective	**Room/board:** $6,974
Acceptance rate: 79%	**Average debt:** $16,250
Student/faculty ratio: 17/1	**Proportion who borrowed:** 95%

UNDERGRADUATE STUDENT BODY STATS

2005-2006 enrollment: 2,994 full-time; 687 part-time. Men: 40%; women: 60%. **Ethnic makeup:** African American: 5%; Asian American: 1%; Hispanic: 1%; White: 91%; International: 1%. **Religious preference:** Roman Catholic: 49%; Protestant: 31%; Jewish: 1%; Muslim: 1%; Methodist: 10%; Mormon, Unitarian: 0%; Other: 8%.

ADMISSIONS FACTS AND FIGURES

Phone: (440) 826-2222. **Email:** admission@bw.edu. **Website:** http://www.bw.edu. **Application deadlines for fall 2007:** Regular decision: Rolling. Early decision: Not offered. Early action: Not offered. Admission can be deferred. **Application fee:** $25. Common application is accepted. **To apply online, go to:** http://www.bw.edu/admission/. **Admissions requirements/recommendations:** High school units required (recommended): English: 4 (4); Mathematics: 3 (4); Science: 3; Foreign language: 2; Social studies: 2; History: 1 (1); Academic electives: (3); Total units: 15 (19). Tests: The college uses SAT or ACT scores in admissions decisions. Either SAT or ACT required. For admission to the fall 2007 entering class, the school will accept: ACT with writing, ACT without writing. Campus visit: Recommended. Admissions interview: Recommended. Off-campus interview: May be arranged. **Factors that count in admissions decisions:** *Academic:* Secondary school record: Very important. Class rank: Important.

Letters of recommendation: Considered. Standardized test scores: Important. Essay: Important. **Nonacademic:** Interview: Considered. Extracurricular activities: Important. Talent/ability: Important. Character/personal qualities: Important. Alumni/ae relationship: Considered. Geographical residence: Considered. State residency: Considered. Religious affiliation/commitment: Not considered. Minority status: Considered. Volunteer work: Considered. Work experience: Considered. **Other schools with the greatest overlap in applicants:** Bowling Green State University; John Carroll University; Kent State University; Mount Union College; Ohio State University–Columbus. **Admissions statistics for the fall 2005 entering class:** Total applicants: 2,366. Total accepted: 1,870. Freshmen enrolled: 599; 14% were from out of state. Overall acceptance rate: 79%. **Credentials of fall 2005 freshmen:** 28% ranked in the top 10 percent of their high school class; 57% were in the top 25 percent, and 87% were in the top half. (Proportion submitting class standing: 90%.) **Average high school grade point average:** 3.5. **First-year students who submitted SAT scores:** 55%. Scores (25/75 percentile): Verbal: 495-610, Math: 500-620, Combined: 995-1230. **First-year students submitting ACT scores:** 87%. Scores (25/75 percentile): English: 20-27, Math: 20-26, Composite: 21-26.

ACADEMICS

Year founded: 1845. **Academic calendar:** Semester. **Degrees offered:** bachelor's, master's. **Most popular majors:** 22% business, management, marketing, and related support services, 15% education, 12% psychology, 7% parks, recreation, leisure, and fitness studies, 6% English language and literature/letters. **Major fields of study:** biological and biomedical sciences; business, management, marketing, and related support services; communication, journalism, and related programs; computer and information sciences and support services; education; English language and literature/letters; foreign languages, literatures, and linguistics; health professions and related clinical sciences; history; mathematics and statistics; multi/interdisciplinary studies; parks, recreation, leisure, and fitness studies; philosophy and religious studies; physical sciences; psychology; security and protective services; social sciences; visual and performing arts. **Areas of required coursework:** arts/fine arts, humanities, mathematics, English (including composition), philosophy, sciences (biological or physical), history, social science, other. **Pre-professional programs:** pre-law, pre-dentistry, pre-medicine, pre-theology, pre-veterinary science, other. **Special academic programs (% participation):** accelerated program (.3%), cross-registration (.3%), distance learning (0%), double major (18%), dual enrollment (0%), exchange student program (domestic) (.3%), honors program (7%), independent study (20%), internships (15%), student-designed major (1%), study abroad (5%), teacher certificate program (16%), weekend college (4%), other (18%). **Teacher certification offered in:** early childhood, special education, middle/junior high, secondary. **Reserve Officers Training Corps (ROTC):** Army ROTC: Offered at cooperating institution (John Carroll University); Air Force ROTC: Offered at cooperating institution (Kent State University). **Faculty and instruction (2005-2006):** Total instructional faculty: 162 full-time, 190 part-time (56% men; 44% women; 8% minorities). Full-time faculty with Ph.D. or other terminal degree: 80%. Student/faculty ratio: 17/1. Classes of fewer than 20 students: 49%; of 20 to 49 students: 51%; of 50 or more students: 0%. **Advanced Placement and International Baccalaureate credit:** AP tests may be used for: Credit and/or placement. Scores accepted: 3, 4, 5. International Baccalaureate exams may be used for: Credit only. **Freshmen returning for sophomore year:** 83%. **Graduation rates:** Four-year: 50%; five-year: 65%; six-year: 67%. **Graduate study:** 19% of students pursue further study within one year. Fields in which graduates pursue further study: Master of Business Administration (MBA), 13%; law, 10%; medicine, 4%; arts and sciences, 32%.

COSTS AND FINANCIAL AID

Financial aid office: (440) 826-2108. **Expenses (2006-2007):** Tuition and fees 2006-2007: $21,236; room/board: $6,974. Estimated books and supplies: $1,000; transportation: $600; personal expenses: $1,500. **Financial aid:** Priority filing date for institution's financial aid form: May 1; deadline: September 1. In 2005-2006, 91% of undergraduates applied for financial aid. Of those, 77% were determined to have financial need; 64% had their need fully met. Average financial aid package (proportion receiving): $13,355 (77%). Average amount of gift aid, such as scholarships or grants (proportion receiving): $9,956 (77%). Average amount of self-help aid, such as work study or loans (proportion receiving): $4,659 (63%). Average need-based loan (excluding PLUS or other private loans): $3,440. Among students who received need-based aid, the average percentage of need met: 87%. Among students who received aid based on merit, the average award (and the proportion receiving): $7,975 (23%). Average amount of debt of borrowers graduating in 2005: $16,250. Proportion who borrowed: 95%.

CAMPUS LIFE AND EXTRACURRICULAR ACTIVITIES

Campus housing available (% using): coed dorms (50%), women's dorms (6%), men's dorms (0%), sorority housing (6%), fraternity housing (4%), apartment for single students (7%), special housing for disabled students (1%), special housing for international students (1%), other housing options (25%). Students who live in college-owned, operated, or affiliated housing: 54%. **Student employment:** During the 2005-2006 academic year, 31% of undergraduates worked on campus. Average per-year earnings: $888. **Clubs and organizations:** Number of student organizations: 118. Activities include: choral groups, concert band, dance, drama/theater, jazz band, literary magazine, music ensembles, musical theater, opera, pep band, radio station, student government, student newspaper, symphony orchestra, television station, yearbook. Number of fraternities: 4; sororities: 7. Proportion of men in fraternities: 1%; of women in sororities: 1%. Average proportion of students who stay on campus on weekends: 50%. **Sports program (2005-2006):** Member of NCAA III. *Men's intercollegiate varsity sports:* baseball, basketball, cross-country, football, golf, soccer, swimming and diving, tennis, track and field (indoor), track and field (outdoor), wrestling. *Women's intercollegiate varsity sports:* basketball, cross-country, golf, soccer, softball, swimming and diving, tennis, track and field (indoor), track and field (outdoor), volleyball.

SERVICES AND FACILITIES

Basic services: nonremedial tutoring, health service, health insurance, other. **Remedial assistance:** math, study skills. **Counseling services:** minority student, career, personal, academic, older student, psychological, birth control, religious. **For learning-disabled students:** School does not offer a structured program with separate admission and additional fees. Total undergraduates in learning-disabled program or receiving services: 37. Services include: remedial math, tape recorders, note-taking services, learning center, readers, extended time for tests, tutors. **Library:** Number of titles: 200,000; number of current serial subscriptions: 22,000. **Information technology resources:** Students are not required to lease or own a computer. Number of campus computers available to all students: 553. School has a wireless network. Approximate number of users that can be accommodated: 4,000. Proportion of college-owned housing units wired for high-speed internet access: 100%. **Campus safety:** Security services offered: 24-hour foot-and-vehicle patrols, late-night transport/escort service, 24-hour emergency telephones, lighted pathways/sidewalks, controlled dormitory access (key, security card, etc).

TRANSFER AND INTERNATIONAL STUDENTS

Transfer students: May apply for admission for the following academic terms: Fall, Spring, Summer. Applicants do not need a minimum number of credits to apply. For fall 2005: Transfer applications received: 494. Transfer applicants offered admission: 327. Transfer applicants enrolled: 217. **International students:** Number of foreign undergraduates: 40 (1% of student body). Number of countries represented: 16. Minimum TOEFL score required: 500 (paper); 177 (computer). Average TOEFL score: 543 (paper).

Bluffton University

- **Address:** 1 University Drive, Bluffton, OH 45817
- **Website:** http://www.bluffton.edu
- **Private; Religious affiliation:** Mennonite Church USA
- **Enrollment:** 1,005 full-time; 74 part-time

KEY STATS

- ✔ **U.S News College Ranking:** 34, Comp. Coll.–Bachelor's (Midwest)
- ✔ **ACT Score (25th/75th percentile):** 19-24
- ✔ **Tuition:** 2006-2007: $20,570

Selectivity: Selective	**Room/board:** $7,082
Acceptance rate: 71%	**Average debt:** $27,441
Student/faculty ratio: 14/1	**Proportion who borrowed:** 77%

UNDERGRADUATE STUDENT BODY STATS

2005-2006 enrollment: 1,005 full-time; 74 part-time. Men: 42%; women: 58%. **Ethnic makeup:** African American: 3%; Asian American: 1%; Hispanic: 2%; White: 92%; International: 2%.

ADMISSIONS FACTS AND FIGURES

Phone: (800) 488-3257. **Email:** admissions@bluffton.edu. **Website:** http://www.bluffton.edu. **Application deadlines for fall 2007:** Regular decision: August 20. Early decision: Not offered. Early action: Not offered. Admission can be deferred. **Application fee:** $20. Common application is not accepted. **To apply online, go to:** http://www.bluffton.edu/admission/apply/index.html. **Admissions requirements/recommendations:** High school units required (recommended): English: 0 (4); Mathematics: 0 (3); Science: 0 (3); Foreign language: 0 (3); Social studies: 0 (3); History: 0 (0); Academic electives: 0 (0); Total units: 0 (16). Tests: The college uses SAT or ACT scores in admissions decisions. Either SAT or ACT required. For admission to the fall 2007 entering class, the school will accept: ACT with writing, ACT without writing. Campus visit: Recommended. Admissions interview: Recommended. Off-campus interview: May be arranged. **Factors that count in admissions decisions:** *Academic:* Secondary school record: Considered. Class rank: Very important. Letters of recommendation: Important. Standardized test scores: Very important. Essay: Considered. *Nonacademic:* Interview: Important. Extracurricular activities: Important. Talent/ability: Considered. Character/personal qualities: Considered. Alumni/ae relationship: Not considered. Geographical residence: Not considered. State residency: Not considered. Religious affiliation/commitment: Considered. Minority status: Not considered. Volunteer work: Considered. Work experience: Considered. **Other schools with the greatest overlap in applicants:** Bowling Green State University; Ohio Northern University; Ohio State University–Columbus; University of Findlay; University of Toledo. **Admissions statistics for the fall 2005 entering class:** Total applicants: 1,074. Total accepted: 765. Freshmen enrolled: 230; 15% were from out of state. Overall acceptance rate: 71%. **Credentials of fall 2005 freshmen:** 14% ranked in the top 10 percent of their high school class; 42% were in the top 25 percent, and 80% were in the top half. (Proportion submitting class standing: 97%.) **Average high school grade point average:** 3.4. **First-year students who submitted SAT scores:** 24%. Scores (25/75 percentile): Verbal: 490-590, Math: 480-560, Combined: 970-1150. **First-year students submitting ACT scores:** 90%. Scores (25/75 percentile): English: 18-25, Math: 18-24, Composite: 19-24.

ACADEMICS

Year founded: 1899. **Academic calendar:** Semester. **Degrees offered:** bachelor's, master's. **Most popular majors:** 30% organizational behavior studies, 11% business administration and management, 11% elementary education and teaching, 4% communication studies/speech communication and rhetoric, 4% junior high/intermediate/middle school education and teaching. **Major fields of study:** biological and biomedical sciences; business, management, marketing, and related support services; communication, journalism, and related programs; computer and information sciences and support services; education; English language and literature/letters; family and consumer sciences/human sciences; foreign languages, literatures, and linguistics; health professions and related clinical sciences; history; mathematics and statistics; multi/interdisciplinary studies; parks, recreation, leisure, and fitness studies; philosophy and religious studies; physical sciences; psychology; public administration and social service professions; security and protective services; social sciences; theology and religious vocations; visual and performing arts. **Areas of required coursework:** arts/fine arts, humanities, mathematics, English (including composition), philosophy, sciences (biological or physical), history, social science, other. **Pre-professional programs:** pre-law, pre-dentistry, pre-medicine, pre-theology, pre-optometry. **Special academic programs (% participation):** double major (5%), dual enrollment (1%), honors program (5%), independent study (20%), internships (30%), student-designed major (1%), study abroad (5%), teacher certificate program (23%), other. **Teacher certification offered in:** early childhood, special education, elementary, vo-tech, middle/junior high, secondary. **Cooperative education programs:** business, education, home economics, social/behavioral science, technologies. **Faculty and instruction (2005-2006):** Total instructional faculty: 67 full-time, 47 part-time (61% men; 39% women; 6% minorities). Full-time faculty with Ph.D. or other terminal degree: 72%. Student/faculty ratio: 14/1. Classes of fewer than 20 students: 51%; of 20 to 49 students: 48%; of 50 or more students: 1%. **Advanced Placement and International Baccalaureate credit:** AP tests may be used for: Credit and/or placement. Scores accepted: 3, 4, 5. **Freshmen returning for sophomore year:** 74%. **Graduation rates:** Four-year: 46%; five-year: 55%; six-year: 60%.

COSTS AND FINANCIAL AID

Financial aid office: (419) 358-3266. **Expenses (2006-2007):** Tuition and fees 2006-2007: $20,570; room/board: $7,082. Estimated books and supplies: $1,100; transportation: $800; personal expenses: $1,300. **Financial aid:**

Priority filing date for institution's financial aid form: May 1; deadline: October 1. In 2005-2006, 78% of undergraduates applied for financial aid. Of those, 74% were determined to have financial need; 48% had their need fully met. Average financial aid package (proportion receiving): $18,106 (74%). Average amount of gift aid, such as scholarships or grants (proportion receiving): $12,147 (74%). Average amount of self-help aid, such as work study or loans (proportion receiving): $6,088 (68%). Average need-based loan (excluding PLUS or other private loans): $4,759. Among students who received need-based aid, the average percentage of need met: 91%. Among students who received aid based on merit, the average award (and the proportion receiving): $8,087 (10%). Average amount of debt of borrowers graduating in 2005: $27,441. Proportion who borrowed: 77%.

CAMPUS LIFE AND EXTRACURRICULAR ACTIVITIES

Campus housing available: coed dorms, women's dorms, men's dorms. Students who live in college-owned, operated, or affiliated housing: 72%. **Student employment:** During the 2005-2006 academic year, 65% of undergraduates worked on campus. Average per-year earnings: $1,500. **Clubs and organizations:** Number of student organizations: 30. Activities include: choral groups, concert band, dance, drama/theater, jazz band, literary magazine, music ensembles, musical theater, radio station, student government, student newspaper, yearbook. Number of fraternities: 0; sororities: 0. Average proportion of students who stay on campus on weekends: 33%. **Sports program (2005-2006):** Member of NCAA III. *Men's intercollegiate varsity sports:* baseball, basketball, cross-country, football, soccer, tennis, track and field (indoor), track and field (outdoor). *Women's intercollegiate varsity sports:* basketball, cross-country, soccer, softball, tennis, track and field (indoor), track and field (outdoor), volleyball.

SERVICES AND FACILITIES

Basic services: nonremedial tutoring, placement service, health service, health insurance. **Remedial assistance:** reading, math, writing, study skills. **Counseling services:** minority student, career, personal, academic, religious. **For learning-disabled students:** School does not offer a structured program with separate admission and additional fees. Services include: remedial math, remedial English, remedial reading, tape recorders, videotaped classes, note-taking services, oral tests, learning center, readers, extended time for tests, tutors. **Library:** Number of titles: 169,056; number of current serial subscriptions: 6,300. **Information technology resources:** Students are not required to lease or own a computer. Number of campus computers available to all students: 150. School has a wireless network. Approximate number of users that can be accommodated: 75. Proportion of college-owned housing units wired for high-speed internet access: 100%. **Campus safety:** Security services offered: 24-hour emergency telephones, lighted pathways/sidewalks, controlled dormitory access (key, security card, etc).

TRANSFER AND INTERNATIONAL STUDENTS

Transfer students: May apply for admission for the following academic terms: Fall, Winter, Spring, Summer. Applicants do not need a minimum number of credits to apply. For fall 2005: Transfer applications received: 113. Transfer applicants offered admission: 65. Transfer applicants enrolled: 44. **International students:** Number of foreign undergraduates: 17 (2% of student body). Minimum TOEFL score required: 500 (paper); 180 (computer).

Bowling Green State University

- **Address:** 110 McFall Center, Bowling Green, OH 43403
- **Website:** http://www.bgsu.edu
- **Public**
- **Enrollment:** 15,014 full-time; 1,065 part-time

KEY STATS

✔ **U.S News College Ranking:** third tier, National Universities
✔ **ACT Score (25th/75th percentile):** 19-24
✔ **Tuition:** 2006-2007: $9,074 in state, $16,382 out of state

Selectivity: Selective	**Room/board:** $6,684
Acceptance rate: 90%	**Average debt:** $21,594
Student/faculty ratio: 19/1	**Proportion who borrowed:** 72%

UNDERGRADUATE STUDENT BODY STATS

2005-2006 enrollment: 15,014 full-time; 1,065 part-time. Men: 45%; women: 55%. **Ethnic makeup:** African American: 8%; American-Indian: 1%; Asian American: 1%; Hispanic: 3%; White: 87%; International: 1%.

ADMISSIONS FACTS AND FIGURES

Phone: (419) 372-2478. **Email:** admissions@bgnet.bgsu.edu. **Website:** http://www.bgsu.edu. **Application deadlines for fall 2007:** Regular decision: July 15. Early decision: Not offered. Early action: Not offered. Admission can be deferred. **Application fee:** $40. Common application is not accepted. **To apply online, go to:** http://go2.bgsu.edu/choose/apply/. **Admissions requirements/recommendations:** High school units required (recommended): English: 4 (4); Mathematics: 3 (3); Science: 3 (3); Foreign language: 2 (2); Social studies: 3 (3); Total units: 16 (16). Tests: The college uses SAT or ACT scores in admissions decisions. Either SAT or ACT required. For admission to the fall 2007 entering class, the school will accept: ACT with writing, ACT without writing. Campus visit: Recommended. Admissions interview: Recommended. Off-campus interview: Not available. **Factors that count in admissions decisions:** *Academic:* Secondary school record: Very important. Class rank: Important. Letters of recommendation: Considered. Standardized test scores: Very important. Essay: Considered. *Nonacademic:* Interview: Considered. Extracurricular activities: Considered. Talent/ability: Important. Character/personal qualities: Considered. Alumni/ae relationship: Considered. Geographical residence: Not considered. State residency: Not considered. Religious affiliation/commitment: Not considered. Minority status: Considered. Volunteer work: Considered. Work experience: Considered. **Other schools with the greatest overlap in applicants:** Kent State University; Miami University–Oxford; Ohio State University–Columbus; Ohio University; University of Toledo. **Admissions statistics for the fall 2005 entering class:** Total applicants: 11,168. Total accepted: 10,058. Freshmen enrolled: 3,603; 12% were from out of state. Overall acceptance rate: 90%. **Credentials of fall 2005 freshmen:** 14% ranked in the top 10 percent of their high school class; 38% were in the top 25 percent, and 71% were in the top half. (Proportion submitting class standing: 80%.) **Average high school grade point average:** 3.2. **First-year students who submitted SAT scores:** 32%. Scores (25/75 percentile): Verbal: 460-570, Math: 460-570, Combined: 920-1140. **First-year students submitting ACT scores:** 91%. Scores (25/75 percentile): English: 18-24, Math: 18-24, Composite: 19-24.

ACADEMICS

Year founded: 1910. **Academic calendar:** Semester. **Degrees offered:** bachelor's, master's, post-master's certificate, doctorate. **Most popular majors:** 7% kindergarten/preschool education and teaching, 5% speech and rhetorical studies, 4% design and visual communications, 4% junior high/intermediate/middle school education and teaching, 4% psychology. **Major fields of study:** architecture and related services; area, ethnic, cultural, and gender studies; biological and biomedical sciences; business, management, marketing, and related support services; communication, journalism, and related programs; computer and information sciences and support services; education; engineering technologies/technicians; English language and literature/letters; family and consumer sciences/human sciences; foreign languages, literatures, and linguistics; health professions and related clinical sciences; history; legal professions and studies; liberal arts and sciences studies, and humanities; mathematics and statistics; multi/interdisciplinary studies; natural resources and conservation; parks, recreation, leisure, and fitness studies; philosophy and religious studies; physical sciences; psychology; public administration and social service professions; security and protective services; social sciences; transportation and materials moving; visual and performing arts. **Areas of required coursework:** humanities, mathematics, English (including composition), sciences (biological or physical), social science, other. **Pre-professional programs:** pre-law, pre-dentistry, pre-medicine, pre-veterinary science, pre-optometry, pre-pharmacy, other. **Special academic programs:** accelerated program, cooperative (work-study plan) program, cross-registration, distance learning, double major, dual enrollment, exchange student program (domestic), honors program, independent study, internships, liberal arts/career combination, student-designed major, study abroad, teacher certificate program. **Teacher certification offered in:** early childhood, special education, elementary, vo-tech, middle/junior high, secondary. **Cooperative education programs:** art, business, computer science, education, health professions, home economics, humanities, natural science, social/behavioral science, technologies, other. **Reserve Officers Training Corps (ROTC):** Army ROTC: Offered on campus; Air Force ROTC: Offered on campus. **Faculty and instruction (2005-2006):** Total instructional faculty: 851 full-time, 196 part-time (55% men; 45% women; 14% minorities). Full-time faculty with Ph.D. or other terminal degree: 77%. Student/faculty ratio: 19/1. Classes of fewer than 20 students: 36%; of 20 to

49 students: 57%; of 50 or more students: 6%. **Advanced Placement and International Baccalaureate credit:** AP tests may be used for: Credit and/or placement. Scores accepted: 3, 4, 5. **Freshmen returning for sophomore year:** 76%. **Graduation rates:** Four-year: 34%; five-year: 57%; six-year: 60%.

COSTS AND FINANCIAL AID

Financial aid office: (419) 372-2651. **Expenses (2006-2007):** Tuition and fees 2006-2007: $9,074 in state, $16,382 out of state; room/board: $6,684. Estimated books and supplies: $1,140; transportation: $778; personal expenses: $2,232. **Financial aid:** Priority filing date for institution's financial aid form: February 15. In 2005-2006, 70% of undergraduates applied for financial aid. Of those, 57% were determined to have financial need; 16% had their need fully met. Average financial aid package (proportion receiving): $8,245 (57%). Average amount of gift aid, such as scholarships or grants (proportion receiving): $3,575 (26%). Average amount of self-help aid, such as work study or loans (proportion receiving): $3,809 (50%). Average need-based loan (excluding PLUS or other private loans): $3,757. Among students who received need-based aid, the average percentage of need met: 53%. Among students who received aid based on merit, the average award (and the proportion receiving): $5,274 (10%). The average athletic scholarship (and the proportion receiving): $14,414 (2%). Average amount of debt of borrowers graduating in 2005: $21,594. Proportion who borrowed: 72%.

CAMPUS LIFE AND EXTRACURRICULAR ACTIVITIES

Campus housing available (% using): coed dorms (71%), sorority housing (5%), fraternity housing (3%), apartment for single students (5%), special housing for disabled students (0%), special housing for international students (1%), other housing options (15%). Students who live in college-owned, operated, or affiliated housing: 45%. **Student employment:** During the 2005-2006 academic year, 26% of undergraduates worked on campus. Average per-year earnings: $2,218. **Clubs and organizations:** Number of student organizations: 300. Activities include: choral groups, concert band, dance, drama/theater, jazz band, literary magazine, marching band, music ensembles, musical theater, pep band, radio station, student government, student newspaper, student film society, symphony orchestra, television station, yearbook. Number of fraternities: 19; sororities: 18. Proportion of men in fraternities: 8%; of women in sororities: 11%. **Sports program (2005-2006):** Member of NCAA I. *Men's intercollegiate varsity sports:* baseball, basketball, cross-country, football, golf, ice hockey, soccer. *Women's intercollegiate varsity sports:* basketball, cross-country, golf, gymnastics, soccer, softball, swimming and diving, tennis, track and field (indoor), track and field (outdoor), volleyball.

SERVICES AND FACILITIES

Basic services: nonremedial tutoring, women's center, placement service, health service, health insurance. **Remedial assistance:** reading, math, writing, study skills. **Counseling services:** minority student, career, military, personal, veteran student, academic, older student, psychological, birth control. **For learning-disabled students:** School does not offer a structured program with separate admission and additional fees. Total undergraduates in learning-disabled program or receiving services: 254. Services include: reading machines, tape recorders, note-taking services, oral tests, readers, extended time for tests, priority registration, texts on tape, other testing accomodations, other. **Library:** Number of titles: 2,468,812; number of current serial subscriptions: 9,502. **Information technology resources:** Students are not required to lease or own a computer. Number of campus computers available to all students: 1,314. School has a wireless network. Proportion of college-owned housing units wired for high-speed internet access: 100%. **Campus safety:** Security services offered: 24-hour foot-and-vehicle patrols, late-night transport/escort service, 24-hour emergency telephones, lighted pathways/sidewalks, controlled dormitory access (key, security card, etc).

TRANSFER AND INTERNATIONAL STUDENTS

Transfer students: May apply for admission for the following academic terms: Fall, Spring, Summer. Applicants need a minimum number of credits to apply. For fall 2005: Transfer applications received: 1,507. Transfer applicants offered admission: 1,069. Transfer applicants enrolled: 718. **International students:** Number of foreign undergraduates: 191 (1% of student body). Minimum TOEFL score required: 500 (paper); 173 (computer).

Capital University

- **Address:** 1 College and Main, Columbus, OH 43209-2394
- **Website:** http://www.capital.edu
- **Private; Religious affiliation:** Lutheran
- **Enrollment:** 2,242 full-time; 620 part-time

KEY STATS

✔ **U.S News College Ranking:** 17, Universities–Master's (Midwest)
✔ **ACT Score (25th/75th percentile):** 21-26
✔ **Tuition:** 2006-2007: $24,500

Selectivity: More selective	**Room/board:** $6,552
Acceptance rate: 78%	**Average debt:** $24,092
Student/faculty ratio: 10/1	**Proportion who borrowed:** 80%

UNDERGRADUATE STUDENT BODY STATS

2005-2006 enrollment: 2,242 full-time; 620 part-time. Men: 36%; women: 64%. **Ethnic makeup:** African American: 12%; Asian American: 2%; Hispanic: 1%; White: 84%; International: 1%. **Religious preference:** Roman Catholic: 19%; Protestant: 37%; No preference: 12%; Lutheran: 15%; Other: 17%.

ADMISSIONS FACTS AND FIGURES

Phone: (866) 544-6175. **Email:** admissions@capital.edu. **Website:** http://www.capital.edu. **Application deadlines for fall 2007:** Regular decision: Rolling. Early decision: Not offered. Early action: Not offered. Admission can be deferred. **Application fee:** $25. Common application is accepted. **To apply online, go to:** http://www.applyweb.com/apply/capital/menu.html. **Admissions requirements/recommendations:** High school units required (recommended): English: (4); Mathematics: (3); Science: (3); Foreign language: (2); Social studies: (3); Academic electives: (1); Total units: (18). Tests: The college uses SAT or ACT scores in admissions decisions. Either SAT or ACT required. For admission to the fall 2007 entering class, the school will accept: ACT with writing, ACT without writing. Campus visit: Recommended. Admissions interview: Recommended. Off-campus interview: Not available. **Factors that count in admissions decisions:** *Academic:* Secondary school record: Very important. Class rank: Important. Letters of recommendation: Considered. Standardized test scores: Very important. Essay: Not considered. *Nonacademic:* Interview: Considered. Extracurricular activities: Considered. Talent/ability: Considered. Character/personal qualities: Considered. Alumni/ae relationship: Considered. Geographical residence: Considered. State residency: Considered. Religious affiliation/commitment: Considered. Minority status: Considered. Volunteer work: Considered. Work experience: Not considered. **Other schools with the greatest overlap in applicants:** Miami University–Oxford; Ohio Dominican University; Ohio State University–Columbus; Ohio University; Otterbein College. **Admissions statistics for the fall 2005 entering class:** Total applicants: 3,023. Total accepted: 2,356. Freshmen enrolled: 602; 9% were from out of state. Overall acceptance rate: 78%. **Credentials of fall 2005 freshmen:** 29% ranked in the top 10 percent of their high school class; 55% were in the top 25 percent, and 86% were in the top half. (Proportion submitting class standing: 93%.) **First-year students who submitted SAT scores:** 33%. Scores (25/75 percentile): Verbal: 490-600, Math: 480-600, Combined: 970-1200. **First-year students submitting ACT scores:** 94%. Scores (25/75 percentile): English: 20-26, Math: 19-26, Composite: 21-26.

ACADEMICS

Year founded: 1830. **Academic calendar:** Semester. **Degrees offered:** certificate, bachelor's, master's, first professional. **Most popular majors:** 15% education, 13% health professions and related clinical sciences, 13% multi/interdisciplinary studies, 12% social sciences, 11% public administration and social service professions. **Major fields of study:** biological and biomedical sciences; business, management, marketing, and related support services; communication, journalism, and related programs; computer and information sciences and support services; education; engineering; English language and literature/letters; foreign languages, literatures, and linguistics; health professions and related clinical sciences; history; mathematics and statistics; multi/interdisciplinary studies; natural resources and conservation; parks, recreation, leisure, and fitness studies; philosophy and religious studies; physical sciences; psychology; public administration and social service professions; social sciences; visual and performing arts. **Areas of required coursework:** arts/fine arts, humanities, mathematics, English (including composition), foreign languages, sciences (biological or physical), social science, other. **Pre-professional programs:** pre-law, pre-dentistry, pre-medicine, pre-theology, pre-veterinary science, pre-optometry, pre-pharmacy. **Special academic programs (% participation):** cross-registration, double major (12.9%), English as a Second Language (ESL), external degree program, honors program (4.4%), independent study (20.5%), internships (20.2%), student-designed major (10.8%), study abroad (3.7%). **Teacher certification offered in:** early childhood, special education, elementary, middle/junior high, secondary. **Reserve Officers Training Corps (ROTC):** Army ROTC: Offered on campus; Air Force ROTC: Offered at cooperating institution (Ohio State University). **Faculty and instruction (2005-2006):** Total instructional faculty: 218 full-time, 242 part-time. Full-time faculty with Ph.D. or other terminal degree: 69%. Student/faculty ratio: 10/1. Classes of fewer than 20 students; 68%; of 20 to 49 students: 31%; of 50 or more students: 0%. **Advanced Placement and International Baccalaureate credit:** AP tests may be used for: Credit only. Scores accepted: 3, 4, 5. International Baccalaureate exams may be used for: Credit only. **Freshmen returning for sophomore year:** 77%. **Graduation rates:** Four-year: 48%; five-year: 56%; six-year: 59%. **Graduate study:** 20% of students pursue further study immediately upon graduation. Fields in which graduates pursue further study: Master of Business Administration (MBA), 1%; law, 6%; medicine, 6%; dentistry, 2%; engineering, 4%; theology (or the seminary), 6%; education, 2%; arts and sciences, 72%; veterinary medicine, 2%.

COSTS AND FINANCIAL AID

Financial aid office: (614) 236-6511. **Expenses (2006-2007):** Tuition and fees 2006-2007: $24,500; room/board: $6,552. Estimated books and supplies: $960; transportation: $560; personal expenses: $1,730. **Financial aid:** Priority filing date for institution's financial aid form: March 1. In 2005-2006, 86% of undergraduates applied for financial aid. Of those, 79% were determined to have financial need; 12% had their need fully met. Average financial aid package (proportion receiving): $17,779 (79%). Average amount of gift aid, such as scholarships or grants (proportion receiving): $13,679 (79%). Average amount of self-help aid, such as work study or loans (proportion receiving): $5,092 (67%). Average need-based loan (excluding PLUS or other private loans): $4,379. Among students who received need-based aid, the average percentage of need met: 73%. Among students who received aid based on merit, the average award (and the proportion receiving): $9,259 (19%). The average athletic scholarship (and the proportion receiving): $0 (0%). Average amount of debt of borrowers graduating in 2005: $24,092. Proportion who borrowed: 80%.

CAMPUS LIFE AND EXTRACURRICULAR ACTIVITIES

Campus housing available: coed dorms, apartment for single students, other housing options. Students who live in college-owned, operated, or affiliated housing: 36%. **Student employment:** During the 2005-2006 academic year, 40% of undergraduates worked on campus. Average per-year earnings: $2,000. **Clubs and organizations:** Number of student organizations: 56. Activities include: choral groups, concert band, dance, drama/theater, jazz band, literary magazine, music ensembles, musical theater, radio station, student government, student newspaper, symphony orchestra, television station, yearbook. Number of fraternities: 3; sororities: 3. Proportion of men in fraternities: 7%; of women in sororities: 8%. Average proportion of students who stay on campus on weekends: 60%. **Sports program (2005-2006):** Member of NCAA III. **Men's intercollegiate varsity sports:** baseball, basketball, cross-country, football, golf, soccer, tennis, track and field (indoor), track and field (outdoor). **Women's intercollegiate varsity sports:** basketball, cross-country, golf, soccer, softball, tennis, track and field (indoor), track and field (outdoor), volleyball.

SERVICES AND FACILITIES

Basic services: nonremedial tutoring, placement service, health service, health insurance. **Remedial assistance:** math, writing, study skills, other. **Counseling services:** minority student, career, military, personal, academic, older student, psychological, birth control, religious. **For learning-disabled students:** School does not offer a structured program with separate admission and additional fees. Total undergraduates in learning-disabled program or receiving services: 60. Services include: remedial English, tape recorders, note-taking services, oral tests, learning center, readers, extended time for tests, tutors, priority registration, texts on tape, other testing accomodations. **Library:** Number of titles: 191,145; number of current serial subscriptions: 6,705. **Information technology resources:** Students are not required to lease or own a computer. Number of campus computers available to all students: 105. School does not have a wireless network. Proportion of college-owned housing units wired for high-speed internet access: 100%. **Campus safety:** Security services offered: 24-hour foot-and-vehicle patrols, late-night trans-port/escort service, lighted pathways/sidewalks, student patrols, controlled dormitory access (key, security card, etc).

TRANSFER AND INTERNATIONAL STUDENTS

Transfer students: May apply for admission for the following academic terms: Fall, Spring, Summer. Applicants need a minimum number of credits to apply. For fall 2005: Transfer applications received: 531. Transfer applicants offered admission: 140. Transfer applicants enrolled: 72. **International students:** Number of foreign undergraduates: 21 (1% of student body). Number of countries represented: 16. Minimum TOEFL score required: 500 (paper); 173 (computer). Average TOEFL score: 554 (paper).

Case Western Reserve University

- **Address:** 10900 Euclid Avenue, Cleveland, OH 44106
- **Website:** http://www.case.edu
- **Private**
- **Enrollment:** 3,714 full-time; 235 part-time

KEY STATS

✔ **U.S News College Ranking:** 38, National Universities
✔ **SAT Score (25th/75th percentile):** 1240-1440
✔ **Tuition:** 2006-2007: $30,538

Selectivity: More selective	**Room/board:** $9,280
Acceptance rate: 68%	**Average debt:** $20,597
Student/faculty ratio: 9/1	**Proportion who borrowed:** 67%

UNDERGRADUATE STUDENT BODY STATS

2005-2006 enrollment: 3,714 full-time; 235 part-time. Men: 59%; women: 41%. **Ethnic makeup:** African American: 5%; Asian American: 15%; Hispanic: 2%; White: 73%; International: 4%.

ADMISSIONS FACTS AND FIGURES

Phone: (216) 368-4450. **Email:** admission@case.edu. **Website:** http://www.case.edu. **Application deadlines for fall 2007:** Regular decision: January 15; decision sent by April 1. Early decision: Not offered. Early action: Send application by: November 1; Decision sent by: January 1. Admission can be deferred. **Application fee:** $35. Common application is accepted. **To apply online, go to:** http://admission.case.edu/admissions/application/default.asp. **Admissions requirements/recommendations:** High school units required (recommended): English: 4; Mathematics: 3 (4); Science: 3; Foreign language: 2 (3); Social studies: 3 (4); Total units: 16. Tests: The college uses SAT or ACT scores in admissions decisions. Either SAT or ACT required. For admission to the fall 2007 entering class, the school will accept: ACT with writing. Campus visit: Recommended. Admissions interview: Recommended. Off-campus interview: May be arranged. **Factors that count in admissions decisions:** *Academic:* Secondary school record: Very important. Class rank: Important. Letters of recommendation: Important. Standardized test scores: Important. Essay: Important. *Nonacademic:* Interview: Important. Extracurricular activities: Very important. Talent/ability: Very important. Character/personal qualities: Important. Alumni/ae relationship: Important. Geographical residence: Not considered. State residency: Not considered. Religious affiliation/commitment: Not considered. Minority status: Important. Volunteer work: Very important. Work experience: Very important. **Other schools with the greatest overlap in applicants:** Carnegie Mellon University; Cornell University; Ohio State University–Columbus; University of Michigan–Ann Arbor; Washington University in St. Louis. **Admissions statistics for the fall 2005 entering class:** Total applicants: 7,181. Total accepted: 4,916. Freshmen enrolled: 1,162; 47% were from out of state. Accepted through early-decision or early-action plans: 39%. Overall acceptance rate: 68%. Non-early acceptance rate: 64%. **Size of waiting list:** N/A applicants; enrolled from waiting list: 45. **Credentials of fall 2005 freshmen:** 63% ranked in the top 10 percent of their high school class; 91% were in the top 25 percent, and 99% were in the top half. (Proportion submitting class standing: 67%.) **First-year students who submitted SAT scores:** 89%. Scores (25/75 percentile): Verbal: 600-700, Math: 640-740, Combined: 1240-1440. **First-year students submitting ACT scores:** 58%. Scores (25/75 percentile): English: 26-32, Math: 27-32, Composite: 27-31.

ACADEMICS

Year founded: 1826. **Academic calendar:** Semester. **Degrees offered:** bachelor's, master's, first professional, doctorate. **Most popular majors:** 11% psychology, 10% biology/biological sciences, 7% biomedical/medical engineering, 7% business administration and management, 6% mechanical engineering. **Major fields of study:** area, ethnic, cultural, and gender studies; biological and biomedical sciences; business, management, marketing, and related support services; computer and information sciences and support services; education; engineering; English language and literature/letters; family and consumer sciences/human sciences; foreign languages, literatures, and linguistics; health professions and related clinical sciences; history; mathematics and statistics; multi/interdisciplinary studies; natural resources and conservation; philosophy and religious studies; physical sciences; psychology; social sciences; visual and performing arts. **Areas of required coursework:** humanities, mathematics, English (including composition), sciences (biological or physical), social science, other. **Pre-professional programs:** pre-law, pre-dentistry, pre-medicine, other. **Special academic programs (% participation):** accelerated program (7%), cooperative (work-study plan) program (15%), cross-registration (5%), double major (23%), dual enrollment, English as a Second Language (ESL), honors program (11%), independent study (66%), internships (28%), liberal arts/career combination (1%), student-designed major (1%), study abroad (12%), teacher certificate program (1%). **Teacher certification offered in:** elementary, secondary. **Cooperative education programs:** business, computer science, engineering, natural science. **Reserve Officers Training Corps (ROTC):** Army ROTC: Offered at cooperating institution (John Carroll University); Air Force ROTC: Offered at cooperating institution (University of Akron). **Faculty and instruction (2005-2006):** Total instructional faculty: 687 full-time, 166 part-time (62% men; 38% women; 14% minorities). Full-time faculty with Ph.D. or other terminal degree: 92%. Student/faculty ratio: 9/1. Classes of fewer than 20 students: 59%; of 20 to 49 students: 30%; of 50 or more students: 12%. **Advanced Placement and International Baccalaureate credit:** AP tests may be used for: Credit and/or placement. Scores accepted: 4, 5. International Baccalaureate exams may be used for: Credit and/or placement. **Freshmen returning for sophomore year:** 92%. **Graduation rates:** Four-year: 57%; five-year: 74%; six-year: 77%. **Graduate study:** 43% of students pursue further study immediately upon graduation. Fields in which graduates pursue further study: Master of Business Administration (MBA), 1%; law, 4%; medicine, 10%; dentistry, 1%; engineering, 10%; education, 2%; arts and sciences, 10%; veterinary medicine, 1%.

COSTS AND FINANCIAL AID

Financial aid office: (216) 368-3866. **Expenses (2006-2007):** Tuition and fees 2006-2007: $30,538; room/board: $9,280. Estimated books and supplies: $1,040; transportation: $950; personal expenses: $1,650. **Financial aid:** Priority filing date for institution's financial aid form: February 1. In 2005-2006, 69% of undergraduates applied for financial aid. Of those, 60% were determined to have financial need; 88% had their need fully met. Average financial aid package (proportion receiving): $28,931 (60%). Average amount of gift aid, such as scholarships or grants (proportion receiving): $18,391 (60%). Average amount of self-help aid, such as work study or loans (proportion receiving): $7,130 (48%). Average need-based loan (excluding PLUS or other private loans): $5,349. Among students who received need-based aid, the average percentage of need met: 92%. Among students who received aid based on merit, the average award (and the proportion receiving): $11,852 (30%). Average amount of debt of borrowers graduating in 2005: $20,597. Proportion who borrowed: 67%.

CAMPUS LIFE AND EXTRACURRICULAR ACTIVITIES

Campus housing available: coed dorms, sorority housing, fraternity housing, apartment for single students, other housing options. Students who live in college-owned, operated, or affiliated housing: 75%. **Student employment:** During the 2005-2006 academic year, 47% of undergraduates worked on campus. Average per-year earnings: $2,500. **Clubs and organizations:** Number of student organizations: 100. Activities include: choral groups, concert band, dance, drama/theater, jazz band, literary magazine, marching band, music ensembles, musical theater, pep band, radio station, student government, student newspaper, student film society, symphony orchestra, yearbook. Number of fraternities: 17; sororities: 6. Proportion of men in fraternities: 34%; of women in sororities: 23%. **Sports program (2005-2006):** Member of NCAA III. *Men's intercollegiate varsity sports:* baseball, basketball, cross-country, football, soccer, swimming and diving, tennis, track and field (indoor), track and field (outdoor), wrestling. *Women's intercollegiate varsity sports:* basketball, cross-country, soccer, softball, swimming and diving, tennis, track and field (indoor), track and field (outdoor), volleyball.

SERVICES AND FACILITIES

Basic services: nonremedial tutoring, women's center, placement service, health service, health insurance. **Counseling services:** minority student, career, personal, veteran student, academic, older student, psychological, birth control, religious. **For learning-disabled students:** School does not offer a structured program with separate admission and additional fees. Total undergraduates in learning-disabled program or receiving services: 47. Services include: reading machines, tape recorders, diagnostic testing service, note-taking services, oral tests, learning center, readers, extended time for tests, tutors, early syllabus, texts on tape, typist/scribe, other testing accomodations, other. **Library:** Number of titles: 2,471,504; number of current serial subscriptions: 20,265. **Information technology resources:** Students are not required to lease or own a computer. Number of campus computers available to all students: 300. School has a wireless network. Approximate number of users that can be accommodated: 50,000. Proportion of college-owned housing units wired for high-speed internet access: 100%. **Campus safety:** Security services offered: 24-hour foot-and-vehicle patrols, late-night transport/escort service, 24-hour emergency telephones, lighted pathways/sidewalks, controlled dormitory access (key, security card, etc).

TRANSFER AND INTERNATIONAL STUDENTS

Transfer students: May apply for admission for the following academic terms: Fall, Spring, Summer. Applicants do not need a minimum number of credits to apply. For fall 2005: Transfer applications received: 408. Transfer applicants offered admission: 132. Transfer applicants enrolled: 75. **International students:** Number of foreign undergraduates: 149 (4% of student body). Number of countries represented: 28. Minimum TOEFL score required: 550 (paper); 213 (computer).

Cedarville University

- **Address:** 251 N. Main Street, Cedarville, OH 45314
- **Website:** http://www.cedarville.edu
- **Private; Religious affiliation:** Baptist
- **Enrollment:** 2,930 full-time; 160 part-time

KEY STATS

✔ U.S News College Ranking: 14, Comp. Coll.–Bachelor's (Midwest)
✔ ACT Score (25th/75th percentile): 22-28
✔ Tuition: 2006-2007: $18,400

Selectivity: More selective	Room/board: $5,010
Acceptance rate: 83%	Average debt: $19,258
Student/faculty ratio: 13/1	Proportion who borrowed: 67%

UNDERGRADUATE STUDENT BODY STATS

2005-2006 enrollment: 2,930 full-time; 160 part-time. Men: 44%; women: 56%. **Ethnic makeup:** African American: 2%; Asian American: 1%; Hispanic: 2%; White: 95%.

ADMISSIONS FACTS AND FIGURES

Phone: (800) 233-2784. **Email:** admissions@cedarville.edu. **Website:** http://www.cedarville.edu. **Application deadlines for fall 2007:** Regular decision: Rolling. Early decision: Not offered. Early action: Not offered. Admission can be deferred. **Application fee:** $30. Common application is not accepted. **To apply online, go to:** https://www.cedarville.edu/myapplication/index.cfm. **Admissions requirements/recommendations:** High school units required (recommended): English: 4 (4); Mathematics: 3 (4); Science: 3 (3); Foreign language: 2 (3); Social studies: 3 (3); Total units: 15 (17). Tests: The college uses SAT or ACT scores in admissions decisions. Either SAT or ACT required. For admission to the fall 2007 entering class, the school will accept: ACT with writing, ACT without writing. Campus visit: Recommended. Admissions interview: Neither required nor recommended. **Factors that count in admissions decisions:** *Academic:* Secondary school record: Very important. Class rank: Considered. Letters of recommendation: Important. Standardized test scores: Very important. Essay: Very important. *Nonacademic:* Interview: Considered. Extracurricular activities: Considered. Talent/ability: Considered. Character/personal qualities: Very important. Alumni/ae relationship: Considered. Geographical residence: Not considered. State residency: Not considered. Religious affiliation/commitment: Very important. Minority status: Important. Volunteer work: Considered. Work experience: Not considered. **Other schools with the greatest overlap in**

applicants: Indiana Wesleyan University; Liberty University; Taylor University. **Admissions statistics for the fall 2005 entering class:** Total applicants: 2,017. Total accepted: 1,679. Freshmen enrolled: 763; 64% were from out of state. Overall acceptance rate: 83%. **Size of waiting list:** 0 applicants; enrolled from waiting list: 0. **Credentials of fall 2005 freshmen:** 34% ranked in the top 10 percent of their high school class; 63% were in the top 25 percent, and 89% were in the top half. (Proportion submitting class standing: 75%.) **Average high school grade point average:** 3.6. **First-year students who submitted SAT scores:** 60%. Scores (25/75 percentile): Verbal: 540-650, Math: 520-640, Combined: 1060-1290. **First-year students submitting ACT scores:** 71%. Scores (25/75 percentile): English: 23-29, Math: 22-27, Composite: 22-28.

ACADEMICS

Year founded: 1887. **Academic calendar:** Semester. **Degrees offered:** certificate, bachelor's, master's. **Most popular majors:** 9% nursing/registered nurse training (R.N., A.S.N., B.S.N., M.S.N.), 6% early childhood education and teaching, 5% business administration and management, 5% communication studies/speech communication and rhetoric, 4% mechanical engineering. **Major fields of study:** area, ethnic, cultural, and gender studies; biological and biomedical sciences; business, management, marketing, and related support services; communications technologies/technicians and support services; computer and information sciences and support services; education; engineering; English language and literature/letters; foreign languages, literatures, and linguistics; health professions and related clinical sciences; history; legal professions and studies; mathematics and statistics; multi/interdisciplinary studies; parks, recreation, leisure, and fitness studies; philosophy and religious studies; physical sciences; psychology; public administration and social service professions; security and protective services; social sciences; theology and religious vocations; visual and performing arts. **Areas of required coursework:** arts/fine arts, humanities, mathematics, English (including composition), sciences (biological or physical), history, social science, other. **Special academic programs (% participation):** accelerated program (2%), cross-registration (.5%), distance learning (38%), double major (10%), honors program (3%), independent study (18%), internships (26%), student-designed major (0%), study abroad (5%), teacher certificate program (18%). **Teacher certification offered in:** early childhood, special education, middle/junior high, secondary. **Reserve Officers Training Corps (ROTC):** Army ROTC: Offered at cooperating institution (Central State University); Air Force ROTC: Offered at cooperating institution (Wright State University). **Faculty and instruction (2005-2006):** Total instructional faculty: 208 full-time, 51 part-time (66% men; 34% women; 5% minorities). Full-time faculty with Ph.D. or other terminal degree: 63%. Student/faculty ratio: 13/1. Classes of fewer than 20 students: 58%; of 20 to 49 students: 35%; of 50 or more students: 7%. **Advanced Placement and International Baccalaureate credit:** AP tests may be used for: Credit and/or placement. Scores accepted: 3, 4, 5. International Baccalaureate exams may be used for: Credit and/or placement. **Freshmen returning for sophomore year:** 82%. **Graduation rates:** Four-year: 57%; five-year: 69%; six-year: 70%. **Graduate study:** 17% of students pursue further study immediately upon graduation; 2% within one year. Fields in which graduates pursue further study: Master of Business Administration (MBA), 5%; law, 1%; medicine, 1%; engineering, 5%; theology (or the seminary), 23%; education, 4%; arts and sciences, 23%.

COSTS AND FINANCIAL AID

Financial aid office: (937) 766-7866. **Expenses (2006-2007):** Tuition and fees 2006-2007: $18,400; room/board: $5,010. Estimated books and supplies: $800 personal expenses: $1,400. **Financial aid:** Priority filing date for institution's financial aid form: March 1. In 2005-2006, 72% of undergraduates applied for financial aid. Of those, 61% were determined to have financial need; 53% had their need fully met. Average financial aid package (proportion receiving): $15,778 (61%). Average amount of gift aid, such as scholarships or grants (proportion receiving): $1,879 (32%). Average amount of self-help aid, such as work study or loans (proportion receiving): $3,626 (53%). Average need-based loan (excluding PLUS or other private loans): $4,129. Among students who received need-based aid, the average percentage of need met: 38%. Among students who received aid based on merit, the average award (and the proportion receiving): $9,457 (19%). The average athletic scholarship (and the proportion receiving): $3,039 (5%). Average amount of debt of borrowers graduating in 2005: $19,258. Proportion who borrowed: 67%.

CAMPUS LIFE AND EXTRACURRICULAR ACTIVITIES

Campus housing available (% using): women's dorms (55%), men's dorms (43%), apartments for married students (2%). Students who live in college-owned, operated, or affiliated housing: 80%. **Student employment:** During the 2005-2006 academic year, 41% of undergraduates worked on campus. Average per-year earnings: $2,500. **Clubs and organizations:** Number of student organizations: 51. Activities include: choral groups, concert band, drama/theater, jazz band, music ensembles, musical theater, pep band, radio station, student government, student newspaper, symphony orchestra, yearbook. Number of fraternities: 0; sororities: 0. Average proportion of students who stay on campus on weekends: 80%. **Sports program (2005-2006):** Member of NAIA. *Men's intercollegiate varsity sports:* baseball, basketball, cross-country, golf, soccer, tennis, track and field (indoor), track and field (outdoor). *Women's intercollegiate varsity sports:* basketball, cross-country, soccer, softball, tennis, track and field (indoor), track and field (outdoor), volleyball.

SERVICES AND FACILITIES

Basic services: nonremedial tutoring, placement service, health service. **Remedial assistance:** reading, math, writing. **Counseling services:** career, military, personal, academic, religious. **For learning-disabled students:** School does not offer a structured program with separate admission and additional fees. Total undergraduates in learning-disabled program or receiving services: 25. Services include: remedial math, remedial English, tape recorders, note-taking services, oral tests, readers, extended time for tests, tutors, priority registration, priority seating, texts on tape, typist/scribe, exams on tape or computer, other testing accomodations, other. **Library:** Number of titles: 166,484; number of current serial subscriptions: 931. **Information technology resources:** Students are not required to lease or own a computer. Number of campus computers available to all students: 1,850. School has a wireless network. Approximate number of users that can be accommodated: 1,000. Proportion of college-owned housing units wired for high-speed internet access: 100%. **Campus safety:** Security services offered: 24-hour foot-and-vehicle patrols, late-night transport/escort service, 24-hour emergency telephones, lighted pathways/sidewalks, controlled dormitory access (key, security card, etc).

TRANSFER AND INTERNATIONAL STUDENTS

Transfer students: May apply for admission for the following academic terms: Fall, Spring, Summer. Applicants need a minimum number of credits to apply. For fall 2005: Transfer applications received: 386. Transfer applicants offered admission: 228. Transfer applicants enrolled: 137. **International students:** Number of foreign undergraduates: 14. Number of countries represented: 16. Minimum TOEFL score required: 550 (paper); 213 (computer).

Central State University

- **Address:** PO Box 1004, Wilberforce, OH 45384
- **Website:** http://www.centralstate.edu
- **Public**
- **Enrollment:** 1,450 full-time; 167 part-time

KEY STATS

✔ **U.S News College Ranking:** fourth tier, Comp. Coll.–Bachelor's (Midwest)
✔ **ACT Score (25th/75th percentile):** 14-18
✔ **Tuition:** 2006-2007: $5,294 in state, $11,462 out of state

Selectivity: Less selective	**Room/board:** $7,402
Acceptance rate: 38%	**Average debt:** N/A
Student/faculty ratio: 13/1	**Proportion who borrowed:** N/A

UNDERGRADUATE STUDENT BODY STATS

2005-2006 enrollment: 1,450 full-time; 167 part-time. Men: 51%; women: 49%. **Ethnic makeup:** African American: 87%; Hispanic: 1%; White: 11%; International: 1%.

ADMISSIONS FACTS AND FIGURES

Phone: (937) 376-6348. **Email:** admissions@centralstate.edu. **Website:** http://www.centralstate.edu. **Application deadlines for fall 2007:** Regular decision: Rolling. Early decision: Not offered. Early action: Not offered. Admission can be deferred. **Application fee:** $20. Common application is not accepted. **To apply online, go to:** http://www.centralstate.edu/admissions/apply2.html. **Admissions requirements/recommendations:** High school units required (recommended): English: 4; Mathematics: 3; Science: 3; Foreign language: 2; Social studies: 3; Academic electives: (2); Total units: 16 (2). Tests: The college uses SAT or ACT scores in admissions decisions.

Either SAT or ACT required. For admission to the fall 2007 entering class, the school will accept: ACT with writing, ACT without writing. Campus visit: Neither required nor recommended. Admissions interview: Neither required nor recommended. Off-campus interview: Not available. **Factors that count in admissions decisions: *Academic:*** Secondary school record: Very important. Class rank: Important. Letters of recommendation: Considered. Standardized test scores: Very important. Essay: Important. ***Nonacademic:*** Interview: Considered. Extracurricular activities: Considered. Talent/ability: Considered. Character/personal qualities: Important. Alumni/ae relationship: Not considered. Geographical residence: Important. State residency: Important. Religious affiliation/commitment: Not considered. Minority status: Not considered. Volunteer work: Not considered. Work experience: Not considered. **Other schools with the greatest overlap in applicants:** Cleveland State University; Ohio State University–Columbus; University of Cincinnati; Wright State University. **Admissions statistics for the fall 2005 entering class:** Total applicants: 4,563. Total accepted: 1,745. Freshmen enrolled: 353; 35% were from out of state. Overall acceptance rate: 38%. **Credentials of fall 2005 freshmen:** 10% ranked in the top 10 percent of their high school class; 25% were in the top 25 percent, and 50% were in the top half. (Proportion submitting class standing: 78%.) **Average high school grade point average:** 2.5. **First-year students who submitted SAT scores:** 21%. Scores (25/75 percentile): Verbal: 270-490, Math: 360-480, Combined: 630-970. **First-year students submitting ACT scores:** 82%. Scores (25/75 percentile): English: 12-17, Math: 14-17, Composite: 14-18.

ACADEMICS

Year founded: 1887. **Academic calendar:** Semester. **Degrees offered:** bachelor's, master's. **Most popular majors:** 30% business, management, marketing, and related support services, 11% education, 10% communication, journalism, and related programs, 10% social sciences, 9% psychology. **Major fields of study:** biological and biomedical sciences; business, management, marketing, and related support services; communication, journalism, and related programs; computer and information sciences and support services; education; engineering; engineering technologies/technicians; English language and literature/letters; history; mathematics and statistics; parks, recreation, leisure, and fitness studies; physical sciences; psychology; public administration and social service professions; social sciences; visual and performing arts. **Areas of required coursework:** arts/fine arts, humanities, computer literacy, mathematics, English (including composition), philosophy, foreign languages, sciences (biological or physical), history, social science. **Pre-professional programs:** pre-law, pre-dentistry, pre-medicine, pre-veterinary science. **Special academic programs:** cooperative (work-study plan) program, cross-registration, double major, English as a Second Language (ESL), honors program, independent study, internships, study abroad, teacher certificate program. **Teacher certification offered in:** early childhood, special education, elementary, middle/junior high, secondary. **Cooperative education programs:** business, computer science, education, engineering, humanities, natural science, social/behavioral science, technologies. **Reserve Officers Training Corps (ROTC):** Army ROTC: Offered on campus; Air Force ROTC: Offered at cooperating institution (Wright State University, Cedarville University). **Faculty and instruction (2005-2006):** Total instructional faculty: 94 full-time, 68 part-time (61% men; 39% women; 73% minorities). Full-time faculty with Ph.D. or other terminal degree: 66%. Student/faculty ratio: 13/1. Classes of fewer than 20 students: 59%; of 20 to 49 students: 39%; of 50 or more students: 1%. **Advanced Placement and International Baccalaureate credit:** AP tests may be used for: Credit and/or placement. Scores accepted: 3, 4, 5. International Baccalaureate exams may be used for: Credit and/or placement. **Freshmen returning for sophomore year:** 52%. **Graduation rates:** Four-year: 16%; five-year: 27%; six-year: 24%. **Graduate study:** 10% of students pursue further study immediately upon graduation; 3% within one year; 1% within five years.

COSTS AND FINANCIAL AID

Financial aid office: (937) 376-6579. **Expenses (2006-2007):** Tuition and fees 2006-2007: $5,294 in state, $11,462 out of state; room/board: $7,402. Estimated books and supplies: $900; transportation: $800; personal expenses: $1,280. **Financial aid:** Priority filing date for institution's financial aid form: February 15. In 2005-2006, 95% of undergraduates applied for financial aid.

CAMPUS LIFE AND EXTRACURRICULAR ACTIVITIES

Campus housing available (% using): coed dorms (66%), women's dorms (14%), men's dorms (20%). Students who live in college-owned, operated, or affiliated housing: 52%. **Student employment:** During the 2005-2006 academic year, 20% of undergraduates worked on campus. Average per-year earnings: $4,800. **Clubs and organizations:** Number of student organiza-

tions: 36. Activities include: choral groups, concert band, dance, drama/theater, jazz band, marching band, music ensembles, opera, pep band, radio station, student government, student newspaper, student film society, symphony orchestra, television station, yearbook. Number of fraternities: 8; sororities: 7. Proportion of men in fraternities: 1%; of women in sororities: 1%. Average proportion of students who stay on campus on weekends: 30%. **Sports program (2005-2006):** Member of NCAA II. ***Men's intercollegiate varsity sports:*** basketball, cheerleading, cross-country, golf, tennis, track and field (indoor), track and field (outdoor), volleyball. ***Women's intercollegiate varsity sports:*** basketball, cheerleading, cross-country, golf, tennis, track and field (indoor), track and field (outdoor), volleyball.

SERVICES AND FACILITIES

Basic services: nonremedial tutoring, placement service, day care, health service, health insurance. **Remedial assistance:** reading, math, writing, study skills. **Counseling services:** career, military, personal, academic, older student, psychological, birth control. **For learning-disabled students:** School does not offer a structured program with separate admission and additional fees. Total undergraduates in learning-disabled program or receiving services: 46. Services include: tape recorders, diagnostic testing service, untimed tests, note-taking services, oral tests, learning center, readers, extended time for tests, tutors, priority seating, other testing accomodations. **Library:** Number of titles: 179,753; number of current serial subscriptions: 375. **Information technology resources:** Students are not required to lease or own a computer. Number of campus computers available to all students: 520. School has a wireless network. Approximate number of users that can be accommodated: 300. Proportion of college-owned housing units wired for high-speed internet access: 100%. **Campus safety:** Security services offered: 24-hour foot-and-vehicle patrols, 24-hour emergency telephones, lighted pathways/sidewalks, controlled dormitory access (key, security card, etc).

TRANSFER AND INTERNATIONAL STUDENTS

Transfer students: May apply for admission for the following academic terms: Fall, Spring, Summer. Applicants need a minimum number of credits to apply. For fall 2005: Transfer applications received: 560. Transfer applicants offered admission: 195. Transfer applicants enrolled: 122. **International students:** Number of foreign undergraduates: 10 (1% of student body). Minimum TOEFL score required: 500 (paper).

Cleveland Institute of Art

- **Address:** 11141 East Boulevard, Cleveland, OH 44106
- **Website:** http://www.cia.edu
- **Private**
- **Enrollment:** 512 full-time; 28 part-time

KEY STATS

✔ **U.S News College Ranking:** Unranked Specialty School–Fine Arts
✔ **ACT Score (25th/75th percentile):** 19-25
✔ **Tuition:** 2006-2007: $28,991

Selectivity: Selective	**Room/board:** $9,444
Acceptance rate: 69%	**Average debt:** $37,543
Student/faculty ratio: 8/1	**Proportion who borrowed:** 89%

UNDERGRADUATE STUDENT BODY STATS

2005-2006 enrollment: 512 full-time; 28 part-time. Men: 48%; women: 52%. **Ethnic makeup:** African American: 5%; Asian American: 3%; Hispanic: 2%; White: 89%; International: 2%.

ADMISSIONS FACTS AND FIGURES

Phone: (216) 421-7418. **Email:** admissions@cia.edu. **Website:** http://www.cia.edu. **Application deadlines for fall 2007:** Regular decision: Rolling. Early decision: Not offered. Early action: Not offered. Admission can be deferred. **Application fee:** $30. Common application is not accepted. **To apply online, go to:** https://www.applyweb.com/aw?cia. **Admissions requirements/recommendations:** High school units required (recommended): English: (4); Mathematics: (3); Science: (3); Social studies: (3); Academic electives: (6); Total units: (20). Tests: The college uses SAT or ACT scores in admissions decisions. Either SAT or ACT required. For admission to the fall 2007 entering class, the school will accept: ACT with writing, ACT without writing. Campus visit: Recommended. Admissions interview: Recommended. Off-campus interview: May be arranged. **Factors that count in admissions decisions: *Academic:*** Secondary school record: Very important. Class rank: Not considered. Letters of recommendation: Important. Standardized test scores: Important. Essay: Important. ***Nonacademic:*** Interview: Important. Extracurricular activities: Not considered. Talent/ability: Very important. Character/personal qualities: Important. Alumni/ae relationship: Not considered. Geographical residence: Not considered. State residency: Not considered. Religious affiliation/commitment: Not considered. Minority status: Not considered. Volunteer work: Not considered. Work experience: Not considered. **Other schools with the greatest overlap in applicants:** Columbus College of Art and Design; Maryland Institute College of Art; Pratt Institute; Rhode Island School of Design; School of the Art Institute of Chicago. **Admissions statistics for the fall 2005 entering class:** Total applicants: 382. Total accepted: 263. Freshmen enrolled: 93; Overall acceptance rate: 69%. **Credentials of fall 2005 freshmen:** 3% ranked in the top 10 percent of their high school class; 12% were in the top 25 percent, and 37% were in the top half. (Proportion submitting class standing: 62%.) **Average high school grade point average:** 3.2. **First-year students who submitted SAT scores:** 24%. Scores (25/75 percentile): Verbal: 500-630, Math: 440-550, Combined: 940-1180. **First-year students submitting ACT scores:** 62%. Scores (25/75 percentile): English: N/A, Math: N/A, Composite: 19-25.

ACADEMICS
Year founded: 1882. **Academic calendar:** Semester. **Degrees offered:** bachelor's, master's. **Most popular majors:** Information not available. **Major fields of study:** health professions and related clinical sciences; visual and performing arts. **Areas of required coursework:** arts/fine arts, humanities, computer literacy, English (including composition), history, social science, other. **Special academic programs (% participation):** cross-registration (8%), exchange student program (domestic) (3%), honors program, independent study (3%), internships (3%), study abroad (3%). **Faculty and instruction (2005-2006):** Total instructional faculty: 47 full-time, 54 part-time (58% men; 42% women; 8% minorities). Full-time faculty with Ph.D. or other terminal degree: 81%. Student/faculty ratio: 8/1. Classes of fewer than 20 students: 75%; of 20 to 49 students: 25%; of 50 or more students: 0%. **Advanced Placement and International Baccalaureate credit:** AP tests may be used for: Credit only. Scores accepted: 3, 4, 5. International Baccalaureate exams may be used for: Credit only. **Freshmen returning for sophomore year:** 81%. **Graduation rates:** Four-year: 0%; five-year: 67%; six-year: 59%.

COSTS AND FINANCIAL AID
Financial aid office: (216) 421-7425. **Expenses (2006-2007):** Tuition and fees 2006-2007: $28,991; room/board: $9,444. Estimated books and supplies: $1,300; transportation: $1,400; personal expenses: $1,940. **Financial aid:** Priority filing date for institution's financial aid form: March 15. In 2005-2006, 88% of undergraduates applied for financial aid. Of those, 81% were determined to have financial need; 6% had their need fully met. Average financial aid package (proportion receiving): $16,015 (81%). Average amount of gift aid, such as scholarships or grants (proportion receiving): $10,431 (81%). Average amount of self-help aid, such as work study or loans (proportion receiving): $6,039 (75%). Average need-based loan (excluding PLUS or other private loans): $4,622. Among students who received need-based aid, the average percentage of need met: 53%. Among students who received aid based on merit, the average award (and the proportion receiving): $12,369 (17%). Average amount of debt of borrowers graduating in 2005: $37,543. Proportion who borrowed: 89%.

CAMPUS LIFE AND EXTRACURRICULAR ACTIVITIES
Campus housing available (% using): coed dorms (20%), apartment for single students, cooperative housing (70%), other housing options. **Student employment:** During the 2005-2006 academic year, 5% of undergraduates worked on campus. Average per-year earnings: $1,200. Activities include: literary magazine, student government. Average proportion of students who stay on campus on weekends: 60%.

SERVICES AND FACILITIES
Basic services: nonremedial tutoring, health service, health insurance. **Remedial assistance:** reading, writing, study skills. **Counseling services:** career, personal, academic. **For learning-disabled students:** School does not offer a structured program with separate admission and additional fees. Services include: remedial English, untimed tests, note-taking services, oral tests, extended time for tests, tutors. **Library:** Number of titles: 42,000; number of current serial subscriptions: 230. **Information technology resources:** Students are not required to lease or own a computer. **Campus**

safety: Security services offered: late-night transport/escort service, 24-hour emergency telephones, controlled dormitory access (key, security card, etc.).

TRANSFER AND INTERNATIONAL STUDENTS
Transfer students: May apply for admission for the following academic terms: Fall, Spring. Applicants need a minimum number of credits to apply. For fall 2005: Transfer applications received: 58. Transfer applicants offered admission: 28. Transfer applicants enrolled: 22. **International students:** Number of foreign undergraduates: 10 (2% of student body). Number of countries represented: 5. Minimum TOEFL score required: 525 (paper); 195 (computer). Average TOEFL score: 569 (paper).

Cleveland Institute of Music

- ■ **Address:** 11021 East Boulevard, Cleveland, OH 44106
- ■ **Website:** http://www.cim.edu/
- ■ **Private**
- ■ **Enrollment:** 243 full-time; 1 part-time

KEY STATS
✔ **U.S News College Ranking:** Unranked Specialty School–Fine Arts
✔ **SAT or ACT Score (25th/75th percentile):** N/A
✔ **Tuition:** 2005-2006: $26,870

Selectivity: Least selective	**Room/board:** $8,726
Acceptance rate: 34%	**Average debt:** N/A
Student/faculty ratio: N/A	**Proportion who borrowed:** N/A

UNDERGRADUATE STUDENT BODY STATS
2005-2006 enrollment: 243 full-time; 1 part-time. Men: 45%; women: 55%. **Ethnic makeup:** African American: 1%; American-Indian: 1%; Asian American: 8%; Hispanic: 4%; White: 76%; International: 10%.

ADMISSIONS FACTS AND FIGURES
Phone: (216) 795-3107. **Email:** cimadmission@case.edu. **Website:** http://www.cim.edu/. **Application deadlines for fall 2007:** Regular decision: December 1; decision sent by April 1. Early decision: Not offered. Early action: Not offered. Admission can be deferred. **Application fee:** $100. Common application is not accepted. **To apply online, go to:** http://www.cim.edu/colAdmisApplication.php. **Admissions requirements/recommendations:** Tests: The college does not use SAT or ACT scores in admissions decisions. Neither SAT nor ACT required. Campus visit: Recommended. Admissions interview: Recommended. **Factors that count in admissions decisions: *Academic:*** Secondary school record: Not considered. Class rank: Considered. Letters of recommendation: Very important. Standardized test scores: Important. Essay: Important. ***Nonacademic:*** Interview: Not considered. Extracurricular activities: Not considered. Talent/ability: Very important. Character/personal qualities: Considered. Alumni/ae relationship: Not considered. Geographical residence: Not considered. State residency: Not considered. Religious affiliation/commitment: Not considered. Minority status: Not considered. Volunteer work: Not considered. Work experience: Not considered. **Admissions statistics for the fall 2005 entering class:** Total applicants: 447. Total accepted: 151. Freshmen enrolled: 0; Overall acceptance rate: 34%.

ACADEMICS
Year founded: 1920. **Academic calendar:** Semester. **Degrees offered:** certificate, bachelor's, master's, doctorate. **Most popular majors:** Information not available. **Major fields of study:** visual and performing arts. **Areas of required coursework:** arts/fine arts, humanities, mathematics, English (including composition), sciences (biological or physical), social science. **Special academic programs:** cross-registration, double major, independent study, study abroad. **Advanced Placement and International Baccalaureate credit:** AP tests may be used for: Credit and/or placement. Scores accepted: 3, 4, 5. International Baccalaureate exams may be used for: Credit and/or placement. **Freshmen returning for sophomore year:** 90%. **Graduation rates:** Four-year: 81%; five-year: 83%; six-year: 77%.

COSTS AND FINANCIAL AID
Financial aid office: (216) 791-5000. **Expenses (2005-2006):** Tuition and fees 2005-2006: $26,870; room/board: $8,726. **Financial aid:** Priority filing date for institution's financial aid form: February 15; deadline: February 15.

CAMPUS LIFE AND EXTRACURRICULAR ACTIVITIES

Campus housing available: coed dorms. Activities include: choral groups, dance, drama/theater, jazz band, music ensembles, opera, student government, student newspaper, symphony orchestra. Number of fraternities: 0; sororities: 0. Average proportion of students who stay on campus on weekends: 98%.

SERVICES AND FACILITIES

Basic services: nonremedial tutoring, placement service, health service, health insurance. **Remedial assistance:** writing, study skills. **Counseling services:** career, personal, academic, psychological, birth control. **For learning-disabled students:** School does not offer a structured program with separate admission and additional fees. Services include: remedial English, remedial reading, tape recorders, diagnostic testing service, untimed tests, note-taking services, learning center, readers, extended time for tests, tutors, other testing accomodations. **Library:** Number of titles: 50,924; number of current serial subscriptions: 110. **Information technology resources:** Students are not required to lease or own a computer. Number of campus computers available to all students: 10. School has a wireless network. Proportion of college-owned housing units wired for high-speed internet access: 100%. **Campus safety:** Security services offered: 24-hour foot-and-vehicle patrols, late-night transport/escort service, 24-hour emergency telephones, lighted pathways/sidewalks, controlled dormitory access (key, security card, etc).

TRANSFER AND INTERNATIONAL STUDENTS

Transfer students: May apply for admission for the following academic terms: Fall, Spring. Applicants do not need a minimum number of credits to apply. **International students:** Number of foreign undergraduates: 17 (10% of student body). Minimum TOEFL score required: 550 (paper); 213 (computer).

Cleveland State University

- **Address:** 2121 Euclid Avenue, Cleveland, OH 44115
- **Website:** http://www.csuohio.edu
- **Public**
- **Enrollment:** 6,536 full-time; 3,022 part-time

KEY STATS

- ✔ **U.S News College Ranking:** fourth tier, National Universities
- ✔ **ACT Score (25th/75th percentile):** 16-22
- ✔ **Tuition:** 2006-2007: $7,970 in state, $10,712 out of state

Selectivity: Less selective	**Room/board:** $7,834
Acceptance rate: 80%	**Average debt:** N/A
Student/faculty ratio: 14/1	**Proportion who borrowed:** N/A

UNDERGRADUATE STUDENT BODY STATS

2005-2006 enrollment: 6,536 full-time; 3,022 part-time. Men: 45%; women: 55%. **Ethnic makeup:** African American: 21%; Asian American: 3%; Hispanic: 3%; White: 70%; International: 2%.

ADMISSIONS FACTS AND FIGURES

Phone: (216) 687-2100. **Email:** admissions@csuohio.edu. **Website:** http://www.csuohio.edu. **Application deadlines for fall 2007:** Regular decision: July 15. Early decision: Not offered. Early action: Not offered. Admission can be deferred. **Application fee:** $30. Common application is accepted. **To apply online, go to:** http://www.csuohio.edu/admissions/application.html. **Admissions requirements/recommendations:** High school units required (recommended): English: (4); Mathematics: (3); Science: (3); Foreign language: (2); Social studies: (3); Total units: (16). Tests: The college uses SAT or ACT scores in admissions decisions. Either SAT or ACT required. For admission to the fall 2007 entering class, the school will accept: ACT without writing. Campus visit: Recommended. Admissions interview: Neither required nor recommended. Off-campus interview: Not available. **Factors that count in admissions decisions:** *Academic:* Secondary school record: Considered. Class rank: Considered. Letters of recommendation: Considered. Standardized test scores: Very important. Essay: Considered. *Nonacademic:* Interview: Not considered. Extracurricular activities: Not considered. Talent/ability: Not considered. Character/personal qualities: Not considered. Alumni/ae relationship: Not considered. Geographical residence: Not considered. State residency: Not considered. Religious affiliation/commitment: Not considered. Minority status: Not considered. Volunteer work: Not considered. Work experience: Not considered. **Other schools with the greatest overlap in applicants:** Baldwin-Wallace College; Bowling Green State University; Kent State University; Ohio State University–Columbus; University of Akron. **Admissions statistics for the fall 2005 entering class:** Total applicants: 3,153. Total accepted: 2,520. Freshmen enrolled: 1,079; 6% were from out of state. Overall acceptance rate: 80%. **Credentials of fall 2005 freshmen:** 9% ranked in the top 10 percent of their high school class; 29% were in the top 25 percent, and 53% were in the top half. (Proportion submitting class standing: 77%.) **Average high school grade point average:** 2.8. First-year students who submitted SAT scores: 39%. Scores (25/75 percentile): Verbal: 410-550, Math: 410-570, Combined: 820-1120. **First-year students submitting ACT scores:** 72%. Scores (25/75 percentile): English: N/A, Math: N/A, Composite: 16-22.

ACADEMICS

Year founded: 1964. **Academic calendar:** Semester. **Degrees offered:** certificate, bachelor's, post-bachelor's certificate, master's, post-master's certificate, first professional, first professional certificate, doctorate. **Most popular majors:** 10% communication studies/speech communication and rhetoric, 7% psychology, 6% early childhood education and teaching, 5% social work, 4% urban studies/affairs. **Major fields of study:** agriculture, agriculture operations, and related sciences; area, ethnic, cultural, and gender studies; biological and biomedical sciences; business, management, marketing, and related support services; communication, journalism, and related programs; computer and information sciences and support services; education; engineering; engineering technologies/technicians; English language and literature/letters; foreign languages, literatures, and linguistics; health professions and related clinical sciences; history; liberal arts and sciences studies, and humanities; mathematics and statistics; multi/interdisciplinary studies; natural resources and conservation; parks, recreation, leisure, and fitness studies; philosophy and religious studies; physical sciences; psychology; public administration and social service professions; social sciences; visual and performing arts. **Areas of required coursework:** arts/fine arts, humanities, mathematics, English (including composition), philosophy, foreign languages, sciences (biological or physical), history, social science, other. **Pre-professional programs:** pre-medicine, pre-pharmacy. **Special academic programs:** accelerated program, cooperative (work-study plan) program, cross-registration, distance learning, double major, dual enrollment, English as a Second Language (ESL), exchange student program (domestic), honors program, internships, student-designed major, study abroad, teacher certificate program. **Teacher certification offered in:** early childhood, special education, elementary, middle/junior high, adult education, secondary. **Cooperative education programs:** art, business, computer science, education, engineering, health professions, humanities, natural science, social/behavioral science, technologies. **Reserve Officers Training Corps (ROTC):** Army ROTC: Offered at cooperating institution (John Carroll University); Navy ROTC: Offered at cooperating institution (Kent State University); Air Force ROTC: Offered at cooperating institution (Kent State University). **Faculty and instruction (2005-2006):** Total instructional faculty: 575 full-time, 422 part-time (59% men; 41% women; 17% minorities). Full-time faculty with Ph.D. or other terminal degree: 86%. Student/faculty ratio: 14/1. Classes of fewer than 20 students: 40%; of 20 to 49 students: 50%; of 50 or more students: 10%. **Advanced Placement and International Baccalaureate credit:** AP tests may be used for: Credit and/or placement. International Baccalaureate exams may be used for: Credit and/or placement. **Freshmen returning for sophomore year:** 61%. **Graduation rates:** Four-year: 11%; five-year: 24%; six-year: 30%.

COSTS AND FINANCIAL AID

Financial aid office: (216) 687-2054. **Expenses (2006-2007):** Tuition and fees 2006-2007: $7,970 in state, $10,712 out of state; room/board: $7,834. Estimated books and supplies: $800; transportation: $1,400; personal expenses: $2,376. **Financial aid:** Priority filing date for institution's financial aid form: February 15. In 2005-2006, 82% of undergraduates applied for financial aid. Of those, 74% were determined to have financial need; 7% had their need fully met. Average financial aid package (proportion receiving): $7,247 (72%). Average amount of gift aid, such as scholarships or grants (proportion receiving): $4,979 (54%). Average amount of self-help aid, such as work study or loans (proportion receiving): $4,067 (63%). Average need-based loan (excluding PLUS or other private loans): $3,901. Among students who received need-based aid, the average percentage of need met: 48%. Among students who received aid based on merit, the average award (and the proportion receiving): $8,133 (11%). The average athletic scholarship (and the proportion receiving): $9,254 (2%).

CAMPUS LIFE AND EXTRACURRICULAR ACTIVITIES

Campus housing available: coed dorms. Students who live in college-owned, operated, or affiliated housing: 5%. **Student employment:** During the 2005-2006 academic year, 8% of undergraduates worked on campus. Average per-year earnings: $6,720. **Clubs and organizations:** Number of student organizations: 118. Activities include: choral groups, dance, drama/theater, jazz band, literary magazine, music ensembles, musical theater, opera, radio station, student government, student newspaper, symphony orchestra. Number of fraternities: 8; sororities: 8. Proportion of men in fraternities: 5%; of women in sororities: 5%. Average proportion of students who stay on campus on weekends: 4%. **Sports program (2005-2006):** Member of NCAA I. *Men's intercollegiate varsity sports:* baseball, basketball, fencing, golf, soccer, swimming and diving, tennis, wrestling. *Women's intercollegiate varsity sports:* basketball, cross-country, fencing, golf, soccer, softball, swimming and diving, tennis, volleyball.

SERVICES AND FACILITIES

Basic services: nonremedial tutoring, women's center, placement service, health service, health insurance. **Remedial assistance:** reading, math, writing, study skills. **Counseling services:** minority student, career, military, personal, veteran student, academic, older student, psychological, birth control. **For learning-disabled students:** School does not offer a structured program with separate admission and additional fees. Services include: remedial math, remedial English, reading machines, tape recorders, note-taking services, oral tests, learning center, readers, extended time for tests, tutors, priority registration, priority seating, texts on tape, typist/scribe, exams on tape or computer, other testing accomodations, other. **Library:** Number of titles: 1,011,471; number of current serial subscriptions: 4,269. **Information technology resources:** Students are not required to lease or own a computer. Number of campus computers available to all students: 740. School has a wireless network. Approximate number of users that can be accommodated: 16,000. Proportion of college-owned housing units wired for high-speed internet access: 100%. **Campus safety:** Security services offered: 24-hour foot-and-vehicle patrols, late-night transport/escort service, 24-hour emergency telephones, lighted pathways/sidewalks, student patrols, controlled dormitory access (key, security card, etc).

TRANSFER AND INTERNATIONAL STUDENTS

Transfer students: May apply for admission for the following academic terms: Fall, Spring, Summer. Applicants do not need a minimum number of credits to apply. For fall 2005: Transfer applications received: 2,896. Transfer applicants offered admission: 2,013. Transfer applicants enrolled: 1,040. **International students:** Number of foreign undergraduates: 191 (2% of student body). Number of countries represented: 52. Minimum TOEFL score required: 525 (paper); 197 (computer). Average TOEFL score: 525 (paper).

College of Mount St. Joseph

- **Address:** 5701 Delhi Road, Cincinnati, OH 45233
- **Website:** http://www.msj.edu
- **Private; Religious affiliation:** Catholic
- **Enrollment:** 1,338 full-time; 597 part-time

KEY STATS

✔ **U.S News College Ranking:** 40, Universities–Master's (Midwest)
✔ **ACT Score (25th/75th percentile):** 18-23
✔ **Tuition:** 2006-2007: $20,090

Selectivity: Selective	**Room/board:** $6,300
Acceptance rate: 73%	**Average debt:** $13,400
Student/faculty ratio: 11/1	**Proportion who borrowed:** 80%

UNDERGRADUATE STUDENT BODY STATS

2005-2006 enrollment: 1,338 full-time; 597 part-time. Men: 31%; women: 69%. **Ethnic makeup:** African American: 10%; Hispanic: 1%; White: 88%. **Religious preference:** Protestant: 19%; No preference: 18%; Unknown: 21%; Catholic: 41%; Other: 1%.

ADMISSIONS FACTS AND FIGURES

Phone: (513) 244-4531. **Email:** admission@mail.msj.edu. **Website:** http://www.msj.edu. **Application deadlines for fall 2007:** Regular decision: August 15. Early decision: Not offered. Early action: Not offered. Admission

can be deferred. **Application fee:** $25. Common application is accepted. **To apply online, go to:** http://www.msj.edu/admission/apply/. **Admissions requirements/recommendations:** High school units required (recommended): English: 4 (4); Mathematics: 2 (4); Science: 2 (4); Foreign language: 2 (2); Social studies: 1 (2); History: 1 (2); Academic electives: 0 (4); Total units: 13 (23). Tests: The college uses SAT or ACT scores in admissions decisions. Either SAT or ACT required. For admission to the fall 2007 entering class, the school will accept: ACT with writing. Campus visit: Recommended. Admissions interview: Recommended. Off-campus interview: May be arranged. **Factors that count in admissions decisions:** *Academic:* Secondary school record: Very important. Class rank: Not considered. Letters of recommendation: Considered. Standardized test scores: Very important. Essay: Considered. *Nonacademic:* Interview: Considered. Extracurricular activities: Important. Talent/ability: Considered. Character/personal qualities: Considered. Alumni/ae relationship: Considered. Geographical residence: Not considered. State residency: Not considered. Religious affiliation/commitment: Not considered. Minority status: Not considered. Volunteer work: Considered. Work experience: Considered. **Other schools with the greatest overlap in applicants:** Northern Kentucky University; University of Cincinnati; Wittenberg University; Xavier University. **Admissions statistics for the fall 2005 entering class:** Total applicants: 1,087. Total accepted: 793. Freshmen enrolled: 315; 13% were from out of state. Overall acceptance rate: 73%. **Credentials of fall 2005 freshmen:** 13% ranked in the top 10 percent of their high school class; 36% were in the top 25 percent, and 69% were in the top half. (Proportion submitting class standing: 87%.) **Average high school grade point average:** 3.2. **First-year students who submitted SAT scores:** 47%. Scores (25/75 percentile): Verbal: 440-560, Math: 430-540, Combined: 870-1100. **First-year students submitting ACT scores:** 82%. Scores (25/75 percentile): English: N/A, Math: N/A, Composite: 18-23.

ACADEMICS

Year founded: 1920. **Academic calendar:** Semester. **Degrees offered:** certificate, associate, bachelor's, post-bachelor's certificate, master's, doctorate. **Most popular majors:** 12% nursing/registered nurse training (R.N., A.S.N., B.S.N., M.S.N.), 11% business administration and management, 7% liberal arts and sciences/liberal studies, 7% rehabilitation and therapeutic professions, 6% communication studies/speech communication and rhetoric. **Major fields of study:** biological and biomedical sciences; business, management, marketing, and related support services; communication, journalism, and related programs; computer and information sciences and support services; education; English language and literature/letters; health professions and related clinical sciences; history; legal professions and studies; liberal arts and sciences studies, and humanities; mathematics and statistics; multi/interdisciplinary studies; philosophy and religious studies; physical sciences; psychology; public administration and social service professions; social sciences; theology and religious vocations; visual and performing arts. **Areas of required coursework:** arts/fine arts, humanities, mathematics, English (including composition), philosophy, sciences (biological or physical), history, social science, other. **Pre-professional programs:** pre-law, pre-dentistry, pre-medicine, pre-theology, pre-veterinary science, pre-optometry, pre-pharmacy, other. **Special academic programs (% participation):** accelerated program (8%), cooperative (work-study plan) program (33%), cross-registration (13%), distance learning (22%), double major (5%), honors program (12%), independent study (46%), internships (33%), liberal arts/career combination (0%), study abroad (3%), teacher certificate program (17%). **Teacher certification offered in:** early childhood, special education, middle/junior high, secondary. **Cooperative education programs:** art, business, education, health professions, humanities, natural science, social/behavioral science, other. **Reserve Officers Training Corps (ROTC):** Army ROTC: Offered at cooperating institution (Xavier University); Air Force ROTC: Offered at cooperating institution (University of Cincinnati). **Faculty and instruction (2005-2006):** Total instructional faculty: 124 full-time, 89 part-time (38% men; 62% women; 4% minorities). Full-time faculty with Ph.D. or other terminal degree: 56%. Student/faculty ratio: 11/1. Classes of fewer than 20 students: 61%; of 20 to 49 students: 39%; of 50 or more students: 0%. **Advanced Placement and International Baccalaureate credit:** AP tests may be used for: Credit and/or placement. Scores accepted: 3, 4, 5. International Baccalaureate exams may be used for: Credit and/or placement. **Freshmen returning for sophomore year:** 75%. **Graduation rates:** Four-year: 53%; five-year: 66%; six-year: 67%. **Graduate study:** 15% of students pursue further study immediately upon graduation. Fields in which graduates pursue further study: Master of Business Administration (MBA), 4%; law, 4%; education, 6%; arts and sciences, 15%.

COSTS AND FINANCIAL AID

Financial aid office: (513) 244-4418. **Expenses (2006-2007):** Tuition and fees 2006-2007: $20,090; room/board: $6,300. Estimated books and supplies: $800; transportation: $400; personal expenses: $600. **Financial aid:** Priority filing date for institution's financial aid form: March 1. In 2005-2006, 96% of undergraduates applied for financial aid. Of those, 68% were determined to have financial need; 53% had their need fully met. Average financial aid package (proportion receiving): $15,832 (68%). Average amount of gift aid, such as scholarships or grants (proportion receiving): $6,998 (57%). Average amount of self-help aid, such as work study or loans (proportion receiving): $6,383 (64%). Average need-based loan (excluding PLUS or other private loans): $4,737. Among students who received need-based aid, the average percentage of need met: 90%. Among students who received aid based on merit, the average award (and the proportion receiving): $6,990 (12%). The average athletic scholarship (and the proportion receiving): $0 (0%). Average amount of debt of borrowers graduating in 2005: $13,400. Proportion who borrowed: 80%.

CAMPUS LIFE AND EXTRACURRICULAR ACTIVITIES

Campus housing available (% using): coed dorms (100%). Students who live in college-owned, operated, or affiliated housing: 21%. **Student employment:** During the 2005-2006 academic year, 13% of undergraduates worked on campus. Average per-year earnings: $892. **Clubs and organizations:** Number of student organizations: 45. Activities include: choral groups, concert band, dance, drama/theater, jazz band, literary magazine, marching band, music ensembles, musical theater, pep band, student government, student newspaper. Number of fraternities: 0; sororities: 0. **Sports program (2005-2006):** Member of NCAA III. *Men's intercollegiate varsity sports:* baseball, basketball, cross-country, football, golf, soccer, tennis, track and field (indoor), track and field (outdoor), wrestling. *Women's intercollegiate varsity sports:* basketball, cross-country, golf, soccer, softball, tennis, track and field (indoor), track and field (outdoor), volleyball.

SERVICES AND FACILITIES

Basic services: nonremedial tutoring, women's center, placement service, day care, health service, health insurance. **Remedial assistance:** reading, math, writing, study skills. **Counseling services:** minority student, career, personal, veteran student, academic, older student, psychological, religious. **For learning-disabled students:** School does not offer a structured program with separate admission and additional fees. Total undergraduates in learning-disabled program or receiving services: 113. Services include: remedial math, remedial English, note-taking services, learning center, readers, extended time for tests, tutors. **Library:** Number of titles: 97,410; number of current serial subscriptions: 8,393. **Information technology resources:** Students are not required to lease or own a computer. Number of campus computers available to all students: 278. School has a wireless network. Approximate number of users that can be accommodated: 4,500. Proportion of college-owned housing units wired for high-speed internet access: 100%. **Campus safety:** Security services offered: 24-hour foot-and-vehicle patrols, late-night transport/escort service, 24-hour emergency telephones, lighted pathways/sidewalks, student patrols, controlled dormitory access (key, security card, etc).

TRANSFER AND INTERNATIONAL STUDENTS

Transfer students: May apply for admission for the following academic terms: Fall, Winter, Spring, Summer. Applicants need a minimum number of credits to apply. For fall 2005: Transfer applications received: 518. Transfer applicants offered admission: 366. Transfer applicants enrolled: 200. **International students:** Number of foreign undergraduates: 7. Number of countries represented: 7. Minimum TOEFL score required: 510 (paper); 180 (computer).

College of Wooster

- **Address:** 1189 Beall Avenue, Wooster, OH 44691
- **Website:** http://www.wooster.edu/
- **Private**
- **Enrollment:** 1,813 full-time; 33 part-time

KEY STATS

✔ **U.S News College Ranking:** 67, Liberal Arts Colleges
✔ **SAT Score (25th/75th percentile):** 1110-1340
✔ **Tuition:** 2006-2007: $30,060
  Selectivity: More selective   **Room/board:** $7,520
  Acceptance rate: 75%   **Average debt:** $19,989
  Student/faculty ratio: 12/1   **Proportion who borrowed:** 55%

UNDERGRADUATE STUDENT BODY STATS

2005-2006 enrollment: 1,813 full-time; 33 part-time. Men: 48%; women: 52%. **Ethnic makeup:** African American: 4%; Asian American: 2%; Hispanic: 2%; White: 87%; International: 5%.

ADMISSIONS FACTS AND FIGURES

Phone: (800) 877-9905. **Email:** admissions@wooster.edu. **Website:** http://www.wooster.edu/. **Application deadlines for fall 2007:** Regular decision: February 15; decision sent by April 1. Early decision: Send application by: December 1; Decision sent by: December 15. Early action: Not offered. Admission can be deferred. **Application fee:** $40. Common application is accepted. **Admissions requirements/recommendations:** High school units required (recommended): English: 4; Mathematics: 3 (4); Science: 3 (4); Foreign language: 2 (3); Social studies: 3 (4); Academic electives: 2. Tests: The college uses SAT or ACT scores in admissions decisions. Either SAT or ACT required. For admission to the fall 2007 entering class, the school will accept: ACT with writing. Campus visit: Recommended. Admissions interview: Recommended. Off-campus interview: May be arranged. **Factors that count in admissions decisions:** *Academic:* Secondary school record: Very important. Class rank: Very important. Letters of recommendation: Important. Standardized test scores: Important. Essay: Important. *Nonacademic:* Interview: Considered. Extracurricular activities: Considered. Talent/ability: Important. Character/personal qualities: Important. Alumni/ae relationship: Considered. Geographical residence: Considered. State residency: Considered. Religious affiliation/commitment: Not considered. Minority status: Considered. Volunteer work: Considered. Work experience: Considered. **Other schools with the greatest overlap in applicants:** Allegheny College; Denison University; Kenyon College; Miami University–Oxford; Ohio Wesleyan University. **Admissions statistics for the fall 2005 entering class:** Total applicants: 2,542. Total accepted: 1,900. Freshmen enrolled: 537; 59% were from out of state. Accepted through early-decision or early-action plans: 12%. Overall acceptance rate: 75%. Early-decision acceptance rate: 93%. Non-early acceptance rate: 74%. **Size of waiting list:** 147 applicants; enrolled from waiting list: 6. **Credentials of fall 2005 freshmen:** 32% ranked in the top 10 percent of their high school class; 66% were in the top 25 percent, and 92% were in the top half. (Proportion submitting class standing: 66%.) **Average high school grade point average:** 3.6. **First-year students who submitted SAT scores:** 73%. Scores (25/75 percentile): Verbal: 560-680, Math: 550-660, Combined: 1110-1340. **First-year students submitting ACT scores:** 58%. Scores (25/75 percentile): English: 22-29, Math: 22-28, Composite: 23-28.

ACADEMICS

Year founded: 1866. **Academic calendar:** Semester. **Degrees offered:** bachelor's. **Most popular majors:** 11% history, 9% English language and literature, 7% communication studies/speech communication and rhetoric, 7% sociology, 6% political science and government. **Major fields of study:** area, ethnic, cultural, and gender studies; biological and biomedical sciences; business, management, marketing, and related support services; communication, journalism, and related programs; computer and information sciences and support services; education; English language and literature/letters; foreign languages, literatures, and linguistics; health professions and related clinical sciences; history; mathematics and statistics; multi/interdisciplinary studies; philosophy and religious studies; physical sciences; psychology; social sciences; visual and performing arts. **Areas of required coursework:** arts/fine arts, humanities, mathematics, English (including composition), foreign languages, sciences (biological or physical), history, social science, other. **Pre-professional programs:** pre-law, pre-medicine, pre-theology, pre-veterinary science, other. **Special academic programs (% participation):** double major, exchange student program (domestic), independent study (100%), internships, student-designed major, study abroad, teacher certificate program. **Teacher certification offered in:** early childhood, elementary, middle/junior high, secondary. **Cooperative education programs:** engineering, health professions, natural science, other. **Faculty and instruction (2005-2006):** Total instructional faculty: 133 full-time, 58 part-time (55% men; 45% women; 6% minorities). Full-time faculty with Ph.D. or other terminal degree: 98%. Student/faculty ratio: 12/1. Classes of fewer than 20 students: 69%; of 20 to 49 students: 31%; of 50 or more students: 1%. **Advanced Placement and International Baccalaureate credit:** AP tests may be used for: Credit only. Scores accepted: 3, 4, 5. International Baccalaureate exams may be used for: Credit only. **Freshmen returning for sophomore year:** 87%. **Graduation rates:** Four-year: 68%; five-year: 74%; six-year: 75%. **Graduate study:** 42% of students pursue further study within one year; 66% within five years. Fields in which graduates pursue further study: Master of Business Administration (MBA), 3%; law, 11%; medicine, 8%; dentistry, 1%; theology (or the seminary), 3%; education, 11%; arts and sciences, 52%.

COSTS AND FINANCIAL AID

Financial aid office: (330) 263-2317. **Expenses (2006-2007):** Tuition and fees 2006-2007: $30,060; room/board: $7,520. Estimated books and supplies: $810; transportation: $150; personal expenses: $600. **Financial aid:** Priority filing date for institution's financial aid form: February 15; deadline: September 1. In 2005-2006, 67% of undergraduates applied for financial aid. Of those, 58% were determined to have financial need; 91% had their need fully met. Average financial aid package (proportion receiving): $23,837 (58%). Average amount of gift aid, such as scholarships or grants (proportion receiving): $17,286 (57%). Average amount of self-help aid, such as work study or loans (proportion receiving): $6,296 (47%). Average need-based loan (excluding PLUS or other private loans): $6,333. Among students who received need-based aid, the average percentage of need met: 93%. Among students who received aid based on merit, the average award (and the proportion receiving): $11,350 (27%). Average amount of debt of borrowers graduating in 2005: $19,989. Proportion who borrowed: 55%.

CAMPUS LIFE AND EXTRACURRICULAR ACTIVITIES

Campus housing available: coed dorms, women's dorms, sorority housing, fraternity housing, other housing options. Students who live in college-owned, operated, or affiliated housing: 99%. **Clubs and organizations:** Number of student organizations: 100. Activities include: choral groups, concert band, dance, drama/theater, jazz band, literary magazine, marching band, music ensembles, musical theater, pep band, radio station, student government, student newspaper, student film society, symphony orchestra, yearbook. Number of fraternities: 5; sororities: 6. Proportion of men in fraternities: 10%; of women in sororities: 17%. **Sports program (2005-2006):** Member of NCAA III. *Men's intercollegiate varsity sports:* baseball, basketball, cross-country, football, golf, lacrosse, soccer, swimming and diving, tennis, track and field (indoor), track and field (outdoor). *Women's intercollegiate varsity sports:* basketball, cross-country, field hockey, lacrosse, soccer, softball, swimming and diving, tennis, track and field (indoor), track and field (outdoor), volleyball.

SERVICES AND FACILITIES

Basic services: nonremedial tutoring, placement service, health service. **Remedial assistance:** reading, math, writing, study skills. **Counseling services:** minority student, career, personal, academic, psychological, birth control, religious. **For learning-disabled students:** School does not offer a structured program with separate admission and additional fees. Services include: tape recorders, untimed tests, oral tests, learning center, readers, tutors. **Information technology resources:** Students are not required to lease or own a computer. Number of campus computers available to all students: 500. School has a wireless network. Proportion of college-owned housing units wired for high-speed internet access: 100%. **Campus safety:** Security services offered: 24-hour foot-and-vehicle patrols, late-night transport/escort service, 24-hour emergency telephones, lighted pathways/sidewalks, student patrols, controlled dormitory access (key, security card, etc).

TRANSFER AND INTERNATIONAL STUDENTS

Transfer students: May apply for admission for the following academic terms: Fall, Spring. Applicants do not need a minimum number of credits to apply. For fall 2005: Transfer applications received: 60. Transfer applicants offered admission: 33. Transfer applicants enrolled: 22. **International students:** Number of foreign undergraduates: 90 (5% of student body). Minimum TOEFL score required: 550 (paper); 213 (computer).

Columbus College of Art and Design

- **Address:** 107 N. Ninth Street, Columbus, OH 43215
- **Website:** http://www.ccad.edu
- **Private**
- **Enrollment:** 1,255 full-time; 199 part-time

KEY STATS

✔ **U.S News College Ranking:** Unranked Specialty School–Fine Arts
✔ **ACT Score (25th/75th percentile):** 18-23
✔ **Tuition:** 2006-2007: $21,296

Selectivity: Selective	Room/board: $6,600
Acceptance rate: 61%	Average debt: $31,078
Student/faculty ratio: 12/1	Proportion who borrowed: 99%

UNDERGRADUATE STUDENT BODY STATS

2005-2006 enrollment: 1,255 full-time; 199 part-time. Men: 48%; women: 52%. **Ethnic makeup:** African American: 7%; Asian American: 2%; Hispanic: 3%; White: 81%; International: 7%.

ADMISSIONS FACTS AND FIGURES

Phone: (614) 222-3261. **Email:** admissions@ccad.edu. **Website:** http://www.ccad.edu. **Application deadlines for fall 2007:** Regular decision: Rolling. Early decision: Not offered. Early action: Not offered. Admission can be deferred. **Application fee:** $25. Common application is not accepted. **Admissions requirements/recommendations:** High school units required (recommended): English: (2); Mathematics: (2); Total units: (4). Tests: The college uses SAT or ACT scores in admissions decisions. Either SAT or ACT required. Campus visit: Recommended. Admissions interview: Required. Off-campus interview: May be arranged. **Factors that count in admissions decisions:** *Academic:* Secondary school record: Important. Class rank: Considered. Letters of recommendation: Important. Standardized test scores: Considered. Essay: Important. *Nonacademic:* Interview: Considered. Extracurricular activities: Considered. Talent/ability: Very important. Character/personal qualities: Important. Alumni/ae relationship: Considered. Geographical residence: Not considered. State residency: Not considered. Religious affiliation/commitment: Not considered. Minority status: Not considered. Volunteer work: Considered. Work experience: Considered. **Admissions statistics for the fall 2005 entering class:** Total applicants: 910. Total accepted: 551. Freshmen enrolled: 207; 18% were from out of state. Overall acceptance rate: 61%. **Credentials of fall 2005 freshmen:** 3% ranked in the top 10 percent of their high school class; 27% were in the top 25 percent, and 48% were in the top half. (Proportion submitting class standing: 74%.) **Average high school grade point average:** 2.9. **First-year students who submitted SAT scores:** 44%. Scores (25/75 percentile): Verbal: 460-590, Math: 430-540, Combined: 890-1130. **First-year students submitting ACT scores:** 94%. Scores (25/75 percentile): English: N/A, Math: N/A, Composite: 18-23.

ACADEMICS

Year founded: 1879. **Academic calendar:** Semester. **Degrees offered:** bachelor's. **Most popular majors:** 23% film/video and photographic arts, 21% illustration, 19% commercial and advertising art, 15% fine arts and art studies, 9% fashion/apparel design. **Major fields of study:** visual and performing arts. **Areas of required coursework:** arts/fine arts, humanities, computer literacy, mathematics, English (including composition), philosophy, sciences (biological or physical), history, social science. **Special academic programs (% participation):** accelerated program (5%), cross-registration (1%), double major (1%), independent study (3%), internships (3%), study abroad (1%). **Faculty and instruction (2005-2006):** Total instructional faculty: 76 full-time, 105 part-time (62% men; 38% women; 9% minorities). Full-time faculty with Ph.D. or other terminal degree: 62%. Student/faculty ratio: 12/1. Classes of fewer than 20 students: 55%; of 20 to 49 students: 45%; of 50 or more students: 0%. **Advanced Placement and International Baccalaureate credit:** AP tests may be used for: Credit and/or placement. Scores accepted: 3, 4, 5. **Freshmen returning for sophomore year:** 82%. **Graduation rates:** Four-year: 43%; five-year: 53%; six-year: 49%.

COSTS AND FINANCIAL AID

Financial aid office: (614) 222-3295. **Expenses (2006-2007):** Tuition and fees 2006-2007: $21,296; room/board: $6,600. Estimated books and supplies: $3,000; transportation: $1,300; personal expenses: $1,300. **Financial aid:** Priority filing date for institution's financial aid form: March 3; deadline:

June 2. In 2005-2006, 88% of undergraduates applied for financial aid. Of those, 76% were determined to have financial need; 20% had their need fully met. Average financial aid package (proportion receiving): $13,698 (76%). Average amount of gift aid, such as scholarships or grants (proportion receiving): $9,215 (75%). Average amount of self-help aid, such as work study or loans (proportion receiving): $5,555 (62%). Average need-based loan (excluding PLUS or other private loans): $5,330. Among students who received need-based aid, the average percentage of need met: 65%. Among students who received aid based on merit, the average award (and the proportion receiving): $11,472 (17%). The average athletic scholarship (and the proportion receiving): $0 (0%). Average amount of debt of borrowers graduating in 2005: $31,078. Proportion who borrowed: 99%.

CAMPUS LIFE AND EXTRACURRICULAR ACTIVITIES

Campus housing available (% using): coed dorms (89%), apartment for single students (11%). Students who live in college-owned, operated, or affiliated housing: 22%. **Student employment:** During the 2005-2006 academic year, 10% of undergraduates worked on campus. Average per-year earnings: $2,790. **Clubs and organizations:** Number of student organizations: 20. Activities include: dance, literary magazine, student government, student film society. Number of fraternities: 0; sororities: 0. Average proportion of students who stay on campus on weekends: 40%.

SERVICES AND FACILITIES

Basic services: placement service, health insurance. **Remedial assistance:** reading, math, writing, study skills. **Counseling services:** career, personal, academic, psychological. **For learning-disabled students:** School does not offer a structured program with separate admission and additional fees. Total undergraduates in learning-disabled program or receiving services: 74. Services include: remedial English, reading machines, tape recorders, note-taking services, oral tests, learning center, readers, extended time for tests, priority registration. **Library:** Number of titles: 50,920; number of current serial subscriptions: 386. **Information technology resources:** Students are not required to lease or own a computer. Number of campus computers available to all students: 206. School has a wireless network. Proportion of college-owned housing units wired for high-speed internet access: 100%. **Campus safety:** Security services offered: 24-hour foot-and-vehicle patrols, late-night transport/escort service, 24-hour emergency telephones, lighted pathways/sidewalks, controlled dormitory access (key, security card, etc).

TRANSFER AND INTERNATIONAL STUDENTS

Transfer students: May apply for admission for the following academic terms: Fall, Spring. Applicants do not need a minimum number of credits to apply. For fall 2005: Transfer applications received: 169. Transfer applicants offered admission: 111. Transfer applicants enrolled: 75. **International students:** Number of foreign undergraduates: 90 (7% of student body). Number of countries represented: 18. Minimum TOEFL score required: 500 (paper); 173 (computer). Average TOEFL score: 550 (paper).

Defiance College

- **Address:** 701 N. Clinton Street, Defiance, OH 43512
- **Website:** http://www.defiance.edu
- **Private; Religious affiliation:** United Church of Christ
- **Enrollment:** 673 full-time; 154 part-time

KEY STATS

✔ **U.S News College Ranking:** 50, Comp. Coll.–Bachelor's (Midwest)
✔ **ACT Score (25th/75th percentile):** 18-24
✔ **Tuition:** 2006-2007: $19,740

Selectivity: Selective	**Room/board:** $6,170
Acceptance rate: 69%	**Average debt:** $17,359
Student/faculty ratio: 15/1	**Proportion who borrowed:** 76%

UNDERGRADUATE STUDENT BODY STATS

2005-2006 enrollment: 673 full-time; 154 part-time. Men: 44%; women: 56%. **Ethnic makeup:** African American: 4%; Hispanic: 3%; White: 92%.

ADMISSIONS FACTS AND FIGURES

Phone: (800) 520-4632. **Email:** admissions@defiance.edu. **Website:** http://www.defiance.edu. **Application deadlines for fall 2007:** Regular decision: August 15. Early decision: Not offered. Early action: Not offered.

Admission cannot be deferred. **Application fee:** $25. Common application is accepted. **Admissions requirements/recommendations:** High school units required (recommended): English: (4); Mathematics: (3); Science: (3); Foreign language: (2); Social studies: (2); Total units: (15). Tests: The college uses SAT or ACT scores in admissions decisions. Either SAT or ACT required. For admission to the fall 2007 entering class, the school will accept ACT with writing, ACT without writing. Campus visit: Recommended. Admissions interview: Neither required nor recommended. Off-campus interview: May be arranged. **Factors that count in admissions decisions:** *Academic:* Secondary school record: Very important. Class rank: Considered. Letters of recommendation: Important. Standardized test scores: Very important. Essay: Important. *Nonacademic:* Interview: Considered. Extracurricular activities: Considered. Talent/ability: Not considered. Character/personal qualities: Considered. Alumni/ae relationship: Not considered. Geographical residence: Not considered. State residency: Not considered. Religious affiliation/commitment: Not considered. Minority status: Not considered. Volunteer work: Considered. Work experience: Not considered. **Admissions statistics for the fall 2005 entering class:** Total applicants: 975. Total accepted: 677. Freshmen enrolled: 208; 22% were from out of state. Overall acceptance rate: 69%. **Credentials of fall 2005 freshmen:** 15% ranked in the top 10 percent of their high school class; 42% were in the top 25 percent, and 69% were in the top half. (Proportion submitting class standing: 94%.) **Average high school grade point average:** 3.2. **First-year students who submitted SAT scores:** 13%. Scores (25/75 percentile): Verbal: 430-510, Math: 400-520, Combined: 830-1030. **First-year students submitting ACT scores:** 87%. Scores (25/75 percentile): English: 17-23, Math: 17-24, Composite: 18-24.

ACADEMICS

Year founded: 1850. **Academic calendar:** Semester. **Degrees offered:** associate, bachelor's, master's. **Most popular majors:** 12% early childhood education and teaching, 8% business administration and management, 7% business/commerce, 7% criminal justice/police science, 7% social work. **Major fields of study:** biological and biomedical sciences; business, management, marketing, and related support services; communication, journalism, and related programs; computer and information sciences and support services; education; health professions and related clinical sciences; history; legal professions and studies; mathematics and statistics; parks, recreation, leisure, and fitness studies; philosophy and religious studies; physical sciences; psychology; public administration and social service professions; security and protective services; theology and religious vocations; visual and performing arts. **Areas of required coursework:** arts/fine arts, humanities, computer literacy, mathematics, English (including composition), philosophy, sciences (biological or physical), history, social science. **Pre-professional programs:** pre-law, pre-dentistry, pre-medicine, pre-theology, pre-veterinary science. **Special academic programs:** accelerated program, cooperative (work-study plan) program, double major, honors program, independent study, internships, student-designed major, study abroad, teacher certificate program, weekend college. **Teacher certification offered in:** early childhood, elementary, middle/junior high, secondary. **Cooperative education programs:** business, computer science, education. **Faculty and instruction (2005-2006):** Total instructional faculty: 38 full-time, 50 part-time (60% men; 40% women; 5% minorities). Full-time faculty with Ph.D. or other terminal degree: 63%. Student/faculty ratio: 15/1. Classes of fewer than 20 students: 74%; of 20 to 49 students: 24%; of 50 or more students: 2%. **Freshmen returning for sophomore year:** 64%. **Graduation rates:** Four-year: 36%; five-year: 45%; six-year: 49%. **Graduate study:** 10% of students pursue further study immediately upon graduation; 10% within one year.

COSTS AND FINANCIAL AID

Financial aid office: (419) 783-2376. **Expenses (2006-2007):** Tuition and fees 2006-2007: $19,740; room/board: $6,170. Estimated books and supplies: $1,000; transportation: $1,300; personal expenses: $1,190. **Financial aid:** Priority filing date for institution's financial aid form: March 1. In 2005-2006, 93% of undergraduates applied for financial aid. Of those, 83% were determined to have financial need; Average financial aid package (proportion receiving): $14,129 (83%). Average amount of gift aid, such as scholarships or grants (proportion receiving): $1,821 (46%). Average amount of self-help aid, such as work study or loans (proportion receiving): $4,091 (65%). Average need-based loan (excluding PLUS or other private loans): $3,401. Among students who received need-based aid, the average percentage of need met: 83%. Among students who received aid based on merit, the average award (and the proportion receiving): $7,863 (8%). The average athletic scholarship (and the proportion receiving): $0 (0%). Average amount of debt of borrowers graduating in 2005: $17,359. Proportion who borrowed: 76%.

CAMPUS LIFE AND EXTRACURRICULAR ACTIVITIES

Campus housing available: coed dorms, apartment for single students. Students who live in college-owned, operated, or affiliated housing: 66%. **Student employment:** During the 2005-2006 academic year, 30% of undergraduates worked on campus. Average per-year earnings: $5. Activities include: choral groups, concert band, dance, drama/theater, literary magazine, student government, student newspaper, yearbook. Number of fraternities: 1; sororities: 2. Proportion of men in fraternities: 3%; of women in sororities: 3%. Average proportion of students who stay on campus on weekends: 40%. **Sports program (2005-2006):** Member of NCAA III. *Men's intercollegiate varsity sports:* baseball, basketball, cross-country, football, soccer, tennis, track and field (indoor), track and field (outdoor). *Women's intercollegiate varsity sports:* basketball, cross-country, soccer, softball, tennis, track and field (indoor), track and field (outdoor), volleyball.

SERVICES AND FACILITIES

Basic services: nonremedial tutoring, placement service, health service, health insurance. **Remedial assistance:** reading, writing. **Counseling services:** minority student, career, personal, academic, psychological, religious. **For learning-disabled students:** Services include: remedial English, remedial reading, tape recorders, untimed tests, learning center, tutors. **Library:** Number of titles: 138,418; number of current serial subscriptions: 331. **Information technology resources:** Students are not required to lease or own a computer. Number of campus computers available to all students: 200. School has a wireless network. Proportion of college-owned housing units wired for high-speed internet access: 100%. **Campus safety:** Security services offered: lighted pathways/sidewalks, controlled dormitory access (key, security card, etc).

TRANSFER AND INTERNATIONAL STUDENTS

Transfer students: May apply for admission for the following academic terms: Fall, Spring, Summer. Applicants need a minimum number of credits to apply. For fall 2005: Transfer applications received: 143. Transfer applicants offered admission: 77. Transfer applicants enrolled: 45. **International students:** Number of countries represented: 1. Minimum TOEFL score required: 550 (paper); 213 (computer).

Denison University

- **Address:** 1 Main Street, Granville, OH 43023
- **Website:** http://www.denison.edu
- **Private**
- **Enrollment:** 2,292 full-time; 37 part-time

KEY STATS

- ✔ **U.S News College Ranking:** 48, Liberal Arts Colleges
- ✔ **SAT Score (25th/75th percentile):** 1150-1330
- ✔ **Tuition:** 2006-2007: $30,660

Selectivity: More selective	**Room/board:** $8,560
Acceptance rate: 39%	**Average debt:** $14,657
Student/faculty ratio: 11/1	**Proportion who borrowed:** 49%

UNDERGRADUATE STUDENT BODY STATS

2005-2006 enrollment: 2,292 full-time; 37 part-time. Men: 44%; women: 56%. **Ethnic makeup:** African American: 5%; Asian American: 3%; Hispanic: 3%; White: 84%; International: 5%. **Religious preference:** Roman Catholic: 33%; Protestant: 33%; Jewish: 5%; Muslim: 2%; Hindu: 1%; Buddhist: 1%; No preference: 6%; Other: 17%.

ADMISSIONS FACTS AND FIGURES

Phone: (740) 587-6276. **Email:** admissions@denison.edu. **Website:** http://www.denison.edu. **Application deadlines for fall 2007:** Regular decision: January 1; decision sent by April 1. Early decision: Send application by: November 1; Decision sent by: N/A. Early action: Not offered. Admission can be deferred. **Application fee:** $40. Common application is accepted. **To apply online, go to:** https://dss.denison.edu/admissions/apppart1ss.php. **Admissions requirements/recommendations:** High school units required (recommended): English: 4; Mathematics: 4; Science: 4; Foreign language: 3; Social studies: 2; History: 1; Academic electives: 1; Total units: 19. Tests: The college uses SAT or ACT scores in admissions decisions. Either SAT or ACT required. For admission to the fall 2007 entering class, the school will accept: ACT with writing. Campus visit: Recommended. Admissions inter-

view: Recommended. Off-campus interview: May be arranged. **Factors that count in admissions decisions:** *Academic:* Secondary school record: Very important. Class rank: Very important. Letters of recommendation: Very important. Standardized test scores: Very important. Essay: Very important. *Nonacademic:* Interview: Important. Extracurricular activities: Important. Talent/ability: Important. Character/personal qualities: Important. Alumni/ae relationship: Important. Geographical residence: Considered. State residency: Considered. Religious affiliation/commitment: Considered. Minority status: Considered. Volunteer work: Considered. Work experience: Considered. **Other schools with the greatest overlap in applicants:** College of Wooster; DePauw University; Kenyon College; Miami University–Oxford; Ohio Wesleyan University. **Admissions statistics for the fall 2005 entering class:** Total applicants: 5,144. Total accepted: 1,997. Freshmen enrolled: 622; 62% were from out of state. Accepted through early-decision or early-action plans: 25%. Overall acceptance rate: 39%. Early-decision acceptance rate: 82%. Non-early acceptance rate: 37%. **Size of waiting list:** 433 applicants; enrolled from waiting list: 13. **Credentials of fall 2005 freshmen:** 54% ranked in the top 10 percent of their high school class; 80% were in the top 25 percent, and 96% were in the top half. (Proportion submitting class standing: 61%.) **Average high school grade point average:** 3.6. **First-year students who submitted SAT scores:** 61%. Scores (25/75 percentile): Verbal: 570-660, Math: 580-670, Combined: 1150-1330. **First-year students submitting ACT scores:** 32%. Scores (25/75 percentile): English: N/A, Math: N/A, Composite: 25-29.

ACADEMICS

Year founded: 1831. **Academic calendar:** Semester. **Degrees offered:** bachelor's. **Most popular majors:** 23% social sciences, 12% communication, journalism, and related programs, 9% English language and literature/letters, 9% biological and biomedical sciences, 9% psychology. **Major fields of study:** area, ethnic, cultural, and gender studies; biological and biomedical sciences; communication, journalism, and related programs; computer and information sciences and support services; education; English language and literature/letters; foreign languages, literatures, and linguistics; history; mathematics and statistics; natural resources and conservation; philosophy and religious studies; physical sciences; psychology; social sciences; visual and performing arts. **Areas of required coursework:** arts/fine arts, humanities, English (including composition), philosophy, foreign languages, sciences (biological or physical), history, social science. **Pre-professional programs:** pre-law, pre-dentistry, pre-medicine, pre-veterinary science, other. **Special academic programs (% participation):** double major (18%), honors program (48%), independent study (52%), internships (30%), student-designed major (1%), study abroad (31%). **Reserve Officers Training Corps (ROTC):** Army ROTC: Offered at cooperating institution (Capital University). **Faculty and instruction (2005-2006):** Total instructional faculty: 183 full-time, 15 part-time (56% men; 44% women; 12% minorities). Full-time faculty with Ph.D. or other terminal degree: 97%. Student/faculty ratio: 11/1. Classes of fewer than 20 students: 62%; of 20 to 49 students: 38%; of 50 or more students: 0%. **Advanced Placement and International Baccalaureate credit:** AP tests may be used for: Placement only. Scores accepted: 4, 5. **Freshmen returning for sophomore year:** 89%. **Graduation rates:** Four-year: 75%; five-year: 78%; six-year: 79%. **Graduate study:** 26% of students pursue further study immediately upon graduation; 28% within one year; 40% within five years. Fields in which graduates pursue further study: Master of Business Administration (MBA), 1%; law, 6%; medicine, 3%; arts and sciences, 11%.

COSTS AND FINANCIAL AID

Financial aid office: (740) 587-6279. **Expenses (2006-2007):** Tuition and fees 2006-2007: $30,660; room/board: $8,560. Estimated books and supplies: $600; transportation: $400; personal expenses: $800. **Financial aid:** Priority filing date for institution's financial aid form: February 15. In 2005-2006, 54% of undergraduates applied for financial aid. Of those, 44% were determined to have financial need; 46% had their need fully met. Average financial aid package (proportion receiving): $25,367 (44%). Average amount of gift aid, such as scholarships or grants (proportion receiving): $19,189 (44%). Average amount of self-help aid, such as work study or loans (proportion receiving): $5,830 (33%). Average need-based loan (excluding PLUS or other private loans): $5,013. Among students who received need-based aid, the average percentage of need met: 93%. Among students who received aid based on merit, the average award (and the proportion receiving): $12,464 (9%). The average athletic scholarship (and the proportion receiving): $0 (0%). Average amount of debt of borrowers graduating in 2005: $14,657. Proportion who borrowed: 49%.

CAMPUS LIFE AND EXTRACURRICULAR ACTIVITIES

Campus housing available (% using): coed dorms (90%), women's dorms (5%), men's dorms (4%), other housing options (1%). Students who live in college-owned, operated, or affiliated housing: 98%. **Student employment:** During the 2005-2006 academic year, 44% of undergraduates worked on campus. Average per-year earnings: $2,100. **Clubs and organizations:** Number of student organizations: 138. Activities include: choral groups, concert band, dance, drama/theater, jazz band, literary magazine, music ensembles, musical theater, pep band, radio station, student government, student newspaper, student film society, symphony orchestra, television station, yearbook. Number of fraternities: 8; sororities: 6. Proportion of men in fraternities: 25%; of women in sororities: 30%. Average proportion of students who stay on campus on weekends: 90%. **Sports program (2005-2006):** Member of NCAA III. *Men's intercollegiate varsity sports:* baseball, basketball, cross-country, football, golf, lacrosse, soccer, swimming and diving, tennis, track and field (indoor), track and field (outdoor). *Women's intercollegiate varsity sports:* basketball, cross-country, field hockey, lacrosse, soccer, softball, swimming and diving, tennis, track and field (indoor), track and field (outdoor), volleyball.

SERVICES AND FACILITIES

Basic services: nonremedial tutoring, women's center, placement service, health service, health insurance. **Counseling services:** minority student, career, personal, academic, psychological, birth control, religious. **For learning-disabled students:** School does not offer a structured program with separate admission and additional fees. Total undergraduates in learning-disabled program or receiving services: 171. Services include: tape recorders, note-taking services, learning center, readers, extended time for tests, tutors, priority seating, texts on tape, other. **Library:** Number of titles: 767,118; number of current serial subscriptions: 6,316. **Information technology resources:** Students are not required to lease or own a computer. Number of campus computers available to all students: 593. School has a wireless network. Approximate number of users that can be accommodated: 500. Proportion of college-owned housing units wired for high-speed internet access: 100%. **Campus safety:** Security services offered: 24-hour foot-and-vehicle patrols, late-night transport/escort service, 24-hour emergency telephones, lighted pathways/sidewalks, student patrols, controlled dormitory access (key, security card, etc).

TRANSFER AND INTERNATIONAL STUDENTS

Transfer students: May apply for admission for the following academic terms: Fall, Spring. Applicants need a minimum number of credits to apply. For fall 2005: Transfer applications received: 42. Transfer applicants offered admission: 23. Transfer applicants enrolled: 13. **International students:** Number of foreign undergraduates: 119 (5% of student body). Number of countries represented: 28. Minimum TOEFL score required: 550 (paper); 213 (computer). Average TOEFL score: 619 (paper).

Franciscan University of Steubenville

- **Address:** 1235 University Boulevard, Steubenville, OH 43952-1763
- **Website:** http://www.franciscan.edu
- **Private; Religious affiliation:** Roman Catholic
- **Enrollment:** 1,818 full-time; 163 part-time

KEY STATS
✔ **U.S News College Ranking:** 30, Universities–Master's (Midwest)
✔ **SAT Score (25th/75th percentile):** 1060-1290
✔ **Tuition:** 2006-2007: $17,350

Selectivity: More selective	**Room/board:** $5,950
Acceptance rate: 81%	**Average debt:** $26,192
Student/faculty ratio: 15/1	**Proportion who borrowed:** 75%

UNDERGRADUATE STUDENT BODY STATS

2005-2006 enrollment: 1,818 full-time; 163 part-time. Men: 39%; women: 61%. **Ethnic makeup:** Asian American: 1%; Hispanic: 3%; White: 94%; International: 1%. **Religious preference:** Protestant: 3%; Unknown: 14%; Roman Catholic: 83%.

ADMISSIONS FACTS AND FIGURES

Phone: (740) 283-6226. **Email:** admissions@franciscan.edu. **Website:** http://www.franciscan.edu. **Application deadlines for fall 2007:** Regular decision: Rolling. Early decision: Not offered. Early action: Not offered. Admission can be deferred. **Application fee:** $20. Common application is accepted. **Admissions requirements/recommendations:** High school units required (recommended): English: (4); Mathematics: (3); Science: (3); Foreign language: (3); Social studies: (2); History: (2); Academic electives: (1); Total units: 15. Tests: The college uses SAT or ACT scores in admissions decisions. Either SAT or ACT required. For admission to the fall 2007 entering class, the school will accept: ACT with writing, ACT without writing. Campus visit: Recommended. Admissions interview: Recommended. Off-campus interview: May be arranged. **Factors that count in admissions decisions:** *Academic:* Secondary school record: Very important. Class rank: Not considered. Letters of recommendation: Considered. Standardized test scores: Very important. Essay: Very important. *Nonacademic:* Interview: Very important. Extracurricular activities: Important. Talent/ability: Important. Character/personal qualities: Very important. Alumni/ae relationship: Not considered. Geographical residence: Not considered. State residency: Not considered. Religious affiliation/commitment: Not considered. Minority status: Not considered. Volunteer work: Not considered. Work experience: Not considered. **Other schools with the greatest overlap in applicants:** Catholic University of America; Christendom College; Ohio State University–Columbus; University of Notre Dame. **Admissions statistics for the fall 2005 entering class:** Total applicants: 1,047. Total accepted: 847. Freshmen enrolled: 402; 77% were from out of state. Overall acceptance rate: 81%. **Size of waiting list:** 17 applicants; enrolled from waiting list: 8. **Credentials of fall 2005 freshmen:** 27% ranked in the top 10 percent of their high school class; 59% were in the top 25 percent, and 85% were in the top half. (Proportion submitting class standing: 62%.) **Average high school grade point average:** 3.6. **First-year students who submitted SAT scores:** 67%. Scores (25/75 percentile): Verbal: 540-660, Math: 520-630, Combined: 1060-1290. **First-year students submitting ACT scores:** 56%. Scores (25/75 percentile): English: 22-29, Math: 20-27, Composite: 22-27.

ACADEMICS

Year founded: 1946. **Academic calendar:** Semester. **Degrees offered:** associate, bachelor's, master's. **Most popular majors:** 27% theology/theological studies, 11% elementary education and teaching, 9% business administration and management, 8% nursing/registered nurse training (R.N., A.S.N., B.S.N., M.S.N.), 7% communication studies/speech communication and rhetoric. **Major fields of study:** biological and biomedical sciences; business, management, marketing, and related support services; communication, journalism, and related programs; computer and information sciences and support services; education; engineering; English language and literature/letters; foreign languages, literatures, and linguistics; health professions and related clinical sciences; history; legal professions and studies; liberal arts and sciences studies, and humanities; mathematics and statistics; philosophy and religious studies; physical sciences; psychology; public administration and social service professions; social sciences; theology and religious vocations. **Areas of required coursework:** humanities, English (including composition), philosophy, foreign languages, sciences (biological or physical), history, social science, other. **Pre-professional programs:** pre-law, pre-dentistry, pre-medicine, pre-theology, pre-veterinary science, pre-optometry, pre-pharmacy, other. **Special academic programs (% participation):** accelerated program (6%), distance learning (6%), double major (18%), honors program (9%), independent study (1%), internships (31%), liberal arts/career combination (4%), study abroad (56%), teacher certificate program (13%). **Teacher certification offered in:** early childhood, special education, elementary, middle/junior high, secondary. **Faculty and instruction (2005-2006):** Total instructional faculty: 104 full-time, 101 part-time (66% men; 34% women; 1% minorities). Full-time faculty with Ph.D. or other terminal degree: 67%. Student/faculty ratio: 15/1. Classes of fewer than 20 students: 46%; of 20 to 49 students: 52%; of 50 or more students: 1%. **Advanced Placement and International Baccalaureate credit:** AP tests may be used for: Credit and/or placement. Scores accepted: 3, 4, 5. International Baccalaureate exams may be used for: Credit and/or placement. **Freshmen returning for sophomore year:** 85%. **Graduation rates:** Four-year: 59%; five-year: 70%; six-year: 70%. **Graduate study:** 16% of students pursue further study immediately upon graduation; 22% within one year. Fields in which graduates pursue further study: Master of Business Administration (MBA), 12%; law, 6%; medicine, 12%; theology (or the seminary), 35%; education, 12%; arts and sciences, 23%.

COSTS AND FINANCIAL AID

Financial aid office: (740) 283-6226. **Expenses (2006-2007):** Tuition and fees 2006-2007: $17,350; room/board: $5,950. Estimated books and supplies: $800; transportation: $1,500; personal expenses: $1,200. **Financial aid:** In 2005-2006, 83% of undergraduates applied for financial aid. Of those, 69%

were determined to have financial need; 11% had their need fully met. Average financial aid package (proportion receiving): $10,542 (69%). Average amount of gift aid, such as scholarships or grants (proportion receiving): $6,485 (65%). Average amount of self-help aid, such as work study or loans (proportion receiving): $4,726 (65%). Average need-based loan (excluding PLUS or other private loans): $4,126. Among students who received need-based aid, the average percentage of need met: 57%. Among students who received aid based on merit, the average award (and the proportion receiving): $8,207 (22%). The average athletic scholarship (and the proportion receiving): $0 (0%). Average amount of debt of borrowers graduating in 2005: $26,192. Proportion who borrowed: 75%.

CAMPUS LIFE AND EXTRACURRICULAR ACTIVITIES

Campus housing available (% using): women's dorms (60%), men's dorms (40%). Students who live in college-owned, operated, or affiliated housing: 63%. **Student employment:** During the 2005-2006 academic year, 50% of undergraduates worked on campus. Average per-year earnings: $1,500. **Clubs and organizations:** Number of student organizations: 20. Activities include: choral groups, drama/theater, literary magazine, music ensembles, radio station, student government, student newspaper, yearbook. Number of fraternities: 1; sororities: 1. Proportion of men in fraternities: 1%; of women in sororities: 1%. Average proportion of students who stay on campus on weekends: 70%.

SERVICES AND FACILITIES

Basic services: nonremedial tutoring, health service, health insurance. **Remedial assistance:** writing, study skills, other. **Counseling services:** career, personal, veteran student, academic, religious. **For learning-disabled students:** School does not offer a structured program with separate admission and additional fees. Services include: reading machines, tape recorders, untimed tests, note-taking services, oral tests, readers, extended time for tests, tutors, priority registration, other. **Library:** Number of titles: 261,686; number of current serial subscriptions: 390. **Information technology resources:** Students are not required to lease or own a computer. Number of campus computers available to all students: 126. School has a wireless network. Approximate number of users that can be accommodated: 250. Proportion of college-owned housing units wired for high-speed internet access: 0%. **Campus safety:** Security services offered: 24-hour foot-and-vehicle patrols, late-night transport/escort service, 24-hour emergency telephones, lighted pathways/sidewalks, student patrols, controlled dormitory access (key, security card, etc).

TRANSFER AND INTERNATIONAL STUDENTS

Transfer students: May apply for admission for the following academic terms: Fall, Spring, Summer. Applicants do not need a minimum number of credits to apply. For fall 2005: Transfer applications received: 423. Transfer applicants offered admission: 316. Transfer applicants enrolled: 196. **International students:** Number of foreign undergraduates: 23 (1% of student body). Number of countries represented: 9. Minimum TOEFL score required: 550 (paper); 213 (computer). Average TOEFL score: 653 (paper).

Franklin University

- **Address:** 201 S. Grant Avenue, Columbus, OH 43215
- **Website:** http://www.franklin.edu
- **Private**
- **Enrollment:** N/A

KEY STATS

✔ **U.S News College Ranking:** Unranked Specialty School–Business
✔ **SAT or ACT Score (25th/75th percentile):** N/A
✔ **Tuition:** N/A
  Selectivity: Least selective   **Room/board:** N/A
  Acceptance rate: N/A   **Average debt:** N/A
  Student/faculty ratio: N/A   **Proportion who borrowed:** N/A

Heidelberg College

- **Address:** 310 E. Market Street, Tiffin, OH 44883
- **Website:** http://www.heidelberg.edu
- **Private; Religious affiliation:** United Church of Christ
- **Enrollment:** 1,179 full-time; 51 part-time

KEY STATS

✔ **U.S News College Ranking:** 30, Universities–Master's (Midwest)
✔ **ACT Score (25th/75th percentile):** 19-24
✔ **Tuition:** 2006-2007: $17,400
  Selectivity: Selective   **Room/board:** $7,530
  Acceptance rate: 75%   **Average debt:** $26,125
  Student/faculty ratio: 13/1   **Proportion who borrowed:** 87%

UNDERGRADUATE STUDENT BODY STATS

2005-2006 enrollment: 1,179 full-time; 51 part-time. Men: 50%; women: 50%. **Ethnic makeup:** African American: 4%; Asian American: 1%; Hispanic: 1%; White: 92%; International: 2%. **Religious preference:** Roman Catholic: 26%; Protestant: 32%; No preference: 5%; Unknown: 32%; United Church of Christ: 5%.

ADMISSIONS FACTS AND FIGURES

Phone: (419) 448-2330. **Email:** adminfo@heidelberg.edu. **Website:** http://www.heidelberg.edu. **Application deadlines for fall 2007:** Regular decision: August 1. Early decision: Not offered. Early action: Not offered. Admission can be deferred. **Application fee:** $25. Common application is accepted. **Admissions requirements/recommendations:** High school units required (recommended): English: (4); Mathematics: (3); Science: (3); Foreign language: (2); Social studies: (3); History: (2); Academic electives: (3); Total units: (21). Tests: The college uses SAT or ACT scores in admissions decisions. Either SAT or ACT required. For admission to the fall 2007 entering class, the school will accept: ACT with writing, ACT without writing. Campus visit: Recommended. Admissions interview: Recommended. Off-campus interview: May be arranged. **Factors that count in admissions decisions:** *Academic:* Secondary school record: Very important. Class rank: Important. Letters of recommendation: Considered. Standardized test scores: Very important. Essay: Considered. *Nonacademic:* Interview: Very important. Extracurricular activities: Important. Talent/ability: Important. Character/personal qualities: Very important. Alumni/ae relationship: Considered. Geographical residence: Considered. State residency: Considered. Religious affiliation/commitment: Considered. Minority status: Not considered. Volunteer work: Important. Work experience: Considered. **Other schools with the greatest overlap in applicants:** Ashland University; Baldwin-Wallace College; Bowling Green State University; Miami University–Oxford; Ohio Northern University. **Admissions statistics for the fall 2005 entering class:** Total applicants: 1,830. Total accepted: 1,370. Freshmen enrolled: 328; 6% were from out of state. Overall acceptance rate: 75%. **Credentials of fall 2005 freshmen:** 14% ranked in the top 10 percent of their high school class; 34% were in the top 25 percent, and 68% were in the top half. (Proportion submitting class standing: 93%.) **Average high school grade point average:** 3.2. **First-year students who submitted SAT scores:** 34%. Scores (25/75 percentile): Verbal: 450-570, Math: 450-580, Combined: 900-1150. **First-year students submitting ACT scores:** 92%. Scores (25/75 percentile): English: 18-24, Math: 18-24, Composite: 19-24.

ACADEMICS

Year founded: 1850. **Academic calendar:** Semester. **Degrees offered:** bachelor's, master's. **Most popular majors:** 28% business, management, marketing, and related support services, 17% education, 11% communication, journalism, and related programs, 9% psychology, 7% biological and biomedical sciences. **Major fields of study:** biological and biomedical sciences; business, management, marketing, and related support services; communication, journalism, and related programs; computer and information sciences and support services; education; English language and literature/letters; foreign languages, literatures, and linguistics; mathematics and statistics; natural resources and conservation; parks, recreation, leisure, and fitness studies; philosophy and religious studies; physical sciences; psychology; social sciences; visual and performing arts. **Areas of required coursework:** arts/fine arts, humanities, computer literacy, mathematics, English (including composition), foreign languages, sciences (biological or physical), history, social science. **Pre-professional programs:** pre-law, pre-dentistry, pre-medicine, pre-theology, pre-veterinary science, pre-optometry, pre-pharmacy. **Special academic programs:** cooperative (work-study plan) program, cross-registration, double major, exchange student program (domestic), honors program, independent study, internships, liberal arts/career combination, study abroad, teacher certificate program. **Teacher certification offered in:** early childhood, special education, elementary, middle/junior high, secondary, bilingual/bicultural. **Reserve Officers Training Corps (ROTC):** Army ROTC: Offered at cooperating institution (Bowling Green State University); Air Force ROTC: Offered at cooperating institution (Bowling Green State University). **Faculty and instruction (2005-2006):** Total instructional faculty: 71 full-time, 63 part-time (56% men; 44% women; 5% minorities). Full-time faculty with Ph.D. or other terminal degree: 70%. Student/faculty ratio: 13/1. Classes of fewer than 20 students: 59%; of 20 to 49 students: 40%; of 50 or more students: 1%. **Advanced Placement and International Baccalaureate credit:** AP tests may be used for: Credit only. Scores accepted: 3. International Baccalaureate exams may be used for: Credit and/or placement. **Freshmen returning for sophomore year:** 69%. **Graduation rates:** Four-year: 48%; five-year: 57%; six-year: 59%. **Graduate study:** 26% of students pursue further study immediately upon graduation; 22% within one year; 28% within five years. Fields in which graduates pursue further study: Master of Business Administration (MBA), 14%; law, 11%; medicine, 1%; theology (or the seminary), 5%; education, 9%; arts and sciences, 27%; veterinary medicine, 2%.

COSTS AND FINANCIAL AID
Financial aid office: (419) 448-2293. **Expenses (2006-2007):** Tuition and fees 2006-2007: $17,400; room/board: $7,530. Estimated books and supplies: $1,250; transportation: $500; personal expenses: $500. **Financial aid:** Priority filing date for institution's financial aid form: March 1. In 2005-2006, 88% of undergraduates applied for financial aid. Of those, 81% were determined to have financial need; 17% had their need fully met. Average financial aid package (proportion receiving): $14,130 (81%). Average amount of gift aid, such as scholarships or grants (proportion receiving): $9,894 (81%). Average amount of self-help aid, such as work study or loans (proportion receiving): $4,973 (68%). Average need-based loan (excluding PLUS or other private loans): $4,349. Among students who received need-based aid, the average percentage of need met: 86%. Among students who received aid based on merit, the average award (and the proportion receiving): $6,518 (7%). The average athletic scholarship (and the proportion receiving): $0 (0%). Average amount of debt of borrowers graduating in 2005: $26,125. Proportion who borrowed: 87%.

CAMPUS LIFE AND EXTRACURRICULAR ACTIVITIES
Campus housing available (% using): coed dorms (75%), women's dorms (8%), apartments for married students (1%), apartment for single students (8%), special housing for disabled students (1%), special housing for international students (1%), cooperative housing (6%). Students who live in college-owned, operated, or affiliated housing: 67%. **Student employment:** During the 2005-2006 academic year, 17% of undergraduates worked on campus. Average per-year earnings: $1,000. **Clubs and organizations:** Number of student organizations: 70. Activities include: choral groups, concert band, dance, drama/theater, jazz band, literary magazine, music ensembles, musical theater, opera, pep band, radio station, student government, student newspaper, student film society, symphony orchestra, television station, yearbook. Number of fraternities: 4; sororities: 4. Proportion of men in fraternities: 18%; of women in sororities: 24%. Average proportion of students who stay on campus on weekends: 65%. **Sports program (2005-2006):** Member of NCAA III. *Men's intercollegiate varsity sports:* baseball, basketball, cheerleading, cross-country, football, golf, soccer, tennis, track and field (indoor), track and field (outdoor), wrestling. *Women's intercollegiate varsity sports:* basketball, cross-country, golf, soccer, softball, tennis, track and field (indoor), track and field (outdoor), volleyball.

SERVICES AND FACILITIES
Basic services: nonremedial tutoring, placement service, health service, health insurance. **Remedial assistance:** reading, math, writing, study skills. **Counseling services:** minority student, career, personal, academic, older student, psychological, religious. **For learning-disabled students:** School does not offer a structured program with separate admission and additional fees. Total undergraduates in learning-disabled program or receiving services: 13. Services include: remedial math, remedial English, remedial reading, tape recorders, other special classes, untimed tests, note-taking services, oral tests, learning center, readers, extended time for tests, tutors. **Library:** Number of titles: 290,595; number of current serial subscriptions: 492. **Information technology resources:** Students are not required to lease or own a computer. Number of campus computers available to all students: 120. School has a wireless network. Approximate number of users that can be accommodated: 50. Proportion of college-owned housing units wired for high-speed internet access: 98%. **Campus safety:** Security services offered: 24-hour foot-and-vehicle patrols, late-night transport/escort service, 24-hour emergency telephones, lighted pathways/sidewalks, student patrols, controlled dormitory access (key, security card, etc).

TRANSFER AND INTERNATIONAL STUDENTS
Transfer students: May apply for admission for the following academic terms: Fall, Spring, Summer. Applicants need a minimum number of credits to apply. For fall 2005: Transfer applications received: 138. Transfer applicants offered admission: 81. Transfer applicants enrolled: 51. **International students:** Number of foreign undergraduates: 25 (2% of student body). Number of countries represented: 12. Minimum TOEFL score required: 550 (paper); 220 (computer).

Hiram College

- **Address:** PO Box 67, Hiram, OH 44234
- **Website:** http://www.hiram.edu
- **Private; Religious affiliation:** Disciples of Christ
- **Enrollment:** 877 full-time; 205 part-time

KEY STATS
✔ **U.S News College Ranking:** third tier, Liberal Arts Colleges
✔ **ACT Score (25th/75th percentile):** 20-26
✔ **Tuition:** N/A

Selectivity: Selective	**Room/board:** N/A
Acceptance rate: 85%	**Average debt:** N/A
Student/faculty ratio: 12/1	**Proportion who borrowed:** N/A

UNDERGRADUATE STUDENT BODY STATS
2005-2006 enrollment: 877 full-time; 205 part-time. Men: 44%; women: 56%. **Ethnic makeup:** African American: 10%; Asian American: 1%; Hispanic: 1%; White: 84%; International: 3%.

ADMISSIONS FACTS AND FIGURES
Phone: (800) 362-5280. **Email:** admission@hiram.edu. **Website:** http://www.hiram.edu. **Application deadlines for fall 2007:** Regular decision: April 15. Early decision: Not offered. Early action: Not offered. Admission can be deferred. **Application fee:** $35. Common application is accepted. **To apply online, go to:** http://www.hiram.edu/apply. **Admissions requirements/recommendations:** High school units required (recommended): English: 4; Mathematics: 3; Science: 3; Foreign language: 2 (3); Social studies: 3; History: 1; Academic electives: 2; Total units: 20 (21). Tests: The college uses SAT or ACT scores in admissions decisions. Either SAT or ACT required. For admission to the fall 2007 entering class, the school will accept: ACT with writing, ACT without writing. Campus visit: Recommended. Admissions interview: Recommended. Off-campus interview: May not be arranged. **Factors that count in admissions decisions:** *Academic:* Secondary school record: Very important. Class rank: Considered. Letters of recommendation: Considered. Standardized test scores: Important. Essay: Considered. *Nonacademic:* Interview: Considered. Extracurricular activities: Important. Talent/ability: Important. Character/personal qualities: Important. Alumni/ae relationship: Considered. Geographical residence: Not considered. State residency: Not considered. Religious affiliation/commitment: Not considered. Minority status: Considered. Volunteer work: Considered. Work experience: Considered. **Other schools with the greatest overlap in applicants:** Allegheny College; Baldwin-Wallace College; Heidelberg College; John Carroll University; Ohio Wesleyan University. **Admissions statistics for the fall 2005 entering class:** Total applicants: 832. Total accepted: 710. Freshmen enrolled: 215; 17% were from out of state. Overall acceptance rate: 85%. **Credentials of fall 2005 freshmen:** 24% ranked in the top 10 percent of their high school class; 52% were in the top 25 percent, and 83% were in the top half. (Proportion submitting class standing: 82%.) **Average high school grade point average:** 3.4. **First-year students who submitted SAT scores:** 57%. Scores (25/75 percentile): Verbal: 480-630, Math: 490-620, Combined: 970-1250. **First-year students submitting ACT scores:** 78%. Scores (25/75 percentile): English: 20-27, Math: 19-26, Composite: 20-26.

ACADEMICS

Year founded: 1850. **Academic calendar:** Other. **Degrees offered:** bachelor's, master's. **Most popular majors:** 16% business, management, marketing, and related support services, 16% social sciences, 9% biological and biomedical sciences, 9% education, 8% communication, journalism, and related programs. **Major fields of study:** biological and biomedical sciences; business, management, marketing, and related support services; communication, journalism, and related programs; education; English language and literature/letters; foreign languages, literatures, and linguistics; history; mathematics and statistics; multi/interdisciplinary studies; natural resources and conservation; philosophy and religious studies; physical sciences; psychology; social sciences; visual and performing arts. **Areas of required coursework:** arts/fine arts, humanities, sciences (biological or physical), social science, other. **Pre-professional programs:** pre-law, pre-medicine, pre-veterinary science. **Special academic programs (% participation):** cross-registration (1%), double major (15%), English as a Second Language (ESL) (.5%), exchange student program (domestic), independent study (20%), internships (30%), student-designed major (.5%), study abroad (45%), teacher certification program (15%), weekend college (10%). **Teacher certification offered in:** early childhood, elementary, middle/junior high, secondary. **Faculty and instruction (2005-2006):** Total instructional faculty: 64 full-time, 39 part-time (54% men; 46% women; 3% minorities). Full-time faculty with Ph.D. or other terminal degree: 94%. Student/faculty ratio: 12/1. **Advanced Placement and International Baccalaureate credit:** AP tests may be used for: Credit and/or placement. Scores accepted: 4. International Baccalaureate exams may be used for: Credit and/or placement. **Freshmen returning for sophomore year:** 79%. **Graduation rates:** Four-year: 55%; five-year: 63%; six-year: 64%. **Graduate study:** 30% of students pursue further study immediately upon graduation; 40% within one year; 50% within five years. Fields in which graduates pursue further study: Master of Business Administration (MBA), 6%; law, 18%; medicine, 5%; dentistry, 1%; engineering, 1%; theology (or the seminary), 2%; education, 9%; arts and sciences, 55%; veterinary medicine, 4%.

COSTS AND FINANCIAL AID

Financial aid office: (330) 569-5107.

CAMPUS LIFE AND EXTRACURRICULAR ACTIVITIES

Campus housing available: coed dorms, women's dorms, special housing for disabled students. Students who live in college-owned, operated, or affiliated housing: 86%. **Student employment:** During the 2005-2006 academic year, 48% of undergraduates worked on campus. Average per-year earnings: $1,600. **Clubs and organizations:** Number of student organizations: 73. Activities include: choral groups, concert band, dance, drama/theater, jazz band, literary magazine, music ensembles, musical theater, opera, pep band, radio station, student government, student newspaper, symphony orchestra, yearbook. Number of fraternities: 3; sororities: 3. Average proportion of students who stay on campus on weekends: 75%. **Sports program (2005-2006):** Member of NCAA III. *Men's intercollegiate varsity sports:* baseball, basketball, cross-country, football, golf, soccer, swimming and diving, tennis, track and field (indoor), track and field (outdoor). *Women's intercollegiate varsity sports:* basketball, cross-country, golf, soccer, softball, swimming and diving, tennis, track and field (indoor), track and field (outdoor), volleyball.

SERVICES AND FACILITIES

Basic services: nonremedial tutoring, women's center, placement service, health service, health insurance. **Remedial assistance:** writing, study skills. **Counseling services:** minority student, career, personal, veteran student, academic, older student, psychological, birth control, religious. **For learning-disabled students:** School does not offer a structured program with separate admission and additional fees. Total undergraduates in learning-disabled program or receiving services: 35. Services include: note-taking services, oral tests, extended time for tests, tutors, proofreading services, texts on tape, exams on tape or computer, other testing accomodations. **Library:** Number of titles: 640,561; number of current serial subscriptions: 6,535. **Information technology resources:** Students are not required to lease or own a computer. Number of campus computers available to all students: 129. School has a wireless network. Approximate number of users that can be accommodated: 1,500. Proportion of college-owned housing units wired for high-speed internet access: 100%. **Campus safety:** Security services offered: late-night transport/escort service, 24-hour emergency telephones, lighted pathways/sidewalks, controlled dormitory access (key, security card, etc).

TRANSFER AND INTERNATIONAL STUDENTS

Transfer students: May apply for admission for the following academic terms: Fall, Spring. Applicants do not need a minimum number of credits to apply. For fall 2005: Transfer applications received: 98. Transfer applicants offered admission: 63. Transfer applicants enrolled: 37. **International students:** Number of foreign undergraduates: 30 (3% of student body). Minimum TOEFL score required: 550 (paper); 213 (computer). Average TOEFL score: 585 (paper).

John Carroll University

- **Address:** 20700 N. Park Boulevard, University Heights, OH 44118
- **Website:** http://www.jcu.edu
- **Private; Religious affiliation:** Roman Catholic (Jesuit)
- **Enrollment:** 3,180 full-time; 133 part-time

KEY STATS

✔ **U.S News College Ranking:** 5, Universities–Master's (Midwest)
✔ **ACT Score (25th/75th percentile):** 21-26
✔ **Tuition:** 2006-2007: $25,072

Selectivity: More selective	**Room/board:** $7,790
Acceptance rate: 85%	**Average debt:** $21,385
Student/faculty ratio: 13/1	**Proportion who borrowed:** 90%

UNDERGRADUATE STUDENT BODY STATS

2005-2006 enrollment: 3,180 full-time; 133 part-time. Men: 47%; women: 53%. **Ethnic makeup:** African American: 4%; Asian American: 2%; Hispanic: 2%; White: 91%. **Religious preference:** Protestant: 14%; Jewish: 1%; Muslim: 1%; Unknown: 13%; Roman Catholic (Jesuit): 69%; Other: 2%.

ADMISSIONS FACTS AND FIGURES

Phone: (216) 397-4294. **Email:** admission@jcu.edu. **Website:** http://www.jcu.edu. **Application deadlines for fall 2007:** Regular decision: February 1. Early decision: Not offered. Early action: Not offered. Admission can be deferred. **Application fee:** $25. Common application is accepted. **To apply online, go to:** http://explore.jcu.edu. **Admissions requirements/recommendations:** High school units required (recommended): English: 4 (4); Mathematics: 3 (4); Science: 2 (3); Foreign language: 2 (3); Social studies: 2 (4); Academic electives: 3 (3); Total units: 16 (21). Tests: The college uses SAT or ACT scores in admissions decisions. Either SAT or ACT required. For admission to the fall 2007 entering class, the school will accept: ACT without writing. Campus visit: Recommended. Admissions interview: Recommended. Off-campus interview: May be arranged. **Factors that count in admissions decisions:** *Academic:* Secondary school record: Very important. Class rank: Considered. Letters of recommendation: Important. Standardized test scores: Important. Essay: Important. *Nonacademic:* Interview: Considered. Extracurricular activities: Important. Talent/ability: Considered. Character/personal qualities: Considered. Alumni/ae relationship: Considered. Geographical residence: Not considered. State residency: Not considered. Religious affiliation/commitment: Not considered. Minority status: Not considered. Volunteer work: Considered. Work experience: Considered. **Other schools with the greatest overlap in applicants:** Baldwin-Wallace College; Miami University–Oxford; Ohio University; University of Dayton; Xavier University. **Admissions statistics for the fall 2005 entering class:** Total applicants: 3,057. Total accepted: 2,604. Freshmen enrolled: 786; 32% were from out of state. Overall acceptance rate: 85%. **Credentials of fall 2005 freshmen:** 28% ranked in the top 10 percent of their high school class; 58% were in the top 25 percent, and 84% were in the top half. (Proportion submitting class standing: 66%.) **Average high school grade point average:** 3.5. First-year students who submitted SAT scores: 42%. Scores (25/75 percentile): Verbal: 530-630, Math: 530-630, Combined: 1060-1260. First-year students submitting ACT scores: 58%. Scores (25/75 percentile): English: 20-26, Math: 20-26, Composite: 21-26.

ACADEMICS

Year founded: 1886. **Academic calendar:** Semester. **Degrees offered:** bachelor's, master's. **Most popular majors:** 16% communication studies/speech communication and rhetoric, 10% education, 9% biology/biological sciences, 8% accounting, 8% marketing/marketing management. **Major fields of study:** biological and biomedical sciences; business, management, marketing, and related support services; communication, journalism, and related programs; computer and information sciences and support services;

education; engineering; English language and literature/letters; foreign languages, literatures, and linguistics; history; liberal arts and sciences studies, and humanities; mathematics and statistics; philosophy and religious studies; physical sciences; psychology; social sciences; visual and performing arts. **Areas of required coursework:** humanities, mathematics, English (including composition), philosophy, foreign languages, sciences (biological or physical), social science, other. **Pre-professional programs:** pre-law, pre-dentistry, pre-medicine. **Special academic programs (% participation):** accelerated program (1%), cooperative (work-study plan) program (25%), cross-registration (4%), double major (7%), exchange student program (domestic) (1%), honors program (3%), independent study (8%), internships (28%), liberal arts/career combination (2%), student-designed major (0%), study abroad (9%), teacher certificate program (18%). **Teacher certification offered in:** early childhood, middle/junior high, secondary. **Cooperative education programs:** art, business, computer science, natural science, other. **Reserve Officers Training Corps (ROTC):** Army ROTC: Offered on campus. **Faculty and instruction (2005-2006):** Total instructional faculty: 222 full-time, 169 part-time (58% men; 42% women; 8% minorities). Full-time faculty with Ph.D. or other terminal degree: 93%. Student/faculty ratio: 13/1. Classes of fewer than 20 students: 40%; of 20 to 49 students: 60%; of 50 or more students: 0%. **Advanced Placement and International Baccalaureate credit:** AP tests may be used for: Credit and/or placement. Scores accepted: 3, 4, 5. International Baccalaureate exams may be used for: Credit only. **Freshmen returning for sophomore year:** 86%. **Graduation rates:** Four-year: 65%; five-year: 73%; six-year: 75%. **Graduate study:** 25% of students pursue further study immediately upon graduation. Fields in which graduates pursue further study: Master of Business Administration (MBA), 16%; law, 12%; medicine, 17%; dentistry, 2%; engineering, 2%; theology (or the seminary), 5%; education, 9%; arts and sciences, 37%.

COSTS AND FINANCIAL AID

Financial aid office: (216) 397-4248. **Expenses (2006-2007):** Tuition and fees 2006-2007: $25,072; room/board: $7,790. Estimated books and supplies: $1,200; transportation: $800; personal expenses: $750. **Financial aid:** Priority filing date for institution's financial aid form: March 1; deadline: March 1. In 2005-2006, 82% of undergraduates applied for financial aid. Of those, 69% were determined to have financial need; 30% had their need fully met. Average financial aid package (proportion receiving): $18,007 (69%). Average amount of gift aid, such as scholarships or grants (proportion receiving): $11,259 (67%). Average amount of self-help aid, such as work study or loans (proportion receiving): $5,407 (58%). Average need-based loan (excluding PLUS or other private loans): $4,418. Among students who received need-based aid, the average percentage of need met: 83%. Among students who received aid based on merit, the average award (and the proportion receiving): $6,829 (9%). The average athletic scholarship (and the proportion receiving): $0 (0%). Average amount of debt of borrowers graduating in 2005: $21,385. Proportion who borrowed: 90%.

CAMPUS LIFE AND EXTRACURRICULAR ACTIVITIES

Campus housing available (% using): coed dorms (71%), women's dorms (11%), men's dorms (12%), other housing options (6%). Students who live in college-owned, operated, or affiliated housing: 45%. **Student employment:** During the 2005-2006 academic year, 29% of undergraduates worked on campus. Average per-year earnings: $1,900. **Clubs and organizations:** Number of student organizations: 87. Activities include: choral groups, concert band, dance, drama/theater, jazz band, literary magazine, music ensembles, musical theater, pep band, radio station, student government, student newspaper, television station, yearbook. Number of fraternities: 3; sororities: 5. Proportion of men in fraternities: 9%; of women in sororities: 14%. Average proportion of students who stay on campus on weekends: 50%. **Sports program (2005-2006):** Member of NCAA III. *Men's intercollegiate varsity sports:* baseball, basketball, cross-country, football, golf, soccer, swimming and diving, tennis, track and field (indoor), track and field (outdoor), wrestling. *Women's intercollegiate varsity sports:* basketball, cross-country, golf, soccer, softball, swimming and diving, tennis, track and field (indoor), track and field (outdoor), volleyball.

SERVICES AND FACILITIES

Basic services: nonremedial tutoring, placement service, health service. **Remedial assistance:** study skills. **Counseling services:** minority student, career, military, personal, veteran student, academic, older student, psychological, religious, other. **For learning-disabled students:** School does not offer a structured program with separate admission and additional fees. Total undergraduates in learning-disabled program or receiving services: 213. Services include: reading machines, note-taking services, oral tests, readers, extended time for tests. **Library:** Number of titles: 740,826; number of cur-

rent serial subscriptions: 8,047. **Information technology resources:** Students are not required to lease or own a computer. Number of campus computers available to all students: 300. School has a wireless network. Approximate number of users that can be accommodated: 3,000. Proportion of college-owned housing units wired for high-speed internet access: 100%. **Campus safety:** Security services offered: 24-hour foot-and-vehicle patrols, late-night transport/escort service, 24-hour emergency telephones, lighted pathways/sidewalks, controlled dormitory access (key, security card, etc).

TRANSFER AND INTERNATIONAL STUDENTS

Transfer students: May apply for admission for the following academic terms: Fall, Spring, Summer. Applicants do not need a minimum number of credits to apply. For fall 2005: Transfer applications received: 334. Transfer applicants offered admission: 196. Transfer applicants enrolled: 110. **International students:** Number of foreign undergraduates: 0. Number of countries represented: 9. Minimum TOEFL score required: 550 (paper); 213 (computer).

Kent State University

- ■ **Address:** PO Box 5190, Kent, OH 44242-0001
- ■ **Website:** http://www.kent.edu
- ■ **Public**
- ■ **Enrollment:** 15,828 full-time; 2,917 part-time

KEY STATS

✔ **U.S News College Ranking:** fourth tier, National Universities
✔ **ACT Score (25th/75th percentile):** 19-24
✔ **Tuition:** 2006-2007: $8,430 in state, $15,862 out of state
  Selectivity: Selective   **Room/board:** $6,880
  Acceptance rate: 94%   **Average debt:** $21,066
  Student/faculty ratio: 19/1   **Proportion who borrowed:** 69%

UNDERGRADUATE STUDENT BODY STATS

2005-2006 enrollment: 15,828 full-time; 2,917 part-time. Men: 40%; women: 60%. **Ethnic makeup:** African American: 8%; Asian American: 1%; Hispanic: 1%; White: 88%; International: 1%.

ADMISSIONS FACTS AND FIGURES

Phone: (330) 672-2444. **Email:** KENTADM@Admissions.Kent.edu. **Website:** http://www.kent.edu. **Application deadlines for fall 2007:** Regular decision: May 1. Early decision: Not offered. Early action: Not offered. Admission cannot be deferred. **Application fee:** $30. Common application is not accepted. **To apply online, go to:** https://www.admissions.kent.edu/apply.asp. **Admissions requirements/recommendations:** High school units required (recommended): English: (4); Mathematics: (3); Science: (3); Foreign language: (2); Social studies: (3); Total units: (16). Tests: The college uses SAT or ACT scores in admissions decisions. Either SAT or ACT required. For admission to the fall 2007 entering class, the school will accept: ACT without writing. Campus visit: Recommended. Admissions interview: Recommended. Off-campus interview: Not available. **Factors that count in admissions decisions:** *Academic:* Secondary school record: Important. Class rank: Considered. Letters of recommendation: Considered. Standardized test scores: Very important. Essay: Not considered. *Nonacademic:* Interview: Not considered. Extracurricular activities: Not considered. Talent/ability: Not considered. Character/personal qualities: Not considered. Alumni/ae relationship: Not considered. Geographical residence: Not considered. State residency: Not considered. Religious affiliation/commitment: Not considered. Minority status: Not considered. Volunteer work: Not considered. Work experience: Not considered. **Other schools with the greatest overlap in applicants:** Bowling Green State University; Ohio State University–Columbus; Ohio University; University of Akron; University of Toledo. **Admissions statistics for the fall 2005 entering class:** Total applicants: 10,774. Total accepted: 10,074. Freshmen enrolled: 3,814; 12% were from out of state. Overall acceptance rate: 94%. **Size of waiting list:** 836 applicants; enrolled from waiting list: 236. **Credentials of fall 2005 freshmen:** 13% ranked in the top 10 percent of their high school class; 34% were in the top 25 percent, and 70% were in the top half. (Proportion submitting class standing: 90%.) **Average high school grade point average:** 3.2. **First-year students who submitted SAT scores:** 39%. Scores (25/75 percentile): Verbal: 460-570, Math: 460-570, Combined: 920-1140. **First-year students submitting ACT scores:**

84%. Scores (25/75 percentile): English: 18-24, Math: 18-24, Composite: 19-24.

ACADEMICS

Year founded: 1910. **Academic calendar:** Semester. **Degrees offered:** certificate, associate, transfer-associate, terminal-associate, bachelor's, post-bachelor's certificate, master's, post-master's certificate, doctorate. **Most popular majors:** 20% business, management, marketing, and related support services, 14% education, 8% communication, journalism, and related programs, 8% health professions and related clinical sciences, 6% psychology. **Major fields of study:** agriculture, agriculture operations, and related sciences; architecture and related services; area, ethnic, cultural, and gender studies; biological and biomedical sciences; business, management, marketing, and related support services; communication, journalism, and related programs; communications technologies/technicians and support services; computer and information sciences and support services; education; engineering; English language and literature/letters; family and consumer sciences/human sciences; foreign languages, literatures, and linguistics; health professions and related clinical sciences; history; legal professions and studies; liberal arts and sciences studies, and humanities; mathematics and statistics; multi/interdisciplinary studies; natural resources and conservation; parks, recreation, leisure, and fitness studies; philosophy and religious studies; physical sciences; psychology; public administration and social service professions; security and protective services; social sciences; theology and religious vocations; transportation and materials moving; visual and performing arts. **Areas of required coursework:** arts/fine arts, humanities, English (including composition), sciences (biological or physical), social science, other. **Pre-professional programs:** pre-dentistry, pre-medicine, pre-veterinary science, pre-pharmacy. **Special academic programs:** accelerated program, cooperative (work-study plan) program, cross-registration, distance learning, double major, dual enrollment, English as a Second Language (ESL), exchange student program (domestic), external degree program, honors program, independent study, internships, liberal arts/career combination, student-designed major, study abroad, teacher certificate program, weekend college, other. **Teacher certification offered in:** early childhood, special education, vo-tech, middle/junior high, secondary, bilingual/bicultural. **Cooperative education programs:** technologies, vocational arts. **Reserve Officers Training Corps (ROTC):** Army ROTC: Offered on campus; Air Force ROTC: Offered on campus. **Faculty and instruction (2005-2006):** Total instructional faculty: 841 full-time, 614 part-time (49% men; 51% women; 13% minorities). Full-time faculty with Ph.D. or other terminal degree: 70%. Student/faculty ratio: 19/1. Classes of fewer than 20 students: 52%; of 20 to 49 students: 41%; of 50 or more students: 8%. **Advanced Placement and International Baccalaureate credit:** AP tests may be used for: Credit and/or placement. Scores accepted: 3, 4, 5. **Freshmen returning for sophomore year:** 72%. **Graduation rates:** Four-year: 19%; five-year: 40%; six-year: 46%.

COSTS AND FINANCIAL AID

Financial aid office: (330) 672-2972. **Expenses (2006-2007):** Tuition and fees 2006-2007: $8,430 in state, $15,862 out of state; room/board: $6,880. Estimated books and supplies: $1,090; transportation: $1,460; personal expenses: $2,190. **Financial aid:** Priority filing date for institution's financial aid form: March 1. In 2005-2006, 70% of undergraduates applied for financial aid. Of those, 58% were determined to have financial need; 13% had their need fully met. Average financial aid package (proportion receiving): $7,040 (58%). Average amount of gift aid, such as scholarships or grants (proportion receiving): $4,670 (40%). Average amount of self-help aid, such as work study or loans (proportion receiving): $3,877 (52%). Average need-based loan (excluding PLUS or other private loans): $3,820. Among students who received need-based aid, the average percentage of need met: 56%. Among students who received aid based on merit, the average award (and the proportion receiving): $3,761 (8%). The average athletic scholarship (and the proportion receiving): $12,658 (1%). Average amount of debt of borrowers graduating in 2005: $21,066. Proportion who borrowed: 69%.

CAMPUS LIFE AND EXTRACURRICULAR ACTIVITIES

Campus housing available: coed dorms, women's dorms, men's dorms, sorority housing, fraternity housing, apartments for married students, apartment for single students. Students who live in college-owned, operated, or affiliated housing: 36%. **Student employment:** During the 2005-2006 academic year, 24% of undergraduates worked on campus. Average per-year earnings: $3,300. **Clubs and organizations:** Number of student organizations: 242. Activities include: choral groups, concert band, dance, drama/theater, jazz band, literary magazine, marching band, music ensembles, musical theater, pep band, radio station, student government, student

newspaper, student film society, television station. Number of fraternities: 17; sororities: 7. Proportion of men in fraternities: 1%; of women in sororities: 1%. Average proportion of students who stay on campus on weekends: 60%. **Sports program (2005-2006):** Member of NCAA I. **Men's intercollegiate varsity sports:** baseball, basketball, cross-country, football, golf, track and field (indoor), track and field (outdoor), wrestling. **Women's intercollegiate varsity sports:** basketball, cross-country, field hockey, golf, gymnastics, soccer, softball, track and field (indoor), track and field (outdoor), volleyball.

SERVICES AND FACILITIES

Basic services: nonremedial tutoring, women's center, placement service, day care, health service, health insurance. **Remedial assistance:** reading, math, writing, study skills. **Counseling services:** minority student, career, military, personal, veteran student, academic, older student, psychological, birth control. **For learning-disabled students:** School does not offer a structured program with separate admission and additional fees. Total undergraduates in learning-disabled program or receiving services: 976. Services include: remedial math, remedial English, remedial reading, tape recorders, note-taking services, oral tests, learning center, readers, extended time for tests, tutors, priority registration, priority seating, texts on tape, other testing accomodations. **Library:** Number of titles: 2,367,222; number of current serial subscriptions: 13,357. **Information technology resources:** Students are not required to lease or own a computer. Number of campus computers available to all students: 1,305. School has a wireless network. Approximate number of users that can be accommodated: 3,500. Proportion of college-owned housing units wired for high-speed internet access: 100%. **Campus safety:** Security services offered: 24-hour foot-and-vehicle patrols, late-night transport/escort service, 24-hour emergency telephones, lighted pathways/sidewalks, student patrols, controlled dormitory access (key, security card, etc).

TRANSFER AND INTERNATIONAL STUDENTS

Transfer students: May apply for admission for the following academic terms: Fall, Spring, Summer. Applicants do not need a minimum number of credits to apply. For fall 2005: Transfer applications received: 1,576. Transfer applicants offered admission: 1,509. Transfer applicants enrolled: 911. **International students:** Number of foreign undergraduates: 153 (1% of student body). Number of countries represented: 94. Minimum TOEFL score required: 525 (paper); 197 (computer). Average TOEFL score: 532 (paper).

Kenyon College

- **Address:** Ransom Hall, Gambier, OH 43022-9623
- **Website:** http://www.kenyon.edu
- **Private; Religious affiliation:** Episcopal nondenominational
- **Enrollment:** 1,640 full-time; 21 part-time

KEY STATS

✔ **U.S News College Ranking:** 32, Liberal Arts Colleges
✔ **SAT Score (25th/75th percentile):** 1240-1420
✔ **Tuition:** 2006-2007: $36,050

Selectivity: Most selective	**Room/board:** $5,900
Acceptance rate: 36%	**Average debt:** $19,190
Student/faculty ratio: 10/1	**Proportion who borrowed:** 60%

UNDERGRADUATE STUDENT BODY STATS

2005-2006 enrollment: 1,640 full-time; 21 part-time. Men: 47%; women: 53%. **Ethnic makeup:** African American: 3%; Asian American: 4%; Hispanic: 3%; White: 87%; International: 2%. **Religious preference:** Roman Catholic: 20%; Protestant: 42%; Jewish: 10%; Muslim: 3%; Hindu: 1%; Buddhist: 1%; No preference: 19%.

ADMISSIONS FACTS AND FIGURES

Phone: (740) 427-5776. **Email:** admissions@kenyon.edu. **Website:** http://www.kenyon.edu. **Application deadlines for fall 2007:** Regular decision: January 15; decision sent by April 1. Early decision: Send application by: December 1; Decision sent by: December 15. Early action: Not offered. Admission can be deferred. **Application fee:** $50. Common application is accepted. **Admissions requirements/recommendations:** High school units required (recommended): English: 4 (4); Mathematics: 3 (4); Science: 3 (4); Foreign language: 3 (4); Social studies: 1 (2); History: 1 (1); Academic electives: 3 (4); Total units: 21 (23). Tests: The college uses SAT or ACT scores in admissions decisions. Either SAT or ACT required. For admission to the fall 2007 entering class, the school will accept: ACT with writing, ACT without writing. Campus visit: Recommended. Admissions interview: Recommended. Off-campus interview: May be arranged. **Factors that count in admissions decisions:** *Academic:* Secondary school record: Very important. Class rank: Important. Letters of recommendation: Very important. Standardized test scores; Important. Essay: Very important. *Nonacademic:* Interview: Important. Extracurricular activities: Important. Talent/ability: Important. Character/personal qualities: Very important. Alumni/ae relationship: Considered. Geographical residence: Considered. State residency: Considered. Religious affiliation/commitment: Not considered. Minority status: Considered. Volunteer work: Considered. Work experience: Considered. **Other schools with the greatest overlap in applicants:** College of Wooster; Denison University; Grinnell College; Macalester College; Oberlin College. **Admissions statistics for the fall 2005 entering class:** Total applicants: 3,928. Total accepted: 1,418. Freshmen enrolled: 440; 80% were from out of state. Accepted through early-decision or early-action plans: 38%. Overall acceptance rate: 36%. Early-decision acceptance rate: 64%. Non-early acceptance rate: 34%. **Size of waiting list:** 586 applicants; enrolled from waiting list: 8. **Credentials of fall 2005 freshmen:** 59% ranked in the top 10 percent of their high school class; 89% were in the top 25 percent, and 100% were in the top half. (Proportion submitting class standing: 40%.) **Average high school grade point average:** 3.8. **First-year students who submitted SAT scores:** 84%. Scores (25/75 percentile): Verbal: 630-720, Math: 610-700, Combined: 1240-1420. **First-year students submitting ACT scores:** 39%. Scores (25/75 percentile): English: N/A, Math: N/A, Composite: 28-31.

ACADEMICS

Year founded: 1824. **Academic calendar:** Semester. **Degrees offered:** bachelor's. **Most popular majors:** 20% social sciences, 19% English language and literature/letters, 14% visual and performing arts, 10% multi/interdisciplinary studies, 9% psychology. **Areas of required coursework:** arts/fine arts, humanities, foreign languages, sciences (biological or physical), social science, other. **Pre-professional programs:** pre-law, pre-dentistry, pre-medicine, pre-theology, pre-veterinary science, other. **Special academic programs (% participation):** double major (15.3%), honors program (15%), independent study (54%), internships, student-designed major (1.7%), study abroad (24%). **Faculty and instruction (2005-2006):** Total instructional faculty: 151 full-time, 35 part-time (59% men; 41% women; 16% minorities). Full-time faculty with Ph.D. or other terminal degree: 99%. Student/faculty ratio: 10/1. Classes of fewer than 20 students: 69%; of 20 to 49 students: 30%; of 50 or more students: 1%. **Advanced Placement and International Baccalaureate credit:** AP tests may be used for: Credit and/or placement. Scores accepted: 4, 5. International Baccalaureate exams may be used for: Credit and/or placement. **Freshmen returning for sophomore year:** 92%. **Graduation rates:** Four-year: 80%; five-year: 83%; six-year: 83%. **Graduate study:** 18% of students pursue further study immediately upon graduation; 25% within one year; 70% within five years. Fields in which graduates pursue further study: Master of Business Administration (MBA), 12%; law, 12%; medicine, 6%; dentistry, 1%; engineering, 1%; theology (or the seminary), 2%; education, 18%; arts and sciences, 27%; veterinary medicine, 1%.

COSTS AND FINANCIAL AID

Financial aid office: (740) 427-5430. **Expenses (2006-2007):** Tuition and fees 2006-2007: $36,050; room/board: $5,900. Estimated books and supplies: $1,200; transportation: $900; personal expenses: $0. **Financial aid:** Priority filing date for institution's financial aid form: February 15; deadline: February 15. In 2005-2006, 52% of undergraduates applied for financial aid. Of those, 43% were determined to have financial need; 54% had their need fully met. Average financial aid package (proportion receiving): $24,982 (43%). Average amount of gift aid, such as scholarships or grants (proportion receiving): $21,897 (41%). Average amount of self-help aid, such as work study or loans (proportion receiving): $4,349 (38%). Average need-based loan (excluding PLUS or other private loans): $3,810. Among students who received need-based aid, the average percentage of need met: 98%. Among students who received aid based on merit, the average award (and the proportion receiving): $12,072 (23%). The average athletic scholarship (and the proportion receiving): $0 (0%). Average amount of debt of borrowers graduating in 2005: $19,190. Proportion who borrowed: 60%.

CAMPUS LIFE AND EXTRACURRICULAR ACTIVITIES

Campus housing available (% using): coed dorms (67%), women's dorms (3%), fraternity housing (9%), apartment for single students (19%), special housing for disabled students, other housing options (2%). Students who live in college-owned, operated, or affiliated housing: 97%. **Student employ-**

ment: During the 2005-2006 academic year, 38% of undergraduates worked on campus. Average per-year earnings: $545. **Clubs and organizations:** Number of student organizations: 138. Activities include: choral groups, concert band, dance, drama/theater, jazz band, literary magazine, music ensembles, musical theater, opera, pep band, radio station, student government, student newspaper, student film society, symphony orchestra, yearbook. Number of fraternities: 7; sororities: 3. Proportion of men in fraternities: 27%; of women in sororities: 9%. Average proportion of students who stay on campus on weekends: 99%. **Sports program (2005-2006):** Member of NCAA III. *Men's intercollegiate varsity sports:* baseball, basketball, cross-country, football, golf, lacrosse, soccer, swimming and diving, tennis, track and field (indoor), track and field (outdoor). *Women's intercollegiate varsity sports:* basketball, cross-country, field hockey, lacrosse, soccer, softball, swimming and diving, tennis, track and field (indoor), track and field (outdoor), volleyball.

SERVICES AND FACILITIES

Basic services: nonremedial tutoring, women's center, placement service, health service, health insurance. **Remedial assistance:** writing, study skills. **Counseling services:** minority student, career, personal, academic, psychological, birth control, religious, other. **For learning-disabled students:** School does not offer a structured program with separate admission and additional fees. Total undergraduates in learning-disabled program or receiving services: 106. Services include: remedial math, remedial English, reading machines, tape recorders, videotaped classes, diagnostic testing service, untimed tests, note-taking services, oral tests, readers, extended time for tests, tutors, early syllabus, priority registration, proofreading services, substitution of courses, texts on tape, typist/scribe, exams on tape or computer, other testing accomodations, other. **Library:** Number of titles: 809,327; number of current serial subscriptions: 8,871. **Information technology resources:** Students are not required to lease or own a computer. Number of campus computers available to all students: 530. School has a wireless network. Approximate number of users that can be accommodated: 2,000. Proportion of college-owned housing units wired for high-speed internet access: 100%. **Campus safety:** Security services offered: 24-hour foot-and-vehicle patrols, late-night transport/escort service, 24-hour emergency telephones, lighted pathways/sidewalks, student patrols.

TRANSFER AND INTERNATIONAL STUDENTS

Transfer students: May apply for admission for the following academic terms: Fall, Spring. Applicants do not need a minimum number of credits to apply. For fall 2005: Transfer applications received: 136. Transfer applicants offered admission: 14. Transfer applicants enrolled: 11. **International students:** Number of foreign undergraduates: 40 (2% of student body). Number of countries represented: 50. Minimum TOEFL score required: 570 (paper); 230 (computer). Average TOEFL score: 630 (paper).

Lake Erie College

- **Address:** 391 W. Washington Street, Painesville, OH 44077
- **Website:** http://www.lec.edu
- **Private**
- **Enrollment:** 574 full-time; 108 part-time

KEY STATS

✔ **U.S News College Ranking:** third tier, Universities–Master's (Midwest)
✔ **ACT Score (25th/75th percentile):** 17-22
✔ **Tuition:** 2006-2007: $22,890

Selectivity: Selective	**Room/board:** $6,778
Acceptance rate: 76%	**Average debt:** $18,000
Student/faculty ratio: 12/1	**Proportion who borrowed:** N/A

UNDERGRADUATE STUDENT BODY STATS

2005-2006 enrollment: 574 full-time; 108 part-time. Men: 27%; women: 73%. **Ethnic makeup:** African American: 7%; Asian American: 1%; Hispanic: 2%; White: 90%.

ADMISSIONS FACTS AND FIGURES

Phone: (800) 916-0904. **Email:** admissions@lec.edu. **Website:** http://www.lec.edu. **Application deadlines for fall 2007:** Regular decision: Rolling. Early decision: Not offered. Early action: Send application by: N/A; Decision sent by: N/A. Admission can be deferred. **Application fee:** $25.

Common application is accepted. **Admissions requirements/recommendations:** High school units required (recommended): English: (4); Mathematics: (3); Science: (3); Foreign language: (2); Social studies: (3). Tests: The college uses SAT or ACT scores in admissions decisions. Either SAT or ACT required. For admission to the fall 2007 entering class, the school will accept: ACT with writing, ACT without writing. Campus visit: Recommended. Admissions interview: Recommended. Off-campus interview: May be arranged. **Factors that count in admissions decisions:** *Academic:* Secondary school record: Very important. Class rank: Important. Letters of recommendation: Considered. Standardized test scores: Very important. Essay: Considered. *Nonacademic:* Interview: Very important. Extracurricular activities: Considered. Talent/ability: Important. Character/personal qualities: Important. Alumni/ae relationship: Considered. Geographical residence: Considered. State residency: Considered. Religious affiliation/commitment: Not considered. Minority status: Not considered. Volunteer work: Considered. Work experience: Considered. **Other schools with the greatest overlap in applicants:** Hiram College; John Carroll University; Kent State University; Notre Dame College; Otterbein College. **Admissions statistics for the fall 2005 entering class:** Total applicants: 532. Total accepted: 404. Freshmen enrolled: 117; 32% were from out of state. Overall acceptance rate: 76%. Non-early acceptance rate: 76%. **Credentials of fall 2005 freshmen:** 15% ranked in the top 10 percent of their high school class; 29% were in the top 25 percent, and 59% were in the top half. (Proportion submitting class standing: 64%.) **Average high school grade point average:** 3.1. **First-year students who submitted SAT scores:** 41%. Scores (25/75 percentile): Verbal: 430-550, Math: 420-530, Combined: 850-1080. **First-year students submitting ACT scores:** 71%. Scores (25/75 percentile): English: 15-22, Math: 16-20, Composite: 17-22.

ACADEMICS
Year founded: 1856. **Academic calendar:** Semester. **Degrees offered:** certificate, bachelor's, post-bachelor's certificate, master's. **Most popular majors:** 22% education, 17% business, management, marketing, and related support services, 10% agriculture, agriculture operations, and related sciences, 10% history, 8% multi/interdisciplinary studies. **Major fields of study:** agriculture, agriculture operations, and related sciences; biological and biomedical sciences; business, management, marketing, and related support services; communication, journalism, and related programs; education; history; legal professions and studies; mathematics and statistics; multi/interdisciplinary studies; natural resources and conservation; psychology; visual and performing arts. **Areas of required coursework:** arts/fine arts, humanities, computer literacy, mathematics, English (including composition), philosophy, foreign languages, sciences (biological or physical), history, social science, other. **Pre-professional programs:** pre-law, pre-dentistry, pre-medicine, pre-veterinary science, pre-pharmacy, other. **Special academic programs:** accelerated program, cross-registration, double major, honors program, independent study, internships, liberal arts/career combination, student-designed major, study abroad, teacher certificate program, weekend college. **Teacher certification offered in:** early childhood, middle/junior high. **Faculty and instruction (2005-2006):** Total instructional faculty: 34 full-time, 59 part-time (51% men; 49% women; 5% minorities). Full-time faculty with Ph.D. or other terminal degree: 76%. Student/faculty ratio: 12/1. Classes of fewer than 20 students: 82%; of 20 to 49 students: 18%; of 50 or more students: 0%. **Advanced Placement and International Baccalaureate credit:** AP tests may be used for: Credit and/or placement. Scores accepted: 3, 4, 5. International Baccalaureate exams may be used for: Credit and/or placement. **Freshmen returning for sophomore year:** 64%. **Graduation rates:** Four-year: 32%; five-year: 40%; six-year: 47%.

COSTS AND FINANCIAL AID
Financial aid office: (440) 375-7100. **Expenses (2006-2007):** Tuition and fees 2006-2007: $22,890; room/board: $6,778. Average amount of debt of borrowers graduating in 2005: $18,000.

CAMPUS LIFE AND EXTRACURRICULAR ACTIVITIES
Campus housing available (% using): coed dorms (25%), women's dorms (50%), men's dorms (25%). Students who live in college-owned, operated, or affiliated housing: 44%. **Student employment:** During the 2005-2006 academic year, 21% of undergraduates worked on campus. Average per-year earnings: $3,090. **Clubs and organizations:** Number of student organizations: 27. Activities include: choral groups, dance, drama/theater, music ensembles, radio station, student government, student newspaper, yearbook. Number of fraternities: 0; sororities: 1. of women in sororities: 4%. Average proportion of students who stay on campus on weekends: 45%. **Sports program (2005-2006):** Member of NCAA III. *Men's intercollegiate*

varsity sports: baseball, basketball, cross-country, golf, soccer. ***Women's intercollegiate varsity sports:*** basketball, cross-country, soccer, softball, volleyball.

SERVICES AND FACILITIES
Basic services: nonremedial tutoring. **Remedial assistance:** reading, math, writing, study skills. **Counseling services:** career, academic. **For learning-disabled students:** School does not offer a structured program with separate admission and additional fees. Total undergraduates in learning-disabled program or receiving services: 64. Services include: remedial math, remedial English, reading machines, tape recorders, other special classes, untimed tests, note-taking services, oral tests, learning center, readers, extended time for tests, tutors, texts on tape, other. **Library:** Number of titles: 87,000; number of current serial subscriptions: 6,050. **Information technology resources:** Students are not required to lease or own a computer. Number of campus computers available to all students: 128. School has a wireless network. Approximate number of users that can be accommodated: 400. Proportion of college-owned housing units wired for high-speed internet access: 100%. **Campus safety:** Security services offered: late-night transport/escort service, 24-hour emergency telephones, lighted pathways/sidewalks, controlled dormitory access (key, security card, etc).

TRANSFER AND INTERNATIONAL STUDENTS
Transfer students: May apply for admission for the following academic terms: Fall, Spring, Summer. Applicants do not need a minimum number of credits to apply. For fall 2005: Transfer applications received: 165. Transfer applicants offered admission: 127. Transfer applicants enrolled: 75. **International students:** Number of foreign undergraduates: 3. Number of countries represented: 6. Minimum TOEFL score required: 550 (paper); 213 (computer).

Lourdes College

- **Address:** 6832 Convent Boulevard, Sylvania, OH 43560-2898
- **Website:** http://www.lourdes.edu
- **Private; Religious affiliation:** Roman Catholic
- **Enrollment:** 849 full-time; 839 part-time

KEY STATS
✔ **U.S News College Ranking:** fourth tier, Comp. Coll.–Bachelor's (Midwest)
✔ **ACT Score (25th/75th percentile):** 17-21
✔ **Tuition:** 2006-2007: $13,200

Selectivity: Less selective   **Room/board:** N/A
Acceptance rate: 41%   **Average debt:** N/A
Student/faculty ratio: 12/1   **Proportion who borrowed:** N/A

UNDERGRADUATE STUDENT BODY STATS
2005-2006 enrollment: 849 full-time; 839 part-time. Men: 18%; women: 82%. **Ethnic makeup:** African American: 14%; American-Indian: 1%; Asian American: 1%; Hispanic: 2%; White: 83%. **Religious preference:** No preference: 10%; Unknown: 15%; Roman Catholic: 40%; Lutheran: 12%; Other: 23%.

ADMISSIONS FACTS AND FIGURES
Phone: (419) 885-5291. **Email:** lcadmits@lourdes.edu. **Website:** http://www.lourdes.edu. **Application deadlines for fall 2007:** Regular decision: Rolling. Early decision: Not offered. Early action: Not offered. Admission can be deferred. **Application fee:** $25. Common application is accepted. **Admissions requirements/recommendations:** Tests: The college uses SAT or ACT scores in admissions decisions. Neither SAT nor ACT required. For admission to the fall 2007 entering class, the school will accept: ACT with writing, ACT without writing. Campus visit: Recommended. Admissions interview: Recommended. Off-campus interview: May be arranged. **Factors that count in admissions decisions:** *Academic:* Secondary school record: Not considered. Class rank: Not considered. Letters of recommendation: Considered. Standardized test scores: Very important. Essay: Not considered. *Nonacademic:* Interview: Considered. Extracurricular activities: Not considered. Talent/ability: Not considered. Character/personal qualities: Not considered. Alumni/ae relationship: Not considered. Geographical residence: Not considered. State residency: Not considered. Religious affiliation/commitment: Not considered. Minority status: Not considered. Volunteer work: Not considered. Work experience: Not considered. **Admissions statistics for the fall 2005 entering**

class: Total applicants: 314. Total accepted: 129. Freshmen enrolled: 129; 7% were from out of state. Overall acceptance rate: 41%. **Credentials of fall 2005 freshmen:** 4% ranked in the top 10 percent of their high school class; 26% were in the top 25 percent, and 64% were in the top half. (Proportion submitting class standing: 81%.) **Average high school grade point average:** 3.0. **First-year students who submitted SAT scores:** 4%. Scores (25/75 percentile): Verbal: 410-560, Math: 430-580, Combined: 840-1140. **First-year students submitting ACT scores:** 81%. Scores (25/75 percentile): English: 16-22, Math: 16-20, Composite: 17-21.

ACADEMICS

Year founded: 1958. **Academic calendar:** Semester. **Degrees offered:** certificate, associate, bachelor's, post-bachelor's certificate, master's. **Most popular majors:** 27% business, management, marketing, and related support services, 26% public administration and social service professions, 13% education, 11% multi/interdisciplinary studies, 5% public administration and social service professions. **Major fields of study:** biological and biomedical sciences; business, management, marketing, and related support services; education; English language and literature/letters; health professions and related clinical sciences; history; multi/interdisciplinary studies; philosophy and religious studies; psychology; public administration and social service professions; security and protective services; social sciences; visual and performing arts. **Areas of required coursework:** arts/fine arts, humanities, computer literacy, mathematics, English (including composition), philosophy, sciences (biological or physical), history, social science. **Pre-professional programs:** pre-law, pre-dentistry, pre-medicine, pre-veterinary science, other. **Special academic programs:** accelerated program, cooperative (work-study plan) program, distance learning, double major, dual enrollment, independent study, internships, liberal arts/career combination, student-designed major, teacher certificate program, weekend college. **Teacher certification offered in:** early childhood, elementary, middle/junior high, secondary. **Reserve Officers Training Corps (ROTC):** Army ROTC: Offered at cooperating institution (University of Toledo); Air Force ROTC: Offered at cooperating institution (Bowling Green State University). **Faculty and instruction (2005-2006):** Total instructional faculty: 65 full-time, 111 part-time (33% men; 67% women; 6% minorities). Full-time faculty with Ph.D. or other terminal degree: 43%. Student/faculty ratio: 12/1. Classes of fewer than 20 students: 65%; of 20 to 49 students: 35%; of 50 or more students: 0%. **Freshmen returning for sophomore year:** 61%. **Graduation rates:** Four-year: 4%; five-year: 25%; six-year: 29%. **Graduate study:** Fields in which graduates pursue further study: Master of Business Administration (MBA), 13%; theology (or the seminary), 3%; education, 27%; arts and sciences, 43%.

COSTS AND FINANCIAL AID

Financial aid office: (419) 824-3732. **Expenses (2006-2007):** Tuition and fees 2006-2007: $13,200; room/board: N/A. **Financial aid:** Priority filing date for institution's financial aid form: March 1. In 2005-2006, 93% of undergraduates applied for financial aid. Of those, 80% were determined to have financial need; Average financial aid package (proportion receiving): $8,768 (80%). Average amount of gift aid, such as scholarships or grants (proportion receiving): $5,048 (65%). Average amount of self-help aid, such as work study or loans (proportion receiving): $4,001 (71%). Average need-based loan (excluding PLUS or other private loans): $3,537. Among students who received aid based on merit, the average award (and the proportion receiving): $0 (0%). The average athletic scholarship (and the proportion receiving): $0 (0%).

CAMPUS LIFE AND EXTRACURRICULAR ACTIVITIES

Students who live in college-owned, operated, or affiliated housing: 0%. **Clubs and organizations:** Number of student organizations: 13. Activities include: choral groups, literary magazine, student government, student film society. Number of fraternities: 0; sororities: 0.

SERVICES AND FACILITIES

Basic services: nonremedial tutoring. **Remedial assistance:** reading, math, writing, study skills. **Counseling services:** career, personal, academic, religious. **For learning-disabled students:** School does not offer a structured program with separate admission and additional fees. Services include: remedial math, remedial English, remedial reading, tape recorders, untimed tests, note-taking services, oral tests, learning center, readers, extended time for tests, tutors, priority seating, texts on tape, other testing accomodations. **Library:** Number of titles: 64,567; number of current serial subscriptions: 449. **Information technology resources:** Students are not required to lease or own a computer. Number of campus computers available to all students: 147. School has a wireless network. **Campus safety:** Security services offered: 24-hour emergency telephones.

TRANSFER AND INTERNATIONAL STUDENTS

Transfer students: May apply for admission for the following academic terms: Fall, Spring, Summer. Applicants need a minimum number of credits to apply. For fall 2005: Transfer applications received: 655. Transfer applicants offered admission: 539. Transfer applicants enrolled: 304. **International students:** Number of foreign undergraduates: 2. Minimum TOEFL score required: 500 (paper); 173 (computer).

Malone College

- **Address:** 515 25th Street NW, Canton, OH 44709
- **Website:** http://www.malone.edu
- **Private; Religious affiliation:** Evangelical Friends
- **Enrollment:** 1,676 full-time; 244 part-time

KEY STATS
- ✔ **U.S News College Ranking:** 55, Universities–Master's (Midwest)
- ✔ **ACT Score (25th/75th percentile):** 19-25
- ✔ **Tuition:** 2006-2007: $17,790

Selectivity: Selective	**Room/board:** $6,400
Acceptance rate: 81%	**Average debt:** $18,482
Student/faculty ratio: 14/1	**Proportion who borrowed:** 72%

UNDERGRADUATE STUDENT BODY STATS

2005-2006 enrollment: 1,676 full-time; 244 part-time. Men: 39%; women: 61%. **Ethnic makeup:** African American: 6%; Hispanic: 1%; White: 91%; International: 1%.

ADMISSIONS FACTS AND FIGURES

Phone: (330) 471-8145. **Email:** admissions@malone.edu. **Website:** http://www.malone.edu. **Application deadlines for fall 2007:** Regular decision: July 1. Early decision: Not offered. Early action: Not offered. Admission can be deferred. **Application fee:** $20. Common application is accepted. **To apply online, go to:** http://www.malone.edu/ugrad_application/. **Admissions requirements/recommendations:** High school units required (recommended): English: 4; Mathematics: 3; Science: 3; Foreign language: 2; Social studies: 2; History: 1; Academic electives: 2; Total units: 18. Tests: The college uses SAT or ACT scores in admissions decisions. Either SAT or ACT required. For admission to the fall 2007 entering class, the school will accept: ACT with writing, ACT without writing. Campus visit: Recommended. Admissions interview: Recommended. Off-campus interview: Not available. **Factors that count in admissions decisions:** *Academic:* Secondary school record: Very important. Class rank: Important. Letters of recommendation: Important. Standardized test scores: Very important. Essay: Important. *Nonacademic:* Interview: Considered, Extracurricular activities: Considered. Talent/ability: Important. Character/personal qualities: Very important. Alumni/ae relationship: Considered. Geographical residence: Not considered. State residency: Not considered. Religious affiliation/commitment: Important. Minority status: Considered. Volunteer work: Considered. Work experience: Not considered. **Other schools with the greatest overlap in applicants:** Indiana Wesleyan University; Kent State University; Mount Union College; Mount Vernon Nazarene University; University of Akron. **Admissions statistics for the fall 2005 entering class:** Total applicants: 1,036. Total accepted: 839. Freshmen enrolled: 361; 13% were from out of state. Overall acceptance rate: 81%. **Credentials of fall 2005 freshmen:** 19% ranked in the top 10 percent of their high school class; 47% were in the top 25 percent, and 76% were in the top half. (Proportion submitting class standing: 82%.) **Average high school grade point average:** 3.3. **First-year students who submitted SAT scores:** 25%. Scores (25/75 percentile): Verbal: 470-590, Math: 450-580, Combined: 920-1170. **First-year students submitting ACT scores:** 88%. Scores (25/75 percentile): English: 19-25, Math: 17-24, Composite: 19-25.

ACADEMICS

Year founded: 1892. **Academic calendar:** Semester. **Degrees offered:** bachelor's, post-bachelor's certificate, master's. **Most popular majors:** 40% business administration, management, and operations, 9% nursing/registered nurse training (R.N., A.S.N., B.S.N., M.S.N.), 8% early childhood education and teaching, 7% business administration and management, 5% communication, journalism, and related programs. **Major fields of study:** biological and biomedical sciences; business, management, marketing, and related support services; communication, journalism, and related programs; communications technologies/technicians and support services; computer and information sciences and support services; education; English language and literature/letters; foreign languages, literatures, and linguistics; health professions and related clinical sciences; history; liberal arts and sciences studies, and humanities; mathematics and statistics; parks, recreation, leisure, and fitness studies; philosophy and religious studies; physical sciences; psychology; public administration and social service professions; social sciences; theology and religious vocations; visual and performing arts. **Areas of required coursework:** arts/fine arts, humanities, mathematics, English (including composition), philosophy, sciences (biological or physical), history, social science, other. **Pre-professional programs:** pre-law, pre-dentistry, pre-medicine, pre-theology, pre-veterinary science. **Special academic programs (% participation):** accelerated program (5.3%), cooperative (work-study plan) program (4.6%), distance learning (47.3%), double major (4.4%), dual enrollment (1.9%), exchange student program (domestic) (3%), honors program (6.8%), independent study (17.8%), internships (22.3%), student-designed major (2.6%), study abroad (3%), teacher certificate program (16.9%), other (43%). **Teacher certification offered in:** early childhood, special education, elementary, middle/junior high, secondary. **Cooperative education programs:** other. **Reserve Officers Training Corps (ROTC):** Army ROTC: Offered at cooperating institution (University of Akron); Air Force ROTC: Offered at cooperating institution (University of Akron). **Faculty and instruction (2005-2006):** Total instructional faculty: 104 full-time, 98 part-time (54% men; 46% women; 4% minorities). Full-time faculty with Ph.D. or other terminal degree: 70%. Student/faculty ratio: 14/1. Classes of fewer than 20 students: 56%; of 20 to 49 students: 42%; of 50 or more students: 2%. **Advanced Placement and International Baccalaureate credit:** AP tests may be used for: Credit only. Scores accepted: 3, 4, 5. International Baccalaureate exams may be used for: Credit and/or placement. **Freshmen returning for sophomore year:** 74%. **Graduation rates:** Four-year: 39%; five-year: 55%; six-year: 55%. **Graduate study:** 23% of students pursue further study within one year. Fields in which graduates pursue further study: Master of Business Administration (MBA), 7%; law, 2%; medicine, 1%; theology (or the seminary), 1%; education, 3%; arts and sciences, 6%.

COSTS AND FINANCIAL AID

Financial aid office: (330) 471-8159. **Expenses (2006-2007):** Tuition and fees 2006-2007: $17,790; room/board: $6,400. Estimated books and supplies: $930; transportation: $900; personal expenses: $1,200. **Financial aid:** Priority filing date for institution's financial aid form: March 1; deadline: July 31. In 2005-2006, 85% of undergraduates applied for financial aid. Of those, 75% were determined to have financial need; 18% had their need fully met. Average financial aid package (proportion receiving): $12,194 (75%). Average amount of gift aid, such as scholarships or grants (proportion receiving): $8,344 (74%). Average amount of self-help aid, such as work study or loans (proportion receiving): $4,305 (68%). Average need-based loan (excluding PLUS or other private loans): $4,074. Among students who received need-based aid, the average percentage of need met: 71%. Among students who received aid based on merit, the average award (and the proportion receiving): $4,524 (11%). The average athletic scholarship (and the proportion receiving): $6,228 (4%). Average amount of debt of borrowers graduating in 2005: $18,482. Proportion who borrowed: 72%.

CAMPUS LIFE AND EXTRACURRICULAR ACTIVITIES

Campus housing available (% using): women's dorms (61%), men's dorms (39%). Students who live in college-owned, operated, or affiliated housing: 51%. **Student employment:** During the 2005-2006 academic year, 5% of undergraduates worked on campus. Average per-year earnings: $925. **Clubs and organizations:** Number of student organizations: 57. Activities include: choral groups, concert band, dance, drama/theater, jazz band, literary magazine, marching band, music ensembles, musical theater, radio station, student government, student newspaper, yearbook. Number of fraternities: 0; sororities: 0. Average proportion of students who stay on campus on weekends: 40%. **Sports program (2005-2006):** Member of NAIA. *Men's intercollegiate varsity sports:* baseball, basketball, cross-country, football, golf, soccer, tennis, track and field (indoor), track and field (outdoor). *Women's intercollegiate varsity sports:* basketball, cheerleading, cross-country, golf, soccer, softball, tennis, track and field (indoor), track and field (outdoor), volleyball.

SERVICES AND FACILITIES

Basic services: nonremedial tutoring, placement service, health service, health insurance. **Remedial assistance:** reading, math, writing, study skills. **Counseling services:** minority student, career, personal, academic, older student, psychological, religious. **For learning-disabled students:** School does not offer a structured program with separate admission and additional fees.

Total undergraduates in learning-disabled program or receiving services: 18. Services include: remedial math, remedial English, remedial reading, tape recorders, note-taking services, oral tests, readers, extended time for tests, tutors, texts on tape, other. **Library:** Number of titles: 241,954; number of current serial subscriptions: 7,116. **Information technology resources:** Students are not required to lease or own a computer. Number of campus computers available to all students: 215. School has a wireless network. Approximate number of users that can be accommodated: 250. Proportion of college-owned housing units wired for high-speed internet access: 100%. **Campus safety:** Security services offered: 24-hour foot-and-vehicle patrols, late-night transport/escort service, 24-hour emergency telephones, lighted pathways/sidewalks, controlled dormitory access (key, security card, etc).

TRANSFER AND INTERNATIONAL STUDENTS

Transfer students: May apply for admission for the following academic terms: Fall, Spring, Summer. Applicants do not need a minimum number of credits to apply. For fall 2005: Transfer applications received: 278. Transfer applicants offered admission: 207. Transfer applicants enrolled: 117. **International students:** Number of foreign undergraduates: 21 (1% of student body). Number of countries represented: 15. Minimum TOEFL score required: 550 (paper); 213 (computer).

Marietta College

- **Address:** 215 Fifth Street, Marietta, OH 45750
- **Website:** http://www.marietta.edu
- **Private**
- **Enrollment:** 1,274 full-time; 71 part-time

KEY STATS

✔ **U.S News College Ranking:** 17, Comp. Coll.–Bachelor's (Midwest)
✔ **ACT Score (25th/75th percentile):** 20-26
✔ **Tuition:** 2005-2006: $22,656

Selectivity: Selective	Room/board: $6,446
Acceptance rate: 78%	Average debt: N/A
Student/faculty ratio: 12/1	Proportion who borrowed: N/A

UNDERGRADUATE STUDENT BODY STATS

2005-2006 enrollment: 1,274 full-time; 71 part-time. Men: 49%; women: 51%. **Ethnic makeup:** African American: 3%; American-Indian: 1%; Asian American: 1%; Hispanic: 1%; White: 89%; International: 5%.

ADMISSIONS FACTS AND FIGURES

Phone: (800) 331-7896. **Email:** admit@marietta.edu. **Website:** http://www.marietta.edu. **Application deadlines for fall 2007:** Regular decision: April 15. Early decision: Not offered. Early action: Not offered. Admission can be deferred. **Application fee:** $25. Common application is accepted. **To apply online, go to:** http://admission.marietta.edu/hs /index.html. **Admissions requirements/recommendations:** High school units required (recommended): English: 4 (4); Mathematics: 3 (4); Science: 3 (4); Foreign language: 2 (4); Social studies: 2 (2); History: 2; Academic electives: 3 (3); Total units: 16 (21). Tests: The college uses SAT or ACT scores in admissions decisions. Either SAT or ACT required. For admission to the fall 2007 entering class, the school will accept: ACT with writing, ACT without writing. Campus visit: Recommended. Admissions interview: Recommended. Off-campus interview: May be arranged. **Factors that count in admissions decisions:** *Academic:* Secondary school record: Very important. Class rank: Very important. Letters of recommendation: Important. Standardized test scores: Very important. Essay: Considered. *Nonacademic:* Interview: Important. Extracurricular activities: Considered. Talent/ability: Considered. Character/personal qualities: Important. Alumni/ae relationship: Considered. Geographical residence: Considered. State residency: Not considered. Religious affiliation/commitment: Not considered. Minority status: Considered. Volunteer work: Considered. Work experience: Considered. **Other schools with the greatest overlap in applicants:** John Carroll University; Miami University–Oxford; Ohio State University–Columbus; Ohio University; Otterbein College. **Admissions statistics for the fall 2005 entering class:** Total applicants: 2,237. Total accepted: 1,748. Freshmen enrolled: 392; 38% were from out of state. Overall acceptance rate: 78%. **Credentials of fall 2005 freshmen:** 20% ranked in the top 10 percent of their high school class; 47% were in the top 25 percent, and 76% were in the top half. (Proportion submitting class standing: 86%.) **Average high school**

grade point average: 3.4. **First-year students who submitted SAT scores:** 51%. Scores (25/75 percentile): Verbal: 480-600, Math: 470-600, Combined: 950-1200. **First-year students submitting ACT scores:** 79%. Scores (25/75 percentile): English: N/A, Math: N/A, Composite: 20-26.

ACADEMICS
Year founded: 1797. **Academic calendar:** Semester. **Degrees offered:** bachelor's, master's. **Most popular majors:** 22% business administration and management, 7% athletic training/trainer, 5% psychology, 4% petroleum engineering, 3% education. **Major fields of study:** biological and biomedical sciences; business, management, marketing, and related support services; communication, journalism, and related programs; computer and information sciences and support services; education; engineering; English language and literature/letters; foreign languages, literatures, and linguistics; health professions and related clinical sciences; history; mathematics and statistics; natural resources and conservation; physical sciences; psychology; social sciences; visual and performing arts. **Areas of required coursework:** arts/fine arts, humanities, computer literacy, mathematics, English (including composition), philosophy, sciences (biological or physical), history, social science, other. **Pre-professional programs:** pre-law, pre-dentistry, pre-medicine, pre-veterinary science. **Special academic programs:** double major, English as a Second Language (ESL), exchange student program (domestic), honors program, independent study, internships, liberal arts/career combination, student-designed major, study abroad, teacher certificate program. **Teacher certification offered in:** early childhood, elementary, middle/junior high, secondary. **Cooperative education programs:** engineering. **Faculty and instruction (2005-2006):** Total instructional faculty: 93 full-time, 40 part-time (60% men; 40% women; 3% minorities). Full-time faculty with Ph.D. or other terminal degree: 77%. Student/faculty ratio: 12/1. Classes of fewer than 20 students: 78%; of 20 to 49 students: 22%; of 50 or more students: 0%. **Advanced Placement and International Baccalaureate credit:** AP tests may be used for: Credit and/or placement. Scores accepted: 3, 4, 5. International Baccalaureate exams may be used for: Credit and/or placement. **Freshmen returning for sophomore year:** 72%. **Graduation rates:** Six-year: 54%. **Graduate study:** 25% of students pursue further study immediately upon graduation; 20% within one year. Fields in which graduates pursue further study: Master of Business Administration (MBA), 5%; law, 7%; medicine, 10%; engineering, 5%; education, 10%; arts and sciences, 65%.

COSTS AND FINANCIAL AID
Financial aid office: (740) 376-4712. **Expenses (2005-2006):** Tuition and fees 2005-2006: $22,656; room/board: $6,446. Estimated books and supplies: $635; transportation: $530; personal expenses: $1,215. **Financial aid:** Priority filing date for institution's financial aid form: March 1; deadline: May 1.

CAMPUS LIFE AND EXTRACURRICULAR ACTIVITIES
Campus housing available (% using): coed dorms (65%), women's dorms (10%), men's dorms (9%), sorority housing (5%), fraternity housing (7%), apartment for single students (4%). Students who live in college-owned, operated, or affiliated housing: 90%. **Student employment:** During the 2005-2006 academic year, 7% of undergraduates worked on campus. Average per-year earnings: $2,000. **Clubs and organizations:** Number of student organizations: 80. Activities include: choral groups, concert band, dance, drama/theater, jazz band, literary magazine, music ensembles, musical theater, radio station, student government, student newspaper, television station, yearbook. Number of fraternities: 4; sororities: 3. Proportion of men in fraternities: 22%; of women in sororities: 22%. Average proportion of students who stay on campus on weekends: 80%. **Sports program (2005-2006):** Member of NCAA III. *Men's intercollegiate varsity sports:* baseball, basketball, crew, cross-country, football, golf, lightweight crew, soccer, tennis, track and field (indoor), track and field (outdoor). *Women's intercollegiate varsity sports:* basketball, crew, cross-country, lightweight crew, rowing, soccer, softball, tennis, track and field (indoor), track and field (outdoor), volleyball.

SERVICES AND FACILITIES
Basic services: nonremedial tutoring, placement service, health service, other. **Remedial assistance:** reading, math, writing, study skills. **Counseling services:** career, personal, academic, psychological. **For learning-disabled students:** School does not offer a structured program with separate admission and additional fees. Total undergraduates in learning-disabled program or receiving services: 56. Services include: remedial math, remedial English, reading machines, tape recorders, untimed tests, note-taking services, oral tests, learning center, readers, extended time for tests, tutors, texts on tape,

other testing accomodations, other. **Library:** Number of titles: 246,706; number of current serial subscriptions: 6,714. **Information technology resources:** Students are not required to lease or own a computer. School has a wireless network. Proportion of college-owned housing units wired for high-speed internet access: 100%. **Campus safety:** Security services offered: 24-hour foot-and-vehicle patrols, late-night transport/escort service, 24-hour emergency telephones, lighted pathways/sidewalks, student patrols, controlled dormitory access (key, security card, etc).

TRANSFER AND INTERNATIONAL STUDENTS
Transfer students: May apply for admission for the following academic terms: Fall, Spring. Applicants need a minimum number of credits to apply. For fall 2005: Transfer applications received: 104. Transfer applicants offered admission: 77. Transfer applicants enrolled: 55. **International students:** Number of foreign undergraduates: 47 (5% of student body). Number of countries represented: 12. Minimum TOEFL score required: 550 (paper); 213 (computer).

Miami University–Oxford

- **Address:** 501 E. High Street, Oxford, OH 45056
- **Website:** http://www.muohio.edu
- **Public**
- **Enrollment:** 14,312 full-time; 331 part-time

KEY STATS
✔ **U.S News College Ranking:** 60, National Universities
✔ **ACT Score (25th/75th percentile):** 25-29
✔ **Tuition:** 2006-2007: $22,997 in state, $23,017 out of state

Selectivity: More selective	**Room/board:** $8,140
Acceptance rate: 69%	**Average debt:** $21,522
Student/faculty ratio: 16/1	**Proportion who borrowed:** 48%

UNDERGRADUATE STUDENT BODY STATS
2005-2006 enrollment: 14,312 full-time; 331 part-time. Men: 47%; women: 53%. **Ethnic makeup:** African American: 3%; American-Indian: 1%; Asian American: 3%; Hispanic: 2%; White: 91%; International: 1%.

ADMISSIONS FACTS AND FIGURES
Phone: (513) 529-2531. **Email:** admission@muohio.edu. **Website:** http://www.muohio.edu. **Application deadlines for fall 2007:** Regular decision: January 31; decision sent by March 15. Early decision: Send application by: November 1; Decision sent by: December 15. Early action: Send application by: December 1; Decision sent by: February 1. Admission can be deferred. **Application fee:** $45. Common application is accepted. **To apply online, go to:** http://www.muohio.edu/admission/apply. **Admissions requirements/recommendations:** High school units required (recommended): English: 4 (4); Mathematics: 3 (3); Science: 3 (3); Foreign language: 2 (2); Social studies: 3 (3); History: 0 (0); Academic electives: 0 (0); Total units: 16 (16). Tests: The college uses SAT or ACT scores in admissions decisions. Either SAT or ACT required. For admission to the fall 2007 entering class, the school will accept: ACT with writing. Campus visit: Neither required nor recommended. Admissions interview: Neither required nor recommended. Off-campus interview: Not available. **Factors that count in admissions decisions:** *Academic:* Secondary school record: Very important. Class rank: Very important. Letters of recommendation: Very important. Standardized test scores: Very important. Essay: Very important. *Nonacademic:* Interview: Not considered. Extracurricular activities: Considered. Talent/ability: Very important. Character/personal qualities: Very important. Alumni/ae relationship: Considered. Geographical residence: Considered. State residency: Considered. Religious affiliation/commitment: Not considered. Minority status: Considered. Volunteer work: Considered. Work experience: Considered. **Other schools with the greatest overlap in applicants:** Indiana University–Bloomington; Ohio State University–Columbus; Ohio University; University of Dayton; University of Michigan–Ann Arbor. **Admissions statistics for the fall 2005 entering class:** Total applicants: 15,579. Total accepted: 10,823. Freshmen enrolled: 3,162; 32% were from out of state. Overall acceptance rate: 69%. Non-early acceptance rate: 69%. **Size of waiting list:** 1777 applicants; enrolled from waiting list: 556. **Credentials of fall 2005 freshmen:** 41% ranked in the top 10 percent of their high school class; 79% were in the top 25 percent, and 99% were in the top half. (Proportion submitting class standing: 65%.) **Average high school grade**

point average: 3.8. **First-year students who submitted SAT scores:** 77%. Scores (25/75 percentile): Verbal: 560-650, Math: 580-670, Combined: 1140-1320. **First-year students submitting ACT scores:** 97%. Scores (25/75 percentile): English: N/A, Math: N/A, Composite: 25-29.

ACADEMICS

Year founded: 1809. **Academic calendar:** Semester. **Degrees offered:** certificate, associate, transfer-associate, terminal-associate, bachelor's, master's, post-master's certificate, doctorate. **Most popular majors:** 30% business, management, marketing, and related support services, 10% education, 10% social sciences, 7% biological and biomedical sciences, 6% psychology. **Major fields of study:** architecture and related services; area, ethnic, cultural, and gender studies; biological and biomedical sciences; business, management, marketing, and related support services; communication, journalism, and related programs; computer and information sciences and support services; education; engineering; engineering technologies/technicians; English language and literature/letters; family and consumer sciences/human sciences; foreign languages, literatures, and linguistics; health professions and related clinical sciences; history; library science; mathematics and statistics; multi/interdisciplinary studies; natural resources and conservation; parks, recreation, leisure, and fitness studies; philosophy and religious studies; physical sciences; psychology; public administration and social service professions; social sciences; visual and performing arts. **Areas of required coursework:** arts/fine arts, humanities, mathematics, English (including composition), philosophy, foreign languages, sciences (biological or physical), history, social science. **Pre-professional programs:** pre-law, pre-dentistry, pre-medicine, pre-veterinary science, pre-optometry, pre-pharmacy, other. **Special academic programs (% participation):** cooperative (work-study plan) program (1%), cross-registration (1%), double major (6%), exchange student program (domestic) (1%), honors program (6%), independent study (60%), internships (30%), liberal arts/career combination (1%), student-designed major (2%), study abroad (33%), teacher certificate program (20%). **Teacher certification offered in:** early childhood, special education, elementary, middle/junior high, secondary. **Cooperative education programs:** computer science, engineering. **Reserve Officers Training Corps (ROTC):** Army ROTC: Offered at cooperating institution (Xavier University); Navy ROTC: Offered on campus; Air Force ROTC: Offered on campus. **Faculty and instruction (2005-2006):** Total instructional faculty: 842 full-time, 356 part-time (60% men; 40% women; 12% minorities). Full-time faculty with Ph.D. or other terminal degree: 90%. Student/faculty ratio: 16/1. Classes of fewer than 20 students: 35%; of 20 to 49 students: 56%; of 50 or more students: 9%. **Advanced Placement and International Baccalaureate credit:** AP tests may be used for: Credit only. Scores accepted: 3, 4. International Baccalaureate exams may be used for: Credit only. **Freshmen returning for sophomore year:** 90%. **Graduation rates:** Four-year: 66%; five-year: 78%; six-year: 80%.

COSTS AND FINANCIAL AID

Financial aid office: (513) 529-8734. **Expenses (2006-2007):** Tuition and fees 2006-2007: $22,997 in state, $23,017 out of state; room/board: $8,140. Estimated books and supplies: $1,140; transportation: $970; personal expenses: $3,174. **Financial aid:** Priority filing date for institution's financial aid form: February 15. In 2005-2006, 51% of undergraduates applied for financial aid. Of those, 41% were determined to have financial need; 29% had their need fully met. Average financial aid package (proportion receiving): $15,665 (40%). Average amount of gift aid, such as scholarships or grants (proportion receiving): $4,005 (17%). Average amount of self-help aid, such as work study or loans (proportion receiving): $4,233 (29%). Average need-based loan (excluding PLUS or other private loans): $3,947. Among students who received need-based aid, the average percentage of need met: 75%. Among students who received aid based on merit, the average award (and the proportion receiving): $11,606 (40%). The average athletic scholarship (and the proportion receiving): $16,442 (2%). Average amount of debt of borrowers graduating in 2005: $21,522. Proportion who borrowed: 48%.

CAMPUS LIFE AND EXTRACURRICULAR ACTIVITIES

Campus housing available: coed dorms, women's dorms, men's dorms, sorority housing, apartments for married students, apartment for single students, special housing for disabled students, special housing for international students, other housing options. Students who live in college-owned, operated, or affiliated housing: 44%. **Student employment:** During the 2005-2006 academic year, 45% of undergraduates worked on campus. Average per-year earnings: $1,650. **Clubs and organizations:** Number of student organizations: 350. Activities include: choral groups, concert band, dance, drama/theater, jazz band, literary magazine, marching band, music ensembles, musical theater, opera, pep band, radio station, student govern-

ment, student newspaper, student film society, symphony orchestra, television station, yearbook. Number of fraternities: 27; sororities: 21. Proportion of men in fraternities: 22%; of women in sororities: 25%. Average proportion of students who stay on campus on weekends: 90%. **Sports program (2005-2006):** Member of NCAA I. *Men's intercollegiate varsity sports:* baseball, basketball, cross-country, football, golf, ice hockey, swimming and diving, track and field (outdoor). *Women's intercollegiate varsity sports:* basketball, cross-country, field hockey, soccer, softball, swimming and diving, tennis, track and field (indoor), track and field (outdoor), volleyball.

SERVICES AND FACILITIES

Basic services: nonremedial tutoring, women's center, placement service, day care, health service, health insurance. **Remedial assistance:** reading, math, writing, study skills. **Counseling services:** minority student, career, military, personal, veteran student, academic, older student, psychological, birth control. **For learning-disabled students:** School does not offer a structured program with separate admission and additional fees. Services include: reading machines, tape recorders, untimed tests, oral tests, learning center, readers, extended time for tests, tutors, other. **Library:** Number of titles: 2,373,050; number of current serial subscriptions: 13,710. **Information technology resources:** Students are not required to lease or own a computer. Number of campus computers available to all students: 3,500. School has a wireless network. Proportion of college-owned housing units wired for high-speed internet access: 100%. **Campus safety:** Security services offered: 24-hour foot-and-vehicle patrols, late-night transport/escort service, 24-hour emergency telephones, lighted pathways/sidewalks, student patrols, controlled dormitory access (key, security card, etc).

TRANSFER AND INTERNATIONAL STUDENTS

Transfer students: May apply for admission for the following academic terms: Fall, Spring, Summer. Applicants do not need a minimum number of credits to apply. For fall 2005: Transfer applications received: 559. Transfer applicants offered admission: 410. Transfer applicants enrolled: 239. **International students:** Number of foreign undergraduates: 110 (1% of student body). Minimum TOEFL score required: 530 (paper); 200 (computer).

Mount Union College

- **Address:** 1972 Clark Avenue, Alliance, OH 44601
- **Website:** http://www.muc.edu/admission/apply_online
- **Private; Religious affiliation:** United Methodist
- **Enrollment:** 2,021 full-time; 184 part-time

KEY STATS

✔ **U.S News College Ranking:** 12, Comp. Coll.–Bachelor's (Midwest)
✔ **ACT Score (25th/75th percentile):** 20-25
✔ **Tuition:** 2006-2007: $20,970

Selectivity: Selective	**Room/board:** $6,350
Acceptance rate: 80%	**Average debt:** $16,139
Student/faculty ratio: 13/1	**Proportion who borrowed:** 84%

UNDERGRADUATE STUDENT BODY STATS

2005-2006 enrollment: 2,021 full-time; 184 part-time. Men: 47%; women: 53%. **Ethnic makeup:** African American: 4%; Hispanic: 1%; White: 93%; International: 2%. **Religious preference:** Roman Catholic: 32%; Protestant: 20%; No preference: 28%; United Methodist: 14%.

ADMISSIONS FACTS AND FIGURES

Phone: (330) 823-2590. **Email:** admission@muc.edu. **Website:** http://www.muc.edu/admission/apply_online. **Application deadlines for fall 2007:** Regular decision: Rolling. Early decision: Not offered. Early action: Not offered. Admission can be deferred. **Application fee:** None. Common application is accepted. **To apply online, go to:** http://www.muc.edu/admissions/apply_for_admission_online. **Admissions requirements/recommendations:** High school units required (recommended): English: (4); Mathematics: (3); Science: (3); Foreign language: (2); Social studies: (3); History: (0); Academic electives: (1); Total units: (18). Tests: The college uses SAT or ACT scores in admissions decisions. Either SAT or ACT required. For admission to the fall 2007 entering class, the school will accept: ACT with writing, ACT without writing. Campus visit: Recommended. Admissions interview: Recommended. Off-campus interview: Not available.

Factors that count in admissions decisions: Academic: Secondary school record: Very important. Class rank: Very important. Letters of recommendation: Important. Standardized test scores: Very important. Essay: Considered. **Nonacademic:** Interview: Considered. Extracurricular activities: Considered. Talent/ability: Considered. Character/personal qualities: Considered. Alumni/ae relationship: Considered. Geographical residence: Not considered. State residency: Not considered. Religious affiliation/commitment: Not considered. Minority status: Considered. Volunteer work: Considered. Work experience: Considered. **Other schools with the greatest overlap in applicants:** Bowling Green State University; Kent State University; Ohio State University–Columbus; Ohio University; University of Akron. **Admissions statistics for the fall 2005 entering class:** Total applicants: 1,768. Total accepted: 1,414. Freshmen enrolled: 503; 9% were from out of state. Overall acceptance rate: 80%. **Credentials of fall 2005 freshmen:** 14% ranked in the top 10 percent of their high school class; 41% were in the top 25 percent, and 78% were in the top half. (Proportion submitting class standing: 82%.) **Average high school grade point average:** 3.2. **First-year students who submitted SAT scores:** 35%. Scores (25/75 percentile): Verbal: 460-560, Math: 450-570, Combined: 910-1130. **First-year students submitting ACT scores:** 91%. Scores (25/75 percentile): English: 18-25, Math: 18-25, Composite: 20-25.

ACADEMICS

Year founded: 1846. **Academic calendar:** Semester. **Degrees offered:** bachelor's. **Most popular majors:** 14% early childhood education and teaching, 13% business administration and management, 6% junior high/intermediate/middle school education and teaching, 6% psychology, 6% sport and fitness administration/management. **Major fields of study:** area, ethnic, cultural, and gender studies; biological and biomedical sciences; business, management, marketing, and related support services; communication, journalism, and related programs; computer and information sciences and support services; education; English language and literature/letters; foreign languages, literatures, and linguistics; health professions and related clinical sciences; history; mathematics and statistics; multi/interdisciplinary studies; parks, recreation, leisure, and fitness studies; philosophy and religious studies; physical sciences; psychology; social sciences; visual and performing arts. **Areas of required coursework:** arts/fine arts, humanities, computer literacy, mathematics, English (including composition), philosophy, foreign languages, sciences (biological or physical), history, social science. **Pre-professional programs:** pre-law, pre-dentistry, pre-medicine, pre-theology, pre-veterinary science, pre-pharmacy, other. **Special academic programs (% participation):** double major (7.3%), English as a Second Language (ESL) (.5%), honors program (3.2%), independent study (16%), internships (14%), student-designed major (0%), study abroad (8%), teacher certificate program (24%). **Teacher certification offered in:** early childhood, elementary, middle/junior high, secondary. **Reserve Officers Training Corps (ROTC):** Army ROTC: Offered at cooperating institution (Kent State University); Air Force ROTC: Offered at cooperating institution (Kent State University). **Faculty and instruction (2005-2006):** Total instructional faculty: 123 full-time, 103 part-time (63% men; 37% women). Full-time faculty with Ph.D. or other terminal degree: 80%. Student/faculty ratio: 13/1. Classes of fewer than 20 students: 57%; of 20 to 49 students: 42%; of 50 or more students: 1%. **Advanced Placement and International Baccalaureate credit:** AP tests may be used for: Credit only. Scores accepted: 3, 4, 5. International Baccalaureate exams may be used for: Credit only. **Freshmen returning for sophomore year:** 79%. **Graduation rates:** Four-year: 49%; five-year: 60%; six-year: 66%. **Graduate study:** 24% of students pursue further study immediately upon graduation; 24% within one year. Fields in which graduates pursue further study: Master of Business Administration (MBA), 7%; law, 8%; medicine, 15%; dentistry, 2%; theology (or the seminary), 2%; education, 20%; arts and sciences, 64%.

COSTS AND FINANCIAL AID

Financial aid office: (877) 543-9185. **Expenses (2006-2007):** Tuition and fees 2006-2007: $20,970; room/board: $6,350. Estimated books and supplies: $600; transportation: $760; personal expenses: $740. **Financial aid:** Priority filing date for institution's financial aid form: May 1. In 2005-2006, 87% of undergraduates applied for financial aid. Of those, 79% were determined to have financial need; 22% had their need fully met. Average financial aid package (proportion receiving): $16,184 (79%). Average amount of gift aid, such as scholarships or grants (proportion receiving): $11,209 (79%). Average amount of self-help aid, such as work study or loans (proportion receiving): $5,552 (71%). Average need-based loan (excluding PLUS or other private loans): $4,811. Among students who received need-based aid, the average percentage of need met: 82%. Among students who received aid based on merit, the average award (and the proportion receiving): $8,759

(20%). The average athletic scholarship (and the proportion receiving): $0 (0%). Average amount of debt of borrowers graduating in 2005: $16,139. Proportion who borrowed: 84%.

CAMPUS LIFE AND EXTRACURRICULAR ACTIVITIES

Campus housing available (% using): coed dorms (37%), women's dorms (24%), men's dorms (22%), fraternity housing (9%), other housing options (8%). Students who live in college-owned, operated, or affiliated housing: 63%. **Student employment:** During the 2005-2006 academic year, 16% of undergraduates worked on campus. Average per-year earnings: $1,231. **Clubs and organizations:** Number of student organizations: 80. Activities include: choral groups, concert band, dance, drama/theater, jazz band, literary magazine, marching band, music ensembles, musical theater, pep band, radio station, student government, student newspaper, symphony orchestra, yearbook. Number of fraternities: 4; sororities: 4. Proportion of men in fraternities: 12%; of women in sororities: 20%. Average proportion of students who stay on campus on weekends: 50%. **Sports program (2005-2006):** Member of NCAA III. **Men's intercollegiate varsity sports:** baseball, basketball, cross-country, football, golf, soccer, swimming and diving, tennis, track and field (indoor), track and field (outdoor), wrestling. **Women's intercollegiate varsity sports:** basketball, cross-country, golf, soccer, softball, swimming and diving, tennis, track and field (indoor), track and field (outdoor), volleyball.

SERVICES AND FACILITIES

Basic services: nonremedial tutoring, placement service, health service, health insurance. **Remedial assistance:** math, writing, study skills. **Counseling services:** minority student, career, military, personal, academic, older student, psychological, religious, other. **For learning-disabled students:** School does not offer a structured program with separate admission and additional fees. Total undergraduates in learning-disabled program or receiving services: 32. Services include: reading machines, tape recorders, note-taking services, oral tests, learning center, readers, extended time for tests, tutors, substitution of courses, texts on tape, typist/scribe, other testing accomodations. **Library:** Number of titles: 242,844; number of current serial subscriptions: 763. **Information technology resources:** Students are not required to lease or own a computer. Number of campus computers available to all students: 220. School has a wireless network. Approximate number of users that can be accommodated: 1,500. Proportion of college-owned housing units wired for high-speed internet access: 98%. **Campus safety:** Security services offered: 24-hour foot-and-vehicle patrols, late-night transport/escort service, 24-hour emergency telephones, lighted pathways/sidewalks, student patrols, controlled dormitory access (key, security card, etc).

TRANSFER AND INTERNATIONAL STUDENTS

Transfer students: May apply for admission for the following academic terms: Fall, Spring, Summer. Applicants do not need a minimum number of credits to apply. For fall 2005: Transfer applications received: 138. Transfer applicants offered admission: 61. Transfer applicants enrolled: 38. **International students:** Number of foreign undergraduates: 47 (2% of student body). Number of countries represented: 8. Minimum TOEFL score required: 550 (paper); 213 (computer). Average TOEFL score: 500 (paper).

Mount Vernon Nazarene University

■ **Address:** 800 Martinsburg Road, Mount Vernon, OH 43050
■ **Website:** http://www.mvnu.edu
■ **Private; Religious affiliation:** Nazarene
■ **Enrollment:** 1,921 full-time; 274 part-time

KEY STATS

✔ **U.S News College Ranking:** 52, Comp. Coll.–Bachelor's (Midwest)
✔ **ACT Score (25th/75th percentile):** 20-25
✔ **Tuition:** 2006-2007: $16,876

Selectivity: Selective	**Room/board:** $5,090
Acceptance rate: 80%	**Average debt:** $20,293
Student/faculty ratio: 17/1	**Proportion who borrowed:** 79%

UNDERGRADUATE STUDENT BODY STATS

2005-2006 enrollment: 1,921 full-time; 274 part-time. Men: 42%; women: 58%. **Ethnic makeup:** African American: 4%; Asian American: 1%;

Hispanic: 1%; White: 94%; International: 1%. **Religious preference:** Roman Catholic: 5%; Nazarene: 31%; Baptist: 8%; Other: 56%.

ADMISSIONS FACTS AND FIGURES

Phone: (866) 462-6868. **Email:** admissions@mvnu.edu. **Website:** http://www.mvnu.edu. **Application deadlines for fall 2007:** Regular decision: May 1. Early decision: Not offered. Early action: Not offered. Admission can be deferred. **Application fee:** $25. Common application is not accepted. **Admissions requirements/recommendations:** High school units required (recommended): English: (4); Mathematics: (3); Science: (3); Foreign language: (3); Social studies: (3); Academic electives: (7); Total units: (21). Tests: The college uses SAT or ACT scores in admissions decisions. Either SAT or ACT required. For admission to the fall 2007 entering class, the school will accept: ACT with writing, ACT without writing. Campus visit: Recommended. Admissions interview: Neither required nor recommended. Off-campus interview: Not available. **Factors that count in admissions decisions:** *Academic:* Secondary school record: Considered. Class rank: Not considered. Letters of recommendation: Considered. Standardized test scores: Very important. Essay: Considered. *Nonacademic:* Interview: Not considered. Extracurricular activities: Not considered. Talent/ability: Not considered. Character/personal qualities: Considered. Alumni/ae relationship: Not considered. Geographical residence: Not considered. State residency: Not considered. Religious affiliation/commitment: Not considered. Minority status: Not considered. Volunteer work: Not considered. Work experience: Not considered. **Other schools with the greatest overlap in applicants:** Cedarville University; Indiana Wesleyan University; Malone College; Ohio State University–Columbus; Olivet Nazarene University. **Admissions statistics for the fall 2005 entering class:** Total applicants: 741. Total accepted: 595. Freshmen enrolled: 380; 16% were from out of state. Overall acceptance rate: 80%. **Credentials of fall 2005 freshmen:** 20% ranked in the top 10 percent of their high school class; 55% were in the top 25 percent, and 93% were in the top half. (Proportion submitting class standing: 87%.) **Average high school grade point average:** 3.4. **First-year students who submitted SAT scores:** 31%. Scores (25/75 percentile): Verbal: 480-580, Math: 450-580, Combined: 930-1160. **First-year students submitting ACT scores:** 92%. Scores (25/75 percentile): English: 19-26, Math: 18-25, Composite: 20-25.

ACADEMICS

Year founded: 1968. **Academic calendar:** 4-1-4. **Degrees offered:** associate, terminal-associate, bachelor's, master's. **Most popular majors:** 59% business, management, marketing, and related support services, 9% education, 6% philosophy and religious studies, 4% biological and biomedical sciences, 4% social sciences. **Major fields of study:** biological and biomedical sciences; business, management, marketing, and related support services; communication, journalism, and related programs; computer and information sciences and support services; education; English language and literature/letters; family and consumer sciences/human sciences; foreign languages, literatures, and linguistics; history; mathematics and statistics; parks, recreation, leisure, and fitness studies; philosophy and religious studies; physical sciences; psychology; security and protective services; social sciences; theology and religious vocations; visual and performing arts. **Areas of required coursework:** arts/fine arts, humanities, mathematics, English (including composition), philosophy, sciences (biological or physical), history, social science. **Pre-professional programs:** pre-law, pre-dentistry, pre-medicine, pre-veterinary science, pre-pharmacy. **Special academic programs (% participation):** cross-registration (2%), double major (9%), dual enrollment (1%), honors program (3%), independent study (2%), internships (7%), study abroad (2%), teacher certificate program (18%). **Teacher certification offered in:** early childhood, special education, vo-tech; middle/junior high, secondary. **Cooperative education programs:** engineering, health professions, vocational arts. **Faculty and instruction (2005-2006):** Total instructional faculty: 101 full-time, 125 part-time (65% men; 35% women; 4% minorities). Full-time faculty with Ph.D. or other terminal degree: 62%. Student/faculty ratio: 17/1. Classes of fewer than 20 students: 61%; of 20 to 49 students: 35%; of 50 or more students: 4%. **Advanced Placement and International Baccalaureate credit:** AP tests may be used for: Credit and/or placement. Scores accepted: 3, 4, 5. International Baccalaureate exams may be used for: Credit and/or placement. **Freshmen returning for sophomore year:** 73%. **Graduation rates:** Four-year: 37%; five-year: 46%; six-year: 51%. **Graduate study:** 21% of students pursue further study immediately upon graduation; 26% within one year. Fields in which graduates pursue further study: Master of Business Administration (MBA), 28%; law, 9%; medicine, 6%; theology (or the seminary), 16%; education, 3%; arts and sciences, 25%.

COSTS AND FINANCIAL AID

Financial aid office: (740) 392-6868. **Expenses (2006-2007):** Tuition and fees 2006-2007: $16,876; room/board: $5,090. Estimated books and supplies: $900; transportation: $1,000; personal expenses: $970. **Financial aid:** Priority filing date for institution's financial aid form: March 15. In 2005-2006, 69% of undergraduates applied for financial aid. Of those, 55% were determined to have financial need; 18% had their need fully met. Average financial aid package (proportion receiving): $12,008 (55%). Average amount of gift aid, such as scholarships or grants (proportion receiving): $6,658 (54%). Average amount of self-help aid, such as work study or loans (proportion receiving): $4,394 (47%). Average need-based loan (excluding PLUS or other private loans): $3,876. Among students who received need-based aid, the average percentage of need met: 85%. Among students who received aid based on merit, the average award (and the proportion receiving): $2,893 (7%). The average athletic scholarship (and the proportion receiving): $3,917 (3%). Average amount of debt of borrowers graduating in 2005: $20,293. Proportion who borrowed: 79%.

CAMPUS LIFE AND EXTRACURRICULAR ACTIVITIES

Campus housing available (% using): women's dorms (21%), men's dorms (21%), apartment for single students (58%), special housing for disabled students. Students who live in college-owned, operated, or affiliated housing: 49%. **Student employment:** During the 2005-2006 academic year, 35% of undergraduates worked on campus. Average per-year earnings: $1,182. **Clubs and organizations:** Number of student organizations: 37. Activities include: choral groups, concert band, drama/theater, jazz band, music ensembles, musical theater, opera, pep band, radio station, student government, student newspaper, symphony orchestra, yearbook. Number of fraternities: 0; sororities: 0. Average proportion of students who stay on campus on weekends: 50%. **Sports program (2005-2006):** Member of NAIA. *Men's intercollegiate varsity sports:* baseball, basketball, golf, soccer. *Women's intercollegiate varsity sports:* basketball, soccer, softball, volleyball.

SERVICES AND FACILITIES

Basic services: health service. **Remedial assistance:** reading, math, writing. **Counseling services:** minority student, career, personal, academic, older student, psychological, religious. **For learning-disabled students:** School does not offer a structured program with separate admission and additional fees. Total undergraduates in learning-disabled program or receiving services: 60. Services include: remedial math, remedial English, remedial reading, tape recorders, note-taking services, oral tests, extended time for tests. **Library:** Number of titles: 98,333; number of current serial subscriptions: 6,724. **Information technology resources:** Students are not required to lease or own a computer. Number of campus computers available to all students: 300. School has a wireless network. Approximate number of users that can be accommodated: 125. Proportion of college-owned housing units wired for high-speed internet access: 100%. **Campus safety:** Security services offered: 24-hour foot-and-vehicle patrols, late-night transport/escort service, 24-hour emergency telephones, lighted pathways/sidewalks, controlled dormitory access (key, security card, etc).

TRANSFER AND INTERNATIONAL STUDENTS

Transfer students: May apply for admission for the following academic terms: Fall, Winter, Spring. Applicants do not need a minimum number of credits to apply. For fall 2005: Transfer applications received: 124. Transfer applicants offered admission: 90. Transfer applicants enrolled: 69. **International students:** Number of foreign undergraduates: 11 (1% of student body). Number of countries represented: 9. Minimum TOEFL score required: 500 (paper); 173 (computer). Average TOEFL score: 550 (paper).

Muskingum College

- **Address:** 163 Stormont Street, New Concord, OH 43762
- **Website:** http://www.muskingum.edu
- **Private; Religious affiliation:** Presbyterian (U.S.A.)
- **Enrollment:** 1,563 full-time; 71 part-time

KEY STATS

- ✔ **U.S News College Ranking:** third tier, Liberal Arts Colleges
- ✔ **ACT Score (25th/75th percentile):** 19-24
- ✔ **Tuition:** 2006-2007: $17,195

Selectivity: Selective	**Room/board:** $6,740
Acceptance rate: 79%	**Average debt:** $17,277
Student/faculty ratio: 15/1	**Proportion who borrowed:** 72%

UNDERGRADUATE STUDENT BODY STATS

2005-2006 enrollment: 1,563 full-time; 71 part-time. Men: 50%; women: 50%. **Ethnic makeup:** African American: 4%; Asian American: 1%; Hispanic: 1%; White: 92%; International: 2%. **Religious preference:** Roman Catholic: 12%; Protestant: 40%; Jewish: 1%; No preference: 31%; Unknown: 5%; Presbyterian (U.S.A.): 9%; Other: 2%.

ADMISSIONS FACTS AND FIGURES

Phone: (740) 826-8137. **Email:** adminfo@muskingum.edu. **Website:** http://www.muskingum.edu. **Application deadlines for fall 2007:** Regular decision: August 1. Early decision: Not offered. Early action: Not offered. Admission can be deferred. Common application is accepted. **Admissions requirements/recommendations:** High school units required (recommended): English: 4 (4); Mathematics: 2 (3); Science: 2 (3); Foreign language: 2 (2); Social studies: 1 (1); History: 2 (2); Total units: 10 (15). Tests: The college uses SAT or ACT scores in admissions decisions. Either SAT or ACT required. For admission to the fall 2007 entering class, the school will accept: ACT with writing, ACT without writing. Campus visit: Recommended. Admissions interview: Recommended. Off-campus interview: Not available. **Factors that count in admissions decisions: *Academic:*** Secondary school record: Very important. Class rank: Important. Letters of recommendation: Important. Standardized test scores: Important. Essay: Considered. ***Nonacademic:*** Interview: Considered. Extracurricular activities: Considered. Talent/ability: Considered. Character/personal qualities: Considered. Alumni/ae relationship: Considered. Geographical residence: Considered. State residency: Not considered. Religious affiliation/commitment: Not considered. Minority status: Considered. Volunteer work: Not considered. Work experience: Not considered. **Other schools with the greatest overlap in applicants:** Marietta College; Mount Union College; Ohio State University–Columbus; Ohio University; Otterbein College. **Admissions statistics for the fall 2005 entering class:** Total applicants: 1,759. Total accepted: 1,396. Freshmen enrolled: 436; 13% were from out of state. Overall acceptance rate: 79%. **Size of waiting list:** 0 applicants; enrolled from waiting list: 0. **Credentials of fall 2005 freshmen:** 25% ranked in the top 10 percent of their high school class; 48% were in the top 25 percent, and 76% were in the top half. (Proportion submitting class standing: 95%.) **Average high school grade point average:** 3.3. **First-year students who submitted SAT scores:** 27%. Scores (25/75 percentile): Verbal: 460-580, Math: 440-570, Combined: 900-1150. **First-year students submitting ACT scores:** 91%. Scores (25/75 percentile): English: 18-24, Math: 19-24, Composite: 19-24.

ACADEMICS

Year founded: 1837. **Academic calendar:** Semester. **Degrees offered:** bachelor's, master's. **Most popular majors:** 23% education, 22% business, management, marketing, and related support services, 10% biological and biomedical sciences, 7% psychology. **Major fields of study:** biological and biomedical sciences; business, management, marketing, and related support services; communication, journalism, and related programs; computer and information sciences and support services; education; English language and literature/letters; foreign languages, literatures, and linguistics; history; liberal arts and sciences studies, and humanities; mathematics and statistics; multi/interdisciplinary studies; philosophy and religious studies; physical sciences; psychology; security and protective services; social sciences; visual and performing arts. **Areas of required coursework:** arts/fine arts, humanities, mathematics, English (including composition), philosophy, sciences (biological or physical), history, social science, other. **Pre-professional programs:** pre-law, pre-dentistry, pre-medicine, pre-theology, pre-veterinary

science, pre-optometry, pre-pharmacy. **Special academic programs (% participation):** accelerated program (2%), double major (25%), dual enrollment (1%), English as a Second Language (ESL) (1%), independent study (23%), internships (42%), student-designed major (1%), study abroad (3%), teacher certificate program (30%). **Teacher certification offered in:** early childhood, special education, elementary, middle/junior high, secondary. **Faculty and instruction (2005-2006):** Total instructional faculty: 98 full-time, 41 part-time (54% men; 46% women; 6% minorities). Full-time faculty with Ph.D. or other terminal degree: 87%. Student/faculty ratio: 15/1. Classes of fewer than 20 students: 61%; of 20 to 49 students: 39%; of 50 or more students: 0%. **Advanced Placement and International Baccalaureate credit:** AP tests may be used for: Credit only. Scores accepted: 3, 4, 5. International Baccalaureate exams may be used for: Credit only. **Freshmen returning for sophomore year:** 73%. **Graduation rates:** Four-year: 49%; five-year: 62%; six-year: 64%. **Graduate study:** 18% of students pursue further study immediately upon graduation; 20% within one year; 50% within five years. Fields in which graduates pursue further study: Master of Business Administration (MBA), 5%; law, 5%; medicine, 3%; dentistry, 2%; theology (or the seminary), 2%; education, 50%; arts and sciences, 32%; veterinary medicine, 1%.

COSTS AND FINANCIAL AID

Financial aid office: (740) 826-8139. **Expenses (2006-2007):** Tuition and fees 2006-2007: $17,195; room/board: $6,740. Estimated books and supplies: $1,000; transportation: $500; personal expenses: $900. **Financial aid:** Priority filing date for institution's financial aid form: March 15. In 2005-2006, 86% of undergraduates applied for financial aid. Of those, 77% were determined to have financial need; 35% had their need fully met. Average financial aid package (proportion receiving): $14,348 (77%). Average amount of gift aid, such as scholarships or grants (proportion receiving): $10,498 (77%). Average amount of self-help aid, such as work study or loans (proportion receiving): $4,504 (66%). Average need-based loan (excluding PLUS or other private loans): $3,981. Among students who received need-based aid, the average percentage of need met: 85%. Among students who received aid based on merit, the average award (and the proportion receiving): $5,271 (18%). The average athletic scholarship (and the proportion receiving): $0 (0%). Average amount of debt of borrowers graduating in 2005: $17,277. Proportion who borrowed: 72%.

CAMPUS LIFE AND EXTRACURRICULAR ACTIVITIES

Campus housing available (% using): coed dorms (50%), women's dorms (11%), men's dorms (9%), sorority housing (7%), fraternity housing (8%), apartment for single students (3%), other housing options (12%). Students who live in college-owned, operated, or affiliated housing: 80%. **Student employment:** During the 2005-2006 academic year, 40% of undergraduates worked on campus. Average per-year earnings: $1,000. **Clubs and organizations:** Number of student organizations: 91. Activities include: choral groups, concert band, dance, drama/theater, jazz band, literary magazine, marching band, music ensembles, musical theater, pep band, radio station, student government, student newspaper, student film society, symphony orchestra, television station, yearbook. Number of fraternities: 6; sororities: 6. Proportion of men in fraternities: 20%; of women in sororities: 25%. Average proportion of students who stay on campus on weekends: 60%. **Sports program (2005-2006):** Member of NCAA III. *Men's intercollegiate varsity sports:* baseball, basketball, cross-country, football, golf, soccer, tennis, track and field (indoor), track and field (outdoor), wrestling. *Women's intercollegiate varsity sports:* basketball, cross-country, golf, soccer, softball, tennis, track and field (indoor), track and field (outdoor), volleyball.

SERVICES AND FACILITIES

Basic services: nonremedial tutoring, women's center, placement service, health service, health insurance. **Remedial assistance:** math, study skills. **Counseling services:** minority student, career, personal, academic, psychological, birth control, religious. **For learning-disabled students:** School does not offer a structured program with separate admission and additional fees. Total undergraduates in learning-disabled program or receiving services: 172. Services include: reading machines, tape recorders, untimed tests, note-taking services, oral tests, learning center, readers, extended time for tests, tutors, texts on tape. **Library:** Number of titles: 216,389; number of current serial subscriptions: 11,947. **Information technology resources:** Students are not required to lease or own a computer. Number of campus computers available to all students: 216. School has a wireless network. Approximate number of users that can be accommodated: 50. Proportion of college-owned housing units wired for high-speed internet access: 100%. **Campus safety:** Security services offered: 24-hour foot-and-vehicle patrols,

late-night transport/escort service, 24-hour emergency telephones, lighted pathways/sidewalks, controlled dormitory access (key, security card, etc).

TRANSFER AND INTERNATIONAL STUDENTS

Transfer students: May apply for admission for the following academic terms: Fall, Spring, Summer. Applicants do not need a minimum number of credits to apply. For fall 2005: Transfer applications received: 174. Transfer applicants offered admission: 103. Transfer applicants enrolled: 72. **International students:** Number of foreign undergraduates: 37 (2% of student body). Number of countries represented: 10. Minimum TOEFL score required: 550 (paper); 213 (computer). Average TOEFL score: 600 (paper).

Myers University

- ■ **Address:** 3921 Chester Avenue, Cleveland, OH 44114
- ■ **Website:** http://www.myers.edu
- ■ **Private**
- ■ **Enrollment:** 568 full-time; 360 part-time

KEY STATS

✔ **U.S News College Ranking:** Unranked Specialty School–Business
✔ **ACT Score:** 17
✔ **Tuition:** 2006-2007: $10,800
Selectivity: Least selective **Room/board:** $7,190
Acceptance rate: 87% **Average debt:** $8,073
Student/faculty ratio: 26/1 **Proportion who borrowed:** 65%

UNDERGRADUATE STUDENT BODY STATS

2005-2006 enrollment: 568 full-time; 360 part-time. Men: 31%; women: 69%. **Ethnic makeup:** African American: 53%; Hispanic: 4%; White: 42%.

ADMISSIONS FACTS AND FIGURES

Phone: (877) 366-9377. **Email:** admissions@myers.edu. **Website:** http://www.myers.edu. **Application deadlines for fall 2007:** Regular decision: Rolling. Early decision: Not offered. Early action: Not offered. Admission can be deferred. **Application fee:** $25. Common application is accepted. **To apply online, go to:** http://myers.edu/forms/formsindex.html. **Admissions requirements/recommendations:** High school units required (recommended): English: 4 (4); Mathematics: 3 (3); Science: 3 (3); Foreign language: 3 (3); Social studies: 3 (3); Academic electives: 1 (1); Total units: 19 (19). Tests: The college uses SAT or ACT scores in admissions decisions. Either SAT or ACT required. For admission to the fall 2007 entering class, the school will accept: ACT with writing, ACT without writing. Campus visit: Recommended. Admissions interview: Required. Off-campus interview: May be arranged. **Factors that count in admissions decisions:** *Academic:* Secondary school record: Very important. Class rank: Not considered. Letters of recommendation: Not considered. Standardized test scores: Very important. Essay: Not considered. *Nonacademic:* Interview: Important. Extracurricular activities: Considered. Talent/ability: Not considered. Character/personal qualities: Considered. Alumni/ae relationship: Not considered. Geographical residence: Not considered. State residency: Not considered. Religious affiliation/commitment: Not considered. Minority status: Not considered. Volunteer work: Not considered. Work experience: Not considered. **Admissions statistics for the fall 2005 entering class:** Total applicants: 333. Total accepted: 290. Freshmen enrolled: 98; Overall acceptance rate: 87%.

ACADEMICS

Year founded: 1848. **Academic calendar:** Semester. **Degrees offered:** certificate, associate, bachelor's, post-bachelor's certificate, master's. **Most popular majors:** 35% business, management, marketing, and related support services, 19% accounting and business/management, 13% criminal justice and corrections. **Major fields of study:** business, management, marketing, and related support services; computer and information sciences and support services; legal professions and studies; public administration and social service professions. **Areas of required coursework:** arts/fine arts, humanities, computer literacy, mathematics, English (including composition), philosophy, history, social science. **Special academic programs:** accelerated program, cooperative (work-study plan) program, cross-registration, distance learning, double major, external degree program, independent study, internships, weekend college. **Cooperative education programs:** business. **Faculty and instruction (2005-2006):** Total instructional faculty: 20 full-time, 85 part-

time. Full-time faculty with Ph.D. or other terminal degree: 45%. Student/faculty ratio: 26/1. Classes of fewer than 20 students: 88%; of 20 to 49 students: 12%. **Advanced Placement and International Baccalaureate credit:** AP tests may be used for: Credit only. Scores accepted: 2, 3. **Freshmen returning for sophomore year:** 39%. **Graduation rates:** Six-year: 25%.

COSTS AND FINANCIAL AID

Financial aid office: (216) 361-2741. **Expenses (2006-2007):** Tuition and fees 2006-2007: $10,800; room/board: $7,190. Estimated books and supplies: $1,500; transportation: $850; personal expenses: $0. **Financial aid:** Priority filing date for institution's financial aid form: March 15. In 2005-2006, 99% of undergraduates applied for financial aid. Of those, 98% were determined to have financial need; 17% had their need fully met. Average financial aid package (proportion receiving): $9,822 (96%). Average amount of gift aid, such as scholarships or grants (proportion receiving): $4,779 (14%). Average amount of self-help aid, such as work study or loans (proportion receiving): $4,456 (92%). Average need-based loan (excluding PLUS or other private loans): $4,295. Among students who received need-based aid, the average percentage of need met: 54%. Among students who received aid based on merit, the average award (and the proportion receiving): $1,500 (0%). The average athletic scholarship (and the proportion receiving): $3,177 (4%). Average amount of debt of borrowers graduating in 2005: $8,073. Proportion who borrowed: 65%.

CAMPUS LIFE AND EXTRACURRICULAR ACTIVITIES

Campus housing available: coed dorms. Students who live in college-owned, operated, or affiliated housing: 3%. **Clubs and organizations:** Number of student organizations: 12. Activities include: student government. Number of fraternities: 0; sororities: 0. Proportion of men in fraternities: 1%; of women in sororities: 1%.

SERVICES AND FACILITIES

Basic services: nonremedial tutoring, placement service. **Remedial assistance:** reading, math, writing, study skills. **Counseling services:** minority student, career, academic. **For learning-disabled students:** School does not offer a structured program with separate admission and additional fees. **Library:** Number of titles: 15,809; number of current serial subscriptions: 141. **Information technology resources:** Students are not required to lease or own a computer. Number of campus computers available to all students: 125. School has a wireless network. **Campus safety:** Security services offered: 24-hour foot-and-vehicle patrols, late-night transport/escort service.

TRANSFER AND INTERNATIONAL STUDENTS

Transfer students: May apply for admission for the following academic terms: Fall, Winter, Spring, Summer. Applicants need a minimum number of credits to apply. **International students:** Number of foreign undergraduates: 0. Minimum TOEFL score required: 500 (paper); 210 (computer). Average TOEFL score: 500 (paper).

Notre Dame College of Ohio

- ■ **Address:** 4545 College Road, Cleveland, OH 44121
- ■ **Website:** http://www.notredamecollege.edu
- ■ **Private; Religious affiliation:** Roman Catholic
- ■ **Enrollment:** 604 full-time; 451 part-time

KEY STATS

✔ **U.S College Ranking:** third tier, Comp. Coll.–Bachelor's (Midwest)
✔ **ACT Score (25th/75th percentile):** 17-21
✔ **Tuition:** 2006-2007: $20,130
Selectivity: Less selective **Room/board:** $6,850
Acceptance rate: 53% **Average debt:** N/A
Student/faculty ratio: 19/1 **Proportion who borrowed:** N/A

UNDERGRADUATE STUDENT BODY STATS

2005-2006 enrollment: 604 full-time; 451 part-time. Men: 33%; women: 67%. **Ethnic makeup:** African American: 19%; Asian American: 1%; Hispanic: 2%; White: 72%; International: 5%.

ADMISSIONS FACTS AND FIGURES

Phone: (216) 373-5355. **Email:** admissions@ndc.edu. **Website:** http://www.notredamecollege.edu. **Application deadlines for fall 2007:** Regular decision: Rolling. Early decision: Not offered. Early action: Not offered. Admission can be deferred. **Application fee:** $30. Common application is not accepted. **To apply online, go to:** http://www.notredamecollege.edu/application/. **Admissions requirements/recommendations:** High school units required (recommended): English: 4 (4); Mathematics: 3 (3); Science: 3 (3); Foreign language: 2 (2); Social studies: 3 (3); History: 0 (0); Academic electives: 0 (0); Total units: 16 (16). Tests: The college uses SAT or ACT scores in admissions decisions. Either SAT or ACT required. For admission to the fall 2007 entering class, the school will accept: ACT with writing, ACT without writing. Campus visit: Recommended. Admissions interview: Recommended. Off-campus interview: May be arranged. **Factors that count in admissions decisions:** *Academic:* Secondary school record: Very important. Class rank: Important. Letters of recommendation: Very important. Standardized test scores: Important. Essay: Considered. *Nonacademic:* Interview: Considered. Extracurricular activities: Considered. Talent/ability: Considered. Character/personal qualities: Considered. Alumni/ae relationship: Considered. Geographical residence: Not considered. State residency: Not considered. Religious affiliation/commitment: Not considered. Minority status: Not considered. Volunteer work: Considered. Work experience: Considered. **Other schools with the greatest overlap in applicants:** Baldwin-Wallace College; Cleveland State University; John Carroll University; Ursuline College. **Admissions statistics for the fall 2005 entering class:** Total applicants: 969. Total accepted: 518. Freshmen enrolled: 168; 7% were from out of state. Overall acceptance rate: 53%. **Credentials of fall 2005 freshmen:** 4% ranked in the top 10 percent of their high school class; 22% were in the top 25 percent, and 62% were in the top half. (Proportion submitting class standing: 79%.) **Average high school grade point average:** 2.9. **First-year students who submitted SAT scores:** 39%. Scores (25/75 percentile): Verbal: 440-528, Math: 393-520, Combined: 833-1048. **First-year students submitting ACT scores:** 86%. Scores (25/75 percentile): English: 15-21, Math: 16-21, Composite: 17-21.

ACADEMICS

Year founded: 1922. **Academic calendar:** Semester. **Degrees offered:** certificate, associate, bachelor's, master's. **Most popular majors:** Information not available. **Major fields of study:** biological and biomedical sciences; business, management, marketing, and related support services; communication, journalism, and related programs; education; English language and literature/letters; health professions and related clinical sciences; history; legal professions and studies; mathematics and statistics; physical sciences; psychology; social sciences; theology and religious vocations; visual and performing arts. **Areas of required coursework:** arts/fine arts, computer literacy, mathematics, English (including composition), philosophy, sciences (biological or physical), social science, other. **Pre-professional programs:** pre-law, pre-dentistry, pre-medicine, pre-veterinary science, pre-pharmacy. **Special academic programs:** cooperative (work-study plan) program, cross-registration, distance learning, double major, independent study, internships, student-designed major, study abroad, teacher certificate program, weekend college. **Teacher certification offered in:** early childhood, special education, elementary, middle/junior high, secondary. **Faculty and instruction (2005-2006):** Total instructional faculty: 36 full-time, 84 part-time (43% men; 57% women; 4% minorities). Full-time faculty with Ph.D. or other terminal degree: 53%. Student/faculty ratio: 19/1. Classes of fewer than 20 students: 74%; of 20 to 49 students: 26%. **Advanced Placement and International Baccalaureate credit:** AP tests may be used for: Credit and/or placement. Scores accepted: 4, 5. **Freshmen returning for sophomore year:** 81%. **Graduation rates:** Four-year: 35%; five-year: 46%; six-year: 36%.

COSTS AND FINANCIAL AID

Financial aid office: (216) 373-5263. **Expenses (2006-2007):** Tuition and fees 2006-2007: $20,130; room/board: $6,850. Estimated books and supplies: $1,270; transportation: $550; personal expenses: $940. **Financial aid:** In 2005-2006, 99% of undergraduates applied for financial aid. Of those, 99% were determined to have financial need; Average financial aid package (proportion receiving): $13,941 (99%). Average amount of gift aid, such as scholarships or grants (proportion receiving): N/A (99%). Average amount of self-help aid, such as work study or loans (proportion receiving): N/A (99%). Among students who received need-based aid, the average percentage of need met: 65%.

CAMPUS LIFE AND EXTRACURRICULAR ACTIVITIES

Campus housing available (% using): coed dorms (100%). Students who live in college-owned, operated, or affiliated housing: 45%. Average per-year earnings: $2,450. **Clubs and organizations:** Number of student organizations: 32. Activities include: choral groups, drama/theater, literary magazine, pep band, student government, student newspaper, yearbook. Number of fraternities: 0; sororities: 0. Average proportion of students who stay on campus on weekends: 65%. **Sports program (2005-2006):** Member of NAIA. *Men's intercollegiate varsity sports:* baseball, basketball, cross-country, golf, soccer, tennis, track and field (indoor), track and field (outdoor). *Women's intercollegiate varsity sports:* basketball, cross-country, golf, soccer, softball, track and field (indoor), track and field (outdoor), volleyball.

SERVICES AND FACILITIES

Basic services: nonremedial tutoring, placement service, health service, health insurance. **Remedial assistance:** reading, math, writing, study skills. **Counseling services:** minority student, career, academic, older student, psychological, religious. **For learning-disabled students:** School does not offer a structured program with separate admission and additional fees. Total undergraduates in learning-disabled program or receiving services: 22. Services include: remedial math, remedial English, reading machines, tape recorders, untimed tests, note-taking services, oral tests, learning center, readers, extended time for tests, tutors, early syllabus, priority registration, priority seating, substitution of courses, texts on tape, typist/scribe, exams on tape or computer, other testing accomodations, other. **Information technology resources:** Students are not required to lease or own a computer. Number of campus computers available to all students: 80. School has a wireless network. Proportion of college-owned housing units wired for high-speed internet access: 100%. **Campus safety:** Security services offered: 24-hour foot-and-vehicle patrols, late-night transport/escort service, 24-hour emergency telephones, lighted pathways/sidewalks, controlled dormitory access (key, security card, etc).

TRANSFER AND INTERNATIONAL STUDENTS

Transfer students: May apply for admission for the following academic terms: Fall, Spring, Summer. Applicants need a minimum number of credits to apply. For fall 2005: Transfer applicants enrolled: 97. **International students:** Number of foreign undergraduates: 33 (5% of student body). Number of countries represented: 17. Minimum TOEFL score required: 550 (paper); 213 (computer).

Oberlin College

- **Address:** 173 W. Lorain Street, Oberlin, OH 44074
- **Website:** http://www.oberlin.edu
- **Private**
- **Enrollment:** 2,755 full-time; 90 part-time

KEY STATS

✔ **U.S News College Ranking:** 22, Liberal Arts Colleges
✔ **SAT Score (25th/75th percentile):** 1270-1460
✔ **Tuition:** 2006-2007: $34,428

Selectivity: Most selective	**Room/board:** $8,720	
Acceptance rate: 34%	**Average debt:** $16,922	
Student/faculty ratio: 9/1	**Proportion who borrowed:** 60%	

UNDERGRADUATE STUDENT BODY STATS

2005-2006 enrollment: 2,755 full-time; 90 part-time. Men: 44%; women: 56%. **Ethnic makeup:** African American: 5%; American-Indian: 1%; Asian American: 8%; Hispanic: 5%; White: 75%; International: 6%.

ADMISSIONS FACTS AND FIGURES

Phone: (440) 775-8411. **Email:** college.admissions@oberlin.edu. **Website:** http://www.oberlin.edu. **Application deadlines for fall 2007:** Regular decision: January 15; decision sent by April 1. Early decision: Send application by: November 15; Decision sent by: December 10. Early action: Not offered. Admission can be deferred. **Application fee:** $35. Common application is accepted. **To apply online, go to:** http://www.oberlin.edu/coladm/onlineapplication. **Admissions requirements/recommendations:** High school units required (recommended): English: 4; Mathematics: 4; Science: 3; Foreign language: 3; Social studies: 3. Tests: The college uses SAT or ACT scores in admissions decisions. Either SAT or ACT required. For admission to the fall

2007 entering class, the school will accept: ACT with writing. Campus visit: Recommended. Admissions interview: Recommended. Off-campus interview: May be arranged. **Factors that count in admissions decisions: Academic:** Secondary school record: Very important. Class rank: Very important. Letters of recommendation: Important. Standardized test scores: Very important. Essay: Important. **Nonacademic:** Interview: Considered. Extracurricular activities: Important. Talent/ability: Important. Character/personal qualities: Important. Alumni/ae relationship: Important. Geographical residence: Considered. State residency: Considered. Religious affiliation/commitment: Not considered. Minority status: Considered. Volunteer work: Considered. Work experience: Considered. **Other schools with the greatest overlap in applicants:** Brown University; Carleton College; Macalester College; Vassar College; Wesleyan College. **Admissions statistics for the fall 2005 entering class:** Total applicants: 6,587. Total accepted: 2,235. Freshmen enrolled: 741; 81% were from out of state. Overall acceptance rate: 34%. Non-early acceptance rate: 34%. **Size of waiting list:** 891 applicants; enrolled from waiting list: 33. **Credentials of fall 2005 freshmen:** 68% ranked in the top 10 percent of their high school class; 93% were in the top 25 percent, and 100% were in the top half. (Proportion submitting class standing: 55%.) **Average high school grade point average:** 3.6. **First-year students who submitted SAT scores:** 90%. Scores (25/75 percentile): Verbal: 650-750, Math: 620-710, Combined: 1270-1460. **First-year students submitting ACT scores:** 29%. Scores (25/75 percentile): English: N/A, Math: N/A, Composite: 27-32.

ACADEMICS

Year founded: 1833. **Academic calendar:** 4-1-4. **Degrees offered:** bachelor's, post-bachelor's certificate, master's. **Most popular majors:** 17% music performance, 13% English language and literature, 7% biology, 7% history, 7% political science and government. **Major fields of study:** area, ethnic, cultural, and gender studies; biological and biomedical sciences; computer and information sciences and support services; education; engineering; English language and literature/letters; foreign languages, literatures, and linguistics; history; legal professions and studies; mathematics and statistics; multi/interdisciplinary studies; natural resources and conservation; philosophy and religious studies; physical sciences; psychology; social sciences; visual and performing arts. **Areas of required coursework:** humanities, sciences (biological or physical), social science, other. **Pre-professional programs:** pre-law, pre-dentistry, pre-medicine, pre-veterinary science. **Special academic programs:** cross-registration, double major, dual enrollment, English as a Second Language (ESL), exchange student program (domestic), honors program, independent study, internships, student-designed major, study abroad, teacher certificate program. **Teacher certification offered in:** elementary, secondary. **Faculty and instruction (2005-2006):** Total instructional faculty 287 full-time, 60 part-time (58% men; 42% women; 16% minorities). Full-time faculty with Ph.D. or other terminal degree: 96%. Student/faculty ratio: 9/1. Classes of fewer than 20 students: 68%; of 20 to 49 students: 29%; of 50 or more students: 3%. **Advanced Placement and International Baccalaureate credit:** AP tests may be used for: Credit and/or placement. Scores accepted: 4, 5. International Baccalaureate exams may be used for: Credit and/or placement. **Freshmen returning for sophomore year:** 91%. **Graduation rates:** Four-year: 68%; five-year: 80%; six-year: 83%. **Graduate study:** 20% of students pursue further study immediately upon graduation; 65% within five years.

COSTS AND FINANCIAL AID

Financial aid office: (440) 775-8142. **Expenses (2006-2007):** Tuition and fees 2006-2007: $34,428; room/board: $8,720. Estimated books and supplies: $830; transportation: $750; personal expenses: $978. **Financial aid:** Priority filing date for institution's financial aid form: January 15; deadline: January 15. In 2005-2006, 67% of undergraduates applied for financial aid. Of those, 59% were determined to have financial need; 100% had their need fully met. Average financial aid package (proportion receiving): $23,710 (59%). Average amount of gift aid, such as scholarships or grants (proportion receiving): $18,007 (50%). Average amount of self-help aid, such as work study or loans (proportion receiving): $5,087 (52%). Average need-based loan (excluding PLUS or other private loans): $4,248. Among students who received need-based aid, the average percentage of need met: 100%. Among students who received aid based on merit, the average award (and the proportion receiving): $11,029 (10%). Average amount of debt of borrowers graduating in 2005: $16,922. Proportion who borrowed: 60%.

CAMPUS LIFE AND EXTRACURRICULAR ACTIVITIES

Campus housing available (% using): coed dorms (77%), women's dorms (1%), apartment for single students (2%), special housing for disabled students, cooperative housing (7%), other housing options (13%). Students who live in college-owned, operated, or affiliated housing: 82%. **Student employment:** During the 2005-2006 academic year, 45% of undergraduates worked on campus. Average per-year earnings: $1,800. **Clubs and organizations:** Number of student organizations: 114. Activities include: choral groups, concert band, dance, drama/theater, jazz band, literary magazine, marching band, music ensembles, musical theater, opera, pep band, radio station, student government, student newspaper, student film society, symphony orchestra, yearbook. Number of fraternities: 0; sororities: 0. Average proportion of students who stay on campus on weekends: 99%. **Sports program (2005-2006):** Member of NCAA III. **Men's intercollegiate varsity sports:** baseball, basketball, cross-country, football, golf, lacrosse, soccer, swimming and diving, tennis, track and field (indoor), track and field (outdoor). **Women's intercollegiate varsity sports:** basketball, cross-country, field hockey, lacrosse, soccer, softball, swimming and diving, tennis, track and field (indoor), track and field (outdoor), volleyball.

SERVICES AND FACILITIES

Basic services: nonremedial tutoring, women's center, placement service, health service, health insurance, other. **Remedial assistance:** math, writing, study skills. **Counseling services:** minority student, career, personal, academic, older student, psychological, birth control, religious. **For learning-disabled students:** School does not offer a structured program with separate admission and additional fees. Total undergraduates in learning-disabled program or receiving services: 270. Services include: reading machines, tape recorders, videotaped classes, untimed tests, note-taking services, oral tests, learning center, readers, extended time for tests, tutors, early syllabus, priority registration, priority seating, texts on tape, typist/scribe, exams on tape or computer, other testing accomodations, other. **Library:** Number of titles: 1,833,737; number of current serial subscriptions: 20,936. **Information technology resources:** Students are not required to lease or own a computer. Number of campus computers available to all students: 395. School has a wireless network. Approximate number of users that can be accommodated: 2,000. Proportion of college-owned housing units wired for high-speed internet access: 100%. **Campus safety:** Security services offered: 24-hour foot-and-vehicle patrols, late-night transport/escort service, 24-hour emergency telephones, lighted pathways/sidewalks, student patrols, controlled dormitory access (key, security card, etc).

TRANSFER AND INTERNATIONAL STUDENTS

Transfer students: May apply for admission for the following academic terms: Fall, Spring. Applicants do not need a minimum number of credits to apply. For fall 2005: Transfer applications received: 268. Transfer applicants offered admission: 83. Transfer applicants enrolled: 37. **International students:** Number of foreign undergraduates: 180 (6% of student body). Number of countries represented: 46. Minimum TOEFL score required: 600 (paper); 250 (computer). Average TOEFL score: 640 (paper).

Ohio Dominican University

- **Address:** 1216 Sunbury Road, Columbus, OH 43219
- **Website:** http://www.ohiodominican.edu
- **Private; Religious affiliation:** Roman Catholic
- **Enrollment:** 1,702 full-time; 857 part-time

KEY STATS

✔ **U.S News College Ranking:** third tier, Comp. Coll.–Bachelor's (Midwest)
✔ **ACT Score (25th/75th percentile):** 19-24
✔ **Tuition:** 2006-2007: $20,570

Selectivity: Selective	Room/board: $6,800
Acceptance rate: 72%	Average debt: N/A
Student/faculty ratio: 15/1	Proportion who borrowed: N/A

UNDERGRADUATE STUDENT BODY STATS

2005-2006 enrollment: 1,702 full-time; 857 part-time. Men: 37%; women: 63%. **Ethnic makeup:** African American: 21%; Asian American: 1%; Hispanic: 1%; White: 76%. **Religious preference:** Roman Catholic: 33%; Protestant: 37%; Jewish: 1%; Muslim: 1%; Buddhist: 1%; No preference: 2%; Unknown: 23%.

ADMISSIONS FACTS AND FIGURES

Phone: (614) 251-4500. **Email:** admissions@ohiodominican.edu. **Website:** http://www.ohiodominican.edu. **Application deadlines for fall 2007:** Regular decision: Rolling. Early decision: Not offered. Early action: Not offered. Admission can be deferred. **Application fee:** $25. Common application is accepted. **Admissions requirements/recommendations:** High school units required (recommended): English: 4 (4); Mathematics: 3 (3); Science: 3 (3); Foreign language: 3 (3); Social studies: 3 (3); Total units: 16 (16). Tests: The college uses SAT or ACT scores in admissions decisions. Either SAT or ACT required. For admission to the fall 2007 entering class, the school will accept: ACT with writing, ACT without writing. Campus visit: Required. Admissions interview: Required. Off-campus interview: May be arranged. **Factors that count in admissions decisions:** *Academic:* Secondary school record: Very important. Class rank: Considered. Letters of recommendation: Considered. Standardized test scores: Very important. Essay: Considered. *Nonacademic:* Interview: Considered. Extracurricular activities: Considered. Talent/ability: Considered. Character/personal qualities: Considered. Alumni/ae relationship: Not considered. Geographical residence: Not considered. State residency: Not considered. Religious affiliation/commitment: Not considered. Minority status: Not considered. Volunteer work: Considered. Work experience: Considered. **Admissions statistics for the fall 2005 entering class:** Total applicants: 1,902. Total accepted: 1,374. Freshmen enrolled: 381; 5% were from out of state. Overall acceptance rate: 72%. **Credentials of fall 2005 freshmen:** 13% ranked in the top 10 percent of their high school class; 33% were in the top 25 percent, and 66% were in the top half. (Proportion submitting class standing: 93%.) **Average high school grade point average:** 3.1. **First-year students who submitted SAT scores:** 30%. Scores (25/75 percentile): Verbal: N/A, Math: N/A, Combined: N/A. **First-year students submitting ACT scores:** 95%. Scores (25/75 percentile): English: N/A, Math: N/A, Composite: 19-24.

ACADEMICS

Year founded: 1911. **Academic calendar:** Semester. **Degrees offered:** associate, bachelor's, master's. **Most popular majors:** 40% business administration and management, 10% elementary education and teaching, 8% junior high/intermediate/middle school education and teaching, 7% general studies, 4% criminal justice/law enforcement administration. **Major fields of study:** biological and biomedical sciences; business, management, marketing, and related support services; communication, journalism, and related programs; computer and information sciences and support services; education; English language and literature/letters; history; liberal arts and sciences studies, and humanities; mathematics and statistics; parks, recreation, leisure, and fitness studies; philosophy and religious studies; physical sciences; psychology; public administration and social service professions; security and protective services; social sciences; theology and religious vocations; visual and performing arts. **Areas of required coursework:** arts/fine arts, humanities, mathematics, English (including composition), philosophy, foreign languages, sciences (biological or physical), social science, other. **Pre-professional programs:** pre-law, pre-dentistry, pre-medicine, pre-veterinary science. **Special academic programs:** cross-registration, distance learning, double major, dual enrollment, honors program, independent study, internships, study abroad, teacher certificate program, weekend college. **Teacher certification offered in:** early childhood, special education, elementary, middle/junior high, secondary. **Reserve Officers Training Corps (ROTC):** Army ROTC: Offered at cooperating institution (Capital University). **Faculty and instruction (2005-2006):** Total instructional faculty: 66 full-time, 135 part-time (50% men; 50% women; 11% minorities). Full-time faculty with Ph.D. or other terminal degree: 88%. Student/faculty ratio: 15/1. Classes of fewer than 20 students: 52%; of 20 to 49 students: 48%; of 50 or more students: 0%. **Advanced Placement and International Baccalaureate credit:** AP tests may be used for: Credit only. Scores accepted: 3, 4, 5. International Baccalaureate exams may be used for: Credit and/or placement. **Freshmen returning for sophomore year:** 61%. **Graduation rates:** Four-year: 37%; five-year: 47%; six-year: 49%.

COSTS AND FINANCIAL AID

Financial aid office: (614) 251-4778. **Expenses (2006-2007):** Tuition and fees 2006-2007: $20,570; room/board: $6,800. Estimated books and supplies: $900; transportation: $500; personal expenses: $1,620. **Financial aid:** Priority filing date for institution's financial aid form: April 6; deadline: June 6.

CAMPUS LIFE AND EXTRACURRICULAR ACTIVITIES

Campus housing available (% using): coed dorms (97%), apartment for single students (3%). Students who live in college-owned, operated, or affiliated housing: 26%. **Student employment:** During the 2005-2006 academic year, 24% of undergraduates worked on campus. Average per-year earnings: $2,500. **Clubs and organizations:** Number of student organizations: 32. Activities include: choral groups, dance, drama/theater, literary magazine,

marching band, music ensembles, radio station, student government, student newspaper. Number of fraternities: 0; sororities: 0. **Sports program (2005-2006):** Member of NAIA. *Men's intercollegiate varsity sports:* baseball, basketball, football, golf, soccer, tennis. *Women's intercollegiate varsity sports:* basketball, golf, soccer, softball, tennis, volleyball.

SERVICES AND FACILITIES

Basic services: nonremedial tutoring, placement service, health service. **Remedial assistance:** reading, math, writing, study skills. **Counseling services:** career, veteran student, academic, older student, psychological, religious. **For learning-disabled students:** School does not offer a structured program with separate admission and additional fees. **Library:** Number of titles: 105,500; number of current serial subscriptions: 588. **Information technology resources:** Students are not required to lease or own a computer. Number of campus computers available to all students: 336. School does not have a wireless network. Proportion of college-owned housing units wired for high-speed internet access: 100%. **Campus safety:** Security services offered: 24-hour foot-and-vehicle patrols, late-night transport/escort service, 24-hour emergency telephones, lighted pathways/sidewalks, controlled dormitory access (key, security card, etc).

TRANSFER AND INTERNATIONAL STUDENTS

Transfer students: May apply for admission for the following academic terms: Fall, Winter, Summer. Applicants do not need a minimum number of credits to apply. For fall 2005: Transfer applications received: 535. Transfer applicants offered admission: 293. Transfer applicants enrolled: 140. **International students:** Number of foreign undergraduates: 9. Minimum TOEFL score required: 550 (paper); 213 (computer).

Ohio Northern University

- **Address:** 525 S. Main Street, Ada, OH 45810
- **Website:** http://www.onu.edu
- **Private; Religious affiliation:** Methodist
- **Enrollment:** 2,525 full-time; 72 part-time

KEY STATS
✔ **U.S News College Ranking:** 5, Comp. Coll.–Bachelor's (Midwest)
✔ **ACT Score (25th/75th percentile):** 23-28
✔ **Tuition:** 2006-2007: $28,260

Selectivity: More selective	**Room/board:** $7,080
Acceptance rate: 80%	**Average debt:** $37,017
Student/faculty ratio: 14/1	**Proportion who borrowed:** 78%

UNDERGRADUATE STUDENT BODY STATS

2005-2006 enrollment: 2,525 full-time; 72 part-time. Men: 53%; women: 47%. **Ethnic makeup:** African American: 2%; Asian American: 1%; Hispanic: 1%; White: 96%. **Religious preference:** Roman Catholic: 28%; No preference: 20%; Methodist: 17%; Other: 35%.

ADMISSIONS FACTS AND FIGURES

Phone: (888) 408-4668. **Email:** admissions-ug@onu.edu. **Website:** http://www.onu.edu. **Application deadlines for fall 2007:** Regular decision: August 15. Early decision: Not offered. Early action: Not offered. Admission can be deferred. **Application fee:** $30. Common application is accepted. **To apply online, go to:** http://admissions.onu.edu/apply/index.shtml. **Admissions requirements/recommendations:** High school units required (recommended): English: 4 (4); Mathematics: 2 (4); Science: 2 (3); Foreign language: (2); Social studies: 2 (3); History: 2 (2); Academic electives: 4 (4); Total units: 16 (22). Tests: The college uses SAT or ACT scores in admissions decisions. Either SAT or ACT required. For admission to the fall 2007 entering class, the school will accept: ACT with writing, ACT without writing. Campus visit: Recommended. Admissions interview: Recommended. Off-campus interview: Not available. **Factors that count in admissions decisions:** *Academic:* Secondary school record: Very important. Class rank: Important. Letters of recommendation: Considered. Standardized test scores: Very important. Essay: Considered. *Nonacademic:* Interview: Important. Extracurricular activities: Important. Talent/ability: Considered. Character/personal qualities: Considered. Alumni/ae relationship: Considered. Geographical residence: Considered. State residency: Considered. Religious affiliation/commitment: Not considered. Minority status: Considered. Volunteer work: Considered. Work experience:

Considered. **Other schools with the greatest overlap in applicants:** Miami University–Oxford; Ohio State University–Columbus; Ohio University; University of Dayton; Wittenberg University. **Admissions statistics for the fall 2005 entering class:** Total applicants: 3,371. Total accepted: 2,698. Freshmen enrolled: 809; 13% were from out of state. Overall acceptance rate: 80%. **Credentials of fall 2005 freshmen:** 38% ranked in the top 10 percent of their high school class; 66% were in the top 25 percent, and 87% were in the top half. (Proportion submitting class standing: 90%.) **Average high school grade point average:** 3.6. **First-year students who submitted SAT scores:** 46%. Scores (25/75 percentile): Verbal: 530-630, Math: 530-650, Combined: 1060-1280. **First-year students submitting ACT scores:** 92%. Scores (25/75 percentile): English: 21-28, Math: 22-28, Composite: 23-28.

ACADEMICS

Year founded: 1871. **Academic calendar:** Quarter. **Degrees offered:** bachelor's, post-bachelor's certificate, master's, first professional. **Most popular majors:** 15% business, management, marketing, and related support services, 13% education, 11% engineering, 9% communication, journalism, and related programs, 7% biological and biomedical sciences. **Major fields of study:** biological and biomedical sciences; business, management, marketing, and related support services; communication, journalism, and related programs; computer and information sciences and support services; education; engineering; engineering technologies/technicians; English language and literature/letters; foreign languages, literatures, and linguistics; health professions and related clinical sciences; history; legal professions and studies; mathematics and statistics; natural resources and conservation; parks, recreation, leisure, and fitness studies; philosophy and religious studies; physical sciences; psychology; security and protective services; social sciences; theology and religious vocations; visual and performing arts. **Areas of required coursework:** arts/fine arts, humanities, computer literacy, mathematics, English (including composition), philosophy, sciences (biological or physical), history, social science. **Pre-professional programs:** pre-law, pre-dentistry, pre-medicine, pre-theology, pre-veterinary science, other. **Special academic programs:** cooperative (work-study plan) program, distance learning, double major, dual enrollment, exchange student program (domestic), honors program, independent study, internships, liberal arts/career combination, study abroad, teacher certificate program. **Teacher certification offered in:** early childhood, middle/junior high, secondary. **Cooperative education programs:** computer science, engineering, technologies, other. **Reserve Officers Training Corps (ROTC):** Army ROTC: Offered at cooperating institution (Bowling Green State University); Air Force ROTC: Offered at cooperating institution (Bowling Green State University). **Faculty and instruction (2005-2006):** Total instructional faculty: 205 full-time, 77 part-time (65% men; 35% women; 6% minorities). Full-time faculty with Ph.D. or other terminal degree: 82%. Student/faculty ratio: 14/1. Classes of fewer than 20 students: 50%; of 20 to 49 students: 47%; of 50 or more students: 3%. **Advanced Placement and International Baccalaureate credit:** AP tests may be used for: Credit and/or placement. Scores accepted: 3, 4, 5. International Baccalaureate exams may be used for: Credit and/or placement. **Freshmen returning for sophomore year:** 83%. **Graduation rates:** Four-year: 49%; five-year: 61%; six-year: 66%. **Graduate study:** 13% of students pursue further study immediately upon graduation; 21% within one year. Fields in which graduates pursue further study: Master of Business Administration (MBA), 6%; law, 16%; medicine, 19%; engineering, 13%; theology (or the seminary), 2%; education, 2%; arts and sciences, 40%.

COSTS AND FINANCIAL AID

Financial aid office: (419) 772-2272. **Expenses (2006-2007):** Tuition and fees 2006-2007: $28,260; room/board: $7,080. Estimated books and supplies: $1,200; transportation: $600; personal expenses: $1,200. **Financial aid:** Priority filing date for institution's financial aid form: April 15. In 2005-2006, 90% of undergraduates applied for financial aid. Of those, 81% were determined to have financial need; 30% had their need fully met. Average financial aid package (proportion receiving): $22,130 (81%). Average amount of gift aid, such as scholarships or grants (proportion receiving): $9,754 (54%). Average amount of self-help aid, such as work study or loans (proportion receiving): $6,162 (65%). Average need-based loan (excluding PLUS or other private loans): $5,034. Among students who received need-based aid, the average percentage of need met: 85%. Among students who received aid based on merit, the average award (and the proportion receiving): $12,417 (16%). The average athletic scholarship (and the proportion receiving): $0 (0%). Average amount of debt of borrowers graduating in 2005: $37,017. Proportion who borrowed: 78%.

CAMPUS LIFE AND EXTRACURRICULAR ACTIVITIES

Campus housing available (% using): coed dorms (59%), women's dorms (6%), men's dorms (2%), sorority housing (6%), fraternity housing (1%), apartments for married students (1%), apartment for single students (23%), special housing for disabled students (1%), other housing options (1%). Students who live in college-owned, operated, or affiliated housing: 61%. **Clubs and organizations:** Number of student organizations: 150. Activities include: choral groups, concert band, dance, drama/theater, jazz band, literary magazine, marching band, music ensembles, musical theater, opera, pep band, radio station, student government, student newspaper, symphony orchestra, television station, yearbook. Number of fraternities: 7; sororities: 4. Proportion of men in fraternities: 18%; of women in sororities: 20%. Average proportion of students who stay on campus on weekends: 70%. **Sports program (2005-2006):** Member of NCAA III. **Men's intercollegiate varsity sports:** baseball, basketball, cross-country, football, golf, soccer, swimming and diving, tennis, track and field (indoor), track and field (outdoor), wrestling. **Women's intercollegiate varsity sports:** basketball, cross-country, golf, soccer, softball, swimming and diving, tennis, track and field (indoor), track and field (outdoor), volleyball.

SERVICES AND FACILITIES

Basic services: nonremedial tutoring, placement service, day care, health service, health insurance. **Remedial assistance:** reading, math, writing, study skills. **Counseling services:** minority student, career, personal, academic, psychological, birth control, religious. **For learning-disabled students:** School does not offer a structured program with separate admission and additional fees. Services include: remedial math, remedial English, remedial reading, tape recorders, other special classes, untimed tests, note-taking services, oral tests, readers, extended time for tests, tutors, other. **Library:** Number of titles: 488,502; number of current serial subscriptions: 9,362. **Information technology resources:** Students are not required to lease or own a computer. Number of campus computers available to all students: 550. School has a wireless network. Proportion of college-owned housing units wired for high-speed internet access: 100%. **Campus safety:** Security services offered: 24-hour foot-and-vehicle patrols, late-night transport/escort service, 24-hour emergency telephones, lighted pathways/sidewalks, controlled dormitory access (key, security card, etc).

TRANSFER AND INTERNATIONAL STUDENTS

Transfer students: May apply for admission for the following academic terms: Fall, Winter, Spring, Summer. Applicants do not need a minimum number of credits to apply. For fall 2005: Transfer applications received: 193. Transfer applicants offered admission: 64. Transfer applicants enrolled: 54. **International students:** Number of foreign undergraduates: 9. Number of countries represented: 14. Minimum TOEFL score required: 550 (paper); 213 (computer).

Ohio State University–Columbus

- **Address:** 154 W. 12th Avenue, Columbus, OH 43210
- **Website:** http://www.osu.edu
- **Public**
- **Enrollment:** 33,817 full-time; 3,594 part-time

KEY STATS

✔ **U.S News College Ranking:** 57, National Universities
✔ **ACT Score (25th/75th percentile):** 24-28
✔ **Tuition:** 2006-2007: $8,667 in state, $20,562 out of state

Selectivity: More selective	**Room/board:** $6,720
Acceptance rate: 74%	**Average debt:** $17,821
Student/faculty ratio: 13/1	**Proportion who borrowed:** 58%

UNDERGRADUATE STUDENT BODY STATS

2005-2006 enrollment: 33,817 full-time; 3,594 part-time. Men: 53%; women: 47%. **Ethnic makeup:** African American: 8%; Asian American: 5%; Hispanic: 3%; White: 81%; International: 3%.

ADMISSIONS FACTS AND FIGURES

Phone: (614) 292-3980. **Email:** askabuckeye@osu.edu. **Website:** http://www.osu.edu. **Application deadlines for fall 2007:** Regular decision: February 1. Early decision: Not offered. Early action: Not offered. Admission cannot be deferred. **Application fee:** $40. Common application is accepted.

To apply online, go to: http://www.applyweb.com/apply/osu/index.html.
Admissions requirements/recommendations: High school units required (recommended): English: 4 (4); Mathematics: 3 (4); Science: 2 (3); Foreign language: 2 (3); Social studies: 2 (3); Academic electives: 1 (1). Tests: The college uses SAT or ACT scores in admissions decisions. Either SAT or ACT required. For admission to the fall 2007 entering class, the school will accept: ACT with writing. Campus visit: Recommended. Admissions interview: Neither required nor recommended. Off-campus interview: Not available. **Factors that count in admissions decisions:** *Academic:* Secondary school record: Very important. Class rank: Very important. Letters of recommendation: Considered. Standardized test scores: Very important. Essay: Important. *Nonacademic:* Interview: Not considered. Extracurricular activities: Important. Talent/ability: Important. Character/personal qualities: Considered. Alumni/ae relationship: Not considered. Geographical residence: Considered. State residency: Considered. Religious affiliation/commitment: Not considered. Minority status: Considered. Volunteer work: Important. Work experience: Important. **Other schools with the greatest overlap in applicants:** Bowling Green State University; Kent State University; Miami University–Oxford; Ohio University; University of Cincinnati. **Admissions statistics for the fall 2005 entering class:** Total applicants: 17,566. Total accepted: 12,945. Freshmen enrolled: 5,954; 12% were from out of state. Overall acceptance rate: 74%. **Size of waiting list:** 404 applicants; enrolled from waiting list: 0. **Credentials of fall 2005 freshmen:** 39% ranked in the top 10 percent of their high school class; 76% were in the top 25 percent, and 97% were in the top half. (Proportion submitting class standing: 75%.) **First-year students who submitted SAT scores:** 60%. Scores (25/75 percentile): Verbal: 530-640, Math: 550-660, Combined: 1080-1300. **First-year students submitting ACT scores:** 87%. Scores (25/75 percentile): English: 23-29, Math: 24-29, Composite: 24-28.

ACADEMICS

Year founded: 1870. **Academic calendar:** Quarter. **Degrees offered:** associate, bachelor's, post-bachelor's certificate, master's, post-master's certificate, first professional, doctorate. **Most popular majors:** 6% psychology, 4% English language and literature, 4% communication studies/speech communication and rhetoric, 4% family resource management studies, 4% human development and family studies. **Major fields of study:** agriculture, agriculture operations, and related sciences; architecture and related services; area, ethnic, cultural, and gender studies; biological and biomedical sciences; business, management, marketing, and related support services; communication, journalism, and related programs; computer and information sciences and support services; education; engineering; engineering technologies/technicians; English language and literature/letters; family and consumer sciences/human sciences; foreign languages, literatures, and linguistics; health professions and related clinical sciences; history; liberal arts and sciences studies, and humanities; mathematics and statistics; multi/interdisciplinary studies; natural resources and conservation; parks, recreation, leisure, and fitness studies; philosophy and religious studies; physical sciences; psychology; public administration and social service professions; social sciences; transportation and materials moving; visual and performing arts. **Areas of required coursework:** arts/fine arts, humanities, mathematics, English (including composition), foreign languages, sciences (biological or physical), history, social science, other. **Pre-professional programs:** pre-law, pre-dentistry, pre-medicine, pre-theology, pre-veterinary science, pre-optometry, pre-pharmacy. **Special academic programs:** accelerated program, cooperative (work-study plan) program, cross-registration, distance learning, double major, dual enrollment, English as a Second Language (ESL), exchange student program (domestic), honors program, independent study, internships, liberal arts/career combination, student-designed major, study abroad, teacher certificate program. **Teacher certification offered in:** secondary. **Cooperative education programs:** agriculture, art, business, computer science, engineering, humanities, natural science, social/behavioral science, vocational arts. **Reserve Officers Training Corps (ROTC):** Army ROTC: Offered on campus; Navy ROTC: Offered on campus; Air Force ROTC: Offered on campus. **Faculty and instruction (2005-2006):** Total instructional faculty: 2,872 full-time, 1,023 part-time (66% men; 34% women; 17% minorities). Full-time faculty with Ph.D. or other terminal degree: 99%. Student/faculty ratio: 13/1. Classes of fewer than 20 students: 43%; of 20 to 49 students: 40%; of 50 or more students: 17%. **Advanced Placement and International Baccalaureate credit:** AP tests may be used for: Credit only. Scores accepted: 3, 4, 5. International Baccalaureate exams may be used for: Credit and/or placement. **Freshmen returning for sophomore year:** 88%. **Graduation rates:** Four-year: 35%; five-year: 63%; six-year: 68%.

COSTS AND FINANCIAL AID

Financial aid office: (614) 292-0300. **Expenses (2006-2007):** Tuition and fees 2006-2007: $8,667 in state, $20,562 out of state; room/board: $6,720. Estimated books and supplies: $1,254; transportation: $144; personal expenses: $3,645. **Financial aid:** Priority filing date for institution's financial aid form: March 1. In 2005-2006, 67% of undergraduates applied for financial aid. Of those, 52% were determined to have financial need; 22% had their need fully met. Average financial aid package (proportion receiving): $9,726 (52%). Average amount of gift aid, such as scholarships or grants (proportion receiving): $5,713 (46%). Average amount of self-help aid, such as work study or loans (proportion receiving): $5,045 (48%). Average need-based loan (excluding PLUS or other private loans): $4,085. Among students who received need-based aid, the average percentage of need met: 69%. Among students who received aid based on merit, the average award (and the proportion receiving): $4,047 (17%). The average athletic scholarship (and the proportion receiving): $19,239 (1%). Average amount of debt of borrowers graduating in 2005: $17,821. Proportion who borrowed: 58%.

CAMPUS LIFE AND EXTRACURRICULAR ACTIVITIES

Campus housing available (% using): coed dorms (87%), apartments for married students (4%), apartment for single students (2%), special housing for disabled students (2%), cooperative housing (4%), other housing options (0%). Students who live in college-owned, operated, or affiliated housing: 24%. **Student employment:** During the 2005-2006 academic year, 19% of undergraduates worked on campus. Average per-year earnings: $5,194. **Clubs and organizations:** Number of student organizations: 800. Activities include: choral groups, concert band, dance, drama/theater, jazz band, literary magazine, marching band, music ensembles, musical theater, opera, pep band, radio station, student government, student newspaper, student film society, symphony orchestra, television station, yearbook. Number of fraternities: 40; sororities: 19. Proportion of men in fraternities: 6%; of women in sororities: 6%. Average proportion of students who stay on campus on weekends: 50%. **Sports program (2005-2006):** Member of NCAA I. *Men's intercollegiate varsity sports:* baseball, basketball, cross-country, fencing, football, golf, gymnastics, ice hockey, lacrosse, riflery, soccer, swimming and diving, tennis, track and field (indoor), track and field (outdoor), volleyball, wrestling, pistol. *Women's intercollegiate varsity sports:* basketball, crew, cross-country, fencing, field hockey, golf, gymnastics, ice hockey, lacrosse, rowing, soccer, swimming and diving, syncronized swimming, tennis, track and field (indoor), track and field (outdoor), volleyball, mixed rifle.

SERVICES AND FACILITIES

Basic services: nonremedial tutoring, women's center, placement service, day care, health service, health insurance. **Remedial assistance:** reading, math, writing, study skills. **Counseling services:** minority student, career, military, personal, veteran student, academic, older student, psychological, birth control, religious. **For learning-disabled students:** School does not offer a structured program with separate admission and additional fees. Total undergraduates in learning-disabled program or receiving services: 1500. Services include: extended time for tests, priority registration, other. **Library:** Number of titles: 5,936,434; number of current serial subscriptions: 34,745. **Information technology resources:** Students are not required to lease or own a computer. Number of campus computers available to all students: 800. School does not have a wireless network. Approximate number of users that can be accommodated: 8,000. Proportion of college-owned housing units wired for high-speed internet access: 100%. **Campus safety:** Security services offered: 24-hour foot-and-vehicle patrols, late-night transport/escort service, 24-hour emergency telephones, lighted pathways/sidewalks, student patrols, controlled dormitory access (key, security card, etc).

TRANSFER AND INTERNATIONAL STUDENTS

Transfer students: May apply for admission for the following academic terms: Fall, Winter, Spring, Summer. Applicants do not need a minimum number of credits to apply. For fall 2005: Transfer applications received: 3,511. Transfer applicants offered admission: 3,020. Transfer applicants enrolled: 1,795. **International students:** Number of foreign undergraduates: 1023 (3% of student body). Number of countries represented: 78. Minimum TOEFL score required: 527 (paper); 197 (computer).

Ohio University

- **Address:** Athens, OH 45701
- **Website:** http://www.ohio.edu
- **Public**
- **Enrollment:** 16,094 full-time; 1,113 part-time

KEY STATS

✔ **U.S News College Ranking:** 110, National Universities
✔ **ACT Score (25th/75th percentile):** 21-25
✔ **Tuition:** 2005-2006: $8,235 in state, $17,199 out of state

Selectivity: Selective	**Room/board:** $7,686
Acceptance rate: 89%	**Average debt:** $18,101
Student/faculty ratio: 19/1	**Proportion who borrowed:** 62%

UNDERGRADUATE STUDENT BODY STATS

2005-2006 enrollment: 16,094 full-time; 1,113 part-time. Men: 47%; women: 53%. **Ethnic makeup:** African American: 4%; Asian American: 1%; Hispanic: 1%; White: 93%; International: 1%. **Religious preference:** Roman Catholic: 31%; Protestant: 42%; Jewish: 2%; No preference: 9%; Unknown: 12%.

ADMISSIONS FACTS AND FIGURES

Phone: (740) 593-4100. **Email:** admissions@ohio.edu. **Website:** http://www.ohio.edu. **Application deadlines for fall 2007:** Regular decision: February 1. Early decision: Not offered. Early action: Not offered. Admission can be deferred. **Application fee:** $45. Common application is not accepted. **To apply online, go to:** http://www.applyweb.com/aw?ohiou. **Admissions requirements/recommendations:** High school units required (recommended): English: 4; Mathematics: 3; Science: 3; Foreign language: 2; Social studies: 3; Total units: 16. Tests: The college uses SAT or ACT scores in admissions decisions. Either SAT or ACT required. For admission to the fall 2007 entering class, the school will accept: ACT without writing. Campus visit: Recommended. Admissions interview: Neither required nor recommended. Off-campus interview: Not available. **Factors that count in admissions decisions:** *Academic:* Secondary school record: Very important. Class rank: Important. Letters of recommendation: Considered. Standardized test scores: Important. Essay: Considered. *Nonacademic:* Interview: Not considered. Extracurricular activities: Considered. Talent/ability: Considered. Character/personal qualities: Considered. Alumni/ae relationship: Considered. Geographical residence: Not considered. State residency: Not considered. Religious affiliation/commitment: Not considered. Minority status: Considered. Volunteer work: Considered. Work experience: Considered. **Other schools with the greatest overlap in applicants:** Bowling Green State University; Kent State University; Miami University–Oxford; Ohio State University–Columbus; University of Cincinnati. **Admissions statistics for the fall 2005 entering class:** Total applicants: 12,367. Total accepted: 11,027. Freshmen enrolled: 4,163; 8% were from out of state. Overall acceptance rate: 89%. **Size of waiting list:** 0 applicants; enrolled from waiting list: 0. **Credentials of fall 2005 freshmen:** 16% ranked in the top 10 percent of their high school class; 42% were in the top 25 percent, and 80% were in the top half. (Proportion submitting class standing: 81%.) **Average high school grade point average:** 3.3. **First-year students who submitted SAT scores:** 54%. Scores (25/75 percentile): Verbal: 490-600, Math: 490-600, Combined: 980-1200. **First-year students submitting ACT scores:** 88%. Scores (25/75 percentile): English: 20-25, Math: 19-25, Composite: 21-25.

ACADEMICS

Year founded: 1804. **Academic calendar:** Quarter. **Degrees offered:** associate, bachelor's, master's, first professional, doctorate. **Most popular majors:** 6% communication studies/speech communication and rhetoric, 6% health and physical education, 5% early childhood education and teaching, 5% journalism, 4% secondary education and teaching. **Major fields of study:** area, ethnic, cultural, and gender studies; biological and biomedical sciences; business, management, marketing, and related support services; communication, journalism, and related programs; computer and information sciences and support services; education; engineering; engineering technologies/technicians; English language and literature/letters; family and consumer sciences/human sciences; foreign languages, literatures, and linguistics; health professions and related clinical sciences; history; liberal arts and sciences studies, and humanities; mathematics and statistics; parks, recreation, leisure, and fitness studies; philosophy and religious studies; physical sciences; psychology; public administration and social service professions; social sciences; transportation and materials moving; visual

and performing arts. **Areas of required coursework:** arts/fine arts, humanities, mathematics, English (including composition), philosophy, foreign languages, sciences (biological or physical), history, social science. **Pre-professional programs:** pre-law, pre-dentistry, pre-medicine, pre-theology, pre-veterinary science, pre-optometry, pre-pharmacy. **Special academic programs (% participation):** accelerated program (1%), cooperative (work-study plan) program (4%), distance learning (3%), double major (6%), dual enrollment (3%), English as a Second Language (ESL) (2%), external degree program (1%), honors program (1%), independent study (1%), internships (6%), liberal arts/career combination (1%), student-designed major (1%), study abroad (17%), teacher certificate program (9%). **Teacher certification offered in:** early childhood, special education, elementary, middle/junior high, secondary. **Reserve Officers Training Corps (ROTC):** Army ROTC: Offered on campus; Air Force ROTC: Offered on campus. **Faculty and instruction (2005-2006):** Total instructional faculty: 869 full-time, 319 part-time (62% men; 38% women; 14% minorities). Full-time faculty with Ph.D. or other terminal degree: 89%. Student/faculty ratio: 19/1. Classes of fewer than 20 students: 45%; of 20 to 49 students: 46%; of 50 or more students: 10%. **Advanced Placement and International Baccalaureate credit:** AP tests may be used for: Credit and/or placement. Scores accepted: 3. **Freshmen returning for sophomore year:** 83%. **Graduation rates:** Four-year: 46%; five-year: 67%; six-year: 71%. **Graduate study:** 26% of students pursue further study within one year; 31% within five years. Fields in which graduates pursue further study: Master of Business Administration (MBA), 2%; law, 2%; medicine, 1%; engineering, 1%; education, 4%; arts and sciences, 8%.

COSTS AND FINANCIAL AID

Financial aid office: (740) 593-4141. **Expenses (2005-2006):** Tuition and fees 2005-2006: $8,235 in state, $17,199 out of state; room/board: $7,686. **Financial aid:** Priority filing date for institution's financial aid form: March 15. In 2005-2006, 71% of undergraduates applied for financial aid. Of those, 50% were determined to have financial need; 16% had their need fully met. Average financial aid package (proportion receiving): $6,870 (48%). Average amount of gift aid, such as scholarships or grants (proportion receiving): N/A (19%). Average amount of self-help aid, such as work study or loans (proportion receiving): N/A (42%). Among students who received need-based aid, the average percentage of need met: 52%. Among students who received aid based on merit, the average award (and the proportion receiving): $3,755 (11%). The average athletic scholarship (and the proportion receiving): $13,755 (2%). Average amount of debt of borrowers graduating in 2005: $18,101. Proportion who borrowed: 62%.

CAMPUS LIFE AND EXTRACURRICULAR ACTIVITIES

Campus housing available (% using): coed dorms (89%), women's dorms (3%), sorority housing (5%), fraternity housing (3%), apartments for married students (0%), apartment for single students (0%), special housing for disabled students, special housing for international students, cooperative housing, other housing options. Students who live in college-owned, operated, or affiliated housing: 45%. **Student employment:** During the 2005-2006 academic year, 40% of undergraduates worked on campus. Average per-year earnings: $1,464. **Clubs and organizations:** Number of student organizations: 333. Activities include: choral groups, concert band, dance, drama/theater, jazz band, literary magazine, marching band, music ensembles, musical theater, opera, pep band, radio station, student government, student newspaper, student film society, symphony orchestra, television station, yearbook. Number of fraternities: 18; sororities: 13. Proportion of men in fraternities: 11%; of women in sororities: 13%. Average proportion of students who stay on campus on weekends: 90%. **Sports program (2005-2006):** Member of NCAA I. *Men's intercollegiate varsity sports:* baseball, basketball, cross-country, football, golf, swimming and diving, track and field (indoor), track and field (outdoor), wrestling. *Women's intercollegiate varsity sports:* basketball, cross-country, field hockey, golf, lacrosse, soccer, softball, swimming and diving, track and field (indoor), track and field (outdoor), volleyball.

SERVICES AND FACILITIES

Basic services: nonremedial tutoring, placement service, health service, health insurance. **Remedial assistance:** reading, math, writing, study skills. **Counseling services:** minority student, career, military, personal, veteran student, academic, psychological, birth control. **For learning-disabled students:** School does not offer a structured program with separate admission and additional fees. Services include: remedial math, reading machines, readers, extended time for tests, tutors, priority registration, typist/scribe. **Library:** Number of titles: 2,599,791; number of current serial subscriptions: 19,928. **Information technology resources:** Students are not required to lease or own a computer. Number of campus computers available to all students: 6,100.

School has a wireless network. Approximate number of users that can be accommodated: 26,000. Proportion of college-owned housing units wired for high-speed internet access: 100%. **Campus safety:** Security services offered: 24-hour foot-and-vehicle patrols, late-night transport/escort service, 24-hour emergency telephones, lighted pathways/sidewalks, controlled dormitory access (key, security card, etc).

TRANSFER AND INTERNATIONAL STUDENTS

Transfer students: May apply for admission for the following academic terms: Fall, Winter, Spring, Summer. Applicants need a minimum number of credits to apply. For fall 2005: Transfer applications received: 1,082. Transfer applicants offered admission: 764. Transfer applicants enrolled: 469. **International students:** Number of foreign undergraduates: 245 (1% of student body). Minimum TOEFL score required: 550 (paper).

Ohio Wesleyan University

- **Address:** 61 S. Sandusky Street, Delaware, OH 43015
- **Website:** http://web.owu.edu
- **Private; Religious affiliation:** Methodist
- **Enrollment:** 1,941 full-time; 35 part-time

KEY STATS

✔ **U.S News College Ranking:** 95, Liberal Arts Colleges
✔ **SAT Score (25th/75th percentile):** 1120-1320
✔ **Tuition:** 2006-2007: $30,290

Selectivity: More selective	**Room/board:** $7,790
Acceptance rate: 75%	**Average debt:** $22,619
Student/faculty ratio: 13/1	**Proportion who borrowed:** 60%

UNDERGRADUATE STUDENT BODY STATS

2005-2006 enrollment: 1,941 full-time; 35 part-time. Men: 47%; women: 53%. **Ethnic makeup:** African American: 5%; Asian American: 2%; Hispanic: 1%; White: 85%; International: 8%.

ADMISSIONS FACTS AND FIGURES

Phone: (740) 368-3020. **Email:** owuadmit@owu.edu. **Website:** http://web.owu.edu. **Application deadlines for fall 2007:** Regular decision: March 1. Early decision: Send application by: December 1; Decision sent by: December 30. Early action: Send application by: December 15; Decision sent by: January 15. Admission can be deferred. **Application fee:** $35. Common application is accepted. **To apply online, go to:** http://admission.owu.edu/apps.html. **Admissions requirements/recommendations:** High school units required (recommended): English: 4; Mathematics: 3 (4); Science: 3 (4); Foreign language: 3 (4); Social studies: 3 (4); Total units: 16. Tests: The college uses SAT or ACT scores in admissions decisions. Either SAT or ACT required. For admission to the fall 2007 entering class, the school will accept: ACT with writing, ACT without writing. Campus visit: Recommended. Admissions interview: Recommended. Off-campus interview: May be arranged. **Factors that count in admissions decisions:** *Academic:* Secondary school record: Very important. Class rank: Important. Letters of recommendation: Very important. Standardized test scores: Important. Essay: Very important. *Nonacademic:* Interview: Very important. Extracurricular activities: Important. Talent/ability: Important. Character/personal qualities: Very important. Alumni/ae relationship: Important. Geographical residence: Important. State residency: Not considered. Religious affiliation/commitment: Not considered. Minority status: Important. Volunteer work: Important. Work experience: Considered. **Other schools with the greatest overlap in applicants:** College of Wooster; DePauw University; Denison University; Kenyon College; Miami University–Oxford. **Admissions statistics for the fall 2005 entering class:** Total applicants: 2,929. Total accepted: 2,187. Freshmen enrolled: 595; 43% were from out of state. Accepted through early-decision or early-action plans: 36%. Overall acceptance rate: 75%. Early-decision acceptance rate: 76%. Non-early acceptance rate: 69%. **Size of waiting list:** 20 applicants; enrolled from waiting list: 1. **Credentials of fall 2005 freshmen:** 30% ranked in the top 10 percent of their high school class; 52% were in the top 25 percent, and 81% were in the top half. (Proportion submitting class standing: 56%.) **Average high school grade point average:** 3.3. **First-year students who submitted SAT scores:** 71%. Scores (25/75 percentile): Verbal: 550-660, Math: 570-660, Combined: 1120-1320. **First-year students submitting ACT scores:** 62%. Scores (25/75 percentile): English: 23-29, Math: 23-28, Composite: 24-29.

ACADEMICS

Year founded: 1842. **Academic calendar:** Semester. **Degrees offered:** bachelor's. **Most popular majors:** 11% psychology, 9% business/managerial economics, 6% zoology/animal biology, 5% political science and government, 5% sociology. **Major fields of study:** area, ethnic, cultural, and gender studies; biological and biomedical sciences; business, management, marketing, and related support services; communication, journalism, and related programs; computer and information sciences and support services; education; English language and literature/letters; foreign languages, literatures, and linguistics; health professions and related clinical sciences; history; legal professions and studies; liberal arts and sciences studies, and humanities; mathematics and statistics; multi/interdisciplinary studies; natural resources and conservation; parks, recreation, leisure, and fitness studies; philosophy and religious studies; physical sciences; psychology; public administration and social service professions; social sciences; theology and religious vocations; visual and performing arts. **Areas of required coursework:** arts/fine arts, humanities, English (including composition), foreign languages, sciences (biological or physical), social science, other. **Pre-professional programs:** pre-law, pre-dentistry, pre-medicine, pre-theology, pre-veterinary science, pre-optometry, other. **Special academic programs (% participation):** double major (23.8%), exchange student program (domestic) (5.8%), honors program (32%), independent study (51.5%), internships (20.3%), student-designed major (.25%), study abroad (8%), teacher certificate program (7%). **Teacher certification offered in:** early childhood, elementary, middle/junior high, secondary. **Reserve Officers Training Corps (ROTC):** Army ROTC: Offered at cooperating institution (Capital University). **Faculty and instruction (2005-2006):** Total instructional faculty: 130 full-time, 61 part-time (60% men; 40% women; 9% minorities). Full-time faculty with Ph.D. or other terminal degree: 100%. Student/faculty ratio: 13/1. Classes of fewer than 20 students: 58%; of 20 to 49 students: 42%; of 50 or more students: 0%. **Advanced Placement and International Baccalaureate credit:** AP tests may be used for: Credit and/or placement. Scores accepted: 4, 5. International Baccalaureate exams may be used for: Credit and/or placement. **Freshmen returning for sophomore year:** 80%. **Graduation rates:** Four-year: 63%; five-year: 68%; six-year: 68%. **Graduate study:** 35% of students pursue further study immediately upon graduation; 52% within five years. Fields in which graduates pursue further study: Master of Business Administration (MBA), 10%; law, 9%; medicine, 10%; dentistry, 2%; education, 19%; arts and sciences, 48%; veterinary medicine, 2%.

COSTS AND FINANCIAL AID

Financial aid office: (740) 368-3050. **Expenses (2006-2007):** Tuition and fees 2006-2007: $30,290; room/board: $7,790. Estimated books and supplies: $2,050; transportation: $60; personal expenses: $0. **Financial aid:** Priority filing date for institution's financial aid form: March 1; deadline: May 1. In 2005-2006, 66% of undergraduates applied for financial aid. Of those, 56% were determined to have financial need; 28% had their need fully met. Average financial aid package (proportion receiving): $20,854 (56%). Average amount of gift aid, such as scholarships or grants (proportion receiving): $14,473 (56%). Average amount of self-help aid, such as work study or loans (proportion receiving): $4,501 (48%). Average need-based loan (excluding PLUS or other private loans): $3,525. Among students who received need-based aid, the average percentage of need met: 82%. Among students who received aid based on merit, the average award (and the proportion receiving): $11,439 (41%). The average athletic scholarship (and the proportion receiving): $0 (0%). Average amount of debt of borrowers graduating in 2005: $22,619. Proportion who borrowed: 60%.

CAMPUS LIFE AND EXTRACURRICULAR ACTIVITIES

Campus housing available (% using): coed dorms (67%), women's dorms (12%), fraternity housing (13%), apartment for single students (1%), special housing for international students (1%), other housing options (6%). Students who live in college-owned, operated, or affiliated housing: 83%. **Student employment:** During the 2005-2006 academic year, 50% of undergraduates worked on campus. Average per-year earnings: $1,500. **Clubs and organizations:** Number of student organizations: 95. Activities include: choral groups, concert band, dance, drama/theater, jazz band, literary magazine, music ensembles, musical theater, opera, pep band, radio station, student government, student newspaper, student film society, symphony orchestra, television station, yearbook. Number of fraternities: 10; sororities: 7. Proportion of men in fraternities: 39%; of women in sororities: 26%. Average proportion of students who stay on campus on weekends: 75%. **Sports program (2005-2006):** Member of NCAA III. *Men's intercollegiate varsity sports:* baseball, basketball, cross-country, football, golf, lacrosse, soccer, swimming and diving, tennis, track and field (indoor), track and field (outdoor). *Women's intercollegiate varsity sports:* basketball, cross-country, field hockey, lacrosse, soccer, softball, swimming and diving, tennis, track and field (indoor), track and field (outdoor), volleyball.

SERVICES AND FACILITIES

Basic services: nonremedial tutoring, placement service, health service, health insurance. **Counseling services:** minority student, career, personal, academic, psychological, birth control, religious. **For learning-disabled students:** School does not offer a structured program with separate admission and additional fees. Total undergraduates in learning-disabled program or receiving services: 189. Services include: remedial math, remedial English, tape recorders, other special classes, note-taking services, oral tests, learning center, extended time for tests, tutors, other. **Library:** Number of titles: 442,843; number of current serial subscriptions: 7,949. **Information technology resources:** Students are not required to lease or own a computer. Number of campus computers available to all students: 300. School has a wireless network. Approximate number of users that can be accommodated: 100. Proportion of college-owned housing units wired for high-speed internet access: 100%. **Campus safety:** Security services offered: 24-hour foot-and-vehicle patrols, late-night transport/escort service, 24-hour emergency telephones, lighted pathways/sidewalks, student patrols, controlled dormitory access (key, security card, etc).

TRANSFER AND INTERNATIONAL STUDENTS

Transfer students: May apply for admission for the following academic terms: Fall, Spring. Applicants need a minimum number of credits to apply. For fall 2005: Transfer applications received: 89. Transfer applicants offered admission: 55. Transfer applicants enrolled: 35. **International students:** Number of foreign undergraduates: 153 (8% of student body). Number of countries represented: 47. Minimum TOEFL score required: 520 (paper); 190 (computer).

Otterbein College

- **Address:** One Otterbein College, Westerville, OH 43081
- **Website:** http://www.otterbein.edu
- **Private; Religious affiliation:** United Methodist
- **Enrollment:** 2,261 full-time; 463 part-time

KEY STATS

✔ **U.S News College Ranking:** 7, Comp. Coll.–Bachelor's (Midwest)
✔ **ACT Score (25th/75th percentile):** 21-26
✔ **Tuition:** 2006-2007: $23,871

Selectivity: More selective	**Room/board:** $6,789
Acceptance rate: 76%	**Average debt:** N/A
Student/faculty ratio: 12/1	**Proportion who borrowed:** N/A

UNDERGRADUATE STUDENT BODY STATS

2005-2006 enrollment: 2,261 full-time; 463 part-time. Men: 35%; women: 65%. **Ethnic makeup:** African American: 6%; Asian American: 1%; Hispanic: 1%; White: 91%; International: 1%. **Religious preference:** Roman Catholic: 21%; Protestant: 5%; Jewish: 1%; Muslim: 1%; Unknown: 25%; United Methodist: 19%; Baptist: 8%; Other: 20%.

ADMISSIONS FACTS AND FIGURES

Phone: (614) 823-1500. **Email:** UOtterB@Otterbein.edu. **Website:** http://www.otterbein.edu. **Application deadlines for fall 2007:** Regular decision: June 1. Early decision: Not offered. Early action: Not offered. Admission can be deferred. **Application fee:** $25. Common application is accepted. **To apply online, go to:** http://www.otterbein.edu/Admission/Applying/application.asp. **Admissions requirements/recommendations:** High school units required (recommended): English: 4 (4); Mathematics: 3 (4); Science: 3 (4); Foreign language: 2 (4); Social studies: 3 (4); History: 2 (2); Academic electives: 0 (0); Total units: 17 (22). Tests: The college uses SAT or ACT scores in admissions decisions. Either SAT or ACT required. For admission to the fall 2007 entering class, the school will accept: ACT with writing, ACT without writing. Campus visit: Recommended. Admissions interview: Recommended. Off-campus interview: May be arranged. **Factors that count in admissions decisions:** *Academic:* Secondary school record: Very important. Class rank: Very important. Letters of recommendation: Important. Standardized test scores: Very important. Essay: Important. *Nonacademic:* Interview: Considered. Extracurricular activities: Important. Talent/ability: Important.

Character/personal qualities: Important. Alumni/ae relationship: Important. Geographical residence: Considered. State residency: Considered. Religious affiliation/commitment: Considered. Minority status: Very important. Volunteer work: Important. Work experience: Considered. **Other schools with the greatest overlap in applicants:** Bowling Green State University; Capital University; Miami University–Oxford; Ohio State University–Columbus; Ohio University. **Admissions statistics for the fall 2005 entering class:** Total applicants: 2,754. Total accepted: 2,103. Freshmen enrolled: 627; 7% were from out of state. Overall acceptance rate: 76%. **Credentials of fall 2005 freshmen:** 26% ranked in the top 10 percent of their high school class; 54% were in the top 25 percent, and 84% were in the top half. (Proportion submitting class standing: 88%.) **Average high school grade point average:** 3.4. **First-year students who submitted SAT scores:** 31%. Scores (25/75 percentile): Verbal: 500-620, Math: 510-620, Combined: 1010-1240. **First-year students submitting ACT scores:** 92%. Scores (25/75 percentile): English: 20-26, Math: 19-26, Composite: 21-26.

ACADEMICS

Year founded: 1847. **Academic calendar:** Quarter. **Degrees offered:** bachelor's, post-bachelor's certificate, master's, post-master's certificate. **Most popular majors:** 14% business administration and management, 9% nursing/registered nurse training (R.N., A.S.N., B.S.N., M.S.N.), 8% early childhood education and teaching, 7% public relations, advertising, and applied communication , 6% psychology. **Major fields of study:** agriculture, agriculture operations, and related sciences; biological and biomedical sciences; business, management, marketing, and related support services; communication, journalism, and related programs; computer and information sciences and support services; English language and literature/letters; foreign languages, literatures, and linguistics; health professions and related clinical sciences; history; liberal arts and sciences studies, and humanities; mathematics and statistics; natural resources and conservation; parks, recreation, leisure, and fitness studies; philosophy and religious studies; physical sciences; psychology; social sciences. **Areas of required coursework:** arts/fine arts, humanities, mathematics, English (including composition), philosophy, foreign languages, sciences (biological or physical), history, social science, other. **Pre-professional programs:** pre-law, pre-dentistry, pre-medicine, pre-theology, pre-veterinary science, pre-optometry. **Special academic programs (% participation):** accelerated program (5%), cross-registration (1%), distance learning (5%), double major (10%), dual enrollment (1%), exchange student program (domestic) (1%), honors program (6%), independent study (2%), internships (2%), liberal arts/career combination (10%), student-designed major (1%), study abroad (1%), teacher certificate program (20%), weekend college (2%). **Teacher certification offered in:** early childhood, elementary, middle/junior high, secondary. **Reserve Officers Training Corps (ROTC):** Army ROTC: Offered at cooperating institution (Ohio State University); Navy ROTC: Offered at cooperating institution (Ohio State University); Air Force ROTC: Offered at cooperating institution (Ohio State University). **Faculty and instruction (2005-2006):** Total instructional faculty: 155 full-time, 134 part-time. Full-time faculty with Ph.D. or other terminal degree: 94%. Student/faculty ratio: 12/1. Classes of fewer than 20 students: 64%; of 20 to 49 students: 33%; of 50 or more students: 3%. **Advanced Placement and International Baccalaureate credit:** AP tests may be used for: Credit and/or placement. Scores accepted: 3, 4, 5. International Baccalaureate exams may be used for: Credit and/or placement. **Freshmen returning for sophomore year:** 81%. **Graduation rates:** Four-year: 50%; five-year: 61%; six-year: 66%. **Graduate study:** 14% of students pursue further study immediately upon graduation; 44% within five years.

COSTS AND FINANCIAL AID

Financial aid office: (614) 823-1502. **Expenses (2006-2007):** Tuition and fees 2006-2007: $23,871; room/board: $6,789. Estimated books and supplies: $909; transportation: $663; personal expenses: $1,338. **Financial aid:** Priority filing date for institution's financial aid form: April 1; deadline: June 1.

CAMPUS LIFE AND EXTRACURRICULAR ACTIVITIES

Campus housing available (% using): coed dorms (24%), women's dorms (30%), men's dorms (16%), sorority housing (5%), fraternity housing (5%), apartment for single students (15%), special housing for disabled students, other housing options (5%). Students who live in college-owned, operated, or affiliated housing: 50%. **Student employment:** During the 2005-2006 academic year, 13% of undergraduates worked on campus. Average per-year earnings: $758. Activities include: choral groups, concert band, dance, drama/theater, jazz band, literary magazine, marching band, music ensembles, musical theater, opera, pep band, radio station, student government, student newspaper, symphony orchestra, television station, yearbook.

Number of fraternities: 7; sororities: 6. Proportion of men in fraternities: 19%; of women in sororities: 11%. Average proportion of students who stay on campus on weekends: 39%. **Sports program (2005-2006):** Member of NCAA III. *Men's intercollegiate varsity sports:* baseball, basketball, cross-country, football, golf, soccer, tennis, track and field (indoor), track and field (outdoor). *Women's intercollegiate varsity sports:* basketball, cross-country, golf, soccer, softball, tennis, track and field (indoor), track and field (outdoor), volleyball.

SERVICES AND FACILITIES

Basic services: nonremedial tutoring, women's center, placement service, health service, health insurance, other. **Remedial assistance:** reading, math, writing, study skills. **Counseling services:** minority student, career, personal, veteran student, academic, older student, psychological, religious. **For learning-disabled students:** School does not offer a structured program with separate admission and additional fees. Total undergraduates in learning-disabled program or receiving services: 83. Services include: remedial math, remedial reading, tape recorders, note-taking services, oral tests, learning center, readers, extended time for tests, tutors, priority registration, priority seating, substitution of courses, texts on tape, typist/scribe, exams on tape or computer. **Library:** Number of titles: 259,290; number of current serial subscriptions: 7,369. **Information technology resources:** Students are not required to lease or own a computer. Number of campus computers available to all students: 150. School has a wireless network. Approximate number of users that can be accommodated: 100. Proportion of college-owned housing units wired for high-speed internet access: 100%. **Campus safety:** Security services offered: 24-hour foot-and-vehicle patrols, late-night transport/escort service, 24-hour emergency telephones, lighted pathways/sidewalks, student patrols, controlled dormitory access (key, security card, etc).

TRANSFER AND INTERNATIONAL STUDENTS

Transfer students: May apply for admission for the following academic terms: Fall, Winter, Spring, Summer. Applicants need a minimum number of credits to apply. For fall 2005: Transfer applications received: 310. Transfer applicants offered admission: 159. Transfer applicants enrolled: 77. **International students:** Number of foreign undergraduates: 36 (1% of student body). Number of countries represented: 9. Minimum TOEFL score required: 523 (paper); 193 (computer).

Shawnee State University

- **Address:** 940 Second Street, Portsmouth, OH 45662
- **Website:** http://www.shawnee.edu
- **Public**
- **Enrollment:** 3,197 full-time; 623 part-time

KEY STATS

✔ **U.S News College Ranking:** fourth tier, Liberal Arts Colleges
✔ **ACT Score (25th/75th percentile):** 17-23
✔ **Tuition:** 2006-2007: $5,436 in state, $9,576 out of state

Selectivity: Less selective	**Room/board:** $6,930
Acceptance rate: 100%	**Average debt:** N/A
Student/faculty ratio: 18/1	**Proportion who borrowed:** N/A

UNDERGRADUATE STUDENT BODY STATS

2005-2006 enrollment: 3,197 full-time; 623 part-time. Men: 39%; women: 61%. **Ethnic makeup:** African American: 3%; American-Indian: 1%; White: 95%; International: 1%.

ADMISSIONS FACTS AND FIGURES

Phone: (800) 959-2778. **Email:** To_SSU@shawnee.edu. **Website:** http://www.shawnee.edu. **Application deadlines for fall 2007:** Regular decision: Rolling. Early decision: Not offered. Early action: Not offered. Admission can be deferred. Common application is not accepted. **To apply online, go to:** http://www.shawnee.edu/offices/adms/application.html. **Admissions requirements/recommendations:** High school units required (recommended): English: (4); Mathematics: (3); Science: (3); Foreign language: (2); Social studies: (3); Total units: (16). Tests: The college does not use SAT or ACT scores in admissions decisions. Neither SAT nor ACT required. For admission to the fall 2007 entering class, the school will accept: ACT with writing, ACT without writing. Campus visit:

Recommended. Admissions interview: Neither required nor recommended. Off-campus interview: Not available. **Factors that count in admissions decisions:** *Academic:* Secondary school record: Not considered. Class rank: Not considered. Letters of recommendation: Not considered. Standardized test scores: Not considered. Essay: Not considered. *Nonacademic:* Interview: Not considered. Extracurricular activities: Not considered. Talent/ability: Not considered. Character/personal qualities: Not considered. Alumni/ae relationship: Not considered. Geographical residence: Not considered. State residency: Not considered. Religious affiliation/commitment: Not considered. Minority status: Not considered. Volunteer work: Not considered. Work experience: Not considered. **Other schools with the greatest overlap in applicants:** Ohio University. **Admissions statistics for the fall 2005 entering class:** Total applicants: 2,917. Total accepted: 2,917. Freshmen enrolled: 870; 8% were from out of state. Overall acceptance rate: 100%. **Credentials of fall 2005 freshmen:** 15% ranked in the top 10 percent of their high school class; 34% were in the top 25 percent, and 67% were in the top half. (Proportion submitting class standing: 89%.) **First-year students submitting ACT scores:** 79%. Scores (25/75 percentile): English: 16-22, Math: 16-23, Composite: 17-23.

ACADEMICS

Year founded: 1986. **Academic calendar:** Quarter. **Degrees offered:** certificate, associate, bachelor's. **Most popular majors:** 15% business administration and management, 12% social sciences, 8% early childhood education and teaching. **Major fields of study:** biological and biomedical sciences; business, management, marketing, and related support services; education; engineering technologies/technicians; English language and literature/letters; health professions and related clinical sciences; history; legal professions and studies; liberal arts and sciences studies, and humanities; mathematics and statistics; parks, recreation, leisure, and fitness studies; physical sciences; psychology; social sciences; visual and performing arts. **Areas of required coursework:** arts/fine arts, humanities, mathematics, English (including composition), philosophy, sciences (biological or physical), social science. **Pre-professional programs:** pre-medicine. **Special academic programs (% participation):** distance learning (2%), double major (4%), dual enrollment, honors program, independent study (2%), internships, student-designed major, study abroad, teacher certificate program (9%). **Teacher certification offered in:** early childhood, special education, elementary, middle/junior high, secondary. **Faculty and instruction (2005-2006):** Total instructional faculty: 138 full-time, 160 part-time (56% men; 44% women; 3% minorities). Full-time faculty with Ph.D. or other terminal degree: 54%. Student/faculty ratio: 18/1. Classes of fewer than 20 students: 60%; of 20 to 49 students: 37%; of 50 or more students: 3%. **Advanced Placement and International Baccalaureate credit:** AP tests may be used for: Credit and/or placement. Scores accepted: 3, 4, 5. **Freshmen returning for sophomore year:** 58%. **Graduation rates:** Four-year: 13%; five-year: 20%; six-year: 24%. **Graduate study:** 28% of students pursue further study within one year. Fields in which graduates pursue further study: Master of Business Administration (MBA), 4%; medicine, 4%; engineering, 1%; education, 6%; arts and sciences, 15%.

COSTS AND FINANCIAL AID

Financial aid office: (740) 351-4243. **Expenses (2006-2007):** Tuition and fees 2006-2007: $5,436 in state, $9,576 out of state; room/board: $6,930.

CAMPUS LIFE AND EXTRACURRICULAR ACTIVITIES

Campus housing available (% using): coed dorms (95%), other housing options (5%). Students who live in college-owned, operated, or affiliated housing: 15%. **Student employment:** During the 2005-2006 academic year, 5% of undergraduates worked on campus. Average per-year earnings: $5,040. **Clubs and organizations:** Number of student organizations: 44. Activities include: choral groups, drama/theater, literary magazine, music ensembles, musical theater, student government, student newspaper. Number of fraternities: 2; sororities: 2. Proportion of men in fraternities: 5%; of women in sororities: 3%. Average proportion of students who stay on campus on weekends: 10%. **Sports program (2005-2006):** Member of NAIA. *Men's intercollegiate varsity sports:* baseball, basketball, cross-country, golf, soccer. *Women's intercollegiate varsity sports:* basketball, cross-country, soccer, softball, tennis, volleyball.

SERVICES AND FACILITIES

Basic services: nonremedial tutoring, women's center, placement service, health service. **Remedial assistance:** reading, math, writing, study skills. **Counseling services:** minority student, career, military, personal, veteran student, academic, older student, psychological. **For learning-disabled students:** School does not offer a structured program with separate admission and additional fees. Total undergraduates in learning-disabled program or receiving services: 82. Services include: remedial math, remedial English, reading machines, remedial reading, tape recorders, other special classes, untimed tests, note-taking services, oral tests, learning center, readers, tutors. **Library:** Number of titles: 150,661; number of current serial subscriptions: 13,820. **Information technology resources:** Students are not required to lease or own a computer. Number of campus computers available to all students: 620. School has a wireless network. Proportion of college-owned housing units wired for high-speed internet access: 100%. **Campus safety:** Security services offered: 24-hour foot-and-vehicle patrols, late-night transport/escort service, 24-hour emergency telephones, lighted pathways/sidewalks, controlled dormitory access (key, security card, etc).

TRANSFER AND INTERNATIONAL STUDENTS

Transfer students: May apply for admission for the following academic terms: Fall, Winter, Spring, Summer. Applicants do not need a minimum number of credits to apply. For fall 2005: Transfer applications received: 625. Transfer applicants offered admission: 625. Transfer applicants enrolled: 223. **International students:** Number of foreign undergraduates: 24 (1% of student body). Number of countries represented: 12. Minimum TOEFL score required: 500 (paper).

Tiffin University

- **Address:** 155 Miami Street, Tiffin, OH 44883
- **Website:** http://www.tiffin.edu
- **Private**
- **Enrollment:** 1,097 full-time; 138 part-time

KEY STATS

✔ **U.S News College Ranking:** Unranked Specialty School–Business
✔ **SAT Score (25th/75th percentile):** 818-1060
✔ **Tuition:** 2006-2007: $15,870
Selectivity: Less selective **Room/board:** $6,775
Acceptance rate: 73% **Average debt:** $19,994
Student/faculty ratio: 16/1 **Proportion who borrowed:** 82%

UNDERGRADUATE STUDENT BODY STATS

2005-2006 enrollment: 1,097 full-time; 138 part-time. Men: 47%; women: 53%. **Ethnic makeup:** African American: 16%; Hispanic: 2%; White: 80%; International: 2%.

ADMISSIONS FACTS AND FIGURES

Phone: (419) 448-3423. **Email:** admiss@tiffin.edu. **Website:** http://www.tiffin.edu. **Application deadlines for fall 2007:** Regular decision: Rolling. Early decision: Not offered. Early action: Not offered. Admission cannot be deferred. **Application fee:** $20. Common application is accepted. **To apply online, go to:** http://www.tiffin.edu/apply. **Admissions requirements/recommendations:** High school units required (recommended): English: 4; Mathematics: 3; Science: 3; Foreign language: 0; Social studies: 3; History: 0; Academic electives: 0; Total units: 13. Tests: The college uses SAT or ACT scores in admissions decisions. Either SAT or ACT required. For admission to the fall 2007 entering class, the school will accept: ACT with writing, ACT without writing. Campus visit: Recommended. Admissions interview: Neither required nor recommended. Off-campus interview: May be arranged. **Factors that count in admissions decisions:** *Academic:* Secondary school record: Important. Class rank: Considered. Letters of recommendation: Considered. Standardized test scores: Very important. Essay: Considered. *Nonacademic:* Interview: Important. Extracurricular activities: Considered. Talent/ability: Considered. Character/personal qualities: Considered. Alumni/ae relationship: Not considered. Geographical residence: Not considered. State residency: Not considered. Religious affiliation/commitment: Not considered. Minority status: Not considered. Volunteer work: Not considered. Work experience: Not considered. **Other schools with the greatest overlap in applicants:** Ashland University; Bowling Green State University; Ohio State University–Columbus; University of Findlay; University of Toledo. **Admissions statistics for the fall 2005 entering class:** Total applicants: 1,563. Total accepted: 1,138. Freshmen enrolled: 252; 1% were from out of state. Overall acceptance rate: 73%. **Credentials of fall 2005 freshmen:** 7% ranked in the top 10 percent of their high school class; 24% were in the top 25 percent. **Average high school grade point average:** 3.0. **First-year students who submitted SAT scores:** 80%. Scores (25/75 per-

centile): Verbal: 388-520, Math: 430-540, Combined: 818-1060. **First-year students submitting ACT scores:** 11%. Scores (25/75 percentile): English: 16-22, Math: 17-23, Composite: 18-22.

ACADEMICS

Year founded: 1888. **Academic calendar:** Semester. **Degrees offered:** associate, bachelor's, master's. **Most popular majors:** 60% marketing/marketing management, 16% security and protective services, 10% psychology, 1% sport and fitness administration/management, 0% information science/studies. **Major fields of study:** business, management, marketing, and related support services; communication, journalism, and related programs; computer and information sciences and support services; English language and literature/letters; liberal arts and sciences studies, and humanities; multi/interdisciplinary studies; parks, recreation, leisure, and fitness studies; psychology; public administration and social service professions; security and protective services; social sciences; visual and performing arts. **Areas of required coursework:** arts/fine arts, humanities, computer literacy, mathematics, English (including composition), philosophy, sciences (biological or physical), history, social science. **Special academic programs (% participation):** accelerated program (40%), cross-registration, distance learning (0%), double major (1%), dual enrollment, English as a Second Language (ESL), honors program, independent study (4%), internships (21%), study abroad (1%), teacher certificate program. **Cooperative education programs:** education. **Reserve Officers Training Corps (ROTC):** Army ROTC: Offered at cooperating institution (Bowling Green State University). **Faculty and instruction (2005-2006):** Total instructional faculty: 51 full-time, 82 part-time (59% men; 41% women; 11% minorities). Full-time faculty with Ph.D. or other terminal degree: 71%. Student/faculty ratio: 16/1. Classes of fewer than 20 students: 66%; of 20 to 49 students: 34%. **Advanced Placement and International Baccalaureate credit:** AP tests may be used for: Credit and/or placement. Scores accepted: 3, 4, 5. International Baccalaureate exams may be used for: Credit and/or placement. **Freshmen returning for sophomore year:** 61%. **Graduation rates:** Four-year: 24%; five-year: 31%; six-year: 30%. **Graduate study:** 25% of students pursue further study immediately upon graduation. Fields in which graduates pursue further study: Master of Business Administration (MBA), 25%; law, 1%.

COSTS AND FINANCIAL AID

Financial aid office: (419) 448-3357. **Expenses (2006-2007):** Tuition and fees 2006-2007: $15,870; room/board: $6,775. Estimated books and supplies: $1,200; transportation: $2,000; personal expenses: $2,200. **Financial aid:** Priority filing date for institution's financial aid form: January 1. 12% had their need fully met. Average financial aid package (proportion receiving): $12,053 (N/A). Average amount of gift aid, such as scholarships or grants (proportion receiving): $4,569 (N/A). Average amount of self-help aid, such as work study or loans (proportion receiving): $4,350 (N/A). Average need-based loan (excluding PLUS or other private loans): $3,818. Among students who received need-based aid, the average percentage of need met: 17%. Among students who received aid based on merit, the average award (and the proportion receiving): $10,062 (N/A). The average athletic scholarship (and the proportion receiving): $5,307 (N/A). Average amount of debt of borrowers graduating in 2005: $19,994. Proportion who borrowed: 82%.

CAMPUS LIFE AND EXTRACURRICULAR ACTIVITIES

Campus housing available (% using): coed dorms (78%), sorority housing (4%), fraternity housing (3%), apartments for married students, apartment for single students (5%), special housing for disabled students, special housing for international students (3%), other housing options (7%). Students who live in college-owned, operated, or affiliated housing: 34%. **Student employment:** During the 2005-2006 academic year, 15% of undergraduates worked on campus. Average per-year earnings: $1,000. **Clubs and organizations:** Number of student organizations: 18. Activities include: choral groups, concert band, dance, drama/theater, jazz band, marching band, music ensembles, musical theater, pep band, student government, student newspaper, student film society. Number of fraternities: 2; sororities: 3. Proportion of men in fraternities: 2%; of women in sororities: 3%. Average proportion of students who stay on campus on weekends: 65%. **Sports program (2005-2006):** Member of NAIA. *Men's intercollegiate varsity sports:* baseball, basketball, cross-country, football, golf, soccer, tennis, track and field (indoor), track and field (outdoor). *Women's intercollegiate varsity sports:* basketball, cross-country, golf, soccer, softball, tennis, track and field (indoor), track and field (outdoor), volleyball.

SERVICES AND FACILITIES

Basic services: nonremedial tutoring. **Remedial assistance:** reading, math, writing, study skills. **Counseling services:** career, military, academic, older student, psychological. **For learning-disabled students:** School does not offer a structured program with separate admission and additional fees. Services include: remedial math, remedial English, oral tests, learning center, extended time for tests, tutors. **Library:** Number of titles: 50,688; number of current serial subscriptions: 250. **Information technology resources:** Students are not required to lease or own a computer. Number of campus computers available to all students: 145. School has a wireless network. Proportion of college-owned housing units wired for high-speed internet access: 100%. **Campus safety:** Security services offered: lighted pathways/sidewalks, student patrols, controlled dormitory access (key, security card, etc).

TRANSFER AND INTERNATIONAL STUDENTS
Transfer students: May apply for admission for the following academic terms: Fall, Spring, Summer. Applicants do not need a minimum number of credits to apply. For fall 2005: Transfer applications received: 163. Transfer applicants offered admission: 82. Transfer applicants enrolled: 67. **International students:** Number of foreign undergraduates: 24 (2% of student body). Minimum TOEFL score required: 500 (paper); 173 (computer). Average TOEFL score: 620 (paper).

Union Institute and University

- **Address:** 440 E. McMillan Street, Cincinnati, OH 45206
- **Website:** http://www.tui.edu
- **Private**
- **Enrollment:** 673 full-time; 449 part-time

KEY STATS
✔ **U.S News College Ranking:** fourth tier, National Universities
✔ **SAT or ACT Score (25th/75th percentile):** N/A
✔ **Tuition:** 2006-2007: $11,080

Selectivity: Selective	**Room/board:** N/A
Acceptance rate: N/A	**Average debt:** N/A
Student/faculty ratio: 23/1	**Proportion who borrowed:** N/A

UNDERGRADUATE STUDENT BODY STATS
2005-2006 enrollment: 673 full-time; 449 part-time. Men: 32%; women: 68%. **Ethnic makeup:** African American: 24%; American-Indian: 1%; Asian American: 1%; Hispanic: 8%; White: 66%.

ADMISSIONS FACTS AND FIGURES
Phone: (513) 487-1239. **Email:** admissions@tui.edu. **Website:** http://www.tui.edu. **Application deadlines for fall 2007:** Regular decision: Rolling. Early decision: Not offered. Early action: Not offered. Admission can be deferred. **Application fee:** $35. Common application is not accepted. **Admissions requirements/recommendations:** Tests: The college does not use SAT or ACT scores in admissions decisions. Neither SAT nor ACT required. Campus visit: Recommended. Admissions interview: Required. Off-campus interview: May be arranged. **Factors that count in admissions decisions:** *Academic:* Secondary school record: Considered. Class rank: Not considered. Letters of recommendation: Very important. Standardized test scores: Considered. Essay: Very important. *Nonacademic:* Interview: Very important. Extracurricular activities: Considered. Talent/ability: Considered. Character/personal qualities: Considered. Alumni/ae relationship: Not considered. Geographical residence: Not considered. State residency: Not considered. Religious affiliation/commitment: Not considered. Minority status: Not considered. Volunteer work: Considered. Work experience: Considered.

ACADEMICS
Year founded: 1964. **Academic calendar:** Semester. **Degrees offered:** bachelor's, master's, post-master's certificate, doctorate. **Most popular majors:** 28% liberal arts and sciences/liberal studies, 28% psychology, 13% business/commerce, 13% education. **Major fields of study:** business, management, marketing, and related support services; communication, journalism, and related programs; education; health professions and related clinical sciences; liberal arts and sciences studies, and humanities; psychology; public administration and social service professions; security and protective services; social sciences. **Areas of required coursework:** arts/fine arts, humanities, mathematics, English (including composition), sciences (biological or physical), social science. **Special academic programs (% participation):** distance learning (11%), double major (1%), independent study (100%), stu-

dent-designed major (100%), teacher certificate program (15%). **Teacher certification offered in:** early childhood, special education, elementary, middle/junior high. **Faculty and instruction (2005-2006):** Total instructional faculty: 50 full-time, 117 part-time (45% men; 55% women; 10% minorities). Full-time faculty with Ph.D. or other terminal degree: 40%. Student/faculty ratio: 23/1. Classes of fewer than 20 students: 99%; of 20 to 49 students: 1%; of 50 or more students: 0%. **Advanced Placement and International Baccalaureate credit:** International Baccalaureate exams may be used for: Credit only. **Freshmen returning for sophomore year:** 68%. **Graduation rates:** Six-year: 28%.

COSTS AND FINANCIAL AID
Financial aid office: (513) 487-1127. **Expenses (2006-2007):** Tuition and fees 2006-2007: $11,080; room/board: N/A. **Financial aid:** Priority filing date for institution's financial aid form: March 15; deadline: June 4.

CAMPUS LIFE AND EXTRACURRICULAR ACTIVITIES
Students who live in college-owned, operated, or affiliated housing: 0%. Number of fraternities: 0; sororities: 0.

SERVICES AND FACILITIES
Remedial assistance: reading, math, writing, study skills. **Counseling services:** career, academic, older student. **For learning-disabled students:** School does not offer a structured program with separate admission and additional fees. Services include: remedial English, remedial reading, tape recorders, other special classes, diagnostic testing service, untimed tests, oral tests, learning center, readers, extended time for tests, tutors. **Information technology resources:** Students are not required to lease or own a computer. Number of campus computers available to all students: 65. School does not have a wireless network. **Campus safety:** Security services offered: late-night transport/escort service, lighted pathways/sidewalks.

TRANSFER AND INTERNATIONAL STUDENTS
Transfer students: May apply for admission for the following academic terms: Fall, Winter, Spring, Summer. Applicants do not need a minimum number of credits to apply. For fall 2005: Transfer applications received: 340. Transfer applicants offered admission: 303. Transfer applicants enrolled: 206. **International students:** Number of foreign undergraduates: 1.

University of Akron

- **Address:** 302 Buchtel Common, Akron, OH 44325
- **Website:** http://www.uakron.edu
- **Public**
- **Enrollment:** 12,635 full-time; 4,505 part-time

KEY STATS
✔ **U.S News College Ranking:** fourth tier, National Universities
✔ **ACT Score (25th/75th percentile):** 17-24
✔ **Tuition:** 2006-2007: $8,382 in state, $17,631 out of state

Selectivity: Less selective	**Room/board:** $7,640
Acceptance rate: 82%	**Average debt:** $15,500
Student/faculty ratio: 18/1	**Proportion who borrowed:** 62%

UNDERGRADUATE STUDENT BODY STATS
2005-2006 enrollment: 12,635 full-time; 4,505 part-time. Men: 47%; women: 53%. **Ethnic makeup:** African American: 15%; Asian American: 2%; Hispanic: 1%; White: 81%; International: 1%.

ADMISSIONS FACTS AND FIGURES
Phone: (330) 972-7077. **Email:** admissions@uakron.edu. **Website:** http://www.uakron.edu. **Application deadlines for fall 2007:** Regular decision: August 1. Early decision: Not offered. Early action: Send application by: November 15; Decision sent by: December 1. Admission can be deferred. **Application fee:** $30. Common application is not accepted. **To apply online, go to:** http://www.uakron.edu/admissions. **Admissions requirements/recommendations:** High school units required (recommended): English: (4); Mathematics: (3); Science: (3); Foreign language: (2); Social studies: (3); Total units: (15). Tests: The college uses SAT or ACT scores in admissions decisions. Either SAT or ACT required. For admission to the fall 2007 entering class, the school will accept: ACT with writing, ACT without writing. Campus visit: Recommended. Admissions interview: Neither required nor

recommended. Off-campus interview: May be arranged. **Factors that count in admissions decisions:** *Academic:* Secondary school record: Very important. Class rank: Very important. Letters of recommendation: Not considered. Standardized test scores: Very important. Essay: Not considered. *Nonacademic:* Interview: Not considered. Extracurricular activities: Not considered. Talent/ability: Not considered. Character/personal qualities: Not considered. Alumni/ae relationship: Not considered. Geographical residence: Not considered. State residency: Not considered. Religious affiliation/commitment: Not considered. Minority status: Not considered. Volunteer work: Not considered. Work experience: Not considered. **Other schools with the greatest overlap in applicants:** Bowling Green State University; Kent State University; Ohio State University–Columbus; Ohio University; University of Toledo. **Admissions statistics for the fall 2005 entering class:** Total applicants: 8,810. Total accepted: 7,267. Freshmen enrolled: 3,082; 3% were from out of state. Accepted through early-decision or early-action plans: 18%. Overall acceptance rate: 82%. Non-early acceptance rate: 87%. **Credentials of fall 2005 freshmen:** 12% ranked in the top 10 percent of their high school class; 29% were in the top 25 percent, and 56% were in the top half. (Proportion submitting class standing: 79%.) **Average high school grade point average:** 3.0. **First-year students who submitted SAT scores:** 8%. Scores (25/75 percentile): Verbal: 440-570, Math: 440-590, Combined: 880-1160. **First-year students submitting ACT scores:** 92%. Scores (25/75 percentile): English: 15-23, Math: 17-24, Composite: 17-24.

ACADEMICS

Year founded: 1870. **Academic calendar:** Semester. **Degrees offered:** certificate, associate, bachelor's, post-bachelor's certificate, master's, first professional, first professional certificate, doctorate. **Most popular majors:** 21% business, management, marketing, and related support services, 17% education, 11% health professions and related clinical sciences, 7% communication, journalism, and related programs, 6% engineering. **Major fields of study:** architecture and related services; biological and biomedical sciences; business, management, marketing, and related support services; communication, journalism, and related programs; computer and information sciences and support services; education; engineering; engineering technologies/technicians; English language and literature/letters; family and consumer sciences/human sciences; foreign languages, literatures, and linguistics; health professions and related clinical sciences; history; liberal arts and sciences studies, and humanities; mathematics and statistics; multi/interdisciplinary studies; parks, recreation, leisure, and fitness studies; philosophy and religious studies; physical sciences; psychology; public administration and social service professions; security and protective services; social sciences; visual and performing arts. **Areas of required coursework:** arts/fine arts, humanities, computer literacy, mathematics, English (including composition), foreign languages, sciences (biological or physical), history, social science, other. **Pre-professional programs:** pre-law, pre-medicine, pre-pharmacy. **Special academic programs (% participation):** accelerated program, cooperative (work-study plan) program (8%), distance learning, double major (4%), dual enrollment, English as a Second Language (ESL), honors program (6%), independent study (13%), internships (15%), student-designed major, study abroad, teacher certificate program, weekend college. **Teacher certification offered in:** early childhood, special education, elementary, vo-tech, middle/junior high, secondary. **Cooperative education programs:** art, business, computer science, engineering, health professions, humanities, natural science, social/behavioral science, technologies. **Reserve Officers Training Corps (ROTC):** Army ROTC: Offered on campus; Air Force ROTC: Offered on campus. **Faculty and instruction (2005-2006):** Total instructional faculty: 701 full-time, 773 part-time (53% men; 47% women; 12% minorities). Full-time faculty with Ph.D. or other terminal degree: 85%. Student/faculty ratio: 18/1. Classes of fewer than 20 students: 44%; of 20 to 49 students: 50%; of 50 or more students: 6%. **Advanced Placement and International Baccalaureate credit:** AP tests may be used for: Credit and/or placement. Scores accepted: 3, 4, 5. International Baccalaureate exams may be used for: Credit only. **Freshmen returning for sophomore year:** 66%. **Graduation rates:** Four-year: 10%; five-year: 28%; six-year: 35%. **Graduate study:** 10% of students pursue further study immediately upon graduation.

COSTS AND FINANCIAL AID

Financial aid office: (330) 972-7032. **Expenses (2006-2007):** Tuition and fees 2006-2007: $8,382 in state, $17,631 out of state; room/board: $7,640. **Financial aid:** Priority filing date for institution's financial aid form: February 1. In 2005-2006, 77% of undergraduates applied for financial aid. Of those, 62% were determined to have financial need; 5% had their need fully met. Average financial aid package (proportion receiving): $6,798 (62%). Average amount of gift aid, such as scholarships or grants (propor-

tion receiving): $4,427 (34%). Average amount of self-help aid, such as work study or loans (proportion receiving): $3,415 (55%). Average need-based loan (excluding PLUS or other private loans): $3,415. Among students who received need-based aid, the average percentage of need met: 49%. Among students who received aid based on merit, the average award (and the proportion receiving): $3,419 (5%). The average athletic scholarship (and the proportion receiving): $9,675 (2%). Average amount of debt of borrowers graduating in 2005: $15,500. Proportion who borrowed: 62%.

CAMPUS LIFE AND EXTRACURRICULAR ACTIVITIES

Campus housing available (% using): coed dorms (82%), women's dorms (5%), men's dorms (5%), sorority housing, fraternity housing, apartment for single students (8%), special housing for disabled students, special housing for international students, other housing options. **Student employment:** During the 2005-2006 academic year, 9% of undergraduates worked on campus. Average per-year earnings: $3,840. **Clubs and organizations:** Number of student organizations: 200. Activities include: choral groups, concert band, dance, drama/theater, jazz band, marching band, music ensembles, musical theater, pep band, radio station, student government, student newspaper, symphony orchestra, television station, yearbook. Number of fraternities: 14; sororities: 8. Average proportion of students who stay on campus on weekends: 30%. **Sports program (2005-2006):** Member of NCAA I. *Men's intercollegiate varsity sports:* baseball, basketball, cross-country, football, golf, riflery, soccer, track and field (indoor), track and field (outdoor). *Women's intercollegiate varsity sports:* basketball, cross-country, riflery, soccer, softball, swimming and diving, tennis, track and field (indoor), track and field (outdoor), volleyball.

SERVICES AND FACILITIES

Basic services: nonremedial tutoring, women's center, placement service, day care, health service, health insurance. **Remedial assistance:** reading, math, writing, study skills. **Counseling services:** minority student, career, military, personal, veteran student, academic, older student, psychological, birth control, religious. **For learning-disabled students:** School does not offer a structured program with separate admission and additional fees. Total undergraduates in learning-disabled program or receiving services: 350. Services include: remedial math, remedial English, reading machines, remedial reading, tape recorders, diagnostic testing service, note-taking services, oral tests, readers, extended time for tests, priority registration, priority seating, texts on tape, other testing accomodations, other. **Library:** Number of titles: 1,233,833; number of current serial subscriptions: 12,438. **Information technology resources:** Students are not required to lease or own a computer. Number of campus computers available to all students: 2,900. School has a wireless network. Approximate number of users that can be accommodated: 4,080. Proportion of college-owned housing units wired for high-speed internet access: 85%. **Campus safety:** Security services offered: 24-hour foot-and-vehicle patrols, late-night transport/escort service, 24-hour emergency telephones, lighted pathways/sidewalks, student patrols, controlled dormitory access (key, security card, etc).

TRANSFER AND INTERNATIONAL STUDENTS

Transfer students: May apply for admission for the following academic terms: Fall, Spring, Summer. Applicants do not need a minimum number of credits to apply. For fall 2005: Transfer applications received: 1,965. Transfer applicants offered admission: 1,304. Transfer applicants enrolled: 836. **International students:** Number of foreign undergraduates: 116 (1% of student body). Number of countries represented: 41. Minimum TOEFL score required: 500 (paper); 173 (computer).

University of Cincinnati

- **Address:** PO Box 210063, Cincinnati, OH 45221-0063
- **Website:** http://www.uc.edu
- **Public**
- **Enrollment:** 16,098 full-time; 3,414 part-time

KEY STATS
✔ **U.S News College Ranking:** third tier, National Universities
✔ **ACT Score (25th/75th percentile):** 21-27
✔ **Tuition:** 2006-2007: $8,883 in state, $22,635 out of state

Selectivity: More selective	**Room/board:** $7,890
Acceptance rate: 76%	**Average debt:** $16,794
Student/faculty ratio: 14/1	**Proportion who borrowed:** 66%

UNDERGRADUATE STUDENT BODY STATS
2005-2006 enrollment: 16,098 full-time; 3,414 part-time. Men: 50%; women: 50%. **Ethnic makeup:** African American: 14%; Asian American: 3%; Hispanic: 2%; White: 81%; International: 1%.

ADMISSIONS FACTS AND FIGURES
Phone: (513) 556-1100. **Email:** admissions@uc.edu. **Website:** http://www.uc.edu. **Application deadlines for fall 2007:** Regular decision: September 1. Early decision: Not offered. Early action: Not offered. Admission can be deferred. **Application fee:** $40. Common application is not accepted. **Admissions requirements/recommendations:** High school units required (recommended): English: 4; Mathematics: 3 (4); Science: 2 (3); Foreign language: 2; Social studies: 2; History: (1); Academic electives: 2; Total units: 16. Tests: The college uses SAT or ACT scores in admissions decisions. Either SAT or ACT required. For admission to the fall 2007 entering class, the school will accept: ACT with writing. **Factors that count in admissions decisions:** *Academic:* Secondary school record: Very important. Class rank: Very important. Letters of recommendation: Not considered. Standardized test scores: Very important. Essay: Considered. *Nonacademic:* Interview: Not considered. Extracurricular activities: Considered. Talent/ability: Not considered. Character/personal qualities: Not considered. Alumni/ae relationship: Not considered. Geographical residence: Not considered. State residency: Not considered. Religious affiliation/commitment: Not considered. Minority status: Not considered. Volunteer work: Not considered. Work experience: Not considered. **Admissions statistics for the fall 2005 entering class:** Total applicants: 11,813. Total accepted: 8,975. Freshmen enrolled: 3,138; 10% were from out of state. Overall acceptance rate: 76%. **Credentials of fall 2005 freshmen:** 19% ranked in the top 10 percent of their high school class; 48% were in the top 25 percent, and 81% were in the top half. (Proportion submitting class standing: 84%.) **Average high school grade point average:** 3.3. **First-year students who submitted SAT scores:** 62%. Scores (25/75 percentile): Verbal: 500-620, Math: 500-640, Combined: 1000-1260. **First-year students submitting ACT scores:** 83%. Scores (25/75 percentile): English: 20-27, Math: 20-27, Composite: 21-27.

ACADEMICS
Year founded: 1819. **Academic calendar:** Quarter. **Degrees offered:** certificate, associate, transfer-associate, terminal-associate, bachelor's, post-bachelor's certificate, master's, first professional, doctorate. **Most popular majors:** 22% business, management, marketing, and related support services, 13% engineering, 10% visual and performing arts, 9% English language and literature/letters, 7% health professions and related clinical sciences. **Major fields of study:** agriculture, agriculture operations, and related sciences; architecture and related services; area, ethnic, cultural, and gender studies; biological and biomedical sciences; business, management, marketing, and related support services; communication, journalism, and related programs; communications technologies/technicians and support services; computer and information sciences and support services; education; engineering; engineering technologies/technicians; English language and literature/letters; family and consumer sciences/human sciences; foreign languages, literatures, and linguistics; health professions and related clinical sciences; history; legal professions and studies; liberal arts and sciences studies, and humanities; mathematics and statistics; multi/interdisciplinary studies; natural resources and conservation; philosophy and religious studies; physical sciences; psychology; public administration and social service professions; security and protective services; social sciences; theology and religious vocations; visual and performing arts. **Areas of required coursework:** arts/fine arts, humanities, computer literacy, mathematics, English (including composition), philosophy, foreign languages, sciences (biological or physical), history, social science, other. **Pre-professional programs:** pre-law, pre-medicine, pre-pharmacy. **Special academic programs:** accelerated program, cooperative (work-study plan) program, distance learning, double major, English as a Second Language (ESL) program, honors program, independent study, internships, liberal arts/career combination, study abroad, teacher certificate program, weekend college. **Teacher certification offered in:** early childhood, special education, elementary, vo-tech, middle/junior high, adult education, secondary, bilingual/bicultural. **Cooperative education programs:** art, business, engineering, other. **Reserve Officers Training Corps (ROTC):** Army ROTC: Offered on campus; Air Force ROTC: Offered on campus. **Faculty and instruction (2005-2006):** Total instructional faculty: 1,200 full-time, 41 part-time (62% men; 38% women; 17% minorities). Full-time faculty with Ph.D. or other terminal degree: 67%. Student/faculty ratio: 14/1. Classes of fewer than 20 students: 47%; of 20 to 49 students: 47%; of 50 or more students: 6%. **Advanced Placement and International Baccalaureate credit:** AP tests may be used for: Credit and/or placement. International Baccalaureate exams may be used for: Credit and/or placement. **Freshmen returning for sophomore year:** 77%. **Graduation rates:** Four-year: 17%; five-year: 43%; six-year: 50%.

COSTS AND FINANCIAL AID
Financial aid office: (513) 556-6982. **Expenses (2006-2007):** Tuition and fees 2006-2007: $8,883 in state, $22,635 out of state; room/board: $7,890. Estimated books and supplies: $1,140; transportation: $800; personal expenses: $4,870. **Financial aid:** In 2005-2006, 68% of undergraduates applied for financial aid. Of those, 56% were determined to have financial need; 6% had their need fully met. Average financial aid package (proportion receiving): $7,476 (54%). Average amount of gift aid, such as scholarships or grants (proportion receiving): $4,449 (26%). Average amount of self-help aid, such as work study or loans (proportion receiving): $3,098 (17%). Average need-based loan (excluding PLUS or other private loans): $3,888. Among students who received need-based aid, the average percentage of need met: 63%. Among students who received aid based on merit, the average award (and the proportion receiving): $4,696 (15%). The average athletic scholarship (and the proportion receiving): $15,205 (1%). Average amount of debt of borrowers graduating in 2005: $16,794. Proportion who borrowed: 66%.

CAMPUS LIFE AND EXTRACURRICULAR ACTIVITIES
Campus housing available: coed dorms, women's dorms, men's dorms, sorority housing, fraternity housing, apartments for married students, apartment for single students, special housing for international students. Students who live in college-owned, operated, or affiliated housing: 20%. Activities include: choral groups, concert band, dance, drama/theater, jazz band, marching band, music ensembles, musical theater, opera, pep band, radio station, student government, student newspaper, student film society, symphony orchestra, yearbook. **Sports program (2005-2006):** Member of NCAA I. *Men's intercollegiate varsity sports:* baseball, basketball, cross-country, football, golf, soccer, swimming and diving, track and field (outdoor). *Women's intercollegiate varsity sports:* basketball, crew, cross-country, golf, soccer, swimming and diving, tennis, track and field (indoor), track and field (outdoor), volleyball.

SERVICES AND FACILITIES
Basic services: women's center, day care, health service, health insurance. **Remedial assistance:** reading, math, writing, study skills. **Counseling services:** career, older student. **For learning-disabled students:** Services include: remedial math, remedial English, remedial reading. **Information technology resources:** Students are not required to lease or own a computer. **Campus safety:** Security services offered: 24-hour foot-and-vehicle patrols, late-night transport/escort service, 24-hour emergency telephones, lighted pathways/sidewalks, controlled dormitory access (key, security card, etc).

TRANSFER AND INTERNATIONAL STUDENTS
Transfer students: May apply for admission for the following academic terms: Fall, Winter, Spring, Summer. Applicants do not need a minimum number of credits to apply. For fall 2005: Transfer applications received: 2,452. Transfer applicants offered admission: 1,660. Transfer applicants enrolled: 1,256. **International students:** Number of foreign undergraduates: 242 (1% of student body). Minimum TOEFL score required: 515 (paper); 185 (computer).

University of Dayton

■ **Address:** 300 College Park, Dayton, OH 45469
■ **Website:** http://www.udayton.edu
■ **Private; Religious affiliation:** Roman Catholic (Marianist)
■ **Enrollment:** 6,913 full-time; 513 part-time

KEY STATS

✔ **U.S News College Ranking:** 105, National Universities
✔ **ACT Score (25th/75th percentile):** 23-28
✔ **Tuition:** 2006-2007: $23,970

Selectivity: More selective	**Room/board:** $7,190
Acceptance rate: 80%	**Average debt:** $20,151
Student/faculty ratio: 13/1	**Proportion who borrowed:** 67%

UNDERGRADUATE STUDENT BODY STATS

2005-2006 enrollment: 6,913 full-time; 513 part-time. Men: 51%; women: 49%. **Ethnic makeup:** African American: 4%; Asian American: 1%; Hispanic: 2%; White: 92%. **Religious preference:** Protestant: 9%; No preference: 3%; Unknown: 18%; Roman Catholic (Marianist): 67%; Other: 3%.

ADMISSIONS FACTS AND FIGURES

Phone: (937) 229-4411. **Email:** admission@udayton.edu. **Website:** http://www.udayton.edu. **Application deadlines for fall 2007:** Regular decision: Rolling. Early decision: Not offered. Early action: Not offered. Admission can be deferred. Common application is not accepted. **To apply online, go to:** http://admission.udayton.edu/apply/application_login.asp. **Admissions requirements/recommendations:** High school units required (recommended): English: (4); Mathematics: (3); Science: (2); Social studies: (3); Academic electives: (4); Total units: (16). Tests: The college uses SAT or ACT scores in admissions decisions. Either SAT or ACT required. For admission to the fall 2007 entering class, the school will accept: ACT with writing, ACT without writing. Campus visit: Recommended. Admissions interview: Recommended. Off-campus interview: May be arranged. **Factors that count in admissions decisions:** *Academic:* Secondary school record: Very important. Class rank: Important. Letters of recommendation: Considered. Standardized test scores: Important. Essay: Considered. *Nonacademic:* Interview: Considered. Extracurricular activities: Considered. Talent/ability: Important. Character/personal qualities: Considered. Alumni/ae relationship: Considered. Geographical residence: Not considered. State residency: Not considered. Religious affiliation/commitment: Not considered. Minority status: Considered. Volunteer work: Considered. Work experience: Considered. **Other schools with the greatest overlap in applicants:** Miami University–Oxford; Ohio State University–Columbus; Ohio University; University of Cincinnati; Xavier University. **Admissions statistics for the fall 2005 entering class:** Total applicants: 8,675. Total accepted: 6,899. Freshmen enrolled: 1,981; 41% were from out of state. Overall acceptance rate: 80%. **Size of waiting list:** 296 applicants; enrolled from waiting list: 4. **Credentials of fall 2005 freshmen:** 24% ranked in the top 10 percent of their high school class; 50% were in the top 25 percent, and 81% were in the top half. (Proportion submitting class standing: 70%.) **Average high school grade point average:** 3.5. **First-year students who submitted SAT scores:** 43%. Scores (25/75 percentile): Verbal: 520-620, Math: 540-650, Combined: 1060-1270. **First-year students submitting ACT scores:** 65%. Scores (25/75 percentile): English: 22-28, Math: 22-27, Composite: 23-28.

ACADEMICS

Year founded: 1850. **Academic calendar:** Semester. **Degrees offered:** bachelor's, master's, post-master's certificate, first professional, doctorate. **Most popular majors:** 23% business, management, marketing, and related support services, 13% education, 11% engineering, 10% communication, journalism, and related programs, 5% psychology. **Major fields of study:** area, ethnic, cultural, and gender studies; biological and biomedical sciences; business, management, marketing, and related support services; communication, journalism, and related programs; computer and information sciences and support services; education; engineering; engineering technologies/technicians; English language and literature/letters; family and consumer sciences/human sciences; foreign languages, literatures, and linguistics; health professions and related clinical sciences; history; legal professions and studies; liberal arts and sciences studies, and humanities; mathematics and statistics; multi/interdisciplinary studies; parks, recreation, leisure, and fitness studies; philosophy and religious studies; physical sciences; psychology; security and protective services; social sciences; visual and performing arts. **Areas of required coursework:** arts/fine arts, humanities, mathematics, English (including composition), philosophy, sciences (biological or physical), history, social science, other. **Pre-professional programs:** pre-law, pre-dentistry, pre-medicine, pre-veterinary science, other. **Special academic programs (% participation):** accelerated program (2%), cooperative (work-study plan) program, cross-registration, distance learning, double major (9%), dual enrollment, English as a Second Language (ESL), exchange student program (domestic), honors program (2%), independent study, internships, liberal arts/career combination, student-designed major, study abroad (41%), teacher certificate program. **Teacher certification offered in:** early childhood, special education, elementary, middle/junior high, secondary, bilingual/bicultural. **Cooperative education programs:** art, business, computer science, engineering, humanities, natural science, social/behavioral science, technologies, other. **Reserve Officers Training Corps (ROTC):** Army ROTC: Offered on campus; Air Force ROTC: Offered at cooperating institution (Wright State University). **Faculty and instruction (2005-2006):** Total instructional faculty: 446 full-time, 499 part-time. Full-time faculty with Ph.D. or other terminal degree: 93%. Student/faculty ratio: 13/1. Classes of fewer than 20 students: 34%; of 20 to 49 students: 62%; of 50 or more students: 4%. **Advanced Placement and International Baccalaureate credit:** AP tests may be used for: Credit and/or placement. Scores accepted: 3, 4, 5. International Baccalaureate exams may be used for: Credit and/or placement. **Freshmen returning for sophomore year:** 87%. **Graduation rates:** Four-year: 60%; five-year: 76%; six-year: 79%. **Graduate study:** 53% of students pursue further study immediately upon graduation. Fields in which graduates pursue further study: Master of Business Administration (MBA), 20%; law, 6%; medicine, 11%; dentistry, 1%; engineering, 2%; education, 20%; arts and sciences, 32%.

COSTS AND FINANCIAL AID

Financial aid office: (937) 229-4311. **Expenses (2006-2007):** Tuition and fees 2006-2007: $23,970; room/board: $7,190. Estimated books and supplies: $800; transportation: $500; personal expenses: $1,770. **Financial aid:** Priority filing date for institution's financial aid form: March 31. In 2005-2006, 92% of undergraduates applied for financial aid. Of those, 59% were determined to have financial need; 52% had their need fully met. Average financial aid package (proportion receiving): $7,187 (57%). Average amount of gift aid, such as scholarships or grants (proportion receiving): $2,381 (56%). Average amount of self-help aid, such as work study or loans (proportion receiving): $3,848 (52%). Average need-based loan (excluding PLUS or other private loans): $3,631. Among students who received need-based aid, the average percentage of need met: 93%. Among students who received aid based on merit, the average award (and the proportion receiving): $8,793 (15%). The average athletic scholarship (and the proportion receiving): $15,236 (1%). Average amount of debt of borrowers graduating in 2005: $20,151. Proportion who borrowed: 67%.

CAMPUS LIFE AND EXTRACURRICULAR ACTIVITIES

Campus housing available (% using): coed dorms (49%), sorority housing (1%), fraternity housing (1%), apartment for single students (19%), special housing for disabled students (0%), special housing for international students (0%), other housing options (30%). Students who live in college-owned, operated, or affiliated housing: 79%. **Student employment:** During the 2005-2006 academic year, 50% of undergraduates worked on campus. Average per-year earnings: $1,090. **Clubs and organizations:** Number of student organizations: 170. Activities include: choral groups, concert band, dance, drama/theater, jazz band, literary magazine, marching band, music ensembles, musical theater, opera, pep band, radio station, student government, student newspaper, symphony orchestra, television station, yearbook. Number of fraternities: 12; sororities: 9. Proportion of men in fraternities: 15%; of women in sororities: 19%. Average proportion of students who stay on campus on weekends: 85%. **Sports program (2005-2006):** Member of NCAA I. *Men's intercollegiate varsity sports:* baseball, basketball, cross-country, football, golf, soccer, tennis. *Women's intercollegiate varsity sports:* basketball, crew, cross-country, golf, soccer, softball, tennis, track and field (indoor), track and field (outdoor), volleyball.

SERVICES AND FACILITIES

Basic services: nonremedial tutoring, women's center, placement service, day care, health service, health insurance. **Remedial assistance:** reading, math, writing, study skills. **Counseling services:** minority student, career, military, personal, veteran student, academic, older student, psychological, religious. **For learning-disabled students:** School does not offer a structured program with separate admission and additional fees. Total undergraduates in learning-disabled program or receiving services: 600. Services include: remedial math, remedial English, reading machines, tape recorders, other special classes, note-taking services, oral tests, learning center, readers, extended time for tests, tutors, priority registration, priority seating, proof-reading services, texts on tape, typist/scribe, other testing accomodations, waiver of foreign language degree requirement, waiver of math degree requirement. **Library:** Number of titles: 1,333,310; number of current serial subscriptions: 8,425. **Information technology resources:** Students are required to lease or own a computer. Number of campus computers available to all students: 7,675. School has a wireless network. Approximate number of users that can be accommodated: 9,000. Proportion of college-owned housing units wired for high-speed internet access: 100%. **Campus safety:** Security services offered: 24-hour foot-and-vehicle patrols, late-night transport/escort service, 24-hour emergency telephones, lighted pathways/sidewalks, student patrols, controlled dormitory access (key, security card, etc.).

TRANSFER AND INTERNATIONAL STUDENTS

Transfer students: May apply for admission for the following academic terms: Fall, Winter, Summer. Applicants need a minimum number of credits to apply. For fall 2005: Transfer applications received: 776. Transfer applicants offered admission: 244. Transfer applicants enrolled: 123. **International students:** Number of foreign undergraduates: 29. Number of countries represented: 20. Minimum TOEFL score required: 523 (paper); 193 (computer). Average TOEFL score: 550 (paper).

University of Findlay

- **Address:** 1000 N. Main Street, Findlay, OH 45840
- **Website:** http://www.findlay.edu
- **Private; Religious affiliation:** Churches of God General Conference
- **Enrollment:** 2,648 full-time; 953 part-time

KEY STATS

✔ **U.S News College Ranking:** third tier, Universities–Master's (Midwest)
✔ **ACT Score (25th/75th percentile):** 20-25
✔ **Tuition:** 2006-2007: $22,796

Selectivity: Selective	**Room/board:** $7,792
Acceptance rate: 70%	**Average debt:** N/A
Student/faculty ratio: 15/1	**Proportion who borrowed:** 84%

UNDERGRADUATE STUDENT BODY STATS

2005-2006 enrollment: 2,648 full-time; 953 part-time. Men: 40%; women: 60%. **Ethnic makeup:** African American: 3%; Asian American: 1%; Hispanic: 1%; White: 90%; International: 4%. **Religious preference:** Roman Catholic: 31%; Protestant: 35%; Jewish: 1%; No preference: 7%; Unknown: 19%; Churches of God General Conference: 5%.

ADMISSIONS FACTS AND FIGURES

Phone: (800) 548-0932. **Email:** admissions@findlay.edu. **Website:** http://www.findlay.edu. **Application deadlines for fall 2007:** Regular decision: July 1. Early decision: Not offered. Early action: Not offered. Admission can be deferred. **Application fee:** None. Common application is accepted. **To apply online, go to:** http://www.findlay.edu/admissions/info/undergraduate/apply/default.htm. **Admissions requirements/recommendations:** High school units required (recommended): English: (4); Mathematics: (2); Science: (4); Foreign language: (2); Social studies: (2); History: (1); Academic electives: (1); Total units: (16). Tests: The college uses SAT or ACT scores in admissions decisions. Either SAT or ACT required. For admission to the fall 2007 entering class, the school will accept: ACT with writing. Campus visit: Recommended. Admissions interview: Recommended. Off-campus interview: May be arranged. **Factors that count in admissions decisions:** *Academic:* Secondary school record: Very important. Class rank: Considered. Letters of recommendation: Important. Standardized test scores: Very important. Essay: Considered. *Nonacademic:* Interview: Important. Extracurricular activities: Considered. Talent/ability: Considered. Character/personal qualities: Considered. Alumni/ae relationship: Considered. Geographical residence: Not considered. State residency: Not considered. Religious affiliation/commitment: Considered. Minority status: Not considered. Volunteer work: Considered. Work experience: Not considered. **Other schools with the greatest overlap in applicants:** Ashland University; Bowling Green State University; Heidelberg College; Ohio Northern University; Tiffin University. **Admissions statistics for the fall 2005 entering class:** Total applicants: 2,485. Total accepted: 1,744. Freshmen

enrolled: 642; 19% were from out of state. Overall acceptance rate: 70%. **Credentials of fall 2005 freshmen:** 22% ranked in the top 10 percent of their high school class; 50% were in the top 25 percent, and 80% were in the top half. (Proportion submitting class standing: 89%.) **Average high school grade point average:** 3.3. **First-year students who submitted SAT scores:** 24%. Scores (25/75 percentile): Verbal: 470-580, Math: 470-580, Combined: 940-1160. **First-year students submitting ACT scores:** 76%. Scores (25/75 percentile): English: N/A, Math: N/A, Composite: 20-25.

ACADEMICS

Year founded: 1882. **Academic calendar:** Semester. **Degrees offered:** associate, bachelor's, master's. **Most popular majors:** 29% business, management, marketing, and related support services, 18% health professions and related clinical sciences, 16% education, 7% agriculture, agriculture operations, and related sciences, 5% computer and information sciences and support services. **Major fields of study:** agriculture, agriculture operations, and related sciences; biological and biomedical sciences; business, management, marketing, and related support services; communication, journalism, and related programs; computer and information sciences and support services; education; engineering technologies/technicians; English language and literature/letters; foreign languages, literatures, and linguistics; health professions and related clinical sciences; history; legal professions and studies; mathematics and statistics; parks, recreation, leisure, and fitness studies; philosophy and religious studies; psychology; public administration and social service professions; security and protective services; social sciences; visual and performing arts. **Areas of required coursework:** arts/fine arts, humanities, computer literacy, mathematics, English (including composition), foreign languages, sciences (biological or physical), social science. **Pre-professional programs:** pre-law, pre-medicine, pre-theology, pre-veterinary science. **Special academic programs (% participation):** accelerated program (6%), cooperative (work-study plan) program, distance learning (12%), double major (24%), dual enrollment (8%), English as a Second Language (ESL) (5%), honors program, independent study (2%), internships (2%), liberal arts/career combination, student-designed major (1%), study abroad (1%), teacher certificate program (2%), weekend college (2%). **Teacher certification offered in:** early childhood, special education, elementary, middle/junior high, adult education, secondary, bilingual/bicultural. **Cooperative education programs:** business, computer science, health professions, social/behavioral science, other. **Reserve Officers Training Corps (ROTC):** Army ROTC: Offered at cooperating institution (Bowling Green State University); Air Force ROTC: Offered at cooperating institution (Bowling Green State University). **Faculty and instruction (2005-2006):** Total instructional faculty: 175 full-time, 156 part-time (54% men; 46% women; 6% minorities). Full-time faculty with Ph.D. or other terminal degree: 53%. Student/faculty ratio: 15/1. Classes of fewer than 20 students: 57%; of 20 to 49 students: 39%; of 50 or more students: 4%. **Advanced Placement and International Baccalaureate credit:** AP tests may be used for: Credit and/or placement. Scores accepted: 4. International Baccalaureate exams may be used for: Credit and/or placement. **Freshmen returning for sophomore year:** 72%. **Graduation rates:** Four-year: 42%; five-year: 52%; six-year: 53%. **Graduate study:** 37% of students pursue further study within one year.

COSTS AND FINANCIAL AID

Financial aid office: (419) 434-4792. **Expenses (2006-2007):** Tuition and fees 2006-2007: $22,796; room/board: $7,792. Estimated books and supplies: $1,050. **Financial aid:** Priority filing date for institution's financial aid form: August 1; deadline: September 1. In 2005-2006, 72% of undergraduates applied for financial aid. Of those, 72% were determined to have financial need; 9% had their need fully met. Average financial aid package (proportion receiving): $19,308 (72%). Average amount of gift aid, such as scholarships or grants (proportion receiving): $8,215 (72%). Average amount of self-help aid, such as work study or loans (proportion receiving): $8,100 (72%). Average need-based loan (excluding PLUS or other private loans): $5,200. Among students who received need-based aid, the average percentage of need met: 75%. Among students who received aid based on merit, the average award (and the proportion receiving): $8,100 (14%). The average athletic scholarship (and the proportion receiving): $7,397 (12%). Proportion who borrowed: 84%.

CAMPUS LIFE AND EXTRACURRICULAR ACTIVITIES

Campus housing available (% using): coed dorms (52%), women's dorms (26%), sorority housing (1%), fraternity housing (1%), apartment for single students (15%), other housing options (5%). Students who live in college-owned, operated, or affiliated housing: 47%. **Student employment:** During the 2005-2006 academic year, 26% of undergraduates worked on campus. Average per-year earnings: $313. **Clubs and organizations:** Number of student organizations: 50. Activities include: choral groups, concert band, dance, drama/theater, jazz band, literary magazine, marching band, music ensembles, musical theater, pep band, radio station, student government, student newspaper, television station. Number of fraternities: 2; sororities: 2. Proportion of men in fraternities: 4%; of women in sororities: 3%. Average proportion of students who stay on campus on weekends: 30%. **Sports program (2005-2006):** Member of NCAA II. *Men's intercollegiate varsity sports:* baseball, basketball, cross-country, equestrian Sports, football, golf, ice hockey, soccer, swimming and diving, tennis, track and field (indoor), track and field (outdoor), volleyball, wrestling. *Women's intercollegiate varsity sports:* basketball, cross-country, equestrian sports, golf, ice hockey, soccer, softball, swimming and diving, tennis, track and field (indoor), track and field (outdoor), volleyball.

SERVICES AND FACILITIES

Basic services: nonremedial tutoring, placement service, health service, health insurance. **Remedial assistance:** reading, math, writing, study skills. **Counseling services:** minority student, career, military, personal, veteran student, academic, older student, psychological, birth control, religious. **For learning-disabled students:** School does not offer a structured program with separate admission and additional fees. Total undergraduates in learning-disabled program or receiving services: 29. Services include: remedial math, remedial English, reading machines, remedial reading, tape recorders, untimed tests, note-taking services, oral tests, readers, extended time for tests, tutors, priority registration, other testing accomodations. **Library:** Number of titles: 143,945; number of current serial subscriptions: 804. **Information technology resources:** Students are not required to lease or own a computer. Number of campus computers available to all students: 274. School has a wireless network. Proportion of college-owned housing units wired for high-speed internet access: 100%. **Campus safety:** Security services offered: 24-hour foot-and-vehicle patrols, 24-hour emergency telephones, lighted pathways/sidewalks, controlled dormitory access (key, security card, etc).

TRANSFER AND INTERNATIONAL STUDENTS

Transfer students: May apply for admission for the following academic terms: Fall, Spring, Summer. Applicants need a minimum number of credits to apply. For fall 2005: Transfer applications received: 265. Transfer applicants offered admission: 366. Transfer applicants enrolled: 138. **International students:** Number of foreign undergraduates: 128 (4% of student body). Number of countries represented: 24. Minimum TOEFL score required: 500 (paper); 173 (computer).

University of Rio Grande

- **Address:** PO Box 500, Rio Grande, OH 45674
- **Website:** http://www.rio.edu
- **Private**
- **Enrollment:** 1,699 full-time; 442 part-time

KEY STATS
- ✔ **U.S News College Ranking:** fourth tier, Universities–Master's (Midwest)
- ✔ **ACT Score (25th/75th percentile):** 17-22
- ✔ **Tuition:** 2006-2007: $13,575

Selectivity: Less selective	**Room/board:** $6,788
Acceptance rate: 100%	**Average debt:** $12,136
Student/faculty ratio: N/A	**Proportion who borrowed:** 80%

UNDERGRADUATE STUDENT BODY STATS

2005-2006 enrollment: 1,699 full-time; 442 part-time. Men: 39%; women: 61%. **Ethnic makeup:** African American: 3%; Asian American: 1%; Hispanic: 1%; White: 96%.

ADMISSIONS FACTS AND FIGURES

Phone: (740) 245-7208. **Email:** admissions@rio.edu. **Website:** http://www.rio.edu. **Application deadlines for fall 2007:** Regular decision: Rolling. Early decision: Not offered. Early action: Not offered. **Application fee:** $15. Common application is accepted. **Admissions requirements/recommendations:** High school units required (recommended): English: 0 (4); Mathematics: 0 (3); Science: 0 (3); Foreign language: 0 (2); Social studies: 0 (2); History: 0 (2); Academic electives: 0 (9); Total units: 0 (21). Tests: The college does not use SAT or ACT scores in admissions decisions. Neither

SAT nor ACT required. For admission to the fall 2007 entering class, the school will accept: ACT with writing, ACT without writing. Campus visit: Recommended. Admissions interview: Recommended. Off-campus interview: May be arranged. **Factors that count in admissions decisions:** *Academic:* Secondary school record: Not considered. Class rank: Not considered. Letters of recommendation: Not considered. Standardized test scores: Not considered. Essay: Not considered. *Nonacademic:* Interview: Not considered. Extracurricular activities: Not considered. Talent/ability: Not considered. Character/personal qualities: Not considered. Alumni/ae relationship: Not considered. Geographical residence: Not considered. State residency: Considered. Religious affiliation/commitment: Not considered. Minority status: Not considered. Volunteer work: Not considered. Work experience: Not considered. **Other schools with the greatest overlap in applicants:** Marshall University; Ohio University; Shawnee State University. **Admissions statistics for the fall 2005 entering class:** Total applicants: 1,575. Total accepted: 1,575. Freshmen enrolled: 473; Overall acceptance rate: 100%. **Credentials of fall 2005 freshmen:** 11% ranked in the top 10 percent of their high school class; 32% were in the top 25 percent.

ACADEMICS

Year founded: 1876. **Academic calendar:** Semester. **Degrees offered:** certificate, associate, bachelor's, master's. **Most popular majors:** 43% health professions and related clinical sciences, 25% business, management, marketing, and related support services, 17% communication, journalism, and related programs, 12% engineering technologies/technicians, 4% computer and information sciences and support services. **Major fields of study:** area, ethnic, cultural, and gender studies; biological and biomedical sciences; business, management, marketing, and related support services; communication, journalism, and related programs; computer and information sciences and support services; education; engineering technologies/technicians; English language and literature/letters; health professions and related clinical sciences; mathematics and statistics; natural resources and conservation; parks, recreation, leisure, and fitness studies; physical sciences; psychology; public administration and social service professions; social sciences; visual and performing arts. **Areas of required coursework:** humanities, computer literacy, mathematics, English (including composition), sciences (biological or physical), history. **Special academic programs (% participation):** cooperative (work-study plan) program (10%), distance learning (2%), double major (5%), English as a Second Language (ESL) (1%), honors program (5%), student-designed major (1%), study abroad (1%). **Teacher certification offered in:** early childhood, special education, vo-tech, middle/junior high, secondary. **Cooperative education programs:** business, technologies. **Reserve Officers Training Corps (ROTC):** Army ROTC: Offered at cooperating institution (Ohio University). **Faculty and instruction (2005-2006):** Total instructional faculty: N/A. Classes of fewer than 20 students: 76%; of 20 to 49 students: 23%; of 50 or more students: 1%. **Freshmen returning for sophomore year:** 62%. **Graduation rates:** Four-year: 25%; five-year: 35%; six-year: 43%.

COSTS AND FINANCIAL AID

Financial aid office: (740) 245-7218. **Expenses (2006-2007):** Tuition and fees 2006-2007: $13,575; room/board: $6,788. Estimated books and supplies: $1,000; transportation: $3,252; personal expenses: $1,750. **Financial aid:** Priority filing date for institution's financial aid form: March 15; deadline: August 10. In 2005-2006, 66% of undergraduates applied for financial aid. Of those, 66% were determined to have financial need; Average financial aid package (proportion receiving): $8,081 (66%). Average amount of gift aid, such as scholarships or grants (proportion receiving): N/A (46%). Average amount of self-help aid, such as work study or loans (proportion receiving): N/A (58%). Among students who received aid based on merit, the average award (and the proportion receiving): $0 (0%). The average athletic scholarship (and the proportion receiving): $0 (0%). Average amount of debt of borrowers graduating in 2005: $12,136. Proportion who borrowed: 80%.

CAMPUS LIFE AND EXTRACURRICULAR ACTIVITIES

Campus housing available: coed dorms, women's dorms, men's dorms. **Student employment:** During the 2005-2006 academic year, 15% of undergraduates worked on campus. Average per-year earnings: $3,000. **Clubs and organizations:** Number of student organizations: 33. Activities include: choral groups, dance, drama/theater, jazz band, literary magazine, music ensembles, musical theater, pep band, radio station, student government, student newspaper. Number of fraternities: 6; sororities: 5. Average proportion of students who stay on campus on weekends: 20%. **Sports program (2005-2006):** Member of NAIA. *Men's intercollegiate varsity sports:* baseball, basketball, cross-country, soccer, track and field (indoor), track and field (outdoor). *Women's intercollegiate varsity sports:* basketball, cross-country, softball, track and field (indoor), track and field (outdoor), volleyball.

SERVICES AND FACILITIES

Basic services: nonremedial tutoring, health service, health insurance. **Remedial assistance:** reading, math, writing, study skills. **Counseling services:** career, personal, veteran student, academic. **For learning-disabled students:** School does not offer a structured program with separate admission and additional fees. Total undergraduates in learning-disabled program or receiving services: 102. Services include: remedial math, remedial English, reading machines, remedial reading, tape recorders, other special classes, untimed tests, note-taking services, oral tests, learning center, readers, extended time for tests, tutors, early syllabus, proofreading services, texts on tape, typist/scribe, exams on tape or computer, other testing accomodations. **Library:** Number of titles: 124,164; number of current serial subscriptions: 320. **Information technology resources:** Students are not required to lease or own a computer. Number of campus computers available to all students: 631. School has a wireless network. Approximate number of users that can be accommodated: 760. Proportion of college-owned housing units wired for high-speed internet access: 100%. **Campus safety:** Security services offered: 24-hour foot-and-vehicle patrols, late-night transport/escort service, 24-hour emergency telephones, lighted pathways/sidewalks, controlled dormitory access (key, security card, etc).

TRANSFER AND INTERNATIONAL STUDENTS

Transfer students: May apply for admission for the following academic terms: Fall, Spring, Summer. Applicants do not need a minimum number of credits to apply. **International students:** Number of foreign undergraduates: 9 (1% of student body). Minimum TOEFL score required: 400 (paper); 97 (computer). Average TOEFL score: 550 (paper).

University of Toledo

■ **Address:** 2801 W. Bancroft, Toledo, OH 43606
■ **Website:** http://www.utoledo.edu
■ **Public**
■ **Enrollment:** 13,078 full-time; 2,980 part-time

KEY STATS

✔ **U.S News College Ranking:** fourth tier, National Universities
✔ **ACT Score (25th/75th percentile):** 19-25
✔ **Tuition:** 2005-2006: $7,494 in state, $16,305 out of state
  Selectivity: Selective   **Room/board:** N/A
  Acceptance rate: 80%   **Average debt:** N/A
  Student/faculty ratio: 18/1   **Proportion who borrowed:** N/A

UNDERGRADUATE STUDENT BODY STATS

2005-2006 enrollment: 13,078 full-time; 2,980 part-time. Men: 50%; women: 50%. **Ethnic makeup:** African American: 13%; Asian American: 2%; Hispanic: 3%; White: 81%; International: 1%.

ADMISSIONS FACTS AND FIGURES

Phone: (419) 530-8888. **Email:** enroll@utnet.utoledo.edu. **Website:** http://www.utoledo.edu. **Application deadlines for fall 2007:** Regular decision: Rolling. Early decision: Not offered. Early action: Not offered. Admission can be deferred. **Application fee:** $40. Common application is not accepted. **To apply online, go to:** http://undergradadmission.utoledo.edu/pages/apply.asp. **Admissions requirements/recommendations:** High school units required (recommended): English: 4 (4); Mathematics: 3 (3); Science: 3 (3); Foreign language: (2); Social studies: 3 (3); History: (1); Total units: 13 (16). Tests: The college uses SAT or ACT scores in admissions decisions. Either SAT or ACT required. For admission to the fall 2007 entering class, the school will accept: ACT with writing. Campus visit: Recommended. Admissions interview: Neither required nor recommended. Off-campus interview: May be arranged. **Factors that count in admissions decisions:** *Academic:* Secondary school record: Very important. Class rank: Not considered. Letters of recommendation: Not considered. Standardized test scores: Very important. Essay: Not considered. *Nonacademic:* Interview: Not considered. Extracurricular activities: Not considered. Talent/ability: Not considered. Character/personal qualities: Not considered. Alumni/ae relationship: Not considered. Geographical residence: Not considered. State residency: Very important.

Religious affiliation/commitment: Not considered. Minority status: Not considered. Volunteer work: Not considered. Work experience: Not considered. **Admissions statistics for the fall 2005 entering class:** Total applicants: 8,126. Total accepted: 6,474. Freshmen enrolled: 3,160; 3% were from out of state. Overall acceptance rate: 80%. **Credentials of fall 2005 freshmen:** 16% ranked in the top 10 percent of their high school class; 37% were in the top 25 percent, and 64% were in the top half. (Proportion submitting class standing: 78%.) **Average high school grade point average:** 3.0. **First-year students who submitted SAT scores:** 27%. Scores (25/75 percentile): Verbal: 450-570, Math: 460-600, Combined: 910-1170. **First-year students submitting ACT scores:** 88%. Scores (25/75 percentile): English: 17-24, Math: 17-25, Composite: 19-25.

ACADEMICS

Year founded: 1872. **Academic calendar:** Semester. **Degrees offered:** certificate, associate, bachelor's, post-bachelor's certificate, master's, post-master's certificate, first professional, doctorate. **Most popular majors:** 22% business, management, marketing, and related support services, 13% education, 12% engineering, 11% health professions and related clinical sciences, 5% engineering technologies/technicians. **Major fields of study:** area, ethnic, cultural, and gender studies; biological and biomedical sciences; business, management, marketing, and related support services; communication, journalism, and related programs; computer and information sciences and support services; education; engineering; engineering technologies/technicians; English language and literature/letters; foreign languages, literatures, and linguistics; health professions and related clinical sciences; history; legal professions and studies; liberal arts and sciences studies, and humanities; mathematics and statistics; multi/interdisciplinary studies; natural resources and conservation; parks, recreation, leisure, and fitness studies; philosophy and religious studies; physical sciences; psychology; public administration and social service professions; security and protective services; social sciences; visual and performing arts. **Areas of required coursework:** arts/fine arts, humanities, mathematics, English (including composition), sciences (biological or physical), social science. **Pre-professional programs:** pre-law, pre-pharmacy. **Special academic programs:** accelerated program, cooperative (work-study plan) program, cross-registration, distance learning, double major, dual enrollment, exchange student program (domestic), honors program, independent study, internships, liberal arts/career combination, student-designed major, study abroad, teacher certificate program, weekend college. **Teacher certification offered in:** early childhood, special education, elementary, middle/junior high, secondary, bilingual/bicultural. **Cooperative education programs:** business, education, engineering. **Reserve Officers Training Corps (ROTC):** Army ROTC: Offered on campus; Air Force ROTC: Offered at cooperating institution (Bowling Green State University). **Faculty and instruction (2005-2006):** Total instructional faculty: 813 full-time, 436 part-time (59% men; 41% women; 15% minorities). Full-time faculty with Ph.D. or other terminal degree: 73%. Student/faculty ratio: 18/1. Classes of fewer than 20 students: 35%; of 20 to 49 students: 55%; of 50 or more students: 10%. **Advanced Placement and International Baccalaureate credit:** AP tests may be used for: Credit and/or placement. Scores accepted: 3. International Baccalaureate exams may be used for: Credit only. **Freshmen returning for sophomore year:** 69%. **Graduation rates:** Four-year: 17%; five-year: 38%; six-year: 43%.

COSTS AND FINANCIAL AID

Financial aid office: (419) 530-8700. **Expenses (2005-2006):** Tuition and fees 2005-2006: $7,494 in state, $16,305 out of state; room/board: N/A. **Financial aid:** Priority filing date for institution's financial aid form: April 1.

CAMPUS LIFE AND EXTRACURRICULAR ACTIVITIES

Campus housing available: coed dorms, women's dorms, men's dorms, sorority housing, fraternity housing, special housing for disabled students, special housing for international students. Students who live in college-owned, operated, or affiliated housing: 18%. **Clubs and organizations:** Number of student organizations: 146. Activities include: choral groups, concert band, dance, drama/theater, jazz band, literary magazine, marching band, music ensembles, musical theater, opera, pep band, radio station, student government, student newspaper, student film society, symphony orchestra, television station. Number of fraternities: 16; sororities: 12. Proportion of men in fraternities: 5%; of women in sororities: 5%. **Sports program (2005-2006):** Member of NCAA I. *Men's intercollegiate varsity sports:* baseball, basketball, cross-country, football, golf, swimming and diving, tennis, track and field (indoor), track and field (outdoor). *Women's intercollegiate varsity sports:* basketball, cross-country, golf, soccer, softball, swimming and diving, tennis, track and field (indoor), track and field (outdoor), volleyball.

SERVICES AND FACILITIES

Basic services: nonremedial tutoring, women's center, placement service, day care, health service, health insurance. **Remedial assistance:** reading, math, writing, study skills. **Counseling services:** minority student, career, military, personal, veteran student, academic, older student, psychological. **For learning-disabled students:** School does not offer a structured program with separate admission and additional fees. Services include: remedial math, remedial English, reading machines, remedial reading, tape recorders, videotaped classes, untimed tests, note-taking services, oral tests, learning center, readers, extended time for tests, tutors, priority registration, substitution of courses, texts on tape, typist/scribe, exams on tape or computer, take home exams, other testing accomodations, other. **Library:** Number of titles: 2,006,000; number of current serial subscriptions: 3,181. **Information technology resources:** Students are not required to lease or own a computer. Number of campus computers available to all students: 2,800. School has a wireless network. Approximate number of users that can be accommodated: 2,500. Proportion of college-owned housing units wired for high-speed internet access: 100%. **Campus safety:** Security services offered: 24-hour foot-and-vehicle patrols, late-night transport/escort service, 24-hour emergency telephones, lighted pathways/sidewalks, student patrols, controlled dormitory access (key, security card, etc).

TRANSFER AND INTERNATIONAL STUDENTS

Transfer students: May apply for admission for the following academic terms: Fall, Spring, Summer. Applicants need a minimum number of credits to apply. For fall 2005: Transfer applications received: 2,643. Transfer applicants offered admission: 2,159. Transfer applicants enrolled: 855. **International students:** Number of foreign undergraduates: 207 (1% of student body). Number of countries represented: 36. Minimum TOEFL score required: 500 (paper); 173 (computer). Average TOEFL score: 457 (paper).

Urbana University

- **Address:** 579 College Way, Urbana, OH 43078
- **Website:** http://www.urbana.edu
- **Private; Religious affiliation:** Swedenborgian Church
- **Enrollment:** N/A

KEY STATS

✔ **U.S News College Ranking:** fourth tier, Comp. Coll.–Bachelor's (Midwest)
✔ **SAT or ACT Score (25th/75th percentile):** N/A
✔ **Tuition:** 2006-2007: $16,804

Selectivity: Less selective	**Room/board:** $6,612
Acceptance rate: N/A	**Average debt:** N/A
Student/faculty ratio: N/A	**Proportion who borrowed:** N/A

Ursuline College

- **Address:** 2550 Lander Road, Pepper Pike, OH 44124
- **Website:** http://www.ursuline.edu
- **Private; Religious affiliation:** Roman Catholic
- **Enrollment:** 755 full-time; 397 part-time

KEY STATS

✔ **U.S News College Ranking:** 62, Universities–Master's (Midwest)
✔ **ACT Score (25th/75th percentile):** 17-23
✔ **Tuition:** 2006-2007: $20,090

Selectivity: Selective	**Room/board:** $6,684
Acceptance rate: 65%	**Average debt:** $23,000
Student/faculty ratio: 9/1	**Proportion who borrowed:** 67%

UNDERGRADUATE STUDENT BODY STATS

2005-2006 enrollment: 755 full-time; 397 part-time. Men: 8%; women: 92%. **Ethnic makeup:** African American: 26%; Asian American: 1%; Hispanic: 2%; White: 70%; International: 1%. **Religious preference:** Protestant: 11%; Jewish: 1%; No preference: 8%; Unknown: 34%; Roman Catholic: 30%; Other: 16%.

ADMISSIONS FACTS AND FIGURES

Phone: (440) 449-4203. **Email:** admission@ursuline.edu. **Website:** http://www.ursuline.edu. **Application deadlines for fall 2007:** Regular decision: Rolling. Early decision: Not offered. Early action: Send application by: November 15; Decision sent by: February 15. Admission can be deferred. **Application fee:** $25. Common application is not accepted. **Admissions requirements/recommendations:** High school units required (recommended): English: 4 (4); Mathematics: 3 (3); Science: 3 (3); Foreign language: 2 (2); Social studies: 3 (3); History: 0 (0); Academic electives: 0 (0); Total units: 17 (17). Tests: The college uses SAT or ACT scores in admissions decisions. Either SAT or ACT required. For admission to the fall 2007 entering class, the school will accept: ACT with writing, ACT without writing. Campus visit: Recommended. Admissions interview: Recommended. Off-campus interview: May be arranged. **Factors that count in admissions decisions: Academic:** Secondary school record: Very important. Class rank: Considered. Letters of recommendation: Very important. Standardized test scores: Very important. Essay: Very important. **Nonacademic:** Interview: Considered. Extracurricular activities: Considered. Talent/ability: Considered. Character/personal qualities: Considered. Alumni/ae relationship: Considered. Geographical residence: Not considered. State residency: Not considered. Religious affiliation/commitment: Not considered. Minority status: Considered. Volunteer work: Considered. Work experience: Considered. **Other schools with the greatest overlap in applicants:** Bowling Green State University; Cleveland State University; John Carroll University; Kent State University; University of Akron. **Admissions statistics for the fall 2005 entering class:** Total applicants: 439. Total accepted: 286. Freshmen enrolled: 141; 1% were from out of state. Accepted through early-decision or early-action plans: 37%. Overall acceptance rate: 65%. Non-early acceptance rate: 58%. **Credentials of fall 2005 freshmen:** 40% ranked in the top 10 percent of their high school class; 51% were in the top 25 percent, and 87% were in the top half. (Proportion submitting class standing: 93%.) **Average high school grade point average:** 3.3. First-year students who submitted SAT scores: 53%. Scores (25/75 percentile): Verbal: 420-540, Math: 440-550, Combined: 860-1090. **First-year students submitting ACT scores:** 87%. Scores (25/75 percentile): English: 17-23, Math: 17-23, Composite: 17-23.

ACADEMICS

Year founded: 1871. **Academic calendar:** Semester. **Degrees offered:** bachelor's, master's, post-master's certificate. **Most popular majors:** 29% health professions and related clinical sciences, 27% business, management, marketing, and related support services, 15% education, 8% visual and performing arts. **Major fields of study:** area, ethnic, cultural, and gender studies; biological and biomedical sciences; business, management, marketing, and related support services; communication, journalism, and related programs; education; English language and literature/letters; family and consumer sciences/human sciences; health professions and related clinical sciences; history; legal professions and studies; liberal arts and sciences studies, and humanities; mathematics and statistics; multi/interdisciplinary studies; philosophy and religious studies; psychology; public administration and social service professions; social sciences; theology and religious vocations; visual and performing arts. **Areas of required coursework:** arts/fine arts, humanities, mathematics, English (including composition), philosophy, sciences (biological or physical), social science, other. **Pre-professional programs:** pre-law, pre-dentistry, pre-medicine, pre-veterinary science. **Special academic programs (% participation):** accelerated program (18%), cooperative (work-study plan) program, cross-registration, double major, independent study, internships, student-designed major. **Teacher certification offered in:** early childhood, special education, middle/junior high, secondary. **Reserve Officers Training Corps (ROTC):** Army ROTC: Offered at cooperating institution (John Carroll University). **Faculty and instruction (2005-2006):** Total instructional faculty: 72 full-time, 140 part-time (27% men; 73% women; 3% minorities). Full-time faculty with Ph.D. or other terminal degree: 63%. Student/faculty ratio: 9/1. Classes of fewer than 20 students: 83%; of 20 to 49 students: 17%. **Advanced Placement and International Baccalaureate credit:** AP tests may be used for: Credit only. Scores accepted: 3, 4, 5. International Baccalaureate exams may be used for: Credit only. **Freshmen returning for sophomore year:** 68%. **Graduation rates:** Four-year: 24%; five-year: 42%; six-year: 48%. **Graduate study:** 8% of students pursue further study immediately upon graduation.

COSTS AND FINANCIAL AID

Financial aid office: (440) 646-8309. **Expenses (2006-2007):** Tuition and fees 2006-2007: $20,090; room/board: $6,684. Estimated books and supplies: $900; transportation: $416; personal expenses: $600. **Financial aid:** Priority filing date for institution's financial aid form: March 1. In 2005-2006, 83% of undergraduates applied for financial aid. Of those, 78% were determined to have financial need; 26% had their need fully met. Average financial aid package (proportion receiving): $15,796 (78%). Average amount of gift aid, such as scholarships or grants (proportion receiving): $5,882 (74%). Average amount of self-help aid, such as work study or loans (proportion receiving): $4,765 (77%). Average need-based loan (excluding PLUS or other private loans): $4,231. Among students who received need-based aid, the average percentage of need met: 78%. Among students who received aid based on merit, the average award (and the proportion receiving): $3,593 (15%). The average athletic scholarship (and the proportion receiving): $4,080 (11%). Average amount of debt of borrowers graduating in 2005: $23,000. Proportion who borrowed: 67%.

CAMPUS LIFE AND EXTRACURRICULAR ACTIVITIES

Campus housing available (% using): coed dorms (67%), women's dorms (33%). Students who live in college-owned, operated, or affiliated housing: 14%. **Student employment:** During the 2005-2006 academic year, 0% of undergraduates worked on campus. Average per-year earnings: $0. **Clubs and organizations:** Number of student organizations: 17. Activities include: choral groups, drama/theater, literary magazine, student government. Number of fraternities: 0; sororities: 0. Average proportion of students who stay on campus on weekends: 60%. **Sports program (2005-2006):** Member of NAIA. **Women's intercollegiate varsity sports:** basketball, cross-country, golf, soccer, softball, tennis, volleyball.

SERVICES AND FACILITIES

Basic services: nonremedial tutoring. **Remedial assistance:** reading, math, writing, study skills. **Counseling services:** career, personal. **For learning-disabled students:** School does not offer a structured program with separate admission and additional fees. Total undergraduates in learning-disabled program or receiving services: 30. Services include: remedial math, remedial English, reading machines, remedial reading, tape recorders, other special classes, diagnostic testing service, untimed tests, note-taking services, oral tests, learning center, readers, extended time for tests, tutors, other. **Library:** Number of titles: 124,614; number of current serial subscriptions: 13,317. **Information technology resources:** Students are not required to lease or own a computer. Number of campus computers available to all students: 72. School has a wireless network. Approximate number of users that can be accommodated: 300. Proportion of college-owned housing units wired for high-speed internet access: 100%. **Campus safety:** Security services offered: 24-hour foot-and-vehicle patrols, late-night transport/escort service, 24-hour emergency telephones, lighted pathways/sidewalks, controlled dormitory access (key, security card, etc).

TRANSFER AND INTERNATIONAL STUDENTS

Transfer students: May apply for admission for the following academic terms: Fall, Spring, Summer. Applicants do not need a minimum number of credits to apply. For fall 2005: Transfer applications received: 288. Transfer applicants offered admission: 250. Transfer applicants enrolled: 160. **International students:** Number of foreign undergraduates: 6 (1% of student body). Minimum TOEFL score required: 500 (paper); 173 (computer).

Walsh University

- **Address:** 2020 E. Maple Street, North Canton, OH 44720
- **Website:** http://www.walsh.edu
- **Private; Religious affiliation:** Roman Catholic
- **Enrollment:** 1,415 full-time; 444 part-time

KEY STATS
✔ **U.S News College Ranking:** third tier, Universities–Master's (Midwest)
✔ **ACT Score (25th/75th percentile):** 19-24
✔ **Tuition:** 2006-2007: $17,720

Selectivity: Selective	**Room/board:** $7,130
Acceptance rate: 80%	**Average debt:** $18,775
Student/faculty ratio: 14/1	**Proportion who borrowed:** 79%

UNDERGRADUATE STUDENT BODY STATS

2005-2006 enrollment: 1,415 full-time; 444 part-time: Men: 36%; women: 64%. **Ethnic makeup:** African American: 6%; Asian American: 1%; Hispanic: 1%; White: 90%; International: 2%. **Religious preference:** Roman Catholic: 37%; Protestant: 3%; No preference: 2%; Unknown: 15%.

ADMISSIONS FACTS AND FIGURES

Phone: (800) 362-9846. **Email:** admissions@walsh.edu. **Website:** http://www.walsh.edu. **Application deadlines for fall 2007:** Regular decision: August 15. Early decision: Not offered. Early action: Not offered. Admission can be deferred. **Application fee:** $25. Common application is not accepted. **Admissions requirements/recommendations:** High school units required (recommended): English: (4); Mathematics: (3); Science: (3); Foreign language: (2); Social studies: (3); Academic electives: (1); Total units: (16). Tests: The college uses SAT or ACT scores in admissions decisions. Either SAT or ACT required. For admission to the fall 2007 entering class, the school will accept: ACT with writing, ACT without writing. Campus visit: Recommended. Admissions interview: Recommended. Off-campus interview: May be arranged. **Factors that count in admissions decisions:** *Academic:* Secondary school record: Very important. Class rank: Important. Letters of recommendation: Important. Standardized test scores: Very important. Essay: Important. *Nonacademic:* Interview: Considered. Extracurricular activities: Considered. Talent/ability: Not considered. Character/personal qualities: Important. Alumni/ae relationship: Not considered. Geographical residence: Not considered. State residency: Not considered. Religious affiliation/commitment: Not considered. Minority status: Not considered. Volunteer work: Important. Work experience: Not considered. **Other schools with the greatest overlap in applicants:** Baldwin-Wallace College; John Carroll University; Kent State University; Malone College; Mount Union College. **Admissions statistics for the fall 2005 entering class:** Total applicants: 1,179. Total accepted: 946. Freshmen enrolled: 618; 4% were from out of state. Overall acceptance rate: 80%. **Credentials of fall 2005 freshmen:** 15% ranked in the top 10 percent of their high school class; 42% were in the top 25 percent, and 75% were in the top half. (Proportion submitting class standing: 97%.) **Average high school grade point average:** 3.3. **First-year students who submitted SAT scores:** 25%. Scores (25/75 percentile): Verbal: 450-560, Math: 440-560, Combined: 890-1120. **First-year students submitting ACT scores:** 95%. Scores (25/75 percentile): English: 18-24, Math: 18-24, Composite: 19-24.

ACADEMICS

Year founded: 1958. **Academic calendar:** Semester. **Degrees offered:** associate, bachelor's, master's. **Most popular majors:** 36% business, management, marketing, and related support services, 23% education, 10% health professions and related clinical sciences, 7% biological and biomedical sciences, 6% communication studies/speech communication and rhetoric. **Major fields of study:** biological and biomedical sciences; business, management, marketing, and related support services; communication, journalism, and related programs; computer and information sciences and support services; education; English language and literature/letters; foreign languages, literatures, and linguistics; health professions and related clinical sciences; history; mathematics and statistics; parks, recreation, leisure, and fitness studies; philosophy and religious studies; physical sciences; psychology; social sciences; theology and religious vocations. **Areas of required coursework:** arts/fine arts, humanities, mathematics, English (including composition), philosophy, foreign languages, sciences (biological or physical), history, social science, other. **Pre-professional programs:** pre-law, pre-dentistry, pre-medicine, pre-theology, pre-veterinary science, pre-optometry, pre-pharmacy, other. **Special academic programs (% participation):** accelerated program (23%), cooperative (work-study plan) program (20%), cross-registration (0%), double major (3%), dual enrollment (0%), English as a Second Language (ESL) (1%), exchange student program (domestic) (0%), external degree program (15%), honors program (5%), independent study (5%), internships (42%), study abroad (1%), teacher certificate program (19%). **Teacher certification offered in:** early childhood, special education, middle/junior high, secondary. **Cooperative education programs:** business, computer science, education, health professions, humanities, natural science, social/behavioral science. **Faculty and instruction (2005-2006):** Total instructional faculty: 80 full-time, 107 part-time (49% men; 51% women; 3% minorities). Full-time faculty with Ph.D. or other terminal degree: 80%. Student/faculty ratio: 14/1. Classes of fewer than 20 students: 70%; of 20 to 49 students: 30%. **Advanced Placement and International Baccalaureate credit:** International Baccalaureate exams may be used for: Credit and/or placement. **Freshmen returning for sophomore year:** 74%. **Graduation rates:** Four-year: 35%; five-year: 56%; six-year: 47%. **Graduate study:** 22% of students pursue further study immediately upon graduation. Fields in which graduates pursue further study: Master of Business Administration (MBA), 16%; arts and sciences, 10%.

COSTS AND FINANCIAL AID

Financial aid office: (330) 490-7150. **Expenses (2006-2007):** Tuition and fees 2006-2007: $17,720; room/board: $7,130. Estimated books and supplies:

$876; transportation: $582; personal expenses: $1,000. **Financial aid:** In 2005-2006, 85% of undergraduates applied for financial aid. Of those, 74% were determined to have financial need; 52% had their need fully met. Average financial aid package (proportion receiving): $11,262 (74%). Average amount of gift aid, such as scholarships or grants (proportion receiving): $5,827 (72%). Average amount of self-help aid, such as work study or loans (proportion receiving): $7,250 (66%). Average need-based loan (excluding PLUS or other private loans): $4,220. Among students who received need-based aid, the average percentage of need met: 83%. Among students who received aid based on merit, the average award (and the proportion receiving): $4,834 (13%). The average athletic scholarship (and the proportion receiving): $3,402 (24%). Average amount of debt of borrowers graduating in 2005: $18,775. Proportion who borrowed: 79%.

CAMPUS LIFE AND EXTRACURRICULAR ACTIVITIES

Campus housing available (% using): coed dorms (79%), women's dorms (0%), men's dorms (0%), apartment for single students (20%), special housing for disabled students (1%). Students who live in college-owned, operated, or affiliated housing: 50%. **Student employment:** During the 2005-2006 academic year, 11% of undergraduates worked on campus. Average per-year earnings: $1,072. **Clubs and organizations:** Number of student organizations: 32. Activities include: choral groups, dance, drama/theater, literary magazine, music ensembles, pep band, radio station, student government, student newspaper, yearbook. Number of fraternities: 0; sororities: 0. Average proportion of students who stay on campus on weekends: 70%. **Sports program (2005-2006):** Member of NAIA. *Men's intercollegiate varsity sports:* baseball, basketball, cross-country, football, golf, soccer, tennis, track and field (indoor), track and field (outdoor). *Women's intercollegiate varsity sports:* basketball, cross-country, golf, soccer, softball, tennis, track and field (indoor), track and field (outdoor), volleyball.

SERVICES AND FACILITIES

Basic services: nonremedial tutoring, placement service, health service, health insurance. **Remedial assistance:** reading, math, writing, study skills. **Counseling services:** minority student, career, personal, veteran student, academic, older student, psychological, religious, other. **For learning-disabled students:** School does not offer a structured program with separate admission and additional fees. Total undergraduates in learning-disabled program or receiving services: 40. Services include: remedial math, remedial English, tape recorders, other special classes, untimed tests, special bookstore section, oral tests, learning center, readers, extended time for tests, tutors, priority seating. **Library:** Number of titles: 139,543; number of current serial subscriptions: 5,412. **Information technology resources:** Students are not required to lease or own a computer. Number of campus computers available to all students: 276. School has a wireless network. Approximate number of users that can be accommodated: 30. Proportion of college-owned housing units wired for high-speed internet access: 100%. **Campus safety:** Security services offered: 24-hour foot-and-vehicle patrols, late-night transport/escort service, 24-hour emergency telephones, lighted pathways/sidewalks, student patrols, controlled dormitory access (key, security card, etc).

TRANSFER AND INTERNATIONAL STUDENTS

Transfer students: May apply for admission for the following academic terms: Fall, Spring, Summer. Applicants do not need a minimum number of credits to apply. For fall 2005: Transfer applications received: 223. Transfer applicants offered admission: 200. Transfer applicants enrolled: 146. **International students:** Number of foreign undergraduates: 33 (2% of student body). Number of countries represented: 16. Minimum TOEFL score required: 500 (paper); 163 (computer).

Wilberforce University

■ **Address:** PO Box 1001, 1055 N. Beckett Road, Wilberforce, OH 45384
■ **Website:** http://www.wilberforce.edu
■ **Private; Religious affiliation:** African Methodist Episcopal
■ **Enrollment:** N/A

KEY STATS
✔ **U.S News College Ranking:** fourth tier, Comp. Coll.–Bachelor's (Midwest)
✔ **SAT or ACT Score (25th/75th percentile):** N/A
✔ **Tuition:** 2006-2007: $11,560

Selectivity: Less selective	**Room/board:** $5,320
Acceptance rate: N/A	**Average debt:** N/A
Student/faculty ratio: N/A	**Proportion who borrowed:** N/A

Wilmington College

■ **Address:** Pyle Center Box 1327, Wilmington, OH 45177
■ **Website:** http://www.wilmington.edu
■ **Private; Religious affiliation:** Quaker
■ **Enrollment:** 1,383 full-time; 340 part-time

KEY STATS
✔ **U.S News College Ranking:** 38, Comp. Coll.–Bachelor's (Midwest)
✔ **ACT Score (25th/75th percentile):** 19-23
✔ **Tuition:** 2006-2007: $20,656

Selectivity: Selective	**Room/board:** $7,406
Acceptance rate: 98%	**Average debt:** N/A
Student/faculty ratio: 14/1	**Proportion who borrowed:** N/A

UNDERGRADUATE STUDENT BODY STATS

2005-2006 enrollment: 1,383 full-time; 340 part-time. Men: 46%; women: 54%. **Ethnic makeup:** African American: 9%; American-Indian: 1%; Hispanic: 1%; White: 88%; International: 1%.

ADMISSIONS FACTS AND FIGURES

Phone: (937) 382-6661. **Email:** admission@wilmington.edu. **Website:** http://www.wilmington.edu. **Application deadlines for fall 2007:** Regular decision: May 1. Early decision: Not offered. Early action: Not offered. Admission can be deferred. Common application is accepted. **Admissions requirements/recommendations:** High school units required (recommended): English: 4 (4); Mathematics: 2 (2); Science: 2 (2); Foreign language: (2); Social studies: 2 (2); History: (0); Academic electives: (0); Total units: 16 (16). Tests: The college uses SAT or ACT scores in admissions decisions. Either SAT or ACT required. For admission to the fall 2007 entering class, the school will accept: ACT without writing. Campus visit: Recommended. Admissions interview: Recommended. Off-campus interview: Not available. **Factors that count in admissions decisions:** *Academic:* Secondary school record: Important. Class rank: Important. Letters of recommendation: Considered. Standardized test scores: Important. Essay: Not considered. *Nonacademic:* Interview: Considered. Extracurricular activities: Considered. Talent/ability: Important. Character/personal qualities: Important. Alumni/ae relationship: Important. Geographical residence: Not considered. State residency: Not considered. Religious affiliation/commitment: Not considered. Minority status: Not considered. Volunteer work: Considered. Work experience: Not considered. **Other schools with the greatest overlap in applicants:** Ohio State University–Columbus; Ohio University; Otterbein College; University of Cincinnati; Wright State University. **Admissions statistics for the fall 2005 entering class:** Total applicants: 1,409. Total accepted: 1,381. Freshmen enrolled: 389; 5% were from out of state. Overall acceptance rate: 98%. **Credentials of fall 2005 freshmen:** 16% ranked in the top 10 percent of their high school class; 46% were in the top 25 percent, and 77% were in the top half. (Proportion submitting class standing: 82%.) **Average high school grade point average:** 3.3. **First-year students who submitted SAT scores:** 22%. Scores (25/75 percentile): Verbal: 430-530, Math: 440-550, Combined: 870-1080. **First-year students submitting ACT scores:** 99%. Scores (25/75 percentile): English: 18-23, Math: 19-25, Composite: 19-23.

ACADEMICS

Year founded: 1870. **Academic calendar:** Semester. **Degrees offered:** bachelor's, master's. **Most popular majors:** 31% business, management, marketing, and related support services, 22% education, 6% agriculture, agriculture operations, and related sciences, 6% communication, journalism, and related programs, 6% social sciences. **Major fields of study:** agriculture, agriculture operations, and related sciences; biological and biomedical sciences; business, management, marketing, and related support services; communication, journalism, and related programs; computer and information sciences and support services; education; English language and literature/letters; foreign languages, literatures, and linguistics; health professions and related clinical sciences; history; liberal arts and sciences studies, and humanities; mathematics and statistics; parks, recreation, leisure, and fitness studies; philosophy and religious studies; physical sciences; psychology; public administration and social service professions; security and protective services; social sciences; visual and performing arts. **Areas of required coursework:** arts/fine arts, humanities, computer literacy, mathematics, English (including composition), sciences (biological or physical), history, social science, other. **Special academic programs (% participation):** accelerated program (4%), cross-registration (1%), double major (23%), dual enrollment, honors program (6%), independent study (11%), internships (27%), liberal arts/career combination, student-designed major (.4%), study abroad (1%), teacher certificate program (26%), weekend college. **Teacher certification offered in:** early childhood, elementary, middle/junior high, secondary. **Faculty and instruction (2005-2006):** Total instructional faculty: 71 full-time, 26 part-time (43% men; 57% women; 5% minorities). Full-time faculty with Ph.D. or other terminal degree: 69%. Student/faculty ratio: 14/1. Classes of fewer than 20 students: 71%; of 20 to 49 students: 29%; of 50 or more students: 0%. **Advanced Placement and International Baccalaureate credit:** AP tests may be used for: Credit only. Scores accepted: 3, 4, 5. International Baccalaureate exams may be used for: Credit only. **Freshmen returning for sophomore year:** 72%. **Graduation rates:** Four-year: 49%; five-year: 57%; six-year: 56%.

COSTS AND FINANCIAL AID

Financial aid office: (937) 382-6661. **Expenses (2006-2007):** Tuition and fees 2006-2007: $20,656; room/board: $7,406. **Financial aid:** Priority filing date for institution's financial aid form: March 15. In 2005-2006, 91% of undergraduates applied for financial aid. Of those, 87% were determined to have financial need; 29% had their need fully met. Average financial aid package (proportion receiving): $16,901 (87%). Average amount of gift aid, such as scholarships or grants (proportion receiving): $6,489 (72%). Average amount of self-help aid, such as work study or loans (proportion receiving): $5,894 (74%). Average need-based loan (excluding PLUS or other private loans): $5,126. Among students who received need-based aid, the average percentage of need met: 86%. Among students who received aid based on merit, the average award (and the proportion receiving): $6,780 (10%). The average athletic scholarship (and the proportion receiving): $0 (0%).

CAMPUS LIFE AND EXTRACURRICULAR ACTIVITIES

Campus housing available: coed dorms, women's dorms, sorority housing, fraternity housing, apartment for single students. Students who live in college-owned, operated, or affiliated housing: 67%. **Student employment:** During the 2005-2006 academic year, 30% of undergraduates worked on campus. Average per-year earnings: $1,000. **Clubs and organizations:** Number of student organizations: 60. Activities include: choral groups, concert band, drama/theater, literary magazine, music ensembles, musical theater, student government, student newspaper, yearbook. Number of fraternities: 5; sororities: 5. Proportion of men in fraternities: 7%; of women in sororities: 11%. Average proportion of students who stay on campus on weekends: 65%. **Sports program (2005-2006):** Member of NCAA III. *Men's intercollegiate varsity sports:* baseball, basketball, cross-country, football, golf, soccer, swimming and diving, tennis, track and field (indoor), track and field (outdoor), wrestling. *Women's intercollegiate varsity sports:* basketball, cross-country, golf, soccer, softball, swimming and diving, tennis, track and field (indoor), track and field (outdoor), volleyball.

SERVICES AND FACILITIES

Basic services: nonremedial tutoring, placement service, health service, health insurance. **Remedial assistance:** math, writing, study skills. **Counseling services:** minority student, career, personal, academic, psychological, birth control, religious. **For learning-disabled students:** School does not offer a structured program with separate admission and additional fees. Services include: remedial math, remedial English, tape recorders, other special classes, diagnostic testing service, untimed tests, note-taking services, oral tests, learning center, readers, extended time for tests, tutors.

Information technology resources: Students are not required to lease or own a computer. Number of campus computers available to all students: 86. School does not have a wireless network. Proportion of college-owned housing units wired for high-speed internet access: 95%. **Campus safety:** Security services offered: 24-hour foot-and-vehicle patrols, late-night transport/escort service, 24-hour emergency telephones, lighted pathways/sidewalks, student patrols, controlled dormitory access (key, security card, etc).

TRANSFER AND INTERNATIONAL STUDENTS

Transfer students: May apply for admission for the following academic terms: Fall, Spring. Applicants need a minimum number of credits to apply. For fall 2005: Transfer applications received: 198. Transfer applicants offered admission: 194. Transfer applicants enrolled: 64. **International students:** Number of foreign undergraduates: 12 (1% of student body). Minimum TOEFL score required: 500 (paper); 173 (computer). Average TOEFL score: 520 (paper).

Wittenberg University

■ **Address:** PO Box 720, Springfield, OH 45501
■ **Website:** http://www.wittenberg.edu
■ **Private; Religious affiliation:** Lutheran
■ **Enrollment:** 1,930 full-time; 148 part-time

KEY STATS

✔ **U.S News College Ranking:** third tier, Liberal Arts Colleges
✔ **ACT Score (25th/75th percentile):** 21-27
✔ **Tuition:** 2006-2007: $29,280

Selectivity: More selective   **Room/board:** $7,498
Acceptance rate: 85%   **Average debt:** $21,615
Student/faculty ratio: 12/1   **Proportion who borrowed:** 69%

UNDERGRADUATE STUDENT BODY STATS

2005-2006 enrollment: 1,930 full-time; 148 part-time. Men: 42%; women: 58%. **Ethnic makeup:** African American: 5%; Asian American: 1%; Hispanic: 1%; White: 91%; International: 2%. **Religious preference:** Roman Catholic: 18%; Protestant: 1%; Jewish: 1%; No preference: 34%; Unknown: 7%; Lutheran: 17%; Other: 19%.

ADMISSIONS FACTS AND FIGURES

Phone: (937) 327-6314. **Email:** admission@wittenberg.edu. **Website:** http://www.wittenberg.edu. **Application deadlines for fall 2007:** Regular decision: March 15. Early decision: Send application by: November 15; Decision sent by: December 1. Early action: Send application by: December 1; Decision sent by: January 1. Admission can be deferred. **Application fee:** $40. Common application is accepted. **To apply online, go to:** http://www.wittenberg.edu/admit/app/appinstr.shtml. **Admissions requirements/recommendations:** High school units required (recommended): English: 4 (4); Mathematics: 3 (4); Science: 3 (4); Foreign language: 2 (3); Social studies: 0 (0); History: 2 (3); Total units: 16 (20). Tests: The college uses SAT or ACT scores in admissions decisions. Either SAT or ACT required. For admission to the fall 2007 entering class, the school will accept: ACT with writing, ACT without writing. Campus visit: Recommended. Admissions interview: Recommended. Off-campus interview: May be arranged. **Factors that count in admissions decisions:** *Academic:* Secondary school record: Very important. Class rank: Very important. Letters of recommendation: Very important. Standardized test scores: Very important. Essay: Very important. *Nonacademic:* Interview: Very important. Extracurricular activities: Important. Talent/ability: Important. Character/personal qualities: Important. Alumni/ae relationship: Important. Geographical residence: Not considered. State residency: Not considered. Religious affiliation/commitment: Not considered. Minority status: Not considered. Volunteer work: Important. Work experience: Considered. **Other schools with the greatest overlap in applicants:** College of Wooster; Denison University; Miami University–Oxford; Ohio Wesleyan University; University of Dayton. **Admissions statistics for the fall 2005 entering class:** Total applicants: 2,479. Total accepted: 2,102. Freshmen enrolled: 496; 29% were from out of state. Accepted through early-decision or early-action plans: 63%. Overall acceptance rate: 85%. Non-early acceptance rate: 73%. **Credentials of fall 2005 freshmen:** 27% ranked in the top 10 percent of their high school class; 56% were in the top 25 percent, and 83% were in the top half. (Proportion submitting class standing: 77%.) **Average**

high school grade point average: 3.5. **First-year students who submitted SAT scores:** 59%. Scores (25/75 percentile): Verbal: 520-630, Math: 500-620, Combined: 1020-1250. **First-year students submitting ACT scores:** 80%. Scores (25/75 percentile): English: 20-27, Math: 20-26, Composite: 21-27.

ACADEMICS

Year founded: 1845. **Academic calendar:** Semester. **Degrees offered:** bachelor's, master's. **Most popular majors:** 17% business/commerce, 14% elementary education and teaching, 10% biology/biological sciences, 10% psychology, 9% English language and literature. **Major fields of study:** area, ethnic, cultural, and gender studies; biological and biomedical sciences; business, management, marketing, and related support services; communication, journalism, and related programs; computer and information sciences and support services; education; English language and literature/letters; foreign languages, literatures, and linguistics; history; liberal arts and sciences studies, and humanities; mathematics and statistics; philosophy and religious studies; physical sciences; psychology; social sciences; visual and performing arts. **Areas of required coursework:** arts/fine arts, humanities, computer literacy, mathematics, English (including composition), philosophy, foreign languages, sciences (biological or physical), history, social science. **Pre-professional programs:** pre-law, pre-dentistry, pre-medicine, pre-theology, pre-veterinary science, pre-optometry, pre-pharmacy. **Special academic programs (% participation):** cross-registration (1%), double major (6%), dual enrollment (1%), honors program (7%), independent study (26%), internships (18%), student-designed major (1%), study abroad (15%), teacher certificate program (31%). **Teacher certification offered in:** early childhood, special education, elementary, middle/junior high, secondary. **Reserve Officers Training Corps (ROTC):** Army ROTC: Offered at cooperating institution (Central State University); Air Force ROTC: Offered at cooperating institution (Wright State University). **Faculty and instruction (2005-2006):** Total instructional faculty: 148 full-time, 54 part-time (58% men; 42% women; 6% minorities). Full-time faculty with Ph.D. or other terminal degree: 89%. Student/faculty ratio: 12/1. Classes of fewer than 20 students: 62%; of 20 to 49 students: 37%; of 50 or more students: 1%. **Advanced Placement and International Baccalaureate credit:** AP tests may be used for: Credit and/or placement. Scores accepted: 3, 4, 5. International Baccalaureate exams may be used for: Credit and/or placement. **Freshmen returning for sophomore year:** 80%. **Graduation rates:** Four-year: 61%; five-year: 64%; six-year: 65%. **Graduate study:** 31% of students pursue further study within one year. Fields in which graduates pursue further study: Master of Business Administration (MBA), 2%; law, 8%; medicine, 6%; dentistry, 2%; theology (or the seminary), 4%; education, 19%; arts and sciences, 44%; veterinary medicine, 2%.

COSTS AND FINANCIAL AID

Financial aid office: (937) 327-7321. **Expenses (2006-2007):** Tuition and fees 2006-2007: $29,280; room/board: $7,498. Estimated books and supplies: $800; transportation: $600; personal expenses: $1,000. **Financial aid:** Priority filing date for institution's financial aid form: March 15. In 2005-2006, 86% of undergraduates applied for financial aid. Of those, 75% were determined to have financial need; 42% had their need fully met. Average financial aid package (proportion receiving): $21,691 (75%). Average amount of gift aid, such as scholarships or grants (proportion receiving): $16,720 (74%). Average amount of self-help aid, such as work study or loans (proportion receiving): $4,639 (73%). Average need-based loan (excluding PLUS or other private loans): $3,465. Among students who received need-based aid, the average percentage of need met: 88%. Among students who received aid based on merit, the average award (and the proportion receiving): $9,776 (18%). The average athletic scholarship (and the proportion receiving): $0 (0%). Average amount of debt of borrowers graduating in 2005: $21,615. Proportion who borrowed: 69%.

CAMPUS LIFE AND EXTRACURRICULAR ACTIVITIES

Campus housing available (% using): coed dorms (47%), women's dorms (7%), sorority housing (8%), fraternity housing (4%), apartment for single students (2%), other housing options (32%). Students who live in college-owned, operated, or affiliated housing: 82%. **Student employment:** During the 2005-2006 academic year, 60% of undergraduates worked on campus. Average per-year earnings: $1,800. **Clubs and organizations:** Number of student organizations: 135. Activities include: choral groups, concert band, dance, drama/theater, jazz band, literary magazine, music ensembles, musical theater, opera, pep band, radio station, student government, student newspaper, student film society, symphony orchestra, yearbook. Number of fraternities: 6; sororities: 6. Proportion of men in fraternities: 30%; of women in sororities: 38%. Average proportion of students who stay on campus on weekends: 81%. **Sports program (2005-2006):** Member of NCAA III.

Men's intercollegiate varsity sports: baseball, basketball, cross-country, football, golf, lacrosse, soccer, swimming and diving, tennis, track and field (indoor), track and field (outdoor). **Women's intercollegiate varsity sports:** basketball, cross-country, field hockey, golf, lacrosse, soccer, softball, swimming and diving, tennis, track and field (indoor), track and field (outdoor), volleyball.

SERVICES AND FACILITIES

Basic services: nonremedial tutoring, women's center, placement service, health service, health insurance. **Remedial assistance:** math, writing, study skills. **Counseling services:** minority student, career, personal, academic, psychological, birth control, religious. **For learning-disabled students:** School does not offer a structured program with separate admission and additional fees. Total undergraduates in learning-disabled program or receiving services: 88. Services include: extended time for tests, tutors. **Library:** Number of titles: 413,947; number of current serial subscriptions: 12,394. **Information technology resources:** Students are not required to lease or own a computer. Number of campus computers available to all students: 800. School has a wireless network. Approximate number of users that can be accommodated: 900. Proportion of college-owned housing units wired for high-speed internet access: 100%. **Campus safety:** Security services offered: 24-hour foot-and-vehicle patrols, late-night transport/escort service, 24-hour emergency telephones, lighted pathways/sidewalks, controlled dormitory access (key, security card, etc.).

TRANSFER AND INTERNATIONAL STUDENTS

Transfer students: May apply for admission for the following academic terms: Fall, Spring, Summer. Applicants do not need a minimum number of credits to apply. For fall 2005: Transfer applications received: 116. Transfer applicants offered admission: 66. Transfer applicants enrolled: 27. **International students:** Number of foreign undergraduates: 35 (2% of student body). Number of countries represented: 16. Minimum TOEFL score required: 550 (paper); 213 (computer).

Wright State University

- **Address:** 3640 Colonel Glenn Highway, Dayton, OH 45435
- **Website:** http://www.wright.edu
- **Public**
- **Enrollment:** 10,450 full-time; 1,818 part-time

KEY STATS

✔ **U.S News College Ranking:** fourth tier, National Universities
✔ **ACT Score (25th/75th percentile):** 18-23
✔ **Tuition:** 2006-2007: $7,278 in state, $14,004 out of state

Selectivity: Selective	**Room/board:** $6,964
Acceptance rate: 87%	**Average debt:** N/A
Student/faculty ratio: 20/1	**Proportion who borrowed:** N/A

UNDERGRADUATE STUDENT BODY STATS

2005-2006 enrollment: 10,450 full-time; 1,818 part-time. Men: 44%; women: 56%. **Ethnic makeup:** African American: 12%; Asian American: 2%; Hispanic: 1%; White: 83%; International: 1%.

ADMISSIONS FACTS AND FIGURES

Phone: (937) 775-5700. **Email:** admissions@wright.edu. **Website:** http://www.wright.edu. **Application deadlines for fall 2007:** Regular decision: Rolling. Early decision: Not offered. Early action: Not offered. Admission can be deferred. **Application fee:** $30. Common application is not accepted. **To apply online, go to:** https://www.applyweb.com/aw?wright. **Admissions requirements/recommendations:** High school units required (recommended): English: 4; Mathematics: 3; Science: 3; Foreign language: 2; Social studies: 3; Total units: 15. Tests: The college uses SAT or ACT scores in admissions decisions. Either SAT or ACT required. For admission to the fall 2007 entering class, the school will accept: ACT with writing, ACT without writing, the new SAT. Campus visit: Recommended. Admissions interview: Recommended. Off-campus interview: Not available. **Factors that count in admissions decisions:** *Academic:* Secondary school record: Very important. Class rank: Important. Letters of recommendation: Considered. Standardized test scores: Very important. Essay: Not considered. *Nonacademic:* Interview: Not considered. Extracurricular activities: Not considered. Talent/ability: Not considered. Character/personal qualities: Not considered. Alumni/ae relationship: Not considered. Geographical residence: Not considered. State residency: Considered. Religious affiliation/commitment: Not considered. Minority status: Not considered. Volunteer work: Not considered. Work experience: Not considered. **Admissions statistics for the fall 2005 entering class:** Total applicants: 5,497. Total accepted: 4,763. Freshmen enrolled: 2,336; 3% were from out of state. Overall acceptance rate: 87%. **Credentials of fall 2005 freshmen:** 15% ranked in the top 10 percent of their high school class; 35% were in the top 25 percent, and 67% were in the top half. (Proportion submitting class standing: 92%.) **Average high school grade point average:** 3.0. **First-year students who submitted SAT scores:** 33%. Scores (25/75 percentile): Verbal: 440-560, Math: 430-570, Combined: 870-1130. **First-year students submitting ACT scores:** 87%. Scores (25/75 percentile): English: N/A, Math: N/A, Composite: 18-23.

ACADEMICS

Year founded: 1964. **Academic calendar:** Quarter. **Degrees offered:** certificate, associate, transfer-associate, terminal-associate, bachelor's, master's, post-master's certificate, first professional, doctorate. **Most popular majors:** 22% education, 20% business/commerce. **Major fields of study:** area, ethnic, cultural, and gender studies; biological and biomedical sciences; business, management, marketing, and related support services; communication, journalism, and related programs; computer and information sciences and support services; education; engineering; English language and literature/letters; foreign languages, literatures, and linguistics; health professions and related clinical sciences; history; liberal arts and sciences studies, and humanities; mathematics and statistics; multi/interdisciplinary studies; philosophy and religious studies; physical sciences; psychology; public administration and social service professions; social sciences; visual and performing arts. **Areas of required coursework:** arts/fine arts, humanities, mathematics, English (including composition), sciences (biological or physical), history, social science. **Pre-professional programs:** pre-law, pre-dentistry, pre-medicine. **Special academic programs:** cooperative (work-study plan) program, cross-registration, distance learning, double major, English as a Second Language (ESL), honors program, independent study, internships, student-designed major, study abroad, teacher certificate program. **Teacher certification offered in:** early childhood, special education, elementary, vo-tech, middle/junior high, secondary. **Cooperative education programs:** art, business, computer science, education, engineering, humanities, technologies, vocational arts. **Reserve Officers Training Corps (ROTC):** Army ROTC: Offered on campus; Air Force ROTC: Offered on campus. **Faculty and instruction (2005-2006):** Total instructional faculty: 722 full-time, 34 part-time (61% men; 39% women; 13% minorities). Student/faculty ratio: 20/1. Classes of fewer than 20 students: 49%; of 20 to 49 students: 45%; of 50 or more students: 6%. **Advanced Placement and International Baccalaureate credit:** AP tests may be used for: Credit and/or placement. Scores accepted: 3, 4, 5. International Baccalaureate exams may be used for: Credit and/or placement. **Freshmen returning for sophomore year:** 71%. **Graduation rates:** Four-year: 16%; five-year: 35%; six-year: 40%.

COSTS AND FINANCIAL AID

Financial aid office: (937) 873-5721. **Expenses (2006-2007):** Tuition and fees 2006-2007: $7,278 in state, $14,004 out of state; room/board: $6,964. **Financial aid:** Priority filing date for institution's financial aid form: February 15.

CAMPUS LIFE AND EXTRACURRICULAR ACTIVITIES

Campus housing available: coed dorms, men's dorms, sorority housing, fraternity housing, apartments for married students, apartment for single students, special housing for disabled students, special housing for international students, other housing options. Students who live in college-owned, operated, or affiliated housing: 24%. Average per-year earnings: $6. **Clubs and organizations:** Number of student organizations: 145. Activities include: choral groups, concert band, dance, drama/theater, jazz band, literary magazine, marching band, music ensembles, musical theater, opera, pep band, radio station, student government, student newspaper, symphony orchestra, television station. Number of fraternities: 11; sororities: 7. Proportion of men in fraternities: 2%; of women in sororities: 2%. **Sports program (2005-2006):** Member of NCAA I. *Men's intercollegiate varsity sports:* baseball, basketball, cross-country, golf, soccer, swimming and diving, tennis. *Women's intercollegiate varsity sports:* basketball, cross-country, soccer, softball, swimming and diving, tennis, track and field (indoor), track and field (outdoor), volleyball.

SERVICES AND FACILITIES

Basic services: nonremedial tutoring, women's center, placement service, day care, health service, other. **Remedial assistance:** reading, math, writing, study skills. **Counseling services:** minority student, career, military, personal, veteran student, academic, psychological, birth control, religious, other. **For learning-disabled students:** School does not offer a structured program with separate admission and additional fees. Total undergraduates in learning-disabled program or receiving services: 500. Services include: remedial math, remedial English, reading machines, remedial reading, tape recorders, other special classes, diagnostic testing service, untimed tests, note-taking services, learning center, readers, extended time for tests, tutors, other. **Library:** Number of titles: 703,000; number of current serial subscriptions: 3,200. **Information technology resources:** Students are not required to lease or own a computer. Number of campus computers available to all students: 3,000. School has a wireless network. Proportion of college-owned housing units wired for high-speed internet access: 100%. **Campus safety:** Security services offered: late-night transport/escort service, 24-hour emergency telephones, lighted pathways/sidewalks.

TRANSFER AND INTERNATIONAL STUDENTS

Transfer students: May apply for admission for the following academic terms: Fall, Winter, Spring, Summer. Applicants need a minimum number of credits to apply. For fall 2005: Transfer applications received: 1,773. Transfer applicants offered admission: 1,384. Transfer applicants enrolled: 899. **International students:** Number of foreign undergraduates: 131 (1% of student body). Number of countries represented: 67. Minimum TOEFL score required: 500 (paper); 173 (computer). Average TOEFL score: 550 (paper).

Xavier University

- **Address:** 3800 Victory Parkway, Cincinnati, OH 45207
- **Website:** http://www.xavier.edu
- **Private; Religious affiliation:** Roman Catholic (Jesuit)
- **Enrollment:** 3,333 full-time; 546 part-time

KEY STATS

✔ **U.S News College Ranking:** 2, Universities–Master's (Midwest)
✔ **ACT Score (25th/75th percentile):** 23-28
✔ **Tuition:** 2006-2007: $23,240

Selectivity: More selective	**Room/board:** $8,380
Acceptance rate: 66%	**Average debt:** $19,300
Student/faculty ratio: 13/1	**Proportion who borrowed:** 58%

UNDERGRADUATE STUDENT BODY STATS

2005-2006 enrollment: 3,333 full-time; 546 part-time. Men: 44%; women: 56%. **Ethnic makeup:** African American: 11%; Asian American: 2%; Hispanic: 2%; White: 83%; International: 1%. **Religious preference:** Protestant: 14%; No preference: 1%; Unknown: 13%; Roman Catholic (Jesuit): 62%; Other: 10%.

ADMISSIONS FACTS AND FIGURES

Phone: (877) 982-3648. **Email:** xuadmit@xavier.edu. **Website:** http://www.xavier.edu. **Application deadlines for fall 2007:** Regular decision: February 1. Early decision: Not offered. Early action: Send application by: December 1; Decision sent by: January 15. Admission can be deferred. **Application fee:** $35. Common application is accepted. **To apply online, go to:** http://www.xavier.edu/applyonline. **Admissions requirements/recommendations:** High school units required (recommended): English: (4); Mathematics: (3); Science: (3); Foreign language: (2); Social studies: (3); History: (0); Academic electives: (5); Total units: (21). Tests: The college uses SAT or ACT scores in admissions decisions. Either SAT or ACT required. For admission to the fall 2007 entering class, the school will accept: ACT with writing, ACT without writing. Campus visit: Recommended. Admissions interview: Recommended. Off-campus interview: May be arranged. **Factors that count in admissions decisions:** *Academic:* Secondary school record: Very important. Class rank: Important. Letters of recommendation: Important. Standardized test scores: Important. Essay: Important. *Nonacademic:* Interview: Not considered. Extracurricular activities: Considered. Talent/ability: Considered. Character/personal qualities: Important. Alumni/ae relationship: Considered. Geographical residence: Not considered. State residency: Not considered. Religious affiliation/commitment: Not considered. Minority status: Considered. Volunteer work: Considered. Work experience: Considered. **Other schools with the greatest overlap in applicants:** Miami University–Oxford; Ohio State University–Columbus; University of Cincinnati; University of Dayton; University of Notre Dame. **Admissions statistics for the fall 2005 entering class:** Total applicants: 5,468. Total accepted: 3,612. Freshmen enrolled: 765; 49% were from out of state. Accepted through early-decision or early-action plans: 68%. Overall acceptance rate: 66%. Non-early acceptance rate: 50%. **Size of waiting list:** 599 applicants; enrolled from waiting list: 47. **Credentials of fall 2005 freshmen:** 30% ranked in the top 10 percent of their high school class; 62% were in the top 25 percent, and 89% were in the top half. (Proportion submitting class standing: 69%.) **Average high school grade point average:** 3.6. **First-year students who submitted SAT scores:** 75%. Scores (25/75 percentile): Verbal: 540-640, Math: 540-640, Combined: 1080-1280. **First-year students submitting ACT scores:** 77%. Scores (25/75 percentile): English: 22-28, Math: 22-28, Composite: 23-28.

ACADEMICS

Year founded: 1831. **Academic calendar:** Semester. **Degrees offered:** certificate, associate, terminal-associate, bachelor's, post-bachelor's certificate, master's, post-master's certificate, doctorate. **Most popular majors:** 26% business, management, marketing, and related support services, 14% liberal arts and sciences studies, and humanities, 9% communication, journalism, and related programs, 6% education, 6% psychology. **Major fields of study:** biological and biomedical sciences; business, management, marketing, and related support services; communication, journalism, and related programs; computer and information sciences and support services; education; English language and literature/letters; foreign languages, literatures, and linguistics; health professions and related clinical sciences; history; liberal arts and sciences studies, and humanities; mathematics and statistics; multi/interdisciplinary studies; natural resources and conservation; parks, recreation, leisure, and fitness studies; philosophy and religious studies; physical sciences; psychology; public administration and social service professions; security and protective services; social sciences; theology and religious vocations; visual and performing arts. **Areas of required coursework:** arts/fine arts, mathematics, English (including composition), philosophy, foreign languages, sciences (biological or physical), history, social science, other. **Pre-professional programs:** pre-pharmacy, other. **Special academic programs:** cooperative (work-study plan) program, cross-registration, double major, dual enrollment, English as a Second Language (ESL), honors program, independent study, internships, study abroad, teacher certificate program, weekend college. **Teacher certification offered in:** early childhood, special education, middle/junior high, secondary. **Cooperative education programs:** business, computer science. **Reserve Officers Training Corps (ROTC):** Army ROTC: Offered on campus; Air Force ROTC: Offered at cooperating institution (University of Cincinnati). **Faculty and instruction (2005-2006):** Total instructional faculty: 294 full-time, 304 part-time (52% men; 48% women; 12% minorities). Full-time faculty with Ph.D. or other terminal degree: 80%. Student/faculty ratio: 13/1. Classes of fewer than 20 students: 50%; of 20 to 49 students: 49%; of 50 or more students: 1%. **Advanced Placement and International Baccalaureate credit:** AP tests may be used for: Credit and/or placement. Scores accepted: 3, 4, 5. International Baccalaureate exams may be used for: Credit and/or placement. **Freshmen returning for sophomore year:** 90%. **Graduation rates:** Four-year: 70%; five-year: 78%; six-year: 76%. **Graduate study:** 27% of students pursue further study within one year. Fields in which graduates pursue further study: Master of Business Administration (MBA), 4%; law, 2%; medicine, 6%; education, 4%; arts and sciences, 12%.

COSTS AND FINANCIAL AID

Financial aid office: (513) 745-3142. **Expenses (2006-2007):** Tuition and fees 2006-2007: $23,240; room/board: $8,380. Estimated books and supplies: $900; transportation: $800; personal expenses: $600. **Financial aid:** Priority filing date for institution's financial aid form: February 15. In 2005-2006, 68% of undergraduates applied for financial aid. Of those, 54% were determined to have financial need; 26% had their need fully met. Average financial aid package (proportion receiving): $14,510 (54%). Average amount of gift aid, such as scholarships or grants (proportion receiving): $9,872 (52%). Average amount of self-help aid, such as work study or loans (proportion receiving): $5,183 (43%). Average need-based loan (excluding PLUS or other private loans): $4,426. Among students who received need-based aid, the average percentage of need met: 75%. Among students who received aid based on merit, the average award (and the proportion receiving): $8,158 (29%). The average athletic scholarship (and the proportion receiving): $13,435 (4%). Average amount of debt of borrowers graduating in 2005: $19,300. Proportion who borrowed: 58%.

CAMPUS LIFE AND EXTRACURRICULAR ACTIVITIES

Campus housing available (% using): coed dorms (66%), apartment for single students (33%), other housing options (1%). Students who live in college-owned, operated, or affiliated housing: 46%. **Student employment:** During the 2005-2006 academic year, 20% of undergraduates worked on campus. Average per-year earnings: $2,070. **Clubs and organizations:** Number of student organizations: 100. Activities include: choral groups, concert band, dance, drama/theater, jazz band, literary magazine, music ensembles, musical theater, opera, pep band, radio station, student government, student newspaper, television station. Number of fraternities: 0; sororities: 0. Average proportion of students who stay on campus on weekends: 70%. **Sports program (2005-2006):** Member of NCAA I. *Men's intercollegiate varsity sports:* baseball, basketball, cross-country, golf, soccer, swimming and diving, tennis, track and field (indoor), track and field (outdoor). *Women's intercollegiate varsity sports:* basketball, cross-country, golf, soccer, swimming and diving, tennis, track and field (indoor), track and field (outdoor), volleyball.

SERVICES AND FACILITIES

Basic services: nonremedial tutoring, health service, health insurance. **Remedial assistance:** math, study skills. **Counseling services:** career, personal, academic, psychological, religious. **For learning-disabled students:** School does not offer a structured program with separate admission and additional fees. Total undergraduates in learning-disabled program or receiving services: 227. Services include: tape recorders, videotaped classes, diagnostic testing service, note-taking services, oral tests, learning center, readers, extended time for tests, tutors, priority registration, priority seating, substitution of courses, other testing accomodations. **Library:** Number of titles: 366,284; number of current serial subscriptions: 9,375. **Information technology resources:** Students are not required to lease or own a computer. Number of campus computers available to all students: 225. School has a wireless network. Approximate number of users that can be accommodated: 450. Proportion of college-owned housing units wired for high-speed internet access: 100%. **Campus safety:** Security services offered: 24-hour foot-and-vehicle patrols, late-night transport/escort service, 24-hour emergency telephones, lighted pathways/sidewalks, controlled dormitory access (key, security card, etc).

TRANSFER AND INTERNATIONAL STUDENTS

Transfer students: May apply for admission for the following academic terms: Fall, Spring. Applicants need a minimum number of credits to apply. For fall 2005: Transfer applications received: 368. Transfer applicants offered admission: 196. Transfer applicants enrolled: 115. **International students:** Number of foreign undergraduates: 51 (1% of student body). Number of countries represented: 31. Minimum TOEFL score required: 530 (paper); 197 (computer). Average TOEFL score: 615 (paper).

Youngstown State University

- **Address:** 1 University Plaza, Youngstown, OH 44555
- **Website:** http://www.ysu.edu
- **Public**
- **Enrollment:** 9,241 full-time; 2,454 part-time

KEY STATS

✔ **U.S News College Ranking:** fourth tier, Universities–Master's (Midwest)
✔ **ACT Score (25th/75th percentile):** 17-22
✔ **Tuition:** 2006-2007: $6,713 in state, $12,233 out of state

Selectivity: Less selective	**Room/board:** $6,490
Acceptance rate: 99%	**Average debt:** N/A
Student/faculty ratio: 18/1	**Proportion who borrowed:** N/A

UNDERGRADUATE STUDENT BODY STATS

2005-2006 enrollment: 9,241 full-time; 2,454 part-time. Men: 44%; women: 56%. **Ethnic makeup:** African American: 12%; Asian American: 1%; Hispanic: 2%; White: 84%; International: 1%.

ADMISSIONS FACTS AND FIGURES

Phone: (877) 468-6978. **Email:** enroll@ysu.edu. **Website:** http://www.ysu.edu. **Application deadlines for fall 2007:** Regular decision: August 15. Early decision: Not offered. Early action: Send application by: February 15; Decision sent by: February 20. Admission can be deferred.

Application fee: $30. Common application is accepted. **Admissions requirements/recommendations:** High school units required (recommended): English: (4); Mathematics: (3); Science: (3); Foreign language: (2); Social studies: (3); Total units: (16). Tests: The college uses SAT or ACT scores in admissions decisions. Either SAT or ACT required. For admission to the fall 2007 entering class, the school will accept: ACT without writing. Campus visit: Recommended. Admissions interview: Neither required nor recommended. Off-campus interview: Not available. **Factors that count in admissions decisions:** *Academic:* Secondary school record: Important. Class rank: Important. Letters of recommendation: Not considered. Standardized test scores: Very important. Essay: Not considered. *Nonacademic:* Interview: Not considered. Extracurricular activities: Not considered. Talent/ability: Not considered. Character/personal qualities: Not considered. Alumni/ae relationship: Not considered. Geographical residence: Very important. State residency: Very important. Religious affiliation/commitment: Not considered. Minority status: Not considered. Volunteer work: Not considered. Work experience: Not considered. **Admissions statistics for the fall 2005 entering class:** Total applicants: 4,019. Total accepted: 3,994. Freshmen enrolled: 2,258; 10% were from out of state. Accepted through early-decision or early-action plans: 33%. Overall acceptance rate: 99%. **Credentials of fall 2005 freshmen:** 9% ranked in the top 10 percent of their high school class; 25% were in the top 25 percent, and 52% were in the top half. (Proportion submitting class standing: 90%.) **Average high school grade point average:** 2.8. **First-year students who submitted SAT scores:** 21%. Scores (25/75 percentile): Verbal: 430-550, Math: 410-550, Combined: 840-1100. **First-year students submitting ACT scores:** 88%. Scores (25/75 percentile): English: 15-22, Math: 16-22, Composite: 17-22.

ACADEMICS

Year founded: 1908. **Academic calendar:** Semester. **Degrees offered:** certificate, diploma, associate, transfer-associate, terminal-associate, bachelor's, post-bachelor's certificate, master's, doctorate. **Most popular majors:** 10% early childhood education and teaching, 5% criminal justice/safety studies, 5% marketing/marketing management, 4% accounting, 4% chemistry. **Major fields of study:** area, ethnic, cultural, and gender studies; biological and biomedical sciences; business, management, marketing, and related support services; communication, journalism, and related programs; computer and information sciences and support services; education; engineering; engineering technologies/technicians; English language and literature/letters; family and consumer sciences/human sciences; foreign languages, literatures, and linguistics; health professions and related clinical sciences; history; legal professions and studies; liberal arts and sciences studies, and humanities; mathematics and statistics; natural resources and conservation; parks, recreation, leisure, and fitness studies; philosophy and religious studies; physical sciences; psychology; public administration and social service professions; security and protective services; social sciences; visual and performing arts. **Areas of required coursework:** arts/fine arts, humanities, mathematics, English (including composition), sciences (biological or physical), social science. **Pre-professional programs:** pre-law, pre-dentistry, pre-medicine, pre-veterinary science, pre-optometry, pre-pharmacy. **Special academic programs:** accelerated program, cooperative (work-study plan) program, cross-registration, distance learning, double major, English as a Second Language (ESL), exchange student program (domestic), honors program, independent study, internships, student-designed major, study abroad, teacher certificate program, weekend college. **Teacher certification offered in:** early childhood, special education, vo-tech, middle/junior high, adult education, secondary. **Cooperative education programs:** business, engineering. **Reserve Officers Training Corps (ROTC):** Army ROTC: Offered on campus; Air Force ROTC: Offered at cooperating institution (Kent State University). **Faculty and instruction (2005-2006):** Total instructional faculty: 427 full-time, 552 part-time (54% men; 46% women; 9% minorities). Full-time faculty with Ph.D. or other terminal degree: 82%. Student/faculty ratio: 18/1. Classes of fewer than 20 students: 38%; of 20 to 49 students: 56%; of 50 or more students: 7%. **Advanced Placement and International Baccalaureate credit:** AP tests may be used for: Credit and/or placement. Scores accepted: 3, 4, 5. International Baccalaureate exams may be used for: Credit and/or placement. **Freshmen returning for sophomore year:** 72%. **Graduation rates:** Four-year: 13%; five-year: 29%; six-year: 37%.

COSTS AND FINANCIAL AID

Financial aid office: (330) 941-3399. **Expenses (2006-2007):** Tuition and fees 2006-2007: $6,713 in state, $12,233 out of state; room/board: $6,490. Estimated books and supplies: $1,057; transportation: $1,370; personal expenses: $500. **Financial aid:** Priority filing date for institution's financial aid form: February 15; deadline: February 15.

CAMPUS LIFE AND EXTRACURRICULAR ACTIVITIES

Campus housing available (% using): coed dorms (65%), women's dorms (4%), sorority housing (0%), fraternity housing (0%), apartment for single students (31%). Students who live in college-owned, operated, or affiliated housing: 11%. **Student employment:** During the 2005-2006 academic year, 20% of undergraduates worked on campus. Average per-year earnings: $6,000. **Clubs and organizations:** Number of student organizations: 160. Activities include: choral groups, concert band, dance, drama/theater, jazz band, literary magazine, marching band, music ensembles, musical theater, opera, pep band, radio station, student government, student newspaper, student film society, symphony orchestra, yearbook. Number of fraternities: 14; sororities: 4. Proportion of men in fraternities: 3%; of women in sororities: 1%. Average proportion of students who stay on campus on weekends: 50%. **Sports program (2005-2006):** Member of NCAA I. *Men's intercollegiate varsity sports:* baseball, basketball, cross-country, football, golf, tennis, track and field (indoor), track and field (outdoor). *Women's intercollegiate varsity sports:* basketball, cross-country, golf, soccer, softball, swimming and diving, tennis, track and field (indoor), track and field (outdoor), volleyball.

SERVICES AND FACILITIES

Basic services: nonremedial tutoring, women's center, placement service, day care, health service, health insurance. **Remedial assistance:** reading, math, writing, study skills. **Counseling services:** minority student, career, military, personal, veteran student, academic, older student, psychological. **For learning-disabled students:** School does not offer a structured program with separate admission and additional fees. Total undergraduates in learning-disabled program or receiving services: 75. Services include: remedial math, remedial English, reading machines, remedial reading, tape recorders, untimed tests, note-taking services, readers, extended time for tests, tutors, priority registration, substitution of courses, texts on tape, typist/scribe, exams on tape or computer, other testing accomodations, waiver of foreign language degree requirement. **Library:** Number of titles: 868,835; number of current serial subscriptions: 22,277. **Information technology resources:** Students are not required to lease or own a computer. Number of campus computers available to all students: 1,618. School has a wireless network. Approximate number of users that can be accommodated: 140. Proportion of college-owned housing units wired for high-speed internet access: 100%. **Campus safety:** Security services offered: 24-hour foot-and-vehicle patrols, late-night transport/escort service, 24-hour emergency telephones, lighted pathways/sidewalks, student patrols, controlled dormitory access (key, security card, etc.).

TRANSFER AND INTERNATIONAL STUDENTS

Transfer students: May apply for admission for the following academic terms: Fall, Spring, Summer. Applicants do not need a minimum number of credits to apply. For fall 2005: Transfer applications received: 930. Transfer applicants offered admission: 805. Transfer applicants enrolled: 581. **International students:** Number of foreign undergraduates: 60 (1% of student body). Number of countries represented: 56. Minimum TOEFL score required: 500 (paper); 173 (computer).

Oklahoma

Cameron University

- **Address:** 2800 W. Gore Boulevard, Lawton, OK 73505-6377
- **Website:** http://www.cameron.edu
- **Public**
- **Enrollment:** 3,173 full-time; 2,266 part-time

KEY STATS
- ✔ **U.S News College Ranking:** fourth tier, Universities–Master's (West)
- ✔ **ACT Score (25th/75th percentile):** 16-22
- ✔ **Tuition:** 2006-2007: $3,538 in state, $8,110 out of state
- **Selectivity:** Less selective
- **Acceptance rate:** 100%
- **Student/faculty ratio:** 17/1
- **Room/board:** $4,092
- **Average debt:** $6,300
- **Proportion who borrowed:** 32%

UNDERGRADUATE STUDENT BODY STATS
2005-2006 enrollment: 3,173 full-time; 2,266 part-time. Men: 40%; women: 60%. **Ethnic makeup:** African American: 19%; American-Indian: 8%; Asian American: 3%; Hispanic: 9%; White: 59%; International: 3%.

ADMISSIONS FACTS AND FIGURES
Phone: (580) 581-2289. **Email:** admissions@cameron.edu. **Website:** http://www.cameron.edu. **Application deadlines for fall 2007:** Regular decision: August 28. Early decision: Not offered. Early action: Not offered. Admission can be deferred. **Application fee:** $15. Common application is not accepted. **Admissions requirements/recommendations:** High school units required (recommended): English: 4; Mathematics: 3; Science: 2 (3); Foreign language: (1); Social studies: 0; History: 2; Academic electives: 3; Total units: 15. Tests: The college uses SAT or ACT scores in admissions decisions. Either SAT or ACT required. For admission to the fall 2007 entering class, the school will accept: ACT with writing, ACT without writing. Campus visit: Neither required nor recommended. Admissions interview: Neither required nor recommended. Off-campus interview: Not available. **Factors that count in admissions decisions:** *Academic:* Secondary school record: Very important. Class rank: Very important. Letters of recommendation: Not considered. Standardized test scores: Very important. Essay: Not considered. *Nonacademic:* Interview: Not considered. Extracurricular activities: Not considered. Talent/ability: Considered. Character/personal qualities: Not considered. Alumni/ae relationship: Not considered. Geographical residence: Considered. State residency: Not considered. Religious affiliation/commitment: Not considered. Minority status: Not considered. Volunteer work: Not considered. Work experience: Not considered. **Other schools with the greatest overlap in applicants:** Midwestern State University; Oklahoma State University; University of Central Oklahoma; University of Oklahoma; University of Science and Arts of Oklahoma. **Admissions statistics for the fall 2005 entering class:** Total applicants: 1,357. Total accepted: 1,356. Freshmen enrolled: 943; 12% were from out of state. Overall acceptance rate: 100%. **Credentials of fall 2005 freshmen:** 8% ranked in the top 10 percent of their high school class; 28% were in the top 25 percent, and 62% were in the top half. (Proportion submitting class standing: 62%.) **Average high school grade point average:** 3.1. **First-year students submitting ACT scores:** 61%. Scores (25/75 percentile): English: 15-22, Math: 16-20, Composite: 16-22.

ACADEMICS
Year founded: 1908. **Academic calendar:** Semester. **Degrees offered:** associate, bachelor's, master's. **Most popular majors:** 10% business administration and management, 7% education, 6% elementary education and teaching, 5% psychology, 4% criminology. **Major fields of study:** agriculture, agriculture operations, and related sciences; biological and biomedical sciences; business, management, marketing, and related support services; computer and information sciences and support services; education; engineering technologies/technicians; English language and literature/letters; family and consumer sciences/human sciences; foreign languages, literatures, and linguistics; health professions and related clinical sciences; history; mathematics and statistics; multi/interdisciplinary studies; physical sciences; psychology; social sciences; visual and performing arts. **Areas of required coursework:** humanities, computer literacy, mathematics, English (including composition), sciences (biological or physical), history, social science. **Special academic programs:** accelerated program, distance learning, double major, dual enrollment, honors program, independent study, internships, liberal arts/career combination, teacher certificate program, weekend college. **Teacher certification offered in:** early childhood, special education, elementary. **Cooperative education programs:** computer science, education, health professions. **Reserve Officers Training Corps (ROTC):** Army ROTC: Offered on campus. **Faculty and instruction (2005-2006):** Total instructional faculty: 168 full-time, 124 part-time (60% men; 40% women; 16% minorities). Full-time faculty with Ph.D. or other terminal degree: 71%. Student/faculty ratio: 17/1. Classes of fewer than 20 students: 42%; of 20 to 49 students: 55%; of 50 or more students: 3%. **Advanced Placement and International Baccalaureate credit:** AP tests may be used for: Credit only. Scores accepted: 3, 4, 5. **Freshmen returning for sophomore year:** 58%. **Graduation rates:** Four-year: 24%; five-year: 29%; six-year: 25%.

COSTS AND FINANCIAL AID
Financial aid office: (580) 581-2293. **Expenses (2006-2007):** Tuition and fees 2006-2007: $3,538 in state, $8,110 out of state; room/board: $4,092. Estimated books and supplies: $1,000; transportation: $1,284; personal expenses: $1,000. **Financial aid:** Priority filing date for institution's financial aid form: May 1. In 2005-2006, 56% of undergraduates applied for financial aid. Of those, 47% were determined to have financial need; 82% had their need fully met. Average financial aid package (proportion receiving): $3,500 (46%). Average amount of gift aid, such as scholarships or grants (proportion receiving): $2,500 (34%). Average amount of self-help aid, such as work study or loans (proportion receiving): $4,130 (35%). Average need-based loan (excluding PLUS or other private loans): $3,930. Among students who received need-based aid, the average percentage of need met: 87%. Among students who received aid based on merit, the average award (and the proportion receiving): $750 (9%). The average athletic scholarship (and the proportion receiving): $3,200 (4%). Average amount of debt of borrowers graduating in 2005: $6,300. Proportion who borrowed: 32%.

CAMPUS LIFE AND EXTRACURRICULAR ACTIVITIES
Campus housing available (% using): women's dorms (20%), men's dorms (20%), apartment for single students (60%). Students who live in college-owned, operated, or affiliated housing: 8%. **Student employment:** During the 2005-2006 academic year, 0% of undergraduates worked on campus. Average per-year earnings: $0. **Clubs and organizations:** Number of student organizations: 64. Activities include: choral groups, concert band, dance, drama/theater, jazz band, literary magazine, music ensembles, musical theater, opera, pep band, radio station, student government, student newspaper, student film society, symphony orchestra, television station. Number of fraternities: 2; sororities: 2. Proportion of men in fraternities: 1%; of women in sororities: 1%. Average proportion of students who stay on campus on weekends: 2%. **Sports program (2005-2006):** Member of NCAA II. *Men's intercollegiate varsity sports:* baseball, basketball, cross-country, golf, tennis. *Women's intercollegiate varsity sports:* basketball, golf, softball, tennis, volleyball.

SERVICES AND FACILITIES
Basic services: placement service. **Remedial assistance:** reading, math, writing, study skills. **Counseling services:** minority student, career, military, veteran student, academic. **For learning-disabled students:** School does not offer a structured program with separate admission and additional fees. **Library:** Number of titles: 267,887; number of current serial subscriptions: 15,928. **Information technology resources:** Students are not required to lease or own a computer. Number of campus computers available to all students: 526. School has a wireless network. Approximate number of users that can be accommodated: 100. Proportion of college-owned housing units wired for high-speed internet access: 100%. **Campus safety:** Security services offered: 24-hour foot-and-vehicle patrols, late-night transport/escort service, lighted pathways/sidewalks, controlled dormitory access (key, security card, etc).

TRANSFER AND INTERNATIONAL STUDENTS

Transfer students: May apply for admission for the following academic terms: Fall, Spring, Summer. Applicants need a minimum number of credits to apply. For fall 2005: Transfer applications received: 559. Transfer applicants offered admission: 557. Transfer applicants enrolled: 399.
International students: Number of foreign undergraduates: 156 (3% of student body). Number of countries represented: 46. Minimum TOEFL score required: 500 (paper); 185 (computer). Average TOEFL score: 525 (paper).

East Central University

- **Address:** 14th Street and Francis Avenue, Ada, OK 74820
- **Website:** http://www.ecok.edu
- **Public**
- **Enrollment:** 3,151 full-time; 668 part-time

KEY STATS

✔ **U.S News College Ranking:** fourth tier, Universities–Master's (West)
✔ **ACT Score (25th/75th percentile):** 18-23
✔ **Tuition:** 2005-2006: $3,042 in state, $7,366 out of state

Selectivity: Selective	**Room/board:** $3,980
Acceptance rate: 55%	**Average debt:** $19,882
Student/faculty ratio: 20/1	**Proportion who borrowed:** 60%

UNDERGRADUATE STUDENT BODY STATS

2005-2006 enrollment: 3,151 full-time; 668 part-time. Men: 39%; women: 61%. **Ethnic makeup:** African American: 5%; American-Indian: 20%; Asian American: 1%; Hispanic: 2%; White: 71%; International: 1%.

ADMISSIONS FACTS AND FIGURES

Phone: (580) 310-5239. **Email:** parmstro@mailclerk.ecok.edu. **Website:** http://www.ecok.edu. **Application deadlines for fall 2007:** Regular decision: Rolling. Early decision: Not offered. Early action: Not offered. Admission cannot be deferred. **Application fee:** $20. Common application is not accepted. **Admissions requirements/recommendations:** High school units required (recommended): English: 4 (4); Mathematics: 3 (3); Science: 2 (2); Social studies: 1 (1); History: 2 (2); Academic electives: 3 (3); Total units: 15 (15). Tests: The college uses SAT or ACT scores in admissions decisions. Either SAT or ACT required. For admission to the fall 2007 entering class, the school will accept: ACT with writing, ACT without writing. Campus visit: Recommended. Admissions interview: Neither required nor recommended. **Factors that count in admissions decisions:** *Academic:* Secondary school record: Not considered. Class rank: Very important. Letters of recommendation: Not considered. Standardized test scores: Very important. Essay: Not considered. *Nonacademic:* Interview: Not considered. Extracurricular activities: Not considered. Talent/ability: Not considered. Character/personal qualities: Not considered. Alumni/ae relationship: Not considered. Geographical residence: Not considered. State residency: Not considered. Religious affiliation/commitment: Not considered. Minority status: Not considered. Volunteer work: Not considered. Work experience: Not considered. **Admissions statistics for the fall 2005 entering class:** Total applicants: 1,103. Total accepted: 607. Freshmen enrolled: 572; 6% were from out of state. Overall acceptance rate: 55%. **Credentials of fall 2005 freshmen:** 17% ranked in the top 10 percent of their high school class; 41% were in the top 25 percent, and 76% were in the top half. (Proportion submitting class standing: 83%.) Average high school grade point average: 3.3. First-year students submitting ACT scores: 100%. Scores (25/75 percentile): English: 17-24, Math: 16-22, Composite: 18-23.

ACADEMICS

Year founded: 1909. **Academic calendar:** Semester. **Degrees offered:** bachelor's, master's. **Most popular majors:** 13% human services, 9% business administration and management, 8% elementary education and teaching, 8% nursing/registered nurse training (R.N., A.S.N., B.S.N., M.S.N.), 5% general studies. **Major fields of study:** biological and biomedical sciences; business, management, marketing, and related support services; communication, journalism, and related programs; computer and information sciences and support services; education; English language and literature/letters; family and consumer sciences/human sciences; health professions and related clinical sciences; history; legal professions and studies; liberal arts and sciences studies, and humanities; mathematics and statistics; physical sciences; psychology; public administration and social service professions; security and protective services; social sciences; visual and performing arts. **Areas of required coursework:** arts/fine arts, humanities, computer literacy, mathematics, English (including composition), foreign languages, sciences (biological or physical), history, social science. **Pre-professional programs:** pre-law, pre-dentistry, pre-medicine, pre-veterinary science, pre-optometry, pre-pharmacy, other. **Special academic programs:** distance learning, double major, dual enrollment, exchange student program (domestic), honors program, independent study, internships, student-designed major, teacher certificate program. **Teacher certification offered in:** early childhood, special education, elementary, middle/junior high, secondary. **Faculty and instruction (2005-2006):** Total instructional faculty: 156 full-time, 87 part-time (52% men; 48% women; 8% minorities). Full-time faculty with Ph.D. or other terminal degree: 71%. Student/faculty ratio: 20/1. Classes of fewer than 20 students: 45%; of 20 to 49 students: 52%; of 50 or more students: 3%. **Advanced Placement and International Baccalaureate credit:** AP tests may be used for: Credit only. Scores accepted: 3, 4, 5. International Baccalaureate exams may be used for: Credit only. **Freshmen returning for sophomore year:** 63%. **Graduation rates:** Four-year: 14%; five-year: 30%; six-year: 34%.

COSTS AND FINANCIAL AID

Financial aid office: (580) 310-5242. **Expenses (2005-2006):** Tuition and fees 2005-2006: $3,042 in state, $7,366 out of state; room/board: $3,980. **Financial aid:** Priority filing date for institution's financial aid form: March 1. In 2005-2006, 78% of undergraduates applied for financial aid. Of those, 69% were determined to have financial need; 16% had their need fully met. Average financial aid package (proportion receiving): $6,325 (66%). Average amount of gift aid, such as scholarships or grants (proportion receiving): $2,946 (49%). Average amount of self-help aid, such as work study or loans (proportion receiving): $3,519 (42%). Average need-based loan (excluding PLUS or other private loans): $3,511. Among students who received need-based aid, the average percentage of need met: 44%. Among students who received aid based on merit, the average award (and the proportion receiving): $1,217 (3%). The average athletic scholarship (and the proportion receiving): $3,522 (3%). Average amount of debt of borrowers graduating in 2005: $19,882. Proportion who borrowed: 60%.

CAMPUS LIFE AND EXTRACURRICULAR ACTIVITIES

Campus housing available (% using): coed dorms (44%), women's dorms (11%), sorority housing (7%), fraternity housing (6%), apartments for married students (15%), apartment for single students (15%), special housing for disabled students (2%). Students who live in college-owned, operated, or affiliated housing: 20%. **Student employment:** During the 2005-2006 academic year, 9% of undergraduates worked on campus. Average per-year earnings: $4,798. **Clubs and organizations:** Number of student organizations: 88. Activities include: choral groups, concert band, dance, drama/theater, jazz band, marching band, music ensembles, musical theater, opera, pep band, student government, student newspaper, yearbook. Number of fraternities: 4; sororities: 3. Proportion of men in fraternities: 2%; of women in sororities: 2%. Average proportion of students who stay on campus on weekends: 5%. **Sports program (2005-2006):** Member of NCAA II. *Men's intercollegiate varsity sports:* baseball, basketball, cross-country, football, golf, tennis. *Women's intercollegiate varsity sports:* basketball, cross-country, soccer, softball, tennis.

SERVICES AND FACILITIES

Basic services: nonremedial tutoring, placement service, day care, health service, health insurance. **Remedial assistance:** reading, math, writing, study skills, other. **Counseling services:** minority student, career, personal, veteran student, academic, older student, psychological. **For learning-disabled students:** School does not offer a structured program with separate admission and additional fees. Total undergraduates in learning-disabled program or receiving services: 31. Services include: remedial math, remedial English, remedial reading, tape recorders, videotaped classes, note-taking services, oral tests, learning center, readers, extended time for tests, tutors, priority registration, priority seating, proofreading services, texts on tape, typist/scribe, exams on tape or computer, other testing accomodations, other. **Library:** Number of titles: 188,771; number of current serial subscriptions: 17,098. **Information technology resources:** Students are not required to lease or own a computer. Number of campus computers available to all students: 700. School has a wireless network. Approximate number of users that can be accommodated: 250. Proportion of college-owned housing units wired for high-speed internet access: 0%. **Campus safety:** Security services offered: 24-hour foot-and-vehicle patrols, 24-hour emergency telephones, lighted pathways/sidewalks, controlled dormitory access (key, security card, etc).

TRANSFER AND INTERNATIONAL STUDENTS

Transfer students: May apply for admission for the following academic terms: Fall, Spring, Summer. Applicants need a minimum number of credits to apply. For fall 2005: Transfer applications received: 454. Transfer applicants offered admission: 444. Transfer applicants enrolled: 366. **International students:** Number of foreign undergraduates: 51 (1% of student body). Number of countries represented: 32. Minimum TOEFL score required: 500 (paper); 173 (computer).

Langston University

- **Address:** PO Box 907, Langston, OK 73050
- **Website:** http://www.lunet.edu
- **Public**
- **Enrollment:** N/A

KEY STATS

✔ **U.S News College Ranking:** fourth tier, Comp. Coll.–Bachelor's (West)
✔ **SAT or ACT Score (25th/75th percentile):** N/A
✔ **Tuition:** N/A
  Selectivity: Less selective   **Room/board:** N/A
  Acceptance rate: N/A   **Average debt:** N/A
  Student/faculty ratio: N/A   **Proportion who borrowed:** N/A

Northeastern State University

- **Address:** 600 N. Grand, Tahlequah, OK 74464
- **Website:** http://www.nsuok.edu
- **Public**
- **Enrollment:** 6,516 full-time; 2,109 part-time

KEY STATS

✔ **U.S News College Ranking:** fourth tier, Universities–Master's (West)
✔ **ACT Score (25th/75th percentile):** 18-23
✔ **Tuition:** 2006-2007: $3,270 in state, $8,040 out of state
  Selectivity: Selective   **Room/board:** $3,080
  Acceptance rate: 76%   **Average debt:** $17,824
  Student/faculty ratio: 21/1   **Proportion who borrowed:** 69%

UNDERGRADUATE STUDENT BODY STATS

2005-2006 enrollment: 6,516 full-time; 2,109 part-time. Men: 39%; women: 61%. **Ethnic makeup:** African American: 6%; American-Indian: 29%; Asian American: 1%; Hispanic: 2%; White: 60%; International: 3%.

ADMISSIONS FACTS AND FIGURES

Phone: (918) 458-2200. **Email:** nsuinfo@nsuok.edu. **Website:** http://www.nsuok.edu. **Application deadlines for fall 2007:** Regular decision: Rolling; decision sent by August 25. Early decision: Not offered. Early action: Not offered. Admission cannot be deferred. Common application is not accepted. **Admissions requirements/recommendations:** High school units required (recommended): English: 4; Mathematics: 3; Science: 2; Foreign language: 0; Social studies: 0; History: 2; Academic electives: 0; Total units: 15. Tests: The college uses SAT or ACT scores in admissions decisions. ACT required. For admission to the fall 2007 entering class, the school will accept: ACT with writing, ACT without writing. Campus visit: Recommended. Admissions interview: Neither required nor recommended. Off-campus interview: Not available. **Factors that count in admissions decisions:** *Academic:* Secondary school record: Very important. Class rank: Very important. Standardized test scores: Very important. Essay: Not considered. *Nonacademic:* Interview: Not considered. Extracurricular activities: Not considered. Talent/ability: Not considered. Character/personal qualities: Not considered. Alumni/ae relationship: Not considered. Geographical residence: Considered. State residency: Considered. Religious affiliation/commitment: Not considered. Minority status: Not considered. Volunteer work: Not considered. Work experience: Not considered. **Admissions statistics for the fall 2005 entering class:** Total applicants: 2,174. Total accepted: 1,650. Freshmen enrolled: 1,104; 12% were from out of state. Overall acceptance rate: 76%. **Credentials of fall 2005 freshmen:** 16% ranked in the top 10 percent of their high school class; 37% were in the top 25 percent, and 72%

were in the top half. (Proportion submitting class standing: 85%.) **Average high school grade point average:** 3.2. **First-year students submitting ACT scores:** 91%. Scores (25/75 percentile): English: N/A, Math: N/A, Composite: 18-23.

ACADEMICS

Year founded: 1846. **Academic calendar:** Semester. **Degrees offered:** bachelor's, post-bachelor's certificate, master's, first professional, doctorate. **Most popular majors:** 16% elementary education and teaching, 8% business administration and management, 8% criminal justice/law enforcement administration, 5% biology/biological sciences, 5% early childhood education and teaching. **Major fields of study:** area, ethnic, cultural, and gender studies; biological and biomedical sciences; business, management, marketing, and related support services; communication, journalism, and related programs; computer and information sciences and support services; education; engineering; engineering technologies/technicians; English language and literature/letters; family and consumer sciences/human sciences; foreign languages, literatures, and linguistics; health professions and related clinical sciences; history; legal professions and studies; liberal arts and sciences studies, and humanities; mathematics and statistics; natural resources and conservation; parks, recreation, leisure, and fitness studies; physical sciences; psychology; public administration and social service professions; security and protective services; social sciences; visual and performing arts. **Areas of required coursework:** humanities, computer literacy, mathematics, English (including composition), sciences (biological or physical), history, social science, other. **Pre-professional programs:** pre-law, predentistry, pre-medicine, pre-theology, pre-veterinary science, pre-optometry, pre-pharmacy. **Special academic programs (% participation):** cooperative (work-study plan) program (.05%), distance learning (2%), double major (1%), dual enrollment (10%), honors program (1%), independent study (1%), internships (15%), student-designed major (.05%), teacher certificate program (29%), weekend college (1%). **Teacher certification offered in:** early childhood, special education, elementary, middle/junior high, secondary. **Cooperative education programs:** business, health professions. **Reserve Officers Training Corps (ROTC):** Army ROTC: Offered on campus. **Faculty and instruction (2005-2006):** Total instructional faculty: 325 full-time, 132 part-time (50% men; 50% women; 12% minorities). Full-time faculty with Ph.D. or other terminal degree: 67%. Student/faculty ratio: 21/1. Classes of fewer than 20 students: 40%; of 20 to 49 students: 53%; of 50 or more students: 7%. **Advanced Placement and International Baccalaureate credit:** AP tests may be used for: Credit and/or placement. Scores accepted: 3, 4, 5. International Baccalaureate exams may be used for: Credit only. **Freshmen returning for sophomore year:** 72%. **Graduation rates:** Four-year: 11%; five-year: 27%; six-year: 34%. **Graduate study:** 7% of students pursue further study immediately upon graduation; 12% within one year; 20% within five years. Fields in which graduates pursue further study: Master of Business Administration (MBA), 25%; law, 1%; medicine, 3%; dentistry, 1%; education, 65%; arts and sciences, 4%.

COSTS AND FINANCIAL AID

Financial aid office: (918) 456-5511. **Expenses (2006-2007):** Tuition and fees 2006-2007: $3,270 in state, $8,040 out of state; room/board: $3,080. Estimated books and supplies: $900; transportation: $1,200; personal expenses: $1,000. **Financial aid:** Priority filing date for institution's financial aid form: April 15. In 2005-2006, 92% of undergraduates applied for financial aid. Of those, 90% were determined to have financial need; 10% had their need fully met. Average financial aid package (proportion receiving): $3,686 (90%). Average amount of gift aid, such as scholarships or grants (proportion receiving): $1,884 (60%). Average amount of self-help aid, such as work study or loans (proportion receiving): $1,895 (59%). Average need-based loan (excluding PLUS or other private loans): $1,758. Among students who received need-based aid, the average percentage of need met: 67%. Among students who received aid based on merit, the average award (and the proportion receiving): $1,933 (2%). The average athletic scholarship (and the proportion receiving): $3,390 (4%). Average amount of debt of borrowers graduating in 2005: $17,824. Proportion who borrowed: 69%.

CAMPUS LIFE AND EXTRACURRICULAR ACTIVITIES

Campus housing available (% using): coed dorms (88%), sorority housing (6%), apartments for married students (5%), special housing for disabled students (1%). Students who live in college-owned, operated, or affiliated housing: 18%. **Student employment:** During the 2005-2006 academic year, 68% of undergraduates worked on campus. Average per-year earnings: $4,100. **Clubs and organizations:** Number of student organizations: 74. Activities include: choral groups, concert band, dance, drama/theater, jazz band, literary magazine, marching band, music ensembles, musical theater, pep band, student government, student newspaper, symphony orchestra, television station. Number of fraternities: 7; sororities: 5. Proportion of men in fraternities: 2%; of women in sororities: 2%. **Sports program (2005-2006):** Member of NCAA II. *Men's intercollegiate varsity sports:* baseball, basketball, football, golf, soccer. *Women's intercollegiate varsity sports:* basketball, golf, soccer, softball, tennis.

SERVICES AND FACILITIES
Basic services: nonremedial tutoring, placement service, health service. **Remedial assistance:** reading, math, writing, other. **Counseling services:** minority student, career, military, personal, veteran student, academic, older student, birth control. **For learning-disabled students:** School does not offer a structured program with separate admission and additional fees. Total undergraduates in learning-disabled program or receiving services: 195. Services include: remedial math, remedial English, remedial reading, tape recorders, untimed tests, note-taking services, oral tests, readers, extended time for tests, tutors. **Library:** Number of titles: 398,798; number of current serial subscriptions: 5,089. **Information technology resources:** Students are not required to lease or own a computer. Number of campus computers available to all students: 772. School has a wireless network. Approximate number of users that can be accommodated: 120. Proportion of college-owned housing units wired for high-speed internet access: 100%. **Campus safety:** Security services offered: 24-hour foot-and-vehicle patrols, late-night transport/escort service, 24-hour emergency telephones, student patrols, controlled dormitory access (key, security card, etc).

TRANSFER AND INTERNATIONAL STUDENTS
Transfer students: May apply for admission for the following academic terms: Fall, Spring, Summer. Applicants need a minimum number of credits to apply. For fall 2005: Transfer applications received: 1,807. Transfer applicants offered admission: 1,475. Transfer applicants enrolled: 1,144. **International students:** Number of foreign undergraduates: 233 (3% of student body). Number of countries represented: 44. Minimum TOEFL score required: 500 (paper); 173 (computer).

Northwestern Oklahoma State University

■ **Address:** 709 Oklahoma Boulevard, Alva, OK 73717
■ **Website:** http://www.nwalva.edu
■ **Public**
■ **Enrollment:** 1,475 full-time; 389 part-time

KEY STATS
✔ **U.S News College Ranking:** fourth tier, Universities–Master's (West)
✔ **ACT Score (25th/75th percentile):** 17-22
✔ **Tuition:** 2006-2007: $3,428 in state, $8,498 out of state

Selectivity: Less selective	**Room/board:** $3,310
Acceptance rate: 99%	**Average debt:** $9,476
Student/faculty ratio: N/A	**Proportion who borrowed:** 47%

UNDERGRADUATE STUDENT BODY STATS
2005-2006 enrollment: 1,475 full-time; 389 part-time. Men: 41%; women: 59%. **Ethnic makeup:** African American: 4%; American-Indian: 4%; Asian American: 1%; Hispanic: 3%; White: 85%; International: 3%.

ADMISSIONS FACTS AND FIGURES
Phone: (580) 327-8545. **Email:** preadm@nwosu.edu. **Website:** http://www.nwalva.edu. **Application deadlines for fall 2007:** Regular decision: Rolling. Early decision: Not offered. Early action: Not offered. **Application fee:** $15. Common application is not accepted. **Admissions requirements/recommendations:** High school units required (recommended): English: 4; Mathematics: 3; Science: 2; Foreign language: (2); History: 2; Academic electives: (3); Total units: 15. Tests: The college uses SAT or ACT scores in admissions decisions. Either SAT or ACT required. For admission to the fall 2007 entering class, the school will accept: ACT with writing, ACT without writing. Campus visit: Recommended. Admissions interview: Neither required nor recommended. **Factors that count in admissions decisions:** *Academic:* Secondary school record: Very important. Class rank: Important. Letters of recommendation: Not considered. Standardized test scores: Very important. Essay: Not considered. *Nonacademic:* Interview: Not considered. Extracurricular activities: Not considered. Talent/ability: Considered. Character/personal qualities: Not consid-

ered. Alumni/ae relationship: Not considered. Geographical residence: Not considered. State residency: Not considered. Religious affiliation/commitment: Not considered. Minority status: Not considered. Volunteer work: Not considered. Work experience: Not considered. **Other schools with the greatest overlap in applicants:** Oklahoma State University; Southwestern Oklahoma State University; University of Central Oklahoma; University of Oklahoma. **Admissions statistics for the fall 2005 entering class:** Total applicants: 438. Total accepted: 434. Freshmen enrolled: 291; 22% were from out of state. Overall acceptance rate: 99%. **Credentials of fall 2005 freshmen:** 12% ranked in the top 10 percent of their high school class; 28% were in the top 25 percent, and 57% were in the top half. (Proportion submitting class standing: 94%.) **Average high school grade point average:** 3.2. **First-year students submitting ACT scores:** 94%. Scores (25/75 percentile): English: N/A, Math: N/A, Composite: 17-22.

ACADEMICS
Year founded: 1897. **Academic calendar:** Semester. **Degrees offered:** bachelor's, master's. **Most popular majors:** 16% business administration and management, 11% elementary education and teaching, 9% nursing/registered nurse training (R.N., A.S.N., B.S.N., M.S.N.), 6% psychology, 5% criminal justice/police science. **Major fields of study:** agriculture, agriculture operations, and related sciences; biological and biomedical sciences; business, management, marketing, and related support services; communication, journalism, and related programs; computer and information sciences and support services; construction trades; education; English language and literature/letters; family and consumer sciences/human sciences; foreign languages, literatures, and linguistics; health professions and related clinical sciences; liberal arts and sciences studies, and humanities; library science; mathematics and statistics; parks, recreation, leisure, and fitness studies; physical sciences; psychology; public administration and social service professions; security and protective services; visual and performing arts. **Areas of required coursework:** humanities, computer literacy, mathematics, English (including composition), sciences (biological or physical), history. **Special academic programs:** cooperative (work-study plan) program, distance learning, double major, independent study, internships, teacher certificate program. **Teacher certification offered in:** early childhood, special education, elementary, middle/junior high, secondary. **Faculty and instruction (2005-2006):** Total instructional faculty: N/A. Classes of fewer than 20 students: 74%; of 20 to 49 students: 25%; of 50 or more students: 1%. **Freshmen returning for sophomore year:** 66%. **Graduation rates:** Four-year: 26%; five-year: 35%; six-year: 30%.

COSTS AND FINANCIAL AID
Financial aid office: (580) 327-8542. **Expenses (2006-2007):** Tuition and fees 2006-2007: $3,428 in state, $8,498 out of state; room/board: $3,310. Estimated books and supplies: $900; transportation: $1,000; personal expenses: $1,200. **Financial aid:** In 2005-2006, 85% of undergraduates applied for financial aid. Of those, 57% were determined to have financial need; 43% had their need fully met. Average financial aid package (proportion receiving): $5,598 (57%). Average amount of gift aid, such as scholarships or grants (proportion receiving): $3,531 (48%). Average amount of self-help aid, such as work study or loans (proportion receiving): $2,883 (35%). Average need-based loan (excluding PLUS or other private loans): $3,053. Among students who received need-based aid, the average percentage of need met: 75%. Among students who received aid based on merit, the average award (and the proportion receiving): $1,104 (15%). The average athletic scholarship (and the proportion receiving): $1,950 (9%). Average amount of debt of borrowers graduating in 2005: $9,476. Proportion who borrowed: 47%.

CAMPUS LIFE AND EXTRACURRICULAR ACTIVITIES
Campus housing available: women's dorms, men's dorms. Students who live in college-owned, operated, or affiliated housing: 20%. Activities include: choral groups, concert band, dance, drama/theater, jazz band, marching band, music ensembles, musical theater, pep band, radio station, student government, student newspaper, television station, yearbook. Number of fraternities: 1; sororities: 2. **Sports program (2005-2006):** Member of NAIA. *Men's intercollegiate varsity sports:* baseball, basketball, cross-country, football, golf. *Women's intercollegiate varsity sports:* basketball, cross-country, golf, soccer, softball.

SERVICES AND FACILITIES
Basic services: nonremedial tutoring, placement service. **Remedial assistance:** reading, math, writing. **Counseling services:** personal, academic. **Information technology resources:** Students are not required to lease or own a computer.

TRANSFER AND INTERNATIONAL STUDENTS

Transfer students: May apply for admission for the following academic terms: Fall, Spring, Summer. Applicants need a minimum number of credits to apply. For fall 2005: Transfer applications received: 349. Transfer applicants offered admission: 349. Transfer applicants enrolled: 252. **International students:** Number of foreign undergraduates: 51 (3% of student body).

Oklahoma Baptist University

- ■ **Address:** 500 W. University, Shawnee, OK 74804
- ■ **Website:** http://www.okbu.edu
- ■ **Private; Religious affiliation:** Southern Baptist Convention
- ■ **Enrollment:** 1,405 full-time; 244 part-time

KEY STATS

- ✔ **U.S News College Ranking:** 5, Comp. Coll.–Bachelor's (West)
- ✔ **ACT Score (25th/75th percentile):** 21-27
- ✔ **Tuition:** 2006-2007: $14,666

Selectivity: More selective	**Room/board:** $4,330
Acceptance rate: 99%	**Average debt:** $16,614
Student/faculty ratio: 15/1	**Proportion who borrowed:** 51%

UNDERGRADUATE STUDENT BODY STATS

2005-2006 enrollment: 1,405 full-time; 244 part-time. Men: 45%; women: 55%. **Ethnic makeup:** African American: 5%; American-Indian: 6%; Asian American: 2%; Hispanic: 3%; White: 81%; International: 3%. **Religious preference:** Roman Catholic: 1%; Protestant: 14%; No preference: 12%; Unknown: 1%; Southern Baptist Convention: 72%.

ADMISSIONS FACTS AND FIGURES

Phone: (405) 878-2023. **Email:** admissions@okbu.edu. **Website:** http://www.okbu.edu. **Application deadlines for fall 2007:** Regular decision: August 1. Early decision: Not offered. Early action: Not offered. Admission can be deferred. **Application fee:** $25. Common application is accepted. **To apply online, go to:** http://www.okbu.edu/admissions/onlineapp.html?section=welcome. **Admissions requirements/recommendations:** High school units required (recommended): English: 4 (4); Mathematics: 3 (3); Science: 3 (3); Foreign language: 2 (2); Social studies: 1 (1); History: 2 (2); Academic electives: 2 (2); Total units: 17 (17). Tests: The college uses SAT or ACT scores in admissions decisions. Either SAT or ACT required. For admission to the fall 2007 entering class, the school will accept: ACT with writing, ACT without writing. Campus visit: Recommended. Admissions interview: Recommended. Off-campus interview: May be arranged. **Factors that count in admissions decisions:** *Academic:* Secondary school record: Very important. Class rank: Important. Letters of recommendation: Important. Standardized test scores: Important. Essay: Considered. *Nonacademic:* Interview: Important. Extracurricular activities: Important. Talent/ability: Important. Character/personal qualities: Important. Alumni/ae relationship: Considered. Geographical residence: Considered. State residency: Not considered. Religious affiliation/commitment: Considered. Minority status: Not considered. Volunteer work: Considered. Work experience: Considered. **Other schools with the greatest overlap in applicants:** East Central University; Oklahoma State University; Southwestern Oklahoma State University; University of Central Oklahoma; University of Oklahoma. **Admissions statistics for the fall 2005 entering class:** Total applicants: 876. Total accepted: 867. Freshmen enrolled: 374; 42% were from out of state. Overall acceptance rate: 99%. **Credentials of fall 2005 freshmen:** 36% ranked in the top 10 percent of their high school class; 60% were in the top 25 percent, and 86% were in the top half. (Proportion submitting class standing: 77%.) Average high school grade point average: 3.6. **First-year students who submitted SAT scores:** 28%. Scores (25/75 percentile): Verbal: 520-610, Math: 500-600, Combined: 1020-1210. **First-year students submitting ACT scores:** 86%. Scores (25/75 percentile): English: 21-28, Math: 18-27, Composite: 21-27.

ACADEMICS

Year founded: 1910. **Academic calendar:** 4-1-4. **Degrees offered:** associate, bachelor's. **Most popular majors:** 11% elementary education and teaching, 8% Bible/biblical studies, 7% nursing, 5% family psychology, 4% business administration, management, and operations. **Major fields of study:** biological and biomedical sciences; business, management, marketing, and related

support services; communication, journalism, and related programs; computer and information sciences and support services; education; English language and literature/letters; family and consumer sciences/human sciences; foreign languages, literatures, and linguistics; health professions and related clinical sciences; history; legal professions and studies; liberal arts and sciences studies, and humanities; mathematics and statistics; multi/interdisciplinary studies; parks, recreation, leisure, and fitness studies; philosophy and religious studies; physical sciences; psychology; social sciences; theology and religious vocations; visual and performing arts. **Areas of required coursework:** arts/fine arts, humanities, computer literacy, mathematics, English (including composition), philosophy, foreign languages, sciences (biological or physical), history, social science, other. **Pre-professional programs:** pre-law, pre-dentistry, pre-medicine, pre-theology, pre-veterinary science, pre-optometry, pre-pharmacy. **Special academic programs (% participation):** cooperative (work-study plan) program (25%), distance learning (1%), double major (1%), dual enrollment (1%), English as a Second Language (ESL) (4%), exchange student program (domestic) (1%), honors program (2%), independent study (4%), internships (5%), liberal arts/career combination (1%), student-designed major (1%), study abroad (11%), teacher certificate program (20%). **Teacher certification offered in:** early childhood, special education, elementary, middle/junior high, secondary. **Cooperative education programs:** art, business, computer science, education, health professions, social/behavioral science, other. **Faculty and instruction (2005-2006):** Total instructional faculty: 103 full-time, 54 part-time (55% men; 45% women; 6% minorities). Full-time faculty with Ph.D. or other terminal degree: 66%. Student/faculty ratio: 15/1. Classes of fewer than 20 students: 67%; of 20 to 49 students: 30%; of 50 or more students: 3%. **Advanced Placement and International Baccalaureate credit:** AP tests may be used for: Credit and/or placement. Scores accepted: 2. International Baccalaureate exams may be used for: Credit and/or placement. **Freshmen returning for sophomore year:** 71%. **Graduation rates:** Four-year: 53%; five-year: 53%; six-year: 54%. **Graduate study:** 39% of students pursue further study within one year. Fields in which graduates pursue further study: Master of Business Administration (MBA), 1%; law, 1%; medicine, 2%; theology (or the seminary), 22%; education, 2%; arts and sciences, 7%.

COSTS AND FINANCIAL AID

Financial aid office: (405) 878-2016. **Expenses (2006-2007):** Tuition and fees 2006-2007: $14,666; room/board: $4,330. Estimated books and supplies: $800; transportation: $150; personal expenses: $250. **Financial aid:** Priority filing date for institution's financial aid form: March 1. In 2005-2006, 79% of undergraduates applied for financial aid. Of those, 58% were determined to have financial need; 52% had their need fully met. Average financial aid package (proportion receiving): $12,278 (58%). Average amount of gift aid, such as scholarships or grants (proportion receiving): $3,700 (54%). Average amount of self-help aid, such as work study or loans (proportion receiving): $4,260 (39%). Average need-based loan (excluding PLUS or other private loans): $3,871. Among students who received need-based aid, the average percentage of need met: 70%. Among students who received aid based on merit, the average award (and the proportion receiving): $5,240 (21%). The average athletic scholarship (and the proportion receiving): $5,535 (17%). Average amount of debt of borrowers graduating in 2005: $16,614. Proportion who borrowed: 51%.

CAMPUS LIFE AND EXTRACURRICULAR ACTIVITIES

Campus housing available (% using): women's dorms (41%), men's dorms (28%), apartments for married students (3%), apartment for single students (28%), special housing for disabled students (0%). Students who live in college-owned, operated, or affiliated housing: 72%. **Student employment:** During the 2005-2006 academic year, 11% of undergraduates worked on campus. Average per-year earnings: $1,500. **Clubs and organizations:** Number of student organizations: 77. Activities include: choral groups, concert band, drama/theater, jazz band, literary magazine, music ensembles, musical theater, opera, pep band, student government, student newspaper, symphony orchestra, yearbook. Number of fraternities: 4; sororities: 4. Proportion of men in fraternities: 5%; of women in sororities: 5%. Average proportion of students who stay on campus on weekends: 55%. **Sports program (2005-2006):** Member of NAIA. *Men's intercollegiate varsity sports:* baseball, basketball, cross-country, golf, soccer, tennis, track and field (indoor), track and field (outdoor). *Women's intercollegiate varsity sports:* basketball, cross-country, golf, soccer, softball, tennis, track and field (indoor), track and field (outdoor).

SERVICES AND FACILITIES

Basic services: nonremedial tutoring, placement service, health service. **Remedial assistance:** reading, math, writing, study skills. **Counseling serv-**

ices: career, personal, religious. **For learning-disabled students:** School does not offer a structured program with separate admission and additional fees. Total undergraduates in learning-disabled program or receiving services: 34. Services include: remedial math, remedial English, reading machines, remedial reading, tape recorders, other special classes, untimed tests, note-taking services, oral tests, readers, extended time for tests, tutors, priority registration, priority seating, texts on tape, other testing accomodations. **Library:** Number of titles: 159,034; number of current serial subscriptions: 295. **Information technology resources:** Students are not required to lease or own a computer. Number of campus computers available to all students: 235. School has a wireless network. Approximate number of users that can be accommodated: 2,000. Proportion of college-owned housing units wired for high-speed internet access: 95%. **Campus safety:** Security services offered: 24-hour foot-and-vehicle patrols, lighted pathways/sidewalks, controlled dormitory access (key, security card, etc).

TRANSFER AND INTERNATIONAL STUDENTS

Transfer students: May apply for admission for the following academic terms: Fall, Winter, Spring, Summer. Applicants do not need a minimum number of credits to apply. For fall 2005: Transfer applications received: 215. Transfer applicants offered admission: 93. Transfer applicants enrolled: 91. **International students:** Number of foreign undergraduates: 51 (3% of student body). Number of countries represented: 13. Minimum TOEFL score required: 500 (paper); 173 (computer). Average TOEFL score: 525 (paper).

Oklahoma Christian University

- **Address:** Box 11000, Oklahoma City, OK 73136-1100
- **Website:** http://www.oc.edu/
- **Private; Religious affiliation:** Church of Christ
- **Enrollment:** 1,744 full-time; 91 part-time

KEY STATS

✔ **U.S News College Ranking:** 10, Comp. Coll.–Bachelor's (West)
✔ **ACT Score (25th/75th percentile):** 20-27
✔ **Tuition:** 2006-2007: $14,976

Selectivity: More selective	**Room/board:** $5,510
Acceptance rate: 100%	**Average debt:** $21,096
Student/faculty ratio: 16/1	**Proportion who borrowed:** 74%

UNDERGRADUATE STUDENT BODY STATS

2005-2006 enrollment: 1,744 full-time; 91 part-time. Men: 50%; women: 50%. **Ethnic makeup:** African American: 6%; American-Indian: 2%; Asian American: 1%; Hispanic: 3%; White: 87%. **Religious preference:** Roman Catholic: 1%; No preference: 1%; Church of Christ: 80%; Baptist: 8%; Other: 10%.

ADMISSIONS FACTS AND FIGURES

Phone: (405) 425-5050. **Email:** info@oc.edu. **Website:** http://www.oc.edu/. **Application deadlines for fall 2007:** Regular decision: September 5; decision sent by August 5. Early decision: Not offered. Early action: Not offered. Admission can be deferred. **Application fee:** $25. Common application is not accepted. **Admissions requirements/recommendations:** High school units required (recommended): English: 4; Mathematics: 3; Science: 2; Foreign language: (1); Social studies: 1; History: 2; Academic electives: 3. Tests: The college uses SAT or ACT scores in admissions decisions. Either SAT or ACT required. For admission to the fall 2007 entering class, the school will accept: ACT with writing. Campus visit: Recommended. Admissions interview: Recommended. Off-campus interview: May be arranged. **Factors that count in admissions decisions:** *Academic:* Secondary school record: Important. Class rank: Important. Letters of recommendation: Important. Standardized test scores: Very important. Essay: Important. *Nonacademic:* Interview: Important. Extracurricular activities: Important. Talent/ability: Important. Character/personal qualities: Very important. Alumni/ae relationship: Considered. Geographical residence: Not considered. State residency: Not considered. Religious affiliation/commitment: Important. Minority status: Important. Volunteer work: Important. Work experience: Considered. **Other schools with the greatest overlap in applicants:** Abilene Christian University; Harding University; Oklahoma State University; Texas A&M University–College Station; University of Oklahoma. **Admissions statistics for the fall 2005 entering class:** Total applicants: 1,419. Total accepted: 1,419. Freshmen enrolled: 611; 59% were from out of state. Overall accept-

ance rate: 100%. **Credentials of fall 2005 freshmen:** 23% ranked in the top 10 percent of their high school class; 46% were in the top 25 percent, and 77% were in the top half. (Proportion submitting class standing: 83%.) **Average high school grade point average:** 3.3. **First-year students who submitted SAT scores:** 28%. Scores (25/75 percentile): Verbal: 580-620, Math: 470-620, Combined: 1050-1240. **First-year students submitting ACT scores:** 100%. Scores (25/75 percentile): English: 20-28, Math: 18-26, Composite: 20-27.

ACADEMICS

Year founded: 1950. **Academic calendar:** Semester. **Degrees offered:** bachelor's, master's. **Most popular majors:** 17% business, management, marketing, and related support services, 16% liberal arts and sciences studies, and humanities, 12% education, 9% engineering, 6% biological and biomedical sciences. **Major fields of study:** biological and biomedical sciences; business, management, marketing, and related support services; communication, journalism, and related programs; computer and information sciences and support services; education; engineering; English language and literature/letters; family and consumer sciences/human sciences; foreign languages, literatures, and linguistics; history; legal professions and studies; liberal arts and sciences studies, and humanities; mathematics and statistics; parks, recreation, leisure, and fitness studies; physical sciences; psychology; social sciences; theology and religious vocations; visual and performing arts. **Areas of required coursework:** arts/fine arts, humanities, mathematics, English (including composition), philosophy, sciences (biological or physical), history, social science. **Pre-professional programs:** pre-law, pre-dentistry, pre-medicine, pre-theology, pre-veterinary science, pre-optometry, pre-pharmacy. **Special academic programs (% participation):** double major (8%), honors program (5%), independent study (5%), internships (1%), student-designed major (6%), study abroad (4%), teacher certificate program (11%). **Teacher certification offered in:** early childhood, elementary, secondary. **Cooperative education programs:** other. **Reserve Officers Training Corps (ROTC):** Army ROTC: Offered at cooperating institution (University of Central Oklahoma); Air Force ROTC: Offered at cooperating institution (University of Oklahoma). **Faculty and instruction (2005-2006):** Total instructional faculty: 78 full-time, 90 part-time (69% men; 31% women; 7% minorities). Full-time faculty with Ph.D. or other terminal degree: 74%. Student/faculty ratio: 16/1. Classes of fewer than 20 students: 35%; of 20 to 49 students: 55%; of 50 or more students: 10%. **Advanced Placement and International Baccalaureate credit:** AP tests may be used for: Credit and/or placement. Scores accepted: 3. International Baccalaureate exams may be used for: Credit and/or placement. **Freshmen returning for sophomore year:** 70%. **Graduation rates:** Four-year: 31%; five-year: 46%; six-year: 41%. **Graduate study:** 10% of students pursue further study immediately upon graduation; 20% within one year; 30% within five years. Fields in which graduates pursue further study: Master of Business Administration (MBA), 20%; law, 10%; medicine, 10%; dentistry, 3%; engineering, 5%; theology (or the seminary), 15%; education, 15%; arts and sciences, 20%; veterinary medicine, 3%.

COSTS AND FINANCIAL AID

Financial aid office: (405) 425-5190. **Expenses (2006-2007):** Tuition and fees 2006-2007: $14,976; room/board: $5,510. Estimated books and supplies: $800; transportation: $1,144; personal expenses: $3,518. **Financial aid:** Priority filing date for institution's financial aid form: March 15. In 2005-2006, 100% of undergraduates applied for financial aid. Of those, 70% were determined to have financial need; 22% had their need fully met. Average financial aid package (proportion receiving): $12,128 (69%). Average amount of gift aid, such as scholarships or grants (proportion receiving): $1,609 (36%). Average amount of self-help aid, such as work study or loans (proportion receiving): $4,342 (51%). Average need-based loan (excluding PLUS or other private loans): $3,677. Among students who received need-based aid, the average percentage of need met: 46%. Among students who received aid based on merit, the average award (and the proportion receiving): $1,827 (21%). The average athletic scholarship (and the proportion receiving): $4,250 (20%). Average amount of debt of borrowers graduating in 2005: $21,096. Proportion who borrowed: 74%.

CAMPUS LIFE AND EXTRACURRICULAR ACTIVITIES

Campus housing available (% using): women's dorms (32%), men's dorms (28%), apartments for married students (4%), apartment for single students (35%), special housing for disabled students (1%). Students who live in college-owned, operated, or affiliated housing: 72%. **Student employment:** During the 2005-2006 academic year, 22% of undergraduates worked on campus. Average per-year earnings: $1,500. **Clubs and organizations:** Number of student organizations: 51. Activities include: choral groups, concert band, drama/theater, jazz band, literary magazine, music ensembles, musical theater, opera, pep band, radio station, student government, student newspaper, symphony orchestra, television station, yearbook. Number of fraternities: 6; sororities: 7. Proportion of men in fraternities: 32%; of women in sororities: 34%. Average proportion of students who stay on campus on weekends: 70%. **Sports program (2005-2006):** Member of NAIA. *Men's intercollegiate varsity sports:* basketball, cross-country, golf, soccer, tennis, track and field (indoor), track and field (outdoor), tennis. *Women's intercollegiate varsity sports:* basketball, cross-country, soccer, softball, tennis, track and field (indoor), track and field (outdoor), tennis.

SERVICES AND FACILITIES

Basic services: nonremedial tutoring, placement service, health service, health insurance. **Remedial assistance:** math, writing. **Counseling services:** minority student, career, personal, veteran student, academic, psychological, religious. **For learning-disabled students:** School does not offer a structured program with separate admission and additional fees. Total undergraduates in learning-disabled program or receiving services: 52. Services include: remedial math, remedial English, tape recorders, untimed tests, note-taking services, oral tests, readers, extended time for tests, tutors, priority seating, texts on tape, typist/scribe, other testing accomodations. **Library:** Number of titles: 82,092; number of current serial subscriptions: 1,171. **Information technology resources:** Students are required to lease or own a computer. Number of campus computers available to all students: 2,200. School has a wireless network. Approximate number of users that can be accommodated: 2,000. Proportion of college-owned housing units wired for high-speed internet access: 100%. **Campus safety:** Security services offered: 24-hour foot-and-vehicle patrols, late-night transport/escort service, 24-hour emergency telephones, lighted pathways/sidewalks, controlled dormitory access (key, security card, etc).

TRANSFER AND INTERNATIONAL STUDENTS

Transfer students: May apply for admission for the following academic terms: Fall, Spring, Summer. Applicants do not need a minimum number of credits to apply. For fall 2005: Transfer applications received: 101. Transfer applicants offered admission: 101. Transfer applicants enrolled: 101. **International students:** Number of foreign undergraduates: 0. Number of countries represented: 26. Minimum TOEFL score required: 500 (paper); 173 (computer). Average TOEFL score: 515 (paper).

Oklahoma City University

- **Address:** 2501 N. Blackwelder, Oklahoma City, OK 73106-1493
- **Website:** http://www.okcu.edu
- **Private; Religious affiliation:** United Methodist
- **Enrollment:** 1,466 full-time; 445 part-time

KEY STATS

✔ **U.S News College Ranking:** 22, Universities–Master's (West)
✔ **ACT Score (25th/75th percentile):** 22-27
✔ **Tuition:** 2006-2007: $19,200

Selectivity: More selective	**Room/board:** $6,560
Acceptance rate: 81%	**Average debt:** $19,178
Student/faculty ratio: 12/1	**Proportion who borrowed:** 47%

UNDERGRADUATE STUDENT BODY STATS

2005-2006 enrollment: 1,466 full-time; 445 part-time. Men: 37%; women: 63%. **Ethnic makeup:** African American: 8%; American-Indian: 4%; Asian American: 2%; Hispanic: 4%; White: 62%; International: 20%. **Religious preference:** Roman Catholic: 10%; Protestant: 21%; Jewish: 1%; Muslim: 1%; Hindu: 1%; Buddhist: 1%; No preference: 14%; Unknown: 4%; United Methodist: 17%.

ADMISSIONS FACTS AND FIGURES

Phone: (405) 208-5050. **Email:** uadmissions@okcu.edu. **Website:** http://www.okcu.edu. **Application deadlines for fall 2007:** Regular decision: August 21. Early decision: Not offered. Early action: Not offered. Admission can be deferred. **Application fee:** $30. Common application is accepted. **To apply online, go to:** http://www.okcu.edu/admissions/online_menu.asp. **Admissions requirements/recommendations:** High school units required (recommended): English: 4; Mathematics: 3; Science: 3; Foreign language: 2; Social studies: 3; History: 3; Total units: 15. Tests: The college uses SAT or ACT scores in admissions decisions. Either SAT or ACT required. For

admission to the fall 2007 entering class, the school will accept: ACT with writing, ACT without writing. Campus visit: Recommended. Admissions interview: Recommended. Off-campus interview: May be arranged. **Factors that count in admissions decisions:** *Academic:* Secondary school record: Very important. Class rank: Very important. Letters of recommendation: Important. Standardized test scores: Very important. Essay: Very important. *Nonacademic:* Interview: Considered. Extracurricular activities: Important. Talent/ability: Very important. Character/personal qualities: Very important. Alumni/ae relationship: Considered. Geographical residence: Not considered. State residency: Not considered. Religious affiliation/commitment: Considered. Minority status: Important. Volunteer work: Important. Work experience: Considered. **Other schools with the greatest overlap in applicants:** Baylor University; New York University; Oklahoma State University; University of Oklahoma; University of Tulsa. **Admissions statistics for the fall 2005 entering class:** Total applicants: 1,044. Total accepted: 846. Freshmen enrolled: 370; 57% were from out of state. Overall acceptance rate: 81%. **Credentials of fall 2005 freshmen:** 30% ranked in the top 10 percent of their high school class; 65% were in the top 25 percent, and 87% were in the top half. (Proportion submitting class standing: 88%.) **Average high school grade point average:** 3.7. **First-year students who submitted SAT scores:** 34%. Scores (25/75 percentile): Verbal: 520-630, Math: 500-610, Combined: 1020-1240. **First-year students submitting ACT scores:** 77%. Scores (25/75 percentile): English: 22-28, Math: 19-26, Composite: 22-27.

ACADEMICS

Year founded: 1904. **Academic calendar:** Semester. **Degrees offered:** bachelor's, master's, first professional. **Most popular majors:** 30% liberal arts and sciences studies, and humanities, 23% visual and performing arts, 11% business, management, marketing, and related support services, 8% health professions and related clinical sciences. **Major fields of study:** biological and biomedical sciences; business, management, marketing, and related support services; communication, journalism, and related programs; computer and information sciences and support services; education; English language and literature/letters; foreign languages, literatures, and linguistics; health professions and related clinical sciences; history; liberal arts and sciences studies, and humanities; mathematics and statistics; philosophy and religious studies; physical sciences; psychology; social sciences; theology and religious vocations; visual and performing arts. **Areas of required coursework:** arts/fine arts, humanities, computer literacy, mathematics, English (including composition), philosophy, foreign languages, sciences (biological or physical), history, social science. **Pre-professional programs:** pre-law, pre-dentistry, pre-medicine, pre-theology, pre-veterinary science, pre-optometry, pre-pharmacy. **Special academic programs (% participation):** accelerated program, cooperative (work-study plan) program (18%), double major (4%), dual enrollment, English as a Second Language (ESL) (11%), exchange student program (domestic), external degree program, honors program (5%), independent study (35%), internships (78%), student-designed major, study abroad (21%), teacher certificate program. **Teacher certification offered in:** early childhood, elementary, middle/junior high, secondary, bilingual/bicultural. **Reserve Officers Training Corps (ROTC):** Army ROTC: Offered at cooperating institution (University of Central Oklahoma); Air Force ROTC: Offered at cooperating institution (University of Oklahoma). **Faculty and instruction (2005-2006):** Total instructional faculty: 170 full-time, 160 part-time (56% men; 44% women; 11% minorities). Full-time faculty with Ph.D. or other terminal degree: 79%. Student/faculty ratio: 12/1. Classes of fewer than 20 students: 65%; of 20 to 49 students: 34%; of 50 or more students: 1%. **Advanced Placement and International Baccalaureate credit:** AP tests may be used for: Credit and/or placement. Scores accepted: 3. International Baccalaureate exams may be used for: Credit only. **Freshmen returning for sophomore year:** 72%. **Graduation rates:** Four-year: 38%; five-year: 48%; six-year: 52%.

COSTS AND FINANCIAL AID

Financial aid office: (405) 208-5211. **Expenses (2006-2007):** Tuition and fees 2006-2007: $19,200; room/board: $6,560. Estimated books and supplies: $1,500; transportation: $1,600; personal expenses: $1,000. **Financial aid:** Priority filing date for institution's financial aid form: March 1. In 2005-2006, 69% of undergraduates applied for financial aid. Of those, 52% were determined to have financial need; 46% had their need fully met. Average financial aid package (proportion receiving): $15,462 (50%). Average amount of gift aid, such as scholarships or grants (proportion receiving): $11,621 (47%). Average amount of self-help aid, such as work study or loans (proportion receiving): $4,060 (36%). Average need-based loan (excluding PLUS or other private loans): $3,769. Among students who received need-based aid, the average percentage of need met: 86%. Among students who received aid based on merit, the average award (and the proportion receiv-

ing): $8,481 (14%). The average athletic scholarship (and the proportion receiving): $9,786 (13%). Average amount of debt of borrowers graduating in 2005: $19,178. Proportion who borrowed: 47%.

CAMPUS LIFE AND EXTRACURRICULAR ACTIVITIES

Campus housing available: women's dorms, men's dorms, fraternity housing, apartments for married students, apartment for single students, special housing for disabled students. Students who live in college-owned, operated, or affiliated housing: 54%. **Clubs and organizations:** Number of student organizations: 66. Activities include: choral groups, concert band, dance, drama/theater, jazz band, literary magazine, music ensembles, musical theater, opera, pep band, student government, student newspaper, symphony orchestra, television station, yearbook. Number of fraternities: 3; sororities: 3. Proportion of men in fraternities: 9%; of women in sororities: 11%. Average proportion of students who stay on campus on weekends: 28%. **Sports program (2005-2006):** Member of NAIA. *Men's intercollegiate varsity sports:* baseball, basketball, golf, soccer. *Women's intercollegiate varsity sports:* basketball, golf, soccer, softball.

SERVICES AND FACILITIES

Basic services: placement service, health service, health insurance. **Remedial assistance:** study skills. **Counseling services:** career, personal, academic, older student. **For learning-disabled students:** School does not offer a structured program with separate admission and additional fees. Total undergraduates in learning-disabled program or receiving services: 2. Services include: remedial math, remedial English, remedial reading, oral tests, learning center, readers, extended time for tests, tutors, priority seating, texts on tape, other testing accomodations. **Library:** Number of titles: 451,966; number of current serial subscriptions: 4,975. **Information technology resources:** Students are not required to lease or own a computer. Number of campus computers available to all students: 312. School has a wireless network. Approximate number of users that can be accommodated: 350. Proportion of college-owned housing units wired for high-speed internet access: 100%. **Campus safety:** Security services offered: 24-hour foot-and-vehicle patrols, late-night transport/escort service, 24-hour emergency telephones, lighted pathways/sidewalks, controlled dormitory access (key, security card, etc).

TRANSFER AND INTERNATIONAL STUDENTS

Transfer students: May apply for admission for the following academic terms: Fall, Spring, Summer. Applicants need a minimum number of credits to apply. For fall 2005: Transfer applications received: 339. Transfer applicants offered admission: 267. Transfer applicants enrolled: 139.
International students: Number of foreign undergraduates: 386 (20% of student body). Number of countries represented: 65. Minimum TOEFL score required: 500 (paper).

Oklahoma Panhandle State University

- **Address:** PO Box 430, Goodwell, OK 73939-0430
- **Website:** http://www.opsu.edu
- **Public**
- **Enrollment:** 921 full-time; 223 part-time

KEY STATS

✔ **U.S News College Ranking:** fourth tier, Comp. Coll.–Bachelor's (West)
✔ **SAT or ACT Score (25th/75th percentile):** N/A
✔ **Tuition:** 2006-2007: $3,461 in state, $5,687 out of state
  Selectivity: Less selective   **Room/board:** $4,100
  Acceptance rate: 100%   **Average debt:** N/A
  Student/faculty ratio: 13/1   **Proportion who borrowed:** N/A

UNDERGRADUATE STUDENT BODY STATS

2005-2006 enrollment: 921 full-time; 223 part-time. Men: 45%; women: 55%. **Ethnic makeup:** African American: 4%; American-Indian: 2%; Hispanic: 11%; White: 79%; International: 3%.

ADMISSIONS FACTS AND FIGURES

Phone: (800) 664-6778. **Email:** opsu@opsu.edu. **Website:** http://www.opsu.edu. **Application deadlines for fall 2007:** Regular decision: Rolling. Early decision: Not offered. Early action: Not offered. Admission can be deferred. Common application is accepted. **To apply online, go to:**

http://www.opsu.edu/require.htm. **Admissions requirements/recommendations:** High school units required (recommended): English: 4 (4); Mathematics: 3 (3); Science: 2 (2); Social studies: 1 (1); History: 2 (2); Academic electives: 3 (3); Total units: 15 (15). Tests: The college does not use SAT or ACT scores in admissions decisions. Neither SAT nor ACT required. For admission to the fall 2007 entering class, the school will accept: ACT without writing. Campus visit: Neither required nor recommended. Admissions interview: Neither required nor recommended. Off-campus interview: May be arranged. **Factors that count in admissions decisions:** *Academic:* Secondary school record: Very important. Class rank: Very important. Letters of recommendation: Not considered. Standardized test scores: Very important. Essay: Not considered. *Nonacademic:* Interview: Not considered. Extracurricular activities: Not considered. Talent/ability: Not considered. Character/personal qualities: Not considered. Alumni/ae relationship: Not considered. Geographical residence: Not considered. State residency: Not considered. Religious affiliation/commitment: Not considered. Minority status: Not considered. Volunteer work: Not considered. Work experience: Not considered. **Admissions statistics for the fall 2005 entering class:** Total applicants: 491. Total accepted: 491. Freshmen enrolled: 212; Overall acceptance rate: 100%.

ACADEMICS

Year founded: 1909. **Academic calendar:** Semester. **Degrees offered:** associate, bachelor's. **Most popular majors:** Information not available. **Major fields of study:** agriculture, agriculture operations, and related sciences; biological and biomedical sciences; business, management, marketing, and related support services; computer and information sciences and support services; education; engineering technologies/technicians; English language and literature/letters; health professions and related clinical sciences; history; liberal arts and sciences studies, and humanities; mathematics and statistics; parks, recreation, leisure, and fitness studies; physical sciences; psychology; social sciences. **Areas of required coursework:** humanities, computer literacy, mathematics, English (including composition), sciences (biological or physical), history, social science. **Special academic programs:** distance learning, double major, dual enrollment, English as a Second Language (ESL), honors program, teacher certificate program. **Faculty and instruction (2005-2006):** Total instructional faculty: 58 full-time, 31 part-time (52% men; 48% women; 3% minorities). Full-time faculty with Ph.D. or other terminal degree: 34%. Student/faculty ratio: 13/1. **Advanced Placement and International Baccalaureate credit:** AP tests may be used for: Credit only. Scores accepted: 3, 4, 5. International Baccalaureate exams may be used for: Credit only. **Freshmen returning for sophomore year:** 56%. **Graduation rates:** Four-year: 18%; five-year: 29%; six-year: 24%.

COSTS AND FINANCIAL AID

Financial aid office: (580) 349-1580. **Expenses (2006-2007):** Tuition and fees 2006-2007: $3,461 in state, $5,687 out of state; room/board: $4,100. **Financial aid:** Priority filing date for institution's financial aid form: March 15.

CAMPUS LIFE AND EXTRACURRICULAR ACTIVITIES

Campus housing available: coed dorms, women's dorms, men's dorms, apartments for married students, apartment for single students. Activities include: choral groups, concert band, jazz band, marching band, radio station, student government, student newspaper, yearbook. Number of fraternities: 0; sororities: 0. **Sports program (2005-2006):** Member of NCAA II. *Men's intercollegiate varsity sports:* baseball, basketball, cross-country, football, golf. *Women's intercollegiate varsity sports:* basketball, cross-country, golf, softball, volleyball.

SERVICES AND FACILITIES

Basic services: health service. **Remedial assistance:** reading, math, writing, study skills. **Information technology resources:** Students are not required to lease or own a computer. Number of campus computers available to all students: 160. School has a wireless network. Approximate number of users that can be accommodated: 250. Proportion of college-owned housing units wired for high-speed internet access: 100%.

TRANSFER AND INTERNATIONAL STUDENTS

Transfer students: May apply for admission for the following academic terms: Fall, Winter, Spring, Summer. Applicants need a minimum number of credits to apply. **International students:** Number of foreign undergraduates: 25 (3% of student body). Minimum TOEFL score required: 500 (paper); 173 (computer).

Oklahoma State University

- **Address:** 101 Whitehurst Hall, Stillwater, OK 74078
- **Website:** http://www.okstate.edu
- **Public**
- **Enrollment:** 16,731 full-time; 2,178 part-time

KEY STATS
✔ **U.S News College Ranking:** third tier, National Universities
✔ **ACT Score (25th/75th percentile):** 22-27
✔ **Tuition:** 2005-2006: $4,365 in state, $12,389 out of state
Selectivity: More selective **Room/board:** $5,848
Acceptance rate: 88% **Average debt:** $17,844
Student/faculty ratio: 19/1 **Proportion who borrowed:** 56%

UNDERGRADUATE STUDENT BODY STATS
2005-2006 enrollment: 16,731 full-time; 2,178 part-time. Men: 52%; women: 48%. **Ethnic makeup:** African American: 4%; American-Indian: 9%; Asian American: 2%; Hispanic: 2%; White: 79%; International: 4%.

ADMISSIONS FACTS AND FIGURES
Phone: (405) 744-6858. **Email:** admit@okstate.edu. **Website:** http://www.okstate.edu. **Application deadlines for fall 2007:** Regular decision: Rolling. Early decision: Not offered. Early action: Not offered. Admission cannot be deferred. **Application fee:** $40. Common application is not accepted. **Admissions requirements/recommendations:** High school units required (recommended): English: 4; Mathematics: 3; Science: 2; Foreign language: (2); Social studies: 2; History: 1; Academic electives: 3; Total units: 15 (3). Tests: The college uses SAT or ACT scores in admissions decisions. Either SAT or ACT required. For admission to the fall 2007 entering class, the school will accept: ACT with writing, ACT without writing. Campus visit: Recommended. Admissions interview: Recommended. Off-campus interview: Not available. **Factors that count in admissions decisions:** *Academic:* Secondary school record: Considered. Class rank: Very important. Letters of recommendation: Considered. Standardized test scores: Very important. Essay: Considered. *Nonacademic:* Interview: Considered. Extracurricular activities: Considered. Talent/ability: Considered. Character/personal qualities: Considered. Alumni/ae relationship: Not considered. Geographical residence: Not considered. State residency: Not considered. Religious affiliation/commitment: Not considered. Minority status: Not considered. Volunteer work: Not considered. Work experience: Not considered. **Other schools with the greatest overlap in applicants:** University of Oklahoma. **Admissions statistics for the fall 2005 entering class:** Total applicants: 6,533. Total accepted: 5,719. Freshmen enrolled: 3,315; 22% were from out of state. Overall acceptance rate: 88%. **Credentials of fall 2005 freshmen:** 27% ranked in the top 10 percent of their high school class; 55% were in the top 25 percent, and 85% were in the top half. (Proportion submitting class standing: 87%.) **Average high school grade point average:** 3.5. **First-year students who submitted SAT scores:** 27%. Scores (25/75 percentile): Verbal: 500-610, Math: 510-620, Combined: 1010-1230. **First-year students submitting ACT scores:** 93%. Scores (25/75 percentile): English: 21-28, Math: 20-26, Composite: 22-27.

ACADEMICS
Year founded: 1890. **Academic calendar:** Semester. **Degrees offered:** certificate, bachelor's, master's, post-master's certificate, first professional, doctorate. **Most popular majors:** 30% business, management, marketing, and related support services, 9% engineering, 8% agriculture, agriculture operations, and related sciences, 8% education, 8% family and consumer sciences/human sciences. **Major fields of study:** agriculture, agriculture operations, and related sciences; architecture and related services; area, ethnic, cultural, and gender studies; biological and biomedical sciences; business, management, marketing, and related support services; communication, journalism, and related programs; computer and information sciences and support services; education; engineering; engineering technologies/technicians; English language and literature/letters; family and consumer sciences/human sciences; foreign languages, literatures, and linguistics; health professions and related clinical sciences; history; liberal arts and sciences studies, and humanities; mathematics and statistics; natural resources and conservation; parks, recreation, leisure, and fitness studies; philosophy and religious studies; physical sciences; psychology; security and protective services; social sciences; transportation and materials moving; visual and performing arts. **Areas of required coursework:** humanities, mathematics, English (including composition), sciences (biological or physical), history, social science, other. **Pre-professional programs:** pre-law, pre-medicine, pre-veterinary science. **Special academic programs:** accelerated program, cooperative (work-study plan) program, cross-registration, distance learning, double major, dual enrollment, English as a Second Language (ESL), exchange student program (domestic), honors program, independent study, internships, student-designed major, study abroad, teacher certificate program. **Teacher certification offered in:** early childhood, elementary, secondary. **Reserve Officers Training Corps (ROTC):** Army ROTC: Offered on campus; Air Force ROTC: Offered on campus. **Faculty and instruction (2005-2006):** Total instructional faculty: 1,000 full-time, 237 part-time (66% men; 34% women; 9% minorities). Full-time faculty with Ph.D. or other terminal degree: 90%. Student/faculty ratio: 19/1. Classes of fewer than 20 students: 28%; of 20 to 49 students: 56%; of 50 or more students: 16%. **Advanced Placement and International Baccalaureate credit:** International Baccalaureate exams may be used for: Credit and/or placement. **Freshmen returning for sophomore year:** 80%. **Graduation rates:** Four-year: 26%; five-year: 53%; six-year: 59%.

COSTS AND FINANCIAL AID
Financial aid office: (405) 744-6604. **Expenses (2005-2006):** Tuition and fees 2005-2006: $4,365 in state, $12,389 out of state; room/board: $5,848. Estimated books and supplies: $880; transportation: $1,620; personal expenses: $2,190. **Financial aid:** Priority filing date for institution's financial aid form: February 1. In 2005-2006, 68% of undergraduates applied for financial aid. Of those, 52% were determined to have financial need; 18% had their need fully met. Average financial aid package (proportion receiving): $8,867 (51%). Average amount of gift aid, such as scholarships or grants (proportion receiving): $3,714 (36%). Average amount of self-help aid, such as work study or loans (proportion receiving): $4,089 (38%). Average need-based loan (excluding PLUS or other private loans): $4,035. Among students who received need-based aid, the average percentage of need met: 73%. Among students who received aid based on merit, the average award (and the proportion receiving): $3,396 (23%). The average athletic scholarship (and the proportion receiving): $7,743 (1%). Average amount of debt of borrowers graduating in 2005: $17,844. Proportion who borrowed: 56%.

CAMPUS LIFE AND EXTRACURRICULAR ACTIVITIES
Campus housing available: coed dorms, women's dorms, men's dorms, sorority housing, fraternity housing, apartments for married students, apartment for single students, special housing for disabled students, other housing options. Students who live in college-owned, operated, or affiliated housing: 37%. **Clubs and organizations:** Number of student organizations: 350. Activities include: choral groups, concert band, dance, drama/theater, jazz band, literary magazine, marching band, music ensembles, musical theater, opera, pep band, radio station, student government, student newspaper, symphony orchestra, television station. Number of fraternities: 34; sororities: 16. Proportion of men in fraternities: 13%; of women in sororities: 17%. **Sports program (2005-2006):** Member of NCAA I. *Men's intercollegiate varsity sports:* baseball, basketball, cross-country, football, golf, tennis, track and field (indoor), track and field (outdoor), wrestling. *Women's intercollegiate varsity sports:* basketball, cross-country, equestrian sports, golf, soccer, softball, tennis, track and field (indoor), track and field (outdoor).

SERVICES AND FACILITIES
Basic services: nonremedial tutoring, women's center, health service, health insurance. **Remedial assistance:** reading, math, writing. **Counseling services:** career, personal, academic, older student, psychological, birth control. **For learning-disabled students:** School does not offer a structured program with separate admission and additional fees. **Library:** Number of titles: 2,538,195; number of current serial subscriptions: 49,655. **Information technology resources:** Students are not required to lease or own a computer. School has a wireless network. Approximate number of users that can be accommodated: 40,000. Proportion of college-owned housing units wired for high-speed internet access: 100%. **Campus safety:** Security services offered: 24-hour foot-and-vehicle patrols, 24-hour emergency telephones, lighted pathways/sidewalks, controlled dormitory access (key, security card, etc).

TRANSFER AND INTERNATIONAL STUDENTS
Transfer students: May apply for admission for the following academic terms: Fall, Spring, Summer. Applicants need a minimum number of credits to apply. For fall 2005: Transfer applications received: 2,739. Transfer applicants offered admission: 2,315. Transfer applicants enrolled: 1,771. **International students:** Number of foreign undergraduates: 679 (4% of stu-

dent body). Number of countries represented: 85. Minimum TOEFL score required: 500 (paper); 173 (computer). Average TOEFL score: 518 (paper).

Oklahoma Wesleyan University

- **Address:** 2201 Silver Lake Road, Bartlesville, OK 74006
- **Website:** http://www.okwu.edu
- **Private; Religious affiliation:** Wesleyan Church
- **Enrollment:** 555 full-time; 509 part-time

KEY STATS

✔ **U.S News College Ranking:** 12, Comp. Coll.–Bachelor's (West)
✔ **ACT Score (25th/75th percentile):** 18-23
✔ **Tuition:** 2006-2007: $14,550

Selectivity: Selective	**Room/board:** $5,350
Acceptance rate: 91%	**Average debt:** $20,684
Student/faculty ratio: 18/1	**Proportion who borrowed:** 98%

UNDERGRADUATE STUDENT BODY STATS

2005-2006 enrollment: 555 full-time; 509 part-time. Men: 33%; women: 67%. **Ethnic makeup:** African American: 4%; American-Indian: 11%; Asian American: 1%; Hispanic: 2%; White: 79%; International: 1%. **Religious preference:** Roman Catholic: 4%; Protestant: 59%; No preference: 16%; Wesleyan Church: 20%.

ADMISSIONS FACTS AND FIGURES

Phone: (866) 222-8226. **Email:** admissions@okwu.edu. **Website:** http://www.okwu.edu. **Application deadlines for fall 2007:** Regular decision: August 15. Early decision: Not offered. Early action: Not offered. Admission can be deferred. **Application fee:** $25. Common application is accepted. **Admissions requirements/recommendations:** High school units required (recommended): English: 4 (4); Mathematics: 2 (2); Science: 1 (1); Foreign language: 0 (0); Social studies: 0 (0); History: 2 (2); Academic electives: 6 (6); Total units: 15 (15). Tests: The college uses SAT or ACT scores in admissions decisions. Either SAT or ACT required. For admission to the fall 2007 entering class, the school will accept: ACT with writing, ACT without writing. Campus visit: Recommended. Admissions interview: Recommended. Off-campus interview: Not available. **Factors that count in admissions decisions:** *Academic:* Secondary school record: Important. Class rank: Very important. Letters of recommendation: Considered. Standardized test scores: Very important. Essay: Considered. *Nonacademic:* Interview: Not considered. Extracurricular activities: Not considered. Talent/ability: Not considered. Character/personal qualities: Not considered. Alumni/ae relationship: Not considered. Geographical residence: Not considered. State residency: Not considered. Religious affiliation/commitment: Very important. Minority status: Not considered. Volunteer work: Not considered. Work experience: Not considered. **Other schools with the greatest overlap in applicants:** MidAmerica Nazarene University; Oklahoma State University; Southern Nazarene University; University of Oklahoma; University of Phoenix. **Admissions statistics for the fall 2005 entering class:** Total applicants: 404. Total accepted: 368. Freshmen enrolled: 133; 46% were from out of state. Overall acceptance rate: 91%. **Credentials of fall 2005 freshmen:** 14% ranked in the top 10 percent of their high school class; 38% were in the top 25 percent, and 67% were in the top half. (Proportion submitting class standing: 68%.) **Average high school grade point average:** 3.3. **First-year students who submitted SAT scores:** 9%. Scores (25/75 percentile): Verbal: 460-590, Math: 430-600, Combined: 890-1190. **First-year students submitting ACT scores:** 78%. Scores (25/75 percentile): English: 17-23, Math: 17-23, Composite: 18-23.

ACADEMICS

Year founded: 1972. **Academic calendar:** Semester. **Degrees offered:** certificate, associate, bachelor's, master's. **Most popular majors:** 36% nursing science (M.S., Ph.D.), 28% business administration and management, 13% human resources management/personnel administration, 5% religion/religious studies, 3% elementary education and teaching. **Major fields of study:** biological and biomedical sciences; business, management, marketing, and related support services; communication, journalism, and related programs; education; English language and literature/letters; health professions and related clinical sciences; history; mathematics and statistics; parks, recreation, leisure, and fitness studies; philosophy and religious studies; physical sciences; psychology; social sciences; theology and religious vocations;

visual and performing arts. **Areas of required coursework:** humanities, mathematics, English (including composition); sciences (biological or physical), history, social science, other. **Pre-professional programs:** pre-law, pre-dentistry, pre-medicine, pre-theology, pre-veterinary science, pre-optometry, pre-pharmacy. **Special academic programs (% participation):** accelerated program (75%), double major (20%), English as a Second Language (ESL) (0%), independent study, internships (7%), teacher certificate program (6%). **Teacher certification offered in:** elementary, middle/junior high, secondary. **Cooperative education programs:** technologies, vocational arts. **Faculty and instruction (2005-2006):** Total instructional faculty: 28 full-time, 4 part-time (78% men; 22% women; 0% minorities). Full-time faculty with Ph.D. or other terminal degree: 54%. Student/faculty ratio: 18/1. Classes of fewer than 20 students: 92%; of 20 to 49 students: 7%; of 50 or more students: 1%. **Advanced Placement and International Baccalaureate credit:** International Baccalaureate exams may be used for: Credit only. **Freshmen returning for sophomore year:** 60%. **Graduation rates:** Four-year: 19%; five-year: 24%; six-year: 41%.

COSTS AND FINANCIAL AID

Financial aid office: (918) 335-6282. **Expenses (2006-2007):** Tuition and fees 2006-2007: $14,550; room/board: $5,350. Estimated books and supplies: $800; transportation: $1,000; personal expenses: $1,800. **Financial aid:** Priority filing-date for institution's financial aid form: March 1. In 2005-2006, 99% of undergraduates applied for financial aid. Of those, 97% were determined to have financial need; 16% had their need fully met. Average financial aid package (proportion receiving): $7,148 (97%). Average amount of gift aid, such as scholarships or grants (proportion receiving): $3,217 (95%). Average amount of self-help aid, such as work study or loans (proportion receiving): $3,387 (96%). Average need-based loan (excluding PLUS or other private loans): $2,742. Among students who received need-based aid, the average percentage of need met: 58%. Among students who received aid based on merit, the average award (and the proportion receiving): $1,958 (4%). The average athletic scholarship (and the proportion receiving): $3,381 (21%). Average amount of debt of borrowers graduating in 2005: $20,684. Proportion who borrowed: 98%.

CAMPUS LIFE AND EXTRACURRICULAR ACTIVITIES

Campus housing available (% using): women's dorms (52%), men's dorms (48%). Students who live in college-owned, operated, or affiliated housing: 31%. **Student employment:** During the 2005-2006 academic year, 4% of undergraduates worked on campus. Average per-year earnings: $1,680. **Clubs and organizations:** Number of student organizations: 19. Activities include: choral groups, concert band, drama/theater, jazz band, music ensembles, musical theater, student government, student newspaper, symphony orchestra, yearbook. Number of fraternities: 0; sororities: 0. Average proportion of students who stay on campus on weekends: 80%. **Sports program (2005-2006):** Member of NAIA. *Men's intercollegiate varsity sports:* baseball, basketball, golf, soccer. *Women's intercollegiate varsity sports:* basketball, soccer, softball, volleyball.

SERVICES AND FACILITIES

Basic services: nonremedial tutoring, placement service, health service, health insurance. **Remedial assistance:** reading, math, writing, study skills. **Counseling services:** career, personal, academic, religious. **For learning-disabled students:** School does not offer a structured program with separate admission and additional fees. Total undergraduates in learning-disabled program or receiving services: 12. Services include: remedial math, remedial English, reading machines, remedial reading, tape recorders, videotaped classes, untimed tests, note-taking services, oral tests, learning center, readers, extended time for tests, tutors, early syllabus, priority seating, proofreading services, texts on tape, typist/scribe, exams on tape or computer, take home exams, other testing accomodations. **Information technology resources:** Students are not required to lease or own a computer. Number of campus computers available to all students: 60. School does not have a wireless network. Proportion of college-owned housing units wired for high-speed internet access: 100%. **Campus safety:** Security services offered: lighted pathways/sidewalks, controlled dormitory access (key, security card, etc).

TRANSFER AND INTERNATIONAL STUDENTS

Transfer students: May apply for admission for the following academic terms: Fall, Spring, Summer. Applicants do not need a minimum number of credits to apply. For fall 2005: Transfer applications received: 184. Transfer applicants offered admission: 170. Transfer applicants enrolled: 136. **International students:** Number of foreign undergraduates: 15 (1% of student body). Minimum TOEFL score required: 500 (paper); 173 (computer). Average TOEFL score: 500 (paper).

Oral Roberts University

- ■ **Address:** 7777 S. Lewis Avenue, Tulsa, OK 74171
- ■ **Website:** http://www.oru.edu
- ■ **Private; Religious affiliation:** Christian interdenominational
- ■ **Enrollment:** 2,393 full-time; 956 part-time

KEY STATS
- ✔ **U.S News College Ranking:** 51, Universities–Master's (West)
- ✔ **ACT Score (25th/75th percentile):** 20-26
- ✔ **Tuition:** 2006-2007: $16,670

Selectivity: Selective	**Room/board:** $7,060
Acceptance rate: 67%	**Average debt:** $30,471
Student/faculty ratio: 14/1	**Proportion who borrowed:** 83%

UNDERGRADUATE STUDENT BODY STATS
2005-2006 enrollment: 2,393 full-time; 956 part-time. Men: 41%; women: 59%. **Ethnic makeup:** African American: 18%; American-Indian: 1%; Asian American: 2%; Hispanic: 5%; White: 59%; International: 15%.

ADMISSIONS FACTS AND FIGURES
Phone: (800) 678-8876. **Email:** admissions@oru.edu. **Website:** http://www.oru.edu. **Application deadlines for fall 2007:** Regular decision: Rolling. Early decision: Not offered. Early action: Send application by: N/A; Decision sent by: N/A. Admission can be deferred. **Application fee:** $35. Common application is not accepted. **To apply online, go to:** http://www.oru.edu/university/departments/admissions/. **Admissions requirements/recommendations:** High school units required (recommended): English: 4 (4); Mathematics: 2 (2); Science: 1 (1); Foreign language: 2 (2); Social studies: 2 (2); Total units: 16 (16). Tests: The college uses SAT or ACT scores in admissions decisions. Either SAT or ACT required. For admission to the fall 2007 entering class, the school will accept: ACT with writing, ACT without writing. Campus visit: Recommended. Admissions interview: Recommended. Off-campus interview: May be arranged. **Factors that count in admissions decisions:** *Academic:* Secondary school record: Very important. Class rank: Important. Letters of recommendation: Important. Standardized test scores: Very important. Essay: Very important. *Nonacademic:* Interview: Not considered. Extracurricular activities: Not considered. Talent/ability: Not considered. Character/personal qualities: Considered. Alumni/ae relationship: Considered. Geographical residence: Not considered. State residency: Not considered. Religious affiliation/commitment: Considered. Minority status: Not considered. Volunteer work: Not considered. Work experience: Not considered. **Admissions statistics for the fall 2005 entering class:** Total applicants: 1,210. Total accepted: 814. Freshmen enrolled: 465. Overall acceptance rate: 67%. Non-early acceptance rate: 67%. **Credentials of fall 2005 freshmen:** 25% ranked in the top 10 percent of their high school class; 47% were in the top 25 percent, and 76% were in the top half. (Proportion submitting class standing: 65%.) **First-year students who submitted SAT scores:** 52%. Scores (25/75 percentile): Verbal: 475-610, Math: 480-600, Combined: 955-1210. **First-year students submitting ACT scores:** 72%. Scores (25/75 percentile): English: 20-26, Math: 18-25, Composite: 20-26.

ACADEMICS
Year founded: 1963. **Academic calendar:** Semester. **Degrees offered:** bachelor's, master's, first professional, doctorate. **Most popular majors:** Information not available. **Major fields of study:** biological and biomedical sciences; business, management, marketing, and related support services; communication, journalism, and related programs; computer and information sciences and support services; education; engineering; English language and literature/letters; foreign languages, literatures, and linguistics; health professions and related clinical sciences; history; legal professions and studies; liberal arts and sciences studies, and humanities; mathematics and statistics; multi/interdisciplinary studies; physical sciences; psychology; public administration and social service professions; social sciences; theology and religious vocations. **Areas of required coursework:** humanities, mathematics, English (including composition), foreign languages, sciences (biological or physical), history, social science, other. **Pre-professional programs:** pre-law, pre-medicine, pre-theology. **Special academic programs (%**

participation): distance learning (1%), double major (1%), dual enrollment (1%), English as a Second Language (ESL) (1%), external degree program (1%), honors program (9%), independent study (10%), internships (20%), liberal arts/career combination (5%), student-designed major (2%), study abroad (10%), teacher certificate program (12%), weekend college (1%). **Teacher certification offered in:** early childhood, special education, elementary, middle/junior high, secondary. **Cooperative education programs:** art, business, computer science, education, engineering, health professions, other. **Reserve Officers Training Corps (ROTC):** Air Force ROTC: Offered at cooperating institution (OSU-Tulsa). **Faculty and instruction (2005-2006):** Total instructional faculty: 197 full-time, 90 part-time (59% men; 41% women; 13% minorities). Full-time faculty with Ph.D. or other terminal degree: 63%. Student/faculty ratio: 14/1. Classes of fewer than 20 students: 65%; of 20 to 49 students: 31%; of 50 or more students: 4%. **Advanced Placement and International Baccalaureate credit:** AP tests may be used for: Placement only. Scores accepted: 3. International Baccalaureate exams may be used for: Credit and/or placement. **Freshmen returning for sophomore year:** 80%. **Graduation rates:** Four-year: 41%; five-year: 53%; six-year: 49%. **Graduate study:** 60% of students pursue further study immediately upon graduation; 20% within one year; 10% within five years.

COSTS AND FINANCIAL AID
Financial aid office: (918) 495-7088. **Expenses (2006-2007):** Tuition and fees 2006-2007: $16,670; room/board: $7,060. Estimated books and supplies: $1,000; transportation: $1,300; personal expenses: $1,500. **Financial aid:** Priority filing date for institution's financial aid form: March 15. In 2005-2006, 79% of undergraduates applied for financial aid. Of those, 69% were determined to have financial need; 50% had their need fully met. Average financial aid package (proportion receiving): $16,503 (69%). Average amount of gift aid, such as scholarships or grants (proportion receiving): $7,880 (64%). Average amount of self-help aid, such as work study or loans (proportion receiving): $10,159 (64%). Average need-based loan (excluding PLUS or other private loans): $9,813. Among students who received need-based aid, the average percentage of need met: 88%. Among students who received aid based on merit, the average award (and the proportion receiving): $7,195 (19%). The average athletic scholarship (and the proportion receiving): $17,769 (5%). Average amount of debt of borrowers graduating in 2005: $30,471. Proportion who borrowed: 83%.

CAMPUS LIFE AND EXTRACURRICULAR ACTIVITIES
Campus housing available (% using): women's dorms (51%), men's dorms (48%), special housing for disabled students (1%). **Student employment:** During the 2005-2006 academic year, 29% of undergraduates worked on campus. Average per-year earnings: $2,000. Activities include: choral groups, concert band, drama/theater, jazz band, literary magazine, music ensembles, musical theater, opera, pep band, radio station, student government, student newspaper, student film society, symphony orchestra, television station, yearbook. Number of fraternities: 0; sororities: 0. Average proportion of students who stay on campus on weekends: 80%. **Sports program (2005-2006):** Member of NCAA I. *Men's intercollegiate varsity sports:* baseball, basketball, cross-country, golf, soccer, tennis, track and field (indoor), track and field (outdoor). *Women's intercollegiate varsity sports:* basketball, cross-country, golf, soccer, tennis, track and field (indoor), track and field (outdoor), volleyball.

SERVICES AND FACILITIES
Basic services: nonremedial tutoring, placement service, health service, health insurance. **Remedial assistance:** reading, math, writing, study skills. **Counseling services:** career, personal, academic, religious. **For learning-disabled students:** School does not offer a structured program with separate admission and additional fees. Services include: remedial math, remedial English, reading machines, remedial reading, tape recorders, diagnostic testing service, note-taking services, special bookstore section, oral tests, learning center, readers, extended time for tests, tutors. **Information technology resources:** Students are not required to lease or own a computer. Number of campus computers available to all students: 180. School does not have a wireless network. Proportion of college-owned housing units wired for high-speed internet access: 100%. **Campus safety:** Security services offered: 24-hour foot-and-vehicle patrols, late-night transport/escort service, 24-hour emergency telephones, lighted pathways/sidewalks, controlled dormitory access (key, security card, etc).

TRANSFER AND INTERNATIONAL STUDENTS
Transfer students: May apply for admission for the following academic terms: Fall, Winter, Spring, Summer. Applicants need a minimum number of credits to apply. **International students:** Number of foreign undergradu-

ates: 493 (15% of student body). Number of countries represented: 66. Minimum TOEFL score required: 500 (paper). Average TOEFL score: 559 (paper).

Southeastern Oklahoma State University

- ■ **Address:** 1405 N. Fourth, PMB 4225, Durant, OK 74701-0609
- ■ **Website:** http://www.sosu.edu
- ■ **Public**
- ■ **Enrollment:** 2,994 full-time; 669 part-time

KEY STATS
✔ **U.S News College Ranking:** fourth tier, Universities–Master's (West)
✔ **ACT Score (25th/75th percentile):** 17-22
✔ **Tuition:** 2006-2007: $3,372 in state, $5,998 out of state
  Selectivity: Selective   **Room/board:** $3,190
  Acceptance rate: 68%   **Average debt:** $6,124
  Student/faculty ratio: 20/1   **Proportion who borrowed:** 30%

UNDERGRADUATE STUDENT BODY STATS
2005-2006 enrollment: 2,994 full-time; 669 part-time. Men: 44%; women: 56%. **Ethnic makeup:** African American: 5%; American-Indian: 29%; Asian American: 1%; Hispanic: 2%; White: 62%; International: 1%.

ADMISSIONS FACTS AND FIGURES
Phone: (580) 745-2060. **Email:** admissions@sosu.edu. **Website:** http://www.sosu.edu. **Application deadlines for fall 2007:** Regular decision: Rolling. Early decision: Not offered. Early action: Not offered. Admission cannot be deferred. **Application fee:** $20. Common application is not accepted. **Admissions requirements/recommendations:** High school units required (recommended): English: 4; Mathematics: 3; Science: 2; History: 2; Academic electives: 3; Total units: 15. Tests: The college uses SAT or ACT scores in admissions decisions. Either SAT or ACT required. For admission to the fall 2007 entering class, the school will accept: ACT with writing, ACT without writing. Campus visit: Recommended. Admissions interview: Neither required nor recommended. Off-campus interview: Not available. **Factors that count in admissions decisions:** *Academic:* Secondary school record: Not considered. Class rank: Very important. Letters of recommendation: Considered. Standardized test scores: Very important. Essay: Not considered. *Nonacademic:* Interview: Considered. Extracurricular activities: Not considered. Talent/ability: Considered. Character/personal qualities: Considered. Alumni/ae relationship: Not considered. Geographical residence: Not considered. State residency: Considered. Religious affiliation/commitment: Not considered. Minority status: Not considered. Volunteer work: Not considered. Work experience: Not considered. **Other schools with the greatest overlap in applicants:** East Central University; Oklahoma State University; University of Central Oklahoma; University of Oklahoma. **Admissions statistics for the fall 2005 entering class:** Total applicants: 1,101. Total accepted: 747. Freshmen enrolled: 619; 17% were from out of state. Overall acceptance rate: 68%. **Credentials of fall 2005 freshmen:** 17% ranked in the top 10 percent of their high school class; 40% were in the top 25 percent, and 74% were in the top half. (Proportion submitting class standing: 90%.) **Average high school grade point average:** 3.3. **First-year students who submitted SAT scores:** 5%. Scores (25/75 percentile): Verbal: N/A, Math: N/A, Combined: N/A. **First-year students submitting ACT scores:** 85%. Scores (25/75 percentile): English: 16-23, Math: 16-21, Composite: 17-22.

ACADEMICS
Year founded: 1909. **Academic calendar:** Semester. **Degrees offered:** bachelor's, master's, post-master's certificate. **Most popular majors:** 23% education, 12% business, management, marketing, and related support services, 6% communication, journalism, and related programs, 6% parks, recreation, leisure, and fitness studies, 6% psychology. **Major fields of study:** biological and biomedical sciences; business, management, marketing, and related support services; communication, journalism, and related programs; computer and information sciences and support services; education; engineering technologies/technicians; English language and literature/letters; foreign languages, literatures, and linguistics; history; liberal arts and sciences studies, and humanities; mathematics and statistics; multi/interdisciplinary studies; natural resources and conservation; parks, recreation, leisure, and fitness studies; physical sciences; psychology; security and pro-

tective services; social sciences; transportation and materials moving; visual and performing arts. **Areas of required coursework:** arts/fine arts, humanities, computer literacy, mathematics, English (including composition), sciences (biological or physical), history, social science. **Pre-professional programs:** pre-law, pre-dentistry, pre-medicine, pre-veterinary science, pre-optometry, pre-pharmacy. **Special academic programs (% participation):** distance learning (10%), double major (5%), honors program (4%), independent study, internships (14%), liberal arts/career combination (1%), student-designed major (2%), teacher certificate program (20%). **Teacher certification offered in:** special education, elementary, middle/junior high, secondary, bilingual/bicultural. **Faculty and instruction (2005-2006):** Total instructional faculty: 141 full-time, 96 part-time (58% men; 42% women; 22% minorities). Full-time faculty with Ph.D. or other terminal degree: 67%. **Student/faculty ratio:** 20/1. Classes of fewer than 20 students: 44%; of 20 to 49 students: 53%; of 50 or more students: 3%. **Advanced Placement and International Baccalaureate credit:** AP tests may be used for: Credit and/or placement. Scores accepted: 3. **Freshmen returning for sophomore year:** 61%. **Graduation rates:** Four-year: 13%; five-year: 25%; six-year: 32%. **Graduate study:** 15% of students pursue further study immediately upon graduation; 14% within one year; 25% within five years. Fields in which graduates pursue further study: Master of Business Administration (MBA), 9%; law, 1%; medicine, 1%; dentistry, 1%; education, 51%; arts and sciences, 35%; veterinary medicine, 1%.

COSTS AND FINANCIAL AID
Financial aid office: (580) 745-2186. **Expenses (2006-2007):** Tuition and fees 2006-2007: $3,372 in state, $5,998 out of state; room/board: $3,190. Estimated books and supplies: $800; transportation: $1,094; personal expenses: $1,447. **Financial aid:** Priority filing date for institution's financial aid form: March 1. Average amount of debt of borrowers graduating in 2005: $6,124. Proportion who borrowed: 30%.

CAMPUS LIFE AND EXTRACURRICULAR ACTIVITIES
Campus housing available (% using): coed dorms (20%), women's dorms (29%), men's dorms (50%). Students who live in college-owned, operated, or affiliated housing: 10%. **Student employment:** During the 2005-2006 academic year, 20% of undergraduates worked on campus. Average per-year earnings: $1,384. **Clubs and organizations:** Number of student organizations: 87. Activities include: choral groups, concert band, dance, drama/theater, jazz band, literary magazine, marching band, music ensembles, musical theater, opera, pep band, radio station, student government, student newspaper, yearbook. Number of fraternities: 3; sororities: 2. Proportion of men in fraternities: 1%; of women in sororities: 2%. Average proportion of students who stay on campus on weekends: 25%. **Sports program (2005-2006):** Member of NCAA II. *Men's intercollegiate varsity sports:* baseball, basketball, football, golf, tennis. *Women's intercollegiate varsity sports:* basketball, cross-country, softball, tennis, volleyball.

SERVICES AND FACILITIES
Basic services: nonremedial tutoring, placement service, health service, other. **Remedial assistance:** reading, math, writing, other. **Counseling services:** minority student, career, personal, veteran student, academic, older student, psychological. **For learning-disabled students:** School does not offer a structured program with separate admission and additional fees. Total undergraduates in learning-disabled program or receiving services: 28. Services include: remedial math, remedial English, reading machines, remedial reading, tape recorders, other special classes, diagnostic testing service, untimed tests, note-taking services, oral tests, learning center, readers, extended time for tests, tutors, texts on tape, other testing accomodations, other. **Library:** Number of titles: 294,968; number of current serial subscriptions: 905. **Information technology resources:** Students are not required to lease or own a computer. Number of campus computers available to all students: 414. School has a wireless network. Approximate number of users that can be accommodated: 100. Proportion of college-owned housing units wired for high-speed internet access: 97%. **Campus safety:** Security services offered: late-night transport/escort service, lighted pathways/sidewalks, controlled dormitory access (key, security card, etc).

TRANSFER AND INTERNATIONAL STUDENTS
Transfer students: May apply for admission for the following academic terms: Fall, Spring, Summer. Applicants need a minimum number of credits to apply. For fall 2005: Transfer applications received: 558. Transfer applicants offered admission: 515. Transfer applicants enrolled: 417. **International students:** Number of foreign undergraduates: 36 (1% of student body). Number of countries represented: 32. Minimum TOEFL score required: 500 (paper); 173 (computer). Average TOEFL score: 500 (paper).

Southern Nazarene University

- **Address:** 6729 N.W. 39th Expressway, Bethany, OK 73008
- **Website:** http://www.snu.edu
- **Private; Religious affiliation:** Nazarene
- **Enrollment:** 1,659 full-time; 134 part-time

KEY STATS

✔ **U.S News College Ranking:** 57, Universities–Master's (West)
✔ **ACT Score (25th/75th percentile):** 19-26
✔ **Tuition:** 2006-2007: $15,024

Selectivity: Selective	**Room/board:** $5,378
Acceptance rate: 100%	**Average debt:** $20,505
Student/faculty ratio: 17/1	**Proportion who borrowed:** N/A

UNDERGRADUATE STUDENT BODY STATS

2005-2006 enrollment: 1,659 full-time; 134 part-time. Men: 49%; women: 51%. **Ethnic makeup:** African American: 9%; American-Indian: 4%; Asian American: 2%; Hispanic: 4%; White: 82%. **Religious preference:** Roman Catholic: 4%; Protestant: 43%; No preference: 12%; Unknown: 4%; Nazarene: 37%.

ADMISSIONS FACTS AND FIGURES

Phone: (405) 491-6324. **Email:** admissions@snu.edu. **Website:** http://www.snu.edu. **Application deadlines for fall 2007:** Regular decision: August 6. Early decision: Not offered. Early action: Not offered. Admission can be deferred. **Application fee:** $25. Common application is not accepted. **Admissions requirements/recommendations:** Tests: The college uses SAT or ACT scores in admissions decisions. Neither SAT nor ACT required. For admission to the fall 2007 entering class, the school will accept: ACT with writing, ACT without writing. Campus visit: Recommended. Admissions interview: Recommended. Off-campus interview: May be arranged. **Factors that count in admissions decisions:** *Academic:* Secondary school record: Important. Class rank: Important. Letters of recommendation: Important. Standardized test scores: Very important. Essay: Not considered. *Nonacademic:* Interview: Not considered. Extracurricular activities: Not considered. Talent/ability: Considered. Character/personal qualities: Important. Alumni/ae relationship: Not considered. Geographical residence: Not considered. State residency: Not considered. Religious affiliation/commitment: Not considered. Minority status: Not considered. Volunteer work: Not considered. Work experience: Not considered. **Admissions statistics for the fall 2005 entering class:** Total applicants: 529. Total accepted: 529. Freshmen enrolled: 284; Overall acceptance rate: 100%. **Credentials of fall 2005 freshmen:** 25% ranked in the top 10 percent of their high school class; 45% were in the top 25 percent, and 74% were in the top half. (Proportion submitting class standing: 83%.) **Average high school grade point average:** 3.5. **First-year students who submitted SAT scores:** 26%. Scores (25/75 percentile): Verbal: N/A, Math: N/A, Combined: N/A. **First-year students submitting ACT scores:** 85%. Scores (25/75 percentile): English: N/A, Math: N/A, Composite: 19-26.

ACADEMICS

Year founded: 1899. **Academic calendar:** Semester. **Degrees offered:** associate, bachelor's, master's. **Most popular majors:** 50% business/commerce, 10% nursing/registered nurse training (R.N., A.S.N., B.S.N., M.S.N.), 9% human development and family studies, 7% education, 5% theology/theological studies. **Major fields of study:** area, ethnic, cultural, and gender studies; biological and biomedical sciences; business, management, marketing, and related support services; communication, journalism, and related programs; communications technologies/technicians and support services; computer and information sciences and support services; education; English language and literature/letters; family and consumer sciences/human sciences; foreign languages, literatures, and linguistics; health professions and related clinical sciences; history; mathematics and statistics; parks, recreation, leisure, and fitness studies; philosophy and religious studies; physical sciences; psychology; social sciences; theology and religious vocations; transportation and materials moving; visual and performing arts. **Areas of required coursework:** arts/fine arts, humanities, computer literacy, mathematics, English (including composition), philosophy, sciences (biological or physical), history, social science. **Pre-professional programs:** pre-law, pre-dentistry, pre-medicine, pre-pharmacy. **Special academic programs:** accelerated program, cross-registration, double major, dual enrollment, English as a Second Language (ESL), honors program, independent study, internships, student-designed major, study abroad, teacher certificate program. **Teacher certification offered in:** early childhood, elementary, middle/junior high, secondary. **Reserve Officers Training Corps (ROTC):** Army ROTC: Offered at cooperating institution (University of Central Oklahoma); Air Force ROTC: Offered at cooperating institution (University of Oklahoma). **Faculty and instruction (2005-2006):** Total instructional faculty: 69 full-time, 107 part-time (51% men; 49% women; 5% minorities). Full-time faculty with Ph.D. or other terminal degree: 70%. Student/faculty ratio: 17/1. Classes of fewer than 20 students: 59%; of 20 to 49 students: 38%; of 50 or more students: 3%. **Advanced Placement and International Baccalaureate credit:** AP tests may be used for: Credit and/or placement. Scores accepted: 3, 4, 5. International Baccalaureate exams may be used for: Credit only. **Freshmen returning for sophomore year:** 69%. **Graduation rates:** Four-year: 26%; five-year: 39%; six-year: 47%.

COSTS AND FINANCIAL AID

Financial aid office: (405) 491-6310. **Expenses (2006-2007):** Tuition and fees 2006-2007: $15,024; room/board: $5,378. Estimated books and supplies: $850; transportation: $400; personal expenses: $2,500. **Financial aid:** Priority filing date for institution's financial aid form: March 1. In 2005-2006, 92% of undergraduates applied for financial aid. Of those, 80% were determined to have financial need; 2% had their need fully met. Average financial aid package (proportion receiving): N/A (80%). Average amount of gift aid, such as scholarships or grants (proportion receiving): N/A (34%). Average amount of self-help aid, such as work study or loans (proportion receiving): N/A (34%). Average amount of debt of borrowers graduating in 2005: $20,505.

CAMPUS LIFE AND EXTRACURRICULAR ACTIVITIES

Campus housing available (% using): women's dorms (45%), men's dorms (35%), apartments for married students (5%), apartment for single students (15%), special housing for disabled students (0%). Students who live in college-owned, operated, or affiliated housing: 43%. **Student employment:** During the 2005-2006 academic year, 10% of undergraduates worked on campus. Average per-year earnings: $2,000. Activities include: choral groups, concert band, drama/theater, jazz band, literary magazine, music ensembles, musical theater, opera, pep band, student government, student newspaper, symphony orchestra, television station, yearbook. Number of fraternities: 0; sororities: 0. Average proportion of students who stay on campus on weekends: 50%. **Sports program (2005-2006):** Member of NAIA. *Men's intercollegiate varsity sports:* baseball, basketball, cross-country, football, golf, soccer, track and field (indoor), track and field (outdoor). *Women's intercollegiate varsity sports:* basketball, cross-country, golf, soccer, softball, tennis, track and field (indoor), track and field (outdoor), volleyball.

SERVICES AND FACILITIES

Basic services: nonremedial tutoring, placement service, health service, health insurance. **Remedial assistance:** reading, math, writing, study skills. **Counseling services:** minority student, career, military, personal, veteran student, academic, older student, psychological, birth control, religious. **For learning-disabled students:** School does not offer a structured program with separate admission and additional fees. Total undergraduates in learning-disabled program or receiving services: 22. Services include: remedial English, reading machines, tape recorders, note-taking services, oral tests, learning center, readers, extended time for tests, tutors, other. **Library:** Number of titles: 97,341; number of current serial subscriptions: 200. **Information technology resources:** Students are not required to lease or own a computer. Number of campus computers available to all students: 170. School has a wireless network. Approximate number of users that can be accommodated: 2,500. Proportion of college-owned housing units wired for high-speed internet access: 100%. **Campus safety:** Security services offered: 24-hour foot-and-vehicle patrols, late-night transport/escort service, lighted pathways/sidewalks, student patrols, controlled dormitory access (key, security card, etc).

TRANSFER AND INTERNATIONAL STUDENTS

Transfer students: May apply for admission for the following academic terms: Fall, Spring. Applicants do not need a minimum number of credits to apply. For fall 2005: Transfer applications received: 197. Transfer applicants offered admission: 197. Transfer applicants enrolled: 114. **International students:** Number of foreign undergraduates: 2. Number of countries represented: 29. Minimum TOEFL score required: 173 (computer).

Southwestern Oklahoma State University

■ **Address:** 100 Campus Drive, Weatherford, OK 73096-3098
■ **Website:** http://www.swosu.edu
■ **Public**
■ **Enrollment:** 3,503 full-time; 454 part-time

KEY STATS
✔ **U.S News College Ranking:** third tier, Universities–Master's (West)
✔ **ACT Score (25th/75th percentile):** 18-24
✔ **Tuition:** 2005-2006: $3,240 in state, $7,740 out of state

Selectivity: Selective	**Room/board:** $3,240
Acceptance rate: 93%	**Average debt:** N/A
Student/faculty ratio: 20/1	**Proportion who borrowed:** N/A

UNDERGRADUATE STUDENT BODY STATS
2005-2006 enrollment: 3,503 full-time; 454 part-time. Men: 45%; women: 55%. **Ethnic makeup:** African American: 5%; American-Indian: 7%; Asian American: 1%; Hispanic: 4%; White: 80%; International: 3%.

ADMISSIONS FACTS AND FIGURES
Phone: (580) 774-3782. **Email:** swosuinfo@swosu.edu. **Website:** http://www.swosu.edu. **Application deadlines for fall 2007:** Regular decision: Rolling. Early decision: Not offered. Early action: Not offered. Admission can be deferred. **Application fee:** $15. Common application is not accepted. **To apply online, go to:** http://www.swosu.edu/resources/forms/regstr/admissi.pdf. **Admissions requirements/recommendations:** High school units required (recommended): English: 4 (4); Mathematics: 3 (3); Science: 2 (2); Social studies: 1 (1); History: 2 (2); Academic electives: 0 (2); Total units: 15 (17). Tests: The college uses SAT or ACT scores in admissions decisions. ACT required. For admission to the fall 2007 entering class, the school will accept: ACT with writing, ACT without writing. Campus visit: Recommended. Admissions interview: Neither required nor recommended. **Factors that count in admissions decisions:** *Academic:* Secondary school record: Very important. Class rank: Very important. Letters of recommendation: Not considered. Standardized test scores: Very important. Essay: Not considered. *Nonacademic:* Interview: Not considered. Extracurricular activities: Not considered. Talent/ability: Not considered. Character/personal qualities: Not considered. Alumni/ae relationship: Not considered. Geographical residence: Not considered. State residency: Not considered. Religious affiliation/commitment: Not considered. Minority status: Not considered. Volunteer work: Not considered. Work experience: Not considered. **Other schools with the greatest overlap in applicants:** Oklahoma State University; University of Central Oklahoma; University of Oklahoma. **Admissions statistics for the fall 2005 entering class:** Total applicants: 1,221. Total accepted: 1,136. Freshmen enrolled: 792; 9% were from out of state. Overall acceptance rate: 93%. **Credentials of fall 2005 freshmen:** 20% ranked in the top 10 percent of their high school class; 45% were in the top 25 percent, and 74% were in the top half. (Proportion submitting class standing: 92%.) **Average high school grade point average:** 3.4. **First-year students submitting ACT scores:** 96%. Scores (25/75 percentile): English: 17-24, Math: 17-24, Composite: 18-24.

ACADEMICS
Year founded: 1901. **Academic calendar:** Semester. **Degrees offered:** associate, bachelor's, master's, first professional. **Most popular majors:** 23% education, 20% business, management, marketing, and related support services, 17% health professions and related clinical sciences, 9% visual and performing arts. **Major fields of study:** biological and biomedical sciences; business, management, marketing, and related support services; computer and information sciences and support services; education; engineering; engineering technologies/technicians; English language and literature/letters; health professions and related clinical sciences; history; mathematics and statistics; multi/interdisciplinary studies; parks, recreation, leisure, and fitness studies; physical sciences; psychology; public administration and social service professions; security and protective services; social sciences; visual and performing arts. **Areas of required coursework:** arts/fine arts, humanities, computer literacy, mathematics, English (including composition), sciences (biological or physical), history, social science, other. **Pre-professional programs:** pre-law, pre-dentistry, pre-medicine, pre-pharmacy. **Special academic programs:** accelerated program, distance learning, double major, dual enrollment, independent study, internships, student-designed major, teacher certificate program, weekend college. **Teacher certification**

offered in: early childhood, special education, elementary, middle/junior high, secondary. **Faculty and instruction (2005-2006):** Total instructional faculty: 195. Full-time faculty with Ph.D. or other terminal degree: 63%. Student/faculty ratio: 20/1. Classes of fewer than 20 students: 36%; of 20 to 49 students: 56%; of 50 or more students: 8%. **Advanced Placement and International Baccalaureate credit:** AP tests may be used for: Credit only. Scores accepted: 3, 4, 5. **Freshmen returning for sophomore year:** 64%. **Graduation rates:** Four-year: 15%; five-year: 28%; six-year: 36%.

COSTS AND FINANCIAL AID
Financial aid office: (580) 774-3786. **Expenses (2005-2006):** Tuition and fees 2005-2006: $3,240 in state, $7,740 out of state; room/board: $3,240. Estimated books and supplies: $1,088; transportation: $1,500; personal expenses: $1,224. **Financial aid:** Priority filing date for institution's financial aid form: March 1; deadline: March 1. In 2005-2006, 75% of undergraduates applied for financial aid. Of those, 58% were determined to have financial need; 35% had their need fully met. Average financial aid package (proportion receiving): $4,368 (57%). Average amount of gift aid, such as scholarships or grants (proportion receiving): $1,187 (52%). Average amount of self-help aid, such as work study or loans (proportion receiving): $1,292 (42%). Average need-based loan (excluding PLUS or other private loans): $1,324. Among students who received need-based aid, the average percentage of need met: 91%. Among students who received aid based on merit, the average award (and the proportion receiving): $400 (25%). The average athletic scholarship (and the proportion receiving): $400 (6%).

CAMPUS LIFE AND EXTRACURRICULAR ACTIVITIES
Campus housing available (% using): women's dorms (50%), men's dorms (44%), apartments for married students (6%). Students who live in college-owned, operated, or affiliated housing: 30%. **Clubs and organizations:** Number of student organizations: 69. Activities include: choral groups, concert band, drama/theater, jazz band, marching band, music ensembles, musical theater, pep band, student government, student newspaper, symphony orchestra, yearbook. Number of fraternities: 2; sororities: 3. **Sports program (2005-2006):** Member of NCAA II. *Men's intercollegiate varsity sports:* baseball, basketball, football, golf, soccer. *Women's intercollegiate varsity sports:* basketball, cross-country, golf, soccer, softball.

SERVICES AND FACILITIES
Basic services: nonremedial tutoring, placement service, health service. **Remedial assistance:** reading, math, writing, study skills. **Counseling services:** minority student, career, personal, veteran student, academic, older student, psychological, birth control, other. **For learning-disabled students:** School does not offer a structured program with separate admission and additional fees. Services include: remedial math, remedial English, remedial reading, untimed tests, learning center, tutors. **Library:** Number of titles: 299,954; number of current serial subscriptions: 1,136. **Information technology resources:** Students are not required to lease or own a computer. Number of campus computers available to all students: 800. School has a wireless network. Approximate number of users that can be accommodated: 2,000. Proportion of college-owned housing units wired for high-speed internet access: 100%. **Campus safety:** Security services offered: 24-hour emergency telephones, lighted pathways/sidewalks, controlled dormitory access (key, security card, etc).

TRANSFER AND INTERNATIONAL STUDENTS
Transfer students: May apply for admission for the following academic terms: Fall, Spring, Summer. Applicants need a minimum number of credits to apply. For fall 2005: Transfer applications received: 620. Transfer applicants enrolled: 303. **International students:** Number of foreign undergraduates: 126 (3% of student body). Number of countries represented: 33. Minimum TOEFL score required: 500 (paper); 173 (computer).

St. Gregory's University

- **Address:** 1900 W. MacArthur Street, Shawnee, OK 74804
- **Website:** http://www.stgregorys.edu
- **Private; Religious affiliation:** Roman Catholic
- **Enrollment:** 490 full-time; 378 part-time

KEY STATS

✔ **U.S News College Ranking:** third tier, Comp. Coll.–Bachelor's (West)
✔ **ACT Score (25th/75th percentile):** 17-22
✔ **Tuition:** 2006-2007: $13,772

Selectivity: Selective	**Room/board:** $5,636
Acceptance rate: 81%	**Average debt:** $10,062
Student/faculty ratio: 16/1	**Proportion who borrowed:** 68%

UNDERGRADUATE STUDENT BODY STATS

2005-2006 enrollment: 490 full-time; 378 part-time. Men: 48%; women: 52%. **Ethnic makeup:** African American: 7%; American-Indian: 11%; Asian American: 1%; Hispanic: 8%; White: 64%; International: 10%.

ADMISSIONS FACTS AND FIGURES

Phone: (405) 878-5444. **Email:** admissions@stgregorys.edu. **Website:** http://www.stgregorys.edu. **Application deadlines for fall 2007:** Regular decision: Rolling. Early decision: Not offered. Early action: Not offered. Admission can be deferred. **Application fee:** $25. Common application is accepted. **Admissions requirements/recommendations:** High school units required (recommended): English: 4; Mathematics: 3; Science: 2; History: 2; Total units: 15. Tests: The college uses SAT or ACT scores in admissions decisions. Neither SAT nor ACT required. For admission to the fall 2007 entering class, the school will accept: ACT with writing, ACT without writing. Campus visit: Recommended. Admissions interview: Recommended. Off-campus interview: May be arranged. **Factors that count in admissions decisions:** *Academic:* Secondary school record: Very important. Class rank: Very important. Letters of recommendation: Considered. Standardized test scores: Very important. Essay: Considered. *Nonacademic:* Interview: Considered. Extracurricular activities: Not considered. Talent/ability: Not considered. Character/personal qualities: Not considered. Alumni/ae relationship: Not considered. Geographical residence: Not considered. State residency: Not considered. Religious affiliation/commitment: Not considered. Minority status: Not considered. Volunteer work: Not considered. Work experience: Not considered. **Admissions statistics for the fall 2005 entering class:** Total applicants: 207. Total accepted: 167. Freshmen enrolled: 101; Overall acceptance rate: 81%. **Credentials of fall 2005 freshmen:** 13% ranked in the top 10 percent of their high school class; 36% were in the top 25 percent, and 65% were in the top half. (Proportion submitting class standing: 85%.) **Average high school grade point average:** 3.2. **First-year students who submitted SAT scores:** 19%. Scores (25/75 percentile): Verbal: 390-550, Math: 420-520, Combined: 810-1070. **First-year students submitting ACT scores:** 62%. Scores (25/75 percentile): English: 15-23, Math: 16-21, Composite: 17-22.

ACADEMICS

Year founded: 1875. **Academic calendar:** Semester. **Degrees offered:** associate, bachelor's, master's. **Most popular majors:** Information not available. **Major fields of study:** biological and biomedical sciences; business, management, marketing, and related support services; communication, journalism, and related programs; education; English language and literature/letters; health professions and related clinical sciences; history; legal professions and studies; liberal arts and sciences studies, and humanities; mathematics and statistics; multi/interdisciplinary studies; philosophy and religious studies; physical sciences; psychology; security and protective services; social sciences; theology and religious vocations; visual and performing arts. **Areas of required coursework:** arts/fine arts, humanities, computer literacy, mathematics, English (including composition), philosophy, sciences (biological or physical), history, social science, other. **Pre-professional programs:** pre-law, pre-dentistry, pre-medicine, pre-theology, pre-veterinary science, pre-pharmacy, other. **Special academic programs:** accelerated program, double major, honors program, independent study, internships, student-designed major, study abroad, teacher certificate program. **Teacher certification offered in:** middle/junior high, secondary. **Reserve Officers Training Corps (ROTC):** Air Force ROTC: Offered at cooperating institution (University of Oklahoma). **Faculty and instruction (2005-2006):** Total instructional faculty: 27 full-time, 34 part-time (48% men; 52% women; 8% minorities). Full-time faculty with Ph.D. or other terminal degree: 48%. Student/faculty ratio: 16/1. Classes of fewer than 20 students: 88%; of 20 to 49 students: 12%. **Advanced Placement and International Baccalaureate credit:** AP tests may be used for: Credit and/or placement. Scores accepted: 3. International Baccalaureate exams may be used for: Credit and/or placement. **Freshmen returning for sophomore year:** 58%. **Graduation rates:** Four-year: 19%; five-year: 31%; six-year: 29%.

COSTS AND FINANCIAL AID

Financial aid office: (405) 878-5412. **Expenses (2006-2007):** Tuition and fees 2006-2007: $13,772; room/board: $5,636. Estimated books and supplies: $800; transportation: $2,100; personal expenses: $1,822. **Financial aid:** Priority filing date for institution's financial aid form: April 1. In 2005-2006, 80% of undergraduates applied for financial aid. Of those, 65% were determined to have financial need; 14% had their need fully met. Average financial aid package (proportion receiving): $9,381 (63%). Average amount of gift aid, such as scholarships or grants (proportion receiving): $4,402 (53%). Average amount of self-help aid, such as work study or loans (proportion receiving): $3,425 (42%). Average need-based loan (excluding PLUS or other private loans): $3,981. Among students who received need-based aid, the average percentage of need met: 79%. Among students who received aid based on merit, the average award (and the proportion receiving): $2,306 (20%). The average athletic scholarship (and the proportion receiving): $3,525 (21%). Average amount of debt of borrowers graduating in 2005: $10,062. Proportion who borrowed: 68%.

CAMPUS LIFE AND EXTRACURRICULAR ACTIVITIES

Campus housing available: women's dorms, men's dorms, special housing for disabled students. **Student employment:** During the 2005-2006 academic year, 10% of undergraduates worked on campus. Average per-year earnings: $900. **Clubs and organizations:** Number of student organizations: 19. Activities include: choral groups, dance, drama/theater, jazz band, music ensembles, musical theater, student government, student newspaper. Number of fraternities: 2; sororities: 2. Average proportion of students who stay on campus on weekends: 30%. **Sports program (2005-2006):** Member of NAIA. *Men's intercollegiate varsity sports:* baseball, basketball, cross-country, golf, soccer, track and field (indoor), track and field (outdoor). *Women's intercollegiate varsity sports:* basketball, cross-country, golf, soccer, softball, track and field (indoor), track and field (outdoor).

SERVICES AND FACILITIES

Basic services: placement service, health service, health insurance. **Remedial assistance:** writing, study skills. **Counseling services:** career, personal, academic, psychological, religious. **For learning-disabled students:** School does not offer a structured program with separate admission and additional fees. Total undergraduates in learning-disabled program or receiving services: 18. Services include: remedial math, remedial reading, tape recorders, videotaped classes, untimed tests, note-taking services, oral tests, learning center, readers, extended time for tests, tutors, priority seating, proofreading services, texts on tape, typist/scribe, other testing accomodations, other. **Library:** Number of titles: 82,715; number of current serial subscriptions: 2,060. **Information technology resources:** Students are required to lease or own a computer. Number of campus computers available to all students: 75. School has a wireless network. Approximate number of users that can be accommodated: 1,000. Proportion of college-owned housing units wired for high-speed internet access: 100%. **Campus safety:** Security services offered: 24-hour foot-and-vehicle patrols, late-night transport/escort service, 24-hour emergency telephones, lighted pathways/sidewalks, controlled dormitory access (key, security card, etc).

TRANSFER AND INTERNATIONAL STUDENTS

Transfer students: May apply for admission for the following academic terms: Fall, Spring, Summer. Applicants do not need a minimum number of credits to apply. For fall 2005: Transfer applications received: 93. Transfer applicants offered admission: 83. Transfer applicants enrolled: 67. **International students:** Number of foreign undergraduates: 80 (10% of student body). Number of countries represented: 22. Minimum TOEFL score required: 500 (paper). Average TOEFL score: 540 (paper).

University of Central Oklahoma

- **Address:** 100 N. University Drive, Edmond, OK 73034
- **Website:** http://www.ucok.edu
- **Public**
- **Enrollment:** 10,512 full-time; 4,117 part-time

KEY STATS
- ✔ **U.S News College Ranking:** fourth tier, Universities–Master's (West)
- ✔ **ACT Score (25th/75th percentile):** 19-23
- ✔ **Tuition:** 2006-2007: $3,539 in state, $8,924 out of state

Selectivity: Selective	**Room/board:** $4,763
Acceptance rate: 95%	**Average debt:** $15,508
Student/faculty ratio: 23/1	**Proportion who borrowed:** 53%

UNDERGRADUATE STUDENT BODY STATS
2005-2006 enrollment: 10,512 full-time; 4,117 part-time. Men: 41%; women: 59%. **Ethnic makeup:** African American: 9%; American-Indian: 6%; Asian American: 3%; Hispanic: 3%; White: 71%; International: 7%.

ADMISSIONS FACTS AND FIGURES
Phone: (405) 974-2338. **Email:** admituco@ucok.edu. **Website:** http://www.ucok.edu. **Application deadlines for fall 2007:** Regular decision: Rolling. Early decision: Not offered. Early action: Not offered. Admission can be deferred. **Application fee:** $25. Common application is not accepted. **To apply online, go to:** http://bronze.ucok.edu/registrar/admit/Admissions.htm. **Admissions requirements/recommendations:** High school units required (recommended): English: 4 (4); Mathematics: 3 (4); Science: 2 (3); Foreign language: (2); Social studies: 1 (1); History: 2 (2); Academic electives: 3; Total units: 15 (16). Tests: The college uses SAT or ACT scores in admissions decisions. Either SAT or ACT required. For admission to the fall 2007 entering class, the school will accept: ACT with writing, ACT without writing. Campus visit: Recommended. Admissions interview: Neither required nor recommended. Off-campus interview: Not available. **Factors that count in admissions decisions:** *Academic:* Secondary school record: Very important. Class rank: Very important. Letters of recommendation: Not considered. Standardized test scores: Very important. Essay: Not considered. *Nonacademic:* Interview: Not considered. Extracurricular activities: Considered. Talent/ability: Considered. Character/personal qualities: Not considered. Alumni/ae relationship: Not considered. Geographical residence: Not considered. State residency: Not considered. Religious affiliation/commitment: Not considered. Minority status: Not considered. Volunteer work: Not considered. Work experience: Not considered. **Other schools with the greatest overlap in applicants:** Oklahoma State University; University of Oklahoma. **Admissions statistics for the fall 2005 entering class:** Total applicants: 4,020. Total accepted: 3,817. Freshmen enrolled: 2,169; 4% were from out of state. Overall acceptance rate: 95%. **Credentials of fall 2005 freshmen:** 14% ranked in the top 10 percent of their high school class; 36% were in the top 25 percent, and 74% were in the top half. (Proportion submitting class standing: 73%.) **Average high school grade point average:** 3.6. **First-year students submitting ACT scores:** 91%. Scores (25/75 percentile): English: 19-24, Math: 17-23, Composite: 19-23.

ACADEMICS
Year founded: 1890. **Academic calendar:** Semester. **Degrees offered:** certificate, bachelor's, master's. **Most popular majors:** 28% business, management, marketing, and related support services, 11% education, 10% liberal arts and sciences studies, and humanities, 8% communication, journalism, and related programs, 5% health professions and related clinical sciences. **Major fields of study:** biological and biomedical sciences; business, management, marketing, and related support services; communication, journalism, and related programs; computer and information sciences and support services; education; engineering; English language and literature/letters; family and consumer sciences/human sciences; foreign languages, literatures, and linguistics; health professions and related clinical sciences; history; liberal arts and sciences studies, and humanities; mathematics and statistics; personal and culinary services; philosophy and religious studies; physical sciences; psychology; security and protective services; social sciences; visual and performing arts. **Areas of required coursework:** humanities, mathematics, English (including composition), philosophy, sciences (biological or physical), history, social science. **Pre-professional programs:** pre-dentistry, pre-medicine, pre-veterinary science, pre-optometry, pre-pharmacy, other. **Special academic programs (% participation):** accelerated program, distance learning, double major (.23%), dual enrollment (0%), independent study (6.18%), internships (10.78%), teacher certificate program (12.04%). **Teacher certification offered in:** early childhood, special education, elementary, vo-tech, secondary, bilingual/bicultural. **Reserve Officers Training Corps (ROTC):** Army ROTC: Offered on campus. **Faculty and instruction (2005-2006):** Total instructional faculty: 411 full-time, 401 part-time (48% men; 52% women; 12% minorities). Full-time faculty with Ph.D. or other terminal degree: 73%. Student/faculty ratio: 23/1. Classes of fewer than 20 students: 26%; of 20 to 49 students: 68%; of 50 or more students: 5%. **Advanced Placement and International Baccalaureate credit:** Scores accepted: 3, 4, 5. International Baccalaureate exams may be used for: Credit and/or placement. **Freshmen returning for sophomore year:** 72%. **Graduation rates:** Four-year: 12%; five-year: 28%; six-year: 31%.

COSTS AND FINANCIAL AID
Financial aid office: (405) 974-3334. **Expenses (2006-2007):** Tuition and fees 2006-2007: $3,539 in state, $8,924 out of state; room/board: $4,763. Estimated books and supplies: $1,000. **Financial aid:** Priority filing date for institution's financial aid form: May 31; deadline: May 31. In 2005-2006, 61% of undergraduates applied for financial aid. Of those, 48% were determined to have financial need; 10% had their need fully met. Average financial aid package (proportion receiving): $6,043 (45%). Average amount of gift aid, such as scholarships or grants (proportion receiving): N/A (43%). Average amount of self-help aid, such as work study or loans (proportion receiving): $3,839 (45%). Average need-based loan (excluding PLUS or other private loans): $3,787. Among students who received need-based aid, the average percentage of need met: 68%. Among students who received aid based on merit, the average award (and the proportion receiving): $2,169 (7%). The average athletic scholarship (and the proportion receiving): $3,754 (2%). Average amount of debt of borrowers graduating in 2005: $15,508. Proportion who borrowed: 53%.

CAMPUS LIFE AND EXTRACURRICULAR ACTIVITIES
Campus housing available (% using): coed dorms (12%), women's dorms (15%), men's dorms (11%), sorority housing (19%), fraternity housing (12%), apartments for married students (4%), apartment for single students (27%). Students who live in college-owned, operated, or affiliated housing: 12%. **Student employment:** During the 2005-2006 academic year, 5% of undergraduates worked on campus. Average per-year earnings: $7,083. **Clubs and organizations:** Number of student organizations: 220. Activities include: choral groups, concert band, dance, drama/theater, jazz band, marching band, music ensembles, musical theater, opera, pep band, radio station, student government, student newspaper, symphony orchestra, television station, yearbook. Number of fraternities: 10; sororities: 9. Proportion of men in fraternities: 2%; of women in sororities: 3%. Average proportion of students who stay on campus on weekends: 9%. **Sports program (2005-2006):** Member of NCAA II. *Men's intercollegiate varsity sports:* baseball, basketball, football, golf, tennis, wrestling. *Women's intercollegiate varsity sports:* basketball, cross-country, golf, soccer, softball, tennis, volleyball.

SERVICES AND FACILITIES
Basic services: nonremedial tutoring, placement service, health service, health insurance. **Remedial assistance:** reading, math, writing, study skills. **Counseling services:** minority student, career, personal, academic, older student, psychological, birth control, other. **For learning-disabled students:** School does not offer a structured program with separate admission and additional fees. Total undergraduates in learning-disabled program or receiving services: 252. Services include: remedial math, remedial English, reading machines, remedial reading, tape recorders, note-taking services, special bookstore section, oral tests, readers, extended time for tests, tutors, priority registration, priority seating, substitution of courses, texts on tape, typist/scribe, exams on tape or computer, take home exams, other testing accomodations, waiver of foreign language degree requirement, waiver of math degree requirement. **Library:** Number of titles: 470,409; number of current serial subscriptions: 3,130. **Information technology resources:** Students are not required to lease or own a computer. Number of campus computers available to all students: 713. School has a wireless network. Approximate number of users that can be accommodated: 350. Proportion of college-owned housing units wired for high-speed internet access: 100%. **Campus safety:** Security services offered: 24-hour foot-and-vehicle patrols, late-night transport/escort service, 24-hour emergency telephones, lighted pathways/sidewalks, controlled dormitory access (key, security card, etc).

TRANSFER AND INTERNATIONAL STUDENTS

Transfer students: May apply for admission for the following academic terms: Fall, Spring, Summer. Applicants need a minimum number of credits to apply. For fall 2005: Transfer applications received: 2,633. Transfer applicants offered admission: 2,481. Transfer applicants enrolled: 1,715. **International students:** Number of foreign undergraduates: 1077 (7% of student body). Number of countries represented: 73. Minimum TOEFL score required: 500 (paper); 173 (computer). Average TOEFL score: 520 (paper).

University of Oklahoma

- **Address:** 660 Parrington Oval, Norman, OK 73019-0390
- **Website:** http://www.ou.edu
- **Public**
- **Enrollment:** 18,493 full-time; 2,786 part-time

KEY STATS

✔ **U.S News College Ranking:** 112, National Universities
✔ **ACT Score (25th/75th percentile):** 23-28
✔ **Tuition:** 2005-2006: $4,408 in state, $12,301 out of state

Selectivity: More selective	**Room/board:** $6,361
Acceptance rate: 86%	**Average debt:** $18,494
Student/faculty ratio: 22/1	**Proportion who borrowed:** 49%

UNDERGRADUATE STUDENT BODY STATS

2005-2006 enrollment: 18,493 full-time; 2,786 part-time. Men: 49%; women: 51%. **Ethnic makeup:** African American: 5%; American-Indian: 7%; Asian American: 5%; Hispanic: 4%; White: 76%; International: 2%.

ADMISSIONS FACTS AND FIGURES

Phone: (405) 325-2252. **Email:** admrec@ou.edu. **Website:** http://www.ou.edu. **Application deadlines for fall 2007:** Regular decision: April 1. Early decision: Not offered. Early action: Not offered. Admission cannot be deferred. **Application fee:** $40. Common application is not accepted. **To apply online, go to:** http://www.ou.edu/admrec/admissions.htm. **Admissions requirements/recommendations:** High school units required (recommended): English: 4; Mathematics: 3; Science: 2; Foreign language: (3); Social studies: 2; History: 1; Academic electives: 3; Total units: 15. Tests: The college uses SAT or ACT scores in admissions decisions. Either SAT or ACT required. For admission to the fall 2007 entering class, the school will accept: ACT with writing, ACT without writing. Campus visit: Neither required nor recommended. Admissions interview: Neither required nor recommended. Off-campus interview: Not available. **Factors that count in admissions decisions:** *Academic:* Secondary school record: Very important. Class rank: Very important. Letters of recommendation: Considered. Standardized test scores: Very important. Essay: Considered. *Nonacademic:* Interview: Not considered. Extracurricular activities: Not considered. Talent/ability: Not considered. Character/personal qualities: Not considered. Alumni/ae relationship: Not considered. Geographical residence: Not considered. State residency: Considered. Religious affiliation/commitment: Not considered. Minority status: Not considered. Volunteer work: Not considered. Work experience: Not considered. **Other schools with the greatest overlap in applicants:** Baylor University; Oklahoma State University; Texas A&M University–College Station; Texas Tech University; University of Texas–Austin. **Admissions statistics for the fall 2005 entering class:** Total applicants: 7,388. Total accepted: 6,331. Freshmen enrolled: 3,245; Overall acceptance rate: 86%. **Size of waiting list:** 950 applicants; enrolled from waiting list: 544. **Credentials of fall 2005 freshmen:** 37% ranked in the top 10 percent of their high school class; 72% were in the top 25 percent, and 93% were in the top half. (Proportion submitting class standing: 85%.) **Average high school grade point average:** 3.6. **First-year students who submitted SAT scores:** 44%. Scores (25/75 percentile): Verbal: N/A, Math: N/A, Combined: N/A. **First-year students submitting ACT scores:** 86%. Scores (25/75 percentile): English: N/A, Math: N/A, Composite: 23-28.

ACADEMICS

Year founded: 1890. **Academic calendar:** Semester. **Degrees offered:** certificate, bachelor's, master's, post-master's certificate, first professional, doctorate. **Most popular majors:** 7% sociology, 6% liberal arts and sciences/liberal studies, 5% psychology, 4% management science, 4% marketing/marketing management. **Major fields of study:** architecture and related services; area, ethnic, cultural, and gender studies; biological and biomedical sciences;

business, management, marketing, and related support services; communication, journalism, and related programs; computer and information sciences and support services; education; engineering; English language and literature/letters; foreign languages, literatures, and linguistics; health professions and related clinical sciences; history; liberal arts and sciences studies, and humanities; mathematics and statistics; multi/interdisciplinary studies; natural resources and conservation; parks, recreation, leisure, and fitness studies; philosophy and religious studies; physical sciences; psychology; public administration and social service professions; social sciences; transportation and materials moving; visual and performing arts. **Areas of required coursework:** arts/fine arts, humanities, computer literacy, mathematics, English (including composition), philosophy, foreign languages, sciences (biological or physical), history, social science, other. **Pre-professional programs:** pre-dentistry, pre-medicine, pre-veterinary science, pre-optometry, pre-pharmacy. **Special academic programs:** accelerated program, cooperative (work-study plan) program, distance learning, double major, dual enrollment, English as a Second Language (ESL), external degree program, honors program, independent study, internships, liberal arts/career combination, student-designed major, study abroad, teacher certificate program, weekend college. **Teacher certification offered in:** early childhood, special education, elementary, secondary. **Cooperative education programs:** business, engineering, health professions, humanities, natural science, social/behavioral science. **Reserve Officers Training Corps (ROTC):** Army ROTC: Offered on campus; Navy ROTC: Offered on campus; Air Force ROTC: Offered on campus. **Faculty and instruction (2005-2006):** Total instructional faculty: 1,276 full-time, 377 part-time (66% men; 40% women; 14% minorities). Full-time faculty with Ph.D. or other terminal degree: 84%. Student/faculty ratio: 22/1. Classes of fewer than 20 students: 39%; of 20 to 49 students: 49%; of 50 or more students: 12%. **Advanced Placement and International Baccalaureate credit:** AP tests may be used for: Credit only. Scores accepted: 3, 4, 5. International Baccalaureate exams may be used for: Credit only. **Freshmen returning for sophomore year:** 84%. **Graduation rates:** Four-year: 19%; five-year: 46%; six-year: 56%.

COSTS AND FINANCIAL AID

Financial aid office: (405) 325-4521. **Expenses (2005-2006):** Tuition and fees 2005-2006: $4,408 in state, $12,301 out of state; room/board: $6,361. Estimated books and supplies: $1,067; transportation: $1,032; personal expenses: $3,176. **Financial aid:** Priority filing date for institution's financial aid form: March 1. In 2005-2006, 56% of undergraduates applied for financial aid. Of those, 53% were determined to have financial need; 83% had their need fully met. Average financial aid package (proportion receiving): $9,782 (53%). Average amount of gift aid, such as scholarships or grants (proportion receiving): $3,686 (18%). Average amount of self-help aid, such as work study or loans (proportion receiving): $4,686 (41%). Average need-based loan (excluding PLUS or other private loans): $4,612. Among students who received need-based aid, the average percentage of need met: 87%. Among students who received aid based on merit, the average award (and the proportion receiving): $3,895 (12%). The average athletic scholarship (and the proportion receiving): $12,508 (1%). Average amount of debt of borrowers graduating in 2005: $18,494. Proportion who borrowed: 49%.

CAMPUS LIFE AND EXTRACURRICULAR ACTIVITIES

Campus housing available (% using): coed dorms (70%), women's dorms, men's dorms, sorority housing, fraternity housing, apartments for married students (13%), apartment for single students (13%), special housing for disabled students (1%), special housing for international students (3%), other housing options. Students who live in college-owned, operated, or affiliated housing: 28%. **Clubs and organizations:** Number of student organizations: 369. Activities include: choral groups, concert band, dance, drama/theater, jazz band, literary magazine, marching band, music ensembles, musical theater, opera, pep band, radio station, student government, student newspaper, student film society, symphony orchestra, television station, yearbook. Number of fraternities: 22; sororities: 17. Proportion of men in fraternities: 14%; of women in sororities: 23%. Average proportion of students who stay on campus on weekends: 80%. **Sports program (2005-2006):** Member of NCAA I. *Men's intercollegiate varsity sports:* baseball, basketball, cross-country, football, golf, gymnastics, tennis, track and field (indoor), track and field (outdoor), wrestling. *Women's intercollegiate varsity sports:* basketball, cross-country, golf, gymnastics, soccer, softball, tennis, track and field (indoor), track and field (outdoor), volleyball.

SERVICES AND FACILITIES

Basic services: nonremedial tutoring, women's center, placement service, day care, health service, health insurance. **Remedial assistance:** math, writing, study skills. **Counseling services:** minority student, career, personal, veteran student, academic, older student, psychological, birth control. **For learning-disabled students:** School does not offer a structured program with separate admission and additional fees. Total undergraduates in learning-disabled program or receiving services: 397. Services include: remedial math, remedial English, reading machines, tape recorders, diagnostic testing service, note-taking services, readers, extended time for tests, tutors, priority registration, substitution of courses, texts on tape, typist/scribe, exams on tape or computer, other testing accomodations, other. **Library:** Number of titles: 4,796,089; number of current serial subscriptions: 31,752.

Information technology resources: Students are not required to lease or own a computer. Number of campus computers available to all students: 2,900. School has a wireless network. Approximate number of users that can be accommodated: 2,000. Proportion of college-owned housing units wired for high-speed internet access: 100%. **Campus safety:** Security services offered: 24-hour foot-and-vehicle patrols, late-night transport/escort service, 24-hour emergency telephones, lighted pathways/sidewalks, student patrols, controlled dormitory access (key, security card, etc).

TRANSFER AND INTERNATIONAL STUDENTS

Transfer students: May apply for admission for the following academic terms: Fall, Spring, Summer. Applicants need a minimum number of credits to apply. For fall 2005: Transfer applications received: 2,793. Transfer applicants offered admission: 2,098. Transfer applicants enrolled: 1,610. **International students:** Number of foreign undergraduates: 413 (2% of student body). Number of countries represented: 98. Minimum TOEFL score required: 550 (paper); 213 (computer). Average TOEFL score: 573 (paper).

Univ. of Science and Arts of Oklahoma

- ■ **Address:** 1727 W. Alabama, Chickasha, OK 73018-5322
- ■ **Website:** http://www.usao.edu
- ■ **Public**
- ■ **Enrollment:** 1,064 full-time; 366 part-time

KEY STATS

✔ **U.S News College Ranking:** third tier, Comp. Coll.–Bachelor's (West)

✔ **ACT Score (25th/75th percentile):** 18-25

✔ **Tuition:** 2006-2007: $3,720 in state, $8,820 out of state

Selectivity: Selective	**Room/board:** $4,510
Acceptance rate: 89%	**Average debt:** $11,378
Student/faculty ratio: 20/1	**Proportion who borrowed:** 67%

UNDERGRADUATE STUDENT BODY STATS

2005-2006 enrollment: 1,064 full-time; 366 part-time. Men: 36%; women: 64%. **Ethnic makeup:** African American: 6%; American-Indian: 13%; Asian American: 1%; Hispanic: 3%; White: 76%; International: 2%.

ADMISSIONS FACTS AND FIGURES

Phone: (405) 574-1204. **Email:** usao-admissions@usao.edu. **Website:** http://www.usao.edu. **Application deadlines for fall 2007:** Regular decision: September 6. Early decision: Not offered. Early action: Not offered. Admission can be deferred. **Application fee:** $15. Common application is accepted. **To apply online, go to:** http://www.usao.edu/usao_easy_intro.htm. **Admissions requirements/recommendations:** High school units required (recommended): English: 4; Mathematics: 3 (4); Science: 2 (3); Foreign language: (2); Social studies: 1; History: 2; Academic electives: 3; Total units: 15 (21). Tests: The college uses SAT or ACT scores in admissions decisions. Neither SAT nor ACT required. For admission to the fall 2007 entering class, the school will accept: ACT with writing, ACT without writing. Campus visit: Recommended. Admissions interview: Neither required nor recommended. Off-campus interview: Not available. **Factors that count in admissions decisions:** *Academic:* Secondary school record: Very important. Class rank: Very important. Letters of recommendation: Considered. Standardized test scores: Very important. Essay: Not considered. *Nonacademic:* Interview: Not considered. Extracurricular activities: Not considered. Talent/ability: Important. Character/personal qualities: Considered. Alumni/ae relationship: Not considered. Geographical residence: Not considered. State residency: Not considered. Religious affiliation/commitment: Not considered. Minority status: Not considered. Volunteer work: Not considered. Work experience: Not considered. **Other schools with the greatest overlap in applicants:** Cameron University; Southwestern Oklahoma State University; University of Central Oklahoma; University of Oklahoma.

Admissions statistics for the fall 2005 entering class: Total applicants: 448. Total accepted: 397. Freshmen enrolled: 282; 6% were from out of state. Overall acceptance rate: 89%. **Credentials of fall 2005 freshmen:** 13% ranked in the top 10 percent of their high school class; 42% were in the top 25 percent, and 75% were in the top half. (Proportion submitting class standing: 88%.) **Average high school grade point average:** 3.4. **First-year students submitting ACT scores:** 90%. Scores (25/75 percentile): English: 17-25, Math: 17-23, Composite: 18-25.

ACADEMICS

Year founded: 1908. **Academic calendar:** Trimester. **Degrees offered:** bachelor's. **Most popular majors:** 21% business, management, marketing, and related support services, 17% education, 11% visual and performing arts, 9% parks, recreation, leisure, and fitness studies, 9% psychology. **Major fields of study:** area, ethnic, cultural, and gender studies; biological and biomedical sciences; business, management, marketing, and related support services; communication, journalism, and related programs; computer and information sciences and support services; education; English language and literature/letters; health professions and related clinical sciences; history; mathematics and statistics; multi/interdisciplinary studies; parks, recreation, leisure, and fitness studies; physical sciences; psychology; social sciences; visual and performing arts. **Areas of required coursework:** arts/fine arts, humanities, computer literacy, mathematics, English (including composition), philosophy, sciences (biological or physical), history, social science, other. **Pre-professional programs:** pre-law, pre-dentistry, pre-medicine, pre-veterinary science, pre-optometry, pre-pharmacy, other. **Special academic programs (% participation):** accelerated program (57%), distance learning, double major, independent study (60%), internships (5%), liberal arts/career combination, student-designed major, study abroad, teacher certification program (23%). **Teacher certification offered in:** early childhood, special education, elementary, secondary. **Faculty and instruction (2005-2006):** Total instructional faculty: 48 full-time, 36 part-time (61% men; 39% women; 12% minorities). Full-time faculty with Ph.D. or other terminal degree: 92%. Student/faculty ratio: 20/1. Classes of fewer than 20 students: 56%; of 20 to 49 students: 37%; of 50 or more students: 7%. **Advanced Placement and International Baccalaureate credit:** AP tests may be used for: Credit and/or placement. Scores accepted: 3, 4, 5. International Baccalaureate exams may be used for: Credit and/or placement. **Freshmen returning for sophomore year:** 58%. **Graduation rates:** Four-year: 12%; five-year: 25%; six-year: 30%. **Graduate study:** 10% of students pursue further study immediately upon graduation; 20% within one year; 25% within five years. Fields in which graduates pursue further study: Master of Business Administration (MBA), 20%; law, 10%; medicine, 25%; dentistry, 5%; education, 10%; arts and sciences, 25%; veterinary medicine, 5%.

COSTS AND FINANCIAL AID

Financial aid office: (405) 574-1240. **Expenses (2006-2007):** Tuition and fees 2006-2007: $3,720 in state, $8,820 out of state; room/board: $4,510. Estimated books and supplies: $1,000; transportation: $2,044; personal expenses: $1,380. **Financial aid:** Priority filing date for institution's financial aid form: March 15. In 2005-2006, 80% of undergraduates applied for financial aid. Of those, 67% were determined to have financial need; 18% had their need fully met. Average financial aid package (proportion receiving): $6,799 (66%). Average amount of gift aid, such as scholarships or grants (proportion receiving): $4,866 (61%). Average amount of self-help aid, such as work study or loans (proportion receiving): $3,387 (44%). Average need-based loan (excluding PLUS or other private loans): $2,884. Among students who received need-based aid, the average percentage of need met: 68%. Among students who received aid based on merit, the average award (and the proportion receiving): $3,857 (18%). The average athletic scholarship (and the proportion receiving): $5,638 (4%). Average amount of debt of borrowers graduating in 2005: $11,378. Proportion who borrowed: 67%.

CAMPUS LIFE AND EXTRACURRICULAR ACTIVITIES

Campus housing available (% using): coed dorms (35%), apartment for single students (65%). Students who live in college-owned, operated, or affiliated housing: 37%. **Student employment:** During the 2005-2006 academic year, 23% of undergraduates worked on campus. Average per-year earnings: $1,012. **Clubs and organizations:** Number of student organizations: 45. Activities include: choral groups, concert band, drama/theater, jazz band, music ensembles, musical theater, pep band, student government, student newspaper, student film society. Number of fraternities: 1; sororities: 1. Proportion of men in fraternities: 2%; of women in sororities: 3%. Average proportion of students who stay on campus on weekends: 45%. **Sports program (2005-2006):** Member of NAIA. *Men's intercollegiate varsity sports:*

baseball, basketball, soccer. *Women's intercollegiate varsity sports:* basketball, soccer, softball.

SERVICES AND FACILITIES

Basic services: nonremedial tutoring, placement service, health service. **Remedial assistance:** reading, math, writing, study skills, other. **Counseling services:** minority student, career, military, personal, veteran student, academic, older student, birth control. **For learning-disabled students:** School does not offer a structured program with separate admission and additional fees. **Library:** Number of titles: 74,256; number of current serial subscriptions: 150. **Information technology resources:** Students are not required to lease or own a computer. Number of campus computers available to all students: 135. School has a wireless network. Approximate number of users that can be accommodated: 1,500. Proportion of college-owned housing units wired for high-speed internet access: 100%. **Campus safety:** Security services offered: 24-hour foot-and-vehicle patrols, lighted pathways/sidewalks, controlled dormitory access (key, security card, etc).

TRANSFER AND INTERNATIONAL STUDENTS

Transfer students: May apply for admission for the following academic terms: Fall, Spring, Summer. Applicants need a minimum number of credits to apply. For fall 2005: Transfer applicants enrolled: 124. **International students:** Number of foreign undergraduates: 25 (2% of student body). Number of countries represented: 13. Minimum TOEFL score required: 500 (paper); 173 (computer). Average TOEFL score: 500 (paper).

University of Tulsa

- **Address:** 600 S. College Avenue, Tulsa, OK 74104
- **Website:** http://www.utulsa.edu
- **Private; Religious affiliation:** Presbyterian
- **Enrollment:** 2,635 full-time; 161 part-time

KEY STATS

✔ **U.S News College Ranking:** 88, National Universities
✔ **ACT Score (25th/75th percentile):** 23-30
✔ **Tuition:** 2006-2007: $20,738

Selectivity: More selective	**Room/board:** $7,052
Acceptance rate: 75%	**Average debt:** $23,824
Student/faculty ratio: 11/1	**Proportion who borrowed:** 59%

UNDERGRADUATE STUDENT BODY STATS

2005-2006 enrollment: 2,635 full-time; 161 part-time. Men: 51%; women: 49%. **Ethnic makeup:** African American: 7%; American-Indian: 5%; Asian American: 2%; Hispanic: 4%; White: 74%; International: 8%. **Religious preference:** Roman Catholic: 14%; Protestant: 36%; Jewish: 1%; Muslim: 1%; No preference: 42%; Presbyterian: 4%; Other: 2%.

ADMISSIONS FACTS AND FIGURES

Phone: (918) 631-2307. **Email:** admission@utulsa.edu. **Website:** http://www.utulsa.edu. **Application deadlines for fall 2007:** Regular decision: Rolling. Early decision: Not offered. Early action: Not offered. Admission can be deferred. **Application fee:** $35. Common application is accepted. **Admissions requirements/recommendations:** High school units required (recommended): English: (4); Mathematics: (3); Science: (3); Foreign language: (2); Social studies: (1); History: (2); Academic electives: (1); Total units: (16). Tests: The college uses SAT or ACT scores in admissions decisions. Either SAT or ACT required. For admission to the fall 2007 entering class, the school will accept: ACT with writing, ACT without writing. Campus visit: Recommended. Admissions interview: Recommended. Off-campus interview: May be arranged. **Factors that count in admissions decisions:** *Academic:* Secondary school record: Very important. Class rank: Very important. Letters of recommendation: Important. Standardized test scores: Important. Essay: Considered. *Nonacademic:* Interview: Very important. Extracurricular activities: Important. Talent/ability: Important. Character/personal qualities: Considered. Alumni/ae relationship: Considered. Geographical residence: Not considered. State residency: Not considered. Religious affiliation/commitment: Not considered. Minority status: Not considered. Volunteer work: Considered. Work experience: Considered. **Other schools with the greatest overlap in applicants:** Rice University; Southern Methodist University; Texas Christian University; University of Oklahoma; Washington University in St. Louis. **Admissions**

statistics for the fall 2005 entering class: Total applicants: 2,687. Total accepted: 2,017. Freshmen enrolled: 631; 45% were from out of state. Overall acceptance rate: 75%. **Size of waiting list:** 272 applicants; enrolled from waiting list: 95. **Credentials of fall 2005 freshmen:** 63% ranked in the top 10 percent of their high school class; 81% were in the top 25 percent, and 94% were in the top half. (Proportion submitting class standing: 94%.) **Average high school grade point average:** 3.7. **First-year students who submitted SAT scores:** 59%. Scores (25/75 percentile): Verbal: 540-700, Math: 550-710, Combined: 1090-1410. **First-year students submitting ACT scores:** 80%. Scores (25/75 percentile): English: 23-32, Math: 22-29, Composite: 23-30.

ACADEMICS

Year founded: 1894. **Academic calendar:** Semester. **Degrees offered:** bachelor's, post-bachelor's certificate, master's, first professional, first professional certificate, doctorate. **Most popular majors:** 24% business, management, marketing, and related support services, 17% engineering, 10% visual and performing arts, 6% biological and biomedical sciences, 6% computer and information sciences and support services. **Major fields of study:** biological and biomedical sciences; business, management, marketing, and related support services; communication, journalism, and related programs; computer and information sciences and support services; education; engineering; English language and literature/letters; foreign languages, literatures, and linguistics; health professions and related clinical sciences; history; legal professions and studies; liberal arts and sciences studies, and humanities; mathematics and statistics; natural resources and conservation; parks, recreation, leisure, and fitness studies; philosophy and religious studies; physical sciences; psychology; social sciences; visual and performing arts. **Areas of required coursework:** arts/fine arts, humanities, computer literacy, mathematics, English (including composition), philosophy, foreign languages, sciences (biological or physical), history, social science. **Pre-professional programs:** pre-law, pre-medicine, other. **Special academic programs (% participation):** accelerated program (3%), double major (14.2%), dual enrollment (0%), English as a Second Language (ESL) (10.8%), honors program (7.2%), independent study (47.9%), internships (15.4%), liberal arts/career combination (2.4%), student-designed major (0%), study abroad (16.9%), teacher certificate program (3.3%). **Teacher certification offered in:** special education, elementary, middle/junior high, secondary. **Reserve Officers Training Corps (ROTC):** Air Force ROTC: Offered at cooperating institution (Oklahoma State University). **Faculty and instruction (2005-2006):** Total instructional faculty: 306 full-time, 116 part-time (64% men; 36% women; 10% minorities). Full-time faculty with Ph.D. or other terminal degree: 96%. Student/faculty ratio: 11/1. Classes of fewer than 20 students: 60%; of 20 to 49 students: 38%; of 50 or more students: 1%. **Advanced Placement and International Baccalaureate credit:** AP tests may be used for: Credit and/or placement. Scores accepted: 3, 4, 5. International Baccalaureate exams may be used for: Credit and/or placement. **Freshmen returning for sophomore year:** 82%. **Graduation rates:** Four-year: 43%; five-year: 59%; six-year: 61%. **Graduate study:** 29% of students pursue further study immediately upon graduation; 31% within one year. Fields in which graduates pursue further study: Master of Business Administration (MBA), 16%; law, 10%; medicine, 10%; engineering, 16%; education, 6%; arts and sciences, 42%.

COSTS AND FINANCIAL AID

Financial aid office: (918) 631-2526. **Expenses (2006-2007):** Tuition and fees 2006-2007: $20,738; room/board: $7,052. Estimated books and supplies: $1,200; transportation: $1,285; personal expenses: $2,570. **Financial aid:** Priority filing date for institution's financial aid form: April 1. In 2005-2006, 90% of undergraduates applied for financial aid. Of those, 47% were determined to have financial need; 55% had their need fully met. Average financial aid package (proportion receiving): $21,719 (47%). Average amount of gift aid, such as scholarships or grants (proportion receiving): $4,339 (24%). Average amount of self-help aid, such as work study or loans (proportion receiving): $7,181 (40%). Average need-based loan (excluding PLUS or other private loans): $5,979. Among students who received need-based aid, the average percentage of need met: 88%. Among students who received aid based on merit, the average award (and the proportion receiving): $10,881 (35%). The average athletic scholarship (and the proportion receiving): $17,578 (13%). Average amount of debt of borrowers graduating in 2005: $23,824. Proportion who borrowed: 59%.

CAMPUS LIFE AND EXTRACURRICULAR ACTIVITIES

Campus housing available (% using): coed dorms (24%), women's dorms (11%), men's dorms (21%), sorority housing (8%), fraternity housing (4%), apartments for married students (10%), apartment for single students

(21%), other housing options (1%). Students who live in college-owned, operated, or affiliated housing: 64%. **Student employment:** During the 2005-2006 academic year, 16% of undergraduates worked on campus. Average per-year earnings: $4,500. **Clubs and organizations:** Number of student organizations: 245. Activities include: choral groups, concert band, drama/theater, jazz band, literary magazine, marching band, music ensembles, musical theater, opera, pep band, radio station, student government, student newspaper, symphony orchestra, television station, yearbook. Number of fraternities: 6; sororities: 9. Proportion of men in fraternities: 21%; of women in sororities: 23%. Average proportion of students who stay on campus on weekends: 95%. **Sports program (2005-2006):** Member of NCAA I. *Men's intercollegiate varsity sports:* basketball, cross-country, football, golf, soccer, tennis, track and field (indoor), track and field (outdoor). *Women's intercollegiate varsity sports:* basketball, crew, cross-country, golf, soccer, softball, tennis, track and field (indoor), track and field (outdoor), volleyball.

SERVICES AND FACILITIES

Basic services: nonremedial tutoring, women's center, placement service, day care, health service, health insurance. **Counseling services:** minority student, career, personal, veteran student, academic, older student, psychological, birth control, religious. **For learning-disabled students:** School does not offer a structured program with separate admission and additional fees. Total undergraduates in learning-disabled program or receiving services: 63. Services include: reading machines, tape recorders, untimed tests, note-taking services, learning center, readers, extended time for tests, tutors, priority registration, priority seating. **Library:** Number of titles: 1,051,430; number of current serial subscriptions: 27,604. **Information technology resources:** Students are not required to lease or own a computer. Number of campus computers available to all students: 792. School has a wireless network. Approximate number of users that can be accommodated: 1,300. Proportion of college-owned housing units wired for high-speed internet access: 100%. **Campus safety:** Security services offered: 24-hour foot-and-vehicle patrols, late-night transport/escort service, 24-hour emergency telephones, lighted pathways/sidewalks, controlled dormitory access (key, security card, etc).

TRANSFER AND INTERNATIONAL STUDENTS

Transfer students: May apply for admission for the following academic terms: Fall, Spring, Summer. Applicants do not need a minimum number of credits to apply. For fall 2005: Transfer applications received: 497. Transfer applicants offered admission: 322. Transfer applicants enrolled: 188. **International students:** Number of foreign undergraduates: 221 (8% of student body). Number of countries represented: 49. Minimum TOEFL score required: 500 (paper); 173 (computer). Average TOEFL score: 563 (paper).

Oregon

Concordia University

- **Address:** 2811 N.E. Holman Street, Portland, OR 97211
- **Website:** http://www.cu-portland.edu
- **Private; Religious affiliation:** Lutheran Church-Missouri Synod
- **Enrollment:** 808 full-time; 198 part-time

KEY STATS
✔ **U.S News College Ranking:** third tier, Universities–Master's (West)
✔ **SAT Score (25th/75th percentile):** 890-1130
✔ **Tuition:** 2006-2007: $20,100

Selectivity: Selective	**Room/board:** $5,900
Acceptance rate: 66%	**Average debt:** N/A
Student/faculty ratio: 17/1	**Proportion who borrowed:** N/A

UNDERGRADUATE STUDENT BODY STATS
2005-2006 enrollment: 808 full-time; 198 part-time. Men: 37%; women: 63%. **Ethnic makeup:** African American: 6%; American-Indian: 2%; Asian American: 5%; Hispanic: 4%; White: 82%; International: 1%. **Religious preference:** Roman Catholic: 9%; Protestant: 46%; No preference: 6%; Unknown: 17%; Lutheran Church-Missouri Synod: 13%; Other: 9%.

ADMISSIONS FACTS AND FIGURES
Phone: (503) 280-8501. **Email:** admissions@cu-portland.edu. **Website:** http://www.cu-portland.edu. **Application deadlines for fall 2007:** Regular decision: July 1. Early decision: Not offered. Early action: Not offered. Admission can be deferred. **Application fee:** $20. Common application is not accepted. **To apply online, go to:** http://www.cu-portland.edu/admissions/applying/. **Admissions requirements/recommendations:** High school units required (recommended): English: (4); Mathematics: (3); Science: (3); Foreign language: (2); Social studies: (3); Academic electives: (3); Total units: (19). Tests: The college uses SAT or ACT scores in admissions decisions. Either SAT or ACT required. For admission to the fall 2007 entering class, the school will accept: ACT with writing, ACT without writing. Campus visit: Recommended. Admissions interview: Recommended. Off-campus interview: May be arranged. **Factors that count in admissions decisions:** **Academic:** Secondary school record: Very important. Class rank: Considered. Letters of recommendation: Very important. Standardized test scores: Very important. Essay: Considered. **Nonacademic:** Character/personal qualities: Considered. Religious affiliation/commitment: Not considered. **Other schools with the greatest overlap in applicants:** George Fox University; Pacific Lutheran University; Portland State University; University of Portland; Whitworth College. **Admissions statistics for the fall 2005 entering class:** Total applicants: 804. Total accepted: 532. Freshmen enrolled: 171; 51% were from out of state. Overall acceptance rate: 66%. **Credentials of fall 2005 freshmen:** 17% ranked in the top 10 percent of their high school class; 49% were in the top 25 percent, and 77% were in the top half. (Proportion submitting class standing: 67%.) **Average high school grade point average:** 3.4. **First-year students who submitted SAT scores:** 85%. Scores (25/75 percentile): Verbal: 430-560, Math: 460-570, Combined: 890-1130. **First-year students submitting ACT scores:** 33%. Scores (25/75 percentile): English: 17-25, Math: 17-24, Composite: 18-24.

ACADEMICS
Year founded: 1905. **Academic calendar:** Semester. **Degrees offered:** associate, bachelor's, post-bachelor's certificate, master's. **Most popular majors:** 37% education, 29% business, management, marketing, and related support services, 15% psychology, 11% biological and biomedical sciences, 9% theology and religious vocations. **Major fields of study:** biological and biomedical sciences; business, management, marketing, and related support services; education; English language and literature/letters; health professions and related clinical sciences; history; liberal arts and sciences studies, and humanities; natural resources and conservation; parks, recreation, leisure, and fitness studies; psychology; public administration and social service professions; theology and religious vocations. **Areas of required**

coursework: arts/fine arts, humanities, mathematics, English (including composition), sciences (biological or physical), history, social science, other. **Pre-professional programs:** pre-law, pre-dentistry, pre-medicine, pre-theology, pre-veterinary science, pre-optometry. **Special academic programs:** accelerated program, cross-registration, double major, honors program, independent study, internships, student-designed major, study abroad, teacher certificate program. **Teacher certification offered in:** early childhood, elementary, middle/junior high, secondary. **Reserve Officers Training Corps (ROTC):** Air Force ROTC: Offered at cooperating institution (University of Portland). **Faculty and instruction (2005-2006):** Total instructional faculty: 42 full-time, 95 part-time (50% men; 50% women; 2% minorities). Full-time faculty with Ph.D. or other terminal degree: 55%. Student/faculty ratio: 17/1. Classes of fewer than 20 students: 68%; of 20 to 49 students: 32%; of 50 or more students: 0%. **Advanced Placement and International Baccalaureate credit:** AP tests may be used for: Credit only. Scores accepted: 3, 4, 5. International Baccalaureate exams may be used for: Credit and/or placement. **Freshmen returning for sophomore year:** 67%. **Graduation rates:** Four-year: 30%; five-year: 40%; six-year: 43%.

COSTS AND FINANCIAL AID
Financial aid office: (503) 280-8514. **Expenses (2006-2007):** Tuition and fees 2006-2007: $20,100; room/board: $5,900. Estimated books and supplies: $750; transportation: $600; personal expenses: $1,350.

CAMPUS LIFE AND EXTRACURRICULAR ACTIVITIES
Campus housing available (% using): coed dorms (60%), apartment for single students (30%), other housing options (10%). Students who live in college-owned, operated, or affiliated housing: 39%. **Clubs and organizations:** Number of student organizations: 30. Activities include: choral groups, drama/theater, literary magazine, music ensembles, radio station, student government, student newspaper. Number of fraternities: 0; sororities: 0. Average proportion of students who stay on campus on weekends: 60%. **Sports program (2005-2006):** Member of NAIA. *Men's intercollegiate varsity sports:* baseball, basketball, golf, soccer. *Women's intercollegiate varsity sports:* basketball, golf, soccer, softball, volleyball.

SERVICES AND FACILITIES
Basic services: nonremedial tutoring, placement service, health service, health insurance. **Remedial assistance:** math, writing. **Counseling services:** minority student, career, personal, academic, older student, psychological, birth control, religious. **For learning-disabled students:** School does not offer a structured program with separate admission and additional fees. Total undergraduates in learning-disabled program or receiving services: 10. Services include: remedial math, remedial English, reading machines, tape recorders, videotaped classes, untimed tests, note-taking services, oral tests, learning center, readers, extended time for tests, tutors, priority registration, priority seating, texts on tape, other testing accomodations. **Library:** Number of titles: 70,738; number of current serial subscriptions: 20,500. **Information technology resources:** Students are required to lease or own a computer. Number of campus computers available to all students: 100. School has a wireless network. Approximate number of users that can be accommodated: 1,000. Proportion of college-owned housing units wired for high-speed internet access: 100%. **Campus safety:** Security services offered: 24-hour foot-and-vehicle patrols, late-night transport/escort service, 24-hour emergency telephones, lighted pathways/sidewalks, student patrols, controlled dormitory access (key, security card, etc).

TRANSFER AND INTERNATIONAL STUDENTS
Transfer students: May apply for admission for the following academic terms: Fall, Spring, Summer. Applicants need a minimum number of credits to apply. For fall 2005: Transfer applications received: 617. Transfer applicants offered admission: 338. Transfer applicants enrolled: 211. **International students:** Number of foreign undergraduates: 8 (1% of student body). Minimum TOEFL score required: 525 (paper); 195 (computer).

Corban College

- **Address:** 5000 Deer Park Drive SE, Salem, OR 97301
- **Website:** http://www.corban.edu
- **Private; Religious affiliation:** Independent Baptist
- **Enrollment:** 653 full-time; 151 part-time

KEY STATS

✔ **U.S News College Ranking:** 8, Comp. Coll.–Bachelor's (West)
✔ **SAT Score (25th/75th percentile):** 869-1318
✔ **Tuition:** 2006-2007: $19,294

Selectivity: Selective	**Room/board:** $7,084
Acceptance rate: 83%	**Average debt:** $23,400
Student/faculty ratio: 16/1	**Proportion who borrowed:** 70%

UNDERGRADUATE STUDENT BODY STATS

2005-2006 enrollment: 653 full-time; 151 part-time. Men: 42%; women: 58%. **Ethnic makeup:** African American: 1%; American-Indian: 1%; Asian American: 2%; Hispanic: 2%; White: 93%. **Religious preference:** Protestant: 100%.

ADMISSIONS FACTS AND FIGURES

Phone: (800) 845-3005. **Email:** admissions@corban.edu. **Website:** http://www.corban.edu. **Application deadlines for fall 2007:** Regular decision: August 1; decision sent by August 1. Early decision: Not offered. Early action: Not offered. Admission cannot be deferred. **Application fee:** $35. Common application is not accepted. **Admissions requirements/recommendations:** High school units required (recommended): English: 4 (4); Mathematics: 3 (3); Science: 2 (2); Foreign language: 1 (1); Social studies: 3 (3); Total units: 13 (13). Tests: The college uses SAT or ACT scores in admissions decisions. Either SAT or ACT required. For admission to the fall 2007 entering class, the school will accept: ACT with writing. Campus visit: Recommended. Admissions interview: Recommended. Off-campus interview: May be arranged. **Factors that count in admissions decisions:** *Academic:* Secondary school record: Important. Class rank: Considered. Letters of recommendation: Very important. Standardized test scores: Important. Essay: Very important. *Nonacademic:* Interview: Considered. Extracurricular activities: Considered. Talent/ability: Not considered. Character/personal qualities: Important. Alumni/ae relationship: Considered. Geographical residence: Not considered. State residency: Not considered. Religious affiliation/commitment: Very important. Minority status: Not considered. Volunteer work: Not considered. Work experience: Not considered. **Other schools with the greatest overlap in applicants:** George Fox University; Master's College and Seminary; Northwest Christian College; Northwest University; Seattle Pacific University. **Admissions statistics for the fall 2005 entering class:** Total applicants: 485. Total accepted: 402. Freshmen enrolled: 205; 31% were from out of state. Overall acceptance rate: 83%. **Credentials of fall 2005 freshmen:** 29% ranked in the top 10 percent of their high school class; 56% were in the top 25 percent, and 75% were in the top half. (Proportion submitting class standing: 71%.) **Average high school grade point average:** 3.6. **First-year students who submitted SAT scores:** 91%. Scores (25/75 percentile): Verbal: 445-669, Math: 424-649, Combined: 869-1318. **First-year students submitting ACT scores:** 5%. Scores (25/75 percentile): English: N/A, Math: N/A, Composite: 20-31.

ACADEMICS

Year founded: 1935. **Academic calendar:** Semester. **Degrees offered:** associate, bachelor's, master's. **Most popular majors:** 27% psychology, 26% business, management, marketing, and related support services, 15% education, 13% theology and religious vocations, 9% liberal arts and sciences studies, and humanities. **Major fields of study:** business, management, marketing, and related support services; communication, journalism, and related programs; computer and information sciences and support services; education; English language and literature/letters; health professions and related clinical sciences; legal professions and studies; liberal arts and sciences studies, and humanities; mathematics and statistics; parks, recreation, leisure, and fitness studies; psychology; social sciences; theology and religious vocations; visual and performing arts. **Areas of required coursework:** arts/fine arts, humanities, computer literacy, mathematics, English (including composition), philosophy, sciences (biological or physical), history, social science, other. **Pre-professional programs:** pre-law, pre-dentistry, pre-medicine, pre-theology, pre-veterinary science, pre-optometry. **Special academic programs (% participation):** accelerated program (30%), cross-registration (4%), dis-

tance learning (9%), double major (5%), honors program (5%), independent study (10%), internships (66%), student-designed major, study abroad (5%), teacher certificate program (18%), weekend college (70%). **Teacher certification offered in:** elementary, middle/junior high, secondary. **Cooperative education programs:** education, other. **Reserve Officers Training Corps (ROTC):** Army ROTC: Offered at cooperating institution (Oregon State University); Air Force ROTC: Offered at cooperating institution (Oregon State University). **Faculty and instruction (2005-2006):** Total instructional faculty: 34 full-time, 37 part-time (70% men; 30% women; 3% minorities). Full-time faculty with Ph.D. or other terminal degree: 41%. Student/faculty ratio: 16/1. Classes of fewer than 20 students: 59%; of 20 to 49 students: 37%; of 50 or more students: 4%. **Advanced Placement and International Baccalaureate credit:** AP tests may be used for: Credit only. Scores accepted: 3. International Baccalaureate exams may be used for: Credit only. **Freshmen returning for sophomore year:** 71%. **Graduation rates:** Four-year: 50%; five-year: 58%; six-year: 52%. **Graduate study:** 5% of students pursue further study immediately upon graduation; 15% within one year; 25% within five years. Fields in which graduates pursue further study: Master of Business Administration (MBA), 5%; theology (or the seminary), 10%; education, 60%; arts and sciences, 25%.

COSTS AND FINANCIAL AID

Financial aid office: (503) 375-7006. **Expenses (2006-2007):** Tuition and fees 2006-2007: $19,294; room/board: $7,084. Estimated transportation: $500; personal expenses: $500. **Financial aid:** Priority filing date for institution's financial aid form: February 15. In 2005-2006, 93% of undergraduates applied for financial aid. Of those, 86% were determined to have financial need; 13% had their need fully met. Average financial aid package (proportion receiving): $12,117 (86%). Average amount of gift aid, such as scholarships or grants (proportion receiving): $8,955 (86%). Average amount of self-help aid, such as work study or loans (proportion receiving): $3,846 (71%). Average need-based loan (excluding PLUS or other private loans): $3,846. Among students who received need-based aid, the average percentage of need met: 61%. Among students who received aid based on merit, the average award (and the proportion receiving): $7,847 (13%). The average athletic scholarship (and the proportion receiving): $3,819 (6%). Average amount of debt of borrowers graduating in 2005: $23,400. Proportion who borrowed: 70%.

CAMPUS LIFE AND EXTRACURRICULAR ACTIVITIES

Campus housing available (% using): women's dorms (58%), men's dorms (33%), apartment for single students (9%). Students who live in college-owned, operated, or affiliated housing: 58%. **Student employment:** During the 2005-2006 academic year, 15% of undergraduates worked on campus. Average per-year earnings: $1,500. **Clubs and organizations:** Number of student organizations: 14. Activities include: choral groups, concert band, drama/theater, jazz band, literary magazine, music ensembles, musical theater, pep band, radio station, student government, student newspaper, symphony orchestra, yearbook. Number of fraternities: 0; sororities: 0. Average proportion of students who stay on campus on weekends: 50%. **Sports program (2005-2006):** Member of NAIA. *Men's intercollegiate varsity sports:* baseball, basketball, cross-country, golf, soccer, track and field (outdoor). *Women's intercollegiate varsity sports:* basketball, cross-country, soccer, softball, track and field (outdoor), volleyball.

SERVICES AND FACILITIES

Basic services: nonremedial tutoring, health service, health insurance. **Remedial assistance:** study skills. **Counseling services:** career, military, personal, veteran student, academic, older student, psychological, religious. **For learning-disabled students:** School does not offer a structured program with separate admission and additional fees. Total undergraduates in learning-disabled program or receiving services: 10. Services include: tape recorders, note-taking services, oral tests, learning center, readers, extended time for tests, tutors, priority seating, texts on tape. **Library:** Number of titles: 103,489; number of current serial subscriptions: 573. **Information technology resources:** Students are not required to lease or own a computer. Number of campus computers available to all students: 30. School has a wireless network. Approximate number of users that can be accommodated: 400. Proportion of college-owned housing units wired for high-speed internet access: 100%. **Campus safety:** Security services offered: late-night transport/escort service, 24-hour emergency telephones, lighted pathways/sidewalks, student patrols, controlled dormitory access (key, security card, etc).

TRANSFER AND INTERNATIONAL STUDENTS

Transfer students: May apply for admission for the following academic terms: Fall, Spring. Applicants need a minimum number of credits to apply. For fall 2005: Transfer applications received: 97. Transfer applicants offered admission: 97. Transfer applicants enrolled: 97. **International students:** Number of foreign undergraduates: 3. Number of countries represented: 2. Minimum TOEFL score required: 500 (paper).

Eastern Oregon University

- **Address:** 1 University Boulevard, La Grande, OR 97850
- **Website:** http://www.eou.edu
- **Public**
- **Enrollment:** 2,029 full-time; 1,168 part-time

KEY STATS

✔ **U.S News College Ranking:** fourth tier, Universities–Master's (West)
✔ **SAT Score (25th/75th percentile):** 860-1100
✔ **Tuition:** 2006-2007: $5,826 in state, $5,826 out of state

Selectivity: Less selective	**Room/board:** $7,776
Acceptance rate: 73%	**Average debt:** N/A
Student/faculty ratio: N/A	**Proportion who borrowed:** N/A

George Fox University

- **Address:** 414 N. Meridian Street, Newberg, OR 97132
- **Website:** http://www.georgefox.edu
- **Private; Religious affiliation:** Evangelical Friends
- **Enrollment:** 1,549 full-time; 322 part-time

KEY STATS

✔ **U.S News College Ranking:** 19, Universities–Master's (West)
✔ **SAT Score (25th/75th percentile):** 990-1240
✔ **Tuition:** 2006-2007: $22,570

Selectivity: More selective	**Room/board:** $7,210
Acceptance rate: 83%	**Average debt:** $15,026
Student/faculty ratio: 13/1	**Proportion who borrowed:** 61%

UNDERGRADUATE STUDENT BODY STATS

2005-2006 enrollment: 1,549 full-time; 322 part-time. Men: 39%; women: 61%. **Ethnic makeup:** African American: 1%; American-Indian: 1%; Asian American: 5%; Hispanic: 2%; White: 88%; International: 2%. **Religious preference:** Roman Catholic: 3%; Protestant: 89%; No preference: 3%; Evangelical Friends: 5%.

ADMISSIONS FACTS AND FIGURES

Phone: (800) 765-4369. **Email:** admissions@georgefox.edu. **Website:** http://www.georgefox.edu. **Application deadlines for fall 2007:** Regular decision: Rolling. Early decision: Not offered. Early action: Send application by: December 1; Decision sent by: January 1. Admission can be deferred. **Application fee:** $40. Common application is accepted. **To apply online, go to:** http://apply.georgefox.edu. **Admissions requirements/recommendations:** High school units required (recommended): English: 0 (4); Mathematics: 0 (3); Science: 0 (3); Foreign language: 0 (2); Social studies: 0 (2); History: 0 (2); Academic electives: (0); Total units: 0 (16). Tests: The college uses SAT or ACT scores in admissions decisions. Either SAT or ACT required. For admission to the fall 2007 entering class, the school will accept: ACT with writing, ACT without writing. Campus visit: Recommended. Admissions interview: Recommended. Off-campus interview: May be arranged. **Factors that count in admissions decisions:** *Academic:* Secondary school record: Very important. Class rank: Not considered. Letters of recommendation: Important. Standardized test scores: Important. Essay: Important. *Nonacademic:* Interview: Considered. Extracurricular activities: Considered. Talent/ability: Considered. Character/personal qualities: Considered. Alumni/ae relationship: Not considered. Geographical residence: Not considered. State residency: Not considered. Religious affiliation/commitment: Not considered. Minority status: Not considered. Volunteer work: Not considered. Work experience: Not considered. **Other schools with the greatest overlap in applicants:** Corban College; Linfield College; Oregon State

University; Seattle Pacific University; Whitworth College. **Admissions statistics for the fall 2005 entering class:** Total applicants: 1,503. Total accepted: 1,251. Freshmen enrolled: 588; 37% were from out of state. Overall acceptance rate: 83%. Non-early acceptance rate: 83%. **Credentials of fall 2005 freshmen:** 37% ranked in the top 10 percent of their high school class; 65% were in the top 25 percent, and 86% were in the top half. (Proportion submitting class standing: 52%.) **Average high school grade point average:** 3.6. **First-year students who submitted SAT scores:** 74%. Scores (25/75 percentile): Verbal: 490-620, Math: 500-620, Combined: 990-1240. **First-year students submitting ACT scores:** 20%. Scores (25/75 percentile): English: 19-26, Math: 18-26, Composite: 20-26.

ACADEMICS

Year founded: 1891. **Academic calendar:** Semester. **Degrees offered:** bachelor's, post-bachelor's certificate, master's, first professional, doctorate. **Most popular majors:** 39% business, management, marketing, and related support services, 13% multi/interdisciplinary studies, 6% history, 6% elementary education and teaching, 4% visual and performing arts. **Major fields of study:** biological and biomedical sciences; business, management, marketing, and related support services; communication, journalism, and related programs; computer and information sciences and support services; education; engineering; English language and literature/letters; family and consumer sciences/human sciences; foreign languages, literatures, and linguistics; health professions and related clinical sciences; history; mathematics and statistics; multi/interdisciplinary studies; parks, recreation, leisure, and fitness studies; philosophy and religious studies; physical sciences; psychology; public administration and social service professions; social sciences; theology and religious vocations; visual and performing arts. **Areas of required coursework:** arts/fine arts, humanities, mathematics, English (including composition), sciences (biological or physical), history, social science, other. **Pre-professional programs:** pre-law, pre-medicine. **Special academic programs (% participation):** accelerated program (6.9%), cross-registration (.3%), double major (9.8%), dual enrollment (.9%), English as a Second Language (ESL) (2.4%), exchange student program (domestic) (1%), honors program (3.7%); independent study (31.1%), internships (55.4%), student-designed major (5.4%), study abroad (58.8%), teacher certificate program (8.1%). **Teacher certification offered in:** early childhood, elementary. **Reserve Officers Training Corps (ROTC):** Air Force ROTC: Offered at cooperating institution (University of Portland). **Faculty and instruction (2005-2006):** Total instructional faculty: 144 full-time, 116 part-time (55% men; 45% women; 4% minorities). Full-time faculty with Ph.D. or other terminal degree: 62%. Student/faculty ratio: 13/1. Classes of fewer than 20 students: 62%; of 20 to 49 students: 37%; of 50 or more students: 2%. **Advanced Placement and International Baccalaureate credit:** AP tests may be used for: Credit and/or placement. Scores accepted: 3, 4, 5. International Baccalaureate exams may be used for: Credit and/or placement. **Freshmen returning for sophomore year:** 80%. **Graduation rates:** Four-year: 54%; five-year: 63%; six-year: 62%. **Graduate study:** 17% of students pursue further study immediately upon graduation; 24% within one year. Fields in which graduates pursue further study: Master of Business Administration (MBA), 3%; medicine, 10%; dentistry, 6%; engineering, 3%; education, 42%; arts and sciences, 32%.

COSTS AND FINANCIAL AID

Financial aid office: (503) 554-2290. **Expenses (2006-2007):** Tuition and fees 2006-2007: $22,570; room/board: $7,210. Estimated books and supplies: $700; transportation: $700; personal expenses: $1,380. **Financial aid:** Priority filing date for institution's financial aid form: February 1. In 2005-2006, 91% of undergraduates applied for financial aid. Of those, 83% were determined to have financial need; 14% had their need fully met. Average financial aid package (proportion receiving): $15,281 (83%). Average amount of gift aid, such as scholarships or grants (proportion receiving): $11,305 (79%). Average amount of self-help aid, such as work study or loans (proportion receiving): $4,889 (76%). Average need-based loan (excluding PLUS or other private loans): $4,267. Among students who received need-based aid, the average percentage of need met: 75%. Among students who received aid based on merit, the average award (and the proportion receiving): $8,863 (15%). The average athletic scholarship (and the proportion receiving): $0 (0%). Average amount of debt of borrowers graduating in 2005: $15,026. Proportion who borrowed: 61%.

CAMPUS LIFE AND EXTRACURRICULAR ACTIVITIES

Campus housing available (% using): women's dorms (39%), men's dorms (24%), apartment for single students (20%), special housing for disabled students (1%), other housing options (16%). Students who live in college-owned, operated, or affiliated housing: 66%. **Student employment:** During the 2005-2006 academic year, 17% of undergraduates worked on campus. Average per-year earnings: $2,100. **Clubs and organizations:** Number of student organizations: 20. Activities include: choral groups, concert band, drama/theater, jazz band, literary magazine, music ensembles, musical theater, pep band, radio station, student government, student newspaper, symphony orchestra, yearbook. Number of fraternities: 0; sororities: 0. Average proportion of students who stay on campus on weekends: 60%. **Sports program (2005-2006):** Member of NCAA III. *Men's intercollegiate varsity sports:* baseball, basketball, cross-country, soccer, tennis, track and field (outdoor). *Women's intercollegiate varsity sports:* basketball, cross-country, soccer, softball, tennis, track and field (outdoor), volleyball.

SERVICES AND FACILITIES

Basic services: nonremedial tutoring, women's center, health service, health insurance. **Remedial assistance:** reading, math, writing, study skills. **Counseling services:** minority student, career, personal, academic, psychological, birth control, religious. **For learning-disabled students:** School does not offer a structured program with separate admission and additional fees. Total undergraduates in learning-disabled program or receiving services: 25. Services include: remedial English, remedial reading, tape recorders, untimed tests, note-taking services, oral tests, learning center, readers, extended time for tests, tutors, priority seating, texts on tape, typist/scribe, other testing accomodations. **Library:** Number of titles: 202,852; number of current serial subscriptions: 2,383. **Information technology resources:** Students are not required to lease or own a computer. Number of campus computers available to all students: 2,900. School has a wireless network. Approximate number of users that can be accommodated: 600. Proportion of college-owned housing units wired for high-speed internet access: 95%. **Campus safety:** Security services offered: 24-hour foot-and-vehicle patrols, late-night transport/escort service, 24-hour emergency telephones, lighted pathways/sidewalks, student patrols, controlled dormitory access (key, security card, etc).

TRANSFER AND INTERNATIONAL STUDENTS

Transfer students: May apply for admission for the following academic terms: Fall, Spring. Applicants need a minimum number of credits to apply. For fall 2005: Transfer applications received: 249. Transfer applicants offered admission: 168. Transfer applicants enrolled: 91. **International students:** Number of foreign undergraduates: 39 (2% of student body). Number of countries represented: 28. Minimum TOEFL score required: 500 (paper); 173 (computer).

Lewis and Clark College

- **Address:** 0615 S.W. Palatine Hill Road, Portland, OR 97219-7899
- **Website:** http://www.lclark.edu
- **Private**
- **Enrollment:** 1,940 full-time; 24 part-time

KEY STATS

✔ **U.S News College Ranking:** 79, Liberal Arts Colleges
✔ **SAT Score (25th/75th percentile):** 1200-1380
✔ **Tuition:** 2006-2007: $29,772

Selectivity: More selective	**Room/board:** $8,048
Acceptance rate: 59%	**Average debt:** $19,156
Student/faculty ratio: 13/1	**Proportion who borrowed:** 57%

UNDERGRADUATE STUDENT BODY STATS

2005-2006 enrollment: 1,940 full-time; 24 part-time. Men: 39%; women: 61%. **Ethnic makeup:** African American: 1%; American-Indian: 1%; Asian American: 6%; Hispanic: 4%; White: 85%; International: 4%. **Religious preference:** Roman Catholic: 8%; Protestant: 20%; Jewish: 4%; Buddhist: 2%; No preference: 28%; Unknown: 31%; Other: 7%.

ADMISSIONS FACTS AND FIGURES

Phone: (800) 444-4111. **Email:** admissions@lclark.edu. **Website:** http://www.lclark.edu. **Application deadlines for fall 2007:** Regular decision: February 1; decision sent by April 1. Early decision: Not offered. Early action: Send application by: November 15; Decision sent by: January 15. Admission can be deferred. **Application fee:** $50. Common application is accepted. **Admissions requirements/recommendations:** High school units required (recommended): English: (4); Mathematics: (3); Science: (3); Foreign lan-

guage: (2); Social studies: (3). Tests: The college uses SAT or ACT scores in admissions decisions. Neither SAT nor ACT required. For admission to the fall 2007 entering class, the school will accept: ACT with writing, ACT without writing. Campus visit: Recommended. Admissions interview: Neither required nor recommended. Off-campus interview: May be arranged. **Factors that count in admissions decisions:** *Academic:* Secondary school record: Very important. Class rank: Important. Letters of recommendation: Important. Standardized test scores: Important. Essay: Important. *Nonacademic:* Interview: Considered. Extracurricular activities: Important. Talent/ability: Important. Character/personal qualities: Important. Alumni/ae relationship: Important. Geographical residence: Considered. State residency: Considered. Religious affiliation/commitment: Not considered. Minority status: Very important. Volunteer work: Important. Work experience: Considered. **Other schools with the greatest overlap in applicants:** Reed College; University of Oregon; University of Puget Sound; Whitman College; Willamette University. **Admissions statistics for the fall 2005 entering class:** Total applicants: 4,196. Total accepted: 2,495. Freshmen enrolled: 490; 83% were from out of state. Accepted through early-decision or early-action plans: 32%. Overall acceptance rate: 59%. Non-early acceptance rate: 56%. **Size of waiting list:** 567 applicants; enrolled from waiting list: 43. **Credentials of fall 2005 freshmen:** 42% ranked in the top 10 percent of their high school class; 78% were in the top 25 percent, and 98% were in the top half. (Proportion submitting class standing: 77%.) **Average high school grade point average:** 3.7. **First-year students who submitted SAT scores:** 75%. Scores (25/75 percentile): Verbal: 610-700, Math: 590-680, Combined: 1200-1380. **First-year students submitting ACT scores:** 37%. Scores (25/75 percentile): English: 25-31, Math: 25-29, Composite: 26-30.

ACADEMICS

Year founded: 1867. **Academic calendar:** Semester. **Degrees offered:** certificate, bachelor's, master's, post-master's certificate, first professional, doctorate. **Most popular majors:** 19% social sciences, 11% biological and biomedical sciences, 11% foreign languages, literatures, and linguistics, 11% psychology, 9% visual and performing arts. **Major fields of study:** area, ethnic, cultural, and gender studies; biological and biomedical sciences; communication, journalism, and related programs; computer and information sciences and support services; English language and literature/letters; foreign languages, literatures, and linguistics; history; liberal arts and sciences studies, and humanities; mathematics and statistics; natural resources and conservation; philosophy and religious studies; physical sciences; psychology; social sciences; visual and performing arts. **Areas of required coursework:** arts/fine arts, humanities, mathematics, foreign languages, sciences (biological or physical), other. **Pre-professional programs:** pre-law, pre-dentistry, pre-medicine, pre-veterinary science, pre-optometry, pre-pharmacy. **Special academic programs (% participation):** accelerated program (0%), cross-registration (0%), double major (11.6%), dual enrollment, English as a Second Language (ESL) (2.5%), honors program (13.5%), independent study (25%), internships (41%), student-designed major (0%), study abroad (61.4%). **Faculty and instruction (2005-2006):** Total instructional faculty: 205 full-time, 118 part-time (52% men; 48% women; 8% minorities). Full-time faculty with Ph.D. or other terminal degree: 91%. Student/faculty ratio: 13/1. Classes of fewer than 20 students: 55%; of 20 to 49 students: 43%; of 50 or more students: 2%. **Advanced Placement and International Baccalaureate credit:** AP tests may be used for: Credit and/or placement. Scores accepted: 4, 5. International Baccalaureate exams may be used for: Credit and/or placement. **Freshmen returning for sophomore year:** 85%. **Graduation rates:** Four-year: 62%; five-year: 69%; six-year: 71%. **Graduate study:** 26% of students pursue further study immediately upon graduation; 26% within one year; 64% within five years. Fields in which graduates pursue further study: Master of Business Administration (MBA), 8%; law, 11%; medicine, 5%; dentistry, 2%; engineering, 1%; theology (or the seminary), 1%; education, 28%; arts and sciences, 43%; veterinary medicine, 1%.

COSTS AND FINANCIAL AID

Financial aid office: (503) 768-7090. **Expenses (2006-2007):** Tuition and fees 2006-2007: $29,772; room/board: $8,048. Estimated books and supplies: $1,000; transportation: $900; personal expenses: $900. **Financial aid:** Priority filing date for institution's financial aid form: March 1. In 2005-2006, 79% of undergraduates applied for financial aid. Of those, 61% were determined to have financial need; 34% had their need fully met. Average financial aid package (proportion receiving): $24,262 (61%). Average amount of gift aid, such as scholarships or grants (proportion receiving): $19,851 (61%). Average amount of self-help aid, such as work study or loans (proportion receiving): $6,130 (44%). Average need-based loan (excluding PLUS or other private loans): $5,020. Among students who received need-based aid, the average percentage of need met: 87%. Among students who received aid based on merit, the average award (and the proportion receiving): $7,913 (14%). The average athletic scholarship (and the proportion receiving): $0 (0%). Average amount of debt of borrowers graduating in 2005: $19,156. Proportion who borrowed: 57%.

CAMPUS LIFE AND EXTRACURRICULAR ACTIVITIES

Campus housing available (% using): coed dorms (74%), women's dorms (5%), other housing options (21%). Students who live in college-owned, operated, or affiliated housing: 66%. **Student employment:** During the 2005-2006 academic year, 25% of undergraduates worked on campus. Average per-year earnings: $619. **Clubs and organizations:** Number of student organizations: 75. Activities include: choral groups, concert band, dance, drama/theater, jazz band, literary magazine, music ensembles, musical theater, radio station, student government, student newspaper, symphony orchestra, television station, yearbook. Number of fraternities: 0; sororities: 0. Average proportion of students who stay on campus on weekends: 97%. **Sports program (2005-2006):** Member of NCAA III. *Men's intercollegiate varsity sports:* baseball, basketball, cross-country, football, golf, swimming and diving, tennis, track and field (outdoor). *Women's intercollegiate varsity sports:* basketball, cross-country, golf, rowing, softball, swimming and diving, tennis, track and field (outdoor), volleyball.

SERVICES AND FACILITIES

Basic services: nonremedial tutoring, placement service, health service, health insurance. **Remedial assistance:** math, writing, study skills, other. **Counseling services:** minority student, career, personal, academic, older student, psychological, birth control, religious. **For learning-disabled students:** School does not offer a structured program with separate admission and additional fees. Total undergraduates in learning-disabled program or receiving services: 151. Services include: tape recorders, diagnostic testing service, note-taking services, readers, extended time for tests, tutors, proofreading services, substitution of courses, texts on tape, other testing accomodations, other. **Library:** Number of titles: 290,000; number of current serial subscriptions: 3,000. **Information technology resources:** Students are not required to lease or own a computer. Number of campus computers available to all students: 130. School has a wireless network. Proportion of college-owned housing units wired for high-speed internet access: 0%. **Campus safety:** Security services offered: 24-hour foot-and-vehicle patrols, late-night transport/escort service, 24-hour emergency telephones, lighted pathways/sidewalks, student patrols, controlled dormitory access (key, security card, etc).

TRANSFER AND INTERNATIONAL STUDENTS

Transfer students: May apply for admission for the following academic terms: Fall, Spring, Summer. Applicants do not need a minimum number of credits to apply. For fall 2005: Transfer applications received: 312. Transfer applicants offered admission: 136. Transfer applicants enrolled: 56. **International students:** Number of foreign undergraduates: 67 (4% of student body). Minimum TOEFL score required: 500 (paper); 173 (computer). Average TOEFL score: 576 (paper).

Linfield College

- **Address:** 900 S.E. Baker Street, McMinnville, OR 97128-6894
- **Website:** http://www.linfield.edu
- **Private; Religious affiliation:** American Baptist
- **Enrollment:** 1,708 full-time; 42 part-time

KEY STATS

✔ **U.S News College Ranking:** 1, Comp. Coll.–Bachelor's (West)
✔ **SAT Score (25th/75th percentile):** 1030-1260
✔ **Tuition:** 2006-2007: $24,174

Selectivity: More selective	**Room/board:** $7,020
Acceptance rate: 73%	**Average debt:** $24,594
Student/faculty ratio: 14/1	**Proportion who borrowed:** 75%

UNDERGRADUATE STUDENT BODY STATS

2005-2006 enrollment: 1,708 full-time; 42 part-time. Men: 46%; women: 54%. **Ethnic makeup:** African American: 1%; American-Indian: 1%; Asian American: 6%; Hispanic: 2%; White: 87%; International: 2%. **Religious preference:** Roman Catholic: 11%; Protestant: 41%; Jewish: 1%; Muslim: 1%;

Hindu: 1%; Buddhist: 1%; No preference: 5%; Unknown: 38%; American Baptist: 1%.

ADMISSIONS FACTS AND FIGURES

Phone: (800) 640-2287. **Email:** admission@linfield.edu. **Website:** http://www.linfield.edu. **Application deadlines for fall 2007:** Regular decision: Rolling; decision sent by April 1. Early decision: Not offered. Early action: Send application by: November 15; Decision sent by: January 15. Admission can be deferred. **Application fee:** $40. Common application is accepted. **To apply online, go to:** http://www.linfield.edu/admission/application/index.php. **Admissions requirements/recommendations:** High school units required (recommended): English: (4); Mathematics: (4); Science: (3); Foreign language: (2); Social studies: (4); Total units: (17). Tests: The college uses SAT or ACT scores in admissions decisions. Either SAT or ACT required. For admission to the fall 2007 entering class, the school will accept: ACT with writing, ACT without writing. Campus visit: Recommended. Admissions interview: Recommended. Off-campus interview: May be arranged. **Factors that count in admissions decisions:** *Academic:* Secondary school record: Very important. Class rank: Important. Letters of recommendation: Important. Standardized test scores: Very important. Essay: Important. *Nonacademic:* Interview: Not considered. Extracurricular activities: Considered. Talent/ability: Considered. Character/personal qualities: Considered. Alumni/ae relationship: Considered. Geographical residence: Considered. State residency: Not considered. Religious affiliation/commitment: Not considered. Minority status: Considered. Volunteer work: Considered. Work experience: Considered. **Other schools with the greatest overlap in applicants:** Gonzaga University; Oregon State University; University of Oregon; University of Puget Sound; Willamette University. **Admissions statistics for the fall 2005 entering class:** Total applicants: 2,131. Total accepted: 1,560. Freshmen enrolled: 488; 41% were from out of state. Accepted through early-decision or early-action plans: 31%. Overall acceptance rate: 73%. Non-early acceptance rate: 68%. **Size of waiting list:** 15 applicants; enrolled from waiting list: 0. **Credentials of fall 2005 freshmen:** 34% ranked in the top 10 percent of their high school class; 67% were in the top 25 percent, and 93% were in the top half. (Proportion submitting class standing: 84%.) **Average high school grade point average:** 3.6. **First-year students who submitted SAT scores:** 85%. Scores (25/75 percentile): Verbal: 510-620, Math: 520-640, Combined: 1030-1260. **First-year students submitting ACT scores:** 16%. Scores (25/75 percentile): English: N/A, Math: N/A, Composite: 21-27.

ACADEMICS

Year founded: 1849. **Academic calendar:** 4-1-4. **Degrees offered:** bachelor's, post-bachelor's certificate. **Most popular majors:** 20% business, management, marketing, and related support services; 11% education, 10% social sciences, 8% parks, recreation, leisure, and fitness studies, 7% physical sciences. **Major fields of study:** biological and biomedical sciences; business, management, marketing, and related support services; communication, journalism, and related programs; computer and information sciences and support services; education; English language and literature/letters; foreign languages, literatures, and linguistics; health professions and related clinical sciences; history; mathematics and statistics; natural resources and conservation; parks, recreation, leisure, and fitness studies; philosophy and religious studies; physical sciences; psychology; social sciences; visual and performing arts. **Areas of required coursework:** arts/fine arts, humanities, mathematics, English (including composition), philosophy, sciences (biological or physical), history, social science, other. **Special academic programs (% participation):** cross-registration (1%), distance learning, double major (12%), English as a Second Language (ESL) (1%), external degree program, independent study (21%), internships (32%), liberal arts/career combination (3%), student-designed major (0%), study abroad (59%), teacher certificate program (12%). **Teacher certification offered in:** early childhood, elementary, middle/junior high, secondary. **Reserve Officers Training Corps (ROTC):** Air Force ROTC: Offered at cooperating institution (University of Portland). **Faculty and instruction (2005-2006):** Total instructional faculty: 107 full-time, 57 part-time (59% men; 41% women; 5% minorities). Full-time faculty with Ph.D. or other terminal degree: 93%. Student/faculty ratio: 14/1. Classes of fewer than 20 students: 60%; of 20 to 49 students: 39%; of 50 or more students: 2%. **Advanced Placement and International Baccalaureate credit:** AP tests may be used for: Credit and/or placement. Scores accepted: 4, 5. International Baccalaureate exams may be used for: Credit only. **Freshmen returning for sophomore year:** 82%. **Graduation rates:** Four-year: 57%; five-year: 66%; six-year: 68%. **Graduate study:** 17% of students pursue further study within one year; 30% within five years. Fields in which graduates pursue further study: Master of Business Administration (MBA), 5%;

law, 14%; medicine, 6%; dentistry, 6%; education, 14%; arts and sciences, 40%; veterinary medicine, 1%.

COSTS AND FINANCIAL AID

Financial aid office: (503) 883-2225. **Expenses (2006-2007):** Tuition and fees 2006-2007: $24,174; room/board: $7,020. Estimated books and supplies: $650; transportation: $200; personal expenses: $1,100. **Financial aid:** Priority filing date for institution's financial aid form: February 1; deadline: February 1. In 2005-2006, 67% of undergraduates applied for financial aid. Of those, 67% were determined to have financial need; 39% had their need fully met. Average financial aid package (proportion receiving): $17,653 (67%). Average amount of gift aid, such as scholarships or grants (proportion receiving): $6,672 (52%). Average amount of self-help aid, such as work study or loans (proportion receiving): $5,668 (53%). Average need-based loan (excluding PLUS or other private loans): $4,457. Among students who received need-based aid, the average percentage of need met: 85%. Among students who received aid based on merit, the average award (and the proportion receiving): $8,946 (22%). The average athletic scholarship (and the proportion receiving): $0 (0%). Average amount of debt of borrowers graduating in 2005: $24,594. Proportion who borrowed: 75%.

CAMPUS LIFE AND EXTRACURRICULAR ACTIVITIES

Campus housing available (% using): coed dorms (54%), women's dorms (7%), men's dorms (4%), apartment for single students (34%), special housing for disabled students, other housing options (1%). Students who live in college-owned, operated, or affiliated housing: 74%. **Student employment:** During the 2005-2006 academic year, 46% of undergraduates worked on campus. Average per-year earnings: $1,800. **Clubs and organizations:** Number of student organizations: 90. Activities include: choral groups, concert band, dance, drama/theater, jazz band, literary magazine, music ensembles, musical theater, opera, pep band, radio station, student government, student newspaper, symphony orchestra, yearbook. Number of fraternities: 4; sororities: 4. Proportion of men in fraternities: 26%; of women in sororities: 30%. Average proportion of students who stay on campus on weekends: 80%. **Sports program (2005-2006):** Member of NCAA III. *Men's intercollegiate varsity sports:* baseball, basketball, cross-country, football, golf, soccer, swimming and diving, tennis, track and field (indoor), track and field (outdoor). *Women's intercollegiate varsity sports:* basketball, cross-country, golf, lacrosse, soccer, softball, swimming and diving, tennis, track and field (indoor), track and field (outdoor), volleyball.

SERVICES AND FACILITIES

Basic services: nonremedial tutoring, women's center, health service, health insurance. **Counseling services:** minority student, career, personal, academic, psychological, birth control, religious. **For learning-disabled students:** School does not offer a structured program with separate admission and additional fees. Total undergraduates in learning-disabled program or receiving services: 241. Services include: reading machines, tape recorders, videotaped classes, untimed tests, note-taking services, oral tests, learning center, readers, extended time for tests, tutors, priority registration, priority seating, texts on tape, other testing accomodations, other. **Library:** Number of titles: 173,960; number of current serial subscriptions: 1,115. **Information technology resources:** Students are not required to lease or own a computer. Number of campus computers available to all students: 266. School has a wireless network. Approximate number of users that can be accommodated: 17,000. Proportion of college-owned housing units wired for high-speed internet access: 100%. **Campus safety:** Security services offered: 24-hour foot-and-vehicle patrols, late-night transport/escort service, 24-hour emergency telephones, lighted pathways/sidewalks, controlled dormitory access (key, security card, etc.).

TRANSFER AND INTERNATIONAL STUDENTS

Transfer students: May apply for admission for the following academic terms: Fall, Spring. Applicants need a minimum number of credits to apply. For fall 2005: Transfer applications received: 166. Transfer applicants offered admission: 112. Transfer applicants enrolled: 55. **International students:** Number of foreign undergraduates: 34 (2% of student body). Number of countries represented: 17. Minimum TOEFL score required: 550 (paper); 213 (computer). Average TOEFL score: 577 (paper).

Marylhurst University

- **Address:** PO Box 261, Marylhurst, OR 97036-0261
- **Website:** http://www.marylhurst.edu
- **Private; Religious affiliation:** Roman Catholic
- **Enrollment:** 238 full-time; 641 part-time

KEY STATS

✔ **U.S News College Ranking:** third tier, Universities–Master's (West)
✔ **ACT Score (25th/75th percentile):** 20-20
✔ **Tuition:** 2006-2007: $14,895

Selectivity: Selective	**Room/board:** N/A
Acceptance rate: 44%	**Average debt:** $23,000
Student/faculty ratio: 7/1	**Proportion who borrowed:** 67%

UNDERGRADUATE STUDENT BODY STATS

2005-2006 enrollment: 238 full-time; 641 part-time. Men: 25%; women: 75%. **Ethnic makeup:** African American: 2%; Asian American: 2%; Hispanic: 2%; White: 91%; International: 4%.

ADMISSIONS FACTS AND FIGURES

Phone: (503) 699-6268. **Email:** admissions@marylhurst.edu. **Website:** http://www.marylhurst.edu. **Application deadlines for fall 2007:** Regular decision: Rolling. Early decision: Not offered. Early action: Not offered. Admission can be deferred. **Application fee:** $20. Common application is accepted. **Admissions requirements/recommendations:** Tests: The college uses SAT or ACT scores in admissions decisions. Neither SAT nor ACT required. For admission to the fall 2007 entering class, the school will accept: ACT with writing, ACT without writing. Campus visit: Recommended. Admissions interview: Recommended. Off-campus interview: May be arranged. **Factors that count in admissions decisions:** *Academic:* Secondary school record: Considered. Class rank: Not considered. Letters of recommendation: Considered. Standardized test scores: Important. Essay: Not considered. *Nonacademic:* Interview: Not considered. Extracurricular activities: Not considered. Talent/ability: Not considered. Character/personal qualities: Not considered. Alumni/ae relationship: Not considered. Geographical residence: Not considered. State residency: Not considered. Religious affiliation/commitment: Not considered. Minority status: Not considered. Volunteer work: Not considered. Work experience: Not considered. **Admissions statistics for the fall 2005 entering class:** Total applicants: 34. Total accepted: 15. Freshmen enrolled: 12; Overall acceptance rate: 44%.

ACADEMICS

Year founded: 1893. **Academic calendar:** Quarter. **Degrees offered:** certificate, bachelor's, post-bachelor's certificate, master's, post-master's certificate. **Most popular majors:** 24% business/commerce, 12% communication studies/speech communication and rhetoric, 10% multi/interdisciplinary studies, 8% humanities/humanistic studies, 7% fine arts and art studies. **Major fields of study:** business, management, marketing, and related support services; communication, journalism, and related programs; English language and literature/letters; health professions and related clinical sciences; liberal arts and sciences studies, and humanities; multi/interdisciplinary studies; natural resources and conservation; philosophy and religious studies; psychology; social sciences; visual and performing arts. **Areas of required coursework:** arts/fine arts, humanities, computer literacy, mathematics, English (including composition), philosophy, sciences (biological or physical), social science, other. **Special academic programs:** accelerated program, distance learning, double major, English as a Second Language (ESL), independent study, internships, student-designed major, weekend college. **Cooperative education programs:** art, business, social/behavioral science, other. **Faculty and instruction (2005-2006):** Total instructional faculty: 42 full-time, 205 part-time (46% men; 54% women; 5% minorities). Full-time faculty with Ph.D. or other terminal degree: 62%. Student/faculty ratio: 7/1. Classes of fewer than 20 students: 97%; of 20 to 49 students: 3%; of 50 or more students: 0%. **Advanced Placement and International Baccalaureate credit:** AP tests may be used for: Credit only. Scores accepted: 4. International Baccalaureate exams may be used for: Credit only. **Freshmen returning for sophomore year:** 61%. **Graduation rates:** Four-year: 0%; five-year: 10%; six-year: 17%.

COSTS AND FINANCIAL AID

Financial aid office: (503) 699-6253. **Expenses (2006-2007):** Tuition and fees 2006-2007: $14,895; room/board: N/A. **Financial aid:** Priority filing date for institution's financial aid form: March 1. In 2005-2006, 93% of undergraduates applied for financial aid. Of those, 90% were determined to have financial need; 6% had their need fully met. Average financial aid package (proportion receiving): $12,368 (90%). Average amount of gift aid, such as scholarships or grants (proportion receiving): $6,723 (48%). Average amount of self-help aid, such as work study or loans (proportion receiving): $5,649 (84%). Average need-based loan (excluding PLUS or other private loans): $4,732. Among students who received need-based aid, the average percentage of need met: 48%. Among students who received aid based on merit, the average award (and the proportion receiving): $0 (0%). The average athletic scholarship (and the proportion receiving): $0 (0%). Average amount of debt of borrowers graduating in 2005: $23,000. Proportion who borrowed: 67%.

CAMPUS LIFE AND EXTRACURRICULAR ACTIVITIES

Students who live in college-owned, operated, or affiliated housing: 0%. **Clubs and organizations:** Number of student organizations: 6. Activities include: choral groups, jazz band, literary magazine, music ensembles, symphony orchestra. Number of fraternities: 0; sororities: 0.

SERVICES AND FACILITIES

Basic services: placement service, health insurance, other. **Remedial assistance:** other. **Counseling services:** career, academic, older student, other. **For learning-disabled students:** School does not offer a structured program with separate admission and additional fees. Total undergraduates in learning-disabled program or receiving services: 5. Services include: tape recorders, untimed tests, note-taking services, oral tests, readers, extended time for tests, priority registration, priority seating, texts on tape, other testing accomodations, other. **Library:** Number of titles: 91,161; number of current serial subscriptions: 479. **Information technology resources:** Students are not required to lease or own a computer. Number of campus computers available to all students: 52. School has a wireless network. Approximate number of users that can be accommodated: 300. Proportion of college-owned housing units wired for high-speed internet access: 100%. **Campus safety:** Security services offered: 24-hour foot-and-vehicle patrols, late-night transport/escort service, lighted pathways/sidewalks, controlled dormitory access (key, security card, etc).

TRANSFER AND INTERNATIONAL STUDENTS

Transfer students: May apply for admission for the following academic terms: Fall, Winter, Spring, Summer. Applicants do not need a minimum number of credits to apply. **International students:** Number of foreign undergraduates: 2 (4% of student body). Number of countries represented: 16. Minimum TOEFL score required: 550 (paper); 213 (computer). Average TOEFL score: 503 (paper).

Northwest Christian College

- **Address:** 828 E. 11th Avenue, Eugene, OR 97401
- **Website:** http://www.nwcc.edu
- **Private; Religious affiliation:** Christian Church (Disciples of Christ/Churches of Christ)
- **Enrollment:** 256 full-time; 146 part-time

KEY STATS

✔ **U.S News College Ranking:** 16, Comp. Coll.–Bachelor's (West)
✔ **SAT Score (25th/75th percentile):** 838-1113
✔ **Tuition:** 2006-2007: $19,890

Selectivity: Less selective	**Room/board:** $6,424
Acceptance rate: 64%	**Average debt:** $17,585
Student/faculty ratio: 9/1	**Proportion who borrowed:** 75%

UNDERGRADUATE STUDENT BODY STATS

2005-2006 enrollment: 256 full-time; 146 part-time. Men: 40%; women: 60%. **Ethnic makeup:** African American: 1%; American-Indian: 1%; Asian American: 1%; Hispanic: 2%; White: 96%.

ADMISSIONS FACTS AND FIGURES

Phone: (541) 684-7201. **Email:** admissions@nwcc.edu. **Website:** http://www.nwcc.edu. **Application deadlines for fall 2007:** Regular decision: Rolling. Early decision: Not offered. Early action: Not offered. Admission can be deferred. Common application is accepted. **To apply online, go to:** http://www.nwcc.edu/admissions/. **Admissions requirements/recommendations:** High school units required (recommended): English: 4; Mathematics: 3; Science: 2; Foreign language: 2; Social studies: 2; History: 1; Total units: 15. Tests: The college uses SAT or ACT scores in admissions decisions. Either SAT or ACT required. For admission to the fall 2007 entering class, the school will accept: ACT without writing. Campus visit: Recommended. Admissions interview: Recommended. Off-campus interview: May be arranged. **Factors that count in admissions decisions:** *Academic:* Secondary school record: Considered. Class rank: Important. Letters of recommendation: Important. Standardized test scores: Important. Essay: Important. *Nonacademic:* Interview: Not considered. Extracurricular activities: Not considered. Talent/ability: Not considered. Character/personal qualities: Considered. Alumni/ae relationship: Not considered. Geographical residence: Not considered. State residency: Not considered. Religious affiliation/commitment: Not considered. Minority status: Not considered. Volunteer work: Not considered. Work experience: Considered. **Other schools with the greatest overlap in applicants:** Concordia College; Corban College; George Fox University; Linfield College; Warner Pacific College. **Admissions statistics for the fall 2005 entering class:** Total applicants: 179. Total accepted: 114. Freshmen enrolled: 47; 18% were from out of state. Overall acceptance rate: 64%. **Credentials of fall 2005 freshmen:** 13% ranked in the top 10 percent of their high school class; 36% were in the top 25 percent, and 67% were in the top half. (Proportion submitting class standing: 90%.) **Average high school grade point average:** 3.2. **First-year students who submitted SAT scores:** 88%. Scores (25/75 percentile): Verbal: 430-590, Math: 408-523, Combined: 838-1113. **First-year students submitting ACT scores:** 28%. Scores (25/75 percentile): English: 18-21, Math: 18-22, Composite: 19-22.

ACADEMICS

Year founded: 1895. **Academic calendar:** Semester. **Degrees offered:** certificate, associate, bachelor's, post-bachelor's certificate, master's. **Most popular majors:** 51% business, management, marketing, and related support services, 27% education, 6% psychology, 5% health professions and related clinical sciences, 4% computer and information sciences and support services. **Major fields of study:** area, ethnic, cultural, and gender studies; biological and biomedical sciences; business, management, marketing, and related support services; communication, journalism, and related programs; computer and information sciences and support services; education; health professions and related clinical sciences; liberal arts and sciences studies, and humanities; multi/interdisciplinary studies; psychology; public administration and social service professions; social sciences; theology and religious vocations; visual and performing arts. **Areas of required coursework:** arts/fine arts, humanities, computer literacy, mathematics, English (including composition), philosophy, sciences (biological or physical), history, social science, other. **Special academic programs (% participation):** accelerated program, distance learning, double major, English as a Second Language (ESL), independent study, internships (100%), liberal arts/career combination, student-designed major, study abroad, teacher certificate program. **Teacher certification offered in:** early childhood, elementary, middle/junior high, secondary. **Reserve Officers Training Corps (ROTC):** Army ROTC: Offered at cooperating institution (University of Oregon). **Faculty and instruction (2005-2006):** Total instructional faculty: 19 full-time, 42 part-time (56% men; 44% women; 5% minorities). Full-time faculty with Ph.D. or other terminal degree: 47%. Student/faculty ratio: 9/1. Classes of fewer than 20 students: 90%; of 20 to 49 students: 9%; of 50 or more students: 1%. **Advanced Placement and International Baccalaureate credit:** AP tests may be used for: Credit only. Scores accepted: 3, 4, 5. International Baccalaureate exams may be used for: Credit only. **Freshmen returning for sophomore year:** 66%. **Graduation rates:** Four-year: 30%; five-year: 38%; six-year: 33%.

COSTS AND FINANCIAL AID

Financial aid office: (541) 684-7203. **Expenses (2006-2007):** Tuition and fees 2006-2007: $19,890; room/board: $6,424. Estimated books and supplies: $825; transportation: $900; personal expenses: $900. **Financial aid:** Priority filing date for institution's financial aid form: March 1. In 2005-2006, 97% of undergraduates applied for financial aid. Of those, 91% were determined to have financial need; 20% had their need fully met. Average financial aid package (proportion receiving): $16,195 (90%). Average amount of gift aid, such as scholarships or grants (proportion receiving): $11,315 (90%).

Average amount of self-help aid, such as work study or loans (proportion receiving): $5,536 (81%). Average need-based loan (excluding PLUS or other private loans): $4,198. Among students who received need-based aid, the average percentage of need met: 76%. Among students who received aid based on merit, the average award (and the proportion receiving): $6,880 (8%). The average athletic scholarship (and the proportion receiving): $3,000 (3%). Average amount of debt of borrowers graduating in 2005: $17,585. Proportion who borrowed: 75%.

CAMPUS LIFE AND EXTRACURRICULAR ACTIVITIES

Campus housing available: coed dorms, apartment for single students. Students who live in college-owned, operated, or affiliated housing: 27%. **Clubs and organizations:** Number of student organizations: 11. Activities include: choral groups, concert band, drama/theater, literary magazine, music ensembles, student government, student newspaper, yearbook. Number of fraternities: 0; sororities: 0.

SERVICES AND FACILITIES

Basic services: nonremedial tutoring, placement service, health insurance. **Remedial assistance:** reading, math, writing, study skills. **Counseling services:** career, personal, academic, psychological, religious. **For learning-disabled students:** School does not offer a structured program with separate admission and additional fees. Services include: remedial math, remedial English, remedial reading, tape recorders, videotaped classes, oral tests, extended time for tests, tutors. **Library:** Number of titles: 62,681; number of current serial subscriptions: 266. **Information technology resources:** Students are not required to lease or own a computer. Number of campus computers available to all students: 46. School has a wireless network. Proportion of college-owned housing units wired for high-speed internet access: 95%. **Campus safety:** Security services offered: 24-hour foot-and-vehicle patrols, late-night transport/escort service, 24-hour emergency telephones, lighted pathways/sidewalks, controlled dormitory access (key, security card, etc).

TRANSFER AND INTERNATIONAL STUDENTS

Transfer students: May apply for admission for the following academic terms: Fall, Spring, Summer. Applicants need a minimum number of credits to apply. For fall 2005: Transfer applications received: 122. Transfer applicants offered admission: 75. Transfer applicants enrolled: 55. **International students:** Number of foreign undergraduates: 0. Number of countries represented: 1. Minimum TOEFL score required: 500 (paper); 173 (computer).

Oregon Institute of Technology

- **Address:** 3201 Campus Drive, Klamath Falls, OR 97601
- **Website:** http://www.oit.edu
- **Public**
- **Enrollment:** 1,880 full-time; 1,450 part-time

KEY STATS

✔ **U.S News College Ranking:** Unranked Specialty School–Engineering
✔ **ACT Score (25th/75th percentile):** 21-26
✔ **Tuition:** 2006-2007: $5,618 in state, $14,690 out of state

Selectivity: More selective	**Room/board:** $7,552
Acceptance rate: 88%	**Average debt:** $22,351
Student/faculty ratio: 15/1	**Proportion who borrowed:** 70%

UNDERGRADUATE STUDENT BODY STATS

2005-2006 enrollment: 1,880 full-time; 1,450 part-time. Men: 53%; women: 47%. **Ethnic makeup:** African American: 1%; American-Indian: 2%; Asian American: 5%; Hispanic: 4%; White: 87%; International: 1%.

ADMISSIONS FACTS AND FIGURES

Phone: (541) 885-1155. **Email:** oit@oit.edu. **Website:** http://www.oit.edu. **Application deadlines for fall 2007:** Regular decision: October 1. Early decision: Not offered. Early action: Not offered. Admission can be deferred. **Application fee:** $50. Common application is not accepted. **Admissions requirements/recommendations:** High school units required (recommended): English: 4; Mathematics: 3; Science: 2; Foreign language: 2; Social studies: 3; Total units: 14. Tests: The college uses SAT or ACT scores in admissions decisions. Either SAT or ACT required. For admission to the fall 2007 entering class, the school will accept: ACT with writing. Campus visit:

Recommended. Admissions interview: Recommended. Off-campus interview: Not available. **Factors that count in admissions decisions:** *Academic:* Secondary school record: Considered. Class rank: Considered. Letters of recommendation: Considered. Standardized test scores: Very important. Essay: Not considered. *Nonacademic:* Interview: Considered. Extracurricular activities: Not considered. Talent/ability: Not considered. Character/personal qualities: Considered. Alumni/ae relationship: Not considered. Geographical residence: Not considered. State residency: Not considered. Religious affiliation/commitment: Not considered. Minority status: Not considered. Volunteer work: Not considered. Work experience: Considered. **Other schools with the greatest overlap in applicants:** Oregon State University; Southern Oregon University. **Admissions statistics for the fall 2005 entering class:** Total applicants: 651. Total accepted: 575. Freshmen enrolled: 265; 10% were from out of state. Overall acceptance rate: 88%. **Credentials of fall 2005 freshmen:** 25% ranked in the top 10 percent of their high school class; 56% were in the top 25 percent, and 92% were in the top half. (Proportion submitting class standing: 88%.) **Average high school grade point average:** 3.5.

ACADEMICS

Year founded: 1947. **Academic calendar:** Quarter. **Degrees offered:** certificate, associate, bachelor's, master's. **Most popular majors:** Information not available. **Major fields of study:** business, management, marketing, and related support services; communication, journalism, and related programs; computer and information sciences and support services; engineering; engineering technologies/technicians; health professions and related clinical sciences; natural resources and conservation; psychology. **Areas of required coursework:** humanities, computer literacy, mathematics, English (including composition), sciences (biological or physical), social science. **Pre-professional programs:** pre-dentistry, pre-medicine, pre-veterinary science, pre-pharmacy. **Special academic programs (% participation):** cooperative (work-study plan) program (1%), distance learning (43%), double major (4%), dual enrollment (7%), internships (23%), study abroad. **Cooperative education programs:** business, computer science, engineering, health professions, natural science, social/behavioral science, technologies, vocational arts. **Reserve Officers Training Corps (ROTC):** Army ROTC: Offered at cooperating institution (Southern Oregon University). **Faculty and instruction (2005-2006):** Total instructional faculty: 126 full-time, 96 part-time (65% men; 35% women; 6% minorities). Full-time faculty with Ph.D. or other terminal degree: 33%. Student/faculty ratio: 15/1. Classes of fewer than 20 students: 56%; of 20 to 49 students: 41%; of 50 or more students: 3%. **Advanced Placement and International Baccalaureate credit:** AP tests may be used for: Credit only. Scores accepted: 3, 4, 5. International Baccalaureate exams may be used for: Credit and/or placement. **Freshmen returning for sophomore year:** 71%. **Graduation rates:** Six-year: 37%. **Graduate study:** 7% of students pursue further study within one year. Fields in which graduates pursue further study: Master of Business Administration (MBA), 1%; engineering, 3%; education, 5%; arts and sciences, 3%.

COSTS AND FINANCIAL AID

Financial aid office: (541) 885-1280. **Expenses (2006-2007):** Tuition and fees 2006-2007: $5,618 in state, $14,690 out of state; room/board: $7,552. **Financial aid:** Priority filing date for institution's financial aid form: February 1. In 2005-2006, 93% of undergraduates applied for financial aid. Of those, 89% were determined to have financial need; 40% had their need fully met. Average financial aid package (proportion receiving): $5,211 (86%). Average amount of gift aid, such as scholarships or grants (proportion receiving): $4,051 (43%). Average amount of self-help aid, such as work study or loans (proportion receiving): $5,083 (64%). Average need-based loan (excluding PLUS or other private loans): $4,096. Among students who received need-based aid, the average percentage of need met: 18%. Among students who received aid based on merit, the average award (and the proportion receiving): $1,000 (0%). The average athletic scholarship (and the proportion receiving): $1,473 (1%). Average amount of debt of borrowers graduating in 2005: $22,351. Proportion who borrowed: 70%.

CAMPUS LIFE AND EXTRACURRICULAR ACTIVITIES

Campus housing available (% using): coed dorms (100%). Students who live in college-owned, operated, or affiliated housing: 14%. **Student employment:** During the 2005-2006 academic year, 13% of undergraduates worked on campus. **Clubs and organizations:** Number of student organizations: 52. Activities include: choral groups, pep band, radio station, student government, student newspaper, symphony orchestra, television station. Number of fraternities: 1; sororities: 0. Average proportion of students who stay on campus on weekends: 75%. **Sports program (2005-2006):** Member of NAIA. *Men's intercollegiate varsity sports:* baseball, basketball, cross-country, track and field (indoor), track and field (outdoor). *Women's intercollegiate varsity sports:* basketball, cross-country, soccer, softball, track and field (indoor), track and field (outdoor), volleyball.

SERVICES AND FACILITIES

Basic services: nonremedial tutoring, placement service, health service, health insurance. **Remedial assistance:** reading, math, writing, study skills. **Counseling services:** minority student, career, personal, veteran student, academic, older student, psychological, birth control. **For learning-disabled students:** School does not offer a structured program with separate admission and additional fees. Services include: remedial math, reading machines, remedial reading, tape recorders, note-taking services, oral tests, learning center, readers, extended time for tests, tutors. **Library:** Number of titles: 260,884; number of current serial subscriptions: 2,451. **Information technology resources:** Students are not required to lease or own a computer. Number of campus computers available to all students: 694. School has a wireless network. Proportion of college-owned housing units wired for high-speed internet access: 100%. **Campus safety:** Security services offered: 24-hour foot-and-vehicle patrols, late-night transport/escort service, 24-hour emergency telephones, lighted pathways/sidewalks, student patrols, controlled dormitory access (key, security card, etc).

TRANSFER AND INTERNATIONAL STUDENTS

Transfer students: May apply for admission for the following academic terms: Fall, Winter, Spring, Summer. Applicants need a minimum number of credits to apply. For fall 2005: Transfer applications received: 566. Transfer applicants offered admission: 538. Transfer applicants enrolled: 405. **International students:** Number of foreign undergraduates: 30 (1% of student body). Minimum TOEFL score required: 520 (paper); 190 (computer).

Oregon State University

■ **Address:** 104 Kerr Administration Building, Corvallis, OR 97331
■ **Website:** http://oregonstate.edu
■ **Public**
■ **Enrollment:** 13,862 full-time; 1,885 part-time

KEY STATS

✔ **U.S News College Ranking:** third tier, National Universities
✔ **SAT Score (25th/75th percentile):** 960-1200
✔ **Tuition:** 2005-2006: $5,442 in state, $17,502 out of state

Selectivity: Selective	**Room/board:** $6,930
Acceptance rate: 89%	**Average debt:** $16,952
Student/faculty ratio: 19/1	**Proportion who borrowed:** 62%

UNDERGRADUATE STUDENT BODY STATS

2005-2006 enrollment: 13,862 full-time; 1,885 part-time. Men: 53%; women: 47%. **Ethnic makeup:** African American: 1%; American-Indian: 1%; Asian American: 8%; Hispanic: 4%; White: 84%; International: 1%.

ADMISSIONS FACTS AND FIGURES

Phone: (541) 737-4411. **Email:** osuadmit@oregonstate.edu. **Website:** http://oregonstate.edu. **Application deadlines for fall 2007:** Regular decision: September 1. Early decision: Not offered. Early action: Send application by: November 1; Decision sent by: December 15. Admission can be deferred. **Application fee:** $50. Common application is not accepted. **To apply online, go to:** http://oregonstate.edu/admissions. **Admissions requirements/recommendations:** High school units required (recommended): English: 4; Mathematics: 3; Science: 2; Foreign language: 2; Social studies: 3; Total units: 14 (0). Tests: The college uses SAT or ACT scores in admissions decisions. Either SAT or ACT required. For admission to the fall 2007 entering class, the school will accept: ACT with writing. Campus visit: Neither required nor recommended. Admissions interview: Neither required nor recommended. Off-campus interview: Not available. **Factors that count in admissions decisions:** *Academic:* Secondary school record: Very important. Class rank: Important. Letters of recommendation: Considered. Standardized test scores: Considered. Essay: Very important. *Nonacademic:* Interview: Considered. Extracurricular activities: Considered. Talent/ability: Important. Character/personal qualities: Important. Alumni/ae relationship: Not considered. Geographical residence: Not considered. State residency: Not considered. Religious affiliation/commitment: Not considered.

Minority status: Not considered. Volunteer work: Important. Work experience: Considered. **Other schools with the greatest overlap in applicants:** Portland State University; University of California–Davis; University of Oregon; University of Washington; Washington State University. **Admissions statistics for the fall 2005 entering class:** Total applicants: 6,822. Total accepted: 6,078. Freshmen enrolled: 2,902; 10% were from out of state. Overall acceptance rate: 89%. Non-early acceptance rate: 89%. **Credentials of fall 2005 freshmen:** 18% ranked in the top 10 percent of their high school class; 46% were in the top 25 percent, and 79% were in the top half. (Proportion submitting class standing: 67%.) **Average high school grade point average:** 3.5. **First-year students who submitted SAT scores:** 93%. Scores (25/75 percentile): Verbal: 470-590, Math: 490-610, Combined: 960-1200. **First-year students submitting ACT scores:** 16%. Scores (25/75 percentile): English: 18-25, Math: 19-26, Composite: 20-26.

ACADEMICS

Year founded: 1858. **Academic calendar:** Quarter. **Degrees offered:** certificate, bachelor's, post-bachelor's certificate, master's, post-master's certificate, first professional, doctorate. **Most popular majors:** 15% business administration and management, 7% human development and family studies, 5% liberal arts and sciences/liberal studies, 4% biological and physical sciences, 4% health and physical education. **Major fields of study:** agriculture, agriculture operations, and related sciences; area, ethnic, cultural, and gender studies; biological and biomedical sciences; business, management, marketing, and related support services; communication, journalism, and related programs; computer and information sciences and support services; education; engineering; English language and literature/letters; family and consumer sciences/human sciences; foreign languages, literatures, and linguistics; health professions and related clinical sciences; history; liberal arts and sciences studies, and humanities; mathematics and statistics; multi/interdisciplinary studies; natural resources and conservation; parks, recreation, leisure, and fitness studies; philosophy and religious studies; physical sciences; psychology; social sciences; visual and performing arts. **Areas of required coursework:** humanities, mathematics, English (including composition), sciences (biological or physical), social science, other. **Pre-professional programs:** pre-dentistry, pre-medicine, pre-veterinary science, pre-optometry, pre-pharmacy, other. **Special academic programs (% participation):** accelerated program, cooperative (work-study plan) program, cross-registration, distance learning (33%), double major (13%), dual enrollment (14%), English as a Second Language (ESL) (1%), exchange student program (domestic) (1%), external degree program, honors program (5%), independent study (5%), internships (54%), liberal arts/career combination, student-designed major, study abroad (13%), teacher certificate program (8%). **Teacher certification offered in:** early childhood, elementary, vo-tech, middle/junior high, adult education, secondary, bilingual/bicultural. **Cooperative education programs:** engineering, other. **Reserve Officers Training Corps (ROTC):** Army ROTC: Offered on campus; Navy ROTC: Offered on campus; Air Force ROTC: Offered on campus. **Faculty and instruction (2005-2006):** Total instructional faculty: 760 full-time, 455 part-time (56% men; 44% women; 12% minorities). Full-time faculty with Ph.D. or other terminal degree: 78%. Student/faculty ratio: 19/1. Classes of fewer than 20 students: 42%; of 20 to 49 students: 40%; of 50 or more students: 18%. **Advanced Placement and International Baccalaureate credit:** AP tests may be used for: Credit and/or placement. Scores accepted: 3, 4, 5. International Baccalaureate exams may be used for: Credit and/or placement. **Freshmen returning for sophomore year:** 81%. **Graduation rates:** Four-year: 31%; five-year: 56%; six-year: 62%. **Graduate study:** 23% of students pursue further study within one year.

COSTS AND FINANCIAL AID

Financial aid office: (541) 737-2241. **Expenses (2005-2006):** Tuition and fees 2005-2006: $5,442 in state, $17,502 out of state; room/board: $6,930. Estimated books and supplies: $1,401 personal expenses: $2,262. **Financial aid:** Priority filing date for institution's financial aid form: February 28. In 2005-2006, 68% of undergraduates applied for financial aid. Of those, 52% were determined to have financial need; 20% had their need fully met. Average financial aid package (proportion receiving): $8,696 (51%). Average amount of gift aid, such as scholarships or grants (proportion receiving): $2,532 (37%). Average amount of self-help aid, such as work study or loans (proportion receiving): $2,606 (47%). Average need-based loan (excluding PLUS or other private loans): $3,145. Among students who received need-based aid, the average percentage of need met: 67%. Among students who received aid based on merit, the average award (and the proportion receiving): $2,327 (0%). The average athletic scholarship (and the proportion receiving): $9,495 (3%). Average amount of debt of borrowers graduating in 2005: $16,952. Proportion who borrowed: 62%.

CAMPUS LIFE AND EXTRACURRICULAR ACTIVITIES

Campus housing available: coed dorms, sorority housing, fraternity housing, apartments for married students, apartment for single students, special housing for disabled students, special housing for international students, cooperative housing, other housing options. Students who live in college-owned, operated, or affiliated housing: 22%. **Student employment:** During the 2005-2006 academic year, 18% of undergraduates worked on campus. Average per-year earnings: $3,300. **Clubs and organizations:** Number of student organizations: 300. Activities include: choral groups, concert band, dance, drama/theater, jazz band, literary magazine, marching band, music ensembles, musical theater, opera, pep band, radio station, student government, student newspaper, student film society, symphony orchestra, television station, yearbook. Number of fraternities: 21; sororities: 14. Proportion of men in fraternities: 9%; of women in sororities: 9%. Average proportion of students who stay on campus on weekends: 65%. **Sports program (2005-2006):** Member of NCAA I. *Men's intercollegiate varsity sports:* baseball, basketball, crew, football, golf, soccer, wrestling. *Women's intercollegiate varsity sports:* basketball, crew, cross-country, golf, gymnastics, soccer, softball, swimming and diving, volleyball.

SERVICES AND FACILITIES

Basic services: nonremedial tutoring, women's center, placement service, day care, health service, health insurance, other. **Remedial assistance:** math, writing, study skills, other. **Counseling services:** minority student, career, military, personal, veteran student, academic, older student, psychological, birth control. **For learning-disabled students:** School does not offer a structured program with separate admission and additional fees. Total undergraduates in learning-disabled program or receiving services: 382. Services include: remedial math, remedial English, reading machines, remedial reading, tape recorders, note-taking services, oral tests, learning center, extended time for tests, tutors. **Library:** Number of titles: 1,403,451; number of current serial subscriptions: 14,777. **Information technology resources:** Students are not required to lease or own a computer. School has a wireless network. Approximate number of users that can be accommodated: 7,500. Proportion of college-owned housing units wired for high-speed internet access: 100%. **Campus safety:** Security services offered: 24-hour foot-and-vehicle patrols, late-night transport/escort service, 24-hour emergency telephones, lighted pathways/sidewalks, student patrols, controlled dormitory access (key, security card, etc).

TRANSFER AND INTERNATIONAL STUDENTS

Transfer students: May apply for admission for the following academic terms: Fall, Winter, Spring, Summer. Applicants need a minimum number of credits to apply. For fall 2005: Transfer applications received: 1,504. Transfer applicants offered admission: 1,338. Transfer applicants enrolled: 872. **International students:** Number of foreign undergraduates: 204 (1% of student body). Number of countries represented: 99. Minimum TOEFL score required: 550 (paper); 213 (computer).

Pacific Northwest College of Art

- **Address:** 1241 N.W. Johnson, Portland, OR 97209
- **Website:** http://www.pnca.edu
- **Private**
- **Enrollment:** N/A

KEY STATS

✔ **U.S News College Ranking:** Unranked Specialty School–Fine Arts
✔ **SAT or ACT Score (25th/75th percentile):** N/A
✔ **Tuition:** N/A

Selectivity: Least selective	**Room/board:** N/A
Acceptance rate: N/A	**Average debt:** N/A
Student/faculty ratio: N/A	**Proportion who borrowed:** N/A

Pacific University

- **Address:** 2043 College Way, Forest Grove, OR 97116
- **Website:** http://www.pacificu.edu
- **Private; Religious affiliation:** United Church of Christ
- **Enrollment:** 1,173 full-time; 59 part-time

KEY STATS

✔ **U.S News College Ranking:** 14, Universities–Master's (West)
✔ **SAT Score (25th/75th percentile):** 1010-1240
✔ **Tuition:** 2006-2007: $22,534

Selectivity: Selective	**Room/board:** $6,468
Acceptance rate: 87%	**Average debt:** $25,581
Student/faculty ratio: 12/1	**Proportion who borrowed:** 84%

UNDERGRADUATE STUDENT BODY STATS

2005-2006 enrollment: 1,173 full-time; 59 part-time. Men: 40%; women: 60%. **Ethnic makeup:** African American: 1%; American-Indian: 1%; Asian American: 20%; Hispanic: 3%; White: 74%.

ADMISSIONS FACTS AND FIGURES

Phone: (800) 677-6712. **Email:** admissions@pacificu.edu. **Website:** http://www.pacificu.edu. **Application deadlines for fall 2007:** Regular decision: August 15. Early decision: Not offered. Early action: Not offered. Admission can be deferred. **Application fee:** $40. Common application is accepted. **To apply online, go to:** http://www.pacificu.edu/admissions/onlineapps.html. **Admissions requirements/recommendations:** High school units required (recommended): English: (4); Mathematics: (3); Science: (3); Foreign language: (2); Social studies: (3); History: (1); Academic electives: (4); Total units: (21). Tests: The college uses SAT or ACT scores in admissions decisions. Either SAT or ACT required. For admission to the fall 2007 entering class, the school will accept: ACT with writing, ACT without writing. Campus visit: Recommended. Admissions interview: Recommended. Off-campus interview: May be arranged. **Factors that count in admissions decisions:** *Academic:* Secondary school record: Very important. Class rank: Important. Letters of recommendation: Very important. Standardized test scores: Very important. Essay: Important. *Nonacademic:* Interview: Important. Extracurricular activities: Considered. Talent/ability: Considered. Character/personal qualities: Considered. Alumni/ae relationship: Considered. Geographical residence: Not considered. State residency: Not considered. Religious affiliation/commitment: Not considered. Minority status: Considered. Volunteer work: Important. Work experience: Considered. **Admissions statistics for the fall 2005 entering class:** Total applicants: 1,324. Total accepted: 1,147. Freshmen enrolled: 326; 55% were from out of state. Overall acceptance rate: 87%. **Credentials of fall 2005 freshmen:** 28% ranked in the top 10 percent of their high school class; 59% were in the top 25 percent, and 87% were in the top half. (Proportion submitting class standing: 70%.) **Average high school grade point average:** 3.5. **First-year students who submitted SAT scores:** 91%. Scores (25/75 percentile): Verbal: 500-620, Math: 510-620, Combined: 1010-1240. **First-year students submitting ACT scores:** 29%. Scores (25/75 percentile): English: 21-28, Math: 20-26, Composite: 23-28.

ACADEMICS

Year founded: 1849. **Academic calendar:** 4-1-4. **Degrees offered:** bachelor's, master's, first professional, doctorate. **Most popular majors:** 14% biology/biological sciences; 12% business administration and management, 11% education, 11% parks, recreation, leisure, and fitness studies, 10% psychology. **Major fields of study:** biological and biomedical sciences; business, management, marketing, and related support services; communication, journalism, and related programs; computer and information sciences and support services; education; English language and literature/letters; foreign languages, literatures, and linguistics; health professions and related clinical sciences; history; liberal arts and sciences studies, and humanities; mathematics and statistics; multi/interdisciplinary studies; natural resources and conservation; parks, recreation, leisure, and fitness studies; philosophy and religious studies; physical sciences; psychology; public administration and social service professions; social sciences; visual and performing arts. **Areas of required coursework:** arts/fine arts, humanities, mathematics, English (including composition), foreign languages, sciences (biological or physical), social science, other. **Pre-professional programs:** pre-medicine, pre-optometry. **Special academic programs (% participation):** cross-registration (0%), double major (13%), English as a Second Language (ESL) (0%), independent study (48%), internships (31%), liberal arts/career combination (0%), study abroad (17%), teacher certificate program (9%). **Teacher certification offered in:** early childhood, elementary, middle/junior high, secondary. **Cooperative education programs:** engineering, health professions, natural science. **Reserve Officers Training Corps (ROTC):** Army ROTC: Offered at cooperating institution (University of Portland); Air Force ROTC: Offered at cooperating institution (Portland State University). **Faculty and instruction (2005-2006):** Total instructional faculty: 82 full-time, 46 part-time (57% men; 43% women; 9% minorities). Full-time faculty with Ph.D. or other terminal degree: 88%. Student/faculty ratio: 12/1. Classes of fewer than 20 students: 66%; of 20 to 49 students: 31%; of 50 or more students: 2%. **Advanced Placement and International Baccalaureate credit:** AP tests may be used for: Credit and/or placement. Scores accepted: 4. International Baccalaureate exams may be used for: Credit and/or placement. **Freshmen returning for sophomore year:** 80%. **Graduation rates:** Four-year: 55%; five-year: 65%; six-year: 62%. **Graduate study:** 34% of students pursue further study immediately upon graduation; 40% within one year. Fields in which graduates pursue further study: Master of Business Administration (MBA), 1%; law, 2%; medicine, 2%; dentistry, 1%; engineering, 1%; theology (or the seminary), 1%; education, 6%; arts and sciences, 6%.

COSTS AND FINANCIAL AID
Financial aid office: (503) 352-2222. **Expenses (2006-2007):** Tuition and fees 2006-2007: $22,534; room/board: $6,468. Estimated books and supplies: $900; transportation: $756; personal expenses: $1,148. **Financial aid:** Priority filing date for institution's financial aid form: February 15. In 2005-2006, 87% of undergraduates applied for financial aid. Of those, 73% were determined to have financial need; 38% had their need fully met. Average financial aid package (proportion receiving): $17,492 (73%). Average amount of gift aid, such as scholarships or grants (proportion receiving): $11,538 (71%). Average amount of self-help aid, such as work study or loans (proportion receiving): $6,724 (62%). Average need-based loan (excluding PLUS or other private loans): $5,429. Among students who received need-based aid, the average percentage of need met: 86%. Among students who received aid based on merit, the average award (and the proportion receiving): $8,645 (23%). The average athletic scholarship (and the proportion receiving): $0 (0%). Average amount of debt of borrowers graduating in 2005: $25,581. Proportion who borrowed: 84%.

CAMPUS LIFE AND EXTRACURRICULAR ACTIVITIES
Campus housing available (% using): coed dorms (98%), apartment for single students (2%), special housing for disabled students, other housing options. Students who live in college-owned, operated, or affiliated housing: 60%. **Student employment:** During the 2005-2006 academic year, 12% of undergraduates worked on campus. Average per-year earnings: $3,000. **Clubs and organizations:** Number of student organizations: 50. Activities include: choral groups, concert band, dance, drama/theater, jazz band, literary magazine, music ensembles, musical theater, radio station, student government, student newspaper, student film society, symphony orchestra, yearbook. Number of fraternities: 3; sororities: 4. Proportion of men in fraternities: 11%; of women in sororities: 10%. Average proportion of students who stay on campus on weekends: 60%. **Sports program (2005-2006):** Member of NCAA III. *Men's intercollegiate varsity sports:* baseball, basketball, cross-country, golf, soccer, swimming and diving, tennis, track and field (outdoor), wrestling. *Women's intercollegiate varsity sports:* basketball, cross-country, golf, soccer, softball, swimming and diving, tennis, track and field (outdoor), volleyball, wrestling.

SERVICES AND FACILITIES
Basic services: nonremedial tutoring, women's center, placement service, health service, health insurance. **Remedial assistance:** math, writing. **Counseling services:** minority student, career, personal, veteran student, academic, older student, psychological, birth control. **For learning-disabled students:** School does not offer a structured program with separate admission and additional fees. Total undergraduates in learning-disabled program or receiving services: 39. Services include: other special classes, untimed tests, note-taking services, oral tests, readers, extended time for tests, tutors, priority seating, substitution of courses, texts on tape, exams on tape or computer. **Library:** Number of titles: 202,409; number of current serial subscriptions: 19,723. **Information technology resources:** Students are not required to lease or own a computer. Number of campus computers available to all students: 200. School has a wireless network. Approximate number of users that can be accommodated: 960. Proportion of college-owned housing units wired for high-speed internet access: 100%. **Campus safety:** Security services offered: 24-hour foot-and-vehicle patrols, late-night trans-port/escort service, 24-hour emergency telephones, lighted pathways/sidewalks, controlled dormitory access (key, security card, etc).

TRANSFER AND INTERNATIONAL STUDENTS
Transfer students: May apply for admission for the following academic terms: Fall, Spring. Applicants need a minimum number of credits to apply. For fall 2005: Transfer applications received: 206. Transfer applicants offered admission: 151. Transfer applicants enrolled: 68. **International students:** Number of foreign undergraduates: 2. Number of countries represented: 15. Minimum TOEFL score required: 550 (paper); 213 (computer). Average TOEFL score: 560 (paper).

Portland State University

- **Address:** PO Box 751, Portland, OR 97207-0751
- **Website:** http://www.pdx.edu
- **Public**
- **Enrollment:** 10,851 full-time; 7,015 part-time

KEY STATS
✔ **U.S News College Ranking:** fourth tier, National Universities
✔ **SAT Score (25th/75th percentile):** 930-1170
✔ **Tuition:** 2006-2007: $5,210 in state, $17,435 out of state

Selectivity: Selective	**Room/board:** $8,445
Acceptance rate: 92%	**Average debt:** $18,085
Student/faculty ratio: 18/1	**Proportion who borrowed:** 70%

UNDERGRADUATE STUDENT BODY STATS
2005-2006 enrollment: 10,851 full-time; 7,015 part-time. Men: 46%; women: 54%. **Ethnic makeup:** African American: 3%; American-Indian: 1%; Asian American: 10%; Hispanic: 5%; White: 77%; International: 3%.

ADMISSIONS FACTS AND FIGURES
Phone: (503) 725-3511. **Email:** admissions@pdx.edu. **Website:** http://www.pdx.edu. **Application deadlines for fall 2007:** Regular decision: Rolling. Early decision: Not offered. Early action: Not offered. Admission can be deferred. **Application fee:** $50. Common application is not accepted. **To apply online, go to:** http://www.pdx.edu/admissions/apply.html/. **Admissions requirements/recommendations:** High school units required (recommended): English: 4; Mathematics: 3; Science: 2; Foreign language: 2; Social studies: 2; History: 1; Academic electives: 0; Total units: 14 (1). Tests: The college uses SAT or ACT scores in admissions decisions. Either SAT or ACT required. For admission to the fall 2007 entering class, the school will accept: ACT with writing. Campus visit: Recommended. Admissions interview: Neither required nor recommended. Off-campus interview: Not available. **Factors that count in admissions decisions:** *Academic:* Secondary school record: Very important. Class rank: Not considered. Letters of recommendation: Not considered. Standardized test scores: Considered. Essay: Not considered. *Nonacademic:* Interview: Not considered. Extracurricular activities: Not considered. Talent/ability: Not considered. Character/personal qualities: Not considered. Alumni/ae relationship: Not considered. Geographical residence: Not considered. State residency: Not considered. Religious affiliation/commitment: Not considered. Minority status: Not considered. Volunteer work: Not considered. Work experience: Not considered. **Other schools with the greatest overlap in applicants:** Oregon State University; University of Oregon. **Admissions statistics for the fall 2005 entering class:** Total applicants: 2,844. Total accepted: 2,623. Freshmen enrolled: 1,427; 17% were from out of state. Overall acceptance rate: 92%. **Average high school grade point average:** 3.3. **First-year students who submitted SAT scores:** 78%. Scores (25/75 percentile): Verbal: 460-590; Math: 470-580, Combined: 930-1170. **First-year students submitting ACT scores:** 13%. Scores (25/75 percentile): English: N/A, Math: N/A, Composite: 20-25.

ACADEMICS
Year founded: 1946. **Academic calendar:** Quarter. **Degrees offered:** certificate, bachelor's, post-bachelor's certificate, master's, doctorate. **Most popular majors:** 24% business administration and management, 19% social sciences, 7% liberal arts and sciences/liberal studies, 7% psychology, 6% physical sciences. **Major fields of study:** architecture and related services; area, ethnic, cultural, and gender studies; biological and biomedical sciences; business, management, marketing, and related support services; communi-

cation, journalism, and related programs; computer and information sciences and support services; engineering; engineering technologies/technicians; English language and literature/letters; family and consumer sciences/human sciences; foreign languages, literatures, and linguistics; health professions and related clinical sciences; liberal arts and sciences studies, and humanities; mathematics and statistics; natural resources and conservation; parks, recreation, leisure, and fitness studies; philosophy and religious studies; physical sciences; psychology; public administration and social service professions; social sciences; visual and performing arts. **Pre-professional programs:** pre-law, pre-dentistry, pre-medicine, pre-veterinary science, pre-optometry, pre-pharmacy, other. **Special academic programs (% participation):** accelerated program, cooperative (work-study plan) program, cross-registration, distance learning (26.3%), double major (13%), dual enrollment, English as a Second Language (ESL) (1.3%), exchange student program (domestic), external degree program, honors program (5%), independent study (25.9%), internships (12%), study abroad (4.5%), teacher certificate program. **Teacher certification offered in:** early childhood, special education, elementary, middle/junior high, adult education, secondary, bilingual/bicultural. **Cooperative education programs:** art, business, computer science, education, engineering, health professions, humanities, natural science, social/behavioral science, technologies. **Reserve Officers Training Corps (ROTC):** Army ROTC: Offered on campus; Air Force ROTC: Offered at cooperating institution (University of Portland). **Faculty and instruction (2005-2006):** Total instructional faculty: 737 full-time, 497 part-time (57% men; 43% women; 14% minorities). Full-time faculty with Ph.D. or other terminal degree: 77%. Student/faculty ratio: 18/1. Classes of fewer than 20 students: 25%; of 20 to 49 students: 59%; of 50 or more students: 16%. **Advanced Placement and International Baccalaureate credit:** AP tests may be used for: Credit and/or placement. International Baccalaureate exams may be used for: Credit and/or placement. **Freshmen returning for sophomore year:** 65%. **Graduation rates:** Four-year: 10%; five-year: 25%; six-year: 33%.

COSTS AND FINANCIAL AID

Financial aid office: (503) 725-3461. **Expenses (2006-2007):** Tuition and fees 2006-2007: $5,210 in state, $17,435 out of state; room/board: $8,445. **Financial aid:** Priority filing date for institution's financial aid form: February 28. In 2005-2006, 63% of undergraduates applied for financial aid. Of those, 54% were determined to have financial need; 10% had their need fully met. Average financial aid package (proportion receiving): $7,576 (53%). Average amount of gift aid, such as scholarships or grants (proportion receiving): $4,420 (35%). Average amount of self-help aid, such as work study or loans (proportion receiving): $4,650 (47%). Average need-based loan (excluding PLUS or other private loans): $4,498. Among students who received need-based aid, the average percentage of need met: 55%. Among students who received aid based on merit, the average award (and the proportion receiving): $2,258 (1%). The average athletic scholarship (and the proportion receiving): $7,225 (0%). Average amount of debt of borrowers graduating in 2005: $18,085. Proportion who borrowed: 70%.

CAMPUS LIFE AND EXTRACURRICULAR ACTIVITIES

Campus housing available: coed dorms, fraternity housing, apartments for married students, apartment for single students, special housing for disabled students, other housing options. Students who live in college-owned, operated, or affiliated housing: 0%. **Clubs and organizations:** Number of student organizations: 150. Activities include: choral groups, concert band, dance, drama/theater, jazz band, literary magazine, music ensembles, musical theater, opera, pep band, radio station, student government, student newspaper, student film society, symphony orchestra. Number of fraternities: 4; sororities: 4. Proportion of men in fraternities: 2%; Average proportion of students who stay on campus on weekends: 10%. **Sports program (2005-2006):** Member of NCAA I. *Men's intercollegiate varsity sports:* basketball, cross-country, football, track and field (indoor), track and field (outdoor), wrestling. *Women's intercollegiate varsity sports:* basketball, cross-country, golf, soccer, softball, track and field (indoor), track and field (outdoor), volleyball.

SERVICES AND FACILITIES

Basic services: women's center, day care, health service, health insurance. **Remedial assistance:** math, writing, study skills. **Counseling services:** minority student, career, military, personal, veteran student, academic, psychological, birth control, religious, other. **For learning-disabled students:** School does not offer a structured program with separate admission and additional fees. **Library:** Number of titles: 1,715,197; number of current serial subscriptions: 4,855. **Information technology resources:** Students are not required to lease or own a computer. Number of campus computers available to all students: 875. School has a wireless network. **Campus safety:** Security services

offered: 24-hour foot-and-vehicle patrols, late-night transport/escort service, 24-hour emergency telephones, lighted pathways/sidewalks, controlled dormitory access (key, security card, etc).

TRANSFER AND INTERNATIONAL STUDENTS

Transfer students: May apply for admission for the following academic terms: Fall, Winter, Spring, Summer. Applicants need a minimum number of credits to apply. For fall 2005: Transfer applications received: 3,659. Transfer applicants offered admission: 3,550. Transfer applicants enrolled: 2,674. **International students:** Number of foreign undergraduates: 470 (3% of student body). Number of countries represented: 72. Minimum TOEFL score required: 525 (paper); 197 (computer).

Reed College

- **Address:** 3203 S.E. Woodstock Boulevard, Portland, OR 97202
- **Website:** http://www.reed.edu/
- **Private**
- **Enrollment:** 1,272 full-time; 37 part-time

KEY STATS
✔ **U.S News College Ranking:** 53, Liberal Arts Colleges
✔ **SAT Score (25th/75th percentile):** 1280-1470
✔ **Tuition:** 2006-2007: $34,530
  Selectivity: More selective **Room/board:** $9,000
  Acceptance rate: 45% **Average debt:** $17,175
  Student/faculty ratio: 10/1 **Proportion who borrowed:** 61%

Southern Oregon University

- **Address:** 1250 Siskiyou Boulevard, Ashland, OR 97520
- **Website:** http://www.sou.edu
- **Public**
- **Enrollment:** 3,475 full-time; 961 part-time

KEY STATS
✔ **U.S News College Ranking:** third tier, Universities–Master's (West)
✔ **SAT Score:** 1036
✔ **Tuition:** 2005-2006: $4,932 in state, $16,362 out of state
  Selectivity: Selective **Room/board:** $7,254
  Acceptance rate: 80% **Average debt:** N/A
  Student/faculty ratio: 19/1 **Proportion who borrowed:** N/A

UNDERGRADUATE STUDENT BODY STATS

2005-2006 enrollment: 3,475 full-time; 961 part-time. Men: 43%; women: 57%. **Ethnic makeup:** African American: 1%; American-Indian: 2%; Asian American: 3%; Hispanic: 4%; White: 87%; International: 2%.

ADMISSIONS FACTS AND FIGURES

Phone: (541) 552-6411. **Email:** admissions@sou.edu. **Website:** http://www.sou.edu. **Application deadlines for fall 2007:** Regular decision: Rolling. Early decision: Not offered. Early action: Not offered. Admission can be deferred. **Application fee:** $50. Common application is accepted. **To apply online, go to:** http://www.sou.edu/admissions/. **Admissions requirements/recommendations:** High school units required (recommended): English: 4; Mathematics: 3; Science: 2; Foreign language: 2; Social studies: 3; Total units: 14. Tests: The college uses SAT or ACT scores in admissions decisions. Either SAT or ACT required. For admission to the fall 2007 entering class, the school will accept: ACT with writing, ACT without writing. Campus visit: Recommended. Admissions interview: Neither required nor recommended. Off-campus interview: Not available. **Factors that count in admissions decisions:** *Academic:* Secondary school record: Very important. Class rank: Not considered. Letters of recommendation: Considered. Standardized test scores: Very important. Essay: Considered. *Nonacademic:* Interview: Not considered. Extracurricular activities: Considered. Talent/ability: Considered. Character/personal qualities: Considered. Alumni/ae relationship: Not considered. Geographical residence: Not considered. State residency: Not considered. Religious affiliation/commitment: Not considered. Minority status: Not considered. Volunteer work: Considered. Work experience: Considered. **Other schools with the greatest overlap in applicants:** Eastern Oregon University; Oregon State University; Portland State University; University of Oregon; Western Oregon University. **Admissions statistics for the fall 2005 entering class:** Total applicants: 2,157. Total accepted: 1,726. Freshmen enrolled: 770; Overall acceptance rate: 80%. **Average high school grade point average:** 3.2. **First-year students who submitted SAT scores:** 90%. Scores (25/75 percentile): Verbal: N/A; Math: N/A; Combined: N/A. **First-year students submitting ACT scores:** 17%. Scores (25/75 percentile): English: N/A, Math: N/A, Composite: N/A.

ACADEMICS

Year founded: 1926. **Academic calendar:** Quarter. **Degrees offered:** bachelor's, post-bachelor's certificate, master's. **Most popular majors:** 19% business, management, marketing, and related support services, 10% communication, journalism, and related programs, 10% social sciences, 9% visual and performing arts, 8% psychology. **Major fields of study:** biological and biomedical sciences; business, management, marketing, and related support services; communication, journalism, and related programs; communications technologies/technicians and support services; computer and information sciences and support services; education; English language and literature/letters; foreign languages, literatures, and linguistics; history; multi/interdisciplinary studies; natural resources and conservation; physical sciences; psychology; security and protective services; social sciences; visual and performing arts. **Areas of required coursework:** arts/fine arts, humanities, computer literacy, mathematics, English (including composition), sciences (biological or physical), social science. **Pre-professional programs:** pre-law, pre-dentistry, pre-medicine, pre-theology, pre-veterinary science, pre-optometry, pre-pharmacy, other. **Special academic programs:** accelerated program, cooperative (work-study plan) program, cross-registration, distance learning, double major, dual enrollment, English as a Second Language (ESL), exchange student program (domestic), external degree program, honors program, independent study, internships, liberal arts/career combination, student-designed major, study abroad, teacher certificate program. **Teacher certification offered in:** early childhood, special education, elementary, middle/junior high, secondary, bilingual/bicultural. **Cooperative education programs:** other. **Reserve Officers Training Corps (ROTC):** Army RQTC: Offered on campus. **Faculty and instruction (2005-2006):** Total instructional faculty: 193 full-time, 96 part-time (54% men; 46% women; 13% minorities). Full-time faculty with Ph.D. or other terminal degree: 85%. Student/faculty ratio: 19/1. Classes of fewer than 20 students: 46%; of 20 to 49 students: 48%; of 50 or more students: 5%. **Advanced Placement and International Baccalaureate credit:** AP tests may be used for: Credit and/or placement. Scores accepted: 3, 4, 5. International Baccalaureate exams may be used for: Credit and/or placement. **Freshmen returning for sophomore year:** 67%. **Graduation rates:** Four-year: 19%; five-year: 36%; six-year: 36%.

COSTS AND FINANCIAL AID

Financial aid office: (541) 552-6754. **Expenses (2005-2006):** Tuition and fees 2005-2006: $4,932 in state, $16,362 out of state; room/board: $7,254. Estimated books and supplies: $1,125; transportation: $900; personal expenses: $3,066. **Financial aid:** Priority filing date for institution's financial aid form: March 1.

CAMPUS LIFE AND EXTRACURRICULAR ACTIVITIES

Campus housing available: coed dorms, apartments for married students, apartment for single students, special housing for disabled students, special housing for international students, other housing options. **Clubs and organizations:** Number of student organizations: 70. Activities include: choral groups, concert band, dance, drama/theater, jazz band, literary magazine, music ensembles, musical theater, opera, pep band, radio station, student government, student newspaper, symphony orchestra, television station. Number of fraternities: 0; sororities: 0. **Sports program (2005-2006):** Member of NAIA. **Men's intercollegiate varsity sports:** basketball, cross-country, football, track and field (indoor), track and field (outdoor), wrestling. **Women's intercollegiate varsity sports:** basketball, cross-country, soccer, softball, tennis, track and field (indoor), track and field (outdoor), volleyball.

SERVICES AND FACILITIES

Basic services: nonremedial tutoring, women's center, placement service, day care, health service, health insurance. **Remedial assistance:** math. **Counseling services:** minority student, career, military, personal, veteran student, academic, older student, psychological, birth control. **For learning-disabled students:** School offers a structured program with separate admission and additional fees. Services include: remedial math, other testing accommodations, reading machines, tape recorders, other special classes, note-tak-

ing services, oral tests, learning center, readers, extended time for tests, tutors, priority registration, substitution of courses, texts on tape, other testing accomodations. **Information technology resources:** Students are not required to lease or own a computer. Number of campus computers available to all students: 1,000. School has a wireless network. Proportion of college-owned housing units wired for high-speed internet access: 95%. **Campus safety:** Security services offered: 24-hour foot-and-vehicle patrols, late-night transport/escort service, 24-hour emergency telephones, lighted pathways/sidewalks, controlled dormitory access (key, security card, etc).

TRANSFER AND INTERNATIONAL STUDENTS

Transfer students: May apply for admission for the following academic terms: Fall, Winter, Spring, Summer. Applicants need a minimum number of credits to apply. For fall 2005: Transfer applications received: 701. Transfer applicants offered admission: 615. Transfer applicants enrolled: 438. **International students:** Number of foreign undergraduates: 93 (2% of student body). Minimum TOEFL score required: 520 (paper).

University of Oregon

- **Address:** 1217 University of Oregon, Eugene, OR 97403-1217
- **Website:** http://www.uoregon.edu
- **Public**
- **Enrollment:** 14,996 full-time; 1,477 part-time

KEY STATS

✔ **U.S News College Ranking:** 120, National Universities
✔ **SAT Score (25th/75th percentile):** 1001-1232
✔ **Tuition:** 2005-2006: $5,613 in state, $17,445 out of state

Selectivity: Selective	**Room/board:** $7,496
Acceptance rate: 90%	**Average debt:** $18,029
Student/faculty ratio: 18/1	**Proportion who borrowed:** 60%

UNDERGRADUATE STUDENT BODY STATS

2005-2006 enrollment: 14,996 full-time; 1,477 part-time. Men: 47%; women: 53%. **Ethnic makeup:** African American: 2%; American-Indian: 1%; Asian American: 6%; Hispanic: 3%; White: 84%; International: 4%.

ADMISSIONS FACTS AND FIGURES

Phone: (800) 232-3825. **Email:** uoadmit@uoregon.edu. **Website:** http://www.uoregon.edu. **Application deadlines for fall 2007:** Regular decision: January 15. Early decision: Not offered. Early action: Not offered. Admission cannot be deferred. **Application fee:** $50. Common application is not accepted. **To apply online, go to:** http://admissions.uoregon.edu/apply/onlineapp.htm. **Admissions requirements/recommendations:** High school units required (recommended): English: 4; Mathematics: 3; Science: 2; Foreign language: 2; Social studies: 3; Total units: 14. Tests: The college uses SAT or ACT scores in admissions decisions. Either SAT or ACT required. For admission to the fall 2007 entering class, the school will accept: ACT with writing. Campus visit: Neither required nor recommended. Admissions interview: Neither required nor recommended. Off-campus interview: Not available. **Factors that count in admissions decisions:** *Academic:* Secondary school record: Very important. Class rank: Considered. Letters of recommendation: Considered. Standardized test scores: Considered. Essay: Considered. *Nonacademic:* Interview: Not considered. Extracurricular activities: Not considered. Talent/ability: Considered. Character/personal qualities: Not considered. Alumni/ae relationship: Not considered. Geographical residence: Considered. State residency: Considered. Religious affiliation/commitment: Not considered. Minority status: Considered. Volunteer work: Considered. Work experience: Considered. **Other schools with the greatest overlap in applicants:** Oregon State University; University of California–Davis; University of California–Santa Barbara; University of Colorado–Boulder; University of Washington. **Admissions statistics for the fall 2005 entering class:** Total applicants: 10,012. Total accepted: 9,048. Freshmen enrolled: 3,207; 27% were from out of state. Overall acceptance rate: 90%. **Credentials of fall 2005 freshmen:** 25% ranked in the top 10 percent of their high school class; 58% were in the top 25 percent, and 91% were in the top half. (Proportion submitting class standing: 70%.) **Average high school grade point average:** 3.5. **First-year students who submitted SAT scores:** 93%. Scores (25/75 percentile): Verbal: 498-617, Math: 503-615, Combined: 1001-1232.

ACADEMICS

Year founded: 1876. **Academic calendar:** Quarter. **Degrees offered:** bachelor's, post-bachelor's certificate, master's, post-master's certificate, first professional, doctorate. **Most popular majors:** 10% business/commerce, 7% political science and government, 7% psychology, 5% sociology, 4% economics. **Major fields of study:** architecture and related services; area, ethnic, cultural, and gender studies; biological and biomedical sciences; business, management, marketing, and related support services; communication, journalism, and related programs; computer and information sciences and support services; education; English language and literature/letters; foreign languages, literatures, and linguistics; health professions and related clinical sciences; history; liberal arts and sciences studies, and humanities; mathematics and statistics; multi/interdisciplinary studies; natural resources and conservation; philosophy and religious studies; physical sciences; psychology; public administration and social service professions; social sciences; visual and performing arts. **Areas of required coursework:** humanities, mathematics, English (including composition), foreign languages, sciences (biological or physical), social science, other. **Pre-professional programs:** pre-law, pre-dentistry, pre-medicine, pre-veterinary science, pre-optometry, pre-pharmacy, other. **Special academic programs:** cross-registration, distance learning, double major, dual enrollment, English as a Second Language (ESL), exchange student program (domestic), honors program, independent study, internships, student-designed major, study abroad, teacher certificate program, other. **Teacher certification offered in:** early childhood, special education, elementary, middle/junior high, secondary, bilingual/bicultural. **Reserve Officers Training Corps (ROTC):** Army ROTC: Offered on campus. **Faculty and instruction (2005-2006):** Total instructional faculty: 785 full-time, 337 part-time (58% men; 42% women; 17% minorities). Full-time faculty with Ph.D. or other terminal degree: 98%. Student/faculty ratio: 18/1. Classes of fewer than 20 students: 39%; of 20 to 49 students: 45%; of 50 or more students: 16%. **Advanced Placement and International Baccalaureate credit:** AP tests may be used for: Credit only. Scores accepted: 3, 4, 5. International Baccalaureate exams may be used for: Credit only. **Freshmen returning for sophomore year:** 84%. **Graduation rates:** Four-year: 39%; five-year: 60%; six-year: 65%. **Graduate study:** 21% of students pursue further study immediately upon graduation.

COSTS AND FINANCIAL AID

Financial aid office: (541) 346-3221. **Expenses (2005-2006):** Tuition and fees 2005-2006: $5,613 in state, $17,445 out of state; room/board: $7,496. Estimated books and supplies: $900 personal expenses: $2,376. **Financial aid:** Priority filing date for institution's financial aid form: March 1. In 2005-2006, 60% of undergraduates applied for financial aid. Of those, 43% were determined to have financial need; 17% had their need fully met. Average financial aid package (proportion receiving): $7,656 (41%). Average amount of gift aid, such as scholarships or grants (proportion receiving): $4,034 (22%). Average amount of self-help aid, such as work study or loans (proportion receiving): $4,958 (36%). Average need-based loan (excluding PLUS or other private loans): $4,489. Among students who received need-based aid, the average percentage of need met: 64%. Among students who received aid based on merit, the average award (and the proportion receiving): $1,701 (6%). The average athletic scholarship (and the proportion receiving): $18,322 (2%). Average amount of debt of borrowers graduating in 2005: $18,029. Proportion who borrowed: 60%.

CAMPUS LIFE AND EXTRACURRICULAR ACTIVITIES

Campus housing available: coed dorms, sorority housing, fraternity housing, apartments for married students, apartment for single students, special housing for disabled students. Students who live in college-owned, operated, or affiliated housing: 21%. **Student employment:** During the 2005-2006 academic year, 9% of undergraduates worked on campus. Average per-year earnings: $2,677. **Clubs and organizations:** Number of student organizations: 250. Activities include: choral groups, concert band, dance, drama/theater, jazz band, literary magazine, marching band, music ensembles, musical theater, opera, pep band, radio station, student government, student newspaper, symphony orchestra. Number of fraternities: 12; sororities: 8. Proportion of men in fraternities: 8%; of women in sororities: 8%. Average proportion of students who stay on campus on weekends: 65%. **Sports program (2005-2006):** Member of NCAA I. *Men's intercollegiate varsity sports:* basketball, cross-country, football, golf, tennis, track and field (indoor), track and field (outdoor), wrestling. *Women's intercollegiate varsity sports:* basketball, cross-country, golf, lacrosse, soccer, softball, tennis, track and field (indoor), track and field (outdoor), volleyball.

SERVICES AND FACILITIES

Basic services: women's center, placement service, day care, health service, health insurance. **Remedial assistance:** reading, math, writing, study skills. **Counseling services:** minority student, career, military, personal, veteran student, academic, older student, psychological, birth control, religious. **For learning-disabled students:** School does not offer a structured program with separate admission and additional fees. Services include: remedial math, remedial English, reading machines, remedial reading, tape recorders, diagnostic testing service, untimed tests, note-taking services, oral tests, learning center, readers, extended time for tests, tutors, priority registration, priority seating, texts on tape, other testing accomodations, other. **Library:** Number of titles: 3,110,956; number of current serial subscriptions: 18,826. **Information technology resources:** Students are not required to lease or own a computer. Number of campus computers available to all students: 1,700. School has a wireless network. Approximate number of users that can be accommodated: 5,000. Proportion of college-owned housing units wired for high-speed internet access: 90%. **Campus safety:** Security services offered: 24-hour foot-and-vehicle patrols, late-night transport/escort service, 24-hour emergency telephones, lighted pathways/sidewalks, student patrols, controlled dormitory access (key, security card, etc).

TRANSFER AND INTERNATIONAL STUDENTS

Transfer students: May apply for admission for the following academic terms: Fall, Winter, Spring, Summer. Applicants need a minimum number of credits to apply. For fall 2005: Transfer applications received: 2,631. Transfer applicants offered admission: 2,086. Transfer applicants enrolled: 1,436. **International students:** Number of foreign undergraduates: 683 (4% of student body). Number of countries represented: 55. Minimum TOEFL score required: 500 (paper); 173 (computer). Average TOEFL score: 569 (paper).

University of Portland

- **Address:** 5000 N. Willamette Boulevard, Portland, OR 97203
- **Website:** http://www.up.edu
- **Private; Religious affiliation:** Roman Catholic
- **Enrollment:** 2,840 full-time; 80 part-time

KEY STATS

✔ **U.S News College Ranking:** 5, Universities–Master's (West)
✔ **SAT Score (25th/75th percentile):** 1080-1280
✔ **Tuition:** 2006-2007: $26,390

Selectivity: More selective	**Room/board:** $7,850
Acceptance rate: 81%	**Average debt:** $22,253
Student/faculty ratio: 13/1	**Proportion who borrowed:** 64%

UNDERGRADUATE STUDENT BODY STATS

2005-2006 enrollment: 2,840 full-time; 80 part-time. Men: 38%; women: 62%. **Ethnic makeup:** African American: 2%; American-Indian: 1%; Asian American: 9%; Hispanic: 4%; White: 84%; International: 1%. **Religious preference:** Protestant: 13%; Buddhist: 2%; Unknown: 18%; Roman Catholic: 51%; Other: 16%.

ADMISSIONS FACTS AND FIGURES

Phone: (888) 627-5601. **Email:** admissio@up.edu. **Website:** http://www.up.edu. **Application deadlines for fall 2007:** Regular decision: June 1. Early decision: Not offered. Early action: Not offered. Admission can be deferred. **Application fee:** $50. Common application is accepted. **Admissions requirements/recommendations:** High school units required (recommended): English: 3 (4); Mathematics: 2 (3); Science: 2 (2); Social studies: 2 (2); History: 2 (2); Academic electives: 7 (7). Tests: The college uses SAT or ACT scores in admissions decisions. Either SAT or ACT required. For admission to the fall 2007 entering class, the school will accept: ACT with writing, ACT without writing. Campus visit: Recommended. Admissions interview: Neither required nor recommended. Off-campus interview: May be arranged. **Factors that count in admissions decisions:** *Academic:* Secondary school record: Very important. Class rank: Important. Letters of recommendation: Important. Standardized test scores: Very important. Essay: Important. *Nonacademic:* Interview: Considered. Extracurricular activities: Important. Talent/ability: Important. Character/personal qualities: Considered. Alumni/ae relationship: Considered. Geographical residence: Considered. State residency: Not considered. Religious affiliation/commitment: Considered. Minority status: Considered. Volunteer work: Important. Work experience: Considered. **Other schools with the greatest overlap in applicants:** Gonzaga University; Santa Clara University; Seattle University; University of Oregon; University of Washington. **Admissions statistics for the fall 2005 entering class:** Total applicants: 3,026. Total accepted: 2,445. Freshmen enrolled: 724; 62% were from out of state. Overall acceptance rate: 81%. **Size of waiting list:** 145 applicants; enrolled from waiting list: 102. **Credentials of fall 2005 freshmen:** 44% ranked in the top 10 percent of their high school class; 76% were in the top 25 percent, and 95% were in the top half. (Proportion submitting class standing: 61%.) **Average high school grade point average:** 3.6. **First-year students who submitted SAT scores:** 100%. Scores (25/75 percentile): Verbal: 540-640, Math: 540-640, Combined: 1080-1280.

ACADEMICS

Year founded: 1901. **Academic calendar:** Semester. **Degrees offered:** bachelor's, master's, post-master's certificate. **Most popular majors:** 18% health professions and related clinical sciences, 17% business, management, marketing, and related support services, 9% biological and biomedical sciences, 9% engineering, 9% social sciences. **Major fields of study:** area, ethnic, cultural, and gender studies; biological and biomedical sciences; business, management, marketing, and related support services; communication, journalism, and related programs; computer and information sciences and support services; education; engineering; English language and literature/letters; foreign languages, literatures, and linguistics; health professions and related clinical sciences; history; mathematics and statistics; multi/interdisciplinary studies; natural resources and conservation; philosophy and religious studies; physical sciences; psychology; public administration and social service professions; social sciences; theology and religious vocations; visual and performing arts. **Areas of required coursework:** arts/fine arts, mathematics, English (including composition), philosophy, sciences (biological or physical), history, social science. **Pre-professional programs:** pre-law, pre-dentistry, pre-medicine, pre-veterinary science, pre-optometry, pre-pharmacy. **Special academic programs:** cross-registration, double major, honors program, independent study, internships, liberal arts/career combination, study abroad, teacher certificate program. **Teacher certification offered in:** early childhood, elementary, middle/junior high, secondary. **Reserve Officers Training Corps (ROTC)** Army ROTC: Offered on campus; Air Force ROTC: Offered on campus. **Faculty and instruction (2005-2006):** Total instructional faculty: 188 full-time, 91 part-time (58% men; 42% women; 3% minorities). Full-time faculty with Ph.D. or other terminal degree: 86%. Student/faculty ratio: 13/1. Classes of fewer than 20 students: 34%; of 20 to 49 students: 62%; of 50 or more students: 4%. **Advanced Placement and International Baccalaureate credit:** International Baccalaureate exams may be used for: Credit and/or placement. **Freshmen returning for sophomore year:** 85%. **Graduation rates:** Four-year: 57%; five-year: 67%; six-year: 69%. **Graduate study:** 25% of students pursue further study immediately upon graduation; 45% within five years.

COSTS AND FINANCIAL AID

Financial aid office: (503) 943-7311. **Expenses (2006-2007):** Tuition and fees 2006-2007: $26,390; room/board: $7,850. Estimated books and supplies: $800; transportation: $1,000; personal expenses: $800. **Financial aid:** Priority filing date for institution's financial aid form: March 1. In 2005-2006, 71% of undergraduates applied for financial aid. Of those, 52% were determined to have financial need; 27% had their need fully met. Average financial aid package (proportion receiving): $21,356 (51%). Average amount of gift aid, such as scholarships or grants (proportion receiving): $14,249 (51%). Average amount of self-help aid, such as work study or loans (proportion receiving): $6,020 (43%). Average need-based loan (excluding PLUS or other private loans): $5,511. Among students who received need-based aid, the average percentage of need met: 84%. Among students who received aid based on merit, the average award (and the proportion receiving): $16,651 (43%). The average athletic scholarship (and the proportion receiving): $22,787 (4%). Average amount of debt of borrowers graduating in 2005: $22,253. Proportion who borrowed: 64%.

CAMPUS LIFE AND EXTRACURRICULAR ACTIVITIES

Campus housing available (% using): coed dorms (53%), women's dorms (23%), men's dorms (17%), other housing options (7%). Students who live in college-owned, operated, or affiliated housing: 49%. **Student employment:** During the 2005-2006 academic year, 45% of undergraduates worked on campus. Average per-year earnings: $2,000. **Clubs and organizations:** Number of student organizations: 48. Activities include: choral groups, concert band, dance, drama/theater, jazz band, literary magazine, music ensembles, musical theater, pep band, radio station, student government, student newspaper, student film society, symphony orchestra, yearbook. Number of fraternities: 0; sororities: 0. **Sports program (2005-2006):** Member of NCAA I. *Men's intercollegiate varsity sports:* baseball, basketball, cross-country, golf, soccer, tennis, track and field (indoor), track and field (outdoor). *Women's intercollegiate varsity sports:* basketball, cross-country, golf, soccer, tennis, track and field (indoor), track and field (outdoor), volleyball.

SERVICES AND FACILITIES

Basic services: nonremedial tutoring, placement service, health service, health insurance. **Remedial assistance:** math, writing. **Counseling services:** career, personal, academic, psychological, religious. **For learning-disabled students:** School does not offer a structured program with separate admission and additional fees. Total undergraduates in learning-disabled program or receiving services: 26. Services include: reading machines, note-taking services, readers, extended time for tests, other. **Library:** Number of titles: 245,905; number of current serial subscriptions: 1,584. **Information technology resources:** Students are not required to lease or own a computer. Number of campus computers available to all students: 329. School has a wireless network. Approximate number of users that can be accommodated: 900. Proportion of college-owned housing units wired for high-speed internet access: 100%. **Campus safety:** Security services offered: 24-hour foot-and-vehicle patrols, late-night transport/escort service, 24-hour emergency telephones, lighted pathways/sidewalks, controlled dormitory access (key, security card, etc).

TRANSFER AND INTERNATIONAL STUDENTS

Transfer students: May apply for admission for the following academic terms: Fall, Spring, Summer. Applicants need a minimum number of credits to apply. For fall 2005: Transfer applications received: 843. Transfer applicants offered admission: 194. Transfer applicants enrolled: 88. **International students:** Number of foreign undergraduates: 34 (1% of student body). Number of countries represented: 33. Minimum TOEFL score required: 197 (computer).

Warner Pacific College

- **Address:** 2219 S.E. 68th Avenue, Portland, OR 97215
- **Website:** http://www.warnerpacific.edu
- **Private; Religious affiliation:** Church of God
- **Enrollment:** 548 full-time; 12 part-time

KEY STATS

✔ **U.S News College Ranking:** fourth tier, Liberal Arts Colleges
✔ **SAT Score (25th/75th percentile):** 913-1146
✔ **Tuition:** 2006-2007: $20,480

Selectivity: Selective	**Room/board:** $5,740
Acceptance rate: 57%	**Average debt:** $18,591
Student/faculty ratio: 15/1	**Proportion who borrowed:** 86%

UNDERGRADUATE STUDENT BODY STATS

2005-2006 enrollment: 548 full-time; 12 part-time. Men: 35%; women: 65%. **Ethnic makeup:** African American: 4%; Asian American: 1%; Hispanic: 3%; White: 90%; International: 1%. **Religious preference:** Roman Catholic: 1%; Protestant: 43%; Unknown: 43%; Church of God: 13%.

ADMISSIONS FACTS AND FIGURES

Phone: (503) 517-1020. **Email:** admissions@warnerpacific.edu. **Website:** http://www.warnerpacific.edu. **Application deadlines for fall 2007:** Regular decision: September 12. Early decision: Not offered. Early action: Send application by: January 31; Decision sent by: N/A. Admission can be deferred. **Application fee:** $25. Common application is accepted. **Admissions requirements/recommendations:** High school units required (recommended): English: (4); Mathematics: (2); Science: (2); Social studies: (3). Tests: The college uses SAT or ACT scores in admissions decisions. Either SAT or ACT required. For admission to the fall 2007 entering class, the school will accept: ACT with writing, ACT without writing. Campus visit: Recommended. Admissions interview: Recommended. Off-campus interview: May be arranged. **Factors that count in admissions decisions:** *Academic:* Secondary school record: Very important. Class rank: Not considered. Letters of recommendation: Considered. Standardized test scores: Very important. Essay: Very important. *Nonacademic:* Interview: Not considered. Extracurricular activities: Not considered. Talent/ability: Not considered. Character/personal qualities: Not considered. Alumni/ae relationship: Not considered. Geographical residence: Not considered. State residency: Not considered. Religious affiliation/commitment: Not considered. Minority status: Not considered. Volunteer work: Not considered. Work experience: Not considered. **Other schools with the greatest overlap in applicants:** Concordia University; Corban College; George Fox University; Seattle Pacific University; Whitworth College. **Admissions statistics for the fall 2005 entering class:** Total applicants: 820. Total accepted: 466. Freshmen enrolled: 104; 25% were from out of state. Overall acceptance rate: 57%. Non-early acceptance rate: 57%. **Average high school grade point average:** 3.4. **First-year students who submitted SAT scores:** 77%. Scores (25/75 percentile): Verbal: 463-578, Math: 450-568, Combined: 913-1146. **First-year students submitting ACT scores:** 23%. Scores (25/75 percentile): English: N/A, Math: N/A, Composite: N/A.

ACADEMICS

Year founded: 1937. **Academic calendar:** Semester. **Degrees offered:** associate, bachelor's, post-bachelor's certificate, master's. **Most popular majors:** 36% human development and family studies, 34% business administration and management, 19% religion/religious studies, 15% social sciences. **Major fields of study:** biological and biomedical sciences; business, management, marketing, and related support services; education; English language and literature/letters; family and consumer sciences/human sciences; history; liberal arts and sciences studies, and humanities; parks, recreation, leisure, and fitness studies; philosophy and religious studies; physical sciences; psychology; public administration and social service professions; social sciences; theology and religious vocations; visual and performing arts. **Areas of required coursework:** arts/fine arts, humanities, mathematics, English (including composition), philosophy, sciences (biological or physical), history, social science, other. **Pre-professional programs:** pre-medicine, pre-theology. **Special academic programs (% participation):** accelerated program (40%), cross-registration (5.7%), double major (5.2%), independent study (13.1%), internships (36%), student-designed major (1.2%), study abroad (2.9%), teacher certificate program (12.1%). **Teacher certification offered in:** early childhood, elementary, middle/junior high, secondary. **Reserve Officers Training Corps (ROTC):** Air Force ROTC: Offered at cooperating institution (University of Portland). **Faculty and instruction (2005-2006):** Total instructional faculty: 24. Full-time faculty with Ph.D. or other terminal degree: 63%. Student/faculty ratio: 15/1. Classes of fewer than 20 students: 76%; of 20 to 49 students: 24%; of 50 or more students: 1%. **Advanced Placement and International Baccalaureate credit:** AP tests may be used for: Credit and/or placement. Scores accepted: 3, 4, 5. International Baccalaureate exams may be used for: Credit and/or placement. **Freshmen returning for sophomore year:** 66%. **Graduation rates:** Four-year: 39%; five-year: 47%; six-year: 47%. **Graduate study:** 15% of students pursue further study immediately upon graduation; 10% within one year; 5% within five years. Fields in which graduates pursue further study: Master of Business Administration (MBA), 25%; law, 2%; medicine, 3%; dentistry, 1%; theology (or the seminary), 30%; education, 30%; arts and sciences, 9%.

COSTS AND FINANCIAL AID

Financial aid office: (503) 517-1017. **Expenses (2006-2007):** Tuition and fees 2006-2007: $20,480; room/board: $5,740. Estimated books and supplies: $905; transportation: $860; personal expenses: $1,458. **Financial aid:** Priority filing date for institution's financial aid form: March 1. In 2005-2006, 96% of undergraduates applied for financial aid. Of those, 89% were determined to have financial need; 14% had their need fully met. Average financial aid package (proportion receiving): $14,048 (89%). Average amount of gift aid, such as scholarships or grants (proportion receiving): $8,146 (83%). Average amount of self-help aid, such as work study or loans (proportion receiving): $4,102 (76%). Average need-based loan (excluding PLUS or other private loans): $3,570. Among students who received need-based aid, the average percentage of need met: 74%. Among students who received aid based on merit, the average award (and the proportion receiving): $6,521 (4%). The average athletic scholarship (and the proportion receiving): $7,721 (4%). Average amount of debt of borrowers graduating in 2005: $18,591. Proportion who borrowed: 86%.

CAMPUS LIFE AND EXTRACURRICULAR ACTIVITIES

Campus housing available (% using): women's dorms (28%), men's dorms (17%), apartments for married students (3%), apartment for single students (42%), other housing options (10%). Students who live in college-owned, operated, or affiliated housing: 30%. **Student employment:** During the 2005-2006 academic year, 2% of undergraduates worked on campus. Average per-year earnings: $5,000. **Clubs and organizations:** Number of student

organizations: 2. Activities include: choral groups, concert band, drama/theater, jazz band, literary magazine, music ensembles, musical theater, student government, yearbook. Number of fraternities: 0; sororities: 0. Average proportion of students who stay on campus on weekends: 70%. **Sports program (2005-2006):** Member of NAIA. *Men's intercollegiate varsity sports:* basketball, cross-country, soccer, track and field (outdoor). *Women's intercollegiate varsity sports:* basketball, cross-country, soccer, track and field (outdoor), volleyball.

SERVICES AND FACILITIES

Basic services: nonremedial tutoring, health service, health insurance. **Remedial assistance:** reading, math, writing, study skills. **Counseling services:** minority student, career, personal, academic, psychological, birth control, religious, other. **For learning-disabled students:** School does not offer a structured program with separate admission and additional fees. Services include: remedial English, other special classes, learning center, readers, extended time for tests, tutors. **Information technology resources:** Students are not required to lease or own a computer. Number of campus computers available to all students: 50. School has a wireless network. Proportion of college-owned housing units wired for high-speed internet access: 100%. **Campus safety:** Security services offered: 24-hour foot-and-vehicle patrols, late-night transport/escort service, 24-hour emergency telephones, lighted pathways/sidewalks, student patrols, controlled dormitory access (key, security card, etc).

TRANSFER AND INTERNATIONAL STUDENTS

Transfer students: May apply for admission for the following academic terms: Fall, Spring, Summer. Applicants need a minimum number of credits to apply. For fall 2005: Transfer applications received: 213. Transfer applicants offered admission: 134. Transfer applicants enrolled: 90. **International students:** Number of foreign undergraduates: 4 (1% of student body). Number of countries represented: 6. Minimum TOEFL score required: 525 (paper); 195 (computer).

Western Oregon University

- **Address:** 345 N. Monmouth Avenue, Monmouth, OR 97361-1394
- **Website:** http://www.wou.edu
- **Public**
- **Enrollment:** 3,783 full-time; 478 part-time

KEY STATS

✔ **U.S News College Ranking:** third tier, Universities–Master's (West)
✔ **SAT Score (25th/75th percentile):** 860-1090
✔ **Tuition:** 2006-2007: $4,662 in state, $14,802 out of state

Selectivity: Less selective	**Room/board:** $7,206
Acceptance rate: 55%	**Average debt:** $19,422
Student/faculty ratio: 17/1	**Proportion who borrowed:** 51%

UNDERGRADUATE STUDENT BODY STATS

2005-2006 enrollment: 3,783 full-time; 478 part-time. Men: 42%; women: 58%. **Ethnic makeup:** African American: 2%; American-Indian: 1%; Asian American: 3%; Hispanic: 6%; White: 86%; International: 2%.

ADMISSIONS FACTS AND FIGURES

Phone: (503) 838-8211. **Email:** wolfgram@wou.edu. **Website:** http://www.wou.edu. **Application deadlines for fall 2007:** Regular decision: Rolling. Early decision: Not offered. Early action: Not offered. Admission can be deferred. **Application fee:** $50. Common application is not accepted. **To apply online, go to:** http://www.wou.edu/studentaffairs/admissions/apply/. **Admissions requirements/recommendations:** High school units required (recommended): English: 4; Mathematics: 3; Science: 2; Foreign language: 2; Social studies: 2; History: 1; Total units: 14. Tests: The college uses SAT or ACT scores in admissions decisions. Either SAT or ACT required. For admission to the fall 2007 entering class, the school will accept: ACT with writing, ACT without writing. Campus visit: Recommended. Admissions interview: Neither required nor recommended. Off-campus interview: Not available. **Factors that count in admissions decisions:** *Academic:* Secondary school record: Very important. Class rank: Considered. Letters of recommendation: Not considered. Standardized test scores: Very important. Essay: Not considered. *Nonacademic:* Interview: Not considered. Extracurricular activities:

Considered. Talent/ability: Considered. Character/personal qualities: Not considered. Alumni/ae relationship: Considered. Geographical residence: Not considered. State residency: Not considered. Religious affiliation/commitment: Not considered. Minority status: Considered. Volunteer work: Not considered. Work experience: Not considered. **Admissions statistics for the fall 2005 entering class:** Total applicants: 1,881. Total accepted: 1,026. Freshmen enrolled: 834; 10% were from out of state. Overall acceptance rate: 55%. **Credentials of fall 2005 freshmen:** 9% ranked in the top 10 percent of their high school class; 27% were in the top 25 percent, and 62% were in the top half. (Proportion submitting class standing: 90%.) **Average high school grade point average:** 3.2. **First-year students who submitted SAT scores:** 90%. Scores (25/75 percentile): Verbal: 430-540, Math: 430-550, Combined: 860-1090. **First-year students submitting ACT scores:** 15%. Scores (25/75 percentile): English: 15-23, Math: 16-24, Composite: 17-23.

ACADEMICS

Year founded: 1856. **Academic calendar:** Quarter. **Degrees offered:** associate, bachelor's, post-bachelor's certificate, master's. **Most popular majors:** 25% education, 12% social sciences, 11% business/commerce, 10% psychology, 9% multi/interdisciplinary studies. **Major fields of study:** biological and biomedical sciences; education; English language and literature/letters; foreign languages, literatures, and linguistics; mathematics and statistics; multi/interdisciplinary studies; natural resources and conservation; philosophy and religious studies; psychology; public administration and social service professions; security and protective services; social sciences; visual and performing arts. **Areas of required coursework:** arts/fine arts, computer literacy, mathematics, English (including composition), philosophy, foreign languages, sciences (biological or physical), social science. **Pre-professional programs:** pre-law, pre-dentistry, pre-medicine, pre-veterinary science, pre-optometry, pre-pharmacy, other. **Special academic programs:** cooperative (work-study plan) program, distance learning, double major, dual enrollment, English as a Second Language (ESL), honors program, independent study, internships, student-designed major, study abroad, teacher certificate program. **Teacher certification offered in:** early childhood, special education, elementary, middle/junior high, secondary, bilingual/bicultural. **Reserve Officers Training Corps (ROTC):** Army ROTC: Offered on campus; Navy ROTC: Offered at cooperating institution (Oregon State University); Air Force ROTC: Offered at cooperating institution (Oregon State University). **Faculty and instruction (2005-2006):** Total instructional faculty: 179 full-time, 175 part-time (49% men; 51% women; 5% minorities). Full-time faculty with Ph.D. or other terminal degree: 72%. Student/faculty ratio: 17/1. Classes of fewer than 20 students: 79%; of 20 to 49 students: 19%; of 50 or more students: 3%. **Advanced Placement and International Baccalaureate credit:** AP tests may be used for: Credit only. Scores accepted: 3, 4, 5. International Baccalaureate exams may be used for: Credit only. **Freshmen returning for sophomore year:** 69%. **Graduation rates:** Four-year: 18%; five-year: 39%; six-year: 38%.

COSTS AND FINANCIAL AID

Financial aid office: (503) 838-8475. **Expenses (2006-2007):** Tuition and fees 2006-2007: $4,662 in state, $14,802 out of state; room/board: $7,206. Estimated books and supplies: $1,125; transportation: $945; personal expenses: $1,890. **Financial aid:** Priority filing date for institution's financial aid form: March 1. In 2005-2006, 92% of undergraduates applied for financial aid. Of those, 73% were determined to have financial need; 11% had their need fully met. Average financial aid package (proportion receiving): $6,412 (73%). Average amount of gift aid, such as scholarships or grants (proportion receiving): $4,261 (53%). Average amount of self-help aid, such as work study or loans (proportion receiving): $3,732 (64%). Average need-based loan (excluding PLUS or other private loans): $3,535. Among students who received need-based aid, the average percentage of need met: 65%. Among students who received aid based on merit, the average award (and the proportion receiving): $7,544 (22%). The average athletic scholarship (and the proportion receiving): $1,288 (2%). Average amount of debt of borrowers graduating in 2005: $19,422. Proportion who borrowed: 51%.

CAMPUS LIFE AND EXTRACURRICULAR ACTIVITIES

Campus housing available (% using): coed dorms (79%), apartments for married students (2%), apartment for single students (16%), special housing for disabled students (3%). Students who live in college-owned, operated, or affiliated housing: 24%. **Clubs and organizations:** Number of student organizations: 67. Activities include: choral groups, concert band, dance, drama/theater, jazz band, literary magazine, music ensembles, musical theater, pep band, student government, student newspaper, symphony orchestra, television station. Average proportion of students who stay on campus on weekends: 50%. **Sports program (2005-2006):** Member of NCAA

II. **Men's intercollegiate varsity sports:** baseball, basketball, cross-country, football, track and field (indoor), track and field (outdoor). **Women's intercollegiate varsity sports:** basketball, cross-country, soccer, softball, track and field (indoor), track and field (outdoor), volleyball.

SERVICES AND FACILITIES

Basic services: nonremedial tutoring, day care, health service, health insurance. **Remedial assistance:** reading, math, writing, study skills. **Counseling services:** minority student, career, personal, academic, older student, psychological, birth control. **For learning-disabled students:** School does not offer a structured program with separate admission and additional fees. Total undergraduates in learning-disabled program or receiving services: 105. Services include: remedial math, remedial English, reading machines, tape recorders, diagnostic testing service, note-taking services, learning center, extended time for tests, tutors, priority registration, substitution of courses, texts on tape, exams on tape or computer, other. **Library:** Number of titles: 200,988; number of current serial subscriptions: 2,577. **Information technology resources:** Students are not required to lease or own a computer. Number of campus computers available to all students: 411. School has a wireless network. Approximate number of users that can be accommodated: 25. Proportion of college-owned housing units wired for high-speed internet access: 100%. **Campus safety:** Security services offered: 24-hour foot-and-vehicle patrols, late-night transport/escort service, 24-hour emergency telephones, lighted pathways/sidewalks.

TRANSFER AND INTERNATIONAL STUDENTS

Transfer students: May apply for admission for the following academic terms: Fall, Winter, Spring, Summer. Applicants need a minimum number of credits to apply. For fall 2005: Transfer applications received: 727. Transfer applicants offered admission: 523. Transfer applicants enrolled: 472. **International students:** Number of foreign undergraduates: 65 (2% of student body). Minimum TOEFL score required: 500 (paper); 173 (computer). Average TOEFL score: 520 (paper).

Willamette University

- **Address:** 900 State Street, Salem, OR 97301
- **Website:** http://www.willamette.edu
- **Private; Religious affiliation:** United Methodist
- **Enrollment:** 1,823 full-time; 131 part-time

KEY STATS

✔ **U.S News College Ranking:** 65, Liberal Arts Colleges
✔ **SAT Score (25th/75th percentile):** 1140-1320
✔ **Tuition:** 2005-2006: $28,416

Selectivity: More selective	**Room/board:** $7,000
Acceptance rate: 74%	**Average debt:** N/A
Student/faculty ratio: 11/1	**Proportion who borrowed:** N/A

UNDERGRADUATE STUDENT BODY STATS

2005-2006 enrollment: 1,823 full-time; 131 part-time. Men: 46%; women: 54%. **Ethnic makeup:** African American: 2%; American-Indian: 1%; Asian American: 7%; Hispanic: 4%; White: 86%; International: 1%. **Religious preference:** Roman Catholic: 19%; Protestant: 9%; Jewish: 1%; No preference: 27%; Unknown: 38%; United Methodist: 3%; Other: 3%.

ADMISSIONS FACTS AND FIGURES

Phone: (503) 370-6303. **Email:** LIBARTS@willamette.edu. **Website:** http://www.willamette.edu. **Application deadlines for fall 2007:** Regular decision: February 1; decision sent by April 1. Early decision: Not offered. Early action: Send application by: December 1; Decision sent by: January 15. Admission can be deferred. **Application fee:** $50. Common application is accepted. **To apply online, go to:** http://www.willamette.edu/admission/application/. **Admissions requirements/recommendations:** High school units required (recommended): English: (4); Mathematics: (4); Science: (3); Foreign language: (3); Social studies: (3). Tests: The college uses SAT or ACT scores in admissions decisions. Either SAT or ACT required. For admission to the fall 2007 entering class, the school will accept: ACT with writing. Campus visit: Recommended. Admissions interview: Recommended. Off-campus interview: May be arranged. **Factors that count in admissions decisions:** *Academic:* Secondary school record: Very important. Class rank: Very important. Letters of recommendation: Very important. Standardized test scores: Very important. Essay: Important. **Nonacademic:** Interview: Important. Extracurricular activities: Important. Talent/ability: Important. Character/personal qualities: Important. Alumni/ae relationship: Considered. Geographical residence: Considered. State residency: Not considered. Religious affiliation/commitment: Not considered. Minority status: Considered. Volunteer work: Considered. Work experience: Considered. **Other schools with the greatest overlap in applicants:** Lewis and Clark College; Linfield College; University of Oregon; University of Puget Sound; Whitman College. **Admissions statistics for the fall 2005 entering class:** Total applicants: 2,790. Total accepted: 2,072. Freshmen enrolled: 444; 67% were from out of state. Accepted through early-decision or early-action plans: 33%. Overall acceptance rate: 74%. Non-early acceptance rate: 70%. **Size of waiting list:** 182 applicants; enrolled from waiting list: 23. **Credentials of fall 2005 freshmen:** 40% ranked in the top 10 percent of their high school class; 73% were in the top 25 percent, and 96% were in the top half. (Proportion submitting class standing: 69%.) **Average high school grade point average:** 3.7. **First-year students who submitted SAT scores:** 91%. Scores (25/75 percentile): Verbal: 570-670, Math: 570-650, Combined: 1140-1320. **First-year students submitting ACT scores:** 38%. Scores (25/75 percentile): English: 24-30, Math: 24-28, Composite: 25-29.

ACADEMICS

Year founded: 1842. **Academic calendar:** Semester. **Degrees offered:** bachelor's, post-bachelor's certificate, master's, first professional, first professional certificate. **Most popular majors:** 10% political science and government, 8% Spanish language and literature, 8% biology/biological sciences, 8% economics, 7% psychology. **Major fields of study:** area, ethnic, cultural, and gender studies; biological and biomedical sciences; computer and information sciences and support services; English language and literature/letters; foreign languages, literatures, and linguistics; history; liberal arts and sciences studies, and humanities; mathematics and statistics; multi/interdisciplinary studies; natural resources and conservation; parks, recreation, leisure, and fitness studies; philosophy and religious studies; physical sciences; psychology; social sciences; visual and performing arts. **Areas of required coursework:** arts/fine arts, humanities, mathematics, English (including composition), foreign languages, sciences (biological or physical), history, social science. **Pre-professional programs:** pre-law, pre-dentistry, pre-medicine, pre-veterinary science. **Special academic programs (% participation):** accelerated program (12%), cooperative (work-study plan) program (20%), double major (17%), exchange student program (domestic) (2%), independent study (32%), internships (68%), student-designed major (1%), study abroad (53%), teacher certificate program. **Reserve Officers Training Corps (ROTC):** Air Force ROTC: Offered at cooperating institution (University of Portland). **Faculty and instruction (2005-2006):** Total instructional faculty: 184 full-time, 117 part-time (58% men; 42% women; 8% minorities). Full-time faculty with Ph.D. or other terminal degree: 97%. Student/faculty ratio: 11/1. Classes of fewer than 20 students: 68%; of 20 to 49 students: 32%; of 50 or more students: 0%. **Advanced Placement and International Baccalaureate credit:** AP tests may be used for: Credit only. Scores accepted: 4, 5. International Baccalaureate exams may be used for: Credit only. **Freshmen returning for sophomore year:** 89%. **Graduation rates:** Four-year: 67%; five-year: 74%; six-year: 74%. **Graduate study:** 26% of students pursue further study immediately upon graduation; 42% within one year; 68% within five years. Fields in which graduates pursue further study: Master of Business Administration (MBA), 15%; law, 10%; medicine, 10%;

engineering, 4%; education, 10%; arts and sciences, 50%; veterinary medicine, 1%.

COSTS AND FINANCIAL AID

Financial aid office: (503) 370-6273. **Expenses (2005-2006):** Tuition and fees 2005-2006: $28,416; room/board: $7,000. Estimated books and supplies: $800 personal expenses: $1,000. **Financial aid:** Priority filing date for institution's financial aid form: February 1.

CAMPUS LIFE AND EXTRACURRICULAR ACTIVITIES

Campus housing available (% using): coed dorms (59%), sorority housing (10%), fraternity housing (11%), apartment for single students (10%), special housing for international students (5%), other housing options (5%). Students who live in college-owned, operated, or affiliated housing: 67%. **Student employment:** During the 2005-2006 academic year, 30% of undergraduates worked on campus. Average per-year earnings: $1,870. **Clubs and organizations:** Number of student organizations: 112. Activities include: choral groups, concert band, dance, drama/theater, jazz band, literary magazine, music ensembles, musical theater, pep band, radio station, student government, student newspaper, symphony orchestra, yearbook. Number of fraternities: 4; sororities: 3. Proportion of men in fraternities: 35%; of women in sororities: 29%. Average proportion of students who stay on campus on weekends: 35%. **Sports program (2005-2006):** Member of NCAA III. **Men's intercollegiate varsity sports:** baseball, basketball, cross-country, football, golf, soccer, swimming and diving, tennis, track and field (outdoor). **Women's intercollegiate varsity sports:** basketball, cross-country, golf, rowing, soccer, softball, swimming and diving, tennis, track and field (outdoor), volleyball.

SERVICES AND FACILITIES

Basic services: nonremedial tutoring, women's center, health service, health insurance. **Remedial assistance:** other. **Counseling services:** minority student, career, military, personal, veteran student, academic, older student, psychological, birth control, religious. **For learning-disabled students:** School does not offer a structured program with separate admission and additional fees. Services include: tape recorders, note-taking services, extended time for tests, tutors, other. **Library:** Number of titles: 372,571; number of current serial subscriptions: 1,623. **Information technology resources:** Students are not required to lease or own a computer. Number of campus computers available to all students: 400. School has a wireless network. Approximate number of users that can be accommodated: 1,500. Proportion of college-owned housing units wired for high-speed internet access: 100%. **Campus safety:** Security services offered: 24-hour foot-and-vehicle patrols, late-night transport/escort service, 24-hour emergency telephones, lighted pathways/sidewalks, student patrols, controlled dormitory access (key, security card, etc).

TRANSFER AND INTERNATIONAL STUDENTS

Transfer students: May apply for admission for the following academic terms: Fall, Spring. Applicants do not need a minimum number of credits to apply. For fall 2005: Transfer applications received: 197. Transfer applicants offered admission: 138. Transfer applicants enrolled: 65. **International students:** Number of foreign undergraduates: 13 (1% of student body). Number of countries represented: 4. Minimum TOEFL score required: 560 (paper); 215 (computer). Average TOEFL score: 590 (paper).

Pennsylvania

Albright College

- **Address:** PO Box 15234, 13th and Bern Streets, Reading, PA 19612-5234
- **Website:** http://www.albright.edu
- **Private; Religious affiliation:** United Methodist
- **Enrollment:** 2,066 full-time; 46 part-time

KEY STATS

✔ **U.S News College Ranking:** third tier, Liberal Arts Colleges
✔ **SAT Score (25th/75th percentile):** 930-1150
✔ **Tuition:** 2006-2007: $27,420

Selectivity: Selective	**Room/board:** $8,158
Acceptance rate: 69%	**Average debt:** $24,671
Student/faculty ratio: 14/1	**Proportion who borrowed:** 88%

UNDERGRADUATE STUDENT BODY STATS

2005-2006 enrollment: 2,066 full-time; 46 part-time. Men: 41%; women: 59%. **Ethnic makeup:** African American: 9%; Asian American: 2%; Hispanic: 4%; White: 81%; International: 3%. **Religious preference:** Roman Catholic: 24%; Protestant: 8%; Jewish: 1%; No preference: 51%; United Methodist: 5%; Other: 11%.

ADMISSIONS FACTS AND FIGURES

Phone: (800) 252-1856. **Email:** admission@alb.edu. **Website:** http://www.albright.edu. **Application deadlines for fall 2007:** Regular decision: Rolling. Early decision: Not offered. Early action: Not offered. Admission can be deferred. **Application fee:** $25. Common application is accepted. **To apply online, go to:** http://www.albright.edu/admission/application.html. **Admissions requirements/recommendations:** High school units required (recommended): English: 4 (4); Mathematics: 2 (3); Science: 3 (4); Foreign language: 2 (3); Social studies: 2 (2); History: 1 (2); Academic electives: 2 (2); Total units: 16 (20). Tests: The college uses SAT or ACT scores in admissions decisions. Either SAT or ACT required. Campus visit: Recommended. Admissions interview: Recommended. Off-campus interview: Not available. **Factors that count in admissions decisions: Academic:** Secondary school record: Very important. Class rank: Important. Letters of recommendation: Important. Standardized test scores: Important. Essay: Important. **Nonacademic:** Interview: Not considered. Extracurricular activities: Considered. Talent/ability: Considered. Character/personal qualities: Important. Alumni/ae relationship: Considered. Geographical residence: Not considered. State residency: Not considered. Religious affiliation/commitment: Not considered. Minority status: Not considered. Volunteer work: Considered. Work experience: Considered. **Other schools with the greatest overlap in applicants:** Elizabethtown College; Moravian College; Muhlenberg College; Susquehanna University; Ursinus College. **Admissions statistics for the fall 2005 entering class:** Total applicants: 3,058. Total accepted: 2,125. Freshmen enrolled: 451; 37% were from out of state. Overall acceptance rate: 69%. **Credentials of fall 2005 freshmen:** 23% ranked in the top 10 percent of their high school class; 48% were in the top 25 percent, and 79% were in the top half. (Proportion submitting class standing: 80%.) **First-year students who submitted SAT scores:** 94%. Scores (25/75 percentile): Verbal: 470-580, Math: 460-570, Combined: 930-1150. **First-year students submitting ACT scores:** 6%. Scores (25/75 percentile): English: N/A, Math: N/A, Composite: 19-23.

ACADEMICS

Year founded: 1856. **Academic calendar:** 4-1-4. **Degrees offered:** certificate, bachelor's, master's. **Most popular majors:** 28% business, management, marketing, and related support services, 15% social sciences, 14% psychology, 11% visual and performing arts, 7% computer and information sciences and support services. **Major fields of study:** area, ethnic, cultural, and gender studies; biological and biomedical sciences; business, management, marketing, and related support services; communication, journalism, and related programs; computer and information sciences and support services; education; English language and literature/letters; family and consumer sci-

ences/human sciences; foreign languages, literatures, and linguistics; history; mathematics and statistics; multi/interdisciplinary studies; natural resources and conservation; philosophy and religious studies; physical sciences; psychology; social sciences; visual and performing arts. **Areas of required coursework:** arts/fine arts, humanities, computer literacy, mathematics, English (including composition), philosophy, foreign languages, sciences (biological or physical), history, social science, other. **Pre-professional programs:** pre-law, pre-dentistry, pre-medicine, pre-theology, pre-veterinary science, pre-optometry. **Special academic programs (% participation):** accelerated program (1%), cross-registration (1%), double major (48%), English as a Second Language (ESL) (1%), exchange student program (domestic) (1%), honors program (15%), independent study (15%), internships (35%), liberal arts/career combination (23%), student-designed major (1%), study abroad (2%), teacher certificate program (14%). **Teacher certification offered in:** early childhood, special education, elementary, secondary. **Faculty and instruction (2005-2006):** Total instructional faculty: 103 full-time, 52 part-time (52% men; 48% women; 5% minorities). Full-time faculty with Ph.D. or other terminal degree: 83%. Student/faculty ratio: 14/1. Classes of fewer than 20 students: 60%; of 20 to 49 students: 40%; of 50 or more students: 0%. **Advanced Placement and International Baccalaureate credit:** AP tests may be used for: Credit and/or placement. Scores accepted: 3, 4, 5. International Baccalaureate exams may be used for: Credit and/or placement. **Freshmen returning for sophomore year:** 78%. **Graduation rates:** Four-year: 52%; five-year: 56%; six-year: 57%. **Graduate study:** 26% of students pursue further study immediately upon graduation. Fields in which graduates pursue further study: Master of Business Administration (MBA), 2%; law, 7%; medicine, 10%; dentistry, 2%; theology (or the seminary), 3%; education, 23%; arts and sciences, 53%; veterinary medicine, 1%.

COSTS AND FINANCIAL AID

Financial aid office: (610) 921-7515. **Expenses (2006-2007):** Tuition and fees 2006-2007: $27,420; room/board: $8,158. Estimated books and supplies: $800; transportation: $200; personal expenses: $1,000. **Financial aid:** Priority filing date for institution's financial aid form: March 1. In 2005-2006, 85% of undergraduates applied for financial aid. Of those, 75% were determined to have financial need; 20% had their need fully met. Average financial aid package (proportion receiving): $17,140 (74%). Average amount of gift aid, such as scholarships or grants (proportion receiving): $13,532 (72%). Average amount of self-help aid, such as work study or loans (proportion receiving): $4,787 (63%). Average need-based loan (excluding PLUS or other private loans): $4,248. Among students who received need-based aid, the average percentage of need met: 75%. Among students who received aid based on merit, the average award (and the proportion receiving): $1,230 (16%). The average athletic scholarship (and the proportion receiving): $0 (0%). Average amount of debt of borrowers graduating in 2005: $24,671. Proportion who borrowed: 88%.

CAMPUS LIFE AND EXTRACURRICULAR ACTIVITIES

Campus housing available (% using): coed dorms (74%), apartment for single students (14%), other housing options (12%). Students who live in college-owned, operated, or affiliated housing: 61%. **Student employment:** During the 2005-2006 academic year, 17% of undergraduates worked on campus. Average per-year earnings: $1,800. **Clubs and organizations:** Number of student organizations: 75. Activities include: choral groups, concert band, dance, drama/theater, jazz band, literary magazine, music ensembles, musical theater, pep band, radio station, student government, student newspaper, student film society, television station, yearbook. Number of fraternities: 4; sororities: 3. Proportion of men in fraternities: 25%; of women in sororities: 30%. Average proportion of students who stay on campus on weekends: 80%. **Sports program (2005-2006):** Member of NCAA III. **Men's intercollegiate varsity sports:** baseball, basketball, cross-country, football, golf, soccer, swimming and diving, tennis, track and field (indoor), track and field (outdoor), wrestling. **Women's intercollegiate varsity sports:** badminton, basketball, cross-country, field hockey, soccer, softball, swimming and diving, tennis, track and field (indoor), track and field (outdoor), volleyball.

SERVICES AND FACILITIES

Basic services: nonremedial tutoring, women's center, health service. **Counseling services:** minority student, career, personal, academic, older student, psychological, religious. **For learning-disabled students:** School does not offer a structured program with separate admission and additional fees. Total undergraduates in learning-disabled program or receiving services: 38. Services include: tape recorders, note-taking services, oral tests, learning center, readers, extended time for tests, tutors, priority registration, priority seating, proofreading services, texts on tape. **Library:** Number of titles: 220,275; number of current serial subscriptions: 748. **Information technology resources:** Students are not required to lease or own a computer. Number of campus computers available to all students: 300. School has a wireless network. Approximate number of users that can be accommodated: 600. Proportion of college-owned housing units wired for high-speed internet access: 100%. **Campus safety:** Security services offered: 24-hour foot-and-vehicle patrols, late-night transport/escort service, 24-hour emergency telephones, lighted pathways/sidewalks, student patrols, controlled dormitory access (key, security card, etc).

TRANSFER AND INTERNATIONAL STUDENTS

Transfer students: May apply for admission for the following academic terms: Fall, Winter, Spring, Summer. Applicants do not need a minimum number of credits to apply. For fall 2005: Transfer applicants enrolled: 51. **International students:** Number of foreign undergraduates: 67 (3% of student body). Number of countries represented: 24. Minimum TOEFL score required: 525 (paper). Average TOEFL score: 548 (paper).

Allegheny College

- **Address:** 520 N. Main Street, Meadville, PA 16335
- **Website:** http://www.allegheny.edu
- **Private; Religious affiliation:** United Methodist
- **Enrollment:** 2,010 full-time; 43 part-time

KEY STATS

✔ **U.S News College Ranking:** 82, Liberal Arts Colleges
✔ **SAT Score (25th/75th percentile):** 1140-1320
✔ **Tuition:** 2006-2007: $28,300

Selectivity: More selective	**Room/board:** $7,000
Acceptance rate: 62%	**Average debt:** $24,825
Student/faculty ratio: 14/1	**Proportion who borrowed:** 78%

UNDERGRADUATE STUDENT BODY STATS

2005-2006 enrollment: 2,010 full-time; 43 part-time. Men: 47%; women: 53%. **Ethnic makeup:** African American: 1%; Asian American: 3%; Hispanic: 1%; White: 93%; International: 1%. **Religious preference:** Roman Catholic: 37%; Protestant: 21%; Jewish: 2%; No preference: 10%; Unknown: 14%; United Methodist: 10%; Non Christian: 2%; Other: 4%.

ADMISSIONS FACTS AND FIGURES

Phone: (800) 521-5293. **Email:** admissions@allegheny.edu. **Website:** http://www.allegheny.edu. **Application deadlines for fall 2007:** Regular decision: February 15; decision sent by April 1. Early decision: Send application by: November 15; Decision sent by: December 15. Early action: Not offered. Admission can be deferred. **Application fee:** $35. Common application is accepted. **To apply online, go to:** https://apply.embark.com/ugrad/Allegheny/. **Admissions requirements/recommendations:** High school units required (recommended): English: 4; Mathematics: 3; Science: 3; Foreign language: 2; Social studies: 3; History: 0; Academic electives: 1; Total units: 16. Tests: The college uses SAT or ACT scores in admissions decisions. Either SAT or ACT required. For admission to the fall 2007 entering class, the school will accept: ACT without writing. Campus visit: Recommended. Admissions interview: Recommended. Off-campus interview: May be arranged. **Factors that count in admissions decisions:** *Academic:* Secondary school record: Very important. Class rank: Very important. Letters of recommendation: Important. Standardized test scores: Important. Essay: Considered. *Nonacademic:* Interview: Important. Extracurricular activities: Important. Talent/ability: Considered. Character/personal qualities: Important. Alumni/ae relationship: Considered. Geographical residence: Considered. State residency: Not considered. Religious affiliation/commitment: Not considered. Minority status: Considered. Volunteer work: Considered. Work experience: Considered. **Other schools with the greatest overlap in applicants:** College of Wooster; Denison University; Pennsylvania State University–University Park; University of Pittsburgh; Washington and Jefferson College. **Admissions statistics for the fall 2005 entering class:** Total applicants: 3,540. Total accepted: 2,206. Freshmen enrolled: 564; 62% were from out of state. Accepted through early-decision or early-action plans: 11%. Overall acceptance rate: 62%. Early-decision acceptance rate: 63%. Non-early acceptance rate: 62%. **Size of waiting list:** 352 applicants; enrolled from waiting list: 32. **Credentials of fall 2005 freshmen:** 45% ranked in the top 10 percent of their high school class; 77% were in the top 25 percent, and 97% were in the top half. (Proportion submitting class standing: 80%.) **Average high school grade point average:** 3.8. **First-year students who submitted SAT scores:** 75%. Scores (25/75 percentile): Verbal: 570-660, Math: 570-660, Combined: 1140-1320. **First-year students submitting ACT scores:** 37%. Scores (25/75 percentile): English: 23-29, Math: 23-27, Composite: 23-28.

ACADEMICS

Year founded: 1815. **Academic calendar:** Semester. **Degrees offered:** bachelor's. **Most popular majors:** 13% biology/biological sciences, 12% psychology, 11% economics, 11% political science and government, 10% English language and literature. **Major fields of study:** area, ethnic, cultural, and gender studies; biological and biomedical sciences; business, management, marketing, and related support services; communication, journalism, and related programs; computer and information sciences and support services; education; engineering; English language and literature/letters; foreign languages, literatures, and linguistics; health professions and related clinical sciences; history; legal professions and studies; mathematics and statistics; multi/interdisciplinary studies; natural resources and conservation; philosophy and religious studies; physical sciences; psychology; social sciences; visual and performing arts. **Areas of required coursework:** humanities, sciences (biological or physical), social science. **Pre-professional programs:** pre-law, pre-dentistry, pre-medicine, pre-veterinary science, pre-optometry, pre-pharmacy, other. **Special academic programs (% participation):** double major (15%), dual enrollment (0%), English as a Second Language (ESL) (0%), independent study (100%), internships (30%), student-designed major (1%), study abroad (24%), other (3%). **Cooperative education programs:** business, education, engineering, health professions, other. **Faculty and instruction (2005-2006):** Total instructional faculty: 135 full-time, 28 part-time (61% men; 39% women; 7% minorities). Full-time faculty with Ph.D. or other terminal degree: 95%. Student/faculty ratio: 14/1. Classes of fewer than 20 students: 58%; of 20 to 49 students: 40%; of 50 or more students: 1%. **Advanced Placement and International Baccalaureate credit:** AP tests may be used for: Credit and/or placement. Scores accepted: 4, 5. International Baccalaureate exams may be used for: Credit and/or placement. **Freshmen returning for sophomore year:** 86%. **Graduation rates:** Four-year: 67%; five-year: 73%; six-year: 73%. **Graduate study:** 52% of students pursue further study immediately upon graduation. Fields in which graduates pursue further study: Master of Business Administration (MBA), 8%; law, 11%; medicine, 31%; dentistry, 4%; engineering, 2%; education, 9%; arts and sciences, 25%; veterinary medicine, 2%.

COSTS AND FINANCIAL AID

Financial aid office: (800) 835-7780. **Expenses (2006-2007):** Tuition and fees 2006-2007: $28,300; room/board: $7,000. Estimated books and supplies: $900; transportation: $800; personal expenses: $800. **Financial aid:** Priority filing date for institution's financial aid form: February 15. In 2005-2006, 79% of undergraduates applied for financial aid. Of those, 68% were determined to have financial need; 45% had their need fully met. Average financial aid package (proportion receiving): $21,250 (68%). Average amount of gift aid, such as scholarships or grants (proportion receiving): $14,950 (68%). Average amount of self-help aid, such as work study or loans (proportion receiving): $6,020 (56%). Average need-based loan (excluding PLUS or other private loans): $4,720. Among students who received need-based aid, the average percentage of need met: 92%. Among students who received aid based on merit, the average award (and the proportion receiving): $10,635 (28%). Average amount of debt of borrowers graduating in 2005: $24,825. Proportion who borrowed: 78%.

CAMPUS LIFE AND EXTRACURRICULAR ACTIVITIES

Campus housing available (% using): coed dorms (64%), women's dorms (13%), men's dorms (6%), fraternity housing (2%), apartment for single students (5%), special housing for disabled students (0%), other housing options (10%). Students who live in college-owned, operated, or affiliated housing: 76%. **Student employment:** During the 2005-2006 academic year, 19% of undergraduates worked on campus. Average per-year earnings: $715. **Clubs and organizations:** Number of student organizations: 100.

Activities include: choral groups, concert band, dance, drama/theater, jazz band, literary magazine, music ensembles, musical theater, pep band, radio station, student government, student newspaper, symphony orchestra, television station, yearbook. Number of fraternities: 5; sororities: 4. Proportion of men in fraternities: 24%; of women in sororities: 26%. Average proportion of students who stay on campus on weekends: 75%. **Sports program (2005-2006):** Member of NCAA III. *Men's intercollegiate varsity sports:* baseball, basketball, cross-country, football, golf, soccer, swimming and diving, tennis, track and field (indoor), track and field (outdoor). *Women's intercollegiate varsity sports:* basketball, cross-country, golf, lacrosse, soccer, softball, swimming and diving, tennis, track and field (indoor), track and field (outdoor), volleyball.

SERVICES AND FACILITIES
Basic services: nonremedial tutoring, placement service, health service, health insurance, other. **Counseling services:** minority student, career, personal, academic, older student, psychological, birth control, religious, other. **For learning-disabled students:** School does not offer a structured program with separate admission and additional fees. Total undergraduates in learning-disabled program or receiving services: 90. Services include: tape recorders, note-taking services, oral tests, learning center, readers, extended time for tests, tutors, priority registration, priority seating, texts on tape, typist/scribe, exams on tape or computer, other. **Library:** Number of titles: 291,922; number of current serial subscriptions: 4,542. **Information technology resources:** Students are not required to lease or own a computer. Number of campus computers available to all students: 311. School has a wireless network. Approximate number of users that can be accommodated: 500. Proportion of college-owned housing units wired for high-speed internet access: 100%. **Campus safety:** Security services offered: 24-hour foot-and-vehicle patrols, late-night transport/escort service, 24-hour emergency telephones, lighted pathways/sidewalks, student patrols, controlled dormitory access (key, security card, etc).

TRANSFER AND INTERNATIONAL STUDENTS
Transfer students: May apply for admission for the following academic terms: Fall, Spring. Applicants need a minimum number of credits to apply. For fall 2005: Transfer applications received: 111. Transfer applicants offered admission: 53. Transfer applicants enrolled: 26. **International students:** Number of foreign undergraduates: 19 (1% of student body). Number of countries represented: 14. Minimum TOEFL score required: 550 (paper); 213 (computer).

Alvernia College

- **Address:** 400 St. Bernardine Street, Reading, PA 19607-1799
- **Website:** http://www.alvernia.edu
- **Private; Religious affiliation:** Roman Catholic
- **Enrollment:** 1,515 full-time; 481 part-time

KEY STATS
- ✔ U.S News College Ranking: 27, Comp. Coll.–Bachelor's (North)
- ✔ SAT Score (25th/75th percentile): 840-1050
- ✔ Tuition: 2006-2007: $20,422

Selectivity: Less selective	Room/board: $8,193
Acceptance rate: 76%	Average debt: $6,985
Student/faculty ratio: 13/1	Proportion who borrowed: 91%

UNDERGRADUATE STUDENT BODY STATS
2005-2006 enrollment: 1,515 full-time; 481 part-time. Men: 31%; women: 69%. **Ethnic makeup:** African American: 14%; Asian American: 1%; Hispanic: 5%; White: 80%.

ADMISSIONS FACTS AND FIGURES
Phone: (610) 796-8220. **Email:** admissions@alvernia.edu. **Website:** http://www.alvernia.edu. **Application deadlines for fall 2007:** Regular decision: Rolling. Early decision: Not offered. Early action: Not offered. Admission can be deferred. **Application fee:** $25. Common application is accepted. **Admissions requirements/recommendations:** High school units required (recommended): English: 4 (0); Mathematics: 2 (0); Science: 2 (0); Foreign language: 2 (0); Social studies: 2 (0); History: 0 (0); Academic electives: 4 (0); Total units: 17 (0). Tests: The college uses SAT or ACT scores in admissions decisions. SAT required. For admission to the fall 2007 entering class, the school will accept: ACT with writing, ACT without writing. Campus visit: Recommended. Admissions interview: Recommended. Off-campus interview: May be arranged. **Factors that count in admissions decisions:** *Academic:* Secondary school record: Important. Class rank: Important. Letters of recommendation: Very important. Standardized test scores: Important. Essay: Important. *Nonacademic:* Interview: Important. Extracurricular activities: Important. Talent/ability: Important. Character/personal qualities: Important. Alumni/ae relationship: Not considered. Geographical residence: Not considered. State residency: Not considered. Religious affiliation/commitment: Considered. Minority status: Not considered. Volunteer work: Important. Work experience: Important. **Other schools with the greatest overlap in applicants:** Cabrini College; Kutztown University of Pennsylvania; Pennsylvania State University–University Park; West Chester University of Pennsylvania; York College of Pennsylvania. **Admissions statistics for the fall 2005 entering class:** Total applicants: 922. Total accepted: 699. Freshmen enrolled: 274; 22% were from out of state. Overall acceptance rate: 76%. **Credentials of fall 2005 freshmen:** 8% ranked in the top 10 percent of their high school class; 27% were in the top 25 percent, and 53% were in the top half. (Proportion submitting class standing: 85%.) **Average high school grade point average:** 2.9. **First-year students who submitted SAT scores:** 97%. Scores (25/75 percentile): Verbal: 420-520, Math: 420-530, Combined: 840-1050. **First-year students submitting ACT scores:** 6%. Scores (25/75 percentile): English: N/A, Math: N/A, Composite: N/A.

ACADEMICS
Year founded: 1958. **Academic calendar:** Semester. **Degrees offered:** certificate, associate, bachelor's, post-bachelor's certificate, master's, post-master's certificate, doctorate. **Most popular majors:** 26% health professions and related clinical sciences, 22% business, management, marketing, and related support services, 14% security and protective services, 12% education. **Major fields of study:** biological and biomedical sciences; business, management, marketing, and related support services; communication, journalism, and related programs; computer and information sciences and support services; education; English language and literature/letters; health professions and related clinical sciences; liberal arts and sciences studies, and humanities; mathematics and statistics; multi/interdisciplinary studies; parks, recreation, leisure, and fitness studies; philosophy and religious studies; physical sciences; psychology; public administration and social service professions; security and protective services; social sciences. **Areas of required coursework:** arts/fine arts, humanities, mathematics, English (including composition), philosophy, foreign languages, sciences (biological or physical), history, social science. **Pre-professional programs:** pre-dentistry. **Special academic programs:** accelerated program, cross-registration, double major, dual enrollment, English as a Second Language (ESL), honors program, independent study, internships, student-designed major, study abroad, teacher certificate program. **Teacher certification offered in:** early childhood, special education, elementary, middle/junior high, secondary. **Reserve Officers Training Corps (ROTC):** Army ROTC: Offered at cooperating institution (Lehigh University). **Faculty and instruction (2005-2006):** Total instructional faculty: 74 full-time, 161 part-time. Full-time faculty with Ph.D. or other terminal degree: 68%. Student/faculty ratio: 13/1. Classes of fewer than 20 students: 58%; of 20 to 49 students: 41%; of 50 or more students: 0%. **Advanced Placement and International Baccalaureate credit:** AP tests may be used for: Credit and/or placement. International Baccalaureate exams may be used for: Credit and/or placement. **Freshmen returning for sophomore year:** 78%. **Graduation rates:** Four-year: 42%; five-year: 45%; six-year: 49%.

COSTS AND FINANCIAL AID
Financial aid office: (610) 796-8356. **Expenses (2006-2007):** Tuition and fees 2006-2007: $20,422; room/board: $8,193. Estimated books and supplies: $1,200; transportation: $1,146; personal expenses: $1,146. **Financial aid:** In 2005-2006, 96% of undergraduates applied for financial aid. Of those, 94% were determined to have financial need; 9% had their need fully met. Average financial aid package (proportion receiving): $12,225 (94%). Average amount of gift aid, such as scholarships or grants (proportion receiving): $6,521 (94%). Average amount of self-help aid, such as work study or loans (proportion receiving): $6,200 (90%). Average need-based loan (excluding PLUS or other private loans): $5,482. Among students who received need-based aid, the average percentage of need met: 79%. Among students who received aid based on merit, the average award (and the proportion receiving): $6,500 (2%). The average athletic scholarship (and the proportion receiving): $0 (0%). Average amount of debt of borrowers graduating in 2005: $6,985. Proportion who borrowed: 91%.

CAMPUS LIFE AND EXTRACURRICULAR ACTIVITIES

Campus housing available: coed dorms, women's dorms, other housing options. Students who live in college-owned, operated, or affiliated housing: 43%. **Clubs and organizations:** Number of student organizations: 37. Activities include: choral groups, dance, drama/theater, literary magazine, music ensembles, musical theater, student government, student newspaper, yearbook. Number of fraternities: 0; sororities: 0. Average proportion of students who stay on campus on weekends: 40%. **Sports program (2005-2006):** Member of NCAA III. *Men's intercollegiate varsity sports:* baseball, basketball, cross-country, golf, lacrosse, soccer, tennis. *Women's intercollegiate varsity sports:* basketball, cross-country, field hockey, lacrosse, soccer, softball, tennis, volleyball.

SERVICES AND FACILITIES

Basic services: health service, health insurance. **Remedial assistance:** reading, math, writing, study skills. **Counseling services:** career, personal, academic, psychological, religious. **For learning-disabled students:** School does not offer a structured program with separate admission and additional fees. Services include: remedial math, remedial English, remedial reading, tape recorders, note-taking services, oral tests, learning center, extended time for tests, tutors. **Information technology resources:** Students are not required to lease or own a computer. Number of campus computers available to all students: 100. School has a wireless network. Approximate number of users that can be accommodated: 60. Proportion of college-owned housing units wired for high-speed internet access: 100%. **Campus safety:** Security services offered: 24-hour foot-and-vehicle patrols, late-night transport/escort service, 24-hour emergency telephones, lighted pathways/sidewalks, controlled dormitory access (key, security card, etc.).

TRANSFER AND INTERNATIONAL STUDENTS

Transfer students: May apply for admission for the following academic terms: Fall, Spring, Summer. Applicants need a minimum number of credits to apply. For fall 2005: Transfer applications received: 235. Transfer applicants offered admission: 133. Transfer applicants enrolled: 107. **International students:** Number of foreign undergraduates: 3. Minimum TOEFL score required: 550 (paper); 213 (computer).

Arcadia University

- **Address:** 450 S. Easton Road, Glenside, PA 19038-3295
- **Website:** http://www.arcadia.edu
- **Private; Religious affiliation:** Presbyterian
- **Enrollment:** 1,750 full-time; 207 part-time

KEY STATS

✔ **U.S News College Ranking:** 22, Universities–Master's (North)
✔ **SAT Score (25th/75th percentile):** 1020-1230
✔ **Tuition:** 2006-2007: $25,990

Selectivity: More selective	**Room/board:** $9,660
Acceptance rate: 79%	**Average debt:** $31,146
Student/faculty ratio: 12/1	**Proportion who borrowed:** 82%

UNDERGRADUATE STUDENT BODY STATS

2005-2006 enrollment: 1,750 full-time; 207 part-time. Men: 28%; women: 72%. **Ethnic makeup:** African American: 8%; Asian American: 2%; Hispanic: 2%; White: 85%; International: 1%. **Religious preference:** Roman Catholic: 31%; Protestant: 16%; Jewish: 3%; Muslim: 1%; Buddhist: 1%; Unknown: 44%; Presbyterian: 2%; Other: 2%.

ADMISSIONS FACTS AND FIGURES

Phone: (215) 572-2910. **Email:** admiss@arcadia.edu. **Website:** http://www.arcadia.edu. **Application deadlines for fall 2007:** Regular decision: Rolling. Early decision: Send application by: November 1; Decision sent by: December 1. Early action: Not offered. Admission can be deferred. **Application fee:** $30. Common application is accepted. **Admissions requirements/recommendations:** High school units required (recommended): English: 4; Mathematics: 3; Science: 3; Foreign language: 3; Social studies: 4; Academic electives: 3; Total units: 19. Tests: The college uses SAT or ACT scores in admissions decisions. Either SAT or ACT required. For admission to the fall 2007 entering class, the school will accept: ACT with writing. Campus visit: Recommended. Admissions interview: Recommended. Off-campus interview: Not available. **Factors that count in admissions decisions:**

Academic: Secondary school record: Very important. Class rank: Important. Letters of recommendation: Very important. Standardized test scores: Very important. Essay: Important. *Nonacademic:* Interview: Considered. Extracurricular activities: Considered. Talent/ability: Considered. Character/personal qualities: Considered. Alumni/ae relationship: Considered. Geographical residence: Not considered. State residency: Not considered. Religious affiliation/commitment: Not considered. Minority status: Not considered. Volunteer work: Considered. Work experience: Considered. **Other schools with the greatest overlap in applicants:** Drexel University; Pennsylvania State University–University Park; Rider University; St. Joseph's University; Temple University. **Admissions statistics for the fall 2005 entering class:** Total applicants: 2,701. Total accepted: 2,122. Freshmen enrolled: 441; 40% were from out of state. Accepted through early-decision or early-action plans: 1%. Overall acceptance rate: 79%. Early-decision acceptance rate: 79%. Non-early acceptance rate: 79%. **Credentials of fall 2005 freshmen:** 31% ranked in the top 10 percent of their high school class; 63% were in the top 25 percent, and 91% were in the top half. (Proportion submitting class standing: 72%.) **First-year students who submitted SAT scores:** 96%. Scores (25/75 percentile): Verbal: 520-620, Math: 500-610, Combined: 1020-1230. **First-year students submitting ACT scores:** 10%. Scores (25/75 percentile): English: N/A, Math: N/A, Composite: 21-26.

ACADEMICS

Year founded: 1853. **Academic calendar:** Semester. **Degrees offered:** certificate, bachelor's, post-bachelor's certificate, master's, post-master's certificate, doctorate. **Most popular majors:** 9% elementary education and teaching, 9% psychology, 8% business administration and management, 7% biology/biological sciences, 6% early childhood education and teaching. **Major fields of study:** biological and biomedical sciences; business, management, marketing, and related support services; communication, journalism, and related programs; computer and information sciences and support services; education; engineering; English language and literature/letters; foreign languages, literatures, and linguistics; health professions and related clinical sciences; history; liberal arts and sciences studies, and humanities; mathematics and statistics; philosophy and religious studies; physical sciences; psychology; social sciences; visual and performing arts. **Areas of required coursework:** arts/fine arts, humanities, mathematics, English (including composition), foreign languages, sciences (biological or physical), social science, other. **Pre-professional programs:** pre-law, pre-dentistry, pre-medicine, pre-veterinary science, pre-optometry, pre-pharmacy, other. **Special academic programs (% participation):** cooperative (work-study plan) program (2.1%), cross-registration (1%), distance learning (6%), double major (4.9%), English as a Second Language (ESL) (0%), exchange student program (domestic) (0%), external degree program (1%), honors program (2.5%), independent study (7.2%), internships (43%), student-designed major (1.8%), study abroad (28%), teacher certificate program (15%). **Teacher certification offered in:** early childhood, special education, elementary, middle/junior high, secondary. **Cooperative education programs:** business, computer science, natural science. **Faculty and instruction (2005-2006):** Total instructional faculty: 110 full-time, 283 part-time (43% men; 57% women; 10% minorities). Full-time faculty with Ph.D. or other terminal degree: 89%. Student/faculty ratio: 12/1. Classes of fewer than 20 students: 67%; of 20 to 49 students: 33%; of 50 or more students: 0%. **Advanced Placement and International Baccalaureate credit:** AP tests may be used for: Credit and/or placement. Scores accepted: 3, 4, 5. International Baccalaureate exams may be used for: Credit and/or placement. **Freshmen returning for sophomore year:** 80%. **Graduation rates:** Four-year: 57%; five-year: 69%; six-year: 65%. **Graduate study:** 20% of students pursue further study immediately upon graduation; 34% within one year; 40% within five years. Fields in which graduates pursue further study: Master of Business Administration (MBA), 5%; law, 5%; medicine, 7%; dentistry, 3%; engineering, 3%; theology (or the seminary), 1%; education, 35%; arts and sciences, 39%; veterinary medicine, 2%.

COSTS AND FINANCIAL AID

Financial aid office: (215) 572-2980. **Expenses (2006-2007):** Tuition and fees 2006-2007: $25,990; room/board: $9,660. Estimated books and supplies: $800; transportation: $250; personal expenses: $650. **Financial aid:** Priority filing date for institution's financial aid form: March 1. In 2005-2006, 97% of undergraduates applied for financial aid. Of those, 88% were determined to have financial need; 50% had their need fully met. Average financial aid package (proportion receiving): $19,214 (88%). Average amount of gift aid, such as scholarships or grants (proportion receiving): $12,731 (71%). Average amount of self-help aid, such as work study or loans (proportion receiving): $5,699 (69%). Average need-based loan (excluding PLUS or other private loans): $4,834. Among students who received need-based aid, the average percentage of need met: 78%. Among students who received aid based on merit, the average award (and the proportion receiving): $7,652 (9%). The average athletic scholarship (and the proportion receiving): $0 (0%). Average amount of debt of borrowers graduating in 2005: $31,146. Proportion who borrowed: 82%.

CAMPUS LIFE AND EXTRACURRICULAR ACTIVITIES

Campus housing available (% using): coed dorms (53%), apartment for single students (47%). Students who live in college-owned, operated, or affiliated housing: 66%. **Student employment:** During the 2005-2006 academic year, 52% of undergraduates worked on campus. Average per-year earnings: $1,200. **Clubs and organizations:** Number of student organizations: 81. Activities include: choral groups, dance, drama/theater, literary magazine, musical theater, radio station, student government, student newspaper, yearbook. Number of fraternities: 0; sororities: 0. Average proportion of students who stay on campus on weekends: 77%. **Sports program (2005-2006):** Member of NCAA III. **Men's intercollegiate varsity sports:** baseball, basketball, cross-country, golf, soccer, swimming and diving, tennis. **Women's intercollegiate varsity sports:** basketball, cross-country, field hockey, lacrosse, soccer, softball, swimming and diving, tennis, volleyball.

SERVICES AND FACILITIES

Basic services: nonremedial tutoring, health service, health insurance, other. **Remedial assistance:** math, writing, study skills. **Counseling services:** minority student, career, personal, academic, psychological, other. **For learning-disabled students:** School does not offer a structured program with separate admission and additional fees. Total undergraduates in learning-disabled program or receiving services: 58. Services include: remedial math, remedial English, reading machines, tape recorders, other special classes, notetaking services, learning center, extended time for tests, tutors, priority seating, substitution of courses, texts on tape, other. **Library:** Number of titles: 143,232; number of current serial subscriptions: 936. **Information technology resources:** Students are not required to lease or own a computer. Number of campus computers available to all students: 350. School has a wireless network. Approximate number of users that can be accommodated: 1,500. Proportion of college-owned housing units wired for high-speed internet access: 100%. **Campus safety:** Security services offered: 24-hour foot-and-vehicle patrols, late-night transport/escort service, 24-hour emergency telephones, lighted pathways/sidewalks, controlled dormitory access (key, security card, etc.).

TRANSFER AND INTERNATIONAL STUDENTS

Transfer students: May apply for admission for the following academic terms: Fall, Spring. Applicants do not need a minimum number of credits to apply. For fall 2005: Transfer applications received: 449. Transfer applicants offered admission: 291. Transfer applicants enrolled: 148.
International students: Number of foreign undergraduates: 26 (1% of student body). Number of countries represented: 20. Minimum TOEFL score required: 520 (paper); 190 (computer). Average TOEFL score: 571 (paper).

Bloomsburg University of Pennsylvania

■ **Address:** 400 E. Second Street, Bloomsburg, PA 17815
■ **Website:** http://www.bloomu.edu
■ **Public**
■ **Enrollment:** 7,257 full-time; 526 part-time

KEY STATS

✔ **U.S News College Ranking:** 83, Universities–Master's (North)
✔ **SAT Score (25th/75th percentile):** 920-1110
✔ **Tuition:** 2006-2007: $0 in state, $0 out of state

Selectivity: Less selective	**Room/board:** $5,616
Acceptance rate: 68%	**Average debt:** $16,442
Student/faculty ratio: 21/1	**Proportion who borrowed:** 68%

UNDERGRADUATE STUDENT BODY STATS

2005-2006 enrollment: 7,257 full-time; 526 part-time. Men: 40%; women: 60%. **Ethnic makeup:** African American: 6%; Asian American: 1%; Hispanic: 2%; White: 90%; International: 1%.

ADMISSIONS FACTS AND FIGURES

Phone: (570) 389-4316. **Email:** buadmiss@bloomu.edu. **Website:** http://www.bloomu.edu. **Application deadlines for fall 2007:** Regular decision: Rolling. Early decision: Send application by: November 15; Decision sent by: N/A. Early action: Send application by: October 31; Decision sent by: N/A. Admission can be deferred. **Application fee:** $30. Common application is not accepted. **To apply online, go to:** http://www.bloomu.edu/admissions. **Admissions requirements/recommendations:** High school units required (recommended): English: 4 (4); Mathematics: 3 (4); Science: 3 (4); Foreign language: 0 (2); Social studies: 2 (2); History: 2 (2); Academic electives: 2 (2); Total units: 16 (20). Tests: The college uses SAT or ACT scores in admissions decisions. Either SAT or ACT required. For admission to the fall 2007 entering class, the school will accept: ACT with writing, ACT without writing. Campus visit: Recommended. Off-campus interview: May be arranged. **Factors that count in admissions decisions:** *Academic:* Secondary school record: Very important. Class rank: Very important. Letters of recommendation: Considered. Standardized test scores: Very important. Essay: Considered. *Nonacademic:* Interview: Considered. Extracurricular activities: Considered. Talent/ability: Considered. Character/personal qualities: Considered. Geographical residence: Considered. State residency: Considered. Religious affiliation/commitment: Not considered. Volunteer work: Considered. Work experience: Considered. **Other schools with the greatest overlap in applicants:** Kutztown University of Pennsylvania; Lock Haven University of Pennsylvania; Millersville University of Pennsylvania; Pennsylvania State University–University Park; Shippensburg University of Pennsylvania. **Admissions statistics for the fall 2005 entering class:** Total applicants: 8,237. Total accepted: 5,570. Freshmen enrolled: 1,697; 13% were from out of state. Accepted through early-decision or early-action plans: 13%. Overall acceptance rate: 68%. Early-decision acceptance rate: 75%. Non-early acceptance rate: 67%. **Size of waiting list:** 71 applicants; enrolled from waiting list: 0. **Credentials of fall 2005 freshmen:** 9% ranked in the top 10 percent of their high school class; 35% were in the top 25 percent, and 75% were in the top half. (Proportion submitting class standing: 89%.) **Average high school grade point average:** 3.3. **First-year students who submitted SAT scores:** 99%. Scores (25/75 percentile): Verbal: 460-550, Math: 460-560, Combined: 920-1110.

ACADEMICS

Year founded: 1839. **Academic calendar:** Semester. **Degrees offered:** associate, terminal-associate, bachelor's, post-bachelor's certificate, master's, doctorate. **Most popular majors:** 15% business administration and management, 13% elementary education and teaching, 6% speech and rhetorical studies, 5% mathematics, 5% special education and teaching. **Major fields of study:** biological and biomedical sciences; business, management, marketing, and related support services; communication, journalism, and related programs; computer and information sciences and support services; education; engineering; English language and literature/letters; foreign languages, literatures, and linguistics; health professions and related clinical sciences; history; mathematics and statistics; parks, recreation, leisure, and fitness studies; philosophy and religious studies; physical sciences; psychology; public administration and social service professions; security and protective services; social sciences; visual and performing arts. **Areas of required coursework:** arts/fine arts, humanities, mathematics, English (including composition), philosophy, sciences (biological or physical), history, social science, other. **Pre-professional programs:** pre-law, pre-dentistry, pre-medicine, pre-veterinary science, pre-optometry, pre-pharmacy, other. **Special academic programs (% participation):** distance learning (2%), double major (6%), honors program (1%), independent study (5%), internships (35%), study abroad (1%), teacher certificate program (27%). **Teacher certification offered in:** early childhood, special education, elementary, secondary. **Reserve Officers Training Corps (ROTC):** Army ROTC: Offered on campus; Air Force ROTC: Offered at cooperating institution (Wilkes University). **Faculty and instruction (2005-2006):** Total instructional faculty: 358 full-time, 39 part-time (59% men; 41% women; 11% minorities). Full-time faculty with Ph.D. or other terminal degree: 83%. Student/faculty ratio: 21/1. Classes of fewer than 20 students: 23%; of 20 to 49 students: 70%; of 50 or more students: 7%. **Advanced Placement and International Baccalaureate credit:** AP tests may be used for: Credit and/or placement. Scores accepted: 3, 4, 5. **Freshmen returning for sophomore year:** 81%. **Graduation rates:** Four-year: 38%; five-year: 61%; six-year: 61%. **Graduate study:** 18% of students pursue further study within one year.

COSTS AND FINANCIAL AID

Financial aid office: (570) 389-4297. **Expenses (2006-2007):** Tuition and fees 2006-2007: $0 in state, $0 out of state; room/board: $5,616. Estimated books and supplies: $1,000; transportation: $974; personal expenses:

$2,650. **Financial aid:** Priority filing date for institution's financial aid form: March 15. In 2005-2006, 88% of undergraduates applied for financial aid. Of those, 84% were determined to have financial need; 84% had their need fully met. Average financial aid package (proportion receiving): $9,356 (78%). Average amount of gift aid, such as scholarships or grants (proportion receiving): $4,105 (39%). Average amount of self-help aid, such as work study or loans (proportion receiving): $4,096 (48%). Average need-based loan (excluding PLUS or other private loans): $3,540. Among students who received need-based aid, the average percentage of need met: 65%. Among students who received aid based on merit, the average award (and the proportion receiving): $1,642 (1%). The average athletic scholarship (and the proportion receiving): $2,201 (3%). Average amount of debt of borrowers graduating in 2005: $16,442. Proportion who borrowed: 68%.

CAMPUS LIFE AND EXTRACURRICULAR ACTIVITIES

Campus housing available (% using): coed dorms (79%), apartment for single students (21%). Students who live in college-owned, operated, or affiliated housing: 46%. **Student employment:** During the 2005-2006 academic year, 15% of undergraduates worked on campus. Average per-year earnings: $1,560. **Clubs and organizations:** Number of student organizations: 200. Activities include: choral groups, concert band, dance, drama/theater, jazz band, literary magazine, marching band, music ensembles, radio station, student government, student newspaper, symphony orchestra, television station, yearbook. Number of fraternities: 15; sororities: 12. Proportion of men in fraternities: 4%; of women in sororities: 6%. **Sports program (2005-2006):** Member of NCAA II. *Men's intercollegiate varsity sports:* baseball, basketball, cross-country, football, soccer, swimming and diving, tennis, track and field (indoor), track and field (outdoor), wrestling. *Women's intercollegiate varsity sports:* basketball, cross-country, field hockey, lacrosse, soccer, softball, swimming and diving, tennis, track and field (indoor), track and field (outdoor).

SERVICES AND FACILITIES

Basic services: nonremedial tutoring, women's center, placement service, day care, health service, health insurance. **Remedial assistance:** reading, math, writing, study skills. **Counseling services:** career, personal, academic, psychological. **For learning-disabled students:** School does not offer a structured program with separate admission and additional fees. Services include: remedial math, remedial English, reading machines, remedial reading, tape recorders, other special classes, note-taking services, oral tests, readers, extended time for tests, tutors, other. **Library:** Number of titles: 460,723; number of current serial subscriptions: 2,976. **Information technology resources:** Students are not required to lease or own a computer. Number of campus computers available to all students: 1,250. School has a wireless network. Approximate number of users that can be accommodated: 4,000. Proportion of college-owned housing units wired for high-speed internet access: 100%. **Campus safety:** Security services offered: 24-hour foot-and-vehicle patrols, late-night transport/escort service, 24-hour emergency telephones, lighted pathways/sidewalks, controlled dormitory access (key, security card, etc).

TRANSFER AND INTERNATIONAL STUDENTS

Transfer students: May apply for admission for the following academic terms: Fall, Spring, Summer. Applicants need a minimum number of credits to apply. For fall 2005: Transfer applications received: 1,014. Transfer applicants offered admission: 629. Transfer applicants enrolled: 413. **International students:** Number of foreign undergraduates: 43 (1% of student body). Number of countries represented: 22. Minimum TOEFL score required: 500 (paper); 173 (computer). Average TOEFL score: 550 (paper).

Bryn Athyn College of the New Church

- **Address:** 2895 College Drive, PO Box 717, Bryn Athyn, PA 19009
- **Website:** http://www.brynathyn.edu
- **Private; Religious affiliation:** General Church of the New Jerusalem
- **Enrollment:** 133 full-time; 9 part-time

KEY STATS

✔ **U.S News College Ranking:** Unranked, Comp. Coll.–Bachelor's (North)
✔ **SAT Score (25th/75th percentile):** 920-1290
✔ **Tuition:** 2006-2007: $10,114

Selectivity: N/A	Room/board: $5,574
Acceptance rate: 96%	Average debt: $5,062
Student/faculty ratio: 7/1	Proportion who borrowed: 37%

UNDERGRADUATE STUDENT BODY STATS

2005-2006 enrollment: 133 full-time; 9 part-time. Men: 40%; women: 60%. **Ethnic makeup:** Asian American: 1%; White: 76%; International: 23%.

ADMISSIONS FACTS AND FIGURES

Phone: (267) 502-2511. **Email:** admissions@brynathyn.edu. **Website:** http://www.brynathyn.edu. **Application deadlines for fall 2007:** Regular decision: July 1. Early decision: Not offered. Early action: Not offered. Admission can be deferred. **Application fee:** $30. Common application is not accepted. **Admissions requirements/recommendations:** High school units required (recommended): English: 4; Mathematics: 3; Science: 3; Foreign language: 2; Total units: 15. Tests: The college uses SAT or ACT scores in admissions decisions. Either SAT or ACT required. For admission to the fall 2007 entering class, the school will accept: ACT with writing. Campus visit: Recommended. Admissions interview: Recommended. Off-campus interview: May be arranged. **Factors that count in admissions decisions:** *Academic:* Secondary school record: Very important. Class rank: Considered. Letters of recommendation: Very important. Standardized test scores: Important. Essay: Important. *Nonacademic:* Interview: Considered. Extracurricular activities: Considered. Talent/ability: Considered. Character/personal qualities: Very important. Alumni/ae relationship: Considered. Geographical residence: Not considered. State residency: Not considered. Religious affiliation/commitment: Very important. Minority status: Not considered. Volunteer work: Considered. Work experience: Considered. **Other schools with the greatest overlap in applicants:** Pennsylvania State University–Abington; Pennsylvania State University–University Park. **Admissions statistics for the fall 2005 entering class:** Total applicants: 52. Total accepted: 50. Freshmen enrolled: 45; 18% were from out of state. Overall acceptance rate: 96%. **Average high school grade point average:** 3.4. **First-year students who submitted SAT scores:** 93%. Scores (25/75 percentile): Verbal: 450-660, Math: 470-630, Combined: 920-1290. **First-year students submitting ACT scores:** 11%. Scores (25/75 percentile): English: 26-34, Math: 24-28, Composite: 22-29.

ACADEMICS

Year founded: 1877. **Academic calendar:** Trimester. **Degrees offered:** associate, bachelor's, master's, first professional, first professional certificate. **Most popular majors:** 50% multi/interdisciplinary studies, 15% education, 15% history, 10% biology/biological sciences, 5% English language and literature. **Major fields of study:** biological and biomedical sciences; education; English language and literature/letters; history; multi/interdisciplinary studies; philosophy and religious studies. **Areas of required coursework:** arts/fine arts, mathematics, English (including composition), philosophy, sciences (biological or physical), history, social science, other. **Special academic programs (% participation):** accelerated program (0%), cooperative (work-study plan) program (40%), cross-registration (10%), English as a Second Language (ESL) (5%), independent study (60%), internships (30%), student-designed major (50%), study abroad (0%), teacher certificate program (0%). **Teacher certification offered in:** early childhood, special education, elementary, secondary. **Cooperative education programs:** other. **Faculty and instruction (2005-2006):** Total instructional faculty: 21 full-time, 27 part-time (58% men; 42% women; 2% minorities). Full-time faculty with Ph.D. or other terminal degree: 71%. Student/faculty ratio: 7/1. Classes of fewer than 20 students: 92%; of 20 to 49 students: 8%. **Advanced Placement and International Baccalaureate credit:** AP tests may be used for: Credit and/or placement. International Baccalaureate exams may be used for: Credit and/or placement. **Freshmen returning for sophomore year:** 65%. **Graduation rates:** Four-year: 13%; five-year: 16%; six-year: 22%.

COSTS AND FINANCIAL AID

Financial aid office: (267) 502-2630. **Expenses (2006-2007):** Tuition and fees 2006-2007: $10,114; room/board: $5,574. Estimated books and supplies: $700 personal expenses: $700. **Financial aid:** In 2005-2006, 62% of undergraduates applied for financial aid. Of those, 50% were determined to have financial need; 50% had their need fully met. Average financial aid package (proportion receiving): $8,008 (49%). Average amount of gift aid, such as scholarships or grants (proportion receiving): $6,687 (47%). Average amount of self-help aid, such as work study or loans (proportion receiving): $2,582 (23%). Average need-based loan (excluding PLUS or other private loans): $2,582. Among students who received need-based aid, the average percentage of need met: 86%. Among students who received aid based on merit, the average award (and the proportion receiving): $900 (8%). The average athletic scholarship (and the proportion receiving): $0 (0%). Average amount of debt of borrowers graduating in 2005: $5,062. Proportion who borrowed: 37%.

CAMPUS LIFE AND EXTRACURRICULAR ACTIVITIES

Campus housing available (% using): women's dorms (42%), men's dorms (36%), other housing options (22%). Students who live in college-owned, operated, or affiliated housing: 62%. **Student employment:** During the 2005-2006 academic year, 25% of undergraduates worked on campus. Average per-year earnings: $1,830. **Clubs and organizations:** Number of student organizations: 13. Activities include: choral groups, drama/theater, student government, student newspaper. Number of fraternities: 0; sororities: 1. of women in sororities: 15%. Average proportion of students who stay on campus on weekends: 70%.

SERVICES AND FACILITIES

Basic services: nonremedial tutoring, health service, health insurance. **Remedial assistance:** math, writing. **Counseling services:** career, personal, academic, psychological, religious. **For learning-disabled students:** School does not offer a structured program with separate admission and additional fees. Total undergraduates in learning-disabled program or receiving services: 0. Services include: remedial math, remedial English, tape recorders, untimed tests, oral tests, extended time for tests, tutors, other. **Library:** Number of titles: 104,358; number of current serial subscriptions: 319. **Information technology resources:** Students are not required to lease or own a computer. Number of campus computers available to all students: 55. School has a wireless network. Approximate number of users that can be accommodated: 50. Proportion of college-owned housing units wired for high-speed internet access: 96%. **Campus safety:** Security services offered: 24-hour emergency telephones, lighted pathways/sidewalks, controlled dormitory access (key, security card, etc).

TRANSFER AND INTERNATIONAL STUDENTS

Transfer students: May apply for admission for the following academic terms: Fall, Winter, Spring. Applicants do not need a minimum number of credits to apply. For fall 2005: Transfer applications received: 5. Transfer applicants offered admission: 5. Transfer applicants enrolled: 5. **International students:** Number of foreign undergraduates: 16 (23% of student body). Number of countries represented: 10. Minimum TOEFL score required: 520 (paper); 190 (computer). Average TOEFL score: 570 (paper).

Bryn Mawr College

- **Address:** 101 N. Merion Avenue, Bryn Mawr, PA 19010
- **Website:** http://www.brynmawr.edu
- **Private**
- **Enrollment:** 1,307 full-time; 39 part-time

KEY STATS

✔ **U.S News College Ranking:** 20, Liberal Arts Colleges
✔ **SAT Score (25th/75th percentile):** 1210-1400
✔ **Tuition:** 2006-2007: $33,010

Selectivity: More selective	**Room/board:** $10,550
Acceptance rate: 46%	**Average debt:** $17,018
Student/faculty ratio: 8/1	**Proportion who borrowed:** 57%

UNDERGRADUATE STUDENT BODY STATS

2005-2006 enrollment: 1,307 full-time; 39 part-time. Men: 3%; women: 97%. **Ethnic makeup:** African American: 5%; Asian American: 12%; Hispanic: 3%; White: 74%; International: 7%.

ADMISSIONS FACTS AND FIGURES

Phone: (610) 526-5152. **Email:** admissions@brynmawr.edu. **Website:** http://www.brynmawr.edu. **Application deadlines for fall 2007:** Regular decision: January 15; decision sent by April 1. Early decision: Send application by: November 15; Decision sent by: December 15. Early action: Not offered. Admission can be deferred. **Application fee:** $50. Common application is accepted. **Admissions requirements/recommendations:** High school units required (recommended): English: (4); Mathematics: (3); Science: (2); Foreign language: (3); Social studies: (2); History: (2); Academic electives: 2; Total units: (16). **Tests:** The college uses SAT or ACT scores in admissions decisions. Either SAT or ACT required. For admission to the fall 2007 entering class, the school will accept: ACT with writing, ACT without writing. Campus visit: Recommended. Admissions interview: Recommended. Off-campus interview: May be arranged. **Factors that count in admissions decisions:** *Academic:* Secondary school record: Very important. Class rank: Considered. Letters of recommendation: Very important. Standardized test scores: Considered. Essay: Important. *Nonacademic:* Interview: Considered. Extracurricular activities: Important. Talent/ability: Considered. Character/personal qualities: Important. Alumni/ae relationship: Considered. Geographical residence: Considered. State residency: Not considered. Religious affiliation/commitment: Not considered. Minority status: Considered. Volunteer work: Considered. Work experience: Considered. **Other schools with the greatest overlap in applicants:** Haverford College; Mount Holyoke College; Smith College; Swarthmore College; Wellesley College. **Admissions statistics for the fall 2005 entering class:** Total applicants: 1,938. Total accepted: 899. Freshmen enrolled: 355; 87% were from out of state. Accepted through early-decision or early-action plans: 26%. Overall acceptance rate: 46%. Early-decision acceptance rate: 67%. Non-early acceptance rate: 45%. **Size of waiting list:** 385 applicants; enrolled from waiting list: 16. **Credentials of fall 2005 freshmen:** 62% ranked in the top 10 percent of their high school class; 87% were in the top 25 percent, and 100% were in the top half. (Proportion submitting class standing: 40%.) **First-year students who submitted SAT scores:** 93%. Scores (25/75 percentile): Verbal: 620-720, Math: 590-680, Combined: 1210-1400. **First-year students submitting ACT scores:** 30%. Scores (25/75 percentile): English: N/A, Math: N/A, Composite: 27-30.

ACADEMICS

Year founded: 1885. **Academic calendar:** Semester. **Degrees offered:** bachelor's, post-bachelor's certificate, master's, doctorate. **Most popular majors:** 11% English language and literature, 9% mathematics, 9% political science and government, 8% biology/biological sciences, 8% psychology. **Major fields of study:** area, ethnic, cultural, and gender studies; biological and biomedical sciences; computer and information sciences and support services; English language and literature/letters; foreign languages, literatures, and linguistics; history; mathematics and statistics; multi/interdisciplinary studies; philosophy and religious studies; physical sciences; psychology; social sciences; visual and performing arts. **Areas of required coursework:** humanities, mathematics, English (including composition), foreign languages, sciences (biological or physical), social science, other. **Pre-professional programs:** pre-law, pre-medicine. **Special academic programs:** accelerated program, cross-registration, double major, dual enrollment, exchange student program (domestic), independent study, internships, liberal arts/career combination, student-designed major, study abroad, teacher certificate program, other. **Teacher certification offered in:** elementary, middle/junior high, secondary. **Cooperative education programs:** engineering. **Reserve Officers Training Corps (ROTC):** Air Force ROTC: Offered at cooperating institution (St. Joseph's University). **Faculty and instruction (2005-2006):** Total instructional faculty: 145 full-time, 37 part-time (46% men; 54% women; 14% minorities). Full-time faculty with Ph.D. or other terminal degree: 97%. Student/faculty ratio: 8/1. Classes of fewer than 20 students: 71%; of 20 to 49 students: 26%; of 50 or more students: 4%. **Advanced Placement and International Baccalaureate credit:** AP tests may be used for: Credit and/or placement. Scores accepted: 4, 5. International Baccalaureate exams may be used for: Placement only. **Freshmen returning for sophomore year:** 93%. **Graduation rates:** Four-year: 80%; five-year: 84%; six-year: 86%. **Graduate study:** 23% of students pursue further study within one year.

COSTS AND FINANCIAL AID

Financial aid office: (610) 526-5245. **Expenses (2006-2007):** Tuition and fees 2006-2007: $33,010; room/board: $10,550. Estimated books and supplies:

$1,000; transportation: $450; personal expenses: $1,000. **Financial aid:** In 2005-2006, 62% of undergraduates applied for financial aid. Of those, 54% were determined to have financial need; 98% had their need fully met. Average financial aid package (proportion receiving): $27,582 (54%). Average amount of gift aid, such as scholarships or grants (proportion receiving): $22,888 (52%). Average amount of self-help aid, such as work study or loans (proportion receiving): $5,800 (45%). Average need-based loan (excluding PLUS or other private loans): $4,479. Among students who received need-based aid, the average percentage of need met: 98%. Among students who received aid based on merit, the average award (and the proportion receiving): $11,082 (2%). The average athletic scholarship (and the proportion receiving): $0 (0%). Average amount of debt of borrowers graduating in 2005: $17,018. Proportion who borrowed: 57%.

CAMPUS LIFE AND EXTRACURRICULAR ACTIVITIES
Campus housing available: coed dorms, women's dorms, apartment for single students, cooperative housing, other housing options. Students who live in college-owned, operated, or affiliated housing: 97%. **Student employment:** During the 2005-2006 academic year, 75% of undergraduates worked on campus. Average per-year earnings: $1,700. **Clubs and organizations:** Number of student organizations: 100. Activities include: choral groups, dance, drama/theater, literary magazine, music ensembles, musical theater, radio station, student government, student newspaper, student film society, yearbook. Number of fraternities: 0; sororities: 0. Average proportion of students who stay on campus on weekends: 90%. **Sports program (2005-2006):** Member of NCAA III. *Women's intercollegiate varsity sports:* badminton, basketball, cross-country, field hockey, lacrosse, rowing, soccer, swimming and diving, tennis, track and field (indoor), track and field (outdoor), volleyball.

SERVICES AND FACILITIES
Basic services: nonremedial tutoring, women's center, health service, health insurance. **Counseling services:** minority student, career, personal, academic, older student, psychological, birth control, religious. **For learning-disabled students:** School does not offer a structured program with separate admission and additional fees. **Information technology resources:** Students are not required to lease or own a computer. Number of campus computers available to all students: 300. School has a wireless network. Approximate number of users that can be accommodated: 600. Proportion of college-owned housing units wired for high-speed internet access: 100%. **Campus safety:** Security services offered: 24-hour foot-and-vehicle patrols, 24-hour emergency telephones, lighted pathways/sidewalks, controlled dormitory access (key, security card, etc).

TRANSFER AND INTERNATIONAL STUDENTS
Transfer students: May apply for admission for the following academic terms: Fall, Spring. Applicants do not need a minimum number of credits to apply. For fall 2005: Transfer applications received: 61. Transfer applicants offered admission: 13. Transfer applicants enrolled: 5. **International students:** Number of foreign undergraduates: 89 (7% of student body). Number of countries represented: 44. Minimum TOEFL score required: 600 (paper); 250 (computer).

Bucknell University

- **Address:** Lewisburg, PA 17837
- **Website:** http://www.bucknell.edu
- **Private**
- **Enrollment:** 3,469 full-time; 36 part-time

KEY STATS
✔ **U.S News College Ranking:** 29, Liberal Arts Colleges
✔ **SAT Score (25th/75th percentile):** 1230-1390
✔ **Tuition:** 2006-2007: $34,574

Selectivity: Most selective	**Room/board:** $7,366
Acceptance rate: 34%	**Average debt:** $17,400
Student/faculty ratio: 12/1	**Proportion who borrowed:** 62%

UNDERGRADUATE STUDENT BODY STATS
2005-2006 enrollment: 3,469 full-time; 36 part-time. Men: 49%; women: 51%. **Ethnic makeup:** African American: 3%; Asian American: 7%; Hispanic:

2%; White: 85%; International: 3%. **Religious preference:** Roman Catholic: 29%; Protestant: 27%; Jewish: 7%; Buddhist: 1%; No preference: 32%.

ADMISSIONS FACTS AND FIGURES
Phone: (570) 577-1101. **Email:** admissions@bucknell.edu. **Website:** http://www.bucknell.edu. **Application deadlines for fall 2007:** Regular decision: January 1; decision sent by April 1. Early decision: Send application by: November 15; Decision sent by: December 15. Early action: Not offered. Admission can be deferred. **Application fee:** $60. Common application is accepted. **To apply online, go to:** http://www.applyweb.com/aw?buckn. **Admissions requirements/recommendations:** High school units required (recommended): English: 4 (4); Mathematics: 3 (4); Science: 2 (3); Foreign language: 2 (4); Social studies: 2 (2); History: 2 (2); Academic electives: 1 (1); Total units: 16 (20). Tests: The college uses SAT or ACT scores in admissions decisions. Either SAT or ACT required. For admission to the fall 2007 entering class, the school will accept: ACT with writing. Campus visit: Recommended. Admissions interview: Recommended. Off-campus interview: May be arranged. **Factors that count in admissions decisions:** *Academic:* Secondary school record: Very important. Class rank: Very important. Letters of recommendation: Important. Standardized test scores: Very important. Essay: Considered. *Nonacademic:* Interview: Considered. Extracurricular activities: Important. Talent/ability: Very important. Character/personal qualities: Very important. Alumni/ae relationship: Considered. Geographical residence: Considered. State residency: Not considered. Religious affiliation/commitment: Considered. Minority status: Important. Volunteer work: Important. Work experience: Considered. **Other schools with the greatest overlap in applicants:** Boston College; Colgate University; Cornell University; Lehigh University; Villanova University. **Admissions statistics for the fall 2005 entering class:** Total applicants: 8,306. Total accepted: 2,820. Freshmen enrolled: 923; 76% were from out of state. Accepted through early-decision or early-action plans: 41%. Overall acceptance rate: 34%. Early-decision acceptance rate: 58%. Non-early acceptance rate: 32%. **Size of waiting list:** 2375 applicants; enrolled from waiting list: 101. **Credentials of fall 2005 freshmen:** 68% ranked in the top 10 percent of their high school class; 93% were in the top 25 percent, and 100% were in the top half. (Proportion submitting class standing: 50%.) **First-year students who submitted SAT scores:** 97%. Scores (25/75 percentile): Verbal: 600-680, Math: 630-710, Combined: 1230-1390. **First-year students submitting ACT scores:** 19%. Scores (25/75 percentile): English: N/A, Math: N/A, Composite: 27-30.

ACADEMICS
Year founded: 1846. **Academic calendar:** Semester. **Degrees offered:** bachelor's, master's. **Most popular majors:** 14% business administration and management, 14% economics, 8% psychology, 7% English language and literature, 7% biological and biomedical sciences. **Major fields of study:** area, ethnic, cultural, and gender studies; biological and biomedical sciences; business, management, marketing, and related support services; computer and information sciences and support services; education; engineering; English language and literature/letters; foreign languages, literatures, and linguistics; history; liberal arts and sciences studies, and humanities; mathematics and statistics; multi/interdisciplinary studies; natural resources and conservation; philosophy and religious studies; physical sciences; psychology; social sciences; visual and performing arts. **Areas of required coursework:** humanities, mathematics, English (including composition), sciences (biological or physical), social science. **Special academic programs (% participation):** double major (24%), dual enrollment, honors program (6%), independent study (10%), internships, liberal arts/career combination, student-designed major (1%), study abroad (40%), teacher certificate program (4%). **Teacher certification offered in:** early childhood, elementary, secondary. **Reserve Officers Training Corps (ROTC):** Army ROTC: Offered on campus. **Faculty and instruction (2005-2006):** Total instructional faculty: 299 full-time, 29 part-time (63% men; 37% women; 11% minorities). Full-time faculty with Ph.D. or other terminal degree: 97%. Student/faculty ratio: 12/1. Classes of fewer than 20 students: 55%; of 20 to 49 students: 43%; of 50 or more students: 2%. **Advanced Placement and International Baccalaureate credit:** AP tests may be used for: Credit and/or placement. Scores accepted: 3, 4, 5. International Baccalaureate exams may be used for: Credit and/or placement. **Freshmen returning for sophomore year:** 95%. **Graduation rates:** Four-year: 85%; five-year: 90%; six-year: 90%. **Graduate study:** 22% of students pursue further study immediately upon graduation. Fields in which graduates pursue further study: Master of Business Administration (MBA), 5%; law, 19%; medicine, 8%; engineering, 12%; education, 8%; arts and sciences, 38%; veterinary medicine, 1%.

COSTS AND FINANCIAL AID

Financial aid office: (570) 577-1331. **Expenses (2006-2007):** Tuition and fees 2006-2007: $34,574; room/board: $7,366. Estimated books and supplies: $750 personal expenses: $982. **Financial aid:** In 2005-2006, 59% of undergraduates applied for financial aid. Of those, 48% were determined to have financial need; 100% had their need fully met. Average financial aid package (proportion receiving): $21,000 (48%). Average amount of gift aid, such as scholarships or grants (proportion receiving): $17,300 (45%). Average amount of self-help aid, such as work study or loans (proportion receiving): $1,700 (48%). Average need-based loan (excluding PLUS or other private loans): $5,200. Among students who received need-based aid, the average percentage of need met: 100%. Among students who received aid based on merit, the average award (and the proportion receiving): $12,356 (1%). The average athletic scholarship (and the proportion receiving): $10,000 (1%). Average amount of debt of borrowers graduating in 2005: $17,400. Proportion who borrowed: 62%.

CAMPUS LIFE AND EXTRACURRICULAR ACTIVITIES

Campus housing available (% using): coed dorms (66%), women's dorms (1%), sorority housing (3%), fraternity housing (9%), apartment for single students (17%), special housing for disabled students, special housing for international students (1%), other housing options (1%). Students who live in college-owned, operated, or affiliated housing: 88%. **Student employment:** During the 2005-2006 academic year, 45% of undergraduates worked on campus. Average per-year earnings: $1,650. **Clubs and organizations:** Number of student organizations: 135. Activities include: choral groups, concert band, dance, drama/theater, jazz band, literary magazine, music ensembles, opera, pep band, radio station, student government, student newspaper, student film society, symphony orchestra, yearbook. Number of fraternities: 11; sororities: 7. Proportion of men in fraternities: 37%; of women in sororities: 39%. Average proportion of students who stay on campus on weekends: 85%. **Sports program (2005-2006):** Member of NCAA I. *Men's intercollegiate varsity sports:* baseball, basketball, cross-country, football, golf, lacrosse, soccer, swimming and diving, tennis, track and field (indoor), track and field (outdoor), water polo. *Women's intercollegiate varsity sports:* basketball, crew, cross-country, field hockey, golf, lacrosse, soccer, softball, swimming and diving, tennis, track and field (indoor), track and field (outdoor), volleyball, water polo.

SERVICES AND FACILITIES

Basic services: nonremedial tutoring, women's center, placement service, health service, health insurance. **Counseling services:** minority student, career, military, personal, academic, psychological, birth control, religious. **For learning-disabled students:** School does not offer a structured program with separate admission and additional fees. Total undergraduates in learning-disabled program or receiving services: 72. Services include: reading machines, tape recorders, oral tests, extended time for tests, tutors, other testing accomodations, other. **Library:** Number of titles: 778,159; number of current serial subscriptions: 4,733. **Information technology resources:** Students are not required to lease or own a computer. Number of campus computers available to all students: 568. School has a wireless network. Approximate number of users that can be accommodated: 5,000. Proportion of college-owned housing units wired for high-speed internet access: 100%. **Campus safety:** Security services offered: 24-hour foot-and-vehicle patrols, late-night transport/escort service, 24-hour emergency telephones, lighted pathways/sidewalks, student patrols, controlled dormitory access (key, security card, etc).

TRANSFER AND INTERNATIONAL STUDENTS

Transfer students: May apply for admission for the following academic terms: Fall, Spring. Applicants need a minimum number of credits to apply. For fall 2005: Transfer applications received: 130. Transfer applicants offered admission: 64. Transfer applicants enrolled: 30. **International students:** Number of foreign undergraduates: 94 (3% of student body). Number of countries represented: 41. Minimum TOEFL score required: 550 (paper); 213 (computer). Average TOEFL score: 617 (paper).

Cabrini College

- **Address:** 610 King of Prussia Road, Radnor, PA 19087-3698
- **Website:** http://www.cabrini.edu
- **Private; Religious affiliation:** Roman Catholic
- **Enrollment:** 1,550 full-time; 189 part-time

KEY STATS

✔ **U.S News College Ranking:** third tier, Universities–Master's (North)
✔ **SAT Score (25th/75th percentile):** 890-1090
✔ **Tuition:** 2006-2007: $25,920

Selectivity: Less selective	**Room/board:** $9,800
Acceptance rate: 65%	**Average debt:** $17,400
Student/faculty ratio: 15/1	**Proportion who borrowed:** 84%

UNDERGRADUATE STUDENT BODY STATS

2005-2006 enrollment: 1,550 full-time; 189 part-time. Men: 32%; women: 68%. **Ethnic makeup:** African American: 5%; Asian American: 2%; Hispanic: 2%; White: 91%; International: 1%. **Religious preference:** Protestant: 13%; Jewish: 1%; No preference: 7%; Roman Catholic: 72%; Other: 7%.

ADMISSIONS FACTS AND FIGURES

Phone: (610) 902-8552. **Email:** admit@cabrini.edu. **Website:** http://www.cabrini.edu. **Application deadlines for fall 2007:** Regular decision: Rolling. Early decision: Not offered. Early action: Not offered. Admission can be deferred. **Application fee:** $35. Common application is accepted. **To apply online, go to:** http://www.applyweb.com/aw?cabrini/. **Admissions requirements/recommendations:** High school units required (recommended): English: 4 (4); Mathematics: 3 (4); Science: 3 (3); Foreign language: 2 (2); Social studies: 3 (3); History: 3 (3); Academic electives: (2); Total units: 18 (21). Tests: The college uses SAT or ACT scores in admissions decisions. Either SAT or ACT required. For admission to the fall 2007 entering class, the school will accept: ACT with writing, ACT without writing. Campus visit: Recommended. Admissions interview: Recommended. Off-campus interview: May be arranged. **Factors that count in admissions decisions:** *Academic:* Secondary school record: Considered. Class rank: Considered. Letters of recommendation: Considered. Standardized test scores: Very important. Essay: Considered. *Nonacademic:* Interview: Considered. Extracurricular activities: Considered. Talent/ability: Considered. Character/personal qualities: Considered. Alumni/ae relationship: Considered. Geographical residence: Not considered. State residency: Not considered. Religious affiliation/commitment: Not considered. Minority status: Not considered. Volunteer work: Considered. Work experience: Considered. **Other schools with the greatest overlap in applicants:** La Salle University; Neumann College; St. Joseph's University; Temple University; West Chester University of Pennsylvania. **Admissions statistics for the fall 2005 entering class:** Total applicants: 2,535. Total accepted: 1,648. Freshmen enrolled: 539; 43% were from out of state. Overall acceptance rate: 65%. **Size of waiting list:** 50 applicants; enrolled from waiting list: 15. **Credentials of fall 2005 freshmen:** 8% ranked in the top 10 percent of their high school class; 27% were in the top 25 percent, and 58% were in the top half. (Proportion submitting class standing: 82%.) **Average high school grade point average:** 3.2. **First-year students who submitted SAT scores:** 99%. Scores (25/75 percentile): Verbal: 450-550, Math: 440-540, Combined: 890-1090. **First-year students submitting ACT scores:** 2%. Scores (25/75 percentile): English: N/A, Math: N/A, Composite: N/A.

ACADEMICS

Year founded: 1957. **Academic calendar:** Semester. **Degrees offered:** certificate, bachelor's, post-bachelor's certificate, master's. **Most popular majors:** 32% business, management, marketing, and related support services, 20% education, 13% communication studies/speech communication and rhetoric, 6% visual and performing arts, 4% social sciences. **Major fields of study:** area, ethnic, cultural, and gender studies; biological and biomedical sciences; business, management, marketing, and related support services; communication, journalism, and related programs; computer and information sciences and support services; education; English language and literature/letters; foreign languages, literatures, and linguistics; health professions and related clinical sciences; history; liberal arts and sciences studies, and humanities; mathematics and statistics; parks, recreation, leisure, and fitness studies; philosophy and religious studies; physical sciences; psychology; public administration and social service professions;

social sciences; visual and performing arts. **Areas of required coursework:** arts/fine arts, humanities, computer literacy, mathematics, English (including composition), philosophy, foreign languages, sciences (biological or physical), history, social science, other. **Pre-professional programs:** pre-law, pre-medicine, pre-pharmacy. **Special academic programs (% participation):** accelerated program (10%), cross-registration (5%), distance learning (14%), double major (7%), honors program (15%), independent study (14%), internships (18%), student-designed major (1%), study abroad (5%), teacher certificate program (15%). **Teacher certification offered in:** early childhood, special education, elementary, middle/junior high, secondary. **Cooperative education programs:** business, humanities. **Reserve Officers Training Corps (ROTC):** Army ROTC: Offered at cooperating institution (Valley Forge Military Academy). **Faculty and instruction (2005-2006):** Total instructional faculty: 65 full-time, 172 part-time (49% men; 51% women; 8% minorities). Full-time faculty with Ph.D. or other terminal degree: 77%. Student/faculty ratio: 15/1. Classes of fewer than 20 students: 55%; of 20 to 49 students: 45%; of 50 or more students: 0%. **Advanced Placement and International Baccalaureate credit:** AP tests may be used for: Credit and/or placement. Scores accepted: 3, 4, 5. **Freshmen returning for sophomore year:** 73%. **Graduation rates:** Four-year: 50%; five-year: 59%; six-year: 58%. **Graduate study:** 18% of students pursue further study within one year. Fields in which graduates pursue further study: Master of Business Administration (MBA), 16%; law, 6%; medicine, 1%; education, 32%; arts and sciences, 45%.

COSTS AND FINANCIAL AID

Financial aid office: (610) 902-8420. **Expenses (2006-2007):** Tuition and fees 2006-2007: $25,920; room/board: $9,800. Estimated books and supplies: $960; transportation: $425; personal expenses: $1,125. **Financial aid:** In 2005-2006, 83% of undergraduates applied for financial aid. Of those, 73% were determined to have financial need; 16% had their need fully met. Average financial aid package (proportion receiving): $19,399 (73%). Average amount of gift aid, such as scholarships or grants (proportion receiving): $5,659 (56%). Average amount of self-help aid, such as work study or loans (proportion receiving): $3,919 (60%). Average need-based loan (excluding PLUS or other private loans): $3,919. Among students who received need-based aid, the average percentage of need met: 84%. Among students who received aid based on merit, the average award (and the proportion receiving): $7,154 (9%). The average athletic scholarship (and the proportion receiving): $0 (0%). Average amount of debt of borrowers graduating in 2005: $17,400. Proportion who borrowed: 84%.

CAMPUS LIFE AND EXTRACURRICULAR ACTIVITIES

Campus housing available (% using): coed dorms (65%), women's dorms (22%), apartment for single students (11%), special housing for disabled students, other housing options. Students who live in college-owned, operated, or affiliated housing: 63%. **Student employment:** During the 2005-2006 academic year, 6% of undergraduates worked on campus. Average per-year earnings: $1,200. **Clubs and organizations:** Number of student organizations: 11. Activities include: choral groups, dance, drama/theater, literary magazine, music ensembles, musical theater, radio station, student government, student newspaper, television station, yearbook. Number of fraternities: 0; sororities: 0. Average proportion of students who stay on campus on weekends: 50%. **Sports program (2005-2006):** Member of NCAA III. *Men's intercollegiate varsity sports:* basketball, cross-country, golf, lacrosse, soccer, tennis, track and field (indoor), track and field (outdoor). *Women's intercollegiate varsity sports:* basketball, cross-country, field hockey, lacrosse, soccer, softball, swimming and diving, tennis, track and field (indoor), track and field (outdoor), volleyball.

SERVICES AND FACILITIES

Basic services: nonremedial tutoring, health service, health insurance. **Remedial assistance:** reading, math, writing, study skills. **Counseling services:** minority student, career, personal, academic, psychological, religious. **For learning-disabled students:** School does not offer a structured program with separate admission and additional fees. Total undergraduates in learning-disabled program or receiving services: 130. Services include: remedial math, tape recorders, note-taking services, learning center, other. **Library:** Number of titles: 96,304; number of current serial subscriptions: 20,963. **Information technology resources:** Students are not required to lease or own a computer. Number of campus computers available to all students: 474. School has a wireless network. Proportion of college-owned housing units wired for high-speed internet access: 100%. **Campus safety:** Security services offered: 24-hour foot-and-vehicle patrols, late-night transport/escort service, 24-hour emergency telephones, lighted pathways/sidewalks, student patrols, controlled dormitory access (key, security card, etc).

TRANSFER AND INTERNATIONAL STUDENTS

Transfer students: May apply for admission for the following academic terms: Fall, Spring, Summer. Applicants need a minimum number of credits to apply. For fall 2005: Transfer applications received: 280. Transfer applicants offered admission: 216. Transfer applicants enrolled: 112. **International students:** Number of foreign undergraduates: 10 (1% of student body). Number of countries represented: 7. Minimum TOEFL score required: 500 (paper); 300 (computer).

California University of Pennsylvania

- **Address:** 250 University Avenue, Box 94, California, PA 15419
- **Website:** http://www.cup.edu
- **Public**
- **Enrollment:** 5,273 full-time; 670 part-time

KEY STATS

✔ **U.S News College Ranking:** fourth tier, Universities–Master's (North)
✔ **SAT Score (25th/75th percentile):** 890-1060
✔ **Tuition:** 2005-2006: $6,432 in state, $8,886 out of state

Selectivity: Less selective	**Room/board:** $7,788
Acceptance rate: 78%	**Average debt:** $21,975
Student/faculty ratio: 22/1	**Proportion who borrowed:** 79%

UNDERGRADUATE STUDENT BODY STATS

2005-2006 enrollment: 5,273 full-time; 670 part-time. Men: 48%; women: 52%. **Ethnic makeup:** African American: 5%; Hispanic: 1%; White: 93%; International: 1%.

ADMISSIONS FACTS AND FIGURES

Phone: (724) 938-4404. **Email:** inquiry@cup.edu. **Website:** http://www.cup.edu. **Application deadlines for fall 2007:** Regular decision: Rolling. Early decision: Not offered. Early action: Not offered. Admission can be deferred. **Application fee:** $25. Common application is not accepted. **Admissions requirements/recommendations:** High school units required (recommended): English: 4 (4); Mathematics: 3 (3); Science: 1 (1); Foreign language: (2); Social studies: 2 (2); History: 2 (2); Academic electives: 6 (6); Total units: 19 (21). Tests: The college uses SAT or ACT scores in admissions decisions. SAT required. For admission to the fall 2007 entering class, the school will accept ACT without writing. Campus visit: Recommended. Admissions interview: Recommended. Off-campus interview: May be arranged. **Factors that count in admissions decisions:** *Academic:* Secondary school record: Very important. Class rank: Very important. Letters of recommendation: Considered. Standardized test scores: Very important. Essay: Considered. *Nonacademic:* Interview: Considered. Extracurricular activities: Considered. Talent/ability: Considered. Character/personal qualities: Considered. Alumni/ae relationship: Not considered. Geographical residence: Not considered. State residency: Not considered. Religious affiliation/commitment: Not considered. Minority status: Not considered. Volunteer work: Not considered. Work experience: Considered. **Other schools with the greatest overlap in applicants:** Clarion University of Pennsylvania; Edinboro University of Pennsylvania; Indiana University of Pennsylvania; Pennsylvania State University–University Park; Slippery Rock University of Pennsylvania. **Admissions statistics for the fall 2005 entering class:** Total applicants: 3,385. Total accepted: 2,633. Freshmen enrolled: 1,259; 4% were from out of state. Overall acceptance rate: 78%. **Credentials of fall 2005 freshmen:** 10% ranked in the top 10 percent of their high school class; 23% were in the top 25 percent, and 52% were in the top half. (Proportion submitting class standing: 91%.) **Average high school grade point average:** 3.0. **First-year students who submitted SAT scores:** 93%. Scores (25/75 percentile): Verbal: 450-530; Math: 440-530; Combined: 890-1060. **First-year students submitting ACT scores:** 13%. Scores (25/75 percentile): English: N/A, Math: N/A, Composite: 17-21.

ACADEMICS

Year founded: 1852. **Academic calendar:** Semester. **Degrees offered:** certificate, associate, terminal-associate, bachelor's, post-bachelor's certificate, master's, post-master's certificate. **Most popular majors:** 14% elementary education and teaching, 12% business administration and management, 8% criminal justice/safety studies, 6% education, 6% psychology. **Major fields of study:** biological and biomedical sciences; business, management, marketing, and related support services; communication, journalism, and related programs; computer and information sciences and support services; education; engineering technologies/technicians; English language and literature/letters; foreign languages, literatures, and linguistics; health professions and related clinical sciences; history; liberal arts and sciences studies, and humanities; mathematics and statistics; multi/interdisciplinary studies; natural resources and conservation; parks, recreation, leisure, and fitness studies; philosophy and religious studies; physical sciences; psychology; public administration and social service professions; security and protective services; social sciences; visual and performing arts. **Areas of required coursework:** arts/fine arts, humanities, computer literacy, mathematics, English (including composition), sciences (biological or physical), other. **Pre-professional programs:** pre-law, pre-dentistry, pre-medicine, pre-veterinary science, pre-optometry, pre-pharmacy. **Special academic programs (% participation):** accelerated program (4%), cooperative (work-study plan) program (1%), cross-registration (2%), distance learning (6%), double major (1%), dual enrollment (2%), exchange student program (domestic) (1%), external degree program (0%), honors program (2%), independent study (10%), internships (12%), student-designed major (2%), study abroad (0%), teacher certificate program (15%), weekend college (1%). **Teacher certification offered in:** early childhood, special education, elementary, middle/junior high, secondary. **Cooperative education programs:** business, education, health professions. **Reserve Officers Training Corps (ROTC):** Army ROTC: Offered on campus. **Faculty and instruction (2005-2006):** Total instructional faculty: 289 full-time, 95 part-time (58% men; 42% women; 11% minorities). Full-time faculty with Ph.D. or other terminal degree: 63%. Student/faculty ratio: 22/1. Classes of fewer than 20 students: 26%; of 20 to 49 students: 63%; of 50 or more students: 12%. **Advanced Placement and International Baccalaureate credit:** AP tests may be used for: Credit only. Scores accepted: 3, 4, 5. International Baccalaureate exams may be used for: Credit and/or placement. **Freshmen returning for sophomore year:** 76%. **Graduation rates:** Four-year: 17%; five-year: 39%; six-year: 45%. **Graduate study:** 14% of students pursue further study immediately upon graduation; 16% within one year. Fields in which graduates pursue further study: Master of Business Administration (MBA), 3%; law, 2%; medicine, 1%; dentistry, 1%; engineering, 1%; education, 5%; arts and sciences, 1%.

COSTS AND FINANCIAL AID
Financial aid office: (724) 938-4415. **Expenses (2005-2006):** Tuition and fees 2005-2006: $6,432 in state, $8,886 out of state; room/board: $7,788. Estimated books and supplies: $800; transportation: $780; personal expenses: $1,522. **Financial aid:** Priority filing date for institution's financial aid form: May 1. In 2005-2006, 93% of undergraduates applied for financial aid. Of those, 76% were determined to have financial need; 1% had their need fully met. Average financial aid package (proportion receiving): $7,799 (75%). Average amount of gift aid, such as scholarships or grants (proportion receiving): $4,025 (55%). Average amount of self-help aid, such as work study or loans (proportion receiving): $4,057 (67%). Average need-based loan (excluding PLUS or other private loans): $3,571. Among students who received need-based aid, the average percentage of need met: 90%. Among students who received aid based on merit, the average award (and the proportion receiving): $3,056 (15%). The average athletic scholarship (and the proportion receiving): $4,947 (4%). Average amount of debt of borrowers graduating in 2005: $21,975. Proportion who borrowed: 79%.

CAMPUS LIFE AND EXTRACURRICULAR ACTIVITIES
Campus housing available (% using): coed dorms (100%). Students who live in college-owned, operated, or affiliated housing: 30%. **Clubs and organizations:** Number of student organizations: 83. Activities include: choral groups, concert band, dance, drama/theater, jazz band, literary magazine, marching band, music ensembles, musical theater, opera, radio station, student government, student newspaper, television station, yearbook. Number of fraternities: 7; sororities: 7. Proportion of men in fraternities: 10%; of women in sororities: 10%. Average proportion of students who stay on campus on weekends: 35%. **Sports program (2005-2006):** Member of NCAA II. **Men's intercollegiate varsity sports:** baseball, basketball, cross-country, football, golf, soccer, track and field (indoor), track and field (outdoor). **Women's intercollegiate varsity sports:** basketball, cross-country, golf, soccer, softball, swimming and diving, tennis, track and field (indoor), track and field (outdoor), volleyball.

SERVICES AND FACILITIES
Basic services: nonremedial tutoring, women's center, placement service, health service, other. **Remedial assistance:** reading, math, writing, study skills. **Counseling services:** minority student, career, military, personal, veteran student, academic, older student, psychological, birth control, religious. **For learning-disabled students:** School does not offer a structured

program with separate admission and additional fees. Total undergraduates in learning-disabled program or receiving services: 75. **Library:** Number of titles: 456,718; number of current serial subscriptions: 373. **Information technology resources:** Students are not required to lease or own a computer. Number of campus computers available to all students: 900. School has a wireless network. Approximate number of users that can be accommodated: 1,000. Proportion of college-owned housing units wired for high-speed internet access: 100%. **Campus safety:** Security services offered: 24-hour foot-and-vehicle patrols, late-night transport/escort service, 24-hour emergency telephones, lighted pathways/sidewalks, controlled dormitory access (key, security card, etc).

TRANSFER AND INTERNATIONAL STUDENTS
Transfer students: May apply for admission for the following academic terms: Fall, Spring, Summer. Applicants do not need a minimum number of credits to apply. For fall 2005: Transfer applications received: 1,036. Transfer applicants offered admission: 827. Transfer applicants enrolled: 619. **International students:** Number of foreign undergraduates: 40 (1% of student body). Minimum TOEFL score required: 450 (paper); 133 (computer). Average TOEFL score: 510 (paper).

Carlow University

- **Address:** 3333 Fifth Avenue, Pittsburgh, PA 15213-3165
- **Website:** http://www.carlow.edu
- **Private; Religious affiliation:** Roman Catholic
- **Enrollment:** 1,167 full-time; 456 part-time

KEY STATS
✔ **U.S News College Ranking:** third tier, Universities–Master's (North)
✔ **SAT Score (25th/75th percentile):** 920-1110
✔ **Tuition:** 2006-2007: $18,598

Selectivity: Selective	**Room/board:** $7,284
Acceptance rate: 64%	**Average debt:** $23,691
Student/faculty ratio: 12/1	**Proportion who borrowed:** 79%

UNDERGRADUATE STUDENT BODY STATS
2005-2006 enrollment: 1,167 full-time; 456 part-time. Men: 6%; women: 94%. **Ethnic makeup:** African American: 18%; American-Indian: 1%; Asian American: 1%; Hispanic: 1%; White: 80%. **Religious preference:** Roman Catholic: 42%; Protestant: 9%; Jewish: 1%; Unknown: 12%; Other: 36%.

ADMISSIONS FACTS AND FIGURES
Phone: (412) 578-6059. **Email:** admissions@carlow.edu. **Website:** http://www.carlow.edu. **Application deadlines for fall 2007:** Regular decision: August 1. Early decision: Not offered. Early action: Send application by: September 30; Decision sent by: October 30. Admission can be deferred. **Application fee:** $20. Common application is accepted. **To apply online, go to:** http://www.carlow.edu/admissions/trad_app_form.html. **Admissions requirements/recommendations:** High school units required (recommended): English: 4; Mathematics: 3 (4); Science: 3 (4); Foreign language: 0; Social studies: 2; History: 2; Academic electives: 4; Total units: 18. Tests: The college uses SAT or ACT scores in admissions decisions. Either SAT or ACT required. For admission to the fall 2007 entering class, the school will accept: ACT with writing. Campus visit: Recommended. Admissions interview: Recommended. Off-campus interview: May be arranged. **Factors that count in admissions decisions:** *Academic:* Secondary school record: Very important. Class rank: Important. Letters of recommendation: Considered. Standardized test scores: Important. Essay: Considered. *Nonacademic:* Interview: Considered. Extracurricular activities: Considered. Talent/ability: Considered. Character/personal qualities: Important. Alumni/ae relationship: Considered. Geographical residence: Not considered. State residency: Not considered. Religious affiliation/commitment: Considered. Minority status: Considered. Volunteer work: Considered. Work experience: Considered. **Other schools with the greatest overlap in applicants:** Duquesne University; Indiana University of Pennsylvania; Pennsylvania State University–University Park; Robert Morris University; University of Pittsburgh. **Admissions statistics for the fall 2005 entering class:** Total applicants: 1,076. Total accepted: 684. Freshmen enrolled: 277; 6% were from out of state. Accepted through early-decision or early-action plans: 18%. Overall acceptance rate: 64%. Non-early acceptance rate: 65%. **Credentials of fall 2005 freshmen:** 16% ranked in the top 10 percent of their high school

class; 43% were in the top 25 percent, and 84% were in the top half. (Proportion submitting class standing: 95%.) **Average high school grade point average:** 3.4. **First-year students who submitted SAT scores:** 85%. Scores (25/75 percentile): Verbal: 470-570, Math: 450-540, Combined: 920-1110. **First-year students submitting ACT scores:** 23%. Scores (25/75 percentile): English: N/A, Math: N/A, Composite: 19-25.

ACADEMICS

Year founded: 1929. **Academic calendar:** Semester. **Degrees offered:** bachelor's, master's, post-master's certificate. **Most popular majors:** 19% nursing/registered nurse training (R.N., A.S.N., B.S.N., M.S.N.), 11% business/commerce, 10% elementary education and teaching, 7% communication, journalism, and related programs, 6% psychology. **Major fields of study:** biological and biomedical sciences; business, management, marketing, and related support services; communication, journalism, and related programs; computer and information sciences and support services; education; English language and literature/letters; foreign languages, literatures, and linguistics; health professions and related clinical sciences; history; liberal arts and sciences studies, and humanities; mathematics and statistics; multi/interdisciplinary studies; natural resources and conservation; philosophy and religious studies; physical sciences; psychology; public administration and social service professions; science technologies/technicians; social sciences; theology and religious vocations; visual and performing arts. **Areas of required coursework:** arts/fine arts, humanities, mathematics, English (including composition), philosophy, sciences (biological or physical), history, social science, other. **Pre-professional programs:** pre-law, pre-dentistry, pre-medicine, pre-veterinary science, pre-optometry, pre-pharmacy, other. **Special academic programs (% participation):** accelerated program (25%), cross-registration (15%), distance learning (5%), double major (30%), honors program (10%), independent study (5%), internships (25%), liberal arts/career combination (10%), student-designed major (3%), study abroad (5%), teacher certificate program (20%), weekend college (20%). **Teacher certification offered in:** early childhood, special education, elementary, middle/junior high, secondary. **Cooperative education programs:** art, engineering, health professions, other. **Reserve Officers Training Corps (ROTC):** Army ROTC: Offered at cooperating institution (University of Pittsburgh); Navy ROTC: Offered at cooperating institution (Carnegie Mellon University); Air Force ROTC: Offered at cooperating institution (University of Pittsburgh). **Faculty and instruction (2005-2006):** Total instructional faculty: 79 full-time, 154 part-time (31% men; 69% women; 7% minorities). Full-time faculty with Ph.D. or other terminal degree: 76%. Student/faculty ratio: 12/1. Classes of fewer than 20 students: 84%; of 20 to 49 students: 16%; of 50 or more students: 1%. **Advanced Placement and International Baccalaureate credit:** AP tests may be used for: Credit and/or placement. International Baccalaureate exams may be used for: Credit only. **Freshmen returning for sophomore year:** 70%. **Graduation rates:** Four-year: 35%; five-year: 51%; six-year: 51%. **Graduate study:** 16% of students pursue further study immediately upon graduation; 22% within one year. Fields in which graduates pursue further study: Master of Business Administration (MBA), 8%; education, 20%; arts and sciences, 70%.

COSTS AND FINANCIAL AID

Financial aid office: (412) 578-6058. **Expenses (2006-2007):** Tuition and fees 2006-2007: $18,598; room/board: $7,284. Estimated books and supplies: $700; transportation: $500; personal expenses: $1,000. **Financial aid:** Priority filing date for institution's financial aid form: April 1. In 2005-2006, 95% of undergraduates applied for financial aid. Average financial aid package (proportion receiving): $15,815 (94%). Average amount of gift aid, such as scholarships or grants (proportion receiving): $6,403 (71%). Average amount of self-help aid, such as work study or loans (proportion receiving): $4,775 (74%). Average need-based loan (excluding PLUS or other private loans): $4,382. The average athletic scholarship (and the proportion receiving): $3,380 (6%). Average amount of debt of borrowers graduating in 2005: $23,691. Proportion who borrowed: 79%.

CAMPUS LIFE AND EXTRACURRICULAR ACTIVITIES

Campus housing available (% using): women's dorms (100%). Students who live in college-owned, operated, or affiliated housing: 21%. **Student employment:** During the 2005-2006 academic year, 4% of undergraduates worked on campus. Average per-year earnings: $1,000. **Clubs and organizations:** Number of student organizations: 30. Activities include: choral groups, drama/theater, literary magazine, student government, student newspaper, yearbook. Number of fraternities: 0; sororities: 0. Average proportion of students who stay on campus on weekends: 55%. **Sports program (2005-2006):** Member of NAIA. *Women's intercollegiate varsity sports:* basketball, soccer, softball, tennis, volleyball.

SERVICES AND FACILITIES

Basic services: nonremedial tutoring, other. **Remedial assistance:** reading, math, writing, study skills. **Counseling services:** minority student, career, personal, academic, psychological, religious. **For learning-disabled students:** School does not offer a structured program with separate admission and additional fees. Total undergraduates in learning-disabled program or receiving services: 15. Services include: tape recorders, videotaped classes, note-taking services, oral tests, learning center, readers, extended time for tests, tutors, early syllabus, priority seating, substitution of courses, texts on tape, typist/scribe, exams on tape or computer, other testing accomodations. **Library:** Number of titles: 127,367; number of current serial subscriptions: 362. **Information technology resources:** Students are not required to lease or own a computer. Number of campus computers available to all students: 162. School has a wireless network. Approximate number of users that can be accommodated: 5,000. Proportion of college-owned housing units wired for high-speed internet access: 100%. **Campus safety:** Security services offered: 24-hour foot-and-vehicle patrols, late-night transport/escort service, 24-hour emergency telephones, lighted pathways/sidewalks, controlled dormitory access (key, security card, etc).

TRANSFER AND INTERNATIONAL STUDENTS

Transfer students: May apply for admission for the following academic terms: Fall, Spring, Summer. Applicants do not need a minimum number of credits to apply. For fall 2005: Transfer applications received: 611. Transfer applicants offered admission: 260. Transfer applicants enrolled: 212. **International students:** Number of foreign undergraduates: 1. Number of countries represented: 9. Minimum TOEFL score required: 500 (paper); 173 (computer). Average TOEFL score: 553 (paper).

Carnegie Mellon University

- **Address:** 5000 Forbes Avenue, Pittsburgh, PA 15213
- **Website:** http://www.cmu.edu
- **Private**
- **Enrollment:** 5,384 full-time; 239 part-time

KEY STATS
✔ **U.S News College Ranking:** 21, National Universities
✔ **SAT Score (25th/75th percentile):** 1290-1470
✔ **Tuition:** 2006-2007: $33,448

Selectivity: Most selective	**Room/board:** $8,970
Acceptance rate: 39%	**Average debt:** $26,500
Student/faculty ratio: 10/1	**Proportion who borrowed:** 48%

UNDERGRADUATE STUDENT BODY STATS

2005-2006 enrollment: 5,384 full-time; 239 part-time. Men: 60%; women: 40%. **Ethnic makeup:** African American: 5%; Asian American: 24%; Hispanic: 5%; White: 54%; International: 12%. **Religious preference:** Roman Catholic: 19%; Protestant: 27%; Jewish: 6%; Muslim: 2%; Hindu: 5%; Buddhist: 3%; No preference: 34%.

ADMISSIONS FACTS AND FIGURES

Phone: (412) 268-2082. **Email:** undergraduate-admissions@andrew.cmu.edu. **Website:** http://www.cmu.edu. **Application deadlines for fall 2007:** Regular decision: January 1; decision sent by April 15. Early decision: Send application by: November 15; Decision sent by: December 15. Early action: Not offered. Admission can be deferred. **Application fee:** $60. Common application is accepted. **To apply online, go to:** http://www.cmu.edu/enrollment/admission. **Admissions requirements/recommendations:** High school units required (recommended): English: 4 (4); Mathematics: 4 (4); Science: 3 (3); Foreign language: 2 (2); Social studies: 0 (0); History: 0 (0); Academic electives: 3 (4). Tests: The college uses SAT or ACT scores in admissions decisions. Either SAT or ACT required. For admission to the fall 2007 entering class, the school will accept: ACT with writing. Campus visit: Recommended. Admissions interview: Recommended. Off-campus interview: May be arranged. **Factors that count in admissions decisions:** *Academic:* Secondary school record: Very important. Class rank: Important. Letters of recommendation: Important. Standardized test scores: Important. Essay: Important. *Nonacademic:* Interview: Considered. Extracurricular activities: Considered. Talent/ability: Considered. Character/personal qualities: Considered. Alumni/ae relationship: Considered. Geographical residence: Considered.

State residency: Not considered. Religious affiliation/commitment: Not considered. Minority status: Considered. Volunteer work: Considered. Work experience: Considered. **Other schools with the greatest overlap in applicants:** Columbia University; Cornell University; Massachusetts Institute of Technology; Stanford University; University of Pennsylvania. **Admissions statistics for the fall 2005 entering class:** Total applicants: 15,777. Total accepted: 6,135. Freshmen enrolled: 1,409; 70% were from out of state. Accepted through early-decision or early-action plans: 18%. Overall acceptance rate: 39%. Early-decision acceptance rate: 58%. Non-early acceptance rate: 38%. **Size of waiting list:** 2704 applicants; enrolled from waiting list: 120. **Credentials of fall 2005 freshmen:** 71% ranked in the top 10 percent of their high school class; 94% were in the top 25 percent, and 99% were in the top half. (Proportion submitting class standing: 38%.) **Average high school grade point average:** 3.6. **First-year students who submitted SAT scores:** 98%. Scores (25/75 percentile): Verbal: 610-710, Math: 680-760, Combined: 1290-1470. **First-year students submitting ACT scores:** 17%. Scores (25/75 percentile): English: 27-33, Math: 28-34, Composite: 28-32.

ACADEMICS

Year founded: 1900. **Academic calendar:** Semester. **Degrees offered:** bachelor's, master's, post-master's certificate, doctorate. **Most popular majors:** 12% computer engineering, 11% computer science, 7% mechanical engineering, 5% systems science and theory, 4% finance. **Major fields of study:** architecture and related services; area, ethnic, cultural, and gender studies; biological and biomedical sciences; business, management, marketing, and related support services; communication, journalism, and related programs; computer and information sciences and support services; education; engineering; English language and literature/letters; foreign languages, literatures, and linguistics; history; liberal arts and sciences studies, and humanities; mathematics and statistics; multi/interdisciplinary studies; natural resources and conservation; philosophy and religious studies; physical sciences; psychology; public administration and social service professions; social sciences; visual and performing arts. **Areas of required coursework:** humanities, computer literacy, mathematics, English (including composition), history, social science. **Special academic programs:** cooperative (work-study plan) program, cross-registration, double major, dual enrollment, English as a Second Language (ESL), independent study, internships, student-designed major, study abroad. **Cooperative education programs:** computer science, engineering. **Reserve Officers Training Corps (ROTC):** Army ROTC: Offered on campus; Navy ROTC: Offered on campus; Air Force ROTC: Offered on campus. **Faculty and instruction (2005-2006):** Total instructional faculty: 822 full-time, 173 part-time (71% men; 29% women; 14% minorities). Full-time faculty with Ph.D. or other terminal degree: 98%. Student/faculty ratio: 10/1. Classes of fewer than 20 students: 66%; of 20 to 49 students: 25%; of 50 or more students: 9%. **Advanced Placement and International Baccalaureate credit:** AP tests may be used for: Credit and/or placement. Scores accepted: 4, 5. International Baccalaureate exams may be used for: Credit and/or placement. **Freshmen returning for sophomore year:** 94%. **Graduation rates:** Four-year: 66%; five-year: 83%; six-year: 86%. **Graduate study:** 31% of students pursue further study immediately upon graduation; 31% within one year; 60% within five years. Fields in which graduates pursue further study: Master of Business Administration (MBA), 3%; law, 3%; medicine, 9%; dentistry, 4%; engineering, 18%; education, 6%; arts and sciences, 30%.

COSTS AND FINANCIAL AID

Financial aid office: (412) 268-8186. **Expenses (2006-2007):** Tuition and fees 2006-2007: $33,448; room/board: $8,970. Estimated books and supplies: $945 personal expenses: $1,315. **Financial aid:** Priority filing date for institution's financial aid form: February 15; deadline: May 1. In 2005-2006, 59% of undergraduates applied for financial aid. Of those, 51% were determined to have financial need; 36% had their need fully met. Average financial aid package (proportion receiving): $22,143 (50%). Average amount of gift aid, such as scholarships or grants (proportion receiving): $16,636 (48%). Average amount of self-help aid, such as work study or loans (proportion receiving): $6,703 (48%). Average need-based loan (excluding PLUS or other private loans): $4,853. Among students who received need-based aid, the average percentage of need met: 81%. Among students who received aid based on merit, the average award (and the proportion receiving): $12,318 (9%). The average athletic scholarship (and the proportion receiving): $0 (0%). Average amount of debt of borrowers graduating in 2005: $26,500. Proportion who borrowed: 48%.

CAMPUS LIFE AND EXTRACURRICULAR ACTIVITIES

Campus housing available (% using): coed dorms (50%), women's dorms (2%), men's dorms (9%), sorority housing (2%), fraternity housing (7%),

apartment for single students (25%), special housing for disabled students, other housing options (5%). Students who live in college-owned, operated, or affiliated housing: 67%. **Student employment:** During the 2005-2006 academic year, 30% of undergraduates worked on campus. Average per-year earnings: $1,100. **Clubs and organizations:** Number of student organizations: 225. Activities include: choral groups, concert band, dance, drama/theater, jazz band, literary magazine, marching band, music ensembles, musical theater, opera, pep band, radio station, student government, student newspaper, student film society, symphony orchestra, television station, yearbook. Number of fraternities: 17; sororities: 8. Proportion of men in fraternities: 18%; of women in sororities: 17%. **Sports program (2005-2006):** Member of NCAA III. *Men's intercollegiate varsity sports:* basketball, cheerleading, cross-country, football, golf, soccer, swimming and diving, tennis, track and field (indoor), track and field (outdoor). *Women's intercollegiate varsity sports:* basketball, cheerleading, cross-country, soccer, swimming and diving, tennis, track and field (indoor), track and field (outdoor), volleyball.

SERVICES AND FACILITIES

Basic services: nonremedial tutoring, women's center, placement service, day care, health service, health insurance, other. **Counseling services:** minority student, career, military, personal, academic, psychological, birth control, religious. **For learning-disabled students:** School does not offer a structured program with separate admission and additional fees. Total undergraduates in learning-disabled program or receiving services: 134. Services include: tape recorders, note-taking services, oral tests, learning center, extended time for tests, tutors, priority seating, proofreading services, texts on tape, exams on tape or computer, other. **Library:** Number of titles: 1,066,057; number of current serial subscriptions: 21,370. **Information technology resources:** Students are not required to lease or own a computer. Number of campus computers available to all students: 388. School has a wireless network. Proportion of college-owned housing units wired for high-speed internet access: 100%. **Campus safety:** Security services offered: 24-hour foot-and-vehicle patrols, late-night transport/escort service, 24-hour emergency telephones, lighted pathways/sidewalks, controlled dormitory access (key, security card, etc).

TRANSFER AND INTERNATIONAL STUDENTS

Transfer students: May apply for admission for the following academic terms: Fall, Spring. Applicants do not need a minimum number of credits to apply. For fall 2005: Transfer applications received: 346. Transfer applicants offered admission: 55. Transfer applicants enrolled: 33. **International students:** Number of foreign undergraduates: 635 (12% of student body). Number of countries represented: 99. Minimum TOEFL score required: 600 (paper); 250 (computer).

Cedar Crest College

- **Address:** 100 College Drive, Allentown, PA 18104-6196
- **Website:** http://www.cedarcrest.edu
- **Private**
- **Enrollment:** 947 full-time; 879 part-time

KEY STATS
✔ **U.S News College Ranking:** 11, Comp. Coll.–Bachelor's (North)
✔ **SAT Score (25th/75th percentile):** 940-1170
✔ **Tuition:** 2006-2007: $23,848

Selectivity: Selective	**Room/board:** $8,256
Acceptance rate: 66%	**Average debt:** $22,820
Student/faculty ratio: 11/1	**Proportion who borrowed:** 97%

UNDERGRADUATE STUDENT BODY STATS
2005-2006 enrollment: 947 full-time; 879 part-time. Men: 5%; women: 95%. **Ethnic makeup:** African American: 6%; Asian American: 3%; Hispanic: 6%; White: 85%.

ADMISSIONS FACTS AND FIGURES
Phone: (800) 360-1222. **Email:** cccadmis@cedarcrest.edu. **Website:** http://www.cedarcrest.edu. **Application deadlines for fall 2007:** Regular decision: Rolling. Early decision: Not offered. Early action: Not offered. Admission can be deferred. **Application fee:** $30. Common application is accepted. **Admissions requirements/recommendations:** High school units

required (recommended): English: 4; Mathematics: 3; Science: 2; Foreign language: 2; Social studies: 3; Academic electives: (3); Total units: 16. Tests: The college uses SAT or ACT scores in admissions decisions. Either SAT or ACT required. For admission to the fall 2007 entering class, the school will accept: ACT with writing, ACT without writing. Campus visit: Recommended. Admissions interview: Recommended. Off-campus interview: May be arranged. **Factors that count in admissions decisions: Academic:** Secondary school record: Very important. Class rank: Very important. Letters of recommendation: Very important. Standardized test scores: Very important. Essay: Very important. **Nonacademic:** Interview: Important. Extracurricular activities: Important. Talent/ability: Important. Character/personal qualities: Important. Alumni/ae relationship: Considered. Geographical residence: Not considered. State residency: Not considered. Religious affiliation/commitment: Not considered. Minority status: Not considered. Volunteer work: Considered. Work experience: Considered. **Other schools with the greatest overlap in applicants:** DeSales University; Moravian College; Muhlenberg College; Pennsylvania State University–University Park; Temple University. **Admissions statistics for the fall 2005 entering class:** Total applicants: 1,444. Total accepted: 955. Freshmen enrolled: 204; Overall acceptance rate: 66%. **Credentials of fall 2005 freshmen:** 21% ranked in the top 10 percent of their high school class; 49% were in the top 25 percent, and 89% were in the top half. (Proportion submitting class standing: 79%.) **Average high school grade point average:** 3.1. **First-year students who submitted SAT scores:** 98%. Scores (25/75 percentile): Verbal: 480-600, Math: 460-570, Combined: 940-1170. **First-year students submitting ACT scores:** 12%. Scores (25/75 percentile): English: 20-28, Math: 19-26, Composite: 22-27.

ACADEMICS

Year founded: 1867. **Academic calendar:** Semester. **Degrees offered:** certificate, bachelor's, master's. **Most popular majors:** 20% health professions and related clinical sciences, 17% business, management, marketing, and related support services, 15% biological and biomedical sciences, 14% psychology, 8% education. **Major fields of study:** biological and biomedical sciences; business, management, marketing, and related support services; communication, journalism, and related programs; computer and information sciences and support services; education; engineering; English language and literature/letters; family and consumer sciences/human sciences; foreign languages, literatures, and linguistics; health professions and related clinical sciences; history; liberal arts and sciences studies, and humanities; mathematics and statistics; physical sciences; psychology; public administration and social service professions; security and protective services; social sciences; visual and performing arts. **Areas of required coursework:** arts/fine arts, humanities, computer literacy, mathematics, English (including composition), sciences (biological or physical), history, social science. **Pre-professional programs:** pre-law, pre-dentistry, pre-medicine, pre-veterinary science. **Special academic programs:** accelerated program, cross-registration, distance learning, double major, dual enrollment, English as a Second Language (ESL), honors program, independent study, internships, liberal arts/career combination, student-designed major, study abroad, teacher certificate program, weekend college. **Teacher certification offered in:** early childhood, special education, elementary, secondary. **Reserve Officers Training Corps (ROTC):** Army ROTC: Offered at cooperating institution (Lehigh University). **Faculty and instruction (2005-2006):** Total instructional faculty: 80 full-time, 77 part-time (32% men; 68% women; 4% minorities). Full-time faculty with Ph.D. or other terminal degree: 70%. Student/faculty ratio: 11/1. Classes of fewer than 20 students: 74%; of 20 to 49 students: 23%; of 50 or more students: 4%. **Advanced Placement and International Baccalaureate credit:** AP tests may be used for: Credit and/or placement. Scores accepted: 3, 4, 5. International Baccalaureate exams may be used for: Credit and/or placement. **Freshmen returning for sophomore year:** 85%. **Graduation rates:** Four-year: 58%; five-year: 58%; six-year: 59%. **Graduate study:** 25% of students pursue further study immediately upon graduation; 42% within one year. Fields in which graduates pursue further study: Master of Business Administration (MBA), 4%; law, 1%; medicine, 5%; dentistry, 1%; education, 25%; arts and sciences, 1%; veterinary medicine, 1%.

COSTS AND FINANCIAL AID

Financial aid office: (610) 740-3785. **Expenses (2006-2007):** Tuition and fees 2006-2007: $23,848; room/board: $8,256. Estimated books and supplies: $1,000; transportation: $0; personal expenses: $500. **Financial aid:** In 2005-2006, 97% of undergraduates applied for financial aid. Of those, 88% were determined to have financial need; 16% had their need fully met. Average financial aid package (proportion receiving): $15,960 (88%). Average amount of gift aid, such as scholarships or grants (proportion receiving):

$12,194 (85%). Average amount of self-help aid, such as work study or loans (proportion receiving): $4,843 (78%). Average need-based loan (excluding PLUS or other private loans): $4,110. Among students who received need-based aid, the average percentage of need met: 74%. Among students who received aid based on merit, the average award (and the proportion receiving): $13,887 (11%). The average athletic scholarship (and the proportion receiving): $0 (0%). Average amount of debt of borrowers graduating in 2005: $22,820. Proportion who borrowed: 97%.

CAMPUS LIFE AND EXTRACURRICULAR ACTIVITIES

Campus housing available (% using): women's dorms (100%). Students who live in college-owned, operated, or affiliated housing: 62%. **Student employment:** During the 2005-2006 academic year, 60% of undergraduates worked on campus. Average per-year earnings: $1,500. **Clubs and organizations:** Number of student organizations: 50. Activities include: choral groups, dance, drama/theater, literary magazine, music ensembles, musical theater, radio station, student government, student newspaper, student film society, television station, yearbook. Number of fraternities: 0; sororities: 0. Average proportion of students who stay on campus on weekends: 80%. **Sports program (2005-2006):** Member of NCAA III. **Women's intercollegiate varsity sports:** basketball, cross-country, field hockey, lacrosse, soccer, softball, tennis, volleyball.

SERVICES AND FACILITIES

Basic services: nonremedial tutoring. **Remedial assistance:** reading, math, writing, study skills. **Counseling services:** career, personal, academic, psychological. **For learning-disabled students:** School does not offer a structured program with separate admission and additional fees. Total undergraduates in learning-disabled program or receiving services: 25. Services include: remedial English, tape recorders, other special classes, note-taking services, learning center, extended time for tests, tutors. **Library:** Number of titles: 140,423; number of current serial subscriptions: 1,126. **Information technology resources:** Students are not required to lease or own a computer. Number of campus computers available to all students: 258. School has a wireless network. Approximate number of users that can be accommodated: 60. Proportion of college-owned housing units wired for high-speed internet access: 100%. **Campus safety:** Security services offered: 24-hour foot-and-vehicle patrols, late-night transport/escort service, 24-hour emergency telephones, lighted pathways/sidewalks, controlled dormitory access (key, security card, etc).

TRANSFER AND INTERNATIONAL STUDENTS

Transfer students: May apply for admission for the following academic terms: Fall, Spring, Summer. Applicants do not need a minimum number of credits to apply. For fall 2005: Transfer applications received: 242. Transfer applicants offered admission: 120. Transfer applicants enrolled: 64. **International students:** Number of foreign undergraduates: 4. Number of countries represented: 7. Minimum TOEFL score required: 500 (paper); 222 (computer). Average TOEFL score: 520 (paper).

Chatham College

- **Address:** Woodland Road, Pittsburgh, PA 15232
- **Website:** http://www.chatham.edu
- **Private**
- **Enrollment:** N/A

KEY STATS
✔ **U.S News College Ranking:** third tier, Liberal Arts Colleges
✔ **ACT Score (25th/75th percentile):** 22-27
✔ **Tuition:** 2005-2006: $23,110

Selectivity: More selective	**Room/board:** $7,410
Acceptance rate: 62%	**Average debt:** N/A
Student/faculty ratio: N/A	**Proportion who borrowed:** N/A

Chestnut Hill College

- **Address:** 9601 Germantown Avenue, Philadelphia, PA 19118-2693
- **Website:** http://www.chc.edu
- **Private; Religious affiliation:** Roman Catholic
- **Enrollment:** 802 full-time; 237 part-time

KEY STATS

✔ **U.S News College Ranking:** third tier, Universities–Master's (North)
✔ **SAT Score (25th/75th percentile):** 880-1070
✔ **Tuition:** 2006-2007: $23,600

Selectivity: Less selective	**Room/board:** $7,950
Acceptance rate: 73%	**Average debt:** $28,250
Student/faculty ratio: 9/1	**Proportion who borrowed:** 67%

UNDERGRADUATE STUDENT BODY STATS

2005-2006 enrollment: 802 full-time; 237 part-time. Men: 28%; women: 72%. **Ethnic makeup:** African American: 38%; Asian American: 3%; Hispanic: 6%; White: 53%; International: 1%. **Religious preference:** Protestant: 24%; Jewish: 1%; Muslim: 1%; Unknown: 30%; Roman Catholic: 40%; Other: 4%.

ADMISSIONS FACTS AND FIGURES

Phone: (215) 248-7001. **Email:** chcapply@chc.edu. **Website:** http://www.chc.edu. **Application deadlines for fall 2007:** Regular decision: July 15. Early decision: Not offered. Early action: Not offered. Admission can be deferred. **Application fee:** $35. Common application is accepted. **Admissions requirements/recommendations:** High school units required (recommended): English: 4 (4); Mathematics: 3 (3); Science: 3 (3); Foreign language: 2 (2); Total units: 16 (16). Tests: The college uses SAT or ACT scores in admissions decisions. Either SAT or ACT required. For admission to the fall 2007 entering class, the school will accept: ACT with writing, ACT without writing. Campus visit: Recommended. Admissions interview: Recommended. Off-campus interview: May be arranged. **Factors that count in admissions decisions:** *Academic:* Secondary school record: Very important. Class rank: Important. Letters of recommendation: Important. Standardized test scores: Important. Essay: Very important. *Nonacademic:* Interview: Important. Extracurricular activities: Important. Talent/ability: Considered. Character/personal qualities: Important. Alumni/ae relationship: Considered. Geographical residence: Not considered. State residency: Not considered. Religious affiliation/commitment: Not considered. Minority status: Not considered. Volunteer work: Considered. Work experience: Considered. **Other schools with the greatest overlap in applicants:** Drexel University; La Salle University; Pennsylvania State University–University Park; Temple University; West Chester University of Pennsylvania. **Admissions statistics for the fall 2005 entering class:** Total applicants: 1,255. Total accepted: 921. Freshmen enrolled: 216; 43% were from out of state. Overall acceptance rate: 73%. **Credentials of fall 2005 freshmen:** 13% ranked in the top 10 percent of their high school class; 30% were in the top 25 percent, and 65% were in the top half. (Proportion submitting class standing: 61%.) Average high school grade point average: 3.0. **First-year students who submitted SAT scores:** 96%. Scores (25/75 percentile): Verbal: 450-550, Math: 430-520, Combined: 880-1070. **First-year students submitting ACT scores:** 6%. Scores (25/75 percentile): English: N/A, Math: N/A, Composite: 18-24.

ACADEMICS

Year founded: 1924. **Academic calendar:** Semester. **Degrees offered:** certificate, associate, transfer-associate, bachelor's, post-bachelor's certificate, master's, post-master's certificate, doctorate. **Most popular majors:** 28% business, management, marketing, and related support services, 13% public administration and social service professions, 10% education, 9% psychology, 9% security and protective services. **Major fields of study:** biological and biomedical sciences; business, management, marketing, and related support services; communication, journalism, and related programs; communications technologies/technicians and support services; computer and information sciences and support services; education; English language and literature/letters; family and consumer sciences/human sciences; foreign languages, literatures, and linguistics; health professions and related clinical sciences; history; liberal arts and sciences studies, and humanities; multi/interdisciplinary studies; natural resources and conservation; physical sciences; psychology; public administration and social service professions; security and protective services; social sciences; visual and performing arts.

Areas of required coursework: arts/fine arts, humanities, computer literacy, mathematics, English (including composition), foreign languages, sciences (biological or physical), history, social science, other. **Pre-professional programs:** pre-law, pre-medicine, pre-veterinary science. **Special academic programs:** cooperative (work-study plan) program, cross-registration, double major, dual enrollment, English as a Second Language (ESL), exchange student program (domestic), honors program, independent study, internships, student-designed major, study abroad, teacher certificate program. **Teacher certification offered in:** early childhood, special education, elementary, middle/junior high, secondary. **Cooperative education programs:** business, computer science, humanities, natural science, social/behavioral science, technologies. **Faculty and instruction (2005-2006):** Total instructional faculty: 72 full-time, 183 part-time (40% men; 60% women; 7% minorities). Full-time faculty with Ph.D. or other terminal degree: 83%. Student/faculty ratio: 9/1. Classes of fewer than 20 students: 85%; of 20 to 49 students: 15%; of 50 or more students: 0%. **Advanced Placement and International Baccalaureate credit:** AP tests may be used for: Credit and/or placement. Scores accepted: 3, 4, 5. International Baccalaureate exams may be used for: Credit and/or placement. **Freshmen returning for sophomore year:** 69%. **Graduation rates:** Four-year: 42%; five-year: 44%; six-year: 57%.

COSTS AND FINANCIAL AID

Financial aid office: (215) 248-7182. **Expenses (2006-2007):** Tuition and fees 2006-2007: $23,600; room/board: $7,950. Estimated books and supplies: $1,160; transportation: $920; personal expenses: $1,240. **Financial aid:** Priority filing date for institution's financial aid form: April 15; deadline: April 15. In 2005-2006, 94% of undergraduates applied for financial aid. Of those, 79% were determined to have financial need; 1% had their need fully met. Average financial aid package (proportion receiving): $8,500 (79%). Average amount of gift aid, such as scholarships or grants (proportion receiving): N/A (79%). Average amount of self-help aid, such as work study or loans (proportion receiving): N/A (74%). Among students who received need-based aid, the average percentage of need met: 56%. Among students who received aid based on merit, the average award (and the proportion receiving): $6,000 (11%). The average athletic scholarship (and the proportion receiving): $0 (0%). Average amount of debt of borrowers graduating in 2005: $28,250. Proportion who borrowed: 67%.

CAMPUS LIFE AND EXTRACURRICULAR ACTIVITIES

Campus housing available (% using): coed dorms (35%), women's dorms (50%), other housing options (15%). Students who live in college-owned, operated, or affiliated housing: 70%. **Student employment:** During the 2005-2006 academic year, 15% of undergraduates worked on campus. **Clubs and organizations:** Number of student organizations: 25. Activities include: choral groups, concert band, drama/theater, jazz band, literary magazine, music ensembles, musical theater, student government, student newspaper, yearbook. Number of fraternities: 0; sororities: 0. Average proportion of students who stay on campus on weekends: 30%. **Sports program (2005-2006):** Member of NCAA III. *Men's intercollegiate varsity sports:* basketball, cross-country, golf, soccer, tennis. *Women's intercollegiate varsity sports:* basketball, cross-country, golf, lacrosse, soccer, softball, tennis, volleyball.

SERVICES AND FACILITIES

Basic services: nonremedial tutoring, placement service, health service, health insurance. **Remedial assistance:** math, writing, study skills, other. **Counseling services:** career, personal, academic, psychological, religious. **For learning-disabled students:** School does not offer a structured program with separate admission and additional fees. Services include: remedial math, remedial English, untimed tests, oral tests, readers, extended time for tests, tutors. **Library:** Number of titles: 129,090; number of current serial subscriptions: 1,401. **Information technology resources:** Students are required to lease or own a computer. Number of campus computers available to all students: 65. School has a wireless network. Proportion of college-owned housing units wired for high-speed internet access: 25%. **Campus safety:** Security services offered: 24-hour foot-and-vehicle patrols, late-night transport/escort service, lighted pathways/sidewalks, controlled dormitory access (key, security card, etc).

TRANSFER AND INTERNATIONAL STUDENTS

Transfer students: May apply for admission for the following academic terms: Fall, Spring, Summer. Applicants do not need a minimum number of credits to apply. For fall 2005: Transfer applications received: 223. Transfer applicants offered admission: 100. Transfer applicants enrolled: 42. **International students:** Number of foreign undergraduates: 8 (1% of student body). Number of countries represented: 8. Minimum TOEFL score required: 500 (paper). Average TOEFL score: 500 (paper).

Cheyney University of Pennsylvania

- **Address:** 1837 University Circle, Cheyney, PA 19319
- **Website:** http://www.cheyney.edu
- **Public**
- **Enrollment:** 1,295 full-time; 106 part-time

KEY STATS

✔ **U.S News College Ranking:** fourth tier, Universities–Master's (North)
✔ **SAT Score:** 787
✔ **Tuition:** N/A

Selectivity: Least selective	**Room/board:** N/A
Acceptance rate: 56%	**Average debt:** N/A
Student/faculty ratio: 14/1	**Proportion who borrowed:** N/A

UNDERGRADUATE STUDENT BODY STATS

2005-2006 enrollment: 1,295 full-time; 106 part-time. Men: 46%; women: 54%. **Ethnic makeup:** African American: 94%; Hispanic: 1%; White: 5%; International: 1%.

ADMISSIONS FACTS AND FIGURES

Phone: (610) 399-2275. **Email:** admissions@cheyney.edu. **Website:** http://www.cheyney.edu. **Application deadlines for fall 2007:** Regular decision: Rolling. Early decision: Not offered. Early action: Not offered. Admission can be deferred. **Application fee:** $20. Common application is not accepted. **Admissions requirements/recommendations:** High school units required (recommended): English: 4; Mathematics: 3; Science: 2; Foreign language: 2; History: 2; Total units: 13. Tests: The college uses SAT or ACT scores in admissions decisions. SAT required. Campus visit: Neither required nor recommended. Admissions interview: Neither required nor recommended. Off-campus interview: Not available. **Factors that count in admissions decisions:** *Academic:* Secondary school record: Very important. Class rank: Important. Letters of recommendation: Very important. Standardized test scores: Important. Essay: Important. *Nonacademic:* Interview: Important. Extracurricular activities: Important. Talent/ability: Considered. Character/personal qualities: Not considered. Alumni/ae relationship: Not considered. Geographical residence: Not considered. State residency: Important. Religious affiliation/commitment: Not considered. Minority status: Considered. Volunteer work: Not considered. Work experience: Not considered. **Other schools with the greatest overlap in applicants:** Drexel University; Lincoln University; Pennsylvania State University–University Park; Temple University; West Chester University of Pennsylvania. **Admissions statistics for the fall 2005 entering class:** Total applicants: 2,751. Total accepted: 1,553. Freshmen enrolled: 675; 17% were from out of state. Overall acceptance rate: 56%. **First-year students who submitted SAT scores:** 56%. Scores (25/75 percentile): Verbal: N/A, Math: N/A, Combined: N/A. **First-year students submitting ACT scores:** 3%. Scores (25/75 percentile): English: N/A, Math: N/A, Composite: N/A.

ACADEMICS

Year founded: 1837. **Academic calendar:** Semester. **Degrees offered:** certificate, bachelor's, post-bachelor's certificate, master's. **Most popular majors:** 30% social sciences, 28% business, management, marketing, and related support services, 12% psychology, 6% communication, journalism, and related programs, 6% parks, recreation, leisure, and fitness studies. **Major fields of study:** biological and biomedical sciences; business, management, marketing, and related support services; communication, journalism, and related programs; communications technologies/technicians and support services; computer and information sciences and support services; education; English language and literature/letters; family and consumer sciences/human sciences; foreign languages, literatures, and linguistics; health professions and related clinical sciences; mathematics and statistics; parks, recreation, leisure, and fitness studies; physical sciences; psychology; social sciences; visual and performing arts. **Areas of required coursework:** arts/fine arts, humanities, computer literacy, mathematics, English (including composition), foreign languages, sciences (biological or physical), social science. **Special academic programs:** cooperative (work-study plan) program, cross-registration, distance learning, double major, honors program, independent study, internships, study abroad, teacher certificate program.

Teacher certification offered in: early childhood, special education, elementary, secondary. **Cooperative education programs:** business, computer science, natural science, social/behavioral science. **Reserve Officers Training Corps (ROTC):** Army ROTC: Offered at cooperating institution (West Chester University). **Faculty and instruction (2005-2006):** Total instructional faculty: 103 full-time, 24 part-time (47% men; 53% women; 61% minorities). Full-time faculty with Ph.D. or other terminal degree: 62%. Student/faculty ratio: 14/1. Classes of fewer than 20 students: 40%; of 20 to 49 students: 58%; of 50 or more students: 2%. **Advanced Placement and International Baccalaureate credit:** AP tests may be used for: Placement only. International Baccalaureate exams may be used for: Credit and/or placement. **Freshmen returning for sophomore year:** 60%. **Graduation rates:** Six-year: 32%.

COSTS AND FINANCIAL AID

Financial aid office: (610) 399-2302.

CAMPUS LIFE AND EXTRACURRICULAR ACTIVITIES

Campus housing available: coed dorms, women's dorms, men's dorms, other housing options. Students who live in college-owned, operated, or affiliated housing: 76%. **Student employment:** During the 2005-2006 academic year, 1% of undergraduates worked on campus. Average per-year earnings: $14,000. Activities include: choral groups, drama/theater, marching band, music ensembles, radio station, student government, student newspaper, student film society, yearbook. Number of fraternities: 5; sororities: 4. Proportion of men in fraternities: 5%; of women in sororities: 8%. **Sports program (2005-2006):** Member of NCAA II. *Men's intercollegiate varsity sports:* basketball, cross-country, football, track and field (indoor), track and field (outdoor). *Women's intercollegiate varsity sports:* basketball, bowling, cross-country, tennis, track and field (indoor), track and field (outdoor), volleyball.

SERVICES AND FACILITIES

Basic services: nonremedial tutoring, placement service, day care. **Remedial assistance:** reading, math, study skills. **Counseling services:** career, academic. **Library:** Number of titles: 291,700; number of current serial subscriptions: 485. **Information technology resources:** Students are not required to lease or own a computer. Number of campus computers available to all students: 450. School has a wireless network. Approximate number of users that can be accommodated: 300. Proportion of college-owned housing units wired for high-speed internet access: 100%. **Campus safety:** Security services offered: 24-hour emergency telephones, lighted pathways/sidewalks.

TRANSFER AND INTERNATIONAL STUDENTS

Transfer students: May apply for admission for the following academic terms: Fall, Spring. Applicants do not need a minimum number of credits to apply. For fall 2005: Transfer applications received: 217. Transfer applicants offered admission: 157. Transfer applicants enrolled: 79. **International students:** Number of foreign undergraduates: 7 (1% of student body). Number of countries represented: 6. Minimum TOEFL score required: 500 (paper).

Clarion University of Pennsylvania

- **Address:** 840 Wood Street, Clarion, PA 16214
- **Website:** http://www.clarion.edu
- **Public**
- **Enrollment:** 5,069 full-time; 675 part-time

KEY STATS

✔ **U.S News College Ranking:** third tier, Universities–Master's (North)
✔ **SAT Score (25th/75th percentile):** 850-1060
✔ **Tuition:** 2006-2007: $5,163 in state, $10,266 out of state

Selectivity: Less selective	**Room/board:** $5,546
Acceptance rate: 78%	**Average debt:** $14,791
Student/faculty ratio: 20/1	**Proportion who borrowed:** 83%

UNDERGRADUATE STUDENT BODY STATS

2005-2006 enrollment: 5,069 full-time; 675 part-time. Men: 39%; women: 61%. **Ethnic makeup:** African American: 5%; Asian American: 1%; Hispanic: 1%; White: 92%; International: 1%.

ADMISSIONS FACTS AND FIGURES

Phone: (814) 393-2306. **Email:** admissions@clarion.edu. **Website:** http://www.clarion.edu. **Application deadlines for fall 2007:** Regular decision: Rolling. Early decision: Not offered. Early action: Not offered. Admission can be deferred. **Application fee:** $30. Common application is accepted. **To apply online, go to:** http://www.applyweb.com/aw?clarion. **Admissions requirements/recommendations:** High school units required (recommended): English: 4 (4); Mathematics: 3 (4); Science: 3 (4); Foreign language: 0 (2); Social studies: 3 (4); History: 0 (0); Academic electives: 0 (0); Total units: 13 (19). Tests: The college uses SAT or ACT scores in admissions decisions. Either SAT or ACT required. For admission to the fall 2007 entering class, the school will accept: ACT with writing, ACT without writing. Campus visit: Recommended. Admissions interview: Recommended. Off-campus interview: Not available. **Factors that count in admissions decisions: Academic:** Secondary school record: Very important. Class rank: Very important. Letters of recommendation: Important. Standardized test scores: Very important. Essay: Important. **Nonacademic:** Interview: Considered. Extracurricular activities: Considered. Talent/ability: Considered. Character/personal qualities: Considered. Alumni/ae relationship: Not considered. Geographical residence: Not considered. State residency: Not considered. Religious affiliation/commitment: Not considered. Minority status: Not considered. Volunteer work: Considered. Work experience: Considered. **Other schools with the greatest overlap in applicants:** California University of Pennsylvania; Edinboro University of Pennsylvania; Indiana University of Pennsylvania; Shippensburg University of Pennsylvania; Slippery Rock University of Pennsylvania. **Admissions statistics for the fall 2005 entering class:** Total applicants: 3,346. Total accepted: 2,609. Freshmen enrolled: 1,241; 4% were from out of state. Overall acceptance rate: 78%. **Credentials of fall 2005 freshmen:** 1% ranked in the top 10 percent of their high school class; 24% were in the top 25 percent, and 60% were in the top half. (Proportion submitting class standing: 94%.) **Average high school grade point average:** 3.2. **First-year students who submitted SAT scores:** 90%. Scores (25/75 percentile): Verbal: 430-530, Math: 420-530, Combined: 850-1060.

ACADEMICS

Year founded: 1867. **Academic calendar:** Semester. **Degrees offered:** certificate, associate, bachelor's, master's, post-master's certificate. **Most popular majors:** 28% education, 18% business, management, marketing, and related support services, 10% communication, journalism, and related programs, 5% computer and information sciences and support services, 4% biological and biomedical sciences. **Major fields of study:** biological and biomedical sciences; business, management, marketing, and related support services; communication, journalism, and related programs; computer and information sciences and support services; education; English language and literature/letters; foreign languages, literatures, and linguistics; health professions and related clinical sciences; history; liberal arts and sciences studies, and humanities; library science; mathematics and statistics; multi/interdisciplinary studies; natural resources and conservation; philosophy and religious studies; physical sciences; psychology; social sciences; visual and performing arts. **Areas of required coursework:** arts/fine arts, humanities, computer literacy, mathematics, English (including composition), sciences (biological or physical), social science, other. **Pre-professional programs:** pre-law, pre-dentistry, pre-medicine, pre-theology, pre-veterinary science, pre-optometry, pre-pharmacy, other. **Special academic programs:** accelerated program, cooperative (work-study plan) program, distance learning, double major, dual enrollment, honors program, independent study, internships, liberal arts/career combination, study abroad, teacher certificate program. **Teacher certification offered in:** early childhood, special education, elementary, middle/junior high, secondary. **Cooperative education programs:** engineering, health professions, social/behavioral science. **Reserve Officers Training Corps (ROTC):** Army ROTC: Offered on campus. **Faculty and instruction (2005-2006):** Total instructional faculty: 254 full-time, 50 part-time (54% men; 46% women; 10% minorities). Full-time faculty with Ph.D. or other terminal degree: 84%. Student/faculty ratio: 20/1. Classes of fewer than 20 students: 24%; of 20 to 49 students: 67%; of 50 or more students: 9%. **Advanced Placement and International Baccalaureate credit:** AP tests may be used for: Credit only. Scores accepted: 3, 4, 5. **Freshmen returning for sophomore year:** 74%. **Graduation rates:** Four-year: 23%; five-year: 48%; six-year: 52%. **Graduate study:** 13% of students pursue further study immediately upon graduation; 13% within one year. Fields in which graduates pursue further study: Master of Business Administration (MBA), 6%; law, 4%; education, 23%; arts and sciences, 12%.

COSTS AND FINANCIAL AID

Financial aid office: (814) 393-2315. **Expenses (2005-2006):** Tuition and fees 2005-2006: $6,447 in state, $11,355 out of state; room/board: $5,246. Estimated books and supplies: $850; transportation: $800; personal expenses: $2,235. **Financial aid:** Priority filing date for institution's financial aid form: April 15; deadline: April 15. In 2005-2006, 84% of undergraduates applied for financial aid. Of those, 71% were determined to have financial need; 16% had their need fully met. Average financial aid package (proportion receiving): $7,008 (69%). Average amount of gift aid, such as scholarships or grants (proportion receiving): $4,535 (55%). Average amount of self-help aid, such as work study or loans (proportion receiving): $3,503 (62%). Average need-based loan (excluding PLUS or other private loans): $3,457. Among students who received need-based aid, the average percentage of need met: 71%. Among students who received aid based on merit, the average award (and the proportion receiving): $1,659 (5%). The average athletic scholarship (and the proportion receiving): $2,818 (4%). Average amount of debt of borrowers graduating in 2005: $14,791. Proportion who borrowed: 83%.

CAMPUS LIFE AND EXTRACURRICULAR ACTIVITIES

Campus housing available (% using): coed dorms (50%), women's dorms (20%), men's dorms (3%), sorority housing, fraternity housing, apartment for single students (27%), other housing options. Students who live in college-owned, operated, or affiliated housing: 80%. **Student employment:** During the 2005-2006 academic year, 14% of undergraduates worked on campus. Average per-year earnings: $1,500. **Clubs and organizations:** Number of student organizations: 150. Activities include: choral groups, concert band, dance, drama/theater, jazz band, marching band, music ensembles, musical theater, pep band, radio station, student government, student newspaper, television station. Number of fraternities: 5; sororities: 8. Proportion of men in fraternities: 5%; of women in sororities: 9%. Average proportion of students who stay on campus on weekends: 50%. **Sports program (2005-2006):** Member of NCAA II. **Men's intercollegiate varsity sports:** baseball, basketball, cross-country, football, golf, swimming and diving, track and field (indoor), track and field (outdoor), wrestling. **Women's intercollegiate varsity sports:** basketball, cross-country, soccer, softball, swimming and diving, tennis, track and field (indoor), track and field (outdoor), volleyball.

SERVICES AND FACILITIES

Basic services: nonremedial tutoring, women's center, placement service, day care, health service, health insurance. **Remedial assistance:** reading, math, writing, study skills. **Counseling services:** minority student, career, military, personal, veteran student, academic, older student, psychological, birth control, religious. **For learning-disabled students:** School does not offer a structured program with separate admission and additional fees. Total undergraduates in learning-disabled program or receiving services: 150. Services include: remedial math, remedial English, reading machines, remedial reading, tape recorders, note-taking services, oral tests, learning center, readers, extended time for tests, tutors, early syllabus, priority seating, substitution of courses, texts on tape, typist/scribe, exams on tape or computer, other testing accomodations, other. **Library:** Number of titles: 439,810; number of current serial subscriptions: 20,684. **Information technology resources:** Students are not required to lease or own a computer. Number of campus computers available to all students: 1,143. School has a wireless network. Approximate number of users that can be accommodated: 300. Proportion of college-owned housing units wired for high-speed internet access: 100%. **Campus safety:** Security services offered: 24-hour foot-and-vehicle patrols, late-night transport/escort service, 24-hour emergency telephones, lighted pathways/sidewalks, student patrols, controlled dormitory access (key, security card, etc).

TRANSFER AND INTERNATIONAL STUDENTS

Transfer students: May apply for admission for the following academic terms: Fall, Winter, Spring, Summer. Applicants need a minimum number of credits to apply. For fall 2005: Transfer applications received: 795. Transfer applicants offered admission: 640. Transfer applicants enrolled: 334. **International students:** Number of foreign undergraduates: 41 (1% of student body). Number of countries represented: 23. Minimum TOEFL score required: 500 (paper); 173 (computer).

College Misericordia

- **Address:** 301 Lake Street, Dallas, PA 18612-1098
- **Website:** http://www.misericordia.edu/
- **Private; Religious affiliation:** Roman Catholic
- **Enrollment:** 1,428 full-time; 644 part-time

KEY STATS

- ✔ **U.S News College Ranking:** 56, Universities–Master's (North)
- ✔ **SAT Score (25th/75th percentile):** 900-1090
- ✔ **Tuition:** 2006-2007: $20,860

Selectivity: Less selective	**Room/board:** $8,640
Acceptance rate: 81%	**Average debt:** $18,013
Student/faculty ratio: 12/1	**Proportion who borrowed:** 87%

UNDERGRADUATE STUDENT BODY STATS

2005-2006 enrollment: 1,428 full-time; 644 part-time. Men: 26%; women: 74%. **Ethnic makeup:** African American: 2%; Asian American: 1%; Hispanic: 2%; White: 96%. **Religious preference:** Protestant: 26%; No preference: 6%; Roman Catholic: 59%; Other: 9%.

ADMISSIONS FACTS AND FIGURES

Phone: (570) 674-6264. **Email:** admiss@misericordia.edu. **Website:** http://www.misericordia.edu/. **Application deadlines for fall 2007:** Regular decision: Rolling. Early decision: Not offered. Early action: Not offered. Admission can be deferred. **Application fee:** $25. Common application is accepted. **To apply online, go to:** https://www.misericordia.edu/apply/app. **Admissions requirements/recommendations:** High school units required (recommended): English: 4; Mathematics: 4; Science: 4; Social studies: 4; Total units: 16. Tests: The college uses SAT or ACT scores in admissions decisions. Either SAT or ACT required. For admission to the fall 2007 entering class, the school will accept: ACT with writing, ACT without writing. Campus visit: Recommended. Admissions interview: Recommended. Off-campus interview: May be arranged. **Factors that count in admissions decisions:** *Academic:* Secondary school record: Very important. Class rank: Important. Letters of recommendation: Considered. Standardized test scores: Important. Essay: Considered. *Nonacademic:* Interview: Important. Extracurricular activities: Important. Talent/ability: Not considered. Character/personal qualities: Very important. Alumni/ae relationship: Not considered. Geographical residence: Not considered. State residency: Not considered. Religious affiliation/commitment: Not considered. Minority status: Considered. Volunteer work: Important. Work experience: Considered. **Other schools with the greatest overlap in applicants:** Bloomsburg University of Pennsylvania; King's College; Pennsylvania State University–University Park; University of Scranton; Wilkes University. **Admissions statistics for the fall 2005 entering class:** Total applicants: 1,071. Total accepted: 865. Freshmen enrolled: 335; 26% were from out of state. Overall acceptance rate: 81%. **Credentials of fall 2005 freshmen:** 11% ranked in the top 10 percent of their high school class; 40% were in the top 25 percent, and 72% were in the top half. (Proportion submitting class standing: 93%.) **Average high school grade point average:** 3.1. **First-year students who submitted SAT scores:** 90%. Scores (25/75 percentile): Verbal: 450-540, Math: 450-550, Combined: 900-1090. **First-year students submitting ACT scores:** 3%. Scores (25/75 percentile): English: 19-24, Math: 16-19, Composite: 19-23.

ACADEMICS

Year founded: 1924. **Academic calendar:** Semester. **Degrees offered:** certificate, bachelor's, post-bachelor's certificate, master's, post-master's certificate, doctorate. **Most popular majors:** 20% nursing, 16% business administration and management, 13% health professions and related clinical sciences, 10% elementary education and teaching, 5% psychology. **Major fields of study:** biological and biomedical sciences; business, management, marketing, and related support services; communication, journalism, and related programs; computer and information sciences and support services; education; English language and literature/letters; health professions and related clinical sciences; history; liberal arts and sciences studies, and humanities; mathematics and statistics; multi/interdisciplinary studies; parks, recreation, leisure, and fitness studies; philosophy and religious studies; physical sciences; psychology; public administration and social service professions. **Areas of required coursework:** arts/fine arts, humanities, computer literacy, mathematics, English (including composition), philosophy, sciences (biological or physical), history, social science, other. **Pre-profes-**

sional programs: pre-law, pre-dentistry, pre-medicine, pre-veterinary science, pre-optometry. **Special academic programs:** accelerated program, cross-registration, distance learning, double major, dual enrollment, honors program, independent study, internships, student-designed major, study abroad, teacher certificate program, weekend college. **Teacher certification offered in:** early childhood, special education, elementary, secondary. **Reserve Officers Training Corps (ROTC):** Army ROTC: Offered at cooperating institution (Kings College); Air Force ROTC: Offered at cooperating institution (Wilkes University). **Faculty and instruction (2005-2006):** Total instructional faculty: 90 full-time, 168 part-time (45% men; 55% women; 2% minorities). Full-time faculty with Ph.D. or other terminal degree: 80%. Student/faculty ratio: 12/1. Classes of fewer than 20 students: 61%; of 20 to 49 students: 39%; of 50 or more students: 0%. **Advanced Placement and International Baccalaureate credit:** AP tests may be used for: Credit only. Scores accepted: 3, 4, 5. International Baccalaureate exams may be used for: Credit only. **Freshmen returning for sophomore year:** 83%. **Graduation rates:** Four-year: 66%; five-year: 72%; six-year: 71%. **Graduate study:** 24% of students pursue further study within one year. Fields in which graduates pursue further study: Master of Business Administration (MBA), 10%; education, 7%; arts and sciences, 44%.

COSTS AND FINANCIAL AID

Financial aid office: (570) 674-6280. **Expenses (2006-2007):** Tuition and fees 2006-2007: $20,860; room/board: $8,640. Estimated books and supplies: $800; transportation: $500; personal expenses: $500. **Financial aid:** Priority filing date for institution's financial aid form: March 1; deadline: May 1. In 2005-2006, 91% of undergraduates applied for financial aid. Of those, 81% were determined to have financial need; 23% had their need fully met. Average financial aid package (proportion receiving): $13,722 (81%). Average amount of gift aid, such as scholarships or grants (proportion receiving): $9,527 (80%). Average amount of self-help aid, such as work study or loans (proportion receiving): $1,400 (68%). Average need-based loan (excluding PLUS or other private loans): $6,244. Among students who received need-based aid, the average percentage of need met: 75%. Among students who received aid based on merit, the average award (and the proportion receiving): $6,008 (10%). The average athletic scholarship (and the proportion receiving): $0 (0%). Average amount of debt of borrowers graduating in 2005: $18,013. Proportion who borrowed: 87%.

CAMPUS LIFE AND EXTRACURRICULAR ACTIVITIES

Campus housing available (% using): coed dorms (96%), other housing options (4%). Students who live in college-owned, operated, or affiliated housing: 39%. **Student employment:** During the 2005-2006 academic year, 5% of undergraduates worked on campus. Average per-year earnings: $500. **Clubs and organizations:** Number of student organizations: 25. Activities include: choral groups, dance, drama/theater, jazz band, literary magazine, music ensembles, radio station, student government, student newspaper, television station. Number of fraternities: 0; sororities: 0. Average proportion of students who stay on campus on weekends: 50%. **Sports program (2005-2006):** Member of NCAA III. *Men's intercollegiate varsity sports:* baseball, basketball, cross-country, golf, lacrosse, soccer, swimming and diving, track and field (indoor), track and field (outdoor). *Women's intercollegiate varsity sports:* basketball, cheerleading, cross-country, field hockey, lacrosse, soccer, softball, swimming and diving, tennis, track and field (indoor), track and field (outdoor), volleyball.

SERVICES AND FACILITIES

Basic services: nonremedial tutoring, placement service, health service. **Remedial assistance:** study skills. **Counseling services:** minority student, career, personal, veteran student, academic, older student, psychological, religious. **For learning-disabled students:** School does not offer a structured program with separate admission and additional fees. Total undergraduates in learning-disabled program or receiving services: 55. Services include: reading machines, tape recorders, untimed tests, note-taking services, oral tests, learning center, readers, extended time for tests, tutors, priority seating, proofreading services, texts on tape, typist/scribe, other testing accommodations, other. **Library:** Number of titles: 73,528; number of current serial subscriptions: 590. **Information technology resources:** Students are not required to lease or own a computer. Number of campus computers available to all students: 100. School has a wireless network. Approximate number of users that can be accommodated: 100. Proportion of college-owned housing units wired for high-speed internet access: 100%. **Campus safety:** Security services offered: 24-hour foot-and-vehicle patrols, late-night transport/escort service, 24-hour emergency telephones, lighted pathways/sidewalks, controlled dormitory access (key, security card, etc.).

TRANSFER AND INTERNATIONAL STUDENTS

Transfer students: May apply for admission for the following academic terms: Fall, Spring, Summer. Applicants need a minimum number of credits to apply. For fall 2005: Transfer applications received: 263. Transfer applicants offered admission: 173. Transfer applicants enrolled: 112.
International students: Number of foreign undergraduates: 3. Number of countries represented: 2. Minimum TOEFL score required: 500 (paper); 175 (computer). Average TOEFL score: 500 (paper).

Curtis Institute of Music

- **Address:** 1726 Locust Street, Philadelphia, PA 19103
- **Website:** http://www.curtis.edu
- **Private**
- **Enrollment:** N/A

KEY STATS
✔ **U.S News College Ranking:** Unranked Specialty School–Fine Arts
✔ **SAT or ACT Score (25th/75th percentile):** N/A
✔ **Tuition:** N/A

Selectivity: Least selective	**Room/board:** N/A
Acceptance rate: N/A	**Average debt:** N/A
Student/faculty ratio: N/A	**Proportion who borrowed:** N/A

Delaware Valley College

- **Address:** 700 E. Butler Avenue, Doylestown, PA 18901
- **Website:** http://www.devalcol.edu
- **Private**
- **Enrollment:** 1,600 full-time; 394 part-time

KEY STATS
✔ **U.S News College Ranking:** 24, Comp. Coll.–Bachelor's (North)
✔ **SAT Score (25th/75th percentile):** 930-1130
✔ **Tuition:** 2006-2007: $22,800

Selectivity: Selective	**Room/board:** $8,536
Acceptance rate: 79%	**Average debt:** $17,482
Student/faculty ratio: 15/1	**Proportion who borrowed:** 68%

UNDERGRADUATE STUDENT BODY STATS

2005-2006 enrollment: 1,600 full-time; 394 part-time. Men: 46%; women: 54%. **Ethnic makeup:** African American: 4%; Asian American: 1%; Hispanic: 1%; White: 94%. **Religious preference:** Roman Catholic: 30%; Protestant: 41%; Jewish: 2%; No preference: 20%; Unknown: 3%.

ADMISSIONS FACTS AND FIGURES

Phone: (215) 489-2211. **Email:** admitme@devalcol.edu. **Website:** http://www.devalcol.edu. **Application deadlines for fall 2007:** Regular decision: Rolling. Early decision: Not offered. Early action: Not offered. Admission can be deferred. **Application fee:** $35. Common application is accepted. **Admissions requirements/recommendations:** High school units required (recommended): English: 3; Mathematics: 2; Science: 2; Social studies: 2; Academic electives: 6; Total units: 15. Tests: The college uses SAT or ACT scores in admissions decisions. Either SAT or ACT required. For admission to the fall 2007 entering class, the school will accept: ACT without writing. Campus visit: Recommended. Admissions interview: Recommended. Off-campus interview: May be arranged. **Factors that count in admissions decisions:** *Academic:* Secondary school record: Important. Class rank: Important. Letters of recommendation: Considered. Standardized test scores: Very important. Essay: Considered. *Nonacademic:* Interview: Important. Extracurricular activities: Considered. Talent/ability: Considered. Character/personal qualities: Considered. Alumni/ae relationship: Considered. Geographical residence: Not considered. State residency: Not considered. Religious affiliation/commitment: Not considered. Minority status: Not considered. Volunteer work: Considered. Work experience: Considered. **Other schools with the greatest overlap in applicants:** DeSales University; Pennsylvania State University–University Park; Temple University; West Chester University of Pennsylvania; Wilkes University. **Admissions statistics for the fall 2005 entering class:** Total applicants: 1,476.

Total accepted: 1,164. Freshmen enrolled: 451; 44% were from out of state. Overall acceptance rate: 79%. **Credentials of fall 2005 freshmen:** 15% ranked in the top 10 percent of their high school class; 41% were in the top 25 percent, and 75% were in the top half. (Proportion submitting class standing: 84%.) **Average high school grade point average:** 3.5. **First-year students who submitted SAT scores:** 96%. Scores (25/75 percentile): Verbal: 460-570, Math: 470-560, Combined: 930-1130. **First-year students submitting ACT scores:** 4%. Scores (25/75 percentile): English: 18-24, Math: 17-22, Composite: 20-25.

ACADEMICS

Year founded: 1896. **Academic calendar:** Semester. **Degrees offered:** certificate, associate, bachelor's, post-bachelor's certificate, master's. **Most popular majors:** 40% agriculture, agriculture operations, and related sciences, 30% business, management, marketing, and related support services, 8% security and protective services, 7% computer and information sciences and support services, 6% biological and biomedical sciences. **Major fields of study:** agriculture, agriculture operations, and related sciences; biological and biomedical sciences; business, management, marketing, and related support services; computer and information sciences and support services; education; English language and literature/letters; mathematics and statistics; natural resources and conservation; physical sciences; security and protective services. **Areas of required coursework:** arts/fine arts, humanities, computer literacy, mathematics, English (including composition), philosophy, sciences (biological or physical), history, social science, other. **Pre-professional programs:** pre-law, pre-dentistry, pre-medicine, pre-veterinary science, pre-optometry, pre-pharmacy. **Special academic programs (% participation):** cooperative (work-study plan) program (100%), cross-registration (17%), distance learning (11%), double major (18%), honors program (19%), independent study (36%), internships (100%), liberal arts/career combination, study abroad (9%), teacher certificate program (14%), weekend college (2%). **Teacher certification offered in:** vo-tech, middle/junior high, secondary. **Cooperative education programs:** agriculture, business, computer science, social/behavioral science. **Faculty and instruction (2005-2006):** Total instructional faculty: 78 full-time, 114 part-time (66% men; 34% women; 6% minorities). Full-time faculty with Ph.D. or other terminal degree: 62%. Student/faculty ratio: 15/1. Classes of fewer than 20 students: 57%; of 20 to 49 students: 40%; of 50 or more students: 3%. **Advanced Placement and International Baccalaureate credit:** AP tests may be used for: Credit and/or placement. Scores accepted: 2, 3. International Baccalaureate exams may be used for: Credit and/or placement. **Freshmen returning for sophomore year:** 72%. **Graduation rates:** Six-year: 52%. **Graduate study:** 23% of students pursue further study immediately upon graduation; 23% within one year.

COSTS AND FINANCIAL AID

Financial aid office: (215) 489-2272. **Expenses (2006-2007):** Tuition and fees 2006-2007: $22,800; room/board: $8,536. Estimated books and supplies: $800; transportation: $720; personal expenses: $1,200. **Financial aid:** Priority filing date for institution's financial aid form: April 1. In 2005-2006, 82% of undergraduates applied for financial aid. Of those, 80% were determined to have financial need; 68% had their need fully met. Average financial aid package (proportion receiving): $17,760 (78%). Average amount of gift aid, such as scholarships or grants (proportion receiving): $13,075 (64%). Average amount of self-help aid, such as work study or loans (proportion receiving): $4,685 (60%). Average need-based loan (excluding PLUS or other private loans): $3,709. Among students who received need-based aid, the average percentage of need met: 85%. Among students who received aid based on merit, the average award (and the proportion receiving): $8,302 (22%). The average athletic scholarship (and the proportion receiving): $0 (0%). Average amount of debt of borrowers graduating in 2005: $17,482. Proportion who borrowed: 68%.

CAMPUS LIFE AND EXTRACURRICULAR ACTIVITIES

Campus housing available (% using): coed dorms (77%), women's dorms (11%), men's dorms (10%). Students who live in college-owned, operated, or affiliated housing: 55%. **Student employment:** During the 2005-2006 academic year, 25% of undergraduates worked on campus. Average per-year earnings: $1,800. **Clubs and organizations:** Number of student organizations: 49. Activities include: choral groups, concert band, drama/theater, literary magazine, music ensembles, radio station, student government, student newspaper, yearbook. Number of fraternities: 5; sororities: 3. Proportion of men in fraternities: 4%; of women in sororities: 5%. Average proportion of students who stay on campus on weekends: 55%. **Sports program (2005-2006):** Member of NCAA III. *Men's intercollegiate varsity sports:* baseball, basketball, cross-country, football, golf, soccer, track and field (indoor), track and field (outdoor), wrestling. *Women's intercollegiate* *varsity sports:* basketball, cheerleading, cross-country, field hockey, soccer, softball, track and field (indoor), track and field (outdoor), volleyball.

SERVICES AND FACILITIES
Basic services: nonremedial tutoring, placement service, health service, health insurance. **Remedial assistance:** reading, math, writing, study skills. **Counseling services:** career, personal, veteran student, academic, older student, psychological. **For learning-disabled students:** School does not offer a structured program with separate admission and additional fees. Services include: reading machines, note-taking services, extended time for tests. **Library:** Number of titles: 50,630; number of current serial subscriptions: 790. **Information technology resources:** Students are not required to lease or own a computer. Number of campus computers available to all students: 150. School has a wireless network. Approximate number of users that can be accommodated: 500. Proportion of college-owned housing units wired for high-speed internet access: 100%. **Campus safety:** Security services offered: 24-hour foot-and-vehicle patrols, late-night transport/escort service, lighted pathways/sidewalks, controlled dormitory access (key, security card, etc).

TRANSFER AND INTERNATIONAL STUDENTS
Transfer students: May apply for admission for the following academic terms: Fall, Spring. Applicants need a minimum number of credits to apply. For fall 2005: Transfer applications received: 243. Transfer applicants offered admission: 157. Transfer applicants enrolled: 86. **International students:** Number of foreign undergraduates: 2. Minimum TOEFL score required: 500 (paper); 173 (computer).

DeSales University

- **Address:** 2755 Station Avenue, Center Valley, PA 18034-9568
- **Website:** http://www.desales.edu
- **Private; Religious affiliation:** Roman Catholic
- **Enrollment:** 1,561 full-time; 723 part-time

KEY STATS
✔ **U.S News College Ranking:** 79, Universities–Master's (North)
✔ **SAT Score (25th/75th percentile):** 980-1180
✔ **Tuition:** 2006-2007: $22,000

Selectivity: Selective	**Room/board:** $8,250
Acceptance rate: 79%	**Average debt:** $22,690
Student/faculty ratio: 17/1	**Proportion who borrowed:** 74%

UNDERGRADUATE STUDENT BODY STATS
2005-2006 enrollment: 1,561 full-time; 723 part-time. Men: 42%; women: 58%. **Ethnic makeup:** African American: 1%; Hispanic: 1%; White: 97%. **Religious preference:** Roman Catholic: 71%; Protestant: 15%; No preference: 8%; Other: 4%.

ADMISSIONS FACTS AND FIGURES
Phone: (610) 282-4443. **Email:** admiss@desales.edu. **Website:** http://www.desales.edu. **Application deadlines for fall 2007:** Regular decision: August 1. Early decision: Not offered. Early action: Not offered. Admission can be deferred. **Application fee:** $30. Common application is accepted. **Admissions requirements/recommendations:** High school units required (recommended): English: 4 (4); Mathematics: 3 (4); Science: 2 (2); Foreign language: 2 (2); Social studies: 3 (4); Total units: 16 (18). Tests: The college uses SAT or ACT scores in admissions decisions. Either SAT or ACT required. Campus visit: Recommended. Admissions interview: Recommended. Off-campus interview: May be arranged. **Factors that count in admissions decisions:** *Academic:* Secondary school record: Very important. Class rank: Very important. Letters of recommendation: Very important. Standardized test scores: Very important. Essay: Considered. *Nonacademic:* Interview: Important. Extracurricular activities: Important. Talent/ability: Important. Character/personal qualities: Important. Alumni/ae relationship: Not considered. Geographical residence: Considered. State residency: Considered. Religious affiliation/commitment: Not considered. Minority status: Considered. Volunteer work: Considered. Work experience: Considered. **Other schools with the greatest overlap in applicants:** King's College; Moravian College; Pennsylvania State University–University Park; St. Joseph's University; University of Scranton. **Admissions statistics for the fall 2005 entering class:** Total applicants: 1,728.

Total accepted: 1,365. Freshmen enrolled: 434; 30% were from out of state. Overall acceptance rate: 79%. **Credentials of fall 2005 freshmen:** 20% ranked in the top 10 percent of their high school class; 48% were in the top 25 percent, and 79% were in the top half. (Proportion submitting class standing: 68%.) **Average high school grade point average:** 3.3. **First-year students who submitted SAT scores:** 96%. Scores (25/75 percentile): Verbal: 490-590, Math: 490-590, Combined: 980-1180. **First-year students submitting ACT scores:** 4%. Scores (25/75 percentile): English: N/A, Math: N/A, Composite: 19-24.

ACADEMICS
Year founded: 1964. **Academic calendar:** Semester. **Degrees offered:** certificate, bachelor's, post-bachelor's certificate, master's, post-master's certificate. **Most popular majors:** 30% business, management, marketing, and related support services, 16% visual and performing arts, 12% health professions and related clinical sciences, 8% security and protective services, 6% computer and information sciences and support services. **Major fields of study:** biological and biomedical sciences; business, management, marketing, and related support services; communication, journalism, and related programs; computer and information sciences and support services; education; English language and literature/letters; family and consumer sciences/human sciences; foreign languages, literatures, and linguistics; health professions and related clinical sciences; history; legal professions and studies; liberal arts and sciences studies, and humanities; mathematics and statistics; parks, recreation, leisure, and fitness studies; philosophy and religious studies; physical sciences; psychology; security and protective services; social sciences; theology and religious vocations; visual and performing arts. **Areas of required coursework:** arts/fine arts, humanities, computer literacy, mathematics, English (including composition), philosophy, foreign languages, sciences (biological or physical), history, social science. **Pre-professional programs:** pre-law, pre-dentistry, pre-medicine, pre-theology, pre-veterinary science, pre-optometry, pre-pharmacy. **Special academic programs:** accelerated program, cross-registration, distance learning, double major, external degree program, honors program, independent study, internships, liberal arts/career combination, study abroad, teacher certificate program, weekend college. **Teacher certification offered in:** early childhood, special education, elementary, middle/junior high, secondary. **Reserve Officers Training Corps (ROTC):** Army ROTC: Offered at cooperating institution (Lehigh University). **Faculty and instruction (2005-2006):** Total instructional faculty: 92 full-time, 71 part-time (55% men; 45% women; 2% minorities). Full-time faculty with Ph.D. or other terminal degree: 72%. Student/faculty ratio: 17/1. Classes of fewer than 20 students: 44%; of 20 to 49 students: 53%; of 50 or more students: 3%. **Advanced Placement and International Baccalaureate credit:** AP tests may be used for: Credit and/or placement. Scores accepted: 3, 4, 5. **Freshmen returning for sophomore year:** 85%. **Graduation rates:** Four-year: 62%; five-year: 69%; six-year: 64%. **Graduate study:** 29% of students pursue further study within one year. Fields in which graduates pursue further study: Master of Business Administration (MBA), 17%; law, 8%; education, 4%; arts and sciences, 46%.

COSTS AND FINANCIAL AID
Financial aid office: (610) 282-1100. **Expenses (2006-2007):** Tuition and fees 2006-2007: $22,000; room/board: $8,250. Estimated books and supplies: $900 personal expenses: $1,800. **Financial aid:** Priority filing date for institution's financial aid form: February 1; deadline: May 1. In 2005-2006, 82% of undergraduates applied for financial aid. Of those, 69% were determined to have financial need; 41% had their need fully met. Average financial aid package (proportion receiving): $14,278 (69%). Average amount of gift aid, such as scholarships or grants (proportion receiving): $11,122 (68%). Average amount of self-help aid, such as work study or loans (proportion receiving): $3,908 (58%). Average need-based loan (excluding PLUS or other private loans): $3,525. Among students who received need-based aid, the average percentage of need met: 75%. Among students who received aid based on merit, the average award (and the proportion receiving): $6,118 (28%). The average athletic scholarship (and the proportion receiving): $0 (0%). Average amount of debt of borrowers graduating in 2005: $22,690. Proportion who borrowed: 74%.

CAMPUS LIFE AND EXTRACURRICULAR ACTIVITIES
Campus housing available (% using): coed dorms (40%), women's dorms (26%), men's dorms (18%), other housing options (16%). Students who live in college-owned, operated, or affiliated housing: 71%. **Student employment:** During the 2005-2006 academic year, 45% of undergraduates worked on campus. Average per-year earnings: $725. **Clubs and organizations:** Number of student organizations: 31. Activities include: choral groups, dance,

drama/theater, literary magazine, radio station, student government, student newspaper, student film society, yearbook. Number of fraternities: 0; sororities: 0. **Sports program (2005-2006):** Member of NCAA III. *Men's intercollegiate varsity sports:* baseball, basketball, cross-country, golf, lacrosse, soccer, tennis, track and field (indoor), track and field (outdoor). *Women's intercollegiate varsity sports:* basketball, cross-country, field hockey, soccer, softball, tennis, track and field (indoor), track and field (outdoor), volleyball.

SERVICES AND FACILITIES

Basic services: nonremedial tutoring, placement service, health service, health insurance. **Remedial assistance:** reading, math, writing, study skills. **Counseling services:** career, personal, academic, older student, religious. **For learning-disabled students:** School does not offer a structured program with separate admission and additional fees. Total undergraduates in learning-disabled program or receiving services: 92. Services include: remedial English, reading machines, remedial reading, tape recorders, untimed tests, note-taking services, oral tests, learning center, readers, extended time for tests, tutors, priority registration, priority seating, texts on tape, typist/scribe, exams on tape or computer, other testing accomodations, other. **Library:** Number of titles: 145,329; number of current serial subscriptions: 12,541. **Information technology resources:** Students are not required to lease or own a computer. Number of campus computers available to all students: 150. School has a wireless network. Approximate number of users that can be accommodated: 500. Proportion of college-owned housing units wired for high-speed internet access: 100%. **Campus safety:** Security services offered: 24-hour foot-and-vehicle patrols, late-night transport/escort service, 24-hour emergency telephones, lighted pathways/sidewalks, controlled dormitory access (key, security card, etc.).

TRANSFER AND INTERNATIONAL STUDENTS

Transfer students: May apply for admission for the following academic terms: Fall, Spring. Applicants need a minimum number of credits to apply. For fall 2005: Transfer applications received: 204. Transfer applicants offered admission: 108. Transfer applicants enrolled: 51. **International students:** Number of foreign undergraduates: 1. Number of countries represented: 3. Minimum TOEFL score required: 550 (paper); 213 (computer). Average TOEFL score: 550 (paper).

Dickinson College

- **Address:** PO Box 1773, Carlisle, PA 17013-2896
- **Website:** http://www.dickinson.edu
- **Private**
- **Enrollment:** 2,311 full-time; 41 part-time

KEY STATS

- ✔ **U.S News College Ranking:** 41, Liberal Arts Colleges
- ✔ **SAT Score (25th/75th percentile):** 1200-1380
- ✔ **Tuition:** 2006-2007: $33,804

Selectivity: More selective	**Room/board:** $8,480
Acceptance rate: 49%	**Average debt:** $20,982
Student/faculty ratio: 12/1	**Proportion who borrowed:** 62%

UNDERGRADUATE STUDENT BODY STATS

2005-2006 enrollment: 2,311 full-time; 41 part-time. Men: 44%; women: 56%. **Ethnic makeup:** African American: 4%; Asian American: 4%; Hispanic: 4%; White: 82%; International: 5%. **Religious preference:** Roman Catholic: 29%; Protestant: 31%; Jewish: 10%; Muslim: 1%; Hindu: 1%; Buddhist: 1%; No preference: 24%.

ADMISSIONS FACTS AND FIGURES

Phone: (800) 644-1773. **Email:** admit@dickinson.edu. **Website:** http://www.dickinson.edu. **Application deadlines for fall 2007:** Regular decision: February 1; decision sent by March 31. Early decision: Send application by: November 15; Decision sent by: December 15. Early action: Send application by: December 1; Decision sent by: January 31. Admission can be deferred. **Application fee:** $60. Common application is accepted. **To apply online, go to:** http://www.dickinson.edu/admit. **Admissions requirements/recommendations:** High school units required (recommended): English: 4; Mathematics: 3; Science: 3; Foreign language: 2 (3); Social studies: 2; Academic electives: 2; Total units: 16. Tests: The college

uses SAT or ACT scores in admissions decisions. Neither SAT nor ACT required. For admission to the fall 2007 entering class, the school will accept: ACT with writing, ACT without writing. Campus visit: Recommended. Admissions interview: Recommended. Off-campus interview: May be arranged. **Factors that count in admissions decisions:** *Academic:* Secondary school record: Very important. Class rank: Important. Letters of recommendation: Important. Standardized test scores: Important. Essay: Considered. *Nonacademic:* Interview: Considered. Extracurricular activities: Very important. Talent/ability: Very important. Character/personal qualities: Considered. Alumni/ae relationship: Important. Geographical residence: Considered. State residency: Considered. Religious affiliation/commitment: Not considered. Minority status: Considered. Volunteer work: Very important. Work experience: Important. **Other schools with the greatest overlap in applicants:** Bucknell University; Franklin and Marshall College; Gettysburg College; Hamilton College; Lafayette College. **Admissions statistics for the fall 2005 entering class:** Total applicants: 4,784. Total accepted: 2,359. Freshmen enrolled: 648; 75% were from out of state. Accepted through early-decision or early-action plans: 62%. Overall acceptance rate: 49%. Early-decision acceptance rate: 74%. Non-early acceptance rate: 45%. **Size of waiting list:** 278 applicants; enrolled from waiting list: 20. **Credentials of fall 2005 freshmen:** 52% ranked in the top 10 percent of their high school class; 81% were in the top 25 percent, and 98% were in the top half. (Proportion submitting class standing: 39%.) **First-year students who submitted SAT scores:** 70%. Scores (25/75 percentile): Verbal: 600-700, Math: 600-680, Combined: 1200-1380. **First-year students submitting ACT scores:** 14%. Scores (25/75 percentile): English: N/A, Math: N/A, Composite: 26-30.

ACADEMICS

Year founded: 1783. **Academic calendar:** Semester. **Degrees offered:** bachelor's. **Most popular majors:** 11% foreign languages and literatures, 9% biology/biological sciences, 9% psychology, 8% political science and government, 7% English language and literature. **Major fields of study:** area, ethnic, cultural, and gender studies; biological and biomedical sciences; business, management, marketing, and related support services; computer and information sciences and support services; engineering; English language and literature/letters; foreign languages, literatures, and linguistics; history; legal professions and studies; mathematics and statistics; multi/interdisciplinary studies; natural resources and conservation; philosophy and religious studies; physical sciences; psychology; public administration and social service professions; social sciences; visual and performing arts. **Areas of required coursework:** humanities, foreign languages, sciences (biological or physical), social science, other. **Pre-professional programs:** pre-law, pre-dentistry, pre-medicine, pre-theology, pre-veterinary science, pre-optometry, pre-pharmacy. **Special academic programs:** accelerated program, cross-registration, double major, English as a Second Language (ESL), exchange student program (domestic), independent study, internships, liberal arts/career combination, student-designed major, study abroad, teacher certificate program. **Teacher certification offered in:** secondary. **Reserve Officers Training Corps (ROTC):** Army ROTC: Offered on campus. **Faculty and instruction (2005-2006):** Total instructional faculty: 175 full-time, 34 part-time (55% men; 45% women; 10% minorities). Full-time faculty with Ph.D. or other terminal degree: 94%. Student/faculty ratio: 12/1. Classes of fewer than 20 students: 68%; of 20 to 49 students: 31%; of 50 or more students: 0%. **Advanced Placement and International Baccalaureate credit:** AP tests may be used for: Credit and/or placement. Scores accepted: 3, 4. International Baccalaureate exams may be used for: Credit and/or placement. **Freshmen returning for sophomore year:** 90%. **Graduation rates:** Four-year: 81%; five-year: 84%; six-year: 84%. **Graduate study:** 24% of students pursue further study immediately upon graduation; 37% within one year; 52% within five years. Fields in which graduates pursue further study: Master of Business Administration (MBA), 5%; law, 17%; medicine, 6%; theology (or the seminary), 4%; education, 15%; arts and sciences, 33%; veterinary medicine, 1%.

COSTS AND FINANCIAL AID

Financial aid office: (717) 245-1308. **Expenses (2006-2007):** Tuition and fees 2006-2007: $33,804; room/board: $8,480. Estimated books and supplies: $1,000; transportation: $310; personal expenses: $1,190. **Financial aid:** Priority filing date for institution's financial aid form: November 15; deadline: February 1. In 2005-2006, 58% of undergraduates applied for financial aid. Of those, 50% were determined to have financial need; 71% had their need fully met. Average financial aid package (proportion receiving): $27,496 (49%). Average amount of gift aid, such as scholarships or grants (proportion receiving): $20,818 (47%). Average amount of self-help aid, such as work study or loans (proportion receiving): $6,600 (47%). Average need-based loan (excluding PLUS or other private loans): $5,224. Among students who received need-based aid, the average percentage of need met: 96%. Among students who received aid based on merit, the average award (and the proportion receiving): $12,318 (12%). The average athletic scholarship (and the proportion receiving): $0 (0%). Average amount of debt of borrowers graduating in 2005: $20,982. Proportion who borrowed: 62%.

CAMPUS LIFE AND EXTRACURRICULAR ACTIVITIES
Campus housing available: coed dorms, sorority housing, fraternity housing, apartment for single students, special housing for disabled students, other housing options. Students who live in college-owned, operated, or affiliated housing: 92%. **Student employment:** During the 2005-2006 academic year, 30% of undergraduates worked on campus. Average per-year earnings: $1,018. **Clubs and organizations:** Number of student organizations: 120. Activities include: choral groups, concert band, dance, drama/theater, jazz band, literary magazine, music ensembles, musical theater, radio station, student government, student newspaper, student film society, symphony orchestra, yearbook. Number of fraternities: 6; sororities: 4. Proportion of men in fraternities: 19%; of women in sororities: 24%. Average proportion of students who stay on campus on weekends: 85%. **Sports program (2005-2006):** Member of NCAA III. **Men's intercollegiate varsity sports:** baseball, basketball, cross-country, football, golf, lacrosse, soccer, swimming and diving, tennis, track and field (indoor), track and field (outdoor). **Women's intercollegiate varsity sports:** basketball, cross-country, field hockey, golf, lacrosse, soccer, softball, swimming and diving, tennis, track and field (indoor), track and field (outdoor), volleyball.

SERVICES AND FACILITIES
Basic services: nonremedial tutoring, women's center, placement service, day care, health service, health insurance, other. **Counseling services:** minority student, career, personal, veteran student, academic, older student, psychological, birth control, religious. **For learning-disabled students:** School does not offer a structured program with separate admission and additional fees. Total undergraduates in learning-disabled program or receiving services: 159. Services include: tape recorders, untimed tests, note-taking services, oral tests, readers, tutors, other. **Library:** Number of titles: 536,776; number of current serial subscriptions: 2,846. **Information technology resources:** Students are not required to lease or own a computer. Number of campus computers available to all students: 581. School has a wireless network. Approximate number of users that can be accommodated: 350. Proportion of college-owned housing units wired for high-speed internet access: 100%. **Campus safety:** Security services offered: 24-hour foot-and-vehicle patrols, late-night transport/escort service, 24-hour emergency telephones, lighted pathways/sidewalks, student patrols, controlled dormitory access (key, security card, etc).

TRANSFER AND INTERNATIONAL STUDENTS
Transfer students: May apply for admission for the following academic terms: Fall, Spring. Applicants need a minimum number of credits to apply. For fall 2005: Transfer applications received: 107. Transfer applicants offered admission: 16. Transfer applicants enrolled: 10. **International students:** Number of foreign undergraduates: 107 (5% of student body). Number of countries represented: 40. Minimum TOEFL score required: 600 (paper); 250 (computer). Average TOEFL score: 620 (paper).

Drexel University

- **Address:** 3141 Chestnut Street, Philadelphia, PA 19104-2875
- **Website:** http://www.drexel.edu
- **Private**
- **Enrollment:** 8,318 full-time; 2,196 part-time

KEY STATS
✔ **U.S News College Ranking:** 112, National Universities
✔ **SAT Score (25th/75th percentile):** 1080-1290
✔ **Tuition:** 2006-2007: $25,450

Selectivity: More selective	**Room/board:** $12,015
Acceptance rate: 82%	**Average debt:** $25,347
Student/faculty ratio: 10/1	**Proportion who borrowed:** 85%

UNDERGRADUATE STUDENT BODY STATS
2005-2006 enrollment: 8,318 full-time; 2,196 part-time. Men: 57%; women: 43%. **Ethnic makeup:** African American: 11%; Asian American: 11%; Hispanic: 3%; White: 69%; International: 6%.

ADMISSIONS FACTS AND FIGURES
Phone: (800) 237-3935. **Email:** enroll@drexel.edu. **Website:** http://www.drexel.edu. **Application deadlines for fall 2007:** Regular decision: March 1. Early decision: Not offered. Early action: Not offered. Admission can be deferred. **Application fee:** $50. Common application is accepted. **To apply online, go to:** http://www.drexel.edu/em/apply/. **Admissions requirements/recommendations:** High school units required (recommended): Mathematics: 3; Science: 1; Foreign language: (1). Tests: The college uses SAT or ACT scores in admissions decisions. Either SAT or ACT required. For admission to the fall 2007 entering class, the school will accept: ACT with writing, ACT without writing. Campus visit: Recommended. Admissions interview: Recommended. Off-campus interview: May be arranged. **Factors that count in admissions decisions:** *Academic:* Secondary school record: Very important. Class rank: Very important. Letters of recommendation: Important. Standardized test scores: Very important. Essay: Very important. *Nonacademic:* Interview: Important. Extracurricular activities: Important. Talent/ability: Important. Character/personal qualities: Important. Alumni/ae relationship: Considered. Geographical residence: Not considered. State residency: Not considered. Religious affiliation/commitment: Not considered. Minority status: Not considered. Volunteer work: Considered. Work experience: Considered. **Admissions statistics for the fall 2005 entering class:** Total applicants: 12,093. Total accepted: 9,946. Freshmen enrolled: 2,476; 51% were from out of state. Overall acceptance rate: 82%. **Size of waiting list:** 891 applicants; enrolled from waiting list: 379. **Credentials of fall 2005 freshmen:** 30% ranked in the top 10 percent of their high school class; 59% were in the top 25 percent, and 86% were in the top half. (Proportion submitting class standing: 61%.) **Average high school grade point average:** 3.5. **First-year students who submitted SAT scores:** 94%. Scores (25/75 percentile): Verbal: 530-630, Math: 550-660, Combined: 1080-1290.

ACADEMICS
Year founded: 1891. **Academic calendar:** Quarter. **Degrees offered:** certificate, associate, bachelor's, post-bachelor's certificate, master's, post-master's certificate, first professional, doctorate. **Most popular majors:** 25% business/commerce, 9% information science/studies, 9% nursing/registered nurse training (R.N., A.S.N., B.S.N., M.S.N.), 4% computer science, 4% electrical, electronics, and communications engineering. **Major fields of study:** architecture and related services; area, ethnic, cultural, and gender studies; business, management, marketing, and related support services; computer and information sciences and support services; construction trades; education; engineering; English language and literature/letters; health professions and related clinical sciences; history; liberal arts and sciences studies, and humanities; mathematics and statistics; multi/interdisciplinary studies; natural resources and conservation; parks, recreation, leisure, and fitness studies; personal and culinary services; physical sciences; psychology; security and protective services; social sciences; visual and performing arts. **Areas of required coursework:** humanities, computer literacy, mathematics, English (including composition), sciences (biological or physical), history. **Pre-professional programs:** pre-medicine, other. **Special academic programs (% participation):** accelerated program (2%), cooperative (work-study plan) program (95%), distance learning, double major (1%), dual enrollment, English as a Second Language (ESL) (6%), honors program (12%), independent study, student-designed major, study abroad, teacher certificate program (2%), weekend college. **Teacher certification offered in:** elementary, middle/junior high, secondary. **Cooperative education programs:** art, business, computer science, education, engineering, health professions, humanities, natural science, social/behavioral science, technologies, other. **Reserve Officers Training Corps (ROTC):** Army ROTC: Offered on campus; Navy ROTC: Offered at cooperating institution (University of Pennsylvania); Air Force ROTC: Offered at cooperating institution (St. Joseph's University). **Faculty and instruction (2005-2006):** Total instructional faculty: 723 full-time, 690 part-time (59% men; 41% women; 13% minorities). Student/faculty ratio: 10/1. Classes of fewer than 20 students: 55%; of 20 to 49 students: 38%; of 50 or more students: 8%. **Advanced Placement and International Baccalaureate credit:** AP tests may be used for: Credit and/or placement. Scores accepted: 4, 5. International Baccalaureate exams may be used for: Credit and/or placement. **Freshmen returning for sophomore year:** 82%. **Graduation rates:** Four-year: 14%; five-year: 54%; six-year: 60%. **Graduate study:** 13% of students pursue further study within one year; 45% within five years. Fields in which graduates pur-

sue further study: Master of Business Administration (MBA), 25%; law, 2%; medicine, 5%; engineering, 35%; education, 5%; arts and sciences, 20%; veterinary medicine, 2%.

COSTS AND FINANCIAL AID

Financial aid office: (215) 895-2537. **Expenses (2006-2007):** Tuition and fees 2006-2007: $25,450; room/board: $12,015. Estimated books and supplies: $1,575; transportation: $625; personal expenses: $2,500. **Financial aid:** In 2005-2006, 86% of undergraduates applied for financial aid. Of those, 64% were determined to have financial need; 11% had their need fully met. Average financial aid package (proportion receiving): $15,076 (63%). Average amount of gift aid, such as scholarships or grants (proportion receiving): $4,672 (26%). Average amount of self-help aid, such as work study or loans (proportion receiving): $5,071 (54%). Average need-based loan (excluding PLUS or other private loans): $4,299. Among students who received need-based aid, the average percentage of need met: 59%. Among students who received aid based on merit, the average award (and the proportion receiving): $9,206 (19%). The average athletic scholarship (and the proportion receiving): $17,163 (2%). Average amount of debt of borrowers graduating in 2005: $25,347. Proportion who borrowed: 85%.

CAMPUS LIFE AND EXTRACURRICULAR ACTIVITIES

Campus housing available (% using): coed dorms (95%), sorority housing (3%), fraternity housing (1%), special housing for disabled students (0%), special housing for international students (1%). Students who live in college-owned, operated, or affiliated housing: 25%. **Student employment:** During the 2005-2006 academic year, 8% of undergraduates worked on campus. **Clubs and organizations:** Number of student organizations: 135. Activities include: choral groups, concert band, dance, drama/theater, jazz band, literary magazine, music ensembles, musical theater, pep band, radio station, student government, student newspaper, student film society, television station, yearbook. Number of fraternities: 12; sororities: 11. Proportion of men in fraternities: 5%; of women in sororities: 5%. Average proportion of students who stay on campus on weekends: 50%. **Sports program (2005-2006):** Member of NCAA I. *Men's intercollegiate varsity sports:* basketball, crew, golf, lacrosse, soccer, swimming and diving, tennis, wrestling. *Women's intercollegiate varsity sports:* basketball, crew, field hockey, lacrosse, soccer, softball, swimming and diving, tennis.

SERVICES AND FACILITIES

Basic services: nonremedial tutoring, women's center, placement service, day care, health service, health insurance. **Remedial assistance:** reading, math, writing, study skills. **Counseling services:** minority student, career, personal, academic, older student, psychological, other. **For learning-disabled students:** School does not offer a structured program with separate admission and additional fees. Total undergraduates in learning-disabled program or receiving services: 275. Services include: reading machines, tape recorders, diagnostic testing service, note-taking services, oral tests, learning center, readers, extended time for tests, tutors, early syllabus, priority registration, priority seating, substitution of courses, texts on tape, typist/scribe, exams on tape or computer, other testing accomodations. **Library:** Number of titles: 570,335; number of current serial subscriptions: 8,321. **Information technology resources:** Students are required to lease or own a computer. Number of campus computers available to all students: 3,000. School has a wireless network. Approximate number of users that can be accommodated: 20,000. Proportion of college-owned housing units wired for high-speed internet access: 100%. **Campus safety:** Security services offered: 24-hour foot-and-vehicle patrols, late-night transport/escort service, 24-hour emergency telephones, lighted pathways/sidewalks, controlled dormitory access (key, security card, etc).

TRANSFER AND INTERNATIONAL STUDENTS

Transfer students: May apply for admission for the following academic terms: Fall, Winter, Spring, Summer. Applicants need a minimum number of credits to apply. For fall 2005: Transfer applications received: 2,815. Transfer applicants offered admission: 2,128. Transfer applicants enrolled: 905. **International students:** Number of foreign undergraduates: 502 (6% of student body). Number of countries represented: 74. Minimum TOEFL score required: 550 (paper); 213 (computer). Average TOEFL score: 570 (paper).

Duquesne University

- **Address:** 600 Forbes Avenue, Pittsburgh, PA 15282
- **Website:** http://www.duq.edu
- **Private; Religious affiliation:** Roman Catholic
- **Enrollment:** 5,323 full-time; 327 part-time

KEY STATS

✔ **U.S News College Ranking:** third tier, National Universities
✔ **SAT Score (25th/75th percentile):** 1020-1230
✔ **Tuition:** 2006-2007: $22,665

Selectivity: Selective	**Room/board:** $8,296
Acceptance rate: 80%	**Average debt:** $21,493
Student/faculty ratio: 15/1	**Proportion who borrowed:** 78%

UNDERGRADUATE STUDENT BODY STATS

2005-2006 enrollment: 5,323 full-time; 327 part-time. Men: 41%; women: 59%. **Ethnic makeup:** African American: 4%; Asian American: 2%; Hispanic: 1%; White: 91%; International: 2%.

ADMISSIONS FACTS AND FIGURES

Phone: (412) 396-6222. **Email:** admissions@duq.edu. **Website:** http://www.duq.edu. **Application deadlines for fall 2007:** Regular decision: July 1. Early decision: Send application by: November 1; Decision sent by: December 15. Early action: Send application by: December 1; Decision sent by: January 15. Admission can be deferred. **Application fee:** $50. Common application is accepted. **To apply online, go to:** http://www2.duq.edu/admissions/applications. **Admissions requirements/recommendations:** High school units required (recommended): English: 4; Mathematics: 2; Science: 2; Foreign language: 2; Social studies: 2; Academic electives: 4; Total units: 16. Tests: The college uses SAT or ACT scores in admissions decisions. Either SAT or ACT required. For admission to the fall 2007 entering class, the school will accept: ACT with writing. Campus visit: Recommended. Admissions interview: Recommended. Off-campus interview: Not available. **Factors that count in admissions decisions:** *Academic:* Secondary school record: Very important. Class rank: Important. Letters of recommendation: Very important. Standardized test scores: Very important. Essay: Very important. *Nonacademic:* Interview: Important. Extracurricular activities: Important. Talent/ability: Important. Character/personal qualities: Important. Alumni/ae relationship: Considered. Geographical residence: Not considered. State residency: Not considered. Religious affiliation/commitment: Not considered. Minority status: Considered. Volunteer work: Important. Work experience: Considered. **Other schools with the greatest overlap in applicants:** Gannon University; Pennsylvania State University–University Park; St. Vincent College; University of Pittsburgh; West Virginia University. **Admissions statistics for the fall 2005 entering class:** Total applicants: 4,740. Total accepted: 3,789. Freshmen enrolled: 1,328; 18% were from out of state. Accepted through early-decision or early-action plans: 21%. Overall acceptance rate: 80%. Non-early acceptance rate: 84%. **Credentials of fall 2005 freshmen:** 28% ranked in the top 10 percent of their high school class; 58% were in the top 25 percent, and 88% were in the top half. (Proportion submitting class standing: 81%.) **Average high school grade point average:** 3.6. **First-year students who submitted SAT scores:** 95%. Scores (25/75 percentile): Verbal: 510-610, Math: 510-620, Combined: 1020-1230. **First-year students submitting ACT scores:** 25%. Scores (25/75 percentile): English: 21-27, Math: 21-27, Composite: 21-26.

ACADEMICS

Year founded: 1878. **Academic calendar:** Semester. **Degrees offered:** bachelor's, post-bachelor's certificate, master's, post-master's certificate, first professional, doctorate. **Most popular majors:** 26% business, management, marketing, and related support services, 17% health professions and related clinical sciences, 10% education, 7% communication, journalism, and related programs, 6% liberal arts and sciences studies, and humanities. **Major fields of study:** biological and biomedical sciences; business, management, marketing, and related support services; communication, journalism, and related programs; computer and information sciences and support services; education; English language and literature/letters; foreign languages, literatures, and linguistics; health professions and related clinical sciences; history; liberal arts and sciences studies, and humanities; mathematics and statistics; natural resources and conservation; philosophy and religious studies; physical sciences; psychology; social sciences; theology and religious vocations; visual and performing arts. **Areas of required coursework:**

arts/fine arts, humanities, computer literacy, mathematics, English (including composition), philosophy, foreign languages, sciences (biological or physical), history, social science, other. **Pre-professional programs:** pre-law, pre-dentistry, pre-medicine, pre-veterinary science, pre-optometry, pre-pharmacy, other. **Special academic programs (% participation):** accelerated program, cross-registration (6.9%), distance learning (17.5%), double major (24.8%), dual enrollment, English as a Second Language (ESL) (.7%), exchange student program (domestic) (.6%), honors program (7.1%), independent study (3.8%), internships (14%), liberal arts/career combination (2.7%), student-designed major (.2%), study abroad (1.1%), teacher certificate program (9.9%), weekend college (8.7%). **Teacher certification offered in:** early childhood, special education, elementary, secondary. **Reserve Officers Training Corps (ROTC):** Army ROTC: Offered on campus; Navy ROTC: Offered at cooperating institution (Carnegie Mellon University); Air Force ROTC: Offered at cooperating institution (University of Pittsburgh). **Faculty and instruction (2005-2006):** Total instructional faculty: 429 full-time, 446 part-time (58% men; 42% women; 5% minorities). Full-time faculty with Ph.D. or other terminal degree: 88%. Student/faculty ratio: 15/1. Classes of fewer than 20 students: 47%; of 20 to 49 students: 46%; of 50 or more students: 7%. **Advanced Placement and International Baccalaureate credit:** AP tests may be used for: Credit only. Scores accepted: 3, 4, 5. International Baccalaureate exams may be used for: Credit only. **Freshmen returning for sophomore year:** 88%. **Graduation rates:** Four-year: 54%; five-year: 66%; six-year: 68%. **Graduate study:** 5% of students pursue further study immediately upon graduation; 15% within five years. Fields in which graduates pursue further study: Master of Business Administration (MBA), 25%; law, 25%; medicine, 5%; dentistry, 5%; education, 25%; arts and sciences, 15%.

COSTS AND FINANCIAL AID

Financial aid office: (412) 396-6607. **Expenses (2006-2007):** Tuition and fees 2006-2007: $22,665; room/board: $8,296. **Financial aid:** In 2005-2006, 77% of undergraduates applied for financial aid. Of those, 67% were determined to have financial need; 58% had their need fully met. Average financial aid package (proportion receiving): $15,919 (66%). Average amount of gift aid, such as scholarships or grants (proportion receiving): $11,275 (56%). Average amount of self-help aid, such as work study or loans (proportion receiving): $5,974 (56%). Average need-based loan (excluding PLUS or other private loans): $4,257. Among students who received need-based aid, the average percentage of need met: 87%. Among students who received aid based on merit, the average award (and the proportion receiving): $8,077 (21%). The average athletic scholarship (and the proportion receiving): $12,274 (6%). Average amount of debt of borrowers graduating in 2005: $21,493. Proportion who borrowed: 78%.

CAMPUS LIFE AND EXTRACURRICULAR ACTIVITIES

Campus housing available (% using): coed dorms (74%), sorority housing (6%), fraternity housing (4%), apartments for married students (0%), apartment for single students (15%), special housing for disabled students (1%). Students who live in college-owned, operated, or affiliated housing: 55%. **Student employment:** During the 2005-2006 academic year, 5% of undergraduates worked on campus. Average per-year earnings: $1,200. **Clubs and organizations:** Number of student organizations: 130. Activities include: choral groups, concert band, dance, drama/theater, jazz band, literary magazine, marching band, music ensembles, musical theater, opera, pep band, radio station, student government, student newspaper, student film society, symphony orchestra, television station, yearbook. Number of fraternities: 9; sororities: 8. Proportion of men in fraternities: 16%; of women in sororities: 20%. Average proportion of students who stay on campus on weekends: 60%. **Sports program (2005-2006):** Member of NCAA I. *Men's intercollegiate varsity sports:* baseball, basketball, cross-country, football, golf, soccer, swimming and diving, tennis, track and field (outdoor), wrestling. *Women's intercollegiate varsity sports:* basketball, cross-country, lacrosse, rowing, soccer, swimming and diving, tennis, track and field (indoor), track and field (outdoor), volleyball.

SERVICES AND FACILITIES

Basic services: nonremedial tutoring, placement service, day care, health service, health insurance, other. **Remedial assistance:** reading, math, writing, study skills, other. **Counseling services:** minority student, career, personal, veteran student, academic, older student, psychological, religious. **For learning-disabled students:** School does not offer a structured program with separate admission and additional fees. Total undergraduates in learning-disabled program or receiving services: 69. Services include: tape recorders, note-taking services, oral tests, learning center, readers, extended time for tests, tutors, priority registration, priority seating, other. **Library:** Number of

titles: 690,904; number of current serial subscriptions: 1,101. **Information technology resources:** Students are not required to lease or own a computer. Number of campus computers available to all students: 800. School has a wireless network. Approximate number of users that can be accommodated: 500. Proportion of college-owned housing units wired for high-speed internet access: 100%. **Campus safety:** Security services offered: 24-hour foot-and-vehicle patrols, late-night transport/escort service, 24-hour emergency telephones, lighted pathways/sidewalks, controlled dormitory access (key, security card, etc).

TRANSFER AND INTERNATIONAL STUDENTS

Transfer students: May apply for admission for the following academic terms: Fall, Spring, Summer. Applicants need a minimum number of credits to apply. For fall 2005: Transfer applications received: 355. Transfer applicants offered admission: 256. Transfer applicants enrolled: 166. **International students:** Number of foreign undergraduates: 119 (2% of student body). Number of countries represented: 67. Minimum TOEFL score required: 525 (paper); 195 (computer).

Eastern University

- **Address:** 1300 Eagle Road, St. Davids, PA 19087-3696
- **Website:** http://www.eastern.edu
- **Private; Religious affiliation:** American Baptist
- **Enrollment:** 1,998 full-time; 279 part-time

KEY STATS
- ✔ **U.S News College Ranking:** third tier, Universities–Master's (North)
- ✔ **SAT Score (25th/75th percentile):** 970-1190
- ✔ **Tuition:** 2006-2007: $20,030

Selectivity: Selective	**Room/board:** $8,080
Acceptance rate: 77%	**Average debt:** $20,541
Student/faculty ratio: N/A	**Proportion who borrowed:** 71%

UNDERGRADUATE STUDENT BODY STATS

2005-2006 enrollment: 1,998 full-time; 279 part-time. Men: 35%; women: 65%. **Ethnic makeup:** African American: 15%; Asian American: 2%; Hispanic: 5%; White: 76%; International: 2%.

ADMISSIONS FACTS AND FIGURES

Phone: (610) 341-5967. **Email:** ugadm@eastern.edu. **Website:** http://www.eastern.edu. **Application deadlines for fall 2007:** Regular decision: Rolling. Early decision: Not offered. Early action: Not offered. Admission can be deferred. **Application fee:** $25. Common application is accepted. **Admissions requirements/recommendations:** High school units required (recommended): English: 0 (4); Mathematics: 0 (3); Science: 0 (3); Foreign language: 0 (3); Social studies: 0 (2); History: 0 (0); Academic electives: 0 (0); Total units: 0 (0). Tests: The college uses SAT or ACT scores in admissions decisions. Either SAT or ACT required. For admission to the fall 2007 entering class, the school will accept: ACT with writing, ACT without writing. Campus visit: Recommended. Admissions interview: Recommended. Off-campus interview: May be arranged. **Factors that count in admissions decisions:** *Academic:* Secondary school record: Very important. Class rank: Important. Letters of recommendation: Considered. Standardized test scores: Important. Essay: Considered. *Nonacademic:* Interview: Considered. Extracurricular activities: Considered. Talent/ability: Considered. Character/personal qualities: Important. Alumni/ae relationship: Considered. Geographical residence: Not considered. State residency: Not considered. Religious affiliation/commitment: Considered. Minority status: Not considered. Volunteer work: Considered. Work experience: Considered. **Other schools with the greatest overlap in applicants:** Liberty University; Messiah College. **Admissions statistics for the fall 2005 entering class:** Total applicants: 1,153. Total accepted: 893. Freshmen enrolled: 404; 47% were from out of state. Overall acceptance rate: 77%. **Size of waiting list:** 0 applicants; enrolled from waiting list: 0. **Credentials of fall 2005 freshmen:** 35% ranked in the top 10 percent of their high school class; 42% were in the top 25 percent, and 78% were in the top half. (Proportion submitting class standing: 69%.) **Average high school grade point average:** 3.4. **First-year students who submitted SAT scores:** 96%. Scores (25/75 percentile): Verbal: 490-600, Math: 480-590, Combined: 970-1190. **First-year students submitting ACT scores:** 3%. Scores (25/75 percentile): English: 22-30, Math: 20-26, Composite: 21-27.

ACADEMICS

Year founded: 1952. **Academic calendar:** Semester. **Degrees offered:** transfer-associate, bachelor's, post-bachelor's certificate, master's, first professional, doctorate. **Most popular majors:** 7% elementary education and teaching, 6% psychology, 5% youth ministry, 4% business administration and management, 4% communication studies/speech communication and rhetoric. **Major fields of study:** biological and biomedical sciences; business, management, marketing, and related support services; communication, journalism, and related programs; education; English language and literature/letters; foreign languages, literatures, and linguistics; health professions and related clinical sciences; history; mathematics and statistics; natural resources and conservation; parks, recreation, leisure, and fitness studies; physical sciences; psychology; public administration and social service professions; social sciences; theology and religious vocations; visual and performing arts. **Areas of required coursework:** arts/fine arts, humanities, English (including composition), philosophy, foreign languages, sciences (biological or physical), history, social science. **Special academic programs (% participation):** cross-registration (2%), double major (10%), honors program (9%), independent study (10%), internships, student-designed major (2%), study abroad (20%), teacher certificate program (20%). **Teacher certification offered in:** early childhood, special education, elementary, secondary. **Reserve Officers Training Corps (ROTC):** Army ROTC: Offered at cooperating institution (Valley Forge Military College); Air Force ROTC: Offered at cooperating institution (St. Joseph's University). **Faculty and instruction (2005-2006):** Total instructional faculty: 115 full-time, 275 part-time (54% men; 46% women; 21% minorities). Full-time faculty with Ph.D. or other terminal degree: 86%. Classes of fewer than 20 students: 70%; of 20 to 49 students: 29%; of 50 or more students: 1%. **Advanced Placement and International Baccalaureate credit:** AP tests may be used for: Credit and/or placement. Scores accepted: 3, 4, 5. International Baccalaureate exams may be used for: Credit and/or placement. **Freshmen returning for sophomore year:** 79%. **Graduation rates:** Four-year: 50%; five-year: 58%; six-year: 61%.

COSTS AND FINANCIAL AID

Financial aid office: (610) 341-5842. **Expenses (2006-2007):** Tuition and fees 2006-2007: $20,030; room/board: $8,080. Estimated books and supplies: $1,000; transportation: $1,500; personal expenses: $1,800. **Financial aid:** Priority filing date for institution's financial aid form: April 1. In 2005-2006, 86% of undergraduates applied for financial aid. Of those, 74% were determined to have financial need; 24% had their need fully met. Average financial aid package (proportion receiving): $13,217 (74%). Average amount of gift aid, such as scholarships or grants (proportion receiving): $11,259 (70%). Average amount of self-help aid, such as work study or loans (proportion receiving): $1,307 (71%). Average need-based loan (excluding PLUS or other private loans): $2,678. Among students who received need-based aid, the average percentage of need met: 72%. Among students who received aid based on merit, the average award (and the proportion receiving): $7,245 (11%). Average amount of debt of borrowers graduating in 2005: $20,541. Proportion who borrowed: 71%.

CAMPUS LIFE AND EXTRACURRICULAR ACTIVITIES

Campus housing available: coed dorms, apartment for single students, other housing options. Students who live in college-owned, operated, or affiliated housing: 66%. Average per-year earnings: $1,500. **Clubs and organizations:** Number of student organizations: 77. Activities include: choral groups, concert band, dance, drama/theater, jazz band, literary magazine, music ensembles, musical theater, pep band, student government, student newspaper, student film society, yearbook. Number of fraternities: 0; sororities: 0. Average proportion of students who stay on campus on weekends: 75%. **Sports program (2005-2006):** Member of NCAA III. *Men's intercollegiate varsity sports:* baseball, basketball, cross-country, golf, lacrosse, soccer, tennis. *Women's intercollegiate varsity sports:* basketball, cross-country, field hockey, lacrosse, soccer, softball, tennis, volleyball.

SERVICES AND FACILITIES

Basic services: nonremedial tutoring, women's center, health service, health insurance. **Remedial assistance:** reading, writing. **Counseling services:** minority student, career, military, personal, academic, psychological, birth control, religious. **For learning-disabled students:** Services include: learning center, tutors, other. **Library:** Number of titles: 187,500; number of current serial subscriptions: 650. **Information technology resources:** Students are not required to lease or own a computer. Number of campus computers available to all students: 87. School has a wireless network. Approximate number of users that can be accommodated: 100. Proportion of college-owned housing units wired for high-speed internet access: 100%. **Campus safety:** Security services offered: 24-hour foot-and-vehicle patrols, late-night transport/escort service, 24-hour emergency telephones, lighted pathways/sidewalks, controlled dormitory access (key, security card, etc).

TRANSFER AND INTERNATIONAL STUDENTS

Transfer students: May apply for admission for the following academic terms: Fall, Spring, Summer. Applicants do not need a minimum number of credits to apply. For fall 2005: Transfer applications received: 275. Transfer applicants offered admission: 186. Transfer applicants enrolled: 112. **International students:** Number of foreign undergraduates: 47 (2% of student body). Minimum TOEFL score required: 550 (paper); 213 (computer).

East Stroudsburg Univ. of Pennsylvania

- **Address:** 200 Prospect Street, East Stroudsburg, PA 18301-2999
- **Website:** http://www.esu.edu
- **Public**
- **Enrollment:** 5,056 full-time; 540 part-time

KEY STATS

✔ **U.S News College Ranking:** third tier, Universities–Master's (North)
✔ **SAT Score (25th/75th percentile):** 900-1080
✔ **Tuition:** 2005-2006: $6,399 in state, $13,719 out of state

Selectivity: Less selective	**Room/board:** $4,794
Acceptance rate: 64%	**Average debt:** $21,900
Student/faculty ratio: 19/1	**Proportion who borrowed:** 69%

UNDERGRADUATE STUDENT BODY STATS

2005-2006 enrollment: 5,056 full-time; 540 part-time. Men: 42%; women: 58%. **Ethnic makeup:** African American: 4%; Asian American: 1%; Hispanic: 4%; White: 90%.

ADMISSIONS FACTS AND FIGURES

Phone: (570) 422-3542. **Email:** undergrads@po-box.esu.edu. **Website:** http://www.esu.edu. **Application deadlines for fall 2007:** Regular decision: April 1. Early decision: Not offered. Early action: Not offered. Admission can be deferred. **Application fee:** $35. Common application is not accepted. **To apply online, go to:** https://www.applyweb.com/public/account?paeast. **Admissions requirements/recommendations:** High school units required (recommended): English: (4); Mathematics: (4); Science: (3); Foreign language: (2); Social studies: (3); History: (3); Total units: (16). The college uses SAT or ACT scores in admissions decisions. Either SAT or ACT required. For admission to the fall 2007 entering class, the school will accept: ACT with writing, ACT without writing. Campus visit: Neither required nor recommended. Admissions interview: Neither required nor recommended. Off-campus interview: Not available. **Factors that count in admissions decisions:** *Academic:* Secondary school record: Very important. Class rank: Important. Letters of recommendation: Considered. Standardized test scores: Very important. Essay: Considered. *Nonacademic:* Interview: Not considered. Extracurricular activities: Considered. Talent/ability: Considered. Character/personal qualities: Considered. Alumni/ae relationship: Considered. Geographical residence: Not considered. State residency: Considered. Religious affiliation/commitment: Not considered. Minority status: Considered. Volunteer work: Considered. Work experience: Considered. **Admissions statistics for the fall 2005 entering class:** Total applicants: 5,063. Total accepted: 3,264. Freshmen enrolled: 1,101; 28% were from out of state. Overall acceptance rate: 64%. **Credentials of fall 2005 freshmen:** 7% ranked in the top 10 percent of their high school class; 26% were in the top 25 percent, and 71% were in the top half. (Proportion submitting class standing: 89%.) **Average high school grade point average:** 2.9. **First-year students who submitted SAT scores:** 99%. Scores (25/75 percentile): Verbal: 450-530, Math: 450-550, Combined: 900-1080.

ACADEMICS

Year founded: 1893. **Academic calendar:** Semester. **Degrees offered:** associate, bachelor's, post-bachelor's certificate, master's. **Most popular majors:** 24% education, 13% business, management, marketing, and related support services, 11% social sciences, 9% parks, recreation, leisure, and fitness studies, 9% psychology. **Major fields of study:** biological and biomedical sciences; business, management, marketing, and related support services; communication, journalism, and related programs; communications technologies/technicians and support services; computer and information sciences and support services; education; English language and literature/letters; foreign languages, literatures, and linguistics; health professions and related clinical sciences; history; liberal arts and sciences studies, and humanities; mathematics and statistics; multi/interdisciplinary studies; parks, recreation, leisure, and fitness studies; philosophy and religious studies; physical sciences; psychology; social sciences; visual and performing arts. **Areas of required coursework:** arts/fine arts, mathematics, English (including composition), sciences (biological or physical), social science. **Pre-professional programs:** pre-law, pre-dentistry, pre-medicine, pre-pharmacy. **Special academic programs (% participation):** accelerated program (1%), double major (3%), exchange student program (domestic) (1%), honors program (2%), independent study (10%), internships (20%), student-designed major (1%), study abroad (1%), teacher certificate program (25%). **Teacher certification offered in:** early childhood, special education, elementary, middle/junior high, secondary. **Reserve Officers Training Corps (ROTC):** Army ROTC: Offered at cooperating institution (Lehigh University); Air Force ROTC: Offered at cooperating institution (Wilkes University). **Faculty and instruction (2005-2006):** Total instructional faculty: 259 full-time, 73 part-time (55% men; 45% women; 10% minorities). Full-time faculty with Ph.D. or other terminal degree: 78%. Student/faculty ratio: 19/1. Classes of fewer than 20 students: 26%; of 20 to 49 students: 71%; of 50 or more students: 3%. **Advanced Placement and International Baccalaureate credit:** AP tests may be used for: Credit only. Scores accepted: 3, 4, 5. International Baccalaureate exams may be used for: Credit only. **Freshmen returning for sophomore year:** 76%. **Graduation rates:** Four-year: 19%; five-year: 43%; six-year: 50%. **Graduate study:** 15% of students pursue further study immediately upon graduation; 25% within one year; 50% within five years. Fields in which graduates pursue further study: law, 1%; medicine, 1%; education, 50%; arts and sciences, 25%.

COSTS AND FINANCIAL AID

Financial aid office: (570) 422-2800. **Expenses (2005-2006):** Tuition and fees 2005-2006: $6,399 in state, $13,719 out of state; room/board: $4,794. Estimated books and supplies: $1,000; transportation: $315; personal expenses: $2,012. **Financial aid:** Priority filing date for institution's financial aid form: March 1; deadline: March 1. In 2005-2006, 78% of undergraduates applied for financial aid. Of those, 58% were determined to have financial need; 74% had their need fully met. Average financial aid package (proportion receiving): $5,224 (57%). Average amount of gift aid, such as scholarships or grants (proportion receiving): $3,489 (33%). Average amount of self-help aid, such as work-study or loans (proportion receiving): $6,057 (47%). Average need-based loan (excluding PLUS or other private loans): $3,780. Among students who received need-based aid, the average percentage of need met: 86%. Among students who received aid based on merit, the average award (and the proportion receiving): $7,415 (18%). The average athletic scholarship (and the proportion receiving): $1,749 (4%). Average amount of debt of borrowers graduating in 2005: $21,900. Proportion who borrowed: 69%.

CAMPUS LIFE AND EXTRACURRICULAR ACTIVITIES

Campus housing available (% using): coed dorms (51%), apartment for single students (29%), special housing for disabled students, special housing for international students, other housing options (20%). Students who live in college-owned, operated, or affiliated housing: 47%. **Clubs and organizations:** Number of student organizations: 103. Activities include: choral groups, concert band, dance, drama/theater, jazz band, literary magazine, marching band, music ensembles, musical theater, opera, pep band, radio station, student government, student newspaper, yearbook. Number of fraternities: 6; sororities: 6. Proportion of men in fraternities: 5%; of women in sororities: 3%. Average proportion of students who stay on campus on weekends: 45%. **Sports program (2005-2006):** Member of NCAA II. *Men's intercollegiate varsity sports:* baseball, basketball, cross-country, football, soccer, tennis, track and field (indoor), track and field (outdoor), volleyball, wrestling. *Women's intercollegiate varsity sports:* basketball, cross-country, field hockey, lacrosse, soccer, softball, swimming and diving, tennis, track and field (indoor), track and field (outdoor), volleyball.

SERVICES AND FACILITIES

Basic services: nonremedial tutoring, women's center, placement service, day care, health service. **Remedial assistance:** reading, math, writing, study skills. **Counseling services:** minority student, career, personal, veteran student, academic, older student, psychological. **For learning-disabled students:** School does not offer a structured program with separate admission and additional fees. Services include: remedial math, remedial English, reading machines, tape recorders, note-taking services, oral tests, readers, extended time for tests, tutors, other. **Library:** Number of titles: 548,965; number of

current serial subscriptions: 1,200. **Information technology resources:** Students are not required to lease or own a computer. Number of campus computers available to all students: 735. School has a wireless network. Approximate number of users that can be accommodated: 220. Proportion of college-owned housing units wired for high-speed internet access: 100%. **Campus safety:** Security services offered: 24-hour foot-and-vehicle patrols, late-night transport/escort service, 24-hour emergency telephones, lighted pathways/sidewalks, student patrols, controlled dormitory access (key, security card, etc).

TRANSFER AND INTERNATIONAL STUDENTS

Transfer students: May apply for admission for the following academic terms: Fall, Spring. Applicants do not need a minimum number of credits to apply. For fall 2005: Transfer applications received: 858. Transfer applicants offered admission: 739. Transfer applicants enrolled: 434. **International students:** Number of foreign undergraduates: 26. Number of countries represented: 11. Minimum TOEFL score required: 550 (paper); 213 (computer). Average TOEFL score: 578 (paper).

Edinboro University of Pennsylvania

- **Address:** Edinboro, PA 16444
- **Website:** http://webs.edinboro.edu/welcome
- **Public**
- **Enrollment:** 5,722 full-time; 801 part-time

KEY STATS
- ✔ **U.S News College Ranking:** fourth tier, Universities–Master's (North)
- ✔ **SAT Score (25th/75th percentile):** 840-1070
- ✔ **Tuition:** 2006-2007: $6,290 in state, $11,198 out of state

Selectivity: Less selective	**Room/board:** $5,518
Acceptance rate: 82%	**Average debt:** $17,034
Student/faculty ratio: 17/1	**Proportion who borrowed:** 67%

UNDERGRADUATE STUDENT BODY STATS

2005-2006 enrollment: 5,722 full-time; 801 part-time. Men: 42%; women: 58%. **Ethnic makeup:** African American: 8%; Asian American: 1%; Hispanic: 1%; White: 88%; International: 2%. **Religious preference:** Roman Catholic: 30%; Protestant: 30%; Jewish: 1%; No preference: 17%; Baptist: 8%; Other: 14%.

ADMISSIONS FACTS AND FIGURES

Phone: (800) 626-2203. **Email:** eup_admissions@edinboro.edu. **Website:** http://webs.edinboro.edu/welcome. **Application deadlines for fall 2007:** Regular decision: August 30; decision sent by July 1. Early decision: Not offered. Early action: Not offered. Admission can be deferred. **Application fee:** $30. Common application is accepted. **To apply online, go to:** http://webs.edinboro.edu/pubrel/admissions/applyonline.html. **Admissions requirements/recommendations:** High school units required (recommended): English: 4 (4); Mathematics: 3 (3); Science: 3 (3); Foreign language: 2 (2); Social studies: 3 (3); History: 0 (0); Academic electives: 4 (4); Total units: 20 (17). Tests: The college uses SAT or ACT scores in admissions decisions. Either SAT or ACT required. For admission to the fall 2007 entering class, the school will accept: ACT with writing. Campus visit: Recommended. Admissions interview: Recommended. Off-campus interview: May be arranged. **Factors that count in admissions decisions:** *Academic:* Secondary school record: Very important. Class rank: Very important. Letters of recommendation: Considered. Standardized test scores: Very important. Essay: Considered. *Nonacademic:* Interview: Considered. Extracurricular activities: Important. Talent/ability: Considered. Character/personal qualities: Considered. Alumni/ae relationship: Considered. Geographical residence: Considered. State residency: Important. Religious affiliation/commitment: Not considered. Minority status: Important. Volunteer work: Considered. Work experience: Considered. **Other schools with the greatest overlap in applicants:** Clarion University of Pennsylvania; Indiana University of Pennsylvania; Pennsylvania State–Erie, The Behrend College; Slippery Rock University of Pennsylvania; University of Pittsburgh. **Admissions statistics for the fall 2005 entering class:** Total applicants: 3,541. Total accepted: 2,903. Freshmen enrolled: 1,325; 10% were from out of state. Overall acceptance rate: 82%. **Credentials of fall 2005 freshmen:** 6% ranked in the top 10 percent of their high school class; 21% were in the top 25 percent, and 55% were in the top half. (Proportion submitting class standing: 92%.) **First-year students who submitted SAT scores:** 81%. Scores (25/75 percentile): Verbal: 420-540, Math: 420-530, Combined: 840-1070. **First-year students submitting ACT scores:** 17%. Scores (25/75 percentile): English: N/A, Math: N/A, Composite: 16-21.

ACADEMICS

Year founded: 1857. **Academic calendar:** Semester. **Degrees offered:** associate, bachelor's, post-bachelor's certificate, master's, post-master's certificate. **Most popular majors:** 15% visual and performing arts, 14% education, 8% communication, journalism, and related programs, 8% health professions and related clinical sciences, 8% security and protective services. **Major fields of study:** biological and biomedical sciences; business, management, marketing, and related support services; communication, journalism, and related programs; computer and information sciences and support services; education; English language and literature/letters; foreign languages, literatures, and linguistics; health professions and related clinical sciences; history; liberal arts and sciences studies, and humanities; mathematics and statistics; multi/interdisciplinary studies; natural resources and conservation; parks, recreation, leisure, and fitness studies; philosophy and religious studies; physical sciences; psychology; public administration and social service professions; security and protective services; social sciences; visual and performing arts. **Areas of required coursework:** arts/fine arts, humanities, computer literacy, mathematics, English (including composition), philosophy, sciences (biological or physical), history, social science. **Pre-professional programs:** pre-law, pre-dentistry, pre-medicine, pre-veterinary science, pre-pharmacy. **Special academic programs (% participation):** distance learning (2.8%), double major (2.4%), dual enrollment, honors program (1.9%), independent study (5.2%), internships (32.3%), liberal arts/career combination, study abroad (1.8%), teacher certificate program, other (2.9%). **Teacher certification offered in:** early childhood, special education, elementary, middle/junior high, secondary. **Cooperative education programs:** engineering, health professions. **Reserve Officers Training Corps (ROTC):** Army ROTC: Offered on campus. **Faculty and instruction (2005-2006):** Total instructional faculty: 363 full-time, 45 part-time (55% men; 45% women; 9% minorities). Full-time faculty with Ph.D. or other terminal degree: 69%. Student/faculty ratio: 17/1. Classes of fewer than 20 students: 32%; of 20 to 49 students: 62%; of 50 or more students: 5%. **Advanced Placement and International Baccalaureate credit:** AP tests may be used for: Credit and/or placement. Scores accepted: 3, 4, 5. **Freshmen returning for sophomore year:** 71%. **Graduation rates:** Four-year: 20%; five-year: 46%; six-year: 49%.

COSTS AND FINANCIAL AID

Financial aid office: (814) 732-5555. **Expenses (2006-2007):** Tuition and fees 2006-2007: $6,290 in state, $11,198 out of state; room/board: $5,518. Estimated books and supplies: $900; transportation: $800; personal expenses: $1,300. **Financial aid:** Priority filing date for institution's financial aid form: March 15; deadline: May 1. In 2005-2006, 91% of undergraduates applied for financial aid. Of those, 79% were determined to have financial need; 7% had their need fully met. Average financial aid package (proportion receiving): $6,402 (77%). Average amount of gift aid, such as scholarships or grants (proportion receiving): $1,825 (77%). Average amount of self-help aid, such as work study or loans (proportion receiving): $3,915 (63%). Average need-based loan (excluding PLUS or other private loans): $3,227. Among students who received need-based aid, the average percentage of need met: 81%. Among students who received aid based on merit, the average award (and the proportion receiving): $1,900 (11%). The average athletic scholarship (and the proportion receiving): $2,960 (2%). Average amount of debt of borrowers graduating in 2005: $17,034. Proportion who borrowed: 67%.

CAMPUS LIFE AND EXTRACURRICULAR ACTIVITIES

Campus housing available (% using): coed dorms (67%), women's dorms (17%), special housing for disabled students (8%), special housing for international students, other housing options (8%). Students who live in college-owned, operated, or affiliated housing: 27%. **Student employment:** During the 2005-2006 academic year, 19% of undergraduates worked on campus. Average per-year earnings: $1,829. **Clubs and organizations:** Number of student organizations: 221. Activities include: choral groups, dance, drama/theater, literary magazine, marching band, pep band, radio station, student government, student newspaper, student film society, television station. Number of fraternities: 12; sororities: 8. Average proportion of students who stay on campus on weekends: 65%. **Sports program (2005-2006):** Member of NCAA II. *Men's intercollegiate varsity sports:* basketball, cross-country, football, swimming and diving, track and field (outdoor), wrestling. *Women's intercollegiate varsity sports:* basketball, cross-country, soccer, soft-

ball, swimming and diving, track and field (indoor), track and field (outdoor), volleyball.

SERVICES AND FACILITIES

Basic services: health service, health insurance. **Remedial assistance:** reading, math, writing, study skills, other. **Counseling services:** minority student, career, military, personal, veteran student, academic, older student, psychological, birth control, religious. **For learning-disabled students:** School does not offer a structured program with separate admission and additional fees. Total undergraduates in learning-disabled program or receiving services: 300. Services include: remedial math, remedial English, tape recorders, note-taking services, readers, extended time for tests, tutors, priority registration, texts on tape, other. **Library:** Number of titles: 501,276; number of current serial subscriptions: 1,523. **Information technology resources:** Students are not required to lease or own a computer. Number of campus computers available to all students: 800. School has a wireless network. Approximate number of users that can be accommodated: 512. Proportion of college-owned housing units wired for high-speed internet access: 100%. **Campus safety:** Security services offered: 24-hour foot-and-vehicle patrols, late-night transport/escort service, 24-hour emergency telephones, lighted pathways/sidewalks, student patrols.

TRANSFER AND INTERNATIONAL STUDENTS

Transfer students: May apply for admission for the following academic terms: Fall, Spring. Applicants do not need a minimum number of credits to apply. For fall 2005: Transfer applications received: 979. Transfer applicants offered admission: 520. Transfer applicants enrolled: 480. **International students:** Number of foreign undergraduates: 121 (2% of student body). Number of countries represented: 41. Minimum TOEFL score required: 500 (paper); 173 (computer).

Elizabethtown College

- **Address:** 1 Alpha Drive, Elizabethtown, PA 17022-2298
- **Website:** http://www.etown.edu
- **Private; Religious affiliation:** Church of the Brethren
- **Enrollment:** 1,861 full-time; 301 part-time

KEY STATS

✔ **U.S News College Ranking:** 3, Comp. Coll.–Bachelor's (North)
✔ **SAT Score (25th/75th percentile):** 1000-1230
✔ **Tuition:** 2006-2007: $26,950

Selectivity: More selective	**Room/board:** $7,300
Acceptance rate: 62%	**Average debt:** $29,233
Student/faculty ratio: 12/1	**Proportion who borrowed:** 77%

UNDERGRADUATE STUDENT BODY STATS

2005-2006 enrollment: 1,861 full-time; 301 part-time. Men: 34%; women: 66%. **Ethnic makeup:** African American: 1%; Asian American: 2%; Hispanic: 1%; White: 93%; International: 2%. **Religious preference:** Roman Catholic: 23%; Protestant: 21%; Jewish: 1%; No preference: 5%; Unknown: 36%; Church of the Brethren: 3%; Other: 10%.

ADMISSIONS FACTS AND FIGURES

Phone: (717) 361-1400. **Email:** admissions@etown.edu. **Website:** http://www.etown.edu. **Application deadlines for fall 2007:** Regular decision: Rolling; decision sent by April 1. Early decision: Not offered. Early action: Not offered. Admission can be deferred. **Application fee:** $30. Common application is accepted. **To apply online, go to:** http://www.etown.edu/admissions/onlineapp.html. **Admissions requirements/recommendations:** High school units required (recommended): English: 4 (4); Mathematics: 3 (4); Science: 2 (4); Foreign language: 2 (2); Social studies: 2 (2); History: 2 (2); Academic electives: 0 (2); Total units: 15 (20). Tests: The college uses SAT or ACT scores in admissions decisions. Either SAT or ACT required. For admission to the fall 2007 entering class, the school will accept: ACT with writing, ACT without writing. Campus visit: Recommended. Admissions interview: Recommended. Off-campus interview: May be arranged. **Factors that count in admissions decisions:** *Academic:* Secondary school record: Very important. Class rank: Important. Letters of recommendation: Important. Standardized test scores: Important. Essay: Considered. *Nonacademic:* Interview: Very important. Extracurricular activities: Considered. Talent/ability: Considered. Character/personal qualities: Considered. Alumni/ae relationship: Considered. Geographical residence: Considered. State residency: Considered. Religious affiliation/commitment: Considered. Minority status: Considered. Volunteer work: Considered. Work experience: Considered. **Other schools with the greatest overlap in applicants:** Albright College; Gettysburg College; Juniata College; Lebanon Valley College; Susquehanna University. **Admissions statistics for the fall 2005 entering class:** Total applicants: 2,708. Total accepted: 1,692. Freshmen enrolled: 538; 31% were from out of state. Overall acceptance rate: 62%. **Size of waiting list:** 226 applicants; enrolled from waiting list: 3. **Credentials of fall 2005 freshmen:** 29% ranked in the top 10 percent of their high school class; 58% were in the top 25 percent, and 85% were in the top half. (Proportion submitting class standing: 82%.) **Average high school grade point average:** 3.6. **First-year students who submitted SAT scores:** 85%. Scores (25/75 percentile): Verbal: 500-610, Math: 500-620, Combined: 1000-1230. **First-year students submitting ACT scores:** 12%. Scores (25/75 percentile): English: 19-25, Math: 19-25, Composite: 19-24.

ACADEMICS

Year founded: 1899. **Academic calendar:** Semester. **Degrees offered:** certificate, diploma, associate, bachelor's, post-bachelor's certificate, master's. **Most popular majors:** 27% business, management, marketing, and related support services, 18% education, 10% health professions and related clinical sciences, 8% communication, journalism, and related programs, 5% social sciences. **Major fields of study:** biological and biomedical sciences; business, management, marketing, and related support services; communication, journalism, and related programs; computer and information sciences and support services; education; engineering; English language and literature/letters; foreign languages, literatures, and linguistics; health professions and related clinical sciences; history; legal professions and studies; mathematics and statistics; natural resources and conservation; philosophy and religious studies; physical sciences; psychology; public administration and social service professions; social sciences; visual and performing arts. **Areas of required coursework:** arts/fine arts, humanities, mathematics, English (including composition), foreign languages, sciences (biological or physical), history, social science. **Pre-professional programs:** pre-law, pre-dentistry, pre-medicine, pre-veterinary science. **Special academic programs (% participation):** accelerated program (9%), distance learning (9%), double major (3%), English as a Second Language (ESL) (.5%), exchange student program (domestic) (3%), external degree program, honors program (12%), independent study (24%), internships (53%), study abroad (8%), teacher certificate program (19%). **Teacher certification offered in:** early childhood, special education, elementary, middle/junior high, secondary. **Cooperative education programs:** engineering, health professions, natural science, other. **Faculty and instruction (2005-2006):** Total instructional faculty: 124 full-time, 114 part-time (55% men; 45% women; 5% minorities). Full-time faculty with Ph.D. or other terminal degree: 85%. Student/faculty ratio: 12/1. Classes of fewer than 20 students: 68%; of 20 to 49 students: 31%; of 50 or more students: 1%. **Advanced Placement and International Baccalaureate credit:** AP tests may be used for: Credit only. Scores accepted: 3, 4, 5. International Baccalaureate exams may be used for: Credit only. **Freshmen returning for sophomore year:** 85%. **Graduation rates:** Four-year: 63%; five-year: 69%; six-year: 69%. **Graduate study:** 42% of students pursue further study immediately upon graduation. Fields in which graduates pursue further study: Master of Business Administration (MBA), 5%; law, 4%; medicine, 10%; theology (or the seminary), 2%; education, 6%; arts and sciences, 69%; veterinary medicine, 2%.

COSTS AND FINANCIAL AID

Financial aid office: (717) 361-1404. **Expenses (2006-2007):** Tuition and fees 2006-2007: $26,950; room/board: $7,300. Estimated books and supplies: $700; transportation: $150; personal expenses: $600. **Financial aid:** Priority filing date for institution's financial aid form: March 15. In 2005-2006, 82% of undergraduates applied for financial aid. Of those, 71% were determined to have financial need; 28% had their need fully met. Average financial aid package (proportion receiving): $16,420 (71%). Average amount of gift aid, such as scholarships or grants (proportion receiving): $14,244 (70%). Average amount of self-help aid, such as work study or loans (proportion receiving): $4,924 (59%). Average need-based loan (excluding PLUS or other private loans): $3,914. Among students who received need-based aid, the average percentage of need met: 79%. Among students who received aid based on merit, the average award (and the proportion receiving): $15,442 (9%). The average athletic scholarship (and the proportion receiving): $0 (0%). Average amount of debt of borrowers graduating in 2005: $29,233. Proportion who borrowed: 77%.

CAMPUS LIFE AND EXTRACURRICULAR ACTIVITIES

Campus housing available (% using): coed dorms (68%), women's dorms (11%), apartment for single students (15%), special housing for disabled students (3%), cooperative housing (3%). Students who live in college-owned, operated, or affiliated housing: 82%. **Student employment:** During the 2005-2006 academic year, 53% of undergraduates worked on campus. Average per-year earnings: $604. **Clubs and organizations:** Number of student organizations: 70. Activities include: choral groups, concert band, dance, drama/theater, jazz band, literary magazine, music ensembles, musical theater, radio station, student government, student newspaper, symphony orchestra, television station, yearbook. Number of fraternities: 0; sororities: 0. Average proportion of students who stay on campus on weekends: 65%. **Sports program (2005-2006):** Member of NCAA III. *Men's intercollegiate varsity sports:* baseball, basketball, cross-country, golf, lacrosse, soccer, swimming and diving, tennis, track and field (indoor), track and field (outdoor), wrestling. *Women's intercollegiate varsity sports:* basketball, cross-country, field hockey, lacrosse, soccer, softball, swimming and diving, tennis, track and field (indoor), track and field (outdoor), volleyball.

SERVICES AND FACILITIES

Basic services: nonremedial tutoring, health service, health insurance. **Remedial assistance:** reading, math, writing, study skills, other. **Counseling services:** minority student, career, personal, academic, psychological, birth control, religious. **For learning-disabled students:** School does not offer a structured program with separate admission and additional fees. Total undergraduates in learning-disabled program or receiving services: 90. Services include: remedial math, reading machines, tape recorders, videotaped classes, note-taking services, oral tests, learning center, readers, extended time for tests, tutors, early syllabus, priority registration, priority seating, substitution of courses, texts on tape, typist/scribe, exams on tape or computer, waiver of foreign language degree requirement, other. **Library:** Number of titles: 194,990; number of current serial subscriptions: 970. **Information technology resources:** Students are not required to lease or own a computer. Number of campus computers available to all students: 200. School has a wireless network. Approximate number of users that can be accommodated: 500. Proportion of college-owned housing units wired for high-speed internet access: 100%. **Campus safety:** Security services offered: 24-hour foot-and-vehicle patrols, late-night transport/escort service, 24-hour emergency telephones, lighted pathways/sidewalks, student patrols, controlled dormitory access (key, security card, etc).

TRANSFER AND INTERNATIONAL STUDENTS

Transfer students: May apply for admission for the following academic terms: Fall, Spring. Applicants do not need a minimum number of credits to apply. For fall 2005: Transfer applications received: 122. Transfer applicants offered admission: 71. Transfer applicants enrolled: 43. **International students:** Number of foreign undergraduates: 44 (2% of student body). Number of countries represented: 36. Minimum TOEFL score required: 525 (paper); 200 (computer). Average TOEFL score: 565 (paper).

Franklin and Marshall College

- **Address:** PO Box 3003, Lancaster, PA 17604
- **Website:** http://www.fandm.edu
- **Private**
- **Enrollment:** 1,982 full-time; 43 part-time

KEY STATS

✔ **U.S News College Ranking:** 41, Liberal Arts Colleges
✔ **SAT Score (25th/75th percentile):** 1180-1370
✔ **Tuition:** 2006-2007: $34,450
Selectivity: More selective **Room/board:** $8,540
Acceptance rate: 45% **Average debt:** $19,391
Student/faculty ratio: 10/1 **Proportion who borrowed:** 61%

UNDERGRADUATE STUDENT BODY STATS

2005-2006 enrollment: 1,982 full-time; 43 part-time. Men: 53%; women: 47%. **Ethnic makeup:** African American: 3%; Asian American: 4%; Hispanic: 4%; White: 83%; International: 7%. **Religious preference:** Roman Catholic: 21%; Protestant: 18%; Jewish: 9%; Muslim: 2%; Hindu: 1%; No preference: 8%; Unknown: 35%.

ADMISSIONS FACTS AND FIGURES

Phone: (717) 291-3953. **Email:** admission@fandm.edu. **Website:** http://www.fandm.edu. **Application deadlines for fall 2007:** Regular decision: February 1; decision sent by April 1. Early decision: Send application by: November 15; Decision sent by: December 15. Early action: Not offered. Admission can be deferred. **Application fee:** $50. Common application is accepted. **To apply online, go to:** http://admission.fandm.edu/admission/process.asp. **Admissions requirements/recommendations:** High school units required (recommended): English: 4; Mathematics: 3 (4); Science: 2 (3); Foreign language: 2 (4); Social studies: 1 (3); History: 2 (3). Tests: The college uses SAT or ACT scores in admissions decisions. Neither SAT nor ACT required. For admission to the fall 2007 entering class, the school will accept: ACT with writing, ACT without writing. Campus visit: Recommended. Admissions interview: Recommended. Off-campus interview: May be arranged. **Factors that count in admissions decisions:** *Academic:* Secondary school record: Very important. Class rank: Very important. Letters of recommendation: Important. Standardized test scores: Important. Essay: Important. *Nonacademic:* Interview: Important. Extracurricular activities: Important. Talent/ability: Important. Character/personal qualities: Very important. Alumni/ae relationship: Considered. Geographical residence: Considered. State residency: Not considered. Religious affiliation/commitment: Not considered. Minority status: Considered. Volunteer work: Important. Work experience: Considered. **Other schools with the greatest overlap in applicants:** Bucknell University; Dickinson College; Gettysburg College; Lafayette College; Pennsylvania State University–University Park. **Admissions statistics for the fall 2005 entering class:** Total applicants: 4,227. Total accepted: 1,921. Freshmen enrolled: 582; 65% were from out of state. Accepted through early-decision or early-action plans: 47%. Overall acceptance rate: 45%. Early-decision acceptance rate: 77%. Non-early acceptance rate: 42%. **Size of waiting list:** 1255 applicants; enrolled from waiting list: 25. **Credentials of fall 2005 freshmen:** 54% ranked in the top 10 percent of their high school class; 83% were in the top 25 percent, and 97% were in the top half. (Proportion submitting class standing: 33%.) **First-year students who submitted SAT scores:** 81%. Scores (25/75 percentile): Verbal: 580-680; Math: 600-690, Combined: 1180-1370. **First-year students submitting ACT scores:** 6%. Scores (25/75 percentile): English: N/A, Math: N/A, Composite: N/A.

ACADEMICS

Year founded: 1787. **Academic calendar:** Semester. **Degrees offered:** bachelor's. **Most popular majors:** 21% political science and government, 15% business administration and management, 11% English language and literature, 6% biology/biological sciences, 6% sociology. **Major fields of study:** area, ethnic, cultural, and gender studies; biological and biomedical sciences; business, management, marketing, and related support services; English language and literature/letters; foreign languages, literatures, and linguistics; history; mathematics and statistics; multi/interdisciplinary studies; natural resources and conservation; philosophy and religious studies; physical sciences; psychology; public administration and social service professions; social sciences; visual and performing arts. **Areas of required coursework:** arts/fine arts, humanities, foreign languages, sciences (biological or physical), social science, other. **Pre-professional programs:** pre-law, pre-dentistry, pre-medicine, pre-veterinary science, pre-optometry. **Special academic programs (% participation):** accelerated program, cross-registration, double major (21%), dual enrollment, exchange student program (domestic), honors program (10%), independent study (38%), internships (26%), liberal arts/career combination, student-designed major (4%), study abroad (20%), teacher certificate program (1%). **Teacher certification offered in:** secondary. **Cooperative education programs:** engineering. **Reserve Officers Training Corps (ROTC):** Army ROTC: Offered at cooperating institution (Millersville University). **Faculty and instruction (2005-2006):** Total instructional faculty: 175 full-time, 48 part-time (61% men; 39% women; 9% minorities). Full-time faculty with Ph.D. or other terminal degree: 97%. Student/faculty ratio: 10/1. Classes of fewer than 20 students: 50%; of 20 to 49 students: 50%; of 50 or more students: 0%. **Advanced Placement and International Baccalaureate credit:** AP tests may be used for: Credit and/or placement. Scores accepted: 4, 5. International Baccalaureate exams may be used for: Credit and/or placement. **Freshmen returning for sophomore year:** 91%. **Graduation rates:** Four-year: 75%; five-year: 81%; six-year: 82%. **Graduate study:** 25% of students pursue further study immediately upon graduation. Fields in which graduates pursue further study: Master of Business Administration (MBA), 35%; law, 18%; medicine, 11%; dentistry, 2%; education, 4%; arts and sciences, 28%; veterinary medicine, 2%.

COSTS AND FINANCIAL AID

Financial aid office: (717) 291-3991. **Expenses (2006-2007):** Tuition and fees 2006-2007: $34,450; room/board: $8,540. Estimated books and supplies: $650; transportation: $100; personal expenses: $750. **Financial aid:** Priority filing date for institution's financial aid form: February 1; deadline: March 1. In 2005-2006, 73% of undergraduates applied for financial aid. Of those, 48% were determined to have financial need; 99% had their need fully met. Average financial aid package (proportion receiving): $24,283 (48%). Average amount of gift aid, such as scholarships or grants (proportion receiving): $19,856 (45%). Average amount of self-help aid, such as work study or loans (proportion receiving): $1,875 (48%). Average need-based loan (excluding PLUS or other private loans): $5,040. Among students who received need-based aid, the average percentage of need met: 100%. Among students who received aid based on merit, the average award (and the proportion receiving): $8,826 (24%). The average athletic scholarship (and the proportion receiving): $0 (0%). Average amount of debt of borrowers graduating in 2005: $19,391. Proportion who borrowed: 61%.

CAMPUS LIFE AND EXTRACURRICULAR ACTIVITIES

Campus housing available (% using): coed dorms (88%), women's dorms (2%), men's dorms (1%), fraternity housing (3%), apartment for single students (2%), special housing for disabled students (0%), special housing for international students (1%), other housing options (3%). Students who live in college-owned, operated, or affiliated housing: 65%. Average per-year earnings: $1,400. **Clubs and organizations:** Number of student organizations: 125. Activities include: choral groups, concert band, dance, drama/theater, jazz band, literary magazine, music ensembles, musical theater, radio station, student government, student newspaper, symphony orchestra, television station, yearbook. Number of fraternities: 7; sororities: 2. Proportion of men in fraternities: 38%; of women in sororities: 8%. Average proportion of students who stay on campus on weekends: 90%. **Sports program (2005-2006):** Member of NCAA III. *Men's intercollegiate varsity sports:* baseball, basketball, cross-country, football, golf, lacrosse, soccer, squash, swimming and diving, tennis, track and field (indoor), track and field (outdoor), wrestling. *Women's intercollegiate varsity sports:* basketball, cross-country, field hockey, golf, lacrosse, soccer, softball, squash, swimming and diving, tennis, track and field (indoor), track and field (outdoor), volleyball.

SERVICES AND FACILITIES

Basic services: nonremedial tutoring, women's center, placement service, day care, health service, health insurance, other. **Remedial assistance:** other. **Counseling services:** minority student, career, personal, academic, psychological, birth control, religious. **For learning-disabled students:** School does not offer a structured program with separate admission and additional fees. **Library:** Number of titles: 499,575; number of current serial subscriptions: 1,986. **Information technology resources:** Students are not required to lease or own a computer. Number of campus computers available to all students: 272. School has a wireless network. Proportion of college-owned housing units wired for high-speed internet access: 100%. **Campus safety:** Security services offered: 24-hour foot-and-vehicle patrols, late-night transport/escort service, 24-hour emergency telephones, lighted pathways/sidewalks, controlled dormitory access (key, security card, etc.).

TRANSFER AND INTERNATIONAL STUDENTS

Transfer students: May apply for admission for the following academic terms: Fall, Spring. Applicants need a minimum number of credits to apply. For fall 2005: Transfer applications received: 74. Transfer applicants offered admission: 27. Transfer applicants enrolled: 15. **International students:** Number of foreign undergraduates: 135 (7% of student body). Number of countries represented: 40. Minimum TOEFL score required: 600 (paper); 250 (computer).

Gannon University

- **Address:** 109 University Square, Erie, PA 16541
- **Website:** http://www.gannon.edu
- **Private; Religious affiliation:** Roman Catholic
- **Enrollment:** 2,184 full-time; 390 part-time

KEY STATS

✔ **U.S News College Ranking:** 40, Universities–Master's (North)
✔ **SAT Score (25th/75th percentile):** 940-1150
✔ **Tuition:** 2006-2007: $19,996

Selectivity: Selective   **Room/board:** $7,880
Acceptance rate: 86%   **Average debt:** $24,148
Student/faculty ratio: 13/1   **Proportion who borrowed:** 75%

UNDERGRADUATE STUDENT BODY STATS

2005-2006 enrollment: 2,184 full-time; 390 part-time. Men: 40%; women: 60%. **Ethnic makeup:** African American: 5%; Asian American: 1%; Hispanic: 1%; White: 92%; International: 1%. **Religious preference:** Protestant: 22%; Unknown: 15%; Roman Catholic: 53%.

ADMISSIONS FACTS AND FIGURES

Phone: (814) 871-7240. **Email:** admissions@gannon.edu. **Website:** http://www.gannon.edu. **Application deadlines for fall 2007:** Regular decision: Rolling. Early decision: Not offered. Early action: Not offered. Admission can be deferred. **Application fee:** $25. Common application is accepted. **To apply online, go to:** http://www.gannon.edu/admiss/undergrad/apply/instruct.asp. **Admissions requirements/recommendations:** High school units required (recommended): English: 4 (4); Mathematics: (4); Science: (4); Foreign language: (2); Social studies: (1); History: (1); Total units: 16 (18). **Tests:** The college uses SAT or ACT scores in admissions decisions. Either SAT or ACT required. For admission to the fall 2007 entering class, the school will accept: ACT with writing, ACT without writing. Campus visit: Recommended. Admissions interview: Recommended. Off-campus interview: Not available. **Factors that count in admissions decisions: *Academic:*** Secondary school record: Very important. Class rank: Very important. Letters of recommendation: Important. Standardized test scores: Important. Essay: Very important. ***Nonacademic:*** Interview: Considered. Extracurricular activities: Considered. Talent/ability: Not considered. Character/personal qualities: Important. Alumni/ae relationship: Considered. Geographical residence: Not considered. State residency: Not considered. Religious affiliation/commitment: Not considered. Minority status: Not considered. Volunteer work: Considered. Work experience: Considered. **Other schools with the greatest overlap in applicants:** Duquesne University; John Carroll University; Pennsylvania State University–University Park; Pennsylvania State–Erie, The Behrend College; University of Pittsburgh. **Admissions statistics for the fall 2005 entering class:** Total applicants: 2,443. Total accepted: 2,111. Freshmen enrolled: 632; 28% were from out of state. Overall acceptance rate: 86%. **Credentials of fall 2005 freshmen:** 21% ranked in the top 10 percent of their high school class; 48% were in the top 25 percent, and 76% were in the top half. (Proportion submitting class standing: 85%.) **Average high school grade point average:** 3.3. **First-year students who submitted SAT scores:** 89%. Scores (25/75 percentile): Verbal: 470-570; Math: 470-580, Combined: 940-1150. **First-year students submitting ACT scores:** 34%. Scores (25/75 percentile): English: 17-24, Math: 18-24, Composite: 18-24.

ACADEMICS

Year founded: 1925. **Academic calendar:** Semester. **Degrees offered:** certificate, associate, bachelor's, post-bachelor's certificate, master's, doctorate. **Most popular majors:** 20% health professions and related clinical sciences, 17% business, management, marketing, and related support services, 12% education, 9% security and protective services, 8% engineering. **Major fields of study:** area, ethnic, cultural, and gender studies; biological and biomedical sciences; business, management, marketing, and related support services; communication, journalism, and related programs; communications technologies/technicians and support services; computer and information sciences and support services; education; engineering; English language and literature/letters; foreign languages, literatures, and linguistics; health professions and related clinical sciences; history; legal professions and studies; liberal arts and sciences studies, and humanities; mathematics and statistics; multi/interdisciplinary studies; natural resources and conservation; personal and culinary services; philosophy and religious studies; physical sciences; psychology; public administration and social service professions; science technologies/technicians; security and protective services; social sciences; theology and religious vocations; visual and performing arts. **Areas of required coursework:** arts/fine arts, humanities, computer literacy, mathematics, English (including composition), philosophy, sciences (biological or physical), history, social science, other. **Pre-professional programs:** pre-law, pre-dentistry, pre-medicine, pre-veterinary science, pre-optometry, pre-pharmacy, other. **Special academic programs:** accelerated program, cooperative (work-study plan) program, distance learning, double major, dual enrollment, honors program, independent study, internships, liberal arts/career combination, study abroad, teacher certificate program. **Teacher certification offered in:** early childhood, special education, elementary, secondary. **Cooperative education programs:** engineering. **Reserve Officers Training Corps (ROTC):** Army ROTC: Offered on campus. **Faculty and instruction (2005-2006):** Total instructional faculty: 180 full-time, 119 part-time (57% men; 43% women; 8% minorities). Full-time faculty with Ph.D. or other terminal degree: 68%. Student/faculty ratio: 13/1. Classes of fewer than 20 students: 57%; of 20 to 49 students: 42%; of 50 or more students: 1%. **Advanced Placement and International Baccalaureate credit:** AP tests may be used for: Credit and/or placement. Scores accepted: 3, 4, 5. International Baccalaureate exams may be used for: Credit and/or placement. **Freshmen returning for sophomore year:** 81%. **Graduation rates:** Four-year: 50%; five-year: 64%; six-year: 65%. **Graduate study:** 27% of students pursue further study immediately upon graduation. Fields in which graduates pursue further study: Master of Business Administration (MBA), 6%; law, 5%; medicine, 10%; dentistry, 1%; engineering, 4%; theology (or the seminary), 1%; education, 5%; arts and sciences, 68%; veterinary medicine, 1%.

COSTS AND FINANCIAL AID

Financial aid office: (814) 871-7337. **Expenses (2006-2007):** Tuition and fees 2006-2007: $19,996; room/board: $7,880. Estimated books and supplies: $1,000; transportation: $615; personal expenses: $1,175. **Financial aid:** Priority filing date for institution's financial aid form: March 15. In 2005-2006, 94% of undergraduates applied for financial aid. Of those, 86% were determined to have financial need; 18% had their need fully met. Average financial aid package (proportion receiving): $15,226 (85%). Average amount of gift aid, such as scholarships or grants (proportion receiving): $11,609 (83%). Average amount of self-help aid, such as work study or loans (proportion receiving): $4,776 (72%). Average need-based loan (excluding PLUS or other private loans): $3,728. Among students who received need-based aid, the average percentage of need met: 72%. Among students who received aid based on merit, the average award (and the proportion receiving): $6,260 (10%). The average athletic scholarship (and the proportion receiving): $15,659 (3%). Average amount of debt of borrowers graduating in 2005: $24,148. Proportion who borrowed: 75%.

CAMPUS LIFE AND EXTRACURRICULAR ACTIVITIES

Campus housing available (% using): coed dorms (42%), apartment for single students (58%), special housing for disabled students. Students who live in college-owned, operated, or affiliated housing: 47%. **Student employment:** During the 2005-2006 academic year, 25% of undergraduates worked on campus. Average per-year earnings: $1,700. **Clubs and organizations:** Number of student organizations: 69. Activities include: choral groups, concert band, dance, drama/theater, literary magazine, music ensembles, pep band, radio station, student government, student newspaper, yearbook. Number of fraternities: 5; sororities: 5. Proportion of men in fraternities: 8%; of women in sororities: 12%. Average proportion of students who stay on campus on weekends: 75%. **Sports program (2005-2006):** Member of NCAA II. ***Men's intercollegiate varsity sports:*** baseball, basketball, cross-country, football, golf, soccer, swimming and diving, water polo, wrestling. ***Women's intercollegiate varsity sports:*** basketball, cross-country, golf, lacrosse, soccer, softball, swimming and diving, volleyball, water polo.

SERVICES AND FACILITIES

Basic services: nonremedial tutoring, placement service, health service, health insurance. **Remedial assistance:** math, writing, other. **Counseling services:** career, personal, academic, older student, psychological, religious. **For learning-disabled students:** School does not offer a structured program with separate admission and additional fees. Total undergraduates in learning-disabled program or receiving services: 24. Services include: remedial English, reading machines, tape recorders, other special classes, oral tests, learning center, readers, extended time for tests, tutors, texts on tape, typist/scribe, other. **Library:** Number of titles: 270,349; number of current serial subscriptions: 14,000. **Information technology resources:** Students are not required to lease or own a computer. Number of campus computers available to all students: 350. School has a wireless network. Approximate number of users that can be accommodated: 800. Proportion of college-owned housing units wired for high-speed internet access: 100%. **Campus safety:** Security services offered: 24-hour foot-and-vehicle patrols, late-night transport/escort service, 24-hour emergency telephones, lighted pathways/sidewalks, controlled dormitory access (key, security card, etc.).

TRANSFER AND INTERNATIONAL STUDENTS

Transfer students: May apply for admission for the following academic terms: Fall, Spring, Summer. Applicants need a minimum number of credits to apply. For fall 2005: Transfer applications received: 222. Transfer applicants offered admission: 132. Transfer applicants enrolled: 59. **International students:** Number of foreign undergraduates: 26 (1% of student body). Number of countries represented: 12. Minimum TOEFL score required: 500 (paper); 173 (computer).

Geneva College

- Address: 3200 College Avenue, Beaver Falls, PA 15010
- Website: http://www.geneva.edu
- Private; Religious affiliation: Reformed Presbyterian of N.A.
- Enrollment: 1,574 full-time; 188 part-time

KEY STATS

✔ **U.S News College Ranking:** third tier, Universities–Master's (North)
✔ **SAT Score (25th/75th percentile):** 980-1210
✔ **Tuition:** 2006-2007: $18,460

Selectivity: Selective	**Room/board:** $6,960
Acceptance rate: 68%	**Average debt:** $23,424
Student/faculty ratio: N/A	**Proportion who borrowed:** 91%

UNDERGRADUATE STUDENT BODY STATS

2005-2006 enrollment: 1,574 full-time; 188 part-time. Men: 43%; women: 57%. **Ethnic makeup:** African American: 9%; Asian American: 1%; White: 88%; International: 1%. **Religious preference:** Roman Catholic: 7%; Protestant: 86%; Unknown: 3%; Reformed Presbyterian of N.A.: 4%.

ADMISSIONS FACTS AND FIGURES

Phone: (724) 847-6500. **Email:** admissions@geneva.edu. **Website:** http://www.geneva.edu. **Application deadlines for fall 2007:** Regular decision: Rolling. Early decision: Not offered. Early action: Not offered. Admission can be deferred. **Application fee:** $25. Common application is accepted. **Admissions requirements/recommendations:** High school units required (recommended): English: 4; Mathematics: 2; Science: 1; Foreign language: 2; Social studies: 3; Academic electives: 4; Total units: 16. Tests: The college uses SAT or ACT scores in admissions decisions. Either SAT or ACT required. For admission to the fall 2007 entering class, the school will accept: ACT with writing. Campus visit: Recommended. Admissions interview: Recommended. Off-campus interview: Not available. **Factors that count in admissions decisions:** *Academic:* Secondary school record: Very important. Class rank: Considered. Letters of recommendation: Very important. Standardized test scores: Very important. Essay: Very important. *Nonacademic:* Interview: Considered. Extracurricular activities: Considered. Talent/ability: Not considered. Character/personal qualities: Considered. Alumni/ae relationship: Considered. Geographical residence: Not considered. State residency: Not considered. Religious affiliation/commitment: Not considered. Minority status: Not considered. Volunteer work: Not considered. Work experience: Not considered. **Other schools with the greatest overlap in applicants:** Grove City College; Messiah College; Pennsylvania State University–University Park; Slippery Rock University of Pennsylvania; University of Pittsburgh. **Admissions statistics for the fall 2005 entering class:** Total applicants: 1,328. Total accepted: 905. Freshmen enrolled: 353; 29% were from out of state. Overall acceptance rate: 68%. **Credentials of fall 2005 freshmen:** 22% ranked in the top 10 percent of their high school class; 45% were in the top 25 percent, and 77% were in the top half. (Proportion submitting class standing: 78%.) **Average high school grade point average:** 3.5. **First-year students who submitted SAT scores:** 90%. Scores (25/75 percentile): Verbal: 490-610, Math: 490-600, Combined: 980-1210. **First-year students submitting ACT scores:** 10%. Scores (25/75 percentile): English: N/A, Math: N/A, Composite: 21-25.

ACADEMICS

Year founded: 1848. **Academic calendar:** Semester. **Degrees offered:** associate, bachelor's, master's. **Most popular majors:** 17% elementary education and teaching, 11% Bible/biblical studies, 11% business administration and management, 8% communication studies/speech communication and rhetoric, 8% social work. **Major fields of study:** biological and biomedical sciences; business, management, marketing, and related support services; communication, journalism, and related programs; computer and information sciences and support services; education; engineering; English language and literature/letters; health professions and related clinical sciences; history; legal professions and studies; mathematics and statistics; philosophy and religious studies; physical sciences; public administration and social service professions; social sciences; theology and religious vocations; transportation and materials moving; visual and performing arts. **Areas of required coursework:** arts/fine arts, humanities, English (including composition), sciences (biological or physical), social science, other. **Pre-professional programs:** pre-law, pre-medicine. **Special academic programs:** accelerated program, cooperative (work-study plan) program, double major, dual enrollment, English as a Second Language (ESL), honors program, independent study, internships, student-designed major, study abroad, teacher certificate program. **Teacher certification offered in:** special education, elementary, secondary. **Cooperative education programs:** other. **Reserve Officers Training Corps (ROTC):** Army ROTC: Offered at cooperating institution (Slippery Rock University). **Faculty and instruction (2005-2006):** Total instructional faculty: 82 full-time, 103 part-time (64% men; 36% women; 7% minorities). Full-time faculty with Ph.D. or other terminal degree: 74%. **Advanced Placement and International Baccalaureate credit:** AP tests may be used for: Credit and/or placement. Scores accepted: 3, 4, 5. International Baccalaureate exams may be used for: Credit and/or placement. **Freshmen returning for sophomore year:** 77%. **Graduation rates:** Four-year: 42%; five-year: 53%; six-year: 56%.

COSTS AND FINANCIAL AID

Financial aid office: (724) 847-6530. **Expenses (2006-2007):** Tuition and fees 2006-2007: $18,460; room/board: $6,960. Estimated books and supplies: $800; transportation: $140; personal expenses: $1,150. **Financial aid:** Priority filing date for institution's financial aid form: March 15. In 2005-2006, 91% of undergraduates applied for financial aid. Of those, 83% were determined to have financial need; 23% had their need fully met. Average financial aid package (proportion receiving): $13,360 (83%). Average amount of gift aid, such as scholarships or grants (proportion receiving): $9,647 (82%). Average amount of self-help aid, such as work study or loans (proportion receiving): $4,370 (72%). Average need-based loan (excluding PLUS or other private loans): $3,634. Among students who received need-based aid, the average percentage of need met: 77%. Among students who received aid based on merit, the average award (and the proportion receiving): $8,558 (15%). The average athletic scholarship (and the proportion receiving): $3,368 (4%). Average amount of debt of borrowers graduating in 2005: $23,424. Proportion who borrowed: 91%.

CAMPUS LIFE AND EXTRACURRICULAR ACTIVITIES

Campus housing available: women's dorms, men's dorms, apartment for single students, other housing options. Students who live in college-owned, operated, or affiliated housing: 71%. Average per-year earnings: $1,500. **Clubs and organizations:** Number of student organizations: 4. Activities include: choral groups, concert band, dance, drama/theater, jazz band, literary magazine, marching band, music ensembles, pep band, radio station, student government, student newspaper, yearbook. Number of fraternities: 0; sororities: 0. Average proportion of students who stay on campus on weekends: 65%. **Sports program (2005-2006):** Member of NAIA. *Men's intercollegiate varsity sports:* baseball, basketball, cross-country, football, soccer, track and field (outdoor). *Women's intercollegiate varsity sports:* basketball, cross-country, soccer, softball, tennis, track and field (outdoor), volleyball.

SERVICES AND FACILITIES

Basic services: health service, health insurance. **Remedial assistance:** reading, math, writing, study skills. **Counseling services:** minority student, career, personal, academic, religious. **For learning-disabled students:** School does not offer a structured program with separate admission and additional fees. Total undergraduates in learning-disabled program or receiving services: 80. Services include: remedial math, remedial English, reading machines, remedial reading, videotaped classes, diagnostic testing service, note-taking services, readers, extended time for tests, tutors, other testing accomodations, other. **Library:** Number of titles: 163,734; number of current serial subscriptions: 857. **Information technology resources:** Students are not

required to lease or own a computer. Number of campus computers available to all students: 150. School has a wireless network. Proportion of college-owned housing units wired for high-speed internet access: 100%.
Campus safety: Security services offered: 24-hour foot-and-vehicle patrols, late-night transport/escort service, lighted pathways/sidewalks, student patrols, controlled dormitory access (key, security card, etc).

TRANSFER AND INTERNATIONAL STUDENTS
Transfer students: May apply for admission for the following academic terms: Fall, Spring, Summer. Applicants need a minimum number of credits to apply. For fall 2005: Transfer applications received: 266. Transfer applicants offered admission: 145. Transfer applicants enrolled: 74.
International students: Number of foreign undergraduates: 16 (1% of student body). Number of countries represented: 17. Minimum TOEFL score required: 480 (paper); 157 (computer). Average TOEFL score: 550 (paper).

Gettysburg College

- **Address:** 300 N. Washington Street, Gettysburg, PA 17325
- **Website:** http://www.gettysburg.edu
- **Private; Religious affiliation:** Lutheran
- **Enrollment:** 2,478 full-time; 26 part-time

KEY STATS
✔ **U.S News College Ranking:** 45, Liberal Arts Colleges
✔ **SAT Score (25th/75th percentile):** 1210-1350
✔ **Tuition:** 2006-2007: $33,795
   Selectivity: More selective   **Room/board:** $8,260
   Acceptance rate: 43%   **Average debt:** $21,810
   Student/faculty ratio: 11/1   **Proportion who borrowed:** 59%

UNDERGRADUATE STUDENT BODY STATS
2005-2006 enrollment: 2,478 full-time; 26 part-time. Men: 48%; women: 52%. **Ethnic makeup:** African American: 4%; Asian American: 1%; Hispanic: 2%; White: 91%; International: 1%. **Religious preference:** Roman Catholic: 28%; Protestant: 20%; Jewish: 2%; No preference: 4%; Unknown: 30%; Lutheran: 6%; Other: 10%.

ADMISSIONS FACTS AND FIGURES
Phone: (800) 431-0803. **Email:** admiss@gettysburg.edu. **Website:** http://www.gettysburg.edu. **Application deadlines for fall 2007:** Regular decision: February 15; decision sent by April 1. Early decision: Send application by: November 15; Decision sent by: December 15. Early action: Not offered. Admission can be deferred. **Application fee:** $45. Common application is accepted. **Admissions requirements/recommendations:** High school units required (recommended): English: 3 (4); Mathematics: 3 (4); Science: 3 (4); Foreign language: 3 (4); Social studies: 3 (4); History: 3 (4); Academic electives: 4 (4); Total units: 4 (4). Tests: The college uses SAT or ACT scores in admissions decisions. Either SAT or ACT required. For admission to the fall 2007 entering class, the school will accept: ACT with writing, ACT without writing. Campus visit: Recommended. Admissions interview: Recommended. **Factors that count in admissions decisions:** *Academic:* Secondary school record: Very important. Class rank: Very important. Letters of recommendation: Very important. Standardized test scores: Important. Essay: Important. *Nonacademic:* Interview: Important. Extracurricular activities: Important. Talent/ability: Important. Character/personal qualities: Important. Alumni/ae relationship: Considered. Geographical residence: Considered. State residency: Not considered. Religious affiliation/commitment: Not considered. Minority status: Considered. Volunteer work: Important. Work experience: Considered. **Other schools with the greatest overlap in applicants:** Bucknell University; Dickinson College; Franklin and Marshall College; Lafayette College; University of Richmond. **Admissions statistics for the fall 2005 entering class:** Total applicants: 5,097. Total accepted: 2,183. Freshmen enrolled: 697; 75% were from out of state. Accepted through early-decision or early-action plans: 35%. Overall acceptance rate: 43%. Early-decision acceptance rate: 75%. Non-early acceptance rate: 41%. **Credentials of fall 2005 freshmen:** 66% ranked in the top 10 percent of their high school class; 89% were in the top 25 percent, and 100% were in the top half. (Proportion submitting class standing: 51%.) **First-year students who submitted SAT scores:** 94%. Scores (25/75 percentile): Verbal: 600-680, Math: 610-670, Combined: 1210-1350.

First-year students submitting ACT scores: 6%. Scores (25/75 percentile): English: N/A, Math: N/A, Composite: 27-30.

ACADEMICS
Year founded: 1832. **Academic calendar:** Semester. **Degrees offered:** bachelor's. **Most popular majors:** 22% business administration and management, 11% political science and government, 9% psychology, 7% English language and literature, 7% biology/biological sciences. **Major fields of study:** agriculture, agriculture operations, and related sciences; area, ethnic, cultural, and gender studies; biological and biomedical sciences; business, management, marketing, and related support services; computer and information sciences and support services; education; English language and literature/letters; foreign languages, literatures, and linguistics; history; mathematics and statistics; multi/interdisciplinary studies; natural resources and conservation; philosophy and religious studies; physical sciences; psychology; social sciences; visual and performing arts. **Areas of required coursework:** arts/fine arts, humanities, computer literacy, mathematics, English (including composition), foreign languages, sciences (biological or physical), history, social science, other. **Pre-professional programs:** pre-law, pre-dentistry, pre-medicine, pre-theology, pre-veterinary science, pre-optometry, pre-pharmacy. **Special academic programs (% participation):** accelerated program (1%), cross-registration (1%), double major (13%), dual enrollment (1%), exchange student program (domestic) (4%), independent study (36%), internships (20%), liberal arts/career combination, student-designed major (3%), study abroad (41%), teacher certificate program (7%). **Teacher certification offered in:** elementary, middle/junior high, secondary. **Reserve Officers Training Corps (ROTC):** Army ROTC: Offered at cooperating institution (Dickinson College). **Faculty and instruction (2005-2006):** Total instructional faculty: 191 full-time, 88 part-time (55% men; 45% women; 13% minorities). Full-time faculty with Ph.D. or other terminal degree: 93%. Student/faculty ratio: 11/1. Classes of fewer than 20 students: 68%; of 20 to 49 students: 31%; of 50 or more students: 0%. **Advanced Placement and International Baccalaureate credit:** AP tests may be used for: Credit only. Scores accepted: 4, 5. International Baccalaureate exams may be used for: Credit and/or placement. **Freshmen returning for sophomore year:** 91%. **Graduation rates:** Four-year: 70%; five-year: 75%; six-year: 76%. **Graduate study:** 30% of students pursue further study immediately upon graduation; 35% within one year; 45% within five years.

COSTS AND FINANCIAL AID
Financial aid office: (717) 337-6611. **Expenses (2006-2007):** Tuition and fees 2006-2007: $33,795; room/board: $8,260. Estimated books and supplies: $500; transportation: $500; personal expenses: $500. **Financial aid:** Priority filing date for institution's financial aid form: January 15; deadline: February 15. In 2005-2006, 65% of undergraduates applied for financial aid. Of those, 56% were determined to have financial need; 100% had their need fully met. Average financial aid package (proportion receiving): $25,089 (56%). Average amount of gift aid, such as scholarships or grants (proportion receiving): $19,711 (56%). Average amount of self-help aid, such as work study or loans (proportion receiving): $5,378 (50%). Average need-based loan (excluding PLUS or other private loans): $4,495. Among students who received need-based aid, the average percentage of need met: 100%. Among students who received aid based on merit, the average award (and the proportion receiving): $9,571 (12%). The average athletic scholarship (and the proportion receiving): $0 (0%). Average amount of debt of borrowers graduating in 2005: $21,810. Proportion who borrowed: 59%.

CAMPUS LIFE AND EXTRACURRICULAR ACTIVITIES
Campus housing available: coed dorms, women's dorms, men's dorms, fraternity housing, apartment for single students, cooperative housing, other housing options. Students who live in college-owned, operated, or affiliated housing: 94%. **Student employment:** During the 2005-2006 academic year, 30% of undergraduates worked on campus. Average per-year earnings: $975. **Clubs and organizations:** Number of student organizations: 109. Activities include: choral groups, concert band, dance, drama/theater, jazz band, literary magazine, marching band, music ensembles, musical theater, radio station, student government, student newspaper, yearbook. Number of fraternities: 11; sororities: 5. Proportion of men in fraternities: 40%; of women in sororities: 26%. Average proportion of students who stay on campus on weekends: 90%. **Sports program (2005-2006):** Member of NCAA III. **Men's intercollegiate varsity sports:** baseball, basketball, cross-country, football, golf, lacrosse, soccer, swimming and diving, tennis, track and field (indoor), track and field (outdoor), wrestling. **Women's intercollegiate varsity sports:** basketball, cross-country, field hockey, golf, lacrosse, soccer, softball, swimming and diving, tennis, track and field (indoor), track and field (outdoor), volleyball.

SERVICES AND FACILITIES

Basic services: nonremedial tutoring, women's center, placement service, health service. **Remedial assistance:** math, writing. **Counseling services:** minority student, career, personal, academic, psychological, birth control, religious, other. **For learning-disabled students:** School does not offer a structured program with separate admission and additional fees. Services include: tape recorders, extended time for tests, tutors. **Library:** Number of titles: 382,603; number of current serial subscriptions: 5,162. **Information technology resources:** Students are not required to lease or own a computer. Number of campus computers available to all students: 239. School has a wireless network. Approximate number of users that can be accommodated: 284. Proportion of college-owned housing units wired for high-speed internet access: 100%. **Campus safety:** Security services offered: 24-hour foot-and-vehicle patrols, late-night transport/escort service, 24-hour emergency telephones, lighted pathways/sidewalks, controlled dormitory access (key, security card, etc).

TRANSFER AND INTERNATIONAL STUDENTS

Transfer students: May apply for admission for the following academic terms: Fall, Spring. For fall 2005: Transfer applications received: 148. Transfer applicants offered admission: 27. Transfer applicants enrolled: 12. **International students:** Number of foreign undergraduates: 35 (1% of student body). Number of countries represented: 27. Minimum TOEFL score required: 550 (paper); 213 (computer).

Gratz College

- **Address:** 7605 Old York Road, Melrose Park, PA 19027
- **Website:** http://www.gratzcollege.edu
- **Private; Religious affiliation:** Jewish
- **Enrollment:** N/A

KEY STATS
✔ **U.S News College Ranking:** Unranked, Universities–Master's (North)
✔ **SAT or ACT Score (25th/75th percentile):** N/A
✔ **Tuition:** N/A

Selectivity: N/A	**Room/board:** N/A
Acceptance rate: N/A	**Average debt:** N/A
Student/faculty ratio: N/A	**Proportion who borrowed:** N/A

Grove City College

- **Address:** 100 Campus Drive, Grove City, PA 16127
- **Website:** http://www.gcc.edu
- **Private; Religious affiliation:** Presbyterian
- **Enrollment:** 2,308 full-time; 33 part-time

KEY STATS
✔ **U.S News College Ranking:** 7, Comp. Coll.–Bachelor's (North)
✔ **SAT Score (25th/75th percentile):** 1161-1396
✔ **Tuition:** 2006-2007: $10,962

Selectivity: More selective	**Room/board:** $5,766
Acceptance rate: 45%	**Average debt:** $23,409
Student/faculty ratio: 16/1	**Proportion who borrowed:** 53%

UNDERGRADUATE STUDENT BODY STATS

2005-2006 enrollment: 2,308 full-time; 33 part-time. Men: 50%; women: 50%. **Ethnic makeup:** Asian American: 2%; White: 97%; International: 1%. **Religious preference:** Roman Catholic: 7%; Protestant: 54%; No preference: 20%; Presbyterian: 19%.

ADMISSIONS FACTS AND FIGURES

Phone: (724) 458-2100. **Email:** admissions@gcc.edu. **Website:** http://www.gcc.edu. **Application deadlines for fall 2007:** Regular decision: February 1; decision sent by March 15. Early decision: Send application by: November 15; Decision sent by: December 15. Early action: Not offered. Admission can be deferred. **Application fee:** $50. Common application is not accepted. **Admissions requirements/recommendations:** High school units required (recommended): English: (4); Mathematics: (3); Science: (3);

Foreign language: (3); Social studies: (2); History: (2); Total units: (17). Tests: The college uses SAT or ACT scores in admissions decisions. Either SAT or ACT required. For admission to the fall 2007 entering class, the school will accept: ACT without writing. Campus visit: Recommended. Admissions interview: Recommended. Off-campus interview: Not available. **Factors that count in admissions decisions:** *Academic:* Secondary school record: Very important. Class rank: Important. Letters of recommendation: Important. Standardized test scores: Important. Essay: Important. *Nonacademic:* Interview: Very important. Extracurricular activities: Very important. Talent/ability: Very important. Character/personal qualities: Very important. Alumni/ae relationship: Considered. Geographical residence: Important. State residency: Considered. Religious affiliation/commitment: Very important. Minority status: Considered. Volunteer work: Important. Work experience: Considered. **Other schools with the greatest overlap in applicants:** Hillsdale College; Messiah College; Pennsylvania State University–University Park; University of Pittsburgh; Wheaton College. **Admissions statistics for the fall 2005 entering class:** Total applicants: 2,077. Total accepted: 925. Freshmen enrolled: 582; 51% were from out of state. Accepted through early-decision or early-action plans: 54%. Overall acceptance rate: 45%. Early-decision acceptance rate: 51%. Non-early acceptance rate: 42%. **Size of waiting list:** 944 applicants; enrolled from waiting list: 32. **Credentials of fall 2005 freshmen:** 54% ranked in the top 10 percent of their high school class; 83% were in the top 25 percent, and 95% were in the top half. (Proportion submitting class standing: 78%.) **Average high school grade point average:** 3.9. **First-year students who submitted SAT scores:** 94%. Scores (25/75 percentile): Verbal: 579-698, Math: 582-698, Combined: 1161-1396. **First-year students submitting ACT scores:** 34%. Scores (25/75 percentile): English: 25-31, Math: 25-29, Composite: 25-30.

ACADEMICS

Year founded: 1876. **Academic calendar:** Semester. **Degrees offered:** bachelor's. **Most popular majors:** 21% business, management, marketing, and related support services, 12% education, 11% biological and biomedical sciences, 8% engineering, 7% English language and literature. **Major fields of study:** biological and biomedical sciences; business, management, marketing, and related support services; communication, journalism, and related programs; computer and information sciences and support services; education; engineering; English language and literature/letters; history; mathematics and statistics; philosophy and religious studies; physical sciences; psychology; social sciences; theology and religious vocations; visual and performing arts. **Areas of required coursework:** arts/fine arts, humanities, mathematics, philosophy, foreign languages, sciences (biological or physical), history, social science. **Pre-professional programs:** pre-law, pre-dentistry, pre-medicine, pre-theology, pre-veterinary science. **Special academic programs:** accelerated program, cross-registration, double major, independent study, internships, student-designed major, study abroad, teacher certificate program. **Teacher certification offered in:** early childhood, elementary, middle/junior high, secondary. **Reserve Officers Training Corps (ROTC):** Army ROTC: Offered at cooperating institution (Slippery Rock University). **Faculty and instruction (2005-2006):** Total instructional faculty: 125 full-time, 59 part-time (71% men; 29% women; 1% minorities). Full-time faculty with Ph.D. or other terminal degree: 81%. Student/faculty ratio: 16/1. Classes of fewer than 20 students: 36%; of 20 to 49 students: 58%; of 50 or more students: 6%. **Advanced Placement and International Baccalaureate credit:** International Baccalaureate exams may be used for: Credit only. **Freshmen returning for sophomore year:** 90%. **Graduation rates:** Four-year: 74%; five-year: 80%; six-year: 81%. **Graduate study:** 20% of students pursue further study immediately upon graduation; 50% within five years. Fields in which graduates pursue further study: Master of Business Administration (MBA), 1%; law, 1%; medicine, 2%; engineering, 1%; education, 2%; arts and sciences, 13%.

COSTS AND FINANCIAL AID

Financial aid office: (724) 458-3300. **Expenses (2006-2007):** Tuition and fees 2006-2007: $10,962; room/board: $5,766. Estimated books and supplies: $900; transportation: $500; personal expenses: $350. **Financial aid:** In 2005-2006, 44% of undergraduates applied for financial aid. Of those, 36% were determined to have financial need; 9% had their need fully met. Average financial aid package (proportion receiving): $5,175 (36%). Average amount of gift aid, such as scholarships or grants (proportion receiving): $4,971 (33%). Average amount of self-help aid, such as work study or loans (proportion receiving): $0 (22%). Average need-based loan (excluding PLUS or other private loans): $0. Among students who received need-based aid, the average percentage of need met: 49%. Among students who received aid based on merit, the average award (and the proportion receiving): $6,260 (34%). The average athletic scholarship (and the proportion receiving): $0 (0%). Average amount of debt of borrowers graduating in 2005: $23,409. Proportion who borrowed: 53%.

CAMPUS LIFE AND EXTRACURRICULAR ACTIVITIES

Campus housing available (% using): women's dorms (46%), men's dorms (46%), apartment for single students (8%). Students who live in college-owned, operated, or affiliated housing: 93%. **Student employment:** During the 2005-2006 academic year, 30% of undergraduates worked on campus. Average per-year earnings: $1,000. **Clubs and organizations:** Number of student organizations: 130. Activities include: choral groups, concert band, dance, drama/theater, jazz band, literary magazine, marching band, music ensembles, musical theater, opera, pep band, radio station, student government, student newspaper, symphony orchestra, yearbook. Number of fraternities: 8; sororities: 9. Proportion of men in fraternities: 15%; of women in sororities: 17%. Average proportion of students who stay on campus on weekends: 80%. **Sports program (2005-2006):** Member of NCAA II. *Men's intercollegiate varsity sports:* baseball, basketball, cross-country, football, golf, soccer, swimming and diving, tennis, track and field (outdoor), water polo. *Women's intercollegiate varsity sports:* basketball, cross-country, golf, soccer, softball, swimming and diving, tennis, track and field (outdoor), volleyball, water polo.

SERVICES AND FACILITIES

Basic services: nonremedial tutoring, placement service, health service, health insurance. **Counseling services:** minority student, career, personal, academic, psychological, birth control, religious. **For learning-disabled students:** School does not offer a structured program with separate admission and additional fees. Total undergraduates in learning-disabled program or receiving services: 0. Services include: tape recorders, tutors. **Library:** Number of titles: 140,000; number of current serial subscriptions: 5,633. **Information technology resources:** Students are required to lease or own a computer. Number of campus computers available to all students: 2,341. School has a wireless network. Approximate number of users that can be accommodated: 3,000. Proportion of college-owned housing units wired for high-speed internet access: 100%. **Campus safety:** Security services offered: 24-hour foot-and-vehicle patrols, late-night transport/escort service, lighted pathways/sidewalks, student patrols, controlled dormitory access (key, security card, etc).

TRANSFER AND INTERNATIONAL STUDENTS

Transfer students: May apply for admission for the following academic terms: Fall, Spring. Applicants do not need a minimum number of credits to apply. For fall 2005: Transfer applications received: 81. Transfer applicants offered admission: 30. Transfer applicants enrolled: 26. **International students:** Number of foreign undergraduates: 13 (1% of student body). Minimum TOEFL score required: 550 (paper); 213 (computer). Average TOEFL score: 650 (paper).

Gwynedd-Mercy College

- **Address:** 1325 Sumneytown Pike, PO Box 901, Gwynedd Valley, PA 19437-0901
- **Website:** http://www.gmc.edu
- **Private; Religious affiliation:** Roman Catholic
- **Enrollment:** 1,273 full-time; 907 part-time

KEY STATS

✔ **U.S News College Ranking:** third tier, Universities–Master's (North)
✔ **SAT Score (25th/75th percentile):** 870-1060
✔ **Tuition:** 2006-2007: $18,945

Selectivity: Less selective	**Room/board:** $8,300
Acceptance rate: 65%	**Average debt:** $18,750
Student/faculty ratio: 13/1	**Proportion who borrowed:** 89%

UNDERGRADUATE STUDENT BODY STATS

2005-2006 enrollment: 1,273 full-time; 907 part-time. Men: 25%; women: 75%. **Ethnic makeup:** African American: 14%; Asian American: 3%; Hispanic: 2%; White: 80%; International: 1%. **Religious preference:** Roman Catholic: 54%; Protestant: 19%; Jewish: 1%; Muslim: 1%; Unknown: 6%; Other: 19%.

ADMISSIONS FACTS AND FIGURES

Phone: (215) 681-5510. **Email:** admissions@gmc.edu. **Website:** http://www.gmc.edu. **Application deadlines for fall 2007:** Regular decision: August 20. Early decision: Not offered. Early action: Not offered. Admission can be deferred. **Application fee:** $25. Common application is accepted. **To apply online, go to:** http://www.gmc.edu/admissions/apply.html. **Admissions requirements/recommendations:** High school units required (recommended): English: 4; Mathematics: 3; Science: 3; History: 1; Academic electives: 3; Total units: 16. Tests: The college uses SAT or ACT scores in admissions decisions. Either SAT or ACT required. Campus visit: Recommended. Admissions interview: Recommended. Off-campus interview: May be arranged. **Factors that count in admissions decisions:** *Academic:* Secondary school record: Very important. Class rank: Important. Letters of recommendation: Important. Standardized test scores: Important. Essay: Not considered. *Nonacademic:* Interview: Considered. Extracurricular activities: Important. Talent/ability: Not considered. Character/personal qualities: Considered. Alumni/ae relationship: Considered. Geographical residence: Not considered. State residency: Not considered. Religious affiliation/commitment: Not considered. Minority status: Not considered. Volunteer work: Considered. Work experience: Considered. **Admissions statistics for the fall 2005 entering class:** Total applicants: 1,622. Total accepted: 1,052. Freshmen enrolled: 345; 13% were from out of state. Overall acceptance rate: 65%. Size of waiting list: 0 applicants; enrolled from waiting list: 0. **Credentials of fall 2005 freshmen:** 4% ranked in the top 10 percent of their high school class; 20% were in the top 25 percent, and 58% were in the top half. (Proportion submitting class standing: 79%.) First-year students who submitted SAT scores: 99%. Scores (25/75 percentile): Verbal: 440-530, Math: 430-530, Combined: 870-1060.

ACADEMICS

Year founded: 1948. **Academic calendar:** Semester. **Degrees offered:** certificate, associate, bachelor's, post-bachelor's certificate, master's, post-master's certificate. **Most popular majors:** 39% business, management, marketing, and related support services, 20% education, 18% health professions and related clinical sciences, 7% computer and information sciences and support services, 6% psychology. **Major fields of study:** biological and biomedical sciences; business, management, marketing, and related support services; communication, journalism, and related programs; computer and information sciences and support services; education; English language and literature/letters; health professions and related clinical sciences; history; mathematics and statistics; psychology; public administration and social service professions; security and protective services; social sciences. **Areas of required coursework:** arts/fine arts, humanities, English (including composition), philosophy, history, social science, other. **Pre-professional programs:** pre-law. **Special academic programs (% participation):** accelerated program (12%), cooperative (work-study plan) program (1%), cross-registration, double major (1%), English as a Second Language (ESL) (3%), honors program (2%), independent study, internships, liberal arts/career combination (100%), study abroad, teacher certificate program (25%), weekend college. **Teacher certification offered in:** early childhood, special education, elementary, secondary. **Faculty and instruction (2005-2006):** Total instructional faculty: 78 full-time, 196 part-time (45% men; 55% women; 5% minorities). Full-time faculty with Ph.D. or other terminal degree: 54%. Student/faculty ratio: 13/1. Classes of fewer than 20 students: 65%; of 20 to 49 students: 32%; of 50 or more students: 3%. **Advanced Placement and International Baccalaureate credit:** AP tests may be used for: Credit only. Scores accepted: 3, 4, 5. **Freshmen returning for sophomore year:** 81%. **Graduation rates:** Four-year: 64%; five-year: 73%; six-year: 74%. **Graduate study:** 28% of students pursue further study within one year.

COSTS AND FINANCIAL AID

Financial aid office: (215) 641-5570. **Expenses (2006-2007):** Tuition and fees 2006-2007: $18,945; room/board: $8,300. Estimated books and supplies: $500; transportation: $500; personal expenses: $1,000. **Financial aid:** Priority filing date for institution's financial aid form: March 1; deadline: July 15. In 2005-2006, 87% of undergraduates applied for financial aid. Of those, 75% were determined to have financial need; 17% had their need fully met. Average financial aid package (proportion receiving): $13,189 (74%). Average amount of gift aid, such as scholarships or grants (proportion receiving): $10,039 (73%). Average amount of self-help aid, such as work study or loans (proportion receiving): $3,963 (62%). Average need-based loan (excluding PLUS or other private loans): $3,352. Among students who received need-based aid, the average percentage of need met: 73%. Among students who received aid based on merit, the average award (and the proportion receiving): $11,737 (19%). The average athletic scholarship (and the proportion receiving): $0 (0%). Average amount of debt of borrowers graduating in 2005: $18,750. Proportion who borrowed: 89%.

CAMPUS LIFE AND EXTRACURRICULAR ACTIVITIES
Campus housing available (% using): coed dorms (100%), special housing for disabled students (0%). Students who live in college-owned, operated, or affiliated housing: 24%. **Clubs and organizations:** Number of student organizations: 22. Activities include: choral groups, literary magazine, student government, student newspaper, yearbook. Number of fraternities: 0; sororities: 0. Average proportion of students who stay on campus on weekends: 35%. **Sports program (2005-2006):** Member of NCAA III. *Men's intercollegiate varsity sports:* baseball, basketball, cross-country, golf, soccer, tennis, track and field (indoor), track and field (outdoor). *Women's intercollegiate varsity sports:* basketball, cross-country, field hockey, lacrosse, soccer, softball, tennis, track and field (indoor), track and field (outdoor), volleyball.

SERVICES AND FACILITIES
Basic services: nonremedial tutoring, day care, health service, health insurance. **Remedial assistance:** math, writing, study skills. **Counseling services:** career, personal, academic, religious. **For learning-disabled students:** School does not offer a structured program with separate admission and additional fees. Services include: remedial math, remedial English, reading machines, tape recorders, untimed tests, oral tests, learning center, readers, extended time for tests, tutors, other. **Library:** Number of titles: 99,493; number of current serial subscriptions: 685. **Information technology resources:** Students are not required to lease or own a computer. Number of campus computers available to all students: 265. School has a wireless network. **Campus safety:** Security services offered: 24-hour foot-and-vehicle patrols, late-night transport/escort service, 24-hour emergency telephones, lighted pathways/sidewalks, controlled dormitory access (key, security card, etc.).

TRANSFER AND INTERNATIONAL STUDENTS
Transfer students: May apply for admission for the following academic terms: Fall, Spring, Summer. Applicants do not need a minimum number of credits to apply. For fall 2005: Transfer applications received: 1,127. Transfer applicants offered admission: 467. Transfer applicants enrolled: 269. **International students:** Number of foreign undergraduates: 20 (1% of student body). Number of countries represented: 51. Minimum TOEFL score required: 525 (paper); 195 (computer).

Haverford College

- **Address:** 370 Lancaster Avenue, Haverford, PA 19041-1392
- **Website:** http://www.haverford.edu
- **Private**
- **Enrollment:** 1,168 full-time

KEY STATS
✔ **U.S News College Ranking:** 9, Liberal Arts Colleges
✔ **SAT Score (25th/75th percentile):** 1290-1470
✔ **Tuition:** 2006-2007: $33,710

Selectivity: Most selective	**Room/board:** $10,390
Acceptance rate: 26%	**Average debt:** $16,330
Student/faculty ratio: 8/1	**Proportion who borrowed:** 36%

UNDERGRADUATE STUDENT BODY STATS
2005-2006 enrollment: 1,168 full-time. Men: 47%; women: 53%. **Ethnic makeup:** African American: 7%; American-Indian: 1%; Asian American: 13%; Hispanic: 8%; White: 69%; International: 4%.

ADMISSIONS FACTS AND FIGURES
Phone: (610) 896-1350. **Email:** admitme@haverford.edu. **Website:** http://www.haverford.edu. **Application deadlines for fall 2007:** Regular decision: January 15; decision sent by April 15. Early decision: Send application by: November 15; Decision sent by: December 15. Early action: Not offered. Admission can be deferred. **Application fee:** $60. Common application is accepted. **To apply online, go to:** http://www.haverford.edu/admissions/how-toapply.html. **Admissions requirements/recommendations:** High school units required (recommended): English: 4; Mathematics: 3 (4); Science: 1 (2); Foreign language: 2 (3); Social studies: 2; Total units: 12. Tests: The college uses SAT or ACT scores in admissions decisions. Either SAT or ACT required. For admission to the fall 2007 entering class, the school will

accept: ACT with writing. Campus visit: Recommended. Admissions interview: Recommended. Off-campus interview: May be arranged. **Factors that count in admissions decisions:** *Academic:* Secondary school record: Very important. Class rank: Important. Letters of recommendation: Important. Standardized test scores: Very important. Essay: Very important. *Nonacademic:* Interview: Considered. Extracurricular activities: Important. Talent/ability: Important. Character/personal qualities: Very important. Alumni/ae relationship: Considered. Geographical residence: Considered. State residency: Not considered. Religious affiliation/commitment: Not considered. Minority status: Considered. Volunteer work: Important. Work experience: Important. **Other schools with the greatest overlap in applicants:** Amherst College; Brown University; Swarthmore College; Tufts University; Wesleyan University. **Admissions statistics for the fall 2005 entering class:** Total applicants: 3,112. Total accepted: 816. Freshmen enrolled: 316; 85% were from out of state. Accepted through early-decision or early-action plans: 33%. Overall acceptance rate: 26%. Early-decision acceptance rate: 50%. Non-early acceptance rate: 25%. **Size of waiting list:** 610 applicants; enrolled from waiting list: 28. **Credentials of fall 2005 freshmen:** 91% ranked in the top 10 percent of their high school class; 96% were in the top 25 percent, and 100% were in the top half. (Proportion submitting class standing: 44%.) **First-year students who submitted SAT scores:** 99%. Scores (25/75 percentile): Verbal: 640-740, Math: 650-730, Combined: 1290-1470. **First-year students submitting ACT scores:** 1%. Scores (25/75 percentile): English: N/A, Math: N/A, Composite: N/A.

ACADEMICS
Year founded: 1833. **Academic calendar:** Semester. **Degrees offered:** bachelor's. **Most popular majors:** 12% biology/biological sciences, 9% English language and literature, 9% history, 8% mathematics, 8% political science and government. **Major fields of study:** area, ethnic, cultural, and gender studies; biological and biomedical sciences; computer and information sciences and support services; English language and literature/letters; foreign languages, literatures, and linguistics; history; liberal arts and sciences studies, and humanities; mathematics and statistics; multi/interdisciplinary studies; philosophy and religious studies; physical sciences; psychology; social sciences; visual and performing arts. **Areas of required coursework:** humanities, mathematics, English (including composition), foreign languages, sciences (biological or physical), social science, other. **Pre-professional programs:** pre-law, pre-medicine. **Special academic programs (% participation):** cross-registration (75%), double major (7%), exchange student program (domestic) (1%), independent study (5%), internships, liberal arts/career combination, student-designed major (2%), study abroad (43%), teacher certificate program (1%). **Teacher certification offered in:** secondary. **Faculty and instruction (2005-2006):** Total instructional faculty: 111 full-time, 5 part-time (53% men; 47% women; 22% minorities). Full-time faculty with Ph.D. or other terminal degree: 98%. Student/faculty ratio: 8/1. Classes of fewer than 20 students: 72%; of 20 to 49 students: 26%; of 50 or more students: 2%. **Advanced Placement and International Baccalaureate credit:** AP tests may be used for: Credit only. Scores accepted: 4, 5. International Baccalaureate exams may be used for: Credit only. **Freshmen returning for sophomore year:** 96%. **Graduation rates:** Four-year: 81%; five-year: 85%; six-year: 88%. **Graduate study:** 18% of students pursue further study immediately upon graduation; 54% within five years. Fields in which graduates pursue further study: law, 3%; medicine, 4%; arts and sciences, 9%.

COSTS AND FINANCIAL AID
Financial aid office: (610) 896-1350. **Expenses (2006-2007):** Tuition and fees 2006-2007: $33,710; room/board: $10,390. Estimated books and supplies: $1,194; transportation: $145; personal expenses: $1,468. **Financial aid:** In 2005-2006, 50% of undergraduates applied for financial aid. Of those, 43% were determined to have financial need; 100% had their need fully met. Average financial aid package (proportion receiving): $26,990 (43%). Average amount of gift aid, such as scholarships or grants (proportion receiving): $24,073 (41%). Average amount of self-help aid, such as work study or loans (proportion receiving): $4,466 (40%). Average need-based loan (excluding PLUS or other private loans): $3,884. Among students who received need-based aid, the average percentage of need met: 100%. Average amount of debt of borrowers graduating in 2005: $16,330. Proportion who borrowed: 36%.

CAMPUS LIFE AND EXTRACURRICULAR ACTIVITIES
Campus housing available (% using): coed dorms (56%), apartment for single students (36%), cooperative housing (1%), other housing options (7%). Students who live in college-owned, operated, or affiliated housing: 99%. **Student employment:** During the 2005-2006 academic year, 20% of undergraduates worked on campus. **Clubs and organizations:** Number of student

organizations: 93. Activities include: choral groups, dance, drama/theater, literary magazine, music ensembles, musical theater, radio station, student government, student newspaper, yearbook. Number of fraternities: 0; sororities: 0. Average proportion of students who stay on campus on weekends: 85%. **Sports program (2005-2006):** Member of NCAA III. ***Men's intercollegiate varsity sports:*** baseball, basketball, cross-country, fencing, lacrosse, soccer, tennis, track and field (indoor), track and field (outdoor). ***Women's intercollegiate varsity sports:*** basketball, cross-country, fencing, field hockey, lacrosse, soccer, softball, squash, tennis, track and field (indoor), track and field (outdoor), volleyball.

SERVICES AND FACILITIES

Basic services: nonremedial tutoring, women's center, placement service, health service, health insurance. **Counseling services:** minority student, career, personal, academic, psychological, birth control. **For learning-disabled students:** School does not offer a structured program with separate admission and additional fees. Total undergraduates in learning-disabled program or receiving services: 41. **Library:** Number of titles: 757,759; number of current serial subscriptions: 4,506. **Information technology resources:** Students are not required to lease or own a computer. Number of campus computers available to all students: 300. Proportion of college-owned housing units wired for high-speed internet access: 100%. **Campus safety:** Security services offered: 24-hour foot-and-vehicle patrols, late-night transport/escort service, 24-hour emergency telephones, lighted pathways/sidewalks, controlled dormitory access (key, security card, etc).

TRANSFER AND INTERNATIONAL STUDENTS

Transfer students: May apply for admission for the following academic terms: Fall. Applicants need a minimum number of credits to apply. For fall 2005: Transfer applications received: 105. Transfer applicants offered admission: 8. Transfer applicants enrolled: 2. **International students:** Number of foreign undergraduates: 44 (4% of student body). Minimum TOEFL score required: 600 (paper); 250 (computer).

Holy Family University

- **Address:** 9701 Frankford Avenue, Philadelphia, PA 19114-2094
- **Website:** http://www.holyfamily.edu
- **Private; Religious affiliation:** Roman Catholic
- **Enrollment:** 1,379 full-time; 856 part-time

KEY STATS

✔ **U.S News College Ranking:** third tier, Universities–Master's (North)
✔ **SAT Score (25th/75th percentile):** 870-1030
✔ **Tuition (2006-2007):** $18,850

Selectivity: Less selective	**Room/board:** $8,300
Acceptance rate: 70%	**Average debt:** $17,125
Student/faculty ratio: 15/1	**Proportion who borrowed:** 68%

UNDERGRADUATE STUDENT BODY STATS

2005-2006 enrollment: 1,379 full-time; 856 part-time. Men: 24%; women: 76%. **Ethnic makeup:** African American: 8%; Asian American: 4%; Hispanic: 3%; White: 82%; International: 2%. **Religious preference:** Roman Catholic: 72%; Protestant: 13%; Jewish: 2%; Buddhist: 1%; No preference: 2%; Unknown: 6%.

ADMISSIONS FACTS AND FIGURES

Phone: (215) 637-3050. **Email:** admissions@holyfamily.edu. **Website:** http://www.holyfamily.edu. **Application deadlines for fall 2007:** Regular decision: Rolling. Early decision: Not offered. Early action: Not offered. Admission can be deferred. **Application fee:** $25. Common application is accepted. **To apply online, go to:** http://my.holyfamily.edu/i2e/app/. **Admissions requirements/recommendations:** High school units required (recommended): English: 4 (4); Mathematics: 3 (3); Science: 2 (2); Foreign language: (2); Social studies: (0); History: 2 (2); Academic electives: 3 (3); Total units: 14 (16). Tests: The college uses SAT or ACT scores in admissions decisions. Either SAT or ACT required. For admission to the fall 2007 entering class, the school will accept: ACT with writing. Campus visit: Recommended. Admissions interview: Recommended. Off-campus interview: May be arranged. **Factors that count in admissions decisions:** *Academic:* Secondary school record: Very important. Class rank: Important. Letters of recommendation: Considered. Standardized test scores:

Important. Essay: Important. *Nonacademic:* Interview: Considered. Extracurricular activities: Important. Talent/ability: Considered. Character/personal qualities: Considered. Alumni/ae relationship: Considered. Geographical residence: Not considered. State residency: Not considered. Religious affiliation/commitment: Not considered. Minority status: Not considered. Volunteer work: Considered. Work experience: Considered. **Other schools with the greatest overlap in applicants:** Arcadia University; Gwynedd-Mercy College; La Salle University; Pennsylvania State University–University Park; Temple University. **Admissions statistics for the fall 2005 entering class:** Total applicants: 859. Total accepted: 597. Freshmen enrolled: 436; 13% were from out of state. Overall acceptance rate: 70%. **Size of waiting list:** 0 applicants; enrolled from waiting list: 0. **Credentials of fall 2005 freshmen:** 11% ranked in the top 10 percent of their high school class; 38% were in the top 25 percent, and 78% were in the top half. (Proportion submitting class standing: 96%.) **Average high school grade point average:** 3.0. **First-year students who submitted SAT scores:** 97%. Scores (25/75 percentile): Verbal: 440-520, Math: 430-510, Combined: 870-1030. **First-year students submitting ACT scores:** 2%. Scores (25/75 percentile): English: 20-24, Math: 16-18, Composite: 19-23.

ACADEMICS

Year founded: 1954. **Academic calendar:** Semester. **Degrees offered:** certificate, associate, bachelor's, post-bachelor's certificate, master's, post-master's certificate. **Most popular majors:** 57% education, 18% business, management, marketing, and related support services, 13% health professions and related clinical sciences, 8% physical sciences, 2% communications technologies/technicians and support services. **Major fields of study:** biological and biomedical sciences; business, management, marketing, and related support services; computer and information sciences and support services; education; English language and literature/letters; foreign languages, literatures, and linguistics; health professions and related clinical sciences; liberal arts and sciences studies, and humanities; mathematics and statistics; parks, recreation, leisure, and fitness studies; philosophy and religious studies; physical sciences; psychology; public administration and social service professions; security and protective services; social sciences; theology and religious vocations; visual and performing arts. **Areas of required coursework:** humanities, computer literacy, English (including composition), philosophy, foreign languages, sciences (biological or physical), social science. **Pre-professional programs:** pre-law, pre-dentistry, pre-medicine, pre-optometry, pre-pharmacy. **Special academic programs (% participation):** accelerated program (7%), cooperative (work-study plan) program (2%), honors program (3%), independent study (2%), internships (8%), study abroad (1%), teacher certificate program (14%). **Teacher certification offered in:** early childhood, special education, elementary, secondary. **Cooperative education programs:** art, business, computer science, education, health professions, humanities, natural science, social/behavioral science. **Faculty and instruction (2005-2006):** Total instructional faculty: 91 full-time, 255 part-time (46% men; 54% women; 6% minorities). Full-time faculty with Ph.D. or other terminal degree: 66%. Student/faculty ratio: 15/1. Classes of fewer than 20 students: 72%; of 20 to 49 students: 28%; of 50 or more students: 0%. **Advanced Placement and International Baccalaureate credit:** AP tests may be used for: Credit and/or placement. Scores accepted: 3, 4, 5. International Baccalaureate exams may be used for: Credit and/or placement. **Freshmen returning for sophomore year:** 80%. **Graduation rates:** Four-year: 70%; five-year: 79%; six-year: 73%. **Graduate study:** 3% of students pursue further study immediately upon graduation; 3% within one year. Fields in which graduates pursue further study: law, 1%; medicine, 1%; education, 2%; arts and sciences, 2%.

COSTS AND FINANCIAL AID

Financial aid office: (215) 637-5538. **Expenses (2006-2007):** Tuition and fees 2006-2007: $18,850; room/board: $8,300. Estimated books and supplies: $926; transportation: $700; personal expenses: $0. **Financial aid:** Priority filing date for institution's financial aid form: March 1. In 2005-2006, 85% of undergraduates applied for financial aid. Of those, 72% were determined to have financial need; 100% had their need fully met. Average financial aid package (proportion receiving): $8,500 (72%). Average amount of gift aid, such as scholarships or grants (proportion receiving): $4,000 (72%). Average amount of self-help aid, such as work study or loans (proportion receiving): $4,000 (6%). Average need-based loan (excluding PLUS or other private loans): $3,875. Among students who received need-based aid, the average percentage of need met: 85%. Among students who received aid based on merit, the average award (and the proportion receiving): $6,000 (3%). The average athletic scholarship (and the proportion receiving): $7,500 (8%). Average amount of debt of borrowers graduating in 2005: $17,125. Proportion who borrowed: 68%.

CAMPUS LIFE AND EXTRACURRICULAR ACTIVITIES

Campus housing available (% using): coed dorms (62%), other housing options (38%). Students who live in college-owned, operated, or affiliated housing: 21%. **Student employment:** During the 2005-2006 academic year, 0% of undergraduates worked on campus. **Clubs and organizations:** Number of student organizations: 24. Activities include: choral groups, literary magazine, student government, student newspaper, yearbook. Number of fraternities: 0; sororities: 0. Average proportion of students who stay on campus on weekends: 7%. **Sports program (2005-2006):** Member of NCAA II. *Men's intercollegiate varsity sports:* basketball, cross-country, golf, soccer. *Women's intercollegiate varsity sports:* basketball, cross-country, soccer, softball, tennis, volleyball.

SERVICES AND FACILITIES

Basic services: placement service. **Remedial assistance:** reading, math, writing, study skills. **Counseling services:** minority student, career, academic, psychological, religious. **For learning-disabled students:** School does not offer a structured program with separate admission and additional fees. Total undergraduates in learning-disabled program or receiving services: 64. Services include: remedial math, remedial English, reading machines, remedial reading, tape recorders, other special classes, note-taking services, oral tests, learning center, readers, extended time for tests, tutors, priority seating, texts on tape, other testing accomodations, other. **Library:** Number of titles: 115,000; number of current serial subscriptions: 575. **Information technology resources:** Students are not required to lease or own a computer. Number of campus computers available to all students: 450. School does not have a wireless network. Proportion of college-owned housing units wired for high-speed internet access: 100%. **Campus safety:** Security services offered: 24-hour foot-and-vehicle patrols, late-night transport/escort service, 24-hour emergency telephones, lighted pathways/sidewalks, controlled dormitory access (key, security card, etc).

TRANSFER AND INTERNATIONAL STUDENTS

Transfer students: May apply for admission for the following academic terms: Fall, Spring, Summer. Applicants do not need a minimum number of credits to apply. For fall 2005: Transfer applications received: 633. Transfer applicants offered admission: 344. Transfer applicants enrolled: 171. **International students:** Number of foreign undergraduates: 38 (2% of student body). Minimum TOEFL score required: 550 (paper); 213 (computer).

Immaculata University

- **Address:** 1145 King Road, Immaculata, PA 19345-0702
- **Website:** http://www.immaculata.edu
- **Private; Religious affiliation:** Roman Catholic
- **Enrollment:** 691 full-time; 2,326 part-time

KEY STATS

- ✔ **U.S News College Ranking:** third tier, Universities–Master's (North)
- ✔ **SAT Score (25th/75th percentile):** 880-1080
- ✔ **Tuition:** 2006-2007: $19,500

Selectivity: Less selective	**Room/board:** $8,850
Acceptance rate: 80%	**Average debt:** $17,125
Student/faculty ratio: 12/1	**Proportion who borrowed:** 85%

UNDERGRADUATE STUDENT BODY STATS

2005-2006 enrollment: 691 full-time; 2,326 part-time. Men: 21%; women: 79%. **Ethnic makeup:** African American: 7%; Asian American: 1%; Hispanic: 2%; White: 89%; International: 1%. **Religious preference:** Roman Catholic: 60%; Other: 40%.

ADMISSIONS FACTS AND FIGURES

Phone: (877) 428-6329. **Email:** admiss@immaculata.edu. **Website:** http://www.immaculata.edu. **Application deadlines for fall 2007:** Regular decision: August 15. Early decision: Not offered. Early action: Not offered. Admission can be deferred. **Application fee:** $35. Common application is not accepted. **To apply online, go to:** http://www.immaculata.edu/ugapp/. **Admissions requirements/recommendations:** High school units required (recommended): English: 4; Mathematics: 2; Science: 2; Foreign language: 2; Social studies: 2; History: 0; Academic electives: 4; Total units: 16. Tests: The college uses SAT or ACT scores in admissions decisions. Either SAT or ACT required. For admission to the fall 2007 entering class, the school will accept: ACT with writing, ACT without writing. Campus visit: Recommended. Admissions interview: Recommended. Off-campus interview: Not available. **Factors that count in admissions decisions:** *Academic:* Secondary school record: Very important. Class rank: Considered. Letters of recommendation: Very important. Standardized test scores: Important. Essay: Not considered. *Nonacademic:* Interview: Considered. Extracurricular activities: Not considered. Talent/ability: Important. Character/personal qualities: Not considered. Alumni/ae relationship: Considered. Geographical residence: Not considered. State residency: Not considered. Religious affiliation/commitment: Not considered. Minority status: Not considered. Volunteer work: Not considered. Work experience: Not considered. **Other schools with the greatest overlap in applicants:** Cabrini College; Marywood University; Millersville University of Pennsylvania; Shippensburg University of Pennsylvania; West Chester University of Pennsylvania. **Admissions statistics for the fall 2005 entering class:** Total applicants: 1,394. Total accepted: 1,119. Freshmen enrolled: 298; 35% were from out of state. Overall acceptance rate: 80%. **Size of waiting list:** 0 applicants; enrolled from waiting list: 0. **Credentials of fall 2005 freshmen:** 16% ranked in the top 10 percent of their high school class; 40% were in the top 25 percent, and 66% were in the top half. (Proportion submitting class standing: 23%.) **Average high school grade point average:** 3.2. **First-year students who submitted SAT scores:** 97%. Scores (25/75 percentile): Verbal: 450-550, Math: 430-530, Combined: 880-1080.

ACADEMICS

Year founded: 1920. **Academic calendar:** Semester. **Degrees offered:** certificate, associate, bachelor's, post-bachelor's certificate, master's, post-master's certificate, doctorate. **Most popular majors:** 37% health professions and related clinical sciences, 34% business, management, marketing, and related support services, 11% psychology, 3% English language and literature/letters, 2% education. **Major fields of study:** biological and biomedical sciences; business, management, marketing, and related support services; communication, journalism, and related programs; computer and information sciences and support services; education; English language and literature/letters; foreign languages, literatures, and linguistics; health professions and related clinical sciences; history; mathematics and statistics; multi/interdisciplinary studies; natural resources and conservation; parks, recreation, leisure, and fitness studies; physical sciences; psychology; public administration and social service professions; security and protective services; social sciences; theology and religious vocations; visual and performing arts. **Areas of required coursework:** humanities, mathematics, English (including composition), philosophy, foreign languages, sciences (biological or physical), history, social science, other. **Pre-professional programs:** pre-law, pre-dentistry, pre-medicine, pre-theology, pre-veterinary science, pre-optometry, pre-pharmacy, other. **Special academic programs (% participation):** accelerated program (75%), cross-registration (1%), double major (20%), honors program (11%), independent study (10%), internships (30%), liberal arts/career combination (85%), study abroad (1%), teacher certificate program (35%). **Teacher certification offered in:** early childhood, special education, elementary, middle/junior high, secondary. **Faculty and instruction (2005-2006):** Total instructional faculty: 87 full-time, 210 part-time (39% men; 61% women; 4% minorities). Full-time faculty with Ph.D. or other terminal degree: 66%. Student/faculty ratio: 12/1. Classes of fewer than 20 students: 74%; of 20 to 49 students: 25%; of 50 or more students: 1%. **Advanced Placement and International Baccalaureate credit:** AP tests may be used for: Credit and/or placement. Scores accepted: 3, 4, 5. **Freshmen returning for sophomore year:** 74%. **Graduation rates:** Four-year: 60%; five-year: 60%; six-year: 57%. **Graduate study:** 24% of students pursue further study immediately upon graduation.

COSTS AND FINANCIAL AID

Financial aid office: (610) 647-4400. **Expenses (2006-2007):** Tuition and fees 2006-2007: $19,500; room/board: $8,850. Estimated books and supplies: $1,050; transportation: $840; personal expenses: $1,576. **Financial aid:** Priority filing date for institution's financial aid form: April 15; deadline: April 15. In 2005-2006, 90% of undergraduates applied for financial aid. Of those, 90% were determined to have financial need; 11% had their need fully met. Average financial aid package (proportion receiving): $13,725 (90%). Average amount of gift aid, such as scholarships or grants (proportion receiving): $7,800 (90%). Average amount of self-help aid, such as work study or loans (proportion receiving): $3,593 (80%). Average need-based loan (excluding PLUS or other private loans): $2,778. Among students who received need-based aid, the average percentage of need met: 50%. Among students who received aid based on merit, the average award (and the proportion receiving): $9,463 (49%). The average athletic scholarship (and the proportion receiving): $0 (0%). Average amount of debt of borrowers graduating in 2005: $17,125. Proportion who borrowed: 85%.

CAMPUS LIFE AND EXTRACURRICULAR ACTIVITIES

Campus housing available (% using): coed dorms (34%), women's dorms (55%), apartment for single students (10%), special housing for disabled students (1%). Students who live in college-owned, operated, or affiliated housing: 76%. **Student employment:** During the 2005-2006 academic year, 40% of undergraduates worked on campus. Average per-year earnings: $1,000. **Clubs and organizations:** Number of student organizations: 46. Activities include: choral groups, concert band, dance, drama/theater, literary magazine, music ensembles, musical theater, student government, student newspaper, symphony orchestra, yearbook. Number of fraternities: 1; sororities: 4. Proportion of men in fraternities: 8%; of women in sororities: 30%. Average proportion of students who stay on campus on weekends: 45%. **Sports program (2005-2006):** Member of NCAA III. *Men's intercollegiate varsity sports:* basketball, golf, soccer, tennis. *Women's intercollegiate varsity sports:* basketball, cross-country, field hockey, lacrosse, soccer, softball, tennis, volleyball.

SERVICES AND FACILITIES

Basic services: nonremedial tutoring, placement service, health service, health insurance, other. **Remedial assistance:** math, writing, study skills. **Counseling services:** minority student, career, personal, academic, older student, psychological, religious. **For learning-disabled students:** School does not offer a structured program with separate admission and additional fees. Total undergraduates in learning-disabled program or receiving services: 21. Services include: tape recorders, untimed tests, note-taking services, oral tests, learning center, extended time for tests, tutors, priority registration, priority seating, other testing accomodations, waiver of foreign language degree requirement, waiver of math degree requirement. **Library:** Number of titles: 158,030; number of current serial subscriptions: 570. **Information technology resources:** Students are not required to lease or own a computer. Number of campus computers available to all students: 254. School has a wireless network. Proportion of college-owned housing units wired for high-speed internet access: 100%. **Campus safety:** Security services offered: 24-hour foot-and-vehicle patrols, late-night transport/escort service, 24-hour emergency telephones, lighted pathways/sidewalks, student patrols, controlled dormitory access (key, security card, etc).

TRANSFER AND INTERNATIONAL STUDENTS

Transfer students: May apply for admission for the following academic terms: Fall, Spring. Applicants do not need a minimum number of credits to apply. For fall 2005: Transfer applications received: 116. Transfer applicants offered admission: 66. Transfer applicants enrolled: 41. **International students:** Number of foreign undergraduates: 23 (1% of student body). Number of countries represented: 9. Minimum TOEFL score required: 550 (paper). Average TOEFL score: 590 (paper).

Indiana University of Pennsylvania

- **Address:** 1011 South Drive, Indiana, PA 15705
- **Website:** http://www.iup.edu
- **Public**
- **Enrollment:** 11,223 full-time; 824 part-time

KEY STATS

✔ **U.S News College Ranking:** fourth tier, National Universities
✔ **SAT Score (25th/75th percentile):** 950-1140
✔ **Tuition:** 2005-2006: $6,085 in state, $13,301 out of state

Selectivity: Selective	**Room/board:** $4,866
Acceptance rate: 55%	**Average debt:** $18,105
Student/faculty ratio: 17/1	**Proportion who borrowed:** 80%

UNDERGRADUATE STUDENT BODY STATS

2005-2006 enrollment: 11,223 full-time; 824 part-time. Men: 45%; women: 55%. **Ethnic makeup:** African American: 7%; Asian American: 1%; Hispanic: 1%; White: 89%; International: 1%.

ADMISSIONS FACTS AND FIGURES

Phone: (800) 442-6830. **Email:** admissions-inquiry@iup.edu. **Website:** http://www.iup.edu. **Application deadlines for fall 2007:** Regular decision:

Rolling. Early decision: Not offered. Early action: Not offered. Admission can be deferred. **Application fee:** $35. Common application is accepted. **To apply online, go to:** http://www.iup.edu/admissions. **Admissions requirements/recommendations:** High school units required (recommended): English: (4); Mathematics: (3); Science: (3); Foreign language: (2); Social studies: (2); History: (1); Academic electives: (1); Total units: (16). Tests: The college uses SAT or ACT scores in admissions decisions. Either SAT or ACT required. For admission to the fall 2007 entering class, the school will accept: ACT with writing, ACT without writing. Campus visit: Recommended. Admissions interview: Neither required nor recommended. Off-campus interview: May be arranged. **Factors that count in admissions decisions:** *Academic:* Secondary school record: Important. Class rank: Important. Letters of recommendation: Considered. Standardized test scores: Very important. Essay: Considered. *Nonacademic:* Interview: Considered. Extracurricular activities: Considered. Talent/ability: Important. Character/personal qualities: Not considered. Alumni/ae relationship: Considered. Geographical residence: Not considered. State residency: Not considered. Religious affiliation/commitment: Not considered. Minority status: Not considered. Volunteer work: Considered. Work experience: Considered. **Other schools with the greatest overlap in applicants:** Pennsylvania State University–University Park; Slippery Rock University of Pennsylvania; University of Pittsburgh. **Admissions statistics for the fall 2005 entering class:** Total applicants: 8,293. Total accepted: 4,583. Freshmen enrolled: 2,509; 3% were from out of state. Overall acceptance rate: 55%. **Credentials of fall 2005 freshmen:** 13% ranked in the top 10 percent of their high school class; 32% were in the top 25 percent, and 70% were in the top half. (Proportion submitting class standing: 93%.) **Average high school grade point average:** 3.4. **First-year students who submitted SAT scores:** 100%. Scores (25/75 percentile): Verbal: 480-570, Math: 470-570, Combined: 950-1140.

ACADEMICS

Year founded: 1875. **Academic calendar:** Semester. **Degrees offered:** certificate, associate, bachelor's, post-bachelor's certificate, master's, post-master's certificate, doctorate. **Most popular majors:** 24% business, management, marketing, and related support services, 17% criminology, 8% visual and performing arts, 5% human development and family studies. **Major fields of study:** architecture and related services; biological and biomedical sciences; business, management, marketing, and related support services; communication, journalism, and related programs; computer and information sciences and support services; education; engineering technologies/technicians; English language and literature/letters; family and consumer sciences/human sciences; foreign languages, literatures, and linguistics; health professions and related clinical sciences; history; liberal arts and sciences studies, and humanities; mathematics and statistics; multi/interdisciplinary studies; parks, recreation, leisure, and fitness studies; philosophy and religious studies; physical sciences; psychology; social sciences; visual and performing arts. **Areas of required coursework:** arts/fine arts, humanities, mathematics, English (including composition), philosophy, sciences (biological or physical), history, social science. **Pre-professional programs:** pre-law, pre-dentistry, pre-medicine, pre-veterinary science, pre-optometry, pre-pharmacy, other. **Special academic programs:** accelerated program, cooperative (work-study plan) program, distance learning, double major, dual enrollment, English as a Second Language (ESL), exchange student program (domestic), honors program, independent study, internships, study abroad, teacher certificate program, weekend college. **Teacher certification offered in:** early childhood, special education, elementary, vo-tech, secondary. **Cooperative education programs:** health professions, natural science, other. **Reserve Officers Training Corps (ROTC):** Army ROTC: Offered on campus. **Faculty and instruction (2005-2006):** Total instructional faculty: 634 (56% men; 44% women; 14% minorities). Full-time faculty with Ph.D. or other terminal degree: 78%. Student/faculty ratio: 17/1. Classes of fewer than 20 students: 28%; of 20 to 49 students: 59%; of 50 or more students: 13%. **Advanced Placement and International Baccalaureate credit:** AP tests may be used for: Credit and/or placement. Scores accepted: 3, 4, 5. Freshmen returning for sophomore year: 76%. Graduation rates: Six-year: 50%.

COSTS AND FINANCIAL AID

Financial aid office: (724) 357-2218. **Expenses (2005-2006):** Tuition and fees 2005-2006: $6,085 in state, $13,301 out of state; room/board: $4,866. Estimated books and supplies: $900 personal expenses: $2,749. **Financial aid:** Priority filing date for institution's financial aid form: April 15. In 2005-2006, 82% of undergraduates applied for financial aid. Of those, 66% were determined to have financial need; 11% had their need fully met. Average financial aid package (proportion receiving): $7,498 (65%). Average amount of gift aid, such as scholarships or grants (proportion receiving): $3,875 (48%). Average amount of self-help aid, such as work study or loans (proportion receiving): $4,306 (61%). Average need-based loan (excluding PLUS or other private loans): $3,698. Among students who received need-based aid, the average percentage of need met: 76%. Among students who received aid based on merit, the average award (and the proportion receiving): $2,249 (3%). The average athletic scholarship (and the proportion receiving): $3,663 (2%). Average amount of debt of borrowers graduating in 2005: $18,105. Proportion who borrowed: 80%.

CAMPUS LIFE AND EXTRACURRICULAR ACTIVITIES

Campus housing available (% using): coed dorms (78%), apartment for single students (7%), special housing for disabled students (1%), special housing for international students (5%), other housing options (9%). Students who live in college-owned, operated, or affiliated housing: 31%. **Student employment:** During the 2005-2006 academic year, 20% of undergraduates worked on campus. Average per-year earnings: $2,300. **Clubs and organizations:** Number of student organizations: 250. Activities include: choral groups, concert band, dance, drama/theater, jazz band, literary magazine, marching band, music ensembles, musical theater, opera, pep band, radio station, student government, student newspaper, symphony orchestra, television station. Number of fraternities: 19; sororities: 14. Proportion of men in fraternities: 10%; of women in sororities: 11%. Average proportion of students who stay on campus on weekends: 32%. **Sports program (2005-2006):** Member of NCAA II. **Men's intercollegiate varsity sports:** baseball, basketball, cross-country, football, golf, swimming and diving, track and field (indoor), track and field (outdoor). **Women's intercollegiate varsity sports:** basketball, cross-country, field hockey, lacrosse, soccer, softball, swimming and diving, tennis, track and field (indoor), track and field (outdoor), volleyball.

SERVICES AND FACILITIES

Basic services: day care, health service. **Remedial assistance:** reading, math, writing, study skills. **Counseling services:** minority student, career, military, personal, veteran student, academic, older student, psychological, birth control. **For learning-disabled students:** School does not offer a structured program with separate admission and additional fees. Total undergraduates in learning-disabled program or receiving services: 250. Services include: remedial math, reading machines, remedial reading, tape recorders, note-taking services, learning center, readers, extended time for tests, proofreading services, texts on tape, other testing accomodations. **Library:** Number of titles: 900,931; number of current serial subscriptions: 15,024. **Information technology resources:** Students are not required to lease or own a computer. Number of campus computers available to all students: 1,649. School has a wireless network. Approximate number of users that can be accommodated: 16,000. Proportion of college-owned housing units wired for high-speed internet access: 100%. **Campus safety:** Security services offered: 24-hour foot-and-vehicle patrols, late-night transport/escort service, 24-hour emergency telephones, lighted pathways/sidewalks, student patrols, controlled dormitory access (key, security card, etc).

TRANSFER AND INTERNATIONAL STUDENTS

Transfer students: May apply for admission for the following academic terms: Fall, Spring, Summer. Applicants need a minimum number of credits to apply. **International students:** Number of foreign undergraduates: 176 (1% of student body). Minimum TOEFL score required: 500 (paper); 173 (computer).

Juniata College

- **Address:** 1700 Moore Street, Huntingdon, PA 16652
- **Website:** http://www.juniata.edu
- **Private; Religious affiliation:** Church of the Brethren
- **Enrollment:** 1,389 full-time; 60 part-time

KEY STATS

✔ **U.S News College Ranking:** 95, Liberal Arts Colleges
✔ **SAT Score (25th/75th percentile):** 1080-1270
✔ **Tuition:** 2006-2007: $27,540

Selectivity: More selective	**Room/board:** $7,680
Acceptance rate: 68%	**Average debt:** $22,131
Student/faculty ratio: 13/1	**Proportion who borrowed:** 77%

UNDERGRADUATE STUDENT BODY STATS

2005-2006 enrollment: 1,389 full-time; 60 part-time. Men: 47%; women: 53%. **Ethnic makeup:** African American: 2%; Asian American: 2%; Hispanic: 1%; White: 92%; International: 3%. **Religious preference:** Roman Catholic: 31%; Protestant: 58%; Jewish: 1%; Muslim: 1%; Church of the Brethren: 6%; Unspecified, Buddhist, Wicca, Hindu: 2%.

ADMISSIONS FACTS AND FIGURES

Phone: (877) 586-4282. **Email:** admissions@juniata.edu. **Website:** http://www.juniata.edu. **Application deadlines for fall 2007:** Regular decision: March 1. Early decision: Send application by: November 1; Decision sent by: December 30. Early action: Send application by; December 1; Decision sent by: January 30. Admission can be deferred. **Application fee:** $30. Common application is accepted. **To apply online, go to:** http://secureweb.juniata.edu/apply/. **Admissions requirements/recommendations:** High school units required (recommended): English: 4 (4); Mathematics: 3 (4); Science: 3 (4); Foreign language: 2 (2); Social studies: 1 (1); History: 3 (3); Total units: 16 (18). Tests: The college uses SAT or ACT scores in admissions decisions. Neither SAT nor ACT required. For admission to the fall 2007 entering class, the school will accept: ACT with writing, ACT without writing. Campus visit: Recommended. Admissions interview: Recommended. Off-campus interview: May be arranged. **Factors that count in admissions decisions:** *Academic:* Secondary school record: Very important. Class rank: Not considered. Letters of recommendation: Very important. Standardized test scores: Very important. Essay: Very important. *Nonacademic:* Interview: Important. Extracurricular activities: Important. Talent/ability: Important. Character/personal qualities: Very important. Alumni/ae relationship: Considered. Geographical residence: Not considered. State residency: Not considered. Religious affiliation/commitment: Not considered. Minority status: Considered. Volunteer work: Important. Work experience: Not considered. **Other schools with the greatest overlap in applicants:** Allegheny College; Dickinson College; Elizabethtown College; Pennsylvania State University–University Park; Susquehanna University. **Admissions statistics for the fall 2005 entering class:** Total applicants: 1,745. Total accepted: 1,184. Freshmen enrolled: 388; 27% were from out of state. Accepted through early-decision or early-action plans: 16%. Overall acceptance rate: 68%. Early-decision acceptance rate: 90%. Non-early acceptance rate: 67%. **Size of waiting list:** 72 applicants; enrolled from waiting list: 2. **Credentials of fall 2005 freshmen:** 43% ranked in the top 10 percent of their high school class; 79% were in the top 25 percent, and 97% were in the top half. (Proportion submitting class standing: 84%.) **Average high school grade point average:** 3.8. **First-year students who submitted SAT scores:** 92%. Scores (25/75 percentile): Verbal: 530-630, Math: 550-640, Combined: 1080-1270. **First-year students submitting ACT scores:** 6%. Scores (25/75 percentile): English: N/A, Math: N/A, Composite: N/A.

ACADEMICS

Year founded: 1876. **Academic calendar:** Semester. **Degrees offered:** bachelor's. **Most popular majors:** 16% biological and biomedical sciences, 14% business, management, marketing, and related support services, 14% education, 11% social sciences, 8% multi/interdisciplinary studies. **Major fields of study:** biological and biomedical sciences; business, management, marketing, and related support services; communication, journalism, and related programs; computer and information sciences and support services; education; engineering; English language and literature/letters; foreign languages, literatures, and linguistics; health professions and related clinical sciences; history; legal professions and studies; liberal arts and sciences studies, and humanities; mathematics and statistics; multi/interdisciplinary studies; natural resources and conservation; philosophy and religious studies; physical sciences; psychology; public administration and social service professions; social sciences; theology and religious vocations; visual and performing arts. **Areas of required coursework:** arts/fine arts, humanities, computer literacy, mathematics, English (including composition), sciences (biological or physical), social science, other. **Pre-professional programs:** pre-law, pre-dentistry, pre-medicine, pre-theology, pre-veterinary science, pre-optometry, pre-pharmacy, other. **Special academic programs (% participation):** accelerated program (2%), double major, dual enrollment, English as a Second Language (ESL) (0%), exchange student program (domestic) (1%), honors program (100%), independent study (33%), internships (78%), student-designed major (52%), study abroad (31%), teacher certificate program (15%), other (1%). **Teacher certification offered in:** early childhood, special education, elementary, secondary. **Cooperative education programs:** engineering, health professions, other. **Faculty and instruction (2005-2006):** Total instructional faculty: 94 full-time, 38 part-time (61% men; 39% women; 5% minorities). Full-time faculty with Ph.D. or other terminal degree: 91%. Student/faculty ratio: 13/1.

Classes of fewer than 20 students: 66%; of 20 to 49 students: 31%; of 50 or more students: 3%. **Advanced Placement and International Baccalaureate credit:** AP tests may be used for: Credit and/or placement. Scores accepted: 4, 5. International Baccalaureate exams may be used for: Credit and/or placement. **Freshmen returning for sophomore year:** 86%. **Graduation rates:** Four-year: 67%; five-year: 74%; six-year: 75%. **Graduate study:** 33% of students pursue further study within one year. Fields in which graduates pursue further study: Master of Business Administration (MBA), 2%; law, 3%; medicine, 5%; dentistry, 1%; engineering, 1%; theology (or the seminary), 1%; education, 2%; arts and sciences, 18%; veterinary medicine, 1%.

COSTS AND FINANCIAL AID
Financial aid office: (814) 641-3142. **Expenses (2006-2007):** Tuition and fees 2006-2007: $27,540; room/board: $7,680. Estimated books and supplies: $600; transportation: $250; personal expenses: $1,000. **Financial aid:** Priority filing date for institution's financial aid form: March 1; deadline: March 1. In 2005-2006, 84% of undergraduates applied for financial aid. Of those, 76% were determined to have financial need; 34% had their need fully met. Average financial aid package (proportion receiving): $18,539 (76%). Average amount of gift aid, such as scholarships or grants (proportion receiving): $14,789 (72%). Average amount of self-help aid, such as work study or loans (proportion receiving): $5,102 (58%). Average need-based loan (excluding PLUS or other private loans): $3,981. Among students who received need-based aid, the average percentage of need met: 77%. Among students who received aid based on merit, the average award (and the proportion receiving): $12,311 (23%). The average athletic scholarship (and the proportion receiving): $0 (0%). Average amount of debt of borrowers graduating in 2005: $22,131. Proportion who borrowed: 77%.

CAMPUS LIFE AND EXTRACURRICULAR ACTIVITIES
Campus housing available (% using): coed dorms (61%), women's dorms (12%), apartment for single students (27%), special housing for international students, other housing options. Students who live in college-owned, operated, or affiliated housing: 83%. **Student employment:** During the 2005-2006 academic year, 54% of undergraduates worked on campus. Average per-year earnings: $626. **Clubs and organizations:** Number of student organizations: 88. Activities include: choral groups, concert band, dance, drama/theater, jazz band, literary magazine, music ensembles, musical theater, pep band, radio station, student government, student newspaper, student film society, symphony orchestra, yearbook. Number of fraternities: 0; sororities: 0. Average proportion of students who stay on campus on weekends: 75%. **Sports program (2005-2006):** Member of NCAA III. *Men's intercollegiate varsity sports:* baseball, basketball, cross-country, football, soccer, tennis, track and field (indoor), track and field (outdoor), volleyball. *Women's intercollegiate varsity sports:* basketball, cross-country, field hockey, soccer, softball, swimming and diving, tennis, track and field (indoor), track and field (outdoor), volleyball.

SERVICES AND FACILITIES
Basic services: nonremedial tutoring, placement service, health service, health insurance, other. **Remedial assistance:** study skills. **Counseling services:** minority student, career, personal, academic, older student, psychological, religious, other. **For learning-disabled students:** School does not offer a structured program with separate admission and additional fees. Services include: untimed tests, extended time for tests, tutors, other. **Library:** Number of titles: 280,000; number of current serial subscriptions: 1,000. **Information technology resources:** Students are not required to lease or own a computer. Number of campus computers available to all students: 340. School has a wireless network. Proportion of college-owned housing units wired for high-speed internet access: 100%. **Campus safety:** Security services offered: 24-hour foot-and-vehicle patrols, late-night transport/escort service, 24-hour emergency telephones, lighted pathways/sidewalks.

TRANSFER AND INTERNATIONAL STUDENTS
Transfer students: May apply for admission for the following academic terms: Fall, Spring. Applicants need a minimum number of credits to apply. For fall 2005: Transfer applications received: 84. Transfer applicants offered admission: 35. Transfer applicants enrolled: 23. **International students:** Number of foreign undergraduates: 40 (3% of student body). Number of countries represented: 79. Minimum TOEFL score required: 550 (paper); 213 (computer). Average TOEFL score: 557 (paper).

King's College

- **Address:** 133 N. River Street, Wilkes-Barre, PA 18711
- **Website:** http://www.kings.edu
- **Private; Religious affiliation:** Roman Catholic
- **Enrollment:** 1,849 full-time; 261 part-time

KEY STATS
✔ **U.S News College Ranking:** 36, Universities–Master's (North)
✔ **SAT Score (25th/75th percentile):** 940-1130
✔ **Tuition:** 2006-2007: $22,280

Selectivity: Selective	**Room/board:** $8,590
Acceptance rate: 84%	**Average debt:** $17,263
Student/faculty ratio: 14/1	**Proportion who borrowed:** 88%

UNDERGRADUATE STUDENT BODY STATS
2005-2006 enrollment: 1,849 full-time; 261 part-time. Men: 52%; women: 48%. **Ethnic makeup:** African American: 2%; Asian American: 1%; Hispanic: 2%; White: 95%. **Religious preference:** Protestant: 13%; Unknown: 21%; Roman Catholic: 59%; Other: 7%.

ADMISSIONS FACTS AND FIGURES
Phone: (888) 546-4772. **Email:** admissions@kings.edu. **Website:** http://www.kings.edu. **Application deadlines for fall 2007:** Regular decision: Rolling. Early decision: Not offered. Early action: Not offered. Admission can be deferred. **Application fee:** $30. Common application is accepted. **To apply online, go to:** http://www.kings.edu/admissions/adm_app.htm. **Admissions requirements/recommendations:** High school units required (recommended): English: 4 (4); Mathematics: 3 (4); Science: 3 (4); Foreign language: 2 (4); Social studies: 3 (3); History: 1 (1); Academic electives: (2); Total units: 16 (22). Tests: The college uses SAT or ACT scores in admissions decisions. Either SAT or ACT required. For admission to the fall 2007 entering class, the school will accept: ACT without writing. Campus visit: Recommended. Admissions interview: Recommended. Off-campus interview: May be arranged. **Factors that count in admissions decisions:** *Academic:* Secondary school record: Important. Class rank: Important. Letters of recommendation: Important. Standardized test scores: Very important. Essay: Important. *Nonacademic:* Interview: Important. Extracurricular activities: Very important. Talent/ability: Very important. Character/personal qualities: Important. Alumni/ae relationship: Important. Geographical residence: Not considered. State residency: Not considered. Religious affiliation/commitment: Not considered. Minority status: Not considered. Volunteer work: Important. Work experience: Not considered. **Other schools with the greatest overlap in applicants:** Bloomsburg University of Pennsylvania; College Misericordia; Pennsylvania State University–University Park; University of Scranton; Wilkes University. **Admissions statistics for the fall 2005 entering class:** Total applicants: 1,654. Total accepted: 1,388. Freshmen enrolled: 480; 32% were from out of state. Overall acceptance rate: 84%. **Credentials of fall 2005 freshmen:** 16% ranked in the top 10 percent of their high school class; 40% were in the top 25 percent, and 71% were in the top half. (Proportion submitting class standing: 88%.) **Average high school grade point average:** 3.3. **First-year students who submitted SAT scores:** 95%. Scores (25/75 percentile): Verbal: 470-560, Math: 470-570, Combined: 940-1130.

ACADEMICS
Year founded: 1946. **Academic calendar:** Semester. **Degrees offered:** certificate, associate, bachelor's, post-bachelor's certificate, master's. **Most popular majors:** 12% elementary education and teaching, 10% business administration and management, 8% accounting, 7% communication and media studies, 6% psychology. **Major fields of study:** biological and biomedical sciences; business, management, marketing, and related support services; communication, journalism, and related programs; computer and information sciences and support services; education; English language and literature/letters; foreign languages, literatures, and linguistics; health professions and related clinical sciences; history; mathematics and statistics; multi/interdisciplinary studies; natural resources and conservation; philosophy and religious studies; physical sciences; psychology; security and protective services; social sciences; theology and religious vocations; visual and performing arts. **Areas of required coursework:** arts/fine arts, humanities, computer literacy, mathematics, English (including composition), philosophy, foreign languages, sciences (biological or physical), history, social science, other. **Pre-professional programs:** pre-law, pre-dentistry, pre-medicine,

pre-theology, pre-veterinary science, pre-optometry, pre-pharmacy. **Special academic programs:** accelerated program, cross-registration, distance learning, double major, dual enrollment, English as a Second Language (ESL), exchange student program (domestic), honors program, independent study, internships, student-designed major, study abroad, teacher certificate program, weekend college. **Teacher certification offered in:** early childhood, special education, elementary, middle/junior high, secondary. **Reserve Officers Training Corps (ROTC):** Army ROTC: Offered on campus; Air Force ROTC: Offered on campus. **Faculty and instruction (2005-2006):** Total instructional faculty: 110 full-time, 91 part-time (59% men; 41% women; 2% minorities). Full-time faculty with Ph.D. or other terminal degree: 83%. Student/faculty ratio: 14/1. Classes of fewer than 20 students: 53%; of 20 to 49 students: 47%; of 50 or more students: 0%. **Advanced Placement and International Baccalaureate credit:** AP tests may be used for: Credit and/or placement. Scores accepted: 3, 4, 5. **Freshmen returning for sophomore year:** 81%. **Graduation rates:** Four-year: 64%; five-year: 70%; six-year: 70%. **Graduate study:** 18% of students pursue further study immediately upon graduation. Fields in which graduates pursue further study: Master of Business Administration (MBA), 3%; law, 16%; medicine, 3%; dentistry, 1%; education, 7%; arts and sciences, 66%; veterinary medicine, 4%.

COSTS AND FINANCIAL AID

Financial aid office: (570) 208-5868. **Expenses (2006-2007):** Tuition and fees 2006-2007: $22,280; room/board: $8,590. Estimated books and supplies: $962; transportation: $530; personal expenses: $1,100. **Financial aid:** Priority filing date for institution's financial aid form: February 15. In 2005-2006, 92% of undergraduates applied for financial aid. Of those, 82% were determined to have financial need; 20% had their need fully met. Average financial aid package (proportion receiving): $15,220 (81%). Average amount of gift aid, such as scholarships or grants (proportion receiving): $6,373 (64%). Average amount of self-help aid, such as work study or loans (proportion receiving): $4,639 (68%). Average need-based loan (excluding PLUS or other private loans): $4,369. Among students who received need-based aid, the average percentage of need met: 71%. Among students who received aid based on merit, the average award (and the proportion receiving): $8,242 (17%). Average amount of debt of borrowers graduating in 2005: $17,263. Proportion who borrowed: 88%.

CAMPUS LIFE AND EXTRACURRICULAR ACTIVITIES

Campus housing available (% using): women's dorms (28%), men's dorms (46%), apartment for single students (25%), special housing for disabled students (1%). Students who live in college-owned, operated, or affiliated housing: 43%. **Student employment:** During the 2005-2006 academic year, 29% of undergraduates worked on campus. Average per-year earnings: $1,800. **Clubs and organizations:** Number of student organizations: 50. Activities include: choral groups, dance, drama/theater, literary magazine, music ensembles, musical theater, pep band, radio station, student government, student newspaper, student film society, yearbook. Average proportion of students who stay on campus on weekends: 83%. **Sports program (2005-2006):** Member of NCAA III. *Men's intercollegiate varsity sports:* baseball, basketball, cross-country, football, golf, lacrosse, soccer, swimming and diving, tennis, wrestling. *Women's intercollegiate varsity sports:* basketball, cross-country, field hockey, lacrosse, soccer, softball, swimming and diving, tennis, volleyball.

SERVICES AND FACILITIES

Basic services: nonremedial tutoring, women's center, placement service, day care, health service. **Remedial assistance:** reading, writing, study skills. **Counseling services:** minority student, career, military, personal, academic, older student, psychological, religious. **For learning-disabled students:** School does not offer a structured program with separate admission and additional fees. Total undergraduates in learning-disabled program or receiving services: 64. Services include: remedial math, remedial English, reading machines, tape recorders, untimed tests, note-taking services, oral tests, learning center, extended time for tests, tutors, priority registration, priority seating, exams on tape or computer. **Library:** Number of titles: 171,558; number of current serial subscriptions: 660. **Information technology resources:** Students are not required to lease or own a computer. Number of campus computers available to all students: 450. School has a wireless network. Proportion of college-owned housing units wired for high-speed internet access: 100%. **Campus safety:** Security services offered: 24-hour foot-and-vehicle patrols, late-night transport/escort service, 24-hour emergency telephones, lighted pathways/sidewalks, controlled dormitory access (key, security card, etc.).

TRANSFER AND INTERNATIONAL STUDENTS

Transfer students: May apply for admission for the following academic terms: Fall, Spring. Applicants need a minimum number of credits to apply. For fall 2005: Transfer applications received: 247. Transfer applicants offered admission: 168. Transfer applicants enrolled: 110. **International students:** Number of foreign undergraduates: 7. Number of countries represented: 6. Minimum TOEFL score required: 530 (paper); 200 (computer). Average TOEFL score: 600 (paper).

Kutztown University of Pennsylvania

■ **Address:** 15200 Kutztown Road, Kutztown, PA 19530-0730
■ **Website:** http://www.kutztown.edu
■ **Public**
■ **Enrollment:** 7,951 full-time; 855 part-time

KEY STATS

✔ **U.S News College Ranking:** third tier, Universities–Master's (North)
✔ **SAT Score (25th/75th percentile):** 1008-1029
✔ **Tuition:** 2005-2006: $6,527 in state, $14,068 out of state

Selectivity: Less selective	**Room/board:** $5,480
Acceptance rate: 65%	**Average debt:** $14,479
Student/faculty ratio: 19/1	**Proportion who borrowed:** 78%

UNDERGRADUATE STUDENT BODY STATS

2005-2006 enrollment: 7,951 full-time; 855 part-time. Men: 41%; women: 59%. **Ethnic makeup:** African American: 8%; Asian American: 1%; Hispanic: 4%; White: 87%; International: 1%.

ADMISSIONS FACTS AND FIGURES

Phone: (610) 683-4060. **Email:** admission@kutztown.edu. **Website:** http://www.kutztown.edu. **Application deadlines for fall 2007:** Regular decision: Rolling. Early decision: Not offered. Early action: Not offered. Admission can be deferred. **Application fee:** $35. Common application is not accepted. **To apply online, go to:** http://www.kutztown.edu/admissions/apply_online.shtml. **Admissions requirements/recommendations:** High school units required (recommended): English: (4); Mathematics: (3); Science: (3); Foreign language: (2); Social studies: (4); Total units: (16). Tests: The college uses SAT or ACT scores in admissions decisions. Either SAT or ACT required. For admission to the fall 2007 entering class, the school will accept: ACT with writing, ACT without writing. Campus visit: Recommended. Admissions interview: Recommended. Off-campus interview: Not available. **Factors that count in admissions decisions:** *Academic:* Secondary school record: Very important. Class rank: Very important. Letters of recommendation: Considered. Standardized test scores: Very important. Essay: Not considered. *Nonacademic:* Interview: Considered. Extracurricular activities: Considered. Talent/ability: Considered. Character/personal qualities: Considered. Alumni/ae relationship: Not considered. Geographical residence: Considered. State residency: Considered. Religious affiliation/commitment: Not considered. Minority status: Considered. Volunteer work: Considered. Work experience: Considered. **Admissions statistics for the fall 2005 entering class:** Total applicants: 8,603. Total accepted: 5,585. 11% were from out of state. Overall acceptance rate: 65%. **Size of waiting list:** 0 applicants; enrolled from waiting list: 0. **Credentials of fall 2005 freshmen:** 6% ranked in the top 10 percent of their high school class; 22% were in the top 25 percent, and 72% were in the top half. (Proportion submitting class standing: 100%.) **First-year students who submitted SAT scores:** 99%. Scores (25/75 percentile): Verbal: 511-514, Math: 497-515, Combined: 1008-1029.

ACADEMICS

Year founded: 1866. **Academic calendar:** Semester. **Degrees offered:** bachelor's, post-bachelor's certificate, master's. **Most popular majors:** 20% education, 16% visual and performing arts, 15% business administration and management, 10% English language and literature, 8% psychology. **Major fields of study:** biological and biomedical sciences; business, management, marketing, and related support services; communication, journalism, and related programs; computer and information sciences and support services; education; English language and literature/letters; foreign languages, literatures, and linguistics; health professions and related clinical sciences; history; liberal arts and sciences studies, and humanities; library science; mathematics and statistics; multi/interdisciplinary studies; natural resources and conservation; philosophy and religious studies; physical sciences; psychology; public administration and social service professions; security and protective services; social sciences; visual and performing arts. **Areas of required coursework:** arts/fine arts, humanities, computer literacy, mathematics, English (including composition), foreign languages, sciences (biological or physical), history, social science. **Pre-professional programs:** pre-law, pre-dentistry, pre-medicine, pre-veterinary science, pre-optometry. **Special academic programs:** cross-registration, distance learning, double major, dual enrollment, honors program, independent study, internships, liberal arts/career combination, student-designed major, study abroad, teacher certificate program. **Teacher certification offered in:** early childhood, special education, elementary, middle/junior high, secondary. **Reserve Officers Training Corps (ROTC):** Army ROTC: Offered at cooperating institution (Lehigh University). **Faculty and instruction (2005-2006):** Total instructional faculty: 295 full-time, 166 part-time (52% men; 48% women; 11% minorities). Full-time faculty with Ph.D. or other terminal degree: 82%. Student/faculty ratio: 19/1. Classes of fewer than 20 students: 26%; of 20 to 49 students: 66%; of 50 or more students: 8%. **Advanced Placement and International Baccalaureate credit:** AP tests may be used for: Credit only. Scores accepted: 3, 4, 5. **Freshmen returning for sophomore year:** 77%. **Graduation rates:** Six-year: 49%.

COSTS AND FINANCIAL AID

Financial aid office: (610) 683-4077. **Expenses (2005-2006):** Tuition and fees 2005-2006: $6,527 in state, $14,068 out of state; room/board: $5,480. Estimated books and supplies: $1,100 personal expenses: $2,600. **Financial aid:** Priority filing date for institution's financial aid form: February 15. In 2005-2006, 80% of undergraduates applied for financial aid. Of those, 60% were determined to have financial need; 46% had their need fully met. Average financial aid package (proportion receiving): $6,189 (60%). Average amount of gift aid, such as scholarships or grants (proportion receiving): $4,133 (43%). Average amount of self-help aid, such as work study or loans (proportion receiving): $3,533 (48%). Average need-based loan (excluding PLUS or other private loans): $3,533. Among students who received need-based aid, the average percentage of need met: 57%. Among students who received aid based on merit, the average award (and the proportion receiving): $2,033 (3%). The average athletic scholarship (and the proportion receiving): $1,464 (2%). Average amount of debt of borrowers graduating in 2005: $14,479. Proportion who borrowed: 78%.

CAMPUS LIFE AND EXTRACURRICULAR ACTIVITIES

Campus housing available: coed dorms, women's dorms, apartment for single students, cooperative housing, other housing options. Students who live in college-owned, operated, or affiliated housing: 47%. **Student employment:** During the 2005-2006 academic year, 22% of undergraduates worked on campus. Average per-year earnings: $1,200. **Clubs and organizations:** Number of student organizations: 136. Activities include: choral groups, concert band, dance, drama/theater, jazz band, literary magazine, marching band, music ensembles, musical theater, radio station, student government, student newspaper, television station, yearbook. Number of fraternities: 6; sororities: 5. Proportion of men in fraternities: 4%; of women in sororities: 4%. Average proportion of students who stay on campus on weekends: 60%. **Sports program (2005-2006):** Member of NCAA II. *Men's intercollegiate varsity sports:* baseball, basketball, cross-country, football, soccer, swimming and diving, tennis, track and field (indoor), track and field (outdoor), wrestling. *Women's intercollegiate varsity sports:* basketball, cross-country, field hockey, golf, soccer, softball, swimming and diving, tennis, track and field (indoor), track and field (outdoor), volleyball.

SERVICES AND FACILITIES

Basic services: women's center, day care, health service. **Remedial assistance:** reading, math, writing, study skills. **Counseling services:** minority student, career, personal, veteran student, older student, psychological, birth control, other. **For learning-disabled students:** School does not offer a structured program with separate admission and additional fees. Services include: note-taking services, oral tests, learning center, readers, extended time for tests, tutors. **Library:** Number of titles: 500,484; number of current serial subscriptions: 15,600. **Information technology resources:** Students are not required to lease or own a computer. Number of campus computers available to all students: 650. School has a wireless network. Proportion of college-owned housing units wired for high-speed internet access: 100%. **Campus safety:** Security services offered: 24-hour foot-and-vehicle patrols, late-night transport/escort service, 24-hour emergency telephones, lighted pathways/sidewalks, controlled dormitory access (key, security card, etc).

TRANSFER AND INTERNATIONAL STUDENTS

Transfer students: May apply for admission for the following academic terms: Fall, Spring. Applicants do not need a minimum number of credits to apply. **International students:** Number of foreign undergraduates: 49 (1% of student body). Number of countries represented: 9. Minimum TOEFL score required: 500 (paper); 173 (computer). Average TOEFL score: 550 (paper).

Lafayette College

- **Address:** 118 Markle Hall, Easton, PA 18042
- **Website:** http://www.lafayette.edu
- **Private; Religious affiliation:** Presbyterian
- **Enrollment:** 2,281 full-time; 65 part-time

KEY STATS
✔ **U.S News College Ranking:** 30, Liberal Arts Colleges
✔ **SAT Score (25th/75th percentile):** 1180-1370
✔ **Tuition:** 2006-2007: $31,669

Selectivity: More selective	**Room/board:** $9,864
Acceptance rate: 37%	**Average debt:** $19,373
Student/faculty ratio: 11/1	**Proportion who borrowed:** 51%

UNDERGRADUATE STUDENT BODY STATS
2005-2006 enrollment: 2,281 full-time; 65 part-time. Men: 52%; women: 48%. **Ethnic makeup:** African American: 5%; Asian American: 2%; Hispanic: 4%; White: 83%; International: 6%.

ADMISSIONS FACTS AND FIGURES
Phone: (610) 330-5100. **Email:** admissions@lafayette.edu. **Website:** http://www.lafayette.edu. **Application deadlines for fall 2007:** Regular decision: January 1; decision sent by April 1. Early decision: Send application by: February 15; Decision sent by: N/A. Early action: Not offered. Admission can be deferred. **Application fee:** $60. Common application is accepted. **Admissions requirements/recommendations:** High school units required (recommended): English: (4); Mathematics: (3); Science: (3); Foreign language: (3); Social studies: (2); Academic electives: (5); Total units: (4). Tests: The college uses SAT or ACT scores in admissions decisions. Either SAT or ACT required. For admission to the fall 2007 entering class, the school will accept: ACT with writing, ACT without writing. Campus visit: Recommended. Admissions interview: Recommended. Off-campus interview: May be arranged. **Factors that count in admissions decisions:** *Academic:* Secondary school record: Very important. Class rank: Important. Letters of recommendation: Important. Standardized test scores: Important. Essay: Important. *Nonacademic:* Interview: Considered. Extracurricular activities: Important. Talent/ability: Important. Character/personal qualities: Important. Alumni/ae relationship: Important. Geographical residence: Considered. State residency: Not considered. Religious affiliation/commitment: Not considered. Minority status: Important. Work experience: Considered. **Other schools with the greatest overlap in applicants:** Bucknell University; Colgate University; Lehigh University; University of Pennsylvania; Villanova University. **Admissions statistics for the fall 2005 entering class:** Total applicants: 5,728. Total accepted: 2,146. Freshmen enrolled: 603; Overall acceptance rate: 37%. Non-early acceptance rate: 37%. **Size of waiting list:** 1643 applicants; enrolled from waiting list: 67. **Credentials of fall 2005 freshmen:** 62% ranked in the top 10 percent of their high school class; 88% were in the top 25 percent, and 98% were in the top half. (Proportion submitting class standing: 52%.) **Average high school grade point average:** 3.7. **First-year students who submitted SAT scores:** 96%. Scores (25/75 percentile): Verbal: 580-670, Math: 600-700, Combined: 1180-1370. **First-year students submitting ACT scores:** 17%. Scores (25/75 percentile): English: N/A, Math: N/A, Composite: 25-30.

ACADEMICS
Year founded: 1826. **Academic calendar:** Semester. **Degrees offered:** bachelor's. **Most popular majors:** 32% social sciences, 18% engineering, 7% English language and literature/letters, 7% psychology, 6% biological and biomedical sciences. **Major fields of study:** area, ethnic, cultural, and gender studies; biological and biomedical sciences; computer and information sciences and support services; engineering; English language and literature/letters; foreign languages, literatures, and linguistics; history; mathematics and statistics; multi/interdisciplinary studies; philosophy and

religious studies; physical sciences; psychology; social sciences; visual and performing arts. **Areas of required coursework:** arts/fine arts, humanities, computer literacy, mathematics, English (including composition), sciences (biological or physical), history, social science. **Pre-professional programs:** pre-law, pre-medicine. **Special academic programs:** cross-registration, distance learning, double major, exchange student program (domestic), honors program, independent study, internships, student-designed major, study abroad. **Cooperative education programs:** health professions. **Reserve Officers Training Corps (ROTC):** Army ROTC: Offered at cooperating institution (Lehigh University). **Faculty and instruction (2005-2006):** Total instructional faculty: 187 full-time, 41 part-time (67% men; 33% women; 7% minorities). Full-time faculty with Ph.D. or other terminal degree: 100%. Student/faculty ratio: 11/1. Classes of fewer than 20 students: 61%; of 20 to 49 students: 37%; of 50 or more students: 2%. **Freshmen returning for sophomore year:** 94%. **Graduation rates:** Four-year: 87%; five-year: 90%; six-year: 90%. **Graduate study:** 24% of students pursue further study immediately upon graduation. Fields in which graduates pursue further study: law, 6%; medicine, 2%; dentistry, 2%; engineering, 5%.

COSTS AND FINANCIAL AID

Financial aid office: (610) 330-5055. **Expenses (2006-2007):** Tuition and fees 2006-2007: $31,669; room/board: $9,864. Estimated books and supplies: $850; transportation: $100; personal expenses: $900. **Financial aid:** Priority filing date for institution's financial aid form: February 15; deadline: March 15. In 2005-2006, 60% of undergraduates applied for financial aid. Of those, 54% were determined to have financial need; 100% had their need fully met. Average financial aid package (proportion receiving): $24,675 (54%). Average amount of gift aid, such as scholarships or grants (proportion receiving): $22,543 (48%). Average amount of self-help aid, such as work study or loans (proportion receiving): $4,747 (38%). Average need-based loan (excluding PLUS or other private loans): $4,114. Among students who received need-based aid, the average percentage of need met: 100%. Among students who received aid based on merit, the average award (and the proportion receiving): $13,141 (7%). Average amount of debt of borrowers graduating in 2005: $19,373. Proportion who borrowed: 51%.

CAMPUS LIFE AND EXTRACURRICULAR ACTIVITIES

Campus housing available: coed dorms, men's dorms, sorority housing, fraternity housing, apartment for single students, special housing for disabled students. Students who live in college-owned, operated, or affiliated housing: 96%. **Student employment:** During the 2005-2006 academic year, 15% of undergraduates worked on campus. **Clubs and organizations:** Number of student organizations: 260. Activities include: choral groups, concert band, dance, drama/theater, jazz band, literary magazine, music ensembles, musical theater, pep band, radio station, student government, student newspaper, symphony orchestra, yearbook. Number of fraternities: 5; sororities: 6. Proportion of men in fraternities: 25%; of women in sororities: 45%. **Sports program (2005-2006):** Member of NCAA I. *Men's intercollegiate varsity sports:* baseball, basketball, cross-country, fencing, football, golf, lacrosse, soccer, swimming and diving, tennis, track and field (indoor), track and field (outdoor). *Women's intercollegiate varsity sports:* basketball, cross-country, fencing, field hockey, lacrosse, soccer, softball, swimming and diving, tennis, track and field (indoor), track and field (outdoor), volleyball.

SERVICES AND FACILITIES

For learning-disabled students: School does not offer a structured program with separate admission and additional fees. **Information technology resources:** Students are not required to lease or own a computer. Number of campus computers available to all students: 600. School has a wireless network. Proportion of college-owned housing units wired for high-speed internet access: 100%.

TRANSFER AND INTERNATIONAL STUDENTS

Transfer students: May apply for admission for the following academic terms: Fall, Spring. Applicants need a minimum number of credits to apply. For fall 2005: Transfer applications received: 115. Transfer applicants offered admission: 27. Transfer applicants enrolled: 14. **International students:** Number of foreign undergraduates: 128 (6% of student body).

La Roche College

- **Address:** 9000 Babcock Boulevard, Pittsburgh, PA 15237
- **Website:** http://www.laroche.edu
- **Private; Religious affiliation:** Roman Catholic
- **Enrollment:** 1,202 full-time; 298 part-time

KEY STATS

✔ **U.S News College Ranking:** fourth tier, Universities–Master's (North)
✔ **SAT Score (25th/75th percentile):** 850-1060
✔ **Tuition:** 2005-2006: $17,180

Selectivity: Less selective	Room/board: $7,344
Acceptance rate: 65%	Average debt: N/A
Student/faculty ratio: 12/1	Proportion who borrowed: N/A

UNDERGRADUATE STUDENT BODY STATS

2005-2006 enrollment: 1,202 full-time; 298 part-time. Men: 32%; women: 68%. **Ethnic makeup:** African American: 4%; American-Indian: 1%; Asian American: 1%; Hispanic: 1%; White: 83%; International: 11%. **Religious preference:** Protestant: 12%; Jewish: 1%; Unknown: 59%; Roman Catholic: 27%; Greek Orthodox, Muslim, Hindu: 1%.

ADMISSIONS FACTS AND FIGURES

Phone: (800) 838-4572. **Email:** admissions@laroche.edu. **Website:** http://www.laroche.edu. **Application deadlines for fall 2007:** Regular decision: Rolling. Early decision: Not offered. Early action: Not offered. Admission can be deferred. **Application fee:** $50. Common application is accepted. **To apply online, go to:** http://apply.laroche.edu/. **Admissions requirements/recommendations:** High school units required (recommended): English: 4 (4); Mathematics: 3 (3); Science: 3 (3); Foreign language: 0 (2); Social studies: 3 (3); History: 3 (3); Total units: 16 (18). Tests: The college uses SAT or ACT scores in admissions decisions. Either SAT or ACT required. For admission to the fall 2007 entering class, the school will accept: ACT with writing, ACT without writing. Campus visit: Neither required nor recommended. Admissions interview: Recommended. Off-campus interview: May be arranged. **Factors that count in admissions decisions:** *Academic:* Secondary school record: Very important. Class rank: Considered. Letters of recommendation: Important. Standardized test scores: Very important. Essay: Important. *Nonacademic:* Interview: Considered. Extracurricular activities: Considered. Talent/ability: Important. Character/personal qualities: Considered. Alumni/ae relationship: Not considered. Geographical residence: Considered. State residency: Not considered. Religious affiliation/commitment: Not considered. Minority status: Not considered. Volunteer work: Considered. Work experience: Considered. **Other schools with the greatest overlap in applicants:** Duquesne University; Indiana University of Pennsylvania; Robert Morris College; Slippery Rock University of Pennsylvania; University of Pittsburgh. **Admissions statistics for the fall 2005 entering class:** Total applicants: 838. Total accepted: 547. Freshmen enrolled: 305; 6% were from out of state. Overall acceptance rate: 65%. **Credentials of fall 2005 freshmen:** 12% ranked in the top 10 percent of their high school class; 31% were in the top 25 percent, and 63% were in the top half. (Proportion submitting class standing: 62%.) **Average high school grade point average:** 3.2. **First-year students who submitted SAT scores:** 90%. Scores (25/75 percentile): Verbal: 420-530, Math: 430-530, Combined: 850-1060. **First-year students submitting ACT scores:** 11%. Scores (25/75 percentile): English: 15-22, Math: 16-23, Composite: 17-22.

ACADEMICS

Year founded: 1963. **Academic calendar:** Semester. **Degrees offered:** certificate, associate, terminal-associate, bachelor's, post-bachelor's certificate, master's. **Most popular majors:** 10% elementary education and teaching, 8% design and visual communications, 7% information technology, 7% management science, 7% psychology. **Major fields of study:** architecture and related services; biological and biomedical sciences; business, management, marketing, and related support services; communication, journalism, and related programs; computer and information sciences and support services; education; English language and literature/letters; health professions and related clinical sciences; history; liberal arts and sciences studies, and humanities; mathematics and statistics; philosophy and religious studies; physical sciences; psychology; public administration and social service professions; security and protective services; social sciences; theology and religious vocations; visual and performing arts. **Areas of required coursework:** arts/fine arts, humanities, computer literacy, mathematics, English (including composition), philosophy, foreign languages, sciences (biological or physical), history, social science. **Special academic programs (% participation):** accelerated program (1%), cross-registration (5%), double major (8%), English as a Second Language (ESL) (17%), honors program (0%), independent study (28%), internships (16%), student-designed major (2%), study abroad (1%). **Teacher certification offered in:** early childhood, special education, elementary, secondary, bilingual/bicultural. **Reserve Officers Training Corps (ROTC):** Army ROTC: Offered at cooperating institution (University of Pittsburgh); Air Force ROTC: Offered at cooperating institution (Duquesne University). **Faculty and instruction (2005-2006):** Total instructional faculty: 62 full-time, 163 part-time (46% men; 54% women; 4% minorities). Full-time faculty with Ph.D. or other terminal degree: 85%. Student/faculty ratio: 12/1. Classes of fewer than 20 students: 75%; of 20 to 49 students: 25%; of 50 or more students: 0%. **Advanced Placement and International Baccalaureate credit:** AP tests may be used for: Credit only. Scores accepted: 4. International Baccalaureate exams may be used for: Credit only. **Freshmen returning for sophomore year:** 72%. **Graduation rates:** Four-year: 43%; five-year: 58%; six-year: 55%. **Graduate study:** 6% of students pursue further study within one year.

COSTS AND FINANCIAL AID

Financial aid office: (412) 536-1120. **Expenses (2005-2006):** Tuition and fees 2005-2006: $17,180; room/board: $7,344. Estimated books and supplies: $800; transportation: $650; personal expenses: $650. **Financial aid:** Priority filing date for institution's financial aid form: January 15; deadline: March 1.

CAMPUS LIFE AND EXTRACURRICULAR ACTIVITIES

Campus housing available (% using): coed dorms (100%). Students who live in college-owned, operated, or affiliated housing: 43%. **Student employment:** During the 2005-2006 academic year, 2% of undergraduates worked on campus. Average per-year earnings: $3,000. **Clubs and organizations:** Number of student organizations: 39. Activities include: choral groups, dance, drama/theater, literary magazine, musical theater, radio station, student government, student newspaper. Number of fraternities: 0; sororities: 0. Average proportion of students who stay on campus on weekends: 45%. **Sports program (2005-2006):** Member of NCAA III. *Men's intercollegiate varsity sports:* baseball, basketball, cross-country, golf, soccer. *Women's intercollegiate varsity sports:* basketball, cross-country, soccer, softball, volleyball.

SERVICES AND FACILITIES

Basic services: nonremedial tutoring, placement service, health service, health insurance. **Remedial assistance:** reading, math, writing, study skills. **Counseling services:** minority student, career, personal, veteran student, academic, psychological. **For learning-disabled students:** School does not offer a structured program with separate admission and additional fees. Total undergraduates in learning-disabled program or receiving services: 49. Services include: remedial math, remedial English, remedial reading, tape recorders, videotaped classes, untimed tests, note-taking services, oral tests, learning center, readers, extended time for tests, tutors, typist/scribe, other testing accomodations. **Library:** Number of titles: 116,955; number of current serial subscriptions: 582. **Information technology resources:** Students are not required to lease or own a computer. Number of campus computers available to all students: 180. School has a wireless network. Approximate number of users that can be accommodated: 200. Proportion of college-owned housing units wired for high-speed internet access: 100%. **Campus safety:** Security services offered: 24-hour foot-and-vehicle patrols, late-night transport/escort service, 24-hour emergency telephones, lighted pathways/sidewalks, student patrols, controlled dormitory access (key, security card, etc).

TRANSFER AND INTERNATIONAL STUDENTS

Transfer students: May apply for admission for the following academic terms: Fall, Spring, Summer. Applicants need a minimum number of credits to apply. For fall 2005: Transfer applications received: 345. Transfer applicants offered admission: 211. Transfer applicants enrolled: 167. **International students:** Number of foreign undergraduates: 153 (11% of student body). Number of countries represented: 33. Minimum TOEFL score required: 550 (paper); 220 (computer). Average TOEFL score: 620 (paper).

■ **Address:** 1900 W. Olney Avenue, Philadelphia, PA 19141-1199
■ **Website:** http://www.lasalle.edu
■ **Private; Religious affiliation:** Roman Catholic
■ **Enrollment:** 3,281 full-time; 1,058 part-time

KEY STATS

✔ **U.S News College Ranking:** 20, Universities–Master's (North)
✔ **SAT Score (25th/75th percentile):** 960-1200
✔ **Tuition:** 2006-2007: $27,700

Selectivity: Selective	**Room/board:** $10,050
Acceptance rate: 70%	**Average debt:** $26,929
Student/faculty ratio: 13/1	**Proportion who borrowed:** 82%

UNDERGRADUATE STUDENT BODY STATS

2005-2006 enrollment: 3,281 full-time; 1,058 part-time. Men: 40%; women: 60%. **Ethnic makeup:** African American: 15%; Asian American: 3%; Hispanic: 8%; White: 73%; International: 1%. **Religious preference:** Protestant: 1%; Buddhist: 1%; Unknown: 23%; Roman Catholic: 62%; Christian: 5%; Other: 8%.

ADMISSIONS FACTS AND FIGURES

Phone: (215) 951-1500. **Email:** admiss@lasalle.edu. **Website:** http://www.lasalle.edu. **Application deadlines for fall 2007:** Regular decision: Rolling. Early decision: Not offered. Early action: Not offered. Admission can be deferred. **Application fee:** $35. Common application is accepted. **Admissions requirements/recommendations:** High school units required (recommended): English: 4; Mathematics: 3; Science: 1 (2); Foreign language: 2; Social studies: 0; History: 1 (3); Academic electives: 5; Total units: 16 (5). Tests: The college uses SAT or ACT scores in admissions decisions. Either SAT or ACT required. For admission to the fall 2007 entering class, the school will accept: ACT with writing, ACT without writing. Campus visit: Recommended. Admissions interview: Recommended. Off-campus interview: Not available. **Factors that count in admissions decisions:** *Academic:* Secondary school record: Very important. Class rank: Very important. Letters of recommendation: Important. Standardized test scores: Important. Essay: Important. *Nonacademic:* Interview: Considered. Extracurricular activities: Important. Talent/ability: Important. Character/personal qualities: Important. Alumni/ae relationship: Important. Geographical residence: Not considered. State residency: Not considered. Religious affiliation/commitment: Not considered. Minority status: Considered. Volunteer work: Considered. Work experience: Considered. **Other schools with the greatest overlap in applicants:** Drexel University; Pennsylvania State University–University Park; St. Joseph's University; Temple University; Villanova University. **Admissions statistics for the fall 2005 entering class:** Total applicants: 4,562. Total accepted: 3,206. Freshmen enrolled: 822; 48% were from out of state. Overall acceptance rate: 70%. **Size of waiting list:** 0 applicants; enrolled from waiting list: 0. **Credentials of fall 2005 freshmen:** 18% ranked in the top 10 percent of their high school class; 47% were in the top 25 percent, and 75% were in the top half. (Proportion submitting class standing: 62%.) **First-year students who submitted SAT scores:** 89%. Scores (25/75 percentile): Verbal: 480-600, Math: 480-600, Combined: 960-1200. **First-year students submitting ACT scores:** 4%. Scores (25/75 percentile): English: N/A, Math: N/A, Composite: N/A.

ACADEMICS

Year founded: 1863. **Academic calendar:** Semester. **Degrees offered:** certificate, associate, bachelor's, post-bachelor's certificate, master's, post-master's certificate, doctorate. **Most popular majors:** 13% communication studies/speech communication and rhetoric, 11% nursing, 9% accounting, 7% marketing, 6% education. **Major fields of study:** area, ethnic, cultural, and gender studies; biological and biomedical sciences; business, management, marketing, and related support services; communication, journalism, and related programs; computer and information sciences and support services; education; English language and literature/letters; foreign languages, literatures, and linguistics; health professions and related clinical sciences; history; mathematics and statistics; multi/interdisciplinary studies; natural resources and conservation; philosophy and religious studies; physical sciences; psychology; public administration and social service professions; security and protective services; social sciences; visual and performing arts. **Areas of required coursework:** arts/fine arts, computer literacy, mathematics, English (including composition), philosophy, foreign languages, sciences (biological or physical), history, social science, other. **Pre-professional programs:** pre-law, pre-dentistry, pre-medicine, pre-veterinary science. **Special academic programs (% participation):** accelerated program (5%), cooperative (work-study plan) program (4%), double major (14%), dual enrollment (1%), English as a Second Language (ESL) (.5%), honors program (6%), independent study (9%), internships (31%), study abroad (2%), teacher certificate program (9%). **Teacher certification offered in:** special education, elementary, secondary. **Cooperative education programs:** business, computer science, education, health professions, social/behavioral science. **Reserve Officers Training Corps (ROTC):** Army ROTC: Offered at cooperating institution (Drexel University); Air Force ROTC: Offered at cooperating institution (St. Joseph's University). **Faculty and instruction (2005-2006):** Total instructional faculty: 210 full-time, 186 part-time (51% men; 49% women; 9% minorities). Full-time faculty with Ph.D. or other terminal degree: 83%. Student/faculty ratio: 13/1. Classes of fewer than 20 students: 51%; of 20 to 49 students: 49%; of 50 or more students: 0%. **Advanced Placement and International Baccalaureate credit:** AP tests may be used for: Credit and/or placement. Scores accepted: 3, 4, 5. International Baccalaureate exams may be used for: Credit only. **Freshmen returning for sophomore year:** 86%. **Graduation rates:** Four-year: 56%; five-year: 68%; six-year: 72%. **Graduate study:** 13% of students pursue further study within one year. Fields in which graduates pursue further study: Master of Business Administration (MBA), 10%; law, 15%; medicine, 11%; dentistry, 1%; theology (or the seminary), 1%; education, 9%; arts and sciences, 41%.

COSTS AND FINANCIAL AID
Financial aid office: (215) 951-1070. **Expenses (2006-2007):** Tuition and fees 2006-2007: $27,700; room/board: $10,050. Estimated books and supplies: $619 personal expenses: $1,000. **Financial aid:** Priority filing date for institution's financial aid form: February 15; deadline: March 15. In 2005-2006, 82% of undergraduates applied for financial aid. Of those, 73% were determined to have financial need; 31% had their need fully met. Average financial aid package (proportion receiving): $17,999 (73%). Average amount of gift aid, such as scholarships or grants (proportion receiving): $12,804 (72%). Average amount of self-help aid, such as work study or loans (proportion receiving): $4,765 (57%). Average need-based loan (excluding PLUS or other private loans): $4,530. Among students who received need-based aid, the average percentage of need met: 86%. Among students who received aid based on merit, the average award (and the proportion receiving): $10,868 (20%). The average athletic scholarship (and the proportion receiving): $15,773 (3%). Average amount of debt of borrowers graduating in 2005: $26,929. Proportion who borrowed: 82%.

CAMPUS LIFE AND EXTRACURRICULAR ACTIVITIES
Campus housing available (% using): coed dorms (96%), special housing for disabled students (1%), other housing options (3%). Students who live in college-owned, operated, or affiliated housing: 60%. **Student employment:** During the 2005-2006 academic year, 13% of undergraduates worked on campus. Average per-year earnings: $2,781. **Clubs and organizations:** Number of student organizations: 121. Activities include: choral groups, dance, drama/theater, jazz band, literary magazine, music ensembles, musical theater, pep band, radio station, student government, student newspaper, student film society, television station, yearbook. Number of fraternities: 7; sororities: 6. Proportion of men in fraternities: 7%; of women in sororities: 10%. Average proportion of students who stay on campus on weekends: 80%. **Sports program (2005-2006):** Member of NCAA I. *Men's intercollegiate varsity sports:* baseball, basketball, cross-country, football, golf, soccer, swimming and diving, tennis, track and field (indoor), track and field (outdoor), rowing . *Women's intercollegiate varsity sports:* basketball, crew, cross-country, field hockey, lacrosse, soccer, softball, swimming and diving, tennis, track and field (indoor), track and field (outdoor), volleyball.

SERVICES AND FACILITIES
Basic services: nonremedial tutoring, women's center, placement service, health service, health insurance. **Remedial assistance:** writing, study skills. **Counseling services:** minority student, career, military, personal, veteran student, academic, older student, psychological, religious, other. **For learning-disabled students:** School does not offer a structured program with separate admission and additional fees. Services include: tape recorders, untimed tests, note-taking services, extended time for tests, tutors. **Library:** Number of titles: 405,000; number of current serial subscriptions: 1,450.
Information technology resources: Students are required to lease or own a computer. Number of campus computers available to all students: 750. School has a wireless network. Approximate number of users that can be accommodated: 500. Proportion of college-owned housing units wired for high-speed internet access: 100%. **Campus safety:** Security services offered: 24-hour foot-and-vehicle patrols, late-night transport/escort service, 24-hour emergency telephones, lighted pathways/sidewalks, controlled dormitory access (key, security card, etc.).

TRANSFER AND INTERNATIONAL STUDENTS
Transfer students: May apply for admission for the following academic terms: Fall, Spring. Applicants do not need a minimum number of credits to apply. For fall 2005: Transfer applications received: 1,330. Transfer applicants offered admission: 534. Transfer applicants enrolled: 277. **International students:** Number of foreign undergraduates: 28 (1% of student body). Number of countries represented: 14. Minimum TOEFL score required: 500 (paper); 175 (computer). Average TOEFL score: 540 (paper).

Lebanon Valley College

- **Address:** 101 N. College Avenue, Annville, PA 17003
- **Website:** http://www.lvc.edu
- **Private; Religious affiliation:** Methodist
- **Enrollment:** 1,614 full-time; 160 part-time

KEY STATS
✔ **U.S News College Ranking:** 25, Universities–Master's (North)
✔ **SAT Score (25th/75th percentile):** 1010-1230
✔ **Tuition:** 2006-2007: $26,385
  Selectivity: More selective   **Room/board:** $7,115
  Acceptance rate: 77%   **Average debt:** $24,236
  Student/faculty ratio: 13/1   **Proportion who borrowed:** 73%

UNDERGRADUATE STUDENT BODY STATS
2005-2006 enrollment: 1,614 full-time; 160 part-time. Men: 44%; women: 56%. **Ethnic makeup:** African American: 2%; Asian American: 2%; Hispanic: 2%; White: 94%.

ADMISSIONS FACTS AND FIGURES
Phone: (717) 867-6181. **Email:** admission@lvc.edu. **Website:** http://www.lvc.edu. **Application deadlines for fall 2007:** Regular decision: Rolling. Early decision: Not offered. Early action: Not offered. Admission cannot be deferred. **Application fee:** $30. Common application is not accepted. **To apply online, go to:** http://www.lvc.edu/admission/full-time.aspx. **Admissions requirements/recommendations:** High school units required (recommended): English: 4 (4); Mathematics: 3 (3); Science: 2 (3); Foreign language: 2 (3); Social studies: 1; History: (2); Total units: 16. Tests: The college uses SAT or ACT scores in admissions decisions. Neither SAT nor ACT required. For admission to the fall 2007 entering class, the school will accept: ACT with writing, ACT without writing. Campus visit: Recommended. Admissions interview: Recommended. Off-campus interview: Not available. **Factors that count in admissions decisions:** *Academic:* Secondary school record: Very important. Class rank: Very important. Letters of recommendation: Considered. Standardized test scores: Important. Essay: Considered. *Nonacademic:* Interview: Important. Extracurricular activities: Important. Talent/ability: Important. Character/personal qualities: Important. Alumni/ae relationship: Considered. Geographical residence: Considered. State residency: Considered. Religious affiliation/commitment: Not considered. Minority status: Considered. Volunteer work: Considered. Work experience: Considered. **Other schools with the greatest overlap in applicants:** Elizabethtown College; Millersville University of Pennsylvania; Pennsylvania State University–University Park; Susquehanna University; West Chester University of Pennsylvania. **Admissions statistics for the fall 2005 entering class:** Total applicants: 2,006. Total accepted: 1,537. Freshmen enrolled: 454; 23% were from out of state. Overall acceptance rate: 77%. **Size of waiting list:** 15 applicants; enrolled from waiting list: 10. **Credentials of fall 2005 freshmen:** 36% ranked in the top 10 percent of their high school class; 70% were in the top 25 percent, and 93% were in the top half. (Proportion submitting class standing: 92%.) **First-year students who submitted SAT scores:** 100%. Scores (25/75 percentile): Verbal: 500-610, Math: 510-620, Combined: 1010-1230. **First-year students submitting ACT scores:** 1%. Scores (25/75 percentile): English: N/A, Math: N/A, Composite: N/A.

ACADEMICS
Year founded: 1866. **Academic calendar:** Semester. **Degrees offered:** certificate, associate, terminal-associate, bachelor's, post-bachelor's certificate,

master's, first professional. **Most popular majors:** 22% education, 18% business, management, marketing, and related support services, 11% psychology, 8% visual and performing arts, 7% health professions and related clinical sciences. **Major fields of study:** area, ethnic, cultural, and gender studies; biological and biomedical sciences; business, management, marketing, and related support services; communication, journalism, and related programs; communications technologies/technicians and support services; computer and information sciences and support services; education; English language and literature/letters; foreign languages, literatures, and linguistics; health professions and related clinical sciences; history; mathematics and statistics; multi/interdisciplinary studies; philosophy and religious studies; physical sciences; psychology; social sciences; visual and performing arts. **Areas of required coursework:** arts/fine arts, humanities, mathematics, English (including composition), philosophy, foreign languages, sciences (biological or physical), history, social science, other. **Preprofessional programs:** pre-law, pre-dentistry, pre-medicine, pre-veterinary science, pre-optometry, pre-pharmacy. **Special academic programs (% participation):** cross-registration (0%), double major (13%), dual enrollment (0%), independent study (13%), internships (27%), liberal arts/career combination, student-designed major (2%), study abroad (15%), teacher certificate program (28%). **Teacher certification offered in:** special education, elementary, secondary. **Cooperative education programs:** engineering, health professions, other. **Reserve Officers Training Corps (ROTC):** Army ROTC: Offered at cooperating institution (Millersville University). **Faculty and instruction (2005-2006):** Total instructional faculty: 100 full-time, 99 part-time (59% men; 41% women; 5% minorities). Full-time faculty with Ph.D. or other terminal degree: 85%. Student/faculty ratio: 13/1. Classes of fewer than 20 students: 59%; of 20 to 49 students: 40%; of 50 or more students: 1%. **Advanced Placement and International Baccalaureate credit:** AP tests may be used for: Credit and/or placement. Scores accepted: 4, 5. International Baccalaureate exams may be used for: Credit only. **Freshmen returning for sophomore year:** 85%. **Graduation rates:** Four-year: 69%; five-year: 73%; six-year: 70%. **Graduate study:** 12% of students pursue further study immediately upon graduation. Fields in which graduates pursue further study: Master of Business Administration (MBA), 1%; law, 1%; medicine, 1%; theology (or the seminary), 1%; arts and sciences, 7%; veterinary medicine, 1%.

COSTS AND FINANCIAL AID
Financial aid office: (717) 867-6126. **Expenses (2006-2007):** Tuition and fees 2006-2007: $26,385; room/board: $7,115. Estimated books and supplies: $900; transportation: $370; personal expenses: $800. **Financial aid:** Priority filing date for institution's financial aid form: March 1. In 2005-2006, 89% of undergraduates applied for financial aid. Of those, 78% were determined to have financial need; 38% had their need fully met. Average financial aid package (proportion receiving): $17,982 (78%). Average amount of gift aid, such as scholarships or grants (proportion receiving): $14,836 (77%). Average amount of self-help aid, such as work study or loans (proportion receiving): $5,223 (63%). Average need-based loan (excluding PLUS or other private loans): $4,222. Among students who received need-based aid, the average percentage of need met: 88%. Among students who received aid based on merit, the average award (and the proportion receiving): $10,104 (18%). The average athletic scholarship (and the proportion receiving): $0 (0%). Average amount of debt of borrowers graduating in 2005: $24,236. Proportion who borrowed: 73%.

CAMPUS LIFE AND EXTRACURRICULAR ACTIVITIES
Campus housing available (% using): coed dorms (49%), women's dorms (12%), men's dorms (7%), apartment for single students (11%), special housing for disabled students (1%), other housing options (20%). Students who live in college-owned, operated, or affiliated housing: 76%. **Student employment:** During the 2005-2006 academic year, 57% of undergraduates worked on campus. Average per-year earnings: $760. **Clubs and organizations:** Number of student organizations: 77. Activities include: choral groups, concert band, drama/theater, jazz band, literary magazine, marching band, music ensembles, musical theater, radio station, student government, student newspaper, symphony orchestra, yearbook. Number of fraternities: 4; sororities: 3. Proportion of men in fraternities: 14%; of women in sororities: 12%. Average proportion of students who stay on campus on weekends: 60%. **Sports program (2005-2006):** Member of NCAA III. *Men's intercollegiate varsity sports:* baseball, basketball, cross-country, football, golf, ice hockey, soccer, swimming and diving, tennis, track and field (indoor), track and field (outdoor). *Women's intercollegiate varsity sports:* basketball, cross-country, field hockey, soccer, softball, swimming and diving, tennis, track and field (indoor), track and field (outdoor), volleyball.

SERVICES AND FACILITIES
Basic services: nonremedial tutoring, placement service, health service, health insurance. **Counseling services:** minority student, career, personal, academic, older student, psychological, birth control, religious, other. **For learning-disabled students:** School does not offer a structured program with separate admission and additional fees. Total undergraduates in learning-disabled program or receiving services: 118. Services include: reading machines, tape recorders, videotaped classes, diagnostic testing service, untimed tests, note-taking services, oral tests, learning center, readers, extended time for tests, tutors, early syllabus, priority registration, priority seating, proofreading services, substitution of courses, texts on tape, typist/scribe, exams on tape or computer, other testing accomodations, waiver of foreign language degree requirement, waiver of math degree requirement. **Library:** Number of titles: 149,724; number of current serial subscriptions: 800. **Information technology resources:** Students are not required to lease or own a computer. Number of campus computers available to all students: 210. School has a wireless network. Proportion of college-owned housing units wired for high-speed internet access: 100%. **Campus safety:** Security services offered: 24-hour foot-and-vehicle patrols, late-night transport/escort service, 24-hour emergency telephones, lighted pathways/sidewalks, student patrols, controlled dormitory access (key, security card, etc).

TRANSFER AND INTERNATIONAL STUDENTS
Transfer students: May apply for admission for the following academic terms: Fall, Spring. Applicants need a minimum number of credits to apply. For fall 2005: Transfer applications received: 159. Transfer applicants offered admission: 80. Transfer applicants enrolled: 50. **International students:** Number of foreign undergraduates: 8. Number of countries represented: 4. Minimum TOEFL score required: 550 (paper); 213 (computer).

Lehigh University

- **Address:** 27 Memorial Drive W, Bethlehem, PA 18015
- **Website:** http://www.lehigh.edu
- **Private**
- **Enrollment:** 4,621 full-time; 58 part-time

KEY STATS
✔ **U.S News College Ranking:** 33, National Universities
✔ **SAT Score (25th/75th percentile):** 1240-1400
✔ **Tuition:** 2006-2007: $33,770

Selectivity: Most selective	**Room/board:** $8,920
Acceptance rate: 41%	**Average debt:** $23,418
Student/faculty ratio: 9/1	**Proportion who borrowed:** 52%

UNDERGRADUATE STUDENT BODY STATS
2005-2006 enrollment: 4,621 full-time; 58 part-time. Men: 59%; women: 41%. **Ethnic makeup:** African American: 2%; Asian American: 5%; Hispanic: 2%; White: 87%; International: 3%.

ADMISSIONS FACTS AND FIGURES
Phone: (610) 758-3100. **Email:** admissions@lehigh.edu. **Website:** http://www.lehigh.edu. **Application deadlines for fall 2007:** Regular decision: January 1; decision sent by April 1. Early decision: Send application by: November 15; Decision sent by: December 15. Early action: Not offered. Admission can be deferred. **Application fee:** $60. Common application is accepted. **To apply online, go to:** http://www3.lehigh.edu/admissions/apply-orinquire.asp. **Admissions requirements/recommendations:** High school units required (recommended): English: 4; Mathematics: 3; Science: 2; Foreign language: 2; Social studies: 2; Academic electives: 3; Total units: 16. Tests: The college uses SAT or ACT scores in admissions decisions. Either SAT or ACT required. For admission to the fall 2007 entering class, the school will accept: ACT with writing. Campus visit: Recommended. Admissions interview: Neither required nor recommended. Off-campus interview: May be arranged. **Factors that count in admissions decisions:** *Academic:* Secondary school record: Very important. Class rank: Considered. Letters of recommendation: Very important. Standardized test scores: Important. Essay: Important. *Nonacademic:* Interview: Not considered. Extracurricular activities: Important. Talent/ability: Important. Character/personal qualities: Important. Alumni/ae relationship: Considered. Geographical residence: Not considered. State residency: Not

considered. Religious affiliation/commitment: Not considered. Minority status: Considered. Volunteer work: Important. Work experience: Considered. **Other schools with the greatest overlap in applicants:** Bucknell University; Carnegie Mellon University; Cornell University; University of Pennsylvania. **Admissions statistics for the fall 2005 entering class:** Total applicants: 10,501. Total accepted: 4,340. Freshmen enrolled: 1,223; 76% were from out of state. Accepted through early-decision or early-action plans: 39%. Overall acceptance rate: 41%. Early-decision acceptance rate: 60%. Non-early acceptance rate: 40%. **Size of waiting list:** 1984 applicants; enrolled from waiting list: 0. **Credentials of fall 2005 freshmen:** 78% ranked in the top 10 percent of their high school class; 95% were in the top 25 percent, and 100% were in the top half. (Proportion submitting class standing: 43%.) **First-year students who submitted SAT scores:** 98%. Scores (25/75 percentile): Verbal: 600-680, Math: 640-720, Combined: 1240-1400. **First-year students submitting ACT scores:** 2%. Scores (25/75 percentile): English: N/A, Math: N/A, Composite: N/A.

ACADEMICS

Year founded: 1865. **Academic calendar:** Semester. **Degrees offered:** bachelor's, post-bachelor's certificate, master's, post-master's certificate, doctorate. **Most popular majors:** 8% finance, 8% mechanical engineering, 7% accounting, 7% psychology, 6% marketing/marketing management. **Major fields of study:** architecture and related services; area, ethnic, cultural, and gender studies; biological and biomedical sciences; business, management, marketing, and related support services; communication, journalism, and related programs; computer and information sciences and support services; engineering; English language and literature/letters; foreign languages, literatures, and linguistics; health professions and related clinical sciences; history; mathematics and statistics; multi/interdisciplinary studies; natural resources and conservation; philosophy and religious studies; physical sciences; psychology; social sciences; visual and performing arts. **Areas of required coursework:** humanities, computer literacy, mathematics, English (including composition), sciences (biological or physical), social science. **Pre-professional programs:** pre-law, pre-dentistry, pre-medicine, pre-optometry. **Special academic programs (% participation):** accelerated program (0%), cooperative (work-study plan) program (4%), cross-registration (5%), double major (13%), English as a Second Language (ESL) (5%), honors program (13%), independent study, internships (30%), study abroad (10%). **Cooperative education programs:** education, engineering. **Reserve Officers Training Corps (ROTC):** Army ROTC: Offered on campus. **Faculty and instruction (2005-2006):** Total instructional faculty: 434 full-time, 187 part-time (69% men; 31% women; 18% minorities). Full-time faculty with Ph.D. or other terminal degree: 99%. Student/faculty ratio: 9/1. Classes of fewer than 20 students: 67%; of 20 to 49 students: 28%; of 50 or more students: 6%. **Advanced Placement and International Baccalaureate credit:** AP tests may be used for: Credit and/or placement. Scores accepted: 4, 5. International Baccalaureate exams may be used for: Credit and/or placement. **Freshmen returning for sophomore year:** 94%. **Graduation rates:** Four-year: 74%; five-year: 84%; six-year: 85%. **Graduate study:** 34% of students pursue further study immediately upon graduation. Fields in which graduates pursue further study: Master of Business Administration (MBA), 7%; law, 18%; medicine, 16%; dentistry, 2%; engineering, 22%; education, 9%; arts and sciences, 26%.

COSTS AND FINANCIAL AID

Financial aid office: (610) 758-3181. **Expenses (2006-2007):** Tuition and fees 2006-2007: $33,770; room/board: $8,920. Estimated books and supplies: $1,000 personal expenses: $1,010. **Financial aid:** In 2005-2006, 55% of undergraduates applied for financial aid. Of those, 47% were determined to have financial need; 53% had their need fully met. Average financial aid package (proportion receiving): $25,403 (46%). Average amount of gift aid, such as scholarships or grants (proportion receiving): $20,441 (42%). Average amount of self-help aid, such as work study or loans (proportion receiving): $5,329 (43%). Average need-based loan (excluding PLUS or other private loans): $4,325. Among students who received need-based aid, the average percentage of need met: 98%. Among students who received aid based on merit, the average award (and the proportion receiving): $9,808 (6%). The average athletic scholarship (and the proportion receiving): $30,543 (1%). Average amount of debt of borrowers graduating in 2005: $23,418. Proportion who borrowed: 52%.

CAMPUS LIFE AND EXTRACURRICULAR ACTIVITIES

Campus housing available (% using): coed dorms (45%), sorority housing (10%), fraternity housing (19%), apartment for single students (18%), special housing for disabled students (1%), cooperative housing (1%), other housing options (6%). Students who live in college-owned, operated, or affiliated housing: 69%. **Student employment:** During the 2005-2006 academic year, 2% of undergraduates worked on campus. Average per-year earnings: $827. **Clubs and organizations:** Number of student organizations: 133. Activities include: choral groups, concert band, dance, drama/theater, jazz band, literary magazine, marching band, music ensembles, musical theater, pep band, radio station, student government, student newspaper, student film society, symphony orchestra, yearbook. Number of fraternities: 22; sororities: 9. Proportion of men in fraternities: 33%; of women in sororities: 39%. Average proportion of students who stay on campus on weekends: 85%. **Sports program (2005-2006):** Member of NCAA I. *Men's intercollegiate varsity sports:* baseball, basketball, cross-country, football, golf, lacrosse, soccer, swimming and diving, tennis, track and field (indoor), track and field (outdoor), wrestling. *Women's intercollegiate varsity sports:* basketball, crew, cross-country, field hockey, golf, lacrosse, rowing, soccer, softball, swimming and diving, tennis, track and field (indoor), track and field (outdoor), volleyball.

SERVICES AND FACILITIES

Basic services: nonremedial tutoring, women's center, placement service, day care, health service, health insurance, other. **Remedial assistance:** reading, math, writing, study skills. **Counseling services:** minority student, career, military, personal, veteran student, academic, older student, psychological, birth control, religious. **For learning-disabled students:** School does not offer a structured program with separate admission and additional fees. Total undergraduates in learning-disabled program or receiving services: 189. Services include: reading machines, learning center, tutors. **Library:** Number of titles: 1,145,980; number of current serial subscriptions: 13,610. **Information technology resources:** Students are not required to lease or own a computer. Number of campus computers available to all students: 572. School has a wireless network. Proportion of college-owned housing units wired for high-speed internet access: 100%. **Campus safety:** Security services offered: 24-hour foot-and-vehicle patrols, late-night transport/escort service, 24-hour emergency telephones, lighted pathways/sidewalks, student patrols, controlled dormitory access (key, security card, etc).

TRANSFER AND INTERNATIONAL STUDENTS

Transfer students: May apply for admission for the following academic terms: Fall, Spring. Applicants need a minimum number of credits to apply. For fall 2005: Transfer applications received: 212. Transfer applicants offered admission: 94. Transfer applicants enrolled: 46. **International students:** Number of foreign undergraduates: 118 (3% of student body). Number of countries represented: 42. Minimum TOEFL score required: 573 (paper); 230 (computer). Average TOEFL score: 627 (paper).

Lincoln University

- **Address:** PO Box 179, Lincoln University, PA 19352
- **Website:** http://www.lincoln.edu
- **Public**
- **Enrollment:** 1,652 full-time; 48 part-time

KEY STATS

✔ **U.S News College Ranking:** fourth tier, Universities–Master's (North)
✔ **SAT Score (25th/75th percentile):** 700-890
✔ **Tuition:** 2005-2006: $6,866 in state, $10,542 out of state

Selectivity: Less selective	**Room/board:** $6,792
Acceptance rate: 35%	**Average debt:** $21,000
Student/faculty ratio: 16/1	**Proportion who borrowed:** 78%

UNDERGRADUATE STUDENT BODY STATS

2005-2006 enrollment: 1,652 full-time; 48 part-time. Men: 39%; women: 61%. **Ethnic makeup:** African American: 93%; White: 1%; International: 6%.

ADMISSIONS FACTS AND FIGURES

Phone: (800) 790-0191. **Email:** admiss@lu.lincoln.edu. **Website:** http://www.lincoln.edu. **Application deadlines for fall 2007:** Regular decision: July 1. Early decision: Not offered. Early action: Not offered. Admission can be deferred. **Application fee:** $20. Common application is accepted. **To apply online, go to:** http://www.lincoln.edu/admissions/application.html#app. **Admissions requirements/recommendations:** High school units required (recommended): English: 4; Mathematics: 3; Science: 3; Social studies: 3; Academic electives: 5; Total units: 21. Tests: The college uses SAT or ACT scores in admissions decisions. Either SAT or ACT required. For admission to the fall 2007 entering class, the school will accept: ACT with writing, ACT without writing. Campus visit: Recommended. Admissions interview: Recommended. Off-campus interview: Not available. **Factors that count in admissions decisions:** *Academic:* Secondary school record: Very important. Class rank: Very important. Letters of recommendation: Important. Standardized test scores: Important. Essay: Considered. *Nonacademic:* Interview: Considered. Extracurricular activities: Considered. Talent/ability: Important. Character/personal qualities: Considered. Alumni/ae relationship: Considered. Geographical residence: Considered. State residency: Considered. Religious affiliation/commitment: Considered. Minority status: Not considered. Volunteer work: Considered. Work experience: Considered. **Admissions statistics for the fall 2005 entering class:** Total applicants: 5,435. Total accepted: 1,914. Freshmen enrolled: 636; 53% were from out of state. Overall acceptance rate: 35%. **Credentials of fall 2005 freshmen:** 7% ranked in the top 10 percent of their high school class; 23% were in the top 25 percent, and 45% were in the top half. (Proportion submitting class standing: 52%.) **Average high school grade point average:** 2.8. **First-year students who submitted SAT scores:** 93%. Scores (25/75 percentile): Verbal: 350-450, Math: 350-440, Combined: 700-890. **First-year students submitting ACT scores:** 5%. Scores (25/75 percentile): English: 12-16, Math: 14-16, Composite: 14-17.

ACADEMICS

Year founded: 1854. **Academic calendar:** Semester. **Degrees offered:** bachelor's, master's. **Most popular majors:** 18% business, management, marketing, and related support services, 16% security and protective services, 15% education, 8% social sciences, 7% parks, recreation, leisure, and fitness studies. **Major fields of study:** area, ethnic, cultural, and gender studies; biological and biomedical sciences; business, management, marketing, and related support services; communication, journalism, and related programs; computer and information sciences and support services; education; engineering; English language and literature/letters; foreign languages, literatures, and linguistics; health professions and related clinical sciences; history; mathematics and statistics; parks, recreation, leisure, and fitness studies; philosophy and religious studies; physical sciences; psychology; public administration and social service professions; security and protective services; social sciences; visual and performing arts. **Areas of required coursework:** arts/fine arts, humanities, computer literacy, mathematics, English (including composition), philosophy, foreign languages, sciences (biological or physical), history, social science. **Pre-professional programs:** pre-law, pre-medicine, other. **Special academic programs:** double major, exchange student program (domestic), honors program, independent study, internships, study abroad, teacher certificate program. **Teacher certification offered in:** early childhood, special education, elementary, secondary. **Reserve Officers Training Corps (ROTC):** Army ROTC: Offered at cooperating institution (University of Delaware). **Faculty and instruction (2005-2006):** Total instructional faculty: 93 full-time, 90 part-time (58% men; 42% women; 74% minorities). Full-time faculty with Ph.D. or other terminal degree: 76%. Student/faculty ratio: 16/1. Classes of fewer than 20 students: 43%; of 20 to 49 students: 56%; of 50 or more students: 1%. **Advanced Placement and International Baccalaureate credit:** AP tests may be used for: Credit only. **Freshmen returning for sophomore year:** 64%. **Graduation rates:** Four-year: 27%; five-year: 34%; six-year: 41%. **Graduate study:** 14% of students pursue further study immediately upon graduation.

COSTS AND FINANCIAL AID

Financial aid office: (800) 561-2606. **Expenses (2005-2006):** Tuition and fees 2005-2006: $6,866 in state, $10,542 out of state; room/board: $6,792. Estimated books and supplies: $1,200; transportation: $210; personal expenses: $1,297. **Financial aid:** Priority filing date for institution's financial aid form: May 1; deadline: May 1. In 2005-2006, 90% of undergraduates applied for financial aid. Of those, 83% were determined to have financial need; 8% had their need fully met. Average financial aid package (proportion receiving): $9,118 (83%). Average amount of gift aid, such as scholarships or grants (proportion receiving): $4,889 (64%). Average amount of self-help aid, such as work study or loans (proportion receiving): $3,811 (78%). Average need-based loan (excluding PLUS or other private loans): $3,490. Among students who received need-based aid, the average percentage of need met: 49%. Among students who received aid based on merit, the average award (and the proportion receiving): $8,509 (6%). The average athletic scholarship (and the proportion receiving): $0 (0%). Average amount of debt of borrowers graduating in 2005: $21,000. Proportion who borrowed: 78%.

CAMPUS LIFE AND EXTRACURRICULAR ACTIVITIES

Campus housing available (% using): coed dorms (33%), women's dorms (44%), men's dorms (23%). Students who live in college-owned, operated, or affiliated housing: 97%. **Student employment:** During the 2005-2006 academic year, 36% of undergraduates worked on campus. Average per-year earnings: $700. **Clubs and organizations:** Number of student organizations: 65. Activities include: choral groups, dance, drama/theater, jazz band, music ensembles, radio station, student government, student newspaper, television station, yearbook. Number of fraternities: 5; sororities: 4. Proportion of men in fraternities: 2%; of women in sororities: 1%. Average proportion of students who stay on campus on weekends: 90%. **Sports program (2005-2006):** Member of NCAA III. **Men's intercollegiate varsity sports:** baseball, basketball, cross-country, soccer, tennis, track and field (indoor), track and field (outdoor). **Women's intercollegiate varsity sports:** basketball, cross-country, soccer, tennis, track and field (indoor), track and field (outdoor), volleyball.

SERVICES AND FACILITIES

Basic services: nonremedial tutoring, women's center, placement service, health service, health insurance. **Remedial assistance:** reading, math, writing, study skills. **Counseling services:** career, personal, academic. **For learning-disabled students:** School does not offer a structured program with separate admission and additional fees. Services include: remedial math, remedial English, remedial reading, tape recorders, videotaped classes, untimed tests, oral tests, learning center, readers, extended time for tests, tutors. **Library:** Number of titles: 188,973; number of current serial subscriptions: 605. **Information technology resources:** Students are not required to lease or own a computer. Number of campus computers available to all students: 200. School has a wireless network. Approximate number of users that can be accommodated: 200. Proportion of college-owned housing units wired for high-speed internet access: 30%. **Campus safety:** Security services offered: 24-hour foot-and-vehicle patrols, late-night transport/escort service, 24-hour emergency telephones, lighted pathways/sidewalks, controlled dormitory access (key, security card, etc).

TRANSFER AND INTERNATIONAL STUDENTS

Transfer students: May apply for admission for the following academic terms: Fall, Spring, Summer. Applicants need a minimum number of credits to apply. For fall 2005: Transfer applications received: 292. Transfer applicants offered admission: 77. Transfer applicants enrolled: 43. **International students:** Number of foreign undergraduates: 100 (6% of student body). Number of countries represented: 39. Minimum TOEFL score required: 500 (paper).

Lock Haven University of Pennsylvania

- **Address:** 401 N. Fairview Street, Lock Haven, PA 17745
- **Website:** http://www.lhup.edu
- **Public**
- **Enrollment:** 4,556 full-time; 421 part-time

KEY STATS

✔ **U.S News College Ranking:** fourth tier, Universities–Master's (North)
✔ **SAT Score (25th/75th percentile):** 850-1050
✔ **Tuition:** 2005-2006: $6,258 in state, $11,618 out of state

Selectivity: Less selective	**Room/board:** $5,840
Acceptance rate: 77%	**Average debt:** $19,500
Student/faculty ratio: 19/1	**Proportion who borrowed:** 75%

UNDERGRADUATE STUDENT BODY STATS

2005-2006 enrollment: 4,556 full-time; 421 part-time. Men: 42%; women: 58%. **Ethnic makeup:** African American: 5%; Asian American: 1%; Hispanic: 2%; White: 90%; International: 1%.

ADMISSIONS FACTS AND FIGURES

Phone: (570) 893-2027. **Email:** admissions@lhup.edu. **Website:** http://www.lhup.edu. **Application deadlines for fall 2007:** Regular decision: Rolling. Early decision: Not offered. Early action: Not offered. Admission can be deferred. **Application fee:** $25. Common application is not accepted. **To apply online, go to:** http://www.lhup.edu/admissions/application_form.html. **Admissions requirements/recommendations:** High school units required (recommended): English: 4 (4); Mathematics: 3 (4);

Science: 3 (4); Foreign language: (2); Social studies: 2 (2); History: 2 (2); Total units: 16 (21). Tests: The college uses SAT or ACT scores in admissions decisions. Either SAT or ACT required. For admission to the fall 2007 entering class, the school will accept: ACT with writing, ACT without writing. Campus visit: Recommended. Admissions interview: Recommended. Off-campus interview: May be arranged. **Factors that count in admissions decisions:** *Academic:* Secondary school record: Very important. Class rank: Very important. Letters of recommendation: Considered. Standardized test scores: Important. Essay: Considered. *Nonacademic:* Interview: Considered. Extracurricular activities: Considered. Talent/ability: Very important. Character/personal qualities: Very important. Alumni/ae relationship: Not considered. Geographical residence: Not considered. State residency: Not considered. Religious affiliation/commitment: Not considered. Minority status: Important. Volunteer work: Considered. Work experience: Considered. **Other schools with the greatest overlap in applicants:** Clarion University of Pennsylvania; Kutztown University of Pennsylvania; Mansfield University of Pennsylvania; Millersville University of Pennsylvania; West Chester University of Pennsylvania. **Admissions statistics for the fall 2005 entering class:** Total applicants: 4,182. Total accepted: 3,208. Freshmen enrolled: 1,247; 10% were from out of state. Overall acceptance rate: 77%. **Credentials of fall 2005 freshmen:** 7% ranked in the top 10 percent of their high school class; 25% were in the top 25 percent, and 62% were in the top half. (Proportion submitting class standing: 89%.) **Average high school grade point average:** 3.1. First-year students who submitted SAT scores: 95%. Scores (25/75 percentile): Verbal: 420-520, Math: 430-530, Combined: 850-1050. **First-year students submitting ACT scores:** 8%. Scores (25/75 percentile): English: N/A, Math: N/A, Composite: 16-21.

ACADEMICS

Year founded: 1870. **Academic calendar:** Semester. **Degrees offered:** associate, bachelor's, master's. **Most popular majors:** 21% education, 19% parks, recreation, leisure, and fitness studies, 11% health professions and related clinical sciences, 9% business, management, marketing, and related support services, 6% security and protective services. **Major fields of study:** biological and biomedical sciences; business, management, marketing, and related support services; communication, journalism, and related programs; computer and information sciences and support services; education; English language and literature/letters; foreign languages, literatures, and linguistics; health professions and related clinical sciences; history; legal professions and studies; liberal arts and sciences studies, and humanities; mathematics and statistics; multi/interdisciplinary studies; parks, recreation, leisure, and fitness studies; philosophy and religious studies; physical sciences; psychology; public administration and social service professions; security and protective services; social sciences; visual and performing arts. **Areas of required coursework:** arts/fine arts, humanities, computer literacy, mathematics, English (including composition), philosophy, sciences (biological or physical), history, social science. **Pre-professional programs:** pre-law, pre-dentistry, pre-medicine, pre-veterinary science, pre-pharmacy, other. **Special academic programs:** cooperative (work-study plan) program, cross-registration, distance learning, double major, dual enrollment, English as a Second Language (ESL), honors program, independent study, internships, student-designed major, study abroad, teacher certificate program. **Teacher certification offered in:** early childhood, special education, elementary, secondary. **Cooperative education programs:** engineering. **Reserve Officers Training Corps (ROTC):** Army ROTC: Offered on campus. **Faculty and instruction (2005-2006):** Total instructional faculty: 254 full-time, 19 part-time (54% men; 46% women; 12% minorities). Full-time faculty with Ph.D. or other terminal degree: 77%. Student/faculty ratio: 19/1. Classes of fewer than 20 students: 30%; of 20 to 49 students: 68%; of 50 or more students: 2%. **Advanced Placement and International Baccalaureate credit:** AP tests may be used for: Credit and/or placement. Scores accepted: 3, 4, 5. International Baccalaureate exams may be used for: Credit only. **Freshmen returning for sophomore year:** 72%. **Graduation rates:** Four-year: 25%; five-year: 49%; six-year: 50%. **Graduate study:** 12% of students pursue further study within one year. Fields in which graduates pursue further study: Master of Business Administration (MBA), 13%; law, 2%; medicine, 41%; theology (or the seminary), 2%; education, 11%; arts and sciences, 28%.

COSTS AND FINANCIAL AID

Financial aid office: (570) 893-2344. **Expenses (2005-2006):** Tuition and fees 2005-2006: $6,258 in state, $11,618 out of state; room/board: $5,840. Estimated books and supplies: $900; transportation: $300; personal expenses: $1,090. **Financial aid:** In 2005-2006, 95% of undergraduates applied for financial aid. Of those, 80% were determined to have financial need; 55% had their need fully met. Average financial aid package (proportion receiving): $6,562 (80%). Average amount of gift aid, such as scholar-

ships or grants (proportion receiving): $4,922 (53%). Average amount of self-help aid, such as work study or loans (proportion receiving): $4,265 (62%). Average need-based loan (excluding PLUS or other private loans): $3,797. Among students who received need-based aid, the average percentage of need met: 77%. Among students who received aid based on merit, the average award (and the proportion receiving): $1,575 (4%). The average athletic scholarship (and the proportion receiving): $2,155 (5%). Average amount of debt of borrowers graduating in 2005: $19,500. Proportion who borrowed: 75%.

CAMPUS LIFE AND EXTRACURRICULAR ACTIVITIES

Campus housing available (% using): coed dorms (85%), women's dorms (7%), apartment for single students (8%). Students who live in college-owned, operated, or affiliated housing: 17%. **Student employment:** During the 2005-2006 academic year, 16% of undergraduates worked on campus. Average per-year earnings: $2,318. **Clubs and organizations:** Number of student organizations: 96. Activities include: choral groups, concert band, dance, drama/theater, jazz band, literary magazine, marching band, music ensembles, radio station, student government, student newspaper, television station. Number of fraternities: 6; sororities: 4. Proportion of men in fraternities: 4%; of women in sororities: 3%. Average proportion of students who stay on campus on weekends: 50%. **Sports program (2005-2006):** Member of NCAA II. *Men's intercollegiate varsity sports:* baseball, basketball, cross-country, football, soccer, track and field (indoor), track and field (outdoor), wrestling. *Women's intercollegiate varsity sports:* basketball, cross-country, field hockey, lacrosse, soccer, softball, swimming and diving, track and field (indoor), track and field (outdoor), volleyball.

SERVICES AND FACILITIES

Basic services: placement service, health service. **Remedial assistance:** math, writing, study skills. **Counseling services:** career, personal, veteran student, academic, psychological. **For learning-disabled students:** School does not offer a structured program with separate admission and additional fees. Services include: reading machines, tape recorders, note-taking services, readers, extended time for tests. **Library:** Number of titles: 422,306; number of current serial subscriptions: 927. **Information technology resources:** Students are not required to lease or own a computer. Number of campus computers available to all students: 290. School has a wireless network. Approximate number of users that can be accommodated: 700. Proportion of college-owned housing units wired for high-speed internet access: 100%. **Campus safety:** Security services offered: 24-hour foot-and-vehicle patrols, late-night transport/escort service, 24-hour emergency telephones, lighted pathways/sidewalks, controlled dormitory access (key, security card, etc).

TRANSFER AND INTERNATIONAL STUDENTS

Transfer students: May apply for admission for the following academic terms: Fall, Spring, Summer. Applicants do not need a minimum number of credits to apply. For fall 2005: Transfer applications received: 437. Transfer applicants offered admission: 316. Transfer applicants enrolled: 168. **International students:** Number of foreign undergraduates: 64 (1% of student body). Number of countries represented: 32. Minimum TOEFL score required: 550 (paper); 213 (computer).

Lycoming College

- **Address:** 700 College Place, Williamsport, PA 17701
- **Website:** http://www.lycoming.edu
- **Private; Religious affiliation:** Methodist
- **Enrollment:** 1,450 full-time; 21 part-time

KEY STATS

✔ **U.S News College Ranking:** third tier, Liberal Arts Colleges
✔ **SAT Score (25th/75th percentile):** 970-1150
✔ **Tuition:** 2006-2007: $25,605

Selectivity: Selective	**Room/board:** $6,826
Acceptance rate: 77%	**Average debt:** $23,343
Student/faculty ratio: 14/1	**Proportion who borrowed:** 87%

UNDERGRADUATE STUDENT BODY STATS

2005-2006 enrollment: 1,450 full-time; 21 part-time. Men: 43%; women: 57%. **Ethnic makeup:** African American: 3%; Asian American: 1%; Hispanic:

1%; White: 94%; International: 1%. **Religious preference:** Roman Catholic: 24%; Protestant: 22%; Jewish: 1%; No preference: 32%; Unknown: 7%; Methodist: 11%; Other: 3%.

ADMISSIONS FACTS AND FIGURES
Phone: (800) 345-3920. **Email:** admissions@lycoming.edu. **Website:** http://www.lycoming.edu. **Application deadlines for fall 2007:** Regular decision: June 1. Early decision: Not offered. Early action: Not offered. Admission can be deferred. **Application fee:** $35. Common application is accepted. **Admissions requirements/recommendations:** High school units required (recommended): English: 4 (4); Mathematics: 3 (4); Science: 2 (4); Foreign language: 2 (4); Social studies: 4 (4); History: 3 (4); Academic electives: 2 (2); Total units: 20 (26). Tests: The college uses SAT or ACT scores in admissions decisions. Either SAT or ACT required. Campus visit: Recommended. Admissions interview: Recommended. Off-campus interview: May be arranged. **Factors that count in admissions decisions:** *Academic:* Secondary school record: Very important. Class rank: Very important. Letters of recommendation: Important. Standardized test scores: Important. Essay: Important. *Nonacademic:* Interview: Important. Extracurricular activities: Important. Talent/ability: Important. Character/personal qualities: Very important. Alumni/ae relationship: Important. Geographical residence: Important. State residency: Considered. Religious affiliation/commitment: Considered. Minority status: Important. Volunteer work: Considered. Work experience: Considered. **Other schools with the greatest overlap in applicants:** Bloomsburg University of Pennsylvania; Bucknell University; Bucknell University; Lock Haven University of Pennsylvania; Lock Haven University of Pennsylvania; Pennsylvania State University–University Park; Pennsylvania State University–University Park; Susquehanna University; Susquehanna University. **Admissions statistics for the fall 2005 entering class:** Total applicants: 1,511. Total accepted: 1,157. Freshmen enrolled: 360; 38% were from out of state. Overall acceptance rate: 77%. **Credentials of fall 2005 freshmen:** 19% ranked in the top 10 percent of their high school class; 45% were in the top 25 percent, and 80% were in the top half. (Proportion submitting class standing: 82%.) **First-year students who submitted SAT scores:** 98%. Scores (25/75 percentile): Verbal: 490-580, Math: 480-570, Combined: 970-1150. **First-year students submitting ACT scores:** 11%. Scores (25/75 percentile): English: N/A, Math: N/A, Composite: 21-25.

ACADEMICS
Year founded: 1812. **Academic calendar:** Semester. **Degrees offered:** bachelor's. **Most popular majors:** 19% psychology, 12% business administration and management, 11% biology/biological sciences, 11% criminology, 7% communication studies/speech communication and rhetoric. **Major fields of study:** area, ethnic, cultural, and gender studies; biological and biomedical sciences; business, management, marketing, and related support services; communication, journalism, and related programs; computer and information sciences and support services; English language and literature/letters; foreign languages, literatures, and linguistics; history; mathematics and statistics; multi/interdisciplinary studies; philosophy and religious studies; physical sciences; psychology; security and protective services; social sciences; visual and performing arts. **Areas of required coursework:** arts/fine arts, humanities, mathematics, English (including composition), foreign languages, sciences (biological or physical), social science. **Special academic programs (% participation):** cross-registration (1%), double major (19%), honors program (19%), independent study (14%), internships (10%), student-designed major (1%), study abroad (2%), teacher certificate program (9%). **Teacher certification offered in:** special education, elementary, secondary. **Reserve Officers Training Corps (ROTC):** Army ROTC: Offered at cooperating institution (Bucknell University). **Faculty and instruction (2005-2006):** Total instructional faculty: 84 full-time, 41 part-time (62% men; 38% women; 4% minorities). Full-time faculty with Ph.D. or other terminal degree: 92%. Student/faculty ratio: 14/1. Classes of fewer than 20 students: 60%; of 20 to 49 students: 39%; of 50 or more students: 2%. **Advanced Placement and International Baccalaureate credit:** AP tests may be used for: Credit only. Scores accepted: 4, 5. International Baccalaureate exams may be used for: Credit only. **Freshmen returning for sophomore year:** 84%. **Graduation rates:** Four-year: 61%; five-year: 65%; six-year: 66%. **Graduate study:** 20% of students pursue further study immediately upon graduation. Fields in which graduates pursue further study: law, 18%; medicine, 7%; education, 10%; arts and sciences, 37%.

COSTS AND FINANCIAL AID
Financial aid office: (570) 321-4040. **Expenses (2006-2007):** Tuition and fees 2006-2007: $25,605; room/board: $6,826. Estimated books and supplies: $800; transportation: $600; personal expenses: $2,200. **Financial aid:**

Priority filing date for institution's financial aid form: March 1. In 2005-2006, 91% of undergraduates applied for financial aid. Of those, 83% were determined to have financial need; 23% had their need fully met. Average financial aid package (proportion receiving): $17,826 (83%). Average amount of gift aid, such as scholarships or grants (proportion receiving): $13,513 (82%). Average amount of self-help aid, such as work study or loans (proportion receiving): $4,774 (73%). Average need-based loan (excluding PLUS or other private loans): $4,261. Among students who received need-based aid, the average percentage of need met: 77%. Among students who received aid based on merit, the average award (and the proportion receiving): $8,949 (13%). The average athletic scholarship (and the proportion receiving): $0 (0%). Average amount of debt of borrowers graduating in 2005: $23,343. Proportion who borrowed: 87%.

CAMPUS LIFE AND EXTRACURRICULAR ACTIVITIES
Campus housing available (% using): coed dorms (70%), women's dorms (10%), sorority housing (6%), fraternity housing (4%), apartment for single students (9%), special housing for disabled students (1%). Students who live in college-owned, operated, or affiliated housing: 84%. **Student employment:** During the 2005-2006 academic year, 40% of undergraduates worked on campus. Average per-year earnings: $1,105. **Clubs and organizations:** Number of student organizations: 71. Activities include: choral groups, concert band, dance, drama/theater, jazz band, literary magazine, music ensembles, pep band, radio station, student government, student newspaper, television station, yearbook. Number of fraternities: 5; sororities: 5. Proportion of men in fraternities: 16%; of women in sororities: 26%. Average proportion of students who stay on campus on weekends: 75%. **Sports program (2005-2006):** Member of NCAA III. *Men's intercollegiate varsity sports:* basketball, cross-country, football, golf, lacrosse, soccer, swimming and diving, tennis, track and field (indoor), track and field (outdoor), wrestling. *Women's intercollegiate varsity sports:* basketball, cross-country, lacrosse, soccer, softball, swimming and diving, tennis, track and field (indoor), track and field (outdoor), volleyball.

SERVICES AND FACILITIES
Basic services: nonremedial tutoring, women's center, placement service, health service, health insurance. **Remedial assistance:** math, writing, study skills, other. **Counseling services:** minority student, career, personal, academic, older student, psychological, religious. **For learning-disabled students:** School does not offer a structured program with separate admission and additional fees. Total undergraduates in learning-disabled program or receiving services: 29. Services include: remedial math, reading machines, tape recorders, other special classes, videotaped classes, untimed tests, note-taking services, oral tests, learning center, readers, extended time for tests, tutors. **Library:** Number of titles: 186,000; number of current serial subscriptions: 717. **Information technology resources:** Students are not required to lease or own a computer. Number of campus computers available to all students: 125. School has a wireless network. Proportion of college-owned housing units wired for high-speed internet access: 100%. **Campus safety:** Security services offered: 24-hour foot-and-vehicle patrols, late-night transport/escort service, 24-hour emergency telephones, lighted pathways/sidewalks, student patrols, controlled dormitory access (key, security card, etc).

TRANSFER AND INTERNATIONAL STUDENTS
Transfer students: May apply for admission for the following academic terms: Fall, Spring. Applicants do not need a minimum number of credits to apply. For fall 2005: Transfer applications received: 102. Transfer applicants offered admission: 58. Transfer applicants enrolled: 23. **International students:** Number of foreign undergraduates: 12 (1% of student body). Minimum TOEFL score required: 500 (paper). Average TOEFL score: 560 (paper).

Mansfield University of Pennsylvania

- **Address:** Alumni Hall, Mansfield, PA 16933
- **Website:** http://www.mansfield.edu
- **Public**
- **Enrollment:** 2,713 full-time; 273 part-time

KEY STATS

✔ **U.S News College Ranking:** third tier, Universities–Master's (North)

✔ **SAT Score (25th/75th percentile):** 870-1080

✔ **Tuition:** 2005-2006: $6,434 in state, $13,794 out of state

Selectivity: Less selective	**Room/board:** $5,868
Acceptance rate: 72%	**Average debt:** $22,821
Student/faculty ratio: 16/1	**Proportion who borrowed:** 77%

UNDERGRADUATE STUDENT BODY STATS

2005-2006 enrollment: 2,713 full-time; 273 part-time. Men: 38%; women: 62%. **Ethnic makeup:** African American: 6%; American-Indian: 1%; Asian American: 1%; Hispanic: 1%; White: 90%; International: 1%.

ADMISSIONS FACTS AND FIGURES

Phone: (800) 577-6826. **Email:** admissns@mansfield.edu. **Website:** http://www.mansfield.edu. **Application deadlines for fall 2007:** Regular decision: July 6. Early decision: Not offered. Early action: Not offered. Admission can be deferred. **Application fee:** $25. Common application is accepted. **Admissions requirements/recommendations:** High school units required (recommended): English: 4 (4); Mathematics: 3 (4); Science: 2 (4); Foreign language: (2); Social studies: 4 (4); Academic electives: 6 (3); Total units: 21 (23). Tests: The college uses SAT or ACT scores in admissions decisions. Either SAT or ACT required. For admission to the fall 2007 entering class, the school will accept: ACT with writing, ACT without writing. Campus visit: Recommended. Admissions interview: Recommended. Off-campus interview: Not available. **Factors that count in admissions decisions: *Academic:*** Secondary school record: Very important. Class rank: Very important. Letters of recommendation: Considered. Standardized test scores: Very important. Essay: Considered. ***Nonacademic:*** Interview: Important. Extracurricular activities: Considered. Talent/ability: Very important. Character/personal qualities: Considered. Alumni/ae relationship: Considered. Geographical residence: Not considered. State residency: Not considered. Religious affiliation/commitment: Not considered. Minority status: Not considered. Volunteer work: Considered. Work experience: Considered. **Other schools with the greatest overlap in applicants:** Bloomsburg University of Pennsylvania; Clarion University of Pennsylvania; Lock Haven University of Pennsylvania; Lycoming College; Pennsylvania State University–University Park. **Admissions statistics for the fall 2005 entering class:** Total applicants: 2,348. Total accepted: 1,689. Freshmen enrolled: 680; 15% were from out of state. Overall acceptance rate: 72%. **Credentials of fall 2005 freshmen:** 12% ranked in the top 10 percent of their high school class; 33% were in the top 25 percent, and 64% were in the top half. (Proportion submitting class standing: 88%.) **Average high school grade point average:** 3.3. **First-year students who submitted SAT scores:** 95%. Scores (25/75 percentile): Verbal: 440-540, Math: 430-540, Combined: 870-1080.

ACADEMICS

Year founded: 1857. **Academic calendar:** Semester. **Degrees offered:** certificate, associate, bachelor's, master's. **Most popular majors:** 14% elementary education and teaching, 12% business administration and management, 10% communication studies/speech communication and rhetoric, 10% criminal justice/law enforcement administration, 9% music. **Major fields of study:** biological and biomedical sciences; business, management, marketing, and related support services; communication, journalism, and related programs; computer and information sciences and support services; education; English language and literature/letters; family and consumer sciences/human sciences; foreign languages, literatures, and linguistics; health professions and related clinical sciences; history; legal professions and studies; liberal arts and sciences studies, and humanities; mathematics and statistics; philosophy and religious studies; physical sciences; psychology; public administration and social service professions; science technologies/technicians; security and protective services; social sciences; visual and performing arts. **Areas of required coursework:** arts/fine arts, humanities, computer literacy, mathematics, English (including composition), foreign languages, sciences (biological or physical), history, social science. **Pre-pro-**

fessional programs: pre-law, pre-dentistry, pre-medicine, pre-veterinary science, pre-optometry, pre-pharmacy. **Special academic programs (% participation):** cooperative (work-study plan) program, cross-registration (19%), distance learning (9%), double major (34%), dual enrollment, exchange student program (domestic) (1.6%), honors program (7%), independent study (74%), internships (10.4%), liberal arts/career combination, student-designed major, study abroad, teacher certificate program (12%). **Teacher certification offered in:** early childhood, special education, elementary, middle/junior high, secondary, bilingual/bicultural. **Cooperative education programs:** education. **Reserve Officers Training Corps (ROTC):** Army ROTC: Offered at cooperating institution (Lock Haven University). **Faculty and instruction (2005-2006):** Total instructional faculty: 165 full-time, 58 part-time (50% men; 50% women; 10% minorities). Full-time faculty with Ph.D. or other terminal degree: 93%. Student/faculty ratio: 16/1. Classes of fewer than 20 students: 42%; of 20 to 49 students: 51%; of 50 or more students: 7%. **Advanced Placement and International Baccalaureate credit:** AP tests may be used for: Credit only. Scores accepted: 3, 4, 5. International Baccalaureate exams may be used for: Credit and/or placement. **Freshmen returning for sophomore year:** 67%. **Graduation rates:** Four-year: 30%; five-year: 48%; six-year: 49%. **Graduate study:** 7% of students pursue further study immediately upon graduation. Fields in which graduates pursue further study: law, 1%; medicine, 1%; engineering, 1%; education, 97%.

COSTS AND FINANCIAL AID

Financial aid office: (570) 662-4878. **Expenses (2005-2006):** Tuition and fees 2005-2006: $6,434 in state, $13,794 out of state; room/board: $5,868. Estimated books and supplies: $1,200; transportation: $1,000; personal expenses: $2,000. **Financial aid:** Priority filing date for institution's financial aid form: March 15; deadline: April 30. In 2005-2006, 90% of undergraduates applied for financial aid. Of those, 74% were determined to have financial need; 44% had their need fully met. Average financial aid package (proportion receiving): $10,934 (74%). Average amount of gift aid, such as scholarships or grants (proportion receiving): $3,924 (55%). Average amount of self-help aid, such as work study or loans (proportion receiving): $3,799 (66%). Average need-based loan (excluding PLUS or other private loans): $3,636. Among students who received need-based aid, the average percentage of need met: 56%. Among students who received aid based on merit, the average award (and the proportion receiving): $1,830 (3%). The average athletic scholarship (and the proportion receiving): $2,077 (6%). Average amount of debt of borrowers graduating in 2005: $22,821. Proportion who borrowed: 77%.

CAMPUS LIFE AND EXTRACURRICULAR ACTIVITIES

Campus housing available (% using): coed dorms (70%), women's dorms (20%), sorority housing (5%), fraternity housing (5%). Students who live in college-owned, operated, or affiliated housing: 48%. **Student employment:** During the 2005-2006 academic year, 15% of undergraduates worked on campus. Average per-year earnings: $1,300. **Clubs and organizations:** Number of student organizations: 97. Activities include: choral groups, concert band, drama/theater, jazz band, literary magazine, marching band, music ensembles, musical theater, pep band, radio station, student government, student newspaper, symphony orchestra, television station. Number of fraternities: 6; sororities: 4. Proportion of men in fraternities: 5%; of women in sororities: 4%. Average proportion of students who stay on campus on weekends: 50%. **Sports program (2005-2006):** Member of NCAA II. ***Men's intercollegiate varsity sports:*** baseball, basketball, cross-country, football, track and field (indoor), track and field (outdoor). ***Women's intercollegiate varsity sports:*** basketball, cross-country, field hockey, soccer, softball, swimming and diving, track and field (indoor), track and field (outdoor).

SERVICES AND FACILITIES

Basic services: nonremedial tutoring, women's center, placement service, day care, health service, health insurance. **Remedial assistance:** reading, math, writing, study skills. **Counseling services:** minority student, career, military, personal, veteran student, academic, older student, psychological, birth control, religious. **For learning-disabled students:** School does not offer a structured program with separate admission and additional fees. Total undergraduates in learning-disabled program or receiving services: 35. Services include: remedial math, remedial English, tape recorders, diagnostic testing service, note-taking services, learning center, extended time for tests, tutors, priority registration, other testing accomodations. **Library:** Number of titles: 246,141; number of current serial subscriptions: 2,948. **Information technology resources:** Students are not required to lease or own a computer. Number of campus computers available to all students: 705. School has a wireless network. Approximate number of users that can be accommodated: 4,000. Proportion of college-owned housing units wired for high-speed internet access: 100%. **Campus safety:** Security services offered: 24-hour foot-and-vehicle patrols, late-night transport/escort service, 24-hour emergency telephones, lighted pathways/sidewalks, student patrols, controlled dormitory access (key, security card, etc).

TRANSFER AND INTERNATIONAL STUDENTS

Transfer students: May apply for admission for the following academic terms: Fall, Spring, Summer. Applicants do not need a minimum number of credits to apply. For fall 2005: Transfer applications received: 653. Transfer applicants offered admission: 410. Transfer applicants enrolled: 248. **International students:** Number of foreign undergraduates: 17 (1% of student body). Number of countries represented: 20. Minimum TOEFL score required: 550 (paper); 213 (computer).

Marywood University

- **Address:** 2300 Adams Avenue, Scranton, PA 18509-1598
- **Website:** http://www.marywood.edu
- **Private; Religious affiliation:** Roman Catholic
- **Enrollment:** 1,662 full-time; 205 part-time

KEY STATS

✔ **U.S News College Ranking:** 46, Universities–Master's (North)
✔ **SAT Score (25th/75th percentile):** 940-1140
✔ **Tuition:** 2006-2007: $22,760

Selectivity: Selective	**Room/board:** $9,690
Acceptance rate: 77%	**Average debt:** $31,073
Student/faculty ratio: 12/1	**Proportion who borrowed:** 89%

UNDERGRADUATE STUDENT BODY STATS

2005-2006 enrollment: 1,662 full-time; 205 part-time. Men: 27%; women: 73%. **Ethnic makeup:** African American: 2%; Asian American: 1%; Hispanic: 3%; White: 92%; International: 1%. **Religious preference:** Roman Catholic: 61%; Protestant: 23%; Muslim: 1%; Hindu: 1%; No preference: 10%.

ADMISSIONS FACTS AND FIGURES

Phone: (800) 348-6234. **Email:** ugadm@marywood.edu. **Website:** http://www.marywood.edu. **Application deadlines for fall 2007:** Regular decision: Rolling. Early decision: Not offered. Early action: Not offered. Admission can be deferred. **Application fee:** $30. Common application is accepted. **To apply online, go to:** http://www.marywood.edu/apply. **Admissions requirements/recommendations:** High school units required (recommended): English: 4; Mathematics: 2; Science: 1; Social studies: 3; Academic electives: 6; Total units: 16. Tests: The college uses SAT or ACT scores in admissions decisions. Either SAT or ACT required. For admission to the fall 2007 entering class, the school will accept: ACT with writing, ACT without writing. Campus visit: Recommended. Admissions interview: Recommended. Off-campus interview: May be arranged. **Factors that count in admissions decisions:** *Academic:* Secondary school record: Very important. Class rank: Very important. Letters of recommendation: Considered. Standardized test scores: Very important. Essay: Considered. *Nonacademic:* Interview: Important. Extracurricular activities: Considered. Talent/ability: Important. Character/personal qualities: Very important. Alumni/ae relationship: Not considered. Geographical residence: Not considered. State residency: Not considered. Religious affiliation/commitment: Not considered. Minority status: Not considered. Volunteer work: Considered. Work experience: Not considered. **Admissions statistics for the fall 2005 entering class:** Total applicants: 1,441. Total accepted: 1,104. Freshmen enrolled: 404; 31% were from out of state. Overall acceptance rate: 77%. **Credentials of fall 2005 freshmen:** 16% ranked in the top 10 percent of their high school class; 41% were in the top 25 percent, and 78% were in the top half. (Proportion submitting class standing: 83%.) **Average high school grade point average:** 3.3. **First-year students who submitted SAT scores:** 98%. Scores (25/75 percentile): Verbal: 470-570, Math: 470-570, Combined: 940-1140. **First-year students submitting ACT scores:** 6%. Scores (25/75 percentile): English: N/A, Math: N/A, Composite: 19-23.

ACADEMICS

Year founded: 1915. **Academic calendar:** Semester. **Degrees offered:** certificate, associate, terminal-associate, bachelor's, post-bachelor's certificate, master's, post-master's certificate, doctorate. **Most popular majors:** 21% edu-

cation, 15% visual and performing arts, 6% psychology, 5% communication, journalism, and related programs, 5% liberal arts and sciences studies, and humanities. **Major fields of study:** biological and biomedical sciences; business, management, marketing, and related support services; communication, journalism, and related programs; communications technologies/technicians and support services; computer and information sciences and support services; education; family and consumer sciences/human sciences; health professions and related clinical sciences; legal professions and studies; mathematics and statistics; multi/interdisciplinary studies; natural resources and conservation; parks, recreation, leisure, and fitness studies; philosophy and religious studies; psychology; public administration and social service professions; security and protective services; social sciences; visual and performing arts. **Areas of required coursework:** arts/fine arts, humanities, mathematics, English (including composition), philosophy, foreign languages, sciences (biological or physical), history, social science, other. **Pre-professional programs:** pre-law, other. **Special academic programs:** accelerated program, cross-registration, distance learning, double major, dual enrollment, English as a Second Language (ESL), honors program, independent study, internships, student-designed major, study abroad, teacher certificate program, weekend college. **Teacher certification offered in:** early childhood, special education, elementary, adult education, secondary, bilingual/bicultural. **Reserve Officers Training Corps (ROTC):** Army ROTC: Offered at cooperating institution (University of Scranton); Air Force ROTC: Offered at cooperating institution (Wilkes University). **Faculty and instruction (2005-2006):** Total instructional faculty: 134 full-time, 175 part-time (43% men; 57% women; 5% minorities). Full-time faculty with Ph.D. or other terminal degree: 81%. Student/faculty ratio: 12/1. Classes of fewer than 20 students: 64%; of 20 to 49 students: 36%; of 50 or more students: 0%. **Advanced Placement and International Baccalaureate credit:** AP tests may be used for: Placement only. Scores accepted: 3, 4, 5. International Baccalaureate exams may be used for: Credit and/or placement. **Freshmen returning for sophomore year:** 80%. Graduation rates: Four-year: 42%; five-year: 61%; six-year: 66%. **Graduate study:** 31% of students pursue further study immediately upon graduation; 60% within five years.

COSTS AND FINANCIAL AID

Financial aid office: (570) 348-6225. **Expenses (2006-2007):** Tuition and fees 2006-2007: $22,760; room/board: $9,690. **Financial aid:** Priority filing date for institution's financial aid form: February 15. In 2005-2006, 90% of undergraduates applied for financial aid. Of those, 82% were determined to have financial need; 21% had their need fully met. Average financial aid package (proportion receiving): $16,474 (82%). Average amount of gift aid, such as scholarships or grants (proportion receiving): $11,226 (81%). Average amount of self-help aid, such as work study or loans (proportion receiving): $5,063 (71%). Average need-based loan (excluding PLUS or other private loans): $4,311. Among students who received need-based aid, the average percentage of need met: 75%. Among students who received aid based on merit, the average award (and the proportion receiving): $7,724 (15%). The average athletic scholarship (and the proportion receiving): $0 (0%). Average amount of debt of borrowers graduating in 2005: $31,073. Proportion who borrowed: 89%.

CAMPUS LIFE AND EXTRACURRICULAR ACTIVITIES

Campus housing available (% using): coed dorms (75%), women's dorms (10%), men's dorms (5%), apartment for single students (10%), special housing for disabled students (0%). Students who live in college-owned, operated, or affiliated housing: 62%. **Clubs and organizations:** Number of student organizations: 55. Activities include: choral groups, dance, drama/theater, jazz band, literary magazine, music ensembles, musical theater, radio station, student government, student newspaper, symphony orchestra, television station. Number of fraternities: 0; sororities: 1. of women in sororities: 1%. Average proportion of students who stay on campus on weekends: 30%. **Sports program (2005-2006):** Member of NCAA III. *Men's intercollegiate varsity sports:* baseball, basketball, cross-country, soccer, tennis. *Women's intercollegiate varsity sports:* basketball, cross-country, field hockey, soccer, softball, tennis, volleyball.

SERVICES AND FACILITIES

Basic services: nonremedial tutoring, day care, health service, other. **Remedial assistance:** math, writing, study skills. **Counseling services:** minority student, career, personal, academic, older student, psychological, religious. **For learning-disabled students:** School does not offer a structured program with separate admission and additional fees. Services include: reading machines, tape recorders, diagnostic testing service, untimed tests, note-taking services, oral tests, learning center, readers, extended time for tests, tutors, other. **Library:** Number of titles: 219,770; number of current serial subscriptions: 8,358. **Information technology resources:** Students are not required to lease or own a computer. Number of campus computers available to all students: 416. School has a wireless network. Approximate number of users that can be accommodated: 100. Proportion of college-owned housing units wired for high-speed internet access: 100%. **Campus safety:** Security services offered: 24-hour foot-and-vehicle patrols, late-night transport/escort service, 24-hour emergency telephones, lighted pathways/sidewalks, controlled dormitory access (key, security card, etc).

TRANSFER AND INTERNATIONAL STUDENTS

Transfer students: May apply for admission for the following academic terms: Fall, Spring, Summer. Applicants need a minimum number of credits to apply. For fall 2005: Transfer applications received: 329. Transfer applicants offered admission: 230. Transfer applicants enrolled: 157. **International students:** Number of foreign undergraduates: 21 (1% of student body). Number of countries represented: 18. Minimum TOEFL score required: 500 (paper); 173 (computer). Average TOEFL score: 567 (paper).

Mercyhurst College

- **Address:** 501 E. 38th Street, Erie, PA 16546
- **Website:** http://www.mercyhurst.edu
- **Private; Religious affiliation:** Roman Catholic
- **Enrollment:** 3,378 full-time; 462 part-time

KEY STATS

- ✔ **U.S News College Ranking:** 14. Comp. Coll.–Bachelor's (North)
- ✔ **SAT Score (25th/75th percentile):** 970-1180
- ✔ **Tuition:** 2006-2007: $20,364

Selectivity: Selective	**Room/board:** $7,458
Acceptance rate: 78%	**Average debt:** $21,000
Student/faculty ratio: 18/1	**Proportion who borrowed:** 93%

UNDERGRADUATE STUDENT BODY STATS

2005-2006 enrollment: 3,378 full-time; 462 part-time. Men: 40%; women: 60%. **Ethnic makeup:** African American: 4%; Asian American: 1%; Hispanic: 2%; White: 90%; International: 4%. **Religious preference:** Roman Catholic: 51%; Protestant: 18%; No preference: 5%; Unknown: 14%; Other: 12%.

ADMISSIONS FACTS AND FIGURES

Phone: (814) 824-2202. **Email:** jcooney@mercyhurst.edu. **Website:** http://www.mercyhurst.edu. **Application deadlines for fall 2007:** Regular decision: Rolling. Early decision: Not offered. Early action: Not offered. Admission can be deferred. **Application fee:** $30. Common application is accepted. **To apply online, go to:** http://apply.mercyhurst.edu. **Admissions requirements/recommendations:** High school units required (recommended): English: 4 (4); Mathematics: 3 (3); Science: 2 (3); Foreign language: 2 (2); Social studies: 5 (2); History: (2); Total units: 16 (16). Tests: The college uses SAT or ACT scores in admissions decisions. Either SAT or ACT required. For admission to the fall 2007 entering class, the school will accept: ACT with writing, ACT without writing. Campus visit: Recommended. Admissions interview: Recommended. Off-campus interview: Not available. **Factors that count in admissions decisions:** *Academic:* Secondary school record: Very important. Class rank: Important. Letters of recommendation: Important. Standardized test scores: Important. Essay: Considered. *Nonacademic:* Interview: Considered. Extracurricular activities: Considered. Talent/ability: Important. Character/personal qualities: Important. Alumni/ae relationship: Considered. Geographical residence: Considered. State residency: Considered. Religious affiliation/commitment: Considered. Minority status: Considered. Volunteer work: Considered. Work experience: Considered. **Other schools with the greatest overlap in applicants:** Allegheny College; Canisius College; Duquesne University; Gannon University; University of Dayton. **Admissions statistics for the fall 2005 entering class:** Total applicants: 2,711. Total accepted: 2,121. Freshmen enrolled: 696; 57% were from out of state. Overall acceptance rate: 78%. **Credentials of fall 2005 freshmen:** 18% ranked in the top 10 percent of their high school class; 43% were in the top 25 percent, and 79% were in the top half. (Proportion submitting class standing: 74%.) **Average high school grade point average:** 3.2. **First-year students who submitted SAT scores:** 86%. Scores (25/75 percentile): Verbal: 480-590, Math: 490-590,

Combined: 970-1180. **First-year students submitting ACT scores:** 41%. Scores (25/75 percentile): English: 18-25, Math: 19-25, Composite: 19-25.

ACADEMICS

Year founded: 1926. **Academic calendar:** Trimester. **Degrees offered:** certificate, associate, terminal-associate, bachelor's, post-bachelor's certificate, master's. **Most popular majors:** 24% business, management, marketing, and related support services, 16% education, 7% family and consumer sciences/human sciences, 7% visual and performing arts, 6% health professions and related clinical sciences. **Major fields of study:** biological and biomedical sciences; business, management, marketing, and related support services; communication, journalism, and related programs; computer and information sciences and support services; education; English language and literature/letters; family and consumer sciences/human sciences; foreign languages, literatures, and linguistics; health professions and related clinical sciences; history; liberal arts and sciences studies, and humanities; mathematics and statistics; multi/interdisciplinary studies; philosophy and religious studies; physical sciences; psychology; public administration and social service professions; security and protective services; social sciences; theology and religious vocations; visual and performing arts. **Areas of required coursework:** arts/fine arts, humanities, computer literacy, mathematics, English (including composition), philosophy, foreign languages, sciences (biological or physical), history, social science. **Pre-professional programs:** pre-law, pre-dentistry, pre-medicine, pre-veterinary science, pre-pharmacy. **Special academic programs (% participation):** cooperative (work-study plan) program (3%), cross-registration (1%), double major (2%), honors program (8%), independent study (1%), internships (12%), liberal arts/career combination (2%), student-designed major (1%), study abroad (1%), teacher certificate program (8%), weekend college (.5%). **Teacher certification offered in:** early childhood, special education, elementary, middle/junior high, secondary. **Cooperative education programs:** art, business, computer science, home economics, natural science, social/behavioral science. **Reserve Officers Training Corps (ROTC):** Army ROTC: Offered at cooperating institution (Gannon University). **Faculty and instruction (2005-2006):** Total instructional faculty: 163 full-time, 85 part-time (54% men; 46% women; 4% minorities). Full-time faculty with Ph.D. or other terminal degree: 60%. Student/faculty ratio: 18/1. Classes of fewer than 20 students: 53%; of 20 to 49 students: 47%; of 50 or more students: 1%. **Advanced Placement and International Baccalaureate credit:** AP tests may be used for: Credit and/or placement. Scores accepted: 4, 5. International Baccalaureate exams may be used for: Credit only. **Freshmen returning for sophomore year:** 83%. **Graduation rates:** Four-year: 52%; five-year: 61%; six-year: 62%. **Graduate study:** 25% of students pursue further study immediately upon graduation; 35% within one year; 60% within five years. Fields in which graduates pursue further study: Master of Business Administration (MBA), 10%; law, 1%; medicine, 2%; dentistry, 2%; theology (or the seminary), 1%; education, 15%; arts and sciences, 40%; veterinary medicine, 15%.

COSTS AND FINANCIAL AID

Financial aid office: (814) 824-2288. **Expenses (2006-2007):** Tuition and fees 2006-2007: $20,364; room/board: $7,458. Estimated books and supplies: $1,000 personal expenses: $2,000. **Financial aid:** Priority filing date for institution's financial aid form: March 1. In 2005-2006, 91% of undergraduates applied for financial aid. Of those, 77% were determined to have financial need; 81% had their need fully met. Average financial aid package (proportion receiving): $10,261 (76%). Average amount of gift aid, such as scholarships or grants (proportion receiving): $5,433 (76%). Average amount of self-help aid, such as work study or loans (proportion receiving): $2,829 (76%). Average need-based loan (excluding PLUS or other private loans): $3,224. Among students who received need-based aid, the average percentage of need met: 89%. Average amount of debt of borrowers graduating in 2005: $21,000. Proportion who borrowed: 93%.

CAMPUS LIFE AND EXTRACURRICULAR ACTIVITIES

Campus housing available (% using): women's dorms (16%), men's dorms (8%), apartment for single students (59%), special housing for disabled students (1%), other housing options (16%). Students who live in college-owned, operated, or affiliated housing: 6%. **Student employment:** During the 2005-2006 academic year, 38% of undergraduates worked on campus. Average per-year earnings: $1,200. **Clubs and organizations:** Number of student organizations: 54. Activities include: choral groups, concert band, dance, drama/theater, jazz band, literary magazine, music ensembles, musical theater, opera, pep band, radio station, student government, student newspaper, symphony orchestra, television station, yearbook. Number of fraternities: 0; sororities: 0. Average proportion of students who stay on campus on weekends: 80%. **Sports program (2005-2006):** Member of

NCAA II. Men's intercollegiate varsity sports: baseball, basketball, cross-country, football, golf, ice hockey, lacrosse, soccer, tennis, volleyball, water polo, wrestling. **Women's intercollegiate varsity sports:** basketball, cross-country, field hockey, golf, ice hockey, lacrosse, soccer, softball, tennis, volleyball, water polo, rowing.

SERVICES AND FACILITIES

Basic services: nonremedial tutoring, placement service, health service. **Remedial assistance:** reading, math, writing, study skills. **Counseling services:** career, personal, veteran student, academic, psychological. **For learning-disabled students:** School does not offer a structured program with separate admission and additional fees. Total undergraduates in learning-disabled program or receiving services: 79. Services include: remedial math, remedial English, reading machines, remedial reading, tape recorders, untimed tests, note-taking services, oral tests, learning center, readers, extended time for tests, tutors, priority registration, texts on tape. **Library:** Number of titles: 187,205; number of current serial subscriptions: 1,013. **Information technology resources:** Students are not required to lease or own a computer. Number of campus computers available to all students: 330. School has a wireless network. Approximate number of users that can be accommodated: 2,000. Proportion of college-owned housing units wired for high-speed internet access: 100%. **Campus safety:** Security services offered: 24-hour foot-and-vehicle patrols, lighted pathways/sidewalks, controlled dormitory access (key, security card, etc).

TRANSFER AND INTERNATIONAL STUDENTS

Transfer students: May apply for admission for the following academic terms: Fall, Winter, Spring, Summer. Applicants do not need a minimum number of credits to apply. For fall 2005: Transfer applications received: 195. Transfer applicants offered admission: 103. Transfer applicants enrolled: 72. **International students:** Number of foreign undergraduates: 161 (4% of student body). Number of countries represented: 20. Minimum TOEFL score required: 550 (paper); 213 (computer). Average TOEFL score: 0 (paper).

Messiah College

- **Address:** 1 College Avenue, Grantham, PA 17027-0800
- **Website:** http://www.messiah.edu
- **Private; Religious affiliation:** Christian interdenominational
- **Enrollment:** 2,864 full-time; 52 part-time

KEY STATS

✔ **U.S News College Ranking:** 4, Comp. Coll.–Bachelor's (North)
✔ **SAT Score (25th/75th percentile):** 1090-1310
✔ **Tuition:** 2006-2007: $23,290

Selectivity: More selective	**Room/board:** $7,060
Acceptance rate: 75%	**Average debt:** $27,322
Student/faculty ratio: 14/1	**Proportion who borrowed:** 70%

UNDERGRADUATE STUDENT BODY STATS

2005-2006 enrollment: 2,864 full-time; 52 part-time. Men: 37%; women: 63%. **Ethnic makeup:** African American: 2%; Asian American: 2%; Hispanic: 2%; White: 91%; International: 3%. **Religious preference:** Protestant: 74%; Unknown: 5%; Christian interdenominational: 16%; Brethren in Christ: 5%.

ADMISSIONS FACTS AND FIGURES

Phone: (717) 691-6000. **Email:** admiss@messiah.edu. **Website:** http://www.messiah.edu. **Application deadlines for fall 2007:** Regular decision: Rolling. Early decision: Not offered. Early action: Not offered. Admission can be deferred. **Application fee:** $30. Common application is accepted. **Admissions requirements/recommendations:** High school units required (recommended): English: 4 (4); Mathematics: 2 (3); Science: 2 (3); Foreign language: 2 (2); Social studies: 2 (2); History: 0 (2); Academic electives: 4 (4); Total units: 16 (20). Tests: The college uses SAT or ACT scores in admissions decisions. Neither SAT nor ACT required. For admission to the fall 2007 entering class, the school will accept: ACT without writing. Campus visit: Recommended. Admissions interview: Recommended. Off-campus interview: Not available. **Factors that count in admissions decisions:** *Academic:* Secondary school record: Very important. Class rank: Very important. Letters of recommendation: Very important. Standardized test scores:

Very important. Essay: Important. *Nonacademic:* Interview: Considered. Extracurricular activities: Very important. Talent/ability: Very important. Character/personal qualities: Very important. Alumni/ae relationship: Considered. Geographical residence: Not considered. State residency: Not considered. Religious affiliation/commitment: Very important. Minority status: Considered. Volunteer work: Important. Work experience: Considered. **Admissions statistics for the fall 2005 entering class:** Total applicants: 2,730. Total accepted: 2,036. Freshmen enrolled: 707; 51% were from out of state. Overall acceptance rate: 75%. **Credentials of fall 2005 freshmen:** 39% ranked in the top 10 percent of their high school class; 71% were in the top 25 percent, and 94% were in the top half. (Proportion submitting class standing: 74%.) **Average high school grade point average:** 3.8. **First-year students who submitted SAT scores:** 94%. Scores (25/75 percentile): Verbal: 550-660, Math: 540-650, Combined: 1090-1310. **First-year students submitting ACT scores:** 18%. Scores (25/75 percentile): English: 22-30, Math: 21-27, Composite: 23-28.

ACADEMICS

Year founded: 1909. **Academic calendar:** Semester. **Degrees offered:** bachelor's. **Most popular majors:** 8% elementary education and teaching, 7% nursing/registered nurse training (R.N., A.S.N., B.S.N., M.S.N.), 7% psychology, 5% communication studies/speech communication and rhetoric, 5% engineering. **Major fields of study:** biological and biomedical sciences; business, management, marketing, and related support services; communication, journalism, and related programs; computer and information sciences and support services; education; engineering; English language and literature/letters; family and consumer sciences/human sciences; foreign languages, literatures, and linguistics; health professions and related clinical sciences; history; liberal arts and sciences studies, and humanities; mathematics and statistics; multi/interdisciplinary studies; natural resources and conservation; parks, recreation, leisure, and fitness studies; philosophy and religious studies; physical sciences; psychology; public administration and social service professions; security and protective services; social sciences; theology and religious vocations; visual and performing arts. **Areas of required coursework:** arts/fine arts, humanities, mathematics, English (including composition), philosophy, foreign languages, sciences (biological or physical), history, social science, other. **Pre-professional programs:** pre-law, pre-dentistry, pre-medicine, pre-veterinary science, other. **Special academic programs:** accelerated program, double major, dual enrollment, English as a Second Language (ESL), exchange student program (domestic), honors program, independent study, internships, student-designed major, study abroad, teacher certificate program, other. **Teacher certification offered in:** early childhood, elementary, secondary. **Faculty and instruction (2005-2006):** Total instructional faculty: 170 full-time, 127 part-time (59% men; 41% women; 6% minorities). Full-time faculty with Ph.D. or other terminal degree: 71%. Student/faculty ratio: 14/1. Classes of fewer than 20 students: 43%; of 20 to 49 students: 54%; of 50 or more students: 2%. **Advanced Placement and International Baccalaureate credit:** AP tests may be used for: Credit and/or placement. Scores accepted: 2, 3, 4, 5. International Baccalaureate exams may be used for: Credit and/or placement. **Freshmen returning for sophomore year:** 86%. **Graduation rates:** Four-year: 69%; five-year: 75%; six-year: 74%. **Graduate study:** 12% of students pursue further study immediately upon graduation; 15% within one year. Fields in which graduates pursue further study: Master of Business Administration (MBA), 1%; engineering, 1%; theology (or the seminary), 1%; education, 2%; arts and sciences, 11%.

COSTS AND FINANCIAL AID

Financial aid office: (717) 691-6007. **Expenses (2006-2007):** Tuition and fees 2006-2007: $23,290; room/board: $7,060. Estimated books and supplies: $890; transportation: $630; personal expenses: $1,200. **Financial aid:** Priority filing date for institution's financial aid form: April 1. In 2005-2006, 80% of undergraduates applied for financial aid. Of those, 68% were determined to have financial need; 27% had their need fully met. Average financial aid package (proportion receiving): $11,017 (68%). Average amount of gift aid, such as scholarships or grants (proportion receiving): $3,910 (63%). Average amount of self-help aid, such as work study or loans (proportion receiving): $3,668 (65%). Average need-based loan (excluding PLUS or other private loans): $3,010. Among students who received need-based aid, the average percentage of need met: 61%. Among students who received aid based on merit, the average award (and the proportion receiving): $7,726 (19%). The average athletic scholarship (and the proportion receiving): $0 (0%). Average amount of debt of borrowers graduating in 2005: $27,322. Proportion who borrowed: 70%.

CAMPUS LIFE AND EXTRACURRICULAR ACTIVITIES

Campus housing available: coed dorms, women's dorms, men's dorms, apartment for single students, special housing for disabled students, special housing for international students. Students who live in college-owned, operated, or affiliated housing: 84%. **Student employment:** During the 2005-2006 academic year, 27% of undergraduates worked on campus. Average per-year earnings: $2,356. **Clubs and organizations:** Number of student organizations: 54. Activities include: choral groups, concert band, dance, drama/theater, jazz band, literary magazine, music ensembles, musical theater, pep band, radio station, student government, student newspaper, student film society, symphony orchestra, yearbook. Number of fraternities: 0; sororities: 0. Average proportion of students who stay on campus on weekends: 70%. **Sports program (2005-2006):** Member of NCAA III. *Men's intercollegiate varsity sports:* baseball, basketball, cross-country, golf, lacrosse, soccer, tennis, track and field (indoor), track and field (outdoor), wrestling. *Women's intercollegiate varsity sports:* basketball, cross-country, field hockey, lacrosse, soccer, softball, tennis, track and field (indoor), track and field (outdoor), volleyball.

SERVICES AND FACILITIES

Basic services: health service. **Remedial assistance:** reading, math, writing, study skills. **Counseling services:** minority student, career, academic, psychological, religious. **For learning-disabled students:** School does not offer a structured program with separate admission and additional fees. Total undergraduates in learning-disabled program or receiving services: 25. Services include: reading machines, tape recorders, untimed tests, note-taking services, oral tests, learning center, readers, extended time for tests, tutors, other. **Library:** Number of titles: 295,518; number of current serial subscriptions: 11,036. **Information technology resources:** Students are not required to lease or own a computer. Number of campus computers available to all students: 527. School has a wireless network. **Campus safety:** Security services offered: 24-hour foot-and-vehicle patrols, late-night transport/escort service, 24-hour emergency telephones, lighted pathways/sidewalks, student patrols, controlled dormitory access (key, security card, etc).

TRANSFER AND INTERNATIONAL STUDENTS

Transfer students: May apply for admission for the following academic terms: Fall, Spring. Applicants need a minimum number of credits to apply. For fall 2005: Transfer applications received: 262. Transfer applicants offered admission: 187. Transfer applicants enrolled: 85. **International students:** Number of foreign undergraduates: 73 (3% of student body). Number of countries represented: 29. Minimum TOEFL score required: 550 (paper); 213 (computer).

Millersville University of Pennsylvania

- **Address:** PO Box 1002, Millersville, PA 17551-0302
- **Website:** http://www.millersville.edu
- **Public**
- **Enrollment:** 6,313 full-time; 622 part-time

KEY STATS

✔ **U.S News College Ranking:** 56, Universities–Master's (North)
✔ **SAT Score (25th/75th percentile):** 970-1150
✔ **Tuition:** 2005-2006: $6,236 in state, $13,596 out of state

Selectivity: Selective	**Room/board:** $5,878
Acceptance rate: 55%	**Average debt:** $17,433
Student/faculty ratio: 18/1	**Proportion who borrowed:** 74%

UNDERGRADUATE STUDENT BODY STATS

2005-2006 enrollment: 6,313 full-time; 622 part-time. Men: 43%; women: 57%. **Ethnic makeup:** African American: 7%; Asian American: 2%; Hispanic: 3%; White: 87%.

ADMISSIONS FACTS AND FIGURES

Phone: (717) 872-3371. **Email:** Admissions@millersville.edu. **Website:** http://www.millersville.edu. **Application deadlines for fall 2007:** Regular decision: Rolling. Early decision: Not offered. Early action: Not offered. Admission can be deferred. **Application fee:** $35. Common application is accepted. **To apply online, go to:** http://www.millersville.edu/~admit/. **Admissions requirements/recommendations:** High school units required (recommended): English: 4 (0); Mathematics: 3 (0); Science: 3 (0); Foreign language: 0 (2); Social studies: 3 (0); History: 2 (0); Academic electives: 0 (4); Total units: 15 (21). Tests: The college uses SAT or ACT scores in admissions decisions. Either SAT or ACT required. For admission to the fall 2007 entering class, the school will accept: ACT without writing. Campus visit: Recommended. Admissions interview: Neither required nor recommended. Off-campus interview: Not available. **Factors that count in admissions decisions:** *Academic:* Secondary school record: Very important. Class rank: Very important. Letters of recommendation: Considered. Standardized test scores: Very important. Essay: Considered. *Nonacademic:* Interview: Considered. Extracurricular activities: Considered. Talent/ability: Considered. Character/personal qualities: Considered. Alumni/ae relationship: Considered. Geographical residence: Considered. State residency: Considered. Religious affiliation/commitment: Not considered. Minority status: Considered. Volunteer work: Considered. Work experience: Considered. **Other schools with the greatest overlap in applicants:** Bloomsburg University of Pennsylvania; Pennsylvania State University–University Park; Shippensburg University of Pennsylvania; Temple University; West Chester University of Pennsylvania. **Admissions statistics for the fall 2005 entering class:** Total applicants: 6,413. Total accepted: 3,555. Freshmen enrolled: 1,320; 4% were from out of state. Overall acceptance rate: 55%. **Size of waiting list:** 905 applicants; enrolled from waiting list: 7. **Credentials of fall 2005 freshmen:** 15% ranked in the top 10 percent of their high school class; 45% were in the top 25 percent, and 83% were in the top half. (Proportion submitting class standing: 89%.) **First-year students who submitted SAT scores:** 99%. Scores (25/75 percentile): Verbal: 480-570, Math: 490-580, Combined: 970-1150.

ACADEMICS

Year founded: 1855. **Academic calendar:** 4-1-4. **Degrees offered:** associate, bachelor's, post-bachelor's certificate, master's, post-master's certificate. **Most popular majors:** 16% education, 12% business, management, marketing, and related support services, 10% social sciences, 8% communication, journalism, and related programs, 7% psychology. **Major fields of study:** biological and biomedical sciences; business, management, marketing, and related support services; communication, journalism, and related programs; computer and information sciences and support services; education; engineering technologies/technicians; English language and literature/letters; foreign languages, literatures, and linguistics; mathematics and statistics; philosophy and religious studies; physical sciences; psychology; public administration and social service professions; social sciences; visual and performing arts. **Areas of required coursework:** humanities, mathematics, English (including composition), sciences (biological or physical), social science, other. **Pre-professional programs:** pre-law, pre-dentistry, pre-medicine, pre-veterinary science, pre-optometry, other. **Special academic programs:** accelerated program, cooperative (work-study plan) program, cross-registration, distance learning, double major, dual enrollment, English as a Second Language (ESL), honors program, independent study, internships, liberal arts/career combination, study abroad, teacher certificate program, other. **Teacher certification offered in:** early childhood, special education, elementary, vo-tech, middle/junior high, secondary, bilingual/bicultural. **Cooperative education programs:** art, business, computer science, education, engineering, health professions, humanities, natural science, social/behavioral science, technologies. **Reserve Officers Training Corps (ROTC):** Army ROTC: Offered on campus. **Faculty and instruction (2005-2006):** Total instructional faculty: 312 full-time, 121 part-time (53% men; 47% women; 14% minorities). Full-time faculty with Ph.D. or other terminal degree: 92%. Student/faculty ratio: 18/1. Classes of fewer than 20 students: 23%; of 20 to 49 students: 72%; of 50 or more students: 5%. **Advanced Placement and International Baccalaureate credit:** AP tests may be used for: Credit and/or placement. Scores accepted: 3. International Baccalaureate exams may be used for: Credit only. **Freshmen returning for sophomore year:** 81%. **Graduation rates:** Four-year: 34%; five-year: 58%; six-year: 62%. **Graduate study:** Fields in which graduates pursue further study: Master of Business Administration (MBA), 1%; law, 1%; medicine, 2%; dentistry, 2%; engineering, 4%; theology (or the seminary), 1%; education, 5%; arts and sciences, 4%; veterinary medicine, 2%.

COSTS AND FINANCIAL AID

Financial aid office: (717) 872-3026. **Expenses (2005-2006):** Tuition and fees 2005-2006: $6,236 in state, $13,596 out of state; room/board: $5,878. Estimated books and supplies: $850; transportation: $700; personal expenses: $1,756. **Financial aid:** In 2005-2006, 75% of undergraduates applied for financial aid. Of those, 51% were determined to have financial need; 26% had their need fully met. Average financial aid package (proportion receiving): $7,172 (50%). Average amount of gift aid, such as scholarships or grants (proportion receiving): $4,002 (38%). Average amount of self-help aid, such as work study or loans (proportion receiving): $3,958 (46%). Average need-based loan (excluding PLUS or other private loans): $3,640. Among students who received need-based aid, the average percentage of need met: 82%. Among students who received aid based on merit, the average award (and the proportion receiving): $2,505 (3%). The average athletic scholarship (and the proportion receiving): $1,396 (1%). Average amount of debt of borrowers graduating in 2005: $17,433. Proportion who borrowed: 74%.

CAMPUS LIFE AND EXTRACURRICULAR ACTIVITIES
Campus housing available (% using): coed dorms (100%), special housing for international students, other housing options. Students who live in college-owned, operated, or affiliated housing: 32%. **Student employment:** During the 2005-2006 academic year, 30% of undergraduates worked on campus. Average per-year earnings: $1,129. **Clubs and organizations:** Number of student organizations: 127. Activities include: choral groups, concert band, dance, drama/theater, jazz band, literary magazine, marching band, music ensembles, musical theater, pep band, radio station, student government, student newspaper, symphony orchestra, television station, yearbook. Number of fraternities: 8; sororities: 8. Proportion of men in fraternities: 3%; of women in sororities: 4%. **Sports program (2005-2006):** Member of NCAA II. *Men's intercollegiate varsity sports:* baseball, basketball, cross-country, football, golf, soccer, tennis, track and field (indoor), track and field (outdoor), wrestling. *Women's intercollegiate varsity sports:* basketball, cross-country, field hockey, lacrosse, soccer, softball, swimming and diving, tennis, track and field (indoor), track and field (outdoor), volleyball.

SERVICES AND FACILITIES
Basic services: nonremedial tutoring, women's center, placement service, day care, health service, health insurance, other. **Remedial assistance:** reading, math, writing, study skills. **Counseling services:** minority student, career, personal, veteran student, academic, older student, psychological. **For learning-disabled students:** School does not offer a structured program with separate admission and additional fees. Total undergraduates in learning-disabled program or receiving services: 182. Services include: remedial math, remedial English, reading machines, tape recorders, diagnostic testing service, untimed tests, note-taking services, oral tests, learning center, readers, extended time for tests, tutors, other testing accomodations, other. **Library:** Number of titles: 505,601; number of current serial subscriptions: 10,776. **Information technology resources:** Students are not required to lease or own a computer. Number of campus computers available to all students: 510. School has a wireless network. Approximate number of users that can be accommodated: 1,000. Proportion of college-owned housing units wired for high-speed internet access: 100%. **Campus safety:** Security services offered: 24-hour foot-and-vehicle patrols, late-night transport/escort service, 24-hour emergency telephones, lighted pathways/sidewalks, student patrols, controlled dormitory access (key, security card, etc).

TRANSFER AND INTERNATIONAL STUDENTS
Transfer students: May apply for admission for the following academic terms: Fall, Winter, Spring, Summer. Applicants need a minimum number of credits to apply. For fall 2005: Transfer applications received: 988. Transfer applicants offered admission: 689. Transfer applicants enrolled: 439. **International students:** Number of foreign undergraduates: 24. Number of countries represented: 24. Minimum TOEFL score required: 500 (paper); 183 (computer). Average TOEFL score: 579 (paper).

Moore College of Art and Design

- **Address:** 20th and the Parkway, Philadelphia, PA 19103
- **Website:** http://www.moore.edu
- **Private**
- **Enrollment:** 421 full-time; 40 part-time

KEY STATS
✔ **U.S News College Ranking:** Unranked Specialty School–Fine Arts
✔ **SAT Score:** 983
✔ **Tuition:** 2006-2007: $24,674

Selectivity: Less selective	**Room/board:** $9,346
Acceptance rate: 55%	**Average debt:** N/A
Student/faculty ratio: 8/1	**Proportion who borrowed:** N/A

UNDERGRADUATE STUDENT BODY STATS
2005-2006 enrollment: 421 full-time; 40 part-time. Men: 0%; women: 100%. **Ethnic makeup:** African American: 10%; Asian American: 6%; Hispanic: 5%; White: 77%; International: 2%.

ADMISSIONS FACTS AND FIGURES
Phone: (215) 965-4015. **Email:** admiss@moore.edu. **Website:** http://www.moore.edu. **Application deadlines for fall 2007:** Regular decision: August 15. Early decision: Send application by: November 15; Decision sent by: December 1. Early action: Not offered. Admission can be deferred. **Application fee:** $40. Common application is not accepted. **Admissions requirements/recommendations:** Tests: The college uses SAT or ACT scores in admissions decisions. Either SAT or ACT required. Campus visit: Recommended. Admissions interview: Recommended. Off-campus interview: May be arranged. **Factors that count in admissions decisions:** *Academic:* Secondary school record: Very important. Class rank: Considered. Letters of recommendation: Important. Standardized test scores: Very important. Essay: Important. *Nonacademic:* Interview: Very important. Extracurricular activities: Important. Talent/ability: Very important. Character/personal qualities: Very important. Alumni/ae relationship: Not considered. Geographical residence: Not considered. State residency: Not considered. Religious affiliation/commitment: Not considered. Minority status: Considered. Volunteer work: Considered. Work experience: Considered. **Other schools with the greatest overlap in applicants:** University of the Arts. **Admissions statistics for the fall 2005 entering class:** Total applicants: 352. Total accepted: 195. Freshmen enrolled: 86; 45% were from out of state. Overall acceptance rate: 55%. Non-early acceptance rate: 55%. **Average high school grade point average:** 3.1. **First-year students who submitted SAT scores:** 93%. Scores (25/75 percentile): Verbal: N/A, Math: N/A, Combined: N/A. **First-year students submitting ACT scores:** 9%. Scores (25/75 percentile): English: N/A, Math: N/A, Composite: N/A.

ACADEMICS
Year founded: 1848. **Academic calendar:** Semester. **Degrees offered:** certificate, bachelor's, post-bachelor's certificate. **Most popular majors:** Information not available. **Major fields of study:** visual and performing arts. **Areas of required coursework:** arts/fine arts, humanities, history. **Special academic programs (% participation):** cooperative (work-study plan) program, double major, internships (100%), study abroad, teacher certificate program. **Faculty and instruction (2005-2006):** Total instructional faculty: 32 full-time, 74 part-time (34% men; 66% women; 11% minorities). Full-time faculty with Ph.D. or other terminal degree: 69%. Student/faculty ratio: 8/1. Classes of fewer than 20 students: 83%; of 20 to 49 students: 17%; of 50 or more students: 0%. **Advanced Placement and International Baccalaureate credit:** International Baccalaureate exams may be used for: Credit only. **Freshmen returning for sophomore year:** 80%. **Graduation rates:** Four-year: 59%; five-year: 69%; six-year: 58%.

COSTS AND FINANCIAL AID
Financial aid office: (215) 965-4042. **Expenses (2006-2007):** Tuition and fees 2006-2007: $24,674; room/board: $9,346. Estimated books and supplies: $2,130; transportation: $750; personal expenses: $675. **Financial aid:** Priority filing date for institution's financial aid form: March 1.

CAMPUS LIFE AND EXTRACURRICULAR ACTIVITIES
Campus housing available (% using): women's dorms (100%). Students who live in college-owned, operated, or affiliated housing: 23%. **Clubs and organizations:** Number of student organizations: 7. Activities include: student government, student newspaper, yearbook. Number of fraternities: 0; sororities: 0.

SERVICES AND FACILITIES
Basic services: nonremedial tutoring, health service. **Remedial assistance:** reading, writing. **Counseling services:** career, personal, academic, psychological. **For learning-disabled students:** School does not offer a structured program with separate admission and additional fees. Services include: remedial English, tape recorders, untimed tests, note-taking services, learning center, extended time for tests, tutors, texts on tape. **Library:** Number of titles: 40,000; number of current serial subscriptions: 130. **Information technology resources:** Students are required to lease or own a computer. School has a wireless network. **Campus safety:** Security services offered: controlled dormitory access (key, security card, etc).

TRANSFER AND INTERNATIONAL STUDENTS
Transfer students: May apply for admission for the following academic terms: Fall, Spring. Applicants do not need a minimum number of credits

to apply. For fall 2005: Transfer applications received: 143. Transfer applicants offered admission: 75. Transfer applicants enrolled: 43. **International students:** Number of foreign undergraduates: 9 (2% of student body). Number of countries represented: 8. Minimum TOEFL score required: 527 (paper); 197 (computer). Average TOEFL score: 560 (paper).

Moravian College

- Address: 1200 Main Street, Bethlehem, PA 18018
- Website: http://www.moravian.edu
- Private; Religious affiliation: Moravian Church in America
- Enrollment: 1,543 full-time; 249 part-time

KEY STATS

✔ U.S News College Ranking: third tier, Liberal Arts Colleges
✔ SAT Score (25th/75th percentile): 1040-1250
✔ Tuition: 2006-2007: $26,775

Selectivity: More selective   Room/board: $7,760
Acceptance rate: 65%   Average debt: N/A
Student/faculty ratio: 11/1   Proportion who borrowed: N/A

UNDERGRADUATE STUDENT BODY STATS

2005-2006 enrollment: 1,543 full-time; 249 part-time. Men: 41%; women: 59%. **Ethnic makeup:** African American: 2%; Asian American: 2%; Hispanic: 3%; White: 91%; International: 1%.

ADMISSIONS FACTS AND FIGURES

Phone: (610) 861-1320. **Email:** admissions@moravian.edu. **Website:** http://www.moravian.edu. **Application deadlines for fall 2007:** Regular decision: February 15; decision sent by March 15. Early decision: Send application by: January 15; Decision sent by: December 15. Early action: Not offered. Admission can be deferred. **Application fee:** $40. Common application is accepted. **To apply online, go to:** http://www.moravian.edu/admission/applying.htm. **Admissions requirements/recommendations:** High school units required (recommended): English: 4; Mathematics: 3 (4); Science: 2; Foreign language: 2 (3); Social studies: 4; Total units: 17 (17). Tests: The college uses SAT or ACT scores in admissions decisions. Either SAT or ACT required. For admission to the fall 2007 entering class, the school will accept: ACT with writing. Campus visit: Recommended. Admissions interview: Recommended. Off-campus interview: May be arranged. **Factors that count in admissions decisions:** *Academic:* Secondary school record: Very important. Class rank: Very important. Letters of recommendation: Important. Standardized test scores: Important. Essay: Important. *Nonacademic:* Interview: Considered. Extracurricular activities: Important. Talent/ability: Considered. Character/personal qualities: Very important. Alumni/ae relationship: Considered. Geographical residence: Considered. State residency: Not considered. Religious affiliation/commitment: Not considered. Minority status: Not considered. Volunteer work: Important. Work experience: Considered. **Admissions statistics for the fall 2005 entering class:** Total applicants: 1,890. Total accepted: 1,231. Freshmen enrolled: 382; 43% were from out of state. Accepted through early-decision or early-action plans: 37%. Overall acceptance rate: 65%. Early-decision acceptance rate: 72%. Non-early acceptance rate: 64%. **Size of waiting list:** 172 applicants; enrolled from waiting list: 17. **Credentials of fall 2005 freshmen:** 31% ranked in the top 10 percent of their high school class; 64% were in the top 25 percent, and 93% were in the top half. (Proportion submitting class standing: 72%.) First-year students who submitted SAT scores: 93%. Scores (25/75 percentile): Verbal: 520-620, Math: 520-630, Combined: 1040-1250. **First-year students submitting ACT scores:** 7%. Scores (25/75 percentile): English: N/A, Math: N/A, Composite: 19-21.

ACADEMICS

Year founded: 1742. **Academic calendar:** Semester. **Degrees offered:** bachelor's, post-bachelor's certificate, master's, first professional. **Most popular majors:** 21% social sciences, 14% business, management, marketing, and related support services, 13% psychology, 10% visual and performing arts, 9% English language and literature/letters. **Major fields of study:** biological and biomedical sciences; business, management, marketing, and related support services; computer and information sciences and support services; education; engineering; English language and literature/letters; foreign languages, literatures, and linguistics; health professions and related clinical sciences; history; mathematics and statistics; multi/interdisciplinary studies;

natural resources and conservation; philosophy and religious studies; physical sciences; psychology; social sciences; visual and performing arts. **Areas of required coursework:** arts/fine arts, humanities, computer literacy, mathematics, English (including composition), philosophy, foreign languages, sciences (biological or physical), history, social science. **Pre-professional programs:** pre-law, pre-dentistry, pre-medicine, pre-veterinary science, other. **Special academic programs (% participation):** cross-registration (20%), double major (17%), honors program (12%), independent study (15%), internships (60%), student-designed major (3%), study abroad (10%), teacher certificate program (10%). **Teacher certification offered in:** elementary, secondary. **Cooperative education programs:** engineering, health professions. **Reserve Officers Training Corps (ROTC):** Army ROTC: Offered at cooperating institution (Lehigh University). **Faculty and instruction (2005-2006):** Total instructional faculty: 118 full-time, 72 part-time (48% men; 52% women; 4% minorities). Full-time faculty with Ph.D. or other terminal degree: 86%. Student/faculty ratio: 11/1. Classes of fewer than 20 students: 66%; of 20 to 49 students: 34%; of 50 or more students: 0%. **Advanced Placement and International Baccalaureate credit:** AP tests may be used for: Credit and/or placement. Scores accepted: 4, 5. International Baccalaureate exams may be used for: Credit and/or placement. **Freshmen returning for sophomore year:** 86%. **Graduation rates:** Four-year: 67%; five-year: 70%; six-year: 71%. **Graduate study:** 20% of students pursue further study immediately upon graduation.

COSTS AND FINANCIAL AID

Financial aid office: (610) 861-1330. **Expenses (2006-2007):** Tuition and fees 2006-2007: $26,775; room/board: $7,760. Estimated books and supplies: $800; transportation: $424; personal expenses: $1,312. **Financial aid:** Priority filing date for institution's financial aid form: February 14; deadline: April 15. In 2005-2006, 86% of undergraduates applied for financial aid. Of those, 74% were determined to have financial need; 21% had their need fully met. Average financial aid package (proportion receiving): $17,118 (74%). Average amount of gift aid, such as scholarships or grants (proportion receiving): $12,278 (73%). Average amount of self-help aid, such as work study or loans (proportion receiving): $5,541 (66%). Average need-based loan (excluding PLUS or other private loans): $4,175. Among students who received need-based aid, the average percentage of need met: 74%. Among students who received aid based on merit, the average award (and the proportion receiving): $13,668 (22%). The average athletic scholarship (and the proportion receiving): $0 (0%).

CAMPUS LIFE AND EXTRACURRICULAR ACTIVITIES

Campus housing available (% using): coed dorms (44%), women's dorms (16%), men's dorms (3%), sorority housing (2%), fraternity housing (2%), apartment for single students (33%). Students who live in college-owned, operated, or affiliated housing: 71%. **Student employment:** During the 2005-2006 academic year, 10% of undergraduates worked on campus. Average per-year earnings: $1,200. **Clubs and organizations:** Number of student organizations: 68. Activities include: choral groups, concert band, dance, drama/theater, jazz band, literary magazine, marching band, music ensembles, radio station, student government, student newspaper, symphony orchestra, yearbook. Number of fraternities: 3; sororities: 4. Proportion of men in fraternities: 15%; of women in sororities: 22%. **Sports program (2005-2006):** Member of NCAA III. *Men's intercollegiate varsity sports:* baseball, basketball, cross-country, football, golf, lacrosse, soccer, tennis, track and field (indoor), track and field (outdoor). *Women's intercollegiate varsity sports:* basketball, cross-country, field hockey, lacrosse, soccer, softball, tennis, track and field (indoor), track and field (outdoor), volleyball.

SERVICES AND FACILITIES

Basic services: nonremedial tutoring, placement service, health service, health insurance. **Counseling services:** minority student, career, personal, academic, older student, psychological, birth control, religious. **For learning-disabled students:** School does not offer a structured program with separate admission and additional fees. Total undergraduates in learning-disabled program or receiving services: 35. Services include: tape recorders, note-taking services, oral tests, learning center, readers, extended time for tests, tutors, other testing accomodations, other. **Library:** Number of titles: 260,000; number of current serial subscriptions: 1,200. **Information technology resources:** Students are not required to lease or own a computer. Number of campus computers available to all students: 175. School has a wireless network. Proportion of college-owned housing units wired for high-speed internet access: 100%. **Campus safety:** Security services offered: 24-hour foot-and-vehicle patrols, late-night transport/escort service, 24-hour emergency telephones, lighted pathways/sidewalks, controlled dormitory access (key, security card, etc).

TRANSFER AND INTERNATIONAL STUDENTS

Transfer students: May apply for admission for the following academic terms: Fall, Spring, Summer. Applicants need a minimum number of credits to apply. For fall 2005: Transfer applications received: 221. Transfer applicants offered admission: 84. Transfer applicants enrolled: 60. **International students:** Number of foreign undergraduates: 17 (1% of student body). Minimum TOEFL score required: 550 (paper); 213 (computer). Average TOEFL score: 608 (paper).

Mount Aloysius College

- **Address:** 7373 Admiral Peary Highway, Cresson, PA 16630
- **Website:** http://www.mtaloy.edu
- **Private; Religious affiliation:** Roman Catholic (Sisters of Mercy)
- **Enrollment:** 1,147 full-time; 335 part-time

KEY STATS
✔ **U.S News College Ranking:** 29, Comp. Coll.–Bachelor's (North)
✔ **SAT Score (25th/75th percentile):** 833-1028
✔ **Tuition:** 2006-2007: $15,350

Selectivity: Less selective	**Room/board:** $7,270
Acceptance rate: 77%	**Average debt:** $20,970
Student/faculty ratio: 14/1	**Proportion who borrowed:** 79%

UNDERGRADUATE STUDENT BODY STATS

2005-2006 enrollment: 1,147 full-time; 335 part-time. Men: 28%; women: 72%. **Ethnic makeup:** African American: 2%; American-Indian: 1%; Hispanic: 1%; White: 95%; International: 2%.

ADMISSIONS FACTS AND FIGURES

Phone: (814) 886-6383. **Email:** admissions@mtaloy.edu. **Website:** http://www.mtaloy.edu. **Application deadlines for fall 2007:** Regular decision: August 3; decision sent by August 1. Early decision: Not offered. Early action: Not offered. Admission can be deferred. **Application fee:** $30. Common application is accepted. **Admissions requirements/recommendations:** High school units required (recommended): English: 4; Mathematics: 3; Science: 3; Foreign language: (2); Social studies: 3; History: (3); Academic electives: 3; Total units: 16 (5). Tests: The college uses SAT or ACT scores in admissions decisions. Either SAT or ACT required. For admission to the fall 2007 entering class, the school will accept: ACT with writing, ACT without writing. Campus visit: Recommended. Admissions interview: Neither required nor recommended. Off-campus interview: Not available. **Factors that count in admissions decisions:** *Academic:* Secondary school record: Very important. Class rank: Important. Letters of recommendation: Important. Standardized test scores: Important. Essay: Considered. *Nonacademic:* Interview: Very important. Extracurricular activities: Very important. Talent/ability: Very important. Character/personal qualities: Very important. Alumni/ae relationship: Not considered. Geographical residence: Not considered. State residency: Not considered. Religious affiliation/commitment: Not considered. Minority status: Not considered. Volunteer work: Very important. Work experience: Not considered. **Admissions statistics for the fall 2005 entering class:** Total applicants: 949. Total accepted: 728. Freshmen enrolled: 297; 3% were from out of state. Overall acceptance rate: 77%. **Size of waiting list:** 60 applicants; enrolled from waiting list: 10. Average high school grade point average: 3.1. **First-year students who submitted SAT scores:** 77%. Scores (25/75 percentile): Verbal: 413-520, Math: 420-508, Combined: 833-1028. **First-year students submitting ACT scores:** 33%. Scores (25/75 percentile): English: 15-20, Math: 15-19, Composite: 16-20.

ACADEMICS

Year founded: 1853. **Academic calendar:** Semester. **Degrees offered:** diploma, associate, bachelor's, master's. **Most popular majors:** 29% health professions and related clinical sciences, 15% business, management, marketing, and related support services, 10% security and protective services, 8% education, 8% multi/interdisciplinary studies. **Major fields of study:** agriculture, agriculture operations, and related sciences; business, management, marketing, and related support services; education; foreign languages, literatures, and linguistics; health professions and related clinical sciences; multi/interdisciplinary studies; psychology; social sciences. **Areas of required coursework:** arts/fine arts, humanities, computer literacy, mathematics, English (including composition), philosophy, sciences (biological or physical), history, social science. **Pre-professional programs:** pre-law. **Special**

academic programs: accelerated program, distance learning, double major, honors program, independent study, internships, student-designed major, teacher certificate program. **Teacher certification offered in:** early childhood, elementary. **Cooperative education programs:** art, business, computer science, education, health professions, humanities, natural science, social/behavioral science. **Faculty and instruction (2005-2006):** Total instructional faculty: 62 full-time, 103 part-time (37% men; 63% women; 1% minorities). Full-time faculty with Ph.D. or other terminal degree: 35%. Student/faculty ratio: 14/1. Classes of fewer than 20 students: 67%; of 20 to 49 students: 33%. **Advanced Placement and International Baccalaureate credit:** AP tests may be used for: Placement only. Scores accepted: 5. International Baccalaureate exams may be used for: Credit only. **Freshmen returning for sophomore year:** 65%. **Graduation rates:** Four-year: 36%; five-year: 55%; six-year: 69%.

COSTS AND FINANCIAL AID

Financial aid office: (814) 886-6357. **Expenses (2006-2007):** Tuition and fees 2006-2007: $15,350; room/board: $7,270. Estimated books and supplies: $1,600 personal expenses: $3,000. **Financial aid:** Priority filing date for institution's financial aid form: February 15; deadline: May 1. In 2005-2006, 100% of undergraduates applied for financial aid. Of those, 94% were determined to have financial need; Average financial aid package (proportion receiving): $11,400 (94%). Average amount of gift aid, such as scholarships or grants (proportion receiving): $2,600 (94%). Average amount of self-help aid, such as work study or loans (proportion receiving): $3,850 (94%). Average need-based loan (excluding PLUS or other private loans): $3,530. Among students who received need-based aid, the average percentage of need met: 25%. Among students who received aid based on merit, the average award (and the proportion receiving): $2,000 (6%). The average athletic scholarship (and the proportion receiving): $2,320 (0%). Average amount of debt of borrowers graduating in 2005: $20,970. Proportion who borrowed: 79%.

CAMPUS LIFE AND EXTRACURRICULAR ACTIVITIES

Campus housing available: women's dorms, men's dorms. Students who live in college-owned, operated, or affiliated housing: 10%. **Clubs and organizations:** Number of student organizations: 60. Activities include: choral groups, drama/theater, student government, student newspaper. Average proportion of students who stay on campus on weekends: 50%. **Sports program (2005-2006):** Member of NCAA III. *Men's intercollegiate varsity sports:* baseball, basketball, cross-country, golf, soccer. *Women's intercollegiate varsity sports:* basketball, cheerleading, cross-country, golf, soccer, volleyball.

SERVICES AND FACILITIES

Basic services: nonremedial tutoring, placement service, day care, health service. **Remedial assistance:** reading, math, writing. **Counseling services:** military, personal, veteran student, academic, psychological, religious. **For learning-disabled students:** Services include: remedial math, remedial English, remedial reading, tape recorders, note-taking services, special bookstore section, oral tests, learning center, readers, extended time for tests, tutors. **Information technology resources:** Students are not required to lease or own a computer. Number of campus computers available to all students: 125. School has a wireless network. Proportion of college-owned housing units wired for high-speed internet access: 100%. **Campus safety:** Security services offered: 24-hour foot-and-vehicle patrols, late-night transport/escort service, 24-hour emergency telephones, lighted pathways/sidewalks, controlled dormitory access (key, security card, etc).

TRANSFER AND INTERNATIONAL STUDENTS

Transfer students: May apply for admission for the following academic terms: Fall, Winter, Spring, Summer. Applicants need a minimum number of credits to apply. For fall 2005: Transfer applicants enrolled: 116. **International students:** Number of foreign undergraduates: 23 (2% of student body). Minimum TOEFL score required: 500 (paper); 173 (computer).

Muhlenberg College

- **Address:** 2400 W. Chew Street, Allentown, PA 18104
- **Website:** http://www.muhlenberg.edu
- **Private; Religious affiliation:** Lutheran
- **Enrollment:** 2,267 full-time; 190 part-time

KEY STATS

- ✔ **U.S News College Ranking:** 74, Liberal Arts Colleges
- ✔ **SAT Score (25th/75th percentile):** 1130-1330
- ✔ **Tuition:** N/A
- **Selectivity:** More selective
- **Acceptance rate:** 43%
- **Student/faculty ratio:** 12/1
- **Room/board:** N/A
- **Average debt:** N/A
- **Proportion who borrowed:** N/A

UNDERGRADUATE STUDENT BODY STATS

2005-2006 enrollment: 2,267 full-time; 190 part-time. Men: 42%; women: 58%. **Ethnic makeup:** African American: 2%; Asian American: 2%; Hispanic: 3%; White: 92%. **Religious preference:** Roman Catholic: 27%; Protestant: 13%; Jewish: 22%; No preference: 16%; Unknown: 14%; Lutheran: 7%; Other: 1%.

ADMISSIONS FACTS AND FIGURES

Phone: (484) 664-3200. **Email:** admissions@muhlenberg.edu. **Website:** http://www.muhlenberg.edu. **Application deadlines for fall 2007:** Regular decision: February 15; decision sent by March 15. Early decision: Send application by: February 1; Decision sent by: N/A. Early action: Not offered. Admission can be deferred. **Application fee:** $45. Common application is accepted. **Admissions requirements/recommendations:** High school units required (recommended): English: 4; Mathematics: 3 (4); Science: 2 (3); Foreign language: 2 (4); Social studies: 0 (2); History: 2; Academic electives: 1; Total units: 16. Tests: The college uses SAT or ACT scores in admissions decisions. Neither SAT nor ACT required. For admission to the fall 2007 entering class, the school will accept: ACT with writing. Campus visit: Recommended. Admissions interview: Recommended. Off-campus interview: May be arranged. **Factors that count in admissions decisions:** *Academic:* Secondary school record: Very important. Class rank: Important. Letters of recommendation: Important. Standardized test scores: Important. Essay: Important. *Nonacademic:* Interview: Important. Extracurricular activities: Important. Talent/ability: Very important. Character/personal qualities: Very important. Alumni/ae relationship: Considered. Geographical residence: Considered. State residency: Not considered. Religious affiliation/commitment: Not considered. Minority status: Considered. Volunteer work: Considered. Work experience: Considered. **Other schools with the greatest overlap in applicants:** Bucknell University; Dickinson College; Franklin and Marshall College; Gettysburg College; Lafayette College. **Admissions statistics for the fall 2005 entering class:** Total applicants: 4,217. Total accepted: 1,809. Freshmen enrolled: 576; 79% were from out of state. Accepted through early-decision or early-action plans: 54%. Overall acceptance rate: 43%. Early-decision acceptance rate: 69%. Non-early acceptance rate: 40%. **Size of waiting list:** 1539 applicants; enrolled from waiting list: 41. **Credentials of fall 2005 freshmen:** 42% ranked in the top 10 percent of their high school class; 82% were in the top 25 percent, and 98% were in the top half. (Proportion submitting class standing: 50%.) **Average high school grade point average:** 3.4. **First-year students who submitted SAT scores:** 93%. Scores (25/75 percentile): Verbal: 560-660, Math: 570-670, Combined: 1130-1330. **First-year students submitting ACT scores:** 5%. Scores (25/75 percentile): English: N/A, Math: N/A, Composite: 26-29.

ACADEMICS

Year founded: 1848. **Academic calendar:** Semester. **Degrees offered:** associate, bachelor's. **Most popular majors:** 27% business, management, marketing, and related support services; 16% social sciences, 11% drama and dramatics/theater arts, 8% communication, journalism, and related programs, 8% psychology. **Major fields of study:** area, ethnic, cultural, and gender studies; biological and biomedical sciences; business, management, marketing, and related support services; communication, journalism, and related programs; computer and information sciences and support services; English language and literature/letters; foreign languages, literatures, and linguistics; history; mathematics and statistics; multi/interdisciplinary studies; natural resources and conservation; philosophy and religious studies; physical sciences; psychology; social sciences; visual and performing arts. **Areas of required coursework:** arts/fine arts, humanities, mathematics, English (including composition), philosophy, foreign languages, sciences (biological or physical), history, social science, other. **Pre-professional programs:** pre-law, pre-medicine. **Special academic programs (% participation):** accelerated program (4%), cross-registration (2%), double major (31%), independent study (19%), internships (18%), student-designed major (1%), study abroad (20%), teacher certificate program (5%). **Teacher certification offered in:** elementary, secondary. **Reserve Officers Training Corps (ROTC):** Army ROTC: Offered at cooperating institution (Lehigh University). **Faculty and instruction (2005-2006):** Total instructional faculty: 152 full-time, 104 part-time (54% men; 46% women; 7% minorities). Full-time faculty with Ph.D. or other terminal degree: 86%. Student/faculty ratio: 12/1. Classes of fewer than 20 students: 57%; of 20 to 49 students: 42%; of 50 or more students: 2%. **Advanced Placement and International Baccalaureate credit:** AP tests may be used for: Credit and/or placement. Scores accepted: 3, 4, 5. International Baccalaureate exams may be used for: Credit and/or placement. **Freshmen returning for sophomore year:** 93%. **Graduation rates:** Four-year: 81%; five-year: 85%; six-year: 85%. **Graduate study:** 29% of students pursue further study within one year. Fields in which graduates pursue further study: Master of Business Administration (MBA), 2%; law, 12%; medicine, 24%; theology (or the seminary), 1%; education, 2%; arts and sciences, 12%.

COSTS AND FINANCIAL AID

Financial aid office: (484) 664-3174. **Financial aid:** Priority filing date for institution's financial aid form: January 15; deadline: February 15.

CAMPUS LIFE AND EXTRACURRICULAR ACTIVITIES

Campus housing available (% using): coed dorms (68%), women's dorms (9%), sorority housing (3%), fraternity housing (3%), special housing for disabled students (1%), special housing for international students (1%), other housing options (15%). Students who live in college-owned, operated, or affiliated housing: 1%. **Student employment:** During the 2005-2006 academic year, 27% of undergraduates worked on campus. Average per-year earnings: $1,800. **Clubs and organizations:** Number of student organizations: 121. Activities include: choral groups, concert band, dance, drama/theater, jazz band, literary magazine, music ensembles, musical theater, opera, radio station, student government, student newspaper, yearbook. Number of fraternities: 4; sororities: 4. Proportion of men in fraternities: 14%; of women in sororities: 18%. Average proportion of students who stay on campus on weekends: 75%. **Sports program (2005-2006):** Member of NCAA III. **Men's intercollegiate varsity sports:** baseball, basketball, cross-country, football, golf, lacrosse, soccer, tennis, track and field (indoor), track and field (outdoor), wrestling. **Women's intercollegiate varsity sports:** basketball, cross-country, field hockey, golf, lacrosse, soccer, softball, tennis, track and field (indoor), track and field (outdoor), volleyball.

SERVICES AND FACILITIES

Basic services: nonremedial tutoring, placement service, health service. **Counseling services:** minority student, career, personal, academic, older student, psychological, birth control, religious. **For learning-disabled students:** School does not offer a structured program with separate admission and additional fees. Services include: reading machines, tape recorders, note-taking services, oral tests, learning center, readers, extended time for tests, tutors. **Library:** Number of titles: 305,094; number of current serial subscriptions: 865. **Information technology resources:** Students are not required to lease or own a computer. Number of campus computers available to all students: 393. School has a wireless network. Approximate number of users that can be accommodated: 450. Proportion of college-owned housing units wired for high-speed internet access: 100%. **Campus safety:** Security services offered: 24-hour foot-and-vehicle patrols, late-night transport/escort service, 24-hour emergency telephones, lighted pathways/sidewalks, controlled dormitory access (key, security card, etc).

TRANSFER AND INTERNATIONAL STUDENTS

Transfer students: May apply for admission for the following academic terms: Fall, Spring. Applicants need a minimum number of credits to apply. For fall 2005: Transfer applications received: 87. Transfer applicants offered admission: 10. Transfer applicants enrolled: 6. **International students:** Number of foreign undergraduates: 10. Minimum TOEFL score required: 550 (paper); 213 (computer). Average TOEFL score: 585 (paper).

Neumann College

- **Address:** 1 Neumann Drive, Aston, PA 19014-1298
- **Website:** http://www.neumann.edu
- **Private; Religious affiliation:** Roman Catholic
- **Enrollment:** 1,832 full-time; 481 part-time

KEY STATS
✔ **U.S News College Ranking:** third tier, Comp. Coll.–Bachelor's (North)
✔ **SAT Score (25th/75th percentile):** 800-980
✔ **Tuition:** 2006-2007: $18,632

Selectivity: Less selective	**Room/board:** $8,418
Acceptance rate: 96%	**Average debt:** $20,000
Student/faculty ratio: 16/1	**Proportion who borrowed:** 80%

UNDERGRADUATE STUDENT BODY STATS
2005-2006 enrollment: 1,832 full-time; 481 part-time. Men: 33%; women: 67%. **Ethnic makeup:** African American: 13%; Asian American: 1%; Hispanic: 2%; White: 81%; International: 2%. **Religious preference:** Protestant: 23%; Jewish: 1%; Muslim: 1%; No preference: 2%; Unknown: 3%; Roman Catholic: 65%; Other: 5%.

ADMISSIONS FACTS AND FIGURES
Phone: (800) 963-8626. **Email:** neumann@neumann.edu. **Website:** http://www.neumann.edu. **Application deadlines for fall 2007:** Regular decision: August 1. Early decision: Not offered. Early action: Not offered. Admission can be deferred. **Application fee:** $35. Common application is not accepted. **To apply online, go to:** http://www.neumann.edu/i2e/app/app_int.asp. **Admissions requirements/recommendations:** High school units required (recommended): English: 4; Mathematics: 2; Science: 2 (3); Foreign language: 2; Social studies: 2; Academic electives: 4; Total units: 16 (17). **Tests:** The college uses SAT or ACT scores in admissions decisions. Either SAT or ACT required. For admission to the fall 2007 entering class, the school will accept: ACT without writing. Campus visit: Recommended. Admissions interview: Recommended. Off-campus interview: May not be arranged. **Factors that count in admissions decisions:** *Academic:* Secondary school record: Very important. Class rank: Important. Letters of recommendation: Important. Standardized test scores: Very important. Essay: Important. *Nonacademic:* Interview: Considered. Extracurricular activities: Considered. Talent/ability: Considered. Character/personal qualities: Important. Alumni/ae relationship: Important. Geographical residence: Considered. State residency: Considered. Religious affiliation/commitment: Not considered. Minority status: Considered. Volunteer work: Considered. Work experience: Not considered. **Other schools with the greatest overlap in applicants:** Cabrini College; Rowan University; Temple University; Villanova University; West Chester University of Pennsylvania. **Admissions statistics for the fall 2005 entering class:** Total applicants: 2,080. Total accepted: 1,996. Freshmen enrolled: 522; 32% were from out of state. Overall acceptance rate: 96%. **Credentials of fall 2005 freshmen:** 10% ranked in the top 10 percent of their high school class; 50% were in the top 25 percent, and 80% were in the top half. (Proportion submitting class standing: 99%.) **Average high school grade point average:** 3.0. **First-year students who submitted SAT scores:** 99%. Scores (25/75 percentile): Verbal: 400-490; Math: 400-490; Combined: 800-980. **First-year students submitting ACT scores:** 1%. Scores (25/75 percentile): English: N/A, Math: N/A, Composite: N/A.

ACADEMICS
Year founded: 1965. **Academic calendar:** Semester. **Degrees offered:** associate, bachelor's, post-bachelor's certificate, master's, first professional, doctorate. **Most popular majors:** 29% liberal arts and sciences/liberal studies, 15% elementary education and teaching, 14% business administration and management, 14% nursing/registered nurse training (R.N., A.S.N., B.S.N., M.S.N.), 8% sport and fitness administration/management. **Major fields of study:** agriculture, agriculture operations, and related sciences; biological and biomedical sciences; business, management, marketing, and related support services; communication, journalism, and related programs; computer and information sciences and support services; education; English language and literature/letters; health professions and related clinical sciences; liberal arts and sciences studies, and humanities; natural resources and conservation; parks, recreation, leisure, and fitness studies; psychology; security and protective services; social sciences. **Areas of required coursework:** arts/fine arts, humanities, mathematics, English (including composition), philosophy, foreign languages, sciences (biological or physical),

history, social science, other. **Special academic programs (% participation):** accelerated program (20%), cooperative (work-study plan) program (50%), distance learning (1%), double major (2%), honors program (2%), independent study (20%), internships (50%), liberal arts/career combination (20%), study abroad (1%), teacher certificate program (15%), weekend college (10%). **Teacher certification offered in:** early childhood, elementary. **Cooperative education programs:** business, computer science, education, health professions. **Reserve Officers Training Corps (ROTC):** Army ROTC: Offered at cooperating institution (Widener University). **Faculty and instruction (2005-2006):** Total instructional faculty: 84 full-time, 131 part-time (43% men; 57% women; 5% minorities). Full-time faculty with Ph.D. or other terminal degree: 64%. Student/faculty ratio: 16/1. Classes of fewer than 20 students: 40%; of 20 to 49 students: 60%; of 50 or more students: 0%. **Advanced Placement and International Baccalaureate credit:** AP tests may be used for: Credit only. Scores accepted: 2, 3, 4, 5. International Baccalaureate exams may be used for: Credit and/or placement. **Freshmen returning for sophomore year:** 72%. **Graduation rates:** Four-year: 33%; five-year: 50%; six-year: 54%. **Graduate study:** 16% of students pursue further study immediately upon graduation; 15% within one year; 10% within five years. Fields in which graduates pursue further study: Master of Business Administration (MBA), 30%; law, 1%; medicine, 1%; theology (or the seminary), 1%; education, 50%; arts and sciences, 17%.

COSTS AND FINANCIAL AID
Financial aid office: (610) 558-5521. **Expenses (2006-2007):** Tuition and fees 2006-2007: $18,632; room/board: $8,418. Estimated books and supplies: $1,600; transportation: $1,200; personal expenses: $1,200. **Financial aid:** Priority filing date for institution's financial aid form: March 15; deadline: May 15. In 2005-2006, 90% of undergraduates applied for financial aid. Of those, 90% were determined to have financial need; 60% had their need fully met. Average financial aid package (proportion receiving): $17,000 (90%). Average amount of gift aid, such as scholarships or grants (proportion receiving): $14,000 (82%). Average amount of self-help aid, such as work study or loans (proportion receiving): $1,800 (14%). Average need-based loan (excluding PLUS or other private loans): $5,000. Among students who received need-based aid, the average percentage of need met: 65%. Average amount of debt of borrowers graduating in 2005: $20,000. Proportion who borrowed: 80%.

CAMPUS LIFE AND EXTRACURRICULAR ACTIVITIES
Campus housing available: coed dorms, other housing options. Students who live in college-owned, operated, or affiliated housing: 48%. **Student employment:** During the 2005-2006 academic year, 20% of undergraduates worked on campus. Average per-year earnings: $1,800. **Clubs and organizations:** Number of student organizations: 18. Activities include: choral groups, dance, drama/theater, jazz band, literary magazine, music ensembles, musical theater, student government, student newspaper, television station, yearbook. Average proportion of students who stay on campus on weekends: 30%. **Sports program (2005-2006):** Member of NCAA III. *Men's intercollegiate varsity sports:* baseball, basketball, golf, ice hockey, lacrosse, soccer, tennis. *Women's intercollegiate varsity sports:* basketball, field hockey, ice hockey, soccer, softball, tennis, volleyball.

SERVICES AND FACILITIES
Basic services: nonremedial tutoring, placement service, day care, health service, health insurance. **Remedial assistance:** reading, math, writing. **Counseling services:** career, personal, academic, religious. **For learning-disabled students:** School does not offer a structured program with separate admission and additional fees. Total undergraduates in learning-disabled program or receiving services: 20. Services include: remedial math, remedial English, remedial reading, tape recorders, note-taking services, oral tests, learning center, readers, extended time for tests, tutors. **Library:** Number of titles: 75,000; number of current serial subscriptions: 400. **Information technology resources:** Students are not required to lease or own a computer. Number of campus computers available to all students: 250. School has a wireless network. Approximate number of users that can be accommodated: 200. Proportion of college-owned housing units wired for high-speed internet access: 100%. **Campus safety:** Security services offered: 24-hour foot-and-vehicle patrols, 24-hour emergency telephones, lighted pathways/sidewalks, controlled dormitory access (key, security card, etc).

TRANSFER AND INTERNATIONAL STUDENTS
Transfer students: May apply for admission for the following academic terms: Fall, Spring. Applicants need a minimum number of credits to apply. For fall 2005: Transfer applications received: 170. Transfer applicants

offered admission: 160. Transfer applicants enrolled: 83. **International students:** Number of foreign undergraduates: 48 (2% of student body). Minimum TOEFL score required: 550 (paper); 213 (computer). Average TOEFL score: 550 (paper).

Pennsylvania College of Technology

- **Address:** 1 College Avenue, Williamsport, PA 17701
- **Website:** http://www.pct.edu
- **Public**
- **Enrollment:** 5,515 full-time; 1,022 part-time

KEY STATS

✔ **U.S News College Ranking:** third tier, Comp. Coll.–Bachelor's (North)
✔ **SAT Score:** 934
✔ **Tuition:** 2005-2006: $10,080 in state, $12,660 out of state

Selectivity: Less selective	Room/board: $5,600
Acceptance rate: 94%	Average debt: N/A
Student/faculty ratio: 19/1	Proportion who borrowed: N/A

UNDERGRADUATE STUDENT BODY STATS

2005-2006 enrollment: 5,515 full-time; 1,022 part-time. Men: 65%; women: 35%. **Ethnic makeup:** African American: 3%; American-Indian: 1%; Asian American: 1%; Hispanic: 1%; White: 94%.

ADMISSIONS FACTS AND FIGURES

Phone: (570) 327-4761. **Email:** admissions@pct.edu. **Website:** http://www.pct.edu. **Application deadlines for fall 2007:** Regular decision: July 1. Early decision: Not offered. Early action: Not offered. Admission can be deferred. **Application fee:** $50. Common application is not accepted. **To apply online, go to:** http://www2.pct.edu/admissio/application_types.html. **Admissions requirements/recommendations:** Tests: The college uses SAT or ACT scores in admissions decisions. Neither SAT nor ACT required. For admission to the fall 2007 entering class, the school will accept: ACT with writing, ACT without writing. Campus visit: Neither required nor recommended. Admissions interview: Neither required nor recommended. Off-campus interview: Not available. **Factors that count in admissions decisions:** *Academic:* Secondary school record: Very important. Class rank: Considered. Letters of recommendation: Considered. Standardized test scores: Considered. Essay: Not considered. *Nonacademic:* Interview: Not considered. Extracurricular activities: Important. Talent/ability: Important. Character/personal qualities: Important. Alumni/ae relationship: Not considered. Geographical residence: Not considered. State residency: Not considered. Religious affiliation/commitment: Not considered. Minority status: Not considered. Volunteer work: Important. Work experience: Considered. **Admissions statistics for the fall 2005 entering class:** Total applicants: 4,776. Total accepted: 4,505. Freshmen enrolled: 1,671; Overall acceptance rate: 94%. **Size of waiting list:** 1030 applicants; enrolled from waiting list: 377. **First-year students who submitted SAT scores:** 65%. Scores (25/75 percentile): Verbal: N/A, Math: N/A, Combined: N/A.

ACADEMICS

Year founded: 1941. **Academic calendar:** Semester. **Degrees offered:** certificate, associate, bachelor's. **Most popular majors:** 4% computer systems networking and telecommunications, 3% business administration and management, 2% commercial and advertising art, 2% electrical and electronic engineering technologies/technicians, 2% health professions and related clinical sciences. **Major fields of study:** business, management, marketing, and related support services; communications technologies/technicians and support services; computer and information sciences and support services; engineering technologies/technicians; health professions and related clinical sciences; legal professions and studies; mechanic and repair technologies/technicians; personal and culinary services; visual and performing arts. **Areas of required coursework:** humanities, computer literacy, mathematics, English (including composition), foreign languages, sciences (biological or physical), social science, other. **Special academic programs:** cooperative (work-study plan) program, cross-registration, distance learning, internships, study abroad, weekend college. **Cooperative education programs:** health professions, technologies, vocational arts. **Reserve Officers Training Corps (ROTC):** Army ROTC: Offered at cooperating institution (Bucknell University). **Faculty and instruction (2005-2006):** Total instructional faculty: 283 full-time, 208 part-time (62% men; 38% women; 3%

minorities). Student/faculty ratio: 19/1. Classes of fewer than 20 students: 58%; of 20 to 49 students: 42%; of 50 or more students: 0%. **Freshmen returning for sophomore year:** 67%. **Graduation rates:** Four-year: 33%; five-year: 45%; six-year: 39%. **Graduate study:** 18% of students pursue further study within one year. Fields in which graduates pursue further study: Master of Business Administration (MBA), 1%; law, 3%; medicine, 1%; engineering, 4%.

COSTS AND FINANCIAL AID

Financial aid office: (570) 327-4766. **Expenses (2005-2006):** Tuition and fees 2005-2006: $10,080 in state, $12,660 out of state; room/board: $5,600. Estimated books and supplies: $1,000 personal expenses: $2,450.

CAMPUS LIFE AND EXTRACURRICULAR ACTIVITIES

Campus housing available (% using): other housing options (100%). Students who live in college-owned, operated, or affiliated housing: 23%. **Clubs and organizations:** Number of student organizations: 46. Activities include: dance, radio station, student government, student newspaper. Number of fraternities: 0; sororities: 0.

SERVICES AND FACILITIES

Basic services: nonremedial tutoring, placement service, day care, health service. **Remedial assistance:** reading, math, writing, study skills. **Counseling services:** career, personal, academic. **For learning-disabled students:** Total undergraduates in learning-disabled program or receiving services: 375. Services include: remedial math, remedial English, remedial reading, tape recorders, other special classes, note-taking services, oral tests, learning center, readers, extended time for tests, tutors, priority registration, priority seating, substitution of courses, typist/scribe, exams on tape or computer, other testing accomodations. **Library:** Number of titles: 93,297; number of current serial subscriptions: 835. **Information technology resources:** Students are not required to lease or own a computer. Number of campus computers available to all students: 1,500. School has a wireless network. Proportion of college-owned housing units wired for high-speed internet access: 100%. **Campus safety:** Security services offered: 24-hour foot-and-vehicle patrols, late-night transport/escort service, 24-hour emergency telephones, lighted pathways/sidewalks, controlled dormitory access (key, security card, etc).

TRANSFER AND INTERNATIONAL STUDENTS

Transfer students: May apply for admission for the following academic terms: Fall, Spring, Summer. Applicants do not need a minimum number of credits to apply. For fall 2005: Transfer applications received: 288. Transfer applicants offered admission: 284. Transfer applicants enrolled: 220. **International students:** Number of foreign undergraduates: 28. Number of countries represented: 18. Minimum TOEFL score required: 500 (paper); 173 (computer).

Penn. State—Erie, The Behrend College

- **Address:** 5091 Station Road, Erie, PA 16563
- **Website:** http://www.pserie.psu.edu/
- **Public**
- **Enrollment:** 3,160 full-time; 222 part-time

KEY STATS

✔ **U.S News College Ranking:** 46, Universities–Master's (North)
✔ **SAT Score (25th/75th percentile):** 980-1170
✔ **Tuition:** 2005-2006: $10,626 in state, $16,024 out of state

Selectivity: Selective	Room/board: $6,530
Acceptance rate: 80%	Average debt: $22,400
Student/faculty ratio: 15/1	Proportion who borrowed: 64%

UNDERGRADUATE STUDENT BODY STATS

2005-2006 enrollment: 3,160 full-time; 222 part-time. Men: 67%; women: 33%. **Ethnic makeup:** African American: 3%; Asian American: 2%; Hispanic: 2%; White: 92%; International: 1%.

ADMISSIONS FACTS AND FIGURES

Phone: (814) 898-6100. **Email:** behrend.admissions@psu.edu. **Website:** http://www.pserie.psu.edu/. **Application deadlines for fall 2007:** Regular decision: Rolling. Early decision: Not offered. Early action: Not offered.

Admission can be deferred. **Application fee:** $50. Common application is not accepted. **To apply online, go to:** http://www.psu.edu/dept/admissions/apply. **Admissions requirements/recommendations:** High school units required (recommended): English: 4 (0); Mathematics: 3 (0); Science: 3 (0); Foreign language: 2 (0); Social studies: 3 (0); History: 0 (0); Academic electives: 0 (0); Total units: 0 (0). Tests: The college uses SAT or ACT scores in admissions decisions. Either SAT or ACT required. For admission to the fall 2007 entering class, the school will accept: ACT with writing, ACT without writing. Campus visit: Recommended. Admissions interview: Recommended. Off-campus interview: May be arranged. **Factors that count in admissions decisions:** *Academic:* Secondary school record: Important. Class rank: Considered. Letters of recommendation: Considered. Standardized test scores: Very important. Essay: Considered. *Nonacademic:* Interview: Not considered. Extracurricular activities: Considered. Talent/ability: Considered. Character/personal qualities: Considered. Alumni/ae relationship: Considered. Geographical residence: Not considered. State residency: Not considered. Religious affiliation/commitment: Not considered. Minority status: Not considered. Volunteer work: Considered. Work experience: Considered. **Other schools with the greatest overlap in applicants:** Edinboro University of Pennsylvania; Grove City College; Pennsylvania State University–University Park; Rochester Institute of Technology; University of Pittsburgh. **Admissions statistics for the fall 2005 entering class:** Total applicants: 2,417. Total accepted: 1,925. Freshmen enrolled: 838; 11% were from out of state. Overall acceptance rate: 80%. **Credentials of fall 2005 freshmen:** 12% ranked in the top 10 percent of their high school class; 36% were in the top 25 percent, and 76% were in the top half. (Proportion submitting class standing: 89%.) **Average high school grade point average:** 3.4. **First-year students who submitted SAT scores:** 93%. Scores (25/75 percentile): Verbal: 480-570, Math: 500-600, Combined: 980-1170. **First-year students submitting ACT scores:** 21%. Scores (25/75 percentile): English: N/A, Math: N/A, Composite: N/A.

ACADEMICS

Year founded: 1948. **Academic calendar:** Semester. **Degrees offered:** transfer-associate, terminal-associate, bachelor's, master's. **Most popular majors:** 42% business, management, marketing, and related support services, 20% engineering, 7% psychology, 6% biological and biomedical sciences, 5% engineering technologies/technicians. **Major fields of study:** biological and biomedical sciences; business, management, marketing, and related support services; communication, journalism, and related programs; computer and information sciences and support services; engineering; engineering technologies/technicians; English language and literature/letters; history; liberal arts and sciences studies, and humanities; mathematics and statistics; physical sciences; psychology; social sciences. **Areas of required coursework:** arts/fine arts, humanities, mathematics, English (including composition), foreign languages, sciences (biological or physical), social science, other. **Pre-professional programs:** pre-law, pre-dentistry, pre-medicine, pre-veterinary science, pre-optometry, pre-pharmacy, other. **Special academic programs (% participation):** accelerated program (1%), cooperative (work-study plan) program, distance learning (1%), double major (4%), dual enrollment (1%), honors program (6.5%), independent study (23%), internships (31%), liberal arts/career combination (1%), study abroad (5%), teacher certificate program (2%). **Teacher certification offered in:** elementary, secondary. **Cooperative education programs:** education, other. **Reserve Officers Training Corps (ROTC):** Army ROTC: Offered at cooperating institution (Gannon University). **Faculty and instruction (2005-2006):** Total instructional faculty: 200 full-time, 61 part-time (68% men; 32% women; 9% minorities). Full-time faculty with Ph.D. or other terminal degree: 60%. Student/faculty ratio: 15/1. Classes of fewer than 20 students: 38%; of 20 to 49 students: 58%; of 50 or more students: 5%. **Advanced Placement and International Baccalaureate credit:** AP tests may be used for: Credit and/or placement. Scores accepted: 3, 4, 5. International Baccalaureate exams may be used for: Credit only. **Freshmen returning for sophomore year:** 83%. **Graduation rates:** Four-year: 39%; five-year: 64%; six-year: 64%. **Graduate study:** 19% of students pursue further study within one year. Fields in which graduates pursue further study: Master of Business Administration (MBA), 2%; law, 7%; engineering, 19%; education, 26%; arts and sciences, 47%.

COSTS AND FINANCIAL AID

Financial aid office: (814) 898-6162. **Expenses (2005-2006):** Tuition and fees 2005-2006: $10,626 in state, $16,024 out of state; room/board: $6,530. Estimated books and supplies: $1,040; transportation: $378; personal expenses: $2,016. **Financial aid:** Priority filing date for institution's financial aid form: February 15. In 2005-2006, 85% of undergraduates applied for financial aid. Of those, 71% were determined to have financial need; 7% had

their need fully met. Average financial aid package (proportion receiving): $7,395 (70%). Average amount of gift aid, such as scholarships or grants (proportion receiving): $4,373 (49%). Average amount of self-help aid, such as work study or loans (proportion receiving): $4,360 (64%). Average need-based loan (excluding PLUS or other private loans): $4,132. Among students who received need-based aid, the average percentage of need met: 63%. Among students who received aid based on merit, the average award (and the proportion receiving): $2,593 (5%). The average athletic scholarship (and the proportion receiving): $0 (0%). Average amount of debt of borrowers graduating in 2005: $22,400. Proportion who borrowed: 64%.

CAMPUS LIFE AND EXTRACURRICULAR ACTIVITIES

Campus housing available (% using): coed dorms (35%), women's dorms (0%), men's dorms (0%), apartment for single students (62%), special housing for disabled students (3%), other housing options (0%). Students who live in college-owned, operated, or affiliated housing: 49%. **Student employment:** During the 2005-2006 academic year, 16% of undergraduates worked on campus. Average per-year earnings: $2,165. **Clubs and organizations:** Number of student organizations: 100. Activities include: choral groups, concert band, dance, drama/theater, jazz band, literary magazine, music ensembles, pep band, radio station, student government, student newspaper, student film society. Number of fraternities: 4; sororities: 3. Proportion of men in fraternities: 4%; of women in sororities: 4%. Average proportion of students who stay on campus on weekends: 60%. **Sports program (2005-2006):** Member of NCAA III. *Men's intercollegiate varsity sports:* baseball, basketball, cross-country, golf, soccer, swimming and diving, tennis, track and field (indoor), track and field (outdoor), water polo. *Women's intercollegiate varsity sports:* basketball, cross-country, golf, soccer, softball, swimming and diving, tennis, track and field (indoor), track and field (outdoor), volleyball, water polo.

SERVICES AND FACILITIES

Basic services: nonremedial tutoring, placement service, day care, health service, health insurance. **Remedial assistance:** reading, math, writing, study skills. **Counseling services:** minority student, career, military, personal, veteran student, academic, older student, psychological, birth control, religious. **For learning-disabled students:** School does not offer a structured program with separate admission and additional fees. Total undergraduates in learning-disabled program or receiving services: 57. Services include: remedial math, remedial English, reading machines, remedial reading, tape recorders, untimed tests, note-taking services, oral tests, learning center, readers, extended time for tests, tutors, priority registration, priority seating, texts on tape, other testing accomodations, other. **Library:** Number of titles: 119,640; number of current serial subscriptions: 596. **Information technology resources:** Students are not required to lease or own a computer. Number of campus computers available to all students: 325. School has a wireless network. Approximate number of users that can be accommodated: 253. Proportion of college-owned housing units wired for high-speed internet access: 100%. **Campus safety:** Security services offered: 24-hour foot-and-vehicle patrols, late-night transport/escort service, 24-hour emergency telephones, lighted pathways/sidewalks, student patrols, controlled dormitory access (key, security card, etc).

TRANSFER AND INTERNATIONAL STUDENTS

Transfer students: May apply for admission for the following academic terms: Fall, Spring, Summer. Applicants need a minimum number of credits to apply. For fall 2005: Transfer applications received: 218. Transfer applicants offered admission: 149. Transfer applicants enrolled: 88. **International students:** Number of foreign undergraduates: 36 (1% of student body). Number of countries represented: 23. Minimum TOEFL score required: 550 (paper); 213 (computer).

Penn. State University—University Park

- **Address:** University Park Campus, University Park, PA 16802
- **Website:** http://www.psu.edu
- **Public**
- **Enrollment:** 33,208 full-time; 1,429 part-time

KEY STATS

- ✔ **U.S News College Ranking:** 47, National Universities
- ✔ **SAT Score (25th/75th percentile):** 1100-1300
- ✔ **Tuition:** 2006-2007: $12,164 in state, $22,712 out of state
- **Selectivity:** More selective   **Room/board:** $6,850
- **Acceptance rate:** 62%   **Average debt:** N/A
- **Student/faculty ratio:** 17/1   **Proportion who borrowed:** N/A

UNDERGRADUATE STUDENT BODY STATS

2005-2006 enrollment: 33,208 full-time; 1,429 part-time. Men: 55%; women: 45%. **Ethnic makeup:** African American: 4%; Asian American: 6%; Hispanic: 3%; White: 85%; International: 2%.

ADMISSIONS FACTS AND FIGURES

Phone: (814) 865-5471. **Website:** http://www.psu.edu. **Application deadlines for fall 2007:** Regular decision: Rolling. Early decision: Not offered. Early action: Not offered. Admission can be deferred. **Application fee:** $50. Common application is not accepted. **To apply online, go to:** http://www.psu.edu/admissions. **Admissions requirements/recommendations:** High school units required (recommended): English: 4 (0); Mathematics: 3 (0); Science: 3 (0); Foreign language: 2 (0); Social studies: 3 (0); History: 0 (0); Academic electives: 0 (0); Total units: 15 (0). Tests: The college uses SAT or ACT scores in admissions decisions. Either SAT or ACT required. For admission to the fall 2007 entering class, the school will accept: ACT with writing, ACT without writing. Campus visit: Recommended. Admissions interview: Neither required nor recommended. Off-campus interview: Not available. **Factors that count in admissions decisions:** *Academic:* Secondary school record: Important. Class rank: Considered. Letters of recommendation: Considered. Standardized test scores: Very important. Essay: Considered. *Nonacademic:* Interview: Not considered. Extracurricular activities: Considered. Talent/ability: Considered. Character/personal qualities: Considered. Alumni/ae relationship: Considered. Geographical residence: Not considered. State residency: Not considered. Religious affiliation/commitment: Not considered. Minority status: Not considered. Volunteer work: Considered. Work experience: Considered. **Other schools with the greatest overlap in applicants:** Rutgers–New Brunswick; Temple University; University of Delaware; University of Maryland–College Park; University of Pittsburgh. **Admissions statistics for the fall 2005 entering class:** Total applicants: 29,904. Total accepted: 18,423. Freshmen enrolled: 6,496; 28% were from out of state. Overall acceptance rate: 62%. **Credentials of fall 2005 freshmen:** 40% ranked in the top 10 percent of their high school class; 78% were in the top 25 percent, and 98% were in the top half. (Proportion submitting class standing: 80%.) **Average high school grade point average:** 3.5. **First-year students who submitted SAT scores:** 97%. Scores (25/75 percentile): Verbal: 530-630, Math: 570-670, Combined: 1100-1300. **First-year students submitting ACT scores:** 12%. Scores (25/75 percentile): English: N/A, Math: N/A, Composite: N/A.

ACADEMICS

Year founded: 1855. **Academic calendar:** Semester. **Degrees offered:** certificate, terminal-associate, bachelor's, post-bachelor's certificate, master's, doctorate. **Most popular majors:** 21% business, management, marketing, and related support services, 13% engineering, 10% communication, journalism, and related programs, 6% education, 6% social sciences. **Major fields of study:** agriculture, agriculture operations, and related sciences; architecture and related services; area, ethnic, cultural, and gender studies; biological and biomedical sciences; business, management, marketing, and related support services; communication, journalism, and related programs; computer and information sciences and support services; education; engineering; English language and literature/letters; family and consumer sciences/human sciences; foreign languages, literatures, and linguistics; health professions and related clinical sciences; history; liberal arts and sciences studies, and humanities; mathematics and statistics; multi/interdisciplinary studies; natural resources and conservation; parks, recreation, leisure, and fitness studies; philosophy and religious studies; physical sci-

ences; psychology; science technologies/technicians; security and protective services; social sciences; visual and performing arts. **Areas of required coursework:** arts/fine arts, humanities, computer literacy, mathematics, English (including composition), foreign languages, sciences (biological or physical), social science, other. **Pre-professional programs:** pre-law, pre-dentistry, pre-medicine, pre-veterinary science, pre-optometry, other. **Special academic programs:** accelerated program, cooperative (work-study plan) program, cross-registration, distance learning, double major, dual enrollment, English as a Second Language (ESL), exchange student program (domestic), external degree program, honors program, independent study, internships, liberal arts/career combination, student-designed major, study abroad, teacher certificate program. **Teacher certification offered in:** early childhood, special education, elementary, vo-tech, secondary, bilingual/bicultural. **Cooperative education programs:** business, engineering, other. **Reserve Officers Training Corps (ROTC):** Army ROTC: Offered on campus; Navy ROTC: Offered on campus; Air Force ROTC: Offered on campus. **Faculty and instruction (2005-2006):** Total instructional faculty: 2,233 full-time, 313 part-time (63% men; 37% women; 17% minorities). Full-time faculty with Ph.D. or other terminal degree: 78%. Student/faculty ratio: 17/1. Classes of fewer than 20 students: 31%; of 20 to 49 students: 51%; of 50 or more students: 18%. **Advanced Placement and International Baccalaureate credit:** AP tests may be used for: Credit only. Scores accepted: 3, 4, 5. International Baccalaureate exams may be used for: Credit and/or placement. **Freshmen returning for sophomore year:** 92%. **Graduation rates:** Four-year: 54%; five-year: 81%; six-year: 84%. **Graduate study:** 24% of students pursue further study within one year.

COSTS AND FINANCIAL AID

Financial aid office: (814) 865-6301. **Expenses (2005-2006):** Tuition and fees 2005-2006: $11,508 in state, $21,744 out of state; room/board: $6,530. Estimated books and supplies: $1,040; transportation: $378; personal expenses: $2,016. **Financial aid:** Priority filing date for institution's financial aid form: February 15. In 2005-2006, 67% of undergraduates applied for financial aid. Of those, 50% were determined to have financial need; 9% had their need fully met. Average financial aid package (proportion receiving): $7,062 (49%). Average amount of gift aid, such as scholarships or grants (proportion receiving): $4,509 (29%). Average amount of self-help aid, such as work study or loans (proportion receiving): $4,453 (43%). Average need-based loan (excluding PLUS or other private loans): $4,247. Among students who received need-based aid, the average percentage of need met: 62%. Among students who received aid based on merit, the average award (and the proportion receiving): $2,506 (11%). The average athletic scholarship (and the proportion receiving): $17,339 (1%).

CAMPUS LIFE AND EXTRACURRICULAR ACTIVITIES

Campus housing available: coed dorms, women's dorms, men's dorms, sorority housing, apartments for married students, apartment for single students, special housing for disabled students, special housing for international students, other housing options. Students who live in college-owned, operated, or affiliated housing: 39%. **Clubs and organizations:** Number of student organizations: 652. Activities include: choral groups, concert band, dance, drama/theater, jazz band, literary magazine, marching band, music ensembles, musical theater, opera, pep band, radio station, student government, student newspaper, student film society, symphony orchestra, television station, yearbook. Number of fraternities: 55; sororities: 30. Proportion of men in fraternities: 12%; of women in sororities: 10%. Average proportion of students who stay on campus on weekends: 90%. **Sports program (2005-2006):** Member of NCAA I. *Men's intercollegiate varsity sports:* baseball, basketball, cross-country, fencing, football, golf, gymnastics, lacrosse, soccer, swimming and diving, tennis, track and field (indoor), track and field (outdoor), volleyball, wrestling. *Women's intercollegiate varsity sports:* basketball, cross-country, fencing, field hockey, golf, gymnastics, lacrosse, soccer, softball, swimming and diving, tennis, track and field (indoor), track and field (outdoor), volleyball.

SERVICES AND FACILITIES

Basic services: nonremedial tutoring, women's center, placement service, day care, health service, health insurance. **Remedial assistance:** reading, math, writing, study skills, other. **Counseling services:** minority student, career, military, personal, veteran student, academic, older student, psychological, birth control, religious. **For learning-disabled students:** School does not offer a structured program with separate admission and additional fees. Services include: remedial math, remedial English, reading machines, remedial reading, tape recorders, note-taking services, learning center, readers, extended time for tests, tutors, priority registration, priority seating, substitution of courses, texts on tape, other testing accomodations. **Library:**

Number of titles: 2,985,177; number of current serial subscriptions: 25,374. **Information technology resources:** Students are not required to lease or own a computer. Number of campus computers available to all students: 6,150. School has a wireless network. Approximate number of users that can be accommodated: 5,000. Proportion of college-owned housing units wired for high-speed internet access: 100%. **Campus safety:** Security services offered: 24-hour foot-and-vehicle patrols, late-night transport/escort service, 24-hour emergency telephones, lighted pathways/sidewalks, student patrols, controlled dormitory access (key, security card, etc).

TRANSFER AND INTERNATIONAL STUDENTS

Transfer students: May apply for admission for the following academic terms: Fall, Spring, Summer. Applicants need a minimum number of credits to apply. For fall 2005: Transfer applications received: 1,252. Transfer applicants offered admission: 640. Transfer applicants enrolled: 348. **International students:** Number of foreign undergraduates: 727 (2% of student body). Number of countries represented: 81. Minimum TOEFL score required: 550 (paper); 213 (computer).

Philadelphia University

- **Address:** School House Lane and Henry Avenue, Philadelphia, PA 19144
- **Website:** http://www.philau.edu
- **Private**
- **Enrollment:** 2,432 full-time; 275 part-time

KEY STATS

✔ **U.S News College Ranking:** 68, Universities–Master's (North)
✔ **SAT Score (25th/75th percentile):** 980-1160
✔ **Tuition:** 2006-2007: $23,818

Selectivity: Selective	**Room/board:** $8,212
Acceptance rate: 64%	**Average debt:** $22,917
Student/faculty ratio: 12/1	**Proportion who borrowed:** 74%

UNDERGRADUATE STUDENT BODY STATS

2005-2006 enrollment: 2,432 full-time; 275 part-time. Men: 31%; women: 69%. **Ethnic makeup:** African American: 9%; Asian American: 4%; Hispanic: 3%; White: 81%; International: 3%.

ADMISSIONS FACTS AND FIGURES

Phone: (215) 951-2800. **Email:** admissions@philau.edu. **Website:** http://www.philau.edu. **Application deadlines for fall 2007:** Regular decision: Rolling. Early decision: Not offered. Early action: Not offered. Admission can be deferred. **Application fee:** $35. Common application is accepted. **Admissions requirements/recommendations:** High school units required (recommended): English: 4 (4); Mathematics: 3 (4); Science: 3 (4); Foreign language: (2); Social studies: 2 (3); History: 1 (2); Academic electives: 2. Tests: The college uses SAT or ACT scores in admissions decisions. Either SAT or ACT required. For admission to the fall 2007 entering class, the school will accept: ACT without writing. Campus visit: Recommended. Admissions interview: Recommended. Off-campus interview: Not available. **Factors that count in admissions decisions:** *Academic:* Secondary school record: Very important. Class rank: Important. Letters of recommendation: Important. Standardized test scores: Very important. Essay: Considered. *Nonacademic:* Interview: Important. Extracurricular activities: Important. Alumni/ae relationship: Not considered. Volunteer work: Not considered. Work experience: Not considered. **Other schools with the greatest overlap in applicants:** Drexel University; Fashion Institute of Technology; Pennsylvania State University–University Park; Syracuse University; Temple University. **Admissions statistics for the fall 2005 entering class:** Total applicants: 4,180. Total accepted: 2,682. Freshmen enrolled: 692; 48% were from out of state. Overall acceptance rate: 64%. **Size of waiting list:** 140 applicants; enrolled from waiting list: 20. **Credentials of fall 2005 freshmen:** 12% ranked in the top 10 percent of their high school class; 38% were in the top 25 percent, and 80% were in the top half. (Proportion submitting class standing: 69%.) **Average high school grade point average:** 3.4. **First-year students who submitted SAT scores:** 96%. Scores (25/75 percentile): Verbal: 490-570, Math: 490-590, Combined: 980-1160. **First-year students submitting ACT scores:** 4%. Scores (25/75 percentile): English: N/A, Math: N/A, Composite: N/A.

ACADEMICS

Year founded: 1884. **Academic calendar:** Semester. **Degrees offered:** certificate, bachelor's, post-bachelor's certificate, master's, post-master's certificate, doctorate. **Most popular majors:** 15% fashion merchandising, 11% architecture (B.Arch., B.A./B.S., M.Arch., M.A./M.S., Ph.D.), 8% graphic design, 7% fashion/apparel design, 7% marketing/marketing management. **Major fields of study:** architecture and related services; biological and biomedical sciences; business, management, marketing, and related support services; communication, journalism, and related programs; communications technologies/technicians and support services; computer and information sciences and support services; engineering; health professions and related clinical sciences; multi/interdisciplinary studies; physical sciences; psychology; visual and performing arts. **Areas of required coursework:** arts/fine arts, humanities, computer literacy, mathematics, English (including composition), sciences (biological or physical), history, social science. **Pre-professional programs:** pre-dentistry, pre-medicine, pre-veterinary science, pre-optometry, pre-pharmacy. **Special academic programs (% participation):** accelerated program, distance learning (1%), double major (1%), honors program (6%), independent study (15%), internships (25%), liberal arts/career combination (100%), study abroad (31%). **Cooperative education programs:** social/behavioral science. **Faculty and instruction (2005-2006):** Total instructional faculty: 104 full-time, 314 part-time (61% men; 39% women; 14% minorities). Full-time faculty with Ph.D. or other terminal degree: 70%. Student/faculty ratio: 12/1. Classes of fewer than 20 students: 64%; of 20 to 49 students: 36%; of 50 or more students: 0%. **Advanced Placement and International Baccalaureate credit:** AP tests may be used for: Credit only. Scores accepted: 3, 4, 5. **Freshmen returning for sophomore year:** 71%. **Graduation rates:** Four-year: 35%; five-year: 51%; six-year: 55%. **Graduate study:** 19% of students pursue further study within one year. Fields in which graduates pursue further study: Master of Business Administration (MBA), 51%; medicine, 8%; arts and sciences, 41%.

COSTS AND FINANCIAL AID

Financial aid office: (215) 951-2940. **Expenses (2006-2007):** Tuition and fees 2006-2007: $23,818; room/board: $8,212. **Financial aid:** Priority filing date for institution's financial aid form: April 15; deadline: April 15. In 2005-2006, 79% of undergraduates applied for financial aid. Of those, 68% were determined to have financial need; 11% had their need fully met. Average financial aid package (proportion receiving): $15,474 (68%). Average amount of gift aid, such as scholarships or grants (proportion receiving): $9,974 (67%). Average amount of self-help aid, such as work study or loans (proportion receiving): $5,356 (62%). Average need-based loan (excluding PLUS or other private loans): $4,045. Among students who received need-based aid, the average percentage of need met: 72%. Among students who received aid based on merit, the average award (and the proportion receiving): $4,066 (26%). The average athletic scholarship (and the proportion receiving): $11,118 (3%). Average amount of debt of borrowers graduating in 2005: $22,917. Proportion who borrowed: 74%.

CAMPUS LIFE AND EXTRACURRICULAR ACTIVITIES

Campus housing available (% using): coed dorms (57%), women's dorms (15%), apartment for single students (28%). Students who live in college-owned, operated, or affiliated housing: 50%. **Student employment:** During the 2005-2006 academic year, 9% of undergraduates worked on campus. Average per-year earnings: $2,000. **Clubs and organizations:** Number of student organizations: 35. Activities include: choral groups, dance, drama/theater, student government, student newspaper, yearbook. Number of fraternities: 2; sororities: 1. Proportion of men in fraternities: 1%; of women in sororities: 1%. Average proportion of students who stay on campus on weekends: 60%. **Sports program (2005-2006):** Member of NCAA II. *Men's intercollegiate varsity sports:* baseball, basketball, cross-country, golf, soccer, tennis. *Women's intercollegiate varsity sports:* basketball, cross-country, field hockey, lacrosse, soccer, softball, tennis, volleyball.

SERVICES AND FACILITIES

Basic services: nonremedial tutoring, placement service, health service. **Remedial assistance:** reading, math, writing, study skills. **Counseling services:** career, personal, academic, psychological. **For learning-disabled students:** School does not offer a structured program with separate admission and additional fees. Services include: remedial math, remedial English, reading machines, remedial reading, tape recorders, videotaped classes, note-taking services, oral tests, learning center, readers, extended time for tests, tutors, priority registration, texts on tape, other testing accomodations. **Library:** Number of titles: 111,484; number of current serial subscriptions: 3,343. **Information technology resources:** Students are not required to lease or own a computer. Number of campus computers available to all students:

675. School has a wireless network. Approximate number of users that can be accommodated: 500. Proportion of college-owned housing units wired for high-speed internet access: 100%. **Campus safety:** Security services offered: 24-hour foot-and-vehicle patrols, late-night transport/escort service, 24-hour emergency telephones, lighted pathways/sidewalks, controlled dormitory access (key, security card, etc).

TRANSFER AND INTERNATIONAL STUDENTS

Transfer students: May apply for admission for the following academic terms: Fall, Spring, Summer. Applicants need a minimum number of credits to apply. For fall 2005: Transfer applications received: 524. Transfer applicants offered admission: 227. Transfer applicants enrolled: 98. **International students:** Number of foreign undergraduates: 68 (3% of student body). Number of countries represented: 24. Minimum TOEFL score required: 500 (paper); 170 (computer).

Point Park University

- Address: 201 Wood Street, Pittsburgh, PA 15222
- Website: http://www.pointpark.edu
- Private
- Enrollment: 2,263 full-time; 699 part-time

KEY STATS
- ✔ **U.S News College Ranking:** fourth tier, Universities–Master's (North)
- ✔ **SAT Score (25th/75th percentile):** 920-1130
- ✔ **Tuition:** 2006-2007: $17,770

Selectivity: Selective	**Room/board:** $7,880
Acceptance rate: 76%	**Average debt:** $25,289
Student/faculty ratio: 15/1	**Proportion who borrowed:** 95%

UNDERGRADUATE STUDENT BODY STATS

2005-2006 enrollment: 2,263 full-time; 699 part-time. Men: 41%; women: 59%. **Ethnic makeup:** African American: 18%; Asian American: 1%; Hispanic: 2%; White: 79%; International: 1%.

ADMISSIONS FACTS AND FIGURES

Phone: (800) 321-0129. **Email:** enroll@pointpark.edu. **Website:** http://www.pointpark.edu. **Application deadlines for fall 2007:** Regular decision: Rolling. Early decision: Not offered. Early action: Not offered. Admission can be deferred. **Application fee:** $40. Common application is accepted. **Admissions requirements/recommendations:** High school units required (recommended): English: (4); Mathematics: (3); Science: (3); Foreign language: (2); Social studies: (3); History: (3); Total units: (18). Tests: The college uses SAT or ACT scores in admissions decisions. Either SAT or ACT required. Campus visit: Recommended. Admissions interview: Recommended. Off-campus interview: Not available. **Factors that count in admissions decisions:** *Academic:* Secondary school record: Considered. Class rank: Considered. Letters of recommendation: Not considered. Standardized test scores: Considered. Essay: Not considered. *Nonacademic:* Interview: Not considered. Extracurricular activities: Considered. Talent/ability: Very important. Character/personal qualities: Considered. Alumni/ae relationship: Not considered. Geographical residence: Not considered. State residency: Not considered. Religious affiliation/commitment: Not considered. Minority status: Not considered. Volunteer work: Not considered. Work experience: Not considered. **Other schools with the greatest overlap in applicants:** Duquesne University; New York University; Pennsylvania State University–University Park; Slippery Rock University of Pennsylvania; University of Pittsburgh. **Admissions statistics for the fall 2005 entering class:** Total applicants: 2,453. Total accepted: 1,866. Freshmen enrolled: 472; 31% were from out of state. Overall acceptance rate: 76%. **Credentials of fall 2005 freshmen:** 12% ranked in the top 10 percent of their high school class; 38% were in the top 25 percent, and 72% were in the top half. (Proportion submitting class standing: 84%.) **Average high school grade point average:** 3.2. **First-year students who submitted SAT scores:** 89%. Scores (25/75 percentile): Verbal: 470-580, Math: 450-550, Combined: 920-1130. **First-year students submitting ACT scores:** 20%. Scores (25/75 percentile): English: 20-26, Math: 17-24, Composite: 20-25.

ACADEMICS

Year founded: 1960. **Academic calendar:** Semester. **Degrees offered:** certificate, associate, bachelor's, master's. **Most popular majors:** 18% business

administration and management, 13% criminal justice/safety studies, 11% drama and dramatics/theater arts, 6% dance, 4% computer/information technology services administration and management. **Major fields of study:** area, ethnic, cultural, and gender studies; biological and biomedical sciences; business, management, marketing, and related support services; communication, journalism, and related programs; computer and information sciences and support services; education; engineering technologies/technicians; English language and literature/letters; health professions and related clinical sciences; history; legal professions and studies; liberal arts and sciences studies, and humanities; multi/interdisciplinary studies; natural resources and conservation; personal and culinary services; psychology; public administration and social service professions; security and protective services; social sciences; visual and performing arts. **Areas of required coursework:** arts/fine arts, humanities, computer literacy, mathematics, English (including composition), sciences (biological or physical), history, social science. **Special academic programs:** accelerated program, cooperative (work-study plan) program, cross-registration, distance learning, double major, English as a Second Language (ESL), honors program, independent study, internships, study abroad, teacher certificate program, weekend college. **Teacher certification offered in:** early childhood, elementary, secondary. **Cooperative education programs:** education. **Reserve Officers Training Corps (ROTC):** Army ROTC: Offered at cooperating institution (Duquesne University); Air Force ROTC: Offered at cooperating institution (University of Pittsburgh). **Faculty and instruction (2005-2006):** Total instructional faculty: 89 full-time, 300 part-time (58% men; 42% women). Full-time faculty with Ph.D. or other terminal degree: 55%. Student/faculty ratio: 15/1. Classes of fewer than 20 students: 75%; of 20 to 49 students: 25%; of 50 or more students: 0%. **Advanced Placement and International Baccalaureate credit:** AP tests may be used for: Credit only. Scores accepted: 3, 4, 5. International Baccalaureate exams may be used for: Credit only. **Freshmen returning for sophomore year:** 71%. **Graduation rates:** Four-year: 36%; five-year: 42%; six-year: 39%.

COSTS AND FINANCIAL AID

Financial aid office: (412) 392-3930. **Expenses (2006-2007):** Tuition and fees 2006-2007: $17,770; room/board: $7,880. Estimated books and supplies: $1,000; transportation: $1,200; personal expenses: $1,000. **Financial aid:** Priority filing date for institution's financial aid form: May 1. In 2005-2006, 89% of undergraduates applied for financial aid. Of those, 80% were determined to have financial need; 18% had their need fully met. Average financial aid package (proportion receiving): $12,906 (80%). Average amount of gift aid, such as scholarships or grants (proportion receiving): $7,234 (77%). Average amount of self-help aid, such as work study or loans (proportion receiving): $6,428 (74%). Average need-based loan (excluding PLUS or other private loans): $5,100. Among students who received need-based aid, the average percentage of need met: 68%. Among students who received aid based on merit, the average award (and the proportion receiving): $9,565 (18%). The average athletic scholarship (and the proportion receiving): $7,798 (2%). Average amount of debt of borrowers graduating in 2005: $25,289. Proportion who borrowed: 95%.

CAMPUS LIFE AND EXTRACURRICULAR ACTIVITIES

Campus housing available (% using): coed dorms (57%), women's dorms (32%), men's dorms (11%), special housing for disabled students, special housing for international students, other housing options. Students who live in college-owned, operated, or affiliated housing: 23%. **Student employment:** During the 2005-2006 academic year, 0% of undergraduates worked on campus. Average per-year earnings: $0. **Clubs and organizations:** Number of student organizations: 29. Activities include: choral groups, dance, drama/theater, literary magazine, musical theater, radio station, student government, student newspaper, student film society, television station. Number of fraternities: 0; sororities: 0. Average proportion of students who stay on campus on weekends: 75%. **Sports program (2005-2006):** Member of NAIA. *Men's intercollegiate varsity sports:* baseball, basketball, cross-country, soccer. *Women's intercollegiate varsity sports:* basketball, cross-country, softball, volleyball.

SERVICES AND FACILITIES

Basic services: nonremedial tutoring, day care, health service, health insurance. **Remedial assistance:** reading, math, writing, study skills. **Counseling services:** career, personal, academic, psychological. **For learning-disabled students:** School does not offer a structured program with separate admission and additional fees. Total undergraduates in learning-disabled program or receiving services: 7. Services include: remedial math, remedial English, remedial reading, tape recorders, note-taking services, oral tests, readers, extended time for tests, tutors, priority seating, exams on tape or computer, other testing accomodations, other. **Library:** Number of titles: 117,000; number of current serial subscriptions: 274. **Information technology resources:** Students are not required to lease or own a computer. Number of campus computers available to all students: 253. School has a wireless network. Approximate number of users that can be accommodated: 400. Proportion of college-owned housing units wired for high-speed internet access: 100%. **Campus safety:** Security services offered: 24-hour emergency telephones, lighted pathways/sidewalks, controlled dormitory access (key, security card, etc).

TRANSFER AND INTERNATIONAL STUDENTS

Transfer students: May apply for admission for the following academic terms: Fall, Spring, Summer. Applicants need a minimum number of credits to apply. For fall 2005: Transfer applications received: 1,154. Transfer applicants offered admission: 763. Transfer applicants enrolled: 458. **International students:** Number of foreign undergraduates: 32 (1% of student body). Number of countries represented: 34. Minimum TOEFL score required: 500 (paper); 173 (computer). Average TOEFL score: 520 (paper).

Robert Morris University

- **Address:** 6001 University Boulevard, Moon Township, PA 15108-1189
- **Website:** http://www.rmu.edu
- **Private**
- **Enrollment:** 3,103 full-time; 868 part-time

KEY STATS

✔ **U.S News College Ranking:** third tier, Universities–Master's (North)
✔ **SAT Score (25th/75th percentile):** 910-1110
✔ **Tuition:** 2006-2007: $16,590

Selectivity: Less selective	**Room/board:** $8,410
Acceptance rate: 78%	**Average debt:** N/A
Student/faculty ratio: 16/1	**Proportion who borrowed:** N/A

UNDERGRADUATE STUDENT BODY STATS

2005-2006 enrollment: 3,103 full-time; 868 part-time. Men: 54%; women: 46%. **Ethnic makeup:** African American: 8%; Asian American: 1%; Hispanic: 1%; White: 89%; International: 2%.

ADMISSIONS FACTS AND FIGURES

Phone: (412) 262-8206. **Email:** enrollmentoffice@rmu.edu. **Website:** http://www.rmu.edu. **Application deadlines for fall 2007:** Regular decision: July 1. Early decision: Not offered. Early action: Not offered. Admission can be deferred. **Application fee:** $30. Common application is accepted. **Admissions requirements/recommendations:** High school units required (recommended): English: 4; Mathematics: 3; Science: 2; Foreign language: (2); Social studies: 4; Academic electives: 3; Total units: 16 (18). Tests: The college uses SAT or ACT scores in admissions decisions. Either SAT or ACT required. For admission to the fall 2007 entering class, the school will accept: ACT with writing, ACT without writing. Campus visit: Recommended. Admissions interview: Recommended. Off-campus interview: May be arranged. **Factors that count in admissions decisions:** *Academic:* Secondary school record: Important. Class rank: Important. Letters of recommendation: Important. Standardized test scores: Very important. Essay: Considered. *Nonacademic:* Interview: Important. Extracurricular activities: Important. Talent/ability: Considered. Character/personal qualities: Important. Alumni/ae relationship: Not considered. Geographical residence: Considered. State residency: Not considered. Religious affiliation/commitment: Not considered. Minority status: Not considered. Volunteer work: Considered. Work experience: Considered. **Other schools with the greatest overlap in applicants:** Duquesne University; Indiana University of Pennsylvania; Pennsylvania State University–University Park; University of Pittsburgh; West Virginia University. **Admissions statistics for the fall 2005 entering class:** Total applicants: 2,584. Total accepted: 2,024. Freshmen enrolled: 695; 19% were from out of state. Overall acceptance rate: 78%. **Credentials of fall 2005 freshmen:** 8% ranked in the top 10 percent of their high school class; 27% were in the top 25 percent, and 66% were in the top half. (Proportion submitting class standing: 84%.) **Average high school grade point average:** 3.2. **First-year students who submitted SAT scores:** 91%. Scores (25/75 percentile): Verbal: 450-540, Math: 460-570, Combined: 910-1110. **First-year students submit-**

ting ACT scores: 7%. Scores (25/75 percentile): English: 17-22, Math: 18-24, Composite: 19-23.

ACADEMICS

Year founded: 1921. **Academic calendar:** Semester. **Degrees offered:** certificate, bachelor's, post-bachelor's certificate, master's, doctorate. **Most popular majors:** 16% business administration and management, 11% marketing/marketing management, 10% accounting, 10% communication studies/speech communication and rhetoric, 8% information science/studies. **Major fields of study:** business, management, marketing, and related support services; communication, journalism, and related programs; computer and information sciences and support services; education; engineering; English language and literature/letters; health professions and related clinical sciences; mathematics and statistics; multi/interdisciplinary studies; natural resources and conservation; parks, recreation, leisure, and fitness studies; psychology; social sciences; transportation and materials moving; visual and performing arts. **Areas of required coursework:** humanities, computer literacy, mathematics, English (including composition), sciences (biological or physical), history, social science. **Pre-professional programs:** pre-law, pre-medicine. **Special academic programs:** cooperative (work-study plan) program, cross-registration, distance learning, double major, honors program, independent study, internships, study abroad, teacher certificate program, weekend college. **Teacher certification offered in:** elementary, middle/junior high, secondary. **Cooperative education programs:** business, computer science, education, engineering. **Reserve Officers Training Corps (ROTC):** Army ROTC: Offered on campus; Air Force ROTC: Offered at cooperating institution (University of Pittsburgh). **Faculty and instruction (2005-2006):** Total instructional faculty: 157 full-time, 227 part-time (57% men; 43% women; 8% minorities). Full-time faculty with Ph.D. or other terminal degree: 82%. Student/faculty ratio: 16/1. Classes of fewer than 20 students: 50%; of 20 to 49 students: 50%; of 50 or more students: 0%. **Advanced Placement and International Baccalaureate credit:** AP tests may be used for: Credit only. Scores accepted: 3. International Baccalaureate exams may be used for: Credit only. Freshmen returning for sophomore year: 76%. **Graduation rates:** Four-year: 30%; five-year: 51%; six-year: 55%. **Graduate study:** 3% of students pursue further study immediately upon graduation; 5% within one year; 15% within five years.

COSTS AND FINANCIAL AID

Financial aid office: (412) 262-8545. **Expenses (2006-2007):** Tuition and fees 2006-2007: $16,590; room/board: $8,410. Estimated books and supplies: $1,000; transportation: $1,000; personal expenses: $1,800. **Financial aid:** Priority filing date for institution's financial aid form: May 1. In 2005-2006, 85% of undergraduates applied for financial aid. Of those, 75% were determined to have financial need; 24% had their need fully met. Average financial aid package (proportion receiving): $12,784 (75%). Average amount of gift aid, such as scholarships or grants (proportion receiving): $6,956 (68%). Average amount of self-help aid, such as work study or loans (proportion receiving): $6,942 (69%). Average need-based loan (excluding PLUS or other private loans): $5,837. Among students who received need-based aid, the average percentage of need met: 70%. Among students who received aid based on merit, the average award (and the proportion receiving): $9,451 (19%). The average athletic scholarship (and the proportion receiving): $9,234 (4%).

CAMPUS LIFE AND EXTRACURRICULAR ACTIVITIES

Campus housing available (% using): coed dorms (57%), women's dorms (13%), men's dorms (13%), apartment for single students (11%), other housing options (6%). Students who live in college-owned, operated, or affiliated housing: 28%. **Clubs and organizations:** Number of student organizations: 50. Activities include: drama/theater, marching band, musical theater, pep band, student government, student newspaper, television station. Number of fraternities: 6; sororities: 3. Proportion of men in fraternities: 4%; of women in sororities: 4%. Average proportion of students who stay on campus on weekends: 25%. **Sports program (2005-2006):** Member of NCAA I. *Men's intercollegiate varsity sports:* basketball, cross-country, football, golf, ice hockey, lacrosse, soccer, tennis, track and field (indoor), track and field (outdoor). *Women's intercollegiate varsity sports:* basketball, crew, cross-country, field hockey, golf, lacrosse, soccer, softball, tennis, track and field (indoor), track and field (outdoor), volleyball.

SERVICES AND FACILITIES

Basic services: nonremedial tutoring, placement service, health service. **Remedial assistance:** reading, math, writing, study skills. **Counseling services:** minority student, career, personal, psychological, religious. **For learning-disabled students:** School does not offer a structured program with separate admission and additional fees. Total undergraduates in learning-disabled program or receiving services: 37. Services include: remedial math, remedial English, reading machines, remedial reading, tape recorders, oral tests, learning center, readers, extended time for tests, priority registration, priority seating, other testing accomodations. **Library:** Number of titles: 135,989; number of current serial subscriptions: 584. **Information technology resources:** Students are not required to lease or own a computer. Number of campus computers available to all students: 300. School has a wireless network. Approximate number of users that can be accommodated: 100. Proportion of college-owned housing units wired for high-speed internet access: 100%. **Campus safety:** Security services offered: 24-hour foot-and-vehicle patrols, late-night transport/escort service, 24-hour emergency telephones, lighted pathways/sidewalks, controlled dormitory access (key, security card, etc.).

TRANSFER AND INTERNATIONAL STUDENTS

Transfer students: May apply for admission for the following academic terms: Fall, Spring, Summer. Applicants do not need a minimum number of credits to apply. For fall 2005: Transfer applications received: 804. Transfer applicants offered admission: 651. Transfer applicants enrolled: 387. **International students:** Number of foreign undergraduates: 64 (2% of student body). Number of countries represented: 20. Minimum TOEFL score required: 500 (paper); 173 (computer).

Rosemont College

- **Address:** 1400 Montgomery Avenue, Rosemont, PA 19010-1699
- **Website:** http://www.rosemont.edu
- **Private; Religious affiliation:** Roman Catholic
- **Enrollment:** 425 full-time; 219 part-time

KEY STATS

✔ **U.S News College Ranking:** third tier, Liberal Arts Colleges
✔ **SAT Score (25th/75th percentile):** 940-1220
✔ **Tuition:** 2006-2007: $21,465

Selectivity: Selective	**Room/board:** $9,200
Acceptance rate: 66%	**Average debt:** $23,091
Student/faculty ratio: 8/1	**Proportion who borrowed:** 78%

UNDERGRADUATE STUDENT BODY STATS

2005-2006 enrollment: 425 full-time; 219 part-time. Men: 13%; women: 87%. **Ethnic makeup:** African American: 28%; Asian American: 7%; Hispanic: 7%; White: 54%; International: 4%. **Religious preference:** Roman Catholic: 60%; Other: 40%.

ADMISSIONS FACTS AND FIGURES

Phone: (800) 331-0708. **Email:** admissions@rosemont.edu. **Website:** http://www.rosemont.edu. **Application deadlines for fall 2007:** Regular decision: August 1. Early decision: Not offered. Early action: Not offered. Admission can be deferred. **Application fee:** $35. Common application is accepted. **Admissions requirements/recommendations:** High school units required (recommended): English: 4; Mathematics: 2; Science: 2; Foreign language: 2; Social studies: 2; History: 2; Academic electives: 2; Total units: 18. Tests: The college uses SAT or ACT scores in admissions decisions. Either SAT or ACT required. Campus visit: Recommended. Admissions interview: Recommended. Off-campus interview: May be arranged. **Factors that count in admissions decisions:** *Academic:* Secondary school record: Very important. Class rank: Very important. Letters of recommendation: Very important. Standardized test scores: Important. Essay: Very important. *Nonacademic:* Interview: Very important. Extracurricular activities: Important. Talent/ability: Important. Character/personal qualities: Very important. Alumni/ae relationship: Considered. Geographical residence: Not considered. State residency: Not considered. Religious affiliation/commitment: Not considered. Minority status: Not considered. Volunteer work: Very important. Work experience: Considered. **Other schools with the greatest overlap in applicants:** Rowan University; Rutgers–New Brunswick; St. Joseph's University; Temple University; Villanova University. **Admissions statistics for the fall 2005 entering class:** Total applicants: 434. Total accepted: 285. Freshmen enrolled: 120; 30% were from out of state. Overall acceptance rate: 66%. **Credentials of fall 2005 freshmen:** 23% ranked in the top 10 percent of their high school class; 47% were in the top 25 percent, and 70% were in the top half. (Proportion submitting class standing: 45%.)

Average high school grade point average: 3.4. **First-year students who submitted SAT scores:** 100%. Scores (25/75 percentile): Verbal: 480-620, Math: 460-600, Combined: 940-1220.

ACADEMICS

Year founded: 1921. **Academic calendar:** Semester. **Degrees offered:** certificate, bachelor's, post-bachelor's certificate, master's. **Most popular majors:** 17% visual and performing arts, 16% business, management, marketing, and related support services, 15% social sciences, 14% English language and literature/letters, 13% psychology. **Major fields of study:** area, ethnic, cultural, and gender studies; biological and biomedical sciences; business, management, marketing, and related support services; communication, journalism, and related programs; English language and literature/letters; foreign languages, literatures, and linguistics; history; liberal arts and sciences studies, and humanities; mathematics and statistics; multi/interdisciplinary studies; natural resources and conservation; philosophy and religious studies; physical sciences; psychology; social sciences; visual and performing arts. **Areas of required coursework:** arts/fine arts, humanities, computer literacy, mathematics, English (including composition), philosophy, foreign languages, sciences (biological or physical), history, social science. **Pre-professional programs:** pre-law, pre-dentistry, pre-medicine, pre-veterinary science. **Special academic programs (% participation):** cross-registration (42%), distance learning (2%), double major (19%), dual enrollment (2%), honors program (12%), independent study (20%), internships (85%), student-designed major (2%), study abroad (40%), teacher certificate program (6%). **Teacher certification offered in:** early childhood, special education, elementary, secondary. **Cooperative education programs:** art, engineering, health professions. **Reserve Officers Training Corps (ROTC):** Army ROTC: Offered at cooperating institution (Valley Forge Military); Navy ROTC: Offered at cooperating institution (Villanova University). **Faculty and instruction (2005-2006):** Total instructional faculty: 33 full-time, 134 part-time (42% men; 58% women; 11% minorities). Full-time faculty with Ph.D. or other terminal degree: 97%. Student/faculty ratio: 8/1. Classes of fewer than 20 students: 92%; of 20 to 49 students: 8%; of 50 or more students: 0%. **Advanced Placement and International Baccalaureate credit:** AP tests may be used for: Credit and/or placement. Scores accepted: 3, 4, 5. International Baccalaureate exams may be used for: Credit and/or placement. **Freshmen returning for sophomore year:** 82%. **Graduation rates:** Four-year: 62%; five-year: 62%; six-year: 62%. **Graduate study:** 15% of students pursue further study immediately upon graduation; 20% within one year; 25% within five years. Fields in which graduates pursue further study: Master of Business Administration (MBA), 10%; law, 3%; medicine, 5%; education, 30%; arts and sciences, 30%.

COSTS AND FINANCIAL AID

Financial aid office: (610) 527-0200. **Expenses (2006-2007):** Tuition and fees 2006-2007: $21,465; room/board: $9,200. Estimated books and supplies: $1,000; transportation: $200; personal expenses: $1,000. **Financial aid:** Priority filing date for institution's financial aid form: February 15. In 2005-2006, 89% of undergraduates applied for financial aid. Of those, 77% were determined to have financial need; 21% had their need fully met. Average financial aid package (proportion receiving): $17,513 (77%). Average amount of gift aid, such as scholarships or grants (proportion receiving): $14,389 (76%). Average amount of self-help aid, such as work study or loans (proportion receiving): $4,128 (60%). Average need-based loan (excluding PLUS or other private loans): $3,550. Among students who received need-based aid, the average percentage of need met: 76%. Among students who received aid based on merit, the average award (and the proportion receiving): $16,134 (22%). The average athletic scholarship (and the proportion receiving): $0 (0%). Average amount of debt of borrowers graduating in 2005: $23,091. Proportion who borrowed: 78%.

CAMPUS LIFE AND EXTRACURRICULAR ACTIVITIES

Campus housing available (% using): women's dorms (100%), special housing for disabled students. Students who live in college-owned, operated, or affiliated housing: 70%. **Student employment:** During the 2005-2006 academic year, 47% of undergraduates worked on campus. Average per-year earnings: $2,000. **Clubs and organizations:** Number of student organizations: 25. Activities include: choral groups, dance, drama/theater, jazz band, literary magazine, radio station, student government, student newspaper, yearbook. Number of fraternities: 0; sororities: 0. Average proportion of students who stay on campus on weekends: 60%. **Sports program (2005-2006):** Member of NCAA III. *Women's intercollegiate varsity sports:* basketball, field hockey, lacrosse, softball, tennis, volleyball.

SERVICES AND FACILITIES

Basic services: nonremedial tutoring, women's center, placement service, health service, health insurance. **Remedial assistance:** reading, math, writing, study skills. **Counseling services:** minority student, career, personal, academic, older student, psychological, religious. **For learning-disabled students:** School does not offer a structured program with separate admission and additional fees. Total undergraduates in learning-disabled program or receiving services: 9. Services include: remedial math, remedial English, tape recorders, diagnostic testing service, untimed tests, note-taking services, oral tests, learning center, readers, extended time for tests, tutors. **Library:** Number of titles: 161,480; number of current serial subscriptions: 891. **Information technology resources:** Students are not required to lease or own a computer. Number of campus computers available to all students: 85. School does not have a wireless network. Proportion of college-owned housing units wired for high-speed internet access: 100%. **Campus safety:** Security services offered: 24-hour foot-and-vehicle patrols, late-night transport/escort service, 24-hour emergency telephones, lighted pathways/sidewalks, controlled dormitory access (key, security card, etc.).

TRANSFER AND INTERNATIONAL STUDENTS

Transfer students: May apply for admission for the following academic terms: Fall, Spring. Applicants do not need a minimum number of credits to apply. For fall 2005: Transfer applications received: 43. Transfer applicants offered admission: 33. Transfer applicants enrolled: 27. **International students:** Number of foreign undergraduates: 23 (4% of student body). Number of countries represented: 17. Minimum TOEFL score required: 500 (paper). Average TOEFL score: 550 (paper).

Seton Hill University

- **Address:** Seton Hill Drive, Greensburg, PA 15601
- **Website:** http://www.setonhill.edu
- **Private; Religious affiliation:** Roman Catholic
- **Enrollment:** 1,226 full-time; 300 part-time

KEY STATS

✔ **U.S News College Ranking:** fourth tier, Liberal Arts Colleges
✔ **SAT Score (25th/75th percentile):** 920-1100
✔ **Tuition:** 2006-2007: $23,380

Selectivity: Selective	**Room/board:** $7,450
Acceptance rate: 70%	**Average debt:** $26,281
Student/faculty ratio: 14/1	**Proportion who borrowed:** 74%

UNDERGRADUATE STUDENT BODY STATS

2005-2006 enrollment: 1,226 full-time; 300 part-time. Men: 36%; women: 64%. **Ethnic makeup:** African American: 8%; Asian American: 1%; Hispanic: 1%; White: 88%; International: 2%.

ADMISSIONS FACTS AND FIGURES

Phone: (724) 838-4255. **Email:** admit@setonhill.edu. **Website:** http://www.setonhill.edu. **Application deadlines for fall 2007:** Regular decision: August 15. Early decision: Not offered. Early action: Not offered. Admission can be deferred. **Application fee:** $35. Common application is accepted. **To apply online, go to:** http://www.setonhill.edu/admissions2/newappo.cfm. **Admissions requirements/recommendations:** High school units required (recommended): English: 4; Mathematics: 2; Science: 1; Foreign language: (2); Social studies: 2; Academic electives: 4; Total units: 15. Tests: The college uses SAT or ACT scores in admissions decisions. Neither SAT nor ACT required. For admission to the fall 2007 entering class, the school will accept: ACT without writing. Campus visit: Recommended. Admissions interview: Recommended. Off-campus interview: May be arranged. **Factors that count in admissions decisions:** *Academic:* Secondary school record: Very important. Class rank: Important. Letters of recommendation: Considered. Standardized test scores: Important. Essay: Considered. *Nonacademic:* Interview: Very important. Extracurricular activities: Important. Talent/ability: Important. Character/personal qualities: Important. Alumni/ae relationship: Considered. Geographical residence: Not considered. State residency: Not considered. Religious affiliation/commitment: Not considered. Minority status: Not considered. Volunteer work: Considered. Work experience: Considered. **Other schools with the greatest overlap in applicants:** Indiana University of Pennsylvania; Pennsylvania State University–University Park;

Slippery Rock University of Pennsylvania; St. Vincent College; Washington and Jefferson College. **Admissions statistics for the fall 2005 entering class:** Total applicants: 2,133. Total accepted: 1,500. Freshmen enrolled: 336; 28% were from out of state. Overall acceptance rate: 70%. **Credentials of fall 2005 freshmen:** 14% ranked in the top 10 percent of their high school class; 39% were in the top 25 percent, and 73% were in the top half. (Proportion submitting class standing: 91%.) **Average high school grade point average:** 3.0. **First-year students who submitted SAT scores:** 92%. Scores (25/75 percentile): Verbal: 460-550, Math: 460-550, Combined: 920-1100. **First-year students submitting ACT scores:** 18%. Scores (25/75 percentile): English: N/A, Math: N/A, Composite: 17-22.

ACADEMICS

Year founded: 1883. **Academic calendar:** Semester. **Degrees offered:** certificate, bachelor's, post-bachelor's certificate, master's, post-master's certificate. **Most popular majors:** 33% business, management, marketing, and related support services, 11% visual and performing arts, 10% public administration and social service professions, 7% psychology, 5% health professions and related clinical sciences. **Major fields of study:** biological and biomedical sciences; business, management, marketing, and related support services; communication, journalism, and related programs; computer and information sciences and support services; education; English language and literature/letters; family and consumer sciences/human sciences; foreign languages, literatures, and linguistics; health professions and related clinical sciences; history; liberal arts and sciences studies, and humanities; mathematics and statistics; philosophy and religious studies; physical sciences; psychology; public administration and social service professions; security and protective services; social sciences; theology and religious vocations; visual and performing arts. **Areas of required coursework:** arts/fine arts, humanities, computer literacy, mathematics, English (including composition), philosophy, foreign languages, sciences (biological or physical), history, other. **Pre-professional programs:** pre-law, pre-dentistry, pre-medicine, pre-veterinary science, pre-optometry. **Special academic programs:** accelerated program, cross-registration, distance learning, double major, English as a Second Language (ESL), exchange student program (domestic), honors program, independent study, internships, liberal arts/career combination, student-designed major, study abroad, teacher certificate program, weekend college. **Teacher certification offered in:** early childhood, special education, elementary, middle/junior high, secondary. **Cooperative education programs:** engineering, health professions. **Reserve Officers Training Corps (ROTC):** Army ROTC: Offered at cooperating institution (University of Pittsburgh). **Faculty and instruction (2005-2006):** Total instructional faculty: 68 full-time, 117 part-time (42% men; 58% women; 3% minorities). Full-time faculty with Ph.D. or other terminal degree: 85%. Student/faculty ratio: 14/1. Classes of fewer than 20 students: 60%; of 20 to 49 students: 40%; of 50 or more students: 0%. **Advanced Placement and International Baccalaureate credit:** AP tests may be used for: Credit and/or placement. Scores accepted: 3, 4, 5. International Baccalaureate exams may be used for: Credit and/or placement. **Freshmen returning for sophomore year:** 77%. **Graduation rates:** Four-year: 44%; five-year: 53%; six-year: 54%. **Graduate study:** 29% of students pursue further study immediately upon graduation. Fields in which graduates pursue further study: Master of Business Administration (MBA), 23%; law, 3%; engineering, 3%; education, 16%; arts and sciences, 48%.

COSTS AND FINANCIAL AID

Financial aid office: (724) 838-4293. **Expenses (2006-2007):** Tuition and fees 2006-2007: $23,380; room/board: $7,450. Estimated books and supplies: $1,000; transportation: $200; personal expenses: $2,400. **Financial aid:** Priority filing date for institution's financial aid form: May 1. In 2005-2006, 79% of undergraduates applied for financial aid. Of those, 75% were determined to have financial need; 20% had their need fully met. Average financial aid package (proportion receiving): $18,903 (75%). Average amount of gift aid, such as scholarships or grants (proportion receiving): $12,100 (75%). Average amount of self-help aid, such as work study or loans (proportion receiving): $4,629 (62%). Average need-based loan (excluding PLUS or other private loans): $3,895. Among students who received need-based aid, the average percentage of need met: 75%. Among students who received aid based on merit, the average award (and the proportion receiving): $7,100 (4%). The average athletic scholarship (and the proportion receiving): $19,107 (3%). Average amount of debt of borrowers graduating in 2005: $26,281. Proportion who borrowed: 74%.

CAMPUS LIFE AND EXTRACURRICULAR ACTIVITIES

Campus housing available: coed dorms, women's dorms, men's dorms. Students who live in college-owned, operated, or affiliated housing: 60%.

Clubs and organizations: Number of student organizations: 40. Activities include: choral groups, concert band, dance, drama/theater, jazz band, literary magazine, music ensembles, musical theater, pep band, student government, student newspaper, symphony orchestra. Number of fraternities: 0; sororities: 0. **Sports program (2005-2006):** Member of NAIA. *Men's intercollegiate varsity sports:* baseball, basketball, cross-country, golf, soccer, tennis. *Women's intercollegiate varsity sports:* basketball, cross-country, equestrian sports, golf, soccer, softball, tennis, volleyball.

SERVICES AND FACILITIES

Basic services: nonremedial tutoring, placement service, health service. **Remedial assistance:** math, writing, study skills. **Counseling services:** minority student, career, personal, veteran student, academic, older student, psychological, religious. **For learning-disabled students:** School does not offer a structured program with separate admission and additional fees. Total undergraduates in learning-disabled program or receiving services: 51. Services include: reading machines, tape recorders, videotaped classes, untimed tests, note-taking services, oral tests, readers, extended time for tests, tutors, early syllabus, priority seating, proofreading services, substitution of courses, texts on tape, typist/scribe, exams on tape or computer, take home exams, other testing accomodations. **Library:** Number of titles: 120,345; number of current serial subscriptions: 380. **Information technology resources:** Students are not required to lease or own a computer. Number of campus computers available to all students: 400. School has a wireless network. Approximate number of users that can be accommodated: 150. Proportion of college-owned housing units wired for high-speed internet access: 100%. **Campus safety:** Security services offered: 24-hour foot-and-vehicle patrols, late-night transport/escort service, 24-hour emergency telephones, lighted pathways/sidewalks, controlled dormitory access (key, security card, etc).

TRANSFER AND INTERNATIONAL STUDENTS

Transfer students: May apply for admission for the following academic terms: Fall, Spring, Summer. Applicants do not need a minimum number of credits to apply. For fall 2005: Transfer applications received: 232. Transfer applicants offered admission: 113. Transfer applicants enrolled: 64. **International students:** Number of foreign undergraduates: 23 (2% of student body). Number of countries represented: 15. Minimum TOEFL score required: 500 (paper); 173 (computer). Average TOEFL score: 530 (paper).

Shippensburg University of Pennsylvania

- **Address:** 1871 Old Main Drive, Shippensburg, PA 17257-2299
- **Website:** http://www.ship.edu
- **Public**
- **Enrollment:** 6,175 full-time; 284 part-time

KEY STATS

- ✔ **U.S News College Ranking:** 56, Universities–Master's (North)
- ✔ **SAT Score (25th/75th percentile):** 940-1140
- ✔ **Tuition:** 2005-2006: $6,175 in state, $13,535 out of state

Selectivity: Selective	Room/board: $5,710
Acceptance rate: 66%	Average debt: $17,976
Student/faculty ratio: 20/1	Proportion who borrowed: 67%

UNDERGRADUATE STUDENT BODY STATS

2005-2006 enrollment: 6,175 full-time; 284 part-time. Men: 48%; women: 52%. **Ethnic makeup:** African American: 5%; Asian American: 1%; Hispanic: 2%; White: 92%.

ADMISSIONS FACTS AND FIGURES

Phone: (717) 477-1231. **Email:** admiss@ship.edu. **Website:** http://www.ship.edu. **Application deadlines for fall 2007:** Regular decision: Rolling. Early decision: Not offered. Early action: Send application by: N/A; Decision sent by: N/A. Admission can be deferred. **Application fee:** $30. Common application is accepted. **To apply online, go to:** http://www.ship.edu/admiss/app.html. **Admissions requirements/recommendations:** High school units required (recommended): English: (4); Mathematics: (3); Science: (3); Foreign language: (2); Social studies: (3); Total units: (15). Tests: The college uses SAT or ACT scores in admissions decisions. Either SAT or ACT required. For admission to the fall 2007 entering class, the school will accept: ACT with writing, ACT without writing.

Campus visit: Recommended. Admissions interview: Neither required nor recommended. Off-campus interview: May be arranged. **Factors that count in admissions decisions:** *Academic:* Secondary school record: Very important. Class rank: Very important. Letters of recommendation: Considered. Standardized test scores: Very important. Essay: Considered. *Nonacademic:* Interview: Considered. Extracurricular activities: Considered. Talent/ability: Considered. Character/personal qualities: Considered. Alumni/ae relationship: Not considered. Geographical residence: Not considered. State residency: Not considered. Religious affiliation/commitment: Not considered. Minority status: Not considered. Volunteer work: Considered. Work experience: Considered. **Other schools with the greatest overlap in applicants:** Drexel University; Millersville University of Pennsylvania; Pennsylvania State University–University Park; Towson University; West Chester University of Pennsylvania. **Admissions statistics for the fall 2005 entering class:** Total applicants: 6,281. Total accepted: 4,131. Freshmen enrolled: 1,503; 5% were from out of state. Overall acceptance rate: 66%. Non-early acceptance rate: 66%. **Credentials of fall 2005 freshmen:** 10% ranked in the top 10 percent of their high school class; 30% were in the top 25 percent, and 70% were in the top half. (Proportion submitting class standing: 87%.) **Average high school grade point average:** 3.2. **First-year students who submitted SAT scores:** 100%. Scores (25/75 percentile): Verbal: 470-570, Math: 470-570, Combined: 940-1140. **First-year students submitting ACT scores:** 6%. Scores (25/75 percentile): English: N/A, Math: N/A, Composite: N/A.

ACADEMICS

Year founded: 1871. **Academic calendar:** Semester. **Degrees offered:** certificate, bachelor's, post-bachelor's certificate, master's, post-master's certificate. **Most popular majors:** 17% elementary education and teaching, 7% business administration and management, 7% criminal justice/safety studies, 7% journalism, 6% marketing/marketing management. **Major fields of study:** biological and biomedical sciences; business, management, marketing, and related support services; communication, journalism, and related programs; computer and information sciences and support services; education; English language and literature/letters; foreign languages, literatures, and linguistics; health professions and related clinical sciences; history; mathematics and statistics; multi/interdisciplinary studies; natural resources and conservation; parks, recreation, leisure, and fitness studies; physical sciences; psychology; public administration and social service professions; security and protective services; social sciences; visual and performing arts. **Areas of required coursework:** humanities, mathematics, English (including composition), sciences (biological or physical), history, social science, other. **Pre-professional programs:** pre-law, pre-dentistry, pre-medicine, pre-veterinary science, pre-optometry, pre-pharmacy, other. **Special academic programs:** accelerated program, cooperative (work-study plan) program, cross-registration, distance learning, double major, dual enrollment, exchange student program (domestic), honors program, independent study, internships, study abroad, teacher certificate program, other. **Teacher certification offered in:** early childhood, special education, elementary, secondary. **Cooperative education programs:** art, engineering, health professions. **Reserve Officers Training Corps (ROTC):** Army ROTC: Offered on campus. **Faculty and instruction (2005-2006):** Total instructional faculty: 305 full-time, 66 part-time (56% men; 44% women; 11% minorities). Full-time faculty with Ph.D. or other terminal degree: 87%. Student/faculty ratio: 20/1. Classes of fewer than 20 students: 25%; of 20 to 49 students: 75%; of 50 or more students: 0%. **Advanced Placement and International Baccalaureate credit:** AP tests may be used for: Credit and/or placement. Scores accepted: 3, 4, 5. **Freshmen returning for sophomore year:** 79%. **Graduation rates:** Four-year: 42%; five-year: 61%; six-year: 61%.

COSTS AND FINANCIAL AID

Financial aid office: (717) 477-1131. **Expenses (2005-2006):** Tuition and fees 2005-2006: $6,175 in state, $13,535 out of state; room/board: $5,710. Estimated books and supplies: $1,000; transportation: $750; personal expenses: $2,502. **Financial aid:** Priority filing date for institution's financial aid form: March 30. In 2005-2006, 72% of undergraduates applied for financial aid. Of those, 48% were determined to have financial need; 22% had their need fully met. Average financial aid package (proportion receiving): $6,256 (46%). Average amount of gift aid, such as scholarships or grants (proportion receiving): $3,943 (36%). Average amount of self-help aid, such as work study or loans (proportion receiving): $3,693 (40%). Average need-based loan (excluding PLUS or other private loans): $3,446. Among students who received need-based aid, the average percentage of need met: 69%. Among students who received aid based on merit, the average award (and the proportion receiving): $615 (32%). The average athletic scholarship (and the proportion receiving): $2,287 (4%). Average amount of

debt of borrowers graduating in 2005: $17,976. Proportion who borrowed: 67%.

CAMPUS LIFE AND EXTRACURRICULAR ACTIVITIES

Campus housing available (% using): coed dorms (68%), women's dorms (9%), apartment for single students (23%), special housing for disabled students (0%). Students who live in college-owned, operated, or affiliated housing: 40%. **Clubs and organizations:** Number of student organizations: 251. Activities include: choral groups, concert band, dance, drama/theater, jazz band, literary magazine, marching band, music ensembles, musical theater, radio station, student government, student newspaper, television station, yearbook. Number of fraternities: 11; sororities: 13. Proportion of men in fraternities: 6%; of women in sororities: 8%. Average proportion of students who stay on campus on weekends: 50%. **Sports program (2005-2006):** Member of NCAA II. *Men's intercollegiate varsity sports:* baseball, basketball, cross-country, football, soccer, swimming and diving, track and field (indoor), track and field (outdoor), wrestling. *Women's intercollegiate varsity sports:* basketball, cross-country, field hockey, lacrosse, soccer, softball, swimming and diving, tennis, track and field (indoor), track and field (outdoor), volleyball.

SERVICES AND FACILITIES

Basic services: nonremedial tutoring, women's center, placement service, day care, health service, health insurance. **Remedial assistance:** reading, math, writing, study skills. **Counseling services:** minority student, career, military, personal, veteran student, academic, older student, psychological, other. **For learning-disabled students:** School does not offer a structured program with separate admission and additional fees. Services include: remedial math, remedial English, reading machines, remedial reading, tape recorders, note-taking services, oral tests, learning center, readers, extended time for tests, tutors, other. **Library:** Number of titles: 450,517; number of current serial subscriptions: 1,243. **Information technology resources:** Students are not required to lease or own a computer. Number of campus computers available to all students: 903. School has a wireless network. Approximate number of users that can be accommodated: 3,000. Proportion of college-owned housing units wired for high-speed internet access: 100%. **Campus safety:** Security services offered: 24-hour foot-and-vehicle patrols, late-night transport/escort service, 24-hour emergency telephones, lighted pathways/sidewalks, student patrols, controlled dormitory access (key, security card, etc).

TRANSFER AND INTERNATIONAL STUDENTS

Transfer students: May apply for admission for the following academic terms: Fall, Spring, Summer. Applicants do not need a minimum number of credits to apply. For fall 2005: Transfer applications received: 958. Transfer applicants offered admission: 600. Transfer applicants enrolled: 401. **International students:** Number of foreign undergraduates: 14. Number of countries represented: 17. Minimum TOEFL score required: 550 (paper); 213 (computer).

Slippery Rock University of Pennsylvania

- **Address:** 1 Morrow Way, Slippery Rock, PA 16057-1383
- **Website:** http://www.sru.edu
- **Public**
- **Enrollment:** 6,883 full-time; 531 part-time

KEY STATS

✔ **U.S News College Ranking:** third tier, Universities–Master's (North)
✔ **SAT Score (25th/75th percentile):** 900-1090
✔ **Tuition:** 2006-2007: $6,212 in state, $8,666 out of state

Selectivity: Selective	**Room/board:** $4,796
Acceptance rate: 41%	**Average debt:** N/A
Student/faculty ratio: 19/1	**Proportion who borrowed:** N/A

UNDERGRADUATE STUDENT BODY STATS

2005-2006 enrollment: 6,883 full-time; 531 part-time. Men: 45%; women: 55%. **Ethnic makeup:** African American: 4%; Asian American: 1%; Hispanic: 1%; White: 93%; International: 1%.

ADMISSIONS FACTS AND FIGURES

Phone: (800) 929-4778. **Email:** asktherock@sru.edu. **Website:** http://www.sru.edu. **Application deadlines for fall 2007:** Regular decision: Rolling. Early decision: Not offered. Early action: Not offered. Admission can be deferred. **Application fee:** $25. Common application is accepted. **To apply online, go to:** http://www.sru.edu/pages/5259.asp. **Admissions requirements/recommendations:** High school units required (recommended): English: (4); Mathematics: (3); Science: (3); Foreign language: (2); Social studies: (3); History: (3); Total units: (16). Tests: The college uses SAT or ACT scores in admissions decisions. Either SAT or ACT required. For admission to the fall 2007 entering class, the school will accept: ACT with writing, ACT without writing. Campus visit: Recommended. Admissions interview: Neither required nor recommended. Off-campus interview: Not available. **Factors that count in admissions decisions:** *Academic:* Secondary school record: Very important. Class rank: Very important. Letters of recommendation: Considered. Standardized test scores: Very important. Essay: Considered. *Nonacademic:* Interview: Considered. Extracurricular activities: Considered. Talent/ability: Considered. Character/personal qualities: Considered. Alumni/ae relationship: Considered. Geographical residence: Considered. State residency: Considered. Religious affiliation/commitment: Not considered. Minority status: Considered. Volunteer work: Considered. Work experience: Considered. **Other schools with the greatest overlap in applicants:** California University of Pennsylvania; Clarion University of Pennsylvania; Edinboro University of Pennsylvania; Indiana University of Pennsylvania; University of Pittsburgh. **Admissions statistics for the fall 2005 entering class:** Total applicants: 4,360. Total accepted: 1,777. Freshmen enrolled: 1,455; 10% were from out of state. Overall acceptance rate: 41%. **Size of waiting list:** 1541 applicants; enrolled from waiting list: 376. **Credentials of fall 2005 freshmen:** 8% ranked in the top 10 percent of their high school class; 28% were in the top 25 percent, and 70% were in the top half. (Proportion submitting class standing: 93%.) **Average high school grade point average:** 3.2. **First-year students who submitted SAT scores:** 94%. Scores (25/75 percentile): Verbal: 450-540, Math: 450-550, Combined: 900-1090. **First-year students submitting ACT scores:** 19%. Scores (25/75 percentile): English: 17-23, Math: 17-24, Composite: 18-23.

ACADEMICS

Year founded: 1889. **Academic calendar:** Semester. **Degrees offered:** certificate, bachelor's, post-bachelor's certificate, master's, post-master's certificate, doctorate. **Most popular majors:** 19% education, 14% business, management, marketing, and related support services, 13% parks, recreation, leisure, and fitness studies, 9% health professions and related clinical sciences, 6% communication, journalism, and related programs. **Major fields of study:** biological and biomedical sciences; business, management, marketing, and related support services; communication, journalism, and related programs; computer and information sciences and support services; education; engineering technologies/technicians; English language and literature/letters; foreign languages, literatures, and linguistics; health professions and related clinical sciences; history; mathematics and statistics; multi/interdisciplinary studies; natural resources and conservation; parks, recreation, leisure, and fitness studies; philosophy and religious studies; physical sciences; psychology; public administration and social service professions; social sciences; visual and performing arts. **Areas of required coursework:** arts/fine arts, humanities, mathematics, English (including composition), sciences (biological or physical), history, social science. **Pre-professional programs:** pre-pharmacy, other. **Special academic programs:** cross-registration, distance learning, double major, dual enrollment, exchange student program (domestic), honors program, independent study, internships, liberal arts/career combination, study abroad, teacher certificate program. **Teacher certification offered in:** early childhood, special education, elementary, middle/junior high, secondary. **Cooperative education programs:** art. **Reserve Officers Training Corps (ROTC):** Army ROTC: Offered on campus. **Faculty and instruction (2005-2006):** Total instructional faculty: 367 full-time, 34 part-time (54% men; 46% women; 16% minorities). Full-time faculty with Ph.D. or other terminal degree: 80%. Student/faculty ratio: 19/1. Classes of fewer than 20 students: 25%; of 20 to 49 students: 68%; of 50 or more students: 7%. **Advanced Placement and International Baccalaureate credit:** AP tests may be used for: Credit only. Scores accepted: 3, 4, 5. **Freshmen returning for sophomore year:** 77%. **Graduation rates:** Four-year: 26%; five-year: 48%; six-year: 50%. **Graduate study:** 11% of students pursue further study immediately upon graduation. Fields in which graduates pursue further study: Master of Business Administration (MBA), 3%; law, 3%; medicine, 1%; dentistry, 1%; engineering, 1%; theology (or the seminary), 1%; education, 70%; arts and sciences, 20%; veterinary medicine, 1%.

COSTS AND FINANCIAL AID

Financial aid office: (724) 738-2044. **Expenses (2006-2007):** Tuition and fees 2006-2007: $6,212 in state, $8,666 out of state; room/board: $4,796. Estimated books and supplies: $1,254; transportation: $686; personal expenses: $648. **Financial aid:** Priority filing date for institution's financial aid form: May 1. In 2005-2006, 88% of undergraduates applied for financial aid. Of those, 62% were determined to have financial need; 64% had their need fully met. Average financial aid package (proportion receiving): $6,938 (60%). Average amount of gift aid, such as scholarships or grants (proportion receiving): $3,015 (46%). Average amount of self-help aid, such as work study or loans (proportion receiving): $3,184 (53%). Average need-based loan (excluding PLUS or other private loans): $3,162. Among students who received need-based aid, the average percentage of need met: 81%. Among students who received aid based on merit, the average award (and the proportion receiving): $5,131 (21%). The average athletic scholarship (and the proportion receiving): $2,556 (4%).

CAMPUS LIFE AND EXTRACURRICULAR ACTIVITIES

Campus housing available (% using): coed dorms (80%), women's dorms (11%), apartment for single students (7%), special housing for disabled students (2%). Students who live in college-owned, operated, or affiliated housing: 23%. **Student employment:** During the 2005-2006 academic year, 20% of undergraduates worked on campus. Average per-year earnings: $3,000. **Clubs and organizations:** Number of student organizations: 161. Activities include: choral groups, concert band, dance, drama/theater, jazz band, literary magazine, marching band, music ensembles, musical theater, radio station, student government, student newspaper, student film society, symphony orchestra, television station, yearbook. Number of fraternities: 11; sororities: 8. Proportion of men in fraternities: 5%; of women in sororities: 7%. Average proportion of students who stay on campus on weekends: 50%. **Sports program (2005-2006):** Member of NCAA II. *Men's intercollegiate varsity sports:* baseball, basketball, cross-country, football, golf, soccer, swimming and diving, tennis, track and field (indoor), track and field (outdoor), water polo, wrestling. *Women's intercollegiate varsity sports:* basketball, cross-country, field hockey, soccer, softball, swimming and diving, tennis, track and field (indoor), track and field (outdoor), volleyball, water polo.

SERVICES AND FACILITIES

Basic services: nonremedial tutoring, women's center, placement service, day care, health service, health insurance, other. **Remedial assistance:** reading, math, writing, study skills, other. **Counseling services:** minority student, career, military, personal, veteran student, academic, older student, psychological, birth control, religious. **For learning-disabled students:** School does not offer a structured program with separate admission and additional fees. Total undergraduates in learning-disabled program or receiving services: 355. Services include: reading machines, tape recorders, untimed tests, note-taking services, oral tests, readers, extended time for tests, tutors, priority registration, priority seating, texts on tape, exams on tape or computer, other. **Library:** Number of titles: 503,376; number of current serial subscriptions: 599. **Information technology resources:** Students are not required to lease or own a computer. Number of campus computers available to all students: 1,024. School has a wireless network. Approximate number of users that can be accommodated: 6,750. Proportion of college-owned housing units wired for high-speed internet access: 100%. **Campus safety:** Security services offered: 24-hour foot-and-vehicle patrols, late-night transport/escort service, 24-hour emergency telephones, lighted pathways/sidewalks, student patrols, controlled dormitory access (key, security card, etc).

TRANSFER AND INTERNATIONAL STUDENTS

Transfer students: May apply for admission for the following academic terms: Fall, Spring, Summer. Applicants do not need a minimum number of credits to apply. For fall 2005: Transfer applications received: 987. Transfer applicants offered admission: 675. Transfer applicants enrolled: 567. **International students:** Number of foreign undergraduates: 92 (1% of student body). Minimum TOEFL score required: 500 (paper); 173 (computer).

St. Francis University

- **Address:** PO Box 600, Loretto, PA 15940
- **Website:** http://www.francis.edu/
- **Private; Religious affiliation:** Roman Catholic
- **Enrollment:** 1,255 full-time; 206 part-time

KEY STATS

✔ **U.S News College Ranking:** 62, Universities–Master's (North)
✔ **SAT Score (25th/75th percentile):** 930-1170
✔ **Tuition:** 2006-2007: $22,224

Selectivity: Selective	**Room/board:** $7,640
Acceptance rate: 91%	**Average debt:** $14,500
Student/faculty ratio: 15/1	**Proportion who borrowed:** 90%

UNDERGRADUATE STUDENT BODY STATS

2005-2006 enrollment: 1,255 full-time; 206 part-time. Men: 37%; women: 63%. **Ethnic makeup:** African American: 7%; Asian American: 1%; Hispanic: 1%; White: 90%. **Religious preference:** Roman Catholic: 55%; Protestant: 45%.

ADMISSIONS FACTS AND FIGURES

Phone: (814) 472-3100. **Email:** admissions@francis.edu. **Website:** http://www.francis.edu/. **Application deadlines for fall 2007:** Regular decision: Rolling. Early decision: Not offered. Early action: Not offered. Admission can be deferred. **Application fee:** $30. Common application is accepted. **To apply online, go to:** http://www.applyweb.com/apply/stfrancis/menu.html. **Admissions requirements/recommendations:** High school units required (recommended): English: 4 (4); Mathematics: 2 (2); Science: 1 (2); Foreign language: (2); Social studies: 2 (2); Academic electives: 7 (6); Total units: 16 (19). Tests: The college uses SAT or ACT scores in admissions decisions. Either SAT or ACT required. For admission to the fall 2007 entering class, the school will accept: ACT without writing. Campus visit: Recommended. Admissions interview: Recommended. Off-campus interview: May be arranged. **Factors that count in admissions decisions:** *Academic:* Secondary school record: Very important. Class rank: Very important. Letters of recommendation: Important. Standardized test scores: Important. Essay: Important. *Nonacademic:* Interview: Important. Extracurricular activities: Very important. Talent/ability: Important. Character/personal qualities: Important. Alumni/ae relationship: Considered. Geographical residence: Considered. State residency: Considered. Religious affiliation/commitment: Not considered. Minority status: Not considered. Volunteer work: Important. Work experience: Important. **Other schools with the greatest overlap in applicants:** Duquesne University; Gannon University; Pennsylvania State University–University Park; St. Vincent College; University of Pittsburgh–Johnstown. **Admissions statistics for the fall 2005 entering class:** Total applicants: 1,246. Total accepted: 1,132. Freshmen enrolled: 366; Overall acceptance rate: 91%. **Credentials of fall 2005 freshmen:** 27% ranked in the top 10 percent of their high school class; 29% were in the top 25 percent, and 80% were in the top half. (Proportion submitting class standing: 77%.) **Average high school grade point average:** 3.4. **First-year students who submitted SAT scores:** 88%. Scores (25/75 percentile): Verbal: 460-580, Math: 470-590, Combined: 930-1170. **First-year students submitting ACT scores:** 10%. Scores (25/75 percentile): English: N/A, Math: N/A, Composite: 20-26.

ACADEMICS

Year founded: 1847. **Academic calendar:** Semester. **Degrees offered:** certificate, associate, bachelor's, master's, doctorate. **Most popular majors:** 10% accounting, 9% physician assistant, 7% business administration and management, 6% elementary education and teaching, 6% occupational therapy/therapist. **Major fields of study:** biological and biomedical sciences; business, management, marketing, and related support services; communication, journalism, and related programs; computer and information sciences and support services; education; engineering; English language and literature/letters; foreign languages, literatures, and linguistics; health professions and related clinical sciences; history; legal professions and studies; mathematics and statistics; natural resources and conservation; philosophy and religious studies; physical sciences; psychology; public administration and social service professions; security and protective services; social sciences. **Areas of required coursework:** arts/fine arts, humanities, computer literacy, mathematics, English (including composition), philosophy, foreign languages, sciences (biological or physical), history, social science. **Pre-pro-**

fessional programs: pre-law, pre-dentistry, pre-medicine, pre-veterinary science, pre-optometry, pre-pharmacy. **Special academic programs (% participation):** accelerated program (2%), distance learning (3%), double major (5%), dual enrollment (2%), English as a Second Language (ESL) (1%), exchange student program (domestic) (5%), honors program (8%), independent study (5%), internships (60%), liberal arts/career combination (5%), student-designed major (2%), study abroad (35%), teacher certificate program (10%), weekend college (10%). **Teacher certification offered in:** special education, elementary, secondary. **Cooperative education programs:** engineering, health professions. **Reserve Officers Training Corps (ROTC):** Army ROTC: Offered at cooperating institution (Indiana University of Pennsylvania). **Faculty and instruction (2005-2006):** Total instructional faculty: 87 full-time, 72 part-time (58% men; 42% women; 3% minorities). Full-time faculty with Ph.D. or other terminal degree: 71%. Student/faculty ratio: 15/1. Classes of fewer than 20 students: 53%; of 20 to 49 students: 44%; of 50 or more students: 3%. **Advanced Placement and International Baccalaureate credit:** AP tests may be used for: Credit and/or placement. **Freshmen returning for sophomore year:** 77%. **Graduation rates:** Four-year: 47%; five-year: 59%; six-year: 60%. **Graduate study:** 25% of students pursue further study immediately upon graduation. Fields in which graduates pursue further study: Master of Business Administration (MBA), 8%; law, 6%; medicine, 6%; dentistry, 1%; engineering, 1%; theology (or the seminary), 1%; education, 4%; arts and sciences, 72%; veterinary medicine, 4%.

COSTS AND FINANCIAL AID

Financial aid office: (814) 472-3010. **Expenses (2006-2007):** Tuition and fees 2006-2007: $22,224; room/board: $7,640. Estimated books and supplies: $1,000 personal expenses: $1,250. **Financial aid:** Priority filing date for institution's financial aid form: May 1. In 2005-2006, 94% of undergraduates applied for financial aid. Of those, 84% were determined to have financial need; 41% had their need fully met. Average financial aid package (proportion receiving): $18,573 (84%). Average amount of gift aid, such as scholarships or grants (proportion receiving): $13,427 (83%). Average amount of self-help aid, such as work study or loans (proportion receiving): $6,313 (70%). Average need-based loan (excluding PLUS or other private loans): $5,511. Among students who received need-based aid, the average percentage of need met: 84%. Among students who received aid based on merit, the average award (and the proportion receiving): $12,433 (15%). The average athletic scholarship (and the proportion receiving): $8,053 (10%). Average amount of debt of borrowers graduating in 2005: $14,500. Proportion who borrowed: 90%.

CAMPUS LIFE AND EXTRACURRICULAR ACTIVITIES

Campus housing available (% using): women's dorms (60%), men's dorms (37%), apartment for single students (3%), special housing for disabled students. Students who live in college-owned, operated, or affiliated housing: 75%. **Student employment:** During the 2005-2006 academic year, 3% of undergraduates worked on campus. **Clubs and organizations:** Number of student organizations: 53. Activities include: choral groups, dance, drama/theater, literary magazine, pep band, radio station, student government, student newspaper, television station, yearbook. Number of fraternities: 3; sororities: 3. Proportion of men in fraternities: 4%; of women in sororities: 6%. Average proportion of students who stay on campus on weekends: 60%. **Sports program (2005-2006):** Member of NCAA I. *Men's intercollegiate varsity sports:* basketball, cheerleading, cross-country, football, golf, soccer, tennis, track and field (indoor), track and field (outdoor), volleyball. *Women's intercollegiate varsity sports:* basketball, cheerleading, cross-country, field hockey, golf, lacrosse, soccer, softball, swimming and diving, tennis, track and field (indoor), track and field (outdoor), volleyball.

SERVICES AND FACILITIES

Basic services: nonremedial tutoring, placement service, health service, health insurance. **Remedial assistance:** math, writing, study skills. **Counseling services:** minority student, career, military, personal, veteran student, academic, older student, psychological, religious, other. **For learning-disabled students:** School does not offer a structured program with separate admission and additional fees. Total undergraduates in learning-disabled program or receiving services: 51. Services include: remedial math, remedial English, reading machines, tape recorders, untimed tests, note-taking services, oral tests, learning center, readers, extended time for tests, tutors, priority registration, priority seating, texts on tape. **Library:** Number of titles: 118,132; number of current serial subscriptions: 9,294. **Information technology resources:** Students are required to lease or own a computer. Number of campus computers available to all students: 1,332. School has a wireless network. Approximate number of users that can be accommodated: 800. Proportion of college-owned housing units wired for high-speed internet

access: 99%. **Campus safety:** Security services offered: 24-hour foot-and-vehicle patrols, late-night transport/escort service, 24-hour emergency telephones, lighted pathways/sidewalks, controlled dormitory access (key, security card, etc).

TRANSFER AND INTERNATIONAL STUDENTS

Transfer students: May apply for admission for the following academic terms: Fall, Spring, Summer. Applicants do not need a minimum number of credits to apply. For fall 2005: Transfer applications received: 451. Transfer applicants offered admission: 201. Transfer applicants enrolled: 102. **International students:** Number of foreign undergraduates: 5. Number of countries represented: 2. Minimum TOEFL score required: 500 (paper); 220 (computer).

St. Joseph's University

- **Address:** 5600 City Avenue, Philadelphia, PA 19131
- **Website:** http://www.sju.edu
- **Private; Religious affiliation:** Roman Catholic-Jesuit
- **Enrollment:** 4,247 full-time; 896 part-time

KEY STATS

✔ **U.S News College Ranking:** 9, Universities–Master's (North)
✔ **SAT Score (25th/75th percentile):** 1050-1250
✔ **Tuition:** 2006-2007: $29,095
   Selectivity: More selective   **Room/board:** $10,170
   Acceptance rate: 47%   **Average debt:** $16,120
   Student/faculty ratio: 15/1   **Proportion who borrowed:** 71%

UNDERGRADUATE STUDENT BODY STATS

2005-2006 enrollment: 4,247 full-time; 896 part-time. Men: 47%; women: 53%. **Ethnic makeup:** African American: 8%; Asian American: 3%; Hispanic: 3%; White: 86%; International: 1%. **Religious preference:** Roman Catholic: 69%; Jewish: 1%; Unknown: 16%; Christian/Non-catholic: 9%; Other: 5%.

ADMISSIONS FACTS AND FIGURES

Phone: (610) 660-1300. **Email:** admit@sju.edu. **Website:** http://www.sju.edu. **Application deadlines for fall 2007:** Regular decision: February 1; decision sent by March 15. Early decision: Not offered. Early action: Send application by: November 15; Decision sent by: January 15. Admission can be deferred. **Application fee:** $55. Common application is accepted. **Admissions requirements/recommendations:** High school units required (recommended): English: 4 (4); Mathematics: 3 (4); Science: 2 (4); Foreign language: 2 (4); Social studies: 0 (1); History: 1 (4); Total units: 12 (20). Tests: The college uses SAT or ACT scores in admissions decisions. Either SAT or ACT required. For admission to the fall 2007 entering class, the school will accept: ACT without writing. Campus visit: Recommended. Admissions interview: Neither required nor recommended. Off-campus interview: Not available. **Factors that count in admissions decisions:** *Academic:* Secondary school record: Very important. Class rank: Considered. Letters of recommendation: Important. Standardized test scores: Very important. Essay: Important. *Nonacademic:* Interview: Considered. Extracurricular activities: Important. Talent/ability: Considered. Character/personal qualities: Very important. Alumni/ae relationship: Considered. Geographical residence: Considered. State residency: Not considered. Religious affiliation/commitment: Not considered. Minority status: Considered. Volunteer work: Important. Work experience: Considered. **Other schools with the greatest overlap in applicants:** Loyola College in Maryland; Pennsylvania State University–University Park; University of Delaware; University of Scranton; Villanova University. **Admissions statistics for the fall 2005 entering class:** Total applicants: 9,021. Total accepted: 4,282. Freshmen enrolled: 1,140; 56% were from out of state. Overall acceptance rate: 47%. Non-early acceptance rate: 47%. **Size of waiting list:** 2932 applicants; enrolled from waiting list: 0. **Credentials of fall 2005 freshmen:** 24% ranked in the top 10 percent of their high school class; 78% were in the top 25 percent, and 87% were in the top half. (Proportion submitting class standing: 30%.) **Average high school grade point average:** 3.3. **First-year students who submitted SAT scores:** 99%. Scores (25/75 percentile): Verbal: 520-620, Math: 530-630, Combined: 1050-1250. **First-year students submitting ACT scores:** 2%. Scores (25/75 percentile): English: N/A, Math: N/A, Composite: 22-24.

ACADEMICS

Year founded: 1851. **Academic calendar:** Semester. **Degrees offered:** certificate, associate, bachelor's, post-bachelor's certificate, master's, post-master's certificate, doctorate. **Most popular majors:** 12% marketing/marketing management, 8% finance, 7% English language and literature, 7% special products marketing operations, 6% psychology. **Major fields of study:** area, ethnic, cultural, and gender studies; biological and biomedical sciences; business, management, marketing, and related support services; communication, journalism, and related programs; computer and information sciences and support services; education; English language and literature/letters; foreign languages, literatures, and linguistics; health professions and related clinical sciences; history; legal professions and studies; liberal arts and sciences studies, and humanities; mathematics and statistics; natural resources and conservation; philosophy and religious studies; physical sciences; psychology; public administration and social service professions; social sciences; visual and performing arts. **Areas of required coursework:** arts/fine arts, humanities, mathematics, English (including composition), philosophy, foreign languages, sciences (biological or physical), history, social science, other. **Special academic programs (% participation):** accelerated program (.5%), cooperative (work-study plan) program (2.3%), distance learning (0%), double major (1.9%), dual enrollment (0%), English as a Second Language (ESL) (.5%), honors program (9.4%), independent study (34.3%), internships (10.8%), student-designed major (0%), study abroad (11.2%), teacher certificate program (8.4%), weekend college (0%). **Teacher certification offered in:** special education, elementary, secondary. **Cooperative education programs:** business. **Reserve Officers Training Corps (ROTC):** Army ROTC: Offered at cooperating institution (University of Pennsylvania, Temple University, Drexel University); Navy ROTC: Offered at cooperating institution (Villanova University, University of Pennsylvania); Air Force ROTC: Offered on campus. **Faculty and instruction (2005-2006):** Total instructional faculty: 226 full-time, 328 part-time (60% men; 40% women; 9% minorities). Full-time faculty with Ph.D. or other terminal degree: 98%. Student/faculty ratio: 15/1. Classes of fewer than 20 students: 37%; of 20 to 49 students: 62%; of 50 or more students: 1%. **Advanced Placement and International Baccalaureate credit:** AP tests may be used for: Credit and/or placement. Scores accepted: 4, 5. International Baccalaureate exams may be used for: Credit only. **Freshmen returning for sophomore year:** 89%. **Graduation rates:** Four-year: 68%; five-year: 75%; six-year: 76%. **Graduate study:** 25% of students pursue further study immediately upon graduation; 89% within one year; 100% within five years. Fields in which graduates pursue further study: Master of Business Administration (MBA), 11%; law, 11%; medicine, 11%; education, 19%; arts and sciences, 25%.

COSTS AND FINANCIAL AID

Financial aid office: (610) 660-1556. **Expenses (2006-2007):** Tuition and fees 2006-2007: $29,095; room/board: $10,170. Estimated books and supplies: $1,500; transportation: $0; personal expenses: $2,500. **Financial aid:** Priority filing date for institution's financial aid form: February 15; deadline: May 1. In 2005-2006, 59% of undergraduates applied for financial aid. Of those, 48% were determined to have financial need; 25% had their need fully met. Average financial aid package (proportion receiving): $13,301 (48%). Average amount of gift aid, such as scholarships or grants (proportion receiving): $7,706 (39%). Average amount of self-help aid, such as work study or loans (proportion receiving): $6,240 (48%). Average need-based loan (excluding PLUS or other private loans): $4,890. Among students who received need-based aid, the average percentage of need met: 80%. Among students who received aid based on merit, the average award (and the proportion receiving): $7,176 (22%). The average athletic scholarship (and the proportion receiving): $11,929 (7%). Average amount of debt of borrowers graduating in 2005: $16,120. Proportion who borrowed: 71%.

CAMPUS LIFE AND EXTRACURRICULAR ACTIVITIES

Campus housing available (% using): coed dorms (47%), women's dorms (8%), men's dorms (6%), apartment for single students (38%), other housing options (1%). Students who live in college-owned, operated, or affiliated housing: 59%. **Student employment:** During the 2005-2006 academic year, 16% of undergraduates worked on campus. **Clubs and organizations:** Number of student organizations: 104. Activities include: choral groups, concert band, dance, drama/theater, jazz band, literary magazine, music ensembles, musical theater, pep band, radio station, student government, student newspaper, yearbook. Number of fraternities: 3; sororities: 4. Proportion of men in fraternities: 8%; of women in sororities: 11%. Average proportion of students who stay on campus on weekends: 40%. **Sports program (2005-2006):** Member of NCAA I. *Men's intercollegiate varsity sports:* baseball, basketball, cross-country, golf, lacrosse, soccer, tennis, track and

field (indoor), track and field (outdoor). *Women's intercollegiate varsity sports:* basketball, cross-country, field hockey, lacrosse, rowing, soccer, softball, tennis, track and field (indoor), track and field (outdoor).

SERVICES AND FACILITIES

Basic services: nonremedial tutoring, health service, other. **Remedial assistance:** other. **Counseling services:** minority student, career, personal, academic, psychological, religious. **For learning-disabled students:** School does not offer a structured program with separate admission and additional fees. Total undergraduates in learning-disabled program or receiving services: 76. Services include: reading machines, tape recorders, diagnostic testing service, note-taking services, oral tests, learning center, readers, extended time for tests, tutors, priority seating, proofreading services, texts on tape, exams on tape or computer, take home exams, other testing accomodations, waiver of foreign language degree requirement, other. **Library:** Number of titles: 352,500; number of current serial subscriptions: 8,917. **Information technology resources:** Students are not required to lease or own a computer. Number of campus computers available to all students: 656. School has a wireless network. Approximate number of users that can be accommodated: 216. Proportion of college-owned housing units wired for high-speed internet access: 100%. **Campus safety:** Security services offered: 24-hour foot-and-vehicle patrols, late-night transport/escort service, 24-hour emergency telephones, lighted pathways/sidewalks, controlled dormitory access (key, security card, etc).

TRANSFER AND INTERNATIONAL STUDENTS

Transfer students: May apply for admission for the following academic terms: Fall, Spring. Applicants need a minimum number of credits to apply. For fall 2005: Transfer applications received: 254. Transfer applicants offered admission: 80. Transfer applicants enrolled: 40. **International students:** Number of foreign undergraduates: 62 (1% of student body). Number of countries represented: 33. Minimum TOEFL score required: 550 (paper); 213 (computer). Average TOEFL score: 610 (paper).

St. Vincent College

- **Address:** 300 Fraser Purchase Road, Latrobe, PA 15650-2690
- **Website:** http://www.stvincent.edu
- **Private; Religious affiliation:** Roman Catholic
- **Enrollment:** 1,471 full-time; 105 part-time

KEY STATS

✔ **U.S News College Ranking:** third tier, Liberal Arts Colleges
✔ **SAT Score (25th/75th percentile):** 960-1180
✔ **Tuition:** 2006-2007: $23,000

Selectivity: Selective	**Room/board:** $7,242
Acceptance rate: 73%	**Average debt:** N/A
Student/faculty ratio: 13/1	**Proportion who borrowed:** N/A

UNDERGRADUATE STUDENT BODY STATS

2005-2006 enrollment: 1,471 full-time; 105 part-time. Men: 48%; women: 52%. **Ethnic makeup:** African American: 2%; Asian American: 1%; Hispanic: 1%; White: 94%; International: 1%. **Religious preference:** Protestant: 21%; No preference: 18%; Roman Catholic: 59%; Other: 2%.

ADMISSIONS FACTS AND FIGURES

Phone: (800) 782-5549. **Email:** admission@stvincent.edu. **Website:** http://www.stvincent.edu. **Application deadlines for fall 2007:** Regular decision: May 1. Early decision: Not offered. Early action: Not offered. Admission can be deferred. **Application fee:** $25. Common application is accepted. **Admissions requirements/recommendations:** High school units required (recommended): English: 4 (4); Mathematics: 3 (3); Science: 1 (3); Foreign language: 0 (2); Social studies: 3 (3); History: 0 (0); Academic electives: 5 (5); Total units: 16 (20). Tests: The college uses SAT or ACT scores in admissions decisions. Either SAT or ACT required. For admission to the fall 2007 entering class, the school will accept: ACT with writing, ACT without writing. Campus visit: Recommended. Admissions interview: Recommended. Off-campus interview: May be arranged. **Factors that count in admissions decisions:** *Academic:* Secondary school record: Very important. Class rank: Very important. Letters of recommendation: Considered. Standardized test scores: Important. Essay: Important. *Nonacademic:* Interview: Considered. Extracurricular activities: Considered. Talent/ability:

Considered. Character/personal qualities: Important. Alumni/ae relationship: Considered. Geographical residence: Not considered. State residency: Not considered. Religious affiliation/commitment: Not considered. Minority status: Not considered. Volunteer work: Considered. Work experience: Not considered. **Admissions statistics for the fall 2005 entering class:** Total applicants: 1,488. Total accepted: 1,088. Freshmen enrolled: 483; 10% were from out of state. Overall acceptance rate: 73%. **Credentials of fall 2005 freshmen:** 21% ranked in the top 10 percent of their high school class; 53% were in the top 25 percent, and 86% were in the top half. (Proportion submitting class standing: 86%.) **Average high school grade point average:** 3.5. First-year students who submitted SAT scores: 97%. Scores (25/75 percentile): Verbal: 480-590, Math: 480-590, Combined: 960-1180. **First-year students submitting ACT scores:** 18%. Scores (25/75 percentile): English: 18-24, Math: 18-24, Composite: 19-24.

ACADEMICS

Year founded: 1846. **Academic calendar:** Semester. **Degrees offered:** certificate, bachelor's, post-bachelor's certificate, master's. **Most popular majors:** 11% communication studies/speech communication and rhetoric, 10% psychology, 8% history, 7% biology/biological sciences, 7% business administration and management. **Major fields of study:** biological and biomedical sciences; business, management, marketing, and related support services; communication, journalism, and related programs; computer and information sciences and support services; education; engineering; English language and literature/letters; foreign languages, literatures, and linguistics; health professions and related clinical sciences; history; liberal arts and sciences studies, and humanities; mathematics and statistics; natural resources and conservation; philosophy and religious studies; physical sciences; psychology; public administration and social service professions; social sciences; theology and religious vocations; visual and performing arts. **Areas of required coursework:** arts/fine arts, mathematics, English (including composition), philosophy, foreign languages, sciences (biological or physical), history, social science, other. **Pre-professional programs:** pre-law, pre-dentistry, pre-medicine, pre-theology, pre-veterinary science, pre-optometry, other. **Special academic programs (% participation):** cooperative (work-study plan) program, cross-registration, double major (4%), dual enrollment, honors program, independent study, internships, liberal arts/career combination, study abroad, teacher certificate program. **Teacher certification offered in:** early childhood, elementary, secondary. **Reserve Officers Training Corps (ROTC):** Air Force ROTC: Offered at cooperating institution (University of Pittsburgh). **Faculty and instruction (2005-2006):** Total instructional faculty: 95 full-time, 72 part-time (71% men; 29% women; 1% minorities). Full-time faculty with Ph.D. or other terminal degree: 78%. Student/faculty ratio: 13/1. Classes of fewer than 20 students: 44%; of 20 to 49 students: 56%; of 50 or more students: 0%. **Advanced Placement and International Baccalaureate credit:** AP tests may be used for: Credit and/or placement. Scores accepted: 3, 4, 5. International Baccalaureate exams may be used for: Credit and/or placement. **Freshmen returning for sophomore year:** 86%. **Graduation rates:** Four-year: 59%; five-year: 67%; six-year: 69%. **Graduate study:** 30% of students pursue further study within one year.

COSTS AND FINANCIAL AID

Financial aid office: (724) 537-4540. **Expenses (2006-2007):** Tuition and fees 2006-2007: $23,000; room/board: $7,242. **Financial aid:** Priority filing date for institution's financial aid form: March 1; deadline: May 1. In 2005-2006, 97% of undergraduates applied for financial aid. Of those, 75% were determined to have financial need; 21% had their need fully met. Average financial aid package (proportion receiving): $16,963 (75%). Average amount of gift aid, such as scholarships or grants (proportion receiving): $12,070 (75%). Average amount of self-help aid, such as work study or loans (proportion receiving): $3,477 (56%). Average need-based loan (excluding PLUS or other private loans): $2,905. Among students who received need-based aid, the average percentage of need met: 85%. Among students who received aid based on merit, the average award (and the proportion receiving): $8,933 (20%). The average athletic scholarship (and the proportion receiving): $4,728 (24%).

CAMPUS LIFE AND EXTRACURRICULAR ACTIVITIES

Campus housing available (% using): coed dorms (100%). Students who live in college-owned, operated, or affiliated housing: 73%. **Student employment:** During the 2005-2006 academic year, 37% of undergraduates worked on campus. Average per-year earnings: $794. **Clubs and organizations:** Number of student organizations: 57. Activities include: choral groups, dance, drama/theater, literary magazine, music ensembles, pep band, radio station, student government, student newspaper, television station, yearbook.

Number of fraternities: 0; sororities: 0. Average proportion of students who stay on campus on weekends: 70%. **Sports program (2005-2006):** Member of NAIA. **Men's intercollegiate varsity sports:** baseball, basketball, cross-country, golf, lacrosse, soccer, tennis. **Women's intercollegiate varsity sports:** basketball, cross-country, golf, lacrosse, soccer, softball, tennis, volleyball.

SERVICES AND FACILITIES

Basic services: nonremedial tutoring, placement service, day care, health service. **Counseling services:** career, personal, psychological, religious. **For learning-disabled students:** School does not offer a structured program with separate admission and additional fees. Total undergraduates in learning-disabled program or receiving services: 23. Services include: reading machines, tape recorders, untimed tests, note-taking services, oral tests, learning center, readers, extended time for tests, tutors, priority registration, priority seating, other testing accomodations. **Library:** Number of titles: 372,656; number of current serial subscriptions: 635. **Information technology resources:** Students are not required to lease or own a computer. Number of campus computers available to all students: 228. School has a wireless network. Approximate number of users that can be accommodated: 500. Proportion of college-owned housing units wired for high-speed internet access: 100%. **Campus safety:** Security services offered: late-night transport/escort service, 24-hour emergency telephones, lighted pathways/sidewalks, controlled dormitory access (key, security card, etc).

TRANSFER AND INTERNATIONAL STUDENTS

Transfer students: May apply for admission for the following academic terms: Fall, Spring, Summer. Applicants do not need a minimum number of credits to apply. For fall 2005: Transfer applications received: 144. Transfer applicants offered admission: 85. Transfer applicants enrolled: 57. **International students:** Number of foreign undergraduates: 18 (1% of student body). Number of countries represented: 22. Minimum TOEFL score required: 550 (paper); 213 (computer).

Susquehanna University

- **Address:** 514 University Avenue, Selinsgrove, PA 17870
- **Website:** http://www.susqu.edu
- **Private; Religious affiliation:** Lutheran
- **Enrollment:** 1,894 full-time; 95 part-time

KEY STATS

✔ **U.S News College Ranking:** 104, Liberal Arts Colleges
✔ **SAT Score (25th/75th percentile):** 1050-1230
✔ **Tuition:** 2006-2007: $27,620

Selectivity: More selective **Room/board:** $7,600
Acceptance rate: 81% **Average debt:** $18,414
Student/faculty ratio: 13/1 **Proportion who borrowed:** 81%

UNDERGRADUATE STUDENT BODY STATS

2005-2006 enrollment: 1,894 full-time; 95 part-time. Men: 44%; women: 56%. **Ethnic makeup:** African American: 3%; Asian American: 2%; Hispanic: 2%; White: 93%; International: 1%. **Religious preference:** Roman Catholic: 38%; Protestant: 36%; Jewish: 2%; Lutheran: 17%.

ADMISSIONS FACTS AND FIGURES

Phone: (800) 326-9672. **Email:** suadmiss@susqu.edu. **Website:** http://www.susqu.edu. **Application deadlines for fall 2007:** Regular decision: March 1. Early decision: Send application by: November 15; Decision sent by: December 1. Early action: Not offered. Admission can be deferred. **Application fee:** $35. Common application is accepted. **To apply online, go to:** http://www.susqu.edu/admissions/. **Admissions requirements/recommendations:** High school units required (recommended): English: 4 (4); Mathematics: 3 (4); Science: 3 (4); Foreign language: 2 (3); Social studies: 1 (3); History: 1 (2); Academic electives: 2 (3); Total units: 18 (26). Tests: The college uses SAT or ACT scores in admissions decisions. Neither SAT nor ACT required. For admission to the fall 2007 entering class, the school will accept: ACT with writing, ACT without writing. Campus visit: Recommended. Admissions interview: Recommended. Off-campus interview: May be arranged. **Factors that count in admissions decisions:** *Academic:* Secondary school record: Very important. Class rank: Very important. Letters of recommendation: Important. Standardized test scores: Very important. Essay: Important. *Nonacademic:* Interview: Important.

Extracurricular activities: Important. Talent/ability: Important. Character/personal qualities: Important. Alumni/ae relationship: Considered. Geographical residence: Considered. State residency: Considered. Religious affiliation/commitment: Considered. Minority status: Important. Volunteer work: Important. Work experience: Considered. **Other schools with the greatest overlap in applicants:** Bucknell University; Dickinson College; Gettysburg College; Muhlenberg College; Pennsylvania State University–University Park. **Admissions statistics for the fall 2005 entering class:** Total applicants: 2,217. Total accepted: 1,801. Freshmen enrolled: 512; 43% were from out of state. Accepted through early-decision or early-action plans: 23%. Overall acceptance rate: 81%. Early-decision acceptance rate: 75%. Non-early acceptance rate: 82%. **Size of waiting list:** 89 applicants; enrolled from waiting list: 7. **Credentials of fall 2005 freshmen:** 29% ranked in the top 10 percent of their high school class; 60% were in the top 25 percent, and 89% were in the top half. (Proportion submitting class standing: 71%.) **First-year students who submitted SAT scores:** 89%. Scores (25/75 percentile): Verbal: 520-610, Math: 530-620, Combined: 1050-1230. **First-year students submitting ACT scores:** 8%. Scores (25/75 percentile): English: N/A, Math: N/A, Composite: N/A.

ACADEMICS

Year founded: 1858. **Academic calendar:** Semester. **Degrees offered:** associate, bachelor's. **Most popular majors:** 23% business administration and management, 15% communication studies/speech communication and rhetoric, 7% elementary education and teaching, 7% psychology, 5% biology. **Major fields of study:** biological and biomedical sciences; business, management, marketing, and related support services; communication, journalism, and related programs; computer and information sciences and support services; education; English language and literature/letters; foreign languages, literatures, and linguistics; history; mathematics and statistics; philosophy and religious studies; physical sciences; psychology; social sciences; theology and religious vocations; visual and performing arts. **Areas of required coursework:** arts/fine arts, humanities, computer literacy, mathematics, English (including composition), foreign languages, sciences (biological or physical), history, social science, other. **Pre-professional programs:** pre-law, pre-dentistry, pre-medicine, pre-theology, pre-veterinary science, pre-optometry. **Special academic programs (% participation):** accelerated program (1%), cross-registration (0%), distance learning (7%), double major (8%), dual enrollment (0%), exchange student program (domestic) (4%), honors program (11%), independent study (44%), internships (40%), student-designed major (1%), study abroad (28%), teacher certificate program (13%). **Teacher certification offered in:** early childhood, elementary, middle/junior high, secondary. **Reserve Officers Training Corps (ROTC):** Army ROTC: Offered at cooperating institution (Bucknell University). **Faculty and instruction (2005-2006):** Total instructional faculty: 122 full-time, 65 part-time (56% men; 44% women; 11% minorities). Full-time faculty with Ph.D. or other terminal degree: 90%. Student/faculty ratio: 13/1. Classes of fewer than 20 students: 49%; of 20 to 49 students: 51%; of 50 or more students: 0%. **Advanced Placement and International Baccalaureate credit:** AP tests may be used for: Credit and/or placement. Scores accepted: 4, 5. International Baccalaureate exams may be used for: Credit and/or placement. **Freshmen returning for sophomore year:** 88%. **Graduation rates:** Four-year: 75%; five-year: 80%; six-year: 80%. **Graduate study:** 21% of students pursue further study immediately upon graduation. Fields in which graduates pursue further study: Master of Business Administration (MBA), 1%; law, 3%; medicine, 1%; arts and sciences, 16%.

COSTS AND FINANCIAL AID

Financial aid office: (570) 372-4450. **Expenses (2006-2007):** Tuition and fees 2006-2007: $27,620; room/board: $7,600. Estimated books and supplies: $700; transportation: $235; personal expenses: $700. **Financial aid:** Priority filing date for institution's financial aid form: March 1; deadline: May 1. In 2005-2006, 75% of undergraduates applied for financial aid. Of those, 65% were determined to have financial need; 23% had their need fully met. Average financial aid package (proportion receiving): $18,578 (64%). Average amount of gift aid, such as scholarships or grants (proportion receiving): $14,698 (64%). Average amount of self-help aid, such as work study or loans (proportion receiving): $4,890 (53%). Average need-based loan (excluding PLUS or other private loans): $3,879. Among students who received need-based aid, the average percentage of need met: 81%. Among students who received aid based on merit, the average award (and the proportion receiving): $9,655 (26%). The average athletic scholarship (and the proportion receiving): $0 (0%). Average amount of debt of borrowers graduating in 2005: $18,414. Proportion who borrowed: 81%.

CAMPUS LIFE AND EXTRACURRICULAR ACTIVITIES

Campus housing available (% using): coed dorms (69%), sorority housing (3%), fraternity housing (3%), apartment for single students (14%), special housing for disabled students (1%), special housing for international students (1%), other housing options (9%). Students who live in college-owned, operated, or affiliated housing: 78%. **Student employment:** During the 2005-2006 academic year, 22% of undergraduates worked on campus. Average per-year earnings: $1,500. **Clubs and organizations:** Number of student organizations: 151. Activities include: choral groups, concert band, dance, drama/theater, jazz band, literary magazine, music ensembles, musical theater, opera, pep band, radio station, student government, student newspaper, student film society, symphony orchestra, yearbook. Number of fraternities: 5; sororities: 4. Proportion of men in fraternities: 16%; of women in sororities: 20%. Average proportion of students who stay on campus on weekends: 65%. **Sports program (2005-2006):** Member of NCAA III. *Men's intercollegiate varsity sports:* baseball, basketball, cross-country, football, golf, lacrosse, soccer, swimming and diving, tennis, track and field (indoor), track and field (outdoor). *Women's intercollegiate varsity sports:* basketball, cross-country, field hockey, golf, lacrosse, soccer, softball, swimming and diving, tennis, track and field (indoor), track and field (outdoor), volleyball.

SERVICES AND FACILITIES

Basic services: nonremedial tutoring, women's center, placement service, day care, health service, health insurance. **Counseling services:** minority student, career, personal, academic, older student, psychological, birth control, religious. **For learning-disabled students:** School does not offer a structured program with separate admission and additional fees. Services include: reading machines, tape recorders, diagnostic testing service, untimed tests, note-taking services, learning center, extended time for tests. **Library:** Number of titles: 290,967; number of current serial subscriptions: 15,935. **Information technology resources:** Students are not required to lease or own a computer. Number of campus computers available to all students: 440. School has a wireless network. Approximate number of users that can be accommodated: 800. Proportion of college-owned housing units wired for high-speed internet access: 100%. **Campus safety:** Security services offered: 24-hour foot-and-vehicle patrols, lighted pathways/sidewalks, controlled dormitory access (key, security card, etc).

TRANSFER AND INTERNATIONAL STUDENTS

Transfer students: May apply for admission for the following academic terms: Fall, Spring. Applicants do not need a minimum number of credits to apply. For fall 2005: Transfer applications received: 106. Transfer applicants offered admission: 55. Transfer applicants enrolled: 36. **International students:** Number of foreign undergraduates: 10 (1% of student body). Number of countries represented: 9. Minimum TOEFL score required: 550 (paper); 213 (computer). Average TOEFL score: 600 (paper).

Swarthmore College

- **Address:** 500 College Avenue, Swarthmore, PA 19081
- **Website:** http://www.swarthmore.edu
- **Private**
- **Enrollment:** 1,472 full-time; 7 part-time

KEY STATS

- ✔ **U.S News College Ranking:** 3, Liberal Arts Colleges
- ✔ **SAT Score (25th/75th percentile):** 1350-1530
- ✔ **Tuition:** 2006-2007: $33,232
- **Selectivity:** Most selective   **Room/board:** $10,300
- **Acceptance rate:** 22%   **Average debt:** $12,413
- **Student/faculty ratio:** 8/1   **Proportion who borrowed:** 36%

UNDERGRADUATE STUDENT BODY STATS

2005-2006 enrollment: 1,472 full-time; 7 part-time. Men: 48%; women: 52%. **Ethnic makeup:** African American: 7%; American-Indian: 1%; Asian American: 15%; Hispanic: 10%; White: 61%; International: 6%.

ADMISSIONS FACTS AND FIGURES

Phone: (610) 328-8300. **Email:** admissions@swarthmore.edu. **Website:** http://www.swarthmore.edu. **Application deadlines for fall 2007:** Regular decision: January 2; decision sent by April 1. Early decision: Send application by: November 15; Decision sent by: December 15. Early action: Not offered. Admission can be deferred. **Application fee:** $60. Common application is accepted. **To apply online, go to:** http://www.commonapp.org. **Admissions requirements/recommendations:** High school units required (recommended): English: (4); Mathematics: (3); Science: (3); Social studies: (3); History: (3). Tests: The college uses SAT or ACT scores in admissions decisions. Either SAT or ACT required. For admission to the fall 2007 entering class, the school will accept: ACT with writing. Campus visit: Recommended. Admissions interview: Recommended. Off-campus interview: May be arranged. **Factors that count in admissions decisions:** *Academic:* Secondary school record: Very important. Class rank: Very important. Letters of recommendation: Very important. Standardized test scores: Important. Essay: Very important. *Nonacademic:* Interview: Considered. Extracurricular activities: Important. Talent/ability: Considered. Character/personal qualities: Very important. Alumni/ae relationship: Considered. Geographical residence: Considered. State residency: Not considered. Religious affiliation/commitment: Not considered. Minority status: Considered. Volunteer work: Considered. Work experience: Considered. **Other schools with the greatest overlap in applicants:** Brown University; Harvard University; Princeton University; Stanford University; Yale University. **Admissions statistics for the fall 2005 entering class:** Total applicants: 4,085. Total accepted: 917. Freshmen enrolled: 389; 81% were from out of state. Accepted through early-decision or early-action plans: 40%. Overall acceptance rate: 22%. Early-decision acceptance rate: 50%. Non-early acceptance rate: 20%. **Size of waiting list:** N/A applicants; enrolled from waiting list: 18. **Credentials of fall 2005 freshmen:** 88% ranked in the top 10 percent of their high school class; 95% were in the top 25 percent, and 100% were in the top half. (Proportion submitting class standing: 52%.) **First-year students who submitted SAT scores:** 99%. Scores (25/75 percentile): Verbal: 680-770, Math: 670-760, Combined: 1350-1530. **First-year students submitting ACT scores:** 15%. Scores (25/75 percentile): English: N/A, Math: N/A, Composite: N/A.

ACADEMICS

Year founded: 1864. **Academic calendar:** Semester. **Degrees offered:** bachelor's. **Most popular majors:** 26% social sciences, 13% biological and biomedical sciences, 8% English language and literature/letters, 7% foreign languages, literatures, and linguistics, 7% history. **Major fields of study:** area, ethnic, cultural, and gender studies; biological and biomedical sciences; computer and information sciences and support services; education; engineering; English language and literature/letters; foreign languages, literatures, and linguistics; history; mathematics and statistics; multi/interdisciplinary studies; philosophy and religious studies; physical sciences; psychology; social sciences; visual and performing arts. **Areas of required coursework:** humanities, foreign languages, sciences (biological or physical), social science. **Special academic programs (% participation):** accelerated program (.5%), cross-registration (20.8%), double major (16.3%), exchange student program (domestic) (.5%), honors program (32.9%), independent study (76.8%), internships (1%), student-designed major (10.8%), study abroad (39%), teacher certificate program (2.9%). **Teacher certification offered in:** secondary. **Reserve Officers Training Corps (ROTC):** Army ROTC: Offered at cooperating institution (Widener University); Navy ROTC: Offered at cooperating institution (University of Pennsylvania); Air Force ROTC: Offered at cooperating institution (St. Joseph's University). **Faculty and instruction (2005-2006):** Total instructional faculty: 168 full-time, 27 part-time (58% men; 42% women; 13% minorities). Full-time faculty with Ph.D. or other terminal degree: 100%. Student/faculty ratio: 8/1. Classes of fewer than 20 students: 76%; of 20 to 49 students: 21%; of 50 or more students: 2%. **Advanced Placement and International Baccalaureate credit:** AP tests may be used for: Credit and/or placement. Scores accepted: 4, 5. International Baccalaureate exams may be used for: Credit and/or placement. **Freshmen returning for sophomore year:** 96%. **Graduation rates:** Four-year: 86%; five-year: 91%; six-year: 92%. **Graduate study:** 26% of students pursue further study immediately upon graduation; 27% within one year; 73% within five years. Fields in which graduates pursue further study: Master of Business Administration (MBA), 8%; law, 14%; medicine, 12%; engineering, 3%; theology (or the seminary), 2%; education, 12%; arts and sciences, 48%.

COSTS AND FINANCIAL AID

Financial aid office: (610) 328-8358. **Expenses (2006-2007):** Tuition and fees 2006-2007: $33,232; room/board: $10,300. Estimated books and supplies: $1,048; transportation: $400; personal expenses: $1,020. **Financial aid:** Priority filing date for institution's financial aid form: February 15; deadline: February 15. In 2005-2006, 55% of undergraduates applied for financial aid. Of those, 48% were determined to have financial need; 100% had their

need fully met. Average financial aid package (proportion receiving): $28,914 (48%). Average amount of gift aid, such as scholarships or grants (proportion receiving): $24,980 (48%). Average amount of self-help aid, such as work study or loans (proportion receiving): $4,096 (47%). Average need-based loan (excluding PLUS or other private loans): $3,179. Among students who received need-based aid, the average percentage of need met: 100%. Among students who received aid based on merit, the average award (and the proportion receiving): $31,196 (1%). The average athletic scholarship (and the proportion receiving): $0 (0%). Average amount of debt of borrowers graduating in 2005: $12,413. Proportion who borrowed: 36%.

CAMPUS LIFE AND EXTRACURRICULAR ACTIVITIES

Campus housing available (% using): coed dorms (88%), women's dorms (8%), men's dorms (4%), fraternity housing (0%), special housing for disabled students (0%). Students who live in college-owned, operated, or affiliated housing: 96%. **Student employment:** During the 2005-2006 academic year, 80% of undergraduates worked on campus. Average per-year earnings: $1,700. **Clubs and organizations:** Number of student organizations: 100. Activities include: choral groups, dance, drama/theater, jazz band, literary magazine, music ensembles, opera, radio station, student government, student newspaper, student film society, symphony orchestra, yearbook. Number of fraternities: 2; sororities: 0. Proportion of men in fraternities: 6%; Average proportion of students who stay on campus on weekends: 90%. **Sports program (2005-2006):** Member of NCAA III. *Men's intercollegiate varsity sports:* baseball, basketball, cross-country, golf, lacrosse, soccer, swimming and diving, tennis, track and field (indoor), track and field (outdoor). *Women's intercollegiate varsity sports:* badminton, basketball, cross-country, field hockey, lacrosse, soccer, softball, swimming and diving, tennis, track and field (indoor), track and field (outdoor), volleyball.

SERVICES AND FACILITIES

Basic services: nonremedial tutoring, women's center, placement service, health service, health insurance, other. **Counseling services:** minority student, career, personal, academic, psychological, birth control, religious, other. **For learning-disabled students:** School does not offer a structured program with separate admission and additional fees. Total undergraduates in learning-disabled program or receiving services: 9. Services include: reading machines, tape recorders, videotaped classes, diagnostic testing service, untimed tests, note-taking services, oral tests, readers, extended time for tests, tutors, early syllabus, priority registration, priority seating, proofreading services, texts on tape, exams on tape or computer. **Library:** Number of titles: 762,747; number of current serial subscriptions: 8,191. **Information technology resources:** Students are not required to lease or own a computer. Number of campus computers available to all students: 250. School has a wireless network. Approximate number of users that can be accommodated: 1,000. Proportion of college-owned housing units wired for high-speed internet access: 100%. **Campus safety:** Security services offered: 24-hour foot-and-vehicle patrols, late-night transport/escort service, 24-hour emergency telephones, lighted pathways/sidewalks, controlled dormitory access (key, security card, etc.).

TRANSFER AND INTERNATIONAL STUDENTS

Transfer students: May apply for admission for the following academic terms: Fall. Applicants need a minimum number of credits to apply. For fall 2005: Transfer applications received: 105. Transfer applicants offered admission: 27. Transfer applicants enrolled: 8. **International students:** Number of foreign undergraduates: 92 (6% of student body). Number of countries represented: 36. Average TOEFL score: 613 (paper).

Temple University

- **Address:** 1801 N. Broad Street, Philadelphia, PA 19122-6096
- **Website:** http://www.temple.edu
- **Public**
- **Enrollment:** 20,936 full-time; 3,258 part-time

KEY STATS
✔ **U.S News College Ranking:** third tier, National Universities
✔ **SAT Score (25th/75th percentile):** 1000-1200
✔ **Tuition:** 2006-2007: $10,180 in state, $18,224 out of state

Selectivity: Selective	**Room/board:** $8,230
Acceptance rate: 63%	**Average debt:** $25,493
Student/faculty ratio: 17/1	**Proportion who borrowed:** 71%

UNDERGRADUATE STUDENT BODY STATS
2005-2006 enrollment: 20,936 full-time; 3,258 part-time. Men: 43%; women: 57%. **Ethnic makeup:** African American: 19%; Asian American: 9%; Hispanic: 3%; White: 66%; International: 3%.

ADMISSIONS FACTS AND FIGURES
Phone: (215) 204-7200. **Email:** tuadm@temple.edu. **Website:** http://www.temple.edu. **Application deadlines for fall 2007:** Regular decision: April 1. Early decision: Not offered. Early action: Not offered. Admission can be deferred. **Application fee:** $35. Common application is not accepted. **To apply online, go to:** http://www.temple.edu/ugapp. **Admissions requirements/recommendations:** High school units required (recommended): English: 4 (4); Mathematics: 3 (4); Science: 2 (3); Foreign language: 2 (2); Social studies: 2 (2); History: 1 (2); Academic electives: 1 (3); Total units: 16 (22). Tests: The college uses SAT or ACT scores in admissions decisions. Either SAT or ACT required. For admission to the fall 2007 entering class, the school will accept: ACT with writing, ACT without writing. Campus visit: Recommended. Admissions interview: Neither required nor recommended. Off-campus interview: Not available. **Factors that count in admissions decisions:** *Academic:* Secondary school record: Very important. Class rank: Very important. Letters of recommendation: Considered. Standardized test scores: Important. Essay: Considered. *Nonacademic:* Interview: Not considered. Extracurricular activities: Considered. Talent/ability: Considered. Character/personal qualities: Considered. Alumni/ae relationship: Considered. Geographical residence: Not considered. State residency: Not considered. Religious affiliation/commitment: Not considered. Minority status: Not considered. Volunteer work: Considered. Work experience: Considered. **Other schools with the greatest overlap in applicants:** Drexel University; Pennsylvania State University–University Park; Rutgers–New Brunswick; University of Delaware; University of Pittsburgh. **Admissions statistics for the fall 2005 entering class:** Total applicants: 17,352. Total accepted: 10,989. Freshmen enrolled: 3,871; 29% were from out of state. Overall acceptance rate: 63%. **Credentials of fall 2005 freshmen:** 19% ranked in the top 10 percent of their high school class; 51% were in the top 25 percent, and 89% were in the top half. (Proportion submitting class standing: 71%.) **Average high school grade point average:** 3.3. **First-year students who submitted SAT scores:** 97%. Scores (25/75 percentile): Verbal: 500-600, Math: 500-600, Combined: 1000-1200. **First-year students submitting ACT scores:** 7%. Scores (25/75 percentile): English: N/A, Math: N/A, Composite: 20-24.

ACADEMICS
Year founded: 1888. **Academic calendar:** Semester. **Degrees offered:** certificate, diploma, associate, transfer-associate, terminal-associate, bachelor's, post-bachelor's certificate, master's, post-master's certificate, first professional, first professional certificate, doctorate. **Most popular majors:** 5% biology, 5% psychology, 4% journalism, 4% marketing, 4% teacher education and professional development. **Major fields of study:** agriculture, agriculture operations, and related sciences; architecture and related services; area, ethnic, cultural, and gender studies; biological and biomedical sciences; business, management, marketing, and related support services; communication, journalism, and related programs; computer and information sciences and support services; education; engineering; English language and literature/letters; foreign languages, literatures, and linguistics; health professions and related clinical sciences; history; legal professions and studies; liberal arts and sciences studies, and humanities; mathematics and statistics; multi/interdisciplinary studies; natural resources and conservation; parks, recreation, leisure, and fitness studies; philosophy and religious studies; physical sciences; psychology; public administration and social service professions; security and protective services; social sciences; visual and performing arts. **Areas of required coursework:** humanities, mathematics, English (including composition), sciences (biological or physical), history, social science. **Pre-professional programs:** pre-law, pre-dentistry, pre-medicine, pre-veterinary science, pre-optometry, pre-pharmacy. **Special academic programs:** cooperative (work-study plan) program, cross-registration, distance learning, double major, dual enrollment, English as a Second Language (ESL), exchange student program (domestic), honors program, independent study, internships, liberal arts/career combination, student-designed major, study abroad, teacher certificate program. **Teacher certification offered in:** early childhood, elementary, vo-tech, middle/junior high, adult education, secondary, bilingual/bicultural. **Cooperative education programs:** business. **Reserve Officers Training Corps (ROTC):** Army ROTC: Offered on campus; Navy ROTC: Offered at cooperating institution (University of Pennsylvania); Air Force ROTC: Offered at cooperating institution (Saint Joseph's University). **Faculty and instruction (2005-2006):** Total instructional faculty: 1,225 full-time, 1,491 part-time (61% men; 39% women; 16% minorities). Full-time faculty with Ph.D. or other terminal degree: 77%. Student/faculty ratio: 17/1. Classes of fewer than 20 students: 37%; of 20 to 49 students: 56%; of 50 or more students: 8%. **Advanced Placement and International Baccalaureate credit:** AP tests may be used for: Credit only. Scores accepted: 3. **Freshmen returning for sophomore year:** 83%. **Graduation rates:** Four-year: 27%; five-year: 52%; six-year: 57%.

COSTS AND FINANCIAL AID
Financial aid office: (215) 204-8760. **Expenses (2006-2007):** Tuition and fees 2006-2007: $10,180 in state, $18,224 out of state; room/board: $8,230. **Financial aid:** Priority filing date for institution's financial aid form: March 1. In 2005-2006, 99% of undergraduates applied for financial aid. Of those, 76% were determined to have financial need; 29% had their need fully met. Average financial aid package (proportion receiving): $13,365 (71%). Average amount of gift aid, such as scholarships or grants (proportion receiving): $4,904 (71%). Average amount of self-help aid, such as work study or loans (proportion receiving): $3,504 (62%). Average need-based loan (excluding PLUS or other private loans): $3,514. Among students who received need-based aid, the average percentage of need met: 83%. Among students who received aid based on merit, the average award (and the proportion receiving): $4,603 (24%). The average athletic scholarship (and the proportion receiving): $13,730 (1%). Average amount of debt of borrowers graduating in 2005: $25,493. Proportion who borrowed: 71%.

CAMPUS LIFE AND EXTRACURRICULAR ACTIVITIES
Campus housing available (% using): coed dorms (100%). Students who live in college-owned, operated, or affiliated housing: 20%. **Student employment:** During the 2005-2006 academic year, 14% of undergraduates worked on campus. Average per-year earnings: $1,194. **Clubs and organizations:** Number of student organizations: 120. Activities include: choral groups, concert band, dance, drama/theater, jazz band, literary magazine, marching band, music ensembles, musical theater, opera, pep band, radio station, student government, student newspaper, student film society, symphony orchestra, yearbook. Number of fraternities: 13; sororities: 12. Proportion of men in fraternities: 1%; of women in sororities: 1%. **Sports program (2005-2006):** Member of NCAA I. *Men's intercollegiate varsity sports:* baseball, basketball, cheerleading, crew, football, golf, gymnastics, heavyweight crew, lightweight crew, soccer, tennis, track and field (indoor), track and field (outdoor). *Women's intercollegiate varsity sports:* basketball, crew, cross-country, fencing, field hockey, gymnastics, lacrosse, rowing, soccer, softball, tennis, track and field (indoor), track and field (outdoor), volleyball.

SERVICES AND FACILITIES
Basic services: nonremedial tutoring, placement service, health service, health insurance. **Remedial assistance:** reading, math, writing, study skills. **Counseling services:** career, personal, academic, older student, psychological, birth control. **For learning-disabled students:** School does not offer a structured program with separate admission and additional fees. Total undergraduates in learning-disabled program or receiving services: 746. Services include: remedial math, remedial English, reading machines, remedial reading, tape recorders, other special classes, videotaped classes, diagnostic testing service, untimed tests, note-taking services, oral tests, learning center, readers, extended time for tests, tutors, other. **Library:** Number of titles: 3,059,609; number of current serial subscriptions: 23,567. **Information technology resources:** Students are not required to lease or own a computer. Number of campus computers available to all students: 3,111. School has a wireless network. Proportion of college-owned housing units wired for high-speed internet access: 100%. **Campus safety:** Security serv-

ices offered: 24-hour foot-and-vehicle patrols, late-night transport/escort service, 24-hour emergency telephones, lighted pathways/sidewalks, controlled dormitory access (key, security card, etc.).

TRANSFER AND INTERNATIONAL STUDENTS
Transfer students: May apply for admission for the following academic terms: Fall, Spring. Applicants need a minimum number of credits to apply. For fall 2005: Transfer applications received: 4,437. Transfer applicants offered admission: 3,810. Transfer applicants enrolled: 2,557. **International students:** Number of foreign undergraduates: 708 (3% of student body). Number of countries represented: 105. Minimum TOEFL score required: 525 (paper); 194 (computer).

Thiel College

- **Address:** 75 College Avenue, Greenville, PA 16125
- **Website:** http://www.thiel.edu
- **Private; Religious affiliation:** Lutheran
- **Enrollment:** 1,253 full-time; 67 part-time

KEY STATS
✔ **U.S News College Ranking:** 31, Comp. Coll.–Bachelor's (North)
✔ **SAT Score (25th/75th percentile):** 850-1070
✔ **Tuition:** 2006-2007: $18,720

Selectivity: Less selective	**Room/board:** $7,574
Acceptance rate: 75%	**Average debt:** $20,000
Student/faculty ratio: 17/1	**Proportion who borrowed:** 87%

UNDERGRADUATE STUDENT BODY STATS
2005-2006 enrollment: 1,253 full-time; 67 part-time. Men: 55%; women: 45%. **Ethnic makeup:** African American: 6%; Asian American: 1%; Hispanic: 1%; White: 88%; International: 5%. **Religious preference:** Roman Catholic: 19%; Protestant: 20%; Jewish: 1%; No preference: 49%; Lutheran: 7%; Other: 1%.

ADMISSIONS FACTS AND FIGURES
Phone: (800) 248-4435. **Email:** admission@thiel.edu. **Website:** http://www.thiel.edu. **Application deadlines for fall 2007:** Regular decision: June 30. Early decision: Not offered. Early action: Not offered. Admission can be deferred. **Application fee:** $25. Common application is accepted. **Admissions requirements/recommendations:** High school units required (recommended): English: 4 (4); Mathematics: 2 (2); Science: 2 (2); Foreign language: 2 (2); Social studies: 3 (3); Total units: 16 (16). Tests: The college uses SAT or ACT scores in admissions decisions. Neither SAT nor ACT required. For admission to the fall 2007 entering class, the school will accept: ACT without writing. Campus visit: Recommended. Admissions interview: Recommended. Off-campus interview: May be arranged. **Factors that count in admissions decisions:** *Academic:* Secondary school record: Very important. Class rank: Important. Letters of recommendation: Considered. Standardized test scores: Very important. Essay: Considered. *Nonacademic:* Interview: Very important. Extracurricular activities: Considered. Talent/ability: Considered. Character/personal qualities: Important. Alumni/ae relationship: Not considered. Geographical residence: Not considered. State residency: Not considered. Religious affiliation/commitment: Not considered. Minority status: Not considered. Volunteer work: Considered. Work experience: Considered. **Other schools with the greatest overlap in applicants:** Clarion University of Pennsylvania; Edinboro University of Pennsylvania; Gannon University; Geneva College; Slippery Rock University of Pennsylvania. **Admissions statistics for the fall 2005 entering class:** Total applicants: 2,397. Total accepted: 1,803. Freshmen enrolled: 427; 25% were from out of state. Overall acceptance rate: 75%. **Credentials of fall 2005 freshmen:** 8% ranked in the top 10 percent of their high school class; 24% were in the top 25 percent, and 57% were in the top half. (Proportion submitting class standing: 84%.) **Average high school grade point average:** 3.0. **First-year students who submitted SAT scores:** 77%. Scores (25/75 percentile): Verbal: 420-530, Math: 430-540, Combined: 850-1070. **First-year students submitting ACT scores:** 30%. Scores (25/75 percentile): English: 14-20, Math: 16-22, Composite: 16-22.

ACADEMICS
Year founded: 1866. **Academic calendar:** Semester. **Degrees offered:** associate, bachelor's. **Most popular majors:** 34% business, management, market-

ing, and related support services, 11% psychology, 11% social sciences, 7% education, 6% biological and biomedical sciences. **Major fields of study:** biological and biomedical sciences; business, management, marketing, and related support services; communication, journalism, and related programs; computer and information sciences and support services; education; engineering; English language and literature/letters; health professions and related clinical sciences; history; legal professions and studies; mathematics and statistics; natural resources and conservation; personal and culinary services; philosophy and religious studies; physical sciences; psychology; social sciences. **Areas of required coursework:** arts/fine arts, humanities, mathematics, English (including composition), foreign languages, sciences (biological or physical), history. **Pre-professional programs:** pre-law, pre-dentistry, pre-medicine, pre-theology, pre-veterinary science, pre-pharmacy. **Special academic programs (% participation):** double major (34%), dual enrollment (1%), English as a Second Language (ESL) (1%), honors program (8%), internships (24%), liberal arts/career combination (92%), study abroad (2%), teacher certificate program (12%). **Teacher certification offered in:** elementary, secondary. **Cooperative education programs:** art, business, computer science, humanities, natural science, social/behavioral science. **Faculty and instruction (2005-2006):** Total instructional faculty: 61 full-time, 61 part-time (56% men; 44% women; 3% minorities). Full-time faculty with Ph.D. or other terminal degree: 64%. Student/faculty ratio: 17/1. Classes of fewer than 20 students: 48%; of 20 to 49 students: 51%; of 50 or more students: 1%. **Advanced Placement and International Baccalaureate credit:** AP tests may be used for: Placement only. Scores accepted: 5. **Freshmen returning for sophomore year:** 64%. **Graduation rates:** Four-year: 31%; five-year: 41%; six-year: 37%. **Graduate study:** 16% of students pursue further study immediately upon graduation. Fields in which graduates pursue further study: Master of Business Administration (MBA), 3%; law, 6%; medicine, 5%; dentistry, 1%; engineering, 3%; theology (or the seminary), 5%; education, 6%; arts and sciences, 70%.

COSTS AND FINANCIAL AID
Financial aid office: (724) 589-2178. **Expenses (2006-2007):** Tuition and fees 2006-2007: $18,720; room/board: $7,574. Estimated books and supplies: $800 personal expenses: $2,000. **Financial aid:** Priority filing date for institution's financial aid form: March 15. In 2005-2006, 97% of undergraduates applied for financial aid. Of those, 87% were determined to have financial need; 20% had their need fully met. Average financial aid package (proportion receiving): $13,265 (87%). Average amount of gift aid, such as scholarships or grants (proportion receiving): $9,236 (87%). Average amount of self-help aid, such as work study or loans (proportion receiving): $4,002 (87%). Average need-based loan (excluding PLUS or other private loans): $3,508. Among students who received need-based aid, the average percentage of need met: 75%. Among students who received aid based on merit, the average award (and the proportion receiving): $7,229 (13%). The average athletic scholarship (and the proportion receiving): $0 (0%). Average amount of debt of borrowers graduating in 2005: $20,000. Proportion who borrowed: 87%.

CAMPUS LIFE AND EXTRACURRICULAR ACTIVITIES
Campus housing available (% using): coed dorms (54%), sorority housing (3%), fraternity housing (3%), apartment for single students (10%), other housing options (30%). Students who live in college-owned, operated, or affiliated housing: 81%. **Student employment:** During the 2005-2006 academic year, 4% of undergraduates worked on campus. Average per-year earnings: $1,225. **Clubs and organizations:** Number of student organizations: 35. Activities include: choral groups, concert band, dance, drama/theater, literary magazine, musical theater, pep band, radio station, student government, student newspaper, symphony orchestra, television station, yearbook. Number of fraternities: 3; sororities: 4. Proportion of men in fraternities: 15%; of women in sororities: 18%. Average proportion of students who stay on campus on weekends: 85%. **Sports program (2005-2006):** Member of NCAA III. *Men's intercollegiate varsity sports:* baseball, basketball, cheerleading, cross-country, football, golf, soccer, tennis, track and field (indoor), track and field (outdoor), wrestling. *Women's intercollegiate varsity sports:* basketball, cheerleading, cross-country, golf, soccer, softball, tennis, track and field (indoor), track and field (outdoor), volleyball.

SERVICES AND FACILITIES
Basic services: nonremedial tutoring, health service. **Remedial assistance:** reading, math, writing, study skills. **Counseling services:** minority student, career, academic, psychological. **For learning-disabled students:** School does not offer a structured program with separate admission and additional fees. Total undergraduates in learning-disabled program or receiving services: 41. Services include: remedial math, remedial English, remedial reading, tape

recorders, videotaped classes, untimed tests, note-taking services, oral tests, learning center, readers, extended time for tests, tutors, priority seating. **Library:** Number of titles: 180,708; number of current serial subscriptions: 460. **Information technology resources:** Students are required to lease or own a computer. Number of campus computers available to all students: 220. School has a wireless network. Approximate number of users that can be accommodated: 2,000. Proportion of college-owned housing units wired for high-speed internet access: 100%. **Campus safety:** Security services offered: 24-hour foot-and-vehicle patrols, late-night transport/escort service, 24-hour emergency telephones, lighted pathways/sidewalks, controlled dormitory access (key, security card, etc).

TRANSFER AND INTERNATIONAL STUDENTS

Transfer students: May apply for admission for the following academic terms: Fall, Spring, Summer. Applicants do not need a minimum number of credits to apply. For fall 2005: Transfer applications received: 217. Transfer applicants offered admission: 111. Transfer applicants enrolled: 55. **International students:** Number of foreign undergraduates: 61 (5% of student body). Number of countries represented: 15. Minimum TOEFL score required: 450 (paper); 173 (computer). Average TOEFL score: 485 (paper).

University of Pennsylvania

- **Address:** 3451 Walnut Street, Philadelphia, PA 19104
- **Website:** http://www.upenn.edu
- **Private**
- **Enrollment:** 9,545 full-time; 296 part-time

KEY STATS
✔ **U.S News College Ranking:** 7, National Universities
✔ **SAT Score (25th/75th percentile):** 1340-1520
✔ **Tuition:** 2006-2007: $34,156

Selectivity: Most selective	**Room/board:** $9,804
Acceptance rate: 21%	**Average debt:** $21,133
Student/faculty ratio: 6/1	**Proportion who borrowed:** 41%

UNDERGRADUATE STUDENT BODY STATS

2005-2006 enrollment: 9,545 full-time; 296 part-time. Men: 50%; women: 50%. **Ethnic makeup:** African American: 7%; Asian American: 18%; Hispanic: 6%; White: 60%; International: 9%. **Religious preference:** Roman Catholic: 20%; Protestant: 22%; Jewish: 19%; Muslim: 1%; Hindu: 4%; Buddhist: 2%; No preference: 25%.

ADMISSIONS FACTS AND FIGURES

Phone: (215) 898-7507. **Email:** info@admissions.ugao.upenn.edu. **Website:** http://www.upenn.edu. **Application deadlines for fall 2007:** Regular decision: January 1; decision sent by April 1. Early decision: Send application by: November 1; Decision sent by: December 15. Early action: Not offered. Admission can be deferred. **Application fee:** $70. Common application is accepted. **To apply online, go to:** http://www.admissionsug.upenn.edu/apply-ing/. **Admissions requirements/recommendations:** High school units required (recommended): English: (4); Mathematics: (4); Science: (4); Foreign language: (4); Social studies: (1); History: (3); Total units: (20). Tests: The college uses SAT or ACT scores in admissions decisions. Either SAT or ACT required. For admission to the fall 2007 entering class, the school will accept: ACT with writing. Campus visit: Recommended. Admissions interview: Recommended. Off-campus interview: May be arranged. **Factors that count in admissions decisions:** *Academic:* Secondary school record: Very important. Class rank: Considered. Letters of recommendation: Very important. Standardized test scores: Important. Essay: Very important. *Nonacademic:* Interview: Considered. Extracurricular activities: Important. Talent/ability: Important. Character/personal qualities: Very important. Alumni/ae relationship: Considered. Geographical residence: Considered. State residency: Not considered. Religious affiliation/commitment: Not considered. Minority status: Considered. Volunteer work: Considered. Work experience: Considered. **Other schools with the greatest overlap in applicants:** Harvard University; Massachusetts Institute of Technology; Princeton University; Stanford University; Yale University. **Admissions statistics for the fall 2005 entering class:** Total applicants: 18,824. Total accepted: 3,913. Freshmen enrolled: 2,552; 81% were from out of state. Accepted through early-decision or early-action plans: 46%. Overall acceptance rate: 21%. Early-decision acceptance rate: 34%. Non-early acceptance rate: 18%. **Size of**

waiting list: 1296 applicants; enrolled from waiting list: 35. **Credentials of fall 2005 freshmen:** 94% ranked in the top 10 percent of their high school class; 99% were in the top 25 percent, and 100% were in the top half. (Proportion submitting class standing: 100%.) **Average high school grade point average:** 3.8. **First-year students who submitted SAT scores:** 97%. Scores (25/75 percentile): Verbal: 660-750, Math: 680-770, Combined: 1340-1520. **First-year students submitting ACT scores:** 24%. Scores (25/75 percentile): English: 28-34, Math: 28-34, Composite: 28-33.

ACADEMICS

Year founded: 1740. **Academic calendar:** Semester. **Degrees offered:** associate, terminal-associate, bachelor's, post-bachelor's certificate, master's, post-master's certificate, first professional, first professional certificate, doctorate. **Most popular majors:** 12% finance, 8% economics, 6% history, 5% psychology, 4% nursing/registered nurse training (R.N., A.S.N., B.S.N., M.S.N.). **Major fields of study:** architecture and related services; area, ethnic, cultural, and gender studies; biological and biomedical sciences; business, management, marketing, and related support services; communication, journalism, and related programs; computer and information sciences and support services; education; engineering; English language and literature/letters; foreign languages, literatures, and linguistics; health professions and related clinical sciences; history; legal professions and studies; liberal arts and sciences studies, and humanities; mathematics and statistics; multi/interdisciplinary studies; natural resources and conservation; philosophy and religious studies; physical sciences; psychology; public administration and social service professions; social sciences; visual and performing arts. **Areas of required coursework:** humanities, English (including composition), foreign languages, sciences (biological or physical), social science. **Pre-professional programs:** pre-law, pre-dentistry, pre-medicine, pre-veterinary science. **Special academic programs (% participation):** accelerated program (6%), cross-registration (0%), distance learning (4%), double major (29%), dual enrollment (3%), English as a Second Language (ESL) (1%), exchange student program (domestic), honors program (19%), independent study (33%), internships (78%), liberal arts/career combination (5%), student-designed major (2%), study abroad (27%), teacher certificate program (.2%). **Teacher certification offered in:** elementary, secondary. **Reserve Officers Training Corps (ROTC):** Army ROTC: Offered at cooperating institution (Drexel University); Navy ROTC: Offered on campus; Air Force ROTC: Offered at cooperating institution (St. Joseph's University). **Faculty and instruction (2005-2006):** Total instructional faculty: 1,388 full-time, 602 part-time (64% men; 36% women; 16% minorities). Full-time faculty with Ph.D. or other terminal degree: 100%. Student/faculty ratio: 6/1. Classes of fewer than 20 students: 73%; of 20 to 49 students: 20%; of 50 or more students: 8%. **Advanced Placement and International Baccalaureate credit:** AP tests may be used for: Credit and/or placement. Scores accepted: 5. International Baccalaureate exams may be used for: Credit and/or placement. **Freshmen returning for sophomore year:** 98%. **Graduation rates:** Four-year: 87%; five-year: 93%; six-year: 94%. **Graduate study:** 19% of students pursue further study immediately upon graduation; 30% within one year; 65% within five years. Fields in which graduates pursue further study: Master of Business Administration (MBA), 21%; law, 24%; medicine, 16%; dentistry, 1%; engineering, 5%; theology (or the seminary), 1%; education, 4%; arts and sciences, 14%; veterinary medicine, 1%.

COSTS AND FINANCIAL AID

Financial aid office: (215) 898-1988. **Expenses (2006-2007):** Tuition and fees 2006-2007: $34,156; room/board: $9,804. Estimated books and supplies: $900; transportation: $550; personal expenses: $1,720. **Financial aid:** Priority filing date for institution's financial aid form: February 15. In 2005-2006, 51% of undergraduates applied for financial aid. Of those, 44% were determined to have financial need; 100% had their need fully met. Average financial aid package (proportion receiving): $28,642 (44%). Average amount of gift aid, such as scholarships or grants (proportion receiving): $23,595 (41%). Average amount of self-help aid, such as work study or loans (proportion receiving): $6,360 (44%). Average need-based loan (excluding PLUS or other private loans): $3,699. Among students who received need-based aid, the average percentage of need met: 100%. Average amount of debt of borrowers graduating in 2005: $21,133. Proportion who borrowed: 41%.

CAMPUS LIFE AND EXTRACURRICULAR ACTIVITIES

Campus housing available (% using): coed dorms (67%), sorority housing (2%), fraternity housing (6%), apartments for married students, apartment for single students (22%), special housing for disabled students, special housing for international students (0%), other housing options (3%). Students who live in college-owned, operated, or affiliated housing: 62%.

Student employment: During the 2005-2006 academic year, 39% of undergraduates worked on campus. Average per-year earnings: $1,744. **Clubs and organizations:** Number of student organizations: 376. Activities include: choral groups, concert band, dance, drama/theater, jazz band, literary magazine, marching band, music ensembles, musical theater, opera, pep band, radio station, student government, student newspaper, student film society, symphony orchestra, television station, yearbook. Number of fraternities: 32; sororities: 14. Proportion of men in fraternities: 24%; of women in sororities: 17%. Average proportion of students who stay on campus on weekends: 95%. **Sports program (2005-2006):** Member of NCAA I. *Men's intercollegiate varsity sports:* baseball, basketball, crew, cross-country, fencing, football, golf, lacrosse, lightweight crew, lightweight football, soccer, squash, swimming and diving, tennis, track and field (indoor), track and field (outdoor), wrestling. *Women's intercollegiate varsity sports:* basketball, crew, cross-country, fencing, field hockey, golf, gymnastics, lacrosse, soccer, softball, squash, swimming and diving, tennis, track and field (indoor), track and field (outdoor), volleyball.

SERVICES AND FACILITIES

Basic services: nonremedial tutoring, women's center, placement service, day care, health service, health insurance, other. **Counseling services:** minority student, career, personal, academic, older student, psychological, birth control, religious, other. **For learning-disabled students:** School does not offer a structured program with separate admission and additional fees. Total undergraduates in learning-disabled program or receiving services: 233. Services include: reading machines, tape recorders, other special classes, note-taking services, oral tests, learning center, readers, extended time for tests, tutors, priority seating, texts on tape. **Library:** Number of titles: 5,475,309; number of current serial subscriptions: 43,931. **Information technology resources:** Students are not required to lease or own a computer. Number of campus computers available to all students: 975. School has a wireless network. Approximate number of users that can be accommodated: 12,500. Proportion of college-owned housing units wired for high-speed internet access: 100%. **Campus safety:** Security services offered: 24-hour foot-and-vehicle patrols, late-night transport/escort service, 24-hour emergency telephones, lighted pathways/sidewalks, controlled dormitory access (key, security card, etc).

TRANSFER AND INTERNATIONAL STUDENTS

Transfer students: May apply for admission for the following academic terms: Fall. Applicants need a minimum number of credits to apply. For fall 2005: Transfer applications received: 1,535. Transfer applicants offered admission: 265. Transfer applicants enrolled: 175. **International students:** Number of foreign undergraduates: 921 (9% of student body). Number of countries represented: 111. Minimum TOEFL score required: 550 (paper); 220 (computer).

University of Pittsburgh

- **Address:** 4200 Fifth Avenue, Pittsburgh, PA 15260
- **Website:** http://www.pitt.edu/
- **Public**
- **Enrollment:** 15,100 full-time; 1,924 part-time

KEY STATS

- ✔ **U.S News College Ranking:** 57, National Universities
- ✔ **SAT Score (25th/75th percentile):** 1130-1330
- ✔ **Tuition:** 2005-2006: $11,436 in state, $20,784 out of state

Selectivity: More selective	**Room/board:** $7,430
Acceptance rate: 53%	**Average debt:** $17,051
Student/faculty ratio: 15/1	**Proportion who borrowed:** 63%

UNDERGRADUATE STUDENT BODY STATS

2005-2006 enrollment: 15,100 full-time; 1,924 part-time. Men: 48%; women: 52%. **Ethnic makeup:** African American: 9%; Asian American: 4%; Hispanic: 1%; White: 85%; International: 1%.

ADMISSIONS FACTS AND FIGURES

Phone: (412) 624-7488. **Email:** oafa@pitt.edu. **Website:** http://www.pitt.edu/. **Application deadlines for fall 2007:** Regular decision: Rolling. Early decision: Not offered. Early action: Not offered. Admission can be deferred. **Application fee:** $35. Common application is accepted. **To apply online, go to:**

https://www.admissions.pitt.edu/freshapp/freshman.asp. **Admissions requirements/recommendations:** High school units required (recommended): English: 4; Mathematics: 3; Science: 3 (4); Foreign language: (3); Social studies: 1 (3); History: (2); Academic electives: 4; Total units: 15. Tests: The college uses SAT or ACT scores in admissions decisions. Either SAT or ACT required. For admission to the fall 2007 entering class, the school will accept: ACT with writing. Campus visit: Recommended. Admissions interview: Neither required nor recommended. Off-campus interview: Not available. **Factors that count in admissions decisions:** *Academic:* Secondary school record: Very important. Class rank: Important. Letters of recommendation: Considered. Standardized test scores: Important. Essay: Considered. *Nonacademic:* Interview: Considered. Extracurricular activities: Considered. Talent/ability: Considered. Character/personal qualities: Considered. Alumni/ae relationship: Not considered. Geographical residence: Not considered. State residency: Not considered. Religious affiliation/commitment: Not considered. Minority status: Considered. Volunteer work: Considered. Work experience: Considered. **Other schools with the greatest overlap in applicants:** Boston University; Duquesne University; Pennsylvania State University–University Park; University of Delaware; University of Maryland–College Park. **Admissions statistics for the fall 2005 entering class:** Total applicants: 18,153. Total accepted: 9,654. Freshmen enrolled: 3,249; 21% were from out of state. Overall acceptance rate: 53%. **Size of waiting list:** 226 applicants; enrolled from waiting list: 24. **Credentials of fall 2005 freshmen:** 43% ranked in the top 10 percent of their high school class; 80% were in the top 25 percent, and 98% were in the top half. (Proportion submitting class standing: 79%.) **First-year students who submitted SAT scores:** 99%. Scores (25/75 percentile): Verbal: 560-660, Math: 570-670, Combined: 1130-1330. **First-year students submitting ACT scores:** 20%. Scores (25/75 percentile): English: N/A, Math: N/A, Composite: 24-29.

ACADEMICS

Year founded: 1787. **Academic calendar:** Semester. **Degrees offered:** certificate, bachelor's, post-bachelor's certificate, master's, post-master's certificate, first professional, doctorate. **Most popular majors:** 14% business, management, marketing, and related support services; 12% English language and literature/letters, 11% health professions and related clinical sciences, 11% social sciences, 10% psychology. **Major fields of study:** area, ethnic, cultural, and gender studies; biological and biomedical sciences; business, management, marketing, and related support services; communication, journalism, and related programs; computer and information sciences and support services; education; engineering; English language and literature/letters; foreign languages, literatures, and linguistics; health professions and related clinical sciences; history; legal professions and studies; liberal arts and sciences studies, and humanities; mathematics and statistics; multi/interdisciplinary studies; philosophy and religious studies; physical sciences; psychology; public administration and social service professions; security and protective services; social sciences; visual and performing arts. **Areas of required coursework:** arts/fine arts, humanities, mathematics, English (including composition), philosophy, foreign languages, sciences (biological or physical), history, social science. **Pre-professional programs:** pre-law, pre-dentistry, pre-medicine, pre-pharmacy, other. **Special academic programs:** accelerated program, cooperative (work-study plan) program, cross-registration, distance learning, double major, dual enrollment, English as a Second Language (ESL), exchange student program (domestic), external degree program, honors program, independent study, internships, liberal arts/career combination, student-designed major, study abroad, teacher certificate program, weekend college. **Teacher certification offered in:** early childhood, special education, elementary, secondary. **Cooperative education programs:** engineering. **Reserve Officers Training Corps (ROTC):** Army ROTC: Offered on campus; Navy ROTC: Offered at cooperating institution (Carnegie Mellon University); Air Force ROTC: Offered on campus. **Faculty and instruction (2005-2006):** Total instructional faculty: 1,574 full-time, 583 part-time (59% men; 41% women; 12% minorities). Full-time faculty with Ph.D. or other terminal degree: 92%. Student/faculty ratio: 15/1. Classes of fewer than 20 students: 46%; of 20 to 49 students: 40%; of 50 or more students: 15%. **Advanced Placement and International Baccalaureate credit:** AP tests may be used for: Credit only. Scores accepted: 3, 4, 5. International Baccalaureate exams may be used for: Credit only. **Freshmen returning for sophomore year:** 89%. **Graduation rates:** Four-year: 46%; five-year: 66%; six-year: 70%. **Graduate study:** 34% of students pursue further study within one year; 73% within five years. Fields in which graduates pursue further study: law, 5%; medicine, 3%; dentistry, 1%; engineering, 2%; education, 8%; arts and sciences, 4%.

COSTS AND FINANCIAL AID

Financial aid office: (412) 624-7488. **Expenses (2005-2006):** Tuition and fees 2005-2006: $11,436 in state, $20,784 out of state; room/board: $7,430. Estimated books and supplies: $1,000; transportation: $1,260; personal expenses: $1,500. **Financial aid:** Priority filing date for institution's financial aid form: March 1; deadline: June 1. In 2005-2006, 69% of undergraduates applied for financial aid. Of those, 55% were determined to have financial need; 35% had their need fully met. Average financial aid package (proportion receiving): $11,605 (52%). Average amount of gift aid, such as scholarships or grants (proportion receiving): $4,486 (34%). Average amount of self-help aid, such as work study or loans (proportion receiving): $5,281 (44%). Average need-based loan (excluding PLUS or other private loans): $4,542. Among students who received need-based aid, the average percentage of need met: 76%. Among students who received aid based on merit, the average award (and the proportion receiving): $9,699 (7%). The average athletic scholarship (and the proportion receiving): $16,140 (2%). Average amount of debt of borrowers graduating in 2005: $17,051. Proportion who borrowed: 63%.

CAMPUS LIFE AND EXTRACURRICULAR ACTIVITIES

Campus housing available (% using): coed dorms (73%), women's dorms (10%), sorority housing (2%), fraternity housing (2%), other housing options (13%). Students who live in college-owned, operated, or affiliated housing: 44%. Average per-year earnings: $6,200. **Clubs and organizations:** Number of student organizations: 270. Activities include: choral groups, concert band, dance, drama/theater, jazz band, literary magazine, marching band, music ensembles, pep band, radio station, student government, student newspaper, student film society, symphony orchestra, television station, yearbook. Number of fraternities: 16; sororities: 11. Proportion of men in fraternities: 9%; of women in sororities: 9%. **Sports program (2005-2006):** Member of NCAA I. *Men's intercollegiate varsity sports:* baseball, basketball, cross-country, football, soccer, swimming and diving, track and field (indoor), track and field (outdoor), wrestling. *Women's intercollegiate varsity sports:* basketball, cross-country, gymnastics, soccer, softball, swimming and diving, tennis, track and field (indoor), track and field (outdoor), volleyball.

SERVICES AND FACILITIES

Basic services: nonremedial tutoring, placement service, health service. **Remedial assistance:** math, writing, study skills. **Counseling services:** minority student, career, personal, academic, older student, psychological. **For learning-disabled students:** School does not offer a structured program with separate admission and additional fees. Total undergraduates in learning-disabled program or receiving services: 280. Services include: reading machines, tape recorders, learning center, readers, extended time for tests, texts on tape, other testing accomodations. **Library:** Number of titles: 4,411,596; number of current serial subscriptions: 42,323. **Information technology resources:** Students are not required to lease or own a computer. Number of campus computers available to all students: 650. School has a wireless network. Approximate number of users that can be accommodated: 1,000. Proportion of college-owned housing units wired for high-speed internet access: 100%. **Campus safety:** Security services offered: 24-hour foot-and-vehicle patrols, late-night transport/escort service, 24-hour emergency telephones, lighted pathways/sidewalks, controlled dormitory access (key, security card, etc).

TRANSFER AND INTERNATIONAL STUDENTS

Transfer students: May apply for admission for the following academic terms: Fall, Spring, Summer. Applicants need a minimum number of credits to apply. For fall 2005: Transfer applications received: 1,970. Transfer applicants offered admission: 836. Transfer applicants enrolled: 613. **International students:** Number of foreign undergraduates: 110 (1% of student body). Number of countries represented: 42. Minimum TOEFL score required: 550 (paper); 213 (computer).

University of Pittsburgh—Bradford

- **Address:** 300 Campus Drive, Bradford, PA 16701
- **Website:** http://www.upb.pitt.edu
- **Public**
- **Enrollment:** 991 full-time; 310 part-time

KEY STATS

✔ **U.S News College Ranking:** fourth tier, Liberal Arts Colleges
✔ **SAT Score (25th/75th percentile):** 910-1110
✔ **Tuition:** 2005-2006: $10,538 in state, $20,426 out of state
Selectivity: Less selective **Room/board:** $6,470
Acceptance rate: 76% **Average debt:** $19,313
Student/faculty ratio: 13/1 **Proportion who borrowed:** 85%

UNDERGRADUATE STUDENT BODY STATS

2005-2006 enrollment: 991 full-time; 310 part-time. Men: 40%; women: 60%. **Ethnic makeup:** African American: 4%; American-Indian: 1%; Asian American: 1%; Hispanic: 1%; White: 94%.

ADMISSIONS FACTS AND FIGURES

Phone: (814) 362-7555. **Email:** admissions@www.upb.pitt.edu. **Website:** http://www.upb.pitt.edu. **Application deadlines for fall 2007:** Regular decision: Rolling. Early decision: Not offered. Early action: Not offered. Admission can be deferred. **Application fee:** $35. Common application is accepted. **To apply online, go to:** http://www.upb.pitt.edu/admissions/applying/applying.htm. **Admissions requirements/recommendations:** High school units required (recommended): English: 4 (4); Mathematics: 2 (2); Science: 1 (2); Foreign language: 2 (2); Social studies: 0 (0); History: 1 (1); Academic electives: 5 (5); Total units: 15 (16). Tests: The college uses SAT or ACT scores in admissions decisions. Either SAT or ACT required. For admission to the fall 2007 entering class, the school will accept: ACT with writing, ACT without writing. Campus visit: Recommended. Admissions interview: Recommended. Off-campus interview: Not available. **Factors that count in admissions decisions:** *Academic:* Secondary school record: Important. Class rank: Considered. Letters of recommendation: Considered. Standardized test scores: Important. Essay: Considered. *Nonacademic:* Interview: Important. Extracurricular activities: Considered. Talent/ability: Considered. Character/personal qualities: Considered. Alumni/ae relationship: Considered. Geographical residence: Not considered. State residency: Not considered. Religious affiliation/commitment: Not considered. Minority status: Not considered. Volunteer work: Considered. Work experience: Considered. **Other schools with the greatest overlap in applicants:** Clarion University of Pennsylvania; Edinboro University of Pennsylvania; Edinboro University of Pennsylvania; Mansfield University of Pennsylvania; Mansfield University of Pennsylvania; Pennsylvania State–Erie, The Behrend College; Pennsylvania State–Erie, The Behrend College; University of Pittsburgh–Greensburg; University of Pittsburgh–Greensburg. **Admissions statistics for the fall 2005 entering class:** Total applicants: 592. Total accepted: 449. Freshmen enrolled: 239; 13% were from out of state. Overall acceptance rate: 76%. **Credentials of fall 2005 freshmen:** 11% ranked in the top 10 percent of their high school class; 32% were in the top 25 percent, and 76% were in the top half. (Proportion submitting class standing: 72%.) **Average high school grade point average:** 3.3. **First-year students who submitted SAT scores:** 90%. Scores (25/75 percentile): Verbal: 450-560, Math: 460-550, Combined: 910-1110. **First-year students submitting ACT scores:** 10%. Scores (25/75 percentile): English: 17-21, Math: 18-21, Composite: 19-23.

ACADEMICS

Year founded: 1963. **Academic calendar:** Semester. **Degrees offered:** associate, transfer-associate, terminal-associate, bachelor's. **Most popular majors:** 19% business, management, marketing, and related support services, 17% social sciences, 15% security and protective services, 9% English language and literature/letters, 7% health professions and related clinical sciences. **Major fields of study:** biological and biomedical sciences; business, management, marketing, and related support services; communication, journalism, and related programs; computer and information sciences and support services; education; engineering; English language and literature/letters; health professions and related clinical sciences; mathematics and statistics; parks, recreation, leisure, and fitness studies; physical sciences; psychology; security and protective services; social sciences; visual and performing arts. **Areas of required coursework:** arts/fine arts, humanities, computer literacy, mathematics, English (including composition), philosophy, sciences (biological or physical), history, social science. **Pre-professional programs:** pre-law, pre-dentistry, pre-medicine, pre-veterinary science, pre-optometry, pre-pharmacy, other. **Special academic programs (% participation):** cross-registration (19%), distance learning (57%), double major (25%), dual enrollment (3%), external degree program (0%), independent study (35%), internships (34%), study abroad (0%), teacher certificate program (18%). **Teacher certification offered in:** elementary, secondary. **Reserve Officers Training Corps (ROTC):** Army ROTC: Offered at cooperating institution (St. Bonaventure University). **Faculty and instruction (2005-2006):** Total instructional faculty: 65 full-time, 57 part-time (55% men; 45% women; 10% minorities). Full-time faculty with Ph.D. or other terminal degree: 62%. Student/faculty ratio: 13/1. Classes of fewer than 20 students: 69%; of 20 to 49 students: 30%; of 50 or more students: 2%. **Advanced Placement and International Baccalaureate credit:** AP tests may be used for: Credit and/or placement. Scores accepted: 2, 3, 4. International Baccalaureate exams may be used for: Credit only. **Freshmen returning for sophomore year:** 64%. **Graduation rates:** Four-year: 17%; five-year: 35%; six-year: 41%. **Graduate study:** 24% of students pursue further study within one year. Fields in which graduates pursue further study: Master of Business Administration (MBA), 2%; law, 5%; medicine, 5%; education, 2%; arts and sciences, 10%.

COSTS AND FINANCIAL AID

Financial aid office: (814) 362-7550. **Expenses (2005-2006):** Tuition and fees 2005-2006: $10,538 in state, $20,426 out of state; room/board: $6,470. Estimated books and supplies: $1,000; transportation: $1,260; personal expenses: $1,500. **Financial aid:** Priority filing date for institution's financial aid form: March 1. In 2005-2006, 95% of undergraduates applied for financial aid. Of those, 83% were determined to have financial need; 22% had their need fully met. Average financial aid package (proportion receiving): $12,000 (83%). Average amount of gift aid, such as scholarships or grants (proportion receiving): $4,000 (59%). Average amount of self-help aid, such as work study or loans (proportion receiving): $5,681 (75%). Average need-based loan (excluding PLUS or other private loans): $4,281. Among students who received need-based aid, the average percentage of need met: 78%. Among students who received aid based on merit, the average award (and the proportion receiving): $4,000 (12%). The average athletic scholarship (and the proportion receiving): $0 (0%). Average amount of debt of borrowers graduating in 2005: $19,313. Proportion who borrowed: 85%.

CAMPUS LIFE AND EXTRACURRICULAR ACTIVITIES

Campus housing available (% using): apartment for single students (100%), special housing for disabled students. Students who live in college-owned, operated, or affiliated housing: 51%. **Student employment:** During the 2005-2006 academic year, 20% of undergraduates worked on campus. Average per-year earnings: $1,500. **Clubs and organizations:** Number of student organizations: 47. Activities include: choral groups, dance, drama/theater, literary magazine, radio station, student government, student newspaper. Number of fraternities: 3; sororities: 2. Proportion of men in fraternities: 7%; of women in sororities: 8%. Average proportion of students who stay on campus on weekends: 43%. **Sports program (2005-2006):** Member of NCAA III. *Men's intercollegiate varsity sports:* baseball, basketball, cross-country, golf, soccer. *Women's intercollegiate varsity sports:* basketball, cross-country, golf, soccer, softball, volleyball.

SERVICES AND FACILITIES

Basic services: nonremedial tutoring, placement service, health service. **Remedial assistance:** math, writing, study skills. **Counseling services:** career, military, personal, veteran student, academic, older student, psychological. **For learning-disabled students:** School does not offer a structured program with separate admission and additional fees. Total undergraduates in learning-disabled program or receiving services: 5. Services include: remedial math, remedial English, reading machines, tape recorders, note-taking services, learning center, extended time for tests, tutors, priority seating, proofreading services, substitution of courses, texts on tape, exams on tape or computer, waiver of math degree requirement. **Library:** Number of titles: 92,740; number of current serial subscriptions: 343. **Information technology resources:** Students are not required to lease or own a computer. Number of campus computers available to all students: 123. School has a wireless network. Approximate number of users that can be accommodated: 200. Proportion of college-owned housing units wired for high-speed internet access: 100%. **Campus safety:** Security services offered: 24-hour foot-and-vehicle patrols, late-night transport/escort service, 24-hour emergency telephones, lighted pathways/sidewalks, controlled dormitory access (key, security card, etc).

TRANSFER AND INTERNATIONAL STUDENTS

Transfer students: May apply for admission for the following academic terms: Fall, Spring, Summer. Applicants do not need a minimum number of credits to apply. For fall 2005: Transfer applications received: 160. Transfer applicants offered admission: 120. Transfer applicants enrolled: 95. **International students:** Number of foreign undergraduates: 3. Number of countries represented: 4. Minimum TOEFL score required: 550 (paper); 213 (computer).

University of Pittsburgh–Greensburg

- **Address:** 1150 Mt. Pleasant Road, Greensburg, PA 15601
- **Website:** http://www.upg.pitt.edu/
- **Public**
- **Enrollment:** 1,641 full-time; 155 part-time

KEY STATS
✔ **U.S News College Ranking:** fourth tier, Liberal Arts Colleges
✔ **SAT Score (25th/75th percentile):** 861-1225
✔ **Tuition:** 2005-2006: $10,562 in state, $20,453 out of state

Selectivity: Less selective	**Room/board:** $7,210
Acceptance rate: 89%	**Average debt:** N/A
Student/faculty ratio: 18/1	**Proportion who borrowed:** N/A

UNDERGRADUATE STUDENT BODY STATS

2005-2006 enrollment: 1,641 full-time; 155 part-time. Men: 49%; women: 51%. **Ethnic makeup:** African American: 3%; Asian American: 2%; Hispanic: 1%; White: 94%.

ADMISSIONS FACTS AND FIGURES

Phone: (724) 836-9880. **Email:** upgadmit@pitt.edu. **Website:** http://www.upg.pitt.edu/. **Application deadlines for fall 2007:** Regular decision: August 1. Early decision: Not offered. Early action: Not offered. Admission can be deferred. **Application fee:** $45. Common application is not accepted. **Admissions requirements/recommendations:** High school units required (recommended): English: 4 (4); Mathematics: 2 (4); Science: 1 (2); Foreign language: (3); Social studies: 2 (2); History: 2 (2); Academic electives: 3 (1); Total units: 15 (20). Tests: The college uses SAT or ACT scores in admissions decisions. Either SAT or ACT required. For admission to the fall 2007 entering class, the school will accept: ACT with writing. Campus visit: Recommended. Admissions interview: Recommended. Off-campus interview: Not available. **Factors that count in admissions decisions:** *Academic:* Secondary school record: Very important. Class rank: Very important. Letters of recommendation: Considered. Standardized test scores: Important. Essay: Considered. *Nonacademic:* Interview: Important. Extracurricular activities: Considered. Talent/ability: Considered. Character/personal qualities: Considered. Alumni/ae relationship: Not considered. Geographical residence: Not considered. State residency: Not considered. Religious affiliation/commitment: Not considered. Minority status: Not considered. Volunteer work: Considered. Work experience: Not considered. **Other schools with the greatest overlap in applicants:** California University of Pennsylvania; Indiana University of Pennsylvania; Pennsylvania State University–University Park; University of Pittsburgh; University of Pittsburgh–Johnstown. **Admissions statistics for the fall 2005 entering class:** Total applicants: 1,580. Total accepted: 1,408. Freshmen enrolled: 424; 2% were from out of state. Overall acceptance rate: 89%. **Credentials of fall 2005 freshmen:** 9% ranked in the top 10 percent of their high school class; 33% were in the top 25 percent, and 76% were in the top half. (Proportion submitting class standing: 83%.) **First-year students who submitted SAT scores:** 99%. Scores (25/75 percentile): Verbal: 429-611, Math: 432-614, Combined: 861-1225. **First-year students submitting ACT scores:** 7%. Scores (25/75 percentile): English: 17-27, Math: 16-27, Composite: 15-26.

ACADEMICS

Year founded: 1963. **Academic calendar:** Semester. **Degrees offered:** certificate, bachelor's. **Most popular majors:** 25% business, management, marketing, and related support services, 21% social sciences, 20% psychology, 8% English language and literature/letters, 6% communications technologies/technicians and support services. **Major fields of study:** biological and biomedical sciences; business, management, marketing, and related support services; English language and literature/letters; history; liberal arts and sciences studies, and humanities; mathematics and statistics; multi/interdisciplinary studies; security and protective services; social sciences. **Areas of required coursework:** arts/fine arts, humanities, computer literacy, mathematics, English (including composition), philosophy, foreign languages, sciences (biological or physical), history, social science. **Pre-professional programs:** pre-law, pre-dentistry, pre-medicine, pre-veterinary science, pre-optometry, pre-pharmacy. **Special academic programs:** cross-registration, double major, dual enrollment, independent study, internships, liberal arts/career combination, student-designed major, study abroad. **Reserve Officers Training Corps (ROTC):** Army ROTC: Offered on campus; Air Force ROTC: Offered at cooperating institution (University of Pittsburgh, Oakland). **Faculty and instruction (2005-2006):** Total instructional faculty: 76 full-time, 62 part-time (52% men; 48% women; 10% minorities). Full-time faculty with Ph.D. or other terminal degree: 82%. Student/faculty ratio: 18/1. Classes of fewer than 20 students: 35%; of 20 to 49 students: 57%; of 50 or more students: 8%. **Advanced Placement and International Baccalaureate credit:** AP tests may be used for: Credit only. Scores accepted: 3, 4, 5. International Baccalaureate exams may be used for: Credit only. **Freshmen returning for sophomore year:** 75%. **Graduation rates:** Six-year: 47%. **Graduate study:** 24% of students pursue further study immediately upon graduation; 50% within five years. Fields in which graduates pursue further study: law, 1%; education, 46%.

COSTS AND FINANCIAL AID

Financial aid office: (724) 836-9881. **Expenses (2005-2006):** Tuition and fees 2005-2006: $10,562 in state, $20,453 out of state; room/board: $7,210. Estimated books and supplies: $1,000; transportation: $1,100; personal expenses: $1,500. **Financial aid:** Priority filing date for institution's financial aid form: March 1; deadline: May 1. In 2005-2006, 100% of undergraduates applied for financial aid. Of those, 84% were determined to have financial need; 30% had their need fully met. Average financial aid package (proportion receiving): $7,063 (77%). Average amount of gift aid, such as scholarships or grants (proportion receiving): $3,970 (51%). Average amount of self-help aid, such as work study or loans (proportion receiving): $3,666 (76%). Average need-based loan (excluding PLUS or other private loans): $3,661. Among students who received need-based aid, the average percentage of need met: 54%. Among students who received aid based on merit, the average award (and the proportion receiving): $2,676 (2%). The average athletic scholarship (and the proportion receiving): $0 (0%).

CAMPUS LIFE AND EXTRACURRICULAR ACTIVITIES

Campus housing available (% using): coed dorms (53%), apartment for single students (44%), special housing for disabled students (1%), special housing for international students (2%). Students who live in college-owned, operated, or affiliated housing: 36%. **Student employment:** During the 2005-2006 academic year, 5% of undergraduates worked on campus. Average per-year earnings: $2,250. **Clubs and organizations:** Number of student organizations: 35. Activities include: choral groups, concert band, dance, drama/theater, literary magazine, music ensembles, musical theater, pep band, student government, student newspaper. Number of fraternities: 0; sororities: 0. Average proportion of students who stay on campus on weekends: 45%. **Sports program (2005-2006):** Member of NCAA III. *Men's intercollegiate varsity sports:* baseball, basketball, cross-country, golf, soccer, tennis. *Women's intercollegiate varsity sports:* basketball, cross-country, golf, soccer, softball, volleyball.

SERVICES AND FACILITIES

Basic services: nonremedial tutoring, placement service, health service. **Remedial assistance:** reading, math, writing, study skills. **Counseling services:** minority student, career, personal, academic, psychological, birth control. **For learning-disabled students:** School does not offer a structured program with separate admission and additional fees. Total undergraduates in learning-disabled program or receiving services: 10. Services include: remedial math, remedial English, reading machines, tape recorders, note-taking services, learning center, readers, extended time for tests, tutors, priority registration, priority seating, texts on tape, other testing accomodations. **Library:** Number of titles: 75,600; number of current serial subscriptions: 350. **Information technology resources:** Students are not required to lease or own a computer. Number of campus computers available to all students: 375. School has a wireless network. Approximate number of users that can be accommodated: 20. Proportion of college-owned housing units wired for high-speed internet access: 100%. **Campus safety:** Security services offered: 24-hour foot-and-vehicle patrols, late-night transport/escort service, 24-hour emergency telephones, lighted pathways/sidewalks, controlled dormitory access (key, security card, etc).

TRANSFER AND INTERNATIONAL STUDENTS

Transfer students: May apply for admission for the following academic terms: Fall, Spring, Summer. Applicants do not need a minimum number of credits to apply. For fall 2005: Transfer applications received: 224. Transfer applicants offered admission: 189. Transfer applicants enrolled: 131. **International students:** Number of foreign undergraduates: 0. Number of countries represented: 3. Minimum TOEFL score required: 550 (paper); 220 (computer).

University of Pittsburgh–Johnstown

- **Address:** 450 Schoolhouse Road, Johnstown, PA 15904
- **Website:** http://www.upj.pitt.edu
- **Public**
- **Enrollment:** 2,915 full-time; 258 part-time

KEY STATS

✔ **U.S News College Ranking:** 29, Comp. Coll.–Bachelor's (North)
✔ **SAT Score (25th/75th percentile):** 940-1130
✔ **Tuition:** 2005-2006: $10,540 in state, $20,428 out of state
Selectivity: Less selective   **Room/board:** $6,240
Acceptance rate: 85%   **Average debt:** $22,362
Student/faculty ratio: 19/1   **Proportion who borrowed:** 89%

UNDERGRADUATE STUDENT BODY STATS

2005-2006 enrollment: 2,915 full-time; 258 part-time. Men: 51%; women: 49%. **Ethnic makeup:** African American: 1%; Asian American: 1%; White: 97%.

ADMISSIONS FACTS AND FIGURES

Phone: (800) 765-4875. **Email:** upjadmit@pitt.edu. **Website:** http://www.upj.pitt.edu. **Application deadlines for fall 2007:** Regular decision: Rolling. Early decision: Not offered. Early action: Not offered. Admission can be deferred. **Application fee:** $35. Common application is not accepted. **Admissions requirements/recommendations:** High school units required (recommended): English: 4; Mathematics: 2 (3); Science: 2; Foreign language: 2; Social studies: 4; Total units: 15. Tests: The college uses SAT or ACT scores in admissions decisions. Either SAT or ACT required. For admission to the fall 2007 entering class, the school will accept: ACT without writing. Campus visit: Recommended. Admissions interview: Recommended. Off-campus interview: Not available. **Factors that count in admissions decisions:** *Academic:* Secondary school record: Very important. Class rank: Very important. Letters of recommendation: Considered. Standardized test scores: Important. Essay: Considered. *Nonacademic:* Interview: Important. Extracurricular activities: Considered. Talent/ability: Considered. Character/personal qualities: Considered. Alumni/ae relationship: Not considered. Geographical residence: Not considered. State residency: Not considered. Religious affiliation/commitment: Not considered. Minority status: Considered. Volunteer work: Considered. Work experience: Considered. **Other schools with the greatest overlap in applicants:** Clarion University of Pennsylvania; Duquesne University; Indiana University of Pennsylvania; Pennsylvania State University–University Park; Slippery Rock University of Pennsylvania. **Admissions statistics for the fall 2005 entering class:** Total applicants: 2,589. Total accepted: 2,189. Freshmen enrolled: 822; 1% were from out of state. Overall acceptance rate: 85%. **Credentials of fall 2005 freshmen:** 13% ranked in the top 10 percent of their high school class; 34% were in the top 25 percent, and 70% were in the top half. (Proportion submitting class standing: 74%.) **Average high school grade point average:** 3.3. **First-year students who submitted SAT scores:** 94%. Scores (25/75 percentile): Verbal: 470-560, Math: 470-570, Combined: 940-1130. **First-year students submitting ACT scores:** 7%. Scores (25/75 percentile): English: 17-22, Math: 17-25, Composite: 18-23.

ACADEMICS

Year founded: 1927. **Academic calendar:** Semester. **Degrees offered:** certificate, associate, bachelor's. **Most popular majors:** 21% business, management, marketing, and related support services, 16% education, 14% social sciences, 11% engineering technologies/technicians, 9% communication, journalism, and related programs. **Major fields of study:** area, ethnic, cultural, and gender studies; biological and biomedical sciences; business, management, marketing, and related support services; communication, journalism, and related programs; computer and information sciences and support services; education; engineering technologies/technicians; English language and literature/letters; health professions and related clinical sciences; history; legal professions and studies; liberal arts and sciences studies, and humanities; mathematics and statistics; natural resources and conservation; physical sciences; psychology; social sciences; visual and performing arts. **Areas of required coursework:** humanities, mathematics, English (including composition), sciences (biological or physical), history, social science. **Pre-professional programs:** pre-law, pre-dentistry, pre-medicine, pre-theology, pre-veterinary science, pre-optometry, pre-pharmacy, other. **Special academic programs:** accelerated program, cooperative (work-study plan) program, cross-registration, distance learning, double major, dual enrollment, independent study, internships, liberal arts/career combination, student-designed major, study abroad, teacher certificate program. **Teacher certification offered in:** elementary, middle/junior high, secondary. **Cooperative education programs:** engineering. **Faculty and instruction (2005-2006):** Total instructional faculty: 139 full-time, 51 part-time (64% men; 36% women; 6% minorities). Full-time faculty with Ph.D. or other terminal degree: 69%. Student/faculty ratio: 19/1. Classes of fewer than 20 students: 28%; of 20 to 49 students: 68%; of 50 or more students: 4%. **Advanced Placement and International Baccalaureate credit:** AP tests may be used for: Credit and/or placement. Scores accepted: 3, 4, 5. International Baccalaureate exams may be used for: Credit and/or placement. **Freshmen returning for sophomore year:** 77%. **Graduation rates:** Four-year: 36%; five-year: 53%; six-year: 60%. **Graduate study:** 15% of students pursue further study within one year. Fields in which graduates pursue further study: Master of Business Administration (MBA), 5%; law, 5%; medicine, 8%; dentistry, 2%; engineering, 5%; education, 58%; arts and sciences, 17%.

COSTS AND FINANCIAL AID
Financial aid office: (814) 269-7045. **Expenses (2005-2006):** Tuition and fees 2005-2006: $10,540 in state; $20,428 out of state; room/board: $6,240. Estimated books and supplies: $1,000; transportation: $1,260; personal expenses: $1,500. **Financial aid:** Priority filing date for institution's financial aid form: April 1. In 2005-2006, 94% of undergraduates applied for financial aid. Of those, 81% were determined to have financial need; 6% had their need fully met. Average financial aid package (proportion receiving): $9,214 (75%). Average amount of gift aid, such as scholarships or grants (proportion receiving): $4,175 (63%). Average amount of self-help aid, such as work study or loans (proportion receiving): $3,882 (69%). Average need-based loan (excluding PLUS or other private loans): $3,034. Among students who received need-based aid, the average percentage of need met: 54%. Among students who received aid based on merit, the average award (and the proportion receiving): $2,806 (3%). The average athletic scholarship (and the proportion receiving): $5,451 (2%). Average amount of debt of borrowers graduating in 2005: $22,362. Proportion who borrowed: 89%.

CAMPUS LIFE AND EXTRACURRICULAR ACTIVITIES
Campus housing available (% using): coed dorms (52%), sorority housing (3%), fraternity housing (4%), apartment for single students (29%), special housing for disabled students, other housing options (12%). Students who live in college-owned, operated, or affiliated housing: 67%. **Student employment:** During the 2005-2006 academic year, 9% of undergraduates worked on campus. Average per-year earnings: $1,834. **Clubs and organizations:** Number of student organizations: 70. Activities include: choral groups, concert band, dance, drama/theater, literary magazine, music ensembles, musical theater, radio station, student government, student newspaper, television station, yearbook. Number of fraternities: 4; sororities: 3. Proportion of men in fraternities: 3%; of women in sororities: 3%. Average proportion of students who stay on campus on weekends: 55%. **Sports program (2005-2006):** Member of NCAA II. *Men's intercollegiate varsity sports:* baseball, basketball, golf, soccer, wrestling. *Women's intercollegiate varsity sports:* basketball, cross-country, golf, soccer, track and field (outdoor), volleyball.

SERVICES AND FACILITIES
Basic services: nonremedial tutoring, health service. **Remedial assistance:** math, study skills. **Counseling services:** minority student, personal, academic, psychological, religious. **For learning-disabled students:** School does not offer a structured program with separate admission and additional fees. Services include: remedial math, reading machines, tape recorders, note-taking services, oral tests, learning center, extended time for tests, tutors, priority registration, priority seating, proofreading services, texts on tape, typist/scribe, exams on tape or computer, other testing accomodations, other. **Library:** Number of titles: 153,516; number of current serial subscriptions: 350. **Information technology resources:** Students are not required to lease or own a computer. Number of campus computers available to all students: 200. School does not have a wireless network. Proportion of college-owned housing units wired for high-speed internet access: 100%. **Campus safety:** Security services offered: 24-hour foot-and-vehicle patrols, late-night transport/escort service, 24-hour emergency telephones, lighted pathways/sidewalks, controlled dormitory access (key, security card, etc).

TRANSFER AND INTERNATIONAL STUDENTS
Transfer students: May apply for admission for the following academic terms: Fall, Spring, Summer. Applicants do not need a minimum number of credits to apply. For fall 2005: Transfer applications received: 204. Transfer applicants offered admission: 150. Transfer applicants enrolled: 128. **International students:** Number of foreign undergraduates: 0. Minimum TOEFL score required: 550 (paper); 213 (computer).

University of Scranton

- **Address:** 800 Linden Street, Scranton, PA 18510-4694
- **Website:** http://www.scranton.edu
- **Private; Religious affiliation:** Roman Catholic (Jesuit)
- **Enrollment:** 3,858 full-time; 226 part-time

KEY STATS
✔ **U.S News College Ranking:** 9, Universities–Master's (North)
✔ **SAT Score (25th/75th percentile):** 1030-1200
✔ **Tuition:** 2006-2007: $25,938

Selectivity: Selective	**Room/board:** $10,224
Acceptance rate: 75%	**Average debt:** $23,222
Student/faculty ratio: 12/1	**Proportion who borrowed:** 70%

UNDERGRADUATE STUDENT BODY STATS
2005-2006 enrollment: 3,858 full-time; 226 part-time. Men: 42%; women: 58%. **Ethnic makeup:** African American: 2%; Asian American: 2%; Hispanic: 5%; White: 91%. **Religious preference:** Roman Catholic: 67%; Protestant: 2%; Unknown: 30%; Other: 1%.

ADMISSIONS FACTS AND FIGURES
Phone: (570) 941-7540. **Email:** admissions@scranton.edu. **Website:** http://www.scranton.edu. **Application deadlines for fall 2007:** Regular decision: March 1. Early decision: Not offered. Early action: Send application by: November 15; Decision sent by: December 15. Admission can be deferred. **Application fee:** $40. Common application is accepted. **To apply online, go to:** http://www.scranton.edu/apply. **Admissions requirements/recommendations:** High school units required (recommended): English: 4 (4); Mathematics: 3 (4); Science: 1 (2); Foreign language: 2 (2); Social studies: 2 (2); Academic electives: 0 (0); Total units: 16 (16). Tests: The college uses SAT or ACT scores in admissions decisions. Either SAT or ACT required. For admission to the fall 2007 entering class, the school will accept: ACT with writing, ACT without writing. Campus visit: Recommended. Admissions interview: Recommended. Off-campus interview: Not available. **Factors that count in admissions decisions:** *Academic:* Secondary school record: Very important. Class rank: Very important. Letters of recommendation: Considered. Standardized test scores: Very important. Essay: Considered. *Nonacademic:* Interview: Considered. Extracurricular activities: Important. Talent/ability: Considered. Character/personal qualities: Considered. Alumni/ae relationship: Considered. Geographical residence: Not considered. State residency: Not considered. Religious affiliation/commitment: Not considered. Minority status: Not considered. Volunteer work: Considered. Work experience: Considered. **Other schools with the greatest overlap in applicants:** Loyola College in Maryland; Pennsylvania State University–University Park; St. Joseph's University; University of Delaware; Villanova University. **Admissions statistics for the fall 2005 entering class:** Total applicants: 6,343. Total accepted: 4,777. Freshmen enrolled: 956; 55% were from out of state. Overall acceptance rate: 75%. Non-early acceptance rate: 75%. **Size of waiting list:** 963 applicants; enrolled from waiting list: 128. **Credentials of fall 2005 freshmen:** 26% ranked in the top 10 percent of their high school class; 57% were in the top 25 percent, and 84% were in the top half. (Proportion submitting class standing: 59%.) **Average high school grade point average:** 3.3. **First-year students who submitted SAT scores:** 93%. Scores (25/75 percentile): Verbal: 520-600, Math: 510-600, Combined: 1030-1200.

ACADEMICS

Year founded: 1888. **Academic calendar:** Semester. **Degrees offered:** certificate, associate, bachelor's, post-bachelor's certificate, master's, post-master's certificate, doctorate. **Most popular majors:** 20% business, management, marketing, and related support services, 13% education, 11% health professions and related clinical sciences, 10% communication, journalism, and related programs, 9% social sciences. **Major fields of study:** biological and biomedical sciences; business, management, marketing, and related support services; communication, journalism, and related programs; computer and information sciences and support services; education; engineering; engineering technologies/technicians; family and consumer sciences/human sciences; foreign languages, literatures, and linguistics; health professions and related clinical sciences; history; liberal arts and sciences studies, and humanities; mathematics and statistics; multi/interdisciplinary studies; parks, recreation, leisure, and fitness studies; philosophy and religious studies; physical sciences; psychology; security and protective services; social sciences; visual and performing arts. **Areas of required coursework:** humanities, computer literacy, mathematics, English (including composition), philosophy, sciences (biological or physical), social science, other. **Pre-professional programs:** pre-law, pre-dentistry, pre-medicine, pre-veterinary science, other. **Special academic programs (% participation):** accelerated program, cross-registration (1%), distance learning (23%), double major (16%), dual enrollment (1.5%), exchange student program (domestic) (.1%), honors program (10%), independent study (15%), internships (29%), study abroad (10%), teacher certificate program (18%), other (.4%). **Teacher certification offered in:** early childhood, special education, elementary, secondary. **Reserve Officers Training Corps (ROTC):** Army ROTC: Offered on campus; Air Force ROTC: Offered at cooperating institution (Wilkes University). **Faculty and instruction (2005-2006):** Total instructional faculty: 250 full-time, 173 part-time (59% men; 41% women; 5% minorities). Full-time faculty with Ph.D. or other terminal degree: 85%. Student/faculty ratio: 12/1. Classes of fewer than 20 students: 48%; of 20 to 49 students: 51%; of 50 or more students: 0%. **Advanced Placement and International Baccalaureate credit:** AP tests may be used for: Credit only. Scores accepted: 3, 4, 5. International Baccalaureate exams may be used for: Credit only. **Freshmen returning for sophomore year:** 88%. **Graduation rates:** Four-year: 72%; five-year: 79%; six-year: 80%. **Graduate study:** 35% of students pursue further study within one year. Fields in which graduates pursue further study: Master of Business Administration (MBA), 10%; law, 7%; medicine, 14%; dentistry, 1%; education, 14%; arts and sciences, 54%.

COSTS AND FINANCIAL AID

Financial aid office: (570) 941-7700. **Expenses (2006-2007):** Tuition and fees 2006-2007: $25,938; room/board: $10,224. Estimated books and supplies: $1,000; transportation: $500; personal expenses: $1,100. **Financial aid:** Priority filing date for institution's financial aid form: February 15. In 2005-2006, 77% of undergraduates applied for financial aid. Of those, 67% were determined to have financial need; 16% had their need fully met. Average financial aid package (proportion receiving): $15,912 (66%). Average amount of gift aid, such as scholarships or grants (proportion receiving): $11,493 (63%). Average amount of self-help aid, such as work study or loans (proportion receiving): $5,299 (57%). Average need-based loan (excluding PLUS or other private loans): $4,572. Among students who received need-based aid, the average percentage of need met: 76%. Among students who received aid based on merit, the average award (and the proportion receiving): $7,494 (6%). The average athletic scholarship (and the proportion receiving): $0 (0%). Average amount of debt of borrowers graduating in 2005: $23,222. Proportion who borrowed: 70%.

CAMPUS LIFE AND EXTRACURRICULAR ACTIVITIES

Campus housing available (% using): coed dorms (58%), women's dorms (16%), men's dorms (12%), apartment for single students (14%), special housing for disabled students, special housing for international students. Students who live in college-owned, operated, or affiliated housing: 51%. **Student employment:** During the 2005-2006 academic year, 17% of undergraduates worked on campus. Average per-year earnings: $1,200. **Clubs and organizations:** Number of student organizations: 75. Activities include: choral groups, concert band, dance, drama/theater, jazz band, literary magazine, music ensembles, radio station, student government, student newspaper, television station, yearbook. Number of fraternities: 0; sororities: 0. Average proportion of students who stay on campus on weekends: 65%. **Sports program (2005-2006):** Member of NCAA III. *Men's intercollegiate varsity sports:* baseball, basketball, cross-country, golf, ice hockey, lacrosse, soccer, swimming and diving, tennis, wrestling. *Women's intercollegiate varsity sports:* basketball, cross-country, field hockey, lacrosse, soccer, softball, swimming and diving, tennis, volleyball.

SERVICES AND FACILITIES

Basic services: nonremedial tutoring, women's center, placement service, health service, other. **Remedial assistance:** reading, math, writing, study skills, other. **Counseling services:** minority student, career, personal, academic, older student, psychological, religious, other. **For learning-disabled students:** School does not offer a structured program with separate admission and additional fees. Total undergraduates in learning-disabled program or receiving services: 180. Services include: remedial math, remedial English, reading machines, remedial reading, tape recorders, diagnostic testing service, untimed tests, oral tests, learning center, extended time for tests, tutors, priority registration, priority seating, texts on tape, exams on tape or computer, other testing accomodations. **Library:** Number of titles: 365,501; number of current serial subscriptions: 1,709. **Information technology resources:** Students are not required to lease or own a computer. Number of campus computers available to all students: 900. School has a wireless network. Approximate number of users that can be accommodated: 1,650. Proportion of college-owned housing units wired for high-speed internet access: 100%. **Campus safety:** Security services offered: 24-hour foot-and-vehicle patrols, late-night transport/escort service, 24-hour emergency telephones, lighted pathways/sidewalks, student patrols, controlled dormitory access (key, security card, etc).

TRANSFER AND INTERNATIONAL STUDENTS

Transfer students: May apply for admission for the following academic terms: Fall, Winter, Spring, Summer. Applicants do not need a minimum number of credits to apply. **International students:** Number of foreign undergraduates: 17. Number of countries represented: 9. Minimum TOEFL score required: 500 (paper); 170 (computer).

University of the Arts

- **Address:** 320 S. Broad Street, Philadelphia, PA 19102
- **Website:** http://www.uarts.edu
- **Private**
- **Enrollment:** 2,035 full-time; 44 part-time

KEY STATS

✔ **U.S News College Ranking:** Unranked Specialty School–Fine Arts
✔ **SAT Score (25th/75th percentile):** 930-1170
✔ **Tuition:** 2006-2007: $25,680

Selectivity: Selective	**Room/board:** $6,345
Acceptance rate: 49%	**Average debt:** N/A
Student/faculty ratio: 9/1	**Proportion who borrowed:** 70%

UNDERGRADUATE STUDENT BODY STATS

2005-2006 enrollment: 2,035 full-time; 44 part-time. Men: 45%; women: 55%. **Ethnic makeup:** African American: 10%; Asian American: 3%; Hispanic: 4%; White: 80%; International: 3%.

ADMISSIONS FACTS AND FIGURES

Phone: (215) 717-6049. **Email:** admissions@uarts.edu. **Website:** http://www.uarts.edu. **Application deadlines for fall 2007:** Regular decision: Rolling. Early decision: Not offered. Early action: Not offered. Admission can be deferred. **Application fee:** $60. Common application is accepted. **To apply online, go to:** http://www.uarts.edu/admission/ugrad/apply.cfm. **Admissions requirements/recommendations:** High school units required (recommended): English: 4; Mathematics: (3); Science: (2); Foreign language: (2); Social studies: (2); History: (2); Total units: 4 (13). Tests: The college uses SAT or ACT scores in admissions decisions. Neither SAT nor ACT required. For admission to the fall 2007 entering class, the school will accept: ACT with writing, ACT without writing. Campus visit: Recommended. Admissions interview: Recommended. **Factors that count in admissions decisions:** *Academic:* Secondary school record: Very important. Class rank: Important. Letters of recommendation: Considered. Standardized test scores: Important. Essay: Important. *Nonacademic:* Interview: Very important. Extracurricular activities: Important. Talent/ability: Very important. Character/personal qualities: Important. Alumni/ae relationship: Considered. Geographical residence: Not considered. State residency: Not considered. Religious affiliation/commitment: Not considered. Minority status: Considered. Volunteer work: Considered. Work experience: Considered. **Other schools with the greatest overlap in applicants:** Drexel University; New York University; Pratt Institute; Rutgers–New Brunswick;

Temple University. **Admissions statistics for the fall 2005 entering class:** Total applicants: 2,285. Total accepted: 1,116. Freshmen enrolled: 510; 64% were from out of state. Overall acceptance rate: 49%. **Size of waiting list:** 44 applicants; enrolled from waiting list: 10. **Credentials of fall 2005 freshmen:** 13% ranked in the top 10 percent of their high school class; 32% were in the top 25 percent, and 66% were in the top half. (Proportion submitting class standing: 67%.) **Average high school grade point average:** 2.9. **First-year students who submitted SAT scores:** 98%. Scores (25/75 percentile): Verbal: 480-600, Math: 450-570, Combined: 930-1170. **First-year students submitting ACT scores:** 9%. Scores (25/75 percentile): English: N/A, Math: N/A, Composite: 19-26.

ACADEMICS

Year founded: 1876. **Academic calendar:** Semester. **Degrees offered:** certificate, diploma, bachelor's, master's. **Most popular majors:** 11% dance, 9% crafts/craft design, folk art, and artisanry, 8% graphic design, 8% illustration, 8% photography. **Major fields of study:** communication, journalism, and related programs; education; multi/interdisciplinary studies; visual and performing arts. **Areas of required coursework:** arts/fine arts, humanities, computer literacy, mathematics, English (including composition), sciences (biological or physical), history, social science. **Special academic programs (% participation):** accelerated program, cross-registration, double major (1%), dual enrollment (1%), exchange student program (domestic) (1%), independent study (10%), internships (5%), study abroad (1%), teacher certificate program (10%). **Faculty and instruction (2005-2006):** Total instructional faculty: 118 full-time, 354 part-time (57% men; 43% women; 5% minorities). Full-time faculty with Ph.D. or other terminal degree: 48%. Student/faculty ratio: 9/1. Classes of fewer than 20 students: 78%; of 20 to 49 students: 22%; of 50 or more students: 0%. **Advanced Placement and International Baccalaureate credit:** AP tests may be used for: Credit only. Scores accepted: 4, 5. **Freshmen returning for sophomore year:** 81%. **Graduation rates:** Four-year: 49%; five-year: 55%; six-year: 58%.

COSTS AND FINANCIAL AID

Financial aid office: (215) 717-6170. **Expenses (2006-2007):** Tuition and fees 2006-2007: $25,680; room/board: $6,345. Estimated books and supplies: $2,000; transportation: $801; personal expenses: $1,622. **Financial aid:** Priority filing date for institution's financial aid form: March 1; deadline: March 1. In 2005-2006, 97% of undergraduates applied for financial aid. Of those, 66% were determined to have financial need; 59% had their need fully met. Average financial aid package (proportion receiving): $16,500 (66%). Average amount of gift aid, such as scholarships or grants (proportion receiving): $5,000 (48%). Average amount of self-help aid, such as work study or loans (proportion receiving): $4,000 (66%). Average need-based loan (excluding PLUS or other private loans): $4,000. Among students who received need-based aid, the average percentage of need met: 65%. Among students who received aid based on merit, the average award (and the proportion receiving): $8,300 (30%). Proportion who borrowed: 70%.

CAMPUS LIFE AND EXTRACURRICULAR ACTIVITIES

Campus housing available (% using): coed dorms (100%). Students who live in college-owned, operated, or affiliated housing: 60%. **Student employment:** During the 2005-2006 academic year, 0% of undergraduates worked on campus. **Clubs and organizations:** Number of student organizations: 5. Activities include: choral groups, concert band, dance, drama/theater, jazz band, music ensembles, musical theater, radio station, student government, student newspaper. Number of fraternities: 0; sororities: 0. Average proportion of students who stay on campus on weekends: 60%.

SERVICES AND FACILITIES

Basic services: nonremedial tutoring, health service. **Remedial assistance:** math, writing. **Counseling services:** minority student, career, personal, academic, psychological, birth control. **For learning-disabled students:** School does not offer a structured program with separate admission and additional fees. Services include: remedial math, remedial English, tape recorders, note-taking services, readers, extended time for tests, tutors. **Library:** Number of titles: 127,036; number of current serial subscriptions: 538. **Information technology resources:** Students are not required to lease or own a computer. Number of campus computers available to all students: 475. School does not have a wireless network. Proportion of college-owned housing units wired for high-speed internet access: 100%. **Campus safety:** Security services offered: 24-hour foot-and-vehicle patrols, late-night transport/escort service, lighted pathways/sidewalks, controlled dormitory access (key, security card, etc.).

TRANSFER AND INTERNATIONAL STUDENTS

Transfer students: May apply for admission for the following academic terms: Fall, Spring. Applicants do not need a minimum number of credits to apply. For fall 2005: Transfer applications received: 461. Transfer applicants offered admission: 201. Transfer applicants enrolled: 120. **International students:** Number of foreign undergraduates: 52 (3% of student body). Number of countries represented: 19. Minimum TOEFL score required: 500 (paper); 173 (computer). Average TOEFL score: 564 (paper).

Ursinus College

- **Address:** Box 1000, Collegeville, PA 19426
- **Website:** http://www.ursinus.edu
- **Private**
- **Enrollment:** 1,552 full-time; 19 part-time

KEY STATS

✔ **U.S News College Ranking:** 69, Liberal Arts Colleges
✔ **SAT Score (25th/75th percentile):** 1110-1325
✔ **Tuition:** 2006-2007: $33,350

Selectivity: More selective   **Room/board:** $7,600
Acceptance rate: 75%   **Average debt:** $21,500
Student/faculty ratio: 12/1   **Proportion who borrowed:** 81%

UNDERGRADUATE STUDENT BODY STATS

2005-2006 enrollment: 1,552 full-time; 19 part-time. Men: 47%; women: 53%. **Ethnic makeup:** African American: 7%; Asian American: 4%; Hispanic: 3%; White: 84%; International: 1%.

ADMISSIONS FACTS AND FIGURES

Phone: (610) 409-3200. **Email:** Admissions@Ursinus.edu. **Website:** http://www.ursinus.edu. **Application deadlines for fall 2007:** Regular decision: February 15; decision sent by April 1. Early decision: Send application by: January 15; Decision sent by: January 31. Early action: Send application by: December 1; Decision sent by: N/A. Admission can be deferred. **Application fee:** $50. Common application is accepted. **To apply online, go to:** http://www.applyweb.com/apply/ursinus/. **Admissions requirements/recommendations:** High school units required (recommended): English: 4; Mathematics: 3 (4); Science: 1 (3); Foreign language: 2 (4); Social studies: 1 (3); History: 0 (0); Academic electives: 5; Total units: 16 (20). Tests: The college uses SAT or ACT scores in admissions decisions. Neither SAT nor ACT required. For admission to the fall 2007 entering class, the school will accept: ACT with writing, ACT without writing. Campus visit: Recommended. Admissions interview: Recommended. Off-campus interview: May be arranged. **Factors that count in admissions decisions:** *Academic:* Secondary school record: Very important. Class rank: Very important. Letters of recommendation: Important. Standardized test scores: Important. Essay: Important. *Nonacademic:* Interview: Considered. Extracurricular activities: Very important. Talent/ability: Important. Character/personal qualities: Considered. Alumni/ae relationship: Important. Geographical residence: Considered. State residency: Not considered. Religious affiliation/commitment: Not considered. Minority status: Important. Volunteer work: Important. Work experience: Important. **Other schools with the greatest overlap in applicants:** Dickinson College; Franklin and Marshall College; Gettysburg College; Haverford College; Lafayette College. **Admissions statistics for the fall 2005 entering class:** Total applicants: 1,776. Total accepted: 1,326. Freshmen enrolled: 426; 40% were from out of state. Accepted through early-decision or early-action plans: 27%. Overall acceptance rate: 75%. Early-decision acceptance rate: 95%. Non-early acceptance rate: 73%. **Size of waiting list:** 26 applicants; enrolled from waiting list: 0. **Credentials of fall 2005 freshmen:** 44% ranked in the top 10 percent of their high school class; 73% were in the top 25 percent, and 93% were in the top half. (Proportion submitting class standing: 65%.) **Average high school grade point average:** 3.5. **First-year students who submitted SAT scores:** 76%. Scores (25/75 percentile): Verbal: 550-660, Math: 560-665, Combined: 1110-1325. **First-year students submitting ACT scores:** 13%. Scores (25/75 percentile): English: N/A, Math: N/A, Composite: 22-28.

ACADEMICS

Year founded: 1869. **Academic calendar:** Semester. **Degrees offered:** bachelor's. **Most popular majors:** 23% economics, 13% biology/biological sciences, 12% psychology, 9% mass communication/media studies, 8% English language and literature. **Major fields of study:** area, ethnic, cultural, and gender studies; biological and biomedical sciences; communication, journalism, and related programs; computer and information sciences and support services; engineering; English language and literature/letters; foreign languages, literatures, and linguistics; history; mathematics and statistics; multi/interdisciplinary studies; natural resources and conservation; parks, recreation, leisure, and fitness studies; philosophy and religious studies; physical sciences; psychology; social sciences; visual and performing arts. **Areas of required coursework:** arts/fine arts, humanities, mathematics, English (including composition), foreign languages, sciences (biological or physical), social science, other. **Pre-professional programs:** pre-law, pre-dentistry, pre-medicine, pre-veterinary science, other. **Special academic programs (% participation):** double major (21%), dual enrollment, exchange student program (domestic) (1%), honors program (15%), independent study (64%), internships (55%), student-designed major (1%), study abroad (28%), teacher certificate program (6%). **Teacher certification offered in:** middle/junior high, secondary. **Faculty and instruction (2005-2006):** Total instructional faculty: 115 full-time, 50 part-time (50% men; 50% women; 7% minorities). Full-time faculty with Ph.D. or other terminal degree: 93%. Student/faculty ratio: 12/1. Classes of fewer than 20 students: 76%; of 20 to 49 students: 24%; of 50 or more students: 1%. **Advanced Placement and International Baccalaureate credit:** AP tests may be used for: Credit and/or placement. Scores accepted: 3, 4, 5. International Baccalaureate exams may be used for: Credit and/or placement. **Freshmen returning for sophomore year:** 90%. **Graduation rates:** Four-year: 72%; five-year: 75%; six-year: 76%. **Graduate study:** 34% of students pursue further study immediately upon graduation. Fields in which graduates pursue further study: Master of Business Administration (MBA), 5%; law, 10%; medicine, 14%; dentistry, 2%; engineering, 2%; theology (or the seminary), 3%; education, 10%; arts and sciences, 46%; veterinary medicine, 4%.

COSTS AND FINANCIAL AID
Financial aid office: (610) 409-3600. **Expenses (2006-2007):** Tuition and fees 2006-2007: $33,350; room/board: $7,600. Estimated books and supplies: $600; transportation: $200; personal expenses: $1,000. **Financial aid:** In 2005-2006, 98% of undergraduates applied for financial aid. Of those, 83% were determined to have financial need; 65% had their need fully met. Average financial aid package (proportion receiving): $23,938 (83%). Average amount of gift aid, such as scholarships or grants (proportion receiving): $18,558 (83%). Average amount of self-help aid, such as work study or loans (proportion receiving): $5,380 (83%). Average need-based loan (excluding PLUS or other private loans): $4,607. Among students who received need-based aid, the average percentage of need met: 85%. Among students who received aid based on merit, the average award (and the proportion receiving): $9,000 (15%). Average amount of debt of borrowers graduating in 2005: $21,500. Proportion who borrowed: 81%.

CAMPUS LIFE AND EXTRACURRICULAR ACTIVITIES
Campus housing available (% using): coed dorms (65%), women's dorms (10%), men's dorms (10%), special housing for international students (5%), other housing options (10%). Students who live in college-owned, operated, or affiliated housing: 95%. **Student employment:** During the 2005-2006 academic year, 43% of undergraduates worked on campus. Average per-year earnings: $1,800. **Clubs and organizations:** Number of student organizations: 80. Activities include: choral groups, concert band, dance, drama/theater, jazz band, literary magazine, music ensembles, pep band, radio station, student government, student newspaper, student film society, television station, yearbook. Number of fraternities: 8; sororities: 7. Proportion of men in fraternities: 17%; of women in sororities: 28%. Average proportion of students who stay on campus on weekends: 85%. **Sports program (2005-2006):** Member of NCAA III. *Men's intercollegiate varsity sports:* baseball, basketball, cross-country, football, golf, lacrosse, soccer, swimming and diving, tennis, track and field (indoor), track and field (outdoor), wrestling. *Women's intercollegiate varsity sports:* basketball, cross-country, field hockey, golf, gymnastics, lacrosse, soccer, softball, swimming and diving, tennis, track and field (indoor), track and field (outdoor), volleyball.

SERVICES AND FACILITIES
Basic services: nonremedial tutoring, placement service, health service, health insurance, other. **Counseling services:** minority student, career, personal, academic, psychological, birth control, religious. **For learning-disabled students:** School does not offer a structured program with separate admission and additional fees. Total undergraduates in learning-disabled program or receiving services: 23. Services include: tape recorders, note-taking services, readers, extended time for tests, tutors, priority seating. **Library:** Number of titles: 406,000; number of current serial subscriptions: 2,269.

Information technology resources: Students are required to lease or own a computer. Number of campus computers available to all students: 1,825. School has a wireless network. Approximate number of users that can be accommodated: 345. Proportion of college-owned housing units wired for high-speed internet access: 100%. **Campus safety:** Security services offered: 24-hour foot-and-vehicle patrols, late-night transport/escort service, 24-hour emergency telephones, lighted pathways/sidewalks, controlled dormitory access (key, security card, etc).

TRANSFER AND INTERNATIONAL STUDENTS
Transfer students: May apply for admission for the following academic terms: Fall, Spring. Applicants do not need a minimum number of credits to apply. For fall 2005: Transfer applications received: 49. Transfer applicants offered admission: 20. Transfer applicants enrolled: 11. **International students:** Number of foreign undergraduates: 18 (1% of student body). Number of countries represented: 14. Minimum TOEFL score required: 500 (paper); 173 (computer). Average TOEFL score: 580 (paper).

Villanova University

- ■ **Address:** 800 Lancaster Avenue, Villanova, PA 19085
- ■ **Website:** http://www.villanova.edu
- ■ **Private; Religious affiliation:** Roman Catholic
- ■ **Enrollment:** 6,540 full-time; 668 part-time

KEY STATS
✔ **U.S News College Ranking:** 1, Universities–Master's (North)
✔ **SAT Score (25th/75th percentile):** 1180-1350
✔ **Tuition:** 2006-2007: $31,525

Selectivity: More selective	**Room/board:** $9,560
Acceptance rate: 51%	**Average debt:** $28,549
Student/faculty ratio: 13/1	**Proportion who borrowed:** 56%

UNDERGRADUATE STUDENT BODY STATS
2005-2006 enrollment: 6,540 full-time; 668 part-time. Men: 49%; women: 51%. **Ethnic makeup:** African American: 4%; Asian American: 6%; Hispanic: 5%; White: 82%; International: 2%. **Religious preference:** Protestant: 14%; Jewish: 1%; Muslim: 1%; Hindu: 1%; Buddhist: 1%; No preference: 4%; Roman Catholic: 76%.

ADMISSIONS FACTS AND FIGURES
Phone: (610) 519-4000. **Email:** gotovu@villanova.edu. **Website:** http://www.villanova.edu. **Application deadlines for fall 2007:** Regular decision: January 7; decision sent by April 1. Early decision: Not offered. Early action: Send application by: November 1; Decision sent by: December 20. Admission can be deferred. **Application fee:** $70. Common application is accepted. **To apply online, go to:** http://www.villanova.edu/enroll/admission. **Admissions requirements/recommendations:** High school units required (recommended): English: 4 (4); Mathematics: 4 (4); Science: 4 (4); Foreign language: 2 (4); Academic electives: 2 (2); Total units: 22 (25). Tests: The college uses SAT or ACT scores in admissions decisions. Either SAT or ACT required. For admission to the fall 2007 entering class, the school will accept: ACT with writing. Campus visit: Recommended. Admissions interview: Neither required nor recommended. Off-campus interview: May be arranged. **Factors that count in admissions decisions:** *Academic:* Secondary school record: Very important. Class rank: Very important. Letters of recommendation: Important. Standardized test scores: Very important. Essay: Important. *Nonacademic:* Interview: Not considered. Extracurricular activities: Important. Talent/ability: Important. Character/personal qualities: Important. Alumni/ae relationship: Considered. Geographical residence: Considered. State residency: Considered. Religious affiliation/commitment: Not considered. Minority status: Considered. Volunteer work: Important. Work experience: Important. **Other schools with the greatest overlap in applicants:** Boston College; Georgetown University; Loyola College in Maryland; Pennsylvania State University–University Park; University of Notre Dame. **Admissions statistics for the fall 2005 entering class:** Total applicants: 10,394. Total accepted: 5,338. Freshmen enrolled: 1,628; 76% were from out of state. Accepted through early-decision or early-action plans: 26%. Overall acceptance rate: 51%. Non-early acceptance rate: 50%. **Size of waiting list:** 2831 applicants; enrolled from waiting list: 116. **Credentials of fall 2005 freshmen:** 47% ranked in the top 10 percent of their high school class; 83% were in the top 25 percent, and 97% were in the top

half. (Proportion submitting class standing: 44%.) **Average high school grade point average:** 3.7. **First-year students who submitted SAT scores:** 98%. Scores (25/75 percentile): Verbal: 580-660, Math: 600-690, Combined: 1180-1350. **First-year students submitting ACT scores:** 17%. Scores (25/75 percentile): English: N/A, Math: N/A, Composite: 27-30.

ACADEMICS

Year founded: 1842. **Academic calendar:** Semester. **Degrees offered:** certificate, associate, bachelor's, post-bachelor's certificate, master's, post-master's certificate, first professional, doctorate. **Most popular majors:** 35% business, management, marketing, and related support services, 11% engineering, 10% social sciences, 9% communication, journalism, and related programs, 7% health professions and related clinical sciences. **Major fields of study:** biological and biomedical sciences; business, management, marketing, and related support services; communication, journalism, and related programs; computer and information sciences and support services; education; engineering; English language and literature/letters; foreign languages, literatures, and linguistics; health professions and related clinical sciences; history; liberal arts and sciences studies, and humanities; mathematics and statistics; philosophy and religious studies; physical sciences; psychology; public administration and social service professions; social sciences; visual and performing arts. **Areas of required coursework:** humanities, mathematics, English (including composition), philosophy, foreign languages, sciences (biological or physical), history, social science, other. **Special academic programs (% participation):** accelerated program (1%), cross-registration (2%), distance learning (21%), double major (20%), English as a Second Language (ESL) (0%), honors program (12%), independent study (14%), internships (23%), study abroad (32%), teacher certificate program (2%). **Teacher certification offered in:** elementary, secondary. **Reserve Officers Training Corps (ROTC):** Army ROTC: Offered on campus; Navy ROTC: Offered on campus; Air Force ROTC: Offered at cooperating institution (St. Joseph's University). **Faculty and instruction (2005-2006):** Total instructional faculty: 570 full-time, 353 part-time (64% men; 36% women; 9% minorities). Full-time faculty with Ph.D. or other terminal degree: 91%. Student/faculty ratio: 13/1. Classes of fewer than 20 students: 42%; of 20 to 49 students: 54%; of 50 or more students: 4%. **Advanced Placement and International Baccalaureate credit:** AP tests may be used for: Credit and/or placement. Scores accepted: 3, 4, 5. International Baccalaureate exams may be used for: Credit and/or placement. **Freshmen returning for sophomore year:** 94%. **Graduation rates:** Four-year: 79%; five-year: 83%; six-year: 85%. **Graduate study:** 20% of students pursue further study immediately upon graduation; 24% within one year. Fields in which graduates pursue further study: Master of Business Administration (MBA), 3%; law, 24%; medicine, 12%; dentistry, 2%; engineering, 7%; theology (or the seminary), 1%; education, 6%; arts and sciences, 41%.

COSTS AND FINANCIAL AID

Financial aid office: (610) 519-4010. **Expenses (2006-2007):** Tuition and fees 2006-2007: $31,525; room/board: $9,560. Estimated books and supplies: $950; transportation: $600; personal expenses: $900. **Financial aid:** In 2005-2006, 56% of undergraduates applied for financial aid. Of those, 45% were determined to have financial need; 18% had their need fully met. Average financial aid package (proportion receiving): $20,503 (44%). Average amount of gift aid, such as scholarships or grants (proportion receiving): $16,202 (39%). Average amount of self-help aid, such as work study or loans (proportion receiving): $5,671 (39%). Average need-based loan (excluding PLUS or other private loans): $4,698. Among students who received need-based aid, the average percentage of need met: 78%. Among students who received aid based on merit, the average award (and the proportion receiving): $10,971 (5%). The average athletic scholarship (and the proportion receiving): $31,286 (2%). Average amount of debt of borrowers graduating in 2005: $28,549. Proportion who borrowed: 56%.

CAMPUS LIFE AND EXTRACURRICULAR ACTIVITIES

Campus housing available (% using): coed dorms (96%), women's dorms (2%), men's dorms (2%). Students who live in college-owned, operated, or affiliated housing: 70%. **Student employment:** During the 2005-2006 academic year, 17% of undergraduates worked on campus. Average per-year earnings: $1,500. **Clubs and organizations:** Number of student organizations: 155. Activities include: choral groups, concert band, dance, drama/theater, jazz band, literary magazine, marching band, music ensembles, musical theater, opera, pep band, radio station, student government, student newspaper, student film society, television station, yearbook. Number of fraternities: 9; sororities: 9. Proportion of men in fraternities: 10%; of women in sororities: 23%. Average proportion of students who stay on campus on weekends: 85%. **Sports program (2005-2006):** Member of NCAA I.

Men's intercollegiate varsity sports: baseball, basketball, cross-country, field hockey, football, golf, lacrosse, soccer, swimming and diving, tennis, track and field (indoor), track and field (outdoor). **Women's intercollegiate varsity sports:** basketball, cross-country, field hockey, lacrosse, lightweight crew, rowing, soccer, softball, swimming and diving, tennis, track and field (indoor), track and field (outdoor), volleyball, water polo.

SERVICES AND FACILITIES

Basic services: health service, health insurance, other. **Remedial assistance:** math, writing, study skills. **Counseling services:** minority student, career, military, personal, veteran student, academic, older student, psychological, religious. **For learning-disabled students:** School does not offer a structured program with separate admission and additional fees. Total undergraduates in learning-disabled program or receiving services: 224. Services include: reading machines, tape recorders, untimed tests, note-taking services, learning center, readers, extended time for tests, tutors, priority seating, texts on tape, exams on tape or computer, other testing accomodations, other. **Library:** Number of titles: 746,500; number of current serial subscriptions: 10,800. **Information technology resources:** Students are not required to lease or own a computer. Number of campus computers available to all students: 1,400. School has a wireless network. Approximate number of users that can be accommodated: 5,000. Proportion of college-owned housing units wired for high-speed internet access: 100%. **Campus safety:** Security services offered: 24-hour foot-and-vehicle patrols, late-night transport/escort service, 24-hour emergency telephones, lighted pathways/sidewalks, student patrols, controlled dormitory access (key, security card, etc).

TRANSFER AND INTERNATIONAL STUDENTS

Transfer students: May apply for admission for the following academic terms: Fall, Spring. Applicants do not need a minimum number of credits to apply. For fall 2005: Transfer applications received: 391. Transfer applicants offered admission: 198. Transfer applicants enrolled: 106. **International students:** Number of foreign undergraduates: 148 (2% of student body). Number of countries represented: 33. Minimum TOEFL score required: 550 (paper); 213 (computer). Average TOEFL score: 596 (paper).

Washington and Jefferson College

- ■ **Address:** 60 S. Lincoln Street, Washington, PA 15301
- ■ **Website:** http://www.washjeff.edu
- ■ **Private**
- ■ **Enrollment:** 1,400 full-time; 18 part-time

KEY STATS

✔ **U.S News College Ranking:** 104, Liberal Arts Colleges
✔ **SAT Score (25th/75th percentile):** 1050-1230
✔ **Tuition:** 2006-2007: $28,680

Selectivity: More selective	**Room/board:** $7,602
Acceptance rate: 39%	**Average debt:** $17,000
Student/faculty ratio: 12/1	**Proportion who borrowed:** 75%

UNDERGRADUATE STUDENT BODY STATS

2005-2006 enrollment: 1,400 full-time; 18 part-time. Men: 52%; women: 48%. **Ethnic makeup:** African American: 2%; Asian American: 1%; Hispanic: 1%; White: 95%.

ADMISSIONS FACTS AND FIGURES

Phone: (724) 223-6025. **Email:** admission@washjeff.edu. **Website:** http://www.washjeff.edu. **Application deadlines for fall 2007:** Regular decision: March 1. Early decision: Send application by: December 1; Decision sent by: December 15. Early action: Send application by: January 15; Decision sent by: February 15. Admission can be deferred. **Application fee:** $25. Common application is accepted. **Admissions requirements/recommendations:** High school units required (recommended): English: 3; Mathematics: 3; Science: 1; Foreign language: 2; Academic electives: 6; Total units: 15. Tests: The college uses SAT or ACT scores in admissions decisions. Either SAT or ACT required. For admission to the fall 2007 entering class, the school will accept: ACT with writing, ACT without writing. Campus visit: Recommended. Admissions interview: Recommended. Off-campus interview: May be arranged. **Factors that count in admissions decisions:** *Academic:* Secondary school record: Very important. Class rank: Important. Letters of recommendation: Considered. Standardized test scores: Important. Essay: Considered. *Nonacademic:* Interview: Considered. Extracurricular activities: Considered. Talent/ability: Considered. Character/personal qualities: Considered. Alumni/ae relationship: Considered. Geographical residence: Considered. State residency: Considered. Religious affiliation/commitment: Not considered. Minority status: Considered. Volunteer work: Considered. Work experience: Not considered. **Other schools with the greatest overlap in applicants:** Allegheny College; College of Wooster; Duquesne University; Pennsylvania State University–University Park; University of Pittsburgh. **Admissions statistics for the fall 2005 entering class:** Total applicants: 4,477. Total accepted: 1,737. Freshmen enrolled: 388; 31% were from out of state. Accepted through early-decision or early-action plans: 74%. Overall acceptance rate: 39%. Early-decision acceptance rate: 30%. Non-early acceptance rate: 21%. **Size of waiting list:** 157 applicants; enrolled from waiting list: 17. **Credentials of fall 2005 freshmen:** 31% ranked in the top 10 percent of their high school class; 65% were in the top 25 percent, and 94% were in the top half. (Proportion submitting class standing: 78%.) **Average high school grade point average:** 3.3. **First-year students who submitted SAT scores:** 85%. Scores (25/75 percentile): Verbal: 520-610, Math: 530-620, Combined: 1050-1230. **First-year students submitting ACT scores:** 29%. Scores (25/75 percentile): English: 22-27, Math: 23-27, Composite: 23-27.

ACADEMICS

Year founded: 1781. **Academic calendar:** 4-1-4. **Degrees offered:** associate, bachelor's. **Most popular majors:** 17% business/commerce, 14% accounting, 13% psychology, 9% history, 8% political science and government. **Major fields of study:** biological and biomedical sciences; business, management, marketing, and related support services; computer and information sciences and support services; education; English language and literature/letters; foreign languages, literatures, and linguistics; history; liberal arts and sciences studies, and humanities; mathematics and statistics; philosophy and religious studies; physical sciences; psychology; social sciences; visual and performing arts. **Areas of required coursework:** arts/fine arts, humanities, mathematics, English (including composition), foreign languages, sciences (biological or physical), social science. **Pre-professional programs:** pre-law, pre-dentistry, pre-medicine, pre-veterinary science, pre-optometry, other. **Special academic programs (% participation):** double major (22%), honors program (2%), independent study (28%), internships (25%), student-designed major (2%), study abroad (26%), teacher certificate program (5%), other (3%). **Teacher certification offered in:** elementary, middle/junior high, secondary. **Reserve Officers Training Corps (ROTC):** Army ROTC: Offered at cooperating institution (University of Pittsburgh); Air Force ROTC: Offered at cooperating institution (University of Pittsburgh). **Faculty and instruction (2005-2006):** Total instructional faculty: 97 full-time, 33 part-time (60% men; 40% women; 12% minorities). Full-time faculty with Ph.D. or other terminal degree: 86%. Student/faculty ratio: 12/1. Classes of fewer than 20 students: 65%; of 20 to 49 students: 35%; of 50 or more students: 1%. **Advanced Placement and International Baccalaureate credit:** AP tests may be used for: Credit and/or placement. Scores accepted: 4, 5. International Baccalaureate exams may be used for: Credit and/or placement. **Freshmen returning for sophomore year:** 84%. **Graduation rates:** Four-year: 66%; five-year: 68%; six-year: 68%. **Graduate study:** 25% of students pursue further study immediately upon graduation. Fields in which graduates pursue further study: Master of Business Administration (MBA), 2%; law, 19%; medicine, 17%; dentistry, 2%; theology (or the seminary), 2%; education, 9%; arts and sciences, 55%.

COSTS AND FINANCIAL AID

Financial aid office: (724) 223-6019. **Expenses (2006-2007):** Tuition and fees 2006-2007: $28,080; room/board: $7,602. Estimated books and supplies: $600; transportation: $200; personal expenses: $700. **Financial aid:** Priority filing date for institution's financial aid form: February 15. In 2005-2006, 84% of undergraduates applied for financial aid. Of those, 73% were determined to have financial need; 29% had their need fully met. Average financial aid package (proportion receiving): $19,096 (73%). Average amount of gift aid, such as scholarships or grants (proportion receiving): $14,301 (71%). Average amount of self-help aid, such as work study or loans (proportion receiving): $4,784 (61%). Average need-based loan (excluding PLUS or other private loans): $3,725. Among students who received need-based aid, the average percentage of need met: 74%. Among students who received aid based on merit, the average award (and the proportion receiving): $9,297 (20%). The average athletic scholarship (and the proportion receiving): $0 (0%). Average amount of debt of borrowers graduating in 2005: $17,000. Proportion who borrowed: 75%.

CAMPUS LIFE AND EXTRACURRICULAR ACTIVITIES

Campus housing available (% using): coed dorms (33%), women's dorms (14%), men's dorms (15%), sorority housing (9%), fraternity housing (9%), special housing for disabled students (1%), special housing for international students (0%), other housing options (19%). Students who live in college-owned, operated, or affiliated housing: 81%. **Student employment:** During the 2005-2006 academic year, 43% of undergraduates worked on campus. Average per-year earnings: $700. **Clubs and organizations:** Number of student organizations: 79. Activities include: choral groups, concert band, dance, drama/theater, jazz band, literary magazine, music ensembles, musical theater, radio station, student government, student newspaper, student film society, yearbook. Number of fraternities: 6; sororities: 4. Proportion of men in fraternities: 43%; of women in sororities: 37%. Average proportion of students who stay on campus on weekends: 75%. **Sports program (2005-2006):** Member of NCAA III. *Men's intercollegiate varsity sports:* baseball, basketball, cross-country, football, golf, lacrosse, soccer, swimming and diving, tennis, track and field (indoor), track and field (outdoor), water polo, wrestling. *Women's intercollegiate varsity sports:* basketball, cross-country, field hockey, golf, soccer, softball, swimming and diving, tennis, track and field (indoor), track and field (outdoor), volleyball, water polo.

SERVICES AND FACILITIES

Basic services: nonremedial tutoring, placement service, health service, health insurance. **Remedial assistance:** study skills. **Counseling services:** minority student, career, personal, academic, psychological, birth control, religious. **For learning-disabled students:** School does not offer a structured program with separate admission and additional fees. Services include: tape recorders, untimed tests, oral tests, learning center, readers, extended time for tests, tutors, priority seating, texts on tape, exams on tape or computer, other testing accomodations. **Library:** Number of titles: 189,848; number of current serial subscriptions: 526. **Information technology resources:** Students are not required to lease or own a computer. Number of campus computers available to all students: 450. School has a wireless network. Proportion of college-owned housing units wired for high-speed internet access: 100%. **Campus safety:** Security services offered: 24-hour foot-and-vehicle patrols, late-night transport/escort service, 24-hour emergency telephones, lighted pathways/sidewalks, controlled dormitory access (key, security card, etc).

TRANSFER AND INTERNATIONAL STUDENTS

Transfer students: May apply for admission for the following academic terms: Fall, Winter, Spring. Applicants do not need a minimum number of credits to apply. For fall 2005: Transfer applications received: 65. Transfer applicants offered admission: 33. Transfer applicants enrolled: 22. **International students:** Number of foreign undergraduates: 0. Number of countries represented: 1. Minimum TOEFL score required: 500 (paper); 213 (computer). Average TOEFL score: 592 (paper).

Waynesburg College

- **Address:** 51 W. College Street, Waynesburg, PA 15370
- **Website:** http://www.waynesburg.edu/
- **Private; Religious affiliation:** Presbyterian
- **Enrollment:** 1,343 full-time; 271 part-time

KEY STATS

✔ **U.S News College Ranking:** third tier, Universities–Master's (North)
✔ **SAT Score (25th/75th percentile):** 860-1070
✔ **Tuition:** 2006-2007: $15,780

Selectivity: Less selective	**Room/board:** $6,370
Acceptance rate: 74%	**Average debt:** $21,000
Student/faculty ratio: 13/1	**Proportion who borrowed:** 89%

UNDERGRADUATE STUDENT BODY STATS

2005-2006 enrollment: 1,343 full-time; 271 part-time. Men: 38%; women: 62%. **Ethnic makeup:** African American: 3%; Hispanic: 1%; White: 96%. **Religious preference:** Roman Catholic: 26%; Protestant: 7%; No preference: 3%; Unknown: 16%; Presbyterian: 10%; Other: 38%.

ADMISSIONS FACTS AND FIGURES

Phone: (800) 225-7393. **Email:** admissions@waynesburg.edu. **Website:** http://www.waynesburg.edu/. **Application deadlines for fall 2007:** Regular decision: Rolling. Early decision: Not offered. Early action: Not offered. Admission cannot be deferred. **Application fee:** $20. Common application is accepted. **To apply online, go to:** http://www.waynesburg.edu/apply.htm. **Admissions requirements/recommendations:** High school units required (recommended): English: 4; Mathematics: 3; Science: 2; Foreign language: (2); Social studies: 2; Academic electives: 5; Total units: 16. Tests: The college uses SAT or ACT scores in admissions decisions. SAT required. For admission to the fall 2007 entering class, the school will accept: ACT with writing. Campus visit: Recommended. Admissions interview: Recommended. Off-campus interview: May be arranged. **Factors that count in admissions decisions:** *Academic:* Secondary school record: Very important. Class rank: Very important. Letters of recommendation: Considered. Standardized test scores: Very important. Essay: Considered. *Nonacademic:* Interview: Very important. Extracurricular activities: Considered. Talent/ability: Not considered. Character/personal qualities: Considered. Alumni/ae relationship: Not considered. Geographical residence: Not considered. State residency: Not considered. Religious affiliation/commitment: Not considered. Minority status: Not considered. Volunteer work: Not considered. Work experience: Considered. **Other schools with the greatest overlap in applicants:** California University of Pennsylvania; Geneva College; Washington and Jefferson College; West Virginia University; Westminster College. **Admissions statistics for the fall 2005 entering class:** Total applicants: 1,518. Total accepted: 1,124. Freshmen enrolled: 341; 15% were from out of state. Overall acceptance rate: 74%. **Credentials of fall 2005 freshmen:** 14% ranked in the top 10 percent of their high school class; 40% were in the top 25 percent, and 77% were in the top half. (Proportion submitting class standing: 92%.) **Average high school grade point average:** 3.4. **First-year students who submitted SAT scores:** 88%. Scores (25/75 percentile): Verbal: 430-530, Math: 430-540, Combined: 860-1070. **First-year students submitting ACT scores:** 21%. Scores (25/75 percentile): English: N/A, Math: N/A, Composite: N/A.

ACADEMICS

Year founded: 1849. **Academic calendar:** Semester. **Degrees offered:** associate, bachelor's, master's. **Most popular majors:** 23% business, management, marketing, and related support services, 22% nursing, 12% education, 9% public administration and social service professions. **Major fields of study:** biological and biomedical sciences; business, management, marketing, and related support services; communication, journalism, and related programs; computer and information sciences and support services; education; English language and literature/letters; health professions and related clinical sciences; history; mathematics and statistics; multi/interdisciplinary studies; physical sciences; psychology; public administration and social service professions; security and protective services; social sciences; visual and performing arts. **Areas of required coursework:** arts/fine arts, computer literacy, mathematics, English (including composition), philosophy, sciences (biological or physical), history, social science, other. **Pre-professional programs:** pre-law, pre-dentistry, pre-medicine, pre-veterinary science, other. **Special academic programs (% participation):** accelerated program (31%), distance learning (1%), double major (3%), dual enrollment (8%), honors program (4%), independent study (64%), internships (18%), liberal arts/career combination (15%), student-designed major (1%), study abroad (1%), teacher certificate program (7%). **Teacher certification offered in:** elementary, secondary. **Reserve Officers Training Corps (ROTC):** Army ROTC: Offered at cooperating institution (West Virginia University). **Faculty and instruction (2005-2006):** Total instructional faculty: 62 full-time, 73 part-time (50% men; 50% women; 1% minorities). Full-time faculty with Ph.D. or other terminal degree: 56%. Student/faculty ratio: 13/1. Classes of fewer than 20 students: 63%; of 20 to 49 students: 36%; of 50 or more students: 1%. **Advanced Placement and International Baccalaureate credit:** AP tests may be used for: Placement only. Scores accepted: 3, 4, 5. International Baccalaureate exams may be used for: Credit and/or placement. **Freshmen returning for sophomore year:** 74%. **Graduation rates:** Four-year: 44%; five-year: 52%; six-year: 52%. **Graduate study:** 9% of students pursue further study immediately upon graduation; 12% within one year; 15% within five years. Fields in which graduates pursue further study: Master of Business Administration (MBA), 53%; law, 10%; medicine, 10%; dentistry, 2%; engineering, 3%; theology (or the seminary), 1%; education, 15%; arts and sciences, 5%; veterinary medicine, 1%.

COSTS AND FINANCIAL AID

Financial aid office: (724) 852-3208. **Expenses (2006-2007):** Tuition and fees 2006-2007: $15,780; room/board: $6,370. Estimated books and supplies: $1,000; transportation: $300; personal expenses: $250. **Financial aid:** Priority filing date for institution's financial aid form: March 15. In 2005-2006, 96% of undergraduates applied for financial aid. Of those, 85% were

determined to have financial need; 29% had their need fully met. Average financial aid package (proportion receiving): $11,919 (84%). Average amount of gift aid, such as scholarships or grants (proportion receiving): $8,890 (82%). Average amount of self-help aid, such as work study or loans (proportion receiving): $3,774 (73%). Average need-based loan (excluding PLUS or other private loans): $3,590. Among students who received need-based aid, the average percentage of need met: 80%. Among students who received aid based on merit, the average award (and the proportion receiving): $10,327 (12%). The average athletic scholarship (and the proportion receiving): $0 (0%). Average amount of debt of borrowers graduating in 2005: $21,000. Proportion who borrowed: 89%.

CAMPUS LIFE AND EXTRACURRICULAR ACTIVITIES

Campus housing available (% using): women's dorms (47%), men's dorms (38%), other housing options (15%). Students who live in college-owned, operated, or affiliated housing: 52%. **Student employment:** During the 2005-2006 academic year, 20% of undergraduates worked on campus. Average per-year earnings: $1,400. **Clubs and organizations:** Number of student organizations: 30. Activities include: choral groups, concert band, drama/theater, literary magazine, music ensembles, musical theater, pep band, radio station, student government, student newspaper, television station, yearbook. Number of fraternities: 0; sororities: 0. Average proportion of students who stay on campus on weekends: 25%. **Sports program (2005-2006):** Member of NCAA III. *Men's intercollegiate varsity sports:* baseball, basketball, football, golf, soccer, tennis, wrestling. *Women's intercollegiate varsity sports:* basketball, cross-country, golf, soccer, softball, tennis, volleyball.

SERVICES AND FACILITIES

Basic services: nonremedial tutoring, placement service, health service. **Remedial assistance:** math, writing, study skills. **Counseling services:** minority student, career, personal, academic, older student, psychological, religious, other. **For learning-disabled students:** School does not offer a structured program with separate admission and additional fees. Total undergraduates in learning-disabled program or receiving services: 35. Services include: remedial math, remedial English, reading machines, tape recorders, oral tests, learning center, readers, extended time for tests, tutors, priority seating, exams on tape or computer. **Library:** Number of titles: 95,953; number of current serial subscriptions: 459. **Information technology resources:** Students are not required to lease or own a computer. Number of campus computers available to all students: 220. School has a wireless network. Approximate number of users that can be accommodated: 140. Proportion of college-owned housing units wired for high-speed internet access: 100%. **Campus safety:** Security services offered: 24-hour foot-and-vehicle patrols, 24-hour emergency telephones, lighted pathways/sidewalks, controlled dormitory access (key, security card, etc).

TRANSFER AND INTERNATIONAL STUDENTS

Transfer students: May apply for admission for the following academic terms: Fall, Spring, Summer. Applicants do not need a minimum number of credits to apply. **International students:** Number of foreign undergraduates: 1. Number of countries represented: 3. Minimum TOEFL score required: 500 (paper); 173 (computer). Average TOEFL score: 550 (paper).

West Chester University of Pennsylvania

- ■ **Address:** West Chester, PA 19383
- ■ **Website:** http://www.wcupa.edu/
- ■ **Public**
- ■ **Enrollment:** 9,788 full-time; 1,050 part-time

KEY STATS

✔ **U.S News College Ranking:** 68, Universities–Master's (North)
✔ **SAT Score (25th/75th percentile):** 980-1150
✔ **Tuition:** 2005-2006: $6,147 in state, $13,507 out of state

Selectivity: Selective	**Room/board:** $6,208
Acceptance rate: 49%	**Average debt:** N/A
Student/faculty ratio: 16/1	**Proportion who borrowed:** N/A

UNDERGRADUATE STUDENT BODY STATS

2005-2006 enrollment: 9,788 full-time; 1,050 part-time. Men: 39%; women: 61%. **Ethnic makeup:** African American: 9%; Asian American: 2%; Hispanic: 3%; White: 87%.

ADMISSIONS FACTS AND FIGURES

Phone: (610) 436-3414. **Email:** ugadmiss@wcupa.edu. **Website:** http://www.wcupa.edu/. **Application deadlines for fall 2007:** Regular decision: Rolling. Early decision: Not offered. Early action: Not offered. Admission can be deferred. **Application fee:** $35. Common application is not accepted. **To apply online, go to:** http://www.wcupa.edu/_ADMISSIONS/SCH_DGR/. **Admissions requirements/recommendations:** High school units required (recommended): English: 4 (4); Mathematics: 3 (4); Science: 2 (3); Foreign language: 0 (2); Social studies: 2 (2); History: 4 (4); Academic electives: 1 (2); Total units: 16 (21). Tests: The college uses SAT or ACT scores in admissions decisions. Either SAT or ACT required. For admission to the fall 2007 entering class, the school will accept: ACT with writing. Campus visit: Recommended. Admissions interview: Neither required nor recommended. Off-campus interview: Not available. **Factors that count in admissions decisions:** *Academic:* Secondary school record: Very important. Class rank: Very important. Letters of recommendation: Not considered. Standardized test scores: Important. Essay: Considered. *Nonacademic:* Interview: Not considered. Extracurricular activities: Considered. Talent/ability: Considered. Character/personal qualities: Considered. Alumni/ae relationship: Not considered. Geographical residence: Not considered. State residency: Not considered. Religious affiliation/commitment: Not considered. Minority status: Considered. Volunteer work: Considered. Work experience: Considered. **Other schools with the greatest overlap in applicants:** Bloomsburg University of Pennsylvania; Kutztown University of Pennsylvania; Pennsylvania State University–University Park; Shippensburg University of Pennsylvania; University of Delaware. **Admissions statistics for the fall 2005 entering class:** Total applicants: 11,013. Total accepted: 5,438. Freshmen enrolled: 1,901; 16% were from out of state. Overall acceptance rate: 49%. **Size of waiting list:** 850 applicants; enrolled from waiting list: 30. **Credentials of fall 2005 freshmen:** 9% ranked in the top 10 percent of their high school class; 31% were in the top 25 percent, and 67% were in the top half. (Proportion submitting class standing: 83%.) **Average high school grade point average:** 3.4. **First-year students who submitted SAT scores:** 100%. Scores (25/75 percentile): Verbal: 490-570, Math: 490-580, Combined: 980-1150.

ACADEMICS

Year founded: 1871. **Academic calendar:** Semester. **Degrees offered:** certificate, bachelor's, post-bachelor's certificate, master's, post-master's certificate. **Most popular majors:** 12% elementary education and teaching, 9% liberal arts and sciences/liberal studies, 7% business administration and management, 5% criminal justice/safety studies, 5% psychology. **Major fields of study:** area, ethnic, cultural, and gender studies; biological and biomedical sciences; business, management, marketing, and related support services; communication, journalism, and related programs; computer and information sciences and support services; education; English language and literature/letters; foreign languages, literatures, and linguistics; health professions and related clinical sciences; history; liberal arts and sciences studies, and humanities; mathematics and statistics; parks, recreation, leisure, and fitness studies; philosophy and religious studies; physical sciences; psychology; public administration and social service professions; security and protective services; social sciences; visual and performing arts. **Areas of required coursework:** arts/fine arts, humanities, computer literacy, mathematics, English (including composition), foreign languages, sciences (biological or physical), history, social science, other. **Pre-professional programs:** pre-law, pre-medicine, pre-theology. **Special academic programs:** cooperative (work-study plan) program, cross-registration, distance learning, double major, dual enrollment, English as a Second Language (ESL), exchange student program (domestic), external degree program, honors program, independent study, internships, student-designed major, study abroad, teacher certificate program, other. **Teacher certification offered in:** early childhood, special education, elementary, middle/junior high, secondary. **Cooperative education programs:** art, business, computer science, education, health professions, humanities, natural science, social/behavioral science. **Reserve Officers Training Corps (ROTC):** Army ROTC: Offered at cooperating institution (Widener University); Air Force ROTC: Offered at cooperating institution (St. Joseph's University). **Faculty and instruction (2005-2006):** Total instructional faculty: 567 full-time, 230 part-time (49% men; 51% women; 13% minorities). Full-time faculty with Ph.D. or other terminal degree: 77%. Student/faculty ratio: 16/1. Classes of fewer than 20 students: 27%; of 20 to

49 students: 69%; of 50 or more students: 4%. **Advanced Placement and International Baccalaureate credit:** AP tests may be used for: Credit only. Scores accepted: 3, 4, 5. International Baccalaureate exams may be used for: Credit only. **Freshmen returning for sophomore year:** 84%. **Graduation rates:** Four-year: 26%; five-year: 55%; six-year: 59%.

COSTS AND FINANCIAL AID

Financial aid office: (610) 436-2627. **Expenses (2005-2006):** Tuition and fees 2005-2006: $6,147 in state, $13,507 out of state; room/board: $6,208. Estimated books and supplies: $1,000. **Financial aid:** Priority filing date for institution's financial aid form: March 1.

CAMPUS LIFE AND EXTRACURRICULAR ACTIVITIES

Campus housing available (% using): coed dorms (68%), women's dorms (6%), apartment for single students (25%), special housing for disabled students (1%), special housing for international students (0%). Students who live in college-owned, operated, or affiliated housing: 31%. **Student employment:** During the 2005-2006 academic year, 5% of undergraduates worked on campus. Average per-year earnings: $1,740. **Clubs and organizations:** Number of student organizations: 215. Activities include: choral groups, concert band, dance, drama/theater, jazz band, literary magazine, marching band, music ensembles, musical theater, opera, radio station, student government, student newspaper, symphony orchestra, television station, yearbook. Number of fraternities: 11; sororities: 12. Average proportion of students who stay on campus on weekends: 50%. **Sports program (2005-2006):** Member of NCAA II. *Men's intercollegiate varsity sports:* baseball, basketball, cross-country, football, golf, lacrosse, soccer, swimming and diving, tennis, track and field (indoor), track and field (outdoor). *Women's intercollegiate varsity sports:* basketball, cross-country, field hockey, golf, gymnastics, lacrosse, soccer, softball, swimming and diving, tennis, track and field (indoor), track and field (outdoor), volleyball.

SERVICES AND FACILITIES

Basic services: nonremedial tutoring, women's center, placement service, day care, health service, health insurance, other. **Remedial assistance:** math, writing, study skills. **Counseling services:** career, personal, academic, psychological. **For learning-disabled students:** School does not offer a structured program with separate admission and additional fees. Total undergraduates in learning-disabled program or receiving services: 326. Services include: remedial math, remedial English, reading machines, remedial reading, tape recorders, untimed tests, note-taking services, oral tests, learning center, readers, extended time for tests, tutors, priority registration, priority seating, substitution of courses, texts on tape, typist/scribe, exams on tape or computer, other testing accomodations. **Library:** Number of titles: 744,976; number of current serial subscriptions: 5,373. **Information technology resources:** Students are not required to lease or own a computer. Number of campus computers available to all students: 1,000. School has a wireless network. Approximate number of users that can be accommodated: 2,400. Proportion of college-owned housing units wired for high-speed internet access: 100%. **Campus safety:** Security services offered: 24-hour foot-and-vehicle patrols, late-night transport/escort service, 24-hour emergency telephones, lighted pathways/sidewalks, controlled dormitory access (key, security card, etc).

TRANSFER AND INTERNATIONAL STUDENTS

Transfer students: May apply for admission for the following academic terms: Fall, Spring. Applicants do not need a minimum number of credits to apply. For fall 2005: Transfer applications received: 2,673. Transfer applicants offered admission: 1,487. Transfer applicants enrolled: 962. **International students:** Number of foreign undergraduates: 41. Number of countries represented: 22. Minimum TOEFL score required: 550 (paper); 213 (computer).

Westminster College

- **Address:** South Market Street, New Wilmington, PA 16172
- **Website:** http://www.westminster.edu
- **Private; Religious affiliation:** Presbyterian (U.S.A.)
- **Enrollment:** 1,410 full-time; 54 part-time

KEY STATS
- ✔ **U.S News College Ranking:** third tier, Liberal Arts Colleges
- ✔ **SAT Score (25th/75th percentile):** 960-1182
- ✔ **Tuition:** 2006-2007: $24,200
- **Selectivity:** Selective
- **Acceptance rate:** 77%
- **Student/faculty ratio:** 12/1
- **Room/board:** $7,070
- **Average debt:** $20,386
- **Proportion who borrowed:** 83%

UNDERGRADUATE STUDENT BODY STATS
2005-2006 enrollment: 1,410 full-time; 54 part-time. Men: 36%; women: 64%. **Ethnic makeup:** African American: 2%; White: 97%. **Religious preference:** Roman Catholic: 29%; Protestant: 40%; Jewish: 1%; Muslim: 1%; Hindu: 1%; Buddhist: 1%; No preference: 20%.

ADMISSIONS FACTS AND FIGURES
Phone: (800) 942-8033. **Email:** admis@westminster.edu. **Website:** http://www.westminster.edu. **Application deadlines for fall 2007:** Regular decision: January 5. Early decision: Not offered. Early action: Send application by: November 15; Decision sent by: December 1. Admission can be deferred. **Application fee:** $35. Common application is accepted. **To apply online, go to:** http://www.commonapp.org. **Admissions requirements/recommendations:** High school units required (recommended): English: 4; Mathematics: 3; Science: 2; Foreign language: 2; Social studies: 2; History: 1; Academic electives: 3; Total units: 16. Tests: The college uses SAT or ACT scores in admissions decisions. Either SAT or ACT required. Campus visit: Recommended. Admissions interview: Recommended. Off-campus interview: May be arranged. **Factors that count in admissions decisions:** *Academic:* Secondary school record: Very important. Class rank: Very important. Letters of recommendation: Important. Standardized test scores: Very important. Essay: Important. *Nonacademic:* Interview: Very important. Extracurricular activities: Considered. Talent/ability: Considered. Character/personal qualities: Important. Alumni/ae relationship: Considered. Geographical residence: Not considered. State residency: Not considered. Religious affiliation/commitment: Considered. Minority status: Considered. Volunteer work: Considered. Work experience: Considered. **Other schools with the greatest overlap in applicants:** Allegheny College; Geneva College; Grove City College; Thiel College; Washington and Jefferson College. **Admissions statistics for the fall 2005 entering class:** Total applicants: 1,302. Total accepted: 1,006. Freshmen enrolled: 359; 19% were from out of state. Overall acceptance rate: 77%. Non-early acceptance rate: 77%. **Credentials of fall 2005 freshmen:** 20% ranked in the top 10 percent of their high school class; 55% were in the top 25 percent, and 87% were in the top half. (Proportion submitting class standing: 93%.) **Average high school grade point average:** 3.4. **First-year students who submitted SAT scores:** 89%. Scores (25/75 percentile): Verbal: 480-592, Math: 480-590, Combined: 960-1182. **First-year students submitting ACT scores:** 37%. Scores (25/75 percentile): English: 19-25, Math: 18-24, Composite: 20-25.

ACADEMICS
Year founded: 1852. **Academic calendar:** Semester. **Degrees offered:** bachelor's, master's. **Most popular majors:** 21% education, 16% business, management, marketing, and related support services, 13% social sciences, 8% communication, journalism, and related programs, 6% English language and literature/letters. **Major fields of study:** biological and biomedical sciences; business, management, marketing, and related support services; communication, journalism, and related programs; computer and information sciences and support services; education; English language and literature/letters; foreign languages, literatures, and linguistics; history; mathematics and statistics; multi/interdisciplinary studies; natural resources and conservation; philosophy and religious studies; physical sciences; psychology; social sciences; theology and religious vocations; visual and performing arts. **Areas of required coursework:** arts/fine arts, humanities, mathematics, English (including composition), philosophy, foreign languages, sciences (biological or physical), history, social science, other. **Pre-professional programs:** pre-law, pre-dentistry, pre-medicine, pre-theology, pre-veterinary science, pre-optometry, pre-pharmacy. **Special academic**

programs (% participation): accelerated program (2%), cross-registration (1%), double major (2%), exchange student program (domestic) (1%), honors program (1%), independent study (2%), internships (70%), liberal arts/career combination (100%), student-designed major (1%), study abroad (6%), teacher certificate program. **Teacher certification offered in:** special education, elementary, middle/junior high, secondary. **Reserve Officers Training Corps (ROTC):** Army ROTC: Offered at cooperating institution (Youngstown State University). **Faculty and instruction (2005-2006):** Total instructional faculty: 100 full-time, 49 part-time (58% men; 42% women; 3% minorities). Full-time faculty with Ph.D. or other terminal degree: 83%. Student/faculty ratio: 12/1. Classes of fewer than 20 students: 68%; of 20 to 49 students: 32%; of 50 or more students: 1%. **Advanced Placement and International Baccalaureate credit:** AP tests may be used for: Credit and/or placement. Scores accepted: 3, 5. International Baccalaureate exams may be used for: Credit and/or placement. **Freshmen returning for sophomore year:** 85%. **Graduation rates:** Four-year: 65%; five-year: 76%; six-year: 76%. **Graduate study:** 35% of students pursue further study within one year. Fields in which graduates pursue further study: Master of Business Administration (MBA), 1%; law, 6%; medicine, 7%; theology (or the seminary), 2%; education, 10%; arts and sciences, 10%; veterinary medicine, 2%.

COSTS AND FINANCIAL AID
Financial aid office: (724) 946-7102. **Expenses (2006-2007):** Tuition and fees 2006-2007: $24,200; room/board: $7,070. Estimated books and supplies: $1,000; transportation: $0; personal expenses: $1,000. **Financial aid:** Priority filing date for institution's financial aid form: May 1. In 2005-2006, 85% of undergraduates applied for financial aid. Of those, 78% were determined to have financial need; 33% had their need fully met. Average financial aid package (proportion receiving): $18,665 (78%). Average amount of gift aid, such as scholarships or grants (proportion receiving): $14,511 (78%). Average amount of self-help aid, such as work study or loans (proportion receiving): $4,557 (63%). Average need-based loan (excluding PLUS or other private loans): $4,031. Among students who received need-based aid, the average percentage of need met: 89%. Among students who received aid based on merit, the average award (and the proportion receiving): $8,818 (20%). Average amount of debt of borrowers graduating in 2005: $20,386. Proportion who borrowed: 83%.

CAMPUS LIFE AND EXTRACURRICULAR ACTIVITIES
Campus housing available (% using): women's dorms (40%), men's dorms (32%), fraternity housing (18%), other housing options (10%). Students who live in college-owned, operated, or affiliated housing: 85%. **Student employment:** During the 2005-2006 academic year, 21% of undergraduates worked on campus. **Clubs and organizations:** Number of student organizations: 69. Activities include: choral groups, concert band, dance, drama/theater, jazz band, literary magazine, marching band, music ensembles, musical theater, opera, pep band, radio station, student government, student newspaper, student film society, symphony orchestra, television station, yearbook. Number of fraternities: 5; sororities: 5. Proportion of men in fraternities: 33%; of women in sororities: 35%. Average proportion of students who stay on campus on weekends: 75%. **Sports program (2005-2006):** Member of NCAA III. *Men's intercollegiate varsity sports:* baseball, basketball, cross-country, football, golf, soccer, swimming and diving, tennis, track and field (indoor), track and field (outdoor). *Women's intercollegiate varsity sports:* basketball, cross-country, golf, soccer, softball, swimming and diving, tennis, track and field (indoor), track and field (outdoor), volleyball.

SERVICES AND FACILITIES
Basic services: nonremedial tutoring, placement service, health service, health insurance. **Remedial assistance:** reading, study skills. **Counseling services:** minority student, career, personal, academic, older student, psychological, religious. **For learning-disabled students:** School does not offer a structured program with separate admission and additional fees. Total undergraduates in learning-disabled program or receiving services: 53. Services include: reading machines, remedial reading, tape recorders, videotaped classes, untimed tests, note-taking services, oral tests, learning center, readers, extended time for tests, tutors, priority seating, other. **Library:** Number of titles: 283,070; number of current serial subscriptions: 848. **Information technology resources:** Students are not required to lease or own a computer. Number of campus computers available to all students: 120. School has a wireless network. Approximate number of users that can be accommodated: 1,200. Proportion of college-owned housing units wired for high-speed internet access: 100%. **Campus safety:** Security services offered: 24-hour foot-and-vehicle patrols, late-night transport/escort service, 24-hour emergency telephones, lighted pathways/sidewalks, controlled dormitory access (key, security card, etc).

TRANSFER AND INTERNATIONAL STUDENTS

Transfer students: May apply for admission for the following academic terms: Fall, Spring. Applicants do not need a minimum number of credits to apply. For fall 2005: Transfer applications received: 54. Transfer applicants offered admission: 27. Transfer applicants enrolled: 20. **International students:** Number of foreign undergraduates: 0. Minimum TOEFL score required: 500 (paper); 173 (computer).

Widener University

- **Address:** 1 University Place, Chester, PA 19013
- **Website:** http://www.widener.edu
- **Private**
- **Enrollment:** 2,375 full-time; 141 part-time

KEY STATS

✔ **U.S News College Ranking:** third tier, National Universities
✔ **SAT Score (25th/75th percentile):** 890-1090
✔ **Tuition:** 2006-2007: $26,750

Selectivity: Less selective	**Room/board:** $9,640
Acceptance rate: 81%	**Average debt:** $26,348
Student/faculty ratio: 11/1	**Proportion who borrowed:** 79%

UNDERGRADUATE STUDENT BODY STATS

2005-2006 enrollment: 2,375 full-time; 141 part-time. Men: 51%; women: 49%. **Ethnic makeup:** African American: 16%; Asian American: 2%; Hispanic: 3%; White: 78%; International: 1%.

ADMISSIONS FACTS AND FIGURES

Phone: (610) 499-4126. **Email:** admissions.office@widener.edu. **Website:** http://www.widener.edu. **Application deadlines for fall 2007:** Regular decision: Rolling. Early decision: Not offered. Early action: Not offered. Admission can be deferred. **Application fee:** $35. Common application is accepted. **To apply online, go to:** https://www.applyweb.com/apply/wideneru/. **Admissions requirements/recommendations:** High school units required (recommended): English: 4 (4); Mathematics: 3 (4); Science: 3 (4); Foreign language: 2 (2); Social studies: 3 (4); History: 0 (0); Academic electives: 3 (3); Total units: 18 (23). Tests: The college uses SAT or ACT scores in admissions decisions. Either SAT or ACT required. For admission to the fall 2007 entering class, the school will accept: ACT with writing, ACT without writing. Campus visit: Recommended. Admissions interview: Recommended. Off-campus interview: May be arranged. **Factors that count in admissions decisions:** *Academic:* Secondary school record: Very important. Class rank: Very important. Letters of recommendation: Considered. Standardized test scores: Very important. Essay: Considered. *Nonacademic:* Interview: Considered. Extracurricular activities: Considered. Talent/ability: Considered. Character/personal qualities: Considered. Alumni/ae relationship: Considered. Geographical residence: Not considered. State residency: Not considered. Religious affiliation/commitment: Not considered. Minority status: Not considered. Volunteer work: Considered. Work experience: Not considered. **Other schools with the greatest overlap in applicants:** Drexel University; La Salle University; St. Joseph's University; Temple University; West Chester University of Pennsylvania. **Admissions statistics for the fall 2005 entering class:** Total applicants: 2,963. Total accepted: 2,406. Freshmen enrolled: 650; 40% were from out of state. Overall acceptance rate: 81%. **Credentials of fall 2005 freshmen:** 13% ranked in the top 10 percent of their high school class; 34% were in the top 25 percent, and 69% were in the top half. (Proportion submitting class standing: 85%.) **Average high school grade point average:** 3.3. **First-year students who submitted SAT scores:** 99%. Scores (25/75 percentile): Verbal: 450-530; Math: 440-560; Combined: 890-1090.

ACADEMICS

Year founded: 1821. **Academic calendar:** Semester. **Degrees offered:** certificate, associate, bachelor's, master's, first professional, doctorate. **Most popular majors:** 34% business administration, management, and operations, 16% health professions and related clinical sciences, 9% engineering, 8% psychology, 8% social sciences. **Major fields of study:** biological and biomedical sciences; business, management, marketing, and related support services; communication, journalism, and related programs; computer and information sciences and support services; education; engineering; English language and literature/letters; foreign languages, literatures, and linguis-

tics; health professions and related clinical sciences; history; legal professions and studies; liberal arts and sciences studies, and humanities; mathematics and statistics; multi/interdisciplinary studies; psychology; public administration and social service professions; security and protective services; social sciences. **Areas of required coursework:** humanities, computer literacy, mathematics, English (including composition), sciences (biological or physical), social science. **Pre-professional programs:** pre-law, pre-dentistry, pre-medicine, pre-veterinary science, pre-optometry, pre-pharmacy, other. **Special academic programs:** accelerated program, cooperative (work-study plan) program, distance learning, double major, English as a Second Language (ESL), honors program, independent study, internships, student-designed major, study abroad, teacher certificate program, weekend college. **Teacher certification offered in:** early childhood, special education, elementary, secondary, bilingual/bicultural. **Cooperative education programs:** business, computer science, engineering, other. **Reserve Officers Training Corps (ROTC):** Army ROTC: Offered on campus; Navy ROTC: Offered at cooperating institution (Villanova University); Air Force ROTC: Offered at cooperating institution (St. Joseph's University). **Faculty and instruction (2005-2006):** Total instructional faculty: 314 full-time, 283 part-time. Full-time faculty with Ph.D. or other terminal degree: 92%. Student/faculty ratio: 11/1. Classes of fewer than 20 students: 70%; of 20 to 49 students: 29%; of 50 or more students: 1%. **Advanced Placement and International Baccalaureate credit:** AP tests may be used for: Credit and/or placement. Scores accepted: 3, 4, 5. International Baccalaureate exams may be used for: Credit only. **Freshmen returning for sophomore year:** 72%. **Graduation rates:** Four-year: 39%; five-year: 53%; six-year: 57%. **Graduate study:** 17% of students pursue further study immediately upon graduation.

COSTS AND FINANCIAL AID

Financial aid office: (610) 499-4174. **Expenses (2006-2007):** Tuition and fees 2006-2007: $26,750; room/board: $9,640. Estimated books and supplies: $940; transportation: $468; personal expenses: $1,170. **Financial aid:** Priority filing date for institution's financial aid form: February 15. In 2005-2006, 89% of undergraduates applied for financial aid. Of those, 81% were determined to have financial need; 48% had their need fully met. Average financial aid package (proportion receiving): $20,192 (81%). Average amount of gift aid, such as scholarships or grants (proportion receiving): $10,799 (73%). Average amount of self-help aid, such as work study or loans (proportion receiving): $6,816 (72%). Average need-based loan (excluding PLUS or other private loans): $4,705. Among students who received need-based aid, the average percentage of need met: 77%. Among students who received aid based on merit, the average award (and the proportion receiving): $8,201 (12%). The average athletic scholarship (and the proportion receiving): $0 (0%). Average amount of debt of borrowers graduating in 2005: $26,348. Proportion who borrowed: 79%.

CAMPUS LIFE AND EXTRACURRICULAR ACTIVITIES

Campus housing available: coed dorms, women's dorms, men's dorms, sorority housing, fraternity housing, apartment for single students, cooperative housing, other housing options. Students who live in college-owned, operated, or affiliated housing: 61%. **Student employment:** During the 2005-2006 academic year, 40% of undergraduates worked on campus. Average per-year earnings: $2,500. **Clubs and organizations:** Number of student organizations: 99. Activities include: choral groups, concert band, dance, drama/theater, jazz band, literary magazine, music ensembles, pep band, radio station, student government, student newspaper, student film society, yearbook. Number of fraternities: 7; sororities: 3. Proportion of men in fraternities: 12%; of women in sororities: 11%. Average proportion of students who stay on campus on weekends: 65%. **Sports program (2005-2006):** Member of NCAA III. *Men's intercollegiate varsity sports:* baseball, basketball, cross-country, football, golf, lacrosse, soccer, swimming and diving, tennis, track and field (indoor), track and field (outdoor). *Women's intercollegiate varsity sports:* basketball, cross-country, field hockey, lacrosse, soccer, softball, swimming and diving, tennis, track and field (indoor), track and field (outdoor), volleyball.

SERVICES AND FACILITIES

Basic services: nonremedial tutoring, placement service, day care, health service, health insurance. **Remedial assistance:** reading, math, writing, study skills. **Counseling services:** minority student, career, military, personal, veteran student, academic, older student, psychological, birth control, religious. **For learning-disabled students:** School does not offer a structured program with separate admission and additional fees. Services include: remedial math, remedial English, reading machines, remedial reading, tape recorders, diagnostic testing service, untimed tests, note-taking services, oral tests, learning center, readers, extended time for tests, tutors, texts on tape. **Library:** Number of titles: 238,349; number of current serial subscriptions: 1,974. **Information technology resources:** Students are not required to lease or own a computer. Number of campus computers available to all students: 720. School has a wireless network. Proportion of college-owned housing units wired for high-speed internet access: 100%. **Campus safety:** Security services offered: 24-hour foot-and-vehicle patrols, late-night transport/escort service, 24-hour emergency telephones, lighted pathways/sidewalks, controlled dormitory access (key, security card, etc).

TRANSFER AND INTERNATIONAL STUDENTS

Transfer students: May apply for admission for the following academic terms: Fall, Spring, Summer. Applicants need a minimum number of credits to apply. For fall 2005: Transfer applications received: 672. Transfer applicants offered admission: 419. Transfer applicants enrolled: 151. **International students:** Number of foreign undergraduates: 5 (1% of student body). Number of countries represented: 38. Minimum TOEFL score required: 500 (paper); 173 (computer). Average TOEFL score: 550 (paper).

Wilkes University

- **Address:** 84 W South Street, Wilkes-Barre, PA 18766
- **Website:** http://www.wilkes.edu
- **Private**
- **Enrollment:** 1,968 full-time; 220 part-time

KEY STATS

✔ **U.S News College Ranking:** 68, Universities–Master's (North)
✔ **SAT Score (25th/75th percentile):** 960-1180
✔ **Tuition:** 2006-2007: $22,990

Selectivity: Selective	**Room/board:** $9,860
Acceptance rate: 77%	**Average debt:** $25,164
Student/faculty ratio: 15/1	**Proportion who borrowed:** 84%

UNDERGRADUATE STUDENT BODY STATS

2005-2006 enrollment: 1,968 full-time; 220 part-time. Men: 47%; women: 53%. **Ethnic makeup:** African American: 2%; Asian American: 2%; Hispanic: 2%; White: 93%.

ADMISSIONS FACTS AND FIGURES

Phone: (570) 408-4400. **Email:** admissions@wilkes.edu. **Website:** http://www.wilkes.edu. **Application deadlines for fall 2007:** Regular decision: Rolling. Early decision: Not offered. Early action: Not offered. Admission can be deferred. **Application fee:** $35. Common application is accepted. **Admissions requirements/recommendations:** High school units required (recommended): English: (4); Mathematics: (3); Science: (2); Social studies: (3). Tests: The college uses SAT or ACT scores in admissions decisions. Either SAT or ACT required. Campus visit: Recommended. Admissions interview: Recommended. Off-campus interview: May be arranged. **Factors that count in admissions decisions:** *Academic:* Secondary school record: Very important. Class rank: Very important. Letters of recommendation: Considered. Standardized test scores: Important. Essay: Considered. *Nonacademic:* Interview: Considered. Extracurricular activities: Important. Talent/ability: Considered. Character/personal qualities: Important. Alumni/ae relationship: Considered. Geographical residence: Not considered. State residency: Not considered. Religious affiliation/commitment: Not considered. Minority status: Not considered. Volunteer work: Considered. Work experience: Considered. **Other schools with the greatest overlap in applicants:** Bloomsburg University of Pennsylvania; East Stroudsburg University of Pennsylvania; King's College; Pennsylvania State University–University Park; University of Scranton. **Admissions statistics for the fall 2005 entering class:** Total applicants: 2,702. Total accepted: 2,084. Freshmen enrolled: 572; 23% were from out of state. Overall acceptance rate: 77%. **Credentials of fall 2005 freshmen:** 20% ranked in the top 10 percent of their high school class; 48% were in the top 25 percent, and 82% were in the top half. (Proportion submitting class standing: 88%.) **Average high school grade point average:** 3.3. **First-year students who submitted SAT scores:** 99%. Scores (25/75 percentile): Verbal: 480-580, Math: 480-600, Combined: 960-1180.

ACADEMICS

Year founded: 1933. **Academic calendar:** Semester. **Degrees offered:** bachelor's, master's, first professional. **Most popular majors:** 16% business, management, marketing, and related support services, 10% education, 9% engineering, 9% psychology, 8% biological and biomedical sciences. **Major fields of study:** biological and biomedical sciences; business, management, marketing, and related support services; communication, journalism, and related programs; computer and information sciences and support services; education; engineering; English language and literature/letters; foreign languages, literatures, and linguistics; health professions and related clinical sciences; history; liberal arts and sciences studies, and humanities; mathematics and statistics; multi/interdisciplinary studies; philosophy and religious studies; physical sciences; psychology; security and protective services; social sciences; visual and performing arts. **Areas of required coursework:** arts/fine arts, humanities, computer literacy, mathematics, English (including composition), sciences (biological or physical), social science. **Pre-professional programs:** pre-law, pre-dentistry, pre-medicine, pre-veterinary science, pre-optometry, pre-pharmacy. **Special academic programs:** cooperative (work-study plan) program, cross-registration, distance learning, double major, dual enrollment, external degree program, honors program, independent study, internships, student-designed major, study abroad, teacher certificate program, weekend college. **Teacher certification offered in:** early childhood, special education, elementary, secondary. **Reserve Officers Training Corps (ROTC):** Army ROTC: Offered at cooperating institution (King's College, University of Scranton); Air Force ROTC: Offered on campus. **Faculty and instruction (2005-2006):** Total full-time faculty: 131 full-time, 86 part-time. Full-time faculty with Ph.D. or other terminal degree: 87%. Student/faculty ratio: 15/1. Classes of fewer than 20 students: 43%; of 20 to 49 students: 52%; of 50 or more students: 5%. **Advanced Placement and International Baccalaureate credit:** AP tests may be used for: Credit and/or placement. Scores accepted: 3, 4, 5. International Baccalaureate exams may be used for: Credit and/or placement. **Freshmen returning for sophomore year:** 79%. **Graduation rates:** Four-year: 44%; five-year: 55%; six-year: 57%.

COSTS AND FINANCIAL AID

Financial aid office: (570) 408-4346. **Expenses (2006-2007):** Tuition and fees 2006-2007: $22,990; room/board: $9,860. Estimated books and supplies: $1,050; transportation: $500; personal expenses: $1,000. **Financial aid:** Priority filing date for institution's financial aid form: March 1. In 2005-2006, 93% of undergraduates applied for financial aid. Of those, 83% were determined to have financial need; 24% had their need fully met. Average financial aid package (proportion receiving): $16,882 (79%). Average amount of gift aid, such as scholarships or grants (proportion receiving): $12,315 (78%). Average amount of self-help aid, such as work study or loans (proportion receiving): $4,366 (75%). Average need-based loan (excluding PLUS or other private loans): $3,787. Among students who received need-based aid, the average percentage of need met: 82%. Among students who received aid based on merit, the average award (and the proportion receiving): $8,838 (13%). The average athletic scholarship (and the proportion receiving): $0 (0%). Average amount of debt of borrowers graduating in 2005: $25,164. Proportion who borrowed: 84%.

CAMPUS LIFE AND EXTRACURRICULAR ACTIVITIES

Campus housing available: coed dorms, women's dorms, men's dorms, apartment for single students. Students who live in college-owned, operated, or affiliated housing: 45%. **Student employment:** During the 2005-2006 academic year, 36% of undergraduates worked on campus. Average per-year earnings: $700. **Clubs and organizations:** Number of student organizations: 60. Activities include: choral groups, dance, drama/theater, jazz band, literary magazine, music ensembles, musical theater, pep band, radio station, student government, student newspaper, television station, yearbook. Number of fraternities: 0; sororities: 0. Average proportion of students who stay on campus on weekends: 85%. **Sports program (2005-2006):** Member of NCAA III. *Men's intercollegiate varsity sports:* baseball, basketball, football, golf, soccer, tennis, wrestling. *Women's intercollegiate varsity sports:* basketball, field hockey, lacrosse, soccer, softball, tennis, volleyball.

SERVICES AND FACILITIES

Basic services: nonremedial tutoring, placement service, health service. **Remedial assistance:** reading, math, writing, study skills. **Counseling services:** minority student, career, military, personal, veteran student, academic, older student, psychological. **For learning-disabled students:** School does not offer a structured program with separate admission and additional fees. Total undergraduates in learning-disabled program or receiving services: 45. Services include: remedial math, remedial English, reading machines, remedial reading, tape recorders, diagnostic testing service, untimed tests, note-taking services, oral tests, learning center, readers, extended time for tests, tutors, priority registration, priority seating, texts on tape, typist/scribe, other testing accomodations, waiver of foreign language degree requirement. **Library:** Number of titles: 185,844; number of current serial subscriptions: 521. **Information technology resources:** Students are not required to lease or own a computer. Number of campus computers available to all students: 655. School has a wireless network. Approximate number of users that can be accommodated: 3,000. Proportion of college-owned housing units wired for high-speed internet access: 100%. **Campus safety:** Security services offered: 24-hour foot-and-vehicle patrols, late-night transport/escort service, 24-hour emergency telephones, lighted pathways/sidewalks, controlled dormitory access (key, security card, etc).

TRANSFER AND INTERNATIONAL STUDENTS

Transfer students: May apply for admission for the following academic terms: Fall, Spring, Summer. Applicants need a minimum number of credits to apply. For fall 2005: Transfer applications received: 507. Transfer applicants offered admission: 271. Transfer applicants enrolled: 137. **International students:** Number of foreign undergraduates: 6. Minimum TOEFL score required: 500 (paper); 173 (computer).

Wilson College

- **Address:** 1015 Philadelphia Avenue, Chambersburg, PA 17201
- **Website:** http://www.wilson.edu
- **Private; Religious affiliation:** Presbyterian
- **Enrollment:** 348 full-time; 384 part-time

KEY STATS

✔ **U.S News College Ranking:** 18, Comp. Coll.–Bachelor's (North)
✔ **SAT Score (25th/75th percentile):** 890-1140
✔ **Tuition:** 2006-2007: $21,830

Selectivity: Selective	**Room/board:** $7,916
Acceptance rate: 57%	**Average debt:** $25,848
Student/faculty ratio: 10/1	**Proportion who borrowed:** 90%

UNDERGRADUATE STUDENT BODY STATS

2005-2006 enrollment: 348 full-time; 384 part-time. Men: 11%; women: 89%. **Ethnic makeup:** African American: 5%; Asian American: 1%; Hispanic: 3%; White: 87%; International: 5%. **Religious preference:** Roman Catholic: 3%; Protestant: 6%; Jewish: 1%; Hindu: 1%; Buddhist: 1%; No preference: 87%; Presbyterian: 1%.

ADMISSIONS FACTS AND FIGURES

Phone: (800) 421-8402. **Email:** admissions@wilson.edu. **Website:** http://www.wilson.edu. **Application deadlines for fall 2007:** Regular decision: Rolling. Early decision: Not offered. Early action: Not offered. Admission can be deferred. **Application fee:** $35. Common application is accepted. **To apply online, go to:** http://www.wilson.edu/apply. **Admissions requirements/recommendations:** High school units required (recommended): English: (4); Mathematics: (3); Science: (2); Foreign language: (2); Social studies: (0); History: (4); Total units: (15). Tests: The college uses SAT or ACT scores in admissions decisions. Either SAT or ACT required. For admission to the fall 2007 entering class, the school will accept: ACT with writing, ACT without writing. Campus visit: Recommended. Admissions interview: Recommended. Off-campus interview: May be arranged. **Factors that count in admissions decisions:** *Academic:* Secondary school record: Very important. Class rank: Important. Letters of recommendation: Important. Standardized test scores: Important. Essay: Important. *Nonacademic:* Interview: Important. Extracurricular activities: Important. Talent/ability: Considered. Character/personal qualities: Important. Alumni/ae relationship: Considered. Geographical residence: Not considered. State residency: Not considered. Religious affiliation/commitment: Not considered. Minority status: Not considered. Volunteer work: Considered. Work experience: Considered. **Other schools with the greatest overlap in applicants:** Delaware Valley College; Lebanon Valley College; Pennsylvania State University–University Park; Shippensburg University of Pennsylvania. **Admissions statistics for the fall 2005 entering class:** Total applicants: 441. Total accepted: 250. Freshmen enrolled: 76; 32% were from out of state. Overall acceptance rate: 57%. **Credentials of fall 2005 freshmen:** 9% ranked in the top 10 percent of their high school class; 39% were in the top 25 per-

cent, and 84% were in the top half. (Proportion submitting class standing: 74%.) **Average high school grade point average:** 3.3. **First-year students who submitted SAT scores:** 96%. Scores (25/75 percentile): Verbal: 460-580, Math: 430-560, Combined: 890-1140. **First-year students submitting ACT scores:** 13%. Scores (25/75 percentile): English: N/A, Math: N/A, Composite: 20-25.

ACADEMICS

Year founded: 1869. **Academic calendar:** 4-1-4. **Degrees offered:** certificate, associate, bachelor's. **Most popular majors:** 21% veterinary/animal health technology/technician and veterinary assistant, 13% business administration and management, 10% elementary education and teaching, 10% social sciences, 9% biology/biological sciences. **Major fields of study:** agriculture, agriculture operations, and related sciences; biological and biomedical sciences; business, management, marketing, and related support services; communication, journalism, and related programs; education; English language and literature/letters; foreign languages, literatures, and linguistics; health professions and related clinical sciences; mathematics and statistics; multi/interdisciplinary studies; natural resources and conservation; parks, recreation, leisure, and fitness studies; philosophy and religious studies; physical sciences; psychology; social sciences; visual and performing arts. **Areas of required coursework:** arts/fine arts, humanities, computer literacy, mathematics, English (including composition), foreign languages, sciences (biological or physical), history, social science, other. **Pre-professional programs:** pre-law, pre-dentistry, pre-medicine, pre-veterinary science, pre-optometry, pre-pharmacy. **Special academic programs (% participation):** double major (6.59%), English as a Second Language (ESL) (1.1%), exchange student program (domestic) (8.79%), honors program (6.59%), independent study (24.18%), internships (28.57%), liberal arts/career combination (49.45%), student-designed major (5.49%), study abroad (1.1%), teacher certificate program (9.89%). **Teacher certification offered in:** elementary, secondary. **Faculty and instruction (2005-2006):** Total instructional faculty: 40 full-time, 35 part-time (45% men; 55% women; 3% minorities). Full-time faculty with Ph.D. or other terminal degree: 78%. Student/faculty ratio: 10/1. Classes of fewer than 20 students: 85%; of 20 to 49 students: 15%. **Advanced Placement and International Baccalaureate credit:** AP tests may be used for: Credit only. Scores accepted: 4, 5. International Baccalaureate exams may be used for: Credit and/or placement. **Freshmen returning for sophomore year:** 67%. **Graduation rates:** Four-year: 42%; five-year: 45%; six-year: 51%. **Graduate study:** 21% of students pursue further study immediately upon graduation. Fields in which graduates pursue further study: Master of Business Administration (MBA), 8%; law, 14%; theology (or the seminary), 5%; education, 29%; arts and sciences, 29%; veterinary medicine, 5%.

COSTS AND FINANCIAL AID

Financial aid office: (717) 262-2016. **Expenses (2006-2007):** Tuition and fees 2006-2007: $21,830; room/board: $7,916. Estimated books and supplies: $800; transportation: $400; personal expenses: $800. **Financial aid:** Priority filing date for institution's financial aid form: April 30. In 2005-2006, 84% of undergraduates applied for financial aid. Of those, 74% were determined to have financial need; 19% had their need fully met. Average financial aid package (proportion receiving): $16,223 (73%). Average amount of gift aid, such as scholarships or grants (proportion receiving): $12,451 (71%). Average amount of self-help aid, such as work study or loans (proportion receiving): $4,747 (62%). Average need-based loan (excluding PLUS or other private loans): $4,407. Among students who received need-based aid, the average percentage of need met: 78%. Among students who received aid based on merit, the average award (and the proportion receiving): $14,565 (23%). The average athletic scholarship (and the proportion receiving): $0 (0%). Average amount of debt of borrowers graduating in 2005: $25,848. Proportion who borrowed: 90%.

CAMPUS LIFE AND EXTRACURRICULAR ACTIVITIES

Campus housing available (% using): women's dorms (87%), other housing options (13%). Students who live in college-owned, operated, or affiliated housing: 41%. **Student employment:** During the 2005-2006 academic year, 5% of undergraduates worked on campus. Average per-year earnings: $2,250. **Clubs and organizations:** Number of student organizations: 24. Activities include: choral groups, dance, drama/theater, literary magazine, music ensembles, student government, student newspaper, yearbook. Number of fraternities: 0; sororities: 0. Average proportion of students who stay on campus on weekends: 30%. **Sports program (2005-2006):** Member of NCAA III. *Women's intercollegiate varsity sports:* basketball, field hockey, gymnastics, soccer, softball, tennis, volleyball.

SERVICES AND FACILITIES

Basic services: nonremedial tutoring, women's center, placement service, day care, health service, health insurance, other. **Remedial assistance:** math, writing, study skills. **Counseling services:** career, personal, academic, older student, psychological, birth control, religious. **For learning-disabled students:** School does not offer a structured program with separate admission and additional fees. Total undergraduates in learning-disabled program or receiving services: 29. Services include: remedial math, tape recorders, note-taking services, oral tests, learning center, readers, extended time for tests, tutors, priority seating, substitution of courses, texts on tape, typist/scribe, other testing accomodations, waiver of foreign language degree requirement, waiver of math degree requirement, other. **Library:** Number of titles: 179,202; number of current serial subscriptions: 253. **Information technology resources:** Students are not required to lease or own a computer. Number of campus computers available to all students: 112. School has a wireless network. Approximate number of users that can be accommodated: 100. Proportion of college-owned housing units wired for high-speed internet access: 100%. **Campus safety:** Security services offered: 24-hour foot-and-vehicle patrols, late-night transport/escort service, 24-hour emergency telephones, lighted pathways/sidewalks, controlled dormitory access (key, security card, etc).

TRANSFER AND INTERNATIONAL STUDENTS

Transfer students: May apply for admission for the following academic terms: Fall, Spring. Applicants do not need a minimum number of credits to apply. For fall 2005: Transfer applications received: 57. Transfer applicants offered admission: 51. Transfer applicants enrolled: 22. **International students:** Number of foreign undergraduates: 24 (5% of student body). Number of countries represented: 10. Minimum TOEFL score required: 500 (paper); 173 (computer). Average TOEFL score: 569 (paper).

York College of Pennsylvania

- **Address:** Country Club Road, York, PA 17405-7199
- **Website:** http://www.ycp.edu
- **Private**
- **Enrollment:** 4,469 full-time; 936 part-time

KEY STATS

✔ **U.S News College Ranking:** 77, Universities–Master's (North)
✔ **SAT Score (25th/75th percentile):** 1000-1190
✔ **Tuition:** 2006-2007: $11,160

Selectivity: Selective	**Room/board:** $6,950
Acceptance rate: 75%	**Average debt:** $18,198
Student/faculty ratio: 21/1	**Proportion who borrowed:** 68%

UNDERGRADUATE STUDENT BODY STATS

2005-2006 enrollment: 4,469 full-time; 936 part-time. Men: 41%; women: 59%. **Ethnic makeup:** African American: 2%; Asian American: 1%; Hispanic: 2%; White: 95%. **Religious preference:** Roman Catholic: 38%; Protestant: 42%; Jewish: 3%; Muslim: 1%.

ADMISSIONS FACTS AND FIGURES

Phone: (717) 849-1600. **Email:** admissions@ycp.edu. **Website:** http://www.ycp.edu. **Application deadlines for fall 2007:** Regular decision: Rolling. Early decision: Not offered. Early action: Not offered. Admission can be deferred. **Application fee:** $30. Common application is accepted. **To apply online, go to:** http://www.ycp.edu/admissions/html/application.html. **Admissions requirements/recommendations:** High school units required (recommended): English: 4; Mathematics: 3 (4); Science: 3; Foreign language: 2; Social studies: 3; Total units: 15. Tests: The college uses SAT or ACT scores in admissions decisions. Either SAT or ACT required. For admission to the fall 2007 entering class, the school will accept: ACT with writing. Campus visit: Recommended. Admissions interview: Recommended. Off-campus interview: May be arranged. **Factors that count in admissions decisions:** *Academic:* Secondary school record: Very important. Class rank: Important. Letters of recommendation: Considered. Standardized test scores: Important. Essay: Considered. *Nonacademic:* Interview: Considered. Extracurricular activities: Considered. Talent/ability: Considered. Character/personal qualities: Important. Alumni/ae relationship: Considered. Geographical residence: Not considered. State residency: Not considered. Religious affiliation/commitment: Not considered. Minority

status: Not considered. Volunteer work: Considered. Work experience: Considered. **Other schools with the greatest overlap in applicants:** Millersville University of Pennsylvania; Pennsylvania State University–University Park; Shippensburg University of Pennsylvania; Towson University; West Chester University of Pennsylvania. **Admissions statistics for the fall 2005 entering class:** Total applicants: 4,152. Total accepted: 3,101. Freshmen enrolled: 1,098; 47% were from out of state. Overall acceptance rate: 75%. **Credentials of fall 2005 freshmen:** 28% ranked in the top 10 percent of their high school class; 65% were in the top 25 percent, and 93% were in the top half. (Proportion submitting class standing: 90%.) **Average high school grade point average:** 3.1. **First-year students who submitted SAT scores:** 91%. Scores (25/75 percentile): Verbal: 500-600, Math: 500-590, Combined: 1000-1190. **First-year students submitting ACT scores:** 8%. Scores (25/75 percentile): English: N/A, Math: N/A, Composite: 21-27.

ACADEMICS

Year founded: 1787. **Academic calendar:** Semester. **Degrees offered:** associate, bachelor's, master's. **Most popular majors:** 21% business, management, marketing, and related support services, 12% education, 10% communication, journalism, and related programs, 10% health professions and related clinical sciences, 9% social sciences. **Major fields of study:** agriculture, agriculture operations, and related sciences; biological and biomedical sciences; business, management, marketing, and related support services; communication, journalism, and related programs; computer and information sciences and support services; education; engineering; engineering technologies/technicians; English language and literature/letters; family and consumer sciences/human sciences; foreign languages, literatures, and linguistics; health professions and related clinical sciences; history; liberal arts and sciences studies, and humanities; mathematics and statistics; multi/interdisciplinary studies; parks, recreation, leisure, and fitness studies; philosophy and religious studies; physical sciences; psychology; public administration and social service professions; security and protective services; social sciences; visual and performing arts. **Areas of required coursework:** arts/fine arts, humanities, computer literacy, mathematics, English (including composition), sciences (biological or physical), history, social science. **Pre-professional programs:** pre-law, pre-dentistry, pre-medicine, pre-veterinary science, pre-optometry, pre-pharmacy. **Special academic programs:** accelerated program, cooperative (work-study plan) program, distance learning, double major, dual enrollment, honors program, independent study, internships, liberal arts/career combination, student-designed major, study abroad, teacher certificate program. **Teacher certification offered in:** early childhood, special education, elementary, middle/junior high, secondary. **Cooperative education programs:** education, engineering, health professions. **Reserve Officers Training Corps (ROTC):** Army ROTC: Offered at cooperating institution (Johns Hopkins University, Dickinson University). **Faculty and instruction (2005-2006):** Total instructional faculty: 134 full-time, 295 part-time (55% men; 45% women; 2% minorities). Full-time faculty with Ph.D. or other terminal degree: 80%. Student/faculty ratio: 21/1. Classes of fewer than 20 students: 34%; of 20 to 49 students: 66%; of 50 or more students: 0%. **Advanced Placement and International Baccalaureate credit:** AP tests may be used for: Credit and/or placement. Scores accepted: 3, 4, 5. **Freshmen returning for sophomore year:** 82%. **Graduation rates:** Four-year: 43%; five-year: 62%; six-year: 63%. **Graduate study:** 15% of students pursue further study immediately upon graduation; 20% within one year; 30% within five years.

COSTS AND FINANCIAL AID

Financial aid office: (717) 849-1682. **Expenses (2006-2007):** Tuition and fees 2006-2007: $11,160; room/board: $6,950. Estimated books and supplies: $800; transportation: $500; personal expenses: $1,000. **Financial aid:** Priority filing date for institution's financial aid form: February 15. In 2005-2006, 76% of undergraduates applied for financial aid. Of those, 51% were determined to have financial need; 25% had their need fully met. Average financial aid package (proportion receiving): $7,015 (50%). Average amount of gift aid, such as scholarships or grants (proportion receiving): $4,138 (35%). Average amount of self-help aid, such as work study or loans (proportion receiving): $3,736 (47%). Average need-based loan (excluding PLUS or other private loans): $3,569. Among students who received need-based aid, the average percentage of need met: 71%. Among students who received aid based on merit, the average award (and the proportion receiving): $3,090 (9%). The average athletic scholarship (and the proportion receiving): $0 (0%). Average amount of debt of borrowers graduating in 2005: $18,198. Proportion who borrowed: 68%.

CAMPUS LIFE AND EXTRACURRICULAR ACTIVITIES

Campus housing available (% using): coed dorms (44%), women's dorms (2%), sorority housing (2%), apartment for single students (52%). Students who live in college-owned, operated, or affiliated housing: 37%. **Student employment:** During the 2005-2006 academic year, 15% of undergraduates worked on campus. Average per-year earnings: $1,600. **Clubs and organizations:** Number of student organizations: 80. Activities include: choral groups, concert band, drama/theater, jazz band, literary magazine, music ensembles, musical theater, radio station, student government, student newspaper, symphony orchestra, television station, yearbook. Number of fraternities: 10; sororities: 7. Proportion of men in fraternities: 9%; of women in sororities: 7%. Average proportion of students who stay on campus on weekends: 70%. **Sports program (2005-2006):** Member of NCAA III. *Men's intercollegiate varsity sports:* baseball, basketball, cross-country, golf, lacrosse, soccer, swimming and diving, tennis, track and field (outdoor), wrestling. *Women's intercollegiate varsity sports:* basketball, cross-country, field hockey, lacrosse, soccer, softball, swimming and diving, tennis, track and field (outdoor), volleyball.

SERVICES AND FACILITIES

Basic services: nonremedial tutoring, placement service, health service, health insurance. **Remedial assistance:** math, writing, study skills. **Counseling services:** minority student, career, personal, veteran student, academic, older student, psychological, birth control, religious. **For learning-disabled students:** School does not offer a structured program with separate admission and additional fees. Total undergraduates in learning-disabled program or receiving services: 87. Services include: remedial math, remedial English, learning center, extended time for tests, tutors. **Library:** Number of titles: 217,025; number of current serial subscriptions: 17,800. **Information technology resources:** Students are not required to lease or own a computer. Number of campus computers available to all students: 450. School has a wireless network. Approximate number of users that can be accommodated: 500. Proportion of college-owned housing units wired for high-speed internet access: 100%. **Campus safety:** Security services offered: 24-hour foot-and-vehicle patrols, late-night transport/escort service, 24-hour emergency telephones, lighted pathways/sidewalks, student patrols, controlled dormitory access (key, security card, etc).

TRANSFER AND INTERNATIONAL STUDENTS

Transfer students: May apply for admission for the following academic terms: Fall, Spring. Applicants do not need a minimum number of credits to apply. For fall 2005: Transfer applications received: 536. Transfer applicants offered admission: 360. Transfer applicants enrolled: 210.
International students: Number of foreign undergraduates: 9. Number of countries represented: 20. Minimum TOEFL score required: 530 (paper); 200 (computer). Average TOEFL score: 600 (paper).

Rhode Island

Brown University

- **Address:** Box 1920, Providence, RI 02912
- **Website:** http://www.brown.edu
- **Private**
- **Enrollment:** 5,931 full-time; 245 part-time

KEY STATS

✔ **U.S News College Ranking:** 15, National Universities
✔ **SAT Score (25th/75th percentile):** 1330-1540
✔ **Tuition:** 2006-2007: $34,620
  Selectivity: Most selective   **Room/board:** $9,134
  Acceptance rate: 15%   **Average debt:** $15,940
  Student/faculty ratio: 9/1   **Proportion who borrowed:** 46%

UNDERGRADUATE STUDENT BODY STATS

2005-2006 enrollment: 5,931 full-time; 245 part-time. Men: 46%; women: 54%. **Ethnic makeup:** African American: 7%; American-Indian: 1%; Asian American: 14%; Hispanic: 7%; White: 66%; International: 6%. **Religious preference:** Roman Catholic: 16%; Protestant: 21%; Jewish: 14%; Muslim: 1%; Hindu: 2%; Buddhist: 1%; No preference: 17%; Unknown: 26%; Orthodox: 1%; Other: 1%.

ADMISSIONS FACTS AND FIGURES

Phone: (401) 863-2378. **Email:** admission_undergraduate@brown.edu. **Website:** http://www.brown.edu. **Application deadlines for fall 2007:** Regular decision: January 1; decision sent by April 1. Early decision: Send application by: November 1; Decision sent by: December 15. Early action: Not offered. Admission can be deferred. **Application fee:** $70. Common application is not accepted. **To apply online, go to:** http://www.brown.edu/Admission. **Admissions requirements/recommendations:** High school units required (recommended): English: 4 (4); Mathematics: 3 (4); Science: 3 (4); Foreign language: 3 (4); History: 2 (2); Academic electives: 1 (1); Total units: 16 (20). Tests: The college uses SAT or ACT scores in admissions decisions. Either SAT or ACT required. For admission to the fall 2007 entering class, the school will accept: ACT with writing. Campus visit: Recommended. Admissions interview: Neither required nor recommended. Off-campus interview: May be arranged. **Factors that count in admissions decisions:** *Academic:* Secondary school record: Very important. Class rank: Important. Letters of recommendation: Important. Standardized test scores: Important. Essay: Important. *Nonacademic:* Interview: Considered. Extracurricular activities: Important. Talent/ability: Very important. Character/personal qualities: Very important. Alumni/ae relationship: Considered. Geographical residence: Considered. State residency: Considered. Religious affiliation/commitment: Not considered. Minority status: Considered. Volunteer work: Considered. Work experience: Considered. **Other schools with the greatest overlap in applicants:** Cornell University; Harvard University; Princeton University; Stanford University; Yale University. **Admissions statistics for the fall 2005 entering class:** Total applicants: 16,911. Total accepted: 2,557. Freshmen enrolled: 1,439; 95% were from out of state. Accepted through early-decision or early-action plans: 39%. Overall acceptance rate: 15%. Early-decision acceptance rate: 28%. Non-early acceptance rate: 13%. **Size of waiting list:** 1735 applicants; enrolled from waiting list: 99. **Credentials of fall 2005 freshmen:** 90% ranked in the top 10 percent of their high school class; 99% were in the top 25 percent, and 100% were in the top half. (Proportion submitting class standing: 47%.) **First-year students who submitted SAT scores:** 96%. Scores (25/75 percentile): Verbal: 660-760, Math: 670-780, Combined: 1330-1540. **First-year students submitting ACT scores:** 22%. Scores (25/75 percentile): English: N/A, Math: N/A, Composite: 27-33.

ACADEMICS

Year founded: 1764. **Academic calendar:** Semester. **Degrees offered:** bachelor's, master's, first professional, doctorate. **Most popular majors:** 8% international relations and affairs, 7% biology, 7% history, 6% business/managerial economics, 4% English language and literature. **Major fields of study:** architecture and related services; area, ethnic, cultural, and gender studies; biological and biomedical sciences; business, management, marketing, and related support services; computer and information sciences and support services; education; engineering; English language and literature/letters; foreign languages, literatures, and linguistics; health professions and related clinical sciences; history; liberal arts and sciences studies, and humanities; mathematics and statistics; multi/interdisciplinary studies; natural resources and conservation; philosophy and religious studies; physical sciences; psychology; public administration and social service professions; social sciences; visual and performing arts. **Areas of required coursework:** English (including composition). **Pre-professional programs:** pre-medicine. **Special academic programs (% participation):** cross-registration (8.2%), double major (20.8%), exchange student program (domestic) (.2%), honors program (26.9%), independent study (56.7%), internships (.1%), student-designed major (.3%), study abroad (32.5%), teacher certificate program (.5%). **Teacher certification offered in:** elementary, middle/junior high, secondary. **Reserve Officers Training Corps (ROTC):** Army ROTC: Offered at cooperating institution (Providence College). **Faculty and instruction (2005-2006):** Total instructional faculty: 687 full-time, 136 part-time (67% men; 33% women; 11% minorities). Full-time faculty with Ph.D. or other terminal degree: 97%. Student/faculty ratio: 9/1. Classes of fewer than 20 students: 67%; of 20 to 49 students: 23%; of 50 or more students: 10%. **Advanced Placement and International Baccalaureate credit:** AP tests may be used for: Placement only. Scores accepted: 4, 5. International Baccalaureate exams may be used for: Credit and/or placement. **Freshmen returning for sophomore year:** 97%. **Graduation rates:** Four-year: 83%; five-year: 93%; six-year: 95%. **Graduate study:** 24% of students pursue further study immediately upon graduation. Fields in which graduates pursue further study: law, 22%; medicine, 25%.

COSTS AND FINANCIAL AID

Financial aid office: (401) 863-2721. **Expenses (2006-2007):** Tuition and fees 2006-2007: $34,620; room/board: $9,134. Estimated books and supplies: $1,128; transportation: $300; personal expenses: $1,458. **Financial aid:** In 2005-2006, 50% of undergraduates applied for financial aid. Of those, 42% were determined to have financial need; 100% had their need fully met. Average financial aid package (proportion receiving): $26,477 (42%). Average amount of gift aid, such as scholarships or grants (proportion receiving): $22,224 (40%). Average amount of self-help aid, such as work study or loans (proportion receiving): $6,062 (39%). Average need-based loan (excluding PLUS or other private loans): $4,935. Among students who received need-based aid, the average percentage of need met: 100%. Among students who received aid based on merit, the average award (and the proportion receiving): $0 (0%). The average athletic scholarship (and the proportion receiving): $0 (0%). Average amount of debt of borrowers graduating in 2005: $15,940. Proportion who borrowed: 46%.

CAMPUS LIFE AND EXTRACURRICULAR ACTIVITIES

Campus housing available (% using): coed dorms (84%), sorority housing (1%), fraternity housing (5%), apartment for single students (9%), special housing for disabled students (1%), cooperative housing. Students who live in college-owned, operated, or affiliated housing: 80%. **Student employment:** During the 2005-2006 academic year, 30% of undergraduates worked on campus. Average per-year earnings: $1,000. **Clubs and organizations:** Number of student organizations: 350. Activities include: choral groups, concert band, dance, drama/theater, jazz band, literary magazine, marching band, music ensembles, musical theater, radio station, student government, student newspaper, student film society, symphony orchestra, television station, yearbook. Number of fraternities: 13; sororities: 5. Proportion of men in fraternities: 10%; of women in sororities: 7%. Average proportion of students who stay on campus on weekends: 85%. **Sports program (2005-2006):** Member of NCAA I. *Men's intercollegiate varsity sports:* baseball, basketball, crew, cross-country, fencing, football, golf, ice hockey, lacrosse, soccer, squash, swimming and diving, tennis, track and field (indoor), track and field (outdoor), water polo, wrestling. *Women's intercollegiate varsity sports:* alpine skiing, basketball, crew, cross-country, equestrian sports, fencing, field hockey, golf, gymnastics, ice hockey, lacrosse, rowing, soccer, softball, squash, swimming and diving, tennis, track and field (indoor), track and field (outdoor), volleyball, water polo.

SERVICES AND FACILITIES
Basic services: nonremedial tutoring, women's center, placement service, health service, health insurance. **Remedial assistance:** writing, study skills. **Counseling services:** minority student, career, personal, academic, older student, psychological, birth control, religious. **For learning-disabled students:** School does not offer a structured program with separate admission and additional fees. Total undergraduates in learning-disabled program or receiving services: 113. Services include: reading machines, tape recorders, note-taking services, learning center, readers, extended time for tests, tutors, priority seating, texts on tape, other testing accomodations, other. **Library:** Number of titles: 3,509,710; number of current serial subscriptions: 21,888. **Information technology resources:** Students are not required to lease or own a computer. Number of campus computers available to all students: 317. School has a wireless network. Approximate number of users that can be accommodated: 6,000. Proportion of college-owned housing units wired for high-speed internet access: 100%. **Campus safety:** Security services offered: 24-hour foot-and-vehicle patrols, late-night transport/escort service, 24-hour emergency telephones, lighted pathways/sidewalks, controlled dormitory access (key, security card, etc).

TRANSFER AND INTERNATIONAL STUDENTS
Transfer students: May apply for admission for the following academic terms: Fall, Spring. Applicants need a minimum number of credits to apply. For fall 2005: Transfer applications received: 823. Transfer applicants offered admission: 202. Transfer applicants enrolled: 135. **International students:** Number of foreign undergraduates: 362 (6% of student body). Number of countries represented: 72. Minimum TOEFL score required: 600 (paper); 250 (computer).

Bryant University

- **Address:** 1150 Douglas Pike, Smithfield, RI 02917
- **Website:** http://www.bryant.edu
- **Private**
- **Enrollment:** 3,012 full-time; 191 part-time

KEY STATS
✔ **U.S News College Ranking:** 19, Universities–Master's (North)
✔ **SAT Score (25th/75th percentile):** 1030-1200
✔ **Tuition:** 2006-2007: $26,099

Selectivity: Selective	**Room/board:** $10,293
Acceptance rate: 58%	**Average debt:** $29,222
Student/faculty ratio: 16/1	**Proportion who borrowed:** 60%

UNDERGRADUATE STUDENT BODY STATS
2005-2006 enrollment: 3,012 full-time; 191 part-time. Men: 59%; women: 41%. **Ethnic makeup:** African American: 3%; Asian American: 2%; Hispanic: 4%; White: 89%; International: 2%.

ADMISSIONS FACTS AND FIGURES
Phone: (800) 622-7001. **Email:** admission@bryant.edu. **Website:** http://www.bryant.edu. **Application deadlines for fall 2007:** Regular decision: February 15; decision sent by March 15. Early decision: Send application by: November 15; Decision sent by: December 15. Early action: Not offered. Admission can be deferred. **Application fee:** $50. Common application is accepted. **To apply online, go to:** http://admission.bryant.edu/application. **Admissions requirements/recommendations:** High school units required (recommended): English: 4; Mathematics: 4; Science: 3; Foreign language: 2; History: 2 (4); Total units: 16. Tests: The college uses SAT or ACT scores in admissions decisions. Either SAT or ACT required. For admission to the fall 2007 entering class, the school will accept: ACT with writing. Campus visit: Recommended. Admissions interview: Neither required nor recommended. Off-campus interview: May be arranged. **Factors that count in admissions decisions:** *Academic:* Secondary school record: Very important. Class rank: Important. Letters of recommendation: Important. Standardized test scores: Important. Essay: Important. *Nonacademic:* Interview: Considered. Extracurricular activities: Considered. Talent/ability: Considered. Character/personal qualities: Considered. Alumni/ae relationship: Considered. Geographical residence: Considered. State residency:

Considered. Religious affiliation/commitment: Not considered. Minority status: Considered. Volunteer work: Considered. Work experience: Considered. **Other schools with the greatest overlap in applicants:** Bentley College; Quinnipiac University; University of Connecticut; University of New Hampshire; University of Rhode Island. **Admissions statistics for the fall 2005 entering class:** Total applicants: 4,214. Total accepted: 2,430. Freshmen enrolled: 822; 87% were from out of state. Accepted through early-decision or early-action plans: 10%. Overall acceptance rate: 58%. Early-decision acceptance rate: 76%. Non-early acceptance rate: 57%. **Size of waiting list:** 664 applicants; enrolled from waiting list: 78. **Credentials of fall 2005 freshmen:** 18% ranked in the top 10 percent of their high school class; 56% were in the top 25 percent, and 90% were in the top half. (Proportion submitting class standing: 71%.) **Average high school grade point average:** 3.3. **First-year students who submitted SAT scores:** 100%. Scores (25/75 percentile): Verbal: 500-580, Math: 530-620, Combined: 1030-1200. **First-year students submitting ACT scores:** 7%. Scores (25/75 percentile): English: N/A, Math: N/A, Composite: 21-25.

ACADEMICS
Year founded: 1863. **Academic calendar:** Semester. **Degrees offered:** bachelor's, master's, post-master's certificate. **Most popular majors:** 26% marketing/marketing management, 23% business administration and management, 17% accounting, 14% finance, 9% computer and information sciences. **Major fields of study:** business, management, marketing, and related support services; communication, journalism, and related programs; computer and information sciences and support services; English language and literature/letters; history; psychology; social sciences. **Areas of required coursework:** humanities, computer literacy, mathematics, English (including composition), sciences (biological or physical), history, social science, other. **Special academic programs (% participation):** double major, honors program, independent study, internships (36%), study abroad (11%). **Reserve Officers Training Corps (ROTC):** Army ROTC: Offered on campus. **Faculty and instruction (2005-2006):** Total instructional faculty: 133 full-time, 129 part-time (58% men; 42% women). Full-time faculty with Ph.D. or other terminal degree: 86%. Student/faculty ratio: 16/1. Classes of fewer than 20 students: 20%; of 20 to 49 students: 80%; of 50 or more students: 0%. **Advanced Placement and International Baccalaureate credit:** AP tests may be used for: Credit and/or placement. Scores accepted: 3, 4, 5. International Baccalaureate exams may be used for: Credit and/or placement. **Freshmen returning for sophomore year:** 84%. **Graduation rates:** Four-year: 63%; five-year: 68%; six-year: 67%. **Graduate study:** 5% of students pursue further study immediately upon graduation. Fields in which graduates pursue further study: Master of Business Administration (MBA), 2%; law, 1%; arts and sciences, 2%.

COSTS AND FINANCIAL AID
Financial aid office: (401) 232-6020. **Expenses (2006-2007):** Tuition and fees 2006-2007: $26,099; room/board: $10,293. Estimated books and supplies: $1,200; transportation: $400; personal expenses: $1,000. **Financial aid:** Priority filing date for institution's financial aid form: February 15; deadline: February 15. In 2005-2006, 75% of undergraduates applied for financial aid. Of those, 65% were determined to have financial need; 11% had their need fully met. Average financial aid package (proportion receiving): $15,270 (65%). Average amount of gift aid, such as scholarships or grants (proportion receiving): $8,615 (51%). Average amount of self-help aid, such as work study or loans (proportion receiving): $6,048 (59%). Average need-based loan (excluding PLUS or other private loans): $4,899. Among students who received need-based aid, the average percentage of need met: 74%. Among students who received aid based on merit, the average award (and the proportion receiving): $7,721 (15%). The average athletic scholarship (and the proportion receiving): $16,546 (2%). Average amount of debt of borrowers graduating in 2005: $29,222. Proportion who borrowed: 60%.

CAMPUS LIFE AND EXTRACURRICULAR ACTIVITIES
Campus housing available: coed dorms, women's dorms, special housing for disabled students, other housing options. Students who live in college-owned, operated, or affiliated housing: 79%. **Student employment:** During the 2005-2006 academic year, 7% of undergraduates worked on campus. Average per-year earnings: $1,385. **Clubs and organizations:** Number of student organizations: 60. Activities include: choral groups, dance, drama/theater, jazz band, literary magazine, pep band, radio station, student government, student newspaper, television station, yearbook. Number of fraternities: 5; sororities: 3. Proportion of men in fraternities: 6%; of women in sororities: 4%. Average proportion of students who stay on campus on weekends: 75%. **Sports program (2005-2006):** Member of NCAA II. *Men's intercollegiate varsity sports:* baseball, basketball, cross-country, football,

golf, lacrosse, soccer, swimming and diving, tennis, track and field (indoor), track and field (outdoor). **Women's intercollegiate varsity sports:** basketball, cross-country, field hockey, lacrosse, soccer, softball, swimming and diving, tennis, track and field (indoor), track and field (outdoor), volleyball.

SERVICES AND FACILITIES

Basic services: nonremedial tutoring, women's center, placement service, health service, health insurance. **Counseling services:** minority student, career, personal, academic, older student, psychological, birth control, religious. **For learning-disabled students:** School does not offer a structured program with separate admission and additional fees. Services include: learning center, extended time for tests, tutors, texts on tape. **Library:** Number of titles: 139,853; number of current serial subscriptions: 200. **Information technology resources:** Students are required to lease or own a computer. Number of campus computers available to all students: 570. School has a wireless network. Approximate number of users that can be accommodated: 12,500. Proportion of college-owned housing units wired for high-speed internet access: 100%. **Campus safety:** Security services offered: 24-hour foot-and-vehicle patrols, late-night transport/escort service, 24-hour emergency telephones, lighted pathways/sidewalks, controlled dormitory access (key, security card, etc).

TRANSFER AND INTERNATIONAL STUDENTS

Transfer students: May apply for admission for the following academic terms: Fall, Spring. Applicants do not need a minimum number of credits to apply. For fall 2005: Transfer applications received: 285. Transfer applicants offered admission: 191. Transfer applicants enrolled: 120. **International students:** Number of foreign undergraduates: 52 (2% of student body). Number of countries represented: 29. Minimum TOEFL score required: 550 (paper); 213 (computer).

Johnson and Wales University

- **Address:** 8 Abbott Park Place, Providence, RI 02903-3703
- **Website:** http://www.jwu.edu
- **Private**
- **Enrollment:** 8,399 full-time; 938 part-time

KEY STATS

- ✔ **U.S News College Ranking:** third tier, Universities–Master's (North)
- ✔ **SAT Score (25th/75th percentile):** 830-1050
- ✔ **Tuition:** 2006-2007: $20,826

Selectivity: Less selective	**Room/board:** $7,300
Acceptance rate: 80%	**Average debt:** $17,704
Student/faculty ratio: 25/1	**Proportion who borrowed:** 68%

UNDERGRADUATE STUDENT BODY STATS

2005-2006 enrollment: 8,399 full-time; 938 part-time. Men: 47%; women: 53%. **Ethnic makeup:** African American: 8%; Asian American: 2%; Hispanic: 5%; White: 81%; International: 4%.

ADMISSIONS FACTS AND FIGURES

Phone: (401) 598-2310. **Email:** admissions@jwu.edu. **Website:** http://www.jwu.edu. **Application deadlines for fall 2007:** Regular decision: Rolling. Early decision: Not offered. Early action: Not offered. Admission can be deferred. Common application is accepted. **Admissions requirements/recommendations:** High school units required (recommended): English: (4); Mathematics: (3); Science: (3); Social studies: (2); Total units: (12). Tests: The college uses SAT or ACT scores in admissions decisions. Neither SAT nor ACT required. For admission to the fall 2007 entering class, the school will accept: ACT with writing, ACT without writing. Campus visit: Recommended. Admissions interview: Neither required nor recommended. Off-campus interview: May be arranged. **Factors that count in admissions decisions:** *Academic:* Secondary school record: Very important. Class rank: Very important. Letters of recommendation: Considered. Standardized test scores: Considered. Essay: Not considered. *Nonacademic:* Interview: Very important. Extracurricular activities: Important. Talent/ability: Not considered. Character/personal qualities: Not considered. Alumni/ae relationship: Considered. Geographical residence: Not considered. State residency: Not considered. Religious affiliation/commitment: Not considered. Minority status: Not considered. Volunteer work: Considered. Work experience: Important. **Admissions statistics for the fall**

2005 entering class: Total applicants: 15,258. Total accepted: 12,235. Freshmen enrolled: 2,792; 22% were from out of state. Overall acceptance rate: 80%. **Credentials of fall 2005 freshmen:** 3% ranked in the top 10 percent of their high school class; 16% were in the top 25 percent. (Proportion submitting class standing: 98%.) **Average high school grade point average:** 2.9. **First-year students who submitted SAT scores:** 53%. Scores (25/75 percentile): Verbal: 420-530, Math: 410-520, Combined: 830-1050.

ACADEMICS

Year founded: 1914. **Academic calendar:** Quarter. **Degrees offered:** certificate, diploma, associate, bachelor's, master's, doctorate. **Most popular majors:** 14% culinary arts/chef training, 5% baking and pastry arts/baker/pastry chef, 5% food-service systems administration/management, 5% hotel/motel administration/management, 4% hotel/motel administration/management. **Major fields of study:** agriculture, agriculture operations, and related sciences; business, management, marketing, and related support services; communication, journalism, and related programs; computer and information sciences and support services; education; engineering; engineering technologies/technicians; family and consumer sciences/human sciences; health professions and related clinical sciences; legal professions and studies; parks, recreation, leisure, and fitness studies; personal and culinary services; security and protective services. **Areas of required coursework:** computer literacy, mathematics, English (including composition), philosophy, sciences (biological or physical), history, social science. **Special academic programs:** accelerated program, cooperative (work-study plan) program, dual enrollment, English as a Second Language (ESL), external degree program, honors program, independent study, internships, study abroad, weekend college. **Cooperative education programs:** business, computer science, technologies, other. **Reserve Officers Training Corps (ROTC):** Army ROTC: Offered at cooperating institution (Providence College). **Faculty and instruction (2005-2006):** Total instructional faculty: 278 full-time, 131 part-time (58% men; 42% women; 5% minorities). Full-time faculty with Ph.D. or other terminal degree: 28%. Student/faculty ratio: 25/1. **Advanced Placement and International Baccalaureate credit:** AP tests may be used for: Credit only. Scores accepted: 3, 4, 5. International Baccalaureate exams may be used for: Credit only. **Freshmen returning for sophomore year:** 72%. **Graduation rates:** Four-year: 47%; five-year: 56%; six-year: 50%. **Graduate study:** 1% of students pursue further study immediately upon graduation.

COSTS AND FINANCIAL AID

Financial aid office: (401) 598-1468. **Expenses (2006-2007):** Tuition and fees 2006-2007: $20,826; room/board: $7,300. Estimated books and supplies: $900; transportation: $750; personal expenses: $500. **Financial aid:** In 2005-2006, 82% of undergraduates applied for financial aid. Of those, 72% were determined to have financial need; 5% had their need fully met. Average financial aid package (proportion receiving): $12,009 (71%). Average amount of gift aid, such as scholarships or grants (proportion receiving): $4,900 (57%). Average amount of self-help aid, such as work study or loans (proportion receiving): $6,509 (69%). Average need-based loan (excluding PLUS or other private loans): $5,788. Among students who received need-based aid, the average percentage of need met: 64%. Among students who received aid based on merit, the average award (and the proportion receiving): $4,455 (13%). Average amount of debt of borrowers graduating in 2005: $17,704. Proportion who borrowed: 68%.

CAMPUS LIFE AND EXTRACURRICULAR ACTIVITIES

Campus housing available: coed dorms. Students who live in college-owned, operated, or affiliated housing: 9%. **Student employment:** During the 2005-2006 academic year, 10% of undergraduates worked on campus. Average per-year earnings: $5,000. **Clubs and organizations:** Number of student organizations: 70. Activities include: choral groups, dance, drama/theater, pep band, student government, student newspaper, student film society, yearbook. Number of fraternities: 7; sororities: 7. Proportion of men in fraternities: 3%; of women in sororities: 4%. Average proportion of students who stay on campus on weekends: 55%. **Sports program (2005-2006):** Member of NCAA III. **Men's intercollegiate varsity sports:** baseball, basketball, cross-country, golf, ice hockey, soccer, tennis, volleyball, wrestling. **Women's intercollegiate varsity sports:** basketball, cross-country, soccer, softball, tennis, volleyball.

SERVICES AND FACILITIES

Basic services: nonremedial tutoring, women's center, placement service, health service, health insurance. **Remedial assistance:** reading, math, writing, study skills. **Counseling services:** minority student, career, personal, academic, psychological. **For learning-disabled students:** School does not offer a structured program with separate admission and additional fees.

Total undergraduates in learning-disabled program or receiving services: 438. Services include: remedial math, reading machines, tape recorders, other special classes, untimed tests, note-taking services, oral tests, learning center, readers, extended time for tests, tutors, early syllabus, priority registration, priority seating, proofreading services, substitution of courses, texts on tape, typist/scribe, exams on tape or computer, other testing accomodations. **Library:** Number of titles: 94,969; number of current serial subscriptions: 2,242. **Information technology resources:** Students are not required to lease or own a computer. Number of campus computers available to all students: 600. School has a wireless network. **Campus safety:** Security services offered: 24-hour foot-and-vehicle patrols, late-night transport/escort service, 24-hour emergency telephones, lighted pathways/sidewalks, controlled dormitory access (key, security card, etc).

TRANSFER AND INTERNATIONAL STUDENTS
Transfer students: May apply for admission for the following academic terms: Fall, Winter, Spring, Summer. Applicants need a minimum number of credits to apply. For fall 2005: Transfer applications received: 1,063. Transfer applicants offered admission: 892. Transfer applicants enrolled: 358. **International students:** Number of foreign undergraduates: 403 (4% of student body). Number of countries represented: 98. Minimum TOEFL score required: 550 (paper); 210 (computer).

Providence College

- **Address:** 549 River Avenue, Providence, RI 02918
- **Website:** http://www.providence.edu
- **Private; Religious affiliation:** Roman Catholic
- **Enrollment:** 3,966 full-time; 621 part-time

KEY STATS
- ✔ **U.S News College Ranking:** 2, Universities–Master's (North)
- ✔ **SAT Score (25th/75th percentile):** 1110-1280
- ✔ **Tuition:** 2006-2007: $27,345
- **Selectivity:** More selective   **Room/board:** $9,765
- **Acceptance rate:** 54%   **Average debt:** $23,000
- **Student/faculty ratio:** 12/1   **Proportion who borrowed:** 65%

UNDERGRADUATE STUDENT BODY STATS
2005-2006 enrollment: 3,966 full-time; 621 part-time. Men: 43%; women: 57%. **Ethnic makeup:** African American: 2%; Asian American: 2%; Hispanic: 2%; White: 93%; International: 1%. **Religious preference:** Protestant: 5%; Roman Catholic: 85%.

ADMISSIONS FACTS AND FIGURES
Phone: (401) 865-2535. **Email:** pcadmiss@providence.edu. **Website:** http://www.providence.edu. **Application deadlines for fall 2007:** Regular decision: January 15; decision sent by April 1. Early decision: Not offered. Early action: Send application by: November 1; Decision sent by: January 1. Admission can be deferred. **Application fee:** $55. Common application is accepted. **Admissions requirements/recommendations:** High school units required (recommended): English: 4 (4); Mathematics: 4 (4); Science: 3 (4); Foreign language: 3 (3); Social studies: 2 (2); History: 2 (2); Total units: 16 (18). Tests: The college uses SAT or ACT scores in admissions decisions. Either SAT or ACT required. For admission to the fall 2007 entering class, the school will accept: ACT with writing. Campus visit: Recommended. Admissions interview: Neither required nor recommended. Off-campus interview: Not available. **Factors that count in admissions decisions:** *Academic:* Secondary school record: Very important. Class rank: Considered. Letters of recommendation: Important. Standardized test scores: Important. Essay: Important. *Nonacademic:* Interview: Not considered. Extracurricular activities: Important. Talent/ability: Considered. Character/personal qualities: Important. Alumni/ae relationship: Considered. Geographical residence: Considered. State residency: Not considered. Religious affiliation/commitment: Not considered. Minority status: Considered. Volunteer work: Considered. Work experience: Considered. **Other schools with the greatest overlap in applicants:** Boston College; College of the Holy Cross; Fairfield University; Stonehill College; Villanova University. **Admissions statistics for the fall 2005 entering class:** Total applicants: 8,237. Total accepted: 4,484. Freshmen enrolled: 1,069; 90% were from out of state. Overall acceptance rate: 54%. Non-early acceptance rate: 54%. **Size of waiting list:** 1647 applicants; enrolled from waiting list: 355. **Credentials of**

fall 2005 freshmen: 38% ranked in the top 10 percent of their high school class; 79% were in the top 25 percent, and 98% were in the top half. (Proportion submitting class standing: 57%.) **Average high school grade point average:** 3.4. **First-year students who submitted SAT scores:** 98%. Scores (25/75 percentile): Verbal: 550-630, Math: 560-650, Combined: 1110-1280. **First-year students submitting ACT scores:** 22%. Scores (25/75 percentile): English: N/A, Math: N/A, Composite: 23-27.

ACADEMICS
Year founded: 1917. **Academic calendar:** Semester. **Degrees offered:** certificate, associate, terminal-associate, bachelor's, post-bachelor's certificate, master's. **Most popular majors:** 10% marketing/marketing management, 8% business administration and management, 7% English language and literature, 7% political science and government, 7% special education and teaching. **Major fields of study:** area, ethnic, cultural, and gender studies; biological and biomedical sciences; business, management, marketing, and related support services; computer and information sciences and support services; education; engineering; English language and literature/letters; foreign languages, literatures, and linguistics; health professions and related clinical sciences; history; liberal arts and sciences studies, and humanities; mathematics and statistics; multi/interdisciplinary studies; philosophy and religious studies; physical sciences; psychology; public administration and social service professions; security and protective services; social sciences; theology and religious vocations; visual and performing arts. **Areas of required coursework:** arts/fine arts, mathematics, English (including composition), philosophy, sciences (biological or physical), social science, other. **Pre-professional programs:** pre-law, pre-dentistry, pre-medicine, pre-veterinary science, pre-optometry, other. **Special academic programs (% participation):** cross-registration (1%), double major (5.02%), honors program (11.32%), independent study (15.64%), internships (68%), student-designed major (0%), study abroad (11.32%). **Teacher certification offered in:** special education, elementary, secondary. **Reserve Officers Training Corps (ROTC):** Army ROTC: Offered on campus. **Faculty and instruction (2005-2006):** Total instructional faculty: 287 full-time, 82 part-time (63% men; 37% women; 8% minorities). Full-time faculty with Ph.D. or other terminal degree: 90%. Student/faculty ratio: 12/1. Classes of fewer than 20 students: 45%; of 20 to 49 students: 52%; of 50 or more students: 3%. **Advanced Placement and International Baccalaureate credit:** AP tests may be used for: Credit only. Scores accepted: 4, 5. International Baccalaureate exams may be used for: Placement only. **Freshmen returning for sophomore year:** 92%. **Graduation rates:** Four-year: 86%; five-year: 87%; six-year: 85%. **Graduate study:** 31% of students pursue further study immediately upon graduation; 37% within one year. Fields in which graduates pursue further study: Master of Business Administration (MBA), 7%; law, 11%; medicine, 5%; education, 22%; arts and sciences, 26%.

COSTS AND FINANCIAL AID
Financial aid office: (401) 865-2286. **Expenses (2006-2007):** Tuition and fees 2006-2007: $27,345; room/board: $9,765. Estimated books and supplies: $750. **Financial aid:** Priority filing date for institution's financial aid form: February 1; deadline: February 1. In 2005-2006, 67% of undergraduates applied for financial aid. Of those, 60% were determined to have financial need; 18% had their need fully met. Average financial aid package (proportion receiving): $17,000 (60%). Average amount of gift aid, such as scholarships or grants (proportion receiving): $11,000 (55%). Average amount of self-help aid, such as work study or loans (proportion receiving): $9,300 (60%). Average need-based loan (excluding PLUS or other private loans): $6,150. Among students who received need-based aid, the average percentage of need met: 86%. Among students who received aid based on merit, the average award (and the proportion receiving): $8,500 (10%). The average athletic scholarship (and the proportion receiving): $20,190 (3%). Average amount of debt of borrowers graduating in 2005: $23,000. Proportion who borrowed: 65%.

CAMPUS LIFE AND EXTRACURRICULAR ACTIVITIES
Campus housing available (% using): coed dorms (10%), women's dorms (27%), men's dorms (23%), apartment for single students (29%), special housing for disabled students, other housing options (11%). Students who live in college-owned, operated, or affiliated housing: 77%. **Student employment:** During the 2005-2006 academic year, 12% of undergraduates worked on campus. Average per-year earnings: $1,800. **Clubs and organizations:** Number of student organizations: 111. Activities include: choral groups, concert band, dance, drama/theater, jazz band, literary magazine, music ensembles, musical theater, pep band, radio station, student government, student newspaper, television station, yearbook. Number of fraternities: 0; sororities: 0. Average proportion of students who stay on campus on week-

ends: 90%. **Sports program (2005-2006):** Member of NCAA I. *Men's inter-collegiate varsity sports:* basketball, cross-country, ice hockey, lacrosse, soccer, swimming and diving, track and field (indoor), track and field (outdoor). *Women's intercollegiate varsity sports:* basketball, cross-country, field hockey, ice hockey, soccer, softball, swimming and diving, tennis, track and field (indoor), track and field (outdoor), volleyball.

SERVICES AND FACILITIES

Basic services: nonremedial tutoring, placement service, health service, other. **Counseling services:** minority student, career, personal, academic, psychological, religious, other. **For learning-disabled students:** School does not offer a structured program with separate admission and additional fees. Total undergraduates in learning-disabled program or receiving services: 150. Services include: reading machines, tape recorders, note-taking services, oral tests, learning center, readers, extended time for tests, tutors, priority registration, priority seating, proofreading services, texts on tape, typist/scribe, exams on tape or computer, other testing accomodations, other. **Library:** Number of titles: 365,982; number of current serial subscriptions: 1,600. **Information technology resources:** Students are not required to lease or own a computer. Number of campus computers available to all students: 199. School has a wireless network. Approximate number of users that can be accommodated: 200. Proportion of college-owned housing units wired for high-speed internet access: 100%. **Campus safety:** Security services offered: 24-hour foot-and-vehicle patrols, late-night transport/escort service, 24-hour emergency telephones, lighted pathways/sidewalks, student patrols, controlled dormitory access (key, security card, etc).

TRANSFER AND INTERNATIONAL STUDENTS

Transfer students: May apply for admission for the following academic terms: Fall, Spring. Applicants need a minimum number of credits to apply. For fall 2005: Transfer applications received: 232. Transfer applicants offered admission: 129. Transfer applicants enrolled: 65. **International students:** Number of foreign undergraduates: 42 (1% of student body). Number of countries represented: 17. Minimum TOEFL score required: 550 (paper); 213 (computer).

Rhode Island College

- **Address:** 600 Mount Pleasant Avenue, Providence, RI 02908
- **Website:** http://www.ric.edu
- **Public**
- **Enrollment:** 5,310 full-time; 2,167 part-time

KEY STATS

✔ **U.S News College Ranking:** third tier, Universities–Master's (North)
✔ **SAT Score (25th/75th percentile):** 860-1080
✔ **Tuition:** 2006-2007: $4,894 in state, $12,574 out of state
  Selectivity: Less selective **Room/board:** $7,350
  Acceptance rate: 78% **Average debt:** N/A
  Student/faculty ratio: 16/1 **Proportion who borrowed:** N/A

UNDERGRADUATE STUDENT BODY STATS

2005-2006 enrollment: 5,310 full-time; 2,167 part-time. Men: 33%; women: 67%. **Ethnic makeup:** African American: 5%; Asian American: 2%; Hispanic: 5%; White: 88%.

ADMISSIONS FACTS AND FIGURES

Phone: (800) 669-5760. **Email:** admissions@ric.edu. **Website:** http://www.ric.edu. **Application deadlines for fall 2007:** Regular decision: May 1. Early decision: Not offered. Early action: Not offered. Admission can be deferred. **Application fee:** $50. Common application is accepted. **Admissions requirements/recommendations:** High school units required (recommended): English: 4; Mathematics: 3; Science: 2; Foreign language: 2; Social studies: 2; Academic electives: 4; Total units: 18. Tests: The college uses SAT or ACT scores in admissions decisions. Either SAT or ACT required. For admission to the fall 2007 entering class, the school will accept: ACT with writing. Campus visit: Recommended. Admissions interview: Recommended. Off-campus interview: May be arranged. **Factors that count in admissions decisions:** *Academic:* Secondary school record: Very important. Class rank: Very important. Letters of recommendation: Important. Standardized test scores: Considered. Essay: Important. *Nonacademic:* Interview: Considered. Extracurricular activities: Considered.

Talent/ability: Considered. Character/personal qualities: Not considered. Alumni/ae relationship: Considered. Geographical residence: Not considered. State residency: Not considered. Religious affiliation/commitment: Not considered. Minority status: Not considered. Volunteer work: Considered. Work experience: Considered. **Admissions statistics for the fall 2005 entering class:** Total applicants: 3,385. Total accepted: 2,625. Freshmen enrolled: 1,098; 16% were from out of state. Overall acceptance rate: 78%. **Credentials of fall 2005 freshmen:** 7% ranked in the top 10 percent of their high school class; 33% were in the top 25 percent, and 77% were in the top half. (Proportion submitting class standing: 85%.) **First-year students who submitted SAT scores:** 99%. Scores (25/75 percentile): Verbal: 430-540, Math: 430-540, Combined: 860-1080.

ACADEMICS

Year founded: 1854. **Academic calendar:** Semester. **Degrees offered:** bachelor's, master's, post-master's certificate, doctorate. **Most popular majors:** 32% education, 13% business, management, marketing, and related support services, 11% psychology, 7% nursing/registered nurse training (R.N., A.S.N., B.S.N., M.S.N.), 6% communication, journalism, and related programs. **Major fields of study:** area, ethnic, cultural, and gender studies; biological and biomedical sciences; business, management, marketing, and related support services; communication, journalism, and related programs; computer and information sciences and support services; education; engineering technologies/technicians; English language and literature/letters; foreign languages, literatures, and linguistics; health professions and related clinical sciences; history; liberal arts and sciences studies, and humanities; mathematics and statistics; multi/interdisciplinary studies; philosophy and religious studies; physical sciences; psychology; public administration and social service professions; security and protective services; social sciences; visual and performing arts. **Areas of required coursework:** arts/fine arts, mathematics, English (including composition), sciences (biological or physical), history, social science. **Pre-professional programs:** prelaw, pre-dentistry, pre-medicine, pre-optometry. **Special academic programs:** double major, English as a Second Language (ESL), exchange student program (domestic), honors program, independent study, internships, student-designed major, study abroad, teacher certificate program. **Teacher certification offered in:** early childhood, special education, elementary, votech, middle/junior high, secondary. **Reserve Officers Training Corps (ROTC):** Army ROTC: Offered at cooperating institution (Providence College). **Faculty and instruction (2005-2006):** Total instructional faculty: 306 full-time, 333 part-time (45% men; 55% women). Full-time faculty with Ph.D. or other terminal degree: 91%. Student/faculty ratio: 16/1. Classes of fewer than 20 students: 47%; of 20 to 49 students: 52%; of 50 or more students: 1%. **Advanced Placement and International Baccalaureate credit:** International Baccalaureate exams may be used for: Credit only. **Freshmen returning for sophomore year:** 78%. **Graduation rates:** Four-year: 16%; five-year: 37%; six-year: 43%.

COSTS AND FINANCIAL AID

Financial aid office: (401) 456-8033. **Expenses (2006-2007):** Tuition and fees 2006-2007: $4,894 in state, $12,574 out of state; room/board: $7,350. Estimated books and supplies: $800; transportation: $440; personal expenses: $1,000. **Financial aid:** Priority filing date for institution's financial aid form: March 1.

CAMPUS LIFE AND EXTRACURRICULAR ACTIVITIES

Campus housing available: coed dorms, women's dorms, special housing for disabled students. Students who live in college-owned, operated, or affiliated housing: 0%. **Student employment:** During the 2005-2006 academic year, 7% of undergraduates worked on campus. **Clubs and organizations:** Number of student organizations: 44. Activities include: choral groups, concert band, dance, drama/theater, jazz band, literary magazine, music ensembles, musical theater, radio station, student government, student newspaper, symphony orchestra, television station, yearbook. Number of fraternities: 2; sororities: 2. **Sports program (2005-2006):** Member of NCAA III. *Men's intercollegiate varsity sports:* baseball, basketball, cross-country, golf, soccer, tennis, track and field (indoor), track and field (outdoor), wrestling. *Women's intercollegiate varsity sports:* basketball, cross-country, gymnastics, lacrosse, soccer, softball, tennis, track and field (indoor), track and field (outdoor), volleyball.

SERVICES AND FACILITIES

Basic services: women's center, placement service, health service. **Counseling services:** minority student, career, personal, academic, older student. **For learning-disabled students:** School does not offer a structured program with separate admission and additional fees. Total undergraduates in learning-disabled program or receiving services: 67. Services include: tape recorders, note-taking services, readers, extended time for tests, tutors, proofreading services, texts on tape, typist/scribe, exams on tape or computer. **Library:** Number of titles: 644,667; number of current serial subscriptions: 2,155. **Information technology resources:** Students are not required to lease or own a computer. Number of campus computers available to all students: 570. School has a wireless network. Approximate number of users that can be accommodated: 250. Proportion of college-owned housing units wired for high-speed internet access: 100%. **Campus safety:** Security services offered: 24-hour foot-and-vehicle patrols, late-night transport/escort service, 24-hour emergency telephones, lighted pathways/sidewalks, controlled dormitory access (key, security card, etc.).

TRANSFER AND INTERNATIONAL STUDENTS

Transfer students: May apply for admission for the following academic terms: Fall, Spring. Applicants need a minimum number of credits to apply. For fall 2005: Transfer applications received: 1,429. Transfer applicants offered admission: 1,097. Transfer applicants enrolled: 752. **International students:** Number of foreign undergraduates: 35. Minimum TOEFL score required: 550 (paper); 213 (computer).

Rhode Island School of Design

- **Address:** 2 College Street, Providence, RI 02903
- **Website:** http://www.risd.edu
- **Private**
- **Enrollment:** 1,878 full-time

KEY STATS

- ✔ **U.S News College Ranking:** Unranked Specialty School–Fine Arts
- ✔ **SAT Score (25th/75th percentile):** 1100-1330
- ✔ **Tuition:** 2006-2007: $31,430

Selectivity: More selective	**Room/board:** $9,360
Acceptance rate: 33%	**Average debt:** $25,400
Student/faculty ratio: 9/1	**Proportion who borrowed:** 53%

UNDERGRADUATE STUDENT BODY STATS

2005-2006 enrollment: 1,878 full-time. Men: 34%; women: 66%. **Ethnic makeup:** African American: 2%; American-Indian: 1%; Asian American: 13%; Hispanic: 5%; White: 66%; International: 13%.

ADMISSIONS FACTS AND FIGURES

Phone: (401) 454-6300. **Email:** admissions@risd.edu. **Website:** http://www.risd.edu. **Application deadlines for fall 2007:** Regular decision: February 15; decision sent by April 1. Early decision: Not offered. Early action: Send application by: December 15; Decision sent by: January 31. Admission can be deferred. **Application fee:** $50. Common application is not accepted. **Admissions requirements/recommendations:** Tests: The college uses SAT or ACT scores in admissions decisions. Either SAT or ACT required. For admission to the fall 2007 entering class, the school will accept: ACT with writing, ACT without writing. Campus visit: Recommended. Admissions interview: Neither required nor recommended. Off-campus interview: Not available. **Factors that count in admissions decisions:** *Academic:* Secondary school record: Very important. Class rank: Considered. Letters of recommendation: Important. Standardized test scores: Important. Essay: Very important. *Nonacademic:* Extracurricular activities: Considered. Talent/ability: Very important. Character/personal qualities: Important. Alumni/ae relationship: Considered. Minority status: Considered. Volunteer work: Considered. Work experience: Considered. **Other schools with the greatest overlap in applicants:** Cooper Union; Maryland Institute College of Art; Pratt Institute. **Admissions statistics for the fall 2005 entering class:** Total applicants: 2,512. Total accepted: 821. Freshmen enrolled: 405; 14% were from out of state. Overall acceptance rate: 33%. Non-early acceptance rate: 33%. **Credentials of fall 2005 freshmen:** 40% ranked in the top 10 percent of their high school class; 72% were in the top 25 percent, and 95% were in the top half. (Proportion submitting class standing: 14%.) **Average high school grade point average:** 3.5. **First-year students who submitted SAT scores:** 94%. Scores (25/75 percentile): Verbal: 530-650, Math: 570-680, Combined: 1100-1330.

ACADEMICS

Year founded: 1877. **Academic calendar:** 4-1-4. **Degrees offered:** bachelor's, master's. **Most popular majors:** 47% fine and studio art, 13% architecture (B.Arch., B.A./B.S., M.Arch., M.A./M.S., Ph.D.), 13% commercial and advertising art, 11% industrial design. **Major fields of study:** visual and performing arts. **Areas of required coursework:** arts/fine arts, humanities, English (including composition), philosophy, history, social science. **Special academic programs (% participation):** cross-registration (10%), double major (5%), English as a Second Language (ESL) (10%), exchange student program (domestic), honors program (2%), independent study (20%), internships (20%), study abroad (20%). **Faculty and instruction (2005-2006):** Total instructional faculty: 140 full-time, 450 part-time (; 3% minorities). Full-time faculty with Ph.D. or other terminal degree: 79%. Student/faculty ratio: 9/1. Classes of fewer than 20 students: 78%; of 20 to 49 students: 21%; of 50 or more students: 1%. **Advanced Placement and International Baccalaureate credit:** AP tests may be used for: Credit only. Scores accepted: 4, 5. International Baccalaureate exams may be used for: Credit only. **Freshmen returning for sophomore year:** 93%. **Graduation rates:** Four-year: 36%; five-year: 76%; six-year: 90%. **Graduate study:** 2% of students pursue further study immediately upon graduation; 6% within one year. Fields in which graduates pursue further study: Master of Business Administration (MBA), 1%; law, 1%; medicine, 1%; dentistry, 1%; engineering, 1%; theology (or the seminary), 1%; education, 5%; arts and sciences, 2%.

COSTS AND FINANCIAL AID

Financial aid office: (401) 454-6636. **Expenses (2006-2007):** Tuition and fees 2006-2007: $31,430; room/board: $9,360. Estimated books and supplies: $2,350; transportation: $760; personal expenses: $2,150. **Financial aid:** In 2005-2006, 57% of undergraduates applied for financial aid. Of those, 51% were determined to have financial need; 8% had their need fully met. Average financial aid package (proportion receiving): $17,150 (50%). Average amount of gift aid, such as scholarships or grants (proportion receiving): $11,250 (44%). Average amount of self-help aid, such as work study or loans (proportion receiving): $6,900 (50%). Average need-based loan (excluding PLUS or other private loans): $5,900. Among students who received need-based aid, the average percentage of need met: 68%. Among students who received aid based on merit, the average award (and the proportion receiving): $4,250 (2%). The average athletic scholarship (and the proportion receiving): $0 (0%). Average amount of debt of borrowers graduating in 2005: $25,400. Proportion who borrowed: 53%.

CAMPUS LIFE AND EXTRACURRICULAR ACTIVITIES

Campus housing available (% using): coed dorms (81%), apartment for single students (19%), special housing for disabled students. Students who live in college-owned, operated, or affiliated housing: 100%. **Student employment:** During the 2005-2006 academic year, 65% of undergraduates worked on campus. Average per-year earnings: $1,700. **Clubs and organizations:** Number of student organizations: 31. Activities include: concert band, dance, drama/theater, literary magazine, student government, student newspaper, student film society, yearbook. Number of fraternities: 0; sororities: 0. Average proportion of students who stay on campus on weekends: 90%.

SERVICES AND FACILITIES

Basic services: placement service, health service, health insurance. **Remedial assistance:** reading, math, writing, study skills, other. **Counseling services:** minority student, career, military, personal, veteran student, academic, older student, psychological, birth control, religious. **For learning-disabled students:** School does not offer a structured program with separate admission and additional fees. Total undergraduates in learning-disabled program or receiving services: 37. Services include: reading machines, untimed tests, note-taking services, oral tests, readers, extended time for tests, tutors, priority seating, other. **Library:** Number of titles: 127,329; number of current serial subscriptions: 422. **Information technology resources:** Students are not required to lease or own a computer. School has a wireless network. Approximate number of users that can be accommodated: 600. Proportion of college-owned housing units wired for high-speed internet access: 100%. **Campus safety:** Security services offered: 24-hour foot-and-vehicle patrols, late-night transport/escort service, 24-hour emergency telephones, lighted pathways/sidewalks, controlled dormitory access (key, security card, etc.).

TRANSFER AND INTERNATIONAL STUDENTS

Transfer students: May apply for admission for the following academic terms: Fall, Spring. Applicants need a minimum number of credits to apply. For fall 2005: Transfer applications received: 588. Transfer applicants offered admission: 161. Transfer applicants enrolled: 110. **International stu-**

dents: Number of foreign undergraduates: 185 (13% of student body). Number of countries represented: 42. Minimum TOEFL score required: 580 (paper); 237 (computer). Average TOEFL score: 614 (paper).

Roger Williams University

- ■ **Address:** 1 Old Ferry Road, Bristol, RI 02809
- ■ **Website:** http://www.rwu.edu
- ■ **Private**
- ■ **Enrollment:** 3,741 full-time; 618 part-time

KEY STATS
✔ **U.S News College Ranking:** 10, Comp. Coll.–Bachelor's (North)
✔ **SAT Score (25th/75th percentile):** 990-1180
✔ **Tuition:** 2006-2007: $24,066

Selectivity: Selective	**Room/board:** $10,693
Acceptance rate: 78%	**Average debt:** $28,147
Student/faculty ratio: 16/1	**Proportion who borrowed:** 80%

UNDERGRADUATE STUDENT BODY STATS
2005-2006 enrollment: 3,741 full-time; 618 part-time. Men: 51%; women: 49%. **Ethnic makeup:** African American: 1%; Asian American: 2%; Hispanic: 2%; White: 93%; International: 2%.

ADMISSIONS FACTS AND FIGURES
Phone: (401) 254-3500. **Email:** admit@rwu.edu. **Website:** http://www.rwu.edu. **Application deadlines for fall 2007:** Regular decision: Rolling. Early decision: Send application by: December 1; Decision sent by: December 15. Early action: Not offered. Admission can be deferred. **Application fee:** $50. Common application is accepted. **Admissions requirements/recommendations:** High school units required (recommended): English: 4 (4); Mathematics: 3 (4); Science: 2 (3); Foreign language: 0 (3); Social studies: 2 (3); History: 2 (3); Academic electives: 2 (3); Total units: 22 (26). Tests: The college uses SAT or ACT scores in admissions decisions. Either SAT or ACT required. For admission to the fall 2007 entering class, the school will accept: ACT without writing. Campus visit: Recommended. Admissions interview: Recommended. Off-campus interview: May be arranged. **Factors that count in admissions decisions:** *Academic:* Secondary school record: Very important. Class rank: Important. Letters of recommendation: Very important. Standardized test scores: Very important. Essay: Very important. *Nonacademic:* Interview: Considered. Extracurricular activities: Important. Talent/ability: Considered. Character/personal qualities: Important. Alumni/ae relationship: Considered. Geographical residence: Not considered. State residency: Not considered. Religious affiliation/commitment: Not considered. Minority status: Not considered. Volunteer work: Important. Work experience: Considered. **Other schools with the greatest overlap in applicants:** Northeastern University; Quinnipiac University; Salve Regina University; University of Connecticut; University of Rhode Island. **Admissions statistics for the fall 2005 entering class:** Total applicants: 6,658. Total accepted: 5,220. Freshmen enrolled: 1,189; 91% were from out of state. Accepted through early-decision or early-action plans: 16%. Overall acceptance rate: 78%. Early-decision acceptance rate: 90%. Non-early acceptance rate: 78%. **Size of waiting list:** 174 applicants; enrolled from waiting list: 1. **Credentials of fall 2005 freshmen:** 11% ranked in the top 10 percent of their high school class; 35% were in the top 25 percent, and 72% were in the top half. (Proportion submitting class standing: 56%.) **Average high school grade point average:** 3.1. **First-year students who submitted SAT scores:** 93%. Scores (25/75 percentile): Verbal: 490-580, Math: 500-600, Combined: 990-1180. **First-year students submitting ACT scores:** 7%. Scores (25/75 percentile): English: N/A, Math: N/A, Composite: 21-25.

ACADEMICS
Year founded: 1956. **Academic calendar:** Semester. **Degrees offered:** certificate, associate, terminal-associate, bachelor's, post-bachelor's certificate, master's, first professional. **Most popular majors:** 23% business, management, marketing, and related support services, 15% security and protective services, 7% architecture and related services, 7% psychology, 6% communication, journalism, and related programs. **Major fields of study:** architecture and related services; biological and biomedical sciences; business, management, marketing, and related support services; communication, journalism, and related programs; computer and information sciences and support services; construction trades; education; engineering; English lan-

guage and literature/letters; foreign languages, literatures, and linguistics; health professions and related clinical sciences; history; legal professions and studies; liberal arts and sciences studies, and humanities; mathematics and statistics; multi/interdisciplinary studies; philosophy and religious studies; physical sciences; psychology; security and protective services; social sciences; visual and performing arts. **Areas of required coursework:** arts/fine arts, humanities, mathematics, English (including composition), philosophy, sciences (biological or physical), history, social science. **Pre-professional programs:** pre-law, pre-medicine, pre-veterinary science. **Special academic programs:** cooperative (work-study plan) program, distance learning, double major, dual enrollment, English as a Second Language (ESL), exchange student program (domestic), external degree program, honors program, independent study, internships, liberal arts/career combination, student-designed major, study abroad, teacher certificate program. **Teacher certification offered in:** elementary, secondary. **Cooperative education programs:** business, humanities, social/behavioral science. **Reserve Officers Training Corps (ROTC):** Army ROTC: Offered at cooperating institution. **Faculty and instruction (2005-2006):** Total instructional faculty: 178 full-time, 220 part-time (60% men; 40% women; 7% minorities). Full-time faculty with Ph.D. or other terminal degree: 80%. Student/faculty ratio: 16/1. Classes of fewer than 20 students: 37%; of 20 to 49 students: 63%; of 50 or more students: 0%. **Advanced Placement and International Baccalaureate credit:** AP tests may be used for: Credit and/or placement. Scores accepted: 3, 4, 5. International Baccalaureate exams may be used for: Credit and/or placement. **Freshmen returning for sophomore year:** 76%. **Graduation rates:** Four-year: 38%; five-year: 52%; six-year: 52%. **Graduate study:** 25% of students pursue further study within one year.

COSTS AND FINANCIAL AID
Financial aid office: (401) 254-3100. **Expenses (2006-2007):** Tuition and fees 2006-2007: $24,066; room/board: $10,693. Estimated books and supplies: $700; transportation: $560; personal expenses: $515. **Financial aid:** Priority filing date for institution's financial aid form: February 1; deadline: February 1. In 2005-2006, 78% of undergraduates applied for financial aid. Of those, 64% were determined to have financial need; 57% had their need fully met. Average financial aid package (proportion receiving): $14,600 (63%). Average amount of gift aid, such as scholarships or grants (proportion receiving): $7,700 (44%). Average amount of self-help aid, such as work study or loans (proportion receiving): $6,900 (54%). Average need-based loan (excluding PLUS or other private loans): $5,100. Among students who received need-based aid, the average percentage of need met: 83%. Among students who received aid based on merit, the average award (and the proportion receiving): $6,017 (9%). The average athletic scholarship (and the proportion receiving): $0 (0%). Average amount of debt of borrowers graduating in 2005: $28,147. Proportion who borrowed: 80%.

CAMPUS LIFE AND EXTRACURRICULAR ACTIVITIES
Campus housing available (% using): coed dorms (66%), apartment for single students (34%). Students who live in college-owned, operated, or affiliated housing: 81%. **Student employment:** During the 2005-2006 academic year, 5% of undergraduates worked on campus. Average per-year earnings: $3,300. **Clubs and organizations:** Number of student organizations: 92. Activities include: choral groups, dance, drama/theater, literary magazine, radio station, student government, student newspaper, student film society, yearbook. Number of fraternities: 0; sororities: 0. Average proportion of students who stay on campus on weekends: 70%. **Sports program (2005-2006):** Member of NCAA III. *Men's intercollegiate varsity sports:* baseball, basketball, cross-country, equestrian Sports, lacrosse, sailing, soccer, swimming and diving, tennis, wrestling. *Women's intercollegiate varsity sports:* basketball, cross-country, equestrian sports, lacrosse, sailing, soccer, softball, swimming and diving, tennis, volleyball.

SERVICES AND FACILITIES
Basic services: nonremedial tutoring, women's center, placement service, health service, health insurance. **Remedial assistance:** reading, math, writing, study skills. **Counseling services:** minority student, career, military, personal, veteran student, academic, older student, psychological, birth control. **For learning-disabled students:** School does not offer a structured program with separate admission and additional fees. Services include: note-taking services, learning center, readers, extended time for tests, tutors. **Library:** Number of titles: 211,709; number of current serial subscriptions: 1,899. **Information technology resources:** Students are not required to lease or own a computer. Number of campus computers available to all students: 400. School has a wireless network. Proportion of college-owned housing units wired for high-speed internet access: 100%. **Campus safety:** Security services offered: 24-hour foot-and-vehicle patrols, late-night transport/escort

service, 24-hour emergency telephones, lighted pathways/sidewalks, controlled dormitory access (key, security card, etc).

TRANSFER AND INTERNATIONAL STUDENTS

Transfer students: May apply for admission for the following academic terms: Fall, Spring. Applicants do not need a minimum number of credits to apply. For fall 2005: Transfer applications received: 339. Transfer applicants offered admission: 219. Transfer applicants enrolled: 91. **International students:** Number of foreign undergraduates: 71 (2% of student body). Number of countries represented: 37.

Salve Regina University

- **Address:** 100 Ochre Point Avenue, Newport, RI 02840-4192
- **Website:** http://www.salve.edu
- **Private; Religious affiliation:** Roman Catholic
- **Enrollment:** 1,987 full-time; 104 part-time

KEY STATS

✔ **U.S News College Ranking:** 37, Universities–Master's (North)
✔ **SAT Score (25th/75th percentile):** 1000-1160
✔ **Tuition:** 2006-2007: $25,175
   Selectivity: Selective   **Room/board:** $9,800
   Acceptance rate: 60%   **Average debt:** $21,925
   Student/faculty ratio: 14/1 **Proportion who borrowed:** 81%

UNDERGRADUATE STUDENT BODY STATS

2005-2006 enrollment: 1,987 full-time; 104 part-time. Men: 29%; women: 71%. **Ethnic makeup:** African American: 1%; Asian American: 1%; Hispanic: 3%; White: 93%; International: 1%.

ADMISSIONS FACTS AND FIGURES

Phone: (888) 467-2583. **Email:** sruadmis@salve.edu. **Website:** http://www.salve.edu. **Application deadlines for fall 2007:** Regular decision: Rolling. Early decision: Not offered. Early action: Send application by: November 1; Decision sent by: December 15. Admission can be deferred. **Application fee:** $40. Common application is accepted. **To apply online, go to:** http://www.salve.edu/office_admissions/index.cfm. **Admissions requirements/recommendations:** High school units required (recommended): English: 4; Mathematics: 3; Science: 2; Foreign language: 2; Social studies: 1; Academic electives: 4; Total units: 16. Tests: The college uses SAT or ACT scores in admissions decisions. Either SAT or ACT required. For admission to the fall 2007 entering class, the school will accept: ACT with writing. Campus visit: Recommended. Admissions interview: Neither required nor recommended. Off-campus interview: May be arranged. **Factors that count in admissions decisions:** *Academic:* Secondary school record: Very important. Class rank: Very important. Letters of recommendation: Important. Standardized test scores: Important. Essay: Important. *Nonacademic:* Interview: Not considered. Extracurricular activities: Considered. Talent/ability: Considered. Character/personal qualities: Considered. Alumni/ae relationship: Considered. Geographical residence: Not considered. State residency: Not considered. Religious affiliation/commitment: Not considered. Minority status: Considered. Volunteer work: Considered. Work experience: Considered. **Other schools with the greatest overlap in applicants:** Assumption College; Providence College; Roger Williams University; Stonehill College; University of Rhode Island. **Admissions statistics for the fall 2005 entering class:** Total applicants: 4,555. Total accepted: 2,727. Freshmen enrolled: 568; 91% were from out of state. Accepted through early-decision or early-action plans: 24%. Overall acceptance rate: 60%. Non-early acceptance rate: 57%. **Size of waiting list:** 479 applicants; enrolled from waiting list: 24. **Credentials of fall 2005 freshmen:** 16% ranked in the top 10 percent of their high school class; 54% were in the top 25 percent, and 89% were in the top half. (Proportion submitting class standing: 60%.) **Average high school grade point average:** 3.3. **First-year students who submitted SAT scores:** 96%. Scores (25/75 percentile): Verbal: 500-580, Math: 500-580, Combined: 1000-1160. **First-year students submitting ACT scores:** 17%. Scores (25/75 percentile): English: 20-26, Math: 20-25, Composite: 21-25.

ACADEMICS

Year founded: 1934. **Academic calendar:** Semester. **Degrees offered:** certificate, associate, bachelor's, post-bachelor's certificate, master's, post-master's

certificate, doctorate. **Most popular majors:** 9% special education and teaching, 8% criminal justice/law enforcement administration, 8% psychology, 6% English language and literature, 5% business administration and management. **Major fields of study:** area, ethnic, cultural, and gender studies; biological and biomedical sciences; business, management, marketing, and related support services; communication, journalism, and related programs; computer and information sciences and support services; education; English language and literature/letters; foreign languages, literatures, and linguistics; health professions and related clinical sciences; history; liberal arts and sciences studies, and humanities; mathematics and statistics; multi/interdisciplinary studies; philosophy and religious studies; physical sciences; psychology; public administration and social service professions; security and protective services; social sciences; visual and performing arts. **Areas of required coursework:** arts/fine arts, humanities, mathematics, English (including composition), philosophy, foreign languages, sciences (biological or physical), history, social science, other. **Pre-professional programs:** pre-law, pre-dentistry, pre-medicine, pre-veterinary science. **Special academic programs (% participation):** accelerated program (3%), distance learning (1%), double major (15%), English as a Second Language (ESL) (0%), honors program (4%), independent study (11%), internships (34%), liberal arts/career combination, study abroad (2%). **Teacher certification offered in:** early childhood, special education, elementary, secondary. **Reserve Officers Training Corps (ROTC):** Army ROTC: Offered at cooperating institution (University of Rhode Island). **Faculty and instruction (2005-2006):** Total instructional faculty: 122 full-time, 118 part-time (45% men; 55% women; 6% minorities). Full-time faculty with Ph.D. or other terminal degree: 77%. Student/faculty ratio: 14/1. Classes of fewer than 20 students: 53%; of 20 to 49 students: 47%; of 50 or more students: 0%. **Advanced Placement and International Baccalaureate credit:** AP tests may be used for: Credit and/or placement. Scores accepted: 3, 4, 5. International Baccalaureate exams may be used for: Credit and/or placement. **Freshmen returning for sophomore year:** 80%. **Graduation rates:** Four-year: 52%; five-year: 59%; six-year: 59%. **Graduate study:** 25% of students pursue further study immediately upon graduation; 32% within one year; 39% within five years. Fields in which graduates pursue further study: Master of Business Administration (MBA), 13%; law, 6%; education, 28%; arts and sciences, 53%.

COSTS AND FINANCIAL AID

Financial aid office: (401) 341-2901. **Expenses (2006-2007):** Tuition and fees 2006-2007: $25,175; room/board: $9,800. Estimated books and supplies: $850; transportation: $700; personal expenses: $1,000. **Financial aid:** Priority filing date for institution's financial aid form: March 1. In 2005-2006, 81% of undergraduates applied for financial aid. Of those, 70% were determined to have financial need; 16% had their need fully met. Average financial aid package (proportion receiving): $16,392 (66%). Average amount of gift aid, such as scholarships or grants (proportion receiving): $11,946 (61%). Average amount of self-help aid, such as work study or loans (proportion receiving): $5,668 (62%). Average need-based loan (excluding PLUS or other private loans): $4,688. Among students who received need-based aid, the average percentage of need met: 69%. Among students who received aid based on merit, the average award (and the proportion receiving): $6,725 (15%). The average athletic scholarship (and the proportion receiving): $0 (0%). Average amount of debt of borrowers graduating in 2005: $21,925. Proportion who borrowed: 81%.

CAMPUS LIFE AND EXTRACURRICULAR ACTIVITIES

Campus housing available (% using): coed dorms (78%), women's dorms (11%), men's dorms (0%), apartment for single students (10%), special housing for disabled students (0%), other housing options (1%). Students who live in college-owned, operated, or affiliated housing: 59%. **Student employment:** During the 2005-2006 academic year, 28% of undergraduates worked on campus. Average per-year earnings: $1,200. **Clubs and organizations:** Number of student organizations: 44. Activities include: choral groups, concert band, dance, drama/theater, jazz band, literary magazine, music ensembles, radio station, student government, student newspaper, yearbook. Number of fraternities: 0; sororities: 0. Average proportion of students who stay on campus on weekends: 67%. **Sports program (2005-2006):** Member of NCAA III. *Men's intercollegiate varsity sports:* baseball, basketball, football, ice hockey, lacrosse, sailing, soccer, tennis. *Women's intercollegiate varsity sports:* basketball, cheerleading, cross-country, field hockey, ice hockey, lacrosse, sailing, soccer, softball, tennis, track and field (outdoor), volleyball.

SERVICES AND FACILITIES

Basic services: nonremedial tutoring, placement service, health service, health insurance. **Remedial assistance:** reading, math, writing, study skills. **Counseling services:** minority student, career, military, personal, academic, psychological, birth control, religious. **For learning-disabled students:** School does not offer a structured program with separate admission and additional fees. Services include: remedial math, reading machines, remedial reading, tape recorders, videotaped classes, untimed tests, note-taking services, oral tests, learning center, readers, extended time for tests, tutors, other testing accomodations. **Library:** Number of titles: 139,441; number of current serial subscriptions: 1,221. **Information technology resources:** Students are required to lease or own a computer. Number of campus computers available to all students: 215. School has a wireless network. Approximate number of users that can be accommodated: 1,675. Proportion of college-owned housing units wired for high-speed internet access: 100%. **Campus safety:** Security services offered: 24-hour foot-and-vehicle patrols, late-night transport/escort service, 24-hour emergency telephones, lighted pathways/sidewalks, controlled dormitory access (key, security card, etc).

TRANSFER AND INTERNATIONAL STUDENTS

Transfer students: May apply for admission for the following academic terms: Fall, Spring. Applicants do not need a minimum number of credits to apply. For fall 2005: Transfer applications received: 201. Transfer applicants offered admission: 120. Transfer applicants enrolled: 57. **International students:** Number of foreign undergraduates: 20 (1% of student body). Number of countries represented: 12. Minimum TOEFL score required: 500 (paper); 173 (computer). Average TOEFL score: 510 (paper).

University of Rhode Island

- **Address:** Kingston, RI 02881-0806
- **Website:** http://www.uri.edu
- **Public**
- **Enrollment:** 9,766 full-time; 1,780 part-time

KEY STATS

✔ **U.S News College Ranking:** third tier, National Universities
✔ **SAT Score (25th/75th percentile):** 1020-1220
✔ **Tuition:** 2006-2007: $7,724 in state, $21,424 out of state

Selectivity: Selective	**Room/board:** $6,882
Acceptance rate: 77%	**Average debt:** $16,200
Student/faculty ratio: 19/1	**Proportion who borrowed:** 56%

UNDERGRADUATE STUDENT BODY STATS

2005-2006 enrollment: 9,766 full-time; 1,780 part-time. Men: 43%; women: 57%. **Ethnic makeup:** African American: 4%; Asian American: 2%; Hispanic: 4%; White: 88%.

ADMISSIONS FACTS AND FIGURES

Phone: (401) 874-7100. **Email:** uriadmit@uri.edu. **Website:** http://www.uri.edu. **Application deadlines for fall 2007:** Regular decision: February 1. Early decision: Not offered. Early action: Send application by: December 15; Decision sent by: January 15. Admission cannot be deferred. **Application fee:** $50. Common application is not accepted. **To apply online, go to:** http://www.uri.edu/admissions. **Admissions requirements/recommendations:** High school units required (recommended): English: 4 (4); Mathematics: 3 (4); Science: 2 (4); Foreign language: 2 (4); Social studies: 2 (4); Academic electives: 5; Total units: 18 (20). Tests: The college uses SAT or ACT scores in admissions decisions. Either SAT or ACT required. For admission to the fall 2007 entering class, the school will accept: ACT with writing. Campus visit: Recommended. Admissions interview: Neither required nor recommended. Off-campus interview: May be arranged. **Factors that count in admissions decisions:** *Academic:* Secondary school record: Very important. Class rank: Very important. Letters of recommendation: Considered. Standardized test scores: Important. Essay: Considered. *Nonacademic:* Interview: Considered. Extracurricular activities: Considered. Talent/ability: Considered. Character/personal qualities: Considered. Alumni/ae relationship: Considered. Geographical residence: Considered. State residency: Considered. Religious affiliation/commitment: Not considered. Minority status: Important. Volunteer work: Considered. Work experience: Considered. **Admissions statistics for the fall 2005 entering class:** Total applicants: 13,388. Total accepted: 10,327. Freshmen enrolled: 2,461; 47%

were from out of state. Overall acceptance rate: 77%. Non-early acceptance rate: 77%. **Credentials of fall 2005 freshmen:** 21% ranked in the top 10 percent of their high school class, and 88% were in the top half. (Proportion submitting class standing: 72%.)

ACADEMICS

Year founded: 1892. **Academic calendar:** Semester. **Degrees offered:** bachelor's, post-bachelor's certificate, master's, first professional, doctorate. **Most popular majors:** 10% communication studies/speech communication and rhetoric, 6% human development and family studies, 6% psychology, 4% finance, 3% apparel and textiles. **Major fields of study:** agriculture, agriculture operations, and related sciences; architecture and related services; area, ethnic, cultural, and gender studies; biological and biomedical sciences; business, management, marketing, and related support services; communication, journalism, and related programs; computer and information sciences and support services; education; engineering; English language and literature/letters; family and consumer sciences/human sciences; foreign languages, literatures, and linguistics; health professions and related clinical sciences; history; liberal arts and sciences studies, and humanities; mathematics and statistics; multi/interdisciplinary studies; natural resources and conservation; philosophy and religious studies; physical sciences; psychology; public administration and social service professions; social sciences; visual and performing arts. **Areas of required coursework:** arts/fine arts, humanities, computer literacy, mathematics, English (including composition), philosophy, foreign languages, sciences (biological or physical), history, social science. **Pre-professional programs:** pre-law, pre-dentistry, pre-medicine, pre-veterinary science. **Special academic programs:** cooperative (work-study plan) program, distance learning, double major, exchange student program (domestic), external degree program, honors program, independent study, internships, liberal arts/career combination, study abroad, teacher certificate program. **Teacher certification offered in:** early childhood, elementary, secondary. **Cooperative education programs:** health professions, other. **Reserve Officers Training Corps (ROTC):** Army ROTC: Offered on campus. **Faculty and instruction (2005-2006):** Total instructional faculty: 668 full-time, 23 part-time (62% men; 38% women; 14% minorities). Full-time faculty with Ph.D. or other terminal degree: 90%. Student/faculty ratio: 19/1. Classes of fewer than 20 students: 36%; of 20 to 49 students: 56%; of 50 or more students: 8%. **Advanced Placement and International Baccalaureate credit:** AP tests may be used for: Credit and/or placement. Scores accepted: 3, 4, 5. International Baccalaureate exams may be used for: Credit and/or placement. **Freshmen returning for sophomore year:** 80%. **Graduation rates:** Four-year: 36%; five-year: 53%; six-year: 56%.

COSTS AND FINANCIAL AID

Financial aid office: (401) 874-9500. **Expenses (2006-2007):** Tuition and fees 2006-2007: $7,724 in state, $21,424 out of state; room/board: $6,882. **Financial aid:** Priority filing date for institution's financial aid form: March 1. In 2005-2006, 83% of undergraduates applied for financial aid. Of those, 69% were determined to have financial need; 52% had their need fully met. Average financial aid package (proportion receiving): $11,659 (51%). Average amount of gift aid, such as scholarships or grants (proportion receiving): $5,883 (49%). Average amount of self-help aid, such as work study or loans (proportion receiving): $6,574 (46%). Average need-based loan (excluding PLUS or other private loans): $6,713. Among students who received need-based aid, the average percentage of need met: 61%. Among students who received aid based on merit, the average award (and the proportion receiving): $4,607 (4%). The average athletic scholarship (and the proportion receiving): $1,372 (0%). Average amount of debt of borrowers graduating in 2005: $16,200. Proportion who borrowed: 56%.

CAMPUS LIFE AND EXTRACURRICULAR ACTIVITIES

Campus housing available (% using): coed dorms (81%), women's dorms (2%), sorority housing (8%), fraternity housing (4%), apartments for married students (1%), apartment for single students (3%), special housing for disabled students (1%). Students who live in college-owned, operated, or affiliated housing: 37%. **Clubs and organizations:** Number of student organizations: 115. Activities include: choral groups, concert band, dance, drama/theater, jazz band, literary magazine, marching band, music ensembles, musical theater, opera, pep band, radio station, student government, student newspaper, student film society, symphony orchestra, television station, yearbook. Number of fraternities: 11; sororities: 9. Proportion of men in fraternities: 10%; of women in sororities: 10%. Average proportion of students who stay on campus on weekends: 62%. **Sports program (2005-2006):** Member of NCAA I. *Men's intercollegiate varsity sports:* baseball, basketball, cross-country, football, golf, soccer, swimming and diving, tennis, track and field (indoor), track and field (outdoor). *Women's intercollegiate varsity*

sports: basketball, crew, cross-country, field hockey, gymnastics, rowing, soccer, softball, swimming and diving, tennis, track and field (indoor), track and field (outdoor), volleyball.

SERVICES AND FACILITIES

Basic services: nonremedial tutoring, women's center, placement service, day care, health service, health insurance, other. **Remedial assistance:** reading, math, writing, study skills. **Counseling services:** minority student, career, military, personal, veteran student, academic, older student, psychological, birth control, religious. **For learning-disabled students:** School does not offer a structured program with separate admission and additional fees. Total undergraduates in learning-disabled program or receiving services: 395. Services include: reading machines, tape recorders, note-taking services, special bookstore section, oral tests, learning center, readers, extended time for tests, priority registration, texts on tape, exams on tape or computer, other testing accomodations, other. **Library:** Number of titles: 1,237,735; number of current serial subscriptions: 6,872. **Information tech-**

nology resources: Students are not required to lease or own a computer. Number of campus computers available to all students: 785. School has a wireless network. Approximate number of users that can be accommodated: 2,000. Proportion of college-owned housing units wired for high-speed internet access: 90%. **Campus safety:** Security services offered: 24-hour foot-and-vehicle patrols, late-night transport/escort service, 24-hour emergency telephones, lighted pathways/sidewalks, controlled dormitory access (key, security card, etc).

TRANSFER AND INTERNATIONAL STUDENTS

Transfer students: May apply for admission for the following academic terms: Fall, Spring. Applicants do not need a minimum number of credits to apply. For fall 2005: Transfer applications received: 1,340. Transfer applicants offered admission: 862. Transfer applicants enrolled: 512.
International students: Number of foreign undergraduates: 29. Minimum TOEFL score required: 550 (paper); 213 (computer).

South Carolina

Allen University

- **Address:** 1530 Harden Street, Columbia, SC 29204
- **Website:** http://www.allenuniversity.edu
- **Private; Religious affiliation:** African Methodist Episcopal
- **Enrollment:** N/A

KEY STATS

✔ **U.S News College Ranking:** fourth tier, Comp. Coll.–Bachelor's (South)
✔ **SAT or ACT Score (25th/75th percentile):** N/A
✔ **Tuition:** 2005-2006: $7,764

Selectivity: Less selective	**Room/board:** $0
Acceptance rate: 60%	**Average debt:** N/A
Student/faculty ratio: N/A	**Proportion who borrowed:** N/A

Anderson University

- **Address:** 316 Boulevard, Anderson, SC 29621
- **Website:** http://www.andersonuniversity.edu
- **Private; Religious affiliation:** South Carolina Baptist Convention
- **Enrollment:** 1,277 full-time; 367 part-time

KEY STATS

✔ **U.S News College Ranking:** 44, Comp. Coll.–Bachelor's (South)
✔ **SAT Score (25th/75th percentile):** 940-1140
✔ **Tuition:** 2006-2007: $16,550

Selectivity: Selective	**Room/board:** $6,400
Acceptance rate: 78%	**Average debt:** $15,125
Student/faculty ratio: 15/1	**Proportion who borrowed:** 76%

UNDERGRADUATE STUDENT BODY STATS

2005-2006 enrollment: 1,277 full-time; 367 part-time. Men: 36%; women: 64%. **Ethnic makeup:** African American: 10%; Asian American: 1%; Hispanic: 1%; White: 86%; International: 2%. **Religious preference:** Roman Catholic: 2%; Protestant: 27%; No preference: 2%; Unknown: 5%; South Carolina Baptist Convention: 62%; Other: 2%.

ADMISSIONS FACTS AND FIGURES

Phone: (864) 231-5607. **Email:** admissions@ac.edu. **Website:** http://www.andersonuniversity.edu. **Application deadlines for fall 2007:** Regular decision: July 1. Early decision: Not offered. Early action: Not offered. Admission can be deferred. **Application fee:** $25. Common application is not accepted. **To apply online, go to:** http://applyweb.com/apply/anderson/menu.html. **Admissions requirements/recommendations:** High school units required (recommended): English: 4 (4); Mathematics: 3 (4); Science: 3 (4); Foreign language: 2 (2); Social studies: 2 (3); History: 2 (2); Academic electives: 4 (4); Total units: 20 (22). Tests: The college uses SAT or ACT scores in admissions decisions. Either SAT or ACT required. For admission to the fall 2007 entering class, the school will accept: ACT with writing, ACT without writing. Campus visit: Recommended. Admissions interview: Recommended. Off-campus interview: May be arranged. **Factors that count in admissions decisions:** *Academic:* Secondary school record: Very important. Class rank: Important. Letters of recommendation: Considered. Standardized test scores: Very important. Essay: Considered. *Nonacademic:* Interview: Considered. Extracurricular activities: Not considered. Talent/ability: Considered. Character/personal qualities: Important. Alumni/ae relationship: Considered. Geographical residence: Not considered. State residency: Not considered. Religious affiliation/commitment: Considered. Minority status: Considered. Volunteer work: Considered. Work experience: Not considered. **Other schools with the greatest overlap in applicants:** Clemson University; College of Charleston; Lander University; University of South Carolina–Columbia;

Winthrop University. **Admissions statistics for the fall 2005 entering class:** Total applicants: 1,079. Total accepted: 838. Freshmen enrolled: 371; 16% were from out of state. Overall acceptance rate: 78%. **Credentials of fall 2005 freshmen:** 17% ranked in the top 10 percent of their high school class; 44% were in the top 25 percent, and 81% were in the top half. (Proportion submitting class standing: 85%.) **Average high school grade point average:** 3.7. **First-year students who submitted SAT scores:** 87%. Scores (25/75 percentile): Verbal: 470-560, Math: 470-580, Combined: 940-1140. **First-year students submitting ACT scores:** 50%. Scores (25/75 percentile): English: 18-24, Math: 18-23, Composite: 18-23.

ACADEMICS

Year founded: 1911. **Academic calendar:** Semester. **Degrees offered:** bachelor's, master's. **Most popular majors:** 34% business, management, marketing, and related support services, 25% education, 11% visual and performing arts, 8% psychology, 7% agriculture, agriculture operations, and related sciences. **Major fields of study:** biological and biomedical sciences; business, management, marketing, and related support services; communication, journalism, and related programs; education; English language and literature/letters; foreign languages, literatures, and linguistics; health professions and related clinical sciences; history; mathematics and statistics; parks, recreation, leisure, and fitness studies; philosophy and religious studies; psychology; security and protective services; theology and religious vocations; visual and performing arts. **Areas of required coursework:** arts/fine arts, humanities, computer literacy, mathematics, English (including composition), foreign languages, sciences (biological or physical), history, social science, other. **Pre-professional programs:** pre-dentistry, pre-medicine, pre-theology, pre-veterinary science, pre-pharmacy, other. **Special academic programs:** accelerated program, cooperative (work-study plan) program, distance learning, double major, dual enrollment, honors program, independent study, internships, liberal arts/career combination, study abroad, teacher certificate program. **Teacher certification offered in:** early childhood, special education, elementary, middle/junior high, secondary. **Reserve Officers Training Corps (ROTC):** Army ROTC: Offered at cooperating institution (Clemson University); Air Force ROTC: Offered at cooperating institution (Clemson University). **Faculty and instruction (2005-2006):** Total instructional faculty: 68 full-time, 82 part-time (57% men; 43% women; 6% minorities). Full-time faculty with Ph.D. or other terminal degree: 60%. Student/faculty ratio: 15/1. Classes of fewer than 20 students: 50%; of 20 to 49 students: 50%; of 50 or more students: 0%. **Advanced Placement and International Baccalaureate credit:** AP tests may be used for: Credit only. Scores accepted: 3, 4, 5. International Baccalaureate exams may be used for: Credit only. **Freshmen returning for sophomore year:** 66%. **Graduation rates:** Four-year: 24%; five-year: 37%; six-year: 42%.

COSTS AND FINANCIAL AID

Financial aid office: (864) 231-2070. **Expenses (2006-2007):** Tuition and fees 2006-2007: $16,550; room/board: $6,400. Estimated books and supplies: $1,650; transportation: $2,000; personal expenses: $2,450. **Financial aid:** Priority filing date for institution's financial aid form: March 1; deadline: July 30. In 2005-2006, 96% of undergraduates applied for financial aid. Of those, 86% were determined to have financial need; 28% had their need fully met. Average financial aid package (proportion receiving): $15,834 (86%). Average amount of gift aid, such as scholarships or grants (proportion receiving): $7,160 (83%). Average amount of self-help aid, such as work study or loans (proportion receiving): $4,701 (50%). Average need-based loan (excluding PLUS or other private loans): $4,596. Among students who received need-based aid, the average percentage of need met: 66%. Among students who received aid based on merit, the average award (and the proportion receiving): $5,652 (8%). The average athletic scholarship (and the proportion receiving): $5,451 (13%). Average amount of debt of borrowers graduating in 2005: $15,125. Proportion who borrowed: 76%.

CAMPUS LIFE AND EXTRACURRICULAR ACTIVITIES

Campus housing available (% using): coed dorms (16%), women's dorms (52%), men's dorms (27%), other housing options (5%). Students who live in college-owned, operated, or affiliated housing: 50%. **Student employment:** During the 2005-2006 academic year, 8% of undergraduates worked on campus. Average per-year earnings: $1,780. **Clubs and organizations:**

Number of student organizations: 29. Activities include: choral groups, concert band, dance, drama/theater, jazz band, literary magazine, music ensembles, musical theater, student government, student newspaper, symphony orchestra, yearbook. Number of fraternities: 0; sororities: 0. Average proportion of students who stay on campus on weekends: 30%. **Sports program (2005-2006):** Member of NCAA II. *Men's intercollegiate varsity sports:* baseball, basketball, cross-country, golf, soccer, tennis, track and field (indoor), track and field (outdoor), wrestling. *Women's intercollegiate varsity sports:* basketball, cross-country, golf, soccer, softball, tennis, track and field (indoor), track and field (outdoor), volleyball.

SERVICES AND FACILITIES

Basic services: nonremedial tutoring, placement service, day care, health service. **Remedial assistance:** reading, math, writing, study skills. **Counseling services:** career, personal, academic, psychological, religious. **For learning-disabled students:** School does not offer a structured program with separate admission and additional fees. Total undergraduates in learning-disabled program or receiving services: 18. Services include: tape recorders, note-taking services, oral tests, readers, extended time for tests. **Library:** Number of titles: 70,844; number of current serial subscriptions: 259. **Information technology resources:** Students are not required to lease or own a computer. Number of campus computers available to all students: 192. School has a wireless network. Approximate number of users that can be accommodated: 879. Proportion of college-owned housing units wired for high-speed internet access: 100%. **Campus safety:** Security services offered: 24-hour foot-and-vehicle patrols, late-night transport/escort service, 24-hour emergency telephones, lighted pathways/sidewalks, student patrols, controlled dormitory access (key, security card, etc).

TRANSFER AND INTERNATIONAL STUDENTS

Transfer students: May apply for admission for the following academic terms: Fall, Spring, Summer. Applicants do not need a minimum number of credits to apply. For fall 2005: Transfer applications received: 205. Transfer applicants offered admission: 142. Transfer applicants enrolled: 96. **International students:** Number of foreign undergraduates: 29 (2% of student body). Number of countries represented: 20. Minimum TOEFL score required: 550 (paper); 220 (computer). Average TOEFL score: 575 (paper).

Benedict College

- **Address:** 1600 Harden Street, Columbia, SC 29204
- **Website:** http://www.benedict.edu
- **Private; Religious affiliation:** Baptist
- **Enrollment:** N/A

KEY STATS

✔ **U.S News College Ranking:** fourth tier, Comp. Coll.–Bachelor's (South)
✔ **ACT Score (25th/75th percentile):** 13-17
✔ **Tuition:** N/A

Selectivity: Least selective	**Room/board:** N/A
Acceptance rate: 73%	**Average debt:** N/A
Student/faculty ratio: N/A	**Proportion who borrowed:** N/A

Charleston Southern University

- **Address:** PO Box 118087, 9200 University Blvd., Charleston, SC 29423
- **Website:** http://www.csuniv.edu
- **Private; Religious affiliation:** Baptist
- **Enrollment:** 2,208 full-time; 374 part-time

KEY STATS

✔ **U.S News College Ranking:** third tier, Universities–Master's (South)
✔ **SAT Score (25th/75th percentile):** 970-1150
✔ **Tuition:** 2006-2007: $16,810

Selectivity: Selective	**Room/board:** $6,450
Acceptance rate: 71%	**Average debt:** $24,251
Student/faculty ratio: 19/1	**Proportion who borrowed:** 90%

UNDERGRADUATE STUDENT BODY STATS

2005-2006 enrollment: 2,208 full-time; 374 part-time. Men: 39%; women: 61%. **Ethnic makeup:** African American: 28%; American-Indian: 1%; Asian American: 2%; Hispanic: 1%; White: 67%; International: 2%.

ADMISSIONS FACTS AND FIGURES

Phone: (843) 863-7050. **Email:** enroll@csuniv.edu. **Website:** http://www.csuniv.edu. **Application deadlines for fall 2007:** Regular decision: August 29. Early decision: Not offered. Early action: Not offered. Admission cannot be deferred. **Application fee:** $30. Common application is not accepted. **Admissions requirements/recommendations:** High school units required (recommended): English: 4; Mathematics: 3 (4); Science: 3; Foreign language: 0 (2); Social studies: 2; History: (2); Total units: 12 (8). Tests: The college uses SAT or ACT scores in admissions decisions. Either SAT or ACT required. For admission to the fall 2007 entering class, the school will accept: ACT with writing. Campus visit: Recommended. Admissions interview: Required. Off-campus interview: Not available. **Factors that count in admissions decisions:** *Academic:* Secondary school record: Important. Class rank: Important. Letters of recommendation: Considered. Standardized test scores: Very important. Essay: Considered. *Nonacademic:* Interview: Considered. Extracurricular activities: Considered. Talent/ability: Considered. Character/personal qualities: Considered. Alumni/ae relationship: Considered. Geographical residence: Not considered. State residency: Not considered. Religious affiliation/commitment: Not considered. Minority status: Not considered. Volunteer work: Not considered. Work experience: Considered. **Other schools with the greatest overlap in applicants:** College of Charleston; Furman University; North Greenville University; University of South Carolina–Columbia. **Admissions statistics for the fall 2005 entering class:** Total applicants: 2,744. Total accepted: 1,955. Freshmen enrolled: 632; 25% were from out of state. Overall acceptance rate: 71%. **Credentials of fall 2005 freshmen:** 16% ranked in the top 10 percent of their high school class; 43% were in the top 25 percent, and 70% were in the top half. (Proportion submitting class standing: 84%.) **Average high school grade point average:** 3.1. **First-year students who submitted SAT scores:** 78%. Scores (25/75 percentile): Verbal: 490-580, Math: 480-570, Combined: 970-1150. **First-year students submitting ACT scores:** 36%. Scores (25/75 percentile): English: N/A, Math: N/A, Composite: 20-24.

ACADEMICS

Year founded: 1964. **Academic calendar:** Other. **Degrees offered:** bachelor's, master's. **Most popular majors:** 17% business, management, marketing, and related support services, 14% education, 13% social sciences, 10% health professions and related clinical sciences, 10% psychology. **Major fields of study:** biological and biomedical sciences; business, management, marketing, and related support services; computer and information sciences and support services; education; engineering; English language and literature/letters; foreign languages, literatures, and linguistics; health professions and related clinical sciences; legal professions and studies; liberal arts and sciences studies, and humanities; mathematics and statistics; multi/interdisciplinary studies; natural resources and conservation; parks, recreation, leisure, and fitness studies; philosophy and religious studies; physical sciences; psychology; science technologies/technicians; security and protective services; social sciences; theology and religious vocations; visual and performing arts. **Areas of required coursework:** arts/fine arts, humanities, computer literacy, mathematics, English (including composition), foreign languages, sciences (biological or physical), history, social science, other. **Pre-professional programs:** pre-law, pre-dentistry, pre-medicine, pre-theology, pre-pharmacy, other. **Special academic programs (% participation):** double major (8.4%), honors program (1.5%), internships (30.2%), teacher certificate program (18.3%). **Teacher certification offered in:** early childhood, elementary, middle/junior high, secondary, bilingual/bicultural. **Cooperative education programs:** engineering. **Reserve Officers Training Corps (ROTC):** Air Force ROTC: Offered on campus. **Faculty and instruction (2005-2006):** Total instructional faculty: 103 full-time, 86 part-time (47% men; 53% women; 6% minorities). Full-time faculty with Ph.D. or other terminal degree: 60%. Student/faculty ratio: 19/1. Classes of fewer than 20 students: 48%; of 20 to 49 students: 48%; of 50 or more students: 4%. **Advanced Placement and International Baccalaureate credit:** AP tests may be used for: Credit only. Scores accepted: 3, 4, 5. **Freshmen returning for sophomore year:** 69%. **Graduation rates:** Four-year: 21%; five-year: 34%; six-year: 34%. **Graduate study:** 15% of students pursue further study immediately upon graduation; 20% within one year. Fields in which graduates pursue further study: Master of Business Administration (MBA), 5%; law, 2%; medicine, 3%; dentistry, 1%; theology (or the seminary), 1%; education, 2%.

COSTS AND FINANCIAL AID

Financial aid office: (843) 863-7050. **Expenses (2006-2007):** Tuition and fees 2006-2007: $16,810; room/board: $6,450. Estimated books and supplies: $1,290; transportation: $1,235; personal expenses: $1,385. **Financial aid:** Priority filing date for institution's financial aid form: April 15. In 2005-2006, 95% of undergraduates applied for financial aid. Of those, 84% were determined to have financial need; 23% had their need fully met. Average financial aid package (proportion receiving): $14,086 (84%). Average amount of gift aid, such as scholarships or grants (proportion receiving): $9,858 (83%). Average amount of self-help aid, such as work study or loans (proportion receiving): $5,197 (70%). Average need-based loan (excluding PLUS or other private loans): $4,534. Among students who received need-based aid, the average percentage of need met: 70%. Among students who received aid based on merit, the average award (and the proportion receiving): $10,704 (14%). The average athletic scholarship (and the proportion receiving): $9,933 (5%). Average amount of debt of borrowers graduating in 2005: $24,251. Proportion who borrowed: 90%.

CAMPUS LIFE AND EXTRACURRICULAR ACTIVITIES

Campus housing available (% using): women's dorms (60%), men's dorms (39%), apartments for married students (1%). Students who live in college-owned, operated, or affiliated housing: 40%. **Student employment:** During the 2005-2006 academic year, 42% of undergraduates worked on campus. Average per-year earnings: $2,000. **Clubs and organizations:** Number of student organizations: 152. Activities include: choral groups, concert band, dance, drama/theater, jazz band, literary magazine, music ensembles, radio station, student government, student newspaper, student film society, symphony orchestra. Number of fraternities: 0; sororities: 0. Average proportion of students who stay on campus on weekends: 55%. **Sports program (2005-2006):** Member of NCAA II. *Men's intercollegiate varsity sports:* baseball, basketball, cross-country, football, golf, tennis, track and field (indoor), track and field (outdoor). *Women's intercollegiate varsity sports:* basketball, cross-country, golf, soccer, softball, tennis, track and field (indoor), track and field (outdoor), volleyball.

SERVICES AND FACILITIES

Basic services: nonremedial tutoring, placement service. **Remedial assistance:** math, writing, study skills. **Counseling services:** personal, veteran student, academic, psychological, religious. **For learning-disabled students:** School does not offer a structured program with separate admission and additional fees. Services include: remedial math, remedial English, tape recorders, note-taking services, oral tests, learning center, readers, extended time for tests, tutors. **Library:** Number of titles: 169,975; number of current serial subscriptions: 1,037. **Information technology resources:** Students are not required to lease or own a computer. Number of campus computers available to all students: 255. School has a wireless network. Proportion of college-owned housing units wired for high-speed internet access: 0%. **Campus safety:** Security services offered: 24-hour foot-and-vehicle patrols, late-night transport/escort service, 24-hour emergency telephones, lighted pathways/sidewalks, controlled dormitory access (key, security card, etc).

TRANSFER AND INTERNATIONAL STUDENTS

Transfer students: May apply for admission for the following academic terms: Fall, Spring, Summer. Applicants need a minimum number of credits to apply. For fall 2005: Transfer applications received: 762. Transfer applicants offered admission: 523. Transfer applicants enrolled: 292. **International students:** Number of foreign undergraduates: 52 (2% of student body). Minimum TOEFL score required: 550 (paper); 213 (computer).

The Citadel

- **Address:** 171 Moultrie Street, Charleston, SC 29409
- **Website:** http://www.citadel.edu
- **Public**
- **Enrollment:** 2,111 full-time; 127 part-time

KEY STATS

✔ **U.S News College Ranking:** 7, Universities–Master's (South)
✔ **SAT Score (25th/75th percentile):** 980-1200
✔ **Tuition:** 2006-2007: $7,168 in state, $17,487 out of state

Selectivity: Selective	Room/board: N/A
Acceptance rate: 78%	Average debt: N/A
Student/faculty ratio: 15/1	Proportion who borrowed: N/A

UNDERGRADUATE STUDENT BODY STATS

2005-2006 enrollment: 2,111 full-time; 127 part-time. Men: 91%; women: 9%. **Ethnic makeup:** African American: 7%; Asian American: 2%; Hispanic: 4%; White: 84%; International: 2%.

ADMISSIONS FACTS AND FIGURES

Phone: (843) 953-5230. **Email:** admissions@citadel.edu. **Website:** http://www.citadel.edu. **Application deadlines for fall 2007:** Regular decision: Rolling. Early decision: Send application by: October 26; Decision sent by: N/A. Early action: Not offered. Admission cannot be deferred. **Application fee:** $40. Common application is not accepted. **To apply online, go to:** http://www.applyweb.com/apply/citadel/. **Admissions requirements/recommendations:** High school units required (recommended): English: 4; Mathematics: 3; Science: 3; Foreign language: 2; Social studies: 2; History: 1; Academic electives: 4; Total units: 20. Tests: The college uses SAT or ACT scores in admissions decisions. Either SAT or ACT required. For admission to the fall 2007 entering class, the school will accept: ACT with writing. Campus visit: Recommended. Admissions interview: Recommended. Off-campus interview: May be arranged. **Factors that count in admissions decisions:** *Academic:* Secondary school record: Important. Class rank: Considered. Letters of recommendation: Considered. Standardized test scores: Very important. Essay: Not considered. *Nonacademic:* Interview: Considered. Extracurricular activities: Important. Talent/ability: Important. Character/personal qualities: Important. Alumni/ae relationship: Considered. Geographical residence: Considered. State residency: Important. Religious affiliation/commitment: Not considered. Minority status: Not considered. Volunteer work: Considered. Work experience: Not considered. **Other schools with the greatest overlap in applicants:** Clemson University; Norwich University; United States Military Academy; University of South Carolina–Columbia; Virginia Military Institute. **Admissions statistics for the fall 2005 entering class:** Total applicants: 1,913. Total accepted: 1,496. Freshmen enrolled: 585; 56% were from out of state. Accepted through early-decision or early-action plans: 19%. Overall acceptance rate: 78%. Early-decision acceptance rate: 99%. Non-early acceptance rate: 77%. **Credentials of fall 2005 freshmen:** 9% ranked in the top 10 percent of their high school class; 31% were in the top 25 percent, and 67% were in the top half. (Proportion submitting class standing: 80%.) **Average high school grade point average:** 3.2. **First-year students who submitted SAT scores:** 82%. Scores (25/75 percentile): Verbal: 480-600, Math: 500-600, Combined: 980-1200. **First-year students submitting ACT scores:** 17%. Scores (25/75 percentile): English: N/A, Math: N/A, Composite: 20-24.

ACADEMICS

Year founded: 1842. **Academic calendar:** Semester. **Degrees offered:** bachelor's, master's, post-master's certificate. **Most popular majors:** 36% business administration and management, 12% criminal justice/law enforcement administration, 10% political science and government, 9% education, 9% engineering. **Major fields of study:** biological and biomedical sciences; business, management, marketing, and related support services; computer and information sciences and support services; education; engineering; English language and literature/letters; foreign languages, literatures, and linguistics; history; mathematics and statistics; physical sciences; psychology; security and protective services; social sciences. **Areas of required coursework:** arts/fine arts, computer literacy, mathematics, English (including composition), foreign languages, sciences (biological or physical), history, social science, other. **Special academic programs:** double major, English as a Second Language (ESL), honors program, independent study, internships, study abroad, teacher certificate program. **Teacher certification offered in:** secondary. **Reserve Officers Training Corps (ROTC):** Army ROTC: Offered on campus; Navy ROTC: Offered on campus; Air Force ROTC: Offered on campus. **Faculty and instruction (2005-2006):** Total instructional faculty: 157 full-time, 75 part-time (69% men; 31% women; 10% minorities). Full-time faculty with Ph.D. or other terminal degree: 94%. Student/faculty ratio: 15/1. Classes of fewer than 20 students: 42%; of 20 to 49 students: 54%; of 50 or more students: 4%. **Advanced Placement and International Baccalaureate credit:** AP tests may be used for: Credit only. Scores accepted: 3, 4, 5. International Baccalaureate exams may be used for: Credit only. **Freshmen returning for sophomore year:** 80%. **Graduation rates:** Four-year: 55%; five-year: 63%; six-year: 67%. **Graduate study:** 15% of students pursue further study immediately upon graduation.

COSTS AND FINANCIAL AID

Financial aid office: (843) 953-5187. **Expenses (2006-2007):** Tuition and fees 2006-2007: $7,168 in state, $17,487 out of state; room/board: N/A. **Financial aid:** Priority filing date for institution's financial aid form: February 28; deadline: February 28. In 2005-2006, 68% of undergraduates applied for financial aid. Of those, 50% were determined to have financial need; 12% had their need fully met. Average financial aid package (proportion receiving): $8,846 (49%). Average amount of gift aid, such as scholarships or grants (proportion receiving): N/A (32%). Average amount of self-help aid, such as work study or loans (proportion receiving): $4,142 (31%). Average need-based loan (excluding PLUS or other private loans): $4,142. Among students who received need-based aid, the average percentage of need met: 58%. Among students who received aid based on merit, the average award (and the proportion receiving): $6,578 (12%). The average athletic scholarship (and the proportion receiving): $14,092 (11%).

CAMPUS LIFE AND EXTRACURRICULAR ACTIVITIES
Campus housing available (% using): coed dorms (100%). Students who live in college-owned, operated, or affiliated housing: 100%. Activities include: choral groups, concert band, drama/theater, jazz band, literary magazine, marching band, music ensembles, pep band, student government, student newspaper, yearbook. Number of fraternities: 0; sororities: 0. **Sports program (2005-2006):** Member of NCAA I. *Men's intercollegiate varsity sports:* baseball, basketball, cross-country, football, golf, riflery, soccer, tennis, track and field (indoor), track and field (outdoor), wrestling, , , , . *Women's intercollegiate varsity sports:* cross-country, golf, riflery, soccer, track and field (indoor), track and field (outdoor), volleyball.

SERVICES AND FACILITIES
Basic services: nonremedial tutoring, health service. **Remedial assistance:** reading, math, writing, study skills. **Counseling services:** minority student, career, personal, academic, psychological. **For learning-disabled students:** School does not offer a structured program with separate admission and additional fees. Services include: tape recorders, untimed tests, note-taking services, oral tests, learning center, readers, extended time for tests, tutors, priority registration, texts on tape, other testing accomodations, other. **Library:** Number of titles: 234,356; number of current serial subscriptions: 494. **Information technology resources:** Students are not required to lease or own a computer. School does not have a wireless network. Proportion of college-owned housing units wired for high-speed internet access: 100%. **Campus safety:** Security services offered: 24-hour foot-and-vehicle patrols, lighted pathways/sidewalks, controlled dormitory access (key, security card, etc).

TRANSFER AND INTERNATIONAL STUDENTS
Transfer students: May apply for admission for the following academic terms: Fall. Applicants need a minimum number of credits to apply. For fall 2005: Transfer applications received: 142. Transfer applicants offered admission: 86. Transfer applicants enrolled: 41. **International students:** Number of foreign undergraduates: 43 (2% of student body). Number of countries represented: 25. Minimum TOEFL score required: 550 (paper); 213 (computer).

Claflin University

- **Address:** 400 Magnolia Street, Orangeburg, SC 29115
- **Website:** http://www.claflin.edu
- **Private; Religious affiliation:** United Methodist
- **Enrollment:** 1,598 full-time; 80 part-time

KEY STATS
✔ **U.S News College Ranking:** 11, Comp. Coll.–Bachelor's (South)
✔ **SAT Score (25th/75th percentile):** 840-1085
✔ **Tuition:** 2006-2007: $11,764

Selectivity: Selective	Room/board: $6,322
Acceptance rate: 40%	Average debt: $21,898
Student/faculty ratio: 14/1	Proportion who borrowed: 95%

UNDERGRADUATE STUDENT BODY STATS
2005-2006 enrollment: 1,598 full-time; 80 part-time. Men: 33%; women: 67%. **Ethnic makeup:** African American: 93%; White: 2%; International: 5%. **Religious preference:** Roman Catholic: 1%; Protestant: 45%; No preference: 6%; Unknown: 35%; United Methodist: 11%.

ADMISSIONS FACTS AND FIGURES
Phone: (803) 535-5747. **Email:** mzeigler@claflin.edu. **Website:** http://www.claflin.edu. **Application deadlines for fall 2007:** Regular decision: June 30. Early decision: Not offered. Early action: Not offered. Admission can be deferred. **Application fee:** $20. Common application is accepted. **Admissions requirements/recommendations:** High school units required (recommended): English: 4 (4); Mathematics: 3 (3); Science: 2 (2); Social studies: 2 (2); History: 1 (1); Academic electives: 7 (7); Total units: 20 (20). Tests: The college uses SAT or ACT scores in admissions decisions. Either SAT or ACT required. For admission to the fall 2007 entering class, the school will accept: ACT with writing, ACT without writing. Campus visit: Recommended. Admissions interview: Neither required nor recommended. Off-campus interview: Not available. **Factors that count in admissions decisions: *Academic:*** Secondary school record: Very important. Class rank: Very important. Letters of recommendation: Considered. Standardized test scores: Very important. Essay: Important. *Nonacademic:* Interview: Not considered. Extracurricular activities: Important. Talent/ability: Important. Character/personal qualities: Very important. Alumni/ae relationship: Important. Geographical residence: Not considered. State residency: Considered. Religious affiliation/commitment: Not considered. Minority status: Not considered. Volunteer work: Considered. Work experience: Considered. **Other schools with the greatest overlap in applicants:** Benedict College; Columbia College; South Carolina State University; University of South Carolina–Columbia; Voorhees College. **Admissions statistics for the fall 2005 entering class:** Total applicants: 2,744. Total accepted: 1,103. Freshmen enrolled: 385; 14% were from out of state. Overall acceptance rate: 40%. **Credentials of fall 2005 freshmen:** 25% ranked in the top 10 percent of their high school class; 46% were in the top 25 percent, and 75% were in the top half. (Proportion submitting class standing: 89%.) **Average high school grade point average:** 3.0. First-year students who submitted SAT scores: 89%. Scores (25/75 percentile): Verbal: 430-575, Math: 410-510, Combined: 840-1085.

ACADEMICS
Year founded: 1869. **Academic calendar:** Semester. **Degrees offered:** bachelor's, master's. **Most popular majors:** 14% criminal justice/safety studies, 12% sociology, 11% child development, 10% business administration and management, 10% organizational behavior studies. **Major fields of study:** area, ethnic, cultural, and gender studies; biological and biomedical sciences; business, management, marketing, and related support services; communication, journalism, and related programs; computer and information sciences and support services; education; engineering; English language and literature/letters; history; mathematics and statistics; natural resources and conservation; parks, recreation, leisure, and fitness studies; philosophy and religious studies; physical sciences; security and protective services; social sciences; visual and performing arts. **Areas of required coursework:** arts/fine arts, humanities, computer literacy, mathematics, English (including composition), philosophy, foreign languages, sciences (biological or physical), history, social science, other. **Special academic programs (% participation):** cooperative (work-study plan) program, cross-registration, distance learning, double major, honors program (12%), independent study, internships, study abroad, teacher certificate program (21%), weekend college (22%), other. **Teacher certification offered in:** early childhood, elementary, middle/junior high, secondary. **Cooperative education programs:** engineering, health professions. **Reserve Officers Training Corps (ROTC):** Army ROTC: Offered at cooperating institution (SCSU). **Faculty and instruction (2005-2006):** Total instructional faculty: 93 full-time, 34 part-time (59% men, 41% women; 72% minorities). Full-time faculty with Ph.D. or other terminal degree: 71%. Student/faculty ratio: 14/1. Classes of fewer than 20 students: 52%; of 20 to 49 students: 48%; of 50 or more students: 0%. **Advanced Placement and International Baccalaureate credit:** AP tests may be used for: Credit and/or placement. International Baccalaureate exams may be used for: Credit and/or placement. **Freshmen returning for sophomore year:** 79%. **Graduation rates:** Four-year: 42%; five-year: 54%; six-year: 68%. **Graduate study:** 20% of students pursue further study immediately upon graduation.

COSTS AND FINANCIAL AID
Financial aid office: (803) 535-5334. **Expenses (2006-2007):** Tuition and fees 2006-2007: $11,764; room/board: $6,322. Estimated books and supplies: $1,200; transportation: $1,800; personal expenses: $1,800. **Financial aid:** Priority filing date for institution's financial aid form: June 1; deadline: June 1. In 2005-2006, 95% of undergraduates applied for financial aid. Of those, 91% were determined to have financial need; Average financial aid package (proportion receiving): N/A (91%). Average amount of gift aid, such as scholarships or grants (proportion receiving): $10,730 (83%). Average amount of self-help aid, such as work study or loans (proportion receiving): $9,500 (83%). Average need-based loan (excluding PLUS or other private loans): $3,700. Average amount of debt of borrowers graduating in 2005: $21,898. Proportion who borrowed: 95%.

CAMPUS LIFE AND EXTRACURRICULAR ACTIVITIES

Campus housing available (% using): women's dorms (67%), men's dorms (33%). Students who live in college-owned, operated, or affiliated housing: 65%. **Student employment:** During the 2005-2006 academic year, 10% of undergraduates worked on campus. Average per-year earnings: $1,500. **Clubs and organizations:** Number of student organizations: 49. Activities include: choral groups, concert band, drama/theater, jazz band, literary magazine, marching band, music ensembles, radio station, student government, student newspaper, student film society, television station, yearbook. Number of fraternities: 4; sororities: 4. Proportion of men in fraternities: 15%; of women in sororities: 15%. Average proportion of students who stay on campus on weekends: 70%. **Sports program (2005-2006):** Member of NAIA. **Men's intercollegiate varsity sports:** baseball, basketball, cross-country, tennis, track and field (indoor), track and field (outdoor). **Women's intercollegiate varsity sports:** basketball, cheerleading, cross-country, softball, tennis, track and field (indoor), track and field (outdoor), volleyball.

SERVICES AND FACILITIES

Basic services: nonremedial tutoring, placement service, health service, health insurance. **Remedial assistance:** reading, math, writing, study skills. **Counseling services:** minority student, career, personal, veteran student, academic, psychological, religious. **For learning-disabled students:** School does not offer a structured program with separate admission and additional fees. Total undergraduates in learning-disabled program or receiving services: 8. **Library:** Number of titles: 157,483; number of current serial subscriptions: 435. **Information technology resources:** Students are not required to lease or own a computer. Number of campus computers available to all students: 500. School has a wireless network. Approximate number of users that can be accommodated: 200. Proportion of college-owned housing units wired for high-speed internet access: 100%. **Campus safety:** Security services offered: 24-hour foot-and-vehicle patrols, late-night transport/escort service, 24-hour emergency telephones, lighted pathways/sidewalks, controlled dormitory access (key, security card, etc).

TRANSFER AND INTERNATIONAL STUDENTS

Transfer students: May apply for admission for the following academic terms: Fall, Spring, Summer. Applicants need a minimum number of credits to apply. For fall 2005: Transfer applications received: 184. Transfer applicants offered admission: 67. Transfer applicants enrolled: 34. **International students:** Number of foreign undergraduates: 80 (5% of student body). Number of countries represented: 16. Minimum TOEFL score required: 500 (paper); 213 (computer).

Clemson University

- **Address:** 105 Sikes Hall, Clemson, SC 29634
- **Website:** http://www.clemson.edu
- **Public**
- **Enrollment:** 13,257 full-time; 839 part-time

KEY STATS

✔ **U.S News College Ranking:** 70, National Universities
✔ **SAT Score (25th/75th percentile):** 1130-1320
✔ **Tuition:** 2006-2007: $9,400 in state, $19,824 out of state

Selectivity: More selective	Room/board: $5,874
Acceptance rate: 57%	Average debt: $17,882
Student/faculty ratio: 15/1	Proportion who borrowed: 44%

UNDERGRADUATE STUDENT BODY STATS

2005-2006 enrollment: 13,257 full-time; 839 part-time. Men: 54%; women: 46%. **Ethnic makeup:** African American: 7%; Asian American: 2%; Hispanic: 1%; White: 90%.

ADMISSIONS FACTS AND FIGURES

Phone: (864) 656-2287. **Email:** cuadmissions@clemson.edu. **Website:** http://www.clemson.edu. **Application deadlines for fall 2007:** Regular decision: May 1. Early decision: Not offered. Early action: Not offered. Admission cannot be deferred. **Application fee:** $50. Common application is not accepted. **To apply online, go to:** http://www.clemson.edu/attend/undrgrd/undergrad.htm. **Admissions requirements/recommendations:** High school units required (recommended): English: 4; Mathematics: 3 (4); Science: 3 (4); Foreign language: 3 (4); Social studies: 3 (4); History: 1 (2);

Academic electives: 2 (2); Total units: 19 (23). **Tests:** The college uses SAT or ACT scores in admissions decisions. Either SAT or ACT required. For admission to the fall 2007 entering class, the school will accept: ACT with writing. **Campus visit:** Recommended. **Admissions interview:** Neither required nor recommended. Off-campus interview: Not available. **Factors that count in admissions decisions:** *Academic:* Secondary school record: Very important. Class rank: Very important. Letters of recommendation: Considered. Standardized test scores: Very important. Essay: Considered. *Nonacademic:* Interview: Not considered. Extracurricular activities: Considered. Talent/ability: Considered. Character/personal qualities: Not considered. Alumni/ae relationship: Important. Geographical residence: Considered. State residency: Very important. Religious affiliation/commitment: Not considered. Minority status: Not considered. Volunteer work: Considered. Work experience: Considered. **Other schools with the greatest overlap in applicants:** College of Charleston; North Carolina State University–Raleigh; University of Georgia; University of North Carolina–Chapel Hill; University of South Carolina–Columbia. **Admissions statistics for the fall 2005 entering class:** Total applicants: 12,463. Total accepted: 7,154. Freshmen enrolled: 2,903; 35% were from out of state. Overall acceptance rate: 57%. **Size of waiting list:** 267 applicants; enrolled from waiting list: 32. **Credentials of fall 2005 freshmen:** 45% ranked in the top 10 percent of their high school class; 79% were in the top 25 percent, and 97% were in the top half. (Proportion submitting class standing: 100%.) **Average high school grade point average:** 3.8. **First-year students who submitted SAT scores:** 86%. Scores (25/75 percentile): Verbal: 550-650, Math: 580-670, Combined: 1130-1320. **First-year students submitting ACT scores:** 14%. Scores (25/75 percentile): English: N/A, Math: N/A, Composite: 24-29.

ACADEMICS

Year founded: 1889. **Academic calendar:** Semester. **Degrees offered:** bachelor's, master's, post-master's certificate, doctorate. **Most popular majors:** 21% business, management, marketing, and related support services, 15% engineering, 10% education, 7% health professions and related clinical sciences, 6% social sciences. **Areas of required coursework:** arts/fine arts, humanities, computer literacy, mathematics, English (including composition), sciences (biological or physical), social science, other. **Pre-professional programs:** pre-law, pre-dentistry, pre-medicine, pre-veterinary science, pre-optometry, pre-pharmacy, other. **Special academic programs (% participation):** cooperative (work-study plan) program (13%), distance learning (20%), double major (3%), honors program (13%), independent study (25%), internships (14%), study abroad (10%), teacher certificate program (8%). **Teacher certification offered in:** early childhood, special education, elementary, votech, secondary. **Cooperative education programs:** agriculture, art, business, computer science, education, engineering, health professions, home economics, humanities, natural science, social/behavioral science, technologies, vocational arts. **Reserve Officers Training Corps (ROTC):** Army ROTC: Offered on campus; Air Force ROTC: Offered on campus. **Faculty and instruction (2005-2006):** Total instructional faculty: 1,015 full-time, 163 part-time (69% men; 31% women; 12% minorities). Full-time faculty with Ph.D. or other terminal degree: 86%. Student/faculty ratio: 15/1. Classes of fewer than 20 students: 39%; of 20 to 49 students: 51%; of 50 or more students: 10%. **Advanced Placement and International Baccalaureate credit:** AP tests may be used for: Credit and/or placement. Scores accepted: 3, 4, 5. International Baccalaureate exams may be used for: Credit and/or placement. **Freshmen returning for sophomore year:** 89%. **Graduation rates:** Four-year: 44%; five-year: 61%; six-year: 75%.

COSTS AND FINANCIAL AID

Financial aid office: (864) 656-2280. **Expenses (2006-2007):** Tuition and fees 2006-2007: $9,400 in state, $19,824 out of state; room/board: $5,874. **Financial aid:** Priority filing date for institution's financial aid form: April 1. In 2005-2006, 53% of undergraduates applied for financial aid. Of those, 39% were determined to have financial need; 25% had their need fully met. Average financial aid package (proportion receiving): $9,154 (38%). Average amount of gift aid, such as scholarships or grants (proportion receiving): $3,337 (18%). Average amount of self-help aid, such as work study or loans (proportion receiving): $4,450 (28%). Average need-based loan (excluding PLUS or other private loans): $4,192. Among students who received need-based aid, the average percentage of need met: 39%. Among students who received aid based on merit, the average award (and the proportion receiving): $3,671 (18%). The average athletic scholarship (and the proportion receiving): $9,881 (3%). Average amount of debt of borrowers graduating in 2005: $17,882. Proportion who borrowed: 44%.

CAMPUS LIFE AND EXTRACURRICULAR ACTIVITIES

Campus housing available: coed dorms, women's dorms, men's dorms, sorority housing, fraternity housing, apartments for married students, apartment for single students, special housing for disabled students, special housing for international students, other housing options. Students who live in college-owned, operated, or affiliated housing: 44%. **Student employment:** During the 2005-2006 academic year, 30% of undergraduates worked on campus. Average per-year earnings: $3,500. **Clubs and organizations:** Number of student organizations: 275. Activities include: choral groups, concert band, dance, drama/theater, jazz band, literary magazine, marching band, music ensembles, pep band, radio station, student government, student newspaper, symphony orchestra, television station, yearbook. Number of fraternities: 24; sororities: 14. Proportion of men in fraternities: 11%; of women in sororities: 17%. Average proportion of students who stay on campus on weekends: 70%. **Sports program (2005-2006):** Member of NCAA I. *Men's intercollegiate varsity sports:* baseball, basketball, cross-country, football, golf, soccer, swimming and diving, tennis, track and field (indoor), track and field (outdoor). *Women's intercollegiate varsity sports:* basketball, cross-country, soccer, swimming and diving, tennis, track and field (indoor), track and field (outdoor), volleyball, rowing.

SERVICES AND FACILITIES

Basic services: nonremedial tutoring, placement service, health service, health insurance. **Remedial assistance:** reading, math, writing, study skills. **Counseling services:** minority student, career, military, veteran student, academic, psychological. **For learning-disabled students:** School does not offer a structured program with separate admission and additional fees. Services include: tape recorders, diagnostic testing service, untimed tests, note-taking services, oral tests, learning center, readers, extended time for tests, tutors, other. **Information technology resources:** Students are required to lease or own a computer. Number of campus computers available to all students: 364. School has a wireless network. Proportion of college-owned housing units wired for high-speed internet access: 100%. **Campus safety:** Security services offered: 24-hour foot-and-vehicle patrols, late-night transport/escort service, 24-hour emergency telephones, lighted pathways/sidewalks, student patrols, controlled dormitory access (key, security card, etc).

TRANSFER AND INTERNATIONAL STUDENTS

Transfer students: May apply for admission for the following academic terms: Fall, Spring. Applicants need a minimum number of credits to apply. For fall 2005: Transfer applications received: 1,488. Transfer applicants offered admission: 1,066. Transfer applicants enrolled: 688. **International students:** Number of foreign undergraduates: 59. Minimum TOEFL score required: 550 (paper); 213 (computer).

Coastal Carolina University

- **Address:** PO Box 261954, Conway, SC 29528-6054
- **Website:** http://www.coastal.edu
- **Public**
- **Enrollment:** 5,753 full-time; 644 part-time

KEY STATS

- ✔ **U.S News College Ranking:** fourth tier, Liberal Arts Colleges
- ✔ **SAT Score (25th/75th percentile):** 950-1120
- ✔ **Tuition:** 2006-2007: $7,580 in state, $16,270 out of state

Selectivity: Selective	**Room/board:** $6,690
Acceptance rate: 74%	**Average debt:** $22,057
Student/faculty ratio: 19/1	**Proportion who borrowed:** 65%

UNDERGRADUATE STUDENT BODY STATS

2005-2006 enrollment: 5,753 full-time; 644 part-time. Men: 47%; women: 53%. **Ethnic makeup:** African American: 12%; American-Indian: 1%; Asian American: 1%; Hispanic: 2%; White: 84%; International: 2%.

ADMISSIONS FACTS AND FIGURES

Phone: (843) 349-2026. **Email:** admissions@coastal.edu. **Website:** http://www.coastal.edu. **Application deadlines for fall 2007:** Regular decision: August 15. Early decision: Not offered. Early action: Not offered. Admission can be deferred. **Application fee:** $45. Common application is accepted. **To apply online, go to:** http://www.coastal.edu/admissions/applications.html. **Admissions requirements/recommendations:** High school units required (recommended): English: 4; Mathematics: 3; Science: 3; Foreign language: 2; Social studies: 2; History: 1; Academic electives: 4; Total units: 20. **Tests:** The college uses SAT or ACT scores in admissions decisions. Either SAT or ACT required. For admission to the fall 2007 entering class, the school will accept: ACT with writing, ACT without writing. Campus visit: Recommended. Admissions interview: Recommended. Off-campus interview: May be arranged. **Factors that count in admissions decisions:** *Academic:* Secondary school record: Very important. Class rank: Important. Letters of recommendation: Considered. Standardized test scores: Very important. Essay: Considered. *Nonacademic:* Interview: Considered. Extracurricular activities: Considered. Talent/ability: Considered. Character/personal qualities: Considered. Alumni/ae relationship: Not considered. Geographical residence: Considered. State residency: Considered. Religious affiliation/commitment: Not considered. Minority status: Not considered. Volunteer work: Not considered. Work experience: Considered. **Other schools with the greatest overlap in applicants:** Clemson University; College of Charleston; University of North Carolina–Wilmington; University of South Carolina–Columbia; Winthrop University. **Admissions statistics for the fall 2005 entering class:** Total applicants: 5,427. Total accepted: 4,015. Freshmen enrolled: 1,498; 51% were from out of state. Overall acceptance rate: 74%. **Credentials of fall 2005 freshmen:** 11% ranked in the top 10 percent of their high school class; 35% were in the top 25 percent, and 72% were in the top half. (Proportion submitting class standing: 85%.) **Average high school grade point average:** 3.3. **First-year students who submitted SAT scores:** 81%. Scores (25/75 percentile): Verbal: 470-550; Math: 480-570, Combined: 950-1120. **First-year students submitting ACT scores:** 19%. Scores (25/75 percentile): English: N/A, Math: N/A, Composite: 20-23.

ACADEMICS

Year founded: 1954. **Academic calendar:** Semester. **Degrees offered:** certificate, bachelor's, master's. **Most popular majors:** 11% business administration and management, 10% marketing/marketing management, 8% marine biology and biological oceanography, 7% psychology, 6% liberal arts and sciences/liberal studies. **Major fields of study:** biological and biomedical sciences; business, management, marketing, and related support services; communication, journalism, and related programs; computer and information sciences and support services; education; English language and literature/letters; foreign languages, literatures, and linguistics; health professions and related clinical sciences; history; liberal arts and sciences studies, and humanities; mathematics and statistics; parks, recreation, leisure, and fitness studies; philosophy and religious studies; physical sciences; psychology; social sciences; visual and performing arts. **Areas of required coursework:** humanities, computer literacy, mathematics, English (including composition), foreign languages, sciences (biological or physical), history, social science, other. **Pre-professional programs:** pre-law, pre-dentistry, pre-medicine, pre-theology, pre-veterinary science, pre-pharmacy. **Special academic programs (% participation):** accelerated program (1%), cooperative (work-study plan) program (19%), distance learning (5%), double major (9%), dual enrollment (2%), honors program (3%), independent study (25%), internships (43%), student-designed major (6%), study abroad (2%), teacher certificate program (18%). **Teacher certification offered in:** early childhood, special education, elementary, middle/junior high, secondary. **Cooperative education programs:** business, computer science, education, humanities, natural science, social/behavioral science, technologies. **Faculty and instruction (2005-2006):** Total instructional faculty: 233 full-time, 181 part-time (57% men; 43% women; 7% minorities). Full-time faculty with Ph.D. or other terminal degree: 78%. Student/faculty ratio: 19/1. Classes of fewer than 20 students: 32%; of 20 to 49 students: 62%; of 50 or more students: 7%. **Advanced Placement and International Baccalaureate credit:** AP tests may be used for: Credit and/or placement. Scores accepted: 3, 4, 5. International Baccalaureate exams may be used for: Credit and/or placement. **Freshmen returning for sophomore year:** 70%. **Graduation rates:** Four-year: 23%; five-year: 38%; six-year: 43%. **Graduate study:** 22% of students pursue further study immediately upon graduation. Fields in which graduates pursue further study: Master of Business Administration (MBA), 9%; law, 4%; medicine, 4%; dentistry, 2%; education, 15%; arts and sciences, 64%; veterinary medicine, 2%.

COSTS AND FINANCIAL AID

Financial aid office: (843) 349-2313. **Expenses (2006-2007):** Tuition and fees 2006-2007: $7,580 in state, $16,270 out of state; room/board: $6,690. **Financial aid:** Priority filing date for institution's financial aid form: March 1. In 2005-2006, 89% of undergraduates applied for financial aid. Of those, 58% were determined to have financial need; 13% had their need fully met. Average financial aid package (proportion receiving): $7,427 (57%). Average amount of gift aid, such as scholarships or grants (proportion receiving): $3,229 (25%). Average amount of self-help aid, such as work study or loans (proportion receiving): $6,781 (51%). Average need-based loan (excluding PLUS or other private loans): $6,524. Among students who received need-based aid, the average percentage of need met: 51%. Among students who received aid based on merit, the average award (and the proportion receiving): $8,872 (22%). The average athletic scholarship (and the proportion receiving): $7,250 (5%). Average amount of debt of borrowers graduating in 2005: $22,057. Proportion who borrowed: 65%.

CAMPUS LIFE AND EXTRACURRICULAR ACTIVITIES

Campus housing available (% using): coed dorms (44%), apartment for single students (53%), special housing for disabled students (3%). Students who live in college-owned, operated, or affiliated housing: 33%. **Student employment:** During the 2005-2006 academic year, 12% of undergraduates worked on campus. Average per-year earnings: $2,000. **Clubs and organizations:** Number of student organizations: 125. Activities include: choral groups, concert band, dance, drama/theater, jazz band, literary magazine, marching band, music ensembles, musical theater, pep band, student government, student newspaper, student film society. Number of fraternities: 10; sororities: 7. Proportion of men in fraternities: 7%; of women in sororities: 6%. Average proportion of students who stay on campus on weekends: 80%. **Sports program (2005-2006):** Member of NCAA I. *Men's intercollegiate varsity sports:* baseball, basketball, cross-country, football, golf, soccer, tennis, track and field (outdoor). *Women's intercollegiate varsity sports:* basketball, cross-country, golf, soccer, softball, tennis, track and field (indoor), track and field (outdoor), volleyball.

SERVICES AND FACILITIES

Basic services: nonremedial tutoring, women's center, placement service, health service, health insurance. **Counseling services:** minority student, career, personal, veteran student, academic, older student, psychological, birth control. **For learning-disabled students:** School does not offer a structured program with separate admission and additional fees. Total undergraduates in learning-disabled program or receiving services: 235. Services include: remedial math, reading machines, tape recorders, other special classes, videotaped classes, untimed tests, note-taking services, oral tests, learning center, readers, extended time for tests, tutors, early syllabus, priority registration, priority seating, substitution of courses, texts on tape, typist/scribe, exams on tape or computer, other testing accomodations, waiver of foreign language degree requirement. **Library:** Number of titles: 146,509; number of current serial subscriptions: 10,858. **Information technology resources:** Students are not required to lease or own a computer. Number of campus computers available to all students: 600. School has a wireless network. Approximate number of users that can be accommodated: 600. Proportion of college-owned housing units wired for high-speed internet access: 100%. **Campus safety:** Security services offered: 24-hour foot-and-vehicle patrols, late-night transport/escort service, 24-hour emergency telephones, lighted pathways/sidewalks, controlled dormitory access (key, security card, etc).

TRANSFER AND INTERNATIONAL STUDENTS

Transfer students: May apply for admission for the following academic terms: Fall, Spring, Summer. Applicants need a minimum number of credits to apply. For fall 2005: Transfer applications received: 1,361. Transfer applicants offered admission: 968. Transfer applicants enrolled: 589. **International students:** Number of foreign undergraduates: 104 (2% of student body). Number of countries represented: 38. Minimum TOEFL score required: 500 (paper); 173 (computer). Average TOEFL score: 569 (paper).

Coker College

- ■ **Address:** 300 E. College Avenue, Hartsville, SC 29550
- ■ **Website:** http://www.coker.edu
- ■ **Private**
- ■ **Enrollment:** 541 full-time; 10 part-time

KEY STATS

✔ **U.S News College Ranking:** 13, Comp. Coll.–Bachelor's (South)
✔ **SAT Score (25th/75th percentile):** 870-1080
✔ **Tuition:** 2006-2007: $17,948

Selectivity: Selective	**Room/board:** $5,776
Acceptance rate: 66%	**Average debt:** $16,859
Student/faculty ratio: 9/1	**Proportion who borrowed:** 87%

UNDERGRADUATE STUDENT BODY STATS

2005-2006 enrollment: 541 full-time; 10 part-time. Men: 41%; women: 59%. **Ethnic makeup:** African American: 20%; Asian American: 1%; Hispanic: 2%; White: 75%; International: 2%.

ADMISSIONS FACTS AND FIGURES

Phone: (843) 383-8050. **Email:** admissions@coker.edu. **Website:** http://www.coker.edu. **Application deadlines for fall 2007:** Regular decision: Rolling. Early decision: Not offered. Early action: Not offered. Admission can be deferred. **Application fee:** $15. Common application is accepted. **To apply online, go to:** http://www.coker.edu/admissions/online_application.html. **Admissions requirements/recommendations:** High school units required (recommended): English: 4; Mathematics: 3; Science: 3; Foreign language: 2; Social studies: 3; Total units: 15. Tests: The college uses SAT or ACT scores in admissions decisions. Either SAT or ACT required. For admission to the fall 2007 entering class, the school will accept: ACT with writing, ACT without writing. Campus visit: Recommended. Admissions interview: Recommended. Off-campus interview: May be arranged. **Factors that count in admissions decisions:** *Academic:* Secondary school record: Important. Class rank: Considered. Letters of recommendation: Considered. Standardized test scores: Very important. Essay: Considered. *Nonacademic:* Interview: Considered. Extracurricular activities: Considered. Talent/ability: Considered. Character/personal qualities: Considered. Alumni/ae relationship: Considered. Geographical residence: Not considered. State residency: Not considered. Religious affiliation/commitment: Not considered. Minority status: Not considered. Volunteer work: Considered. Work experience: Considered. **Admissions statistics for the fall 2005 entering class:** Total applicants: 649. Total accepted: 426. Freshmen enrolled: 148; 21% were from out of state. Overall acceptance rate: 66%. **Credentials of fall 2005 freshmen:** 20% ranked in the top 10 percent of their high school class; 50% were in the top 25 percent, and 82% were in the top half. (Proportion submitting class standing: 93%.) **Average high school grade point average:** 3.3. **First-year students who submitted SAT scores:** 68%. Scores (25/75 percentile): Verbal: 430-530, Math: 440-550, Combined: 870-1080. **First-year students submitting ACT scores:** 33%. Scores (25/75 percentile): English: N/A, Math: N/A, Composite: 17-22.

ACADEMICS

Year founded: 1908. **Academic calendar:** Semester. **Degrees offered:** bachelor's. **Most popular majors:** 18% business administration and management, 8% counseling psychology, 7% communication studies/speech communication and rhetoric, 6% English language and literature, 5% biology/biological sciences. **Major fields of study:** biological and biomedical sciences; business, management, marketing, and related support services; communication, journalism, and related programs; computer and information sciences and support services; education; English language and literature/letters; foreign languages, literatures, and linguistics; health professions and related clinical sciences; history; mathematics and statistics; parks, recreation, leisure, and fitness studies; physical sciences; psychology; public administration and social service professions; security and protective services; social sciences; visual and performing arts. **Areas of required coursework:** arts/fine arts, humanities, mathematics, English (including composition), philosophy, foreign languages, sciences (biological or physical), history, social science, other. **Pre-professional programs:** pre-law. **Special academic programs:** cooperative (work-study plan) program, double major, dual enrollment, honors program, independent study, internships, student-designed major, study abroad, teacher certificate program. **Teacher certification offered in:** early childhood, elementary, secondary. **Cooperative education programs:** health professions. **Faculty and instruction (2005-2006):** Total instructional faculty: 55 full-time, 10 part-time (55% men; 45% women; 11% minorities). Full-time faculty with Ph.D. or other terminal degree: 85%. Student/faculty ratio: 9/1. Classes of fewer than 20 students: 73%; of 20 to 49 students: 27%; of 50 or more students: 0%. **Advanced Placement and International Baccalaureate credit:** AP tests may be used for: Credit and/or placement. Scores accepted: 3, 4, 5. International Baccalaureate exams may be used for: Credit only. **Freshmen returning for sophomore year:** 69%. **Graduation rates:** Four-year: 37%; five-year: 42%; six-year: 49%.

COSTS AND FINANCIAL AID

Financial aid office: (843) 383-8055. **Expenses (2006-2007):** Tuition and fees 2006-2007: $17,948; room/board: $5,776. Estimated books and supplies: $1,000 personal expenses: $650. **Financial aid:** Priority filing date for institution's financial aid form: April 1; deadline: June 1. In 2005-2006, 91% of undergraduates applied for financial aid. Of those, 81% were determined to have financial need; 47% had their need fully met. Average financial aid package (proportion receiving): $16,829 (81%). Average amount of gift aid, such as scholarships or grants (proportion receiving): $5,674 (74%). Average amount of self-help aid, such as work study or loans (proportion receiving): $4,103 (72%). Average need-based loan (excluding PLUS or other private loans): $3,861. Among students who received need-based aid, the average percentage of need met: 91%. Among students who received aid based on merit, the average award (and the proportion receiving): $6,161 (18%). The average athletic scholarship (and the proportion receiving): $4,951 (10%). Average amount of debt of borrowers graduating in 2005: $16,859. Proportion who borrowed: 87%.

CAMPUS LIFE AND EXTRACURRICULAR ACTIVITIES
Campus housing available (% using): coed dorms (100%), special housing for disabled students (0%), other housing options. Students who live in college-owned, operated, or affiliated housing: 65%. **Student employment:** During the 2005-2006 academic year, 1% of undergraduates worked on campus. Average per-year earnings: $800. **Clubs and organizations:** Number of student organizations: 24. Activities include: choral groups, concert band, dance, drama/theater, literary magazine, music ensembles, musical theater, student government, student newspaper, yearbook. Number of fraternities: 0; sororities: 0. Average proportion of students who stay on campus on weekends: 75%. **Sports program (2005-2006):** Member of NCAA II. *Men's intercollegiate varsity sports:* baseball, basketball, cross-country, golf, soccer, tennis. *Women's intercollegiate varsity sports:* basketball, cross-country, soccer, softball, tennis, volleyball.

SERVICES AND FACILITIES
Basic services: nonremedial tutoring, placement service, health service, health insurance. **Remedial assistance:** other. **Counseling services:** minority student, career, personal, veteran student, academic, older student, psychological, birth control, other. **For learning-disabled students:** School does not offer a structured program with separate admission and additional fees. Services include: remedial math, remedial English, tape recorders, untimed tests, oral tests, extended time for tests, tutors, priority seating, other. **Library:** Number of titles: 73,328; number of current serial subscriptions: 230. **Information technology resources:** Students are not required to lease or own a computer. Number of campus computers available to all students: 65. School has a wireless network. Approximate number of users that can be accommodated: 255. Proportion of college-owned housing units wired for high-speed internet access: 100%. **Campus safety:** Security services offered: 24-hour foot-and-vehicle patrols, lighted pathways/sidewalks, controlled dormitory access (key, security card, etc).

TRANSFER AND INTERNATIONAL STUDENTS
Transfer students: May apply for admission for the following academic terms: Fall, Spring, Summer. Applicants need a minimum number of credits to apply. For fall 2005: Transfer applications received: 120. Transfer applicants offered admission: 53. Transfer applicants enrolled: 35.
International students: Number of foreign undergraduates: 9 (2% of student body). Number of countries represented: 10. Minimum TOEFL score required: 500 (paper); 173 (computer).

College of Charleston

- **Address:** 66 George Street, Charleston, SC 29424-0001
- **Website:** http://www.cofc.edu
- **Public**
- **Enrollment:** 9,055 full-time; 823 part-time

KEY STATS
✔ **U.S News College Ranking:** 11, Universities–Master's (South)
✔ **SAT Score (25th/75th percentile):** 1140-1290
✔ **Tuition:** 2005-2006: $6,668 in state, $15,342 out of state

Selectivity: More selective	**Room/board:** N/A
Acceptance rate: 66%	**Average debt:** $16,143
Student/faculty ratio: 14/1	**Proportion who borrowed:** 46%

UNDERGRADUATE STUDENT BODY STATS
2005-2006 enrollment: 9,055 full-time; 823 part-time. Men: 36%; women: 64%. **Ethnic makeup:** African American: 7%; Asian American: 2%; Hispanic: 2%; White: 87%; International: 2%.

ADMISSIONS FACTS AND FIGURES
Phone: (843) 953-5670. **Email:** admissions@cofc.edu. **Website:** http://www.cofc.edu. **Application deadlines for fall 2007:** Regular decision: April 1. Early decision: Not offered. Early action: Send application by: November 1; Decision sent by: December 15. Admission can be deferred. **Application fee:** $35. Common application is accepted. **Admissions requirements/recommendations:** High school units required (recommended): English: 4; Mathematics: 3 (4); Science: 3 (4); Foreign language: 2 (3); Social studies: 3; History: (2); Academic electives: 4; Total units: 20. Tests: The college uses SAT or ACT scores in admissions decisions. Either SAT or ACT required. For admission to the fall 2007 entering class, the school will accept: ACT with writing, ACT without writing. Campus visit: Recommended. Admissions interview: Neither required nor recommended. Off-campus interview: Not available. **Factors that count in admissions decisions:** *Academic:* Secondary school record: Important. Class rank: Important. Letters of recommendation: Considered. Standardized test scores: Very important. Essay: Considered. *Nonacademic:* Interview: Not considered. Extracurricular activities: Considered. Talent/ability: Important. Character/personal qualities: Important. Alumni/ae relationship: Considered. Geographical residence: Considered. State residency: Very important. Religious affiliation/commitment: Not considered. Minority status: Considered. Volunteer work: Considered. Work experience: Considered. **Other schools with the greatest overlap in applicants:** Clemson University; James Madison University; University of Georgia; University of North Carolina–Chapel Hill; University of South Carolina–Columbia. **Admissions statistics for the fall 2005 entering class:** Total applicants: 8,217. Total accepted: 5,436. Freshmen enrolled: 1,993; 42% were from out of state. Overall acceptance rate: 66%. Non-early acceptance rate: 66%. **Size of waiting list:** 244 applicants; enrolled from waiting list: 17. **Credentials of fall 2005 freshmen:** 25% ranked in the top 10 percent of their high school class; 58% were in the top 25 percent, and 91% were in the top half. (Proportion submitting class standing: 71%.) **Average high school grade point average:** 3.6. **First-year students who submitted SAT scores:** 78%. Scores (25/75 percentile): Verbal: 570-650, Math: 570-640, Combined: 1140-1290. **First-year students submitting ACT scores:** 22%. Scores (25/75 percentile): English: 22-26, Math: 20-25, Composite: 22-25.

ACADEMICS
Year founded: 1770. **Academic calendar:** Semester. **Degrees offered:** bachelor's, post-bachelor's certificate, master's. **Most popular majors:** 15% communication studies/speech communication and rhetoric, 14% business administration and management, 9% psychology, 7% biology/biological sciences, 4% political science and government. **Major fields of study:** area, ethnic, cultural, and gender studies; biological and biomedical sciences; business, management, marketing, and related support services; communication, journalism, and related programs; computer and information sciences and support services; education; English language and literature/letters; foreign languages, literatures, and linguistics; health professions and related clinical sciences; history; mathematics and statistics; multi/interdisciplinary studies; philosophy and religious studies; physical sciences; psychology; social sciences; visual and performing arts. **Areas of required coursework:** humanities, mathematics, English (including composition), foreign languages, sciences (biological or physical), history, social science. **Pre-professional programs:** pre-dentistry, pre-medicine. **Special academic programs:** accelerated program, cooperative (work-study plan) program, cross-registration, distance learning, double major, dual enrollment, English as a Second Language (ESL), exchange student program (domestic), external degree program, honors program, independent study, internships, study abroad, teacher certificate program. **Teacher certification offered in:** early childhood, special education, elementary, middle/junior high, secondary. **Reserve Officers Training Corps (ROTC):** Air Force ROTC: Offered at cooperating institution (Charleston Southern University). **Faculty and instruction (2005-2006):** Total instructional faculty: 515 full-time, 343 part-time (52% men; 48% women; 12% minorities). Full-time faculty with Ph.D. or other terminal degree: 85%. Student/faculty ratio: 14/1. Classes of fewer than 20 students: 33%; of 20 to 49 students: 63%; of 50 or more students: 3%. **Advanced Placement and International Baccalaureate credit:** AP tests may be used for: Credit and/or placement. Scores accepted: 3, 4, 5. International Baccalaureate exams may be used for: Credit and/or placement. **Freshmen returning for sophomore year:** 83%. **Graduation rates:** Four-year: 41%; five-year: 55%; six-year: 56%. **Graduate study:** 28% of students pursue further study within one year. Fields in which graduates pursue further study: Master of Business Administration (MBA), 10%; law, 14%; medicine, 10%; dentistry, 7%; education, 16%; arts and sciences, 43%.

COSTS AND FINANCIAL AID

Financial aid office: (843) 953-5540. **Expenses (2005-2006):** Tuition and fees 2005-2006: $6,668 in state, $15,342 out of state; room/board: N/A. Estimated books and supplies: $933; transportation: $864; personal expenses: $1,879. **Financial aid:** Priority filing date for institution's financial aid form: March 15. In 2005-2006, 53% of undergraduates applied for financial aid. Of those, 39% were determined to have financial need; 24% had their need fully met. Average financial aid package (proportion receiving): $8,971 (37%). Average amount of gift aid, such as scholarships or grants (proportion receiving): $2,897 (23%). Average amount of self-help aid, such as work study or loans (proportion receiving): $3,467 (31%). Average need-based loan (excluding PLUS or other private loans): $3,563. Among students who received need-based aid, the average percentage of need met: 62%. Among students who received aid based on merit, the average award (and the proportion receiving): $10,293 (10%). The average athletic scholarship (and the proportion receiving): $13,946 (2%). Average amount of debt of borrowers graduating in 2005: $16,143. Proportion who borrowed: 46%.

CAMPUS LIFE AND EXTRACURRICULAR ACTIVITIES

Campus housing available (% using): coed dorms (41%), women's dorms (24%), men's dorms (7%), sorority housing (2%), fraternity housing (2%), apartment for single students (18%), other housing options (6%). Students who live in college-owned, operated, or affiliated housing: 30%. **Student employment:** During the 2005-2006 academic year, 18% of undergraduates worked on campus. Average per-year earnings: $5,070. **Clubs and organizations:** Number of student organizations: 150. Activities include: choral groups, concert band, dance, drama/theater, jazz band, literary magazine, music ensembles, musical theater, opera, pep band, radio station, student government, student newspaper, student film society, television station, yearbook. Number of fraternities: 13; sororities: 12. Proportion of men in fraternities: 13%; of women in sororities: 16%. Average proportion of students who stay on campus on weekends: 50%. **Sports program (2005-2006):** Member of NCAA I. *Men's intercollegiate varsity sports:* baseball, basketball, cheerleading, cross-country, golf, sailing, soccer, swimming and diving, tennis, coed sailing. *Women's intercollegiate varsity sports:* basketball, cheerleading, cross-country, equestrian sports, golf, sailing, soccer, softball, swimming and diving, tennis, track and field (indoor), track and field (outdoor), volleyball.

SERVICES AND FACILITIES

Basic services: nonremedial tutoring, placement service, health service, health insurance. **Remedial assistance:** reading, math, writing, study skills. **Counseling services:** minority student, career, military, personal, veteran student, academic, older student, psychological, birth control, religious. **For learning-disabled students:** School does not offer a structured program with separate admission and additional fees. Total undergraduates in learning-disabled program or receiving services: 568. Services include: reading machines, tape recorders, diagnostic testing service, learning center, extended time for tests, tutors, priority registration, texts on tape, other. **Library:** Number of titles: 603,413; number of current serial subscriptions: 4,099. **Information technology resources:** Students are not required to lease or own a computer. Number of campus computers available to all students: 900. School has a wireless network. Approximate number of users that can be accommodated: 3,320. Proportion of college-owned housing units wired for high-speed internet access: 100%. **Campus safety:** Security services offered: 24-hour foot-and-vehicle patrols, late-night transport/escort service, 24-hour emergency telephones, lighted pathways/sidewalks, controlled dormitory access (key, security card, etc).

TRANSFER AND INTERNATIONAL STUDENTS

Transfer students: May apply for admission for the following academic terms: Fall, Spring. Applicants need a minimum number of credits to apply. For fall 2005: Transfer applications received: 1,870. Transfer applicants offered admission: 1,322. Transfer applicants enrolled: 689. **International students:** Number of foreign undergraduates: 169 (2% of student body). Minimum TOEFL score required: 550 (paper); 213 (computer).

Columbia College

- **Address:** 1301 Columbia College Drive, Columbia, SC 29203
- **Website:** http://www.columbiacollegesc.edu
- **Private; Religious affiliation:** United Methodist
- **Enrollment:** 867 full-time; 241 part-time

KEY STATS

✔ **U.S News College Ranking:** 17, Comp. Coll.–Bachelor's (South)
✔ **SAT Score (25th/75th percentile):** 910-1180
✔ **Tuition:** 2006-2007: $20,302
  Selectivity: Selective   **Room/board:** $6,022
  Acceptance rate: 84%   **Average debt:** N/A
  Student/faculty ratio: 10/1   **Proportion who borrowed:** N/A

UNDERGRADUATE STUDENT BODY STATS

2005-2006 enrollment: 867 full-time; 241 part-time. Men: 2%; women: 98%. **Ethnic makeup:** African American: 43%; Asian American: 1%; Hispanic: 2%; White: 51%; International: 2%. **Religious preference:** Roman Catholic: 5%; Protestant: 44%; Jewish: 1%; No preference: 17%; Unknown: 6%; United Methodist: 12%; Pentecostal Holiness: 5%; Other: 10%.

ADMISSIONS FACTS AND FIGURES

Phone: (800) 277-1301. **Email:** admissions@colacoll.edu. **Website:** http://www.columbiacollegesc.edu. **Application deadlines for fall 2007:** Regular decision: August 1. Early decision: Not offered. Early action: Not offered. Admission can be deferred. **Application fee:** $25. Common application is accepted. **To apply online, go to:** http://www.columbiacollegesc.edu/apply.html. **Admissions requirements/recommendations:** High school units required (recommended): English: (4); Mathematics: (4); Science: (3); Foreign language: (2); Social studies: (2); History: (1). Tests: The college uses SAT or ACT scores in admissions decisions. Either SAT or ACT required. For admission to the fall 2007 entering class, the school will accept: ACT without writing. Campus visit: Recommended. Admissions interview: Neither required nor recommended. Off-campus interview: May be arranged. **Factors that count in admissions decisions:** *Academic:* Secondary school record: Very important. Class rank: Very important. Letters of recommendation: Very important. Standardized test scores: Very important. Essay: Considered. *Nonacademic:* Interview: Not considered. Extracurricular activities: Not considered. Talent/ability: Not considered. Character/personal qualities: Not considered. Alumni/ae relationship: Not considered. Geographical residence: Not considered. State residency: Not considered. Religious affiliation/commitment: Not considered. Minority status: Not considered. Volunteer work: Not considered. Work experience: Not considered. **Other schools with the greatest overlap in applicants:** Clemson University; College of Charleston; Furman University; University of South Carolina–Columbia; Winthrop University. **Admissions statistics for the fall 2005 entering class:** Total applicants: 763. Total accepted: 640. Freshmen enrolled: 210; 8% were from out of state. Overall acceptance rate: 84%. **Size of waiting list:** 0 applicants; enrolled from waiting list: 0. **Credentials of fall 2005 freshmen:** 15% ranked in the top 10 percent of their high school class; 42% were in the top 25 percent, and 71% were in the top half. (Proportion submitting class standing: 73%.) **Average high school grade point average:** 3.3. **First-year students who submitted SAT scores:** 88%. Scores (25/75 percentile): Verbal: 460-600, Math: 450-580, Combined: 910-1180. **First-year students submitting ACT scores:** 63%. Scores (25/75 percentile): English: 17-24, Math: 16-22, Composite: 18-23.

ACADEMICS

Year founded: 1854. **Academic calendar:** Semester. **Degrees offered:** bachelor's, post-bachelor's certificate, master's. **Most popular majors:** 12% business administration and management, 8% elementary education and teaching, 7% psychology, 7% public administration and social service professions, 6% human development, family studies, and related services. **Major fields of study:** biological and biomedical sciences; business, management, marketing, and related support services; communication, journalism, and related programs; computer and information sciences and support services; education; English language and literature/letters; family and consumer sciences/human sciences; foreign languages, literatures, and linguistics; health professions and related clinical sciences; history; liberal arts and sciences studies, and humanities; mathematics and statistics; multi/interdisciplinary studies; philosophy and religious studies; physical sciences; psychology; public administration and social service professions; social sciences; theology and religious vocations; visual and performing arts. **Areas of required coursework:** arts/fine arts, humanities, computer literacy, mathematics, English (including composition), foreign languages, sciences (biological or physical), history, social science, other. **Pre-professional programs:** pre-medicine, pre-pharmacy. **Special academic programs (% participation):** cross-registration (8%), distance learning (5%), double major (8%), dual enrollment (2%), honors program (15%), independent study (1%), internships (10%), student-designed major (1%), study abroad (1%), teacher certificate program (23%). **Teacher certification offered in:** early childhood, special education, elementary, secondary. **Reserve Officers Training Corps (ROTC):** Army ROTC: Offered at cooperating institution (University of South Carolina). **Faculty and instruction (2005-2006):** Total instructional faculty: 82 full-time, 72 part-time (37% men; 63% women; 11% minorities). Full-time faculty with Ph.D. or other terminal degree: 76%. Student/faculty ratio: 10/1. Classes of fewer than 20 students: 74%; of 20 to 49 students: 26%; of 50 or more students: 0%. **Advanced Placement and International Baccalaureate credit:** AP tests may be used for: Credit and/or placement. Scores accepted: 4, 5. International Baccalaureate exams may be used for: Credit and/or placement. **Freshmen returning for sophomore year:** 64%. Graduation rates: Four-year: 36%; five-year: 48%; six-year: 53%. **Graduate study:** 20% of students pursue further study immediately upon graduation; 15% within one year; 53% within five years.

COSTS AND FINANCIAL AID
Financial aid office: (803) 786-3612. **Expenses (2006-2007):** Tuition and fees 2006-2007: $20,302; room/board: $6,022. Estimated books and supplies: $800. **Financial aid:** Priority filing date for institution's financial aid form: March 15. In 2005-2006, 89% of undergraduates applied for financial aid. Of those, 78% were determined to have financial need; 44% had their need fully met. Average financial aid package (proportion receiving): $20,051 (78%). Average amount of gift aid, such as scholarships or grants (proportion receiving): $8,495 (75%). Average amount of self-help aid, such as work study or loans (proportion receiving): $4,454 (61%). Average need-based loan (excluding PLUS or other private loans): $3,810. Among students who received need-based aid, the average percentage of need met: 70%. Among students who received aid based on merit, the average award (and the proportion receiving): $7,775 (17%).

CAMPUS LIFE AND EXTRACURRICULAR ACTIVITIES
Campus housing available (% using): women's dorms (100%). Students who live in college-owned, operated, or affiliated housing: 47%. **Student employment:** During the 2005-2006 academic year, 23% of undergraduates worked on campus. Average per-year earnings: $1,000. **Clubs and organizations:** Number of student organizations: 50. Activities include: choral groups, concert band, dance, drama/theater, literary magazine, music ensembles, musical theater, opera, student government, student newspaper, yearbook. Number of fraternities: 0; sororities: 0. Average proportion of students who stay on campus on weekends: 60%. **Sports program (2005-2006):** Member of NAIA. *Women's intercollegiate varsity sports:* basketball, soccer, tennis, volleyball.

SERVICES AND FACILITIES
Basic services: nonremedial tutoring, health service, health insurance, other. **Remedial assistance:** reading, math, writing, study skills. **Counseling services:** career, personal, academic, psychological, birth control, religious. **For learning-disabled students:** School does not offer a structured program with separate admission and additional fees. **Library:** Number of titles: 144,671; number of current serial subscriptions: 339. **Information technology resources:** Students are not required to lease or own a computer. Number of campus computers available to all students: 150. School does not have a wireless network. Proportion of college-owned housing units wired for high-speed internet access: 100%. **Campus safety:** Security services offered: 24-hour foot-and-vehicle patrols, late-night transport/escort service, 24-hour emergency telephones, lighted pathways/sidewalks, controlled dormitory access (key, security card, etc).

TRANSFER AND INTERNATIONAL STUDENTS
Transfer students: May apply for admission for the following academic terms: Fall, Spring, Summer. Applicants need a minimum number of credits to apply. For fall 2005: Transfer applications received: 124. Transfer applicants offered admission: 117. Transfer applicants enrolled: 67. **International students:** Number of foreign undergraduates: 27 (2% of student body). Number of countries represented: 14. Minimum TOEFL score required: 550 (paper); 213 (computer).

Converse College

■ **Address:** 580 E. Main Street, Spartanburg, SC 29302
■ **Website:** http://www.converse.edu
■ **Private**
■ **Enrollment:** 648 full-time; 128 part-time

KEY STATS
✔ **U.S News College Ranking:** 19, Universities–Master's (South)
✔ **SAT Score (25th/75th percentile):** 980-1210
✔ **Tuition:** 2006-2007: $22,234
  Selectivity: Selective   **Room/board:** $6,848
  Acceptance rate: 84%   **Average debt:** $16,641
  Student/faculty ratio: 11/1   **Proportion who borrowed:** 58%

UNDERGRADUATE STUDENT BODY STATS
2005-2006 enrollment: 648 full-time; 128 part-time. Men: 0%; women: 100%. **Ethnic makeup:** African American: 14%; Asian American: 1%; Hispanic: 1%; White: 80%; International: 4%.

ADMISSIONS FACTS AND FIGURES
Phone: (864) 596-9040. **Email:** info@converse.edu. **Website:** http://www.converse.edu. **Application deadlines for fall 2007:** Regular decision: April 1. Early decision: Not offered. Early action: Not offered. Admission can be deferred. **Application fee:** $40. Common application is accepted. **Admissions requirements/recommendations:** High school units required (recommended): English: 4 (4); Mathematics: 3 (4); Science: 3 (4); Foreign language: 1 (2); Social studies: 2 (2); History: 2 (2); Academic electives: 6 (2); Total units: 15 (20). Tests: The college uses SAT or ACT scores in admissions decisions. Either SAT or ACT required. For admission to the fall 2007 entering class, the school will accept: ACT with writing, ACT without writing. Campus visit: Recommended. Admissions interview: Recommended. Off-campus interview: May be arranged. **Factors that count in admissions decisions:** *Academic:* Secondary school record: Very important. Class rank: Considered. Letters of recommendation: Important. Standardized test scores: Important. Essay: Important. *Nonacademic:* Interview: Considered. Extracurricular activities: Important. Talent/ability: Important. Character/personal qualities: Important. Alumni/ae relationship: Important. Geographical residence: Not considered. State residency: Not considered. Religious affiliation/commitment: Not considered. Minority status: Not considered. Volunteer work: Important. Work experience: Important. **Other schools with the greatest overlap in applicants:** Clemson University; College of Charleston; University of South Carolina–Columbia; Wofford College. **Admissions statistics for the fall 2005 entering class:** Total applicants: 423. Total accepted: 355. Freshmen enrolled: 177; 33% were from out of state. Overall acceptance rate: 84%. **Size of waiting list:** 0 applicants; enrolled from waiting list: 0. **Credentials of fall 2005 freshmen:** 28% ranked in the top 10 percent of their high school class; 62% were in the top 25 percent, and 88% were in the top half. (Proportion submitting class standing: 81%.) **Average high school grade point average:** 3.8. **First-year students who submitted SAT scores:** 89%. Scores (25/75 percentile): Verbal: 490-610, Math: 490-600, Combined: 980-1210. **First-year students submitting ACT scores:** 49%. Scores (25/75 percentile): English: 20-27, Math: 19-24, Composite: 19-25.

ACADEMICS
Year founded: 1889. **Academic calendar:** 4-1-4. **Degrees offered:** bachelor's, master's, post-master's certificate. **Most popular majors:** 34% education, 16% visual and performing arts, 13% business, management, marketing, and related support services, 6% English language and literature/letters, 6% psychology. **Major fields of study:** biological and biomedical sciences; business, management, marketing, and related support services; computer and information sciences and support services; education; English language and literature/letters; foreign languages, literatures, and linguistics; history; mathematics and statistics; philosophy and religious studies; physical sciences; psychology; social sciences; visual and performing arts. **Areas of required coursework:** arts/fine arts, humanities, computer literacy, mathematics, English (including composition), foreign languages, sciences (biological or physical), history, social science, other. **Pre-professional programs:** pre-law, pre-medicine, pre-theology, pre-veterinary science, pre-pharmacy. **Special academic programs:** cross-registration, double major, English as a Second Language (ESL), honors program, independent study, internships, liberal arts/career combination, student-designed major, study abroad,

teacher certificate program, other. **Teacher certification offered in:** early childhood, special education, elementary, middle/junior high, secondary. **Reserve Officers Training Corps (ROTC):** Army ROTC: Offered at cooperating institution (Wofford). **Faculty and instruction (2005-2006):** Total instructional faculty: 77 full-time, 65 part-time (41% men; 59% women; 8% minorities). Full-time faculty with Ph.D. or other terminal degree: 94%. Student/faculty ratio: 11/1. Classes of fewer than 20 students: 82%; of 20 to 49 students: 18%. **Advanced Placement and International Baccalaureate credit:** AP tests may be used for: Credit and/or placement. Scores accepted: 3, 4, 5. International Baccalaureate exams may be used for: Credit and/or placement. **Freshmen returning for sophomore year;** 75%. **Graduation rates:** Four-year: 55%; five-year: 57%; six-year: 54%. **Graduate study:** 20% of students pursue further study immediately upon graduation; 25% within one year; 30% within five years. Fields in which graduates pursue further study: Master of Business Administration (MBA), 3%; law, 2%; medicine, 2%; education, 18%; arts and sciences, 5%.

COSTS AND FINANCIAL AID

Financial aid office: (864) 596-9019. **Expenses (2006-2007):** Tuition and fees 2006-2007: $22,234; room/board: $6,848. Estimated books and supplies: $855; transportation: $810; personal expenses: $1,650. **Financial aid:** Priority filing date for institution's financial aid form: March 1. In 2005-2006, 78% of undergraduates applied for financial aid. Of those, 71% were determined to have financial need; 36% had their need fully met. Average financial aid package (proportion receiving): $18,431 (71%). Average amount of gift aid, such as scholarships or grants (proportion receiving): $15,292 (70%). Average amount of self-help aid, such as work study or loans (proportion receiving): $4,961 (45%). Average need-based loan (excluding PLUS or other private loans): $4,426. Among students who received need-based aid, the average percentage of need met: 87%. Among students who received aid based on merit, the average award (and the proportion receiving): $16,637 (29%). The average athletic scholarship (and the proportion receiving): $6,499 (4%). Average amount of debt of borrowers graduating in 2005: $16,641. Proportion who borrowed: 58%.

CAMPUS LIFE AND EXTRACURRICULAR ACTIVITIES

Campus housing available (% using): women's dorms (100%). Students who live in college-owned, operated, or affiliated housing: 85%. **Student employment:** During the 2005-2006 academic year, 5% of undergraduates worked on campus. **Clubs and organizations:** Number of student organizations: 60. Activities include: choral groups, concert band, dance, drama/theater, literary magazine, music ensembles, musical theater, opera, student government, student newspaper, symphony orchestra, yearbook. Number of fraternities: 0; sororities: 0. Average proportion of students who stay on campus on weekends: 50%. **Sports program (2005-2006):** Member of NCAA II. *Women's intercollegiate varsity sports:* basketball, cross-country, soccer, tennis, volleyball.

SERVICES AND FACILITIES

Basic services: nonremedial tutoring, placement service, health service. **Remedial assistance:** reading, math, writing, study skills. **Counseling services:** career, personal, academic, psychological, religious. **For learning-disabled students:** School does not offer a structured program with separate admission and additional fees. Services include: remedial math, remedial English, tape recorders, untimed tests, oral tests, readers, extended time for tests, tutors. **Library:** Number of titles: 148,459; number of current serial subscriptions: 590. **Information technology resources:** Students are not required to lease or own a computer. Number of campus computers available to all students: 65. School does not have a wireless network. Proportion of college-owned housing units wired for high-speed internet access: 100%. **Campus safety:** Security services offered: 24-hour foot-and-vehicle patrols, late-night transport/escort service, 24-hour emergency telephones, lighted pathways/sidewalks, controlled dormitory access (key, security card, etc).

TRANSFER AND INTERNATIONAL STUDENTS

Transfer students: May apply for admission for the following academic terms: Fall, Spring, Summer. Applicants need a minimum number of credits to apply. For fall 2005: Transfer applications received: 48. Transfer applicants offered admission: 36. Transfer applicants enrolled: 21. **International students:** Number of foreign undergraduates: 29 (4% of student body). Number of countries represented: 10.

- **Address:** PO Box 338, Due West, SC 29639
- **Website:** http://www.erskine.edu
- **Private; Religious affiliation:** Associate Reformed Presbyterian
- **Enrollment:** 585 full-time; 9 part-time

KEY STATS

✔ **U.S News College Ranking:** third tier, Liberal Arts Colleges
✔ **SAT Score (25th/75th percentile):** 990-1230
✔ **Tuition:** 2006-2007: $20,275
Selectivity: More selective **Room/board:** $6,951
Acceptance rate: 70% **Average debt:** $17,100
Student/faculty ratio: 12/1 **Proportion who borrowed:** 78%

UNDERGRADUATE STUDENT BODY STATS

2005-2006 enrollment: 585 full-time; 9 part-time. Men: 45%; women: 55%. **Ethnic makeup:** African American: 6%; Asian American: 1%; Hispanic: 1%; White: 91%; International: 2%.

ADMISSIONS FACTS AND FIGURES

Phone: (864) 379-8838. **Email:** admissions@erskine.edu. **Website:** http://www.erskine.edu. **Application deadlines for fall 2007:** Regular decision: Rolling. Early decision: Not offered. Early action: Not offered. Admission cannot be deferred. **Application fee:** $25. Common application is not accepted. **To apply online, go to:** http://www.erskine.edu/v2/admissions/application.shtml. **Admissions requirements/recommendations:** High school units required (recommended): Mathematics: (4); Science: (3); Foreign language: (2); Social studies: (2). Tests: The college uses SAT or ACT scores in admissions decisions. Either SAT or ACT required. For admission to the fall 2007 entering class, the school will accept: ACT with writing. Campus visit: Recommended. Admissions interview: Recommended. Off-campus interview: Not available. **Factors that count in admissions decisions:** *Academic:* Secondary school record: Very important. Class rank: Considered. Letters of recommendation: Very important. Standardized test scores: Very important. Essay: Considered. *Nonacademic:* Interview: Considered. Extracurricular activities: Considered. Talent/ability: Considered. Character/personal qualities: Considered. Alumni/ae relationship: Very important. Geographical residence: Not considered. State residency: Not considered. Religious affiliation/commitment: Not considered. Minority status: Not considered. Volunteer work: Considered. Work experience: Considered. **Other schools with the greatest overlap in applicants:** Anderson University; Clemson University; College of Charleston; Presbyterian College; Wofford College. **Admissions statistics for the fall 2005 entering class:** Total applicants: 854. Total accepted: 596. Freshmen enrolled: 181; 34% were from out of state. Overall acceptance rate: 70%. **Credentials of fall 2005 freshmen:** 31% ranked in the top 10 percent of their high school class; 58% were in the top 25 percent, and 84% were in the top half. (Proportion submitting class standing: 80%.) **Average high school grade point average:** 3.8. **First-year students who submitted SAT scores:** 83%. Scores (25/75 percentile): Verbal: 480-620, Math: 510-610, Combined: 990-1230. **First-year students submitting ACT scores:** 17%. Scores (25/75 percentile): English: N/A, Math: N/A, Composite: 21-27.

ACADEMICS

Year founded: 1839. **Academic calendar:** 4-1-4. **Degrees offered:** certificate, bachelor's, master's, first professional, doctorate. **Most popular majors:** 23% business, management, marketing, and related support services, 14% education, 10% biological and biomedical sciences, 9% psychology, 8% history. **Major fields of study:** area, ethnic, cultural, and gender studies; biological and biomedical sciences; business, management, marketing, and related support services; education; English language and literature/letters; foreign languages, literatures, and linguistics; health professions and related clinical sciences; history; mathematics and statistics; parks, recreation, leisure, and fitness studies; philosophy and religious studies; physical sciences; psychology; theology and religious vocations; visual and performing arts. **Areas of required coursework:** arts/fine arts, humanities, computer literacy, mathematics, English (including composition), foreign languages, sciences (biological or physical), history. **Pre-professional programs:** pre-law, pre-dentistry, pre-medicine, pre-theology, pre-veterinary science, pre-pharmacy. **Special academic programs:** cross-registration, double major, independent study, internships, study abroad, teacher certificate program. **Teacher certification offered in:** early childhood, special education, elementary, secondary. **Faculty and instruction (2005-2006):** Total instructional faculty: 37 full-time, 31 part-time (62% men; 38% women; 4% minorities). Full-time faculty with Ph.D. or other terminal degree: 92%. Student/faculty ratio: 12/1. Classes of fewer than 20 students: 72%; of 20 to 49 students: 28%; of 50 or more students: 0%. **Advanced Placement and International Baccalaureate credit:** AP tests may be used for: Credit only. Scores accepted: 4. International Baccalaureate exams may be used for: Credit only. **Freshmen returning for sophomore year:** 75%. **Graduation rates:** Four-year: 64%; five-year: 65%; six-year: 65%. **Graduate study:** 29% of students pursue further study immediately upon graduation; 26% within one year. Fields in which graduates pursue further study: arts and sciences, 40%.

COSTS AND FINANCIAL AID

Financial aid office: (864) 379-8832. **Expenses (2006-2007):** Tuition and fees 2006-2007: $20,275; room/board: $6,951. Estimated books and supplies: $1,000; transportation: $1,750; personal expenses: $850. **Financial aid:** Priority filing date for institution's financial aid form: April 1. In 2005-2006, 95% of undergraduates applied for financial aid. Of those, 80% were determined to have financial need; 33% had their need fully met. Average financial aid package (proportion receiving): $18,100 (80%). Average amount of gift aid, such as scholarships or grants (proportion receiving): $10,500 (77%). Average amount of self-help aid, such as work study or loans (proportion receiving): $4,750 (77%). Average need-based loan (excluding PLUS or other private loans): $4,250. Among students who received need-based aid, the average percentage of need met: 88%. Among students who received aid based on merit, the average award (and the proportion receiving): $10,360 (16%). The average athletic scholarship (and the proportion receiving): $4,275 (19%). Average amount of debt of borrowers graduating in 2005: $17,100. Proportion who borrowed: 78%.

CAMPUS LIFE AND EXTRACURRICULAR ACTIVITIES

Campus housing available (% using): women's dorms (57%), men's dorms (43%). Students who live in college-owned, operated, or affiliated housing: 90%. **Student employment:** During the 2005-2006 academic year, 3% of undergraduates worked on campus. Average per-year earnings: $1,200. **Clubs and organizations:** Number of student organizations: 49. Activities include: choral groups, concert band, dance, drama/theater, jazz band, literary magazine, music ensembles, musical theater, radio station, student government, student newspaper, yearbook. Number of fraternities: 3; sororities: 4. Proportion of men in fraternities: 14%; of women in sororities: 25%. Average proportion of students who stay on campus on weekends: 25%. **Sports program (2005-2006):** Member of NCAA II. *Men's intercollegiate varsity sports:* baseball, basketball, cross-country, tennis. *Women's intercollegiate varsity sports:* basketball, cross-country, soccer, softball, tennis.

SERVICES AND FACILITIES

Basic services: nonremedial tutoring, placement service, health service. **Remedial assistance:** math, writing. **Counseling services:** career, personal, academic, psychological, religious. **For learning-disabled students:** School does not offer a structured program with separate admission and additional fees. Services include: tape recorders, untimed tests, extended time for tests, tutors. **Library:** Number of titles: 263,976; number of current serial subscriptions: 1,040. **Information technology resources:** Students are not required to lease or own a computer. School has a wireless network. Proportion of college-owned housing units wired for high-speed internet access: 100%. **Campus safety:** Security services offered: late-night transport/escort service, lighted pathways/sidewalks, controlled dormitory access (key, security card, etc).

TRANSFER AND INTERNATIONAL STUDENTS

Transfer students: May apply for admission for the following academic terms: Fall, Winter, Spring, Summer. Applicants do not need a minimum number of credits to apply. For fall 2005: Transfer applications received: 14. Transfer applicants offered admission: 14. Transfer applicants enrolled: 12. **International students:** Number of foreign undergraduates: 9 (2% of student body). Number of countries represented: 7. Minimum TOEFL score required: 550 (paper).

Francis Marion University

- **Address:** PO Box 100547, Florence, SC 29501
- **Website:** http://www.fmarion.edu
- **Public**
- **Enrollment:** 3,058 full-time; 442 part-time

KEY STATS
- ✔ **U.S News College Ranking:** third tier, Universities–Master's (South)
- ✔ **SAT Score (25th/75th percentile):** 880-1070
- ✔ **Tuition:** 2006-2007: $6,512 in state, $12,839 out of state
- **Selectivity:** Less selective **Room/board:** $5,430
- **Acceptance rate:** 71% **Average debt:** N/A
- **Student/faculty ratio:** 17/1 **Proportion who borrowed:** N/A

UNDERGRADUATE STUDENT BODY STATS

2005-2006 enrollment: 3,058 full-time; 442 part-time. Men: 35%; women: 65%. **Ethnic makeup:** African American: 42%; Asian American: 1%; Hispanic: 1%; White: 55%; International: 1%.

ADMISSIONS FACTS AND FIGURES

Phone: (843) 661-1231. **Email:** admission@fmarion.edu. **Website:** http://www.fmarion.edu. **Application deadlines for fall 2007:** Regular decision: Rolling. Early decision: Not offered. Early action: Not offered. Admission can be deferred. **Application fee:** $30. Common application is accepted. **To apply online, go to:** http://www.admissions.fmarion.edu/jump/apply.asp. **Admissions requirements/recommendations:** High school units required (recommended): English: 4; Mathematics: 3 (4); Science: 3 (3); Foreign language: 2; Social studies: 2; History: 1; Academic electives: 4; Total units: 20. Tests: The college uses SAT or ACT scores in admissions decisions. Either SAT or ACT required. For admission to the fall 2007 entering class, the school will accept: ACT with writing, ACT without writing. Campus visit: Recommended. Admissions interview: Neither required nor recommended. Off-campus interview: May be arranged. **Factors that count in admissions decisions:** *Academic:* Secondary school record: Very important. Class rank: Important. Letters of recommendation: Considered. Standardized test scores: Very important. Essay: Not considered. *Nonacademic:* Interview: Not considered. Extracurricular activities: Not considered. Talent/ability: Not considered. Character/personal qualities: Not considered. Alumni/ae relationship: Not considered. Geographical residence: Not considered. State residency: Not considered. Religious affiliation/commitment: Not considered. Minority status: Not considered. Volunteer work: Not considered. Work experience: Not considered. **Other schools with the greatest overlap in applicants:** Clemson University; Coastal Carolina University; College of Charleston; University of South Carolina–Columbia; Winthrop University. **Admissions statistics for the fall 2005 entering class:** Total applicants: 2,524. Total accepted: 1,804. Freshmen enrolled: 803; 4% were from out of state. Overall acceptance rate: 71%. **Credentials of fall 2005 freshmen:** 14% ranked in the top 10 percent of their high school class; 39% were in the top 25 percent, and 72% were in the top half. (Proportion submitting class standing: 96%.) **Average high school grade point average:** 3.4. **First-year students who submitted SAT scores:** 73%. Scores (25/75 percentile): Verbal: 440-540, Math: 440-530, Combined: 880-1070. **First-year students submitting ACT scores:** 27%. Scores (25/75 percentile): English: 17-21, Math: 16-21, Composite: 18-21.

ACADEMICS

Year founded: 1970. **Academic calendar:** Semester. **Degrees offered:** bachelor's, master's. **Most popular majors:** 33% business, management, marketing, and related support services, 11% biological and biomedical sciences, 11% education, 9% psychology, 9% social sciences. **Major fields of study:** biological and biomedical sciences; business, management, marketing, and related support services; communication, journalism, and related programs; computer and information sciences and support services; education; English language and literature/letters; foreign languages, literatures, and linguistics; health professions and related clinical sciences; history; liberal arts and sciences studies, and humanities; mathematics and statistics; physical sciences; psychology; social sciences; visual and performing arts. **Areas of required coursework:** arts/fine arts, humanities, computer literacy, mathematics, English (including composition), philosophy, foreign languages, sciences (biological or physical), history, social science. **Pre-professional programs:** pre-law, pre-dentistry, pre-medicine, pre-veterinary science, pre-pharmacy. **Special academic programs (% participation):** accelerated program (1%), cross-registration (2%), distance learning (19%), double major (2%), dual enrollment (6%), honors program (5%), independent study (1%), internships (1%), study abroad (.1%), teacher certificate program (13%). **Teacher certification offered in:** early childhood, elementary, secondary. **Cooperative education programs:** engineering, natural science, other. **Faculty and instruction (2005-2006):** Total instructional faculty: 176 full-time, 105 part-time (57% men; 43% women; 8% minorities). Full-time faculty with Ph.D. or other terminal degree: 81%. Student/faculty ratio: 17/1. Classes of fewer than 20 students: 40%; of 20 to 49 students: 56%; of 50 or more students: 4%. **Advanced Placement and International Baccalaureate credit:** AP tests may be used for: Credit only. Scores accepted: 3, 4, 5. International Baccalaureate exams may be used for: Credit only. **Freshmen returning for sophomore year:** 66%. **Graduation rates:** Four-year: 17%; five-year: 32%; six-year: 39%.

COSTS AND FINANCIAL AID
Financial aid office: (843) 661-1190. **Expenses (2006-2007):** Tuition and fees 2006-2007: $6,512 in state, $12,839 out of state; room/board: $5,430. Estimated books and supplies: $800; transportation: $2,636; personal expenses: $2,064. **Financial aid:** Priority filing date for institution's financial aid form: March 1; deadline: June 30. In 2005-2006, 80% of undergraduates applied for financial aid. Of those, 67% were determined to have financial need; Average financial aid package (proportion receiving): N/A (76%). Average amount of gift aid, such as scholarships or grants (proportion receiving): N/A (46%). Average amount of self-help aid, such as work study or loans (proportion receiving): N/A (53%).

CAMPUS LIFE AND EXTRACURRICULAR ACTIVITIES
Campus housing available: women's dorms, men's dorms, apartment for single students, special housing for disabled students. Students who live in college-owned, operated, or affiliated housing: 39%. **Student employment:** During the 2005-2006 academic year, 17% of undergraduates worked on campus. Average per-year earnings: $5,720. **Clubs and organizations:** Number of student organizations: 56. Activities include: choral groups, drama/theater, jazz band, literary magazine, music ensembles, student government, student newspaper, television station. Number of fraternities: 7; sororities: 7. Proportion of men in fraternities: 3%; of women in sororities: 4%. Average proportion of students who stay on campus on weekends: 35%. **Sports program (2005-2006):** Member of NCAA II. *Men's intercollegiate varsity sports:* baseball, basketball, cross-country, golf, soccer, tennis, track and field (outdoor). *Women's intercollegiate varsity sports:* basketball, cross-country, soccer, softball, tennis, track and field (outdoor), volleyball.

SERVICES AND FACILITIES
Basic services: health service, health insurance. **Remedial assistance:** study skills. **Counseling services:** career, personal, academic, psychological, birth control. **For learning-disabled students:** School does not offer a structured program with separate admission and additional fees. Services include: tape recorders, note-taking services, oral tests, readers, extended time for tests. **Library:** Number of titles: 391,457; number of current serial subscriptions: 1,538. **Information technology resources:** Students are not required to lease or own a computer. Number of campus computers available to all students: 551. School does not have a wireless network. Proportion of college-owned housing units wired for high-speed internet access: 100%. **Campus safety:** Security services offered: 24-hour foot-and-vehicle patrols, late-night transport/escort service, 24-hour emergency telephones, lighted pathways/sidewalks, controlled dormitory access (key, security card, etc).

TRANSFER AND INTERNATIONAL STUDENTS
Transfer students: May apply for admission for the following academic terms: Fall, Spring, Summer. Applicants need a minimum number of credits to apply. For fall 2005: Transfer applications received: 492. Transfer applicants offered admission: 326. Transfer applicants enrolled: 201. **International students:** Number of foreign undergraduates: 30 (1% of student body). Number of countries represented: 24. Minimum TOEFL score required: 500 (paper); 173 (computer). Average TOEFL score: 530 (paper).

Furman University

- **Address:** 3300 Poinsett Highway, Greenville, SC 29613
- **Website:** http://www.furman.edu/
- **Private**
- **Enrollment:** 2,699 full-time; 105 part-time

KEY STATS
✔ **U.S News College Ranking:** 41, Liberal Arts Colleges
✔ **SAT Score (25th/75th percentile):** 1200-1390
✔ **Tuition:** 2006-2007: $28,840
  Selectivity: More selective   **Room/board:** $7,552
  Acceptance rate: 53%   **Average debt:** $21,860
  Student/faculty ratio: 12/1   **Proportion who borrowed:** 38%

UNDERGRADUATE STUDENT BODY STATS
2005-2006 enrollment: 2,699 full-time; 105 part-time. Men: 44%; women: 56%. **Ethnic makeup:** African American: 6%; Asian American: 2%; Hispanic: 1%; White: 89%; International: 1%. **Religious preference:** Roman Catholic: 9%; Protestant: 55%; No preference: 4%; Unknown: 32%.

ADMISSIONS FACTS AND FIGURES
Phone: (864) 294-2034. **Email:** admissions@furman.edu. **Website:** http://www.furman.edu/. **Application deadlines for fall 2007:** Regular decision: January 15; decision sent by March 15. Early decision: Send application by: November 15; Decision sent by: December 15. Early action: Not offered. Admission cannot be deferred. **Application fee:** $40. Common application is accepted. **To apply online, go to:** http://www.engagefurman.com/application/. **Admissions requirements/recommendations:** High school units required (recommended): English: 4 (4); Mathematics: 3 (4); Science: 2 (3); Foreign language: 2 (3); Social studies: 3 (4); Total units: 14 (18). Tests: The college uses SAT or ACT scores in admissions decisions. Either SAT or ACT required. For admission to the fall 2007 entering class, the school will accept: ACT with writing. Campus visit: Recommended. Admissions interview: Neither required nor recommended. Off-campus interview: May be arranged. **Factors that count in admissions decisions:** *Academic:* Secondary school record: Very important. Class rank: Very important. Letters of recommendation: Considered. Standardized test scores: Important. Essay: Important. *Nonacademic:* Interview: Not considered. Extracurricular activities: Important. Talent/ability: Considered. Character/personal qualities: Important. Alumni/ae relationship: Considered. Geographical residence: Not considered. State residency: Not considered. Religious affiliation/commitment: Not considered. Minority status: Considered. Volunteer work: Considered. Work experience: Considered. **Other schools with the greatest overlap in applicants:** Davidson College; Duke University; University of North Carolina–Chapel Hill; Vanderbilt University; Wake Forest University. **Admissions statistics for the fall 2005 entering class:** Total applicants: 4,007. Total accepted: 2,119. Freshmen enrolled: 689; 72% were from out of state. Accepted through early-decision or early-action plans: 41%. Overall acceptance rate: 53%. Early-decision acceptance rate: 69%. Non-early acceptance rate: 50%. **Size of waiting list:** 699 applicants; enrolled from waiting list: 3. **Credentials of fall 2005 freshmen:** 64% ranked in the top 10 percent of their high school class; 88% were in the top 25 percent, and 98% were in the top half. (Proportion submitting class standing: 65%.) **Average high school grade point average:** 3.8. **First-year students who submitted SAT scores:** 95%. Scores (25/75 percentile): Verbal: 600-700, Math: 600-690, Combined: 1200-1390. **First-year students submitting ACT scores:** 47%. Scores (25/75 percentile): English: 25-32, Math: 25-29, Composite: 25-30.

ACADEMICS
Year founded: 1826. **Academic calendar:** Other. **Degrees offered:** bachelor's, post-bachelor's certificate, master's. **Most popular majors:** 13% political science and government, 10% business administration, management, and operations, 9% history, 8% biology, 7% communication and media studies. **Major fields of study:** area, ethnic, cultural, and gender studies; biological and biomedical sciences; business, management, marketing, and related support services; communication, journalism, and related programs; computer and information sciences and support services; education; English language and literature/letters; foreign languages, literatures, and linguistics; health professions and related clinical sciences; history; mathematics and statistics; multi/interdisciplinary studies; parks, recreation, leisure, and fitness studies; philosophy and religious studies; physical sciences; psychology; social sciences; theology and religious vocations; visual and performing

arts. **Areas of required coursework:** arts/fine arts, humanities, mathematics, English (including composition), philosophy, foreign languages, sciences (biological or physical), history, social science, other. **Pre-professional programs:** pre-law, pre-dentistry, pre-medicine, pre-theology, pre-veterinary science, pre-optometry, pre-pharmacy, other. **Special academic programs (% participation):** double major (15%), independent study (33%), internships (50%), student-designed major (1%), study abroad (40%), teacher certificate program (4%). **Teacher certification offered in:** early childhood, special education, elementary, middle/junior high, secondary. **Reserve Officers Training Corps (ROTC):** Army ROTC: Offered on campus. **Faculty and instruction (2005-2006):** Total instructional faculty: 220 full-time, 52 part-time (63% men; 37% women; 7% minorities). Full-time faculty with Ph.D. or other terminal degree: 97%. Student/faculty ratio: 12/1. Classes of fewer than 20 students: 53%; of 20 to 49 students: 47%; of 50 or more students: 0%. **Advanced Placement and International Baccalaureate credit:** AP tests may be used for: Credit and/or placement. Scores accepted: 4, 5. International Baccalaureate exams may be used for: Credit and/or placement. **Freshmen returning for sophomore year:** 92%. **Graduation rates:** Four-year: 79%; five-year: 84%; six-year: 84%. **Graduate study:** 40% of students pursue further study immediately upon graduation; 45% within one year. Fields in which graduates pursue further study: Master of Business Administration (MBA), 4%; law, 16%; medicine, 16%; dentistry, 2%; engineering, 2%; theology (or the seminary), 4%; education, 12%; arts and sciences, 43%; veterinary medicine, 1%.

COSTS AND FINANCIAL AID
Financial aid office: (864) 294-2204. **Expenses (2006-2007):** Tuition and fees 2006-2007: $28,840; room/board: $7,552. Estimated books and supplies: $775; transportation: $1,033; personal expenses: $750. **Financial aid:** In 2005-2006, 55% of undergraduates applied for financial aid. Of those, 44% were determined to have financial need; 43% had their need fully met. Average financial aid package (proportion receiving): $22,162 (44%). Average amount of gift aid, such as scholarships or grants (proportion receiving): $18,486 (44%). Average amount of self-help aid, such as work study or loans (proportion receiving): $6,035 (27%). Average need-based loan (excluding PLUS or other private loans): $5,083. Among students who received need-based aid, the average percentage of need met: 86%. Among students who received aid based on merit, the average award (and the proportion receiving): $10,198 (28%). The average athletic scholarship (and the proportion receiving): $21,362 (6%). Average amount of debt of borrowers graduating in 2005: $21,860. Proportion who borrowed: 38%.

CAMPUS LIFE AND EXTRACURRICULAR ACTIVITIES
Campus housing available (% using): coed dorms (35%), women's dorms (11%), men's dorms (11%), apartment for single students (43%), special housing for disabled students (0%), other housing options (0%). Students who live in college-owned, operated, or affiliated housing: 90%. **Student employment:** During the 2005-2006 academic year, 5% of undergraduates worked on campus. Average per-year earnings: $1,250. **Clubs and organizations:** Number of student organizations: 130. Activities include: choral groups, concert band, dance, drama/theater, jazz band, literary magazine, marching band, music ensembles, musical theater, opera, pep band, radio station, student government, student newspaper, student film society, symphony orchestra, television station, yearbook. Number of fraternities: 8; sororities: 8. Proportion of men in fraternities: 35%; of women in sororities: 40%. Average proportion of students who stay on campus on weekends: 80%. **Sports program (2005-2006):** Member of NCAA I. *Men's intercollegiate varsity sports:* baseball, basketball, cross-country, football, golf, soccer, tennis, track and field (outdoor). *Women's intercollegiate varsity sports:* basketball, cross-country, golf, soccer, softball, tennis, track and field (indoor), track and field (outdoor), volleyball.

SERVICES AND FACILITIES
Basic services: nonremedial tutoring, placement service, health service, health insurance. **Remedial assistance:** study skills. **Counseling services:** minority student, career, personal, veteran student, academic, psychological, religious. **For learning-disabled students:** School does not offer a structured program with separate admission and additional fees. Total undergraduates in learning-disabled program or receiving services: 145. Services include: tape recorders, note-taking services, oral tests, readers, extended time for tests, tutors, other. **Library:** Number of titles: 422,200; number of current serial subscriptions: 3,398. **Information technology resources:** Students are not required to lease or own a computer. Number of campus computers available to all students: 425. School has a wireless network. Approximate number of users that can be accommodated: 1,900. Proportion of college-owned housing units wired for high-speed internet access: 100%. **Campus

safety: Security services offered: 24-hour foot-and-vehicle patrols, late-night transport/escort service, 24-hour emergency telephones, lighted pathways/sidewalks, controlled dormitory access (key, security card, etc).

TRANSFER AND INTERNATIONAL STUDENTS
Transfer students: May apply for admission for the following academic terms: Fall, Winter, Spring, Summer. Applicants need a minimum number of credits to apply. For fall 2005: Transfer applications received: 101. Transfer applicants offered admission: 20. Transfer applicants enrolled: 14. **International students:** Number of foreign undergraduates: 37 (1% of student body). Number of countries represented: 15. Minimum TOEFL score required: 570 (paper); 230 (computer). Average TOEFL score: 630 (paper).

Lander University

- **Address:** 320 Stanley Avenue, Greenwood, SC 29649-2099
- **Website:** http://www.lander.edu
- **Public**
- **Enrollment:** 2,373 full-time; 239 part-time

KEY STATS
✔ **U.S News College Ranking:** third tier, Universities–Master's (South)
✔ **SAT Score (25th/75th percentile):** 855-1070
✔ **Tuition:** 2006-2007: $7,312 in state, $13,628 out of state

Selectivity: Less selective	**Room/board:** $5,651
Acceptance rate: 84%	**Average debt:** N/A
Student/faculty ratio: 16/1	**Proportion who borrowed:** N/A

UNDERGRADUATE STUDENT BODY STATS
2005-2006 enrollment: 2,373 full-time; 239 part-time. Men: 34%; women: 66%. **Ethnic makeup:** African American: 23%; Asian American: 1%; Hispanic: 1%; White: 73%; International: 2%.

ADMISSIONS FACTS AND FIGURES
Phone: (864) 388-8307. **Email:** admissions@lander.edu. **Website:** http://www.lander.edu. **Application deadlines for fall 2007:** Regular decision: August 15. Early decision: Not offered. Early action: Not offered. Admission can be deferred. **Application fee:** $35. Common application is not accepted. **To apply online, go to:** http://www.lander.edu/admissions/apply.html. **Admissions requirements/recommendations:** High school units required (recommended): English: 4 (4); Mathematics: 4 (4); Science: 3 (3); Foreign language: 2 (2); Social studies: 2 (2); History: 1 (1); Academic electives: 2 (2); Total units: 20 (20). Tests: The college uses SAT or ACT scores in admissions decisions. Either SAT or ACT required. For admission to the fall 2007 entering class, the school will accept: ACT with writing, ACT without writing. Campus visit: Recommended. Admissions interview: Recommended. Off-campus interview: May be arranged. **Factors that count in admissions decisions:** *Academic:* Secondary school record: Very important. Class rank: Very important. Letters of recommendation: Considered. Standardized test scores: Very important. Essay: Considered. *Nonacademic:* Interview: Considered. Extracurricular activities: Considered. Talent/ability: Considered. Character/personal qualities: Considered. Alumni/ae relationship: Considered. Geographical residence: Not considered. State residency: Not considered. Religious affiliation/commitment: Not considered. Minority status: Not considered. Volunteer work: Considered. Work experience: Considered. **Other schools with the greatest overlap in applicants:** Francis Marion University; University of South Carolina–Upstate; Winthrop University. **Admissions statistics for the fall 2005 entering class:** Total applicants: 1,469. Total accepted: 1,227. Freshmen enrolled: 577; 3% were from out of state. Overall acceptance rate: 84%. **Credentials of fall 2005 freshmen:** 11% ranked in the top 10 percent of their high school class; 33% were in the top 25 percent, and 72% were in the top half. (Proportion submitting class standing: 96%.) **Average high school grade point average:** 3.4. **First-year students who submitted SAT scores:** 72%. Scores (25/75 percentile): Verbal: 420-530, Math: 435-540, Combined: 855-1070. **First-year students submitting ACT scores:** 28%. Scores (25/75 percentile): English: N/A, Math: N/A, Composite: 17-21.

ACADEMICS
Year founded: 1872. **Academic calendar:** Semester. **Degrees offered:** certificate, bachelor's, master's. **Most popular majors:** 23% business administration and management, 11% elementary education and teaching, 9%

nursing/registered nurse training (R.N., A.S.N., B.S.N., M.S.N.), 8% sociology, 7% psychology. **Major fields of study:** biological and biomedical sciences; business, management, marketing, and related support services; computer and information sciences and support services; education; English language and literature/letters; foreign languages, literatures, and linguistics; health professions and related clinical sciences; history; liberal arts and sciences studies, and humanities; mathematics and statistics; multi/interdisciplinary studies; natural resources and conservation; parks, recreation, leisure, and fitness studies; physical sciences; social sciences; visual and performing arts. **Areas of required coursework:** arts/fine arts, humanities, mathematics, English (including composition), foreign languages, sciences (biological or physical), history, social science. **Pre-professional programs:** pre-law, pre-dentistry, pre-medicine, pre-veterinary science, pre-optometry, pre-pharmacy, other. **Special academic programs:** cooperative (work-study plan) program, distance learning, double major, dual enrollment, honors program, independent study, internships, liberal arts/career combination, student-designed major, study abroad, teacher certificate program, other. **Teacher certification offered in:** early childhood, special education, elementary, secondary. **Cooperative education programs:** art, business, computer science, education, health professions, humanities, natural science, social/behavioral science. **Reserve Officers Training Corps (ROTC):** Army ROTC: Offered on campus. **Faculty and instruction (2005-2006):** Total instructional faculty: 126 full-time, 64 part-time (51% men; 49% women; 11% minorities). Full-time faculty with Ph.D. or other terminal degree: 74%. Student/faculty ratio: 16/1. Classes of fewer than 20 students: 37%; of 20 to 49 students: 62%; of 50 or more students: 1%. **Advanced Placement and International Baccalaureate credit:** AP tests may be used for: Credit only. Scores accepted: 3, 4, 5. International Baccalaureate exams may be used for: Credit only. **Freshmen returning for sophomore year:** 64%. **Graduation rates:** Four-year: 22%; five-year: 40%; six-year: 47%. **Graduate study:** 17% of students pursue further study within five years. Fields in which graduates pursue further study: Master of Business Administration (MBA), 25%; law, 10%; education, 20%; arts and sciences, 5%.

COSTS AND FINANCIAL AID
Financial aid office: (864) 388-8340. **Expenses (2006-2007):** Tuition and fees 2006-2007: $7,312 in state, $13,628 out of state; room/board: $5,651. **Financial aid:** Priority filing date for institution's financial aid form: April 15.

CAMPUS LIFE AND EXTRACURRICULAR ACTIVITIES
Campus housing available: coed dorms, women's dorms. Students who live in college-owned, operated, or affiliated housing: 35%. **Student employment:** During the 2005-2006 academic year, 20% of undergraduates worked on campus. Average per-year earnings: $1,000. **Clubs and organizations:** Number of student organizations: 63. Activities include: choral groups, concert band, dance, drama/theater, jazz band, literary magazine, music ensembles, student government, student newspaper. Number of fraternities: 6; sororities: 6. Proportion of men in fraternities: 11%; of women in sororities: 12%. Average proportion of students who stay on campus on weekends: 30%. **Sports program (2005-2006):** Member of NCAA II. *Men's intercollegiate varsity sports:* baseball, basketball, golf, soccer, tennis. *Women's intercollegiate varsity sports:* basketball, cross-country, soccer, softball, volleyball.

SERVICES AND FACILITIES
Basic services: nonremedial tutoring, placement service, health service, health insurance. **Remedial assistance:** reading, math, writing, study skills, other. **Counseling services:** minority student, career, personal, veteran student, academic. **For learning-disabled students:** School does not offer a structured program with separate admission and additional fees. Total undergraduates in learning-disabled program or receiving services: 101. Services include: remedial math, reading machines, tape recorders, untimed tests, note-taking services, oral tests, learning center, readers, extended time for tests, tutors, priority registration, priority seating, texts on tape, other testing accomodations, other. **Library:** Number of titles: 183,724; number of current serial subscriptions: 823. **Information technology resources:** Students are not required to lease or own a computer. Number of campus computers available to all students: 230. School has a wireless network. Approximate number of users that can be accommodated: 3,000. Proportion of college-owned housing units wired for high-speed internet access: 86%. **Campus safety:** Security services offered: 24-hour foot-and-vehicle patrols, late-night transport/escort service, 24-hour emergency telephones, lighted pathways/sidewalks.

TRANSFER AND INTERNATIONAL STUDENTS
Transfer students: May apply for admission for the following academic terms: Fall, Spring, Summer. Applicants need a minimum number of credits to apply. For fall 2005: Transfer applications received: 395. Transfer applicants offered admission: 334. Transfer applicants enrolled: 224. **International students:** Number of foreign undergraduates: 46 (2% of student body). Minimum TOEFL score required: 550 (paper); 213 (computer).

Limestone College

- **Address:** 1115 College Drive, Gaffney, SC 29340-3799
- **Website:** http://www.limestone.edu
- **Private; Religious affiliation:** Christian Non-Denominational
- **Enrollment:** 2,039 full-time; 1,179 part-time

KEY STATS
✔ **U.S News College Ranking:** third tier, Comp. Coll.–Bachelor's (South)
✔ **SAT Score (25th/75th percentile):** 910-1060
✔ **Tuition:** 2006-2007: $15,000

Selectivity: Less selective	**Room/board:** $6,000
Acceptance rate: 58%	**Average debt:** $16,175
Student/faculty ratio: 10/1	**Proportion who borrowed:** 66%

UNDERGRADUATE STUDENT BODY STATS
2005-2006 enrollment: 2,039 full-time; 1,179 part-time. Men: 37%; women: 63%. **Ethnic makeup:** African American: 46%; Asian American: 1%; Hispanic: 2%; White: 51%; International: 1%. **Religious preference:** Roman Catholic: 11%; Protestant: 53%; No preference: 36%.

ADMISSIONS FACTS AND FIGURES
Phone: (864) 488-4554. **Email:** admiss@limestone.edu. **Website:** http://www.limestone.edu. **Application deadlines for fall 2007:** Regular decision: August 26. Early decision: Not offered. Early action: Not offered. Admission can be deferred. **Application fee:** $25. Common application is accepted. **Admissions requirements/recommendations:** High school units required (recommended): English: (4); Mathematics: (3); Science: (2); Social studies: (3); Total units: (12). Tests: The college uses SAT or ACT scores in admissions decisions. Either SAT or ACT required. For admission to the fall 2007 entering class, the school will accept: ACT with writing, ACT without writing. Campus visit: Recommended. Admissions interview: Neither required nor recommended. Off-campus interview: May be arranged. **Factors that count in admissions decisions:** *Academic:* Secondary school record: Very important. Class rank: Important. Letters of recommendation: Considered. Standardized test scores: Very important. Essay: Not considered. *Nonacademic:* Interview: Considered. Extracurricular activities: Not considered. Talent/ability: Not considered. Character/personal qualities: Not considered. Alumni/ae relationship: Not considered. Geographical residence: Not considered. State residency: Not considered. Religious affiliation/commitment: Not considered. Minority status: Not considered. Volunteer work: Not considered. Work experience: Not considered. **Other schools with the greatest overlap in applicants:** Anderson University; Gardner-Webb University; Lees-McRae College; Newberry College; University of South Carolina–Upstate. **Admissions statistics for the fall 2005 entering class:** Total applicants: 884. Total accepted: 512. Freshmen enrolled: 172; 19% were from out of state. Overall acceptance rate: 58%. **Size of waiting list:** 0 applicants; enrolled from waiting list: 0. **Credentials of fall 2005 freshmen:** 7% ranked in the top 10 percent of their high school class; 20% were in the top 25 percent, and 54% were in the top half. (Proportion submitting class standing: 78%.) **Average high school grade point average:** 3.0. **First-year students who submitted SAT scores:** 69%. Scores (25/75 percentile): Verbal: 450-520, Math: 460-540, Combined: 910-1060. **First-year students submitting ACT scores:** 28%. Scores (25/75 percentile): English: 14-21, Math: 16-19, Composite: 17-21.

ACADEMICS
Year founded: 1845. **Academic calendar:** Semester. **Degrees offered:** associate, bachelor's. **Most popular majors:** 22% business, management, marketing, and related support services, 21% education, 7% parks, recreation, leisure, and fitness studies, 7% security and protective services, 6% public administration and social service professions. **Major fields of study:** biological and biomedical sciences; business, management, marketing, and related support services; computer and information sciences and support services; edu-

cation; English language and literature/letters; health professions and related clinical sciences; history; legal professions and studies; liberal arts and sciences studies, and humanities; mathematics and statistics; parks, recreation, leisure, and fitness studies; physical sciences; psychology; public administration and social service professions; security and protective services; social sciences; visual and performing arts. **Areas of required coursework:** arts/fine arts, humanities, computer literacy, mathematics, English (including composition), sciences (biological or physical), history, social science, other. **Pre-professional programs:** pre-law, pre-dentistry, pre-medicine, pre-veterinary science, pre-pharmacy, other. **Special academic programs (% participation):** accelerated program (14%), distance learning (77%), double major (6%), honors program (14%), independent study (39%), internships (21%), teacher certificate program (14%). **Teacher certification offered in:** elementary, secondary. **Reserve Officers Training Corps (ROTC):** Army ROTC: Offered at cooperating institution (Wofford College). **Faculty and instruction (2005-2006):** Total instructional faculty: 55 full-time, 32 part-time (67% men; 33% women; 0% minorities). Full-time faculty with Ph.D. or other terminal degree: 62%. Student/faculty ratio: 10/1. Classes of fewer than 20 students: 71%; of 20 to 49 students: 29%; of 50 or more students: 0%. **Advanced Placement and International Baccalaureate credit:** AP tests may be used for: Credit only. Scores accepted: 3, 4, 5. International Baccalaureate exams may be used for: Credit only. **Freshmen returning for sophomore year:** 65%. **Graduation rates:** Four-year: 38%; five-year: 50%; six-year: 34%.

COSTS AND FINANCIAL AID

Financial aid office: (864) 488-8231. **Expenses (2006-2007):** Tuition and fees 2006-2007: $15,000; room/board: $6,000. Estimated books and supplies: $1,660; transportation: $1,470; personal expenses: $1,640. **Financial aid:** Priority filing date for institution's financial aid form: February 1. In 2005-2006, 98% of undergraduates applied for financial aid. Of those, 88% were determined to have financial need; 18% had their need fully met. Average financial aid package (proportion receiving): $10,813 (88%). Average amount of gift aid, such as scholarships or grants (proportion receiving): $7,807 (87%). Average amount of self-help aid, such as work study or loans (proportion receiving): $3,841 (73%). Average need-based loan (excluding PLUS or other private loans): $3,309. Among students who received need-based aid, the average percentage of need met: 60%. Among students who received aid based on merit, the average award (and the proportion receiving): $8,131 (18%). The average athletic scholarship (and the proportion receiving): $4,898 (15%). Average amount of debt of borrowers graduating in 2005: $16,175. Proportion who borrowed: 66%.

CAMPUS LIFE AND EXTRACURRICULAR ACTIVITIES

Campus housing available (% using): women's dorms (41%), men's dorms (59%). Students who live in college-owned, operated, or affiliated housing: 50%. **Student employment:** During the 2005-2006 academic year, 17% of undergraduates worked on campus. Average per-year earnings: $601. **Clubs and organizations:** Number of student organizations: 33. Activities include: choral groups, concert band, drama/theater, jazz band, literary magazine, music ensembles, musical theater, student government, yearbook. Number of fraternities: 0; sororities: 1. of women in sororities: 2%. Average proportion of students who stay on campus on weekends: 60%. **Sports program (2005-2006):** Member of NCAA II. *Men's intercollegiate varsity sports:* baseball, basketball, cross-country, golf, lacrosse, soccer, tennis, wrestling. *Women's intercollegiate varsity sports:* basketball, cross-country, golf, lacrosse, soccer, softball, swimming and diving, tennis, volleyball.

SERVICES AND FACILITIES

Basic services: nonremedial tutoring, placement service, health service, health insurance. **Remedial assistance:** math, writing, study skills, other. **Counseling services:** career, personal, veteran student, academic, older student, psychological, birth control, religious, other. **For learning-disabled students:** School does not offer a structured program with separate admission and additional fees. Total undergraduates in learning-disabled program or receiving services: 26. Services include: remedial math, remedial English, remedial reading, other special classes, untimed tests, note-taking services, oral tests, learning center, readers, extended time for tests, tutors, priority seating, texts on tape, other testing accomodations, other. **Library:** Number of titles: 64,936; number of current serial subscriptions: 281. **Information technology resources:** Students are not required to lease or own a computer. Number of campus computers available to all students: 86. School has a wireless network. Approximate number of users that can be accommodated: 50. Proportion of college-owned housing units wired for high-speed internet access: 100%. **Campus safety:** Security services offered: 24-hour foot-and-vehicle patrols, late-night transport/escort service, lighted pathways/sidewalks, controlled dormitory access (key, security card, etc).

TRANSFER AND INTERNATIONAL STUDENTS

Transfer students: May apply for admission for the following academic terms: Fall, Spring, Summer. Applicants need a minimum number of credits to apply. For fall 2005: Transfer applications received: 219. Transfer applicants offered admission: 125. Transfer applicants enrolled: 72. **International students:** Number of foreign undergraduates: 21 (1% of student body). Number of countries represented: 11. Minimum TOEFL score required: 500 (paper); 173 (computer). Average TOEFL score: 657 (paper).

Morris College

- **Address:** 100 W. College Street, Sumter, SC 29150
- **Website:** http://www.morris.edu
- **Private; Religious affiliation:** Baptist
- **Enrollment:** 844 full-time; 19 part-time

KEY STATS

✔ **U.S News College Ranking:** third tier, Comp. Coll.–Bachelor's (South)
✔ **SAT Score (25th/75th percentile):** N/A
✔ **Tuition:** 2006-2007: $8,812

Selectivity: Less selective	**Room/board:** $3,982
Acceptance rate: 85%	**Average debt:** $20,000
Student/faculty ratio: 16/1	**Proportion who borrowed:** 99%

UNDERGRADUATE STUDENT BODY STATS

2005-2006 enrollment: 844 full-time; 19 part-time. Men: 36%; women: 64%. **Ethnic makeup:** African American: 100%.

ADMISSIONS FACTS AND FIGURES

Phone: (803) 934-3225. **Email:** dcalhoun@morris.edu. **Website:** http://www.morris.edu. **Application deadlines for fall 2007:** Regular decision: Rolling. Early decision: Not offered. Early action: Not offered. Admission can be deferred. **Application fee:** $20. Common application is accepted. **To apply online, go to:** http://www.morris.edu/admissions/applications.html. **Admissions requirements/recommendations:** High school units required (recommended): English: 4; Mathematics: 4; Science: 3; Foreign language: 1 (2); Social studies: 2; History: 1; Academic electives: 7; Total units: 24. Tests: The college does not use SAT or ACT scores in admissions decisions. Neither SAT nor ACT required. Campus visit: Recommended. Admissions interview: Recommended. Off-campus interview: May be arranged. **Factors that count in admissions decisions:** *Academic:* Secondary school record: Very important. Class rank: Not considered. Standardized test scores: Not considered. **Other schools with the greatest overlap in applicants:** Allen University; Benedict College; Claflin University; South Carolina State University; Voorhees College. **Admissions statistics for the fall 2005 entering class:** Total applicants: 892. Total accepted: 756. Freshmen enrolled: 208; 20% were from out of state. Overall acceptance rate: 85%. **Average high school grade point average:** 2.5.

ACADEMICS

Year founded: 1908. **Academic calendar:** Semester. **Degrees offered:** bachelor's. **Most popular majors:** 18% health services/allied health/health sciences, 14% criminal justice/law enforcement administration, 14% sociology, 12% business administration and management, 12% business administration, management, and operations. **Major fields of study:** biological and biomedical sciences; business, management, marketing, and related support services; communication, journalism, and related programs; education; English language and literature/letters; health professions and related clinical sciences; history; liberal arts and sciences studies, and humanities; mathematics and statistics; parks, recreation, leisure, and fitness studies; security and protective services; social sciences; theology and religious vocations. **Areas of required coursework:** arts/fine arts, humanities, computer literacy, mathematics, English (including composition), foreign languages, sciences (biological or physical), history, social science, other. **Pre-professional programs:** pre-law, pre-dentistry, pre-medicine, pre-pharmacy, other. **Special academic programs (% participation):** accelerated program (7.4%), cooperative (work-study plan) program (30%), double major (0%), honors program (2.5%), internships (46.8%), teacher certificate program (2.5%). **Teacher certification offered in:** early childhood, elementary, secondary. **Cooperative education programs:** business, health professions, humanities, natural science, social/behavioral science. **Reserve Officers Training Corps (ROTC):** Army ROTC: Offered on campus. **Faculty and instruction (2005-**

2006): Total instructional faculty: 47 full-time, 12 part-time (51% men; 49% women; 63% minorities). Full-time faculty with Ph.D. or other terminal degree: 64%. Student/faculty ratio: 16/1. Classes of fewer than 20 students: 60%; of 20 to 49 students: 40%. **Advanced Placement and International Baccalaureate credit:** AP tests may be used for: Credit only. **Freshmen returning for sophomore year:** 57%. **Graduation rates:** Four-year: 19%; five-year: 38%; six-year: 37%. **Graduate study:** 10% of students pursue further study immediately upon graduation; 5% within one year; 5% within five years. Fields in which graduates pursue further study: Master of Business Administration (MBA), 2%; law, 1%; medicine, 1%; dentistry, 1%; engineering, 1%; theology (or the seminary), 2%; education, 2%; arts and sciences, 22%.

COSTS AND FINANCIAL AID

Financial aid office: (803) 934-3238. **Expenses (2006-2007):** Tuition and fees 2006-2007: $8,812; room/board: $3,982. Estimated books and supplies: $1,500; transportation: $1,300; personal expenses: $1,200. **Financial aid:** Priority filing date for institution's financial aid form: March 30. In 2005-2006, 100% of undergraduates applied for financial aid. Of those, 99% were determined to have financial need; 7% had their need fully met. Average financial aid package (proportion receiving): $12,400 (99%). Average amount of gift aid, such as scholarships or grants (proportion receiving): $3,500 (96%). Average amount of self-help aid, such as work study or loans (proportion receiving): $3,500 (99%). Average need-based loan (excluding PLUS or other private loans): $3,500. Among students who received need-based aid, the average percentage of need met: 87%. Among students who received aid based on merit, the average award (and the proportion receiving): $0 (0%). The average athletic scholarship (and the proportion receiving): $0 (0%). Average amount of debt of borrowers graduating in 2005: $20,000. Proportion who borrowed: 99%.

CAMPUS LIFE AND EXTRACURRICULAR ACTIVITIES

Campus housing available (% using): women's dorms (61%), men's dorms (39%). Students who live in college-owned, operated, or affiliated housing: 71%. **Clubs and organizations:** Number of student organizations: 55. Activities include: choral groups, dance, drama/theater, literary magazine, pep band, radio station, student government, student newspaper, yearbook. Number of fraternities: 4; sororities: 4. Proportion of men in fraternities: 12%; of women in sororities: 11%. Average proportion of students who stay on campus on weekends: 25%. **Sports program (2005-2006):** Member of NCAA II. *Men's intercollegiate varsity sports:* baseball, basketball, cross-country, golf, tennis, track and field (indoor), track and field (outdoor). *Women's intercollegiate varsity sports:* basketball, cross-country, softball, tennis, track and field (indoor), track and field (outdoor), volleyball.

SERVICES AND FACILITIES

Basic services: nonremedial tutoring, placement service, health service, health insurance. **Remedial assistance:** reading, math, writing, study skills, other. **Counseling services:** minority student, career, military, personal, veteran student, academic, older student, birth control, religious. **Library:** Number of titles: 76,456; number of current serial subscriptions: 371. **Information technology resources:** Students are not required to lease or own a computer. Number of campus computers available to all students: 202. School does not have a wireless network. Proportion of college-owned housing units wired for high-speed internet access: 100%. **Campus safety:** Security services offered: 24-hour foot-and-vehicle patrols, late-night transport/escort service, lighted pathways/sidewalks, controlled dormitory access (key, security card, etc).

TRANSFER AND INTERNATIONAL STUDENTS

Transfer students: May apply for admission for the following academic terms: Fall, Spring, Summer. Applicants do not need a minimum number of credits to apply. For fall 2005: Transfer applications received: 112. Transfer applicants offered admission: 63. Transfer applicants enrolled: 52. **International students:** Minimum TOEFL score required: 500 (paper); 300 (computer).

Newberry College

- **Address:** 2100 College Street, Newberry, SC 29108
- **Website:** http://www.newberry.edu/
- **Private; Religious affiliation:** Evangelical Lutheran Church of America
- **Enrollment:** 821 full-time; 20 part-time

KEY STATS

✔ **U.S News College Ranking:** 38, Comp. Coll.–Bachelor's (South)
✔ **SAT Score (25th/75th percentile):** 870-1070
✔ **Tuition:** N/A

Selectivity: Less selective	**Room/board:** N/A
Acceptance rate: 59%	**Average debt:** N/A
Student/faculty ratio: 14/1	**Proportion who borrowed:** N/A

UNDERGRADUATE STUDENT BODY STATS

2005-2006 enrollment: 821 full-time; 20 part-time. Men: 60%; women: 40%. **Ethnic makeup:** African American: 26%; Asian American: 1%; Hispanic: 2%; White: 68%; International: 3%. **Religious preference:** Roman Catholic: 7%; Protestant: 51%; No preference: 10%; Unknown: 2%; Evangelical Lutheran Church of America: 18%.

ADMISSIONS FACTS AND FIGURES

Phone: (800) 845-4955. **Email:** admissions@newberry.edu. **Website:** http://www.newberry.edu/. **Application deadlines for fall 2007:** Regular decision: Rolling. Early decision: Not offered. Early action: Not offered. Admission can be deferred. **Application fee:** $30. Common application is accepted. **To apply online, go to:** http://www.newberry.edu/forms/application_adm.htm. **Admissions requirements/recommendations:** High school units required (recommended): English: 4 (4); Mathematics: 3 (3); Science: 2 (2); Foreign language: 2 (2); Social studies: 2 (2); History: 1 (1); Academic electives: 1 (1); Total units: 15 (15). Tests: The college uses SAT or ACT scores in admissions decisions. Either SAT or ACT required. For admission to the fall 2007 entering class, the school will accept: ACT with writing, ACT without writing. Campus visit: Recommended. Admissions interview: Recommended. Off-campus interview: Not available. **Factors that count in admissions decisions:** *Academic:* Secondary school record: Very important. Class rank: Important. Letters of recommendation: Considered. Standardized test scores: Very important. Essay: Considered. *Nonacademic:* Interview: Considered. Extracurricular activities: Considered. Talent/ability: Considered. Character/personal qualities: Considered. Alumni/ae relationship: Considered. Geographical residence: Considered. State residency: Considered. Religious affiliation/commitment: Considered. Minority status: Considered. Volunteer work: Considered. Work experience: Considered. **Other schools with the greatest overlap in applicants:** Catawba College; Lenoir-Rhyne College; Presbyterian College; Winthrop University; Wofford College. **Admissions statistics for the fall 2005 entering class:** Total applicants: 1,102. Total accepted: 654. Freshmen enrolled: 276; Overall acceptance rate: 59%. **Size of waiting list:** 0 applicants; enrolled from waiting list: 0. **Credentials of fall 2005 freshmen:** 8% ranked in the top 10 percent of their high school class; 24% were in the top 25 percent, and 56% were in the top half. (Proportion submitting class standing: 95%.) **Average high school grade point average:** 3.2. **First-year students who submitted SAT scores:** 87%. Scores (25/75 percentile): Verbal: 430-530, Math: 440-540, Combined: 870-1070. **First-year students submitting ACT scores:** 54%. Scores (25/75 percentile): English: N/A, Math: N/A, Composite: 17-20.

ACADEMICS

Year founded: 1856. **Academic calendar:** Semester. **Degrees offered:** bachelor's. **Most popular majors:** 29% education, 23% business/commerce, 18% physical education teaching and coaching, 15% biology, 15% social sciences. **Major fields of study:** biological and biomedical sciences; business, management, marketing, and related support services; communication, journalism, and related programs; education; English language and literature/letters; foreign languages, literatures, and linguistics; health professions and related clinical sciences; history; mathematics and statistics; multi/interdisciplinary studies; parks, recreation, leisure, and fitness studies; philosophy and religious studies; physical sciences; psychology; social sciences; theology and religious vocations; visual and performing arts. **Areas of required coursework:** arts/fine arts, humanities, computer literacy, mathematics, English (including composition), foreign languages, sciences (biological or physical), history, social science, other. **Pre-professional programs:** pre-law, pre-medicine, pre-theology. **Special academic programs (% participation):**

cooperative (work-study plan) program (0%), double major (3%), dual enrollment (0%), honors program (6%), independent study (3%), internships (2%), liberal arts/career combination, student-designed major (0%), study abroad (0%), teacher certificate program. **Teacher certification offered in:** early childhood, elementary, secondary. **Cooperative education programs:** engineering, health professions, other. **Reserve Officers Training Corps (ROTC):** Army ROTC: Offered at cooperating institution (Presbyterian College). **Faculty and instruction (2005-2006):** Total instructional faculty: 52 full-time, 26 part-time (63% men; 37% women; 9% minorities). Full-time faculty with Ph.D. or other terminal degree: 71%. Student/faculty ratio: 14/1. Classes of fewer than 20 students: 66%; of 20 to 49 students: 34%; of 50 or more students: 1%. **Advanced Placement and International Baccalaureate credit:** AP tests may be used for: Credit and/or placement. Scores accepted: 3, 4, 5. International Baccalaureate exams may be used for: Credit and/or placement. **Freshmen returning for sophomore year:** 61%. **Graduation rates:** Four-year: 33%; five-year: 49%; six-year: 51%. **Graduate study:** 21% of students pursue further study immediately upon graduation; 11% within one year. Fields in which graduates pursue further study: law, 7%; medicine, 1%; theology (or the seminary), 4%; education, 7%; arts and sciences, 6%; veterinary medicine, 1%.

COSTS AND FINANCIAL AID
Financial aid office: (803) 321-5120.

CAMPUS LIFE AND EXTRACURRICULAR ACTIVITIES
Campus housing available (% using): coed dorms (19%), women's dorms (32%), men's dorms (49%), special housing for disabled students. **Student employment:** During the 2005-2006 academic year, 8% of undergraduates worked on campus. Average per-year earnings: $500. **Clubs and organizations:** Number of student organizations: 50. Activities include: choral groups, concert band, drama/theater, jazz band, literary magazine, marching band, music ensembles, musical theater, radio station, student government, student newspaper, television station, yearbook. Number of fraternities: 5; sororities: 4. Average proportion of students who stay on campus on weekends: 60%. **Sports program (2005-2006):** Member of NCAA II. *Men's intercollegiate varsity sports:* baseball, basketball, cross-country, football, golf, soccer, tennis, wrestling. *Women's intercollegiate varsity sports:* basketball, cross-country, golf, soccer, softball, tennis, volleyball.

SERVICES AND FACILITIES
Basic services: placement service, health insurance. **Remedial assistance:** math, writing, study skills. **Counseling services:** career, personal, academic, religious. **For learning-disabled students:** School does not offer a structured program with separate admission and additional fees. Total undergraduates in learning-disabled program or receiving services: 20. Services include: remedial math, remedial English, reading machines, untimed tests, note-taking services, oral tests, learning center, extended time for tests, tutors, priority seating. **Library:** Number of titles: 79,899; number of current serial subscriptions: 258. **Information technology resources:** Students are not required to lease or own a computer. Number of campus computers available to all students: 90. School has a wireless network. Approximate number of users that can be accommodated: 45. Proportion of college-owned housing units wired for high-speed internet access: 100%. **Campus safety:** Security services offered: 24-hour foot-and-vehicle patrols, late-night transport/escort service, 24-hour emergency telephones, controlled dormitory access (key, security card, etc).

TRANSFER AND INTERNATIONAL STUDENTS
Transfer students: May apply for admission for the following academic terms: Fall, Spring, Summer. Applicants need a minimum number of credits to apply. For fall 2005: Transfer applicants enrolled: 78. **International students:** Number of foreign undergraduates: 26 (3% of student body). Number of countries represented: 24. Minimum TOEFL score required: 520 (paper); 197 (computer). Average TOEFL score: 525 (paper).

North Greenville University

- **Address:** PO Box 1892, Tigerville, SC 29688
- **Website:** http://www.ngc.edu
- **Private; Religious affiliation:** Southern Baptist
- **Enrollment:** 1,634 full-time; 210 part-time

KEY STATS
✔ **U.S News College Ranking:** 49, Comp. Coll.–Bachelor's (South)
✔ **SAT Score (25th/75th percentile):** 880-1160
✔ **Tuition:** N/A

Selectivity: Selective	**Room/board:** N/A
Acceptance rate: 88%	**Average debt:** N/A
Student/faculty ratio: 19/1	**Proportion who borrowed:** N/A

UNDERGRADUATE STUDENT BODY STATS
2005-2006 enrollment: 1,634 full-time; 210 part-time. Men: 49%; women: 51%. **Ethnic makeup:** African American: 7%; Hispanic: 1%; White: 90%; International: 1%. **Religious preference:** Roman Catholic: 4%; Protestant: 20%; Unknown: 18%; Southern Baptist: 58%.

ADMISSIONS FACTS AND FIGURES
Phone: (864) 977-7001. **Email:** admissions@ngc.edu. **Website:** http://www.ngc.edu. **Application deadlines for fall 2007:** Regular decision: August 26. Early decision: Not offered. Early action: Not offered. Admission can be deferred. **Application fee:** $25. Common application is not accepted. **Admissions requirements/recommendations:** High school units required (recommended): English: 4 (4); Mathematics: 2 (4); Science: 2 (2); Foreign language: 2 (2); Social studies: 1 (2); History: 1 (2); Academic electives: 2 (4); Total units: 14 (20). Tests: The college uses SAT or ACT scores in admissions decisions. Either SAT or ACT required. For admission to the fall 2007 entering class, the school will accept: ACT with writing, ACT without writing. Campus visit: Recommended. Admissions interview: Neither required nor recommended. **Factors that count in admissions decisions:** *Academic:* Secondary school record: Very important. Class rank: Very important. Letters of recommendation: Considered. Standardized test scores: Very important. Essay: Considered. *Nonacademic:* Interview: Not considered. Extracurricular activities: Important. Talent/ability: Important. Character/personal qualities: Very important. Alumni/ae relationship: Considered. Geographical residence: Not considered. State residency: Not considered. Religious affiliation/commitment: Considered. Minority status: Not considered. Volunteer work: Considered. Work experience: Considered. **Admissions statistics for the fall 2005 entering class:** Total applicants: 753. Total accepted: 660. Freshmen enrolled: 439; Overall acceptance rate: 88%. **Credentials of fall 2005 freshmen:** 12% ranked in the top 10 percent of their high school class; 34% were in the top 25 percent, and 67% were in the top half. **Average high school grade point average:** 3.4. **First-year students who submitted SAT scores:** 83%. Scores (25/75 percentile): Verbal: 440-580, Math: 440-580, Combined: 880-1160. **First-year students submitting ACT scores:** 45%. Scores (25/75 percentile): English: 12-23, Math: 16-23, Composite: 15-23.

ACADEMICS
Year founded: 1892. **Academic calendar:** Semester. **Degrees offered:** associate, bachelor's. **Most popular majors:** 21% Christian studies, 15% education, 10% business administration and management, 5% mass communication/media studies, 4% youth ministry. **Major fields of study:** biological and biomedical sciences; business, management, marketing, and related support services; communication, journalism, and related programs; education; English language and literature/letters; health professions and related clinical sciences; history; mathematics and statistics; multi/interdisciplinary studies; parks, recreation, leisure, and fitness studies; philosophy and religious studies; psychology; theology and religious vocations; visual and performing arts. **Areas of required coursework:** arts/fine arts, humanities, computer literacy, mathematics, English (including composition), foreign languages, sciences (biological or physical), history, social science. **Pre-professional programs:** pre-law, pre-dentistry, pre-medicine, pre-theology, pre-pharmacy. **Special academic programs (% participation):** double major, dual enrollment (1%), English as a Second Language (ESL), honors program (3%), independent study (10%), internships (26%), study abroad, teacher certificate program (14%). **Teacher certification offered in:** early childhood, elementary, middle/junior high. **Reserve Officers Training Corps (ROTC):** Army ROTC: Offered at cooperating institution (Furman University).

Faculty and instruction (2005-2006): Total instructional faculty: 75 full-time, 53 part-time (55% men; 45% women; 4% minorities). Full-time faculty with Ph.D. or other terminal degree: 97%. Student/faculty ratio: 19/1. Classes of fewer than 20 students: 65%; of 20 to 49 students: 35%; of 50 or more students: 1%. Advanced Placement and International Baccalaureate credit: AP tests may be used for: Credit and/or placement. Scores accepted: 3, 4, 5. International Baccalaureate exams may be used for: Credit and/or placement. Freshmen returning for sophomore year: 71%. Graduation rates: Four-year: 24%; five-year: 41%; six-year: 42%.

COSTS AND FINANCIAL AID
Financial aid office: (864) 977-7058.

CAMPUS LIFE AND EXTRACURRICULAR ACTIVITIES
Campus housing available: women's dorms, men's dorms, special housing for disabled students. Students who live in college-owned, operated, or affiliated housing: 66%. Student employment: During the 2005-2006 academic year, 6% of undergraduates worked on campus. Average per-year earnings: $3,150. Activities include: choral groups, concert band, drama/theater, jazz band, literary magazine, marching band, music ensembles, pep band, radio station, student government, student newspaper, television station, yearbook. Number of fraternities: 0; sororities: 0. Average proportion of students who stay on campus on weekends: 30%. Sports program (2005-2006): Member of NCAA II. *Men's intercollegiate varsity sports:* baseball, basketball, cross-country, football, golf, soccer, tennis. *Women's intercollegiate varsity sports:* basketball, cross-country, soccer, softball, tennis, volleyball.

SERVICES AND FACILITIES
Basic services: nonremedial tutoring, placement service, health service, health insurance. Remedial assistance: reading, math, writing, study skills. Counseling services: career, military, personal, veteran student, academic, psychological, religious. For learning-disabled students: School does not offer a structured program with separate admission and additional fees. Services include: remedial math, remedial English, remedial reading, untimed tests, note-taking services, oral tests, extended time for tests, tutors. Information technology resources: Students are not required to lease or own a computer. Number of campus computers available to all students: 60. School has a wireless network. Approximate number of users that can be accommodated: 100. Proportion of college-owned housing units wired for high-speed internet access: 95%. Campus safety: Security services offered: 24-hour foot-and-vehicle patrols, late-night transport/escort service, 24-hour emergency telephones, lighted pathways/sidewalks, controlled dormitory access (key, security card, etc).

TRANSFER AND INTERNATIONAL STUDENTS
Transfer students: May apply for admission for the following academic terms: Fall, Spring, Summer. Applicants need a minimum number of credits to apply. For fall 2005: Transfer applications received: 192. Transfer applicants offered admission: 100. Transfer applicants enrolled: 95. International students: Number of foreign undergraduates: 19 (1% of student body). Minimum TOEFL score required: 500 (paper); 174 (computer). Average TOEFL score: 500 (paper).

Presbyterian College

- ■ **Address:** 503 S. Broad Street, Clinton, SC 29325
- ■ **Website:** http://www.presby.edu
- ■ **Private; Religious affiliation:** Presbyterian (U.S.A.)
- ■ **Enrollment:** 1,138 full-time; 58 part-time

KEY STATS
- ✔ **U.S News College Ranking:** third tier, Liberal Arts Colleges
- ✔ **SAT Score (25th/75th percentile):** 1030-1240
- ✔ **Tuition:** 2006-2007: $24,626

Selectivity: Selective	Room/board: $7,246
Acceptance rate: 76%	Average debt: $19,998
Student/faculty ratio: 12/1	Proportion who borrowed: 64%

UNDERGRADUATE STUDENT BODY STATS
2005-2006 enrollment: 1,138 full-time; 58 part-time. Men: 48%; women: 52%. Ethnic makeup: African American: 5%; Asian American: 1%; Hispanic:

1%; White: 93%. Religious preference: Roman Catholic: 6%; Protestant: 57%; No preference: 6%; Presbyterian (U.S.A.): 31%.

ADMISSIONS FACTS AND FIGURES
Phone: (864) 833-8230. Email: admissions@presby.edu. Website: http://www.presby.edu. Application deadlines for fall 2007: Regular decision: Rolling. Early decision: Send application by: December 5; Decision sent by: N/A. Early action: Not offered. Admission can be deferred. Application fee: $30. Common application is accepted. To apply online, go to: http://apply-web.com/apply/pc/indexa.html. Admissions requirements/recommendations: High school units required (recommended): English: 4; Mathematics: 3; Science: 2; Foreign language: 2; History: 2; Academic electives: 2; Total units: 17. Tests: The college uses SAT or ACT scores in admissions decisions. Either SAT or ACT required. For admission to the fall 2007 entering class, the school will accept: ACT with writing, ACT without writing. Campus visit: Recommended. Admissions interview: Recommended. Off-campus interview: Not available. Factors that count in admissions decisions: *Academic:* Secondary school record: Important. Class rank: Important. Letters of recommendation: Considered. Standardized test scores: Important. Essay: Important. *Nonacademic:* Interview: Considered. Extracurricular activities: Considered. Talent/ability: Considered. Character/personal qualities: Considered. Alumni/ae relationship: Considered. Geographical residence: Not considered. State residency: Not considered. Religious affiliation/commitment: Not considered. Minority status: Not considered. Volunteer work: Not considered. Work experience: Not considered. Other schools with the greatest overlap in applicants: Clemson University; College of Charleston; Furman University; University of South Carolina–Columbia; Wofford College. Admissions statistics for the fall 2005 entering class: Total applicants: 1,110. Total accepted: 846. Freshmen enrolled: 313; 33% were from out of state. Overall acceptance rate: 76%. Early-decision acceptance rate: 91%. Non-early acceptance rate: 75%. Credentials of fall 2005 freshmen: 31% ranked in the top 10 percent of their high school class; 62% were in the top 25 percent, and 87% were in the top half. (Proportion submitting class standing: 83%.) Average high school grade point average: 3.3. First-year students who submitted SAT scores: 96%. Scores (25/75 percentile): Verbal: 510-620, Math: 520-620, Combined: 1030-1240. First-year students submitting ACT scores: 50%. Scores (25/75 percentile): English: N/A, Math: N/A, Composite: 21-26.

ACADEMICS
Year founded: 1880. Academic calendar: Semester. Degrees offered: bachelor's. Most popular majors: 22% business, management, marketing, and related support services, 14% biological and biomedical sciences, 12% psychology, 11% education, 10% social sciences. Major fields of study: biological and biomedical sciences; computer and information sciences and support services; education; English language and literature/letters; foreign languages, literatures, and linguistics; mathematics and statistics; philosophy and religious studies; physical sciences; psychology; social sciences; theology and religious vocations; visual and performing arts. Areas of required coursework: arts/fine arts, humanities, mathematics, English (including composition), philosophy, foreign languages, sciences (biological or physical), history, social science. Pre-professional programs: pre-law, pre-dentistry, pre-medicine, pre-theology, pre-veterinary science, pre-pharmacy, other. Special academic programs (% participation): accelerated program, double major (12%), honors program (9%), independent study (16%), internships (20%), study abroad (14%), teacher certificate program (9%). Teacher certification offered in: early childhood, special education, middle/junior high, secondary. Reserve Officers Training Corps (ROTC): Army ROTC: Offered on campus. Faculty and instruction (2005-2006): Total instructional faculty: 83 full-time, 29 part-time (68% men; 32% women; 5% minorities). Full-time faculty with Ph.D. or other terminal degree: 94%. Student/faculty ratio: 12/1. Classes of fewer than 20 students: 67%; of 20 to 49 students: 33%; of 50 or more students: 0%. Advanced Placement and International Baccalaureate credit: AP tests may be used for: Credit and/or placement. Scores accepted: 3, 4, 5. International Baccalaureate exams may be used for: Credit only. Freshmen returning for sophomore year: 84%. Graduation rates: Four-year: 62%; five-year: 72%; six-year: 73%. Graduate study: 30% of students pursue further study immediately upon graduation. Fields in which graduates pursue further study: Master of Business Administration (MBA), 1%; law, 10%; medicine, 8%; dentistry, 2%; theology (or the seminary), 10%; education, 15%; arts and sciences, 5%.

COSTS AND FINANCIAL AID
Financial aid office: (864) 833-8289. Expenses (2006-2007): Tuition and fees 2006-2007: $24,626; room/board: $7,246. Estimated books and supplies: $1,110; transportation: $1,390; personal expenses: $2,774. Financial aid:

Priority filing date for institution's financial aid form: March 15. In 2005-2006, 73% of undergraduates applied for financial aid. Of those, 61% were determined to have financial need; 30% had their need fully met. Average financial aid package (proportion receiving): $21,609 (61%). Average amount of gift aid, such as scholarships or grants (proportion receiving): N/A (61%). Average amount of self-help aid, such as work study or loans (proportion receiving): N/A (36%). Among students who received need-based aid, the average percentage of need met: 91%. Among students who received aid based on merit, the average award (and the proportion receiving): $8,614 (32%). The average athletic scholarship (and the proportion receiving): $7,145 (24%). Average amount of debt of borrowers graduating in 2005: $19,998. Proportion who borrowed: 64%.

CAMPUS LIFE AND EXTRACURRICULAR ACTIVITIES

Campus housing available (% using): coed dorms (20%), women's dorms (28%), men's dorms (33%), fraternity housing (2%), apartment for single students (14%), special housing for international students (3%). Students who live in college-owned, operated, or affiliated housing: 92%. **Clubs and organizations:** Number of student organizations: 45. Activities include: choral groups, concert band, dance, drama/theater, jazz band, literary magazine, music ensembles, musical theater, opera, pep band, radio station, student government, student newspaper, symphony orchestra, yearbook. Number of fraternities: 9; sororities: 3. Proportion of men in fraternities: 44%; of women in sororities: 36%. Average proportion of students who stay on campus on weekends: 75%. **Sports program (2005-2006):** Member of NCAA II. *Men's intercollegiate varsity sports:* baseball, basketball, cross-country, football, golf, lacrosse, soccer, tennis. *Women's intercollegiate varsity sports:* basketball, cross-country, golf, lacrosse, soccer, softball, tennis, volleyball.

SERVICES AND FACILITIES

Basic services: nonremedial tutoring, placement service, health service. **Remedial assistance:** writing. **Counseling services:** minority student, career, personal, academic, psychological, religious. **For learning-disabled students:** School does not offer a structured program with separate admission and additional fees. Total undergraduates in learning-disabled program or receiving services: 104. Services include: remedial English, tape recorders, diagnostic testing service, oral tests, learning center, extended time for tests, tutors. **Library:** Number of titles: 154,730; number of current serial subscriptions: 684. **Information technology resources:** Students are not required to lease or own a computer. Number of campus computers available to all students: 120. School has a wireless network. Approximate number of users that can be accommodated: 500. Proportion of college-owned housing units wired for high-speed internet access: 99%. **Campus safety:** Security services offered: 24-hour foot-and-vehicle patrols, lighted pathways/sidewalks, controlled dormitory access (key, security card, etc).

TRANSFER AND INTERNATIONAL STUDENTS

Transfer students: May apply for admission for the following academic terms: Fall, Spring, Summer. Applicants need a minimum number of credits to apply. For fall 2005: Transfer applications received: 36. Transfer applicants offered admission: 24. Transfer applicants enrolled: 14. **International students:** Number of foreign undergraduates: 0. Number of countries represented: 7. Minimum TOEFL score required: 550 (paper). Average TOEFL score: 580 (paper).

South Carolina State University

- Address: 300 College Street NE, Orangeburg, SC 29117
- Website: http://www.scsu.edu
- Public
- Enrollment: 3,560 full-time; 328 part-time

KEY STATS

✔ **U.S News College Ranking:** fourth tier, National Universities
✔ **SAT Score (25th/75th percentile):** 780-940
✔ **Tuition:** 2006-2007: $3,639 in state, $7,161 out of state

Selectivity: Less selective	**Room/board:** $2,559
Acceptance rate: 69%	**Average debt:** N/A
Student/faculty ratio: N/A	**Proportion who borrowed:** N/A

UNDERGRADUATE STUDENT BODY STATS

2005-2006 enrollment: 3,560 full-time; 328 part-time. Men: 42%; women: 58%. **Ethnic makeup:** African American: 98%; White: 1%.

ADMISSIONS FACTS AND FIGURES

Phone: (803) 536-7185. **Email:** admissions@scsu.edu. **Website:** http://www.scsu.edu. **Application deadlines for fall 2007:** Regular decision: July 1; decision sent by September 30. Early decision: Not offered. Early action: Not offered. Admission can be deferred. **Application fee:** $25. Common application is accepted. **Admissions requirements/recommendations:** High school units required (recommended): English: 4; Mathematics: 3; Science: 3; Foreign language: 2; Social studies: 3; Academic electives: 4; Total units: 20. Tests: The college uses SAT or ACT scores in admissions decisions. Neither SAT nor ACT required. Campus visit: Recommended. Admissions interview: Recommended. Off-campus interview: May be arranged. **Factors that count in admissions decisions:** *Academic:* Secondary school record: Very important. Class rank: Considered. Letters of recommendation: Considered. Standardized test scores: Very important. *Nonacademic:* Interview: Considered. Extracurricular activities: Considered. Talent/ability: Considered. Character/personal qualities: Considered. Alumni/ae relationship: Considered. Geographical residence: Considered. State residency: Considered. Religious affiliation/commitment: Not considered. Minority status: Not considered. Volunteer work: Not considered. Work experience: Not considered. **Admissions statistics for the fall 2005 entering class:** Total applicants: 4,277. Total accepted: 2,963. Freshmen enrolled: 1,013; 17% were from out of state. Overall acceptance rate: 69%. **Credentials of fall 2005 freshmen:** 8% ranked in the top 10 percent of their high school class; 23% were in the top 25 percent, and 59% were in the top half. (Proportion submitting class standing: 84%.) **First-year students who submitted SAT scores:** 61%. Scores (25/75 percentile): Verbal: 390-470, Math: 390-470, Combined: 780-940. **First-year students submitting ACT scores:** 39%. Scores (25/75 percentile): English: N/A, Math: N/A, Composite: 15-18.

ACADEMICS

Year founded: 1896. **Academic calendar:** Semester. **Degrees offered:** bachelor's, post-bachelor's certificate, master's, post-master's certificate, doctorate. **Most popular majors:** 12% family and consumer sciences/human sciences, 10% business administration and management, 7% biology/biological sciences, 7% early childhood education and teaching, 6% computer and information sciences. **Major fields of study:** agriculture, agriculture operations, and related sciences; biological and biomedical sciences; business, management, marketing, and related support services; computer and information sciences and support services; education; engineering; engineering technologies/technicians; English language and literature/letters; family and consumer sciences/human sciences; foreign languages, literatures, and linguistics; health professions and related clinical sciences; history; mathematics and statistics; parks, recreation, leisure, and fitness studies; physical sciences; psychology; public administration and social service professions; security and protective services; social sciences; visual and performing arts. **Areas of required coursework:** arts/fine arts, humanities, computer literacy, mathematics, English (including composition), philosophy, foreign languages, sciences (biological or physical), history, social science. **Pre-professional programs:** pre-law, pre-dentistry, pre-medicine, pre-veterinary science, pre-optometry, other. **Special academic programs (% participation):** accelerated program, cooperative (work-study plan) program (20%), cross-registration (2%), distance learning (8%), double major (1%), dual enrollment (8%), honors program (2%), independent study (8%), internships (2%), teacher certificate program (8%). **Teacher certification offered in:** early childhood, special education, elementary, secondary. **Reserve Officers Training Corps (ROTC):** Army ROTC: Offered on campus; Navy ROTC: Offered on campus. **Faculty and instruction (2005-2006):** Total instructional faculty: N/A. Classes of fewer than 20 students: 34%; of 20 to 49 students: 65%; of 50 or more students: 0%. **Advanced Placement and International Baccalaureate credit:** AP tests may be used for: Credit and/or placement. International Baccalaureate exams may be used for: Credit and/or placement. **Freshmen returning for sophomore year:** 73%. **Graduation rates:** Four-year: 32%; five-year: 46%; six-year: 49%. **Graduate study:** 20% of students pursue further study immediately upon graduation; 50% within one year; 30% within five years. Fields in which graduates pursue further study: Master of Business Administration (MBA), 20%; law, 10%; medicine, 10%; dentistry, 5%; engineering, 10%; education, 40%; arts and sciences, 5%.

COSTS AND FINANCIAL AID

Financial aid office: (803) 536-7067. **Expenses (2006-2007):** Tuition and fees 2006-2007: $3,639 in state, $7,161 out of state; room/board: $2,559. **Financial aid:** Priority filing date for institution's financial aid form: May 1.

CAMPUS LIFE AND EXTRACURRICULAR ACTIVITIES

Campus housing available: women's dorms, men's dorms, apartment for single students. Students who live in college-owned, operated, or affiliated housing: 85%. **Student employment:** During the 2005-2006 academic year, 3% of undergraduates worked on campus. Average per-year earnings: $1,500. Activities include: choral groups, concert band, dance, drama/theater, jazz band, literary magazine, marching band, music ensembles, pep band, radio station, student government, student newspaper, yearbook. Number of fraternities: 4; sororities: 4. Proportion of men in fraternities: 20%; of women in sororities: 22%. Average proportion of students who stay on campus on weekends: 80%. **Sports program (2005-2006):** Member of NCAA I. *Men's intercollegiate varsity sports:* basketball, cross-country, football, golf, tennis, track and field (indoor), track and field (outdoor). *Women's intercollegiate varsity sports:* basketball, bowling, cross-country, golf, soccer, softball, tennis, track and field (indoor), track and field (outdoor), volleyball.

SERVICES AND FACILITIES

Basic services: placement service, health service. **Counseling services:** minority student, career, military, personal, veteran student, academic. **For learning-disabled students:** School does not offer a structured program with separate admission and additional fees. **Information technology resources:** Students are not required to lease or own a computer. Number of campus computers available to all students: 600. School has a wireless network. Proportion of college-owned housing units wired for high-speed internet access: 100%. **Campus safety:** Security services offered: 24-hour foot-and-vehicle patrols, 24-hour emergency telephones, lighted pathways/sidewalks, controlled dormitory access (key, security card, etc).

TRANSFER AND INTERNATIONAL STUDENTS

Transfer students: May apply for admission for the following academic terms: Fall, Spring, Summer. Applicants do not need a minimum number of credits to apply. For fall 2005: Transfer applications received: 247. Transfer applicants offered admission: 233. Transfer applicants enrolled: 233. **International students:** Number of foreign undergraduates: 0. Minimum TOEFL score required: 500 (paper).

Southern Wesleyan University

- **Address:** PO Box 1020, SWU, Wesleyan Drive, Central, SC 29630
- **Website:** http://www.swu.edu
- **Private; Religious affiliation:** Wesleyan Church
- **Enrollment:** 1,909 full-time; 86 part-time

KEY STATS

✔ **U.S News College Ranking:** third tier, Universities–Master's (South)
✔ **SAT Score (25th/75th percentile):** 925-1140
✔ **Tuition:** 2006-2007: $16,150

Selectivity: Selective	**Room/board:** $5,800
Acceptance rate: 66%	**Average debt:** $24,032
Student/faculty ratio: 18/1	**Proportion who borrowed:** 99%

UNDERGRADUATE STUDENT BODY STATS

2005-2006 enrollment: 1,909 full-time; 86 part-time. Men: 34%; women: 66%. **Ethnic makeup:** African American: 37%; American-Indian: 1%; Asian American: 1%; Hispanic: 1%; White: 60%; International: 1%. **Religious preference:** Roman Catholic: 3%; Protestant: 66%; Unknown: 21%; Wesleyan Church: 10%.

ADMISSIONS FACTS AND FIGURES

Phone: (864) 644-5550. **Email:** admissions@swu.edu. **Website:** http://www.swu.edu. **Application deadlines for fall 2007:** Regular decision: August 11. Early decision: Not offered. Early action: Not offered. Admission can be deferred. **Application fee:** $25. Common application is not accepted. **Admissions requirements/recommendations:** High school units required (recommended): English: 4; Mathematics: 2; Science: 2; Social studies: 2; Total units: 10. Tests: The college uses SAT or ACT scores in admissions decisions. Either SAT or ACT required. For admission to the fall 2007

entering class, the school will accept: ACT with writing, ACT without writing. Campus visit: Recommended. Admissions interview: Neither required nor recommended. Off-campus interview: Not available. **Factors that count in admissions decisions: *Academic:*** Secondary school record: Very important. Class rank: Important. Letters of recommendation: Important. Standardized test scores: Important. Essay: Not considered. ***Nonacademic:*** Interview: Considered. Extracurricular activities: Considered. Talent/ability: Considered. Character/personal qualities: Considered. Alumni/ae relationship: Not considered. Geographical residence: Not considered. State residency: Not considered. Religious affiliation/commitment: Not considered. Minority status: Not considered. Volunteer work: Considered. Work experience: Considered. **Other schools with the greatest overlap in applicants:** Anderson University; Charleston Southern University; Clemson University; North Greenville University; University of South Carolina–Columbia. **Admissions statistics for the fall 2005 entering class:** Total applicants: 401. Total accepted: 264. Freshmen enrolled: 138; 38% were from out of state. Overall acceptance rate: 66%. **Credentials of fall 2005 freshmen:** 12% ranked in the top 10 percent of their high school class; 34% were in the top 25 percent, and 75% were in the top half. (Proportion submitting class standing: 85%.) **Average high school grade point average:** 3.4. **First-year students who submitted SAT scores:** 83%. Scores (25/75 percentile): Verbal: 465-570, Math: 460-570, Combined: 925-1140. **First-year students submitting ACT scores:** 40%. Scores (25/75 percentile): English: N/A, Math: N/A, Composite: 17-23.

ACADEMICS

Year founded: 1906. **Academic calendar:** Semester. **Degrees offered:** associate, bachelor's, master's. **Most popular majors:** 68% business, management, marketing, and related support services, 24% education. **Major fields of study:** biological and biomedical sciences; business, management, marketing, and related support services; communication, journalism, and related programs; computer and information sciences and support services; education; English language and literature/letters; health professions and related clinical sciences; history; mathematics and statistics; parks, recreation, leisure, and fitness studies; philosophy and religious studies; physical sciences; psychology; security and protective services; social sciences; visual and performing arts. **Areas of required coursework:** arts/fine arts, humanities, computer literacy, mathematics, English (including composition), philosophy, sciences (biological or physical), history, social science, other. **Pre-professional programs:** pre-dentistry, pre-medicine, pre-theology. **Special academic programs:** cross-registration, distance learning, double major, dual enrollment, English as a Second Language (ESL), honors program, independent study, internships, student-designed major, study abroad, teacher certificate program. **Teacher certification offered in:** early childhood, special education, elementary, secondary. **Cooperative education programs:** health professions. **Reserve Officers Training Corps (ROTC):** Army ROTC: Offered at cooperating institution (Clemson University); Air Force ROTC: Offered at cooperating institution (Clemson University). **Faculty and instruction (2005-2006):** Total instructional faculty: 50 full-time, 187 part-time (65% men; 35% women; 14% minorities). Full-time faculty with Ph.D. or other terminal degree: 76%. Student/faculty ratio: 18/1. Classes of fewer than 20 students: 85%; of 20 to 49 students: 15%; of 50 or more students: 0%. **Freshmen returning for sophomore year:** 65%. **Graduation rates:** Four-year: 35%; five-year: 49%; six-year: 42%. **Graduate study:** 24% of students pursue further study immediately upon graduation; 11% within one year; 32% within five years. Fields in which graduates pursue further study: Master of Business Administration (MBA), 50%; law, 3%; medicine, 1%; dentistry, 1%; theology (or the seminary), 6%; education, 25%; arts and sciences, 13%.

COSTS AND FINANCIAL AID

Financial aid office: (864) 644-5500. **Expenses (2006-2007):** Tuition and fees 2006-2007: $16,150; room/board: $5,800. Estimated books and supplies: $950; transportation: $800; personal expenses: $1,000. **Financial aid:** Priority filing date for institution's financial aid form: March 31; deadline: June 30. In 2005-2006, 85% of undergraduates applied for financial aid. Of those, 27% were determined to have financial need; 18% had their need fully met. Average financial aid package (proportion receiving): $9,649 (27%). Average amount of gift aid, such as scholarships or grants (proportion receiving): $6,873 (24%). Average amount of self-help aid, such as work study or loans (proportion receiving): $4,157 (23%). Average need-based loan (excluding PLUS or other private loans): $3,673. Among students who received need-based aid, the average percentage of need met: 65%. Among students who received aid based on merit, the average award (and the proportion receiving): $10,101 (5%). The average athletic scholarship (and the proportion receiving): $5,150 (2%). Average amount of debt of borrowers graduating in 2005: $24,032. Proportion who borrowed: 99%.

CAMPUS LIFE AND EXTRACURRICULAR ACTIVITIES

Campus housing available (% using): coed dorms (66%), women's dorms (6%), apartment for single students (28%). Students who live in college-owned, operated, or affiliated housing: 17%. **Clubs and organizations:** Number of student organizations: 14. Activities include: choral groups, concert band, drama/theater, jazz band, literary magazine, music ensembles, musical theater, student government, yearbook. Number of fraternities: 0; sororities: 0. Average proportion of students who stay on campus on weekends: 50%. **Sports program (2005-2006):** Member of NAIA. *Men's intercollegiate varsity sports:* baseball, basketball, cross-country, golf, soccer. *Women's intercollegiate varsity sports:* basketball, cross-country, soccer, softball, volleyball.

SERVICES AND FACILITIES

Basic services: nonremedial tutoring, health service. **Remedial assistance:** reading, math, writing, study skills. **Counseling services:** minority student, career, personal, academic, psychological, religious. **For learning-disabled students:** School does not offer a structured program with separate admission and additional fees. Total undergraduates in learning-disabled program or receiving services: 27. Services include: remedial math, remedial English, remedial reading, tape recorders, untimed tests, note-taking services, oral tests, learning center, readers, extended time for tests, tutors, early syllabus, priority registration, priority seating, substitution of courses, exams on tape or computer, other. **Library:** Number of titles: 103,860; number of current serial subscriptions: 530. **Information technology resources:** Students are not required to lease or own a computer. Number of campus computers available to all students: 256. School has a wireless network. Approximate number of users that can be accommodated: 600. Proportion of college-owned housing units wired for high-speed internet access: 100%. **Campus safety:** Security services offered: 24-hour foot-and-vehicle patrols, 24-hour emergency telephones, lighted pathways/sidewalks, controlled dormitory access (key, security card, etc).

TRANSFER AND INTERNATIONAL STUDENTS

Transfer students: May apply for admission for the following academic terms: Fall, Spring, Summer. Applicants need a minimum number of credits to apply. For fall 2005: Transfer applications received: 146. Transfer applicants offered admission: 93. Transfer applicants enrolled: 60. **International students:** Number of foreign undergraduates: 15 (1% of student body). Number of countries represented: 4. Minimum TOEFL score required: 500 (paper); 173 (computer).

University of South Carolina–Aiken

- **Address:** 471 University Parkway, Aiken, SC 29801
- **Website:** http://www.usca.edu
- **Public**
- **Enrollment:** 2,270 full-time; 880 part-time

KEY STATS

✔ **U.S News College Ranking:** 32, Comp. Coll.–Bachelor's (South)
✔ **SAT Score (25th/75th percentile):** 890-1090
✔ **Tuition:** 2006-2007: $6,590 in state, $13,170 out of state

Selectivity: Selective	Room/board: $5,580
Acceptance rate: 48%	Average debt: $13,963
Student/faculty ratio: 16/1	Proportion who borrowed: 80%

UNDERGRADUATE STUDENT BODY STATS

2005-2006 enrollment: 2,270 full-time; 880 part-time. Men: 33%; women: 67%. **Ethnic makeup:** African American: 26%; Asian American: 1%; Hispanic: 2%; White: 69%; International: 2%.

ADMISSIONS FACTS AND FIGURES

Phone: (803) 641-3366. **Email:** admit@sc.edu. **Website:** http://www.usca.edu. **Application deadlines for fall 2007:** Regular decision: August 1. Early decision: Not offered. Early action: Not offered. Admission can be deferred. **Application fee:** $35. Common application is not accepted. To apply online, go to: http://web.csd.sc.edu/app/ugrad_aiken/. **Admissions requirements/recommendations:** High school units required (recommended): English: 4; Mathematics: 4; Science: 3; Foreign language: 2; Social studies: 2; History: 1; Academic electives: 4; Total units: 21. Tests: The college uses SAT or ACT scores in admissions decisions. Either SAT or ACT

required. For admission to the fall 2007 entering class, the school will accept: ACT without writing. Campus visit: Recommended. Admissions interview: Neither required nor recommended. Off-campus interview: Not available. **Factors that count in admissions decisions:** *Academic:* Secondary school record: Very important. Class rank: Not considered. Letters of recommendation: Not considered. Standardized test scores: Very important. Essay: Not considered. *Nonacademic:* Interview: Not considered. Extracurricular activities: Not considered. Talent/ability: Not considered. Character/personal qualities: Not considered. Alumni/ae relationship: Not considered. Geographical residence: Not considered. State residency: Not considered. Religious affiliation/commitment: Not considered. Minority status: Not considered. Volunteer work: Not considered. Work experience: Not considered. **Other schools with the greatest overlap in applicants:** Clemson University; College of Charleston; Lander University; University of South Carolina–Columbia; Winthrop University. **Admissions statistics for the fall 2005 entering class:** Total applicants: 2,064. Total accepted: 982. Freshmen enrolled: 610; 9% were from out of state. Overall acceptance rate: 48%. **Credentials of fall 2005 freshmen:** 15% ranked in the top 10 percent of their high school class; 39% were in the top 25 percent, and 79% were in the top half. (Proportion submitting class standing: 95%.) **Average high school grade point average:** 3.5. **First-year students who submitted SAT scores:** 77%. Scores (25/75 percentile): Verbal: 440-540, Math: 450-550, Combined: 890-1090. **First-year students submitting ACT scores:** 23%. Scores (25/75 percentile): English: 16-22, Math: 17-22, Composite: 18-22.

ACADEMICS

Year founded: 1961. **Academic calendar:** Semester. **Degrees offered:** bachelor's, master's. **Most popular majors:** 28% business administration and management, 16% education, 10% social sciences, 8% nursing/registered nurse training (R.N., A.S.N., B.S.N., M.S.N.), 7% communication, journalism, and related programs. **Major fields of study:** biological and biomedical sciences; business, management, marketing, and related support services; communication, journalism, and related programs; education; English language and literature/letters; health professions and related clinical sciences; history; mathematics and statistics; multi/interdisciplinary studies; parks, recreation, leisure, and fitness studies; physical sciences; psychology; social sciences; visual and performing arts. **Areas of required coursework:** humanities, mathematics, English (including composition), foreign languages, sciences (biological or physical), history, social science, other. **Pre-professional programs:** pre-law, pre-dentistry, pre-medicine, pre-veterinary science, pre-pharmacy. **Special academic programs:** cooperative (work-study plan) program, distance learning, double major, dual enrollment, English as a Second Language (ESL), exchange student program (domestic), honors program, independent study, internships, liberal arts/career combination, student-designed major, study abroad, teacher certificate program. **Teacher certification offered in:** early childhood, special education, elementary, secondary. **Cooperative education programs:** art, business, computer science, engineering, humanities, natural science, social/behavioral science, technologies. **Faculty and instruction (2005-2006):** Total instructional faculty: 146 full-time, 107 part-time (49% men; 51% women; 14% minorities). Full-time faculty with Ph.D. or other terminal degree: 77%. Student/faculty ratio: 16/1. Classes of fewer than 20 students: 51%; of 20 to 49 students: 49%; of 50 or more students: 1%. **Advanced Placement and International Baccalaureate credit:** AP tests may be used for: Credit and/or placement. Scores accepted: 3, 4, 5. International Baccalaureate exams may be used for: Credit and/or placement. **Freshmen returning for sophomore year:** 67%. **Graduation rates:** Four-year: 21%; five-year: 39%; six-year: 41%.

COSTS AND FINANCIAL AID

Financial aid office: (803) 641-3476. **Expenses (2006-2007):** Tuition and fees 2006-2007: $6,590 in state, $13,170 out of state; room/board: $5,580. Estimated books and supplies: $1,080; transportation: $1,365; personal expenses: $1,670. **Financial aid:** Priority filing date for institution's financial aid form: March 15. Average amount of debt of borrowers graduating in 2005: $13,963. Proportion who borrowed: 80%.

CAMPUS LIFE AND EXTRACURRICULAR ACTIVITIES

Campus housing available: apartment for single students, special housing for disabled students. Students who live in college-owned, operated, or affiliated housing: 19%. **Student employment:** During the 2005-2006 academic year, 5% of undergraduates worked on campus. **Clubs and organizations:** Number of student organizations: 60. Activities include: choral groups, concert band, dance, drama/theater, literary magazine, music ensembles, pep band, student government, student newspaper, symphony orchestra. Number of fraternities: 5; sororities: 7. Average proportion of students who stay on campus on weekends: 50%. **Sports program (2005-2006):** Member of NCAA II. **Men's intercollegiate varsity sports:** baseball, basketball, golf, soccer, tennis. **Women's intercollegiate varsity sports:** basketball, cross-country, soccer, softball, tennis, volleyball.

SERVICES AND FACILITIES
Basic services: nonremedial tutoring, day care, health service. **Counseling services:** minority student, career, personal, academic, psychological. **For learning-disabled students:** School does not offer a structured program with separate admission and additional fees. Total undergraduates in learning-disabled program or receiving services: 107. Services include: reading machines, tape recorders, videotaped classes, note-taking services, oral tests, learning center, readers, extended time for tests, tutors, priority registration, priority seating, texts on tape, typist/scribe, exams on tape or computer, other testing accomodations. **Library:** Number of titles: 213,173; number of current serial subscriptions: 724. **Information technology resources:** Students are not required to lease or own a computer. Number of campus computers available to all students: 784. School has a wireless network. Approximate number of users that can be accommodated: 700. Proportion of college-owned housing units wired for high-speed internet access: 100%. **Campus safety:** Security services offered: 24-hour foot-and-vehicle patrols, late-night transport/escort service, 24-hour emergency telephones, lighted pathways/sidewalks, controlled dormitory access (key, security card, etc).

TRANSFER AND INTERNATIONAL STUDENTS
Transfer students: May apply for admission for the following academic terms: Fall, Spring, Summer. Applicants need a minimum number of credits to apply. For fall 2005: Transfer applications received: 674. Transfer applicants offered admission: 316. Transfer applicants enrolled: 250. **International students:** Number of foreign undergraduates: 45 (2% of student body). Number of countries represented: 19. Minimum TOEFL score required: 550 (paper); 213 (computer).

University of South Carolina–Columbia

- **Address:** Columbia, SC 29208
- **Website:** http://www.sc.edu
- **Public**
- **Enrollment:** 16,399 full-time; 1,963 part-time

KEY STATS
- ✔ U.S News College Ranking: 112, National Universities
- ✔ SAT Score (25th/75th percentile): 1060-1270
- ✔ Tuition: 2006-2007: $0 in state, $0 out of state
  - Selectivity: More selective   Room/board: $6,520
  - Acceptance rate: 68%   Average debt: $18,699
  - Student/faculty ratio: 18/1   Proportion who borrowed: 50%

UNDERGRADUATE STUDENT BODY STATS
2005-2006 enrollment: 16,399 full-time; 1,963 part-time. Men: 46%; women: 54%. **Ethnic makeup:** African American: 14%; Asian American: 3%; Hispanic: 2%; White: 80%; International: 1%.

ADMISSIONS FACTS AND FIGURES
Phone: (803) 777-7700. **Email:** admissions-ugrad@sc.edu. **Website:** http://www.sc.edu. **Application deadlines for fall 2007:** Regular decision: December 1. Early decision: Not offered. Early action: Not offered. Admission cannot be deferred. **Application fee:** $50. Common application is not accepted. **To apply online, go to:** http://www.applyweb.com/apply/uscf/. **Admissions requirements/recommendations:** High school units required (recommended): English: 4; Mathematics: 3; Science: 3; Foreign language: 2; Social studies: 2; History: 1; Academic electives: 4; Total units: 20. **Tests:** The college uses SAT or ACT scores in admissions decisions. Either SAT or ACT required. For admission to the fall 2007 entering class, the school will accept: ACT with writing. Campus visit: Recommended. Admissions interview: Neither required nor recommended. Off-campus interview: Not available. **Factors that count in admissions decisions:** *Academic:* Secondary school record: Very important. Class rank: Considered. Letters of recommendation: Considered. Standardized test scores: Very important. Essay: Considered. *Nonacademic:* Interview: Not considered. Extracurricular activities: Considered. Talent/ability: Considered. Character/personal qualities: Considered. Alumni/ae relationship: Considered. Geographical residence: Not considered. State residency: Considered. Religious affiliation/commit-

ment: Not considered. Minority status: Considered. Volunteer work: Considered. Work experience: Considered. **Other schools with the greatest overlap in applicants:** Clemson University; College of Charleston; Furman University; University of Georgia; University of North Carolina–Chapel Hill. **Admissions statistics for the fall 2005 entering class:** Total applicants: 13,023. Total accepted: 8,812. Freshmen enrolled: 3,734; 32% were from out of state. Overall acceptance rate: 68%. **Size of waiting list:** 674 applicants; enrolled from waiting list: 23. **Credentials of fall 2005 freshmen:** 26% ranked in the top 10 percent of their high school class; 60% were in the top 25 percent, and 91% were in the top half. (Proportion submitting class standing: 85%.) **Average high school grade point average:** 3.8. **First-year students who submitted SAT scores:** 82%. Scores (25/75 percentile): Verbal: 520-630, Math: 540-640, Combined: 1060-1270. **First-year students submitting ACT scores:** 18%. Scores (25/75 percentile): English: N/A, Math: N/A, Composite: 22-27.

ACADEMICS
Year founded: 1801. **Academic calendar:** Semester. **Degrees offered:** associate, bachelor's, post-bachelor's certificate, master's, post-master's certificate, first professional, doctorate. **Most popular majors:** 8% business administration, management, and operations, 7% experimental psychology, 7% public relations, advertising, and applied communication , 5% criminal justice and corrections, 5% health and physical education/fitness. **Major fields of study:** area, ethnic, cultural, and gender studies; biological and biomedical sciences; business, management, marketing, and related support services; communication, journalism, and related programs; computer and information sciences and support services; education; engineering; English language and literature/letters; foreign languages, literatures, and linguistics; health professions and related clinical sciences; history; liberal arts and sciences studies, and humanities; mathematics and statistics; parks, recreation, leisure, and fitness studies; philosophy and religious studies; physical sciences; psychology; security and protective services; social sciences; visual and performing arts. **Areas of required coursework:** arts/fine arts, humanities, computer literacy, mathematics, English (including composition), philosophy, foreign languages, sciences (biological or physical), history, social science. **Pre-professional programs:** pre-law, pre-dentistry, pre-medicine, pre-theology, other. **Special academic programs:** accelerated program, cooperative (work-study plan) program, cross-registration, distance learning, double major, dual enrollment, English as a Second Language (ESL), exchange student program (domestic), external degree program, honors program, independent study, internships, liberal arts/career combination, student-designed major, study abroad, teacher certificate program, weekend college, other. **Teacher certification offered in:** early childhood, special education, elementary, middle/junior high, secondary, bilingual/bicultural. **Cooperative education programs:** art, business, computer science, education, engineering, health professions, humanities, natural science, social/behavioral science. **Reserve Officers Training Corps (ROTC):** Army ROTC: Offered on campus; Navy ROTC: Offered on campus; Air Force ROTC: Offered on campus. **Faculty and instruction (2005-2006):** Total instructional faculty: 1,166 full-time, 386 part-time (64% men; 36% women; 11% minorities). Full-time faculty with Ph.D. or other terminal degree: 86%. Student/faculty ratio: 18/1. Classes of fewer than 20 students: 38%; of 20 to 49 students: 51%; of 50 or more students: 11%. **Advanced Placement and International Baccalaureate credit:** AP tests may be used for: Credit only. Scores accepted: 3. International Baccalaureate exams may be used for: Credit only. **Freshmen returning for sophomore year:** 84%. **Graduation rates:** Four-year: 41%; five-year: 61%; six-year: 65%.

COSTS AND FINANCIAL AID
Financial aid office: (803) 777-8134. **Expenses (2006-2007):** Tuition and fees 2006-2007: $0 in state, $0 out of state; room/board: $6,520. Estimated books and supplies: $838. **Financial aid:** Priority filing date for institution's financial aid form: April 1. In 2005-2006, 63% of undergraduates applied for financial aid. Of those, 49% were determined to have financial need; 24% had their need fully met. Average financial aid package (proportion receiving): $9,501 (49%). Average amount of gift aid, such as scholarships or grants (proportion receiving): $3,426 (26%). Average amount of self-help aid, such as work study or loans (proportion receiving): $3,634 (41%). Average need-based loan (excluding PLUS or other private loans): $3,486. Among students who received need-based aid, the average percentage of need met: 71%. Among students who received aid based on merit, the average award (and the proportion receiving): $5,950 (32%). The average athletic scholarship (and the proportion receiving): $9,669 (3%). Average amount of debt of borrowers graduating in 2005: $18,699. Proportion who borrowed: 50%.

CAMPUS LIFE AND EXTRACURRICULAR ACTIVITIES

Campus housing available (% using): coed dorms (29%), women's dorms (8%), men's dorms (7%), sorority housing (5%), fraternity housing (6%), apartments for married students (3%), apartment for single students (27%), special housing for disabled students (0%), special housing for international students (0%), other housing options (15%). Students who live in college-owned, operated, or affiliated housing: 40%. **Student employment:** During the 2005-2006 academic year, 16% of undergraduates worked on campus. Average per-year earnings: $2,858. **Clubs and organizations:** Number of student organizations: 300. Activities include: choral groups, concert band, dance, drama/theater, jazz band, literary magazine, marching band, music ensembles, musical theater, opera, pep band, radio station, student government, student newspaper, symphony orchestra. Number of fraternities: 18; sororities: 14. Proportion of men in fraternities: 14%; of women in sororities: 15%. Average proportion of students who stay on campus on weekends: 70%. **Sports program (2005-2006):** Member of NCAA I. *Men's intercollegiate varsity sports:* baseball, basketball, football, golf, soccer, swimming and diving, tennis, track and field (indoor), track and field (outdoor). *Women's intercollegiate varsity sports:* basketball, cross-country, equestrian sports, golf, soccer, softball, swimming and diving, tennis, track and field (indoor), track and field (outdoor), volleyball.

SERVICES AND FACILITIES

Basic services: nonremedial tutoring, placement service, day care, health service, health insurance. **Remedial assistance:** reading, math, writing, study skills. **Counseling services:** minority student, military, personal, veteran student, older student, psychological. **For learning-disabled students:** School does not offer a structured program with separate admission and additional fees. Total undergraduates in learning-disabled program or receiving services: 327. Services include: reading machines, tape recorders, untimed tests, note-taking services, readers, extended time for tests. **Library:** Number of titles: 3,498,445; number of current serial subscriptions: 23,740.
Information technology resources: Students are not required to lease or own a computer. Number of campus computers available to all students: 2,800. School has a wireless network. Approximate number of users that can be accommodated: 800. Proportion of college-owned housing units wired for high-speed internet access: 100%. **Campus safety:** Security services offered: 24-hour foot-and-vehicle patrols, late-night transport/escort service, 24-hour emergency telephones, lighted pathways/sidewalks, controlled dormitory access (key, security card, etc.).

TRANSFER AND INTERNATIONAL STUDENTS

Transfer students: May apply for admission for the following academic terms: Fall, Spring, Summer. Applicants need a minimum number of credits to apply. For fall 2005: Transfer applications received: 3,454. Transfer applicants offered admission: 1,994. Transfer applicants enrolled: 944. **International students:** Number of foreign undergraduates: 191 (1% of student body). Number of countries represented: 67. Minimum TOEFL score required: 550 (paper); 213 (computer).

University of South Carolina—Upstate

- **Address:** 800 University Way, Spartanburg, SC 29303
- **Website:** http://www.uscupstate.edu/
- **Public**
- **Enrollment:** 3,564 full-time; 845 part-time

KEY STATS

- ✔ **U.S News College Ranking:** 38, Comp. Coll.–Bachelor's (South)
- ✔ **SAT Score (25th/75th percentile):** 890-1090
- ✔ **Tuition:** 2006-2007: $7,670 in state, $15,108 out of state

Selectivity: Selective	**Room/board:** $5,940
Acceptance rate: 33%	**Average debt:** $17,238
Student/faculty ratio: 17/1	**Proportion who borrowed:** 67%

UNDERGRADUATE STUDENT BODY STATS

2005-2006 enrollment: 3,564 full-time; 845 part-time. Men: 34%; women: 66%. **Ethnic makeup:** African American: 27%; American-Indian: 1%; Asian American: 3%; Hispanic: 2%; White: 66%; International: 2%. **Religious preference:** Roman Catholic: 6%; Protestant: 80%; Hindu: 1%; Buddhist: 1%; No preference: 7%; Other: 5%.

ADMISSIONS FACTS AND FIGURES

Phone: (864) 503-5246. **Email:** admissions@uscupstate.edu. **Website:** http://www.uscupstate.edu/. **Application deadlines for fall 2007:** Regular decision: Rolling; decision sent by May 1. Early decision: Not offered. Early action: Not offered. Admission can be deferred. **Application fee:** $40. Common application is accepted. **To apply online, go to:** http://www.uscs.edu/admn/admis/appl.html. **Admissions requirements/recommendations:** High school units required (recommended): English: 4; Mathematics: 3 (4); Science: 3; Foreign language: 2 (3); Social studies: 2; History: 1; Academic electives: 4; Total units: 20. Tests: The college uses SAT or ACT scores in admissions decisions. Either SAT or ACT required. For admission to the fall 2007 entering class, the school will accept: ACT with writing, ACT without writing. Campus visit: Recommended. Admissions interview: Recommended. Off-campus interview: May be arranged. **Factors that count in admissions decisions:** *Academic:* Secondary school record: Very important. Class rank: Important. Letters of recommendation: Considered. Standardized test scores: Very important. Essay: Considered. *Nonacademic:* Interview: Considered. Extracurricular activities: Considered. Talent/ability: Not considered. Character/personal qualities: Not considered. Alumni/ae relationship: Not considered. Geographical residence: Not considered. State residency: Not considered. Religious affiliation/commitment: Not considered. Minority status: Not considered. Volunteer work: Not considered. Work experience: Not considered. **Other schools with the greatest overlap in applicants:** Coastal Carolina University; College of Charleston; University of South Carolina–Columbia; Winthrop University. **Admissions statistics for the fall 2005 entering class:** Total applicants: 2,296. Total accepted: 749. Freshmen enrolled: 749; Overall acceptance rate: 33%. **Credentials of fall 2005 freshmen:** 13% ranked in the top 10 percent of their high school class; 38% were in the top 25 percent, and 71% were in the top half. (Proportion submitting class standing: 100%.) **Average high school grade point average:** 3.5. **First-year students who submitted SAT scores:** 87%. Scores (25/75 percentile): Verbal: 440-540, Math: 450-550, Combined: 890-1090. **First-year students submitting ACT scores:** 48%. Scores (25/75 percentile): English: 17-22, Math: 17-21, Composite: 18-22.

ACADEMICS

Year founded: 1967. **Academic calendar:** Semester. **Degrees offered:** bachelor's, master's. **Most popular majors:** 19% nursing/registered nurse training (R.N., A.S.N., B.S.N., M.S.N.), 14% business administration and management, 11% liberal arts and sciences/liberal studies, 9% computer and information sciences, 6% elementary education and teaching. **Major fields of study:** biological and biomedical sciences; business, management, marketing, and related support services; communication, journalism, and related programs; computer and information sciences and support services; education; English language and literature/letters; foreign languages, literatures, and linguistics; health professions and related clinical sciences; history; liberal arts and sciences studies, and humanities; mathematics and statistics; multi/interdisciplinary studies; physical sciences; psychology; security and protective services; social sciences; visual and performing arts. **Areas of required coursework:** arts/fine arts, humanities, computer literacy, mathematics, English (including composition), foreign languages, sciences (biological or physical), history, social science, other. **Pre-professional programs:** pre-law, pre-dentistry, pre-medicine, pre-veterinary science, pre-optometry, pre-pharmacy, other. **Special academic programs:** accelerated program, cooperative (work-study plan) program, cross-registration, distance learning, double major, dual enrollment, English as a Second Language (ESL), honors program, independent study, internships, liberal arts/career combination, student-designed major, study abroad, teacher certificate program. **Teacher certification offered in:** early childhood, special education, elementary, middle/junior high, secondary. **Cooperative education programs:** engineering. **Reserve Officers Training Corps (ROTC):** Army ROTC: Offered at cooperating institution (Wofford College). **Faculty and instruction (2005-2006):** Total instructional faculty: 183 full-time, 143 part-time (49% men; 51% women; 12% minorities). Full-time faculty with Ph.D. or other terminal degree: 74%. Student/faculty ratio: 17/1. Classes of fewer than 20 students: 52%; of 20 to 49 students: 48%; of 50 or more students: 1%. **Advanced Placement and International Baccalaureate credit:** AP tests may be used for: Credit and/or placement. Scores accepted: 3, 4, 5. **Freshmen returning for sophomore year:** 65%. **Graduation rates:** Four-year: 16%; five-year: 33%; six-year: 38%.

COSTS AND FINANCIAL AID

Financial aid office: (864) 503-5340. **Expenses (2006-2007):** Tuition and fees 2006-2007: $7,670 in state, $15,108 out of state; room/board: $5,940. **Financial aid:** Priority filing date for institution's financial aid form: March 1. In 2005-2006, 77% of undergraduates applied for financial aid. Of those, 64% were determined to have financial need; 14% had their need fully met.

Average financial aid package (proportion receiving): $7,400 (64%). Average amount of gift aid, such as scholarships or grants (proportion receiving): $3,340 (41%). Average amount of self-help aid, such as work study or loans (proportion receiving): $3,671 (52%). Average need-based loan (excluding PLUS or other private loans): $3,610. Among students who received need-based aid, the average percentage of need met: 42%. Among students who received aid based on merit, the average award (and the proportion receiving): $3,003 (2%). The average athletic scholarship (and the proportion receiving): $3,427 (9%). Average amount of debt of borrowers graduating in 2005: $17,238. Proportion who borrowed: 67%.

CAMPUS LIFE AND EXTRACURRICULAR ACTIVITIES

Campus housing available (% using): coed dorms (50%), apartment for single students (50%), other housing options. Students who live in college-owned, operated, or affiliated housing: 14%. **Student employment:** During the 2005-2006 academic year, 1% of undergraduates worked on campus. Average per-year earnings: $5,000. **Clubs and organizations:** Number of student organizations: 58. Activities include: choral groups, dance, drama/theater, jazz band, literary magazine, music ensembles, student government, student newspaper. Number of fraternities: 5; sororities: 7. Proportion of men in fraternities: 2%; of women in sororities: 3%. Average proportion of students who stay on campus on weekends: 60%. **Sports program (2005-2006):** Member of NCAA II. *Men's intercollegiate varsity sports:* baseball, basketball, cross-country, soccer, tennis. *Women's intercollegiate varsity sports:* basketball, cross-country, soccer, softball, tennis, volleyball.

SERVICES AND FACILITIES

Basic services: nonremedial tutoring, women's center, placement service, day care, health service, health insurance. **Remedial assistance:** reading, math, writing, study skills. **Counseling services:** minority student, career, personal, veteran student, academic, older student, psychological. **For learning-disabled students:** School does not offer a structured program with separate admission and additional fees. Total undergraduates in learning-disabled program or receiving services: 20. Services include: reading machines, tape recorders, note-taking services, learning center, extended time for tests, tutors, priority registration, priority seating, texts on tape, exams on tape or computer, other testing accomodations. **Library:** Number of titles: 235,576; number of current serial subscriptions: 14,953. **Information technology resources:** Students are not required to lease or own a computer. Number of campus computers available to all students: 600. School has a wireless network. Approximate number of users that can be accommodated: 500. Proportion of college-owned housing units wired for high-speed internet access: 100%. **Campus safety:** Security services offered: 24-hour foot-and-vehicle patrols, late-night transport/escort service, 24-hour emergency telephones, lighted pathways/sidewalks, controlled dormitory access (key, security card, etc).

TRANSFER AND INTERNATIONAL STUDENTS

Transfer students: May apply for admission for the following academic terms: Fall, Winter, Spring, Summer. Applicants need a minimum number of credits to apply. For fall 2005: Transfer applications received: 1,171. Transfer applicants offered admission: 819. Transfer applicants enrolled: 614. **International students:** Number of foreign undergraduates: 70 (2% of student body). Minimum TOEFL score required: 500 (paper); 173 (computer). Average TOEFL score: 600 (paper).

Voorhees College

- **Address:** 1411 Voorhees Road, PO Box 678, Denmark, SC 29042
- **Website:** http://www.voorhees.edu
- **Private; Religious affiliation:** Episcopal
- **Enrollment:** N/A

KEY STATS

✔ **U.S News College Ranking:** fourth tier, Comp. Coll.–Bachelor's (South)
✔ **SAT or ACT Score (25th/75th percentile):** N/A
✔ **Tuition:** 2006-2007: $13,162

Selectivity: Less selective	**Room/board:** $5,201
Acceptance rate: N/A	**Average debt:** N/A
Student/faculty ratio: N/A	**Proportion who borrowed:** N/A

Winthrop University

- **Address:** 701 Oakland Avenue, Rock Hill, SC 29733
- **Website:** http://www.winthrop.edu
- **Public**
- **Enrollment:** 4,587 full-time; 600 part-time

KEY STATS

✔ **U.S News College Ranking:** 23, Universities–Master's (South)
✔ **SAT Score (25th/75th percentile):** 960-1180
✔ **Tuition:** 2005-2006: $8,756 in state, $16,150 out of state

Selectivity: Selective	**Room/board:** $5,352
Acceptance rate: 69%	**Average debt:** $18,793
Student/faculty ratio: 14/1	**Proportion who borrowed:** 63%

UNDERGRADUATE STUDENT BODY STATS

2005-2006 enrollment: 4,587 full-time; 600 part-time. Men: 31%; women: 69%. **Ethnic makeup:** African American: 28%; Asian American: 1%; Hispanic: 1%; White: 67%; International: 2%.

ADMISSIONS FACTS AND FIGURES

Phone: (803) 323-2191. **Email:** admissions@winthrop.edu. **Website:** http://www.winthrop.edu. **Application deadlines for fall 2007:** Regular decision: Rolling. Early decision: Not offered. Early action: Not offered. Admission can be deferred. **Application fee:** $40. Common application is accepted. **Admissions requirements/recommendations:** High school units required (recommended): English: 4 (4); Mathematics: 3 (4); Science: 3 (3); Foreign language: 2 (2); Social studies: 2 (2); History: 1 (1); Academic electives: 4 (4); Total units: 20 (21). Tests: The college uses SAT or ACT scores in admissions decisions. Either SAT or ACT required. For admission to the fall 2007 entering class, the school will accept: ACT with writing, ACT without writing. Campus visit: Recommended. Admissions interview: Neither required nor recommended. Off-campus interview: May be arranged. **Factors that count in admissions decisions:** *Academic:* Secondary school record: Very important. Class rank: Important. Letters of recommendation: Considered. Standardized test scores: Important. Essay: Considered. *Nonacademic:* Interview: Considered. Extracurricular activities: Considered. Talent/ability: Considered. Character/personal qualities: Not considered. Alumni/ae relationship: Not considered. Geographical residence: Not considered. State residency: Not considered. Religious affiliation/commitment: Not considered. Minority status: Not considered. Volunteer work: Considered. Work experience: Not considered. **Other schools with the greatest overlap in applicants:** Clemson University; Coastal Carolina University; Francis Marion University; University of South Carolina–Columbia; University of South Carolina–Upstate. **Admissions statistics for the fall 2005 entering class:** Total applicants: 4,304. Total accepted: 2,985. Freshmen enrolled: 1,017; 15% were from out of state. Overall acceptance rate: 69%. **Credentials of fall 2005 freshmen:** 22% ranked in the top 10 percent of their high school class; 56% were in the top 25 percent, and 92% were in the top half. (Proportion submitting class standing: 94%.) **First-year students who submitted SAT scores:** 76%. Scores (25/75 percentile): Verbal: 480-590, Math: 480-590, Combined: 960-1180. **First-year students submitting ACT scores:** 24%. Scores (25/75 percentile): English: N/A, Math: N/A, Composite: 20-24.

ACADEMICS

Year founded: 1886. **Academic calendar:** Semester. **Degrees offered:** certificate, bachelor's, post-bachelor's certificate, master's. **Most popular majors:** Information not available. **Major fields of study:** biological and biomedical sciences; business, management, marketing, and related support services; communication, journalism, and related programs; computer and information sciences and support services; education; English language and literature/letters; family and consumer sciences/human sciences; foreign languages, literatures, and linguistics; health professions and related clinical sciences; history; mathematics and statistics; natural resources and conservation; parks, recreation, leisure, and fitness studies; philosophy and religious studies; physical sciences; psychology; public administration and social service professions; social sciences; visual and performing arts. **Areas of required coursework:** humanities, computer literacy, mathematics, English (including composition), foreign languages, sciences (biological or physical), history, social science. **Pre-professional programs:** pre-law, other. **Special academic programs (% participation):** cooperative (work-study plan) program (11%), cross-registration (1%), distance learning (2%), double major (3%), dual enrollment (6%), exchange student program (domestic) (1%), honors program (1%), independent study (29%), internships (46%), study abroad (2%), teacher certificate program (19%). **Teacher certification offered in:** early childhood, special education, elementary, middle/junior high, secondary. **Cooperative education programs:** business. **Faculty and instruction (2005-2006):** Total instructional faculty: 270 full-time, 272 part-time (44% men; 56% women; 10% minorities). Full-time faculty with Ph.D. or other terminal degree: 84%. Student/faculty ratio: 14/1. Classes of fewer than 20 students: 45%; of 20 to 49 students: 53%; of 50 or more students: 3%. **Advanced Placement and International Baccalaureate credit:** AP tests may be used for: Credit and/or placement. Scores accepted: 4, 5. International Baccalaureate exams may be used for: Credit and/or placement. **Freshmen returning for sophomore year:** 75%. **Graduation rates:** Four-year: 33%; five-year: 55%; six-year: 57%. **Graduate study:** Fields in which graduates pursue further study: Master of Business Administration (MBA), 12%; law, 2%; education, 27%; arts and sciences, 27%.

COSTS AND FINANCIAL AID

Financial aid office: (803) 323-2189. **Expenses (2005-2006):** Tuition and fees 2005-2006: $8,756 in state, $16,150 out of state; room/board: $5,352. Estimated books and supplies: $900; transportation: $1,250; personal expenses: $1,250. **Financial aid:** Priority filing date for institution's financial aid form: March 1. In 2005-2006, 73% of undergraduates applied for financial aid. Of those, 59% were determined to have financial need; 21% had their need fully met. Average financial aid package (proportion receiving): $8,437 (59%). Average amount of gift aid, such as scholarships or grants (proportion receiving): $6,441 (48%). Average amount of self-help aid, such as work study or loans (proportion receiving): $4,081 (47%). Average need-based loan (excluding PLUS or other private loans): $3,970. Among students who received need-based aid, the average percentage of need met: 64%. Among students who received aid based on merit, the average award (and the proportion receiving): $5,409 (11%). The average athletic scholarship (and the proportion receiving): $3,437 (3%). Average amount of debt of borrowers graduating in 2005: $18,793. Proportion who borrowed: 63%.

CAMPUS LIFE AND EXTRACURRICULAR ACTIVITIES

Campus housing available (% using): coed dorms (12%), women's dorms (52%), men's dorms (16%), sorority housing (5%), fraternity housing (5%), apartments for married students (5%), apartment for single students (5%). Students who live in college-owned, operated, or affiliated housing: 42%. **Clubs and organizations:** Number of student organizations: 115. Activities include: choral groups, concert band, dance, drama/theater, jazz band, literary magazine, music ensembles, opera, pep band, radio station, student government, student newspaper, yearbook. Number of fraternities: 16; sororities: 5. Average proportion of students who stay on campus on weekends: 60%. **Sports program (2005-2006):** Member of NCAA I. **Men's intercollegiate varsity sports:** baseball, basketball, cross-country, golf, soccer, tennis, track and field (indoor), track and field (outdoor). **Women's intercollegiate varsity sports:** basketball, cross-country, golf, soccer, softball, tennis, track and field (indoor), track and field (outdoor), volleyball.

SERVICES AND FACILITIES

Basic services: placement service, health service, health insurance. **Counseling services:** minority student, career, personal, veteran student, academic, older student, psychological, birth control, religious. **For learning-disabled students:** School does not offer a structured program with separate admission and additional fees. Services include: tape recorders, note-taking services, oral tests, readers, extended time for tests. **Library:** Number of titles: 421,505; number of current serial subscriptions: 1,421. **Information technology resources:** Students are not required to lease or own a computer. Number of campus computers available to all students: 1,014. School has a wireless network. Approximate number of users that can be accommodated: 300. Proportion of college-owned housing units wired for high-speed internet access: 100%. **Campus safety:** Security services offered: 24-hour foot-and-vehicle patrols, 24-hour emergency telephones, lighted pathways/sidewalks, controlled dormitory access (key, security card, etc).

TRANSFER AND INTERNATIONAL STUDENTS

Transfer students: May apply for admission for the following academic terms: Fall, Winter, Spring, Summer. Applicants do not need a minimum number of credits to apply. For fall 2005: Transfer applications received: 743. Transfer applicants offered admission: 568. Transfer applicants enrolled: 359. **International students:** Number of foreign undergraduates: 92 (2% of student body). Number of countries represented: 45. Minimum TOEFL score required: 520 (paper); 190 (computer).

Wofford College

- **Address:** 429 N. Church Street, Spartanburg, SC 29303-3663
- **Website:** http://www.wofford.edu
- **Private; Religious affiliation:** United Methodist
- **Enrollment:** 1,158 full-time; 16 part-time

KEY STATS

✔ **U.S News College Ranking:** 57, Liberal Arts Colleges
✔ **SAT Score (25th/75th percentile):** 1150-1340
✔ **Tuition:** 2006-2007: $26,110

Selectivity: More selective	**Room/board:** $7,260
Acceptance rate: 66%	**Average debt:** $10,242
Student/faculty ratio: 12/1	**Proportion who borrowed:** 49%

UNDERGRADUATE STUDENT BODY STATS

2005-2006 enrollment: 1,158 full-time; 16 part-time. Men: 52%; women: 48%. **Ethnic makeup:** African American: 6%; Asian American: 2%; Hispanic: 1%; White: 90%; International: 1%. **Religious preference:** Roman Catholic: 11%; Protestant: 46%; No preference: 5%; United Methodist: 22%; Other: 16%.

ADMISSIONS FACTS AND FIGURES

Phone: (864) 597-4130. **Email:** admissions@wofford.edu. **Website:** http://www.wofford.edu. **Application deadlines for fall 2007:** Regular decision: February 1; decision sent by March 15. Early decision: Send application by: November 15; Decision sent by: December 1. Early action: Not offered. Admission can be deferred. **Application fee:** $40. Common application is accepted. **Admissions requirements/recommendations:** High school units required (recommended): English: (4); Mathematics: (4); Science: (3); Foreign language: (3); Social studies: (2); History: (1); Academic electives: (3); Total units: (20). Tests: The college uses SAT or ACT scores in admissions decisions. Either SAT or ACT required. For admission to the fall 2007 entering class, the school will accept: ACT with writing. Campus visit: Recommended. Admissions interview: Recommended. Off-campus interview: May be arranged. **Factors that count in admissions decisions:** **Academic:** Secondary school record: Very important. Class rank: Important. Letters of recommendation: Considered. Standardized test scores: Important. Essay: Important. **Nonacademic:** Interview: Considered. Extracurricular activities: Important. Talent/ability: Important. Character/personal qualities: Important. Alumni/ae relationship: Considered. Geographical residence: Considered. State residency: Not considered. Religious affiliation/commitment: Not considered. Minority status: Considered. Volunteer work: Considered. Work experience: Considered. **Other schools with the greatest overlap in applicants:** Clemson University; Furman University; University of South Carolina–Columbia. **Admissions statistics for the fall 2005 entering class:** Total applicants: 1,871. Total accepted: 1,237. Freshmen enrolled: 321; 47% were from out of state. Accepted through early-decision or early-action plans: 47%. Overall acceptance rate: 66%. Early-decision acceptance rate: 82%. Non-early acceptance rate: 61%. **Size of waiting list:** 134 applicants; enrolled from waiting list: 7. **Credentials of fall 2005 freshmen:** 58% ranked in the top 10 percent of their high school class; 83% were in the top 25 percent, and 99% were in the top half. (Proportion submitting class standing: 67%.) **Average high school grade point average:** 3.5. **First-year students who submitted SAT scores:** 61%. Scores (25/75 percentile): Verbal: 570-660, Math: 580-680, Combined: 1150-1340. **First-year students submitting ACT scores:** 39%. Scores (25/75 percentile): English: N/A, Math: N/A, Composite: 22-27.

ACADEMICS

Year founded: 1854. **Academic calendar:** 4-1-4. **Degrees offered:** bachelor's. **Most popular majors:** 16% biology/biological sciences, 15% business/managerial economics, 10% political science and government, 7% English language and literature, 7% finance. **Major fields of study:** biological and biomedical sciences; business, management, marketing, and related support services; English language and literature/letters; foreign languages, literatures, and linguistics; history; liberal arts and sciences studies, and humanities; mathematics and statistics; multi/interdisciplinary studies; philosophy and religious studies; physical sciences; psychology; social sciences; visual and performing arts. **Areas of required coursework:** arts/fine arts, humanities, computer literacy, mathematics, English (including composition), philosophy, foreign languages, sciences (biological or physical), history, social science. **Pre-professional programs:** pre-law, pre-dentistry, pre-medicine, pre-theology, pre-veterinary science, pre-pharmacy, other. **Special academic programs:** accelerated program, cross-registration, double major, dual enrollment, independent study, internships, student-designed major, study abroad, teacher certificate program. **Teacher certification offered in:** middle/junior high, secondary. **Reserve Officers Training Corps (ROTC):** Army ROTC: Offered on campus. **Faculty and instruction (2005-2006):** Total instructional faculty: 89 full-time, 33 part-time (66% men; 34% women; 7% minorities). Full-time faculty with Ph.D. or other terminal degree: 92%. Student/faculty ratio: 12/1. Classes of fewer than 20 students: 76%; of 20 to 49 students: 24%; of 50 or more students: 0%. **Advanced Placement and International Baccalaureate credit:** AP tests may be used for: Credit and/or placement. Scores accepted: 4. **Freshmen returning for sophomore year:** 90%. **Graduation rates:** Four-year: 74%; five-year: 77%; six-year: 78%. **Graduate study:** 40% of students pursue further study immediately upon graduation. Fields in which graduates pursue further study: Master of Business Administration (MBA), 1%; law, 9%; medicine, 9%; dentistry, 2%; theology (or the seminary), 2%; education, 2%; arts and sciences, 15%.

COSTS AND FINANCIAL AID

Financial aid office: (864) 597-4160. **Expenses (2006-2007):** Tuition and fees 2006-2007: $26,110; room/board: $7,260. Estimated books and supplies: $885; transportation: $750; personal expenses: $1,800. **Financial aid:** Priority filing date for institution's financial aid form: March 15. In 2005-2006, 64% of undergraduates applied for financial aid. Of those, 52% were determined to have financial need; 56% had their need fully met. Average financial aid package (proportion receiving): $22,401 (52%). Average amount of gift aid, such as scholarships or grants (proportion receiving): $16,648 (52%). Average amount of self-help aid, such as work study or loans (proportion receiving): $4,761 (27%). Average need-based loan (excluding PLUS or other private loans): $4,371. Among students who received need-based aid, the average percentage of need met: 89%. Among students who received aid based on merit, the average award (and the proportion receiving): $9,884 (25%). The average athletic scholarship (and the proportion receiving): $15,320 (8%). Average amount of debt of borrowers graduating in 2005: $10,242. Proportion who borrowed: 49%.

CAMPUS LIFE AND EXTRACURRICULAR ACTIVITIES

Campus housing available (% using): coed dorms (56%), women's dorms (18%), men's dorms (20%), fraternity housing (1%), special housing for disabled students (0%), other housing options (5%). Students who live in college-owned, operated, or affiliated housing: 91%. **Student employment:** During the 2005-2006 academic year, 21% of undergraduates worked on campus. Average per-year earnings: $1,368. **Clubs and organizations:** Number of student organizations: 66. Activities include: choral groups, concert band, dance, drama/theater, literary magazine, music ensembles, pep band, student government, student newspaper, yearbook. Number of fraternities: 8; sororities: 4. Proportion of men in fraternities: 51%; of women in sororities: 59%. Average proportion of students who stay on campus on weekends: 75%. **Sports program (2005-2006):** Member of NCAA I. **Men's intercollegiate varsity sports:** baseball, basketball, cross-country, football, golf, riflery, soccer, tennis, track and field (indoor), track and field (outdoor). **Women's intercollegiate varsity sports:** basketball, cross-country, golf, riflery, soccer, tennis, track and field (indoor), track and field (outdoor), volleyball.

SERVICES AND FACILITIES

Basic services: nonremedial tutoring, placement service, health service. **Remedial assistance:** reading, math, writing, study skills. **Counseling services:** minority student, career, personal, academic, psychological, birth control, religious. **For learning-disabled students:** School does not offer a structured program with separate admission and additional fees. Total undergraduates in learning-disabled program or receiving services: 63. Services include: tape recorders, oral tests, extended time for tests, tutors, priority seating, proofreading services, substitution of courses, exams on tape or computer, other testing accomodations, waiver of foreign language degree requirement, waiver of math degree requirement. **Library:** Number of titles: 197,077; number of current serial subscriptions: 539. **Information technology resources:** Students are not required to lease or own a computer. **Campus safety:** Security services offered: 24-hour foot-and-vehicle patrols, late-night transport/escort service, 24-hour emergency telephones, lighted pathways/sidewalks, controlled dormitory access (key, security card, etc).

TRANSFER AND INTERNATIONAL STUDENTS

Transfer students: May apply for admission for the following academic terms: Fall, Winter, Spring. Applicants do not need a minimum number of credits to apply. For fall 2005: Transfer applications received: 65. Transfer applicants offered admission: 22. Transfer applicants enrolled: 10. **International students:** Number of foreign undergraduates: 8 (1% of student body). Number of countries represented: 5. Minimum TOEFL score required: 550 (paper); 213 (computer). Average TOEFL score: 550 (paper).

South Dakota

Augustana College

- **Address:** 2001 S. Summit Avenue, Sioux Falls, SD 57197
- **Website:** http://www.augie.edu
- **Private; Religious affiliation:** Lutheran
- **Enrollment:** 1,621 full-time; 93 part-time

KEY STATS

✔ **U.S News College Ranking:** 12, Comp. Coll.–Bachelor's (Midwest)

✔ **ACT Score (25th/75th percentile):** 22-27

✔ **Tuition:** 2006-2007: $19,986

Selectivity: More selective	**Room/board:** $5,472
Acceptance rate: 80%	**Average debt:** $18,956
Student/faculty ratio: 13/1	**Proportion who borrowed:** 79%

UNDERGRADUATE STUDENT BODY STATS

2005-2006 enrollment: 1,621 full-time; 93 part-time. Men: 38%; women: 62%. **Ethnic makeup:** African American: 1%; Asian American: 1%; White: 95%; International: 2%. **Religious preference:** Roman Catholic: 20%; Protestant: 26%; Lutheran: 49%; Other: 5%.

ADMISSIONS FACTS AND FIGURES

Phone: (605) 274-5516. **Email:** admission@augie.edu. **Website:** http://www.augie.edu. **Application deadlines for fall 2007:** Regular decision: Rolling. Early decision: Not offered. Early action: Not offered. Admission can be deferred. **Application fee:** None. Common application is not accepted. **Admissions requirements/recommendations:** High school units required (recommended): English: (4); Mathematics: (4); Science: (4); Foreign language: (2); Social studies: (2). Tests: The college uses SAT or ACT scores in admissions decisions. Either SAT or ACT required. For admission to the fall 2007 entering class, the school will accept: ACT with writing, ACT without writing. Campus visit: Recommended. Admissions interview: Recommended. Off-campus interview: May be arranged. **Factors that count in admissions decisions:** *Academic:* Secondary school record: Very important. Class rank: Important. Letters of recommendation: Important. Standardized test scores: Very important. Essay: Considered. *Nonacademic:* Interview: Considered. Extracurricular activities: Important. Talent/ability: Considered. Character/personal qualities: Considered. Alumni/ae relationship: Not considered. Geographical residence: Not considered. State residency: Not considered. Religious affiliation/commitment: Not considered. Minority status: Not considered. Volunteer work: Not considered. Work experience: Not considered. **Other schools with the greatest overlap in applicants:** Concordia College–Moorhead; Gustavus Adolphus College; South Dakota State University; University of Sioux Falls; University of South Dakota. **Admissions statistics for the fall 2005 entering class:** Total applicants: 1,544. Total accepted: 1,229. Freshmen enrolled: 405; 59% were from out of state. Overall acceptance rate: 80%. **Credentials of fall 2005 freshmen:** 26% ranked in the top 10 percent of their high school class; 58% were in the top 25 percent, and 86% were in the top half. (Proportion submitting class standing: 97%.) **Average high school grade point average:** 3.6. **First-year students who submitted SAT scores:** 3%. Scores (25/75 percentile): Verbal: 520-700, Math: 510-710, Combined: 1030-1410. **First-year students submitting ACT scores:** 97%. Scores (25/75 percentile): English: 21-27, Math: 20-26, Composite: 22-27.

ACADEMICS

Year founded: 1860. **Academic calendar:** 4-1-4. **Degrees offered:** bachelor's, master's. **Most popular majors:** 18% education, 14% business, management, marketing, and related support services, 13% science technologies/technicians, 11% social sciences, 9% biological and biomedical sciences. **Major fields of study:** biological and biomedical sciences; business, management, marketing, and related support services; communication, journalism, and related programs; computer and information sciences and support services; education; English language and literature/letters; foreign languages, literatures, and linguistics; health professions and related clinical sciences; his-

tory; liberal arts and sciences studies, and humanities; mathematics and statistics; parks, recreation, leisure, and fitness studies; philosophy and religious studies; psychology; social sciences; visual and performing arts. **Areas of required coursework:** arts/fine arts, humanities, computer literacy, mathematics, English (including composition), foreign languages, sciences (biological or physical), history, social science, other. **Pre-professional programs:** pre-law, pre-dentistry, pre-medicine, pre-theology, pre-veterinary science, pre-optometry, pre-pharmacy, other. **Special academic programs (% participation):** cross-registration (6%), double major (29%), independent study (17%), internships (65%), student-designed major, study abroad (55%), **Teacher certification offered in:** special education, elementary, middle/junior high, secondary. **Cooperative education programs:** engineering. **Faculty and instruction (2005-2006):** Total instructional faculty: 108 full-time, 72 part-time (52% men; 48% women; 1% minorities). Full-time faculty with Ph.D. or other terminal degree: 76%. Student/faculty ratio: 13/1. Classes of fewer than 20 students: 44%; of 20 to 49 students: 51%; of 50 or more students: 4%. **Advanced Placement and International Baccalaureate credit:** AP tests may be used for: Credit and/or placement. Scores accepted: 4, 5. International Baccalaureate exams may be used for: Credit and/or placement. **Freshmen returning for sophomore year:** 81%. **Graduation rates:** Four-year: 48%; five-year: 62%; six-year: 66%. **Graduate study:** 28% of students pursue further study immediately upon graduation. Fields in which graduates pursue further study: Master of Business Administration (MBA), 9%; law, 10%; medicine, 20%; theology (or the seminary), 5%.

COSTS AND FINANCIAL AID

Financial aid office: (605) 274-5216. **Expenses (2006-2007):** Tuition and fees 2006-2007: $19,986; room/board: $5,472. Estimated books and supplies: $800; transportation: $400; personal expenses: $800. **Financial aid:** Priority filing date for institution's financial aid form: March 1. In 2005-2006, 80% of undergraduates applied for financial aid. Of those, 68% were determined to have financial need; 16% had their need fully met. Average financial aid package (proportion receiving): $15,183 (68%). Average amount of gift aid, such as scholarships or grants (proportion receiving): $10,674 (68%). Average amount of self-help aid, such as work study or loans (proportion receiving): $5,525 (56%). Average need-based loan (excluding PLUS or other private loans): $5,007. Among students who received need-based aid, the average percentage of need met: 89%. Among students who received aid based on merit, the average award (and the proportion receiving): $7,223 (30%). The average athletic scholarship (and the proportion receiving): $6,635 (9%). Average amount of debt of borrowers graduating in 2005: $18,956. Proportion who borrowed: 79%.

CAMPUS LIFE AND EXTRACURRICULAR ACTIVITIES

Campus housing available (% using): coed dorms (96%), apartments for married students (1%), other housing options (3%). Students who live in college-owned, operated, or affiliated housing: 64%. **Student employment:** During the 2005-2006 academic year, 35% of undergraduates worked on campus. Average per-year earnings: $1,472. **Clubs and organizations:** Number of student organizations: 59. Activities include: choral groups, concert band, dance, drama/theater, jazz band, literary magazine, music ensembles, musical theater, pep band, radio station, student government, student newspaper, symphony orchestra, yearbook. Number of fraternities: 0; sororities: 0. Average proportion of students who stay on campus on weekends: 80%. **Sports program (2005-2006):** Member of NCAA II. *Men's intercollegiate varsity sports:* baseball, basketball, cross-country, football, golf, tennis, track and field (indoor), track and field (outdoor), wrestling. *Women's intercollegiate varsity sports:* basketball, cross-country, golf, soccer, softball, tennis, track and field (indoor), track and field (outdoor), volleyball.

SERVICES AND FACILITIES

Basic services: nonremedial tutoring, placement service, day care, health service, health insurance. **Remedial assistance:** writing. **Counseling services:** minority student, career, personal, veteran student, academic, older student, psychological, birth control, religious. **For learning-disabled students:** School does not offer a structured program with separate admission and additional fees. Total undergraduates in learning-disabled program or receiving services: 7. Services include: remedial English, tape recorders, videotaped classes, untimed tests, note-taking services, oral tests, learning center, readers, extended time for tests, tutors, proofreading services, other testing accomodations, other. **Library:** Number of titles: 261,426; number of current serial subscriptions: 510. **Information technology resources:** Students are not required to lease or own a computer. Number of campus computers available to all students: 375. School has a wireless network. Approximate number of users that can be accommodated: 300. Proportion of college-owned housing units wired for high-speed internet access: 100%. **Campus safety:** Security services offered: 24-hour foot-and-vehicle patrols, late-night transport/escort service, lighted pathways/sidewalks, controlled dormitory access (key, security card, etc).

TRANSFER AND INTERNATIONAL STUDENTS

Transfer students: May apply for admission for the following academic terms: Fall, Winter, Spring, Summer. Applicants need a minimum number of credits to apply. For fall 2005: Transfer applications received: 205. Transfer applicants offered admission: 134. Transfer applicants enrolled: 76. **International students:** Number of foreign undergraduates: 32 (2% of student body). Number of countries represented: 8. Minimum TOEFL score required: 550 (paper); 213 (computer). Average TOEFL score: 590 (paper).

Black Hills State University

■ **Address:** 1200 University Street, Unit 9500, Spearfish, SD 57799-9500
■ **Website:** http://www.bhsu.edu
■ **Public**
■ **Enrollment:** N/A

KEY STATS

✔ **U.S News College Ranking:** fourth tier, Comp. Coll.–Bachelor's (Midwest)
✔ **SAT or ACT Score (25th/75th percentile):** N/A
✔ **Tuition:** 2006-2007: $5,001 in state, $10,188 out of state

Selectivity: Less selective	**Room/board:** $4,667
Acceptance rate: N/A	**Average debt:** N/A
Student/faculty ratio: N/A	**Proportion who borrowed:** N/A

Dakota State University

■ **Address:** 820 N. Washington Avenue, Madison, SD 57042
■ **Website:** http://www.dsu.edu
■ **Public**
■ **Enrollment:** 1,162 full-time; 919 part-time

KEY STATS

✔ **U.S News College Ranking:** third tier, Comp. Coll.–Bachelor's (Midwest)
✔ **ACT Score (25th/75th percentile):** 18-24
✔ **Tuition:** 2006-2007: $5,699 in state, $10,886 out of state

Selectivity: Less selective	**Room/board:** $3,927
Acceptance rate: 98%	**Average debt:** $20,977
Student/faculty ratio: 17/1	**Proportion who borrowed:** 90%

UNDERGRADUATE STUDENT BODY STATS

2005-2006 enrollment: 1,162 full-time; 919 part-time. Men: 47%; women: 53%. **Ethnic makeup:** African American: 1%; American-Indian: 1%; Asian American: 1%; Hispanic: 1%; White: 95%; International: 1%.

ADMISSIONS FACTS AND FIGURES

Phone: (888) 378-9988. **Email:** dsuinfo@dsu.edu. **Website:** http://www.dsu.edu. **Application deadlines for fall 2007:** Regular decision: Rolling. Early decision: Not offered. Early action: Not offered. Admission can be deferred. **Application fee:** $20. Common application is not accepted. **To apply online, go to:** http://www.dsu.edu/applications.htm. **Admissions requirements/recommendations:** High school units required (recommended): English: (4); Mathematics: (3); Science: (3); Social studies: (3). Tests: The college uses SAT or ACT scores in admissions decisions. Either SAT or ACT required. For admission to the fall 2007 entering class, the school will accept: ACT with writing, ACT without writing. Campus visit: Recommended. Admissions interview: Neither required nor recommended.

Off-campus interview: Not available. **Factors that count in admissions decisions: Academic:** Secondary school record: Important. Class rank: Important. Letters of recommendation: Not considered. Standardized test scores: Important. Essay: Not considered. **Nonacademic:** Interview: Not considered. Extracurricular activities: Not considered. Talent/ability: Not considered. Character/personal qualities: Not considered. Alumni/ae relationship: Not considered. Geographical residence: Not considered. State residency: Not considered. Religious affiliation/commitment: Not considered. Minority status: Not considered. Volunteer work: Not considered. Work experience: Not considered. **Other schools with the greatest overlap in applicants:** Black Hills State University; Northern State University; South Dakota School of Mines and Technology; South Dakota State University; University of South Dakota. **Admissions statistics for the fall 2005 entering class:** Total applicants: 539. Total accepted: 528. Freshmen enrolled: 285; 18% were from out of state. Overall acceptance rate: 98%. **Credentials of fall 2005 freshmen:** 6% ranked in the top 10 percent of their high school class; 20% were in the top 25 percent, and 50% were in the top half. (Proportion submitting class standing: 98%.) **Average high school grade point average:** 3.1. **First-year students submitting ACT scores:** 99%. Scores (25/75 percentile): English: 17-23, Math: 17-24, Composite: 18-24.

ACADEMICS

Year founded: 1881. **Academic calendar:** Semester. **Degrees offered:** certificate, associate, bachelor's, master's. **Most popular majors:** 35% computer and information sciences and support services, 28% business, management, marketing, and related support services, 20% education, 4% English language and literature/letters, 4% parks, recreation, leisure, and fitness studies. **Major fields of study:** biological and biomedical sciences; business, management, marketing, and related support services; computer and information sciences and support services; education; English language and literature/letters; health professions and related clinical sciences; mathematics and statistics; parks, recreation, leisure, and fitness studies; physical sciences; science technologies/technicians. **Areas of required coursework:** arts/fine arts, humanities, computer literacy, mathematics, English (including composition), sciences (biological or physical), history, social science. **Special academic programs:** cooperative (work-study plan) program, cross-registration, distance learning, double major, dual enrollment, English as a Second Language (ESL), honors program, independent study, internships, teacher certificate program. **Teacher certification offered in:** special education, elementary, middle/junior high, secondary. **Cooperative education programs:** education. **Reserve Officers Training Corps (ROTC):** Army ROTC: Offered on campus; Air Force ROTC: Offered at cooperating institution (South Dakota State University). **Faculty and instruction (2005-2006):** Total instructional faculty: 77 full-time, 31 part-time (60% men; 40% women; 5% minorities). Full-time faculty with Ph.D. or other terminal degree: 61%. Student/faculty ratio: 17/1. Classes of fewer than 20 students: 52%; of 20 to 49 students: 45%; of 50 or more students: 3%. **Advanced Placement and International Baccalaureate credit:** AP tests may be used for: Credit only. Scores accepted: 3, 4, 5. International Baccalaureate exams may be used for: Placement only. **Freshmen returning for sophomore year:** 68%. **Graduation rates:** Four-year: 18%; five-year: 46%; six-year: 46%. **Graduate study:** 6% of students pursue further study immediately upon graduation. Fields in which graduates pursue further study: Master of Business Administration (MBA), 3%; medicine, 1%; education, 2%.

COSTS AND FINANCIAL AID

Financial aid office: (605) 256-5152. **Expenses (2006-2007):** Tuition and fees 2006-2007: $5,699 in state, $10,886 out of state; room/board: $3,927. Estimated books and supplies: $850; transportation: $750; personal expenses: $1,937. **Financial aid:** Priority filing date for institution's financial aid form: March 1. In 2005-2006, 87% of undergraduates applied for financial aid. Of those, 64% were determined to have financial need; 21% had their need fully met. Average financial aid package (proportion receiving): $6,308 (64%). Average amount of gift aid, such as scholarships or grants (proportion receiving): $3,192 (31%). Average amount of self-help aid, such as work study or loans (proportion receiving): $5,134 (60%). Average need-based loan (excluding PLUS or other private loans): $4,755. Among students who received need-based aid, the average percentage of need met: 85%. Among students who received aid based on merit, the average award (and the proportion receiving): $5,840 (22%). The average athletic scholarship (and the proportion receiving): $1,199 (12%). Average amount of debt of borrowers graduating in 2005: $20,977. Proportion who borrowed: 90%.

CAMPUS LIFE AND EXTRACURRICULAR ACTIVITIES

Campus housing available: coed dorms, women's dorms, men's dorms, apartment for single students. Students who live in college-owned, operated, or affiliated housing: 36%. **Student employment:** During the 2005-2006 academic year, 12% of undergraduates worked on campus. Average per-year earnings: $1,800. **Clubs and organizations:** Number of student organizations: 31. Activities include: choral groups, concert band, dance, drama/theater, jazz band, literary magazine, music ensembles, musical theater, pep band, radio station, student government, student newspaper. Average proportion of students who stay on campus on weekends: 35%. **Sports program (2005-2006):** Member of NAIA. *Men's intercollegiate varsity sports:* baseball, basketball, cross-country, football, track and field (indoor), track and field (outdoor). *Women's intercollegiate varsity sports:* basketball, cross-country, soccer, softball, track and field (indoor), track and field (outdoor), volleyball.

SERVICES AND FACILITIES

Basic services: nonremedial tutoring, placement service, health service. **Remedial assistance:** reading, math, writing, study skills. **Counseling services:** minority student, career, personal, veteran student, academic, older student, psychological, birth control, religious. **For learning-disabled students:** School does not offer a structured program with separate admission and additional fees. Total undergraduates in learning-disabled program or receiving services: 24. Services include: remedial math, other testing accommodations, remedial English, reading machines, remedial reading, tape recorders, other special classes, videotaped classes, untimed tests, note-taking services, special bookstore section, oral tests, learning center, readers, extended time for tests, tutors, priority seating, texts on tape, typist/scribe, exams on tape or computer. **Library:** Number of titles: 98,156; number of current serial subscriptions: 21,234. **Information technology resources:** Students are not required to lease or own a computer. Number of campus computers available to all students: 275. School has a wireless network. Approximate number of users that can be accommodated: 3,500. Proportion of college-owned housing units wired for high-speed internet access: 100%. **Campus safety:** Security services offered: late-night transport/escort service, lighted pathways/sidewalks, controlled dormitory access (key, security card, etc).

TRANSFER AND INTERNATIONAL STUDENTS

Transfer students: May apply for admission for the following academic terms: Fall, Spring, Summer. Applicants do not need a minimum number of credits to apply. For fall 2005: Transfer applications received: 328. Transfer applicants offered admission: 296. Transfer applicants enrolled: 115. **International students:** Number of foreign undergraduates: 11 (1% of student body). Number of countries represented: 5. Minimum TOEFL score required: 550 (paper); 213 (computer).

Dakota Wesleyan University

- **Address:** 1200 W. University Avenue, Mitchell, SD 57301
- **Website:** http://www.dwu.edu
- **Private; Religious affiliation:** United Methodist
- **Enrollment:** 705 full-time; 53 part-time

KEY STATS

✔ **U.S News College Ranking:** third tier, Comp. Coll.–Bachelor's (Midwest)
✔ **ACT Score (25th/75th percentile):** 18-23
✔ **Tuition:** 2006-2007: $16,650

Selectivity: Selective	**Room/board:** $5,100
Acceptance rate: 76%	**Average debt:** $20,068
Student/faculty ratio: 13/1	**Proportion who borrowed:** 93%

UNDERGRADUATE STUDENT BODY STATS

2005-2006 enrollment: 705 full-time; 53 part-time. Men: 42%; women: 58%. **Ethnic makeup:** African American: 5%; American-Indian: 4%; Asian American: 1%; Hispanic: 4%; White: 83%; International: 2%. **Religious preference:** Roman Catholic: 35%; Protestant: 55%; No preference: 10%.

ADMISSIONS FACTS AND FIGURES

Phone: (800) 333-8506. **Email:** admissions@dwu.edu. **Website:** http://www.dwu.edu. **Application deadlines for fall 2007:** Regular decision: August 30. Early decision: Not offered. Early action: Not offered. Admission cannot be deferred. **Application fee:** $25. Common application is not accepted. **Admissions requirements/recommendations:** High school units required (recommended): English: (4); Mathematics: (4); Science: (3);

Foreign language: (2); Social studies: (4); History: (3). Tests: The college uses SAT or ACT scores in admissions decisions. Either SAT or ACT required. For admission to the fall 2007 entering class, the school will accept: ACT with writing, ACT without writing. Campus visit: Recommended. Admissions interview: Neither required nor recommended. Off-campus interview: May be arranged. **Factors that count in admissions decisions:** *Academic:* Secondary school record: Very important. Class rank: Very important. Letters of recommendation: Considered. Standardized test scores: Very important. Essay: Considered. *Nonacademic:* Interview: Not considered. Extracurricular activities: Not considered. Talent/ability: Not considered. Character/personal qualities: Not considered. Alumni/ae relationship: Not considered. Geographical residence: Not considered. State residency: Not considered. Religious affiliation/commitment: Not considered. Minority status: Not considered. Volunteer work: Not considered. Work experience: Not considered. **Other schools with the greatest overlap in applicants:** Augustana College; Northern State University; South Dakota State University; University of Sioux Falls; University of South Dakota. **Admissions statistics for the fall 2005 entering class:** Total applicants: 799. Total accepted: 609. Freshmen enrolled: 346; Overall acceptance rate: 76%. **Credentials of fall 2005 freshmen:** 18% ranked in the top 10 percent of their high school class; 41% were in the top 25 percent, and 81% were in the top half. (Proportion submitting class standing: 81%.) **Average high school grade point average:** 3.0. First-year students who submitted SAT scores: 2%. Scores (25/75 percentile): Verbal: N/A, Math: N/A, Combined: N/A. **First-year students submitting ACT scores:** 98%. Scores (25/75 percentile): English: N/A, Math: N/A, Composite: 18-23.

ACADEMICS

Year founded: 1885. **Academic calendar:** Semester. **Degrees offered:** associate, terminal-associate, bachelor's, master's. **Most popular majors:** 32% education, 24% business/commerce, 12% biology/biological sciences, 9% sport and fitness administration/management. **Major fields of study:** biological and biomedical sciences; business, management, marketing, and related support services; communication, journalism, and related programs; communications technologies/technicians and support services; computer and information sciences and support services; education; English language and literature/letters; health professions and related clinical sciences; history; legal professions and studies; liberal arts and sciences studies, and humanities; mathematics and statistics; multi/interdisciplinary studies; parks, recreation, leisure, and fitness studies; philosophy and religious studies; psychology; public administration and social service professions; security and protective services; social sciences; theology and religious vocations; visual and performing arts. **Areas of required coursework:** arts/fine arts, humanities, computer literacy, mathematics, English (including composition), philosophy, sciences (biological or physical), history, social science, other. **Pre-professional programs:** pre-law, pre-dentistry, pre-medicine, pre-theology, pre-optometry, pre-pharmacy, other. **Special academic programs (% participation):** distance learning (1%), double major (16%), dual enrollment (1%), honors program (10%), independent study (15%), internships (70%), liberal arts/career combination (90%), student-designed major (1%), study abroad (1%), teacher certificate program (15%). **Teacher certification offered in:** special education, elementary, middle/junior high, secondary. **Faculty and instruction (2005-2006):** Total instructional faculty: 50 full-time, 32 part-time (52% men; 48% women; 4% minorities). Full-time faculty with Ph.D. or other terminal degree: 62%. Student/faculty ratio: 13/1. Classes of fewer than 20 students: 65%; of 20 to 49 students: 34%; of 50 or more students: 0%. **Advanced Placement and International Baccalaureate credit:** AP tests may be used for: Credit and/or placement. Scores accepted: 3, 4, 5. International Baccalaureate exams may be used for: Credit and/or placement. **Freshmen returning for sophomore year:** 62%. **Graduation rates:** Six-year: 46%. **Graduate study:** 10% of students pursue further study immediately upon graduation; 2% within one year; 1% within five years. Fields in which graduates pursue further study: Master of Business Administration (MBA), 2%; law, 1%; medicine, 9%; theology (or the seminary), 1%; education, 2%.

COSTS AND FINANCIAL AID

Financial aid office: (605) 995-2656. **Expenses (2006-2007):** Tuition and fees 2006-2007: $16,650; room/board: $5,100. Estimated books and supplies: $920; transportation: $750; personal expenses: $1,700. **Financial aid:** Priority filing date for institution's financial aid form: April 15. In 2005-2006, 94% of undergraduates applied for financial aid. Of those, 90% were determined to have financial need; 45% had their need fully met. Average financial aid package (proportion receiving): $14,500 (90%). Average amount of gift aid, such as scholarships or grants (proportion receiving): $9,500 (90%). Average amount of self-help aid, such as work study or loans (proportion receiving): $4,000 (83%). Average need-based loan (excluding PLUS or other private loans): $3,700. Among students who received need-based aid, the average percentage of need met: 63%. Among students who received aid based on merit, the average award (and the proportion receiving): $0 (0%). The average athletic scholarship (and the proportion receiving): $3,952 (41%). Average amount of debt of borrowers graduating in 2005: $20,068. Proportion who borrowed: 93%.

CAMPUS LIFE AND EXTRACURRICULAR ACTIVITIES
Campus housing available: coed dorms, women's dorms, men's dorms, apartments for married students, apartment for single students, special housing for disabled students, other housing options. **Student employment:** During the 2005-2006 academic year, 0% of undergraduates worked on campus. **Clubs and organizations:** Number of student organizations: 26. Activities include: choral groups, concert band, dance, drama/theater, jazz band, literary magazine, music ensembles, student government, student newspaper, yearbook. Number of fraternities: 0; sororities: 0. Average proportion of students who stay on campus on weekends: 30%. **Sports program (2005-2006):** Member of NAIA. *Men's intercollegiate varsity sports:* baseball, basketball, cheerleading, cross-country, football, golf, track and field (indoor), track and field (outdoor), wrestling. *Women's intercollegiate varsity sports:* basketball, cheerleading, cross-country, golf, softball, track and field (indoor), track and field (outdoor), volleyball.

SERVICES AND FACILITIES
Basic services: nonremedial tutoring, women's center, placement service, day care, health service, health insurance. **Remedial assistance:** reading, math, writing, study skills. **Counseling services:** minority student, career, personal, academic, older student, psychological, religious, other. **For learning-disabled students:** School does not offer a structured program with separate admission and additional fees. Total undergraduates in learning-disabled program or receiving services: 7. Services include: remedial math, remedial English, reading machines, remedial reading, tape recorders, videotaped classes, untimed tests, oral tests, learning center, readers, extended time for tests, tutors, proofreading services. **Information technology resources:** Students are not required to lease or own a computer. Number of campus computers available to all students: 85. School has a wireless network. Proportion of college-owned housing units wired for high-speed internet access: 100%. **Campus safety:** Security services offered: late-night transport/escort service, 24-hour emergency telephones, lighted pathways/sidewalks, controlled dormitory access (key, security card, etc).

TRANSFER AND INTERNATIONAL STUDENTS
Transfer students: May apply for admission for the following academic terms: Fall, Spring, Summer. Applicants do not need a minimum number of credits to apply. For fall 2005: Transfer applicants enrolled: 133. **International students:** Number of foreign undergraduates: 16 (2% of student body). Minimum TOEFL score required: 500 (paper); 200 (computer). Average TOEFL score: 550 (paper).

Mount Marty College

- **Address:** 1105 W. Eighth Street, Yankton, SD 57078
- **Website:** http://www.mtmc.edu
- **Private; Religious affiliation:** Roman Catholic
- **Enrollment:** 712 full-time; 377 part-time

KEY STATS
✔ **U.S News College Ranking:** third tier, Universities–Master's (Midwest)
✔ **ACT Score (25th/75th percentile):** 19-25
✔ **Tuition:** 2006-2007: $16,582

Selectivity: Selective	**Room/board:** $4,958
Acceptance rate: 85%	**Average debt:** $26,304
Student/faculty ratio: 12/1	**Proportion who borrowed:** 85%

UNDERGRADUATE STUDENT BODY STATS
2005-2006 enrollment: 712 full-time; 377 part-time. Men: 33%; women: 67%. **Ethnic makeup:** African American: 1%; American-Indian: 2%; Hispanic: 2%; White: 95%; International: 1%. **Religious preference:** Roman Catholic: 38%; Protestant: 23%; Muslim: 1%; Unknown: 30%; Other: 8%.

ADMISSIONS FACTS AND FIGURES
Phone: (800) 658-4552. **Email:** mmcadmit@mtmc.edu. **Website:** http://www.mtmc.edu. **Application deadlines for fall 2007:** Regular decision: August 30. Early decision: Not offered. Early action: Not offered. Admission can be deferred. **Application fee:** $35. Common application is not accepted. **To apply online, go to:** http://www.applyweb.com/aw?mtmc. **Admissions requirements/recommendations:** Tests: The college uses SAT or ACT scores in admissions decisions. Either SAT or ACT required. For admission to the fall 2007 entering class, the school will accept: ACT with writing, ACT without writing. Campus visit: Recommended. Admissions interview: Recommended. Off-campus interview: May be arranged. **Factors that count in admissions decisions:** *Academic:* Secondary school record: Very important. Class rank: Important. Letters of recommendation: Considered. Standardized test scores: Very important. Essay: Considered. *Nonacademic:* Interview: Considered. Extracurricular activities: Considered. Talent/ability: Considered. Character/personal qualities: Considered. Alumni/ae relationship: Considered. Geographical residence: Considered. State residency: Considered. Religious affiliation/commitment: Considered. Minority status: Considered. Volunteer work: Considered. Work experience: Considered. **Other schools with the greatest overlap in applicants:** Dakota Wesleyan University; South Dakota State University; University of South Dakota; Wayne State College. **Admissions statistics for the fall 2005 entering class:** Total applicants: 317. Total accepted: 268. Freshmen enrolled: 148; 23% were from out of state. Overall acceptance rate: 85%. **Size of waiting list:** 0 applicants; enrolled from waiting list: N/A. **Credentials of fall 2005 freshmen:** 13% ranked in the top 10 percent of their high school class; 51% were in the top 25 percent, and 81% were in the top half. (Proportion submitting class standing: 85%.) **Average high school grade point average:** 3.3. **First-year students submitting ACT scores:** 78%. Scores (25/75 percentile): English: 18-25, Math: 17-25, Composite: 19-25.

ACADEMICS
Year founded: 1936. **Academic calendar:** Semester. **Degrees offered:** certificate, associate, bachelor's, master's. **Most popular majors:** 21% education, 20% business, management, marketing, and related support services, 16% health professions and related clinical sciences. **Major fields of study:** biological and biomedical sciences; business, management, marketing, and related support services; communications technologies/technicians and support services; computer and information sciences and support services; education; English language and literature/letters; health professions and related clinical sciences; history; liberal arts and sciences studies, and humanities; mathematics and statistics; parks, recreation, leisure, and fitness studies; philosophy and religious studies; physical sciences; psychology; security and protective services; social sciences; visual and performing arts. **Areas of required coursework:** arts/fine arts, humanities, computer literacy, mathematics, English (including composition), philosophy, sciences (biological or physical), history, social science. **Pre-professional programs:** pre-law, pre-dentistry, pre-medicine, pre-veterinary science, pre-optometry, pre-pharmacy. **Special academic programs (% participation):** accelerated program (2%), cooperative (work-study plan) program (50%), double major (5%), honors program (5%), independent study (10%), internships (25%), student-designed major (2%), teacher certificate program (15%), weekend college (1%). **Teacher certification offered in:** special education, elementary, middle/junior high, secondary. **Reserve Officers Training Corps (ROTC):** Army ROTC: Offered at cooperating institution (University of South Dakota). **Faculty and instruction (2005-2006):** Total full-time faculty: 48 full-time, 65 part-time (49% men; 51% women; 1% minorities). Full-time faculty with Ph.D. or other terminal degree: 54%. Student/faculty ratio: 12/1. Classes of fewer than 20 students: 83%; of 20 to 49 students: 17%; of 50 or more students: 0%. **Advanced Placement and International Baccalaureate credit:** AP tests may be used for: Credit and/or placement. International Baccalaureate exams may be used for: Credit and/or placement. **Freshmen returning for sophomore year:** 73%. **Graduation rates:** Four-year: 28%; five-year: 43%; six-year: 49%. **Graduate study:** 10% of students pursue further study immediately upon graduation; 3% within one year; 3% within five years. Fields in which graduates pursue further study: law, 5%; medicine, 60%; theology (or the seminary), 5%; arts and sciences, 30%.

COSTS AND FINANCIAL AID
Financial aid office: (605) 668-1589. **Expenses (2006-2007):** Tuition and fees 2006-2007: $16,582; room/board: $4,958. Estimated books and supplies: $800; transportation: $1,236; personal expenses: $1,682. **Financial aid:** Priority filing date for institution's financial aid form: March 1. In 2005-2006, 96% of undergraduates applied for financial aid. Of those, 88% were determined to have financial need; 20% had their need fully met. Average financial aid package (proportion receiving): $13,253 (88%). Average amount

of gift aid, such as scholarships or grants (proportion receiving): $8,552 (87%). Average amount of self-help aid, such as work study or loans (proportion receiving): $5,103 (83%). Average need-based loan (excluding PLUS or other private loans): $4,632. Among students who received need-based aid, the average percentage of need met: 75%. Among students who received aid based on merit, the average award (and the proportion receiving): $9,217 (10%). The average athletic scholarship (and the proportion receiving): $3,554 (4%). Average amount of debt of borrowers graduating in 2005: $26,304. Proportion who borrowed: 85%.

CAMPUS LIFE AND EXTRACURRICULAR ACTIVITIES
Campus housing available (% using): women's dorms (73%), men's dorms (27%). Students who live in college-owned, operated, or affiliated housing: 85%. **Student employment:** During the 2005-2006 academic year, 3% of undergraduates worked on campus. Average per-year earnings: $2,000. **Clubs and organizations:** Number of student organizations: 40. Activities include: choral groups, concert band, drama/theater, jazz band, literary magazine, music ensembles, musical theater, pep band, student government, student newspaper. Number of fraternities: 0; sororities: 0. Average proportion of students who stay on campus on weekends: 20%. **Sports program (2005-2006):** Member of NAIA. *Men's intercollegiate varsity sports:* baseball, basketball, cross-country, golf, soccer, track and field (indoor), track and field (outdoor). *Women's intercollegiate varsity sports:* basketball, cross-country, golf, soccer, softball, track and field (indoor), track and field (outdoor), volleyball.

SERVICES AND FACILITIES
Basic services: nonremedial tutoring, placement service, day care, health service, health insurance. **Remedial assistance:** reading, math, writing, study skills. **Counseling services:** career, personal, academic, older student, psychological, religious. **For learning-disabled students:** School does not offer a structured program with separate admission and additional fees. Services include: remedial math, other testing accommodations, remedial English, remedial reading, tape recorders, untimed tests, note-taking services, oral tests, learning center, readers, extended time for tests, tutors. **Library:** Number of titles: 76,152; number of current serial subscriptions: 400. **Information technology resources:** Students are required to lease or own a computer. Number of campus computers available to all students: 21. School has a wireless network. Approximate number of users that can be accommodated: 700. Proportion of college-owned housing units wired for high-speed internet access: 100%. **Campus safety:** Security services offered: 24-hour emergency telephones, lighted pathways/sidewalks, controlled dormitory access (key, security card, etc).

TRANSFER AND INTERNATIONAL STUDENTS
Transfer students: May apply for admission for the following academic terms: Fall, Spring, Summer. Applicants do not need a minimum number of credits to apply. For fall 2005: Transfer applications received: 100. Transfer applicants offered admission: 100. Transfer applicants enrolled: 100. **International students:** Number of foreign undergraduates: 3 (1% of student body). Minimum TOEFL score required: 500 (paper); 173 (computer).

Northern State University

- **Address:** 1200 S. Jay Street, Aberdeen, SD 57401-7198
- **Website:** http://www.northern.edu
- **Public**
- **Enrollment:** 1,595 full-time; 830 part-time

KEY STATS
✔ **U.S News College Ranking:** fourth tier, Universities–Master's (Midwest)
✔ **ACT Score (25th/75th percentile):** 19-24
✔ **Tuition:** 2006-2007: $4,962 in state, $6,153 out of state

Selectivity: Selective	**Room/board:** $4,102
Acceptance rate: 94%	**Average debt:** $19,864
Student/faculty ratio: 20/1	**Proportion who borrowed:** 80%

UNDERGRADUATE STUDENT BODY STATS
2005-2006 enrollment: 1,595 full-time; 830 part-time. Men: 41%; women: 59%. **Ethnic makeup:** African American: 2%; American-Indian: 3%; Asian American: 1%; Hispanic: 1%; White: 89%; International: 4%.

ADMISSIONS FACTS AND FIGURES
Phone: (800) 678-5330. **Email:** admissions@northern.edu. **Website:** http://www.northern.edu. **Application deadlines for fall 2007:** Regular decision: September 1. Early decision: Not offered. Early action: Not offered. Admission can be deferred. **Application fee:** $15. Common application is accepted. **To apply online, go to:** http://www.northern.edu/prospective/index.html. **Admissions requirements/recommendations:** High school units required (recommended): English: 4; Mathematics: 3; Science: 3; Social studies: 3; Total units: 13. Tests: The college uses SAT or ACT scores in admissions decisions. Neither SAT nor ACT required. For admission to the fall 2007 entering class, the school will accept: ACT with writing, ACT without writing. Campus visit: Recommended. Admissions interview: Recommended. Off-campus interview: May be arranged. **Factors that count in admissions decisions:** *Academic:* Secondary school record: Very important. Class rank: Very important. Letters of recommendation: Not considered. Standardized test scores: Very important. Essay: Not considered. *Nonacademic:* Interview: Considered. Extracurricular activities: Not considered. Talent/ability: Considered. Character/personal qualities: Not considered. Alumni/ae relationship: Not considered. Geographical residence: Not considered. State residency: Not considered. Religious affiliation/commitment: Not considered. Minority status: Not considered. Volunteer work: Not considered. Work experience: Not considered. **Other schools with the greatest overlap in applicants:** South Dakota State University; University of South Dakota. **Admissions statistics for the fall 2005 entering class:** Total applicants: 783. Total accepted: 737. Freshmen enrolled: 381; Overall acceptance rate: 94%. **Credentials of fall 2005 freshmen:** 20% ranked in the top 10 percent of their high school class; 46% were in the top 25 percent, and 69% were in the top half. (Proportion submitting class standing: 94%.) **Average high school grade point average:** 3.1. First-year students who submitted SAT scores: 1%. Scores (25/75 percentile): Verbal: N/A, Math: N/A, Combined: N/A. **First-year students submitting ACT scores:** 95%. Scores (25/75 percentile): English: N/A, Math: N/A, Composite: 19-24.

ACADEMICS
Year founded: 1901. **Academic calendar:** Semester. **Degrees offered:** certificate, associate, bachelor's, post-bachelor's certificate, master's. **Most popular majors:** 34% business/commerce, 34% education, 11% sociology, 6% biology, 3% psychology. **Major fields of study:** biological and biomedical sciences; business, management, marketing, and related support services; computer and information sciences and support services; education; English language and literature/letters; foreign languages, literatures, and linguistics; health professions and related clinical sciences; history; liberal arts and sciences studies, and humanities; mathematics and statistics; parks, recreation, leisure, and fitness studies; physical sciences; psychology; public administration and social service professions; social sciences; visual and performing arts. **Areas of required coursework:** arts/fine arts, humanities, computer literacy, mathematics, English (including composition), philosophy, foreign languages, sciences (biological or physical), history, social science. **Pre-professional programs:** pre-law, pre-dentistry, pre-medicine, pre-veterinary science. **Special academic programs:** accelerated program, cooperative (work-study plan) program, cross-registration, distance learning, double major, dual enrollment, English as a Second Language (ESL), exchange student program (domestic), external degree program, honors program, independent study, internships, liberal arts/career combination, student-designed major, study abroad, teacher certificate program, weekend college. **Teacher certification offered in:** early childhood, special education, elementary, middle/junior high, secondary. **Cooperative education programs:** business, education. **Faculty and instruction (2005-2006):** Total instructional faculty: 94. Full-time faculty with Ph.D. or other terminal degree: 81%. Student/faculty ratio: 20/1. **Advanced Placement and International Baccalaureate credit:** AP tests may be used for: Credit and/or placement. International Baccalaureate exams may be used for: Credit only. **Freshmen returning for sophomore year:** 70%. **Graduation rates:** Six-year: 42%. **Graduate study:** 10% of students pursue further study immediately upon graduation.

COSTS AND FINANCIAL AID
Financial aid office: (605) 626-2640. **Expenses (2006-2007):** Tuition and fees 2006-2007: $4,962 in state, $6,153 out of state; room/board: $4,102. Estimated books and supplies: $850; transportation: $1,200; personal expenses: $1,600. **Financial aid:** Priority filing date for institution's financial aid form: March 1. In 2005-2006, 77% of undergraduates applied for financial aid. Of those, 60% were determined to have financial need; 99% had their need fully met. Average financial aid package (proportion receiving): $6,076 (59%). Average amount of gift aid, such as scholarships or grants

(proportion receiving): $2,540 (46%). Average amount of self-help aid, such as work study or loans (proportion receiving): $4,273 (50%). Average need-based loan (excluding PLUS or other private loans): $3,505. Among students who received aid based on merit, the average award (and the proportion receiving): $1,692 (7%). The average athletic scholarship (and the proportion receiving): $2,369 (11%). Average amount of debt of borrowers graduating in 2005: $19,864. Proportion who borrowed: 80%.

CAMPUS LIFE AND EXTRACURRICULAR ACTIVITIES

Campus housing available: coed dorms, women's dorms, men's dorms, apartments for married students, special housing for international students. **Student employment:** During the 2005-2006 academic year, 10% of undergraduates worked on campus. Average per-year earnings: $2,000. **Clubs and organizations:** Number of student organizations: 100. Activities include: choral groups, concert band, dance, drama/theater, jazz band, marching band, music ensembles, musical theater, pep band, student government, student newspaper, symphony orchestra, television station, yearbook. Average proportion of students who stay on campus on weekends: 35%. **Sports program (2005-2006):** Member of NCAA II. *Men's intercollegiate varsity sports:* baseball, basketball, cross-country, football, golf, track and field (indoor), track and field (outdoor), wrestling. *Women's intercollegiate varsity sports:* basketball, cross-country, golf, soccer, softball, track and field (indoor), track and field (outdoor), volleyball.

SERVICES AND FACILITIES

Basic services: nonremedial tutoring, placement service, day care, health service, health insurance. **Remedial assistance:** reading, math, writing, study skills. **Counseling services:** minority student, career, military, personal, veteran student, academic, older student, psychological, religious. **For learning-disabled students:** School does not offer a structured program with separate admission and additional fees. Total undergraduates in learning-disabled program or receiving services: 28. Services include: remedial math, remedial English, remedial reading, tape recorders, diagnostic testing service, untimed tests, note-taking services, oral tests, readers, extended time for tests, tutors. **Library:** Number of titles: 204,804; number of current serial subscriptions: 150. **Information technology resources:** Students are not required to lease or own a computer. Number of campus computers available to all students: 900. School has a wireless network. Proportion of college-owned housing units wired for high-speed internet access: 100%. **Campus safety:** Security services offered: 24-hour foot-and-vehicle patrols, late-night transport/escort service, 24-hour emergency telephones, lighted pathways/sidewalks, student patrols, controlled dormitory access (key, security card, etc).

TRANSFER AND INTERNATIONAL STUDENTS

Transfer students: May apply for admission for the following academic terms: Fall, Spring, Summer. Applicants do not need a minimum number of credits to apply. For fall 2005: Transfer applications received: 369. Transfer applicants offered admission: 336. Transfer applicants enrolled: 253. **International students:** Number of foreign undergraduates: 70 (4% of student body). Minimum TOEFL score required: 500 (paper); 173 (computer).

South Dakota School of Mines and Tech.

- **Address:** 501 E. St. Joseph Street, Rapid City, SD 57701
- **Website:** http://www.sdsmt.edu
- **Public**
- **Enrollment:** 1,592 full-time; 465 part-time

KEY STATS

✔ **U.S News College Ranking:** Unranked Specialty School–Engineering
✔ **ACT Score (25th/75th percentile):** 22-27
✔ **Tuition:** 2006-2007: $4,757 in state, $9,744 out of state

Selectivity: More selective	**Room/board:** $3,095
Acceptance rate: 94%	**Average debt:** N/A
Student/faculty ratio: 16/1	**Proportion who borrowed:** N/A

UNDERGRADUATE STUDENT BODY STATS

2005-2006 enrollment: 1,592 full-time; 465 part-time. Men: 68%; women: 32%. **Ethnic makeup:** African American: 1%; American-Indian: 3%; Asian American: 1%; Hispanic: 1%; White: 93%; International: 2%.

ADMISSIONS FACTS AND FIGURES

Phone: (605) 394-2414. **Email:** admissions@sdsmt.edu. **Website:** http://www.sdsmt.edu. **Application deadlines for fall 2007:** Regular decision: Rolling. Early decision: Not offered. Early action: Not offered. Admission can be deferred. **Application fee:** $20. Common application is not accepted. **To apply online, go to:** http://www.applyweb.com. **Admissions requirements/recommendations:** High school units required (recommended): English: 4; Mathematics: 3; Science: 6; Social studies: 3; Total units: 18. Tests: The college uses SAT or ACT scores in admissions decisions. Either SAT or ACT required. For admission to the fall 2007 entering class, the school will accept: ACT without writing. Campus visit: Recommended. Admissions interview: Neither required nor recommended. Off-campus interview: May be arranged. **Factors that count in admissions decisions:** *Academic:* Secondary school record: Very important. Class rank: Very important. Letters of recommendation: Not considered. Standardized test scores: Very important. Essay: Not considered. *Nonacademic:* Interview: Not considered. Extracurricular activities: Not considered. Talent/ability: Not considered. Character/personal qualities: Not considered. Alumni/ae relationship: Not considered. Geographical residence: Not considered. State residency: Not considered. Religious affiliation/commitment: Not considered. Minority status: Not considered. Volunteer work: Considered. Work experience: Considered. **Other schools with the greatest overlap in applicants:** Black Hills State University; Colorado School of Mines; South Dakota State University; University of South Dakota. **Admissions statistics for the fall 2005 entering class:** Total applicants: 727. Total accepted: 682. Freshmen enrolled: 365; 33% were from out of state. Overall acceptance rate: 94%. **Credentials of fall 2005 freshmen:** 21% ranked in the top 10 percent of their high school class; 50% were in the top 25 percent, and 81% were in the top half. (Proportion submitting class standing: 95%.) **Average high school grade point average:** 3.4. **First-year students who submitted SAT scores:** 14%. Scores (25/75 percentile): Verbal: 480-570, Math: 510-610, Combined: 990-1180. **First-year students submitting ACT scores:** 97%. Scores (25/75 percentile): English: 20-26, Math: 22-28, Composite: 22-27.

ACADEMICS

Year founded: 1885. **Academic calendar:** Semester. **Degrees offered:** associate, bachelor's, master's, doctorate. **Most popular majors:** 22% mechanical engineering, 13% civil engineering, 11% multi/interdisciplinary studies, 10% electrical, electronics, and communications engineering, 9% computer and information sciences. **Major fields of study:** computer and information sciences and support services; engineering; mathematics and statistics; multi/interdisciplinary studies; physical sciences. **Areas of required coursework:** arts/fine arts, humanities, mathematics, English (including composition), sciences (biological or physical), history, social science. **Pre-professional programs:** pre-dentistry, pre-medicine, pre-optometry, other. **Special academic programs:** cooperative (work-study plan) program, cross-registration, distance learning, dual enrollment, independent study, internships, study abroad, other. **Cooperative education programs:** other. **Reserve Officers Training Corps (ROTC):** Army ROTC: Offered on campus. **Faculty and instruction (2005-2006):** Total instructional faculty: 107 full-time, 33 part-time (80% men; 20% women; 11% minorities). Full-time faculty with Ph.D. or other terminal degree: 85%. Student/faculty ratio: 16/1. Classes of fewer than 20 students: 32%; of 20 to 49 students: 59%; of 50 or more students: 9%. **Advanced Placement and International Baccalaureate credit:** International Baccalaureate exams may be used for: Credit and/or placement. **Freshmen returning for sophomore year:** 70%. **Graduation rates:** Four-year: 12%; five-year: 32%; six-year: 41%.

COSTS AND FINANCIAL AID

Financial aid office: (605) 394-2274. **Expenses (2006-2007):** Tuition and fees 2006-2007: $4,757 in state, $9,744 out of state; room/board: $3,095. Estimated books and supplies: $1,000; transportation: $500; personal expenses: $1,500. **Financial aid:** Priority filing date for institution's financial aid form: March 15. In 2005-2006, 92% of undergraduates applied for financial aid. Of those, 54% were determined to have financial need; 26% had their need fully met. Average financial aid package (proportion receiving): $6,673 (54%). Average amount of gift aid, such as scholarships or grants (proportion receiving): $3,289 (30%). Average amount of self-help aid, such as work study or loans (proportion receiving): $3,901 (49%). Average need-based loan (excluding PLUS or other private loans): $3,658. Among students who received need-based aid, the average percentage of need met: 68%. Among students who received aid based on merit, the average award (and the proportion receiving): $2,559 (17%). The average athletic scholarship (and the proportion receiving): $2,123 (4%).

CAMPUS LIFE AND EXTRACURRICULAR ACTIVITIES

Campus housing available: coed dorms, sorority housing, fraternity housing. Students who live in college-owned, operated, or affiliated housing: 32%. **Clubs and organizations:** Number of student organizations: 75. Activities include: choral groups, drama/theater, music ensembles, pep band, radio station, student government, student newspaper. Number of fraternities: 4; sororities: 2. Proportion of men in fraternities: 22%; of women in sororities: 23%. Average proportion of students who stay on campus on weekends: 30%. **Sports program (2005-2006):** Member of NAIA. *Men's intercollegiate varsity sports:* basketball, cross-country, football, golf, track and field (indoor), track and field (outdoor). *Women's intercollegiate varsity sports:* basketball, cross-country, golf, track and field (indoor), track and field (outdoor), volleyball.

SERVICES AND FACILITIES

Basic services: health service, other. **Counseling services:** minority student, career, military, personal, veteran student, academic, older student, psychological, birth control. **For learning-disabled students:** School does not offer a structured program with separate admission and additional fees. Services include: reading machines, learning center. **Library:** Number of titles: 97,691; number of current serial subscriptions: 27,332. **Information technology resources:** Students are not required to lease or own a computer. Number of campus computers available to all students: 275. School has a wireless network. Proportion of college-owned housing units wired for high-speed internet access: 100%. **Campus safety:** Security services offered: 24-hour emergency telephones, lighted pathways/sidewalks, controlled dormitory access (key, security card, etc).

TRANSFER AND INTERNATIONAL STUDENTS

Transfer students: May apply for admission for the following academic terms: Fall, Spring, Summer. Applicants do not need a minimum number of credits to apply. For fall 2005: Transfer applications received: 197. Transfer applicants offered admission: 171. Transfer applicants enrolled: 110. **International students:** Number of foreign undergraduates: 26 (2% of student body). Minimum TOEFL score required: 530 (paper); 200 (computer).

South Dakota State University

- **Address:** Box 2201, Brookings, SD 57007
- **Website:** http://www3.sdstate.edu
- **Public**
- **Enrollment:** 7,749 full-time; 1,845 part-time

KEY STATS

✔ **U.S News College Ranking:** third tier, National Universities
✔ **ACT Score (25th/75th percentile):** 20-25
✔ **Tuition:** 2006-2007: $5,052 in state, $10,239 out of state

Selectivity: Selective	Room/board: $5,029
Acceptance rate: 93%	Average debt: $19,520
Student/faculty ratio: 18/1	Proportion who borrowed: 81%

UNDERGRADUATE STUDENT BODY STATS

2005-2006 enrollment: 7,749 full-time; 1,845 part-time. Men: 48%; women: 52%. **Ethnic makeup:** African American: 1%; American-Indian: 1%; Asian American: 1%; Hispanic: 1%; White: 96%.

ADMISSIONS FACTS AND FIGURES

Phone: (605) 688-4121. **Email:** SDSU_Admissions@sdstate.edu. **Website:** http://www3.sdstate.edu. **Application deadlines for fall 2007:** Regular decision: Rolling. Early decision: Not offered. Early action: Not offered. Admission can be deferred. **Application fee:** $20. Common application is not accepted. **To apply online, go to:** http://www.applyweb.com/aw?sdksd/. **Admissions requirements/recommendations:** High school units required (recommended): English: 4; Mathematics: 3; Science: 3; Foreign language: 0; Social studies: 3; History: 0; Academic electives: 0; Total units: 14. **Tests:** The college uses SAT or ACT scores in admissions decisions. Either SAT or ACT required. For admission to the fall 2007 entering class, the school will accept: ACT with writing, ACT without writing. Campus visit: Recommended. Admissions interview: Neither required nor recommended. Off-campus interview: Not available. **Factors that count in admissions decisions:** *Academic:* Secondary school record: Very important. Class rank: Very important. Letters of recommendation: Considered. Standardized test

scores: Very important. Essay: Not considered. *Nonacademic:* Interview: Not considered. Extracurricular activities: Not considered. Talent/ability: Not considered. Character/personal qualities: Not considered. Alumni/ae relationship: Not considered. Geographical residence: Not considered. State residency: Not considered. Religious affiliation/commitment: Not considered. Minority status: Not considered. Volunteer work: Not considered. Work experience: Not considered. **Other schools with the greatest overlap in applicants:** Iowa State University; North Dakota State University; University of Nebraska–Lincoln; University of South Dakota. **Admissions statistics for the fall 2005 entering class:** Total applicants: 3,641. Total accepted: 3,376. Freshmen enrolled: 1,869; 33% were from out of state. Overall acceptance rate: 93%. **Credentials of fall 2005 freshmen:** 15% ranked in the top 10 percent of their high school class; 37% were in the top 25 percent, and 70% were in the top half. (Proportion submitting class standing: 98%.) **Average high school grade point average:** 3.4. **First-year students submitting ACT scores:** 98%. Scores (25/75 percentile): English: 19-25, Math: 19-26, Composite: 20-25.

ACADEMICS

Year founded: 1881. **Academic calendar:** Semester. **Degrees offered:** associate, terminal-associate, bachelor's, master's, post-master's certificate, first professional, doctorate. **Most popular majors:** 17% nursing/registered nurse training (R.N., A.S.N., B.S.N., M.S.N.), 5% economics, 4% biology/biological sciences, 4% pharmaceutics and drug design (M.S., Ph.D.), 3% sociology. **Major fields of study:** agriculture, agriculture operations, and related sciences; biological and biomedical sciences; business, management, marketing, and related support services; communication, journalism, and related programs; computer and information sciences and support services; education; engineering; engineering technologies/technicians; English language and literature/letters; family and consumer sciences/human sciences; foreign languages, literatures, and linguistics; health professions and related clinical sciences; history; liberal arts and sciences studies, and humanities; mathematics and statistics; multi/interdisciplinary studies; natural resources and conservation; parks, recreation, leisure, and fitness studies; physical sciences; psychology; social sciences; visual and performing arts. **Areas of required coursework:** arts/fine arts, humanities, computer literacy, mathematics, English (including composition), sciences (biological or physical), social science, other. **Pre-professional programs:** pre-law, pre-dentistry, pre-medicine, pre-theology, pre-veterinary science, pre-optometry, pre-pharmacy, other. **Special academic programs:** accelerated program, cooperative (work-study plan) program, cross-registration, distance learning, double major, dual enrollment, exchange student program (domestic), honors program, independent study, internships, study abroad, teacher certificate program, other. **Teacher certification offered in:** early childhood, elementary, vo-tech, middle/junior high, secondary, bilingual/bicultural. **Cooperative education programs:** agriculture, business, computer science, education, engineering, health professions, home economics, natural science, social/behavioral science, technologies. **Reserve Officers Training Corps (ROTC):** Army ROTC: Offered on campus; Air Force ROTC: Offered on campus. **Faculty and instruction (2005-2006):** Total instructional faculty: 411 full-time, 173 part-time (53% men; 47% women; 8% minorities). Full-time faculty with Ph.D. or other terminal degree: 78%. Student/faculty ratio: 18/1. Classes of fewer than 20 students: 38%; of 20 to 49 students: 49%; of 50 or more students: 13%. **Advanced Placement and International Baccalaureate credit:** AP tests may be used for: Credit only. Scores accepted: 3, 4, 5. International Baccalaureate exams may be used for: Credit only. **Freshmen returning for sophomore year:** 75%. **Graduation rates:** Four-year: 24%; five-year: 49%; six-year: 54%.

COSTS AND FINANCIAL AID

Financial aid office: (605) 688-4695. **Expenses (2006-2007):** Tuition and fees 2006-2007: $5,052 in state, $10,239 out of state; room/board: $5,029. Estimated books and supplies: $896; transportation: $1,130; personal expenses: $1,854. **Financial aid:** Priority filing date for institution's financial aid form: March 15. In 2005-2006, 86% of undergraduates applied for financial aid. Of those, 80% were determined to have financial need; 77% had their need fully met. Average financial aid package (proportion receiving): $7,550 (79%). Average amount of gift aid, such as scholarships or grants (proportion receiving): $3,128 (40%). Average amount of self-help aid, such as work study or loans (proportion receiving): $4,631 (78%). Average need-based loan (excluding PLUS or other private loans): $4,486. Among students who received need-based aid, the average percentage of need met: 83%. Among students who received aid based on merit, the average award (and the proportion receiving): $1,002 (13%). The average athletic scholarship (and the proportion receiving): $4,062 (3%). Average amount of

debt of borrowers graduating in 2005: $19,520. Proportion who borrowed: 81%.

CAMPUS LIFE AND EXTRACURRICULAR ACTIVITIES
Campus housing available: coed dorms, apartments for married students, apartment for single students, special housing for disabled students. Students who live in college-owned, operated, or affiliated housing: 33%. **Student employment:** During the 2005-2006 academic year, 21% of undergraduates worked on campus. **Clubs and organizations:** Number of student organizations: 205. Activities include: choral groups, concert band, dance, drama/theater, jazz band, literary magazine, marching band, music ensembles, musical theater, pep band, radio station, student government, student newspaper, symphony orchestra, television station, yearbook. Number of fraternities: 7; sororities: 3. Proportion of men in fraternities: 5%; of women in sororities: 2%. Average proportion of students who stay on campus on weekends: 68%. **Sports program (2005-2006):** Member of NCAA II. *Men's intercollegiate varsity sports:* baseball, basketball, cross-country, football, golf, swimming and diving, tennis, track and field (indoor), track and field (outdoor), wrestling. *Women's intercollegiate varsity sports:* basketball, cross-country, equestrian sports, golf, soccer, softball, swimming and diving, tennis, track and field (indoor), track and field (outdoor), volleyball.

SERVICES AND FACILITIES
Basic services: nonremedial tutoring, placement service, health service, health insurance, other. **Remedial assistance:** reading, math, writing, study skills. **Counseling services:** minority student, career, military, personal, veteran student, academic, older student, other. **For learning-disabled students:** School does not offer a structured program with separate admission and additional fees. Total undergraduates in learning-disabled program or receiving services: 65. Services include: remedial math, remedial English, reading machines, remedial reading, tape recorders, videotaped classes, diagnostic testing service, untimed tests, note-taking services, oral tests, readers, extended time for tests, tutors, priority seating, texts on tape, exams on tape or computer, other testing accomodations. **Library:** Number of titles: 890,319; number of current serial subscriptions: 27,646. **Information technology resources:** Students are not required to lease or own a computer. Number of campus computers available to all students: 1,022. School has a wireless network. Proportion of college-owned housing units wired for high-speed internet access: 100%. **Campus safety:** Security services offered: 24-hour foot-and-vehicle patrols, late-night transport/escort service, 24-hour emergency telephones, lighted pathways/sidewalks, student patrols, controlled dormitory access (key, security card, etc).

TRANSFER AND INTERNATIONAL STUDENTS
Transfer students: May apply for admission for the following academic terms: Fall, Spring, Summer. Applicants do not need a minimum number of credits to apply. For fall 2005: Transfer applications received: 1,226. Transfer applicants offered admission: 1,030. Transfer applicants enrolled: 661. **International students:** Number of foreign undergraduates: 16. Number of countries represented: 21. Minimum TOEFL score required: 500 (paper); 173 (computer).

University of Sioux Falls

- **Address:** 1101 W. 22nd Street, Sioux Falls, SD 57105
- **Website:** http://www.usiouxfalls.edu
- **Private; Religious affiliation:** American Baptist
- **Enrollment:** 1,168 full-time; 128 part-time

KEY STATS
✔ **U.S News College Ranking:** 70, Universities–Master's (Midwest)
✔ **ACT Score (25th/75th percentile):** 19-25
✔ **Tuition:** 2006-2007: $16,720

Selectivity: Selective	Room/board: $5,100
Acceptance rate: 95%	Average debt: N/A
Student/faculty ratio: 17/1	Proportion who borrowed: N/A

UNDERGRADUATE STUDENT BODY STATS
2005-2006 enrollment: 1,168 full-time; 128 part-time. Men: 46%; women: 54%. **Ethnic makeup:** African American: 2%; Hispanic: 1%; White: 97%. **Religious preference:** Roman Catholic: 12%; No preference: 3%; Unknown: 30%; American Baptist: 19%; Lutheran: 17%; Other: 19%.

ADMISSIONS FACTS AND FIGURES
Phone: (605) 331-6600. **Email:** admissions@usiouxfalls.edu. **Website:** http://www.usiouxfalls.edu. **Application deadlines for fall 2007:** Regular decision: Rolling. Early decision: Not offered. Early action: Not offered. Admission can be deferred. **Application fee:** $25. Common application is not accepted. **To apply online, go to:** http://www.usiouxfalls.edu/admissions/index.html. **Admissions requirements/recommendations:** High school units required (recommended): English: (4); Mathematics: (3); Science: (2); Social studies: (3); History: (3). Tests: The college uses SAT or ACT scores in admissions decisions. ACT required. For admission to the fall 2007 entering class, the school will accept: ACT with writing, ACT without writing. Campus visit: Recommended. Admissions interview: Neither required nor recommended. Off-campus interview: May be arranged. **Factors that count in admissions decisions:** *Academic:* Secondary school record: Very important. Class rank: Very important. Letters of recommendation: Considered. Standardized test scores: Very important. Essay: Not considered. *Nonacademic:* Interview: Considered. Extracurricular activities: Not considered. Talent/ability: Not considered. Character/personal qualities: Not considered. Alumni/ae relationship: Not considered. Geographical residence: Not considered. State residency: Not considered. Religious affiliation/commitment: Not considered. Minority status: Not considered. Volunteer work: Not considered. Work experience: Not considered. **Other schools with the greatest overlap in applicants:** Bethel College; Dakota Wesleyan University; Dordt College; Northwestern College; South Dakota State University. **Admissions statistics for the fall 2005 entering class:** Total applicants: 552. Total accepted: 526. Freshmen enrolled: 224; 37% were from out of state. Overall acceptance rate: 95%. **Credentials of fall 2005 freshmen:** 16% ranked in the top 10 percent of their high school class; 39% were in the top 25 percent, and 69% were in the top half. (Proportion submitting class standing: 96%.) **Average high school grade point average:** 3.3. **First-year students who submitted SAT scores:** 2%. Scores (25/75 percentile): Verbal: 395-500, Math: 400-550, Combined: 795-1050. **First-year students submitting ACT scores:** 98%. Scores (25/75 percentile): English: N/A, Math: N/A, Composite: 19-25.

ACADEMICS
Year founded: 1883. **Academic calendar:** 4-1-4. **Degrees offered:** associate, bachelor's, master's. **Most popular majors:** 20% business administration and management, 20% organizational behavior studies, 16% elementary education and teaching, 6% philosophy and religious studies, 5% criminal justice/safety studies. **Major fields of study:** biological and biomedical sciences; business, management, marketing, and related support services; communication, journalism, and related programs; computer and information sciences and support services; education; English language and literature/letters; health professions and related clinical sciences; history; liberal arts and sciences studies, and humanities; mathematics and statistics; parks, recreation, leisure, and fitness studies; philosophy and religious studies; physical sciences; psychology; public administration and social service professions; security and protective services; social sciences; theology and religious vocations; visual and performing arts. **Areas of required coursework:** arts/fine arts, humanities, computer literacy, mathematics, English (including composition), philosophy, sciences (biological or physical), history, social science, other. **Pre-professional programs:** pre-law, pre-dentistry, pre-medicine, pre-theology, pre-veterinary science, other. **Special academic programs (% participation):** accelerated program (1%), cross-registration (1%), distance learning (5%), double major (15%), honors program (5%), independent study (15%), internships (10%), student-designed major (1%), study abroad (1%), teacher certificate program (2%), weekend college (10%). **Teacher certification offered in:** early childhood, elementary, middle/junior high, secondary. **Faculty and instruction (2005-2006):** Total instructional faculty: 62 full-time, 75 part-time (54% men; 46% women; 3% minorities). Full-time faculty with Ph.D. or other terminal degree: 71%. Student/faculty ratio: 17/1. Classes of fewer than 20 students: 60%; of 20 to 49 students: 39%; of 50 or more students: 2%. **Advanced Placement and International Baccalaureate credit:** AP tests may be used for: Credit only. Scores accepted: 4, 5. International Baccalaureate exams may be used for: Credit only. **Freshmen returning for sophomore year:** 67%. **Graduation rates:** Four-year: 27%; five-year: 42%; six-year: 49%. **Graduate study:** 10% of students pursue further study immediately upon graduation; 10% within one year. Fields in which graduates pursue further study: Master of Business Administration (MBA), 1%; law, 1%; medicine, 1%; theology (or the seminary), 2%; education, 1%; arts and sciences, 4%.

COSTS AND FINANCIAL AID
Financial aid office: (605) 331-6623. **Expenses (2006-2007):** Tuition and fees 2006-2007: $16,720; room/board: $5,100. Estimated books and supplies:

$750; transportation: $500; personal expenses: $2,070. **Financial aid:** Priority filing date for institution's financial aid form: March 1.

CAMPUS LIFE AND EXTRACURRICULAR ACTIVITIES
Campus housing available (% using): coed dorms (55%), women's dorms (18%), men's dorms (14%), apartments for married students (10%), apartment for single students (3%). Students who live in college-owned, operated, or affiliated housing: 39%. **Student employment:** During the 2005-2006 academic year, 12% of undergraduates worked on campus. Average per-year earnings: $1,200. **Clubs and organizations:** Number of student organizations: 16. Activities include: choral groups, concert band, drama/theater, jazz band, literary magazine, music ensembles, musical theater, radio station, student government, student newspaper, student film society, television station. Number of fraternities: 0; sororities: 0. Average proportion of students who stay on campus on weekends: 70%. **Sports program (2005-2006):** Member of NAIA. *Men's intercollegiate varsity sports:* baseball, basketball, cross-country, football, golf, soccer, tennis, track and field (indoor), track and field (outdoor). *Women's intercollegiate varsity sports:* basketball, cross-country, golf, soccer, softball, tennis, track and field (indoor), track and field (outdoor), volleyball.

SERVICES AND FACILITIES
Basic services: nonremedial tutoring, women's center, placement service, health insurance. **Remedial assistance:** reading, math, writing, study skills. **Counseling services:** minority student, career, personal, academic, older student, psychological, religious. **For learning-disabled students:** School does not offer a structured program with separate admission and additional fees. Total undergraduates in learning-disabled program or receiving services: 33. Services include: remedial math, tape recorders, untimed tests, note-taking services, special bookstore section, oral tests, learning center, readers, extended time for tests, tutors, priority seating, texts on tape. **Library:** Number of titles: 87,446; number of current serial subscriptions: 403. **Information technology resources:** Students are not required to lease or own a computer. Number of campus computers available to all students: 155. School has a wireless network. Approximate number of users that can be accommodated: 120. Proportion of college-owned housing units wired for high-speed internet access: 100%. **Campus safety:** Security services offered: late-night transport/escort service, 24-hour emergency telephones, lighted pathways/sidewalks, controlled dormitory access (key, security card, etc).

TRANSFER AND INTERNATIONAL STUDENTS
Transfer students: May apply for admission for the following academic terms: Fall, Spring, Summer. Applicants do not need a minimum number of credits to apply. For fall 2005: Transfer applications received: 218. Transfer applicants offered admission: 185. Transfer applicants enrolled: 121. **International students:** Number of foreign undergraduates: 1. Number of countries represented: 1. Minimum TOEFL score required: 500 (paper); 173 (computer).

University of South Dakota

- ■ **Address:** 414 E. Clark Street, Vermillion, SD 57069
- ■ **Website:** http://www.usd.edu
- ■ **Public**
- ■ **Enrollment:** 4,274 full-time; 2,134 part-time

KEY STATS
- ✔ **U.S News College Ranking:** third tier, National Universities
- ✔ **ACT Score (25th/75th percentile):** 19-25
- ✔ **Tuition:** 2006-2007: $5,072 in state, $10,259 out of state

Selectivity: Selective	**Room/board:** $4,964
Acceptance rate: 86%	**Average debt:** $19,535
Student/faculty ratio: 15/1	**Proportion who borrowed:** 80%

UNDERGRADUATE STUDENT BODY STATS
2005-2006 enrollment: 4,274 full-time; 2,134 part-time. Men: 38%; women: 62%. **Ethnic makeup:** African American: 1%; American-Indian: 2%; Asian American: 1%; Hispanic: 1%; White: 94%; International: 1%.

ADMISSIONS FACTS AND FIGURES
Phone: (605) 677-5434. **Email:** admiss@usd.edu. **Website:** http://www.usd.edu. **Application deadlines for fall 2007:** Regular decision: Rolling. Early decision: Not offered. Early action: Not offered. Admission can be deferred. **Application fee:** $20. Common application is not accepted. **To apply online, go to:** http://usd.edu/admissions/forms/ugAdmissionApplication.cfm. **Admissions requirements/recommendations:** High school units required (recommended): English: 4 (4); Mathematics: 3 (4); Science: 3 (4); Foreign language: 0 (2); Social studies: 3 (3); History: 0 (0); Academic electives: 0 (0); Total units: 14 (18). Tests: The college uses SAT or ACT scores in admissions decisions. Either SAT or ACT required. For admission to the fall 2007 entering class, the school will accept: ACT with writing, ACT without writing. Campus visit: Recommended. Admissions interview: Neither required nor recommended. Off-campus interview: May be arranged. **Factors that count in admissions decisions:** *Academic:* Secondary school record: Very important. Class rank: Very important. Letters of recommendation: Considered. Standardized test scores: Very important. Essay: Considered. *Nonacademic:* Interview: Not considered. Extracurricular activities: Considered. Talent/ability: Considered. Character/personal qualities: Not considered. Alumni/ae relationship: Not considered. Geographical residence: Not considered. State residency: Not considered. Religious affiliation/commitment: Not considered. Minority status: Considered. Volunteer work: Not considered. Work experience: Not considered. **Other schools with the greatest overlap in applicants:** Augustana College; Dakota State University; Mount Marty College; South Dakota State University; University of Nebraska–Lincoln. **Admissions statistics for the fall 2005 entering class:** Total applicants: 2,829. Total accepted: 2,439. Freshmen enrolled: 1,165; 27% were from out of state. Overall acceptance rate: 86%. **Credentials of fall 2005 freshmen:** 13% ranked in the top 10 percent of their high school class; 35% were in the top 25 percent, and 67% were in the top half. (Proportion submitting class standing: 95%.) **Average high school grade point average:** 3.2. **First-year students who submitted SAT scores:** 6%. Scores (25/75 percentile): Verbal: 440-610, Math: 450-600, Combined: 890-1210. **First-year students submitting ACT scores:** 97%. Scores (25/75 percentile): English: 19-25, Math: 18-24, Composite: 19-25.

ACADEMICS
Year founded: 1862. **Academic calendar:** Semester. **Degrees offered:** certificate, associate, terminal-associate, bachelor's, post-bachelor's certificate, master's, post-master's certificate, first professional, first professional certificate, doctorate. **Most popular majors:** 21% business, management, marketing, and related support services, 13% education, 10% health professions and related clinical sciences, 10% psychology, 7% social sciences. **Major fields of study:** area, ethnic, cultural, and gender studies; biological and biomedical sciences; business, management, marketing, and related support services; communication, journalism, and related programs; computer and information sciences and support services; education; English language and literature/letters; foreign languages, literatures, and linguistics; health professions and related clinical sciences; history; liberal arts and sciences studies, and humanities; mathematics and statistics; multi/interdisciplinary studies; parks, recreation, leisure, and fitness studies; philosophy and religious studies; physical sciences; psychology; security and protective services; social sciences; visual and performing arts. **Areas of required coursework:** arts/fine arts, humanities, computer literacy, mathematics, English (including composition), sciences (biological or physical), social science, other. **Preprofessional programs:** pre-law, pre-dentistry, pre-medicine, pre-veterinary science, pre-optometry, pre-pharmacy, other. **Special academic programs (% participation):** accelerated program (21%), cross-registration (24.7%), distance learning (60.5%), double major (11.3%), dual enrollment (7%), English as a Second Language (ESL) (1.3%), exchange student program (domestic) (2.3%), external degree program (5%), honors program (9.6%), independent study (1%), internships (42.7%), liberal arts/career combination (20%), student-designed major (1%), study abroad (.4%), teacher certificate program (17%). **Teacher certification offered in:** early childhood, special education, elementary, middle/junior high, adult education, secondary, bilingual/bicultural. **Reserve Officers Training Corps (ROTC):** Army ROTC: Offered on campus. **Faculty and instruction (2005-2006):** Total instructional faculty: 285 full-time, 37 part-time (59% men; 41% women; 10% minorities). Full-time faculty with Ph.D. or other terminal degree: 79%. Student/faculty ratio: 15/1. Classes of fewer than 20 students: 54%; of 20 to 49 students: 40%; of 50 or more students: 6%. **Advanced Placement and International Baccalaureate credit:** AP tests may be used for: Credit only. Scores accepted: 3, 4, 5. International Baccalaureate exams may be used for: Credit only. **Freshmen returning for sophomore year:** 69%. **Graduation rates:** Four-year: 21%; five-year: 42%; six-year: 46%. **Graduate study:** 21% of students pursue further study within one year. Fields in which graduates pursue further study: Master of Business Administration (MBA), 3%; law, 7%;

medicine, 4%; dentistry, 1%; theology (or the seminary), 1%; education, 11%; arts and sciences, 36%.

COSTS AND FINANCIAL AID

Financial aid office: (605) 677-5446. **Expenses (2006-2007):** Tuition and fees 2006-2007: $5,072 in state, $10,259 out of state; room/board: $4,964. Estimated books and supplies: $750; transportation: $1,100; personal expenses: $2,000. **Financial aid:** Priority filing date for institution's financial aid form: March 15; deadline: March 15. In 2005-2006, 81% of undergraduates applied for financial aid. Of those, 63% were determined to have financial need; 65% had their need fully met. Average financial aid package (proportion receiving): $5,545 (60%). Average amount of gift aid, such as scholarships or grants (proportion receiving): $3,061 (31%). Average amount of self-help aid, such as work study or loans (proportion receiving): $3,823 (59%). Average need-based loan (excluding PLUS or other private loans): $3,790. Among students who received need-based aid, the average percentage of need met: 75%. Among students who received aid based on merit, the average award (and the proportion receiving): $2,954 (17%). The average athletic scholarship (and the proportion receiving): $3,321 (6%). Average amount of debt of borrowers graduating in 2005: $19,535. Proportion who borrowed: 80%.

CAMPUS LIFE AND EXTRACURRICULAR ACTIVITIES

Campus housing available (% using): coed dorms (74%), sorority housing (10%), fraternity housing (10%), apartments for married students (2%), apartment for single students (4%), special housing for disabled students, other housing options. Students who live in college-owned, operated, or affiliated housing: 31%. **Student employment:** During the 2005-2006 academic year, 15% of undergraduates worked on campus. Average per-year earnings: $1,225. **Clubs and organizations:** Number of student organizations: 120. Activities include: choral groups, concert band, dance, drama/theater, jazz band, literary magazine, marching band, music ensembles, musical theater, opera, pep band, radio station, student government, student newspaper, symphony orchestra, television station. Number of fraternities: 8; sororities: 4. Proportion of men in fraternities: 9%; of women in sororities: 8%. Average proportion of students who stay on campus on weekends: 60%. **Sports program (2005-2006):** Member of NCAA II. *Men's intercollegiate varsity sports:* baseball, basketball, cross-country, football, golf, swimming and diving, track and field (indoor), track and field (outdoor). *Women's intercollegiate varsity sports:* basketball, cross-country, golf, soccer, softball, swimming and diving, tennis, track and field (indoor), track and field (outdoor), volleyball.

SERVICES AND FACILITIES

Basic services: nonremedial tutoring, placement service, day care, health service, health insurance, other. **Remedial assistance:** reading, math, writing, study skills. **Counseling services:** minority student, career, military, personal, veteran student, academic, psychological, birth control. **For learning-disabled students:** School does not offer a structured program with separate admission and additional fees. Services include: remedial math, remedial English, reading machines, tape recorders, other special classes, diagnostic testing service, untimed tests, note-taking services, oral tests, learning center, readers, extended time for tests, tutors, other. **Library:** Number of titles: 844,842; number of current serial subscriptions: 2,233. **Information technology resources:** Students are not required to lease or own a computer. Number of campus computers available to all students: 493. School has a wireless network. Approximate number of users that can be accommodated: 1,920. Proportion of college-owned housing units wired for high-speed internet access: 100%. **Campus safety:** Security services offered: 24-hour foot-and-vehicle patrols, late-night transport/escort service, 24-hour emergency telephones, lighted pathways/sidewalks, controlled dormitory access (key, security card, etc).

TRANSFER AND INTERNATIONAL STUDENTS

Transfer students: May apply for admission for the following academic terms: Fall, Spring, Summer. Applicants do not need a minimum number of credits to apply. For fall 2005: Transfer applications received: 1,591. Transfer applicants offered admission: 1,064. Transfer applicants enrolled: 707. **International students:** Number of foreign undergraduates: 30 (1% of student body). Number of countries represented: 28. Minimum TOEFL score required: 550 (paper); 213 (computer). Average TOEFL score: 550 (paper).

Tennessee

Austin Peay State University

- **Address:** PO Box 4675, Clarksville, TN 37044
- **Website:** http://www.apsu.edu
- **Public**
- **Enrollment:** 6,348 full-time; 1,868 part-time

KEY STATS
✔ **U.S News College Ranking:** third tier, Universities–Master's (South)
✔ **ACT Score (25th/75th percentile):** 19-24
✔ **Tuition:** 2006-2007: $4,635 in state, $13,947 out of state

Selectivity: Selective	**Room/board:** $4,800
Acceptance rate: 91%	**Average debt:** N/A
Student/faculty ratio: 21/1	**Proportion who borrowed:** N/A

UNDERGRADUATE STUDENT BODY STATS
2005-2006 enrollment: 6,348 full-time; 1,868 part-time. Men: 37%; women: 63%. **Ethnic makeup:** African American: 18%; American-Indian: 1%; Asian American: 2%; Hispanic: 4%; White: 74%.

ADMISSIONS FACTS AND FIGURES
Phone: (931) 221-7661. **Email:** admissions@apsu01.apsu.edu. **Website:** http://www.apsu.edu. **Application deadlines for fall 2007:** Regular decision: August 28. Early decision: Not offered. Early action: Not offered. Admission can be deferred. **Application fee:** $15. Common application is not accepted. **To apply online, go to:** http://www.apsu.edu/admissions. **Admissions requirements/recommendations:** High school units required (recommended): English: 4 (4); Mathematics: 3 (3); Science: 2 (2); Foreign language: 2 (2); Social studies: 1 (1); History: 1 (1); Total units: 14 (14). Tests: The college uses SAT or ACT scores in admissions decisions. Neither SAT nor ACT required. For admission to the fall 2007 entering class, the school will accept: ACT with writing, ACT without writing. Campus visit: Recommended. Admissions interview: Neither required nor recommended. Off-campus interview: Not available. **Factors that count in admissions decisions: Academic:** Secondary school record: Not considered. Class rank: Not considered. Letters of recommendation: Not considered. Standardized test scores: Very important. Essay: Not considered. **Nonacademic:** Interview: Not considered. Extracurricular activities: Not considered. Talent/ability: Not considered. Character/personal qualities: Not considered. Alumni/ae relationship: Not considered. Geographical residence: Not considered. State residency: Not considered. Religious affiliation/commitment: Not considered. Minority status: Not considered. Volunteer work: Not considered. Work experience: Not considered. **Admissions statistics for the fall 2005 entering class:** Total applicants: 2,608. Total accepted: 2,367. Freshmen enrolled: 1,408; 5% were from out of state. Overall acceptance rate: 91%. **Credentials of fall 2005 freshmen:** 14% ranked in the top 10 percent of their high school class; 36% were in the top 25 percent, and 68% were in the top half. (Proportion submitting class standing: 89%.) **Average high school grade point average:** 3.1. **First-year students who submitted SAT scores:** 6%. Scores (25/75 percentile): Verbal: 445-580, Math: 420-555, Combined: 865-1135. **First-year students submitting ACT scores:** 80%. Scores (25/75 percentile): English: 19-25, Math: 17-23, Composite: 19-24.

ACADEMICS
Year founded: 1927. **Academic calendar:** Semester. **Degrees offered:** certificate, associate, transfer-associate, terminal-associate, bachelor's, post-bachelor's certificate, master's, post-master's certificate. **Most popular majors:** 25% business, management, marketing, and related support services, 9% health professions and related clinical sciences, 8% communication, journalism, and related programs, 7% multi/interdisciplinary studies, 6% liberal arts and sciences studies, and humanities. **Major fields of study:** agriculture, agriculture operations, and related sciences; biological and biomedical sciences; business, management, marketing, and related support services; communication, journalism, and related programs; computer and information sciences and support services; education; engineering technologies/technicians; English language and literature/letters; foreign languages, literatures, and linguistics; health professions and related clinical sciences; history; liberal arts and sciences studies, and humanities; mathematics and statistics; multi/interdisciplinary studies; parks, recreation, leisure, and fitness studies; philosophy and religious studies; physical sciences; psychology; public administration and social service professions; security and protective services; social sciences; visual and performing arts. **Areas of required coursework:** arts/fine arts, humanities, mathematics, English (including composition), foreign languages, sciences (biological or physical), history, social science. **Pre-professional programs:** pre-law, pre-dentistry, pre-medicine, pre-veterinary science, pre-optometry, pre-pharmacy, other. **Special academic programs:** accelerated program, cooperative (work-study plan) program, distance learning, double major, dual enrollment, English as a Second Language (ESL), honors program, independent study, internships, study abroad, teacher certificate program, other. **Teacher certification offered in:** early childhood, special education, elementary, middle/junior high, secondary. **Cooperative education programs:** agriculture, art, business, computer science, education, engineering, health professions, humanities, natural science, social/behavioral science, technologies, vocational arts. **Reserve Officers Training Corps (ROTC):** Army ROTC: Offered on campus. **Faculty and instruction (2005-2006):** Total instructional faculty: 290 full-time, 174 part-time (52% men; 48% women; 12% minorities). Student/faculty ratio: 21/1. Classes of fewer than 20 students: 41%; of 20 to 49 students: 56%; of 50 or more students: 3%. **Advanced Placement and International Baccalaureate credit:** AP tests may be used for: Credit and/or placement. Scores accepted: 3, 4, 5. **Freshmen returning for sophomore year:** 63%. **Graduation rates:** Four-year: 10%; five-year: 25%; six-year: 31%.

COSTS AND FINANCIAL AID
Financial aid office: (931) 221-7907. **Expenses (2006-2007):** Tuition and fees 2006-2007: $4,635 in state, $13,947 out of state; room/board: $4,800. Estimated books and supplies: $1,350; transportation: $1,600; personal expenses: $3,000. **Financial aid:** Priority filing date for institution's financial aid form: April 1. In 2005-2006, 84% of undergraduates applied for financial aid. Of those, 74% were determined to have financial need; Average financial aid package (proportion receiving): $6,367 (72%). Average amount of gift aid, such as scholarships or grants (proportion receiving): $3,641 (43%). Average amount of self-help aid, such as work study or loans (proportion receiving): N/A (3%). Among students who received aid based on merit, the average award (and the proportion receiving): $4,457 (7%). The average athletic scholarship (and the proportion receiving): $4,481 (2%).

CAMPUS LIFE AND EXTRACURRICULAR ACTIVITIES
Campus housing available (% using): coed dorms (64%), women's dorms (20%), men's dorms (8%), sorority housing (0%), apartments for married students (2%), apartment for single students (6%), special housing for disabled students (0%). Students who live in college-owned, operated, or affiliated housing: 16%. **Clubs and organizations:** Number of student organizations: 90. Activities include: choral groups, concert band, dance, drama/theater, jazz band, literary magazine, marching band, music ensembles, musical theater, opera, pep band, radio station, student government, student newspaper, student film society, symphony orchestra, television station. Number of fraternities: 8; sororities: 7. Proportion of men in fraternities: 7%; of women in sororities: 5%. Average proportion of students who stay on campus on weekends: 30%. **Sports program (2005-2006):** Member of NCAA I. **Men's intercollegiate varsity sports:** baseball, basketball, cross-country, football, golf, tennis. **Women's intercollegiate varsity sports:** basketball, cross-country, golf, riflery, soccer, softball, tennis, track and field (indoor), track and field (outdoor), volleyball.

SERVICES AND FACILITIES
Basic services: nonremedial tutoring, placement service, day care, health service, health insurance. **Remedial assistance:** reading, math, writing, study skills. **Counseling services:** minority student, career, military, personal, veteran student, academic, older student, birth control, religious, other. **For learning-disabled students:** School does not offer a structured program with separate admission and additional fees. Total undergraduates in learning-disabled program or receiving services: 34. Services include: remedial math,

remedial English, reading machines, remedial reading, tape recorders, videotaped classes, note-taking services, oral tests, learning center, readers, extended time for tests, tutors, priority seating, proofreading services, texts on tape, exams on tape or computer, other testing accomodations. **Library:** Number of titles: 345,000; number of current serial subscriptions: 1,240. **Information technology resources:** Students are not required to lease or own a computer. Number of campus computers available to all students: 719. School has a wireless network. Approximate number of users that can be accommodated: 2,000. Proportion of college-owned housing units wired for high-speed internet access: 0%. **Campus safety:** Security services offered: 24-hour foot-and-vehicle patrols, late-night transport/escort service, 24-hour emergency telephones, lighted pathways/sidewalks, student patrols, controlled dormitory access (key, security card, etc.).

TRANSFER AND INTERNATIONAL STUDENTS

Transfer students: May apply for admission for the following academic terms: Fall, Spring, Summer. Applicants do not need a minimum number of credits to apply. For fall 2005: Transfer applications received: 1,204. Transfer applicants offered admission: 1,165. Transfer applicants enrolled: 914. **International students:** Number of foreign undergraduates: 39. Number of countries represented: 15. Minimum TOEFL score required: 500 (paper); 173 (computer).

Belmont University

- **Address:** 1900 Belmont Boulevard, Nashville, TN 37212
- **Website:** http://www.belmont.edu
- **Private; Religious affiliation:** Baptist
- **Enrollment:** 3,287 full-time; 358 part-time

KEY STATS
- ✔ **U.S News College Ranking:** 10, Universities–Master's (South)
- ✔ **ACT Score (25th/75th percentile):** 23-28
- ✔ **Tuition:** 2006-2007: $18,420

Selectivity: More selective	**Room/board:** $9,170
Acceptance rate: 72%	**Average debt:** $18,007
Student/faculty ratio: 13/1	**Proportion who borrowed:** 56%

UNDERGRADUATE STUDENT BODY STATS

2005-2006 enrollment: 3,287 full-time; 358 part-time. Men: 39%; women: 61%. **Ethnic makeup:** African American: 4%; American-Indian: 1%; Asian American: 1%; Hispanic: 2%; White: 92%; International: 1%. **Religious preference:** Roman Catholic: 8%; Protestant: 22%; No preference: 16%; Unknown: 23%; Baptist: 23%.

ADMISSIONS FACTS AND FIGURES

Phone: (615) 460-6785. **Email:** buadmission@mail.belmont.edu. **Website:** http://www.belmont.edu. **Application deadlines for fall 2007:** Regular decision: August 1. Early decision: Not offered. Early action: Not offered. Admission can be deferred. **Application fee:** $35. Common application is accepted. **To apply online, go to:** http://www.xap.com/applications/Belmont_University/apply.html. **Admissions requirements/recommendations:** High school units required (recommended): English: 4 (4); Mathematics: 3 (4); Science: 2 (3); Foreign language: 2 (2); Social studies: 2 (2); Academic electives: 5 (3); Total units: 18 (18). Tests: The college uses SAT or ACT scores in admissions decisions. Either SAT or ACT required. For admission to the fall 2007 entering class, the school will accept: ACT with writing, ACT without writing. Campus visit: Neither required nor recommended. Admissions interview: Neither required nor recommended. Off-campus interview: Not available. **Factors that count in admissions decisions:** *Academic:* Secondary school record: Very important. Class rank: Very important. Letters of recommendation: Important. Standardized test scores: Very important. Essay: Important. *Nonacademic:* Interview: Not considered. Extracurricular activities: Considered. Talent/ability: Considered. Character/personal qualities: Considered. Alumni/ae relationship: Considered. Geographical residence: Not considered. State residency: Not considered. Religious affiliation/commitment: Not considered. Minority status: Considered. Volunteer work: Considered. Work experience: Considered. **Other schools with the greatest overlap in applicants:** Lipscomb University; Middle Tennessee State University; Samford University; University of Tennessee; Vanderbilt University. **Admissions statistics for the fall 2005 entering class:** Total applicants: 2,184. Total accepted: 1,579. Freshmen

enrolled: 797; 64% were from out of state. Overall acceptance rate: 72%. **Credentials of fall 2005 freshmen:** 36% ranked in the top 10 percent of their high school class; 67% were in the top 25 percent, and 91% were in the top half. (Proportion submitting class standing: 78%.) **Average high school grade point average:** 3.5. **First-year students who submitted SAT scores:** 56%. Scores (25/75 percentile): Verbal: 530-640, Math: 540-640, Combined: 1070-1280. **First-year students submitting ACT scores:** 75%. Scores (25/75 percentile): English: 24-30, Math: 21-27, Composite: 23-28.

ACADEMICS

Year founded: 1890. **Academic calendar:** Semester. **Degrees offered:** bachelor's, master's, post-master's certificate, doctorate. **Most popular majors:** 24% music management and merchandising, 17% business administration, management, and operations, 11% music, 11% nursing/registered nurse training (R.N., A.S.N., B.S.N., M.S.N.), 4% broadcast journalism. **Major fields of study:** biological and biomedical sciences; business, management, marketing, and related support services; communication, journalism, and related programs; computer and information sciences and support services; education; engineering; English language and literature/letters; foreign languages, literatures, and linguistics; health professions and related clinical sciences; history; liberal arts and sciences studies, and humanities; mathematics and statistics; parks, recreation, leisure, and fitness studies; philosophy and religious studies; physical sciences; psychology; public administration and social service professions; social sciences; visual and performing arts. **Areas of required coursework:** arts/fine arts, humanities, computer literacy, mathematics, English (including composition), sciences (biological or physical), history, social science. **Pre-professional programs:** pre-law, pre-dentistry, pre-medicine, pre-theology, pre-veterinary science, pre-optometry, pre-pharmacy. **Special academic programs (% participation):** accelerated program (12%), cooperative (work-study plan) program (17%), distance learning (35%), double major (5%), honors program (8%), independent study (7%), internships (40%), liberal arts/career combination (80%), student-designed major (4%), study abroad (38%), teacher certificate program (7%), weekend college (15%). **Teacher certification offered in:** early childhood, elementary, middle/junior high, secondary. **Reserve Officers Training Corps (ROTC):** Army ROTC: Offered at cooperating institution (Vanderbilt University); Navy ROTC: Offered at cooperating institution (Vanderbilt University). **Faculty and instruction (2005-2006):** Total instructional faculty: 214 full-time, 247 part-time (50% men; 50% women; 3% minorities). Full-time faculty with Ph.D. or other terminal degree: 75%. Student/faculty ratio: 13/1. Classes of fewer than 20 students: 47%; of 20 to 49 students: 53%; of 50 or more students: 0%. **Advanced Placement and International Baccalaureate credit:** AP tests may be used for: Placement only. Scores accepted: 3, 4, 5. **Freshmen returning for sophomore year:** 79%. **Graduation rates:** Four-year: 46%; five-year: 60%; six-year: 59%. **Graduate study:** 9% of students pursue further study immediately upon graduation; 23% within one year. Fields in which graduates pursue further study: Master of Business Administration (MBA), 40%; law, 3%; medicine, 6%; dentistry, 4%; engineering, 1%; theology (or the seminary), 3%; education, 25%; arts and sciences, 19%; veterinary medicine, 1%.

COSTS AND FINANCIAL AID

Financial aid office: (615) 460-6403. **Expenses (2006-2007):** Tuition and fees 2006-2007: $18,420; room/board: $9,170. Estimated books and supplies: $1,100; transportation: $1,100; personal expenses: $1,600. **Financial aid:** Priority filing date for institution's financial aid form: March 1. In 2005-2006, 83% of undergraduates applied for financial aid. Of those, 51% were determined to have financial need; 22% had their need fully met. Average financial aid package (proportion receiving): $9,696 (49%). Average amount of gift aid, such as scholarships or grants (proportion receiving): $4,909 (35%). Average amount of self-help aid, such as work study or loans (proportion receiving): $7,242 (38%). Average need-based loan (excluding PLUS or other private loans): $7,215. Among students who received need-based aid, the average percentage of need met: 64%. Among students who received aid based on merit, the average award (and the proportion receiving): $5,704 (11%). The average athletic scholarship (and the proportion receiving): $11,822 (7%). Average amount of debt of borrowers graduating in 2005: $18,007. Proportion who borrowed: 56%.

CAMPUS LIFE AND EXTRACURRICULAR ACTIVITIES

Campus housing available (% using): women's dorms (28%), men's dorms (21%), apartment for single students (49%), special housing for disabled students (0%), other housing options (2%). Students who live in college-owned, operated, or affiliated housing: 48%. **Student employment:** During the 2005-2006 academic year, 15% of undergraduates worked on campus. Average per-year earnings: $1,600. **Clubs and organizations:** Number of student organizations: 71. Activities include: choral groups, concert band, dance, drama/theater, jazz band, literary magazine, marching band, music ensembles, musical theater, opera, pep band, radio station, student government, student newspaper, symphony orchestra, television station. Number of fraternities: 3; sororities: 4. Proportion of men in fraternities: 3%; of women in sororities: 3%. Average proportion of students who stay on campus on weekends: 60%. **Sports program (2005-2006):** Member of NCAA I. *Men's intercollegiate varsity sports:* baseball, basketball, cross-country, golf, soccer, tennis, track and field (indoor), track and field (outdoor). *Women's intercollegiate varsity sports:* basketball, cross-country, golf, soccer, softball, tennis, track and field (indoor), track and field (outdoor), volleyball.

SERVICES AND FACILITIES
Basic services: placement service, health service. **Remedial assistance:** math, writing. **Counseling services:** minority student, career, personal, veteran student, academic, older student, psychological, birth control, religious. **For learning-disabled students:** School does not offer a structured program with separate admission and additional fees. Total undergraduates in learning-disabled program or receiving services: 27. Services include: remedial math, remedial English, tape recorders, untimed tests, note-taking services, oral tests, readers, extended time for tests, priority seating, other testing accomodations. **Library:** Number of titles: 200,630; number of current serial subscriptions: 1,415. **Information technology resources:** Students are not required to lease or own a computer. Number of campus computers available to all students: 550. School has a wireless network. Approximate number of users that can be accommodated: 800. Proportion of college-owned housing units wired for high-speed internet access: 100%. **Campus safety:** Security services offered: 24-hour foot-and-vehicle patrols, late-night transport/escort service, 24-hour emergency telephones, lighted pathways/sidewalks, controlled dormitory access (key, security card, etc).

TRANSFER AND INTERNATIONAL STUDENTS
Transfer students: May apply for admission for the following academic terms: Fall, Spring, Summer. Applicants need a minimum number of credits to apply. For fall 2005: Transfer applications received: 721. Transfer applicants offered admission: 410. Transfer applicants enrolled: 376.
International students: Number of foreign undergraduates: 38 (1% of student body). Number of countries represented: 27. Minimum TOEFL score required: 550 (paper); 213 (computer). Average TOEFL score: 520 (paper).

Bethel College

- **Address:** 325 Cherry Street, McKenzie, TN 38201
- **Website:** http://www.bethel-college.edu
- **Private; Religious affiliation:** Cumberland Presbyterian
- **Enrollment:** N/A

KEY STATS
✔ **U.S News College Ranking:** fourth tier, Liberal Arts Colleges
✔ **SAT or ACT Score (25th/75th percentile):** N/A
✔ **Tuition:** 2006-2007: $10,826

Selectivity: Selective	Room/board: $6,048
Acceptance rate: 60%	Average debt: N/A
Student/faculty ratio: N/A	Proportion who borrowed: N/A

Bryan College

- **Address:** PO Box 7000, Dayton, TN 37321-7000
- **Website:** http://www.bryan.edu
- **Private; Religious affiliation:** Christian nondenominational
- **Enrollment:** 733 full-time; 33 part-time

KEY STATS
✔ **U.S News College Ranking:** 14, Comp. Coll.–Bachelor's (South)
✔ **ACT Score (25th/75th percentile):** 22-27
✔ **Tuition:** 2006-2007: $15,450

Selectivity: More selective	Room/board: $4,540
Acceptance rate: 95%	Average debt: $16,521
Student/faculty ratio: 12/1	Proportion who borrowed: 60%

UNDERGRADUATE STUDENT BODY STATS
2005-2006 enrollment: 733 full-time; 33 part-time. Men: 43%; women: 57%.
Ethnic makeup: African American: 6%; Hispanic: 2%; White: 91%; International: 1%.

ADMISSIONS FACTS AND FIGURES
Phone: (800) 277-9522. **Email:** admissions@bryan.edu. **Website:** http://www.bryan.edu. **Application deadlines for fall 2007:** Regular decision: July 31. Early decision: Not offered. Early action: Send application by: N/A; Decision sent by: N/A. Admission can be deferred. **Application fee:** $30. Common application is accepted. **Admissions requirements/recommendations:** High school units required (recommended): English: (4); Mathematics: (3); Science: (3); Foreign language: (2); Social studies: (3); Total units: (18). Tests: The college uses SAT or ACT scores in admissions decisions. Either SAT or ACT required. For admission to the fall 2007 entering class, the school will accept: ACT with writing, ACT without writing. Campus visit: Recommended. Admissions interview: Recommended. Off-campus interview: May be arranged. **Factors that count in admissions decisions:** *Academic:* Secondary school record: Very important. Class rank: Considered. Letters of recommendation: Very important. Standardized test scores: Very important. Essay: Considered. *Nonacademic:* Interview: Considered. Extracurricular activities: Considered. Talent/ability: Considered. Character/personal qualities: Important. Alumni/ae relationship: Considered. Geographical residence: Not considered. State residency: Not considered. Religious affiliation/commitment: Important. Minority status: Not considered. Volunteer work: Considered. Work experience: Not considered. **Other schools with the greatest overlap in applicants:** Cedarville University; Covenant College; Lee University; University of Tennessee–Chattanooga. **Admissions statistics for the fall 2005 entering class:** Total applicants: 367. Total accepted: 347. Freshmen enrolled: 184; 60% were from out of state. Overall acceptance rate: 95%. Non-early acceptance rate: 95%. **Credentials of fall 2005 freshmen:** 44% ranked in the top 10 percent of their high school class; 66% were in the top 25 percent; and 82% were in the top half. (Proportion submitting class standing: 60%.) **Average high school grade point average:** 3.6. **First-year students who submitted SAT scores:** 51%. Scores (25/75 percentile): Verbal: 545-680, Math: 505-640, Combined: 1050-1320. **First-year students submitting ACT scores:** 78%. Scores (25/75 percentile): English: 21-29, Math: 18-25, Composite: 22-27.

ACADEMICS
Year founded: 1930. **Academic calendar:** Semester. **Degrees offered:** associate, bachelor's, master's. **Most popular majors:** 22% business, management, marketing, and related support services, 15% communication, journalism, and related programs, 14% education, 8% theology and religious vocations, 7% visual and performing arts. **Major fields of study:** communication, journalism, and related programs; computer and information sciences and support services; education; English language and literature/letters; foreign languages, literatures, and linguistics; health professions and related clinical sciences; history; liberal arts and sciences studies, and humanities; parks, recreation, leisure, and fitness studies; philosophy and religious studies; psychology; social sciences; theology and religious vocations; visual and performing arts. **Areas of required coursework:** arts/fine arts, humanities, mathematics, English (including composition), foreign languages, sciences (biological or physical), history, social science. **Special academic programs:** distance learning, double major, honors program, independent study, internships, liberal arts/career combination, study abroad, teacher certificate program. **Teacher certification offered in:** elementary, secondary. **Faculty and instruction (2005-2006):** Total instructional faculty: 36 full-time, 32 part-time (78% men; 22% women; 0% minorities). Full-time faculty with Ph.D. or other terminal degree: 72%. Student/faculty ratio: 12/1. Classes of fewer than 20 students: 68%; of 20 to 49 students: 27%; of 50 or more students: 4%. **Advanced Placement and International Baccalaureate credit:** AP tests may be used for: Credit and/or placement. Scores accepted: 3, 4, 5. International Baccalaureate exams may be used for: Credit and/or placement. **Freshmen returning for sophomore year:** 74%. **Graduation rates:** Four-year: 61%; five-year: 70%; six-year: 59%. **Graduate study:** 60% of students pursue further study immediately upon graduation; 50% within one year; 85% within five years.

COSTS AND FINANCIAL AID
Financial aid office: (423) 775-7339. **Expenses (2006-2007):** Tuition and fees 2006-2007: $15,450; room/board: $4,540. Estimated books and supplies: $1,000; transportation: $1,500; personal expenses: $1,500. **Financial aid:** Priority filing date for institution's financial aid form: March 1. In 2005-2006, 97% of undergraduates applied for financial aid. Of those, 86% were determined to have financial need; 48% had their need fully met. Average

financial aid package (proportion receiving): $9,832 (86%). Average amount of gift aid, such as scholarships or grants (proportion receiving): $3,721 (45%). Average amount of self-help aid, such as work study or loans (proportion receiving): $4,865 (64%). Average need-based loan (excluding PLUS or other private loans): $4,054. Among students who received need-based aid, the average percentage of need met: 67%. Among students who received aid based on merit, the average award (and the proportion receiving): $5,339 (12%). The average athletic scholarship (and the proportion receiving): $5,030 (16%). Average amount of debt of borrowers graduating in 2005: $16,521. Proportion who borrowed: 60%.

CAMPUS LIFE AND EXTRACURRICULAR ACTIVITIES

Campus housing available (% using): women's dorms (53%), men's dorms (43%), apartments for married students (2%), apartment for single students (2%). Students who live in college-owned, operated, or affiliated housing: 82%. **Student employment:** During the 2005-2006 academic year, 2% of undergraduates worked on campus. Average per-year earnings: $1,000. Activities include: choral groups, drama/theater, music ensembles, musical theater, student government, student newspaper, yearbook. Number of fraternities: 0; sororities: 0. Average proportion of students who stay on campus on weekends: 50%. **Sports program (2005-2006):** Member of NAIA. *Men's intercollegiate varsity sports:* baseball, basketball, soccer. *Women's intercollegiate varsity sports:* basketball, soccer, volleyball.

SERVICES AND FACILITIES

Basic services: nonremedial tutoring, placement service. **Remedial assistance:** reading, math, writing, study skills. **Counseling services:** minority student, career, personal, academic, psychological, religious. **For learning-disabled students:** School does not offer a structured program with separate admission and additional fees. Total undergraduates in learning-disabled program or receiving services: 7. Services include: remedial math, remedial English, remedial reading, tape recorders, untimed tests, note-taking services, oral tests, learning center, readers, extended time for tests, tutors, texts on tape. **Library:** Number of titles: 154,375; number of current serial subscriptions: 10,000. **Information technology resources:** Students are not required to lease or own a computer. Number of campus computers available to all students: 203. School has a wireless network. Approximate number of users that can be accommodated: 858. Proportion of college-owned housing units wired for high-speed internet access: 100%. **Campus safety:** Security services offered: 24-hour emergency telephones, lighted pathways/sidewalks, controlled dormitory access (key, security card, etc).

TRANSFER AND INTERNATIONAL STUDENTS

Transfer students: May apply for admission for the following academic terms: Fall, Spring. Applicants need a minimum number of credits to apply. For fall 2005: Transfer applications received: 76. Transfer applicants offered admission: 76. Transfer applicants enrolled: 44. **International students:** Number of foreign undergraduates: 9 (1% of student body). Number of countries represented: 5. Minimum TOEFL score required: 533 (paper); 200 (computer).

Carson-Newman College

- **Address:** 1646 Russell Avenue, Jefferson City, TN 37760
- **Website:** http://www.cn.edu
- **Private; Religious affiliation:** Baptist
- **Enrollment:** 1,759 full-time; 92 part-time

KEY STATS

✔ **U.S News College Ranking:** 33, Universities–Master's (South)
✔ **ACT Score (25th/75th percentile):** 19-26
✔ **Tuition:** 2006-2007: $16,040

Selectivity: More selective	**Room/board:** $5,200
Acceptance rate: 78%	**Average debt:** $16,512
Student/faculty ratio: 13/1	**Proportion who borrowed:** 71%

UNDERGRADUATE STUDENT BODY STATS

2005-2006 enrollment: 1,759 full-time; 92 part-time. Men: 46%; women: 54%. **Ethnic makeup:** African American: 9%; Hispanic: 1%; White: 88%; International: 2%. **Religious preference:** Roman Catholic: 3%; Protestant: 21%; No preference: 8%; Baptist: 63%; Other: 5%.

ADMISSIONS FACTS AND FIGURES

Phone: (800) 678-9061. **Email:** thuebner@cn.edu. **Website:** http://www.cn.edu. **Application deadlines for fall 2007:** Regular decision: August 1. Early decision: Not offered. Early action: Not offered. Admission can be deferred. **Application fee:** $25. Common application is not accepted. **Admissions requirements/recommendations:** High school units required (recommended): English: 4; Mathematics: 2 (3); Science: 2; Foreign language: (2); Social studies: 3; History: 2; Total units: 20. Tests: The college uses SAT or ACT scores in admissions decisions. Either SAT or ACT required. For admission to the fall 2007 entering class, the school will accept: ACT with writing, ACT without writing. Campus visit: Recommended. Admissions interview: Recommended. Off-campus interview: Not available. **Factors that count in admissions decisions:** *Academic:* Secondary school record: Very important. Class rank: Considered. Letters of recommendation: Important. Standardized test scores: Important. Essay: Considered. *Nonacademic:* Interview: Considered. Extracurricular activities: Important. Talent/ability: Considered. Character/personal qualities: Important. Alumni/ae relationship: Considered. Geographical residence: Not considered. State residency: Not considered. Religious affiliation/commitment: Considered. Minority status: Considered. Volunteer work: Considered. Work experience: Considered. **Admissions statistics for the fall 2005 entering class:** Total applicants: 1,066. Total accepted: 828. Freshmen enrolled: 449; 39% were from out of state. Overall acceptance rate: 78%. **Credentials of fall 2005 freshmen:** 27% ranked in the top 10 percent of their high school class; 47% were in the top 25 percent, and 73% were in the top half. (Proportion submitting class standing: 78%.) **Average high school grade point average:** 3.3. **First-year students who submitted SAT scores:** 40%. Scores (25/75 percentile): Verbal: N/A; Math: N/A; Combined: N/A. **First-year students submitting ACT scores:** 60%. Scores (25/75 percentile): English: N/A; Math: N/A, Composite: 19-26.

ACADEMICS

Year founded: 1851. **Academic calendar:** Semester. **Degrees offered:** bachelor's, master's. **Most popular majors:** 19% education, 18% business/commerce, 7% nursing, 7% psychology, 6% communication studies/speech communication and rhetoric. **Major fields of study:** biological and biomedical sciences; business, management, marketing, and related support services; communication, journalism, and related programs; computer and information sciences and support services; education; English language and literature/letters; family and consumer sciences/human sciences; foreign languages, literatures, and linguistics; health professions and related clinical sciences; history; liberal arts and sciences studies, and humanities; mathematics and statistics; multi/interdisciplinary studies; parks, recreation, leisure, and fitness studies; philosophy and religious studies; physical sciences; psychology; social sciences; theology and religious vocations; visual and performing arts. **Areas of required coursework:** arts/fine arts, mathematics, English (including composition), foreign languages, sciences (biological or physical). **Special academic programs:** accelerated program, double major, dual enrollment, English as a Second Language (ESL), exchange student program (domestic), honors program, independent study, internships, liberal arts/career combination, student-designed major, study abroad, teacher certificate program, weekend college. **Teacher certification offered in:** early childhood, special education, elementary, middle/junior high, secondary. **Reserve Officers Training Corps (ROTC):** Army ROTC: Offered on campus; Air Force ROTC: Offered on campus. **Faculty and instruction (2005-2006):** Total instructional faculty: 128 full-time, 67 part-time. Full-time faculty with Ph.D. or other terminal degree: 66%. Student/faculty ratio: 13/1. Classes of fewer than 20 students: 59%; of 20 to 49 students: 40%; of 50 or more students: 0%. **Advanced Placement and International Baccalaureate credit:** AP tests may be used for: Credit and/or placement. Scores accepted: 4. International Baccalaureate exams may be used for: Credit only. **Freshmen returning for sophomore year:** 72%. **Graduation rates:** Four-year: 45%; five-year: 55%; six-year: 58%. **Graduate study:** 30% of students pursue further study immediately upon graduation; 41% within one year; 64% within five years.

COSTS AND FINANCIAL AID

Financial aid office: (865) 471-3247. **Expenses (2006-2007):** Tuition and fees 2006-2007: $16,040; room/board: $5,200. Estimated books and supplies: $990; transportation: $1,600; personal expenses: $1,500. **Financial aid:** In 2005-2006, 89% of undergraduates applied for financial aid. Of those, 72% were determined to have financial need; 37% had their need fully met. Average financial aid package (proportion receiving): $12,839 (72%). Average amount of gift aid, such as scholarships or grants (proportion receiving): $8,983 (69%). Average amount of self-help aid, such as work study or loans (proportion receiving): $4,075 (55%). Average need-based loan (excluding PLUS or other private loans): $3,790. Among students who received need-based aid, the average percentage of need met: 82%. Among students who received aid based on merit, the average award (and the proportion receiving): $9,120 (26%). The average athletic scholarship (and the proportion receiving): $5,977 (5%). Average amount of debt of borrowers graduating in 2005: $16,512. Proportion who borrowed: 71%.

CAMPUS LIFE AND EXTRACURRICULAR ACTIVITIES

Campus housing available: women's dorms, men's dorms, apartments for married students. Students who live in college-owned, operated, or affiliated housing: 57%. Activities include: choral groups, concert band, dance, drama/theater, jazz band, literary magazine, marching band, music ensembles, musical theater, pep band, radio station, student government, student newspaper, student film society, television station, yearbook. Average proportion of students who stay on campus on weekends: 25%. **Sports program (2005-2006):** Member of NCAA II. *Men's intercollegiate varsity sports:* baseball, basketball, cross-country, football, golf, soccer, tennis, track and field (indoor), track and field (outdoor), wrestling. *Women's intercollegiate varsity sports:* basketball, cross-country, soccer, softball, tennis, track and field (indoor), track and field (outdoor), volleyball.

SERVICES AND FACILITIES

For learning-disabled students: School does not offer a structured program with separate admission and additional fees. **Library:** Number of titles: 218,371; number of current serial subscriptions: 3,966. **Information technology resources:** Students are not required to lease or own a computer. Number of campus computers available to all students: 300.

TRANSFER AND INTERNATIONAL STUDENTS

Transfer students: May apply for admission for the following academic terms: Fall, Spring, Summer. Applicants need a minimum number of credits to apply. For fall 2005: Transfer applications received: 218. Transfer applicants offered admission: 195. Transfer applicants enrolled: 134. **International students:** Number of foreign undergraduates: 28 (2% of student body). Number of countries represented: 22. Minimum TOEFL score required: 550 (paper). Average TOEFL score: 570 (paper).

Christian Brothers University

- **Address:** 650 East Parkway S, Memphis, TN 38104
- **Website:** http://www.cbu.edu
- **Private; Religious affiliation:** Roman Catholic
- **Enrollment:** 1,151 full-time; 346 part-time

KEY STATS

✔ **U.S News College Ranking:** 22, Universities–Master's (South)
✔ **ACT Score (25th/75th percentile):** 21-27
✔ **Tuition:** 2006-2007: $20,080

Selectivity: More selective	**Room/board:** $5,650
Acceptance rate: 72%	**Average debt:** $24,463
Student/faculty ratio: 12/1	**Proportion who borrowed:** 63%

UNDERGRADUATE STUDENT BODY STATS

2005-2006 enrollment: 1,151 full-time; 346 part-time. Men: 45%; women: 55%. **Ethnic makeup:** African American: 36%; Asian American: 5%; Hispanic: 2%; White: 55%; International: 2%. **Religious preference:** Protestant: 42%; Unknown: 36%; Roman Catholic: 20%; Other: 2%.

ADMISSIONS FACTS AND FIGURES

Phone: (901) 321-3205. **Email:** admissions@cbu.edu. **Website:** http://www.cbu.edu. **Application deadlines for fall 2007:** Regular decision: Rolling. Early decision: Not offered. Early action: Send application by: December 1; Decision sent by: December 20. Admission can be deferred. **Application fee:** $25. Common application is accepted. **To apply online, go to:** http://www.cbu.edu/Admissions/apply.html. **Admissions requirements/recommendations:** High school units required (recommended): English: 4; Mathematics: 3 (4); Science: 3; Foreign language: (2); History: (1). Tests: The college uses SAT or ACT scores in admissions decisions. Either SAT or ACT required. For admission to the fall 2007 entering class, the school will accept: ACT with writing, ACT without writing. Campus visit: Recommended. Admissions interview: Recommended. Off-campus interview: May be arranged. **Factors that count in admissions decisions:**

Academic: Secondary school record: Very important. Class rank: Important. Letters of recommendation: Important. Standardized test scores: Very important. Essay: Important. **Nonacademic:** Interview: Important. Extracurricular activities: Important. Talent/ability: Considered. Character/personal qualities: Important. Alumni/ae relationship: Considered. Geographical residence: Not considered. State residency: Not considered. Religious affiliation/commitment: Not considered. Minority status: Not considered. Volunteer work: Considered. Work experience: Considered. **Other schools with the greatest overlap in applicants:** Rhodes College; University of Memphis; University of Mississippi; University of Tennessee. **Admissions statistics for the fall 2005 entering class:** Total applicants: 963. Total accepted: 693. Freshmen enrolled: 261; 22% were from out of state. Overall acceptance rate: 72%. Non-early acceptance rate: 72%. **Credentials of fall 2005 freshmen:** 35% ranked in the top 10 percent of their high school class; 60% were in the top 25 percent, and 83% were in the top half. (Proportion submitting class standing: 80%.) **Average high school grade point average:** 3.4. **First-year students who submitted SAT scores:** 26%. Scores (25/75 percentile): Verbal: 490-630, Math: 480-620, Combined: 970-1250. **First-year students submitting ACT scores:** 95%. Scores (25/75 percentile): English: 22-29, Math: 21-26, Composite: 21-27.

ACADEMICS

Year founded: 1871. **Academic calendar:** Semester. **Degrees offered:** bachelor's, master's. **Most popular majors:** 39% business, management, marketing, and related support services, 22% psychology, 15% engineering, 6% education, 6% physical sciences. **Major fields of study:** biological and biomedical sciences; business, management, marketing, and related support services; communication, journalism, and related programs; computer and information sciences and support services; engineering; English language and literature/letters; history; liberal arts and sciences studies, and humanities; mathematics and statistics; multi/interdisciplinary studies; philosophy and religious studies; physical sciences; psychology. **Areas of required coursework:** computer literacy, mathematics, English (including composition), sciences (biological or physical), history, social science, other. **Pre-professional programs:** pre-law, pre-dentistry, pre-medicine, pre-theology, pre-pharmacy. **Special academic programs (% participation):** accelerated program (32%), cooperative (work-study plan) program (35%), cross-registration (1%), double major (1%), honors program (5%), independent study (25%), internships (15%), study abroad (10%), teacher certificate program (5%). **Teacher certification offered in:** elementary, secondary. **Reserve Officers Training Corps (ROTC):** Army ROTC: Offered at cooperating institution (The University of Memphis); Navy ROTC: Offered at cooperating institution (The University of Memphis); Air Force ROTC: Offered at cooperating institution (The University of Memphis). **Faculty and instruction (2005-2006):** Total instructional faculty: 102 full-time, 52 part-time (64% men; 36% women; 15% minorities). Full-time faculty with Ph.D. or other terminal degree: 88%. Student/faculty ratio: 12/1. Classes of fewer than 20 students: 65%; of 20 to 49 students: 35%; of 50 or more students: 0%. **Advanced Placement and International Baccalaureate credit:** AP tests may be used for: Credit only. **Freshmen returning for sophomore year:** 80%. **Graduation rates:** Four-year: 49%; five-year: 58%; six-year: 62%. **Graduate study:** 11% of students pursue further study immediately upon graduation; 30% within one year. Fields in which graduates pursue further study: Master of Business Administration (MBA), 30%; law, 5%; medicine, 5%; dentistry, 2%; education, 30%; arts and sciences, 30%.

COSTS AND FINANCIAL AID

Financial aid office: (901) 321-3305. **Expenses (2006-2007):** Tuition and fees 2006-2007: $20,080; room/board: $5,650. Estimated books and supplies: $1,000. **Financial aid:** Priority filing date for institution's financial aid form: February 15. In 2005-2006, 84% of undergraduates applied for financial aid. Of those, 68% were determined to have financial need; 22% had their need fully met. Average financial aid package (proportion receiving): $14,897 (68%). Average amount of gift aid, such as scholarships or grants (proportion receiving): $6,028 (36%). Average amount of self-help aid, such as work study or loans (proportion receiving): $4,203 (50%). Average need-based loan (excluding PLUS or other private loans): $4,054. Among students who received need-based aid, the average percentage of need met: 79%. Among students who received aid based on merit, the average award (and the proportion receiving): $9,419 (25%). The average athletic scholarship (and the proportion receiving): $7,587 (11%). Average amount of debt of borrowers graduating in 2005: $24,463. Proportion who borrowed: 63%.

CAMPUS LIFE AND EXTRACURRICULAR ACTIVITIES

Campus housing available (% using): coed dorms (32%), women's dorms (17%), men's dorms (24%), apartment for single students (27%). Students who live in college-owned, operated, or affiliated housing: 44%. **Clubs and organizations:** Number of student organizations: 34. Activities include: choral groups, drama/theater, literary magazine, student government, yearbook. Number of fraternities: 5; sororities: 6. Proportion of men in fraternities: 13%; of women in sororities: 13%. Average proportion of students who stay on campus on weekends: 40%. **Sports program (2005-2006):** Member of NCAA II. *Men's intercollegiate varsity sports:* baseball, basketball, cross-country, golf, soccer, tennis. *Women's intercollegiate varsity sports:* basketball, cross-country, golf, soccer, softball, tennis, volleyball.

SERVICES AND FACILITIES

Basic services: nonremedial tutoring, placement service, health service, health insurance. **Remedial assistance:** other. **Counseling services:** career, personal, academic, older student, psychological, religious. **For learning-disabled students:** School does not offer a structured program with separate admission and additional fees. Total undergraduates in learning-disabled program or receiving services: 32. Services include: other testing accommodations, tape recorders, untimed tests, note-taking services, oral tests, readers, extended time for tests, tutors, priority seating, texts on tape, typist/scribe, exams on tape or computer, other. **Library:** Number of titles: 168,680; number of current serial subscriptions: 532. **Information technology resources:** Students are not required to lease or own a computer. Number of campus computers available to all students: 246. School has a wireless network. Approximate number of users that can be accommodated: 500. Proportion of college-owned housing units wired for high-speed internet access: 100%. **Campus safety:** Security services offered: 24-hour foot-and-vehicle patrols, late-night transport/escort service, 24-hour emergency telephones, lighted pathways/sidewalks, controlled dormitory access (key, security card, etc).

TRANSFER AND INTERNATIONAL STUDENTS

Transfer students: May apply for admission for the following academic terms: Fall, Spring, Summer. Applicants do not need a minimum number of credits to apply. For fall 2005: Transfer applications received: 181. Transfer applicants offered admission: 90. Transfer applicants enrolled: 62. **International students:** Number of foreign undergraduates: 30 (2% of student body). Number of countries represented: 21. Minimum TOEFL score required: 500 (paper); 173 (computer). Average TOEFL score: 629 (paper).

Crichton College

- **Address:** 255 N. Highland, Memphis, TN 38111-1375
- **Website:** http://www.crichton.edu
- **Private; Religious affiliation:** Christian nondenominational
- **Enrollment:** 503 full-time; 469 part-time

KEY STATS

✔ **U.S News College Ranking:** fourth tier, Comp. Coll.–Bachelor's (South)
✔ **ACT Score (25th/75th percentile):** 20-26
✔ **Tuition:** 2005-2006: $10,248

Selectivity: Selective	**Room/board:** $5,844
Acceptance rate: 60%	**Average debt:** N/A
Student/faculty ratio: N/A	**Proportion who borrowed:** N/A

UNDERGRADUATE STUDENT BODY STATS

2005-2006 enrollment: 503 full-time; 469 part-time. Men: 35%; women: 65%. **Ethnic makeup:** African American: 44%; Hispanic: 1%; White: 54%; International: 1%.

ADMISSIONS FACTS AND FIGURES

Phone: (901) 320-9797. **Email:** info@crichton.edu. **Website:** http://www.crichton.edu. **Application deadlines for fall 2007:** Regular decision: August 21. Early decision: Not offered. Early action: Not offered. Admission can be deferred. **Application fee:** $25. Common application is accepted. **To apply online, go to:** http://www.crichton.edu/admissions/onlineapp2002.html. **Admissions requirements/recommendations:** High school units required (recommended): English: 3; Mathematics: 3; Science: 2; Foreign language: 3; Social studies: 3. Tests: The college uses SAT or ACT scores in admissions decisions. Either SAT or ACT required. For admission to the fall 2007 entering class, the school will accept: ACT with writing, ACT without writing. Campus visit: Recommended. Admissions interview: Recommended. Off-campus interview: May be arranged. **Factors that count**

in admissions decisions: *Academic:* Secondary school record: Very important. Class rank: Considered. Letters of recommendation: Considered. Standardized test scores: Very important. Essay: Not considered. *Nonacademic:* Interview: Considered. Extracurricular activities: Considered. Talent/ability: Considered. Character/personal qualities: Considered. Alumni/ae relationship: Not considered. Geographical residence: Not considered. State residency: Not considered. Religious affiliation/commitment: Important. Minority status: Not considered. Volunteer work: Not considered. Work experience: Not considered. **Other schools with the greatest overlap in applicants:** Bethel College; Union University; University of Memphis. **Admissions statistics for the fall 2005 entering class:** Freshmen enrolled: 80; Overall acceptance rate: 60%. **First-year students submitting ACT scores:** 100%. Scores (25/75 percentile): English: N/A, Math: N/A, Composite: 20-26.

ACADEMICS

Year founded: 1941. **Academic calendar:** Semester. **Degrees offered:** certificate, bachelor's, post-bachelor's certificate. **Most popular majors:** Information not available. **Major fields of study:** biological and biomedical sciences; business, management, marketing, and related support services; education; English language and literature/letters; health professions and related clinical sciences; history; legal professions and studies; liberal arts and sciences studies, and humanities; physical sciences; psychology; theology and religious vocations. **Areas of required coursework:** humanities, computer literacy, mathematics, English (including composition), sciences (biological or physical), other. **Pre-professional programs:** pre-law, other. **Special academic programs:** accelerated program, cooperative (work-study plan) program, distance learning, double major, dual enrollment, honors program, independent study, internships, student-designed major, study abroad, teacher certificate program, weekend college, other. **Teacher certification offered in:** elementary, secondary. **Faculty and instruction (2005-2006):** Total instructional faculty: 34 full-time, 73 part-time (63% men; 37% women; 14% minorities). Full-time faculty with Ph.D. or other terminal degree: 59%. Classes of fewer than 20 students: 82%; of 20 to 49 students: 18%; of 50 or more students: 0%. **Advanced Placement and International Baccalaureate credit:** AP tests may be used for: Credit and/or placement. International Baccalaureate exams may be used for: Credit only. **Freshmen returning for sophomore year:** 56%. **Graduation rates:** Six-year: 19%.

COSTS AND FINANCIAL AID

Financial aid office: (901) 320-9787. **Expenses (2005-2006):** Tuition and fees 2005-2006: $10,248; room/board: $5,844. Estimated books and supplies: $600; transportation: $1,494; personal expenses: $78. **Financial aid:** Priority filing date for institution's financial aid form: March 31. In 2005-2006, 82% of undergraduates applied for financial aid. Of those, 69% were determined to have financial need; 20% had their need fully met. Average financial aid package (proportion receiving): $8,381 (69%). Average amount of gift aid, such as scholarships or grants (proportion receiving): N/A (59%). Among students who received need-based aid, the average percentage of need met: 61%. Among students who received aid based on merit, the average award (and the proportion receiving): $6,173 (10%). The average athletic scholarship (and the proportion receiving): $4,951 (8%).

CAMPUS LIFE AND EXTRACURRICULAR ACTIVITIES

Campus housing available: apartment for single students, special housing for disabled students. **Student employment:** During the 2005-2006 academic year, 9% of undergraduates worked on campus. Average per-year earnings: $3,389. **Clubs and organizations:** Number of student organizations: 9. Activities include: choral groups, drama/theater, music ensembles, musical theater, student government, student film society. Number of fraternities: 0; sororities: 0. **Sports program (2005-2006):** Member of NAIA. *Men's intercollegiate varsity sports:* baseball, basketball. *Women's intercollegiate varsity sports:* soccer.

SERVICES AND FACILITIES

Basic services: nonremedial tutoring, health insurance. **Remedial assistance:** reading, math. **Counseling services:** career, academic, older student, other. **For learning-disabled students:** School does not offer a structured program with separate admission and additional fees. Services include: remedial math, remedial English, tape recorders, videotaped classes, diagnostic testing service, untimed tests, note-taking services, oral tests, readers, extended time for tests, tutors, other. **Library:** Number of titles: 55,833; number of current serial subscriptions: 303. **Information technology resources:** Students are not required to lease or own a computer. Number of campus computers available to all students: 33. School has a wireless network. Approximate number of users that can be accommodated: 1,000. Proportion of college-owned housing units wired for high-speed internet access: 0%. **Campus safety:** Security services offered: late-night transport/escort service, lighted pathways/sidewalks, controlled dormitory access (key, security card, etc).

TRANSFER AND INTERNATIONAL STUDENTS
Transfer students: May apply for admission for the following academic terms: Fall, Spring, Summer. Applicants need a minimum number of credits to apply. **International students:** Number of foreign undergraduates: 8 (1% of student body). Number of countries represented: 6. Minimum TOEFL score required: 500 (paper); 173 (computer).

Cumberland University

- **Address:** 1 Cumberland Square, Lebanon, TN 37087-3408
- **Website:** http://www.cumberland.edu
- **Private**
- **Enrollment:** 937 full-time; 146 part-time

KEY STATS
- ✔ **U.S News College Ranking:** fourth tier, Universities–Master's (South)
- ✔ **ACT Score (25th/75th percentile):** 18-23
- ✔ **Tuition:** 2006-2007: $14,810

Selectivity: Selective	**Room/board:** $5,060
Acceptance rate: 69%	**Average debt:** $18,456
Student/faculty ratio: 18/1	**Proportion who borrowed:** 67%

UNDERGRADUATE STUDENT BODY STATS
2005-2006 enrollment: 937 full-time; 146 part-time. Men: 43%; women: 57%. **Ethnic makeup:** African American: 10%; American-Indian: 1%; Asian American: 1%; Hispanic: 2%; White: 83%; International: 4%.

ADMISSIONS FACTS AND FIGURES
Phone: (615) 444-2562. **Email:** admissions@cumberland.edu. **Website:** http://www.cumberland.edu. **Application deadlines for fall 2007:** Regular decision: Rolling; decision sent by June 15. Early decision: Not offered. Early action: Not offered. Admission can be deferred. **Application fee:** $25. Common application is not accepted. **Admissions requirements/recommendations:** High school units required (recommended): English: 4 (4); Mathematics: 3 (3); Science: 3 (3); Foreign language: 2 (2); Social studies: 2 (2); History: 1 (2); Academic electives: 12 (12); Total units: 27 (28). Tests: The college uses SAT or ACT scores in admissions decisions. ACT required. For admission to the fall 2007 entering class, the school will accept: ACT without writing. Campus visit: Recommended. Admissions interview: Neither required nor recommended. Off-campus interview: May be arranged. **Factors that count in admissions decisions:** *Academic:* Secondary school record: Very important. Class rank: Considered. Letters of recommendation: Considered. Standardized test scores: Very important. Essay: Considered. *Nonacademic:* Interview: Considered. Extracurricular activities: Considered. Talent/ability: Considered. Character/personal qualities: Considered. Alumni/ae relationship: Important. Geographical residence: Not considered. State residency: Not considered. Religious affiliation/commitment: Not considered. Minority status: Not considered. Volunteer work: Not considered. Work experience: Considered. **Other schools with the greatest overlap in applicants:** Belmont University; Freed-Hardeman University; Middle Tennessee State University; Trevecca Nazarene University; Union University. **Admissions statistics for the fall 2005 entering class:** Total applicants: 1,038. Total accepted: 717. Freshmen enrolled: 262; 12% were from out of state. Overall acceptance rate: 69%. **Credentials of fall 2005 freshmen:** 15% ranked in the top 10 percent of their high school class; 38% were in the top 25 percent, and 69% were in the top half. (Proportion submitting class standing: 85%.) **Average high school grade point average:** 3.3. **First-year students who submitted SAT scores:** 8%. Scores (25/75 percentile): Verbal: 410-540, Math: 460-520, Combined: 870-1060. **First-year students submitting ACT scores:** 82%. Scores (25/75 percentile): English: 18-21, Math: 19-23, Composite: 18-23.

ACADEMICS
Year founded: 1842. **Academic calendar:** Semester. **Degrees offered:** associate, bachelor's, master's. **Most popular majors:** 28% nursing/registered nurse training (R.N., A.S.N., B.S.N., M.S.N.), 20% education, 18% business/commerce, 9% liberal arts and sciences/liberal studies, 7% corrections and criminal justice. **Major fields of study:** area, ethnic, cultural, and gender

studies; biological and biomedical sciences; business, management, marketing, and related support services; computer and information sciences and support services; education; English language and literature/letters; health professions and related clinical sciences; history; liberal arts and sciences studies, and humanities; mathematics and statistics; parks, recreation, leisure, and fitness studies; psychology; security and protective services; social sciences; visual and performing arts. **Areas of required coursework:** arts/fine arts, humanities, computer literacy, mathematics, English (including composition), philosophy, foreign languages, sciences (biological or physical), history, social science, other. **Pre-professional programs:** pre-law, pre-dentistry, pre-medicine, pre-veterinary science, pre-optometry, pre-pharmacy, other. **Special academic programs (% participation):** accelerated program (1%), double major (4%), dual enrollment (3%), honors program (9%), independent study (3%), internships (2%), teacher certificate program (21%). **Teacher certification offered (% participation):** early childhood, special education, elementary, secondary. **Reserve Officers Training Corps (ROTC):** Army ROTC: Offered at cooperating institution (Middle TN State University). **Faculty and instruction (2005-2006):** Total instructional faculty: 54 full-time, 50 part-time (58% men; 42% women; 7% minorities). Full-time faculty with Ph.D. or other terminal degree: 56%. Student/faculty ratio: 18/1. Classes of fewer than 20 students: 56%; of 20 to 49 students: 40%; of 50 or more students: 4%. **Advanced Placement and International Baccalaureate credit:** AP tests may be used for: Credit and/or placement. Scores accepted: 3, 4, 5. International Baccalaureate exams may be used for: Credit only. **Freshmen returning for sophomore year:** 63%. **Graduation rates:** Four-year: 21%; five-year: 37%; six-year: 39%. **Graduate study:** 20% of students pursue further study immediately upon graduation; 30% within one year; 10% within five years. Fields in which graduates pursue further study: Master of Business Administration (MBA), 10%; law, 1%; medicine, 1%; dentistry, 1%; education, 60%; arts and sciences, 3%; veterinary medicine, 1%.

COSTS AND FINANCIAL AID
Financial aid office: (615) 444-2562. **Expenses (2006-2007):** Tuition and fees 2006-2007: $14,810; room/board: $5,060. Estimated books and supplies: $1,131; transportation: $708; personal expenses: $2,827. **Financial aid:** Priority filing date for institution's financial aid form: February 15; deadline: May 1. In 2005-2006, 89% of undergraduates applied for financial aid. Of those, 75% were determined to have financial need; 30% had their need fully met. Average financial aid package (proportion receiving): $14,455 (75%). Average amount of gift aid, such as scholarships or grants (proportion receiving): $5,348 (34%). Average amount of self-help aid, such as work study or loans (proportion receiving): $3,679 (49%). Average need-based loan (excluding PLUS or other private loans): $7,143. Among students who received need-based aid, the average percentage of need met: 84%. Among students who received aid based on merit, the average award (and the proportion receiving): $4,497 (17%). The average athletic scholarship (and the proportion receiving): $6,620 (13%). Average amount of debt of borrowers graduating in 2005: $18,456. Proportion who borrowed: 67%.

CAMPUS LIFE AND EXTRACURRICULAR ACTIVITIES
Campus housing available (% using): women's dorms (45%), men's dorms (55%), special housing for disabled students. Students who live in college-owned, operated, or affiliated housing: 39%. **Student employment:** During the 2005-2006 academic year, 2% of undergraduates worked on campus. Average per-year earnings: $1,500. **Clubs and organizations:** Number of student organizations: 38. Activities include: choral groups, concert band, dance, drama/theater, jazz band, marching band, music ensembles, musical theater, pep band, radio station, student government, student newspaper, yearbook. Number of fraternities: 3; sororities: 2. Proportion of men in fraternities: 6%; of women in sororities: 3%. Average proportion of students who stay on campus on weekends: 30%. **Sports program (2005-2006):** Member of NAIA. *Men's intercollegiate varsity sports:* baseball, basketball, cross-country, football, golf, soccer, tennis, wrestling. *Women's intercollegiate varsity sports:* basketball, cross-country, golf, soccer, softball, tennis, volleyball.

SERVICES AND FACILITIES
Basic services: placement service. **Remedial assistance:** reading, math, writing, study skills. **Counseling services:** minority student, career, personal, academic, psychological. **For learning-disabled students:** School does not offer a structured program with separate admission and additional fees. Total undergraduates in learning-disabled program or receiving services: 6. Services include: remedial math, remedial English, reading machines, remedial reading, tape recorders, other special classes, videotaped classes, untimed tests, note-taking services, oral tests, learning center, readers, extended time for tests, tutors, priority seating, substitution of courses, texts

on tape, exams on tape or computer, take home exams, other testing accomodations. **Library:** Number of titles: 35,000; number of current serial subscriptions: 379. **Information technology resources:** Students are not required to lease or own a computer. Number of campus computers available to all students: 142. School has a wireless network. Approximate number of users that can be accommodated: 10,752. Proportion of college-owned housing units wired for high-speed internet access: 100%. **Campus safety:** Security services offered: 24-hour foot-and-vehicle patrols, 24-hour emergency telephones, lighted pathways/sidewalks, controlled dormitory access (key, security card, etc).

TRANSFER AND INTERNATIONAL STUDENTS

Transfer students: May apply for admission for the following academic terms: Fall, Spring, Summer. Applicants need a minimum number of credits to apply. For fall 2005: Transfer applications received: 265. Transfer applicants offered admission: 200. Transfer applicants enrolled: 119. **International students:** Number of foreign undergraduates: 48 (4% of student body). Minimum TOEFL score required: 500 (paper); 173 (computer). Average TOEFL score: 550 (paper).

East Tennessee State University

- **Address:** 807 University Parkway, Johnson City, TN 37614-0000
- **Website:** http://www.etsu.edu
- **Public**
- **Enrollment:** 8,183 full-time; 1,587 part-time

KEY STATS
- ✔ **U.S News College Ranking:** fourth tier, National Universities
- ✔ **ACT Score (25th/75th percentile):** 20-25
- ✔ **Tuition:** 2006-2007: $4,637 in state, $809 out of state

Selectivity: Selective	**Room/board:** $4,852
Acceptance rate: 81%	**Average debt:** $17,988
Student/faculty ratio: 17/1	**Proportion who borrowed:** 58%

UNDERGRADUATE STUDENT BODY STATS

2005-2006 enrollment: 8,183 full-time; 1,587 part-time. Men: 42%; women: 58%. **Ethnic makeup:** African American: 4%; Asian American: 1%; Hispanic: 1%; White: 92%; International: 1%.

ADMISSIONS FACTS AND FIGURES

Phone: (423) 439-4213. **Email:** go2etsu@etsu.edu. **Website:** http://www.etsu.edu. **Application deadlines for fall 2007:** Regular decision: Rolling. Early decision: Not offered. Early action: Not offered. Admission cannot be deferred. **Application fee:** $15. Common application is not accepted. **To apply online, go to:** http://www.etsu.edu/admissions/apply.asp. **Admissions requirements/recommendations:** High school units required (recommended): English: 4; Mathematics: 3 (4); Science: 2 (3); Foreign language: 2; Social studies: 1; History: 1; Total units: 14 (16). Tests: The college uses SAT or ACT scores in admissions decisions. Either SAT or ACT required. For admission to the fall 2007 entering class, the school will accept: ACT with writing, ACT without writing. Campus visit: Recommended. Admissions interview: Recommended. Off-campus interview: May be arranged. **Factors that count in admissions decisions:** *Academic:* Secondary school record: Important. Class rank: Considered. Letters of recommendation: Not considered. Standardized test scores: Very important. Essay: Not considered. *Nonacademic:* Interview: Not considered. Extracurricular activities: Not considered. Talent/ability: Not considered. Character/personal qualities: Not considered. Alumni/ae relationship: Not considered. Geographical residence: Considered. State residency: Considered. Religious affiliation/commitment: Not considered. Minority status: Not considered. Volunteer work: Not considered. Work experience: Not considered. **Other schools with the greatest overlap in applicants:** Appalachian State University; University of Tennessee; University of Tennessee–Chattanooga; University of Virginia–Wise; Virginia Tech. **Admissions statistics for the fall 2005 entering class:** Total applicants: 3,601. Total accepted: 2,925. Freshmen enrolled: 1,595; 9% were from out of state. Overall acceptance rate: 81%. **Credentials of fall 2005 freshmen:** 18% ranked in the top 10 percent of their high school class; 38% were in the top 25 percent, and 71% were in the top half. (Proportion submitting class standing: 50%.) **Average high school grade point average:** 3.3. **First-year students who submitted SAT scores:** 22%. Scores (25/75 percentile): Verbal: 450-590,

Math: 450-570, Combined: 900-1160. **First-year students submitting ACT scores:** 94%. Scores (25/75 percentile): English: 19-25, Math: 18-24, Composite: 20-25.

ACADEMICS

Year founded: 1911. **Academic calendar:** Semester. **Degrees offered:** associate, terminal-associate, bachelor's, post-bachelor's certificate, master's, post-master's certificate, first professional, doctorate. **Most popular majors:** 17% health professions and related clinical sciences, 16% business, management, marketing, and related support services, 6% liberal arts and sciences studies, and humanities, 5% family and consumer sciences/human sciences, 5% security and protective services. **Major fields of study:** biological and biomedical sciences; business, management, marketing, and related support services; communication, journalism, and related programs; communications technologies/technicians and support services; computer and information sciences and support services; education; engineering technologies/technicians; English language and literature/letters; family and consumer sciences/human sciences; foreign languages, literatures, and linguistics; health professions and related clinical sciences; history; liberal arts and sciences studies, and humanities; mathematics and statistics; multi/interdisciplinary studies; parks, recreation, leisure, and fitness studies; philosophy and religious studies; physical sciences; psychology; public administration and social service professions; security and protective services; social sciences; visual and performing arts. **Areas of required coursework:** arts/fine arts, humanities, computer literacy, mathematics, English (including composition), philosophy, sciences (biological or physical), history, social science. **Pre-professional programs:** pre-law, pre-dentistry, pre-medicine, pre-veterinary science, pre-optometry, pre-pharmacy, other. **Special academic programs:** accelerated program, cooperative (work-study plan) program, distance learning, double major, dual enrollment, exchange student program (domestic), honors program, independent study, internships, study abroad, teacher certificate program. **Teacher certification offered in:** early childhood, special education, elementary, middle/junior high, secondary. **Cooperative education programs:** art, business, computer science, education, health professions, home economics, humanities, natural science, social/behavioral science, technologies, other. **Reserve Officers Training Corps (ROTC):** Army ROTC: Offered on campus. **Faculty and instruction (2005-2006):** Total instructional faculty: 480 full-time, 309 part-time (52% men; 48% women; 4% minorities). Full-time faculty with Ph.D. or other terminal degree: 70%. Student/faculty ratio: 17/1. Classes of fewer than 20 students: 43%; of 20 to 49 students: 49%; of 50 or more students: 8%. **Advanced Placement and International Baccalaureate credit:** AP tests may be used for: Credit only. Scores accepted: 3, 4, 5. International Baccalaureate exams may be used for: Credit only. **Freshmen returning for sophomore year:** 68%. **Graduation rates:** Four-year: 15%; five-year: 33%; six-year: 39%.

COSTS AND FINANCIAL AID

Financial aid office: (423) 439-4300. **Expenses (2005-2006):** Tuition and fees 2005-2006: $4,507 in state, $10,141 out of state; room/board: $5,048. Estimated books and supplies: $943; transportation: $2,625; personal expenses: $2,170. **Financial aid:** Priority filing date for institution's financial aid form: April 15. In 2005-2006, 82% of undergraduates applied for financial aid. Of those, 57% were determined to have financial need; 44% had their need fully met. Average financial aid package (proportion receiving): $4,762 (56%). Average amount of gift aid, such as scholarships or grants (proportion receiving): $3,009 (41%). Average amount of self-help aid, such as work study or loans (proportion receiving): $3,010 (38%). Average need-based loan (excluding PLUS or other private loans): $3,216. Among students who received need-based aid, the average percentage of need met: 82%. Among students who received aid based on merit, the average award (and the proportion receiving): $3,054 (14%). The average athletic scholarship (and the proportion receiving): $10,726 (2%). Average amount of debt of borrowers graduating in 2005: $17,988. Proportion who borrowed: 58%.

CAMPUS LIFE AND EXTRACURRICULAR ACTIVITIES

Campus housing available: coed dorms, women's dorms, men's dorms, fraternity housing, apartments for married students, apartment for single students, special housing for disabled students, special housing for international students. Students who live in college-owned, operated, or affiliated housing: 21%. **Clubs and organizations:** Number of student organizations: 200. Activities include: choral groups, concert band, drama/theater, jazz band, literary magazine, music ensembles, pep band, radio station, student government, student newspaper, television station. Number of fraternities: 8; sororities: 8. Proportion of men in fraternities: 7%; of women in sororities: 7%. Average proportion of students who stay on campus on weekends: 10%. **Sports program (2005-2006):** Member of NCAA I. *Men's intercollegiate varsity sports:* baseball, basketball, cross-country, golf, tennis, track and field (indoor), track and field (outdoor). *Women's intercollegiate varsity sports:* basketball, cross-country, golf, soccer, softball, tennis, track and field (indoor), track and field (outdoor), volleyball.

SERVICES AND FACILITIES
Basic services: nonremedial tutoring, women's center, placement service, day care, health service, health insurance. **Counseling services:** minority student, career, military, personal, veteran student, academic, older student, psychological, birth control, religious. **For learning-disabled students:** School does not offer a structured program with separate admission and additional fees. Services include: untimed tests, note-taking services, oral tests, tutors. **Library:** Number of titles: 1,011,552; number of current serial subscriptions: 8,523. **Information technology resources:** Students are not required to lease or own a computer. Number of campus computers available to all students: 600. School does not have a wireless network. **Campus safety:** Security services offered: 24-hour foot-and-vehicle patrols, late-night transport/escort service, 24-hour emergency telephones, lighted pathways/sidewalks, controlled dormitory access (key, security card, etc).

TRANSFER AND INTERNATIONAL STUDENTS
Transfer students: May apply for admission for the following academic terms: Fall, Spring, Summer. Applicants need a minimum number of credits to apply. For fall 2005: Transfer applications received: 2,011. Transfer applicants offered admission: 1,242. Transfer applicants enrolled: 907. **International students:** Number of foreign undergraduates: 128 (1% of student body). Number of countries represented: 52. Minimum TOEFL score required: 500 (paper); 173 (computer). Average TOEFL score: 545 (paper).

Fisk University

■ **Address:** 1000 17th Avenue N, Nashville, TN 37208-3051
■ **Website:** http://www.fisk.edu
■ **Private**
■ **Enrollment:** 818 full-time; 46 part-time

KEY STATS
✔ **U.S News College Ranking:** third tier, Liberal Arts Colleges
✔ **ACT Score (25th/75th percentile):** 18-23
✔ **Tuition:** 2006-2007: $13,968

Selectivity: Selective	**Room/board:** $7,012
Acceptance rate: 79%	**Average debt:** N/A
Student/faculty ratio: 12/1	**Proportion who borrowed:** N/A

UNDERGRADUATE STUDENT BODY STATS
2005-2006 enrollment: 818 full-time; 46 part-time. Men: 30%; women: 70%. **Ethnic makeup:** African American: 92%; White: 3%; International: 4%.

ADMISSIONS FACTS AND FIGURES
Phone: (888) 702-0022. **Email:** admissions@fisk.edu. **Website:** http://www.fisk.edu. **Application deadlines for fall 2007:** Regular decision: June 1. Early decision: Not offered. Early action: Not offered. Admission can be deferred. **Application fee:** $50. Common application is accepted. **Admissions requirements/recommendations:** High school units required (recommended): English: (4); Mathematics: (3); Science: (1); Foreign language: (1); Social studies: (3); History: (1); Academic electives: (6); Total units: (20). Tests: The college uses SAT or ACT scores in admissions decisions. Either SAT or ACT required. For admission to the fall 2007 entering class, the school will accept: ACT with writing. Campus visit: Neither required nor recommended. Admissions interview: Recommended. Off-campus interview: May be arranged. **Factors that count in admissions decisions:** *Academic:* Secondary school record: Very important. Class rank: Very important. Letters of recommendation: Important. Standardized test scores: Important. Essay: Important. *Nonacademic:* Interview: Important. Talent/ability: Important. Character/personal qualities: Important. State residency: Not considered. Religious affiliation/commitment: Not considered. Minority status: Not considered. **Other schools with the greatest overlap in applicants:** Clark Atlanta University; Morehouse College; Spelman College; Tennessee State University; University of Chicago. **Admissions statistics for the fall 2005 entering class:** Total applicants: 1,717. Total accepted: 1,362. Freshmen enrolled: 214; 74% were from out of state. Overall acceptance

rate: 79%. **Credentials of fall 2005 freshmen:** 17% ranked in the top 10 percent of their high school class; 69% were in the top 25 percent, and 74% were in the top half. (Proportion submitting class standing: 70%.) **Average high school grade point average:** 3.0. **First-year students who submitted SAT scores:** 47%. Scores (25/75 percentile): Verbal: 435-560, Math: 425-540, Combined: 860-1100. **First-year students submitting ACT scores:** 73%. Scores (25/75 percentile): English: N/A, Math: N/A, Composite: 18-23.

ACADEMICS
Year founded: 1866. **Academic calendar:** Semester. **Degrees offered:** bachelor's, master's. **Most popular majors:** 25% psychology, 19% business/commerce, 12% biology, 10% political science and government, 6% pharmacology. **Major fields of study:** biological and biomedical sciences; business, management, marketing, and related support services; computer and information sciences and support services; education; English language and literature/letters; foreign languages, literatures, and linguistics; history; philosophy and religious studies; physical sciences; psychology; social sciences; visual and performing arts. **Areas of required coursework:** arts/fine arts, humanities, mathematics, English (including composition), philosophy, foreign languages, sciences (biological or physical), history, social science. **Pre-professional programs:** pre-dentistry, pre-medicine, pre-pharmacy. **Special academic programs (% participation):** cross-registration (2%), double major (10%), exchange student program (domestic) (1%), honors program (6%), independent study (.5%), internships (7%), student-designed major (0%), study abroad (.5%), teacher certificate program (4%). **Teacher certification offered in:** special education, secondary. **Reserve Officers Training Corps (ROTC):** Army ROTC: Offered at cooperating institution (Vanderbilt University); Navy ROTC: Offered at cooperating institution (Vanderbilt University); Air Force ROTC: Offered at cooperating institution (Tennessee State University). **Faculty and instruction (2005-2006):** Total instructional faculty: 58 full-time, 43 part-time (56% men; 44% women; 75% minorities). Full-time faculty with Ph.D. or other terminal degree: 76%. Student/faculty ratio: 12/1. Classes of fewer than 20 students: 65%; of 20 to 49 students: 33%; of 50 or more students: 2%. **Advanced Placement and International Baccalaureate credit:** AP tests may be used for: Credit and/or placement. Scores accepted: 4, 5. **Freshmen returning for sophomore year:** 85%. **Graduation rates:** Four-year: 44%; five-year: 54%; six-year: 58%. **Graduate study:** 28% of students pursue further study immediately upon graduation; 40% within one year; 45% within five years.

COSTS AND FINANCIAL AID
Financial aid office: (615) 329-8585. **Expenses (2006-2007):** Tuition and fees 2006-2007: $13,968; room/board: $7,012. Estimated books and supplies: $1,400; transportation: $1,600; personal expenses: $1,750. **Financial aid:** Priority filing date for institution's financial aid form: March 1; deadline: June 1.

CAMPUS LIFE AND EXTRACURRICULAR ACTIVITIES
Campus housing available: coed dorms, women's dorms, men's dorms. Students who live in college-owned, operated, or affiliated housing: 67%. **Clubs and organizations:** Number of student organizations: 85. Activities include: choral groups, dance, drama/theater, jazz band, music ensembles, radio station, student government, yearbook. Number of fraternities: 4; sororities: 4. Proportion of men in fraternities: 10%; of women in sororities: 10%. Average proportion of students who stay on campus on weekends: 90%. **Sports program (2005-2006):** Member of NCAA III. *Men's intercollegiate varsity sports:* baseball, basketball, cross-country, soccer, tennis, track and field (indoor), track and field (outdoor). *Women's intercollegiate varsity sports:* basketball, cross-country, soccer, softball, tennis, track and field (indoor), track and field (outdoor), volleyball.

SERVICES AND FACILITIES
Basic services: nonremedial tutoring, health insurance. **Remedial assistance:** reading, math, writing, study skills. **Counseling services:** personal, academic, psychological, religious. **For learning-disabled students:** School does not offer a structured program with separate admission and additional fees. Total undergraduates in learning-disabled program or receiving services: 9. Services include: untimed tests, oral tests, learning center, readers, extended time for tests, tutors, substitution of courses, waiver of foreign language degree requirement, waiver of math degree requirement. **Library:** Number of titles: 207,352; number of current serial subscriptions: 1,722. **Information technology resources:** Students are not required to lease or own a computer. Number of campus computers available to all students: 105. School has a wireless network. Proportion of college-owned housing units wired for high-speed internet access: 100%. **Campus safety:** Security services offered:

24-hour foot-and-vehicle patrols, 24-hour emergency telephones, lighted pathways/sidewalks, controlled dormitory access (key, security card, etc).

TRANSFER AND INTERNATIONAL STUDENTS
Transfer students: May apply for admission for the following academic terms: Fall, Spring. Applicants do not need a minimum number of credits to apply. For fall 2005: Transfer applications received: 73. Transfer applicants offered admission: 67. Transfer applicants enrolled: 42. **International students:** Number of foreign undergraduates: 34 (4% of student body). Number of countries represented: 8. Minimum TOEFL score required: 225 (paper); 250 (computer).

Freed-Hardeman University

- **Address:** 158 E. Main Street, Henderson, TN 38340-2399
- **Website:** http://www.fhu.edu
- **Private; Religious affiliation:** Church of Christ
- **Enrollment:** 1,402 full-time; 98 part-time

KEY STATS
✔ **U.S News College Ranking:** 50, Universities–Master's (South)
✔ **ACT Score (25th/75th percentile):** 20-26
✔ **Tuition:** 2006-2007: $13,192

Selectivity: More selective	**Room/board:** N/A
Acceptance rate: 99%	**Average debt:** N/A
Student/faculty ratio: 14/1	**Proportion who borrowed:** N/A

UNDERGRADUATE STUDENT BODY STATS
2005-2006 enrollment: 1,402 full-time; 98 part-time. Men: 46%; women: 54%. **Ethnic makeup:** African American: 4%; American-Indian: 1%; Asian American: 1%; White: 92%; International: 2%. **Religious preference:** Church of Christ: 88%; Other: 12%.

ADMISSIONS FACTS AND FIGURES
Phone: (800) 630-3480. **Email:** admissions@fhu.edu. **Website:** http://www.fhu.edu. **Application deadlines for fall 2007:** Regular decision: Rolling. Early decision: Not offered. Early action: Not offered. Admission can be deferred. Common application is not accepted. **To apply online, go to:** http://www.fhu.edu/admissions/application.asp. **Admissions requirements/recommendations:** High school units required (recommended): English: (4); Mathematics: (2); Science: (2); Social studies: (2); Academic electives: (10); Total units: (20). Tests: The college uses SAT or ACT scores in admissions decisions. Either SAT or ACT required. For admission to the fall 2007 entering class, the school will accept: ACT with writing, ACT without writing. Campus visit: Recommended. Admissions interview: Neither required nor recommended. Off-campus interview: Not available. **Factors that count in admissions decisions:** *Academic:* Secondary school record: Very important. Class rank: Not considered. Letters of recommendation: Considered. Standardized test scores: Very important. Essay: Not considered. *Nonacademic:* Interview: Not considered. Extracurricular activities: Considered. Talent/ability: Not considered. Character/personal qualities: Considered. Alumni/ae relationship: Considered. Geographical residence: Not considered. State residency: Not considered. Religious affiliation/commitment: Considered. Minority status: Considered. Volunteer work: Considered. Work experience: Considered. **Other schools with the greatest overlap in applicants:** Harding University; Lipscomb University; Middle Tennessee State University; University of Tennessee–Martin.
Admissions statistics for the fall 2005 entering class: Total applicants: 1,230. Total accepted: 1,223. Freshmen enrolled: 374; 51% were from out of state. Overall acceptance rate: 99%. **Credentials of fall 2005 freshmen:** 30% ranked in the top 10 percent of their high school class; 57% were in the top 25 percent, and 78% were in the top half. (Proportion submitting class standing: 55%.) **Average high school grade point average:** 3.5. **First-year students who submitted SAT scores:** 16%. Scores (25/75 percentile): Verbal: 510-600, Math: 490-610, Combined: 1000-1210. **First-year students submitting ACT scores:** 90%. Scores (25/75 percentile): English: 20-28, Math: 19-26, Composite: 20-26.

ACADEMICS
Year founded: 1869. **Academic calendar:** Semester. **Degrees offered:** bachelor's, post-bachelor's certificate, master's, post-master's certificate. **Most popular majors:** 15% theology and religious vocations; 13% business, man-

agement, marketing, and related support services, 13% multi/interdisciplinary studies, 9% biological and biomedical sciences, 7% psychology. **Major fields of study:** biological and biomedical sciences; business, management, marketing, and related support services; communication, journalism, and related programs; computer and information sciences and support services; education; English language and literature/letters; family and consumer sciences/human sciences; health professions and related clinical sciences; history; mathematics and statistics; multi/interdisciplinary studies; parks, recreation, leisure, and fitness studies; philosophy and religious studies; physical sciences; psychology; public administration and social service professions; theology and religious vocations; visual and performing arts. **Areas of required coursework:** arts/fine arts, humanities, computer literacy, mathematics, English (including composition), sciences (biological or physical), history, social science. **Pre-professional programs:** other. **Special academic programs (% participation):** accelerated program, cooperative (work-study plan) program, cross-registration, distance learning, double major, dual enrollment, honors program (8%), independent study, internships, liberal arts/career combination, student-designed major, study abroad (2%), teacher certificate program. **Teacher certification offered in:** early childhood, special education, elementary, middle/junior high, secondary. **Faculty and instruction (2005-2006):** Total instructional faculty: 106 full-time, 41 part-time (70% men; 30% women; 5% minorities). Full-time faculty with Ph.D. or other terminal degree: 71%. Student/faculty ratio: 14/1. Classes of fewer than 20 students: 51%; of 20 to 49 students: 46%; of 50 or more students: 4%. **Advanced Placement and International Baccalaureate credit:** AP tests may be used for: Credit only. Scores accepted: 3, 4, 5. International Baccalaureate exams may be used for: Credit only. **Freshmen returning for sophomore year:** 77%. **Graduation rates:** Four-year: 39%; five-year: 54%; six-year: 53%. **Graduate study:** Fields in which graduates pursue further study: Master of Business Administration (MBA), 10%; law, 3%; medicine, 5%; dentistry, 2%; theology (or the seminary), 30%; education, 30%; arts and sciences, 15%.

COSTS AND FINANCIAL AID
Financial aid office: (731) 989-6662. **Expenses (2006-2007):** Tuition and fees 2006-2007: $13,192; room/board: N/A. Estimated books and supplies: $1,500; transportation: $1,390; personal expenses: $1,610. **Financial aid:** Priority filing date for institution's financial aid form: March 1. In 2005-2006, 90% of undergraduates applied for financial aid. Of those, 77% were determined to have financial need; 19% had their need fully met. Average financial aid package (proportion receiving): $10,706 (75%). Average amount of gift aid, such as scholarships or grants (proportion receiving): $7,795 (69%). Average amount of self-help aid, such as work study or loans (proportion receiving): $4,368 (61%). Average need-based loan (excluding PLUS or other private loans): $3,875. Among students who received need-based aid, the average percentage of need met: 62%. Among students who received aid based on merit, the average award (and the proportion receiving): $12,850 (20%). The average athletic scholarship (and the proportion receiving): $0 (0%).

CAMPUS LIFE AND EXTRACURRICULAR ACTIVITIES
Campus housing available (% using): women's dorms (44%), men's dorms (39%), apartment for single students (16%), special housing for international students (1%). Students who live in college-owned, operated, or affiliated housing: 71%. **Student employment:** During the 2005-2006 academic year, 33% of undergraduates worked on campus. Average per-year earnings: $1,000. **Clubs and organizations:** Number of student organizations: 53. Activities include: choral groups, concert band, drama/theater, jazz band, music ensembles, musical theater, pep band, radio station, student government, student newspaper, television station, yearbook. Number of fraternities: 6; sororities: 6. Average proportion of students who stay on campus on weekends: 66%. **Sports program (2005-2006):** Member of NAIA. *Men's intercollegiate varsity sports:* baseball, basketball, cross-country, golf, soccer, tennis. *Women's intercollegiate varsity sports:* basketball, cheerleading, cross-country, golf, soccer, softball, tennis, volleyball.

SERVICES AND FACILITIES
Basic services: placement service, day care, health service, health insurance. **Remedial assistance:** reading, math, writing, study skills. **Counseling services:** minority student, career, personal, academic, psychological, religious. **For learning-disabled students:** School does not offer a structured program with separate admission and additional fees. Services include: remedial math, remedial English, remedial reading, oral tests, extended time for tests, tutors, priority seating. **Library:** Number of titles: 129,595; number of current serial subscriptions: 690. **Information technology resources:** Students are not required to lease or own a computer. Number of campus

computers available to all students: 240. School has a wireless network. Proportion of college-owned housing units wired for high-speed internet access: 100%. **Campus safety:** Security services offered: 24-hour foot-and-vehicle patrols, lighted pathways/sidewalks, controlled dormitory access (key, security card, etc).

TRANSFER AND INTERNATIONAL STUDENTS

Transfer students: May apply for admission for the following academic terms: Fall, Spring, Summer. Applicants need a minimum number of credits to apply. **International students:** Number of foreign undergraduates: 36 (2% of student body). Number of countries represented: 18. Minimum TOEFL score required: 500 (paper); 185 (computer).

King College

- Address: 1350 King College Road, Bristol, TN 37620
- Website: http://www.king.edu
- Private; Religious affiliation: Presbyterian
- Enrollment: 803 full-time; 70 part-time

KEY STATS

✔ **U.S News College Ranking:** fourth tier, Liberal Arts Colleges
✔ **ACT Score (25th/75th percentile):** 20-24
✔ **Tuition:** 2006-2007: $18,345
  Selectivity: Selective **Room/board:** $6,200
  Acceptance rate: 95% **Average debt:** $16,635
  Student/faculty ratio: 13/1 **Proportion who borrowed:** 99%

UNDERGRADUATE STUDENT BODY STATS

2005-2006 enrollment: 803 full-time; 70 part-time. Men: 40%; women: 60%. **Ethnic makeup:** African American: 3%; Hispanic: 2%; White: 91%; International: 3%. **Religious preference:** Roman Catholic: 1%; Protestant: 70%; Unknown: 5%; Other: 24%.

ADMISSIONS FACTS AND FIGURES

Phone: (423) 652-4861. **Email:** admissions@king.edu. **Website:** http://www.king.edu. **Application deadlines for fall 2007:** Regular decision: Rolling. Early decision: Not offered. Early action: Not offered. Admission can be deferred. **Application fee:** $20. Common application is accepted. **To apply online, go to:** http://www.king.edu/admissions/apply/index.asp. **Admissions requirements/recommendations:** High school units required (recommended): English: 4; Mathematics: 3; Science: 1; Foreign language: 2; Social studies: 2; History: 2; Academic electives: 4; Total units: 16. Tests: The college uses SAT or ACT scores in admissions decisions. Either SAT or ACT required. For admission to the fall 2007 entering class, the school will accept: ACT with writing, ACT without writing. Campus visit: Recommended. Admissions interview: Recommended. Off-campus interview: Not available. **Factors that count in admissions decisions:** *Academic:* Secondary school record: Considered. Class rank: Considered. Letters of recommendation: Considered. Standardized test scores: Very important. Essay: Considered. *Nonacademic:* Interview: Not considered. Extracurricular activities: Not considered. Talent/ability: Not considered. Character/personal qualities: Not considered. Alumni/ae relationship: Not considered. Geographical residence: Not considered. State residency: Not considered. Religious affiliation/commitment: Not considered. Minority status: Not considered. Volunteer work: Not considered. Work experience: Not considered. **Other schools with the greatest overlap in applicants:** Carson-Newman College; East Tennessee State University; Milligan College; Tusculum College; University of Tennessee. **Admissions statistics for the fall 2005 entering class:** Total applicants: 550. Total accepted: 524. Freshmen enrolled: 209; 44% were from out of state. Overall acceptance rate: 95%. **Size of waiting list:** 0 applicants; enrolled from waiting list: 0. **Credentials of fall 2005 freshmen:** 19% ranked in the top 10 percent of their high school class; 43% were in the top 25 percent, and 78% were in the top half. (Proportion submitting class standing: 62%.) **Average high school grade point average:** 3.4. First-year students who submitted SAT scores: 49%. Scores (25/75 percentile): Verbal: 460-570, Math: 490-570, Combined: 950-1140. **First-year students submitting ACT scores:** 68%. Scores (25/75 percentile): English: 20-25, Math: 18-24, Composite: 20-24.

ACADEMICS

Year founded: 1867. **Academic calendar:** Semester. **Degrees offered:** bachelor's, master's. **Most popular majors:** 24% business administration and management, 22% health professions and related clinical sciences, 9% English language and literature, 7% biological and biomedical sciences, 7% history. **Major fields of study:** biological and biomedical sciences; business, management, marketing, and related support services; communication, journalism, and related programs; computer and information sciences and support services; education; engineering; English language and literature/letters; foreign languages, literatures, and linguistics; health professions and related clinical sciences; history; mathematics and statistics; multi/interdisciplinary studies; physical sciences; psychology; security and protective services; social sciences; theology and religious vocations; visual and performing arts. **Areas of required coursework:** arts/fine arts, humanities, mathematics, English (including composition), foreign languages, sciences (biological or physical), history, social science, other. **Pre-professional programs:** pre-law, pre-dentistry, pre-medicine, pre-theology, pre-veterinary science, pre-pharmacy, other. **Special academic programs (% participation):** accelerated program (20%), cross-registration (10%), double major, dual enrollment, English as a Second Language (ESL) (5%), exchange student program (domestic), honors program (5%), independent study (20%), internships (25%), student-designed major (5%), study abroad (25%), teacher certificate program (15%). **Teacher certification offered in:** early childhood, special education, elementary, middle/junior high, secondary. **Faculty and instruction (2005-2006):** Total instructional faculty: 50 full-time, 44 part-time (52% men; 48% women; 4% minorities). Full-time faculty with Ph.D. or other terminal degree: 76%. Student/faculty ratio: 13/1. Classes of fewer than 20 students: 77%; of 20 to 49 students: 23%; of 50 or more students: 1%. **Advanced Placement and International Baccalaureate credit:** AP tests may be used for: Credit only. Scores accepted: 4, 5. International Baccalaureate exams may be used for: Credit only. **Freshmen returning for sophomore year:** 72%. **Graduation rates:** Four-year: 47%; five-year: 59%; six-year: 59%. **Graduate study:** 24% of students pursue further study immediately upon graduation. Fields in which graduates pursue further study: Master of Business Administration (MBA), 42%; law, 3%; medicine, 5%; theology (or the seminary), 5%; education, 5%; arts and sciences, 39%.

COSTS AND FINANCIAL AID

Financial aid office: (423) 652-4725. **Expenses (2006-2007):** Tuition and fees 2006-2007: $18,345; room/board: $6,200. Estimated books and supplies: $850; transportation: $1,000; personal expenses: $2,000. **Financial aid:** Priority filing date for institution's financial aid form: March 1. In 2005-2006, 88% of undergraduates applied for financial aid. Of those, 76% were determined to have financial need; 24% had their need fully met. Average financial aid package (proportion receiving): $15,045 (76%). Average amount of gift aid, such as scholarships or grants (proportion receiving): $12,080 (74%). Average amount of self-help aid, such as work study or loans (proportion receiving): $4,481 (56%). Average need-based loan (excluding PLUS or other private loans): $4,335. Among students who received need-based aid, the average percentage of need met: 77%. Among students who received aid based on merit, the average award (and the proportion receiving): $9,793 (16%). The average athletic scholarship (and the proportion receiving): $5,795 (15%). Average amount of debt of borrowers graduating in 2005: $16,635. Proportion who borrowed: 99%.

CAMPUS LIFE AND EXTRACURRICULAR ACTIVITIES

Campus housing available (% using): women's dorms (53%), men's dorms (47%). Students who live in college-owned, operated, or affiliated housing: 52%. **Student employment:** During the 2005-2006 academic year, 28% of undergraduates worked on campus. Average per-year earnings: $1,236. **Clubs and organizations:** Number of student organizations: 35. Activities include: choral groups, dance, drama/theater, literary magazine, music ensembles, musical theater, pep band, student government, student newspaper, yearbook. Number of fraternities: 0; sororities: 0. Average proportion of students who stay on campus on weekends: 60%. **Sports program (2005-2006):** Member of NAIA. **Men's intercollegiate varsity sports:** baseball, basketball, cross-country, golf, soccer, tennis, track and field (indoor), track and field (outdoor). **Women's intercollegiate varsity sports:** basketball, cross-country, golf, soccer, softball, tennis, track and field (indoor), track and field (outdoor), volleyball.

SERVICES AND FACILITIES

Basic services: nonremedial tutoring, placement service, health insurance. **Remedial assistance:** reading, math, writing, study skills. **Counseling services:** minority student, career, personal, academic, older student, psychological, religious. **For learning-disabled students:** School does not offer a structured program with separate admission and additional fees. Total undergraduates in learning-disabled program or receiving services: 10. Services include: remedial math, remedial English, remedial reading, tape recorders, other special classes, untimed tests, oral tests, learning center, extended time for tests, tutors, other. **Library:** Number of titles: 129,020; number of current serial subscriptions: 389. **Information technology resources:** Students are required to lease or own a computer. Number of campus computers available to all students: 90. School has a wireless network. Approximate number of users that can be accommodated: 250. Proportion of college-owned housing units wired for high-speed internet access: 100%. **Campus safety:** Security services offered: late-night transport/escort service, 24-hour emergency telephones, lighted pathways/sidewalks, controlled dormitory access (key, security card, etc).

TRANSFER AND INTERNATIONAL STUDENTS

Transfer students: May apply for admission for the following academic terms: Fall, Spring, Summer. Applicants need a minimum number of credits to apply. For fall 2005: Transfer applications received: 381. Transfer applicants offered admission: 224. Transfer applicants enrolled: 120. **International students:** Number of foreign undergraduates: 24 (3% of student body). Number of countries represented: 17. Minimum TOEFL score required: 523 (paper); 193 (computer).

Lambuth University

■ **Address:** 705 Lambuth Boulevard, Jackson, TN 38301
■ **Website:** http://www.lambuth.edu
■ **Private; Religious affiliation:** United Methodist
■ **Enrollment:** 766 full-time; 39 part-time

KEY STATS
✔ **U.S News College Ranking:** 27, Comp. Coll.–Bachelor's (South)
✔ **ACT Score (25th/75th percentile):** 21-26
✔ **Tuition:** 2006-2007: $16,380
  Selectivity: More selective   **Room/board:** $6,710
  Acceptance rate: 65%   **Average debt:** $17,000
  Student/faculty ratio: 13/1   **Proportion who borrowed:** 80%

UNDERGRADUATE STUDENT BODY STATS

2005-2006 enrollment: 766 full-time; 39 part-time. Men: 46%; women: 54%. **Ethnic makeup:** African American: 19%; Asian American: 1%; Hispanic: 3%; White: 75%; International: 3%. **Religious preference:** Roman Catholic: 8%; Protestant: 20%; Unknown: 28%; United Methodist: 23%; Baptist: 21%.

ADMISSIONS FACTS AND FIGURES

Phone: (731) 425-3223. **Email:** admit@lambuth.edu. **Website:** http://www.lambuth.edu. **Application deadlines for fall 2007:** Regular decision: Rolling. Early decision: Not offered. Early action: Not offered. Admission can be deferred. **Application fee:** $25. Common application is accepted. **Admissions requirements/recommendations:** High school units required (recommended): English: (4); Mathematics: (4); Science: (3); Foreign language: (2); Social studies: (2); History: (2). Tests: The college uses SAT or ACT scores in admissions decisions. Either SAT or ACT required. For admission to the fall 2007 entering class, the school will accept: ACT with writing, ACT without writing. Campus visit: Recommended. Admissions interview: Neither required nor recommended. Off-campus interview: Not available. **Factors that count in admissions decisions:** *Academic:* Secondary school record: Very important. Class rank: Considered. Letters of recommendation: Considered. Standardized test scores: Very important. Essay: Considered. *Nonacademic:* Interview: Not considered. Extracurricular activities: Considered. Talent/ability: Very important. Character/personal qualities: Important. Alumni/ae relationship: Considered. Geographical residence: Not considered. State residency: Not considered. Religious affiliation/commitment: Considered. Minority status: Not considered. Volunteer work: Not considered. Work experience: Not considered. **Other schools with the greatest overlap in applicants:** Bethel University; Freed-Hardeman University; Freed-Hardeman University; Union University; Union University; University of Memphis; University of Memphis; University of Tennessee–Martin; University of Tennessee–Martin. **Admissions statistics for the fall 2005 entering class:** Total applicants: 1,333. Total accepted: 861. Freshmen enrolled: 234; 28%

were from out of state. Overall acceptance rate: 65%. **Credentials of fall 2005 freshmen:** 29% ranked in the top 10 percent of their high school class; 52% were in the top 25 percent, and 79% were in the top half. (Proportion submitting class standing: 84%.) **Average high school grade point average:** 3.4. **First-year students who submitted SAT scores:** 15%. Scores (25/75 percentile): Verbal: 480-600, Math: 500-590, Combined: 980-1190. **First-year students submitting ACT scores:** 84%. Scores (25/75 percentile): English: 22-28, Math: 19-25, Composite: 21-26.

ACADEMICS

Year founded: 1843. **Academic calendar:** Semester. **Degrees offered:** bachelor's. **Most popular majors:** 30% business, management, marketing, and related support services, 10% education, 9% parks, recreation, leisure, and fitness studies, 6% communication, journalism, and related programs, 6% visual and performing arts. **Major fields of study:** biological and biomedical sciences; business, management, marketing, and related support services; communication, journalism, and related programs; education; English language and literature/letters; family and consumer sciences/human sciences; foreign languages, literatures, and linguistics; health professions and related clinical sciences; history; legal professions and studies; liberal arts and sciences studies, and humanities; mathematics and statistics; multi/interdisciplinary studies; natural resources and conservation; parks, recreation, leisure, and fitness studies; philosophy and religious studies; physical sciences; psychology; security and protective services; social sciences; theology and religious vocations; visual and performing arts. **Areas of required coursework:** arts/fine arts, humanities, computer literacy, mathematics, English (including composition), philosophy, sciences (biological or physical), history, social science, other. **Pre-professional programs:** pre-law, pre-dentistry, pre-medicine, pre-theology, pre-veterinary science, pre-optometry, pre-pharmacy, other. **Special academic programs (% participation):** accelerated program (8%), cross-registration (4%), double major (4%), English as a Second Language (ESL) (3%), honors program (2%), independent study (10%), internships (75%), liberal arts/career combination (100%), student-designed major (1%), study abroad (6%), teacher certificate program (17%). **Teacher certification offered in:** special education, elementary, middle/junior high, secondary. **Faculty and instruction (2005-2006):** Total instructional faculty: 52 full-time, 35 part-time (55% men; 45% women; 6% minorities). Full-time faculty with Ph.D. or other terminal degree: 73%. Student/faculty ratio: 13/1. Classes of fewer than 20 students: 72%; of 20 to 49 students: 28%; of 50 or more students: 0%. **Advanced Placement and International Baccalaureate credit:** AP tests may be used for: Credit and/or placement. Scores accepted: 3, 4, 5. International Baccalaureate exams may be used for: Credit and/or placement. **Freshmen returning for sophomore year:** 60%. **Graduation rates:** Four-year: 25%; five-year: 37%; six-year: 41%. **Graduate study:** 40% of students pursue further study immediately upon graduation; 12% within one year; 19% within five years. Fields in which graduates pursue further study: Master of Business Administration (MBA), 7%; law, 6%; medicine, 2%; dentistry, 1%; engineering, 1%; theology (or the seminary), 3%; education, 7%; arts and sciences, 6%.

COSTS AND FINANCIAL AID

Financial aid office: (731) 425-3332. **Expenses (2006-2007):** Tuition and fees 2006-2007: $16,380; room/board: $6,710. Estimated books and supplies: $1,200; transportation: $1,600; personal expenses: $1,810. **Financial aid:** Priority filing date for institution's financial aid form: February 15. In 2005-2006, 89% of undergraduates applied for financial aid. Of those, 75% were determined to have financial need; 65% had their need fully met. Average financial aid package (proportion receiving): $16,084 (75%). Average amount of gift aid, such as scholarships or grants (proportion receiving): $10,520 (72%). Average amount of self-help aid, such as work study or loans (proportion receiving): $5,156 (51%). Average need-based loan (excluding PLUS or other private loans): $5,022. Among students who received need-based aid, the average percentage of need met: 75%. Among students who received aid based on merit, the average award (and the proportion receiving): $6,781 (13%). The average athletic scholarship (and the proportion receiving): $7,168 (5%). Average amount of debt of borrowers graduating in 2005: $17,000. Proportion who borrowed: 80%.

CAMPUS LIFE AND EXTRACURRICULAR ACTIVITIES

Campus housing available (% using): coed dorms (14%), women's dorms (30%), men's dorms (36%), sorority housing (2%), fraternity housing (2%), apartment for single students (15%), special housing for disabled students (1%). Students who live in college-owned, operated, or affiliated housing: 62%. **Student employment:** During the 2005-2006 academic year, 12% of undergraduates worked on campus. Average per-year earnings: $1,712. **Clubs and organizations:** Number of student organizations: 30. Activities include: choral groups, concert band, dance, drama/theater, jazz band, literary magazine, music ensembles, musical theater, pep band, radio station, student government, student newspaper, student film society, yearbook. Number of fraternities: 3; sororities: 4. Proportion of men in fraternities: 11%; of women in sororities: 15%. Average proportion of students who stay on campus on weekends: 60%. **Sports program (2005-2006):** Member of NAIA. **Men's intercollegiate varsity sports:** baseball, basketball, cross-country, football, golf, soccer, swimming and diving, tennis, track and field (outdoor). **Women's intercollegiate varsity sports:** basketball, cross-country, golf, soccer, softball, swimming and diving, tennis, track and field (outdoor), volleyball.

SERVICES AND FACILITIES
Basic services: nonremedial tutoring, placement service, health service, other. **Remedial assistance:** reading, math, writing, study skills. **Counseling services:** minority student, career, personal, academic, birth control, religious. **For learning-disabled students:** School does not offer a structured program with separate admission and additional fees. Total undergraduates in learning-disabled program or receiving services: 3. Services include: remedial math, remedial English, remedial reading, tape recorders, diagnostic testing service, untimed tests, oral tests, learning center, extended time for tests, tutors. **Library:** Number of titles: 272,435; number of current serial subscriptions: 139,999. **Information technology resources:** Students are not required to lease or own a computer. Number of campus computers available to all students: 72. School has a wireless network. Approximate number of users that can be accommodated: 500. Proportion of college-owned housing units wired for high-speed internet access: 50%. **Campus safety:** Security services offered: 24-hour foot-and-vehicle patrols, late-night transport/escort service, 24-hour emergency telephones, lighted pathways/sidewalks, controlled dormitory access (key, security card, etc).

TRANSFER AND INTERNATIONAL STUDENTS
Transfer students: May apply for admission for the following academic terms: Fall, Spring, Summer. Applicants need a minimum number of credits to apply. For fall 2005: Transfer applications received: 214. Transfer applicants offered admission: 122. Transfer applicants enrolled: 74. **International students:** Number of foreign undergraduates: 14 (3% of student body). Number of countries represented: 8. Minimum TOEFL score required: 500 (paper); 173 (computer).

Lane College

- **Address:** 545 Lane Avenue, Jackson, TN 38301-4598
- **Website:** http://www.lanecollege.edu
- **Private; Religious affiliation:** Methodist
- **Enrollment:** 1,202 full-time; 11 part-time

KEY STATS
✔ **U.S News College Ranking:** fourth tier, Liberal Arts Colleges
✔ **ACT Score (25th/75th percentile):** 18-23
✔ **Tuition:** 2006-2007: $7,620

Selectivity: Selective	**Room/board:** $4,800
Acceptance rate: 35%	**Average debt:** $20,000
Student/faculty ratio: 23/1	**Proportion who borrowed:** 98%

UNDERGRADUATE STUDENT BODY STATS
2005-2006 enrollment: 1,202 full-time; 11 part-time. Men: 50%; women: 50%. **Ethnic makeup:** African American: 100%.

ADMISSIONS FACTS AND FIGURES
Phone: (731) 426-7533. **Email:** admissions@lanecollege.edu. **Website:** http://www.lanecollege.edu. **Application deadlines for fall 2007:** Regular decision: August 1. Early decision: Send application by: May 15; Decision sent by: N/A. Early action: Not offered. Admission can be deferred. Common application is accepted. **Admissions requirements/recommendations:** High school units required (recommended): English: 4; Mathematics: 2; Science: 2; Foreign language: (2); Social studies: 2; History: 2; Total units: 16. Tests: The college uses SAT or ACT scores in admissions decisions. Either SAT or ACT required. For admission to the fall 2007 entering class, the school will accept: ACT with writing, ACT without writing. Campus visit: Recommended. Admissions interview: Recommended. Off-campus interview: May be arranged. **Factors that count in admissions decisions:**

Academic: Secondary school record: Very important. Class rank: Considered. Letters of recommendation: Very important. Standardized test scores: Important. Essay: Considered. **Nonacademic:** Interview: Considered. Extracurricular activities: Important. Talent/ability: Important. Character/personal qualities: Very important. **Admissions statistics for the fall 2005 entering class:** Total applicants: 3,817. Total accepted: 1,340. Freshmen enrolled: 504; 15% were from out of state. Overall acceptance rate: 35%. Non-early acceptance rate: 35%. **Credentials of fall 2005 freshmen:** 43% ranked in the top 10 percent of their high school class; 57% were in the top 25 percent, and 79% were in the top half. (Proportion submitting class standing: 96%.) **Average high school grade point average:** 2.9. **First-year students who submitted SAT scores:** 1%. Scores (25/75 percentile): Verbal: N/A, Math: N/A, Combined: N/A. **First-year students submitting ACT scores:** 99%. Scores (25/75 percentile): English: N/A, Math: N/A, Composite: 18-23.

ACADEMICS
Year founded: 1882. **Academic calendar:** Semester. **Degrees offered:** bachelor's, post-bachelor's certificate. **Most popular majors:** 16% business administration and management, 16% multi/interdisciplinary studies, 14% criminal justice/safety studies, 11% biology/biological sciences, 9% computer and information sciences. **Major fields of study:** biological and biomedical sciences; business, management, marketing, and related support services; communication, journalism, and related programs; computer and information sciences and support services; education; English language and literature/letters; foreign languages, literatures, and linguistics; history; mathematics and statistics; multi/interdisciplinary studies; philosophy and religious studies; physical sciences; security and protective services; social sciences; visual and performing arts. **Areas of required coursework:** arts/fine arts, humanities, computer literacy, mathematics, English (including composition), foreign languages, sciences (biological or physical), history, social science, other. **Pre-professional programs:** pre-law, pre-dentistry, pre-medicine, pre-theology, pre-veterinary science, pre-optometry, pre-pharmacy, other. **Special academic programs (% participation):** accelerated program (2%), double major (5%), dual enrollment (1%), internships (18%), study abroad (1%), teacher certificate program (15%). **Teacher certification offered in:** elementary, middle/junior high, secondary. **Faculty and instruction (2005-2006):** Total instructional faculty: 54 (69% men; 31% women; 76% minorities). Full-time faculty with Ph.D. or other terminal degree: 59%. Student/faculty ratio: 23/1. Classes of fewer than 20 students: 41%; of 20 to 49 students: 58%; of 50 or more students: 1%. **Advanced Placement and International Baccalaureate credit:** AP tests may be used for: Credit and/or placement. Scores accepted: 3. International Baccalaureate exams may be used for: Credit and/or placement. **Freshmen returning for sophomore year:** 67%. **Graduation rates:** Four-year: 50%; five-year: 54%; six-year: 56%. **Graduate study:** 40% of students pursue further study immediately upon graduation; 45% within one year; 65% within five years. Fields in which graduates pursue further study: Master of Business Administration (MBA), 4%; law, 3%; medicine, 1%; education, 30%; arts and sciences, 23%.

COSTS AND FINANCIAL AID
Financial aid office: (731) 426-7535. **Expenses (2006-2007):** Tuition and fees 2006-2007: $7,620; room/board: $4,800. Estimated books and supplies: $700; transportation: $455; personal expenses: $625. **Financial aid:** Priority filing date for institution's financial aid form: April 1. In 2005-2006, 100% of undergraduates applied for financial aid. Of those, 82% were determined to have financial need; 11% had their need fully met. Average financial aid package (proportion receiving): $9,403 (82%). Average amount of gift aid, such as scholarships or grants (proportion receiving): $3,852 (12%). Average amount of self-help aid, such as work study or loans (proportion receiving): $3,653 (78%). Average need-based loan (excluding PLUS or other private loans): $3,465. Among students who received need-based aid, the average percentage of need met: 80%. Among students who received aid based on merit, the average award (and the proportion receiving): $0 (0%). The average athletic scholarship (and the proportion receiving): $0 (0%). Average amount of debt of borrowers graduating in 2005: $20,000. Proportion who borrowed: 98%.

CAMPUS LIFE AND EXTRACURRICULAR ACTIVITIES
Campus housing available (% using): women's dorms (49%), men's dorms (51%). Students who live in college-owned, operated, or affiliated housing: 75%. **Student employment:** During the 2005-2006 academic year, 3% of undergraduates worked on campus. Average per-year earnings: $1,545. **Clubs and organizations:** Number of student organizations: 25. Activities include: choral groups, concert band, dance, drama/theater, marching band, music ensembles, pep band, student government, student newspaper, yearbook. Number of fraternities: 4; sororities: 4. Average proportion of stu-

dents who stay on campus on weekends: 40%. **Sports program (2005-2006):** Member of NCAA II. *Men's intercollegiate varsity sports:* baseball, basketball, cross-country, football, tennis, track and field (outdoor). *Women's intercollegiate varsity sports:* basketball, cross-country, softball, tennis, track and field (outdoor), volleyball.

SERVICES AND FACILITIES

Basic services: nonremedial tutoring, placement service, health service. **Remedial assistance:** reading, math, writing, study skills. **Counseling services:** career, personal, veteran student, academic, psychological, religious, other. **Library:** Number of titles: 151,744; number of current serial subscriptions: 1,046. **Information technology resources:** Students are not required to lease or own a computer. Number of campus computers available to all students: 500. School has a wireless network. Approximate number of users that can be accommodated: 150. Proportion of college-owned housing units wired for high-speed internet access: 100%. **Campus safety:** Security services offered: 24-hour foot-and-vehicle patrols, late-night transport/escort service, lighted pathways/sidewalks, controlled dormitory access (key, security card, etc).

TRANSFER AND INTERNATIONAL STUDENTS

Transfer students: May apply for admission for the following academic terms: Fall, Spring, Summer. Applicants need a minimum number of credits to apply. For fall 2005: Transfer applications received: 454. Transfer applicants offered admission: 121. Transfer applicants enrolled: 94. **International students:** Minimum TOEFL score required: 325 (paper). Average TOEFL score: 339 (paper).

Lee University

- **Address:** PO Box 3450, Cleveland, TN 37320
- **Website:** http://www.leeuniversity.edu
- **Private; Religious affiliation:** Pentecostal
- **Enrollment:** 3,316 full-time; 332 part-time

KEY STATS

✔ **U.S News College Ranking:** 19, Comp. Coll.–Bachelor's (South)
✔ **ACT Score (25th/75th percentile):** 19-26
✔ **Tuition:** 2006-2007: $10,258

Selectivity: Selective	**Room/board:** $5,024
Acceptance rate: 61%	**Average debt:** $26,482
Student/faculty ratio: 17/1	**Proportion who borrowed:** 71%

UNDERGRADUATE STUDENT BODY STATS

2005-2006 enrollment: 3,316 full-time; 332 part-time. Men: 42%; women: 58%. **Ethnic makeup:** African American: 4%; American-Indian: 1%; Asian American: 1%; Hispanic: 3%; White: 87%; International: 5%.

ADMISSIONS FACTS AND FIGURES

Phone: (423) 614-8500. **Email:** admissions@leeuniversity.edu. **Website:** http://www.leeuniversity.edu. **Application deadlines for fall 2007:** Regular decision: September 1. Early decision: Not offered. Early action: Not offered. Admission can be deferred. **Application fee:** $25. Common application is accepted. **Admissions requirements/recommendations:** High school units required (recommended): English: 4 (4); Mathematics: 3 (3); Science: 2 (2); Foreign language: 1 (1); Social studies: 2 (2); History: 1 (1); Academic electives: 0 (0); Total units: 13 (14). Tests: The college uses SAT or ACT scores in admissions decisions. Either SAT or ACT required. For admission to the fall 2007 entering class, the school will accept: ACT with writing, ACT without writing. Campus visit: Recommended. Admissions interview: Neither required nor recommended. Off-campus interview: May be arranged. **Factors that count in admissions decisions:** *Academic:* Secondary school record: Very important. Class rank: Very important. Letters of recommendation: Considered. Standardized test scores: Very important. Essay: Not considered. *Nonacademic:* Interview: Considered. Extracurricular activities: Considered. Talent/ability: Considered. Character/personal qualities: Important. Alumni/ae relationship: Not considered. Geographical residence: Not considered. State residency: Not considered. Religious affiliation/commitment: Not considered. Minority status: Not considered. Volunteer work: Not considered. Work experience: Not considered. **Other schools with the greatest overlap in applicants:** University of Georgia; University of Tennessee; University of Tennessee–Chattanooga. **Admissions**

statistics for the fall 2005 entering class: Total applicants: 1,465. Total accepted: 895. Freshmen enrolled: 761; 67% were from out of state. Overall acceptance rate: 61%. **Credentials of fall 2005 freshmen:** 19% ranked in the top 10 percent of their high school class; 43% were in the top 25 percent, and 69% were in the top half. (Proportion submitting class standing: 72%.) **Average high school grade point average:** 3.3. **First-year students who submitted SAT scores:** 51%. Scores (25/75 percentile): Verbal: 480-610, Math: 450-600, Combined: 930-1210. **First-year students submitting ACT scores:** 73%. Scores (25/75 percentile): English: 19-28, Math: 17-25, Composite: 19-26.

ACADEMICS

Year founded: 1918. **Academic calendar:** Semester. **Degrees offered:** bachelor's, master's. **Most popular majors:** 21% education, 16% philosophy and religious studies, 13% communications technologies/technicians and support services, 11% psychology, 10% business, management, marketing, and related support services. **Major fields of study:** biological and biomedical sciences; business, management, marketing, and related support services; communication, journalism, and related programs; communications technologies/technicians and support services; computer and information sciences and support services; education; English language and literature/letters; foreign languages, literatures, and linguistics; health professions and related clinical sciences; mathematics and statistics; multi/interdisciplinary studies; parks, recreation, leisure, and fitness studies; philosophy and religious studies; physical sciences; psychology; social sciences; visual and performing arts. **Areas of required coursework:** arts/fine arts, humanities, computer literacy, mathematics, English (including composition), foreign languages, sciences (biological or physical), history, social science, other. **Pre-professional programs:** pre-law, pre-dentistry, pre-medicine, pre-theology, pre-veterinary science, pre-pharmacy. **Special academic programs (% participation):** distance learning, double major (6%), dual enrollment (1%), English as a Second Language (ESL) (1%), external degree program (3%), honors program (4%), independent study (31%), internships (74%), liberal arts/career combination, study abroad (100%), teacher certificate program. **Teacher certification offered in:** early childhood, special education, elementary, vo-tech, middle/junior high, secondary, bilingual/bicultural. **Faculty and instruction (2005-2006):** Total instructional faculty: 148 full-time, 164 part-time (64% men; 36% women; 8% minorities). Full-time faculty with Ph.D. or other terminal degree: 75%. Student/faculty ratio: 17/1. Classes of fewer than 20 students: 52%; of 20 to 49 students: 42%; of 50 or more students: 6%. **Advanced Placement and International Baccalaureate credit:** AP tests may be used for: Credit and/or placement. Scores accepted: 3, 4, 5. International Baccalaureate exams may be used for: Credit only. **Freshmen returning for sophomore year:** 73%. **Graduation rates:** Four-year: 31%; five-year: 45%; six-year: 44%.

COSTS AND FINANCIAL AID

Financial aid office: (423) 614-8300. **Expenses (2006-2007):** Tuition and fees 2006-2007: $10,258; room/board: $5,024. Estimated books and supplies: $800; transportation: $1,340; personal expenses: $1,424. **Financial aid:** Priority filing date for institution's financial aid form: March 15. In 2005-2006, 70% of undergraduates applied for financial aid. Of those, 57% were determined to have financial need; 17% had their need fully met. Average financial aid package (proportion receiving): $7,911 (56%). Average amount of gift aid, such as scholarships or grants (proportion receiving): $5,752 (45%). Average amount of self-help aid, such as work study or loans (proportion receiving): $4,229 (44%). Average need-based loan (excluding PLUS or other private loans): $4,041. Among students who received need-based aid, the average percentage of need met: 54%. Among students who received aid based on merit, the average award (and the proportion receiving): $7,114 (24%). The average athletic scholarship (and the proportion receiving): $6,735 (3%). Average amount of debt of borrowers graduating in 2005: $26,482. Proportion who borrowed: 71%.

CAMPUS LIFE AND EXTRACURRICULAR ACTIVITIES

Campus housing available (% using): women's dorms (41%), men's dorms (28%), apartments for married students (2%), apartment for single students (29%), special housing for disabled students. Students who live in college-owned, operated, or affiliated housing: 48%. **Student employment:** During the 2005-2006 academic year, 13% of undergraduates worked on campus. Average per-year earnings: $2,000. **Clubs and organizations:** Number of student organizations: 72. Activities include: choral groups, concert band, drama/theater, jazz band, literary magazine, music ensembles, musical theater, opera, pep band, student government, student newspaper, symphony orchestra, yearbook. Number of fraternities: 5; sororities: 5. Proportion of men in fraternities: 13%; of women in sororities: 10%. Average proportion of students who stay on campus on weekends: 70%. **Sports program (2005-2006):** Member of NAIA. **Men's intercollegiate varsity sports:** baseball, basketball, cross-country, golf, soccer, tennis. **Women's intercollegiate varsity sports:** basketball, cross-country, soccer, softball, tennis, volleyball.

SERVICES AND FACILITIES
Basic services: nonremedial tutoring, women's center, placement service, health service, health insurance. **Remedial assistance:** reading, math, writing, study skills. **Counseling services:** minority student, career, military, personal, veteran student, academic, older student, psychological, birth control, religious. **For learning-disabled students:** School does not offer a structured program with separate admission and additional fees. Total undergraduates in learning-disabled program or receiving services: 105. Services include: remedial math, remedial English, reading machines, remedial reading, tape recorders, videotaped classes, untimed tests, note-taking services, oral tests, learning center, readers, extended time for tests, tutors, other testing accomodations. **Library:** Number of titles: 138,428; number of current serial subscriptions: 2,564. **Information technology resources:** Students are not required to lease or own a computer. Number of campus computers available to all students: 463. School has a wireless network. Approximate number of users that can be accommodated: 1,950. Proportion of college-owned housing units wired for high-speed internet access: 50%. **Campus safety:** Security services offered: 24-hour foot-and-vehicle patrols, late-night transport/escort service, 24-hour emergency telephones, lighted pathways/sidewalks, student patrols, controlled dormitory access (key, security card, etc).

TRANSFER AND INTERNATIONAL STUDENTS
Transfer students: May apply for admission for the following academic terms: Fall, Spring, Summer. Applicants need a minimum number of credits to apply. For fall 2005: Transfer applications received: 522. Transfer applicants offered admission: 335. Transfer applicants enrolled: 301. **International students:** Number of foreign undergraduates: 177 (5% of student body). Number of countries represented: 48. Minimum TOEFL score required: 450 (paper); 133 (computer). Average TOEFL score: 522 (paper).

LeMoyne-Owen College

- **Address:** 807 Walker Avenue, Memphis, TN 38126
- **Website:** http://www.loc.edu/
- **Private; Religious affiliation:** United Church of Christ/Baptist
- **Enrollment:** 684 full-time; 125 part-time

KEY STATS
✔ **U.S News College Ranking:** fourth tier, Comp. Coll.–Bachelor's (South)
✔ **ACT Score:** 16
✔ **Tuition:** 2006-2007: $10,373

Selectivity: Less selective	**Room/board:** $4,852
Acceptance rate: 38%	**Average debt:** $15,528
Student/faculty ratio: N/A	**Proportion who borrowed:** 94%

UNDERGRADUATE STUDENT BODY STATS
2005-2006 enrollment: 684 full-time; 125 part-time. Men: 32%; women: 68%. **Ethnic makeup:** African American: 97%; White: 1%; International: 1%.

ADMISSIONS FACTS AND FIGURES
Phone: (901) 435-1500. **Email:** admission@loc.edu. **Website:** http://www.loc.edu/. **Application deadlines for fall 2007:** Regular decision: April 1. Early decision: Not offered. Early action: Not offered. Admission can be deferred. **Application fee:** $25. Common application is accepted. **Admissions requirements/recommendations:** High school units required (recommended): English: 4 (4); Mathematics: 4 (4); Science: 3 (3); Foreign language: 2 (2); Social studies: 3 (3); History: 3 (3); Total units: 19. Tests: The college uses SAT or ACT scores in admissions decisions. Either SAT or ACT required. For admission to the fall 2007 entering class, the school will accept: ACT with writing, ACT without writing. Campus visit: Recommended. Admissions interview: Neither required nor recommended. Off-campus interview: Not available. **Factors that count in admissions decisions:** *Academic:* Secondary school record: Very important. Class rank: Considered. Letters of recommendation: Considered. Standardized test scores: Considered. Essay: Considered. *Nonacademic:* Extracurricular activities: Considered. Talent/ability: Considered. Character/personal qualities: Considered. Alumni/ae relationship: Considered. Geographical residence:

Not considered. State residency: Not considered. Religious affiliation/commitment: Not considered. Minority status: Not considered. Volunteer work: Considered. Work experience: Not considered. **Admissions statistics for the fall 2005 entering class:** Total applicants: 1,562. Total accepted: 587. Freshmen enrolled: 112; 17% were from out of state. Overall acceptance rate: 38%. **Size of waiting list:** 0 applicants; enrolled from waiting list: 0. **Average high school grade point average:** 2.5. **First-year students submitting ACT scores:** 76%. Scores (25/75 percentile): English: N/A, Math: N/A, Composite: N/A.

ACADEMICS
Year founded: 1862. **Academic calendar:** Semester. **Degrees offered:** bachelor's. **Most popular majors:** 40% business, management, marketing, and related support services, 27% social sciences, 14% liberal arts and sciences studies, and humanities, 10% biological and biomedical sciences, 9% education. **Major fields of study:** biological and biomedical sciences; business, management, marketing, and related support services; computer and information sciences and support services; education; English language and literature/letters; history; liberal arts and sciences studies, and humanities; mathematics and statistics; multi/interdisciplinary studies; physical sciences; social sciences; visual and performing arts. **Areas of required coursework:** humanities, computer literacy, mathematics, English (including composition), foreign languages, sciences (biological or physical), history, social science. **Special academic programs (% participation):** accelerated program (15%), double major (0%), honors program (5%), internships (20%), student-designed major, study abroad (0%), teacher certificate program (7%). **Teacher certification offered in:** early childhood, elementary, middle/junior high, secondary. **Reserve Officers Training Corps (ROTC):** Army ROTC: Offered at cooperating institution (University of Memphis); Navy ROTC: Offered at cooperating institution (University of Memphis); Air Force ROTC: Offered at cooperating institution (University of Memphis). **Faculty and instruction (2005-2006):** Total instructional faculty: 60. Full-time faculty with Ph.D. or other terminal degree: 52%. Classes of fewer than 20 students: 83%; of 20 to 49 students: 17%. **Advanced Placement and International Baccalaureate credit:** AP tests may be used for: Credit only. Scores accepted: 3, 4, 5. International Baccalaureate exams may be used for: Credit only. **Freshmen returning for sophomore year:** 54%. **Graduation rates:** Six-year: 18%.

COSTS AND FINANCIAL AID
Financial aid office: (901) 942-7313. **Expenses (2006-2007):** Tuition and fees 2006-2007: $10,373; room/board: $4,852. **Financial aid:** Priority filing date for institution's financial aid form: April 1. In 2005-2006, 97% of undergraduates applied for financial aid. Of those, 94% were determined to have financial need; 6% had their need fully met. Average financial aid package (proportion receiving): $9,421 (91%). Average amount of gift aid, such as scholarships or grants (proportion receiving): $6,750 (86%). Average amount of self-help aid, such as work study or loans (proportion receiving): $3,622 (77%). Average need-based loan (excluding PLUS or other private loans): $3,158. Among students who received need-based aid, the average percentage of need met: 55%. Among students who received aid based on merit, the average award (and the proportion receiving): $8,701 (6%). The average athletic scholarship (and the proportion receiving): $5,278 (3%). Average amount of debt of borrowers graduating in 2005: $15,528. Proportion who borrowed: 94%.

CAMPUS LIFE AND EXTRACURRICULAR ACTIVITIES
Campus housing available: women's dorms, men's dorms. Students who live in college-owned, operated, or affiliated housing: 10%. **Clubs and organizations:** Number of student organizations: 28. Activities include: choral groups, music ensembles, student government, student newspaper, yearbook. Number of fraternities: 4; sororities: 4. Proportion of men in fraternities: 10%; of women in sororities: 20%. Average proportion of students who stay on campus on weekends: 20%. **Sports program (2005-2006):** Member of NCAA II. **Men's intercollegiate varsity sports:** baseball, basketball, cross-country, golf, tennis. **Women's intercollegiate varsity sports:** basketball, cross-country, softball, tennis, volleyball.

SERVICES AND FACILITIES
Basic services: placement service. **Remedial assistance:** reading, math, writing, study skills. **Counseling services:** career, personal, birth control, religious. **For learning-disabled students:** Total undergraduates in learning-disabled program or receiving services: 12. **Information technology resources:** Students are not required to lease or own a computer. Number of campus computers available to all students: 125. School does not have a wireless network. Proportion of college-owned housing units wired for

high-speed internet access: 90%. **Campus safety:** Security services offered: 24-hour foot-and-vehicle patrols, late-night transport/escort service, 24-hour emergency telephones, lighted pathways/sidewalks.

TRANSFER AND INTERNATIONAL STUDENTS
Transfer students: May apply for admission for the following academic terms: Fall, Winter, Spring, Summer. Applicants need a minimum number of credits to apply. For fall 2005: Transfer applications received: 353. Transfer applicants offered admission: 134. Transfer applicants enrolled: 90. **International students:** Number of foreign undergraduates: 10 (1% of student body). Number of countries represented: 11. Minimum TOEFL score required: 550 (paper).

Lincoln Memorial University

- **Address:** Cumberland Gap Parkway, Harrogate, TN 37752-1901
- **Website:** http://www.lmunet.edu
- **Private**
- **Enrollment:** N/A

KEY STATS
- ✔ **U.S News College Ranking:** fourth tier, Universities–Master's (South)
- ✔ **SAT or ACT Score (25th/75th percentile):** N/A
- ✔ **Tuition:** N/A
  - **Selectivity:** Less selective **Room/board:** N/A
  - **Acceptance rate:** N/A **Average debt:** N/A
  - **Student/faculty ratio:** N/A **Proportion who borrowed:** N/A

Lipscomb University

- **Address:** 3901 Granny White Pike, Nashville, TN 37204-3951
- **Website:** http://www.lipscomb.edu
- **Private; Religious affiliation:** Church of Christ
- **Enrollment:** 2,070 full-time; 227 part-time

KEY STATS
- ✔ **U.S News College Ranking:** 28, Universities–Master's (South)
- ✔ **ACT Score (25th/75th percentile):** 21-27
- ✔ **Tuition:** 2006-2007: $15,566
  - **Selectivity:** More selective **Room/board:** $6,730
  - **Acceptance rate:** 76% **Average debt:** $33,000
  - **Student/faculty ratio:** 15/1 **Proportion who borrowed:** 56%

UNDERGRADUATE STUDENT BODY STATS
2005-2006 enrollment: 2,070 full-time; 227 part-time. Men: 43%; women: 57%. **Ethnic makeup:** African American: 5%; Asian American: 1%; Hispanic: 2%; White: 91%; International: 1%. **Religious preference:** Roman Catholic: 2%; Protestant: 20%; Unknown: 14%; Church of Christ: 64%.

ADMISSIONS FACTS AND FIGURES
Phone: (615) 269-1776. **Email:** admissions@lipscomb.edu. **Website:** http://www.lipscomb.edu. **Application deadlines for fall 2007:** Regular decision: Rolling. Early decision: Not offered. Early action: Not offered. Admission cannot be deferred. **Application fee:** $50. Common application is not accepted. **To apply online, go to:** http://admissions.lipscomb.edu/. **Admissions requirements/recommendations:** High school units required (recommended): English: 4; Mathematics: 2; Science: 2; Foreign language: 2; Social studies: 2; Academic electives: 2; Total units: 14. Tests: The college uses SAT or ACT scores in admissions decisions. Either SAT or ACT required. For admission to the fall 2007 entering class, the school will accept: ACT with writing, ACT without writing. Campus visit: Recommended. Admissions interview: Recommended. Off-campus interview: May be arranged. **Factors that count in admissions decisions:** *Academic:* Secondary school record: Considered. Class rank: Important. Letters of recommendation: Important. Standardized test scores: Very important. Essay: Considered. *Nonacademic:* Interview: Considered. Extracurricular activities: Considered. Talent/ability: Considered. Character/personal qualities: Important. Alumni/ae relationship:

Considered. Geographical residence: Not considered. State residency: Not considered. Religious affiliation/commitment: Not considered. Minority status: Not considered. Volunteer work: Considered. Work experience: Not considered. **Other schools with the greatest overlap in applicants:** Belmont University; Harding University; Middle Tennessee State University; University of Tennessee; Vanderbilt University. **Admissions statistics for the fall 2005 entering class:** Total applicants: 1,599. Total accepted: 1,210. Freshmen enrolled: 526; 37% were from out of state. Overall acceptance rate: 76%. **Credentials of fall 2005 freshmen:** 25% ranked in the top 10 percent of their high school class; 51% were in the top 25 percent, and 82% were in the top half. (Proportion submitting class standing: 92%.) **Average high school grade point average:** 3.5. **First-year students who submitted SAT scores:** 36%. Scores (25/75 percentile): Verbal: 510-630, Math: 490-630, Combined: 1000-1260. **First-year students submitting ACT scores:** 85%. Scores (25/75 percentile): English: 21-29, Math: 20-26, Composite: 21-27.

ACADEMICS
Year founded: 1891. **Academic calendar:** Semester. **Degrees offered:** bachelor's, master's, first professional. **Most popular majors:** 34% business, management, marketing, and related support services, 10% education, 8% biological and biomedical sciences, 7% communication, journalism, and related programs, 6% psychology. **Major fields of study:** architecture and related services; area, ethnic, cultural, and gender studies; biological and biomedical sciences; business, management, marketing, and related support services; communication, journalism, and related programs; computer and information sciences and support services; education; engineering; English language and literature/letters; family and consumer sciences/human sciences; foreign languages, literatures, and linguistics; health professions and related clinical sciences; history; legal professions and studies; liberal arts and sciences studies, and humanities; mathematics and statistics; natural resources and conservation; parks, recreation, leisure, and fitness studies; philosophy and religious studies; physical sciences; psychology; public administration and social service professions; social sciences; theology and religious vocations; visual and performing arts. **Areas of required coursework:** arts/fine arts, humanities, computer literacy, mathematics, English (including composition), sciences (biological or physical), history, social science, other. **Pre-professional programs:** pre-law, pre-dentistry, pre-medicine, pre-theology, pre-veterinary science, pre-optometry, pre-pharmacy, other. **Special academic programs:** accelerated program, cooperative (work-study plan) program, distance learning, double major, dual enrollment, honors program, independent study, internships, study abroad, teacher certificate program. **Teacher certification offered in:** early childhood, special education, elementary, middle/junior high, secondary. **Cooperative education programs:** art, business, computer science, education, engineering, health professions, home economics, humanities, natural science, social/behavioral science, technologies. **Reserve Officers Training Corps (ROTC):** Army ROTC: Offered at cooperating institution (Vanderbilt University); Air Force ROTC: Offered at cooperating institution (Tennessee State University). **Faculty and instruction (2005-2006):** Total instructional faculty: 119 full-time, 77 part-time (67% men; 33% women; 4% minorities). Full-time faculty with Ph.D. or other terminal degree: 84%. Student/faculty ratio: 15/1. Classes of fewer than 20 students: 50%; of 20 to 49 students: 47%; of 50 or more students: 3%. **Advanced Placement and International Baccalaureate credit:** AP tests may be used for: Credit and/or placement. Scores accepted: 3, 4, 5. **Freshmen returning for sophomore year:** 76%. **Graduation rates:** Four-year: 29%; five-year: 50%; six-year: 52%. **Graduate study:** Fields in which graduates pursue further study: Master of Business Administration (MBA), 6%; law, 4%; medicine, 15%; dentistry, 2%; engineering, 2%; theology (or the seminary), 13%; education, 16%; veterinary medicine, 1%.

COSTS AND FINANCIAL AID
Financial aid office: (615) 269-1791. **Expenses (2006-2007):** Tuition and fees 2006-2007: $15,566; room/board: $6,730. Estimated books and supplies: $1,000; transportation: $1,250; personal expenses: $1,250. **Financial aid:** Priority filing date for institution's financial aid form: March 1. In 2005-2006, 75% of undergraduates applied for financial aid. Of those, 61% were determined to have financial need; 85% had their need fully met. Average financial aid package (proportion receiving): $10,316 (52%). Average amount of gift aid, such as scholarships or grants (proportion receiving): $2,916 (42%). Average amount of self-help aid, such as work study or loans (proportion receiving): $4,085 (36%). Average need-based loan (excluding PLUS or other private loans): $4,004. Among students who received need-based aid, the average percentage of need met: 79%. Among students who received aid based on merit, the average award (and the proportion receiving): $5,495 (46%). The average athletic scholarship (and the proportion

receiving): $23,216 (10%). Average amount of debt of borrowers graduating in 2005: $33,000. Proportion who borrowed: 56%.

CAMPUS LIFE AND EXTRACURRICULAR ACTIVITIES

Campus housing available (% using): women's dorms (59%), men's dorms (41%). Students who live in college-owned, operated, or affiliated housing: 54%. **Student employment:** During the 2005-2006 academic year, 31% of undergraduates worked on campus. Average per-year earnings: $1,080. **Clubs and organizations:** Number of student organizations: 53. Activities include: choral groups, concert band, drama/theater, jazz band, literary magazine, marching band, music ensembles, musical theater, radio station, student government, student newspaper, yearbook. Number of fraternities: 7; sororities: 6. Proportion of men in fraternities: 8%; of women in sororities: 12%. **Sports program (2005-2006):** Member of NCAA I. *Men's intercollegiate varsity sports:* baseball, basketball, cross-country, golf, soccer, tennis, track and field (indoor), track and field (outdoor). *Women's intercollegiate varsity sports:* basketball, cross-country, golf, soccer, softball, tennis, track and field (indoor), track and field (outdoor), volleyball.

SERVICES AND FACILITIES

Basic services: placement service, health service. **Remedial assistance:** reading, math, writing, study skills. **Counseling services:** minority student, career, personal, academic, psychological, religious. **For learning-disabled students:** School does not offer a structured program with separate admission and additional fees. Services include: remedial math, remedial English, reading machines, tape recorders, diagnostic testing service, untimed tests, note-taking services, oral tests, readers, extended time for tests, tutors, priority registration, priority seating, proofreading services, substitution of courses, texts on tape, other testing accomodations, waiver of foreign language degree requirement, waiver of math degree requirement. **Library:** Number of titles: 252,765; number of current serial subscriptions: 882. **Information technology resources:** Students are not required to lease or own a computer. Number of campus computers available to all students: 330. School has a wireless network. Approximate number of users that can be accommodated: 3,750. Proportion of college-owned housing units wired for high-speed internet access: 100%. **Campus safety:** Security services offered: 24-hour foot-and-vehicle patrols, late-night transport/escort service, 24-hour emergency telephones, lighted pathways/sidewalks, student patrols, controlled dormitory access (key, security card, etc).

TRANSFER AND INTERNATIONAL STUDENTS

Transfer students: May apply for admission for the following academic terms: Fall, Winter, Spring, Summer. Applicants need a minimum number of credits to apply. For fall 2005: Transfer applications received: 346. Transfer applicants offered admission: 226. Transfer applicants enrolled: 146. **International students:** Number of foreign undergraduates: 33 (1% of student body). Number of countries represented: 35. Minimum TOEFL score required: 550 (paper); 213 (computer). Average TOEFL score: 635 (paper).

Martin Methodist College

- **Address:** 433 W. Madison Street, Pulaski, TN 38478
- **Website:** http://www.martinmethodist.edu
- **Private; Religious affiliation:** Methodist
- **Enrollment:** 580 full-time; 242 part-time

KEY STATS

✔ **U.S News College Ranking:** third tier, Comp. Coll.–Bachelor's (South)
✔ **ACT Score (25th/75th percentile):** 17-23
✔ **Tuition:** 2006-2007: $15,391

Selectivity: Selective	**Room/board:** $5,800
Acceptance rate: 96%	**Average debt:** $15,473
Student/faculty ratio: 17/1	**Proportion who borrowed:** 68%

UNDERGRADUATE STUDENT BODY STATS

2005-2006 enrollment: 580 full-time; 242 part-time. Men: 40%; women: 60%. **Ethnic makeup:** African American: 14%; Hispanic: 2%; White: 73%; International: 10%. **Religious preference:** Roman Catholic: 4%; No preference: 42%; Methodist: 16%; Baptist: 27%; Other: 12%.

ADMISSIONS FACTS AND FIGURES

Phone: (931) 363-9804. **Email:** admit@martinmethodist.edu. **Website:** http://www.martinmethodist.edu. **Application deadlines for fall 2007:** Regular decision: August 1. Early decision: Send application by: N/A; Decision sent by: N/A. Early action: Not offered. Admission can be deferred. **Application fee:** $30. Common application is accepted. **Admissions requirements/recommendations:** High school units required (recommended): English: 4 (4); Mathematics: 2 (2); Science: 1 (1); Foreign language: 0 (1); Social studies: 1 (1); History: 1 (1); Academic electives: 6 (6); Total units: 20 (24). Tests: The college uses SAT or ACT scores in admissions decisions. Either SAT or ACT required. For admission to the fall 2007 entering class, the school will accept: ACT with writing, ACT without writing. Campus visit: Recommended. Admissions interview: Recommended. Off-campus interview: May be arranged. **Factors that count in admissions decisions:** *Academic:* Secondary school record: Very important. Class rank: Very important. Letters of recommendation: Considered. Standardized test scores: Important. Essay: Considered. *Nonacademic:* Interview: Not considered. Extracurricular activities: Considered. Talent/ability: Not considered. Character/personal qualities: Considered. Alumni/ae relationship: Considered. Geographical residence: Considered. State residency: Not considered. Religious affiliation/commitment: Not considered. Minority status: Not considered. Volunteer work: Not considered. Work experience: Not considered. **Other schools with the greatest overlap in applicants:** Cumberland University; Middle Tennessee State University; Trevecca Nazarene University; University of North Alabama. **Admissions statistics for the fall 2005 entering class:** Total applicants: 585. Total accepted: 559. Freshmen enrolled: 221; Overall acceptance rate: 96%. Non-early acceptance rate: 96%. **Credentials of fall 2005 freshmen:** 21% ranked in the top 10 percent of their high school class; 36% were in the top 25 percent, and 80% were in the top half. (Proportion submitting class standing: 52%.) **Average high school grade point average:** 2.9.

ACADEMICS

Year founded: 1870. **Academic calendar:** Semester. **Degrees offered:** associate, bachelor's. **Most popular majors:** 21% business administration and management, 8% psychology, 7% human services, 6% accounting, 6% education. **Major fields of study:** biological and biomedical sciences; business, management, marketing, and related support services; education; English language and literature/letters; parks, recreation, leisure, and fitness studies; psychology; public administration and social service professions; theology and religious vocations. **Areas of required coursework:** arts/fine arts, humanities, computer literacy, mathematics, English (including composition), philosophy, sciences (biological or physical), history, social science, other. **Pre-professional programs:** pre-dentistry, pre-medicine. **Special academic programs (% participation):** double major (13%), dual enrollment, English as a Second Language (ESL), independent study (72%), study abroad, teacher certificate program (8%). **Teacher certification offered in:** elementary, secondary. **Faculty and instruction (2005-2006):** Total instructional faculty: N/A. Student/faculty ratio: 17/1. Classes of fewer than 20 students: 71%; of 20 to 49 students: 28%; of 50 or more students: 1%. **Advanced Placement and International Baccalaureate credit:** AP tests may be used for: Credit only. Scores accepted: 3, 4, 5. **Freshmen returning for sophomore year:** 58%. **Graduation rates:** Six-year: 19%.

COSTS AND FINANCIAL AID

Financial aid office: (931) 363-9821. **Expenses (2006-2007):** Tuition and fees 2006-2007: $15,391; room/board: $5,800. Estimated books and supplies: $1,000; transportation: $750; personal expenses: $2,000. **Financial aid:** Priority filing date for institution's financial aid form: February 1; deadline: August 1. In 2005-2006, 100% of undergraduates applied for financial aid. Of those, 83% were determined to have financial need; 36% had their need fully met. Average financial aid package (proportion receiving): N/A (64%). Average amount of gift aid, such as scholarships or grants (proportion receiving): N/A (64%). Average amount of self-help aid, such as work study or loans (proportion receiving): N/A (54%). Among students who received need-based aid, the average percentage of need met: 41%. Among students who received aid based on merit, the average award (and the proportion receiving): $4,000 (44%). The average athletic scholarship (and the proportion receiving): $11,484 (22%). Average amount of debt of borrowers graduating in 2005: $15,473. Proportion who borrowed: 68%.

CAMPUS LIFE AND EXTRACURRICULAR ACTIVITIES

Campus housing available (% using): women's dorms (34%), men's dorms (36%), apartment for single students (30%), special housing for disabled students (0%). **Student employment:** During the 2005-2006 academic year, 16% of undergraduates worked on campus. Average per-year earnings:

$1,500. **Clubs and organizations:** Number of student organizations: 20. Activities include: choral groups, concert band, drama/theater, music ensembles, musical theater, pep band, student government, student newspaper, yearbook. Number of fraternities: 0; sororities: 0. Average proportion of students who stay on campus on weekends: 50%. **Sports program (2005-2006):** Member of NAIA. *Men's intercollegiate varsity sports:* baseball, basketball, golf, soccer, tennis. *Women's intercollegiate varsity sports:* basketball, soccer, softball, tennis, volleyball.

SERVICES AND FACILITIES

Basic services: nonremedial tutoring. **Remedial assistance:** reading, math, writing, study skills. **Counseling services:** minority student, career, personal, psychological, religious. **For learning-disabled students:** School does not offer a structured program with separate admission and additional fees. Services include: remedial math, remedial English, remedial reading, tape recorders, diagnostic testing service, untimed tests, note-taking services, learning center, extended time for tests, tutors. **Library:** Number of titles: 46,543; number of current serial subscriptions: 804. **Information technology resources:** Students are not required to lease or own a computer. Number of campus computers available to all students: 85. School does not have a wireless network. Proportion of college-owned housing units wired for high-speed internet access: 100%. **Campus safety:** Security services offered: lighted pathways/sidewalks, controlled dormitory access (key, security card, etc).

TRANSFER AND INTERNATIONAL STUDENTS

Transfer students: May apply for admission for the following academic terms: Fall, Spring, Summer. Applicants do not need a minimum number of credits to apply. **International students:** Number of foreign undergraduates: 76 (10% of student body). Minimum TOEFL score required: 450 (paper); 250 (computer). Average TOEFL score: 474 (paper).

Maryville College

- **Address:** 502 E. Lamar Alexander Parkway, Maryville, TN 37804-5907
- **Website:** http://www.maryvillecollege.edu
- **Private; Religious affiliation:** Presbyterian
- **Enrollment:** 1,120 full-time; 26 part-time

KEY STATS

✔ **U.S News College Ranking:** 3, Comp. Coll.–Bachelor's (South)
✔ **ACT Score (25th/75th percentile):** 21-28
✔ **Tuition:** 2006-2007: $23,800

Selectivity: More selective	**Room/board:** $7,400
Acceptance rate: 79%	**Average debt:** $17,026
Student/faculty ratio: N/A	**Proportion who borrowed:** 90%

UNDERGRADUATE STUDENT BODY STATS

2005-2006 enrollment: 1,120 full-time; 26 part-time. Men: 46%; women: 54%. **Ethnic makeup:** African American: 6%; Asian American: 1%; Hispanic: 1%; White: 87%; International: 4%. **Religious preference:** Roman Catholic: 9%; Protestant: 73%; Unknown: 7%; Presbyterian: 11%.

ADMISSIONS FACTS AND FIGURES

Phone: (865) 981-8092. **Email:** admissions@maryvillecollege.edu. **Website:** http://www.maryvillecollege.edu. **Application deadlines for fall 2007:** Regular decision: March 1; decision sent by April 1. Early decision: Send application by: November 15; Decision sent by: December 1. Early action: Send application by: N/A; Decision sent by: N/A. Admission can be deferred. **Application fee:** $25. Common application is accepted. **Admissions requirements/recommendations:** High school units required (recommended): English: 4; Mathematics: 3; Science: 2; Foreign language: 2; Social studies: 2; History: (1); Academic electives: 1; Total units: 15. Tests: The college uses SAT or ACT scores in admissions decisions. Either SAT or ACT required. For admission to the fall 2007 entering class, the school will accept: ACT with writing, ACT without writing. Campus visit: Recommended. Admissions interview: Recommended. Off-campus interview: May be arranged. **Factors that count in admissions decisions:** *Academic:* Secondary school record: Very important. Class rank: Very important. Letters of recommendation: Important. Standardized test scores: Very important. Essay: Important. *Nonacademic:* Interview: Important. Extracurricular activities: Considered. Talent/ability: Considered. Character/personal qualities: Important.

Alumni/ae relationship: Not considered. Geographical residence: Not considered. State residency: Not considered. Religious affiliation/commitment: Not considered. Minority status: Not considered. Volunteer work: Considered. Work experience: Not considered. **Other schools with the greatest overlap in applicants:** Carson-Newman College; Centre College; Rhodes College; University of Tennessee. **Admissions statistics for the fall 2005 entering class:** Total applicants: 1,496. Total accepted: 1,183. Freshmen enrolled: 333; Overall acceptance rate: 79%. Non-early acceptance rate: 79%. **Credentials of fall 2005 freshmen:** 33% ranked in the top 10 percent of their high school class; 63% were in the top 25 percent. **First-year students who submitted SAT scores:** 42%. Scores (25/75 percentile): Verbal: 490-620, Math: 460-600, Combined: 950-1220. **First-year students submitting ACT scores:** 85%. Scores (25/75 percentile): English: 21-28, Math: 19-26, Composite: 21-28.

ACADEMICS

Year founded: 1819. **Academic calendar:** 4-1-4. **Degrees offered:** bachelor's. **Most popular majors:** Information not available. **Major fields of study:** biological and biomedical sciences; business, management, marketing, and related support services; computer and information sciences and support services; education; engineering; English language and literature/letters; foreign languages, literatures, and linguistics; health professions and related clinical sciences; history; mathematics and statistics; multi/interdisciplinary studies; natural resources and conservation; parks, recreation, leisure, and fitness studies; philosophy and religious studies; physical sciences; psychology; social sciences; visual and performing arts. **Areas of required coursework:** arts/fine arts, humanities, computer literacy, mathematics, English (including composition), philosophy, foreign languages, sciences (biological or physical), history, social science, other. **Pre-professional programs:** pre-law, pre-dentistry, pre-medicine, pre-theology, pre-veterinary science, pre-pharmacy. **Special academic programs (% participation):** double major (8%), English as a Second Language (ESL) (2%), honors program (15%), independent study (100%), internships (16%), liberal arts/career combination (40%), student-designed major (1%), study abroad (10%), teacher certificate program (18%). **Teacher certification offered in:** elementary, middle/junior high, secondary. **Advanced Placement and International Baccalaureate credit:** AP tests may be used for: Credit only. Scores accepted: 3. International Baccalaureate exams may be used for: Credit only. **Freshmen returning for sophomore year:** 70%. **Graduation rates:** Four-year: 45%; five-year: 53%; six-year: 57%. **Graduate study:** 25% of students pursue further study within one year; 30% within five years. Fields in which graduates pursue further study: Master of Business Administration (MBA), 5%; law, 6%; medicine, 5%; dentistry, 1%; engineering, 5%; theology (or the seminary), 3%; education, 8%; arts and sciences, 66%.

COSTS AND FINANCIAL AID

Financial aid office: (865) 981-8100. **Expenses (2006-2007):** Tuition and fees 2006-2007: $23,800; room/board: $7,400. Estimated books and supplies: $650; transportation: $700; personal expenses: $800. **Financial aid:** Priority filing date for institution's financial aid form: March 1. In 2005-2006, 100% of undergraduates applied for financial aid. Of those, 77% were determined to have financial need; 56% had their need fully met. Average financial aid package (proportion receiving): $20,380 (77%). Average amount of gift aid, such as scholarships or grants (proportion receiving): $13,670 (74%). Average amount of self-help aid, such as work study or loans (proportion receiving): $6,627 (37%). Average need-based loan (excluding PLUS or other private loans): $5,086. Among students who received need-based aid, the average percentage of need met: 92%. Among students who received aid based on merit, the average award (and the proportion receiving): $1,535 (22%). The average athletic scholarship (and the proportion receiving): $0 (0%). Average amount of debt of borrowers graduating in 2005: $17,026. Proportion who borrowed: 90%.

CAMPUS LIFE AND EXTRACURRICULAR ACTIVITIES

Campus housing available (% using): coed dorms (59%), women's dorms (14%), men's dorms (13%), apartment for single students (13%), special housing for disabled students (1%). **Student employment:** During the 2005-2006 academic year, 15% of undergraduates worked on campus. Average per-year earnings: $1,200. **Clubs and organizations:** Number of student organizations: 55. Activities include: choral groups, concert band, dance, drama/theater, jazz band, literary magazine, music ensembles, radio station, student government, student newspaper, symphony orchestra, yearbook. Number of fraternities: 0; sororities: 0. Average proportion of students who stay on campus on weekends: 50%. **Sports program (2005-2006):** Member of NCAA III. *Men's intercollegiate varsity sports:* baseball, basketball, cross-country, football, soccer, tennis. **Women's intercollegiate varsity sports:** basketball, cross-country, soccer, softball, tennis, volleyball.

SERVICES AND FACILITIES
Basic services: nonremedial tutoring, placement service, health service, health insurance. **Remedial assistance:** reading, math, writing, study skills, other. **Counseling services:** minority student, career, personal, academic, older student, psychological, religious. **For learning-disabled students:** School does not offer a structured program with separate admission and additional fees. Total undergraduates in learning-disabled program or receiving services: 32. Services include: remedial math, remedial English, reading machines, remedial reading, tape recorders, untimed tests, note-taking services, oral tests, learning center, readers, extended time for tests, tutors, priority seating, texts on tape. **Library:** Number of titles: 128,022; number of current serial subscriptions: 1,118. **Information technology resources:** Students are not required to lease or own a computer. Number of campus computers available to all students: 96. School has a wireless network. Proportion of college-owned housing units wired for high-speed internet access: 100%. **Campus safety:** Security services offered: 24-hour foot-and-vehicle patrols, late-night transport/escort service, lighted pathways/sidewalks, controlled dormitory access (key, security card, etc).

TRANSFER AND INTERNATIONAL STUDENTS
Transfer students: May apply for admission for the following academic terms: Fall, Winter, Spring, Summer. Applicants need a minimum number of credits to apply. **International students:** Number of foreign undergraduates: 49 (4% of student body). Number of countries represented: 20. Minimum TOEFL score required: 525 (paper); 200 (computer).

Memphis College of Art

- **Address:** Overton Park, 1930 Poplar Avenue, Memphis, TN 38104
- **Website:** http://www.mca.edu
- **Private**
- **Enrollment:** 270 full-time; 44 part-time

KEY STATS
✔ **U.S News College Ranking:** Unranked Specialty School–Fine Arts
✔ **ACT Score (25th/75th percentile):** 17-28
✔ **Tuition:** 2006-2007: $19,760

Selectivity: Less selective	**Room/board:** $7,600
Acceptance rate: 45%	**Average debt:** $20,000
Student/faculty ratio: 11/1	**Proportion who borrowed:** 90%

UNDERGRADUATE STUDENT BODY STATS
2005-2006 enrollment: 270 full-time; 44 part-time. Men: 50%; women: 50%. **Ethnic makeup:** African American: 15%; American-Indian: 1%; Asian American: 2%; Hispanic: 4%; White: 77%; International: 1%.

ADMISSIONS FACTS AND FIGURES
Phone: (800) 727-1088. **Email:** info@mca.edu. **Website:** http://www.mca.edu. **Application deadlines for fall 2007:** Regular decision: August 3. Early decision: Not offered. Early action: Not offered. Admission can be deferred. **Application fee:** $25. Common application is accepted. **Admissions requirements/recommendations:** Tests: The college uses SAT or ACT scores in admissions decisions. Either SAT or ACT required. For admission to the fall 2007 entering class, the school will accept: ACT with writing, ACT without writing. Campus visit: Recommended. Admissions interview: Recommended. Off-campus interview: May be arranged. **Factors that count in admissions decisions:** *Academic:* Secondary school record: Very important. Class rank: Important. Letters of recommendation: Considered. Standardized test scores: Important. Essay: Considered. *Nonacademic:* Interview: Very important. Extracurricular activities: Considered. Talent/ability: Very important. Character/personal qualities: Considered. Alumni/ae relationship: Not considered. Geographical residence: Not considered. State residency: Not considered. Religious affiliation/commitment: Not considered. Minority status: Not considered. Volunteer work: Considered. Work experience: Considered. **Other schools with the greatest overlap in applicants:** Columbus College of Art and Design; Kansas City Art Institute; Maryland Institute College of Art; University of Memphis. **Admissions statistics for the fall 2005 entering class:** Total applicants: 505. Total accepted: 226. Freshmen enrolled: 64; Overall acceptance rate: 45%. **Average high**

school grade point average: 2.9. **First-year students who submitted SAT scores:** 10%. Scores (25/75 percentile): Verbal: N/A, Math: N/A, Combined: N/A. **First-year students submitting ACT scores:** 90%. Scores (25/75 percentile): English: N/A, Math: N/A, Composite: 17-28.

ACADEMICS
Year founded: 1936. **Academic calendar:** Semester. **Degrees offered:** bachelor's, master's. **Most popular majors:** 54% design and applied arts, 46% fine and studio art. **Major fields of study:** visual and performing arts. **Areas of required coursework:** arts/fine arts, humanities, computer literacy, mathematics, English (including composition), sciences (biological or physical), social science. **Special academic programs (% participation):** cross-registration (3%), double major (2%), exchange student program (domestic) (5%), independent study (6%), internships (5%), study abroad (1%). **Cooperative education programs:** art. **Faculty and instruction (2005-2006):** Total instructional faculty: 23 full-time, 15 part-time (53% men; 47% women; 5% minorities). Full-time faculty with Ph.D. or other terminal degree: 83%. Student/faculty ratio: 11/1. Classes of fewer than 20 students: 88%; of 20 to 49 students: 12%; of 50 or more students: 0%. **Advanced Placement and International Baccalaureate credit:** AP tests may be used for: Credit and/or placement. International Baccalaureate exams may be used for: Credit and/or placement. **Freshmen returning for sophomore year:** 67%. **Graduation rates:** Four-year: 32%; five-year: 38%; six-year: 28%. **Graduate study:** 6% of students pursue further study immediately upon graduation; 10% within one year; 15% within five years. Fields in which graduates pursue further study: arts and sciences, 100%.

COSTS AND FINANCIAL AID
Financial aid office: (901) 272-5136. **Expenses (2006-2007):** Tuition and fees 2006-2007: $19,760; room/board: $7,600. Estimated books and supplies: $1,600; transportation: $1,375; personal expenses: $1,465. **Financial aid:** Priority filing date for institution's financial aid form: March 1. In 2005-2006, 86% of undergraduates applied for financial aid. Of those, 77% were determined to have financial need; 54% had their need fully met. Average financial aid package (proportion receiving): $7,000 (77%). Average amount of gift aid, such as scholarships or grants (proportion receiving): $3,000 (48%). Average amount of self-help aid, such as work study or loans (proportion receiving): $5,500 (67%). Average need-based loan (excluding PLUS or other private loans): $5,500. Among students who received need-based aid, the average percentage of need met: 90%. Among students who received aid based on merit, the average award (and the proportion receiving): $5,500 (23%). The average athletic scholarship (and the proportion receiving): $0 (0%). Average amount of debt of borrowers graduating in 2005: $20,000. Proportion who borrowed: 90%.

CAMPUS LIFE AND EXTRACURRICULAR ACTIVITIES
Campus housing available: coed dorms, apartment for single students. Students who live in college-owned, operated, or affiliated housing: 34%. Activities include: student government, student newspaper, yearbook. Number of fraternities: 0; sororities: 0. Average proportion of students who stay on campus on weekends: 33%.

SERVICES AND FACILITIES
Basic services: placement service. **Remedial assistance:** writing, study skills. **Counseling services:** career, personal, academic, psychological. **For learning-disabled students:** School does not offer a structured program with separate admission and additional fees. Services include: remedial English, learning center. **Information technology resources:** Students are not required to lease or own a computer. School does not have a wireless network. Proportion of college-owned housing units wired for high-speed internet access: 100%. **Campus safety:** Security services offered: late-night transport/escort service, 24-hour emergency telephones, controlled dormitory access (key, security card, etc).

TRANSFER AND INTERNATIONAL STUDENTS
Transfer students: May apply for admission for the following academic terms: Fall, Spring. Applicants need a minimum number of credits to apply. For fall 2005: Transfer applications received: 109. Transfer applicants offered admission: 85. Transfer applicants enrolled: 45. **International students:** Number of foreign undergraduates: 4 (1% of student body). Number of countries represented: 6. Minimum TOEFL score required: 500 (paper); 197 (computer).

Middle Tennessee State University

- **Address:** 1301 E. Main Street, CAB Room 205, Murfreesboro, TN 37132
- **Website:** http://www.mtsu.edu
- **Public**
- **Enrollment:** 17,291 full-time; 3,098 part-time

KEY STATS

✔ **U.S News College Ranking:** fourth tier, National Universities
✔ **ACT Score (25th/75th percentile):** 20-24
✔ **Tuition:** 2005-2006: $2,258 in state, $7,149 out of state

Selectivity: Selective	**Room/board:** $3,722
Acceptance rate: 85%	**Average debt:** N/A
Student/faculty ratio: 22/1	**Proportion who borrowed:** N/A

UNDERGRADUATE STUDENT BODY STATS

2005-2006 enrollment: 17,291 full-time; 3,098 part-time. Men: 47%; women: 53%. **Ethnic makeup:** African American: 12%; Asian American: 3%; Hispanic: 2%; White: 83%. **Religious preference:** Roman Catholic: 6%; Protestant: 42%; No preference: 1%; Unknown: 45%; Non-Denominational: 3%; Other: 3%.

ADMISSIONS FACTS AND FIGURES

Phone: (615) 898-2111. **Email:** admissions@mtsu.edu. **Website:** http://www.mtsu.edu. **Application deadlines for fall 2007:** Regular decision: July 1. Early decision: Not offered. Early action: Not offered. Admission can be deferred. **Application fee:** $25. Common application is not accepted. **To apply online, go to:** http://www.mtsu.edu/~admissn/index.htm. **Admissions requirements/recommendations:** High school units required (recommended): English: 4; Mathematics: 3; Science: 2; Foreign language: 2; Social studies: 1; History: 1; Total units: 14. Tests: The college uses SAT or ACT scores in admissions decisions. Either SAT or ACT required. For admission to the fall 2007 entering class, the school will accept: ACT with writing, ACT without writing. Campus visit: Recommended. Admissions interview: Neither required nor recommended. Off-campus interview: Not available. **Factors that count in admissions decisions:** *Academic:* Secondary school record: Very important. Class rank: Considered. Letters of recommendation: Considered. Standardized test scores: Very important. Essay: Not considered. *Nonacademic:* Interview: Not considered. Extracurricular activities: Considered. Talent/ability: Considered. Character/personal qualities: Considered. Alumni/ae relationship: Not considered. Geographical residence: Not considered. State residency: Not considered. Religious affiliation/commitment: Not considered. Minority status: Important. Volunteer work: Considered. Work experience: Considered. **Other schools with the greatest overlap in applicants:** University of Alabama–Huntsville; University of Memphis; University of Tennessee; University of Tennessee–Chattanooga; Western Kentucky University. **Admissions statistics for the fall 2005 entering class:** Total applicants: 6,392. Total accepted: 5,430. Freshmen enrolled: 3,208; 7% were from out of state. Overall acceptance rate: 85%. **Credentials of fall 2005 freshmen:** 13% ranked in the top 10 percent of their high school class; 33% were in the top 25 percent, and 59% were in the top half. (Proportion submitting class standing: 75%.) **First-year students who submitted SAT scores:** 7%. Scores (25/75 percentile): Verbal: 480-590; Math: 500-590, Combined: 980-1180. **First-year students submitting ACT scores:** 92%. Scores (25/75 percentile): English: 20-26, Math: 18-24, Composite: 20-24.

ACADEMICS

Year founded: 1911. **Academic calendar:** Semester. **Degrees offered:** bachelor's, post-bachelor's certificate, master's, post-master's certificate, doctorate. **Most popular majors:** 19% business, management, marketing, and related support services, 10% visual and performing arts, 9% communication, journalism, and related programs, 8% liberal arts and sciences studies, and humanities, 5% health professions and related clinical sciences. **Major fields of study:** agriculture, agriculture operations, and related sciences; biological and biomedical sciences; business, management, marketing, and related support services; communication, journalism, and related programs; computer and information sciences and support services; education; engineering technologies/technicians; English language and literature/letters; family and consumer sciences/human sciences; foreign languages, literatures, and linguistics; health professions and related clinical sciences; history; liberal arts and sciences studies, and humanities; mathematics and statistics; multi/interdisciplinary studies; parks, recreation, leisure, and fitness studies; philosophy and religious studies; physical sciences; psychology; public administration and social service professions; security and protective services; social sciences; transportation and materials moving; visual and performing arts. **Areas of required coursework:** arts/fine arts, humanities, computer literacy, mathematics, English (including composition), philosophy, foreign languages, sciences (biological or physical), history, social science. **Pre-professional programs:** pre-dentistry, pre-medicine, pre-pharmacy. **Special academic programs:** accelerated program, cooperative (work-study plan) program, cross-registration, distance learning, double major, dual enrollment, English as a Second Language (ESL), honors program, independent study, internships, student-designed major, study abroad, teacher certificate program. **Teacher certification offered in:** early childhood, special education, elementary, vo-tech, middle/junior high, secondary. **Cooperative education programs:** agriculture, business, computer science, education, engineering, humanities, social/behavioral science, technologies. **Reserve Officers Training Corps (ROTC):** Army ROTC: Offered on campus; Air Force ROTC: Offered at cooperating institution (Tennessee State University). **Faculty and instruction (2005-2006):** Total instructional faculty: 881 full-time, 317 part-time (53% men; 47% women; 13% minorities). Full-time faculty with Ph.D. or other terminal degree: 68%. Student/faculty ratio: 22/1. Classes of fewer than 20 students: 38%; of 20 to 49 students: 57%; of 50 or more students: 5%. **Advanced Placement and International Baccalaureate credit:** AP tests may be used for: Placement only. Scores accepted: 3. **Freshmen returning for sophomore year:** 75%. **Graduation rates:** Four-year: 23%; five-year: 38%; six-year: 40%. **Graduate study:** 18% of students pursue further study immediately upon graduation; 15% within one year.

COSTS AND FINANCIAL AID

Financial aid office: (615) 898-2830. **Expenses (2005-2006):** Tuition and fees 2005-2006: $2,258 in state, $7,149 out of state; room/board: $3,722. Estimated books and supplies: $1,000; transportation: $1,800; personal expenses: $1,350. **Financial aid:** Priority filing date for institution's financial aid form: May 1.

CAMPUS LIFE AND EXTRACURRICULAR ACTIVITIES

Campus housing available (% using): coed dorms (28%), women's dorms (23%), men's dorms (23%), fraternity housing (4%), apartments for married students (2%), apartment for single students (20%), special housing for disabled students. Students who live in college-owned, operated, or affiliated housing: 15%. **Student employment:** During the 2005-2006 academic year, 8% of undergraduates worked on campus. Average per-year earnings: $3,400. **Clubs and organizations:** Number of student organizations: 209. Activities include: choral groups, concert band, dance, drama/theater, jazz band, literary magazine, marching band, music ensembles, musical theater, opera, pep band, radio station, student government, student newspaper, student film society, symphony orchestra, television station. Number of fraternities: 16; sororities: 12. Proportion of men in fraternities: 7%; of women in sororities: 8%. Average proportion of students who stay on campus on weekends: 15%. **Sports program (2005-2006):** Member of NAIA. *Men's intercollegiate varsity sports:* baseball, basketball, cheerleading, cross-country, football, golf, tennis, track and field (indoor), track and field (outdoor). *Women's intercollegiate varsity sports:* basketball, cheerleading, cross-country, golf, soccer, softball, tennis, track and field (indoor), track and field (outdoor), volleyball.

SERVICES AND FACILITIES

Basic services: nonremedial tutoring, women's center, placement service, day care, health service, health insurance. **Remedial assistance:** reading, math, writing, study skills, other. **Counseling services:** minority student, career, military, personal, veteran student, academic, older student, psychological. **For learning-disabled students:** School does not offer a structured program with separate admission and additional fees. Total undergraduates in learning-disabled program or receiving services: 934. Services include: remedial math, remedial English, reading machines, remedial reading, tape recorders, note-taking services, oral tests, learning center, readers, extended time for tests, tutors, priority registration, priority seating, substitution of courses, texts on tape, typist/scribe, exams on tape or computer, other testing accomodations, other. **Library:** Number of titles: 748,888; number of current serial subscriptions: 4,144. **Information technology resources:** Students are not required to lease or own a computer. Number of campus computers available to all students: 2,300. School has a wireless network. Approximate number of users that can be accommodated: 5,000. Proportion of college-owned housing units wired for high-speed internet access: 100%. **Campus safety:** Security services offered: 24-hour foot-and-vehicle patrols, late-night transport/escort service, 24-hour emergency telephones, lighted pathways/sidewalks, controlled dormitory access (key, security card, etc).

TRANSFER AND INTERNATIONAL STUDENTS
Transfer students: May apply for admission for the following academic terms: Fall, Spring, Summer. Applicants need a minimum number of credits to apply. For fall 2005: Transfer applications received: 2,630. Transfer applicants offered admission: 2,495. Transfer applicants enrolled: 1,996. **International students:** Minimum TOEFL score required: 500 (paper); 173 (computer).

Milligan College

- **Address:** PO Box 500, Milligan College, TN 37682
- **Website:** http://www.milligan.edu
- **Private; Religious affiliation:** Independent Christian Churches
- **Enrollment:** 730 full-time; 23 part-time

KEY STATS
✔ **U.S News College Ranking:** 44, Universities–Master's (South)
✔ **ACT Score (25th/75th percentile):** 21-26
✔ **Tuition:** 2006-2007: $18,320

Selectivity: Selective	**Room/board:** $5,030
Acceptance rate: 78%	**Average debt:** $18,769
Student/faculty ratio: 12/1	**Proportion who borrowed:** 65%

UNDERGRADUATE STUDENT BODY STATS
2005-2006 enrollment: 730 full-time; 23 part-time. Men: 39%; women: 61%. **Ethnic makeup:** African American: 1%; American-Indian: 1%; Asian American: 1%; Hispanic: 1%; White: 94%; International: 2%. **Religious preference:** Roman Catholic: 2%; Protestant: 41%; Unknown: 4%; Independent Christian Churches: 53%.

ADMISSIONS FACTS AND FIGURES
Phone: (423) 461-8730. **Email:** admissions@milligan.edu. **Website:** http://www.milligan.edu. **Application deadlines for fall 2007:** Regular decision: August 1. Early decision: Not offered. Early action: Not offered. Admission can be deferred. **Application fee:** $30. Common application is not accepted. **To apply online, go to:** http://www.applyweb.com/aw?millgn. **Admissions requirements/recommendations:** High school units required (recommended): English: (4); Mathematics: (3); Science: (3); Foreign language: (2); Social studies: (2); History: (3); Total units: (17). Tests: The college uses SAT or ACT scores in admissions decisions. Either SAT or ACT required. For admission to the fall 2007 entering class, the school will accept: ACT with writing, ACT without writing. Campus visit: Recommended. Admissions interview: Neither required nor recommended. Off-campus interview: Not available. **Factors that count in admissions decisions:** *Academic:* Secondary school record: Very important. Class rank: Considered. Letters of recommendation: Important. Standardized test scores: Very important. Essay: Very important. *Nonacademic:* Interview: Considered. Extracurricular activities: Important. Talent/ability: Considered. Character/personal qualities: Very important. Alumni/ae relationship: Considered. Geographical residence: Not considered. State residency: Not considered. Religious affiliation/commitment: Very important. Minority status: Considered. Volunteer work: Considered. Work experience: Considered. **Admissions statistics for the fall 2005 entering class:** Total applicants: 686. Total accepted: 536. Freshmen enrolled: 168; 62% were from out of state. Overall acceptance rate: 78%. **Average high school grade point average:** 3.6. First-year students who submitted SAT scores: 56%. Scores (25/75 percentile): Verbal: 500-600, Math: 480-590, Combined: 980-1190. **First-year students submitting ACT scores:** 66%. Scores (25/75 percentile): English: 22-28, Math: 19-26, Composite: 21-26.

ACADEMICS
Year founded: 1866. **Academic calendar:** Semester. **Degrees offered:** bachelor's, master's. **Most popular majors:** 25% business, management, marketing, and related support services, 10% communications technologies/technicians and support services, 8% psychology, 7% biological and biomedical sciences, 7% visual and performing arts. **Major fields of study:** biological and biomedical sciences; business, management, marketing, and related support services; communication, journalism, and related programs; computer and information sciences and support services; educa-

tion; English language and literature/letters; health professions and related clinical sciences; history; liberal arts and sciences studies, and humanities; mathematics and statistics; parks, recreation, leisure, and fitness studies; physical sciences; psychology; public administration and social service professions; social sciences; theology and religious vocations; visual and performing arts. **Areas of required coursework:** arts/fine arts, humanities, computer literacy, mathematics, English (including composition), philosophy, sciences (biological or physical), history, social science, other. **Pre-professional programs:** pre-law, pre-dentistry, pre-medicine, pre-theology, pre-veterinary science, pre-pharmacy. **Special academic programs (% participation):** double major (25%), independent study (15%), internships (50%), study abroad (2%), teacher certificate program (20%). **Teacher certification offered in:** early childhood, elementary, middle/junior high, secondary. **Reserve Officers Training Corps (ROTC):** Army ROTC: Offered at cooperating institution (East Tennessee State University). **Faculty and instruction (2005-2006):** Total instructional faculty: 69 full-time, 39 part-time (51% men; 49% women; 1% minorities). Full-time faculty with Ph.D. or other terminal degree: 71%. Student/faculty ratio: 12/1. Classes of fewer than 20 students: 69%; of 20 to 49 students: 29%; of 50 or more students: 2%. **Advanced Placement and International Baccalaureate credit:** AP tests may be used for: Credit and/or placement. Scores accepted: 3, 4, 5. International Baccalaureate exams may be used for: Credit and/or placement. **Freshmen returning for sophomore year:** 76%. **Graduation rates:** Four-year: 49%; five-year: 60%; six-year: 54%.

COSTS AND FINANCIAL AID
Financial aid office: (423) 461-8949. **Expenses (2006-2007):** Tuition and fees 2006-2007: $18,320; room/board: $5,030. Estimated books and supplies: $750; transportation: $900; personal expenses: $1,100. **Financial aid:** Priority filing date for institution's financial aid form: March 1. In 2005-2006, 90% of undergraduates applied for financial aid. Of those, 84% were determined to have financial need; 49% had their need fully met. Average financial aid package (proportion receiving): $14,512 (84%). Average amount of gift aid, such as scholarships or grants (proportion receiving): $6,051 (42%). Average amount of self-help aid, such as work study or loans (proportion receiving): $4,472 (53%). Average need-based loan (excluding PLUS or other private loans): $4,098. Among students who received need-based aid, the average percentage of need met: 62%. Among students who received aid based on merit, the average award (and the proportion receiving): $5,980 (12%). The average athletic scholarship (and the proportion receiving): $6,337 (22%). Average amount of debt of borrowers graduating in 2005: $18,769. Proportion who borrowed: 65%.

CAMPUS LIFE AND EXTRACURRICULAR ACTIVITIES
Campus housing available (% using): women's dorms (54%), men's dorms (36%), apartments for married students (6%), apartment for single students (4%). Students who live in college-owned, operated, or affiliated housing: 77%. **Clubs and organizations:** Number of student organizations: 40. Activities include: choral groups, concert band, drama/theater, jazz band, literary magazine, music ensembles, musical theater, pep band, radio station, student government, student newspaper, symphony orchestra, yearbook. Number of fraternities: 0; sororities: 0. Average proportion of students who stay on campus on weekends: 65%. **Sports program (2005-2006):** Member of NAIA. *Men's intercollegiate varsity sports:* baseball, basketball, cross-country, golf, soccer, tennis, track and field (indoor), track and field (outdoor). *Women's intercollegiate varsity sports:* basketball, cross-country, soccer, softball, tennis, track and field (indoor), track and field (outdoor), volleyball.

SERVICES AND FACILITIES
Basic services: nonremedial tutoring, health service, health insurance. **Remedial assistance:** reading, math, writing, study skills. **Counseling services:** career, personal, academic, psychological. **For learning-disabled students:** School does not offer a structured program with separate admission and additional fees. Total undergraduates in learning-disabled program or receiving services: 9. Services include: remedial math, remedial English, remedial reading, untimed tests, note-taking services, special bookstore section, oral tests, learning center, extended time for tests, tutors, early syllabus, priority seating, texts on tape, exams on tape or computer, take home exams, other testing accomodations. **Library:** Number of titles: 171,596; number of current serial subscriptions: 7,313. **Information technology resources:** Students are not required to lease or own a computer. Number of campus computers available to all students: 123. School has a wireless network. Approximate number of users that can be accommodated: 408. Proportion of college-owned housing units wired for high-speed internet

access: 100%. **Campus safety:** Security services offered: lighted pathways/sidewalks, controlled dormitory access (key, security card, etc).

TRANSFER AND INTERNATIONAL STUDENTS

Transfer students: May apply for admission for the following academic terms: Fall, Spring, Summer. Applicants need a minimum number of credits to apply. For fall 2005: Transfer applications received: 156. Transfer applicants offered admission: 90. Transfer applicants enrolled: 57. **International students:** Number of foreign undergraduates: 17 (2% of student body). Number of countries represented: 10. Minimum TOEFL score required: 550 (paper); 213 (computer). Average TOEFL score: 527 (paper).

Rhodes College

■ **Address:** 2000 N. Parkway, Memphis, TN 38112
■ **Website:** http://www.rhodes.edu
■ **Private; Religious affiliation:** Presbyterian
■ **Enrollment:** 1,641 full-time; 36 part-time

KEY STATS

✔ **U.S News College Ranking:** 45, Liberal Arts Colleges
✔ **SAT Score (25th/75th percentile):** 1160-1350
✔ **Tuition:** 2006-2007: $27,874

Selectivity: More selective	**Room/board:** $7,180
Acceptance rate: 50%	**Average debt:** $22,575
Student/faculty ratio: 11/1	**Proportion who borrowed:** 46%

UNDERGRADUATE STUDENT BODY STATS

2005-2006 enrollment: 1,641 full-time; 36 part-time. Men: 42%; women: 58%. **Ethnic makeup:** African American: 5%; Asian American: 3%; Hispanic: 1%; White: 90%.

ADMISSIONS FACTS AND FIGURES

Phone: (800) 844-5969. **Email:** adminfo@rhodes.edu. **Website:** http://www.rhodes.edu. **Application deadlines for fall 2007:** Regular decision: Rolling. Early decision: Send application by: November 1; Decision sent by: December 1. Early action: Not offered. Admission can be deferred. **Application fee:** $45. Common application is accepted. **Admissions requirements/recommendations:** High school units required (recommended): English: 4; Mathematics: 3 (4); Science: 2; Foreign language: 2; Social studies: 2; History: 2; Academic electives: 3; Total units: 16. Tests: The college uses SAT or ACT scores in admissions decisions. Either SAT or ACT required. For admission to the fall 2007 entering class, the school will accept: ACT with writing, ACT without writing. Campus visit: Recommended. Admissions interview: Recommended. Off-campus interview: May be arranged. **Factors that count in admissions decisions:** *Academic:* Secondary school record: Very important. Class rank: Very important. Letters of recommendation: Important. Standardized test scores: Important. Essay: Important. *Nonacademic:* Interview: Considered. Extracurricular activities: Considered. Talent/ability: Considered. Character/personal qualities: Important. Alumni/ae relationship: Important. Geographical residence: Considered. State residency: Considered. Religious affiliation/commitment: Not considered. Minority status: Important. Volunteer work: Considered. Work experience: Considered. **Other schools with the greatest overlap in applicants:** Davidson College; Emory University; Sewanee–University of the South; Vanderbilt University; Washington University in St. Louis. **Admissions statistics for the fall 2005 entering class:** Total applicants: 3,539. Total accepted: 1,780. Freshmen enrolled: 444; 77% were from out of state. Overall acceptance rate: 50%. Non-early acceptance rate: 50%. **Size of waiting list:** 506 applicants; enrolled from waiting list: 73. **Credentials of fall 2005 freshmen:** 50% ranked in the top 10 percent of their high school class; 79% were in the top 25 percent, and 96% were in the top half. (Proportion submitting class standing: 51%.) **Average high school grade point average:** 3.6. **First-year students who submitted SAT scores:** 78%. Scores (25/75 percentile): Verbal: 580-680, Math: 580-670, Combined: 1160-1350. **First-year students submitting ACT scores:** 66%. Scores (25/75 percentile): English: 26-31, Math: 24-29, Composite: 25-30.

ACADEMICS

Year founded: 1848. **Academic calendar:** Semester. **Degrees offered:** bachelor's, master's. **Most popular majors:** Information not available. **Major fields**

of study: area, ethnic, cultural, and gender studies; biological and biomedical sciences; business, management, marketing, and related support services; computer and information sciences and support services; English language and literature/letters; foreign languages, literatures, and linguistics; history; mathematics and statistics; multi/interdisciplinary studies; philosophy and religious studies; physical sciences; psychology; social sciences; visual and performing arts. **Areas of required coursework:** arts/fine arts, humanities, mathematics, English (including composition), philosophy, foreign languages, sciences (biological or physical), history, social science, other. **Pre-professional programs:** pre-law, pre-dentistry, pre-medicine, pre-theology, pre-pharmacy. **Special academic programs (% participation):** cross-registration (3%), double major (6.25%), dual enrollment (0%), honors program (3%), independent study (10%), internships (60%), student-designed major (1%), study abroad (62%). **Cooperative education programs:** art, engineering, health professions. **Reserve Officers Training Corps (ROTC):** Army ROTC: Offered at cooperating institution (University of Memphis); Air Force ROTC: Offered at cooperating institution (University of Memphis). **Faculty and instruction (2005-2006):** Total instructional faculty: 141 full-time, 43 part-time (59% men; 41% women; 12% minorities). Full-time faculty with Ph.D. or other terminal degree: 95%. Student/faculty ratio: 11/1. Classes of fewer than 20 students: 74%; of 20 to 49 students: 26%; of 50 or more students: 1%. **Advanced Placement and International Baccalaureate credit:** AP tests may be used for: Credit and/or placement. Scores accepted: 4, 5. International Baccalaureate exams may be used for: Credit and/or placement. **Freshmen returning for sophomore year:** 86%. **Graduation rates:** Four-year: 77%; five-year: 80%; six-year: 80%. **Graduate study:** 35% of students pursue further study within one year. Fields in which graduates pursue further study: Master of Business Administration (MBA), 2%; law, 43%; medicine, 13%; dentistry, 2%; engineering, 1%; theology (or the seminary), 7%; education, 12%; arts and sciences, 20%.

COSTS AND FINANCIAL AID

Financial aid office: (901) 843-3810. **Expenses (2006-2007):** Tuition and fees 2006-2007: $27,874; room/board: $7,180. Estimated books and supplies: $904; transportation: $691; personal expenses: $1,295. **Financial aid:** In 2005-2006, 53% of undergraduates applied for financial aid. Of those, 35% were determined to have financial need; 55% had their need fully met. Average financial aid package (proportion receiving): $24,349 (35%). Average amount of gift aid, such as scholarships or grants (proportion receiving): $13,966 (34%). Average amount of self-help aid, such as work study or loans (proportion receiving): $6,658 (21%). Average need-based loan (excluding PLUS or other private loans): $6,015. Among students who received need-based aid, the average percentage of need met: 88%. Among students who received aid based on merit, the average award (and the proportion receiving): $9,887 (42%). The average athletic scholarship (and the proportion receiving): $0 (0%). Average amount of debt of borrowers graduating in 2005: $22,575. Proportion who borrowed: 46%.

CAMPUS LIFE AND EXTRACURRICULAR ACTIVITIES

Campus housing available (% using): coed dorms (12%), women's dorms (30%), men's dorms (40%), apartment for single students (18%). Students who live in college-owned, operated, or affiliated housing: 77%. **Student employment:** During the 2005-2006 academic year, 40% of undergraduates worked on campus. Average per-year earnings: $1,000. **Clubs and organizations:** Number of student organizations: 90. Activities include: choral groups, dance, drama/theater, literary magazine, music ensembles, musical theater, pep band, student government, student newspaper, student film society, symphony orchestra, yearbook. Number of fraternities: 7; sororities: 6. Proportion of men in fraternities: 48%; of women in sororities: 53%. Average proportion of students who stay on campus on weekends: 90%. **Sports program (2005-2006):** Member of NCAA III. *Men's intercollegiate varsity sports:* baseball, basketball, cross-country, football, golf, soccer, swimming and diving, tennis, track and field (indoor), track and field (outdoor). *Women's intercollegiate varsity sports:* basketball, cross-country, field hockey, golf, soccer, softball, swimming and diving, tennis, track and field (indoor), track and field (outdoor), volleyball.

SERVICES AND FACILITIES

Basic services: nonremedial tutoring, women's center, placement service, health service, health insurance. **Counseling services:** minority student, career, personal, academic, psychological, religious. **For learning-disabled students:** School does not offer a structured program with separate admission and additional fees. Services include: reading machines, tape recorders, note-taking services, readers, extended time for tests, tutors, priority seating, texts on tape. **Library:** Number of titles: 274,886; number of current serial subscriptions: 1,669. **Information technology resources:** Students are not required to lease or own a computer. Number of campus computers available to all students: 220. School has a wireless network. Proportion of college-owned housing units wired for high-speed internet access: 100%. **Campus safety:** Security services offered: 24-hour foot-and-vehicle patrols, late-night transport/escort service, 24-hour emergency telephones, lighted pathways/sidewalks, student patrols, controlled dormitory access (key, security card, etc).

TRANSFER AND INTERNATIONAL STUDENTS

Transfer students: May apply for admission for the following academic terms: Fall, Spring. Applicants need a minimum number of credits to apply. For fall 2005: Transfer applications received: 151. Transfer applicants offered admission: 40. Transfer applicants enrolled: 18. **International students:** Number of foreign undergraduates: 4. Number of countries represented: 7. Minimum TOEFL score required: 550 (paper); 213 (computer).

Sewanee—University of the South

- **Address:** 735 University Avenue, Sewanee, TN 37383
- **Website:** http://www.sewanee.edu
- **Private; Religious affiliation:** Episcopal
- **Enrollment:** 1,410 full-time; 22 part-time

KEY STATS

✔ **U.S News College Ranking:** 34, Liberal Arts Colleges
✔ **SAT Score (25th/75th percentile):** 1158-1330
✔ **Tuition:** 2006-2007: $28,750
   Selectivity: More selective   **Room/board:** $8,160
   Acceptance rate: 67%   **Average debt:** $14,926
   Student/faculty ratio: 10/1   **Proportion who borrowed:** 36%

UNDERGRADUATE STUDENT BODY STATS

2005-2006 enrollment: 1,410 full-time; 22 part-time. Men: 45%; women: 55%. **Ethnic makeup:** African American: 4%; Asian American: 2%; Hispanic: 2%; White: 90%; International: 2%. **Religious preference:** Roman Catholic: 7%; Protestant: 14%; Jewish: 1%; Unknown: 28%; Episcopal: 36%; Other: 14%.

ADMISSIONS FACTS AND FIGURES

Phone: (800) 522-2234. **Email:** admiss@sewanee.edu. **Website:** http://www.sewanee.edu. **Application deadlines for fall 2007:** Regular decision: February 1; decision sent by April 1. Early decision: Send application by: November 15; Decision sent by: December 15. Early action: Not offered. Admission can be deferred. **Application fee:** $45. Common application is accepted. **To apply online, go to:** http://admission.sewanee.edu/apply. **Admissions requirements/recommendations:** High school units required (recommended): English: 4 (4); Mathematics: 3 (4); Science: 2 (4); Foreign language: 2 (4); Social studies: 1 (2); History: 1 (2); Total units: 13 (20). Tests: The college uses SAT or ACT scores in admissions decisions. Either SAT or ACT required. For admission to the fall 2007 entering class, the school will accept: ACT with writing. Campus visit: Recommended. Admissions interview: Recommended. Off-campus interview: May be arranged. **Factors that count in admissions decisions:** *Academic:* Secondary school record: Very important. Class rank: Considered. Letters of recommendation: Very important. Standardized test scores: Important. Essay: Important. *Nonacademic:* Interview: Considered. Extracurricular activities: Important. Talent/ability: Considered. Character/personal qualities: Important. Alumni/ae relationship: Considered. Geographical residence: Considered. State residency: Not considered. Religious affiliation/commitment: Not considered. Minority status: Considered. Volunteer work: Important. Work experience: Important. **Other schools with the greatest overlap in applicants:** Furman University; Rhodes College; University of Georgia; Vanderbilt University; Washington and Lee University. **Admissions statistics for the fall 2005 entering class:** Total applicants: 2,027. Total accepted: 1,358. Freshmen enrolled: 421; 80% were from out of state. Overall acceptance rate: 67%. Early-decision acceptance rate: 82%. Non-early acceptance rate: 66%. **Size of waiting list:** 203 applicants; enrolled from waiting list: 2. **Credentials of fall 2005 freshmen:** 42% ranked in the top 10 percent of their high school class; 78% were in the top 25 percent, and 94% were in the top half. (Proportion submitting class standing: 40%.) **Average high school grade point average:** 3.6. **First-year students who submitted SAT scores:** 86%. Scores (25/75 percentile): Verbal: 588-670, Math: 570-660, Combined: 1158-1330. **First-year students**

submitting ACT scores: 52%. Scores (25/75 percentile): English: N/A, Math: N/A, Composite: 25-29.

ACADEMICS

Year founded: 1857. **Academic calendar:** Semester. **Degrees offered:** bachelor's, master's, first professional, doctorate. **Most popular majors:** 18% English language and literature/letters, 15% history, 15% social sciences, 9% visual and performing arts, 7% natural resources and conservation. **Major fields of study:** area, ethnic, cultural, and gender studies; biological and biomedical sciences; computer and information sciences and support services; English language and literature/letters; foreign languages, literatures, and linguistics; history; mathematics and statistics; natural resources and conservation; philosophy and religious studies; physical sciences; psychology; social sciences; visual and performing arts. **Areas of required coursework:** arts/fine arts, humanities, mathematics, English (including composition), philosophy, foreign languages, sciences (biological or physical), history, social science, other. **Pre-professional programs:** pre-law, pre-dentistry, pre-medicine, pre-veterinary science, other. **Special academic programs:** double major, independent study, internships, student-designed major, study abroad, teacher certificate program. **Teacher certification offered in:** elementary, middle/junior high, secondary. **Faculty and instruction (2005-2006):** Total instructional faculty: 132 full-time, 44 part-time (63% men; 38% women; 9% minorities). Full-time faculty with Ph.D. or other terminal degree: 94%. Student/faculty ratio: 10/1. Classes of fewer than 20 students: 72%; of 20 to 49 students: 28%; of 50 or more students: 0%. **Advanced Placement and International Baccalaureate credit:** AP tests may be used for: Credit only. Scores accepted: 4, 5. International Baccalaureate exams may be used for: Credit only. **Freshmen returning for sophomore year:** 86%. **Graduation rates:** Four-year: 79%; five-year: 82%; six-year: 82%. **Graduate study:** 14% of students pursue further study immediately upon graduation; 24% within one year; 45% within five years. Fields in which graduates pursue further study: Master of Business Administration (MBA), 8%; law, 13%; medicine, 5%; dentistry, 1%; engineering, 1%; theology (or the seminary), 3%; education, 4%; arts and sciences, 21%; veterinary medicine, 1%.

COSTS AND FINANCIAL AID

Financial aid office: (931) 598-1312. **Expenses (2006-2007):** Tuition and fees 2006-2007: $28,750; room/board: $8,160. Estimated books and supplies: $850 personal expenses: $900. **Financial aid:** Priority filing date for institution's financial aid form: March 1. In 2005-2006, 50% of undergraduates applied for financial aid. Of those, 47% were determined to have financial need; 84% had their need fully met. Average financial aid package (proportion receiving): $19,574 (47%). Average amount of gift aid, such as scholarships or grants (proportion receiving): $16,156 (45%). Average amount of self-help aid, such as work study or loans (proportion receiving): $3,128 (35%). Average need-based loan (excluding PLUS or other private loans): $3,311. Among students who received need-based aid, the average percentage of need met: 97%. Among students who received aid based on merit, the average award (and the proportion receiving): $11,581 (20%). Average amount of debt of borrowers graduating in 2005: $14,926. Proportion who borrowed: 36%.

CAMPUS LIFE AND EXTRACURRICULAR ACTIVITIES

Campus housing available (% using): coed dorms (44%), women's dorms (27%), men's dorms (21%), sorority housing (4%), fraternity housing (2%), apartments for married students (1%), other housing options (1%). Students who live in college-owned, operated, or affiliated housing: 94%. **Student employment:** During the 2005-2006 academic year, 15% of undergraduates worked on campus. Average per-year earnings: $1,500. **Clubs and organizations:** Number of student organizations: 110. Activities include: choral groups, dance, drama/theater, jazz band, literary magazine, music ensembles, musical theater, radio station, student government, student newspaper, student film society, symphony orchestra, yearbook. Number of fraternities: 11; sororities: 6. Proportion of men in fraternities: 70%; of women in sororities: 68%. Average proportion of students who stay on campus on weekends: 90%. **Sports program (2005-2006):** Member of NCAA III. *Men's intercollegiate varsity sports:* baseball, basketball, cross-country, football, golf, soccer, swimming and diving, tennis, track and field (indoor), track and field (outdoor). *Women's intercollegiate varsity sports:* basketball, cross-country, equestrian sports, field hockey, golf, soccer, softball, swimming and diving, tennis, track and field (indoor), track and field (outdoor), volleyball.

SERVICES AND FACILITIES

Basic services: nonremedial tutoring, women's center, day care, health service, health insurance, other. **Counseling services:** minority student, career, personal, academic, older student, psychological, birth control, religious. **For**

learning-disabled students: School does not offer a structured program with separate admission and additional fees. Services include: untimed tests, note-taking services, extended time for tests. **Library:** Number of titles: 676,342; number of current serial subscriptions: 3,896. **Information technology resources:** Students are not required to lease or own a computer. Number of campus computers available to all students: 170. School has a wireless network. Approximate number of users that can be accommodated: 650. Proportion of college-owned housing units wired for high-speed internet access: 100%. **Campus safety:** Security services offered: 24-hour foot-and-vehicle patrols, late-night transport/escort service, 24-hour emergency telephones, lighted pathways/sidewalks, controlled dormitory access (key, security card, etc).

TRANSFER AND INTERNATIONAL STUDENTS

Transfer students: May apply for admission for the following academic terms: Fall, Spring. Applicants do not need a minimum number of credits to apply. For fall 2005: Transfer applications received: 42. Transfer applicants offered admission: 4. Transfer applicants enrolled: 3. **International students:** Number of foreign undergraduates: 24 (2% of student body). Number of countries represented: 23. Minimum TOEFL score required: 550 (paper); 220 (computer).

Southern Adventist University

- **Address:** PO Box 370, Collegedale, TN 37315
- **Website:** http://www.southern.edu
- **Private; Religious affiliation:** Seventh-day Adventist
- **Enrollment:** 2,083 full-time; 307 part-time

KEY STATS

✔ **U.S News College Ranking:** 29, Comp. Coll.–Bachelor's (South)
✔ **ACT Score (25th/75th percentile):** 19-24
✔ **Tuition:** 2006-2007: $14,784

Selectivity: Selective	**Room/board:** $4,604
Acceptance rate: 69%	**Average debt:** $10,935
Student/faculty ratio: 16/1	**Proportion who borrowed:** 67%

UNDERGRADUATE STUDENT BODY STATS

2005-2006 enrollment: 2,083 full-time; 307 part-time. Men: 46%; women: 54%. **Ethnic makeup:** African American: 11%; Asian American: 5%; Hispanic: 12%; White: 67%; International: 5%. **Religious preference:** Protestant: 2%; Seventh-day Adventist: 97%.

ADMISSIONS FACTS AND FIGURES

Phone: (423) 236-2844. **Email:** admissions@southern.edu. **Website:** http://www.southern.edu. **Application deadlines for fall 2007:** Regular decision: September 7. Early decision: Not offered. Early action: Not offered. Admission can be deferred. **Application fee:** $25. Common application is not accepted. **To apply online, go to:** http://www.collegenet.com. **Admissions requirements/recommendations:** High school units required (recommended): English: 3 (4); Mathematics: 2 (3); Science: 2 (3); Foreign language: 0 (2); Social studies: 1 (1); History: 2 (2); Academic electives: 7 (7); Total units: 18 (24). Tests: The college uses SAT or ACT scores in admissions decisions. Either SAT or ACT required. For admission to the fall 2007 entering class, the school will accept: ACT with writing, ACT without writing. Campus visit: Recommended. Admissions interview: Recommended. Off-campus interview: May be arranged. **Factors that count in admissions decisions:** *Academic:* Secondary school record: Very important. Class rank: Not considered. Letters of recommendation: Not considered. Standardized test scores: Very important. Essay: Not considered. *Nonacademic:* Interview: Not considered. Extracurricular activities: Not considered. Talent/ability: Not considered. Character/personal qualities: Not considered. Alumni/ae relationship: Not considered. Geographical residence: Not considered. State residency: Not considered. Religious affiliation/commitment: Not considered. Minority status: Not considered. Volunteer work: Not considered. Work experience: Not considered. **Other schools with the greatest overlap in applicants:** Andrews University; Columbia Union College. **Admissions statistics for the fall 2005 entering class:** Total applicants: 1,471. Total accepted: 1,022. Freshmen enrolled: 605; 79% were from out of state. Overall acceptance rate: 69%. **Average high school grade point average:** 3.4. **First-year students who submitted SAT scores:** 46%. Scores (25/75 percentile): Verbal: N/A,

Math: N/A, Combined: N/A. **First-year students submitting ACT scores:** 73%. Scores (25/75 percentile): English: 19-25, Math: 17-24, Composite: 19-24.

ACADEMICS

Year founded: 1892. **Academic calendar:** Semester. **Degrees offered:** certificate, associate, bachelor's, master's. **Most popular majors:** 15% business, management, marketing, and related support services, 15% health professions and related clinical sciences, 12% visual and performing arts, 9% theology and religious vocations, 8% education. **Major fields of study:** area, ethnic, cultural, and gender studies; biological and biomedical sciences; business, management, marketing, and related support services; communication, journalism, and related programs; communications technologies/technicians and support services; computer and information sciences and support services; education; English language and literature/letters; family and consumer sciences/human sciences; foreign languages, literatures, and linguistics; health professions and related clinical sciences; mathematics and statistics; multi/interdisciplinary studies; parks, recreation, leisure, and fitness studies; philosophy and religious studies; physical sciences; psychology; public administration and social service professions; social sciences; theology and religious vocations; visual and performing arts. **Areas of required coursework:** arts/fine arts, computer literacy, mathematics, English (including composition), philosophy, sciences (biological or physical), history, social science. **Pre-professional programs:** pre-law, pre-dentistry, pre-medicine, pre-theology, pre-optometry, pre-pharmacy. **Special academic programs:** double major, dual enrollment, English as a Second Language (ESL), honors program, independent study, internships, study abroad, teacher certificate program. **Teacher certification offered in:** elementary, secondary. **Faculty and instruction (2005-2006):** Total instructional faculty: 131 full-time, 86 part-time (57% men; 43% women; 13% minorities). Full-time faculty with Ph.D. or other terminal degree: 66%. Student/faculty ratio: 16/1. **Advanced Placement and International Baccalaureate credit:** AP tests may be used for: Credit only. Scores accepted: 3, 4, 5. International Baccalaureate exams may be used for: Credit and/or placement. **Freshmen returning for sophomore year:** 71%. **Graduation rates:** Four-year: 24%; five-year: 41%; six-year: 54%. **Graduate study:** 10% of students pursue further study immediately upon graduation. Fields in which graduates pursue further study: medicine, 33%; dentistry, 8%; theology (or the seminary), 21%; education, 4%; arts and sciences, 34%.

COSTS AND FINANCIAL AID

Financial aid office: (423) 236-2835. **Expenses (2006-2007):** Tuition and fees 2006-2007: $14,784; room/board: $4,604. Estimated books and supplies: $1,000; transportation: $1,500; personal expenses: $2,000. **Financial aid:** Priority filing date for institution's financial aid form: March 1. In 2005-2006, 77% of undergraduates applied for financial aid. Of those, 66% were determined to have financial need; 18% had their need fully met. Average financial aid package (proportion receiving): $12,500 (66%). Average amount of gift aid, such as scholarships or grants (proportion receiving): $3,000 (40%). Average amount of self-help aid, such as work study or loans (proportion receiving): $4,300 (53%). Average need-based loan (excluding PLUS or other private loans): $2,600. Among students who received need-based aid, the average percentage of need met: 67%. Among students who received aid based on merit, the average award (and the proportion receiving): $3,000 (28%). The average athletic scholarship (and the proportion receiving): $0 (0%). Average amount of debt of borrowers graduating in 2005: $10,935. Proportion who borrowed: 67%.

CAMPUS LIFE AND EXTRACURRICULAR ACTIVITIES

Campus housing available (% using): women's dorms (48%), men's dorms (44%), apartments for married students (8%). Students who live in college-owned, operated, or affiliated housing: 65%. **Student employment:** During the 2005-2006 academic year, 50% of undergraduates worked on campus. Average per-year earnings: $3,000. **Clubs and organizations:** Number of student organizations: 38. Activities include: choral groups, concert band, drama/theater, music ensembles, radio station, student government, student newspaper, student film society, symphony orchestra, television station, yearbook. Number of fraternities: 0; sororities: 0.

SERVICES AND FACILITIES

Basic services: nonremedial tutoring, placement service, health service, health insurance. **Remedial assistance:** reading, math, writing, study skills. **Counseling services:** career, personal, academic, psychological, religious. **For learning-disabled students:** School does not offer a structured program with separate admission and additional fees. Total undergraduates in learning-disabled program or receiving services: 40. Services include: remedial math, remedial English, reading machines, tape recorders, diagnostic testing service, note-taking services, oral tests, learning center, readers, extended time for tests, tutors, priority seating, texts on tape, other testing accomodations. **Library:** Number of titles: 153,283; number of current serial subscriptions: 18,429. **Information technology resources:** Students are not required to lease or own a computer. Number of campus computers available to all students: 150. School has a wireless network. Approximate number of users that can be accommodated: 2,000. Proportion of college-owned housing units wired for high-speed internet access: 95%. **Campus safety:** Security services offered: 24-hour foot-and-vehicle patrols, late-night transport/escort service, 24-hour emergency telephones, lighted pathways/sidewalks, student patrols, controlled dormitory access (key, security card, etc).

TRANSFER AND INTERNATIONAL STUDENTS
Transfer students: May apply for admission for the following academic terms: Fall, Winter, Summer. Applicants need a minimum number of credits to apply. For fall 2005: Transfer applicants enrolled: 185. **International students:** Number of foreign undergraduates: 119 (5% of student body). Minimum TOEFL score required: 450 (paper); 133 (computer).

Tennessee State University

- **Address:** 3500 John Merritt Boulevard, Nashville, TN 37209-1561
- **Website:** http://www.tnstate.edu
- **Public**
- **Enrollment:** 5,873 full-time; 1,164 part-time

KEY STATS
✔ **U.S News College Ranking:** fourth tier, National Universities
✔ **ACT Score (25th/75th percentile):** 16-21
✔ **Tuition:** 2005-2006: $4,274 in state, $13,356 out of state

Selectivity: Selective	**Room/board:** $4,567
Acceptance rate: 43%	**Average debt:** $23,434
Student/faculty ratio: N/A	**Proportion who borrowed:** 84%

UNDERGRADUATE STUDENT BODY STATS
2005-2006 enrollment: 5,873 full-time; 1,164 part-time. Men: 35%; women: 65%. **Ethnic makeup:** African American: 84%; Asian American: 1%; White: 13%; International: 1%.

ADMISSIONS FACTS AND FIGURES
Phone: (615) 963-5101. **Email:** jcade@tnstate.edu. **Website:** http://www.tnstate.edu. **Application deadlines for fall 2007:** Regular decision: August 11. Early decision: Not offered. Early action: Not offered. Admission cannot be deferred. **Application fee:** $15. Common application is not accepted. **Admissions requirements/recommendations:** High school units required (recommended): English: 4; Mathematics: 3; Science: 2; Foreign language: 2; Social studies: 1; History: 1; Academic electives: 1; Total units: 14. Tests: The college uses SAT or ACT scores in admissions decisions. Either SAT or ACT required. Campus visit: Recommended. Admissions interview: Neither required nor recommended. Off-campus interview: May be arranged. **Factors that count in admissions decisions:** *Academic:* Secondary school record: Very important. Class rank: Important. Letters of recommendation: Important. Standardized test scores: Very important. *Nonacademic:* Interview: Not considered. Extracurricular activities: Not considered. Talent/ability: Not considered. Character/personal qualities: Not considered. Alumni/ae relationship: Important. Geographical residence: Not considered. State residency: Important. Religious affiliation/commitment: Not considered. Minority status: Not considered. Volunteer work: Not considered. Work experience: Not considered. **Other schools with the greatest overlap in applicants:** Alabama State University; Austin Peay State University; Dillard University; Lipscomb University; Middle Tennessee State University. **Admissions statistics for the fall 2005 entering class:** Total applicants: 6,950. Total accepted: 2,962. Freshmen enrolled: 1,205; 31% were from out of state. Overall acceptance rate: 43%.

ACADEMICS
Year founded: 1912. **Academic calendar:** Semester. **Degrees offered:** associate, bachelor's, master's, doctorate. **Most popular majors:** 31% education, 8% biological and biomedical sciences, 7% engineering, 2% mathematics and statistics, 0% physical sciences. **Major fields of study:** agriculture, agriculture operations, and related sciences; area, ethnic, cultural, and gender studies; biological and biomedical sciences; business, management, marketing,

and related support services; computer and information sciences and support services; education; engineering; engineering technologies/technicians; English language and literature/letters; family and consumer sciences/human sciences; foreign languages, literatures, and linguistics; health professions and related clinical sciences; history; liberal arts and sciences studies, and humanities; mathematics and statistics; parks, recreation, leisure, and fitness studies; physical sciences; psychology; public administration and social service professions; security and protective services; social sciences; visual and performing arts. **Areas of required coursework:** arts/fine arts, humanities, mathematics, English (including composition), philosophy, foreign languages, sciences (biological or physical), history, social science. **Special academic programs (% participation):** cooperative (work-study plan) program (12%), cross-registration, distance learning (2%), double major (1%), exchange student program (domestic) (2%), honors program (16%), independent study (1%), internships (14%), teacher certificate program (17%). **Teacher certification offered in:** early childhood, special education, elementary, adult education, secondary. **Cooperative education programs:** business, computer science, engineering. **Reserve Officers Training Corps (ROTC):** Air Force ROTC: Offered on campus. **Faculty and instruction (2005-2006):** Total instructional faculty: 405 full-time, 171 part-time (56% men; 44% women; 65% minorities). Full-time faculty with Ph.D. or other terminal degree: 96%. Classes of fewer than 20 students: 46%; of 20 to 49 students: 51%; of 50 or more students: 2%. Freshmen returning for sophomore year: 74%. **Graduation rates:** Six-year: 46%. **Graduate study:** 3% of students pursue further study immediately upon graduation; 4% within one year; 2% within five years. Fields in which graduates pursue further study: Master of Business Administration (MBA), 12%; law, 2%; medicine, 4%; engineering, 5%; education, 8%.

COSTS AND FINANCIAL AID
Financial aid office: (615) 963-5701. **Expenses (2005-2006):** Tuition and fees 2005-2006: $4,274 in state, $13,356 out of state; room/board: $4,567. Estimated books and supplies: $1,030; transportation: $1,744; personal expenses: $4,089. **Financial aid:** Priority filing date for institution's financial aid form: April 1; deadline: August 1. 59% had their need fully met. Average financial aid package (proportion receiving): $2,875 (N/A). Average amount of gift aid, such as scholarships or grants (proportion receiving): $108 (N/A). Average amount of self-help aid, such as work study or loans (proportion receiving): $1,010 (N/A). Average need-based loan (excluding PLUS or other private loans): $777. Among students who received need-based aid, the average percentage of need met: 82%. Among students who received aid based on merit, the average award (and the proportion receiving): $8,370 (N/A). The average athletic scholarship (and the proportion receiving): $12,024 (N/A). Average amount of debt of borrowers graduating in 2005: $23,434. Proportion who borrowed: 84%.

CAMPUS LIFE AND EXTRACURRICULAR ACTIVITIES
Campus housing available (% using): coed dorms (23%), women's dorms (37%), men's dorms (28%), apartment for single students (12%). Students who live in college-owned, operated, or affiliated housing: 73%. **Student employment:** During the 2005-2006 academic year, 33% of undergraduates worked on campus. Average per-year earnings: $2,500. **Clubs and organizations:** Number of student organizations: 18. Activities include: choral groups, drama/theater, jazz band, marching band, music ensembles, pep band, radio station, student government, student newspaper, yearbook. Number of fraternities: 13; sororities: 12. Proportion of men in fraternities: 9%; of women in sororities: 14%. Average proportion of students who stay on campus on weekends: 71%. **Sports program (2005-2006):** Member of NCAA I. *Men's intercollegiate varsity sports:* basketball, cross-country, football, golf, tennis, track and field (indoor), track and field (outdoor). *Women's intercollegiate varsity sports:* basketball, cross-country, golf, softball, tennis, track and field (indoor), track and field (outdoor), volleyball.

SERVICES AND FACILITIES
Basic services: placement service, day care, health service. **Remedial assistance:** reading, math, writing, study skills. **Counseling services:** minority student, career, military, veteran student, academic, older student, psychological. **For learning-disabled students:** School does not offer a structured program with separate admission and additional fees. Services include: remedial math, remedial English, remedial reading, tape recorders, diagnostic testing service, untimed tests, learning center, tutors. **Information technology resources:** Students are not required to lease or own a computer. Number of campus computers available to all students: 1,200. School has a wireless network. **Campus safety:** Security services offered: 24-hour foot-and-vehicle patrols, late-night transport/escort service, 24-hour emergency

telephones, lighted pathways/sidewalks, controlled dormitory access (key, security card, etc).

TRANSFER AND INTERNATIONAL STUDENTS

Transfer students: May apply for admission for the following academic terms: Fall, Winter, Spring, Summer. Applicants need a minimum number of credits to apply. **International students:** Number of foreign undergraduates: 49 (1% of student body). Minimum TOEFL score required: 500 (paper), Average TOEFL score: 525 (paper).

Tennessee Technological University

- **Address:** Campus Box 5006 USPS 077-460, Cookeville, TN 38505
- **Website:** http://www.tntech.edu
- **Public**
- **Enrollment:** 6,453 full-time; 802 part-time

KEY STATS

✔ **U.S News College Ranking:** 33, Universities–Master's (South)
✔ **ACT Score (25th/75th percentile):** 20-26
✔ **Tuition:** 2006-2007: $4,660 in state, $9,960 out of state

Selectivity: More selective	**Room/board:** $6,450
Acceptance rate: 75%	**Average debt:** $14,164
Student/faculty ratio: 18/1	**Proportion who borrowed:** 35%

UNDERGRADUATE STUDENT BODY STATS

2005-2006 enrollment: 6,453 full-time; 802 part-time. Men: 54%; women: 46%. **Ethnic makeup:** African American: 4%; Asian American: 1%; Hispanic: 1%; White: 93%; International: 1%.

ADMISSIONS FACTS AND FIGURES

Phone: (800) 255-8881. **Email:** admissions@tntech.edu. **Website:** http://www.tntech.edu. **Application deadlines for fall 2007:** Regular decision: August 1. Early decision: Not offered. Early action: Not offered. Admission can be deferred. **Application fee:** $15. Common application is not accepted. **Admissions requirements/recommendations:** High school units required (recommended): English: 4; Mathematics: 3 (4); Science: 2 (3); Foreign language: 2; Social studies: 1; History: 1; Total units: 14. Tests: The college uses SAT or ACT scores in admissions decisions. Either SAT or ACT required. For admission to the fall 2007 entering class, the school will accept: ACT with writing, ACT without writing. Campus visit: Recommended. Admissions interview: Recommended. Off-campus interview: May be arranged. **Factors that count in admissions decisions:** *Academic:* Secondary school record: Very important. Class rank: Important. Letters of recommendation: Not considered. Standardized test scores: Very important. Essay: Not considered. *Nonacademic:* Interview: Not considered. Extracurricular activities: Not considered. Talent/ability: Not considered. Character/personal qualities: Not considered. Alumni/ae relationship: Not considered. Geographical residence: Not considered. State residency: Considered. Religious affiliation/commitment: Not considered. Minority status: Not considered. Volunteer work: Not considered. Work experience: Not considered. **Admissions statistics for the fall 2005 entering class:** Total applicants: 3,292. Total accepted: 2,475. Freshmen enrolled: 1,424; 4% were from out of state. Overall acceptance rate: 75%. **Credentials of fall 2005 freshmen:** 24% ranked in the top 10 percent of their high school class; 53% were in the top 25 percent, and 84% were in the top half. (Proportion submitting class standing: 76%.) **Average high school grade point average:** 3.2. **First-year students who submitted SAT scores:** 14%. Scores (25/75 percentile): Verbal: 490-600, Math: 500-630, Combined: 990-1230. **First-year students submitting ACT scores:** 97%. Scores (25/75 percentile): English: 20-26, Math: 19-25, Composite: 20-26.

ACADEMICS

Year founded: 1915. **Academic calendar:** Semester. **Degrees offered:** bachelor's, post-bachelor's certificate, master's, doctorate. **Most popular majors:** 13% multi/interdisciplinary studies, 10% business administration and management, 6% mechanical engineering, 4% agriculture, 4% sociology. **Major fields of study:** agriculture, agriculture operations, and related sciences; area, ethnic, cultural, and gender studies; biological and biomedical sciences; business, management, marketing, and related support services; communication, journalism, and related programs; computer and information sciences and support services; education; engineering; engineering

technologies/technicians; English language and literature/letters; family and consumer sciences/human sciences; foreign languages, literatures, and linguistics; health professions and related clinical sciences; history; mathematics and statistics; multi/interdisciplinary studies; natural resources and conservation; parks, recreation, leisure, and fitness studies; physical sciences; psychology; social sciences; visual and performing arts. **Areas of required coursework:** arts/fine arts, humanities, computer literacy, mathematics, English (including composition), foreign languages, sciences (biological or physical), history, social science, other. **Pre-professional programs:** pre-law, pre-dentistry, pre-medicine, pre-veterinary science, pre-optometry, pre-pharmacy, other. **Special academic programs (% participation):** cooperative (work-study plan) program (15%), distance learning (15.6%), double major (3.8%), dual enrollment (3.8%), English as a Second Language (ESL) (.02%), exchange student program (domestic) (.001%), honors program (4.2%), independent study (5.1%), internships (19.6%), liberal arts/career combination (.8%), study abroad (.9%), teacher certificate program (8.6%). **Teacher certification offered in:** early childhood, special education, elementary, vo-tech, middle/junior high, secondary, bilingual/bicultural. **Cooperative education programs:** business, computer science, engineering. **Reserve Officers Training Corps (ROTC):** Army ROTC: Offered on campus; Air Force ROTC: Offered at cooperating institution (Tennessee State University). **Faculty and instruction (2005-2006):** Total instructional faculty: 380 full-time, 180 part-time (60% men; 40% women; 11% minorities). Full-time faculty with Ph.D. or other terminal degree: 83%. Student/faculty ratio: 18/1. Classes of fewer than 20 students: 47%; of 20 to 49 students: 46%; of 50 or more students: 6%. **Advanced Placement and International Baccalaureate credit:** AP tests may be used for: Credit only. Scores accepted: 4, 5. International Baccalaureate exams may be used for: Credit only. **Freshmen returning for sophomore year:** 72%. **Graduation rates:** Four-year: 13%; five-year: 36%; six-year: 45%. **Graduate study:** 21% of students pursue further study immediately upon graduation.

COSTS AND FINANCIAL AID

Financial aid office: (931) 372-3073. **Expenses (2006-2007):** Tuition and fees 2006-2007: $4,660 in state, $9,960 out of state; room/board: $6,450. Estimated books and supplies: $1,330; transportation: $1,500; personal expenses: $1,290. **Financial aid:** Priority filing date for institution's financial aid form: March 15. In 2005-2006, 82% of undergraduates applied for financial aid. Of those, 51% were determined to have financial need; 27% had their need fully met. Average financial aid package (proportion receiving): $3,502 (51%). Average amount of gift aid, such as scholarships or grants (proportion receiving): $2,632 (29%). Average amount of self-help aid, such as work study or loans (proportion receiving): $2,895 (32%). Average need-based loan (excluding PLUS or other private loans): $3,223. Among students who received need-based aid, the average percentage of need met: 80%. Among students who received aid based on merit, the average award (and the proportion receiving): $3,481 (22%). The average athletic scholarship (and the proportion receiving): $9,162 (4%). Average amount of debt of borrowers graduating in 2005: $14,164. Proportion who borrowed: 35%.

CAMPUS LIFE AND EXTRACURRICULAR ACTIVITIES

Campus housing available (% using): coed dorms (76%), women's dorms (8%), men's dorms (10%), apartments for married students (3%), apartment for single students (3%). Students who live in college-owned, operated, or affiliated housing: 28%. **Student employment:** During the 2005-2006 academic year, 10% of undergraduates worked on campus. Average per-year earnings: $3,160. **Clubs and organizations:** Number of student organizations: 190. Activities include: choral groups, concert band, dance, drama/theater, jazz band, marching band, music ensembles, musical theater, pep band, radio station, student government, student newspaper, symphony orchestra, yearbook. Number of fraternities: 13; sororities: 8. Proportion of men in fraternities: 11%; of women in sororities: 10%. Average proportion of students who stay on campus on weekends: 30%. **Sports program (2005-2006):** Member of NCAA I. *Men's intercollegiate varsity sports:* baseball, basketball, cheerleading, cross-country, football, golf, riflery, tennis. *Women's intercollegiate varsity sports:* basketball, cheerleading, cross-country, golf, soccer, softball, tennis, track and field (indoor), track and field (outdoor), volleyball.

SERVICES AND FACILITIES

Basic services: nonremedial tutoring, women's center, placement service, day care, health service, health insurance. **Remedial assistance:** reading, math, writing, study skills. **Counseling services:** minority student, career, military, personal, veteran student, academic, older student, psychological, birth control. **For learning-disabled students:** School does not offer a structured program with separate admission and additional fees. Total under-graduates in learning-disabled program or receiving services: 45. Services include: reading machines, tape recorders, videotaped classes, note-taking services, oral tests, learning center, readers, extended time for tests, tutors, priority registration, priority seating, typist/scribe, exams on tape or computer, other. **Library:** Number of titles: 648,377; number of current serial subscriptions: 3,155. **Information technology resources:** Students are not required to lease or own a computer. Number of campus computers available to all students: 1,114. School has a wireless network. Proportion of college-owned housing units wired for high-speed internet access: 100%. **Campus safety:** Security services offered: 24-hour foot-and-vehicle patrols, late-night transport/escort service, 24-hour emergency telephones, lighted pathways/sidewalks, controlled dormitory access (key, security card, etc).

TRANSFER AND INTERNATIONAL STUDENTS

Transfer students: May apply for admission for the following academic terms: Fall, Spring, Summer. Applicants need a minimum number of credits to apply. For fall 2005: Transfer applications received: 1,825. Transfer applicants offered admission: 1,274. Transfer applicants enrolled: 641. **International students:** Number of foreign undergraduates: 62 (1% of student body). Minimum TOEFL score required: 500 (paper); 173 (computer). Average TOEFL score: 525 (paper).

Tennessee Wesleyan College

- **Address:** PO Box 40, Athens, TN 37371-0040
- **Website:** http://www.twcnet.edu
- **Private; Religious affiliation:** United Methodist
- **Enrollment:** N/A

KEY STATS

✔ **U.S News College Ranking:** third tier, Comp. Coll.–Bachelor's (South)
✔ **ACT Score (25th/75th percentile):** 19-24
✔ **Tuition:** 2006-2007: $14,550

Selectivity: Selective	**Room/board:** $5,500
Acceptance rate: 84%	**Average debt:** $15,154
Student/faculty ratio: N/A	**Proportion who borrowed:** 82%

Trevecca Nazarene University

- **Address:** 333 Murfreesboro Road, Nashville, TN 37210
- **Website:** http://www.trevecca.edu
- **Private; Religious affiliation:** Nazarene
- **Enrollment:** 987 full-time; 258 part-time

KEY STATS

✔ **U.S News College Ranking:** third tier, Universities–Master's (South)
✔ **ACT Score (25th/75th percentile):** 19-25
✔ **Tuition:** 2006-2007: $14,774

Selectivity: Selective	**Room/board:** $6,470
Acceptance rate: 69%	**Average debt:** $24,000
Student/faculty ratio: 16/1	**Proportion who borrowed:** 73%

UNDERGRADUATE STUDENT BODY STATS

2005-2006 enrollment: 987 full-time; 258 part-time. Men: 45%; women: 55%. **Ethnic makeup:** African American: 8%; Asian American: 1%; Hispanic: 2%; White: 86%; International: 2%. **Religious preference:** Roman Catholic: 2%; Protestant: 28%; No preference: 1%; Unknown: 5%; Nazarene: 64%.

ADMISSIONS FACTS AND FIGURES

Phone: (615) 248-1320. **Email:** admissions_und@trevecca.edu. **Website:** http://www.trevecca.edu. **Application deadlines for fall 2007:** Regular decision: Rolling. Early decision: Not offered. Early action: Not offered. Admission can be deferred. **Application fee:** $25. Common application is not accepted. **Admissions requirements/recommendations:** High school units required (recommended): English: (4); Mathematics: (2); Science: (1); Foreign language: (2); Social studies: (1); History: (1); Academic electives: (4); Total units: (15). Tests: The college uses SAT or ACT scores in admis-sions decisions. Either SAT or ACT required. For admission to the fall 2007 entering class, the school will accept: ACT with writing, ACT without writing. **Factors that count in admissions decisions:** *Academic:* Secondary school record: Not considered. Class rank: Considered. Letters of recommendation: Considered. Standardized test scores: Very important. Essay: Considered. *Nonacademic:* Interview: Considered. Extracurricular activities: Considered. Talent/ability: Considered. Character/personal qualities: Very important. Alumni/ae relationship: Not considered. Geographical residence: Not considered. State residency: Not considered. Religious affiliation/commitment: Not considered. Minority status: Not considered. Volunteer work: Not considered. Work experience: Not considered. **Admissions statistics for the fall 2005 entering class:** Total applicants: 762. Total accepted: 522. Freshmen enrolled: 250; 59% were from out of state. Overall acceptance rate: 69%. **Credentials of fall 2005 freshmen:** 20% ranked in the top 10 percent of their high school class; 48% were in the top 25 percent, and 71% were in the top half. (Proportion submitting class standing: 74%.) **Average high school grade point average:** 3.2. **First-year students who submitted SAT scores:** 36%. Scores (25/75 percentile): Verbal: 470-580, Math: 450-590, Combined: 920-1170. **First-year students submitting ACT scores:** 84%. Scores (25/75 percentile): English: 19-26, Math: 17-24, Composite: 19-25.

ACADEMICS

Year founded: 1901. **Academic calendar:** Semester. **Degrees offered:** associate, bachelor's, master's, doctorate. **Most popular majors:** 68% business, management, marketing, and related support services, 5% education, 5% visual and performing arts, 4% biological and biomedical sciences, 4% philosophy and religious studies. **Major fields of study:** biological and biomedical sciences; business, management, marketing, and related support services; communication, journalism, and related programs; computer and information sciences and support services; education; English language and literature/letters; health professions and related clinical sciences; history; mathematics and statistics; parks, recreation, leisure, and fitness studies; philosophy and religious studies; physical sciences; psychology; public administration and social service professions; social sciences; theology and religious vocations; visual and performing arts. **Areas of required course-work:** arts/fine arts, humanities, computer literacy, mathematics, English (including composition), philosophy, foreign languages, sciences (biological or physical), history, social science, other. **Special academic programs:** double major, internships, study abroad, teacher certificate program, other. **Teacher certification offered in:** early childhood, elementary, middle/junior high, secondary. **Reserve Officers Training Corps (ROTC):** Army ROTC: Offered at cooperating institution (Vanderbilt University). **Faculty and instruction (2005-2006):** Total instructional faculty: 73 full-time, 144 part-time (61% men; 39% women; 1% minorities). Full-time faculty with Ph.D. or other terminal degree: 74%. Student/faculty ratio: 16/1. Classes of fewer than 20 students: 62%; of 20 to 49 students: 35%; of 50 or more students: 2%. **Advanced Placement and International Baccalaureate credit:** AP tests may be used for: Credit only. **Freshmen returning for sophomore year:** 69%. **Graduation rates:** Four-year: 23%; five-year: 34%; six-year: 37%.

COSTS AND FINANCIAL AID

Financial aid office: (615) 248-1242. **Expenses (2006-2007):** Tuition and fees 2006-2007: $14,774; room/board: $6,470. Estimated books and supplies: $888; transportation: $907; personal expenses: $1,381. **Financial aid:** Priority filing date for institution's financial aid form: March 1. In 2005-2006, 95% of undergraduates applied for financial aid. Of those, 82% were determined to have financial need; 14% had their need fully met. Average financial aid package (proportion receiving): $8,846 (67%). Average amount of gift aid, such as scholarships or grants (proportion receiving): $6,388 (57%). Average amount of self-help aid, such as work study or loans (proportion receiving): $4,436 (52%). Average need-based loan (excluding PLUS or other private loans): $4,342. Among students who received need-based aid, the average percentage of need met: 52%. Among students who received aid based on merit, the average award (and the proportion receiving): $8,622 (31%). The average athletic scholarship (and the proportion receiving): $16,173 (1%). Average amount of debt of borrowers graduating in 2005: $24,000. Proportion who borrowed: 73%.

CAMPUS LIFE AND EXTRACURRICULAR ACTIVITIES

Campus housing available: women's dorms, men's dorms, apartments for married students, apartment for single students. Students who live in college-owned, operated, or affiliated housing: 56%. **Clubs and organizations:** Number of student organizations: 31. Activities include: choral groups, concert band, drama/theater, jazz band, literary magazine, marching band, music ensembles, musical theater, pep band, radio station, student government, student newspaper, symphony orchestra, yearbook. Number of fraternities: o; sororities: o. **Sports program (2005-2006):** Member of NAIA. *Men's intercollegiate varsity sports:* baseball, basketball, golf, soccer. *Women's intercollegiate varsity sports:* basketball, golf, soccer, softball, volleyball.

SERVICES AND FACILITIES

Basic services: nonremedial tutoring, placement service, health service. **Remedial assistance:** reading, math, writing, study skills. **Counseling services:** career, personal, academic, religious. **For learning-disabled students:** School does not offer a structured program with separate admission and additional fees. Total undergraduates in learning-disabled program or receiving services: 10. Services include: remedial math, remedial English, reading machines, remedial reading, tape recorders, note-taking services, oral tests, learning center, extended time for tests, texts on tape, other testing accomodations. **Library:** Number of titles: 108,570; number of current serial subscriptions: 703. **Information technology resources:** Students are not required to lease or own a computer. Number of campus computers available to all students: 239. School has a wireless network. Approximate number of users that can be accommodated: 150. Proportion of college-owned housing units wired for high-speed internet access: 85%.

TRANSFER AND INTERNATIONAL STUDENTS

Transfer students: May apply for admission for the following academic terms: Fall, Spring, Summer. Applicants need a minimum number of credits to apply. For fall 2005: Transfer applications received: 223. Transfer applicants offered admission: 112. Transfer applicants enrolled: 61. **International students:** Number of foreign undergraduates: 21 (2% of student body). Number of countries represented: 14. Minimum TOEFL score required: 500 (paper); 173 (computer).

Tusculum College

- **Address:** PO Box 5035, Greeneville, TN 37743
- **Website:** http://www.tusculum.edu
- **Private; Religious affiliation:** Presbyterian (U.S.A.)
- **Enrollment:** 2,268 full-time; 21 part-time

KEY STATS

✔ **U.S News College Ranking:** fourth tier, Universities–Master's (South)
✔ **ACT Score (25th/75th percentile):** 17-23
✔ **Tuition:** 2006-2007: $16,215

Selectivity: Selective	Room/board: $6,500
Acceptance rate: 67%	Average debt: $20,928
Student/faculty ratio: 17/1	Proportion who borrowed: 72%

UNDERGRADUATE STUDENT BODY STATS

2005-2006 enrollment: 2,268 full-time; 21 part-time. Men: 44%; women: 56%. **Ethnic makeup:** African American: 12%; Asian American: 1%; Hispanic: 1%; White: 83%; International: 3%.

ADMISSIONS FACTS AND FIGURES

Phone: (800) 729-0256. **Email:** admissions@tusculum.edu. **Website:** http://www.tusculum.edu. **Application deadlines for fall 2007:** Regular decision: Rolling. Early decision: Not offered. Early action: Not offered. Admission can be deferred. Common application is not accepted. **Admissions requirements/recommendations:** High school units required (recommended): English: 4; Mathematics: 3; Science: 2; Social studies: 3; Total units: 12. Tests: The college uses SAT or ACT scores in admissions decisions. Either SAT or ACT required. For admission to the fall 2007 entering class, the school will accept: ACT with writing, ACT without writing. Campus visit: Recommended. Admissions interview: Recommended. Off-campus interview: May be arranged. **Factors that count in admissions decisions:** *Academic:* Secondary school record: Very important. Class rank: Considered. Letters of recommendation: Considered. Standardized test scores: Very important. Essay: Important. *Nonacademic:* Interview: Considered. Extracurricular activities: Considered. Talent/ability: Considered. Character/personal qualities: Considered. Alumni/ae relationship: Not considered. Geographical residence: Not considered. State residency: Not considered. Religious affiliation/commitment: Not considered. Minority status: Not considered. Volunteer work: Considered. Work experience: Not considered. **Other schools with the greatest overlap in applicants:** Carson-Newman College; Catawba College; Mars Hill College; Southern

Wesleyan University; Wingate University. **Admissions statistics for the fall 2005 entering class:** Total applicants: 1,969. Total accepted: 1,320. Freshmen enrolled: 259; 45% were from out of state. Overall acceptance rate: 67%. **Credentials of fall 2005 freshmen:** 10% ranked in the top 10 percent of their high school class; 27% were in the top 25 percent, and 61% were in the top half. (Proportion submitting class standing: 50%.) **Average high school grade point average:** 2.9. **First-year students who submitted SAT scores:** 42%. Scores (25/75 percentile): Verbal: 410-530, Math: 440-522, Combined: 850-1052. **First-year students submitting ACT scores:** 74%. Scores (25/75 percentile): English: 17-23, Math: 17-23, Composite: 17-23.

ACADEMICS

Year founded: 1794. **Academic calendar:** Other. **Degrees offered:** bachelor's, master's. **Most popular majors:** 35% elementary education and teaching, 15% business administration and management, 15% sport and fitness administration/management, 8% biology/biological sciences, 5% psychology. **Major fields of study:** biological and biomedical sciences; business, management, marketing, and related support services; communication, journalism, and related programs; education; English language and literature/letters; health professions and related clinical sciences; history; mathematics and statistics; multi/interdisciplinary studies; natural resources and conservation; parks, recreation, leisure, and fitness studies; physical sciences; psychology; science technologies/technicians; social sciences; visual and performing arts. **Areas of required coursework:** humanities, computer literacy, mathematics, English (including composition), sciences (biological or physical), history, social science, other. **Pre-professional programs:** pre-law, pre-medicine, pre-pharmacy. **Special academic programs:** double major, honors program, internships, student-designed major, teacher certificate program. **Teacher certification offered in:** early childhood, special education, elementary, secondary. **Faculty and instruction (2005-2006):** Total instructional faculty: 80 full-time, 70 part-time (56% men; 44% women; 3% minorities). Full-time faculty with Ph.D. or other terminal degree: 69%. Student/faculty ratio: 17/1. Classes of fewer than 20 students: 65%; of 20 to 49 students: 35%; of 50 or more students: 0%. **Advanced Placement and International Baccalaureate credit:** AP tests may be used for: Credit and/or placement. Scores accepted: 4. International Baccalaureate exams may be used for: Credit and/or placement. **Freshmen returning for sophomore year:** 61%. **Graduation rates:** Four-year: 33%; five-year: 38%; six-year: 43%. **Graduate study:** 10% of students pursue further study immediately upon graduation; 12% within one year.

COSTS AND FINANCIAL AID

Financial aid office: (423) 636-7377. **Expenses (2006-2007):** Tuition and fees 2006-2007: $16,215; room/board: $6,500. Estimated books and supplies: $955; transportation: $1,200; personal expenses: $1,200. **Financial aid:** Priority filing date for institution's financial aid form: February 15. In 2005-2006, 90% of undergraduates applied for financial aid. Of those, 68% were determined to have financial need; 10% had their need fully met. Average financial aid package (proportion receiving): $9,092 (68%). Average amount of gift aid, such as scholarships or grants (proportion receiving): $6,313 (28%). Average amount of self-help aid, such as work study or loans (proportion receiving): $3,863 (55%). Among students who received need-based aid, the average percentage of need met: 61%. Among students who received aid based on merit, the average award (and the proportion receiving): $6,043 (12%). Average amount of debt of borrowers graduating in 2005: $20,928. Proportion who borrowed: 72%.

CAMPUS LIFE AND EXTRACURRICULAR ACTIVITIES

Campus housing available (% using): coed dorms (13%), women's dorms (13%), men's dorms (42%), apartment for single students (32%). Students who live in college-owned, operated, or affiliated housing: 26%. **Student employment:** During the 2005-2006 academic year, 5% of undergraduates worked on campus. **Clubs and organizations:** Number of student organizations: 20. Activities include: dance, drama/theater, pep band, radio station, student government, student newspaper, television station, yearbook. Number of fraternities: 1; sororities: 1. Proportion of men in fraternities: 1%; of women in sororities: 1%. Average proportion of students who stay on campus on weekends: 60%. **Sports program (2005-2006):** Member of NCAA II. *Men's intercollegiate varsity sports:* baseball, basketball, cross-country, football, golf, soccer, tennis. *Women's intercollegiate varsity sports:* basketball, cross-country, golf, soccer, softball, tennis, volleyball.

SERVICES AND FACILITIES

Basic services: nonremedial tutoring, health service. **Remedial assistance:** reading, math, writing, study skills. **Counseling services:** career, academic. **For learning-disabled students:** School does not offer a structured program with separate admission and additional fees. Total undergraduates in learning-disabled program or receiving services: 42. Services include: remedial math, remedial English, reading machines, remedial reading, tape recorders, videotaped classes, note-taking services, oral tests, learning center, readers, extended time for tests, tutors, early syllabus. **Library:** Number of titles: 53,094; number of current serial subscriptions: 254. **Information technology resources:** Students are not required to lease or own a computer. Number of campus computers available to all students: 164. School has a wireless network. Approximate number of users that can be accommodated: 300. Proportion of college-owned housing units wired for high-speed internet access: 100%. **Campus safety:** Security services offered: 24-hour foot-and-vehicle patrols, controlled dormitory access (key, security card, etc).

TRANSFER AND INTERNATIONAL STUDENTS

Transfer students: May apply for admission for the following academic terms: Fall, Winter, Spring, Summer. Applicants do not need a minimum number of credits to apply. For fall 2005: Transfer applications received: 196. Transfer applicants offered admission: 112. Transfer applicants enrolled: 83. **International students:** Number of foreign undergraduates: 75 (3% of student body). Minimum TOEFL score required: 550 (paper).

Union University

- **Address:** 1050 Union University Drive, Jackson, TN 38305
- **Website:** http://www.uu.edu
- **Private; Religious affiliation:** Baptist
- **Enrollment:** 1,611 full-time; 475 part-time

KEY STATS
✔ **U.S News College Ranking:** 25, Universities–Master's (South)
✔ **ACT Score (25th/75th percentile):** 22-27
✔ **Tuition:** 2006-2007: $17,590

Selectivity: More selective	**Room/board:** $6,200
Acceptance rate: 86%	**Average debt:** $19,506
Student/faculty ratio: 12/1	**Proportion who borrowed:** 59%

UNDERGRADUATE STUDENT BODY STATS

2005-2006 enrollment: 1,611 full-time; 475 part-time. Men: 39%; women: 61%. **Ethnic makeup:** African American: 8%; Asian American: 1%; Hispanic: 1%; White: 88%; International: 2%. **Religious preference:** Roman Catholic: 1%; Protestant: 16%; Baptist: 61%; Other: 22%.

ADMISSIONS FACTS AND FIGURES

Phone: (800) 338-6466. **Email:** info@uu.edu. **Website:** http://www.uu.edu. **Application deadlines for fall 2007:** Regular decision: August 1. Early decision: Not offered. Early action: Not offered. Admission can be deferred. **Application fee:** $25. Common application is accepted. **To apply online, go to:** http://www.uu.edu/union/admiss/apps.htm. **Admissions requirements/recommendations:** High school units required (recommended): English: 4 (4); Mathematics: 3 (4); Science: 3 (4); Foreign language: 1 (2); Social studies: 2 (2); History: 1 (2); Academic electives: 1 (4); Total units: 15 (22). Tests: The college uses SAT or ACT scores in admissions decisions. Either SAT or ACT required. For admission to the fall 2007 entering class, the school will accept: ACT with writing, ACT without writing. Campus visit: Recommended. Admissions interview: Recommended. Off-campus interview: May be arranged. **Factors that count in admissions decisions:** *Academic:* Secondary school record: Very important. Class rank: Important. Letters of recommendation: Important. Standardized test scores: Very important. Essay: Considered. *Nonacademic:* Interview: Important. Extracurricular activities: Considered. Talent/ability: Important. Character/personal qualities: Very important. Alumni/ae relationship: Important. Geographical residence: Not considered. State residency: Not considered. Religious affiliation/commitment: Important. Minority status: Not considered. Volunteer work: Considered. Work experience: Considered. **Other schools with the greatest overlap in applicants:** Belmont University; Carson-Newman College; Samford University; University of Tennessee; Wheaton College. **Admissions statistics for the fall 2005 entering class:** Total applicants: 1,090. Total accepted: 936. Freshmen enrolled: 408; 39% were from out of state. Overall acceptance rate: 86%. **Credentials of fall 2005 freshmen:** 37% ranked in the top 10 percent of their high school class; 66% were in the top 25 percent, and 89% were in the top half. (Proportion submitting class standing: 73%.) **Average high school grade point average:** 3.6.

First-year students who submitted SAT scores: 29%. Scores (25/75 percentile): Verbal: 550-650, Math: 520-620, Combined: 1070-1270. **First-year students submitting ACT scores:** 86%. Scores (25/75 percentile): English: 21-29, Math: 19-26, Composite: 22-27.

ACADEMICS

Year founded: 1823. **Academic calendar:** 4-1-4. **Degrees offered:** diploma, associate, bachelor's, master's, post-master's certificate, doctorate. **Most popular majors:** 27% health professions and related clinical sciences, 21% business, management, marketing, and related support services, 11% philosophy and religious studies, 9% education, 5% psychology. **Major fields of study:** area, ethnic, cultural, and gender studies; biological and biomedical sciences; business, management, marketing, and related support services; communication, journalism, and related programs; computer and information sciences and support services; education; engineering; English language and literature/letters; family and consumer sciences/human sciences; foreign languages, literatures, and linguistics; health professions and related clinical sciences; history; mathematics and statistics; parks, recreation, leisure, and fitness studies; philosophy and religious studies; physical sciences; psychology; public administration and social service professions; social sciences; theology and religious vocations; visual and performing arts. **Areas of required coursework:** arts/fine arts, humanities, computer literacy, mathematics, English (including composition), sciences (biological or physical), history, social science, other. **Pre-professional programs:** pre-law, pre-dentistry, pre-medicine, pre-theology, pre-veterinary science, pre-optometry, pre-pharmacy, other. **Special academic programs (% participation):** accelerated program, cross-registration, distance learning, double major (7%), dual enrollment, English as a Second Language (ESL), exchange student program (domestic), honors program (1%), independent study, internships, study abroad, teacher certificate program (11%). **Teacher certification offered in:** early childhood, special education, elementary, middle/junior high, secondary. **Cooperative education programs:** business, education. **Faculty and instruction (2005-2006):** Total instructional faculty: 152 full-time, 126 part-time (50% men; 50% women; 10% minorities). Full-time faculty with Ph.D. or other terminal degree: 82%. Student/faculty ratio: 12/1. Classes of fewer than 20 students: 73%; of 20 to 49 students: 26%; of 50 or more students: 1%. **Advanced Placement and International Baccalaureate credit:** AP tests may be used for: Credit only. Scores accepted: 3, 4, 5. International Baccalaureate exams may be used for: Credit only. **Freshmen returning for sophomore year:** 74%. **Graduation rates:** Four-year: 43%; five-year: 60%; six-year: 57%. **Graduate study:** 23% of students pursue further study immediately upon graduation; 19% within one year; 8% within five years. Fields in which graduates pursue further study: Master of Business Administration (MBA), 20%; law, 1%; medicine, 3%; engineering, 1%; theology (or the seminary), 24%; education, 9%; arts and sciences, 36%; veterinary medicine, 1%.

COSTS AND FINANCIAL AID

Financial aid office: (731) 661-5015. **Expenses (2006-2007):** Tuition and fees 2006-2007: $17,590; room/board: $6,200. Estimated books and supplies: $1,000; transportation: $1,400; personal expenses: $2,860. **Financial aid:** Priority filing date for institution's financial aid form: January 30. In 2005-2006, 65% of undergraduates applied for financial aid. Of those, 53% were determined to have financial need; Average financial aid package (proportion receiving): $13,650 (53%). Average amount of gift aid, such as scholarships or grants (proportion receiving): $4,350 (39%). Average amount of self-help aid, such as work study or loans (proportion receiving): $4,675 (36%). Average need-based loan (excluding PLUS or other private loans): $4,500. Among students who received aid based on merit, the average award (and the proportion receiving): $6,700 (22%). The average athletic scholarship (and the proportion receiving): $9,775 (9%). Average amount of debt of borrowers graduating in 2005: $19,506. Proportion who borrowed: 59%.

CAMPUS LIFE AND EXTRACURRICULAR ACTIVITIES

Campus housing available (% using): women's dorms, men's dorms, apartments for married students (2%), apartment for single students (98%), special housing for disabled students (0%). Students who live in college-owned, operated, or affiliated housing: 69%. **Student employment:** During the 2005-2006 academic year, 26% of undergraduates worked on campus. Average per-year earnings: $800. **Clubs and organizations:** Number of student organizations: 47. Activities include: choral groups, concert band, drama/theater, jazz band, literary magazine, music ensembles, musical theater, opera, pep band, student government, student newspaper, student film society, symphony orchestra, television station, yearbook. Number of fraternities: 3; sororities: 3. Proportion of men in fraternities: 12%; of women in sororities: 15%. Average proportion of students who stay on campus on weekends: 65%. **Sports program (2005-2006):** Member of NAIA. **Men's intercollegiate varsity sports:** baseball, basketball, cross-country, golf, soccer. **Women's intercollegiate varsity sports:** basketball, cross-country, softball, volleyball.

SERVICES AND FACILITIES

Basic services: nonremedial tutoring, placement service, health service, health insurance. **Remedial assistance:** study skills. **Counseling services:** minority student, career, personal, veteran student, academic, psychological, religious. **For learning-disabled students:** School does not offer a structured program with separate admission and additional fees. Total undergraduates in learning-disabled program or receiving services: 24. Services include: tape recorders, other special classes, diagnostic testing service, untimed tests, note-taking services, oral tests, learning center, extended time for tests, tutors, priority seating. **Library:** Number of titles: 145,935; number of current serial subscriptions: 718. **Information technology resources:** Students are not required to lease or own a computer. Number of campus computers available to all students: 200. School has a wireless network. Proportion of college-owned housing units wired for high-speed internet access: 100%. **Campus safety:** Security services offered: 24-hour foot-and-vehicle patrols, late-night transport/escort service, 24-hour emergency telephones, lighted pathways/sidewalks, student patrols, controlled dormitory access (key, security card, etc).

TRANSFER AND INTERNATIONAL STUDENTS

Transfer students: May apply for admission for the following academic terms: Fall, Winter, Spring, Summer. Applicants need a minimum number of credits to apply. For fall 2005: Transfer applications received: 303. Transfer applicants offered admission: 201. Transfer applicants enrolled: 122. **International students:** Number of foreign undergraduates: 44 (2% of student body). Number of countries represented: 40. Minimum TOEFL score required: 500 (paper); 173 (computer). Average TOEFL score: 545 (paper).

University of Memphis

- **Address:** Memphis, TN 38152
- **Website:** http://www.memphis.edu
- **Public**
- **Enrollment:** 11,568 full-time; 4,197 part-time

KEY STATS

✔ **U.S News College Ranking:** fourth tier, National Universities
✔ **ACT Score (25th/75th percentile):** 18-24
✔ **Tuition:** 2005-2006: $5,084 in state, $14,898 out of state

Selectivity: Selective	**Room/board:** $5,049
Acceptance rate: 71%	**Average debt:** $22,962
Student/faculty ratio: 17/1	**Proportion who borrowed:** 23%

UNDERGRADUATE STUDENT BODY STATS

2005-2006 enrollment: 11,568 full-time; 4,197 part-time. Men: 39%; women: 61%. **Ethnic makeup:** African American: 38%; Asian American: 2%; Hispanic: 1%; White: 56%; International: 2%.

ADMISSIONS FACTS AND FIGURES

Phone: (901) 678-2111. **Email:** recruitment@memphis.edu. **Website:** http://www.memphis.edu. **Application deadlines for fall 2007:** Regular decision: July 1. Early decision: Not offered. Early action: Not offered. Admission cannot be deferred. **Application fee:** $25. Common application is not accepted. **To apply online, go to:** http://www.enrollment.memphis.edu/Admissions/. **Admissions requirements/recommendations:** High school units required (recommended): English: 4; Mathematics: 3 (4); Science: 2; Foreign language: 2; Social studies: 2; History: 1; Academic electives: 0; Total units: 15. Tests: The college uses SAT or ACT scores in admissions decisions. Either SAT or ACT required. For admission to the fall 2007 entering class, the school will accept: ACT with writing, ACT without writing. Campus visit: Recommended. Admissions interview: Recommended. Off-campus interview: May be arranged. **Factors that count in admissions decisions: Academic:** Secondary school record: Very important. Class rank: Not considered. Letters of recommendation: Considered. Standardized test scores:

Very important. Essay: Considered. **Nonacademic:** Interview: Not considered. Extracurricular activities: Not considered. Talent/ability: Considered. Character/personal qualities: Considered. Alumni/ae relationship: Not considered. Geographical residence: Not considered. State residency: Not considered. Religious affiliation/commitment: Not considered. Minority status: Not considered. Volunteer work: Not considered. Work experience: Considered. **Other schools with the greatest overlap in applicants:** Middle Tennessee State University; Tennessee State University; University of Arkansas; University of Mississippi; University of Tennessee. **Admissions statistics for the fall 2005 entering class:** Total applicants: 5,131. Total accepted: 3,665. Freshmen enrolled: 2,073; 7% were from out of state. Overall acceptance rate: 71%. **Credentials of fall 2005 freshmen:** 18% ranked in the top 10 percent of their high school class; 45% were in the top 25 percent, and 81% were in the top half. (Proportion submitting class standing: 72%.) **Average high school grade point average:** 3.1. **First-year students who submitted SAT scores:** 10%. Scores (25/75 percentile): Verbal: 460-600, Math: 475-600, Combined: 935-1200. **First-year students submitting ACT scores:** 90%. Scores (25/75 percentile): English: 19-25, Math: 17-23, Composite: 18-24.

ACADEMICS

Year founded: 1912. **Academic calendar:** Semester. **Degrees offered:** certificate, bachelor's, post-bachelor's certificate, master's, post-master's certificate, first professional, first professional certificate, doctorate. **Most popular majors:** 20% business, management, marketing, and related support services, 10% multi/interdisciplinary studies, 8% communication, journalism, and related programs, 8% education, 7% social sciences. **Major fields of study:** architecture and related services; area, ethnic, cultural, and gender studies; biological and biomedical sciences; business, management, marketing, and related support services; communication, journalism, and related programs; computer and information sciences and support services; education; engineering; engineering technologies/technicians; English language and literature/letters; foreign languages, literatures, and linguistics; health professions and related clinical sciences; history; liberal arts and sciences studies, and humanities; mathematics and statistics; multi/interdisciplinary studies; parks, recreation, leisure, and fitness studies; philosophy and religious studies; physical sciences; psychology; public administration and social service professions; security and protective services; social sciences; visual and performing arts. **Areas of required coursework:** arts/fine arts, humanities, computer literacy, mathematics, English (including composition), philosophy, foreign languages, sciences (biological or physical), history, social science. **Pre-professional programs:** pre-law, pre-dentistry, pre-medicine, pre-veterinary science, pre-optometry, pre-pharmacy, other. **Special academic programs (% participation):** accelerated program, cooperative (work-study plan) program, cross-registration, distance learning (11%), double major, dual enrollment, English as a Second Language (ESL), exchange student program (domestic) (1%), external degree program, honors program (10%), independent study, internships (55%), liberal arts/career combination, student-designed major (4%), study abroad (5%), teacher certification program (9.25%). **Teacher certification offered in:** early childhood, special education, elementary, middle/junior high, secondary. **Reserve Officers Training Corps (ROTC):** Army ROTC: Offered on campus; Navy ROTC: Offered on campus; Air Force ROTC: Offered on campus. **Faculty and instruction (2005-2006):** Total instructional faculty: 743 full-time, 514 part-time (56% men; 44% women; 19% minorities). Full-time faculty with Ph.D. or other terminal degree: 84%. Student/faculty ratio: 17/1. Classes of fewer than 20 students: 39%; of 20 to 49 students: 51%; of 50 or more students: 10%. **Advanced Placement and International Baccalaureate credit:** AP tests may be used for: Credit only. Scores accepted: 3, 4, 5. International Baccalaureate exams may be used for: Credit only. **Freshmen returning for sophomore year:** 73%. **Graduation rates:** Four-year: 11%; five-year: 26%; six-year: 35%. **Graduate study:** 26% of students pursue further study immediately upon graduation. Fields in which graduates pursue further study: Master of Business Administration (MBA), 7%; law, 3%; medicine, 3%; engineering, 6%; education, 9%; arts and sciences, 4%.

COSTS AND FINANCIAL AID

Financial aid office: (901) 678-4825. **Expenses (2005-2006):** Tuition and fees 2005-2006: $5,084 in state, $14,898 out of state; room/board: $5,049. Estimated books and supplies: $900; transportation: $1,500; personal expenses: $2,277. **Financial aid:** Priority filing date for institution's financial aid form: March 1; deadline: June 1. In 2005-2006, 80% of undergraduates applied for financial aid. Of those, 54% were determined to have financial need; 18% had their need fully met. Average financial aid package (proportion receiving): $4,056 (52%). Average amount of gift aid, such as scholarships or grants (proportion receiving): $2,665 (36%). Average amount of self-help aid, such as work study or loans (proportion receiving): $2,727 (37%). Average need-based loan (excluding PLUS or other private loans): $3,169. Among students who received need-based aid, the average percentage of need met: 80%. Among students who received need-based aid based on merit, the average award (and the proportion receiving): $4,193 (16%). The average athletic scholarship (and the proportion receiving): $7,469 (7%). Average amount of debt of borrowers graduating in 2005: $22,962. Proportion who borrowed: 23%.

CAMPUS LIFE AND EXTRACURRICULAR ACTIVITIES

Campus housing available (% using): women's dorms (40%), men's dorms (32%), fraternity housing (1%), apartments for married students (4%), apartment for single students (20%), special housing for disabled students (3%). Students who live in college-owned, operated, or affiliated housing: 13%. **Student employment:** During the 2005-2006 academic year, 9% of undergraduates worked on campus. Average per-year earnings: $3,083. **Clubs and organizations:** Number of student organizations: 176. Activities include: choral groups, concert band, dance, drama/theater, jazz band, literary magazine, marching band, music ensembles, musical theater, opera, pep band, radio station, student government, student newspaper, student film society, symphony orchestra, television station. Number of fraternities: 13; sororities: 11. Proportion of men in fraternities: 2%; of women in sororities: 3%. Average proportion of students who stay on campus on weekends: 30%. **Sports program (2005-2006):** Member of NCAA I. *Men's intercollegiate varsity sports:* baseball, basketball, cross-country, football, golf, riflery, soccer, tennis, track and field (indoor), track and field (outdoor). *Women's intercollegiate varsity sports:* basketball, cross-country, golf, riflery, soccer, tennis, track and field (indoor), track and field (outdoor), volleyball.

SERVICES AND FACILITIES

Basic services: nonremedial tutoring, women's center, placement service, day care, health service, health insurance. **Remedial assistance:** reading, math, writing, study skills. **Counseling services:** minority student, career, military, personal, veteran student, academic, older student, psychological, birth control, religious. **For learning-disabled students:** School does not offer a structured program with separate admission and additional fees. Total undergraduates in learning-disabled program or receiving services: 403. Services include: reading machines, tape recorders, diagnostic testing service, learning center, extended time for tests, tutors, priority registration, priority seating, proofreading services, texts on tape, other testing accomodations, other. **Library:** Number of titles: 1,904,734; number of current serial subscriptions: 9,392. **Information technology resources:** Students are not required to lease or own a computer. Number of campus computers available to all students: 2,000. School has a wireless network. Approximate number of users that can be accommodated: 45,000. Proportion of college-owned housing units wired for high-speed internet access: 100%. **Campus safety:** Security services offered: 24-hour foot-and-vehicle patrols, late-night transport/escort service, 24-hour emergency telephones, lighted pathways/sidewalks, student patrols, controlled dormitory access (key, security card, etc).

TRANSFER AND INTERNATIONAL STUDENTS

Transfer students: May apply for admission for the following academic terms: Fall, Spring, Summer. Applicants need a minimum number of credits to apply. For fall 2005: Transfer applications received: 3,643. Transfer applicants offered admission: 2,553. Transfer applicants enrolled: 1,787. **International students:** Number of foreign undergraduates: 317 (2% of student body). Number of countries represented: 44. Minimum TOEFL score required: 500 (paper); 173 (computer).

University of Tennessee

■ **Address:** 800 Andy Holt Tower, Knoxville, TN 37996
■ **Website:** http://www.tennessee.edu
■ **Public**
■ **Enrollment:** 18,739 full-time; 1,493 part-time

KEY STATS

✔ **U.S News College Ranking:** 88, National Universities
✔ **ACT Score (25th/75th percentile):** 23-28
✔ **Tuition:** 2005-2006: $5,626 in state, $16,696 out of state
  Selectivity: More selective   **Room/board:** $5,756
  Acceptance rate: 74%   **Average debt:** $18,433
  Student/faculty ratio: 15/1   **Proportion who borrowed:** 49%

UNDERGRADUATE STUDENT BODY STATS

2005-2006 enrollment: 18,739 full-time; 1,493 part-time. Men: 49%; women: 51%. **Ethnic makeup:** African American: 9%; Asian American: 3%; Hispanic: 1%; White: 85%; International: 1%.

ADMISSIONS FACTS AND FIGURES

Phone: (865) 974-2184. **Email:** admissions@tennessee.edu. **Website:** http://www.tennessee.edu. **Application deadlines for fall 2007:** Regular decision: Rolling. Early decision: Not offered. Early action: Send application by: November 1; Decision sent by: January 1. Admission can be deferred. **Application fee:** $30. Common application is not accepted. **To apply online, go to:** http://www.applyweb.com/aw?utk. **Admissions requirements/recommendations:** High school units required (recommended): English: 4; Mathematics: 3; Science: 2; Foreign language: 2; Social studies: 1; History: 1; Total units: 14. Tests: The college uses SAT or ACT scores in admissions decisions. Either SAT or ACT required. For admission to the fall 2007 entering class, the school will accept: ACT with writing, ACT without writing. Campus visit: Recommended. Admissions interview: Neither required nor recommended. Off-campus interview: Not available. **Factors that count in admissions decisions:** *Academic:* Secondary school record: Very important. Class rank: Considered. Letters of recommendation: Considered. Standardized test scores: Very important. Essay: Considered. *Nonacademic:* Interview: Not considered. Extracurricular activities: Considered. Talent/ability: Considered. Character/personal qualities: Considered. Alumni/ae relationship: Considered. Geographical residence: Considered. State residency: Considered. Religious affiliation/commitment: Not considered. Minority status: Considered. Volunteer work: Considered. Work experience: Considered. **Other schools with the greatest overlap in applicants:** East Tennessee State University; Middle Tennessee State University; Tennessee Technological University; University of Tennessee–Chattanooga; Vanderbilt University. **Admissions statistics for the fall 2005 entering class:** Total applicants: 12,251. Total accepted: 9,060. Freshmen enrolled: 4,265; 15% were from out of state. Overall acceptance rate: 74%. Non-early acceptance rate: 74%. **Size of waiting list:** 1800 applicants; enrolled from waiting list: 50. **Credentials of fall 2005 freshmen:** 34% ranked in the top 10 percent of their high school class; 63% were in the top 25 percent, and 90% were in the top half. (Proportion submitting class standing: 51%.) **Average high school grade point average:** 3.6. **First-year students who submitted SAT scores:** 41%. Scores (25/75 percentile): Verbal: 520-630, Math: 530-640, Combined: 1050-1270. **First-year students submitting ACT scores:** 87%. Scores (25/75 percentile): English: 23-29, Math: 22-27, Composite: 23-28.

ACADEMICS

Year founded: 1794. **Academic calendar:** Semester. **Degrees offered:** bachelor's, post-bachelor's certificate, master's, post-master's certificate, first professional, doctorate. **Most popular majors:** 11% psychology, 5% English language and literature, 4% finance, 4% marketing/marketing management, 4% political science and government. **Major fields of study:** agriculture, agriculture operations, and related sciences; architecture and related services; area, ethnic, cultural, and gender studies; biological and biomedical sciences; business, management, marketing, and related support services; communication, journalism, and related programs; computer and information sciences and support services; education; engineering; English language and literature/letters; family and consumer sciences/human sciences; foreign languages, literatures, and linguistics; health professions and related clinical sciences; history; mathematics and statistics; natural resources and conservation; parks, recreation, leisure, and fitness studies; philosophy and religious studies; physical sciences; psychology; public administration and social service professions; social sciences; visual and performing arts. **Areas of required coursework:** humanities, mathematics, English (including composition), foreign languages, sciences (biological or physical), history, social science. **Pre-professional programs:** pre-law, pre-dentistry, pre-medicine, pre-veterinary science, pre-pharmacy. **Special academic programs:** cooperative (work-study plan) program, distance learning, double major, dual enrollment, English as a Second Language (ESL), exchange student program (domestic), honors program, independent study, internships, liberal arts/career combination, student-designed major, study abroad, teacher certificate program. **Teacher certification offered in:** early childhood, special education, elementary, secondary. **Cooperative education programs:** business, engineering. **Reserve Officers Training Corps (ROTC):** Army ROTC: Offered on campus; Air Force ROTC: Offered on campus. **Faculty and instruction (2005-2006):** Total instructional faculty: 1,518 full-time, 79 part-time (64% men; 36% women; 15% minorities). Full-time faculty with Ph.D. or other terminal degree: 81%. Student/faculty ratio: 15/1. Classes of fewer than 20 students: 35%; of 20 to 49 students: 57%; of 50 or more students: 8%. **Advanced Placement and International Baccalaureate credit:** AP tests may be used for: Credit and/or placement. Scores accepted: 4, 5. International Baccalaureate exams may be used for: Credit and/or placement. **Freshmen returning for sophomore year:** 78%. **Graduation rates:** Four-year: 29%; five-year: 52%; six-year: 57%.

COSTS AND FINANCIAL AID

Financial aid office: (865) 974-3131. **Expenses (2005-2006):** Tuition and fees 2005-2006: $5,626 in state, $16,696 out of state; room/board: $5,756. Estimated books and supplies: $1,190 personal expenses: $4,732. **Financial aid:** Priority filing date for institution's financial aid form: March 1. In 2005-2006, 93% of undergraduates applied for financial aid. Of those, 53% were determined to have financial need; 28% had their need fully met. Average financial aid package (proportion receiving): $7,531 (53%). Average amount of gift aid, such as scholarships or grants (proportion receiving): $5,168 (42%). Average amount of self-help aid, such as work study or loans (proportion receiving): $3,682 (37%). Average need-based loan (excluding PLUS or other private loans): $3,775. Among students who received need-based aid, the average percentage of need met: 65%. Among students who received aid based on merit, the average award (and the proportion receiving): $10,145 (1%). The average athletic scholarship (and the proportion receiving): $12,206 (3%). Average amount of debt of borrowers graduating in 2005: $18,433. Proportion who borrowed: 49%.

CAMPUS LIFE AND EXTRACURRICULAR ACTIVITIES

Campus housing available (% using): coed dorms (44%), women's dorms (21%), men's dorms (19%), sorority housing, fraternity housing, apartments for married students (7%), apartment for single students (9%). Students who live in college-owned, operated, or affiliated housing: 33%. **Student employment:** During the 2005-2006 academic year, 15% of undergraduates worked on campus. **Clubs and organizations:** Number of student organizations: 355. Activities include: choral groups, concert band, dance, drama/theater, jazz band, literary magazine, marching band, music ensembles, musical theater, opera, pep band, radio station, student government, student newspaper, student film society, symphony orchestra, yearbook. Number of fraternities: 21; sororities: 19. Proportion of men in fraternities: 15%; of women in sororities: 20%. **Sports program (2005-2006):** Member of NCAA I. **Men's intercollegiate varsity sports:** baseball, basketball, cross-country, football, golf, swimming and diving, tennis, track and field (indoor), track and field (outdoor). **Women's intercollegiate varsity sports:** basketball, crew, cross-country, golf, soccer, softball, swimming and diving, tennis, track and field (indoor), track and field (outdoor), volleyball.

SERVICES AND FACILITIES

Basic services: nonremedial tutoring, women's center, placement service, day care, health service, health insurance. **Remedial assistance:** study skills. **Counseling services:** minority student, career, military, personal, veteran student, academic, older student, psychological, birth control. **For learning-disabled students:** School does not offer a structured program with separate admission and additional fees. Services include: reading machines, tape recorders, diagnostic testing service, note-taking services, oral tests, readers, extended time for tests. **Library:** Number of titles: 2,273,524; number of current serial subscriptions: 15,430. **Information technology resources:** Students are not required to lease or own a computer. Number of campus computers available to all students: 1,500. School has a wireless network. Proportion of college-owned housing units wired for high-speed internet access: 100%. **Campus safety:** Security services offered: 24-hour foot-and-vehicle patrols, late-night transport/escort service, 24-hour emergency telephones, lighted pathways/sidewalks, controlled dormitory access (key, security card, etc).

TRANSFER AND INTERNATIONAL STUDENTS

Transfer students: May apply for admission for the following academic terms: Fall, Spring, Summer. Applicants need a minimum number of credits to apply. For fall 2005: Transfer applications received: 2,796. Transfer applicants offered admission: 1,996. Transfer applicants enrolled: 1,327. **International students:** Number of foreign undergraduates: 279 (1% of student body). Number of countries represented: 100. Minimum TOEFL score required: 523 (paper); 193 (computer).

University of Tennessee–Chattanooga

- **Address:** 615 McCallie Avenue, Chattanooga, TN 37403
- **Website:** http://www.utc.edu
- **Public**
- **Enrollment:** 6,190 full-time; 1,087 part-time

KEY STATS
✔ **U.S News College Ranking:** 40, Universities–Master's (South)
✔ **ACT Score (25th/75th percentile):** 19-24
✔ **Tuition:** 2006-2007: $4,688 in state, $14,084 out of state
  Selectivity: Selective   **Room/board:** $7,560
  Acceptance rate: 84%   **Average debt:** $15,348
  Student/faculty ratio: 16/1   **Proportion who borrowed:** 48%

UNDERGRADUATE STUDENT BODY STATS
2005-2006 enrollment: 6,190 full-time; 1,087 part-time. Men: 42%; women: 58%. **Ethnic makeup:** African American: 23%; American-Indian: 1%; Asian American: 3%; Hispanic: 1%; White: 72%; International: 1%.

ADMISSIONS FACTS AND FIGURES
Phone: (423) 425-4662. **Email:** yancy-freeman@utc.edu. **Website:** http://www.utc.edu. **Application deadlines for fall 2007:** Regular decision: Rolling. Early decision: Not offered. Early action: Not offered. Admission can be deferred. **Application fee:** $25. Common application is not accepted. **To apply online, go to:** https://secure.utc.edu/admissions/secure/. **Admissions requirements/recommendations:** High school units required (recommended): English: 4; Mathematics: 3; Science: 2; Foreign language: 2; Social studies: 2; History: 1; Total units: 15. Tests: The college uses SAT or ACT scores in admissions decisions. Either SAT or ACT required. For admission to the fall 2007 entering class, the school will accept: ACT with writing, ACT without writing. Campus visit: Neither required nor recommended. Admissions interview: Neither required nor recommended. Off-campus interview: May be arranged. **Factors that count in admissions decisions:** *Academic:* Secondary school record: Very important. Class rank: Not considered. Letters of recommendation: Considered. Standardized test scores: Very important. Essay: Considered. *Nonacademic:* Interview: Not considered. Extracurricular activities: Considered. Talent/ability: Considered. Character/personal qualities: Important. Alumni/ae relationship: Not considered. Geographical residence: Not considered. State residency: Not considered. Religious affiliation/commitment: Not considered. Minority status: Not considered. Volunteer work: Considered. Work experience: Considered. **Other schools with the greatest overlap in applicants:** East Tennessee State University; Middle Tennessee State University; Tennessee State University; Tennessee Technological University; University of Tennessee. **Admissions statistics for the fall 2005 entering class:** Total applicants: 3,580. Total accepted: 3,021. Freshmen enrolled: 1,454; 5% were from out of state. Overall acceptance rate: 84%. **Credentials of fall 2005 freshmen:** 44% were in the top 25 percent. **Average high school grade point average:** 3.2. **First-year students who submitted SAT scores:** 9%. Scores (25/75 percentile): Verbal: N/A, Math: N/A, Combined: N/A. **First-year students submitting ACT scores:** 91%. Scores (25/75 percentile): English: 18-25, Math: 17-24, Composite: 19-24.

ACADEMICS
Year founded: 1886. **Academic calendar:** Semester. **Degrees offered:** bachelor's, post-bachelor's certificate, master's, post-master's certificate, first professional, doctorate. **Most popular majors:** 27% business/commerce, 9% family and consumer sciences/human sciences, 7% education, 6% psychology, 5% biology/biological sciences. **Major fields of study:** biological and biomedical sciences; business, management, marketing, and related support services; communication, journalism, and related programs; computer and information sciences and support services; education; engineering; English

language and literature/letters; family and consumer sciences/human sciences; foreign languages, literatures, and linguistics; health professions and related clinical sciences; history; legal professions and studies; liberal arts and sciences studies, and humanities; mathematics and statistics; natural resources and conservation; parks, recreation, leisure, and fitness studies; philosophy and religious studies; physical sciences; psychology; public administration and social service professions; security and protective services; social sciences; visual and performing arts. **Areas of required coursework:** arts/fine arts, humanities, computer literacy, mathematics, English (including composition), sciences (biological or physical), social science. **Pre-professional programs:** pre-law, pre-dentistry, pre-medicine, pre-veterinary science, pre-pharmacy, other. **Special academic programs:** cooperative (work-study plan) program, cross-registration, double major, dual enrollment, English as a Second Language (ESL), exchange student program (domestic), honors program, independent study, internships, study abroad, teacher certificate program. **Teacher certification offered in:** early childhood, special education, elementary, middle/junior high, secondary. **Cooperative education programs:** business, engineering, health professions, home economics, social/behavioral science. **Faculty and instruction (2005-2006):** Total instructional faculty: 371 full-time, 252 part-time (53% men; 47% women; 10% minorities). Full-time faculty with Ph.D. or other terminal degree: 77%. Student/faculty ratio: 16/1. Classes of fewer than 20 students: 38%; of 20 to 49 students: 59%; of 50 or more students: 3%. **Advanced Placement and International Baccalaureate credit:** AP tests may be used for: Credit only. Scores accepted: 3. **Freshmen returning for sophomore year:** 69%. **Graduation rates:** Four-year: 16%; five-year: 37%; six-year: 47%.

COSTS AND FINANCIAL AID

Financial aid office: (423) 425-4677. **Expenses (2006-2007):** Tuition and fees 2006-2007: $4,688 in state, $14,084 out of state; room/board: $7,560. **Financial aid:** Priority filing date for institution's financial aid form: April 1. In 2005-2006, 80% of undergraduates applied for financial aid. Of those, 67% were determined to have financial need; 13% had their need fully met. Average financial aid package (proportion receiving): $8,301 (59%). Average amount of gift aid, such as scholarships or grants (proportion receiving): $3,630 (49%). Average amount of self-help aid, such as work study or loans (proportion receiving): $5,450 (44%). Average need-based loan (excluding PLUS or other private loans): $4,671. Among students who received need-based aid, the average percentage of need met: 78%. Among students who received aid based on merit, the average award (and the proportion receiving): $3,518 (14%). The average athletic scholarship (and the proportion receiving): $11,057 (4%). Average amount of debt of borrowers graduating in 2005: $15,348. Proportion who borrowed: 48%.

CAMPUS LIFE AND EXTRACURRICULAR ACTIVITIES

Campus housing available (% using): apartments for married students (1%), apartment for single students (97%), special housing for disabled students (1%), special housing for international students (1%). Students who live in college-owned, operated, or affiliated housing: 33%. **Student employment:** During the 2005-2006 academic year, 15% of undergraduates worked on campus. Average per-year earnings: $5,500. **Clubs and organizations:** Number of student organizations: 130. Activities include: choral groups, concert band, dance, drama/theater, jazz band, literary magazine, marching band, music ensembles, musical theater, pep band, radio station, student government, student newspaper, student film society, symphony orchestra. Number of fraternities: 12; sororities: 7. Proportion of men in fraternities: 3%; of women in sororities: 3%. **Sports program (2005-2006):** Member of NCAA I. **Men's intercollegiate varsity sports:** basketball, cross-country, football, golf, tennis, track and field (indoor), track and field (outdoor), wrestling. **Women's intercollegiate varsity sports:** basketball, cross-country, soccer, softball, tennis, track and field (indoor), track and field (outdoor), volleyball.

SERVICES AND FACILITIES

Basic services: nonremedial tutoring, placement service, health service, health insurance. **Remedial assistance:** reading, math, writing, study skills. **Counseling services:** career, psychological. **For learning-disabled students:** School does not offer a structured program with separate admission and additional fees. Total undergraduates in learning-disabled program or receiving services: 281. Services include: remedial math, remedial English, untimed tests, oral tests, readers, extended time for tests, tutors. **Library:** Number of titles: 571,957; number of current serial subscriptions: 12,393. **Information technology resources:** Students are not required to lease or own a computer. Number of campus computers available to all students: 1,374. School has a wireless network. Approximate number of users that can be accommodated: 350. Proportion of college-owned housing units wired for

high-speed internet access: 100%. **Campus safety:** Security services offered: 24-hour foot-and-vehicle patrols, late-night transport/escort service, 24-hour emergency telephones, lighted pathways/sidewalks.

TRANSFER AND INTERNATIONAL STUDENTS

Transfer students: May apply for admission for the following academic terms: Fall, Spring, Summer. Applicants do not need a minimum number of credits to apply. For fall 2005: Transfer applications received: 1,185. Transfer applicants offered admission: 863. Transfer applicants enrolled: 577. **International students:** Number of foreign undergraduates: 61 (1% of student body). Number of countries represented: 63. Minimum TOEFL score required: 500 (paper); 173 (computer). Average TOEFL score: 512 (paper).

University of Tennessee–Martin

- **Address:** University Street, Martin, TN 38238
- **Website:** http://www.utm.edu
- **Public**
- **Enrollment:** 5,016 full-time; 926 part-time

KEY STATS

✔ **U.S News College Ranking:** 56, Universities–Master's (South)
✔ **ACT Score (25th/75th percentile):** 19-24
✔ **Tuition:** 2006-2007: $4,644 in state, $14,124 out of state
  Selectivity: Selective   **Room/board:** $4,310
  Acceptance rate: 78%   **Average debt:** $16,749
  Student/faculty ratio: 19/1   **Proportion who borrowed:** 57%

UNDERGRADUATE STUDENT BODY STATS

2005-2006 enrollment: 5,016 full-time; 926 part-time. Men: 43%; women: 57%. **Ethnic makeup:** African American: 15%; Hispanic: 1%; White: 80%; International: 2%.

ADMISSIONS FACTS AND FIGURES

Phone: (800) 829-8861. **Email:** admitme@utm.edu. **Website:** http://www.utm.edu. **Application deadlines for fall 2007:** Regular decision: August 1. Early decision: Not offered. Early action: Not offered. Admission can be deferred. **Application fee:** $25. Common application is accepted. **Admissions requirements/recommendations:** High school units required (recommended): English: 4; Mathematics: 3; Science: 2; Foreign language: 2; Social studies: 0; History: 2; Academic electives: 0; Total units: 14. Tests: The college uses SAT or ACT scores in admissions decisions. Either SAT or ACT required. For admission to the fall 2007 entering class, the school will accept: ACT with writing, ACT without writing. Campus visit: Neither required nor recommended. Admissions interview: Neither required nor recommended. Off-campus interview: Not available. **Factors that count in admissions decisions: Academic:** Secondary school record: Very important. Class rank: Not considered. Letters of recommendation: Not considered. Standardized test scores: Very important. Essay: Not considered. **Nonacademic:** Interview: Not considered. Extracurricular activities: Not considered. Talent/ability: Not considered. Character/personal qualities: Not considered. Alumni/ae relationship: Not considered. Geographical residence: Not considered. State residency: Not considered. Religious affiliation/commitment: Not considered. Minority status: Not considered. Volunteer work: Not considered. Work experience: Not considered. **Other schools with the greatest overlap in applicants:** Austin Peay State University; Middle Tennessee State University; Murray State University; University of Tennessee; University of Tennessee–Chattanooga. **Admissions statistics for the fall 2005 entering class:** Total applicants: 2,803. Total accepted: 2,184. Freshmen enrolled: 1,250; 5% were from out of state. Overall acceptance rate: 78%. **Credentials of fall 2005 freshmen:** 20% ranked in the top 10 percent of their high school class; 50% were in the top 25 percent, and 83% were in the top half. (Proportion submitting class standing: 82%.) **Average high school grade point average:** 3.3. **First-year students submitting ACT scores:** 90%. Scores (25/75 percentile): English: 19-25, Math: 17-23, Composite: 19-24.

ACADEMICS

Year founded: 1900. **Academic calendar:** Semester. **Degrees offered:** bachelor's, master's. **Most popular majors:** 22% marketing/marketing management, 20% multi/interdisciplinary studies, 6% agriculture, 5%

communication studies/speech communication and rhetoric, 5% health professions and related clinical sciences. **Major fields of study:** agriculture, agriculture operations, and related sciences; biological and biomedical sciences; business, management, marketing, and related support services; communication, journalism, and related programs; computer and information sciences and support services; education; engineering; engineering technologies/technicians; English language and literature/letters; family and consumer sciences/human sciences; foreign languages, literatures, and linguistics; health professions and related clinical sciences; history; mathematics and statistics; multi/interdisciplinary studies; natural resources and conservation; parks, recreation, leisure, and fitness studies; philosophy and religious studies; physical sciences; psychology; public administration and social service professions; security and protective services; social sciences; visual and performing arts. **Areas of required coursework:** arts/fine arts, humanities, computer literacy, mathematics, English (including composition), foreign languages, sciences (biological or physical), history, social science, other. **Special academic programs (% participation):** accelerated program, cooperative (work-study plan) program (.002%), distance learning (5%), double major (.019%), dual enrollment (5%), English as a Second Language (ESL), honors program (8%), independent study (.031%), internships (32%), student-designed major (12%), study abroad (11%), teacher certification program (12.09%). **Teacher certification offered in:** early childhood, special education, elementary, middle/junior high, secondary. **Cooperative education programs:** agriculture, art, business, education, home economics. **Reserve Officers Training Corps (ROTC):** Army ROTC: Offered on campus. **Faculty and instruction (2005-2006):** Total instructional faculty: 245 full-time, 171 part-time (55% men; 45% women; 10% minorities). Full-time faculty with Ph.D. or other terminal degree: 69%. Student/faculty ratio: 19/1. Classes of fewer than 20 students: 49%; of 20 to 49 students: 43%; of 50 or more students: 8%. **Advanced Placement and International Baccalaureate credit:** AP tests may be used for: Credit only. Scores accepted: 3, 4, 5. **Freshmen returning for sophomore year:** 71%. **Graduation rates:** Four-year: 19%; five-year: 35%; six-year: 40%. **Graduate study:** 20% of students pursue further study immediately upon graduation.

COSTS AND FINANCIAL AID
Financial aid office: (731) 587-7040. **Expenses (2006-2007):** Tuition and fees 2006-2007: $4,644 in state, $14,124 out of state; room/board: $4,310. Estimated books and supplies: $1,200; transportation: $1,020; personal expenses: $2,100. **Financial aid:** Priority filing date for institution's financial aid form: March 1. In 2005-2006, 92% of undergraduates applied for financial aid. Of those, 59% were determined to have financial need; 38% had their need fully met. Average financial aid package (proportion receiving): $8,443 (58%). Average amount of gift aid, such as scholarships or grants (proportion receiving): $4,252 (37%). Average amount of self-help aid, such as work study or loans (proportion receiving): $3,744 (38%). Average need-based loan (excluding PLUS or other private loans): $3,613. Among students who received need-based aid, the average percentage of need met: 77%. Among students who received aid based on merit, the average award (and the proportion receiving): $4,449 (24%). The average athletic scholarship (and the proportion receiving): $10,042 (2%). Average amount of debt of borrowers graduating in 2005: $16,749. Proportion who borrowed: 57%.

CAMPUS LIFE AND EXTRACURRICULAR ACTIVITIES
Campus housing available (% using): coed dorms (51%), apartments for married students (12%), apartment for single students (37%), special housing for disabled students, other housing options (0%). Students who live in college-owned, operated, or affiliated housing: 40%. **Student employment:** During the 2005-2006 academic year, 22% of undergraduates worked on campus. Average per-year earnings: $4,000. **Clubs and organizations:** Number of student organizations: 127. Activities include: choral groups, concert band, dance, drama/theater, jazz band, literary magazine, marching band, music ensembles, musical theater, opera, pep band, radio station, student government, student newspaper, television station, yearbook. Number of fraternities: 11; sororities: 8. Proportion of men in fraternities: 7%; of women in sororities: 5%. Average proportion of students who stay on campus on weekends: 51%. **Sports program (2005-2006):** Member of NCAA I. *Men's intercollegiate varsity sports:* baseball, basketball, cross-country, football, golf, riflery, tennis. *Women's intercollegiate varsity sports:* basketball, cross-country, riflery, soccer, softball, tennis, track and field (indoor), track and field (outdoor), volleyball.

SERVICES AND FACILITIES
Basic services: nonremedial tutoring, placement service, day care, health service, health insurance. **Remedial assistance:** math. **Counseling services:** minority student, career, personal, veteran student, academic, older student,

psychological, birth control. **For learning-disabled students:** School does not offer a structured program with separate admission and additional fees. Total undergraduates in learning-disabled program or receiving services: 39. Services include: remedial math, reading machines, tape recorders, oral tests, learning center, readers, extended time for tests, tutors, texts on tape, exams on tape or computer, other testing accomodations, other. **Library:** Number of titles: 486,595; number of current serial subscriptions: 1,990. **Information technology resources:** Students are not required to lease or own a computer. Number of campus computers available to all students: 693. School has a wireless network. Approximate number of users that can be accommodated: 1,000. Proportion of college-owned housing units wired for high-speed internet access: 100%. **Campus safety:** Security services offered: 24-hour foot-and-vehicle patrols, 24-hour emergency telephones, lighted pathways/sidewalks, controlled dormitory access (key, security card, etc).

TRANSFER AND INTERNATIONAL STUDENTS
Transfer students: May apply for admission for the following academic terms: Fall, Spring, Summer. Applicants need a minimum number of credits to apply. For fall 2005: Transfer applications received: 902. Transfer applicants offered admission: 670. Transfer applicants enrolled: 421. **International students:** Number of foreign undergraduates: 115 (2% of student body). Number of countries represented: 28. Minimum TOEFL score required: 500 (paper); 173 (computer). Average TOEFL score: 525 (paper).

Vanderbilt University

- **Address:** Nashville, TN 37240
- **Website:** http://www.vanderbilt.edu
- **Private**
- **Enrollment:** 6,293 full-time; 107 part-time

KEY STATS
- ✔ **U.S News College Ranking:** 18, National Universities
- ✔ **SAT Score (25th/75th percentile):** 1280-1460
- ✔ **Tuition:** 2006-2007: $33,440

Selectivity: Most selective	**Room/board:** $10,890
Acceptance rate: 35%	**Average debt:** $19,585
Student/faculty ratio: 9/1	**Proportion who borrowed:** 31%

UNDERGRADUATE STUDENT BODY STATS
2005-2006 enrollment: 6,293 full-time; 107 part-time. Men: 48%; women: 52%. **Ethnic makeup:** African American: 8%; Asian American: 6%; Hispanic: 5%; White: 79%; International: 2%.

ADMISSIONS FACTS AND FIGURES
Phone: (800) 288-0432. **Email:** admissions@vanderbilt.edu. **Website:** http://www.vanderbilt.edu. **Application deadlines for fall 2007:** Regular decision: January 3; decision sent by April 1. Early decision: Send application by: November 1; Decision sent by: December 15. Early action: Not offered. Admission can be deferred. **Application fee:** $50. Common application is accepted. **To apply online, go to:** http://www.vanderbilt.edu/admissions. **Admissions requirements/recommendations:** High school units required (recommended): English: 4 (4); Mathematics: 3 (4); Science: 2 (4); Foreign language: 2 (4); Social studies: 2 (4); History: 0 (0); Academic electives: 0 (0); Total units: 13 (20). Tests: The college uses SAT or ACT scores in admissions decisions. Either SAT or ACT required. For admission to the fall 2007 entering class, the school will accept: ACT with writing. Campus visit: Recommended. Admissions interview: Neither required nor recommended. Off-campus interview: May not be arranged. **Factors that count in admissions decisions:** *Academic:* Secondary school record: Very important. Class rank: Very important. Letters of recommendation: Important. Standardized test scores: Very important. Essay: Important. *Nonacademic:* Interview: Considered. Extracurricular activities: Very important. Talent/ability: Considered. Character/personal qualities: Considered. Alumni/ae relationship: Not considered. Geographical residence: Not considered. State residency: Not considered. Religious affiliation/commitment: Not considered. Minority status: Considered. Volunteer work: Considered. Work experience: Considered. **Other schools with the greatest overlap in applicants:** Duke University; Emory University; Harvard University; University of Virginia; Washington University in St. Louis. **Admissions statistics for the fall 2005 entering class:** Total applicants: 11,663. Total accepted: 4,115. Freshmen enrolled: 1,620; 84% were from out of state. Overall acceptance rate: 35%.

Early-decision acceptance rate: 48%. Non-early acceptance rate: 34%. **Size of waiting list:** 1361 applicants; enrolled from waiting list: 50. **Credentials of fall 2005 freshmen:** 77% ranked in the top 10 percent of their high school class; 93% were in the top 25 percent, and 99% were in the top half. (Proportion submitting class standing: 55%.) **First-year students who submitted SAT scores:** 89%. Scores (25/75 percentile): Verbal: 630-720, Math: 650-740, Combined: 1280-1460. **First-year students submitting ACT scores:** 53%. Scores (25/75 percentile): English: 29-34, Math: 27-33, Composite: 28-33.

ACADEMICS

Year founded: 1873. **Academic calendar:** Semester. **Degrees offered:** bachelor's, master's, first professional, doctorate. **Most popular majors:** 27% social sciences, 14% engineering, 7% psychology, 6% English language and literature/letters, 6% foreign languages, literatures, and linguistics. **Major fields of study:** area, ethnic, cultural, and gender studies; biological and biomedical sciences; communication, journalism, and related programs; computer and information sciences and support services; education; engineering; English language and literature/letters; foreign languages, literatures, and linguistics; history; mathematics and statistics; multi/interdisciplinary studies; philosophy and religious studies; physical sciences; psychology; social sciences; visual and performing arts. **Areas of required coursework:** humanities, mathematics, English (including composition), foreign languages, sciences (biological or physical), social science. **Pre-professional programs:** pre-law, pre-medicine, other. **Special academic programs:** accelerated program, cooperative (work-study plan) program, cross-registration, distance learning, double major, dual enrollment, English as a Second Language (ESL), honors program, independent study, internships, student-designed major, study abroad, teacher certificate program. **Teacher certification offered in:** early childhood, special education, elementary, middle/junior high, secondary. **Reserve Officers Training Corps (ROTC):** Army ROTC: Offered on campus; Navy ROTC: Offered on campus; Air Force ROTC: Offered at cooperating institution (University of Tennessee). **Faculty and instruction (2005-2006):** Total instructional faculty: 785 full-time, 113 part-time. Full-time faculty with Ph.D. or other terminal degree: 97%. Student/faculty ratio: 9/1. Classes of fewer than 20 students: 66%; of 20 to 49 students: 27%; of 50 or more students: 7%. **Freshmen returning for sophomore year:** 95%. **Graduation rates:** Four-year: 83%; five-year: 87%; six-year: 88%. **Graduate study:** 53% of students pursue further study immediately upon graduation.

COSTS AND FINANCIAL AID

Financial aid office: (615) 322-3591. **Expenses (2006-2007):** Tuition and fees 2006-2007: $33,440; room/board: $10,890. **Financial aid:** Priority filing date for institution's financial aid form: February 1. In 2005-2006, 43% of undergraduates applied for financial aid. Of those, 40% were determined to have financial need; 95% had their need fully met. Average financial aid package (proportion receiving): $31,840 (40%). Average amount of gift aid, such as scholarships or grants (proportion receiving): $24,806 (38%). Average amount of self-help aid, such as work study or loans (proportion receiving): $4,806 (25%). Average need-based loan (excluding PLUS or other private loans): $3,870. Among students who received need-based aid, the average percentage of need met: 99%. Among students who received aid based on merit, the average award (and the proportion receiving):

$17,602 (13%). The average athletic scholarship (and the proportion receiving): $32,280 (4%). Average amount of debt of borrowers graduating in 2005: $19,585. Proportion who borrowed: 31%.

CAMPUS LIFE AND EXTRACURRICULAR ACTIVITIES

Campus housing available: coed dorms, women's dorms, men's dorms, apartments for married students, apartment for single students, special housing for disabled students, special housing for international students. Students who live in college-owned, operated, or affiliated housing: 83%. **Student employment:** During the 2005-2006 academic year, 23% of undergraduates worked on campus. Average per-year earnings: $2,700. **Clubs and organizations:** Number of student organizations: 300. Activities include: choral groups, concert band, dance, drama/theater, jazz band, literary magazine, marching band, music ensembles, musical theater, opera, pep band, radio station, student government, student newspaper, student film society, symphony orchestra, yearbook. Number of fraternities: 16; sororities: 14. Proportion of men in fraternities: 34%; of women in sororities: 50%. Average proportion of students who stay on campus on weekends: 90%. **Sports program (2005-2006):** Member of NCAA I. *Men's intercollegiate varsity sports:* baseball, basketball, cross-country, football, golf, soccer, tennis. *Women's intercollegiate varsity sports:* basketball, bowling, cross-country, golf, lacrosse, soccer, tennis, track and field (indoor), track and field (outdoor).

SERVICES AND FACILITIES

Basic services: nonremedial tutoring, women's center, placement service, day care, health service, health insurance. **Remedial assistance:** writing, study skills. **Counseling services:** minority student, career, military, personal, veteran student, academic, older student, psychological, birth control, religious. **For learning-disabled students:** School does not offer a structured program with separate admission and additional fees. Total undergraduates in learning-disabled program or receiving services: 280. Services include: tape recorders, diagnostic testing service, note-taking services, oral tests, learning center, readers, extended time for tests, tutors, priority seating, texts on tape, other testing accomodations. **Library:** Number of titles: 3,056,707; number of current serial subscriptions: 33,883. **Information technology resources:** Students are not required to lease or own a computer. Number of campus computers available to all students: 500. School has a wireless network. Approximate number of users that can be accommodated: 10,000. Proportion of college-owned housing units wired for high-speed internet access: 100%. **Campus safety:** Security services offered: 24-hour foot-and-vehicle patrols, late-night transport/escort service, 24-hour emergency telephones, lighted pathways/sidewalks, student patrols, controlled dormitory access (key, security card, etc).

TRANSFER AND INTERNATIONAL STUDENTS

Transfer students: May apply for admission for the following academic terms: Fall, Spring. Applicants need a minimum number of credits to apply. For fall 2005: Transfer applications received: 378. Transfer applicants offered admission: 93. Transfer applicants enrolled: 55. **International students:** Number of foreign undergraduates: 132 (2% of student body). Number of countries represented: 33. Minimum TOEFL score required: 570 (paper); 230 (computer).

Texas

Abilene Christian University

- **Address:** ACU Box 29100, Abilene, TX 79699-9000
- **Website:** http://www.acu.edu
- **Private; Religious affiliation:** Church of Christ
- **Enrollment:** 3,929 full-time; 191 part-time

KEY STATS

✔ **U.S News College Ranking:** 25, Universities–Master's (West)
✔ **SAT Score (25th/75th percentile):** 980-1253
✔ **Tuition:** 2006-2007: $16,330

Selectivity: Selective	**Room/board:** $6,129
Acceptance rate: 55%	**Average debt:** $26,413
Student/faculty ratio: 16/1	**Proportion who borrowed:** 71%

UNDERGRADUATE STUDENT BODY STATS

2005-2006 enrollment: 3,929 full-time; 191 part-time. Men: 45%; women: 55%. **Ethnic makeup:** African American: 7%; American-Indian: 1%; Asian American: 1%; Hispanic: 7%; White: 80%; International: 4%. **Religious preference:** Roman Catholic: 3%; Protestant: 16%; Unknown: 3%; Church of Christ: 62%; Baptist: 12%; Other: 4%.

ADMISSIONS FACTS AND FIGURES

Phone: (800) 460-6228. **Email:** info@admissions.acu.edu. **Website:** http://www.acu.edu. **Application deadlines for fall 2007:** Regular decision: August 1. Early decision: Not offered. Early action: Not offered. Admission cannot be deferred. **Application fee:** $25. Common application is accepted. **To apply online, go to:** http://www.acu.edu/admissions/ugrad/applyonline.html. **Admissions requirements/recommendations:** High school units required (recommended): English: 4 (4); Mathematics: 3 (3); Science: 3 (3); Foreign language: 2 (2); Total units: 12 (12). Tests: The college uses SAT or ACT scores in admissions decisions. Either SAT or ACT required. For admission to the fall 2007 entering class, the school will accept: ACT without writing. Campus visit: Recommended. Admissions interview: Recommended. Off-campus interview: May be arranged. **Factors that count in admissions decisions: Academic:** Secondary school record: Very important. Class rank: Important. Letters of recommendation: Important. Standardized test scores: Very important. Essay: Not considered. **Nonacademic:** Interview: Important. Extracurricular activities: Considered. Talent/ability: Important. Character/personal qualities: Very important. Alumni/ae relationship: Considered. Geographical residence: Not considered. State residency: Not considered. Religious affiliation/commitment: Important. Minority status: Considered. Volunteer work: Considered. Work experience: Considered. **Other schools with the greatest overlap in applicants:** Baylor University; Harding University; Oklahoma Christian University; Texas A&M University–College Station; Texas Tech University. **Admissions statistics for the fall 2005 entering class:** Total applicants: 3,785. Total accepted: 2,097. Freshmen enrolled: 1,031; 18% were from out of state. Overall acceptance rate: 55%. **Size of waiting list:** 0 applicants; enrolled from waiting list: N/A. **Credentials of fall 2005 freshmen:** 20% ranked in the top 10 percent of their high school class; 48% were in the top 25 percent, and 79% were in the top half. (Proportion submitting class standing: 71%.) **Average high school grade point average:** 3.5. **First-year students who submitted SAT scores:** 58%. Scores (25/75 percentile): Verbal: 490-623, Math: 490-630, Combined: 980-1253. **First-year students submitting ACT scores:** 42%. Scores (25/75 percentile): English: 20-27, Math: 19-25, Composite: 20-26.

ACADEMICS

Year founded: 1906. **Academic calendar:** Semester. **Degrees offered:** certificate, associate, bachelor's, post-bachelor's certificate, master's, post-master's certificate, first professional, doctorate. **Most popular majors:** 9% management science, 7% marketing/marketing management, 5% accounting, 5% elementary education and teaching, 4% psychology. **Major fields of study:** agriculture, agriculture operations, and related sciences; biological and bio-

medical sciences; business, management, marketing, and related support services; communication, journalism, and related programs; computer and information sciences and support services; education; engineering; English language and literature/letters; family and consumer sciences/human sciences; foreign languages, literatures, and linguistics; health professions and related clinical sciences; history; legal professions and studies; liberal arts and sciences studies, and humanities; mathematics and statistics; multi/interdisciplinary studies; natural resources and conservation; parks, recreation, leisure, and fitness studies; physical sciences; psychology; public administration and social service professions; social sciences; theology and religious vocations; visual and performing arts. **Areas of required coursework:** arts/fine arts, humanities, mathematics, English (including composition), foreign languages, sciences (biological or physical), history, social science, other. **Pre-professional programs:** pre-law, pre-dentistry, pre-medicine, pre-theology, pre-veterinary science, pre-optometry, pre-pharmacy, other. **Special academic programs (% participation):** cross-registration, distance learning, double major (9%), dual enrollment, English as a Second Language (ESL), honors program (6%), independent study, internships (50%), student-designed major (3%), study abroad (13%), teacher certificate program (14%). **Teacher certification offered in:** early childhood, special education, elementary, middle/junior high, secondary. **Cooperative education programs:** engineering, natural science. **Faculty and instruction (2005-2006):** Total instructional faculty: 218 full-time, 141 part-time (62% men; 38% women; 7% minorities). Full-time faculty with Ph.D. or other terminal degree: 78%. Student/faculty ratio: 16/1. Classes of fewer than 20 students: 45%; of 20 to 49 students: 47%; of 50 or more students: 8%. **Advanced Placement and International Baccalaureate credit:** AP tests may be used for: Credit only. Scores accepted: 3, 4, 5. International Baccalaureate exams may be used for: Credit only. **Freshmen returning for sophomore year:** 75%. **Graduation rates:** Four-year: 36%; five-year: 53%; six-year: 55%. **Graduate study:** 35% of students pursue further study immediately upon graduation; 34% within one year.

COSTS AND FINANCIAL AID

Financial aid office: (325) 674-2643. **Expenses (2006-2007):** Tuition and fees 2006-2007: $16,330; room/board: $6,129. Estimated books and supplies: $1,050; transportation: $1,312; personal expenses: $1,690. **Financial aid:** Priority filing date for institution's financial aid form: March 1. In 2005-2006, 97% of undergraduates applied for financial aid. Of those, 60% were determined to have financial need; 29% had their need fully met. Average financial aid package (proportion receiving): $11,055 (60%). Average amount of gift aid, such as scholarships or grants (proportion receiving): $7,814 (58%). Average amount of self-help aid, such as work study or loans (proportion receiving): $4,181 (48%). Average need-based loan (excluding PLUS or other private loans): $3,996. Among students who received need-based aid, the average percentage of need met: 71%. Among students who received aid based on merit, the average award (and the proportion receiving): $5,767 (28%). The average athletic scholarship (and the proportion receiving): $10,495 (5%). Average amount of debt of borrowers graduating in 2005: $26,413. Proportion who borrowed: 71%.

CAMPUS LIFE AND EXTRACURRICULAR ACTIVITIES

Campus housing available (% using): women's dorms (47%), men's dorms (38%), apartments for married students (1%), apartment for single students (14%), special housing for disabled students. Students who live in college-owned, operated, or affiliated housing: 44%. **Student employment:** During the 2005-2006 academic year, 20% of undergraduates worked on campus. Average per-year earnings: $1,500. **Clubs and organizations:** Number of student organizations: 100. Activities include: choral groups, concert band, drama/theater, jazz band, literary magazine, marching band, music ensembles, musical theater, opera, radio station, student government, student newspaper, symphony orchestra, television station, yearbook. Number of fraternities: 6; sororities: 5. Proportion of men in fraternities: 18%; of women in sororities: 22%. Average proportion of students who stay on campus on weekends: 25%. **Sports program (2005-2006):** Member of NCAA II. **Men's intercollegiate varsity sports:** baseball, basketball, cross-country, football, golf, tennis, track and field (indoor), track and field (outdoor). **Women's**

intercollegiate varsity sports: basketball, cheerleading, cross-country, softball, tennis, track and field (indoor), track and field (outdoor), volleyball.

SERVICES AND FACILITIES

Basic services: nonremedial tutoring, placement service, health service, health insurance, other. **Remedial assistance:** reading, math, study skills. **Counseling services:** minority student, career, military, personal, veteran student, academic, older student, psychological, religious. **For learning-disabled students:** School does not offer a structured program with separate admission and additional fees. Total undergraduates in learning-disabled program or receiving services: 112. Services include: remedial math, remedial English, tape recorders, diagnostic testing service, note-taking services, oral tests, readers, extended time for tests, tutors. **Library:** Number of titles: 503,707; number of current serial subscriptions: 2,771. **Information technology resources:** Students are not required to lease or own a computer. Number of campus computers available to all students: 700. School has a wireless network. Approximate number of users that can be accommodated: 500. Proportion of college-owned housing units wired for high-speed internet access: 97%. **Campus safety:** Security services offered: 24-hour foot-and-vehicle patrols, late-night transport/escort service, 24-hour emergency telephones, lighted pathways/sidewalks, student patrols, controlled dormitory access (key, security card, etc).

TRANSFER AND INTERNATIONAL STUDENTS

Transfer students: May apply for admission for the following academic terms: Fall, Spring, Summer. Applicants do not need a minimum number of credits to apply. For fall 2005: Transfer applications received: 537. Transfer applicants offered admission: 258. Transfer applicants enrolled: 191. **International students:** Number of foreign undergraduates: 169 (4% of student body). Number of countries represented: 46. Minimum TOEFL score required: 525 (paper); 197 (computer).

Angelo State University

- **Address:** 2601 W. Avenue N, San Angelo, TX 76909
- **Website:** http://www.angelo.edu
- **Public**
- **Enrollment:** 4,840 full-time; 869 part-time

KEY STATS

✔ **U.S News College Ranking:** fourth tier, Universities–Master's (West)
✔ **ACT Score (25th/75th percentile):** 17-23
✔ **Tuition:** 2006-2007: $3,180 in state, $11,460 out of state

Selectivity: Less selective	**Room/board:** $5,314
Acceptance rate: 100%	**Average debt:** N/A
Student/faculty ratio: 20/1	**Proportion who borrowed:** N/A

UNDERGRADUATE STUDENT BODY STATS

2005-2006 enrollment: 4,840 full-time; 869 part-time. Men: 46%; women: 54%. **Ethnic makeup:** African American: 6%; Asian American: 1%; Hispanic: 23%; White: 68%; International: 1%.

ADMISSIONS FACTS AND FIGURES

Phone: (325) 942-2041. **Email:** admissions@angelo.edu. **Website:** http://www.angelo.edu. **Application deadlines for fall 2007:** Regular decision: August 15. Early decision: Not offered. Early action: Not offered. Admission can be deferred. **Application fee:** $20. Common application is not accepted. **To apply online, go to:** https://www.applytexas.org. **Admissions requirements/recommendations:** High school units required (recommended): English: 4 (4); Mathematics: 3 (3); Science: 3 (3); Foreign language: 2 (2); Social studies: 3 (3); History: 0 (0); Academic electives: 0 (0); Total units: 23 (23). Tests: The college uses SAT or ACT scores in admissions decisions. Either SAT or ACT required. For admission to the fall 2007 entering class, the school will accept: ACT with writing, ACT without writing. Campus visit: Recommended. Admissions interview: Neither required nor recommended. Off-campus interview: Not available. **Factors that count in admissions decisions:** *Academic:* Secondary school record: Very important. Class rank: Very important. Letters of recommendation: Not considered. Standardized test scores: Important. Essay: Not considered. *Nonacademic:* Interview: Not considered. Extracurricular activities: Not considered. Talent/ability: Not considered. Character/personal qualities: Not considered. Alumni/ae relationship: Not considered. Geographical residence: Not con-

sidered. State residency: Not considered. Religious affiliation/commitment: Not considered. Minority status: Not considered. Volunteer work: Not considered. Work experience: Not considered. **Other schools with the greatest overlap in applicants:** Texas A&M University–College Station; Texas State University–San Marcos; Texas Tech University; University of Texas–Austin. **Admissions statistics for the fall 2005 entering class:** Total applicants: 2,224. Total accepted: 2,216. Freshmen enrolled: 1,304; 2% were from out of state. Overall acceptance rate: 100%. **Credentials of fall 2005 freshmen:** 12% ranked in the top 10 percent of their high school class; 40% were in the top 25 percent, and 74% were in the top half. (Proportion submitting class standing: 97%.) **First-year students who submitted SAT scores:** 56%. Scores (25/75 percentile): Verbal: 420-540, Math: 430-550, Combined: 850-1090. **First-year students submitting ACT scores:** 63%. Scores (25/75 percentile): English: 16-22, Math: 16-23, Composite: 17-23.

ACADEMICS

Year founded: 1928. **Academic calendar:** Semester. **Degrees offered:** associate, bachelor's, master's, first professional. **Most popular majors:** 23% business, management, marketing, and related support services, 14% multi/interdisciplinary studies, 11% health professions and related clinical sciences, 10% parks, recreation, leisure, and fitness studies, 10% psychology. **Major fields of study:** agriculture, agriculture operations, and related sciences; biological and biomedical sciences; business, management, marketing, and related support services; communication, journalism, and related programs; computer and information sciences and support services; English language and literature/letters; foreign languages, literatures, and linguistics; health professions and related clinical sciences; history; liberal arts and sciences studies, and humanities; mathematics and statistics; multi/interdisciplinary studies; natural resources and conservation; parks, recreation, leisure, and fitness studies; physical sciences; psychology; security and protective services; social sciences; visual and performing arts. **Areas of required coursework:** arts/fine arts, computer literacy, mathematics, English (including composition), sciences (biological or physical), history, social science, other. **Pre-professional programs:** other. **Special academic programs:** distance learning, double major, dual enrollment, honors program, independent study, internships, study abroad, teacher certificate program. **Teacher certification offered in:** early childhood, special education, elementary, middle/junior high, secondary. **Reserve Officers Training Corps (ROTC):** Air Force ROTC: Offered on campus. **Faculty and instruction (2005-2006):** Total instructional faculty: 226 full-time, 116 part-time (54% men; 46% women; 11% minorities). Full-time faculty with Ph.D. or other terminal degree: 73%. Student/faculty ratio: 20/1. Classes of fewer than 20 students: 25%; of 20 to 49 students: 63%; of 50 or more students: 12%. **Advanced Placement and International Baccalaureate credit:** AP tests may be used for: Credit only. Scores accepted: 3, 4, 5. **Freshmen returning for sophomore year:** 63%. **Graduation rates:** Four-year: 22%; five-year: 33%; six-year: 35%.

COSTS AND FINANCIAL AID

Financial aid office: (325) 942-2246. **Expenses (2006-2007):** Tuition and fees 2006-2007: $3,180 in state, $11,460 out of state; room/board: $5,314. Estimated transportation: $620; personal expenses: $2,496. **Financial aid:** Priority filing date for institution's financial aid form: May 1. In 2005-2006, 92% of undergraduates applied for financial aid. Of those, 67% were determined to have financial need; 77% had their need fully met. Average financial aid package (proportion receiving): $6,531 (67%). Average amount of gift aid, such as scholarships or grants (proportion receiving): $2,161 (59%). Average amount of self-help aid, such as work study or loans (proportion receiving): $2,431 (53%). Average need-based loan (excluding PLUS or other private loans): $2,566. Among students who received need-based aid, the average percentage of need met: 65%. Among students who received aid based on merit, the average award (and the proportion receiving): $2,343 (6%). The average athletic scholarship (and the proportion receiving): $2,770 (1%).

CAMPUS LIFE AND EXTRACURRICULAR ACTIVITIES

Campus housing available: coed dorms, women's dorms, men's dorms, apartment for single students, special housing for disabled students. Students who live in college-owned, operated, or affiliated housing: 26%. Average per-year earnings: $2,750. **Clubs and organizations:** Number of student organizations: 91. Activities include: choral groups, concert band, dance, drama/theater, jazz band, literary magazine, marching band, music ensembles, musical theater, pep band, radio station, student government, student newspaper, television station. Number of fraternities: 4; sororities: 2. Proportion of men in fraternities: 3%; of women in sororities: 4%. Average proportion of students who stay on campus on weekends: 20%. **Sports program (2005-2006):** Member of NCAA II. *Men's intercollegiate var-*

sity sports: baseball, basketball, cross-country, football, track and field (outdoor). **Women's intercollegiate varsity sports:** basketball, cross-country, soccer, softball, track and field (outdoor), volleyball.

SERVICES AND FACILITIES

Basic services: nonremedial tutoring, placement service, health service, health insurance. **Remedial assistance:** reading, math, writing. **Counseling services:** career, personal, veteran student, academic, psychological. **For learning-disabled students:** Services include: remedial math, remedial English, remedial reading, tape recorders, diagnostic testing service, note-taking services, oral tests, learning center, extended time for tests. **Library:** Number of titles: 481,826; number of current serial subscriptions: 1,628. **Information technology resources:** Students are not required to lease or own a computer. Number of campus computers available to all students: 600. **Campus safety:** Security services offered: 24-hour foot-and-vehicle patrols, late-night transport/escort service, 24-hour emergency telephones, lighted pathways/sidewalks, controlled dormitory access (key, security card, etc).

TRANSFER AND INTERNATIONAL STUDENTS

Transfer students: May apply for admission for the following academic terms: Fall, Spring, Summer. Applicants need a minimum number of credits to apply. For fall 2005: Transfer applications received: 582. Transfer applicants offered admission: 559. Transfer applicants enrolled: 429. **International students:** Number of foreign undergraduates: 43 (1% of student body). Minimum TOEFL score required: 550 (paper); 213 (computer).

Austin College

- **Address:** 900 N. Grand Avenue, Sherman, TX 75090-4400
- **Website:** http://www.austincollege.edu
- **Private; Religious affiliation:** Presbyterian
- **Enrollment:** 1,286 full-time; 12 part-time

KEY STATS

✔ **U.S News College Ranking:** 74, Liberal Arts Colleges
✔ **SAT Score (25th/75th percentile):** 1160-1350
✔ **Tuition:** 2006-2007: $21,586

Selectivity: More selective	**Room/board:** $7,741
Acceptance rate: 67%	**Average debt:** N/A
Student/faculty ratio: 13/1	**Proportion who borrowed:** N/A

UNDERGRADUATE STUDENT BODY STATS

2005-2006 enrollment: 1,286 full-time; 12 part-time. Men: 45%; women: 55%. **Ethnic makeup:** African American: 4%; American-Indian: 1%; Asian American: 12%; Hispanic: 9%; White: 74%; International: 1%. **Religious preference:** Roman Catholic: 19%; Protestant: 49%; Jewish: 1%; Muslim: 2%; Hindu: 3%; Buddhist: 1%; No preference: 1%; Unknown: 4%; Presbyterian: 14%.

ADMISSIONS FACTS AND FIGURES

Phone: (800) 442-5363. **Email:** admission@austincollege.edu. **Website:** http://www.austincollege.edu. **Application deadlines for fall 2007:** Regular decision: May 1. Early decision: Send application by: December 1; Decision sent by: January 10. Early action: Send application by: January 15; Decision sent by: March 1. Admission can be deferred. **Application fee:** $35. Common application is accepted. **To apply online, go to:** http://www.austincollege.edu/info.asp?713. **Admissions requirements/recommendations:** High school units required (recommended): English: 4 (4); Mathematics: 3 (4); Science: 3 (4); Foreign language: 2 (3); Social studies: 2 (3); History: 0 (0); Academic electives: 1 (1); Total units: 16 (21). Tests: The college uses SAT or ACT scores in admissions decisions. Either SAT or ACT required. For admission to the fall 2007 entering class, the school will accept: ACT with writing. Campus visit: Recommended. Admissions interview: Recommended. Off-campus interview: May be arranged. **Factors that count in admissions decisions: *Academic:*** Secondary school record: Very important. Class rank: Important. Letters of recommendation: Important. Standardized test scores: Important. Essay: Important. ***Nonacademic:*** Interview: Considered. Extracurricular activities: Important. Talent/ability: Important. Character/personal qualities: Important. Alumni/ae relationship: Considered. Geographical residence: Considered. State residency: Considered. Religious affiliation/commitment: Considered. Minority status: Considered. Volunteer work: Considered. Work experience: Considered.

Other schools with the greatest overlap in applicants: Baylor University; Southern Methodist University; Southwestern University; Texas A&M University–College Station; Trinity University. **Admissions statistics for the fall 2005 entering class:** Total applicants: 1,530. Total accepted: 1,029. Freshmen enrolled: 348; 8% were from out of state. Accepted through early-decision or early-action plans: 72%. Overall acceptance rate: 67%. Early-decision acceptance rate: 84%. Non-early acceptance rate: 50%. **Size of waiting list:** 56 applicants; enrolled from waiting list: 9. **Credentials of fall 2005 freshmen:** 44% ranked in the top 10 percent of their high school class; 75% were in the top 25 percent, and 97% were in the top half. (Proportion submitting class standing: 87%.) **First-year students who submitted SAT scores:** 75%. Scores (25/75 percentile): Verbal: 580-680, Math: 580-670, Combined: 1160-1350. **First-year students submitting ACT scores:** 56%. Scores (25/75 percentile): English: N/A, Math: N/A, Composite: 23-28.

ACADEMICS

Year founded: 1849. **Academic calendar:** 4-1-4. **Degrees offered:** bachelor's, master's. **Most popular majors:** 14% psychology, 13% business/commerce, 8% English language and literature, 8% biology/biological sciences, 7% political science and government. **Major fields of study:** area, ethnic, cultural, and gender studies; biological and biomedical sciences; business, management, marketing, and related support services; communication, journalism, and related programs; computer and information sciences and support services; education; English language and literature/letters; foreign languages, literatures, and linguistics; history; mathematics and statistics; multi/interdisciplinary studies; philosophy and religious studies; physical sciences; psychology; social sciences; visual and performing arts. **Areas of required coursework:** humanities, mathematics, English (including composition), foreign languages, sciences (biological or physical), social science. **Pre-professional programs:** pre-law, pre-dentistry, pre-medicine, pre-theology, other. **Special academic programs (% participation):** double major (27%), exchange student program (domestic) (0%), honors program (7%), independent study (57%), internships (28%), student-designed major (3%), study abroad (70%), teacher certificate program (20%). **Teacher certification offered in:** early childhood, elementary, middle/junior high, secondary. **Faculty and instruction (2005-2006):** Total instructional faculty: 91 full-time, 40 part-time (62% men; 38% women; 9% minorities). Full-time faculty with Ph.D. or other terminal degree: 98%. Student/faculty ratio: 13/1. Classes of fewer than 20 students: 60%; of 20 to 49 students: 38%; of 50 or more students: 2%. **Advanced Placement and International Baccalaureate credit:** AP tests may be used for: Credit and/or placement. Scores accepted: 4, 5. International Baccalaureate exams may be used for: Credit and/or placement. **Freshmen returning for sophomore year:** 86%. **Graduation rates:** Four-year: 69%; five-year: 74%; six-year: 75%. **Graduate study:** 41% of students pursue further study immediately upon graduation; 12% within one year. Fields in which graduates pursue further study: Master of Business Administration (MBA), 1%; law, 14%; medicine, 18%; dentistry, 1%; engineering, 4%; theology (or the seminary), 3%; education, 24%; arts and sciences, 29%.

COSTS AND FINANCIAL AID

Financial aid office: (903) 813-2900. **Expenses (2006-2007):** Tuition and fees 2006-2007: $21,586; room/board: $7,741. Estimated books and supplies: $800; transportation: $250; personal expenses: $950. **Financial aid:** Priority filing date for institution's financial aid form: April 1. In 2005-2006, 69% of undergraduates applied for financial aid. Of those, 54% were determined to have financial need; 96% had their need fully met. Average financial aid package (proportion receiving): $20,989 (54%). Average amount of gift aid, such as scholarships or grants (proportion receiving): $13,446 (54%). Average amount of self-help aid, such as work study or loans (proportion receiving): $7,513 (42%). Average need-based loan (excluding PLUS or other private loans): $5,857. Among students who received need-based aid, the average percentage of need met: 99%. Among students who received aid based on merit, the average award (and the proportion receiving): $9,199 (38%). The average athletic scholarship (and the proportion receiving): $0 (0%).

CAMPUS LIFE AND EXTRACURRICULAR ACTIVITIES

Campus housing available (% using): coed dorms (25%), women's dorms (31%), men's dorms (16%), apartment for single students (23%), other housing options (5%). Students who live in college-owned, operated, or affiliated housing: 70%. **Student employment:** During the 2005-2006 academic year, 31% of undergraduates worked on campus. Average per-year earnings: $1,600. **Clubs and organizations:** Number of student organizations: 77. Activities include: choral groups, dance, drama/theater, jazz band, literary magazine, music ensembles, musical theater, pep band, student government, student newspaper, symphony orchestra, yearbook. Number of fraternities: 9; sororities: 7. Proportion of men in fraternities: 29%; of women in sororities: 28%. Average proportion of students who stay on campus on weekends: 60%. **Sports program (2005-2006):** Member of NCAA III. *Men's intercollegiate varsity sports:* baseball, basketball, football, soccer, swimming and diving, tennis. *Women's intercollegiate varsity sports:* basketball, soccer, swimming and diving, tennis, volleyball.

SERVICES AND FACILITIES
Basic services: nonremedial tutoring, health service, health insurance, other. **Remedial assistance:** other. **Counseling services:** minority student, career, military, personal, veteran student, academic, older student, psychological, birth control, religious, other. **For learning-disabled students:** School does not offer a structured program with separate admission and additional fees. Total undergraduates in learning-disabled program or receiving services: 41. Services include: reading machines, tape recorders, note-taking services, learning center, extended time for tests, tutors, texts on tape, other. **Library:** Number of titles: 239,986; number of current serial subscriptions: 2,835. **Information technology resources:** Students are not required to lease or own a computer. Number of campus computers available to all students: 160. School has a wireless network. Approximate number of users that can be accommodated: 200. Proportion of college-owned housing units wired for high-speed internet access: 100%. **Campus safety:** Security services offered: 24-hour foot-and-vehicle patrols, late-night transport/escort service, 24-hour emergency telephones, lighted pathways/sidewalks, controlled dormitory access (key, security card, etc).

TRANSFER AND INTERNATIONAL STUDENTS
Transfer students: May apply for admission for the following academic terms: Fall, Spring, Summer. Applicants do not need a minimum number of credits to apply. For fall 2005: Transfer applications received: 117. Transfer applicants offered admission: 64. Transfer applicants enrolled: 32. **International students:** Number of foreign undergraduates: 15 (1% of student body). Number of countries represented: 18. Minimum TOEFL score required: 550 (paper); 213 (computer). Average TOEFL score: 600 (paper).

Baylor University

- **Address:** 1 Bear Place, Waco, TX 76798
- **Website:** http://www.baylor.edu
- **Private; Religious affiliation:** Baptist
- **Enrollment:** 11,465 full-time; 360 part-time

KEY STATS
- ✔ **U.S News College Ranking:** 81, National Universities
- ✔ **SAT Score (25th/75th percentile):** 1090-1310
- ✔ **Tuition:** 2006-2007: $22,814

Selectivity: More selective	**Room/board:** $7,125
Acceptance rate: 66%	**Average debt:** N/A
Student/faculty ratio: 16/1	**Proportion who borrowed:** N/A

UNDERGRADUATE STUDENT BODY STATS
2005-2006 enrollment: 11,465 full-time; 360 part-time. Men: 42%; women: 58%. **Ethnic makeup:** African American: 8%; American-Indian: 1%; Asian American: 7%; Hispanic: 10%; White: 74%; International: 1%.

ADMISSIONS FACTS AND FIGURES
Phone: (800) 229-5678. **Email:** Admissions@Baylor.edu. **Website:** http://www.baylor.edu. **Application deadlines for fall 2007:** Regular decision: February 1. Early decision: Not offered. Early action: Send application by: N/A; Decision sent by: N/A. Admission can be deferred. **Application fee:** $50. Common application is accepted. **To apply online, go to:** http://www.baylor.edu/admissions/undergrad_apply.asp. **Admissions requirements/recommendations:** High school units required (recommended): English: 4; Mathematics: 3; Science: 2; Foreign language: 2; Social studies: 1; History: 1; Academic electives: 3; Total units: 16. Tests: The college uses SAT or ACT scores in admissions decisions. Either SAT or ACT required. For admission to the fall 2007 entering class, the school will accept: ACT with writing. Campus visit: Recommended. **Factors that count in admissions decisions:** *Academic:* Secondary school record: Important. Class rank: Very important. Letters of recommendation: Considered. Standardized test scores: Very important. Essay: Important. *Nonacademic:*

Interview: Considered. Extracurricular activities: Considered. Talent/ability: Considered. Character/personal qualities: Considered. Alumni/ae relationship: Considered. Geographical residence: Not considered. State residency: Not considered. Religious affiliation/commitment: Considered. Minority status: Not considered. Volunteer work: Considered. Work experience: Considered. **Other schools with the greatest overlap in applicants:** Rice University; Texas A&M University–College Station; Texas Christian University; Texas Tech University; University of Texas–Austin. **Admissions statistics for the fall 2005 entering class:** Total applicants: 15,443. Total accepted: 10,157. Freshmen enrolled: 3,168; 18% were from out of state. Overall acceptance rate: 66%. Non-early acceptance rate: 66%. **Credentials of fall 2005 freshmen:** 38% ranked in the top 10 percent of their high school class; 68% were in the top 25 percent, and 91% were in the top half. (Proportion submitting class standing: 89%.) **First-year students who submitted SAT scores:** 72%. Scores (25/75 percentile): Verbal: 540-650, Math: 550-660, Combined: 1090-1310. **First-year students submitting ACT scores:** 28%. Scores (25/75 percentile): English: 21-28, Math: 20-26, Composite: 22-27.

ACADEMICS
Year founded: 1845. **Academic calendar:** Semester. **Degrees offered:** bachelor's, master's, post-master's certificate, first professional, doctorate. **Most popular majors:** 6% biology/biological sciences; 6% marketing/marketing management; 6% psychology; 5% accounting; 4% journalism. **Major fields of study:** architecture and related services; area, ethnic, cultural, and gender studies; biological and biomedical sciences; business, management, marketing, and related support services; communication, journalism, and related programs; computer and information sciences and support services; education; engineering; English language and literature/letters; family and consumer sciences/human sciences; foreign languages, literatures, and linguistics; health professions and related clinical sciences; history; liberal arts and sciences studies, and humanities; mathematics and statistics; multi/interdisciplinary studies; natural resources and conservation; parks, recreation, leisure, and fitness studies; philosophy and religious studies; physical sciences; psychology; public administration and social service professions; security and protective services; social sciences; theology and religious vocations; transportation and materials moving; visual and performing arts. **Areas of required coursework:** arts/fine arts, humanities, mathematics, English (including composition), philosophy, foreign languages, sciences (biological or physical), history, social science, other. **Pre-professional programs:** pre-law, pre-dentistry, pre-medicine, pre-veterinary science, pre-optometry, pre-pharmacy, other. **Special academic programs:** accelerated program, double major, honors program, independent study, internships, student-designed major, study abroad, teacher certificate program. **Teacher certification offered in:** early childhood, special education, elementary, middle/junior high, secondary. **Cooperative education programs:** health professions. **Reserve Officers Training Corps (ROTC):** Air Force ROTC: Offered on campus. **Faculty and instruction (2005-2006):** Total instructional faculty: 755 full-time, 155 part-time (63% men; 37% women; 8% minorities). Full-time faculty with Ph.D. or other terminal degree: 77%. Student/faculty ratio: 16/1. Classes of fewer than 20 students: 36%; of 20 to 49 students: 54%; of 50 or more students: 10%. **Advanced Placement and International Baccalaureate credit:** AP tests may be used for: Credit and/or placement. Scores accepted: 4, 5. International Baccalaureate exams may be used for: Credit and/or placement. **Freshmen returning for sophomore year:** 83%. **Graduation rates:** Four-year: 45%; five-year: 69%; six-year: 72%.

COSTS AND FINANCIAL AID
Financial aid office: (254) 710-2611. **Expenses (2006-2007):** Tuition and fees 2006-2007: $22,814; room/board: $7,125. Estimated books and supplies: $1,502; transportation: $1,625; personal expenses: $2,108. **Financial aid:** Priority filing date for institution's financial aid form: March 1. In 2005-2006, 63% of undergraduates applied for financial aid. Of those, 51% were determined to have financial need; 18% had their need fully met. Average financial aid package (proportion receiving): $15,392 (51%). Average amount of gift aid, such as scholarships or grants (proportion receiving): $10,925 (48%). Average amount of self-help aid, such as work study or loans (proportion receiving): $5,477 (40%). Average need-based loan (excluding PLUS or other private loans): $2,394. Among students who received need-based aid, the average percentage of need met: 67%. Among students who received aid based on merit, the average award (and the proportion receiving): $6,981 (31%). The average athletic scholarship (and the proportion receiving): $18,982 (3%).

CAMPUS LIFE AND EXTRACURRICULAR ACTIVITIES

Campus housing available: women's dorms, men's dorms, apartments for married students, apartment for single students, special housing for disabled students. Students who live in college-owned, operated, or affiliated housing: 34%. **Student employment:** During the 2005-2006 academic year, 13% of undergraduates worked on campus. Average per-year earnings: $1,100. **Clubs and organizations:** Number of student organizations: 300. Activities include: choral groups, concert band, dance, drama/theater, jazz band, literary magazine, marching band, music ensembles, musical theater, opera, pep band, radio station, student government, student newspaper, student film society, symphony orchestra, television station, yearbook. Number of fraternities: 22; sororities: 18. Proportion of men in fraternities: 13%; of women in sororities: 17%. Average proportion of students who stay on campus on weekends: 80%. **Sports program (2005-2006):** Member of NCAA I. **Men's intercollegiate varsity sports:** baseball, basketball, cross-country, football, golf, tennis, track and field (indoor), track and field (outdoor). **Women's intercollegiate varsity sports:** basketball, cross-country, equestrian sports, golf, soccer, softball, tennis, track and field (indoor), track and field (outdoor), volleyball.

SERVICES AND FACILITIES

Basic services: nonremedial tutoring, health service, health insurance, other. **Remedial assistance:** math, writing, study skills. **Counseling services:** career, personal, academic, psychological, religious. **For learning-disabled students:** School does not offer a structured program with separate admission and additional fees. Total undergraduates in learning-disabled program or receiving services: 425. Services include: reading machines, tape recorders, note-taking services, oral tests, readers, extended time for tests, tutors, priority registration, priority seating, typist/scribe, exams on tape or computer, other testing accomodations. **Library:** Number of titles: 2,165,992; number of current serial subscriptions: 20,027. **Information technology resources:** Students are not required to lease or own a computer. Number of campus computers available to all students: 1,696. School has a wireless network. Approximate number of users that can be accommodated: 10,000. Proportion of college-owned housing units wired for high-speed internet access: 98%. **Campus safety:** Security services offered: 24-hour foot-and-vehicle patrols, late-night transport/escort service, 24-hour emergency telephones, lighted pathways/sidewalks, controlled dormitory access (key, security card, etc).

TRANSFER AND INTERNATIONAL STUDENTS

Transfer students: May apply for admission for the following academic terms: Fall, Spring, Summer. Applicants need a minimum number of credits to apply. For fall 2005: Transfer applications received: 1,636. Transfer applicants offered admission: 832. Transfer applicants enrolled: 422. **International students:** Number of foreign undergraduates: 173 (1% of student body). Number of countries represented: 76. Minimum TOEFL score required: 540 (paper); 207 (computer).

Concordia University–Austin

- **Address:** 3400 I-35 N, Austin, TX 78705
- **Website:** http://www.concordia.edu
- **Private; Religious affiliation:** Lutheran Church-Missouri Synod
- **Enrollment:** 756 full-time; 373 part-time

KEY STATS

✔ **U.S News College Ranking:** 16, Comp. Coll.–Bachelor's (West)
✔ **SAT Score (25th/75th percentile):** 910-1120
✔ **Tuition:** 2006-2007: $18,070

Selectivity: Selective	**Room/board:** $7,100
Acceptance rate: 73%	**Average debt:** $20,202
Student/faculty ratio: 13/1	**Proportion who borrowed:** 68%

UNDERGRADUATE STUDENT BODY STATS

2005-2006 enrollment: 756 full-time; 373 part-time. Men: 43%; women: 57%. **Ethnic makeup:** African American: 9%; Asian American: 1%; Hispanic: 16%; White: 74%.

ADMISSIONS FACTS AND FIGURES

Phone: (800) 865-4282. **Email:** admissions@concordia.edu. **Website:** http://www.concordia.edu. **Application deadlines for fall 2007:** Regular decision: Rolling. Early decision: Not offered. Early action: Not offered. Admission can be deferred. **Application fee:** $25. Common application is not accepted. **Admissions requirements/recommendations:** High school units required (recommended): English: 4 (4); Mathematics: 3 (3); Science: 3 (3); Total units: 10 (10). Tests: The college uses SAT or ACT scores in admissions decisions. Either SAT or ACT required. For admission to the fall 2007 entering class, the school will accept: ACT with writing, ACT without writing. Campus visit: Recommended. Admissions interview: Recommended. Off-campus interview: May be arranged. **Factors that count in admissions decisions:** *Academic:* Secondary school record: Very important. Class rank: Important. Letters of recommendation: Considered. Standardized test scores: Very important. Essay: Considered. *Nonacademic:* Interview: Not considered. Extracurricular activities: Not considered. Talent/ability: Not considered. Geographical residence: Not considered. State residency: Not considered. Religious affiliation/commitment: Not considered. Minority status: Not considered. Volunteer work: Not considered. Work experience: Not considered. **Other schools with the greatest overlap in applicants:** St. Edward's University; Texas State University–San Marcos; University of Houston; University of Mary Hardin-Baylor. **Admissions statistics for the fall 2005 entering class:** Total applicants: 728. Total accepted: 532. Freshmen enrolled: 195; Overall acceptance rate: 73%. **Credentials of fall 2005 freshmen:** 10% ranked in the top 10 percent of their high school class; 36% were in the top 25 percent, and 74% were in the top half. (Proportion submitting class standing: 82%.) **Average high school grade point average:** 3.3. **First-year students who submitted SAT scores:** 75%. Scores (25/75 percentile): Verbal: 450-560, Math: 460-560, Combined: 910-1120. **First-year students submitting ACT scores:** 41%. Scores (25/75 percentile): English: 17-25, Math: 18-23, Composite: 18-23.

ACADEMICS

Year founded: 1926. **Academic calendar:** Semester. **Degrees offered:** certificate, associate, bachelor's, post-bachelor's certificate, master's. **Most popular majors:** Information not available. **Major fields of study:** biological and biomedical sciences; business, management, marketing, and related support services; communication, journalism, and related programs; computer and information sciences and support services; education; English language and literature/letters; history; liberal arts and sciences studies, and humanities; mathematics and statistics; natural resources and conservation; parks, recreation, leisure, and fitness studies; security and protective services; social sciences; theology and religious vocations. **Areas of required coursework:** arts/fine arts, humanities, computer literacy, mathematics, English (including composition), sciences (biological or physical), history, social science, other. **Pre-professional programs:** pre-law, pre-dentistry, pre-medicine, pre-theology, pre-veterinary science. **Special academic programs:** cooperative (work-study plan) program, distance learning, double major, dual enrollment, exchange student program (domestic), honors program, independent study, internships, teacher certificate program. **Teacher certification offered in:** early childhood, elementary, middle/junior high, secondary. **Reserve Officers Training Corps (ROTC):** Army ROTC: Offered at cooperating institution (University of Texas); Air Force ROTC: Offered at cooperating institution (University of Texas). **Faculty and instruction (2005-2006):** Total instructional faculty: 35 full-time, 100 part-time (61% men; 39% women; 8% minorities). Full-time faculty with Ph.D. or other terminal degree: 74%. Student/faculty ratio: 13/1. Classes of fewer than 20 students: 81%; of 20 to 49 students: 19%; of 50 or more students: 0%. **Advanced Placement and International Baccalaureate credit:** AP tests may be used for: Credit only. Scores accepted: 3. International Baccalaureate exams may be used for: Credit only. **Freshmen returning for sophomore year:** 57%. **Graduation rates:** Four-year: 20%; five-year: 30%; six-year: 33%.

COSTS AND FINANCIAL AID

Financial aid office: (512) 486-1283. **Expenses (2006-2007):** Tuition and fees 2006-2007: $18,070; room/board: $7,100. Estimated books and supplies: $1,000; transportation: $700; personal expenses: $1,130. **Financial aid:** Priority filing date for institution's financial aid form: May 1. In 2005-2006, 87% of undergraduates applied for financial aid. Of those, 66% were determined to have financial need; 45% had their need fully met. Average financial aid package (proportion receiving): $15,222 (66%). Average amount of gift aid, such as scholarships or grants (proportion receiving): $8,735 (54%). Average amount of self-help aid, such as work study or loans (proportion receiving): $6,636 (60%). Average need-based loan (excluding PLUS or other private loans): $6,411. Among students who received need-based aid, the average percentage of need met: 81%. Among students who received aid based on merit, the average award (and the proportion receiving): $6,844 (18%). The average athletic scholarship (and the proportion receiving): $0 (0%). Average amount of debt of borrowers graduating in 2005: $20,202. Proportion who borrowed: 68%.

CAMPUS LIFE AND EXTRACURRICULAR ACTIVITIES
Campus housing available: coed dorms, women's dorms, men's dorms, special housing for disabled students. Activities include: choral groups, drama/theater, jazz band, music ensembles, student government, yearbook. Number of fraternities: 0; sororities: 0. **Sports program (2005-2006):** Member of NCAA III. *Men's intercollegiate varsity sports:* baseball, basketball, cross-country, golf, soccer, tennis. *Women's intercollegiate varsity sports:* basketball, cross-country, soccer, softball, tennis, volleyball.

SERVICES AND FACILITIES
Counseling services: academic, psychological. **For learning-disabled students:** School does not offer a structured program with separate admission and additional fees. Services include: remedial math, remedial English, extended time for tests, tutors. **Campus safety:** Security services offered: 24-hour foot-and-vehicle patrols, controlled dormitory access (key, security card, etc).

TRANSFER AND INTERNATIONAL STUDENTS
Transfer students: May apply for admission for the following academic terms: Fall, Spring, Summer. Applicants need a minimum number of credits to apply. **International students:** Number of foreign undergraduates: 1. Minimum TOEFL score required: 550 (paper).

Dallas Baptist University

- **Address:** 3000 Mountain Creek Parkway, Dallas, TX 75211-9299
- **Website:** http://www.dbu.edu
- **Private; Religious affiliation:** Baptist
- **Enrollment:** 2,100 full-time; 1,467 part-time

KEY STATS
✔ **U.S News College Ranking:** 61, Universities–Master's (West)
✔ **SAT Score (25th/75th percentile):** 962-1163
✔ **Tuition:** 2006-2007: $13,050

Selectivity: Selective	**Room/board:** $4,959
Acceptance rate: 64%	**Average debt:** $18,763
Student/faculty ratio: 17/1	**Proportion who borrowed:** 55%

UNDERGRADUATE STUDENT BODY STATS
2005-2006 enrollment: 2,100 full-time; 1,467 part-time. Men: 40%; women: 60%. **Ethnic makeup:** African American: 17%; American-Indian: 1%; Asian American: 1%; Hispanic: 10%; White: 64%; International: 7%. **Religious preference:** Roman Catholic: 4%; Protestant: 17%; No preference: 17%; Baptist: 47%; Non-Denominational: 15%.

ADMISSIONS FACTS AND FIGURES
Phone: (214) 333-5360. **Email:** admiss@dbu.edu. **Website:** http://www.dbu.edu. **Application deadlines for fall 2007:** Regular decision: Rolling. Early decision: Not offered. Early action: Not offered. Admission can be deferred. **Application fee:** $25. Common application is accepted. **Admissions requirements/recommendations:** High school units required (recommended): English: (4); Mathematics: (3); Science: (2); Foreign language: (2); Social studies: (3); History: (2); Total units: (16). Tests: The college uses SAT or ACT scores in admissions decisions. Either SAT or ACT required. For admission to the fall 2007 entering class, the school will accept: ACT with writing. Campus visit: Recommended. Admissions interview: Recommended. Off-campus interview: May be arranged. **Factors that count in admissions decisions:** *Academic:* Secondary school record: Very important. Class rank: Very important. Letters of recommendation: Considered. Standardized test scores: Very important. Essay: Very important. *Nonacademic:* Interview: Considered. Extracurricular activities: Important. Talent/ability: Very important. Character/personal qualities: Very important. Alumni/ae relationship: Considered. Geographical residence: Not considered. State residency: Not considered. Religious affiliation/commitment: Very important. Minority status: Not considered. Volunteer work: Considered. Work experience: Considered. **Other schools with the greatest overlap in applicants:** Baylor University; Hardin-Simmons University; Texas A&M University–College Station; Texas Christian University; University of

North Texas. **Admissions statistics for the fall 2005 entering class:** Total applicants: 937. Total accepted: 599. Freshmen enrolled: 362; 10% were from out of state. Overall acceptance rate: 64%. **Credentials of fall 2005 freshmen:** 23% ranked in the top 10 percent of their high school class; 53% were in the top 25 percent, and 83% were in the top half. (Proportion submitting class standing: 82%.) **Average high school grade point average:** 3.6. **First-year students who submitted SAT scores:** 60%. Scores (25/75 percentile): Verbal: 484-581, Math: 478-582, Combined: 962-1163. **First-year students submitting ACT scores:** 40%. Scores (25/75 percentile): English: N/A, Math: N/A, Composite: 19-24.

ACADEMICS
Year founded: 1898. **Academic calendar:** 4-1-4. **Degrees offered:** certificate, associate, bachelor's, post-bachelor's certificate, master's, post-master's certificate, doctorate. **Most popular majors:** 23% business administration and management, 17% general studies, 8% communication studies/speech communication and rhetoric, 8% psychology, 7% management information systems. **Major fields of study:** biological and biomedical sciences; business, management, marketing, and related support services; communication, journalism, and related programs; computer and information sciences and support services; education; English language and literature/letters; health professions and related clinical sciences; liberal arts and sciences studies, and humanities; mathematics and statistics; multi/interdisciplinary studies; philosophy and religious studies; psychology; public administration and social service professions; security and protective services; social sciences; theology and religious vocations; visual and performing arts. **Areas of required coursework:** arts/fine arts, humanities, computer literacy, mathematics, English (including composition), foreign languages, sciences (biological or physical), history, social science, other. **Pre-professional programs:** pre-law, pre-dentistry, pre-medicine, pre-theology, pre-veterinary science, pre-optometry, pre-pharmacy, other. **Special academic programs:** accelerated program, distance learning, double major, dual enrollment, English as a Second Language (ESL), independent study, internships, study abroad, teacher certificate program, weekend college. **Teacher certification offered in:** early childhood, special education, elementary, middle/junior high, secondary. **Reserve Officers Training Corps (ROTC):** Army ROTC: Offered at cooperating institution (Univ. of Texas at Arlington); Air Force ROTC: Offered at cooperating institution (Texas Christian University). **Faculty and instruction (2005-2006):** Total instructional faculty: 100 full-time, 356 part-time (58% men; 42% women; 9% minorities). Full-time faculty with Ph.D. or other terminal degree: 81%. Student/faculty ratio: 17/1. Classes of fewer than 20 students: 60%; of 20 to 49 students: 36%; of 50 or more students: 4%. **Advanced Placement and International Baccalaureate credit:** AP tests may be used for: Credit and/or placement. Scores accepted: 3, 4. International Baccalaureate exams may be used for: Credit only. **Freshmen returning for sophomore year:** 67%. **Graduation rates:** Four-year: 33%; five-year: 44%; six-year: 45%.

COSTS AND FINANCIAL AID
Financial aid office: (214) 333-5460. **Expenses (2006-2007):** Tuition and fees 2006-2007: $13,050; room/board: $4,959. Estimated books and supplies: $1,020; transportation: $675; personal expenses: $1,503. **Financial aid:** Priority filing date for institution's financial aid form: March 20. In 2005-2006, 84% of undergraduates applied for financial aid. Of those, 57% were determined to have financial need; 41% had their need fully met. Average financial aid package (proportion receiving): $10,262 (56%). Average amount of gift aid, such as scholarships or grants (proportion receiving): $2,767 (41%). Average amount of self-help aid, such as work study or loans (proportion receiving): $3,163 (44%). Average need-based loan (excluding PLUS or other private loans): $3,398. Among students who received need-based aid, the average percentage of need met: 79%. Among students who received aid based on merit, the average award (and the proportion receiving): $9,093 (21%). The average athletic scholarship (and the proportion receiving): $6,659 (5%). Average amount of debt of borrowers graduating in 2005: $18,763. Proportion who borrowed: 55%.

CAMPUS LIFE AND EXTRACURRICULAR ACTIVITIES
Campus housing available (% using): women's dorms (36%), men's dorms (26%), apartments for married students (1%), apartment for single students (37%), special housing for disabled students (0%). Students who live in college-owned, operated, or affiliated housing: 34%. **Student employment:** During the 2005-2006 academic year, 23% of undergraduates worked on campus. Average per-year earnings: $2,880. **Clubs and organizations:** Number of student organizations: 36. Activities include: choral groups, drama/theater, music ensembles, musical theater, opera, student government, yearbook. Number of fraternities: 0; sororities: 0. Average proportion

of students who stay on campus on weekends: 75%. **Sports program (2005-2006):** Member of NCAA II. *Men's intercollegiate varsity sports:* baseball, cross-country, golf, soccer, tennis, track and field (indoor), track and field (outdoor). *Women's intercollegiate varsity sports:* cross-country, golf, soccer, tennis, track and field (indoor), track and field (outdoor), volleyball.

SERVICES AND FACILITIES

Basic services: nonremedial tutoring, placement service, health service, health insurance. **Remedial assistance:** math, writing, study skills, other. **Counseling services:** minority student, career, military, personal, veteran student, academic, older student, psychological, religious. **For learning-disabled students:** School does not offer a structured program with separate admission and additional fees. Total undergraduates in learning-disabled program or receiving services: 54. Services include: remedial math, other testing accommodations, reading machines, tape recorders, videotaped classes, untimed tests, note-taking services, oral tests, learning center, readers, extended time for tests, tutors, priority seating, texts on tape. **Library:** Number of titles: 276,945; number of current serial subscriptions: 637. **Information technology resources:** Students are not required to lease or own a computer. Number of campus computers available to all students: 220. School has a wireless network. Approximate number of users that can be accommodated: 2,200. Proportion of college-owned housing units wired for high-speed internet access: 100%. **Campus safety:** Security services offered: 24-hour foot-and-vehicle patrols, late-night transport/escort service, 24-hour emergency telephones, lighted pathways/sidewalks, controlled dormitory access (key, security card, etc).

TRANSFER AND INTERNATIONAL STUDENTS

Transfer students: May apply for admission for the following academic terms: Fall, Winter, Spring, Summer. Applicants do not need a minimum number of credits to apply. For fall 2005: Transfer applications received: 577. Transfer applicants offered admission: 354. Transfer applicants enrolled: 308. **International students:** Number of foreign undergraduates: 240 (7% of student body). Number of countries represented: 43. Minimum TOEFL score required: 525 (paper); 197 (computer). Average TOEFL score: 525 (paper).

East Texas Baptist University

- Address: 1209 N. Grove, Marshall, TX 75670
- Website: http://www.etbu.edu
- Private; Religious affiliation: Baptist
- Enrollment: 1,176 full-time; 150 part-time

KEY STATS

✔ U.S News College Ranking: 11, Comp. Coll.–Bachelor's (West)
✔ ACT Score (25th/75th percentile): 18-24
✔ Tuition: 2006-2007: $13,720

Selectivity: Selective	Room/board: $4,190
Acceptance rate: 79%	Average debt: $16,777
Student/faculty ratio: 15/1	Proportion who borrowed: 81%

UNDERGRADUATE STUDENT BODY STATS

2005-2006 enrollment: 1,176 full-time; 150 part-time. Men: 45%; women: 55%. **Ethnic makeup:** African American: 15%; American-Indian: 1%; Hispanic: 4%; White: 80%; International: 1%. **Religious preference:** Roman Catholic: 2%; Protestant: 7%; No preference: 16%; Baptist: 72%; Other: 3%.

ADMISSIONS FACTS AND FIGURES

Phone: (800) 804-3828. **Email:** admissions@etbu.edu. **Website:** http://www.etbu.edu. **Application deadlines for fall 2007:** Regular decision: August 17. Early decision: Not offered. Early action: Not offered. Admission can be deferred. **Application fee:** $25. Common application is accepted. **Admissions requirements/recommendations:** High school units required (recommended): English: (4); Mathematics: (3); Science: (2); Social studies: (3); Academic electives: (1); Total units: (22). Tests: The college uses SAT or ACT scores in admissions decisions. Either SAT or ACT required. For admission to the fall 2007 entering class, the school will accept: ACT with writing, ACT without writing. Campus visit: Recommended. Admissions interview: Neither required nor recommended. Off-campus interview: May be arranged. **Factors that count in admissions decisions:** *Academic:* Secondary school record: Very important. Class rank: Very important.

Letters of recommendation: Not considered. Standardized test scores: Very important. Essay: Not considered. *Nonacademic:* Interview: Not considered. Extracurricular activities: Not considered. Talent/ability: Not considered. Character/personal qualities: Important. Alumni/ae relationship: Considered. Geographical residence: Not considered. State residency: Not considered. Religious affiliation/commitment: Considered. Minority status: Not considered. Volunteer work: Not considered. Work experience: Not considered. **Other schools with the greatest overlap in applicants:** Baylor University; Dallas Baptist University; Stephen F. Austin State University; Texas A&M University–College Station; University of Texas–Tyler. **Admissions statistics for the fall 2005 entering class:** Total applicants: 851. Total accepted: 670. Freshmen enrolled: 303; 1% were from out of state. Overall acceptance rate: 79%. **Credentials of fall 2005 freshmen:** 16% ranked in the top 10 percent of their high school class; 44% were in the top 25 percent, and 78% were in the top half. (Proportion submitting class standing: 92%.) **First-year students who submitted SAT scores:** 49%. Scores (25/75 percentile): Verbal: 440-530, Math: 440-540, Combined: 880-1070. **First-year students submitting ACT scores:** 68%. Scores (25/75 percentile): English: 17-25, Math: 17-24, Composite: 18-24.

ACADEMICS

Year founded: 1912. **Academic calendar:** Other. **Degrees offered:** certificate, bachelor's. **Most popular majors:** 22% education, 16% business, management, marketing, and related support services, 14% theology and religious vocations, 9% security and protective services, 7% health professions and related clinical sciences. **Major fields of study:** biological and biomedical sciences; business, management, marketing, and related support services; communication, journalism, and related programs; education; English language and literature/letters; foreign languages, literatures, and linguistics; health professions and related clinical sciences; history; liberal arts and sciences studies, and humanities; mathematics and statistics; parks, recreation, leisure, and fitness studies; philosophy and religious studies; physical sciences; psychology; social sciences; theology and religious vocations; visual and performing arts. **Areas of required coursework:** arts/fine arts, humanities, mathematics, English (including composition), sciences (biological or physical), history, social science, other. **Pre-professional programs:** pre-law, pre-dentistry, pre-medicine, pre-theology, pre-veterinary science, pre-optometry, pre-pharmacy. **Special academic programs:** accelerated program, double major, dual enrollment, exchange student program (domestic), honors program, independent study, internships, liberal arts/career combination, study abroad, teacher certificate program. **Teacher certification offered in:** early childhood, elementary, middle/junior high, secondary. **Faculty and instruction (2005-2006):** Total instructional faculty: 66 full-time, 41 part-time (59% men; 41% women; 10% minorities). Full-time faculty with Ph.D. or other terminal degree: 85%. Student/faculty ratio: 15/1. Classes of fewer than 20 students: 43%; of 20 to 49 students: 54%; of 50 or more students: 3%. **Advanced Placement and International Baccalaureate credit:** AP tests may be used for: Credit only. Scores accepted: 3, 4, 5. International Baccalaureate exams may be used for: Credit and/or placement. **Freshmen returning for sophomore year:** 60%. **Graduation rates:** Four-year: 26%; five-year: 45%; six-year: 42%. **Graduate study:** 44% of students pursue further study within five years.

COSTS AND FINANCIAL AID

Financial aid office: (903) 923-2137. **Expenses (2006-2007):** Tuition and fees 2006-2007: $13,720; room/board: $4,190. Estimated books and supplies: $800; transportation: $639; personal expenses: $1,319. **Financial aid:** Priority filing date for institution's financial aid form: June 1. In 2005-2006, 92% of undergraduates applied for financial aid. Of those, 77% were determined to have financial need; 26% had their need fully met. Average financial aid package (proportion receiving): $11,930 (77%). Average amount of gift aid, such as scholarships or grants (proportion receiving): $7,492 (61%). Average amount of self-help aid, such as work study or loans (proportion receiving): $3,927 (59%). Average need-based loan (excluding PLUS or other private loans): $3,743. Among students who received need-based aid, the average percentage of need met: 85%. Among students who received aid based on merit, the average award (and the proportion receiving): $5,768 (16%). Average amount of debt of borrowers graduating in 2005: $16,777. Proportion who borrowed: 81%.

CAMPUS LIFE AND EXTRACURRICULAR ACTIVITIES

Campus housing available (% using): women's dorms (26%), men's dorms (18%), apartments for married students (4%), apartment for single students (52%). Students who live in college-owned, operated, or affiliated housing: 71%. **Student employment:** During the 2005-2006 academic year, 20% of undergraduates worked on campus. Average per-year earnings: $1,604.

Clubs and organizations: Number of student organizations: 36. Activities include: choral groups, concert band, drama/theater, jazz band, literary magazine, marching band, music ensembles, musical theater, opera, pep band, student government, student newspaper, symphony orchestra, yearbook. Number of fraternities: 2; sororities: 2. Proportion of men in fraternities: 2%; of women in sororities: 3%. Average proportion of students who stay on campus on weekends: 20%. **Sports program (2005-2006):** Member of NCAA II. **Men's intercollegiate varsity sports:** baseball, basketball, cross-country, football, soccer. **Women's intercollegiate varsity sports:** basketball, cross-country, soccer, softball, volleyball.

SERVICES AND FACILITIES

Basic services: nonremedial tutoring, placement service, health insurance. **Remedial assistance:** math, writing, study skills. **Counseling services:** minority student, career, personal, academic, psychological, religious. **For learning-disabled students:** School does not offer a structured program with separate admission and additional fees. Total undergraduates in learning-disabled program or receiving services: 24. Services include: reading machines, tape recorders, note-taking services, oral tests, extended time for tests, tutors, priority seating, texts on tape, other testing accomodations. **Library:** Number of titles: 115,354; number of current serial subscriptions: 300. **Information technology resources:** Students are not required to lease or own a computer. Number of campus computers available to all students: 206. School has a wireless network. Approximate number of users that can be accommodated: 800. Proportion of college-owned housing units wired for high-speed internet access: 100%. **Campus safety:** Security services offered: 24-hour foot-and-vehicle patrols, late-night transport/escort service, 24-hour emergency telephones, lighted pathways/sidewalks, controlled dormitory access (key, security card, etc).

TRANSFER AND INTERNATIONAL STUDENTS

Transfer students: May apply for admission for the following academic terms: Fall, Spring, Summer. Applicants need a minimum number of credits to apply. For fall 2005: Transfer applications received: 249. Transfer applicants offered admission: 180. Transfer applicants enrolled: 104. **International students:** Number of foreign undergraduates: 7 (1% of student body). Number of countries represented: 11. Minimum TOEFL score required: 500 (paper); 173 (computer). Average TOEFL score: 575 (paper).

Hardin-Simmons University

- **Address:** 2200 Hickory, Abilene, TX 79698-1000
- **Website:** http://www.hsutx.edu/
- **Private; Religious affiliation:** Baptist
- **Enrollment:** 1,779 full-time; 212 part-time

KEY STATS

✔ **U.S News College Ranking:** 38, Universities–Master's (West)
✔ **SAT Score (25th/75th percentile):** 930-1150
✔ **Tuition:** 2006-2007: $15,626

Selectivity: Selective	**Room/board:** $4,580
Acceptance rate: 66%	**Average debt:** $26,144
Student/faculty ratio: 15/1	**Proportion who borrowed:** 72%

UNDERGRADUATE STUDENT BODY STATS

2005-2006 enrollment: 1,779 full-time; 212 part-time. Men: 45%; women: 55%. **Ethnic makeup:** African American: 5%; American-Indian: 1%; Asian American: 1%; Hispanic: 10%; White: 83%. **Religious preference:** Roman Catholic: 6%; Protestant: 12%; No preference: 2%; Unknown: 15%; Baptist: 55%; Non denominational : 10%.

ADMISSIONS FACTS AND FIGURES

Phone: (325) 670-1206. **Email:** enroll@hsutx.edu. **Website:** http://www.hsutx.edu/. **Application deadlines for fall 2007:** Regular decision: Rolling. Early decision: Not offered. Early action: Not offered. Admission can be deferred. **Application fee:** $50. Common application is not accepted. **To apply online, go to:** http://www.hsutx.edu/admissions/apply/. **Admissions requirements/recommendations:** High school units required (recommended): English: 3; Mathematics: 2; Science: 2; Social studies: 2; Academic electives: 7; Total units: 16. Tests: The college uses SAT or ACT scores in admissions decisions. Either SAT or ACT required. For admission to the fall 2007 entering class, the school will accept: ACT with writing.

Campus visit: Recommended. Admissions interview: Neither required nor recommended. Off-campus interview: Not available. **Factors that count in admissions decisions:** *Academic:* Secondary school record: Considered. Class rank: Very important. Letters of recommendation: Important. Standardized test scores: Very important. Essay: Not considered. *Nonacademic:* Interview: Not considered. Extracurricular activities: Considered. Talent/ability: Important. Character/personal qualities: Important. Alumni/ae relationship: Considered. Geographical residence: Not considered. State residency: Not considered. Religious affiliation/commitment: Considered. Minority status: Not considered. Volunteer work: Not considered. Work experience: Not considered. **Other schools with the greatest overlap in applicants:** Abilene Christian University; Baylor University; Texas A&M University–College Station; Texas Tech University; University of Texas–Austin. **Admissions statistics for the fall 2005 entering class:** Total applicants: 1,179. Total accepted: 782. Freshmen enrolled: 436; 3% were from out of state. Overall acceptance rate: 66%. **Credentials of fall 2005 freshmen:** 21% ranked in the top 10 percent of their high school class; 45% were in the top 25 percent, and 77% were in the top half. (Proportion submitting class standing: 92%.) **Average high school grade point average:** 3.6. **First-year students who submitted SAT scores:** 70%. Scores (25/75 percentile): Verbal: 460-580, Math: 470-570, Combined: 930-1150. **First-year students submitting ACT scores:** 66%. Scores (25/75 percentile): English: 18-24, Math: 18-25, Composite: 19-24.

ACADEMICS

Year founded: 1891. **Academic calendar:** Semester. **Degrees offered:** bachelor's, post-bachelor's certificate, master's, first professional, doctorate. **Most popular majors:** 18% education, 13% business, management, marketing, and related support services, 9% health professions and related clinical sciences, 8% parks, recreation, leisure, and fitness studies, 8% visual and performing arts. **Major fields of study:** agriculture, agriculture operations, and related sciences; biological and biomedical sciences; business, management, marketing, and related support services; communication, journalism, and related programs; computer and information sciences and support services; education; English language and literature/letters; foreign languages, literatures, and linguistics; health professions and related clinical sciences; history; legal professions and studies; mathematics and statistics; natural resources and conservation; parks, recreation, leisure, and fitness studies; philosophy and religious studies; physical sciences; psychology; public administration and social service professions; security and protective services; social sciences; theology and religious vocations; visual and performing arts. **Areas of required coursework:** arts/fine arts, humanities, computer literacy, mathematics, English (including composition), sciences (biological or physical), history, social science, other. **Pre-professional programs:** pre-law, pre-dentistry, pre-medicine, pre-theology, pre-pharmacy, other. **Special academic programs (% participation):** accelerated program (2.9%), cross-registration (16.3%), distance learning (0%), double major (8.2%), dual enrollment (1%), honors program, independent study (17.3%), internships (34.3%), study abroad (8.8%), teacher certificate program (18%). **Teacher certification offered in:** early childhood, special education, elementary, middle/junior high, secondary. **Cooperative education programs:** agriculture, other. **Faculty and instruction (2005-2006):** Total instructional faculty: 138 full-time, 48 part-time (61% men; 39% women; 3% minorities). Full-time faculty with Ph.D. or other terminal degree: 74%. Student/faculty ratio: 15/1. Classes of fewer than 20 students: 54%; of 20 to 49 students: 45%; of 50 or more students: 1%. **Advanced Placement and International Baccalaureate credit:** AP tests may be used for: Credit only. Scores accepted: 3, 4, 5. **Freshmen returning for sophomore year:** 67%. **Graduation rates:** Four-year: 27%; five-year: 48%; six-year: 48%. **Graduate study:** 34% of students pursue further study immediately upon graduation; 20% within one year; 22% within five years. Fields in which graduates pursue further study: Master of Business Administration (MBA), 13%; law, 2%; medicine, 19%; dentistry, 1%; engineering, 1%; theology (or the seminary), 14%; education, 21%; arts and sciences, 7%.

COSTS AND FINANCIAL AID

Financial aid office: (325) 670-5891. **Expenses (2006-2007):** Tuition and fees 2006-2007: $15,626; room/board: $4,580. Estimated books and supplies: $750; transportation: $1,056; personal expenses: $1,482. **Financial aid:** Priority filing date for institution's financial aid form: March 15. In 2005-2006, 95% of undergraduates applied for financial aid. Of those, 69% were determined to have financial need; 20% had their need fully met. Average financial aid package (proportion receiving): $13,530 (69%). Average amount of gift aid, such as scholarships or grants (proportion receiving): $4,812 (52%). Average amount of self-help aid, such as work study or loans (proportion receiving): $5,308 (64%). Average need-based loan (excluding

PLUS or other private loans): $3,803. Among students who received need-based aid, the average percentage of need met: 70%. Among students who received aid based on merit, the average award (and the proportion receiving): $3,751 (13%). Average amount of debt of borrowers graduating in 2005: $26,144. Proportion who borrowed: 72%.

CAMPUS LIFE AND EXTRACURRICULAR ACTIVITIES
Campus housing available (% using): women's dorms (45%), men's dorms (40%), apartments for married students (0%), apartment for single students (9%), other housing options (6%). Students who live in college-owned, operated, or affiliated housing: 43%. **Student employment:** During the 2005-2006 academic year, 0% of undergraduates worked on campus. Average per-year earnings: $0. **Clubs and organizations:** Number of student organizations: 0. Activities include: choral groups, concert band, drama/theater, jazz band, literary magazine, marching band, music ensembles, musical theater, opera, student government, student newspaper, symphony orchestra, yearbook. Number of fraternities: 4; sororities: 4. Proportion of men in fraternities: 8%; of women in sororities: 11%. Average proportion of students who stay on campus on weekends: 80%. **Sports program (2005-2006):** Member of NCAA III. *Men's intercollegiate varsity sports:* baseball, basketball, cheerleading, football, golf, soccer, tennis. *Women's intercollegiate varsity sports:* basketball, golf, soccer, softball, tennis, volleyball.

SERVICES AND FACILITIES
Basic services: nonremedial tutoring, placement service, health service. **Remedial assistance:** reading, math, writing, study skills, other. **Counseling services:** minority student, career, military, personal, veteran student, academic, older student, psychological, birth control, religious. **For learning-disabled students:** School does not offer a structured program with separate admission and additional fees. Total undergraduates in learning-disabled program or receiving services: 30. Services include: remedial math, remedial English, remedial reading, tape recorders, untimed tests, note-taking services, oral tests, readers, extended time for tests, tutors, other. **Library:** Number of titles: 216,429; number of current serial subscriptions: 35,567. **Information technology resources:** Students are not required to lease or own a computer. Number of campus computers available to all students: 200. School has a wireless network. Approximate number of users that can be accommodated: 300. Proportion of college-owned housing units wired for high-speed internet access: 100%. **Campus safety:** Security services offered: 24-hour foot-and-vehicle patrols, late-night transport/escort service, 24-hour emergency telephones, lighted pathways/sidewalks, controlled dormitory access (key, security card, etc.).

TRANSFER AND INTERNATIONAL STUDENTS
Transfer students: May apply for admission for the following academic terms: Fall, Spring, Summer. Applicants need a minimum number of credits to apply. For fall 2005: Transfer applications received: 382. Transfer applicants offered admission: 255. Transfer applicants enrolled: 168. **International students:** Number of foreign undergraduates: 9. Number of countries represented: 8. Minimum TOEFL score required: 550 (paper); 213 (computer). Average TOEFL score: 590 (paper).

Houston Baptist University

- **Address:** 7502 Fondren Road, Houston, TX 77074-3298
- **Website:** http://www.hbu.edu
- **Private; Religious affiliation:** Baptist
- **Enrollment:** 1,653 full-time; 279 part-time

KEY STATS
✔ **U.S News College Ranking:** 49, Universities–Master's (West)
✔ **SAT Score (25th/75th percentile):** 1000-1230
✔ **Tuition:** 2006-2007: $16,500

Selectivity: Selective	Room/board: $4,500
Acceptance rate: 65%	Average debt: $18,238
Student/faculty ratio: 15/1	Proportion who borrowed: 75%

UNDERGRADUATE STUDENT BODY STATS
2005-2006 enrollment: 1,653 full-time; 279 part-time. Men: 33%; women: 67%. **Ethnic makeup:** African American: 20%; Asian American: 13%; Hispanic: 14%; White: 46%; International: 6%. **Religious preference:**

Roman Catholic: 15%; Protestant: 8%; Jewish: 1%; Baptist: 42%; Other: 34%.

ADMISSIONS FACTS AND FIGURES
Phone: (281) 649-3211. **Email:** unadm@hbu.edu. **Website:** http://www.hbu.edu. **Application deadlines for fall 2007:** Regular decision: Rolling. Early decision: Not offered. Early action: Not offered. Admission can be deferred. **Application fee:** $25. Common application is not accepted. **Admissions requirements/recommendations:** High school units required (recommended): English: (4); Mathematics: (3); Science: (3); Foreign language: (2); Social studies: (2); History: (2); Academic electives: (2); Total units: (18). Tests: The college uses SAT or ACT scores in admissions decisions. Either SAT or ACT required. For admission to the fall 2007 entering class, the school will accept: ACT with writing, ACT without writing. Campus visit: Recommended. Admissions interview: Recommended. Off-campus interview: May be arranged. **Factors that count in admissions decisions:** *Academic:* Secondary school record: Very important. Class rank: Important. Letters of recommendation: Very important. Standardized test scores: Very important. Essay: Very important. *Nonacademic:* Interview: Considered. Extracurricular activities: Important. Talent/ability: Important. Character/personal qualities: Considered. Alumni/ae relationship: Considered. Geographical residence: Important. State residency: Not considered. Religious affiliation/commitment: Important. Minority status: Not considered. Volunteer work: Important. Work experience: Not considered. **Admissions statistics for the fall 2005 entering class:** Total applicants: 867. Total accepted: 567. Freshmen enrolled: 313; 2% were from out of state. Overall acceptance rate: 65%. **Credentials of fall 2005 freshmen:** 24% ranked in the top 10 percent of their high school class; 44% were in the top 25 percent, and 79% were in the top half. (Proportion submitting class standing: 73%.) **First-year students who submitted SAT scores:** 88%. Scores (25/75 percentile): Verbal: 500-610, Math: 500-620, Combined: 1000-1230. **First-year students submitting ACT scores:** 39%. Scores (25/75 percentile): English: 18-25, Math: 18-25, Composite: 19-25.

ACADEMICS
Year founded: 1960. **Academic calendar:** Quarter. **Degrees offered:** associate, bachelor's, master's. **Most popular majors:** 32% business, management, marketing, and related support services, 12% biological and biomedical sciences, 11% psychology, 10% education, 2% philosophy and religious studies. **Major fields of study:** biological and biomedical sciences; business, management, marketing, and related support services; communication, journalism, and related programs; education; English language and literature/letters; family and consumer sciences/human sciences; foreign languages, literatures, and linguistics; health professions and related clinical sciences; history; liberal arts and sciences studies, and humanities; mathematics and statistics; multi/interdisciplinary studies; parks, recreation, leisure, and fitness studies; philosophy and religious studies; physical sciences; psychology; social sciences; visual and performing arts. **Areas of required coursework:** arts/fine arts, humanities, computer literacy, mathematics, English (including composition), foreign languages, sciences (biological or physical), social science, other. **Pre-professional programs:** pre-law, pre-dentistry, pre-medicine, pre-optometry, pre-pharmacy, other. **Special academic programs (% participation):** accelerated program (1%), double major (81%), English as a Second Language (ESL) (2%), honors program (0%), internships (25%), study abroad (5%), teacher certificate program (14%). **Teacher certification offered in:** early childhood, special education, elementary, middle/junior high, secondary, bilingual/bicultural. **Reserve Officers Training Corps (ROTC):** Army ROTC: Offered at cooperating institution (University of Houston); Navy ROTC: Offered at cooperating institution (Rice University). **Faculty and instruction (2005-2006):** Total instructional faculty: 103 full-time, 66 part-time (53% men; 47% women; 17% minorities). Full-time faculty with Ph.D. or other terminal degree: 81%. Student/faculty ratio: 15/1. Classes of fewer than 20 students: 56%; of 20 to 49 students: 43%; of 50 or more students: 1%. **Advanced Placement and International Baccalaureate credit:** AP tests may be used for: Credit only. Scores accepted: 3, 4, 5. International Baccalaureate exams may be used for: Credit and/or placement. **Freshmen returning for sophomore year:** 72%. **Graduation rates:** Four-year: 33%; five-year: 52%; six-year: 50%.

COSTS AND FINANCIAL AID
Financial aid office: (281) 649-3389. **Expenses (2006-2007):** Tuition and fees 2006-2007: $16,500; room/board: $4,500. Estimated books and supplies: $1,131; transportation: $866; personal expenses: $1,738. **Financial aid:** Priority filing date for institution's financial aid form: March 1; deadline: April 15. In 2005-2006, 100% of undergraduates applied for financial aid. Of those, 87% were determined to have financial need; 14% had their need

fully met. Average financial aid package (proportion receiving): $10,935 (87%). Average amount of gift aid, such as scholarships or grants (proportion receiving): $7,531 (84%). Average amount of self-help aid, such as work study or loans (proportion receiving): $4,412 (72%). Average need-based loan (excluding PLUS or other private loans): $3,434. Among students who received need-based aid, the average percentage of need met: 61%. Among students who received aid based on merit, the average award (and the proportion receiving): $14,816 (13%). The average athletic scholarship (and the proportion receiving): $6,440 (1%). Average amount of debt of borrowers graduating in 2005: $18,238. Proportion who borrowed: 75%.

CAMPUS LIFE AND EXTRACURRICULAR ACTIVITIES

Campus housing available (% using): women's dorms (25%), men's dorms (15%), apartment for single students (60%). Students who live in college-owned, operated, or affiliated housing: 32%. **Student employment:** During the 2005-2006 academic year, 15% of undergraduates worked on campus. Average per-year earnings: $1,075. **Clubs and organizations:** Number of student organizations: 52. Activities include: choral groups, concert band, drama/theater, music ensembles, pep band, student government, student newspaper, symphony orchestra, yearbook. Number of fraternities: 3; sororities: 2. Proportion of men in fraternities: 5%; of women in sororities: 5%. Average proportion of students who stay on campus on weekends: 50%. **Sports program (2005-2006):** Member of NAIA. *Men's intercollegiate varsity sports:* baseball, basketball. *Women's intercollegiate varsity sports:* basketball, softball, volleyball.

SERVICES AND FACILITIES

Basic services: nonremedial tutoring, placement service, health service, health insurance. **Remedial assistance:** study skills. **Counseling services:** minority student, career, personal, academic, older student, psychological, religious. **For learning-disabled students:** School does not offer a structured program with separate admission and additional fees. Total undergraduates in learning-disabled program or receiving services: 39. Services include: remedial math, remedial English, remedial reading, diagnostic testing service, untimed tests, oral tests, learning center, extended time for tests. **Library:** Number of titles: 218,505; number of current serial subscriptions: 25,000. **Information technology resources:** Students are not required to lease or own a computer. Number of campus computers available to all students: 100. School has a wireless network. Proportion of college-owned housing units wired for high-speed internet access: 75%. **Campus safety:** Security services offered: 24-hour foot-and-vehicle patrols, late-night transport/escort service, 24-hour emergency telephones, lighted pathways/sidewalks, controlled dormitory access (key, security card, etc.).

TRANSFER AND INTERNATIONAL STUDENTS

Transfer students: May apply for admission for the following academic terms: Fall, Winter, Spring, Summer. Applicants need a minimum number of credits to apply. For fall 2005: Transfer applicants enrolled: 298. **International students:** Number of foreign undergraduates: 109 (6% of student body). Number of countries represented: 37. Minimum TOEFL score required: 550 (paper); 213 (computer).

Howard Payne University

- **Address:** 1000 Fisk Avenue, Brownwood, TX 76801
- **Website:** http://www.hputx.edu
- **Private; Religious affiliation:** Baptist
- **Enrollment:** 1,043 full-time; 321 part-time

KEY STATS
- ✔ **U.S News College Ranking:** 16, Comp. Coll.–Bachelor's (West)
- ✔ **SAT Score (25th/75th percentile):** 783-1270
- ✔ **Tuition:** 2006-2007: $12,530

Selectivity: Selective	**Room/board:** $4,794
Acceptance rate: 71%	**Average debt:** $19,100.
Student/faculty ratio: 12/1	**Proportion who borrowed:** 64%

UNDERGRADUATE STUDENT BODY STATS

2005-2006 enrollment: 1,043 full-time; 321 part-time. Men: 49%; women: 51%. **Ethnic makeup:** African American: 6%; American-Indian: 1%; Asian American: 1%; Hispanic: 14%; White: 78%. **Religious preference:** Roman Catholic: 4%; Protestant: 22%; No preference: 7%; Unknown: 4%; Baptist: 63%.

ADMISSIONS FACTS AND FIGURES

Phone: (325) 649-8027. **Email:** enroll@hputx.edu. **Website:** http://www.hputx.edu. **Application deadlines for fall 2007:** Regular decision: August 15. Early decision: Not offered. Early action: Not offered. Admission can be deferred. **Application fee:** $25. Common application is accepted. **Admissions requirements/recommendations:** High school units required (recommended): English: (4); Mathematics: (3); Science: (2); Social studies: (3); History: (10); Total units: 15 (22). Tests: The college uses SAT or ACT scores in admissions decisions. Either SAT or ACT required. For admission to the fall 2007 entering class, the school will accept ACT without writing. Campus visit: Recommended. Admissions interview: Neither required nor recommended. Off-campus interview: May be arranged. **Factors that count in admissions decisions:** *Academic:* Secondary school record: Very important. Class rank: Considered. Letters of recommendation: Important. Standardized test scores: Very important. Essay: Not considered. *Nonacademic:* Interview: Important. Extracurricular activities: Not considered. Talent/ability: Not considered. Character/personal qualities: Considered. Alumni/ae relationship: Not considered. Geographical residence: Not considered. State residency: Not considered. Religious affiliation/commitment: Not considered. Minority status: Not considered. Volunteer work: Not considered. Work experience: Not considered. **Other schools with the greatest overlap in applicants:** East Texas Baptist University; Hardin-Simmons University; MacMurray College; University of Mary Hardin-Baylor; Wayland Baptist University. **Admissions statistics for the fall 2005 entering class:** Total applicants: 1,076. Total accepted: 763. Freshmen enrolled: 297; 6% were from out of state. Overall acceptance rate: 71%. **Credentials of fall 2005 freshmen:** 16% ranked in the top 10 percent of their high school class; 39% were in the top 25 percent, and 73% were in the top half. (Proportion submitting class standing: 84%.) **Average high school grade point average:** 3.5. **First-year students who submitted SAT scores:** 62%. Scores (25/75 percentile): Verbal: 397-645, Math: 386-625, Combined: 783-1270. **First-year students submitting ACT scores:** 58%. Scores (25/75 percentile): English: 14-27, Math: 16-25, Composite: 16-26.

ACADEMICS

Year founded: 1889. **Academic calendar:** Semester. **Degrees offered:** certificate, associate, bachelor's. **Most popular majors:** 9% elementary education and teaching, 7% communication studies/speech communication and rhetoric, 7% marketing/marketing management, 7% social sciences, 6% psychology. **Major fields of study:** biological and biomedical sciences; business, management, marketing, and related support services; communication, journalism, and related programs; computer and information sciences and support services; education; English language and literature/letters; foreign languages, literatures, and linguistics; health professions and related clinical sciences; history; legal professions and studies; liberal arts and sciences studies, and humanities; mathematics and statistics; parks, recreation, leisure, and fitness studies; philosophy and religious studies; physical sciences; psychology; social sciences; theology and religious vocations; visual and performing arts. **Areas of required coursework:** arts/fine arts, humanities, computer literacy, mathematics, English (including composition), sciences (biological or physical), social science. **Pre-professional programs:** pre-law, pre-medicine, pre-theology. **Special academic programs:** accelerated program, cooperative (work-study plan) program, distance learning, double major, dual enrollment, English as a Second Language (ESL), honors program, independent study, study abroad, teacher certificate program. **Teacher certification offered in:** elementary, middle/junior high, secondary, bilingual/bicultural. **Faculty and instruction (2005-2006):** Total instructional faculty: 75 full-time, 61 part-time. Full-time faculty with Ph.D. or other terminal degree: 49%. Student/faculty ratio: 12/1. Classes of fewer than 20 students: 76%; of 20 to 49 students: 24%; of 50 or more students: 0%. **Advanced Placement and International Baccalaureate credit:** AP tests may be used for: Credit only. Scores accepted: 3, 4, 5. **Freshmen returning for sophomore year:** 59%. **Graduation rates:** Four-year: 24%; five-year: 36%; six-year: 37%.

COSTS AND FINANCIAL AID

Financial aid office: (325) 649-8014. **Expenses (2006-2007):** Tuition and fees 2006-2007: $12,530; room/board: $4,794. Estimated books and supplies: $1,000; transportation: $800; personal expenses: $1,500. **Financial aid:** Priority filing date for institution's financial aid form: March 15. In 2005-2006, 87% of undergraduates applied for financial aid. Of those, 75% were determined to have financial need; 24% had their need fully met. Average financial aid package (proportion receiving): $11,638 (75%). Average amount of gift aid, such as scholarships or grants (proportion receiving): $7,582 (73%). Average amount of self-help aid, such as work study or loans (proportion receiving): $4,841 (60%). Average need-based loan (excluding PLUS or other private loans): $3,475. Among students who received need-based aid, the average percentage of need met: 81%. Among students who received aid based on merit, the average award (and the proportion receiving): $5,252 (19%). The average athletic scholarship (and the proportion receiving): $0 (0%). Average amount of debt of borrowers graduating in 2005: $19,100. Proportion who borrowed: 64%.

CAMPUS LIFE AND EXTRACURRICULAR ACTIVITIES
Campus housing available (% using): women's dorms (39%), men's dorms (45%), apartment for single students (16%). Students who live in college-owned, operated, or affiliated housing: 46%. Average per-year earnings: $1,200. **Clubs and organizations:** Number of student organizations: 31. Activities include: choral groups, concert band, drama/theater, jazz band, literary magazine, marching band, music ensembles, musical theater, opera, radio station, student government, student newspaper, yearbook. Number of fraternities: 5; sororities: 6. Proportion of men in fraternities: 14%; of women in sororities: 16%. Average proportion of students who stay on campus on weekends: 50%. **Sports program (2005-2006):** Member of NCAA III. *Men's intercollegiate varsity sports:* baseball, basketball, football, tennis, track and field (outdoor). *Women's intercollegiate varsity sports:* basketball, softball, tennis, track and field (outdoor), volleyball.

SERVICES AND FACILITIES
Basic services: nonremedial tutoring, health service. **Remedial assistance:** reading, math, writing, study skills. **Counseling services:** personal, academic, older student, religious. **For learning-disabled students:** School does not offer a structured program with separate admission and additional fees. Services include: remedial math, remedial English, remedial reading, tape recorders, untimed tests, note-taking services, oral tests, learning center, extended time for tests, tutors, priority seating, other testing accomodations. **Library:** Number of titles: 118,825; number of current serial subscriptions: 598. **Information technology resources:** Students are not required to lease or own a computer. Number of campus computers available to all students: 250. School has a wireless network. Approximate number of users that can be accommodated: 800. Proportion of college-owned housing units wired for high-speed internet access: 100%. **Campus safety:** Security services offered: 24-hour foot-and-vehicle patrols, 24-hour emergency telephones, controlled dormitory access (key, security card, etc).

TRANSFER AND INTERNATIONAL STUDENTS
Transfer students: May apply for admission for the following academic terms: Fall, Spring, Summer. Applicants do not need a minimum number of credits to apply. For fall 2005: Transfer applications received: 202. Transfer applicants offered admission: 114. Transfer applicants enrolled: 83. **International students:** Number of countries represented: 6. Minimum TOEFL score required: 500 (paper); 173 (computer). Average TOEFL score: 550 (paper).

Huston-Tillotson University

- **Address:** 900 Chicon Street, Austin, TX 78702
- **Website:** http://www.htu.edu/
- **Private; Religious affiliation:** United Church of Christ/Methodist
- **Enrollment:** 625 full-time; 50 part-time

KEY STATS
✔ **U.S News College Ranking:** fourth tier, Comp. Coll.–Bachelor's (West)
✔ **ACT Score (25th/75th percentile):** 14-17
✔ **Tuition:** 2006-2007: $9,210

Selectivity: Least selective	**Room/board:** $8,450
Acceptance rate: 56%	**Average debt:** N/A
Student/faculty ratio: N/A	**Proportion who borrowed:** N/A

UNDERGRADUATE STUDENT BODY STATS
2005-2006 enrollment: 625 full-time; 50 part-time. Men: 47%; women: 53%. **Ethnic makeup:** African American: 75%; Asian American: 1%; Hispanic: 13%; White: 9%; International: 2%.

ADMISSIONS FACTS AND FIGURES
Phone: (512) 505-3028. **Email:** admission@htu.edu. **Website:** http://www.htu.edu/. **Application deadlines for fall 2007:** Regular decision: August 1. Early decision: Not offered. Early action: Not offered. Admission can be deferred. **Application fee:** $25. Common application is not accepted. **Admissions requirements/recommendations:** High school units required (recommended): English: 4; Mathematics: 3; Science: 2; Foreign language: (2); Social studies: 3; Academic electives: 1; Total units: 22. Tests: The college uses SAT or ACT scores in admissions decisions. Either SAT or ACT required. For admission to the fall 2007 entering class, the school will accept: ACT with writing, ACT without writing. Campus visit: Recommended. Admissions interview: Recommended. Off-campus interview: May be arranged. **Factors that count in admissions decisions:** *Academic:* Secondary school record: Very important. Class rank: Considered. Letters of recommendation: Considered. Standardized test scores: Very important. Essay: Important. *Nonacademic:* Interview: Important. Extracurricular activities: Considered. Talent/ability: Considered. Character/personal qualities: Not considered. Alumni/ae relationship: Considered. Geographical residence: Not considered. State residency: Not considered. Religious affiliation/commitment: Important. Minority status: Not considered. Volunteer work: Not considered. Work experience: Not considered. **Other schools with the greatest overlap in applicants:** Paul Quinn College; Prairie View A&M University; Texas State University–San Marcos; Wiley College. **Admissions statistics for the fall 2005 entering class:** Total applicants: 409. Total accepted: 227. Freshmen enrolled: 168; Overall acceptance rate: 56%. **First-year students who submitted SAT scores:** 50%. Scores (25/75 percentile): Verbal: 360-440, Math: 340-468, Combined: 700-908. **First-year students submitting ACT scores:** 70%. Scores (25/75 percentile): English: 10-16, Math: 15-17, Composite: 14-17.

ACADEMICS
Year founded: 1875. **Academic calendar:** Semester. **Degrees offered:** certificate, bachelor's. **Most popular majors:** 23% business, management, marketing, and related support services, 16% computer and information sciences and support services, 11% parks, recreation, leisure, and fitness studies. **Major fields of study:** biological and biomedical sciences; computer and information sciences and support services; education; English language and literature/letters; history; mathematics and statistics; parks, recreation, leisure, and fitness studies; physical sciences; psychology; security and protective services; social sciences; visual and performing arts. **Areas of required coursework:** arts/fine arts, humanities, computer literacy, mathematics, English (including composition), philosophy, foreign languages, sciences (biological or physical), history, social science. **Special academic programs:** cross-registration, distance learning, double major, dual enrollment, external degree program, honors program, independent study, internships, liberal arts/career combination, student-designed major, study abroad. **Teacher certification offered in:** early childhood, special education, elementary, middle/junior high, secondary. **Reserve Officers Training Corps (ROTC):** Army ROTC: Offered at cooperating institution (University of Texas at Austin); Navy ROTC: Offered at cooperating institution (University of Texas at Austin); Air Force ROTC: Offered at cooperating institution (University of Texas at Austin). **Advanced Placement and International Baccalaureate credit:** Scores accepted: 4, 5. **Freshmen returning for sophomore year:** 52%. **Graduation rates:** Four-year: 5%; five-year: 12%; six-year: 17%.

COSTS AND FINANCIAL AID
Financial aid office: (512) 505-3031. **Expenses (2006-2007):** Tuition and fees 2006-2007: $9,210; room/board: $8,450.

CAMPUS LIFE AND EXTRACURRICULAR ACTIVITIES
Campus housing available: women's dorms, men's dorms. **Clubs and organizations:** Number of student organizations: 17. Activities include: choral groups, literary magazine, music ensembles, student government, student newspaper. Number of fraternities: 4; sororities: 4. Average proportion of students who stay on campus on weekends: 25%. **Sports program (2005-2006):** Member of NAIA. *Men's intercollegiate varsity sports:* baseball, basketball, soccer, track and field (indoor), track and field (outdoor). *Women's intercollegiate varsity sports:* basketball, cross-country, soccer, swimming and diving, track and field (indoor), track and field (outdoor), volleyball.

SERVICES AND FACILITIES
Basic services: nonremedial tutoring, placement service, health service, health insurance. **Remedial assistance:** reading, math, writing, study skills. **Counseling services:** career, personal, academic, birth control, religious. **For learning-disabled students:** School does not offer a structured program with

separate admission and additional fees. Services include: remedial math, remedial English, remedial reading, diagnostic testing service, untimed tests, oral tests, tutors. **Library:** Number of titles: 88,455; number of current serial subscriptions: 2,353. **Information technology resources:** Students are not required to lease or own a computer. Number of campus computers available to all students: 400. School has a wireless network. **Campus safety:** Security services offered: 24-hour foot-and-vehicle patrols, 24-hour emergency telephones, lighted pathways/sidewalks, controlled dormitory access (key, security card, etc).

TRANSFER AND INTERNATIONAL STUDENTS

Transfer students: May apply for admission for the following academic terms: Fall, Spring, Summer. Applicants do not need a minimum number of credits to apply. **International students:** Number of foreign undergraduates: 14 (2% of student body). Minimum TOEFL score required: 500 (paper); 173 (computer).

Jarvis Christian College

- ■ **Address:** PO Box 1470, Hawkins, TX 75765-1470
- ■ **Website:** http://www.jarvis.edu
- ■ **Private; Religious affiliation:** Disciples of Christ
- ■ **Enrollment:** 559 full-time; 13 part-time

KEY STATS

✔ **U.S News College Ranking:** fourth tier, Comp. Coll.–Bachelor's (West)
✔ **SAT Score:** 740
✔ **Tuition:** 2006-2007: $7,585

Selectivity: Least selective	**Room/board:** $4,810
Acceptance rate: 76%	**Average debt:** $14,600
Student/faculty ratio: 13/1	**Proportion who borrowed:** 74%

UNDERGRADUATE STUDENT BODY STATS

2005-2006 enrollment: 559 full-time; 13 part-time. Men: 46%; women: 54%. **Ethnic makeup:** African American: 98%; Hispanic: 1%; White: 1%. **Religious preference:** Roman Catholic: 2%; Protestant: 68%; No preference: 27%; Disciples of Christ: 3%.

ADMISSIONS FACTS AND FIGURES

Phone: (903) 769-5730. **Email:** Recruitment@jarvis.edu. **Website:** http://www.jarvis.edu. **Application deadlines for fall 2007:** Regular decision: August 1. Early decision: Not offered. Early action: Not offered. Admission cannot be deferred. **Application fee:** $25. Common application is not accepted. **Admissions requirements/recommendations:** High school units required (recommended): English: 3 (3); Mathematics: 2 (2); Science: 1 (1); Foreign language: 0 (0); Social studies: 3 (3); History: 0 (0); Academic electives: 7 (7); Total units: 16 (16). Tests: The college uses SAT or ACT scores in admissions decisions. Neither SAT nor ACT required. For admission to the fall 2007 entering class, the school will accept: ACT with writing, ACT without writing. Campus visit: Recommended. Admissions interview: Recommended. Off-campus interview: May be arranged. **Factors that count in admissions decisions:** *Academic:* Secondary school record: Important. Class rank: Not considered. Letters of recommendation: Considered. Standardized test scores: Important. Essay: Not considered. *Nonacademic:* Interview: Not considered. Extracurricular activities: Considered. Talent/ability: Considered. Character/personal qualities: Considered. Alumni/ae relationship: Not considered. Geographical residence: Not considered. State residency: Not considered. Religious affiliation/commitment: Not considered. Minority status: Not considered. Volunteer work: Not considered. Work experience: Not considered. **Other schools with the greatest overlap in applicants:** Huston-Tillotson University; Paul Quinn College; Texas College; Wiley College. **Admissions statistics for the fall 2005 entering class:** Total applicants: 225. Total accepted: 171. Freshmen enrolled: 98; 0% were from out of state. Overall acceptance rate: 76%. **Size of waiting list:** 0 applicants; enrolled from waiting list: 0. **Credentials of fall 2005 freshmen:** 7% ranked in the top 10 percent of their high school class; 14% were in the top 25 percent, and 29% were in the top half. (Proportion submitting class standing: 73%.) **Average high school grade point average:** 2.6. **First-year students who submitted SAT scores:** 29%. Scores (25/75 percentile): Verbal: N/A, Math: N/A, Combined: N/A. **First-year students submitting ACT scores:** 23%. Scores (25/75 percentile): English: N/A, Math: N/A, Composite: N/A.

ACADEMICS

Year founded: 1912. **Academic calendar:** Semester. **Degrees offered:** bachelor's. **Most popular majors:** 37% business administration and management, 18% social sciences, 16% computer and information sciences, 16% health and physical education, 9% education. **Major fields of study:** biological and biomedical sciences; business, management, marketing, and related support services; computer and information sciences and support services; education; English language and literature/letters; health professions and related clinical sciences; history; mathematics and statistics; philosophy and religious studies; physical sciences; social sciences. **Areas of required coursework:** humanities, computer literacy, mathematics, English (including composition), foreign languages, sciences (biological or physical), history, social science, other. **Pre-professional programs:** pre-law, pre-medicine. **Special academic programs (% participation):** cooperative (work-study plan) program (85%), cross-registration (1%), distance learning (10%), double major (1%), dual enrollment (1%), honors program (1%), internships (5%), student-designed major (1%), study abroad, teacher certificate program (9%). **Teacher certification offered in:** special education, elementary, middle/junior high, secondary. **Cooperative education programs:** business, health professions, social/behavioral science. **Faculty and instruction (2005-2006):** Total instructional faculty: 37 full-time, 8 part-time (62% men; 38% women; 58% minorities). Full-time faculty with Ph.D. or other terminal degree: 49%. Student/faculty ratio: 13/1. Classes of fewer than 20 students: 58%; of 20 to 49 students: 41%; of 50 or more students: 1%. **Advanced Placement and International Baccalaureate credit:** International Baccalaureate exams may be used for: Credit and/or placement. **Freshmen returning for sophomore year:** 54%. **Graduation rates:** Four-year: 11%; five-year: 23%; six-year: 16%. **Graduate study:** 1% of students pursue further study immediately upon graduation; 2% within one year; 3% within five years. Fields in which graduates pursue further study: law, 1%; medicine, 1%; education, 3%.

COSTS AND FINANCIAL AID

Financial aid office: (903) 769-5740. **Expenses (2006-2007):** Tuition and fees 2006-2007: $7,585; room/board: $4,810. Estimated books and supplies: $800; transportation: $0; personal expenses: $1,650. **Financial aid:** Priority filing date for institution's financial aid form: May 15. In 2005-2006, 99% of undergraduates applied for financial aid. Of those, 94% were determined to have financial need; 94% had their need fully met. Average financial aid package (proportion receiving): $9,800 (93%). Average amount of gift aid, such as scholarships or grants (proportion receiving): N/A (85%). Average amount of self-help aid, such as work study or loans (proportion receiving): $1,650 (84%). Average need-based loan (excluding PLUS or other private loans): $3,700. Among students who received need-based aid, the average percentage of need met: 87%. Among students who received aid based on merit, the average award (and the proportion receiving): $11,500 (2%). The average athletic scholarship (and the proportion receiving): $9,200 (1%). Average amount of debt of borrowers graduating in 2005: $14,600. Proportion who borrowed: 74%.

CAMPUS LIFE AND EXTRACURRICULAR ACTIVITIES

Campus housing available (% using): women's dorms (45%), men's dorms (50%), apartments for married students (5%). Students who live in college-owned, operated, or affiliated housing: 84%. **Student employment:** During the 2005-2006 academic year, 2% of undergraduates worked on campus. Average per-year earnings: $5,000. **Clubs and organizations:** Number of student organizations: 20. Activities include: choral groups, drama/theater, music ensembles, student government. Number of fraternities: 4; sororities: 4. Proportion of men in fraternities: 10%; of women in sororities: 10%. Average proportion of students who stay on campus on weekends: 50%. **Sports program (2005-2006):** Member of NAIA. *Men's intercollegiate varsity sports:* baseball, basketball, track and field (outdoor). *Women's intercollegiate varsity sports:* basketball, volleyball.

SERVICES AND FACILITIES

Basic services: nonremedial tutoring, placement service, health service, health insurance. **Remedial assistance:** reading, math, writing, study skills. **Counseling services:** minority student, career, personal, veteran student, academic, older student, psychological, birth control, religious. **For learning-disabled students:** School does not offer a structured program with separate admission and additional fees. Total undergraduates in learning-disabled program or receiving services: 0. Services include: remedial math, remedial English, remedial reading, tape recorders, videotaped classes, diagnostic testing service, oral tests, extended time for tests, tutors. **Library:** Number of titles: 54,170; number of current serial subscriptions: 121. **Information technology resources:** Students are not required to lease or own a computer. Number of campus computers available to all students: 318. School has a wireless network. Approximate number of users that can be accommodated: 850. Proportion of college-owned housing units wired for high-speed internet access: 85%. **Campus safety:** Security services offered: 24-hour foot-and-vehicle patrols, 24-hour emergency telephones, lighted pathways/sidewalks, student patrols, controlled dormitory access (key, security card, etc).

TRANSFER AND INTERNATIONAL STUDENTS
Transfer students: May apply for admission for the following academic terms: Fall, Spring. Applicants do not need a minimum number of credits to apply. For fall 2005: Transfer applications received: 76. Transfer applicants offered admission: 76. Transfer applicants enrolled: 41. **International students:** Number of foreign undergraduates: 0. Number of countries represented: 3. Minimum TOEFL score required: 500 (paper); 173 (computer). Average TOEFL score: 535 (paper).

Lamar University

- **Address:** Lamar Station, Box 10001, Beaumont, TX 77710
- **Website:** http://www.lamar.edu
- **Public**
- **Enrollment:** 6,708 full-time; 2,976 part-time

KEY STATS
✔ **U.S News College Ranking:** fourth tier, Universities–Master's (West)
✔ **SAT Score (25th/75th percentile):** 810-1040
✔ **Tuition:** 2006-2007: $4,722 in state, $12,972 out of state
  Selectivity: Less selective   **Room/board:** $5,888
  Acceptance rate: 67%   **Average debt:** $13,000
  Student/faculty ratio: 21/1   **Proportion who borrowed:** 54%

UNDERGRADUATE STUDENT BODY STATS
2005-2006 enrollment: 6,708 full-time; 2,976 part-time. Men: 40%; women: 60%. **Ethnic makeup:** African American: 27%; American-Indian: 1%; Asian American: 3%; Hispanic: 6%; White: 63%; International: 1%.

ADMISSIONS FACTS AND FIGURES
Phone: (409) 880-8888. **Email:** admissions@hal.lamar.edu. **Website:** http://www.lamar.edu. **Application deadlines for fall 2007:** Regular decision: August 1. Early decision: Not offered. Early action: Not offered. Admission can be deferred. **Application fee:** $25. Common application is accepted. **Admissions requirements/recommendations:** High school units required (recommended): English: 4; Mathematics: 3; Science: 2; Foreign language: 0 (2); Social studies: 3; History: 0; Academic electives: 2; Total units: 14. Tests: The college uses SAT or ACT scores in admissions decisions. Either SAT or ACT required. For admission to the fall 2007 entering class, the school will accept: ACT without writing. Campus visit: Recommended. Admissions interview: Neither required nor recommended. **Factors that count in admissions decisions:** *Academic:* Secondary school record: Very important. Class rank: Very important. Letters of recommendation: Considered. Standardized test scores: Very important. Essay: Considered. *Nonacademic:* Interview: Not considered. Extracurricular activities: Considered. Talent/ability: Considered. Alumni/ae relationship: Not considered. Geographical residence: Not considered. State residency: Not considered. Religious affiliation/commitment: Not considered. Minority status: Not considered. Volunteer work: Not considered. Work experience: Not considered. **Admissions statistics for the fall 2005 entering class:** Total applicants: 5,213. Total accepted: 3,513. Freshmen enrolled: 1,683; 1% were from out of state. Overall acceptance rate: 67%. **Credentials of fall 2005 freshmen:** 12% ranked in the top 10 percent of their high school class; 34% were in the top 25 percent, and 75% were in the top half. (Proportion submitting class standing: 93%.) **First-year students who submitted SAT scores:** 95%. Scores (25/75 percentile): Verbal: 410-520, Math: 400-520, Combined: 810-1040. **First-year students submitting ACT scores:** 5%. Scores (25/75 percentile): English: 15-20, Math: 16-20, Composite: 16-20.

ACADEMICS
Year founded: 1923. **Academic calendar:** Semester. **Degrees offered:** associate, bachelor's, master's, doctorate. **Most popular majors:** 15% multi/interdisciplinary studies, 10% general studies, 4% communication studies/speech communication and rhetoric, 4% management information systems, 4% marketing/marketing management. **Major fields of study:** biological and biomedical sciences; business, management, marketing, and related sup-

port services; communication, journalism, and related programs; computer and information sciences and support services; education; engineering; engineering technologies/technicians; English language and literature/letters; foreign languages, literatures, and linguistics; health professions and related clinical sciences; history; mathematics and statistics; natural resources and conservation; physical sciences; psychology; security and protective services; social sciences; visual and performing arts. **Areas of required coursework:** arts/fine arts, humanities, mathematics, English (including composition), philosophy, sciences (biological or physical), history, social science, other. **Pre-professional programs:** pre-law, pre-dentistry, pre-medicine, pre-veterinary science, pre-optometry, pre-pharmacy. **Teacher certification offered in:** early childhood, special education, elementary, secondary. **Cooperative education programs:** computer science, education, natural science. **Faculty and instruction (2005-2006):** Total instructional faculty: 340 full-time, 158 part-time (53% men; 47% women; 19% minorities). Full-time faculty with Ph.D. or other terminal degree: 71%. Student/faculty ratio: 21/1. Classes of fewer than 20 students: 27%; of 20 to 49 students: 61%; of 50 or more students: 12%. **Advanced Placement and International Baccalaureate credit:** AP tests may be used for: Credit and/or placement. International Baccalaureate exams may be used for: Credit and/or placement. **Freshmen returning for sophomore year:** 68%. **Graduation rates:** Four-year: 9%; five-year: 24%; six-year: 29%.

COSTS AND FINANCIAL AID
Financial aid office: (409) 880-8450. **Expenses (2006-2007):** Tuition and fees 2006-2007: $4,722 in state, $12,972 out of state; room/board: $5,888. Estimated books and supplies: $1,328; transportation: $2,076; personal expenses: $1,948. **Financial aid:** Priority filing date for institution's financial aid form: April 1. In 2005-2006, 70% of undergraduates applied for financial aid. Of those, 47% were determined to have financial need; 6% had their need fully met. Average financial aid package (proportion receiving): $1,237 (40%). Average amount of self-help aid, such as work study or loans (proportion receiving): N/A (16%). Among students who received need-based aid, the average percentage of need met: 30%. Among students who received aid based on merit, the average award (and the proportion receiving): $900 (17%). Average amount of debt of borrowers graduating in 2005: $13,000. Proportion who borrowed: 54%.

CAMPUS LIFE AND EXTRACURRICULAR ACTIVITIES
Campus housing available (% using): coed dorms (100%). Students who live in college-owned, operated, or affiliated housing: 17%. **Clubs and organizations:** Number of student organizations: 119. Activities include: choral groups, concert band, dance, drama/theater, jazz band, literary magazine, music ensembles, musical theater, opera, pep band, radio station, student government, student newspaper, student film society, symphony orchestra, television station. Number of fraternities: 9; sororities: 7. Proportion of men in fraternities: 2%; of women in sororities: 2%. **Sports program (2005-2006):** Member of NCAA I. *Men's intercollegiate varsity sports:* baseball, basketball, cross-country, golf, tennis, track and field (indoor), track and field (outdoor). *Women's intercollegiate varsity sports:* basketball, cross-country, golf, tennis, track and field (indoor), track and field (outdoor), volleyball.

SERVICES AND FACILITIES
Basic services: nonremedial tutoring, placement service, health service, health insurance. **Remedial assistance:** reading, math, writing, study skills. **Counseling services:** minority student, career, veteran student, academic. **For learning-disabled students:** School does not offer a structured program with separate admission and additional fees. Total undergraduates in learning-disabled program or receiving services: 50. Services include: remedial math, remedial English, reading machines, remedial reading, tape recorders, note-taking services, oral tests, readers, extended time for tests, priority registration, priority seating, substitution of courses, texts on tape, exams on tape or computer, other. **Library:** Number of titles: 697,385; number of current serial subscriptions: 2,749. **Information technology resources:** Students are not required to lease or own a computer. Proportion of college-owned housing units wired for high-speed internet access: 100%. **Campus safety:** Security services offered: 24-hour foot-and-vehicle patrols, late-night transport/escort service, 24-hour emergency telephones, lighted pathways/sidewalks, controlled dormitory access (key, security card, etc).

TRANSFER AND INTERNATIONAL STUDENTS
Transfer students: May apply for admission for the following academic terms: Fall, Spring, Summer. Applicants need a minimum number of credits to apply. For fall 2005: Transfer applications received: 1,618. Transfer applicants offered admission: 1,179. Transfer applicants enrolled: 704. **International students:** Number of foreign undergraduates: 73 (1% of stu-

dent body). Minimum TOEFL score required: 525 (paper); 197 (computer). Average TOEFL score: 586 (paper).

LeTourneau University

- **Address:** PO Box 7001, Longview, TX 75607-7001
- **Website:** http://www.letu.edu
- **Private; Religious affiliation:** Christian nondenominational
- **Enrollment:** 1,405 full-time; 2,201 part-time

KEY STATS

✔ **U.S News College Ranking:** 28, Universities–Master's (West)
✔ **SAT Score (25th/75th percentile):** 1020-1300
✔ **Tuition:** 2006-2007: $16,920

Selectivity: More selective	**Room/board:** $6,590
Acceptance rate: 76%	**Average debt:** $28,426
Student/faculty ratio: 14/1	**Proportion who borrowed:** 87%

UNDERGRADUATE STUDENT BODY STATS

2005-2006 enrollment: 1,405 full-time; 2,201 part-time. Men: 44%; women: 56%. **Ethnic makeup:** African American: 22%; Asian American: 1%; Hispanic: 8%; White: 68%; International: 1%. **Religious preference:** Roman Catholic: 2%; Protestant: 93%; Unknown: 3%; Other: 2%.

ADMISSIONS FACTS AND FIGURES

Phone: (903) 233-3400. **Email:** admissions@letu.edu. **Website:** http://www.letu.edu. **Application deadlines for fall 2007:** Regular decision: August 1. Early decision: Not offered. Early action: Not offered. Admission can be deferred. **Application fee:** $25. Common application is not accepted. **Admissions requirements/recommendations:** High school units required (recommended): English: 4 (0); Mathematics: 3 (0); Science: 3 (0); Foreign language: 0 (1); Social studies: 2 (0); History: 1 (0); Academic electives: 0 (2); Total units: 16 (0). Tests: The college uses SAT or ACT scores in admissions decisions. Either SAT or ACT required. For admission to the fall 2007 entering class, the school will accept: ACT with writing, ACT without writing. Campus visit: Recommended. Admissions interview: Neither required nor recommended. Off-campus interview: May be arranged. **Factors that count in admissions decisions:** *Academic:* Secondary school record: Very important. Class rank: Important. Letters of recommendation: Considered. Standardized test scores: Very important. Essay: Important. *Nonacademic:* Interview: Considered. Extracurricular activities: Considered. Talent/ability: Considered. Character/personal qualities: Important. Alumni/ae relationship: Considered. Geographical residence: Not considered. State residency: Not considered. Religious affiliation/commitment: Important. Minority status: Not considered. Volunteer work: Considered. Work experience: Considered. **Other schools with the greatest overlap in applicants:** Baylor University; Texas A&M University–College Station; University of Texas–Tyler. **Admissions statistics for the fall 2005 entering class:** Total applicants: 920. Total accepted: 703. Freshmen enrolled: 352; 55% were from out of state. Overall acceptance rate: 76%. **Credentials of fall 2005 freshmen:** 32% ranked in the top 10 percent of their high school class; 60% were in the top 25 percent, and 86% were in the top half. (Proportion submitting class standing: 64%.) **Average high school grade point average:** 3.5. **First-year students who submitted SAT scores:** 70%. Scores (25/75 percentile): Verbal: 500-650, Math: 520-650, Combined: 1020-1300. **First-year students submitting ACT scores:** 47%. Scores (25/75 percentile): English: 21-28, Math: 22-29, Composite: 22-28.

ACADEMICS

Year founded: 1946. **Academic calendar:** Semester. **Degrees offered:** associate, bachelor's, master's. **Most popular majors:** 23% business, management, marketing, and related support services, 22% engineering, 13% transportation and materials moving, 11% education, 11% engineering technologies/technicians. **Major fields of study:** biological and biomedical sciences; business, management, marketing, and related support services; computer and information sciences and support services; education; engineering; engineering technologies/technicians; English language and literature/letters; history; mathematics and statistics; multi/interdisciplinary studies; parks, recreation, leisure, and fitness studies; physical sciences; psychology; social sciences; theology and religious vocations; transportation and materials moving. **Areas of required coursework:** humanities, computer literacy, mathematics, English (including composition), sciences (biological

or physical), history, social science, other. **Pre-professional programs:** pre-law, pre-dentistry, pre-medicine, pre-theology, pre-veterinary science, pre-optometry. **Special academic programs:** accelerated program, cooperative (work-study plan) program, distance learning, double major, dual enrollment, honors program, independent study, internships, study abroad, teacher certificate program, weekend college. **Teacher certification offered in:** early childhood, special education, elementary, middle/junior high, secondary. **Cooperative education programs:** business, computer science, education, engineering, technologies, other. **Faculty and instruction (2005-2006):** Total instructional faculty: 72 full-time, 243 part-time (58% men; 42% women; 12% minorities). Full-time faculty with Ph.D. or other terminal degree: 72%. Student/faculty ratio: 14/1. Classes of fewer than 20 students: 80%; of 20 to 49 students: 20%; of 50 or more students: 0%. **Advanced Placement and International Baccalaureate credit:** AP tests may be used for: Credit only. Scores accepted: 3, 4, 5. International Baccalaureate exams may be used for: Credit only. **Freshmen returning for sophomore year:** 72%. **Graduation rates:** Four-year: 29%; five-year: 51%; six-year: 50%.

COSTS AND FINANCIAL AID

Financial aid office: (903) 233-3430. **Expenses (2006-2007):** Tuition and fees 2006-2007: $16,920; room/board: $6,590. Estimated books and supplies: $1,240; transportation: $1,095; personal expenses: $1,000. **Financial aid:** Priority filing date for institution's financial aid form: February 15. In 2005-2006, 75% of undergraduates applied for financial aid. Of those, 63% were determined to have financial need; 17% had their need fully met. Average financial aid package (proportion receiving): $11,288 (63%). Average amount of gift aid, such as scholarships or grants (proportion receiving): $7,757 (60%). Average amount of self-help aid, such as work study or loans (proportion receiving): $4,114 (63%). Average need-based loan (excluding PLUS or other private loans): $3,931. Among students who received need-based aid, the average percentage of need met: 69%. Among students who received aid based on merit, the average award (and the proportion receiving): $4,134 (17%). Average amount of debt of borrowers graduating in 2005: $28,426. Proportion who borrowed: 87%.

CAMPUS LIFE AND EXTRACURRICULAR ACTIVITIES

Campus housing available (% using): women's dorms (22%), men's dorms (59%), apartments for married students (5%), apartment for single students (11%). Students who live in college-owned, operated, or affiliated housing: 76%. **Student employment:** During the 2005-2006 academic year, 27% of undergraduates worked on campus. Average per-year earnings: $1,375. **Clubs and organizations:** Number of student organizations: 22. Activities include: choral groups, drama/theater, jazz band, music ensembles, student government, student newspaper, yearbook. Number of fraternities: 0; sororities: 0. Average proportion of students who stay on campus on weekends: 75%. **Sports program (2005-2006):** Member of NCAA III. *Men's intercollegiate varsity sports:* baseball, basketball, cross-country, golf, soccer, tennis. *Women's intercollegiate varsity sports:* basketball, cross-country, golf, soccer, softball, tennis, volleyball.

SERVICES AND FACILITIES

Basic services: nonremedial tutoring, health service, health insurance, other. **Remedial assistance:** math, writing. **Counseling services:** career, academic, religious. **Library:** Number of titles: 118,143; number of current serial subscriptions: 565. **Information technology resources:** Students are not required to lease or own a computer. Number of campus computers available to all students: 210. School has a wireless network. Approximate number of users that can be accommodated: 600. Proportion of college-owned housing units wired for high-speed internet access: 100%. **Campus safety:** Security services offered: 24-hour foot-and-vehicle patrols, late-night transport/escort service, 24-hour emergency telephones, lighted pathways/sidewalks, student patrols, controlled dormitory access (key, security card, etc).

TRANSFER AND INTERNATIONAL STUDENTS

Transfer students: May apply for admission for the following academic terms: Fall, Spring, Summer. Applicants need a minimum number of credits to apply. For fall 2005: Transfer applications received: 249. Transfer applicants offered admission: 153. Transfer applicants enrolled: 101. **International students:** Number of foreign undergraduates: 27 (1% of student body). Number of countries represented: 22. Minimum TOEFL score required: 500 (paper); 173 (computer).

Lubbock Christian University

- **Address:** 5601 19th Street, Lubbock, TX 79407
- **Website:** http://www.lcu.edu
- **Private; Religious affiliation:** Church of Christ
- **Enrollment:** 1,383 full-time; 449 part-time

KEY STATS

✔ **U.S News College Ranking:** 20, Comp. Coll.–Bachelor's (West)
✔ **ACT Score (25th/75th percentile):** 18-24
✔ **Tuition:** 2006-2007: $13,644

Selectivity: Selective	**Room/board:** $4,600
Acceptance rate: 74%	**Average debt:** $22,192
Student/faculty ratio: 15/1	**Proportion who borrowed:** 81%

UNDERGRADUATE STUDENT BODY STATS

2005-2006 enrollment: 1,383 full-time; 449 part-time. Men: 43%; women: 57%. **Ethnic makeup:** African American: 7%; Asian American: 1%; Hispanic: 15%; White: 77%; International: 1%. **Religious preference:** Roman Catholic: 7%; Protestant: 41%; Unknown: 2%; Church of Christ: 46%.

ADMISSIONS FACTS AND FIGURES

Phone: (806) 720-7151. **Email:** admissions@lcu.edu. **Website:** http://www.lcu.edu. **Application deadlines for fall 2007:** Regular decision: August 15. Early decision: Not offered. Early action: Not offered. Admission cannot be deferred. **Application fee:** $25. Common application is accepted. **Admissions requirements/recommendations:** High school units required (recommended): English: (4); Mathematics: (3); Science: (3); Foreign language: (2); Social studies: (2); History: (2); Academic electives: (4); Total units: (22). Tests: The college uses SAT or ACT scores in admissions decisions. Either SAT or ACT required. For admission to the fall 2007 entering class, the school will accept: ACT without writing. Campus visit: Recommended. Admissions interview: Neither required nor recommended. Off-campus interview: May not be arranged. **Factors that count in admissions decisions:** *Academic:* Secondary school record: Considered. Class rank: Considered. Letters of recommendation: Considered. Standardized test scores: Very important. Essay: Not considered. *Nonacademic:* Interview: Not considered. Extracurricular activities: Considered. Talent/ability: Considered. Character/personal qualities: Very important. Alumni/ae relationship: Important. Geographical residence: Not considered. State residency: Not considered. Religious affiliation/commitment: Not considered. Minority status: Not considered. Volunteer work: Important. Work experience: Considered. **Other schools with the greatest overlap in applicants:** Abilene Christian University; Harding University; Oklahoma Christian University; Texas Tech University; West Texas A&M University. **Admissions statistics for the fall 2005 entering class:** Total applicants: 912. Total accepted: 671. Freshmen enrolled: 320; 13% were from out of state. Overall acceptance rate: 74%. **Credentials of fall 2005 freshmen:** 14% ranked in the top 10 percent of their high school class; 41% were in the top 25 percent, and 71% were in the top half. (Proportion submitting class standing: 82%.) **Average high school grade point average:** 3.4. **First-year students who submitted SAT scores:** 58%. Scores (25/75 percentile): Verbal: 430-570, Math: 430-560, Combined: 860-1130. **First-year students submitting ACT scores:** 76%. Scores (25/75 percentile): English: 17-24, Math: 17-24, Composite: 18-24.

ACADEMICS

Year founded: 1957. **Academic calendar:** Semester. **Degrees offered:** associate, bachelor's, master's, first professional. **Most popular majors:** 29% business, management, marketing, and related support services, 23% education, 7% public administration and social service professions, 6% health professions and related clinical sciences, 6% liberal arts and sciences studies, and humanities. **Major fields of study:** agriculture, agriculture operations, and related sciences; biological and biomedical sciences; business, management, marketing, and related support services; communication, journalism, and related programs; computer and information sciences and support services; education; engineering; family and consumer sciences/human sciences; foreign languages, literatures, and linguistics; health professions and related clinical sciences; liberal arts and sciences studies, and humanities; mathematics and statistics; parks, recreation, leisure, and fitness studies; physical sciences; psychology; public administration and social service professions; security and protective services; theology and religious vocations; visual and performing arts. **Areas of required coursework:** arts/fine arts, humanities, computer literacy, mathematics, English (including composition), sciences (biological or physical), history, social science. **Pre-professional programs:** pre-law, pre-dentistry, pre-medicine, pre-veterinary science, pre-optometry, pre-pharmacy. **Special academic programs (% participation):** double major (1%), honors program (11%), internships (14%), liberal arts/career combination (5%), student-designed major (5%), study abroad (3%), teacher certificate program (20%). **Teacher certification offered in:** early childhood, special education, elementary, middle/junior high, secondary. **Cooperative education programs:** agriculture, engineering, health professions, other. **Reserve Officers Training Corps (ROTC):** Army ROTC: Offered at cooperating institution (Texas Tech University). **Faculty and instruction (2005-2006):** Total instructional faculty: 81 full-time, 73 part-time (59% men; 41% women; 3% minorities). Full-time faculty with Ph.D. or other terminal degree: 59%. Student/faculty ratio: 15/1. Classes of fewer than 20 students: 57%; of 20 to 49 students: 40%; of 50 or more students: 2%. **Advanced Placement and International Baccalaureate credit:** AP tests may be used for: Credit only. Scores accepted: 3, 4, 5. International Baccalaureate exams may be used for: Credit only. **Freshmen returning for sophomore year:** 66%. **Graduation rates:** Four-year: 22%; five-year: 35%; six-year: 34%. **Graduate study:** 40% of students pursue further study immediately upon graduation. Fields in which graduates pursue further study: Master of Business Administration (MBA), 7%; medicine, 4%; dentistry, 2%; theology (or the seminary), 7%; education, 19%; arts and sciences, 4%.

COSTS AND FINANCIAL AID

Financial aid office: (800) 933-7601. **Expenses (2006-2007):** Tuition and fees 2006-2007: $13,644; room/board: $4,600. Estimated books and supplies: $1,032; transportation: $1,726; personal expenses: $1,932. **Financial aid:** Priority filing date for institution's financial aid form: June 1. In 2005-2006, 71% of undergraduates applied for financial aid. Of those, 61% were determined to have financial need; 10% had their need fully met. Average financial aid package (proportion receiving): $11,163 (61%). Average amount of gift aid, such as scholarships or grants (proportion receiving): $7,409 (59%). Average amount of self-help aid, such as work study or loans (proportion receiving): $4,407 (55%). Average need-based loan (excluding PLUS or other private loans): $3,655. Among students who received need-based aid, the average percentage of need met: 73%. Among students who received aid based on merit, the average award (and the proportion receiving): $10,592 (15%). The average athletic scholarship (and the proportion receiving): $7,392 (4%). Average amount of debt of borrowers graduating in 2005: $22,192. Proportion who borrowed: 81%.

CAMPUS LIFE AND EXTRACURRICULAR ACTIVITIES

Campus housing available (% using): women's dorms (49%), men's dorms (38%), apartments for married students (2%), apartment for single students (11%). Students who live in college-owned, operated, or affiliated housing: 31%. **Student employment:** During the 2005-2006 academic year, 18% of undergraduates worked on campus. Average per-year earnings: $967. **Clubs and organizations:** Number of student organizations: 17. Activities include: choral groups, drama/theater, music ensembles, student government, student newspaper, yearbook. Number of fraternities: 4; sororities: 4. Proportion of men in fraternities: 17%; of women in sororities: 20%. Average proportion of students who stay on campus on weekends: 26%. **Sports program (2005-2006):** Member of NAIA. *Men's intercollegiate varsity sports:* baseball, basketball, golf. *Women's intercollegiate varsity sports:* basketball, golf, volleyball.

SERVICES AND FACILITIES

Basic services: nonremedial tutoring, placement service. **Remedial assistance:** reading, math, writing, study skills. **Counseling services:** minority student, career, personal, veteran student, academic, older student, psychological, religious. **For learning-disabled students:** School does not offer a structured program with separate admission and additional fees. Total undergraduates in learning-disabled program or receiving services: 45. Services include: remedial math, remedial English, reading machines, remedial reading, tape recorders, untimed tests, note-taking services, oral tests, learning center, readers, extended time for tests, tutors, priority registration, priority seating, other testing accomodations. **Library:** Number of titles: 117,508; number of current serial subscriptions: 543. **Information technology resources:** Students are not required to lease or own a computer. Number of campus computers available to all students: 169. School has a wireless network. Proportion of college-owned housing units wired for high-speed internet access: 100%. **Campus safety:** Security services offered: 24-hour foot-and-vehicle patrols, late-night transport/escort service, lighted pathways/sidewalks, controlled dormitory access (key, security card, etc).

TRANSFER AND INTERNATIONAL STUDENTS

Transfer students: May apply for admission for the following academic terms: Fall, Spring, Summer. Applicants need a minimum number of credits to apply. For fall 2005: Transfer applications received: 560. Transfer applicants offered admission: 387. Transfer applicants enrolled: 272. **International students:** Number of foreign undergraduates: 15 (1% of student body). Minimum TOEFL score required: 500 (paper); 173 (computer). Average TOEFL score: 550 (paper).

McMurry University

- **Address:** S. 14th and Sayles Boulevard, Abilene, TX 79697
- **Website:** http://www.mcm.edu
- **Private; Religious affiliation:** Methodist
- **Enrollment:** 1,187 full-time; 243 part-time

KEY STATS

✔ **U.S News College Ranking:** 12, Comp. Coll.–Bachelor's (West)
✔ **SAT Score (25th/75th percentile):** 860-1110
✔ **Tuition:** 2006-2007: $15,170

Selectivity: Less selective	**Room/board:** $5,918
Acceptance rate: 86%	**Average debt:** $24,854
Student/faculty ratio: 14/1	**Proportion who borrowed:** 82%

UNDERGRADUATE STUDENT BODY STATS

2005-2006 enrollment: 1,187 full-time; 243 part-time. Men: 50%; women: 50%. **Ethnic makeup:** African American: 11%; American-Indian: 1%; Asian American: 1%; Hispanic: 14%; White: 72%; International: 1%. **Religious preference:** Roman Catholic: 15%; Protestant: 34%; No preference: 1%; Unknown: 21%; Methodist: 20%; Other: 9%.

ADMISSIONS FACTS AND FIGURES

Phone: (325) 793-4700. **Email:** admissions@mcm.edu. **Website:** http://www.mcm.edu. **Application deadlines for fall 2007:** Regular decision: August 15. Early decision: Not offered. Early action: Not offered. Admission can be deferred. **Application fee:** $20. Common application is accepted. **Admissions requirements/recommendations:** High school units required (recommended): English: 4 (4); Mathematics: 3 (3); Science: 2 (3); Foreign language: (2); Social studies: 3 (4); Total units: 12 (16). Tests: The college uses SAT or ACT scores in admissions decisions. Either SAT or ACT required. For admission to the fall 2007 entering class, the school will accept: ACT without writing. Campus visit: Recommended. Admissions interview: Neither required nor recommended. Off-campus interview: May be arranged. **Factors that count in admissions decisions:** *Academic:* Secondary school record: Very important. Class rank: Very important. Letters of recommendation: Considered. Standardized test scores: Very important. Essay: Considered. *Nonacademic:* Interview: Considered. Extracurricular activities: Important. Talent/ability: Important. Character/personal qualities: Important. Alumni/ae relationship: Considered. Geographical residence: Considered. State residency: Considered. Religious affiliation/commitment: Considered. Minority status: Not considered. Volunteer work: Important. Work experience: Considered. **Admissions statistics for the fall 2005 entering class:** Total applicants: 917. Total accepted: 785. Freshmen enrolled: 292; 6% were from out of state. Overall acceptance rate: 86%. **Credentials of fall 2005 freshmen:** 17% ranked in the top 10 percent of their high school class; 41% were in the top 25 percent, and 74% were in the top half. (Proportion submitting class standing: 95%.) **Average high school grade point average:** 3.4. **First-year students who submitted SAT scores:** 78%. Scores (25/75 percentile): Verbal: 420-540, Math: 440-570, Combined: 860-1110. **First-year students submitting ACT scores:** 52%. Scores (25/75 percentile): English: 16-23, Math: 17-24, Composite: 18-23.

ACADEMICS

Year founded: 1923. **Academic calendar:** Semester. **Degrees offered:** bachelor's. **Most popular majors:** 27% education, 14% business, management, marketing, and related support services, 11% health professions and related clinical sciences, 9% social sciences, 7% communication, journalism, and related programs. **Major fields of study:** biological and biomedical sciences; business, management, marketing, and related support services; computer and information sciences and support services; education; English language and literature/letters; foreign languages, literatures, and linguistics; health

professions and related clinical sciences; history; mathematics and statistics; multi/interdisciplinary studies; natural resources and conservation; philosophy and religious studies; physical sciences; psychology; public administration and social service professions; social sciences; visual and performing arts. **Areas of required coursework:** arts/fine arts, humanities, computer literacy, mathematics, English (including composition), philosophy, foreign languages, sciences (biological or physical), history, social science, other. **Pre-professional programs:** pre-law, pre-dentistry, pre-medicine, pre-theology, pre-veterinary science, pre-pharmacy, other. **Special academic programs:** accelerated program, cross-registration, double major, dual enrollment, honors program, independent study, internships, liberal arts/career combination, study abroad, teacher certificate program, other. **Teacher certification offered in:** early childhood, special education, elementary, middle/junior high, secondary, bilingual/bicultural. **Reserve Officers Training Corps (ROTC):** Air Force ROTC: Offered at cooperating institution (Angelo State University). **Faculty and instruction (2005-2006):** Total instructional faculty: 77 full-time, 51 part-time (59% men; 41% women; 7% minorities). Full-time faculty with Ph.D. or other terminal degree: 78%. Student/faculty ratio: 14/1. Classes of fewer than 20 students: 64%; of 20 to 49 students: 35%; of 50 or more students: 1%. **Advanced Placement and International Baccalaureate credit:** AP tests may be used for: Placement only. Scores accepted: 3, 4, 5. International Baccalaureate exams may be used for: Credit and/or placement. **Freshmen returning for sophomore year:** 62%. **Graduation rates:** Four-year: 25%; five-year: 39%; six-year: 41%. **Graduate study:** 22% of students pursue further study immediately upon graduation. Fields in which graduates pursue further study: Master of Business Administration (MBA), 17%; law, 7%; theology (or the seminary), 17%; education, 7%; arts and sciences, 53%.

COSTS AND FINANCIAL AID

Financial aid office: (325) 793-4709. **Expenses (2006-2007):** Tuition and fees 2006-2007: $15,170; room/board: $5,918. Estimated books and supplies: $1,000; transportation: $600; personal expenses: $1,400. **Financial aid:** Priority filing date for institution's financial aid form: March 15. In 2005-2006, 90% of undergraduates applied for financial aid. Of those, 81% were determined to have financial need; 15% had their need fully met. Average financial aid package (proportion receiving): $15,032 (81%). Average amount of gift aid, such as scholarships or grants (proportion receiving): $7,919 (78%). Average amount of self-help aid, such as work study or loans (proportion receiving): $4,433 (66%). Average need-based loan (excluding PLUS or other private loans): $4,128. Among students who received need-based aid, the average percentage of need met: 84%. Among students who received aid based on merit, the average award (and the proportion receiving): $4,201 (6%). The average athletic scholarship (and the proportion receiving): $0 (0%). Average amount of debt of borrowers graduating in 2005: $24,854. Proportion who borrowed: 82%.

CAMPUS LIFE AND EXTRACURRICULAR ACTIVITIES

Campus housing available (% using): women's dorms (35%), men's dorms (49%), apartment for single students (16%), special housing for disabled students (0%). Students who live in college-owned, operated, or affiliated housing: 41%. **Student employment:** During the 2005-2006 academic year, 8% of undergraduates worked on campus. Average per-year earnings: $1,650. **Clubs and organizations:** Number of student organizations: 45. Activities include: choral groups, concert band, drama/theater, jazz band, literary magazine, marching band, music ensembles, musical theater, student government, student newspaper, yearbook. Number of fraternities: 7; sororities: 6. Proportion of men in fraternities: 15%; of women in sororities: 20%. Average proportion of students who stay on campus on weekends: 50%. **Sports program (2005-2006):** Member of NCAA III. *Men's intercollegiate varsity sports:* baseball, basketball, cross-country, football, golf, soccer, swimming and diving, tennis, track and field (indoor), track and field (outdoor). *Women's intercollegiate varsity sports:* basketball, cross-country, golf, soccer, swimming and diving, tennis, track and field (indoor), track and field (outdoor), volleyball.

SERVICES AND FACILITIES

Basic services: nonremedial tutoring, placement service, health service, other. **Remedial assistance:** reading, math, writing, study skills. **Counseling services:** minority student, career, military, personal, veteran student, academic, older student, psychological, birth control, religious, other. **For learning-disabled students:** School does not offer a structured program with separate admission and additional fees. Total undergraduates in learning-disabled program or receiving services: 29. Services include: remedial math, remedial English, remedial reading, note-taking services, oral tests, learning center, readers, extended time for tests, tutors, priority seating, other testing accomodations. **Library:** Number of titles: 155,305; number of current serial subscriptions: 405. **Information technology resources:** Students are not required to lease or own a computer. Number of campus computers available to all students: 236. School has a wireless network. Approximate number of users that can be accommodated: 2,100. Proportion of college-owned housing units wired for high-speed internet access: 100%. **Campus safety:** Security services offered: 24-hour foot-and-vehicle patrols, late-night transport/escort service, lighted pathways/sidewalks, controlled dormitory access (key, security card, etc.).

TRANSFER AND INTERNATIONAL STUDENTS
Transfer students: May apply for admission for the following academic terms: Fall, Spring, Summer. Applicants need a minimum number of credits to apply. For fall 2005: Transfer applications received: 410. Transfer applicants offered admission: 282. Transfer applicants enrolled: 184. **International students:** Number of foreign undergraduates: 14 (1% of student body). Number of countries represented: 11. Minimum TOEFL score required: 550 (paper); 213 (computer).

Midwestern State University

- **Address:** 3410 Taft Boulevard, Wichita Falls, TX 76308-2099
- **Website:** http://www.mwsu.edu
- **Public**
- **Enrollment:** 4,013 full-time; 1,531 part-time

KEY STATS
✔ **U.S News College Ranking:** fourth tier, Universities–Master's (West)
✔ **SAT Score (25th/75th percentile):** 870-1080
✔ **Tuition:** 2006-2007: $4,566 in state, $12,816 out of state

Selectivity: Less selective	**Room/board:** $5,220
Acceptance rate: 83%	**Average debt:** $16,041
Student/faculty ratio: 20/1	**Proportion who borrowed:** 46%

UNDERGRADUATE STUDENT BODY STATS
2005-2006 enrollment: 4,013 full-time; 1,531 part-time. Men: 43%; women: 57%. **Ethnic makeup:** African American: 13%; American-Indian: 1%; Asian American: 3%; Hispanic: 9%; White: 68%; International: 5%.

ADMISSIONS FACTS AND FIGURES
Phone: (800) 842-1922. **Email:** admissions@mwsu.edu. **Website:** http://www.mwsu.edu. **Application deadlines for fall 2007:** Regular decision: August 7. Early decision: Not offered. Early action: Send application by: N/A; Decision sent by: N/A. Admission cannot be deferred. **Application fee:** $25. Common application is accepted. **To apply online, go to:** https://www.applytexas.org/adappc/commonapp.wb. **Admissions requirements/recommendations:** High school units required (recommended): English: 4; Mathematics: 3; Science: 2; Academic electives: 6; Total units: 15. Tests: The college uses SAT or ACT scores in admissions decisions. Either SAT or ACT required. For admission to the fall 2007 entering class, the school will accept: ACT with writing. Campus visit: Recommended. Admissions interview: Neither required nor recommended. **Factors that count in admissions decisions:** *Academic:* Secondary school record: Very important. Class rank: Very important. Letters of recommendation: Not considered. Standardized test scores: Very important. Essay: Considered. *Nonacademic:* Interview: Considered. Extracurricular activities: Considered. Talent/ability: Considered. Character/personal qualities: Considered. Alumni/ae relationship: Considered. Geographical residence: Considered. State residency: Considered. Religious affiliation/commitment: Not considered. Minority status: Considered. Volunteer work: Considered. Work experience: Considered. **Other schools with the greatest overlap in applicants:** Angelo State University; Tarleton State University; Texas Tech University. **Admissions statistics for the fall 2005 entering class:** Total applicants: 1,561. Total accepted: 1,291. Freshmen enrolled: 876; 4% were from out of state. Overall acceptance rate: 83%. Non-early acceptance rate: 83%. **Credentials of fall 2005 freshmen:** 12% ranked in the top 10 percent of their high school class; 33% were in the top 25 percent, and 68% were in the top half. (Proportion submitting class standing: 97%.) **Average high school grade point average:** 3.3. **First-year students who submitted SAT scores:** 74%. Scores (25/75 percentile): Verbal: 430-540, Math: 440-540, Combined: 870-1080. **First-year students submitting ACT scores:** 58%. Scores (25/75 percentile): English: 16-23, Math: 17-23, Composite: 18-23.

ACADEMICS
Year founded: 1922. **Academic calendar:** Semester. **Degrees offered:** certificate, associate, bachelor's, post-bachelor's certificate, master's. **Most popular majors:** 18% multi/interdisciplinary studies, 8% early childhood education and teaching, 6% criminal justice/safety studies, 5% business administration and management, 5% nursing/registered nurse training (R.N., A.S.N., B.S.N., M.S.N.). **Major fields of study:** biological and biomedical sciences; business, management, marketing, and related support services; communication, journalism, and related programs; computer and information sciences and support services; education; engineering; engineering technologies/technicians; English language and literature/letters; foreign languages, literatures, and linguistics; health professions and related clinical sciences; history; legal professions and studies; liberal arts and sciences studies, and humanities; mathematics and statistics; multi/interdisciplinary studies; natural resources and conservation; parks, recreation, leisure, and fitness studies; physical sciences; psychology; public administration and social service professions; security and protective services; social sciences; visual and performing arts. **Areas of required coursework:** arts/fine arts, humanities, computer literacy, mathematics, English (including composition), philosophy, foreign languages, sciences (biological or physical), history, social science. **Pre-professional programs:** pre-law, pre-dentistry, pre-medicine, pre-veterinary science, pre-optometry, pre-pharmacy, other. **Special academic programs (% participation):** distance learning (10%), double major (1%), dual enrollment, English as a Second Language (ESL) (1%), honors program (1%), independent study, internships, liberal arts/career combination, study abroad (.1%), teacher certificate program (1.4%). **Teacher certification offered in:** early childhood, special education, elementary, middle/junior high, secondary, bilingual/bicultural. **Reserve Officers Training Corps (ROTC):** Air Force ROTC: Offered at cooperating institution (University of North Texas). **Faculty and instruction (2005-2006):** Total instructional faculty: 208 full-time, 112 part-time (53% men; 47% women; 8% minorities). Full-time faculty with Ph.D. or other terminal degree: 70%. Student/faculty ratio: 20/1. Classes of fewer than 20 students: 35%; of 20 to 49 students: 54%; of 50 or more students: 11%. **Advanced Placement and International Baccalaureate credit:** AP tests may be used for: Credit and/or placement. Scores accepted: 3, 4, 5. International Baccalaureate exams may be used for: Credit and/or placement. **Freshmen returning for sophomore year:** 64%. **Graduation rates:** Four-year: 9%; five-year: 24%; six-year: 30%.

COSTS AND FINANCIAL AID
Financial aid office: (940) 397-4214. **Expenses (2006-2007):** Tuition and fees 2006-2007: $4,566 in state, $12,816 out of state; room/board: $5,220. Estimated books and supplies: $1,050; transportation: $1,189; personal expenses: $1,275. **Financial aid:** Priority filing date for institution's financial aid form: May 1. In 2005-2006, 73% of undergraduates applied for financial aid. Of those, 47% were determined to have financial need; 20% had their need fully met. Average financial aid package (proportion receiving): $6,459 (47%). Average amount of gift aid, such as scholarships or grants (proportion receiving): $4,038 (40%). Average amount of self-help aid, such as work study or loans (proportion receiving): $3,364 (37%). Average need-based loan (excluding PLUS or other private loans): $3,304. Among students who received need-based aid, the average percentage of need met: 70%. Among students who received aid based on merit, the average award (and the proportion receiving): $1,472 (21%). The average athletic scholarship (and the proportion receiving): $2,390 (3%). Average amount of debt of borrowers graduating in 2005: $16,041. Proportion who borrowed: 46%.

CAMPUS LIFE AND EXTRACURRICULAR ACTIVITIES
Campus housing available (% using): coed dorms (3%), women's dorms (29%), men's dorms (16%), apartments for married students (6%), apartment for single students (35%), special housing for disabled students, cooperative housing (1%), other housing options (10%). Students who live in college-owned, operated, or affiliated housing: 20%. **Student employment:** During the 2005-2006 academic year, 6% of undergraduates worked on campus. Average per-year earnings: $4,961. **Clubs and organizations:** Number of student organizations: 124. Activities include: choral groups, concert band, drama/theater, jazz band, literary magazine, marching band, music ensembles, musical theater, pep band, student government, student newspaper, student film society, television station, yearbook. Number of fraternities: 8; sororities: 8. Average proportion of students who stay on campus on weekends: 20%. **Sports program (2005-2006):** Member of NCAA II. *Men's intercollegiate varsity sports:* basketball, football, soccer, tennis. *Women's intercollegiate varsity sports:* basketball, soccer, softball, tennis, volleyball.

SERVICES AND FACILITIES

Basic services: nonremedial tutoring, placement service, health service, health insurance. **Remedial assistance:** reading, math, writing, study skills. **Counseling services:** minority student, career, military, personal, veteran student, academic, older student, psychological, birth control. **For learning-disabled students:** School does not offer a structured program with separate admission and additional fees. Total undergraduates in learning-disabled program or receiving services: 121. Services include: remedial math, remedial English, reading machines, remedial reading, tape recorders, untimed tests, note-taking services, oral tests, learning center, readers, extended time for tests, tutors, priority seating, other testing accomodations. **Library:** Number of titles: 441,251; number of current serial subscriptions: 1,246. **Information technology resources:** Students are not required to lease or own a computer. Number of campus computers available to all students: 472. School does not have a wireless network. Proportion of college-owned housing units wired for high-speed internet access: 100%. **Campus safety:** Security services offered: 24-hour foot-and-vehicle patrols, late-night transport/escort service, 24-hour emergency telephones, lighted pathways/sidewalks, controlled dormitory access (key, security card, etc).

TRANSFER AND INTERNATIONAL STUDENTS

Transfer students: May apply for admission for the following academic terms: Fall, Winter, Spring, Summer. Applicants need a minimum number of credits to apply. For fall 2005: Transfer applications received: 1,263. Transfer applicants offered admission: 906. Transfer applicants enrolled: 586. **International students:** Number of foreign undergraduates: 303 (5% of student body). Number of countries represented: 36. Minimum TOEFL score required: 530 (paper); 197 (computer). Average TOEFL score: 593 (paper).

Our Lady of the Lake University

- **Address:** 411 S. W. 24th Street, San Antonio, TX 78207-4689
- **Website:** http://www.ollusa.edu
- **Private; Religious affiliation:** Roman Catholic
- **Enrollment:** 1,242 full-time; 550 part-time

KEY STATS

- ✔ **U.S News College Ranking:** third tier, Universities–Master's (West)
- ✔ **SAT Score (25th/75th percentile):** 850-1040
- ✔ **Tuition:** 2006-2007: $18,400

Selectivity: Less selective	**Room/board:** $5,768
Acceptance rate: 53%	**Average debt:** $26,058
Student/faculty ratio: 13/1	**Proportion who borrowed:** 83%

UNDERGRADUATE STUDENT BODY STATS

2005-2006 enrollment: 1,242 full-time; 550 part-time. Men: 24%; women: 76%. **Ethnic makeup:** African American: 8%; Asian American: 1%; Hispanic: 71%; White: 19%; International: 1%.

ADMISSIONS FACTS AND FIGURES

Phone: (800) 436-6558. **Email:** admission@lake.ollusa.edu. **Website:** http://www.ollusa.edu. **Application deadlines for fall 2007:** Regular decision: July 15. Early decision: Not offered. Early action: Not offered. Admission can be deferred. **Application fee:** $25. Common application is accepted. **Admissions requirements/recommendations:** High school units required (recommended): English: 4; Mathematics: 2 (3); Science: 2; Foreign language: 3; Social studies: 3; Academic electives: 2 (3); Total units: 16. Tests: The college uses SAT or ACT scores in admissions decisions. Either SAT or ACT required. For admission to the fall 2007 entering class, the school will accept: ACT without writing. Campus visit: Recommended. Admissions interview: Neither required nor recommended. Off-campus interview: May be arranged. **Factors that count in admissions decisions:** *Academic:* Secondary school record: Very important. Class rank: Important. Letters of recommendation: Considered. Standardized test scores: Very important. Essay: Considered. *Nonacademic:* Interview: Considered. Extracurricular activities: Considered. Talent/ability: Considered. Character/personal qualities: Considered. Alumni/ae relationship: Considered. Geographical residence: Not considered. State residency: Not considered. Religious affiliation/commitment: Not considered. Minority status: Not considered. Volunteer work: Considered. Work experience: Considered. **Other schools with the greatest overlap in applicants:** St. Mary's University of San Antonio;

University of the Incarnate Word. **Admissions statistics for the fall 2005 entering class:** Total applicants: 2,214. Total accepted: 1,173. Freshmen enrolled: 271; 2% were from out of state. Overall acceptance rate: 53%. **Credentials of fall 2005 freshmen:** 22% ranked in the top 10 percent of their high school class; 47% were in the top 25 percent, and 76% were in the top half. (Proportion submitting class standing: 86%.) **Average high school grade point average:** 3.2. **First-year students who submitted SAT scores:** 83%. Scores (25/75 percentile): Verbal: 430-520, Math: 420-520, Combined: 850-1040. **First-year students submitting ACT scores:** 42%. Scores (25/75 percentile): English: 16-21, Math: 18-21, Composite: 16-21.

ACADEMICS

Year founded: 1895. **Academic calendar:** Semester. **Degrees offered:** bachelor's, master's, doctorate. **Most popular majors:** 16% psychology, 13% business, management, marketing, and related support services, 8% elementary education and teaching, 8% social work, 4% liberal arts and sciences studies, and humanities. **Major fields of study:** biological and biomedical sciences; business, management, marketing, and related support services; communication, journalism, and related programs; computer and information sciences and support services; education; English language and literature/letters; family and consumer sciences/human sciences; foreign languages, literatures, and linguistics; health professions and related clinical sciences; history; liberal arts and sciences studies, and humanities; mathematics and statistics; philosophy and religious studies; physical sciences; psychology; public administration and social service professions; social sciences; visual and performing arts. **Areas of required coursework:** arts/fine arts, mathematics, English (including composition), philosophy, foreign languages, sciences (biological or physical), history, social science, other. **Special academic programs:** cooperative (work-study plan) program, cross-registration, distance learning, double major, dual enrollment, independent study, study abroad, teacher certificate program, weekend college. **Teacher certification offered in:** early childhood, special education, elementary, middle/junior high, secondary, bilingual/bicultural. **Reserve Officers Training Corps (ROTC):** Army ROTC: Offered at cooperating institution (St. Mary's University of San Antonio); Air Force ROTC: Offered at cooperating institution (University of Texas at San Antonio). **Faculty and instruction (2005-2006):** Total instructional faculty: 118 full-time, 107 part-time (50% men; 50% women; 35% minorities). Student/faculty ratio: 13/1. Classes of fewer than 20 students: 72%; of 20 to 49 students: 27%; of 50 or more students: 0%. **Advanced Placement and International Baccalaureate credit:** AP tests may be used for: Credit and/or placement. Scores accepted: 3, 4, 5. **Freshmen returning for sophomore year:** 61%. **Graduation rates:** Four-year: 14%; five-year: 30%; six-year: 35%.

COSTS AND FINANCIAL AID

Financial aid office: (210) 434-6711. **Expenses (2006-2007):** Tuition and fees 2006-2007: $18,400; room/board: $5,768. Estimated books and supplies: $1,000; transportation: $950; personal expenses: $1,800. **Financial aid:** Priority filing date for institution's financial aid form: April 1. In 2005-2006, 100% of undergraduates applied for financial aid. Of those, 92% were determined to have financial need; 10% had their need fully met. Average financial aid package (proportion receiving): $15,760 (91%). Average amount of gift aid, such as scholarships or grants (proportion receiving): $6,439 (78%). Average amount of self-help aid, such as work study or loans (proportion receiving): $4,680 (17%). Average need-based loan (excluding PLUS or other private loans): $4,009. Among students who received need-based aid, the average percentage of need met: 80%. Among students who received aid based on merit, the average award (and the proportion receiving): $3,768 (8%). Average amount of debt of borrowers graduating in 2005: $26,058. Proportion who borrowed: 83%.

CAMPUS LIFE AND EXTRACURRICULAR ACTIVITIES

Campus housing available: coed dorms, women's dorms, men's dorms, special housing for disabled students. Students who live in college-owned, operated, or affiliated housing: 27%. **Clubs and organizations:** Number of student organizations: 47. Activities include: choral groups, dance, drama/theater, jazz band, literary magazine, marching band, music ensembles, musical theater, student government, student newspaper, symphony orchestra, television station. Number of fraternities: 0; sororities: 0.

SERVICES AND FACILITIES

Basic services: women's center, placement service, health service. **Remedial assistance:** reading, math, writing, study skills. **Counseling services:** career, personal, academic, religious. **For learning-disabled students:** School does not offer a structured program with separate admission and additional fees. Total undergraduates in learning-disabled program or receiving services: 30.

Services include: tape recorders, other special classes, note-taking services, oral tests, learning center, readers, extended time for tests, tutors, early syllabus, priority registration, priority seating, texts on tape, typist/scribe, exams on tape or computer, other testing accomodations. **Library:** Number of titles: 127,441; number of current serial subscriptions: 557. **Information technology resources:** Students are not required to lease or own a computer. Number of campus computers available to all students: 208. School has a wireless network. Approximate number of users that can be accommodated: 1,080. Proportion of college-owned housing units wired for high-speed internet access: 100%. **Campus safety:** Security services offered: 24-hour foot-and-vehicle patrols, late-night transport/escort service, 24-hour emergency telephones, lighted pathways/sidewalks, controlled dormitory access (key, security card, etc).

TRANSFER AND INTERNATIONAL STUDENTS
Transfer students: May apply for admission for the following academic terms: Fall, Spring, Summer. Applicants need a minimum number of credits to apply. For fall 2005: Transfer applications received: 563. Transfer applicants offered admission: 348. Transfer applicants enrolled: 152. **International students:** Number of foreign undergraduates: 10 (1% of student body). Minimum TOEFL score required: 525 (paper); 197 (computer).

Paul Quinn College

- **Address:** 3837 Simpson Stuart Road, Dallas, TX 75241
- **Website:** http://www.pqc.edu/
- **Private; Religious affiliation:** African Methodist Episcopal
- **Enrollment:** N/A

KEY STATS
✔ **U.S News College Ranking:** fourth tier, Comp. Coll.–Bachelor's (West)
✔ **SAT or ACT Score (25th/75th percentile):** N/A
✔ **Tuition:** N/A

Selectivity: Less selective	**Room/board:** N/A
Acceptance rate: N/A	**Average debt:** N/A
Student/faculty ratio: N/A	**Proportion who borrowed:** N/A

Prairie View A&M University

- **Address:** PO Box 188, Prairie View, TX 77446
- **Website:** http://www.pvamu.edu
- **Public; Religious affiliation:**
- **Enrollment:** 5,140 full-time; 562 part-time

KEY STATS
✔ **U.S News College Ranking:** fourth tier, Universities–Master's (West)
✔ **SAT Score (25th/75th percentile):** 780-940
✔ **Tuition:** 2006-2007: $5,461 in state, $13,711 out of state

Selectivity: Less selective	**Room/board:** $6,474
Acceptance rate: 60%	**Average debt:** $25,000
Student/faculty ratio: 16/1	**Proportion who borrowed:** 80%

UNDERGRADUATE STUDENT BODY STATS
2005-2006 enrollment: 5,140 full-time; 562 part-time. Men: 43%; women: 57%. **Ethnic makeup:** African American: 90%; Asian American: 1%; Hispanic: 3%; White: 4%; International: 2%.

ADMISSIONS FACTS AND FIGURES
Phone: (936) 857-2626. **Email:** admissions@pvamu.edu. **Website:** http://www.pvamu.edu. **Application deadlines for fall 2007:** Regular decision: June 1. Early decision: Not offered. Early action: Not offered. Admission can be deferred. **Application fee:** $25. Common application is accepted. **To apply online, go to:** https://www.applytexas.org/adappc/commonapp.wb. **Admissions requirements/recommendations:** High school units required (recommended): English: 4; Mathematics: 3 (4); Science: 3; Foreign language: (2); Social studies: 2; Academic electives: 4; Total units: 16 (18). **Tests:** The college uses SAT or ACT scores in admissions decisions. Either SAT or ACT required. Campus visit: Recommended. Admissions interview:

Neither required nor recommended. Off-campus interview: Not available. **Factors that count in admissions decisions: Academic:** Secondary school record: Very important. Class rank: Very important. Letters of recommendation: Not considered. Standardized test scores: Very important. Essay: Not considered. **Nonacademic:** Interview: Not considered. Extracurricular activities: Considered. Talent/ability: Not considered. Character/personal qualities: Not considered. Alumni/ae relationship: Not considered. Geographical residence: Not considered. State residency: Not considered. Religious affiliation/commitment: Not considered. Minority status: Not considered. Volunteer work: Considered. Work experience: Considered. **Admissions statistics for the fall 2005 entering class:** Total applicants: 4,325. Total accepted: 2,583. Freshmen enrolled: 1,101; 0% were from out of state. Overall acceptance rate: 60%. **Credentials of fall 2005 freshmen:** 4% ranked in the top 10 percent of their high school class; 17% were in the top 25 percent, and 50% were in the top half. (Proportion submitting class standing: 98%.) **Average high school grade point average:** 2.9. **First-year students who submitted SAT scores:** 99%. Scores (25/75 percentile): Verbal: 390-470, Math: 390-470, Combined: 780-940. **First-year students submitting ACT scores:** 70%. Scores (25/75 percentile): English: 17-21, Math: 16-19, Composite: 16-19.

ACADEMICS
Year founded: 1876. **Academic calendar:** Semester. **Degrees offered:** bachelor's, master's, doctorate. **Most popular majors:** 7% biology/biological sciences, 7% nursing/registered nurse training (R.N., A.S.N., B.S.N., M.S.N.), 6% health services/allied health/health sciences, 5% criminal justice/safety studies, 5% health services/allied health/health sciences. **Major fields of study:** agriculture, agriculture operations, and related sciences; architecture and related services; biological and biomedical sciences; business, management, marketing, and related support services; communication, journalism, and related programs; computer and information sciences and support services; engineering; engineering technologies/technicians; English language and literature/letters; family and consumer sciences/human sciences; foreign languages, literatures, and linguistics; health professions and related clinical sciences; history; mathematics and statistics; multi/interdisciplinary studies; parks, recreation, leisure, and fitness studies; physical sciences; psychology; public administration and social service professions; security and protective services; social sciences; visual and performing arts. **Areas of required coursework:** arts/fine arts, humanities, computer literacy, mathematics, English (including composition), philosophy, foreign languages, sciences (biological or physical), history, social science. **Pre-professional programs:** pre-medicine. **Special academic programs:** accelerated program, cooperative (work-study plan) program, distance learning, double major, dual enrollment, English as a Second Language (ESL), honors program, independent study, internships, liberal arts/career combination, teacher certificate program, weekend college. **Teacher certification offered in:** early childhood, special education, elementary, vo-tech, middle/junior high, adult education, secondary, bilingual/bicultural. **Cooperative education programs:** agriculture, business, computer science, education, engineering, natural science, social/behavioral science, technologies. **Reserve Officers Training Corps (ROTC):** Army ROTC: Offered on campus; Navy ROTC: Offered on campus. **Faculty and instruction (2005-2006):** Total instructional faculty: 367 full-time, 118 part-time (61% men; 39% women; 75% minorities). Student/faculty ratio: 16/1. Classes of fewer than 20 students: 53%; of 20 to 49 students: 43%; of 50 or more students: 4%. **Freshmen returning for sophomore year:** 67%. **Graduation rates:** Four-year: 12%; five-year: 27%; six-year: 37%.

COSTS AND FINANCIAL AID
Financial aid office: (936) 857-2424. **Expenses (2006-2007):** Tuition and fees 2006-2007: $5,461 in state, $13,711 out of state; room/board: $6,474. **Financial aid:** Priority filing date for institution's financial aid form: March 1; deadline: March 1. In 2005-2006, 90% of undergraduates applied for financial aid. Of those, 88% were determined to have financial need; 43% had their need fully met. Average financial aid package (proportion receiving): $6,920 (88%). Average amount of gift aid, such as scholarships or grants (proportion receiving): $3,350 (86%). Average amount of self-help aid, such as work study or loans (proportion receiving): $3,225 (88%). Average need-based loan (excluding PLUS or other private loans): $4,000. Among students who received need-based aid, the average percentage of need met: 73%. Among students who received aid based on merit, the average award (and the proportion receiving): $1,300 (6%). The average athletic scholarship (and the proportion receiving): $9,200 (3%). Average amount of debt of borrowers graduating in 2005: $25,000. Proportion who borrowed: 80%.

CAMPUS LIFE AND EXTRACURRICULAR ACTIVITIES

Campus housing available (% using): coed dorms (39%), apartment for single students (61%). Students who live in college-owned, operated, or affiliated housing: 38%. **Student employment:** During the 2005-2006 academic year, 46% of undergrads worked on campus. Average per-year earnings: $1,120. **Clubs and organizations:** Number of student organizations: 82. Activities include: choral groups, concert band, dance, drama/theater, jazz band, marching band, music ensembles, pep band, radio station, student government, student newspaper, symphony orchestra, yearbook. Number of fraternities: 11; sororities: 10. Proportion of men in fraternities: 3%; of women in sororities: 4%. Average proportion of students who stay on campus on weekends: 60%. **Sports program (2005-2006):** Member of NCAA I. *Men's intercollegiate varsity sports:* baseball, basketball, cross-country, football, golf, tennis, track and field (indoor), track and field (outdoor). *Women's intercollegiate varsity sports:* basketball, bowling, cross-country, golf, soccer, softball, tennis, track and field (indoor), track and field (outdoor), volleyball.

SERVICES AND FACILITIES

Basic services: nonremedial tutoring, placement service, health service, health insurance. **Remedial assistance:** reading, math, writing, study skills. **Counseling services:** minority student, career, military, personal, veteran student, academic. **For learning-disabled students:** School does not offer a structured program with separate admission and additional fees. Total undergraduates in learning-disabled program or receiving services: 82. Services include: remedial math, remedial English, remedial reading, tape recorders, diagnostic testing service, untimed tests, note-taking services, learning center, readers, extended time for tests, tutors, priority seating, typist/scribe, other testing accomodations, other. **Library:** Number of titles: 347,477; number of current serial subscriptions: 830. **Information technology resources:** Students are not required to lease or own a computer. Number of campus computers available to all students: 974. School has a wireless network. Proportion of college-owned housing units wired for high-speed internet access: 100%. **Campus safety:** Security services offered: 24-hour foot-and-vehicle patrols, late-night transport/escort service, 24-hour emergency telephones, lighted pathways/sidewalks, controlled dormitory access (key, security card, etc).

TRANSFER AND INTERNATIONAL STUDENTS

Transfer students: May apply for admission for the following academic terms: Fall, Spring, Summer. Applicants do not need a minimum number of credits to apply. For fall 2005: Transfer applications received: 1,089. Transfer applicants offered admission: 614. Transfer applicants enrolled: 325. **International students:** Number of foreign undergraduates: 102 (2% of student body). Minimum TOEFL score required: 500 (paper); 173 (computer).

Rice University

- **Address:** PO Box 1892, Houston, TX 77251-1892
- **Website:** http://www.rice.edu
- **Private**
- **Enrollment:** 3,057 full-time; 128 part-time

KEY STATS

✔ **U.S News College Ranking:** 17, National Universities
✔ **SAT Score (25th/75th percentile):** 1330-1540
✔ **Tuition:** 2006-2007: $23,500

Selectivity: Most selective	Room/board: $9,590
Acceptance rate: 25%	Average debt: $14,166
Student/faculty ratio: 5/1	Proportion who borrowed: 34%

UNDERGRADUATE STUDENT BODY STATS

2005-2006 enrollment: 3,057 full-time; 128 part-time. Men: 51%; women: 49%. **Ethnic makeup:** African American: 7%; American-Indian: 1%; Asian American: 16%; Hispanic: 12%; White: 62%; International: 3%.

ADMISSIONS FACTS AND FIGURES

Phone: (713) 348-7423. **Website:** http://www.rice.edu. **Application deadlines for fall 2007:** Regular decision: January 10; decision sent by April 1. Early decision: Send application by: November 1; Decision sent by: December 15. Early action: Send application by: December 1; Decision sent by: February 10. Admission can be deferred. **Application fee:** $50. Common application is

accepted. **Admissions requirements/recommendations:** High school units required (recommended): English: 4 (4); Mathematics: 3 (4); Science: 2 (4); Foreign language: 2 (4); Social studies: 2 (2); Academic electives: 3 (2); Total units: 16 (20). Tests: The college uses SAT or ACT scores in admissions decisions. Either SAT or ACT required. For admission to the fall 2007 entering class, the school will accept: ACT with writing. Campus visit: Recommended. Admissions interview: Recommended. Off-campus interview: May be arranged. **Factors that count in admissions decisions:** *Academic:* Secondary school record: Very important. Class rank: Very important. Letters of recommendation: Very important. Standardized test scores: Very important. Essay: Very important. *Nonacademic:* Interview: Considered. Extracurricular activities: Very important. Talent/ability: Very important. Character/personal qualities: Very important. Alumni/ae relationship: Considered. Geographical residence: Considered. State residency: Considered. Religious affiliation/commitment: Not considered. Minority status: Considered. Volunteer work: Considered. Work experience: Considered. **Other schools with the greatest overlap in applicants:** Duke University; Harvard University; Stanford University; University of Texas–Austin; Washington University in St. Louis. **Admissions statistics for the fall 2005 entering class:** Total applicants: 7,890. Total accepted: 1,970. Freshmen enrolled: 722; 54% were from out of state. Accepted through early-decision or early-action plans: 57%. Overall acceptance rate: 25%. Early-decision acceptance rate: 32%. Non-early acceptance rate: 22%. **Size of waiting list:** N/A applicants; enrolled from waiting list: 47. **Credentials of fall 2005 freshmen:** 88% ranked in the top 10 percent of their high school class; 96% were in the top 25 percent, and 99% were in the top half. (Proportion submitting class standing: 63%.) **First-year students who submitted SAT scores:** 97%. Scores (25/75 percentile): Verbal: 660-760, Math: 670-780, Combined: 1330-1540. **First-year students submitting ACT scores:** 36%. Scores (25/75 percentile): English: N/A, Math: N/A, Composite: 30-34.

ACADEMICS

Year founded: 1912. **Academic calendar:** Semester. **Degrees offered:** bachelor's, master's, doctorate. **Most popular majors:** 8% biological and biomedical sciences, 7% economics, 6% English language and literature/letters, 6% political science and government, 6% psychology. **Major fields of study:** architecture and related services; area, ethnic, cultural, and gender studies; biological and biomedical sciences; business, management, marketing, and related support services; computer and information sciences and support services; engineering; English language and literature/letters; foreign languages, literatures, and linguistics; history; mathematics and statistics; multi/interdisciplinary studies; parks, recreation, leisure, and fitness studies; philosophy and religious studies; physical sciences; psychology; public administration and social service professions; social sciences; visual and performing arts. **Pre-professional programs:** pre-law, pre-dentistry, pre-medicine, other. **Special academic programs (% participation):** cross-registration, double major (36%), dual enrollment, honors program, independent study, internships, liberal arts/career combination, student-designed major, study abroad, teacher certificate program, other. **Teacher certification offered in:** secondary. **Reserve Officers Training Corps (ROTC):** Army ROTC: Offered at cooperating institution (University of Houston); Navy ROTC: Offered on campus; Air Force ROTC: Offered at cooperating institution (University of Houston). **Faculty and instruction (2005-2006):** Total instructional faculty: 567 full-time, 143 part-time (72% men; 28% women; 14% minorities). Full-time faculty with Ph.D. or other terminal degree: 95%. Student/faculty ratio: 5/1. Classes of fewer than 20 students: 61%; of 20 to 49 students: 29%; of 50 or more students: 10%. **Advanced Placement and International Baccalaureate credit:** AP tests may be used for: Credit and/or placement. Scores accepted: 4, 5. International Baccalaureate exams may be used for: Credit and/or placement. **Freshmen returning for sophomore year:** 96%. **Graduation rates:** Four-year: 76%; five-year: 89%; six-year: 90%. **Graduate study:** 44% of students pursue further study immediately upon graduation; 80% within five years. Fields in which graduates pursue further study: Master of Business Administration (MBA), 1%; law, 15%; medicine, 35%; engineering, 13%; education, 1%; arts and sciences, 24%; veterinary medicine, 1%.

COSTS AND FINANCIAL AID

Financial aid office: (713) 348-4958. **Expenses (2006-2007):** Tuition and fees 2006-2007: $23,500; room/board: $9,590. Estimated books and supplies: $800 personal expenses: $1,550. **Financial aid:** Priority filing date for institution's financial aid form: March 1. In 2005-2006, 53% of undergraduates applied for financial aid. Of those, 35% were determined to have financial need; 100% had their need fully met. Average financial aid package (proportion receiving): $20,140 (35%). Average amount of gift aid, such as scholarships or grants (proportion receiving): $16,889 (34%). Average amount of self-help aid, such as work study or loans (proportion receiving): $3,788 (26%). Average need-based loan (excluding PLUS or other private loans): $3,044. Among students who received need-based aid, the average percentage of need met: 100%. Among students who received aid based on merit, the average award (and the proportion receiving): $6,154 (18%). The average athletic scholarship (and the proportion receiving): $23,521 (10%). Average amount of debt of borrowers graduating in 2005: $14,166. Proportion who borrowed: 34%.

CAMPUS LIFE AND EXTRACURRICULAR ACTIVITIES

Campus housing available (% using): coed dorms (100%), special housing for disabled students. Students who live in college-owned, operated, or affiliated housing: 69%. **Student employment:** During the 2005-2006 academic year, 41% of undergraduates worked on campus. Average per-year earnings: $1,800. **Clubs and organizations:** Number of student organizations: 216. Activities include: choral groups, concert band, dance, drama/theater, jazz band, literary magazine, marching band, music ensembles, musical theater, opera, pep band, radio station, student government, student newspaper, student film society, symphony orchestra, television station, yearbook. Number of fraternities: 0; sororities: 0. Average proportion of students who stay on campus on weekends: 99%. **Sports program (2005-2006):** Member of NCAA I. *Men's intercollegiate varsity sports:* baseball, basketball, cross-country, football, golf, tennis, track and field (indoor), track and field (outdoor). *Women's intercollegiate varsity sports:* basketball, cross-country, soccer, swimming and diving, tennis, track and field (indoor), track and field (outdoor), volleyball.

SERVICES AND FACILITIES

Basic services: nonremedial tutoring, women's center, placement service, health service, health insurance. **Counseling services:** minority student, career, personal, academic, psychological. **For learning-disabled students:** School does not offer a structured program with separate admission and additional fees. Total undergraduates in learning-disabled program or receiving services: 11. Services include: reading machines, tape recorders, note-taking services, extended time for tests, tutors, early syllabus, priority seating, texts on tape, exams on tape or computer, take home exams, other testing accomodations, other. **Library:** Number of titles: 2,437,177; number of current serial subscriptions: 18,409. **Information technology resources:** Students are not required to lease or own a computer. Number of campus computers available to all students: 523. School has a wireless network. Approximate number of users that can be accommodated: 250. Proportion of college-owned housing units wired for high-speed internet access: 100%. **Campus safety:** Security services offered: 24-hour foot-and-vehicle patrols, late-night transport/escort service; 24-hour emergency telephones, lighted pathways/sidewalks, controlled dormitory access (key, security card, etc).

TRANSFER AND INTERNATIONAL STUDENTS

Transfer students: May apply for admission for the following academic terms: Fall, Spring. Applicants need a minimum number of credits to apply. For fall 2005: Transfer applications received: 368. Transfer applicants offered admission: 93. Transfer applicants enrolled: 62. **International students:** Number of foreign undergraduates: 96 (3% of student body). Number of countries represented: 32. Minimum TOEFL score required: 600 (paper); 250 (computer).

Sam Houston State University

- **Address:** 1803 Avenue I, Huntsville, TX 77341
- **Website:** http://www.shsu.edu
- **Public**
- **Enrollment:** 11,120 full-time; 1,893 part-time

KEY STATS

✔ **U.S News College Ranking:** third tier, Universities–Master's (West)
✔ **SAT Score (25th/75th percentile):** 890-1110
✔ **Tuition:** 2006-2007: $4,928 in state, $13,178 out of state

Selectivity: Selective	**Room/board:** $5,598
Acceptance rate: 88%	**Average debt:** $16,636
Student/faculty ratio: 21/1	**Proportion who borrowed:** 61%

UNDERGRADUATE STUDENT BODY STATS

2005-2006 enrollment: 11,120 full-time; 1,893 part-time. Men: 42%; women: 58%. **Ethnic makeup:** African American: 15%; American-Indian: 1%; Asian American: 1%; Hispanic: 11%; White: 72%.

ADMISSIONS FACTS AND FIGURES

Phone: (936) 294-1828. **Email:** admissions@shsu.edu. **Website:** http://www.shsu.edu. **Application deadlines for fall 2007:** Regular decision: August 1. Early decision: Not offered. Early action: Not offered. Admission cannot be deferred. **Application fee:** $35. Common application is accepted. **To apply online, go to:** http://www.Applytexas.org. **Admissions requirements/recommendations:** High school units required (recommended): English: 4 (4); Mathematics: 3 (3); Science: 2 (3); Foreign language: (2); Social studies: 3 (4); Academic electives: 1 (4); Total units: 22 (24). Tests: The college uses SAT or ACT scores in admissions decisions. Either SAT or ACT required. For admission to the fall 2007 entering class, the school will accept: ACT with writing, ACT without writing. Campus visit: Recommended. Admissions interview: Neither required nor recommended. Off-campus interview: Not available. **Factors that count in admissions decisions:** *Academic:* Secondary school record: Very important. Class rank: Very important. Letters of recommendation: Considered. Standardized test scores: Very important. Essay: Considered. *Nonacademic:* Interview: Not considered. Extracurricular activities: Not considered. Talent/ability: Not considered. Character/personal qualities: Not considered. Alumni/ae relationship: Not considered. Geographical residence: Not considered. State residency: Not considered. Religious affiliation/commitment: Not considered. Minority status: Not considered. Volunteer work: Not considered. Work experience: Not considered. **Admissions statistics for the fall 2005 entering class:** Total applicants: 7,411. Total accepted: 6,500. Freshmen enrolled: 2,167; 1% were from out of state. Overall acceptance rate: 88%. **Size of waiting list:** 0 applicants; enrolled from waiting list: 0. **Credentials of fall 2005 freshmen:** 13% ranked in the top 10 percent of their high school class; 43% were in the top 25 percent. **First-year students who submitted SAT scores:** 88%. Scores (25/75 percentile): Verbal: 440-550, Math: 450-560, Combined: 890-1110. **First-year students submitting ACT scores:** 47%. Scores (25/75 percentile): English: 16-22, Math: 17-23, Composite: 18-22.

ACADEMICS

Year founded: 1879. **Academic calendar:** Semester. **Degrees offered:** certificate, diploma, bachelor's, post-bachelor's certificate, master's, doctorate. **Most popular majors:** Information not available. **Major fields of study:** agriculture, agriculture operations, and related sciences; architecture and related services; biological and biomedical sciences; business, management, marketing, and related support services; communication, journalism, and related programs; education; engineering technologies/technicians; English language and literature/letters; family and consumer sciences/human sciences; foreign languages, literatures, and linguistics; health professions and related clinical sciences; history; mathematics and statistics; multi/interdisciplinary studies; natural resources and conservation; parks, recreation, leisure, and fitness studies; philosophy and religious studies; physical sciences; psychology; security and protective services; social sciences; visual and performing arts. **Areas of required coursework:** arts/fine arts, humanities, computer literacy, mathematics, English (including composition), philosophy, sciences (biological or physical), history, social science, other. **Pre-professional programs:** pre-law, pre-dentistry, pre-medicine, pre-veterinary science, pre-pharmacy. **Special academic programs:** distance learning, double major, dual enrollment, English as a Second Language (ESL), honors program, independent study, internships, study abroad, teacher certificate program, weekend college. **Teacher certification offered in:** special education, elementary, secondary, bilingual/bicultural. **Reserve Officers Training Corps (ROTC):** Army ROTC: Offered on campus. **Faculty and instruction (2005-2006):** Total instructional faculty: 471 full-time, 210 part-time (55% men; 45% women; 10% minorities). Student/faculty ratio: 21/1. **Advanced Placement and International Baccalaureate credit:** AP tests may be used for: Credit only. Scores accepted: 3. **Freshmen returning for sophomore year:** 66%. **Graduation rates:** Four-year: 16%; five-year: 31%; six-year: 37%.

COSTS AND FINANCIAL AID

Financial aid office: (936) 294-1774. **Expenses (2006-2007):** Tuition and fees 2006-2007: $4,928 in state, $13,178 out of state; room/board: $5,598. Estimated books and supplies: $972; transportation: $1,550; personal expenses: $1,707. **Financial aid:** Priority filing date for institution's financial aid form: March 31; deadline: May 31. In 2005-2006, 66% of undergraduates applied for financial aid. Of those, 50% were determined to have financial need; 7% had their need fully met. Average financial aid package (proportion receiving): $6,108 (48%). Average amount of gift aid, such as scholarships or grants (proportion receiving): $3,494 (38%). Average amount of self-help aid, such as work study or loans (proportion receiving): $3,523 (42%). Average need-based loan (excluding PLUS or other private loans): $3,517. Among students who received need-based aid, the average percentage of need met: 50%. Among students who received aid based on merit, the average award (and the proportion receiving): $1,893 (7%). The average athletic scholarship (and the proportion receiving): $5,750 (3%). Average amount of debt of borrowers graduating in 2005: $16,636. Proportion who borrowed: 61%.

CAMPUS LIFE AND EXTRACURRICULAR ACTIVITIES

Campus housing available: coed dorms, women's dorms, men's dorms, sorority housing, fraternity housing, apartment for single students. Students who live in college-owned, operated, or affiliated housing: 26%. **Student employment:** During the 2005-2006 academic year, 8% of undergraduates worked on campus. Average per-year earnings: $3,790. **Clubs and organizations:** Number of student organizations: 188. Activities include: choral groups, concert band, dance, drama/theater, jazz band, marching band, music ensembles, musical theater, pep band, radio station, student government, student newspaper, symphony orchestra, television station, yearbook. Number of fraternities: 15; sororities: 8. Proportion of men in fraternities: 11%; of women in sororities: 6%. **Sports program (2005-2006):** Member of NCAA I. **Men's intercollegiate varsity sports:** baseball, basketball, cross-country, football, golf, track and field (indoor), track and field (outdoor). **Women's intercollegiate varsity sports:** basketball, cross-country, golf, soccer, softball, tennis, track and field (indoor), track and field (outdoor), volleyball.

SERVICES AND FACILITIES

Basic services: placement service, health service. **Remedial assistance:** reading, math, writing, study skills. **Counseling services:** minority student, career, personal, academic, older student, psychological. **For learning-disabled students:** School does not offer a structured program with separate admission and additional fees. Services include: remedial math, remedial English, reading machines, remedial reading, tape recorders, note-taking services, oral tests, learning center, extended time for tests, texts on tape. **Library:** Number of titles: 2,461,625; number of current serial subscriptions: 4,771. **Information technology resources:** Students are not required to lease or own a computer. Number of campus computers available to all students: 700. School has a wireless network. Proportion of college-owned housing units wired for high-speed internet access: 100%. **Campus safety:** Security services offered: late-night transport/escort service, 24-hour emergency telephones, lighted pathways/sidewalks, controlled dormitory access (key, security card, etc).

TRANSFER AND INTERNATIONAL STUDENTS

Transfer students: May apply for admission for the following academic terms: Fall, Spring, Summer. Applicants need a minimum number of credits to apply. For fall 2005: Transfer applications received: 4,488. Transfer applicants offered admission: 1,488. Transfer applicants enrolled: 1,488. **International students:** Number of foreign undergraduates: 59. Number of countries represented: 29. Minimum TOEFL score required: 550 (paper); 213 (computer). Average TOEFL score: 599 (paper).

Schreiner University

- **Address:** 2100 Memorial Boulevard, Kerrville, TX 78028
- **Website:** http://www.schreiner.edu
- **Private; Religious affiliation:** Presbyterian
- **Enrollment:** 695 full-time; 75 part-time

KEY STATS

✔ **U.S News College Ranking:** fourth tier, Liberal Arts Colleges
✔ **SAT Score (25th/75th percentile):** 850-1060
✔ **Tuition:** 2006-2007: $15,880

Selectivity: Less selective	**Room/board:** $7,566
Acceptance rate: 69%	**Average debt:** $21,455
Student/faculty ratio: 12/1	**Proportion who borrowed:** 83%

UNDERGRADUATE STUDENT BODY STATS

2005-2006 enrollment: 695 full-time; 75 part-time. Men: 40%; women: 60%. **Ethnic makeup:** African American: 4%; American-Indian: 1%; Asian

American: 1%; Hispanic: 20%; White: 74%; International: 1%. **Religious preference:** Roman Catholic: 23%; Protestant: 54%; Jewish: 1%; No preference: 12%; Presbyterian: 8%; Eastern Orthodox: 0%; Other: 2%.

ADMISSIONS FACTS AND FIGURES

Phone: (800) 343-4919. **Email:** admissions@schreiner.edu. **Website:** http://www.schreiner.edu. **Application deadlines for fall 2007:** Regular decision: August 1. Early decision: Not offered. Early action: Not offered. Admission can be deferred. **Application fee:** $25. Common application is accepted. **To apply online, go to:** http://www.schreiner.edu/ADMISSION/APPLYING.HTML. **Admissions requirements/recommendations:** High school units required (recommended): English: (4); Mathematics: (3); Science: (2); Social studies: (2). Tests: The college uses SAT or ACT scores in admissions decisions. Either SAT or ACT required. For admission to the fall 2007 entering class, the school will accept: ACT with writing. Campus visit: Recommended. Admissions interview: Recommended. Off-campus interview: May be arranged. **Factors that count in admissions decisions:** *Academic:* Secondary school record: Important. Class rank: Important. Letters of recommendation: Considered. Standardized test scores: Important. Essay: Important. *Nonacademic:* Interview: Important. Extracurricular activities: Considered. Talent/ability: Considered. Character/personal qualities: Considered. Alumni/ae relationship: Not considered. Geographical residence: Not considered. State residency: Not considered. Religious affiliation/commitment: Not considered. Minority status: Not considered. Volunteer work: Considered. Work experience: Considered. **Other schools with the greatest overlap in applicants:** Austin College; Baylor University; Texas A&M University–College Station; Texas State University–San Marcos; Trinity University. **Admissions statistics for the fall 2005 entering class:** Total applicants: 565. Total accepted: 387. Freshmen enrolled: 173; 0% were from out of state. Overall acceptance rate: 69%. **Credentials of fall 2005 freshmen:** 10% ranked in the top 10 percent of their high school class; 18% were in the top 25 percent, and 63% were in the top half. (Proportion submitting class standing: 82%.) **Average high school grade point average:** 3.4. **First-year students who submitted SAT scores:** 74%. Scores (25/75 percentile): Verbal: 420-520, Math: 430-540, Combined: 850-1060. **First-year students submitting ACT scores:** 59%. Scores (25/75 percentile): English: 15-21, Math: 17-21, Composite: 17-21.

ACADEMICS

Year founded: 1923. **Academic calendar:** Semester. **Degrees offered:** certificate, associate, bachelor's, post-bachelor's certificate, master's. **Most popular majors:** 28% business, management, marketing, and related support services, 14% education, 12% psychology, 11% multi/interdisciplinary studies, 10% biological and biomedical sciences. **Major fields of study:** biological and biomedical sciences; business, management, marketing, and related support services; education; engineering; English language and literature/letters; history; legal professions and studies; liberal arts and sciences studies, and humanities; mathematics and statistics; multi/interdisciplinary studies; parks, recreation, leisure, and fitness studies; philosophy and religious studies; physical sciences; psychology; social sciences; visual and performing arts. **Areas of required coursework:** arts/fine arts, humanities, computer literacy, mathematics, English (including composition), philosophy, foreign languages, sciences (biological or physical), history, social science. **Pre-professional programs:** pre-law, pre-dentistry, pre-medicine, pre-theology, pre-veterinary science, pre-pharmacy. **Special academic programs (% participation):** accelerated program, double major, dual enrollment, honors program (13.3%), independent study (27.5%), internships (38.3%), liberal arts/career combination, student-designed major (.8%), study abroad (.8%), teacher certificate program (14.2%). **Teacher certification offered in:** elementary, middle/junior high, secondary. **Faculty and instruction (2005-2006):** Total instructional faculty: 52 full-time, 31 part-time (57% men; 43% women; 8% minorities). Full-time faculty with Ph.D. or other terminal degree: 65%. Student/faculty ratio: 12/1. Classes of fewer than 20 students: 66%; of 20 to 49 students: 34%. **Advanced Placement and International Baccalaureate credit:** AP tests may be used for: Credit only. Scores accepted: 3, 4, 5. International Baccalaureate exams may be used for: Credit only. **Freshmen returning for sophomore year:** 62%. **Graduation rates:** Four-year: 27%; five-year: 34%; six-year: 36%.

COSTS AND FINANCIAL AID

Financial aid office: (830) 792-7217. **Expenses (2006-2007):** Tuition and fees 2006-2007: $15,880; room/board: $7,566. Estimated books and supplies: $1,000; transportation: $500; personal expenses: $1,000. **Financial aid:** Priority filing date for institution's financial aid form: April 1; deadline: August 1. In 2005-2006, 92% of undergraduates applied for financial aid.

Of those, 82% were determined to have financial need; 18% had their need fully met. Average financial aid package (proportion receiving): $11,682 (82%). Average amount of gift aid, such as scholarships or grants (proportion receiving): $8,981 (82%). Average amount of self-help aid, such as work study or loans (proportion receiving): $3,195 (69%). Average need-based loan (excluding PLUS or other private loans): $2,795. Among students who received need-based aid, the average percentage of need met: 33%. Among students who received aid based on merit, the average award (and the proportion receiving): $12,968 (19%). Average amount of debt of borrowers graduating in 2005: $21,455. Proportion who borrowed: 83%.

CAMPUS LIFE AND EXTRACURRICULAR ACTIVITIES

Campus housing available (% using): coed dorms (50%), apartments for married students (0%), apartment for single students (50%), special housing for disabled students (0%). Students who live in college-owned, operated, or affiliated housing: 55%. **Student employment:** During the 2005-2006 academic year, 10% of undergraduates worked on campus. Average per-year earnings: $1,500. **Clubs and organizations:** Number of student organizations: 30. Activities include: choral groups, drama/theater, literary magazine, music ensembles, musical theater, pep band, student government, student newspaper, symphony orchestra. Number of fraternities: 2; sororities: 2. Proportion of men in fraternities: 14%; of women in sororities: 19%. Average proportion of students who stay on campus on weekends: 40%. **Sports program (2005-2006):** Member of NCAA III. *Men's intercollegiate varsity sports:* baseball, basketball, golf, soccer, tennis. *Women's intercollegiate varsity sports:* basketball, soccer, softball, tennis, volleyball.

SERVICES AND FACILITIES

Basic services: nonremedial tutoring, placement service, health service. **Counseling services:** career, personal, older student, psychological, birth control, religious. **For learning-disabled students:** School does not offer a structured program with separate admission and additional fees. Total undergraduates in learning-disabled program or receiving services: 66. Services include: remedial math, remedial English, reading machines, tape recorders, note-taking services, oral tests, readers, extended time for tests, tutors, texts on tape, other testing accomodations. **Library:** Number of titles: 69,873; number of current serial subscriptions: 225. **Information technology resources:** Students are not required to lease or own a computer. Number of campus computers available to all students: 106. School has a wireless network. Proportion of college-owned housing units wired for high-speed internet access: 100%. **Campus safety:** Security services offered: 24-hour foot-and-vehicle patrols, late-night transport/escort service, 24-hour emergency telephones, lighted pathways/sidewalks.

TRANSFER AND INTERNATIONAL STUDENTS

Transfer students: May apply for admission for the following academic terms: Fall, Spring, Summer. Applicants need a minimum number of credits to apply. For fall 2005: Transfer applications received: 441. Transfer applicants offered admission: 296. Transfer applicants enrolled: 85. **International students:** Number of foreign undergraduates: 7 (1% of student body). Number of countries represented: 10. Minimum TOEFL score required: 550 (paper); 213 (computer). Average TOEFL score: 584 (paper).

Southern Methodist University

- **Address:** PO Box 750181, Dallas, TX 75275-0181
- **Website:** http://www.smu.edu
- **Private; Religious affiliation:** United Methodist
- **Enrollment:** 6,126 full-time; 363 part-time

KEY STATS

✔ **U.S News College Ranking:** 70, National Universities
✔ **SAT Score (25th/75th percentile):** 1130-1330
✔ **Tuition:** 2006-2007: $28,630

Selectivity: More selective	**Room/board:** $9,695
Acceptance rate: 58%	**Average debt:** $18,571
Student/faculty ratio: 12/1	**Proportion who borrowed:** 43%

UNDERGRADUATE STUDENT BODY STATS

2005-2006 enrollment: 6,126 full-time; 363 part-time. Men: 45%; women: 55%. **Ethnic makeup:** African American: 5%; American-Indian: 1%; Asian American: 6%; Hispanic: 8%; White: 75%; International: 5%. **Religious preference:** Roman Catholic: 16%; Protestant: 21%; Jewish: 1%; Muslim: 1%; Unknown: 35%; United Methodist: 14%; Non-Denominational, Christian: 10%; Other: 2%.

ADMISSIONS FACTS AND FIGURES

Phone: (800) 323-0672. **Email:** enrol_serv@mail.smu.edu. **Website:** http://www.smu.edu. **Application deadlines for fall 2007:** Regular decision: March 15. Early decision: Not offered. Early action: Send application by: November 1; Decision sent by: December 31. Admission can be deferred. **Application fee:** $50. Common application is accepted. **To apply online, go to:** http://www.smu.edu/apply. **Admissions requirements/recommendations:** High school units required (recommended): English: 4 (4); Mathematics: 3 (4); Science: 3 (4); Foreign language: 2 (3); Social studies: 1 (2); History: 2 (3); Total units: 15. Tests: The college uses SAT or ACT scores in admissions decisions. Either SAT or ACT required. For admission to the fall 2007 entering class, the school will accept: ACT with writing, ACT without writing. Campus visit: Recommended. Admissions interview: Neither required nor recommended. Off-campus interview: May be arranged. **Factors that count in admissions decisions:** *Academic:* Secondary school record: Very important. Class rank: Very important. Letters of recommendation: Very important. Standardized test scores: Very important. Essay: Very important. *Nonacademic:* Interview: Considered. Extracurricular activities: Important. Talent/ability: Important. Character/personal qualities: Important. Alumni/ae relationship: Considered. Geographical residence: Not considered. State residency: Not considered. Religious affiliation/commitment: Not considered. Minority status: Not considered. Volunteer work: Important. Work experience: Important. **Other schools with the greatest overlap in applicants:** Texas A&M University–College Station; Texas Christian University; University of Southern California; University of Texas–Austin; Vanderbilt University. **Admissions statistics for the fall 2005 entering class:** Total applicants: 6,981. Total accepted: 4,076. Freshmen enrolled: 1,402; 45% were from out of state. Accepted through early-decision or early-action plans: 52%. Overall acceptance rate: 58%. Non-early acceptance rate: 55%. **Size of waiting list:** 715 applicants; enrolled from waiting list: 76. **Credentials of fall 2005 freshmen:** 35% ranked in the top 10 percent of their high school class; 64% were in the top 25 percent, and 92% were in the top half. (Proportion submitting class standing: 52%.) **Average high school grade point average:** 3.5. **First-year students who submitted SAT scores:** 83%. Scores (25/75 percentile): Verbal: 560-660, Math: 570-670, Combined: 1130-1330. **First-year students submitting ACT scores:** 46%. Scores (25/75 percentile): English: 23-29, Math: 23-28, Composite: 24-28.

ACADEMICS

Year founded: 1911. **Academic calendar:** Semester. **Degrees offered:** certificate, bachelor's, post-bachelor's certificate, master's, first professional, doctorate. **Most popular majors:** 26% business, management, marketing, and related support services, 15% social sciences, 12% communication, journalism, and related programs, 8% psychology, 8% visual and performing arts. **Major fields of study:** area, ethnic, cultural, and gender studies; biological and biomedical sciences; business, management, marketing, and related support services; communication, journalism, and related programs; computer and information sciences and support services; education; engineering; English language and literature/letters; foreign languages, literatures, and linguistics; health professions and related clinical sciences; history; liberal arts and sciences studies, and humanities; mathematics and statistics; multi/interdisciplinary studies; natural resources and conservation; philosophy and religious studies; physical sciences; psychology; public administration and social service professions; social sciences; visual and performing arts. **Areas of required coursework:** arts/fine arts, humanities, computer literacy, mathematics, English (including composition), philosophy, sciences (biological or physical), history, social science. **Pre-professional programs:** pre-law, pre-dentistry, pre-medicine, pre-theology, pre-optometry, pre-pharmacy. **Special academic programs (% participation):** accelerated program, cooperative (work-study plan) program, distance learning, double major (30%), English as a Second Language (ESL) (5%), exchange student program (domestic), honors program (12%), independent study, internships, student-designed major, study abroad, teacher certificate program. **Teacher certification offered in:** elementary, secondary, bilingual/bicultural. **Cooperative education programs:** business, engineering. **Reserve Officers Training Corps (ROTC):** Army ROTC: Offered at cooperating institution (Univ of Texas at Arlington); Air Force ROTC: Offered at cooperating institution (University of North Texas). **Faculty and instruction (2005-2006):** Total instructional faculty: 603 full-time, 322 part-time (66% men; 34% women; 12% minorities). Full-time faculty with Ph.D. or other terminal degree: 84%. Student/faculty ratio: 12/1. Classes of fewer than 20 students: 50%; of

20 to 49 students: 39%; of 50 or more students: 11%. **Advanced Placement and International Baccalaureate credit:** AP tests may be used for: Placement only. Scores accepted: 4, 5. International Baccalaureate exams may be used for: Credit only. **Freshmen returning for sophomore year:** 87%. **Graduation rates:** Four-year: 55%; five-year: 69%; six-year: 71%.

COSTS AND FINANCIAL AID

Financial aid office: (214) 768-3016. **Expenses (2006-2007):** Tuition and fees 2006-2007: $28,630; room/board: $9,695. Estimated books and supplies: $600; transportation: $300; personal expenses: $1,100. **Financial aid:** Priority filing date for institution's financial aid form: February 15. In 2005-2006, 45% of undergraduates applied for financial aid. Of those, 38% were determined to have financial need; 37% had their need fully met. Average financial aid package (proportion receiving): $23,699 (38%). Average amount of gift aid, such as scholarships or grants (proportion receiving): $13,766 (34%). Average amount of self-help aid, such as work study or loans (proportion receiving): $5,595 (30%). Average need-based loan (excluding PLUS or other private loans): $3,924. Among students who received need-based aid, the average percentage of need met: 88%. Among students who received aid based on merit, the average award (and the proportion receiving): $5,311 (30%). The average athletic scholarship (and the proportion receiving): $29,383 (5%). Average amount of debt of borrowers graduating in 2005: $18,571. Proportion who borrowed: 43%.

CAMPUS LIFE AND EXTRACURRICULAR ACTIVITIES

Campus housing available (% using): coed dorms (68%), sorority housing (11%), fraternity housing (11%), apartments for married students (2%), apartment for single students (8%). Students who live in college-owned, operated, or affiliated housing: 45%. Average per-year earnings: $2,500. **Clubs and organizations:** Number of student organizations: 200. Activities include: choral groups, concert band, dance, drama/theater, jazz band, literary magazine, marching band, music ensembles, musical theater, opera, pep band, radio station, student government, student newspaper, student film society, symphony orchestra, television station, yearbook. Number of fraternities: 15; sororities: 14. Proportion of men in fraternities: 29%; of women in sororities: 40%. Average proportion of students who stay on campus on weekends: 85%. **Sports program (2005-2006):** Member of NCAA I. **Men's intercollegiate varsity sports:** basketball, football, golf, soccer, swimming and diving, tennis. **Women's intercollegiate varsity sports:** basketball, cross-country, equestrian sports, golf, rowing, soccer, swimming and diving, tennis, track and field (indoor), track and field (outdoor), volleyball, rowing.

SERVICES AND FACILITIES

Basic services: nonremedial tutoring, women's center, placement service, health service, health insurance. **Remedial assistance:** reading, math, writing, study skills. **Counseling services:** minority student, career, personal, academic, older student, psychological, birth control, religious. **For learning-disabled students:** School does not offer a structured program with separate admission and additional fees. Total undergraduates in learning-disabled program or receiving services: 165. Services include: reading machines, tape recorders, diagnostic testing service, note-taking services, oral tests, learning center, readers, extended time for tests, tutors, priority registration, texts on tape, other. **Library:** Number of titles: 2,807,991; number of current serial subscriptions: 11,635. **Information technology resources:** Students are not required to lease or own a computer. Number of campus computers available to all students: 409. School has a wireless network. **Campus safety:** Security services offered: 24-hour foot-and-vehicle patrols, late-night transport/escort service, 24-hour emergency telephones, lighted pathways/sidewalks, controlled dormitory access (key, security card, etc).

TRANSFER AND INTERNATIONAL STUDENTS

Transfer students: May apply for admission for the following academic terms: Fall, Spring, Summer. Applicants do not need a minimum number of credits to apply. For fall 2005: Transfer applications received: 752. Transfer applicants offered admission: 478. Transfer applicants enrolled: 291. **International students:** Number of foreign undergraduates: 290 (5% of student body). Number of countries represented: 68. Minimum TOEFL score required: 550 (paper); 213 (computer).

Southwestern Adventist University

- **Address:** PO Box 567, Keene, TX 76059
- **Website:** http://www.swau.edu
- **Private; Religious affiliation:** Seventh-day Adventist
- **Enrollment:** 735 full-time; 145 part-time

KEY STATS

✔ **U.S News College Ranking:** third tier, Comp. Coll.–Bachelor's (West)
✔ **SAT or ACT Score (25th/75th percentile):** N/A
✔ **Tuition:** 2006-2007: $13,636

Selectivity: Less selective	**Room/board:** $6,124
Acceptance rate: N/A	**Average debt:** N/A
Student/faculty ratio: N/A	**Proportion who borrowed:** N/A

UNDERGRADUATE STUDENT BODY STATS

2005-2006 enrollment: 735 full-time; 145 part-time. Men: 44%; women: 56%.

ADMISSIONS FACTS AND FIGURES

Phone: (817) 645-3921. **Email:** admissions@swau.edu. **Website:** http://www.swau.edu. **Application deadlines for fall 2007:** Regular decision: September 1. Early decision: Not offered. Early action: Not offered. Common application is not accepted. **To apply online, go to:** http://www.swau.edu/admissions/apply.asp. **Admissions requirements/recommendations:** High school units required (recommended): English: 4; Mathematics: 3; Science: 2; Social studies: 3; History: 2. Tests: The college uses SAT or ACT scores in admissions decisions. SAT required. Campus visit: Recommended. Admissions interview: Neither required nor recommended. **Factors that count in admissions decisions:** *Academic:* Secondary school record: Very important. Class rank: Not considered. Letters of recommendation: Not considered. Standardized test scores: Very important. Essay: Not considered. *Nonacademic:* Interview: Not considered. Extracurricular activities: Considered. Talent/ability: Considered. Character/personal qualities: Important. Alumni/ae relationship: Considered. Geographical residence: Not considered. State residency: Not considered. Religious affiliation/commitment: Very important. Minority status: Not considered. Volunteer work: Considered. Work experience: Considered. **Other schools with the greatest overlap in applicants:** Pacific Union College; Southern Adventist University; Union College; University of Texas–Arlington; Walla Walla College. **Admissions statistics for the fall 2005 entering class:** Freshmen enrolled: 190; **Size of waiting list:** 0 applicants; enrolled from waiting list: N/A.

ACADEMICS

Year founded: 1893. **Academic calendar:** Semester. **Degrees offered:** associate, bachelor's, master's. **Most popular majors:** Information not available. **Major fields of study:** biological and biomedical sciences; business, management, marketing, and related support services; communication, journalism, and related programs; computer and information sciences and support services; education; English language and literature/letters; foreign languages, literatures, and linguistics; history; legal professions and studies; liberal arts and sciences studies; and humanities; mathematics and statistics; philosophy and religious studies; physical sciences; psychology; public administration and social service professions; security and protective services; theology and religious vocations; visual and performing arts. **Areas of required coursework:** arts/fine arts, humanities, computer literacy, mathematics, English (including composition), sciences (biological or physical), history, social science, other. **Pre-professional programs:** pre-law, pre-dentistry, pre-medicine. **Special academic programs (% participation):** distance learning (10%), English as a Second Language (ESL) (1%), honors program (1%), student-designed major (1%), study abroad (1%), teacher certificate program (16%). **Teacher certification offered in:** elementary, middle/junior high, secondary. **Faculty and instruction (2005-2006):** Total instructional faculty: 51 full-time, 22 part-time (62% men; 38% women; 14% minorities). Full-time faculty with Ph.D. or other terminal degree: 59%. **Advanced Placement and International Baccalaureate credit:** AP tests may be used for: Credit only. Scores accepted: 4, 5. **Graduation rates:** Six-year: 32%.

COSTS AND FINANCIAL AID

Financial aid office: (817) 645-3921. **Expenses (2006-2007):** Tuition and fees 2006-2007: $13,636; room/board: $6,124.

CAMPUS LIFE AND EXTRACURRICULAR ACTIVITIES

Campus housing available: women's dorms, men's dorms, apartments for married students. Activities include: choral groups, concert band, radio station, student government, television station, yearbook. Number of fraternities: 0; sororities: 0.

SERVICES AND FACILITIES

Basic services: health service, health insurance. **Remedial assistance:** math, writing. **Counseling services:** academic, religious. **For learning-disabled students:** School does not offer a structured program with separate admission and additional fees. Services include: diagnostic testing service, extended time for tests. **Information technology resources:** Students are not required to lease or own a computer. Number of campus computers available to all students: 300. School has a wireless network. Proportion of college-owned housing units wired for high-speed internet access: 100%.

TRANSFER AND INTERNATIONAL STUDENTS

Transfer students: May apply for admission for the following academic terms: Fall, Spring, Summer. Applicants need a minimum number of credits to apply.

Southwestern University

- **Address:** PO Box 770, Georgetown, TX 78627-0770
- **Website:** http://www.southwestern.edu
- **Private; Religious affiliation:** United Methodist
- **Enrollment:** 1,286 full-time; 23 part-time

KEY STATS

✔ **U.S News College Ranking:** 57, Liberal Arts Colleges
✔ **SAT Score (25th/75th percentile):** 1130-1330
✔ **Tuition:** 2006-2007: $23,650

Selectivity: More selective	**Room/board:** $8,040
Acceptance rate: 67%	**Average debt:** $18,446
Student/faculty ratio: 10/1	**Proportion who borrowed:** 52%

UNDERGRADUATE STUDENT BODY STATS

2005-2006 enrollment: 1,286 full-time; 23 part-time. Men: 41%; women: 59%. **Ethnic makeup:** African American: 3%; American-Indian: 1%; Asian American: 5%; Hispanic: 14%; White: 77%. **Religious preference:** Roman Catholic: 19%; Protestant: 40%; Jewish: 2%; Hindu: 1%; No preference: 7%; Unknown: 6%; United Methodist: 25%.

ADMISSIONS FACTS AND FIGURES

Phone: (800) 252-3166. **Email:** admission@southwestern.edu. **Website:** http://www.southwestern.edu. **Application deadlines for fall 2007:** Regular decision: February 15; decision sent by April 1. Early decision: Send application by: November 1; Decision sent by: December 1. Early action: Not offered. Admission can be deferred. **Application fee:** $40. Common application is accepted. **To apply online, go to:** http://www.southwestern.edu/admission-finaid/adm-apply.html. **Admissions requirements/recommendations:** High school units required (recommended): English: 4 (4); Mathematics: 4 (4); Science: 3 (4); Foreign language: 2 (3); Social studies: 2 (2); History: 2 (2); Total units: 17 (19). Tests: The college uses SAT or ACT scores in admissions decisions. Either SAT or ACT required. For admission to the fall 2007 entering class, the school will accept: ACT with writing. Campus visit: Recommended. Admissions interview: Recommended. Off-campus interview: May be arranged. **Factors that count in admissions decisions: Academic:** Secondary school record: Very important. Class rank: Very important. Letters of recommendation: Very important. Standardized test scores: Very important. Essay: Very important. **Nonacademic:** Interview: Important. Extracurricular activities: Important. Talent/ability: Important. Character/personal qualities: Important. Alumni/ae relationship: Important. Geographical residence: Important. State residency: Not considered. Religious affiliation/commitment: Not considered. Minority status: Important. Volunteer work: Important. Work experience: Important. **Other schools with the greatest overlap in applicants:** Austin College; Baylor University; Texas A&M University–College Station; Trinity University; University of Texas–Austin. **Admissions statistics for the fall 2005 entering class:** Total applicants: 1,760. Total accepted: 1,178. Freshmen enrolled: 329; 7% were from out of state. Accepted through early-decision or early-action plans: 18%. Overall acceptance rate: 67%. Non-early

acceptance rate: 63%. **Size of waiting list:** 88 applicants; enrolled from waiting list: 17. **Credentials of fall 2005 freshmen:** 49% ranked in the top 10 percent of their high school class; 82% were in the top 25 percent, and 97% were in the top half. (Proportion submitting class standing: 87%.) **First-year students who submitted SAT scores:** 95%. Scores (25/75 percentile): Verbal: 560-670, Math: 570-660, Combined: 1130-1330. **First-year students submitting ACT scores:** 53%. Scores (25/75 percentile): English: N/A, Math: N/A, Composite: 24-29.

ACADEMICS

Year founded: 1840. **Academic calendar:** Semester. **Degrees offered:** bachelor's. **Most popular majors:** 18% biological and biomedical sciences, 17% social sciences, 15% communication, journalism, and related programs, 12% business, management, marketing, and related support services, 7% English language and literature/letters. **Major fields of study:** agriculture, agriculture operations, and related sciences; area, ethnic, cultural, and gender studies; biological and biomedical sciences; business, management, marketing, and related support services; communication, journalism, and related programs; computer and information sciences and support services; education; English language and literature/letters; foreign languages, literatures, and linguistics; health professions and related clinical sciences; history; liberal arts and sciences studies, and humanities; mathematics and statistics; multi/interdisciplinary studies; philosophy and religious studies; physical sciences; psychology; social sciences; visual and performing arts. **Areas of required coursework:** arts/fine arts, humanities, computer literacy, mathematics, English (including composition), foreign languages, sciences (biological or physical), social science. **Pre-professional programs:** pre-law, pre-dentistry, pre-medicine, pre-theology, pre-veterinary science, pre-optometry, pre-pharmacy, other. **Special academic programs (% participation):** double major (14%), honors program (24%), independent study (29%), internships (28%), liberal arts/career combination, student-designed major (1%), study abroad (45%), teacher certificate program (8%). **Teacher certification offered in:** early childhood, special education, elementary, middle/junior high, secondary. **Cooperative education programs:** engineering. **Faculty and instruction (2005-2006):** Total instructional faculty: 118 full-time, 49 part-time (50% men; 50% women; 13% minorities). Full-time faculty with Ph.D. or other terminal degree: 99%. Student/faculty ratio: 10/1. Classes of fewer than 20 students: 79%; of 20 to 49 students: 21%; of 50 or more students: 0%. **Advanced Placement and International Baccalaureate credit:** AP tests may be used for: Credit and/or placement. Scores accepted: 4, 5. International Baccalaureate exams may be used for: Credit and/or placement. **Freshmen returning for sophomore year:** 87%. **Graduation rates:** Four-year: 67%; five-year: 77%; six-year: 78%. **Graduate study:** 27% of students pursue further study immediately upon graduation. Fields in which graduates pursue further study: law, 13%; medicine, 4%; theology (or the seminary), 6%.

COSTS AND FINANCIAL AID

Financial aid office: (512) 863-1259. **Expenses (2006-2007):** Tuition and fees 2006-2007: $23,650; room/board: $8,040. Estimated books and supplies: $1,000; transportation: $310; personal expenses: $870. **Financial aid:** Priority filing date for institution's financial aid form: March 1; deadline: March 1. In 2005-2006, 62% of undergraduates applied for financial aid. Of those, 50% were determined to have financial need; 54% had their need fully met. Average financial aid package (proportion receiving): $19,315 (50%). Average amount of gift aid, such as scholarships or grants (proportion receiving): $13,251 (50%). Average amount of self-help aid, such as work study or loans (proportion receiving): $5,287 (44%). Average need-based loan (excluding PLUS or other private loans): $4,530. Among students who received need-based aid, the average percentage of need met: 97%. Among students who received aid based on merit, the average award (and the proportion receiving): $7,935 (29%). The average athletic scholarship (and the proportion receiving): $0 (0%). Average amount of debt of borrowers graduating in 2005: $18,446. Proportion who borrowed: 52%.

CAMPUS LIFE AND EXTRACURRICULAR ACTIVITIES

Campus housing available (% using): coed dorms (27%), women's dorms (20%), men's dorms (16%), fraternity housing (7%), apartment for single students (30%). Students who live in college-owned, operated, or affiliated housing: 80%. **Student employment:** During the 2005-2006 academic year, 24% of undergraduates worked on campus. Average per-year earnings: $1,200. **Clubs and organizations:** Number of student organizations: 105. Activities include: choral groups, concert band, dance, drama/theater, jazz band, literary magazine, music ensembles, musical theater, opera, student government, student newspaper, student film society, symphony orchestra, television station, yearbook. Number of fraternities: 4; sororities: 4.

Proportion of men in fraternities: 29%; of women in sororities: 31%.
Average proportion of students who stay on campus on weekends: 75%.
Sports program (2005-2006): Member of NCAA III. *Men's intercollegiate varsity sports:* baseball, basketball, cross-country, golf, soccer, swimming and diving, tennis. *Women's intercollegiate varsity sports:* basketball, cross-country, golf, soccer, swimming and diving, tennis, volleyball.

SERVICES AND FACILITIES

Basic services: nonremedial tutoring, placement service, health service, health insurance. **Remedial assistance:** writing, study skills, other. **Counseling services:** minority student, career, personal, academic, psychological, religious. **For learning-disabled students:** School does not offer a structured program with separate admission and additional fees. Total undergraduates in learning-disabled program or receiving services: 70. Services include: tape recorders, note-taking services, oral tests, learning center, readers, extended time for tests, tutors, priority seating, substitution of courses, texts on tape, exams on tape or computer, other testing accomodations. **Library:** Number of titles: 342,020; number of current serial subscriptions: 2,973. **Information technology resources:** Students are not required to lease or own a computer. Number of campus computers available to all students: 410. School has a wireless network. Approximate number of users that can be accommodated: 300. Proportion of college-owned housing units wired for high-speed internet access: 100%. **Campus safety:** Security services offered: 24-hour foot-and-vehicle patrols, late-night transport/escort service, 24-hour emergency telephones, lighted pathways/sidewalks, controlled dormitory access (key, security card, etc).

TRANSFER AND INTERNATIONAL STUDENTS

Transfer students: May apply for admission for the following academic terms: Fall, Spring. Applicants do not need a minimum number of credits to apply. For fall 2005: Transfer applications received: 111. Transfer applicants offered admission: 65. Transfer applicants enrolled: 38. **International students:** Number of foreign undergraduates: 4. Number of countries represented: 4. Minimum TOEFL score required: 570 (paper); 230 (computer).

St. Edward's University

- **Address:** 3001 S. Congress Avenue, Austin, TX 78704
- **Website:** http://www.stedwards.edu
- **Private; Religious affiliation:** Roman Catholic
- **Enrollment:** 2,997 full-time; 967 part-time

KEY STATS

✔ **U.S News College Ranking:** 25, Universities–Master's (West)
✔ **SAT Score (25th/75th percentile):** 1010-1210
✔ **Tuition:** 2006-2007: $18,800

Selectivity: Selective	**Room/board:** $6,900
Acceptance rate: 69%	**Average debt:** $24,280
Student/faculty ratio: 14/1	**Proportion who borrowed:** 62%

UNDERGRADUATE STUDENT BODY STATS

2005-2006 enrollment: 2,997 full-time; 967 part-time. Men: 42%; women: 58%. **Ethnic makeup:** African American: 5%; American-Indian: 1%; Asian American: 2%; Hispanic: 30%; White: 60%; International: 2%.

ADMISSIONS FACTS AND FIGURES

Phone: (512) 448-8500. **Email:** seu.admit@admin.stedwards.edu. **Website:** http://www.stedwards.edu. **Application deadlines for fall 2007:** Regular decision: May 1. Early decision: Not offered. Early action: Not offered. Admission can be deferred. **Application fee:** $45. Common application is accepted. **To apply online, go to:** http://www.stedwards.edu/apply_online.htm. **Admissions requirements/recommendations:** High school units required (recommended): English: 4 (4); Mathematics: 3 (4); Science: 2 (3); Foreign language: 2 (3); Social studies: 1 (1); History: 2 (3); Academic electives: 0 (1); Total units: 14 (19). Tests: The college uses SAT or ACT scores in admissions decisions. Either SAT or ACT required. For admission to the fall 2007 entering class, the school will accept: ACT with writing. Campus visit: Recommended. Admissions interview: Recommended. Off-campus interview: Not available. **Factors that count in admissions decisions:** *Academic:* Secondary school record: Very important. Class rank: Very important. Letters of recommendation: Important. Standardized test scores: Very important. Essay: Very important.

Nonacademic: Interview: Considered. Extracurricular activities: Important. Talent/ability: Considered. Character/personal qualities: Considered. Alumni/ae relationship: Not considered. Geographical residence: Considered. State residency: Considered. Religious affiliation/commitment: Not considered. Minority status: Not considered. Volunteer work: Important. Work experience: Considered. **Other schools with the greatest overlap in applicants:** Baylor University; Texas A&M University–College Station; Texas State University–San Marcos; University of Texas–Austin; University of Texas–San Antonio. **Admissions statistics for the fall 2005 entering class:** Total applicants: 2,217. Total accepted: 1,530. Freshmen enrolled: 650; 8% were from out of state. Overall acceptance rate: 69%. **Size of waiting list:** 258 applicants; enrolled from waiting list: 49. **Credentials of fall 2005 freshmen:** 15% ranked in the top 10 percent of their high school class; 45% were in the top 25 percent, and 80% were in the top half. (Proportion submitting class standing: 79%.) **First-year students who submitted SAT scores:** 80%. Scores (25/75 percentile): Verbal: 510-620, Math: 500-590, Combined: 1010-1210. **First-year students submitting ACT scores:** 19%. Scores (25/75 percentile): English: 21-27, Math: 19-25, Composite: 21-26.

ACADEMICS

Year founded: 1885. **Academic calendar:** Semester. **Degrees offered:** bachelor's, post-bachelor's certificate, master's. **Most popular majors:** 16% business administration and management, 8% communication and media studies, 7% psychology, 5% management information systems, 4% marketing/marketing management. **Major fields of study:** area, ethnic, cultural, and gender studies; biological and biomedical sciences; business, management, marketing, and related support services; communication, journalism, and related programs; computer and information sciences and support services; education; English language and literature/letters; foreign languages, literatures, and linguistics; history; liberal arts and sciences studies, and humanities; mathematics and statistics; multi/interdisciplinary studies; natural resources and conservation; parks, recreation, leisure, and fitness studies; philosophy and religious studies; physical sciences; psychology; public administration and social service professions; security and protective services; social sciences; theology and religious vocations; visual and performing arts. **Areas of required coursework:** arts/fine arts, humanities, computer literacy, mathematics, English (including composition), philosophy, foreign languages, sciences (biological or physical), history, social science. **Pre-professional programs:** pre-law, pre-dentistry, pre-medicine, other. **Special academic programs:** double major, honors program, internships, liberal arts/career combination, study abroad, teacher certificate program. **Teacher certification offered in:** early childhood, elementary, middle/junior high, secondary, bilingual/bicultural. **Cooperative education programs:** business, education, humanities, natural science, social/behavioral science. **Reserve Officers Training Corps (ROTC):** Army ROTC: Offered at cooperating institution (University of Texas–Austin); Air Force ROTC: Offered at cooperating institution (University of Texas–Austin). **Faculty and instruction (2005-2006):** Total instructional faculty: 155 full-time, 285 part-time (55% men; 45% women; 14% minorities). Full-time faculty with Ph.D. or other terminal degree: 83%. Student/faculty ratio: 14/1. Classes of fewer than 20 students: 49%; of 20 to 49 students: 51%; of 50 or more students: 0%. **Advanced Placement and International Baccalaureate credit:** AP tests may be used for: Credit only. Scores accepted: 3, 4, 5. International Baccalaureate exams may be used for: Credit only. **Freshmen returning for sophomore year:** 81%. **Graduation rates:** Four-year: 28%; five-year: 48%; six-year: 53%.

COSTS AND FINANCIAL AID

Financial aid office: (512) 448-8520. **Expenses (2006-2007):** Tuition and fees 2006-2007: $18,800; room/board: $6,900. Estimated books and supplies: $1,000; transportation: $870; personal expenses: $2,730. **Financial aid:** Priority filing date for institution's financial aid form: March 1. In 2005-2006, 74% of undergraduates applied for financial aid. Of those, 60% were determined to have financial need; 39% had their need fully met. Average financial aid package (proportion receiving): $14,680 (60%). Average amount of gift aid, such as scholarships or grants (proportion receiving): $10,054 (55%). Average amount of self-help aid, such as work study or loans (proportion receiving): $4,124 (45%). Average need-based loan (excluding PLUS or other private loans): $4,324. Among students who received need-based aid, the average percentage of need met: 76%. Among students who received aid based on merit, the average award (and the proportion receiving): $5,826 (10%). The average athletic scholarship (and the proportion receiving): $9,413 (5%). Average amount of debt of borrowers graduating in 2005: $24,280. Proportion who borrowed: 62%.

CAMPUS LIFE AND EXTRACURRICULAR ACTIVITIES

Campus housing available (% using): coed dorms (58%), women's dorms (12%), apartment for single students (30%), special housing for disabled students, other housing options. Students who live in college-owned, operated, or affiliated housing: 37%. **Student employment:** During the 2005-2006 academic year, 23% of undergraduates worked on campus. Average per-year earnings: $1,692. **Clubs and organizations:** Number of student organizations: 84. Activities include: choral groups, dance, drama/theater, literary magazine, music ensembles, musical theater, student government, student newspaper. Number of fraternities: 0; sororities: 0. Average proportion of students who stay on campus on weekends: 40%. **Sports program (2005-2006):** Member of NCAA II. *Men's intercollegiate varsity sports:* baseball, basketball, cross-country, golf, soccer, tennis. *Women's intercollegiate varsity sports:* basketball, cross-country, golf, soccer, softball, tennis, volleyball.

SERVICES AND FACILITIES

Basic services: nonremedial tutoring, health service, health insurance. **Remedial assistance:** reading, math, writing, study skills. **Counseling services:** career, personal, academic, psychological, religious. **For learning-disabled students:** School does not offer a structured program with separate admission and additional fees. Total undergraduates in learning-disabled program or receiving services: 55. Services include: remedial math, remedial English, remedial reading, other special classes, oral tests, learning center, readers, extended time for tests, tutors. **Library:** Number of titles: 186,226; number of current serial subscriptions: 619. **Information technology resources:** Students are not required to lease or own a computer. Number of campus computers available to all students; 428. School has a wireless network. Approximate number of users that can be accommodated: 1,500. Proportion of college-owned housing units wired for high-speed internet access: 100%. **Campus safety:** Security services offered: 24-hour foot-and-vehicle patrols, late-night transport/escort service, 24-hour emergency telephones, lighted pathways/sidewalks, controlled dormitory access (key, security card, etc).

TRANSFER AND INTERNATIONAL STUDENTS

Transfer students: May apply for admission for the following academic terms: Fall, Spring, Summer. Applicants do not need a minimum number of credits to apply. For fall 2005: Transfer applications received: 504. Transfer applicants offered admission: 342. Transfer applicants enrolled: 263. **International students:** Number of foreign undergraduates: 84 (2% of student body). Number of countries represented: 36. Minimum TOEFL score required: 500 (paper); 173 (computer). Average TOEFL score: 553 (paper).

Stephen F. Austin State University

- **Address:** SFA Station 13051, Nacogdoches, TX 75962
- **Website:** http://www.sfasu.edu
- **Public**
- **Enrollment:** 8,490 full-time; 1,316 part-time

KEY STATS

- ✔ **U.S News College Ranking:** third tier, Universities–Master's (West)
- ✔ **SAT Score (25th/75th percentile):** 880-1120
- ✔ **Tuition:** 2006-2007: $5,232 in state, $13,482 out of state

Selectivity: Less selective	**Room/board:** $6,544
Acceptance rate: 74%	**Average debt:** $14,007
Student/faculty ratio: 18/1	**Proportion who borrowed:** 70%

UNDERGRADUATE STUDENT BODY STATS

2005-2006 enrollment: 8,490 full-time; 1,316 part-time. Men: 40%; women: 60%. **Ethnic makeup:** African American: 17%; American-Indian: 1%; Asian American: 1%; Hispanic: 8%; White: 73%; International: 1%.

ADMISSIONS FACTS AND FIGURES

Phone: (936) 468-2504. **Email:** admissions@sfasu.edu. **Website:** http://www.sfasu.edu. **Application deadlines for fall 2007:** Regular decision: Rolling. Early decision: Not offered. Early action: Not offered. Admission cannot be deferred. **Application fee:** $35. Common application is not accepted. **To apply online, go to:** http://www.sfasu.edu/admissions. **Admissions requirements/recommendations:** High school units required

(recommended): English: 4; Mathematics: 3; Science: 3; Foreign language: 2; Social studies: (3); Total units: 12 (18). **Tests:** The college uses SAT or ACT scores in admissions decisions. Either SAT or ACT required. For admission to the fall 2007 entering class, the school will accept: ACT with writing. Campus visit: Recommended. Admissions interview: Neither required nor recommended. Off-campus interview: Not available. **Factors that count in admissions decisions:** *Academic:* Secondary school record: Very important. Class rank: Very important. Letters of recommendation: Not considered. Standardized test scores: Very important. Essay: Not considered. *Nonacademic:* Interview: Not considered. Extracurricular activities: Considered. Talent/ability: Considered. Character/personal qualities: Considered. Alumni/ae relationship: Not considered. Geographical residence: Considered. State residency: Not considered. Religious affiliation/commitment: Not considered. Minority status: Not considered. Volunteer work: Considered. Work experience: Considered. **Other schools with the greatest overlap in applicants:** Sam Houston State University; Texas A&M University–College Station; Texas State University–San Marcos; University of Houston; University of Texas–Austin. **Admissions statistics for the fall 2005 entering class:** Total applicants: 6,506. Total accepted: 4,823. Freshmen enrolled: 1,921; 2% were from out of state. Overall acceptance rate: 74%. **Credentials of fall 2005 freshmen:** 14% ranked in the top 10 percent of their high school class; 42% were in the top 25 percent, and 81% were in the top half. (Proportion submitting class standing: 96%.) **First-year students who submitted SAT scores:** 81%. Scores (25/75 percentile): Verbal: 430-560, Math: 450-560, Combined: 880-1120. **First-year students submitting ACT scores:** 52%. Scores (25/75 percentile): English: N/A, Math: N/A, Composite: 17-23.

ACADEMICS

Year founded: 1923. **Academic calendar:** Semester. **Degrees offered:** bachelor's, master's, doctorate. **Most popular majors:** 13% multi/interdisciplinary studies, 6% health and physical education, 4% biology/biological sciences, 4% business/commerce, 4% nursing/registered nurse training (R.N., A.S.N., B.S.N., M.S.N.). **Major fields of study:** agriculture, agriculture operations, and related sciences; architecture and related services; biological and biomedical sciences; business, management, marketing, and related support services; communication, journalism, and related programs; computer and information sciences and support services; English language and literature/letters; family and consumer sciences/human sciences; foreign languages, literatures, and linguistics; health professions and related clinical sciences; history; legal professions and studies; liberal arts and sciences studies, and humanities; mathematics and statistics; multi/interdisciplinary studies; natural resources and conservation; parks, recreation, leisure, and fitness studies; physical sciences; psychology; public administration and social service professions; security and protective services; social sciences; visual and performing arts. **Areas of required coursework:** arts/fine arts, humanities, computer literacy, mathematics, English (including composition), sciences (biological or physical), history, social science. **Pre-professional programs:** pre-dentistry, pre-medicine, pre-veterinary science, pre-optometry, pre-pharmacy, other. **Special academic programs:** accelerated program, distance learning, double major, dual enrollment, honors program, independent study, internships, liberal arts/career combination, student-designed major, study abroad, teacher certificate program. **Teacher certification offered in:** early childhood, special education, elementary, middle/junior high, secondary, bilingual/bicultural. **Reserve Officers Training Corps (ROTC):** Army ROTC: Offered on campus. **Faculty and instruction (2005-2006):** Total instructional faculty: 450 full-time, 176 part-time (55% men; 45% women; 8% minorities). Full-time faculty with Ph.D. or other terminal degree: 76%. Student/faculty ratio: 18/1. Classes of fewer than 20 students: 29%; of 20 to 49 students: 62%; of 50 or more students: 9%. **Advanced Placement and International Baccalaureate credit:** AP tests may be used for: Credit only. Scores accepted: 3, 4, 5. International Baccalaureate exams may be used for: Credit only. **Freshmen returning for sophomore year:** 63%. **Graduation rates:** Four-year: 15%; five-year: 31%; six-year: 36%.

COSTS AND FINANCIAL AID

Financial aid office: (936) 468-2403. **Expenses (2006-2007):** Tuition and fees 2006-2007: $5,232 in state, $13,482 out of state; room/board: $6,544. Estimated books and supplies: $957; transportation: $1,983; personal expenses: $1,494. **Financial aid:** Priority filing date for institution's financial aid form: April 1. In 2005-2006, 73% of undergraduates applied for financial aid. Of those, 55% were determined to have financial need; 25% had their need fully met. Average financial aid package (proportion receiving): $5,059 (54%). Average amount of gift aid, such as scholarships or grants (proportion receiving): $2,871 (47%). Average amount of self-help aid, such as work study or loans (proportion receiving): $2,391 (45%). Average need-based loan (excluding PLUS or other private loans): $2,166. Among students who received need-based aid, the average percentage of need met: 70%. Among students who received aid based on merit, the average award (and the proportion receiving): $2,882 (6%). The average athletic scholarship (and the proportion receiving): $6,413 (4%). Average amount of debt of borrowers graduating in 2005: $14,007. Proportion who borrowed: 70%.

CAMPUS LIFE AND EXTRACURRICULAR ACTIVITIES
Campus housing available: coed dorms, women's dorms, men's dorms, sorority housing, fraternity housing, apartments for married students, apartment for single students, special housing for disabled students, other housing options. Students who live in college-owned, operated, or affiliated housing: 38%. Average per-year earnings: $4,100. **Clubs and organizations:** Number of student organizations: 217. Activities include: choral groups, concert band, dance, drama/theater, jazz band, literary magazine, marching band, music ensembles, musical theater, opera, pep band, radio station, student government, student newspaper, student film society, symphony orchestra, television station, yearbook. Number of fraternities: 25; sororities: 14. Proportion of men in fraternities: 13%; of women in sororities: 9%.
Sports program (2005-2006): Member of NCAA I. *Men's intercollegiate varsity sports:* baseball, basketball, cross-country, football, golf, track and field (indoor), track and field (outdoor). *Women's intercollegiate varsity sports:* basketball, cross-country, equestrian sports, soccer, softball, tennis, track and field (indoor), track and field (outdoor), volleyball.

SERVICES AND FACILITIES
Basic services: placement service, health service. **Remedial assistance:** reading, math, writing, study skills. **Counseling services:** minority student, career, military, personal, veteran student, academic, older student, psychological. **For learning-disabled students:** School does not offer a structured program with separate admission and additional fees. Total undergraduates in learning-disabled program or receiving services: 134. Services include: remedial math, remedial English, reading machines, remedial reading, tape recorders, other special classes, diagnostic testing service, note-taking services, oral tests, learning center, readers, extended time for tests, tutors, exams on tape or computer, other. **Information technology resources:** Students are not required to lease or own a computer. Number of campus computers available to all students: 1,000. School has a wireless network. Proportion of college-owned housing units wired for high-speed internet access: 100%. **Campus safety:** Security services offered: 24-hour foot-and-vehicle patrols, late-night transport/escort service, 24-hour emergency telephones, lighted pathways/sidewalks, controlled dormitory access (key, security card, etc).

TRANSFER AND INTERNATIONAL STUDENTS
Transfer students: May apply for admission for the following academic terms: Fall, Spring, Summer. Applicants need a minimum number of credits to apply. For fall 2005: Transfer applications received: 2,262. Transfer applicants offered admission: 1,865. Transfer applicants enrolled: 801.
International students: Number of foreign undergraduates: 66 (1% of student body). Number of countries represented: 40. Minimum TOEFL score required: 550 (paper); 213 (computer). Average TOEFL score: 602 (paper).

St. Mary's University of San Antonio

- **Address:** 1 Camino Santa Maria, San Antonio, TX 78228
- **Website:** http://www.stmarytx.edu
- **Private; Religious affiliation:** Roman Catholic
- **Enrollment:** 2,185 full-time; 200 part-time

KEY STATS
✔ **U.S News College Ranking:** 15, Universities–Master's (West)
✔ **SAT Score (25th/75th percentile):** 950-1145
✔ **Tuition:** 2006-2007: $20,534

Selectivity: Selective	**Room/board:** $6,780
Acceptance rate: 72%	**Average debt:** $25,736
Student/faculty ratio: 13/1	**Proportion who borrowed:** 83%

UNDERGRADUATE STUDENT BODY STATS
2005-2006 enrollment: 2,185 full-time; 200 part-time. Men: 40%; women: 60%. **Ethnic makeup:** African American: 4%; Asian American: 3%;

Hispanic: 70%; White: 20%; International: 4%. **Religious preference:** Protestant: 14%; No preference: 3%; Roman Catholic: 66%; Other: 17%.

ADMISSIONS FACTS AND FIGURES
Phone: (210) 436-3126. **Email:** uadm@stmarytx.edu. **Website:** http://www.stmarytx.edu. **Application deadlines for fall 2007:** Regular decision: Rolling. Early decision: Not offered. Early action: Not offered. Admission can be deferred. **Application fee:** $30. Common application is accepted. **To apply online, go to:** http://www.texasmentor.org/Applications/St._Marys_University/apply.html.
Admissions requirements/recommendations: High school units required (recommended): English: 4 (4); Mathematics: 3 (4); Science: 3 (4); Foreign language: 2 (4); Social studies: 3 (4); Academic electives: 1; Total units: 16 (20). Tests: The college uses SAT or ACT scores in admissions decisions. Either SAT or ACT required. For admission to the fall 2007 entering class, the school will accept: ACT with writing. Campus visit: Recommended. Admissions interview: Recommended. Off-campus interview: May be arranged. **Factors that count in admissions decisions:** *Academic:* Secondary school record: Important. Class rank: Very important. Letters of recommendation: Considered. Standardized test scores: Important. Essay: Considered. *Nonacademic:* Interview: Considered. Extracurricular activities: Considered. Talent/ability: Considered. Character/personal qualities: Considered. Alumni/ae relationship: Not considered. Geographical residence: Not considered. State residency: Not considered. Religious affiliation/commitment: Not considered. Minority status: Not considered. Volunteer work: Considered. Work experience: Considered. **Other schools with the greatest overlap in applicants:** Our Lady of the Lake University; Texas A&M University–College Station; University of Texas–Austin; University of Texas–San Antonio; University of the Incarnate Word. **Admissions statistics for the fall 2005 entering class:** Total applicants: 1,942. Total accepted: 1,400. Freshmen enrolled: 494; 3% were from out of state. Overall acceptance rate: 72%. **Credentials of fall 2005 freshmen:** 32% ranked in the top 10 percent of their high school class; 63% were in the top 25 percent, and 89% were in the top half. (Proportion submitting class standing: 94%.) **Average high school grade point average:** 3.4. **First-year students who submitted SAT scores:** 67%. Scores (25/75 percentile): Verbal: 470-565, Math: 480-580, Combined: 950-1145. **First-year students submitting ACT scores:** 59%. Scores (25/75 percentile): English: 19-24, Math: 17-24, Composite: 20-24.

ACADEMICS
Year founded: 1852. **Academic calendar:** Semester. **Degrees offered:** bachelor's, master's, first professional, doctorate. **Most popular majors:** 9% biology/biological sciences, 9% political science and government, 6% marketing/marketing management, 5% English language and literature, 5% communication studies/speech communication and rhetoric. **Major fields of study:** biological and biomedical sciences; business, management, marketing, and related support services; communication, journalism, and related programs; computer and information sciences and support services; education; engineering; English language and literature/letters; foreign languages, literatures, and linguistics; history; mathematics and statistics; multi/interdisciplinary studies; parks, recreation, leisure, and fitness studies; philosophy and religious studies; physical sciences; psychology; public administration and social service professions; social sciences; theology and religious vocations; visual and performing arts. **Areas of required coursework:** arts/fine arts, humanities, computer literacy, mathematics, English (including composition), philosophy, foreign languages, sciences (biological or physical), history, social science, other. **Pre-professional programs:** pre-law, pre-dentistry, pre-medicine, pre-veterinary science, pre-pharmacy, other. **Special academic programs (% participation):** cooperative (work-study plan) program (31%), cross-registration (.1%), double major (12%), English as a Second Language (ESL) (1%), honors program (5%), independent study (12%), internships (5%), study abroad (12%), teacher certificate program (3%). **Teacher certification offered in:** early childhood, elementary, middle/junior high, secondary. **Reserve Officers Training Corps (ROTC):** Army ROTC: Offered on campus; Air Force ROTC: Offered at cooperating institution (University of Texas at San Antonio). **Faculty and instruction (2005-2006):** Total instructional faculty: 184 full-time, 149 part-time (65% men; 35% women; 22% minorities). Full-time faculty with Ph.D. or other terminal degree: 92%. Student/faculty ratio: 13/1. Classes of fewer than 20 students: 39%; of 20 to 49 students: 60%; of 50 or more students: 1%. **Advanced Placement and International Baccalaureate credit:** AP tests may be used for: Credit and/or placement. Scores accepted: 3, 4, 5. International Baccalaureate exams may be used for: Credit and/or placement. **Freshmen returning for sophomore year:** 79%. **Graduation rates:** Four-year: 34%; five-year: 56%; six-year: 60%. **Graduate study:** 44% of students pursue further study within one year. Fields in which graduates pursue further study:

Master of Business Administration (MBA), 12%; law, 5%; medicine, 2%; arts and sciences, 25%.

COSTS AND FINANCIAL AID
Financial aid office: (210) 436-3141. **Expenses (2006-2007):** Tuition and fees 2006-2007: $20,534; room/board: $6,780. Estimated books and supplies: $1,200; transportation: $600; personal expenses: $1,177. **Financial aid:** Priority filing date for institution's financial aid form: February 15. In 2005-2006, 79% of undergraduates applied for financial aid. Of those, 63% were determined to have financial need; 29% had their need fully met. Average financial aid package (proportion receiving): $19,472 (63%). Average amount of gift aid, such as scholarships or grants (proportion receiving): $12,330 (61%). Average amount of self-help aid, such as work study or loans (proportion receiving): $6,860 (57%). Average need-based loan (excluding PLUS or other private loans): $5,559. Among students who received need-based aid, the average percentage of need met: 81%. Among students who received aid based on merit, the average award (and the proportion receiving): $6,866 (15%). The average athletic scholarship (and the proportion receiving): $11,758 (7%). Average amount of debt of borrowers graduating in 2005: $25,736. Proportion who borrowed: 83%.

CAMPUS LIFE AND EXTRACURRICULAR ACTIVITIES
Campus housing available (% using): coed dorms (91%), women's dorms (8%), special housing for disabled students (1%). Students who live in college-owned, operated, or affiliated housing: 43%. **Student employment:** During the 2005-2006 academic year, 8% of undergraduates worked on campus. Average per-year earnings: $4,800. **Clubs and organizations:** Number of student organizations: 68. Activities include: choral groups, concert band, dance, drama/theater, jazz band, literary magazine, music ensembles, pep band, student government, student newspaper, yearbook. Number of fraternities: 5; sororities: 4. Proportion of men in fraternities: 13%; of women in sororities: 13%. Average proportion of students who stay on campus on weekends: 80%. **Sports program (2005-2006):** Member of NCAA II. *Men's intercollegiate varsity sports:* baseball, basketball, golf, soccer, tennis. *Women's intercollegiate varsity sports:* basketball, cross-country, golf, soccer, softball, tennis, volleyball.

SERVICES AND FACILITIES
Basic services: placement service, health service, health insurance, other. **Remedial assistance:** math, study skills. **Counseling services:** career, personal, academic, psychological, religious, other. **For learning-disabled students:** School does not offer a structured program with separate admission and additional fees. Services include: diagnostic testing service, oral tests, learning center, extended time for tests, tutors, texts on tape, exams on tape or computer, other testing accomodations. **Library:** Number of titles: 497,729; number of current serial subscriptions: 1,027. **Information technology resources:** Students are required to lease or own a computer. Number of campus computers available to all students: 100. School has a wireless network. Approximate number of users that can be accommodated: 3,080. Proportion of college-owned housing units wired for high-speed internet access: 100%. **Campus safety:** Security services offered: 24-hour foot-and-vehicle patrols, late-night transport/escort service, 24-hour emergency telephones, lighted pathways/sidewalks, controlled dormitory access (key, security card, etc).

TRANSFER AND INTERNATIONAL STUDENTS
Transfer students: May apply for admission for the following academic terms: Fall, Spring, Summer. Applicants need a minimum number of credits to apply. For fall 2005: Transfer applications received: 374. Transfer applicants offered admission: 235. Transfer applicants enrolled: 138. **International students:** Number of foreign undergraduates: 87 (4% of student body). Number of countries represented: 40. Minimum TOEFL score required: 550 (paper); 213 (computer). Average TOEFL score: 575 (paper).

Sul Ross State University

- **Address:** PO Box C-114, Alpine, TX 79832
- **Website:** http://www.sulross.edu
- **Public**
- **Enrollment:** N/A

KEY STATS
✔ **U.S News College Ranking:** fourth tier, Universities–Master's (West)
✔ **SAT or ACT Score (25th/75th percentile):** N/A
✔ **Tuition:** 2006-2007: $4,336 in state, $12,586 out of state

Selectivity: Less selective	**Room/board:** $4,260
Acceptance rate: N/A	**Average debt:** N/A
Student/faculty ratio: N/A	**Proportion who borrowed:** N/A

Tarleton State University

- **Address:** Box T 0001, Tarleton Station, Stephenville, TX 76402
- **Website:** http://www.tarleton.edu
- **Public**
- **Enrollment:** N/A

KEY STATS
✔ **U.S News College Ranking:** third tier, Universities–Master's (West)
✔ **ACT Score (25th/75th percentile):** 18-22
✔ **Tuition:** 2006-2007: $3,990 in state, $12,240 out of state

Selectivity: Selective	**Room/board:** $3,148
Acceptance rate: 68%	**Average debt:** N/A
Student/faculty ratio: N/A	**Proportion who borrowed:** N/A

Texas A&M International University

- **Address:** 5201 University Boulevard, Laredo, TX 78041-1900
- **Website:** http://www.tamiu.edu
- **Public**
- **Enrollment:** 2,236 full-time; 1,098 part-time

KEY STATS
✔ **U.S News College Ranking:** third tier, Universities–Master's (West)
✔ **SAT Score (25th/75th percentile):** 810-1010
✔ **Tuition:** 2006-2007: $4,738 in state, $12,988 out of state

Selectivity: Less selective	**Room/board:** $6,500
Acceptance rate: 60%	**Average debt:** $10,627
Student/faculty ratio: 15/1	**Proportion who borrowed:** 57%

UNDERGRADUATE STUDENT BODY STATS
2005-2006 enrollment: 2,236 full-time; 1,098 part-time. Men: 37%; women: 63%. **Ethnic makeup:** Asian American: 1%; Hispanic: 92%; White: 3%; International: 4%.

ADMISSIONS FACTS AND FIGURES
Phone: (956) 326-2200. **Email:** enroll@tamiu.edu. **Website:** http://www.tamiu.edu. **Application deadlines for fall 2007:** Regular decision: July 1. Early decision: Not offered. Early action: Not offered. Admission can be deferred. Common application is not accepted. **Admissions requirements/recommendations:** High school units required (recommended): English: 4; Mathematics: 3; Science: 2; Foreign language: (2); Social studies: 3; Total units: 13 (3). Tests: The college uses SAT or ACT scores in admissions decisions. Either SAT or ACT required. For admission to the fall 2007 entering class, the school will accept: ACT with writing, ACT without writing. Campus visit: Neither required nor recommended. Admissions interview: Neither required nor recommended. Off-campus interview: May be arranged. **Factors that count in admissions decisions:** *Academic:* Secondary school record: Very important. Class rank: Very important. Letters of recommendation: Not considered. Standardized test scores: Very important. Essay:

Not considered. *Nonacademic:* Interview: Not considered. Extracurricular activities: Not considered. Talent/ability: Not considered. Character/personal qualities: Not considered. Alumni/ae relationship: Not considered. Geographical residence: Not considered. State residency: Not considered. Religious affiliation/commitment: Not considered. Minority status: Not considered. Volunteer work: Not considered. Work experience: Not considered. **Other schools with the greatest overlap in applicants:** Texas A&M University–College Station; Texas A&M University–Kingsville; Texas State University–San Marcos; University of Texas–Austin; University of Texas–San Antonio. **Admissions statistics for the fall 2005 entering class:** Total applicants: 1,741. Total accepted: 1,045. Freshmen enrolled: 486; 1% were from out of state. Overall acceptance rate: 60%. **Credentials of fall 2005 freshmen:** 24% ranked in the top 10 percent of their high school class; 53% were in the top 25 percent, and 85% were in the top half. (Proportion submitting class standing: 97%.) **Average high school grade point average:** 3.6. **First-year students who submitted SAT scores:** 74%. Scores (25/75 percentile): Verbal: 400-490, Math: 410-520, Combined: 810-1010. **First-year students submitting ACT scores:** 45%. Scores (25/75 percentile): English: 15-20, Math: 16-21, Composite: 16-20.

ACADEMICS

Year founded: 1970. **Academic calendar:** Semester. **Degrees offered:** bachelor's, master's, doctorate. **Most popular majors:** 20% business administration and management, 13% bilingual and multilingual education, 9% criminal justice/police science, 6% accounting, 5% health and physical education. **Major fields of study:** area, ethnic, cultural, and gender studies; biological and biomedical sciences; business, management, marketing, and related support services; communication, journalism, and related programs; computer and information sciences and support services; English language and literature/letters; foreign languages, literatures, and linguistics; health professions and related clinical sciences; history; mathematics and statistics; multi/interdisciplinary studies; natural resources and conservation; parks, recreation, leisure, and fitness studies; physical sciences; psychology; public administration and social service professions; security and protective services; social sciences; visual and performing arts. **Areas of required coursework:** arts/fine arts, mathematics, English (including composition), sciences (biological or physical), history, social science. **Pre-professional programs:** pre-law, pre-dentistry, pre-medicine. **Special academic programs (% participation):** distance learning (1%), double major (5%), dual enrollment (3%), honors program (3%), independent study (3%), internships (3%), study abroad (1%), teacher certificate program (23%). **Teacher certification offered in:** early childhood, special education, elementary, middle/junior high, secondary, bilingual/bicultural. **Reserve Officers Training Corps (ROTC):** Army ROTC: Offered on campus. **Faculty and instruction (2005-2006):** Total instructional faculty: 161 full-time, 112 part-time (60% men; 40% women; 48% minorities). Full-time faculty with Ph.D. or other terminal degree: 78%. Student/faculty ratio: 15/1. Classes of fewer than 20 students: 50%; of 20 to 49 students: 43%; of 50 or more students: 8%. **Advanced Placement and International Baccalaureate credit:** AP tests may be used for: Credit only. Scores accepted: 3, 4, 5. **Freshmen returning for sophomore year:** 66%. **Graduation rates:** Four-year: 16%; five-year: 31%; six-year: 35%. **Graduate study:** 27% of students pursue further study within one year.

COSTS AND FINANCIAL AID

Financial aid office: (956) 326-2225. **Expenses (2006-2007):** Tuition and fees 2006-2007: $4,738 in state, $12,988 out of state; room/board: $6,500. Estimated books and supplies: $1,300; transportation: $867; personal expenses: $2,161. **Financial aid:** Priority filing date for institution's financial aid form: March 15. In 2005-2006, 88% of undergraduates applied for financial aid. Of those, 82% were determined to have financial need; 1% had their need fully met. Average financial aid package (proportion receiving): $3,818 (78%). Average amount of gift aid, such as scholarships or grants (proportion receiving): $2,844 (74%). Average amount of self-help aid, such as work study or loans (proportion receiving): $2,139 (32%). Average need-based loan (excluding PLUS or other private loans): $2,165. Among students who received need-based aid, the average percentage of need met: 29%. Among students who received aid based on merit, the average award (and the proportion receiving): $1,603 (3%). The average athletic scholarship (and the proportion receiving): $0 (0%). Average amount of debt of borrowers graduating in 2005: $10,627. Proportion who borrowed: 57%.

CAMPUS LIFE AND EXTRACURRICULAR ACTIVITIES

Campus housing available (% using): coed dorms (50%), apartments for married students (2%), apartment for single students (38%), special housing for disabled students (1%), other housing options (9%). Students who live in college-owned, operated, or affiliated housing: 6%. **Student employment:** During the 2005-2006 academic year, 5% of undergraduates worked on campus. Average per-year earnings: $4,800. **Clubs and organizations:** Number of student organizations: 49. Activities include: choral groups, dance, marching band, music ensembles, student government, student newspaper, student film society. Number of fraternities: 0; sororities: 0. Average proportion of students who stay on campus on weekends: 9%. **Sports program (2005-2006):** Member of NAIA. *Men's intercollegiate varsity sports:* basketball, cross-country, golf, soccer. *Women's intercollegiate varsity sports:* basketball, cross-country, golf, soccer, volleyball.

SERVICES AND FACILITIES

Basic services: nonremedial tutoring, placement service, day care, health service. **Remedial assistance:** reading, math, writing, study skills. **Counseling services:** minority student, career, personal, veteran student, academic. **For learning-disabled students:** School does not offer a structured program with separate admission and additional fees. Total undergraduates in learning-disabled program or receiving services: 4. Services include: remedial math, remedial English, reading machines, remedial reading, tape recorders, other special classes, videotaped classes, untimed tests, note-taking services, oral tests, readers, extended time for tests, tutors, priority seating, substitution of courses, texts on tape, typist/scribe, exams on tape or computer, other testing accomodations. **Library:** Number of titles: 278,525; number of current serial subscriptions: 5,459. **Information technology resources:** Students are not required to lease or own a computer. Number of campus computers available to all students: 388. School has a wireless network. Approximate number of users that can be accommodated: 400. Proportion of college-owned housing units wired for high-speed internet access: 100%. **Campus safety:** Security services offered: 24-hour foot-and-vehicle patrols, late-night transport/escort service, 24-hour emergency telephones, lighted pathways/sidewalks, student patrols, controlled dormitory access (key, security card, etc).

TRANSFER AND INTERNATIONAL STUDENTS

Transfer students: May apply for admission for the following academic terms: Fall, Spring, Summer. Applicants need a minimum number of credits to apply. For fall 2005: Transfer applications received: 937. Transfer applicants offered admission: 681. Transfer applicants enrolled: 499. **International students:** Number of foreign undergraduates: 137 (4% of student body). Number of countries represented: 18. Minimum TOEFL score required: 550 (paper); 213 (computer). Average TOEFL score: 567 (paper).

Texas A&M University–College Station

- **Address:** College Station, TX 77843
- **Website:** http://www.tamu.edu
- **Public**
- **Enrollment:** 33,085 full-time; 3,283 part-time

KEY STATS

✔ **U.S News College Ranking:** 60, National Universities
✔ **SAT Score (25th/75th percentile):** 1090-1310
✔ **Tuition:** 2006-2007: $6,966 in state, $15,216 out of state

Selectivity: More selective	**Room/board:** $7,052
Acceptance rate: 70%	**Average debt:** $16,027
Student/faculty ratio: 20/1	**Proportion who borrowed:** 32%

UNDERGRADUATE STUDENT BODY STATS

2005-2006 enrollment: 33,085 full-time; 3,283 part-time. Men: 51%; women: 49%. **Ethnic makeup:** African American: 3%; Asian American: 4%; Hispanic: 11%; White: 81%; International: 1%.

ADMISSIONS FACTS AND FIGURES

Phone: (979) 845-3741. **Email:** admissions@tamu.edu. **Website:** http://www.tamu.edu. **Application deadlines for fall 2007:** Regular decision: February 1. Early decision: Not offered. Early action: Send application by: December 1; Decision sent by: N/A. Admission cannot be deferred. **Application fee:** $50. Common application is not accepted. **To apply online, go to:** http://www.tamu.edu/admissions. **Admissions requirements/recommendations:** High school units required (recommended): English: 4 (4); Mathematics: 4 (4); Science: 3 (3); Foreign language: 2 (2); Social studies: 2 (2); History: 1 (1); Total units: 18 (19). Tests: The college uses SAT or ACT scores in admissions decisions. Either SAT or ACT required. For admission to the fall 2007 entering class, the school will accept: ACT with writing. Campus visit: Recommended. Admissions interview: Neither required nor recommended. Off-campus interview: Not available. **Factors that count in admissions decisions:** *Academic:* Secondary school record: Very important. Class rank: Very important. Letters of recommendation: Considered. Standardized test scores: Very important. Essay: Important. *Nonacademic:* Interview: Not considered. Extracurricular activities: Very important. Talent/ability: Very important. Character/personal qualities: Considered. Alumni/ae relationship: Considered. Geographical residence: Considered. State residency: Very important. Religious affiliation/commitment: Not considered. Minority status: Not considered. Volunteer work: Important. Work experience: Important. **Other schools with the greatest overlap in applicants:** Baylor University; Rice University; Texas State University–San Marcos; Texas Tech University; University of Texas–Austin. **Admissions statistics for the fall 2005 entering class:** Total applicants: 17,871. Total accepted: 12,503. Freshmen enrolled: 7,104; 4% were from out of state. Overall acceptance rate: 70%. Non-early acceptance rate: 70%. **Size of waiting list:** 3866 applicants; enrolled from waiting list: 1109. **Credentials of fall 2005 freshmen:** 50% ranked in the top 10 percent of their high school class; 79% were in the top 25 percent, and 91% were in the top half. (Proportion submitting class standing: 92%.) **First-year students who submitted SAT scores:** 79%. Scores (25/75 percentile): Verbal: 530-640, Math: 560-670, Combined: 1090-1310. **First-year students submitting ACT scores:** 21%. Scores (25/75 percentile): English: 22-28, Math: 23-28, Composite: 23-28.

ACADEMICS
Year founded: 1876. **Academic calendar:** Semester. **Degrees offered:** bachelor's, post-bachelor's certificate, master's, first professional, doctorate. **Most popular majors:** 17% business, management, marketing, and related support services, 12% agriculture, agriculture operations, and related sciences, 12% engineering, 9% biological and biomedical sciences, 9% social sciences. **Major fields of study:** agriculture, agriculture operations, and related sciences; architecture and related services; area, ethnic, cultural, and gender studies; biological and biomedical sciences; business, management, marketing, and related support services; communication, journalism, and related programs; communications technologies/technicians and support services; computer and information sciences and support services; education; engineering; engineering technologies/technicians; English language and literature/letters; family and consumer sciences/human sciences; foreign languages, literatures, and linguistics; health professions and related clinical sciences; history; mathematics and statistics; multi/interdisciplinary studies; natural resources and conservation; parks, recreation, leisure, and fitness studies; philosophy and religious studies; physical sciences; psychology; social sciences; visual and performing arts. **Areas of required coursework:** arts/fine arts, humanities, computer literacy, mathematics, English (including composition), foreign languages, sciences (biological or physical), history, social science, other. **Pre-professional programs:** pre-law, pre-dentistry, pre-medicine, pre-veterinary science, pre-optometry, pre-pharmacy. **Special academic programs (% participation):** accelerated program (2.57%), cooperative (work-study plan) program (3.24%), cross-registration, distance learning, double major (1.9%), dual enrollment (.49%), English as a Second Language (ESL) (.31%), exchange student program (domestic) (.49%), honors program (17.68%), independent study (32.64%), internships (17.39%), liberal arts/career combination (.16%), study abroad (8.16%), teacher certificate program (9.62%), other (2.89%). **Teacher certification offered in:** early childhood, special education, elementary, middle/junior high, secondary, bilingual/bicultural. **Cooperative education programs:** agriculture, business, computer science, engineering, health professions, humanities, natural science, social/behavioral science, technologies. **Reserve Officers Training Corps (ROTC):** Army ROTC: Offered on campus; Navy ROTC: Offered on campus; Air Force ROTC: Offered on campus. **Faculty and instruction (2005-2006):** Total instructional faculty: 1,922 full-time, 398 part-time (72% men; 28% women; 18% minorities). Full-time faculty with Ph.D. or other terminal degree: 90%. Student/faculty ratio: 20/1. Classes of fewer than 20 students: 20%; of 20 to 49 students: 56%; of 50 or more students: 25%. **Advanced Placement and International Baccalaureate credit:** AP tests may be used for: Credit only. Scores accepted: 3, 4, 5. International Baccalaureate exams may be used for: Credit and/or placement. **Freshmen returning for sophomore year:** 90%. **Graduation rates:** Four-year: 35%; five-year: 71%; six-year: 77%.

COSTS AND FINANCIAL AID
Financial aid office: (979) 845-3236. **Expenses (2006-2007):** Tuition and fees 2006-2007: $6,966 in state, $15,216 out of state; room/board: $7,052. Estimated books and supplies: $1,180; transportation: $714; personal expenses: $1,476. **Financial aid:** Priority filing date for institution's financial aid form: April 1. In 2005-2006, 54% of undergraduates applied for financial aid. Of those, 37% were determined to have financial need; 55% had their need fully met. Average financial aid package (proportion receiving): $10,747 (36%). Average amount of gift aid, such as scholarships or grants (proportion receiving): $6,795 (30%). Average amount of self-help aid, such as work study or loans (proportion receiving): $5,299 (27%). Average need-based loan (excluding PLUS or other private loans): $4,984. Among students who received need-based aid, the average percentage of need met: 87%. Among students who received aid based on merit, the average award (and the proportion receiving): $4,406 (23%). The average athletic scholarship (and the proportion receiving): $8,815 (1%). Average amount of debt of borrowers graduating in 2005: $16,027. Proportion who borrowed: 32%.

CAMPUS LIFE AND EXTRACURRICULAR ACTIVITIES
Campus housing available (% using): coed dorms (23%), women's dorms (30%), men's dorms (44%), apartment for single students (0%), special housing for disabled students (0%), other housing options (3%). Students who live in college-owned, operated, or affiliated housing: 25%. **Student employment:** During the 2005-2006 academic year, 30% of undergraduates worked on campus. Average per-year earnings: $2,626. **Clubs and organizations:** Number of student organizations: 700. Activities include: choral groups, concert band, dance, drama/theater, jazz band, literary magazine, marching band, music ensembles, musical theater, pep band, radio station, student government, student newspaper, student film society, symphony orchestra, television station, yearbook. Number of fraternities: 30; sororities: 22. Proportion of men in fraternities: 6%; of women in sororities: 12%. **Sports program (2005-2006):** Member of NCAA I. *Men's intercollegiate varsity sports:* baseball, basketball, cross-country, football, golf, swimming and diving, tennis, track and field (indoor), track and field (outdoor). *Women's intercollegiate varsity sports:* archery, basketball, cross-country, equestrian sports, golf, soccer, softball, swimming and diving, tennis, track and field (indoor), track and field (outdoor), volleyball.

SERVICES AND FACILITIES
Basic services: women's center, placement service, day care, health service. **Remedial assistance:** study skills. **Counseling services:** minority student, career, personal, academic, older student, psychological. **For learning-disabled students:** School does not offer a structured program with separate admission and additional fees. Total undergraduates in learning-disabled program or receiving services: 760. Services include: reading machines, tape recorders, diagnostic testing service, untimed tests, note-taking services, extended time for tests, priority registration, priority seating, substitution of courses, texts on tape, other. **Library:** Number of titles: 3,302,468; number of current serial subscriptions: 56,903. **Information technology resources:** Students are not required to lease or own a computer. Number of campus computers available to all students: 1,307. School has a wireless network. Approximate number of users that can be accommodated: 2,000. Proportion of college-owned housing units wired for high-speed internet access: 100%. **Campus safety:** Security services offered: 24-hour foot-and-vehicle patrols, late-night transport/escort service, 24-hour emergency telephones, lighted pathways/sidewalks, controlled dormitory access (key, security card, etc).

TRANSFER AND INTERNATIONAL STUDENTS
Transfer students: May apply for admission for the following academic terms: Fall, Spring, Summer. Applicants need a minimum number of credits to apply. For fall 2005: Transfer applications received: 3,021. Transfer applicants offered admission: 1,881. Transfer applicants enrolled: 1,568. **International students:** Number of foreign undergraduates: 522 (1% of student body). Number of countries represented: 90. Minimum TOEFL score required: 550 (paper); 213 (computer). Average TOEFL score: 633 (paper).

Texas A&M University–Commerce

- **Address:** PO Box 3011, Commerce, TX 75429
- **Website:** http://www.tamu-commerce.edu
- **Public**
- **Enrollment:** 4,022 full-time; 1,239 part-time

KEY STATS

✔ **U.S News College Ranking:** fourth tier, National Universities
✔ **SAT Score (25th/75th percentile):** 880-1100
✔ **Tuition:** 2006-2007: $4,616 in state, $12,866 out of state

Selectivity: Less selective	**Room/board:** N/A
Acceptance rate: 51%	**Average debt:** $18,182
Student/faculty ratio: N/A	**Proportion who borrowed:** 66%

UNDERGRADUATE STUDENT BODY STATS

2005-2006 enrollment: 4,022 full-time; 1,239 part-time. Men: 39%; women: 61%. **Ethnic makeup:** African American: 19%; American-Indian: 1%; Asian American: 2%; Hispanic: 7%; White: 70%; International: 1%.

ADMISSIONS FACTS AND FIGURES

Phone: (903) 886-5106. **Email:** Admissions@tamu-commerce.edu. **Website:** http://www.tamu-commerce.edu. **Application deadlines for fall 2007:** Regular decision: August 1. Early decision: Not offered. Early action: Not offered. Admission can be deferred. **Application fee:** $25. Common application is accepted. **To apply online, go to:** http://www7.tamu-commerce.edu/future_students.asp. **Admissions requirements/recommendations:** High school units required (recommended): English: 4; Mathematics: 3; Science: 2; Foreign language: (2); Social studies: 2; History: 2; Total units: 12. Tests: The college uses SAT or ACT scores in admissions decisions. Either SAT or ACT required. Campus visit: Neither required nor recommended. Admissions interview: Neither required nor recommended. Off-campus interview: Not available. **Factors that count in admissions decisions:** *Academic:* Secondary school record: Very important. Class rank: Very important. Letters of recommendation: Not considered. Standardized test scores: Very important. Essay: Not considered. *Nonacademic:* Interview: Not considered. Extracurricular activities: Not considered. Talent/ability: Not considered. Character/personal qualities: Not considered. Alumni/ae relationship: Not considered. Geographical residence: Not considered. State residency: Not considered. Religious affiliation/commitment: Not considered. Minority status: Not considered. Volunteer work: Not considered. Work experience: Considered. **Admissions statistics for the fall 2005 entering class:** Total applicants: 1,899. Total accepted: 966. Freshmen enrolled: 563; Overall acceptance rate: 51%. **First-year students who submitted SAT scores:** 65%. Scores (25/75 percentile): Verbal: 440-540, Math: 440-560, Combined: 880-1100. **First-year students submitting ACT scores:** 58%. Scores (25/75 percentile): English: 16-23, Math: 17-22, Composite: 17-23.

ACADEMICS

Year founded: 1889. **Academic calendar:** Semester. **Degrees offered:** certificate, bachelor's, master's, doctorate. **Most popular majors:** Information not available. **Major fields of study:** agriculture, agriculture operations, and related sciences; biological and biomedical sciences; business, management, marketing, and related support services; communication, journalism, and related programs; communications technologies/technicians and support services; computer and information sciences and support services; engineering technologies/technicians; English language and literature/letters; health professions and related clinical sciences; history; legal professions and studies; mathematics and statistics; multi/interdisciplinary studies; parks, recreation, leisure, and fitness studies; physical sciences; psychology; public administration and social service professions; security and protective services; social sciences; visual and performing arts. **Areas of required coursework:** humanities, mathematics, English (including composition), sciences (biological or physical), history. **Special academic programs:** cooperative (work-study plan) program, distance learning, double major, dual enrollment, honors program, independent study, internships, study abroad, teacher certificate program, weekend college, other. **Teacher certification offered in:** early childhood, special education, elementary, secondary. **Cooperative education programs:** agriculture, art, business, computer science, education, engineering, humanities, natural science, social/behavioral science, technologies. **Faculty and instruction (2005-2006):** Total instructional faculty: 298 full-time, 203 part-time (55% men; 45% women; 9%

minorities). Full-time faculty with Ph.D. or other terminal degree: 63%. **Advanced Placement and International Baccalaureate credit:** AP tests may be used for: Placement only. Scores accepted: 3, 4, 5. International Baccalaureate exams may be used for: Credit and/or placement. **Graduation rates:** Six-year: 36%.

COSTS AND FINANCIAL AID

Financial aid office: (903) 886-5096. **Expenses (2006-2007):** Tuition and fees 2006-2007: $4,616 in state, $12,866 out of state; room/board: N/A. Estimated books and supplies: $1,010; transportation: $1,300; personal expenses: $1,630. **Financial aid:** Priority filing date for institution's financial aid form: April 1. In 2005-2006, 78% of undergraduates applied for financial aid. Of those, 67% were determined to have financial need; 18% had their need fully met. Average financial aid package (proportion receiving): $7,254 (65%). Average amount of gift aid, such as scholarships or grants (proportion receiving): $4,697 (58%). Average amount of self-help aid, such as work study or loans (proportion receiving): $3,791 (54%). Average need-based loan (excluding PLUS or other private loans): $3,599. Among students who received need-based aid, the average percentage of need met: 68%. Among students who received aid based on merit, the average award (and the proportion receiving): $1,953 (13%). The average athletic scholarship (and the proportion receiving): $2,788 (0%). Average amount of debt of borrowers graduating in 2005: $18,182. Proportion who borrowed: 66%.

CAMPUS LIFE AND EXTRACURRICULAR ACTIVITIES

Campus housing available: coed dorms, women's dorms, men's dorms, sorority housing, fraternity housing, apartments for married students, special housing for international students. Activities include: choral groups, concert band, dance, drama/theater, marching band, music ensembles, musical theater, pep band, radio station, student government, student newspaper. **Sports program (2005-2006):** Member of NCAA II. ***Men's intercollegiate varsity sports:*** basketball, cheerleading, cross-country, football, golf, track and field (outdoor). ***Women's intercollegiate varsity sports:*** basketball, cheerleading, cross-country, golf, soccer, track and field (outdoor), volleyball.

SERVICES AND FACILITIES

Basic services: nonremedial tutoring, women's center, placement service, day care, health service, health insurance. **Remedial assistance:** reading, math, writing, study skills. **Counseling services:** career, personal, veteran student, academic, psychological. **Information technology resources:** Students are not required to lease or own a computer. School has a wireless network. **Campus safety:** Security services offered: 24-hour foot-and-vehicle patrols, 24-hour emergency telephones, lighted pathways/sidewalks, controlled dormitory access (key, security card, etc).

TRANSFER AND INTERNATIONAL STUDENTS

Transfer students: May apply for admission for the following academic terms: Fall, Winter, Spring, Summer. Applicants need a minimum number of credits to apply. **International students:** Number of foreign undergraduates: 70 (1% of student body). Minimum TOEFL score required: 500 (paper); 175 (computer). Average TOEFL score: 550 (paper).

Texas A&M University–Corpus Christi

- **Address:** 6300 Ocean Drive, Corpus Christi, TX 78412-5503
- **Website:** http://www.tamucc.edu
- **Public**
- **Enrollment:** 5,416 full-time; 1,352 part-time

KEY STATS

✔ **U.S News College Ranking:** third tier, Universities–Master's (West)
✔ **SAT Score (25th/75th percentile):** 840-1040
✔ **Tuition:** 2006-2007: $4,946 in state, $13,196 out of state

Selectivity: Less selective	**Room/board:** N/A
Acceptance rate: 85%	**Average debt:** $17,367
Student/faculty ratio: 20/1	**Proportion who borrowed:** 60%

UNDERGRADUATE STUDENT BODY STATS

2005-2006 enrollment: 5,416 full-time; 1,352 part-time. Men: 40%; women: 60%. **Ethnic makeup:** African American: 3%; American-Indian: 1%; Asian American: 2%; Hispanic: 38%; White: 55%; International: 1%.

ADMISSIONS FACTS AND FIGURES

Phone: (361) 825-2624. **Email:** admiss@falcon.tamucc.edu. **Website:** http://www.tamucc.edu. **Application deadlines for fall 2007:** Regular decision: July 1. Early decision: Not offered. Early action: Not offered. Admission cannot be deferred. **Application fee:** $20. Common application is not accepted. **To apply online, go to:** http://www.applytexas.org. **Admissions requirements/recommendations:** High school units required (recommended): English: 4; Mathematics: 3; Science: 3; Foreign language: 2; Social studies: 3; Total units: 15. Tests: The college uses SAT or ACT scores in admissions decisions. Either SAT or ACT required. Campus visit: Recommended. Admissions interview: Neither required nor recommended. Off-campus interview: Not available. **Factors that count in admissions decisions:** *Academic:* Secondary school record: Very important. Class rank: Very important. Letters of recommendation: Considered. Standardized test scores: Important. Essay: Not considered. *Nonacademic:* Interview: Not considered. Extracurricular activities: Considered. Talent/ability: Considered. Character/personal qualities: Considered. Alumni/ae relationship: Not considered. Geographical residence: Not considered. State residency: Not considered. Religious affiliation/commitment: Not considered. Minority status: Not considered. Volunteer work: Considered. Work experience: Considered. **Other schools with the greatest overlap in applicants:** Texas A&M University–Kingsville. **Admissions statistics for the fall 2005 entering class:** Total applicants: 4,093. Total accepted: 3,464. Freshmen enrolled: 1,256; 3% were from out of state. Overall acceptance rate: 85%. **Credentials of fall 2005 freshmen:** 22% ranked in the top 10 percent of their high school class; 50% were in the top 25 percent, and 84% were in the top half. (Proportion submitting class standing: 100%.) **First-year students who submitted SAT scores:** 77%. Scores (25/75 percentile): Verbal: 410-520, Math: 430-520, Combined: 840-1040. **First-year students submitting ACT scores:** 56%. Scores (25/75 percentile): English: 15-19, Math: 17-25, Composite: 16-21.

ACADEMICS

Year founded: 1947. **Academic calendar:** Semester. **Degrees offered:** bachelor's, post-bachelor's certificate, master's, doctorate. **Most popular majors:** 24% business, management, marketing, and related support services, 14% health professions and related clinical sciences, 12% multi/interdisciplinary studies, 8% biological and biomedical sciences, 6% psychology. **Major fields of study:** biological and biomedical sciences; business, management, marketing, and related support services; communication, journalism, and related programs; computer and information sciences and support services; engineering technologies/technicians; English language and literature/letters; foreign languages, literatures, and linguistics; health professions and related clinical sciences; history; mathematics and statistics; multi/interdisciplinary studies; natural resources and conservation; parks, recreation, leisure, and fitness studies; physical sciences; psychology; security and protective services; social sciences; visual and performing arts. **Areas of required coursework:** arts/fine arts, computer literacy, mathematics, English (including composition), philosophy, foreign languages, sciences (biological or physical), history, social science. **Pre-professional programs:** pre-law, pre-dentistry, pre-medicine, pre-veterinary science, pre-optometry, pre-pharmacy. **Special academic programs (% participation):** cooperative (work-study plan) program, distance learning, double major, independent study, internships, teacher certificate program. **Teacher certification offered in:** early childhood, special education, elementary, vo-tech, middle/junior high, secondary, bilingual/bicultural. **Cooperative education programs:** education, health professions. **Reserve Officers Training Corps (ROTC):** Army ROTC: Offered on campus. **Faculty and instruction (2005-2006):** Total instructional faculty: 264 full-time, 212 part-time (53% men; 47% women; 21% minorities). Full-time faculty with Ph.D. or other terminal degree: 80%. Student/faculty ratio: 20/1. Classes of fewer than 20 students: 28%; of 20 to 49 students: 57%; of 50 or more students: 15%. **Freshmen returning for sophomore year:** 63%. **Graduation rates:** Four-year: 19%; five-year: 33%; six-year: 37%.

COSTS AND FINANCIAL AID

Financial aid office: (361) 825-2338. **Expenses (2006-2007):** Tuition and fees 2006-2007: $4,946 in state, $13,196 out of state; room/board: N/A. Estimated books and supplies: $865; transportation: $828; personal expenses: $1,282. **Financial aid:** Priority filing date for institution's financial aid form: April 1. In 2005-2006, 71% of undergraduates applied for financial aid. Of those, 63% were determined to have financial need; 17% had their need fully met. Average financial aid package (proportion receiving): $6,524 (60%). Average amount of gift aid, such as scholarships or grants (proportion receiving): $3,826 (44%). Average amount of self-help aid, such as work study or loans (proportion receiving): $3,867 (44%). Average need-based loan (excluding PLUS or other private loans): $3,753. Among students who received need-based aid, the average percentage of need met: 63%. Among students who received aid based on merit, the average award (and the proportion receiving): $4,689 (7%). The average athletic scholarship (and the proportion receiving): $5,651 (0%). Average amount of debt of borrowers graduating in 2005: $17,367. Proportion who borrowed: 60%.

CAMPUS LIFE AND EXTRACURRICULAR ACTIVITIES

Campus housing available (% using): coed dorms (100%), apartment for single students. Students who live in college-owned, operated, or affiliated housing: 25%. **Student employment:** During the 2005-2006 academic year, 12% of undergraduates worked on campus. Average per-year earnings: $5,500. Activities include: choral groups, concert band, dance, drama/theater, jazz band, literary magazine, marching band, music ensembles, musical theater, opera, pep band, student government, student newspaper, student film society, symphony orchestra, yearbook. Average proportion of students who stay on campus on weekends: 40%. **Sports program (2005-2006):** Member of NCAA I. *Men's intercollegiate varsity sports:* baseball, basketball, cheerleading, cross-country, tennis, track and field (indoor), track and field (outdoor). *Women's intercollegiate varsity sports:* basketball, cheerleading, cross-country, golf, softball, tennis, track and field (indoor), track and field (outdoor), volleyball.

SERVICES AND FACILITIES

Basic services: nonremedial tutoring, women's center, placement service, health service. **Remedial assistance:** reading, math, writing, study skills. **Counseling services:** minority student, career, veteran student, academic. **For learning-disabled students:** School does not offer a structured program with separate admission and additional fees. Total undergraduates in learning-disabled program or receiving services: 39. Services include: remedial math, remedial English, remedial reading, tape recorders, videotaped classes, note-taking services, oral tests, learning center, readers, extended time for tests, tutors, texts on tape. **Library:** Number of titles: 474,085; number of current serial subscriptions: 1,661. **Information technology resources:** Students are not required to lease or own a computer. Number of campus computers available to all students: 850. School has a wireless network. Approximate number of users that can be accommodated: 10,000. Proportion of college-owned housing units wired for high-speed internet access: 90%. **Campus safety:** Security services offered: 24-hour foot-and-vehicle patrols, late-night transport/escort service, 24-hour emergency telephones, lighted pathways/sidewalks, controlled dormitory access (key, security card, etc).

TRANSFER AND INTERNATIONAL STUDENTS

Transfer students: May apply for admission for the following academic terms: Fall, Spring, Summer. Applicants need a minimum number of credits to apply. For fall 2005: Transfer applications received: 1,855. Transfer applicants offered admission: 1,470. Transfer applicants enrolled: 1,435. **International students:** Number of foreign undergraduates: 42 (1% of student body). Number of countries represented: 36. Minimum TOEFL score required: 550 (paper); 213 (computer). Average TOEFL score: 584 (paper).

Texas A&M University–Galveston

- **Address:** PO Box 1675, Galveston, TX 77553-1675
- **Website:** http://www.tamug.edu
- **Public**
- **Enrollment:** 1,488 full-time; 148 part-time

KEY STATS

- ✔ **U.S News College Ranking:** fourth tier, Liberal Arts Colleges
- ✔ **SAT Score (25th/75th percentile):** 1074-1088
- ✔ **Tuition:** 2006-2007: $5,651 in state, $13,901 out of state

Selectivity: Selective	**Room/board:** $4,870
Acceptance rate: 96%	**Average debt:** $15,793
Student/faculty ratio: 16/1	**Proportion who borrowed:** 63%

UNDERGRADUATE STUDENT BODY STATS

2005-2006 enrollment: 1,488 full-time; 148 part-time. Men: 58%; women: 42%. **Ethnic makeup:** African American: 3%; American-Indian: 1%; Asian American: 2%; Hispanic: 10%; White: 84%.

ADMISSIONS FACTS AND FIGURES

Phone: (409) 740-4414. **Email:** seaaggie@tamug.edu. **Website:** http://www.tamug.edu. **Application deadlines for fall 2007:** Regular decision: Rolling. Early decision: Not offered. Early action: Not offered. Admission can be deferred. **Application fee:** $35. Common application is not accepted. **To apply online, go to:** http://www.applytexas.org. **Admissions requirements/recommendations:** High school units required (recommended): English: 4 (4); Mathematics: 3 (4); Science: 3 (4); Foreign language: (3); Social studies: (3). Tests: The college uses SAT or ACT scores in admissions decisions. Either SAT or ACT required. For admission to the fall 2007 entering class, the school will accept: ACT with writing, ACT without writing. Campus visit: Recommended. Admissions interview: Recommended. Off-campus interview: Not available. **Factors that count in admissions decisions:** *Academic:* Secondary school record: Very important. Class rank: Very important. Letters of recommendation: Important. Standardized test scores: Very important. Essay: Important. *Nonacademic:* Interview: Considered. Extracurricular activities: Important. Talent/ability: Important. Character/personal qualities: Important. Alumni/ae relationship: Considered. Geographical residence: Not considered. State residency: Not considered. Religious affiliation/commitment: Not considered. Minority status: Not considered. Volunteer work: Important. Work experience: Important. **Other schools with the greatest overlap in applicants:** Texas A&M University–College Station; Texas A&M University–Corpus Christi; Texas State University–San Marcos; University of Houston; University of Texas–Austin. **Admissions statistics for the fall 2005 entering class:** Total applicants: 1,171. Total accepted: 1,119. Freshmen enrolled: 466; 27% were from out of state. Overall acceptance rate: 96%. **Credentials of fall 2005 freshmen:** 9% ranked in the top 10 percent of their high school class; 36% were in the top 25 percent, and 81% were in the top half. (Proportion submitting class standing: 91%.) First-year students who submitted SAT scores: 89%. Scores (25/75 percentile): Verbal: 533-538, Math: 541-550, Combined: 1074-1088. **First-year students submitting ACT scores:** 52%. Scores (25/75 percentile): English: 22-23, Math: 23-24, Composite: 23-24.

ACADEMICS

Year founded: 1962. **Academic calendar:** Semester. **Degrees offered:** bachelor's, master's. **Most popular majors:** 30% business administration and management, 28% marine biology and biological oceanography, 12% marine science/merchant marine officer, 11% chemical and physical oceanography, 7% chemical and physical oceanography. **Major fields of study:** area, ethnic, cultural, and gender studies; biological and biomedical sciences; business, management, marketing, and related support services; engineering; engineering technologies/technicians; liberal arts and sciences studies, and humanities; natural resources and conservation; physical sciences; transportation and materials moving. **Areas of required coursework:** humanities, computer literacy, mathematics, English (including composition), foreign languages, sciences (biological or physical), history, social science, other. **Pre-professional programs:** pre-medicine, pre-veterinary science. **Special academic programs:** cooperative (work-study plan) program, double major, dual enrollment, internships, teacher certificate program, other. **Teacher certification offered in:** elementary, middle/junior high, secondary. **Cooperative education programs:** other. **Reserve Officers Training Corps (ROTC):** Navy ROTC: Offered on campus. **Faculty and instruction (2005-2006):** Total instructional faculty: 86 full-time, 55 part-time (79% men; 21% women; 17% minorities). Full-time faculty with Ph.D. or other terminal degree: 73%. Student/faculty ratio: 16/1. Classes of fewer than 20 students: 57%; of 20 to 49 students: 41%; of 50 or more students: 3%. **Advanced Placement and International Baccalaureate credit:** AP tests may be used for: Credit only. Scores accepted: 3, 4, 5. International Baccalaureate exams may be used for: Credit only. **Freshmen returning for sophomore year:** 71%. **Graduation rates:** Four-year: 11%; five-year: 22%; six-year: 25%. **Graduate study:** 11% of students pursue further study immediately upon graduation; 21% within one year; 25% within five years. Fields in which graduates pursue further study: Master of Business Administration (MBA), 20%; law, 20%; medicine, 3%; dentistry, 1%; engineering, 5%; theology (or the seminary), 1%; education, 5%; arts and sciences, 40%; veterinary medicine, 5%.

COSTS AND FINANCIAL AID

Financial aid office: (409) 740-4500. **Expenses (2006-2007):** Tuition and fees 2006-2007: $5,651 in state, $13,901 out of state; room/board: $4,870. Estimated books and supplies: $1,180; transportation: $803; personal expenses: $1,660. **Financial aid:** In 2005-2006, 58% of undergraduates applied for financial aid. Of those, 53% were determined to have financial need; 28% had their need fully met. Average financial aid package (proportion receiving): $10,288 (50%). Average amount of gift aid, such as scholarships or grants (proportion receiving): $4,413 (29%). Average amount of

self-help aid, such as work study or loans (proportion receiving): $3,079 (1%). Average need-based loan (excluding PLUS or other private loans): $3,102. Among students who received need-based aid, the average percentage of need met: 22%. Among students who received aid based on merit, the average award (and the proportion receiving): $7,103 (2%). The average athletic scholarship (and the proportion receiving): $0 (0%). Average amount of debt of borrowers graduating in 2005: $15,793. Proportion who borrowed: 63%.

CAMPUS LIFE AND EXTRACURRICULAR ACTIVITIES

Campus housing available (% using): coed dorms (54%), other housing options (46%). Students who live in college-owned, operated, or affiliated housing: 25%. **Student employment:** During the 2005-2006 academic year, 12% of undergraduates worked on campus. Average per-year earnings: $4,944. **Clubs and organizations:** Number of student organizations: 31. Activities include: choral groups, dance, drama/theater, literary magazine, student government, student newspaper, yearbook. Number of fraternities: 0; sororities: 0. Average proportion of students who stay on campus on weekends: 75%. **Sports program (2005-2006):** *Men's intercollegiate varsity sports:* crew, sailing. *Women's intercollegiate varsity sports:* crew, sailing.

SERVICES AND FACILITIES

Basic services: nonremedial tutoring, placement service, health insurance. **Remedial assistance:** reading, math, writing, study skills, other. **Counseling services:** career, military, personal, veteran student, academic. **For learning-disabled students:** School does not offer a structured program with separate admission and additional fees. Total undergraduates in learning-disabled program or receiving services: 40. Services include: remedial math, remedial English, remedial reading, tape recorders, videotaped classes, note-taking services, oral tests, extended time for tests, tutors. **Library:** Number of titles: 91,305; number of current serial subscriptions: 647. **Information technology resources:** Students are not required to lease or own a computer. Number of campus computers available to all students: 135. School has a wireless network. Approximate number of users that can be accommodated: 50. Proportion of college-owned housing units wired for high-speed internet access: 100%. **Campus safety:** Security services offered: 24-hour foot-and-vehicle patrols, late-night transport/escort service, 24-hour emergency telephones, lighted pathways/sidewalks, student patrols, controlled dormitory access (key, security card, etc.).

TRANSFER AND INTERNATIONAL STUDENTS

Transfer students: May apply for admission for the following academic terms: Fall, Spring, Summer. Applicants do not need a minimum number of credits to apply. For fall 2005: Transfer applications received: 218. Transfer applicants offered admission: 210. Transfer applicants enrolled: 156. **International students:** Number of foreign undergraduates: 4. Number of countries represented: 6. Minimum TOEFL score required: 550 (paper); 213 (computer).

Texas A&M University–Kingsville

- **Address:** MSC 105, Kingsville, TX 78363
- **Website:** http://www.tamuk.edu
- **Public**
- **Enrollment:** 3,700 full-time; 1,422 part-time

KEY STATS

✔ **U.S News College Ranking:** fourth tier, National Universities
✔ **ACT Score (25th/75th percentile):** 16-22
✔ **Tuition:** 2005-2006: $4,566 in state, $12,846 out of state

Selectivity: Less selective	**Room/board:** $4,672
Acceptance rate: 78%	**Average debt:** N/A
Student/faculty ratio: 15/1	**Proportion who borrowed:** N/A

UNDERGRADUATE STUDENT BODY STATS

2005-2006 enrollment: 3,700 full-time; 1,422 part-time. Men: 49%; women: 51%. **Ethnic makeup:** African American: 6%; Asian American: 1%; Hispanic: 66%; White: 25%; International: 2%.

ADMISSIONS FACTS AND FIGURES

Phone: (361) 593-2315. **Email:** kapamoo@tamuk.edu. **Website:** http://www.tamuk.edu. **Application deadlines for fall 2007:** Regular decision:

Rolling. Early decision: Not offered. Early action: Not offered. Admission can be deferred. **Application fee:** $15. Common application is accepted. **To apply online, go to:** http://www.tamuk.edu/general/applyonline.html. **Admissions requirements/recommendations:** High school units required (recommended): English: (4); Mathematics: (3); Science: (3); Foreign language: (3); Social studies: (4); History: (3); Academic electives: (3); Total units: (24). Tests: The college uses SAT or ACT scores in admissions decisions. Either SAT or ACT required. For admission to the fall 2007 entering class, the school will accept: ACT with writing, ACT without writing. Campus visit: Recommended. Admissions interview: Neither required nor recommended. Off-campus interview: May be arranged. **Factors that count in admissions decisions:** *Academic:* Secondary school record: Important. Class rank: Important. Letters of recommendation: Not considered. Standardized test scores: Important. Essay: Not considered. *Nonacademic:* Interview: Not considered. Extracurricular activities: Not considered. Talent/ability: Not considered. Character/personal qualities: Not considered. Alumni/ae relationship: Not considered. Geographical residence: Not considered. State residency: Not considered. Religious affiliation/commitment: Not considered. Minority status: Not considered. Volunteer work: Not considered. Work experience: Not considered. **Other schools with the greatest overlap in applicants:** Texas A&M University–College Station; Texas A&M University–Corpus Christi; Texas State University–San Marcos; University of Texas–Pan American. **Admissions statistics for the fall 2005 entering class:** Total applicants: 2,400. Total accepted: 1,865. Freshmen enrolled: 783; Overall acceptance rate: 78%. **Credentials of fall 2005 freshmen:** 10% ranked in the top 10 percent of their high school class; 35% were in the top 25 percent, and 70% were in the top half. (Proportion submitting class standing: 98%.) **Average high school grade point average:** 3.4. **First-year students who submitted SAT scores:** 50%. Scores (25/75 percentile): Verbal: 410-520, Math: 410-545, Combined: 820-1065. **First-year students submitting ACT scores:** 50%. Scores (25/75 percentile): English: 14-21, Math: 15-20, Composite: 16-22.

ACADEMICS

Year founded: 1925. **Academic calendar:** Semester. **Degrees offered:** bachelor's, master's, doctorate. **Most popular majors:** Information not available. **Major fields of study:** agriculture, agriculture operations, and related sciences; biological and biomedical sciences; business, management, marketing, and related support services; communication, journalism, and related programs; computer and information sciences and support services; education; engineering; engineering technologies/technicians; English language and literature/letters; family and consumer sciences/human sciences; foreign languages, literatures, and linguistics; health professions and related clinical sciences; history; mathematics and statistics; multi/interdisciplinary studies; natural resources and conservation; parks, recreation, leisure, and fitness studies; personal and culinary services; physical sciences; psychology; public administration and social service professions; security and protective services; social sciences; visual and performing arts. **Areas of required coursework:** arts/fine arts, humanities, computer literacy, mathematics, English (including composition), sciences (biological or physical), history, social science. **Pre-professional programs:** pre-law, pre-dentistry, pre-medicine, pre-veterinary science, pre-pharmacy, other. **Special academic programs (% participation):** accelerated program (2%), cooperative (work-study plan) program (15%), distance learning (1%), double major (2%), English as a Second Language (ESL) (1%), honors program (1%), internships (22%), study abroad (1%), teacher certificate program (20%). **Teacher certification offered in:** early childhood, special education, elementary, middle/junior high, adult education, secondary, bilingual/bicultural. **Cooperative education programs:** agriculture, education, home economics. **Reserve Officers Training Corps (ROTC):** Army ROTC: Offered on campus. **Faculty and instruction (2005-2006):** Total instructional faculty: N/A. Student/faculty ratio: 15/1. **Advanced Placement and International Baccalaureate credit:** AP tests may be used for: Credit only. Scores accepted: 3, 4, 5. International Baccalaureate exams may be used for: Credit only. **Freshmen returning for sophomore year:** 56%. **Graduation rates:** Four-year: 7%; five-year: 20%; six-year: 29%.

COSTS AND FINANCIAL AID

Financial aid office: (361) 593-3911. **Expenses (2005-2006):** Tuition and fees 2005-2006: $4,566 in state, $12,846 out of state; room/board: $4,672. Estimated books and supplies: $1,027; transportation: $602; personal expenses: $2,286. **Financial aid:** Priority filing date for institution's financial aid form: April 15.

CAMPUS LIFE AND EXTRACURRICULAR ACTIVITIES

Campus housing available (% using): coed dorms (80%), women's dorms (10%), men's dorms (5%), apartments for married students (5%). **Student employment:** During the 2005-2006 academic year, 18% of undergraduates worked on campus. Average per-year earnings: $1,752. **Clubs and organizations:** Number of student organizations: 150. Activities include: choral groups, concert band, dance, drama/theater, jazz band, literary magazine, marching band, music ensembles, musical theater, pep band, radio station, student government, student newspaper, television station. Number of fraternities: 5; sororities: 5. Average proportion of students who stay on campus on weekends: 10%. **Sports program (2005-2006):** Member of NCAA II. **Men's intercollegiate varsity sports:** baseball, basketball, cross-country, football, track and field (indoor), track and field (outdoor). **Women's intercollegiate varsity sports:** basketball, cross-country, softball, track and field (indoor), track and field (outdoor), volleyball.

SERVICES AND FACILITIES

Basic services: nonremedial tutoring, women's center, placement service, day care, health service, health insurance. **Remedial assistance:** reading, math, writing. **Counseling services:** minority student, career, military, personal, veteran student, academic, older student, psychological, birth control. **For learning-disabled students:** School does not offer a structured program with separate admission and additional fees. Services include: remedial math, remedial English, reading machines, remedial reading, tape recorders, other special classes, videotaped classes, note-taking services, oral tests, learning center, readers, extended time for tests, tutors. **Information technology resources:** Students are not required to lease or own a computer. Number of campus computers available to all students: 500. **Campus safety:** Security services offered: 24-hour foot-and-vehicle patrols, late-night transport/escort service, 24-hour emergency telephones, lighted pathways/sidewalks, controlled dormitory access (key, security card, etc).

TRANSFER AND INTERNATIONAL STUDENTS

Transfer students: May apply for admission for the following academic terms: Fall, Spring, Summer. Applicants need a minimum number of credits to apply. For fall 2005: Transfer applications received: 850. Transfer applicants offered admission: 600. Transfer applicants enrolled: 563. **International students:** Number of foreign undergraduates: 68 (2% of student body). Number of countries represented: 18. Minimum TOEFL score required: 500 (paper). Average TOEFL score: 567 (paper).

Texas Christian University

- **Address:** 2800 S. University Drive, Fort Worth, TX 76129
- **Website:** http://www.tcu.edu
- **Private; Religious affiliation:** Christian Church (Disciples of Christ)
- **Enrollment:** 6,718 full-time; 453 part-time

KEY STATS

- ✔ **U.S News College Ranking:** 105, National Universities
- ✔ **SAT Score (25th/75th percentile):** 1060-1270
- ✔ **Tuition:** 2006-2007: $23,020

Selectivity: More selective	**Room/board:** $7,520
Acceptance rate: 67%	**Average debt:** N/A
Student/faculty ratio: 14/1	**Proportion who borrowed:** N/A

UNDERGRADUATE STUDENT BODY STATS

2005-2006 enrollment: 6,718 full-time; 453 part-time. Men: 40%; women: 60%. **Ethnic makeup:** African American: 5%; American-Indian: 1%; Asian American: 2%; Hispanic: 6%; White: 82%; International: 4%. **Religious preference:** Roman Catholic: 16%; Protestant: 1%; Jewish: 1%; No preference: 20%; Unknown: 2%; Christian Church (Disciples of Christ): 4%; Other: 56%.

ADMISSIONS FACTS AND FIGURES

Phone: (817) 257-7490. **Email:** frogmail@tcu.edu. **Website:** http://www.tcu.edu. **Application deadlines for fall 2007:** Regular decision: February 15; decision sent by April 1. Early decision: Not offered. Early action: Send application by: November 15; Decision sent by: January 1. Admission can be deferred. **Application fee:** $40. Common application is accepted. **Admissions requirements/recommendations:** High school units required (recommended): English: 4 (4); Mathematics: 3 (4); Science: 3 (4);

Foreign language: 2 (4); Social studies: 3 (4); Academic electives: 2 (4); Total units: 17 (24). Tests: The college uses SAT or ACT scores in admissions decisions. Either SAT or ACT required. For admission to the fall 2007 entering class, the school will accept: ACT with writing, ACT without writing. Campus visit: Recommended. Admissions interview: Recommended. Off-campus interview: May be arranged. **Factors that count in admissions decisions:** *Academic:* Secondary school record: Very important. Class rank: Very important. Letters of recommendation: Very important. Standardized test scores: Very important. Essay: Very important. *Nonacademic:* Interview: Considered. Extracurricular activities: Important. Talent/ability: Important. Character/personal qualities: Very important. Alumni/ae relationship: Considered. Geographical residence: Important. State residency: Not considered. Religious affiliation/commitment: Important. Minority status: Important. Volunteer work: Important. Work experience: Important. **Other schools with the greatest overlap in applicants:** Baylor University; Southern Methodist University; Texas A&M University–College Station; Texas Tech University; University of Texas–Austin. **Admissions statistics for the fall 2005 entering class:** Total applicants: 8,155. Total accepted: 5,471. Freshmen enrolled: 1,610; 24% were from out of state. Overall acceptance rate: 67%. Non-early acceptance rate: 67%. **Size of waiting list:** 583 applicants; enrolled from waiting list: 148. **Credentials of fall 2005 freshmen:** 28% ranked in the top 10 percent of their high school class; 61% were in the top 25 percent, and 94% were in the top half. (Proportion submitting class standing: 68%.) **First-year students who submitted SAT scores:** 69%. Scores (25/75 percentile): Verbal: 520-630, Math: 540-640, Combined: 1060-1270. **First-year students submitting ACT scores:** 31%. Scores (25/75 percentile): English: N/A, Math: N/A, Composite: 23-28.

ACADEMICS

Year founded: 1873. **Academic calendar:** Semester. **Degrees offered:** certificate, bachelor's, post-bachelor's certificate, master's, first professional, first professional certificate, doctorate. **Most popular majors:** 27% business, management, marketing, and related support services, 20% communication, journalism, and related programs, 8% education, 8% health professions and related clinical sciences, 7% visual and performing arts. **Major fields of study:** agriculture, agriculture operations, and related sciences; area, ethnic, cultural, and gender studies; biological and biomedical sciences; business, management, marketing, and related support services; communication, journalism, and related programs; computer and information sciences and support services; education; engineering; English language and literature/letters; foreign languages, literatures, and linguistics; health professions and related clinical sciences; history; liberal arts and sciences studies, and humanities; mathematics and statistics; multi/interdisciplinary studies; natural resources and conservation; parks, recreation, leisure, and fitness studies; philosophy and religious studies; physical sciences; psychology; public administration and social service professions; security and protective services; social sciences; theology and religious vocations; visual and performing arts. **Areas of required coursework:** arts/fine arts, humanities, mathematics, English (including composition), foreign languages, sciences (biological or physical), history, social science. **Pre-professional programs:** pre-law, pre-dentistry, pre-medicine, pre-veterinary science, pre-optometry, other. **Special academic programs:** accelerated program, cross-registration, distance learning, double major, English as a Second Language (ESL), honors program, independent study, internships, liberal arts/career combination, study abroad, teacher certificate program. **Teacher certification offered in:** early childhood, special education, elementary, middle/junior high, secondary, bilingual/bicultural. **Reserve Officers Training Corps (ROTC):** Army ROTC: Offered on campus; Air Force ROTC: Offered on campus. **Faculty and instruction (2005-2006):** Total instructional faculty: 465 full-time, 345 part-time (56% men; 44% women; 10% minorities). Full-time faculty with Ph.D. or other terminal degree: 90%. Student/faculty ratio: 14/1. Classes of fewer than 20 students: 50%; of 20 to 49 students: 43%; of 50 or more students: 7%. **Advanced Placement and International Baccalaureate credit:** AP tests may be used for: Credit only. Scores accepted: 3, 4, 5. International Baccalaureate exams may be used for: Credit only. **Freshmen returning for sophomore year:** 82%. **Graduation rates:** Six-year: 69%. **Graduate study:** 33% of students pursue further study within one year. Fields in which graduates pursue further study: Master of Business Administration (MBA), 10%; law, 10%; medicine, 4%; engineering, 2%; theology (or the seminary), 2%; education, 12%; arts and sciences, 11%.

COSTS AND FINANCIAL AID

Financial aid office: (817) 257-7858. **Expenses (2006-2007):** Tuition and fees 2006-2007: $23,020; room/board: $7,520. Estimated books and supplies: $810; transportation: $340; personal expenses: $2,810. **Financial aid:** Priority filing date for institution's financial aid form: May 1; deadline: May

1. In 2005-2006, 54% of undergraduates applied for financial aid. Of those, 43% were determined to have financial need; 42% had their need fully met. Average financial aid package (proportion receiving): $14,589 (43%). Average amount of gift aid, such as scholarships or grants (proportion receiving): $10,253 (37%). Average amount of self-help aid, such as work study or loans (proportion receiving): $7,199 (34%). Average need-based loan (excluding PLUS or other private loans): $5,957. Among students who received need-based aid, the average percentage of need met: 67%. Among students who received aid based on merit, the average award (and the proportion receiving): $8,800 (22%). The average athletic scholarship (and the proportion receiving): $17,887 (4%).

CAMPUS LIFE AND EXTRACURRICULAR ACTIVITIES

Campus housing available: coed dorms, women's dorms, men's dorms, sorority housing, fraternity housing, apartments for married students, apartment for single students, other housing options. Students who live in college-owned, operated, or affiliated housing: 46%. **Clubs and organizations:** Number of student organizations: 193. Activities include: choral groups, concert band, dance, drama/theater, jazz band, literary magazine, marching band, music ensembles, musical theater, opera, pep band, radio station, student government, student newspaper, television station, yearbook. Number of fraternities: 13; sororities: 16. Proportion of men in fraternities: 34%; of women in sororities: 36%. **Sports program (2005-2006):** Member of NCAA I. *Men's intercollegiate varsity sports:* baseball, basketball, cross-country, football, golf, swimming and diving, tennis, track and field (indoor), track and field (outdoor). *Women's intercollegiate varsity sports:* basketball, cross-country, golf, riflery, soccer, swimming and diving, tennis, track and field (indoor), track and field (outdoor), volleyball.

SERVICES AND FACILITIES

Basic services: nonremedial tutoring, women's center, health service, health insurance. **Counseling services:** minority student, career, military, personal, veteran student, academic, older student, psychological, birth control, religious. **For learning-disabled students:** School does not offer a structured program with separate admission and additional fees. **Library:** Number of titles: 1,371,620; number of current serial subscriptions: 28,747. **Information technology resources:** Students are not required to lease or own a computer. Number of campus computers available to all students: 1,170. School has a wireless network. Approximate number of users that can be accommodated: 1,500. Proportion of college-owned housing units wired for high-speed internet access: 100%. **Campus safety:** Security services offered: 24-hour foot-and-vehicle patrols, late-night transport/escort service, 24-hour emergency telephones, lighted pathways/sidewalks, student patrols, controlled dormitory access (key, security card, etc).

TRANSFER AND INTERNATIONAL STUDENTS

Transfer students: May apply for admission for the following academic terms: Fall, Spring, Summer. Applicants do not need a minimum number of credits to apply. For fall 2005: Transfer applications received: 1,162. Transfer applicants offered admission: 498. Transfer applicants enrolled: 388. **International students:** Number of foreign undergraduates: 269 (4% of student body). Number of countries represented: 80. Minimum TOEFL score required: 550 (paper); 213 (computer).

Texas College

- **Address:** 2404 N. Grand Avenue, Box 4500, Tyler, TX 75712
- **Website:** http://www.texascollege.edu
- **Private; Religious affiliation:** Christian Methodist Episcopal Church
- **Enrollment:** 739 full-time; 55 part-time

KEY STATS

✔ **U.S News College Ranking:** fourth tier, Comp. Coll.–Bachelor's (West)
✔ **SAT or ACT Score (25th/75th percentile):** N/A
✔ **Tuition:** 2006-2007: $8,746

Selectivity: Less selective	**Room/board:** $5,600
Acceptance rate: 25%	**Average debt:** N/A
Student/faculty ratio: 16/1	**Proportion who borrowed:** N/A

UNDERGRADUATE STUDENT BODY STATS

2005-2006 enrollment: 739 full-time; 55 part-time. Men: 55%; women: 45%. **Ethnic makeup:** African American: 89%; Hispanic: 9%; White: 2%.

ADMISSIONS FACTS AND FIGURES

Phone: (903) 593-8311. **Email:** afrancis@texascollege.edu. **Website:** http://www.texascollege.edu. **Application deadlines for fall 2007:** Regular decision: Rolling. Early decision: Not offered. Early action: Not offered. Admission can be deferred. **Application fee:** $20. Common application is accepted. **Admissions requirements/recommendations:** High school units required (recommended): English: 4 (4); Mathematics: 2 (2); Science: 2 (2); Foreign language: 0 (0); Social studies: 2 (2); History: 0 (0); Academic electives: 6 (6); Total units: 16 (16). Tests: The college does not use SAT or ACT scores in admissions decisions. Neither SAT nor ACT required. Campus visit: Recommended. Admissions interview: Recommended. Off-campus interview: May be arranged. **Factors that count in admissions decisions:** *Academic:* Secondary school record: Not considered. Class rank: Not considered. Letters of recommendation: Not considered. Standardized test scores: Not considered. Essay: Not considered. *Nonacademic:* Interview: Not considered. Extracurricular activities: Not considered. Talent/ability: Not considered. Character/personal qualities: Not considered. Alumni/ae relationship: Not considered. Geographical residence: Not considered. State residency: Not considered. Religious affiliation/commitment: Not considered. Minority status: Not considered. Volunteer work: Not considered. Work experience: Not considered. **Other schools with the greatest overlap in applicants:** Jarvis Christian College; University of Texas–Tyler; Wiley College. **Admissions statistics for the fall 2005 entering class:** Total accepted: 353. Freshmen enrolled: 212; Overall acceptance rate: 25%. **Credentials of fall 2005 freshmen:** 3% ranked in the top 10 percent of their high school class; 10% were in the top 25 percent.

ACADEMICS

Year founded: 1894. **Academic calendar:** Semester. **Degrees offered:** associate, bachelor's, post-bachelor's certificate. **Most popular majors:** 60% business administration and management, 10% health and physical education, 8% social work, 7% biology/biological sciences, 3% sociology. **Major fields of study:** biological and biomedical sciences; business, management, marketing, and related support services; computer and information sciences and support services; education; English language and literature/letters; history; liberal arts and sciences studies, and humanities; mathematics and statistics; parks, recreation, leisure, and fitness studies; public administration and social service professions; social sciences; visual and performing arts. **Areas of required coursework:** arts/fine arts, computer literacy, mathematics, English (including composition), foreign languages, sciences (biological or physical), history, social science, other. **Special academic programs (% participation):** accelerated program (47%), cooperative (work-study plan) program (20%), distance learning (0%), double major (0%), dual enrollment (0%), independent study, internships (27%), teacher certificate program (0%). **Teacher certification offered in:** early childhood, elementary, middle/junior high, secondary. **Faculty and instruction (2005-2006):** Total instructional faculty: 30 full-time, 20 part-time (54% men; 46% women; 72% minorities). Full-time faculty with Ph.D. or other terminal degree: 53%. Student/faculty ratio: 16/1. Classes of fewer than 20 students: 59%; of 20 to 49 students: 36%; of 50 or more students: 5%. **Advanced Placement and International Baccalaureate credit:** AP tests may be used for: Credit only. Scores accepted: 3. **Freshmen returning for sophomore year:** 50%. **Graduation rates:** Four-year: 9%; five-year: 23%; six-year: 26%. **Graduate study:** 11% of students pursue further study immediately upon graduation; 13% within one year; 10% within five years. Fields in which graduates pursue further study: Master of Business Administration (MBA), 15%; medicine, 5%; theology (or the seminary), 5%; education, 25%; arts and sciences, 6%; veterinary medicine, 2%.

COSTS AND FINANCIAL AID

Financial aid office: (903) 593-8311. **Expenses (2006-2007):** Tuition and fees 2006-2007: $8,746; room/board: $5,600. Estimated books and supplies: $800; transportation: $650; personal expenses: $1,740. **Financial aid:** Priority filing date for institution's financial aid form: April 15; deadline: April 15.

CAMPUS LIFE AND EXTRACURRICULAR ACTIVITIES

Campus housing available (% using): women's dorms (27%), men's dorms (56%), apartment for single students (17%). Students who live in college-owned, operated, or affiliated housing: 49%. **Student employment:** During the 2005-2006 academic year, 5% of undergraduates worked on campus. Average per-year earnings: $1,733. **Clubs and organizations:** Number of student organizations: 37. Activities include: choral groups, concert band, jazz band, marching band, student government, student newspaper, yearbook. Number of fraternities: 4; sororities: 4. Proportion of men in fraternities: 7%; of women in sororities: 14%. Average proportion of students who stay on campus on weekends: 20%. **Sports program (2005-2006):** Member of NAIA. *Men's intercollegiate varsity sports:* baseball, basketball, track and field (outdoor). *Women's intercollegiate varsity sports:* basketball, soccer, softball, track and field (outdoor), volleyball.

SERVICES AND FACILITIES

Basic services: nonremedial tutoring, day care, health service, health insurance. **Remedial assistance:** reading, math, writing, study skills. **Counseling services:** career, personal, veteran student, academic, religious. **For learning-disabled students:** School does not offer a structured program with separate admission and additional fees. **Library:** Number of titles: 74,592; number of current serial subscriptions: 18. **Information technology resources:** Students are not required to lease or own a computer. Number of campus computers available to all students: 105. School has a wireless network. Approximate number of users that can be accommodated: 1,000. Proportion of college-owned housing units wired for high-speed internet access: 83%. **Campus safety:** Security services offered: 24-hour foot-and-vehicle patrols, 24-hour emergency telephones, lighted pathways/sidewalks.

TRANSFER AND INTERNATIONAL STUDENTS

Transfer students: May apply for admission for the following academic terms: Fall, Spring, Summer. Applicants do not need a minimum number of credits to apply. For fall 2005: Transfer applicants enrolled: 108. **International students:** Number of foreign undergraduates: 0. Number of countries represented: 1. Minimum TOEFL score required: 500 (paper).

Texas Lutheran University

- **Address:** 1000 W. Court, Seguin, TX 78155-5999
- **Website:** http://www.tlu.edu
- **Private; Religious affiliation:** Evangelical Lutheran Church in America
- **Enrollment:** 1,328 full-time; 107 part-time

KEY STATS

✔ **U.S News College Ranking:** 5, Comp. Coll.–Bachelor's (West)
✔ **SAT Score (25th/75th percentile):** 940-1160
✔ **Tuition:** 2006-2007: $18,840

Selectivity: Selective	Room/board: $5,600
Acceptance rate: 72%	Average debt: $27,139
Student/faculty ratio: 16/1	Proportion who borrowed: 63%

UNDERGRADUATE STUDENT BODY STATS

2005-2006 enrollment: 1,328 full-time; 107 part-time. Men: 46%; women: 54%. **Ethnic makeup:** African American: 8%; Asian American: 2%; Hispanic: 16%; White: 73%; International: 1%. **Religious preference:** Roman Catholic: 19%; Protestant: 30%; Unknown: 19%; Evangelical Lutheran Church in America: 21%; Other: 11%.

ADMISSIONS FACTS AND FIGURES

Phone: (800) 771-8521. **Email:** admissions@tlu.edu. **Website:** http://www.tlu.edu. **Application deadlines for fall 2007:** Regular decision: August 1. Early decision: Not offered. Early action: Not offered. Admission can be deferred. **Application fee:** $25. Common application is accepted. **Admissions requirements/recommendations:** High school units required (recommended): English: 0 (4); Mathematics: 0 (3); Science: 0 (3); Foreign language: 0 (2); Social studies: 0 (3); History: 0 (3); Academic electives: 0 (4); Total units: 0 (22). Tests: The college uses SAT or ACT scores in admissions decisions. Either SAT or ACT required. For admission to the fall 2007 entering class, the school will accept: ACT with writing, ACT without writing. Campus visit: Recommended. Admissions interview: Recommended. Off-campus interview: May be arranged. **Factors that count in admissions decisions:** *Academic:* Secondary school record: Very important. Class rank: Important. Letters of recommendation: Important. Standardized test scores: Very important. Essay: Important. *Nonacademic:* Interview: Considered. Extracurricular activities: Considered. Talent/ability: Not considered. Character/personal qualities: Considered. Alumni/ae relationship: Not considered. Geographical residence: Not considered. State residency: Not considered. Religious affiliation/commitment: Not considered. Minority status: Not considered. Volunteer work: Important. Work experience: Considered. **Other schools with the greatest overlap in applicants:** Concordia University–Austin; St. Mary's University of San Antonio; Texas A&M University–College Station; Texas State University–San Marcos; University of Texas–San Antonio. **Admissions statistics for the fall 2005 entering class:** Total applicants: 1,150. Total accepted: 833. Freshmen enrolled: 380; 3% were from out of state. Overall acceptance rate: 72%. **Size of waiting list:** 0 applicants; enrolled from waiting list: 0. **Credentials of fall 2005 freshmen:** 24% ranked in the top 10 percent of their high school class; 57% were in the top 25 percent, and 90% were in the top half. (Proportion submitting class standing: 95%.) **Average high school grade point average:** 3.6. **First-year students who submitted SAT scores:** 87%. Scores (25/75 percentile): Verbal: 460-570, Math: 480-590, Combined: 940-1160. **First-year students submitting ACT scores:** 54%. Scores (25/75 percentile): English: 18-24, Math: 18-24, Composite: 18-24.

ACADEMICS

Year founded: 1891. **Academic calendar:** Semester. **Degrees offered:** bachelor's. **Most popular majors:** 36% business, management, marketing, and related support services, 11% biological and biomedical sciences, 10% parks, recreation, leisure, and fitness studies, 8% psychology, 7% English language and literature/letters. **Major fields of study:** biological and biomedical sciences; business, management, marketing, and related support services; communication, journalism, and related programs; computer and information sciences and support services; education; English language and literature/letters; foreign languages, literatures, and linguistics; health professions and related clinical sciences; history; mathematics and statistics; parks, recreation, leisure, and fitness studies; philosophy and religious studies; physical sciences; psychology; social sciences; theology and religious vocations; visual and performing arts. **Areas of required coursework:** arts/fine arts, humanities, mathematics, English (including composition), sciences (biological or physical), history, social science. **Pre-professional programs:** pre-law, pre-dentistry, pre-medicine, pre-theology, pre-veterinary science, pre-pharmacy, other. **Special academic programs (% participation):** double major (9%), honors program (7%), independent study (10%), internships (45%), study abroad (5%), teacher certificate program (11%). **Teacher certification offered in:** elementary, middle/junior high, secondary. **Reserve Officers Training Corps (ROTC):** Army ROTC: Offered at cooperating institution (Texas State University); Air Force ROTC: Offered at cooperating institution (Texas State University). **Faculty and instruction (2005-2006):** Total instructional faculty: 68 full-time, 49 part-time (56% men; 44% women; 11% minorities). Full-time faculty with Ph.D. or other terminal degree: 76%. Student/faculty ratio: 16/1. Classes of fewer than 20 students: 54%; of 20 to 49 students: 46%; of 50 or more students: 0%. **Advanced Placement and International Baccalaureate credit:** AP tests may be used for: Credit and/or placement. Scores accepted: 3, 4, 5. International Baccalaureate exams may be used for: Credit and/or placement. **Freshmen returning for sophomore year:** 71%. **Graduation rates:** Four-year: 29%; five-year: 39%; six-year: 49%. **Graduate study:** 27% of students pursue further study immediately upon graduation. Fields in which graduates pursue further study: Master of Business Administration (MBA), 5%; law, 5%; medicine, 30%; engineering, 5%; theology (or the seminary), 5%; education, 5%; arts and sciences, 45%.

COSTS AND FINANCIAL AID

Financial aid office: (830) 372-8075. **Expenses (2006-2007):** Tuition and fees 2006-2007: $18,840; room/board: $5,600. Estimated books and supplies: $800; transportation: $800; personal expenses: $1,100. **Financial aid:** Priority filing date for institution's financial aid form: April 1. In 2005-2006, 86% of undergraduates applied for financial aid. Of those, 73% were determined to have financial need; 23% had their need fully met. Average financial aid package (proportion receiving): $13,740 (73%). Average amount of gift aid, such as scholarships or grants (proportion receiving): $6,040 (63%). Average amount of self-help aid, such as work study or loans (proportion receiving): $4,667 (56%). Average need-based loan (excluding PLUS or other private loans): $4,191. Among students who received need-based aid, the average percentage of need met: 72%. Among students who received aid based on merit, the average award (and the proportion receiving): $5,881 (24%). The average athletic scholarship (and the proportion receiving): $0 (0%). Average amount of debt of borrowers graduating in 2005: $27,139. Proportion who borrowed: 63%.

CAMPUS LIFE AND EXTRACURRICULAR ACTIVITIES

Campus housing available (% using): coed dorms (31%), women's dorms (29%), men's dorms (23%), apartments for married students (2%), apartment for single students (15%). Students who live in college-owned, operated, or affiliated housing: 35%. **Student employment:** During the 2005-2006 academic year, 19% of undergraduates worked on campus. Average per-year earnings: $1,998. **Clubs and organizations:** Number of student organizations: 65. Activities include: choral groups, concert band, dance, drama/theater, jazz band, literary magazine, music ensembles, musi-

cal theater, pep band, student government, student newspaper, symphony orchestra, yearbook. Number of fraternities: 4; sororities: 3. Proportion of men in fraternities: 1%; Average proportion of students who stay on campus on weekends: 40%. **Sports program (2005-2006):** Member of NCAA III. **Men's intercollegiate varsity sports:** baseball, basketball, football, golf, soccer, tennis. **Women's intercollegiate varsity sports:** basketball, cross-country, golf, soccer, softball, tennis, track and field (indoor), track and field (outdoor), volleyball.

SERVICES AND FACILITIES

Basic services: nonremedial tutoring, women's center, placement service, health service, other. **Remedial assistance:** other. **Counseling services:** career, personal, veteran student, academic, psychological, birth control, religious. **For learning-disabled students:** School does not offer a structured program with separate admission and additional fees. Total undergraduates in learning-disabled program or receiving services: 36. Services include: tape recorders, note-taking services, oral tests, extended time for tests, tutors, priority registration, priority seating, other testing accomodations. **Library:** Number of titles: 171,134; number of current serial subscriptions: 603. **Information technology resources:** Students are not required to lease or own a computer. Number of campus computers available to all students: 110. School has a wireless network. Approximate number of users that can be accommodated: 600. Proportion of college-owned housing units wired for high-speed internet access: 100%. **Campus safety:** Security services offered: 24-hour foot-and-vehicle patrols, late-night transport/escort service, lighted pathways/sidewalks, controlled dormitory access (key, security card, etc).

TRANSFER AND INTERNATIONAL STUDENTS

Transfer students: May apply for admission for the following academic terms: Fall, Spring, Summer. Applicants need a minimum number of credits to apply. For fall 2005: Transfer applications received: 162. Transfer applicants offered admission: 110. Transfer applicants enrolled: 69. **International students:** Number of foreign undergraduates: 11 (1% of student body). Number of countries represented: 3. Minimum TOEFL score required: 550 (paper); 213 (computer). Average TOEFL score: 585 (paper).

Texas Southern University

- **Address:** 3100 Cleburne, Houston, TX 77004
- **Website:** http://www.tsu.edu
- **Public**
- **Enrollment:** N/A

KEY STATS

- ✔ **U.S News College Ranking:** fourth tier, National Universities
- ✔ **SAT or ACT Score (25th/75th percentile):** N/A
- ✔ **Tuition:** 2006-2007: $5,428 in state, $13,678 out of state

Selectivity: Selective	Room/board: $12,112
Acceptance rate: N/A	Average debt: N/A
Student/faculty ratio: N/A	Proportion who borrowed: N/A

Texas State University–San Marcos

- **Address:** 601 University Drive, San Marcos, TX 78666
- **Website:** http://www.txstate.edu
- **Public**
- **Enrollment:** 18,472 full-time; 4,514 part-time

KEY STATS

- ✔ **U.S News College Ranking:** 41, Universities–Master's (West)
- ✔ **SAT Score (25th/75th percentile):** 990-1170
- ✔ **Tuition:** 2006-2007: $5,652 in state, $13,902 out of state

Selectivity: Selective	Room/board: $5,505
Acceptance rate: 76%	Average debt: $16,863
Student/faculty ratio: 24/1	Proportion who borrowed: 59%

UNDERGRADUATE STUDENT BODY STATS

2005-2006 enrollment: 18,472 full-time; 4,514 part-time. Men: 45%; women: 55%. **Ethnic makeup:** African American: 5%; American-Indian: 1%; Asian American: 2%; Hispanic: 20%; White: 71%; International: 1%.

ADMISSIONS FACTS AND FIGURES

Phone: (512) 245-2364. **Email:** admissions@txstate.edu. **Website:** http://www.txstate.edu. **Application deadlines for fall 2007:** Regular decision: May 1. Early decision: Not offered. Early action: Not offered. Admission can be deferred. **Application fee:** $40. Common application is not accepted. **To apply online, go to:** http://www.admission.txstate.edu/index.htm. **Admissions requirements/recommendations:** High school units required (recommended): English: 4 (4); Mathematics: 3 (3); Science: 3 (3); Foreign language: 2 (2); Social studies: 4 (4); History: (2); Academic electives: 4 (4); Total units: 24 (24). Tests: The college uses SAT or ACT scores in admissions decisions. Either SAT or ACT required. For admission to the fall 2007 entering class, the school will accept: ACT with writing. Campus visit: Required. Admissions interview: Neither required nor recommended. Off-campus interview: Not available. **Factors that count in admissions decisions:** *Academic:* Secondary school record: Considered. Class rank: Very important. Letters of recommendation: Not considered. Standardized test scores: Very important. Essay: Considered. *Nonacademic:* Interview: Not considered. Extracurricular activities: Not considered. Talent/ability: Considered. Character/personal qualities: Not considered. Alumni/ae relationship: Not considered. Geographical residence: Not considered. State residency: Not considered. Religious affiliation/commitment: Not considered. Minority status: Not considered. Volunteer work: Not considered. Work experience: Not considered. **Other schools with the greatest overlap in applicants:** Texas A&M University–College Station; Texas Tech University; University of North Texas; University of Texas–Austin; University of Texas–San Antonio. **Admissions statistics for the fall 2005 entering class:** Total applicants: 9,284. Total accepted: 7,095. Freshmen enrolled: 3,073; 2% were from out of state. Overall acceptance rate: 76%. **Credentials of fall 2005 freshmen:** 13% ranked in the top 10 percent of their high school class; 50% were in the top 25 percent, and 94% were in the top half. (Proportion submitting class standing: 99%.) **First-year students who submitted SAT scores:** 79%. Scores (25/75 percentile): Verbal: 490-580, Math: 500-590, Combined: 990-1170. **First-year students submitting ACT scores:** 20%. Scores (25/75 percentile): English: 20-25, Math: 19-24, Composite: 21-25.

ACADEMICS

Year founded: 1899. **Academic calendar:** Semester. **Degrees offered:** bachelor's, post-bachelor's certificate, master's, doctorate. **Most popular majors:** 10% multi/interdisciplinary studies, 6% business administration and management, 5% marketing/marketing management, 4% finance, 4% psychology. **Major fields of study:** agriculture, agriculture operations, and related sciences; architecture and related services; area, ethnic, cultural, and gender studies; biological and biomedical sciences; business, management, marketing, and related support services; communication, journalism, and related programs; communications technologies/technicians and support services; computer and information sciences and support services; engineering; engineering technologies/technicians; English language and literature/letters; family and consumer sciences/human sciences; foreign languages, literatures, and linguistics; health professions and related clinical sciences; history; mathematics and statistics; multi/interdisciplinary studies; natural resources and conservation; parks, recreation, leisure, and fitness studies; philosophy and religious studies; physical sciences; psychology; public administration and social service professions; security and protective services; social sciences; visual and performing arts. **Areas of required coursework:** humanities, mathematics, English (including composition), philosophy, sciences (biological or physical), history, social science. **Pre-professional programs:** pre-law, pre-dentistry, pre-medicine, pre-veterinary science, pre-pharmacy, other. **Special academic programs (% participation):** cross-registration, distance learning (16.8%), double major (3.2%), dual enrollment (.0004%), English as a Second Language (ESL), exchange student program (domestic), honors program (1%), independent study, internships, study abroad (3.2%), teacher certificate program (19.2%), weekend college. **Teacher certification offered in:** early childhood, special education, elementary, vo-tech, secondary, bilingual/bicultural. **Cooperative education programs:** agriculture, home economics, technologies, vocational arts. **Reserve Officers Training Corps (ROTC):** Army ROTC: Offered on campus; Air Force ROTC: Offered on campus. **Faculty and instruction (2005-2006):** Total instructional faculty: 775 full-time, 522 part-time (54% men; 46% women; 15% minorities). Full-time faculty with Ph.D. or other terminal degree: 76%. Student/faculty ratio: 24/1. Classes of fewer than 20 students: 15%; of 20 to 49 students: 65%; of 50 or more students: 20%. **Freshmen**

returning for sophomore year: 76%. **Graduation rates:** Four-year: 21%; five-year: 45%; six-year: 48%. **Graduate study:** 19% of students pursue further study within one year. Fields in which graduates pursue further study: education, 6%.

COSTS AND FINANCIAL AID

Financial aid office: (512) 245-2315. **Expenses (2006-2007):** Tuition and fees 2006-2007: $5,652 in state, $13,902 out of state; room/board: $5,505. Estimated books and supplies: $950; transportation: $870; personal expenses: $2,430. **Financial aid:** Priority filing date for institution's financial aid form: April 1. In 2005-2006, 68% of undergraduates applied for financial aid. Of those, 53% were determined to have financial need; 15% had their need fully met. Average financial aid package (proportion receiving): $7,545 (51%). Average amount of gift aid, such as scholarships or grants (proportion receiving): $4,059 (37%). Average amount of self-help aid, such as work study or loans (proportion receiving): $4,066 (45%). Average need-based loan (excluding PLUS or other private loans): $3,362. Among students who received need-based aid, the average percentage of need met: 67%. Among students who received aid based on merit, the average award (and the proportion receiving): $2,165 (2%). The average athletic scholarship (and the proportion receiving): $6,848 (1%). Average amount of debt of borrowers graduating in 2005: $16,863. Proportion who borrowed: 59%.

CAMPUS LIFE AND EXTRACURRICULAR ACTIVITIES

Campus housing available (% using): coed dorms (75%), women's dorms (14%), men's dorms (1%), sorority housing, fraternity housing, apartments for married students (1%), apartment for single students (9%), special housing for disabled students. Students who live in college-owned, operated, or affiliated housing: 23%. **Student employment:** During the 2005-2006 academic year, 4% of undergraduates worked on campus. Average per-year earnings: $1,981. **Clubs and organizations:** Number of student organizations: 312. Activities include: choral groups, concert band, dance, drama/theater, jazz band, literary magazine, marching band, music ensembles, musical theater, opera, pep band, radio station, student government, student newspaper, student film society, symphony orchestra, yearbook. Number of fraternities: 13; sororities: 7. Proportion of men in fraternities: 5%; of women in sororities: 5%. **Sports program (2005-2006):** Member of NCAA I. *Men's intercollegiate varsity sports:* baseball, basketball, cheerleading, cross-country, football, golf, track and field (indoor), track and field (outdoor). *Women's intercollegiate varsity sports:* basketball, cheerleading, cross-country, golf, soccer, softball, tennis, track and field (indoor), track and field (outdoor), volleyball.

SERVICES AND FACILITIES

Basic services: nonremedial tutoring, women's center, placement service, health service, health insurance. **Remedial assistance:** reading, math, writing, study skills. **Counseling services:** minority student, career, military, personal, veteran student, academic, psychological, birth control. **For learning-disabled students:** School does not offer a structured program with separate admission and additional fees. Total undergraduates in learning-disabled program or receiving services: 657. Services include: remedial math, remedial English, reading machines, remedial reading, tape recorders, diagnostic testing service, untimed tests, note-taking services, oral tests, learning center, readers, extended time for tests, tutors. **Library:** Number of titles: 1,358,459; number of current serial subscriptions: 8,330. **Information technology resources:** Students are not required to lease or own a computer. Number of campus computers available to all students: 1,483. School has a wireless network. Proportion of college-owned housing units wired for high-speed internet access: 100%. **Campus safety:** Security services offered: 24-hour foot-and-vehicle patrols, late-night transport/escort service, 24-hour emergency telephones, lighted pathways/sidewalks, student patrols, controlled dormitory access (key, security card, etc).

TRANSFER AND INTERNATIONAL STUDENTS

Transfer students: May apply for admission for the following academic terms: Fall, Spring, Summer. Applicants need a minimum number of credits to apply. For fall 2005: Transfer applications received: 4,716. Transfer applicants offered admission: 4,256. Transfer applicants enrolled: 2,978. **International students:** Number of foreign undergraduates: 242 (1% of student body). Number of countries represented: 47. Minimum TOEFL score required: 550 (paper); 213 (computer).

Texas Tech University

- **Address:** Box 42013, Lubbock, TX 79409
- **Website:** http://www.ttu.edu
- **Public**
- **Enrollment:** 20,821 full-time; 2,181 part-time

KEY STATS

✔ **U.S News College Ranking:** third tier, National Universities
✔ **SAT Score (25th/75th percentile):** 1040-1220
✔ **Tuition:** 2006-2007: $6,339 in state, $14,589 out of state
- Selectivity: Selective
- Room/board: $7,288
- Acceptance rate: 71%
- Average debt: $19,195
- Student/faculty ratio: 19/1
- Proportion who borrowed: 57%

UNDERGRADUATE STUDENT BODY STATS

2005-2006 enrollment: 20,821 full-time; 2,181 part-time. Men: 55%; women: 45%. **Ethnic makeup:** African American: 3%; American-Indian: 1%; Asian American: 2%; Hispanic: 11%; White: 81%; International: 1%.

ADMISSIONS FACTS AND FIGURES

Phone: (806) 742-1480. **Email:** admissions@ttu.edu. **Website:** http://www.ttu.edu. **Application deadlines for fall 2007:** Regular decision: May 1. Early decision: Not offered. Early action: Not offered. Admission cannot be deferred. **Application fee:** $50. Common application is not accepted. **To apply online, go to:** http://www.applytexas.org. **Admissions requirements/recommendations:** High school units required (recommended): English: 4; Mathematics: 3; Science: 2; Foreign language: 2; Social studies: 0; History: 0; Academic electives: 0; Total units: 11. Tests: The college uses SAT or ACT scores in admissions decisions. Either SAT or ACT required. For admission to the fall 2007 entering class, the school will accept: ACT with writing. Campus visit: Recommended. Admissions interview: Neither required nor recommended. Off-campus interview: Not available. **Factors that count in admissions decisions:** *Academic:* Secondary school record: Very important. Class rank: Very important. Letters of recommendation: Considered. Standardized test scores: Very important. Essay: Important. *Nonacademic:* Interview: Not considered. Extracurricular activities: Important. Talent/ability: Important. Character/personal qualities: Important. Alumni/ae relationship: Important. Geographical residence: Not considered. State residency: Not considered. Religious affiliation/commitment: Not considered. Minority status: Considered. Volunteer work: Important. Work experience: Important. **Other schools with the greatest overlap in applicants:** Baylor University; Texas A&M University–College Station; Texas Christian University; Texas State University–San Marcos; University of Texas–Austin. **Admissions statistics for the fall 2005 entering class:** Total applicants: 12,583. Total accepted: 8,927. Freshmen enrolled: 3,779; 5% were from out of state. Overall acceptance rate: 71%. **Credentials of fall 2005 freshmen:** 22% ranked in the top 10 percent of their high school class; 55% were in the top 25 percent, and 88% were in the top half. (Proportion submitting class standing: 99%.) **First-year students who submitted SAT scores:** 68%. Scores (25/75 percentile): Verbal: 510-600, Math: 530-620, Combined: 1040-1220. **First-year students submitting ACT scores:** 32%. Scores (25/75 percentile): English: 20-26, Math: 20-26, Composite: 22-26.

ACADEMICS

Year founded: 1923. **Academic calendar:** Semester. **Degrees offered:** bachelor's, master's, post-master's certificate, first professional, doctorate. **Most popular majors:** 28% business, management, marketing, and related support services, 14% family and consumer sciences/human sciences, 7% engineering, 6% communication, journalism, and related programs, 5% English language and literature/letters. **Major fields of study:** agriculture, agriculture operations, and related sciences; architecture and related services; area, ethnic, cultural, and gender studies; biological and biomedical sciences; business, management, marketing, and related support services; communication, journalism, and related programs; computer and information sciences and support services; engineering; engineering technologies/technicians; English language and literature/letters; family and consumer sciences/human sciences; foreign languages, literatures, and linguistics; health professions and related clinical sciences; history; liberal arts and sciences studies, and humanities; mathematics and statistics; multi/interdisciplinary studies; natural resources and conservation; parks, recreation, leisure, and fitness studies; philosophy and religious studies;

physical sciences; psychology; public administration and social service professions; social sciences; visual and performing arts. **Areas of required coursework:** arts/fine arts, humanities, mathematics, English (including composition), philosophy, foreign languages, sciences (biological or physical), history, social science, other. **Pre-professional programs:** pre-law, pre-dentistry, pre-medicine, pre-veterinary science, pre-optometry, pre-pharmacy, other. **Special academic programs (% participation):** accelerated program, cooperative (work-study plan) program, cross-registration, distance learning, double major (5.6%), dual enrollment, English as a Second Language (ESL), exchange student program (domestic), external degree program, honors program (13.37%), independent study (27.13%), internships, liberal arts/career combination, student-designed major (.88%), study abroad, teacher certificate program. **Teacher certification offered in:** early childhood, special education, elementary, middle/junior high, secondary, bilingual/bicultural. **Cooperative education programs:** agriculture, art, business, computer science, education, engineering, health professions, home economics, humanities, natural science, social/behavioral science, technologies, other. **Reserve Officers Training Corps (ROTC):** Army ROTC: Offered on campus; Air Force ROTC: Offered on campus. **Faculty and instruction (2005-2006):** Total instructional faculty: 1,046 full-time, 77 part-time (65% men; 35% women; 14% minorities). Full-time faculty with Ph.D. or other terminal degree: 88%. Student/faculty ratio: 19/1. Classes of fewer than 20 students: 23%; of 20 to 49 students: 57%; of 50 or more students: 21%. **Advanced Placement and International Baccalaureate credit:** AP tests may be used for: Credit only. Scores accepted: 3, 4, 5. International Baccalaureate exams may be used for: Credit only. **Freshmen returning for sophomore year:** 83%. **Graduation rates:** Four-year: 23%; five-year: 48%; six-year: 55%. **Graduate study:** 26% of students pursue further study immediately upon graduation; 30% within one year. Fields in which graduates pursue further study: Master of Business Administration (MBA), 16%; law, 11%; medicine, 7%; dentistry, 1%; engineering, 5%; theology (or the seminary), 1%; education, 13%; arts and sciences, 30%; veterinary medicine, 1%.

COSTS AND FINANCIAL AID

Financial aid office: (806) 742-3681. **Expenses (2006-2007):** Tuition and fees 2006-2007: $6,339 in state, $14,589 out of state; room/board: $7,288. Estimated books and supplies: $900; transportation: $1,400; personal expenses: $1,850. **Financial aid:** Priority filing date for institution's financial aid form: April 15. In 2005-2006, 64% of undergraduates applied for financial aid. Of those, 40% were determined to have financial need; 4% had their need fully met. Average financial aid package (proportion receiving): $7,220 (39%). Average amount of gift aid, such as scholarships or grants (proportion receiving): $4,499 (25%). Average amount of self-help aid, such as work study or loans (proportion receiving): $3,947 (35%). Average need-based loan (excluding PLUS or other private loans): $3,906. Among students who received need-based aid, the average percentage of need met: 66%. Among students who received aid based on merit, the average award (and the proportion receiving): $1,847 (3%). The average athletic scholarship (and the proportion receiving): $9,745 (2%). Average amount of debt of borrowers graduating in 2005: $19,195. Proportion who borrowed: 57%.

CAMPUS LIFE AND EXTRACURRICULAR ACTIVITIES

Campus housing available (% using): coed dorms (28%), women's dorms (33%), men's dorms (33%), apartment for single students (6%), special housing for disabled students. Students who live in college-owned, operated, or affiliated housing: 24%. **Student employment:** During the 2005-2006 academic year, 12% of undergraduates worked on campus. Average per-year earnings: $4,466. **Clubs and organizations:** Number of student organizations: 411. Activities include: choral groups, concert band, dance, drama/theater, jazz band, literary magazine, marching band, music ensembles, musical theater, opera, pep band, radio station, student government, student newspaper, student film society, symphony orchestra, television station, yearbook. Number of fraternities: 28; sororities: 21. Proportion of men in fraternities: 11%; of women in sororities: 17%. **Sports program (2005-2006):** Member of NCAA I. *Men's intercollegiate varsity sports:* baseball, basketball, cross-country, football, golf, tennis, track and field (indoor), track and field (outdoor). *Women's intercollegiate varsity sports:* basketball, cross-country, golf, soccer, softball, tennis, track and field (indoor), track and field (outdoor), volleyball.

SERVICES AND FACILITIES

Basic services: nonremedial tutoring, placement service, health service, health insurance. **Remedial assistance:** reading, math, writing, study skills, other. **Counseling services:** minority student, career, personal, academic, psychological, other. **For learning-disabled students:** School does not offer a structured program with separate admission and additional fees. Total undergraduates in learning-disabled program or receiving services: 735. Services include: remedial math, remedial English, remedial reading, tape recorders, note-taking services, learning center, readers, extended time for tests, priority registration, priority seating, texts on tape. **Library:** Number of titles: 2,478,489; number of current serial subscriptions: 26,690. **Information technology resources:** Students are not required to lease or own a computer. Number of campus computers available to all students: 2,000. School has a wireless network. Approximate number of users that can be accommodated: 19,600. Proportion of college-owned housing units wired for high-speed internet access: 100%. **Campus safety:** Security services offered: 24-hour foot-and-vehicle patrols, late-night transport/escort service, 24-hour emergency telephones, lighted pathways/sidewalks, controlled dormitory access (key, security card, etc).

TRANSFER AND INTERNATIONAL STUDENTS

Transfer students: May apply for admission for the following academic terms: Fall, Spring, Summer. Applicants need a minimum number of credits to apply. For fall 2005: Transfer applications received: 3,599. Transfer applicants offered admission: 2,600. Transfer applicants enrolled: 1,968. **International students:** Number of foreign undergraduates: 197 (1% of student body). Number of countries represented: 88. Minimum TOEFL score required: 550 (paper); 213 (computer). Average TOEFL score: 587 (paper).

Texas Wesleyan University

- **Address:** 1201 Wesleyan, Fort Worth, TX 76105-1536
- **Website:** http://www.txwesleyan.edu
- **Private; Religious affiliation:** Methodist
- **Enrollment:** 985 full-time; 392 part-time

KEY STATS

✔ **U.S News College Ranking:** third tier, Universities–Master's (West)
✔ **SAT or ACT Score (25th/75th percentile):** N/A
✔ **Tuition:** 2006-2007: $14,875

Selectivity: Less selective	**Room/board:** $5,470
Acceptance rate: 46%	**Average debt:** N/A
Student/faculty ratio: 14/1	**Proportion who borrowed:** N/A

UNDERGRADUATE STUDENT BODY STATS

2005-2006 enrollment: 985 full-time; 392 part-time. Men: 34%; women: 66%. **Ethnic makeup:** African American: 18%; American-Indian: 1%; Asian American: 2%; Hispanic: 21%; White: 59%. **Religious preference:** Roman Catholic: 6%; Protestant: 19%; Methodist: 5%; Other: 70%.

ADMISSIONS FACTS AND FIGURES

Phone: (817) 531-4458. **Email:** freshman@txwesleyan.edu. **Website:** http://www.txwesleyan.edu. **Application deadlines for fall 2007:** Regular decision: Rolling. Early decision: Not offered. Early action: Not offered. Admission can be deferred. **Application fee:** $25. Common application is accepted. **Admissions requirements/recommendations:** High school units required (recommended): English: 4 (4); Mathematics: 4 (4); Science: 2 (2); Foreign language: (0); Social studies: 3 (3); History: 1 (1); Academic electives: 7 (7); Total units: 21 (21). Tests: The college does not use SAT or ACT scores in admissions decisions. Neither SAT nor ACT required. Campus visit: Neither required nor recommended. Admissions interview: Recommended. Off-campus interview: May be arranged. **Factors that count in admissions decisions:** *Academic:* Secondary school record: Considered. Class rank: Considered. Letters of recommendation: Considered. Standardized test scores: Important. Essay: Considered. *Nonacademic:* Interview: Considered. Extracurricular activities: Not considered. Talent/ability: Not considered. Character/personal qualities: Considered. Alumni/ae relationship: Not considered. Geographical residence: Not considered. State residency: Not considered. Religious affiliation/commitment: Not considered. Minority status: Not considered. Volunteer work: Not considered. Work experience: Not considered. **Other schools with the greatest overlap in applicants:** Dallas Baptist University; University of Dallas; University of St. Mary; University of Texas–Arlington; University of Texas–Dallas. **Admissions statistics for the fall 2005 entering class:** Total applicants: 590. Total accepted: 273. Freshmen enrolled: 196; 1% were from out of state. Overall acceptance rate: 46%. **Size of waiting list:** 0 applicants; enrolled from waiting list: 0.

ACADEMICS

Year founded: 1890. **Academic calendar:** Semester. **Degrees offered:** bachelor's, master's, first professional. **Most popular majors:** 22% elementary education and teaching, 8% psychology, 5% business/commerce, 4% multi/interdisciplinary studies. **Major fields of study:** biological and biomedical sciences; business, management, marketing, and related support services; communication, journalism, and related programs; computer and information sciences and support services; education; English language and literature/letters; foreign languages, literatures, and linguistics; health professions and related clinical sciences; legal professions and studies; mathematics and statistics; multi/interdisciplinary studies; parks, recreation, leisure, and fitness studies; philosophy and religious studies; physical sciences; psychology; science technologies/technicians; security and protective services; social sciences; theology and religious vocations; visual and performing arts. **Areas of required coursework:** arts/fine arts, humanities, computer literacy, mathematics, English (including composition), sciences (biological or physical), history, social science. **Pre-professional programs:** pre-law, pre-medicine, pre-theology. **Special academic programs (% participation):** double major (2%), honors program (1%), independent study (10%), internships (10%), teacher certificate program (12%), weekend college (1%). **Teacher certification offered in:** early childhood, elementary, middle/junior high, bilingual/bicultural. **Reserve Officers Training Corps (ROTC):** Army ROTC: Offered at cooperating institution (Texas Christian University); Air Force ROTC: Offered at cooperating institution (Texas Christian University). **Faculty and instruction (2005-2006):** Total instructional faculty: 139 full-time, 198 part-time (51% men; 49% women; 7% minorities). Student/faculty ratio: 14/1. Classes of fewer than 20 students: 61%; of 20 to 49 students: 39%. **Advanced Placement and International Baccalaureate credit:** International Baccalaureate exams may be used for: Placement only. **Freshmen returning for sophomore year:** 64%. **Graduation rates:** Four-year: 14%; five-year: 27%; six-year: 24%.

COSTS AND FINANCIAL AID

Financial aid office: (817) 531-4420. **Expenses (2006-2007):** Tuition and fees 2006-2007: $14,875; room/board: $5,470. **Financial aid:** Priority filing date for institution's financial aid form: April 15.

CAMPUS LIFE AND EXTRACURRICULAR ACTIVITIES

Campus housing available: coed dorms, women's dorms, men's dorms, apartments for married students. Students who live in college-owned, operated, or affiliated housing: 10%. **Student employment:** During the 2005-2006 academic year, 1% of undergraduates worked on campus. Average per-year earnings: $2,500. **Clubs and organizations:** Number of student organizations: 27. Activities include: choral groups, drama/theater, jazz band, music ensembles, musical theater, student government, student newspaper. Number of fraternities: 4; sororities: 4. Average proportion of students who stay on campus on weekends: 70%. **Sports program (2005-2006):** Member of NAIA. *Men's intercollegiate varsity sports:* baseball, basketball, golf, soccer. *Women's intercollegiate varsity sports:* basketball, soccer, softball, volleyball.

SERVICES AND FACILITIES

Basic services: nonremedial tutoring, health service. **Remedial assistance:** reading, math, writing, study skills. **Counseling services:** minority student, personal, academic, older student, psychological, religious. **For learning-disabled students:** School does not offer a structured program with separate admission and additional fees. Services include: remedial math, remedial English. **Information technology resources:** Students are not required to lease or own a computer. Number of campus computers available to all students: 150. School has a wireless network. Proportion of college-owned housing units wired for high-speed internet access: 100%. **Campus safety:** Security services offered: 24-hour foot-and-vehicle patrols, late-night transport/escort service, 24-hour emergency telephones, lighted pathways/sidewalks, controlled dormitory access (key, security card, etc).

TRANSFER AND INTERNATIONAL STUDENTS

Transfer students: May apply for admission for the following academic terms: Fall, Winter, Spring, Summer. Applicants need a minimum number of credits to apply. For fall 2005: Transfer applications received: 499. Transfer applicants offered admission: 368. Transfer applicants enrolled: 254. **International students:** Minimum TOEFL score required: 520 (paper); 190 (computer). Average TOEFL score: 535 (paper).

Texas Woman's University

- **Address:** Box 425619, Denton, TX 76204-5587
- **Website:** http://www.twu.edu
- **Public**
- **Enrollment:** 4,554 full-time; 1,712 part-time

KEY STATS

✔ **U.S News College Ranking:** fourth tier, National Universities
✔ **SAT Score (25th/75th percentile):** 850-1080
✔ **Tuition:** 2006-2007: $5,160 in state, $13,440 out of state

Selectivity: Less selective	Room/board: $5,624
Acceptance rate: 64%	Average debt: $18,125
Student/faculty ratio: 15/1	Proportion who borrowed: 54%

UNDERGRADUATE STUDENT BODY STATS

2005-2006 enrollment: 4,554 full-time; 1,712 part-time. Men: 7%; women: 93%. **Ethnic makeup:** African American: 21%; American-Indian: 1%; Asian American: 6%; Hispanic: 14%; White: 55%; International: 3%.

ADMISSIONS FACTS AND FIGURES

Phone: (940) 898-3188. **Email:** admissions@twu.edu. **Website:** http://www.twu.edu. **Application deadlines for fall 2007:** Regular decision: July 15. Early decision: Not offered. Early action: Send application by: February 1; Decision sent by: March 1. Admission can be deferred. **Application fee:** $30. Common application is not accepted. **To apply online, go to:** https://www.applytexas.org/adappc/general/c_start.wb. **Admissions requirements/recommendations:** High school units required (recommended): English: 4; Mathematics: 3; Science: 2; Foreign language: 0; Social studies: 2; Academic electives: 11; Total units: 22. Tests: The college uses SAT or ACT scores in admissions decisions. Neither SAT nor ACT required. For admission to the fall 2007 entering class, the school will accept: ACT with writing, ACT without writing. Campus visit: Recommended. Admissions interview: Neither required nor recommended. Off-campus interview: Not available. **Factors that count in admissions decisions:** *Academic:* Secondary school record: Very important. Class rank: Very important. Letters of recommendation: Not considered. Standardized test scores: Very important. Essay: Not considered. *Nonacademic:* Interview: Not considered. Extracurricular activities: Not considered. Talent/ability: Not considered. Character/personal qualities: Not considered. Alumni/ae relationship: Not considered. Geographical residence: Not considered. State residency: Not considered. Religious affiliation/commitment: Not considered. Minority status: Not considered. Volunteer work: Not considered. Work experience: Not considered. **Admissions statistics for the fall 2005 entering class:** Total applicants: 2,796. Total accepted: 1,794. Freshmen enrolled: 744; 2% were from out of state. Overall acceptance rate: 64%. Non-early acceptance rate: 64%. **Credentials of fall 2005 freshmen:** 17% ranked in the top 10 percent of their high school class; 30% were in the top 25 percent, and 76% were in the top half. (Proportion submitting class standing: 94%.) **Average high school grade point average:** 3.3. **First-year students who submitted SAT scores:** 74%. Scores (25/75 percentile): Verbal: 430-540, Math: 420-540, Combined: 850-1080. **First-year students submitting ACT scores:** 7%. Scores (25/75 percentile): English: N/A, Math: N/A, Composite: 17-24.

ACADEMICS

Year founded: 1901. **Academic calendar:** Semester. **Degrees offered:** bachelor's, post-bachelor's certificate, master's, post-master's certificate, doctorate. **Most popular majors:** 33% nursing/registered nurse training (R.N., A.S.N., B.S.N., M.S.N.), 13% multi/interdisciplinary studies, 5% psychology, 3% biology/biological sciences, 3% social work. **Major fields of study:** biological and biomedical sciences; business, management, marketing, and related support services; communication, journalism, and related programs; computer and information sciences and support services; English language and literature/letters; family and consumer sciences/human sciences; health professions and related clinical sciences; history; legal professions and studies; liberal arts and sciences studies, and humanities; mathematics and statistics; multi/interdisciplinary studies; parks, recreation, leisure, and fitness studies; physical sciences; psychology; public administration and social service professions; security and protective services; social sciences; visual and performing arts. **Areas of required coursework:** arts/fine arts, humanities, computer literacy, mathematics, English (including composition), sciences (biological or physical), history, social science, other. **Pre-professional programs:** pre-law, pre-dentistry, pre-medicine, other. **Special academic pro-**

grams (% participation): accelerated program, cooperative (work-study plan) program (7%), cross-registration (1%), distance learning (0%), double major (1%), dual enrollment (0%), honors program (2%), independent study (27%), internships (52%), liberal arts/career combination, study abroad, teacher certificate program (17%). **Teacher certification offered in:** early childhood, special education, elementary, middle/junior high, secondary, bilingual/bicultural. **Cooperative education programs:** art, business, computer science, health professions, humanities, social/behavioral science. **Reserve Officers Training Corps (ROTC):** Army ROTC: Offered at cooperating institution (University of Texas-Arlington); Air Force ROTC: Offered at cooperating institution (University of North Texas). **Faculty and instruction (2005-2006):** Total instructional faculty: 426 full-time, 266 part-time (24% men; 76% women; 9% minorities). Student/faculty ratio: 15/1. Classes of fewer than 20 students: 46%; of 20 to 49 students: 47%; of 50 or more students: 6%. **Advanced Placement and International Baccalaureate credit:** AP tests may be used for: Credit and/or placement. Scores accepted: 3, 4, 5. International Baccalaureate exams may be used for: Credit and/or placement. **Freshmen returning for sophomore year:** 72%. **Graduation rates:** Four-year: 12%; five-year: 29%; six-year: 36%.

COSTS AND FINANCIAL AID

Financial aid office: (940) 898-3050. **Expenses (2006-2007):** Tuition and fees 2006-2007: $5,160 in state, $13,440 out of state; room/board: $5,624. Estimated books and supplies: $930; transportation: $774; personal expenses: $1,818. **Financial aid:** Priority filing date for institution's financial aid form: March 1. In 2005-2006, 73% of undergraduates applied for financial aid. Of those, 59% were determined to have financial need; 87% had their need fully met. Average financial aid package (proportion receiving): $9,718 (58%). Average amount of gift aid, such as scholarships or grants (proportion receiving): $4,011 (42%). Average amount of self-help aid, such as work study or loans (proportion receiving): $4,028 (53%). Average need-based loan (excluding PLUS or other private loans): $3,775. Among students who received need-based aid, the average percentage of need met: 95%. Among students who received aid based on merit, the average award (and the proportion receiving): $2,705 (5%). The average athletic scholarship (and the proportion receiving): $4,571 (2%). Average amount of debt of borrowers graduating in 2005: $18,125. Proportion who borrowed: 54%.

CAMPUS LIFE AND EXTRACURRICULAR ACTIVITIES

Campus housing available (% using): coed dorms (42%), women's dorms (36%), sorority housing (2%), apartments for married students (3%), apartment for single students (13%), special housing for disabled students (2%), special housing for international students (2%), other housing options. Students who live in college-owned, operated, or affiliated housing: 14%. **Student employment:** During the 2005-2006 academic year, 18% of undergraduates worked on campus. Average per-year earnings: $4,430. **Clubs and organizations:** Number of student organizations: 117. Activities include: choral groups, dance, drama/theater, jazz band, music ensembles, musical theater, opera, student government, student newspaper. Number of fraternities: 0; sororities: 9. of women in sororities: 4%. Average proportion of students who stay on campus on weekends: 50%. **Sports program (2005-2006):** Member of NCAA II. *Women's intercollegiate varsity sports:* basketball, gymnastics, soccer, softball, volleyball.

SERVICES AND FACILITIES

Basic services: nonremedial tutoring, placement service, day care, health service, health insurance. **Remedial assistance:** reading, math, writing, study skills, other. **Counseling services:** minority student, career, personal, veteran student, academic, older student, psychological, birth control. **For learning-disabled students:** School does not offer a structured program with separate admission and additional fees. Total undergraduates in learning-disabled program or receiving services: 48. Services include: remedial math, remedial English, tape recorders, note-taking services, oral tests, learning center, readers, extended time for tests, early syllabus, priority registration, priority seating, texts on tape, typist/scribe, exams on tape or computer. **Library:** Number of titles: 636,281; number of current serial subscriptions: 2,626. **Information technology resources:** Students are not required to lease or own a computer. Number of campus computers available to all students: 1,500. School has a wireless network. Approximate number of users that can be accommodated: 3,000. Proportion of college-owned housing units wired for high-speed internet access: 100%. **Campus safety:** Security services offered: 24-hour foot-and-vehicle patrols, late-night transport/escort service, 24-hour emergency telephones, lighted pathways/sidewalks, controlled dormitory access (key, security card, etc).

TRANSFER AND INTERNATIONAL STUDENTS

Transfer students: May apply for admission for the following academic terms: Fall, Spring, Summer. Applicants need a minimum number of credits to apply. For fall 2005: Transfer applications received: 3,436. Transfer applicants offered admission: 2,527. Transfer applicants enrolled: 967.
International students: Number of foreign undergraduates: 197 (3% of student body). Number of countries represented: 65. Minimum TOEFL score required: 550 (paper); 213 (computer). Average TOEFL score: 565 (paper).

Trinity University

- **Address:** 1 Trinity Place, San Antonio, TX 78212-7200
- **Website:** http://www.trinity.edu
- **Private; Religious affiliation:** Presbyterian
- **Enrollment:** 2,485 full-time; 39 part-time

KEY STATS

- ✔ **U.S News College Ranking:** 1, Universities–Master's (West)
- ✔ **SAT Score (25th/75th percentile):** 1210-1380
- ✔ **Tuition:** 2006-2007: $24,131

Selectivity: More selective	**Room/board:** $8,198
Acceptance rate: 63%	**Average debt:** N/A
Student/faculty ratio: 10/1	**Proportion who borrowed:** N/A

UNDERGRADUATE STUDENT BODY STATS

2005-2006 enrollment: 2,485 full-time; 39 part-time. Men: 46%; women: 54%. **Ethnic makeup:** African American: 3%; Asian American: 6%; Hispanic: 11%; White: 77%; International: 2%. **Religious preference:** Roman Catholic: 20%; Jewish: 1%; Hindu: 1%; Buddhist: 2%; No preference: 28%; Presbyterian: 6%; Baptist, Eastern Orthodox, Episcopal, Muslim, LDS(Mormon)... : 28%; Other: 14%.

ADMISSIONS FACTS AND FIGURES

Phone: (800) 874-6489. **Email:** admissions@trinity.edu. **Website:** http://www.trinity.edu. **Application deadlines for fall 2007:** Regular decision: February 1; decision sent by April 1. Early decision: Send application by: N/A; Decision sent by: N/A. Early action: Send application by: November 1; Decision sent by: December 15. Admission can be deferred. **Application fee:** $50. Common application is accepted. **To apply online, go to:** http://www.trinity.edu/departments/admissions/apply3.htm. **Admissions requirements/recommendations:** High school units required (recommended): English: 4 (4); Mathematics: 4 (4); Science: 3 (3); Foreign language: 2 (3); Social studies: 3 (3); Academic electives: 1; Total units: 19 (20). Tests: The college uses SAT or ACT scores in admissions decisions. Either SAT or ACT required. For admission to the fall 2007 entering class, the school will accept: ACT with writing, ACT without writing. Campus visit: Recommended. Admissions interview: Neither required nor recommended. Off-campus interview: May be arranged. **Factors that count in admissions decisions:** *Academic:* Secondary school record: Very important. Class rank: Very important. Letters of recommendation: Important. Standardized test scores: Very important. Essay: Important. *Nonacademic:* Interview: Considered. Extracurricular activities: Important. Talent/ability: Important. Character/personal qualities: Very important. Alumni/ae relationship: Considered. Geographical residence: Considered. State residency: Considered. Religious affiliation/commitment: Not considered. Minority status: Not considered. Volunteer work: Considered. Work experience: Considered. **Admissions statistics for the fall 2005 entering class:** Total applicants: 3,864. Total accepted: 2,442. Freshmen enrolled: 651; 27% were from out of state. Accepted through early-decision or early-action plans: 68%. Overall acceptance rate: 63%. Early-decision acceptance rate: 56%. Non-early acceptance rate: 51%. **Size of waiting list:** 210 applicants; enrolled from waiting list: 0. **Credentials of fall 2005 freshmen:** 47% ranked in the top 10 percent of their high school class; 81% were in the top 25 percent, and 98% were in the top half. (Proportion submitting class standing: 70%.) **Average high school grade point average:** 3.5. **First-year students who submitted SAT scores:** 74%. Scores (25/75 percentile): Verbal: 600-690, Math: 610-690, Combined: 1210-1380. **First-year students submitting ACT scores:** 26%. Scores (25/75 percentile): English: 26-32, Math: 25-29, Composite: 27-30.

ACADEMICS

Year founded: 1869. **Academic calendar:** Semester. **Degrees offered:** bachelor's, master's. **Most popular majors:** 21% business, management, market-

ing, and related support services, 16% social sciences, 11% foreign languages, literatures, and linguistics, 6% English language and literature/letters, 5% engineering. **Major fields of study:** area, ethnic, cultural, and gender studies; biological and biomedical sciences; business, management, marketing, and related support services; communication, journalism, and related programs; communications technologies/technicians and support services; computer and information sciences and support services; education; engineering; engineering technologies/technicians; English language and literature/letters; foreign languages, literatures, and linguistics; history; philosophy and religious studies; physical sciences; psychology; social sciences; theology and religious vocations; visual and performing arts. **Areas of required coursework:** arts/fine arts, humanities, computer literacy, English (including composition), foreign languages, sciences (biological or physical), social science, other. **Special academic programs:** accelerated program, double major, honors program, independent study, internships, liberal arts/career combination, study abroad, teacher certificate program. **Reserve Officers Training Corps (ROTC):** Air Force ROTC: Offered at cooperating institution (University of Texas at San Antonio). **Faculty and instruction (2005-2006):** Total instructional faculty: 222 full-time, 67 part-time (64% men; 36% women; 11% minorities). Full-time faculty with Ph.D. or other terminal degree: 96%. Student/faculty ratio: 10/1. Classes of fewer than 20 students: 51%; of 20 to 49 students: 47%; of 50 or more students: 1%. **Freshmen returning for sophomore year:** 89%. **Graduation rates:** Four-year: 63%; five-year: 73%; six-year: 76%. **Graduate study:** 52% of students pursue further study immediately upon graduation. Fields in which graduates pursue further study: law, 78%; medicine, 73%.

COSTS AND FINANCIAL AID

Financial aid office: (210) 999-8315. **Expenses (2006-2007):** Tuition and fees 2006-2007: $24,131; room/board: $8,198. Estimated books and supplies: $900; transportation: $600; personal expenses: $900. **Financial aid:** Priority filing date for institution's financial aid form: February 1; deadline: April 1. In 2005-2006, 53% of undergraduates applied for financial aid. Of those, 40% were determined to have financial need; 44% had their need fully met. Average financial aid package (proportion receiving): $17,845 (40%). Average amount of gift aid, such as scholarships or grants (proportion receiving): $11,415 (38%). Average amount of self-help aid, such as work study or loans (proportion receiving): $6,988 (34%). Average need-based loan (excluding PLUS or other private loans): $6,105. Among students who received need-based aid, the average percentage of need met: 89%. Among students who received aid based on merit, the average award (and the proportion receiving): $7,869 (31%). The average athletic scholarship (and the proportion receiving): $0 (0%).

CAMPUS LIFE AND EXTRACURRICULAR ACTIVITIES

Campus housing available: coed dorms, special housing for disabled students, special housing for international students, other housing options. Students who live in college-owned, operated, or affiliated housing: 73%. **Student employment:** During the 2005-2006 academic year, 25% of undergraduates worked on campus. Average per-year earnings: $1,650. Activities include: choral groups, concert band, dance, drama/theater, jazz band, literary magazine, music ensembles, musical theater, opera, pep band, radio station, student government, student newspaper, student film society, symphony orchestra, television station, yearbook. Number of fraternities: 9; sororities: 6. Proportion of men in fraternities: 24%; of women in sororities: 29%. Average proportion of students who stay on campus on weekends: 70%. **Sports program (2005-2006):** Member of NCAA III. *Men's intercollegiate varsity sports:* baseball, basketball, cross-country, football, golf, soccer, swimming and diving, tennis, track and field (outdoor). *Women's intercollegiate varsity sports:* basketball, cross-country, golf, soccer, softball, swimming and diving, tennis, track and field (indoor), track and field (outdoor), volleyball.

SERVICES AND FACILITIES

Library: Number of titles: 927,349; number of current serial subscriptions: 2,681. **Information technology resources:** Students are not required to lease or own a computer. Number of campus computers available to all students: 450. School has a wireless network. Approximate number of users that can be accommodated: 2,500. Proportion of college-owned housing units wired for high-speed internet access: 100%. **Campus safety:** Security services offered: 24-hour foot-and-vehicle patrols, late-night transport/escort service, 24-hour emergency telephones, lighted pathways/sidewalks, controlled dormitory access (key, security card, etc).

TRANSFER AND INTERNATIONAL STUDENTS

Transfer students: May apply for admission for the following academic terms: Fall, Winter, Summer. Applicants do not need a minimum number of credits to apply. For fall 2005: Transfer applications received: 49. Transfer applicants offered admission: 32. Transfer applicants enrolled: 32.
International students: Number of foreign undergraduates: 59 (2% of student body). Number of countries represented: 26. Minimum TOEFL score required: 600 (paper); 250 (computer). Average TOEFL score: 605 (paper).

University of Dallas

- **Address:** 1845 E. Northgate Drive, Irving, TX 75062-4736
- **Website:** http://www.udallas.edu
- **Private; Religious affiliation:** Roman Catholic
- **Enrollment:** 1,070 full-time; 96 part-time

KEY STATS

✔ **U.S News College Ranking:** third tier, Liberal Arts Colleges
✔ **SAT Score (25th/75th percentile):** 1120-1350
✔ **Tuition:** 2006-2007: $21,805
  Selectivity: More selective   **Room/board:** $7,332
  Acceptance rate: 81%   **Average debt:** $22,850
  Student/faculty ratio: 12/1   **Proportion who borrowed:** 67%

UNDERGRADUATE STUDENT BODY STATS

2005-2006 enrollment: 1,070 full-time; 96 part-time. Men: 44%; women: 56%. **Ethnic makeup:** African American: 2%; Asian American: 5%; Hispanic: 15%; White: 76%; International: 1%. **Religious preference:** Protestant: 7%; Unknown: 16%; Roman Catholic: 73%; Other: 4%.

ADMISSIONS FACTS AND FIGURES

Phone: (972) 721-5266. **Email:** ugadmis@udallas.edu. **Website:** http://www.udallas.edu. **Application deadlines for fall 2007:** Regular decision: August 1. Early decision: Not offered. Early action: Send application by: December 1; Decision sent by: January 15. Admission can be deferred.
Application fee: $40. Common application is accepted. **To apply online, go to:** http://www.udallas.edu/admiss/index.cfm. **Admissions requirements/recommendations:** High school units required (recommended): English: 4 (4); Mathematics: 3 (4); Science: 3 (3); Foreign language: 2 (3); Social studies: 3 (4); History: 3 (4); Academic electives: 4 (4); Total units: 24 (28). Tests: The college uses SAT or ACT scores in admissions decisions. Either SAT or ACT required. For admission to the fall 2007 entering class, the school will accept: ACT with writing. Campus visit: Recommended. Admissions interview: Recommended. Off-campus interview: May be arranged. **Factors that count in admissions decisions:** *Academic:* Secondary school record: Very important. Class rank: Considered. Letters of recommendation: Very important. Standardized test scores: Very important. Essay: Very important. *Nonacademic:* Interview: Considered. Extracurricular activities: Considered. Talent/ability: Important. Character/personal qualities: Very important. Alumni/ae relationship: Considered. Geographical residence: Not considered. State residency: Not considered. Religious affiliation/commitment: Not considered. Minority status: Not considered. Volunteer work: Considered. Work experience: Considered. **Other schools with the greatest overlap in applicants:** Austin College; Rice University; Southern Methodist University; Trinity University; University of Notre Dame. **Admissions statistics for the fall 2005 entering class:** Total applicants: 817. Total accepted: 662. Freshmen enrolled: 256; 49% were from out of state. Overall acceptance rate: 81%. Non-early acceptance rate: 81%. **Size of waiting list:** 0 applicants; enrolled from waiting list: 0. **Credentials of fall 2005 freshmen:** 34% ranked in the top 10 percent of their high school class; 66% were in the top 25 percent, and 91% were in the top half. (Proportion submitting class standing: 60%.) **Average high school grade point average:** 3.6. **First-year students who submitted SAT scores:** 86%. Scores (25/75 percentile): Verbal: 580-700, Math: 540-650, Combined: 1120-1350. **First-year students submitting ACT scores:** 49%. Scores (25/75 percentile): English: 24-31, Math: 22-28, Composite: 23-29.

ACADEMICS

Year founded: 1956. **Academic calendar:** Semester. **Degrees offered:** bachelor's, post-bachelor's certificate, master's, post-master's certificate, doctorate.
Most popular majors: 14% English language and literature, 11% political science and government, 9% biology/biological sciences, 8% drama and dra-

matics/theater arts, 8% history. **Major fields of study:** architecture and related services; biological and biomedical sciences; business, management, marketing, and related support services; education; engineering; English language and literature/letters; foreign languages, literatures, and linguistics; health professions and related clinical sciences; history; legal professions and studies; mathematics and statistics; multi/interdisciplinary studies; philosophy and religious studies; physical sciences; psychology; social sciences; theology and religious vocations; visual and performing arts. **Areas of required coursework:** arts/fine arts, humanities, mathematics, English (including composition), philosophy, foreign languages, sciences (biological or physical), history, social science, other. **Pre-professional programs:** pre-law, pre-dentistry, pre-medicine, pre-theology, other. **Special academic programs (% participation):** accelerated program, double major, dual enrollment, independent study, internships, liberal arts/career combination, student-designed major, study abroad (80%), teacher certificate program.
Teacher certification offered in: early childhood, elementary, middle/junior high, secondary. **Reserve Officers Training Corps (ROTC):** Army ROTC: Offered at cooperating institution (University of Texas at Arlington); Air Force ROTC: Offered at cooperating institution (University of North Texas).
Faculty and instruction (2005-2006): Total instructional faculty: 116 full-time, 105 part-time (76% men; 24% women; 9% minorities). Full-time faculty with Ph.D. or other terminal degree: 91%. Student/faculty ratio: 12/1. Classes of fewer than 20 students: 49%; of 20 to 49 students: 49%; of 50 or more students: 1%. **Advanced Placement and International Baccalaureate credit:** AP tests may be used for: Credit and/or placement. Scores accepted: 3, 4. International Baccalaureate exams may be used for: Credit and/or placement. **Freshmen returning for sophomore year:** 81%. **Graduation rates:** Four-year: 61%; five-year: 64%; six-year: 66%. **Graduate study:** 50% of students pursue further study immediately upon graduation. Fields in which graduates pursue further study: Master of Business Administration (MBA), 18%; law, 9%; medicine, 13%; theology (or the seminary), 6%; education, 35%; arts and sciences, 19%.

COSTS AND FINANCIAL AID

Financial aid office: (972) 721-5266. **Expenses (2006-2007):** Tuition and fees 2006-2007: $21,805; room/board: $7,332. Estimated books and supplies: $1,200; transportation: $1,800; personal expenses: $1,200. **Financial aid:** Priority filing date for institution's financial aid form: March 1. In 2005-2006, 73% of undergraduates applied for financial aid. Of those, 61% were determined to have financial need; 30% had their need fully met. Average financial aid package (proportion receiving): $17,561 (61%). Average amount of gift aid, such as scholarships or grants (proportion receiving): $12,117 (60%). Average amount of self-help aid, such as work study or loans (proportion receiving): $4,678 (49%). Average need-based loan (excluding PLUS or other private loans): $5,041. Among students who received need-based aid, the average percentage of need met: 86%. Among students who received aid based on merit, the average award (and the proportion receiving): $9,023 (33%). Average amount of debt of borrowers graduating in 2005: $22,850. Proportion who borrowed: 67%.

CAMPUS LIFE AND EXTRACURRICULAR ACTIVITIES

Campus housing available (% using): coed dorms (8%), women's dorms (42%), men's dorms (30%), apartment for single students (20%). Students who live in college-owned, operated, or affiliated housing: 61%. **Student employment:** During the 2005-2006 academic year, 10% of undergraduates worked on campus. Average per-year earnings: $1,500. **Clubs and organizations:** Number of student organizations: 34. Activities include: choral groups, dance, drama/theater, literary magazine, music ensembles, musical theater, student government, student newspaper, student film society, yearbook. Number of fraternities: 0; sororities: 0. Average proportion of students who stay on campus on weekends: 80%. **Sports program (2005-2006):** Member of NCAA III. **Men's intercollegiate varsity sports:** baseball, basketball, cross-country, golf, soccer, track and field (outdoor). **Women's intercollegiate varsity sports:** basketball, cross-country, lacrosse, soccer, softball, track and field (outdoor), volleyball.

SERVICES AND FACILITIES

Basic services: health service, health insurance. **Counseling services:** career, personal, academic, religious. **For learning-disabled students:** School does not offer a structured program with separate admission and additional fees. Services include: reading machines. **Library:** Number of titles: 223,350; number of current serial subscriptions: 583. **Information technology resources:** Students are not required to lease or own a computer. Number of campus computers available to all students: 125. School has a wireless network. Proportion of college-owned housing units wired for high-speed internet access: 100%. **Campus safety:** Security services offered: 24-hour foot-and-vehicle patrols, late-night transport/escort service, 24-hour emergency telephones, lighted pathways/sidewalks, controlled dormitory access (key, security card, etc).

TRANSFER AND INTERNATIONAL STUDENTS

Transfer students: May apply for admission for the following academic terms: Fall, Spring. Applicants need a minimum number of credits to apply. For fall 2005: Transfer applications received: 81. Transfer applicants offered admission: 63. Transfer applicants enrolled: 39. **International students:** Number of foreign undergraduates: 14 (1% of student body). Number of countries represented: 13. Minimum TOEFL score required: 550 (paper); 213 (computer). Average TOEFL score: 592 (paper).

University of Houston

- **Address:** 212 E. Cullen Building, Houston, TX 77204
- **Website:** http://www.uh.edu
- **Public**
- **Enrollment:** 19,866 full-time; 8,320 part-time

KEY STATS

✔ **U.S News College Ranking:** fourth tier, National Universities
✔ **SAT Score (25th/75th percentile):** 950-1190
✔ **Tuition:** 2005-2006: $6,506 in state, $14,786 out of state
  Selectivity: Selective   **Room/board:** $6,058
  Acceptance rate: 80%   **Average debt:** $15,004
  Student/faculty ratio: 21/1   **Proportion who borrowed:** 55%

UNDERGRADUATE STUDENT BODY STATS

2005-2006 enrollment: 19,866 full-time; 8,320 part-time. Men: 48%; women: 52%. **Ethnic makeup:** African American: 16%; Asian American: 21%; Hispanic: 21%; White: 37%; International: 5%.

ADMISSIONS FACTS AND FIGURES

Phone: (713) 743-1010. **Email:** admissions@uh.edu. **Website:** http://www.uh.edu. **Application deadlines for fall 2007:** Regular decision: April 1. Early decision: Not offered. Early action: Not offered. Admission can be deferred. **Application fee:** $50. Common application is not accepted. **To apply online, go to:** http://www.uh.edu/enroll/admis. **Admissions requirements/recommendations:** High school units required (recommended): English: 4; Mathematics: 3; Science: 2; Foreign language: (2); Social studies: 2; History: 2. Tests: The college uses SAT or ACT scores in admissions decisions. Either SAT or ACT required. For admission to the fall 2007 entering class, the school will accept: ACT with writing, ACT without writing. Campus visit: Recommended. Admissions interview: Neither required nor recommended. Off-campus interview: Not available. **Factors that count in admissions decisions:** *Academic:* Secondary school record: Very important. Class rank: Very important. Letters of recommendation: Considered. Standardized test scores: Very important. Essay: Considered. *Nonacademic:* Interview: Not considered. Extracurricular activities: Not considered. Talent/ability: Important. Character/personal qualities: Not considered. Alumni/ae relationship: Considered. Geographical residence: Considered. State residency: Not considered. Religious affiliation/commitment: Not considered. Minority status: Not considered. Volunteer work: Not considered. Work experience: Not considered. **Other schools with the greatest overlap in applicants:** Baylor University; Rice University; Sam Houston State University; Texas A&M University–College Station; University of Texas–Austin. **Admissions statistics for the fall 2005 entering class:** Total applicants: 8,875. Total accepted: 7,130. Freshmen enrolled: 3,445; 2% were from out of state. Overall acceptance rate: 80%. **Credentials of fall 2005 freshmen:** 21% ranked in the top 10 percent of their high school class; 50% were in the top 25 percent, and 80% were in the top half. (Proportion submitting class standing: 93%.) **Average high school grade point average:** 3.2. **First-year students who submitted SAT scores:** 91%. Scores (25/75 percentile): Verbal: 460-580, Math: 490-610, Combined: 950-1190. **First-year students submitting ACT scores:** 30%. Scores (25/75 percentile): English: 17-24, Math: 18-25, Composite: 19-24.

ACADEMICS

Year founded: 1927. **Academic calendar:** Semester. **Degrees offered:** bachelor's, master's, first professional, doctorate. **Most popular majors:** 34% business, management, marketing, and related support services, 9% psychology,

7% social sciences, 6% engineering, 6% engineering technologies/technicians. **Major fields of study:** architecture and related services; area, ethnic, cultural, and gender studies; biological and biomedical sciences; business, management, marketing, and related support services; communication, journalism, and related programs; computer and information sciences and support services; engineering; engineering technologies/technicians; English language and literature/letters; family and consumer sciences/human sciences; foreign languages, literatures, and linguistics; health professions and related clinical sciences; history; mathematics and statistics; multi/interdisciplinary studies; natural resources and conservation; parks, recreation, leisure, and fitness studies; philosophy and religious studies; physical sciences; psychology; social sciences; visual and performing arts. **Areas of required coursework:** arts/fine arts, humanities, mathematics, English (including composition), sciences (biological or physical), history, social science. **Pre-professional programs:** pre-law, pre-dentistry, pre-medicine, pre-veterinary science, pre-optometry, pre-pharmacy. **Special academic programs (% participation):** accelerated program, cooperative (work-study plan) program (2%), cross-registration, distance learning (67%), double major (8%), dual enrollment, English as a Second Language (ESL) (2%), honors program (6%), independent study (20%), internships (5%), study abroad (2%), teacher certificate program (5%). **Teacher certification offered in:** early childhood, special education, elementary, vo-tech, middle/junior high, secondary, bilingual/bicultural. **Cooperative education programs:** business, computer science, education, engineering, natural science, technologies, other. **Reserve Officers Training Corps (ROTC):** Army ROTC: Offered on campus; Navy ROTC: Offered at cooperating institution (Rice University); Air Force ROTC: Offered on campus. **Faculty and instruction (2005-2006):** Total instructional faculty: 1,218 full-time, 427 part-time (65% men; 35% women; 20% minorities). Full-time faculty with Ph.D. or other terminal degree: 84%. Student/faculty ratio: 21/1. Classes of fewer than 20 students: 31%; of 20 to 49 students: 48%; of 50 or more students: 22%. **Advanced Placement and International Baccalaureate credit:** AP tests may be used for: Credit and/or placement. Scores accepted: 3, 4. International Baccalaureate exams may be used for: Credit and/or placement. **Freshmen returning for sophomore year:** 79%. **Graduation rates:** Four-year: 10%; five-year: 29%; six-year: 40%.

COSTS AND FINANCIAL AID

Financial aid office: (713) 743-1010. **Expenses (2005-2006):** Tuition and fees 2005-2006: $6,506 in state, $14,786 out of state; room/board: $6,058. Estimated books and supplies: $1,050; transportation: $1,200; personal expenses: $2,900. **Financial aid:** Priority filing date for institution's financial aid form: April 1. In 2005-2006, 62% of undergraduates applied for financial aid. Of those, 56% were determined to have financial need; 3% had their need fully met. Average financial aid package (proportion receiving): $7,775 (52%). Average amount of gift aid, such as scholarships or grants (proportion receiving): $4,975 (43%). Average amount of self-help aid, such as work study or loans (proportion receiving): $4,481 (37%). Average need-based loan (excluding PLUS or other private loans): $4,133. Among students who received need-based aid, the average percentage of need met: 52%. Among students who received aid based on merit, the average award (and the proportion receiving): $3,884 (1%). The average athletic scholarship (and the proportion receiving): $11,059 (1%). Average amount of debt of borrowers graduating in 2005: $15,004. Proportion who borrowed: 55%.

CAMPUS LIFE AND EXTRACURRICULAR ACTIVITIES

Campus housing available (% using): coed dorms (52%), sorority housing (3%), fraternity housing (3%), apartment for single students (39%), special housing for disabled students (2%). Students who live in college-owned, operated, or affiliated housing: 7%. **Student employment:** During the 2005-2006 academic year, 75% of undergraduates worked on campus. Average per-year earnings: $5,900. **Clubs and organizations:** Number of student organizations: 350. Activities include: choral groups, concert band, dance, drama/theater, jazz band, literary magazine, marching band, music ensembles, musical theater, opera, pep band, radio station, student government, student newspaper, student film society, symphony orchestra, television station, yearbook. Number of fraternities: 20; sororities: 18. Proportion of men in fraternities: 4%; of women in sororities: 3%. Average proportion of students who stay on campus on weekends: 20%. **Sports program (2005-2006):** Member of NCAA I. *Men's intercollegiate varsity sports:* baseball, basketball, cross-country, football, golf, track and field (indoor), track and field (outdoor). *Women's intercollegiate varsity sports:* basketball, cross-country, soccer, softball, swimming and diving, tennis, track and field (indoor), track and field (outdoor), volleyball.

SERVICES AND FACILITIES

Basic services: nonremedial tutoring, women's center, placement service, day care, health service, health insurance. **Remedial assistance:** reading, math, writing, study skills. **Counseling services:** minority student, career, military, personal, veteran student, academic, older student, psychological, birth control, religious. **For learning-disabled students:** School does not offer a structured program with separate admission and additional fees. Total undergraduates in learning-disabled program or receiving services: 546. Services include: remedial math, remedial English, reading machines, remedial reading, tape recorders, videotaped classes, diagnostic testing service, note-taking services, oral tests, learning center, readers, extended time for tests, tutors, priority registration, priority seating, exams on tape or computer, other. **Library:** Number of titles: 3,037,980; number of current serial subscriptions: 21,845. **Information technology resources:** Students are not required to lease or own a computer. School has a wireless network. **Campus safety:** Security services offered: 24-hour foot-and-vehicle patrols, late-night transport/escort service, 24-hour emergency telephones, lighted pathways/sidewalks, controlled dormitory access (key, security card, etc).

TRANSFER AND INTERNATIONAL STUDENTS

Transfer students: May apply for admission for the following academic terms: Fall, Spring, Summer. Applicants need a minimum number of credits to apply. For fall 2005: Transfer applications received: 5,471. Transfer applicants offered admission: 5,080. Transfer applicants enrolled: 3,330. **International students:** Number of foreign undergraduates: 1322 (5% of student body). Number of countries represented: 119. Minimum TOEFL score required: 550 (paper); 213 (computer).

University of Houston–Downtown

- **Address:** 1 Main Street, Houston, TX 77002
- **Website:** http://www.uhd.edu
- **Public**
- **Enrollment:** 5,904 full-time; 5,455 part-time

KEY STATS

- ✔ **U.S News College Ranking:** third tier, Comp. Coll.–Bachelor's (West)
- ✔ **SAT or ACT Score (25th/75th percentile):** N/A
- ✔ **Tuition:** 2005-2006: $4,139 in state, $12,419 out of state

Selectivity: Less selective	**Room/board:** $0
Acceptance rate: 98%	**Average debt:** N/A
Student/faculty ratio: 21/1	**Proportion who borrowed:** N/A

UNDERGRADUATE STUDENT BODY STATS

2005-2006 enrollment: 5,904 full-time; 5,455 part-time. Men: 41%; women: 59%. **Ethnic makeup:** African American: 26%; Asian American: 10%; Hispanic: 37%; White: 23%; International: 4%.

ADMISSIONS FACTS AND FIGURES

Phone: (713) 221-8522. **Email:** uhdadmit@uhd.edu. **Website:** http://www.uhd.edu. **Application deadlines for fall 2007:** Regular decision: July 1. Early decision: Not offered. Early action: Not offered. Admission can be deferred. **Application fee:** $25. Common application is not accepted. **To apply online, go to:** http://www.uhd.edu/admissions/application.htm. **Admissions requirements/recommendations:** High school units required (recommended): English: 4 (4); Mathematics: 3 (3); Science: 3 (3); Foreign language: 3 (3); Social studies: 4 (4); Academic electives: 1 (1); Total units: 25 (25). Tests: The college does not use SAT or ACT scores in admissions decisions. Neither SAT nor ACT required. Campus visit: Recommended. Admissions interview: Neither required nor recommended. Off-campus interview: Not available. **Factors that count in admissions decisions:** *Academic:* Secondary school record: Not considered. Class rank: Not considered. Letters of recommendation: Not considered. Standardized test scores: Not considered. Essay: Not considered. *Nonacademic:* Interview: Not considered. Extracurricular activities: Not considered. Talent/ability: Not considered. Character/personal qualities: Not considered. Alumni/ae relationship: Not considered. Geographical residence: Not considered. State residency: Not considered. Religious affiliation/commitment: Not considered. Minority status: Not considered. Volunteer work: Not considered. Work experience: Not considered. **Admissions statistics for the fall 2005 entering class:** Total applicants: 1,754. Total accepted: 1,726. Freshmen enrolled: 1,029; 2% were from out of state. Overall acceptance rate: 98%.

ACADEMICS

Year founded: 1974. **Academic calendar:** Semester. **Degrees offered:** bachelor's, master's. **Most popular majors:** 43% business, management, marketing, and related support services, 22% liberal arts and sciences studies, and humanities, 7% multi/interdisciplinary studies, 7% psychology, 7% security and protective services. **Major fields of study:** biological and biomedical sciences; business, management, marketing, and related support services; computer and information sciences and support services; engineering technologies/technicians; English language and literature/letters; foreign languages, literatures, and linguistics; history; liberal arts and sciences studies, and humanities; mathematics and statistics; multi/interdisciplinary studies; philosophy and religious studies; physical sciences; psychology; security and protective services; social sciences. **Areas of required coursework:** arts/fine arts, humanities, computer literacy, mathematics, English (including composition), sciences (biological or physical), history, social science, other. **Special academic programs:** cooperative (work-study plan) program, distance learning, double major, dual enrollment, English as a Second Language (ESL), honors program, independent study, internships, study abroad, weekend college, other. **Reserve Officers Training Corps (ROTC):** Army ROTC: Offered at cooperating institution (University of Houston Central Campus). **Faculty and instruction (2005-2006):** Total instructional faculty: 277 full-time, 296 part-time (53% men; 47% women; 32% minorities). Full-time faculty with Ph.D. or other terminal degree: 82%. Student/faculty ratio: 21/1. Classes of fewer than 20 students: 26%; of 20 to 49 students: 71%; of 50 or more students: 3%. **Advanced Placement and International Baccalaureate credit:** International Baccalaureate exams may be used for: Placement only. **Freshmen returning for sophomore year:** 61%. **Graduation rates:** Four-year: 2%; five-year: 9%; six-year: 14%. **Graduate study:** 60% of students pursue further study within five years.

COSTS AND FINANCIAL AID

Financial aid office: (713) 221-8041. **Expenses (2005-2006):** Tuition and fees 2005-2006: $4,139 in state, $12,419 out of state; room/board: $0. Estimated books and supplies: $1,020; transportation: $3,140; personal expenses: $3,588. **Financial aid:** Priority filing date for institution's financial aid form: April 1.

CAMPUS LIFE AND EXTRACURRICULAR ACTIVITIES

Students who live in college-owned, operated, or affiliated housing: 0%. **Student employment:** During the 2005-2006 academic year, 3% of undergraduates worked on campus. Average per-year earnings: $6,886. **Clubs and organizations:** Number of student organizations: 55. Activities include: drama/theater, jazz band, literary magazine, student government, student newspaper. Number of fraternities: 4; sororities: 4. **Sports program (2005-2006):** Member of NCAA I.

SERVICES AND FACILITIES

Basic services: nonremedial tutoring, placement service, health service, other. **Remedial assistance:** reading, math, writing, study skills. **Counseling services:** career, personal, academic, psychological. **For learning-disabled students:** Services include: remedial math, remedial English, reading machines, remedial reading, learning center, extended time for tests, tutors, priority registration, priority seating, other testing accomodations. **Library:** Number of titles: 262,812; number of current serial subscriptions: 1,108. **Information technology resources:** Students are not required to lease or own a computer. Number of campus computers available to all students: 1,075. School has a wireless network. Approximate number of users that can be accommodated: 400. **Campus safety:** Security services offered: 24-hour foot-and-vehicle patrols, late-night transport/escort service, 24-hour emergency telephones, lighted pathways/sidewalks.

TRANSFER AND INTERNATIONAL STUDENTS

Transfer students: May apply for admission for the following academic terms: Fall, Spring, Summer. Applicants need a minimum number of credits to apply. For fall 2005: Transfer applications received: 2,969. Transfer applicants offered admission: 2,968. Transfer applicants enrolled: 1,692. **International students:** Number of foreign undergraduates: 492 (4% of student body). Minimum TOEFL score required: 550 (paper); 213 (computer).

University of Mary Hardin-Baylor

- **Address:** 900 College Street, UMHB Box 8425, Belton, TX 76513
- **Website:** http://www.umhb.edu
- **Private; Religious affiliation:** Baptist
- **Enrollment:** 2,270 full-time; 321 part-time

KEY STATS

✔ **U.S News College Ranking:** 57, Universities–Master's (West)
✔ **SAT Score (25th/75th percentile):** 910-1120
✔ **Tuition:** 2006-2007: $15,710

Selectivity: Selective	**Room/board:** $4,200
Acceptance rate: 75%	**Average debt:** $16,725
Student/faculty ratio: 15/1	**Proportion who borrowed:** 80%

UNDERGRADUATE STUDENT BODY STATS

2005-2006 enrollment: 2,270 full-time; 321 part-time. Men: 37%; women: 63%. **Ethnic makeup:** African American: 11%; Asian American: 1%; Hispanic: 11%; White: 76%; International: 1%. **Religious preference:** Roman Catholic: 11%; Protestant: 29%; No preference: 9%; Baptist: 51%.

ADMISSIONS FACTS AND FIGURES

Phone: (254) 295-4520. **Email:** admission@umhb.edu. **Website:** http://www.umhb.edu. **Application deadlines for fall 2007:** Regular decision: Rolling. Early decision: Not offered. Early action: Not offered. Admission can be deferred. **Application fee:** $35. Common application is accepted. **Admissions requirements/recommendations:** High school units required (recommended): English: 4; Mathematics: 3; Social studies: 2; Total units: 22. Tests: The college uses SAT or ACT scores in admissions decisions. Either SAT or ACT required. For admission to the fall 2007 entering class, the school will accept: ACT with writing. Campus visit: Recommended. Admissions interview: Recommended. Off-campus interview: May be arranged. **Factors that count in admissions decisions:** *Academic:* Secondary school record: Considered. Class rank: Important. Letters of recommendation: Considered. Standardized test scores: Very important. Essay: Considered. *Nonacademic:* Interview: Considered. Extracurricular activities: Considered. Talent/ability: Considered. Character/personal qualities: Considered. Alumni/ae relationship: Considered. Geographical residence: Considered. State residency: Considered. Religious affiliation/commitment: Considered. Minority status: Considered. Volunteer work: Considered. Work experience: Considered. **Admissions statistics for the fall 2005 entering class:** Total applicants: 1,261. Total accepted: 942. Freshmen enrolled: 502; 1% were from out of state. Overall acceptance rate: 75%. **Credentials of fall 2005 freshmen:** 19% ranked in the top 10 percent of their high school class; 46% were in the top 25 percent, and 79% were in the top half. (Proportion submitting class standing: 89%.) **First-year students who submitted SAT scores:** 81%. Scores (25/75 percentile): Verbal: 450-560, Math: 460-560, Combined: 910-1120. **First-year students submitting ACT scores:** 60%. Scores (25/75 percentile): English: 18-25, Math: 18-24, Composite: 20-25.

ACADEMICS

Year founded: 1845. **Academic calendar:** Semester. **Degrees offered:** bachelor's, master's. **Most popular majors:** 13% nursing/registered nurse training (R.N., A.S.N., B.S.N., M.S.N.), 8% elementary education and teaching, 8% general studies, 6% biology/biological sciences, 6% psychology. **Major fields of study:** biological and biomedical sciences; business, management, marketing, and related support services; communication, journalism, and related programs; computer and information sciences and support services; education; English language and literature/letters; foreign languages, literatures, and linguistics; health professions and related clinical sciences; history; liberal arts and sciences studies, and humanities; mathematics and statistics; parks, recreation, leisure, and fitness studies; philosophy and religious studies; physical sciences; psychology; public administration and social service professions; security and protective services; social sciences; theology and religious vocations; visual and performing arts. **Areas of required coursework:** mathematics, English (including composition), foreign languages, sciences (biological or physical), social science, other. **Pre-professional programs:** pre-law, pre-dentistry, pre-medicine, pre-theology, pre-veterinary science, pre-optometry, pre-pharmacy, other. **Special academic programs:** accelerated program, double major, dual enrollment, English as a Second Language (ESL), honors program, independent study, internships, study abroad, teacher certificate program, other. **Teacher certification offered in:** early childhood, special education, elementary, middle/junior high, sec-

ondary. **Reserve Officers Training Corps (ROTC):** Air Force ROTC: Offered at cooperating institution (Baylor University). **Faculty and instruction (2005-2006):** Total instructional faculty: 133 full-time, 94 part-time (47% men; 53% women; 5% minorities). Full-time faculty with Ph.D. or other terminal degree: 69%. Student/faculty ratio: 15/1. Classes of fewer than 20 students: 50%; of 20 to 49 students: 49%; of 50 or more students: 1%. **Advanced Placement and International Baccalaureate credit:** AP tests may be used for: Credit only. Scores accepted: 4, 5. **Freshmen returning for sophomore year:** 61%. **Graduation rates:** Four-year: 26%; five-year: 39%; six-year: 43%.

COSTS AND FINANCIAL AID

Financial aid office: (254) 295-4517. **Expenses (2006-2007):** Tuition and fees 2006-2007: $15,710; room/board: $4,200. Estimated books and supplies: $1,200; transportation: $1,364; personal expenses: $1,684. **Financial aid:** Priority filing date for institution's financial aid form: March 1. In 2005-2006, 93% of undergraduates applied for financial aid. Of those, 75% were determined to have financial need; 22% had their need fully met. Average financial aid package (proportion receiving): $12,511 (74%). Average amount of gift aid, such as scholarships or grants (proportion receiving): $5,134 (61%). Average amount of self-help aid, such as work study or loans (proportion receiving): $5,301 (59%). Average need-based loan (excluding PLUS or other private loans): $4,948. Among students who received need-based aid, the average percentage of need met: 73%. Among students who received aid based on merit, the average award (and the proportion receiving): $3,314 (23%). The average athletic scholarship (and the proportion receiving): $0 (0%). Average amount of debt of borrowers graduating in 2005: $16,725. Proportion who borrowed: 80%.

CAMPUS LIFE AND EXTRACURRICULAR ACTIVITIES

Campus housing available (% using): women's dorms (38%), men's dorms (20%), apartment for single students (42%), special housing for disabled students (0%). Students who live in college-owned, operated, or affiliated housing: 46%. **Student employment:** During the 2005-2006 academic year, 18% of undergraduates worked on campus. Average per-year earnings: $2,300. **Clubs and organizations:** Number of student organizations: 44. Activities include: choral groups, concert band, dance, drama/theater, jazz band, literary magazine, marching band, music ensembles, musical theater, opera, student government, student newspaper, symphony orchestra, yearbook. Number of fraternities: 0; sororities: 0. Average proportion of students who stay on campus on weekends: 60%. **Sports program (2005-2006):** Member of NCAA III. *Men's intercollegiate varsity sports:* baseball, basketball, football, golf, soccer, tennis. *Women's intercollegiate varsity sports:* basketball, golf, soccer, softball, tennis, volleyball.

SERVICES AND FACILITIES

Basic services: nonremedial tutoring, health service. **Remedial assistance:** reading, math, writing, study skills. **Counseling services:** minority student, career, military, personal, veteran student, academic, older student, psychological, religious. **For learning-disabled students:** School does not offer a structured program with separate admission and additional fees. Total undergraduates in learning-disabled program or receiving services: 50. Services include: remedial math, remedial English, remedial reading, tape recorders, other special classes, diagnostic testing service, untimed tests, note-taking services, oral tests, learning center, readers, extended time for tests, tutors, priority registration, priority seating, texts on tape, typist/scribe, other testing accomodations. **Library:** Number of titles: 178,807; number of current serial subscriptions: 1,526. **Information technology resources:** Students are not required to lease or own a computer. Number of campus computers available to all students: 77. School does not have a wireless network. Proportion of college-owned housing units wired for high-speed internet access: 100%. **Campus safety:** Security services offered: 24-hour foot-and-vehicle patrols, 24-hour emergency telephones, lighted pathways/sidewalks, controlled dormitory access (key, security card, etc).

TRANSFER AND INTERNATIONAL STUDENTS

Transfer students: May apply for admission for the following academic terms: Fall, Spring, Summer. Applicants need a minimum number of credits to apply. For fall 2005: Transfer applications received: 691. Transfer applicants offered admission: 592. Transfer applicants enrolled: 368. **International students:** Number of foreign undergraduates: 13 (1% of student body). Number of countries represented: 10.

University of North Texas

- **Address:** PO Box 311277, Denton, TX 76203
- **Website:** http://www.unt.edu
- **Public**
- **Enrollment:** 19,830 full-time; 5,478 part-time

KEY STATS

✔ **U.S News College Ranking:** fourth tier, National Universities
✔ **SAT Score (25th/75th percentile):** 1000-1210
✔ **Tuition:** 2006-2007: $6,112 in state, $14,362 out of state
- **Selectivity:** Selective   **Room/board:** $5,610
- **Acceptance rate:** 69%   **Average debt:** $17,950
- **Student/faculty ratio:** 18/1   **Proportion who borrowed:** 42%

UNDERGRADUATE STUDENT BODY STATS

2005-2006 enrollment: 19,830 full-time; 5,478 part-time. Men: 44%; women: 56%. **Ethnic makeup:** African American: 12%; American-Indian: 1%; Asian American: 5%; Hispanic: 11%; White: 69%; International: 3%.

ADMISSIONS FACTS AND FIGURES

Phone: (940) 565-2681. **Email:** undergrad@unt.edu. **Website:** http://www.unt.edu. **Application deadlines for fall 2007:** Regular decision: August 1. Early decision: Not offered. Early action: Not offered. Admission can be deferred. **Application fee:** $40. Common application is accepted. **To apply online, go to:** http://www.unt.edu/admissions.html. **Admissions requirements/recommendations:** High school units required (recommended): English: 4; Mathematics: 4; Science: 3; Foreign language: 3; Social studies: 4; History: 0; Academic electives: 3; Total units: 24. Tests: The college uses SAT or ACT scores in admissions decisions. Either SAT or ACT required. For admission to the fall 2007 entering class, the school will accept: ACT with writing, ACT without writing. Campus visit: Recommended. Admissions interview: Neither required nor recommended. Off-campus interview: Not available. **Factors that count in admissions decisions:** *Academic:* Secondary school record: Considered. Class rank: Very important. Letters of recommendation: Important. Standardized test scores: Very important. Essay: Considered. *Nonacademic:* Interview: Not considered. Extracurricular activities: Considered. Talent/ability: Considered. Character/personal qualities: Considered. Alumni/ae relationship: Not considered. Geographical residence: Not considered. State residency: Not considered. Religious affiliation/commitment: Not considered. Minority status: Not considered. Volunteer work: Considered. Work experience: Not considered. **Other schools with the greatest overlap in applicants:** Texas A&M University–College Station; Texas State University–San Marcos; Texas Tech University; Texas Woman's University; University of Texas–Arlington. **Admissions statistics for the fall 2005 entering class:** Total applicants: 11,282. Total accepted: 7,834. Freshmen enrolled: 3,635; 3% were from out of state. Overall acceptance rate: 69%. **Credentials of fall 2005 freshmen:** 19% ranked in the top 10 percent of their high school class; 48% were in the top 25 percent, and 86% were in the top half. (Proportion submitting class standing: 94%.) **First-year students who submitted SAT scores:** 87%. Scores (25/75 percentile): Verbal: 500-600, Math: 500-610, Combined: 1000-1210. **First-year students submitting ACT scores:** 44%. Scores (25/75 percentile): English: N/A, Math: N/A, Composite: 20-24.

ACADEMICS

Year founded: 1890. **Academic calendar:** Semester. **Degrees offered:** bachelor's, post-bachelor's certificate, master's, doctorate. **Most popular majors:** 26% business, management, marketing, and related support services, 9% education, 9% visual and performing arts, 8% social sciences, 7% communication, journalism, and related programs. **Major fields of study:** architecture and related services; biological and biomedical sciences; business, management, marketing, and related support services; communication, journalism, and related programs; computer and information sciences and support services; engineering; engineering technologies/technicians; English language and literature/letters; family and consumer sciences/human sciences; foreign languages, literatures, and linguistics; health professions and related clinical sciences; history; liberal arts and sciences studies, and humanities; mathematics and statistics; multi/interdisciplinary studies; parks, recreation, leisure, and fitness studies; philosophy and religious studies; physical sciences; psychology; public administration and social service professions; science technologies/technicians; security and protective services; social sciences; visual and performing arts. **Areas of**

required coursework: arts/fine arts, humanities, computer literacy, mathematics, English (including composition), philosophy, foreign languages, sciences (biological or physical), history, social science. **Pre-professional programs:** pre-law, pre-dentistry, pre-medicine, pre-theology, other. **Special academic programs:** accelerated program, cooperative (work-study plan) program, cross-registration, distance learning, double major, dual enrollment, English as a Second Language (ESL), exchange student program (domestic), external degree program, honors program, independent study, internships, liberal arts/career combination, study abroad, teacher certificate program, weekend college. **Teacher certification offered in:** early childhood, special education, elementary, middle/junior high, secondary, bilingual/bicultural. **Cooperative education programs:** art, business, computer science, education, engineering, health professions, humanities, natural science, social/behavioral science, technologies. **Reserve Officers Training Corps (ROTC):** Army ROTC: Offered at cooperating institution (UT Arlington); Air Force ROTC: Offered on campus. **Faculty and instruction (2005-2006):** Total instructional faculty: 936 full-time, 477 part-time (58% men; 42% women; 15% minorities). Full-time faculty with Ph.D. or other terminal degree: 85%. Student/faculty ratio: 18/1. Classes of fewer than 20 students: 19%; of 20 to 49 students: 58%; of 50 or more students: 23%. **Advanced Placement and International Baccalaureate credit:** International Baccalaureate exams may be used for: Credit only. **Freshmen returning for sophomore year:** 76%. **Graduation rates:** Four-year: 15%; five-year: 35%; six-year: 43%.

COSTS AND FINANCIAL AID

Financial aid office: (940) 565-2302. **Expenses (2006-2007):** Tuition and fees 2006-2007: $6,112 in state, $14,362 out of state; room/board: $5,610. Estimated books and supplies: $1,080; transportation: $1,760; personal expenses: $1,750. **Financial aid:** Priority filing date for institution's financial aid form: June 1. In 2005-2006, 63% of undergraduates applied for financial aid. Of those, 47% were determined to have financial need; 20% had their need fully met. Average financial aid package (proportion receiving): $7,830 (45%). Average amount of gift aid, such as scholarships or grants (proportion receiving): $3,960 (37%). Average amount of self-help aid, such as work study or loans (proportion receiving): $4,369 (39%). Average need-based loan (excluding PLUS or other private loans): $3,923. Among students who received need-based aid, the average percentage of need met: 68%. Among students who received aid based on merit, the average award (and the proportion receiving): $3,001 (7%). The average athletic scholarship (and the proportion receiving): $10,585 (1%). Average amount of debt of borrowers graduating in 2005: $17,950. Proportion who borrowed: 42%.

CAMPUS LIFE AND EXTRACURRICULAR ACTIVITIES

Campus housing available (% using): coed dorms (90%), women's dorms (4%), sorority housing (3%), fraternity housing (1%), apartments for married students (0%), apartment for single students (0%), special housing for disabled students (2%). Students who live in college-owned, operated, or affiliated housing: 21%. **Student employment:** During the 2005-2006 academic year, 14% of undergraduates worked on campus. Average per-year earnings: $5,000. **Clubs and organizations:** Number of student organizations: 269. Activities include: choral groups, concert band, dance, drama/theater, jazz band, literary magazine, marching band, music ensembles, musical theater, opera, pep band, radio station, student government, student newspaper, student film society, symphony orchestra, television station, yearbook. Number of fraternities: 16; sororities: 13. Proportion of men in fraternities: 1%; of women in sororities: 1%. Average proportion of students who stay on campus on weekends: 50%. **Sports program (2005-2006):** Member of NCAA I. *Men's intercollegiate varsity sports:* basketball, cheerleading, cross-country, football, golf, track and field (indoor), track and field (outdoor). *Women's intercollegiate varsity sports:* basketball, cheerleading, cross-country, golf, soccer, softball, swimming and diving, tennis, track and field (indoor), track and field (outdoor), volleyball.

SERVICES AND FACILITIES

Basic services: nonremedial tutoring, women's center, placement service, health service, health insurance. **Remedial assistance:** reading, math, writing, study skills. **Counseling services:** minority student, career, personal, academic, older student, psychological, birth control. **For learning-disabled students:** School does not offer a structured program with separate admission and additional fees. Total undergraduates in learning-disabled program or receiving services: 281. Services include: remedial math, reading machines, diagnostic testing service, learning center, readers, extended time for tests, tutors, priority seating, other. **Library:** Number of titles: 2,125,264; number of current serial subscriptions: 19,487. **Information technology resources:** Students are not required to lease or own a computer. Number of campus computers available to all students: 2,136. School has a wireless network. Approximate number of users that can be accommodated: 800. Proportion of college-owned housing units wired for high-speed internet access: 100%. **Campus safety:** Security services offered: 24-hour foot-and-vehicle patrols, late-night transport/escort service, 24-hour emergency telephones, lighted pathways/sidewalks, controlled dormitory access (key, security card, etc).

TRANSFER AND INTERNATIONAL STUDENTS

Transfer students: May apply for admission for the following academic terms: Fall, Spring, Summer. Applicants need a minimum number of credits to apply. For fall 2005: Transfer applications received: 6,546. Transfer applicants offered admission: 4,949. Transfer applicants enrolled: 3,420. **International students:** Number of foreign undergraduates: 663 (3% of student body). Number of countries represented: 111. Minimum TOEFL score required: 550 (paper); 213 (computer).

University of St. Thomas

- **Address:** 3800 Montrose Boulevard, Houston, TX 77006-4696
- **Website:** http://www.stthom.edu
- **Private; Religious affiliation:** Roman Catholic
- **Enrollment:** 1,365 full-time; 519 part-time

KEY STATS

✔ **U.S News College Ranking:** 29, Universities–Master's (West)
✔ **SAT Score (25th/75th percentile):** 1050-1280
✔ **Tuition:** 2006-2007: $17,860

Selectivity: More selective	**Room/board:** $6,700
Acceptance rate: 92%	**Average debt:** $21,626
Student/faculty ratio: 14/1	**Proportion who borrowed:** 63%

UNDERGRADUATE STUDENT BODY STATS

2005-2006 enrollment: 1,365 full-time; 519 part-time. Men: 38%; women: 62%. **Ethnic makeup:** African American: 6%; American-Indian: 1%; Asian American: 12%; Hispanic: 30%; White: 49%; International: 3%. **Religious preference:** Protestant: 18%; Muslim: 2%; Buddhist: 2%; Unknown: 23%; Roman Catholic: 51%.

ADMISSIONS FACTS AND FIGURES

Phone: (713) 525-3500. **Email:** admissions@stthom.edu. **Website:** http://www.stthom.edu. **Application deadlines for fall 2007:** Regular decision: August 19. Early decision: Not offered. Early action: Not offered. Admission can be deferred. **Application fee:** $35. Common application is accepted. **To apply online, go to:** http://www.texasmentor.org/applications/St._Thomas/apply.html. **Admissions requirements/recommendations:** High school units required (recommended): English: 4 (4); Mathematics: 3 (3); Science: 3 (3); Foreign language: 2 (2); Social studies: 2 (2); History: 1 (1); Academic electives: 3 (3); Total units: 18 (18). Tests: The college uses SAT or ACT scores in admissions decisions. Either SAT or ACT required. For admission to the fall 2007 entering class, the school will accept: ACT with writing. Campus visit: Recommended. Admissions interview: Neither required nor recommended. Off-campus interview: May be arranged. **Factors that count in admissions decisions:** *Academic:* Secondary school record: Very important. Class rank: Very important. Letters of recommendation: Considered. Standardized test scores: Very important. Essay: Very important. *Nonacademic:* Interview: Considered. Extracurricular activities: Considered. Talent/ability: Considered. Character/personal qualities: Considered. Alumni/ae relationship: Not considered. Geographical residence: Not considered. State residency: Not considered. Religious affiliation/commitment: Not considered. Minority status: Not considered. Volunteer work: Considered. Work experience: Considered. **Admissions statistics for the fall 2005 entering class:** Total applicants: 807. Total accepted: 744. Freshmen enrolled: 295; 4% were from out of state. Overall acceptance rate: 92%. **Credentials of fall 2005 freshmen:** 29% ranked in the top 10 percent of their high school class; 58% were in the top 25 percent, and 82% were in the top half. (Proportion submitting class standing: 86%.) **Average high school grade point average:** 3.0. **First-year students who submitted SAT scores:** 84%. Scores (25/75 percentile): Verbal: 530-640, Math: 520-640, Combined: 1050-1280. **First-year students submitting ACT scores:** 16%. Scores (25/75 percentile): English: 20-27, Math: 20-29; Composite: 22-28.

ACADEMICS

Year founded: 1947. **Academic calendar:** Semester. **Degrees offered:** diploma, bachelor's, master's, first professional, doctorate. **Most popular majors:** 27% business, management, marketing, and related support services, 16% liberal arts and sciences studies, and humanities, 12% social sciences, 7% psychology, 6% biological and biomedical sciences. **Major fields of study:** biological and biomedical sciences; business, management, marketing, and related support services; communication, journalism, and related programs; education; English language and literature/letters; foreign languages, literatures, and linguistics; history; liberal arts and sciences studies, and humanities; mathematics and statistics; natural resources and conservation; philosophy and religious studies; physical sciences; psychology; social sciences; theology and religious vocations; visual and performing arts. **Areas of required coursework:** arts/fine arts, mathematics, English (including composition), philosophy, foreign languages, sciences (biological or physical), history, social science, other. **Pre-professional programs:** pre-law, pre-dentistry, pre-medicine, pre-veterinary science, pre-optometry, pre-pharmacy, other. **Special academic programs:** cross-registration, distance learning, double major, honors program, independent study, internships, study abroad, teacher certificate program, other. **Teacher certification offered in:** special education, elementary, middle/junior high, secondary, bilingual/bicultural. **Reserve Officers Training Corps (ROTC):** Army ROTC: Offered at cooperating institution (University of Houston). **Faculty and instruction (2005-2006):** Total instructional faculty: 121 full-time, 151 part-time (56% men; 44% women; 8% minorities). Full-time faculty with Ph.D. or other terminal degree: 88%. Student/faculty ratio: 14/1. Classes of fewer than 20 students: 52%; of 20 to 49 students: 48%; of 50 or more students: 0%. **Advanced Placement and International Baccalaureate credit:** AP tests may be used for: Credit only. Scores accepted: 3, 4, 5. International Baccalaureate exams may be used for: Credit only. **Freshmen returning for sophomore year:** 71%. **Graduation rates:** Four-year: 24%; five-year: 43%; six-year: 49%.

COSTS AND FINANCIAL AID

Financial aid office: (713) 942-3465. **Expenses (2006-2007):** Tuition and fees 2006-2007: $17,860; room/board: $6,700. Estimated books and supplies: $800 personal expenses: $1,740. **Financial aid:** Priority filing date for institution's financial aid form: March 1. In 2005-2006, 65% of undergraduates applied for financial aid. Of those, 57% were determined to have financial need; 11% had their need fully met. Average financial aid package (proportion receiving): $12,487 (57%). Average amount of gift aid, such as scholarships or grants (proportion receiving): $8,653 (54%). Average amount of self-help aid, such as work study or loans (proportion receiving): $4,280 (48%). Average need-based loan (excluding PLUS or other private loans): $4,199. Among students who received need-based aid, the average percentage of need met: 64%. Among students who received aid based on merit, the average award (and the proportion receiving): $6,613 (18%). The average athletic scholarship (and the proportion receiving): $0 (0%): Average amount of debt of borrowers graduating in 2005: $21,626. Proportion who borrowed: 63%.

CAMPUS LIFE AND EXTRACURRICULAR ACTIVITIES

Campus housing available (% using): coed dorms (90%), apartment for single students (8%), other housing options (2%). Students who live in college-owned, operated, or affiliated housing: 14%. **Clubs and organizations:** Number of student organizations: 80. Activities include: choral groups, concert band, drama/theater, jazz band, literary magazine, music ensembles, musical theater, student government, student newspaper. Number of fraternities: 0; sororities: 0.

SERVICES AND FACILITIES

Basic services: nonremedial tutoring, placement service, health service, other. **Remedial assistance:** reading, math, writing, study skills. **Counseling services:** minority student, career, personal, academic, older student, psychological, religious. **For learning-disabled students:** School does not offer a structured program with separate admission and additional fees. Total undergraduates in learning-disabled program or receiving services: 22. Services include: remedial math, remedial English, tape recorders, other special classes, note-taking services, oral tests, learning center, extended time for tests, tutors, early syllabus, priority registration, priority seating, exams on tape or computer, other testing accomodations, other. **Library:** Number of titles: 254,142; number of current serial subscriptions: 16,450. **Information technology resources:** Students are not required to lease or own a computer. Number of campus computers available to all students: 347. School has a wireless network. Approximate number of users that can be accommodated: 800. Proportion of college-owned housing units wired for high-speed internet access: 80%. **Campus safety:** Security services offered:

24-hour foot-and-vehicle patrols, late-night transport/escort service, 24-hour emergency telephones, lighted pathways/sidewalks, controlled dormitory access (key, security card, etc).

TRANSFER AND INTERNATIONAL STUDENTS

Transfer students: May apply for admission for the following academic terms: Fall, Spring, Summer. Applicants need a minimum number of credits to apply. For fall 2005: Transfer applications received: 327. Transfer applicants offered admission: 297. Transfer applicants enrolled: 177. **International students:** Number of foreign undergraduates: 51 (3% of student body). Number of countries represented: 36. Minimum TOEFL score required: 550 (paper); 213 (computer).

University of Texas–Arlington

- **Address:** 701 S. Nedderman Drive, Arlington, TX 76019-0111
- **Website:** http://www.uta.edu
- **Public**
- **Enrollment:** 13,995 full-time; 5,654 part-time

KEY STATS

✔ **U.S News College Ranking:** fourth tier, National Universities
✔ **SAT Score (25th/75th percentile):** 940-1160
✔ **Tuition:** 2006-2007: $6,400 in state, $14,760 out of state

Selectivity: Selective	**Room/board:** $5,820
Acceptance rate: 79%	**Average debt:** $16,780
Student/faculty ratio: 22/1	**Proportion who borrowed:** 42%

UNDERGRADUATE STUDENT BODY STATS

2005-2006 enrollment: 13,995 full-time; 5,654 part-time. Men: 47%; women: 53%. **Ethnic makeup:** African American: 14%; American-Indian: 1%; Asian American: 11%; Hispanic: 15%; White: 54%; International: 5%.

ADMISSIONS FACTS AND FIGURES

Phone: (817) 272-6287. **Email:** admissions@uta.edu. **Website:** http://www.uta.edu. **Application deadlines for fall 2007:** Regular decision: Rolling. Early decision: Not offered. Early action: Not offered. Admission can be deferred. **Application fee:** $35. Common application is not accepted. **To apply online, go to:** http://www.applytexas.org. **Admissions requirements/recommendations:** High school units required (recommended): English: 4 (4); Mathematics: 3 (4); Science: 3 (3); Foreign language: 2 (3); Social studies: 3 (4); Academic electives: 5 (0); Total units: 20. Tests: The college uses SAT or ACT scores in admissions decisions. Either SAT or ACT required. For admission to the fall 2007 entering class, the school will accept: ACT without writing. Campus visit: Recommended. Admissions interview: Neither required nor recommended. Off-campus interview: Not available. **Factors that count in admissions decisions:** *Academic:* Secondary school record: Very important. Class rank: Very important. Letters of recommendation: Considered. Standardized test scores: Very important. Essay: Considered. *Nonacademic:* Interview: Not considered. Extracurricular activities: Considered. Talent/ability: Considered. Character/personal qualities: Considered. Alumni/ae relationship: Not considered. Geographical residence: Not considered. State residency: Not considered. Religious affiliation/commitment: Not considered. Minority status: Not considered. Volunteer work: Considered. Work experience: Considered. **Admissions statistics for the fall 2005 entering class:** Total applicants: 5,465. Total accepted: 4,320. Freshmen enrolled: 2,130; 2% were from out of state. Overall acceptance rate: 79%. **Credentials of fall 2005 freshmen:** 20% ranked in the top 10 percent of their high school class; 60% were in the top 25 percent, and 89% were in the top half. (Proportion submitting class standing: 95%.) **First-year students who submitted SAT scores:** 89%. Scores (25/75 percentile): Verbal: 460-570, Math: 480-590, Combined: 940-1160. **First-year students submitting ACT scores:** 38%. Scores (25/75 percentile): English: 18-24, Math: 18-24, Composite: 19-24.

ACADEMICS

Year founded: 1895. **Academic calendar:** Other. **Degrees offered:** bachelor's, post-bachelor's certificate, master's, post-master's certificate, doctorate. **Most popular majors:** 28% business, management, marketing, and related support services, 9% engineering, 9% health professions and related clinical sciences, 9% multi/interdisciplinary studies, 7% biological and biomedical sciences. **Major fields of study:** architecture and related services;

biological and biomedical sciences; business, management, marketing, and related support services; communication, journalism, and related programs; computer and information sciences and support services; engineering; English language and literature/letters; family and consumer sciences/human sciences; foreign languages, literatures, and linguistics; health professions and related clinical sciences; history; mathematics and statistics; multi/interdisciplinary studies; parks, recreation, leisure, and fitness studies; philosophy and religious studies; physical sciences; psychology; public administration and social service professions; security and protective services; social sciences; visual and performing arts. **Areas of required coursework:** arts/fine arts, computer literacy, mathematics, English (including composition), foreign languages, sciences (biological or physical), history, social science, other. **Pre-professional programs:** pre-law, pre-dentistry, pre-medicine, pre-pharmacy. **Special academic programs:** cooperative (work-study plan) program, cross-registration, distance learning, double major, dual enrollment, English as a Second Language (ESL), honors program, independent study, internships, student-designed major, study abroad, teacher certificate program. **Teacher certification offered in:** early childhood, middle/junior high, secondary, bilingual/bicultural. **Cooperative education programs:** business, engineering, other. **Reserve Officers Training Corps (ROTC):** Army ROTC: Offered on campus; Air Force ROTC: Offered at cooperating institution (Texas Christian University). **Faculty and instruction (2005-2006):** Total instructional faculty: 781 full-time, 332 part-time (60% men; 40% women; 18% minorities). Student/faculty ratio: 22/1. Classes of fewer than 20 students: 27%; of 20 to 49 students: 48%; of 50 or more students: 25%. **Advanced Placement and International Baccalaureate credit:** AP tests may be used for: Credit only. Scores accepted: 3, 4, 5. International Baccalaureate exams may be used for: Credit only. **Freshmen returning for sophomore year:** 70%. **Graduation rates:** Four-year: 15%; five-year: 33%; six-year: 40%.

COSTS AND FINANCIAL AID

Financial aid office: (817) 272-3568. **Expenses (2006-2007):** Tuition and fees 2006-2007: $6,400 in state, $14,760 out of state; room/board: $5,820. **Financial aid:** Priority filing date for institution's financial aid form: May 15. In 2005-2006, 67% of undergraduates applied for financial aid. Of those, 52% were determined to have financial need; 19% had their need fully met. Average financial aid package (proportion receiving): $9,016 (52%). Average amount of gift aid, such as scholarships or grants (proportion receiving): $4,229 (37%). Average amount of self-help aid, such as work study or loans (proportion receiving): $6,023 (45%). Average need-based loan (excluding PLUS or other private loans): $5,798. Among students who received need-based aid, the average percentage of need met: 74%. Among students who received aid based on merit, the average award (and the proportion receiving): $2,323 (13%). The average athletic scholarship (and the proportion receiving): $7,264 (1%). Average amount of debt of borrowers graduating in 2005: $16,780. Proportion who borrowed: 42%.

CAMPUS LIFE AND EXTRACURRICULAR ACTIVITIES

Campus housing available: coed dorms, women's dorms, men's dorms, sorority housing, fraternity housing, apartments for married students, apartment for single students, other housing options. Students who live in college-owned, operated, or affiliated housing: 14%. **Clubs and organizations:** Number of student organizations: 459. Activities include: choral groups, concert band, dance, drama/theater, jazz band, literary magazine, marching band, music ensembles, opera, radio station, student government, student newspaper, student film society, symphony orchestra. Number of fraternities: 12; sororities: 13. Proportion of men in fraternities: 4%; of women in sororities: 3%. Average proportion of students who stay on campus on weekends: 60%. **Sports program (2005-2006):** Member of NCAA I. *Men's intercollegiate varsity sports:* baseball, basketball, cross-country, golf, tennis, track and field (indoor), track and field (outdoor). *Women's intercollegiate varsity sports:* basketball, cross-country, softball, tennis, track and field (indoor), track and field (outdoor), volleyball.

SERVICES AND FACILITIES

Basic services: nonremedial tutoring, placement service, day care, health service, health insurance. **Remedial assistance:** reading, math, writing, study skills. **Counseling services:** minority student, career, military, personal, veteran student, academic, older student, psychological, birth control. **For learning-disabled students:** School does not offer a structured program with separate admission and additional fees. Total undergraduates in learning-disabled program or receiving services: 95. Services include: remedial math, remedial English, reading machines, remedial reading, tape recorders, note-taking services, readers, extended time for tests, tutors, priority seating, other testing accomodations. **Library:** Number of titles: 1,144,133; number of current serial subscriptions: 37,437. **Information technology resources:** Students are not required to lease or own a computer. Number of campus computers available to all students: 1,000. School has a wireless network. Approximate number of users that can be accommodated: 10,000. Proportion of college-owned housing units wired for high-speed internet access: 60%. **Campus safety:** Security services offered: 24-hour foot-and-vehicle patrols, late-night transport/escort service, 24-hour emergency telephones, lighted pathways/sidewalks, controlled dormitory access (key, security card, etc).

TRANSFER AND INTERNATIONAL STUDENTS

Transfer students: May apply for admission for the following academic terms: Fall, Winter, Spring, Summer. Applicants need a minimum number of credits to apply. For fall 2005: Transfer applications received: 5,564. . Transfer applicants offered admission: 5,337. Transfer applicants enrolled: 3,400. **International students:** Number of foreign undergraduates: 935 (5% of student body). Number of countries represented: 147. Minimum TOEFL score required: 550 (paper); 213 (computer).

University of Texas–Austin

- ■ **Address:** Main Building, Room 7, Austin, TX 78712-1111
- ■ **Website:** http://www.utexas.edu
- ■ **Public**
- ■ **Enrollment:** 33,682 full-time; 3,196 part-time

KEY STATS
- ✔ **U.S News College Ranking:** 47, National Universities
- ✔ **SAT Score (25th/75th percentile):** 1110-1360
- ✔ **Tuition:** 2006-2007: $7,630 in state, $20,364 out of state
- **Selectivity:** More selective   **Room/board:** $8,176
- **Acceptance rate:** 51%   **Average debt:** $16,850
- **Student/faculty ratio:** 18/1   **Proportion who borrowed:** 39%

UNDERGRADUATE STUDENT BODY STATS
2005-2006 enrollment: 33,682 full-time; 3,196 part-time. Men: 48%; women: 52%. **Ethnic makeup:** African American: 4%; Asian American: 17%; Hispanic: 16%; White: 59%; International: 3%.

ADMISSIONS FACTS AND FIGURES
Phone: (512) 475-7440. **Email:** askadmit@uts.cc.utexas.edu. **Website:** http://www.utexas.edu. **Application deadlines for fall 2007:** Regular decision: February 1. Early decision: Not offered. Early action: Not offered. Admission can be deferred. **Application fee:** $60. Common application is accepted. **To apply online, go to:** http://bealonghorn.utexas.edu/freshmen/admission/requirements/. **Admissions requirements/recommendations:** High school units required (recommended): English: 4; Mathematics: 3 (4); Science: 2 (3); Foreign language: 2 (3); Social studies: 3; Academic electives: 2; Total units: 16. Tests: The college uses SAT or ACT scores in admissions decisions. Either SAT or ACT required. For admission to the fall 2007 entering class, the school will accept: ACT with writing. Campus visit: Recommended. Admissions interview: Neither required nor recommended. Off-campus interview: Not available. **Factors that count in admissions decisions:** *Academic:* Secondary school record: Very important. Class rank: Very important. Letters of recommendation: Considered. Standardized test scores: Important. Essay: Important. *Nonacademic:* Interview: Not considered. Extracurricular activities: Important. Talent/ability: Important. Character/personal qualities: Considered. Alumni/ae relationship: Not considered. Geographical residence: Considered. State residency: Considered. Religious affiliation/commitment: Not considered. Minority status: Considered. Volunteer work: Important. Work experience: Important. **Other schools with the greatest overlap in applicants:** Baylor University; Rice University; Texas A&M University–College Station; Texas State University–San Marcos; Texas Tech University. **Admissions statistics for the fall 2005 entering class:** Total applicants: 23,925. Total accepted: 12,207. Freshmen enrolled: 6,836; 5% were from out of state. Overall acceptance rate: 51%. **Credentials of fall 2005 freshmen:** 68% ranked in the top 10 percent of their high school class; 92% were in the top 25 percent, and 99% were in the top half. (Proportion submitting class standing: 98%.) **First-year students who submitted SAT scores:** 94%. Scores (25/75 percentile): Verbal: 540-670, Math: 570-690, Combined: 1110-

1360. **First-year students submitting ACT scores:** 29%. Scores (25/75 percentile): English: 22-29, Math: 23-29, Composite: 23-29.

ACADEMICS
Year founded: 1883. **Academic calendar:** Semester. **Degrees offered:** bachelor's, master's, first professional, doctorate. **Most popular majors:** 16% social sciences, 13% business, management, marketing, and related support services, 13% communication, journalism, and related programs, 10% engineering, 8% biological and biomedical sciences. **Major fields of study:** architecture and related services; area, ethnic, cultural, and gender studies; biological and biomedical sciences; business, management, marketing, and related support services; communication, journalism, and related programs; computer and information sciences and support services; engineering; English language and literature/letters; family and consumer sciences/human sciences; foreign languages, literatures, and linguistics; health professions and related clinical sciences; history; liberal arts and sciences studies, and humanities; mathematics and statistics; multi/interdisciplinary studies; parks, recreation, leisure, and fitness studies; philosophy and religious studies; physical sciences; psychology; public administration and social service professions; social sciences; visual and performing arts. **Areas of required coursework:** arts/fine arts, humanities, mathematics, English (including composition), foreign languages, sciences (biological or physical), history, social science. **Pre-professional programs:** pre-pharmacy. **Special academic programs:** accelerated program, cooperative (work-study plan) program, distance learning, double major, dual enrollment, English as a Second Language (ESL), honors program, independent study, internships, liberal arts/career combination, student-designed major, study abroad, teacher certificate program. **Teacher certification offered in:** early childhood, special education, elementary, middle/junior high, secondary, bilingual/bicultural. **Cooperative education programs:** engineering. **Reserve Officers Training Corps (ROTC):** Army ROTC: Offered on campus; Navy ROTC: Offered on campus; Air Force ROTC: Offered on campus. **Faculty and instruction (2005-2006):** Total instructional faculty: 2,482 full-time, 252 part-time (64% men; 36% women; 17% minorities). Full-time faculty with Ph.D. or other terminal degree: 91%. Student/faculty ratio: 18/1. Classes of fewer than 20 students: 34%; of 20 to 49 students: 43%; of 50 or more students: 22%. **Advanced Placement and International Baccalaureate credit:** AP tests may be used for: Credit only. Scores accepted: 2, 3, 4, 5. International Baccalaureate exams may be used for: Credit only. **Freshmen returning for sophomore year:** 92%. **Graduation rates:** Four-year: 42%; five-year: 69%; six-year: 75%.

COSTS AND FINANCIAL AID
Financial aid office: (512) 475-6203. **Expenses (2006-2007):** Tuition and fees 2006-2007: $7,630 in state, $20,364 out of state; room/board: $8,176. Estimated books and supplies: $800; transportation: $894; personal expenses: $2,258. **Financial aid:** Priority filing date for institution's financial aid form: April 1. In 2005-2006, 74% of undergraduates applied for financial aid. Of those, 57% were determined to have financial need; 88% had their need fully met. Average financial aid package (proportion receiving): $9,210 (54%). Average amount of gift aid, such as scholarships or grants (proportion receiving): $5,890 (47%). Average amount of self-help aid, such as work study or loans (proportion receiving): $4,650 (51%). Average need-based loan (excluding PLUS or other private loans): $4,660. Among students who received need-based aid, the average percentage of need met: 90%. Among students who received aid based on merit, the average award (and the proportion receiving): $3,120 (29%). Average amount of debt of borrowers graduating in 2005: $16,850. Proportion who borrowed: 39%.

CAMPUS LIFE AND EXTRACURRICULAR ACTIVITIES
Campus housing available (% using): coed dorms (83%), women's dorms (14%), men's dorms (3%), apartments for married students (0%), apartment for single students (0%), other housing options. Students who live in college-owned, operated, or affiliated housing: 19%. **Clubs and organizations:** Number of student organizations: 900. Activities include: choral groups, concert band, dance, drama/theater, jazz band, literary magazine, marching band, music ensembles, musical theater, opera, pep band, radio station, student government, student newspaper, student film society, symphony orchestra, television station, yearbook. Number of fraternities: 27; sororities: 26. Proportion of men in fraternities: 9%; of women in sororities: 13%. **Sports program (2005-2006):** Member of NCAA I. *Men's intercollegiate varsity sports:* baseball, basketball, cross-country, football, golf, swimming and diving, tennis, track and field (indoor), track and field (outdoor). *Women's intercollegiate varsity sports:* basketball, cross-country, golf, rowing, soccer, softball, swimming and diving, tennis, track and field (indoor), track and field (outdoor), volleyball.

SERVICES AND FACILITIES

Basic services: nonremedial tutoring, women's center, placement service, day care, health service, health insurance. **Remedial assistance:** reading, math, writing, study skills. **Counseling services:** minority student, career, personal, academic, older student, psychological, birth control. **For learning-disabled students:** School does not offer a structured program with separate admission and additional fees. Services include: learning center, extended time for tests, tutors, priority registration, other. **Library:** Number of titles: 8,937,002; number of current serial subscriptions: 46,857. **Information technology resources:** Students are not required to lease or own a computer. Number of campus computers available to all students: 3,797. School has a wireless network. Approximate number of users that can be accommodated: 15,000. Proportion of college-owned housing units wired for high-speed internet access: 100%. **Campus safety:** Security services offered: 24-hour foot-and-vehicle patrols, late-night transport/escort service, 24-hour emergency telephones, lighted pathways/sidewalks, controlled dormitory access (key, security card, etc).

TRANSFER AND INTERNATIONAL STUDENTS

Transfer students: May apply for admission for the following academic terms: Fall, Spring, Summer. Applicants need a minimum number of credits to apply. For fall 2005: Transfer applications received: 7,108. Transfer applicants offered admission: 2,746. Transfer applicants enrolled: 2,160. **International students:** Number of foreign undergraduates: 1220 (3% of student body). Number of countries represented: 125. Minimum TOEFL score required: 550 (paper); 213 (computer).

University of Texas–Brownsville

- **Address:** 80 Fort Brown, Brownsville, TX 78520
- **Website:** http://www.utb.edu
- **Public**
- **Enrollment:** 5,560 full-time; 6,907 part-time

KEY STATS

- ✔ **U.S News College Ranking:** fourth tier, Universities–Master's (West)
- ✔ **SAT or ACT Score (25th/75th percentile):** N/A
- ✔ **Tuition:** 2006-2007: $4,025 in state, $12,543 out of state

Selectivity: Less selective	**Room/board:** $5,166
Acceptance rate: 100%	**Average debt:** N/A
Student/faculty ratio: 18/1	**Proportion who borrowed:** N/A

UNDERGRADUATE STUDENT BODY STATS

2005-2006 enrollment: 5,560 full-time; 6,907 part-time. Men: 40%; women: 60%. **Ethnic makeup:** Hispanic: 91%; White: 5%; International: 3%.

ADMISSIONS FACTS AND FIGURES

Phone: (956) 882-8295. **Email:** admissions@utb.edu. **Website:** http://www.utb.edu. **Application deadlines for fall 2007:** Regular decision: August 1; decision sent by August 1. Early decision: Not offered. Early action: Not offered. Admission can be deferred. **Application fee:** $25. Common application is not accepted. **Admissions requirements/recommendations:** High school units required (recommended): English: 4 (4); Mathematics: 2 (4); Science: 2 (3); Foreign language: 3 (3); Social studies: 4 (4); History: 2 (2); Academic electives: 1 (4); Total units: 19 (25). Tests: The college does not use SAT or ACT scores in admissions decisions. Neither SAT nor ACT required. Campus visit: Neither required nor recommended. Admissions interview: Neither required nor recommended. Off-campus interview: May be arranged. **Factors that count in admissions decisions:** *Academic:* Secondary school record: Not considered. Class rank: Not considered. Letters of recommendation: Not considered. Standardized test scores: Not considered. Essay: Not considered. *Nonacademic:* Interview: Not considered. Extracurricular activities: Not considered. Talent/ability: Not considered. Character/personal qualities: Not considered. Alumni/ae relationship: Not considered. Geographical residence: Not considered. State residency: Not considered. Religious affiliation/commitment: Not considered. Minority status: Not considered. Volunteer work: Not considered. Work experience: Not considered. **Admissions statistics for the fall 2005 entering class:** Total applicants: 3,191. Total accepted: 3,191. Freshmen enrolled: 1,415; 1% were from out of state. Overall acceptance rate: 100%. **Credentials of fall 2005 freshmen:** 5% ranked in the top 10 percent of their high school class; 19%

were in the top 25 percent, and 53% were in the top half. (Proportion submitting class standing: 72%.)

ACADEMICS

Year founded: 1926. **Academic calendar:** Semester. **Degrees offered:** certificate, associate, bachelor's, master's, first professional certificate. **Most popular majors:** 15% business administration and management, 15% multi/interdisciplinary studies, 8% psychology, 6% criminal justice/law enforcement administration, 5% mathematics. **Major fields of study:** biological and biomedical sciences; business, management, marketing, and related support services; communication, journalism, and related programs; computer and information sciences and support services; engineering; engineering technologies/technicians; English language and literature/letters; foreign languages, literatures, and linguistics; health professions and related clinical sciences; history; mathematics and statistics; multi/interdisciplinary studies; natural resources and conservation; parks, recreation, leisure, and fitness studies; physical sciences; psychology; security and protective services; social sciences; visual and performing arts. **Areas of required coursework:** arts/fine arts, humanities, computer literacy, mathematics, English (including composition), philosophy, foreign languages, sciences (biological or physical), history, social science. **Special academic programs:** cooperative (work-study plan) program, distance learning, double major, dual enrollment, English as a Second Language (ESL), independent study, internships, teacher certificate program. **Teacher certification offered in:** early childhood, special education, elementary, vo-tech, middle/junior high, adult education, secondary, bilingual/bicultural. **Cooperative education programs:** business, computer science, engineering, health professions, social/behavioral science, technologies, vocational arts. **Faculty and instruction (2005-2006):** Total instructional faculty: 344 full-time, 315 part-time (54% men; 46% women; 57% minorities). Full-time faculty with Ph.D. or other terminal degree: 52%. Student/faculty ratio: 18/1. Classes of fewer than 20 students: 51%; of 20 to 49 students: 42%; of 50 or more students: 7%. **Advanced Placement and International Baccalaureate credit:** AP tests may be used for: Credit only. Scores accepted: 3, 4, 5. **Freshmen returning for sophomore year:** 67%. **Graduation rates:** Six-year: 35%.

COSTS AND FINANCIAL AID

Financial aid office: (956) 882-8277. **Expenses (2006-2007):** Tuition and fees 2006-2007: $4,025 in state, $12,543 out of state; room/board: $5,166. Estimated books and supplies: $577; transportation: $1,480; personal expenses: $2,368. **Financial aid:** Priority filing date for institution's financial aid form: March 1. In 2005-2006, 84% of undergraduates applied for financial aid. Of those, 80% were determined to have financial need; Average financial aid package (proportion receiving): $3,269 (78%). Average amount of gift aid, such as scholarships or grants (proportion receiving): $2,404 (72%). Average amount of self-help aid, such as work study or loans (proportion receiving): $1,968 (41%). Average need-based loan (excluding PLUS or other private loans): $1,858. Among students who received need-based aid, the average percentage of need met: 29%. Among students who received aid based on merit, the average award (and the proportion receiving): $964 (1%). The average athletic scholarship (and the proportion receiving): $2,196 (1%).

CAMPUS LIFE AND EXTRACURRICULAR ACTIVITIES

Campus housing available: women's dorms, men's dorms, special housing for disabled students. **Clubs and organizations:** Number of student organizations: 70. Activities include: choral groups, concert band, dance, drama/theater, jazz band, music ensembles, opera, radio station, student government, student newspaper. Average proportion of students who stay on campus on weekends: 1%.

SERVICES AND FACILITIES

Basic services: nonremedial tutoring, placement service, day care, health service, health insurance. **Remedial assistance:** reading, math, writing, study skills. **Counseling services:** minority student, career, military, personal, veteran student, academic, older student, psychological, birth control. **For learning-disabled students:** School does not offer a structured program with separate admission and additional fees. **Information technology resources:** Students are not required to lease or own a computer. Number of campus computers available to all students: 700. School has a wireless network. **Campus safety:** Security services offered: 24-hour foot-and-vehicle patrols, 24-hour emergency telephones, lighted pathways/sidewalks, controlled dormitory access (key, security card, etc).

TRANSFER AND INTERNATIONAL STUDENTS

Transfer students: May apply for admission for the following academic terms: Fall, Winter, Spring, Summer. Applicants need a minimum number of credits to apply. For fall 2005: Transfer applications received: 1,114. Transfer applicants offered admission: 1,114. Transfer applicants enrolled: 549. **International students:** Number of foreign undergraduates: 323 (3% of student body). Number of countries represented: 20.

University of Texas–Dallas

- **Address:** PO Box 830688, Richardson, TX 75083-0688
- **Website:** http://www.utdallas.edu
- **Public**
- **Enrollment:** 6,613 full-time; 2,799 part-time

KEY STATS

- ✔ **U.S News College Ranking:** third tier, National Universities
- ✔ **SAT Score (25th/75th percentile):** 1120-1370
- ✔ **Tuition:** 2006-2007: $7,330 in state, $15,580 out of state

Selectivity: More selective	**Room/board:** $6,540
Acceptance rate: 51%	**Average debt:** N/A
Student/faculty ratio: 20/1	**Proportion who borrowed:** N/A

UNDERGRADUATE STUDENT BODY STATS

2005-2006 enrollment: 6,613 full-time; 2,799 part-time. Men: 54%; women: 46%. **Ethnic makeup:** African American: 7%; American-Indian: 1%; Asian American: 20%; Hispanic: 10%; White: 58%; International: 5%.

ADMISSIONS FACTS AND FIGURES

Phone: (972) 883-2270. **Email:** interest@utdallas.edu. **Website:** http://www.utdallas.edu. **Application deadlines for fall 2007:** Regular decision: July 1. Early decision: Not offered. Early action: Not offered. Admission can be deferred. **Application fee:** $50. Common application is not accepted. **To apply online, go to:** http://www.utdallas.edu/student/admissions/prospective/index.html. **Admissions requirements/recommendations:** High school units required (recommended): English: 4 (4); Mathematics: 4 (4); Science: 3 (3); Foreign language: 2 (3); Social studies: 3 (4); Academic electives: 2 (3); Total units: 18 (25). Tests: The college uses SAT or ACT scores in admissions decisions. Either SAT or ACT required. For admission to the fall 2007 entering class, the school will accept: ACT with writing. Campus visit: Recommended. Admissions interview: Neither required nor recommended. Off-campus interview: Not available. **Factors that count in admissions decisions:** *Academic:* Secondary school record: Very important. Class rank: Very important. Letters of recommendation: Considered. Standardized test scores: Very important. Essay: Important. *Nonacademic:* Interview: Not considered. Extracurricular activities: Important. Talent/ability: Considered. Character/personal qualities: Considered. Alumni/ae relationship: Not considered. Geographical residence: Considered. State residency: Considered. Religious affiliation/commitment: Not considered. Minority status: Not considered. Volunteer work: Considered. Work experience: Considered. **Other schools with the greatest overlap in applicants:** Texas A&M University–College Station; University of North Texas; University of Oklahoma; University of Texas–Austin. **Admissions statistics for the fall 2005 entering class:** Total applicants: 5,584. Total accepted: 2,850. Freshmen enrolled: 1,060; 4% were from out of state. Overall acceptance rate: 51%. **Credentials of fall 2005 freshmen:** 41% ranked in the top 10 percent of their high school class; 74% were in the top 25 percent, and 96% were in the top half. (Proportion submitting class standing: 90%.) **Average high school grade point average:** 3.6. **First-year students who submitted SAT scores:** 96%. Scores (25/75 percentile): Verbal: 540-670, Math: 580-700, Combined: 1120-1370. **First-year students submitting ACT scores:** 39%. Scores (25/75 percentile): English: 22-29, Math: 24-29, Composite: 24-29.

ACADEMICS

Year founded: 1969. **Academic calendar:** Semester. **Degrees offered:** certificate, bachelor's, post-bachelor's certificate, master's, doctorate. **Most popular majors:** 31% business, management, marketing, and related support services, 15% multi/interdisciplinary studies, 11% computer and information sciences and support services, 9% engineering, 7% psychology. **Major fields of study:** area, ethnic, cultural, and gender studies; biological and biomedical sciences; business, management, marketing, and related support serv-ices; computer and information sciences and support services; engineering; health professions and related clinical sciences; liberal arts and sciences studies, and humanities; mathematics and statistics; multi/interdisciplinary studies; physical sciences; psychology; public administration and social service professions; social sciences; visual and performing arts. **Areas of required coursework:** arts/fine arts, humanities, computer literacy, mathematics, English (including composition), sciences (biological or physical), history, social science. **Pre-professional programs:** pre-law, pre-dentistry, pre-medicine. **Special academic programs:** accelerated program, cooperative (work-study plan) program, cross-registration, distance learning, double major, dual enrollment, honors program, independent study, internships, liberal arts/career combination, student-designed major, study abroad, teacher certificate program, other. **Teacher certification offered in:** early childhood, elementary, middle/junior high, secondary. **Cooperative education programs:** other. **Reserve Officers Training Corps (ROTC):** Army ROTC: Offered at cooperating institution (University of Texas at Arlington); Air Force ROTC: Offered at cooperating institution (University of North Texas). **Faculty and instruction (2005-2006):** Total instructional faculty: 457 full-time, 239 part-time (67% men; 33% women; 24% minorities). Full-time faculty with Ph.D. or other terminal degree: 92%. Student/faculty ratio: 20/1. Classes of fewer than 20 students: 28%; of 20 to 49 students: 41%; of 50 or more students: 31%. **Advanced Placement and International Baccalaureate credit:** AP tests may be used for: Credit only. Scores accepted: 3, 4, 5. International Baccalaureate exams may be used for: Credit only. **Freshmen returning for sophomore year:** 82%. **Graduation rates:** Four-year: 30%; five-year: 50%; six-year: 56%. **Graduate study:** 17% of students pursue further study immediately upon graduation. Fields in which graduates pursue further study: Master of Business Administration (MBA), 3%; law, 1%; medicine, 5%; engineering, 3%; education, 1%; arts and sciences, 2%.

COSTS AND FINANCIAL AID

Financial aid office: (972) 883-2941. **Expenses (2006-2007):** Tuition and fees 2006-2007: $7,330 in state, $15,580 out of state; room/board: $6,540. Estimated books and supplies: $1,200; transportation: $2,146; personal expenses: $1,848. **Financial aid:** Priority filing date for institution's financial aid form: March 31; deadline: September 29. In 2005-2006, 68% of undergraduates applied for financial aid. Of those, 40% were determined to have financial need; 29% had their need fully met. Average financial aid package (proportion receiving): $9,016 (40%). Average amount of gift aid, such as scholarships or grants (proportion receiving): $4,208 (30%). Average amount of self-help aid, such as work study or loans (proportion receiving): $5,246 (36%). Average need-based loan (excluding PLUS or other private loans): $4,670. Among students who received need-based aid, the average percentage of need met: 72%. Among students who received aid based on merit, the average award (and the proportion receiving): $8,114 (19%). The average athletic scholarship (and the proportion receiving): $0 (0%).

CAMPUS LIFE AND EXTRACURRICULAR ACTIVITIES

Campus housing available (% using): other housing options (100%). Students who live in college-owned, operated, or affiliated housing: 21%. **Student employment:** During the 2005-2006 academic year, 9% of undergraduates worked on campus. Average per-year earnings: $3,052. **Clubs and organizations:** Number of student organizations: 264. Activities include: dance, drama/theater, radio station, student government, student newspaper. Number of fraternities: 6; sororities: 5. Proportion of men in fraternities: 5%; of women in sororities: 3%. Average proportion of students who stay on campus on weekends: 18%. **Sports program (2005-2006):** Member of NCAA III. *Men's intercollegiate varsity sports:* baseball, basketball, cheerleading, cross-country, golf, soccer, tennis. *Women's intercollegiate varsity sports:* basketball, cheerleading, cross-country, golf, soccer, softball, tennis.

SERVICES AND FACILITIES

Basic services: nonremedial tutoring, women's center, health service, other. **Remedial assistance:** reading, math, writing, study skills. **Counseling services:** minority student, career, personal, veteran student, academic, older student, psychological, birth control. **For learning-disabled students:** School does not offer a structured program with separate admission and additional fees. Total undergraduates in learning-disabled program or receiving services: 52. Services include: remedial math, reading machines, remedial reading, tape recorders, other special classes, note-taking services, oral tests, readers, extended time for tests, tutors, other testing accomodations, other. **Library:** Number of titles: 947,305; number of current serial subscriptions: 28,554. **Information technology resources:** Students are not required to lease or own a computer. Number of campus computers available to all students: 700. School has a wireless network. Approximate number of users that can be accommodated: 5,000. Proportion of college-owned housing units wired for high-speed internet access: 0%. **Campus safety:** Security services offered: 24-hour foot-and-vehicle patrols, late-night transport/escort service, 24-hour emergency telephones, lighted pathways/sidewalks.

TRANSFER AND INTERNATIONAL STUDENTS

Transfer students: May apply for admission for the following academic terms: Fall, Spring, Summer. Applicants do not need a minimum number of credits to apply. For fall 2005: Transfer applications received: 4,925. Transfer applicants offered admission: 3,125. Transfer applicants enrolled: 1,563. **International students:** Number of foreign undergraduates: 432 (5% of student body). Number of countries represented: 77. Minimum TOEFL score required: 550 (paper); 213 (computer).

University of Texas–El Paso

- **Address:** 500 W. University Avenue, El Paso, TX 79968
- **Website:** http://www.utep.edu
- **Public**
- **Enrollment:** 10,975 full-time; 5,062 part-time

KEY STATS

✔ **U.S News College Ranking:** fourth tier, National Universities
✔ **SAT Score (25th/75th percentile):** 800-1030
✔ **Tuition:** 2005-2006: $4,888 in state, $13,168 out of state
  Selectivity: Less selective   **Room/board:** N/A
  Acceptance rate: 99%   **Average debt:** $6,546
  Student/faculty ratio: 19/1   **Proportion who borrowed:** 47%

UNDERGRADUATE STUDENT BODY STATS

2005-2006 enrollment: 10,975 full-time; 5,062 part-time. Men: 45%; women: 55%. **Ethnic makeup:** African American: 2%; Asian American: 1%; Hispanic: 76%; White: 11%; International: 10%.

ADMISSIONS FACTS AND FIGURES

Phone: (915) 747-5890. **Email:** futureminer@utep.edu. **Website:** http://www.utep.edu. **Application deadlines for fall 2007:** Regular decision: July 31. Early decision: Not offered. Early action: Send application by: N/A; Decision sent by: N/A. Admission can be deferred. Common application is not accepted. **To apply online, go to:** https://www.applytexas.org/adappc/commonapp.WBX. **Admissions requirements/recommendations:** High school units required (recommended): English: (4); Mathematics: (4); Science: (3); Foreign language: (2); Social studies: (2); History: (2); Total units: (22). Tests: The college uses SAT or ACT scores in admissions decisions. Neither SAT nor ACT required. Campus visit: Recommended. **Factors that count in admissions decisions:** *Academic:* Secondary school record: Very important. Class rank: Very important. Letters of recommendation: Considered. Standardized test scores: Important. Essay: Not considered. *Nonacademic:* Interview: Considered. Extracurricular activities: Considered. Talent/ability: Considered. Character/personal qualities: Considered. Alumni/ae relationship: Considered. Geographical residence: Considered. State residency: Important. Religious affiliation/commitment: Not considered. Minority status: Not considered. Volunteer work: Considered. Work experience: Considered. **Admissions statistics for the fall 2005 entering class:** Total applicants: 4,012. Total accepted: 3,984. Freshmen enrolled: 2,289; 3% were from out of state. Overall acceptance rate: 99%. Non-early acceptance rate: 99%. **Credentials of fall 2005 freshmen:** 17% ranked in the top 10 percent of their high school class; 41% were in the top 25 percent, and 70% were in the top half. (Proportion submitting class standing: 83%.) **Average high school grade point average:** 3.5. **First-year students who submitted SAT scores:** 75%. Scores (25/75 percentile): Verbal: 400-520, Math: 400-510, Combined: 800-1030. **First-year students submitting ACT scores:** 19%. Scores (25/75 percentile): English: 13-20, Math: 15-20, Composite: 15-20.

ACADEMICS

Year founded: 1913. **Academic calendar:** Semester. **Degrees offered:** bachelor's, master's, doctorate. **Most popular majors:** 21% business, management, marketing, and related support services, 16% multi/interdisciplinary studies, 10% engineering, 10% health professions and related clinical sciences, 6% biological and biomedical sciences. **Major fields of study:** area, ethnic, cultural, and gender studies; biological and biomedical sciences; business, management, marketing, and related support services; communication,

journalism, and related programs; computer and information sciences and support services; engineering; English language and literature/letters; foreign languages, literatures, and linguistics; health professions and related clinical sciences; history; mathematics and statistics; multi/interdisciplinary studies; natural resources and conservation; parks, recreation, leisure, and fitness studies; philosophy and religious studies; physical sciences; psychology; public administration and social service professions; security and protective services; social sciences; visual and performing arts. **Areas of required coursework:** arts/fine arts, humanities, computer literacy, mathematics, English (including composition), foreign languages, sciences (biological or physical), history, social science, other. **Pre-professional programs:** pre-law, pre-dentistry, pre-medicine, pre-veterinary science, pre-optometry, pre-pharmacy, other. **Special academic programs:** accelerated program, cooperative (work-study plan) program, cross-registration, distance learning, double major, dual enrollment, English as a Second Language (ESL), exchange student program (domestic), honors program, independent study, internships, study abroad, teacher certificate program, weekend college. **Teacher certification offered in:** early childhood, special education, elementary, vo-tech, middle/junior high, secondary, bilingual/bicultural. **Cooperative education programs:** health professions, other. **Reserve Officers Training Corps (ROTC):** Army ROTC: Offered on campus; Air Force ROTC: Offered on campus. **Faculty and instruction (2005-2006):** Total instructional faculty: 680 full-time, 379 part-time (59% men; 41% women; 37% minorities). Student/faculty ratio: 19/1. Classes of fewer than 20 students: 31%; of 20 to 49 students: 56%; of 50 or more students: 13%. **Advanced Placement and International Baccalaureate credit:** AP tests may be used for: Credit and/or placement. Scores accepted: 3, 4, 5. International Baccalaureate exams may be used for: Credit and/or placement. **Freshmen returning for sophomore year:** 69%. **Graduation rates:** Four-year: 5%; five-year: 18%; six-year: 28%.

COSTS AND FINANCIAL AID

Financial aid office: (915) 747-5204. **Expenses (2005-2006):** Tuition and fees 2005-2006: $4,888 in state, $13,168 out of state; room/board: N/A. Estimated books and supplies: $890 personal expenses: $1,376. **Financial aid:** Priority filing date for institution's financial aid form: March 15. In 2005-2006, 68% of undergraduates applied for financial aid. Of those, 55% were determined to have financial need; 32% had their need fully met. Average financial aid package (proportion receiving): $9,294 (54%). Average amount of gift aid, such as scholarships or grants (proportion receiving): $4,846 (47%). Average amount of self-help aid, such as work study or loans (proportion receiving): $5,157 (51%). Average need-based loan (excluding PLUS or other private loans): $4,922. Among students who received need-based aid, the average percentage of need met: 78%. Among students who received aid based on merit, the average award (and the proportion receiving): $1,482 (6%). The average athletic scholarship (and the proportion receiving): $9,357 (2%). Average amount of debt of borrowers graduating in 2005: $6,546. Proportion who borrowed: 47%.

CAMPUS LIFE AND EXTRACURRICULAR ACTIVITIES

Campus housing available: apartment for single students, special housing for disabled students. **Student employment:** During the 2005-2006 academic year, 10% of undergraduates worked on campus. Average per-year earnings: $6,000. **Clubs and organizations:** Number of student organizations: 155. Activities include: choral groups, concert band, dance, drama/theater, jazz band, literary magazine, marching band, music ensembles, musical theater, opera, pep band, radio station, student government, student newspaper, student film society, symphony orchestra. Number of fraternities: 6; sororities: 8. Average proportion of students who stay on campus on weekends: 2%. **Sports program (2005-2006):** Member of NCAA I. *Men's intercollegiate varsity sports:* basketball, cross-country, football, golf, track and field (indoor), track and field (outdoor). *Women's intercollegiate varsity sports:* basketball, cross-country, golf, riflery, soccer, softball, tennis, track and field (indoor), track and field (outdoor), volleyball.

SERVICES AND FACILITIES

Basic services: nonremedial tutoring, women's center, day care, health service, health insurance. **Remedial assistance:** reading, math, writing, study skills. **Counseling services:** minority student, career, personal, older student, psychological. **For learning-disabled students:** Services include: reading machines, tape recorders, diagnostic testing service, note-taking services, oral tests, readers, extended time for tests, tutors. **Library:** Number of titles: 1,042,847; number of current serial subscriptions: 16,330. **Information technology resources:** Students are not required to lease or own a computer. Number of campus computers available to all students: 10,100. **Campus safety:** Security services offered: 24-hour foot-and-vehicle patrols, late-night transport/escort service, 24-hour emergency telephones, lighted pathways/sidewalks, student patrols, controlled dormitory access (key, security card, etc).

TRANSFER AND INTERNATIONAL STUDENTS

Transfer students: May apply for admission for the following academic terms: Fall, Spring, Summer. Applicants need a minimum number of credits to apply. For fall 2005: Transfer applications received: 1,863. Transfer applicants offered admission: 1,793. Transfer applicants enrolled: 1,126. **International students:** Number of foreign undergraduates: 1570 (10% of student body). Number of countries represented: 77. Minimum TOEFL score required: 500 (paper); 173 (computer).

University of Texas of the Permian Basin

- ■ **Address:** 4901 E. University Boulevard, Odessa, TX 79762-0001
- ■ **Website:** http://www.utpb.edu
- ■ **Public**
- ■ **Enrollment:** 1,886 full-time; 735 part-time

KEY STATS

✔ **U.S News College Ranking:** fourth tier, Universities–Master's (West)
✔ **SAT Score (25th/75th percentile):** 860-1080
✔ **Tuition:** 2006-2007: $4,650 in state, $12,540 out of state

Selectivity: Selective	**Room/board:** $4,088
Acceptance rate: 86%	**Average debt:** $14,870
Student/faculty ratio: 18/1	**Proportion who borrowed:** 48%

UNDERGRADUATE STUDENT BODY STATS

2005-2006 enrollment: 1,886 full-time; 735 part-time. Men: 39%; women: 61%. **Ethnic makeup:** African American: 4%; American-Indian: 1%; Asian American: 1%; Hispanic: 37%; White: 56%.

ADMISSIONS FACTS AND FIGURES

Phone: (432) 552-2605. **Email:** admissions@utpb.edu. **Website:** http://www.utpb.edu. **Application deadlines for fall 2007:** Regular decision: August 15. Early decision: Not offered. Early action: Not offered. Admission can be deferred. **Application fee:** None. Common application is not accepted. **Admissions requirements/recommendations:** High school units required (recommended): English: 4 (0); Mathematics: 3 (4); Science: 2 (3); Foreign language: 2 (0); Social studies: 2 (0); History: 1 (0); Academic electives: 6 (0); Total units: 20 (0). **Tests:** The college uses SAT or ACT scores in admissions decisions. Either SAT or ACT required. For admission to the fall 2007 entering class, the school will accept: ACT with writing, ACT without writing. Campus visit: Recommended. Admissions interview: Neither required nor recommended. Off-campus interview: Not available. **Factors that count in admissions decisions:** *Academic:* Secondary school record: Considered. Class rank: Very important. Letters of recommendation: Important. Standardized test scores: Very important. Essay: Not considered. *Nonacademic:* Interview: Not considered. Extracurricular activities: Not considered. Talent/ability: Not considered. Character/personal qualities: Not considered. Alumni/ae relationship: Not considered. Geographical residence: Not considered. State residency: Not considered. Religious affiliation/commitment: Not considered. Minority status: Not considered. Volunteer work: Not considered. Work experience: Not considered. **Other schools with the greatest overlap in applicants:** Angelo State University; Sul Ross State University; Texas A&M University–College Station; Texas Tech University; University of Texas–Austin. **Admissions statistics for the fall 2005 entering class:** Total applicants: 882. Total accepted: 758. Freshmen enrolled: 307; 2% were from out of state. Overall acceptance rate: 86%. **Credentials of fall 2005 freshmen:** 20% ranked in the top 10 percent of their high school class; 50% were in the top 25 percent, and 84% were in the top half. (Proportion submitting class standing: 83%.) **First-year students who submitted SAT scores:** 72%. Scores (25/75 percentile): Verbal: 430-540, Math: 430-540, Combined: 860-1080. **First-year students submitting ACT scores:** 24%. Scores (25/75 percentile): English: 18-24, Math: 17-24, Composite: 19-23.

ACADEMICS

Year founded: 1969. **Academic calendar:** Semester. **Degrees offered:** bachelor's, master's. **Most popular majors:** 16% business, management, marketing, and related support services, 12% family and consumer

sciences/human sciences, 10% history, 10% social sciences, 8% psychology. **Major fields of study:** biological and biomedical sciences; business, management, marketing, and related support services; communication, journalism, and related programs; computer and information sciences and support services; engineering technologies/technicians; English language and literature/letters; family and consumer sciences/human sciences; foreign languages, literatures, and linguistics; history; liberal arts and sciences studies, and humanities; mathematics and statistics; multi/interdisciplinary studies; natural resources and conservation; parks, recreation, leisure, and fitness studies; physical sciences; psychology; public administration and social service professions; security and protective services; social sciences; visual and performing arts. **Areas of required coursework:** arts/fine arts, humanities, computer literacy, mathematics, English (including composition), sciences (biological or physical), history, social science, other. **Special academic programs (% participation):** accelerated program, cross-registration, distance learning (34.7%), double major, English as a Second Language (ESL), honors program, independent study, internships, study abroad, teacher certificate program. **Teacher certification offered in:** early childhood, special education, elementary, middle/junior high, secondary, bilingual/bicultural. **Faculty and instruction (2005-2006):** Total instructional faculty: 110 full-time, 74 part-time (52% men; 48% women; 11% minorities). Full-time faculty with Ph.D. or other terminal degree: 88%. Student/faculty ratio: 18/1. Classes of fewer than 20 students: 45%; of 20 to 49 students: 46%; of 50 or more students: 9%. **Advanced Placement and International Baccalaureate credit:** AP tests may be used for: Credit and/or placement. Scores accepted: 4, 5. **Freshmen returning for sophomore year:** 63%. **Graduation rates:** Four-year: 15%; five-year: 32%; six-year: 30%.

COSTS AND FINANCIAL AID

Financial aid office: (432) 552-2620. **Expenses (2006-2007):** Tuition and fees 2006-2007: $4,650 in state, $12,540 out of state; room/board: $4,088. Estimated books and supplies: $855; transportation: $705; personal expenses: $1,763. **Financial aid:** Priority filing date for institution's financial aid form: May 1. In 2005-2006, 76% of undergraduates applied for financial aid. Of those, 67% were determined to have financial need; 13% had their need fully met. Average financial aid package (proportion receiving): $3,302 (67%). Average amount of gift aid, such as scholarships or grants (proportion receiving): $2,327 (37%). Average amount of self-help aid, such as work study or loans (proportion receiving): $2,013 (11%). Average need-based loan (excluding PLUS or other private loans): $1,105. Among students who received need-based aid, the average percentage of need met: 51%. Among students who received aid based on merit, the average award (and the proportion receiving): $765 (7%). The average athletic scholarship (and the proportion receiving): $1,262 (1%). Average amount of debt of borrowers graduating in 2005: $14,870. Proportion who borrowed: 48%.

CAMPUS LIFE AND EXTRACURRICULAR ACTIVITIES

Campus housing available (% using): apartments for married students (4%), apartment for single students (96%). Students who live in college-owned, operated, or affiliated housing: 16%. **Student employment:** During the 2005-2006 academic year, 10% of undergraduates worked on campus. Average per-year earnings: $3,000. **Clubs and organizations:** Number of student organizations: 25. Activities include: choral groups, dance, drama/theater, jazz band, literary magazine, music ensembles, pep band, radio station, student government, student newspaper, television station. Number of fraternities: 1; sororities: 0. Proportion of men in fraternities: 1%; Average proportion of students who stay on campus on weekends: 80%. **Sports program (2005-2006):** Member of NAIA. *Men's intercollegiate varsity sports:* baseball, basketball, cross-country, soccer, swimming and diving, track and field (indoor), track and field (outdoor). *Women's intercollegiate varsity sports:* basketball, cheerleading, cross-country, soccer, softball, swimming and diving, track and field (indoor), track and field (outdoor), volleyball.

SERVICES AND FACILITIES

Basic services: nonremedial tutoring, placement service, day care, health service, health insurance, other. **Remedial assistance:** reading, math, writing, study skills, other. **Counseling services:** career, personal, academic, psychological, other. **For learning-disabled students:** School does not offer a structured program with separate admission and additional fees. Total undergraduates in learning-disabled program or receiving services: 20. Services include: remedial math, remedial English, reading machines, remedial reading, tape recorders, videotaped classes, diagnostic testing service, untimed tests, note-taking services, special bookstore section, oral tests, learning center, readers, extended time for tests, tutors, priority registration, priority seating, texts on tape, other testing accomodations, other. **Library:** Number of titles: 287,000; number of current serial subscriptions: 698.

Information technology resources: Students are not required to lease or own a computer. Number of campus computers available to all students: 250. School has a wireless network. Approximate number of users that can be accommodated: 100. Proportion of college-owned housing units wired for high-speed internet access: 100%. **Campus safety:** Security services offered: 24-hour foot-and-vehicle patrols, late-night transport/escort service, 24-hour emergency telephones, lighted pathways/sidewalks, student patrols, controlled dormitory access (key, security card, etc).

TRANSFER AND INTERNATIONAL STUDENTS

Transfer students: May apply for admission for the following academic terms: Fall, Spring, Summer. Applicants need a minimum number of credits to apply. For fall 2005: Transfer applications received: 745. Transfer applicants offered admission: 685. Transfer applicants enrolled: 364. **International students:** Number of foreign undergraduates: 3. Number of countries represented: 6. Minimum TOEFL score required: 550 (paper); 213 (computer). Average TOEFL score: 580 (paper).

University of Texas–Pan American

- **Address:** 1201 W. University Drive, Edinburg, TX 78541-2999
- **Website:** http://www.utpa.edu
- **Public**
- **Enrollment:** 10,617 full-time; 4,325 part-time

KEY STATS

✔ **U.S News College Ranking:** fourth tier, Universities–Master's (West)
✔ **ACT Score (25th/75th percentile):** 16-21
✔ **Tuition:** 2006-2007: $4,160 in state, $12,410 out of state

Selectivity: Selective	**Room/board:** $4,700
Acceptance rate: N/A	**Average debt:** $12,453
Student/faculty ratio: 21/1	**Proportion who borrowed:** 84%

UNDERGRADUATE STUDENT BODY STATS

2005-2006 enrollment: 10,617 full-time; 4,325 part-time. Men: 42%; women: 58%. **Ethnic makeup:** Asian American: 1%; Hispanic: 88%; White: 6%; International: 4%.

ADMISSIONS FACTS AND FIGURES

Phone: (956) 381-2206. **Email:** admissions@panam.edu. **Website:** http://www.utpa.edu. **Application deadlines for fall 2007:** Regular decision: August 11. Early decision: Not offered. Early action: Not offered. Admission cannot be deferred. Common application is not accepted. **To apply online, go to:** http://admissions.panam.edu. **Admissions requirements/recommendations:** High school units required (recommended): English: 4 (4); Mathematics: 3 (3); Science: 3 (3); Foreign language: 2 (2); Social studies: 4 (4); Academic electives: 4 (4); Total units: 24 (24). Tests: The college uses SAT or ACT scores in admissions decisions. Either SAT or ACT required. For admission to the fall 2007 entering class, the school will accept: ACT with writing, ACT without writing. Campus visit: Recommended. Admissions interview: Neither required nor recommended. Off-campus interview: Not available. **Factors that count in admissions decisions:** *Academic:* Secondary school record: Important. Class rank: Important. Letters of recommendation: Not considered. Standardized test scores: Very important. Essay: Not considered. *Nonacademic:* Interview: Not considered. Extracurricular activities: Not considered. Talent/ability: Not considered. Character/personal qualities: Not considered. Alumni/ae relationship: Not considered. Geographical residence: Not considered. State residency: Not considered. Religious affiliation/commitment: Not considered. Minority status: Not considered. Volunteer work: Not considered. Work experience: Not considered. **Admissions statistics for the fall 2005 entering class:** Freshmen enrolled: 2,434; 1% were from out of state. **Credentials of fall 2005 freshmen:** 21% ranked in the top 10 percent of their high school class; 48% were in the top 25 percent, and 79% were in the top half. (Proportion submitting class standing: 92%.) **First-year students who submitted SAT scores:** 45%. Scores (25/75 percentile): Verbal: 410-520, Math: 420-530, Combined: 830-1050. **First-year students submitting ACT scores:** 100%. Scores (25/75 percentile): English: 15-21, Math: 16-21, Composite: 16-21.

ACADEMICS

Year founded: 1927. **Academic calendar:** Semester. **Degrees offered:** bachelor's, master's, doctorate. **Most popular majors:** 20% multi/interdisciplinary

studies, 18% business, management, marketing, and related support services, 11% health professions and related clinical sciences, 7% biological and biomedical sciences, 7% social sciences. **Major fields of study:** area, ethnic, cultural, and gender studies; biological and biomedical sciences; business, management, marketing, and related support services; communication, journalism, and related programs; computer and information sciences and support services; engineering; English language and literature/letters; foreign languages, literatures, and linguistics; health professions and related clinical sciences; history; liberal arts and sciences studies, and humanities; mathematics and statistics; multi/interdisciplinary studies; parks, recreation, leisure, and fitness studies; philosophy and religious studies; physical sciences; psychology; public administration and social service professions; security and protective services; social sciences; visual and performing arts. **Areas of required coursework:** arts/fine arts, humanities, computer literacy, mathematics, English (including composition), philosophy, foreign languages, sciences (biological or physical), history, social science, other. **Pre-professional programs:** pre-law, pre-dentistry, pre-medicine, pre-optometry, pre-pharmacy. **Special academic programs:** accelerated program, cooperative (work-study plan) program, distance learning, double major, dual enrollment, English as a Second Language (ESL), exchange student program (domestic), honors program, independent study, internships, study abroad, teacher certificate program, weekend college. **Teacher certification offered in:** early childhood, special education, elementary, middle/junior high, secondary, bilingual/bicultural. **Cooperative education programs:** health professions. **Reserve Officers Training Corps (ROTC):** Army ROTC: Offered on campus. **Faculty and instruction (2005-2006):** Total instructional faculty: 587 full-time, 119 part-time (59% men; 41% women; 49% minorities). Student/faculty ratio: 21/1. Classes of fewer than 20 students: 19%; of 20 to 49 students: 67%; of 50 or more students: 15%. **Advanced Placement and International Baccalaureate credit:** International Baccalaureate exams may be used for: Credit and/or placement. **Freshmen returning for sophomore year:** 67%. **Graduation rates:** Four-year: 8%; five-year: 21%; six-year: 27%.

COSTS AND FINANCIAL AID

Financial aid office: (956) 381-2501. **Expenses (2006-2007):** Tuition and fees 2006-2007: $4,160 in state, $12,410 out of state; room/board: $4,700. Estimated books and supplies: $620; transportation: $600; personal expenses: $3,000. **Financial aid:** Priority filing date for institution's financial aid form: March 1. In 2005-2006, 89% of undergraduates applied for financial aid. Of those, 85% were determined to have financial need; 7% had their need fully met. Average financial aid package (proportion receiving): $7,488 (83%). Average amount of gift aid, such as scholarships or grants (proportion receiving): N/A (79%). Average amount of self-help aid, such as work study or loans (proportion receiving): N/A (45%). Among students who received need-based aid, the average percentage of need met: 76%. Among students who received aid based on merit, the average award (and the proportion receiving): $4,658 (5%). Average amount of debt of borrowers graduating in 2005: $12,453. Proportion who borrowed: 84%.

CAMPUS LIFE AND EXTRACURRICULAR ACTIVITIES

Campus housing available: women's dorms, men's dorms, apartments for married students, apartment for single students, special housing for disabled students. Students who live in college-owned, operated, or affiliated housing: 3%. Average per-year earnings: $5,602. **Clubs and organizations:** Number of student organizations: 102. Activities include: choral groups, concert band, dance, drama/theater, jazz band, music ensembles, student government, student newspaper, symphony orchestra. Number of fraternities: 7; sororities: 6. Proportion of men in fraternities: 1%; of women in sororities: 1%. **Sports program (2005-2006):** Member of NCAA I. *Men's intercollegiate varsity sports:* baseball, basketball, cross-country, golf, tennis, track and field (indoor), track and field (outdoor). *Women's intercollegiate varsity sports:* basketball, cross-country, golf, tennis, track and field (indoor), track and field (outdoor), volleyball.

SERVICES AND FACILITIES

Basic services: nonremedial tutoring, placement service, day care, health service, health insurance. **Remedial assistance:** reading, math, writing. **Counseling services:** minority student, career, personal, veteran student, academic. **For learning-disabled students:** School does not offer a structured program with separate admission and additional fees. Services include: remedial math, reading machines, remedial reading, tape recorders, videotaped classes, diagnostic testing service, untimed tests, note-taking services, oral tests, learning center, readers, extended time for tests, tutors, priority registration, priority seating, other testing accomodations, other. **Library:** Number of titles: 573,803; number of current serial subscriptions: 8,838. **Information technology resources:** Students are not required to lease or own a computer. Number of campus computers available to all students: 900. School has a wireless network. Proportion of college-owned housing units wired for high-speed internet access: 100%. **Campus safety:** Security services offered: 24-hour foot-and-vehicle patrols, late-night transport/escort service, 24-hour emergency telephones, lighted pathways/sidewalks, controlled dormitory access (key, security card, etc).

TRANSFER AND INTERNATIONAL STUDENTS

Transfer students: May apply for admission for the following academic terms: Fall, Spring, Summer. Applicants do not need a minimum number of credits to apply. For fall 2005: Transfer applicants enrolled: 818. **International students:** Number of foreign undergraduates: 592 (4% of student body). Number of countries represented: 26. Minimum TOEFL score required: 500 (paper); 173 (computer). Average TOEFL score: 549 (paper).

University of Texas–San Antonio

- ■ **Address:** 6900 N. Loop 1604 W, San Antonio, TX 78249
- ■ **Website:** http://www.utsa.edu
- ■ **Public**
- ■ **Enrollment:** 17,554 full-time; 5,877 part-time

KEY STATS

✔ **U.S News College Ranking:** third tier, Universities–Master's (West)
✔ **SAT Score (25th/75th percentile):** 910-1130
✔ **Tuition:** 2006-2007: $6,186 in state, $14,436 out of state
  Selectivity: Less selective   **Room/board:** $7,902
  Acceptance rate: 99%   **Average debt:** $18,000
  Student/faculty ratio: 23/1   **Proportion who borrowed:** 63%

UNDERGRADUATE STUDENT BODY STATS

2005-2006 enrollment: 17,554 full-time; 5,877 part-time. Men: 47%; women: 53%. **Ethnic makeup:** African American: 7%; American-Indian: 1%; Asian American: 5%; Hispanic: 46%; White: 39%; International: 2%.

ADMISSIONS FACTS AND FIGURES

Phone: (800) 669-0919. **Email:** prospects@utsa.edu. **Website:** http://www.utsa.edu. **Application deadlines for fall 2007:** Regular decision: July 1. Early decision: Not offered. Early action: Not offered. Admission can be deferred. **Application fee:** $30. Common application is not accepted. **To apply online, go to:** https://www.applytexas.org/adappc/commonapp.wb. **Admissions requirements/recommendations:** High school units required (recommended): English: (4); Mathematics: (3); Science: (3); Foreign language: (2); Social studies: (4); Total units: (17). Tests: The college uses SAT or ACT scores in admissions decisions. Either SAT or ACT required. For admission to the fall 2007 entering class, the school will accept: ACT with writing. Campus visit: Recommended. Admissions interview: Neither required nor recommended. Off-campus interview: Not available. **Factors that count in admissions decisions:** *Academic:* Secondary school record: Not considered. Class rank: Very important. Letters of recommendation: Considered. Standardized test scores: Very important. Essay: Considered. *Nonacademic:* Interview: Not considered. Extracurricular activities: Important. Talent/ability: Considered. Character/personal qualities: Considered. Alumni/ae relationship: Not considered. Geographical residence: Not considered. State residency: Considered. Religious affiliation/commitment: Not considered. Minority status: Not considered. Volunteer work: Considered. Work experience: Considered. **Other schools with the greatest overlap in applicants:** Texas A&M University–College Station; Texas A&M University–Corpus Christi; Texas State University–San Marcos; University of Texas–Austin; University of Texas–Pan American. **Admissions statistics for the fall 2005 entering class:** Total applicants: 9,144. Total accepted: 9,087. Freshmen enrolled: 4,452; 3% were from out of state. Overall acceptance rate: 99%. **Credentials of fall 2005 freshmen:** 9% ranked in the top 10 percent of their high school class; 35% were in the top 25 percent, and 71% were in the top half. (Proportion submitting class standing: 94%.) **First-year students who submitted SAT scores:** 87%. Scores (25/75 percentile): Verbal: 450-560, Math: 460-570, Combined: 910-1130. **First-year students submitting ACT scores:** 39%. Scores (25/75 percentile): English: 17-23, Math: 17-23, Composite: 18-23.

ACADEMICS

Year founded: 1969. **Academic calendar:** Semester. **Degrees offered:** bachelor's, master's, doctorate. **Most popular majors:** 30% business, management, marketing, and related support services, 12% multi/interdisciplinary studies, 9% biological and biomedical sciences, 8% psychology, 6% security and protective services. **Major fields of study:** architecture and related services; area, ethnic, cultural, and gender studies; biological and biomedical sciences; business, management, marketing, and related support services; communication, journalism, and related programs; computer and information sciences and support services; engineering; English language and literature/letters; foreign languages, literatures, and linguistics; health professions and related clinical sciences; history; liberal arts and sciences studies, and humanities; mathematics and statistics; multi/interdisciplinary studies; natural resources and conservation; parks, recreation, leisure, and fitness studies; philosophy and religious studies; physical sciences; psychology; security and protective services; social sciences; visual and performing arts. **Areas of required coursework:** arts/fine arts, humanities, computer literacy, mathematics, English (including composition), philosophy, foreign languages, sciences (biological or physical), history, social science. **Pre-professional programs:** pre-law, pre-dentistry, pre-medicine. **Special academic programs:** distance learning, double major, dual enrollment, English as a Second Language (ESL), exchange student program (domestic), honors program, independent study, internships, study abroad, teacher certificate program, other. **Teacher certification offered in:** early childhood, special education, elementary, middle/junior high, adult education, secondary, bilingual/bicultural. **Reserve Officers Training Corps (ROTC):** Army ROTC: Offered on campus; Air Force ROTC: Offered on campus. **Faculty and instruction (2005-2006):** Total instructional faculty: 860 full-time, 223 part-time (58% men; 42% women; 32% minorities). Full-time faculty with Ph.D. or other terminal degree: 83%. Student/faculty ratio: 23/1. Classes of fewer than 20 students: 25%; of 20 to 49 students: 52%; of 50 or more students: 23%. **Advanced Placement and International Baccalaureate credit:** AP tests may be used for: Credit only. Scores accepted: 3. International Baccalaureate exams may be used for: Credit and/or placement. **Freshmen returning for sophomore year:** 57%. **Graduation rates:** Four-year: 6%; five-year: 22%; six-year: 28%. **Graduate study:** 8% of students pursue further study within one year. Fields in which graduates pursue further study: law, 13%; medicine, 10%.

COSTS AND FINANCIAL AID

Financial aid office: (210) 458-8000. **Expenses (2006-2007):** Tuition and fees 2006-2007: $6,186 in state, $14,436 out of state; room/board: $7,902. Estimated books and supplies: $1,000; transportation: $880; personal expenses: $2,202. **Financial aid:** Priority filing date for institution's financial aid form: March 1. In 2005-2006, 77% of undergraduates applied for financial aid. Of those, 62% were determined to have financial need; 11% had their need fully met. Average financial aid package (proportion receiving): $6,381 (60%). Average amount of gift aid, such as scholarships or grants (proportion receiving): $3,807 (46%). Average amount of self-help aid, such as work study or loans (proportion receiving): $3,788 (50%). Average need-based loan (excluding PLUS or other private loans): $3,669. Among students who received need-based aid, the average percentage of need met: 52%. Among students who received aid based on merit, the average award (and the proportion receiving): $1,539 (3%). The average athletic scholarship (and the proportion receiving): $8,329 (1%). Average amount of debt of borrowers graduating in 2005: $18,000. Proportion who borrowed: 63%.

CAMPUS LIFE AND EXTRACURRICULAR ACTIVITIES

Campus housing available (% using): coed dorms (83%), apartment for single students, special housing for disabled students (2%), special housing for international students (15%). Students who live in college-owned, operated, or affiliated housing: 11%. **Clubs and organizations:** Number of student organizations: 180. Activities include: choral groups, concert band, dance, drama/theater, jazz band, music ensembles, opera, pep band, student government, student newspaper, symphony orchestra, yearbook. Number of fraternities: 10; sororities: 9. Proportion of men in fraternities: 4%; of women in sororities: 2%. Average proportion of students who stay on campus on weekends: 35%. **Sports program (2005-2006):** Member of NCAA I. *Men's intercollegiate varsity sports:* baseball, basketball, cross-country, golf, tennis, track and field (indoor), track and field (outdoor). *Women's intercollegiate varsity sports:* basketball, cross-country, golf, softball, tennis, track and field (indoor), track and field (outdoor), volleyball.

SERVICES AND FACILITIES

Basic services: nonremedial tutoring, women's center, placement service, day care, health service, other. **Remedial assistance:** reading, math, writing, study skills. **Counseling services:** career, personal, academic. **For learning-disabled students:** Services include: remedial math, remedial English, reading machines, tape recorders, note-taking services, readers. **Library:** Number of titles: 668,000; number of current serial subscriptions: 35,000. **Information technology resources:** Students are not required to lease or own a computer. Number of campus computers available to all students: 800. School has a wireless network. Proportion of college-owned housing units wired for high-speed internet access: 100%. **Campus safety:** Security services offered: 24-hour foot-and-vehicle patrols, late-night transport/escort service, 24-hour emergency telephones, lighted pathways/sidewalks, controlled dormitory access (key, security card, etc).

TRANSFER AND INTERNATIONAL STUDENTS

Transfer students: May apply for admission for the following academic terms: Fall, Spring, Summer. Applicants need a minimum number of credits to apply. For fall 2005: Transfer applications received: 3,168. Transfer applicants offered admission: 2,941. Transfer applicants enrolled: 2,029. **International students:** Number of foreign undergraduates: 471 (2% of student body). Number of countries represented: 471. Minimum TOEFL score required: 500 (paper); 173 (computer). Average TOEFL score: 525 (paper).

University of Texas–Tyler

- **Address:** 3900 University Boulevard, Tyler, TX 75799
- **Website:** http://www.uttyler.edu
- **Public**
- **Enrollment:** 3,600 full-time; 1,102 part-time

KEY STATS

- ✔ **U.S News College Ranking:** 51, Universities–Master's (West)
- ✔ **SAT Score (25th/75th percentile):** 970-1180
- ✔ **Tuition:** 2006-2007: $4,942 in state, $13,192 out of state
  - **Selectivity:** Selective   **Room/board:** $7,350
  - **Acceptance rate:** 75%   **Average debt:** $14,581
  - **Student/faculty ratio:** 17/1   **Proportion who borrowed:** 55%

UNDERGRADUATE STUDENT BODY STATS

2005-2006 enrollment: 3,600 full-time; 1,102 part-time. Men: 41%; women: 59%. **Ethnic makeup:** African American: 10%; American-Indian: 1%; Asian American: 2%; Hispanic: 6%; White: 81%; International: 1%.

ADMISSIONS FACTS AND FIGURES

Phone: (903) 566-7202. **Email:** admissions@mail.uttyl.edu. **Website:** http://www.uttyler.edu. **Application deadlines for fall 2007:** Regular decision: Rolling. Early decision: Not offered. Early action: Not offered. Admission can be deferred. **Application fee:** None. Common application is accepted. **To apply online, go to:** http://www.uttyler.edu/mainsite/onlineapp.html. **Admissions requirements/recommendations:** High school units required (recommended): English: 4; Mathematics: 3; Science: 3 (4); Foreign language: 2; Social studies: 3. Tests: The college uses SAT or ACT scores in admissions decisions. Either SAT or ACT required. For admission to the fall 2007 entering class, the school will accept: ACT with writing, ACT without writing. Campus visit: Recommended. Admissions interview: Neither required nor recommended. Off-campus interview: Not available. **Factors that count in admissions decisions:** *Academic:* Secondary school record: Very important. Class rank: Very important. Letters of recommendation: Not considered. Standardized test scores: Very important. Essay: Not considered. *Nonacademic:* Interview: Not considered. Extracurricular activities: Considered. Talent/ability: Considered. Character/personal qualities: Considered. Alumni/ae relationship: Not considered. Geographical residence: Not considered. State residency: Not considered. Religious affiliation/commitment: Not considered. Minority status: Not considered. Volunteer work: Considered. Work experience: Considered. **Other schools with the greatest overlap in applicants:** Stephen F. Austin State University; Texas A&M University–College Station; University of North Texas; University of Texas–Arlington; University of Texas–Austin. **Admissions statistics for the fall 2005 entering class:** Total applicants: 1,497. Total accepted: 1,127. Freshmen enrolled: 549; 3% were from out of state. Overall acceptance rate: 75%. **Credentials of fall 2005 freshmen:** 22% ranked in the top 10 percent of their high school class; 42% were in the top 25 percent. **First-year students who submitted SAT scores:** 74%. Scores (25/75 percentile): Verbal: 480-580, Math: 490-600, Combined: 970-1180. **First-year students submit-**

ting ACT scores: 54%. Scores (25/75 percentile): English: 20-25, Math: 19-25, Composite: 20-25.

ACADEMICS

Year founded: 1971. **Academic calendar:** Semester. **Degrees offered:** bachelor's, master's. **Most popular majors:** 20% business, management, marketing, and related support services, 18% health professions and related clinical sciences, 18% multi/interdisciplinary studies, 5% English language and literature/letters, 5% social sciences. **Major fields of study:** biological and biomedical sciences; business, management, marketing, and related support services; communication, journalism, and related programs; computer and information sciences and support services; engineering; engineering technologies/technicians; English language and literature/letters; foreign languages, literatures, and linguistics; health professions and related clinical sciences; history; liberal arts and sciences studies, and humanities; mathematics and statistics; multi/interdisciplinary studies; parks, recreation, leisure, and fitness studies; physical sciences; psychology; security and protective services; social sciences; visual and performing arts. **Areas of required coursework:** arts/fine arts, humanities, mathematics, English (including composition), sciences (biological or physical), history, social science, other. **Pre-professional programs:** pre-law, pre-dentistry, pre-medicine, pre-theology. **Special academic programs:** cooperative (work-study plan) program, distance learning, double major, English as a Second Language (ESL), exchange student program (domestic), independent study, internships, student-designed major, study abroad, teacher certificate program, weekend college. **Teacher certification offered in:** early childhood, special education, vo-tech, middle/junior high, secondary, bilingual/bicultural. **Faculty and instruction (2005-2006):** Total instructional faculty: 218 full-time, 142 part-time (51% men; 49% women; 8% minorities). Full-time faculty with Ph.D. or other terminal degree: 72%. Student/faculty ratio: 17/1. Classes of fewer than 20 students: 42%; of 20 to 49 students: 45%; of 50 or more students: 13%. **Advanced Placement and International Baccalaureate credit:** AP tests may be used for: Credit only. Scores accepted: 3, 4, 5. International Baccalaureate exams may be used for: Credit only. **Freshmen returning for sophomore year:** 58%. **Graduation rates:** Four-year: 38%; five-year: 51%; six-year: 48%.

COSTS AND FINANCIAL AID

Financial aid office: (903) 566-7180. **Expenses (2006-2007):** Tuition and fees 2006-2007: $4,942 in state, $13,192 out of state; room/board: $7,350. Estimated books and supplies: $800; transportation: $702; personal expenses: $1,104. **Financial aid:** Priority filing date for institution's financial aid form: April 1. In 2005-2006, 64% of undergraduates applied for financial aid. Of those, 50% were determined to have financial need; 21% had their need fully met. Average financial aid package (proportion receiving): $7,270 (50%). Average amount of gift aid, such as scholarships or grants (proportion receiving): $4,160 (42%). Average amount of self-help aid, such as work study or loans (proportion receiving): $3,609 (46%). Average need-based loan (excluding PLUS or other private loans): $3,512. Among students who received need-based aid, the average percentage of need met: 68%. Among students who received aid based on merit, the average award (and the proportion receiving): $2,496 (11%). The average athletic scholarship (and the proportion receiving): $0 (0%). Average amount of debt of borrowers graduating in 2005: $14,581. Proportion who borrowed: 55%.

CAMPUS LIFE AND EXTRACURRICULAR ACTIVITIES

Campus housing available: apartment for single students, other housing options. Students who live in college-owned, operated, or affiliated housing: 10%. **Student employment:** During the 2005-2006 academic year, 6% of undergraduates worked on campus. Average per-year earnings: $3,803. **Clubs and organizations:** Number of student organizations: 68. Activities include: choral groups, concert band, drama/theater, jazz band, literary magazine, music ensembles, musical theater, opera, student government, student newspaper, student film society. Number of fraternities: 0; sororities: 3. of women in sororities: 2%. Average proportion of students who stay on campus on weekends: 40%. **Sports program (2005-2006):** Member of NCAA III. *Men's intercollegiate varsity sports:* baseball, basketball, cross-country, golf, soccer, tennis. *Women's intercollegiate varsity sports:* basketball, cross-country, golf, soccer, softball, tennis, volleyball.

SERVICES AND FACILITIES

Basic services: nonremedial tutoring, placement service, health service, health insurance. **Remedial assistance:** writing, study skills. **Counseling services:** minority student, career, military, personal, veteran student, academic, older student, psychological, birth control. **For learning-disabled students:** School does not offer a structured program with separate admission and additional fees. Total undergraduates in learning-disabled program or receiving services: 13. Services include: reading machines, tape recorders, videotaped classes, note-taking services, oral tests, readers, extended time for tests, priority seating, other testing accomodations. **Library:** Number of titles: 195,334; number of current serial subscriptions: 334. **Information technology resources:** Students are not required to lease or own a computer. Number of campus computers available to all students: 192. School has a wireless network. Approximate number of users that can be accommodated: 350. Proportion of college-owned housing units wired for high-speed internet access: 100%. **Campus safety:** Security services offered: 24-hour foot-and-vehicle patrols, late-night transport/escort service, 24-hour emergency telephones, lighted pathways/sidewalks, student patrols.

TRANSFER AND INTERNATIONAL STUDENTS

Transfer students: May apply for admission for the following academic terms: Fall, Spring, Summer. Applicants need a minimum number of credits to apply. For fall 2005: Transfer applications received: 1,629. Transfer applicants offered admission: 1,561. Transfer applicants enrolled: 900. **International students:** Number of foreign undergraduates: 39 (1% of student body). Number of countries represented: 44. Minimum TOEFL score required: 550 (paper); 213 (computer).

University of the Incarnate Word

- **Address:** 4301 Broadway, San Antonio, TX 78209-6397
- **Website:** http://www.uiw.edu
- **Private; Religious affiliation:** Roman Catholic
- **Enrollment:** 2,597 full-time; 1,773 part-time

KEY STATS

✔ **U.S News College Ranking:** third tier, Universities–Master's (West)
✔ **SAT Score (25th/75th percentile):** 860-1080
✔ **Tuition:** 2006-2007: $18,272

Selectivity: Less selective	**Room/board:** $6,475
Acceptance rate: 75%	**Average debt:** $23,383
Student/faculty ratio: 14/1	**Proportion who borrowed:** 80%

UNDERGRADUATE STUDENT BODY STATS

2005-2006 enrollment: 2,597 full-time; 1,773 part-time. Men: 34%; women: 66%. **Ethnic makeup:** African American: 7%; American-Indian: 1%; Asian American: 2%; Hispanic: 56%; White: 31%; International: 3%. **Religious preference:** Protestant: 5%; Jewish: 1%; Buddhist: 1%; No preference: 14%; Unknown: 18%; Roman Catholic: 45%; Other: 11%.

ADMISSIONS FACTS AND FIGURES

Phone: (210) 829-6005. **Email:** admis@uiwtx.edu. **Website:** http://www.uiw.edu. **Application deadlines for fall 2007:** Regular decision: Rolling. Early decision: Not offered. Early action: Not offered. Admission can be deferred. **Application fee:** $20. Common application is not accepted. **To apply online, go to:** http://www.uiw.edu/admissions/apply.html. **Admissions requirements/recommendations:** High school units required (recommended): English: 4 (4); Mathematics: 3 (4); Science: 3 (3); Foreign language: 2 (2); Social studies: 3 (4); History: 0 (0); Academic electives: 0 (0); Total units: 16 (18). Tests: The college uses SAT or ACT scores in admissions decisions. Either SAT or ACT required. For admission to the fall 2007 entering class, the school will accept: ACT with writing, ACT without writing. Campus visit: Recommended. Admissions interview: Recommended. Off-campus interview: May be arranged. **Factors that count in admissions decisions:** *Academic:* Secondary school record: Important. Class rank: Considered. Letters of recommendation: Considered. Standardized test scores: Important. Essay: Not considered. *Nonacademic:* Interview: Considered. Extracurricular activities: Considered. Talent/ability: Considered. Character/personal qualities: Considered. Alumni/ae relationship: Considered. Geographical residence: Considered. State residency: Not considered. Religious affiliation/commitment: Not considered. Minority status: Considered. Volunteer work: Considered. Work experience: Considered. **Other schools with the greatest overlap in applicants:** St. Mary's University of San Antonio; Texas Lutheran University; Texas State University–San Marcos; University of Texas–San Antonio. **Admissions statistics for the fall 2005 entering class:** Total applicants: 2,070. Total accepted: 1,560. Freshmen enrolled: 578; 2% were from out of state. Overall acceptance rate: 75%. **Credentials of fall 2005 freshmen:** 17% ranked in the top 10 percent of their high school class; 42% were in the top 25

percent, and 72% were in the top half. (Proportion submitting class standing: 76%.) **Average high school grade point average:** 3.4. **First-year students who submitted SAT scores:** 89%. Scores (25/75 percentile): Verbal: 430-540, Math: 430-540, Combined: 860-1080. **First-year students submitting ACT scores:** 42%. Scores (25/75 percentile): English: 16-23, Math: 16-22, Composite: 17-22.

ACADEMICS

Year founded: 1881. **Academic calendar:** Semester. **Degrees offered:** associate, bachelor's, post-bachelor's certificate, master's, post-master's certificate, first professional, doctorate. **Most popular majors:** 46% business, management, marketing, and related support services, 9% health professions and related clinical sciences, 8% liberal arts and sciences studies, and humanities, 7% visual and performing arts, 6% communication, journalism, and related programs. **Major fields of study:** area, ethnic, cultural, and gender studies; biological and biomedical sciences; business, management, marketing, and related support services; communication, journalism, and related programs; computer and information sciences and support services; education; engineering; English language and literature/letters; family and consumer sciences/human sciences; foreign languages, literatures, and linguistics; health professions and related clinical sciences; history; mathematics and statistics; multi/interdisciplinary studies; natural resources and conservation; parks, recreation, leisure, and fitness studies; philosophy and religious studies; physical sciences; psychology; social sciences; visual and performing arts. **Areas of required coursework:** arts/fine arts, humanities, computer literacy, mathematics, English (including composition), philosophy, foreign languages, sciences (biological or physical), history, social science, other. **Pre-professional programs:** pre-law, pre-pharmacy. **Special academic programs:** accelerated program, cooperative (work-study plan) program, cross-registration, distance learning, double major, dual enrollment, English as a Second Language (ESL), exchange student program (domestic), honors program, independent study, internships, study abroad, teacher certificate program. **Teacher certification offered in:** elementary, secondary. **Reserve Officers Training Corps (ROTC):** Army ROTC: Offered on campus; Air Force ROTC: Offered at cooperating institution (University of Texas at San Antonio). **Faculty and instruction (2005-2006):** Total instructional faculty: 160 full-time, 284 part-time (51% men; 49% women; 30% minorities). Full-time faculty with Ph.D. or other terminal degree: 74%. Student/faculty ratio: 14/1. Classes of fewer than 20 students: 46%; of 20 to 49 students: 53%; of 50 or more students: 1%. **Advanced Placement and International Baccalaureate credit:** AP tests may be used for: Credit and/or placement. Scores accepted: 3, 4, 5. International Baccalaureate exams may be used for: Credit only. **Freshmen returning for sophomore year:** 66%. **Graduation rates:** Four-year: 13%; five-year: 29%; six-year: 38%.

COSTS AND FINANCIAL AID

Financial aid office: (210) 829-6008. **Expenses (2006-2007):** Tuition and fees 2006-2007: $18,272; room/board: $6,475. Estimated books and supplies: $1,000; transportation: $890; personal expenses: $1,500. **Financial aid:** In 2005-2006, 82% of undergraduates applied for financial aid. Of those, 59% were determined to have financial need; 37% had their need fully met. Average financial aid package (proportion receiving): $13,991 (75%). Average amount of gift aid, such as scholarships or grants (proportion receiving): $7,877 (65%). Average amount of self-help aid, such as work study or loans (proportion receiving): $4,710 (53%). Average need-based loan (excluding PLUS or other private loans): $4,229. Among students who received need-based aid, the average percentage of need met: 58%. Among students who received aid based on merit, the average award (and the proportion receiving): $6,108 (15%). The average athletic scholarship (and the proportion receiving): $12,340 (4%). Average amount of debt of borrowers graduating in 2005: $23,383. Proportion who borrowed: 80%.

CAMPUS LIFE AND EXTRACURRICULAR ACTIVITIES

Campus housing available (% using): coed dorms (55%), women's dorms (10%), men's dorms, apartment for single students (35%). Students who live in college-owned, operated, or affiliated housing: 19%. **Student employment:** During the 2005-2006 academic year, 7% of undergraduates worked on campus. Average per-year earnings: $2,030. **Clubs and organizations:** Number of student organizations: 47. Activities include: choral groups, concert band, dance, drama/theater, jazz band, literary magazine, music ensembles, musical theater, radio station, student government, student newspaper. Number of fraternities: 2; sororities: 2. Proportion of men in fraternities: 3%; of women in sororities: 1%. Average proportion of students who stay on campus on weekends: 40%. **Sports program (2005-2006):** Member of NCAA II. *Men's intercollegiate varsity sports:* baseball, basketball, cross-country, golf, soccer, tennis, track and field (outdoor). *Women's intercollegiate varsity sports:* basketball, cross-country, golf, soccer, softball, swimming and diving, syncronized swimming, tennis, track and field (outdoor), volleyball.

SERVICES AND FACILITIES

Basic services: placement service, health service, health insurance. **Remedial assistance:** reading, math, writing, study skills. **Counseling services:** minority student, career, military, personal, veteran student, academic, older student, psychological, birth control, religious. **For learning-disabled students:** School does not offer a structured program with separate admission and additional fees. Total undergraduates in learning-disabled program or receiving services: 100. Services include: remedial math, remedial English, reading machines, remedial reading, tape recorders, videotaped classes, untimed tests, note-taking services, oral tests, learning center, readers, extended time for tests, tutors, priority registration, priority seating, texts on tape, other testing accomodations, other. **Library:** Number of titles: 263,601; number of current serial subscriptions: 19,000. **Information technology resources:** Students are required to lease or own a computer. Number of campus computers available to all students: 599. School has a wireless network. Approximate number of users that can be accommodated: 2,500. Proportion of college-owned housing units wired for high-speed internet access: 100%. **Campus safety:** Security services offered: 24-hour foot-and-vehicle patrols, late-night transport/escort service, 24-hour emergency telephones, lighted pathways/sidewalks, controlled dormitory access (key, security card, etc).

TRANSFER AND INTERNATIONAL STUDENTS

Transfer students: May apply for admission for the following academic terms: Fall, Spring, Summer. Applicants do not need a minimum number of credits to apply. **International students:** Number of foreign undergraduates: 146 (3% of student body). Number of countries represented: 40. Minimum TOEFL score required: 560 (paper); 220 (computer). Average TOEFL score: 560 (paper).

Wayland Baptist University

- **Address:** 1900 W. Seventh Street, Plainview, TX 79072
- **Website:** http://www.wbu.edu
- **Private; Religious affiliation:** Southern Baptist Convention
- **Enrollment:** 840 full-time; 164 part-time

KEY STATS

✔ **U.S News College Ranking:** third tier, Universities–Master's (West)
✔ **ACT Score (25th/75th percentile):** 17-25
✔ **Tuition:** 2006-2007: $10,800

Selectivity: Selective	**Room/board:** $3,441
Acceptance rate: 65%	**Average debt:** $13,972
Student/faculty ratio: 12/1	**Proportion who borrowed:** 78%

UNDERGRADUATE STUDENT BODY STATS

2005-2006 enrollment: 840 full-time; 164 part-time. Men: 43%; women: 57%. **Ethnic makeup:** African American: 4%; American-Indian: 1%; Asian American: 1%; Hispanic: 24%; White: 68%; International: 2%. **Religious preference:** Roman Catholic: 11%; Protestant: 20%; No preference: 4%; Unknown: 14%; Southern Baptist Convention: 34%; Other Baptist: 17%.

ADMISSIONS FACTS AND FIGURES

Phone: (806) 291-3500. **Email:** admityou@wbu.edu. **Website:** http://www.wbu.edu. **Application deadlines for fall 2007:** Regular decision: Rolling. Early decision: Not offered. Early action: Not offered. Admission cannot be deferred. **Application fee:** $35. Common application is not accepted. **Admissions requirements/recommendations:** High school units required (recommended): English: 3; Mathematics: 2 (3); Science: 2 (3); History: 2; Total units: 9 (6). Tests: The college uses SAT or ACT scores in admissions decisions. Either SAT or ACT required. For admission to the fall 2007 entering class, the school will accept: ACT with writing, ACT without writing. Campus visit: Recommended. Admissions interview: Recommended. Off-campus interview: May be arranged. **Factors that count in admissions decisions:** *Academic:* Secondary school record: Important. Class rank: Very important. Letters of recommendation: Not considered. Standardized test scores: Very important. Essay: Not considered. *Nonacademic:* Interview: Not considered. Extracurricular activities: Not considered. Talent/ability: Not considered. Character/personal qualities: Not considered. Alumni/ae relationship: Not considered. Geographical residence: Not considered. State residency: Not considered. Religious affiliation/commitment: Not considered. Minority status: Not considered. Volunteer work: Not considered. Work experience: Not considered. **Other schools with the greatest overlap in appli-**

cants: Hardin-Simmons University; Lubbock Christian University; Texas Tech University; West Texas A&M University. **Admissions statistics for the fall 2005 entering class:** Total applicants: 511. Total accepted: 333. Freshmen enrolled: 226; 16% were from out of state. Overall acceptance rate: 65%. **Credentials of fall 2005 freshmen:** 23% ranked in the top 10 percent of their high school class; 53% were in the top 25 percent, and 83% were in the top half. (Proportion submitting class standing: 78%.) **Average high school grade point average:** 3.5. **First-year students who submitted SAT scores:** 41%. Scores (25/75 percentile): Verbal: 430-580, Math: 450-570, Combined: 880-1150. **First-year students submitting ACT scores:** 80%. Scores (25/75 percentile): English: 16-24, Math: 17-24, Composite: 17-25.

ACADEMICS

Year founded: 1908. **Academic calendar:** Semester. **Degrees offered:** transfer-associate, bachelor's, master's. **Most popular majors:** 24% elementary education and teaching, 21% business administration and management, 10% Christian studies, 7% criminal justice/safety studies, 7% religious education. **Major fields of study:** biological and biomedical sciences; business, management, marketing, and related support services; communication, journalism, and related programs; education; English language and literature/letters; foreign languages, literatures, and linguistics; history; mathematics and statistics; philosophy and religious studies; physical sciences; psychology; security and protective services; social sciences; theology and religious vocations; visual and performing arts. **Areas of required coursework:** arts/fine arts, humanities, computer literacy, mathematics, English (including composition), foreign languages, sciences (biological or physical), history, social science. **Special academic programs:** accelerated program, distance learning, double major, dual enrollment, external degree program, honors program, internships, teacher certificate program. **Teacher certification offered in:** elementary, vo-tech, middle/junior high, secondary. **Cooperative education programs:** computer science, engineering. **Reserve Officers Training Corps (ROTC):** Army ROTC: Offered at cooperating institution (Texas Tech University); Air Force ROTC: Offered at cooperating institution (Texas Tech University). **Faculty and instruction (2005-2006):** Total instructional faculty: 67 full-time, 35 part-time (67% men; 33% women; 4% minorities). Full-time faculty with Ph.D. or other terminal degree: 70%. Student/faculty ratio: 12/1. Classes of fewer than 20 students: 72%; of 20 to 49 students: 28%; of 50 or more students: 0%. **Advanced Placement and International Baccalaureate credit:** AP tests may be used for: Credit only. Scores accepted: 3, 4, 5. International Baccalaureate exams may be used for: Credit only. **Freshmen returning for sophomore year:** 67%. **Graduation rates:** Four-year: 18%; five-year: 28%; six-year: 32%.

COSTS AND FINANCIAL AID

Financial aid office: (806) 291-3520. **Expenses (2006-2007):** Tuition and fees 2006-2007: $10,800; room/board: $3,441. Estimated books and supplies: $800; transportation: $800; personal expenses: $1,684. **Financial aid:** Priority filing date for institution's financial aid form: May 1. In 2005-2006, 92% of undergraduates applied for financial aid. Of those, 75% were determined to have financial need; 23% had their need fully met. Average financial aid package (proportion receiving): $9,012 (75%). Average amount of gift aid, such as scholarships or grants (proportion receiving): $6,770 (71%). Average amount of self-help aid, such as work study or loans (proportion receiving): $3,293 (59%). Average need-based loan (excluding PLUS or other private loans): $3,037. Among students who received need-based aid, the average percentage of need met: 76%. Among students who received aid based on merit, the average award (and the proportion receiving): $8,514 (20%). The average athletic scholarship (and the proportion receiving): $7,289 (8%). Average amount of debt of borrowers graduating in 2005: $13,972. Proportion who borrowed: 78%.

CAMPUS LIFE AND EXTRACURRICULAR ACTIVITIES

Campus housing available (% using): women's dorms (48%), men's dorms (44%), apartments for married students (8%). Students who live in college-owned, operated, or affiliated housing: 55%. **Clubs and organizations:** Number of student organizations: 38. Activities include: choral groups, concert band, drama/theater, marching band, music ensembles, musical theater, pep band, radio station, student government, student newspaper, television station, yearbook. Number of fraternities: 1; sororities: 1. Proportion of men in fraternities: 3%; of women in sororities: 4%. **Sports program (2005-2006):** Member of NAIA. *Men's intercollegiate varsity sports:* baseball, basketball, cross-country, golf, track and field (indoor), track and field (outdoor). *Women's intercollegiate varsity sports:* basketball, cross-country, track and field (indoor), track and field (outdoor), volleyball.

SERVICES AND FACILITIES

Basic services: nonremedial tutoring, placement service, health service. **Remedial assistance:** reading, math, writing, study skills. **Counseling serv-**

ices: career, personal, academic, psychological, religious. **For learning-disabled students:** School does not offer a structured program with separate admission and additional fees. Services include: remedial math, remedial English, remedial reading, tutors. **Library:** Number of titles: 119,015; number of current serial subscriptions: 540. **Information technology resources:** Students are not required to lease or own a computer. Number of campus computers available to all students: 123. School does not have a wireless network. **Campus safety:** Security services offered: 24-hour emergency telephones, lighted pathways/sidewalks, controlled dormitory access (key, security card, etc).

TRANSFER AND INTERNATIONAL STUDENTS

Transfer students: May apply for admission for the following academic terms: Fall, Winter, Spring, Summer. Applicants need a minimum number of credits to apply. For fall 2005: Transfer applications received: 154. Transfer applicants offered admission: 91. Transfer applicants enrolled: 71. **International students:** Number of foreign undergraduates: 19 (2% of student body). Number of countries represented: 12. Minimum TOEFL score required: 500 (paper); 173 (computer).

West Texas A&M University

- **Address:** 2501 Fourth Avenue, Canyon, TX 79016-0001
- **Website:** http://www.wtamu.edu
- **Public**
- **Enrollment:** 4,461 full-time; 1,334 part-time

KEY STATS
✔ **U.S News College Ranking:** third tier, Universities–Master's (West)
✔ **ACT Score (25th/75th percentile):** 17-26
✔ **Tuition:** 2006-2007: $4,314 in state, $12,564 out of state
  Selectivity: Selective   **Room/board:** $4,944
  Acceptance rate: 73%   **Average debt:** N/A
  Student/faculty ratio: 24/1   **Proportion who borrowed:** N/A

UNDERGRADUATE STUDENT BODY STATS

2005-2006 enrollment: 4,461 full-time; 1,334 part-time. Men: 42%; women: 58%. **Ethnic makeup:** African American: 4%; American-Indian: 1%; Asian American: 1%; Hispanic: 16%; White: 76%; International: 1%.

ADMISSIONS FACTS AND FIGURES

Phone: (806) 651-2020. **Email:** admissions@mail.wtamu.edu. **Website:** http://www.wtamu.edu. **Application deadlines for fall 2007:** Regular decision: Rolling. Early decision: Not offered. Early action: Not offered. Admission can be deferred. **Application fee:** $25. Common application is accepted. **To apply online, go to:** http://www.applytexas.org. **Admissions requirements/recommendations:** High school units required (recommended): English: 4 (4); Mathematics: 3 (4); Science: 3 (3); Foreign language: (2); Social studies: (4); History: (2); Academic electives: (8); Total units: (24). Tests: The college uses SAT or ACT scores in admissions decisions. Either SAT or ACT required. For admission to the fall 2007 entering class, the school will accept: ACT with writing, ACT without writing. Campus visit: Recommended. Admissions interview: Neither required nor recommended. Off-campus interview: Not available. **Factors that count in admissions decisions:** *Academic:* Secondary school record: Very important. Class rank: Very important. Letters of recommendation: Not considered. Standardized test scores: Very important. Essay: Not considered. *Nonacademic:* Interview: Not considered. Extracurricular activities: Not considered. Talent/ability: Not considered. Character/personal qualities: Not considered. Alumni/ae relationship: Not considered. Geographical residence: Not considered. State residency: Not considered. Religious affiliation/commitment: Not considered. Minority status: Not considered. Volunteer work: Not considered. Work experience: Not considered. **Other schools with the greatest overlap in applicants:** Angelo State University; Midwestern State University; Tarleton State University; Texas Tech University. **Admissions statistics for the fall 2005 entering class:** Total applicants: 1,903. Total accepted: 1,392. Freshmen enrolled: 780; 12% were from out of state. Overall acceptance rate: 73%. **Credentials of fall 2005 freshmen:** 14% ranked in the top 10 percent of their high school class; 42% were in the top 25 percent, and 78% were in the top half. (Proportion submitting class standing: 93%.) **First-year students who submitted SAT scores:** 37%. Scores (25/75 percentile): Verbal: 400-625, Math: 403-618, Combined: 803-1243. **First-year students submitting ACT scores:** 76%. Scores (25/75 percentile): English: 15-26, Math: 17-26, Composite: 17-26.

ACADEMICS

Year founded: 1910. **Academic calendar:** Semester. **Degrees offered:** bachelor's, master's, doctorate. **Most popular majors:** 17% business, management, marketing, and related support services, 17% multi/interdisciplinary studies, 15% liberal arts and sciences studies, and humanities, 7% biological and biomedical sciences, 6% visual and performing arts. **Major fields of study:** agriculture, agriculture operations, and related sciences; biological and biomedical sciences; business, management, marketing, and related support services; communication, journalism, and related programs; computer and information sciences and support services; engineering; engineering technologies/technicians; English language and literature/letters; foreign languages, literatures, and linguistics; health professions and related clinical sciences; legal professions and studies; liberal arts and sciences studies, and humanities; mathematics and statistics; multi/interdisciplinary studies; natural resources and conservation; parks, recreation, leisure, and fitness studies; physical sciences; psychology; public administration and social service professions; security and protective services; social sciences; visual and performing arts. **Areas of required coursework:** arts/fine arts, humanities, mathematics, English (including composition), sciences (biological or physical), history, social science, other. **Pre-professional programs:** pre-dentistry, pre-medicine, pre-veterinary science. **Special academic programs:** cooperative (work-study plan) program, distance learning, double major, English as a Second Language (ESL), honors program, independent study, internships, liberal arts/career combination, study abroad, teacher certificate program. **Teacher certification offered in:** early childhood, special education, elementary, middle/junior high, secondary, bilingual/bicultural. **Cooperative education programs:** agriculture, business, computer science, engineering, health professions, humanities, natural science, social/behavioral science, technologies. **Faculty and instruction (2005-2006):** Total instructional faculty: 243 full-time, 65 part-time (56% men; 44% women; 7% minorities). Full-time faculty with Ph.D. or other terminal degree: 71%. Student/faculty ratio: 24/1. Classes of fewer than 20 students: 41%; of 20 to 49 students: 51%; of 50 or more students: 8%. **Advanced Placement and International Baccalaureate credit:** AP tests may be used for: Credit only. Scores accepted: 3, 4, 5. International Baccalaureate exams may be used for: Credit only. **Freshmen returning for sophomore year:** 66%. **Graduation rates:** Four-year: 13%; five-year: 28%; six-year: 35%.

COSTS AND FINANCIAL AID

Financial aid office: (806) 651-2055. **Expenses (2006-2007):** Tuition and fees 2006-2007: $4,314 in state, $12,564 out of state; room/board: $4,944. Estimated books and supplies: $900; transportation: $1,160; personal expenses: $1,668. **Financial aid:** Priority filing date for institution's financial aid form: May 1.

CAMPUS LIFE AND EXTRACURRICULAR ACTIVITIES

Campus housing available (% using): coed dorms (22%), women's dorms (42%), men's dorms (30%), sorority housing (3%), special housing for disabled students, other housing options (3%). **Student employment:** During the 2005-2006 academic year, 10% of undergraduates worked on campus. Average per-year earnings: $6,125. **Clubs and organizations:** Number of student organizations: 110. Activities include: choral groups, concert band, dance, drama/theater, jazz band, literary magazine, marching band, music ensembles, musical theater, opera, pep band, radio station, student government, student newspaper, symphony orchestra, yearbook. Number of fraternities: 5; sororities: 5. Average proportion of students who stay on campus on weekends: 12%. **Sports program (2005-2006):** Member of NCAA II. *Men's intercollegiate varsity sports:* baseball, basketball, cross-country, football, golf, soccer. *Women's intercollegiate varsity sports:* basketball, cross-country, equestrian sports, golf, soccer, volleyball.

SERVICES AND FACILITIES

Basic services: nonremedial tutoring, placement service, day care, health service, health insurance. **Counseling services:** minority student, career, military, personal, veteran student, academic, older student, birth control. **For learning-disabled students:** School does not offer a structured program with separate admission and additional fees. Total undergraduates in learning-disabled program or receiving services: 137. Services include: remedial math, remedial English, reading machines, remedial reading, tape recorders, untimed tests, note-taking services, special bookstore section, oral tests, readers, extended time for tests, tutors, other. **Library:** Number of titles: 1,085,760; number of current serial subscriptions: 16,973. **Information technology resources:** Students are not required to lease or own a computer. Number of campus computers available to all students: 560. School has a wireless network. Approximate number of users that can be accommodated: 50. Proportion of college-owned housing units wired for high-speed internet access: 90%. **Campus safety:** Security services offered: 24-hour foot-and-vehicle patrols, late-night transport/escort service, 24-hour emergency telephones, lighted pathways/sidewalks, controlled dormitory access (key, security card, etc).

TRANSFER AND INTERNATIONAL STUDENTS

Transfer students: May apply for admission for the following academic terms: Fall, Winter, Spring, Summer. Applicants need a minimum number of credits to apply. For fall 2005: Transfer applications received: 1,330. Transfer applicants offered admission: 0. Transfer applicants enrolled: 0. **International students:** Number of foreign undergraduates: 77 (1% of student body). Minimum TOEFL score required: 525 (paper); 197 (computer). Average TOEFL score: 525 (paper).

Wiley College

- **Address:** 711 Wiley Avenue, Marshall, TX 75670
- **Website:** http://www.wileyc.edu
- **Private; Religious affiliation:** United Methodist
- **Enrollment:** 774 full-time; 53 part-time

KEY STATS

✔ **U.S News College Ranking:** fourth tier, Comp. Coll.–Bachelor's (West)
✔ **SAT Score (25th/75th percentile):** 680-900
✔ **Tuition:** 2006-2007: $8,978

Selectivity: Least selective	**Room/board:** $4,826
Acceptance rate: 48%	**Average debt:** N/A
Student/faculty ratio: 14/1	**Proportion who borrowed:** 15%

UNDERGRADUATE STUDENT BODY STATS

2005-2006 enrollment: 774 full-time; 53 part-time. Men: 38%; women: 62%. **Ethnic makeup:** African American: 90%; Hispanic: 3%; White: 3%; International: 4%. **Religious preference:** Roman Catholic: 4%; Protestant: 69%; No preference: 19%; United Methodist: 8%.

ADMISSIONS FACTS AND FIGURES

Phone: (800) 658-6889. **Email:** admissions@wileyc.edu. **Website:** http://www.wileyc.edu. **Application deadlines for fall 2007:** Regular decision: September 3. Early decision: Not offered. Early action: Not offered. Admission can be deferred. **Application fee:** $25. Common application is accepted. **Admissions requirements/recommendations:** High school units required (recommended): English: 4 (4); Mathematics: 2 (2); Science: 2; Social studies: 2 (2); Academic electives: 6 (6); Total units: 16 (16). Tests: The college uses SAT or ACT scores in admissions decisions. Neither SAT nor ACT required. Campus visit: Recommended. Admissions interview: Neither required nor recommended. Off-campus interview: May be arranged. **Factors that count in admissions decisions: Academic:** Secondary school record: Considered. Class rank: Considered. Letters of recommendation: Important. Standardized test scores: Important. Essay: Considered. **Nonacademic:** Interview: Considered. Extracurricular activities: Important. Talent/ability: Very important. Character/personal qualities: Very important. Alumni/ae relationship: Not considered. Geographical residence: Considered. State residency: Not considered. Religious affiliation/commitment: Not considered. Minority status: Not considered. Volunteer work: Not considered. Work experience: Considered. **Admissions statistics for the fall 2005 entering class:** Total applicants: 1,542. Total accepted: 740. Freshmen enrolled: 151; 32% were from out of state. Overall acceptance rate: 48%. **Credentials of fall 2005 freshmen:** 6% ranked in the top 10 percent of their high school class; 16% were in the top 25 percent, and 47% were in the top half. (Proportion submitting class standing: 59%.) **Average high school grade point average:** 2.6. **First-year students who submitted SAT scores:** 31%. Scores (25/75 percentile): Verbal: 340-470, Math: 340-430, Combined: 680-900. **First-year students submitting ACT scores:** 30%. Scores (25/75 percentile): English: 11-16, Math: 14-17, Composite: 13-17.

ACADEMICS

Year founded: 1873. **Academic calendar:** Semester. **Degrees offered:** associate, bachelor's. **Most popular majors:** 73% business, management, marketing, and related support services; 11% business administration and management, 10% criminal justice and corrections, 5% elementary education and teaching, 5% sociology. **Major fields of study:** biological and biomedical sciences; business, management, marketing, and related support services; communication, journalism, and related programs; computer and information sciences and support services; education; English language and literature/letters; history; mathematics and statistics; physical sciences; security

and protective services; social sciences; visual and performing arts. **Areas of required coursework:** humanities, computer literacy, mathematics, English (including composition), foreign languages, sciences (biological or physical), history, social science, other. **Pre-professional programs:** pre-medicine, other. **Special academic programs (% participation):** distance learning (10%), double major (1.5%), dual enrollment (1%), internships (2%), study abroad (1%), teacher certificate program (11%). **Teacher certification offered in:** early childhood, elementary, secondary. **Faculty and instruction (2005-2006):** Total instructional faculty: 53 full-time, 19 part-time (63% men; 38% women; 72% minorities). Full-time faculty with Ph.D. or other terminal degree: 64%. Student/faculty ratio: 14/1. Classes of fewer than 20 students: 62%; of 20 to 49 students: 38%. **Freshmen returning for sophomore year:** 55%. **Graduation rates:** Four-year: 6%; five-year: 15%; six-year: 26%. **Graduate study:** 8% of students pursue further study immediately upon graduation; 12% within one year; 17% within five years. Fields in which graduates pursue further study: Master of Business Administration (MBA), 3%; law, 5%; medicine, 20%; dentistry, 5%; theology (or the seminary), 10%; education, 50%; arts and sciences, 7%.

COSTS AND FINANCIAL AID

Financial aid office: (903) 927-3210. **Expenses (2006-2007):** Tuition and fees 2006-2007: $8,978; room/board: $4,826. Estimated books and supplies: $1,400; transportation: $568; personal expenses: $1,002. **Financial aid:** Priority filing date for institution's financial aid form: April 15; deadline: April 15. In 2005-2006, 89% of undergraduates applied for financial aid. Of those, 89% were determined to have financial need; 70% had their need fully met. Average financial aid package (proportion receiving): $10,645 (89%). Average amount of gift aid, such as scholarships or grants (proportion receiving): $2,500 (72%). Average amount of self-help aid, such as work study or loans (proportion receiving): $2,864 (7%). Average need-based loan (excluding PLUS or other private loans): $3,229. Among students who received need-based aid, the average percentage of need met: 79%. Among students who received aid based on merit, the average award (and the proportion receiving): $2,787 (6%). The average athletic scholarship (and the proportion receiving): $2,414 (3%). Proportion who borrowed: 15%.

CAMPUS LIFE AND EXTRACURRICULAR ACTIVITIES

Campus housing available (% using): women's dorms (50%), men's dorms (50%). Students who live in college-owned, operated, or affiliated housing: 49%. **Student employment:** During the 2005-2006 academic year, 34% of undergraduates worked on campus. Average per-year earnings: $1,500. **Clubs and organizations:** Number of student organizations: 25. Activities include: choral groups, music ensembles, radio station, student government, student newspaper, yearbook. Number of fraternities: 4; sororities: 4. Average proportion of students who stay on campus on weekends: 40%. **Sports program (2005-2006):** Member of NAIA. *Men's intercollegiate varsity sports:* baseball, basketball, soccer, track and field (outdoor). *Women's intercollegiate varsity sports:* basketball, track and field (outdoor), volleyball.

SERVICES AND FACILITIES

Basic services: placement service, health service, health insurance. **Remedial assistance:** reading, math, writing. **Counseling services:** career, personal, academic, religious. **For learning-disabled students:** School does not offer a structured program with separate admission and additional fees. Total undergraduates in learning-disabled program or receiving services: 158. Services include: remedial math, remedial English, remedial reading, diagnostic testing service, untimed tests, learning center, extended time for tests, tutors, substitution of courses, exams on tape or computer. **Library:** Number of titles: 79,755; number of current serial subscriptions: 306. **Information technology resources:** Students are required to lease or own a computer. Number of campus computers available to all students: 182. School has a wireless network. Approximate number of users that can be accommodated: 85. Proportion of college-owned housing units wired for high-speed internet access: 100%. **Campus safety:** Security services offered: 24-hour foot-and-vehicle patrols, 24-hour emergency telephones, controlled dormitory access (key, security card, etc).

TRANSFER AND INTERNATIONAL STUDENTS

Transfer students: May apply for admission for the following academic terms: Fall, Spring, Summer. Applicants do not need a minimum number of credits to apply. For fall 2005: Transfer applications received: 1,542. Transfer applicants offered admission: 740. Transfer applicants enrolled: 151. **International students:** Number of foreign undergraduates: 30 (4% of student body). Number of countries represented: 8. Minimum TOEFL score required: 500 (paper).

Utah

UNDERGRADUATE STUDENT BODY STATS

2005-2006 enrollment: 27,460 full-time; 3,338 part-time. Men: 51%; women: 49%. **Ethnic makeup:** African American: 1%; American-Indian: 1%; Asian American: 3%; Hispanic: 4%; White: 89%; International: 3%. **Religious preference:** No preference: 1%; Church of Jesus Christ of Latter-day Saints: 98%; Other: 1%.

ADMISSIONS FACTS AND FIGURES

Phone: (801) 422-2507. **Email:** admissions@byu.edu. **Website:** http://www.byu.edu. **Application deadlines for fall 2007:** Regular decision: February 15. Early decision: Not offered. Early action: Not offered. Admission can be deferred. **Application fee:** $30. Common application is not accepted. **To apply online, go to:** http://saas.byu.edu/depts/admissions/. **Admissions requirements/recommendations:** High school units required (recommended): English: 4 (4); Mathematics: 3 (4); Science: 2 (3); Foreign language: 2 (4); History: 2. Tests: The college uses SAT or ACT scores in admissions decisions. ACT required. For admission to the fall 2007 entering class, the school will accept: ACT with writing, ACT without writing. Campus visit: Neither required nor recommended. Admissions interview: Neither required nor recommended. Off-campus interview: Not available. **Factors that count in admissions decisions:** *Academic:* Secondary school record: Very important. Class rank: Not considered. Letters of recommendation: Important. Standardized test scores: Very important. Essay: Important. *Nonacademic:* Interview: Very important. Extracurricular activities: Important. Talent/ability: Considered. Character/personal qualities: Very important. Alumni/ae relationship: Not considered. Geographical residence: Not considered. State residency: Not considered. Religious affiliation/commitment: Very important. Minority status: Important. Volunteer work: Important. Work experience: Considered. **Other schools with the greatest overlap in applicants:** Brigham Young University–Hawaii; University of Utah; Utah State University. **Admissions statistics for the fall 2005 entering class:** Total applicants: 8,696. Total accepted: 6,794. Freshmen enrolled: 5,335; 72% were from out of state. Overall acceptance rate: 78%. **Credentials of fall 2005 freshmen:** 49% ranked in the top 10 percent of their high school class; 84% were in the top 25 percent; and 99% were in the top half. (Proportion submitting class standing: 86%.) **Average high school grade point average:** 3.7. **First-year students who submitted SAT scores:** 43%. Scores (25/75 percentile): Verbal: 550-660, Math: 570-670, Combined: 1120-1330. **First-year students submitting ACT scores:** 94%. Scores (25/75 percentile): English: 24-30, Math: 24-29, Composite: 25-29.

ACADEMICS

Year founded: 1875. **Academic calendar:** Semester. **Degrees offered:** bachelor's, master's, first professional, doctorate. **Most popular majors:** 16% business, management, marketing, and related support services, 12% education, 7% visual and performing arts, 6% engineering, 5% psychology. **Major fields of study:** agriculture, agriculture operations, and related sciences; area, ethnic, cultural, and gender studies; biological and biomedical sciences; business, management, marketing, and related support services; communication, journalism, and related programs; communications tech-

nologies/technicians and support services; computer and information sciences and support services; education; engineering; English language and literature/letters; family and consumer sciences/human sciences; foreign languages, literatures, and linguistics; health professions and related clinical sciences; history; liberal arts and sciences studies, and humanities; mathematics and statistics; multi/interdisciplinary studies; natural resources and conservation; parks, recreation, leisure, and fitness studies; philosophy and religious studies; physical sciences; psychology; public administration and social service professions; social sciences; visual and performing arts. **Areas of required coursework:** arts/fine arts, mathematics, English (including composition), foreign languages, sciences (biological or physical), history, social science, other. **Pre-professional programs:** pre-law, pre-dentistry, pre-medicine, pre-veterinary science. **Special academic programs:** accelerated program, cooperative (work-study plan) program, cross-registration, distance learning, double major, English as a Second Language (ESL), external degree program, honors program, independent study, internships, liberal arts/career combination, study abroad, teacher certificate program. **Teacher certification offered in:** early childhood, special education, elementary, vo-tech, middle/junior high, secondary, bilingual/bicultural. **Cooperative education programs:** agriculture, art, business, computer science, education, engineering, health professions, home economics, humanities, natural science, social/behavioral science, technologies, vocational arts, other. **Reserve Officers Training Corps (ROTC):** Army ROTC: Offered on campus; Air Force ROTC: Offered on campus. **Faculty and instruction (2005-2006):** Total instructional faculty: 1,321 full-time, 441 part-time (71% men; 29% women; 4% minorities). Student/faculty ratio: 21/1. Classes of fewer than 20 students: 39%; of 20 to 49 students: 48%; of 50 or more students: 12%. **Advanced Placement and International Baccalaureate credit:** AP tests may be used for: Credit and/or placement. Scores accepted: 3, 4, 5. International Baccalaureate exams may be used for: Placement only. **Freshmen returning for sophomore year:** 94%. **Graduation rates:** Six-year: 72%.

COSTS AND FINANCIAL AID

Financial aid office: (801) 422-4104. **Expenses (2006-2007):** Tuition and fees 2006-2007: $3,620; room/board: $5,640. Estimated books and supplies: $1,380; transportation: $1,600; personal expenses: $1,740. **Financial aid:** Priority filing date for institution's financial aid form: April 15. In 2005-2006, 86% of undergraduates applied for financial aid. Of those, 39% were determined to have financial need; Average financial aid package (proportion receiving): $4,302 (36%). Average amount of gift aid, such as scholarships or grants (proportion receiving): $2,533 (29%). Average amount of self-help aid, such as work study or loans (proportion receiving): $1,769 (15%). Average need-based loan (excluding PLUS or other private loans): $1,769. Among students who received need-based aid, the average percentage of need met: 43%. Among students who received aid based on merit, the average award (and the proportion receiving): $2,914 (29%). The average athletic scholarship (and the proportion receiving): $6,848 (1%). Average amount of debt of borrowers graduating in 2005: $12,955. Proportion who borrowed: 35%.

CAMPUS LIFE AND EXTRACURRICULAR ACTIVITIES

Campus housing available: women's dorms, men's dorms, apartments for married students, apartment for single students, other housing options. Students who live in college-owned, operated, or affiliated housing: 20%. **Student employment:** During the 2005-2006 academic year, 39% of undergraduates worked on campus. Average per-year earnings: $4,800. **Clubs and organizations:** Number of student organizations: 390. Activities include: choral groups, concert band, dance, drama/theater, jazz band, literary magazine, marching band, music ensembles, musical theater, opera, pep band, radio station, student government, student newspaper, student film society, symphony orchestra, television station. Number of fraternities: 0; sororities: 0. **Sports program (2005-2006):** Member of NCAA I. *Men's intercollegiate varsity sports:* baseball, basketball, cross-country, football, golf, swimming and diving, tennis, track and field (indoor), track and field (outdoor), volleyball. *Women's intercollegiate varsity sports:* basketball, cross-country, golf, gymnastics, soccer, softball, swimming and diving, tennis, track and field (indoor), track and field (outdoor), volleyball.

SERVICES AND FACILITIES

Basic services: nonremedial tutoring, women's center, placement service, health service, health insurance, other. **Remedial assistance:** reading, math, writing, study skills, other. **Counseling services:** minority student, career, military, personal, veteran student, academic, older student, psychological, religious. **For learning-disabled students:** School does not offer a structured program with separate admission and additional fees. Total undergraduates in learning-disabled program or receiving services: 187. Services include: reading machines, tape recorders, diagnostic testing service, note-taking services, oral tests, learning center, readers, extended time for tests, tutors, priority registration, proofreading services, substitution of courses, texts on tape, typist/scribe, exams on tape or computer, other testing accomodations, other. **Library:** Number of titles: 2,511,155; number of current serial subscriptions: 26,722. **Information technology resources:** Students are not required to lease or own a computer. Number of campus computers available to all students: 2,000. School has a wireless network. Approximate number of users that can be accommodated: 4,100. Proportion of college-owned housing units wired for high-speed internet access: 100%. **Campus safety:** Security services offered: 24-hour foot-and-vehicle patrols, late-night transport/escort service, 24-hour emergency telephones, lighted pathways/sidewalks, student patrols, controlled dormitory access (key, security card, etc).

TRANSFER AND INTERNATIONAL STUDENTS

Transfer students: May apply for admission for the following academic terms: Fall, Winter, Spring, Summer. Applicants need a minimum number of credits to apply. For fall 2005: Transfer applications received: 2,259. Transfer applicants offered admission: 1,117. Transfer applicants enrolled: 841. **International students:** Number of foreign undergraduates: 684 (3% of student body). Number of countries represented: 103. Minimum TOEFL score required: 500 (paper); 173 (computer).

Southern Utah University

- **Address:** 351 W. Center Street, Cedar City, UT 84720
- **Website:** http://www.suu.edu
- **Public**
- **Enrollment:** 4,589 full-time; 1,842 part-time

KEY STATS

✔ **U.S News College Ranking:** third tier, Universities–Master's (West)
✔ **ACT Score (25th/75th percentile):** 18-24
✔ **Tuition:** 2006-2007: $3,565 in state, $10,603 out of state

Selectivity: Selective	**Room/board:** $4,124
Acceptance rate: 80%	**Average debt:** $11,239
Student/faculty ratio: 23/1	**Proportion who borrowed:** 64%

UNDERGRADUATE STUDENT BODY STATS

2005-2006 enrollment: 4,589 full-time; 1,842 part-time. Men: 43%; women: 57%. **Ethnic makeup:** African American: 1%; American-Indian: 2%; Asian American: 2%; Hispanic: 2%; White: 92%; International: 1%.

ADMISSIONS FACTS AND FIGURES

Phone: (435) 586-7740. **Email:** adminfo@suu.edu. **Website:** http://www.suu.edu. **Application deadlines for fall 2007:** Regular decision: August 1. Early decision: Not offered. Early action: Send application by: N/A; Decision sent by: N/A. Admission can be deferred. **Application fee:** $35. Common application is not accepted. **Admissions requirements/recommendations:** High school units required (recommended): English: (4); Mathematics: (3); Science: (2); Social studies: (2). Tests: The college uses SAT or ACT scores in admissions decisions. Either SAT or ACT required. For admission to the fall 2007 entering class, the school will accept: ACT with writing, ACT without writing. Campus visit: Recommended. Admissions interview: Neither required nor recommended. Off-campus interview: Not available. **Factors that count in admissions decisions:** *Academic:* Secondary school record: Not considered. Class rank: Not considered. Letters of recommendation: Not considered. Standardized test scores: Very important. Essay: Not considered. *Nonacademic:* Interview: Not considered. Extracurricular activities: Not considered. Talent/ability: Not considered. Character/personal qualities: Not considered. Alumni/ae relationship: Not considered. Geographical residence: Not considered. State residency: Not considered. Religious affiliation/commitment: Not considered. Minority status: Considered. Volunteer work: Not considered. Work experience: Not

considered. **Admissions statistics for the fall 2005 entering class:** Total applicants: 2,483. Total accepted: 1,995. Freshmen enrolled: 1,074; Overall acceptance rate: 80%. Non-early acceptance rate: 80%. **Credentials of fall 2005 freshmen:** 28% ranked in the top 10 percent of their high school class; 51% were in the top 25 percent, and 81% were in the top half. (Proportion submitting class standing: 75%.) **First-year students who submitted SAT scores:** 10%. Scores (25/75 percentile): Verbal: 440-560, Math: 430-560, Combined: 870-1120. **First-year students submitting ACT scores:** 90%. Scores (25/75 percentile): English: 17-24, Math: 16-23, Composite: 18-24.

ACADEMICS

Year founded: 1897. **Academic calendar:** Semester. **Degrees offered:** certificate, diploma, associate, transfer-associate, terminal-associate, bachelor's, master's. **Most popular majors:** 28% education, 13% business, management, marketing, and related support services, 9% communication, journalism, and related programs, 8% social sciences, 6% psychology. **Major fields of study:** agriculture, agriculture operations, and related sciences; biological and biomedical sciences; business, management, marketing, and related support services; communication, journalism, and related programs; computer and information sciences and support services; construction trades; education; engineering; engineering technologies/technicians; English language and literature/letters; family and consumer sciences/human sciences; foreign languages, literatures, and linguistics; health professions and related clinical sciences; history; mathematics and statistics; multi/interdisciplinary studies; physical sciences; psychology; security and protective services; social sciences; visual and performing arts. **Areas of required coursework:** arts/fine arts, humanities, computer literacy, mathematics, English (including composition), philosophy, sciences (biological or physical), history, social science. **Pre-professional programs:** pre-law, pre-dentistry, pre-medicine, pre-veterinary science, pre-optometry, pre-pharmacy. **Special academic programs:** cooperative (work-study plan) program, distance learning, double major, English as a Second Language (ESL), honors program, independent study, internships, liberal arts/career combination, teacher certificate program, weekend college. **Teacher certification offered in:** early childhood, special education, elementary, secondary. **Reserve Officers Training Corps (ROTC):** Army ROTC: Offered on campus. **Faculty and instruction (2005-2006):** Total instructional faculty: 211 full-time, 63 part-time (66% men; 34% women; 5% minorities). Full-time faculty with Ph.D. or other terminal degree: 73%. Student/faculty ratio: 23/1. Classes of fewer than 20 students: 46%; of 20 to 49 students: 48%; of 50 or more students: 6%. **Freshmen returning for sophomore year:** 57%. **Graduation rates:** Four-year: 18%; five-year: 26%; six-year: 31%.

COSTS AND FINANCIAL AID

Financial aid office: (435) 586-7735. **Expenses (2006-2007):** Tuition and fees 2006-2007: $3,565 in state, $10,603 out of state; room/board: $4,124. Average amount of debt of borrowers graduating in 2005: $11,239. Proportion who borrowed: 64%.

CAMPUS LIFE AND EXTRACURRICULAR ACTIVITIES

Campus housing available: coed dorms, women's dorms, men's dorms, sorority housing, fraternity housing, apartment for single students, special housing for disabled students. Activities include: choral groups, concert band, dance, drama/theater, jazz band, literary magazine, marching band, music ensembles, musical theater, opera, pep band, radio station, student government, student newspaper, symphony orchestra, television station, yearbook. Number of fraternities: 2; sororities: 1. **Sports program (2005-2006):** Member of NCAA I. *Men's intercollegiate varsity sports:* baseball, basketball, cross-country, football, golf, track and field (indoor), track and field (outdoor). *Women's intercollegiate varsity sports:* basketball, cross-country, gymnastics, soccer, softball, tennis, track and field (indoor), track and field (outdoor).

SERVICES AND FACILITIES

Basic services: placement service, health service, health insurance. **Remedial assistance:** reading, math, writing, study skills. **Counseling services:** career, personal, veteran student, academic, older student, psychological. **For learning-disabled students:** Services include: remedial math, remedial English, tape recorders, diagnostic testing service, note-taking services, oral tests, learning center, readers, extended time for tests, tutors. **Information technology resources:** Students are not required to lease or own a computer. Number of campus computers available to all students: 771. Proportion of college-owned housing units wired for high-speed internet access: 100%. **Campus safety:** Security services offered: 24-hour emergency telephones, lighted pathways/sidewalks.

TRANSFER AND INTERNATIONAL STUDENTS

Transfer students: May apply for admission for the following academic terms: Fall, Spring, Summer. Applicants do not need a minimum number of credits to apply. For fall 2005: Transfer applications received: 1,141. Transfer applicants offered admission: 874. Transfer applicants enrolled: 652. **International students:** Number of foreign undergraduates: 67 (1% of student body). Minimum TOEFL score required: 500 (paper); 173 (computer). Average TOEFL score: 510 (paper).

University of Utah

- **Address:** 201 S. Presidents Circle, Salt Lake City, UT 84112
- **Website:** http://www.utah.edu
- **Public**
- **Enrollment:** 15,551 full-time; 7,110 part-time

KEY STATS
- ✔ **U.S News College Ranking:** 120, National Universities
- ✔ **ACT Score (25th/75th percentile):** 21-26
- ✔ **Tuition:** 2006-2007: $3,948 in state, $12,298 out of state

Selectivity: More selective	**Room/board:** $8,964
Acceptance rate: 85%	**Average debt:** $12,806
Student/faculty ratio: 15/1	**Proportion who borrowed:** 45%

UNDERGRADUATE STUDENT BODY STATS

2005-2006 enrollment: 15,551 full-time; 7,110 part-time. Men: 55%; women: 45%. **Ethnic makeup:** African American: 1%; American-Indian: 1%; Asian American: 4%; Hispanic: 4%; White: 89%; International: 2%.

ADMISSIONS FACTS AND FIGURES

Phone: (801) 581-7281. **Email:** Admissions@sa.utah.edu. **Website:** http://www.utah.edu. **Application deadlines for fall 2007:** Regular decision: April 1. Early decision: Not offered. Early action: Not offered. Admission cannot be deferred. **Application fee:** $35. Common application is not accepted. **To apply online, go to:** http://www.sa.utah.edu/admiss/appdownload/. **Admissions requirements/recommendations:** High school units required (recommended): English: 4; Mathematics: 2; Science: 3; Foreign language: 2; History: 1; Academic electives: 4; Total units: 15. Tests: The college uses SAT or ACT scores in admissions decisions. Either SAT or ACT required. For admission to the fall 2007 entering class, the school will accept: ACT with writing, ACT without writing. Campus visit: Recommended. Admissions interview: Neither required nor recommended. Off-campus interview: May be arranged. **Factors that count in admissions decisions: _Academic:_** Secondary school record: Very important. Class rank: Considered. Letters of recommendation: Considered. Standardized test scores: Very important. Essay: Not considered. _Nonacademic:_ Interview: Considered. Extracurricular activities: Considered. Talent/ability: Important. Character/personal qualities: Not considered. Alumni/ae relationship: Not considered. Geographical residence: Not considered. State residency: Not considered. Religious affiliation/commitment: Not considered. Minority status: Considered. Volunteer work: Not considered. Work experience: Not considered. **Other schools with the greatest overlap in applicants:** Brigham Young University–Provo; Utah State University; Utah Valley State College; Weber State University. **Admissions statistics for the fall 2005 entering class:** Total applicants: 6,687. Total accepted: 5,684. Freshmen enrolled: 2,821; 17% were from out of state. Overall acceptance rate: 85%. **Credentials of fall 2005 freshmen:** 27% ranked in the top 10 percent of their high school class; 51% were in the top 25 percent, and 82% were in the top half. (Proportion submitting class standing: 64%.) **Average high school grade point average:** 3.5. **First-year students who submitted SAT scores:** 25%. Scores (25/75 percentile): Verbal: 495-630, Math: 500-630, Combined: 995-1260. **First-year students submitting ACT scores:** 89%. Scores (25/75 percentile): English: 20-27, Math: 19-26, Composite: 21-26.

ACADEMICS

Year founded: 1850. **Academic calendar:** Semester. **Degrees offered:** certificate, bachelor's, post-bachelor's certificate, master's, post-master's certificate, first professional, doctorate. **Most popular majors:** 20% social sciences, 13% business, management, marketing, and related support services, 9% communication, journalism, and related programs, 7% visual and performing arts, 6% engineering. **Major fields of study:** architecture and related services; area, ethnic, cultural, and gender studies; biological and biomed-

ical sciences; business, management, marketing, and related support services; communication, journalism, and related programs; computer and information sciences and support services; education; engineering; English language and literature/letters; family and consumer sciences/human sciences; foreign languages, literatures, and linguistics; health professions and related clinical sciences; history; legal professions and studies; liberal arts and sciences studies, and humanities; mathematics and statistics; multi/interdisciplinary studies; natural resources and conservation; parks, recreation, leisure, and fitness studies; philosophy and religious studies; physical sciences; psychology; public administration and social service professions; social sciences; visual and performing arts. **Areas of required coursework:** arts/fine arts, humanities, mathematics, English (including composition), sciences (biological or physical), history, social science. **Pre-professional programs:** pre-law, pre-dentistry, pre-medicine, pre-pharmacy. **Special academic programs (% participation):** accelerated program (7.13%), cooperative (work-study plan) program (4.6%), distance learning (68.01%), double major (6.51%), English as a Second Language (ESL) (.63%), exchange student program (domestic) (.16%), honors program (6.12%), independent study (17.86%), internships (31.23%), student-designed major (.31%), study abroad (3.36%), teacher certificate program (1.29%). **Teacher certification offered in:** early childhood, special education, elementary, middle/junior high, adult education, secondary. **Cooperative education programs:** agriculture, art, business, computer science, education, engineering, health professions, home economics, humanities, natural science, social/behavioral science, technologies. **Reserve Officers Training Corps (ROTC):** Army ROTC: Offered on campus; Navy ROTC: Offered on campus; Air Force ROTC: Offered on campus. **Faculty and instruction (2005-2006):** Total instructional faculty: 1,175 full-time, 512 part-time (61% men; 39% women; 10% minorities). Full-time faculty with Ph.D. or other terminal degree: 86%. Student/faculty ratio: 15/1. Classes of fewer than 20 students: 35%; of 20 to 49 students: 47%; of 50 or more students: 18%. **Advanced Placement and International Baccalaureate credit:** AP tests may be used for: Credit and/or placement. Scores accepted: 3, 4, 5. International Baccalaureate exams may be used for: Credit and/or placement. **Freshmen returning for sophomore year:** 81%. **Graduation rates:** Four-year: 20%; five-year: 41%; six-year: 55%.

COSTS AND FINANCIAL AID

Financial aid office: (801) 581-8788. **Expenses (2006-2007):** Tuition and fees 2006-2007: $3,948 in state, $12,298 out of state; room/board: $8,964. Estimated books and supplies: $1,080; transportation: $1,188; personal expenses: $4,032. **Financial aid:** Priority filing date for institution's financial aid form: March 15. In 2005-2006, 59% of undergraduates applied for financial aid. Of those, 41% were determined to have financial need; 11% had their need fully met. Average financial aid package (proportion receiving): $8,086 (41%). Average amount of gift aid, such as scholarships or grants (proportion receiving): $3,970 (30%). Average amount of self-help aid, such as work study or loans (proportion receiving): $5,501 (30%). Average need-based loan (excluding PLUS or other private loans): $4,622. Among students who received need-based aid, the average percentage of need met: 50%. Among students who received aid based on merit, the average award (and the proportion receiving): $3,471 (4%). The average athletic scholarship (and the proportion receiving): $10,295 (0%). Average amount of debt of borrowers graduating in 2005: $12,806. Proportion who borrowed: 45%.

CAMPUS LIFE AND EXTRACURRICULAR ACTIVITIES

Campus housing available (% using): coed dorms (52%), sorority housing (5%), fraternity housing (4%), apartments for married students (19%), apartment for single students (11%), special housing for disabled students (9%). Students who live in college-owned, operated, or affiliated housing: 8%. **Student employment:** During the 2005-2006 academic year, 17% of undergraduates worked on campus. Average per-year earnings: $5,958. **Clubs and organizations:** Number of student organizations: 300. Activities include: choral groups, concert band, dance, drama/theater, jazz band, literary magazine, marching band, music ensembles, musical theater, opera, pep band, radio station, student government, student newspaper, student film society, symphony orchestra, television station. Number of fraternities: 8; sororities: 7. Proportion of men in fraternities: 1%; of women in sororities: 1%. Average proportion of students who stay on campus on weekends: 10%. **Sports program (2005-2006):** Member of NCAA I. _Men's intercollegiate varsity sports:_ alpine skiing, baseball, basketball, football, golf, nordic skiing, skiing, swimming and diving, tennis. _Women's intercollegiate varsity sports:_ alpine skiing, basketball, cross-country, gymnastics, nordic skiing, skiing, soccer, softball, swimming and diving, tennis, track and field (indoor), track and field (outdoor), volleyball.

SERVICES AND FACILITIES

Basic services: nonremedial tutoring, women's center, placement service, day care, health service, health insurance. **Remedial assistance:** math. **Counseling services:** minority student, career, military, personal, veteran student, academic, older student, psychological, birth control. **For learning-disabled students:** School does not offer a structured program with separate admission and additional fees. Total undergraduates in learning-disabled program or receiving services: 171. Services include: reading machines, tape recorders, note-taking services, oral tests, readers, extended time for tests, tutors, priority registration, priority seating, substitution of courses, texts on tape, exams on tape or computer, other testing accomodations, other. **Library:** Number of titles: 3,038,589; number of current serial subscriptions: 31,904. **Information technology resources:** Students are not required to lease or own a computer. Number of campus computers available to all students: 8,000. School has a wireless network. Approximate number of users that can be accommodated: 5,000. Proportion of college-owned housing units wired for high-speed internet access: 100%. **Campus safety:** Security services offered: 24-hour foot-and-vehicle patrols, late-night transport/escort service, 24-hour emergency telephones, lighted pathways/sidewalks, controlled dormitory access (key, security card, etc).

TRANSFER AND INTERNATIONAL STUDENTS

Transfer students: May apply for admission for the following academic terms: Fall, Spring, Summer. Applicants need a minimum number of credits to apply. For fall 2005: Transfer applications received: 3,497. Transfer applicants offered admission: 2,928. Transfer applicants enrolled: 2,260. **International students:** Number of foreign undergraduates: 490 (2% of student body). Number of countries represented: 112. Minimum TOEFL score required: 500 (paper); 173 (computer). Average TOEFL score: 550 (paper).

Utah State University

- **Address:** Old Main Hill, Logan, UT 84322
- **Website:** http://www.usu.edu
- **Public**
- **Enrollment:** 10,728 full-time; 2,009 part-time

KEY STATS

- ✔ **U.S News College Ranking:** third tier, National Universities
- ✔ **ACT Score (25th/75th percentile):** 21-27
- ✔ **Tuition:** 2006-2007: $3,799 in state, $11,249 out of state

Selectivity: More selective	**Room/board:** $4,400
Acceptance rate: 94%	**Average debt:** $12,430
Student/faculty ratio: 17/1	**Proportion who borrowed:** 50%

UNDERGRADUATE STUDENT BODY STATS

2005-2006 enrollment: 10,728 full-time; 2,009 part-time. Men: 51%; women: 49%. **Ethnic makeup:** African American: 1%; Asian American: 1%; Hispanic: 2%; White: 92%; International: 3%.

ADMISSIONS FACTS AND FIGURES

Phone: (435) 797-1079. **Email:** admit@cc.usu.edu. **Website:** http://www.usu.edu. **Application deadlines for fall 2007:** Regular decision: Rolling. Early decision: Not offered. Early action: Not offered. Admission can be deferred. **Application fee:** $40. Common application is not accepted. **To apply online, go to:** http://www.usu.edu/admissions/apply. **Admissions requirements/recommendations:** High school units required (recommended): English: 4; Mathematics: 3; Science: 3; Foreign language: (2); History: 1; Academic electives: 4. Tests: The college uses SAT or ACT scores in admissions decisions. Either SAT or ACT required. For admission to the fall 2007 entering class, the school will accept: ACT with writing; ACT without writing. Campus visit: Recommended. Admissions interview: Neither required nor recommended. Off-campus interview: Not available. **Factors that count in admissions decisions: Academic:** Secondary school record: Important. Class rank: Considered. Letters of recommendation: Considered. Standardized test scores: Very important. Essay: Not considered. *Nonacademic:* Interview: Not considered. Extracurricular activities: Not considered. Talent/ability: Not considered. Character/personal qualities: Not considered. Alumni/ae relationship: Not considered. Geographical residence: Not considered. State residency: Not considered. Religious affiliation/commitment: Not considered. Minority status: Not considered. Volunteer work: Not considered. Work experience: Not considered. **Other**

schools with the greatest overlap in applicants: Brigham Young University–Provo; University of Utah. **Admissions statistics for the fall 2005 entering class:** Total applicants: 4,666. Total accepted: 4,365. Freshmen enrolled: 2,054; 17% were from out of state. Overall acceptance rate: 94%. **Credentials of fall 2005 freshmen:** 25% ranked in the top 10 percent of their high school class; 51% were in the top 25 percent, and 81% were in the top half. (Proportion submitting class standing: 80%.) **Average high school grade point average:** 3.5. **First-year students who submitted SAT scores:** 9%. Scores (25/75 percentile): Verbal: 470-620, Math: 490-620, Combined: 960-1240. **First-year students submitting ACT scores:** 93%. Scores (25/75 percentile): English: 20-27, Math: 20-27, Composite: 21-27.

ACADEMICS

Year founded: 1888. **Academic calendar:** Semester. **Degrees offered:** certificate, associate, transfer-associate, terminal-associate, bachelor's, post-bachelor's certificate, master's, post-master's certificate, doctorate. **Most popular majors:** 4% accounting, 4% finance, 4% human development and family studies, 4% marketing/marketing management, 4% physical education teaching and coaching. **Major fields of study:** agriculture, agriculture operations, and related sciences; architecture and related services; area, ethnic, cultural, and gender studies; biological and biomedical sciences; business, management, marketing, and related support services; communication, journalism, and related programs; computer and information sciences and support services; education; engineering; engineering technologies/technicians; English language and literature/letters; family and consumer sciences/human sciences; foreign languages, literatures, and linguistics; health professions and related clinical sciences; legal professions and studies; liberal arts and sciences studies, and humanities; mathematics and statistics; mechanic and repair technologies/technicians; multi/interdisciplinary studies; natural resources and conservation; parks, recreation, leisure, and fitness studies; philosophy and religious studies; physical sciences; precision production; psychology; public administration and social service professions; social sciences; transportation and materials moving; visual and performing arts. **Areas of required coursework:** arts/fine arts, humanities, computer literacy, mathematics, English (including composition), sciences (biological or physical), history, social science, other. **Pre-professional programs:** pre-law, pre-dentistry, pre-medicine, pre-veterinary science. **Special academic programs:** accelerated program, cooperative (work-study plan) program, cross-registration, distance learning, double major, dual enrollment, English as a Second Language (ESL), exchange student program (domestic), honors program, independent study, internships, liberal arts/career combination, student-designed major, study abroad, teacher certificate program, weekend college. **Teacher certification offered in:** early childhood, special education, elementary, vo-tech, middle/junior high, secondary, bilingual/bicultural. **Cooperative education programs:** agriculture, business, education, engineering, home economics, humanities, natural science, social/behavioral science. **Reserve Officers Training Corps (ROTC):** Army ROTC: Offered on campus; Air Force ROTC: Offered on campus. **Faculty and instruction (2005-2006):** Total instructional faculty: 727 full-time, 37 part-time (68% men; 32% women; 6% minorities). Full-time faculty with Ph.D. or other terminal degree: 88%. Student/faculty ratio: 17/1. Classes of fewer than 20 students: 41%; of 20 to 49 students: 45%; of 50 or more students: 14%. **Advanced Placement and International Baccalaureate credit:** AP tests may be used for: Placement only. Scores accepted: 3, 4, 5. International Baccalaureate exams may be used for: Credit only. **Freshmen returning for sophomore year:** 72%. **Graduation rates:** Four-year: 21%; five-year: 35%; six-year: 47%. **Graduate study:** 23% of students pursue further study within one year. Fields in which graduates pursue further study: Master of Business Administration (MBA), 15%; law, 8%; medicine, 8%; dentistry, 4%; engineering, 10%; education, 7%.

COSTS AND FINANCIAL AID

Financial aid office: (435) 797-0173. **Expenses (2006-2007):** Tuition and fees 2006-2007: $3,799 in state, $11,249 out of state; room/board: $4,400. Estimated books and supplies: $1,080; transportation: $1,340; personal expenses: $1,960. **Financial aid:** In 2005-2006, 51% of undergraduates applied for financial aid. Of those, 47% were determined to have financial need; 12% had their need fully met. Average financial aid package (proportion receiving): $5,000 (45%). Average amount of gift aid, such as scholarships or grants (proportion receiving): $3,100 (36%). Average amount of self-help aid, such as work study or loans (proportion receiving): $4,200 (27%). Average need-based loan (excluding PLUS or other private loans): $3,800. Among students who received need-based aid, the average percentage of need met: 59%. Among students who received aid based on merit, the average award (and the proportion receiving): $2,900 (9%). The average athletic scholarship (and the proportion receiving): $7,000 (2%). Average amount of debt of borrowers graduating in 2005: $12,430. Proportion who borrowed: 50%.

CAMPUS LIFE AND EXTRACURRICULAR ACTIVITIES
Campus housing available: coed dorms, women's dorms, men's dorms, sorority housing, fraternity housing, apartments for married students, apartment for single students, special housing for disabled students, special housing for international students, other housing options. **Student employment:** During the 2005-2006 academic year, 29% of undergraduates worked on campus. Average per-year earnings: $7,000. **Clubs and organizations:** Number of student organizations: 200. Activities include: choral groups, concert band, drama/theater, jazz band, marching band, music ensembles, musical theater, opera, pep band, student government, student newspaper, symphony orchestra. Number of fraternities: 5; sororities: 3. Proportion of men in fraternities: 2%; of women in sororities: 2%. **Sports program (2005-2006):** Member of NCAA I. *Men's intercollegiate varsity sports:* basketball, cross-country, football, golf, tennis, track and field (indoor), track and field (outdoor). *Women's intercollegiate varsity sports:* basketball, cross-country, gymnastics, soccer, softball, tennis, track and field (indoor), track and field (outdoor), volleyball.

SERVICES AND FACILITIES
Basic services: nonremedial tutoring, women's center, placement service, day care, health service, health insurance, other. **Remedial assistance:** reading, math, writing, study skills. **Counseling services:** minority student, career, military, personal, veteran student, academic, older student, psychological, birth control, religious. **For learning-disabled students:** Services include: reading machines, tape recorders, note-taking services, readers, extended time for tests, other. **Library:** Number of titles: 1,549,866; number of current serial subscriptions: 12,533. **Information technology resources:** Students are not required to lease or own a computer. Number of campus computers available to all students: 850. School has a wireless network. Approximate number of users that can be accommodated: 1,500. Proportion of college-owned housing units wired for high-speed internet access: 100%. **Campus safety:** Security services offered: 24-hour foot-and-vehicle patrols, late-night transport/escort service, 24-hour emergency telephones, lighted pathways/sidewalks.

TRANSFER AND INTERNATIONAL STUDENTS
Transfer students: May apply for admission for the following academic terms: Fall, Spring, Summer. Applicants need a minimum number of credits to apply. For fall 2005: Transfer applications received: 1,657. Transfer applicants offered admission: 1,543. Transfer applicants enrolled: 928. **International students:** Number of foreign undergraduates: 438 (4% of student body). Number of countries represented: 74. Minimum TOEFL score required: 500 (paper); 173 (computer). Average TOEFL score: 500 (paper).

Utah Valley State College

- **Address:** 800 W. University Parkway, Orem, UT 84058-5999
- **Website:** http://www.uvsc.edu
- **Public**
- **Enrollment:** 11,565 full-time; 12,922 part-time

KEY STATS
✔ **U.S News College Ranking:** fourth tier, Comp. Coll.–Bachelor's (West)
✔ **ACT Score:** 20
✔ **Tuition:** 2006-2007: $3,308 in state, $10,338 out of state

Selectivity: Less selective	**Room/board:** N/A
Acceptance rate: 100%	**Average debt:** $9,046
Student/faculty ratio: N/A	**Proportion who borrowed:** 54%

UNDERGRADUATE STUDENT BODY STATS
2005-2006 enrollment: 11,565 full-time; 12,922 part-time. Men: 56%; women: 44%. **Ethnic makeup:** African American: 1%; American-Indian: 1%; Asian American: 2%; Hispanic: 4%; White: 91%; International: 1%.

ADMISSIONS FACTS AND FIGURES
Phone: (801) 863-8466. **Email:** info@uvsc.edu. **Website:** http://www.uvsc.edu. **Application deadlines for fall 2007:** Regular decision: August 15. Early decision: Not offered. Early action: Not offered. Admission can be deferred. **Application fee:** $30. Common application is not accepted.

To apply online, go to: http://www.uvsc.edu/apply.html. **Admissions requirements/recommendations:** High school units required (recommended): English: (4); Mathematics: (3); Science: (2); Foreign language: (2); Total units: (11). Tests: The college does not use SAT or ACT scores in admissions decisions. Neither SAT nor ACT required. For admission to the fall 2007 entering class, the school will accept: ACT with writing, ACT without writing. Campus visit: Neither required nor recommended. Admissions interview: Neither required nor recommended. Off-campus interview: Not available. **Factors that count in admissions decisions:** *Academic:* Secondary school record: Not considered. Class rank: Not considered. Letters of recommendation: Not considered. Standardized test scores: Not considered. Essay: Not considered. *Nonacademic:* Interview: Not considered. Extracurricular activities: Not considered. Talent/ability: Not considered. Character/personal qualities: Not considered. Alumni/ae relationship: Not considered. Geographical residence: Not considered. State residency: Not considered. Religious affiliation/commitment: Not considered. Minority status: Not considered. Volunteer work: Not considered. Work experience: Not considered. **Other schools with the greatest overlap in applicants:** Brigham Young University–Provo; University of Utah; Utah State University; Weber State University. **Admissions statistics for the fall 2005 entering class:** Total applicants: 4,473. Total accepted: 4,473. Freshmen enrolled: 3,713; 20% were from out of state. Overall acceptance rate: 100%. **Credentials of fall 2005 freshmen:** 6% ranked in the top 10 percent of their high school class; 19% were in the top 25 percent, and 48% were in the top half. (Proportion submitting class standing: 19%.) **Average high school grade point average:** 2.7. **First-year students who submitted SAT scores:** 1%. Scores (25/75 percentile): Verbal: N/A, Math: N/A, Combined: N/A. **First-year students submitting ACT scores:** 53%. Scores (25/75 percentile): English: N/A, Math: N/A, Composite: N/A.

ACADEMICS
Year founded: 1941. **Academic calendar:** Semester. **Degrees offered:** certificate, diploma, associate, transfer-associate, terminal-associate, bachelor's. **Most popular majors:** Information not available. **Major fields of study:** biological and biomedical sciences; business, management, marketing, and related support services; communication, journalism, and related programs; computer and information sciences and support services; education; English language and literature/letters; foreign languages, literatures, and linguistics; health professions and related clinical sciences; history; legal professions and studies; mathematics and statistics; multi/interdisciplinary studies; parks, recreation, leisure, and fitness studies; philosophy and religious studies; physical sciences; psychology; security and protective services; transportation and materials moving; visual and performing arts. **Areas of required coursework:** arts/fine arts, humanities, mathematics, English (including composition), sciences (biological or physical), history, social science, other. **Special academic programs (% participation):** accelerated program, cooperative (work-study plan) program (25%), cross-registration, distance learning (53%), dual enrollment (18%), English as a Second Language (ESL) (2%), honors program (5%), independent study (4%), internships (8%), liberal arts/career combination (2%), student-designed major (28%), study abroad (1%), teacher certificate program (6%), weekend college (24%). **Teacher certification offered in:** early childhood, elementary, middle/junior high, secondary. **Cooperative education programs:** art, business, computer science, education, engineering, health professions, humanities, natural science, social/behavioral science, technologies, vocational arts. **Reserve Officers Training Corps (ROTC):** Army ROTC: Offered on campus; Air Force ROTC: Offered at cooperating institution (Brigham Young University). **Advanced Placement and International Baccalaureate credit:** AP tests may be used for: Credit and/or placement. Scores accepted: 3, 4, 5. International Baccalaureate exams may be used for: Credit and/or placement. **Freshmen returning for sophomore year:** 49%. **Graduation rates:** Four-year: 2%; five-year: 20%; six-year: 33%. **Graduate study:** 10% of students pursue further study within one year.

COSTS AND FINANCIAL AID
Financial aid office: (801) 863-8442. **Expenses (2006-2007):** Tuition and fees 2006-2007: $3,308 in state, $10,338 out of state; room/board: N/A. Estimated books and supplies: $1,532; transportation: $1,352; personal expenses: $1,598. **Financial aid:** Priority filing date for institution's financial aid form: May 1. In 2005-2006, 65% of undergraduates applied for financial aid. Of those, 59% were determined to have financial need; 6% had their need fully met. Average financial aid package (proportion receiving): $7,554 (51%). Average amount of gift aid, such as scholarships or grants (proportion receiving): $3,283 (40%). Average amount of self-help aid, such as work study or loans (proportion receiving): $3,813 (38%). Average need-based loan (excluding PLUS or other private loans): $3,391. Among students

who received need-based aid, the average percentage of need met: 70%. Among students who received aid based on merit, the average award (and the proportion receiving): $2,043 (14%). The average athletic scholarship (and the proportion receiving): $3,070 (1%). Average amount of debt of borrowers graduating in 2005: $9,046. Proportion who borrowed: 54%.

CAMPUS LIFE AND EXTRACURRICULAR ACTIVITIES

Campus housing available: other housing options. **Student employment:** During the 2005-2006 academic year, 2% of undergraduates worked on campus. Average per-year earnings: $7. **Clubs and organizations:** Number of student organizations: 69. Activities include: choral groups, concert band, dance, drama/theater, jazz band, literary magazine, music ensembles, musical theater, pep band, student government, student newspaper, symphony orchestra, television station. Number of fraternities: 0; sororities: 0. **Sports program (2005-2006):** Member of NCAA I. *Men's intercollegiate varsity sports:* baseball, basketball, cross-country, golf, track and field (indoor), track and field (outdoor), wrestling. *Women's intercollegiate varsity sports:* basketball, cross-country, golf, soccer, softball, track and field (indoor), track and field (outdoor), volleyball.

SERVICES AND FACILITIES

Basic services: nonremedial tutoring, women's center, placement service, day care, health service, health insurance. **Remedial assistance:** reading, math, writing, study skills, other. **Counseling services:** minority student, career, military, personal, veteran student, academic, older student, psychological. **For learning-disabled students:** School does not offer a structured program with separate admission and additional fees. Total undergraduates in learning-disabled program or receiving services: 432. Services include: remedial math, remedial English, remedial reading, tape recorders, other special classes, diagnostic testing service, untimed tests, note-taking services, oral tests, readers, extended time for tests, tutors, other testing accomodations, other. **Library:** Number of titles: 183,944; number of current serial subscriptions: 811. **Information technology resources:** Students are not required to lease or own a computer. Number of campus computers available to all students: 1,000. School has a wireless network. **Campus safety:** Security services offered: 24-hour foot-and-vehicle patrols, 24-hour emergency telephones, lighted pathways/sidewalks.

TRANSFER AND INTERNATIONAL STUDENTS

Transfer students: May apply for admission for the following academic terms: Fall, Spring, Summer. Applicants do not need a minimum number of credits to apply. For fall 2005: Transfer applications received: 2,534. Transfer applicants offered admission: 2,534. Transfer applicants enrolled: 1,035. **International students:** Number of foreign undergraduates: 150 (1% of student body). Number of countries represented: 68. Minimum TOEFL score required: 500 (paper); 173 (computer). Average TOEFL score: 520 (paper).

Weber State University

- **Address:** 1103 University Circle, Ogden, UT 84408-1103
- **Website:** http://weber.edu
- **Public**
- **Enrollment:** 10,250 full-time; 7,488 part-time

KEY STATS

✔ **U.S News College Ranking:** 41, Universities–Master's (West)
✔ **ACT Score (25th/75th percentile):** 18-24
✔ **Tuition:** 2006-2007: $3,432 in state, $10,415 out of state

Selectivity: Selective	**Room/board:** $6,500
Acceptance rate: 100%	**Average debt:** N/A
Student/faculty ratio: 22/1	**Proportion who borrowed:** N/A

UNDERGRADUATE STUDENT BODY STATS

2005-2006 enrollment: 10,250 full-time; 7,488 part-time. Men: 50%; women: 50%. **Ethnic makeup:** African American: 1%; American-Indian: 1%; Asian American: 2%; Hispanic: 4%; White: 93%; International: 1%. **Religious preference:** Roman Catholic: 5%; Protestant: 6%; Jewish: 1%; No preference: 12%; Unknown: 16%; LDS: 60%.

ADMISSIONS FACTS AND FIGURES

Phone: (801) 626-6744. **Email:** admissions@weber.edu. **Website:** http://weber.edu. **Application deadlines for fall 2007:** Regular decision: August 23. Early decision: Not offered. Early action: Not offered. Admission can be deferred. **Application fee:** $30. Common application is not accepted. **To apply online, go to:** http://weber.edu/admissions/apply.htm. **Admissions requirements/recommendations:** High school units required (recommended): English: (4); Mathematics: (2); Science: (2); Foreign language: (2); History: (1); Academic electives: (4); Total units: (15). Tests: The college does not use SAT or ACT scores in admissions decisions. Neither SAT nor ACT required. Campus visit: Recommended. Admissions interview: Neither required nor recommended. Off-campus interview: Not available. **Factors that count in admissions decisions:** *Academic:* Secondary school record: Important. Class rank: Not considered. Letters of recommendation: Not considered. Standardized test scores: Important. Essay: Not considered. *Nonacademic:* Interview: Considered. Extracurricular activities: Considered. Talent/ability: Not considered. Character/personal qualities: Considered. Alumni/ae relationship: Not considered. Geographical residence: Not considered. State residency: Not considered. Religious affiliation/commitment: Not considered. Minority status: Not considered. Volunteer work: Not considered. Work experience: Not considered. **Other schools with the greatest overlap in applicants:** Brigham Young University–Provo; University of Utah; Utah State University; Utah Valley State College. **Admissions statistics for the fall 2005 entering class:** Total applicants: 5,196. Total accepted: 5,196. Freshmen enrolled: 2,759; 7% were from out of state. Overall acceptance rate: 100%. **Credentials of fall 2005 freshmen:** 63% were in the top 25 percent, and 93% were in the top half. **Average high school grade point average:** 3.3.

ACADEMICS

Year founded: 1889. **Academic calendar:** Semester. **Degrees offered:** certificate, associate, transfer-associate, terminal-associate, bachelor's, post-bachelor's certificate, master's. **Most popular majors:** 10% selling skills and sales operations, 5% psychology, 3% English language and literature, 3% accounting, 3% nursing/registered nurse training (R.N., A.S.N., B.S.N., M.S.N.). **Major fields of study:** biological and biomedical sciences; business, management, marketing, and related support services; communication, journalism, and related programs; computer and information sciences and support services; construction trades; education; engineering; engineering technologies/technicians; English language and literature/letters; family and consumer sciences/human sciences; foreign languages, literatures, and linguistics; health professions and related clinical sciences; mathematics and statistics; physical sciences; psychology; public administration and social service professions; security and protective services; social sciences; visual and performing arts. **Areas of required coursework:** arts/fine arts, humanities, computer literacy, mathematics, English (including composition), sciences (biological or physical), history, social science. **Pre-professional programs:** pre-law, pre-dentistry, pre-medicine, pre-pharmacy. **Special academic programs:** accelerated program, cooperative (work-study plan) program, distance learning, double major, dual enrollment, English as a Second Language (ESL), exchange student program (domestic), external degree program, honors program, independent study, internships, student-designed major, study abroad, teacher certificate program. **Teacher certification offered in:** early childhood, special education, elementary, middle/junior high, secondary. **Cooperative education programs:** health professions, social/behavioral science, technologies. **Reserve Officers Training Corps (ROTC):** Army ROTC: Offered on campus; Navy ROTC: Offered on campus; Air Force ROTC: Offered on campus. **Faculty and instruction (2005-2006):** Total instructional faculty: 465 full-time, 205 part-time. Full-time faculty with Ph.D. or other terminal degree: 85%. Student/faculty ratio: 22/1. Classes of fewer than 20 students: 40%; of 20 to 49 students: 54%; of 50 or more students: 6%. **Advanced Placement and International Baccalaureate credit:** AP tests may be used for: Placement only. International Baccalaureate exams may be used for: Placement only. **Freshmen returning for sophomore year:** 71%. **Graduation rates:** Four-year: 15%; five-year: 29%; six-year: 43%. **Graduate study:** 40% of students pursue further study immediately upon graduation.

COSTS AND FINANCIAL AID

Financial aid office: (801) 626-7569. **Expenses (2006-2007):** Tuition and fees 2006-2007: $3,432 in state, $10,415 out of state; room/board: $6,500. Estimated books and supplies: $900; transportation: $1,108; personal expenses: $1,275. **Financial aid:** Priority filing date for institution's financial aid form: March 1. In 2005-2006, 53% of undergraduates applied for financial aid. Of those, 48% were determined to have financial need; 7% had their need fully met. Average financial aid package (proportion receiving):

$4,763 (44%). Average amount of gift aid, such as scholarships or grants (proportion receiving): $2,951 (32%). Average amount of self-help aid, such as work study or loans (proportion receiving): $3,814 (25%). Average need-based loan (excluding PLUS or other private loans): $3,523. Among students who received need-based aid, the average percentage of need met: 56%. Among students who received aid based on merit, the average award (and the proportion receiving): $1,527 (25%). The average athletic scholarship (and the proportion receiving): $2,844 (3%).

CAMPUS LIFE AND EXTRACURRICULAR ACTIVITIES

Campus housing available: women's dorms, men's dorms, apartments for married students, apartment for single students, special housing for dis-abled students. Students who live in college-owned, operated, or affiliated housing: 3%. **Student employment:** During the 2005-2006 academic year, 5% of undergraduates worked on campus. Average per-year earnings: $6,000. **Clubs and organizations:** Number of student organizations: 121. Activities include: choral groups, concert band, dance, drama/theater, jazz band, literary magazine, marching band, music ensembles, musical theater, opera, pep band, radio station, student government, student newspaper, stu-dent film society, symphony orchestra, television station. Number of frater-nities: 0; sororities: 0. Proportion of men in fraternities: 1%; of women in sororities: 1%. Average proportion of students who stay on campus on weekends: 3%. **Sports program (2005-2006):** Member of NCAA I. *Men's intercollegiate varsity sports:* basketball, cross-country, football, golf, tennis, track and field (indoor), track and field (outdoor). *Women's intercollegiate varsity sports:* basketball, cross-country, golf, soccer, tennis, track and field (indoor), track and field (outdoor), volleyball.

SERVICES AND FACILITIES

Basic services: nonremedial tutoring, women's center, placement service, day care, health service, health insurance. **Remedial assistance:** math, other. **Counseling services:** minority student, career, military, personal, veteran stu-dent, academic, older student, psychological, birth control, religious. **For learning-disabled students:** School does not offer a structured program with separate admission and additional fees. Total undergraduates in learning-disabled program or receiving services: 290. Services include: remedial math, remedial English, reading machines, untimed tests, note-taking serv-ices, oral tests, readers, extended time for tests, tutors. **Library:** Number of titles: 520,538; number of current serial subscriptions: 1,711. **Information technology resources:** Students are not required to lease or own a computer. Number of campus computers available to all students: 600. School has a wireless network. Approximate number of users that can be accommodated: 60,000. Proportion of college-owned housing units wired for high-speed internet access: 75%. **Campus safety:** Security services offered: 24-hour foot-and-vehicle patrols, late-night transport/escort service, 24-hour emergency telephones, lighted pathways/sidewalks, controlled dormitory access (key, security card, etc).

TRANSFER AND INTERNATIONAL STUDENTS

Transfer students: May apply for admission for the following academic terms: Fall, Spring, Summer. Applicants need a minimum number of cred-its to apply. For fall 2005: Transfer applications received: 3,142. Transfer applicants offered admission: 3,142. Transfer applicants enrolled: 1,942. **International students:** Number of foreign undergraduates: 152 (1% of stu-dent body). Number of countries represented: 37.

Westminster College

■ Address: 1840 S. 1300 E, Salt Lake City, UT 84105-3697
■ Website: http://www.westminstercollege.edu
■ Private
■ Enrollment: 1,633 full-time; 245 part-time

KEY STATS

✔ U.S News College Ranking: 20, Universities–Master's (West)
✔ ACT Score (25th/75th percentile): 21-26
✔ Tuition: 2006-2007: $21,030

Selectivity: More selective	Room/board: $5,726
Acceptance rate: 89%	Average debt: $16,450
Student/faculty ratio: 10/1	Proportion who borrowed: 64%

UNDERGRADUATE STUDENT BODY STATS

2005-2006 enrollment: 1,633 full-time; 245 part-time. Men: 42%; women: 58%. **Ethnic makeup:** African American: 1%; Asian American: 3%; Hispanic: 6%; White: 89%; International: 2%. **Religious preference:** Roman Catholic: 8%; Unknown: 54%; Church of Jesus Christ of Latter-day Saints: 24%; Other: 14%.

ADMISSIONS FACTS AND FIGURES

Phone: (801) 832-2200. **Email:** admission@westminstercollege.edu. **Website:** http://www.westminstercollege.edu. **Application deadlines for fall 2007:** Regular decision: Rolling. Early decision: Not offered. Early action: Not offered. Admission can be deferred. **Application fee:** $40. Common application is accepted. **To apply online, go to:** http://www.westminstercol-lege.edu/prospective_undergraduate/. **Admissions requirements/recommen-dations:** High school units required (recommended): English: 4 (4); Mathematics: 2 (3); Science: 3 (3); Foreign language: 2 (3); Social studies: 2 (2); History: 1 (1); Academic electives: 2 (3); Total units: 16 (19). Tests: The college uses SAT or ACT scores in admissions decisions. Either SAT or ACT required. For admission to the fall 2007 entering class, the school will accept: ACT without writing. Campus visit: Recommended. Admissions interview: Recommended. Off-campus interview: May be arranged. **Factors that count in admissions decisions:** *Academic:* Secondary school record: Very important. Class rank: Important. Letters of recommendation: Considered. Standardized test scores: Important. Essay: Important. *Nonacademic:* Interview: Important. Extracurricular activities: Considered. Talent/ability: Considered. Character/personal qualities: Considered. Alumni/ae relation-ship: Considered. Geographical residence: Considered. State residency: Not considered. Religious affiliation/commitment: Not considered. Minority sta-tus: Not considered. Volunteer work: Not considered. Work experience: Not considered. **Other schools with the greatest overlap in applicants:** Brigham Young University–Provo; University of Utah; Utah State University; Utah Valley State College; Weber State University. **Admissions statistics for the fall 2005 entering class:** Total applicants: 897. Total accepted: 801. Freshmen enrolled: 350; 20% were from out of state. Overall acceptance rate: 89%. **Credentials of fall 2005 freshmen:** 30% ranked in the top 10 percent of their high school class; 57% were in the top 25 percent, and 86% were in the top half. (Proportion submitting class standing: 71%.) **Average high school grade point average:** 3.5. **First-year students who submitted SAT scores:** 33%. Scores (25/75 percentile): Verbal: 493-630, Math: 470-613, Combined: 963-1243. **First-year students submitting ACT scores:** 83%. Scores (25/75 per-centile): English: 20-27, Math: 19-26, Composite: 21-26.

ACADEMICS

Year founded: 1875. **Academic calendar:** Other. **Degrees offered:** bachelor's, post-bachelor's certificate, master's. **Most popular majors:** 36% business, management, marketing, and related support services, 12% education, 11% health professions and related clinical sciences, 8% psychology, 7% commu-nication, journalism, and related programs. **Major fields of study:** biological and biomedical sciences; business, management, marketing, and related support services; communication, journalism, and related programs; com-puter and information sciences and support services; education; English language and literature/letters; health professions and related clinical sci-ences; history; mathematics and statistics; philosophy and religious studies; physical sciences; psychology; social sciences; transportation and materials moving; visual and performing arts. **Areas of required coursework:** arts/fine arts, humanities, computer literacy, mathematics, English (including com-position), philosophy, foreign languages, sciences (biological or physical), history, social science, other. **Pre-professional programs:** pre-law, pre-den-tistry, pre-medicine, pre-veterinary science. **Special academic programs (% participation):** cross-registration (6%), double major (7%), honors program (4%), independent study (16%), internships (53%), liberal arts/career combi-nation (1%), study abroad (3%), teacher certificate program (3%). **Teacher certification offered in:** early childhood, special education, elementary, adult education, secondary. **Cooperative education programs:** art, business, com-puter science, education, health professions, humanities, natural science, social/behavioral science, other. **Reserve Officers Training Corps (ROTC):** Army ROTC: Offered at cooperating institution (University of Utah); Navy ROTC: Offered at cooperating institution (University of Utah); Air Force ROTC: Offered at cooperating institution (University of Utah). **Faculty and instruction (2005-2006):** Total instructional faculty: 121 full-time, 138 part-time (46% men; 54% women; 6% minorities). Full-time faculty with Ph.D. or other terminal degree: 91%. Student/faculty ratio: 10/1. Classes of fewer than 20 students: 69%; of 20 to 49 students: 31%; of 50 or more students: 0%. **Advanced Placement and International Baccalaureate credit:** AP tests may be used for: Credit and/or placement. Scores accepted: 3, 4, 5. International Baccalaureate exams may be used for: Credit and/or placement. **Freshmen returning for sophomore year:** 72%. **Graduation rates:** Four-year: 34%; five-year: 51%; six-year: 53%. **Graduate study:** 35% of students pursue further study immediately upon graduation; 35% within one year. Fields in which graduates pursue further study: Master of Business Administration (MBA), 27%; law, 10%; medicine, 10%; engineering, 5%; theology (or the seminary), 5%; education, 10%; arts and sciences, 25%; veterinary medicine, 5%.

COSTS AND FINANCIAL AID
Financial aid office: (801) 832-2500. **Expenses (2006-2007):** Tuition and fees 2006-2007: $21,030; room/board: $5,726. Estimated books and supplies: $1,000; transportation: $900; personal expenses: $1,225.
Financial aid: Priority filing date for institution's financial aid form: April 15. In 2005-2006, 75% of undergraduates applied for financial aid. Of those, 66% were determined to have financial need; 41% had their need fully met. Average financial aid package (proportion receiving): $18,917 (66%). Average amount of gift aid, such as scholarships or grants (proportion receiving): $10,210 (65%). Average amount of self-help aid, such as work study or loans (proportion receiving): $8,707 (58%). Average need-based loan (excluding PLUS or other private loans): $6,221. Among students who received need-based aid, the average percentage of need met: 87%. Among students who received aid based on merit, the average award (and the proportion receiving): $8,663 (29%). The average athletic scholarship (and the proportion receiving): $4,250 (0%). Average amount of debt of borrowers graduating in 2005: $16,450. Proportion who borrowed: 64%.

CAMPUS LIFE AND EXTRACURRICULAR ACTIVITIES
Campus housing available (% using): coed dorms (28%), apartment for single students (60%), special housing for disabled students (5%), other housing options (7%). Students who live in college-owned, operated, or affiliated housing: 26%. **Student employment:** During the 2005-2006 academic year, 12% of undergraduates worked on campus. Average per-year earnings: $1,700. **Clubs and organizations:** Number of student organizations: 36. Activities include: choral groups, dance, drama/theater, jazz band, literary magazine, music ensembles, musical theater, student government, student newspaper, student film society, symphony orchestra. Number of fraternities: 0; sororities: 0. Average proportion of students who stay on campus on weekends: 55%. **Sports program (2005-2006):** Member of NAIA. *Men's intercollegiate varsity sports:* basketball, cross-country, golf, soccer. *Women's intercollegiate varsity sports:* basketball, cross-country, golf, volleyball.

SERVICES AND FACILITIES
Basic services: nonremedial tutoring, placement service, health insurance. **Remedial assistance:** math, writing, study skills. **Counseling services:** minority student, career, military, personal, veteran student, academic, older student, psychological, religious. **For learning-disabled students:** School does not offer a structured program with separate admission and additional fees. Total undergraduates in learning-disabled program or receiving services: 26. Services include: tape recorders, untimed tests, note-taking services, readers, extended time for tests, tutors, priority registration, priority seating, texts on tape, exams on tape or computer, other testing accomodations. **Library:** Number of titles: 135,083; number of current serial subscriptions: 4,394. **Information technology resources:** Students are not required to lease or own a computer. Number of campus computers available to all students: 450. School has a wireless network. Approximate number of users that can be accommodated: 2,500. Proportion of college-owned housing units wired for high-speed internet access: 100%. **Campus safety:** Security services offered: 24-hour foot-and-vehicle patrols, late-night transport/escort service, 24-hour emergency telephones, lighted pathways/sidewalks, controlled dormitory access (key, security card, etc).

TRANSFER AND INTERNATIONAL STUDENTS
Transfer students: May apply for admission for the following academic terms: Fall, Winter, Spring, Summer. Applicants need a minimum number of credits to apply. For fall 2005: Transfer applications received: 632. Transfer applicants offered admission: 485. Transfer applicants enrolled: 222. **International students:** Number of foreign undergraduates: 30 (2% of student body). Number of countries represented: 4. Minimum TOEFL score required: 550 (paper); 213 (computer).

Vermont

Bennington College

- **Address:** 1 College Drive, Bennington, VT 05201
- **Website:** http://www.bennington.edu
- **Private**
- **Enrollment:** 608 full-time; 4 part-time

KEY STATS

✔ **U.S News College Ranking:** 91, Liberal Arts Colleges
✔ **SAT Score (25th/75th percentile):** 1150-1340
✔ **Tuition:** 2006-2007: $35,250

Selectivity: More selective	**Room/board:** $8,730
Acceptance rate: 62%	**Average debt:** $20,340
Student/faculty ratio: 8/1	**Proportion who borrowed:** 72%

UNDERGRADUATE STUDENT BODY STATS

2005-2006 enrollment: 608 full-time; 4 part-time. Men: 33%; women: 67%. **Ethnic makeup:** African American: 2%; Asian American: 2%; Hispanic: 3%; White: 89%; International: 3%.

ADMISSIONS FACTS AND FIGURES

Phone: (800) 833-6845. **Email:** admissions@bennington.edu. **Website:** http://www.bennington.edu. **Application deadlines for fall 2007:** Regular decision: January 3; decision sent by April 1. Early decision: Send application by: November 15; Decision sent by: December 15. Early action: Not offered. Admission can be deferred. **Application fee:** $60. Common application is accepted. **To apply online, go to:** http://www.bennington.edu/admis_applying.asp. **Admissions requirements/recommendations:** High school units required (recommended): English: (4); Mathematics: (3); Science: (3); Foreign language: (2); Social studies: (3); History: (3); Total units: (18). Tests: The college uses SAT or ACT scores in admissions decisions. Neither SAT nor ACT required. For admission to the fall 2007 entering class, the school will accept: ACT with writing, ACT without writing. Campus visit: Recommended. Admissions interview: Required. Off-campus interview: May be arranged. **Factors that count in admissions decisions:** *Academic:* Secondary school record: Very important. Class rank: Very important. Letters of recommendation: Very important. Standardized test scores: Considered. Essay: Very important. *Nonacademic:* Interview: Very important. Extracurricular activities: Very important. Talent/ability: Very important. Character/personal qualities: Very important. Alumni/ae relationship: Considered. Geographical residence: Considered. State residency: Considered. Religious affiliation/commitment: Not considered. Minority status: Considered. Volunteer work: Considered. Work experience: Considered. **Other schools with the greatest overlap in applicants:** Bard College; New York University; Oberlin College; Sarah Lawrence College; Smith College. **Admissions statistics for the fall 2005 entering class:** Total applicants: 723. Total accepted: 445. Freshmen enrolled: 137; 98% were from out of state. Accepted through early-decision or early-action plans: 16%. Overall acceptance rate: 62%. Early-decision acceptance rate: 54%. Non-early acceptance rate: 62%. **Size of waiting list:** 16 applicants; enrolled from waiting list: 4. **Credentials of fall 2005 freshmen:** 30% ranked in the top 10 percent of their high school class; 74% were in the top 25 percent, and 99% were in the top half. (Proportion submitting class standing: 39%.) **Average high school grade point average:** 3.5. **First-year students who submitted SAT scores:** 96%. Scores (25/75 percentile): Verbal: 610-700, Math: 540-640, Combined: 1150-1340. **First-year students submitting ACT scores:** 18%. Scores (25/75 percentile): English: 25-31, Math: 23-28, Composite: 25-28.

ACADEMICS

Year founded: 1925. **Academic calendar:** Semester. **Degrees offered:** bachelor's, post-bachelor's certificate, master's. **Most popular majors:** 19% visual and performing arts, 15% English language and literature, 9% social sciences, 8% drama and dramatics/theater arts, 6% music. **Major fields of study:** architecture and related services; area, ethnic, cultural, and gender studies; biological and biomedical sciences; communication, journalism, and related programs; communications technologies/technicians and support services; computer and information sciences and support services; education; English language and literature/letters; foreign languages, literatures, and linguistics; health professions and related clinical sciences; history; legal professions and studies; liberal arts and sciences studies, and humanities; mathematics and statistics; multi/interdisciplinary studies; natural resources and conservation; philosophy and religious studies; physical sciences; psychology; social sciences; visual and performing arts. **Pre-professional programs:** pre-law, pre-medicine, pre-veterinary science, other. **Special academic programs (% participation):** accelerated program (1%), cross-registration (5%), double major (40%), English as a Second Language (ESL) (1%), exchange student program (domestic) (1%), honors program (25%), independent study (35%), internships (100%), student-designed major (100%), study abroad (20%), teacher certificate program (7%). **Teacher certification offered in:** early childhood, elementary, middle/junior high, secondary, bilingual/bicultural. **Cooperative education programs:** other. **Faculty and instruction (2005-2006):** Total instructional faculty: 66 full-time, 24 part-time (62% men; 38% women; 14% minorities). Full-time faculty with Ph.D. or other terminal degree: 74%. Student/faculty ratio: 8/1. Classes of fewer than 20 students: 90%; of 20 to 49 students: 10%; of 50 or more students: 0%. **Freshmen returning for sophomore year:** 82%. **Graduation rates:** Four-year: 45%; five-year: 58%; six-year: 60%.

COSTS AND FINANCIAL AID

Financial aid office: (802) 440-4325. **Expenses (2006-2007):** Tuition and fees 2006-2007: $35,250; room/board: $8,730. Estimated books and supplies: $800; transportation: $450; personal expenses: $1,600. **Financial aid:** Priority filing date for institution's financial aid form: March 1. In 2005-2006, 72% of undergraduates applied for financial aid. Of those, 69% were determined to have financial need; 3% had their need fully met. Average financial aid package (proportion receiving): $25,712 (69%). Average amount of gift aid, such as scholarships or grants (proportion receiving): $21,449 (67%). Average amount of self-help aid, such as work study or loans (proportion receiving): $4,842 (67%). Average need-based loan (excluding PLUS or other private loans): $3,798. Among students who received need-based aid, the average percentage of need met: 74%. Among students who received aid based on merit, the average award (and the proportion receiving): $7,498 (5%). The average athletic scholarship (and the proportion receiving): $0 (0%). Average amount of debt of borrowers graduating in 2005: $20,340. Proportion who borrowed: 72%.

CAMPUS LIFE AND EXTRACURRICULAR ACTIVITIES

Campus housing available (% using): coed dorms (96%), special housing for disabled students (0%), cooperative housing (3%), other housing options (1%). Students who live in college-owned, operated, or affiliated housing: 98%. **Student employment:** During the 2005-2006 academic year, 25% of undergraduates worked on campus. Average per-year earnings: $2,037. **Clubs and organizations:** Number of student organizations: 30. Activities include: choral groups, concert band, dance, drama/theater, jazz band, literary magazine, music ensembles, musical theater, radio station, student government, student newspaper, student film society, symphony orchestra, yearbook. Number of fraternities: 0; sororities: 0. Average proportion of students who stay on campus on weekends: 85%. **Sports program (2005-2006):** *Men's intercollegiate varsity sports:* soccer. *Women's intercollegiate varsity sports:* soccer.

SERVICES AND FACILITIES

Basic services: nonremedial tutoring, day care, health service, health insurance. **Counseling services:** career, personal, academic, psychological. **For learning-disabled students:** School does not offer a structured program with separate admission and additional fees. Total undergraduates in learning-disabled program or receiving services: 12. **Library:** Number of titles: 113,125; number of current serial subscriptions: 8,682. **Information technology resources:** Students are not required to lease or own a computer. Number of campus computers available to all students: 75. School has a wireless network. Approximate number of users that can be accommodated: 250. Proportion of college-owned housing units wired for high-speed internet access: 100%. **Campus safety:** Security services offered: 24-hour foot-and-vehicle patrols, late-night transport/escort service, 24-hour emergency telephones, lighted pathways/sidewalks.

TRANSFER AND INTERNATIONAL STUDENTS

Transfer students: May apply for admission for the following academic terms: Fall, Spring. Applicants need a minimum number of credits to apply. For fall 2005: Transfer applications received: 50. Transfer applicants offered admission: 26. Transfer applicants enrolled: 13. **International students:** Number of foreign undergraduates: 19 (3% of student body). Number of countries represented: 8. Minimum TOEFL score required: 577 (paper); 233 (computer).

Burlington College

- **Address:** 95 North Avenue, Burlington, VT 05401
- **Website:** http://www.burlington.edu
- **Private**
- **Enrollment:** 103 full-time; 81 part-time

KEY STATS

- ✔ **U.S News College Ranking:** Unranked, Liberal Arts Colleges
- ✔ **SAT or ACT Score (25th/75th percentile):** N/A
- ✔ **Tuition:** 2006-2007: $16,400

Selectivity: N/A	**Room/board:** N/A
Acceptance rate: 77%	**Average debt:** $21,577
Student/faculty ratio: 4/1	**Proportion who borrowed:** 85%

UNDERGRADUATE STUDENT BODY STATS

2005-2006 enrollment: 103 full-time; 81 part-time. Men: 45%; women: 55%. **Ethnic makeup:** African American: 2%; American-Indian: 3%; Asian American: 1%; Hispanic: 4%; White: 90%.

ADMISSIONS FACTS AND FIGURES

Phone: (802) 862-9616. **Email:** admissions@burlington.edu. **Website:** http://www.burlington.edu. **Application deadlines for fall 2007:** Regular decision: Rolling. Early decision: Not offered. Early action: Not offered. Admission can be deferred. **Application fee:** $50. Common application is accepted. **To apply online, go to:** http://www.commonapp.org. **Admissions requirements/recommendations:** High school units required (recommended): English: (4); Mathematics: (3); Science: (3); Foreign language: (2); Social studies: (4); History: (3); Academic electives: (4); Total units: (24). Tests: The college uses SAT or ACT scores in admissions decisions. Neither SAT nor ACT required. For admission to the fall 2007 entering class, the school will accept: ACT with writing, ACT without writing. Campus visit: Recommended. Admissions interview: Required. Off-campus interview: May be arranged. **Factors that count in admissions decisions:** *Academic:* Secondary school record: Important. Class rank: Not considered. Letters of recommendation: Important. Standardized test scores: Considered. Essay: Very important. *Nonacademic:* Interview: Very important. Extracurricular activities: Considered. Talent/ability: Considered. Character/personal qualities: Very important. Alumni/ae relationship: Not considered. Geographical residence: Not considered. State residency: Not considered. Religious affiliation/commitment: Not considered. Minority status: Not considered. Volunteer work: Considered. Work experience: Considered. **Admissions statistics for the fall 2005 entering class:** Total applicants: 22. Total accepted: 17. Freshmen enrolled: 10; 10% were from out of state. Overall acceptance rate: 77%. **Credentials of fall 2005 freshmen:** (Proportion submitting class standing: 50%.) **Average high school grade point average:** 2.6.

ACADEMICS

Year founded: 1972. **Academic calendar:** Semester. **Degrees offered:** certificate, associate, bachelor's. **Most popular majors:** 29% psychology, 18% liberal arts and sciences/liberal studies, 16% creative writing, 13% psychology, 11% film/cinema studies. **Major fields of study:** area, ethnic, cultural, and gender studies; English language and literature/letters; legal professions and studies; liberal arts and sciences studies, and humanities; psychology; public administration and social service professions; visual and performing arts. **Areas of required coursework:** arts/fine arts, humanities, computer literacy, mathematics, English (including composition), philosophy, sciences (biological or physical), history, social science, other. **Pre-professional programs:** pre-law. **Special academic programs (% participation):** cross-registra-

tion (18%), distance learning (47%), double major (0%), dual enrollment (0%), external degree program (47%), honors program (0%), independent study (92%), internships (89%), liberal arts/career combination (0%), student-designed major (18%), study abroad (3%). **Cooperative education programs:** art, humanities, social/behavioral science, technologies. **Faculty and instruction (2005-2006):** Total instructional faculty: 6 full-time, 79 part-time (49% men; 51% women). Full-time faculty with Ph.D. or other terminal degree: 50%. Student/faculty ratio: 4/1. Classes of fewer than 20 students: 100%; of 20 to 49 students: 0%; of 50 or more students: 0%. **Advanced Placement and International Baccalaureate credit:** AP tests may be used for: Credit and/or placement. Scores accepted: 3, 4, 5. International Baccalaureate exams may be used for: Credit and/or placement. **Freshmen returning for sophomore year:** 55%. **Graduation rates:** Four-year: 17%; five-year: 25%; six-year: 26%. **Graduate study:** 35% of students pursue further study immediately upon graduation. Fields in which graduates pursue further study: law, 10%; theology (or the seminary), 5%; education, 5%; arts and sciences, 80%.

COSTS AND FINANCIAL AID

Financial aid office: (802) 862-9616. **Expenses (2005-2006):** Tuition and fees 2005-2006: $14,670; room/board: N/A. **Financial aid:** In 2005-2006, 68% of undergraduates applied for financial aid. Of those, 65% were determined to have financial need; 3% had their need fully met. Average financial aid package (proportion receiving): $10,170 (64%). Average amount of gift aid, such as scholarships or grants (proportion receiving): $4,927 (45%). Average amount of self-help aid, such as work study or loans (proportion receiving): $6,946 (62%). Average need-based loan (excluding PLUS or other private loans): $6,495. Among students who received need-based aid, the average percentage of need met: 58%. Among students who received aid based on merit, the average award (and the proportion receiving): $250 (1%). The average athletic scholarship (and the proportion receiving): $0 (0%). Average amount of debt of borrowers graduating in 2005: $21,577. Proportion who borrowed: 85%.

CAMPUS LIFE AND EXTRACURRICULAR ACTIVITIES

Campus housing available (% using): apartments for married students (0%), apartment for single students (50%), cooperative housing (50%). Students who live in college-owned, operated, or affiliated housing: 5%. **Student employment:** During the 2005-2006 academic year, 0% of undergraduates worked on campus. Average per-year earnings: $0. **Clubs and organizations:** Number of student organizations: 1. Activities include: drama/theater, literary magazine, student government, student newspaper, student film society. Number of fraternities: 0; sororities: 0.

SERVICES AND FACILITIES

Basic services: nonremedial tutoring. **Remedial assistance:** reading, math, writing, study skills. **Counseling services:** career, personal, academic, psychological. **For learning-disabled students:** School does not offer a structured program with separate admission and additional fees. Total undergraduates in learning-disabled program or receiving services: 6. Services include: tape recorders, oral tests, tutors. **Library:** Number of titles: 13,876; number of current serial subscriptions: 59. **Information technology resources:** Students are not required to lease or own a computer. Number of campus computers available to all students: 26. School has a wireless network. Approximate number of users that can be accommodated: 20. Proportion of college-owned housing units wired for high-speed internet access: 0%. **Campus safety:** Security services offered: lighted pathways/sidewalks.

TRANSFER AND INTERNATIONAL STUDENTS

Transfer students: May apply for admission for the following academic terms: Fall, Spring, Summer. Transfer applicants do not need a minimum number of credits to apply. For fall 2005: Transfer applications received: 34. Transfer applicants offered admission: 34. Transfer applicants enrolled: 30. **International students:** Number of foreign undergraduates: 0. Number of countries represented: 1. Minimum TOEFL score required: 500 (paper).

Castleton State College

- **Address:** Castleton, VT 05735
- **Website:** http://www.castleton.edu
- **Public**
- **Enrollment:** 1,684 full-time; 207 part-time

KEY STATS

✔ **U.S News College Ranking:** fourth tier, Universities–Master's (North)
✔ **SAT Score (25th/75th percentile):** 890-1090
✔ **Tuition:** 2006-2007: $6,828 in state, $14,556 out of state

Selectivity: Less selective	**Room/board:** $6,942
Acceptance rate: 79%	**Average debt:** N/A
Student/faculty ratio: 14/1	**Proportion who borrowed:** N/A

UNDERGRADUATE STUDENT BODY STATS

2005-2006 enrollment: 1,684 full-time; 207 part-time. Men: 41%; women: 59%. **Ethnic makeup:** African American: 1%; American-Indian: 1%; Asian American: 1%; Hispanic: 1%; White: 97%.

ADMISSIONS FACTS AND FIGURES

Phone: (800) 639-8521. **Email:** info@castleton.edu. **Website:** http://www.castleton.edu. **Application deadlines for fall 2007:** Regular decision: Rolling. Early decision: Not offered. Early action: Not offered. Admission can be deferred. **Application fee:** $35. Common application is accepted. **To apply online, go to:** https://www.applyweb.com/aw?castle. **Admissions requirements/recommendations:** High school units required (recommended): English: 4; Mathematics: 3; Science: 2 (3); Social studies: 3 (4); Total units: 14 (2). Tests: The college uses SAT or ACT scores in admissions decisions. Either SAT or ACT required. For admission to the fall 2007 entering class, the school will accept: ACT with writing. Campus visit: Recommended. Admissions interview: Recommended. Off-campus interview: May be arranged. **Factors that count in admissions decisions:** *Academic:* Secondary school record: Very important. Class rank: Considered. Letters of recommendation: Important. Standardized test scores: Important. Essay: Very important. *Nonacademic:* Interview: Considered. Extracurricular activities: Important. Talent/ability: Considered. Character/personal qualities: Considered. Alumni/ae relationship: Considered. Geographical residence: Not considered. State residency: Not considered. Religious affiliation/commitment: Not considered. Minority status: Not considered. Volunteer work: Considered. Work experience: Considered. **Admissions statistics for the fall 2005 entering class:** Total applicants: 1,715. Total accepted: 1,348. Freshmen enrolled: 467; 43% were from out of state. Overall acceptance rate: 79%. **Credentials of fall 2005 freshmen:** 5% ranked in the top 10 percent of their high school class; 20% were in the top 25 percent, and 57% were in the top half. (Proportion submitting class standing: 77%.) **Average high school grade point average:** 2.8. **First-year students who submitted SAT scores:** 92%. Scores (25/75 percentile): Verbal: 430-550, Math: 460-540, Combined: 890-1090. **First-year students submitting ACT scores:** 10%. Scores (25/75 percentile): English: N/A, Math: N/A, Composite: 17-21.

ACADEMICS

Year founded: 1787. **Academic calendar:** Semester. **Degrees offered:** certificate, associate, bachelor's, master's. **Most popular majors:** 18% business, management, marketing, and related support services, 14% visual and performing arts, 10% parks, recreation, leisure, and fitness studies, 8% communication, journalism, and related programs, 7% psychology. **Major fields of study:** biological and biomedical sciences; business, management, marketing, and related support services; communication, journalism, and related programs; computer and information sciences and support services; education; English language and literature/letters; foreign languages, literatures, and linguistics; history; mathematics and statistics; parks, recreation, leisure, and fitness studies; physical sciences; psychology; public administration and social service professions; security and protective services; social sciences; visual and performing arts. **Areas of required coursework:** arts/fine arts, humanities, computer literacy, mathematics, English (including composition), sciences (biological or physical), social science. **Special academic programs:** cooperative (work-study plan) program, double major, dual enrollment, honors program, independent study, internships, liberal arts/career combination, study abroad, teacher certificate program. **Teacher certification offered in:** elementary, middle/junior high, secondary. **Reserve Officers Training Corps (ROTC):** Army ROTC: Offered at cooperating institution (University of Vermont). **Faculty and instruction (2005-2006):** Total

instructional faculty: 89 full-time, 112 part-time (53% men; 47% women; 3% minorities). Full-time faculty with Ph.D. or other terminal degree: 93%. Student/faculty ratio: 14/1. Classes of fewer than 20 students: 73%; of 20 to 49 students: 26%; of 50 or more students: 1%. **Advanced Placement and International Baccalaureate credit:** AP tests may be used for: Credit only. Scores accepted: 3. **Freshmen returning for sophomore year:** 69%. **Graduation rates:** Four-year: 26%; five-year: 37%; six-year: 43%.

COSTS AND FINANCIAL AID

Financial aid office: (802) 468-1292. **Expenses (2006-2007):** Tuition and fees 2006-2007: $6,828 in state, $14,556 out of state; room/board: $6,942. **Financial aid:** Priority filing date for institution's financial aid form: March 31.

CAMPUS LIFE AND EXTRACURRICULAR ACTIVITIES

Campus housing available: coed dorms. Students who live in college-owned, operated, or affiliated housing: 50%. **Clubs and organizations:** Number of student organizations: 40. Activities include: choral groups, concert band, drama/theater, jazz band, literary magazine, music ensembles, radio station, student government, student newspaper, television station, yearbook. Number of fraternities: 0; sororities: 0. Average proportion of students who stay on campus on weekends: 66%. **Sports program (2005-2006):** Member of NCAA III. *Men's intercollegiate varsity sports:* baseball, basketball, crosscountry, golf, ice hockey, lacrosse, soccer, tennis. *Women's intercollegiate varsity sports:* basketball, cross-country, field hockey, ice hockey, lacrosse, soccer, softball, tennis, volleyball.

SERVICES AND FACILITIES

Basic services: health service, health insurance. **Remedial assistance:** math, writing, study skills. **Counseling services:** career, military, academic, birth control. **For learning-disabled students:** School does not offer a structured program with separate admission and additional fees. Services include: reading machines, tape recorders, note-taking services, oral tests, learning center, readers, extended time for tests, tutors. **Library:** Number of titles: 166,011; number of current serial subscriptions: 739. **Information technology resources:** Students are not required to lease or own a computer. Number of campus computers available to all students: 225. School does not have a wireless network. Proportion of college-owned housing units wired for high-speed internet access: 100%. **Campus safety:** Security services offered: 24-hour foot-and-vehicle patrols, late-night transport/escort service, 24-hour emergency telephones, lighted pathways/sidewalks, controlled dormitory access (key, security card, etc).

TRANSFER AND INTERNATIONAL STUDENTS

Transfer students: May apply for admission for the following academic terms: Fall, Spring. Applicants do not need a minimum number of credits to apply. **International students:** Number of foreign undergraduates: 7. Minimum TOEFL score required: 500 (paper); 173 (computer).

Champlain College

- **Address:** 163 S. Willard Street, Burlington, VT 05401
- **Website:** http://www.champlain.edu
- **Private**
- **Enrollment:** 1,716 full-time; 754 part-time

KEY STATS

✔ **U.S News College Ranking:** 17, Comp. Coll.–Bachelor's (North)
✔ **SAT Score (25th/75th percentile):** 1000-1180
✔ **Tuition:** 2006-2007: $16,250

Selectivity: Selective	**Room/board:** $10,200
Acceptance rate: 64%	**Average debt:** N/A
Student/faculty ratio: 15/1	**Proportion who borrowed:** N/A

UNDERGRADUATE STUDENT BODY STATS

2005-2006 enrollment: 1,716 full-time; 754 part-time. Men: 52%; women: 48%. **Ethnic makeup:** Asian American: 1%; Hispanic: 1%; White: 97%.

ADMISSIONS FACTS AND FIGURES

Phone: (800) 570-5858. **Email:** admission@champlain.edu. **Website:** http://www.champlain.edu. **Application deadlines for fall 2007:** Regular decision: August 20. Early decision: Not offered. Early action: Not offered.

Admission cannot be deferred. **Application fee:** $40. Common application is accepted. **To apply online, go to:** https://www.applyweb.com/apply/champln/indexa.html. **Admissions requirements/recommendations:** High school units required (recommended): English: 4; Mathematics: 3; Science: 3; Foreign language: (2); Social studies: 1; History: 3; Academic electives: 4; Total units: 20. Tests: The college uses SAT or ACT scores in admissions decisions. Either SAT or ACT required. For admission to the fall 2007 entering class, the school will accept: ACT with writing, ACT without writing. Campus visit: Recommended. Admissions interview: Recommended. Off-campus interview: May be arranged. **Factors that count in admissions decisions:** *Academic:* Secondary school record: Very important. Class rank: Important. Letters of recommendation: Important. Standardized test scores: Important. Essay: Very important. *Nonacademic:* Interview: Important. Extracurricular activities: Important. Talent/ability: Considered. Character/personal qualities: Considered. Alumni/ae relationship: Considered. Geographical residence: Considered. State residency: Not considered. Religious affiliation/commitment: Not considered. Minority status: Not considered. Volunteer work: Considered. Work experience: Considered. **Other schools with the greatest overlap in applicants:** Colby-Sawyer College; Quinnipiac University; St. Michael's College; University of Southern Maine; University of Vermont. **Admissions statistics for the fall 2005 entering class:** Total applicants: 1,850. Total accepted: 1,176. Freshmen enrolled: 466; 70% were from out of state. Overall acceptance rate: 64%. **Credentials of fall 2005 freshmen:** 10% ranked in the top 10 percent of their high school class; 31% were in the top 25 percent, and 77% were in the top half. (Proportion submitting class standing: 76%.) **First-year students who submitted SAT scores:** 98%. Scores (25/75 percentile): Verbal: 500-590, Math: 500-590, Combined: 1000-1180. **First-year students submitting ACT scores:** 8%. Scores (25/75 percentile): English: N/A, Math: N/A, Composite: 18-23.

ACADEMICS
Year founded: 1878. **Academic calendar:** Semester. **Degrees offered:** certificate, associate, bachelor's, master's. **Most popular majors:** 13% business administration and management, 12% intermedia/multimedia, 10% elementary education and teaching, 8% accounting, 6% criminal justice/safety studies. **Major fields of study:** business, management, marketing, and related support services; communication, journalism, and related programs; computer and information sciences and support services; education; engineering; health professions and related clinical sciences; legal professions and studies; liberal arts and sciences studies, and humanities; psychology; public administration and social service professions; security and protective services; visual and performing arts. **Areas of required coursework:** arts/fine arts, humanities, computer literacy, mathematics, English (including composition), philosophy, sciences (biological or physical), history, social science, other. **Pre-professional programs:** pre-law. **Special academic programs (% participation):** accelerated program (5.4%), cross-registration (.3%), distance learning (70%), double major (1.5%), honors program (6.1%), independent study (.3%), internships (47.8%), liberal arts/career combination (100%), student-designed major (0%), study abroad (.8%). **Teacher certification offered in:** elementary, middle/junior high, secondary. **Reserve Officers Training Corps (ROTC):** Army ROTC: Offered at cooperating institution (University of Vermont). **Faculty and instruction (2005-2006):** Total instructional faculty: 66 full-time, 207 part-time (58% men; 42% women; 1% minorities). Full-time faculty with Ph.D. or other terminal degree: 33%. Student/faculty ratio: 15/1. Classes of fewer than 20 students: 37%; of 20 to 49 students: 63%. **Advanced Placement and International Baccalaureate credit:** AP tests may be used for: Credit and/or placement. Scores accepted: 3. International Baccalaureate exams may be used for: Credit and/or placement. **Freshmen returning for sophomore year:** 80%. **Graduation rates:** Four-year: 59%; five-year: 70%; six-year: 72%. **Graduate study:** 5% of students pursue further study immediately upon graduation. Fields in which graduates pursue further study: Master of Business Administration (MBA), 16%; education, 22%; arts and sciences, 33%.

COSTS AND FINANCIAL AID
Financial aid office: (800) 570-5858. **Expenses (2006-2007):** Tuition and fees 2006-2007: $16,250; room/board: $10,200. Estimated books and supplies: $600. **Financial aid:** Priority filing date for institution's financial aid form: May 1. In 2005-2006, 76% of undergraduates applied for financial aid. Of those, 60% were determined to have financial need; 20% had their need fully met. Average financial aid package (proportion receiving): $9,185 (57%). Average amount of gift aid, such as scholarships or grants (proportion receiving): $5,134 (44%). Average amount of self-help aid, such as work study or loans (proportion receiving): $5,528 (55%). Average need-based loan (excluding PLUS or other private loans): $5,218. Among students who received need-based aid, the average percentage of need met: 63%. Among students who received aid based on merit, the average award (and the proportion receiving): $11,912 (16%). The average athletic scholarship (and the proportion receiving): $0 (0%).

CAMPUS LIFE AND EXTRACURRICULAR ACTIVITIES
Campus housing available (% using): coed dorms (95%), women's dorms (1%), special housing for international students (4%). Students who live in college-owned, operated, or affiliated housing: 40%. **Student employment:** During the 2005-2006 academic year, 7% of undergraduates worked on campus. Average per-year earnings: $2,100. **Clubs and organizations:** Number of student organizations: 30. Activities include: choral groups, dance, drama/theater, literary magazine, music ensembles, musical theater, radio station, student government, student newspaper. Number of fraternities: 0; sororities: 0. Average proportion of students who stay on campus on weekends: 82%.

SERVICES AND FACILITIES
Basic services: nonremedial tutoring, women's center, health service, health insurance. **Remedial assistance:** other. **Counseling services:** career, personal, academic. **For learning-disabled students:** School does not offer a structured program with separate admission and additional fees. Services include: untimed tests, note-taking services, oral tests, extended time for tests, tutors, priority seating, exams on tape or computer, other testing accomodations. **Library:** Number of titles: 40,797; number of current serial subscriptions: 549. **Information technology resources:** Students are not required to lease or own a computer. Number of campus computers available to all students: 380. School has a wireless network. Approximate number of users that can be accommodated: 1,380. Proportion of college-owned housing units wired for high-speed internet access: 100%. **Campus safety:** Security services offered: 24-hour foot-and-vehicle patrols, late-night transport/escort service, 24-hour emergency telephones, lighted pathways/sidewalks, controlled dormitory access (key, security card, etc).

TRANSFER AND INTERNATIONAL STUDENTS
Transfer students: May apply for admission for the following academic terms: Fall, Spring. Applicants do not need a minimum number of credits to apply. For fall 2005: Transfer applications received: 316. Transfer applicants offered admission: 208. Transfer applicants enrolled: 104. **International students:** Number of foreign undergraduates: 6. Number of countries represented: 19. Minimum TOEFL score required: 500 (paper); 173 (computer). Average TOEFL score: 525 (paper).

College of St. Joseph

- **Address:** 71 Clement Road, Rutland, VT 05701
- **Website:** http://www.csj.edu
- **Private; Religious affiliation:** Roman Catholic
- **Enrollment:** 176 full-time; 95 part-time

KEY STATS
✔ **U.S News College Ranking:** fourth tier, Universities–Master's (North)
✔ **SAT Score (25th/75th percentile):** 920-1090
✔ **Tuition:** 2006-2007: $14,900

Selectivity: Less selective	**Room/board:** $7,150
Acceptance rate: 68%	**Average debt:** $21,967
Student/faculty ratio: N/A	**Proportion who borrowed:** 69%

UNDERGRADUATE STUDENT BODY STATS
2005-2006 enrollment: 176 full-time; 95 part-time. Men: 39%; women: 61%. **Ethnic makeup:** African American: 5%; Asian American: 1%; Hispanic: 2%; White: 91%; International: 1%. **Religious preference:** Roman Catholic: 43%; Protestant: 38%; Jewish: 1%; No preference: 16%; Unknown: 2%.

ADMISSIONS FACTS AND FIGURES
Phone: (802) 773-5900. **Email:** admissions@csj.edu. **Website:** http://www.csj.edu. **Application deadlines for fall 2007:** Regular decision: Rolling. Early decision: Not offered. Early action: Not offered. Admission can be deferred. **Application fee:** $25. Common application is accepted. **Admissions requirements/recommendations:** High school units required (recommended): English: 4; Mathematics: 3; Science: 2; Foreign language: 0; Social studies: 2; History: 1; Academic electives: 6. Tests: The college uses SAT or ACT scores in admissions decisions. Either SAT or ACT required.

Campus visit: Recommended. Admissions interview: Recommended. Off-campus interview: May be arranged. **Factors that count in admissions decisions:** *Academic:* Secondary school record: Very important. Class rank: Considered. Letters of recommendation: Very important. Standardized test scores: Considered. Essay: Important. *Nonacademic:* Interview: Considered. Extracurricular activities: Considered. Talent/ability: Considered. Character/personal qualities: Important. Alumni/ae relationship: Considered. Geographical residence: Not considered. State residency: Not considered. Religious affiliation/commitment: Not considered. Minority status: Not considered. Volunteer work: Considered. Work experience: Considered. **Other schools with the greatest overlap in applicants:** Castleton State College; Lyndon State College. **Admissions statistics for the fall 2005 entering class:** Total applicants: 157. Total accepted: 107. Freshmen enrolled: 44; Overall acceptance rate: 68%. **Credentials of fall 2005 freshmen:** 5% ranked in the top 10 percent of their high school class; 29% were in the top 25 percent, and 68% were in the top half. (Proportion submitting class standing: 100%.) **Average high school grade point average:** 3.1. **First-year students who submitted SAT scores:** 93%. Scores (25/75 percentile): Verbal: 460-550, Math: 460-540, Combined: 920-1090. **First-year students submitting ACT scores:** 7%. Scores (25/75 percentile): English: N/A, Math: N/A, Composite: 21-21.

ACADEMICS

Year founded: 1956. **Academic calendar:** Semester. **Degrees offered:** associate, bachelor's, post-bachelor's certificate, master's. **Most popular majors:** 30% psychology, 27% education, 26% business, management, marketing, and related support services. **Major fields of study:** business, management, marketing, and related support services; communication, journalism, and related programs; computer and information sciences and support services; education; English language and literature/letters; liberal arts and sciences studies, and humanities; parks, recreation, leisure, and fitness studies; psychology; public administration and social service professions. **Areas of required coursework:** arts/fine arts, humanities, computer literacy, mathematics, English (including composition), philosophy, sciences (biological or physical), history, social science, other. **Special academic programs (% participation):** accelerated program (8%), double major (5%), independent study (1%), internships (40%), liberal arts/career combination (90%), teacher certificate program (30%). **Teacher certification offered in:** special education, elementary, secondary. **Faculty and instruction (2005-2006):** Total instructional faculty: 11 full-time, 57 part-time (59% men; 41% women; 3% minorities). Full-time faculty with Ph.D. or other terminal degree: 73%. **Advanced Placement and International Baccalaureate credit:** AP tests may be used for: Credit and/or placement. Scores accepted: 4, 5. **Freshmen returning for sophomore year:** 57%. **Graduation rates:** Six-year: 34%. **Graduate study:** 18% of students pursue further study immediately upon graduation; 8% within one year. Fields in which graduates pursue further study: Master of Business Administration (MBA), 28%; education, 64%; arts and sciences, 5%.

COSTS AND FINANCIAL AID

Financial aid office: (802) 773-5900. **Expenses (2006-2007):** Tuition and fees 2006-2007: $14,900; room/board: $7,150. Estimated books and supplies: $1,000; transportation: $650; personal expenses: $675. **Financial aid:** In 2005-2006, 100% of undergraduates applied for financial aid. Of those, 91% were determined to have financial need; 28% had their need fully met. Average financial aid package (proportion receiving): $12,874 (91%). Average amount of gift aid, such as scholarships or grants (proportion receiving): $7,430 (90%). Average amount of self-help aid, such as work study or loans (proportion receiving): $5,727 (87%). Average need-based loan (excluding PLUS or other private loans): $5,046. Among students who received need-based aid, the average percentage of need met: 76%. Among students who received aid based on merit, the average award (and the proportion receiving): $11,020 (9%). The average athletic scholarship (and the proportion receiving): $0 (0%). Average amount of debt of borrowers graduating in 2005: $21,967. Proportion who borrowed: 69%.

CAMPUS LIFE AND EXTRACURRICULAR ACTIVITIES

Campus housing available (% using): women's dorms (55%), men's dorms (45%), special housing for disabled students. **Student employment:** During the 2005-2006 academic year, 0% of undergraduates worked on campus. Average per-year earnings: $0. **Clubs and organizations:** Number of student organizations: 22. Activities include: choral groups, dance, drama/theater, student government. Number of fraternities: 0; sororities: 0. Average proportion of students who stay on campus on weekends: 45%. **Sports program (2005-2006):** Member of NAIA. *Men's intercollegiate varsity sports:* baseball,

basketball, cross-country, soccer. *Women's intercollegiate varsity sports:* basketball, cross-country, soccer, softball.

SERVICES AND FACILITIES

Basic services: nonremedial tutoring, placement service, health insurance. **Remedial assistance:** reading, math, writing, study skills, other. **Counseling services:** career, personal, academic, psychological, religious. **For learning-disabled students:** School does not offer a structured program with separate admission and additional fees. Total undergraduates in learning-disabled program or receiving services: 75. Services include: remedial math, remedial English, tape recorders, untimed tests, note-taking services, oral tests, learning center, extended time for tests, tutors, priority seating, proofreading services. **Library:** Number of titles: 77,707; number of current serial subscriptions: 100. **Information technology resources:** Students are not required to lease or own a computer. Number of campus computers available to all students: 40. School does not have a wireless network. Proportion of college-owned housing units wired for high-speed internet access: 100%. **Campus safety:** Security services offered: 24-hour emergency telephones, lighted pathways/sidewalks, controlled dormitory access (key, security card, etc).

TRANSFER AND INTERNATIONAL STUDENTS

Transfer students: May apply for admission for the following academic terms: Fall, Spring, Summer. Applicants do not need a minimum number of credits to apply. For fall 2005: Transfer applications received: 72. Transfer applicants offered admission: 50. Transfer applicants enrolled: 31. **International students:** Number of foreign undergraduates: 1 (1% of student body). Number of countries represented: 1. Minimum TOEFL score required: 550 (paper); 213 (computer).

Goddard College

- **Address:** 123 Pitkin Road, Plainfield, VT 05667
- **Website:** http://www.goddard.edu
- **Private**
- **Enrollment:** N/A

KEY STATS

✔ **U.S News College Ranking:** fourth tier, Universities–Master's (North)
✔ **SAT or ACT Score (25th/75th percentile):** N/A
✔ **Tuition:** 2005-2006: $9,806

Selectivity: Less selective	**Room/board:** $878
Acceptance rate: N/A	**Average debt:** N/A
Student/faculty ratio: N/A	**Proportion who borrowed:** N/A

Green Mountain College

- **Address:** 1 College Circle, Poultney, VT 05764-1199
- **Website:** http://www.greenmtn.edu
- **Private; Religious affiliation:** United Methodist
- **Enrollment:** 662 full-time; 34 part-time

KEY STATS

✔ **U.S News College Ranking:** third tier, Comp. Coll.–Bachelor's (North)
✔ **SAT Score (25th/75th percentile):** 900-1160
✔ **Tuition:** 2006-2007: $23,264

Selectivity: Less selective	**Room/board:** $8,400
Acceptance rate: 84%	**Average debt:** $23,894
Student/faculty ratio: 14/1	**Proportion who borrowed:** 93%

UNDERGRADUATE STUDENT BODY STATS

2005-2006 enrollment: 662 full-time; 34 part-time. Men: 52%; women: 48%. **Ethnic makeup:** African American: 3%; American-Indian: 2%; Asian American: 1%; Hispanic: 3%; White: 92%; International: 1%. **Religious preference:** Roman Catholic: 15%; Protestant: 1%; Jewish: 2%; No preference: 6%; Unknown: 64%; United Methodist: 3%; Christian: 2%; Other: 7%.

ADMISSIONS FACTS AND FIGURES

Phone: (802) 287-8208. **Email:** admiss@greenmtn.edu. **Website:** http://www.greenmtn.edu. **Application deadlines for fall 2007:** Regular decision: Rolling. Early decision: Not offered. Early action: Not offered. Admission can be deferred. **Application fee:** $30. Common application is accepted. **Admissions requirements/recommendations:** High school units required (recommended): English: 4; Mathematics: 3; Science: 3; Foreign language: 0 (2); Social studies: 3; History: 2; Academic electives: 5; Total units: 18. Tests: The college uses SAT or ACT scores in admissions decisions. Either SAT or ACT required. For admission to the fall 2007 entering class, the school will accept: ACT with writing, ACT without writing. Campus visit: Recommended. Admissions interview: Recommended. Off-campus interview: Not available. **Factors that count in admissions decisions:** *Academic:* Secondary school record: Very important. Class rank: Important. Letters of recommendation: Very important. Standardized test scores: Important. Essay: Very important. *Nonacademic:* Interview: Important. Extracurricular activities: Important. Talent/ability: Considered. Character/personal qualities: Very important. Alumni/ae relationship: Not considered. Geographical residence: Not considered. State residency: Not considered. Religious affiliation/commitment: Not considered. Minority status: Not considered. Volunteer work: Considered. Work experience: Considered. **Admissions statistics for the fall 2005 entering class:** Total applicants: 1,162. Total accepted: 973. Freshmen enrolled: 254; 11% were from out of state. Overall acceptance rate: 84%. **Credentials of fall 2005 freshmen:** 9% ranked in the top 10 percent of their high school class; 24% were in the top 25 percent, and 50% were in the top half. (Proportion submitting class standing: 70%.) **First-year students who submitted SAT scores:** 87%. Scores (25/75 percentile): Verbal: 470-600, Math: 430-560, Combined: 900-1160. **First-year students submitting ACT scores:** 12%. Scores (25/75 percentile): English: N/A, Math: N/A, Composite: 18-23.

ACADEMICS

Year founded: 1834. **Academic calendar:** Semester. **Degrees offered:** certificate, bachelor's. **Most popular majors:** Information not available. **Major fields of study:** biological and biomedical sciences; business, management, marketing, and related support services; communication, journalism, and related programs; education; English language and literature/letters; health professions and related clinical services; history; liberal arts and sciences studies, and humanities; multi/interdisciplinary studies; natural resources and conservation; parks, recreation, leisure, and fitness studies; philosophy and religious studies; psychology; social sciences; visual and performing arts. **Areas of required coursework:** arts/fine arts, mathematics, English (including composition), philosophy, sciences (biological or physical), history, social science, other. **Pre-professional programs:** pre-law, pre-medicine, pre-veterinary science. **Special academic programs (% participation):** double major (1%), honors program, independent study (10%), internships (10%), student-designed major (.5%). **Teacher certification offered in:** special education, elementary, secondary. **Faculty and instruction (2005-2006):** Total instructional faculty: 43 full-time, 1 part-time. Full-time faculty with Ph.D. or other terminal degree: 77%. Student/faculty ratio: 14/1. Classes of fewer than 20 students: 54%; of 20 to 49 students: 46%; of 50 or more students: 0%. **Advanced Placement and International Baccalaureate credit:** AP tests may be used for: Credit only. Scores accepted: 3, 4, 5. International Baccalaureate exams may be used for: Credit only. **Freshmen returning for sophomore year:** 63%. **Graduation rates:** Six-year: 36%.

COSTS AND FINANCIAL AID

Financial aid office: (802) 287-8210. **Expenses (2006-2007):** Tuition and fees 2006-2007: $23,264; room/board: $8,400. **Financial aid:** Priority filing date for institution's financial aid form: March 1. In 2005-2006, 86% of undergraduates applied for financial aid. Of those, 76% were determined to have financial need; 28% had their need fully met. Average financial aid package (proportion receiving): $19,049 (75%). Average amount of gift aid, such as scholarships or grants (proportion receiving): $12,939 (71%). Average amount of self-help aid, such as work study or loans (proportion receiving): $7,336 (68%). Average need-based loan (excluding PLUS or other private loans): $6,251. Among students who received need-based aid, the average percentage of need met: 78%. Among students who received aid based on merit, the average award (and the proportion receiving): $15,767 (13%). The average athletic scholarship (and the proportion receiving): $0 (0%). Average amount of debt of borrowers graduating in 2005: $23,894. Proportion who borrowed: 93%.

CAMPUS LIFE AND EXTRACURRICULAR ACTIVITIES

Campus housing available (% using): coed dorms (86%), apartment for single students (2%), cooperative housing (3%), other housing options (9%). Students who live in college-owned, operated, or affiliated housing: 90%. **Student employment:** During the 2005-2006 academic year, 15% of under-graduates worked on campus. Average per-year earnings: $1,300. **Clubs and organizations:** Number of student organizations: 20. Activities include: choral groups, concert band, drama/theater, jazz band, music ensembles, radio station, student government, student newspaper. Number of fraternities: 0; sororities: 0. Average proportion of students who stay on campus on weekends: 75%. **Sports program (2005-2006):** Member of NAIA. *Men's intercollegiate varsity sports:* alpine skiing, basketball, cross-country, golf, lacrosse, soccer, tennis. *Women's intercollegiate varsity sports:* alpine skiing, basketball, cross-country, soccer, softball, tennis, volleyball.

SERVICES AND FACILITIES

Basic services: nonremedial tutoring, health service, health insurance. **Remedial assistance:** reading, math, writing, study skills. **Counseling services:** minority student, career, personal, academic, psychological, birth control, religious. **For learning-disabled students:** School does not offer a structured program with separate admission and additional fees. Total undergraduates in learning-disabled program or receiving services: 90. Services include: remedial math, reading machines, tape recorders, other special classes, diagnostic testing service, untimed tests, note-taking services, oral tests, learning center, readers, extended time for tests, tutors, priority seating, proofreading services, texts on tape, typist/scribe, exams on tape or computer, other. **Library:** Number of titles: 63,000; number of current serial subscriptions: 284. **Information technology resources:** Students are not required to lease or own a computer. Number of campus computers available to all students: 107. School has a wireless network. Approximate number of users that can be accommodated: 120. Proportion of college-owned housing units wired for high-speed internet access: 100%. **Campus safety:** Security services offered: 24-hour foot-and-vehicle patrols, late-night transport/escort service, lighted pathways/sidewalks, controlled dormitory access (key, security card, etc).

TRANSFER AND INTERNATIONAL STUDENTS

Transfer students: May apply for admission for the following academic terms: Fall, Spring. Applicants need a minimum number of credits to apply. For fall 2005: Transfer applications received: 154. Transfer applicants offered admission: 96. Transfer applicants enrolled: 44. **International students:** Number of foreign undergraduates: 5 (1% of student body). Number of countries represented: 8. Minimum TOEFL score required: 500 (paper); 173 (computer). Average TOEFL score: 526 (paper).

Johnson State College

- **Address:** 337 College Hill, Johnson, VT 05656-9405
- **Website:** http://www.johnsonstatecollege.com
- **Public**
- **Enrollment:** N/A

KEY STATS
✔ **U.S News College Ranking:** fourth tier, Universities–Master's (North)
✔ **SAT Score :** 900
✔ **Tuition:** 2006-2007: $6,484 in state, $13,804 out of state

Selectivity: Less selective	Room/board: $6,674
Acceptance rate: 86%	Average debt: N/A
Student/faculty ratio: N/A	Proportion who borrowed: N/A

Lyndon State College

- **Address:** PO Box 919, Lyndonville, VT 05851
- **Website:** http://www.lyndonstate.edu
- **Public**
- **Enrollment:** 1,140 full-time; 133 part-time

KEY STATS
✔ **U.S News College Ranking:** third tier, Comp. Coll.–Bachelor's (North)
✔ **SAT Score (25th/75th percentile):** 828-1050
✔ **Tuition:** 2006-2007: $7,078 in state, $14,806 out of state

Selectivity: Less selective	Room/board: $6,942
Acceptance rate: 94%	Average debt: N/A
Student/faculty ratio: 20/1	Proportion who borrowed: N/A

UNDERGRADUATE STUDENT BODY STATS

2005-2006 enrollment: 1,140 full-time; 133 part-time. Men: 51%; women: 49%. **Ethnic makeup:** African American: 2%; American-Indian: 1%; Hispanic: 1%; White: 96%.

ADMISSIONS FACTS AND FIGURES

Phone: (802) 626-6413. **Email:** admissions@lyndonstate.edu. **Website:** http://www.lyndonstate.edu. **Application deadlines for fall 2007:** Regular decision: Rolling. Early decision: Not offered. Early action: Send application by: N/A; Decision sent by: N/A. Admission can be deferred. **Application fee:** $35. Common application is accepted. **Admissions requirements/recommendations:** High school units required (recommended): English: 4 (4); Mathematics: 3 (4); Science: 2 (3); Foreign language: 2 (2); Social studies: 2 (2); History: 2 (2); Total units: 15 (13). Tests: The college uses SAT or ACT scores in admissions decisions. Neither SAT nor ACT required. For admission to the fall 2007 entering class, the school will accept: ACT with writing, ACT without writing. Campus visit: Recommended. Admissions interview: Recommended. Off-campus interview: May be arranged. **Factors that count in admissions decisions:** *Academic:* Secondary school record: Very important. Class rank: Important. Letters of recommendation: Important. Standardized test scores: Considered. Essay: Considered. *Nonacademic:* Interview: Important. Extracurricular activities: Considered. Talent/ability: Important. Character/personal qualities: Important. Alumni/ae relationship: Considered. Geographical residence: Not considered. State residency: Not considered. Religious affiliation/commitment: Not considered. Minority status: Not considered. Volunteer work: Considered. Work experience: Considered. **Other schools with the greatest overlap in applicants:** Castleton State College; Johnson State College; Keene State College; Plymouth State University; University of Vermont. **Admissions statistics for the fall 2005 entering class:** Total applicants: 994. Total accepted: 938. Freshmen enrolled: 333; 58% were from out of state. Overall acceptance rate: 94%. Non-early acceptance rate: 94%. **Size of waiting list:** 0 applicants; enrolled from waiting list: 0. **Credentials of fall 2005 freshmen:** 12% ranked in the top 10 percent of their high school class; 22% were in the top 25 percent, and 69% were in the top half. (Proportion submitting class standing: 93%.) **Average high school grade point average:** 2.5. **First-year students who submitted SAT scores:** 90%. Scores (25/75 percentile): Verbal: 418-520, Math: 410-530, Combined: 828-1050. **First-year students submitting ACT scores:** 3%. Scores (25/75 percentile): English: N/A, Math: N/A, Composite: N/A.

ACADEMICS

Year founded: 1911. **Academic calendar:** Semester. **Degrees offered:** certificate, associate, bachelor's, master's. **Most popular majors:** 16% psychology, 13% business, management, marketing, and related support services, 13% liberal arts and sciences studies, and humanities, 13% parks, recreation, leisure, and fitness studies, 11% education. **Major fields of study:** business, management, marketing, and related support services; communication, journalism, and related programs; communications technologies/technicians and support services; computer and information sciences and support services; education; English language and literature/letters; liberal arts and sciences studies, and humanities; mathematics and statistics; multi/interdisciplinary studies; parks, recreation, leisure, and fitness studies; physical sciences; psychology; social sciences; visual and performing arts. **Areas of required coursework:** arts/fine arts, humanities, computer literacy, mathematics, English (including composition), sciences (biological or physical), social science. **Special academic programs (% participation):** accelerated program (0%), cooperative (work-study plan) program (55%), double major (30%), dual enrollment (5%), exchange student program (domestic) (0%), independent study (65%), internships (85%), liberal arts/career combination (18%), student-designed major (1%), study abroad (0%), teacher certificate program (20%). **Teacher certification offered in:** early childhood, special education, elementary, middle/junior high, secondary. **Cooperative education programs:** business, computer science, education, humanities, natural science, social/behavioral science. **Reserve Officers Training Corps (ROTC):** Air Force ROTC: Offered at cooperating institution (Norwich University). **Faculty and instruction (2005-2006):** Total instructional faculty: 59 full-time, 86 part-time (59% men; 41% women; 1% minorities). Full-time faculty with Ph.D. or other terminal degree: 90%. Student/faculty ratio: 20/1. Classes of fewer than 20 students: 75%; of 20 to 49 students: 25%. **Advanced Placement and International Baccalaureate credit:** AP tests may be used for: Credit and/or placement. Scores accepted: 3, 4, 5. International Baccalaureate exams may be used for: Credit and/or placement. **Freshmen returning for sophomore year:** 62%. **Graduation rates:** Four-year: 24%; five-year: 41%; six-year: 37%. **Graduate study:** 7% of students pursue further study within one year. Fields in which graduates pursue further study: Master of Business Administration (MBA), 1%; law, 1%; education, 1%; arts and sciences, 1%.

COSTS AND FINANCIAL AID

Financial aid office: (802) 626-6218. **Expenses (2006-2007):** Tuition and fees 2006-2007: $7,078 in state, $14,806 out of state; room/board: $6,942. Estimated books and supplies: $600 personal expenses: $900. **Financial aid:** Priority filing date for institution's financial aid form: February 15. In 2005-2006, 86% of undergraduates applied for financial aid. Of those, 71% were determined to have financial need; Average financial aid package (proportion receiving): N/A (71%). Average amount of self-help aid, such as work study or loans (proportion receiving): N/A (71%). Among students who received aid based on merit, the average award (and the proportion receiving): $1,519 (6%). The average athletic scholarship (and the proportion receiving): $0 (0%).

CAMPUS LIFE AND EXTRACURRICULAR ACTIVITIES

Campus housing available (% using): coed dorms (97%), women's dorms (1%), special housing for disabled students (1%), other housing options (1%). Students who live in college-owned, operated, or affiliated housing: 50%. **Student employment:** During the 2005-2006 academic year, 3% of undergraduates worked on campus. Average per-year earnings: $1,000. **Clubs and organizations:** Number of student organizations: 26. Activities include: choral groups, dance, drama/theater, literary magazine, music ensembles, musical theater, radio station, student government, student newspaper, symphony orchestra, television station. Number of fraternities: 0; sororities: 0. Average proportion of students who stay on campus on weekends: 60%. **Sports program (2005-2006):** Member of NAIA. *Men's intercollegiate varsity sports:* baseball, basketball, cross-country, soccer, tennis. *Women's intercollegiate varsity sports:* basketball, cross-country, soccer, softball, tennis.

SERVICES AND FACILITIES

Basic services: nonremedial tutoring, health service, health insurance. **Remedial assistance:** reading, math, writing, study skills. **Counseling services:** minority student, career, military, personal, veteran student, academic, psychological, birth control. **For learning-disabled students:** School does not offer a structured program with separate admission and additional fees. Services include: other testing accommodations, reading machines, tape recorders, untimed tests, note-taking services, oral tests, learning center, readers, extended time for tests, tutors. **Library:** Number of titles: 109,629; number of current serial subscriptions: 16,468. **Information technology resources:** Students are not required to lease or own a computer. Number of campus computers available to all students: 230. School has a wireless network. Proportion of college-owned housing units wired for high-speed internet access: 100%. **Campus safety:** Security services offered: 24-hour foot-and-vehicle patrols, late-night transport/escort service, 24-hour emergency telephones, lighted pathways/sidewalks, student patrols, controlled dormitory access (key, security card, etc).

TRANSFER AND INTERNATIONAL STUDENTS

Transfer students: May apply for admission for the following academic terms: Fall, Spring, Summer. Applicants do not need a minimum number of credits to apply. For fall 2005: Transfer applications received: 198. Transfer applicants offered admission: 172. Transfer applicants enrolled: 114. **International students:** Number of foreign undergraduates: 1. Number of countries represented: 1. Minimum TOEFL score required: 500 (paper); 173 (computer). Average TOEFL score: 510 (paper).

Marlboro College

- **Address:** PO Box A, 2582 South Road, Marlboro, VT 05344-0300
- **Website:** http://www.marlboro.edu
- **Private**
- **Enrollment:** 327 full-time; 13 part-time

KEY STATS

✔ **U.S News College Ranking:** third tier, Liberal Arts Colleges
✔ **SAT Score (25th/75th percentile):** 1100-1340
✔ **Tuition:** 2006-2007: $29,240

Selectivity: More selective	**Room/board:** $8,600
Acceptance rate: 58%	**Average debt:** $19,758
Student/faculty ratio: N/A	**Proportion who borrowed:** 85%

UNDERGRADUATE STUDENT BODY STATS

2005-2006 enrollment: 327 full-time; 13 part-time. Men: 39%; women: 61%. **Ethnic makeup:** African American: 1%; Asian American: 3%; Hispanic: 4%; White: 91%; International: 1%.

ADMISSIONS FACTS AND FIGURES

Phone: (800) 343-0049. **Email:** admissions@marlboro.edu. **Website:** http://www.marlboro.edu. **Application deadlines for fall 2007:** Regular decision: February 15. Early decision: Send application by: November 15; Decision sent by: December 15. Early action: Send application by: January 15; Decision sent by: February 1. Admission can be deferred. **Application fee:** $50. Common application is accepted. **To apply online, go to:** http://www.marlboro.edu/admissions/applying.html. **Admissions requirements/recommendations:** High school units required (recommended): English: 4 (4); Mathematics: 3 (3); Science: 3 (3); Foreign language: 3 (3); Social studies: 1 (2); History: 2 (2); Academic electives: 5 (5). Tests: The college uses SAT or ACT scores in admissions decisions. Either SAT or ACT required. For admission to the fall 2007 entering class, the school will accept: ACT with writing, ACT without writing. Campus visit: Recommended. Admissions interview: Recommended. Off-campus interview: May be arranged. **Factors that count in admissions decisions:** *Academic:* Secondary school record: Very important. Class rank: Considered. Letters of recommendation: Important. Standardized test scores: Considered. Essay: Very important. *Nonacademic:* Interview: Considered. Extracurricular activities: Important. Talent/ability: Important. Character/personal qualities: Very important. Alumni/ae relationship: Considered. Geographical residence: Not considered. State residency: Not considered. Religious affiliation/commitment: Not considered. Minority status: Considered. Volunteer work: Important. Work experience: Considered. **Other schools with the greatest overlap in applicants:** Bennington College; College of the Atlantic; Hampshire College; Reed College; Sarah Lawrence College. **Admissions statistics for the fall 2005 entering class:** Total applicants: 497. Total accepted: 289. Freshmen enrolled: 75; Accepted through early-decision or early-action plans: 49%. Overall acceptance rate: 58%. Early-decision acceptance rate: 65%. Non-early acceptance rate: 52%. **Credentials of fall 2005 freshmen:** 33% ranked in the top 10 percent of their high school class; 62% were in the top 25 percent, and 97% were in the top half. (Proportion submitting class standing: 58%.) **Average high school grade point average:** 3.2. **First-year students who submitted SAT scores:** 82%. Scores (25/75 percentile): Verbal: 590-690, Math: 510-650, Combined: 1100-1340. **First-year students submitting ACT scores:** 18%. Scores (25/75 percentile): English: 26-32, Math: 22-30, Composite: 24-32.

ACADEMICS

Year founded: 1946. **Academic calendar:** Semester. **Degrees offered:** certificate, bachelor's, master's. **Most popular majors:** Information not available. **Major fields of study:** area, ethnic, cultural, and gender studies; biological and biomedical sciences; English language and literature/letters; foreign languages, literatures, and linguistics; history; legal professions and studies; liberal arts and sciences studies, and humanities; mathematics and statistics; physical sciences; psychology; social sciences; visual and performing arts. **Areas of required coursework:** English (including composition), other. **Pre-professional programs:** pre-law, pre-medicine, pre-veterinary science. **Special academic programs (% participation):** double major (72%), independent study (45%), internships (21%), student-designed major (100%), study abroad (38%). **Faculty and instruction (2005-2006):** Total instructional faculty: N/A. Classes of fewer than 20 students: 89%; of 20 to 49 students: 11%. **Advanced Placement and International Baccalaureate credit:** AP tests may be used for: Credit only. Scores accepted: 4, 5. International Baccalaureate exams may be used for: Credit only. **Freshmen returning for sophomore year:** 75%. **Graduation rates:** Four-year: 45%; five-year: 51%; six-year: 57%. **Graduate study:** 30% of students pursue further study immediately upon graduation; 40% within one year; 68% within five years.

COSTS AND FINANCIAL AID

Financial aid office: (802) 258-9237. **Expenses (2006-2007):** Tuition and fees 2006-2007: $29,240; room/board: $8,600. Estimated books and supplies: $600; transportation: $800; personal expenses: $1,200. **Financial aid:** Priority filing date for institution's financial aid form: February 15; deadline: March 1. In 2005-2006, 80% of undergraduates applied for financial aid. Of those, 75% were determined to have financial need; Average financial aid package (proportion receiving): $10,057 (75%). Average amount of gift aid, such as scholarships or grants (proportion receiving): $7,621 (68%). Average amount of self-help aid, such as work study or loans (proportion receiving): $2,050 (67%). Average need-based loan (excluding PLUS or other private loans): $3,728. Among students who received need-based aid,

the average percentage of need met: 80%. Among students who received aid based on merit, the average award (and the proportion receiving): $8,834 (91%). The average athletic scholarship (and the proportion receiving): $0 (0%). Average amount of debt of borrowers graduating in 2005: $19,758. Proportion who borrowed: 85%.

CAMPUS LIFE AND EXTRACURRICULAR ACTIVITIES

Campus housing available (% using): coed dorms (80%), women's dorms (5%), apartments for married students (10%), apartment for single students (5%). **Student employment:** During the 2005-2006 academic year, 75% of undergraduates worked on campus. Average per-year earnings: $2,050. **Clubs and organizations:** Number of student organizations: 15. Activities include: choral groups, dance, drama/theater, literary magazine, music ensembles, musical theater, student government, student newspaper, student film society. Number of fraternities: 0; sororities: 0. Average proportion of students who stay on campus on weekends: 85%.

SERVICES AND FACILITIES

Basic services: nonremedial tutoring, health service, health insurance. **Remedial assistance:** writing. **Counseling services:** minority student, career, personal, academic, older student, psychological, birth control. **For learning-disabled students:** School does not offer a structured program with separate admission and additional fees. Services include: untimed tests, learning center, extended time for tests, tutors. **Information technology resources:** Students are not required to lease or own a computer. Number of campus computers available to all students: 50. School has a wireless network. Proportion of college-owned housing units wired for high-speed internet access: 100%.

TRANSFER AND INTERNATIONAL STUDENTS

Transfer students: May apply for admission for the following academic terms: Fall, Spring. Applicants do not need a minimum number of credits to apply. For fall 2005: Transfer applications received: 57. Transfer applicants offered admission: 40. Transfer applicants enrolled: 26. **International students:** Number of foreign undergraduates: 3 (1% of student body). Number of countries represented: 3. Minimum TOEFL score required: 550 (paper); 220 (computer). Average TOEFL score: 600 (paper).

Middlebury College

- **Address:** Middlebury, VT 05753
- **Website:** http://www.middlebury.edu
- **Private**
- **Enrollment:** 2,420 full-time; 35 part-time

KEY STATS

✔ **U.S News College Ranking:** 5, Liberal Arts Colleges
✔ **SAT Score (25th/75th percentile):** 1280-1475
✔ **Tuition:** N/A

Selectivity: Most selective	**Room/board:** N/A
Acceptance rate: 24%	**Average debt:** $20,957
Student/faculty ratio: 9/1	**Proportion who borrowed:** 42%

UNDERGRADUATE STUDENT BODY STATS

2005-2006 enrollment: 2,420 full-time; 35 part-time. Men: 49%; women: 51%. **Ethnic makeup:** African American: 3%; American-Indian: 1%; Asian American: 7%; Hispanic: 5%; White: 76%; International: 9%.

ADMISSIONS FACTS AND FIGURES

Phone: (802) 443-3000. **Email:** admissions@middlebury.edu. **Website:** http://www.middlebury.edu. **Application deadlines for fall 2007:** Regular decision: January 1; decision sent by April 1. Early decision: Send application by: November 15; Decision sent by: December 15. Early action: Not offered. Admission can be deferred. **Application fee:** $55. Common application is accepted. **To apply online, go to:** http://www.middlebury.edu/admissions/applying/. **Admissions requirements/recommendations:** High school units required (recommended): English: (4); Mathematics: (4); Science: (3); Foreign language: (4); Social studies: (3). Tests: The college uses SAT or ACT scores in admissions decisions. ACT required. For admission to the fall 2007 entering class, the school will accept: ACT with writing, ACT without writing. Campus visit: Recommended. Admissions interview: Neither required nor recommended.

Off-campus interview: May be arranged. **Factors that count in admissions decisions:** *Academic:* Secondary school record: Very important. Class rank: Very important. Letters of recommendation: Important. Standardized test scores: Important. Essay: Important. *Nonacademic:* Interview: Not considered. Extracurricular activities: Very important. Talent/ability: Very important. Character/personal qualities: Very important. Alumni/ae relationship: Considered. Geographical residence: Considered. State residency: Not considered. Religious affiliation/commitment: Not considered. Minority status: Important. Volunteer work: Considered. Work experience: Considered. **Admissions statistics for the fall 2005 entering class:** Total applicants: 5,254. Total accepted: 1,241. Freshmen enrolled: 553; 94% were from out of state. Accepted through early-decision or early-action plans: 47%. Overall acceptance rate: 24%. Early-decision acceptance rate: 35%. Non-early acceptance rate: 22%. **Size of waiting list:** 950 applicants; enrolled from waiting list: 38. **Credentials of fall 2005 freshmen:** 84% ranked in the top 10 percent of their high school class; 96% were in the top 25 percent, and 99% were in the top half. (Proportion submitting class standing: 44%.) **First-year students who submitted SAT scores:** 78%. Scores (25/75 percentile): Verbal: 630-745, Math: 650-730, Combined: 1280-1475. **First-year students submitting ACT scores:** 35%. Scores (25/75 percentile): English: N/A, Math: N/A, Composite: 27-32.

ACADEMICS

Year founded: 1800. **Academic calendar:** 4-1-4. **Degrees offered:** bachelor's, master's, doctorate. **Most popular majors:** 14% economics, 9% English language and literature/letters, 9% psychology, 8% international relations and affairs, 8% political science and government. **Major fields of study:** area, ethnic, cultural, and gender studies; biological and biomedical sciences; computer and information sciences and support services; English language and literature/letters; foreign languages, literatures, and linguistics; history; liberal arts and sciences studies, and humanities; mathematics and statistics; multi/interdisciplinary studies; natural resources and conservation; philosophy and religious studies; physical sciences; psychology; social sciences; visual and performing arts. **Areas of required coursework:** arts/fine arts, English (including composition), philosophy, foreign languages, sciences (biological or physical), history, social science, other. **Pre-professional programs:** pre-law, pre-dentistry, pre-medicine, other. **Special academic programs (% participation):** accelerated program, double major (17%), exchange student program (domestic) (2%), honors program, independent study, internships (50%), student-designed major, study abroad (60%), teacher certificate program (1%), other. **Teacher certification offered in:** elementary, secondary. **Reserve Officers Training Corps (ROTC):** Army ROTC: Offered at cooperating institution (University of Vermont). **Faculty and instruction (2005-2006):** Total instructional faculty: 254 full-time, 46 part-time (61% men; 39% women; 12% minorities). Full-time faculty with Ph.D. or other terminal degree: 94%. Student/faculty ratio: 9/1. Classes of fewer than 20 students: 73%; of 20 to 49 students: 23%; of 50 or more students: 4%. **Advanced Placement and International Baccalaureate credit:** AP tests may be used for: Credit and/or placement. Scores accepted: 4, 5. International Baccalaureate exams may be used for: Credit and/or placement. **Freshmen returning for sophomore year:** 96%. **Graduation rates:** Four-year: 85%; five-year: 93%; six-year: 94%.

COSTS AND FINANCIAL AID

Financial aid office: (802) 443-5158. **Financial aid:** Priority filing date for institution's financial aid form: November 15; deadline: December 31. In 2005-2006, 49% of undergraduates applied for financial aid. Of those, 44% were determined to have financial need; 100% had their need fully met. Average financial aid package (proportion receiving): $28,295 (44%). Average amount of gift aid, such as scholarships or grants (proportion receiving): $24,854 (44%). Average amount of self-help aid, such as work study or loans (proportion receiving): $4,901 (44%). Average need-based loan (excluding PLUS or other private loans): $3,963. Among students who received need-based aid, the average percentage of need met: 100%. Among students who received aid based on merit, the average award (and the proportion receiving): $0 (0%). The average athletic scholarship (and the proportion receiving): $0 (0%). Average amount of debt of borrowers graduating in 2005: $20,957. Proportion who borrowed: 42%.

CAMPUS LIFE AND EXTRACURRICULAR ACTIVITIES

Campus housing available: coed dorms, apartment for single students, special housing for disabled students, other housing options. Students who live in college-owned, operated, or affiliated housing: 94%. **Student employment:** During the 2005-2006 academic year, 30% of undergraduates worked on campus. Average per-year earnings: $2,600. **Clubs and organizations:** Number of student organizations: 120. Activities include: choral

groups, dance, drama/theater, jazz band, literary magazine, music ensembles, musical theater, opera, radio station, student government, student newspaper, student film society, symphony orchestra, yearbook. Number of fraternities: 0; sororities: 0. Average proportion of students who stay on campus on weekends: 98%. **Sports program (2005-2006):** Member of NCAA III. *Men's intercollegiate varsity sports:* baseball, basketball, cross-country, football, golf, ice hockey, lacrosse, skiing, soccer, swimming and diving, tennis, track and field (indoor), track and field (outdoor). *Women's intercollegiate varsity sports:* basketball, cross-country, field hockey, golf, ice hockey, lacrosse, skiing, soccer, softball, squash, swimming and diving, tennis, track and field (indoor), track and field (outdoor), volleyball.

SERVICES AND FACILITIES

Basic services: nonremedial tutoring, health service, health insurance, other. **For learning-disabled students:** School does not offer a structured program with separate admission and additional fees. Services include: reading machines, tape recorders, diagnostic testing service, note-taking services, oral tests, learning center, readers, extended time for tests, tutors, other. **Library:** Number of titles: 853,000; number of current serial subscriptions: 2,908. **Information technology resources:** Students are not required to lease or own a computer. Number of campus computers available to all students: 494. School has a wireless network. Approximate number of users that can be accommodated: 6,072. Proportion of college-owned housing units wired for high-speed internet access: 100%. **Campus safety:** Security services offered: late-night transport/escort service, 24-hour emergency telephones, lighted pathways/sidewalks, controlled dormitory access (key, security card, etc).

TRANSFER AND INTERNATIONAL STUDENTS

Transfer students: May apply for admission for the following academic terms: Fall, Spring. Applicants do not need a minimum number of credits to apply. For fall 2005: Transfer applications received: 230. Transfer applicants offered admission: 1. Transfer applicants enrolled: 0. **International students:** Number of foreign undergraduates: 216 (9% of student body). Number of countries represented: 244. Average TOEFL score: 627 (paper).

Norwich University

- **Address:** 158 Harmon Drive, Northfield, VT 05663
- **Website:** http://www.norwich.edu
- **Private**
- **Enrollment:** 1,933 full-time; 62 part-time

KEY STATS

✔ **U.S News College Ranking:** 62, Universities–Master's (North)
✔ **SAT Score (25th/75th percentile):** 1010-1200
✔ **Tuition:** 2006-2007: $22,830

Selectivity: Selective	**Room/board:** $7,964
Acceptance rate: 74%	**Average debt:** $26,294
Student/faculty ratio: 13/1	**Proportion who borrowed:** 91%

UNDERGRADUATE STUDENT BODY STATS

2005-2006 enrollment: 1,933 full-time; 62 part-time. Men: 72%; women: 28%. **Ethnic makeup:** African American: 3%; Asian American: 2%; Hispanic: 3%; White: 91%.

ADMISSIONS FACTS AND FIGURES

Phone: (800) 468-6679. **Email:** nuadm@norwich.edu. **Website:** http://www.norwich.edu. **Application deadlines for fall 2007:** Regular decision: Rolling. Early decision: Not offered. Early action: Not offered. Admission cannot be deferred. **Application fee:** $35. Common application is not accepted. **To apply online, go to:** http://www.norwich.edu/admiss/undergraduate. **Admissions requirements/recommendations:** High school units required (recommended): English: (4); Mathematics: (3); Science: (3); Foreign language: (2); Social studies: (0); History: 0 (3); Academic electives: (0); Total units: (12). Tests: The college uses SAT or ACT scores in admissions decisions. Either SAT or ACT required. For admission to the fall 2007 entering class, the school will accept ACT without writing. Campus visit: Recommended. Admissions interview: Recommended. Off-campus interview: May be arranged. **Factors that count in admissions decisions:** *Academic:* Secondary school record: Very important. Class rank: Important. Letters of recommendation: Important. Standardized test scores: Important.

Essay: Important. *Nonacademic:* Interview: Important. Extracurricular activities: Very important. Talent/ability: Very important. Character/personal qualities: Very important. Alumni/ae relationship: Important. Geographical residence: Considered. State residency: Not considered. Religious affiliation/commitment: Not considered. Minority status: Considered. Volunteer work: Important. Work experience: Considered. **Other schools with the greatest overlap in applicants:** Northeastern University; Pennsylvania State University–University Park; United States Military Academy; United States Naval Academy; Virginia Military Institute. **Admissions statistics for the fall 2005 entering class:** Total applicants: 1,981. Total accepted: 1,470. Freshmen enrolled: 578; Overall acceptance rate: 74%. **Credentials of fall 2005 freshmen:** 16% ranked in the top 10 percent of their high school class; 34% were in the top 25 percent, and 66% were in the top half. (Proportion submitting class standing: 75%.) **Average high school grade point average:** 3.0. **First-year students who submitted SAT scores:** 95%. Scores (25/75 percentile): Verbal: 530-600, Math: 480-600, Combined: 1010-1200. **First-year students submitting ACT scores:** 5%. Scores (25/75 percentile): English: N/A, Math: N/A, Composite: N/A.

ACADEMICS

Year founded: 1819. **Academic calendar:** Semester. **Degrees offered:** bachelor's, post-bachelor's certificate, master's, post-master's certificate. **Most popular majors:** 30% criminal justice and corrections, 22% business administration and management, 12% civil engineering, 12% nursing/registered nurse training (R.N., A.S.N., B.S.N., M.S.N.), 11% architecture (B.Arch., B.A./B.S., M.Arch., M.A./M.S., Ph.D.). **Major fields of study:** architecture and related services; area, ethnic, cultural, and gender studies; biological and biomedical sciences; business, management, marketing, and related support services; communication, journalism, and related programs; computer and information sciences and support services; engineering; English language and literature/letters; health professions and related clinical sciences; history; mathematics and statistics; physical sciences; psychology; social sciences. **Areas of required coursework:** humanities, mathematics, English (including composition), sciences (biological or physical), history, social science, other. **Pre-professional programs:** pre-law, pre-dentistry, pre-medicine, other. **Special academic programs (% participation):** distance learning (2%), double major (4%), dual enrollment (0%), English as a Second Language (ESL) (.5%), independent study (4%), internships (2%), study abroad (1%), teacher certificate program (.5%). **Teacher certification offered in:** elementary, secondary. **Reserve Officers Training Corps (ROTC):** Army ROTC: Offered on campus; Navy ROTC: Offered on campus; Air Force ROTC: Offered on campus. **Faculty and instruction (2005-2006):** Total instructional faculty: 125 full-time, 137 part-time. Full-time faculty with Ph.D. or other terminal degree: 86%. Student/faculty ratio: 13/1. Classes of fewer than 20 students: 57%; of 20 to 49 students: 42%; of 50 or more students: 0%. **Advanced Placement and International Baccalaureate credit:** AP tests may be used for: Credit and/or placement. Scores accepted: 3, 4, 5. **Freshmen returning for sophomore year:** 75%. **Graduation rates:** Six-year: 50%.

COSTS AND FINANCIAL AID

Financial aid office: (802) 485-2015. **Expenses (2006-2007):** Tuition and fees 2006-2007: $22,830; room/board: $7,964. Estimated books and supplies: $1,000; transportation: $300; personal expenses: $500. **Financial aid:** Priority filing date for institution's financial aid form: March 1. In 2005-2006, 92% of undergraduates applied for financial aid. Of those, 78% were determined to have financial need; 28% had their need fully met. Average financial aid package (proportion receiving): $16,159 (78%). Average amount of gift aid, such as scholarships or grants (proportion receiving): $12,289 (77%). Average amount of self-help aid, such as work study or loans (proportion receiving): $5,272 (60%). Average need-based loan (excluding PLUS or other private loans): $4,611. Among students who received need-based aid, the average percentage of need met: 77%. Among students who received aid based on merit, the average award (and the proportion receiving): $17,951 (24%). The average athletic scholarship (and the proportion receiving): $0 (0%). Average amount of debt of borrowers graduating in 2005: $26,294. Proportion who borrowed: 91%.

CAMPUS LIFE AND EXTRACURRICULAR ACTIVITIES

Campus housing available (% using): coed dorms (99%), other housing options (1%). Students who live in college-owned, operated, or affiliated housing: 86%. **Student employment:** During the 2005-2006 academic year, 44% of undergraduates worked on campus. Average per-year earnings: $1,500. **Clubs and organizations:** Number of student organizations: 50. Activities include: choral groups, concert band, drama/theater, jazz band, literary magazine, marching band, music ensembles, pep band, radio sta-

tion, student government, student newspaper, yearbook. Number of fraternities: 0; sororities: 0. Average proportion of students who stay on campus on weekends: 60%. **Sports program (2005-2006):** Member of NCAA III. *Men's intercollegiate varsity sports:* baseball, basketball, cross-country, football, ice hockey, lacrosse, riflery, soccer, swimming and diving, tennis, wrestling. *Women's intercollegiate varsity sports:* basketball, cross-country, riflery, soccer, softball, swimming and diving.

SERVICES AND FACILITIES

Basic services: nonremedial tutoring, placement service, health service, health insurance. **Remedial assistance:** math, writing, study skills. **Counseling services:** career, military, personal, veteran student, academic, psychological, religious. **For learning-disabled students:** School does not offer a structured program with separate admission and additional fees. Total undergraduates in learning-disabled program or receiving services: 65. Services include: remedial math, remedial English, oral tests, learning center, readers, extended time for tests, tutors, priority registration, texts on tape, other testing accomodations, other. **Library:** Number of titles: 305,264; number of current serial subscriptions: 12,387. **Information technology resources:** Students are not required to lease or own a computer. Number of campus computers available to all students: 305. School has a wireless network. Proportion of college-owned housing units wired for high-speed internet access: 100%. **Campus safety:** Security services offered: 24-hour foot-and-vehicle patrols, 24-hour emergency telephones, lighted pathways/sidewalks.

TRANSFER AND INTERNATIONAL STUDENTS

Transfer students: May apply for admission for the following academic terms: Fall, Spring. Applicants need a minimum number of credits to apply. For fall 2005: Transfer applicants enrolled: 91. **International students:** Number of foreign undergraduates: 0. Number of countries represented: 6. Minimum TOEFL score required: 500 (paper); 173 (computer).

Southern Vermont College

- **Address:** 982 Mansion Drive, Bennington, VT 05201
- **Website:** http://www.svc.edu
- Private
- **Enrollment:** N/A

KEY STATS

✔ **U.S News College Ranking:** fourth tier, Comp. Coll.–Bachelor's (North)
✔ **SAT or ACT Score (25th/75th percentile):** N/A
✔ **Tuition:** 2006-2007: $15,100

Selectivity: Less selective	**Room/board:** $7,350
Acceptance rate: N/A	**Average debt:** N/A
Student/faculty ratio: N/A	**Proportion who borrowed:** N/A

St. Michael's College

- **Address:** 1 Winooski Park, Colchester, VT 05439
- **Website:** http://www.smcvt.edu
- **Private; Religious affiliation:** Roman Catholic
- **Enrollment:** 1,945 full-time; 61 part-time

KEY STATS

✔ **U.S News College Ranking:** 11, Universities–Master's (North)
✔ **SAT Score (25th/75th percentile):** 1040-1230
✔ **Tuition:** 2006-2007: $28,515

Selectivity: More selective	**Room/board:** $6,990
Acceptance rate: 72%	**Average debt:** $20,706
Student/faculty ratio: 12/1	**Proportion who borrowed:** 72%

UNDERGRADUATE STUDENT BODY STATS

2005-2006 enrollment: 1,945 full-time; 61 part-time. Men: 46%; women: 54%. **Ethnic makeup:** African American: 1%; Asian American: 1%; Hispanic: 1%; White: 95%; International: 2%.

ADMISSIONS FACTS AND FIGURES

Phone: (800) 762-8000. **Email:** admission@smcvt.edu. **Website:** http://www.smcvt.edu. **Application deadlines for fall 2007:** Regular decision: February 1; decision sent by April 1. Early decision: Not offered. Early action: Send application by: November 1; Decision sent by: January 1. Admission can be deferred. **Application fee:** $45. Common application is accepted. **To apply online, go to:** http://www.smcvt.edu/admissions. **Admissions requirements/recommendations:** High school units required (recommended): English: 4 (4); Mathematics: 3 (4); Science: 3 (4); Foreign language: 3 (4); Social studies: 3 (4); Total units: 16 (20). Tests: The college uses SAT or ACT scores in admissions decisions. Either SAT or ACT required. For admission to the fall 2007 entering class, the school will accept: ACT with writing. Campus visit: Recommended. Admissions interview: Recommended. Off-campus interview: May be arranged. **Factors that count in admissions decisions:** *Academic:* Secondary school record: Very important. Class rank: Very important. Letters of recommendation: Important. Standardized test scores: Important. Essay: Important. *Nonacademic:* Interview: Considered. Extracurricular activities: Important. Talent/ability: Important. Character/personal qualities: Important. Alumni/ae relationship: Considered. Geographical residence: Considered. State residency: Not considered. Religious affiliation/commitment: Not considered. Minority status: Considered. Volunteer work: Considered. Work experience: Considered. **Other schools with the greatest overlap in applicants:** Boston College; Fairfield University; Providence College; St. Anselm College; Stonehill College. **Admissions statistics for the fall 2005 entering class:** Total applicants: 2,924. Total accepted: 2,119. Freshmen enrolled: 597; 79% were from out of state. Accepted through early-decision or early-action plans: 62%. Overall acceptance rate: 72%. Non-early acceptance rate: 60%. **Size of waiting list:** 265 applicants; enrolled from waiting list: 0. **Credentials of fall 2005 freshmen:** 26% ranked in the top 10 percent of their high school class; 58% were in the top 25 percent, and 88% were in the top half. (Proportion submitting class standing: 78%.) **Average high school grade point average:** 3.5. **First-year students who submitted SAT scores:** 99%. Scores (25/75 percentile): Verbal: 520-620, Math: 520-610, Combined: 1040-1230. **First-year students submitting ACT scores:** 20%. Scores (25/75 percentile): English: N/A, Math: N/A, Composite: N/A.

ACADEMICS

Year founded: 1904. **Academic calendar:** Semester. **Degrees offered:** bachelor's, post-bachelor's certificate, master's, post-master's certificate. **Most popular majors:** 20% business, management, marketing, and related support services, 15% psychology, 12% social sciences, 10% English language and literature/letters, 8% biological and biomedical sciences. **Major fields of study:** area, ethnic, cultural, and gender studies; biological and biomedical sciences; business, management, marketing, and related support services; communication, journalism, and related programs; computer and information sciences and support services; education; engineering; English language and literature/letters; foreign languages, literatures, and linguistics; history; mathematics and statistics; natural resources and conservation; physical sciences; psychology; social sciences; visual and performing arts. **Areas of required coursework:** arts/fine arts, humanities, mathematics, English (including composition), philosophy, foreign languages, sciences (biological or physical), history, social science, other. **Pre-professional programs:** pre-law, pre-dentistry, pre-medicine, pre-veterinary science, pre-optometry, pre-pharmacy. **Special academic programs (% participation):** cross-registration (1%), double major (15.8%), dual enrollment (2%), English as a Second Language (ESL) (1%), honors program (26%), independent study (9.3%), internships (42%), liberal arts/career combination (1%), student-designed major (1%), study abroad (32%), teacher certificate program (10.9%). **Teacher certification offered in:** elementary, middle/junior high, secondary. **Cooperative education programs:** education. **Reserve Officers Training Corps (ROTC):** Army ROTC: Offered at cooperating institution (University of Vermont). **Faculty and instruction (2005-2006):** Total instructional faculty: 150 full-time, 67 part-time (52% men; 48% women; 5% minorities). Full-time faculty with Ph.D. or other terminal degree: 86%. Student/faculty ratio: 12/1. Classes of fewer than 20 students: 60%; of 20 to 49 students: 39%; of 50 or more students: 1%. **Advanced Placement and International Baccalaureate credit:** AP tests may be used for: Credit and/or placement. Scores accepted: 3, 4, 5. International Baccalaureate exams may be used for: Credit and/or placement. **Freshmen returning for sophomore year:** 89%. **Graduation rates:** Four-year: 68%; five-year: 75%; six-year: 77%. **Graduate study:** 13% of students pursue further study immediately upon graduation; 46% within five years. Fields in which graduates pursue further study: Master of Business Administration (MBA), 14%; law, 7%; medicine, 5%; dentistry, 2%; engineering, 2%; education, 35%; arts and sciences, 35%.

COSTS AND FINANCIAL AID

Financial aid office: (802) 654-3243. **Expenses (2006-2007):** Tuition and fees 2006-2007: $28,515; room/board: $6,990. Estimated books and supplies: $1,400; transportation: $500; personal expenses: $200. **Financial aid:** Priority filing date for institution's financial aid form: March 15. In 2005-2006, 75% of undergraduates applied for financial aid. Of those, 65% were determined to have financial need; 30% had their need fully met. Average financial aid package (proportion receiving): $19,222 (65%). Average amount of gift aid, such as scholarships or grants (proportion receiving): $13,953 (63%). Average amount of self-help aid, such as work study or loans (proportion receiving): $5,526 (59%). Average need-based loan (excluding PLUS or other private loans): $4,744. Among students who received need-based aid, the average percentage of need met: 83%. Among students who received aid based on merit, the average award (and the proportion receiving): $7,840 (17%). The average athletic scholarship (and the proportion receiving): $31,497 (1%). Average amount of debt of borrowers graduating in 2005: $20,706. Proportion who borrowed: 72%.

CAMPUS LIFE AND EXTRACURRICULAR ACTIVITIES

Campus housing available (% using): coed dorms (42%), women's dorms (10%), apartment for single students (47%), special housing for disabled students (1%), other housing options. Students who live in college-owned, operated, or affiliated housing: 97%. **Student employment:** During the 2005-2006 academic year, 14% of undergraduates worked on campus. Average per-year earnings: $1,494. **Clubs and organizations:** Number of student organizations: 40. Activities include: choral groups, concert band, dance, drama/theater, jazz band, literary magazine, music ensembles, musical theater, radio station, student government, student newspaper, yearbook. Number of fraternities: 0; sororities: 0. Average proportion of students who stay on campus on weekends: 85%. **Sports program (2005-2006):** Member of NCAA II. *Men's intercollegiate varsity sports:* alpine skiing, baseball, basketball, cross-country, golf, ice hockey, lacrosse, nordic skiing, soccer, swimming and diving, tennis. *Women's intercollegiate varsity sports:* alpine skiing, basketball, cross-country, field hockey, ice hockey, lacrosse, nordic skiing, soccer, softball, swimming and diving, tennis, volleyball.

SERVICES AND FACILITIES

Basic services: nonremedial tutoring, women's center, placement service, health service, health insurance. **Remedial assistance:** writing, study skills. **Counseling services:** career, personal, academic, psychological, religious. **For learning-disabled students:** School does not offer a structured program with separate admission and additional fees. Total undergraduates in learning-disabled program or receiving services: 208. Services include: reading machines, tape recorders, note-taking services, learning center, readers, extended time for tests, tutors, texts on tape, typist/scribe, other. **Library:** Number of titles: 227,019; number of current serial subscriptions: 1,435. **Information technology resources:** Students are not required to lease or own a computer. Number of campus computers available to all students: 233. School has a wireless network. Approximate number of users that can be accommodated: 300. Proportion of college-owned housing units wired for high-speed internet access: 100%. **Campus safety:** Security services offered: 24-hour foot-and-vehicle patrols, late-night transport/escort service, 24-hour emergency telephones, lighted pathways/sidewalks, student patrols, controlled dormitory access (key, security card, etc).

TRANSFER AND INTERNATIONAL STUDENTS

Transfer students: May apply for admission for the following academic terms: Fall, Spring. Applicants do not need a minimum number of credits to apply. For fall 2005: Transfer applications received: 80. Transfer applicants offered admission: 45. Transfer applicants enrolled: 18. **International students:** Number of foreign undergraduates: 34 (2% of student body). Number of countries represented: 12. Minimum TOEFL score required: 550 (paper); 213 (computer).

University of Vermont

- **Address:** South Prospect Street, Burlington, VT 05405-0160
- **Website:** http://www.uvm.edu
- **Public**
- **Enrollment:** 8,652 full-time; 1,207 part-time

KEY STATS

✔ **U.S News College Ranking:** 88, National Universities
✔ **SAT Score (25th/75th percentile):** 1070-1260
✔ **Tuition:** 2006-2007: $11,324 in state, $26,308 out of state

Selectivity: More selective	**Room/board:** $7,642
Acceptance rate: 80%	**Average debt:** $23,328
Student/faculty ratio: 15/1	**Proportion who borrowed:** 62%

UNDERGRADUATE STUDENT BODY STATS

2005-2006 enrollment: 8,652 full-time; 1,207 part-time. Men: 45%; women: 55%. **Ethnic makeup:** African American: 1%; Asian American: 2%; Hispanic: 2%; White: 94%; International: 1%.

ADMISSIONS FACTS AND FIGURES

Phone: (802) 656-3370. **Email:** admissions@uvm.edu. **Website:** http://www.uvm.edu. **Application deadlines for fall 2007:** Regular decision: January 15; decision sent by March 31. Early decision: Not offered. Early action: Send application by: November 1; Decision sent by: December 15. Admission can be deferred. **Application fee:** $45. Common application is accepted. **Admissions requirements/recommendations:** High school units required (recommended): English: 4; Mathematics: 3; Science: 2; Foreign language: 2; Social studies: 3; Total units: 16. Tests: The college uses SAT or ACT scores in admissions decisions. Either SAT or ACT required. For admission to the fall 2007 entering class, the school will accept: ACT with writing. Campus visit: Recommended. Admissions interview: Recommended. Off-campus interview: May be arranged. **Factors that count in admissions decisions:** *Academic:* Secondary school record: Very important. Class rank: Important. Letters of recommendation: Considered. Standardized test scores: Important. Essay: Important. *Nonacademic:* Interview: Considered. Extracurricular activities: Considered. Talent/ability: Considered. Character/personal qualities: Important. Alumni/ae relationship: Considered. Geographical residence: Considered. State residency: Important. Religious affiliation/commitment: Not considered. Minority status: Considered. Volunteer work: Considered. Work experience: Considered. **Other schools with the greatest overlap in applicants:** Boston University; Northeastern University; University of Connecticut; University of Massachusetts–Amherst; University of New Hampshire. **Admissions statistics for the fall 2005 entering class:** Total applicants: 13,015. Total accepted: 10,439. Freshmen enrolled: 2,394; 72% were from out of state. Accepted through early-decision or early-action plans: 27%. Overall acceptance rate: 80%. Non-early acceptance rate: 79%. **Size of waiting list:** 924 applicants; enrolled from waiting list: 1. **Credentials of fall 2005 freshmen:** 21% ranked in the top 10 percent of their high school class; 55% were in the top 25 percent, and 91% were in the top half. (Proportion submitting class standing: 59%.) **First-year students who submitted SAT scores:** 96%. Scores (25/75 percentile): Verbal: 530-630, Math: 540-630, Combined: 1070-1260. **First-year students submitting ACT scores:** 20%. Scores (25/75 percentile): English: N/A, Math: N/A, Composite: 22-27.

ACADEMICS

Year founded: 1791. **Academic calendar:** Semester. **Degrees offered:** certificate, bachelor's, post-bachelor's certificate, master's, post-master's certificate, first professional, doctorate. **Most popular majors:** 10% business administration and management, 9% psychology, 7% English language and literature, 6% political science and government, 5% nursing/registered nurse training (R.N., A.S.N., B.S.N., M.S.N.). **Major fields of study:** agriculture, agriculture operations, and related sciences; area, ethnic, cultural, and gender studies; biological and biomedical sciences; business, management, marketing, and related support services; communication, journalism, and related programs; computer and information sciences and support services; education; engineering; English language and literature/letters; family and consumer sciences/human sciences; foreign languages, literatures, and linguistics; health professions and related clinical sciences; history; liberal arts and sciences studies, and humanities; mathematics and statistics; multi/interdisciplinary studies; natural resources and conservation; parks, recreation, leisure, and fitness studies; philosophy and religious studies;

physical sciences; psychology; public administration and social service professions; social sciences; visual and performing arts. **Areas of required coursework:** arts/fine arts, humanities, mathematics, English (including composition), sciences (biological or physical), social science, other. **Pre-professional programs:** pre-law, pre-dentistry, pre-medicine, pre-veterinary science, other. **Special academic programs (% participation):** cooperative (work-study plan) program (1%), distance learning (9%), double major (8%), dual enrollment, exchange student program (domestic) (1%), honors program (4%), independent study (17%), internships (13%), liberal arts/career combination (1%), student-designed major (1%), study abroad (20%), teacher certificate program (7%), other. **Teacher certification offered in:** early childhood, special education, elementary, middle/junior high, secondary. **Cooperative education programs:** agriculture, business, computer science, education, engineering, natural science. **Reserve Officers Training Corps (ROTC):** Army ROTC: Offered on campus. **Faculty and instruction (2005-2006):** Total instructional faculty: 560 full-time, 163 part-time (57% men; 43% women; 10% minorities). Full-time faculty with Ph.D. or other terminal degree: 87%. Student/faculty ratio: 15/1. Classes of fewer than 20 students: 47%; of 20 to 49 students: 42%; of 50 or more students: 11%. **Advanced Placement and International Baccalaureate credit:** AP tests may be used for: Credit only. Scores accepted: 4, 5. International Baccalaureate exams may be used for: Credit only. **Freshmen returning for sophomore year:** 85%. **Graduation rates:** Four-year: 49%; five-year: 63%; six-year: 65%. **Graduate study:** 23% of students pursue further study within one year. Fields in which graduates pursue further study: Master of Business Administration (MBA), 10%; law, 13%; medicine, 10%; dentistry, 3%; engineering, 5%; education, 13%; arts and sciences, 30%; veterinary medicine, 6%.

COSTS AND FINANCIAL AID

Financial aid office: (802) 656-5700. **Expenses (2006-2007):** Tuition and fees 2006-2007: $11,324 in state, $26,308 out of state; room/board: $7,642. Estimated books and supplies: $900 personal expenses: $1,465. **Financial aid:** Priority filing date for institution's financial aid form: February 10. In 2005-2006, 67% of undergraduates applied for financial aid. Of those, 56% were determined to have financial need; 20% had their need fully met. Average financial aid package (proportion receiving): $15,408 (55%). Average amount of gift aid, such as scholarships or grants (proportion receiving): $10,770 (48%). Average amount of self-help aid, such as work study or loans (proportion receiving): $6,282 (46%). Average need-based loan (excluding PLUS or other private loans): $5,978. Among students who received need-based aid, the average percentage of need met: 78%. Among students who received aid based on merit, the average award (and the proportion receiving): $2,157 (16%). The average athletic scholarship (and the proportion receiving): $19,065 (1%). Average amount of debt of borrowers graduating in 2005: $23,328. Proportion who borrowed: 62%.

CAMPUS LIFE AND EXTRACURRICULAR ACTIVITIES

Campus housing available (% using): coed dorms (94%), sorority housing (1%), fraternity housing (1%), apartments for married students (1%), apartment for single students (3%). Students who live in college-owned, operated, or affiliated housing: 53%. **Student employment:** During the 2005-2006 academic year, 15% of undergraduates worked on campus. Average per-year earnings: $1,650. **Clubs and organizations:** Number of student organizations: 110. Activities include: choral groups, concert band, dance, drama/theater, jazz band, literary magazine, music ensembles, musical theater, pep band, radio station, student government, student newspaper, student film society, symphony orchestra, television station. Number of fraternities: 9; sororities: 5. Proportion of men in fraternities: 7%; of women in sororities: 5%. Average proportion of students who stay on campus on weekends: 85%. **Sports program (2005-2006):** Member of NCAA I. *Men's intercollegiate varsity sports:* alpine skiing, baseball, basketball, cross-country, golf, ice hockey, lacrosse, nordic skiing, soccer, swimming and diving, tennis. *Women's intercollegiate varsity sports:* alpine skiing, basketball, cross-country, field hockey, ice hockey, lacrosse, nordic skiing, soccer, softball, swimming and diving, tennis, track and field (indoor), track and field (outdoor).

SERVICES AND FACILITIES

Basic services: nonremedial tutoring, women's center, placement service, health service, health insurance. **Remedial assistance:** reading, math, writing, study skills. **Counseling services:** minority student, career, personal, veteran student, academic, older student, psychological, birth control, religious. **For learning-disabled students:** School does not offer a structured program with separate admission and additional fees. Total undergraduates in learning-disabled program or receiving services: 235. Services include:

reading machines, other special classes, learning center, tutors, priority registration, other. **Library:** Number of titles: 1,420,000; number of current serial subscriptions: 6,600. **Information technology resources:** Students are not required to lease or own a computer. Number of campus computers available to all students: 930. School has a wireless network. Approximate number of users that can be accommodated: 1,000. Proportion of college-owned housing units wired for high-speed internet access: 100%. **Campus safety:** Security services offered: 24-hour foot-and-vehicle patrols, late-night transport/escort service, 24-hour emergency telephones, lighted pathways/sidewalks, controlled dormitory access (key, security card, etc).

TRANSFER AND INTERNATIONAL STUDENTS

Transfer students: May apply for admission for the following academic terms: Fall, Spring. Applicants do not need a minimum number of credits to apply. For fall 2005: Transfer applications received: 1,020. Transfer applicants offered admission: 705. Transfer applicants enrolled: 392. **International students:** Number of foreign undergraduates: 54 (1% of student body). Number of countries represented: 21. Minimum TOEFL score required: 550 (paper); 213 (computer). Average TOEFL score: 600 (paper).

Vermont Technical College

- **Address:** PO Box 500, Randolph Center, VT 05061
- **Website:** http://www.vtc.edu
- **Public**
- **Enrollment:** 1,033 full-time; 323 part-time

KEY STATS

✔ **U.S News College Ranking:** Unranked Specialty School–Engineering
✔ **SAT Score (25th/75th percentile):** 910-1150
✔ **Tuition:** 2006-2007: $8,514 in state, $15,930 out of state

Selectivity: Less selective	**Room/board:** $6,942
Acceptance rate: 70%	**Average debt:** $12,600
Student/faculty ratio: 12/1	**Proportion who borrowed:** 80%

UNDERGRADUATE STUDENT BODY STATS

2005-2006 enrollment: 1,033 full-time; 323 part-time. Men: 60%; women: 40%. **Ethnic makeup:** African American: 1%; American-Indian: 1%; Asian American: 2%; Hispanic: 1%; White: 95%.

ADMISSIONS FACTS AND FIGURES

Phone: (802) 728-1244. **Email:** admissions@vtc.edu. **Website:** http://www.vtc.edu. **Application deadlines for fall 2007:** Regular decision: Rolling. Early decision: Not offered. Early action: Send application by: November 1; Decision sent by: December 1. Admission can be deferred. **Application fee:** $35. Common application is not accepted. **Admissions requirements/recommendations:** High school units required (recommended): English: 4; Mathematics: 3 (4); Science: 2 (3); Foreign language: 0 (2); Social studies: 2; History: 2; Academic electives: 2; Total units: 16. Tests: The college uses SAT or ACT scores in admissions decisions. Either SAT or ACT required. Campus visit: Recommended. Admissions interview: Recommended. Off-campus interview: May be arranged. **Factors that count in admissions decisions:** *Academic:* Secondary school record: Very important. Class rank: Important. Letters of recommendation: Important. Standardized test scores: Very important. Essay: Considered. *Nonacademic:* Interview: Important. Extracurricular activities: Considered. Talent/ability: Considered. Character/personal qualities: Important. Alumni/ae relationship: Important. Geographical residence: Not considered. State residency: Not considered. Religious affiliation/commitment: Not considered. Minority status: Considered. Volunteer work: Considered. Work experience: Considered. **Other schools with the greatest overlap in applicants:** SUNY College of A&T–Cobleskill; University of Maine–Orono; University of Massachusetts–Amherst; University of Vermont; Wentworth Institute of Technology. **Admissions statistics for the fall 2005 entering class:** Total applicants: 757. Total accepted: 528. Freshmen enrolled: 258; Overall acceptance rate: 70%. Non-early acceptance rate: 70%. **Size of waiting list:** 150 applicants; enrolled from waiting list: 25. **Credentials of fall 2005 freshmen:** 9% ranked in the top 10 percent of their high school class; 25% were in the top 25 percent, and 78% were in the top half. (Proportion submitting class standing: 70%.) **Average high school grade point average:** 3.0. **First-year students who submitted SAT scores:** 93%. Scores (25/75 percentile): Verbal: 440-560, Math: 470-590, Combined: 910-1150.

ACADEMICS

Year founded: 1866. **Academic calendar:** Semester. **Degrees offered:** certificate, associate, bachelor's. **Most popular majors:** Information not available. **Major fields of study:** business, management, marketing, and related support services; computer and information sciences and support services; engineering; engineering technologies/technicians. **Areas of required coursework:** arts/fine arts, humanities, computer literacy, mathematics, English (including composition), sciences (biological or physical), social science. **Special academic programs (% participation):** double major, dual enrollment, internships. **Cooperative education programs:** health professions. **Faculty and instruction (2005-2006):** Total instructional faculty: 78 full-time, 61 part-time (56% men; 44% women). Full-time faculty with Ph.D. or other terminal degree: 53%. Student/faculty ratio: 12/1. Classes of fewer than 20 students: 63%; of 20 to 49 students: 36%; of 50 or more students: 1%. **Advanced Placement and International Baccalaureate credit:** International Baccalaureate exams may be used for: Credit only. **Freshmen returning for sophomore year:** 65%. **Graduation rates:** Five-year: 0%; six-year: 64%.

COSTS AND FINANCIAL AID

Financial aid office: (800) 965-8790. **Expenses (2006-2007):** Tuition and fees 2006-2007: $8,514 in state, $15,930 out of state; room/board: $6,942. Estimated books and supplies: $1,000; transportation: $800; personal expenses: $650. **Financial aid:** Priority filing date for institution's financial aid form: March 1. In 2005-2006, 84% of undergraduates applied for financial aid. Of those, 71% were determined to have financial need; 16% had their need fully met. Average financial aid package (proportion receiving): $10,112 (70%). Average amount of gift aid, such as scholarships or grants (proportion receiving): $4,580 (55%). Average amount of self-help aid, such as work study or loans (proportion receiving): $2,980 (68%). Average need-based loan (excluding PLUS or other private loans): $2,740. Among students who received need-based aid, the average percentage of need met: 73%. Among students who received aid based on merit, the average award (and the proportion receiving): $4,266 (1%). The average athletic scholarship (and the proportion receiving): $0 (0%). Average amount of debt of borrowers graduating in 2005: $12,600. Proportion who borrowed: 80%.

CAMPUS LIFE AND EXTRACURRICULAR ACTIVITIES

Campus housing available (% using): coed dorms (100%), special housing for disabled students. **Student employment:** During the 2005-2006 academic year, 20% of undergraduates worked on campus. Average per-year earnings: $850. **Clubs and organizations:** Number of student organizations: 6. Activities include: drama/theater, radio station, student government, yearbook. Number of fraternities: 0; sororities: 0. Average proportion of students who stay on campus on weekends: 35%. **Sports program (2005-2006):** *Men's intercollegiate varsity sports:* baseball, basketball, soccer, volleyball. *Women's intercollegiate varsity sports:* basketball, soccer, volleyball.

SERVICES AND FACILITIES

Basic services: placement service, health service, health insurance. **Remedial assistance:** reading, math, writing, study skills. **Counseling services:** career, veteran student, academic, psychological. **For learning-disabled students:** School does not offer a structured program with separate admission and additional fees. Services include: remedial math, remedial English, reading machines, remedial reading, tape recorders, diagnostic testing service, untimed tests, note-taking services, oral tests, learning center, readers, extended time for tests, tutors. **Library:** Number of titles: 59,480; number of current serial subscriptions: 1,156. **Information technology resources:** Students are not required to lease or own a computer. Number of campus computers available to all students: 400. School has a wireless network. Proportion of college-owned housing units wired for high-speed internet access: 100%. **Campus safety:** Security services offered: 24-hour foot-and-vehicle patrols, 24-hour emergency telephones, lighted pathways/sidewalks, controlled dormitory access (key, security card, etc).

TRANSFER AND INTERNATIONAL STUDENTS

Transfer students: May apply for admission for the following academic terms: Fall, Spring. Applicants do not need a minimum number of credits to apply. For fall 2005: Transfer applications received: 901. Transfer applicants offered admission: 506. Transfer applicants enrolled: 409. **International students:** Number of foreign undergraduates: 0. Minimum TOEFL score required: 500 (paper); 173 (computer). Average TOEFL score: 525 (paper).

Virginia

Averett University

- **Address:** 420 W. Main Street, Danville, VA 24541
- **Website:** http://www.averett.edu
- **Private**
- **Enrollment:** 1,185 full-time; 746 part-time

KEY STATS

✔ **U.S News College Ranking:** third tier, Universities–Master's (South)
✔ **SAT Score (25th/75th percentile):** 888-1070
✔ **Tuition:** 2006-2007: $19,762

Selectivity: Less selective	**Room/board:** $6,448
Acceptance rate: 84%	**Average debt:** $16,398
Student/faculty ratio: 14/1	**Proportion who borrowed:** 70%

UNDERGRADUATE STUDENT BODY STATS

2005-2006 enrollment: 1,185 full-time; 746 part-time. Men: 44%; women: 56%. **Ethnic makeup:** African American: 32%; Asian American: 1%; Hispanic: 2%; White: 63%; International: 1%. **Religious preference:** Roman Catholic: 7%; Protestant: 57%; No preference: 3%; Unknown: 32%; Other Non-Christian: 1%.

ADMISSIONS FACTS AND FIGURES

Phone: (800) 283-7388. **Email:** admit@averett.edu. **Website:** http://www.averett.edu. **Application deadlines for fall 2007:** Regular decision: July 1. Early decision: Not offered. Early action: Not offered. Admission can be deferred. **Application fee:** None. Common application is accepted. **To apply online, go to:** http://www.averett.edu/admissions/applications.html. **Admissions requirements/recommendations:** High school units required (recommended): English: 4 (4); Mathematics: 2 (3); Science: 2 (3); Foreign language: 0 (2); Social studies: 3 (3); History: 3 (3); Academic electives: 3 (5); Total units: 15 (23). Tests: The college uses SAT or ACT scores in admissions decisions. Either SAT or ACT required. For admission to the fall 2007 entering class, the school will accept: ACT with writing, ACT without writing. Campus visit: Recommended. Admissions interview: Recommended. Off-campus interview: May be arranged. **Factors that count in admissions decisions:** *Academic:* Secondary school record: Very important. Class rank: Very important. Letters of recommendation: Considered. Standardized test scores: Very important. Essay: Considered. *Nonacademic:* Interview: Considered. Extracurricular activities: Important. Talent/ability: Considered. Character/personal qualities: Considered. Alumni/ae relationship: Considered. Geographical residence: Not considered. State residency: Not considered. Religious affiliation/commitment: Not considered. Minority status: Not considered. Volunteer work: Considered. Work experience: Considered. **Other schools with the greatest overlap in applicants:** Appalachian State University; Christopher Newport University; East Carolina University; James Madison University; Virginia Tech. **Admissions statistics for the fall 2005 entering class:** Total applicants: 1,202. Total accepted: 1,006. Freshmen enrolled: 258; 49% were from out of state. Overall acceptance rate: 84%. **Size of waiting list:** 0 applicants; enrolled from waiting list: 0. **Credentials of fall 2005 freshmen:** 9% ranked in the top 10 percent of their high school class; 34% were in the top 25 percent, and 67% were in the top half. (Proportion submitting class standing: 79%.) **Average high school grade point average:** 3.1. **First-year students who submitted SAT scores:** 85%. Scores (25/75 percentile): Verbal: 438-530, Math: 450-540, Combined: 888-1070. **First-year students submitting ACT scores:** 19%. Scores (25/75 percentile): English: N/A, Math: N/A, Composite: 17-22.

ACADEMICS

Year founded: 1859. **Academic calendar:** Semester. **Degrees offered:** associate, transfer-associate, bachelor's, master's. **Most popular majors:** 70% business, management, marketing, and related support services, 4% education, 4% liberal arts and sciences studies, and humanities, 4% security and protective services, 3% parks, recreation, leisure, and fitness studies. **Major fields of study:** agriculture, agriculture operations, and related sciences; biological and biomedical sciences; business, management, marketing, and related support services; communication, journalism, and related programs; computer and information sciences and support services; education; English language and literature/letters; health professions and related clinical sciences; history; liberal arts and sciences studies, and humanities; mathematics and statistics; multi/interdisciplinary studies; natural resources and conservation; parks, recreation, leisure, and fitness studies; philosophy and religious studies; physical sciences; psychology; security and protective services; social sciences; transportation and materials moving; visual and performing arts. **Areas of required coursework:** arts/fine arts, humanities, computer literacy, mathematics, English (including composition), sciences (biological or physical), history, social science, other. **Pre-professional programs:** pre-law, pre-dentistry, pre-medicine, pre-theology, pre-pharmacy, other. **Special academic programs (% participation):** accelerated program, cooperative (work-study plan) program (33%), cross-registration (0%), distance learning (15%), double major (9%), dual enrollment (14%), exchange student program (domestic) (0%), external degree program (11%), honors program (7%), independent study (43%), internships (25%), student-designed major (1%), study abroad (4%), teacher certificate program (10%), other (5%). **Teacher certification offered in:** early childhood, elementary, middle/junior high, secondary. **Cooperative education programs:** business, computer science, education, health professions, humanities, natural science, social/behavioral science, technologies, other. **Faculty and instruction (2005-2006):** Total instructional faculty: 65 full-time, 174 part-time (64% men; 36% women; 16% minorities). Full-time faculty with Ph.D. or other terminal degree: 77%. Student/faculty ratio: 14/1. Classes of fewer than 20 students: 84%; of 20 to 49 students: 16%; of 50 or more students: 0%. **Advanced Placement and International Baccalaureate credit:** AP tests may be used for: Credit and/or placement. Scores accepted: 3, 4, 5. International Baccalaureate exams may be used for: Credit and/or placement. **Freshmen returning for sophomore year:** 60%. **Graduation rates:** Six-year: 44%.

COSTS AND FINANCIAL AID

Financial aid office: (434) 791-5646. **Expenses (2006-2007):** Tuition and fees 2006-2007: $19,762; room/board: $6,448. Estimated books and supplies: $900; transportation: $700; personal expenses: $1,400. **Financial aid:** Priority filing date for institution's financial aid form: April 1. In 2005-2006, 93% of undergraduates applied for financial aid. Of those, 82% were determined to have financial need; 17% had their need fully met. Average financial aid package (proportion receiving): $11,583 (81%). Average amount of gift aid, such as scholarships or grants (proportion receiving): $8,803 (73%). Average amount of self-help aid, such as work study or loans (proportion receiving): $4,190 (71%). Average need-based loan (excluding PLUS or other private loans): $4,001. Among students who received need-based aid, the average percentage of need met: 68%. Among students who received aid based on merit, the average award (and the proportion receiving): $11,412 (18%). The average athletic scholarship (and the proportion receiving): $0 (0%). Average amount of debt of borrowers graduating in 2005: $16,398. Proportion who borrowed: 70%.

CAMPUS LIFE AND EXTRACURRICULAR ACTIVITIES

Campus housing available (% using): coed dorms (50%), women's dorms (0%), men's dorms (34%), apartment for single students (16%). Students who live in college-owned, operated, or affiliated housing: 53%. **Student employment:** During the 2005-2006 academic year, 9% of undergraduates worked on campus. Average per-year earnings: $1,351. **Clubs and organizations:** Number of student organizations: 34. Activities include: choral groups, drama/theater, literary magazine, musical theater, student government, student newspaper. Number of fraternities: 1; sororities: 1. Proportion of men in fraternities: 3%; of women in sororities: 2%. Average proportion of students who stay on campus on weekends: 75%. **Sports program (2005-2006):** Member of NCAA III. *Men's intercollegiate varsity sports:* baseball, basketball, cheerleading, cross-country, football, golf, soccer, tennis. *Women's intercollegiate varsity sports:* basketball, cheerleading, cross-country, lacrosse, soccer, softball, tennis, volleyball.

SERVICES AND FACILITIES

Basic services: nonremedial tutoring, placement service, health service, other. **Remedial assistance:** reading, math, writing, study skills. **Counseling services:** minority student, career, personal, veteran student, academic, older student, psychological, religious, other. **For learning-disabled students:** School does not offer a structured program with separate admission and additional fees. Total undergraduates in learning-disabled program or receiving services: 30. Services include: remedial math, remedial English, tape recorders, untimed tests, note-taking services, oral tests, learning center, readers, extended time for tests, tutors, early syllabus, priority seating, texts on tape, exams on tape or computer. **Library:** Number of titles: 104,864; number of current serial subscriptions: 11,362. **Information technology resources:** Students are not required to lease or own a computer. Number of campus computers available to all students: 166. School has a wireless network. Approximate number of users that can be accommodated: 60. Proportion of college-owned housing units wired for high-speed internet access: 50%. **Campus safety:** Security services offered: 24-hour foot-and-vehicle patrols, late-night transport/escort service, 24-hour emergency telephones, lighted pathways/sidewalks, controlled dormitory access (key, security card, etc).

TRANSFER AND INTERNATIONAL STUDENTS

Transfer students: May apply for admission for the following academic terms: Fall, Spring, Summer. Applicants need a minimum number of credits to apply. For fall 2005: Transfer applications received: 267. Transfer applicants offered admission: 260. Transfer applicants enrolled: 188. **International students:** Number of foreign undergraduates: 19 (1% of student body). Number of countries represented: 17. Minimum TOEFL score required: 500 (paper); 173 (computer).

Bluefield College

- **Address:** 3000 College Drive, Bluefield, VA 24605
- **Website:** http://www.bluefield.edu
- **Private; Religious affiliation:** Baptist
- **Enrollment:** 692 full-time; 84 part-time

KEY STATS

✔ **U.S News College Ranking:** 49, Comp. Coll.–Bachelor's (South)
✔ **SAT Score (25th/75th percentile):** 860-1050
✔ **Tuition:** 2006-2007: $12,305

Selectivity: Less selective	**Room/board:** $6,032
Acceptance rate: 50%	**Average debt:** $14,191
Student/faculty ratio: 12/1	**Proportion who borrowed:** 84%

UNDERGRADUATE STUDENT BODY STATS

2005-2006 enrollment: 692 full-time; 84 part-time. Men: 40%; women: 60%. **Ethnic makeup:** African American: 18%; Asian American: 1%; Hispanic: 1%; White: 80%.

ADMISSIONS FACTS AND FIGURES

Phone: (276) 326-4214. **Email:** admissions@bluefield.edu. **Website:** http://www.bluefield.edu. **Application deadlines for fall 2007:** Regular decision: Rolling. Early decision: Not offered. Early action: Not offered. Admission can be deferred. **Application fee:** $30. Common application is not accepted. **Admissions requirements/recommendations:** High school units required (recommended): English: 4; Mathematics: 3; Science: 3; Social studies: 3; Academic electives: 6; Total units: 22. Tests: The college uses SAT or ACT scores in admissions decisions. Either SAT or ACT required. For admission to the fall 2007 entering class, the school will accept: ACT with writing, ACT without writing. Campus visit: Recommended. Admissions interview: Recommended. Off-campus interview: May be arranged. **Factors that count in admissions decisions:** *Academic:* Secondary school record: Very important. Class rank: Important. Letters of recommendation: Considered. Standardized test scores: Very important. Essay: Considered. *Nonacademic:* Interview: Important. Extracurricular activities: Considered. Talent/ability: Considered. Character/personal qualities: Very important. Alumni/ae relationship: Considered. Geographical residence: Not considered. State residency: Not considered. Religious affiliation/commitment: Not considered. Minority status: Not considered. Volunteer work: Considered. Work experience: Considered. **Other schools with the greatest overlap in applicants:** Emory

and Henry College; Liberty University; Radford University; University of Virginia–Wise; Virginia Tech. **Admissions statistics for the fall 2005 entering class:** Total applicants: 537. Total accepted: 268. Freshmen enrolled: 107; 22% were from out of state. Overall acceptance rate: 50%. **Credentials of fall 2005 freshmen:** 23% ranked in the top 10 percent of their high school class; 44% were in the top 25 percent, and 83% were in the top half. (Proportion submitting class standing: 81%.) **Average high school grade point average:** 3.2. **First-year students who submitted SAT scores:** 85%. Scores (25/75 percentile): Verbal: 440-530, Math: 420-520, Combined: 860-1050. **First-year students submitting ACT scores:** 22%. Scores (25/75 percentile): English: 18-23, Math: 17-22, Composite: 19-24.

ACADEMICS

Year founded: 1922. **Academic calendar:** Semester. **Degrees offered:** bachelor's. **Most popular majors:** Information not available. **Major fields of study:** biological and biomedical sciences; business, management, marketing, and related support services; communication, journalism, and related programs; education; English language and literature/letters; history; mathematics and statistics; parks, recreation, leisure, and fitness studies; philosophy and religious studies; physical sciences; psychology; security and protective services; social sciences; theology and religious vocations; visual and performing arts. **Areas of required coursework:** arts/fine arts, computer literacy, mathematics, English (including composition), sciences (biological or physical), history, social science. **Pre-professional programs:** pre-law, pre-medicine, pre-veterinary science. **Special academic programs (% participation):** accelerated program (48%), double major (3%), dual enrollment (1%), honors program (5%), internships (5%), student-designed major (2%), study abroad (2%), teacher certificate program (25%), weekend college (10%). **Teacher certification offered in:** elementary, middle/junior high, secondary. **Faculty and instruction (2005-2006):** Total instructional faculty: 33 full-time, 77 part-time (68% men; 32% women; 6% minorities). Full-time faculty with Ph.D. or other terminal degree: 64%. Student/faculty ratio: 12/1. Classes of fewer than 20 students: 86%; of 20 to 49 students: 14%; of 50 or more students: 0%. **Advanced Placement and International Baccalaureate credit:** AP tests may be used for: Credit and/or placement. Scores accepted: 3, 4, 5. Freshmen returning for sophomore year: 62%. **Graduation rates:** Four-year: 38%; five-year: 38%; six-year: 41%. **Graduate study:** 20% of students pursue further study immediately upon graduation; 15% within one year. Fields in which graduates pursue further study: Master of Business Administration (MBA), 13%; law, 3%; medicine, 3%; dentistry, 3%; theology (or the seminary), 10%; education, 3%; arts and sciences, 2%.

COSTS AND FINANCIAL AID

Financial aid office: (276) 326-4215. **Expenses (2006-2007):** Tuition and fees 2006-2007: $12,305; room/board: $6,032. Estimated books and supplies: $1,300; transportation: $1,410; personal expenses: $1,652. **Financial aid:** Priority filing date for institution's financial aid form: March 31. In 2005-2006, 86% of undergraduates applied for financial aid. Of those, 74% were determined to have financial need; 17% had their need fully met. Average financial aid package (proportion receiving): $8,308 (72%). Average amount of gift aid, such as scholarships or grants (proportion receiving): $5,283 (65%). Average amount of self-help aid, such as work study or loans (proportion receiving): $4,256 (60%). Average need-based loan (excluding PLUS or other private loans): $4,099. Among students who received need-based aid, the average percentage of need met: 56%. Among students who received aid based on merit, the average award (and the proportion receiving): $6,306 (21%). The average athletic scholarship (and the proportion receiving): $2,931 (4%). Average amount of debt of borrowers graduating in 2005: $14,191. Proportion who borrowed: 84%.

CAMPUS LIFE AND EXTRACURRICULAR ACTIVITIES

Campus housing available: coed dorms, women's dorms, men's dorms. Students who live in college-owned, operated, or affiliated housing: 45%. **Student employment:** During the 2005-2006 academic year, 2% of undergraduates worked on campus. Average per-year earnings: $1,300. **Clubs and organizations:** Number of student organizations: 10. Activities include: choral groups, drama/theater, literary magazine, music ensembles, musical theater, student government, student newspaper, yearbook. Number of fraternities: 4; sororities: 2. Proportion of men in fraternities: 2%; of women in sororities: 2%. Average proportion of students who stay on campus on weekends: 60%. **Sports program (2005-2006):** Member of NAIA. *Men's intercollegiate varsity sports:* baseball, basketball, golf, soccer. *Women's intercollegiate varsity sports:* basketball, soccer, softball, volleyball.

SERVICES AND FACILITIES

Basic services: nonremedial tutoring, other. **Remedial assistance:** math, writing. **Counseling services:** career, academic. **For learning-disabled students:** School does not offer a structured program with separate admission and additional fees. Total undergraduates in learning-disabled program or receiving services: 14. Services include: remedial math, remedial English, tape recorders, untimed tests, note-taking services, oral tests, extended time for tests, tutors. **Library:** Number of titles: 76,750; number of current serial subscriptions: 14,500. **Information technology resources:** Students are not required to lease or own a computer. Number of campus computers available to all students: 80. School has a wireless network. Approximate number of users that can be accommodated: 10,254. Proportion of college-owned housing units wired for high-speed internet access: 100%. **Campus safety:** Security services offered: late-night transport/escort service, lighted pathways/sidewalks, student patrols, controlled dormitory access (key, security card, etc).

TRANSFER AND INTERNATIONAL STUDENTS

Transfer students: May apply for admission for the following academic terms: Fall, Spring, Summer. Applicants do not need a minimum number of credits to apply. For fall 2005: Transfer applications received: 164. Transfer applicants offered admission: 72. Transfer applicants enrolled: 40. **International students:** Number of foreign undergraduates: 3. Minimum TOEFL score required: 500 (paper); 173 (computer). Average TOEFL score: 510 (paper).

Bridgewater College

- **Address:** 402 E. College Street, Bridgewater, VA 22812-1599
- **Website:** http://www.bridgewater.edu
- **Private; Religious affiliation:** Church of the Brethren
- **Enrollment:** 1,495 full-time; 11 part-time

KEY STATS

✔ **U.S News College Ranking:** fourth tier, Liberal Arts Colleges
✔ **SAT Score (25th/75th percentile):** 960-1150
✔ **Tuition:** 2006-2007: $20,190

Selectivity: Selective	**Room/board:** $9,060
Acceptance rate: 86%	**Average debt:** $25,780
Student/faculty ratio: 14/1	**Proportion who borrowed:** 69%

UNDERGRADUATE STUDENT BODY STATS

2005-2006 enrollment: 1,495 full-time; 11 part-time. Men: 43%; women: 57%. **Ethnic makeup:** African American: 8%; Asian American: 1%; Hispanic: 1%; White: 89%; International: 1%. **Religious preference:** Roman Catholic: 12%; Protestant: 59%; No preference: 4%; Unknown: 5%; Church of the Brethren: 11%; Other: 9%.

ADMISSIONS FACTS AND FIGURES

Phone: (800) 759-8328. **Email:** admissions@bridgewater.edu. **Website:** http://www.bridgewater.edu. **Application deadlines for fall 2007:** Regular decision: Rolling. Early decision: Not offered. Early action: Not offered. Admission can be deferred. **Application fee:** $30. Common application is accepted. **To apply online, go to:** http://www.bridgewater.edu/departments/admissions/online_app.html. **Admissions requirements/recommendations:** High school units required (recommended): English: 4 (4); Mathematics: 3 (4); Science: 2 (4); Foreign language: 0 (3); Academic electives: 4 (4); Total units: 15 (22). Tests: The college uses SAT or ACT scores in admissions decisions. Either SAT or ACT required. For admission to the fall 2007 entering class, the school will accept: ACT with writing, ACT without writing. Campus visit: Recommended. Admissions interview: Recommended. Off-campus interview: May be arranged. **Factors that count in admissions decisions:** *Academic:* Secondary school record: Very important. Class rank: Important. Letters of recommendation: Important. Standardized test scores: Very important. Essay: Not considered. *Nonacademic:* Interview: Important. Extracurricular activities: Important. Talent/ability: Important. Character/personal qualities: Important. Alumni/ae relationship: Not considered. Geographical residence: Considered. State residency: Considered. Religious affiliation/commitment: Not considered. Minority status: Considered. Volunteer work: Considered. Work experience: Considered. **Other schools with the greatest overlap in applicants:** James Madison

University; Radford University; Virginia Tech. **Admissions statistics for the fall 2005 entering class:** Total applicants: 1,502. Total accepted: 1,292. Freshmen enrolled: 394; 24% were from out of state. Overall acceptance rate: 86%. **Credentials of fall 2005 freshmen:** 17% ranked in the top 10 percent of their high school class; 45% were in the top 25 percent, and 85% were in the top half. (Proportion submitting class standing: 87%.) **Average high school grade point average:** 3.5. **First-year students who submitted SAT scores:** 96%. Scores (25/75 percentile): Verbal: 480-570, Math: 480-580, Combined: 960-1150. **First-year students submitting ACT scores:** 23%. Scores (25/75 percentile): English: 18-24, Math: 18-25, Composite: 19-24.

ACADEMICS

Year founded: 1880. **Academic calendar:** 4-1-4. **Degrees offered:** bachelor's. **Most popular majors:** 16% business administration and management, 13% biology/biological sciences, 9% elementary education and teaching, 8% mass communication/media studies, 6% psychology. **Major fields of study:** biological and biomedical sciences; business, management, marketing, and related support services; communication, journalism, and related programs; computer and information sciences and support services; education; English language and literature/letters; family and consumer sciences/human sciences; foreign languages, literatures, and linguistics; health professions and related clinical sciences; history; liberal arts and sciences studies, and humanities; mathematics and statistics; natural resources and conservation; parks, recreation, leisure, and fitness studies; philosophy and religious studies; physical sciences; psychology; social sciences; visual and performing arts. **Areas of required coursework:** arts/fine arts, humanities, computer literacy, mathematics, English (including composition), philosophy, foreign languages, sciences (biological or physical), history, social science, other. **Pre-professional programs:** pre-law, pre-dentistry, pre-medicine, pre-veterinary science, pre-pharmacy, other. **Special academic programs (% participation):** double major (8%), honors program (8%), independent study (10%), internships (22%), liberal arts/career combination (0%), study abroad (3%), teacher certificate program (20%). **Teacher certification offered in:** special education, elementary, secondary. **Faculty and instruction (2005-2006):** Total instructional faculty: 96 full-time, 30 part-time (56% men; 44% women; 2% minorities). Full-time faculty with Ph.D. or other terminal degree: 79%. Student/faculty ratio: 14/1. Classes of fewer than 20 students: 56%; of 20 to 49 students: 42%; of 50 or more students: 2%. **Advanced Placement and International Baccalaureate credit:** AP tests may be used for: Credit and/or placement. Scores accepted: 3, 4, 5. International Baccalaureate exams may be used for: Credit and/or placement. **Freshmen returning for sophomore year:** 77%. **Graduation rates:** Four-year: 65%; five-year: 67%; six-year: 68%. **Graduate study:** Fields in which graduates pursue further study: Master of Business Administration (MBA), 6%; medicine, 2%; theology (or the seminary), 4%; education, 27%; arts and sciences, 59%; veterinary medicine, 2%.

COSTS AND FINANCIAL AID

Financial aid office: (540) 828-5376. **Expenses (2006-2007):** Tuition and fees 2006-2007: $20,190; room/board: $9,060. Estimated books and supplies: $960; transportation: $600; personal expenses: $990. **Financial aid:** Priority filing date for institution's financial aid form: March 1. In 2005-2006, 82% of undergraduates applied for financial aid. Of those, 68% were determined to have financial need; 31% had their need fully met. Average financial aid package (proportion receiving): $17,309 (68%). Average amount of gift aid, such as scholarships or grants (proportion receiving): $13,371 (68%). Average amount of self-help aid, such as work study or loans (proportion receiving): $3,938 (53%). Average need-based loan (excluding PLUS or other private loans): $3,537. Among students who received need-based aid, the average percentage of need met: 84%. Among students who received aid based on merit, the average award (and the proportion receiving): $7,895 (30%). The average athletic scholarship (and the proportion receiving): $0 (0%). Average amount of debt of borrowers graduating in 2005: $25,780. Proportion who borrowed: 69%.

CAMPUS LIFE AND EXTRACURRICULAR ACTIVITIES

Campus housing available (% using): women's dorms (45%), men's dorms (34%), apartment for single students (17%), special housing for disabled students, other housing options (4%). Students who live in college-owned, operated, or affiliated housing: 80%. **Student employment:** During the 2005-2006 academic year, 9% of undergraduates worked on campus. Average per-year earnings: $796. **Clubs and organizations:** Number of student organizations: 75. Activities include: choral groups, concert band, dance, drama/theater, jazz band, literary magazine, music ensembles, musical theater, pep band, radio station, student government, student newspaper, yearbook. Number of fraternities: 0; sororities: 0. Average proportion of students who stay on campus on weekends: 60%. **Sports program (2005-2006):** Member of NCAA III. *Men's intercollegiate varsity sports:* baseball, basketball, cross-country, football, golf, soccer, tennis, track and field (indoor), track and field (outdoor). *Women's intercollegiate varsity sports:* basketball, cross-country, equestrian sports, field hockey, lacrosse, soccer, softball, tennis, track and field (indoor), track and field (outdoor), volleyball.

SERVICES AND FACILITIES

Basic services: nonremedial tutoring, placement service, health service, health insurance. **Counseling services:** minority student, career, personal, academic, psychological, birth control, religious. **For learning-disabled students:** School does not offer a structured program with separate admission and additional fees. Total undergraduates in learning-disabled program or receiving services: 60. Services include: tape recorders, untimed tests, note-taking services, special bookstore section, readers, extended time for tests, tutors, early syllabus, priority seating, proofreading services, substitution of courses, texts on tape, waiver of foreign language degree requirement, waiver of math degree requirement. **Library:** Number of titles: 140,366; number of current serial subscriptions: 650. **Information technology resources:** Students are not required to lease or own a computer. Number of campus computers available to all students: 176. School has a wireless network. Approximate number of users that can be accommodated: 200. Proportion of college-owned housing units wired for high-speed internet access: 100%. **Campus safety:** Security services offered: 24-hour foot-and-vehicle patrols, 24-hour emergency telephones, lighted pathways/sidewalks, controlled dormitory access (key, security card, etc).

TRANSFER AND INTERNATIONAL STUDENTS

Transfer students: May apply for admission for the following academic terms: Fall, Spring, Summer. Applicants do not need a minimum number of credits to apply. For fall 2005: Transfer applications received: 108. Transfer applicants offered admission: 100. Transfer applicants enrolled: 68. **International students:** Number of foreign undergraduates: 9 (1% of student body). Number of countries represented: 8. Minimum TOEFL score required: 500 (paper); 173 (computer). Average TOEFL score: 560 (paper).

Christendom College

- Address: 134 Christendom Drive, Front Royal, VA 22630
- Website: http://www.christendom.edu
- Private; Religious affiliation: Roman Catholic
- Enrollment: 372 full-time; 7 part-time

KEY STATS

✔ U.S News College Ranking: fourth tier, Liberal Arts Colleges
✔ SAT Score (25th/75th percentile): 1130-1330
✔ Tuition: 2005-2006: $15,818

Selectivity: More selective	Room/board: $5,776
Acceptance rate: 76%	Average debt: N/A
Student/faculty ratio: 13/1	Proportion who borrowed: N/A

UNDERGRADUATE STUDENT BODY STATS

2005-2006 enrollment: 372 full-time; 7 part-time. Men: 43%; women: 57%. **Ethnic makeup:** African American: 1%; Asian American: 2%; Hispanic: 3%; White: 93%; International: 2%. **Religious preference:** Roman Catholic: 100%.

ADMISSIONS FACTS AND FIGURES

Phone: (800) 877-5456. **Email:** admissions@christendom.edu. **Website:** http://www.christendom.edu. **Application deadlines for fall 2007:** Regular decision: Rolling; decision sent by April 1. Early decision: Not offered. Early action: Send application by: December 1; Decision sent by: December 15. Admission cannot be deferred. **Application fee:** $25. Common application is accepted. **Admissions requirements/recommendations:** High school units required (recommended): English: (4); Mathematics: (2); Science: (2); Foreign language: (2); Social studies: (1); History: (2); Academic electives: (1); Total units: (14). Tests: The college uses SAT or ACT scores in admissions decisions. Either SAT or ACT required. For admission to the fall 2007 entering class, the school will accept: ACT with writing, ACT without writing. Campus visit: Recommended. Admissions interview: Recommended. Off-campus interview: Not available. **Factors that count in admissions decisions:** *Academic:* Secondary school record: Important. Class rank:

Important. Letters of recommendation: Important. Standardized test scores: Very important. Essay: Very important. *Nonacademic:* Interview: Important. Extracurricular activities: Considered. Talent/ability: Considered. Character/personal qualities: Very important. Alumni/ae relationship: Considered. Geographical residence: Not considered. State residency: Not considered. Religious affiliation/commitment: Very important. Minority status: Not considered. Volunteer work: Considered. Work experience: Considered. **Other schools with the greatest overlap in applicants:** Franciscan University of Steubenville; Thomas Aquinas College. **Admissions statistics for the fall 2005 entering class:** Total applicants: 249. Total accepted: 190. Freshmen enrolled: 105; 73% were from out of state. Overall acceptance rate: 76%. Non-early acceptance rate: 76%. **Size of waiting list:** 15 applicants; enrolled from waiting list: 5. **Credentials of fall 2005 freshmen:** 15% ranked in the top 10 percent of their high school class; 75% were in the top 25 percent, and 100% were in the top half. (Proportion submitting class standing: 20%.) **Average high school grade point average:** 3.6. **First-year students who submitted SAT scores:** 70%. Scores (25/75 percentile): Verbal: 600-700, Math: 530-630, Combined: 1130-1330. **First-year students submitting ACT scores:** 30%. Scores (25/75 percentile): English: N/A, Math: N/A, Composite: N/A.

ACADEMICS

Year founded: 1977. **Academic calendar:** Semester. **Degrees offered:** associate, bachelor's, master's. **Most popular majors:** Information not available. **Major fields of study:** English language and literature/letters; foreign languages, literatures, and linguistics; history; philosophy and religious studies; social sciences; theology and religious vocations. **Areas of required coursework:** arts/fine arts, humanities, computer literacy, mathematics, English (including composition), philosophy, foreign languages, sciences (biological or physical), history, social science. **Pre-professional programs:** pre-theology. **Special academic programs (% participation):** double major (5%), honors program (10%), independent study (5%), internships (5%), study abroad (10%). **Faculty and instruction (2005-2006):** Total instructional faculty: 23 full-time, 16 part-time (85% men; 15% women). Full-time faculty with Ph.D. or other terminal degree: 78%. Student/faculty ratio: 13/1. Classes of fewer than 20 students: 59%; of 20 to 49 students: 39%; of 50 or more students: 2%. **Advanced Placement and International Baccalaureate credit:** AP tests may be used for: Credit only. Scores accepted: 4, 5. **Freshmen returning for sophomore year:** 84%. **Graduation rates:** Six-year: 66%.

COSTS AND FINANCIAL AID

Financial aid office: (540) 636-2900. **Expenses (2005-2006):** Tuition and fees 2005-2006: $15,818; room/board: $5,776. **Financial aid:** Priority filing date for institution's financial aid form: March 15.

CAMPUS LIFE AND EXTRACURRICULAR ACTIVITIES

Campus housing available: women's dorms, men's dorms. Students who live in college-owned, operated, or affiliated housing: 95%. **Student employment:** During the 2005-2006 academic year, 0% of undergraduates worked on campus. Average per-year earnings: $0. Activities include: choral groups, drama/theater, literary magazine, student government, student newspaper, student film society, yearbook. Number of fraternities: 0; sororities: 0. Average proportion of students who stay on campus on weekends: 90%.

SERVICES AND FACILITIES

Basic services: health service. **Remedial assistance:** writing. **Counseling services:** career, academic, religious. **For learning-disabled students:** School does not offer a structured program with separate admission and additional fees. **Information technology resources:** Students are not required to lease or own a computer. Number of campus computers available to all students: 75. School does not have a wireless network. Proportion of college-owned housing units wired for high-speed internet access: 0%. **Campus safety:** Security services offered: late-night transport/escort service, lighted pathways/sidewalks, controlled dormitory access (key, security card, etc).

TRANSFER AND INTERNATIONAL STUDENTS

Transfer students: May apply for admission for the following academic terms: Fall, Spring. Applicants do not need a minimum number of credits to apply. For fall 2005: Transfer applications received: 34. Transfer applicants offered admission: 23. Transfer applicants enrolled: 18. **International students:** Number of foreign undergraduates: 7 (2% of student body). Minimum TOEFL score required: 500 (paper).

Christopher Newport University

- **Address:** 1 University Place, Newport News, VA 23606
- **Website:** http://www.cnu.edu
- **Public**
- **Enrollment:** 4,204 full-time; 332 part-time

KEY STATS
✔ **U.S News College Ranking:** fourth tier, Liberal Arts Colleges
✔ **SAT Score (25th/75th percentile):** 1060-1230
✔ **Tuition:** 2006-2007: $6,460 in state, $13,482 out of state

Selectivity: Selective	**Room/board:** $8,100
Acceptance rate: 52%	**Average debt:** $13,772
Student/faculty ratio: 20/1	**Proportion who borrowed:** 53%

UNDERGRADUATE STUDENT BODY STATS
2005-2006 enrollment: 4,204 full-time; 332 part-time. Men: 46%; women: 54%. **Ethnic makeup:** African American: 8%; American-Indian: 1%; Asian American: 2%; Hispanic: 2%; White: 87%.

ADMISSIONS FACTS AND FIGURES
Phone: (757) 594-7015. **Email:** admit@cnu.edu. **Website:** http://www.cnu.edu. **Application deadlines for fall 2007:** Regular decision: March 1. Early decision: Not offered. Early action: Send application by: December 1; Decision sent by: N/A. Admission can be deferred. **Application fee:** $45. Common application is accepted. **To apply online, go to:** http://www.cnu.edu/admissions/. **Admissions requirements/recommendations:** High school units required (recommended): English: 4 (4); Mathematics: 4 (4); Science: 4 (3); Foreign language: 3 (3); Social studies: 4 (4); Total units: 19 (18). Tests: The college uses SAT or ACT scores in admissions decisions. Either SAT or ACT required. For admission to the fall 2007 entering class, the school will accept: ACT with writing, ACT without writing. Campus visit: Recommended. Admissions interview: Neither required nor recommended. Off-campus interview: May be arranged. **Factors that count in admissions decisions:** *Academic:* Secondary school record: Very important. Class rank: Considered. Letters of recommendation: Considered. Standardized test scores: Important. Essay: Considered. *Nonacademic:* Interview: Not considered. Extracurricular activities: Considered. Talent/ability: Considered. Character/personal qualities: Not considered. Alumni/ae relationship: Considered. Geographical residence: Not considered. State residency: Not considered. Religious affiliation/commitment: Not considered. Minority status: Not considered. Volunteer work: Not considered. Work experience: Not considered. **Other schools with the greatest overlap in applicants:** George Mason University; James Madison University; University of Mary Washington; University of Virginia; Virginia Tech. **Admissions statistics for the fall 2005 entering class:** Total applicants: 6,104. Total accepted: 3,186. Freshmen enrolled: 1,250; 4% were from out of state. Overall acceptance rate: 52%. Non-early acceptance rate: 52%. **Credentials of fall 2005 freshmen:** 15% ranked in the top 10 percent of their high school class; 48% were in the top 25 percent, and 90% were in the top half. (Proportion submitting class standing: 72%.) **Average high school grade point average:** 3.4. **First-year students who submitted SAT scores:** 99%. Scores (25/75 percentile): Verbal: 530-620, Math: 530-610, Combined: 1060-1230. **First-year students submitting ACT scores:** 22%. Scores (25/75 percentile): English: N/A, Math: N/A, Composite: 21-25.

ACADEMICS
Year founded: 1960. **Academic calendar:** Semester. **Degrees offered:** bachelor's, master's. **Most popular majors:** 15% business administration and management, 13% psychology, 11% political science and government, 8% biology/biological sciences, 7% communication studies/speech communication and rhetoric. **Major fields of study:** agriculture, agriculture operations, and related sciences; biological and biomedical sciences; business, management, marketing, and related support services; communication, journalism, and related programs; computer and information sciences and support services; engineering; English language and literature/letters; foreign languages, literatures, and linguistics; history; mathematics and statistics; multi/interdisciplinary studies; natural resources and conservation; philosophy and religious studies; physical sciences; psychology; public administration and social service professions; social sciences; visual and performing arts. **Areas of required coursework:** arts/fine arts, humanities, mathematics, English (including composition), philosophy, foreign languages, sciences (biological or physical), history, social science. **Pre-professional programs:**

pre-law, pre-dentistry, pre-medicine, pre-theology, pre-veterinary science. **Special academic programs:** cross-registration, double major, dual enrollment, honors program, independent study, internships, student-designed major, study abroad. **Reserve Officers Training Corps (ROTC):** Army ROTC: Offered on campus. **Faculty and instruction (2005-2006):** Total instructional faculty: 218 full-time, 21 part-time (59% men; 41% women; 11% minorities). Full-time faculty with Ph.D. or other terminal degree: 89%. Student/faculty ratio: 20/1. Classes of fewer than 20 students: 42%; of 20 to 49 students: 55%; of 50 or more students: 3%. **Advanced Placement and International Baccalaureate credit:** AP tests may be used for: Credit only. Scores accepted: 2, 3, 4, 5. International Baccalaureate exams may be used for: Credit only. **Freshmen returning for sophomore year:** 74%. **Graduation rates:** Four-year: 18%; five-year: 40%; six-year: 45%.

COSTS AND FINANCIAL AID
Financial aid office: (757) 594-7170. **Expenses (2006-2007):** Tuition and fees 2006-2007: $6,460 in state, $13,482 out of state; room/board: $8,100. Estimated books and supplies: $850; transportation: $812; personal expenses: $1,964. **Financial aid:** Priority filing date for institution's financial aid form: March 1. In 2005-2006, 72% of undergraduates applied for financial aid. Of those, 43% were determined to have financial need; 24% had their need fully met. Average financial aid package (proportion receiving): $6,229 (35%). Average amount of gift aid, such as scholarships or grants (proportion receiving): $4,086 (26%). Average amount of self-help aid, such as work study or loans (proportion receiving): $3,297 (30%). Average need-based loan (excluding PLUS or other private loans): $3,191. Among students who received need-based aid, the average percentage of need met: 76%. Among students who received aid based on merit, the average award (and the proportion receiving): $1,661 (3%). The average athletic scholarship (and the proportion receiving): $0 (0%). Average amount of debt of borrowers graduating in 2005: $13,772. Proportion who borrowed: 53%.

CAMPUS LIFE AND EXTRACURRICULAR ACTIVITIES
Campus housing available (% using): coed dorms (69%), apartment for single students (30%), other housing options (1%). Students who live in college-owned, operated, or affiliated housing: 61%. **Student employment:** During the 2005-2006 academic year, 21% of undergraduates worked on campus. Average per-year earnings: $1,448. **Clubs and organizations:** Number of student organizations: 116. Activities include: choral groups, concert band, dance, drama/theater, jazz band, literary magazine, marching band, music ensembles, musical theater, opera, pep band, radio station, student government, student newspaper, student film society, symphony orchestra, television station. Number of fraternities: 5; sororities: 5. Proportion of men in fraternities: 4%; of women in sororities: 6%. Average proportion of students who stay on campus on weekends: 65%. **Sports program (2005-2006):** Member of NCAA III. *Men's intercollegiate varsity sports:* baseball, basketball, cheerleading, cross-country, football, golf, sailing, soccer, tennis, track and field (indoor), track and field (outdoor). *Women's intercollegiate varsity sports:* basketball, cheerleading, cross-country, field hockey, lacrosse, sailing, soccer, softball, tennis, track and field (indoor), track and field (outdoor), volleyball.

SERVICES AND FACILITIES
Basic services: health service. **Counseling services:** minority student, career, personal, veteran student, academic, religious. **For learning-disabled students:** School does not offer a structured program with separate admission and additional fees. Total undergraduates in learning-disabled program or receiving services: 210. Services include: reading machines, tape recorders, oral tests, extended time for tests, other. **Library:** Number of titles: 206,965; number of current serial subscriptions: 11,086. **Information technology resources:** Students are not required to lease or own a computer. Number of campus computers available to all students: 302. School has a wireless network. Approximate number of users that can be accommodated: 5,000. Proportion of college-owned housing units wired for high-speed internet access: 100%. **Campus safety:** Security services offered: 24-hour foot-and-vehicle patrols, late-night transport/escort service, 24-hour emergency telephones, lighted pathways/sidewalks, student patrols, controlled dormitory access (key, security card, etc).

TRANSFER AND INTERNATIONAL STUDENTS
Transfer students: May apply for admission for the following academic terms: Fall, Spring, Summer. Applicants need a minimum number of credits to apply. For fall 2005: Transfer applications received: 506. Transfer applicants offered admission: 176. Transfer applicants enrolled: 98. **International students:** Number of foreign undergraduates: 1. Number of

countries represented: 1. Minimum TOEFL score required: 530 (paper); 197 (computer).

College of William and Mary

- **Address:** PO Box 8795, Williamsburg, VA 23187-8795
- **Website:** http://www.wm.edu
- **Public**
- **Enrollment:** 5,527 full-time; 67 part-time

KEY STATS

✔ **U.S News College Ranking:** 31, National Universities
✔ **SAT Score (25th/75th percentile):** 1260-1440
✔ **Tuition:** 2006-2007: $8,490 in state, $25,048 out of state

Selectivity: Most selective	Room/board: $6,932
Acceptance rate: 31%	Average debt: $14,524
Student/faculty ratio: 11/1	Proportion who borrowed: 34%

UNDERGRADUATE STUDENT BODY STATS

2005-2006 enrollment: 5,527 full-time; 67 part-time. Men: 45%; women: 55%. **Ethnic makeup:** African American: 6%; American-Indian: 1%; Asian American: 7%; Hispanic: 5%; White: 80%; International: 1%.

ADMISSIONS FACTS AND FIGURES

Phone: (757) 221-4223. **Email:** admiss@wm.edu. **Website:** http://www.wm.edu. **Application deadlines for fall 2007:** Regular decision: January 1. Early decision: Send application by: November 1; Decision sent by: December 1. Early action: Not offered. Admission can be deferred. **Application fee:** $60. Common application is accepted. **To apply online, go to:** http://www.wm.edu/admission. **Admissions requirements/recommendations:** High school units required (recommended): English: (4); Mathematics: (4); Science: (4); Foreign language: (4); Social studies: (4). Tests: The college uses SAT or ACT scores in admissions decisions. Either SAT or ACT required. For admission to the fall 2007 entering class, the school will accept: ACT with writing, ACT without writing. Campus visit: Recommended. Admissions interview: Neither required nor recommended. Off-campus interview: Not available. **Factors that count in admissions decisions:** *Academic:* Secondary school record: Very important. Class rank: Important. Letters of recommendation: Important. Standardized test scores: Important. Essay: Important. *Nonacademic:* Interview: Not considered. Extracurricular activities: Considered. Talent/ability: Considered. Character/personal qualities: Considered. Alumni/ae relationship: Considered. Geographical residence: Considered. State residency: Very important. Religious affiliation/commitment: Not considered. Minority status: Considered. Volunteer work: Considered. Work experience: Considered. **Admissions statistics for the fall 2005 entering class:** Total applicants: 10,610. Total accepted: 3,292. Freshmen enrolled: 1,344; 33% were from out of state. Overall acceptance rate: 31%. Non-early acceptance rate: 31%. **Size of waiting list:** 1812 applicants; enrolled from waiting list: 113. **Credentials of fall 2005 freshmen:** 79% ranked in the top 10 percent of their high school class; 97% were in the top 25 percent, and 100% were in the top half. (Proportion submitting class standing: 50%.) **Average high school grade point average:** 4.0. **First-year students who submitted SAT scores:** 97%. Scores (25/75 percentile): Verbal: 630-730, Math: 630-710, Combined: 1260-1440. **First-year students submitting ACT scores:** 3%. Scores (25/75 percentile): English: 27-33, Math: 27-29, Composite: 28-31.

ACADEMICS

Year founded: 1693. **Academic calendar:** Semester. **Degrees offered:** bachelor's, master's, post-master's certificate, first professional, doctorate. **Most popular majors:** 24% political science and government, 12% business administration and management, 9% English language and literature, 9% psychology, 8% biology/biological sciences. **Major fields of study:** area, ethnic, cultural, and gender studies; biological and biomedical sciences; business, management, marketing, and related support services; computer and information sciences and support services; English language and literature/letters; foreign languages, literatures, and linguistics; history; legal professions and studies; mathematics and statistics; multi/interdisciplinary studies; parks, recreation, leisure, and fitness studies; philosophy and religious studies; physical sciences; psychology; public administration and social service professions; social sciences; visual and performing arts. **Areas of required coursework:** arts/fine arts, humanities, computer literacy,

mathematics, English (including composition), philosophy, foreign languages, sciences (biological or physical), history, social science. **Pre-professional programs:** pre-law, pre-medicine. **Special academic programs:** accelerated program, double major, dual enrollment, exchange student program (domestic), external degree program, honors program, independent study, internships, student-designed major, study abroad, teacher certificate program, other. **Teacher certification offered in:** special education, elementary, middle/junior high, secondary. **Cooperative education programs:** art, business, computer science, education, engineering, health professions, humanities, natural science, social/behavioral science. **Reserve Officers Training Corps (ROTC):** Army ROTC: Offered on campus. **Faculty and instruction (2005-2006):** Total instructional faculty: 596 full-time, 167 part-time (63% men; 37% women; 9% minorities). Full-time faculty with Ph.D. or other terminal degree: 89%. Student/faculty ratio: 11/1. Classes of fewer than 20 students: 47%; of 20 to 49 students: 46%; of 50 or more students: 7%. **Advanced Placement and International Baccalaureate credit:** AP tests may be used for: Credit and/or placement. Scores accepted: 3, 4, 5. International Baccalaureate exams may be used for: Credit and/or placement. **Freshmen returning for sophomore year:** 95%. **Graduation rates:** Four-year: 81%; five-year: 90%; six-year: 91%. **Graduate study:** 30% of students pursue further study immediately upon graduation.

COSTS AND FINANCIAL AID

Financial aid office: (757) 221-2420. **Expenses (2006-2007):** Tuition and fees 2006-2007: $8,490 in state, $25,048 out of state; room/board: $6,932. Estimated books and supplies: $900; transportation: $250; personal expenses: $1,050. **Financial aid:** Priority filing date for institution's financial aid form: February 15; deadline: March 15. In 2005-2006, 47% of undergraduates applied for financial aid. Of those, 27% were determined to have financial need; 46% had their need fully met. Average financial aid package (proportion receiving): $10,682 (27%). Average amount of gift aid, such as scholarships or grants (proportion receiving): $9,613 (22%). Average amount of self-help aid, such as work study or loans (proportion receiving): $2,756 (24%). Average need-based loan (excluding PLUS or other private loans): $2,648. Among students who received need-based aid, the average percentage of need met: 87%. Among students who received aid based on merit, the average award (and the proportion receiving): $5,237 (5%). The average athletic scholarship (and the proportion receiving): $14,280 (5%). Average amount of debt of borrowers graduating in 2005: $14,524. Proportion who borrowed: 34%.

CAMPUS LIFE AND EXTRACURRICULAR ACTIVITIES

Campus housing available: coed dorms, women's dorms, men's dorms, sorority housing, fraternity housing, apartments for married students, apartment for single students, special housing for disabled students, special housing for international students, other housing options. Students who live in college-owned, operated, or affiliated housing: 75%. **Student employment:** During the 2005-2006 academic year, 35% of undergraduates worked on campus. Average per-year earnings: $1,200. **Clubs and organizations:** Number of student organizations: 358. Activities include: choral groups, concert band, dance, drama/theater, jazz band, literary magazine, music ensembles, musical theater, opera, pep band, radio station, student government, student newspaper, student film society, symphony orchestra, television station, yearbook. Number of fraternities: 15; sororities: 12. Proportion of men in fraternities: 24%; of women in sororities: 28%. Average proportion of students who stay on campus on weekends: 95%. **Sports program (2005-2006):** Member of NCAA I. *Men's intercollegiate varsity sports:* baseball, basketball, cross-country, football, golf, gymnastics, soccer, swimming and diving, tennis, track and field (indoor), track and field (outdoor). *Women's intercollegiate varsity sports:* basketball, cross-country, field hockey, golf, gymnastics, lacrosse, soccer, swimming and diving, tennis, track and field (indoor), track and field (outdoor), volleyball.

SERVICES AND FACILITIES

Basic services: nonremedial tutoring, placement service, day care, health service. **Counseling services:** minority student, career, personal, veteran student, academic. **For learning-disabled students:** School does not offer a structured program with separate admission and additional fees. Services include: tape recorders, diagnostic testing service, note-taking services, readers, extended time for tests. **Library:** Number of titles: 2,128,645; number of current serial subscriptions: 11,313. **Information technology resources:** Students are not required to lease or own a computer. Number of campus computers available to all students: 350. School has a wireless network. Approximate number of users that can be accommodated: 1,700. Proportion of college-owned housing units wired for high-speed internet access: 100%. **Campus safety:** Security services offered: 24-hour foot-and-vehicle patrols, late-night transport/escort service, 24-hour emergency telephones, lighted pathways/sidewalks, student patrols, controlled dormitory access (key, security card, etc).

TRANSFER AND INTERNATIONAL STUDENTS

Transfer students: May apply for admission for the following academic terms: Fall, Spring. Applicants need a minimum number of credits to apply. For fall 2005: Transfer applications received: 582. Transfer applicants offered admission: 306. Transfer applicants enrolled: 158. **International students:** Number of foreign undergraduates: 74 (1% of student body). Number of countries represented: 35. Minimum TOEFL score required: 600 (paper); 250 (computer). Average TOEFL score: 658 (paper).

Eastern Mennonite University

- **Address:** 1200 Park Road, Harrisonburg, VA 22802-2462
- **Website:** http://www.emu.edu
- **Private; Religious affiliation:** Mennonite
- **Enrollment:** 970 full-time; 42 part-time

KEY STATS

✔ **U.S News College Ranking:** third tier, Liberal Arts Colleges
✔ **SAT Score (25th/75th percentile):** 960-1260
✔ **Tuition:** N/A

Selectivity: Selective	**Room/board:** N/A
Acceptance rate: 77%	**Average debt:** N/A
Student/faculty ratio: 9/1	**Proportion who borrowed:** N/A

UNDERGRADUATE STUDENT BODY STATS

2005-2006 enrollment: 970 full-time; 42 part-time. Men: 37%; women: 63%. **Ethnic makeup:** African American: 7%; Asian American: 2%; Hispanic: 3%; White: 85%; International: 4%. **Religious preference:** Roman Catholic: 2%; Protestant: 34%; No preference: 7%; Mennonite: 56%; Mormon: 0%; Other: 1%.

ADMISSIONS FACTS AND FIGURES

Phone: (800) 368-2665. **Email:** admiss@emu.edu. **Website:** http://www.emu.edu. **Application deadlines for fall 2007:** Regular decision: Rolling. Early decision: Not offered. Early action: Not offered. Admission can be deferred. **Application fee:** $25. Common application is accepted. **To apply online, go to:** http://www.emu.edu/admissions/apply/. **Admissions requirements/recommendations:** High school units required (recommended): English: 4 (4); Mathematics: 3 (3); Science: 3 (3); Foreign language: 2 (2); Social studies: 3 (3); Academic electives: 6 (6); Total units: 21 (21). Tests: The college uses SAT or ACT scores in admissions decisions. Either SAT or ACT required. For admission to the fall 2007 entering class, the school will accept: ACT with writing. Campus visit: Recommended. Admissions interview: Recommended. Off-campus interview: May be arranged. **Factors that count in admissions decisions:** *Academic:* Secondary school record: Important. Class rank: Not considered. Letters of recommendation: Important. Standardized test scores: Very important. Essay: Very important. *Nonacademic:* Interview: Not considered. Extracurricular activities: Not considered. Talent/ability: Not considered. Character/personal qualities: Considered. Alumni/ae relationship: Not considered. Geographical residence: Not considered. State residency: Not considered. Religious affiliation/commitment: Important. Minority status: Not considered. Volunteer work: Not considered. Work experience: Not considered. **Other schools with the greatest overlap in applicants:** Bridgewater College; Goshen College; Messiah College. **Admissions statistics for the fall 2005 entering class:** Total applicants: 636. Total accepted: 490. Freshmen enrolled: 202; 57% were from out of state. Overall acceptance rate: 77%. **Credentials of fall 2005 freshmen:** 21% ranked in the top 10 percent of their high school class; 44% were in the top 25 percent, and 77% were in the top half. (Proportion submitting class standing: 67%.) **Average high school grade point average:** 3.4. **First-year students who submitted SAT scores:** 86%. Scores (25/75 percentile): Verbal: 480-630; Math: 480-630; Combined: 960-1260. **First-year students submitting ACT scores:** 23%. Scores (25/75 percentile): English: 22-31; Math: 22-26; Composite: 22-28.

ACADEMICS

Year founded: 1917. **Academic calendar:** Semester. **Degrees offered:** certificate, associate, terminal-associate, bachelor's, post-bachelor's certificate,

master's, first professional. **Most popular majors:** 26% business, management, marketing, and related support services, 17% liberal arts and sciences studies, and humanities, 14% health professions and related clinical sciences, 10% education, 4% public administration and social service professions. **Major fields of study:** agriculture, agriculture operations, and related sciences; biological and biomedical sciences; business, management, marketing, and related support services; communication, journalism, and related programs; computer and information sciences and support services; education; English language and literature/letters; foreign languages, literatures, and linguistics; health professions and related clinical sciences; history; liberal arts and sciences studies, and humanities; mathematics and statistics; multi/interdisciplinary studies; natural resources and conservation; parks, recreation, leisure, and fitness studies; philosophy and religious studies; physical sciences; psychology; public administration and social service professions; social sciences; theology and religious vocations; visual and performing arts. **Areas of required coursework:** humanities, computer literacy, mathematics, English (including composition), foreign languages, sciences (biological or physical), social science, other. **Pre-professional programs:** pre-law, pre-dentistry, pre-medicine, pre-theology, pre-veterinary science, pre-optometry, pre-pharmacy, other. **Special academic programs (% participation):** double major (10.3%), English as a Second Language (ESL) (2%), honors program (7.4%), independent study (23.2%), internships (43.8%), study abroad (68.2%), teacher certificate program (17.8%). **Teacher certification offered in:** early childhood, special education, elementary, middle/junior high, secondary, bilingual/bicultural. **Faculty and instruction (2005-2006):** Total instructional faculty: 116 full-time, 47 part-time (58% men; 42% women; 10% minorities). Full-time faculty with Ph.D. or other terminal degree: 71%. Student/faculty ratio: 9/1. Classes of fewer than 20 students: 62%; of 20 to 49 students: 35%; of 50 or more students: 3%. **Advanced Placement and International Baccalaureate credit:** AP tests may be used for: Credit and/or placement. Scores accepted: 3, 4, 5. International Baccalaureate exams may be used for: Credit and/or placement. **Freshmen returning for sophomore year:** 78%. **Graduation rates:** Four-year: 51%; five-year: 66%; six-year: 67%. **Graduate study:** 7% of students pursue further study immediately upon graduation. Fields in which graduates pursue further study: Master of Business Administration (MBA), 4%; medicine, 8%; theology (or the seminary), 15%; education, 8%; arts and sciences, 65%.

COSTS AND FINANCIAL AID

Financial aid office: (540) 432-4139. **Financial aid:** Priority filing date for institution's financial aid form: April 15.

CAMPUS LIFE AND EXTRACURRICULAR ACTIVITIES

Campus housing available (% using): coed dorms (35%), women's dorms (24%), men's dorms (11%), apartments for married students (1%), apartment for single students (27%), special housing for disabled students (0%), other housing options (2%). Students who live in college-owned, operated, or affiliated housing: 56%. **Student employment:** During the 2005-2006 academic year, 6% of undergraduates worked on campus. Average per-year earnings: $1,485. **Clubs and organizations:** Number of student organizations: 38. Activities include: choral groups, dance, drama/theater, jazz band, literary magazine, music ensembles, musical theater, pep band, radio station, student government, student newspaper, symphony orchestra, yearbook. Number of fraternities: 0; sororities: 0. Average proportion of students who stay on campus on weekends: 80%. **Sports program (2005-2006):** Member of NCAA III. *Men's intercollegiate varsity sports:* baseball, basketball, cross-country, soccer, tennis, track and field (indoor), track and field (outdoor), volleyball. *Women's intercollegiate varsity sports:* basketball, cross-country, field hockey, soccer, softball, track and field (indoor), track and field (outdoor), volleyball.

SERVICES AND FACILITIES

Basic services: nonremedial tutoring, health service. **Remedial assistance:** reading, math, writing, study skills. **Counseling services:** minority student, career, personal, veteran student, academic, older student, psychological, birth control, religious, other. **For learning-disabled students:** School does not offer a structured program with separate admission and additional fees. Total undergraduates in learning-disabled program or receiving services: 81. Services include: remedial math, remedial English, reading machines, remedial reading, tape recorders, other special classes, videotaped classes, diagnostic testing service, untimed tests, note-taking services, oral tests, learning center, readers, extended time for tests, tutors, priority registration, priority seating, texts on tape, other testing accomodations, other. **Library:** Number of titles: 167,242; number of current serial subscriptions: 1,168. **Information technology resources:** Students are not required to lease or own a computer. Number of campus computers available to all students: 100.

School has a wireless network. Approximate number of users that can be accommodated: 200. Proportion of college-owned housing units wired for high-speed internet access: 100%. **Campus safety:** Security services offered: late-night transport/escort service, 24-hour emergency telephones, lighted pathways/sidewalks, controlled dormitory access (key, security card, etc).

TRANSFER AND INTERNATIONAL STUDENTS

Transfer students: May apply for admission for the following academic terms: Fall, Spring, Summer. Applicants need a minimum number of credits to apply. For fall 2005: Transfer applications received: 276. Transfer applicants offered admission: 156. Transfer applicants enrolled: 83. **International students:** Number of foreign undergraduates: 35 (4% of student body). Number of countries represented: 20. Minimum TOEFL score required: 550 (paper); 213 (computer).

Emory and Henry College

- **Address:** PO Box 947, Emory, VA 24327
- **Website:** http://www.ehc.edu
- **Private; Religious affiliation:** United Methodist
- **Enrollment:** 1,000 full-time; 27 part-time

KEY STATS
✔ **U.S News College Ranking:** third tier, Liberal Arts Colleges
✔ **SAT Score (25th/75th percentile):** 950-1170
✔ **Tuition:** 2006-2007: $20,860

Selectivity: Selective	**Room/board:** $7,360
Acceptance rate: 76%	**Average debt:** $15,465
Student/faculty ratio: 13/1	**Proportion who borrowed:** 76%

UNDERGRADUATE STUDENT BODY STATS

2005-2006 enrollment: 1,000 full-time; 27 part-time. Men: 51%; women: 49%. **Ethnic makeup:** African American: 4%; Asian American: 1%; Hispanic: 1%; White: 92%.

ADMISSIONS FACTS AND FIGURES

Phone: (800) 848-5493. **Email:** ehadmiss@ehc.edu. **Website:** http://www.ehc.edu. **Application deadlines for fall 2007:** Regular decision: Rolling. Early decision: Send application by: November 1; Decision sent by: December 15. Early action: Not offered. Admission can be deferred. **Application fee:** $30. Common application is accepted. **Admissions requirements/recommendations:** High school units required (recommended): English: 4; Mathematics: 3; Science: 3; Foreign language: 2; Social studies: 2; Total units: 14. Tests: The college uses SAT or ACT scores in admissions decisions. Either SAT or ACT required. For admission to the fall 2007 entering class, the school will accept: ACT with writing, ACT without writing. Campus visit: Recommended. Admissions interview: Recommended. Off-campus interview: May be arranged. **Factors that count in admissions decisions:** *Academic:* Secondary school record: Very important. Class rank: Considered. Letters of recommendation: Important. Standardized test scores: Considered. Essay: Considered. *Nonacademic:* Interview: Considered. Extracurricular activities: Considered. Talent/ability: Considered. Character/personal qualities: Considered. Alumni/ae relationship: Considered. Geographical residence: Considered. State residency: Considered. Religious affiliation/commitment: Considered. Minority status: Considered. Volunteer work: Considered. Work experience: Considered. **Admissions statistics for the fall 2005 entering class:** Total applicants: 1,329. Total accepted: 1,009. Freshmen enrolled: 338; 30% were from out of state. Overall acceptance rate: 76%. Non-early acceptance rate: 76%. **Credentials of fall 2005 freshmen:** 18% ranked in the top 10 percent of their high school class; 44% were in the top 25 percent, and 82% were in the top half. (Proportion submitting class standing: 100%.) **Average high school grade point average:** 3.4. **First-year students who submitted SAT scores:** 82%. Scores (25/75 percentile): Verbal: 480-590, Math: 470-580, Combined: 950-1170. **First-year students submitting ACT scores:** 22%. Scores (25/75 percentile): English: 20-26, Math: 19-24, Composite: 20-26.

ACADEMICS

Year founded: 1836. **Academic calendar:** Semester. **Degrees offered:** bachelor's, master's. **Most popular majors:** 16% social sciences, 13% education, 13% multi/interdisciplinary studies, 6% physical sciences, 6% psychology. **Major fields of study:** area, ethnic, cultural, and gender studies; biological and biomedical sciences; business, management, marketing, and related support services; communication, journalism, and related programs; computer and information sciences and support services; education; English language and literature/letters; foreign languages, literatures, and linguistics; history; mathematics and statistics; multi/interdisciplinary studies; natural resources and conservation; parks, recreation, leisure, and fitness studies; philosophy and religious studies; physical sciences; psychology; public administration and social service professions; social sciences; visual and performing arts. **Areas of required coursework:** humanities, computer literacy, mathematics, English (including composition), sciences (biological or physical), social science. **Pre-professional programs:** pre-law, pre-dentistry, pre-medicine, pre-theology, pre-veterinary science, pre-pharmacy, other. **Special academic programs:** cooperative (work-study plan) program, double major, dual enrollment, honors program, independent study, internships, study abroad, teacher certificate program. **Teacher certification offered in:** early childhood, elementary, middle/junior high, secondary. **Faculty and instruction (2005-2006):** Total instructional faculty: 68 full-time, 27 part-time (65% men; 35% women; 6% minorities). Full-time faculty with Ph.D. or other terminal degree: 88%. Student/faculty ratio: 13/1. Classes of fewer than 20 students: 72%; of 20 to 49 students: 28%; of 50 or more students: 0%. **Advanced Placement and International Baccalaureate credit:** International Baccalaureate exams may be used for: Credit only. **Freshmen returning for sophomore year:** 72%. **Graduation rates:** Four-year: 43%; five-year: 51%; six-year: 52%. **Graduate study:** 28% of students pursue further study immediately upon graduation; 37% within one year. Fields in which graduates pursue further study: Master of Business Administration (MBA), 23%; law, 31%; medicine, 12%; theology (or the seminary), 8%; education, 2%; arts and sciences, 24%.

COSTS AND FINANCIAL AID

Financial aid office: (276) 944-6229. **Expenses (2006-2007):** Tuition and fees 2006-2007: $20,860; room/board: $7,360. **Financial aid:** Priority filing date for institution's financial aid form: April 1; deadline: August 1. In 2005-2006, 88% of undergraduates applied for financial aid. Of those, 79% were determined to have financial need; 25% had their need fully met. Average financial aid package (proportion receiving): $14,362 (79%). Average amount of gift aid, such as scholarships or grants (proportion receiving): $10,834 (79%). Average amount of self-help aid, such as work study or loans (proportion receiving): $3,979 (70%). Average need-based loan (excluding PLUS or other private loans): $3,197. Among students who received need-based aid, the average percentage of need met: 72%. Among students who received aid based on merit, the average award (and the proportion receiving): $10,072 (20%). The average athletic scholarship (and the proportion receiving): $0 (0%). Average amount of debt of borrowers graduating in 2005: $15,465. Proportion who borrowed: 76%.

CAMPUS LIFE AND EXTRACURRICULAR ACTIVITIES

Campus housing available: women's dorms, men's dorms, special housing for disabled students, other housing options. Students who live in college-owned, operated, or affiliated housing: 66%. **Clubs and organizations:** Number of student organizations: 50. Activities include: choral groups, dance, drama/theater, literary magazine, music ensembles, musical theater, opera, pep band, radio station, student government, student newspaper, television station, yearbook. Number of fraternities: 6; sororities: 6. Proportion of men in fraternities: 11%; of women in sororities: 26%. Average proportion of students who stay on campus on weekends: 65%. **Sports program (2005-2006):** Member of NCAA III. *Men's intercollegiate varsity sports:* baseball, basketball, cross-country, football, golf, soccer, tennis. *Women's intercollegiate varsity sports:* basketball, cross-country, soccer, softball, swimming and diving, tennis, volleyball.

SERVICES AND FACILITIES

Basic services: nonremedial tutoring, health service, health insurance. **Remedial assistance:** reading, math, writing, study skills. **Counseling services:** minority student, career, military, personal, veteran student, academic, older student, psychological, birth control, religious. **For learning-disabled students:** School does not offer a structured program with separate admission and additional fees. Total undergraduates in learning-disabled program or receiving services: 70. Services include: remedial English, reading machines, tape recorders, note-taking services, readers, extended time for tests, tutors. **Library:** Number of titles: 278,749; number of current serial subscriptions: 14,054. **Information technology resources:** Students are not required to lease or own a computer. Number of campus computers available to all students: 250. School has a wireless network. Approximate number of users that can be accommodated: 150. Proportion of college-owned housing units wired for high-speed internet access: 95%. **Campus safety:**

Security services offered: 24-hour foot-and-vehicle patrols, late-night transport/escort service, 24-hour emergency telephones, lighted pathways/sidewalks, controlled dormitory access (key, security card, etc).

TRANSFER AND INTERNATIONAL STUDENTS

Transfer students: May apply for admission for the following academic terms: Fall, Spring, Summer. Applicants need a minimum number of credits to apply. For fall 2005: Transfer applications received: 136. Transfer applicants offered admission: 108. Transfer applicants enrolled: 64. **International students:** Number of foreign undergraduates: 3. Number of countries represented: 3. Minimum TOEFL score required: 550 (paper); 213 (computer).

Ferrum College

- **Address:** 215 Ferrum Mountain Road, Ferrum, VA 24088
- **Website:** http://www.ferrum.edu
- **Private; Religious affiliation:** United Methodist
- **Enrollment:** 962 full-time; 29 part-time

KEY STATS

✔ **U.S News College Ranking:** 46, Comp. Coll.–Bachelor's (South)
✔ **SAT Score (25th/75th percentile):** 810-980
✔ **Tuition:** 2006-2007: $19,520

Selectivity: Less selective	**Room/board:** $6,500
Acceptance rate: 72%	**Average debt:** $16,300
Student/faculty ratio: 13/1	**Proportion who borrowed:** 74%

UNDERGRADUATE STUDENT BODY STATS

2005-2006 enrollment: 962 full-time; 29 part-time. Men: 58%; women: 42%. **Ethnic makeup:** African American: 20%; American-Indian: 1%; Asian American: 1%; Hispanic: 2%; White: 76%; International: 1%. **Religious preference:** Roman Catholic: 1%; Protestant: 53%; No preference: 33%; United Methodist: 13%.

ADMISSIONS FACTS AND FIGURES

Phone: (800) 868-9797. **Email:** admissions@ferrum.edu. **Website:** http://www.ferrum.edu. **Application deadlines for fall 2007:** Regular decision: Rolling. Early decision: Not offered. Early action: Not offered. Admission can be deferred. **Application fee:** $25. Common application is accepted. **Admissions requirements/recommendations:** High school units required (recommended): English: (4); Mathematics: (3); Science: (2); Foreign language: (2); Social studies: (3); Academic electives: (2); Total units: (16). Tests: The college uses SAT or ACT scores in admissions decisions. Either SAT or ACT required. For admission to the fall 2007 entering class, the school will accept: ACT with writing, ACT without writing. Campus visit: Recommended. Admissions interview: Recommended. Off-campus interview: May not be arranged. **Factors that count in admissions decisions:** *Academic:* Secondary school record: Very important. Class rank: Considered. Letters of recommendation: Considered. Standardized test scores: Important. Essay: Considered. *Nonacademic:* Interview: Considered. Extracurricular activities: Important. Talent/ability: Important. Character/personal qualities: Very important. Alumni/ae relationship: Considered. Geographical residence: Not considered. State residency: Not considered. Religious affiliation/commitment: Not considered. Minority status: Not considered. Volunteer work: Considered. Work experience: Considered. **Other schools with the greatest overlap in applicants:** Bridgewater College; Lynchburg College; Radford University; Roanoke College; Virginia Tech. **Admissions statistics for the fall 2005 entering class:** Total applicants: 1,248. Total accepted: 896. Freshmen enrolled: 347; 16% were from out of state. Overall acceptance rate: 72%. **Credentials of fall 2005 freshmen:** 1% ranked in the top 10 percent of their high school class; 13% were in the top 25 percent, and 40% were in the top half. (Proportion submitting class standing: 17%.) **Average high school grade point average:** 2.7. **First-year students who submitted SAT scores:** 87%. Scores (25/75 percentile): Verbal: 410-490, Math: 400-490, Combined: 810-980. **First-year students submitting ACT scores:** 19%. Scores (25/75 percentile): English: N/A, Math: N/A, Composite: 15-19.

ACADEMICS

Year founded: 1913. **Academic calendar:** Other. **Degrees offered:** bachelor's. **Most popular majors:** 23% business administration and management, 14% parks, recreation, and leisure studies, 10% psychology, 9% liberal arts and

sciences/liberal studies, 8% history. **Major fields of study:** agriculture, agriculture operations, and related sciences; biological and biomedical sciences; business, management, marketing, and related support services; computer and information sciences and support services; education; English language and literature/letters; foreign languages, literatures, and linguistics; health professions and related clinical sciences; history; liberal arts and sciences studies, and humanities; mathematics and statistics; natural resources and conservation; parks, recreation, leisure, and fitness studies; philosophy and religious studies; physical sciences; psychology; public administration and social service professions; science technologies/technicians; security and protective services; social sciences; visual and performing arts. **Areas of required coursework:** arts/fine arts, humanities, computer literacy, mathematics, English (including composition), sciences (biological or physical), history, social science, other. **Pre-professional programs:** other. **Special academic programs (% participation):** double major (11%), dual enrollment, honors program (5%), independent study, internships (45%), liberal arts/career combination (5%), student-designed major (5%), study abroad (5%), teacher certificate program (9%). **Teacher certification offered in:** elementary, middle/junior high, secondary. **Faculty and instruction (2005-2006):** Total instructional faculty: 62 full-time, 20 part-time (59% men; 41% women; 4% minorities). Full-time faculty with Ph.D. or other terminal degree: 81%. Student/faculty ratio: 13/1. Classes of fewer than 20 students: 71%; of 20 to 49 students: 29%; of 50 or more students: 0%. **Freshmen returning for sophomore year:** 62%. **Graduation rates:** Four-year: 18%; five-year: 31%; six-year: 35%.

COSTS AND FINANCIAL AID

Financial aid office: (540) 365-4282. **Expenses (2006-2007):** Tuition and fees 2006-2007: $19,520; room/board: $6,500. Estimated books and supplies: $800; transportation: $430; personal expenses: $1,300. **Financial aid:** Priority filing date for institution's financial aid form: March 1. In 2005-2006, 100% of undergraduates applied for financial aid. Of those, 76% were determined to have financial need; 11% had their need fully met. Average financial aid package (proportion receiving): $14,639 (76%). Average amount of gift aid, such as scholarships or grants (proportion receiving): $10,075 (76%). Average amount of self-help aid, such as work study or loans (proportion receiving): $4,507 (65%). Average need-based loan (excluding PLUS or other private loans): $3,829. Among students who received need-based aid, the average percentage of need met: 85%. Among students who received aid based on merit, the average award (and the proportion receiving): $6,487 (18%). The average athletic scholarship (and the proportion receiving): $0 (0%). Average amount of debt of borrowers graduating in 2005: $16,300. Proportion who borrowed: 74%.

CAMPUS LIFE AND EXTRACURRICULAR ACTIVITIES

Campus housing available (% using): coed dorms (63%), women's dorms (12%), men's dorms (20%), apartments for married students (2%), apartment for single students (3%). Students who live in college-owned, operated, or affiliated housing: 74%. **Student employment:** During the 2005-2006 academic year, 20% of undergraduates worked on campus. Average per-year earnings: $1,500. **Clubs and organizations:** Number of student organizations: 60. Activities include: choral groups, dance, drama/theater, literary magazine, music ensembles, musical theater, radio station, student government, student newspaper, student film society, yearbook. Number of fraternities: 0; sororities: 0. Average proportion of students who stay on campus on weekends: 75%. **Sports program (2005-2006):** Member of NCAA III. *Men's intercollegiate varsity sports:* baseball, basketball, cheerleading, cross-country, football, golf, soccer, tennis. *Women's intercollegiate varsity sports:* basketball, cheerleading, cross-country, lacrosse, soccer, softball, tennis, volleyball.

SERVICES AND FACILITIES

Basic services: nonremedial tutoring, placement service, health service, health insurance. **Remedial assistance:** reading, math, writing, study skills. **Counseling services:** minority student, career, personal, veteran student, academic, psychological, birth control, religious. **For learning-disabled students:** School does not offer a structured program with separate admission and additional fees. Services include: remedial math, remedial English, tape recorders, videotaped classes, untimed tests, learning center, extended time for tests. **Library:** Number of titles: 114,370; number of current serial subscriptions: 10,618. **Information technology resources:** Students are not required to lease or own a computer. Number of campus computers available to all students: 500. School has a wireless network. Approximate number of users that can be accommodated: 2,000. Proportion of college-owned housing units wired for high-speed internet access: 100%. **Campus safety:** Security services offered: 24-hour foot-and-vehicle patrols, late-night transport/escort service, 24-hour emergency telephones, lighted pathways/sidewalks.

TRANSFER AND INTERNATIONAL STUDENTS

Transfer students: May apply for admission for the following academic terms: Fall, Spring. Applicants do not need a minimum number of credits to apply. For fall 2005: Transfer applications received: 243. Transfer applicants offered admission: 136. Transfer applicants enrolled: 73. **International students:** Number of foreign undergraduates: 10 (1% of student body). Number of countries represented: 10. Minimum TOEFL score required: 550 (paper).

George Mason University

- **Address:** 4400 University Drive, Fairfax, VA 22030
- **Website:** http://www.gmu.edu
- **Public**
- **Enrollment:** 13,578 full-time; 4,513 part-time

KEY STATS

✔ **U.S News College Ranking:** third tier, National Universities
✔ **SAT Score (25th/75th percentile):** 1000-1210
✔ **Tuition:** 2006-2007: $6,408 in state, $18,548 out of state

Selectivity: Selective	**Room/board:** $6,750
Acceptance rate: 69%	**Average debt:** $13,607
Student/faculty ratio: 16/1	**Proportion who borrowed:** 47%

UNDERGRADUATE STUDENT BODY STATS

2005-2006 enrollment: 13,578 full-time; 4,513 part-time. Men: 46%; women: 54%. **Ethnic makeup:** African American: 8%; Asian American: 17%; Hispanic: 8%; White: 64%; International: 4%.

ADMISSIONS FACTS AND FIGURES

Phone: (703) 993-2400. **Email:** admissions@gmu.edu. **Website:** http://www.gmu.edu. **Application deadlines for fall 2007:** Regular decision: January 15; decision sent by April 1. Early decision: Not offered. Early action: Send application by: November 1; Decision sent by: December 15. Admission can be deferred. **Application fee:** $50. Common application is accepted. **To apply online, go to:** http://admissions.gmu.edu. **Admissions requirements/recommendations:** High school units required (recommended): English: 4 (4); Mathematics: 3 (4); Science: 3 (4); Foreign language: 2 (3); Social studies: 3 (4); History: 0 (0); Academic electives: 3 (5); Total units: 18 (24). Tests: The college uses SAT or ACT scores in admissions decisions. Either SAT or ACT required. For admission to the fall 2007 entering class, the school will accept: ACT with writing, ACT without writing. Campus visit: Recommended. Admissions interview: Neither required nor recommended. Off-campus interview: May be arranged. **Factors that count in admissions decisions:** *Academic:* Secondary school record: Very important. Class rank: Considered. Letters of recommendation: Important. Standardized test scores: Important. Essay: Important. *Nonacademic:* Interview: Not considered. Extracurricular activities: Considered. Talent/ability: Important. Character/personal qualities: Important. Alumni/ae relationship: Considered. Geographical residence: Considered. State residency: Considered. Religious affiliation/commitment: Not considered. Minority status: Not considered. Volunteer work: Considered. Work experience: Considered. **Other schools with the greatest overlap in applicants:** George Washington University; James Madison University; University of Maryland–College Park; University of Virginia; Virginia Tech. **Admissions statistics for the fall 2005 entering class:** Total applicants: 10,344. Total accepted: 7,109. Freshmen enrolled: 2,529; 17% were from out of state. Accepted through early-decision or early-action plans: 44%. Overall acceptance rate: 69%. Non-early acceptance rate: 62%. **Size of waiting list:** 477 applicants; enrolled from waiting list: 26. **Credentials of fall 2005 freshmen:** 14% ranked in the top 10 percent of their high school class; 44% were in the top 25 percent, and 90% were in the top half. (Proportion submitting class standing: 50%.) **Average high school grade point average:** 3.4. **First-year students who submitted SAT scores:** 97%. Scores (25/75 percentile): Verbal: 490-600, Math: 510-610, Combined: 1000-1210. **First-year students submitting ACT scores:** 17%. Scores (25/75 percentile): English: 19-25, Math: 19-24, Composite: 20-24.

ACADEMICS

Year founded: 1957. **Academic calendar:** Semester. **Degrees offered:** bachelor's, post-bachelor's certificate, master's, post-master's certificate, first professional, doctorate. **Most popular majors:** 9% communication studies/speech communication and rhetoric, 8% psychology, 7% nursing/registered nurse training (R.N., A.S.N., B.S.N., M.S.N.), 6% political science and government, 5% accounting. **Major fields of study:** area, ethnic, cultural, and gender studies; biological and biomedical sciences; business, management, marketing, and related support services; communication, journalism, and related programs; computer and information sciences and support services; education; engineering; English language and literature/letters; foreign languages, literatures, and linguistics; health professions and related clinical sciences; history; liberal arts and sciences studies, and humanities; mathematics and statistics; multi/interdisciplinary studies; parks, recreation, leisure, and fitness studies; philosophy and religious studies; physical sciences; psychology; public administration and social service professions; security and protective services; social sciences; visual and performing arts. **Areas of required coursework:** arts/fine arts, humanities, computer literacy, mathematics, English (including composition), philosophy, foreign languages, sciences (biological or physical), history, social science, other. **Pre-professional programs:** pre-law, pre-dentistry, pre-medicine, pre-veterinary science, other. **Special academic programs:** accelerated program, cooperative (work-study plan) program, cross-registration, distance learning, double major, dual enrollment, English as a Second Language (ESL), exchange student program (domestic), external degree program, honors program, independent study, internships, liberal arts/career combination, student-designed major, study abroad, teacher certificate program. **Teacher certification offered in:** early childhood, special education, elementary, adult education, secondary, bilingual/bicultural. **Cooperative education programs:** art, business, computer science, education, engineering, health professions, humanities, natural science, social/behavioral science, technologies. **Reserve Officers Training Corps (ROTC):** Army ROTC: Offered on campus; Navy ROTC: Offered at cooperating institution (George Washington); Air Force ROTC: Offered at cooperating institution (University of Maryland – College Park). **Faculty and instruction (2005-2006):** Total instructional faculty: 989 full-time, 914 part-time (54% men; 46% women; 15% minorities). Full-time faculty with Ph.D. or other terminal degree: 92%. Student/faculty ratio: 16/1. Classes of fewer than 20 students: 32%; of 20 to 49 students: 55%; of 50 or more students: 13%. **Advanced Placement and International Baccalaureate credit:** AP tests may be used for: Credit and/or placement. Scores accepted: 4, 5. International Baccalaureate exams may be used for: Credit and/or placement. **Freshmen returning for sophomore year:** 82%. **Graduation rates:** Four-year: 26%; five-year: 46%; six-year: 53%. **Graduate study:** 50% of students pursue further study within one year; 41% within five years.

COSTS AND FINANCIAL AID

Financial aid office: (703) 993-2353. **Expenses (2006-2007):** Tuition and fees 2006-2007: $6,408 in state, $18,548 out of state; room/board: $6,750. Estimated books and supplies: $810; transportation: $1,215; personal expenses: $1,336. **Financial aid:** Priority filing date for institution's financial aid form: March 1. In 2005-2006, 53% of undergraduates applied for financial aid. Of those, 37% were determined to have financial need; 15% had their need fully met. Average financial aid package (proportion receiving): $7,991 (36%). Average amount of gift aid, such as scholarships or grants (proportion receiving): $4,434 (26%). Average amount of self-help aid, such as work study or loans (proportion receiving): $3,966 (29%). Average need-based loan (excluding PLUS or other private loans): $3,830. Among students who received need-based aid, the average percentage of need met: 68%. Among students who received aid based on merit, the average award (and the proportion receiving): $4,116 (2%). The average athletic scholarship (and the proportion receiving): $11,939 (2%). Average amount of debt of borrowers graduating in 2005: $13,607. Proportion who borrowed: 47%.

CAMPUS LIFE AND EXTRACURRICULAR ACTIVITIES

Campus housing available (% using): coed dorms (59%), apartment for single students (40%), special housing for disabled students (1%). Students who live in college-owned, operated, or affiliated housing: 28%. Average per-year earnings: $2,895. **Clubs and organizations:** Number of student organizations: 185. Activities include: choral groups, concert band, dance, drama/theater, jazz band, literary magazine, music ensembles, musical theater, opera, pep band, radio station, student government, student newspaper, student film society, symphony orchestra, television station, yearbook. Number of fraternities: 14; sororities: 12. Proportion of men in fraternities: 5%; of women in sororities: 5%. Average proportion of students who stay on campus on weekends: 97%. **Sports program (2005-2006):** Member of NCAA

I. Men's intercollegiate varsity sports: baseball, basketball, cheerleading, cross-country, golf, soccer, swimming and diving, tennis, track and field (indoor), track and field (outdoor), volleyball, wrestling. **Women's intercollegiate varsity sports:** basketball, cheerleading, crew, cross-country, lacrosse, soccer, softball, swimming and diving, tennis, track and field (indoor), track and field (outdoor), volleyball.

SERVICES AND FACILITIES

Basic services: nonremedial tutoring, women's center, placement service, day care, health service, health insurance, other. **Remedial assistance:** reading, math, writing, study skills, other. **Counseling services:** minority student, career, military, personal, veteran student, academic, older student, psychological, birth control, religious. **For learning-disabled students:** School does not offer a structured program with separate admission and additional fees. Total undergraduates in learning-disabled program or receiving services: 1125. Services include: remedial math, remedial English, reading machines, remedial reading, tape recorders, note-taking services, oral tests, learning center, readers, extended time for tests, priority registration, priority seating, substitution of courses, texts on tape, typist/scribe, exams on tape or computer, other testing accomodations, other. **Library:** Number of titles: 1,506,566; number of current serial subscriptions: 24,234. **Information technology resources:** Students are not required to lease or own a computer. Number of campus computers available to all students: 1,504. School has a wireless network. Approximate number of users that can be accommodated: 7,000. Proportion of college-owned housing units wired for high-speed internet access: 100%. **Campus safety:** Security services offered: 24-hour foot-and-vehicle patrols, late-night transport/escort service, 24-hour emergency telephones, lighted pathways/sidewalks, student patrols, controlled dormitory access (key, security card, etc).

TRANSFER AND INTERNATIONAL STUDENTS

Transfer students: May apply for admission for the following academic terms: Fall, Spring, Summer. Applicants need a minimum number of credits to apply. For fall 2005: Transfer applications received: 5,564. Transfer applicants offered admission: 3,416. Transfer applicants enrolled: 1,974. **International students:** Number of foreign undergraduates: 690 (4% of student body). Number of countries represented: 113. Minimum TOEFL score required: 570 (paper); 230 (computer). Average TOEFL score: 583 (paper).

Hampden-Sydney College

- **Address:** PO Box 667, Hampden-Sydney, VA 23943
- **Website:** http://www.hsc.edu
- **Private; Religious affiliation:** Presbyterian
- **Enrollment:** 1,060 full-time

KEY STATS

- ✔ **U.S News College Ranking:** 104, Liberal Arts Colleges
- ✔ **SAT Score (25th/75th percentile):** 1050-1270
- ✔ **Tuition:** 2006-2007: $25,354

Selectivity: Selective	**Room/board:** $8,126
Acceptance rate: 67%	**Average debt:** $16,244
Student/faculty ratio: 10/1	**Proportion who borrowed:** 54%

UNDERGRADUATE STUDENT BODY STATS

2005-2006 enrollment: 1,060 full-time. Men: 100%; women: 0%. **Ethnic makeup:** African American: 4%; Asian American: 1%; Hispanic: 1%; White: 92%; International: 1%. **Religious preference:** Roman Catholic: 12%; Protestant: 50%; Jewish: 1%; No preference: 25%; Presbyterian: 12%.

ADMISSIONS FACTS AND FIGURES

Phone: (800) 755-0733. **Email:** hsapp@hsc.edu. **Website:** http://www.hsc.edu. **Application deadlines for fall 2007:** Regular decision: March 1; decision sent by April 15. Early decision: Send application by: November 15; Decision sent by: December 15. Early action: Send application by: January 15; Decision sent by: February 15. Admission cannot be deferred. **Application fee:** $30. Common application is accepted. **To apply online, go to:** http://www.hsc.edu/admissions/apply/. **Admissions requirements/recommendations:** High school units required (recommended): English: 4; Mathematics: 3 (4); Science: 2 (3); Foreign language: 2 (3); Social studies: 1; History: 1; Academic electives: 3; Total units: 16. Tests: The college uses SAT or ACT scores in admissions decisions. Either SAT or ACT required. For

admission to the fall 2007 entering class, the school will accept: ACT without writing. Campus visit: Recommended. Admissions interview: Recommended. Off-campus interview: Not available. **Factors that count in admissions decisions: Academic:** Secondary school record: Very important. Class rank: Important. Letters of recommendation: Very important. Standardized test scores: Very important. Essay: Considered. **Nonacademic:** Interview: Considered. Extracurricular activities: Important. Talent/ability: Considered. Character/personal qualities: Very important. Alumni/ae relationship: Considered. Geographical residence: Not considered. State residency: Not considered. Religious affiliation/commitment: Not considered. Minority status: Considered. Volunteer work: Considered. Work experience: Considered. **Other schools with the greatest overlap in applicants:** James Madison University; Randolph-Macon College; University of North Carolina–Chapel Hill; University of Virginia; Virginia Tech. **Admissions statistics for the fall 2005 entering class:** Total applicants: 1,376. Total accepted: 922. Freshmen enrolled: 322; Overall acceptance rate: 67%. Early-decision acceptance rate: 69%. Non-early acceptance rate: 67%. **Credentials of fall 2005 freshmen:** 12% ranked in the top 10 percent of their high school class; 25% were in the top 25 percent, and 50% were in the top half. (Proportion submitting class standing: 98%.) **Average high school grade point average:** 2.7. **First-year students who submitted SAT scores:** 100%. Scores (25/75 percentile): Verbal: 520-630, Math: 530-640, Combined: 1050-1270. **First-year students submitting ACT scores:** 20%. Scores (25/75 percentile): English: 20-21, Math: 22-27, Composite: 21-27.

ACADEMICS

Year founded: 1775. **Academic calendar:** Semester. **Degrees offered:** bachelor's. **Most popular majors:** 15% economics, 12% economics, 12% history, 11% biology, 9% political science and government. **Major fields of study:** biological and biomedical sciences; business, management, marketing, and related support services; computer and information sciences and support services; English language and literature/letters; foreign languages, literatures, and linguistics; history; liberal arts and sciences studies, and humanities; mathematics and statistics; multi/interdisciplinary studies; philosophy and religious studies; physical sciences; psychology; social sciences; visual and performing arts. **Areas of required coursework:** arts/fine arts, humanities, mathematics, English (including composition), philosophy, foreign languages, sciences (biological or physical), history, social science, other. **Special academic programs (% participation):** cooperative (work-study plan) program, cross-registration, double major (19%), exchange student program (domestic) (1%), honors program (18%), independent study, internships, study abroad (7%). **Cooperative education programs:** other. **Reserve Officers Training Corps (ROTC):** Army ROTC: Offered at cooperating institution (Longwood University). **Faculty and instruction (2005-2006):** Total instructional faculty: 101 full-time, 9 part-time (73% men; 27% women; 2% minorities). Full-time faculty with Ph.D. or other terminal degree: 84%. Student/faculty ratio: 10/1. Classes of fewer than 20 students: 67%; of 20 to 49 students: 33%; of 50 or more students: 0%. **Advanced Placement and International Baccalaureate credit:** AP tests may be used for: Credit only. Scores accepted: 4. International Baccalaureate exams may be used for: Credit only. **Freshmen returning for sophomore year:** 81%. **Graduation rates:** Four-year: 58%; five-year: 61%; six-year: 61%. **Graduate study:** 15% of students pursue further study immediately upon graduation; 30% within one year; 55% within five years. Fields in which graduates pursue further study: Master of Business Administration (MBA), 20%; law, 6%; medicine, 7%; education, 1%; arts and sciences, 30%.

COSTS AND FINANCIAL AID

Financial aid office: (434) 223-6119. **Expenses (2006-2007):** Tuition and fees 2006-2007: $25,354; room/board: $8,126. Estimated books and supplies: $1,000 personal expenses: $1,200. **Financial aid:** Priority filing date for institution's financial aid form: March 1; deadline: May 1. In 2005-2006, 62% of undergraduates applied for financial aid. Of those, 47% were determined to have financial need; 37% had their need fully met. Average financial aid package (proportion receiving): $17,891 (47%). Average amount of gift aid, such as scholarships or grants (proportion receiving): $14,035 (47%). Average amount of self-help aid, such as work study or loans (proportion receiving): $5,195 (35%). Average need-based loan (excluding PLUS or other private loans): $4,134. Among students who received need-based aid, the average percentage of need met: 83%. Among students who received aid based on merit, the average award (and the proportion receiving): $16,595 (50%). The average athletic scholarship (and the proportion receiving): $0 (0%). Average amount of debt of borrowers graduating in 2005: $16,244. Proportion who borrowed: 54%.

CAMPUS LIFE AND EXTRACURRICULAR ACTIVITIES

Campus housing available: men's dorms, fraternity housing, apartments for married students, apartment for single students. Students who live in college-owned, operated, or affiliated housing: 95%. **Student employment:** During the 2005-2006 academic year, 33% of undergraduates worked on campus. Average per-year earnings: $975. **Clubs and organizations:** Number of student organizations: 40. Activities include: choral groups, drama/theater, literary magazine, music ensembles, pep band, radio station, student government, student newspaper, yearbook. Number of fraternities: 11Proportion of men in fraternities: 34%; Average proportion of students who stay on campus on weekends: 65%. **Sports program (2005-2006):** Member of NCAA III. *Men's intercollegiate varsity sports:* baseball, basketball, cross-country, football, golf, lacrosse, soccer, tennis.

SERVICES AND FACILITIES

Basic services: nonremedial tutoring, health service. **Remedial assistance:** study skills. **Counseling services:** minority student, career, personal, academic, psychological, religious. **For learning-disabled students:** Services include: reading machines, tape recorders, videotaped classes, note-taking services, oral tests, extended time for tests, tutors, other. **Library:** Number of titles: 299,416; number of current serial subscriptions: 19,004. **Information technology resources:** Students are not required to lease or own a computer. Number of campus computers available to all students: 98. School has a wireless network. **Campus safety:** Security services offered: 24-hour foot-and-vehicle patrols, 24-hour emergency telephones, lighted pathways/sidewalks.

TRANSFER AND INTERNATIONAL STUDENTS

Transfer students: May apply for admission for the following academic terms: Fall, Spring. Applicants need a minimum number of credits to apply. For fall 2005: Transfer applications received: 45. Transfer applicants offered admission: 24. Transfer applicants enrolled: 20. **International students:** Number of foreign undergraduates: 12. (1% of student body). Minimum TOEFL score required: 570 (paper); 230 (computer). Average TOEFL score: 590 (paper).

Hampton University

- **Address:** Tyler Street, Hampton, VA 23668
- **Website:** http://www.hamptonu.edu
- **Private**
- **Enrollment:** 4,913 full-time; 412 part-time

KEY STATS

✔ **U.S News College Ranking:** 25, Universities–Master's (South)
✔ **SAT Score (25th/75th percentile):** 942-1225
✔ **Tuition:** 2005-2006: $14,182

Selectivity: Selective	**Room/board:** $6,746
Acceptance rate: 77%	**Average debt:** N/A
Student/faculty ratio: 16/1	**Proportion who borrowed:** N/A

UNDERGRADUATE STUDENT BODY STATS

2005-2006 enrollment: 4,913 full-time; 412 part-time. Men: 36%; women: 64%. **Ethnic makeup:** African American: 96%; Asian American: 1%; Hispanic: 1%; White: 3%. **Religious preference:** Roman Catholic: 8%; Protestant: 75%; Muslim: 8%; No preference: 8%; Other: 1%.

ADMISSIONS FACTS AND FIGURES

Phone: (757) 727-5328. **Email:** admissions@hamptonu.edu. **Website:** http://www.hamptonu.edu. **Application deadlines for fall 2007:** Regular decision: March 1. Early decision: Not offered. Early action: Send application by: December 1; Decision sent by: December 15. Admission can be deferred. **Application fee:** $25. Common application is accepted. **To apply online, go to:** http://www.hamptonu.edu/Admissions/admiss.htm. **Admissions requirements/recommendations:** High school units required (recommended): English: 4 (4); Mathematics: 3 (3); Science: 2 (2); Foreign language: (2); Social studies: 2 (2); Academic electives: 6 (6); Total units: 17 (17). Tests: The college uses SAT or ACT scores in admissions decisions. Either SAT or ACT required. Campus visit: Recommended. Admissions interview: Neither required nor recommended. Off-campus interview: May be arranged. **Factors that count in admissions decisions:** *Academic:* Secondary school record: Very important. Class rank: Important. Letters of recommendation: Important. Standardized test scores: Very important. Essay: Very important. *Nonacademic:* Interview: Not considered. Extracurricular activities: Considered. Talent/ability: Considered. Character/personal qualities: Very important. Alumni/ae relationship: Considered. Geographical residence: Not considered. State residency: Not considered. Religious affiliation/commitment: Not considered. Minority status: Not considered. Volunteer work: Considered. Work experience: Considered. **Other schools with the greatest overlap in applicants:** Howard University; Norfolk State University; North Carolina A&T State University; Old Dominion University; University of Virginia. **Admissions statistics for the fall 2005 entering class:** Total applicants: 5,401. Total accepted: 4,150. Freshmen enrolled: 1,201; 79% were from out of state. Overall acceptance rate: 77%. Non-early acceptance rate: 77%. **Credentials of fall 2005 freshmen:** 11% ranked in the top 10 percent of their high school class; 66% were in the top 25 percent, and 96% were in the top half. (Proportion submitting class standing: 100%.) **Average high school grade point average:** 3.2. **First-year students who submitted SAT scores:** 68%. Scores (25/75 percentile): Verbal: 478-626, Math: 464-599, Combined: 942-1225. **First-year students submitting ACT scores:** 32%. Scores (25/75 percentile): English: 18-27, Math: 19-24, Composite: 19-25.

ACADEMICS

Year founded: 1868. **Academic calendar:** Semester. **Degrees offered:** associate, bachelor's, master's, first professional, doctorate. **Most popular majors:** 10% business administration and management, 10% nursing/registered nurse training (R.N., A.S.N., B.S.N., M.S.N.), 9% journalism, 8% psychology, 6% biology/biological sciences. **Major fields of study:** architecture and related services; biological and biomedical sciences; business, management, marketing, and related support services; communication, journalism, and related programs; communications technologies/technicians and support services; computer and information sciences and support services; engineering; English language and literature/letters; foreign languages, literatures, and linguistics; health professions and related clinical sciences; history; mathematics and statistics; mechanic and repair technologies/technicians; natural resources and conservation; parks, recreation, leisure, and fitness studies; physical sciences; psychology; public administration and social service professions; social sciences; transportation and materials moving; visual and performing arts. **Areas of required coursework:** arts/fine arts, humanities, computer literacy, mathematics, English (including composition), foreign languages, sciences (biological or physical), history, social science, other. **Pre-professional programs:** pre-pharmacy. **Special academic programs:** accelerated program, cooperative (work-study plan) program, cross-registration, distance learning, double major, dual enrollment, honors program, independent study, internships, study abroad, teacher certificate program. **Teacher certification offered in:** early childhood, special education, elementary, middle/junior high. **Cooperative education programs:** art, business, computer science, education, engineering, health professions, humanities, natural science, social/behavioral science, technologies, other. **Reserve Officers Training Corps (ROTC):** Army ROTC: Offered on campus; Navy ROTC: Offered on campus. **Faculty and instruction (2005-2006):** Total instructional faculty: 305 full-time, 83 part-time (53% men; 47% women; 80% minorities). Full-time faculty with Ph.D. or other terminal degree: 76%. Student/faculty ratio: 16/1. **Advanced Placement and International Baccalaureate credit:** AP tests may be used for: Placement only. Scores accepted: 3, 4, 5. International Baccalaureate exams may be used for: Credit and/or placement. **Freshmen returning for sophomore year:** 85%. **Graduation rates:** Four-year: 35%; five-year: 48%; six-year: 55%. **Graduate study:** 42% of students pursue further study within five years.

COSTS AND FINANCIAL AID

Financial aid office: (800) 624-3341. **Expenses (2005-2006):** Tuition and fees 2005-2006: $14,182; room/board: $6,746. **Financial aid:** Priority filing date for institution's financial aid form: March 1. In 2005-2006, 82% of undergraduates applied for financial aid. Of those, 77% were determined to have financial need; Average financial aid package (proportion receiving): $3,220 (67%). Average amount of gift aid, such as scholarships or grants (proportion receiving): N/A (31%). Average amount of self-help aid, such as work study or loans (proportion receiving): N/A (50%). Among students who received need-based aid, the average percentage of need met: 46%. Among students who received aid based on merit, the average award (and the proportion receiving): $7,474 (6%). The average athletic scholarship (and the proportion receiving): $17,244 (0%).

CAMPUS LIFE AND EXTRACURRICULAR ACTIVITIES

Campus housing available: women's dorms, men's dorms. Students who live in college-owned, operated, or affiliated housing: 43%. **Student employment:** During the 2005-2006 academic year, 1% of undergraduates worked on campus. Average per-year earnings: $1,500. **Clubs and organizations:** Number of student organizations: 85. Activities include: choral groups, concert band, dance, drama/theater, jazz band, marching band, music ensembles, musical theater, opera, pep band, radio station, student government, student newspaper, symphony orchestra, television station, yearbook. Number of fraternities: 6; sororities: 3. Proportion of men in fraternities: 5%; of women in sororities: 4%. Average proportion of students who stay on campus on weekends: 68%. **Sports program (2005-2006):** Member of NCAA I. *Men's intercollegiate varsity sports:* basketball, cross-country, football, golf, sailing, tennis, track and field (indoor), track and field (outdoor). *Women's intercollegiate varsity sports:* basketball, bowling, cross-country, golf, sailing, softball, tennis, track and field (indoor), track and field (outdoor), volleyball.

SERVICES AND FACILITIES

Basic services: nonremedial tutoring, placement service, day care, health service, health insurance. **Remedial assistance:** reading, math, writing, study skills. **Counseling services:** career, military, personal, veteran student, academic, older student, religious. **For learning-disabled students:** School does not offer a structured program with separate admission and additional fees. Total undergraduates in learning-disabled program or receiving services: 20. Services include: remedial math, remedial English, remedial reading, tape recorders, untimed tests, note-taking services, oral tests, readers, extended time for tests, tutors, other. **Library:** Number of titles: 265,000; number of current serial subscriptions: 1,100. **Information technology resources:** Students are not required to lease or own a computer. Number of campus computers available to all students: 1,500. **Campus safety:** Security services offered: 24-hour foot-and-vehicle patrols, 24-hour emergency telephones, lighted pathways/sidewalks, controlled dormitory access (key, security card, etc).

TRANSFER AND INTERNATIONAL STUDENTS

Transfer students: May apply for admission for the following academic terms: Fall, Spring. Applicants need a minimum number of credits to apply. **International students:** Number of foreign undergraduates: 10. Minimum TOEFL score required: 550 (paper). Average TOEFL score: 575 (paper).

Hollins University

- Address: PO Box 9707, Roanoke, VA 24020
- Website: http://www.hollins.edu
- Private
- Enrollment: 790 full-time; 58 part-time

KEY STATS

✔ **U.S News College Ranking:** 104, Liberal Arts Colleges
✔ **SAT Score (25th/75th percentile):** 1020-1230
✔ **Tuition:** 2006-2007: $24,325

Selectivity: Selective	Room/board: $8,650
Acceptance rate: 86%	Average debt: $16,853
Student/faculty ratio: 10/1	Proportion who borrowed: 64%

UNDERGRADUATE STUDENT BODY STATS

2005-2006 enrollment: 790 full-time; 58 part-time. Men: 1%; women: 99%. **Ethnic makeup:** African American: 8%; American-Indian: 1%; Asian American: 1%; Hispanic: 2%; White: 85%; International: 2%. **Religious preference:** Roman Catholic: 7%; Protestant: 26%; Jewish: 1%; Buddhist: 1%; No preference: 5%; Unknown: 54%; Other: 3%.

ADMISSIONS FACTS AND FIGURES

Phone: (800) 456-9595. **Email:** huadm@hollins.edu. **Website:** http://www.hollins.edu. **Application deadlines for fall 2007:** Regular decision: Rolling. Early decision: Send application by: December 1; Decision sent by: December 15. Early action: Not offered. Admission can be deferred. **Application fee:** $35. Common application is accepted. **Admissions requirements/recommendations:** High school units required (recommended): English: 4 (4); Mathematics: 3 (3); Science: 3 (3); Foreign language: 3 (3); Social studies: 3 (3); Total units: 16. Tests: The college uses SAT or ACT scores in admissions decisions. Either SAT or ACT required. For admission to the fall 2007 entering class, the school will accept: ACT with writing, ACT without writing. Campus visit: Recommended. Admissions interview: Recommended. Off-campus interview: May be arranged. **Factors that count**

in admissions decisions: *Academic:* Secondary school record: Considered. Class rank: Considered. Letters of recommendation: Very important. Standardized test scores: Important. Essay: Important. *Nonacademic:* Interview: Considered. Extracurricular activities: Considered. Talent/ability: Important. Character/personal qualities: Considered. Alumni/ae relationship: Considered. Geographical residence: Not considered. State residency: Not considered. Religious affiliation/commitment: Not considered. Minority status: Considered. Volunteer work: Considered. Work experience: Considered. **Other schools with the greatest overlap in applicants:** James Madison University; Randolph-Macon Woman's College; Roanoke College; Sweet Briar College; University of Mary Washington. **Admissions statistics for the fall 2005 entering class:** Total applicants: 686. Total accepted: 589. Freshmen enrolled: 184; 56% were from out of state. Overall acceptance rate: 86%. Early-decision acceptance rate: 97%. Non-early acceptance rate: 85%. **Size of waiting list:** 10 applicants; enrolled from waiting list: 2. **Credentials of fall 2005 freshmen:** 19% ranked in the top 10 percent of their high school class; 55% were in the top 25 percent, and 87% were in the top half. (Proportion submitting class standing: 61%.) **Average high school grade point average:** 3.5. **First-year students who submitted SAT scores:** 91%. Scores (25/75 percentile): Verbal: 530-640, Math: 490-590, Combined: 1020-1230. **First-year students submitting ACT scores:** 35%. Scores (25/75 percentile): English: N/A, Math: N/A, Composite: 22-27.

ACADEMICS

Year founded: 1842. **Academic calendar:** 4-1-4. **Degrees offered:** bachelor's, master's, post-master's certificate. **Most popular majors:** 16% visual and performing arts, 15% English language and literature/letters, 15% social sciences, 9% psychology, 8% communication, journalism, and related programs. **Major fields of study:** area, ethnic, cultural, and gender studies; biological and biomedical sciences; business, management, marketing, and related support services; communication, journalism, and related programs; English language and literature/letters; foreign languages, literatures, and linguistics; history; mathematics and statistics; multi/interdisciplinary studies; natural resources and conservation; philosophy and religious studies; physical sciences; psychology; social sciences; visual and performing arts. **Areas of required coursework:** arts/fine arts, computer literacy, mathematics, English (including composition), foreign languages, sciences (biological or physical), other. **Pre-professional programs:** pre-law, pre-medicine, pre-veterinary science. **Special academic programs (% participation):** accelerated program (3.5%), cooperative (work-study plan) program, cross-registration (0%), double major (16.4%), dual enrollment, exchange student program (domestic), independent study (72.3%), internships (78%), student-designed major (7.3%), study abroad (42.2%), teacher certificate program (2.8%). **Teacher certification offered in:** elementary, middle/junior high, secondary. **Faculty and instruction (2005-2006):** Total instructional faculty: 68 full-time, 41 part-time (49% men; 51% women; 7% minorities). Full-time faculty with Ph.D. or other terminal degree: 99%. Student/faculty ratio: 10/1. Classes of fewer than 20 students: 79%; of 20 to 49 students: 21%; of 50 or more students: 0%. **Advanced Placement and International Baccalaureate credit:** AP tests may be used for: Credit only. Scores accepted: 4, 5. International Baccalaureate exams may be used for: Credit and/or placement. **Freshmen returning for sophomore year:** 77%. **Graduation rates:** Four-year: 55%; five-year: 61%; six-year: 62%. **Graduate study:** 33% of students pursue further study within one year. Fields in which graduates pursue further study: law, 11%; medicine, 4%; education, 6%; arts and sciences, 79%; veterinary medicine, 3%.

COSTS AND FINANCIAL AID

Financial aid office: (540) 362-6332. **Expenses (2006-2007):** Tuition and fees 2006-2007: $24,325; room/board: $8,650. Estimated books and supplies: $800; transportation: $800; personal expenses: $1,000. **Financial aid:** Priority filing date for institution's financial aid form: February 15. In 2005-2006, 96% of undergraduates applied for financial aid. Of those, 61% were determined to have financial need; 21% had their need fully met. Average financial aid package (proportion receiving): $17,913 (61%). Average amount of gift aid, such as scholarships or grants (proportion receiving): $14,983 (61%). Average amount of self-help aid, such as work study or loans (proportion receiving): $5,875 (56%). Average need-based loan (excluding PLUS or other private loans): $4,761. Among students who received need-based aid, the average percentage of need met: 75%. Among students who received aid based on merit, the average award (and the proportion receiving): $9,830 (25%). The average athletic scholarship (and the proportion receiving): $0 (0%). Average amount of debt of borrowers graduating in 2005: $16,853. Proportion who borrowed: 64%.

CAMPUS LIFE AND EXTRACURRICULAR ACTIVITIES

Campus housing available (% using): women's dorms (78%), apartment for single students (15%), special housing for disabled students (1%), special housing for international students (3%), other housing options (3%). Students who live in college-owned, operated, or affiliated housing: 80%. **Clubs and organizations:** Number of student organizations: 32. Activities include: choral groups, dance, drama/theater, literary magazine, music ensembles, musical theater, student government, student newspaper, student film society, television station, yearbook. Number of fraternities: 0; sororities: 0. Average proportion of students who stay on campus on weekends: 40%. **Sports program (2005-2006):** Member of NCAA III. *Women's intercollegiate varsity sports:* basketball, cross-country, equestrian sports, golf, lacrosse, soccer, swimming and diving, tennis, volleyball.

SERVICES AND FACILITIES

Basic services: nonremedial tutoring, placement service, health service, health insurance. **Remedial assistance:** reading, math, writing, study skills. **Counseling services:** minority student, career, personal, academic, older student, psychological, birth control, religious. **For learning-disabled students:** School does not offer a structured program with separate admission and additional fees. Total undergraduates in learning-disabled program or receiving services: 37. Services include: tape recorders, untimed tests, note-taking services, oral tests, learning center, readers, extended time for tests, tutors, texts on tape, other testing accomodations, other. **Library:** Number of titles: 224,881; number of current serial subscriptions: 18,720. **Information technology resources:** Students are not required to lease or own a computer. Number of campus computers available to all students: 113. School has a wireless network. Approximate number of users that can be accommodated: 400. Proportion of college-owned housing units wired for high-speed internet access: 100%. **Campus safety:** Security services offered: 24-hour foot-and-vehicle patrols, late-night transport/escort service, 24-hour emergency telephones, lighted pathways/sidewalks, controlled dormitory access (key, security card, etc).

TRANSFER AND INTERNATIONAL STUDENTS

Transfer students: May apply for admission for the following academic terms: Fall, Spring. Applicants do not need a minimum number of credits to apply. For fall 2005: Transfer applications received: 85. Transfer applicants offered admission: 70. Transfer applicants enrolled: 39. **International students:** Number of foreign undergraduates: 17 (2% of student body). Number of countries represented: 11. Minimum TOEFL score required: 550 (paper); 213 (computer). Average TOEFL score: 567 (paper).

James Madison University

- **Address:** 800 S. Main Street, Harrisonburg, VA 22807
- **Website:** http://www.jmu.edu
- **Public**
- **Enrollment:** 14,885 full-time; 733 part-time

KEY STATS

✔ **U.S News College Ranking:** 2, Universities–Master's (South)
✔ **SAT Score (25th/75th percentile):** 1070-1250
✔ **Tuition:** 2006-2007: $6,290 in state; $16,236 out of state

Selectivity: More selective	**Room/board:** $6,756
Acceptance rate: 68%	**Average debt:** $12,591
Student/faculty ratio: 17/1	**Proportion who borrowed:** 53%

UNDERGRADUATE STUDENT BODY STATS

2005-2006 enrollment: 14,885 full-time; 733 part-time. Men: 40%; women: 60%. **Ethnic makeup:** African American: 3%; Asian American: 5%; Hispanic: 2%; White: 89%; International: 1%. **Religious preference:** Roman Catholic: 27%; Protestant: 33%; Jewish: 3%; Muslim: 1%; Hindu: 1%; No preference: 19%; Other: 16%.

ADMISSIONS FACTS AND FIGURES

Phone: (540) 568-5681. **Email:** admissions@jmu.edu. **Website:** http://www.jmu.edu. **Application deadlines for fall 2007:** Regular decision: January 15; decision sent by April 1. Early decision: Not offered. Early action: Send application by: November 1; Decision sent by: January 15. Admission can be deferred. **Application fee:** $40. Common application is not accepted. **To apply online, go to:** http://www.jmu.edu/admissions. **Admissions require-**

ments/recommendations: High school units required (recommended): English: 4 (4); Mathematics: 4 (4); Science: 3 (4); Foreign language: 3 (4); Social studies: 1 (2); History: 2 (2). Tests: The college uses SAT or ACT scores in admissions decisions. Either SAT or ACT required. For admission to the fall 2007 entering class, the school will accept: ACT with writing, ACT without writing. Campus visit: Recommended. Admissions interview: Neither required nor recommended. Off-campus interview: Not available. **Factors that count in admissions decisions:** *Academic:* Secondary school record: Very important. Class rank: Considered. Letters of recommendation: Considered. Standardized test scores: Important. Essay: Considered. *Nonacademic:* Interview: Not considered. Extracurricular activities: Considered. Talent/ability: Considered. Character/personal qualities: Considered. Alumni/ae relationship: Considered. Geographical residence: Considered. State residency: Considered. Religious affiliation/commitment: Not considered. Minority status: Not considered. Volunteer work: Considered. Work experience: Considered. **Other schools with the greatest overlap in applicants:** College of William and Mary; George Mason University; University of Virginia; Virginia Tech. **Admissions statistics for the fall 2005 entering class:** Total applicants: 16,388. Total accepted: 11,094. Freshmen enrolled: 3,798; 37% were from out of state. Accepted through early-decision or early-action plans: 28%. Overall acceptance rate: 68%. Non-early acceptance rate: 73%. **Size of waiting list:** 1179 applicants; enrolled from waiting list: 4. **Credentials of fall 2005 freshmen:** 28% ranked in the top 10 percent of their high school class; 74% were in the top 25 percent, and 98% were in the top half. (Proportion submitting class standing: 62%.) **Average high school grade point average:** 3.7. **First-year students who submitted SAT scores:** 99%. Scores (25/75 percentile): Verbal: 530-620, Math: 540-630, Combined: 1070-1250. **First-year students submitting ACT scores:** 20%. Scores (25/75 percentile): English: N/A, Math: N/A, Composite: 21-26.

ACADEMICS

Year founded: 1908. **Academic calendar:** Semester. **Degrees offered:** bachelor's, master's, post-master's certificate, doctorate. **Most popular majors:** 21% business, management, marketing, and related support services, 12% social sciences, 9% health professions and related clinical sciences, 8% communication, journalism, and related programs, 7% psychology. **Major fields of study:** biological and biomedical sciences; business, management, marketing, and related support services; communication, journalism, and related programs; computer and information sciences and support services; education; English language and literature/letters; family and consumer sciences/human sciences; foreign languages, literatures, and linguistics; health professions and related clinical sciences; history; legal professions and studies; liberal arts and sciences studies, and humanities; mathematics and statistics; multi/interdisciplinary studies; parks, recreation, leisure, and fitness studies; philosophy and religious studies; physical sciences; psychology; public administration and social service professions; social sciences; visual and performing arts. **Areas of required coursework:** arts/fine arts, humanities, computer literacy, mathematics, English (including composition), philosophy, sciences (biological or physical), history, social science, other. **Pre-professional programs:** pre-law, pre-dentistry, pre-medicine, pre-theology, pre-veterinary science, pre-optometry, pre-pharmacy, other. **Special academic programs:** accelerated program, distance learning, double major, honors program, independent study, internships, study abroad, teacher certificate program. **Teacher certification offered in:** early childhood, special education, elementary, middle/junior high, secondary. **Cooperative education programs:** other. **Reserve Officers Training Corps (ROTC):** Army ROTC: Offered on campus; Air Force ROTC: Offered at cooperating institution (U. of Virginia). **Faculty and instruction (2005-2006):** Total instructional faculty: 795 full-time, 369 part-time (56% men; 44% women; 6% minorities). Full-time faculty with Ph.D. or other terminal degree: 80%. Student/faculty ratio: 17/1. Classes of fewer than 20 students: 29%; of 20 to 49 students: 57%; of 50 or more students: 14%. **Advanced Placement and International Baccalaureate credit:** International Baccalaureate exams may be used for: Credit only. **Freshmen returning for sophomore year:** 92%. **Graduation rates:** Four-year: 62%; five-year: 77%; six-year: 80%. **Graduate study:** 10% of students pursue further study immediately upon graduation; 30% within five years. Fields in which graduates pursue further study: Master of Business Administration (MBA), 2%; law, 8%; medicine, 18%; dentistry, 1%; engineering, 7%; theology (or the seminary), 7%; education, 13%.

COSTS AND FINANCIAL AID

Financial aid office: (540) 568-7820. **Expenses (2006-2007):** Tuition and fees 2006-2007: $6,290 in state, $16,236 out of state; room/board: $6,756. Estimated books and supplies: $820; transportation: $1,496; personal expenses: $1,778. **Financial aid:** Priority filing date for institution's financial aid form: March 1. In 2005-2006, 82% of undergraduates applied for financial aid. Of those, 49% were determined to have financial need; 43% had their need fully met. Average financial aid package (proportion receiving): $6,822 (30%). Average amount of gift aid, such as scholarships or grants (proportion receiving): $5,332 (12%). Average amount of self-help aid, such as work study or loans (proportion receiving): $3,712 (24%). Average need-based loan (excluding PLUS or other private loans): $3,640. Among students who received need-based aid, the average percentage of need met: 50%. Among students who received aid based on merit, the average award (and the proportion receiving): $2,049 (1%). The average athletic scholarship (and the proportion receiving): $12,559 (2%). Average amount of debt of borrowers graduating in 2005: $12,591. Proportion who borrowed: 53%.

CAMPUS LIFE AND EXTRACURRICULAR ACTIVITIES

Campus housing available: coed dorms, sorority housing, apartment for single students, other housing options. Students who live in college-owned, operated, or affiliated housing: 38%. **Student employment:** During the 2005-2006 academic year, 19% of undergraduates worked on campus. Average per-year earnings: $1,680. **Clubs and organizations:** Number of student organizations: 287. Activities include: choral groups, concert band, dance, drama/theater, jazz band, literary magazine, marching band, music ensembles, musical theater, opera, pep band, radio station, student government, student newspaper, symphony orchestra, yearbook. Number of fraternities: 13; sororities: 8. Proportion of men in fraternities: 9%; of women in sororities: 11%. Average proportion of students who stay on campus on weekends: 72%. **Sports program (2005-2006):** Member of NCAA I. *Men's intercollegiate varsity sports:* archery, baseball, basketball, cross-country, football, golf, gymnastics, soccer, swimming and diving, tennis, track and field (indoor), track and field (outdoor), wrestling. *Women's intercollegiate varsity sports:* archery, basketball, cross-country, fencing, field hockey, golf, gymnastics, lacrosse, soccer, softball, swimming and diving, tennis, track and field (indoor), track and field (outdoor), volleyball.

SERVICES AND FACILITIES

Basic services: nonremedial tutoring, women's center, placement service, health service, other. **Counseling services:** minority student, career, personal, academic, older student, other. **For learning-disabled students:** School does not offer a structured program with separate admission and additional fees. Total undergraduates in learning-disabled program or receiving services: 165. **Library:** Number of titles: 641,039; number of current serial subscriptions: 8,804. **Information technology resources:** Students are not required to lease or own a computer. Number of campus computers available to all students: 1,583. School has a wireless network. Approximate number of users that can be accommodated: 1,000. Proportion of college-owned housing units wired for high-speed internet access: 100%. **Campus safety:** Security services offered: 24-hour foot-and-vehicle patrols, late-night transport/escort service, 24-hour emergency telephones, lighted pathways/sidewalks, student patrols, controlled dormitory access (key, security card, etc).

TRANSFER AND INTERNATIONAL STUDENTS

Transfer students: May apply for admission for the following academic terms: Fall, Spring, Summer. Applicants need a minimum number of credits to apply. For fall 2005: Transfer applications received: 1,926. Transfer applicants offered admission: 1,147. Transfer applicants enrolled: 639. **International students:** Number of foreign undergraduates: 106 (1% of student body). Number of countries represented: 39. Minimum TOEFL score required: 570 (paper); 230 (computer).

Liberty University

- **Address:** 1971 University Boulevard, Lynchburg, VA 24502-2269
- **Website:** http://www.liberty.edu
- **Private; Religious affiliation:** Baptist
- **Enrollment:** 8,427 full-time; 1,548 part-time

KEY STATS

✔ **U.S News College Ranking:** fourth tier, Universities–Master's (South)
✔ **SAT Score (25th/75th percentile):** 870-1120
✔ **Tuition:** 2006-2007: $15,350

Selectivity: Less selective	**Room/board:** $5,400
Acceptance rate: 58%	**Average debt:** $11,885
Student/faculty ratio: 27/1	**Proportion who borrowed:** 42%

UNDERGRADUATE STUDENT BODY STATS

2005-2006 enrollment: 8,427 full-time; 1,548 part-time. Men: 48%; women: 52%. **Ethnic makeup:** African American: 10%; American-Indian: 1%; Asian American: 2%; Hispanic: 3%; White: 80%; International: 4%. **Religious preference:** Roman Catholic: 1%; Protestant: 1%; No preference: 27%; Baptist: 43%; Southern Baptist: 15%; Other: 13%.

ADMISSIONS FACTS AND FIGURES

Phone: (800) 543-5317. **Email:** admissions@liberty.edu. **Website:** http://www.liberty.edu. **Application deadlines for fall 2007:** Regular decision: Rolling. Early decision: Not offered. Early action: Not offered. Admission can be deferred. **Application fee:** $35. Common application is not accepted. **To apply online, go to:** http://www.liberty.edu/apply. **Admissions requirements/recommendations:** High school units required (recommended): English: 4 (4); Mathematics: 3 (3); Science: 2 (2); Foreign language: 2 (2); Social studies: 2 (2); Academic electives: 4 (4); Total units: 17 (17). Tests: The college uses SAT or ACT scores in admissions decisions. Either SAT or ACT required. For admission to the fall 2007 entering class, the school will accept ACT with writing, ACT without writing. Campus visit: Recommended. Admissions interview: Neither required nor recommended. Off-campus interview: May be arranged. **Factors that count in admissions decisions:** *Academic:* Secondary school record: Very important. Class rank: Considered. Letters of recommendation: Considered. Standardized test scores: Very important. Essay: Important. *Nonacademic:* Interview: Not considered. Extracurricular activities: Considered. Talent/ability: Considered. Character/personal qualities: Considered. Alumni/ae relationship: Not considered. Geographical residence: Not considered. State residency: Not considered. Religious affiliation/commitment: Not considered. Minority status: Not considered. Volunteer work: Not considered. Work experience: Not considered. **Admissions statistics for the fall 2005 entering class:** Total applicants: 7,504. Total accepted: 4,376. Freshmen enrolled: 1,985; 67% were from out of state. Overall acceptance rate: 58%. **Credentials of fall 2005 freshmen:** 4% ranked in the top 10 percent of their high school class; 14% were in the top 25 percent, and 41% were in the top half. (Proportion submitting class standing: 27%.) **Average high school grade point average:** 3.1. **First-year students who submitted SAT scores:** 79%. Scores (25/75 percentile): Verbal: 440-570, Math: 430-550, Combined: 870-1120. **First-year students submitting ACT scores:** 27%. Scores (25/75 percentile): English: 18-25, Math: 17-23, Composite: 18-24.

ACADEMICS

Year founded: 1971. **Academic calendar:** Semester. **Degrees offered:** certificate, diploma, associate, terminal-associate, bachelor's, master's, post-master's certificate, first professional, doctorate. **Most popular majors:** 16% psychology, 14% religion/religious studies, 13% business/commerce, 11% multi/interdisciplinary studies, 7% communication studies/speech communication and rhetoric. **Major fields of study:** biological and biomedical sciences; business, management, marketing, and related support services; communication, journalism, and related programs; communications technologies/technicians and support services; computer and information sciences and support services; education; English language and literature/letters; family and consumer sciences/human sciences; foreign languages, literatures, and linguistics; health professions and related clinical sciences; history; legal professions and studies; liberal arts and sciences studies, and humanities; mathematics and statistics; multi/interdisciplinary studies; parks, recreation, leisure, and fitness studies; philosophy and religious studies; psychology; security and protective services; social sciences; theology and religious vocations; transportation and materials moving; visual and performing arts. **Areas of required coursework:** humanities, computer literacy, mathematics, English (including composition), philosophy, sciences (biological or physical), history, social science, other. **Pre-professional programs:** pre-law, pre-theology. **Special academic programs:** accelerated program, cooperative (work-study plan) program, distance learning, double major, dual enrollment, English as a Second Language (ESL), external degree program, honors program, independent study, internships, student-designed major, teacher certificate program, weekend college. **Teacher certification offered in:** early childhood, special education, elementary, middle/junior high, secondary. **Reserve Officers Training Corps (ROTC):** Army ROTC: Offered on campus; Air Force ROTC: Offered at cooperating institution (University of Virginia). **Faculty and instruction (2005-2006):** Total instructional faculty: 336 full-time, 165 part-time (65% men; 35% women; 5% minorities). Full-time faculty with Ph.D. or other terminal degree: 64%. Student/faculty ratio: 27/1. Classes of fewer than 20 students: 25%; of 20 to 49 students: 62%; of 50 or more students: 13%. **Advanced Placement and International Baccalaureate credit:** AP tests may be used for: Credit and/or placement. Scores accepted: 3, 4, 5. International Baccalaureate exams may be used for: Credit only. **Freshmen returning for sophomore year:** 74%. **Graduation rates:** Four-year: 25%; five-year: 36%; six-year: 44%.

COSTS AND FINANCIAL AID

Financial aid office: (434) 582-2270. **Expenses (2006-2007):** Tuition and fees 2006-2007: $15,350; room/board: $5,400. Estimated books and supplies: $1,000; transportation: $2,000; personal expenses: $1,000. **Financial aid:** Priority filing date for institution's financial aid form: March 1; deadline: March 1. In 2005-2006, 92% of undergraduates applied for financial aid. Of those, 76% were determined to have financial need; 17% had their need fully met. Average financial aid package (proportion receiving): $10,001 (75%). Average amount of gift aid, such as scholarships or grants (proportion receiving): $2,885 (38%). Average amount of self-help aid, such as work study or loans (proportion receiving): $3,864 (51%). Average need-based loan (excluding PLUS or other private loans): $3,737. Among students who received need-based aid, the average percentage of need met: 62%. Among students who received aid based on merit, the average award (and the proportion receiving): $5,247 (20%). The average athletic scholarship (and the proportion receiving): $10,206 (3%). Average amount of debt of borrowers graduating in 2005: $11,885. Proportion who borrowed: 42%.

CAMPUS LIFE AND EXTRACURRICULAR ACTIVITIES

Campus housing available: women's dorms, men's dorms, apartment for single students, special housing for disabled students. Students who live in college-owned, operated, or affiliated housing: 53%. **Student employment:** During the 2005-2006 academic year, 7% of undergraduates worked on campus. Average per-year earnings: $1,125. **Clubs and organizations:** Number of student organizations: 25. Activities include: choral groups, concert band, drama/theater, marching band, music ensembles, musical theater, opera, pep band, radio station, student government, student newspaper, television station, yearbook. Number of fraternities: 0; sororities: 0. Average proportion of students who stay on campus on weekends: 85%. **Sports program (2005-2006):** Member of NCAA I. *Men's intercollegiate varsity sports:* baseball, basketball, cross-country, football, golf, soccer, tennis, track and field (indoor), track and field (outdoor). *Women's intercollegiate varsity sports:* basketball, cross-country, soccer, softball, tennis, track and field (indoor), track and field (outdoor), volleyball.

SERVICES AND FACILITIES

Basic services: nonremedial tutoring, women's center, placement service, health service. **Remedial assistance:** reading, math, writing, study skills. **Counseling services:** minority student, career, personal, veteran student, academic, religious. **For learning-disabled students:** School does not offer a structured program with separate admission and additional fees. Services include: remedial math, remedial English, remedial reading, oral tests, learning center, extended time for tests, tutors. **Library:** Number of titles: 199,692; number of current serial subscriptions: 33,201. **Information technology resources:** Students are not required to lease or own a computer. Number of campus computers available to all students: 484. School has a wireless network. Proportion of college-owned housing units wired for high-speed internet access: 100%. **Campus safety:** Security services offered: 24-hour foot-and-vehicle patrols, lighted pathways/sidewalks, controlled dormitory access (key, security card, etc).

TRANSFER AND INTERNATIONAL STUDENTS

Transfer students: May apply for admission for the following academic terms: Fall, Winter, Spring, Summer. Applicants do not need a minimum number of credits to apply. For fall 2005: Transfer applications received: 3,883. Transfer applicants offered admission: 3,566. Transfer applicants enrolled: 1,116. **International students:** Number of foreign undergraduates: 414 (4% of student body). Number of countries represented: 72. Minimum TOEFL score required: 500 (paper); 173 (computer). Average TOEFL score: 557 (paper).

Longwood University

- **Address:** 201 High Street, Farmville, VA 23909
- **Website:** http://www.longwood.edu
- **Public**
- **Enrollment:** 3,599 full-time; 150 part-time

KEY STATS

✔ **U.S News College Ranking:** 33, Universities–Master's (South)
✔ **SAT Score (25th/75th percentile):** 1000-1150
✔ **Tuition:** 2006-2007: $7,589 in state, $15,209 out of state

Selectivity: Selective	**Room/board:** $6,058
Acceptance rate: 76%	**Average debt:** N/A
Student/faculty ratio: 20/1	**Proportion who borrowed:** N/A

UNDERGRADUATE STUDENT BODY STATS

2005-2006 enrollment: 3,599 full-time; 150 part-time. Men: 34%; women: 66%. **Ethnic makeup:** African American: 6%; Asian American: 2%; Hispanic: 2%; White: 89%; International: 1%.

ADMISSIONS FACTS AND FIGURES

Phone: (434) 395-2060. **Email:** admit@longwood.edu. **Website:** http://www.longwood.edu. **Application deadlines for fall 2007:** Regular decision: Rolling. Early decision: Not offered. Early action: Send application by: December 1; Decision sent by: January 1. Admission can be deferred. **Application fee:** $40. Common application is accepted. **To apply online, go to:** http://www.whylongwood.com/applynow/applyonline.htm. **Admissions requirements/recommendations:** High school units required (recommended): English: 4; Mathematics: 3 (4); Science: 3 (4); Foreign language: 2 (3); Social studies: 1; History: 2; Academic electives: 3 (4); Total units: 18 (23). Tests: The college uses SAT or ACT scores in admissions decisions. Either SAT or ACT required. For admission to the fall 2007 entering class, the school will accept: ACT with writing, ACT without writing. Campus visit: Recommended. Admissions interview: Neither required nor recommended. Off-campus interview: Not available. **Factors that count in admissions decisions:** *Academic:* Secondary school record: Very important. Class rank: Considered. Letters of recommendation: Considered. Standardized test scores: Very important. Essay: Important. *Nonacademic:* Interview: Not considered. Extracurricular activities: Considered. Talent/ability: Considered. Character/personal qualities: Considered. Alumni/ae relationship: Considered. Geographical residence: Considered. State residency: Considered. Religious affiliation/commitment: Not considered. Minority status: Considered. Volunteer work: Considered. Work experience: Considered. **Other schools with the greatest overlap in applicants:** Christopher Newport University; James Madison University; Radford University; Virginia Tech. **Admissions statistics for the fall 2005 entering class:** Total applicants: 3,369. Total accepted: 2,574. Freshmen enrolled: 958; 10% were from out of state. Accepted through early-decision or early-action plans: 19%. Overall acceptance rate: 76%. Non-early acceptance rate: 92%. **Size of waiting list:** 0 applicants; enrolled from waiting list: 0. **Credentials of fall 2005 freshmen:** 10% ranked in the top 10 percent of their high school class; 39% were in the top 25 percent, and 84% were in the top half. (Proportion submitting class standing: 83%.) **Average high school grade point average:** 3.3. **First-year students who submitted SAT scores:** 86%. Scores (25/75 percentile): Verbal: 500-580, Math: 500-570, Combined: 1000-1150. **First-year students submitting ACT scores:** 14%. Scores (25/75 percentile): English: N/A, Math: N/A, Composite: N/A.

ACADEMICS

Year founded: 1839. **Academic calendar:** Semester. **Degrees offered:** bachelor's, master's. **Most popular majors:** 23% business administration and management, 22% liberal arts and sciences/liberal studies, 7% visual and performing arts, 6% psychology, 5% communication studies/speech communication and rhetoric. **Major fields of study:** biological and biomedical sciences; business, management, marketing, and related support services; communication, journalism, and related programs; computer and information sciences and support services; education; English language and literature/letters; foreign languages, literatures, and linguistics; health professions and related clinical sciences; history; liberal arts and sciences studies, and humanities; mathematics and statistics; parks, recreation, leisure, and fitness studies; physical sciences; psychology; public administration and social service professions; security and protective services; social sciences; visual and performing arts. **Areas of required coursework:** arts/fine arts, humanities, computer literacy, mathematics, English (including composition), philosophy, foreign languages, sciences (biological or physical), history, social science, other. **Pre-professional programs:** pre-law, pre-dentistry, pre-medicine, pre-veterinary science, pre-pharmacy, other. **Special academic programs (% participation):** accelerated program (5%), cross-registration (5%), distance learning (5%), double major (1%), dual enrollment (5%), exchange student program (domestic) (5%), honors program (5%), independent study (5%), internships (100%), study abroad (5%), teacher certificate program (23%). **Teacher certification offered in:** early childhood, special education, elementary, middle/junior high, secondary. **Reserve Officers Training Corps (ROTC):** Army ROTC: Offered on campus. **Faculty and instruction (2005-2006):** Total instructional faculty: 201 full-time, 35 part-time (53% men; 47% women). Full-time faculty with Ph.D. or other terminal degree: 84%. Student/faculty ratio: 20/1. Classes of fewer than 20 students: 38%; of 20 to 49 students: 59%; of 50 or more students: 4%. **Advanced Placement and International Baccalaureate credit:** AP tests may be used for: Credit only. Scores accepted: 3, 4, 5. International Baccalaureate exams may be used for: Credit only. **Freshmen returning for sophomore year:** 79%. **Graduation rates:** Four-year: 48%; five-year: 61%; six-year: 61%. **Graduate study:** 31% of students pursue further study within one year; 31% within five years. Fields in which graduates pursue further study: Master of Business Administration (MBA), 10%; law, 1%; medicine, 1%; dentistry, 1%; engineering, 2%; theology (or the seminary), 1%; education, 38%; arts and sciences, 18%; veterinary medicine, 1%.

COSTS AND FINANCIAL AID
Financial aid office: (434) 395-2077. **Expenses (2006-2007):** Tuition and fees 2006-2007: $7,589 in state, $15,209 out of state; room/board: $6,058. Estimated books and supplies: $700; transportation: $1,000; personal expenses: $2,200. **Financial aid:** Priority filing date for institution's financial aid form: March 1.

CAMPUS LIFE AND EXTRACURRICULAR ACTIVITIES
Campus housing available (% using): coed dorms (75%), women's dorms (7%), sorority housing (7%), apartment for single students (5%), special housing for disabled students (2%), special housing for international students (1%), other housing options. Students who live in college-owned, operated, or affiliated housing: 69%. **Student employment:** During the 2005-2006 academic year, 17% of undergraduates worked on campus. Average per-year earnings: $2,000. **Clubs and organizations:** Number of student organizations: 125. Activities include: choral groups, concert band, dance, drama/theater, jazz band, literary magazine, music ensembles, musical theater, opera, radio station, student government, student newspaper, yearbook. Number of fraternities: 9; sororities: 13. Proportion of men in fraternities: 14%; of women in sororities: 16%. Average proportion of students who stay on campus on weekends: 65%. **Sports program (2005-2006):** Member of NCAA II. *Men's intercollegiate varsity sports:* baseball, basketball, cross-country, golf, soccer, tennis. *Women's intercollegiate varsity sports:* basketball, cross-country, field hockey, golf, lacrosse, soccer, softball, tennis.

SERVICES AND FACILITIES
Basic services: nonremedial tutoring, placement service, health service, health insurance. **Counseling services:** career, personal, academic, psychological, birth control, religious. **For learning-disabled students:** School does not offer a structured program with separate admission and additional fees. Total undergraduates in learning-disabled program or receiving services: 128. Services include: reading machines, tape recorders, untimed tests, note-taking services, oral tests, learning center, readers, extended time for tests, tutors, priority registration, texts on tape, typist/scribe, other testing accomodations, waiver of foreign language degree requirement, other. **Library:** Number of titles: 331,538; number of current serial subscriptions: 4,804. **Information technology resources:** Students are required to lease or own a computer. Number of campus computers available to all students: 350. School has a wireless network. Approximate number of users that can be accommodated: 3,000. Proportion of college-owned housing units wired for high-speed internet access: 100%. **Campus safety:** Security services offered: 24-hour foot-and-vehicle patrols, late-night transport/escort service, 24-hour emergency telephones, lighted pathways/sidewalks, student patrols, controlled dormitory access (key, security card, etc).

TRANSFER AND INTERNATIONAL STUDENTS
Transfer students: May apply for admission for the following academic terms: Fall, Spring, Summer. Applicants need a minimum number of credits to apply. For fall 2005: Transfer applications received: 404. Transfer applicants offered admission: 315. Transfer applicants enrolled: 213.

International students: Number of foreign undergraduates: 22 (1% of student body). Number of countries represented: 10. Minimum TOEFL score required: 550 (paper); 213 (computer).

Lynchburg College

- **Address:** 1501 Lakeside Drive, Lynchburg, VA 24501
- **Website:** http://www.lynchburg.edu
- **Private; Religious affiliation:** Christian Church (Disciples of Christ)
- **Enrollment:** 1,924 full-time; 125 part-time

KEY STATS
✔ **U.S News College Ranking:** 44, Universities–Master's (South)
✔ **SAT Score (25th/75th percentile):** 930-1120
✔ **Tuition:** 2005-2006: $23,945

Selectivity: Selective	**Room/board:** $6,400
Acceptance rate: 72%	**Average debt:** N/A
Student/faculty ratio: 13/1	**Proportion who borrowed:** N/A

UNDERGRADUATE STUDENT BODY STATS
2005-2006 enrollment: 1,924 full-time; 125 part-time. Men: 41%; women: 59%. **Ethnic makeup:** African American: 8%; American-Indian: 1%; Asian American: 2%; Hispanic: 3%; White: 86%. **Religious preference:** Roman Catholic: 18%; Protestant: 40%; Jewish: 1%; No preference: 8%; Unknown: 26%; Christian Church (Disciples of Christ): 5%.

ADMISSIONS FACTS AND FIGURES
Phone: (434) 544-8300. **Email:** admissions@lynchburg.edu. **Website:** http://www.lynchburg.edu. **Application deadlines for fall 2007:** Regular decision: Rolling. Early decision: Send application by: November 15; Decision sent by: December 15. Early action: Not offered. Admission can be deferred. **Application fee:** $30. Common application is accepted. **Admissions requirements/recommendations:** High school units required (recommended): English: 4 (4); Mathematics: 3 (4); Science: 3 (4); Foreign language: 2 (3); Social studies: 2 (2); History: 2 (2); Academic electives: 0 (1); Total units: 16 (20). Tests: The college uses SAT or ACT scores in admissions decisions. Either SAT or ACT required. For admission to the fall 2007 entering class, the school will accept: ACT with writing, ACT without writing. Campus visit: Recommended. Admissions interview: Recommended. Off-campus interview: May be arranged. **Factors that count in admissions decisions:** *Academic:* Secondary school record: Very important. Class rank: Important. Letters of recommendation: Considered. Standardized test scores: Very important. Essay: Considered. *Nonacademic:* Interview: Important. Extracurricular activities: Considered. Talent/ability: Considered. Character/personal qualities: Considered. Alumni/ae relationship: Not considered. Geographical residence: Not considered. State residency: Not considered. Religious affiliation/commitment: Not considered. Minority status: Not considered. Volunteer work: Considered. Work experience: Not considered. **Other schools with the greatest overlap in applicants:** Elon University; Longwood University; Randolph-Macon Woman's College. **Admissions statistics for the fall 2005 entering class:** Total applicants: 4,009. Total accepted: 2,883. Freshmen enrolled: 554; 45% were from out of state. Accepted through early-decision or early-action plans: 8%. Overall acceptance rate: 72%. Early-decision acceptance rate: 55%. Non-early acceptance rate: 73%. **Credentials of fall 2005 freshmen:** 13% ranked in the top 10 percent of their high school class; 39% were in the top 25 percent, and 72% were in the top half. (Proportion submitting class standing: 67%.) **Average high school grade point average:** 3.1. **First-year students who submitted SAT scores:** 98%. Scores (25/75 percentile): Verbal: 470-560, Math: 460-560, Combined: 930-1120. **First-year students submitting ACT scores:** 19%. Scores (25/75 percentile): English: 16-24, Math: 18-24, Composite: 18-22.

ACADEMICS
Year founded: 1903. **Academic calendar:** Semester. **Degrees offered:** bachelor's, master's. **Most popular majors:** 14% business, management, marketing, and related support services, 13% communication, journalism, and related programs, 12% education, 7% health professions and related clinical sciences, 7% psychology. **Major fields of study:** biological and biomedical sciences; business, management, marketing, and related support services; communication, journalism, and related programs; computer and information sciences and support services; education; English language and literature/letters; family and consumer sciences/human sciences; foreign

languages, literatures, and linguistics; health professions and related clinical sciences; history; mathematics and statistics; natural resources and conservation; parks, recreation, leisure, and fitness studies; philosophy and religious studies; physical sciences; psychology; social sciences; visual and performing arts. **Areas of required coursework:** arts/fine arts, humanities, mathematics, English (including composition), philosophy, foreign languages, sciences (biological or physical), history, social science, other. **Pre-professional programs:** pre-law, pre-dentistry, pre-medicine, pre-theology, pre-veterinary science, pre-optometry, pre-pharmacy, other. **Special academic programs (% participation):** accelerated program (1.5%), cross-registration, double major (2.3%), dual enrollment, honors program, independent study, internships (38%), study abroad (20%), teacher certificate program (8%). **Teacher certification offered in:** early childhood, special education, elementary, middle/junior high, secondary. **Faculty and instruction (2005-2006):** Total instructional faculty: 148 full-time, 72 part-time (53% men; 47% women; 7% minorities). Full-time faculty with Ph.D. or other terminal degree: 76%. Student/faculty ratio: 13/1. Classes of fewer than 20 students: 49%; of 20 to 49 students: 51%. **Advanced Placement and International Baccalaureate credit:** AP tests may be used for: Credit and/or placement. Scores accepted: 3, 4, 5. International Baccalaureate exams may be used for: Credit and/or placement. **Freshmen returning for sophomore year:** 72%. **Graduation rates:** Four-year: 47%; five-year: 55%; six-year: 58%.

COSTS AND FINANCIAL AID
Financial aid office: (434) 544-8228. **Expenses (2005-2006):** Tuition and fees 2005-2006: $23,945; room/board: $6,400. Estimated books and supplies: $600; transportation: $400; personal expenses: $500. **Financial aid:** Priority filing date for institution's financial aid form: March 1.

CAMPUS LIFE AND EXTRACURRICULAR ACTIVITIES
Campus housing available (% using): coed dorms (65%), sorority housing (2%), fraternity housing (1%), apartment for single students (17%), special housing for disabled students (2%), special housing for international students (1%), other housing options (12%). Students who live in college-owned, operated, or affiliated housing: 78%. **Student employment:** During the 2005-2006 academic year, 23% of undergraduates worked on campus. Average per-year earnings: $1,363. **Clubs and organizations:** Number of student organizations: 88. Activities include: choral groups, concert band, dance, drama/theater, jazz band, literary magazine, music ensembles, pep band, student government, student newspaper, yearbook. Number of fraternities: 4; sororities: 5. Proportion of men in fraternities: 10%; of women in sororities: 11%. Average proportion of students who stay on campus on weekends: 90%. **Sports program (2005-2006):** Member of NCAA III. *Men's intercollegiate varsity sports:* baseball, basketball, cross-country, equestrian Sports, golf, lacrosse, soccer, tennis, track and field (indoor), track and field (outdoor). *Women's intercollegiate varsity sports:* basketball, cheerleading, cross-country, equestrian sports, field hockey, lacrosse, soccer, softball, tennis, track and field (indoor), track and field (outdoor), volleyball.

SERVICES AND FACILITIES
Basic services: nonremedial tutoring, health service, health insurance. **Counseling services:** minority student, career, personal, academic, older student, psychological, birth control, religious. **For learning-disabled students:** School does not offer a structured program with separate admission and additional fees. Total undergraduates in learning-disabled program or receiving services: 215. Services include: reading machines, tape recorders, untimed tests, note-taking services, oral tests, learning center, readers, extended time for tests, tutors, early syllabus, priority registration, priority seating, proofreading services, substitution of courses, texts on tape, typist/scribe, exams on tape or computer, other testing accomodations, other. **Library:** Number of titles: 192,076; number of current serial subscriptions: 604. **Information technology resources:** Students are not required to lease or own a computer. Number of campus computers available to all students: 300. School has a wireless network. Proportion of college-owned housing units wired for high-speed internet access: 99%. **Campus safety:** Security services offered: 24-hour foot-and-vehicle patrols, late-night transport/escort service, 24-hour emergency telephones, lighted pathways/sidewalks, controlled dormitory access (key, security card, etc).

TRANSFER AND INTERNATIONAL STUDENTS
Transfer students: May apply for admission for the following academic terms: Fall, Spring, Summer. Applicants need a minimum number of credits to apply. For fall 2005: Transfer applications received: 279. Transfer applicants offered admission: 153. Transfer applicants enrolled: 69. **International students:** Number of foreign undergraduates: 8. Number of

countries represented: 4. Minimum TOEFL score required: 525 (paper); 197 (computer). Average TOEFL score: 559 (paper).

Mary Baldwin College

■ **Address:** New and Frederick Streets, Staunton, VA 24401
■ **Website:** http://www.mbc.edu
■ **Private; Religious affiliation:** Presbyterian
■ **Enrollment:** 1,002 full-time; 533 part-time

KEY STATS
✔ **U.S News College Ranking:** 25, Universities–Master's (South)
✔ **SAT Score (25th/75th percentile):** 920-1190
✔ **Tuition:** 2006-2007: $21,450

Selectivity: Selective	**Room/board:** $6,100
Acceptance rate: 77%	**Average debt:** $21,266
Student/faculty ratio: 10/1	**Proportion who borrowed:** 75%

UNDERGRADUATE STUDENT BODY STATS
2005-2006 enrollment: 1,002 full-time; 533 part-time. Men: 8%; women: 92%. **Ethnic makeup:** African American: 20%; American-Indian: 1%; Asian American: 2%; Hispanic: 3%; White: 72%; International: 2%. **Religious preference:** Roman Catholic: 15%; Protestant: 3%; No preference: 3%; Unknown: 33%; Presbyterian: 5%; Other: 41%.

ADMISSIONS FACTS AND FIGURES
Phone: (800) 468-2262. **Email:** admit@mbc.edu. **Website:** http://www.mbc.edu. **Application deadlines for fall 2007:** Regular decision: Rolling. Early decision: Send application by: November 15; Decision sent by: December 1. Early action: Not offered. Admission can be deferred. **Application fee:** $35. Common application is accepted. **To apply online, go to:** http://www.mbc.edu/admission/. **Admissions requirements/recommendations:** High school units required (recommended): English: 4; Mathematics: 3; Science: 2; Foreign language: 2 (3); Social studies: 3; Academic electives: (2). Tests: The college uses SAT or ACT scores in admissions decisions. Either SAT or ACT required. For admission to the fall 2007 entering class, the school will accept: ACT with writing, ACT without writing. Campus visit: Recommended. Admissions interview: Recommended. Off-campus interview: May be arranged. **Factors that count in admissions decisions:** *Academic:* Secondary school record: Very important. Class rank: Considered. Letters of recommendation: Considered. Standardized test scores: Very important. Essay: Considered. *Nonacademic:* Interview: Important. Extracurricular activities: Important. Talent/ability: Considered. Character/personal qualities: Important. Alumni/ae relationship: Considered. Geographical residence: Not considered. State residency: Not considered. Religious affiliation/commitment: Not considered. Minority status: Not considered. Volunteer work: Considered. Work experience: Considered. **Other schools with the greatest overlap in applicants:** Hollins University; James Madison University; Randolph-Macon Woman's College; University of Mary Washington; University of Virginia. **Admissions statistics for the fall 2005 entering class:** Total applicants: 1,255. Total accepted: 969. Freshmen enrolled: 267; 44% were from out of state. Overall acceptance rate: 77%. Non-early acceptance rate: 77%. **Credentials of fall 2005 freshmen:** 14% ranked in the top 10 percent of their high school class; 29% were in the top 25 percent, and 72% were in the top half. (Proportion submitting class standing: 57%.) **Average high school grade point average:** 3.2. **First-year students who submitted SAT scores:** 82%. Scores (25/75 percentile): Verbal: 470-630, Math: 450-560, Combined: 920-1190. **First-year students submitting ACT scores:** 15%. Scores (25/75 percentile): English: N/A, Math: N/A, Composite: 18-26.

ACADEMICS
Year founded: 1842. **Academic calendar:** Other. **Degrees offered:** certificate, bachelor's, master's. **Most popular majors:** 15% psychology, 11% business administration, management, and operations, 10% sociology, 7% English language and literature, 7% history. **Major fields of study:** area, ethnic, cultural, and gender studies; biological and biomedical sciences; business, management, marketing, and related support services; communication, journalism, and related programs; computer and information sciences and support services; English language and literature/letters; foreign languages, literatures, and linguistics; health professions and related clinical sciences; history; mathematics and statistics; multi/interdisciplinary studies; philoso-

phy and religious studies; physical sciences; psychology; public administration and social service professions; social sciences; visual and performing arts. **Areas of required coursework:** arts/fine arts, humanities, computer literacy, mathematics, English (including composition), philosophy, sciences (biological or physical), history, social science, other. **Pre-professional programs:** pre-law, pre-medicine. **Special academic programs (% participation):** accelerated program (15%), cross-registration (15%), distance learning (35%), double major (4%), dual enrollment (8%), English as a Second Language (ESL) (2%), exchange student program (domestic) (1%), external degree program (35%), honors program (10%), independent study (5%), internships (75%), liberal arts/career combination (100%), student-designed major (3%), study abroad (33%), teacher certificate program (17%), other. **Teacher certification offered in:** early childhood, special education, elementary, middle/junior high, secondary. **Cooperative education programs:** computer science, engineering, other. **Reserve Officers Training Corps (ROTC):** Army ROTC: Offered on campus; Navy ROTC: Offered at cooperating institution (Virginia Military Institute); Air Force ROTC: Offered on campus. **Faculty and instruction (2005-2006):** Total instructional faculty: 76 full-time, 58 part-time (43% men; 57% women; 8% minorities). Full-time faculty with Ph.D. or other terminal degree: 93%. Student/faculty ratio: 10/1. Classes of fewer than 20 students: 67%; of 20 to 49 students: 33%; of 50 or more students: 0%. **Advanced Placement and International Baccalaureate credit:** AP tests may be used for: Credit only. Scores accepted: 4, 5. International Baccalaureate exams may be used for: Credit and/or placement. **Freshmen returning for sophomore year:** 65%. **Graduation rates:** Four-year: 49%; five-year: 53%; six-year: 50%. **Graduate study:** 23% of students pursue further study within one year; 35% within five years. Fields in which graduates pursue further study: Master of Business Administration (MBA), 15%; law, 15%; medicine, 15%; dentistry, 2%; theology (or the seminary), 5%; education, 25%; arts and sciences, 20%; veterinary medicine, 3%.

COSTS AND FINANCIAL AID
Financial aid office: (540) 887-7022. **Expenses (2006-2007):** Tuition and fees 2006-2007: $21,450; room/board: $6,100. Estimated books and supplies: $900; transportation: $400; personal expenses: $915. **Financial aid:** Priority filing date for institution's financial aid form: May 15. In 2005-2006, 85% of undergraduates applied for financial aid. Of those, 72% were determined to have financial need; 45% had their need fully met. Average financial aid package (proportion receiving): $19,803 (71%). Average amount of gift aid, such as scholarships or grants (proportion receiving): $9,693 (70%). Average amount of self-help aid, such as work study or loans (proportion receiving): $5,650 (61%). Average need-based loan (excluding PLUS or other private loans): $3,406. Among students who received need-based aid, the average percentage of need met: 86%. Among students who received aid based on merit, the average award (and the proportion receiving): $13,381 (24%). The average athletic scholarship (and the proportion receiving): $0 (0%). Average amount of debt of borrowers graduating in 2005: $21,266. Proportion who borrowed: 75%.

CAMPUS LIFE AND EXTRACURRICULAR ACTIVITIES
Campus housing available (% using): women's dorms (85%), other housing options (15%). Students who live in college-owned, operated, or affiliated housing: 83%. **Student employment:** During the 2005-2006 academic year, 28% of undergraduates worked on campus. Average per-year earnings: $1,700. **Clubs and organizations:** Number of student organizations: 34. Activities include: choral groups, dance, drama/theater, literary magazine, marching band, music ensembles, musical theater, radio station, student government, student newspaper, student film society, television station, yearbook. Number of fraternities: 0; sororities: 0. Average proportion of students who stay on campus on weekends: 40%. **Sports program (2005-2006):** Member of NCAA III. *Women's intercollegiate varsity sports:* basketball, cross-country, field hockey, soccer, softball, swimming and diving, tennis, volleyball.

SERVICES AND FACILITIES
Basic services: women's center, health service. **Remedial assistance:** reading, math, writing, study skills. **Counseling services:** minority student, career, military, personal, academic, psychological, birth control, religious. **For learning-disabled students:** School does not offer a structured program with separate admission and additional fees. Total undergraduates in learning-disabled program or receiving services: 29. Services include: tape recorders, videotaped classes, untimed tests, note-taking services, oral tests, learning center, readers, extended time for tests, tutors. **Library:** Number of titles: 140,466; number of current serial subscriptions: 11,889. **Information technology resources:** Students are not required to lease or own a computer. Number of campus computers available to all students: 227. School has a

wireless network. Approximate number of users that can be accommodated: 890. Proportion of college-owned housing units wired for high-speed internet access: 100%. **Campus safety:** Security services offered: 24-hour foot-and-vehicle patrols, late-night transport/escort service, 24-hour emergency telephones, lighted pathways/sidewalks, controlled dormitory access (key, security card, etc.).

TRANSFER AND INTERNATIONAL STUDENTS
Transfer students: May apply for admission for the following academic terms: Fall, Spring. Applicants need a minimum number of credits to apply. For fall 2005: Transfer applications received: 217. Transfer applicants offered admission: 176. Transfer applicants enrolled: 141. **International students:** Number of foreign undergraduates: 23 (2% of student body). Minimum TOEFL score required: 500 (paper). Average TOEFL score: 500 (paper).

Marymount University

- **Address:** 2807 N. Glebe Road, Arlington, VA 22207
- **Website:** http://www.marymount.edu
- **Private; Religious affiliation:** Roman Catholic
- **Enrollment:** 1,871 full-time; 456 part-time

KEY STATS
✔ **U.S News College Ranking:** 54, Universities–Master's (South)
✔ **SAT Score (25th/75th percentile):** 890-1113
✔ **Tuition:** 2006-2007: $19,199

Selectivity: Less selective	**Room/board:** $8,212
Acceptance rate: 83%	**Average debt:** $24,950
Student/faculty ratio: 13/1	**Proportion who borrowed:** 71%

UNDERGRADUATE STUDENT BODY STATS
2005-2006 enrollment: 1,871 full-time; 456 part-time. Men: 25%; women: 75%. **Ethnic makeup:** African American: 14%; Asian American: 9%; Hispanic: 11%; White: 59%; International: 7%. **Religious preference:** Protestant: 20%; Jewish: 1%; Muslim: 6%; Hindu: 1%; Buddhist: 1%; Unknown: 31%; Roman Catholic: 38%; Greek Orthodox: 1%; Other: 1%.

ADMISSIONS FACTS AND FIGURES
Phone: (703) 284-1500. **Email:** admissions@marymount.edu. **Website:** http://www.marymount.edu. **Application deadlines for fall 2007:** Regular decision: Rolling. Early decision: Not offered. Early action: Not offered. Admission can be deferred. **Application fee:** $35. Common application is not accepted. **To apply online, go to:** http://www.marymount.edu/application/. **Admissions requirements/recommendations:** High school units required (recommended): English: (4); Mathematics: (3); Science: (2); Foreign language: (3); Social studies: (3); Total units: 15. Tests: The college uses SAT or ACT scores in admissions decisions. Either SAT or ACT required. For admission to the fall 2007 entering class, the school will accept: ACT with writing, ACT without writing. Campus visit: Recommended. Admissions interview: Recommended. Off-campus interview: May be arranged. **Factors that count in admissions decisions:** *Academic:* Secondary school record: Very important. Class rank: Important. Letters of recommendation: Important. Standardized test scores: Very important. Essay: Considered. *Nonacademic:* Interview: Considered. Extracurricular activities: Important. Talent/ability: Important. Character/personal qualities: Considered. Alumni/ae relationship: Considered. Geographical residence: Not considered. State residency: Not considered. Religious affiliation/commitment: Not considered. Minority status: Not considered. Volunteer work: Considered. Work experience: Considered. **Admissions statistics for the fall 2005 entering class:** Total applicants: 1,802. Total accepted: 1,491. Freshmen enrolled: 426; 54% were from out of state. Overall acceptance rate: 83%. **Credentials of fall 2005 freshmen:** 12% ranked in the top 10 percent of their high school class; 30% were in the top 25 percent, and 72% were in the top half. (Proportion submitting class standing: 38%.) **Average high school grade point average:** 3.0. **First-year students who submitted SAT scores:** 94%. Scores (25/75 percentile): Verbal: 450-563, Math: 440-550, Combined: 890-1113. **First-year students submitting ACT scores:** 17%. Scores (25/75 percentile): English: 16-22, Math: 17-22, Composite: 17-23.

ACADEMICS

Year founded: 1950. **Academic calendar:** Semester. **Degrees offered:** certificate, associate, bachelor's, post-bachelor's certificate, master's, post-master's certificate, doctorate. **Most popular majors:** 11% interior design, 8% social psychology, 7% commercial and advertising art, 7% computer and information sciences, 7% liberal arts and sciences/liberal studies. **Major fields of study:** biological and biomedical sciences; business, management, marketing, and related support services; communication, journalism, and related programs; computer and information sciences and support services; English language and literature/letters; health professions and related clinical sciences; history; legal professions and studies; liberal arts and sciences studies, and humanities; mathematics and statistics; natural resources and conservation; parks, recreation, leisure, and fitness studies; philosophy and religious studies; psychology; security and protective services; social sciences; visual and performing arts. **Areas of required coursework:** humanities, mathematics, English (including composition), philosophy, sciences (biological or physical), history, social science, other. **Pre-professional programs:** other. **Special academic programs (% participation):** cross-registration (8%), double major (2%), independent study (10%), internships (85%), student-designed major (7%), study abroad (8%), teacher certificate program (9%). **Teacher certification offered in:** early childhood, special education, elementary, secondary. **Reserve Officers Training Corps (ROTC):** Army ROTC: Offered at cooperating institution (Georgetown University). **Faculty and instruction (2005-2006):** Total instructional faculty: 134 full-time, 218 part-time (37% men; 63% women; 6% minorities). Full-time faculty with Ph.D. or other terminal degree: 85%. Student/faculty ratio: 13/1. Classes of fewer than 20 students: 45%; of 20 to 49 students: 53%; of 50 or more students: 2%. **Advanced Placement and International Baccalaureate credit:** AP tests may be used for: Credit and/or placement. Scores accepted: 3, 4, 5. International Baccalaureate exams may be used for: Credit only. **Freshmen returning for sophomore year:** 73%. **Graduation rates:** Four-year: 38%; five-year: 47%; six-year: 54%. **Graduate study:** 27% of students pursue further study within one year; 42% within five years. Fields in which graduates pursue further study: Master of Business Administration (MBA), 12%; law, 2%; medicine, 2%; education, 18%; arts and sciences, 8%; veterinary medicine, 2%.

COSTS AND FINANCIAL AID

Financial aid office: (703) 284-1530. **Expenses (2006-2007):** Tuition and fees 2006-2007: $19,199; room/board: $8,212. Estimated books and supplies: $800; transportation: $470; personal expenses: $900. **Financial aid:** Priority filing date for institution's financial aid form: March 1. In 2005-2006, 71% of undergraduates applied for financial aid. Of those, 57% were determined to have financial need; 16% had their need fully met. Average financial aid package (proportion receiving): $12,511 (56%). Average amount of gift aid, such as scholarships or grants (proportion receiving): $6,834 (41%). Average amount of self-help aid, such as work study or loans (proportion receiving): $4,693 (47%). Average need-based loan (excluding PLUS or other private loans): $3,805. Among students who received need-based aid, the average percentage of need met: 70%. Among students who received aid based on merit, the average award (and the proportion receiving): $8,343 (17%). Average amount of debt of borrowers graduating in 2005: $24,950. Proportion who borrowed: 71%.

CAMPUS LIFE AND EXTRACURRICULAR ACTIVITIES

Campus housing available (% using): coed dorms (43%), women's dorms (53%), apartment for single students (4%). Students who live in college-owned, operated, or affiliated housing: 31%. **Student employment:** During the 2005-2006 academic year, 10% of undergraduates worked on campus. Average per-year earnings: $1,800. **Clubs and organizations:** Number of student organizations: 35. Activities include: choral groups, dance, drama/theater, literary magazine, student government, student newspaper, yearbook. Number of fraternities: 0; sororities: 0. **Sports program (2005-2006):** Member of NCAA III. *Men's intercollegiate varsity sports:* basketball, cross-country, golf, lacrosse, soccer, swimming and diving. *Women's intercollegiate varsity sports:* basketball, cross-country, lacrosse, soccer, swimming and diving, volleyball.

SERVICES AND FACILITIES

Basic services: nonremedial tutoring, health service, health insurance. **Remedial assistance:** math, writing, study skills. **Counseling services:** career, personal, academic, religious. **For learning-disabled students:** School does not offer a structured program with separate admission and additional fees. Total undergraduates in learning-disabled program or receiving services: 38. Services include: remedial math, remedial English, remedial reading, tape recorders, note-taking services, oral tests, learning center, readers, extended

time for tests, tutors, texts on tape, other testing accomodations. **Library:** Number of titles: 196,019; number of current serial subscriptions: 1,536. **Information technology resources:** Students are not required to lease or own a computer. Number of campus computers available to all students: 260. School has a wireless network. Approximate number of users that can be accommodated: 500. Proportion of college-owned housing units wired for high-speed internet access: 100%. **Campus safety:** Security services offered: 24-hour foot-and-vehicle patrols, late-night transport/escort service, 24-hour emergency telephones, lighted pathways/sidewalks, controlled dormitory access (key, security card, etc).

TRANSFER AND INTERNATIONAL STUDENTS

Transfer students: May apply for admission for the following academic terms: Fall, Spring, Summer. Applicants need a minimum number of credits to apply. For fall 2005: Transfer applications received: 695. Transfer applicants offered admission: 578. Transfer applicants enrolled: 354. **International students:** Number of foreign undergraduates: 162 (7% of student body). Number of countries represented: 67. Minimum TOEFL score required: 550 (paper); 213 (computer). Average TOEFL score: 558 (paper).

Norfolk State University

- **Address:** 700 Park Avenue, Norfolk, VA 23504
- **Website:** http://www.nsu.edu
- **Public**
- **Enrollment:** 4,420 full-time; 917 part-time

KEY STATS
- ✔ **U.S News College Ranking:** fourth tier, Universities–Master's (South)
- ✔ **SAT Score (25th/75th percentile):** 820-980
- ✔ **Tuition:** 2006-2007: $5,056 in state, $15,376 out of state

Selectivity: Less selective	**Room/board:** $6,623
Acceptance rate: 71%	**Average debt:** N/A
Student/faculty ratio: 17/1	**Proportion who borrowed:** N/A

UNDERGRADUATE STUDENT BODY STATS

2005-2006 enrollment: 4,420 full-time; 917 part-time. Men: 38%; women: 62%. **Ethnic makeup:** African American: 89%; Asian American: 1%; Hispanic: 2%; White: 8%; International: 1%.

ADMISSIONS FACTS AND FIGURES

Phone: (757) 823-8396. **Email:** admissions@nsu.edu. **Website:** http://www.nsu.edu. **Application deadlines for fall 2007:** Regular decision: May 31. Early decision: Not offered. Early action: Not offered. Admission can be deferred. **Application fee:** $25. Common application is not accepted. **To apply online, go to:** https://www.applyweb.com/apply/norfolk/. **Admissions requirements/recommendations:** High school units required (recommended): English: 4; Mathematics: 3; Science: 3; History: 3; Academic electives: 9; Total units: 22. Tests: The college uses SAT or ACT scores in admissions decisions. Either SAT or ACT required. For admission to the fall 2007 entering class, the school will accept ACT without writing. Campus visit: Recommended. Admissions interview: Neither required nor recommended. Off-campus interview: Not available. **Factors that count in admissions decisions:** *Academic:* Secondary school record: Very important. Class rank: Important. Letters of recommendation: Very important. Standardized test scores: Very important. Essay: Considered. *Nonacademic:* Interview: Considered. Extracurricular activities: Considered. Talent/ability: Considered. Character/personal qualities: Considered. Alumni/ae relationship: Not considered. Geographical residence: Not considered. State residency: Not considered. Religious affiliation/commitment: Not considered. Minority status: Not considered. Volunteer work: Not considered. Work experience: Not considered. **Other schools with the greatest overlap in applicants:** Hampton University; Howard University; Old Dominion University; Virginia Commonwealth University; Virginia State University. **Admissions statistics for the fall 2005 entering class:** Total applicants: 4,696. Total accepted: 3,315. Freshmen enrolled: 1,001; 35% were from out of state. Overall acceptance rate: 71%. **Credentials of fall 2005 freshmen:** 5% ranked in the top 10 percent of their high school class; 20% were in the top 25 percent, and 56% were in the top half. (Proportion submitting class standing: 58%.) **Average high school grade point average:** 2.6. **First-year students who submitted SAT scores:** 95%. Scores (25/75 percentile): Verbal: 410-490, Math: 410-490, Combined: 820-980. **First-year students submitting ACT**

scores: 5%. Scores (25/75 percentile): English: N/A, Math: N/A, Composite: 17-19.

ACADEMICS

Year founded: 1935. **Academic calendar:** Semester. **Degrees offered:** certificate, associate, transfer-associate, terminal-associate, bachelor's, master's, doctorate. **Most popular majors:** 12% multi/interdisciplinary studies, 9% business/commerce, 9% nursing/registered nurse training (R.N., A.S.N., B.S.N., M.S.N.), 9% social work, 8% teacher education and professional development. **Major fields of study:** biological and biomedical sciences; business, management, marketing, and related support services; communication, journalism, and related programs; computer and information sciences and support services; education; engineering; engineering technologies/technicians; English language and literature/letters; family and consumer sciences/human sciences; health professions and related clinical sciences; history; mathematics and statistics; multi/interdisciplinary studies; parks, recreation, leisure, and fitness studies; physical sciences; psychology; public administration and social service professions; social sciences; visual and performing arts. **Areas of required coursework:** humanities, computer literacy, mathematics, English (including composition), sciences (biological or physical), history, social science, other. **Special academic programs:** cooperative (work-study plan) program, cross-registration, distance learning, double major, dual enrollment, English as a Second Language (ESL), honors program, independent study, internships, liberal arts/career combination, teacher certificate program. **Teacher certification offered in:** early childhood, special education, elementary, vo-tech, middle/junior high, adult education, secondary. **Cooperative education programs:** technologies. **Reserve Officers Training Corps (ROTC):** Army ROTC: Offered on campus; Navy ROTC: Offered on campus. **Faculty and instruction (2005-2006):** Total instructional faculty: 280 full-time, 106 part-time (47% men; 53% women; 81% minorities). Student/faculty ratio: 17/1. Classes of fewer than 20 students: 57%; of 20 to 49 students: 40%; of 50 or more students: 3%. **Advanced Placement and International Baccalaureate credit:** AP tests may be used for: Credit and/or placement. Scores accepted: 3. **Freshmen returning for sophomore year:** 67%. **Graduation rates:** Four-year: 12%; five-year: 24%; six-year: 28%.

COSTS AND FINANCIAL AID

Financial aid office: (757) 823-8381. **Expenses (2006-2007):** Tuition and fees 2006-2007: $5,056 in state, $15,376 out of state; room/board: $6,623.

CAMPUS LIFE AND EXTRACURRICULAR ACTIVITIES

Campus housing available: women's dorms, men's dorms, apartment for single students, special housing for disabled students. Students who live in college-owned, operated, or affiliated housing: 34%. **Student employment:** During the 2005-2006 academic year, 11% of undergraduates worked on campus. Average per-year earnings: $1,713. **Clubs and organizations:** Number of student organizations: 154. Activities include: choral groups, concert band, dance, drama/theater, jazz band, marching band, music ensembles, opera, pep band, radio station, student government, student newspaper, symphony orchestra, television station, yearbook. Number of fraternities: 8; sororities: 8. Proportion of men in fraternities: 10%; of women in sororities: 10%. **Sports program (2005-2006):** Member of NCAA I. *Men's intercollegiate varsity sports:* baseball, basketball, cross-country, football, tennis, track and field (indoor), track and field (outdoor). *Women's intercollegiate varsity sports:* basketball, bowling, cross-country, softball, tennis, track and field (indoor), track and field (outdoor), volleyball.

SERVICES AND FACILITIES

Basic services: nonremedial tutoring, placement service, day care, health service, health insurance. **Counseling services:** career, military, personal, veteran student, academic, older student, religious. **For learning-disabled students:** School does not offer a structured program with separate admission and additional fees. Services include: reading machines, tape recorders, videotaped classes, diagnostic testing service, untimed tests, note-taking services, oral tests, learning center, readers, extended time for tests, tutors, other. **Library:** Number of titles: 340,000; number of current serial subscriptions: 1,195. **Information technology resources:** Students are not required to lease or own a computer. Number of campus computers available to all students: 978. School has a wireless network. Approximate number of users that can be accommodated: 1,000. Proportion of college-owned housing units wired for high-speed internet access: 99%. **Campus safety:** Security services offered: 24-hour foot-and-vehicle patrols, late-night transport/escort service, 24-hour emergency telephones, lighted pathways/sidewalks, student patrols, controlled dormitory access (key, security card, etc).

TRANSFER AND INTERNATIONAL STUDENTS

Transfer students: May apply for admission for the following academic terms: Fall, Spring, Summer. Applicants do not need a minimum number of credits to apply. **International students:** Number of foreign undergraduates: 36 (1% of student body). Number of countries represented: 14. Minimum TOEFL score required: 500 (paper). Average TOEFL score: 525 (paper).

Old Dominion University

- **Address:** 5115 Hampton Boulevard, Norfolk, VA 23529
- **Website:** http://www.odu.edu
- **Public**
- **Enrollment:** 10,828 full-time; 4,447 part-time

KEY STATS

✔ **U.S News College Ranking:** fourth tier, National Universities
✔ **SAT Score (25th/75th percentile):** 960-1160
✔ **Tuition:** 2006-2007: $6,098 in state, $16,658 out of state
  Selectivity: Selective   **Room/board:** $6,640
  Acceptance rate: 69%   **Average debt:** $16,775
  Student/faculty ratio: 18/1   **Proportion who borrowed:** 80%

UNDERGRADUATE STUDENT BODY STATS

2005-2006 enrollment: 10,828 full-time; 4,447 part-time. Men: 42%; women: 58%. **Ethnic makeup:** African American: 23%; American-Indian: 1%; Asian American: 6%; Hispanic: 3%; White: 66%; International: 2%.

ADMISSIONS FACTS AND FIGURES

Phone: (757) 683-3685. **Email:** admit@odu.edu. **Website:** http://www.odu.edu. **Application deadlines for fall 2007:** Regular decision: March 15. Early decision: Not offered. Early action: Send application by: December 15; Decision sent by: January 15. Admission can be deferred. **Application fee:** $40. Common application is accepted. **To apply online, go to:** http://admissions.odu.edu/undergraduate.php. **Admissions requirements/recommendations:** High school units required (recommended): English: 4; Mathematics: 3; Science: 3; Foreign language: 3; Social studies: 0 (3); History: 3; Academic electives: 1; Total units: 17. Tests: The college uses SAT or ACT scores in admissions decisions. Either SAT or ACT required. For admission to the fall 2007 entering class, the school will accept: ACT with writing. Campus visit: Recommended. Admissions interview: Neither required nor recommended. Off-campus interview: Not available. **Factors that count in admissions decisions:** *Academic:* Secondary school record: Very important. Class rank: Important. Letters of recommendation: Important. Standardized test scores: Very important. Essay: Important. *Nonacademic:* Interview: Considered. Extracurricular activities: Very important. Talent/ability: Considered. Character/personal qualities: Considered. Alumni/ae relationship: Considered. Geographical residence: Not considered. State residency: Not considered. Religious affiliation/commitment: Not considered. Minority status: Not considered. Volunteer work: Important. Work experience: Important. **Other schools with the greatest overlap in applicants:** Christopher Newport University; College of William and Mary; James Madison University; University of Virginia; Virginia Tech. **Admissions statistics for the fall 2005 entering class:** Total applicants: 7,067. Total accepted: 4,904. Freshmen enrolled: 2,094; 9% were from out of state. Accepted through early-decision or early-action plans: 45%. Overall acceptance rate: 69%. Non-early acceptance rate: 78%. **Credentials of fall 2005 freshmen:** 15% ranked in the top 10 percent of their high school class; 44% were in the top 25 percent, and 88% were in the top half. (Proportion submitting class standing: 74%.) **Average high school grade point average:** 3.3. **First-year students who submitted SAT scores:** 86%. Scores (25/75 percentile): Verbal: 480-580, Math: 480-580, Combined: 960-1160. **First-year students submitting ACT scores:** 15%. Scores (25/75 percentile): English: 18-23, Math: 17-23, Composite: 19-23.

ACADEMICS

Year founded: 1930. **Academic calendar:** Semester. **Degrees offered:** bachelor's, master's, post-master's certificate, doctorate. **Most popular majors:** 21% business, management, marketing, and related support services, 18% health professions and related clinical sciences, 10% English language and literature/letters, 6% engineering, 6% multi/interdisciplinary studies. **Major fields of study:** area, ethnic, cultural, and gender studies; biological and biomedical sciences; business, management, marketing, and related support services; communication, journalism, and related programs; computer and information sciences and support services; education; engineering; engineering technologies/technicians; English language and literature/letters; foreign languages, literatures, and linguistics; health professions and related clinical sciences; history; mathematics and statistics; multi/interdisciplinary studies; parks, recreation, leisure, and fitness studies; philosophy and religious studies; physical sciences; psychology; social sciences; visual and performing arts. **Areas of required coursework:** arts/fine arts, humanities, computer literacy, mathematics, English (including composition), philosophy, foreign languages, sciences (biological or physical), history, social science, other. **Pre-professional programs:** pre-law, pre-dentistry, pre-medicine, pre-veterinary science, pre-optometry, pre-pharmacy. **Special academic programs:** accelerated program, cooperative (work-study plan) program, cross-registration, distance learning, double major, dual enrollment, English as a Second Language (ESL), exchange student program (domestic), honors program, independent study, internships, liberal arts/career combination, student-designed major, study abroad, teacher certificate program, weekend college, other. **Teacher certification offered in:** early childhood, special education, elementary, vo-tech, middle/junior high, secondary. **Cooperative education programs:** art, business, computer science, education, engineering, health professions, humanities, natural science, social/behavioral science, technologies, vocational arts. **Reserve Officers Training Corps (ROTC):** Army ROTC: Offered on campus; Navy ROTC: Offered on campus. **Faculty and instruction (2005-2006):** Total instructional faculty: 620 full-time, 311 part-time (57% men; 43% women; 19% minorities). Full-time faculty with Ph.D. or other terminal degree: 80%. Student/faculty ratio: 18/1. Classes of fewer than 20 students: 41%; of 20 to 49 students: 50%; of 50 or more students: 9%. **Advanced Placement and International Baccalaureate credit:** AP tests may be used for: Credit and/or placement. Scores accepted: 3, 4, 5. International Baccalaureate exams may be used for: Credit only. **Freshmen returning for sophomore year:** 78%. **Graduation rates:** Four-year: 22%; five-year: 42%; six-year: 48%. **Graduate study:** 19% of students pursue further study within one year. Fields in which graduates pursue further study: Master of Business Administration (MBA), 10%; law, 6%; medicine, 8%; dentistry, 1%; engineering, 3%; education, 32%; arts and sciences, 14%; veterinary medicine, 1%.

COSTS AND FINANCIAL AID

Financial aid office: (757) 683-3683. **Expenses (2006-2007):** Tuition and fees 2006-2007: $6,098 in state, $16,658 out of state; room/board: $6,640. Estimated books and supplies: $900; transportation: $1,000; personal expenses: $1,875. **Financial aid:** Priority filing date for institution's financial aid form: February 15; deadline: March 15. In 2005-2006, 71% of undergraduates applied for financial aid. Of those, 60% were determined to have financial need; 48% had their need fully met. Average financial aid package (proportion receiving): $6,417 (56%). Average amount of gift aid, such as scholarships or grants (proportion receiving): $3,610 (29%). Average amount of self-help aid, such as work study or loans (proportion receiving): $3,982 (35%). Average need-based loan (excluding PLUS or other private loans): $3,744. Among students who received need-based aid, the average percentage of need met: 72%. Among students who received aid based on merit, the average award (and the proportion receiving): $3,481 (4%). The average athletic scholarship (and the proportion receiving): $10,251 (2%). Average amount of debt of borrowers graduating in 2005: $16,775. Proportion who borrowed: 80%.

CAMPUS LIFE AND EXTRACURRICULAR ACTIVITIES

Campus housing available (% using): coed dorms (44%), apartment for single students (23%), special housing for disabled students (2%), special housing for international students (3%). Students who live in college-owned, operated, or affiliated housing: 25%. **Student employment:** During the 2005-2006 academic year, 7% of undergraduates worked on campus. Average per-year earnings: $1,854. **Clubs and organizations:** Number of student organizations: 175. Activities include: choral groups, concert band, dance, drama/theater, jazz band, literary magazine, music ensembles, musical theater, pep band, radio station, student government, student newspaper, television station, yearbook. Number of fraternities: 13; sororities: 10. Proportion of men in fraternities: 4%; of women in sororities: 3%. Average proportion of students who stay on campus on weekends: 20%. **Sports program (2005-2006):** Member of NCAA I. *Men's intercollegiate varsity sports:* baseball, basketball, golf, soccer, swimming and diving, tennis, wrestling. *Women's intercollegiate varsity sports:* basketball, field hockey, golf, lacrosse, soccer, swimming and diving, tennis.

SERVICES AND FACILITIES

Basic services: nonremedial tutoring, women's center, placement service, day care, health service, health insurance. **Counseling services:** minority student, career, military, personal, veteran student, academic, older student, psychological, birth control, religious, other. **For learning-disabled students:** School does not offer a structured program with separate admission and additional fees. Total undergraduates in learning-disabled program or receiving services: 165. Services include: tape recorders, other special classes, note-taking services, readers, extended time for tests, priority registration, priority seating, substitution of courses, texts on tape, typist/scribe, exams on tape or computer, other testing accomodations, other. **Library:** Number of titles: 1,110,719; number of current serial subscriptions: 14,607. **Information technology resources:** Students are not required to lease or own a computer. Number of campus computers available to all students: 2,035. School has a wireless network. Approximate number of users that can be accommodated: 2,500. Proportion of college-owned housing units wired for high-speed internet access: 100%. **Campus safety:** Security services offered: 24-hour foot-and-vehicle patrols, late-night transport/escort service, 24-hour emergency telephones, lighted pathways/sidewalks, controlled dormitory access (key, security card, etc).

TRANSFER AND INTERNATIONAL STUDENTS

Transfer students: May apply for admission for the following academic terms: Fall, Spring, Summer. Applicants need a minimum number of credits to apply. For fall 2005: Transfer applications received: 3,109. Transfer applicants offered admission: 2,836. Transfer applicants enrolled: 1,766. **International students:** Number of foreign undergraduates: 281 (2% of student body). Number of countries represented: 81. Minimum TOEFL score required: 550 (paper); 213 (computer).

Radford University

- **Address:** PO Box 6890, RU Station, Radford, VA 24142
- **Website:** http://www.radford.edu
- **Public**
- **Enrollment:** 8,028 full-time; 454 part-time

KEY STATS

✔ **U.S News College Ranking:** 47, Universities–Master's (South)
✔ **SAT Score (25th/75th percentile):** 910-1100
✔ **Tuition:** 2006-2007: $5,746 in state, $13,494 out of state

Selectivity: Less selective	Room/board: $6,218
Acceptance rate: 81%	Average debt: $17,264
Student/faculty ratio: 20/1	Proportion who borrowed: 88%

UNDERGRADUATE STUDENT BODY STATS

2005-2006 enrollment: 8,028 full-time; 454 part-time. Men: 42%; women: 58%. **Ethnic makeup:** African American: 6%; Asian American: 2%; Hispanic: 3%; White: 88%; International: 1%.

ADMISSIONS FACTS AND FIGURES

Phone: (540) 831-5371. **Email:** ruadmiss@radford.edu. **Website:** http://www.radford.edu. **Application deadlines for fall 2007:** Regular decision: February 1; decision sent by March 20. Early decision: Not offered. Early action: Not offered. Admission cannot be deferred. **Application fee:** $35. Common application is accepted. **To apply online, go to:** https://www.applyweb.com/apply/runet/menu.html. **Admissions requirements/recommendations:** High school units required (recommended): English: (4); Mathematics: (4); Science: (4); Foreign language: (3); Social studies: (2); History: (2); Academic electives: (5); Total units: (24). Tests: The college uses SAT or ACT scores in admissions decisions. Either SAT or ACT required. For admission to the fall 2007 entering class, the school will accept: ACT with writing, ACT without writing. Campus visit: Recommended. Admissions interview: Neither required nor recommended. **Factors that count in admissions decisions:** *Academic:* Secondary school record: Very important. Class rank: Considered. Letters of recommendation: Considered. Standardized test scores: Considered. Essay: Considered. *Nonacademic:* Interview: Not considered. Extracurricular activities: Considered. Talent/ability: Considered. Character/personal qualities: Considered. Alumni/ae relationship: Considered. Geographical residence: Considered. State residency: Considered. Religious affiliation/commitment: Not considered. Minority status: Considered. Volunteer work: Considered.

Work experience: Considered. **Admissions statistics for the fall 2005 entering class:** Total applicants: 5,792. Total accepted: 4,719. Freshmen enrolled: 1,896; 9% were from out of state. Overall acceptance rate: 81%. **Credentials of fall 2005 freshmen:** 4% ranked in the top 10 percent of their high school class; 22% were in the top 25 percent, and 69% were in the top half. (Proportion submitting class standing: 76%.) **Average high school grade point average:** 3.1. **First-year students who submitted SAT scores:** 95%. Scores (25/75 percentile): Verbal: 460-550, Math: 450-550, Combined: 910-1100. **First-year students submitting ACT scores:** 4%. Scores (25/75 percentile): English: N/A, Math: N/A, Composite: 18-22.

ACADEMICS

Year founded: 1910. **Academic calendar:** Semester. **Degrees offered:** bachelor's, post-bachelor's certificate, master's, post-master's certificate. **Most popular majors:** 12% multi/interdisciplinary studies, 10% criminal justice/safety studies, 9% marketing/marketing management, 7% business administration and management, 5% psychology. **Major fields of study:** biological and biomedical sciences; business, management, marketing, and related support services; communication, journalism, and related programs; computer and information sciences and support services; education; English language and literature/letters; family and consumer sciences/human sciences; foreign languages, literatures, and linguistics; health professions and related clinical sciences; liberal arts and sciences studies, and humanities; mathematics and statistics; multi/interdisciplinary studies; parks, recreation, leisure, and fitness studies; philosophy and religious studies; physical sciences; psychology; public administration and social service professions; security and protective services; social sciences; visual and performing arts. **Areas of required coursework:** arts/fine arts, humanities, computer literacy, mathematics, English (including composition), philosophy, foreign languages, sciences (biological or physical), history. **Pre-professional programs:** pre-law, pre-dentistry, pre-medicine, pre-veterinary science, pre-pharmacy. **Special academic programs (% participation):** accelerated program (.4%), distance learning (8%), double major (3%), dual enrollment (1%), English as a Second Language (ESL) (.5%), exchange student program (domestic) (.1%), honors program (2%), independent study (2%), internships (69%), study abroad (1%), teacher certificate program (8%). **Teacher certification offered in:** early childhood, special education, elementary, middle/junior high, secondary. **Reserve Officers Training Corps (ROTC):** Army ROTC: Offered on campus. **Faculty and instruction (2005-2006):** Total instructional faculty: 377 full-time, 193 part-time (49% men; 51% women; 8% minorities). Full-time faculty with Ph.D. or other terminal degree: 83%. Student/faculty ratio: 20/1. Classes of fewer than 20 students: 30%; of 20 to 49 students: 64%; of 50 or more students: 6%. **Advanced Placement and International Baccalaureate credit:** AP tests may be used for: Credit and/or placement. Scores accepted: 3, 4, 5. International Baccalaureate exams may be used for: Credit only. **Freshmen returning for sophomore year:** 78%. **Graduation rates:** Four-year: 37%; five-year: 50%; six-year: 54%. **Graduate study:** 8% of students pursue further study immediately upon graduation; 9% within one year; 20% within five years.

COSTS AND FINANCIAL AID

Financial aid office: (540) 831-5408. **Expenses (2006-2007):** Tuition and fees 2006-2007: $5,746 in state, $13,494 out of state; room/board: $6,218. **Financial aid:** Priority filing date for institution's financial aid form: March 1. In 2005-2006, 59% of undergraduates applied for financial aid. Of those, 40% were determined to have financial need; Average financial aid package (proportion receiving): $6,990 (39%). Average amount of gift aid, such as scholarships or grants (proportion receiving): $4,529 (25%). Average amount of self-help aid, such as work study or loans (proportion receiving): $3,678 (35%). Average need-based loan (excluding PLUS or other private loans): $3,481. Among students who received need-based aid, the average percentage of need met: 74%. Among students who received aid based on merit, the average award (and the proportion receiving): $2,787 (3%). The average athletic scholarship (and the proportion receiving): $6,929 (2%). Average amount of debt of borrowers graduating in 2005: $17,264. Proportion who borrowed: 88%.

CAMPUS LIFE AND EXTRACURRICULAR ACTIVITIES

Campus housing available (% using): coed dorms (96%), apartment for single students (4%), special housing for disabled students. Students who live in college-owned, operated, or affiliated housing: 39%. **Student employment:** During the 2005-2006 academic year, 11% of undergraduates worked on campus. Average per-year earnings: $1,627. **Clubs and organizations:** Number of student organizations: 200. Activities include: choral groups, dance, drama/theater, literary magazine, radio station, student government,

student newspaper, television station, yearbook. Number of fraternities: 13; sororities: 11. Proportion of men in fraternities: 6%; of women in sororities: 8%. Average proportion of students who stay on campus on weekends: 70%. **Sports program (2005-2006):** Member of NCAA I. *Men's intercollegiate varsity sports:* baseball, basketball, cross-country, golf, soccer, tennis, track and field (indoor), track and field (outdoor). *Women's intercollegiate varsity sports:* basketball, cross-country, field hockey, golf, soccer, softball, swimming and diving, tennis, track and field (indoor), track and field (outdoor), volleyball.

SERVICES AND FACILITIES

Basic services: nonremedial tutoring, placement service, health service. **Remedial assistance:** reading, math, writing, study skills, other. **Counseling services:** minority student, career, personal, academic, older student, other. **For learning-disabled students:** School does not offer a structured program with separate admission and additional fees. Total undergraduates in learning-disabled program or receiving services: 312. Services include: reading machines, tape recorders, note-taking services, oral tests, learning center, readers, extended time for tests, tutors, early syllabus, priority registration, priority seating, texts on tape, typist/scribe, exams on tape or computer, other testing accomodations. **Library:** Number of titles: 356,675; number of current serial subscriptions: 6,796. **Information technology resources:** Students are not required to lease or own a computer. Number of campus computers available to all students: 620. School has a wireless network. Approximate number of users that can be accommodated: 4,000. Proportion of college-owned housing units wired for high-speed internet access: 100%. **Campus safety:** Security services offered: 24-hour foot-and-vehicle patrols, late-night transport/escort service, 24-hour emergency telephones, lighted pathways/sidewalks, controlled dormitory access (key, security card, etc).

TRANSFER AND INTERNATIONAL STUDENTS

Transfer students: May apply for admission for the following academic terms: Fall, Spring, Summer. Applicants do not need a minimum number of credits to apply. For fall 2005: Transfer applications received: 1,256. Transfer applicants offered admission: 1,090. Transfer applicants enrolled: 677. **International students:** Number of foreign undergraduates: 54 (1% of student body). Number of countries represented: 37. Minimum TOEFL score required: 520 (paper); 190 (computer).

Randolph-Macon College

- **Address:** PO Box 5005, Ashland, VA 23005-5505
- **Website:** http://www.rmc.edu
- **Private; Religious affiliation:** United Methodist
- **Enrollment:** 1,102 full-time; 23 part-time

KEY STATS

✔ **U.S News College Ranking:** 104, Liberal Arts Colleges
✔ **SAT Score (25th/75th percentile):** 1010-1180
✔ **Tuition:** 2006-2007: $25,345

Selectivity: Selective	**Room/board:** $7,695
Acceptance rate: 79%	**Average debt:** $15,130
Student/faculty ratio: 10/1	**Proportion who borrowed:** 70%

UNDERGRADUATE STUDENT BODY STATS

2005-2006 enrollment: 1,102 full-time; 23 part-time. Men: 49%; women: 51%. **Ethnic makeup:** African American: 7%; Asian American: 1%; Hispanic: 1%; White: 89%; International: 1%. **Religious preference:** Roman Catholic: 17%; Protestant: 38%; Jewish: 1%; No preference: 7%; Unknown: 21%; United Methodist: 14%; Other: 2%.

ADMISSIONS FACTS AND FIGURES

Phone: (800) 888-1762. **Email:** admissions@rmc.edu. **Website:** http://www.rmc.edu. **Application deadlines for fall 2007:** Regular decision: March 1; decision sent by April 1. Early decision: Send application by: November 15; Decision sent by: December 1. Early action: Send application by: December 1; Decision sent by: January 1. Admission can be deferred. **Application fee:** $30. Common application is accepted. **To apply online, go to:** http://www.rmc.edu/apply/. **Admissions requirements/recommendations:** High school units required (recommended): English: 4 (4); Mathematics: 3 (4); Science: 3 (4); Foreign language: 2 (4); Social studies: 1

(2); History: 2 (2); Academic electives: 1 (2); Total units: 16 (22). **Tests:** The college uses SAT or ACT scores in admissions decisions. Either SAT or ACT required. For admission to the fall 2007 entering class, the school will accept: ACT without writing. Campus visit: Recommended. Admissions interview: Recommended. Off-campus interview: May be arranged. **Factors that count in admissions decisions:** *Academic:* Secondary school record: Very important. Class rank: Important. Letters of recommendation: Important. Standardized test scores: Important. Essay: Important. *Nonacademic:* Interview: Considered. Extracurricular activities: Considered. Talent/ability: Considered. Character/personal qualities: Considered. Alumni/ae relationship: Considered. Geographical residence: Not considered. State residency: Not considered. Religious affiliation/commitment: Not considered. Minority status: Considered. Volunteer work: Considered. Work experience: Considered. **Other schools with the greatest overlap in applicants:** Christopher Newport University; James Madison University; University of Mary Washington; University of Virginia; Virginia Tech. **Admissions statistics for the fall 2005 entering class:** Total applicants: 1,727. Total accepted: 1,357. Freshmen enrolled: 305; 30% were from out of state. Accepted through early-decision or early-action plans: 9%. Overall acceptance rate: 79%. Early-decision acceptance rate: 79%. Non-early acceptance rate: 79%. **Size of waiting list:** 49 applicants; enrolled from waiting list: 9. **Credentials of fall 2005 freshmen:** 20% ranked in the top 10 percent of their high school class; 43% were in the top 25 percent, and 82% were in the top half. (Proportion submitting class standing: 70%.) **Average high school grade point average:** 3.3. **First-year students who submitted SAT scores:** 82%. Scores (25/75 percentile): Verbal: 510-600, Math: 500-580, Combined: 1010-1180. **First-year students submitting ACT scores:** 21%. Scores (25/75 percentile): English: N/A, Math: N/A, Composite: N/A.

ACADEMICS

Year founded: 1830. **Academic calendar:** 4-1-4. **Degrees offered:** bachelor's. **Most popular majors:** 16% business/managerial economics, 13% sociology, 12% psychology, 11% political science and government, 8% English language and literature. **Major fields of study:** area, ethnic, cultural, and gender studies; biological and biomedical sciences; business, management, marketing, and related support services; computer and information sciences and support services; English language and literature/letters; foreign languages, literatures, and linguistics; history; mathematics and statistics; multi/interdisciplinary studies; natural resources and conservation; philosophy and religious studies; physical sciences; psychology; social sciences; visual and performing arts. **Areas of required coursework:** arts/fine arts, humanities, computer literacy, mathematics, English (including composition), foreign languages, sciences (biological or physical), history, social science, other. **Pre-professional programs:** pre-law, pre-dentistry, pre-medicine, pre-theology, pre-veterinary science, pre-pharmacy, other. **Special academic programs (% participation):** accelerated program (4%), cross-registration (1%), double major (11%), exchange student program (domestic) (1%), honors program (10%), independent study (5%), internships (60%), study abroad (50%), teacher certificate program (5%). **Teacher certification offered in:** elementary, middle/junior high, secondary. **Reserve Officers Training Corps (ROTC):** Army ROTC: Offered at cooperating institution (University of Richmond). **Faculty and instruction (2005-2006):** Total instructional faculty: 90 full-time, 53 part-time (53% men; 47% women; 7% minorities). Full-time faculty with Ph.D. or other terminal degree: 96%. Student/faculty ratio: 10/1. Classes of fewer than 20 students: 74%; of 20 to 49 students: 26%; of 50 or more students: 0%. **Advanced Placement and International Baccalaureate credit:** AP tests may be used for: Credit and/or placement. Scores accepted: 4, 5. International Baccalaureate exams may be used for: Credit and/or placement. **Freshmen returning for sophomore year:** 75%. **Graduation rates:** Four-year: 62%; five-year: 73%; six-year: 74%. **Graduate study:** 27% of students pursue further study immediately upon graduation; 30% within one year; 70% within five years. Fields in which graduates pursue further study: Master of Business Administration (MBA), 10%; law, 15%; medicine, 10%; dentistry, 5%; theology (or the seminary), 1%; education, 8%; arts and sciences, 50%; veterinary medicine, 1%.

COSTS AND FINANCIAL AID

Financial aid office: (804) 752-7259. **Expenses (2006-2007):** Tuition and fees 2006-2007: $25,345; room/board: $7,695. Estimated books and supplies: $1,000; transportation: $780; personal expenses: $720. **Financial aid:** Priority filing date for institution's financial aid form: February 1; deadline: March 1. In 2005-2006, 72% of undergraduates applied for financial aid. Of those, 60% were determined to have financial need; 24% had their need fully met. Average financial aid package (proportion receiving): $17,459 (60%). Average amount of gift aid, such as scholarships or grants (proportion receiving): $12,821 (60%). Average amount of self-help aid, such as

work study or loans (proportion receiving): $5,668 (49%). Average need-based loan (excluding PLUS or other private loans): $4,996. Among students who received need-based aid, the average percentage of need met: 82%. Among students who received aid based on merit, the average award (and the proportion receiving): $12,387 (36%). The average athletic scholarship (and the proportion receiving): $0 (0%). Average amount of debt of borrowers graduating in 2005: $15,130. Proportion who borrowed: 70%.

CAMPUS LIFE AND EXTRACURRICULAR ACTIVITIES

Campus housing available (% using): coed dorms (51%), women's dorms (14%), men's dorms (8%), sorority housing (5%), fraternity housing (8%), apartment for single students (6%), special housing for disabled students (2%), special housing for international students (0%), other housing options (6%). Students who live in college-owned, operated, or affiliated housing: 85%. **Student employment:** During the 2005-2006 academic year, 44% of undergraduates worked on campus. Average per-year earnings: $1,100. **Clubs and organizations:** Number of student organizations: 104. Activities include: choral groups, dance, drama/theater, jazz band, literary magazine, musical theater, pep band, radio station, student government, student newspaper, student film society, yearbook. Number of fraternities: 6; sororities: 4. Proportion of men in fraternities: 35%; of women in sororities: 36%. Average proportion of students who stay on campus on weekends: 80%. **Sports program (2005-2006):** Member of NCAA III. *Men's intercollegiate varsity sports:* baseball, basketball, football, golf, lacrosse, soccer, swimming and diving, tennis. *Women's intercollegiate varsity sports:* basketball, field hockey, soccer, softball, swimming and diving, tennis, volleyball.

SERVICES AND FACILITIES

Basic services: nonremedial tutoring, women's center, placement service, health service, health insurance. **Remedial assistance:** reading, math, writing, study skills. **Counseling services:** minority student, career, personal, academic, psychological, religious. **For learning-disabled students:** School does not offer a structured program with separate admission and additional fees. Total undergraduates in learning-disabled program or receiving services: 70. Services include: reading machines, tape recorders, untimed tests, note-taking services, oral tests, learning center, extended time for tests, tutors, substitution of courses, texts on tape, exams on tape or computer, other testing accomodations. **Library:** Number of titles: 184,872; number of current serial subscriptions: 1,467. **Information technology resources:** Students are not required to lease or own a computer. Number of campus computers available to all students: 350. School has a wireless network. Approximate number of users that can be accommodated: 50. Proportion of college-owned housing units wired for high-speed internet access: 100%. **Campus safety:** Security services offered: 24-hour foot-and-vehicle patrols, late-night transport/escort service, 24-hour emergency telephones, lighted pathways/sidewalks, controlled dormitory access (key, security card, etc).

TRANSFER AND INTERNATIONAL STUDENTS

Transfer students: May apply for admission for the following academic terms: Fall, Spring. Applicants do not need a minimum number of credits to apply. For fall 2005: Transfer applications received: 125. Transfer applicants offered admission: 56. Transfer applicants enrolled: 29. **International students:** Number of foreign undergraduates: 13 (1% of student body). Number of countries represented: 17. Minimum TOEFL score required: 550 (paper); 213 (computer).

Randolph-Macon Woman's College

- **Address:** 2500 Rivermont Avenue, Lynchburg, VA 24503-1526
- **Website:** http://www.rmwc.edu
- **Private; Religious affiliation:** United Methodist
- **Enrollment:** 685 full-time; 27 part-time

KEY STATS

✔ **U.S News College Ranking:** 86, Liberal Arts Colleges
✔ **SAT Score (25th/75th percentile):** 1050-1300
✔ **Tuition:** 2006-2007: $24,380

Selectivity: More selective   **Room/board:** $8,800
Acceptance rate: 87%   **Average debt:** $25,500
Student/faculty ratio: 9/1   **Proportion who borrowed:** 70%

UNDERGRADUATE STUDENT BODY STATS

2005-2006 enrollment: 685 full-time; 27 part-time. Men: 0%; women: 100%. **Ethnic makeup:** African American: 9%; American-Indian: 1%; Asian American: 3%; Hispanic: 4%; White: 74%; International: 10%. **Religious preference:** Roman Catholic: 14%; Protestant: 38%; Jewish: 2%; Muslim: 1%; Hindu: 1%; Buddhist: 1%; No preference: 11%; Unknown: 20%; United Methodist: 9%; Other: 3%.

ADMISSIONS FACTS AND FIGURES

Phone: (800) 745-7692. **Email:** admissions@rmwc.edu. **Website:** http://www.rmwc.edu. **Application deadlines for fall 2007:** Regular decision: Rolling. Early decision: Send application by: November 15; Decision sent by: December 15. Early action: Not offered. Admission can be deferred. **Application fee:** $35. Common application is accepted. **To apply online, go to:** http://www.rmwc.edu/admissions/apply.asp. **Admissions requirements/recommendations:** High school units required (recommended): English: 4 (4); Mathematics: 3 (3); Science: 2 (3); Foreign language: 2 (3); Social studies: 0 (0); History: 2 (2); Academic electives: 1 (2); Total units: 16 (16). Tests: The college uses SAT or ACT scores in admissions decisions. Either SAT or ACT required. For admission to the fall 2007 entering class, the school will accept: ACT with writing, ACT without writing. Campus visit: Recommended. Admissions interview: Recommended. Off-campus interview: May be arranged. **Factors that count in admissions decisions:** *Academic:* Secondary school record: Very important. Class rank: Considered. Letters of recommendation: Important. Standardized test scores: Important. Essay: Important. *Nonacademic:* Interview: Considered. Extracurricular activities: Considered. Talent/ability: Considered. Character/personal qualities: Very important. Alumni/ae relationship: Considered. Geographical residence: Not considered. State residency: Not considered. Religious affiliation/commitment: Not considered. Minority status: Not considered. Volunteer work: Important. Work experience: Considered. **Other schools with the greatest overlap in applicants:** College of William and Mary; Hollins University; Sweet Briar College; University of Mary Washington; University of Virginia. **Admissions statistics for the fall 2005 entering class:** Total applicants: 774. Total accepted: 675. Freshmen enrolled: 184; 65% were from out of state. Accepted through early-decision or early-action plans: 7%. Overall acceptance rate: 87%. Early-decision acceptance rate: 84%. Non-early acceptance rate: 87%. **Size of waiting list:** 0 applicants; enrolled from waiting list: 0. **Credentials of fall 2005 freshmen:** 36% ranked in the top 10 percent of their high school class; 70% were in the top 25 percent, and 93% were in the top half. (Proportion submitting class standing: 58%.) **Average high school grade point average:** 3.4. **First-year students who submitted SAT scores:** 90%. Scores (25/75 percentile): Verbal: 540-670, Math: 510-630, Combined: 1050-1300. **First-year students submitting ACT scores:** 21%. Scores (25/75 percentile): English: 22-31, Math: 21-27, Composite: 23-29.

ACADEMICS

Year founded: 1891. **Academic calendar:** Semester. **Degrees offered:** bachelor's, master's. **Most popular majors:** 14% biology, 12% political science and government, 11% psychology, 10% communication studies/speech communication and rhetoric, 10% history. **Major fields of study:** area, ethnic, cultural, and gender studies; biological and biomedical sciences; communication, journalism, and related programs; education; engineering; English language and literature/letters; foreign languages, literatures, and linguistics; history; mathematics and statistics; multi/interdisciplinary studies; philosophy and religious studies; physical sciences; psychology; social sciences; visual and performing arts. **Areas of required coursework:** arts/fine arts, humanities, mathematics, English (including composition), philosophy, foreign languages, sciences (biological or physical), history, social science, other. **Pre-professional programs:** pre-law, pre-medicine, pre-veterinary science. **Special academic programs (% participation):** accelerated program (5%), cross-registration (9%), double major (13%), dual enrollment (0%), exchange student program (domestic) (1%), honors program (8%), independent study (7%), internships (34%), liberal arts/career combination (1%), student-designed major (2%), study abroad (46%), teacher certificate program (6%), other (0%). **Teacher certification offered in:** early childhood, special education, elementary, secondary. **Faculty and instruction (2005-2006):** Total instructional faculty: 72 full-time, 18 part-time (39% men; 61% women; 10% minorities). Full-time faculty with Ph.D. or other terminal degree: 94%. Student/faculty ratio: 9/1. Classes of fewer than 20 students: 82%; of 20 to 49 students: 18%; of 50 or more students: 0%. **Advanced Placement and International Baccalaureate credit:** AP tests may be used for: Credit and/or placement. Scores accepted: 3, 4, 5. International Baccalaureate exams may be used for: Credit and/or placement. **Freshmen returning for sophomore year:** 78%. **Graduation rates:** Four-year: 63%; five-year: 63%; six-year: 63%. **Graduate study:** 20% of students pursue further study immediately upon graduation; 40% within five years. Fields in which graduates pursue further study: Master of Business Administration (MBA), 2%; law, 10%; medicine, 6%; engineering, 1%; theology (or the seminary), 2%; education, 20%; arts and sciences, 55%; veterinary medicine, 6%.

COSTS AND FINANCIAL AID

Financial aid office: (434) 947-8128. **Expenses (2006-2007):** Tuition and fees 2006-2007: $24,380; room/board: $8,800. Estimated books and supplies: $800; transportation: $500; personal expenses: $1,000. **Financial aid:** Priority filing date for institution's financial aid form: March 1. In 2005-2006, 75% of undergraduates applied for financial aid. Of those, 67% were determined to have financial need; 36% had their need fully met. Average financial aid package (proportion receiving): $21,368 (67%). Average amount of gift aid, such as scholarships or grants (proportion receiving): $16,016 (67%). Average amount of self-help aid, such as work study or loans (proportion receiving): $5,663 (56%). Average need-based loan (excluding PLUS or other private loans): $4,379. Among students who received need-based aid, the average percentage of need met: 88%. Among students who received aid based on merit, the average award (and the proportion receiving): $14,855 (33%). The average athletic scholarship (and the proportion receiving): $0 (0%). Average amount of debt of borrowers graduating in 2005: $25,500. Proportion who borrowed: 70%.

CAMPUS LIFE AND EXTRACURRICULAR ACTIVITIES

Campus housing available (% using): women's dorms (96%), other housing options (4%). Students who live in college-owned, operated, or affiliated housing: 88%. **Student employment:** During the 2005-2006 academic year, 65% of undergraduates worked on campus. Average per-year earnings: $1,860. **Clubs and organizations:** Number of student organizations: 40. Activities include: choral groups, dance, drama/theater, literary magazine, music ensembles, opera, radio station, student government, student newspaper, student film society, yearbook. Number of fraternities: 0; sororities: 0. Average proportion of students who stay on campus on weekends: 60%. **Sports program (2005-2006):** Member of NCAA III. *Women's intercollegiate varsity sports:* basketball, equestrian sports, field hockey, soccer, softball, swimming and diving, tennis, volleyball.

SERVICES AND FACILITIES

Basic services: nonremedial tutoring, health service. **Remedial assistance:** writing, study skills. **Counseling services:** minority student, career, personal, academic, older student, psychological, birth control. **For learning-disabled students:** School does not offer a structured program with separate admission and additional fees. Total undergraduates in learning-disabled program or receiving services: 18. Services include: reading machines, tape recorders, other special classes, note-taking services, oral tests, learning center, readers, extended time for tests, tutors, early syllabus, priority registration, priority seating, proofreading services, substitution of courses, texts on tape, typist/scribe, exams on tape or computer, other testing accomodations, other. **Library:** Number of titles: 198,000; number of current serial subscriptions: 520. **Information technology resources:** Students are not required to lease or own a computer. Number of campus computers available to all students: 150. School has a wireless network. Approximate number of users that can be accommodated: 100. Proportion of college-owned housing units wired for high-speed internet access: 100%. **Campus safety:** Security services offered: 24-hour foot-and-vehicle patrols, late-night transport/escort service, 24-hour emergency telephones, lighted pathways/sidewalks, controlled dormitory access (key, security card, etc).

TRANSFER AND INTERNATIONAL STUDENTS

Transfer students: May apply for admission for the following academic terms: Fall, Spring. Applicants need a minimum number of credits to apply. For fall 2005: Transfer applications received: 47. Transfer applicants offered admission: 45. Transfer applicants enrolled: 29. **International students:** Number of foreign undergraduates: 65 (10% of student body). Number of countries represented: 29. Minimum TOEFL score required: 550 (paper); 213 (computer). Average TOEFL score: 600 (paper).

Regent University

■ **Address:** 1000 Regent University Drive, Virginia Beach, VA 23464-5037
■ **Website:** http://www.regent.edu
■ **Private**
■ **Enrollment:** 496 full-time; 1,022 part-time

KEY STATS

✔ **U.S News College Ranking:** Unranked, Universities–Master's (South)
✔ **ACT Score:** 19
✔ **Tuition:** 2006-2007: $12,000

Selectivity: N/A	**Room/board:** N/A
Acceptance rate: 60%	**Average debt:** N/A
Student/faculty ratio: 20/1	**Proportion who borrowed:** N/A

UNDERGRADUATE STUDENT BODY STATS

2005-2006 enrollment: 496 full-time; 1,022 part-time. Men: 40%; women: 60%. **Ethnic makeup:** African American: 25%; American-Indian: 1%; Asian American: 2%; Hispanic: 4%; White: 69%; International: 1%. **Religious preference:** Roman Catholic: 4%; Protestant: 58%; Unknown: 8%; None: 30%.

ADMISSIONS FACTS AND FIGURES

Phone: (757) 226-4127. **Email:** admissions@regent.edu. **Website:** http://www.regent.edu. **Application deadlines for fall 2007:** Regular decision: Rolling; decision sent by July 31. Early decision: Not offered. Early action: Not offered. Admission can be deferred. **Application fee:** $40. Common application is not accepted. **Admissions requirements/recommendations:** Tests: The college uses SAT or ACT scores in admissions decisions. Neither SAT nor ACT required. For admission to the fall 2007 entering class, the school will accept: ACT with writing, ACT without writing. Campus visit: Neither required nor recommended. Admissions interview: Neither required nor recommended. Off-campus interview: Not available. **Factors that count in admissions decisions:** *Academic:* Secondary school record: Not considered. Class rank: Not considered. Letters of recommendation: Considered. Standardized test scores: Very important. Essay: Important. *Nonacademic:* Religious affiliation/commitment: Important. Work experience: Important. **Other schools with the greatest overlap in applicants:** Norfolk State University; Old Dominion University; University of Maryland–University College. **Admissions statistics for the fall 2005 entering class:** Total applicants: 1,495. Total accepted: 900. Freshmen enrolled: 94; 45% were from out of state. Overall acceptance rate: 60%. **Average high school grade point average:** 2.9.

ACADEMICS

Year founded: 1977. **Academic calendar:** Semester. **Degrees offered:** certificate, bachelor's, post-bachelor's certificate, master's, post-master's certificate, first professional, doctorate. **Most popular majors:** 82% organizational behavior studies, 10% divinity/ministry (B.D., M.Div.), 8% education. **Major fields of study:** business, management, marketing, and related support services; communication, journalism, and related programs; education; theology and religious vocations. **Areas of required coursework:** arts/fine arts, humanities, computer literacy, mathematics, English (including composition), sciences (biological or physical), history, social science. **Pre-professional programs:** pre-theology. **Special academic programs (% participation):** accelerated program (100%), distance learning (50%), independent study, internships (12%), study abroad, teacher certificate program (12%). **Teacher certification offered in:** elementary. **Faculty and instruction (2005-2006):** Total instructional faculty: 10 full-time, 89 part-time (52% men; 48% women; 32% minorities). Full-time faculty with Ph.D. or other terminal degree: 50%. Student/faculty ratio: 20/1. **Advanced Placement and International Baccalaureate credit:** Scores accepted: 3. International Baccalaureate exams may be used for: Credit only.

COSTS AND FINANCIAL AID

Financial aid office: (757) 226-4125. **Expenses (2006-2007):** Tuition and fees 2006-2007: $12,000; room/board: N/A. Estimated books and supplies: $552; transportation: $2,403. **Financial aid:** Priority filing date for institution's financial aid form: March 15. The average athletic scholarship (and the proportion receiving): $0 (N/A).

CAMPUS LIFE AND EXTRACURRICULAR ACTIVITIES

Campus housing available (% using): apartments for married students (50%), apartment for single students (50%). Students who live in college-owned, operated, or affiliated housing: 0%. **Clubs and organizations:** Number of student organizations: 25. Activities include: student government. Number of fraternities: 0; sororities: 0. Average proportion of students who stay on campus on weekends: 95%.

SERVICES AND FACILITIES

Remedial assistance: writing. **Counseling services:** career, personal, academic, older student, psychological, religious. **For learning-disabled students:** School does not offer a structured program with separate admission and additional fees. **Library:** Number of titles: 1,039,089; number of current serial subscriptions: 1,155. **Information technology resources:** Students are not required to lease or own a computer. Number of campus computers available to all students: 130. School has a wireless network. Approximate number of users that can be accommodated: 420. Proportion of college-owned housing units wired for high-speed internet access: 0%. **Campus safety:** Security services offered: 24-hour foot-and-vehicle patrols, 24-hour emergency telephones, lighted pathways/sidewalks.

TRANSFER AND INTERNATIONAL STUDENTS

Transfer students: May apply for admission for the following academic terms: Fall, Spring, Summer. Applicants need a minimum number of credits to apply. For fall 2005: Transfer applications received: 532. Transfer applicants offered admission: 393. Transfer applicants enrolled: 332. **International students:** Number of foreign undergraduates: 6 (1% of student body). Number of countries represented: 5. Minimum TOEFL score required: 577 (paper); 233 (computer).

Roanoke College

■ **Address:** 221 College Lane, Salem, VA 24153-3794
■ **Website:** http://www.roanoke.edu
■ **Private; Religious affiliation:** Lutheran
■ **Enrollment:** 1,833 full-time; 103 part-time

KEY STATS

✔ **U.S News College Ranking:** third tier, Liberal Arts Colleges
✔ **SAT Score (25th/75th percentile):** 1030-1210
✔ **Tuition:** 2006-2007: $24,653

Selectivity: Selective	**Room/board:** $8,152
Acceptance rate: 74%	**Average debt:** $18,543
Student/faculty ratio: 14/1	**Proportion who borrowed:** 72%

UNDERGRADUATE STUDENT BODY STATS

2005-2006 enrollment: 1,833 full-time; 103 part-time. Men: 44%; women: 56%. **Ethnic makeup:** African American: 4%; American-Indian: 1%; Asian American: 2%; Hispanic: 2%; White: 91%; International: 1%. **Religious preference:** Roman Catholic: 18%; Protestant: 45%; Jewish: 1%; No preference: 16%; Unknown: 8%; Lutheran: 8%; Other: 4%.

ADMISSIONS FACTS AND FIGURES

Phone: (540) 375-2270. **Email:** admissions@roanoke.edu. **Website:** http://www.roanoke.edu. **Application deadlines for fall 2007:** Regular decision: March 15; decision sent by April 1. Early decision: Not offered. Early action: Not offered. Admission can be deferred. **Application fee:** $30. Common application is accepted. **To apply online, go to:** http://web.roanoke.edu/x218.xml. **Admissions requirements/recommendations:** High school units required (recommended): English: 4; Mathematics: 3; Science: 2; Foreign language: (4); Social studies: 2; Academic electives: 5; Total units: 18. Tests: The college uses SAT or ACT scores in admissions decisions. Either SAT or ACT required. For admission to the fall 2007 entering class, the school will accept: ACT with writing, ACT without writing. Campus visit: Recommended. Admissions interview: Recommended. Off-campus interview: May be arranged. **Factors that count in admissions decisions:** *Academic:* Secondary school record: Very important. Class rank: Very important. Letters of recommendation: Important. Standardized test scores: Very important. Essay: Considered. *Nonacademic:* Interview: Important. Extracurricular activities: Important. Talent/ability: Considered. Character/personal qualities: Very important. Alumni/ae relationship: Considered. Geographical residence: Not considered. State residency: Not considered. Religious affiliation/commitment: Not considered. Minority status: Considered. Volunteer work: Considered. Work experience: Considered. Admissions statistics for the fall 2005 entering class: Total applicants: 3,016. Total accepted: 2,220. Freshmen enrolled: 534; 46% were from out of state. Overall acceptance rate: 74%. Size of waiting list: 172 applicants; enrolled from waiting list: 3. Credentials of fall 2005 freshmen: 23% ranked in the top 10 percent of their high school class; 50% were in the top 25 percent, and 85% were in the top half. (Proportion submitting class standing: 56%.) Average high school grade point average: 3.2. First-year students who submitted SAT scores: 84%. Scores (25/75 percentile): Verbal: 520-610, Math: 510-600, Combined: 1030-1210. First-year students submitting ACT scores: 16%. Scores (25/75 percentile): English: N/A, Math: N/A, Composite: N/A.

ACADEMICS

Year founded: 1842. Academic calendar: Semester. Degrees offered: bachelor's. Most popular majors: 22% business administration and management, 12% English language and literature, 11% history, 9% social sciences, 8% psychology. Major fields of study: biological and biomedical sciences; business, management, marketing, and related support services; computer and information sciences and support services; English language and literature/letters; foreign languages, literatures, and linguistics; health professions and related clinical sciences; history; mathematics and statistics; natural resources and conservation; parks, recreation, leisure, and fitness studies; philosophy and religious studies; physical sciences; psychology; security and protective services; social sciences; theology and religious vocations; visual and performing arts. Areas of required coursework: arts/fine arts, humanities, computer literacy, mathematics, English (including composition), philosophy, foreign languages, sciences (biological or physical), history, social science, other. Pre-professional programs: pre-law, pre-dentistry, pre-medicine, pre-theology, pre-veterinary science, pre-pharmacy. Special academic programs: accelerated program, cross-registration, double major, dual enrollment, English as a Second Language (ESL), external degree program, honors program, independent study, internships, liberal arts/career combination, study abroad, teacher certificate program. Teacher certification offered in: elementary, secondary. Faculty and instruction (2005-2006): Total instructional faculty: 133 full-time, 41 part-time (53% men; 47% women; 9% minorities). Full-time faculty with Ph.D. or other terminal degree: 84%. Student/faculty ratio: 14/1. Classes of fewer than 20 students: 57%; of 20 to 49 students: 43%; of 50 or more students: 0%. Advanced Placement and International Baccalaureate credit: AP tests may be used for: Credit and/or placement. Scores accepted: 3, 4, 5. International Baccalaureate exams may be used for: Credit and/or placement. Freshmen returning for sophomore year: 79%. Graduation rates: Four-year: 57%; five-year: 64%; six-year: 65%. Graduate study: 40% of students pursue further study within five years.

COSTS AND FINANCIAL AID

Financial aid office: (540) 375-2235. Expenses (2006-2007): Tuition and fees 2006-2007: $24,653; room/board: $8,152. Estimated books and supplies: $850; transportation: $1,000; personal expenses: $750. Financial aid: Priority filing date for institution's financial aid form: March 1. In 2005-2006, 79% of undergraduates applied for financial aid. Of those, 73% were determined to have financial need; 30% had their need fully met. Average financial aid package (proportion receiving): $18,931 (73%). Average amount of gift aid, such as scholarships or grants (proportion receiving): $15,168 (61%). Average amount of self-help aid, such as work study or loans (proportion receiving): $5,093 (44%). Average need-based loan (excluding PLUS or other private loans): $4,267. Among students who received need-based aid, the average percentage of need met: 89%. Among students who received aid based on merit, the average award (and the proportion receiving): $10,255 (23%). Average amount of debt of borrowers graduating in 2005: $18,543. Proportion who borrowed: 72%.

CAMPUS LIFE AND EXTRACURRICULAR ACTIVITIES

Campus housing available: coed dorms, women's dorms, men's dorms, sorority housing, fraternity housing, apartment for single students, other housing options. Students who live in college-owned, operated, or affiliated housing: 65%. Student employment: During the 2005-2006 academic year, 30% of undergraduates worked on campus. Average per-year earnings: $1,500. Clubs and organizations: Number of student organizations: 85. Activities include: choral groups, dance, drama/theater, jazz band, literary magazine, music ensembles, musical theater, pep band, radio station, student government, student newspaper, student film society, yearbook. Number of fraternities: 4; sororities: 4. Proportion of men in fraternities: 22%; of women in sororities: 27%. Sports program (2005-2006): Member of NCAA III. Men's intercollegiate varsity sports: baseball, basketball, cross-

country, golf, lacrosse, soccer, tennis, track and field (indoor), track and field (outdoor). Women's intercollegiate varsity sports: basketball, cross-country, field hockey, lacrosse, soccer, softball, tennis, track and field (indoor), track and field (outdoor), volleyball.

SERVICES AND FACILITIES

Basic services: nonremedial tutoring, placement service, health service. Remedial assistance: study skills. Counseling services: minority student, career, personal, academic, older student, psychological, religious. For learning-disabled students: School does not offer a structured program with separate admission and additional fees. Services include: other testing accommodations, tape recorders, untimed tests, note-taking services, oral tests, learning center, extended time for tests, tutors, other testing accommodations. Library: Number of titles: 215,000; number of current serial subscriptions: 3,791. Information technology resources: Students are not required to lease or own a computer. Number of campus computers available to all students: 170. School has a wireless network. Proportion of college-owned housing units wired for high-speed internet access: 100%. Campus safety: Security services offered: 24-hour foot-and-vehicle patrols, late-night transport/escort service, 24-hour emergency telephones, lighted pathways/sidewalks, controlled dormitory access (key, security card, etc).

TRANSFER AND INTERNATIONAL STUDENTS

Transfer students: May apply for admission for the following academic terms: Fall, Spring, Summer. Applicants need a minimum number of credits to apply. For fall 2005: Transfer applications received: 306. Transfer applicants offered admission: 161. Transfer applicants enrolled: 80. International students: Number of foreign undergraduates: 25 (1% of student body). Number of countries represented: 26. Minimum TOEFL score required: 520 (paper); 190 (computer).

Shenandoah University

- Address: 1460 University Drive, Winchester, VA 22601
- Website: http://www.su.edu
- Private; Religious affiliation: United Methodist
- Enrollment: 1,530 full-time; 76 part-time

KEY STATS

✔ U.S News College Ranking: 47, Universities–Master's (South)
✔ SAT Score (25th/75th percentile): 900-1160
✔ Tuition: 2006-2007: $21,290

Selectivity: Selective	Room/board: $7,650
Acceptance rate: 70%	Average debt: $21,125
Student/faculty ratio: 8/1	Proportion who borrowed: 85%

UNDERGRADUATE STUDENT BODY STATS

2005-2006 enrollment: 1,530 full-time; 76 part-time. Men: 40%; women: 60%. Ethnic makeup: African American: 2%; Asian American: 1%; White: 93%; International: 4%. Religious preference: Roman Catholic: 16%; Protestant: 29%; Jewish: 1%; No preference: 42%; United Methodist: 10%; Orthodox: 0%; Other: 2%.

ADMISSIONS FACTS AND FIGURES

Phone: (540) 665-4581. Email: admit@su.edu. Website: http://www.su.edu. Application deadlines for fall 2007: Regular decision: Rolling. Early decision: Not offered. Early action: Not offered. Admission can be deferred. Application fee: $30. Common application is accepted. To apply online, go to: http://www.su.edu/apps.htm. Admissions requirements/recommendations: High school units required (recommended): English: 4; Mathematics: 3 (4); Science: 2 (4); Foreign language: 2 (3); Social studies: 2; History: 2; Academic electives: 2 (4); Total units: 15. Tests: The college uses SAT or ACT scores in admissions decisions. Either SAT or ACT required. For admission to the fall 2007 entering class, the school will accept: ACT with writing, ACT without writing. Campus visit: Recommended. Admissions interview: Recommended. Off-campus interview: May be arranged. Factors that count in admissions decisions: Academic: Secondary school record: Very important. Class rank: Not considered. Letters of recommendation: Important. Standardized test scores: Important. Essay: Considered. Nonacademic: Interview: Very important. Extracurricular activities: Important. Talent/ability: Very important. Character/personal qualities: Considered. Alumni/ae relationship: Not considered. Geographical residence: Not considered. State residency: Not considered. Religious affiliation/commitment: Not considered. Minority status: Not considered. Volunteer work: Important. Work experience: Considered. **Other schools with the greatest overlap in applicants:** Bridgewater College; Christopher Newport University; George Mason University; James Madison University; Lynchburg College. **Admissions statistics for the fall 2005 entering class:** Total applicants: 1,479. Total accepted: 1,036. Freshmen enrolled: 370; 45% were from out of state. Overall acceptance rate: 70%. **Size of waiting list:** 5 applicants; enrolled from waiting list: 0. **Credentials of fall 2005 freshmen:** 17% ranked in the top 10 percent of their high school class; 40% were in the top 25 percent, and 71% were in the top half. (Proportion submitting class standing: 69%.) **Average high school grade point average:** 3.2. **First-year students who submitted SAT scores:** 94%. Scores (25/75 percentile): Verbal: 450-580, Math: 450-580, Combined: 900-1160. **First-year students submitting ACT scores:** 14%. Scores (25/75 percentile): English: 16-24, Math: 17-23, Composite: 17-24.

ACADEMICS

Year founded: 1875. **Academic calendar:** Semester. **Degrees offered:** certificate, diploma, associate, bachelor's, post-bachelor's certificate, master's, post-master's certificate, first professional, doctorate. **Most popular majors:** 29% visual and performing arts, 17% business, management, marketing, and related support services, 15% education, 13% health professions and related clinical sciences, 6% biological and biomedical sciences. **Major fields of study:** area, ethnic, cultural, and gender studies; biological and biomedical sciences; business, management, marketing, and related support services; communication, journalism, and related programs; education; English language and literature/letters; foreign languages, literatures, and linguistics; health professions and related clinical sciences; history; liberal arts and sciences studies, and humanities; mathematics and statistics; natural resources and conservation; philosophy and religious studies; physical sciences; psychology; public administration and social service professions; security and protective services; social sciences; visual and performing arts. **Areas of required coursework:** humanities, computer literacy, mathematics, English (including composition), philosophy, foreign languages, sciences (biological or physical), history, social science, other. **Pre-professional programs:** pre-law, pre-dentistry, pre-medicine, pre-theology, pre-veterinary science, pre-pharmacy, other. **Special academic programs:** accelerated program, cooperative (work-study plan) program, distance learning, double major, dual enrollment, English as a Second Language (ESL), independent study, internships, liberal arts/career combination, student-designed major, study abroad, teacher certificate program. **Teacher certification offered in:** elementary, middle/junior high, secondary. **Cooperative education programs:** health professions. **Faculty and instruction (2005-2006):** Total instructional faculty: 194 full-time, 165 part-time (48% men; 52% women; 8% minorities). Full-time faculty with Ph.D. or other terminal degree: 79%. Student/faculty ratio: 8/1. Classes of fewer than 20 students: 63%; of 20 to 49 students: 36%; of 50 or more students: 1%. **Advanced Placement and International Baccalaureate credit:** AP tests may be used for: Credit only. Scores accepted: 3, 4, 5. International Baccalaureate exams may be used for: Credit only. **Freshmen returning for sophomore year:** 70%. **Graduation rates:** Four-year: 31%; five-year: 38%; six-year: 43%. **Graduate study:** 15% of students pursue further study immediately upon graduation; 20% within one year; 40% within five years. Fields in which graduates pursue further study: Master of Business Administration (MBA), 5%; law, 1%; medicine, 1%; theology (or the seminary), 1%; education, 20%; arts and sciences, 10%.

COSTS AND FINANCIAL AID

Financial aid office: (540) 665-4538. **Expenses (2006-2007):** Tuition and fees 2006-2007: $21,290; room/board: $7,650. Estimated books and supplies: $1,000; transportation: $600; personal expenses: $1,500. **Financial aid:** Priority filing date for institution's financial aid form: February 15. In 2005-2006, 61% of undergraduates applied for financial aid. Of those, 61% were determined to have financial need; 18% had their need fully met. Average financial aid package (proportion receiving): $14,013 (61%). Average amount of gift aid, such as scholarships or grants (proportion receiving): $7,053 (54%). Average amount of self-help aid, such as work study or loans (proportion receiving): $6,650 (52%). Average need-based loan (excluding PLUS or other private loans): $5,702. Among students who received need-based aid, the average percentage of need met: 85%. Among students who received aid based on merit, the average award (and the proportion receiving): $3,950 (10%). The average athletic scholarship (and the proportion receiving): $0 (0%). Average amount of debt of borrowers graduating in 2005: $21,125. Proportion who borrowed: 85%.

CAMPUS LIFE AND EXTRACURRICULAR ACTIVITIES

Campus housing available (% using): coed dorms (100%), special housing for disabled students, special housing for international students. Students who live in college-owned, operated, or affiliated housing: 45%. **Student employment:** During the 2005-2006 academic year, 3% of undergraduates worked on campus. Average per-year earnings: $940. **Clubs and organizations:** Number of student organizations: 51. Activities include: choral groups, concert band, dance, drama/theater, jazz band, literary magazine, music ensembles, musical theater, opera, radio station, student government, student newspaper, symphony orchestra, television station. Number of fraternities: 0; sororities: 0. Proportion of men in fraternities: 2%; Average proportion of students who stay on campus on weekends: 65%. **Sports program (2005-2006):** Member of NCAA III. *Men's intercollegiate varsity sports:* baseball, basketball, cross-country, football, golf, lacrosse, soccer, tennis. *Women's intercollegiate varsity sports:* basketball, cross-country, field hockey, lacrosse, soccer, softball, tennis, volleyball.

SERVICES AND FACILITIES

Basic services: nonremedial tutoring, placement service, day care, health service, health insurance. **Remedial assistance:** math, study skills. **Counseling services:** minority student, career, military, personal, veteran student, academic, older student, psychological, birth control, religious. **For learning-disabled students:** School does not offer a structured program with separate admission and additional fees. Total undergraduates in learning-disabled program or receiving services: 40. Services include: remedial math, reading machines, tape recorders, other special classes, videotaped classes, note-taking services, oral tests, learning center, readers, extended time for tests, tutors, priority registration, priority seating, texts on tape, typist/scribe, other testing accomodations, other. **Library:** Number of titles: 127,164; number of current serial subscriptions: 1,621. **Information technology resources:** Students are not required to lease or own a computer. Number of campus computers available to all students: 175. School has a wireless network. Approximate number of users that can be accommodated: 3,500. Proportion of college-owned housing units wired for high-speed internet access: 100%. **Campus safety:** Security services offered: 24-hour foot-and-vehicle patrols, late-night transport/escort service, 24-hour emergency telephones, lighted pathways/sidewalks, student patrols, controlled dormitory access (key, security card, etc).

TRANSFER AND INTERNATIONAL STUDENTS

Transfer students: May apply for admission for the following academic terms: Fall, Spring, Summer. Applicants do not need a minimum number of credits to apply. For fall 2005: Transfer applications received: 582. Transfer applicants offered admission: 423. Transfer applicants enrolled: 206. **International students:** Number of foreign undergraduates: 55 (4% of student body). Number of countries represented: 27. Minimum TOEFL score required: 527 (paper); 197 (computer).

St. Paul's College

- **Address:** 115 College Drive, Lawrenceville, VA 23868
- **Website:** http://www.saintpauls.edu
- **Private; Religious affiliation:** Episcopal
- **Enrollment:** 690 full-time; 27 part-time

KEY STATS

✔ **U.S News College Ranking:** fourth tier, Comp. Coll.–Bachelor's (South)
✔ **SAT Score (25th/75th percentile):** 650-780
✔ **Tuition:** 2006-2007: $11,500

Selectivity: Least selective	**Room/board:** $5,890
Acceptance rate: 72%	**Average debt:** $12,011
Student/faculty ratio: N/A	**Proportion who borrowed:** 86%

UNDERGRADUATE STUDENT BODY STATS

2005-2006 enrollment: 690 full-time; 27 part-time. Men: 48%; women: 52%. **Ethnic makeup:** African American: 98%; White: 2%.

ADMISSIONS FACTS AND FIGURES

Phone: (434) 848-1856. **Email:** admissions@saintpauls.edu. **Website:** http://www.saintpauls.edu. **Application deadlines for fall 2007:** Regular decision: Rolling. Early decision: Not offered. Early action: Not offered. Admission cannot be deferred. **Application fee:** $20. Common application is accepted. **Admissions requirements/recommendations:** High school units required (recommended): English: 4 (4); Mathematics: 2 (2); Science: 2 (2); Social studies: (2); Total units: 8 (10). Tests: The college uses SAT or ACT scores in admissions decisions. Either SAT or ACT required. For admission to the fall 2007 entering class, the school will accept: ACT with writing, ACT without writing. Campus visit: Recommended. Admissions interview: Neither required nor recommended. Off-campus interview: May be arranged. **Factors that count in admissions decisions:** *Academic:* Secondary school record: Important. Class rank: Important. Letters of recommendation: Important. Standardized test scores: Important. Essay: Important. *Nonacademic:* Interview: Important. Extracurricular activities: Important. Talent/ability: Important. Character/personal qualities: Important. Alumni/ae relationship: Considered. Geographical residence: Considered. State residency: Considered. Religious affiliation/commitment: Considered. Minority status: Considered. Volunteer work: Important. Work experience: Important. **Admissions statistics for the fall 2005 entering class:** Total applicants: 542. Total accepted: 390. Freshmen enrolled: 224; Overall acceptance rate: 72%. **Credentials of fall 2005 freshmen:** 1% ranked in the top 10 percent of their high school class; 1% were in the top 25 percent.

ACADEMICS

Year founded: 1888. **Academic calendar:** Semester. **Degrees offered:** bachelor's. **Most popular majors:** Information not available. **Major fields of study:** business, management, marketing, and related support services; English language and literature/letters; liberal arts and sciences studies, and humanities; philosophy and religious studies; security and protective services. **Areas of required coursework:** arts/fine arts, humanities, computer literacy, mathematics, English (including composition), sciences (biological or physical), history. **Special academic programs (% participation):** double major (2%), honors program (11%), independent study (7%), internships (25%), study abroad (0%), teacher certificate program (8%). **Teacher certification offered in:** early childhood, special education, elementary, secondary. **Reserve Officers Training Corps (ROTC):** Army ROTC: Offered at cooperating institution (Virginia State). **Freshmen returning for sophomore year:** 46%. **Graduation rates:** Four-year: 0%; five-year: 11%; six-year: 25%.

COSTS AND FINANCIAL AID

Financial aid office: (434) 848-6497. **Expenses (2006-2007):** Tuition and fees 2006-2007: $11,500; room/board: $5,890. Estimated books and supplies: $1,400; transportation: $1,500; personal expenses: $1,400. **Financial aid:** In 2005-2006, 100% of undergraduates applied for financial aid. Of those, 92% were determined to have financial need; 1% had their need fully met. Average financial aid package (proportion receiving): $10,704 (92%). Average amount of gift aid, such as scholarships or grants (proportion receiving): $2,456 (13%). Average amount of self-help aid, such as work study or loans (proportion receiving): $1,890 (88%). Average need-based loan (excluding PLUS or other private loans): $2,627. Among students who received need-based aid, the average percentage of need met: 85%. Among students who received aid based on merit, the average award (and the proportion receiving): $0 (0%). The average athletic scholarship (and the proportion receiving): $0 (0%). Average amount of debt of borrowers graduating in 2005: $12,011. Proportion who borrowed: 86%.

CAMPUS LIFE AND EXTRACURRICULAR ACTIVITIES

Campus housing available: women's dorms, men's dorms, apartment for single students. **Student employment:** During the 2005-2006 academic year, 2% of undergraduates worked on campus. Average per-year earnings: $3,200. **Clubs and organizations:** Number of student organizations: 16. Activities include: student government. Number of fraternities: 5; sororities: 3. Average proportion of students who stay on campus on weekends: 50%. **Sports program (2005-2006):** Member of NCAA II. *Men's intercollegiate varsity sports:* baseball, basketball, cross-country, football, golf, tennis, track and field (indoor), track and field (outdoor). *Women's intercollegiate varsity sports:* basketball, bowling, cross-country, softball, tennis, track and field (indoor), track and field (outdoor), volleyball.

SERVICES AND FACILITIES

Basic services: nonremedial tutoring, placement service, day care, health insurance. **Remedial assistance:** reading, math, writing, study skills. **Counseling services:** minority student, career, personal, academic. **For learning-disabled students:** School does not offer a structured program with separate admission and additional fees. Total undergraduates in learning-disabled program or receiving services: 12. Services include: remedial math, remedial English, remedial reading, tape recorders, diagnostic testing service, untimed tests, note-taking services, learning center, extended time for tests, tutors, other testing accomodations. **Library:**

Number of titles: 55,100; number of current serial subscriptions: 167. **Information technology resources:** Students are not required to lease or own a computer. Number of campus computers available to all students: 250. School does not have a wireless network. Proportion of college-owned housing units wired for high-speed internet access: 90%. **Campus safety:** Security services offered: 24-hour foot-and-vehicle patrols, 24-hour emergency telephones, lighted pathways/sidewalks, controlled dormitory access (key, security card, etc).

TRANSFER AND INTERNATIONAL STUDENTS

Transfer students: May apply for admission for the following academic terms: Fall, Spring, Summer. Applicants need a minimum number of credits to apply. **International students:** Number of foreign undergraduates: 0.

Sweet Briar College

- **Address:** 134 Chapel Road, Sweet Briar, VA 24595
- **Website:** http://www.sbc.edu
- **Private**
- **Enrollment:** 703 full-time; 36 part-time

KEY STATS

✔ **U.S News College Ranking:** 74, Liberal Arts Colleges
✔ **SAT Score (25th/75th percentile):** 1030-1230
✔ **Tuition:** 2006-2007: $23,540

Selectivity: More selective	**Room/board:** $9,480
Acceptance rate: 79%	**Average debt:** $17,808
Student/faculty ratio: 9/1	**Proportion who borrowed:** 56%

UNDERGRADUATE STUDENT BODY STATS

2005-2006 enrollment: 703 full-time; 36 part-time. Men: 4%; women: 96%. **Ethnic makeup:** African American: 3%; American-Indian: 1%; Asian American: 2%; Hispanic: 2%; White: 91%; International: 2%.

ADMISSIONS FACTS AND FIGURES

Phone: (800) 381-6142. **Email:** admissions@sbc.edu. **Website:** http://www.sbc.edu. **Application deadlines for fall 2007:** Regular decision: February 1; decision sent by March 15. Early decision: Send application by December 1; Decision sent by: December 15. Early action: Not offered. Admission can be deferred. **Application fee:** $40. Common application is accepted. **To apply online, go to:** http://www.admissions.sbc.edu/apply/. **Admissions requirements/recommendations:** High school units required (recommended): English: 4 (4); Mathematics: 3 (4); Science: 3 (4); Foreign language: 2 (4); Social studies: 3 (4); Total units: 16 (20). Tests: The college uses SAT or ACT scores in admissions decisions. Either SAT or ACT required. For admission to the fall 2007 entering class, the school will accept: ACT with writing. Campus visit: Recommended. Admissions interview: Recommended. Off-campus interview: May be arranged. **Factors that count in admissions decisions:** *Academic:* Secondary school record: Very important. Class rank: Important. Letters of recommendation: Important. Standardized test scores: Important. Essay: Important. *Nonacademic:* Interview: Important. Extracurricular activities: Important. Talent/ability: Considered. Character/personal qualities: Considered. Alumni/ae relationship: Considered. Geographical residence: Not considered. State residency: Not considered. Religious affiliation/commitment: Not considered. Minority status: Considered. Volunteer work: Considered. Work experience: Considered. **Other schools with the greatest overlap in applicants:** Hollins University; Mount Holyoke College; Randolph-Macon Woman's College; University of Mary Washington; University of Virginia. **Admissions statistics for the fall 2005 entering class:** Total applicants: 623. Total accepted: 495. Freshmen enrolled: 182; 53% were from out of state. Accepted through early-decision or early-action plans: 34%. Overall acceptance rate: 79%. Early-decision acceptance rate: 92%. Non-early acceptance rate: 78%. **Credentials of fall 2005 freshmen:** 25% ranked in the top 10 percent of their high school class; 64% were in the top 25 percent, and 94% were in the top half. (Proportion submitting class standing: 63%.) **Average high school grade point average:** 3.5. **First-year students who submitted SAT scores:** 93%. Scores (25/75 percentile): Verbal: 530-640, Math: 500-590, Combined: 1030-1230. **First-year students submitting ACT scores:** 41%. Scores (25/75 percentile): English: 22-28, Math: 20-25, Composite: 22-27.

ACADEMICS

Year founded: 1901. **Academic calendar:** Semester. **Degrees offered:** bachelor's, master's. **Most popular majors:** 25% social sciences, 10% psychology, 10% visual and performing arts, 9% English language and literature/letters, 6% biological and biomedical sciences. **Major fields of study:** area, ethnic, cultural, and gender studies; biological and biomedical sciences; business, management, marketing, and related support services; computer and information sciences and support services; engineering; engineering technologies/technicians; English language and literature/letters; foreign languages, literatures, and linguistics; history; liberal arts and sciences studies, and humanities; mathematics and statistics; multi/interdisciplinary studies; natural resources and conservation; philosophy and religious studies; physical sciences; psychology; social sciences; visual and performing arts. **Areas of required coursework:** arts/fine arts, humanities, English (including composition), foreign languages, sciences (biological or physical), social science, other. **Special academic programs (% participation):** accelerated program (4%), cross-registration (3%), double major (13%), dual enrollment (15%), exchange student program (domestic) (4%), honors program (24%), independent study (31%), internships (23%), liberal arts/career combination (0%), student-designed major (2%), study abroad (27%), teacher certificate program (7%). **Teacher certification offered in:** elementary, secondary. **Faculty and instruction (2005-2006):** Total instructional faculty: 64 full-time, 35 part-time (47% men; 53% women; 2% minorities). Full-time faculty with Ph.D. or other terminal degree: 100%. Student/faculty ratio: 9/1. Classes of fewer than 20 students: 91%; of 20 to 49 students: 9%. **Advanced Placement and International Baccalaureate credit:** AP tests may be used for: Credit and/or placement. Scores accepted: 4, 5. International Baccalaureate exams may be used for: Credit and/or placement. **Freshmen returning for sophomore year:** 79%. **Graduation rates:** Four-year: 65%; five-year: 67%; six-year: 67%. **Graduate study:** 45% of students pursue further study immediately upon graduation. Fields in which graduates pursue further study: law, 11%; engineering, 3%; education, 3%; arts and sciences, 83%.

COSTS AND FINANCIAL AID

Financial aid office: (434) 381-6156. **Expenses (2006-2007):** Tuition and fees 2006-2007: $23,540; room/board: $9,480. Estimated books and supplies: $600; transportation: $600; personal expenses: $750. **Financial aid:** Priority filing date for institution's financial aid form: March 1. In 2005-2006, 65% of undergraduates applied for financial aid. Of those, 65% were determined to have financial need; 99% had their need fully met. Average financial aid package (proportion receiving): $15,293 (64%). Average amount of gift aid, such as scholarships or grants (proportion receiving): $13,706 (46%). Average amount of self-help aid, such as work study or loans (proportion receiving): $5,044 (42%). Average need-based loan (excluding PLUS or other private loans): $4,755. Among students who received need-based aid, the average percentage of need met: 39%. Among students who received aid based on merit, the average award (and the proportion receiving): $11,213 (46%). Average amount of debt of borrowers graduating in 2005: $17,808. Proportion who borrowed: 56%.

CAMPUS LIFE AND EXTRACURRICULAR ACTIVITIES

Campus housing available (% using): women's dorms (50%), other housing options (50%). Students who live in college-owned, operated, or affiliated housing: 90%. **Student employment:** During the 2005-2006 academic year, 50% of undergraduates worked on campus. Average per-year earnings: $1,000. **Clubs and organizations:** Number of student organizations: 54. Activities include: choral groups, dance, drama/theater, literary magazine, music ensembles, musical theater, radio station, student government, student newspaper, student film society, symphony orchestra, yearbook. Number of fraternities: 0; sororities: 0. Average proportion of students who stay on campus on weekends: 45%. **Sports program (2005-2006):** Member of NCAA III. **Women's intercollegiate varsity sports:** field hockey, lacrosse, soccer, softball, swimming and diving, tennis, volleyball.

SERVICES AND FACILITIES

Basic services: nonremedial tutoring, placement service, health service, health insurance. **Counseling services:** career, personal, academic, psychological, religious. **For learning-disabled students:** School does not offer a structured program with separate admission and additional fees. Total undergraduates in learning-disabled program or receiving services: 100. Services include: learning center, extended time for tests, tutors. **Library:** Number of titles: 257,815; number of current serial subscriptions: 42,813. **Information technology resources:** Students are not required to lease or own a computer. Number of campus computers available to all students: 70. School has a wireless network. Proportion of college-owned housing units wired for high-speed internet access: 99%. **Campus safety:** Security services offered: 24-hour foot-and-vehicle patrols, late-night transport/escort service, 24-hour emergency telephones, lighted pathways/sidewalks, student patrols, controlled dormitory access (key, security card, etc).

TRANSFER AND INTERNATIONAL STUDENTS

Transfer students: May apply for admission for the following academic terms: Fall, Spring. Applicants need a minimum number of credits to apply. For fall 2005: Transfer applications received: 53. Transfer applicants offered admission: 26. Transfer applicants enrolled: 15. **International students:** Number of foreign undergraduates: 10 (2% of student body). Number of countries represented: 13. Minimum TOEFL score required: 550 (paper); 213 (computer).

University of Mary Washington

- **Address:** 1301 College Avenue, Fredericksburg, VA 22401
- **Website:** http://www.umw.edu
- **Public**
- **Enrollment:** 3,519 full-time; 566 part-time

KEY STATS

✔ **U.S News College Ranking:** 6, Universities–Master's (South)
✔ **SAT Score (25th/75th percentile):** 1140-1310
✔ **Tuition:** 2006-2007: $6,084 in state, $15,964 out of state
  Selectivity: More selective   **Room/board:** $6,244
  Acceptance rate: 64%   **Average debt:** $11,800
  Student/faculty ratio: 17/1   **Proportion who borrowed:** 57%

UNDERGRADUATE STUDENT BODY STATS

2005-2006 enrollment: 3,519 full-time; 566 part-time. Men: 34%; women: 66%. **Ethnic makeup:** African American: 4%; Asian American: 5%; Hispanic: 4%; White: 87%.

ADMISSIONS FACTS AND FIGURES

Phone: (540) 654-2000. **Email:** admit@umw.edu. **Website:** http://www.umw.edu. **Application deadlines for fall 2007:** Regular decision: February 1; decision sent by April 1. Early decision: Not offered. Early action: Send application by: January 15; Decision sent by: N/A. Admission can be deferred. **Application fee:** $45. Common application is accepted. **To apply online, go to:** https://www.applyweb.com/apply/umw. **Admissions requirements/recommendations:** High school units required (recommended): English: 4 (4); Mathematics: 3 (4); Science: 3 (4); Foreign language: (4); Social studies: 2 (2); History: 2 (2); Total units: 14 (20). Tests: The college uses SAT or ACT scores in admissions decisions. Either SAT or ACT required. For admission to the fall 2007 entering class, the school will accept: ACT with writing, ACT without writing. Campus visit: Recommended. Admissions interview: Neither required nor recommended. Off-campus interview: Not available. **Factors that count in admissions decisions:** *Academic:* Secondary school record: Very important. Class rank: Very important. Letters of recommendation: Considered. Standardized test scores: Very important. Essay: Important. *Nonacademic:* Interview: Not considered. Extracurricular activities: Important. Talent/ability: Considered. Character/personal qualities: Important. Alumni/ae relationship: Considered. Geographical residence: Not considered. State residency: Considered. Religious affiliation/commitment: Not considered. Minority status: Considered. Volunteer work: Important. Work experience: Considered. **Other schools with the greatest overlap in applicants:** College of William and Mary; James Madison University; Longwood University; University of Richmond; University of Virginia. **Admissions statistics for the fall 2005 entering class:** Total applicants: 4,635. Total accepted: 2,979. Freshmen enrolled: 914; 36% were from out of state. Overall acceptance rate: 64%. Non-early acceptance rate: 64%. Size of waiting list: 601 applicants; enrolled from waiting list: 102. **Credentials of fall 2005 freshmen:** 38% ranked in the top 10 percent of their high school class; 82% were in the top 25 percent, and 97% were in the top half. (Proportion submitting class standing: 50%.) **Average high school grade point average:** 3.7. **First-year students who submitted SAT scores:** 97%. Scores (25/75 percentile): Verbal: 580-670, Math: 560-640, Combined: 1140-1310. **First-year students submitting ACT scores:** 8%. Scores (25/75 percentile): English: 26-32, Math: 23-27, Composite: 25-29.

ACADEMICS

Year founded: 1908. **Academic calendar:** Semester. **Degrees offered:** certificate, bachelor's, post-bachelor's certificate, master's, post-master's certificate. **Most popular majors:** 14% business administration and management, 10% English language and literature, 9% liberal arts and sciences, general studies, and humanities, 9% psychology, 6% biology/biological sciences. **Major fields of study:** area, ethnic, cultural, and gender studies; biological and biomedical sciences; business, management, marketing, and related support services; computer and information sciences and support services; English language and literature/letters; foreign languages, literatures, and linguistics; liberal arts and sciences studies, and humanities; mathematics and statistics; multi/interdisciplinary studies; philosophy and religious studies; physical sciences; psychology; social sciences; visual and performing arts. **Areas of required coursework:** arts/fine arts, humanities, computer literacy, mathematics, English (including composition), philosophy, foreign languages, sciences (biological or physical), history, social science. **Pre-professional programs:** pre-law, pre-dentistry, pre-medicine, pre-veterinary science, pre-pharmacy. **Special academic programs:** double major, independent study, internships, student-designed major, study abroad, teacher certificate program. **Teacher certification offered in:** elementary, secondary. **Faculty and instruction (2005-2006):** Total instructional faculty: 235 full-time, 100 part-time (56% men; 44% women; 10% minorities). Full-time faculty with Ph.D. or other terminal degree: 85%. Student/faculty ratio: 17/1. Classes of fewer than 20 students: 47%; of 20 to 49 students: 52%; of 50 or more students: 0%. **Advanced Placement and International Baccalaureate credit:** AP tests may be used for: Credit and/or placement. Scores accepted: 3, 4, 5. International Baccalaureate exams may be used for: Credit and/or placement. **Freshmen returning for sophomore year:** 87%. **Graduation rates:** Four-year: 70%; five-year: 75%; six-year: 73%. **Graduate study:** 30% of students pursue further study immediately upon graduation; 21% within one year. Fields in which graduates pursue further study: Master of Business Administration (MBA), 5%; law, 10%; medicine, 7%; theology (or the seminary), 3%; education, 25%; arts and sciences, 54%; veterinary medicine, 1%.

COSTS AND FINANCIAL AID

Financial aid office: (540) 654-2468. **Expenses (2006-2007):** Tuition and fees 2006-2007: $6,084 in state, $15,964 out of state; room/board: $6,244. Estimated books and supplies: $1,000; transportation: $900; personal expenses: $1,450. **Financial aid:** Priority filing date for institution's financial aid form: March 15. In 2005-2006, 88% of undergraduates applied for financial aid. Of those, 58% were determined to have financial need; 4% had their need fully met. Average financial aid package (proportion receiving): $4,050 (51%). Average amount of gift aid, such as scholarships or grants (proportion receiving): $2,500 (36%). Average amount of self-help aid, such as work study or loans (proportion receiving): $2,450 (44%). Average need-based loan (excluding PLUS or other private loans): $2,400. Among students who received need-based aid, the average percentage of need met: 56%. Among students who received aid based on merit, the average award (and the proportion receiving): $1,200 (11%). The average athletic scholarship (and the proportion receiving): $0 (0%). Average amount of debt of borrowers graduating in 2005: $11,800. Proportion who borrowed: 57%.

CAMPUS LIFE AND EXTRACURRICULAR ACTIVITIES

Campus housing available (% using): coed dorms (71%), women's dorms (13%), men's dorms (1%), apartment for single students (14%), special housing for disabled students, other housing options (1%). Students who live in college-owned, operated, or affiliated housing: 61%. **Student employment:** During the 2005-2006 academic year, 24% of undergraduates worked on campus. Average per-year earnings: $1,545. **Clubs and organizations:** Number of student organizations: 95. Activities include: choral groups, dance, drama/theater, jazz band, literary magazine, music ensembles, musical theater, opera, radio station, student government, student newspaper, student film society, symphony orchestra, yearbook. Number of fraternities: 0; sororities: 0. **Sports program (2005-2006):** Member of NCAA III. *Men's intercollegiate varsity sports:* baseball, basketball, cross-country, equestrian sports, lacrosse, soccer, swimming and diving, tennis, track and field (indoor), track and field (outdoor). *Women's intercollegiate varsity sports:* basketball, cross-country, equestrian sports, field hockey, lacrosse, soccer, softball, swimming and diving, tennis, track and field (indoor), track and field (outdoor), volleyball, rowing.

SERVICES AND FACILITIES

Basic services: nonremedial tutoring, women's center, health service, health insurance. **Remedial assistance:** writing, study skills, other. **Counseling services:** minority student, career, personal, academic, older student, psychological, birth control, religious. **For learning-disabled students:** School does not offer a structured program with separate admission and additional fees. Total undergraduates in learning-disabled program or receiving services: 54. Services include: reading machines, tape recorders, note-taking services, oral tests, readers, extended time for tests, tutors, substitution of courses, texts on tape, typist/scribe, exams on tape or computer, other testing accomodations, waiver of foreign language degree requirement, waiver of math degree requirement, other. **Library:** Number of titles: 370,615; number of current serial subscriptions: 5,784. **Information technology resources:** Students are not required to lease or own a computer. Number of campus computers available to all students: 40. School has a wireless network. Approximate number of users that can be accommodated: 4,000. Proportion of college-owned housing units wired for high-speed internet access: 100%. **Campus safety:** Security services offered: 24-hour foot-and-vehicle patrols, late-night transport/escort service, 24-hour emergency telephones, lighted pathways/sidewalks, controlled dormitory access (key, security card, etc).

TRANSFER AND INTERNATIONAL STUDENTS

Transfer students: May apply for admission for the following academic terms: Fall, Spring. Applicants need a minimum number of credits to apply. For fall 2005: Transfer applications received: 543. Transfer applicants offered admission: 328. Transfer applicants enrolled: 174. **International students:** Number of foreign undergraduates: 9. Minimum TOEFL score required: 570 (paper); 230 (computer). Average TOEFL score: 620 (paper).

University of Richmond

- **Address:** 28 Westhampton Way, Univ. of Richmond, VA 23173
- **Website:** http://www.richmond.edu
- **Private**
- **Enrollment:** 2,881 full-time; 39 part-time

KEY STATS

✔ **U.S News College Ranking:** 34, Liberal Arts Colleges
✔ **SAT Score (25th/75th percentile):** 1240-1390
✔ **Tuition:** 2006-2007: $36,550

Selectivity: More selective	**Room/board:** $6,060
Acceptance rate: 47%	**Average debt:** $18,500
Student/faculty ratio: 10/1	**Proportion who borrowed:** 41%

UNDERGRADUATE STUDENT BODY STATS

2005-2006 enrollment: 2,881 full-time; 39 part-time. Men: 49%; women: 51%. **Ethnic makeup:** African American: 4%; Asian American: 3%; Hispanic: 2%; White: 87%; International: 4%.

ADMISSIONS FACTS AND FIGURES

Phone: (804) 289-8640. **Email:** admissions@richmond.edu. **Website:** http://www.richmond.edu. **Application deadlines for fall 2007:** Regular decision: January 15; decision sent by April 1. Early decision: Send application by: November 15; Decision sent by: December 15. Early action: Not offered. Admission can be deferred. **Application fee:** $50. Common application is accepted. **Admissions requirements/recommendations:** High school units required (recommended): English: 4 (4); Mathematics: 3 (4); Science: 2 (4); Foreign language: 2 (4); Social studies: 0 (0); History: 2 (4); Academic electives: 0 (0); Total units: 16 (20). Tests: The college uses SAT or ACT scores in admissions decisions. Either SAT or ACT required. For admission to the fall 2007 entering class, the school will accept: ACT with writing, ACT without writing. Campus visit: Recommended. Admissions interview: Neither required nor recommended. Off-campus interview: Not available. **Factors that count in admissions decisions:** *Academic:* Secondary school record: Very important. Class rank: Important. Letters of recommendation: Important. Standardized test scores: Important. Essay: Important. *Nonacademic:* Interview: Not considered. Extracurricular activities: Considered. Talent/ability: Important. Character/personal qualities: Important. Alumni/ae relationship: Considered. Geographical residence: Considered. State residency: Considered. Religious affiliation/commitment: Not considered. Minority status: Considered. Volunteer work: Considered. Work experience: Considered. **Other schools with the greatest overlap in applicants:** Boston College; College of William and Mary; University of Virginia; Vanderbilt University; Wake Forest University. **Admissions statistics for the fall 2005 entering class:** Total applicants: 5,778. Total accepted: 2,743. Freshmen enrolled: 772; 87% were from out of state. Accepted through early-decision or early-action plans: 19%. Overall acceptance rate: 47%. Early-decision acceptance rate: 55%. Non-early acceptance rate: 47%. **Size of waiting list:** 1092 applicants; enrolled from waiting list: 267. **Credentials of fall 2005 freshmen:** 58% ranked in the top 10 percent of their high school class; 88% were in the top 25 percent, and 98% were in the top half. (Proportion submitting class standing: 38%.) **Average high school grade point average:** 3.5. **First-year students who submitted SAT scores:** 82%. Scores (25/75 percentile): Verbal: 610-690, Math: 630-700, Combined: 1240-1390. **First-year students submitting ACT scores:** 34%. Scores (25/75 percentile): English: N/A, Math: N/A, Composite: 26-30.

ACADEMICS
Year founded: 1830. **Academic calendar:** Semester. **Degrees offered:** certificate, diploma, associate, bachelor's, post-bachelor's certificate, master's, first professional. **Most popular majors:** 24% business, management, marketing, and related support services, 19% social sciences, 8% English language and literature/letters, 7% biological and biomedical sciences, 7% history. **Major fields of study:** area, ethnic, cultural, and gender studies; biological and biomedical sciences; business, management, marketing, and related support services; communication, journalism, and related programs; computer and information sciences and support services; English language and literature/letters; foreign languages, literatures, and linguistics; history; liberal arts and sciences studies, and humanities; mathematics and statistics; multi/interdisciplinary studies; natural resources and conservation; philosophy and religious studies; physical sciences; psychology; security and protective services; social sciences; visual and performing arts. **Areas of required coursework:** arts/fine arts, humanities, mathematics, English (including composition), foreign languages, sciences (biological or physical), history, social science, other. **Special academic programs:** accelerated program, cross-registration, distance learning, double major, English as a Second Language (ESL), exchange student program (domestic), honors program, independent study, internships, student-designed major, study abroad, teacher certificate program. **Teacher certification offered in:** elementary, secondary. **Reserve Officers Training Corps (ROTC):** Army ROTC: Offered on campus. **Faculty and instruction (2005-2006):** Total instructional faculty: 262 full-time, 58 part-time (60% men; 40% women; 10% minorities). Full-time faculty with Ph.D. or other terminal degree: 90%. Student/faculty ratio: 10/1. Classes of fewer than 20 students: 64%; of 20 to 49 students: 35%; of 50 or more students: 1%. **Advanced Placement and International Baccalaureate credit:** AP tests may be used for: Credit and/or placement. Scores accepted: 3, 4, 5. International Baccalaureate exams may be used for: Credit only. **Freshmen returning for sophomore year:** 93%. **Graduation rates:** Four-year: 78%; five-year: 84%; six-year: 84%. **Graduate study:** 27% of students pursue further study immediately upon graduation. Fields in which graduates pursue further study: law, 25%; medicine, 8%; dentistry, 1%; theology (or the seminary), 1%; education, 4%; arts and sciences, 61%; veterinary medicine, 1%.

COSTS AND FINANCIAL AID
Financial aid office: (804) 289-8438. **Expenses (2006-2007):** Tuition and fees 2006-2007: $36,550; room/board: $6,060. Estimated books and supplies: $1,050 personal expenses: $990. **Financial aid:** In 2005-2006, 46% of undergraduates applied for financial aid. Of those, 34% were determined to have financial need; 93% had their need fully met. Average financial aid package (proportion receiving): $23,258 (34%). Average amount of gift aid, such as scholarships or grants (proportion receiving): $20,314 (33%). Average amount of self-help aid, such as work study or loans (proportion receiving): $3,169 (30%). Average need-based loan (excluding PLUS or other private loans): $2,755. Among students who received need-based aid, the average percentage of need met: 100%. Among students who received aid based on merit, the average award (and the proportion receiving): $15,469 (14%). The average athletic scholarship (and the proportion receiving): $23,892 (7%). Average amount of debt of borrowers graduating in 2005: $18,500. Proportion who borrowed: 41%.

CAMPUS LIFE AND EXTRACURRICULAR ACTIVITIES
Campus housing available (% using): women's dorms (39%), men's dorms (34%), apartment for single students (24%), special housing for disabled students, special housing for international students. Students who live in college-owned, operated, or affiliated housing: 92%. **Student employment:** During the 2005-2006 academic year, 37% of undergraduates worked on campus. Average per-year earnings: $1,162. **Clubs and organizations:** Number of student organizations: 250. Activities include: choral groups, concert band, dance, drama/theater, jazz band, literary magazine, music ensembles, musical theater, pep band, radio station, student government,

student newspaper, symphony orchestra, yearbook. Number of fraternities: 8; sororities: 8. Proportion of men in fraternities: 45%; of women in sororities: 45%. Average proportion of students who stay on campus on weekends: 90%. **Sports program (2005-2006):** Member of NCAA I. *Men's intercollegiate varsity sports:* baseball, basketball, cross-country, football, golf, soccer, tennis, track and field (indoor), track and field (outdoor). *Women's intercollegiate varsity sports:* basketball, cross-country, field hockey, golf, lacrosse, soccer, swimming and diving, tennis, track and field (indoor), track and field (outdoor).

SERVICES AND FACILITIES
Basic services: nonremedial tutoring, placement service, health service, other. **Counseling services:** minority student, career, military, personal, academic, psychological, birth control, religious. **Library:** Number of titles: 805,503; number of current serial subscriptions: 43,747. **Information technology resources:** Students are not required to lease or own a computer. Number of campus computers available to all students: 750. School has a wireless network. Approximate number of users that can be accommodated: 10,000. Proportion of college-owned housing units wired for high-speed internet access: 100%. **Campus safety:** Security services offered: 24-hour foot-and-vehicle patrols, late-night transport/escort service, 24-hour emergency telephones, lighted pathways/sidewalks, controlled dormitory access (key, security card, etc).

TRANSFER AND INTERNATIONAL STUDENTS
Transfer students: May apply for admission for the following academic terms: Fall, Spring. Applicants need a minimum number of credits to apply. For fall 2005: Transfer applications received: 198. Transfer applicants offered admission: 91. Transfer applicants enrolled: 41. **International students:** Number of foreign undergraduates: 109 (4% of student body). Number of countries represented: 76. Minimum TOEFL score required: 550 (paper); 213 (computer). Average TOEFL score: 597 (paper).

University of Virginia

- **Address:** Charlottesville, VA 22904
- **Website:** http://www.virginia.edu
- **Public**
- **Enrollment:** 13,395 full-time; 818 part-time

KEY STATS
✔ **U.S News College Ranking:** 24, National Universities
✔ **SAT Score (25th/75th percentile):** 1220-1430
✔ **Tuition:** 2006-2007: $7,845 in state, $25,945 out of state
  Selectivity: Most selective   **Room/board:** $6,909
  Acceptance rate: 38%   **Average debt:** $15,176
  Student/faculty ratio: 15/1   **Proportion who borrowed:** 30%

UNDERGRADUATE STUDENT BODY STATS
2005-2006 enrollment: 13,395 full-time; 818 part-time. Men: 46%; women: 54%. **Ethnic makeup:** African American: 9%; Asian American: 11%; Hispanic: 4%; White: 72%; International: 4%.

ADMISSIONS FACTS AND FIGURES
Phone: (434) 982-3200. **Email:** undergrad-admission@virginia.edu. **Website:** http://www.virginia.edu. **Application deadlines for fall 2007:** Regular decision: January 2; decision sent by April 1. Early decision: Send application by: November 1; Decision sent by: December 1. Early action: Not offered. Admission can be deferred. **Application fee:** $60. Common application is not accepted. **To apply online, go to:** http://www.virginia.edu/~admiss/ugadmiss/home.shtml. **Admissions requirements/recommendations:** High school units required (recommended): English: 4; Mathematics: 4 (5); Science: 2 (4); Foreign language: 2 (5); Social studies: 1 (4); Total units: 16. Tests: The college uses SAT or ACT scores in admissions decisions. Either SAT or ACT required. For admission to the fall 2007 entering class, the school will accept: ACT with writing. Campus visit: Recommended. Admissions interview: Neither required nor recommended. Off-campus interview: Not available. **Factors that count in admissions decisions:** *Academic:* Secondary school record: Very important. Class rank: Very important. Letters of recommendation: Important. Standardized test scores: Important. Essay: Very important. *Nonacademic:* Interview: Not considered. Extracurricular activities: Important. Talent/ability: Important.

Character/personal qualities: Important. Alumni/ae relationship: Very important. Geographical residence: Considered. State residency: Very important. Religious affiliation/commitment: Not considered. Minority status: Very important. Volunteer work: Considered. Work experience: Considered. **Other schools with the greatest overlap in applicants:** College of William and Mary; Cornell University; Duke University; University of North Carolina–Chapel Hill; Virginia Tech. **Admissions statistics for the fall 2005 entering class:** Total applicants: 15,657. Total accepted: 5,898. Freshmen enrolled: 3,112; 29% were from out of state. Accepted through early-decision or early-action plans: 31%. Overall acceptance rate: 38%. Early-decision acceptance rate: 42%. Non-early acceptance rate: 37%. **Size of waiting list:** 3247 applicants; enrolled from waiting list: 83. **Credentials of fall 2005 freshmen:** 86% ranked in the top 10 percent of their high school class; 97% were in the top 25 percent, and 99% were in the top half. (Proportion submitting class standing: 52%.) **Average high school grade point average:** 4.0. **First-year students who submitted SAT scores:** 99%. Scores (25/75 percentile): Verbal: 600-710, Math: 620-720, Combined: 1220-1430. **First-year students submitting ACT scores:** 14%. Scores (25/75 percentile): English: 25-32, Math: 25-31, Composite: 25-30.

ACADEMICS

Year founded: 1819. **Academic calendar:** Semester. **Degrees offered:** certificate, bachelor's, master's, post-master's certificate, first professional, doctorate. **Most popular majors:** 11% economics, 10% business/commerce, 9% psychology, 8% English language and literature, 8% international relations and affairs. **Major fields of study:** architecture and related services; area, ethnic, cultural, and gender studies; biological and biomedical sciences; business, management, marketing, and related support services; computer and information sciences and support services; education; engineering; English language and literature/letters; foreign languages, literatures, and linguistics; health professions and related clinical sciences; history; liberal arts and sciences studies, and humanities; mathematics and statistics; multi/interdisciplinary studies; natural resources and conservation; philosophy and religious studies; physical sciences; psychology; social sciences; visual and performing arts. **Areas of required coursework:** humanities, mathematics, English (including composition), foreign languages, sciences (biological or physical), history, social science, other. **Pre-professional programs:** pre-law, pre-medicine. **Special academic programs:** accelerated program, cooperative (work-study plan) program, double major, English as a Second Language (ESL), honors program, independent study, internships, student-designed major, study abroad, teacher certificate program. **Teacher certification offered in:** special education, elementary, middle/junior high, secondary. **Cooperative education programs:** engineering. **Reserve Officers Training Corps (ROTC):** Army ROTC: Offered on campus; Navy ROTC: Offered on campus; Air Force ROTC: Offered on campus. **Faculty and instruction (2005-2006):** Total instructional faculty: 1,193 full-time, 137 part-time (67% men; 33% women; 10% minorities). Full-time faculty with Ph.D. or other terminal degree: 90%. Student/faculty ratio: 15/1. Classes of fewer than 20 students: 47%; of 20 to 49 students: 37%; of 50 or more students: 16%. **Advanced Placement and International Baccalaureate credit:** AP tests may be used for: Credit and/or placement. Scores accepted: 3, 4, 5. International Baccalaureate exams may be used for: Credit and/or placement. **Freshmen returning for sophomore year:** 97%. **Graduation rates:** Four-year: 84%; five-year: 92%; six-year: 93%.

COSTS AND FINANCIAL AID

Financial aid office: (434) 982-6000. **Expenses (2006-2007):** Tuition and fees 2006-2007: $7,845 in state, $25,945 out of state; room/board: $6,909. Estimated books and supplies: $1,000; transportation: $220; personal expenses: $1,754. **Financial aid:** Priority filing date for institution's financial aid form: March 1. In 2005-2006, 41% of undergraduates applied for financial aid. Of those, 24% were determined to have financial need; 100% had their need fully met. Average financial aid package (proportion receiving): $14,974 (24%). Average amount of gift aid, such as scholarships or grants (proportion receiving): $10,916 (20%). Average amount of self-help aid, such as work study or loans (proportion receiving): $5,003 (17%). Average need-based loan (excluding PLUS or other private loans): $4,617. Among students who received need-based aid, the average percentage of need met: 100%. Among students who received aid based on merit, the average award (and the proportion receiving): $8,535 (14%). The average athletic scholarship (and the proportion receiving): $18,529 (3%). Average amount of debt of borrowers graduating in 2005: $15,176. Proportion who borrowed: 30%.

CAMPUS LIFE AND EXTRACURRICULAR ACTIVITIES

Campus housing available: coed dorms, sorority housing, fraternity housing, apartments for married students, apartment for single students, cooperative housing. Students who live in college-owned, operated, or affiliated housing: 45%. **Clubs and organizations:** Number of student organizations: 530. Activities include: choral groups, concert band, dance, drama/theater, jazz band, literary magazine, marching band, music ensembles, musical theater, opera, pep band, radio station, student government, student newspaper, student film society, symphony orchestra, television station, yearbook. Number of fraternities: 32; sororities: 22. Proportion of men in fraternities: 30%; of women in sororities: 30%. **Sports program (2005-2006):** Member of NCAA I. *Men's intercollegiate varsity sports:* baseball, basketball, cross-country, football, golf, lacrosse, soccer, swimming and diving, tennis, track and field (indoor), track and field (outdoor), wrestling. *Women's intercollegiate varsity sports:* basketball, crew, cross-country, field hockey, golf, lacrosse, soccer, softball, swimming and diving, tennis, track and field (indoor), track and field (outdoor), volleyball.

SERVICES AND FACILITIES

Basic services: nonremedial tutoring, women's center, placement service, day care, health service, health insurance. **Remedial assistance:** reading, math, writing, study skills. **Counseling services:** minority student, career, military, personal, veteran student, academic, older student, psychological, birth control. **For learning-disabled students:** School does not offer a structured program with separate admission and additional fees. Services include: tape recorders, diagnostic testing service, untimed tests, note-taking services, oral tests, learning center, readers, extended time for tests, tutors. **Library:** Number of titles: 5,053,162; number of current serial subscriptions: 52,802. **Information technology resources:** Students are not required to lease or own a computer. Number of campus computers available to all students: 1,859. School has a wireless network. Proportion of college-owned housing units wired for high-speed internet access: 100%. **Campus safety:** Security services offered: 24-hour foot-and-vehicle patrols, late-night transport/escort service, 24-hour emergency telephones, lighted pathways/sidewalks, controlled dormitory access (key, security card, etc).

TRANSFER AND INTERNATIONAL STUDENTS

Transfer students: May apply for admission for the following academic terms: Fall, Spring. Applicants need a minimum number of credits to apply. For fall 2005: Transfer applications received: 2,102. Transfer applicants offered admission: 849. Transfer applicants enrolled: 577. **International students:** Number of foreign undergraduates: 567 (4% of student body). Number of countries represented: 109. Minimum TOEFL score required: 550 (paper); 213 (computer). Average TOEFL score: 620 (paper).

University of Virginia–Wise

- **Address:** 1 College Avenue, Wise, VA 24293
- **Website:** http://www.uvawise.edu
- **Public**
- **Enrollment:** 1,456 full-time; 497 part-time

KEY STATS
✔ **U.S News College Ranking:** fourth tier, Liberal Arts Colleges
✔ **SAT Score (25th/75th percentile):** 870-1090
✔ **Tuition:** 2006-2007: $5,692 in state, $16,678 out of state

Selectivity: Selective	**Room/board:** $6,580
Acceptance rate: 76%	**Average debt:** $9,157
Student/faculty ratio: 17/1	**Proportion who borrowed:** 70%

UNDERGRADUATE STUDENT BODY STATS
2005-2006 enrollment: 1,456 full-time; 497 part-time. Men: 43%; women: 57%. **Ethnic makeup:** African American: 6%; Asian American: 1%; Hispanic: 2%; White: 90%; International: 1%.

ADMISSIONS FACTS AND FIGURES
Phone: (888) 282-9324. **Email:** admissions@uvawise.edu. **Website:** http://www.uvawise.edu. **Application deadlines for fall 2007:** Regular decision: August 15. Early decision: Not offered. Early action: Send application by: December 1; Decision sent by: December 15. Admission can be deferred. **Application fee:** $25. Common application is not accepted. **Admissions requirements/recommendations:** High school units required (recommended): English: 4; Mathematics: 3; Science: 2; Foreign language: 2; Social studies: 1; History: 1; Academic electives: 5; Total units: 18. Tests: The college uses SAT or ACT scores in admissions decisions. Either SAT or ACT

required. For admission to the fall 2007 entering class, the school will accept: ACT without writing. Campus visit: Recommended. Admissions interview: Recommended. Off-campus interview: May be arranged. **Factors that count in admissions decisions:** *Academic:* Secondary school record: Very important. Class rank: Important. Letters of recommendation: Considered. Standardized test scores: Important. Essay: Considered. *Nonacademic:* Interview: Considered. Extracurricular activities: Considered. Talent/ability: Important. Character/personal qualities: Considered. Alumni/ae relationship: Not considered. Geographical residence: Not considered. State residency: Not considered. Religious affiliation/commitment: Not considered. Minority status: Considered. Volunteer work: Considered. Work experience: Considered. **Admissions statistics for the fall 2005 entering class:** Total applicants: 1,085. Total accepted: 824. Freshmen enrolled: 366; 6% were from out of state. Accepted through early-decision or early-action plans: 62%. Overall acceptance rate: 76%. Non-early acceptance rate: 63%. **Credentials of fall 2005 freshmen:** 25% ranked in the top 10 percent of their high school class; 49% were in the top 25 percent, and 86% were in the top half. (Proportion submitting class standing: 84%.) **Average high school grade point average:** 3.3. **First-year students who submitted SAT scores:** 96%. Scores (25/75 percentile): Verbal: 440-550, Math: 430-540, Combined: 870-1090. **First-year students submitting ACT scores:** 18%. Scores (25/75 percentile): English: 17-22, Math: 16-22, Composite: 18-22.

ACADEMICS

Year founded: 1954. **Academic calendar:** Semester. **Degrees offered:** bachelor's. **Most popular majors:** 17% business, management, marketing, and related support services, 12% history, 12% liberal arts and sciences studies, and humanities, 9% psychology, 8% criminal justice/law enforcement administration. **Major fields of study:** biological and biomedical sciences; business, management, marketing, and related support services; communication, journalism, and related programs; computer and information sciences and support services; English language and literature/letters; foreign languages, literatures, and linguistics; history; liberal arts and sciences studies, and humanities; mathematics and statistics; multi/interdisciplinary studies; physical sciences; psychology; science technologies/technicians; social sciences; visual and performing arts. **Areas of required coursework:** arts/fine arts, humanities, computer literacy, mathematics, English (including composition), foreign languages, sciences (biological or physical), history, social science. **Pre-professional programs:** pre-law, pre-dentistry, pre-medicine, pre-veterinary science, pre-pharmacy. **Special academic programs (% participation):** accelerated program (.5%), cooperative (work-study plan) program (4%), distance learning (3%), double major (5.8%), dual enrollment (9.7%), honors program (2%), independent study (10%), internships (2%), liberal arts/career combination (10%), student-designed major (.3%), study abroad (0%), teacher certificate program (5%). **Teacher certification offered in:** early childhood, special education, elementary, middle/junior high, secondary. **Cooperative education programs:** other. **Faculty and instruction (2005-2006):** Total instructional faculty: 89 full-time, 51 part-time (55% men; 45% women; 7% minorities). Full-time faculty with Ph.D. or other terminal degree: 70%. Student/faculty ratio: 17/1. Classes of fewer than 20 students: 63%; of 20 to 49 students: 37%; of 50 or more students: 0%. **Advanced Placement and International Baccalaureate credit:** AP tests may be used for: Credit and/or placement. Scores accepted: 3, 4, 5. International Baccalaureate exams may be used for: Credit and/or placement. **Freshmen returning for sophomore year:** 73%. **Graduation rates:** Four-year: 28%; five-year: 38%; six-year: 41%. **Graduate study:** 15% of students pursue further study immediately upon graduation; 20% within one year.

COSTS AND FINANCIAL AID

Financial aid office: (276) 328-0103. **Expenses (2006-2007):** Tuition and fees 2006-2007: $5,692 in state, $16,678 out of state; room/board: $6,580. Estimated books and supplies: $800; transportation: $750; personal expenses: $950. **Financial aid:** Priority filing date for institution's financial aid form: February 15; deadline: April 1. In 2005-2006, 91% of undergraduates applied for financial aid. Of those, 70% were determined to have financial need; 95% had their need fully met. Average financial aid package (proportion receiving): $7,102 (70%). Average amount of gift aid, such as scholarships or grants (proportion receiving): $3,750 (54%). Average amount of self-help aid, such as work study or loans (proportion receiving): $3,259 (44%). Average need-based loan (excluding PLUS or other private loans): $3,068. Among students who received need-based aid, the average percentage of need met: 94%. Among students who received aid based on merit, the average award (and the proportion receiving): $1,581 (17%). The average athletic scholarship (and the proportion receiving): $1,780 (10%). Average amount of debt of borrowers graduating in 2005: $9,157. Proportion who borrowed: 70%.

CAMPUS LIFE AND EXTRACURRICULAR ACTIVITIES

Campus housing available (% using): coed dorms (99%), special housing for disabled students (1%). Students who live in college-owned, operated, or affiliated housing: 25%. **Clubs and organizations:** Number of student organizations: 56. Activities include: choral groups, concert band, dance, drama/theater, literary magazine, music ensembles, musical theater, pep band, radio station, student government, student newspaper, television station. Number of fraternities: 3; sororities: 4. Proportion of men in fraternities: 7%; of women in sororities: 7%. Average proportion of students who stay on campus on weekends: 44%. **Sports program (2005-2006):** Member of NAIA. *Men's intercollegiate varsity sports:* baseball, basketball, cross-country, football, golf, tennis. *Women's intercollegiate varsity sports:* basketball, cross-country, softball, tennis, volleyball.

SERVICES AND FACILITIES

Basic services: nonremedial tutoring, placement service, health service. **Remedial assistance:** reading, math, writing, study skills. **Counseling services:** career, personal, academic, older student, psychological. **For learning-disabled students:** School does not offer a structured program with separate admission and additional fees. Total undergraduates in learning-disabled program or receiving services: 44. Services include: remedial math, remedial English, reading machines, remedial reading, tape recorders, learning center, readers, extended time for tests, tutors, priority seating, other testing accomodations, other. **Library:** Number of titles: 143,265; number of current serial subscriptions: 3,990. **Information technology resources:** Students are not required to lease or own a computer. Number of campus computers available to all students: 173. School does not have a wireless network. Proportion of college-owned housing units wired for high-speed internet access: 100%. **Campus safety:** Security services offered: 24-hour foot-and-vehicle patrols, late-night transport/escort service, 24-hour emergency telephones, lighted pathways/sidewalks.

TRANSFER AND INTERNATIONAL STUDENTS

Transfer students: May apply for admission for the following academic terms: Fall, Spring, Summer. Applicants need a minimum number of credits to apply. For fall 2005: Transfer applications received: 262. Transfer applicants offered admission: 200. Transfer applicants enrolled: 160. **International students:** Number of foreign undergraduates: 9 (1% of student body). Number of countries represented: 7. Minimum TOEFL score required: 550 (paper); 234 (computer). Average TOEFL score: 570 (paper).

Virginia Commonwealth University

- **Address:** Box 842527, Richmond, VA 23284
- **Website:** http://www.vcu.edu
- **Public**
- **Enrollment:** 16,109 full-time; 4,399 part-time

KEY STATS

✔ **U.S News College Ranking:** third tier, National Universities
✔ **SAT Score (25th/75th percentile):** 960-1190
✔ **Tuition:** 2006-2007: $5,383 in state, $17,318 out of state

Selectivity: Selective	**Room/board:** $7,960
Acceptance rate: 68%	**Average debt:** $20,069
Student/faculty ratio: 19/1	**Proportion who borrowed:** 66%

UNDERGRADUATE STUDENT BODY STATS

2005-2006 enrollment: 16,109 full-time; 4,399 part-time. Men: 40%; women: 60%. **Ethnic makeup:** African American: 20%; American-Indian: 1%; Asian American: 9%; Hispanic: 3%; White: 64%; International: 2%.

ADMISSIONS FACTS AND FIGURES

Phone: (800) 841-3638. **Email:** ugrad@vcu.edu. **Website:** http://www.vcu.edu. **Application deadlines for fall 2007:** Regular decision: Rolling. Early decision: Not offered. Early action: Not offered. Admission can be deferred. **Application fee:** $30. Common application is accepted. **To apply online, go to:** http://www.vcu.edu/ugrad. **Admissions requirements/recommendations:** High school units required (recommended): English: 4 (4); Mathematics: 3 (4); Science: 3 (4); Foreign language: 3 (3); Social studies: 1 (1); History: 2 (3); Academic electives: 3 (4); Total units: 20 (24). Tests: The college uses SAT or ACT scores in admissions decisions. Either SAT or ACT required. For admission to the fall 2007 entering class, the school will accept: ACT with writing, ACT without writing. Campus visit: Recommended. Admissions interview: Neither required nor recommended. Off-campus interview: Not available. **Factors that count in admissions decisions:** *Academic:* Secondary school record: Very important. Class rank: Considered. Letters of recommendation: Important. Standardized test scores: Very important. Essay: Considered. ***Nonacademic:*** Interview: Considered. Extracurricular activities: Considered. Talent/ability: Considered. Character/personal qualities: Not considered. Alumni/ae relationship: Not considered. Geographical residence: Not considered. State residency: Not considered. Religious affiliation/commitment: Not considered. Minority status: Not considered. Volunteer work: Not considered. Work experience: Not considered. **Other schools with the greatest overlap in applicants:** George Mason University; James Madison University; Old Dominion University; University of Virginia; Virginia Tech. **Admissions statistics for the fall 2005 entering class:** Total applicants: 11,764. Total accepted: 8,020. Freshmen enrolled: 3,540; 8% were from out of state. Overall acceptance rate: 68%. **Size of waiting list:** 0 applicants; enrolled from waiting list: 0. **Credentials of fall 2005 freshmen:** 16% ranked in the top 10 percent of their high school class; 44% were in the top 25 percent, and 82% were in the top half. (Proportion submitting class standing: 70%.) **Average high school grade point average:** 3.2. **First-year students who submitted SAT scores:** 95%. Scores (25/75 percentile): Verbal: 480-600, Math: 480-590, Combined: 960-1190. **First-year students submitting ACT scores:** 15%. Scores (25/75 percentile): English: 18-24, Math: 17-23, Composite: 18-23.

ACADEMICS

Year founded: 1838. **Academic calendar:** Semester. **Degrees offered:** certificate, bachelor's, post-bachelor's certificate, master's, post-master's certificate, first professional, first professional certificate, doctorate. **Most popular majors:** 20% visual and performing arts, 15% business, management, marketing, and related support services, 11% health professions and related clinical sciences, 10% psychology, 5% security and protective services. **Major fields of study:** area, ethnic, cultural, and gender studies; biological and biomedical sciences; business, management, marketing, and related support services; communication, journalism, and related programs; computer and information sciences and support services; education; engineering; English language and literature/letters; foreign languages, literatures, and linguistics; health professions and related clinical sciences; history; liberal arts and sciences studies, and humanities; mathematics and statistics; multi/interdisciplinary studies; natural resources and conservation; parks, recreation, leisure, and fitness studies; philosophy and religious studies; physical sciences; psychology; public administration and social service professions; security and protective services; social sciences; visual and performing arts. **Areas of required coursework:** arts/fine arts, humanities, mathematics, English (including composition), sciences (biological or physical), social science. **Pre-professional programs:** pre-law, pre-dentistry, pre-medicine, pre-veterinary science, pre-optometry, pre-pharmacy, other. **Special academic programs:** accelerated program, cooperative (work-study plan) program, cross-registration, distance learning, double major, dual enrollment, English as a Second Language (ESL), exchange student program (domestic), external degree program, honors program, independent study, internships, liberal arts/career combination, student-designed major, study abroad, teacher certificate program. **Teacher certification offered in:** early childhood, special education, elementary, middle/junior high, adult education, secondary. **Cooperative education programs:** engineering. **Reserve Officers Training Corps (ROTC):** Army ROTC: Offered on campus. **Faculty and instruction (2005-2006):** Total instructional faculty: 1,744 full-time, 1,069 part-time (55% men; 45% women; 17% minorities). Full-time faculty with Ph.D. or other terminal degree: 80%. Student/faculty ratio: 19/1. Classes of fewer than 20 students: 43%; of 20 to 49 students: 46%; of 50 or more students: 12%. **Advanced Placement and International Baccalaureate credit:** AP tests may be used for: Credit and/or placement. Scores accepted: 3, 4, 5. International Baccalaureate exams may be used for: Credit only. **Freshmen returning for sophomore year:** 79%. **Graduation rates:** Four-year: 21%; five-year: 37%; six-year: 43%.

COSTS AND FINANCIAL AID

Financial aid office: (804) 828-6669. **Expenses (2006-2007):** Tuition and fees 2006-2007: $5,383 in state, $17,318 out of state; room/board: $7,960. Estimated books and supplies: $980; transportation: $1,220; personal expenses: $1,350. **Financial aid:** Priority filing date for institution's financial aid form: March 1. In 2005-2006, 64% of undergraduates applied for financial aid. Of those, 49% were determined to have financial need; 19% had their need fully met. Average financial aid package (proportion receiving): $7,932 (49%). Average amount of gift aid, such as scholarships or grants (proportion receiving): $4,008 (34%). Average amount of self-help aid, such as work study or loans (proportion receiving): $4,782 (44%). Average need-based loan (excluding PLUS or other private loans): $3,780. Among students who received need-based aid, the average percentage of need met: 65%. Among students who received aid based on merit, the average award (and the proportion receiving): $4,785 (4%). The average athletic scholarship (and the proportion receiving): $12,232 (1%). Average amount of debt of borrowers graduating in 2005: $20,069. Proportion who borrowed: 66%.

CAMPUS LIFE AND EXTRACURRICULAR ACTIVITIES

Campus housing available (% using): coed dorms (78%), apartment for single students (20%), special housing for disabled students (1%), special housing for international students (1%). Students who live in college-owned, operated, or affiliated housing: 24%. **Student employment:** During the 2005-2006 academic year, 10% of undergraduates worked on campus. **Clubs and organizations:** Number of student organizations: 317. Activities include: choral groups, concert band, dance, drama/theater, jazz band, literary magazine, marching band, music ensembles, opera, pep band, radio station, student government, student newspaper, symphony orchestra, yearbook. Number of fraternities: 11; sororities: 13. Proportion of men in fraternities: 3%; of women in sororities: 3%. Average proportion of students who stay on campus on weekends: 80%. **Sports program (2005-2006):** Member of NCAA I. *Men's intercollegiate varsity sports:* baseball, basketball, cross-country, field hockey, golf, soccer, tennis, track and field (indoor), track and field (outdoor). *Women's intercollegiate varsity sports:* basketball, cross-country, field hockey, soccer, tennis, track and field (indoor), track and field (outdoor), volleyball.

SERVICES AND FACILITIES

Basic services: nonremedial tutoring, day care, health service. **Remedial assistance:** reading, math, writing, other. **Counseling services:** minority student, career, military, personal, veteran student, psychological, birth control, religious, other. **For learning-disabled students:** School does not offer a structured program with separate admission and additional fees. Total undergraduates in learning-disabled program or receiving services: 350. Services include: remedial English, tape recorders, note-taking services, oral tests, extended time for tests, tutors, priority registration, priority seating, substitution of courses, texts on tape, exams on tape or computer, other testing accomodations. **Library:** Number of titles: 1,576,602; number of current serial subscriptions: 16,800. **Information technology resources:** Students are required to lease or own a computer. Number of campus computers available to all students: 2,500. School has a wireless network. Approximate number of users that can be accommodated: 1,000. Proportion of college-owned housing units wired for high-speed internet access: 100%. **Campus safety:** Security services offered: 24-hour foot-and-vehicle patrols, late-night transport/escort service, 24-hour emergency telephones, lighted pathways/sidewalks, student patrols, controlled dormitory access (key, security card, etc).

TRANSFER AND INTERNATIONAL STUDENTS

Transfer students: May apply for admission for the following academic terms: Fall, Spring. Applicants do not need a minimum number of credits to apply. For fall 2005: Transfer applications received: 3,730. Transfer applicants offered admission: 2,582. Transfer applicants enrolled: 1,789. **International students:** Number of foreign undergraduates: 375 (2% of student body). Number of countries represented: 95. Minimum TOEFL score required: 550 (paper); 213 (computer). Average TOEFL score: 525 (paper).

Virginia Intermont College

- **Address:** 1013 Moore Street, Bristol, VA 24201
- **Website:** http://www.vic.edu
- **Private; Religious affiliation:** Baptist
- **Enrollment:** 986 full-time; 152 part-time

KEY STATS
✔ **U.S News College Ranking:** third tier, Comp. Coll.–Bachelor's (South)
✔ **SAT Score (25th/75th percentile):** 840-1060
✔ **Tuition:** 2006-2007: $17,845

Selectivity: Less selective	Room/board: $6,095
Acceptance rate: 63%	Average debt: $18,700
Student/faculty ratio: N/A	Proportion who borrowed: 83%

UNDERGRADUATE STUDENT BODY STATS

2005-2006 enrollment: 986 full-time; 152 part-time. Men: 30%; women: 70%. **Ethnic makeup:** African American: 7%; American-Indian: 1%; Asian American: 1%; Hispanic: 2%; White: 89%; International: 1%. **Religious preference:** Roman Catholic: 11%; Protestant: 27%; Jewish: 1%; Unknown: 42%; Baptist: 17%.

ADMISSIONS FACTS AND FIGURES

Phone: (276) 466-7856. **Email:** viadmit@vic.edu. **Website:** http://www.vic.edu. **Application deadlines for fall 2007:** Regular decision: Rolling. Early decision: Not offered. Early action: Not offered. Admission can be deferred. **Application fee:** $15. Common application is not accepted. **To apply online, go to:** http://www.vic.edu/admiss/application/index.html. **Admissions requirements/recommendations:** High school units required (recommended): English: 4 (4); Mathematics: 2 (3); Science: 1 (3); Foreign language: 0 (2); Social studies: 2 (2); History: 0 (2); Academic electives: 6 (8); Total units: 15 (24). Tests: The college uses SAT or ACT scores in admissions decisions. Either SAT or ACT required. For admission to the fall 2007 entering class, the school will accept: ACT with writing. Campus visit: Recommended. Admissions interview: Neither required nor recommended. Off-campus interview: May be arranged. **Factors that count in admissions decisions:** *Academic:* Secondary school record: Very important. Class rank: Considered. Letters of recommendation: Considered. Standardized test scores: Very important. Essay: Considered. *Nonacademic:* Interview: Considered. Extracurricular activities: Considered. Talent/ability: Considered. Character/personal qualities: Considered. Alumni/ae relationship: Considered. Geographical residence: Not considered. State residency: Not considered. Religious affiliation/commitment: Not considered. Minority status: Not considered. Volunteer work: Not considered. Work experience: Considered. **Other schools with the greatest overlap in applicants:** Averett University; East Tennessee State University; Radford University; St. Andrews Presbyterian College; Sweet Briar College. **Admissions statistics for the fall 2005 entering class:** Total applicants: 802. Total accepted: 505. Freshmen enrolled: 182; Overall acceptance rate: 63%. **Credentials of fall 2005 freshmen:** 11% ranked in the top 10 percent of their high school class; 24% were in the top 25 percent, and 70% were in the top half. (Proportion submitting class standing: 61%.) **Average high school grade point average:** 3.1. **First-year students who submitted SAT scores:** 71%. Scores (25/75 percentile): Verbal: 430-550, Math: 410-510, Combined: 840-1060. **First-year students submitting ACT scores:** 29%. Scores (25/75 percentile): English: 17-23, Math: 16-22, Composite: 18-22.

ACADEMICS

Year founded: 1884. **Academic calendar:** Semester. **Degrees offered:** associate, bachelor's. **Most popular majors:** Information not available. **Major fields of study:** agriculture, agriculture operations, and related sciences; biological and biomedical sciences; business, management, marketing, and related support services; communication, journalism, and related programs; computer and information sciences and support services; education; English language and literature/letters; health professions and related clinical sciences; history; legal professions and studies; liberal arts and sciences studies, and humanities; natural resources and conservation; parks, recreation, leisure, and fitness studies; personal and culinary services; philosophy and religious studies; psychology; public administration and social service professions; security and protective services; social sciences; visual and performing arts. **Areas of required coursework:** arts/fine arts, humanities, computer literacy, mathematics, English (including composition), philosophy, sciences (biological or physical), history, social science. **Pre-professional programs:** pre-law, pre-medicine, pre-veterinary science. **Special academic programs:** accelerated program, distance learning, double major, English as a Second Language (ESL), honors program, independent study, internships, liberal arts/career combination, teacher certificate program. **Teacher certification offered in:** special education, elementary, secondary. **Advanced Placement and International Baccalaureate credit:** AP tests may be used for: Credit only. Scores accepted: 3. International Baccalaureate exams may be used for: Credit only. **Freshmen returning for sophomore year:** 66%. **Graduation rates:** Four-year: 19%; five-year: 28%; six-year: 36%. **Graduate study:** 7% of students pursue further study within one year. Fields in which graduates pursue further study: Master of Business Administration (MBA), 2%; law, 1%; medicine, 1%; arts and sciences, 2%; veterinary medicine, 1%.

COSTS AND FINANCIAL AID

Financial aid office: (276) 466-7873. **Expenses (2006-2007):** Tuition and fees 2006-2007: $17,845; room/board: $6,095. Estimated books and supplies: $1,000; transportation: $3,000; personal expenses: $2,700. **Financial aid:** Priority filing date for institution's financial aid form: March 1. In 2005-2006, 81% of undergraduates applied for financial aid. Of those, 75% were determined to have financial need; 9% had their need fully met. Average financial aid package (proportion receiving): $10,961 (75%). Average amount of gift aid, such as scholarships or grants (proportion receiving): N/A (70%). Average amount of self-help aid, such as work study or loans (proportion receiving): $4,177 (66%). Average need-based loan (excluding PLUS or other private loans): $3,855. Among students who received need-based aid, the average percentage of need met: 55%. Among students who received aid based on merit, the average award (and the proportion receiving): $8,508 (16%). The average athletic scholarship (and the proportion receiving): $12,054 (9%). Average amount of debt of borrowers graduating in 2005: $18,700. Proportion who borrowed: 83%.

CAMPUS LIFE AND EXTRACURRICULAR ACTIVITIES

Campus housing available: coed dorms, women's dorms, men's dorms, apartments for married students, apartment for single students, special housing for disabled students, other housing options. **Student employment:** During the 2005-2006 academic year, 25% of undergraduates worked on campus. Average per-year earnings: $1,500. **Clubs and organizations:** Number of student organizations: 25. Activities include: choral groups, dance, drama/theater, musical theater, student government, yearbook. Number of fraternities: 0; sororities: 0. Average proportion of students who stay on campus on weekends: 50%. **Sports program (2005-2006):** Member of NAIA. *Men's intercollegiate varsity sports:* baseball, basketball, cross-country, golf, soccer, tennis, track and field (indoor), track and field (outdoor). *Women's intercollegiate varsity sports:* basketball, cross-country, equestrian sports, soccer, softball, tennis, track and field (indoor), track and field (outdoor), volleyball.

SERVICES AND FACILITIES

Basic services: nonremedial tutoring, placement service, health service, health insurance. **Remedial assistance:** reading, math, writing, study skills. **Counseling services:** minority student, career, military, personal, veteran student, academic, older student, psychological, birth control, religious. **For learning-disabled students:** School does not offer a structured program with separate admission and additional fees. Total undergraduates in learning-disabled program or receiving services: 23. Services include: remedial reading, tape recorders, other special classes, diagnostic testing service, untimed tests, note-taking services, oral tests, learning center, readers, extended time for tests, tutors, texts on tape, other. **Library:** Number of titles: 93,382; number of current serial subscriptions: 75. **Information technology resources:** Students are not required to lease or own a computer. Number of campus computers available to all students: 100. School has a wireless network. Proportion of college-owned housing units wired for high-speed internet access: 100%. **Campus safety:** Security services offered: 24-hour foot-and-vehicle patrols, late-night transport/escort service, 24-hour emergency telephones, lighted pathways/sidewalks, controlled dormitory access (key, security card, etc).

TRANSFER AND INTERNATIONAL STUDENTS

Transfer students: May apply for admission for the following academic terms: Fall, Spring, Summer. Applicants need a minimum number of credits to apply. For fall 2005: Transfer applications received: 353. Transfer applicants offered admission: 183. Transfer applicants enrolled: 106. **International students:** Number of foreign undergraduates: 12 (1% of student body). Number of countries represented: 38. Minimum TOEFL score required: 500 (paper); 300 (computer). Average TOEFL score: 500 (paper).

Virginia Military Institute

- **Address:** VMI Parade, Lexington, VA 24450-0304
- **Website:** http://www.vmi.edu
- **Public**
- **Enrollment:** 1,369 full-time

KEY STATS

✔ **U.S News College Ranking:** 86, Liberal Arts Colleges
✔ **SAT Score (25th/75th percentile):** 1050-1250
✔ **Tuition:** 2006-2007: $9,473 in state, $24,282 out of state

Selectivity: Selective	**Room/board:** $5,930
Acceptance rate: 50%	**Average debt:** $14,367
Student/faculty ratio: 11/1	**Proportion who borrowed:** 34%

UNDERGRADUATE STUDENT BODY STATS

2005-2006 enrollment: 1,369 full-time. Men: 92%; women: 8%. **Ethnic makeup:** African American: 5%; Asian American: 3%; Hispanic: 3%; White: 86%; International: 2%.

ADMISSIONS FACTS AND FIGURES

Phone: (800) 767-4207. **Email:** admissions@vmi.edu. **Website:** http://www.vmi.edu. **Application deadlines for fall 2007:** Regular decision: February 15. Early decision: Send application by: November 15; Decision sent by: December 15. Early action: Not offered. Admission cannot be deferred. **Application fee:** $35. Common application is not accepted. **To apply online, go to:** http://www.vmi.edu/admissions. **Admissions requirements/recommendations:** High school units required (recommended): English: 4 (4); Mathematics: 3 (4); Science: 3 (3); Foreign language: 3 (4); Total units: 16 (18). Tests: The college uses SAT or ACT scores in admissions decisions. Either SAT or ACT required. For admission to the fall 2007 entering class, the school will accept: ACT with writing, ACT without writing. Campus visit: Recommended. Admissions interview: Recommended. Off-campus interview: May be arranged. **Factors that count in admissions decisions:** *Academic:* Secondary school record: Very important. Class rank: Very important. Letters of recommendation: Considered. Standardized test scores: Very important. *Nonacademic:* Interview: Important. Extracurricular activities: Important. Talent/ability: Considered. Character/personal qualities: Very important. Alumni/ae relationship: Considered. Geographical residence: Considered. State residency: Important. Minority status: Important. Volunteer work: Important. **Other schools with the greatest overlap in applicants:** The Citadel; United States Air Force Academy; United States Military Academy; United States Naval Academy. **Admissions statistics for the fall 2005 entering class:** Total applicants: 1,811. Total accepted: 913. Freshmen enrolled: 391; 44% were from out of state. Accepted through early-decision or early-action plans: 42%. Overall acceptance rate: 50%. Non-early acceptance rate: 35%. **Size of waiting list:** 68 applicants; enrolled from waiting list: 31. **Credentials of fall 2005 freshmen:** 12% ranked in the top 10 percent of their high school class; 44% were in the top 25 percent, and 85% were in the top half. (Proportion submitting class standing: 79%.) **First-year students who submitted SAT scores:** 86%. Scores (25/75 percentile): Verbal: 520-630, Math: 530-620, Combined: 1050-1250. **First-year students submitting ACT scores:** 13%. Scores (25/75 percentile): English: N/A, Math: N/A, Composite: 22-26.

ACADEMICS

Year founded: 1839. **Academic calendar:** Semester. **Degrees offered:** bachelor's. **Most popular majors:** 29% social sciences, 20% engineering, 8% psychology, 3% English language and literature/letters, 3% computer and information sciences and support services. **Major fields of study:** biological and biomedical sciences; computer and information sciences and support services; engineering; English language and literature/letters; foreign languages, literatures, and linguistics; history; mathematics and statistics; physical sciences; psychology; social sciences. **Areas of required coursework:** mathematics, English (including composition), foreign languages, sciences (biological or physical), history, other. **Special academic programs:** accelerated program, double major, exchange student program (domestic), honors program, independent study, internships, study abroad, teacher certificate program, other. **Teacher certification offered in:** secondary. **Reserve Officers Training Corps (ROTC):** Army ROTC: Offered on campus; Navy ROTC: Offered on campus; Air Force ROTC: Offered on campus. **Faculty and instruction (2005-2006):** Total instructional faculty: 107 full-time, 53 part-time (77% men; 23% women; 6% minorities). Full-time faculty with Ph.D. or other terminal degree: 95%. Student/faculty ratio: 11/1. Classes of fewer than 20 students: 67%; of 20 to 49 students: 33%. **Advanced Placement and International Baccalaureate credit:** AP tests may be used for: Credit and/or placement. Scores accepted: 3, 4, 5. International Baccalaureate exams may be used for: Credit and/or placement. **Freshmen returning for sophomore year:** 86%. **Graduation rates:** Six-year: 66%. **Graduate study:** 13% of students pursue further study immediately upon graduation; 39% within five years.

COSTS AND FINANCIAL AID

Financial aid office: (540) 464-7208. **Expenses (2006-2007):** Tuition and fees 2006-2007: $9,473 in state, $24,282 out of state; room/board: $5,930. Estimated books and supplies: $775; transportation: $300; personal expenses: $1,500. **Financial aid:** Priority filing date for institution's financial aid form: March 1; deadline: March 1. In 2005-2006, 54% of undergraduates applied for financial aid. Of those, 41% were determined to have financial need; 32% had their need fully met. Average financial aid package (proportion receiving): $14,334 (40%). Average amount of gift aid, such as scholarships or grants (proportion receiving): $12,636 (39%). Average

amount of self-help aid, such as work study or loans (proportion receiving): $3,682 (24%). Average need-based loan (excluding PLUS or other private loans): $3,708. Among students who received need-based aid, the average percentage of need met: 94%. Among students who received aid based on merit, the average award (and the proportion receiving): $5,817 (15%). The average athletic scholarship (and the proportion receiving): $12,626 (9%). Average amount of debt of borrowers graduating in 2005: $14,367. Proportion who borrowed: 34%.

CAMPUS LIFE AND EXTRACURRICULAR ACTIVITIES

Campus housing available (% using): other housing options (100%). Students who live in college-owned, operated, or affiliated housing: 100%. **Student employment:** During the 2005-2006 academic year, 15% of undergraduates worked on campus. Average per-year earnings: $7. Activities include: choral groups, concert band, drama/theater, jazz band, literary magazine, marching band, music ensembles, musical theater, pep band, student government, student newspaper, yearbook. Number of fraternities: 0; sororities: 0. Average proportion of students who stay on campus on weekends: 85%. **Sports program (2005-2006):** Member of NCAA I. *Men's intercollegiate varsity sports:* baseball, basketball, cross-country, football, lacrosse, riflery, soccer, swimming and diving, track and field (indoor), track and field (outdoor), wrestling. *Women's intercollegiate varsity sports:* cross-country, soccer, swimming and diving, track and field (indoor), track and field (outdoor).

SERVICES AND FACILITIES

Basic services: nonremedial tutoring, health service. **Remedial assistance:** reading, math, writing, study skills. **Counseling services:** minority student, career, military, personal, veteran student, academic, older student, psychological, birth control, religious. **For learning-disabled students:** School does not offer a structured program with separate admission and additional fees. Total undergraduates in learning-disabled program or receiving services: 6. Services include: reading machines, tape recorders, note-taking services, learning center, extended time for tests, tutors, priority registration, priority seating, texts on tape, other testing accomodations, other. **Library:** Number of titles: 430,854; number of current serial subscriptions: 16,500. **Information technology resources:** Students are not required to lease or own a computer. Number of campus computers available to all students: 167. School has a wireless network. Approximate number of users that can be accommodated: 500. Proportion of college-owned housing units wired for high-speed internet access: 100%. **Campus safety:** Security services offered: 24-hour foot-and-vehicle patrols, 24-hour emergency telephones, lighted pathways/sidewalks, controlled dormitory access (key, security card, etc).

TRANSFER AND INTERNATIONAL STUDENTS

Transfer students: May apply for admission for the following academic terms: Fall. Applicants do not need a minimum number of credits to apply. For fall 2005: Transfer applications received: 132. Transfer applicants offered admission: 52. Transfer applicants enrolled: 43. **International students:** Number of foreign undergraduates: 27 (2% of student body). Minimum TOEFL score required: 500 (paper); 173 (computer). Average TOEFL score: 548 (paper).

Virginia State University

- **Address:** 1 Hayden Street, Petersburg, VA 23806
- **Website:** http://www.vsu.edu
- **Public**
- **Enrollment:** 4,060 full-time; 272 part-time

KEY STATS

✔ **U.S News College Ranking:** third tier, Universities–Master's (South)
✔ **SAT Score (25th/75th percentile):** 750-920
✔ **Tuition:** 2006-2007: $5,556 in state, $12,628 out of state

Selectivity: Least selective	**Room/board:** $6,884
Acceptance rate: 83%	**Average debt:** $25,600
Student/faculty ratio: 17/1	**Proportion who borrowed:** 92%

UNDERGRADUATE STUDENT BODY STATS

2005-2006 enrollment: 4,060 full-time; 272 part-time. Men: 39%; women: 61%. **Ethnic makeup:** African American: 96%; Hispanic: 1%; White: 2%.

ADMISSIONS FACTS AND FIGURES

Phone: (804) 524-5902. **Email:** admiss@vsu.edu. **Website:** http://www.vsu.edu. **Application deadlines for fall 2007:** Regular decision: May 1. Early decision: Not offered. Early action: Not offered. Admission cannot be deferred. **Application fee:** $25. Common application is accepted. **Admissions requirements/recommendations:** High school units required (recommended): English: 4; Mathematics: 3; Science: 2; Foreign language: (2); Social studies: 2; Total units: 11. Tests: The college uses SAT or ACT scores in admissions decisions. Either SAT or ACT required. For admission to the fall 2007 entering class, the school will accept: ACT with writing, ACT without writing. Campus visit: Recommended. Admissions interview: Neither required nor recommended. Off-campus interview: Not available. **Factors that count in admissions decisions:** *Academic:* Secondary school record: Very important. Class rank: Considered. Letters of recommendation: Very important. Standardized test scores: Very important. Essay: Very important. *Nonacademic:* Interview: Not considered. Extracurricular activities: Considered. Talent/ability: Considered. Character/personal qualities: Considered. Alumni/ae relationship: Considered. Geographical residence: Considered. State residency: Considered. Religious affiliation/commitment: Not considered. Minority status: Not considered. Volunteer work: Considered. Work experience: Considered. **Admissions statistics for the fall 2005 entering class:** Total applicants: 3,782. Total accepted: 3,143. Freshmen enrolled: 1,107; 36% were from out of state. Overall acceptance rate: 83%. **Credentials of fall 2005 freshmen:** 4% ranked in the top 10 percent of their high school class; 15% were in the top 25 percent, and 56% were in the top half. (Proportion submitting class standing: 59%.) **Average high school grade point average:** 2.7. **First-year students who submitted SAT scores:** 98%. Scores (25/75 percentile): Verbal: 380-460, Math: 370-460, Combined: 750-920. **First-year students submitting ACT scores:** 1%. Scores (25/75 percentile): English: N/A, Math: N/A, Composite: 16-19.

ACADEMICS

Year founded: 1882. **Academic calendar:** Semester. **Degrees offered:** associate, bachelor's, master's, post-master's certificate, doctorate. **Most popular majors:** 10% liberal arts and sciences/liberal studies, 8% physical education teaching and coaching, 7% business administration and management, 7% multi/interdisciplinary studies, 6% criminal justice/safety studies. **Major fields of study:** agriculture, agriculture operations, and related sciences; biological and biomedical sciences; business, management, marketing, and related support services; communication, journalism, and related programs; computer and information sciences and support services; education; engineering; engineering technologies/technicians; English language and literature/letters; family and consumer sciences/human sciences; health professions and related clinical sciences; history; liberal arts and sciences studies, and humanities; mathematics and statistics; multi/interdisciplinary studies; physical sciences; psychology; public administration and social service professions; security and protective services; social sciences; visual and performing arts. **Areas of required coursework:** arts/fine arts, humanities, computer literacy, mathematics, English (including composition), philosophy, foreign languages, sciences (biological or physical), history, social science. **Pre-professional programs:** other. **Special academic programs:** cooperative (work-study plan) program, double major, dual enrollment, exchange student program (domestic), honors program, independent study, internships, teacher certificate program. **Teacher certification offered in:** early childhood, special education, elementary, middle/junior high, secondary. **Cooperative education programs:** agriculture, art, business, computer science, education, engineering, home economics, humanities, natural science, social/behavioral science, technologies, vocational arts. **Reserve Officers Training Corps (ROTC):** Army ROTC: Offered on campus. **Faculty and instruction (2005-2006):** Total instructional faculty: 226 full-time, 101 part-time (58% men; 42% women; 70% minorities). Full-time faculty with Ph.D. or other terminal degree: 81%. Student/faculty ratio: 17/1. Classes of fewer than 20 students: 39%; of 20 to 49 students: 54%; of 50 or more students: 6%. **Advanced Placement and International Baccalaureate credit:** AP tests may be used for: Credit only. Scores accepted: 3. **Freshmen returning for sophomore year:** 72%. **Graduation rates:** Four-year: 18%; five-year: 34%; six-year: 41%.

COSTS AND FINANCIAL AID

Financial aid office: (804) 524-5992. **Expenses (2006-2007):** Tuition and fees 2006-2007: $5,556 in state, $12,628 out of state; room/board: $6,884. Estimated books and supplies: $850; transportation: $800; personal expenses: $532. **Financial aid:** Priority filing date for institution's financial aid form: March 31; deadline: May 1. In 2005-2006, 96% of undergraduates applied for financial aid. Of those, 88% were determined to have financial need; Average financial aid package (proportion receiving): $7,120 (88%).

Average amount of gift aid, such as scholarships or grants (proportion receiving): $3,255 (62%). Average amount of self-help aid, such as work study or loans (proportion receiving): $4,256 (71%). Average need-based loan (excluding PLUS or other private loans): $4,025. Among students who received need-based aid, the average percentage of need met: 75%. Among students who received aid based on merit, the average award (and the proportion receiving): $4,576 (10%). The average athletic scholarship (and the proportion receiving): $3,250 (5%). Average amount of debt of borrowers graduating in 2005: $25,600. Proportion who borrowed: 92%.

CAMPUS LIFE AND EXTRACURRICULAR ACTIVITIES

Campus housing available (% using): coed dorms (14%), women's dorms (40%), men's dorms (21%), apartment for single students (15%). Students who live in college-owned, operated, or affiliated housing: 61%. **Clubs and organizations:** Number of student organizations: 70. Activities include: choral groups, concert band, dance, drama/theater, jazz band, literary magazine, marching band, music ensembles, pep band, radio station, student government, student newspaper, television station, yearbook. Number of fraternities: 5; sororities: 4. Proportion of men in fraternities: 2%; of women in sororities: 5%. **Sports program (2005-2006):** Member of NCAA II. *Men's intercollegiate varsity sports:* baseball, basketball, cross-country, football, golf, tennis, track and field (indoor), track and field (outdoor). *Women's intercollegiate varsity sports:* basketball, bowling, cross-country, golf, softball, tennis, track and field (indoor), track and field (outdoor), volleyball.

SERVICES AND FACILITIES

Basic services: nonremedial tutoring, placement service, health service. **Counseling services:** veteran student, academic, psychological. **For learning-disabled students:** School does not offer a structured program with separate admission and additional fees. Services include: reading machines, tape recorders, untimed tests, note-taking services, special bookstore section, oral tests, learning center, readers, extended time for tests, tutors, early syllabus, priority registration, priority seating, texts on tape, typist/scribe, exams on tape or computer, other testing accomodations. **Library:** Number of titles: 303,757; number of current serial subscriptions: 1,598. **Information technology resources:** Students are not required to lease or own a computer. Number of campus computers available to all students: 700. School has a wireless network. Approximate number of users that can be accommodated: 1,200. Proportion of college-owned housing units wired for high-speed internet access: 100%. **Campus safety:** Security services offered: late-night transport/escort service, 24-hour emergency telephones, lighted pathways/sidewalks.

TRANSFER AND INTERNATIONAL STUDENTS

Transfer students: May apply for admission for the following academic terms: Fall, Spring, Summer. Applicants need a minimum number of credits to apply. For fall 2005: Transfer applications received: 472. Transfer applicants offered admission: 424. Transfer applicants enrolled: 213. **International students:** Number of foreign undergraduates: 0. Minimum TOEFL score required: 500 (paper); 173 (computer).

Virginia Tech

- **Address:** Blacksburg, VA 24061
- **Website:** http://www.vt.edu
- Public
- **Enrollment:** 21,087 full-time; 540 part-time

KEY STATS

- ✔ **U.S News College Ranking:** 77, National Universities
- ✔ **SAT Score (25th/75th percentile):** 1110-1290
- ✔ **Tuition:** 2006-2007: $6,973 in state, $18,929 out of state

Selectivity: More selective	**Room/board:** $7,020
Acceptance rate: 72%	**Average debt:** $18,385
Student/faculty ratio: 16/1	**Proportion who borrowed:** 54%

UNDERGRADUATE STUDENT BODY STATS

2005-2006 enrollment: 21,087 full-time; 540 part-time. Men: 59%; women: 41%. **Ethnic makeup:** African American: 5%; Asian American: 7%; Hispanic: 2%; White: 83%; International: 2%. **Religious preference:** Roman Catholic: 27%; Protestant: 58%; Jewish: 2%; Muslim: 1%; Hindu: 1%; Buddhist: 1%; No preference: 8%; Other: 2%.

ADMISSIONS FACTS AND FIGURES

Phone: (540) 231-6267. **Email:** vtadmiss@vt.edu. **Website:** http://www.vt.edu. **Application deadlines for fall 2007:** Regular decision: January 15; decision sent by April 1. Early decision: Send application by: November 1; Decision sent by: December 15. Early action: Not offered. Admission can be deferred. **Application fee:** $40. Common application is not accepted. **To apply online, go to:** http://www.admiss.vt.edu/apply.html. **Admissions requirements/recommendations:** High school units required (recommended): English: 4; Mathematics: 3 (4); Science: 2 (3); Foreign language: (3); Social studies: 1; History: 1; Academic electives: 3; Total units: 18. Tests: The college uses SAT or ACT scores in admissions decisions. Either SAT or ACT required. For admission to the fall 2007 entering class, the school will accept: ACT with writing. Campus visit: Recommended. Admissions interview: Neither required nor recommended. **Factors that count in admissions decisions:** *Academic:* Secondary school record: Very important. Class rank: Not considered. Letters of recommendation: Considered. Standardized test scores: Very important. Essay: Not considered. *Nonacademic:* Interview: Not considered. Extracurricular activities: Considered. Talent/ability: Considered. Character/personal qualities: Considered. Alumni/ae relationship: Considered. Geographical residence: Considered. State residency: Considered. Religious affiliation/commitment: Not considered. Minority status: Considered. Volunteer work: Considered. Work experience: Considered. **Admissions statistics for the fall 2005 entering class:** Total applicants: 17,681. Total accepted: 12,714. Freshmen enrolled: 5,049; 29% were from out of state. Accepted through early-decision or early-action plans: 21%. Overall acceptance rate: 72%. Early-decision acceptance rate: 56%. Non-early acceptance rate: 74%. **Size of waiting list:** 1150 applicants; enrolled from waiting list: 0. **Credentials of fall 2005 freshmen:** 37% ranked in the top 10 percent of their high school class; 79% were in the top 25 percent, and 97% were in the top half. (Proportion submitting class standing: 64%.) **Average high school grade point average:** 3.7. **First-year students who submitted SAT scores:** 98%. Scores (25/75 percentile): Verbal: 540-630, Math: 570-660, Combined: 1110-1290. **First-year students submitting ACT scores:** 19%. Scores (25/75 percentile): English: N/A, Math: N/A, Composite: 22-27.

ACADEMICS

Year founded: 1872. **Academic calendar:** Semester. **Degrees offered:** certificate, associate, bachelor's, master's, post-master's certificate, first professional, doctorate. **Most popular majors:** 22% engineering, 21% business, management, marketing, and related support services, 6% biological and biomedical sciences, 5% psychology, 4% communication, journalism, and related programs. **Major fields of study:** agriculture, agriculture operations, and related sciences; architecture and related services; biological and biomedical sciences; business, management, marketing, and related support services; communication, journalism, and related programs; computer and information sciences and support services; education; engineering; engineering technologies/technicians; English language and literature/letters; family and consumer sciences/human sciences; foreign languages, literatures, and linguistics; history; liberal arts and sciences studies, and humanities; mathematics and statistics; natural resources and conservation; philosophy and religious studies; physical sciences; psychology; public administration and social service professions; social sciences; visual and performing arts. **Areas of required coursework:** arts/fine arts, humanities, computer literacy, mathematics, English (including composition), foreign languages, sciences (biological or physical), history, social science. **Pre-professional programs:** pre-law, pre-dentistry, pre-medicine, pre-veterinary science. **Special academic programs:** accelerated program, cooperative (work-study plan) program, cross-registration, distance learning, double major, dual enrollment, English as a Second Language (ESL), honors program, independent study, internships, liberal arts/career combination, student-designed major, study abroad, teacher certificate program. **Teacher certification offered in:** early childhood, elementary, vo-tech, middle/junior high, secondary. **Cooperative education programs:** agriculture, business, computer science, education, engineering, natural science. **Reserve Officers Training Corps (ROTC):** Army ROTC: Offered on campus; Navy ROTC: Offered on campus; Air Force ROTC: Offered on campus. **Faculty and instruction (2005-2006):** Total instructional faculty: 1,304 full-time, 228 part-time (69% men; 31% women; 13% minorities). Full-time faculty with Ph.D. or other terminal degree: 89%. Student/faculty ratio: 16/1. Classes of fewer than 20 students: 24%; of 20 to 49 students: 56%; of 50 or more students: 21%. **Advanced Placement and International Baccalaureate credit:** AP tests may be used for: Credit and/or placement. Scores accepted: 3, 4, 5. International Baccalaureate exams may be used for: Credit and/or placement. **Freshmen returning for sophomore year:** 87%. **Graduation rates:** Four-year: 47%; five-year: 72%; six-year: 76%. **Graduate study:** 22% of students pursue further study immediately upon graduation.

COSTS AND FINANCIAL AID

Financial aid office: (540) 231-5179. **Expenses (2006-2007):** Tuition and fees 2006-2007: $6,973 in state, $18,929 out of state; room/board: $7,020. Estimated books and supplies: $1,067; transportation: $1,534; personal expenses: $1,460. **Financial aid:** Priority filing date for institution's financial aid form: March 11; deadline: March 11. In 2005-2006, 62% of undergraduates applied for financial aid. Of those, 39% were determined to have financial need; 20% had their need fully met. Average financial aid package (proportion receiving): $8,064 (35%). Average amount of gift aid, such as scholarships or grants (proportion receiving): $4,213 (28%). Average amount of self-help aid, such as work study or loans (proportion receiving): $3,765 (31%). Average need-based loan (excluding PLUS or other private loans): $3,570. Among students who received need-based aid, the average percentage of need met: 77%. Among students who received aid based on merit, the average award (and the proportion receiving): $2,122 (5%). The average athletic scholarship (and the proportion receiving): $11,307 (2%). Average amount of debt of borrowers graduating in 2005: $18,385. Proportion who borrowed: 54%.

CAMPUS LIFE AND EXTRACURRICULAR ACTIVITIES

Campus housing available (% using): coed dorms (59%), women's dorms (10%), men's dorms (22%), sorority housing (5%), fraternity housing (2%). Students who live in college-owned, operated, or affiliated housing: 41%. **Clubs and organizations:** Number of student organizations: 795. Activities include: choral groups, concert band, dance, drama/theater, jazz band, literary magazine, marching band, music ensembles, musical theater, pep band, radio station, student government, student newspaper, yearbook. Number of fraternities: 33; sororities: 22. Proportion of men in fraternities: 13%; of women in sororities: 17%. **Sports program (2005-2006):** Member of NCAA I. *Men's intercollegiate varsity sports:* baseball, basketball, cross-country, football, golf, soccer, swimming and diving, tennis, track and field (indoor), track and field (outdoor), wrestling. *Women's intercollegiate varsity sports:* basketball, cross-country, lacrosse, soccer, softball, swimming and diving, tennis, track and field (indoor), track and field (outdoor), volleyball.

SERVICES AND FACILITIES

Basic services: nonremedial tutoring, women's center, placement service, health service, health insurance. **Counseling services:** minority student, career, military, personal, academic, older student, psychological, birth control, religious. **For learning-disabled students:** School does not offer a structured program with separate admission and additional fees. Total undergraduates in learning-disabled program or receiving services: 193. Services include: reading machines, tape recorders, note-taking services, oral tests, learning center, readers, extended time for tests, tutors, early syllabus, priority registration, priority seating, substitution of courses, texts on tape, typist/scribe, exams on tape or computer, other testing accomodations. **Library:** Number of titles: 2,210,645; number of current serial subscriptions: 30,072. **Information technology resources:** Students are required to lease or own a computer. School has a wireless network. Approximate number of users that can be accommodated: 8,000. Proportion of college-owned housing units wired for high-speed internet access: 100%. **Campus safety:** Security services offered: 24-hour foot-and-vehicle patrols, late-night transport/escort service, 24-hour emergency telephones, lighted pathways/sidewalks, controlled dormitory access (key, security card, etc).

TRANSFER AND INTERNATIONAL STUDENTS

Transfer students: May apply for admission for the following academic terms: Fall, Spring, Summer. Applicants need a minimum number of credits to apply. For fall 2005: Transfer applications received: 2,703. Transfer applicants offered admission: 1,171. Transfer applicants enrolled: 740. **International students:** Number of foreign undergraduates: 492 (2% of student body). Number of countries represented: 69. Minimum TOEFL score required: 550 (paper); 207 (computer).

Virginia Union University

- **Address:** 1500 N. Lombardy Street, Richmond, VA 23220
- **Website:** http://www.vuu.edu/
- **Private; Religious affiliation:** Baptist
- **Enrollment:** 1,309 full-time; 35 part-time

KEY STATS

✔ **U.S News College Ranking:** fourth tier, Liberal Arts Colleges
✔ **ACT Score (25th/75th percentile):** 14-16
✔ **Tuition:** 2006-2007: $13,154

Selectivity: Least selective	**Room/board:** $5,888
Acceptance rate: 71%	**Average debt:** $17,560
Student/faculty ratio: N/A	**Proportion who borrowed:** 98%

UNDERGRADUATE STUDENT BODY STATS

2005-2006 enrollment: 1,309 full-time; 35 part-time. Men: 42%; women: 58%. **Ethnic makeup:** African American: 96%; Hispanic: 1%; White: 3%.

ADMISSIONS FACTS AND FIGURES

Phone: (804) 257-5600. **Email:** admissions@vuu.edu. **Website:** http://www.vuu.edu/. **Application deadlines for fall 2007:** Regular decision: August 9; decision sent by April 1. Early decision: Not offered. Early action: Not offered. Admission cannot be deferred. **Application fee:** $25. Common application is not accepted. **To apply online, go to:** http://www.vuu.edu/admissions/apply.htm. **Admissions requirements/recommendations:** High school units required (recommended): English: 4 (4); Mathematics: 3 (3); Science: 2 (2); Foreign language: 2 (2); Social studies: 1 (1); History: 1 (1); Academic electives: 3 (3); Total units: 18 (18). Tests: The college uses SAT or ACT scores in admissions decisions. Either SAT or ACT required. Campus visit: Neither required nor recommended. Admissions interview: Neither required nor recommended. Off-campus interview: May be arranged. **Factors that count in admissions decisions:** *Academic:* Secondary school record: Considered. Class rank: Considered. Letters of recommendation: Considered. Standardized test scores: Important. Essay: Considered. *Nonacademic:* Interview: Not considered. Extracurricular activities: Considered. Talent/ability: Not considered. Character/personal qualities: Not considered. Alumni/ae relationship: Not considered. Geographical residence: Not considered. State residency: Not considered. Religious affiliation/commitment: Not considered. Minority status: Not considered. Volunteer work: Considered. Work experience: Not considered. **Other schools with the greatest overlap in applicants:** Miami University–Oxford; University of California–San Diego; Virginia Commonwealth University; Virginia Tech. **Admissions statistics for the fall 2005 entering class:** 50% were from out of state. Overall acceptance rate: 71%. **Size of waiting list:** 0 applicants; enrolled from waiting list: 0. **Credentials of fall 2005 freshmen:** 4% ranked in the top 10 percent of their high school class; 8% were in the top 25 percent, and 36% were in the top half. (Proportion submitting class standing: 74%.) **Average high school grade point average:** 2.4.

ACADEMICS

Year founded: 1865. **Academic calendar:** Semester. **Degrees offered:** certificate, bachelor's, master's, doctorate. **Most popular majors:** Information not available. **Major fields of study:** communication, journalism, and related programs; computer and information sciences and support services; education. **Areas of required coursework:** arts/fine arts, humanities, computer literacy, mathematics, English (including composition), foreign languages, sciences (biological or physical), history, social science. **Pre-professional programs:** pre-medicine, pre-theology. **Special academic programs (% participation):** honors program (1%), internships (15%), teacher certificate program (10%), weekend college (12%). **Teacher certification offered in:** early childhood, special education, elementary, adult education, secondary. **Advanced Placement and International Baccalaureate credit:** Scores accepted: 4, 5. International Baccalaureate exams may be used for: Credit and/or placement. **Freshmen returning for sophomore year:** 54%. **Graduation rates:** Four-year: 19%; five-year: 29%; six-year: 31%.

COSTS AND FINANCIAL AID

Financial aid office: (804) 257-5882. **Expenses (2006-2007):** Tuition and fees 2006-2007: $13,154; room/board: $5,888. Estimated books and supplies: $600; transportation: $500; personal expenses: $1,000. **Financial aid:** Priority filing date for institution's financial aid form: March 1. In 2005-2006, 91% of undergraduates applied for financial aid. Of those, 83% were determined to have financial need; 28% had their need fully met. Average financial aid package (proportion receiving): $12,687 (82%). Average amount of gift aid, such as scholarships or grants (proportion receiving): $3,681 (55%). Average amount of self-help aid, such as work study or loans (proportion receiving): $5,384 (73%). Average need-based loan (excluding PLUS or other private loans): $3,968. Among students who received need-based aid, the average percentage of need met: 67%. Among students who received aid based on merit, the average award (and the proportion receiving): $5,096 (1%). The average athletic scholarship (and the proportion receiving): $8,482 (8%). Average amount of debt of borrowers graduating in 2005: $17,560. Proportion who borrowed: 98%.

CAMPUS LIFE AND EXTRACURRICULAR ACTIVITIES

Campus housing available (% using): coed dorms (17%), women's dorms (53%), men's dorms (30%), sorority housing, fraternity housing. Students who live in college-owned, operated, or affiliated housing: 44%. **Student employment:** During the 2005-2006 academic year, 30% of undergraduates worked on campus. Average per-year earnings: $1,800. **Clubs and organizations:** Number of student organizations: 24. Activities include: choral groups, concert band, marching band, pep band, radio station, student government, student newspaper, yearbook. Average proportion of students who stay on campus on weekends: 80%. **Sports program (2005-2006):** Member of NCAA II. *Men's intercollegiate varsity sports:* basketball, cross-country, football, golf, tennis, track and field (outdoor). *Women's intercollegiate varsity sports:* basketball, bowling, cross-country, softball, tennis, track and field (outdoor), volleyball.

SERVICES AND FACILITIES

Basic services: placement service, health service, health insurance. **Remedial assistance:** writing. **Counseling services:** career, academic, religious. **For learning-disabled students:** School does not offer a structured program with separate admission and additional fees. Services include: remedial math, remedial English, reading machines, remedial reading, learning center, tutors. **Information technology resources:** Students are not required to lease or own a computer. Number of campus computers available to all students: 200. School has a wireless network. Proportion of college-owned housing units wired for high-speed internet access: 100%. **Campus safety:** Security services offered: 24-hour foot-and-vehicle patrols, 24-hour emergency telephones, lighted pathways/sidewalks, controlled dormitory access (key, security card, etc).

TRANSFER AND INTERNATIONAL STUDENTS

Transfer students: May apply for admission for the following academic terms: Fall, Winter, Summer. Applicants do not need a minimum number of credits to apply.

Virginia Wesleyan College

- **Address:** 1584 Wesleyan Drive, Norfolk, VA 23502-5599
- **Website:** http://www.vwc.edu
- **Private; Religious affiliation:** United Methodist
- **Enrollment:** 1,121 full-time; 271 part-time

KEY STATS

✔ **U.S News College Ranking:** fourth tier, Liberal Arts Colleges
✔ **SAT Score (25th/75th percentile):** 890-1130
✔ **Tuition:** 2006-2007: $23,136

Selectivity: Selective	**Room/board:** $6,850
Acceptance rate: 78%	**Average debt:** $20,386
Student/faculty ratio: 12/1	**Proportion who borrowed:** 79%

UNDERGRADUATE STUDENT BODY STATS

2005-2006 enrollment: 1,121 full-time; 271 part-time. Men: 36%; women: 64%. **Ethnic makeup:** African American: 15%; Asian American: 2%; Hispanic: 3%; White: 79%; International: 1%. **Religious preference:** Roman Catholic: 27%; Protestant: 15%; Jewish: 2%; No preference: 4%; United Methodist: 17%; Baptist: 17%; Other: 18%.

ADMISSIONS FACTS AND FIGURES

Phone: (800) 737-8684. **Email:** admissions@vwc.edu. **Website:** http://www.vwc.edu. **Application deadlines for fall 2007:** Regular decision: Rolling. Early decision: Not offered. Early action: Not offered. Admission cannot be deferred. **Application fee:** $40. Common application is accepted. **To apply online, go to:** http://www.vwc.edu/admissions/. **Admissions requirements/recommendations:** High school units required (recommended): English: 4 (0); Mathematics: 3 (0); Science: 2 (3); Foreign language: 0 (3); Social studies: 0 (2); History: 1 (0); Academic electives: 0 (0); Total units: 12 (19). Tests: The college uses SAT or ACT scores in admissions decisions. Either SAT or ACT required. For admission to the fall 2007 entering class, the school will accept: ACT with writing, ACT without writing. Campus visit: Recommended. Admissions interview: Recommended. Off-campus interview: May be arranged. **Factors that count in admissions decisions:** *Academic:* Secondary school record: Very important. Class rank: Considered. Letters of recommendation: Important. Standardized test scores: Important. Essay: Important. *Nonacademic:* Interview: Considered. Extracurricular activities: Important. Talent/ability: Considered. Character/personal qualities: Considered. Alumni/ae relationship: Considered. Geographical residence: Not considered. State residency: Not considered. Religious affiliation/commitment: Not considered. Minority status: Not considered. Volunteer work: Considered. Work experience: Considered. **Other schools with the greatest overlap in applicants:** Christopher Newport University; College of William and Mary; Lynchburg College; Old Dominion University; Randolph-Macon College. **Admissions statistics for the fall 2005 entering class:** Total applicants: 1,357. Total accepted: 1,065. Freshmen enrolled: 323; 33% were from out of state. Overall acceptance rate: 78%. **Credentials of fall 2005 freshmen:** 13% ranked in the top 10 percent of their high school class; 31% were in the top 25 percent, and 66% were in the top half. (Proportion submitting class standing: 70%.) **Average high school grade point average:** 3.1. **First-year students who submitted SAT scores:** 97%. Scores (25/75 percentile): Verbal: 450-560, Math: 440-570, Combined: 890-1130. **First-year students submitting ACT scores:** 21%. Scores (25/75 percentile): English: 16-22, Math: 16-22, Composite: 17-22.

ACADEMICS
Year founded: 1961. **Academic calendar:** Semester. **Degrees offered:** bachelor's. **Most popular majors:** 22% business, management, marketing, and related support services; 11% communication, journalism, and related programs, 9% education, 8% criminology, 7% parks, recreation, and leisure studies. **Major fields of study:** area, ethnic, cultural, and gender studies; biological and biomedical sciences; business, management, marketing, and related support services; communication, journalism, and related programs; computer and information sciences and support services; education; English language and literature/letters; foreign languages, literatures, and linguistics; history; liberal arts and sciences studies, and humanities; mathematics and statistics; multi/interdisciplinary studies; natural resources and conservation; parks, recreation, leisure, and fitness studies; philosophy and religious studies; physical sciences; psychology; public administration and social service professions; social sciences; visual and performing arts. **Areas of required coursework:** arts/fine arts, humanities, mathematics, English (including composition), foreign languages, sciences (biological or physical), history, social science, other. **Pre-professional programs:** pre-law, pre-dentistry, pre-medicine, pre-theology, pre-veterinary science, pre-pharmacy, other. **Special academic programs (% participation):** accelerated program (1%), cross-registration (1%), distance learning (1%), double major (5%), honors program (4%), independent study (15%), internships (55%), liberal arts/career combination (33%), student-designed major (1%), study abroad (1%), teacher certificate program (9%), other. **Teacher certification offered in:** early childhood, special education, elementary, middle/junior high, secondary. **Reserve Officers Training Corps (ROTC):** Army ROTC: Offered at cooperating institution (Old Dominion University). **Faculty and instruction (2005-2006):** Total instructional faculty: 80 full-time, 58 part-time (49% men; 51% women; 10% minorities). Full-time faculty with Ph.D. or other terminal degree: 85%. Student/faculty ratio: 12/1. Classes of fewer than 20 students: 75%; of 20 to 49 students: 25%; of 50 or more students: 0%. **Advanced Placement and International Baccalaureate credit:** AP tests may be used for: Credit only. Scores accepted: 3, 4, 5. International Baccalaureate exams may be used for: Credit and/or placement. **Freshmen returning for sophomore year:** 66%. **Graduation rates:** Four-year: 30%; five-year: 36%; six-year: 37%. **Graduate study:** 18% of students pursue further study immediately upon graduation.

COSTS AND FINANCIAL AID
Financial aid office: (757) 455-3345. **Expenses (2006-2007):** Tuition and fees 2006-2007: $23,136; room/board: $6,850. Estimated books and supplies: $750; transportation: $1,300; personal expenses: $1,800. **Financial aid:** Priority filing date for institution's financial aid form: March 1. In 2005-2006, 65% of undergraduates applied for financial aid. Of those, 65% were determined to have financial need; 5% had their need fully met. Average financial aid package (proportion receiving): $14,385 (63%). Average amount of gift aid, such as scholarships or grants (proportion receiving): $3,239 (26%). Average amount of self-help aid, such as work study or loans (proportion receiving): $4,311 (58%). Average need-based loan (excluding PLUS or other private loans): $4,077. Among students who received need-based aid, the average percentage of need met: 66%. Among students who received aid based on merit, the average award (and the proportion receiving): $5,992 (22%). Average amount of debt of borrowers graduating in 2005: $20,386. Proportion who borrowed: 79%.

CAMPUS LIFE AND EXTRACURRICULAR ACTIVITIES
Campus housing available (% using): coed dorms (57%), women's dorms (7%), sorority housing (5%), fraternity housing (2%), apartment for single students (13%), special housing for disabled students (2%), special housing for international students (7%), other housing options (7%). Students who live in college-owned, operated, or affiliated housing: 51%. **Student employment:** During the 2005-2006 academic year, 10% of undergraduates worked on campus. Average per-year earnings: $1,500. **Clubs and organizations:** Number of student organizations: 72. Activities include: choral groups, dance, drama/theater, literary magazine, music ensembles, musical theater, radio station, student government, student newspaper, yearbook. Number of fraternities: 3; sororities: 4. Proportion of men in fraternities: 3%; of women in sororities: 6%. Average proportion of students who stay on campus on weekends: 70%. **Sports program (2005-2006):** Member of NCAA III. *Men's intercollegiate varsity sports:* baseball, basketball, cross-country, golf, lacrosse, soccer, tennis, track and field (indoor), track and field (outdoor). *Women's intercollegiate varsity sports:* basketball, cross-country, field hockey, lacrosse, soccer, softball, tennis, track and field (indoor), track and field (outdoor), volleyball.

SERVICES AND FACILITIES
Basic services: nonremedial tutoring, women's center, health service, health insurance. **Remedial assistance:** reading, math, writing, study skills. **Counseling services:** minority student, career, military, personal, veteran student, academic, older student, psychological, birth control, religious. **For learning-disabled students:** School does not offer a structured program with separate admission and additional fees. Total undergraduates in learning-disabled program or receiving services: 50. Services include: remedial math, remedial English, remedial reading, tape recorders, untimed tests, note-taking services, oral tests, learning center, readers, extended time for tests, tutors, priority registration, priority seating, texts on tape, other testing accomodations, other. **Library:** Number of titles: 123,359; number of current serial subscriptions: 800. **Information technology resources:** Students are not required to lease or own a computer. Number of campus computers available to all students: 99. School has a wireless network. Approximate number of users that can be accommodated: 600. Proportion of college-owned housing units wired for high-speed internet access: 100%. **Campus safety:** Security services offered: 24-hour foot-and-vehicle patrols, late-night transport/escort service, 24-hour emergency telephones, lighted pathways/sidewalks, controlled dormitory access (key, security card, etc).

TRANSFER AND INTERNATIONAL STUDENTS
Transfer students: May apply for admission for the following academic terms: Fall, Spring, Summer. Applicants need a minimum number of credits to apply. For fall 2005: Transfer applications received: 220. Transfer applicants offered admission: 155. Transfer applicants enrolled: 94. **International students:** Number of foreign undergraduates: 8 (1% of student body). Number of countries represented: 8. Minimum TOEFL score required: 550 (paper); 213 (computer).

Washington and Lee University

■ **Address:** 204 West Washington Street, Lexington, VA 24450-2116
■ **Website:** http://www.wlu.edu
■ **Private**
■ **Enrollment:** 1,766 full-time; 4 part-time

KEY STATS
✔ **U.S News College Ranking:** 17, Liberal Arts Colleges
✔ **SAT Score (25th/75th percentile):** 1300-1450
✔ **Tuition:** 2006-2007: $31,850

Selectivity: Most selective	**Room/board:** $7,940
Acceptance rate: 29%	**Average debt:** $17,105
Student/faculty ratio: 10/1	**Proportion who borrowed:** 25%

UNDERGRADUATE STUDENT BODY STATS

2005-2006 enrollment: 1,766 full-time; 4 part-time. Men: 50%; women: 50%. **Ethnic makeup:** African American: 4%; Asian American: 3%; Hispanic: 1%; White: 87%; International: 3%. **Religious preference:** Roman Catholic: 15%; Protestant: 34%; Jewish: 2%; No preference: 48%; Other: 1%.

ADMISSIONS FACTS AND FIGURES

Phone: (540) 463-8710. **Email:** admissions@wlu.edu. **Website:** http://www.wlu.edu. **Application deadlines for fall 2007:** Regular decision: January 15; decision sent by April 1. Early decision: Send application by: November 15; Decision sent by: December 22. Early action: Not offered. Admission can be deferred. **Application fee:** $50. Common application is accepted. **To apply online, go to:** http://admissions.wlu.edu/web/page/normal/101.html. **Admissions requirements/recommendations:** High school units required (recommended): English: 4; Mathematics: 3 (4); Science: 1 (3); Foreign language: 3 (3); Social studies: 1; History: 1 (2); Academic electives: 4; Total units: 16. Tests: The college uses SAT or ACT scores in admissions decisions. Either SAT or ACT required. For admission to the fall 2007 entering class, the school will accept: ACT with writing. Campus visit: Recommended. Admissions interview: Recommended. Off-campus interview: May be arranged. **Factors that count in admissions decisions:** *Academic:* Secondary school record: Very important. Class rank: Very important. Letters of recommendation: Important. Standardized test scores: Very important. Essay: Considered. *Nonacademic:* Interview: Considered. Extracurricular activities: Very important. Talent/ability: Considered. Character/personal qualities: Very important. Alumni/ae relationship: Considered. Geographical residence: Considered. State residency: Considered. Religious affiliation/commitment: Not considered. Minority status: Considered. Volunteer work: Considered. Work experience: Considered. **Other schools with the greatest overlap in applicants:** College of William and Mary; Davidson College; Duke University; University of Virginia; Vanderbilt University. **Admissions statistics for the fall 2005 entering class:** Total applicants: 3,950. Total accepted: 1,141. Freshmen enrolled: 465; 87% were from out of state. Accepted through early-decision or early-action plans: 40%. Overall acceptance rate: 29%. Early-decision acceptance rate: 35%. Non-early acceptance rate: 28%. **Size of waiting list:** 912 applicants; enrolled from waiting list: 97. **Credentials of fall 2005 freshmen:** 76% ranked in the top 10 percent of their high school class; 96% were in the top 25 percent, and 100% were in the top half. (Proportion submitting class standing: 53%.) **First-year students who submitted SAT scores:** 81%. Scores (25/75 percentile): Verbal: 650-730, Math: 650-720, Combined: 1300-1450. **First-year students submitting ACT scores:** 18%. Scores (25/75 percentile): English: N/A, Math: N/A, Composite: 28-30.

ACADEMICS

Year founded: 1749. **Academic calendar:** Other. **Degrees offered:** bachelor's, master's, first professional. **Most popular majors:** 11% business administration and management, 10% economics, 9% political science and government, 8% history, 8% journalism. **Major fields of study:** area, ethnic, cultural, and gender studies; biological and biomedical sciences; business, management, marketing, and related support services; communication, journalism, and related programs; computer and information sciences and support services; engineering; English language and literature/letters; foreign languages, literatures, and linguistics; history; mathematics and statistics; multi/interdisciplinary studies; philosophy and religious studies; physical sciences; psychology; public administration and social service professions; social sciences; visual and performing arts. **Areas of required coursework:** humanities, English (including composition), foreign languages, sciences (biological or physical), social science, other. **Pre-professional programs:** other. **Special academic programs (% participation):** accelerated program (.5%), double major (27%), exchange student program (domestic) (2%), honors program (5%), independent study (48%), internships, liberal arts/career combination, student-designed major (1%), study abroad (50%), teacher certificate program (2%). **Reserve Officers Training Corps (ROTC):** Army ROTC: Offered at cooperating institution (Virginia Military Institute). **Faculty and instruction (2005-2006):** Total instructional faculty: 212 full-time, 2 part-time (67% men; 33% women; 8% minorities). Full-time faculty with Ph.D. or other terminal degree: 95%. Student/faculty ratio: 10/1. Classes of fewer than 20 students: 64%; of 20 to 49 students: 35%; of 50 or more students: 0%. **Advanced Placement and International Baccalaureate credit:** AP tests may be used for: Credit and/or placement. Scores accepted: 4, 5. International Baccalaureate exams may be used for: Credit and/or placement. **Freshmen returning for sophomore year:** 95%. **Graduation rates:** Four-year: 84%; five-year: 87%; six-year: 87%. **Graduate study:** 30% of students pursue further study immediately upon graduation. Fields in which graduates pursue further study: Master of Business

Administration (MBA), 7%; law, 31%; medicine, 30%; engineering, 1%; theology (or the seminary), 2%; arts and sciences, 27%.

COSTS AND FINANCIAL AID

Financial aid office: (540) 458-8717. **Expenses (2006-2007):** Tuition and fees 2006-2007: $31,850; room/board: $7,940. Estimated books and supplies: $1,550 personal expenses: $1,660. **Financial aid:** Priority filing date for institution's financial aid form: February 1. In 2005-2006, 39% of undergraduates applied for financial aid. Of those, 33% were determined to have financial need; 85% had their need fully met. Average financial aid package (proportion receiving): $25,158 (33%). Average amount of gift aid, such as scholarships or grants (proportion receiving): $19,037 (27%). Average amount of self-help aid, such as work study or loans (proportion receiving): $5,515 (14%). Average need-based loan (excluding PLUS or other private loans): $4,708. Among students who received need-based aid, the average percentage of need met: 99%. Among students who received aid based on merit, the average award (and the proportion receiving): $13,824 (13%). The average athletic scholarship (and the proportion receiving): $0 (0%). Average amount of debt of borrowers graduating in 2005: $17,105. Proportion who borrowed: 25%.

CAMPUS LIFE AND EXTRACURRICULAR ACTIVITIES

Campus housing available (% using): coed dorms (57%), sorority housing (8%), fraternity housing (27%), apartment for single students (2%), special housing for international students (2%), other housing options (4%). Students who live in college-owned, operated, or affiliated housing: 61%. **Clubs and organizations:** Number of student organizations: 124. Activities include: choral groups, dance, drama/theater, jazz band, literary magazine, music ensembles, radio station, student government, student newspaper, student film society, symphony orchestra, television station, yearbook. Number of fraternities: 15; sororities: 6. Proportion of men in fraternities: 83%; of women in sororities: 77%. **Sports program (2005-2006):** Member of NCAA III. *Men's intercollegiate varsity sports:* baseball, basketball, cross-country, football, golf, lacrosse, soccer, swimming and diving, tennis, track and field (indoor), track and field (outdoor), wrestling. *Women's intercollegiate varsity sports:* basketball, cross-country, equestrian sports, field hockey, lacrosse, soccer, swimming and diving, tennis, track and field (indoor), track and field (outdoor), volleyball.

SERVICES AND FACILITIES

Basic services: nonremedial tutoring, women's center, placement service, health service, health insurance. **Counseling services:** minority student, career, personal, veteran student, academic, older student, psychological, birth control, religious. **For learning-disabled students:** School does not offer a structured program with separate admission and additional fees. Total undergraduates in learning-disabled program or receiving services: 53. Services include: reading machines, tape recorders, untimed tests, note-taking services, extended time for tests, tutors, texts on tape. **Library:** Number of titles: 924,524; number of current serial subscriptions: 8,226. **Information technology resources:** Students are not required to lease or own a computer. Number of campus computers available to all students: 320. School has a wireless network. Approximate number of users that can be accommodated: 750. Proportion of college-owned housing units wired for high-speed internet access: 100%. **Campus safety:** Security services offered: 24-hour foot-and-vehicle patrols, late-night transport/escort service, 24-hour emergency telephones, lighted pathways/sidewalks, controlled dormitory access (key, security card, etc.).

TRANSFER AND INTERNATIONAL STUDENTS

Transfer students: May apply for admission for the following academic terms: Fall, Winter. Applicants need a minimum number of credits to apply. For fall 2005: Transfer applications received: 74. Transfer applicants offered admission: 13. Transfer applicants enrolled: 4. **International students:** Number of foreign undergraduates: 60 (3% of student body). Number of countries represented: 45. Minimum TOEFL score required: 600 (paper); 250 (computer).

Washington

Central Washington University

- **Address:** 400 E. University Way, Ellensburg, WA 98926-7501
- **Website:** http://www.cwu.edu
- **Public**
- **Enrollment:** 8,532 full-time; 1,090 part-time

KEY STATS
- ✔ **U.S News College Ranking:** 41, Universities–Master's (West)
- ✔ **SAT Score (25th/75th percentile):** 915-1140
- ✔ **Tuition:** 2006-2007: $5,238 in state, $13,949 out of state

Selectivity: Less selective	**Room/board:** $7,140
Acceptance rate: 76%	**Average debt:** $15,824
Student/faculty ratio: 22/1	**Proportion who borrowed:** 65%

UNDERGRADUATE STUDENT BODY STATS
2005-2006 enrollment: 8,532 full-time; 1,090 part-time. Men: 47%; women: 53%. **Ethnic makeup:** African American: 2%; American-Indian: 2%; Asian American: 6%; Hispanic: 7%; White: 81%; International: 2%.

ADMISSIONS FACTS AND FIGURES
Phone: (866) 298-4968. **Email:** cwuadmis@cwu.edu. **Website:** http://www.cwu.edu. **Application deadlines for fall 2007:** Regular decision: April 1. Early decision: Not offered. Early action: Not offered. Admission cannot be deferred. **Application fee:** $50. Common application is not accepted. **To apply online, go to:** http://www.cwu.edu/~cwuadmis/. **Admissions requirements/recommendations:** High school units required (recommended): English: 4 (4); Mathematics: 3 (3); Science: 2 (3); Foreign language: 2 (3); Social studies: 3 (3); Total units: 15 (17). Tests: The college uses SAT or ACT scores in admissions decisions. Either SAT or ACT required. For admission to the fall 2007 entering class, the school will accept: ACT with writing, ACT without writing. Campus visit: Recommended. Admissions interview: Recommended. Off-campus interview: Not available. **Factors that count in admissions decisions:** *Academic:* Secondary school record: Very important. Class rank: Considered. Letters of recommendation: Considered. Standardized test scores: Important. Essay: Considered. *Nonacademic:* Interview: Considered. Extracurricular activities: Considered. Talent/ability: Considered. Character/personal qualities: Considered. Alumni/ae relationship: Not considered. Geographical residence: Not considered. State residency: Not considered. Religious affiliation/commitment: Not considered. Minority status: Not considered. Volunteer work: Considered. Work experience: Considered. **Other schools with the greatest overlap in applicants:** Eastern Washington University; Pacific Lutheran University; University of Washington; Washington State University; Western Washington University. **Admissions statistics for the fall 2005 entering class:** Total applicants: 4,656. Total accepted: 3,554. Freshmen enrolled: 1,435; 3% were from out of state. Overall acceptance rate: 76%. **Size of waiting list:** 0 applicants; enrolled from waiting list: N/A. **Credentials of fall 2005 freshmen:** 15% ranked in the top 10 percent of their high school class; 36% were in the top 25 percent, and 77% were in the top half. (Proportion submitting class standing: 16%.) **Average high school grade point average:** 3.2. **First-year students who submitted SAT scores:** 89%. Scores (25/75 percentile): Verbal: 460-570, Math: 455-570, Combined: 915-1140. **First-year students submitting ACT scores:** 27%. Scores (25/75 percentile): English: 17-24, Math: 17-23, Composite: 18-24.

ACADEMICS
Year founded: 1891. **Academic calendar:** Quarter. **Degrees offered:** certificate, bachelor's, post-bachelor's certificate, master's. **Most popular majors:** 25% business, management, marketing, and related support services, 25% education, 9% security and protective services, 8% social sciences, 4% visual and performing arts. **Major fields of study:** area, ethnic, cultural, and gender studies; biological and biomedical sciences; business, management, marketing, and related support services; communication, journalism, and related programs; computer and information sciences and support services; educa-

tion; engineering technologies/technicians; English language and literature/letters; family and consumer sciences/human sciences; foreign languages, literatures, and linguistics; health professions and related clinical sciences; history; liberal arts and sciences studies, and humanities; mathematics and statistics; multi/interdisciplinary studies; parks, recreation, leisure, and fitness studies; philosophy and religious studies; physical sciences; psychology; public administration and social service professions; security and protective services; social sciences; transportation and materials moving; visual and performing arts. **Areas of required coursework:** arts/fine arts, humanities, computer literacy, mathematics, English (including composition), philosophy, foreign languages, sciences (biological or physical), history, social science. **Pre-professional programs:** pre-law, pre-dentistry, pre-medicine, pre-veterinary science, pre-optometry, pre-pharmacy, other. **Special academic programs (% participation):** cooperative (work-study plan) program (16%), distance learning (36%), double major (9%), dual enrollment (1%), English as a Second Language (ESL) (.4%), exchange student program (domestic), honors program (1%), independent study (28%), internships (53%), student-designed major (2%), study abroad (3%), teacher certificate program (24%), weekend college (1%). **Teacher certification offered in:** early childhood, special education, elementary, vo-tech, middle/junior high, secondary, bilingual/bicultural. **Cooperative education programs:** art, business, computer science, education, health professions, home economics, humanities, natural science, social/behavioral science, technologies, vocational arts, other. **Reserve Officers Training Corps (ROTC):** Army ROTC: Offered on campus; Air Force ROTC: Offered on campus. **Faculty and instruction (2005-2006):** Total instructional faculty: 372 full-time, 175 part-time (60% men; 40% women; 11% minorities). Full-time faculty with Ph.D. or other terminal degree: 86%. Student/faculty ratio: 22/1. Classes of fewer than 20 students: 33%; of 20 to 49 students: 62%; of 50 or more students: 6%. **Advanced Placement and International Baccalaureate credit:** AP tests may be used for: Credit and/or placement. Scores accepted: 3, 4, 5. International Baccalaureate exams may be used for: Credit and/or placement. **Freshmen returning for sophomore year:** 78%. **Graduation rates:** Four-year: 21%; five-year: 45%; six-year: 51%. **Graduate study:** 68% of students pursue further study within one year; 72% within five years.

COSTS AND FINANCIAL AID
Financial aid office: (509) 963-1611. **Expenses (2006-2007):** Tuition and fees 2006-2007: $5,238 in state, $13,949 out of state; room/board: $7,140. Estimated books and supplies: $924; transportation: $1,362; personal expenses: $1,683. **Financial aid:** Priority filing date for institution's financial aid form: March 1. In 2005-2006, 70% of undergraduates applied for financial aid. Of those, 53% were determined to have financial need; 25% had their need fully met. Average financial aid package (proportion receiving): $7,996 (51%). Average amount of gift aid, such as scholarships or grants (proportion receiving): $2,309 (36%). Average amount of self-help aid, such as work study or loans (proportion receiving): $3,290 (44%). Average need-based loan (excluding PLUS or other private loans): $3,387. Among students who received need-based aid, the average percentage of need met: 73%. Among students who received aid based on merit, the average award (and the proportion receiving): $731 (0%). The average athletic scholarship (and the proportion receiving): $0 (0%). Average amount of debt of borrowers graduating in 2005: $15,824. Proportion who borrowed: 65%.

CAMPUS LIFE AND EXTRACURRICULAR ACTIVITIES
Campus housing available (% using): coed dorms (77%), women's dorms (1%), apartments for married students (4%), apartment for single students (17%), special housing for disabled students (1%), special housing for international students, other housing options. Students who live in college-owned, operated, or affiliated housing: 43%. **Student employment:** During the 2005-2006 academic year, 24% of undergraduates worked on campus. Average per-year earnings: $3,000. **Clubs and organizations:** Number of student organizations: 138. Activities include: choral groups, concert band, dance, drama/theater, jazz band, literary magazine, marching band, music ensembles, musical theater, opera, pep band, radio station, student government, student newspaper, student film society, symphony orchestra, television station. Number of fraternities: 0; sororities: 0. Average proportion of students who stay on campus on weekends: 35%. **Sports program (2005-**

2006): Member of NCAA II. **Men's intercollegiate varsity sports:** baseball, basketball, cross-country, football, track and field (indoor), track and field (outdoor). **Women's intercollegiate varsity sports:** basketball, cross-country, soccer, softball, track and field (indoor), track and field (outdoor), volleyball.

SERVICES AND FACILITIES

Basic services: nonremedial tutoring, placement service, day care, health service, health insurance. **Remedial assistance:** reading, math, writing. **Counseling services:** minority student, career, military, personal, veteran student, academic, older student, psychological, birth control, other. **For learning-disabled students:** School does not offer a structured program with separate admission and additional fees. Services include: remedial math, remedial English, reading machines, remedial reading, tape recorders, other special classes, note-taking services, oral tests, readers, extended time for tests, tutors, priority registration, priority seating, substitution of courses, texts on tape, typist/scribe, exams on tape or computer, other testing accomodations. **Library:** Number of titles: 536,469; number of current serial subscriptions: 900. **Information technology resources:** Students are not required to lease or own a computer. Number of campus computers available to all students: 687. School has a wireless network. Approximate number of users that can be accommodated: 1,400. Proportion of college-owned housing units wired for high-speed internet access: 84%. **Campus safety:** Security services offered: 24-hour foot-and-vehicle patrols, late-night transport/escort service, 24-hour emergency telephones, lighted pathways/sidewalks, controlled dormitory access (key, security card, etc).

TRANSFER AND INTERNATIONAL STUDENTS

Transfer students: May apply for admission for the following academic terms: Fall, Winter, Spring, Summer. Applicants need a minimum number of credits to apply. For fall 2005: Transfer applications received: 2,339. Transfer applicants offered admission: 1,884. Transfer applicants enrolled: 1,203. **International students:** Number of foreign undergraduates: 145 (2% of student body). Number of countries represented: 26. Minimum TOEFL score required: 525 (paper); 195 (computer).

City University

- **Address:** 11900 N.E. First Street, Bellevue, WA 98005
- **Website:** http://www.cityu.edu
- **Private**
- **Enrollment:** 1,007 full-time; 787 part-time

KEY STATS
- ✔ **U.S News College Ranking:** Unranked, Universities–Master's (West)
- ✔ **SAT or ACT Score (25th/75th percentile):** N/A
- ✔ **Tuition:** N/A

Selectivity: N/A	Room/board: N/A
Acceptance rate: N/A	Average debt: N/A
Student/faculty ratio: 7/1	Proportion who borrowed: N/A

UNDERGRADUATE STUDENT BODY STATS

2005-2006 enrollment: 1,007 full-time; 787 part-time. Men: 44%; women: 56%. **Ethnic makeup:** African American: 4%; American-Indian: 1%; Asian American: 6%; Hispanic: 3%; White: 80%; International: 6%.

ADMISSIONS FACTS AND FIGURES

Phone: (888) 422-4898. **Email:** info@cityu.edu. **Website:** http://www.cityu.edu. **Application deadlines for fall 2007:** Regular decision: Rolling. Early decision: Not offered. Early action: Not offered. Admission can be deferred. **Application fee:** $80. Common application is not accepted. **Admissions requirements/recommendations:** Tests: The college does not use SAT or ACT scores in admissions decisions. Neither SAT nor ACT required. Campus visit: Neither required nor recommended. Admissions interview: Neither required nor recommended. Off-campus interview: May be arranged. **Factors that count in admissions decisions:** *Academic:* Secondary school record: Not considered. Class rank: Not considered. Letters of recommendation: Not considered. Standardized test scores: Not considered. Essay: Not considered. *Nonacademic:* Interview: Not considered. Extracurricular activities: Not considered. Talent/ability: Not considered. Character/personal qualities: Not considered. Alumni/ae relationship: Not considered. Geographical residence: Not considered. State residency: Not considered. Religious affiliation/commitment: Not considered. Minority sta-

tus: Not considered. Volunteer work: Not considered. Work experience: Not considered.

ACADEMICS

Year founded: 1973. **Academic calendar:** Quarter. **Degrees offered:** certificate, associate, transfer-associate, bachelor's, master's. **Most popular majors:** Information not available. **Major fields of study:** business, management, marketing, and related support services; communication, journalism, and related programs; computer and information sciences and support services; education; psychology. **Areas of required coursework:** humanities, mathematics, English (including composition), sciences (biological or physical), social science. **Special academic programs:** distance learning, double major, English as a Second Language (ESL), independent study, internships, student-designed major, teacher certificate program, weekend college. **Teacher certification offered in:** special education, elementary. **Faculty and instruction (2005-2006):** Total instructional faculty: 52 full-time, 1,189 part-time (47% men; 53% women; 13% minorities). Full-time faculty with Ph.D. or other terminal degree: 38%. Student/faculty ratio: 7/1. Classes of fewer than 20 students: 68%; of 20 to 49 students: 32%. **Advanced Placement and International Baccalaureate credit:** AP tests may be used for: Credit only. Scores accepted: 3. International Baccalaureate exams may be used for: Credit only.

COSTS AND FINANCIAL AID

Financial aid office: (800) 426-5596.

CAMPUS LIFE AND EXTRACURRICULAR ACTIVITIES

Student employment: During the 2005-2006 academic year, 0% of undergraduates worked on campus. Average per-year earnings: $0. **Clubs and organizations:** Number of student organizations: 3. Number of fraternities: 0; sororities: 0.

SERVICES AND FACILITIES

Basic services: nonremedial tutoring, health insurance. **Counseling services:** academic, psychological. **For learning-disabled students:** School does not offer a structured program with separate admission and additional fees. Total undergraduates in learning-disabled program or receiving services: 11. Services include: tape recorders, videotaped classes, untimed tests, note-taking services, oral tests, extended time for tests, tutors, priority seating, texts on tape. **Library:** Number of titles: 44,036; number of current serial subscriptions: 18,000. **Information technology resources:** Students are required to lease or own a computer. Number of campus computers available to all students: 269. School has a wireless network. **Campus safety:** Security services offered: late-night transport/escort service, lighted pathways/sidewalks.

TRANSFER AND INTERNATIONAL STUDENTS

Transfer students: May apply for admission for the following academic terms: Fall, Winter, Spring, Summer. Applicants do not need a minimum number of credits to apply. **International students:** Number of foreign undergraduates: 101 (6% of student body). Number of countries represented: 22. Minimum TOEFL score required: 540 (paper); 207 (computer).

Cornish College of the Arts

- **Address:** 1000 Lenora Street, Seattle, WA 98121
- **Website:** http://www.cornish.edu
- **Private**
- **Enrollment:** 739 full-time; 29 part-time

KEY STATS
- ✔ **U.S News College Ranking:** Unranked Specialty School–Fine Arts
- ✔ **SAT or ACT Score (25th/75th percentile):** N/A
- ✔ **Tuition:** 2006-2007: $22,750

Selectivity: Least selective	Room/board: N/A
Acceptance rate: 61%	Average debt: N/A
Student/faculty ratio: 9/1	Proportion who borrowed: N/A

UNDERGRADUATE STUDENT BODY STATS

2005-2006 enrollment: 739 full-time; 29 part-time. Men: 35%; women: 65%. **Ethnic makeup:** African American: 2%; American-Indian: 1%; Asian American: 3%; Hispanic: 5%; White: 85%; International: 4%.

ADMISSIONS FACTS AND FIGURES

Phone: (800) 726-2787. **Email:** admissions@cornish.edu. **Website:** http://www.cornish.edu. **Application deadlines for fall 2007:** Regular decision: August 15. Early decision: Not offered. Early action: Not offered. Admission can be deferred. **Application fee:** $35. Common application is not accepted. **Admissions requirements/recommendations:** High school units required (recommended): English: (4); Mathematics: (2); Science: (2); Foreign language: (2); Social studies: (2); History: (2); Academic electives: (0); Total units: (18). Tests: The college does not use SAT or ACT scores in admissions decisions. Neither SAT nor ACT required. Campus visit: Recommended. Admissions interview: Recommended. Off-campus interview: May be arranged. **Factors that count in admissions decisions:** *Academic:* Secondary school record: Important. Class rank: Not considered. Letters of recommendation: Important. Standardized test scores: Considered. Essay: Very important. *Nonacademic:* Interview: Important. Extracurricular activities: Important. Talent/ability: Very important. Character/personal qualities: Important. Alumni/ae relationship: Important. Geographical residence: Not considered. State residency: Not considered. Religious affiliation/commitment: Not considered. Minority status: Considered. Volunteer work: Not considered. Work experience: Not considered. **Other schools with the greatest overlap in applicants:** California Institute of the Arts; Central Washington University; College of Santa Fe; San Francisco Art Institute; Western Washington University. **Admissions statistics for the fall 2005 entering class:** Total applicants: 958. Total accepted: 580. Freshmen enrolled: 165; Overall acceptance rate: 61%. **Size of waiting list:** 7 applicants; enrolled from waiting list: 2.

ACADEMICS

Year founded: 1914. **Academic calendar:** Semester. **Degrees offered:** bachelor's. **Most popular majors:** 31% design and visual communications, 23% music performance, 20% fine/studio arts, 12% dance, 12% drama and dramatics/theater arts. **Major fields of study:** visual and performing arts. **Areas of required coursework:** humanities, English (including composition), sciences (biological or physical), history, social science, other. **Special academic programs (% participation):** independent study (34%), internships (21%), student-designed major (5%), study abroad (2%). **Faculty and instruction (2005-2006):** Total instructional faculty: 55 full-time, 93 part-time (52% men; 48% women; 8% minorities). Student/faculty ratio: 9/1. Classes of fewer than 20 students: 83%; of 20 to 49 students: 17%; of 50 or more students: 0%. **Advanced Placement and International Baccalaureate credit:** AP tests may be used for: Credit only. Scores accepted: 3, 4, 5. **Freshmen returning for sophomore year:** 67%. **Graduation rates:** Four-year: 39%; five-year: 44%; six-year: 43%.

COSTS AND FINANCIAL AID

Financial aid office: (206) 726-5014. **Expenses (2006-2007):** Tuition and fees 2006-2007: $22,750; room/board: N/A. **Financial aid:** Priority filing date for institution's financial aid form: February 15. In 2005-2006, 84% of undergraduates applied for financial aid. Of those, 71% were determined to have financial need; 50% had their need fully met. Average financial aid package (proportion receiving): $23,829 (71%). Average amount of gift aid, such as scholarships or grants (proportion receiving): $6,393 (59%). Average amount of self-help aid, such as work study or loans (proportion receiving): $6,957 (71%). Average need-based loan (excluding PLUS or other private loans): $2,958. Among students who received need-based aid, the average percentage of need met: 88%. Among students who received aid based on merit, the average award (and the proportion receiving): $1,854 (4%).

CAMPUS LIFE AND EXTRACURRICULAR ACTIVITIES

Student employment: During the 2005-2006 academic year, 0% of undergraduates worked on campus. **Clubs and organizations:** Number of student organizations: 13. Activities include: choral groups, concert band, dance, drama/theater, jazz band, literary magazine, music ensembles, musical theater, opera, student government, student film society, symphony orchestra. Number of fraternities: 0; sororities: 0. Average proportion of students who stay on campus on weekends: 25%.

SERVICES AND FACILITIES

Basic services: health insurance. **Counseling services:** minority student, career, personal, academic, psychological. **For learning-disabled students:** School does not offer a structured program with separate admission and additional fees. Total undergraduates in learning-disabled program or receiving services: 16. Services include: reading machines, tape recorders, untimed tests, note-taking services, oral tests, readers, extended time for tests, early syllabus, priority registration, texts on tape, typist/scribe, exams on tape or computer, other testing accomodations, other. **Library:** Number of

titles: 23,500; number of current serial subscriptions: 100. **Information technology resources:** Students are not required to lease or own a computer. Number of campus computers available to all students: 50. School has a wireless network. Approximate number of users that can be accommodated: 150. Proportion of college-owned housing units wired for high-speed internet access: 0%. **Campus safety:** Security services offered: late-night transport/escort service, lighted pathways/sidewalks.

TRANSFER AND INTERNATIONAL STUDENTS

Transfer students: May apply for admission for the following academic terms: Fall, Spring. Applicants do not need a minimum number of credits to apply. For fall 2005: Transfer applications received: 412. Transfer applicants offered admission: 224. Transfer applicants enrolled: 112. **International students:** Number of foreign undergraduates: 27 (4% of student body). Minimum TOEFL score required: 525 (paper); 195 (computer).

Eastern Washington University

- **Address:** 526 Fifth Street, Cheney, WA 99004
- **Website:** http://www.ewu.edu
- **Public**
- **Enrollment:** 8,174 full-time; 1,429 part-time

KEY STATS
✔ **U.S News College Ranking:** 51, Universities–Master's (West)
✔ **SAT Score (25th/75th percentile):** 880-1590
✔ **Tuition:** 2006-2007: $4,575 in state, $13,605 out of state
  Selectivity: Less selective   **Room/board:** $6,020
  Acceptance rate: 83%   **Average debt:** $18,600
  Student/faculty ratio: 21/1   **Proportion who borrowed:** 65%

UNDERGRADUATE STUDENT BODY STATS

2005-2006 enrollment: 8,174 full-time; 1,429 part-time. Men: 42%; women: 58%. **Ethnic makeup:** African American: 3%; American-Indian: 2%; Asian American: 4%; Hispanic: 6%; White: 84%; International: 1%.

ADMISSIONS FACTS AND FIGURES

Phone: (509) 359-2397. **Email:** admissions@mail.ewu.edu. **Website:** http://www.ewu.edu. **Application deadlines for fall 2007:** Regular decision: August 15. Early decision: Not offered. Early action: Not offered. Admission can be deferred. **Application fee:** $50. Common application is accepted. **To apply online, go to:** http://www.ewu.edu/x5203.xml. **Admissions requirements/recommendations:** High school units required (recommended): English: 4; Mathematics: 3 (4); Science: 2; Foreign language: 2; Social studies: 3; Total units: 15. Tests: The college uses SAT or ACT scores in admissions decisions. Either SAT or ACT required. For admission to the fall 2007 entering class, the school will accept: ACT with writing. Campus visit: Recommended. Admissions interview: Neither required nor recommended. Off-campus interview: Not available. **Factors that count in admissions decisions:** *Academic:* Secondary school record: Very important. Class rank: Not considered. Letters of recommendation: Considered. Standardized test scores: Very important. Essay: Considered. *Nonacademic:* Interview: Considered. Extracurricular activities: Considered. Talent/ability: Considered. Character/personal qualities: Considered. Alumni/ae relationship: Not considered. Geographical residence: Not considered. State residency: Not considered. Religious affiliation/commitment: Not considered. Minority status: Not considered. Volunteer work: Considered. Work experience: Considered. **Other schools with the greatest overlap in applicants:** Central Washington University; University of Washington; Washington State University; Western Washington University. **Admissions statistics for the fall 2005 entering class:** Total applicants: 4,365. Total accepted: 3,602. Freshmen enrolled: 1,637; 8% were from out of state. Overall acceptance rate: 83%. **Credentials of fall 2005 freshmen:** 19% ranked in the top 10 percent of their high school class; 44% were in the top 25 percent. **Average high school grade point average:** 3.3. First-year students who submitted SAT scores: 87%. Scores (25/75 percentile): Verbal: 440-800, Math: 440-790, Combined: 880-1590. **First-year students submitting ACT scores:** 32%. Scores (25/75 percentile): English: 17-34, Math: 17-43, Composite: 18-32.

ACADEMICS

Year founded: 1882. **Academic calendar:** Quarter. **Degrees offered:** certificate, bachelor's, master's, post-master's certificate, doctorate. **Most popular**

majors: 20% business, management, marketing, and related support services, 17% education, 9% health professions and related clinical sciences, 8% social sciences, 7% psychology. **Major fields of study:** architecture and related services; biological and biomedical sciences; business, management, marketing, and related support services; communication, journalism, and related programs; computer and information sciences and support services; education; engineering; engineering technologies/technicians; English language and literature/letters; family and consumer sciences/human sciences; foreign languages, literatures, and linguistics; health professions and related clinical sciences; history; liberal arts and sciences studies, and humanities; mathematics and statistics; military technologies; multi/inter-disciplinary studies; natural resources and conservation; parks, recreation, leisure, and fitness studies; physical sciences; psychology; public administration and social service professions; social sciences; visual and performing arts. **Areas of required coursework:** arts/fine arts, humanities, computer literacy, mathematics, English (including composition), philosophy, sciences (biological or physical), history, social science, other. **Pre-professional programs:** pre-law, pre-dentistry, pre-medicine, pre-veterinary science, pre-optometry, pre-pharmacy. **Special academic programs:** cooperative (work-study plan) program, distance learning, double major, English as a Second Language (ESL), honors program, independent study, internships, student-designed major, study abroad, teacher certificate program, weekend college. **Teacher certification offered in:** early childhood, special education, elementary, middle/junior high, adult education, secondary. **Reserve Officers Training Corps (ROTC):** Army ROTC: Offered on campus. **Faculty and instruction (2005-2006):** Total instructional faculty: 411 full-time, 164 part-time (52% men; 48% women; 9% minorities). Full-time faculty with Ph.D. or other terminal degree: 97%. Student/faculty ratio: 21/1. Classes of fewer than 20 students: 37%; of 20 to 49 students: 51%; of 50 or more students: 11%. **Advanced Placement and International Baccalaureate credit:** AP tests may be used for: Credit and/or placement. Scores accepted: 3, 4, 5. International Baccalaureate exams may be used for: Credit only. **Freshmen returning for sophomore year:** 76%. **Graduation rates:** Four-year: 18%; five-year: 40%; six-year: 46%.

COSTS AND FINANCIAL AID

Financial aid office: (509) 359-2314. **Expenses (2006-2007):** Tuition and fees 2006-2007: $4,575 in state, $13,605 out of state; room/board: $6,020. Estimated books and supplies: $930; transportation: $1,500. **Financial aid:** Priority filing date for institution's financial aid form: April 1. In 2005-2006, 76% of undergraduates applied for financial aid. Of those, 63% were determined to have financial need; 15% had their need fully met. Average financial aid package (proportion receiving): $11,418 (61%). Average amount of gift aid, such as scholarships or grants (proportion receiving): $5,089 (46%). Average amount of self-help aid, such as work study or loans (proportion receiving): $6,439 (49%). Average need-based loan (excluding PLUS or other private loans): $4,052. Among students who received need-based aid, the average percentage of need met: 37%. Among students who received aid based on merit, the average award (and the proportion receiving): $3,450 (2%). The average athletic scholarship (and the proportion receiving): $7,413 (1%). Average amount of debt of borrowers graduating in 2005: $18,600. Proportion who borrowed: 65%.

CAMPUS LIFE AND EXTRACURRICULAR ACTIVITIES

Campus housing available (% using): coed dorms (90%), sorority housing (3%), fraternity housing (2%), apartments for married students (5%), special housing for disabled students. Students who live in college-owned, operated, or affiliated housing: 21%. **Student employment:** During the 2005-2006 academic year, 42% of undergraduates worked on campus. Average per-year earnings: $2,074. **Clubs and organizations:** Number of student organizations: 109. Activities include: choral groups, concert band, dance, drama/theater, jazz band, literary magazine, marching band, music ensembles, musical theater, opera, pep band, radio station, student government, student newspaper, student film society, symphony orchestra, television station. Number of fraternities: 7; sororities: 6. Average proportion of students who stay on campus on weekends: 70%. **Sports program (2005-2006):** Member of NCAA I. *Men's intercollegiate varsity sports:* basketball, cross-country, football, tennis, track and field (indoor), track and field (outdoor). *Women's intercollegiate varsity sports:* basketball, cross-country, golf, soccer, tennis, track and field (indoor), track and field (outdoor), volleyball.

SERVICES AND FACILITIES

Basic services: women's center, placement service, day care, health service, health insurance. **Remedial assistance:** math, writing, study skills, other. **Counseling services:** minority student, career, military, personal, veteran student, academic, older student, psychological. **For learning-disabled students:** School does not offer a structured program with separate admission and additional fees. Total undergraduates in learning-disabled program or receiving services: 99. Services include: other testing accommodations, reading machines, tape recorders, other special classes, untimed tests, note-taking services, oral tests, learning center, readers, extended time for tests, tutors, other testing accomodations, other. **Library:** Number of titles: 895,928; number of current serial subscriptions: 6,392. **Information technology resources:** Students are not required to lease or own a computer. Number of campus computers available to all students: 825. School has a wireless network. Approximate number of users that can be accommodated: 1,000. Proportion of college-owned housing units wired for high-speed internet access: 100%. **Campus safety:** Security services offered: late-night transport/escort service, 24-hour emergency telephones, lighted pathways/sidewalks, controlled dormitory access (key, security card, etc).

TRANSFER AND INTERNATIONAL STUDENTS

Transfer students: May apply for admission for the following academic terms: Fall, Winter, Spring, Summer. Applicants do not need a minimum number of credits to apply. For fall 2005: Transfer applications received: 2,154. Transfer applicants offered admission: 1,705. Transfer applicants enrolled: 1,054. **International students:** Number of foreign undergraduates: 144 (2% of student body). Number of countries represented: 30. Minimum TOEFL score required: 525 (paper); 195 (computer).

Evergreen State College

- **Address:** 2700 Evergreen Parkway NW, Olympia, WA 98505
- **Website:** http://www.evergreen.edu
- **Public**
- **Enrollment:** 3,655 full-time; 516 part-time

KEY STATS

✔ **U.S News College Ranking:** fourth tier, Liberal Arts Colleges
✔ **SAT Score (25th/75th percentile):** 1010-1250
✔ **Tuition:** 2006-2007: $4,551 in state, $14,739 out of state

Selectivity: Selective	**Room/board:** $7,140
Acceptance rate: 97%	**Average debt:** $13,818
Student/faculty ratio: 21/1	**Proportion who borrowed:** 59%

UNDERGRADUATE STUDENT BODY STATS

2005-2006 enrollment: 3,655 full-time; 516 part-time. Men: 45%; women: 55%. **Ethnic makeup:** African American: 5%; American-Indian: 4%; Asian American: 5%; Hispanic: 4%; White: 82%.

ADMISSIONS FACTS AND FIGURES

Phone: (360) 867-6170. **Email:** admissions@evergreen.edu. **Website:** http://www.evergreen.edu. **Application deadlines for fall 2007:** Regular decision: Rolling. Early decision: Not offered. Early action: Not offered. Admission can be deferred. **Application fee:** $50. Common application is not accepted. **To apply online, go to:** http://www.evergreen.edu/admissions/apply.htm. **Admissions requirements/recommendations:** High school units required (recommended): English: 4; Mathematics: 3; Science: 2; Foreign language: 2; Social studies: 3; History: 0; Academic electives: 0; Total units: 15. Tests: The college uses SAT or ACT scores in admissions decisions. Either SAT or ACT required. For admission to the fall 2007 entering class, the school will accept: ACT with writing, ACT without writing. Campus visit: Recommended. Admissions interview: Neither required nor recommended. Off-campus interview: May be arranged. **Factors that count in admissions decisions:** *Academic:* Secondary school record: Very important. Class rank: Not considered. Letters of recommendation: Considered. Standardized test scores: Very important. Essay: Important. *Nonacademic:* Interview: Not considered. Extracurricular activities: Considered. Talent/ability: Considered. Character/personal qualities: Not considered. Alumni/ae relationship: Not considered. Geographical residence: Not considered. State residency: Considered. Religious affiliation/commitment: Not considered. Minority status: Not considered. Volunteer work: Considered. Work experience: Considered. **Other schools with the greatest overlap in applicants:** Lewis and Clark College; University of California–Santa Cruz; University of Washington; Washington State University; Western Washington University. **Admissions statistics for the fall 2005 entering class:** Total applicants: 1,657. Total accepted: 1,611. Freshmen enrolled: 605; 40% were from out of state. Overall acceptance rate: 97%.

Credentials of fall 2005 freshmen: 8% ranked in the top 10 percent of their high school class; 24% were in the top 25 percent, and 60% were in the top half. (Proportion submitting class standing: 30%.) **Average high school grade point average:** 3.1. **First-year students who submitted SAT scores:** 85%. Scores (25/75 percentile): Verbal: 530-650, Math: 480-600, Combined: 1010-1250. **First-year students submitting ACT scores:** 25%. Scores (25/75 percentile): English: N/A, Math: 18-25, Composite: 21-27.

ACADEMICS

Year founded: 1967. **Academic calendar:** Quarter. **Degrees offered:** bachelor's, post-bachelor's certificate, master's. **Most popular majors:** 28% social sciences, 17% liberal arts and sciences studies, and humanities, 14% visual and performing arts, 12% biological and biomedical sciences, 12% natural resources and conservation. **Major fields of study:** area, ethnic, cultural, and gender studies; biological and biomedical sciences; business, management, marketing, and related support services; communication, journalism, and related programs; computer and information sciences and support services; English language and literature/letters; foreign languages, literatures, and linguistics; health professions and related clinical sciences; liberal arts and sciences studies, and humanities; multi/interdisciplinary studies; natural resources and conservation; physical sciences; psychology; social sciences; visual and performing arts. **Special academic programs (% participation):** cooperative (work-study plan) program, double major (4%), exchange student program (domestic), independent study (67%), internships (61%), student-designed major (100%), study abroad (27%), teacher certificate program. **Faculty and instruction (2005-2006):** Total instructional faculty: 158 full-time, 63 part-time (49% men; 51% women; 22% minorities). Full-time faculty with Ph.D. or other terminal degree: 87%. Student/faculty ratio: 21/1. Classes of fewer than 20 students: 43%; of 20 to 49 students: 46%; of 50 or more students: 11%. **Advanced Placement and International Baccalaureate credit:** AP tests may be used for: Credit and/or placement. Scores accepted: 3, 4, 5. International Baccalaureate exams may be used for: Credit only. **Freshmen returning for sophomore year:** 72%. **Graduation rates:** Four-year: 42%; five-year: 51%; six-year: 56%. **Graduate study:** 29% of students pursue further study within one year; 51% within five years. Fields in which graduates pursue further study: Master of Business Administration (MBA), 9%; law, 5%; medicine, 12%; theology (or the seminary), 1%; education, 19%; arts and sciences, 53%; veterinary medicine, 1%.

COSTS AND FINANCIAL AID

Financial aid office: (360) 867-6205. **Expenses (2006-2007):** Tuition and fees 2006-2007: $4,551 in state, $14,739 out of state; room/board: $7,140. Estimated books and supplies: $924; transportation: $1,362; personal expenses: $1,824. **Financial aid:** Priority filing date for institution's financial aid form: March 15. In 2005-2006, 81% of undergraduates applied for financial aid. Of those, 61% were determined to have financial need; 40% had their need fully met. Average financial aid package (proportion receiving): $11,066 (58%). Average amount of gift aid, such as scholarships or grants (proportion receiving): $5,672 (44%). Average amount of self-help aid, such as work study or loans (proportion receiving): $4,450 (48%). Average need-based loan (excluding PLUS or other private loans): $4,071. Among students who received need-based aid, the average percentage of need met: 81%. Among students who received aid based on merit, the average award (and the proportion receiving): $3,793 (0%). The average athletic scholarship (and the proportion receiving): $1,599 (1%). Average amount of debt of borrowers graduating in 2005: $13,818. Proportion who borrowed: 59%.

CAMPUS LIFE AND EXTRACURRICULAR ACTIVITIES

Campus housing available (% using): coed dorms (46%), apartments for married students (2%), apartment for single students (46%), special housing for disabled students (2%), special housing for international students (4%), other housing options. Students who live in college-owned, operated, or affiliated housing: 22%. **Student employment:** During the 2005-2006 academic year, 25% of undergraduates worked on campus. Average per-year earnings: $4,100. **Clubs and organizations:** Number of student organizations: 87. Activities include: choral groups, dance, drama/theater, literary magazine, music ensembles, radio station, student newspaper, student film society, television station. Number of fraternities: 0; sororities: 0. Average proportion of students who stay on campus on weekends: 80%. **Sports program (2005-2006):** Member of NAIA. *Men's intercollegiate varsity sports:* basketball, cross-country, soccer, track and field (indoor), track and field (outdoor). *Women's intercollegiate varsity sports:* basketball, cross-country, soccer, track and field (indoor), track and field (outdoor), volleyball.

SERVICES AND FACILITIES

Basic services: nonremedial tutoring, women's center, placement service, day care, health service. **Counseling services:** minority student, career, personal, veteran student, academic, psychological, birth control, other. **For learning-disabled students:** School does not offer a structured program with separate admission and additional fees. Services include: tape recorders, diagnostic testing service, note-taking services, learning center, extended time for tests, tutors, texts on tape, other testing accomodations. **Library:** Number of titles: 471,105; number of current serial subscriptions: 2,731. **Information technology resources:** Students are not required to lease or own a computer. Number of campus computers available to all students: 300. School has a wireless network. Proportion of college-owned housing units wired for high-speed internet access: 100%. **Campus safety:** Security services offered: 24-hour foot-and-vehicle patrols, late-night transport/escort service, 24-hour emergency telephones, lighted pathways/sidewalks, controlled dormitory access (key, security card, etc).

TRANSFER AND INTERNATIONAL STUDENTS

Transfer students: May apply for admission for the following academic terms: Fall, Winter, Spring. Applicants need a minimum number of credits to apply. For fall 2005: Transfer applications received: 1,301. Transfer applicants offered admission: 1,257. Transfer applicants enrolled: 807. **International students:** Number of foreign undergraduates: 15. Number of countries represented: 3. Minimum TOEFL score required: 525 (paper); 197 (computer). Average TOEFL score: 552 (paper).

Gonzaga University

- **Address:** 502 E. Boone Avenue, Spokane, WA 99258-0001
- **Website:** http://www.gonzaga.edu
- **Private; Religious affiliation:** Roman Catholic
- **Enrollment:** 3,986 full-time; 166 part-time

KEY STATS

✔ **U.S News College Ranking:** 3, Universities–Master's (West)
✔ **SAT Score (25th/75th percentile):** 1090-1290
✔ **Tuition:** 2006-2007: $25,010

Selectivity: More selective	**Room/board:** $6,980
Acceptance rate: 73%	**Average debt:** $23,164
Student/faculty ratio: 12/1	**Proportion who borrowed:** 69%

UNDERGRADUATE STUDENT BODY STATS

2005-2006 enrollment: 3,986 full-time; 166 part-time. Men: 46%; women: 54%. **Ethnic makeup:** African American: 1%; American-Indian: 1%; Asian American: 6%; Hispanic: 4%; White: 87%; International: 1%. **Religious preference:** Protestant: 22%; No preference: 1%; Unknown: 29%; Roman Catholic: 47%.

ADMISSIONS FACTS AND FIGURES

Phone: (800) 322-2584. **Email:** mcculloh@gu.gonzaga.edu. **Website:** http://www.gonzaga.edu. **Application deadlines for fall 2007:** Regular decision: February 1; decision sent by March 15. Early decision: Not offered. Early action: Send application by: November 15; Decision sent by: January 15. Admission can be deferred. **Application fee:** $45. Common application is accepted. **Admissions requirements/recommendations:** High school units required (recommended): English: 4 (4); Mathematics: 3 (4); Science: 3 (4); Foreign language: 3 (4); Social studies: 2 (3); History: 2 (3); Academic electives: 3 (3); Total units: 20 (25). Tests: The college uses SAT or ACT scores in admissions decisions. Either SAT or ACT required. For admission to the fall 2007 entering class, the school will accept: ACT with writing, ACT without writing. Campus visit: Recommended. Admissions interview: Recommended. Off-campus interview: May be arranged. **Factors that count in admissions decisions:** *Academic:* Secondary school record: Very important. Class rank: Important. Letters of recommendation: Important. Standardized test scores: Important. Essay: Important. *Nonacademic:* Interview: Considered. Extracurricular activities: Important. Talent/ability: Important. Character/personal qualities: Very important. Alumni/ae relationship: Considered. Geographical residence: Not considered. State residency: Not considered. Religious affiliation/commitment: Not considered. Minority status: Considered. Volunteer work: Considered. Work experience: Considered. **Other schools with the greatest overlap in applicants:** Santa Clara University; Seattle University; University of Portland; University of Washington;

Washington State University. **Admissions statistics for the fall 2005 entering class:** Total applicants: 4,328. Total accepted: 3,173. Freshmen enrolled: 986; 45% were from out of state. Overall acceptance rate: 73%. Non-early acceptance rate: 73%. **Size of waiting list:** 462 applicants; enrolled from waiting list: 58. **Credentials of fall 2005 freshmen:** 40% ranked in the top 10 percent of their high school class; 71% were in the top 25 percent, and 94% were in the top half. (Proportion submitting class standing: 84%.) **Average high school grade point average:** 3.6. **First-year students who submitted SAT scores:** 93%. Scores (25/75 percentile): Verbal: 540-640, Math: 550-650, Combined: 1090-1290. **First-year students submitting ACT scores:** 46%. Scores (25/75 percentile): English: N/A, Math: N/A, Composite: 24-29.

ACADEMICS

Year founded: 1887. **Academic calendar:** Semester. **Degrees offered:** bachelor's, master's, first professional, doctorate. **Most popular majors:** 23% business, management, marketing, and related support services, 20% social sciences, 10% engineering, 7% communication, journalism, and related programs, 6% psychology. **Major fields of study:** area, ethnic, cultural, and gender studies; biological and biomedical sciences; business, management, marketing, and related support services; communication, journalism, and related programs; communications technologies/technicians and support services; computer and information sciences and support services; education; engineering; English language and literature/letters; foreign languages, literatures, and linguistics; health professions and related clinical sciences; history; liberal arts and sciences studies, and humanities; mathematics and statistics; multi/interdisciplinary studies; philosophy and religious studies; physical sciences; psychology; security and protective services; social sciences; visual and performing arts. **Areas of required coursework:** arts/fine arts, humanities, mathematics, English (including composition), philosophy, foreign languages, sciences (biological or physical), history, social science. **Pre-professional programs:** pre-law, pre-dentistry, pre-medicine. **Special academic programs (% participation):** double major (11%), English as a Second Language (ESL), honors program (3%), internships, study abroad (30%), teacher certificate program (11%), weekend college. **Teacher certification offered in:** special education, elementary, middle/junior high, secondary. **Reserve Officers Training Corps (ROTC):** Army ROTC: Offered on campus. **Faculty and instruction (2005-2006):** Total instructional faculty: 325 full-time, 300 part-time (61% men; 39% women; 5% minorities). Full-time faculty with Ph.D. or other terminal degree: 86%. Student/faculty ratio: 12/1. Classes of fewer than 20 students: 51%; of 20 to 49 students: 47%; of 50 or more students: 2%. **Advanced Placement and International Baccalaureate credit:** AP tests may be used for: Credit and/or placement. Scores accepted: 4, 5. International Baccalaureate exams may be used for: Credit only. **Freshmen returning for sophomore year:** 91%. **Graduation rates:** Four-year: 58%; five-year: 72%; six-year: 76%.

COSTS AND FINANCIAL AID

Financial aid office: (509) 323-4049. **Expenses (2006-2007):** Tuition and fees 2006-2007: $25,010; room/board: $6,980. Estimated books and supplies: $875; transportation: $1,200; personal expenses: $1,700. **Financial aid:** Priority filing date for institution's financial aid form: February 1. In 2005-2006, 76% of undergraduates applied for financial aid. Of those, 61% were determined to have financial need; 33% had their need fully met. Average financial aid package (proportion receiving): $18,255 (59%). Average amount of gift aid, such as scholarships or grants (proportion receiving): $12,374 (57%). Average amount of self-help aid, such as work study or loans (proportion receiving): $6,657 (44%). Average need-based loan (excluding PLUS or other private loans): $5,358. Among students who received need-based aid, the average percentage of need met: 89%. Among students who received aid based on merit, the average award (and the proportion receiving): $7,205 (34%). The average athletic scholarship (and the proportion receiving): $15,619 (4%). Average amount of debt of borrowers graduating in 2005: $23,164. Proportion who borrowed: 69%.

CAMPUS LIFE AND EXTRACURRICULAR ACTIVITIES

Campus housing available (% using): coed dorms (53%), women's dorms (8%), men's dorms (13%), apartment for single students (24%), special housing for international students (1%), other housing options (1%). Students who live in college-owned, operated, or affiliated housing: 52%. **Student employment:** During the 2005-2006 academic year, 11% of undergraduates worked on campus. Average per-year earnings: $2,700. **Clubs and organizations:** Number of student organizations: 102. Activities include: choral groups, concert band, dance, drama/theater, jazz band, literary magazine, music ensembles, pep band, radio station, student government, student newspaper, symphony orchestra, television station, yearbook. Number of fraternities: 0; sororities: 0. Average proportion of students who stay on campus on weekends: 75%.

Sports program (2005-2006): Member of NCAA I. *Men's intercollegiate varsity sports:* baseball, basketball, cross-country, golf, soccer, tennis, track and field (outdoor), rowing. *Women's intercollegiate varsity sports:* basketball, cross-country, golf, rowing, soccer, tennis, track and field (outdoor), volleyball.

SERVICES AND FACILITIES

Basic services: health service, health insurance. **Counseling services:** minority student, career, military, personal, veteran student, academic, older student, psychological, religious. **For learning-disabled students:** School does not offer a structured program with separate admission and additional fees. Total undergraduates in learning-disabled program or receiving services: 110. Services include: reading machines, tape recorders, note-taking services, oral tests, readers, extended time for tests, priority registration, priority seating, substitution of courses, texts on tape, typist/scribe, exams on tape or computer, other testing accomodations, other. **Library:** Number of titles: 291,978; number of current serial subscriptions: 2,529. **Information technology resources:** Students are not required to lease or own a computer. Number of campus computers available to all students: 425. School has a wireless network. Approximate number of users that can be accommodated: 2,500. Proportion of college-owned housing units wired for high-speed internet access: 99%. **Campus safety:** Security services offered: 24-hour foot-and-vehicle patrols, late-night transport/escort service, 24-hour emergency telephones, lighted pathways/sidewalks, student patrols, controlled dormitory access (key, security card, etc).

TRANSFER AND INTERNATIONAL STUDENTS

Transfer students: May apply for admission for the following academic terms: Fall, Spring. Applicants need a minimum number of credits to apply. For fall 2005: Transfer applications received: 410. Transfer applicants offered admission: 291. Transfer applicants enrolled: 170. **International students:** Number of foreign undergraduates: 46 (1% of student body). Number of countries represented: 15. Minimum TOEFL score required: 550 (paper); 213 (computer). Average TOEFL score: 596 (paper).

Henry Cogswell College

- **Address:** 3002 Colby Avenue, Everett, WA 98201
- **Website:** http://www.henrycogswell.edu
- **Private**
- **Enrollment:** 118 full-time; 82 part-time

KEY STATS

✔ **U.S News College Ranking:** Unranked Specialty School–Engineering
✔ **SAT Score (25th/75th percentile):** 1070-1170
✔ **Tuition:** 2006-2007: $17,570

Selectivity: Less selective	**Room/board:** N/A
Acceptance rate: 84%	**Average debt:** $32,000
Student/faculty ratio: 7/1	**Proportion who borrowed:** 50%

UNDERGRADUATE STUDENT BODY STATS

2005-2006 enrollment: 118 full-time; 82 part-time. Men: 75%; women: 26%. **Ethnic makeup:** African American: 3%; American-Indian: 1%; Asian American: 8%; Hispanic: 7%; White: 82%.

ADMISSIONS FACTS AND FIGURES

Phone: (425) 258-3351. **Email:** admissions@henrycogswell.edu. **Website:** http://www.henrycogswell.edu. **Application deadlines for fall 2007:** Regular decision: September 1. Early decision: Not offered. Early action: Not offered. Admission can be deferred. **Application fee:** $50. Common application is accepted. To apply online, go to: https://www.applyweb.com/apply/hcc/menu.html. **Admissions requirements/recommendations:** High school units required (recommended): English: 4; Mathematics: 2 (3); Science: 2 (3); Foreign language: 0 (1); Social studies: 3; History: 0 (1); Academic electives: 2; Total units: 13 (16). Tests: The college uses SAT or ACT scores in admissions decisions. Neither SAT nor ACT required. For admission to the fall 2007 entering class, the school will accept: ACT with writing, ACT without writing. Campus visit: Recommended. Admissions interview: Recommended. Off-campus interview: May be arranged. **Factors that count in admissions decisions:** *Academic:* Secondary school record: Very important. Class rank: Not considered. Letters of recommendation: Important. Standardized test scores: Very important. Essay: Very important. *Nonacademic:* Interview: Important.

Extracurricular activities: Important. Talent/ability: Important. Character/personal qualities: Important. Alumni/ae relationship: Not considered. Geographical residence: Not considered. State residency: Not considered. Religious affiliation/commitment: Not considered. Minority status: Not considered. Volunteer work: Not considered. Work experience: Not considered. **Other schools with the greatest overlap in applicants:** University of Washington; Western Washington University. **Admissions statistics for the fall 2005 entering class:** Total applicants: 86. Total accepted: 72. Freshmen enrolled: 56; 1% were from out of state. Overall acceptance rate: 84%. **Average high school grade point average:** 2.8. **First-year students who submitted SAT scores:** 18%. Scores (25/75 percentile): Verbal: 510-560, Math: 560-610, Combined: 1070-1170. **First-year students submitting ACT scores:** 4%. Scores (25/75 percentile): English: 11-14, Math: 19-23, Composite: 12-20.

ACADEMICS

Year founded: 1979. **Academic calendar:** Trimester. **Degrees offered:** bachelor's. **Most popular majors:** 48% visual and performing arts, 24% engineering, 16% business, management, marketing, and related support services, 12% computer and information sciences and support services. **Major fields of study:** business, management, marketing, and related support services; computer and information sciences and support services; engineering; engineering technologies/technicians; visual and performing arts. **Areas of required coursework:** arts/fine arts, humanities, computer literacy, mathematics, English (including composition), sciences (biological or physical), social science. **Special academic programs (% participation):** accelerated program (100%), cooperative (work-study plan) program (6%), double major (1%), independent study (1%), internships (1%). **Faculty and instruction (2005-2006):** Total instructional faculty: 14 full-time, 18 part-time (75% men; 25% women). Full-time faculty with Ph.D. or other terminal degree: 43%. Student/faculty ratio: 7/1. Classes of fewer than 20 students: 88%; of 20 to 49 students: 12%. **Freshmen returning for sophomore year:** 79%. **Graduation rates:** Four-year: 33%; five-year: 33%; six-year: 51%. **Graduate study:** 9% of students pursue further study immediately upon graduation; 91% within one year. Fields in which graduates pursue further study: Master of Business Administration (MBA), 25%; arts and sciences, 75%.

COSTS AND FINANCIAL AID

Financial aid office: (425) 258-3351. **Expenses (2006-2007):** Tuition and fees 2006-2007: $17,570; room/board: N/A. **Financial aid:** Priority filing date for institution's financial aid form: March 1. In 2005-2006, 85% of undergraduates applied for financial aid. Of those, 69% were determined to have financial need; 3% had their need fully met. Average financial aid package (proportion receiving): $7,250 (61%). Average amount of gift aid, such as scholarships or grants (proportion receiving): $6,000 (24%). Average amount of self-help aid, such as work study or loans (proportion receiving): N/A (32%). Average need-based loan (excluding PLUS or other private loans): $5,000. Among students who received need-based aid, the average percentage of need met: 30%. Average amount of debt of borrowers graduating in 2005: $32,000. Proportion who borrowed: 50%.

CAMPUS LIFE AND EXTRACURRICULAR ACTIVITIES

Student employment: During the 2005-2006 academic year, 0% of undergraduates worked on campus. Average per-year earnings: $6,000. **Clubs and organizations:** Number of student organizations: 6. Activities include: student government, student newspaper. Number of fraternities: 0; sororities: 0. Average proportion of students who stay on campus on weekends: 25%.

SERVICES AND FACILITIES

Basic services: nonremedial tutoring. **Counseling services:** career. **For learning-disabled students:** School does not offer a structured program with separate admission and additional fees. Total undergraduates in learning-disabled program or receiving services: 2. Services include: tutors. **Library:** Number of titles: 9,424; number of current serial subscriptions: 5,295. **Information technology resources:** Students are not required to lease or own a computer. Number of campus computers available to all students: 190. School does not have a wireless network. **Campus safety:** Security services offered: lighted pathways/sidewalks.

TRANSFER AND INTERNATIONAL STUDENTS

Transfer students: May apply for admission for the following academic terms: Fall, Spring, Summer. Applicants do not need a minimum number of credits to apply. For fall 2005: Transfer applications received: 16. Transfer applicants offered admission: 16. Transfer applicants enrolled: 16. **International students:** Number of countries represented: 0. Minimum TOEFL score required: 525 (paper); 195 (computer). Average TOEFL score: 570 (paper).

Heritage University

- **Address:** 3240 Fort Road, Toppenish, WA 98948
- **Website:** http://www.heritage.edu
- **Private**
- **Enrollment:** 568 full-time; 238 part-time

KEY STATS

✔ **U.S News College Ranking:** fourth tier, Universities–Master's (West)
✔ **SAT or ACT Score (25th/75th percentile):** N/A
✔ **Tuition:** 2006-2007: $8,450

Selectivity: Less selective	**Room/board:** N/A
Acceptance rate: 60%	**Average debt:** $19,120
Student/faculty ratio: 9/1	**Proportion who borrowed:** 98%

UNDERGRADUATE STUDENT BODY STATS

2005-2006 enrollment: 568 full-time; 238 part-time. Men: 27%; women: 73%. **Ethnic makeup:** African American: 1%; American-Indian: 10%; Asian American: 1%; Hispanic: 54%; White: 34%. **Religious preference:** Roman Catholic: 45%; Protestant: 25%; Muslim: 1%; No preference: 15%; Unknown: 12%; Yakama Indian Traditional Religions: 2%.

ADMISSIONS FACTS AND FIGURES

Phone: (509) 865-8508. **Email:** 3w_Admissions@heritage.edu. **Website:** http://www.heritage.edu. **Application deadlines for fall 2007:** Regular decision: September 1. Early decision: Not offered. Early action: Not offered. Admission can be deferred. Common application is accepted. **Admissions requirements/recommendations:** High school units required (recommended): English: (3); Mathematics: (2); Science: (1); History: (3); Academic electives: (4); Total units: (13). Tests: The college does not use SAT or ACT scores in admissions decisions. Neither SAT nor ACT required. Campus visit: Recommended. Admissions interview: Recommended. Off-campus interview: May be arranged. **Factors that count in admissions decisions:** *Academic:* Secondary school record: Not considered. Class rank: Not considered. Letters of recommendation: Not considered. Standardized test scores: Considered. Essay: Not considered. *Nonacademic:* Interview: Not considered. Extracurricular activities: Not considered. Talent/ability: Not considered. Character/personal qualities: Not considered. Alumni/ae relationship: Not considered. Geographical residence: Not considered. State residency: Not considered. Religious affiliation/commitment: Not considered. Minority status: Not considered. Volunteer work: Not considered. Work experience: Not considered. **Other schools with the greatest overlap in applicants:** Central Washington University; Eastern Washington University; Washington State University. **Admissions statistics for the fall 2005 entering class:** Total applicants: 475. Total accepted: 285. Freshmen enrolled: 89; Overall acceptance rate: 60%.

ACADEMICS

Year founded: 1982. **Academic calendar:** Semester. **Degrees offered:** certificate, associate, bachelor's, post-bachelor's certificate, master's. **Most popular majors:** 29% education, 19% social work, 16% psychology, 15% business administration and management, 7% English language and literature. **Major fields of study:** agriculture, agriculture operations, and related sciences; area, ethnic, cultural, and gender studies; biological and biomedical sciences; business, management, marketing, and related support services; computer and information sciences and support services; education; English language and literature/letters; liberal arts and sciences studies, and humanities; mathematics and statistics; multi/interdisciplinary studies; natural resources and conservation; physical sciences; psychology; public administration and social service professions; visual and performing arts. **Areas of required coursework:** arts/fine arts, humanities, computer literacy, mathematics, English (including composition), philosophy, foreign languages, sciences (biological or physical), history, social science, other. **Special academic programs (% participation):** cooperative (work-study plan) program (5%), distance learning (5%), double major (3%), English as a Second Language (ESL) (25%), honors program (5%), independent study (15%), internships (70%), liberal arts/career combination (100%), student-designed major (3%), teacher certificate program (40%). **Teacher certification offered in:** early childhood, special education, elementary, middle/junior high, secondary, bilingual/bicultural. **Faculty and instruction (2005-2006):** Total instructional faculty: 47 full-time, 140 part-time (58% men; 42% women; 20% minorities). Full-time faculty with Ph.D. or other terminal degree: 38%. Student/faculty ratio: 9/1. Classes of fewer than 20 students: 76%; of 20 to 49 students: 24%. **Advanced Placement and International Baccalaureate credit:** AP tests may be used for: Credit and/or placement.

Scores accepted: 4, 5. International Baccalaureate exams may be used for: Credit and/or placement. **Freshmen returning for sophomore year:** 63%. **Graduation rates:** Five-year: 7%; six-year: 38%. **Graduate study:** 5% of students pursue further study immediately upon graduation; 5% within one year. Fields in which graduates pursue further study: Master of Business Administration (MBA), 7%; law, 3%; engineering, 1%; education, 60%; arts and sciences, 5%.

COSTS AND FINANCIAL AID

Financial aid office: (509) 865-8502. **Expenses (2006-2007):** Tuition and fees 2006-2007: $8,450; room/board: N/A. Estimated books and supplies: $0; transportation: $0; personal expenses: $0. **Financial aid:** Priority filing date for institution's financial aid form: February 10. In 2005-2006, 80% of undergraduates applied for financial aid. Of those, 79% were determined to have financial need; 10% had their need fully met. Average financial aid package (proportion receiving): $12,333 (79%). Average amount of gift aid, such as scholarships or grants (proportion receiving): $8,812 (74%). Average amount of self-help aid, such as work study or loans (proportion receiving): $4,566 (71%). Average need-based loan (excluding PLUS or other private loans): $3,840. Among students who received need-based aid, the average percentage of need met: 69%. Among students who received aid based on merit, the average award (and the proportion receiving): $6,641 (1%). The average athletic scholarship (and the proportion receiving): $0 (0%). Average amount of debt of borrowers graduating in 2005: $19,120. Proportion who borrowed: 98%.

CAMPUS LIFE AND EXTRACURRICULAR ACTIVITIES

Student employment: During the 2005-2006 academic year, 15% of undergraduates worked on campus. Average per-year earnings: $7,000. **Clubs and organizations:** Number of student organizations: 15. Activities include: dance, drama/theater, literary magazine, music ensembles, student government, student newspaper. Number of fraternities: 0; sororities: 0.

SERVICES AND FACILITIES

Basic services: nonremedial tutoring, placement service, day care. **Remedial assistance:** reading, math, writing, study skills. **Counseling services:** minority student, career, military, personal, veteran student, academic, older student, psychological, birth control, religious. **For learning-disabled students:** School does not offer a structured program with separate admission and additional fees. Total undergraduates in learning-disabled program or receiving services: 3. Services include: remedial math, remedial English, reading machines, remedial reading, tape recorders, untimed tests, note-taking services, oral tests, learning center, readers, extended time for tests, tutors, priority seating, texts on tape, other testing accomodations. **Library:** Number of titles: 50,000; number of current serial subscriptions: 15,000. **Information technology resources:** Students are not required to lease or own a computer. Number of campus computers available to all students: 265. School has a wireless network. Approximate number of users that can be accommodated: 100. **Campus safety:** Security services offered: late-night transport/escort service, 24-hour emergency telephones, lighted pathways/sidewalks.

TRANSFER AND INTERNATIONAL STUDENTS

Transfer students: May apply for admission for the following academic terms: Fall, Spring, Summer. Applicants need a minimum number of credits to apply. For fall 2005: Transfer applications received: 153. Transfer applicants offered admission: 106. Transfer applicants enrolled: 101. **International students:** Number of foreign undergraduates: 0. Number of countries represented: 2. Minimum TOEFL score required: 500 (paper); 173 (computer).

Northwest University

- **Address:** 5520 108th Avenue NE, Kirkland, WA 98083
- **Website:** http://www.northwestu.edu
- **Private; Religious affiliation:** Assemblies of God
- **Enrollment:** 1,051 full-time; 102 part-time

KEY STATS

✔ **U.S News College Ranking:** 14, Comp. Coll.–Bachelor's (West)
✔ **SAT Score:** 1045
✔ **Tuition:** 2006-2007: $18,144

Selectivity: Less selective	**Room/board:** $6,450
Acceptance rate: 83%	**Average debt:** $19,171
Student/faculty ratio: 16/1	**Proportion who borrowed:** 88%

UNDERGRADUATE STUDENT BODY STATS

2005-2006 enrollment: 1,051 full-time; 102 part-time. Men: 37%; women: 63%. **Ethnic makeup:** African American: 4%; American-Indian: 2%; Asian American: 6%; Hispanic: 4%; White: 84%; International: 2%.

ADMISSIONS FACTS AND FIGURES

Phone: (425) 889-5231. **Email:** admissions@northwestu.edu. **Website:** http://www.northwestu.edu. **Application deadlines for fall 2007:** Regular decision: August 1. Early decision: Not offered. Early action: Not offered. Admission can be deferred. **Application fee:** $30. Common application is accepted. **Admissions requirements/recommendations:** High school units required (recommended): English: (4); Mathematics: (3); Science: (2); Foreign language: (2); Social studies: (2); History: (2); Academic electives: (3); Total units: (16). Tests: The college uses SAT or ACT scores in admissions decisions. Either SAT or ACT required. Campus visit: Recommended. Admissions interview: Neither required nor recommended. Off-campus interview: May be arranged. **Factors that count in admissions decisions:** *Academic:* Secondary school record: Very important. Class rank: Important. Letters of recommendation: Very important. Standardized test scores: Very important. Essay: Very important. *Nonacademic:* Interview: Considered. Extracurricular activities: Important. Talent/ability: Considered. Character/personal qualities: Very important. Alumni/ae relationship: Considered. Geographical residence: Not considered. State residency: Not considered. Religious affiliation/commitment: Very important. Minority status: Not considered. Volunteer work: Considered. Work experience: Not considered. **Other schools with the greatest overlap in applicants:** Seattle Pacific University; Vanguard University of Southern California. **Admissions statistics for the fall 2005 entering class:** Total applicants: 427. Total accepted: 356. Freshmen enrolled: 132; 18% were from out of state. Overall acceptance rate: 83%. **First-year students who submitted SAT scores:** 81%. Scores (25/75 percentile): Verbal: N/A, Math: N/A, Combined: N/A. **First-year students submitting ACT scores:** 24%. Scores (25/75 percentile): English: N/A, Math: N/A, Composite: N/A.

ACADEMICS

Year founded: 1934. **Academic calendar:** Semester. **Degrees offered:** associate, bachelor's, master's. **Most popular majors:** 26% business, management, marketing, and related support services, 18% theology and religious vocations, 15% psychology, 13% education, 10% health professions and related clinical sciences. **Major fields of study:** business, management, marketing, and related support services; communication, journalism, and related programs; education; English language and literature/letters; health professions and related clinical sciences; history; natural resources and conservation; philosophy and religious studies; psychology; social sciences; theology and religious vocations. **Areas of required coursework:** arts/fine arts, humanities, mathematics, English (including composition), sciences (biological or physical), history, social science, other. **Pre-professional programs:** pre-law, pre-theology. **Special academic programs (% participation):** double major (2%), independent study (3%), internships (10%), study abroad (2%), teacher certificate program (5%). **Teacher certification offered in:** elementary, secondary. **Reserve Officers Training Corps (ROTC):** Army ROTC: Offered at cooperating institution (University of Washington). **Faculty and instruction (2005-2006):** Total instructional faculty: 52 full-time, 47 part-time (48% men; 52% women; 6% minorities). Full-time faculty with Ph.D. or other terminal degree: 56%. Student/faculty ratio: 16/1. Classes of fewer than 20 students: 53%; of 20 to 49 students: 43%; of 50 or more students: 4%. **Advanced Placement and International Baccalaureate credit:** AP tests may be used for: Credit and/or placement. International Baccalaureate exams may be used for: Credit and/or placement. **Freshmen returning for sophomore year:** 69%. **Graduation rates:** Six-year: 40%.

COSTS AND FINANCIAL AID

Financial aid office: (425) 889-5336. **Expenses (2006-2007):** Tuition and fees 2006-2007: $18,144; room/board: $6,450. Estimated books and supplies: $900; transportation: $400; personal expenses: $1,600. **Financial aid:** Priority filing date for institution's financial aid form: March 1. In 2005-2006, 87% of undergraduates applied for financial aid. Of those, 74% were determined to have financial need; 16% had their need fully met. Average financial aid package (proportion receiving): $12,446 (73%). Average amount of gift aid, such as scholarships or grants (proportion receiving): $8,054 (71%). Average amount of self-help aid, such as work study or loans (proportion receiving): $5,088 (66%). Average need-based loan (excluding PLUS or other private loans): $4,068. Among students who received need-based aid, the average percentage of need met: 68%. Among students who received aid based on merit, the average award (and the proportion receiving): $10,199 (17%). The average athletic scholarship (and the proportion

receiving): $8,875 (3%). Average amount of debt of borrowers graduating in 2005: $19,171. Proportion who borrowed: 88%.

CAMPUS LIFE AND EXTRACURRICULAR ACTIVITIES

Campus housing available: women's dorms, men's dorms, apartments for married students, apartment for single students. Students who live in college-owned, operated, or affiliated housing: 47%. **Student employment:** During the 2005-2006 academic year, 16% of undergraduates worked on campus. Average per-year earnings: $4,896. Activities include: choral groups, concert band, drama/theater, jazz band, music ensembles, student government, student newspaper, yearbook. Number of fraternities: 0; sororities: 0. Average proportion of students who stay on campus on weekends: 50%. **Sports program (2005-2006):** Member of NAIA. *Men's intercollegiate varsity sports:* basketball, soccer, track and field (indoor), track and field (outdoor). *Women's intercollegiate varsity sports:* basketball, cross-country, track and field (indoor), track and field (outdoor), volleyball.

SERVICES AND FACILITIES

Basic services: nonremedial tutoring, placement service, health service, health insurance. **Remedial assistance:** reading, math, writing, study skills. **Counseling services:** career, personal, academic, psychological, religious, other. **For learning-disabled students:** School does not offer a structured program with separate admission and additional fees. Services include: tape recorders, untimed tests, oral tests, learning center, readers, extended time for tests, tutors, priority registration, priority seating, other testing accomodations, other. **Library:** Number of titles: 78,682; number of current serial subscriptions: 598. **Information technology resources:** Students are not required to lease or own a computer. Number of campus computers available to all students: 100. School has a wireless network. Approximate number of users that can be accommodated: 900. Proportion of college-owned housing units wired for high-speed internet access: 100%. **Campus safety:** Security services offered: 24-hour foot-and-vehicle patrols, late-night transport/escort service, 24-hour emergency telephones, lighted pathways/sidewalks, controlled dormitory access (key, security card, etc).

TRANSFER AND INTERNATIONAL STUDENTS

Transfer students: May apply for admission for the following academic terms: Fall, Spring, Summer. Applicants do not need a minimum number of credits to apply. For fall 2005: Transfer applications received: 355. Transfer applicants offered admission: 226. Transfer applicants enrolled: 172. **International students:** Number of foreign undergraduates: 14 (2% of student body). Number of countries represented: 12. Minimum TOEFL score required: 500 (paper); 173 (computer). Average TOEFL score: 575 (paper).

Pacific Lutheran University

- **Address:** 12180 Park Street S., Tacoma, WA 98447
- **Website:** http://www.plu.edu
- **Private; Religious affiliation:** Lutheran
- **Enrollment:** 3,171 full-time; 198 part-time

KEY STATS

✔ **U.S News College Ranking:** 13, Universities–Master's (West)
✔ **SAT Score (25th/75th percentile):** 1000-1240
✔ **Tuition:** 2006-2007: $23,450

Selectivity: More selective	**Room/board:** $7,140
Acceptance rate: 76%	**Average debt:** $22,372
Student/faculty ratio: 15/1	**Proportion who borrowed:** 69%

UNDERGRADUATE STUDENT BODY STATS

2005-2006 enrollment: 3,171 full-time; 198 part-time. Men: 36%; women: 64%. **Ethnic makeup:** African American: 2%; American-Indian: 1%; Asian American: 6%; Hispanic: 2%; White: 84%; International: 6%. **Religious preference:** Roman Catholic: 10%; Protestant: 37%; Jewish: 1%; Muslim: 1%; Buddhist: 1%; No preference: 5%; Unknown: 17%; Lutheran: 28%.

ADMISSIONS FACTS AND FIGURES

Phone: (800) 274-6758. **Email:** admission@plu.edu. **Website:** http://www.plu.edu. **Application deadlines for fall 2007:** Regular decision: Rolling. Early decision: Not offered. Early action: Not offered. Admission

can be deferred. **Application fee:** $40. Common application is accepted. **Admissions requirements/recommendations:** High school units required (recommended): English: 4; Mathematics: 2 (3); Science: 2; Foreign language: 2 (3); Social studies: 2; Academic electives: 3; Total units: 17 (6). Tests: The college uses SAT or ACT scores in admissions decisions. Either SAT or ACT required. For admission to the fall 2007 entering class, the school will accept: ACT without writing. Campus visit: Recommended. Admissions interview: Recommended. Off-campus interview: May be arranged. **Factors that count in admissions decisions:** *Academic:* Secondary school record: Very important. Class rank: Important. Letters of recommendation: Important. Standardized test scores: Important. Essay: Very important. *Nonacademic:* Interview: Considered. Extracurricular activities: Important. Talent/ability: Important. Character/personal qualities: Important. Alumni/ae relationship: Not considered. Geographical residence: Not considered. State residency: Not considered. Religious affiliation/commitment: Not considered. Minority status: Not considered. Volunteer work: Important. Work experience: Considered. **Other schools with the greatest overlap in applicants:** University of Portland; University of Washington; Washington State University; Western Washington University; Whitworth College. **Admissions statistics for the fall 2005 entering class:** Total applicants: 2,112. Total accepted: 1,614. Freshmen enrolled: 690; 24% were from out of state. Overall acceptance rate: 76%. **Credentials of fall 2005 freshmen:** 33% ranked in the top 10 percent of their high school class; 65% were in the top 25 percent, and 89% were in the top half. (Proportion submitting class standing: 33%.) **Average high school grade point average:** 3.6. **First-year students who submitted SAT scores:** 82%. Scores (25/75 percentile): Verbal: 500-620, Math: 500-620, Combined: 1000-1240. **First-year students submitting ACT scores:** 18%. Scores (25/75 percentile): English: 21-27, Math: 20-26, Composite: 21-27.

ACADEMICS

Year founded: 1890. **Academic calendar:** 4-1-4. **Degrees offered:** bachelor's, post-bachelor's certificate, master's. **Most popular majors:** 15% education, 14% business administration and management, 9% nursing/registered nurse training (R.N., A.S.N., B.S.N., M.S.N.), 8% psychology, 7% communication studies/speech communication and rhetoric. **Major fields of study:** biological and biomedical sciences; business, management, marketing, and related support services; communication, journalism, and related programs; computer and information sciences and support services; education; engineering; English language and literature/letters; foreign languages, literatures, and linguistics; health professions and related clinical sciences; history; legal professions and studies; mathematics and statistics; multi/interdisciplinary studies; parks, recreation, leisure, and fitness studies; philosophy and religious studies; physical sciences; psychology; public administration and social service professions; social sciences; visual and performing arts. **Areas of required coursework:** arts/fine arts, humanities, mathematics, English (including composition), philosophy, foreign languages, sciences (biological or physical), history, social science, other. **Pre-professional programs:** pre-law, pre-dentistry, pre-medicine, pre-theology, pre-veterinary science, pre-optometry, pre-pharmacy. **Special academic programs (% participation):** cooperative (work-study plan) program (40%), double major (6.6%), English as a Second Language (ESL) (1%), honors program (2.3%), independent study (40%), internships (17%), liberal arts/career combination (2.2%), student-designed major (1%), study abroad (30.3%), teacher certificate program (11%). **Teacher certification offered in:** special education, elementary, secondary. **Cooperative education programs:** art, business, computer science, education, humanities, natural science, social/behavioral science. **Reserve Officers Training Corps (ROTC):** Army ROTC: Offered on campus. **Faculty and instruction (2005-2006):** Total instructional faculty: 238 full-time, 12 part-time (53% men; 47% women; 13% minorities). Full-time faculty with Ph.D. or other terminal degree: 87%. Student/faculty ratio: 15/1. Classes of fewer than 20 students: 44%; of 20 to 49 students: 52%; of 50 or more students: 4%. **Advanced Placement and International Baccalaureate credit:** AP tests may be used for: Credit and/or placement. Scores accepted: 3, 4, 5. International Baccalaureate exams may be used for: Credit only. **Freshmen returning for sophomore year:** 82%. **Graduation rates:** Four-year: 47%; five-year: 64%; six-year: 65%.

COSTS AND FINANCIAL AID

Financial aid office: (253) 535-7134. **Expenses (2006-2007):** Tuition and fees 2006-2007: $23,450; room/board: $7,140. Estimated books and supplies: $924; transportation: $315; personal expenses: $1,608. **Financial aid:** Priority filing date for institution's financial aid form: January 31. In 2005-2006, 82% of undergraduates applied for financial aid. Of those, 69% were determined to have financial need; 34% had their need fully met. Average financial aid package (proportion receiving): $19,269 (67%). Average amount of gift aid, such as scholarships or grants (proportion receiving): $7,987 (51%). Average amount of self-help aid, such as work study or loans (proportion receiving): $8,753 (61%). Average need-based loan (excluding PLUS or other private loans): $7,132. Among students who received need-based aid, the average percentage of need met: 89%. Among students who received aid based on merit, the average award (and the proportion receiving): $8,086 (20%). The average athletic scholarship (and the proportion receiving): $0 (0%). Average amount of debt of borrowers graduating in 2005: $22,372. Proportion who borrowed: 69%.

CAMPUS LIFE AND EXTRACURRICULAR ACTIVITIES
Campus housing available (% using): coed dorms (69%), women's dorms (11%), apartments for married students (1%), apartment for single students (13%), special housing for disabled students (1%), other housing options (5%). Students who live in college-owned, operated, or affiliated housing: 50%. **Student employment:** During the 2005-2006 academic year, 40% of undergraduates worked on campus. Average per-year earnings: $3,000. **Clubs and organizations:** Number of student organizations: 62. Activities include: choral groups, concert band, dance, drama/theater, jazz band, literary magazine, music ensembles, musical theater, opera, pep band, radio station, student government, student newspaper, student film society, symphony orchestra, television station, yearbook. Number of fraternities: 0; sororities: 0. Average proportion of students who stay on campus on weekends: 75%. **Sports program (2005-2006):** Member of NCAA III. *Men's intercollegiate varsity sports:* baseball, basketball, cross-country, football, golf, soccer, swimming and diving, tennis, track and field (indoor), track and field (outdoor). *Women's intercollegiate varsity sports:* basketball, cross-country, golf, rowing, soccer, softball, swimming and diving, tennis, track and field (indoor), track and field (outdoor), volleyball.

SERVICES AND FACILITIES
Basic services: nonremedial tutoring, women's center, placement service, health service, health insurance. **Counseling services:** minority student, career, military, personal, veteran student, academic, psychological, religious. **For learning-disabled students:** School does not offer a structured program with separate admission and additional fees. Services include: reading machines, tape recorders, other special classes, videotaped classes, untimed tests, note-taking services, oral tests, learning center, readers, extended time for tests, tutors, other. **Library:** Number of titles: 340,842; number of current serial subscriptions: 3,370. **Information technology resources:** Students are not required to lease or own a computer. Number of campus computers available to all students: 200. School has a wireless network. Approximate number of users that can be accommodated: 500. Proportion of college-owned housing units wired for high-speed internet access: 100%. **Campus safety:** Security services offered: 24-hour foot-and-vehicle patrols, late-night transport/escort service, 24-hour emergency telephones, lighted pathways/sidewalks, student patrols, controlled dormitory access (key, security card, etc).

TRANSFER AND INTERNATIONAL STUDENTS
Transfer students: May apply for admission for the following academic terms: Fall, Winter, Spring, Summer. Applicants do not need a minimum number of credits to apply. For fall 2005: Transfer applications received: 933. Transfer applicants offered admission: 635. Transfer applicants enrolled: 262. **International students:** Number of foreign undergraduates: 187 (6% of student body). Number of countries represented: 23. Minimum TOEFL score required: 550 (paper); 213 (computer). Average TOEFL score: 583 (paper).

Seattle Pacific University

■ **Address:** 3307 Third Avenue W, Seattle, WA 98119-1997
■ **Website:** http://www.spu.edu
■ **Private; Religious affiliation:** Free Methodist
■ **Enrollment:** 2,880 full-time; 142 part-time

KEY STATS
✔ **U.S News College Ranking:** 12, Universities–Master's (West)
✔ **SAT Score (25th/75th percentile):** 1050-1280
✔ **Tuition:** 2006-2007: $23,391

Selectivity: More selective	**Room/board:** $7,818
Acceptance rate: 85%	**Average debt:** $22,569
Student/faculty ratio: 14/1	**Proportion who borrowed:** 68%

UNDERGRADUATE STUDENT BODY STATS
2005-2006 enrollment: 2,880 full-time; 142 part-time. Men: 33%; women: 67%. **Ethnic makeup:** African American: 2%; American-Indian: 1%; Asian American: 6%; Hispanic: 3%; White: 87%; International: 1%. **Religious preference:** Roman Catholic: 4%; Protestant: 80%; Unknown: 10%; Free Methodist: 4%; Other: 2%.

ADMISSIONS FACTS AND FIGURES
Phone: (800) 366-3344. **Email:** admissions@spu.edu. **Website:** http://www.spu.edu. **Application deadlines for fall 2007:** Regular decision: March 1; decision sent by March 1. Early decision: Not offered. Early action: Send application by: November 15; Decision sent by: January 6. Admission cannot be deferred. **Application fee:** $45. Common application is not accepted. **To apply online, go to:** http://www.spu.edu/depts/ugadm/applyonline. **Admissions requirements/recommendations:** High school units required (recommended): English: 4 (4); Mathematics: 3 (3); Science: 2 (3); Foreign language: (3); Social studies: 3 (1); History: 2 (2). Tests: The college uses SAT or ACT scores in admissions decisions. Either SAT or ACT required. For admission to the fall 2007 entering class, the school will accept: ACT with writing. Campus visit: Recommended. Admissions interview: Recommended. Off-campus interview: May be arranged. **Factors that count in admissions decisions:** *Academic:* Secondary school record: Very important. Class rank: Considered. Letters of recommendation: Very important. Standardized test scores: Very important. Essay: Very important. *Nonacademic:* Interview: Important. Extracurricular activities: Important. Talent/ability: Important. Character/personal qualities: Important. Alumni/ae relationship: Considered. Geographical residence: Important. State residency: Not considered. Religious affiliation/commitment: Important. Minority status: Important. Volunteer work: Important. Work experience: Important. **Other schools with the greatest overlap in applicants:** Azusa Pacific University; Pacific Lutheran University; University of Washington; Western Washington University; Whitworth College. **Admissions statistics for the fall 2005 entering class:** Total applicants: 1,858. Total accepted: 1,576. Freshmen enrolled: 710; 58% were from out of state. Overall acceptance rate: 85%. Non-early acceptance rate: 85%. **Size of waiting list:** 519 applicants; enrolled from waiting list: 346. **Credentials of fall 2005 freshmen:** 39% ranked in the top 10 percent of their high school class; 67% were in the top 25 percent, and 91% were in the top half. (Proportion submitting class standing: 40%.) **Average high school grade point average:** 3.7. **First-year students who submitted SAT scores:** 93%. Scores (25/75 percentile): Verbal: 530-650, Math: 520-630, Combined: 1050-1280. **First-year students submitting ACT scores:** 36%. Scores (25/75 percentile): English: 21-29, Math: 21-27, Composite: 22-28.

ACADEMICS
Year founded: 1891. **Academic calendar:** Quarter. **Degrees offered:** certificate, bachelor's, master's, post-master's certificate, doctorate. **Most popular majors:** 16% business, management, marketing, and related support services, 11% health professions and related clinical sciences, 9% family and consumer sciences/human sciences, 9% social sciences, 8% communication, journalism, and related programs. **Major fields of study:** biological and biomedical sciences; communication, journalism, and related programs; computer and information sciences and support services; education; engineering; English language and literature/letters; family and consumer sciences/human sciences; foreign languages, literatures, and linguistics; health professions and related clinical sciences; mathematics and statistics; philosophy and religious studies; physical sciences; psychology; social sciences; theology and religious vocations; visual and performing arts. **Areas of required coursework:** arts/fine arts, humanities, mathematics, English (including composition), philosophy, foreign languages, sciences (biological or physical), history, social science, other. **Pre-professional programs:** pre-law, pre-dentistry, pre-medicine, pre-optometry. **Special academic programs:** cooperative (work-study plan) program, cross-registration, distance learning, double major, English as a Second Language (ESL), exchange student program (domestic), external degree program, honors program, independent study, internships, liberal arts/career combination, student-designed major, study abroad, teacher certificate program, weekend college. **Reserve Officers Training Corps (ROTC):** Army ROTC: Offered at cooperating institution (University of Washington); Navy ROTC: Offered at cooperating institution (University of Washington); Air Force ROTC: Offered at cooperating institution (University of Washington). **Faculty and instruction (2005-2006):** Total instructional faculty: 181 full-time, 152 part-time (51% men; 49% women; 7% minorities). Full-time faculty with Ph.D. or other terminal degree: 85%. Student/faculty ratio: 14/1. Classes of fewer than 20 students: 46%; of 20 to 49 students: 50%; of 50 or more students: 4%. **Freshmen returning for**

sophomore year: 82%. **Graduation rates:** Four-year: 48%; five-year: 64%; six-year: 62%.

COSTS AND FINANCIAL AID

Financial aid office: (206) 281-2061. **Expenses (2006-2007):** Tuition and fees 2006-2007: $23,391; room/board: $7,818. Estimated books and supplies: $813; transportation: $897; personal expenses: $1,635. **Financial aid:** Priority filing date for institution's financial aid form: April 1. In 2005-2006, 74% of undergraduates applied for financial aid. Of those, 62% were determined to have financial need; 23% had their need fully met. Average financial aid package (proportion receiving): $18,525 (61%). Average amount of gift aid, such as scholarships or grants (proportion receiving): $14,723 (60%). Average amount of self-help aid, such as work study or loans (proportion receiving): $7,299 (57%). Average need-based loan (excluding PLUS or other private loans): $5,452. Among students who received need-based aid, the average percentage of need met: 82%. Among students who received aid based on merit, the average award (and the proportion receiving): $9,748 (28%). The average athletic scholarship (and the proportion receiving): $13,484 (2%). Average amount of debt of borrowers graduating in 2005: $22,569. Proportion who borrowed: 68%.

CAMPUS LIFE AND EXTRACURRICULAR ACTIVITIES

Campus housing available: coed dorms, apartments for married students, apartment for single students, other housing options. Students who live in college-owned, operated, or affiliated housing: 59%. Activities include: choral groups, drama/theater, jazz band, literary magazine, music ensembles, pep band, radio station, student government, student newspaper, symphony orchestra, yearbook. Number of fraternities: 0; sororities: 0. **Sports program (2005-2006):** Member of NCAA II. *Men's intercollegiate varsity sports:* basketball, crew, cross-country, soccer, track and field (indoor), track and field (outdoor). *Women's intercollegiate varsity sports:* basketball, cross-country, gymnastics, rowing, soccer, track and field (indoor), track and field (outdoor), volleyball.

SERVICES AND FACILITIES

Basic services: health service, health insurance. **Remedial assistance:** reading, math, writing, study skills. **Information technology resources:** Students are not required to lease or own a computer. School has a wireless network. **Campus safety:** Security services offered: 24-hour foot-and-vehicle patrols, late-night transport/escort service, 24-hour emergency telephones, lighted pathways/sidewalks, controlled dormitory access (key, security card, etc).

TRANSFER AND INTERNATIONAL STUDENTS

Transfer students: May apply for admission for the following academic terms: Fall, Winter, Spring, Summer. Applicants do not need a minimum number of credits to apply. For fall 2005: Transfer applications received: 492. Transfer applicants offered admission: 380. Transfer applicants enrolled: 224. **International students:** Number of foreign undergraduates: 26 (1% of student body). Minimum TOEFL score required: 550 (paper); 213 (computer). Average TOEFL score: 582 (paper).

Seattle University

- **Address:** 901 12th Avenue, Seattle, WA 98122-4340
- **Website:** http://www.seattleu.edu
- **Private; Religious affiliation:** Roman Catholic (Jesuit)
- **Enrollment:** 3,877 full-time; 305 part-time

KEY STATS

✔ **U.S News College Ranking:** 7, Universities–Master's (West)
✔ **SAT Score (25th/75th percentile):** 1050-1250
✔ **Tuition:** 2006-2007: $24,615

Selectivity: More selective	**Room/board:** $7,503
Acceptance rate: 68%	**Average debt:** $25,311
Student/faculty ratio: 13/1	**Proportion who borrowed:** 68%

UNDERGRADUATE STUDENT BODY STATS

2005-2006 enrollment: 3,877 full-time; 305 part-time. Men: 39%; women: 61%. **Ethnic makeup:** African American: 5%; American-Indian: 1%; Asian American: 20%; Hispanic: 7%; White: 58%; International: 7%. **Religious preference:** Protestant: 17%; Jewish: 1%; Muslim: 1%; Buddhist: 2%; No preference: 4%; Unknown: 31%; Roman Catholic (Jesuit): 37%; Other: 7%.

ADMISSIONS FACTS AND FIGURES

Phone: (206) 296-2000. **Email:** admissions@seattleu.edu. **Website:** http://www.seattleu.edu. **Application deadlines for fall 2007:** Regular decision: July 1. Early decision: Not offered. Early action: Not offered. Admission can be deferred. **Application fee:** $45. Common application is accepted. **To apply online, go to:** http://www.seattleu.edu/home/prospective_students/freshmen/how_to_apply/application_instructions/. **Admissions requirements/recommendations:** High school units required (recommended): English: 4 (4); Mathematics: 3 (4); Science: 2 (3); Foreign language: 2 (2); Social studies: 3 (4); Academic electives: 2 (2). Tests: The college uses SAT or ACT scores in admissions decisions. Either SAT or ACT required. For admission to the fall 2007 entering class, the school will accept: ACT with writing. Campus visit: Recommended. Admissions interview: Neither required nor recommended. Off-campus interview: May be arranged. **Factors that count in admissions decisions:** *Academic:* Secondary school record: Very important. Class rank: Important. Letters of recommendation: Very important. Standardized test scores: Very important. Essay: Important. *Nonacademic:* Interview: Considered. Extracurricular activities: Important. Talent/ability: Important. Character/personal qualities: Important. Alumni/ae relationship: Considered. Geographical residence: Considered. State residency: Considered. Religious affiliation/commitment: Not considered. Minority status: Considered. Volunteer work: Very important. Work experience: Considered. **Other schools with the greatest overlap in applicants:** Gonzaga University; University of Portland; University of San Diego; University of Washington; Western Washington University. **Admissions statistics for the fall 2005 entering class:** Total applicants: 4,339. Total accepted: 2,935. Freshmen enrolled: 763; 50% were from out of state. Overall acceptance rate: 68%. **Size of waiting list:** 440 applicants; enrolled from waiting list: 3. **Credentials of fall 2005 freshmen:** 32% ranked in the top 10 percent of their high school class; 60% were in the top 25 percent, and 88% were in the top half. (Proportion submitting class standing: 71%.) **Average high school grade point average:** 3.6. **First-year students who submitted SAT scores:** 94%. Scores (25/75 percentile): Verbal: 520-630, Math: 530-620, Combined: 1050-1250. **First-year students submitting ACT scores:** 37%. Scores (25/75 percentile): English: 22-28, Math: 22-27, Composite: 23-27.

ACADEMICS

Year founded: 1891. **Academic calendar:** Quarter. **Degrees offered:** bachelor's, post-bachelor's certificate, master's, post-master's certificate, first professional, first professional certificate, doctorate. **Most popular majors:** 10% nursing/registered nurse training (R.N., A.S.N., B.S.N., M.S.N.), 7% psychology, 6% accounting, 6% finance, 4% marketing/marketing management. **Major fields of study:** area, ethnic, cultural, and gender studies; biological and biomedical sciences; business, management, marketing, and related support services; communication, journalism, and related programs; computer and information sciences and support services; engineering; English language and literature/letters; foreign languages, literatures, and linguistics; health professions and related clinical sciences; liberal arts and sciences studies, and humanities; mathematics and statistics; multi/interdisciplinary studies; natural resources and conservation; philosophy and religious studies; physical sciences; psychology; public administration and social service professions; security and protective services; social sciences; visual and performing arts. **Areas of required coursework:** arts/fine arts, mathematics, English (including composition), philosophy, sciences (biological or physical), history, social science, other. **Pre-professional programs:** pre-law, pre-medicine. **Special academic programs:** double major, honors program, independent study, internships, study abroad, teacher certificate program. **Teacher certification offered in:** special education, elementary, middle/junior high, adult education, secondary. **Reserve Officers Training Corps (ROTC):** Army ROTC: Offered on campus; Navy ROTC: Offered at cooperating institution (University of Washington); Air Force ROTC: Offered at cooperating institution (University of Washington). **Faculty and instruction (2005-2006):** Total instructional faculty: 387 full-time, 195 part-time (53% men; 47% women; 14% minorities). Full-time faculty with Ph.D. or other terminal degree: 85%. Student/faculty ratio: 13/1. Classes of fewer than 20 students: 49%; of 20 to 49 students: 50%; of 50 or more students: 1%. **Advanced Placement and International Baccalaureate credit:** AP tests may be used for: Credit and/or placement. Scores accepted: 4, 5. International Baccalaureate exams may be used for: Credit and/or placement. **Freshmen returning for sophomore year:** 84%. **Graduation rates:** Four-year: 43%; five-year: 59%; six-year: 65%.

COSTS AND FINANCIAL AID

Financial aid office: (206) 296-2000. **Expenses (2006-2007):** Tuition and fees 2006-2007: $24,615; room/board: $7,503. Estimated books and supplies: $1,260; transportation: $1,425; personal expenses: $1,995. **Financial**

aid: Priority filing date for institution's financial aid form: February 1. In 2005-2006, 81% of undergraduates applied for financial aid. Of those, 67% were determined to have financial need; 51% had their need fully met. Average financial aid package (proportion receiving): $22,535 (67%). Average amount of gift aid, such as scholarships or grants (proportion receiving): N/A (65%). Average amount of self-help aid, such as work study or loans (proportion receiving): $6,590 (54%). Average need-based loan (excluding PLUS or other private loans): $4,818. Among students who received need-based aid, the average percentage of need met: 84%. Among students who received aid based on merit, the average award (and the proportion receiving): $7,847 (4%). The average athletic scholarship (and the proportion receiving): $6,370 (1%). Average amount of debt of borrowers graduating in 2005: $25,311. Proportion who borrowed: 68%.

CAMPUS LIFE AND EXTRACURRICULAR ACTIVITIES
Campus housing available: coed dorms, apartment for single students, special housing for disabled students. Students who live in college-owned, operated, or affiliated housing: 37%. **Student employment:** During the 2005-2006 academic year, 11% of undergraduates worked on campus. Average per-year earnings: $4,500. **Clubs and organizations:** Number of student organizations: 90. Activities include: choral groups, concert band, drama/theater, jazz band, literary magazine, music ensembles, musical theater, radio station, student government, student newspaper. Number of fraternities: 0; sororities: 0. **Sports program (2005-2006):** Member of NCAA II. *Men's intercollegiate varsity sports:* basketball, cross-country, soccer, swimming and diving, track and field (indoor), track and field (outdoor). *Women's intercollegiate varsity sports:* basketball, cross-country, soccer, softball, swimming and diving, track and field (indoor), track and field (outdoor), volleyball.

SERVICES AND FACILITIES
Basic services: nonremedial tutoring, women's center, health service, health insurance. **Remedial assistance:** reading, writing, study skills. **Counseling services:** minority student, career, personal, academic, psychological, religious. **For learning-disabled students:** School does not offer a structured program with separate admission and additional fees. Total undergraduates in learning-disabled program or receiving services: 101. Services include: reading machines, tape recorders, note-taking services, oral tests, learning center, readers, extended time for tests, tutors, early syllabus, priority registration, priority seating, substitution of courses, texts on tape, typist/scribe, exams on tape or computer, other testing accomodations, other. **Information technology resources:** Students are not required to lease or own a computer. Number of campus computers available to all students: 355. School has a wireless network. Proportion of college-owned housing units wired for high-speed internet access: 100%. **Campus safety:** Security services offered: 24-hour foot-and-vehicle patrols, late-night transport/escort service, 24-hour emergency telephones, lighted pathways/sidewalks, controlled dormitory access (key, security card, etc).

TRANSFER AND INTERNATIONAL STUDENTS
Transfer students: May apply for admission for the following academic terms: Fall, Winter, Spring, Summer. Applicants need a minimum number of credits to apply. For fall 2005: Transfer applications received: 1,558. Transfer applicants offered admission: 828. Transfer applicants enrolled: 439. **International students:** Number of foreign undergraduates: 306 (7% of student body). Minimum TOEFL score required: 520 (paper); 190 (computer). Average TOEFL score: 567 (paper).

St. Martin's University

- ■ **Address:** 5300 Pacific Avenue SE, Lacey, WA 98503
- ■ **Website:** http://www.stmartin.edu
- ■ **Private; Religious affiliation:** Roman Catholic (Benedictine)
- ■ **Enrollment:** 936 full-time; 242 part-time

KEY STATS
- ✔ **U.S News College Ranking:** 61, Universities–Master's (West)
- ✔ **SAT Score (25th/75th percentile):** 900-1160
- ✔ **Tuition:** 2006-2007: $21,005

Selectivity: Selective	**Room/board:** $6,400
Acceptance rate: 73%	**Average debt:** $27,846
Student/faculty ratio: 11/1	**Proportion who borrowed:** 60%

UNDERGRADUATE STUDENT BODY STATS
2005-2006 enrollment: 936 full-time; 242 part-time. Men: 43%; women: 57%. **Ethnic makeup:** African American: 6%; American-Indian: 1%; Asian American: 9%; Hispanic: 6%; White: 72%; International: 5%. **Religious preference:** Protestant: 25%; Unknown: 25%; Roman Catholic (Benedictine): 50%.

ADMISSIONS FACTS AND FIGURES
Phone: (800) 368-8803. **Email:** admissions@stmartin.edu. **Website:** http://www.stmartin.edu. **Application deadlines for fall 2007:** Regular decision: Rolling. Early decision: Not offered. Early action: Not offered. Admission cannot be deferred. **Application fee:** $35. Common application is accepted. **Admissions requirements/recommendations:** High school units required (recommended): English: (4); Mathematics: (3); Science: (3); Foreign language: (4); Social studies: (2); Academic electives: (3); Total units: (20). Tests: The college uses SAT or ACT scores in admissions decisions. Either SAT or ACT required. For admission to the fall 2007 entering class, the school will accept: ACT with writing. Campus visit: Recommended. Admissions interview: Recommended. Off-campus interview: May be arranged. **Factors that count in admissions decisions:** *Academic:* Secondary school record: Very important. Class rank: Considered. Letters of recommendation: Important. Standardized test scores: Important. Essay: Important. *Nonacademic:* Interview: Considered. Extracurricular activities: Important. Talent/ability: Considered. Character/personal qualities: Important. Alumni/ae relationship: Considered. Geographical residence: Not considered. State residency: Not considered. Religious affiliation/commitment: Not considered. Minority status: Not considered. Volunteer work: Important. Work experience: Considered. **Other schools with the greatest overlap in applicants:** Evergreen State College; Pacific Lutheran University; University of Portland; University of Washington; Washington State University. **Admissions statistics for the fall 2005 entering class:** Total applicants: 522. Total accepted: 382. Freshmen enrolled: 173; 18% were from out of state. Overall acceptance rate: 73%. **Credentials of fall 2005 freshmen:** 18% ranked in the top 10 percent of their high school class; 42% were in the top 25 percent, and 82% were in the top half. (Proportion submitting class standing: 60%.) **Average high school grade point average:** 3.3. **First-year students who submitted SAT scores:** 86%. Scores (25/75 percentile): Verbal: 450-590, Math: 450-570, Combined: 900-1160. **First-year students submitting ACT scores:** 30%. Scores (25/75 percentile): English: N/A, Math: N/A, Composite: 19-23.

ACADEMICS
Year founded: 1895. **Academic calendar:** Semester. **Degrees offered:** certificate, bachelor's, post-bachelor's certificate, master's. **Most popular majors:** 26% business, management, marketing, and related support services, 20% social sciences, 14% psychology, 11% public administration and social service professions, 9% engineering technologies/technicians. **Major fields of study:** biological and biomedical sciences; business, management, marketing, and related support services; computer and information sciences and support services; education; engineering; English language and literature/letters; history; liberal arts and sciences studies, and humanities; mathematics and statistics; philosophy and religious studies; physical sciences; psychology; public administration and social service professions; social sciences; visual and performing arts. **Areas of required coursework:** arts/fine arts, humanities, computer literacy, mathematics, English (including composition), philosophy, foreign languages, sciences (biological or physical), history, social science, other. **Pre-professional programs:** pre-law, pre-dentistry, pre-medicine, pre-optometry, pre-pharmacy. **Special academic programs:** distance learning, double major, English as a Second Language (ESL), exchange student program (domestic), independent study, internships, study abroad, teacher certificate program. **Teacher certification offered in:** special education, elementary, middle/junior high, secondary, bilingual/bicultural. **Reserve Officers Training Corps (ROTC):** Army ROTC: Offered at cooperating institution (Pacific Lutheran University). **Faculty and instruction (2005-2006):** Total instructional faculty: 66 full-time, 96 part-time (59% men; 41% women; 16% minorities). Full-time faculty with Ph.D. or other terminal degree: 74%. Student/faculty ratio: 11/1. Classes of fewer than 20 students: 60%; of 20 to 49 students: 40%; of 50 or more students: 0%. **Advanced Placement and International Baccalaureate credit:** AP tests may be used for: Credit only. Scores accepted: 3, 4, 5. International Baccalaureate exams may be used for: Credit only. **Freshmen returning for sophomore year:** 73%. **Graduation rates:** Four-year: 24%; five-year: 37%; six-year: 38%. **Graduate study:** 29% of students pursue further study within one year.

COSTS AND FINANCIAL AID

Financial aid office: (360) 438-4397. **Expenses (2006-2007):** Tuition and fees 2006-2007: $21,005; room/board: $6,400. Estimated books and supplies: $924; transportation: $1,362; personal expenses: $1,524. **Financial aid:** Priority filing date for institution's financial aid form: March 1. In 2005-2006, 94% of undergraduates applied for financial aid. Of those, 86% were determined to have financial need; 34% had their need fully met. Average financial aid package (proportion receiving): $17,572 (86%). Average amount of gift aid, such as scholarships or grants (proportion receiving): $11,679 (83%). Average amount of self-help aid, such as work study or loans (proportion receiving): $6,999 (77%). Average need-based loan (excluding PLUS or other private loans): $5,197. Among students who received need-based aid, the average percentage of need met: 85%. Among students who received aid based on merit, the average award (and the proportion receiving): $9,545 (14%). The average athletic scholarship (and the proportion receiving): $4,391 (4%). Average amount of debt of borrowers graduating in 2005: $27,846. Proportion who borrowed: 60%.

CAMPUS LIFE AND EXTRACURRICULAR ACTIVITIES

Campus housing available (% using): coed dorms (100%), special housing for disabled students (0%). Students who live in college-owned, operated, or affiliated housing: 22%. **Student employment:** During the 2005-2006 academic year, 13% of undergraduates worked on campus. Average per-year earnings: $1,500. **Clubs and organizations:** Number of student organizations: 26. Activities include: choral groups, concert band, drama/theater, jazz band, pep band, student government, student newspaper, yearbook. Number of fraternities: 0; sororities: 0. Average proportion of students who stay on campus on weekends: 40%. **Sports program (2005-2006):** Member of NCAA II. *Men's intercollegiate varsity sports:* baseball, basketball, cross-country, golf, track and field (indoor), track and field (outdoor). *Women's intercollegiate varsity sports:* basketball, cross-country, golf, softball, track and field (indoor), track and field (outdoor), volleyball.

SERVICES AND FACILITIES

Basic services: nonremedial tutoring, placement service, health insurance. **Remedial assistance:** study skills, other. **Counseling services:** career, personal, veteran student, academic, older student, psychological, religious. **For learning-disabled students:** School does not offer a structured program with separate admission and additional fees. Total undergraduates in learning-disabled program or receiving services: 23. Services include: tape recorders, untimed tests, note-taking services, oral tests, learning center, readers, extended time for tests, tutors, texts on tape, typist/scribe, exams on tape or computer, other testing accomodations, other. **Library:** Number of titles: 87,818; number of current serial subscriptions: 1,423. **Information technology resources:** Students are not required to lease or own a computer. Number of campus computers available to all students: 100. School has a wireless network. Approximate number of users that can be accommodated: 100. Proportion of college-owned housing units wired for high-speed internet access: 100%. **Campus safety:** Security services offered: 24-hour foot-and-vehicle patrols, late-night transport/escort service, lighted pathways/sidewalks, student patrols, controlled dormitory access (key, security card, etc).

TRANSFER AND INTERNATIONAL STUDENTS

Transfer students: May apply for admission for the following academic terms: Fall, Spring, Summer. Applicants need a minimum number of credits to apply. For fall 2005: Transfer applications received: 457. Transfer applicants offered admission: 350. Transfer applicants enrolled: 149. **International students:** Number of foreign undergraduates: 63 (5% of student body). Number of countries represented: 14. Minimum TOEFL score required: 525 (paper); 197 (computer). Average TOEFL score: 550 (paper).

University of Puget Sound

- **Address:** 1500 N. Warner Street, Tacoma, WA 98416
- **Website:** http://www.ups.edu
- **Private**
- **Enrollment:** 2,571 full-time; 33 part-time

KEY STATS

✔ **U.S News College Ranking:** 82, Liberal Arts Colleges
✔ **SAT Score (25th/75th percentile):** 1140-1350
✔ **Tuition:** 2006-2007: $30,425

Selectivity: More selective	**Room/board:** $7,670
Acceptance rate: 71%	**Average debt:** $25,842
Student/faculty ratio: 11/1	**Proportion who borrowed:** 60%

UNDERGRADUATE STUDENT BODY STATS

2005-2006 enrollment: 2,571 full-time; 33 part-time. Men: 42%; women: 58%. **Ethnic makeup:** African American: 2%; American-Indian: 1%; Asian American: 9%; Hispanic: 4%; White: 83%. **Religious preference:** Roman Catholic: 11%; Protestant: 34%; Jewish: 7%; Buddhist: 2%; No preference: 41%; Other: 5%.

ADMISSIONS FACTS AND FIGURES

Phone: (253) 879-3211. **Email:** admission@ups.edu. **Website:** http://www.ups.edu. **Application deadlines for fall 2007:** Regular decision: February 1; decision sent by April 1. Early decision: Send application by: November 15; Decision sent by: December 15. Early action: Not offered. Admission can be deferred. **Application fee:** $40. Common application is accepted. **Admissions requirements/recommendations:** High school units required (recommended): English: 0 (4); Mathematics: 0 (4); Science: 0 (4); Foreign language: 0 (3); Social studies: 0 (3); History: 0 (3); Academic electives: 0 (0); Total units: 0 (19). Tests: The college uses SAT or ACT scores in admissions decisions. Either SAT or ACT required. For admission to the fall 2007 entering class, the school will accept: ACT without writing. Campus visit: Recommended. Admissions interview: Recommended. Off-campus interview: May be arranged. **Factors that count in admissions decisions:** *Academic:* Secondary school record: Very important. Class rank: Considered. Letters of recommendation: Important. Standardized test scores: Very important. Essay: Important. *Nonacademic:* Interview: Considered. Extracurricular activities: Important. Talent/ability: Important. Character/personal qualities: Important. Alumni/ae relationship: Important. Geographical residence: Not considered. State residency: Not considered. Religious affiliation/commitment: Not considered. Minority status: Important. Volunteer work: Considered. Work experience: Considered. **Other schools with the greatest overlap in applicants:** Colorado College; Lewis and Clark College; University of Washington; Whitman College; Willamette University. **Admissions statistics for the fall 2005 entering class:** Total applicants: 4,711. Total accepted: 3,343. Freshmen enrolled: 670; 73% were from out of state. Accepted through early-decision or early-action plans: 17%. Overall acceptance rate: 71%. Early-decision acceptance rate: 91%. Non-early acceptance rate: 70%. **Size of waiting list:** 359 applicants; enrolled from waiting list: 54. **Credentials of fall 2005 freshmen:** 37% ranked in the top 10 percent of their high school class; 68% were in the top 25 percent, and 93% were in the top half. (Proportion submitting class standing: 64%.) **Average high school grade point average:** 3.5. **First-year students who submitted SAT scores:** 91%. Scores (25/75 percentile): Verbal: 580-690, Math: 560-660, Combined: 1140-1350. **First-year students submitting ACT scores:** 46%. Scores (25/75 percentile): English: 24-30, Math: 23-28, Composite: 24-29.

ACADEMICS

Year founded: 1888. **Academic calendar:** Semester. **Degrees offered:** bachelor's, master's, post-master's certificate, first professional. **Most popular majors:** 11% business administration and management, 8% English language and literature, 8% biology/biological sciences, 7% economics, 7% psychology. **Major fields of study:** area, ethnic, cultural, and gender studies; biological and biomedical sciences; business, management, marketing, and related support services; communication, journalism, and related programs; computer and information sciences and support services; education; English language and literature/letters; foreign languages, literatures, and linguistics; history; mathematics and statistics; multi/interdisciplinary studies; parks, recreation, leisure, and fitness studies; philosophy and religious studies; physical sciences; psychology; social sciences; visual and performing arts. **Areas of required coursework:** arts/fine arts, humanities, mathematics, English (including composition), foreign languages, sciences (biological or physical), history, social science. **Pre-professional programs:** pre-law, pre-dentistry, pre-medicine, pre-veterinary science, pre-optometry, pre-pharmacy. **Special academic programs (% participation):** cooperative (work-study plan) program (3%), double major (9%), honors program (5%), independent study (12%), internships (12%), student-designed major (0%), study abroad (32%), teacher certificate program. **Teacher certification offered in:** elementary, middle/junior high, secondary. **Cooperative education programs:** agriculture, art, business, computer science, education, engineering, health professions, humanities, natural science, social/behavioral science. **Reserve Officers Training Corps (ROTC):** Army ROTC: Offered at cooperating institution (Seattle University @ Pacific Lutheran University). **Faculty and instruction (2005-2006):** Total instructional faculty: 224 full-time, 59 part-time (54% men; 46% women; 7% minorities). Full-time faculty with Ph.D. or other terminal degree: 88%. Student/faculty ratio: 11/1. Classes of fewer than 20 students: 52%; of 20 to 49 students: 48%; of 50 or more students: 1%. **Advanced Placement and International Baccalaureate credit:** AP tests may be used for: Credit and/or placement. Scores accepted: 3, 4, 5. International Baccalaureate exams may be used for: Credit and/or placement. **Freshmen returning for sophomore year:** 87%. **Graduation rates:** Four-year: 65%; five-year: 72%; six-year: 73%. **Graduate study:** 26% of students pursue further study immediately upon graduation; 34% within one year; 44% within five years. Fields in which graduates pursue further study: Master of Business Administration (MBA), 10%; law, 9%; medicine, 7%; dentistry, 1%; engineering, 4%; theology (or the seminary), 2%; education, 17%; arts and sciences, 44%; veterinary medicine, 1%.

COSTS AND FINANCIAL AID
Financial aid office: (800) 396-7192. **Expenses (2006-2007):** Tuition and fees 2006-2007: $30,425; room/board: $7,670. Estimated books and supplies: $800; transportation: $500; personal expenses: $1,800. **Financial aid:** Priority filing date for institution's financial aid form: February 1. In 2005-2006, 68% of undergraduates applied for financial aid. Of those, 59% were determined to have financial need; 23% had their need fully met. Average financial aid package (proportion receiving): $20,466 (59%). Average amount of gift aid, such as scholarships or grants (proportion receiving): $15,106 (57%). Average amount of self-help aid, such as work study or loans (proportion receiving): $6,815 (48%). Average need-based loan (excluding PLUS or other private loans): $5,274. Among students who received need-based aid, the average percentage of need met: 80%. Among students who received aid based on merit, the average award (and the proportion receiving): $7,210 (27%). The average athletic scholarship (and the proportion receiving): $0 (0%). Average amount of debt of borrowers graduating in 2005: $25,842. Proportion who borrowed: 60%.

CAMPUS LIFE AND EXTRACURRICULAR ACTIVITIES
Campus housing available (% using): coed dorms (59%), women's dorms (5%), sorority housing (8%), fraternity housing (8%), special housing for disabled students (0%), other housing options (20%). Students who live in college-owned, operated, or affiliated housing: 60%. **Student employment:** During the 2005-2006 academic year, 25% of undergraduates worked on campus. Average per-year earnings: $2,000. **Clubs and organizations:** Number of student organizations: 72. Activities include: choral groups, concert band, dance, drama/theater, jazz band, literary magazine, music ensembles, musical theater, opera, pep band, radio station, student government, student newspaper, student film society, symphony orchestra, yearbook. Number of fraternities: 4; sororities: 4. Proportion of men in fraternities: 22%; of women in sororities: 23%. Average proportion of students who stay on campus on weekends: 90%. **Sports program (2005-2006):** Member of NCAA III. *Men's intercollegiate varsity sports:* baseball, basketball, cross-country, football, golf, skiing, soccer, swimming and diving, tennis, track and field (indoor), track and field (outdoor). *Women's intercollegiate varsity sports:* basketball, cross-country, golf, lacrosse, rowing, skiing, soccer, softball, swimming and diving, tennis, track and field (indoor), track and field (outdoor), volleyball.

SERVICES AND FACILITIES
Basic services: nonremedial tutoring, placement service, health service, health insurance, other. **Remedial assistance:** study skills. **Counseling services:** minority student, career, personal, veteran student, academic, older student, psychological, birth control, religious. **For learning-disabled students:** School does not offer a structured program with separate admission and additional fees. Total undergraduates in learning-disabled program or receiving services: 120. Services include: reading machines, tape recorders, note-taking services, learning center, extended time for tests, tutors, texts on

tape, exams on tape or computer, waiver of foreign language degree requirement. **Library:** Number of titles: 506,419; number of current serial subscriptions: 10,732. **Information technology resources:** Students are not required to lease or own a computer. Number of campus computers available to all students: 314. School has a wireless network. Approximate number of users that can be accommodated: 1,000. Proportion of college-owned housing units wired for high-speed internet access: 100%. **Campus safety:** Security services offered: 24-hour foot-and-vehicle patrols, late-night transport/escort service, 24-hour emergency telephones, lighted pathways/sidewalks, student patrols, controlled dormitory access (key, security card, etc).

TRANSFER AND INTERNATIONAL STUDENTS
Transfer students: May apply for admission for the following academic terms: Fall, Winter, Summer. Applicants need a minimum number of credits to apply. For fall 2005: Transfer applications received: 271. Transfer applicants offered admission: 192. Transfer applicants enrolled: 89. **International students:** Number of foreign undergraduates: 11. Number of countries represented: 12. Minimum TOEFL score required: 550 (paper); 213 (computer). Average TOEFL score: 601 (paper).

University of Washington

- **Address:** Seattle, WA 98195
- **Website:** http://www.washington.edu
- **Public**
- **Enrollment:** 23,216 full-time; 4,272 part-time

KEY STATS
✔ **U.S News College Ranking:** 42, National Universities
✔ **SAT Score (25th/75th percentile):** 1100-1320
✔ **Tuition:** 2006-2007: $5,985 in state, $20,198 out of state
Selectivity: More selective   **Room/board:** $8,001
Acceptance rate: 67%   **Average debt:** $15,700
Student/faculty ratio: 11/1   **Proportion who borrowed:** 50%

UNDERGRADUATE STUDENT BODY STATS
2005-2006 enrollment: 23,216 full-time; 4,272 part-time. Men: 48%; women: 52%. **Ethnic makeup:** African American: 3%; American-Indian: 1%; Asian American: 27%; Hispanic: 4%; White: 61%; International: 3%.

ADMISSIONS FACTS AND FIGURES
Phone: (206) 543-9686. **Email:** askuwadm@u.washington.edu. **Website:** http://www.washington.edu. **Application deadlines for fall 2007:** Regular decision: January 15; decision sent by April 15. Early decision: Not offered. Early action: Not offered. Admission cannot be deferred. **Application fee:** $50. Common application is not accepted. **To apply online, go to:** http://www.washington.edu/students/uga/. **Admissions requirements/recommendations:** High school units required (recommended): English: 4 (4); Mathematics: 3 (4); Science: 2 (3); Foreign language: 2 (3); Social studies: 3 (4); History: 0 (0); Academic electives: 1 (1); Total units: 15. Tests: The college uses SAT or ACT scores in admissions decisions. Either SAT or ACT required. For admission to the fall 2007 entering class, the school will accept: ACT with writing. Campus visit: Neither required nor recommended. Admissions interview: Neither required nor recommended. Off-campus interview: Not available. **Factors that count in admissions decisions:** *Academic:* Secondary school record: Very important. Class rank: Not considered. Letters of recommendation: Not considered. Standardized test scores: Important. Essay: Very important. *Nonacademic:* Interview: Not considered. Extracurricular activities: Important. Talent/ability: Important. Character/personal qualities: Important. Alumni/ae relationship: Not considered. Geographical residence: Not considered. State residency: Considered. Religious affiliation/commitment: Not considered. Minority status: Not considered. Volunteer work: Important. Work experience: Important. **Other schools with the greatest overlap in applicants:** Seattle University; University of Oregon; University of Southern California; Washington State University; Western Washington University. **Admissions statistics for the fall 2005 entering class:** Total applicants: 15,923. Total accepted: 10,681. Freshmen enrolled: 4,924; 23% were from out of state. Overall acceptance rate: 67%. **Size of waiting list:** 912 applicants; enrolled from waiting list: 204. **Credentials of fall 2005 freshmen:** 82% ranked in the top 10 percent of their high school class; 96% were in the top 25 percent, and 100% were in the top half. (Proportion submitting class standing:

46%.) **Average high school grade point average:** 3.7. **First-year students who submitted SAT scores:** 95%. Scores (25/75 percentile): Verbal: 530-650, Math: 570-670, Combined: 1100-1320. **First-year students submitting ACT scores:** 27%. Scores (25/75 percentile): English: 23-28, Math: 22-29, Composite: 23-28.

ACADEMICS

Year founded: 1861. **Academic calendar:** Quarter. **Degrees offered:** bachelor's, master's, first professional, doctorate. **Most popular majors:** 19% social sciences, 11% business, management, marketing, and related support services, 8% multi/interdisciplinary studies, 6% biological and biomedical sciences, 6% engineering. **Major fields of study:** architecture and related services; area, ethnic, cultural, and gender studies; biological and biomedical sciences; business, management, marketing, and related support services; communication, journalism, and related programs; computer and information sciences and support services; engineering; English language and literature/letters; foreign languages, literatures, and linguistics; health professions and related clinical sciences; history; liberal arts and sciences studies, and humanities; library science; mathematics and statistics; multi/interdisciplinary studies; natural resources and conservation; philosophy and religious studies; physical sciences; psychology; public administration and social service professions; security and protective services; social sciences; theology and religious vocations; visual and performing arts. **Areas of required coursework:** arts/fine arts, humanities, computer literacy, mathematics, English (including composition), foreign languages, sciences (biological or physical), history, social science. **Pre-professional programs:** pre-law, pre-dentistry, pre-medicine, pre-theology, pre-veterinary science, pre-optometry, pre-pharmacy. **Special academic programs:** accelerated program, cooperative (work-study plan) program, cross-registration, distance learning, double major, dual enrollment, English as a Second Language (ESL), exchange student program (domestic), external degree program, honors program, independent study, internships, liberal arts/career combination, student-designed major, study abroad, teacher certificate program, weekend college. **Teacher certification offered in:** early childhood, special education, elementary, middle/junior high, secondary, bilingual/bicultural. **Cooperative education programs:** business, engineering. **Reserve Officers Training Corps (ROTC):** Army ROTC: Offered on campus; Navy ROTC: Offered on campus; Air Force ROTC: Offered on campus. **Faculty and instruction (2005-2006):** Total instructional faculty: 2,879 full-time, 639 part-time (63% men; 37% women; 17% minorities). Full-time faculty with Ph.D. or other terminal degree: 93%. Student/faculty ratio: 11/1. Classes of fewer than 20 students: 37%; of 20 to 49 students: 46%; of 50 or more students: 17%. **Advanced Placement and International Baccalaureate credit:** AP tests may be used for: Credit only. Scores accepted: 4, 5. International Baccalaureate exams may be used for: Credit and/or placement. **Freshmen returning for sophomore year:** 92%. **Graduation rates:** Four-year: 46%; five-year: 70%; six-year: 74%. **Graduate study:** 19% of students pursue further study immediately upon graduation.

COSTS AND FINANCIAL AID

Financial aid office: (206) 543-6101. **Expenses (2006-2007):** Tuition and fees 2006-2007: $5,985 in state, $20,198 out of state; room/board: $8,001. Estimated books and supplies: $945; transportation: $396; personal expenses: $2,265. **Financial aid:** Priority filing date for institution's financial aid form: February 28. In 2005-2006, 74% of undergraduates applied for financial aid. Of those, 52% were determined to have financial need; 50% had their need fully met. Average financial aid package (proportion receiving): $10,900 (48%). Average amount of gift aid, such as scholarships or grants (proportion receiving): $6,500 (33%). Average amount of self-help aid, such as work study or loans (proportion receiving): $5,000 (38%). Average need-based loan (excluding PLUS or other private loans): $4,500. Among students who received need-based aid, the average percentage of need met: 86%. Among students who received aid based on merit, the average award (and the proportion receiving): $4,400 (2%). The average athletic scholarship (and the proportion receiving): $15,000 (2%). Average amount of debt of borrowers graduating in 2005: $15,700. Proportion who borrowed: 50%.

CAMPUS LIFE AND EXTRACURRICULAR ACTIVITIES

Campus housing available (% using): coed dorms (57%), sorority housing (17%), fraternity housing (16%), apartments for married students, apartment for single students (4%), special housing for disabled students, other housing options (6%). Students who live in college-owned, operated, or affiliated housing: 17%. Average per-year earnings: $3,600. **Clubs and organizations:** Number of student organizations: 370. Activities include: choral groups, concert band, dance, drama/theater, jazz band, literary maga-

zine, marching band, music ensembles, musical theater, opera, radio station, student government, student newspaper, television station. Number of fraternities: 28; sororities: 16. Proportion of men in fraternities: 12%; of women in sororities: 11%. Average proportion of students who stay on campus on weekends: 100%. **Sports program (2005-2006):** Member of NCAA I. **Men's intercollegiate varsity sports:** baseball, basketball, crew, cross-country, football, golf, soccer, swimming and diving, tennis, track and field (indoor), track and field (outdoor). **Women's intercollegiate varsity sports:** basketball, crew, cross-country, golf, gymnastics, rowing, soccer, softball, swimming and diving, tennis, track and field (indoor), track and field (outdoor), volleyball.

SERVICES AND FACILITIES

Basic services: nonremedial tutoring, women's center, placement service, day care, health service, health insurance. **Remedial assistance:** reading, math, writing, study skills. **Counseling services:** minority student, career, military, personal, veteran student, academic, older student, psychological, birth control, religious. **For learning-disabled students:** School does not offer a structured program with separate admission and additional fees. Total undergraduates in learning-disabled program or receiving services: 237. Services include: reading machines, tape recorders, note-taking services, oral tests, learning center, readers, extended time for tests, early syllabus, priority registration, proofreading services, substitution of courses, texts on tape, typist/scribe, exams on tape or computer, other testing accomodations, waiver of foreign language degree requirement. **Library:** Number of titles: 6,546,072; number of current serial subscriptions: 55,932. **Information technology resources:** Students are not required to lease or own a computer. Number of campus computers available to all students: 5,000. School has a wireless network. Approximate number of users that can be accommodated: 5,500. Proportion of college-owned housing units wired for high-speed internet access: 100%. **Campus safety:** Security services offered: 24-hour foot-and-vehicle patrols, late-night transport/escort service, 24-hour emergency telephones, lighted pathways/sidewalks, student patrols, controlled dormitory access (key, security card, etc).

TRANSFER AND INTERNATIONAL STUDENTS

Transfer students: May apply for admission for the following academic terms: Fall, Winter, Spring, Summer. Applicants do not need a minimum number of credits to apply. For fall 2005: Transfer applications received: 3,597. Transfer applicants offered admission: 1,868. Transfer applicants enrolled: 1,433. **International students:** Number of foreign undergraduates: 882 (3% of student body). Minimum TOEFL score required: 540 (paper); 207 (computer).

Walla Walla College

- **Address:** 204 S. College Avenue, College Place, WA 99324-1198
- **Website:** http://www.wwc.edu
- **Private; Religious affiliation:** Seventh-day Adventist
- **Enrollment:** 1,528 full-time; 142 part-time

KEY STATS

✔ **U.S News College Ranking:** 41, Universities–Master's (West)
✔ **ACT Score (25th/75th percentile):** 19-25
✔ **Tuition:** 2006-2007: $19,917

Selectivity: Selective	**Room/board:** $4,572
Acceptance rate: 78%	**Average debt:** $23,668
Student/faculty ratio: 13/1	**Proportion who borrowed:** 72%

UNDERGRADUATE STUDENT BODY STATS

2005-2006 enrollment: 1,528 full-time; 142 part-time. Men: 52%; women: 48%. **Ethnic makeup:** African American: 3%; American-Indian: 1%; Asian American: 5%; Hispanic: 7%; White: 83%; International: 1%.

ADMISSIONS FACTS AND FIGURES

Phone: (509) 527-2327. **Email:** info@wwc.edu. **Website:** http://www.wwc.edu. **Application deadlines for fall 2007:** Regular decision: Rolling. Early decision: Not offered. Early action: Send application by: N/A; Decision sent by: N/A. Admission can be deferred. **Application fee:** $40. Common application is accepted. **To apply online, go to:** http://www.wwc.edu/enrollment/requirements/. **Admissions requirements/recommendations:** High school units required (recommended): English: 4; Mathematics: 3 (1); Science: 1 (1); Foreign language: (2); Social studies: (1); History: 2; Total units: 10 (5). **Tests:** The college uses SAT or ACT scores in admissions decisions. Either SAT or ACT required. For admission to the fall 2007 entering class, the school will accept: ACT with writing, ACT without writing. Campus visit: Neither required nor recommended. Admissions interview: Neither required nor recommended. Off-campus interview: Not available. **Factors that count in admissions decisions:** *Academic:* Secondary school record: Very important. Class rank: Not considered. Letters of recommendation: Very important. Standardized test scores: Important. Essay: Not considered. *Nonacademic:* Interview: Not considered. Extracurricular activities: Considered. Talent/ability: Considered. Character/personal qualities: Very important. Alumni/ae relationship: Not considered. Geographical residence: Not considered. State residency: Not considered. Religious affiliation/commitment: Not considered. Minority status: Not considered. Volunteer work: Not considered. Work experience: Not considered. **Other schools with the greatest overlap in applicants:** Andrews University; La Sierra University; Pacific Union College; Southern Adventist University; Southwestern Adventist University. **Admissions statistics for the fall 2005 entering class:** Total applicants: 452. Total accepted: 351. Freshmen enrolled: 291; 69% were from out of state. Overall acceptance rate: 78%. Non-early acceptance rate: 78%. **Size of waiting list:** 0 applicants; enrolled from waiting list: 0. **Credentials of fall 2005 freshmen:** 8% ranked in the top 10 percent of their high school class; 19% were in the top 25 percent, and 37% were in the top half. (Proportion submitting class standing: 51%.) **First-year students who submitted SAT scores:** 63%. Scores (25/75 percentile): Verbal: N/A, Math: N/A, Combined: N/A. **First-year students submitting ACT scores:** 73%. Scores (25/75 percentile): English: 17-25, Math: 17-25, Composite: 19-25.

ACADEMICS

Year founded: 1892. **Academic calendar:** Quarter. **Degrees offered:** associate, terminal-associate, bachelor's, master's. **Most popular majors:** Information not available. **Major fields of study:** biological and biomedical sciences; business, management, marketing, and related support services; communication, journalism, and related programs; communications technologies/technicians and support services; computer and information sciences and support services; education; engineering; English language and literature/letters; foreign languages, literatures, and linguistics; health professions and related clinical sciences; history; liberal arts and sciences studies, and humanities; mathematics and statistics; mechanic and repair technologies/technicians; natural resources and conservation; parks, recreation, leisure, and fitness studies; philosophy and religious studies; physical sciences; psychology; theology and religious vocations; visual and performing arts. **Areas of required coursework:** humanities, mathematics, English (including composition), philosophy, sciences (biological or physical), history, social science, other. **Special academic programs:** cooperative (work-study plan) program, distance learning, double major, honors program, internships, liberal arts/career combination, study abroad, teacher certificate program. **Teacher certification offered in:** elementary, secondary. **Faculty and instruction (2005-2006):** Total instructional faculty: 122 full-time, 72 part-time (54% men; 46% women; 6% minorities). Full-time faculty with Ph.D. or other terminal degree: 68%. Student/faculty ratio: 13/1. Classes of fewer than 20 students: 60%; of 20 to 49 students: 37%; of 50 or more students: 2%. **Advanced Placement and International Baccalaureate credit:** AP tests may be used for: Credit and/or placement. Scores accepted: 3, 4. International Baccalaureate exams may be used for: Credit and/or placement. **Freshmen returning for sophomore year:** 69%. **Graduation rates:** Four-year: 18%; five-year: 38%; six-year: 46%.

COSTS AND FINANCIAL AID

Financial aid office: (800) 656-2815. **Expenses (2006-2007):** Tuition and fees 2006-2007: $19,917; room/board: $4,572. **Financial aid:** In 2005-2006, 94% of undergraduates applied for financial aid. Of those, 71% were determined to have financial need; 17% had their need fully met. Average financial aid package (proportion receiving): $17,349 (71%). Average amount of gift aid, such as scholarships or grants (proportion receiving): $6,500 (58%). Average amount of self-help aid, such as work study or loans (proportion receiving): $7,108 (68%). Average need-based loan (excluding PLUS or other private loans): $5,751. Among students who received need-based aid, the average percentage of need met: 86%. Among students who received aid based on merit, the average award (and the proportion receiving): $3,308 (18%). The average athletic scholarship (and the proportion receiving): $0 (0%). Average amount of debt of borrowers graduating in 2005: $23,668. Proportion who borrowed: 72%.

CAMPUS LIFE AND EXTRACURRICULAR ACTIVITIES

Campus housing available (% using): women's dorms (21%), men's dorms (27%), apartments for married students (2%), apartment for single students (15%), other housing options (35%). Students who live in college-owned, operated, or affiliated housing: 44%. **Student employment:** During the 2005-2006 academic year, 71% of undergraduates worked on campus. Average per-year earnings: $3,000. Activities include: choral groups, concert band, drama/theater, literary magazine, music ensembles, radio station, student government, student newspaper, television station, yearbook. Number of fraternities: 0; sororities: 0. **Sports program (2005-2006):** *Men's intercollegiate varsity sports:* basketball, golf, soccer, volleyball. *Women's intercollegiate varsity sports:* basketball, golf, softball, volleyball.

SERVICES AND FACILITIES

Basic services: nonremedial tutoring, health service, health insurance. **Remedial assistance:** reading, math, writing, study skills. **Counseling services:** minority student, career, personal, academic, older student, psychological, birth control, religious. **For learning-disabled students:** School does not offer a structured program with separate admission and additional fees. Total undergraduates in learning-disabled program or receiving services: 31. Services include: remedial math, remedial English, remedial reading, tape recorders, other special classes, videotaped classes, untimed tests, note-taking services, oral tests, learning center, readers, extended time for tests, tutors, early syllabus, priority registration, priority seating, substitution of courses, texts on tape, typist/scribe, exams on tape or computer, other testing accomodations, waiver of foreign language degree requirement, waiver of math degree requirement, other. **Library:** Number of titles: 184,493; number of current serial subscriptions: 2,169. **Information technology resources:** Students are not required to lease or own a computer. Number of campus computers available to all students: 150. School has a wireless network. Proportion of college-owned housing units wired for high-speed internet access: 70%. **Campus safety:** Security services offered: 24-hour foot-and-vehicle patrols, late-night transport/escort service, 24-hour emergency telephones, lighted pathways/sidewalks, student patrols.

TRANSFER AND INTERNATIONAL STUDENTS

Transfer students: May apply for admission for the following academic terms: Fall, Winter, Spring, Summer. Applicants need a minimum number of credits to apply. For fall 2005: Transfer applications received: 1,165. Transfer applicants offered admission: 531. Transfer applicants enrolled: 146. **International students:** Number of foreign undergraduates: 15 (1% of student body). Number of countries represented: 17. Minimum TOEFL score required: 550 (paper); 213 (computer).

Washington State University

- **Address:** French Administration Building, Pullman, WA 99164
- **Website:** http://www.wsu.edu
- **Public**
- **Enrollment:** 16,786 full-time; 2,799 part-time

KEY STATS

✔ **U.S News College Ranking:** 112, National Universities
✔ **SAT Score (25th/75th percentile):** 1000-1210
✔ **Tuition:** 2006-2007: $6,390 in state, $16,030 out of state
  Selectivity: More selective   **Room/board:** $6,890
  Acceptance rate: 74%   **Average debt:** $20,494
  Student/faculty ratio: 15/1   **Proportion who borrowed:** 49%

UNDERGRADUATE STUDENT BODY STATS

2005-2006 enrollment: 16,786 full-time; 2,799 part-time. Men: 48%; women: 52%. **Ethnic makeup:** African American: 3%; American-Indian: 1%; Asian American: 6%; Hispanic: 4%; White: 83%; International: 3%.

ADMISSIONS FACTS AND FIGURES

Phone: (888) 468-6978. **Email:** admiss2@wsu.edu. **Website:** http://www.wsu.edu. **Application deadlines for fall 2007:** Regular decision: Rolling. Early decision: Not offered. Early action: Not offered. Admission cannot be deferred. **Application fee:** $50. Common application is accepted. **To apply online, go to:** http://www.wsu.edu/future-students/admission/apply.html. **Admissions requirements/recommendations:** High school units required (recommended): English: 4 (4);

Mathematics: 3 (4); Science: 2 (2); Foreign language: 2 (2); Social studies: 2 (2); History: 1 (1); Academic electives: 1 (1); Total units: 15 (16). Tests: The college uses SAT or ACT scores in admissions decisions. Either SAT or ACT required. For admission to the fall 2007 entering class, the school will accept: ACT with writing. Campus visit: Recommended. Admissions interview: Neither required nor recommended. Off-campus interview: Not available. **Factors that count in admissions decisions:** *Academic:* Secondary school record: Important. Class rank: Not considered. Letters of recommendation: Considered. Standardized test scores: Very important. Essay: Important. *Nonacademic:* Interview: Not considered. Extracurricular activities: Considered. Talent/ability: Considered. Character/personal qualities: Not considered. Alumni/ae relationship: Not considered. Geographical residence: Not considered. State residency: Not considered. Religious affiliation/commitment: Not considered. Minority status: Not considered. Volunteer work: Not considered. Work experience: Not considered. **Other schools with the greatest overlap in applicants:** Central Washington University; Eastern Washington University; Oregon State University; University of Washington; Western Washington University. **Admissions statistics for the fall 2005 entering class:** Total applicants: 9,193. Total accepted: 6,793. Freshmen enrolled: 2,885; 7% were from out of state. Overall acceptance rate: 74%. **Size of waiting list:** N/A applicants; enrolled from waiting list: 174. **Credentials of fall 2005 freshmen:** 37% ranked in the top 10 percent of their high school class; 57% were in the top 25 percent, and 90% were in the top half. (Proportion submitting class standing: 51%.) **Average high school grade point average:** 3.5. **First-year students who submitted SAT scores:** 95%. Scores (25/75 percentile): Verbal: 490-600, Math: 510-610, Combined: 1000-1210. **First-year students submitting ACT scores:** 25%. Scores (25/75 percentile): English: N/A, Math: N/A, Composite: 20-26.

ACADEMICS

Year founded: 1890. **Academic calendar:** Semester. **Degrees offered:** bachelor's, post-bachelor's certificate, master's, first professional, doctorate. **Most popular majors:** 19% business administration and management, 9% communication studies/speech communication and rhetoric, 9% nursing/registered nurse training (R.N., A.S.N., B.S.N., M.S.N.), 7% education, 2% criminal justice/police science. **Major fields of study:** agriculture, agriculture operations, and related sciences; architecture and related services; area, ethnic, cultural, and gender studies; biological and biomedical sciences; business, management, marketing, and related support services; communication, journalism, and related programs; computer and information sciences and support services; education; engineering; engineering technologies/technicians; English language and literature/letters; family and consumer sciences/human sciences; foreign languages, literatures, and linguistics; health professions and related clinical sciences; history; liberal arts and sciences studies, and humanities; mathematics and statistics; multi/interdisciplinary studies; natural resources and conservation; parks, recreation, leisure, and fitness studies; philosophy and religious studies; physical sciences; psychology; public administration and social service professions; security and protective services; social sciences; visual and performing arts. **Areas of required coursework:** arts/fine arts, humanities, mathematics, English (including composition), foreign languages, sciences (biological or physical), history, social science. **Pre-professional programs:** pre-law, pre-medicine, pre-veterinary science, pre-pharmacy. **Special academic programs:** cooperative (work-study plan) program, cross-registration, distance learning, double major, dual enrollment, English as a Second Language (ESL), exchange student program (domestic), external degree program, honors program, independent study, internships, liberal arts/career combination, student-designed major, study abroad, teacher certificate program. **Teacher certification offered in:** early childhood, special education, elementary, secondary, bilingual/bicultural. **Cooperative education programs:** health professions. **Reserve Officers Training Corps (ROTC):** Army ROTC: Offered on campus; Navy ROTC: Offered at cooperating institution (University of Idaho); Air Force ROTC: Offered on campus. **Faculty and instruction (2005-2006):** Total instructional faculty: 1,057 full-time, 392 part-time (60% men; 40% women; 10% minorities). Full-time faculty with Ph.D. or other terminal degree: 92%. Student/faculty ratio: 15/1. Classes of fewer than 20 students: 40%; of 20 to 49 students: 43%; of 50 or more students: 17%. **Advanced Placement and International Baccalaureate credit:** AP tests may be used for: Credit and/or placement. Scores accepted: 3, 4, 5. International Baccalaureate exams may be used for: Credit only. **Freshmen returning for sophomore year:** 84%. **Graduation rates:** Four-year: 32%; five-year: 58%; six-year: 63%.

COSTS AND FINANCIAL AID

Financial aid office: (509) 335-9711. **Expenses (2006-2007):** Tuition and fees 2006-2007: $6,390 in state, $16,030 out of state; room/board: $6,890.

Estimated books and supplies: $912; transportation: $1,434; personal expenses: $2,108. **Financial aid:** Priority filing date for institution's financial aid form: March 1. In 2005-2006, 67% of undergraduates applied for financial aid. Of those, 50% were determined to have financial need; 36% had their need fully met. Average financial aid package (proportion receiving): $9,141 (48%). Average amount of gift aid, such as scholarships or grants (proportion receiving): $5,820 (33%). Average amount of self-help aid, such as work study or loans (proportion receiving): $4,426 (39%). Average need-based loan (excluding PLUS or other private loans): $4,258. Among students who received need-based aid, the average percentage of need met: 80%. Among students who received aid based on merit, the average award (and the proportion receiving): $3,026 (5%). The average athletic scholarship (and the proportion receiving): $12,338 (2%). Average amount of debt of borrowers graduating in 2005: $20,494. Proportion who borrowed: 49%.

CAMPUS LIFE AND EXTRACURRICULAR ACTIVITIES

Campus housing available (% using): coed dorms (44%), women's dorms (10%), men's dorms (5%), sorority housing (11%), fraternity housing (8%), apartments for married students (11%), apartment for single students (10%), special housing for international students (1%). Students who live in college-owned, operated, or affiliated housing: 35%. **Student employment:** During the 2005-2006 academic year, 24% of undergraduates worked on campus. Average per-year earnings: $1,676. **Clubs and organizations:** Number of student organizations: 329. Activities include: choral groups, concert band, dance, drama/theater, jazz band, literary magazine, marching band, music ensembles, opera, pep band, radio station, student government, student newspaper, student film society, symphony orchestra, television station, yearbook. Number of fraternities: 24; sororities: 15. Proportion of men in fraternities: 14%; of women in sororities: 18%. Average proportion of students who stay on campus on weekends: 75%. **Sports program (2005-2006):** Member of NCAA I. *Men's intercollegiate varsity sports:* baseball, basketball, cross-country, football, golf, track and field (indoor), track and field (outdoor). *Women's intercollegiate varsity sports:* basketball, cross-country, golf, rowing, soccer, swimming and diving, tennis, track and field (indoor), track and field (outdoor), volleyball.

SERVICES AND FACILITIES

Basic services: nonremedial tutoring, women's center, placement service, day care, health service, health insurance. **Counseling services:** minority student, career, personal, veteran student, academic, older student, psychological, birth control, religious. **For learning-disabled students:** School does not offer a structured program with separate admission and additional fees. Total undergraduates in learning-disabled program or receiving services: 859. Services include: reading machines, tape recorders, videotaped classes, diagnostic testing service, note-taking services, oral tests, learning center, readers, extended time for tests, priority registration, priority seating, texts on tape. **Library:** Number of titles: 2,195,306; number of current serial subscriptions: 30,936. **Information technology resources:** Students are not required to lease or own a computer. Number of campus computers available to all students: 2,400. School has a wireless network. Approximate number of users that can be accommodated: 6,000. Proportion of college-owned housing units wired for high-speed internet access: 100%. **Campus safety:** Security services offered: 24-hour foot-and-vehicle patrols, late-night transport/escort service, 24-hour emergency telephones, lighted pathways/sidewalks, student patrols, controlled dormitory access (key, security card, etc).

TRANSFER AND INTERNATIONAL STUDENTS

Transfer students: May apply for admission for the following academic terms: Fall, Spring, Summer. Applicants need a minimum number of credits to apply. For fall 2005: Transfer applications received: 4,229. Transfer applicants offered admission: 3,471. Transfer applicants enrolled: 2,006. **International students:** Number of foreign undergraduates: 541 (3% of student body). Number of countries represented: 99. Minimum TOEFL score required: 520 (paper); 190 (computer).

Western Washington University

- **Address:** 516 High Street, Bellingham, WA 98225
- **Website:** http://www.wwu.edu
- **Public**
- **Enrollment:** 11,943 full-time; 1,059 part-time

KEY STATS

✔ **U.S News College Ranking:** 18, Universities–Master's (West)
✔ **SAT Score (25th/75th percentile):** 1030-1240
✔ **Tuition:** 2006-2007: $5,003 in state, $15,550 out of state
  Selectivity: Selective   **Room/board:** $6,785
  Acceptance rate: 67%   **Average debt:** $15,784
  Student/faculty ratio: 20/1   **Proportion who borrowed:** 58%

UNDERGRADUATE STUDENT BODY STATS

2005-2006 enrollment: 11,943 full-time; 1,059 part-time. Men: 44%; women: 56%. **Ethnic makeup:** African American: 2%; American-Indian: 2%; Asian American: 8%; Hispanic: 3%; White: 84%.

ADMISSIONS FACTS AND FIGURES

Phone: (360) 650-3440. **Email:** admit@cc.wwu.edu. **Website:** http://www.wwu.edu. **Application deadlines for fall 2007:** Regular decision: March 1. Early decision: Not offered. Early action: Not offered. Admission can be deferred. **Application fee:** $50. Common application is accepted. **To apply online, go to:** http://www.ac.wwu.edu/~admit/applynow.html. **Admissions requirements/recommendations:** High school units required (recommended): English: 4; Mathematics: 3; Science: 2; Foreign language: 2; Social studies: 3; Academic electives: 1; Total units: 15. Tests: The college uses SAT or ACT scores in admissions decisions. Either SAT or ACT required. For admission to the fall 2007 entering class, the school will accept: ACT with writing, ACT without writing. Campus visit: Recommended. Admissions interview: Neither required nor recommended. Off-campus interview: Not available. **Factors that count in admissions decisions:** *Academic:* Secondary school record: Very important. Class rank: Important. Letters of recommendation: Considered. Standardized test scores: Important. Essay: Important. *Nonacademic:* Interview: Not considered. Extracurricular activities: Important. Talent/ability: Important. Character/personal qualities: Important. Alumni/ae relationship: Not considered. Geographical residence: Considered. State residency: Considered. Religious affiliation/commitment: Not considered. Minority status: Not considered. Volunteer work: Important. Work experience: Important. **Other schools with the greatest overlap in applicants:** Gonzaga University; Pacific Lutheran University; Seattle University; University of Washington; Washington State University. **Admissions statistics for the fall 2005 entering class:** Total applicants: 8,645. Total accepted: 5,778. Freshmen enrolled: 2,382; 9% were from out of state. Overall acceptance rate: 67%. **Size of waiting list:** 227 applicants; enrolled from waiting list: 3. **Credentials of fall 2005 freshmen:** 28% ranked in the top 10 percent of their high school class; 64% were in the top 25 percent, and 95% were in the top half. (Proportion submitting class standing: 75%.) **Average high school grade point average:** 3.6. **First-year students who submitted SAT scores:** 96%. Scores (25/75 percentile): Verbal: 510-620, Math: 520-620, Combined: 1030-1240. **First-year students submitting ACT scores:** 26%. Scores (25/75 percentile): English: 20-27, Math: 20-26, Composite: 20-26.

ACADEMICS

Year founded: 1893. **Academic calendar:** Quarter. **Degrees offered:** bachelor's, post-bachelor's certificate, master's. **Most popular majors:** 6% child development, 6% psychology, 4% English language and literature, 4% general studies, 4% human services. **Major fields of study:** area, ethnic, cultural, and gender studies; biological and biomedical sciences; business, management, marketing, and related support services; communication, journalism, and related programs; computer and information sciences and support services; education; engineering technologies/technicians; English language and literature/letters; family and consumer sciences/human sciences; foreign languages, literatures, and linguistics; health professions and related clinical sciences; history; liberal arts and sciences studies, and humanities; mathematics and statistics; multi/interdisciplinary studies; natural resources and conservation; parks, recreation, leisure, and fitness studies; philosophy and religious studies; physical sciences; psychology; public administration and social service professions; social sciences; visual and performing arts. **Areas of required coursework:** humanities, mathematics, English (including com-

position), philosophy, sciences (biological or physical), social science, other. **Pre-professional programs:** pre-dentistry, pre-medicine, pre-pharmacy, other. **Special academic programs (% participation):** distance learning (26%), double major (3%), English as a Second Language (ESL) (5%), exchange student program (domestic) (1%), honors program (1%), independent study (38%), internships (27%), liberal arts/career combination, student-designed major (3%), study abroad (9%), teacher certificate program (10%). **Teacher certification offered in:** early childhood, special education, elementary, secondary. **Faculty and instruction (2005-2006):** Total instructional faculty: 472 full-time, 156 part-time (59% men; 41% women; 12% minorities). Full-time faculty with Ph.D. or other terminal degree: 84%. Student/faculty ratio: 20/1. Classes of fewer than 20 students: 52%; of 20 to 49 students: 37%; of 50 or more students: 11%. **Advanced Placement and International Baccalaureate credit:** AP tests may be used for: Credit and/or placement. Scores accepted: 3, 4, 5. **Freshmen returning for sophomore year:** 83%. **Graduation rates:** Four-year: 30%; five-year: 58%; six-year: 64%. **Graduate study:** 15% of students pursue further study within one year.

COSTS AND FINANCIAL AID

Financial aid office: (360) 650-3470. **Expenses (2006-2007):** Tuition and fees 2006-2007: $5,003 in state, $15,550 out of state; room/board: $6,785. **Financial aid:** Priority filing date for institution's financial aid form: February 15. In 2005-2006, 60% of undergraduates applied for financial aid. Of those, 40% were determined to have financial need; 32% had their need fully met. Average financial aid package (proportion receiving): $8,981 (39%). Average amount of gift aid, such as scholarships or grants (proportion receiving): $5,602 (31%). Average amount of self-help aid, such as work study or loans (proportion receiving): $4,475 (32%). Average need-based loan (excluding PLUS or other private loans): $4,150. Among students who received need-based aid, the average percentage of need met: 87%. Among students who received aid based on merit, the average award (and the proportion receiving): $1,586 (2%). The average athletic scholarship (and the proportion receiving): $3,988 (1%). Average amount of debt of borrowers graduating in 2005: $15,784. Proportion who borrowed: 58%.

CAMPUS LIFE AND EXTRACURRICULAR ACTIVITIES

Campus housing available (% using): coed dorms (86%), apartments for married students (0%), apartment for single students (14%). Students who live in college-owned, operated, or affiliated housing: 25%. **Student employment:** During the 2005-2006 academic year, 11% of undergraduates worked on campus. Average per-year earnings: $1,860. **Clubs and organizations:** Number of student organizations: 163. Activities include: choral groups, concert band, dance, drama/theater, jazz band, literary magazine, music ensembles, musical theater, opera, radio station, student government, student newspaper, symphony orchestra. Number of fraternities: 0; sororities: 0. Average proportion of students who stay on campus on weekends: 65%. **Sports program (2005-2006):** Member of NCAA II. *Men's intercollegiate varsity sports:* basketball, cross-country, football, golf, soccer, track and field (indoor), track and field (outdoor). *Women's intercollegiate varsity sports:* basketball, cross-country, golf, rowing, soccer, softball, track and field (indoor), track and field (outdoor), volleyball.

SERVICES AND FACILITIES

Basic services: nonremedial tutoring, women's center, placement service, day care, health service, health insurance. **Remedial assistance:** math, writing, study skills. **Counseling services:** minority student, career, personal, academic, psychological, birth control. **For learning-disabled students:** School does not offer a structured program with separate admission and additional fees. Total undergraduates in learning-disabled program or receiving services: 232. Services include: remedial math, remedial English, reading machines, tape recorders, note-taking services, oral tests, readers, extended time for tests, tutors, priority registration, priority seating, proof-reading services, substitution of courses, texts on tape, typist/scribe, exams on tape or computer, other testing accomodations, other. **Library:** Number of titles: 1,402,135; number of current serial subscriptions: 4,806. **Information technology resources:** Students are not required to lease or own a computer. Number of campus computers available to all students: 2,080. School has a wireless network. Approximate number of users that can be accommodated: 4,800. Proportion of college-owned housing units wired for high-speed internet access: 99%. **Campus safety:** Security services offered: 24-hour foot-and-vehicle patrols, late-night transport/escort service, 24-hour emergency telephones, lighted pathways/sidewalks, student patrols, controlled dormitory access (key, security card, etc).

TRANSFER AND INTERNATIONAL STUDENTS

Transfer students: May apply for admission for the following academic terms: Fall, Winter, Spring, Summer. Applicants do not need a minimum number of credits to apply. For fall 2005: Transfer applications received: 2,513. Transfer applicants offered admission: 1,377. Transfer applicants enrolled: 880. **International students:** Number of foreign undergraduates: 51. Number of countries represented: 27. Minimum TOEFL score required: 550 (paper); 213 (computer).

Whitman College

- **Address:** 345 Boyer Avenue, Walla Walla, WA 99362-2083
- **Website:** http://www.whitman.edu
- **Private**
- **Enrollment:** 1,480 full-time; 32 part-time

KEY STATS
- ✔ **U.S News College Ranking:** 36, Liberal Arts Colleges
- ✔ **SAT Score (25th/75th percentile):** 1240-1450
- ✔ **Tuition:** 2006-2007: $30,806

Selectivity: More selective	**Room/board:** $7,840
Acceptance rate: 49%	**Average debt:** $16,200
Student/faculty ratio: 10/1	**Proportion who borrowed:** 45%

UNDERGRADUATE STUDENT BODY STATS

2005-2006 enrollment: 1,480 full-time; 32 part-time. Men: 46%; women: 54%. **Ethnic makeup:** African American: 2%; American-Indian: 1%; Asian American: 9%; Hispanic: 4%; White: 81%; International: 3%.

ADMISSIONS FACTS AND FIGURES

Phone: (509) 527-5176. **Email:** admission@whitman.edu. **Website:** http://www.whitman.edu. **Application deadlines for fall 2007:** Regular decision: January 15; decision sent by April 1. Early decision: Send application by: November 15; Decision sent by: December 15. Early action: Not offered. Admission can be deferred. **Application fee:** $45. Common application is accepted. **To apply online, go to:** https://www.applyweb.com/apply/whitman/menu.html. **Admissions requirements/recommendations:** High school units required (recommended): English: 4 (4); Mathematics: 4 (4); Science: 3 (3); Foreign language: 2 (2); Social studies: 2 (2); History: 2 (2); Academic electives: 0 (0); Total units: 16 (18). Tests: The college uses SAT or ACT scores in admissions decisions. Either SAT or ACT required. For admission to the fall 2007 entering class, the school will accept: ACT with writing. Campus visit: Recommended. Admissions interview: Recommended. Off-campus interview: May be arranged. **Factors that count in admissions decisions:** *Academic:* Secondary school record: Very important. Class rank: Considered. Letters of recommendation: Important. Standardized test scores: Important. Essay: Very important. *Nonacademic:* Interview: Considered. Extracurricular activities: Important. Talent/ability: Important. Character/personal qualities: Very important. Alumni/ae relationship: Considered. Geographical residence: Considered. State residency: Considered. Religious affiliation/commitment: Not considered. Minority status: Important. Volunteer work: Considered. Work experience: Considered. **Other schools with the greatest overlap in applicants:** Lewis and Clark College; Pomona College; University of Puget Sound; University of Washington; Willamette University. **Admissions statistics for the fall 2005 entering class:** Total applicants: 2,544. Total accepted: 1,251. Freshmen enrolled: 361; 60% were from out of state. Overall acceptance rate: 49%. Early-decision acceptance rate: 71%. Non-early acceptance rate: 47%. **Size of waiting list:** 343 applicants; enrolled from waiting list: 47. **Credentials of fall 2005 freshmen:** 60% ranked in the top 10 percent of their high school class; 91% were in the top 25 percent, and 98% were in the top half. (Proportion submitting class standing: 68%.) **Average high school grade point average:** 3.7. **First-year students who submitted SAT scores:** 82%. Scores (25/75 percentile): Verbal: 620-750, Math: 620-700, Combined: 1240-1450. **First-year students submitting ACT scores:** 18%. Scores (25/75 percentile): English: N/A, Math: N/A, Composite: 27-31.

ACADEMICS

Year founded: 1883. **Academic calendar:** Semester. **Degrees offered:** bachelor's. **Most popular majors:** 11% biology technician/biotechnology laboratory technician, 11% psychology, 10% political science and government, 8% English language and literature, 7% history. **Major fields of study:** area, eth-

nic, cultural, and gender studies; biological and biomedical sciences; communication, journalism, and related programs; English language and literature/letters; foreign languages, literatures, and linguistics; history; mathematics and statistics; philosophy and religious studies; physical sciences; psychology; social sciences; visual and performing arts. **Areas of required coursework:** arts/fine arts, humanities, computer literacy, mathematics, English (including composition), philosophy, foreign languages, sciences (biological or physical), history, social science, other. **Special academic programs:** accelerated program, cooperative (work-study plan) program, cross-registration, double major, dual enrollment, exchange student program (domestic), honors program, independent study, liberal arts/career combination, student-designed major, study abroad, other. **Teacher certification offered in:** early childhood, elementary. **Cooperative education programs:** computer science, education, engineering. **Faculty and instruction (2005-2006):** Total instructional faculty: 115 full-time, 72 part-time (59% men; 41% women; 9% minorities). Full-time faculty with Ph.D. or other terminal degree: 97%. Student/faculty ratio: 10/1. Classes of fewer than 20 students: 70%; of 20 to 49 students: 30%; of 50 or more students: 1%. **Advanced Placement and International Baccalaureate credit:** AP tests may be used for: Credit and/or placement. Scores accepted: 4, 5. International Baccalaureate exams may be used for: Credit and/or placement. **Freshmen returning for sophomore year:** 94%. **Graduation rates:** Four-year: 78%; five-year: 85%; six-year: 86%.

COSTS AND FINANCIAL AID

Financial aid office: (509) 527-5178. **Expenses (2006-2007):** Tuition and fees 2006-2007: $30,806; room/board: $7,840. Estimated books and supplies: $1,400. **Financial aid:** Priority filing date for institution's financial aid form: January 15; deadline: February 1. In 2005-2006, 65% of undergraduates applied for financial aid. Of those, 55% were determined to have financial need; 78% had their need fully met. Average financial aid package (proportion receiving): $22,050 (55%). Average amount of gift aid, such as scholarships or grants (proportion receiving): $16,850 (55%). Average amount of self-help aid, such as work study or loans (proportion receiving): $5,975 (46%). Average need-based loan (excluding PLUS or other private loans): $4,250. Among students who received need-based aid, the average percentage of need met: 89%. Among students who received aid based on merit, the average award (and the proportion receiving): $8,250 (38%). The average athletic scholarship (and the proportion receiving): $0 (6%). Average amount of debt of borrowers graduating in 2005: $16,200. Proportion who borrowed: 45%.

CAMPUS LIFE AND EXTRACURRICULAR ACTIVITIES

Campus housing available: coed dorms, women's dorms, sorority housing, fraternity housing, apartment for single students, other housing options. Students who live in college-owned, operated, or affiliated housing: 63%. **Student employment:** During the 2005-2006 academic year, 67% of undergraduates worked on campus. Average per-year earnings: $1,126. **Clubs and organizations:** Number of student organizations: 60. Activities include: choral groups, concert band, dance, drama/theater, jazz band, literary magazine, music ensembles, musical theater, radio station, student government, student newspaper, student film society, symphony orchestra. Number of fraternities: 4; sororities: 4. Proportion of men in fraternities: 34%; of women in sororities: 26%. Average proportion of students who stay on campus on weekends: 95%. **Sports program (2005-2006):** Member of NCAA III. *Men's intercollegiate varsity sports:* alpine skiing, baseball, basketball, cross-country, golf, nordic skiing, skiing, soccer, swimming and diving, tennis. *Women's intercollegiate varsity sports:* alpine skiing, basketball, cross-country, golf, nordic skiing, skiing, soccer, swimming and diving, tennis, volleyball.

SERVICES AND FACILITIES

Basic services: health service, health insurance. **Remedial assistance:** reading, math, writing, study skills. **Counseling services:** minority student, career, military, personal, veteran student, academic, older student, psychological, birth control, religious. **For learning-disabled students:** School does not offer a structured program with separate admission and additional fees. Total undergraduates in learning-disabled program or receiving services: 114. Services include: reading machines, tape recorders, videotaped classes, diagnostic testing service, note-taking services, oral tests, learning center, readers, extended time for tests, tutors, early syllabus, priority seating, proofreading services, texts on tape, typist/scribe, take home exams, other testing accomodations. **Library:** Number of titles: 374,131; number of current serial subscriptions: 2,200. **Information technology resources:** Students are not required to lease or own a computer. Number of campus computers available to all students: 410. School has a wireless network. Approximate number of users that can be accommodated: 1,200. Proportion of college-owned housing units wired for high-speed internet access: 100%. **Campus safety:** Security services offered: 24-hour foot-and-vehicle patrols, late-night transport/escort service, 24-hour emergency telephones, lighted pathways/sidewalks, student patrols, controlled dormitory access (key, security card, etc).

TRANSFER AND INTERNATIONAL STUDENTS

Transfer students: May apply for admission for the following academic terms: Fall, Spring. Applicants do not need a minimum number of credits to apply. For fall 2005: Transfer applications received: 99. Transfer applicants offered admission: 49. Transfer applicants enrolled: 29. **International students:** Number of foreign undergraduates: 42 (3% of student body). Number of countries represented: 34. Minimum TOEFL score required: 560 (paper); 220 (computer). Average TOEFL score: 650 (paper).

Whitworth College

- **Address:** 300 W. Hawthorne, Spokane, WA 99251
- **Website:** http://www.whitworth.edu
- **Private; Religious affiliation:** Presbyterian Church (USA)
- **Enrollment:** 2,065 full-time; 114 part-time

KEY STATS
✔ **U.S News College Ranking:** 5, Universities–Master's (West)
✔ **SAT or ACT Score (25th/75th percentile):** 1080-1300
✔ **Tuition:** 2006-2007: $24,154
   Selectivity: More selective   **Room/board:** $7,030
   Acceptance rate: 67%   **Average debt:** $18,246
   Student/faculty ratio: 13/1   **Proportion who borrowed:** 73%

UNDERGRADUATE STUDENT BODY STATS
2005-2006 enrollment: 2,065 full-time; 114 part-time. Men: 40%; women: 60%. **Ethnic makeup:** African American: 2%; American-Indian: 1%; Asian American: 4%; Hispanic: 2%; White: 89%; International: 1%.

ADMISSIONS FACTS AND FIGURES
Phone: (800) 533-4668. **Email:** admissions@whitworth.edu. **Website:** http://www.whitworth.edu. **Application deadlines for fall 2007:** Regular decision: March 1; decision sent by April 1. Early decision: Not offered. Early action: Send application by: November 30; Decision sent by: December 24. Admission can be deferred. Common application is accepted. **Admissions requirements/recommendations:** High school units required (recommended): English: (4); Mathematics: (4); Science: (4); Foreign language: (3); Social studies: (3); History: (3); Academic electives: (4). Tests: The college uses SAT or ACT scores in admissions decisions. Either SAT or ACT required. For admission to the fall 2007 entering class, the school will accept: ACT with writing, ACT without writing. Campus visit: Recommended. Admissions interview: Recommended. Off-campus interview: May be arranged. **Factors that count in admissions decisions: Academic:** Secondary school record: Very important. Class rank: Considered. Letters of recommendation: Very important. Standardized test scores: Important. Essay: Very important. *Nonacademic:* Interview: Very important. Extracurricular activities: Very important. Talent/ability: Very important. Character/personal qualities: Very important. Alumni/ae relationship: Important. Geographical residence: Considered. State residency: Considered. Religious affiliation/commitment: Considered. Minority status: Important. Volunteer work: Considered. Work experience: Considered. **Other schools with the greatest overlap in applicants:** Pacific Lutheran University; Seattle Pacific University; University of Washington; Washington State University; Western Washington University. **Admissions statistics for the fall 2005 entering class:** Total applicants: 2,062. Total accepted: 1,372. Freshmen enrolled: 451; 33% were from out of state. Accepted through early-decision or early-action plans: 63%. Overall acceptance rate: 67%. Non-early acceptance rate: 57%. **Size of waiting list:** 120 applicants; enrolled from waiting list: 38. **Credentials of fall 2005 freshmen:** 40% ranked in the top 10 percent of their high school class; 70% were in the top 25 percent, and 90% were in the top half. (Proportion submitting class standing: 75%.) **Average high school grade point average:** 3.7. **First-year students who submitted SAT scores:** 93%. Scores (25/75 percentile): Verbal: 540-650, Math: 540-650, Combined: 1080-1300. **First-year students submit-**

ting ACT scores: 31%. Scores (25/75 percentile): English: 23-30, Math: 23-28, Composite: 24-29.

ACADEMICS
Year founded: 1890. **Academic calendar:** 4-1-4. **Degrees offered:** bachelor's, master's. **Most popular majors:** 21% business, management, marketing, and related support services, 13% education, 8% visual and performing arts, 7% English language and literature/letters, 7% psychology. **Major fields of study:** area, ethnic, cultural, and gender studies; biological and biomedical sciences; business, management, marketing, and related support services; communication, journalism, and related programs; computer and information sciences and support services; education; English language and literature/letters; foreign languages, literatures, and linguistics; health professions and related clinical sciences; history; liberal arts and sciences studies, and humanities; mathematics and statistics; multi/interdisciplinary studies; philosophy and religious studies; physical sciences; psychology; social sciences; visual and performing arts. **Areas of required coursework:** arts/fine arts, humanities, mathematics, English (including composition), foreign languages, sciences (biological or physical), social science, other. **Pre-professional programs:** pre-law, pre-dentistry, pre-medicine, pre-theology, pre-veterinary science, pre-pharmacy. **Special academic programs (% participation):** accelerated program, cooperative (work-study plan) program, cross-registration, double major (19%), dual enrollment, English as a Second Language (ESL), exchange student program (domestic), independent study, internships (24%), student-designed major, study abroad (33%), teacher certificate program (15%). **Teacher certification offered in:** special education, elementary, middle/junior high, secondary. **Cooperative education programs:** business. **Reserve Officers Training Corps (ROTC):** Army ROTC: Offered at cooperating institution (Gonzaga University). **Faculty and instruction (2005-2006):** Total instructional faculty: 120 full-time, 168 part-time (53% men; 47% women; 7% minorities). Full-time faculty with Ph.D. or other terminal degree: 74%. Student/faculty ratio: 13/1. Classes of fewer than 20 students: 59%; of 20 to 49 students: 38%; of 50 or more students: 3%. **Advanced Placement and International Baccalaureate credit:** AP tests may be used for: Credit and/or placement. Scores accepted: 3, 4, 5. International Baccalaureate exams may be used for: Credit and/or placement. **Freshmen returning for sophomore year:** 86%. **Graduation rates:** Four-year: 58%; five-year: 74%; six-year: 70%. **Graduate study:** 23% of students pursue further study immediately upon graduation; 61% within five years.

COSTS AND FINANCIAL AID
Financial aid office: (800) 533-4668. **Expenses (2006-2007):** Tuition and fees 2006-2007: $24,154; room/board: $7,030. Estimated books and supplies: $792; transportation: $1,008; personal expenses: $1,279. **Financial aid:** Priority filing date for institution's financial aid form: March 1. In 2005-2006, 85% of undergraduates applied for financial aid. Of those, 74% were determined to have financial need; 17% had their need fully met. Average financial aid package (proportion receiving): $17,441 (74%). Average amount of gift aid, such as scholarships or grants (proportion receiving): $12,423 (71%). Average amount of self-help aid, such as work study or loans (proportion receiving): $5,861 (61%). Average need-based loan (excluding PLUS or other private loans): $4,572. Among students who received need-based aid, the average percentage of need met: 79%. Among students who received aid based on merit, the average award (and the proportion receiving): $7,382 (23%). Average amount of debt of borrowers graduating in 2005: $18,246. Proportion who borrowed: 73%.

CAMPUS LIFE AND EXTRACURRICULAR ACTIVITIES
Campus housing available (% using): coed dorms (80%), women's dorms (6%), men's dorms (7%), apartment for single students (0%), special housing for disabled students (0%), other housing options (7%). Students who live in college-owned, operated, or affiliated housing: 61%. **Student employment:** During the 2005-2006 academic year, 51% of undergraduates worked on campus. Average per-year earnings: $3,000. **Clubs and organizations:** Number of student organizations: 29. Activities include: choral groups, concert band, dance, drama/theater, jazz band, literary magazine, music ensembles, musical theater, radio station, student government, student newspaper, symphony orchestra, yearbook. Number of fraternities: 0; sororities: 0. Average proportion of students who stay on campus on weekends: 78%. **Sports program (2005-2006):** Member of NCAA III. *Men's intercollegiate varsity sports:* baseball, basketball, cross-country, football, golf, soccer, swimming and diving, tennis, track and field (indoor), track and field (outdoor). *Women's intercollegiate varsity sports:* basketball, cross-country, golf, soccer, softball, swimming and diving, tennis, track and field (indoor), track and field (outdoor), volleyball.

SERVICES AND FACILITIES

Basic services: nonremedial tutoring, placement service, health service, health insurance. **Remedial assistance:** reading, math, writing, study skills. **Counseling services:** minority student, career, personal, academic, older student, psychological, birth control, religious. **For learning-disabled students:** School does not offer a structured program with separate admission and additional fees. Services include: remedial math, remedial English, tape recorders, videotaped classes, untimed tests, note-taking services, readers, extended time for tests, tutors, priority seating, texts on tape, other testing accomodations. **Library:** Number of titles: 178,043; number of current serial subscriptions: 1,478. **Information technology resources:** Students are not required to lease or own a computer. Number of campus computers available to all students: 195. School has a wireless network. Approximate number of users that can be accommodated: 750. Proportion of college-owned housing units wired for high-speed internet access: 95%.

Campus safety: Security services offered: 24-hour foot-and-vehicle patrols, late-night transport/escort service, 24-hour emergency telephones, lighted pathways/sidewalks, student patrols, controlled dormitory access (key, security card, etc).

TRANSFER AND INTERNATIONAL STUDENTS

Transfer students: May apply for admission for the following academic terms: Fall, Winter, Spring. Applicants do not need a minimum number of credits to apply. For fall 2005: Transfer applications received: 233. Transfer applicants offered admission: 175. Transfer applicants enrolled: 93.
International students: Number of foreign undergraduates: 16 (1% of student body). Number of countries represented: 25. Minimum TOEFL score required: 525 (paper); 193 (computer). Average TOEFL score: 525 (paper).

West Virginia

Alderson-Broaddus College

- **Address:** College Hill, Philippi, WV 26416
- **Website:** http://www.ab.edu
- **Private; Religious affiliation:** American Baptist
- **Enrollment:** 592 full-time; 56 part-time

KEY STATS

✔ **U.S News College Ranking:** 27, Comp. Coll.–Bachelor's (South)
✔ **ACT Score (25th/75th percentile):** 19-24
✔ **Tuition:** 2006-2007: $19,090

Selectivity: Selective	**Room/board:** $6,150
Acceptance rate: 75%	**Average debt:** $23,579
Student/faculty ratio: 11/1	**Proportion who borrowed:** 80%

UNDERGRADUATE STUDENT BODY STATS

2005-2006 enrollment: 592 full-time; 56 part-time. Men: 32%; women: 68%. **Ethnic makeup:** African American: 2%; Asian American: 1%; Hispanic: 1%; White: 93%; International: 2%. **Religious preference:** Roman Catholic: 2%; Protestant: 1%; No preference: 23%; Unknown: 14%; American Baptist: 9%.

ADMISSIONS FACTS AND FIGURES

Phone: (800) 263-1549. **Email:** admissions@ab.edu. **Website:** http://www.ab.edu. **Application deadlines for fall 2007:** Regular decision: August 25. Early decision: Not offered. Early action: Not offered. Admission can be deferred. **Application fee:** $10. Common application is not accepted. **To apply online, go to:** http://www.wvmentor.org/applications/wv_common_app/apply/alderson_broaddus.html. **Admissions requirements/recommendations:** High school units required (recommended): English: 4 (4); Mathematics: 3 (3); Science: (3); Foreign language: 1 (1); Social studies: 2 (2); History: (2); Total units: 10 (15). Tests: The college uses SAT or ACT scores in admissions decisions. ACT required. For admission to the fall 2007 entering class, the school will accept: ACT with writing, ACT without writing. Campus visit: Recommended. Admissions interview: Recommended. Off-campus interview: May be arranged. **Factors that count in admissions decisions:** *Academic:* Secondary school record: Considered. Class rank: Not considered. Letters of recommendation: Considered. Standardized test scores: Very important. Essay: Important. *Nonacademic:* Interview: Important. Extracurricular activities: Not considered. Talent/ability: Considered. Character/personal qualities: Not considered. Alumni/ae relationship: Considered. Geographical residence: Not considered. State residency: Not considered. Religious affiliation/commitment: Considered. Minority status: Not considered. Volunteer work: Not considered. Work experience: Considered. **Other schools with the greatest overlap in applicants:** Davis and Elkins College; Fairmont State University; West Virginia University; West Virginia University–Parkersburg; West Virginia Wesleyan College. **Admissions statistics for the fall 2005 entering class:** Total applicants: 480. Total accepted: 362. Freshmen enrolled: 125; 22% were from out of state. Overall acceptance rate: 75%. **Credentials of fall 2005 freshmen:** 20% ranked in the top 10 percent of their high school class; 45% were in the top 25 percent, and 78% were in the top half. (Proportion submitting class standing: 77%.) **Average high school grade point average:** 3.3. **First-year students who submitted SAT scores:** 31%. Scores (25/75 percentile): Verbal: 420-560, Math: 390-530, Combined: 810-1090. **First-year students submitting ACT scores:** 87%. Scores (25/75 percentile): English: 19-24, Math: 17-23, Composite: 19-24.

ACADEMICS

Year founded: 1871. **Academic calendar:** Semester. **Degrees offered:** certificate, associate, bachelor's, master's. **Most popular majors:** 32% nursing/registered nurse training (R.N., A.S.N., B.S.N., M.S.N.), 23% physician assistant, 10% biology/biological sciences, 6% elementary education and teaching, 6% health services/allied health/health sciences. **Major fields of study:** biological and biomedical sciences; business, management, marketing, and related support services; communication, journalism, and related programs; computer and information sciences and support services; education; English language and literature/letters; family and consumer sciences/human sciences; health professions and related clinical sciences; history; liberal arts and sciences studies, and humanities; mathematics and statistics; natural resources and conservation; parks, recreation, leisure, and fitness studies; philosophy and religious studies; physical sciences; psychology; social sciences; visual and performing arts. **Areas of required coursework:** arts/fine arts, humanities, computer literacy, mathematics, English (including composition), philosophy, sciences (biological or physical), history, social science, other. **Pre-professional programs:** pre-law, pre-dentistry, pre-medicine, pre-theology, pre-veterinary science, pre-pharmacy, other. **Special academic programs (% participation):** double major (10%), dual enrollment, honors program (1%), independent study (23%), internships (8%), liberal arts/career combination (100%), student-designed major (1%), study abroad (5%), teacher certificate program (13%). **Teacher certification offered in:** special education, elementary, middle/junior high, secondary. **Faculty and instruction (2005-2006):** Total instructional faculty: 58 full-time, 23 part-time (53% men; 47% women; 10% minorities). Full-time faculty with Ph.D. or other terminal degree: 34%. Student/faculty ratio: 11/1. Classes of fewer than 20 students: 84%; of 20 to 49 students: 16%; of 50 or more students: 0%. **Advanced Placement and International Baccalaureate credit:** AP tests may be used for: Credit and/or placement. Scores accepted: 5. **Freshmen returning for sophomore year:** 80%. **Graduation rates:** Six-year: 42%. **Graduate study:** 15% of students pursue further study immediately upon graduation; 16% within one year; 20% within five years. Fields in which graduates pursue further study: Master of Business Administration (MBA), 5%; law, 5%; medicine, 20%; dentistry, 5%; theology (or the seminary), 20%; education, 85%; arts and sciences, 5%; veterinary medicine, 5%.

COSTS AND FINANCIAL AID

Financial aid office: (304) 457-6354. **Expenses (2006-2007):** Tuition and fees 2006-2007: $19,090; room/board: $6,150. Estimated books and supplies: $800; transportation: $820; personal expenses: $1,500. **Financial aid:** Priority filing date for institution's financial aid form: March 1. In 2005-2006, 100% of undergraduates applied for financial aid. Of those, 95% were determined to have financial need; 31% had their need fully met. Average financial aid package (proportion receiving): $17,211 (95%). Average amount of gift aid, such as scholarships or grants (proportion receiving): $4,961 (91%). Average amount of self-help aid, such as work study or loans (proportion receiving): $4,382 (85%). Average need-based loan (excluding PLUS or other private loans): $3,947. Among students who received need-based aid, the average percentage of need met: 87%. Among students who received aid based on merit, the average award (and the proportion receiving): $5,694 (6%). The average athletic scholarship (and the proportion receiving): $16,734 (1%). Average amount of debt of borrowers graduating in 2005: $23,579. Proportion who borrowed: 80%.

CAMPUS LIFE AND EXTRACURRICULAR ACTIVITIES

Campus housing available (% using): coed dorms (70%), women's dorms (20%), apartments for married students (10%). Students who live in college-owned, operated, or affiliated housing: 47%. **Clubs and organizations:** Number of student organizations: 41. Activities include: choral groups, concert band, dance, drama/theater, jazz band, literary magazine, music ensembles, musical theater, opera, radio station, student government, student newspaper, television station, yearbook. Number of fraternities: 1; sororities: 3. Proportion of men in fraternities: 2%; of women in sororities: 3%. Average proportion of students who stay on campus on weekends: 40%. **Sports program (2005-2006):** Member of NCAA III. *Men's intercollegiate varsity sports:* baseball, basketball, cross-country, soccer, track and field (indoor), track and field (outdoor). *Women's intercollegiate varsity sports:* basketball, cross-country, softball, track and field (indoor), track and field (outdoor), volleyball.

SERVICES AND FACILITIES

Basic services: nonremedial tutoring, placement service, health service, health insurance. **Remedial assistance:** reading, math, writing, study skills. **Counseling services:** minority student, career, military, personal, veteran student, academic, older student, psychological, birth control, religious. **For**

learning-disabled students: School does not offer a structured program with separate admission and additional fees. Total undergraduates in learning-disabled program or receiving services: 16. Services include: remedial math, remedial English, remedial reading, tape recorders, untimed tests, note-taking services, oral tests, learning center, readers, extended time for tests, tutors, priority seating, other testing accomodations. **Library:** Number of titles: 100,000; number of current serial subscriptions: 9,000. **Information technology resources:** Students are not required to lease or own a computer. Number of campus computers available to all students: 95. School has a wireless network. Approximate number of users that can be accommodated: 30. Proportion of college-owned housing units wired for high-speed internet access: 100%. **Campus safety:** Security services offered: late-night transport/escort service, lighted pathways/sidewalks, controlled dormitory access (key, security card, etc.).

TRANSFER AND INTERNATIONAL STUDENTS

Transfer students: May apply for admission for the following academic terms: Fall, Spring, Summer. Applicants need a minimum number of credits to apply. For fall 2005: Transfer applications received: 133. Transfer applicants offered admission: 88. Transfer applicants enrolled: 49. **International students:** Number of foreign undergraduates: 10 (2% of student body). Number of countries represented: 5. Minimum TOEFL score required: 500 (paper); 173 (computer).

Bethany College

- **Address:** PO Box 419, Bethany, WV 26032
- **Website:** http://www.bethanywv.edu
- **Private; Religious affiliation:** Christian Church (Disciples of Christ)
- **Enrollment:** 893 full-time; 9 part-time

KEY STATS

- ✔ **U.S News College Ranking:** fourth tier, Liberal Arts Colleges
- ✔ **SAT Score (25th/75th percentile):** 870-1100
- ✔ **Tuition:** 2006-2007: $16,550

Selectivity: Less selective	**Room/board:** $7,770
Acceptance rate: 89%	**Average debt:** N/A
Student/faculty ratio: 15/1	**Proportion who borrowed:** N/A

UNDERGRADUATE STUDENT BODY STATS

2005-2006 enrollment: 893 full-time; 9 part-time. Men: 45%; women: 55%. **Ethnic makeup:** African American: 3%; Hispanic: 1%; White: 92%; International: 3%. **Religious preference:** Roman Catholic: 29%; Protestant: 38%; No preference: 1%; Unknown: 26%; Christian Church (Disciples of Christ): 6%.

ADMISSIONS FACTS AND FIGURES

Phone: (304) 829-7611. **Email:** admission@bethanywv.edu. **Website:** http://www.bethanywv.edu. **Application deadlines for fall 2007:** Regular decision: Rolling. Early decision: Not offered. Early action: Not offered. Admission can be deferred. **Application fee:** $25. Common application is accepted. **To apply online, go to:** http://www.bethanywv.edu/admission/apply/. **Admissions requirements/recommendations:** High school units required (recommended): English: 4 (0); Mathematics: 3 (0); Science: 3 (0); Foreign language: 2 (0); Social studies: 3 (0); History: 0 (0); Academic electives: 0 (0); Total units: 15 (0). Tests: The college uses SAT or ACT scores in admissions decisions. Either SAT or ACT required. For admission to the fall 2007 entering class, the school will accept: ACT with writing, ACT without writing. Campus visit: Recommended. Admissions interview: Recommended. Off-campus interview: May be arranged. **Factors that count in admissions decisions:** *Academic:* Secondary school record: Very important. Class rank: Very important. Letters of recommendation: Very important. Standardized test scores: Very important. Essay: Very important. *Nonacademic:* Interview: Important. Extracurricular activities: Important. Talent/ability: Considered. Character/personal qualities: Important. Alumni/ae relationship: Considered. Geographical residence: Not considered. State residency: Not considered. Religious affiliation/commitment: Not considered. Minority status: Not considered. Volunteer work: Considered. Work experience: Considered. **Other schools with the greatest overlap in applicants:** Muskingum College; Thiel College; Washington and Jefferson College; Waynesburg College; West Liberty State College. **Admissions statistics for**

the fall 2005 entering class: Total applicants: 728. Total accepted: 646. Freshmen enrolled: 219; 72% were from out of state. Overall acceptance rate: 89%. **Credentials of fall 2005 freshmen:** 11% ranked in the top 10 percent of their high school class; 28% were in the top 25 percent, and 58% were in the top half. (Proportion submitting class standing: 87%.) **Average high school grade point average:** 3.2. **First-year students who submitted SAT scores:** 61%. Scores (25/75 percentile): Verbal: 430-550, Math: 440-550, Combined: 870-1100. **First-year students submitting ACT scores:** 59%. Scores (25/75 percentile): English: 18-24, Math: 17-23, Composite: 19-24.

ACADEMICS

Year founded: 1840. **Academic calendar:** 4-1-4. **Degrees offered:** bachelor's. **Most popular majors:** 16% education, 16% psychology, 12% communication, journalism, and related programs, 8% social work, 7% physical education teaching and coaching. **Major fields of study:** agriculture, agriculture operations, and related sciences; biological and biomedical sciences; business, management, marketing, and related support services; communication, journalism, and related programs; computer and information sciences and support services; education; English language and literature/letters; foreign languages, literatures, and linguistics; history; mathematics and statistics; multi/interdisciplinary studies; natural resources and conservation; philosophy and religious studies; physical sciences; psychology; public administration and social service professions; social sciences; visual and performing arts. **Areas of required coursework:** arts/fine arts, humanities, mathematics, English (including composition), philosophy, foreign languages, sciences (biological or physical), history, social science. **Pre-professional programs:** pre-law, pre-dentistry, pre-medicine, pre-veterinary science. **Special academic programs (% participation):** double major (1%), English as a Second Language (ESL) (1%), independent study (13%), internships (43%), student-designed major (1%), study abroad (1%), teacher certificate program (10%), other (100%). **Teacher certification offered in:** special education, elementary, middle/junior high, secondary. **Faculty and instruction (2005-2006):** Total instructional faculty: 60 full-time, 23 part-time (61% men; 39% women; 7% minorities). Full-time faculty with Ph.D. or other terminal degree: 62%. Student/faculty ratio: 15/1. Classes of fewer than 20 students: 74%; of 20 to 49 students: 23%; of 50 or more students: 4%. **Advanced Placement and International Baccalaureate credit:** AP tests may be used for: Credit only. Scores accepted: 3, 4, 5. International Baccalaureate exams may be used for: Credit and/or placement. **Freshmen returning for sophomore year:** 79%. **Graduation rates:** Four-year: 53%; five-year: 68%; six-year: 69%. **Graduate study:** 43% of students pursue further study within one year. Fields in which graduates pursue further study: Master of Business Administration (MBA), 3%; medicine, 7%; dentistry, 7%; theology (or the seminary), 7%; education, 15%; arts and sciences, 41%.

COSTS AND FINANCIAL AID

Financial aid office: (304) 829-7141. **Expenses (2006-2007):** Tuition and fees 2006-2007: $16,550; room/board: $7,770. Estimated books and supplies: $1,000; transportation: $800; personal expenses: $1,100. **Financial aid:** Priority filing date for institution's financial aid form: March 1; deadline: May 1. In 2005-2006, 67% of undergraduates applied for financial aid. Of those, 48% were determined to have financial need; Average financial aid package (proportion receiving): N/A (48%). Average amount of gift aid, such as scholarships or grants (proportion receiving): N/A (48%). Average amount of self-help aid, such as work study or loans (proportion receiving): N/A (48%). The average athletic scholarship (and the proportion receiving): $0 (0%).

CAMPUS LIFE AND EXTRACURRICULAR ACTIVITIES

Campus housing available (% using): coed dorms (58%), women's dorms (14%), men's dorms (7%), sorority housing (10%), fraternity housing (11%), special housing for disabled students. Students who live in college-owned, operated, or affiliated housing: 96%. **Student employment:** During the 2005-2006 academic year, 85% of undergraduates worked on campus. Average per-year earnings: $1,000. **Clubs and organizations:** Number of student organizations: 97. Activities include: choral groups, concert band, drama/theater, jazz band, literary magazine, music ensembles, pep band, radio station, student government, student newspaper, student film society, television station, yearbook. Number of fraternities: 5; sororities: 3. Proportion of men in fraternities: 40%; of women in sororities: 45%. Average proportion of students who stay on campus on weekends: 65%. **Sports program (2005-2006):** Member of NCAA III. *Men's intercollegiate varsity sports:* baseball, basketball, cross-country, football, soccer, swimming and diving, tennis, track and field (indoor), track and field (outdoor). *Women's intercollegiate varsity sports:* basketball, cross-country, soccer, softball, swimming and diving, tennis, track and field (indoor), track and field (outdoor), volleyball.

SERVICES AND FACILITIES
Basic services: nonremedial tutoring, placement service, health service, health insurance. **Remedial assistance:** reading, math, writing, study skills. **Counseling services:** career, personal, academic, psychological, religious. **For learning-disabled students:** School does not offer a structured program with separate admission and additional fees. Total undergraduates in learning-disabled program or receiving services: 16. Services include: remedial math, remedial English, remedial reading, tape recorders, other special classes, untimed tests, note-taking services, oral tests, learning center, readers, extended time for tests, tutors, other. **Library:** Number of titles: 122,327; number of current serial subscriptions: 91. **Information technology resources:** Students are not required to lease or own a computer. Number of campus computers available to all students: 150. School has a wireless network. Approximate number of users that can be accommodated: 224. Proportion of college-owned housing units wired for high-speed internet access: 100%. **Campus safety:** Security services offered: 24-hour foot-and-vehicle patrols, late-night transport/escort service, 24-hour emergency telephones, lighted pathways/sidewalks, student patrols, controlled dormitory access (key, security card, etc).

TRANSFER AND INTERNATIONAL STUDENTS
Transfer students: May apply for admission for the following academic terms: Fall, Spring. Applicants need a minimum number of credits to apply. For fall 2005: Transfer applications received: 73. Transfer applicants offered admission: 71. Transfer applicants enrolled: 44. **International students:** Number of foreign undergraduates: 22 (3% of student body). Number of countries represented: 11. Minimum TOEFL score required: 550 (paper); 173 (computer). Average TOEFL score: 600 (paper).

Bluefield State College

- **Address:** 219 Rock Street, Bluefield, WV 24701
- **Website:** http://www.bluefieldstate.edu
- **Public**
- **Enrollment:** 1,400 full-time; 308 part-time

KEY STATS
✔ **U.S News College Ranking:** third tier, Comp. Coll.–Bachelor's (South)
✔ **ACT Score (25th/75th percentile):** 16-22
✔ **Tuition:** 2006-2007: $3,682 in state, $7,760 out of state
  Selectivity: Less selective **Room/board:** N/A
  Acceptance rate: 96% **Average debt:** $15,200
  Student/faculty ratio: 17/1 **Proportion who borrowed:** 45%

UNDERGRADUATE STUDENT BODY STATS
2005-2006 enrollment: 1,400 full-time; 308 part-time. Men: 40%; women: 60%. **Ethnic makeup:** African American: 11%; Hispanic: 1%; White: 87%; International: 1%.

ADMISSIONS FACTS AND FIGURES
Phone: (304) 327-4065. **Email:** bscadmit@bluefieldstate.edu. **Website:** http://www.bluefieldstate.edu. **Application deadlines for fall 2007:** Regular decision: Rolling. Early decision: Not offered. Early action: Not offered. Admission can be deferred. Common application is accepted. **Admissions requirements/recommendations:** High school units required (recommended): English: 4; Mathematics: 3; Science: 3; Foreign language: 0 (2); Social studies: 3; History: 1; Academic electives: 1; Total units: 17. Tests: The college uses SAT or ACT scores in admissions decisions. Either SAT or ACT required. For admission to the fall 2007 entering class, the school will accept: ACT with writing, ACT without writing. Campus visit: Neither required nor recommended. Admissions interview: Neither required nor recommended. Off-campus interview: May be arranged. **Factors that count in admissions decisions:** *Academic:* Secondary school record: Important. Class rank: Not considered. Letters of recommendation: Not considered. Standardized test scores: Important. Essay: Not considered. *Nonacademic:* Interview: Not considered. Extracurricular activities: Not considered. Talent/ability: Not considered. Character/personal qualities: Not considered. Alumni/ae relationship: Not considered. Geographical residence: Not considered. State residency: Not considered. Religious affiliation/commitment:

Not considered. Minority status: Not considered. Volunteer work: Not considered. Work experience: Not considered. **Other schools with the greatest overlap in applicants:** Concord University; Marshall University; Mountain State University; West Virginia University; West Virginia University Institute of Technology. **Admissions statistics for the fall 2005 entering class:** Total applicants: 615. Total accepted: 591. Freshmen enrolled: 251; 12% were from out of state. Overall acceptance rate: 96%. **Credentials of fall 2005 freshmen:** 10% ranked in the top 10 percent of their high school class; 34% were in the top 25 percent, and 79% were in the top half. (Proportion submitting class standing: 64%.) **Average high school grade point average:** 3.1. **First-year students who submitted SAT scores:** 11%. Scores (25/75 percentile): Verbal: 430-500, Math: 420-520, Combined: 850-1020. **First-year students submitting ACT scores:** 66%. Scores (25/75 percentile): English: N/A, Math: N/A, Composite: 16-22.

ACADEMICS
Year founded: 1895. **Academic calendar:** Semester. **Degrees offered:** associate, bachelor's. **Most popular majors:** 21% education, 16% health professions and related clinical sciences, 14% business, management, marketing, and related support services, 14% engineering technologies/technicians. **Major fields of study:** business, management, marketing, and related support services; computer and information sciences and support services; education; engineering technologies/technicians; health professions and related clinical sciences; liberal arts and sciences studies, and humanities; multi/interdisciplinary studies; security and protective services; social sciences. **Areas of required coursework:** arts/fine arts, humanities, computer literacy, mathematics, English (including composition), sciences (biological or physical), history, social science. **Pre-professional programs:** pre-law, pre-medicine. **Special academic programs (% participation):** distance learning (12%), double major (1%), dual enrollment (1%), honors program (1%), independent study (1%), internships (1%), teacher certificate program (10%). **Teacher certification offered in:** elementary, middle/junior high. **Faculty and instruction (2005-2006):** Total instructional faculty: 69 full-time, 51 part-time (51% men; 49% women; 9% minorities). Full-time faculty with Ph.D. or other terminal degree: 71%. Student/faculty ratio: 17/1. Classes of fewer than 20 students: 62%; of 20 to 49 students: 38%; of 50 or more students: 0%. **Advanced Placement and International Baccalaureate credit:** AP tests may be used for: Credit only. Scores accepted: 3, 4, 5. International Baccalaureate exams may be used for: Credit only. **Freshmen returning for sophomore year:** 66%. **Graduation rates:** Four-year: 33%; five-year: 39%; six-year: 35%. **Graduate study:** 6% of students pursue further study within one year. Fields in which graduates pursue further study: Master of Business Administration (MBA), 23%; law, 15%; medicine, 15%; dentistry, 8%; engineering, 31%; education, 8%; arts and sciences, 15%.

COSTS AND FINANCIAL AID
Financial aid office: (304) 327-4020. **Expenses (2006-2007):** Tuition and fees 2006-2007: $3,682 in state, $7,760 out of state; room/board: N/A. Estimated books and supplies: $1,200; transportation: $1,000; personal expenses: $1,040. **Financial aid:** Priority filing date for institution's financial aid form: March 1. 13% had their need fully met. Average financial aid package (proportion receiving): $5,600 (N/A). Among students who received need-based aid, the average percentage of need met: 68%. Among students who received aid based on merit, the average award (and the proportion receiving): $1,400 (N/A). The average athletic scholarship (and the proportion receiving): $2,900 (N/A). Average amount of debt of borrowers graduating in 2005: $15,200. Proportion who borrowed: 45%.

CAMPUS LIFE AND EXTRACURRICULAR ACTIVITIES
Students who live in college-owned, operated, or affiliated housing: 0%. **Student employment:** During the 2005-2006 academic year, 2% of undergraduates worked on campus. Average per-year earnings: $3,000. **Clubs and organizations:** Number of student organizations: 49. Activities include: choral groups, drama/theater, radio station, student government, student newspaper, yearbook. Number of fraternities: 4; sororities: 3. Proportion of men in fraternities: 5%; of women in sororities: 8%. **Sports program (2005-2006):** Member of NCAA II. *Men's intercollegiate varsity sports:* baseball, basketball, cross-country, golf, tennis. *Women's intercollegiate varsity sports:* basketball, cross-country, softball, tennis, volleyball.

SERVICES AND FACILITIES
Basic services: nonremedial tutoring, placement service, health service, health insurance. **Remedial assistance:** reading, math, writing, study skills. **Counseling services:** minority student, career, military, personal, veteran student, academic, older student, psychological, birth control. **For learning-disabled students:** School does not offer a structured program with separate

admission and additional fees. Total undergraduates in learning-disabled program or receiving services: 4. Services include: remedial math, remedial English, reading machines, remedial reading, tape recorders, untimed tests, note-taking services, oral tests, readers, extended time for tests, tutors. **Library:** Number of titles: 77,046; number of current serial subscriptions: 118. **Information technology resources:** Students are not required to lease or own a computer. Number of campus computers available to all students: 450. School has a wireless network. Approximate number of users that can be accommodated: 100. **Campus safety:** Security services offered: late-night transport/escort service, lighted pathways/sidewalks, student patrols.

TRANSFER AND INTERNATIONAL STUDENTS

Transfer students: May apply for admission for the following academic terms: Fall, Spring, Summer. Applicants do not need a minimum number of credits to apply. For fall 2005: Transfer applications received: 290. Transfer applicants offered admission: 264. Transfer applicants enrolled: 107. **International students:** Number of foreign undergraduates: 9 (1% of student body). Number of countries represented: 8. Minimum TOEFL score required: 500 (paper). Average TOEFL score: 525 (paper).

Concord University

■ **Address:** Vermillion Street, Athens, WV 24712
■ **Website:** http://www.concord.edu
■ **Public**
■ **Enrollment:** 2,444 full-time; 508 part-time

KEY STATS

✔ **U.S News College Ranking:** 49, Comp. Coll.–Bachelor's (South)
✔ **ACT Score (25th/75th percentile):** 18-24
✔ **Tuition:** 2006-2007: $4,204 in state, $9,338 out of state
  Selectivity: Selective   **Room/board:** $6,070
  Acceptance rate: 74%   **Average debt:** $11,178
  Student/faculty ratio: 21/1   **Proportion who borrowed:** 79%

UNDERGRADUATE STUDENT BODY STATS

2005-2006 enrollment: 2,444 full-time; 508 part-time. Men: 41%; women: 59%. **Ethnic makeup:** African American: 5%; Asian American: 1%; Hispanic: 1%; White: 93%.

ADMISSIONS FACTS AND FIGURES

Phone: (304) 384-5249. **Email:** admissions@concord.edu. **Website:** http://www.concord.edu. **Application deadlines for fall 2007:** Regular decision: Rolling. Early decision: Not offered. Early action: Not offered. Admission can be deferred. Common application is accepted. **To apply online, go to:** http://www.concord.edu/Pages/admissions/admissions/online_applications.htm. **Admissions requirements/recommendations:** High school units required (recommended): English: 4; Mathematics: 2; Science: 2; Foreign language: 0; Social studies: 2; History: 1; Academic electives: 0; Total units: 13. Tests: The college uses SAT or ACT scores in admissions decisions. Either SAT or ACT required. For admission to the fall 2007 entering class, the school will accept: ACT with writing, ACT without writing. Campus visit: Recommended. Admissions interview: Neither required nor recommended. Off-campus interview: May be arranged. **Factors that count in admissions decisions:** *Academic:* Secondary school record: Very important. Class rank: Considered. Letters of recommendation: Considered. Standardized test scores: Very important. Essay: Considered. *Nonacademic:* Interview: Considered. Extracurricular activities: Considered. Talent/ability: Considered. Character/personal qualities: Considered. Alumni/ae relationship: Considered. Geographical residence: Considered. State residency: Considered. Religious affiliation/commitment: Considered. Minority status: Considered. Volunteer work: Considered. Work experience: Considered. **Other schools with the greatest overlap in applicants:** Bluefield State College; Marshall University; West Virginia University. **Admissions statistics for the fall 2005 entering class:** Total applicants: 3,032. Total accepted: 2,236. Freshmen enrolled: 654; 18% were from out of state. Overall acceptance rate: 74%. **Credentials of fall 2005 freshmen:** 20% ranked in the top 10 percent of their high school class; 43% were in the top 25 percent, and 75% were in the top half. (Proportion submitting class standing: 86%.) **Average high school grade point average:** 3.3. **First-year students who submitted SAT scores:** 35%. Scores (25/75 percentile): Verbal: 420-540, Math: 410-540,

Combined: 830-1080. **First-year students submitting ACT scores:** 82%. Scores (25/75 percentile): English: 18-24, Math: 16-22, Composite: 18-24.

ACADEMICS

Year founded: 1872. **Academic calendar:** Semester. **Degrees offered:** associate, bachelor's, master's. **Most popular majors:** 29% education, 21% business, management, marketing, and related support services, 8% social sciences, 6% liberal arts and sciences studies, and humanities, 6% public administration and social service professions. **Major fields of study:** biological and biomedical sciences; business, management, marketing, and related support services; communication, journalism, and related programs; computer and information sciences and support services; education; English language and literature/letters; health professions and related clinical sciences; history; liberal arts and sciences studies, and humanities; mathematics and statistics; multi/interdisciplinary studies; physical sciences; psychology; public administration and social service professions; social sciences; visual and performing arts. **Areas of required coursework:** arts/fine arts, computer literacy, mathematics, English (including composition), foreign languages, sciences (biological or physical), history, social science. **Pre-professional programs:** pre-law, pre-dentistry, pre-medicine, pre-veterinary science, pre-pharmacy. **Special academic programs:** cross-registration, distance learning, double major, dual enrollment, English as a Second Language (ESL), honors program, independent study, internships, student-designed major, teacher certificate program. **Teacher certification offered in:** early childhood, special education, elementary, secondary. **Faculty and instruction (2005-2006):** Total instructional faculty: 97 full-time, 88 part-time (50% men; 50% women; 3% minorities). Full-time faculty with Ph.D. or other terminal degree: 66%. Student/faculty ratio: 21/1. Classes of fewer than 20 students: 59%; of 20 to 49 students: 36%; of 50 or more students: 5%. **Freshmen returning for sophomore year:** 65%. **Graduation rates:** Four-year: 15%; five-year: 28%; six-year: 34%.

COSTS AND FINANCIAL AID

Financial aid office: (304) 384-6069. **Expenses (2006-2007):** Tuition and fees 2006-2007: $4,204 in state, $9,338 out of state; room/board: $6,070. Estimated books and supplies: $1,000; transportation: $1,075; personal expenses: $1,465. **Financial aid:** Priority filing date for institution's financial aid form: April 15. In 2005-2006, 84% of undergraduates applied for financial aid. Of those, 65% were determined to have financial need; 37% had their need fully met. Average financial aid package (proportion receiving): $7,202 (65%). Average amount of gift aid, such as scholarships or grants (proportion receiving): $3,688 (50%). Average amount of self-help aid, such as work study or loans (proportion receiving): $3,446 (50%). Average need-based loan (excluding PLUS or other private loans): $3,219. Among students who received need-based aid, the average percentage of need met: 79%. Among students who received aid based on merit, the average award (and the proportion receiving): $3,232 (13%). The average athletic scholarship (and the proportion receiving): $2,020 (3%). Average amount of debt of borrowers graduating in 2005: $11,178. Proportion who borrowed: 79%.

CAMPUS LIFE AND EXTRACURRICULAR ACTIVITIES

Campus housing available (% using): coed dorms (8%), women's dorms (46%), men's dorms (46%), special housing for disabled students. Students who live in college-owned, operated, or affiliated housing: 34%. **Student employment:** During the 2005-2006 academic year, 19% of undergraduates worked on campus. Average per-year earnings: $1,275. **Clubs and organizations:** Number of student organizations: 61. Activities include: choral groups, concert band, dance, drama/theater, jazz band, literary magazine, marching band, music ensembles, musical theater, pep band, radio station, student government, student newspaper, student film society, television station, yearbook. Number of fraternities: 6; sororities: 5. Proportion of men in fraternities: 20%; of women in sororities: 25%. Average proportion of students who stay on campus on weekends: 30%. **Sports program (2005-2006):** Member of NCAA II. ***Men's intercollegiate varsity sports:*** baseball, basketball, cross-country, football, golf, tennis, track and field (indoor), track and field (outdoor). ***Women's intercollegiate varsity sports:*** basketball, cheerleading, cross-country, soccer, softball, tennis, track and field (indoor), track and field (outdoor), volleyball.

SERVICES AND FACILITIES

Basic services: nonremedial tutoring, placement service, day care, health service. **Remedial assistance:** reading, math, writing, study skills. **Counseling services:** minority student, career, military, personal, veteran student, academic, older student, psychological, birth control. **For learning-disabled students:** School does not offer a structured program with separate admission and additional fees. Total undergraduates in learning-disabled program or receiving services: 45. Services include: remedial math, remedial English, remedial reading, tape recorders, untimed tests, note-taking services, oral tests, readers, extended time for tests, tutors, texts on tape, other testing accomodations. **Library:** Number of titles: 152,000; number of current serial subscriptions: 221. **Information technology resources:** Students are not required to lease or own a computer. Number of campus computers available to all students: 350. School has a wireless network. Approximate number of users that can be accommodated: 500. Proportion of college-owned housing units wired for high-speed internet access: 100%. **Campus safety:** Security services offered: 24-hour foot-and-vehicle patrols, late-night transport/escort service, 24-hour emergency telephones, lighted pathways/sidewalks, controlled dormitory access (key, security card, etc).

TRANSFER AND INTERNATIONAL STUDENTS
Transfer students: May apply for admission for the following academic terms: Fall, Winter, Spring, Summer. Applicants do not need a minimum number of credits to apply. For fall 2005: Transfer applications received: 342. Transfer applicants offered admission: 333. Transfer applicants enrolled: 140. **International students:** Number of foreign undergraduates: 0. Number of countries represented: 11. Minimum TOEFL score required: 500 (paper); 173 (computer). Average TOEFL score: 562 (paper).

Davis and Elkins College

- **Address:** 100 Campus Drive, Elkins, WV 26241
- **Website:** http://www.davisandelkins.edu
- **Private; Religious affiliation:** Presbyterian
- **Enrollment:** 560 full-time; 64 part-time

KEY STATS
✔ **U.S News College Ranking:** 23, Comp. Coll.–Bachelor's (South)
✔ **ACT Score (25th/75th percentile):** 18-22
✔ **Tuition:** 2006-2007: $17,730

Selectivity: Selective	**Room/board:** $6,300
Acceptance rate: 55%	**Average debt:** $20,651
Student/faculty ratio: 11/1	**Proportion who borrowed:** 81%

UNDERGRADUATE STUDENT BODY STATS
2005-2006 enrollment: 560 full-time; 64 part-time. Men: 37%; women: 63%. **Ethnic makeup:** African American: 3%; American-Indian: 1%; Asian American: 1%; Hispanic: 1%; White: 91%; International: 4%.

ADMISSIONS FACTS AND FIGURES
Phone: (304) 637-1230. **Email:** admiss@davisandelkins.edu. **Website:** http://www.davisandelkins.edu. **Application deadlines for fall 2007:** Regular decision: Rolling. Early decision: Not offered. Early action: Not offered. Admission can be deferred. **Application fee:** $35. Common application is accepted. **Admissions requirements/recommendations:** High school units required (recommended): English: 4 (4); Mathematics: 3 (4); Science: 3 (4); Foreign language: 1 (2); Social studies: 3 (4); History: 0 (0); Academic electives: 0 (4); Total units: 15 (24). Tests: The college uses SAT or ACT scores in admissions decisions. Either SAT or ACT required. For admission to the fall 2007 entering class, the school will accept: ACT with writing. Campus visit: Recommended. Admissions interview: Recommended. Off-campus interview: May be arranged. **Factors that count in admissions decisions:** *Academic:* Secondary school record: Very important. Class rank: Important. Letters of recommendation: Important. Standardized test scores: Important. Essay: Considered. *Nonacademic:* Interview: Considered. Extracurricular activities: Important. Talent/ability: Important. Character/personal qualities: Important. Alumni/ae relationship: Considered. Geographical residence: Not considered. State residency: Not considered. Religious affiliation/commitment: Not considered. Minority status: Not considered. Volunteer work: Considered. Work experience: Considered. **Other schools with the greatest overlap in applicants:** Alderson-Broaddus College; Fairmont State University; Glenville State College; West Virginia University; West Virginia Wesleyan College. **Admissions statistics for the fall 2005 entering class:** Total applicants: 563. Total accepted: 307. Freshmen enrolled: 104; 38% were from out of state. Overall acceptance rate: 55%. **Credentials of fall 2005 freshmen:** 12% ranked in the top 10 percent of their high school class; 33% were in the top 25 percent, and 71% were in the top half. (Proportion submitting class standing: 59%.) **Average high school grade point average:** 3.0. **First-year students who submitted SAT scores:** 38%. Scores (25/75 percentile): Verbal:

420-530, Math: 420-510, Combined: 840-1040. **First-year students submitting ACT scores:** 59%. Scores (25/75 percentile): English: 16-23, Math: 16-22, Composite: 18-22.

ACADEMICS
Year founded: 1904. **Academic calendar:** 4-1-4. **Degrees offered:** associate, bachelor's. **Most popular majors:** 11% elementary education and teaching, 10% business administration and management, 10% marketing/marketing management, 6% English language and literature, 6% psychology. **Major fields of study:** biological and biomedical sciences; business, management, marketing, and related support services; communication, journalism, and related programs; computer and information sciences and support services; education; engineering technologies/technicians; English language and literature/letters; foreign languages, literatures, and linguistics; history; mathematics and statistics; natural resources and conservation; parks, recreation, leisure, and fitness studies; philosophy and religious studies; physical sciences; psychology; social sciences; theology and religious vocations; visual and performing arts. **Areas of required coursework:** arts/fine arts, humanities, computer literacy, mathematics, English (including composition), philosophy, sciences (biological or physical), history, social science, other. **Special academic programs (% participation):** cooperative (work-study plan) program (35.4%), cross-registration (0%), double major (7.6%), external degree program (0%), honors program (7.6%), independent study (8.9%), internships (68.4%), student-designed major (6.3%), study abroad (3.8%), teacher certificate program (24%). **Teacher certification offered in:** elementary, middle/junior high, secondary. **Cooperative education programs:** other. **Faculty and instruction (2005-2006):** Total instructional faculty: 44 full-time, 40 part-time (51% men; 49% women; 6% minorities). Full-time faculty with Ph.D. or other terminal degree: 84%. Student/faculty ratio: 11/1. Classes of fewer than 20 students: 80%; of 20 to 49 students: 18%; of 50 or more students: 2%. **Advanced Placement and International Baccalaureate credit:** AP tests may be used for: Credit and/or placement. Scores accepted: 3, 4, 5. International Baccalaureate exams may be used for: Credit and/or placement. **Freshmen returning for sophomore year:** 67%. **Graduation rates:** Four-year: 29%; five-year: 47%; six-year: 45%. **Graduate study:** Fields in which graduates pursue further study: Master of Business Administration (MBA), 11%; law, 6%; education, 44%; arts and sciences, 39%.

COSTS AND FINANCIAL AID
Financial aid office: (304) 637-1373. **Expenses (2006-2007):** Tuition and fees 2006-2007: $17,730; room/board: $6,300. Estimated books and supplies: $800; transportation: $0; personal expenses: $0. **Financial aid:** In 2005-2006, 74% of undergraduates applied for financial aid. Of those, 74% were determined to have financial need; 22% had their need fully met. Average financial aid package (proportion receiving): $12,846 (74%). Average amount of gift aid, such as scholarships or grants (proportion receiving): $4,247 (55%). Average amount of self-help aid, such as work study or loans (proportion receiving): $4,232 (72%). Average need-based loan (excluding PLUS or other private loans): $4,388. Among students who received need-based aid, the average percentage of need met: 71%. Among students who received aid based on merit, the average award (and the proportion receiving): $5,476 (20%). The average athletic scholarship (and the proportion receiving): $5,255 (22%). Average amount of debt of borrowers graduating in 2005: $20,651. Proportion who borrowed: 81%.

CAMPUS LIFE AND EXTRACURRICULAR ACTIVITIES
Campus housing available (% using): coed dorms (45%), women's dorms (27%), men's dorms (28%). Students who live in college-owned, operated, or affiliated housing: 48%. **Student employment:** During the 2005-2006 academic year, 5% of undergraduates worked on campus. Average per-year earnings: $1,000. **Clubs and organizations:** Number of student organizations: 42. Activities include: choral groups, concert band, drama/theater, jazz band, literary magazine, music ensembles, musical theater, radio station, student government, student newspaper, yearbook. Number of fraternities: 2; sororities: 2. Proportion of men in fraternities: 4%; of women in sororities: 7%. Average proportion of students who stay on campus on weekends: 70%. **Sports program (2005-2006):** Member of NCAA II. *Men's intercollegiate varsity sports:* baseball, basketball, cross-country, golf, soccer. *Women's intercollegiate varsity sports:* basketball, cross-country, soccer, softball, volleyball.

SERVICES AND FACILITIES
Basic services: nonremedial tutoring, placement service, health service, health insurance. **Remedial assistance:** reading, math, writing, study skills. **Counseling services:** minority student, career, personal, veteran student, academic, older student, psychological, birth control. **For learning-disabled stu-

dents: School does not offer a structured program with separate admission and additional fees. Total undergraduates in learning-disabled program or receiving services: 40. Services include: remedial math, remedial English, reading machines, remedial reading, tape recorders, untimed tests, note-taking services, oral tests, learning center, readers, extended time for tests, tutors, texts on tape, typist/scribe, exams on tape or computer. **Library:** Number of titles: 226,752; number of current serial subscriptions: 312. **Information technology resources:** Students are not required to lease or own a computer. Number of campus computers available to all students: 81. School has a wireless network. Approximate number of users that can be accommodated: 256. Proportion of college-owned housing units wired for high-speed internet access: 100%. **Campus safety:** Security services offered: late-night transport/escort service, 24-hour emergency telephones, lighted pathways/sidewalks, controlled dormitory access (key, security card, etc).

TRANSFER AND INTERNATIONAL STUDENTS
Transfer students: May apply for admission for the following academic terms: Fall, Winter, Spring, Summer. Applicants do not need a minimum number of credits to apply. For fall 2005: Transfer applications received: 160. Transfer applicants offered admission: 89. Transfer applicants enrolled: 65. **International students:** Number of foreign undergraduates: 21 (4% of student body). Number of countries represented: 15. Minimum TOEFL score required: 450 (paper); 133 (computer). Average TOEFL score: 531 (paper).

Fairmont State University

- **Address:** 1201 Locust Avenue, Fairmont, W.V 26554
- **Website:** http://www.fairmontstate.edu
- **Public**
- **Enrollment:** 3,831 full-time; 670 part-time

KEY STATS
- ✔ **U.S News College Ranking:** third tier, Comp. Coll.–Bachelor's (South)
- ✔ **SAT or ACT Score (25th/75th percentile):** N/A
- ✔ **Tuition:** 2005-2006: $4,218 in state, $7,524 out of state

Selectivity: Less selective	**Room/board:** N/A
Acceptance rate: 42%	**Average debt:** N/A
Student/faculty ratio: 20/1	**Proportion who borrowed:** N/A

UNDERGRADUATE STUDENT BODY STATS
2005-2006 enrollment: 3,831 full-time; 670 part-time. Men: 45%; women: 55%. **Ethnic makeup:** African American: 3%; Asian American: 1%; Hispanic: 1%; White: 95%.

ADMISSIONS FACTS AND FIGURES
Phone: (304) 367-4892. **Email:** admit@fairmontstate.edu. **Website:** http://www.fairmontstate.edu. **Application deadlines for fall 2007:** Regular decision: Rolling. Early decision: Not offered. Early action: Not offered. Admission can be deferred. **Application fee:** None. Common application is accepted. **To apply online, go to:** http://www.fairmontstate.edu/admissions/undergraduate/applying.asp. **Admissions requirements/recommendations:** High school units required (recommended): English: 4; Mathematics: 3; Science: 3; Foreign language: (2) Social studies: 3; Total units: 11. Tests: The college uses SAT or ACT scores in admissions decisions. Either SAT or ACT required. For admission to the fall 2007 entering class, the school will accept: ACT with writing. Campus visit: Recommended. Admissions interview: Recommended. Off-campus interview: Not available. **Factors that count in admissions decisions:** *Academic:* Secondary school record: Very important. Class rank: Not considered. Letters of recommendation: Considered. Standardized test scores: Very important. Essay: Not considered. *Nonacademic:* Interview: Not considered. Extracurricular activities: Not considered. Talent/ability: Not considered. Character/personal qualities: Not considered. Alumni/ae relationship: Not considered. Geographical residence: Not considered. State residency: Not considered. Religious affiliation/commitment: Not considered. Minority status: Not considered. Volunteer work: Not considered. Work experience: Not considered. **Other schools with the greatest overlap in applicants:** Glenville State College; Marshall University; Shepherd University; West Virginia University; West Virginia Wesleyan College. **Admissions statistics for the fall 2005 entering class:** Total applicants: 3,319. Total accepted: 1,391. Freshmen enrolled: 731; 6% were from out of state. Overall acceptance rate: 42%. **Average high**

school grade point average: 3.1. **First-year students who submitted SAT scores:** 6%. Scores (25/75 percentile): Verbal: N/A, Math: N/A, Combined: N/A. **First-year students submitting ACT scores:** 92%. Scores (25/75 percentile): English: N/A, Math: N/A, Composite: N/A.

ACADEMICS
Year founded: 1865. **Academic calendar:** Semester. **Degrees offered:** associate, bachelor's, master's. **Most popular majors:** 25% business/commerce, 24% education, 9% security and protective services, 7% engineering, 7% psychology. **Major fields of study:** biological and biomedical sciences; business, management, marketing, and related support services; communication, journalism, and related programs; communications technologies/technicians and support services; computer and information sciences and support services; education; engineering technologies/technicians; English language and literature/letters; family and consumer sciences/human sciences; health professions and related clinical sciences; history; mathematics and statistics; multi/interdisciplinary studies; physical sciences; psychology; security and protective services; social sciences; visual and performing arts. **Areas of required coursework:** arts/fine arts, humanities, computer literacy, mathematics, English (including composition), foreign languages, sciences (biological or physical), history, social science. **Pre-professional programs:** pre-law, pre-dentistry, pre-medicine, pre-pharmacy, other. **Special academic programs:** accelerated program, cooperative (work-study plan) program, cross-registration, distance learning, double major, dual enrollment, exchange student program (domestic), honors program, independent study, internships, liberal arts/career combination, student-designed major, study abroad, teacher certificate program, weekend college. **Teacher certification offered in:** special education, elementary, secondary. **Cooperative education programs:** education, health professions. **Reserve Officers Training Corps (ROTC):** Army ROTC: Offered at cooperating institution (West Virginia University); Air Force ROTC: Offered at cooperating institution (West Virginia University). **Faculty and instruction (2005-2006):** Total instructional faculty: 163 full-time, 122 part-time. Full-time faculty with Ph.D. or other terminal degree: 63%. Student/faculty ratio: 20/1. Classes of fewer than 20 students: 59%; of 20 to 49 students: 38%; of 50 or more students: 4%. **Advanced Placement and International Baccalaureate credit:** AP tests may be used for: Credit and/or placement. Scores accepted: 3, 4, 5. International Baccalaureate exams may be used for: Credit and/or placement. **Freshmen returning for sophomore year:** 73%. **Graduation rates:** Four-year: 14%; five-year: 30%; six-year: 40%. **Graduate study:** 40% of students pursue further study immediately upon graduation.

COSTS AND FINANCIAL AID
Financial aid office: (304) 367-4213. **Expenses (2005-2006):** Tuition and fees 2005-2006: $4,218 in state, $7,524 out of state; room/board: N/A. Estimated books and supplies: $1,350; transportation: $1,900. **Financial aid:** Priority filing date for institution's financial aid form: March 1; deadline: March 1.

CAMPUS LIFE AND EXTRACURRICULAR ACTIVITIES
Campus housing available (% using): coed dorms (80%), women's dorms (10%), apartment for single students. Students who live in college-owned, operated, or affiliated housing: 10%. **Student employment:** During the 2005-2006 academic year, 0% of undergraduates worked on campus. Average per-year earnings: $2,500. **Clubs and organizations:** Number of student organizations: 81. Activities include: choral groups, concert band, dance, drama/theater, jazz band, literary magazine, marching band, music ensembles, musical theater, pep band, student government, student newspaper, symphony orchestra, yearbook. Number of fraternities: 5; sororities: 4. Average proportion of students who stay on campus on weekends: 20%. **Sports program (2005-2006):** Member of NCAA II. *Men's intercollegiate varsity sports:* baseball, basketball, cross-country, football, golf, swimming and diving, tennis. *Women's intercollegiate varsity sports:* basketball, cheerleading, cross-country, golf, softball, swimming and diving, tennis, volleyball.

SERVICES AND FACILITIES
Basic services: nonremedial tutoring, placement service, health service. **Remedial assistance:** reading, math, writing, study skills. **Counseling services:** minority student, career, military, personal, veteran student, academic, psychological. **For learning-disabled students:** School does not offer a structured program with separate admission and additional fees. Total undergraduates in learning-disabled program or receiving services: 170. Services include: remedial math, remedial English, reading machines, remedial reading, tape recorders, diagnostic testing service, note-taking services, special bookstore section, oral tests, learning center, readers, extended time for tests, tutors, priority registration, priority seating, proofreading services, typ-

ist/scribe, exams on tape or computer, other testing accomodations. **Library:** Number of titles: 224,122; number of current serial subscriptions: 27,267. **Information technology resources:** Students are not required to lease or own a computer. Number of campus computers available to all students: 850. School has a wireless network. Approximate number of users that can be accommodated: 200. Proportion of college-owned housing units wired for high-speed internet access: 100%. **Campus safety:** Security services offered: 24-hour foot-and-vehicle patrols, late-night transport/escort service, 24-hour emergency telephones, lighted pathways/sidewalks, student patrols, controlled dormitory access (key, security card, etc).

TRANSFER AND INTERNATIONAL STUDENTS

Transfer students: May apply for admission for the following academic terms: Fall, Spring, Summer. Applicants need a minimum number of credits to apply. For fall 2005: Transfer applications received: 782. Transfer applicants offered admission: 550. Transfer applicants enrolled: 318. **International students:** Number of foreign undergraduates: 0. Number of countries represented: 15. Minimum TOEFL score required: 500 (paper); 173 (computer).

Glenville State College

- **Address:** 200 High Street, Glenville, WV 26351
- **Website:** http://www.glenville.edu
- **Public**
- **Enrollment:** 1,128 full-time; 264 part-time

KEY STATS

✔ **U.S News College Ranking:** fourth tier, Comp. Coll.–Bachelor's (South)
✔ **ACT Score (25th/75th percentile):** 16-22
✔ **Tuition:** 2006-2007: $3,900 in state, $9,300 out of state

Selectivity: Less selective	**Room/board:** $5,370
Acceptance rate: 100%	**Average debt:** $16,079
Student/faculty ratio: 26/1	**Proportion who borrowed:** 71%

UNDERGRADUATE STUDENT BODY STATS

2005-2006 enrollment: 1,128 full-time; 264 part-time. Men: 52%; women: 48%. **Ethnic makeup:** African American: 6%; Asian American: 1%; White: 92%.

ADMISSIONS FACTS AND FIGURES

Phone: (304) 462-4128. **Email:** admissions@glenville.edu. **Website:** http://www.glenville.edu. **Application deadlines for fall 2007:** Regular decision: Rolling. Early decision: Not offered. Early action: Not offered. Admission can be deferred. Common application is accepted. **To apply online, go to:** http://www.wvmentor.org/applications/wv_common_app/apply/glenville.html. **Admissions requirements/recommendations:** High school units required (recommended): English: 4; Mathematics: 3; Science: 3; Social studies: 3. Tests: The college uses SAT or ACT scores in admissions decisions. Either SAT or ACT required. For admission to the fall 2007 entering class, the school will accept: ACT with writing. Campus visit: Neither required nor recommended. Admissions interview: Neither required nor recommended. Off-campus interview: May be arranged. **Factors that count in admissions decisions:** *Academic:* Secondary school record: Very important. Class rank: Considered. Letters of recommendation: Not considered. Standardized test scores: Very important. Essay: Not considered. *Nonacademic:* Interview: Not considered. Extracurricular activities: Not considered. Talent/ability: Not considered. Character/personal qualities: Not considered. Alumni/ae relationship: Not considered. Geographical residence: Not considered. State residency: Not considered. Religious affiliation/commitment: Not considered. Minority status: Not considered. Volunteer work: Not considered. Work experience: Not considered. **Admissions statistics for the fall 2005 entering class:** Total applicants: 1,329. Total accepted: 1,329. Freshmen enrolled: 270; Overall acceptance rate: 100%. **Size of waiting list:** 0 applicants; enrolled from waiting list: 0. **Credentials of fall 2005 freshmen:** 10% ranked in the top 10 percent of their high school class; 27% were in the top 25 percent, and 66% were in the top half. (Proportion submitting class standing: 90%.) **Average high school grade point average:** 3.0. **First-year students who submitted SAT scores:** 15%. Scores (25/75 percentile): Verbal: 380-460, Math: 370-500, Combined: 750-960. **First-year students submitting ACT scores:** 85%. Scores (25/75 percentile): English: 15-22, Math: 16-20, Composite: 16-22.

ACADEMICS

Year founded: 1872. **Academic calendar:** Semester. **Degrees offered:** associate, bachelor's. **Most popular majors:** 36% business, management, marketing, and related support services, 25% education, 21% liberal arts and sciences studies, and humanities, 9% health professions and related clinical sciences, 6% natural resources and conservation. **Major fields of study:** biological and biomedical sciences; business, management, marketing, and related support services; education; English language and literature/letters; health professions and related clinical sciences; history; liberal arts and sciences studies, and humanities; multi/interdisciplinary studies; natural resources and conservation; physical sciences; social sciences. **Areas of required coursework:** arts/fine arts, computer literacy, mathematics, English (including composition), sciences (biological or physical), history, social science. **Special academic programs:** accelerated program, cooperative (work-study plan) program, distance learning, double major, English as a Second Language (ESL), honors program, internships, student-designed major, teacher certificate program. **Teacher certification offered in:** early childhood, special education, elementary, middle/junior high, secondary. **Cooperative education programs:** health professions. **Faculty and instruction (2005-2006):** Total instructional faculty: 51 full-time, 29 part-time (58% men; 43% women; 3% minorities). Full-time faculty with Ph.D. or other terminal degree: 51%. Student/faculty ratio: 26/1. Classes of fewer than 20 students: 39%; of 20 to 49 students: 57%; of 50 or more students: 4%. **Advanced Placement and International Baccalaureate credit:** AP tests may be used for: Credit only. Scores accepted: 3, 4, 5. **Freshmen returning for sophomore year:** 58%. **Graduation rates:** Four-year: 12%; five-year: 24%; six-year: 30%.

COSTS AND FINANCIAL AID

Financial aid office: (304) 462-4103. **Expenses (2006-2007):** Tuition and fees 2006-2007: $3,900 in state, $9,300 out of state; room/board: $5,370. Estimated books and supplies: $950; transportation: $1,950; personal expenses: $1,810. **Financial aid:** Priority filing date for institution's financial aid form: February 1. In 2005-2006, 88% of undergraduates applied for financial aid. Of those, 75% were determined to have financial need; 29% had their need fully met. Average financial aid package (proportion receiving): $8,736 (73%). Average amount of gift aid, such as scholarships or grants (proportion receiving): $4,455 (55%). Average amount of self-help aid, such as work study or loans (proportion receiving): $3,705 (53%). Average need-based loan (excluding PLUS or other private loans): $4,087. Among students who received need-based aid, the average percentage of need met: 82%. Among students who received aid based on merit, the average award (and the proportion receiving): $2,387 (8%). The average athletic scholarship (and the proportion receiving): $3,444 (3%). Average amount of debt of borrowers graduating in 2005: $16,079. Proportion who borrowed: 71%.

CAMPUS LIFE AND EXTRACURRICULAR ACTIVITIES

Campus housing available: women's dorms, men's dorms, apartments for married students, apartment for single students, special housing for disabled students. Students who live in college-owned, operated, or affiliated housing: 34%. **Student employment:** During the 2005-2006 academic year, 32% of undergraduates worked on campus. Average per-year earnings: $1,068. **Clubs and organizations:** Number of student organizations: 31. Activities include: choral groups, concert band, drama/theater, jazz band, literary magazine, marching band, music ensembles, pep band, student government, student newspaper. Number of fraternities: 2; sororities: 3. Proportion of men in fraternities: 3%; of women in sororities: 9%. Average proportion of students who stay on campus on weekends: 10%. **Sports program (2005-2006):** Member of NCAA II. **Men's intercollegiate varsity sports:** basketball, cross-country, football, golf, track and field (outdoor). **Women's intercollegiate varsity sports:** basketball, cross-country, golf, softball, track and field (outdoor), volleyball.

SERVICES AND FACILITIES

Basic services: nonremedial tutoring, placement service, health service. **Remedial assistance:** math, writing, study skills. **Counseling services:** career, academic, psychological. **For learning-disabled students:** School does not offer a structured program with separate admission and additional fees. Total undergraduates in learning-disabled program or receiving services: 21. Services include: remedial math, remedial English, reading machines, tape recorders, note-taking services, oral tests, learning center, readers, extended time for tests, tutors, priority seating, proofreading services, texts on tape, other testing accomodations. **Library:** Number of titles: 126,464; number of current serial subscriptions: 13,070. **Information technology resources:**

Students are not required to lease or own a computer. Number of campus computers available to all students: 178. School has a wireless network. Proportion of college-owned housing units wired for high-speed internet access: 100%. **Campus safety:** Security services offered: late-night transport/escort service, 24-hour emergency telephones, lighted pathways/sidewalks, student patrols, controlled dormitory access (key, security card, etc).

TRANSFER AND INTERNATIONAL STUDENTS

Transfer students: May apply for admission for the following academic terms: Fall, Spring, Summer. Applicants do not need a minimum number of credits to apply. For fall 2005: Transfer applications received: 130. Transfer applicants offered admission: 84. Transfer applicants enrolled: 56. **International students:** Number of foreign undergraduates: 0. Number of countries represented: 5. Minimum TOEFL score required: 550 (paper); 213 (computer). Average TOEFL score: 472 (paper).

Marshall University

- **Address:** 1 John Marshall Drive, Huntington, WV 25755
- **Website:** http://www.marshall.edu
- **Public**
- **Enrollment:** 8,190 full-time; 1,651 part-time

KEY STATS

✔ **U.S News College Ranking:** 41, Universities–Master's (South)
✔ **ACT Score (25th/75th percentile):** 20-25
✔ **Tuition:** 2005-2006: $3,932 in state, $10,634 out of state

Selectivity: Selective	**Room/board:** $6,272
Acceptance rate: 82%	**Average debt:** $17,053
Student/faculty ratio: 20/1	**Proportion who borrowed:** 60%

UNDERGRADUATE STUDENT BODY STATS

2005-2006 enrollment: 8,190 full-time; 1,651 part-time. Men: 44%; women: 56%. **Ethnic makeup:** African American: 5%; Asian American: 1%; Hispanic: 1%; White: 92%; International: 1%.

ADMISSIONS FACTS AND FIGURES

Phone: (800) 642-3499. **Email:** admissions@marshall.edu. **Website:** http://www.marshall.edu. **Application deadlines for fall 2007:** Regular decision: Rolling. Early decision: Not offered. Early action: Not offered. Admission can be deferred. **Application fee:** $25. Common application is accepted. **To apply online, go to:** http://www.marshall.edu/www/ugadmiss/ugadmiss.asp. **Admissions requirements/recommendations:** High school units required (recommended): English: 4; Mathematics: 3; Science: 3; Social studies: 3; Total units: 15. Tests: The college uses SAT or ACT scores in admissions decisions. Either SAT or ACT required. For admission to the fall 2007 entering class, the school will accept: ACT with writing, ACT without writing. Campus visit: Recommended. Admissions interview: Neither required nor recommended. Off-campus interview: Not available. **Factors that count in admissions decisions: Academic:** Secondary school record: Very important. Class rank: Not considered. Letters of recommendation: Not considered. Standardized test scores: Very important. Essay: Not considered. *Nonacademic:* Interview: Not considered. Extracurricular activities: Not considered. Talent/ability: Not considered. Character/personal qualities: Not considered. Alumni/ae relationship: Not considered. Geographical residence: Not considered. State residency: Not considered. Religious affiliation/commitment: Not considered. Minority status: Not considered. Volunteer work: Not considered. Work experience: Not considered. **Admissions statistics for the fall 2005 entering class:** Total applicants: 2,412. Total accepted: 1,982. Freshmen enrolled: 1,715; 21% were from out of state. Overall acceptance rate: 82%. **Average high school grade point average:** 3.3. **First-year students who submitted SAT scores:** 30%. Scores (25/75 percentile): Verbal: 460-570, Math: 450-570, Combined: 910-1140. **First-year students submitting ACT scores:** 89%. Scores (25/75 percentile): English: 20-26, Math: 18-24, Composite: 20-25.

ACADEMICS

Year founded: 1837. **Academic calendar:** Semester. **Degrees offered:** associate, bachelor's, post-bachelor's certificate, master's, post-master's certificate, first professional, doctorate. **Most popular majors:** 9% elementary education and teaching, 7% business administration and management, 6% psychology,

6% secondary education and teaching, 5% biology/biological sciences. **Major fields of study:** biological and biomedical sciences; business, management, marketing, and related support services; communication, journalism, and related programs; computer and information sciences and support services; education; engineering technologies/technicians; English language and literature/letters; family and consumer sciences/human sciences; foreign languages, literatures, and linguistics; health professions and related clinical sciences; history; liberal arts and sciences studies, and humanities; mathematics and statistics; multi/interdisciplinary studies; natural resources and conservation; parks, recreation, leisure, and fitness studies; physical sciences; psychology; public administration and social service professions; security and protective services; social sciences; visual and performing arts. **Areas of required coursework:** arts/fine arts, humanities, computer literacy, mathematics, English (including composition), foreign languages, sciences (biological or physical), social science. **Pre-professional programs:** pre-dentistry, pre-medicine, pre-veterinary science, pre-pharmacy, other. **Special academic programs:** accelerated program, cooperative (work-study plan) program, cross-registration, distance learning, double major, English as a Second Language (ESL), exchange student program (domestic), honors program, independent study, internships, study abroad, teacher certificate program. **Teacher certification offered in:** early childhood, special education, elementary, middle/junior high, secondary. **Cooperative education programs:** education, other. **Reserve Officers Training Corps (ROTC):** Army ROTC: Offered on campus. **Faculty and instruction (2005-2006):** Total instructional faculty: 469 full-time, 253 part-time (56% men; 44% women; 10% minorities). Full-time faculty with Ph.D. or other terminal degree: 80%. Student/faculty ratio: 20/1. Classes of fewer than 20 students: 36%; of 20 to 49 students: 59%; of 50 or more students: 4%. **Advanced Placement and International Baccalaureate credit:** AP tests may be used for: Credit and/or placement. Scores accepted: 3, 4, 5. International Baccalaureate exams may be used for: Credit only. **Freshmen returning for sophomore year:** 73%. **Graduation rates:** Four-year: 17%; five-year: 34%; six-year: 39%.

COSTS AND FINANCIAL AID

Financial aid office: (304) 696-3162. **Expenses (2005-2006):** Tuition and fees 2005-2006: $3,932 in state, $10,634 out of state; room/board: $6,272. Estimated books and supplies: $800 personal expenses: $2,453. **Financial aid:** Priority filing date for institution's financial aid form: March 1. In 2005-2006, 68% of undergraduates applied for financial aid. Of those, 50% were determined to have financial need; 42% had their need fully met. Average financial aid package (proportion receiving): $7,230 (49%). Average amount of gift aid, such as scholarships or grants (proportion receiving): $3,992 (31%). Average amount of self-help aid, such as work study or loans (proportion receiving): $4,983 (38%). Average need-based loan (excluding PLUS or other private loans): $4,894. Among students who received need-based aid, the average percentage of need met: 58%. Among students who received aid based on merit, the average award (and the proportion receiving): $5,115 (20%). The average athletic scholarship (and the proportion receiving): $10,165 (4%). Average amount of debt of borrowers graduating in 2005: $17,053. Proportion who borrowed: 60%.

CAMPUS LIFE AND EXTRACURRICULAR ACTIVITIES

Campus housing available: coed dorms, women's dorms, men's dorms, sorority housing, fraternity housing, apartments for married students, special housing for disabled students. **Student employment:** During the 2005-2006 academic year, 3% of undergraduates worked on campus. Average per-year earnings: $2,306. **Clubs and organizations:** Number of student organizations: 155. Activities include: choral groups, concert band, dance, drama/theater, jazz band, literary magazine, marching band, music ensembles, musical theater, opera, pep band, radio station, student government, student newspaper, student film society, symphony orchestra, television station. Number of fraternities: 13; sororities: 8. **Sports program (2005-2006):** Member of NCAA I. *Men's intercollegiate varsity sports:* baseball, basketball, cheerleading, cross-country, football, golf, soccer. *Women's intercollegiate varsity sports:* basketball, cheerleading, cross-country, golf, soccer, softball, swimming and diving, tennis, track and field (indoor), track and field (outdoor), volleyball.

SERVICES AND FACILITIES

Basic services: nonremedial tutoring, women's center, placement service, day care, health service, health insurance. **Remedial assistance:** reading, math, writing, study skills. **Counseling services:** minority student, career, personal, academic, older student, psychological, birth control, religious. **For learning-disabled students:** School does not offer a structured program with separate admission and additional fees. Total undergraduates in learning-disabled program or receiving services: 187. Services include: remedial math, remedial English, remedial reading, tape recorders, diagnostic testing service, untimed tests, note-taking services, oral tests, learning center, readers, extended time for tests, tutors, priority registration, proofreading services, substitution of courses, texts on tape, typist/scribe, waiver of foreign language degree requirement, waiver of math degree requirement, other. **Library:** Number of titles: 1,599,793; number of current serial subscriptions: 20,582. **Information technology resources:** Students are not required to lease or own a computer. Number of campus computers available to all students: 1,854. School has a wireless network. Proportion of college-owned housing units wired for high-speed internet access: 100%. **Campus safety:** Security services offered: 24-hour foot-and-vehicle patrols, late-night transport/escort service, 24-hour emergency telephones, lighted pathways/sidewalks, controlled dormitory access (key, security card, etc).

TRANSFER AND INTERNATIONAL STUDENTS

Transfer students: May apply for admission for the following academic terms: Fall, Spring, Summer. Applicants do not need a minimum number of credits to apply. For fall 2005: Transfer applications received: 704. Transfer applicants offered admission: 650. Transfer applicants enrolled: 533. **International students:** Number of foreign undergraduates: 80 (1% of student body). Number of countries represented: 50. Minimum TOEFL score required: 500 (paper); 173 (computer).

Mountain State University

- **Address:** 609 S. Kanawha Street, Beckley, WV 25802
- **Website:** http://www.mountainstate.edu
- **Private**
- **Enrollment:** 2,954 full-time; 1,024 part-time

KEY STATS

- ✔ **U.S News College Ranking:** fourth tier, Comp. Coll.–Bachelor's (South)
- ✔ **ACT Score (25th/75th percentile):** 16-21
- ✔ **Tuition:** 2006-2007: $7,800

Selectivity: Less selective	**Room/board:** $5,636
Acceptance rate: 100%	**Average debt:** $23,570
Student/faculty ratio: 23/1	**Proportion who borrowed:** 69%

UNDERGRADUATE STUDENT BODY STATS

2005-2006 enrollment: 2,954 full-time; 1,024 part-time. Men: 34%; women: 66%. **Ethnic makeup:** African American: 10%; American-Indian: 1%; Asian American: 1%; Hispanic: 2%; White: 84%; International: 2%.

ADMISSIONS FACTS AND FIGURES

Phone: (304) 929-4636. **Email:** gomsu@mountainstate.edu. **Website:** http://www.mountainstate.edu. **Application deadlines for fall 2007:** Regular decision: Rolling. Early decision: Not offered. Early action: Not offered. Admission can be deferred. **Application fee:** $25. Common application is accepted. **Admissions requirements/recommendations:** High school units required (recommended): English: 4 (4); Mathematics: 2 (2); Science: 2 (2); Foreign language: 0 (0); Social studies: 3 (3); History: 0 (2); Academic electives: 0 (0); Total units: 13 (15). Tests: The college uses SAT or ACT scores in admissions decisions. Neither SAT nor ACT required. For admission to the fall 2007 entering class, the school will accept: ACT with writing, ACT without writing. Campus visit: Recommended. Admissions interview: Recommended. Off-campus interview: May be arranged. **Factors that count in admissions decisions:** *Academic:* Secondary school record: Very important. Class rank: Very important. Letters of recommendation: Very important. Standardized test scores: Very important. Essay: Very important. *Nonacademic:* Interview: Very important. Extracurricular activities: Very important. Talent/ability: Very important. Character/personal qualities: Very important. Alumni/ae relationship: Very important. Geographical residence: Very important. State residency: Very important. Religious affiliation/commitment: Very important. Minority status: Very important. Volunteer work: Very important. Work experience: Very important. **Other schools with the greatest overlap in applicants:** Bluefield State College; Concord University; Marshall University; West Virginia University; West Virginia University Institute of Technology. **Admissions statistics for the fall 2005 entering class:** Total applicants: 1,224. Total accepted: 1,224. Freshmen enrolled: 365; 16% were from out of state. Overall acceptance rate: 100%. **Credentials of fall 2005 freshmen:** 2% ranked in the top 10 percent of their high school class; 13% were in the top 25 percent, and 40% were in the top half. (Proportion

submitting class standing: 35%.) **Average high school grade point average:** 2.8. **First-year students who submitted SAT scores:** 3%. Scores (25/75 percentile): Verbal: 450-520, Math: 420-640, Combined: 870-1160. **First-year students submitting ACT scores:** 27%. Scores (25/75 percentile): English: 15-22, Math: 15-20, Composite: 16-21.

ACADEMICS

Year founded: 1933. **Academic calendar:** Semester. **Degrees offered:** certificate, associate, transfer-associate, terminal-associate, bachelor's, post-bachelor's certificate, master's, post-master's certificate. **Most popular majors:** 43% business, management, marketing, and related support services, 18% health professions and related clinical sciences, 18% security and protective services, 9% multi/interdisciplinary studies, 7% biological and biomedical sciences. **Major fields of study:** business, management, marketing, and related support services; computer and information sciences and support services; health professions and related clinical sciences; legal professions and studies; multi/interdisciplinary studies; parks, recreation, leisure, and fitness studies; personal and culinary services; public administration and social service professions; security and protective services; visual and performing arts. **Areas of required coursework:** arts/fine arts, humanities, computer literacy, mathematics, English (including composition), sciences (biological or physical), social science, other. **Pre-professional programs:** pre-law, pre-medicine. **Special academic programs (% participation):** accelerated program (46.2%), distance learning (54.5%), double major (1.2%), dual enrollment (.002%), English as a Second Language (ESL) (.002%), independent study (69.4%), internships (83.2%), liberal arts/career combination (.002%), student-designed major (10%). **Cooperative education programs:** business, computer science, engineering, health professions, natural science, social/behavioral science, technologies. **Faculty and instruction (2005-2006):** Total instructional faculty: 79 full-time, 237 part-time (44% men; 56% women; 5% minorities). Full-time faculty with Ph.D. or other terminal degree: 34%. Student/faculty ratio: 23/1. Classes of fewer than 20 students: 65%; of 20 to 49 students: 35%; of 50 or more students: 0%. **Advanced Placement and International Baccalaureate credit:** AP tests may be used for: Credit only. Scores accepted: 3. International Baccalaureate exams may be used for: Credit only. **Freshmen returning for sophomore year:** 57%. Graduation rates: Four-year: 13%; five-year: 21%; six-year: 21%. **Graduate study:** 19% of students pursue further study immediately upon graduation; 31% within one year; 10% within five years. Fields in which graduates pursue further study: Master of Business Administration (MBA), 3%; law, 2%; medicine, 2%; education, 9%.

COSTS AND FINANCIAL AID

Financial aid office: (304) 929-1595. **Expenses (2006-2007):** Tuition and fees 2006-2007: $7,800; room/board: $5,636. Estimated books and supplies: $1,300; transportation: $0; personal expenses: $0. **Financial aid:** Priority filing date for institution's financial aid form: March 1. In 2005-2006, 73% of undergraduates applied for financial aid. Of those, 69% were determined to have financial need; Average financial aid package (proportion receiving): $6,280 (69%). Average amount of gift aid, such as scholarships or grants (proportion receiving): $3,878 (50%). Average amount of self-help aid, such as work study or loans (proportion receiving): $3,941 (62%). Average need-based loan (excluding PLUS or other private loans): $3,864. Among students who received need-based aid, the average percentage of need met: 47%. Among students who received aid based on merit, the average award (and the proportion receiving): $4,044 (1%). The average athletic scholarship (and the proportion receiving): $7,899 (1%). Average amount of debt of borrowers graduating in 2005: $23,570. Proportion who borrowed: 69%.

CAMPUS LIFE AND EXTRACURRICULAR ACTIVITIES

Campus housing available (% using): coed dorms (4%), other housing options (96%). Students who live in college-owned, operated, or affiliated housing: 4%. **Student employment:** During the 2005-2006 academic year, 4% of undergraduates worked on campus. Average per-year earnings: $1,751. **Clubs and organizations:** Number of student organizations: 16. Activities include: choral groups, drama/theater, literary magazine, pep band, student government, student newspaper, yearbook. Number of fraternities: 0; sororities: 0. Average proportion of students who stay on campus on weekends: 80%. **Sports program (2005-2006):** Member of NAIA. *Men's intercollegiate varsity sports:* basketball. *Women's intercollegiate varsity sports:* softball, volleyball.

SERVICES AND FACILITIES

Remedial assistance: reading, math, writing, study skills. **Counseling services:** veteran student, academic. **For learning-disabled students:** School does not offer a structured program with separate admission and additional fees.

Total undergraduates in learning-disabled program or receiving services: 21. Services include: remedial math, remedial English, reading machines, remedial reading, tape recorders, videotaped classes, diagnostic testing service, untimed tests, note-taking services, oral tests, learning center, readers, extended time for tests, tutors. **Library:** Number of titles: 95,458; number of current serial subscriptions: 201. **Information technology resources:** Students are not required to lease or own a computer. Number of campus computers available to all students: 167. School has a wireless network. Approximate number of users that can be accommodated: 1,000. Proportion of college-owned housing units wired for high-speed internet access: 100%. **Campus safety:** Security services offered: lighted pathways/sidewalks, student patrols, controlled dormitory access (key, security card, etc.).

TRANSFER AND INTERNATIONAL STUDENTS
Transfer students: May apply for admission for the following academic terms: Fall, Winter, Spring, Summer. Applicants do not need a minimum number of credits to apply. For fall 2005: Transfer applications received: 1,463. Transfer applicants offered admission: 1,463. Transfer applicants enrolled: 757. **International students:** Number of foreign undergraduates: 84 (2% of student body). Number of countries represented: 43. Minimum TOEFL score required: 500 (paper); 173 (computer). Average TOEFL score: 520 (paper).

Ohio Valley University

- **Address:** 1 Campus View Drive, Vienna, WV 26105-8000
- **Website:** http://www.ovu.edu
- **Private; Religious affiliation:** Church of Christ
- **Enrollment:** 506 full-time; 34 part-time

KEY STATS
✔ **U.S News College Ranking:** third tier, Comp. Coll.–Bachelor's (South)
✔ **ACT Score (25th/75th percentile):** 18-24
✔ **Tuition:** 2006-2007: $14,262

Selectivity: Less selective	**Room/board:** $5,860
Acceptance rate: 86%	**Average debt:** $18,741
Student/faculty ratio: 15/1	**Proportion who borrowed:** 94%

UNDERGRADUATE STUDENT BODY STATS
2005-2006 enrollment: 506 full-time; 34 part-time. Men: 47%; women: 53%. **Ethnic makeup:** African American: 4%; American-Indian: 1%; Asian American: 1%; Hispanic: 1%; White: 87%; International: 7%. **Religious preference:** Church of Christ: 60%; Other: 40%.

ADMISSIONS FACTS AND FIGURES
Phone: (877) 446-8668. **Email:** admissions@ovu.edu. **Website:** http://www.ovu.edu. **Application deadlines for fall 2007:** Regular decision: July 31. Early decision: Not offered. Early action: Not offered. Admission can be deferred. **Application fee:** $20. Common application is not accepted. **Admissions requirements/recommendations:** High school units required (recommended): English: (3); Mathematics: (3); Science: (3); Foreign language: (0); Social studies: (2); History: (1); Academic electives: (0); Total units: (12). Tests: The college uses SAT or ACT scores in admissions decisions. Either SAT or ACT required. For admission to the fall 2007 entering class, the school will accept: ACT with writing, ACT without writing. Campus visit: Recommended. Admissions interview: Neither required nor recommended. Off-campus interview: May be arranged. **Factors that count in admissions decisions:** *Academic:* Secondary school record: Very important. Class rank: Important. Letters of recommendation: Considered. Standardized test scores: Very important. Essay: Considered. *Nonacademic:* Interview: Considered. Extracurricular activities: Not considered. Talent/ability: Not considered. Character/personal qualities: Very important. Alumni/ae relationship: Considered. Geographical residence: Not considered. State residency: Not considered. Religious affiliation/commitment: Considered. Minority status: Not considered. Volunteer work: Not considered. Work experience: Not considered. **Other schools with the greatest overlap in applicants:** Freed-Hardeman University; Harding University; Lipscomb University; Marshall University; West Virginia University–Parkersburg. **Admissions statistics for the fall 2005 entering class:** Total applicants: 236. Total accepted: 203. Freshmen enrolled: 89; 26% were from out of state. Overall acceptance rate: 86%. **Size of waiting list:** 0 applicants; enrolled from waiting list: 0. **Credentials of fall 2005 freshmen:** 9% ranked in the top 10 percent of their high school class; 32% were in the top 25 percent, and 58% were in the top half. (Proportion submitting class standing: 79%.) **Average high school grade point average:** 3.3. **First-year students who submitted SAT scores:** 34%. Scores (25/75 percentile): Verbal: 510-590, Math: 490-540, Combined: 1000-1130. **First-year students submitting ACT scores:** 80%. Scores (25/75 percentile): English: 18-24, Math: 17-23, Composite: 18-24.

ACADEMICS
Year founded: 1958. **Academic calendar:** Semester. **Degrees offered:** certificate, associate, bachelor's. **Most popular majors:** 46% business administration and management, 16% psychology, 15% elementary education and teaching, 10% secondary education and teaching, 6% Bible/biblical studies. **Major fields of study:** business, management, marketing, and related support services; education; liberal arts and sciences studies, and humanities; psychology; theology and religious vocations. **Areas of required coursework:** arts/fine arts, humanities, computer literacy, mathematics, English (including composition), sciences (biological or physical), history, social science, other. **Pre-professional programs:** pre-law. **Special academic programs (% participation):** accelerated program, double major (.5%), English as a Second Language (ESL) (0%), independent study, internships (32%), study abroad (20%), teacher certificate program (32%), weekend college. **Teacher certification offered in:** special education, elementary, middle/junior high, secondary. **Faculty and instruction (2005-2006):** Total instructional faculty: 25 full-time, 29 part-time (61% men; 39% women). Full-time faculty with Ph.D. or other terminal degree: 44%. Student/faculty ratio: 15/1. Classes of fewer than 20 students: 78%; of 20 to 49 students: 22%. **Advanced Placement and International Baccalaureate credit:** AP tests may be used for: Credit and/or placement. Scores accepted: 3, 4, 5. International Baccalaureate exams may be used for: Credit only. **Freshmen returning for sophomore year:** 66%. **Graduation rates:** Four-year: 27%; five-year: 40%; six-year: 28%.

COSTS AND FINANCIAL AID
Financial aid office: (304) 865-6075. **Expenses (2006-2007):** Tuition and fees 2006-2007: $14,262; room/board: $5,860. Estimated books and supplies: $1,000; transportation: $1,000; personal expenses: $1,000. **Financial aid:** Priority filing date for institution's financial aid form: March 1. In 2005-2006, 87% of undergraduates applied for financial aid. Of those, 74% were determined to have financial need; 18% had their need fully met. Average financial aid package (proportion receiving): $10,304 (74%). Average amount of gift aid, such as scholarships or grants (proportion receiving): $6,518 (71%). Average amount of self-help aid, such as work study or loans (proportion receiving): $4,615 (64%). Average need-based loan (excluding PLUS or other private loans): $4,230. Among students who received need-based aid, the average percentage of need met: 67%. Among students who received aid based on merit, the average award (and the proportion receiving): $8,660 (23%). The average athletic scholarship (and the proportion receiving): $5,739 (15%). Average amount of debt of borrowers graduating in 2005: $18,741. Proportion who borrowed: 94%.

CAMPUS LIFE AND EXTRACURRICULAR ACTIVITIES
Campus housing available (% using): women's dorms (42%), men's dorms (48%), apartments for married students (10%). Students who live in college-owned, operated, or affiliated housing: 55%. **Clubs and organizations:** Number of student organizations: 2. Activities include: choral groups, concert band, drama/theater, jazz band, literary magazine, music ensembles, musical theater, student government, student newspaper, symphony orchestra. Number of fraternities: 4; sororities: 4. Average proportion of students who stay on campus on weekends: 60%. **Sports program (2005-2006):** Member of NCAA II. *Men's intercollegiate varsity sports:* baseball, basketball, cross-country, golf, soccer. *Women's intercollegiate varsity sports:* basketball, cross-country, soccer, softball, volleyball.

SERVICES AND FACILITIES
Basic services: nonremedial tutoring, women's center, placement service, health service, health insurance. **Remedial assistance:** reading, math, writing, study skills, other. **Counseling services:** minority student, career, personal, academic, older student, psychological, religious. **For learning-disabled students:** School does not offer a structured program with separate admission and additional fees. Total undergraduates in learning-disabled program or receiving services: 8. Services include: remedial math, remedial English, remedial reading, tape recorders, untimed tests, oral tests, learning center, readers, extended time for tests, tutors, priority seating, other testing accomodations. **Library:** Number of titles: 33,988; number

of current serial subscriptions: 142. **Information technology resources:** Students are not required to lease or own a computer. Number of campus computers available to all students: 75. School has a wireless network. Approximate number of users that can be accommodated: 200. Proportion of college-owned housing units wired for high-speed internet access: 97%. **Campus safety:** Security services offered: 24-hour emergency telephones, lighted pathways/sidewalks, controlled dormitory access (key, security card, etc).

TRANSFER AND INTERNATIONAL STUDENTS

Transfer students: May apply for admission for the following academic terms: Fall, Spring. Applicants need a minimum number of credits to apply. For fall 2005: Transfer applications received: 78. Transfer applicants offered admission: 59. Transfer applicants enrolled: 43. **International students:** Number of foreign undergraduates: 33 (7% of student body). Number of countries represented: 8. Minimum TOEFL score required: 500 (paper); 173 (computer). Average TOEFL score: 500 (paper).

Shepherd University

- **Address:** PO Box 3210, Shepherdstown, WV 25443-3210
- **Website:** http://www.shepherd.edu
- **Public**
- **Enrollment:** 2,949 full-time; 860 part-time

KEY STATS

✔ **U.S News College Ranking:** third tier, Comp. Coll.–Bachelor's (South)
✔ **ACT Score (25th/75th percentile):** 19-24
✔ **Tuition:** 2006-2007: $4,400 in state, $11,464 out of state

Selectivity: Selective	**Room/board:** $6,456
Acceptance rate: 93%	**Average debt:** $14,887
Student/faculty ratio: 21/1	**Proportion who borrowed:** 68%

UNDERGRADUATE STUDENT BODY STATS

2005-2006 enrollment: 2,949 full-time; 860 part-time. Men: 43%; women: 57%. **Ethnic makeup:** African American: 5%; Asian American: 1%; Hispanic: 2%; White: 90%; International: 1%.

ADMISSIONS FACTS AND FIGURES

Phone: (304) 876-5212. **Email:** admissions@shepherd.edu. **Website:** http://www.shepherd.edu. **Application deadlines for fall 2007:** Regular decision: Rolling. Early decision: Not offered. Early action: Not offered. Admission can be deferred. **Application fee:** $35. Common application is accepted. **To apply online, go to:** http://www.shepherd.edu/admweb/. **Admissions requirements/recommendations:** High school units required (recommended): English: 4; Mathematics: 3; Science: 3; Foreign language: (2); Social studies: 3; History: 1; Academic electives: 7. Tests: The college uses SAT or ACT scores in admissions decisions. Either SAT or ACT required. For admission to the fall 2007 entering class, the school will accept: ACT with writing. Campus visit: Recommended. Admissions interview: Recommended. Off-campus interview: Not available. **Factors that count in admissions decisions:** *Academic:* Secondary school record: Very important. Class rank: Considered. Letters of recommendation: Considered. Standardized test scores: Very important. Essay: Considered. *Nonacademic:* Interview: Considered. Extracurricular activities: Considered. Talent/ability: Considered. Character/personal qualities: Considered. Alumni/ae relationship: Not considered. Geographical residence: Not considered. State residency: Not considered. Religious affiliation/commitment: Not considered. Minority status: Not considered. Volunteer work: Considered. Work experience: Considered. **Other schools with the greatest overlap in applicants:** Fairmont State University; Marshall University; Shippensburg University of Pennsylvania; Virginia Commonwealth University; West Virginia University. **Admissions statistics for the fall 2005 entering class:** Total applicants: 1,593. Total accepted: 1,485. Freshmen enrolled: 675; 39% were from out of state. Overall acceptance rate: 93%. **Average high school grade point average:** 3.2. **First-year students who submitted SAT scores:** 47%. Scores (25/75 percentile): Verbal: 470-560, Math: 460-550, Combined: 930-1110. **First-year students submitting ACT scores:** 51%. Scores (25/75 percentile): English: 19-25, Math: 17-23, Composite: 19-24.

ACADEMICS

Year founded: 1871. **Academic calendar:** Semester. **Degrees offered:** bachelor's, master's. **Most popular majors:** 16% liberal arts and sciences studies, and humanities, 15% education, 13% business, management, marketing, and related support services, 8% parks, recreation, leisure, and fitness studies, 7% social sciences. **Major fields of study:** biological and biomedical sciences; business, management, marketing, and related support services; communication, journalism, and related programs; computer and information sciences and support services; education; English language and literature/letters; family and consumer sciences/human sciences; health professions and related clinical sciences; history; mathematics and statistics; natural resources and conservation; parks, recreation, leisure, and fitness studies; physical sciences; psychology; public administration and social service professions; social sciences; visual and performing arts. **Areas of required coursework:** arts/fine arts, humanities, computer literacy, mathematics, English (including composition), sciences (biological or physical), history, social science, other. **Special academic programs (% participation):** cooperative (work-study plan) program, distance learning, double major, honors program (6%), independent study, internships, study abroad (5%), teacher certificate program. **Teacher certification offered in:** early childhood, elementary, middle/junior high, secondary. **Cooperative education programs:** art, business, computer science, education, humanities, natural science, social/behavioral science. **Reserve Officers Training Corps (ROTC):** Air Force ROTC: Offered at cooperating institution (University of Maryland, College Park). **Faculty and instruction (2005-2006):** Total instructional faculty: 109 full-time, 144 part-time (57% men; 43% women; 8% minorities). Full-time faculty with Ph.D. or other terminal degree: 83%. Student/faculty ratio: 21/1. Classes of fewer than 20 students: 37%; of 20 to 49 students: 62%; of 50 or more students: 1%. **Advanced Placement and International Baccalaureate credit:** AP tests may be used for: Credit only. Scores accepted: 3, 4, 5. International Baccalaureate exams may be used for: Credit and/or placement. **Freshmen returning for sophomore year:** 68%. **Graduation rates:** Four-year: 16%; five-year: 35%; six-year: 41%. **Graduate study:** 15% of students pursue further study immediately upon graduation. Fields in which graduates pursue further study: Master of Business Administration (MBA), 15%; law, 1%; theology (or the seminary), 1%; education, 13%; arts and sciences, 65%.

COSTS AND FINANCIAL AID

Financial aid office: (304) 876-5470. **Expenses (2006-2007):** Tuition and fees 2006-2007: $4,400 in state, $11,464 out of state; room/board: $6,456. Estimated books and supplies: $850; transportation: $1,100; personal expenses: $2,000. **Financial aid:** Priority filing date for institution's financial aid form: March 1. In 2005-2006, 80% of undergraduates applied for financial aid. Of those, 50% were determined to have financial need; 19% had their need fully met. Average financial aid package (proportion receiving): $8,674 (48%). Average amount of gift aid, such as scholarships or grants (proportion receiving): $3,529 (25%). Average amount of self-help aid, such as work study or loans (proportion receiving): $3,687 (38%). Average need-based loan (excluding PLUS or other private loans): $3,584. Among students who received need-based aid, the average percentage of need met: 74%. Among students who received aid based on merit, the average award (and the proportion receiving): $7,458 (20%). The average athletic scholarship (and the proportion receiving): $5,170 (5%). Average amount of debt of borrowers graduating in 2005: $14,887. Proportion who borrowed: 68%.

CAMPUS LIFE AND EXTRACURRICULAR ACTIVITIES

Campus housing available (% using): coed dorms (72%), other housing options (28%). Students who live in college-owned, operated, or affiliated housing: 27%. **Student employment:** During the 2005-2006 academic year, 8% of undergraduates worked on campus. Average per-year earnings: $2,152. **Clubs and organizations:** Number of student organizations: 70. Activities include: choral groups, concert band, dance, drama/theater, jazz band, literary magazine, marching band, music ensembles, musical theater, pep band, radio station, student government, student newspaper, student film society, symphony orchestra. Number of fraternities: 4; sororities: 3. Proportion of men in fraternities: 6%; of women in sororities: 5%. Average proportion of students who stay on campus on weekends: 33%. **Sports program (2005-2006):** Member of NCAA II. *Men's intercollegiate varsity sports:* baseball, basketball, cross-country, football, golf, soccer, tennis. *Women's intercollegiate varsity sports:* basketball, cross-country, soccer, softball, tennis, volleyball.

SERVICES AND FACILITIES

Basic services: health service, other. **Remedial assistance:** reading, math, writing, study skills, other. **Counseling services:** minority student, career, military, personal, veteran student, academic, older student, psychological, birth control. **For learning-disabled students:** School does not offer a structured program with separate admission and additional fees. Total undergraduates in learning-disabled program or receiving services: 60. Services include: tape recorders, untimed tests, note-taking services, oral tests, readers, extended time for tests, tutors, priority registration, priority seating, texts on tape, other. **Library:** Number of titles: 189,055; number of current serial subscriptions: 539. **Information technology resources:** Students are not required to lease or own a computer. Number of campus computers available to all students: 350. School does not have a wireless network. Proportion of college-owned housing units wired for high-speed internet access: 100%. **Campus safety:** Security services offered: 24-hour foot-and-vehicle patrols, late-night transport/escort service, 24-hour emergency telephones, lighted pathways/sidewalks, controlled dormitory access (key, security card, etc).

TRANSFER AND INTERNATIONAL STUDENTS

Transfer students: May apply for admission for the following academic terms: Fall, Spring, Summer. Applicants need a minimum number of credits to apply. For fall 2005: Transfer applications received: 551. Transfer applicants offered admission: 537. Transfer applicants enrolled: 351. **International students:** Number of foreign undergraduates: 23 (1% of student body). Number of countries represented: 22. Minimum TOEFL score required: 550 (paper); 213 (computer).

University of Charleston

- **Address:** 2300 MacCorkle Avenue SE, Charleston, WV 25304
- **Website:** http://www.ucwv.edu
- **Private**
- **Enrollment:** 852 full-time; 135 part-time

KEY STATS

✔ **U.S News College Ranking:** 21, Comp. Coll.–Bachelor's (South)
✔ **ACT Score (25th/75th percentile):** 19-25
✔ **Tuition:** 2006-2007: $21,000

Selectivity: Selective	Room/board: $7,600
Acceptance rate: 64%	Average debt: $22,500
Student/faculty ratio: 13/1	Proportion who borrowed: 80%

UNDERGRADUATE STUDENT BODY STATS

2005-2006 enrollment: 852 full-time; 135 part-time. Men: 40%; women: 60%. **Ethnic makeup:** African American: 6%; Asian American: 1%; Hispanic: 1%; White: 84%; International: 9%.

ADMISSIONS FACTS AND FIGURES

Phone: (800) 995-4682. **Email:** admissions@ucwv.edu. **Website:** http://www.ucwv.edu. **Application deadlines for fall 2007:** Regular decision: Rolling. Early decision: Not offered. Early action: Not offered. Admission can be deferred. **Application fee:** $25. Common application is accepted. **To apply online, go to:** http://www.ucwv.edu/admissions/online_application.aspx. **Admissions requirements/recommendations:** High school units required (recommended): English: (4); Mathematics: (3); Science: (3); Foreign language: (1); Social studies: (3); History: (2); Total units: (16). Tests: The college uses SAT or ACT scores in admissions decisions. Neither SAT nor ACT required. For admission to the fall 2007 entering class, the school will accept: ACT with writing, ACT without writing. Campus visit: Recommended. Admissions interview: Recommended. Off-campus interview: May be arranged. **Factors that count in admissions decisions:** *Academic:* Secondary school record: Important. Class rank: Considered. Letters of recommendation: Considered. Standardized test scores: Very important. Essay: Considered. *Nonacademic:* Interview: Considered. Extracurricular activities: Important. Talent/ability: Considered. Character/personal qualities: Important. Alumni/ae relationship: Not considered. Geographical residence: Not considered. State residency: Not considered. Religious affiliation/commitment: Not considered. Minority status: Not considered. Volunteer work: Considered. Work experience: Considered. **Other schools with the greatest overlap in applicants:** Elon University; Marshall University; Wesleyan University; West Virginia University. **Admissions statistics for the fall 2005 entering class:** Total applicants: 1,262. Total accepted: 802. Freshmen enrolled: 287; 38% were from out of state. Overall acceptance rate: 64%. **Credentials of fall 2005 freshmen:**

25% ranked in the top 10 percent of their high school class; 50% were in the top 25 percent, and 77% were in the top half. (Proportion submitting class standing: 59%.) **Average high school grade point average:** 3.4. **First-year students who submitted SAT scores:** 46%. Scores (25/75 percentile): Verbal: 430-530, Math: 420-540, Combined: 850-1070. **First-year students submitting ACT scores:** 68%. Scores (25/75 percentile): English: 18-25, Math: 17-24, Composite: 19-25.

ACADEMICS

Year founded: 1888. **Academic calendar:** Semester. **Degrees offered:** associate, terminal-associate, bachelor's, master's. **Most popular majors:** 26% nursing/registered nurse training (R.N., A.S.N., B.S.N., M.S.N.), 18% business administration and management, 11% elementary education and teaching, 9% acting, 7% communication, journalism, and related programs. **Major fields of study:** biological and biomedical sciences; business, management, marketing, and related support services; computer and information sciences and support services; education; English language and literature/letters; health professions and related clinical sciences; history; liberal arts and sciences studies, and humanities; natural resources and conservation; parks, recreation, leisure, and fitness studies; physical sciences; psychology; social sciences; visual and performing arts. **Areas of required coursework:** humanities, computer literacy, mathematics, English (including composition), sciences (biological or physical), history, social science, other. **Pre-professional programs:** pre-pharmacy, other. **Special academic programs:** accelerated program, cooperative (work-study plan) program, distance learning, double major, dual enrollment, independent study, internships, liberal arts/career combination, student-designed major, study abroad, teacher certificate program. **Teacher certification offered in:** elementary, middle/junior high, secondary. **Reserve Officers Training Corps (ROTC):** Army ROTC: Offered at cooperating institution (West Virginia State College). **Faculty and instruction (2005-2006):** Total instructional faculty: 60 full-time, 39 part-time (53% men; 47% women; 8% minorities). Full-time faculty with Ph.D. or other terminal degree: 43%. Student/faculty ratio: 13/1. Classes of fewer than 20 students: 69%; of 20 to 49 students: 30%; of 50 or more students: 2%. **Advanced Placement and International Baccalaureate credit:** AP tests may be used for: Credit only. Scores accepted: 3, 4, 5. **Freshmen returning for sophomore year:** 65%. **Graduation rates:** Four-year: 31%; five-year: 43%; six-year: 43%.

COSTS AND FINANCIAL AID

Financial aid office: (304) 357-4759. **Expenses (2006-2007):** Tuition and fees 2006-2007: $21,000; room/board: $7,600. Estimated books and supplies: $1,000; transportation: $750; personal expenses: $250. **Financial aid:** Priority filing date for institution's financial aid form: March 1; deadline: August 15. In 2005-2006, 82% of undergraduates applied for financial aid. Of those, 72% were determined to have financial need; 67% had their need fully met. Average financial aid package (proportion receiving): $19,575 (72%). Average amount of gift aid, such as scholarships or grants (proportion receiving): $3,550 (50%). Average amount of self-help aid, such as work study or loans (proportion receiving): $4,245 (71%). Average need-based loan (excluding PLUS or other private loans): $8,500. Among students who received need-based aid, the average percentage of need met: 68%. Among students who received aid based on merit, the average award (and the proportion receiving): $3,850 (13%). The average athletic scholarship (and the proportion receiving): $8,570 (10%). Average amount of debt of borrowers graduating in 2005: $22,500. Proportion who borrowed: 80%.

CAMPUS LIFE AND EXTRACURRICULAR ACTIVITIES

Campus housing available: coed dorms, other housing options. Students who live in college-owned, operated, or affiliated housing: 48%. **Student employment:** During the 2005-2006 academic year, 19% of undergraduates worked on campus. Average per-year earnings: $500. **Clubs and organizations:** Number of student organizations: 42. Activities include: choral groups, drama/theater, music ensembles, musical theater, pep band, radio station, student government, student newspaper. Number of fraternities: 2; sororities: 2. Average proportion of students who stay on campus on weekends: 70%. **Sports program (2005-2006):** Member of NCAA II. *Men's intercollegiate varsity sports:* baseball, basketball, cross-country, football, golf, soccer, swimming and diving, tennis, track and field (outdoor). *Women's intercollegiate varsity sports:* basketball, cross-country, soccer, softball, swimming and diving, tennis, track and field (outdoor), volleyball, rowing.

SERVICES AND FACILITIES

Basic services: nonremedial tutoring, placement service. **Remedial assistance:** reading, math, writing, study skills. **Counseling services:** career, personal, academic, psychological. **For learning-disabled students:** School does not offer a structured program with separate admission and additional fees. Total undergraduates in learning-disabled program or receiving services: 15. Services include: remedial English, reading machines, remedial reading, tape recorders, other special classes, untimed tests, note-taking services, oral tests, learning center, readers, extended time for tests, tutors, priority seating, texts on tape, other. **Library:** Number of titles: 120,000; number of current serial subscriptions: 308. **Information technology resources:** Students are not required to lease or own a computer. Number of campus computers available to all students: 220. School has a wireless network. Proportion of college-owned housing units wired for high-speed internet access: 100%. **Campus safety:** Security services offered: 24-hour foot-and-vehicle patrols, late-night transport/escort service, 24-hour emergency telephones, lighted pathways/sidewalks, controlled dormitory access (key, security card, etc).

TRANSFER AND INTERNATIONAL STUDENTS
Transfer students: May apply for admission for the following academic terms: Fall, Spring, Summer. Applicants need a minimum number of credits to apply. For fall 2005: Transfer applications received: 287. Transfer applicants offered admission: 197. Transfer applicants enrolled: 90. **International students:** Number of foreign undergraduates: 78 (9% of student body). Number of countries represented: 10. Minimum TOEFL score required: 500 (paper); 173 (computer).

West Liberty State College

- ■ **Address:** Route 88, PO Box 295, West Liberty, WV 26074-0295
- ■ **Website:** http://www.wlsc.edu
- ■ **Public**
- ■ **Enrollment:** 1,974 full-time; 267 part-time

KEY STATS
✔ **U.S News College Ranking:** third tier, Comp. Coll.–Bachelor's (South)
✔ **ACT Score (25th/75th percentile):** 17-22
✔ **Tuition:** 2005-2006: $3,686 in state, $9,054 out of state

Selectivity: Less selective	Room/board: $5,006
Acceptance rate: 81%	Average debt: N/A
Student/faculty ratio: 17/1	Proportion who borrowed: N/A

UNDERGRADUATE STUDENT BODY STATS
2005-2006 enrollment: 1,974 full-time; 267 part-time. Men: 43%; women: 57%. **Ethnic makeup:** African American: 3%; Hispanic: 1%; White: 96%.

ADMISSIONS FACTS AND FIGURES
Phone: (304) 336-8076. **Email:** wladmsn1@wlsc.edu. **Website:** http://www.wlsc.edu. **Application deadlines for fall 2007:** Regular decision: January 9. Early decision: Not offered. Early action: Not offered. Admission cannot be deferred. Common application is not accepted. **Admissions requirements/recommendations:** High school units required (recommended): English: 4; Mathematics: 2; Science: 2; Foreign language: (2); Social studies: 2; History: 1. Tests: The college uses SAT or ACT scores in admissions decisions. Either SAT or ACT required. For admission to the fall 2007 entering class, the school will accept: ACT with writing. Campus visit: Recommended. Admissions interview: Neither required nor recommended. **Factors that count in admissions decisions:** *Academic:* Secondary school record: Very important. Class rank: Not considered. Letters of recommendation: Not considered. Standardized test scores: Very important. Essay: Not considered. *Nonacademic:* Interview: Not considered. Extracurricular activities: Not considered. Talent/ability: Not considered. Character/personal qualities: Not considered. Alumni/ae relationship: Not considered. Geographical residence: Not considered. State residency: Not considered. Religious affiliation/commitment: Not considered. Minority status: Not considered. Volunteer work: Not considered. Work experience: Not considered. **Other schools with the greatest overlap in applicants:** Bethany College; Fairmont State University; Ohio University; West Virginia University; Wheeling Jesuit University. **Admissions statistics for the fall 2005 entering class:** Total applicants: 1,379. Total accepted: 1,113. Freshmen enrolled: 421; Overall acceptance rate: 81%. **Credentials of fall 2005 freshmen:** 6% ranked in the top 10 percent of their high school class; 33% were in the top 25 percent, and 58% were in the top half. (Proportion submitting class standing: 93%.) **Average high school grade point average:** 3.1. **First-year students who submitted SAT scores:** 11%. Scores (25/75 percentile): Verbal: 410-490,

Math: 390-520, Combined: 800-1010. **First-year students submitting ACT scores:** 85%. Scores (25/75 percentile): English: 16-23, Math: 16-21, Composite: 17-22.

ACADEMICS
Year founded: 1837. **Academic calendar:** Semester. **Degrees offered:** associate, bachelor's. **Most popular majors:** 25% business, management, marketing, and related support services, 25% education, 13% health professions and related clinical sciences, 9% liberal arts and sciences studies, and humanities, 8% security and protective services. **Major fields of study:** biological and biomedical sciences; business, management, marketing, and related support services; communication, journalism, and related programs; education; engineering technologies/technicians; English language and literature/letters; health professions and related clinical sciences; history; liberal arts and sciences studies, and humanities; mathematics and statistics; multi/inter-disciplinary studies; physical sciences; psychology; security and protective services; social sciences; visual and performing arts. **Areas of required coursework:** arts/fine arts, humanities, computer literacy, mathematics, English (including composition), philosophy, sciences (biological or physical), history, social science. **Pre-professional programs:** pre-law, pre-dentistry, pre-medicine, pre-veterinary science, pre-optometry, pre-pharmacy. **Special academic programs:** accelerated program, distance learning, double major, dual enrollment, honors program, independent study, internships, liberal arts/career combination, student-designed major, teacher certificate program, weekend college. **Teacher certification offered in:** early childhood, special education, elementary, middle/junior high, secondary. **Faculty and instruction (2005-2006):** Total instructional faculty: 100 full-time, 61 part-time (52% men; 48% women; 7% minorities). Full-time faculty with Ph.D. or other terminal degree: 56%. Student/faculty ratio: 17/1. Classes of fewer than 20 students: 56%; of 20 to 49 students: 44%; of 50 or more students: 0%. **Advanced Placement and International Baccalaureate credit:** AP tests may be used for: Credit only. **Freshmen returning for sophomore year:** 67%. **Graduation rates:** Six-year: 42%.

COSTS AND FINANCIAL AID
Financial aid office: (304) 336-8016. **Expenses (2005-2006):** Tuition and fees 2005-2006: $3,686 in state, $9,054 out of state; room/board: $5,006. Estimated books and supplies: $1,000. **Financial aid:** Priority filing date for institution's financial aid form: March 1.

CAMPUS LIFE AND EXTRACURRICULAR ACTIVITIES
Campus housing available: coed dorms, women's dorms, men's dorms, apartments for married students, apartment for single students, special housing for disabled students. **Clubs and organizations:** Number of student organizations: 23. Activities include: choral groups, concert band, drama/theater, jazz band, literary magazine, marching band, music ensembles, musical theater, pep band, radio station, student government, student newspaper, television station. Number of fraternities: 4; sororities: 10. Average proportion of students who stay on campus on weekends: 20%. **Sports program (2005-2006):** Member of NCAA II. *Men's intercollegiate varsity sports:* baseball, basketball, cross-country, football, golf, tennis, track and field (outdoor), wrestling. *Women's intercollegiate varsity sports:* basketball, cross-country, golf, softball, tennis, track and field (outdoor), volleyball.

SERVICES AND FACILITIES
Basic services: placement service, health service. **Remedial assistance:** math, writing. **Counseling services:** career, personal, veteran student. **For learning-disabled students:** School does not offer a structured program with separate admission and additional fees. Total undergraduates in learning-disabled program or receiving services: 14. Services include: remedial math, remedial English, tape recorders, untimed tests, note-taking services, oral tests, learning center, readers, extended time for tests, tutors, priority registration, priority seating, texts on tape. **Library:** Number of titles: 193,538; number of current serial subscriptions: 420. **Information technology resources:** Students are not required to lease or own a computer. Number of campus computers available to all students: 400. School has a wireless network. Approximate number of users that can be accommodated: 200. Proportion of college-owned housing units wired for high-speed internet access: 90%. **Campus safety:** Security services offered: 24-hour foot-and-vehicle patrols, 24-hour emergency telephones, lighted pathways/sidewalks, controlled dormitory access (key, security card, etc).

TRANSFER AND INTERNATIONAL STUDENTS
Transfer students: May apply for admission for the following academic terms: Fall, Spring. Applicants do not need a minimum number of credits to apply. For fall 2005: Transfer applications received: 549. Transfer appli-

cants offered admission: 398. Transfer applicants enrolled: 247.
International students: Number of foreign undergraduates: 10. Number of countries represented: 9. Minimum TOEFL score required: 500 (paper); 173 (computer).

West Virginia State University

■ **Address:** PO Box 1000, Institute, WV 25112
■ **Website:** http://www.wvstateu.edu
■ **Public**
■ **Enrollment:** 2,396 full-time; 1,059 part-time

KEY STATS
✔ **U.S News College Ranking:** third tier, Comp. Coll.–Bachelor's (South)
✔ **ACT Score :** 18
✔ **Tuition:** 2006-2007: $3,776 in state, $8,874 out of state
  Selectivity: Less selective   **Room/board:** $5,300
  Acceptance rate: 50%   **Average debt:** N/A
  Student/faculty ratio: 19/1   **Proportion who borrowed:** N/A

UNDERGRADUATE STUDENT BODY STATS
2005-2006 enrollment: 2,396 full-time; 1,059 part-time. Men: 41%; women: 59%.

ADMISSIONS FACTS AND FIGURES
Phone: (304) 766-3221. **Email:** go2wvu@mail.wvu.edu. **Website:** http://www.wvstateu.edu. **Application deadlines for fall 2007:** Regular decision: August 10. Early decision: Not offered. Early action: Not offered. **Admissions requirements/recommendations:** Tests: The college uses SAT or ACT scores in admissions decisions. ACT required. **Admissions statistics for the fall 2005 entering class:** Total applicants: 862. Total accepted: 428. Freshmen enrolled: 363; Overall acceptance rate: 50%. **First-year students who submitted SAT scores:** 11%. Scores (25/75 percentile): Verbal: N/A, Math: N/A, Combined: N/A. **First-year students submitting ACT scores:** 85%. Scores (25/75 percentile): English: N/A, Math: N/A, Composite: N/A.

ACADEMICS
Year founded: 1891. **Academic calendar:** Semester. **Degrees offered:** certificate, bachelor's, master's. **Most popular majors:** Information not available. **Major fields of study:** biological and biomedical sciences; business, management, marketing, and related support services; communication, journalism, and related programs; education; English language and literature/letters; health professions and related clinical sciences; history; mathematics and statistics; parks, recreation, leisure, and fitness studies; physical sciences; psychology; public administration and social service professions; security and protective services; social sciences; visual and performing arts. **Reserve Officers Training Corps (ROTC):** Army ROTC: Offered on campus. **Faculty and instruction (2005-2006):** Total instructional faculty: 120 full-time, 74 part-time (53% men; 47% women; 21% minorities). Full-time faculty with Ph.D. or other terminal degree: 64%. Student/faculty ratio: 19/1. **Freshmen returning for sophomore year:** 58%. **Graduation rates:** Four-year: 8%; five-year: 18%; six-year: 25%.

COSTS AND FINANCIAL AID
Financial aid office: (304) 766-3131. **Expenses (2006-2007):** Tuition and fees 2006-2007: $3,776 in state, $8,874 out of state; room/board: $5,300.

CAMPUS LIFE AND EXTRACURRICULAR ACTIVITIES
Sports program (2005-2006): Member of NCAA II. *Men's intercollegiate varsity sports:* baseball, basketball, football, tennis, track and field (outdoor). *Women's intercollegiate varsity sports:* basketball, golf, softball, tennis, volleyball.

West Virginia University

■ **Address:** PO Box 6201, Morgantown, WV 26506-6201
■ **Website:** http://www.wvu.edu
■ **Public**
■ **Enrollment:** 18,449 full-time; 1,061 part-time

KEY STATS
✔ **U.S News College Ranking:** third tier, National Universities
✔ **SAT Score (25th/75th percentile):** 950-1140
✔ **Tuition:** 2006-2007: $4,476 in state, $13,840 out of state
  Selectivity: Selective   **Room/board:** $6,422
  Acceptance rate: 92%   **Average debt:** $13,798
  Student/faculty ratio: 22/1   **Proportion who borrowed:** 62%

UNDERGRADUATE STUDENT BODY STATS
2005-2006 enrollment: 18,449 full-time; 1,061 part-time. Men: 54%; women: 46%. **Ethnic makeup:** African American: 4%; Asian American: 2%; Hispanic: 2%; White: 91%; International: 2%.

ADMISSIONS FACTS AND FIGURES
Phone: (800) 344-9881. **Email:** wvuadmissions@arc.wvu.edu. **Website:** http://www.wvu.edu. **Application deadlines for fall 2007:** Regular decision: August 1. Early decision: Not offered. Early action: Not offered. Admission can be deferred. **Application fee:** $25. Common application is accepted. **To apply online, go to:** http://www.arc.wvu.edu/admissions/applications.html. **Admissions requirements/recommendations:** High school units required (recommended): English: 4; Mathematics: 3; Science: 3; Foreign language: (2); Social studies: 3; Total units: 13 (2). Tests: The college uses SAT or ACT scores in admissions decisions. Either SAT or ACT required. For admission to the fall 2007 entering class, the school will accept ACT with writing. Campus visit: Recommended. Admissions interview: Neither required nor recommended. Off-campus interview: Not available. **Factors that count in admissions decisions:** *Academic:* Secondary school record: Very important. Class rank: Not considered. Letters of recommendation: Considered. Standardized test scores: Very important. Essay: Not considered. *Nonacademic:* Interview: Not considered. Extracurricular activities: Considered. Talent/ability: Not considered. Character/personal qualities: Not considered. Alumni/ae relationship: Not considered. Geographical residence: Not considered. State residency: Important. Religious affiliation/commitment: Not considered. Minority status: Not considered. Volunteer work: Considered. Work experience: Not considered. **Other schools with the greatest overlap in applicants:** Ohio State University–Columbus; Pennsylvania State University–University Park; Rutgers–New Brunswick; University of Pittsburgh; Virginia Tech. **Admissions statistics for the fall 2005 entering class:** Total applicants: 10,957. Total accepted: 10,110. Freshmen enrolled: 4,574; 49% were from out of state. Overall acceptance rate: 92%. **Credentials of fall 2005 freshmen:** 18% ranked in the top 10 percent of their high school class; 43% were in the top 25 percent, and 74% were in the top half. (Proportion submitting class standing: 71%.) **Average high school grade point average:** 3.3. **First-year students who submitted SAT scores:** 51%. Scores (25/75 percentile): Verbal: 470-560, Math: 480-580, Combined: 950-1140. **First-year students submitting ACT scores:** 49%. Scores (25/75 percentile): English: 20-26, Math: 18-25, Composite: 20-26.

ACADEMICS
Year founded: 1867. **Academic calendar:** Semester. **Degrees offered:** bachelor's, master's, first professional, doctorate. **Most popular majors:** 12% business, management, marketing, and related support services, 11% liberal arts and sciences studies, and humanities, 10% communication, journalism, and related programs, 9% engineering, 8% social sciences. **Major fields of study:** agriculture, agriculture operations, and related sciences; architecture and related services; biological and biomedical sciences; business, management, marketing, and related support services; communication, journalism, and related programs; computer and information sciences and support services; education; engineering; English language and literature/letters; family and consumer sciences/human sciences; foreign languages, literatures, and linguistics; health professions and related clinical sciences; history; liberal arts and sciences studies, and humanities; mathematics and statistics; multi/interdisciplinary studies; natural resources and conservation; parks, recreation, leisure, and fitness studies; philosophy and religious studies; physical sciences; psychology; public administration and social service pro-

fessions; security and protective services; social sciences; visual and performing arts. **Areas of required coursework:** humanities, mathematics, English (including composition), sciences (biological or physical), social science. **Pre-professional programs:** pre-pharmacy. **Special academic programs:** accelerated program, cooperative (work-study plan) program, distance learning, double major, English as a Second Language (ESL), exchange student program (domestic), external degree program, honors program, independent study, internships, student-designed major, study abroad, teacher certificate program, weekend college. **Teacher certification offered in:** early childhood, special education, elementary, middle/junior high, secondary. **Cooperative education programs:** engineering. **Reserve Officers Training Corps (ROTC):** Army ROTC: Offered on campus; Air Force ROTC: Offered on campus. **Faculty and instruction (2005-2006):** Total instructional faculty: 785 full-time, 337 part-time (60% men; 40% women; 9% minorities). Full-time faculty with Ph.D. or other terminal degree: 82%. Student/faculty ratio: 22/1. Classes of fewer than 20 students: 34%; of 20 to 49 students: 48%; of 50 or more students: 18%. **Advanced Placement and International Baccalaureate credit:** AP tests may be used for: Credit and/or placement. Scores accepted: 3, 4, 5. International Baccalaureate exams may be used for: Credit only. **Freshmen returning for sophomore year:** 79%. **Graduation rates:** Four-year: 26%; five-year: 48%; six-year: 55%. **Graduate study:** 8% of students pursue further study immediately upon graduation; 10% within one year; 14% within five years. Fields in which graduates pursue further study: Master of Business Administration (MBA), 1%; law, 2%; education, 1%; arts and sciences, 1%.

COSTS AND FINANCIAL AID
Financial aid office: (800) 344-9881. **Expenses (2006-2007):** Tuition and fees 2006-2007: $4,476 in state, $13,840 out of state; room/board: $6,422. Estimated books and supplies: $900; transportation: $1,126; personal expenses: $1,316. **Financial aid:** In 2005-2006, 72% of undergraduates applied for financial aid. Of those, 54% were determined to have financial need; 24% had their need fully met. Average financial aid package (proportion receiving): $7,011 (50%). Average amount of gift aid, such as scholarships or grants (proportion receiving): $3,225 (35%). Average amount of self-help aid, such as work study or loans (proportion receiving): $4,181 (41%). Average need-based loan (excluding PLUS or other private loans): $4,034. Among students who received need-based aid, the average percentage of need met: 88%. Among students who received aid based on merit, the average award (and the proportion receiving): $3,036 (37%). The average athletic scholarship (and the proportion receiving): $13,573 (2%). Average amount of debt of borrowers graduating in 2005: $13,798. Proportion who borrowed: 62%.

CAMPUS LIFE AND EXTRACURRICULAR ACTIVITIES
Campus housing available: coed dorms, women's dorms, men's dorms, sorority housing, fraternity housing, apartments for married students, apartment for single students, special housing for disabled students, special housing for international students, other housing options. Students who live in college-owned, operated, or affiliated housing: 27%. **Student employment:** During the 2005-2006 academic year, 17% of undergraduates worked on campus. Average per-year earnings: $2,045. **Clubs and organizations:** Number of student organizations: 300. Activities include: choral groups, concert band, dance, drama/theater, jazz band, literary magazine, marching band, music ensembles, musical theater, pep band, radio station, student government, student newspaper, symphony orchestra, television station, yearbook. Number of fraternities: 14; sororities: 13. Proportion of men in fraternities: 9%; of women in sororities: 10%. **Sports program (2005-2006):** Member of NCAA I. *Men's intercollegiate varsity sports:* baseball, basketball, football, riflery, soccer, swimming and diving, wrestling. *Women's intercollegiate varsity sports:* basketball, crew, cross-country, gymnastics, riflery, soccer, swimming and diving, tennis, track and field (indoor), track and field (outdoor), volleyball.

SERVICES AND FACILITIES
Basic services: nonremedial tutoring, women's center, placement service, health service, health insurance. **Remedial assistance:** reading, math, writing, study skills. **Counseling services:** minority student, career, military, personal, veteran student, academic, older student, psychological, birth control, religious. **For learning-disabled students:** School does not offer a structured program with separate admission and additional fees. Total undergraduates in learning-disabled program or receiving services: 600. Services include: reading machines, tape recorders, diagnostic testing service, untimed tests, note-taking services, oral tests, learning center, extended time for tests, tutors. **Library:** Number of titles: 1,525,163; number of current serial subscriptions: 31,150. **Information technology resources:** Students are not

required to lease or own a computer. Number of campus computers available to all students: 3,500. School has a wireless network. Approximate number of users that can be accommodated: 7,100. Proportion of college-owned housing units wired for high-speed internet access: 100%. **Campus safety:** Security services offered: 24-hour foot-and-vehicle patrols, late-night transport/escort service, 24-hour emergency telephones, lighted pathways/sidewalks, controlled dormitory access (key, security card, etc).

TRANSFER AND INTERNATIONAL STUDENTS
Transfer students: May apply for admission for the following academic terms: Fall, Spring, Summer. Applicants need a minimum number of credits to apply. For fall 2005: Transfer applications received: 1,956. Transfer applicants offered admission: 1,430. Transfer applicants enrolled: 897. **International students:** Number of foreign undergraduates: 306 (2% of student body). Number of countries represented: 67. Minimum TOEFL score required: 550 (paper); 213 (computer).

West Virginia University Institute of Tech.

- **Address:** 405 Fayette Pike, Montgomery, WV 25136
- **Website:** http://www.wvutech.edu
- **Public**
- **Enrollment:** 1,015 full-time; 500 part-time

KEY STATS
✔ **U.S News College Ranking:** third tier, Comp. Coll.–Bachelor's (South)
✔ **ACT Score (25th/75th percentile):** 17-24
✔ **Tuition:** N/A

Selectivity: Selective	**Room/board:** N/A
Acceptance rate: 65%	**Average debt:** N/A
Student/faculty ratio: 14/1	**Proportion who borrowed:** N/A

UNDERGRADUATE STUDENT BODY STATS
2005-2006 enrollment: 1,015 full-time; 500 part-time. Men: 58%; women: 42%. **Ethnic makeup:** African American: 8%; Asian American: 1%; White: 88%; International: 2%.

ADMISSIONS FACTS AND FIGURES
Phone: (304) 442-3167. **Email:** admissions@wvutech.edu. **Website:** http://www.wvutech.edu. **Application deadlines for fall 2007:** Regular decision: August 11. Early decision: Not offered. Early action: Not offered. Admission can be deferred. Common application is accepted. **Admissions requirements/recommendations:** High school units required (recommended): English: 17; Mathematics: 4; Science: 2; Social studies: 3; Academic electives: (3). Tests: The college uses SAT or ACT scores in admissions decisions. Either SAT or ACT required. Campus visit: Recommended. Admissions interview: Neither required nor recommended. **Factors that count in admissions decisions:** *Academic:* Secondary school record: Very important. Class rank: Considered. Letters of recommendation: Considered. Standardized test scores: Very important. Essay: Not considered. *Nonacademic:* Interview: Not considered. Extracurricular activities: Not considered. Talent/ability: Not considered. Character/personal qualities: Not considered. Alumni/ae relationship: Not considered. Geographical residence: Not considered. State residency: Considered. Religious affiliation/commitment: Not considered. Minority status: Not considered. Volunteer work: Not considered. Work experience: Not considered. **Admissions statistics for the fall 2005 entering class:** Total applicants: 749. Total accepted: 485. Freshmen enrolled: 183; Overall acceptance rate: 65%. **Size of waiting list:** 0 applicants; enrolled from waiting list: 0. **Credentials of fall 2005 freshmen:** 14% ranked in the top 10 percent of their high school class; 22% were in the top 25 percent, and 42% were in the top half. (Proportion submitting class standing: 16%.) **Average high school grade point average:** 3.0. **First-year students who submitted SAT scores:** 20%. Scores (25/75 percentile): Verbal: 430-550, Math: 430-570, Combined: 860-1120. **First-year students submitting ACT scores:** 87%. Scores (25/75 percentile): English: 18-24, Math: 17-24, Composite: 17-24.

ACADEMICS
Year founded: 1895. **Academic calendar:** Semester. **Degrees offered:** associate, bachelor's, master's. **Most popular majors:** Information not available. **Major fields of study:** biological and biomedical sciences; business, management, marketing, and related support services; communications

technologies/technicians and support services; computer and information sciences and support services; education; engineering; health professions and related clinical sciences; liberal arts and sciences studies, and humanities; mathematics and statistics; multi/interdisciplinary studies; physical sciences; public administration and social service professions; social sciences. **Reserve Officers Training Corps (ROTC):** Army ROTC: Offered on campus. **Faculty and instruction (2005-2006):** Total instructional faculty: N/A. Student/faculty ratio: 14/1. Classes of fewer than 20 students: 64%; of 20 to 49 students: 34%; of 50 or more students: 2%. **Freshmen returning for sophomore year:** 58%. **Graduation rates:** Four-year: 14%; five-year: 29%; six-year: 38%.

COSTS AND FINANCIAL AID
Financial aid office: (304) 442-3228. **Financial aid:** Priority filing date for institution's financial aid form: February 1; deadline: April 1.

CAMPUS LIFE AND EXTRACURRICULAR ACTIVITIES
Campus housing available (% using): coed dorms (46%), women's dorms (20%), men's dorms (34%). **Student employment:** During the 2005-2006 academic year, 23% of undergraduates worked on campus. Average per-year earnings: $6. **Clubs and organizations:** Number of student organizations: 45. Activities include: choral groups, concert band, marching band, musical theater, student government, student newspaper. Number of fraternities: 3; sororities: 0. Average proportion of students who stay on campus on weekends: 25%. **Sports program (2005-2006):** Member of NCAA II. *Men's intercollegiate varsity sports:* baseball, basketball, football, golf, tennis. *Women's intercollegiate varsity sports:* basketball, soccer, softball, tennis, volleyball.

SERVICES AND FACILITIES
Basic services: placement service, day care. **Remedial assistance:** reading, math, study skills. **Information technology resources:** Students are not required to lease or own a computer. Number of campus computers available to all students: 300. Proportion of college-owned housing units wired for high-speed internet access: 80%. **Campus safety:** Security services offered: 24-hour foot-and-vehicle patrols, 24-hour emergency telephones, lighted pathways/sidewalks, controlled dormitory access (key, security card, etc).

TRANSFER AND INTERNATIONAL STUDENTS
Transfer students: May apply for admission for the following academic terms: Fall, Spring, Summer. Applicants need a minimum number of credits to apply. For fall 2005: Transfer applications received: 238. Transfer applicants offered admission: 163. Transfer applicants enrolled: 109.
International students: Number of foreign undergraduates: 31 (2% of student body). Minimum TOEFL score required: 500 (paper); 173 (computer). Average TOEFL score: 520 (paper).

West Virginia University–Parkersburg

- **Address:** 300 Campus Drive, Parkersburg, WV 26101-9577
- **Website:** http://www.wvup.edu
- **Public**
- **Enrollment:** 2,200 full-time; 1,572 part-time

KEY STATS
✔ **U.S News College Ranking:** fourth tier, Comp. Coll.–Bachelor's (South)
✔ **SAT or ACT Score (25th/75th percentile):** N/A
✔ **Tuition:** 2006-2007: $1,668 in state, $5,892 out of state
Selectivity: Less selective   **Room/board:** N/A
Acceptance rate: 100%   **Average debt:** $12,000
Student/faculty ratio: 19/1   **Proportion who borrowed:** 83%

UNDERGRADUATE STUDENT BODY STATS
2005-2006 enrollment: 2,200 full-time; 1,572 part-time. Men: 36%; women: 64%. **Ethnic makeup:** African American: 1%; Asian American: 1%; Hispanic: 1%; White: 98%.

ADMISSIONS FACTS AND FIGURES
Phone: (304) 424-8220. **Email:** info@mail.wvup.edu. **Website:** http://www.wvup.edu. **Application deadlines for fall 2007:** Regular decision: Rolling. Early decision: Not offered. Early action: Not offered. Admission cannot be deferred. Common application is accepted. **To apply online, go to:**

http://www.scusco.wvnet.edu/www/stserv/commapp/commonapp.htm.
Admissions requirements/recommendations: High school units required (recommended): English: 0 (4); Mathematics: 0 (3); Science: 0 (3); Foreign language: 0 (0); Social studies: 0 (4); History: 0 (0); Academic electives: 0 (0); Total units: 0 (16). Tests: The college does not use SAT or ACT scores in admissions decisions. Neither SAT nor ACT required. Campus visit: Recommended. Admissions interview: Neither required nor recommended. Off-campus interview: May be arranged. **Factors that count in admissions decisions:** *Academic:* Secondary school record: Not considered. Class rank: Not considered. Letters of recommendation: Not considered. Standardized test scores: Not considered. Essay: Not considered. *Nonacademic:* Interview: Not considered. Extracurricular activities: Not considered. Talent/ability: Not considered. Character/personal qualities: Not considered. Alumni/ae relationship: Not considered. Geographical residence: Not considered. State residency: Not considered. Religious affiliation/commitment: Not considered. Minority status: Not considered. Volunteer work: Not considered. Work experience: Not considered. **Other schools with the greatest overlap in applicants:** Fairmont State University; Glenville State College; Marshall University; West Virginia State University; West Virginia University.
Admissions statistics for the fall 2005 entering class: Total applicants: 659. Total accepted: 659. Freshmen enrolled: 659; 3% were from out of state. Overall acceptance rate: 100%. **Size of waiting list:** 0 applicants; enrolled from waiting list: 0. **Credentials of fall 2005 freshmen:** 18% ranked in the top 10 percent of their high school class; 33% were in the top 25 percent, and 72% were in the top half. (Proportion submitting class standing: 8%.)
Average high school grade point average: 2.9. **First-year students submitting ACT scores:** 71%. Scores (25/75 percentile): English: N/A, Math: N/A, Composite: N/A.

ACADEMICS
Year founded: 1961. **Academic calendar:** Semester. **Degrees offered:** certificate, associate, transfer-associate, terminal-associate, bachelor's. **Most popular majors:** 11% business administration and management, 5% elementary education and teaching, 4% engineering/industrial management. **Major fields of study:** business, management, marketing, and related support services; education; engineering technologies/technicians. **Areas of required coursework:** arts/fine arts, humanities, computer literacy, mathematics, English (including composition), sciences (biological or physical), history, social science. **Special academic programs (% participation):** cooperative (work-study plan) program (2%), cross-registration (4%), distance learning (15%), dual enrollment (5%), independent study (1%), internships (3%).
Teacher certification offered in: elementary. **Cooperative education programs:** business, computer science, education, engineering, health professions, natural science, social/behavioral science, technologies, vocational arts. **Faculty and instruction (2005-2006):** Total instructional faculty: 86 full-time, 148 part-time (48% men; 52% women; 3% minorities). Full-time faculty with Ph.D. or other terminal degree: 22%. Student/faculty ratio: 19/1. Classes of fewer than 20 students: 55%; of 20 to 49 students: 43%; of 50 or more students: 2%. **Freshmen returning for sophomore year:** 65%. **Graduation rates:** Four-year: 3%; five-year: 11%; six-year: 19%. **Graduate study:** 5% of students pursue further study immediately upon graduation; 10% within one year; 15% within five years. Fields in which graduates pursue further study: Master of Business Administration (MBA), 20%; law, 10%; medicine, 10%; dentistry, 5%; engineering, 25%; theology (or the seminary), 5%; education, 25%.

COSTS AND FINANCIAL AID
Financial aid office: (304) 424-8210. **Expenses (2006-2007):** Tuition and fees 2006-2007: $1,668 in state, $5,892 out of state; room/board: N/A. Estimated books and supplies: $800; transportation: $1,818; personal expenses: $1,400. **Financial aid:** Priority filing date for institution's financial aid form: March 1. In 2005-2006, 100% of undergraduates applied for financial aid. Of those, 85% were determined to have financial need; 35% had their need fully met. Average financial aid package (proportion receiving): $5,700 (85%). Average amount of gift aid, such as scholarships or grants (proportion receiving): $5,000 (68%). Average amount of self-help aid, such as work study or loans (proportion receiving): $8,700 (63%). Average need-based loan (excluding PLUS or other private loans): $3,200. Among students who received need-based aid, the average percentage of need met: 82%. Among students who received aid based on merit, the average award (and the proportion receiving): $850 (4%). Average amount of debt of borrowers graduating in 2005: $12,000. Proportion who borrowed: 83%.

CAMPUS LIFE AND EXTRACURRICULAR ACTIVITIES

Students who live in college-owned, operated, or affiliated housing: 0%. **Student employment:** During the 2005-2006 academic year, 2% of undergraduates worked on campus. Average per-year earnings: $2,000. Activities include: choral groups, drama/theater, literary magazine, student government, student newspaper. Number of fraternities: 0; sororities: 0.

SERVICES AND FACILITIES

Basic services: nonremedial tutoring, placement service, day care, health service. **Remedial assistance:** reading, math, writing, study skills. **Counseling services:** career, personal, veteran student, academic. **For learning-disabled students:** School does not offer a structured program with separate admission and additional fees. Total undergraduates in learning-disabled program or receiving services: 14. Services include: remedial math, remedial English, reading machines, remedial reading, tape recorders, diagnostic testing service, oral tests, learning center, readers, extended time for tests, tutors, other testing accomodations. **Library:** Number of titles: 54,891; number of current serial subscriptions: 364. **Information technology resources:** Students are not required to lease or own a computer. Number of campus computers available to all students: 400. School has a wireless network. Approximate number of users that can be accommodated: 50. **Campus safety:** Security services offered: lighted pathways/sidewalks.

TRANSFER AND INTERNATIONAL STUDENTS

Transfer students: May apply for admission for the following academic terms: Fall, Winter, Spring, Summer. Applicants do not need a minimum number of credits to apply. For fall 2005: Transfer applications received: 189. Transfer applicants offered admission: 189. Transfer applicants enrolled: 189. **International students:** Number of foreign undergraduates: 0. Minimum TOEFL score required: 213 (paper). Average TOEFL score: 220 (paper).

West Virginia Wesleyan College

- ■ **Address:** 59 College Avenue, Buckhannon, WV 26201
- ■ **Website:** http://www.wvwc.edu
- ■ **Private; Religious affiliation:** United Methodist
- ■ **Enrollment:** 1,297 full-time; 27 part-time

KEY STATS

- ✔ **U.S News College Ranking:** fourth tier, Liberal Arts Colleges
- ✔ **ACT Score (25th/75th percentile):** 20-25
- ✔ **Tuition:** 2006-2007: $21,330

Selectivity: More selective	**Room/board:** $5,550
Acceptance rate: 77%	**Average debt:** $19,750
Student/faculty ratio: 13/1	**Proportion who borrowed:** 63%

UNDERGRADUATE STUDENT BODY STATS

2005-2006 enrollment: 1,297 full-time; 27 part-time. Men: 46%; women: 54%. **Ethnic makeup:** African American: 5%; Asian American: 1%; Hispanic: 1%; White: 89%; International: 3%.

ADMISSIONS FACTS AND FIGURES

Phone: (800) 722-9933. **Email:** admissions@wvwc.edu. **Website:** http://www.wvwc.edu. **Application deadlines for fall 2007:** Regular decision: July 1. Early decision: Send application by: December 1; Decision sent by: N/A. Early action: Not offered. Admission can be deferred. **Application fee:** $35. Common application is accepted. **To apply online, go to:** http://www.applyweb.com/apply/wvwc/. **Admissions requirements/recommendations:** High school units required (recommended): English: 4; Mathematics: 3; Science: 3; Foreign language: 2 (3); Social studies: 2; History: 2; Academic electives: (3); Total units: 24. Tests: The college uses SAT or ACT scores in admissions decisions. Either SAT or ACT required. For admission to the fall 2007 entering class, the school will accept ACT with writing. Campus visit: Recommended. Admissions interview: Recommended. Off-campus interview: May be arranged. **Factors that count in admissions decisions:** *Academic:* Secondary school record: Very important. Class rank: Considered. Letters of recommendation: Considered. Standardized test scores: Very important. Essay: Important. *Nonacademic:* Interview: Important. Extracurricular activities: Important. Talent/ability: Important. Character/personal qualities: Very important. Alumni/ae relationship: Considered. Geographical residence: Not considered. State residency: Not considered. Religious affiliation/commitment: Not considered. Minority status: Considered. Volunteer work: Considered. Work experience: Considered. **Other schools with the greatest overlap in applicants:** Bethany College; Bridgewater College; Marietta College; Marshall University; Westminster College. **Admissions statistics for the fall 2005 entering class:**, Total applicants: 1,268. Total accepted: 982. Freshmen enrolled: 371; 46% were from out of state. Overall acceptance rate: 77%. Non-early acceptance rate: 77%. **Credentials of fall 2005 freshmen:** 22% ranked in the top 10 percent of their high school class; 53% were in the top 25 percent, and 81% were in the top half. (Proportion submitting class standing: 81%.) **Average high school grade point average:** 3.3. **First-year students who submitted SAT scores:** 61%. Scores (25/75 percentile): Verbal: 460-580, Math: 460-570, Combined: 920-1150. **First-year students submitting ACT scores:** 63%. Scores (25/75 percentile): English: N/A, Math: N/A, Composite: 20-25.

ACADEMICS

Year founded: 1890. **Academic calendar:** Semester. **Degrees offered:** bachelor's, master's. **Most popular majors:** 23% business, management, marketing, and related support services, 12% education, 8% visual and performing arts, 7% health professions and related clinical sciences, 5% biological and biomedical sciences. **Major fields of study:** biological and biomedical sciences; business, management, marketing, and related support services; communication, journalism, and related programs; computer and information sciences and support services; education; English language and literature/letters; health professions and related clinical sciences; history; legal professions and studies; natural resources and conservation; parks, recreation, leisure, and fitness studies; philosophy and religious studies; physical sciences; psychology; security and protective services; social sciences; theology and religious vocations; visual and performing arts. **Areas of required coursework:** arts/fine arts, humanities, computer literacy, mathematics, English (including composition), philosophy, sciences (biological or physical), history, social science. **Pre-professional programs:** pre-law, pre-medicine, pre-theology, pre-pharmacy. **Special academic programs (% participation):** double major (18%), English as a Second Language (ESL), exchange student program (domestic), honors program, independent study, internships, student-designed major, study abroad, teacher certificate program. **Teacher certification offered in:** special education, elementary, middle/junior high, secondary. **Cooperative education programs:** engineering. **Faculty and instruction (2005-2006):** Total instructional faculty: 75 full-time, 80 part-time (; 1% minorities). Full-time faculty with Ph.D. or other terminal degree: 83%. Student/faculty ratio: 13/1. **Advanced Placement and International Baccalaureate credit:** AP tests may be used for: Credit only. Scores accepted: 3. **Freshmen returning for sophomore year:** 78%. **Graduation rates:** Four-year: 45%; five-year: 51%; six-year: 53%. **Graduate study:** 27% of students pursue further study immediately upon graduation; 36% within one year. Fields in which graduates pursue further study: Master of Business Administration (MBA), 13%; law, 5%; medicine, 14%; theology (or the seminary), 5%; education, 5%; arts and sciences, 58%.

COSTS AND FINANCIAL AID

Financial aid office: (304) 473-8080. **Expenses (2006-2007):** Tuition and fees 2006-2007: $21,330; room/board: $5,550. Estimated books and supplies: $1,000; transportation: $1,000; personal expenses: $2,500. **Financial aid:** Priority filing date for institution's financial aid form: March 15. In 2005-2006, 79% of undergraduates applied for financial aid. Of those, 74% were determined to have financial need; 38% had their need fully met. Average financial aid package (proportion receiving): $21,518 (74%). Average amount of gift aid, such as scholarships or grants (proportion receiving): $16,286 (74%). Average amount of self-help aid, such as work study or loans (proportion receiving): $835 (70%). Average need-based loan (excluding PLUS or other private loans): $4,397. Among students who received need-based aid, the average percentage of need met: 88%. Among students who received aid based on merit, the average award (and the proportion receiving): $11,945 (23%). The average athletic scholarship (and the proportion receiving): $8,800 (18%). Average amount of debt of borrowers graduating in 2005: $19,750. Proportion who borrowed: 63%.

CAMPUS LIFE AND EXTRACURRICULAR ACTIVITIES

Campus housing available: coed dorms, women's dorms, men's dorms, fraternity housing, apartment for single students, special housing for disabled students. Students who live in college-owned, operated, or affiliated housing: 80%. **Student employment:** During the 2005-2006 academic year, 70% of undergraduates worked on campus. Average per-year earnings: $1,000. Activities include: choral groups, concert band, dance, drama/theater, jazz band, literary magazine, music ensembles, musical theater, radio station, student government, student newspaper, yearbook. Number of fraternities:

5; sororities: 4. Proportion of men in fraternities: 25%; of women in sororities: 25%. Average proportion of students who stay on campus on weekends: 50%. **Sports program (2005-2006):** Member of NCAA II, *Men's intercollegiate varsity sports:* baseball, basketball, cross-country, football, golf, soccer, swimming and diving, tennis, track and field (indoor), track and field (outdoor). *Women's intercollegiate varsity sports:* basketball, cross-country, soccer, softball, swimming and diving, tennis, track and field (indoor), track and field (outdoor), volleyball.

SERVICES AND FACILITIES
Basic services: nonremedial tutoring, placement service, health service, health insurance. **Remedial assistance:** reading, math, writing, study skills. **Counseling services:** minority student, career, personal, academic, older student, psychological, religious. **For learning-disabled students:** School does not offer a structured program with separate admission and additional fees. Services include: remedial math, remedial English, reading machines, remedial reading, tape recorders, other special classes, diagnostic testing service, untimed tests, note-taking services, oral tests, learning center, readers, extended time for tests, tutors. **Library:** Number of titles: 135,896; number of current serial subscriptions: 1,069. **Information technology resources:** Students are required to lease or own a computer. School has a wireless network. Proportion of college-owned housing units wired for high-speed internet access: 100%. **Campus safety:** Security services offered: 24-hour foot-and-vehicle patrols, late-night transport/escort service, 24-hour emergency telephones, lighted pathways/sidewalks, student patrols, controlled dormitory access (key, security card, etc).

TRANSFER AND INTERNATIONAL STUDENTS
Transfer students: May apply for admission for the following academic terms: Fall, Spring. Applicants need a minimum number of credits to apply. For fall 2005: Transfer applications received: 144. Transfer applicants offered admission: 106. Transfer applicants enrolled: 65. **International students:** Number of foreign undergraduates: 44 (3% of student body). Minimum TOEFL score required: 500 (paper).

Wheeling Jesuit University

- **Address:** 316 Washington Avenue, Wheeling, WV 26003
- **Website:** http://www.wju.edu
- **Private; Religious affiliation:** Roman Catholic
- **Enrollment:** 1,048 full-time; 170 part-time

KEY STATS
- ✔ **U.S News College Ranking:** 21, Universities–Master's (South)
- ✔ **ACT Score (25th/75th percentile):** 19-24
- ✔ **Tuition:** 2006-2007: $22,810

Selectivity: Selective	**Room/board:** $6,910
Acceptance rate: 75%	**Average debt:** $20,227
Student/faculty ratio: 14/1	**Proportion who borrowed:** 74%

UNDERGRADUATE STUDENT BODY STATS
2005-2006 enrollment: 1,048 full-time; 170 part-time. Men: 41%; women: 59%. **Ethnic makeup:** African American: 3%; Asian American: 1%; Hispanic: 2%; White: 91%; International: 3%. **Religious preference:** Roman Catholic: 63%; Other: 37%.

ADMISSIONS FACTS AND FIGURES
Phone: (800) 624-6992. **Email:** admiss@wju.edu. **Website:** http://www.wju.edu. **Application deadlines for fall 2007:** Regular decision: Rolling; decision sent by August 15. Early decision: Not offered. Early action: Not offered. Admission can be deferred. **Application fee:** $25. Common application is accepted. **To apply online, go to:** http://www.wju.edu/admissions/adm_apply.asp. **Admissions requirements/recommendations:** High school units required (recommended): English: 4 (4); Mathematics: 2 (2); Science: 1 (1); Foreign language: (2); Social studies: 2 (2); History: 2; Academic electives: 6 (6); Total units: 15 (15). Tests: The college uses SAT or ACT scores in admissions decisions. Either SAT or ACT required. For admission to the fall 2007 entering class, the school will accept: ACT with writing, ACT without writing. Campus visit: Recommended. Admissions interview: Recommended. Off-campus interview: May be arranged. **Factors that count in admissions decisions:** *Academic:* Secondary school record: Very important. Class rank: Considered. Letters of recommendation: Considered.

Standardized test scores: Very important. Essay: Important. *Nonacademic:* Interview: Important. Extracurricular activities: Considered. Talent/ability: Considered. Character/personal qualities: Important. Alumni/ae relationship: Considered. Geographical residence: Not considered. State residency: Not considered. Religious affiliation/commitment: Not considered. Minority status: Not considered. Volunteer work: Considered. Work experience: Considered. **Other schools with the greatest overlap in applicants:** Bethany College; Duquesne University; Ohio State University–Columbus; Ohio University; West Virginia University. **Admissions statistics for the fall 2005 entering class:** Total applicants; 1,132. Total accepted: 853. Freshmen enrolled: 285; 62% were from out of state. Overall acceptance rate: 75%. **Credentials of fall 2005 freshmen:** 20% ranked in the top 10 percent of their high school class; 41% were in the top 25 percent, and 73% were in the top half. (Proportion submitting class standing: 80%.) **Average high school grade point average:** 3.4. **First-year students who submitted SAT scores:** 51%. Scores (25/75 percentile): Verbal: 480-580, Math: 450-570, Combined: 930-1150. **First-year students submitting ACT scores:** 78%. Scores (25/75 percentile): English: 18-25, Math: 17-25, Composite: 19-24.

ACADEMICS
Year founded: 1954. **Academic calendar:** Semester. **Degrees offered:** bachelor's, master's, first professional. **Most popular majors:** 16% human resources management and services, 14% nursing/registered nurse training (R.N., A.S.N., B.S.N., M.S.N.), 7% psychology, 6% accounting, 6% criminal justice/safety studies. **Major fields of study:** biological and biomedical sciences; business, management, marketing, and related support services; computer and information sciences and support services; English language and literature/letters; foreign languages, literatures, and linguistics; health professions and related clinical sciences; history; liberal arts and sciences studies, and humanities; mathematics and statistics; multi/interdisciplinary studies; philosophy and religious studies; physical sciences; psychology; security and protective services; social sciences; theology and religious vocations. **Areas of required coursework:** arts/fine arts, humanities, mathematics, English (including composition), philosophy, foreign languages, sciences (biological or physical), history, social science, other. **Pre-professional programs:** pre-law, pre-dentistry, pre-medicine, pre-veterinary science, pre-pharmacy, other. **Special academic programs (% participation):** double major (5%), English as a Second Language (ESL) (2%), honors program (8%), independent study (40%), internships (42%), liberal arts/career combination (12%), student-designed major (2%), study abroad (4%), teacher certificate program (10%). **Teacher certification offered in:** special education, elementary, secondary. **Faculty and instruction (2005-2006):** Total instructional faculty: 75 full-time, 73 part-time (55% men; 45% women; 4% minorities). Full-time faculty with Ph.D. or other terminal degree: 80%. Student/faculty ratio: 14/1. Classes of fewer than 20 students: 57%; of 20 to 49 students: 43%; of 50 or more students: 0%. **Advanced Placement and International Baccalaureate credit:** AP tests may be used for: Credit only. Scores accepted: 3, 4, 5. Freshmen returning for sophomore year: 73%. **Graduation rates:** Four-year: 52%; five-year: 59%; six-year: 58%. **Graduate study:** 32% of students pursue further study immediately upon graduation; 32% within one year. Fields in which graduates pursue further study: Master of Business Administration (MBA); 16%; law, 1%; medicine, 26%; dentistry, 6%; engineering, 6%; theology (or the seminary), 6%; education, 12%; arts and sciences, 26%; veterinary medicine, 1%.

COSTS AND FINANCIAL AID
Financial aid office: (304) 243-2304. **Expenses (2006-2007):** Tuition and fees 2006-2007: $22,810; room/board: $6,910. Estimated books and supplies: $800; transportation: $500; personal expenses: $600. **Financial aid:** Priority filing date for institution's financial aid form: March 1. In 2005-2006, 91% of undergraduates applied for financial aid. Of those, 77% were determined to have financial need; 38% had their need fully met. Average financial aid package (proportion receiving): $17,907 (77%). Average amount of gift aid, such as scholarships or grants (proportion receiving): $5,451 (58%). Average amount of self-help aid, such as work study or loans (proportion receiving): $4,321 (62%). Average need-based loan (excluding PLUS or other private loans): $3,758. Among students who received need-based aid, the average percentage of need met: 84%. Among students who received aid based on merit, the average award (and the proportion receiving): $8,021 (17%). The average athletic scholarship (and the proportion receiving): $3,694 (17%). Average amount of debt of borrowers graduating in 2005: $20,227. Proportion who borrowed: 74%.

CAMPUS LIFE AND EXTRACURRICULAR ACTIVITIES
Campus housing available (% using): coed dorms (43%), women's dorms (26%), men's dorms (22%), apartments for married students (3%), apart-

ment for single students (5%), special housing for disabled students (1%). Students who live in college-owned, operated, or affiliated housing: 60%. **Student employment:** During the 2005-2006 academic year, 23% of undergraduates worked on campus. Average per-year earnings: $1,550. **Clubs and organizations:** Number of student organizations: 40. Activities include: choral groups, dance, drama/theater, literary magazine, pep band, student government, student newspaper, television station, yearbook. Number of fraternities: 0; sororities: 0. Average proportion of students who stay on campus on weekends: 70%. **Sports program (2005-2006):** Member of NCAA II. *Men's intercollegiate varsity sports:* baseball, basketball, cheerleading, cross-country, golf, lacrosse, soccer, swimming and diving, track and field (indoor), track and field (outdoor). *Women's intercollegiate varsity sports:* basketball, cheerleading, cross-country, golf, soccer, softball, swimming and diving, track and field (indoor), track and field (outdoor), volleyball.

SERVICES AND FACILITIES

Basic services: nonremedial tutoring, women's center, placement service, health service, health insurance. **Remedial assistance:** reading, math, writing, study skills. **Counseling services:** minority student, career, personal, academic, older student, psychological, religious. **For learning-disabled students:** School does not offer a structured program with separate admission and additional fees. Total undergraduates in learning-disabled program or receiving services: 36. Services include: remedial math, remedial English, remedial reading, untimed tests, note-taking services, oral tests, learning center, readers, extended time for tests, tutors, priority seating, proofreading services. **Library:** Number of titles: 305,154; number of current serial subscriptions: 456. **Information technology resources:** Students are not required to lease or own a computer. Number of campus computers available to all students: 325. School has a wireless network. Approximate number of users that can be accommodated: 150. Proportion of college-owned housing units wired for high-speed internet access: 100%. **Campus safety:** Security services offered: 24-hour foot-and-vehicle patrols, late-night transport/escort service, 24-hour emergency telephones, lighted pathways/sidewalks, student patrols, controlled dormitory access (key, security card, etc).

TRANSFER AND INTERNATIONAL STUDENTS

Transfer students: May apply for admission for the following academic terms: Fall, Spring. Applicants need a minimum number of credits to apply. For fall 2005: Transfer applications received: 167. Transfer applicants offered admission: 95. Transfer applicants enrolled: 51. **International students:** Number of foreign undergraduates: 35 (3% of student body). Number of countries represented: 16. Minimum TOEFL score required: 550 (paper); 213 (computer). Average TOEFL score: 585 (paper).

Wisconsin

Alverno College

- **Address:** 3400 S. 43rd Street, PO Box 343922, Milwaukee, WI 53234-3922
- **Website:** http://www.alverno.edu
- **Private; Religious affiliation:** Roman Catholic
- **Enrollment:** 1,515 full-time; 661 part-time

KEY STATS

✔ **U.S News College Ranking:** 31, Comp. Coll.–Bachelor's (Midwest)
✔ **ACT Score (25th/75th percentile):** 17-22
✔ **Tuition:** 2006-2007: $16,334

Selectivity: Selective	**Room/board:** $5,954
Acceptance rate: 55%	**Average debt:** $29,542
Student/faculty ratio: 12/1	**Proportion who borrowed:** 88%

UNDERGRADUATE STUDENT BODY STATS

2005-2006 enrollment: 1,515 full-time; 661 part-time. Men: 1%; women: 99%. **Ethnic makeup:** African American: 20%; American-Indian: 1%; Asian American: 5%; Hispanic: 11%; White: 63%; International: 1%. **Religious preference:** Protestant: 22%; Muslim: 1%; No preference: 24%; Unknown: 5%; Roman Catholic: 33%; Orthodox: 1%; Other: 14%.

ADMISSIONS FACTS AND FIGURES

Phone: (414) 382-6100. **Email:** admissions@alverno.edu. **Website:** http://www.alverno.edu. **Application deadlines for fall 2007:** Regular decision: Rolling. Early decision: Not offered. Early action: Not offered. Admission can be deferred. **Application fee:** $20. Common application is accepted. **Admissions requirements/recommendations:** High school units required (recommended): English: 4; Mathematics: 3; Science: 3; Foreign language: (2); Social studies: 3; Total units: 17. Tests: The college uses SAT or ACT scores in admissions decisions. Either SAT or ACT required. For admission to the fall 2007 entering class, the school will accept: ACT with writing, ACT without writing. Campus visit: Recommended. Admissions interview: Recommended. Off-campus interview: May be arranged. **Factors that count in admissions decisions:** *Academic:* Secondary school record: Important. Class rank: Important. Letters of recommendation: Considered. Standardized test scores: Very important. Essay: Important. *Nonacademic:* Interview: Not considered. Extracurricular activities: Not considered. Talent/ability: Not considered. Character/personal qualities: Not considered. Alumni/ae relationship: Not considered. Geographical residence: Not considered. State residency: Not considered. Religious affiliation/commitment: Not considered. Minority status: Not considered. Volunteer work: Not considered. Work experience: Not considered. **Other schools with the greatest overlap in applicants:** Cardinal Stritch University; Carroll College; Mount Mary College; University of Wisconsin–Milwaukee. **Admissions statistics for the fall 2005 entering class:** Total applicants: 886. Total accepted: 484. Freshmen enrolled: 280; 3% were from out of state. Overall acceptance rate: 55%. **Credentials of fall 2005 freshmen:** 13% ranked in the top 10 percent of their high school class; 31% were in the top 25 percent, and 66% were in the top half. (Proportion submitting class standing: 92%.) **Average high school grade point average:** 3.0. **First-year students submitting ACT scores:** 96%. Scores (25/75 percentile): English: N/A, Math: N/A, Composite: 17-22.

ACADEMICS

Year founded: 1887. **Academic calendar:** Semester. **Degrees offered:** associate, bachelor's, post-bachelor's certificate, master's. **Most popular majors:** 23% business, management, marketing, and related support services, 20% health professions and related clinical sciences, 12% communication, journalism, and related programs, 11% education, 7% psychology. **Major fields of study:** biological and biomedical sciences; business, management, marketing, and related support services; communication, journalism, and related programs; communications technologies/technicians and support services; computer and information sciences and support services; education; English language and literature/letters; health professions and related clini-

cal sciences; history; liberal arts and sciences studies, and humanities; mathematics and statistics; multi/interdisciplinary studies; natural resources and conservation; philosophy and religious studies; physical sciences; psychology; public administration and social service professions; social sciences; visual and performing arts. **Areas of required coursework:** arts/fine arts, humanities, computer literacy, mathematics, English (including composition), sciences (biological or physical), social science, other. **Preprofessional programs:** pre-law, pre-dentistry, pre-medicine, pre-veterinary science, pre-optometry, pre-pharmacy, other. **Special academic programs (% participation):** double major (3.6%), independent study (10%), internships (65.3%), student-designed major (1.2%), study abroad (2%), teacher certificate program (10.8%), weekend college (33.5%), other (6%). **Teacher certification offered in:** early childhood, elementary, middle/junior high, secondary. **Reserve Officers Training Corps (ROTC):** Army ROTC: Offered at cooperating institution (Marquette University); Air Force ROTC: Offered at cooperating institution (Marquette University). **Faculty and instruction (2005-2006):** Total instructional faculty: 104 full-time, 121 part-time (23% men; 77% women; 7% minorities). Full-time faculty with Ph.D. or other terminal degree: 88%. Student/faculty ratio: 12/1. Classes of fewer than 20 students: 62%; of 20 to 49 students: 38%; of 50 or more students: 0%. **Advanced Placement and International Baccalaureate credit:** AP tests may be used for: Credit and/or placement. Scores accepted: 3, 4, 5. International Baccalaureate exams may be used for: Credit only. **Freshmen returning for sophomore year:** 74%. **Graduation rates:** Four-year: 35%; five-year: 42%; six-year: 46%. **Graduate study:** 18% of students pursue further study immediately upon graduation. Fields in which graduates pursue further study: Master of Business Administration (MBA), 15%; engineering, 2%; education, 40%; arts and sciences, 11%.

COSTS AND FINANCIAL AID

Financial aid office: (414) 382-6046. **Expenses (2006-2007):** Tuition and fees 2006-2007: $16,334; room/board: $5,954. Estimated books and supplies: $1,050; transportation: $1,300; personal expenses: $1,620. **Financial aid:** Priority filing date for institution's financial aid form: April 15. In 2005-2006, 98% of undergraduates applied for financial aid. Average financial aid package (proportion receiving): N/A (98%). Average amount of debt of borrowers graduating in 2005: $29,542. Proportion who borrowed: 88%.

CAMPUS LIFE AND EXTRACURRICULAR ACTIVITIES

Campus housing available (% using): women's dorms (100%). Students who live in college-owned, operated, or affiliated housing: 13%. **Clubs and organizations:** Number of student organizations: 30. Activities include: choral groups, dance, drama/theater, literary magazine, music ensembles, student newspaper. ; sororities: 3. of women in sororities: 2%. Average proportion of students who stay on campus on weekends: 30%. **Sports program (2005-2006):** Member of NCAA III. *Women's intercollegiate varsity sports:* basketball, cross-country, soccer, softball, volleyball.

SERVICES AND FACILITIES

Basic services: nonremedial tutoring, day care, health service. **Remedial assistance:** reading, math, writing, study skills. **Counseling services:** career, personal, academic, psychological, religious. **For learning-disabled students:** School does not offer a structured program with separate admission and additional fees. Total undergraduates in learning-disabled program or receiving services: 45. Services include: remedial math, remedial English, reading machines, remedial reading, tape recorders, note-taking services, learning center, extended time for tests, tutors, proofreading services, texts on tape. **Library:** Number of titles: 82,416; number of current serial subscriptions: 115,084. **Information technology resources:** Students are not required to lease or own a computer. Number of campus computers available to all students: 470. School has a wireless network. Approximate number of users that can be accommodated: 150. Proportion of college-owned housing units wired for high-speed internet access: 100%. **Campus safety:** Security services offered: 24-hour foot-and-vehicle patrols, late-night transport/escort service, 24-hour emergency telephones, lighted pathways/sidewalks, controlled dormitory access (key, security card, etc).

TRANSFER AND INTERNATIONAL STUDENTS

Transfer students: May apply for admission for the following academic terms: Fall, Spring. Applicants do not need a minimum number of credits to apply. For fall 2005: Transfer applications received: 692. Transfer applicants offered admission: 377. Transfer applicants enrolled: 219. **International students:** Number of foreign undergraduates: 13 (1% of student body). Number of countries represented: 12. Minimum TOEFL score required: 520 (paper); 190 (computer).

Beloit College

- **Address:** 700 College Avenue, Beloit, WI 53511
- **Website:** http://www.beloit.edu
- **Private**
- **Enrollment:** 1,330 full-time; 55 part-time

KEY STATS

✔ **U.S News College Ranking:** 61, Liberal Arts Colleges
✔ **SAT Score (25th/75th percentile):** 1140-1360
✔ **Tuition:** 2006-2007: $28,350

Selectivity: More selective	**Room/board:** $6,162
Acceptance rate: 64%	**Average debt:** $20,339
Student/faculty ratio: 11/1	**Proportion who borrowed:** 62%

UNDERGRADUATE STUDENT BODY STATS

2005-2006 enrollment: 1,330 full-time; 55 part-time. Men: 41%; women: 59%. **Ethnic makeup:** African American: 3%; American-Indian: 1%; Asian American: 4%; Hispanic: 2%; White: 86%; International: 5%.

ADMISSIONS FACTS AND FIGURES

Phone: (608) 363-2500. **Email:** admiss@beloit.edu. **Website:** http://www.beloit.edu. **Application deadlines for fall 2007:** Regular decision: Rolling. Early decision: Not offered. Early action: Send application by: December 1; Decision sent by: January 15. Admission can be deferred. **Application fee:** $35. Common application is accepted. **To apply online, go to:** http://www.beloit.edu/apply. **Admissions requirements/recommendations:** High school units required (recommended): English: (4); Mathematics: (4); Science: (4); Foreign language: (3); Social studies: (4); History: (4). Tests: The college uses SAT or ACT scores in admissions decisions. Either SAT or ACT required. For admission to the fall 2007 entering class, the school will accept: ACT with writing, ACT without writing. Campus visit: Recommended. Admissions interview: Recommended. Off-campus interview: May be arranged. **Factors that count in admissions decisions:** *Academic:* Secondary school record: Very important. Class rank: Important. Letters of recommendation: Very important. Standardized test scores: Important. Essay: Very important. *Nonacademic:* Interview: Considered. Extracurricular activities: Considered. Talent/ability: Considered. Character/personal qualities: Considered. Alumni/ae relationship: Considered. Geographical residence: Considered. State residency: Not considered. Religious affiliation/commitment: Not considered. Minority status: Not considered. Volunteer work: Considered. Work experience: Considered. **Other schools with the greatest overlap in applicants:** Carleton College; Grinnell College; Lawrence University; Macalester College; Oberlin College. **Admissions statistics for the fall 2005 entering class:** Total applicants: 2,054. Total accepted: 1,324. Freshmen enrolled: 326; 83% were from out of state. Accepted through early-decision or early-action plans: 56%. Overall acceptance rate: 64%. Non-early acceptance rate: 53%. **Size of waiting list:** 99 applicants; enrolled from waiting list: 7. **Credentials of fall 2005 freshmen:** 37% ranked in the top 10 percent of their high school class; 64% were in the top 25 percent, and 94% were in the top half. (Proportion submitting class standing: 71%.) **Average high school grade point average:** 3.5. **First-year students who submitted SAT scores:** 70%. Scores (25/75 percentile): Verbal: 580-700, Math: 560-660, Combined: 1140-1360. **First-year students submitting ACT scores:** 55%. Scores (25/75 percentile): English: 24-31, Math: 23-28, Composite: 25-29.

ACADEMICS

Year founded: 1846. **Academic calendar:** Semester. **Degrees offered:** bachelor's. **Most popular majors:** 14% psychology, 13% English language and literature, 12% biological and physical sciences, 9% economics, 7% international relations and affairs. **Major fields of study:** area, ethnic, cultural, and gender studies; biological and biomedical sciences; business,

management, marketing, and related support services; computer and information sciences and support services; education; engineering; English language and literature/letters; foreign languages, literatures, and linguistics; history; mathematics and statistics; multi/interdisciplinary studies; philosophy and religious studies; physical sciences; psychology; social sciences; visual and performing arts. **Areas of required coursework:** arts/fine arts, humanities, English (including composition), sciences (biological or physical), social science, other. **Pre-professional programs:** pre-law, pre-dentistry, pre-medicine, pre-veterinary science, pre-optometry. **Special academic programs (% participation):** double major (30%), English as a Second Language (ESL) (3%), exchange student program (domestic) (6%), independent study (60%), internships (35%), liberal arts/career combination (22%), student-designed major (3%), study abroad (56%), teacher certificate program (9%). **Teacher certification offered in:** elementary, middle/junior high, secondary, bilingual/bicultural. **Cooperative education programs:** engineering, health professions, other. **Faculty and instruction (2005-2006):** Total instructional faculty: 103 full-time, 24 part-time (55% men; 45% women; 13% minorities). Full-time faculty with Ph.D. or other terminal degree: 95%. Student/faculty ratio: 11/1. Classes of fewer than 20 students: 73%; of 20 to 49 students: 27%. **Advanced Placement and International Baccalaureate credit:** AP tests may be used for: Placement only. Scores accepted: 4, 5. International Baccalaureate exams may be used for: Credit and/or placement. **Freshmen returning for sophomore year:** 94%. **Graduation rates:** Four-year: 62%; five-year: 70%; six-year: 72%. **Graduate study:** 9% of students pursue further study immediately upon graduation; 20% within one year; 65% within five years. Fields in which graduates pursue further study: Master of Business Administration (MBA), 12%; law, 10%; medicine, 9%; engineering, 3%; education, 6%; arts and sciences, 60%.

COSTS AND FINANCIAL AID

Financial aid office: (608) 363-2663. **Expenses (2006-2007):** Tuition and fees 2006-2007: $28,350; room/board: $6,162. Estimated books and supplies: $500 personal expenses: $900. **Financial aid:** Priority filing date for institution's financial aid form: March 1; deadline: March 1. In 2005-2006, 94% of undergraduates applied for financial aid. Of those, 77% were determined to have financial need; 100% had their need fully met. Average financial aid package (proportion receiving): $19,108 (77%). Average amount of gift aid, such as scholarships or grants (proportion receiving): $14,736 (76%). Average amount of self-help aid, such as work study or loans (proportion receiving): $4,694 (74%). Average need-based loan (excluding PLUS or other private loans): $5,872. Among students who received need-based aid, the average percentage of need met: 100%. Among students who received aid based on merit, the average award (and the proportion receiving): $13,410 (14%). Average amount of debt of borrowers graduating in 2005: $20,339. Proportion who borrowed: 62%.

CAMPUS LIFE AND EXTRACURRICULAR ACTIVITIES

Campus housing available (% using): coed dorms (70%), women's dorms (4%), sorority housing (2%), fraternity housing (7%), apartment for single students (6%), other housing options (11%). Students who live in college-owned, operated, or affiliated housing: 93%. **Student employment:** During the 2005-2006 academic year, 69% of undergraduates worked on campus. Average per-year earnings: $1,500. **Clubs and organizations:** Number of student organizations: 60. Activities include: choral groups, dance, drama/theater, jazz band, literary magazine, music ensembles, musical theater, pep band, radio station, student government, student newspaper, student film society, symphony orchestra, television station. Number of fraternities: 3; sororities: 3. Proportion of men in fraternities: 15%; of women in sororities: 5%. Average proportion of students who stay on campus on weekends: 98%. **Sports program (2005-2006):** Member of NCAA III. *Men's intercollegiate varsity sports:* baseball, basketball, cross-country, football, golf, soccer, swimming and diving, tennis, track and field (indoor), track and field (outdoor). *Women's intercollegiate varsity sports:* basketball, cross-country, golf, soccer, softball, swimming and diving, tennis, track and field (indoor), track and field (outdoor), volleyball.

SERVICES AND FACILITIES

Basic services: nonremedial tutoring, women's center, day care, health service. **Remedial assistance:** study skills. **Counseling services:** minority student, career, personal, academic, psychological, birth control. **For learning-disabled students:** School does not offer a structured program with separate admission and additional fees. Total undergraduates in learning-disabled program or receiving services: 93. Services include: reading machines, tape recorders, note-taking services, oral tests, learning center, readers, extended time for tests, tutors, texts on tape, typist/scribe, exams on tape or computer, other testing accomodations, other. **Library:** Number of titles: 710,023;

number of current serial subscriptions: 1,732. **Information technology resources:** Students are not required to lease or own a computer. Number of campus computers available to all students: 250. School has a wireless network. Approximate number of users that can be accommodated: 600. Proportion of college-owned housing units wired for high-speed internet access: 100%. **Campus safety:** Security services offered: 24-hour foot-and-vehicle patrols, late-night transport/escort service, 24-hour emergency telephones, lighted pathways/sidewalks, student patrols, controlled dormitory access (key, security card, etc.).

TRANSFER AND INTERNATIONAL STUDENTS

Transfer students: May apply for admission for the following academic terms: Fall, Spring. Applicants do not need a minimum number of credits to apply. For fall 2005: Transfer applications received: 100. Transfer applicants offered admission: 46. Transfer applicants enrolled: 28. **International students:** Number of foreign undergraduates: 68 (5% of student body). Number of countries represented: 34. Minimum TOEFL score required: 525 (paper); 197 (computer). Average TOEFL score: 592 (paper).

Cardinal Stritch University

- **Address:** 6801 N. Yates Road, Milwaukee, WI 53217
- **Website:** http://www.stritch.edu
- **Private; Religious affiliation:** Roman Catholic
- **Enrollment:** 2,767 full-time; 254 part-time

KEY STATS

✔ **U.S News College Ranking:** fourth tier, Universities–Master's (Midwest)
✔ **ACT Score (25th/75th percentile):** 19-24
✔ **Tuition:** 2006-2007: $17,600

Selectivity: Selective	**Room/board:** $5,590
Acceptance rate: 92%	**Average debt:** N/A
Student/faculty ratio: 16/1	**Proportion who borrowed:** N/A

UNDERGRADUATE STUDENT BODY STATS

2005-2006 enrollment: 2,767 full-time; 254 part-time. Men: 30%; women: 70%. **Ethnic makeup:** African American: 21%; American-Indian: 1%; Asian American: 1%; Hispanic: 3%; White: 72%; International: 2%. **Religious preference:** Protestant: 22%; Jewish: 1%; Unknown: 55%; Roman Catholic: 20%; Other: 2%.

ADMISSIONS FACTS AND FIGURES

Phone: (414) 410-4040. **Email:** admityou@stritch.edu. **Website:** http://www.stritch.edu. **Application deadlines for fall 2007:** Regular decision: August 1. Early decision: Not offered. Early action: Not offered. Admission cannot be deferred. **Application fee:** $25. Common application is accepted. **Admissions requirements/recommendations:** High school units required (recommended): English: 4; Mathematics: 2; Science: 2; Social studies: 2. Tests: The college uses SAT or ACT scores in admissions decisions. Either SAT or ACT required. For admission to the fall 2007 entering class, the school will accept: ACT with writing, ACT without writing. Campus visit: Recommended. Admissions interview: Recommended. Off-campus interview: May be arranged. **Factors that count in admissions decisions:** *Academic:* Secondary school record: Very important. Class rank: Considered. Letters of recommendation: Considered. Standardized test scores: Very important. **Admissions statistics for the fall 2005 entering class:** Total applicants: 701. Total accepted: 646. Freshmen enrolled: 176; 6% were from out of state. Overall acceptance rate: 92%. **Credentials of fall 2005 freshmen:** 14% ranked in the top 10 percent of their high school class; 31% were in the top 25 percent, and 72% were in the top half. (Proportion submitting class standing: 66%.) **Average high school grade point average:** 3.1. **First-year students who submitted SAT scores:** 5%. Scores (25/75 percentile): Verbal: 470-510, Math: 480-520, Combined: 950-1030. **First-year students submitting ACT scores:** 65%. Scores (25/75 percentile): English: 18-24, Math: 17-25, Composite: 19-24.

ACADEMICS

Year founded: 1937. **Academic calendar:** Semester. **Degrees offered:** certificate, associate, bachelor's, post-bachelor's certificate, master's, doctorate. **Most popular majors:** 48% business administration and management, 10% business/commerce, 8% educational leadership and administration, 8% nursing, 5% education. **Major fields of study:** biological and biomedical sci-

ences; business, management, marketing, and related support services; communication, journalism, and related programs; computer and information sciences and support services; education; English language and literature/letters; foreign languages, literatures, and linguistics; mathematics and statistics; philosophy and religious studies; physical sciences; psychology; social sciences; visual and performing arts. **Areas of required coursework:** humanities, mathematics, English (including composition), social science. **Pre-professional programs:** pre-law, pre-dentistry, pre-medicine, pre-veterinary science, pre-optometry, pre-pharmacy, other. **Special academic programs:** accelerated program, cooperative (work-study plan) program, distance learning, dual enrollment, English as a Second Language (ESL), honors program, independent study, internships, study abroad, teacher certification program. **Teacher certification offered in:** early childhood, special education, elementary, middle/junior high, secondary. **Faculty and instruction (2005-2006):** Total instructional faculty: 93 full-time, 769 part-time. Student/faculty ratio: 16/1. Classes of fewer than 20 students: 92%; of 20 to 49 students: 8%; of 50 or more students: 0%. **Freshmen returning for sophomore year:** 75%. **Graduation rates:** Four-year: 16%; five-year: 36%; six-year: 42%.

COSTS AND FINANCIAL AID

Financial aid office: (414) 410-4048. **Expenses (2006-2007):** Tuition and fees 2006-2007: $17,600; room/board: $5,590. Estimated books and supplies: $672; transportation: $1,200; personal expenses: $3,612. **Financial aid:** Priority filing date for institution's financial aid form: April 15. In 2005-2006, 97% of undergraduates applied for financial aid. Of those, 89% were determined to have financial need; 5% had their need fully met. Average financial aid package (proportion receiving): $8,480 (89%). Average amount of gift aid, such as scholarships or grants (proportion receiving): $6,069 (56%). Average amount of self-help aid, such as work study or loans (proportion receiving): $4,846 (86%). Average need-based loan (excluding PLUS or other private loans): $3,725. Among students who received need-based aid, the average percentage of need met: 47%. Among students who received aid based on merit, the average award (and the proportion receiving): $10,074 (11%).

CAMPUS LIFE AND EXTRACURRICULAR ACTIVITIES

Campus housing available: coed dorms, apartment for single students. Students who live in college-owned, operated, or affiliated housing: 2%. **Clubs and organizations:** Number of student organizations: 20. Activities include: concert band, drama/theater, jazz band, music ensembles, musical theater, radio station, student government, student newspaper. Number of fraternities: 0; sororities: 0. **Sports program (2005-2006):** Member of NAIA. *Men's intercollegiate varsity sports:* baseball, basketball, cross-country, soccer. *Women's intercollegiate varsity sports:* basketball, cross-country, soccer, softball, volleyball.

SERVICES AND FACILITIES

Basic services: nonremedial tutoring, placement service, health service, health insurance. **Remedial assistance:** reading, math, writing, study skills. **Counseling services:** career, personal, veteran student, academic, religious. **Library:** Number of titles: 132,775; number of current serial subscriptions: 3,533. **Information technology resources:** Students are not required to lease or own a computer. Number of campus computers available to all students: 241. School has a wireless network. **Campus safety:** Security services offered: 24-hour foot-and-vehicle patrols, late-night transport/escort service, 24-hour emergency telephones, lighted pathways/sidewalks, controlled dormitory access (key, security card, etc.).

TRANSFER AND INTERNATIONAL STUDENTS

Transfer students: May apply for admission for the following academic terms: Fall, Spring. Applicants need a minimum number of credits to apply. **International students:** Number of foreign undergraduates: 62 (2% of student body).

Carroll College

- **Address:** 100 N. East Avenue, Waukesha, WI 53186
- **Website:** http://www.cc.edu
- **Private; Religious affiliation:** Presbyterian (U.S.A.)
- **Enrollment:** 2,293 full-time; 568 part-time

KEY STATS

- ✔ **U.S News College Ranking:** 28, Comp. Coll.–Bachelor's (Midwest)
- ✔ **ACT Score (25th/75th percentile):** 21-24
- ✔ **Tuition:** 2006-2007: $19,910

Selectivity: Selective	**Room/board:** $6,070
Acceptance rate: 79%	**Average debt:** $18,404
Student/faculty ratio: 17/1	**Proportion who borrowed:** 57%

UNDERGRADUATE STUDENT BODY STATS

2005-2006 enrollment: 2,293 full-time; 568 part-time. Men: 34%; women: 66%. **Ethnic makeup:** African American: 2%; Asian American: 1%; Hispanic: 3%; White: 92%; International: 2%. **Religious preference:** Roman Catholic: 14%; Protestant: 7%; Unknown: 70%; Presbyterian (U.S.A.): 1%; Lutheran: 8%.

ADMISSIONS FACTS AND FIGURES

Phone: (262) 524-7220. **Email:** ccinfo@carroll1.cc.edu. **Website:** http://www.cc.edu. **Application deadlines for fall 2007:** Regular decision: Rolling. Early decision: Not offered. Early action: Not offered. Admission can be deferred. Common application is accepted. **Admissions requirements/recommendations:** High school units required (recommended): English: (4); Mathematics: (4); Science: (2); Foreign language: (0); Social studies: (2); History: (3). Tests: The college uses SAT or ACT scores in admissions decisions. Either SAT or ACT required. For admission to the fall 2007 entering class, the school will accept: ACT with writing, ACT without writing. Campus visit: Recommended. Admissions interview: Recommended. Off-campus interview: Not available. **Factors that count in admissions decisions:** *Academic:* Secondary school record: Very important. Class rank: Very important. Letters of recommendation: Considered. Standardized test scores: Very important. Essay: Considered. *Nonacademic:* Interview: Considered. Extracurricular activities: Not considered. Talent/ability: Not considered. Character/personal qualities: Considered. Alumni/ae relationship: Not considered. Geographical residence: Not considered. State residency: Not considered. Religious affiliation/commitment: Not considered. Minority status: Not considered. Volunteer work: Not considered. Work experience: Not considered. **Other schools with the greatest overlap in applicants:** Carthage College; Marquette University; University of Wisconsin–Madison; University of Wisconsin–Milwaukee; University of Wisconsin–Whitewater. **Admissions statistics for the fall 2005 entering class:** Total applicants: 2,429. Total accepted: 1,912. Freshmen enrolled: 610; 26% were from out of state. Overall acceptance rate: 79%. **Credentials of fall 2005 freshmen:** 15% ranked in the top 10 percent of their high school class; 51% were in the top 25 percent, and 75% were in the top half. (Proportion submitting class standing: 84%.) **First-year students who submitted SAT scores:** 2%. Scores (25/75 percentile): Verbal: N/A, Math: N/A, Combined: N/A. **First-year students submitting ACT scores:** 98%. Scores (25/75 percentile): English: N/A, Math: N/A, Composite: 21-24.

ACADEMICS

Year founded: 1846. **Academic calendar:** Semester. **Degrees offered:** bachelor's, master's. **Most popular majors:** 17% business administration and management, 15% nursing/registered nurse training (R.N., A.S.N., B.S.N., M.S.N.), 11% elementary education and teaching, 8% communication studies/speech communication and rhetoric, 8% psychology. **Major fields of study:** biological and biomedical sciences; business, management, marketing, and related support services; communication, journalism, and related programs; communications technologies/technicians and support services; computer and information sciences and support services; education; engineering; English language and literature/letters; foreign languages, literatures, and linguistics; health professions and related clinical sciences; history; mathematics and statistics; natural resources and conservation; parks, recreation, leisure, and fitness studies; philosophy and religious studies; physical sciences; psychology; security and protective services; social sciences; visual and performing arts. **Areas of required coursework:** arts/fine arts, humanities, computer literacy, mathematics, English (including composition), sciences (biological or physical), social science. **Pre-professional programs:** pre-law, pre-dentistry, pre-medicine, pre-theology, pre-veterinary science, pre-optometry, pre-pharmacy. **Special academic programs (% participation):** distance learning (1%), double major (9%), exchange student program (domestic) (1%), honors program (8%), independent study (5%), internships (65%), student-designed major, study abroad (7%), teacher certificate program (20%). **Teacher certification offered in:** early childhood, elementary, middle/junior high, secondary. **Reserve Officers Training Corps (ROTC):** Army ROTC: Offered at cooperating institution (Marquette University); Air Force ROTC: Offered at cooperating institution (Marquette University). **Faculty and instruction (2005-2006):** Total instructional faculty: 99 full-time, 147 part-time (45% men; 55% women; 1% minorities). Full-time faculty with Ph.D. or other terminal degree: 74%. Student/faculty ratio: 17/1. Classes of fewer than 20 students: 59%; of 20 to 49 students: 37%; of 50 or more students: 4%. **Advanced Placement and International Baccalaureate credit:** AP tests may be used for: Credit and/or placement. Scores accepted: 3, 4, 5. International Baccalaureate exams may be used for: Credit and/or placement. **Freshmen returning for sophomore year:** 76%. **Graduation rates:** Four-year: 45%; five-year: 59%; six-year: 60%. **Graduate study:** 33% of students pursue further study within five years.

COSTS AND FINANCIAL AID

Financial aid office: (262) 524-7296. **Expenses (2006-2007):** Tuition and fees 2006-2007: $19,910; room/board: $6,070. Estimated books and supplies: $872; transportation: $1,065; personal expenses: $1,460. **Financial aid:** In 2005-2006, 87% of undergraduates applied for financial aid. Of those, 75% were determined to have financial need; 70% had their need fully met. Average financial aid package (proportion receiving): $15,075 (75%). Average amount of gift aid, such as scholarships or grants (proportion receiving): $9,401 (75%). Average amount of self-help aid, such as work study or loans (proportion receiving): $4,793 (58%). Average need-based loan (excluding PLUS or other private loans): $4,013. Among students who received need-based aid, the average percentage of need met: 96%. Among students who received aid based on merit, the average award (and the proportion receiving): $7,258 (22%). The average athletic scholarship (and the proportion receiving): $0 (0%). Average amount of debt of borrowers graduating in 2005: $18,404. Proportion who borrowed: 57%.

CAMPUS LIFE AND EXTRACURRICULAR ACTIVITIES

Campus housing available (% using): coed dorms (54%), women's dorms (15%), other housing options (31%). Students who live in college-owned, operated, or affiliated housing: 49%. **Student employment:** During the 2005-2006 academic year, 46% of undergraduates worked on campus. Average per-year earnings: $1,600. **Clubs and organizations:** Number of student organizations: 40. Activities include: choral groups, concert band, dance, drama/theater, jazz band, literary magazine, music ensembles, radio station, student government, student newspaper. Number of fraternities: 2; sororities: 4. Proportion of men in fraternities: 5%; of women in sororities: 6%. Average proportion of students who stay on campus on weekends: 45%. **Sports program (2005-2006):** Member of NCAA III. *Men's intercollegiate varsity sports:* baseball, basketball, cross-country, football, golf, soccer, swimming and diving, tennis, track and field (indoor), track and field (outdoor). *Women's intercollegiate varsity sports:* basketball, cross-country, golf, soccer, softball, swimming and diving, tennis, track and field (indoor), track and field (outdoor), volleyball.

SERVICES AND FACILITIES

Basic services: nonremedial tutoring, placement service, health service, health insurance. **Remedial assistance:** math, writing. **Counseling services:** minority student, career, personal, academic, religious. **For learning-disabled students:** School does not offer a structured program with separate admission and additional fees. Total undergraduates in learning-disabled program or receiving services: 21. Services include: remedial math, remedial English, reading machines, note-taking services, oral tests, learning center, extended time for tests, tutors. **Library:** Number of titles: 150,000; number of current serial subscriptions: 390. **Information technology resources:** Students are not required to lease or own a computer. Number of campus computers available to all students: 250. School has a wireless network. Approximate number of users that can be accommodated: 320. Proportion of college-owned housing units wired for high-speed internet access: 95%. **Campus safety:** Security services offered: 24-hour foot-and-vehicle patrols, late-night transport/escort service, 24-hour emergency telephones, lighted pathways/sidewalks, student patrols, controlled dormitory access (key, security card, etc).

TRANSFER AND INTERNATIONAL STUDENTS

Transfer students: May apply for admission for the following academic terms: Fall, Winter, Spring, Summer. Applicants need a minimum number of credits to apply. For fall 2005: Transfer applications received: 435. Transfer applicants offered admission: 204. Transfer applicants enrolled: 126. **International students:** Number of foreign undergraduates: 51 (2% of student body). Number of countries represented: 26. Minimum TOEFL score required: 550 (paper); 213 (computer). Average TOEFL score: 575 (paper).

Carthage College

- **Address:** 2001 Alford Park Drive, Kenosha, WI 53140
- **Website:** http://www.carthage.edu
- **Private; Religious affiliation:** Evangelical Lutheran Church in America
- **Enrollment:** 2,145 full-time; 449 part-time

KEY STATS

- ✔ **U.S News College Ranking:** 30, Universities–Master's (Midwest)
- ✔ **ACT Score (25th/75th percentile):** 21-27
- ✔ **Tuition:** 2006-2007: $23,650

Selectivity: Selective	**Room/board:** $6,800
Acceptance rate: 76%	**Average debt:** N/A
Student/faculty ratio: 15/1	**Proportion who borrowed:** 92%

UNDERGRADUATE STUDENT BODY STATS

2005-2006 enrollment: 2,145 full-time; 449 part-time. Men: 41%; women: 59%. **Ethnic makeup:** African American: 5%; Asian American: 1%; Hispanic: 4%; White: 89%; International: 1%. **Religious preference:** Roman Catholic: 29%; Protestant: 19%; No preference: 3%; Unknown: 30%; Evangelical Lutheran Church in America: 10%.

ADMISSIONS FACTS AND FIGURES

Phone: (262) 551-6000. **Email:** admissions@carthage.edu. **Website:** http://www.carthage.edu. **Application deadlines for fall 2007:** Regular decision: Rolling. Early decision: Not offered. Early action: Not offered. Admission can be deferred. **Application fee:** $25. Common application is accepted. **To apply online, go to:** http://www.carthage.edu/apply. **Admissions requirements/recommendations:** High school units required (recommended): English: (4); Mathematics: (3); Science: (3); Foreign language: (2); Social studies: (3); History: (0); Academic electives: (3); Total units: (18). **Tests:** The college uses SAT or ACT scores in admissions decisions. Either SAT or ACT required. For admission to the fall 2007 entering class, the school will accept: ACT with writing, ACT without writing. Campus visit: Recommended. Admissions interview: Recommended. Off-campus interview: May be arranged. **Factors that count in admissions decisions:** *Academic:* Secondary school record: Very important. Class rank: Important. Letters of recommendation: Considered. Standardized test scores: Very important. Essay: Considered. *Nonacademic:* Interview: Considered. Extracurricular activities: Considered. Talent/ability: Considered. Character/personal qualities: Considered. Alumni/ae relationship: Not considered. Geographical residence: Not considered. State residency: Not considered. Religious affiliation/commitment: Not considered. Minority status: Not considered. Volunteer work: Considered. Work experience: Considered. **Other schools with the greatest overlap in applicants:** Augustana College; Marquette University; Northern Illinois University; University of Illinois–Urbana-Champaign; University of Wisconsin–Madison. **Admissions statistics for the fall 2005 entering class:** Total applicants: 4,000. Total accepted: 3,036. Freshmen enrolled: 598; 71% were from out of state. Overall acceptance rate: 76%. **Credentials of fall 2005 freshmen:** 18% ranked in the top 10 percent of their high school class; 43% were in the top 25 percent, and 76% were in the top half. (Proportion submitting class standing: 90%.) **Average high school grade point average:** 3.2. **First-year students who submitted SAT scores:** 8%. Scores (25/75 percentile): Verbal: 500-630, Math: 500-620, Combined: 1000-1250. **First-year students submitting ACT scores:** 97%. Scores (25/75 percentile): English: 19-26, Math: 20-27, Composite: 21-27.

ACADEMICS

Year founded: 1847. **Academic calendar:** 4-1-4. **Degrees offered:** bachelor's, master's. **Most popular majors:** 26% business administration and management, 11% social sciences, 8% elementary education and teaching, 5%

visual and performing arts, 4% biology/biological sciences. **Major fields of study:** biological and biomedical sciences; business, management, marketing, and related support services; communication, journalism, and related programs; computer and information sciences and support services; education; English language and literature/letters; foreign languages, literatures, and linguistics; history; liberal arts and sciences studies, and humanities; mathematics and statistics; multi/interdisciplinary studies; natural resources and conservation; parks, recreation, leisure, and fitness studies; philosophy and religious studies; physical sciences; psychology; public administration and social service professions; security and protective services; social sciences; visual and performing arts. **Areas of required coursework:** arts/fine arts, humanities, mathematics, English (including composition), foreign languages, sciences (biological or physical), social science, other. **Pre-professional programs:** pre-law, pre-dentistry, pre-medicine, pre-theology, pre-veterinary science, pre-optometry, pre-pharmacy, other. **Special academic programs (% participation):** accelerated program, cross-registration, double major (34%), honors program (2%), independent study, internships (20%), student-designed major, study abroad, teacher certificate program (21%). **Teacher certification offered in:** special education, elementary, middle/junior high, secondary. **Reserve Officers Training Corps (ROTC):** Army ROTC: Offered at cooperating institution (Marquette University); Air Force ROTC: Offered at cooperating institution (Marquette University). **Faculty and instruction (2005-2006):** Total instructional faculty: 125 full-time, 85 part-time (62% men; 38% women; 5% minorities). Full-time faculty with Ph.D. or other terminal degree: 86%. Student/faculty ratio: 15/1. Classes of fewer than 20 students: 47%; of 20 to 49 students: 53%; of 50 or more students: 0%. **Advanced Placement and International Baccalaureate credit:** AP tests may be used for: Credit and/or placement. Scores accepted: 3, 4, 5. International Baccalaureate exams may be used for: Credit only. **Freshmen returning for sophomore year:** 74%. **Graduation rates:** Four-year: 44%; five-year: 52%; six-year: 55%. **Graduate study:** 15% of students pursue further study immediately upon graduation; 15% within one year; 20% within five years. Fields in which graduates pursue further study: Master of Business Administration (MBA), 28%; law, 8%; medicine, 1%; dentistry, 1%; theology (or the seminary), 2%; education, 46%; arts and sciences, 13%; veterinary medicine, 1%.

COSTS AND FINANCIAL AID

Financial aid office: (262) 551-6001. **Expenses (2006-2007):** Tuition and fees 2006-2007: $23,650; room/board: $6,800. Estimated books and supplies: $1,200; transportation: $1,000; personal expenses: $1,500. **Financial aid:** Priority filing date for institution's financial aid form: February 15. In 2005-2006, 86% of undergraduates applied for financial aid. Of those, 72% were determined to have financial need; 32% had their need fully met. Average financial aid package (proportion receiving): $15,278 (72%). Average amount of gift aid, such as scholarships or grants (proportion receiving): $10,586 (72%). Average amount of self-help aid, such as work study or loans (proportion receiving): $5,849 (59%). Average need-based loan (excluding PLUS or other private loans): $5,672. Among students who received need-based aid, the average percentage of need met: 73%. Among students who received aid based on merit, the average award (and the proportion receiving): $11,549 (25%). The average athletic scholarship (and the proportion receiving): $0 (0%). Proportion who borrowed: 92%.

CAMPUS LIFE AND EXTRACURRICULAR ACTIVITIES

Campus housing available (% using): coed dorms (61%), women's dorms (17%), men's dorms (2%), sorority housing (6%), fraternity housing (4%), apartment for single students (2%), special housing for disabled students (1%), other housing options (7%). Students who live in college-owned, operated, or affiliated housing: 70%. **Student employment:** During the 2005-2006 academic year, 52% of undergraduates worked on campus. Average per-year earnings: $1,200. **Clubs and organizations:** Number of student organizations: 90. Activities include: choral groups, concert band, dance, drama/theater, jazz band, literary magazine, music ensembles, musical theater, opera, pep band, radio station, student government, student newspaper, student film society, symphony orchestra, yearbook. Number of fraternities: 8; sororities: 6. Proportion of men in fraternities: 22%; of women in sororities: 25%. Average proportion of students who stay on campus on weekends: 75%. **Sports program (2005-2006):** Member of NCAA III. *Men's intercollegiate varsity sports:* baseball, basketball, cross-country, football, golf, soccer, swimming and diving, tennis, track and field (indoor), track and field (outdoor), volleyball. *Women's intercollegiate varsity sports:* basketball, cross-country, golf, soccer, softball, swimming and diving, tennis, track and field (indoor), track and field (outdoor), volleyball.

SERVICES AND FACILITIES

Basic services: nonremedial tutoring, placement service, health service. **Remedial assistance:** math, writing, study skills. **Counseling services:** career, personal, academic, psychological, religious. **For learning-disabled students:** School does not offer a structured program with separate admission and additional fees. Services include: reading machines, diagnostic testing service, untimed tests, note-taking services, oral tests, readers, extended time for tests, tutors, substitution of courses. **Library:** Number of titles: 125,488; number of current serial subscriptions: 425. **Information technology resources:** Students are not required to lease or own a computer. Number of campus computers available to all students: 115. School has a wireless network. Proportion of college-owned housing units wired for high-speed internet access: 96%. **Campus safety:** Security services offered: 24-hour foot-and-vehicle patrols, late-night transport/escort service, 24-hour emergency telephones, lighted pathways/sidewalks, student patrols, controlled dormitory access (key, security card, etc).

TRANSFER AND INTERNATIONAL STUDENTS

Transfer students: May apply for admission for the following academic terms: Fall, Winter, Spring, Summer. Applicants do not need a minimum number of credits to apply. **International students:** Number of foreign undergraduates: 18 (1% of student body). Number of countries represented: 18. Minimum TOEFL score required: 500 (paper); 173 (computer). Average TOEFL score: 515 (paper).

Concordia University Wisconsin

- ■ **Address:** 12800 N. Lake Shore Drive, Mequon, WI 53097
- ■ **Website:** http://www.cuw.edu
- ■ **Private; Religious affiliation:** Lutheran
- ■ **Enrollment:** 2,007 full-time; 1,975 part-time

KEY STATS

- ✔ **U.S News College Ranking:** 65, Universities–Master's (Midwest)
- ✔ **ACT Score (25th/75th percentile):** 19-26
- ✔ **Tuition:** 2006-2007: $18,140

Selectivity: Selective	**Room/board:** $6,860
Acceptance rate: 84%	**Average debt:** $17,269
Student/faculty ratio: 12/1	**Proportion who borrowed:** 68%

UNDERGRADUATE STUDENT BODY STATS

2005-2006 enrollment: 2,007 full-time; 1,975 part-time. Men: 37%; women: 63%. **Ethnic makeup:** African American: 13%; American-Indian: 1%; Asian American: 1%; Hispanic: 3%; White: 81%; International: 1%.

ADMISSIONS FACTS AND FIGURES

Phone: (262) 243-4300. **Email:** admissions@cuw.edu. **Website:** http://www.cuw.edu. **Application deadlines for fall 2007:** Regular decision: August 1. Early decision: Not offered. Early action: Not offered. Admission cannot be deferred. **Application fee:** $35. Common application is accepted. **Admissions requirements/recommendations:** High school units required (recommended): English: 3 (4); Mathematics: 2 (3); Science: 2; Foreign language: (2); Social studies: 2; Total units: 16. Tests: The college uses SAT or ACT scores in admissions decisions. ACT required. For admission to the fall 2007 entering class, the school will accept: ACT with writing, ACT without writing. Campus visit: Recommended. Admissions interview: Recommended. Off-campus interview: May be arranged. **Factors that count in admissions decisions:** *Academic:* Secondary school record: Very important. Class rank: Important. Letters of recommendation: Considered. Standardized test scores: Very important. Essay: Considered. *Nonacademic:* Interview: Not considered. Extracurricular activities: Important. Talent/ability: Very important. Character/personal qualities: Very important. Alumni/ae relationship: Not considered. Geographical residence: Not considered. State residency: Not considered. Religious affiliation/commitment: Important. Minority status: Important. Volunteer work: Considered. Work experience: Considered. **Admissions statistics for the fall 2005 entering class:** Total applicants: 1,274. Total accepted: 1,076. Freshmen enrolled: 387; 33% were from out of state. Overall acceptance rate: 84%. **Credentials of fall 2005 freshmen:** 19% ranked in the top 10 percent of their high school class; 38% were in the top 25 percent, and 68% were in the top half. (Proportion submitting class standing: 75%.) **Average high school grade point average:**

3.3. First-year students submitting ACT scores: 100%. Scores (25/75 percentile): English: 19-26, Math: 19-26, Composite: 19-26.

ACADEMICS

Year founded: 1881. **Academic calendar:** 4-1-4. **Degrees offered:** certificate, associate, bachelor's, post-bachelor's certificate, master's, doctorate. **Most popular majors:** 38% business, management, marketing, and related support services, 20% liberal arts and sciences studies, and humanities, 16% education, 15% health professions and related clinical sciences, 11% legal professions and studies. **Major fields of study:** biological and biomedical sciences; business, management, marketing, and related support services; communication, journalism, and related programs; computer and information sciences and support services; education; English language and literature/letters; foreign languages, literatures, and linguistics; health professions and related clinical sciences; liberal arts and sciences studies, and humanities; mathematics and statistics; parks, recreation, leisure, and fitness studies; psychology; public administration and social service professions; social sciences; theology and religious vocations; visual and performing arts. **Areas of required coursework:** arts/fine arts, humanities, computer literacy, mathematics, English (including composition), philosophy, foreign languages, sciences (biological or physical), history, social science, other. **Pre-professional programs:** pre-law, pre-medicine. **Special academic programs (% participation):** accelerated program (40%), cooperative (work-study plan) program (1%), distance learning, double major (7%), dual enrollment (.05%), English as a Second Language (ESL) (1%), exchange student program (domestic) (1%), honors program, independent study (1%), internships (1%), liberal arts/career combination (3%), student-designed major (1%), study abroad (1%), teacher certificate program (1%). **Teacher certification offered in:** early childhood, elementary, middle/junior high, secondary. **Cooperative education programs:** other. **Faculty and instruction (2005-2006):** Total instructional faculty: 89 full-time, 110 part-time (48% men; 52% women; 3% minorities). Full-time faculty with Ph.D. or other terminal degree: 70%. Student/faculty ratio: 12/1. Classes of fewer than 20 students: 51%; of 20 to 49 students: 48%; of 50 or more students: 2%. **Advanced Placement and International Baccalaureate credit:** AP tests may be used for: Credit only. **Freshmen returning for sophomore year:** 77%. **Graduation rates:** Four-year: 44%; five-year: 64%; six-year: 64%. **Graduate study:** 19% of students pursue further study immediately upon graduation. Fields in which graduates pursue further study: theology (or the seminary), 64%.

COSTS AND FINANCIAL AID

Financial aid office: (262) 243-4569. **Expenses (2006-2007):** Tuition and fees 2006-2007: $18,140; room/board: $6,860. Estimated books and supplies: $1,050; transportation: $260; personal expenses: $1,500. **Financial aid:** Priority filing date for institution's financial aid form: May 1; deadline: May 1. In 2005-2006, 93% of undergraduates applied for financial aid. Of those, 77% were determined to have financial need; 35% had their need fully met. Average financial aid package (proportion receiving): $17,213 (77%). Average amount of gift aid, such as scholarships or grants (proportion receiving): $9,147 (72%). Average amount of self-help aid, such as work study or loans (proportion receiving): $5,570 (62%). Average need-based loan (excluding PLUS or other private loans): $5,570. Among students who received need-based aid, the average percentage of need met: 78%. Among students who received aid based on merit, the average award (and the proportion receiving): $7,181 (15%). The average athletic scholarship (and the proportion receiving): $0 (0%). Average amount of debt of borrowers graduating in 2005: $17,269. Proportion who borrowed: 68%.

CAMPUS LIFE AND EXTRACURRICULAR ACTIVITIES

Campus housing available (% using): women's dorms (56%), men's dorms (44%). Students who live in college-owned, operated, or affiliated housing: 79%. **Student employment:** During the 2005-2006 academic year, 38% of undergraduates worked on campus. Average per-year earnings: $2,500. Activities include: choral groups, concert band, drama/theater, jazz band, music ensembles, musical theater, pep band, radio station, student government, student newspaper. Number of fraternities: 0; sororities: 0. Average proportion of students who stay on campus on weekends: 60%. **Sports program (2005-2006):** Member of NCAA III. *Men's intercollegiate varsity sports:* baseball, basketball, cheerleading, cross-country, football, golf, soccer, tennis, track and field (indoor), track and field (outdoor), wrestling. *Women's intercollegiate varsity sports:* basketball, cheerleading, cross-country, golf, soccer, softball, tennis, track and field (indoor), track and field (outdoor), volleyball.

SERVICES AND FACILITIES

Basic services: nonremedial tutoring, placement service, health service. **Remedial assistance:** reading, writing, study skills. **Counseling services:** minority student, career, personal, academic, older student, psychological, religious. **Library:** Number of titles: 74,907; number of current serial subscriptions: 4,434. **Information technology resources:** Students are not required to lease or own a computer. Number of campus computers available to all students: 200. School has a wireless network. Approximate number of users that can be accommodated: 250. Proportion of college-owned housing units wired for high-speed internet access: 100%. **Campus safety:** Security services offered: 24-hour emergency telephones, lighted pathways/sidewalks, controlled dormitory access (key, security card, etc).

TRANSFER AND INTERNATIONAL STUDENTS

Transfer students: May apply for admission for the following academic terms: Fall, Winter, Spring, Summer. Applicants do not need a minimum number of credits to apply. For fall 2005: Transfer applications received: 287. Transfer applicants offered admission: 209. Transfer applicants enrolled: 103. **International students:** Number of foreign undergraduates: 35 (1% of student body). Minimum TOEFL score required: 500 (paper); 173 (computer). Average TOEFL score: 509 (paper).

Edgewood College

- **Address:** 1000 Edgewood College Drive, Madison, WI 53711-1997
- **Website:** http://www.edgewood.edu
- **Private; Religious affiliation:** Roman Catholic
- **Enrollment:** 1,517 full-time; 506 part-time

KEY STATS

- ✔ **U.S News College Ranking:** 70, Universities–Master's (Midwest)
- ✔ **ACT Score (25th/75th percentile):** 19-25
- ✔ **Tuition:** 2006-2007: $18,000

Selectivity: Selective	**Room/board:** $6,056
Acceptance rate: 81%	**Average debt:** $22,710
Student/faculty ratio: 13/1	**Proportion who borrowed:** 73%

UNDERGRADUATE STUDENT BODY STATS

2005-2006 enrollment: 1,517 full-time; 506 part-time. Men: 27%; women: 73%. **Ethnic makeup:** African American: 2%; Asian American: 2%; Hispanic: 2%; White: 92%; International: 1%.

ADMISSIONS FACTS AND FIGURES

Phone: (608) 663-2294. **Email:** admissions@edgewood.edu. **Website:** http://www.edgewood.edu. **Application deadlines for fall 2007:** Regular decision: August 26. Early decision: Not offered. Early action: Not offered. Admission can be deferred. **Application fee:** $25. Common application is accepted. **To apply online, go to:** http://www.applyweb.com/aw?edgewd. **Admissions requirements/recommendations:** High school units required (recommended): English: 4 (4); Mathematics: 2 (2); Science: 2 (2); Foreign language: 2; Social studies: 2 (2); History: 1 (1); Total units: 16 (16). Tests: The college uses SAT or ACT scores in admissions decisions. Either SAT or ACT required. For admission to the fall 2007 entering class, the school will accept: ACT with writing, ACT without writing. Campus visit: Recommended. Admissions interview: Neither required nor recommended. Off-campus interview: Not available. **Factors that count in admissions decisions:** *Academic:* Secondary school record: Very important. Class rank: Very important. Letters of recommendation: Considered. Standardized test scores: Very important. Essay: Considered. *Nonacademic:* Interview: Important. Extracurricular activities: Considered. Talent/ability: Important. Character/personal qualities: Considered. Alumni/ae relationship: Considered. Geographical residence: Considered. State residency: Not considered. Religious affiliation/commitment: Not considered. Minority status: Considered. Volunteer work: Considered. Work experience: Not considered. **Other schools with the greatest overlap in applicants:** University of Wisconsin–Madison. **Admissions statistics for the fall 2005 entering class:** Total applicants: 1,035. Total accepted: 835. Freshmen enrolled: 353; 8% were from out of state. Overall acceptance rate: 81%. **Credentials of fall 2005 freshmen:** 11% ranked in the top 10 percent of their high school class; 34% were in the top 25 percent, and 73% were in the top half. (Proportion submitting class standing: 83%.) **Average high school grade point average:** 3.3. **First-year students who submitted SAT scores:** 2%. Scores (25/75 percentile):

Verbal: N/A, Math: N/A, Combined: N/A. **First-year students submitting ACT scores:** 97%. Scores (25/75 percentile): English: 18-24, Math: 18-24, Composite: 19-25.

ACADEMICS

Year founded: 1927. **Academic calendar:** 4-1-4. **Degrees offered:** associate, bachelor's, master's, doctorate. **Most popular majors:** Information not available. **Major fields of study:** biological and biomedical sciences; business, management, marketing, and related support services; communication, journalism, and related programs; computer and information sciences and support services; education; English language and literature/letters; foreign languages, literatures, and linguistics; health professions and related clinical sciences; history; mathematics and statistics; multi/interdisciplinary studies; philosophy and religious studies; physical sciences; psychology; security and protective services; social sciences; visual and performing arts. **Areas of required coursework:** arts/fine arts, humanities, computer literacy, mathematics, English (including composition), philosophy, foreign languages, sciences (biological or physical), history, social science, other. **Special academic programs:** accelerated program, cross-registration, distance learning, double major, dual enrollment, honors program, independent study, internships, liberal arts/career combination, student-designed major, study abroad, teacher certificate program, weekend college. **Teacher certification offered in:** early childhood, special education, elementary, middle/junior high, secondary, bilingual/bicultural. **Faculty and instruction (2005-2006):** Total instructional faculty: N/A. Student/faculty ratio: 13/1. Classes of fewer than 20 students: 69%; of 20 to 49 students: 31%; of 50 or more students: 0%. **Advanced Placement and International Baccalaureate credit:** International Baccalaureate exams may be used for: Credit and/or placement. **Freshmen returning for sophomore year:** 72%. **Graduation rates:** Four-year: 25%; five-year: 46%; six-year: 45%.

COSTS AND FINANCIAL AID

Financial aid office: (608) 663-2305. **Expenses (2006-2007):** Tuition and fees 2006-2007: $18,000; room/board: $6,056. Estimated books and supplies: $800; transportation: $405; personal expenses: $2,066. **Financial aid:** Priority filing date for institution's financial aid form: March 15. In 2005-2006, 87% of undergraduates applied for financial aid. Of those, 76% were determined to have financial need; 19% had their need fully met. Average financial aid package (proportion receiving): $12,229 (76%). Average amount of gift aid, such as scholarships or grants (proportion receiving): $7,391 (72%). Average amount of self-help aid, such as work study or loans (proportion receiving): $5,602 (70%). Average need-based loan (excluding PLUS or other private loans): $4,360. Among students who received need-based aid, the average percentage of need met: 75%. Among students who received aid based on merit, the average award (and the proportion receiving): $8,895 (18%). Average amount of debt of borrowers graduating in 2005: $22,710. Proportion who borrowed: 73%.

CAMPUS LIFE AND EXTRACURRICULAR ACTIVITIES

Campus housing available: coed dorms, women's dorms, apartment for single students, special housing for disabled students, other housing options. Students who live in college-owned, operated, or affiliated housing: 19%. Average per-year earnings: $1,800. **Clubs and organizations:** Number of student organizations: 38. Activities include: choral groups, concert band, dance, drama/theater, jazz band, literary magazine, music ensembles, musical theater, pep band, student government, student newspaper, symphony orchestra. Number of fraternities: 0; sororities: 0. Average proportion of students who stay on campus on weekends: 10%. **Sports program (2005-2006):** Member of NCAA III. ***Men's intercollegiate varsity sports:*** baseball, basketball, cross-country, golf, soccer, track and field (indoor), track and field (outdoor). ***Women's intercollegiate varsity sports:*** basketball, cross-country, golf, soccer, softball, tennis, track and field (indoor), track and field (outdoor), volleyball.

SERVICES AND FACILITIES

Basic services: nonremedial tutoring, placement service, health service. **Remedial assistance:** reading, math, writing, study skills. **Counseling services:** minority student, career, personal, academic, psychological, birth control, religious. **For learning-disabled students:** School does not offer a structured program with separate admission and additional fees. Services include: remedial math, remedial English, reading machines, tape recorders, note-taking services, oral tests, learning center, readers, extended time for tests, other. **Information technology resources:** Students are not required to lease or own a computer. Number of campus computers available to all students: 146. School does not have a wireless network. Proportion of college-owned housing units wired for high-speed internet access: 100%. **Campus safety:** Security services offered: 24-hour foot-and-vehicle patrols, 24-hour emergency telephones, lighted pathways/sidewalks, controlled dormitory access (key, security card, etc.).

TRANSFER AND INTERNATIONAL STUDENTS

Transfer students: May apply for admission for the following academic terms: Fall, Spring, Summer. Applicants need a minimum number of credits to apply. For fall 2005: Transfer applicants enrolled: 200. **International students:** Number of foreign undergraduates: 22 (1% of student body). Minimum TOEFL score required: 525 (paper); 197 (computer).

Lakeland College

- **Address:** W3711 South Drive, Plymouth, WI 53073
- **Website:** http://www.lakeland.edu
- **Private; Religious affiliation:** United Church of Christ
- **Enrollment:** 1,400 full-time; 1,973 part-time

KEY STATS

✔ **U.S News College Ranking:** third tier, Comp. Coll.–Bachelor's (Midwest)
✔ **ACT Score (25th/75th percentile):** 18-23
✔ **Tuition:** 2006-2007: $16,796

Selectivity: Less selective	**Room/board:** $5,920
Acceptance rate: 71%	**Average debt:** $14,210
Student/faculty ratio: 17/1	**Proportion who borrowed:** 85%

UNDERGRADUATE STUDENT BODY STATS

2005-2006 enrollment: 1,400 full-time; 1,973 part-time. Men: 39%; women: 61%. **Ethnic makeup:** African American: 6%; American-Indian: 1%; Asian American: 2%; Hispanic: 2%; White: 84%; International: 5%.

ADMISSIONS FACTS AND FIGURES

Phone: (920) 565-1226. **Email:** admissions@lakeland.edu. **Website:** http://www.lakeland.edu. **Application deadlines for fall 2007:** Regular decision: September 1; decision sent by September 1. Early decision: Not offered. Early action: Not offered. Admission can be deferred. **Application fee:** $20. Common application is accepted. **To apply online, go to:** http://www.lakeland.edu/Application/Home.asp. **Admissions requirements/recommendations:** High school units required (recommended): English: (4); Mathematics: (4); Science: (2); Foreign language: (2); Social studies: (1); History: (2); Total units: (4). Tests: The college uses SAT or ACT scores in admissions decisions. Either SAT or ACT required. For admission to the fall 2007 entering class, the school will accept: ACT with writing, ACT without writing. Campus visit: Recommended. Admissions interview: Recommended. Off-campus interview: May be arranged. **Factors that count in admissions decisions:** *Academic:* Secondary school record: Considered. Class rank: Important. Letters of recommendation: Considered. Standardized test scores: Very important. Essay: Important. *Nonacademic:* Interview: Considered. Extracurricular activities: Important. Talent/ability: Not considered. Character/personal qualities: Important. Alumni/ae relationship: Considered. Geographical residence: Not considered. State residency: Not considered. Religious affiliation/commitment: Considered. Minority status: Not considered. Volunteer work: Considered. Work experience: Not considered. **Admissions statistics for the fall 2005 entering class:** Total applicants: 872. Total accepted: 617. Freshmen enrolled: 243; Overall acceptance rate: 71%. **Credentials of fall 2005 freshmen:** 7% ranked in the top 10 percent of their high school class; 21% were in the top 25 percent, and 64% were in the top half. (Proportion submitting class standing: 96%.) **Average high school grade point average:** 3.0. **First-year students who submitted SAT scores:** 7%. Scores (25/75 percentile): Verbal: N/A, Math: N/A, Combined: N/A. **First-year students submitting ACT scores:** 97%. Scores (25/75 percentile): English: N/A, Math: N/A, Composite: 18-23.

ACADEMICS

Year founded: 1862. **Academic calendar:** Semester. **Degrees offered:** bachelor's, master's. **Most popular majors:** 69% business/commerce, 16% computer science, 12% education. **Major fields of study:** biological and biomedical sciences; business, management, marketing, and related support services; computer and information sciences and support services; education; English language and literature/letters; foreign languages, literatures, and linguistics; history; mathematics and statistics; philosophy and religious studies; physical sciences; psychology; security and protective

services; social sciences; visual and performing arts. **Areas of required coursework:** arts/fine arts, humanities, mathematics, English (including composition), sciences (biological or physical), history, social science. **Pre-professional programs:** pre-law, pre-dentistry, pre-medicine, other. **Special academic programs (% participation):** cross-registration (10%), distance learning (25%), double major (10%), English as a Second Language (ESL), honors program, independent study, internships, study abroad, teacher certificate program. **Teacher certification offered in:** early childhood, elementary, middle/junior high, secondary. **Faculty and instruction (2005-2006):** Total instructional faculty: 54 full-time, 15 part-time (64% men; 36% women; 9% minorities). Full-time faculty with Ph.D. or other terminal degree: 74%. Student/faculty ratio: 17/1. Classes of fewer than 20 students: 69%; of 20 to 49 students: 31%; of 50 or more students: 0%. **Advanced Placement and International Baccalaureate credit:** AP tests may be used for: Credit only. Scores accepted: 3. International Baccalaureate exams may be used for: Credit and/or placement. **Freshmen returning for sophomore year:** 68%. **Graduation rates:** Four-year: 25%; five-year: 36%; six-year: 41%. **Graduate study:** 15% of students pursue further study immediately upon graduation; 20% within one year. Fields in which graduates pursue further study: Master of Business Administration (MBA), 60%; law, 5%; education, 35%.

COSTS AND FINANCIAL AID

Financial aid office: (920) 565-1298. **Expenses (2006-2007):** Tuition and fees 2006-2007: $16,796; room/board: $5,920. Estimated books and supplies: $700; transportation: $1,924; personal expenses: $1,100. **Financial aid:** Priority filing date for institution's financial aid form: April 1; deadline: April 1. In 2005-2006, 85% of undergraduates applied for financial aid. Of those, 72% were determined to have financial need; 25% had their need fully met. Average financial aid package (proportion receiving): $11,325 (71%). Average amount of gift aid, such as scholarships or grants (proportion receiving): $8,146 (64%). Average amount of self-help aid, such as work study or loans (proportion receiving): $4,577 (63%). Average need-based loan (excluding PLUS or other private loans): $4,123. Among students who received need-based aid, the average percentage of need met: 75%. Among students who received aid based on merit, the average award (and the proportion receiving): $8,232 (22%). The average athletic scholarship (and the proportion receiving): $0 (0%). Average amount of debt of borrowers graduating in 2005: $14,210. Proportion who borrowed: 85%.

CAMPUS LIFE AND EXTRACURRICULAR ACTIVITIES

Campus housing available: coed dorms, women's dorms, men's dorms, sorority housing, fraternity housing, apartment for single students. Students who live in college-owned, operated, or affiliated housing: 66%. **Student employment:** During the 2005-2006 academic year, 25% of undergraduates worked on campus. Average per-year earnings: $4,600. **Clubs and organizations:** Number of student organizations: 32. Activities include: choral groups, concert band, drama/theater, literary magazine, music ensembles, student government, student newspaper, yearbook. Number of fraternities: 3; sororities: 3. Proportion of men in fraternities: 15%; of women in sororities: 15%. **Sports program (2005-2006):** Member of NCAA III. *Men's intercollegiate varsity sports:* baseball, basketball, cross-country, football, golf, soccer, tennis, wrestling. *Women's intercollegiate varsity sports:* basketball, cross-country, golf, soccer, softball, tennis, volleyball.

SERVICES AND FACILITIES

Basic services: nonremedial tutoring, day care, health service. **Remedial assistance:** reading, math, writing, study skills. **Counseling services:** career, personal, academic, psychological, religious. **For learning-disabled students:** School does not offer a structured program with separate admission and additional fees. Services include: remedial math, remedial English, reading machines, remedial reading, tape recorders, untimed tests, note-taking services, oral tests, learning center, readers, extended time for tests, tutors. **Library:** Number of titles: 54,455; number of current serial subscriptions: 306. **Information technology resources:** Students are not required to lease or own a computer. Number of campus computers available to all students: 250. School does not have a wireless network. Proportion of college-owned housing units wired for high-speed internet access: 100%. **Campus safety:** Security services offered: late-night transport/escort service, 24-hour emergency telephones, lighted pathways/sidewalks, student patrols, controlled dormitory access (key, security card, etc.).

TRANSFER AND INTERNATIONAL STUDENTS

Transfer students: May apply for admission for the following academic terms: Fall, Spring, Summer. Applicants do not need a minimum number of credits to apply. **International students:** Number of foreign undergraduates: 167 (5% of student body). Number of countries represented: 35.

Minimum TOEFL score required: 500 (paper); 173 (computer). Average TOEFL score: 550 (paper).

Lawrence University

- **Address:** PO Box 599, Appleton, WI 54912
- **Website:** http://www.lawrence.edu
- **Private**
- **Enrollment:** 1,383 full-time; 67 part-time

KEY STATS
✔ **U.S News College Ranking:** 53, Liberal Arts Colleges
✔ **ACT Score (25th/75th percentile):** 25-30
✔ **Tuition:** 2006-2007: $29,598

Selectivity: More selective	**Room/board:** $6,382
Acceptance rate: 68%	**Average debt:** $19,294
Student/faculty ratio: 9/1	**Proportion who borrowed:** 66%

UNDERGRADUATE STUDENT BODY STATS
2005-2006 enrollment: 1,383 full-time; 67 part-time. Men: 46%; women: 54%. **Ethnic makeup:** African American: 2%; Asian American: 3%; Hispanic: 3%; White: 84%; International: 7%.

ADMISSIONS FACTS AND FIGURES
Phone: (800) 227-0982. **Email:** excel@lawrence.edu. **Website:** http://www.lawrence.edu. **Application deadlines for fall 2007:** Regular decision: January 15; decision sent by April 1. Early decision: Send application by: November 15; Decision sent by: December 1. Early action: Send application by: December 1; Decision sent by: January 15. Admission can be deferred. **Application fee:** $40. Common application is accepted. **To apply online, go to:** http://app.commonapp.org/. **Admissions requirements/recommendations:** High school units required (recommended): English: (4); Mathematics: (3); Science: (3); Foreign language: (2); Total units: 16. Tests: The college uses SAT or ACT scores in admissions decisions. Neither SAT nor ACT required. For admission to the fall 2007 entering class, the school will accept: ACT with writing, ACT without writing. Campus visit: Recommended. Admissions interview: Recommended. Off-campus interview: May be arranged. **Factors that count in admissions decisions:** *Academic:* Secondary school record: Very important. Class rank: Very important. Letters of recommendation: Important. Standardized test scores: Considered. Essay: Important. *Nonacademic:* Interview: Considered. Extracurricular activities: Important. Talent/ability: Important. Character/personal qualities: Important. Alumni/ae relationship: Considered. Geographical residence: Not considered. State residency: Not considered. Religious affiliation/commitment: Not considered. Minority status: Considered. Volunteer work: Considered. Work experience: Considered. **Other schools with the greatest overlap in applicants:** Beloit College; Carleton College; Grinnell College; Oberlin College; University of Wisconsin–Madison. **Admissions statistics for the fall 2005 entering class:** Total applicants: 2,060. Total accepted: 1,407. Freshmen enrolled: 401; 59% were from out of state. Accepted through early-decision or early-action plans: 28%. Overall acceptance rate: 68%. Early-decision acceptance rate: 95%. Non-early acceptance rate: 65%. **Size of waiting list:** 60 applicants; enrolled from waiting list: 2. **Credentials of fall 2005 freshmen:** 41% ranked in the top 10 percent of their high school class; 72% were in the top 25 percent, and 97% were in the top half. (Proportion submitting class standing: 72%.) **Average high school grade point average:** 3.5. **First-year students who submitted SAT scores:** 55%. Scores (25/75 percentile): Verbal: 590-700, Math: 600-690, Combined: 1190-1390. **First-year students submitting ACT scores:** 79%. Scores (25/75 percentile): English: 25-31, Math: 24-29, Composite: 25-30.

ACADEMICS
Year founded: 1847. **Academic calendar:** Trimester. **Degrees offered:** bachelor's. **Most popular majors:** 11% music performance, 9% English language and literature, 9% biology/biological sciences, 9% political science and government, 8% psychology. **Major fields of study:** area, ethnic, cultural, and gender studies; biological and biomedical sciences; computer and information sciences and support services; education; English language and literature/letters; foreign languages, literatures, and linguistics; history; legal professions and studies; liberal arts and sciences studies, and humanities; mathematics and statistics; multi/interdisciplinary studies; natural resources and conservation; philosophy and religious studies; physical sciences; psychology; social sciences; visual and performing arts. **Areas of required coursework:** arts/fine arts, humanities, foreign languages, sciences (biological or physical), social science, other. **Pre-professional programs:** pre-law, pre-dentistry, pre-medicine, pre-veterinary science, pre-optometry, pre-pharmacy. **Special academic programs (% participation):** double major (27%), independent study (81%), internships (11%), student-designed major (1%), study abroad (20%), teacher certificate program (9%). **Teacher certification offered in:** middle/junior high, secondary. **Cooperative education programs:** engineering, health professions, other. **Faculty and instruction (2005-2006):** Total instructional faculty: 144 full-time, 32 part-time (65% men; 35% women; 8% minorities). Full-time faculty with Ph.D. or other terminal degree: 99%. Student/faculty ratio: 9/1. Classes of fewer than 20 students: 73%; of 20 to 49 students: 26%; of 50 or more students: 1%. **Advanced Placement and International Baccalaureate credit:** AP tests may be used for: Credit and/or placement. Scores accepted: 4, 5. International Baccalaureate exams may be used for: Credit and/or placement. **Freshmen returning for sophomore year:** 90%. **Graduation rates:** Four-year: 59%; five-year: 75%; six-year: 76%. **Graduate study:** 33% of students pursue further study immediately upon graduation; 2% within one year; 1% within five years. Fields in which graduates pursue further study: Master of Business Administration (MBA), 1%; law, 10%; medicine, 5%; dentistry, 1%; engineering, 3%; education, 1%; arts and sciences, 37%.

COSTS AND FINANCIAL AID
Financial aid office: (920) 832-6583. **Expenses (2006-2007):** Tuition and fees 2006-2007: $29,598; room/board: $6,382. Estimated books and supplies: $675; transportation: $200; personal expenses: $1,005. **Financial aid:** Priority filing date for institution's financial aid form: March 15. In 2005-2006, 76% of undergraduates applied for financial aid. Of those, 61% were determined to have financial need; 100% had their need fully met. Average financial aid package (proportion receiving): $22,900 (61%). Average amount of gift aid, such as scholarships or grants (proportion receiving): $16,061 (61%). Average amount of self-help aid, such as work study or loans (proportion receiving): $7,540 (56%). Average need-based loan (excluding PLUS or other private loans): $5,660. Among students who received need-based aid, the average percentage of need met: 100%. Among students who received aid based on merit, the average award (and the proportion receiving): $9,270 (31%). The average athletic scholarship (and the proportion receiving): $0 (0%). Average amount of debt of borrowers graduating in 2005: $19,294. Proportion who borrowed: 66%.

CAMPUS LIFE AND EXTRACURRICULAR ACTIVITIES
Campus housing available (% using): coed dorms (79%), women's dorms (2%), other housing options (19%). Students who live in college-owned, operated, or affiliated housing: 96%. **Student employment:** During the 2005-2006 academic year, 20% of undergraduates worked on campus. Average per-year earnings: $2,000. **Clubs and organizations:** Number of student organizations: 117. Activities include: choral groups, concert band, dance, drama/theater, jazz band, literary magazine, music ensembles, musical theater, opera, pep band, radio station, student government, student newspaper, student film society, symphony orchestra, yearbook. Number of fraternities: 5; sororities: 3. Proportion of men in fraternities: 23%; of women in sororities: 10%. Average proportion of students who stay on campus on weekends: 90%. **Sports program (2005-2006):** Member of NCAA III. *Men's intercollegiate varsity sports:* baseball, basketball, cross-country, fencing, football, golf, ice hockey, soccer, swimming and diving, tennis, track and field (indoor), track and field (outdoor), wrestling. *Women's intercollegiate varsity sports:* basketball, cross-country, fencing, soccer, softball, swimming and diving, tennis, track and field (indoor), track and field (outdoor), volleyball.

SERVICES AND FACILITIES
Basic services: nonremedial tutoring, placement service, health service, health insurance. **Remedial assistance:** other. **Counseling services:** minority student, career, personal, academic, older student, psychological, birth control, religious. **For learning-disabled students:** School does not offer a structured program with separate admission and additional fees. Total undergraduates in learning-disabled program or receiving services: 30. Services include: other testing accommodations, tape recorders, untimed tests, note-taking services, oral tests, learning center, readers, extended time for tests, tutors, other testing accomodations, waiver of foreign language degree requirement, other. **Library:** Number of titles: 690,871; number of current serial subscriptions: 1,787. **Information technology resources:** Students are not required to lease or own a computer. Number of campus computers available to all students: 184. School has a wireless network.

Approximate number of users that can be accommodated: 26. Proportion of college-owned housing units wired for high-speed internet access: 100%.
Campus safety: Security services offered: 24-hour foot-and-vehicle patrols, late-night transport/escort service, 24-hour emergency telephones, lighted pathways/sidewalks, controlled dormitory access (key, security card, etc).

TRANSFER AND INTERNATIONAL STUDENTS
Transfer students: May apply for admission for the following academic terms: Fall, Winter, Spring. Applicants need a minimum number of credits to apply. For fall 2005: Transfer applications received: 70. Transfer applicants offered admission: 44. Transfer applicants enrolled: 27. **International students:** Number of foreign undergraduates: 99 (7% of student body). Number of countries represented: 54. Minimum TOEFL score required: 577 (paper); 233 (computer). Average TOEFL score: 617 (paper).

Marian College of Fond du Lac

- **Address:** 45 S. National Avenue, Fond du Lac, WI 54935
- **Website:** http://www.mariancollege.edu
- **Private; Religious affiliation:** Roman Catholic
- **Enrollment:** 1,361 full-time; 716 part-time

KEY STATS
✔ **U.S News College Ranking:** third tier, Universities–Master's (Midwest)
✔ **ACT Score (25th/75th percentile):** 18-22
✔ **Tuition:** 2006-2007: $17,625

Selectivity: Less selective	**Room/board:** $5,200
Acceptance rate: 86%	**Average debt:** $20,800
Student/faculty ratio: 13/1	**Proportion who borrowed:** 90%

UNDERGRADUATE STUDENT BODY STATS
2005-2006 enrollment: 1,361 full-time; 716 part-time. Men: 27%; women: 73%. **Ethnic makeup:** African American: 4%; American-Indian: 1%; Asian American: 1%; Hispanic: 1%; White: 92%; International: 1%. **Religious preference:** Protestant: 30%; Unknown: 15%; Roman Catholic: 41%; Other: 14%.

ADMISSIONS FACTS AND FIGURES
Phone: (920) 923-7650. **Email:** admissions@mariancollege.edu. **Website:** http://www.mariancollege.edu. **Application deadlines for fall 2007:** Regular decision: Rolling. Early decision: Not offered. Early action: Not offered. Admission can be deferred. **Application fee:** $20. Common application is accepted. **To apply online, go to:** http://www.mariancollege.edu/ProspectiveStudents/applicationchoice.htm. **Admissions requirements/recommendations:** High school units required (recommended): English: 4; Mathematics: 2 (3); Science: 1 (2); Foreign language: (2); History: 1; Total units: 17. Tests: The college uses SAT or ACT scores in admissions decisions. Either SAT or ACT required. For admission to the fall 2007 entering class, the school will accept: ACT without writing. Campus visit: Recommended. Admissions interview: Recommended. Off-campus interview: May be arranged. **Factors that count in admissions decisions:** *Academic:* Secondary school record: Very important. Class rank: Very important. Letters of recommendation: Considered. Standardized test scores: Very important. Essay: Considered. *Nonacademic:* Interview: Important. Extracurricular activities: Considered. Talent/ability: Considered. Character/personal qualities: Important. Alumni/ae relationship: Considered. Geographical residence: Not considered. State residency: Not considered. Religious affiliation/commitment: Not considered. Minority status: Not considered. Volunteer work: Considered. Work experience: Considered. **Other schools with the greatest overlap in applicants:** Carroll College; Ripon College; University of Wisconsin–Milwaukee; University of Wisconsin–Oshkosh. **Admissions statistics for the fall 2005 entering class:** Total applicants: 766. Total accepted: 661. Freshmen enrolled: 262; 10% were from out of state. Overall acceptance rate: 86%. **Credentials of fall 2005 freshmen:** 11% ranked in the top 10 percent of their high school class; 31% were in the top 25 percent, and 62% were in the top half. (Proportion submitting class standing: 89%.) **Average high school grade point average:** 3.0. **First-year students submitting ACT scores:** 91%. Scores (25/75 percentile): English: 16-22, Math: 17-23, Composite: 18-22.

ACADEMICS
Year founded: 1936. **Academic calendar:** Semester. **Degrees offered:** bachelor's, master's, doctorate. **Most popular majors:** 36% business, manage-

ment, marketing, and related support services, 16% nursing, 14% education, 10% criminal justice/law enforcement administration, 3% social work. **Major fields of study:** biological and biomedical sciences; business, management, marketing, and related support services; communication, journalism, and related programs; computer and information sciences and support services; education; English language and literature/letters; foreign languages, literatures, and linguistics; health professions and related clinical sciences; history; liberal arts and sciences studies, and humanities; mathematics and statistics; multi/interdisciplinary studies; parks, recreation, leisure, and fitness studies; physical sciences; psychology; public administration and social service professions; security and protective services; visual and performing arts. **Areas of required coursework:** arts/fine arts, humanities, mathematics, English (including composition), philosophy, sciences (biological or physical), history, social science. **Pre-professional programs:** pre-law, pre-dentistry, pre-medicine, pre-veterinary science, other. **Special academic programs:** accelerated program, cooperative (work-study plan) program, distance learning, double major, dual enrollment, honors program, independent study, internships, liberal arts/career combination, student-designed major, study abroad, teacher certificate program, weekend college. **Teacher certification offered in:** early childhood, elementary, middle/junior high, secondary. **Cooperative education programs:** business, computer science, education, health professions, social/behavioral science, other. **Reserve Officers Training Corps (ROTC):** Army ROTC: Offered on campus. **Faculty and instruction (2005-2006):** Total instructional faculty: 78 full-time, 201 part-time (52% men; 48% women; 6% minorities). Full-time faculty with Ph.D. or other terminal degree: 60%. Student/faculty ratio: 13/1. Classes of fewer than 20 students: 71%; of 20 to 49 students: 29%; of 50 or more students: 0%. **Advanced Placement and International Baccalaureate credit:** AP tests may be used for: Credit only. Scores accepted: 3, 4, 5. **Freshmen returning for sophomore year:** 71%. **Graduation rates:** Four-year: 32%; five-year: 46%; six-year: 49%. **Graduate study:** 8% of students pursue further study immediately upon graduation.

COSTS AND FINANCIAL AID
Financial aid office: (920) 923-7614. **Expenses (2006-2007):** Tuition and fees 2006-2007: $17,625; room/board: $5,200. Estimated books and supplies: $700; transportation: $2,000; personal expenses: $1,530. **Financial aid:** Priority filing date for institution's financial aid form: March 1. In 2005-2006, 95% of undergraduates applied for financial aid. Of those, 79% were determined to have financial need; 40% had their need fully met. Average financial aid package (proportion receiving): $16,359 (79%). Average amount of gift aid, such as scholarships or grants (proportion receiving): $8,986 (75%). Average amount of self-help aid, such as work study or loans (proportion receiving): $6,412 (72%). Average need-based loan (excluding PLUS or other private loans): $5,309. Among students who received need-based aid, the average percentage of need met: 92%. Among students who received aid based on merit, the average award (and the proportion receiving): $4,484 (14%). The average athletic scholarship (and the proportion receiving): $0 (0%). Average amount of debt of borrowers graduating in 2005: $20,800. Proportion who borrowed: 90%.

CAMPUS LIFE AND EXTRACURRICULAR ACTIVITIES
Campus housing available: coed dorms, sorority housing, fraternity housing, apartment for single students, special housing for disabled students. Students who live in college-owned, operated, or affiliated housing: 34%. **Student employment:** During the 2005-2006 academic year, 21% of undergraduates worked on campus. Average per-year earnings: $1,300. **Clubs and organizations:** Number of student organizations: 36. Activities include: choral groups, concert band, drama/theater, jazz band, literary magazine, music ensembles, student government, student newspaper, symphony orchestra. Number of fraternities: 2; sororities: 3. Proportion of men in fraternities: 13%; of women in sororities: 11%. Average proportion of students who stay on campus on weekends: 40%. **Sports program (2005-2006):** Member of NCAA III. *Men's intercollegiate varsity sports:* baseball, basketball, golf, ice hockey, soccer, tennis. *Women's intercollegiate varsity sports:* basketball, golf, soccer, softball, tennis, volleyball.

SERVICES AND FACILITIES
Basic services: nonremedial tutoring, placement service, day care, health service, health insurance. **Remedial assistance:** reading, math, writing, study skills, other. **Counseling services:** minority student, career, military, personal, academic, older student, religious. **For learning-disabled students:** School does not offer a structured program with separate admission and additional fees. Total undergraduates in learning-disabled program or receiving services: 10. Services include: remedial math, remedial English, reading machines, remedial reading, tape recorders, other special classes,

untimed tests, note-taking services, oral tests, learning center, readers, extended time for tests, tutors, early syllabus, priority registration, priority seating, proofreading services, texts on tape, typist/scribe, exams on tape or computer, other testing accomodations, other. **Library:** Number of titles: 92,431; number of current serial subscriptions: 775. **Information technology resources:** Students are not required to lease or own a computer. Number of campus computers available to all students: 275. School does not have a wireless network. Proportion of college-owned housing units wired for high-speed internet access: 100%. **Campus safety:** Security services offered: late-night transport/escort service, 24-hour emergency telephones, lighted pathways/sidewalks, student patrols, controlled dormitory access (key, security card, etc.).

TRANSFER AND INTERNATIONAL STUDENTS

Transfer students: May apply for admission for the following academic terms: Fall, Winter, Spring, Summer. Applicants do not need a minimum number of credits to apply. For fall 2005: Transfer applications received: 411. Transfer applicants offered admission: 308. Transfer applicants enrolled: 140. **International students:** Number of foreign undergraduates: 12 (1% of student body). Number of countries represented: 11. Minimum TOEFL score required: 525 (paper); 193 (computer). Average TOEFL score: 700 (paper).

Marquette University

- **Address:** PO Box 1881, Milwaukee, WI 53201-1881
- **Website:** http://www.marquette.edu
- **Private; Religious affiliation:** Roman Catholic (Jesuit)
- **Enrollment:** 7,530 full-time; 480 part-time

KEY STATS

- ✔ **U.S News College Ranking:** 81, National Universities
- ✔ **ACT Score (25th/75th percentile):** 24-29
- ✔ **Tuition:** 2006-2007: $25,074

Selectivity: More selective	**Room/board:** $8,120
Acceptance rate: 70%	**Average debt:** $26,345
Student/faculty ratio: 15/1	**Proportion who borrowed:** 52%

UNDERGRADUATE STUDENT BODY STATS

2005-2006 enrollment: 7,530 full-time; 480 part-time. Men: 45%; women: 55%. **Ethnic makeup:** African American: 5%; Asian American: 4%; Hispanic: 4%; White: 85%; International: 2%. **Religious preference:** Roman Catholic: 63%; Protestant: 17%; Muslim: 1%; No preference: 10%; Other: 9%.

ADMISSIONS FACTS AND FIGURES

Phone: (800) 222-6544. **Email:** admissions@marquette.edu. **Website:** http://www.marquette.edu. **Application deadlines for fall 2007:** Regular decision: Rolling. Early decision: Not offered. Early action: Not offered. Admission can be deferred. **Application fee:** $30. Common application is accepted. **To apply online, go to:** http://www.marquette.edu/apply@mu. **Admissions requirements/recommendations:** High school units required (recommended): English: 4 (4); Mathematics: 2 (4); Science: 2 (3); Foreign language: 2 (2); Social studies: 2 (3); History: 0 (0); Academic electives: 2 (4); Total units: 14 (20). Tests: The college uses SAT or ACT scores in admissions decisions. Either SAT or ACT required. For admission to the fall 2007 entering class, the school will accept: ACT without writing. Campus visit: Recommended. Admissions interview: Neither required nor recommended. Off-campus interview: Not available. **Factors that count in admissions decisions:** *Academic:* Secondary school record: Very important. Class rank: Important. Letters of recommendation: Important. Standardized test scores: Important. Essay: Important. *Nonacademic:* Interview: Not considered. Extracurricular activities: Considered. Talent/ability: Considered. Character/personal qualities: Considered. Alumni/ae relationship: Considered. Geographical residence: Considered. State residency: Considered. Religious affiliation/commitment: Considered. Minority status: Considered. Volunteer work: Considered. Work experience: Not considered. **Other schools with the greatest overlap in applicants:** Loyola University Chicago; St. Louis University; University of Illinois–Urbana-Champaign; University of Wisconsin–Madison; University of Wisconsin–Milwaukee. **Admissions statistics for the fall 2005 entering class:** Total applicants: 10,348. Total accepted: 7,257. Freshmen enrolled: 1,784; 59% were from out

of state. Overall acceptance rate: 70%. **Size of waiting list:** 1516 applicants; enrolled from waiting list: 334. **Credentials of fall 2005 freshmen:** 34% ranked in the top 10 percent of their high school class; 65% were in the top 25 percent, and 94% were in the top half. (Proportion submitting class standing: 51%.) **First-year students who submitted SAT scores:** 21%. Scores (25/75 percentile): Verbal: 540-650, Math: 540-660, Combined: 1080-1310. **First-year students submitting ACT scores:** 82%. Scores (25/75 percentile): English: 24-30, Math: 24-28, Composite: 24-29.

ACADEMICS

Year founded: 1881. **Academic calendar:** Semester. **Degrees offered:** bachelor's, post-bachelor's certificate, master's, post-master's certificate, first professional, doctorate. **Most popular majors:** 22% business, management, marketing, and related support services, 14% communication, journalism, and related programs, 10% engineering, 10% social sciences, 8% health professions and related clinical sciences. **Major fields of study:** biological and biomedical sciences; business, management, marketing, and related support services; communication, journalism, and related programs; computer and information sciences and support services; education; engineering; engineering technologies/technicians; English language and literature/letters; foreign languages, literatures, and linguistics; health professions and related clinical sciences; history; mathematics and statistics; multi/interdisciplinary studies; philosophy and religious studies; physical sciences; psychology; public administration and social service professions; social sciences; theology and religious vocations; visual and performing arts. **Areas of required coursework:** humanities, mathematics, English (including composition), philosophy, foreign languages, sciences (biological or physical), history, social science, other. **Pre-professional programs:** pre-law, pre-dentistry, pre-medicine. **Special academic programs (% participation):** accelerated program (1%), cooperative (work-study plan) program (5%), cross-registration (1%), double major (25%), dual enrollment, English as a Second Language (ESL) (2%), honors program (4%), independent study (29%), internships (8%), liberal arts/career combination, study abroad (16%), teacher certificate program (6%), weekend college (2%). **Teacher certification offered in:** elementary, middle/junior high, secondary. **Cooperative education programs:** business, engineering. **Reserve Officers Training Corps (ROTC):** Army ROTC: Offered on campus; Navy ROTC: Offered on campus; Air Force ROTC: Offered on campus. **Faculty and instruction (2005-2006):** Total instructional faculty: 592 full-time, 454 part-time (62% men; 38% women; 11% minorities). Full-time faculty with Ph.D. or other terminal degree: 88%. Student/faculty ratio: 15/1. Classes of fewer than 20 students: 44%; of 20 to 49 students: 46%; of 50 or more students: 11%. **Advanced Placement and International Baccalaureate credit:** AP tests may be used for: Credit and/or placement. Scores accepted: 3, 4, 5. International Baccalaureate exams may be used for: Credit and/or placement. **Freshmen returning for sophomore year:** 89%. **Graduation rates:** Four-year: 62%; five-year: 78%; six-year: 80%. **Graduate study:** 30% of students pursue further study within one year; 41% within five years. Fields in which graduates pursue further study: Master of Business Administration (MBA): 5%; law, 9%; medicine, 12%; dentistry, 2%; engineering, 7%; theology (or the seminary), 1%; education, 9%.

COSTS AND FINANCIAL AID

Financial aid office: (414) 288-0200. **Expenses (2006-2007):** Tuition and fees 2006-2007: $25,074; room/board: $8,120. Estimated books and supplies: $900; transportation: $500; personal expenses: $1,350. **Financial aid:** Priority filing date for institution's financial aid form: March 1. In 2005-2006, 73% of undergraduates applied for financial aid. Of those, 61% were determined to have financial need; 31% had their need fully met. Average financial aid package (proportion receiving): $16,770 (58%). Average amount of gift aid, such as scholarships or grants (proportion receiving): $11,445 (52%). Average amount of self-help aid, such as work study or loans (proportion receiving): $10,999 (49%). Average need-based loan (excluding PLUS or other private loans): $4,991. Among students who received need-based aid, the average percentage of need met: 74%. Among students who received aid based on merit, the average award (and the proportion receiving): $7,953 (7%). The average athletic scholarship (and the proportion receiving): $19,428 (2%). Average amount of debt of borrowers graduating in 2005: $26,345. Proportion who borrowed: 52%.

CAMPUS LIFE AND EXTRACURRICULAR ACTIVITIES

Campus housing available (% using): coed dorms (51%), women's dorms (9%), men's dorms (7%), sorority housing, fraternity housing (1%), apartments for married students, apartment for single students (26%), special housing for disabled students (1%), special housing for international students (1%), other housing options (4%). Students who live in college-owned, operated, or affiliated housing: 52%. **Student employment:** During the 2005-2006 academic year, 34% of undergraduates worked on campus. Average per-year earnings: $2,500. **Clubs and organizations:** Number of student organizations: 227. Activities include: choral groups, concert band, dance, drama/theater, jazz band, literary magazine, music ensembles, musical theater, pep band, radio station, student government, student newspaper, symphony orchestra, television station, yearbook. Number of fraternities: 11; sororities: 10. Proportion of men in fraternities: 5%; of women in sororities: 7%. Average proportion of students who stay on campus on weekends: 90%. **Sports program (2005-2006):** Member of NCAA I. *Men's intercollegiate varsity sports:* basketball, cross-country, golf, soccer, tennis, track and field (indoor), track and field (outdoor). *Women's intercollegiate varsity sports:* basketball, cross-country, soccer, tennis, track and field (indoor), track and field (outdoor), volleyball.

SERVICES AND FACILITIES

Basic services: nonremedial tutoring, placement service, health service, health insurance, other. **Counseling services:** minority student, career, military, personal, veteran student, academic, older student, psychological, religious. **For learning-disabled students:** School does not offer a structured program with separate admission and additional fees. Total undergraduates in learning-disabled program or receiving services: 50. Services include: other testing accommodations, reading machines, tape recorders, diagnostic testing service, note-taking services, oral tests, extended time for tests, priority registration, texts on tape, other. **Library:** Number of titles: 1,401,953; number of current serial subscriptions: 21,006. **Information technology resources:** Students are not required to lease or own a computer. Number of campus computers available to all students: 1,700. School has a wireless network. Approximate number of users that can be accommodated: 3,500. Proportion of college-owned housing units wired for high-speed internet access: 100%. **Campus safety:** Security services offered: 24-hour foot-and-vehicle patrols, late-night transport/escort service, 24-hour emergency telephones, lighted pathways/sidewalks, student patrols, controlled dormitory access (key, security card, etc).

TRANSFER AND INTERNATIONAL STUDENTS

Transfer students: May apply for admission for the following academic terms: Fall, Spring, Summer. Applicants need a minimum number of credits to apply. For fall 2005: Transfer applications received: 729. Transfer applicants offered admission: 412. Transfer applicants enrolled: 176. **International students:** Number of foreign undergraduates: 137 (2% of student body). Number of countries represented: 51. Minimum TOEFL score required: 550 (paper); 213 (computer). Average TOEFL score: 582 (paper).

Milwaukee Institute of Art and Design

- **Address:** 273 E. Erie Street, Milwaukee, WI 53202
- **Website:** http://www.miad.edu
- **Private**
- **Enrollment:** 606 full-time; 39 part-time

KEY STATS

✔ **U.S News College Ranking:** Unranked Specialty School–Fine Arts
✔ **SAT or ACT Score (25th/75th percentile):** N/A
✔ **Tuition:** 2006-2007: $23,600

Selectivity: Least selective	**Room/board:** $7,000
Acceptance rate: 82%	**Average debt:** N/A
Student/faculty ratio: 10/1	**Proportion who borrowed:** N/A

UNDERGRADUATE STUDENT BODY STATS

2005-2006 enrollment: 606 full-time; 39 part-time. Men: 53%; women: 47%. **Ethnic makeup:** African American: 3%; Asian American: 5%; Hispanic: 6%; White: 83%; International: 3%.

ADMISSIONS FACTS AND FIGURES

Phone: (414) 291-8070. **Email:** admissions@miad.edu. **Website:** http://www.miad.edu. **Application deadlines for fall 2007:** Regular decision: Rolling. Early decision: Not offered. Early action: Not offered. Admission can be deferred. **Application fee:** $25. Common application is accepted. **Admissions requirements/recommendations:** High school units required (recommended): English: 0 (0); Mathematics: 0 (0); Science: 0 (0); Foreign language: 0 (0); Social studies: 0 (0); History: 0 (0); Academic electives: 0

(0); Total units: 0 (0). Tests: The college does not use SAT or ACT scores in admissions decisions. Neither SAT nor ACT required. Campus visit: Recommended. Admissions interview: Recommended. Off-campus interview: Not available. **Factors that count in admissions decisions:** *Academic:* Secondary school record: Considered. Class rank: Considered. Letters of recommendation: Considered. Standardized test scores: Considered. Essay: Very important. *Nonacademic:* Interview: Very important. Extracurricular activities: Considered. Talent/ability: Very important. Character/personal qualities: Very important. Alumni/ae relationship: Not considered. Geographical residence: Not considered. State residency: Not considered. Religious affiliation/commitment: Not considered. Minority status: Not considered. Volunteer work: Considered. Work experience: Considered. **Other schools with the greatest overlap in applicants:** Kansas City Art Institute; Maryland Institute College of Art; Minneapolis College of Art and Design; University of Wisconsin–Milwaukee. **Admissions statistics for the fall 2005 entering class:** Total applicants: 308. Total accepted: 252. Freshmen enrolled: 162; 35% were from out of state. Overall acceptance rate: 82%. **Credentials of fall 2005 freshmen:** 8% ranked in the top 10 percent of their high school class; 21% were in the top 25 percent, and 48% were in the top half. (Proportion submitting class standing: 100%.) **Average high school grade point average:** 2.9. **First-year students who submitted SAT scores:** 6%. Scores (25/75 percentile): Verbal: N/A, Math: N/A, Combined: N/A. **First-year students submitting ACT scores:** 44%. Scores (25/75 percentile): English: N/A, Math: N/A, Composite: N/A.

ACADEMICS

Year founded: 1974. **Academic calendar:** Semester. **Degrees offered:** bachelor's. **Most popular majors:** Information not available. **Major fields of study:** visual and performing arts. **Areas of required coursework:** arts/fine arts, humanities, computer literacy, English (including composition), sciences (biological or physical), history, social science. **Special academic programs:** cross-registration, double major, exchange student program (domestic), independent study, internships, study abroad. **Faculty and instruction (2005-2006):** Total instructional faculty: 34 full-time, 95 part-time (56% men; 44% women). Full-time faculty with Ph.D. or other terminal degree: 65%. Student/faculty ratio: 10/1. Classes of fewer than 20 students: 86%; of 20 to 49 students: 14%; of 50 or more students: 0%. **Advanced Placement and International Baccalaureate credit:** AP tests may be used for: Credit only. Scores accepted: 3, 4, 5. International Baccalaureate exams may be used for: Credit only. **Freshmen returning for sophomore year:** 70%. **Graduation rates:** Four-year: 30%; five-year: 41%; six-year: 51%.

COSTS AND FINANCIAL AID

Financial aid office: (414) 291-3272. **Expenses (2006-2007):** Tuition and fees 2006-2007: $23,600; room/board: $7,000. **Financial aid:** Priority filing date for institution's financial aid form: March 1. In 2005-2006, 90% of undergraduates applied for financial aid. Of those, 83% were determined to have financial need; 28% had their need fully met. Average financial aid package (proportion receiving): $17,423 (83%). Average amount of gift aid, such as scholarships or grants (proportion receiving): $9,792 (81%). Average amount of self-help aid, such as work study or loans (proportion receiving): $8,353 (79%). Average need-based loan (excluding PLUS or other private loans): $7,662. Among students who received need-based aid, the average percentage of need met: 73%. Among students who received aid based on merit, the average award (and the proportion receiving): $10,217 (17%). The average athletic scholarship (and the proportion receiving): $0 (0%).

CAMPUS LIFE AND EXTRACURRICULAR ACTIVITIES

Campus housing available (% using): coed dorms (100%). Students who live in college-owned, operated, or affiliated housing: 23%. **Student employment:** During the 2005-2006 academic year, 30% of undergraduates worked on campus. Average per-year earnings: $1,500. Activities include: drama/theater, literary magazine, student government, student newspaper. Number of fraternities: 0; sororities: 0. Average proportion of students who stay on campus on weekends: 85%.

SERVICES AND FACILITIES

Basic services: nonremedial tutoring, placement service, health service, health insurance. **Remedial assistance:** reading, writing, study skills. **Counseling services:** minority student, career, personal, academic, psychological, birth control. **For learning-disabled students:** School does not offer a structured program with separate admission and additional fees. Services include: remedial English, remedial reading, oral tests, learning center, extended time for tests, tutors. **Information technology resources:** Students are not required to lease or own a computer. Number of campus computers available to all students: 145. School has a wireless network. Approximate number of users that can be accommodated: 500. Proportion of college-owned housing units wired for high-speed internet access: 100%. **Campus safety:** Security services offered: 24-hour foot-and-vehicle patrols, 24-hour emergency telephones, lighted pathways/sidewalks, controlled dormitory access (key, security card, etc).

TRANSFER AND INTERNATIONAL STUDENTS

Transfer students: May apply for admission for the following academic terms: Fall, Spring, Summer. Applicants do not need a minimum number of credits to apply. For fall 2005: Transfer applications received: 89. Transfer applicants offered admission: 70. Transfer applicants enrolled: 43. **International students:** Number of foreign undergraduates: 13 (3% of student body). Minimum TOEFL score required: 550 (paper); 213 (computer).

Milwaukee School of Engineering

- **Address:** 1025 N. Broadway, Milwaukee, WI 53202-3109
- **Website:** http://www.msoe.edu
- **Private**
- **Enrollment:** 1,819 full-time; 273 part-time

KEY STATS

✔ **U.S News College Ranking:** Unranked Specialty School–Engineering
✔ **ACT Score (25th/75th percentile):** 23-28
✔ **Tuition:** 2006-2007: $26,100

Selectivity: Selective	**Room/board:** $6,189
Acceptance rate: 69%	**Average debt:** $31,818
Student/faculty ratio: 12/1	**Proportion who borrowed:** 85%

UNDERGRADUATE STUDENT BODY STATS

2005-2006 enrollment: 1,819 full-time; 273 part-time. Men: 83%; women: 17%. **Ethnic makeup:** African American: 4%; American-Indian: 1%; Asian American: 3%; Hispanic: 3%; White: 88%; International: 2%.

ADMISSIONS FACTS AND FIGURES

Phone: (800) 332-6763. **Email:** explore@msoe.edu. **Website:** http://www.msoe.edu. **Application deadlines for fall 2007:** Regular decision: Rolling. Early decision: Not offered. Early action: Not offered. Admission can be deferred. **Application fee:** $25. Common application is accepted. **To apply online, go to:** http://www.msoe.edu/admiss/app_selector.shtml. **Admissions requirements/recommendations:** High school units required (recommended): English: 4 (4); Mathematics: 4 (4); Science: 2 (2); Foreign language: 0 (0); Social studies: 0 (0); History: 0 (0); Academic electives: 0 (0); Total units: 10 (12). Tests: The college uses SAT or ACT scores in admissions decisions. Either SAT or ACT required. For admission to the fall 2007 entering class, the school will accept: ACT with writing, ACT without writing. Campus visit: Recommended. Admissions interview: Neither required nor recommended. Off-campus interview: May be arranged. **Factors that count in admissions decisions:** *Academic:* Secondary school record: Important. Class rank: Not considered. Letters of recommendation: Considered. Standardized test scores: Very important. Essay: Considered. *Nonacademic:* Interview: Considered. Extracurricular activities: Considered. Talent/ability: Considered. Character/personal qualities: Not considered. Alumni/ae relationship: Not considered. Geographical residence: Not considered. State residency: Not considered. Religious affiliation/commitment: Not considered. Minority status: Not considered. Volunteer work: Considered. Work experience: Considered. **Other schools with the greatest overlap in applicants:** Marquette University; Michigan Technological University; University of Wisconsin–Madison; University of Wisconsin–Milwaukee; University of Wisconsin–Platteville. **Admissions statistics for the fall 2005 entering class:** Total applicants: 1,742. Total accepted: 1,203. Freshmen enrolled: 456; 34% were from out of state. Overall acceptance rate: 69%. **Average high school grade point average:** 3.4. **First-year students who submitted SAT scores:** 11%. Scores (25/75 percentile): Verbal: 530-650, Math: 570-660, Combined: 1100-1310. **First-year students submitting ACT scores:** 97%. Scores (25/75 percentile): English: 21-27, Math: 24-29, Composite: 23-28.

ACADEMICS

Year founded: 1903. **Academic calendar:** Quarter. **Degrees offered:** bachelor's, master's. **Most popular majors:** 69% engineering, 20% business, management, marketing, and related support services, 8% engineering technolo-

gies/technicians, 2% health professions and related clinical sciences, 1% communication, journalism, and related programs. **Major fields of study:** business, management, marketing, and related support services; communication, journalism, and related programs; engineering; engineering technologies/technicians; health professions and related clinical sciences. **Areas of required coursework:** humanities, computer literacy, mathematics, English (including composition), sciences (biological or physical), social science, other. **Special academic programs (% participation):** distance learning (1%), double major (8%), dual enrollment (2%), English as a Second Language (ESL) (1%), independent study (15%), internships (70%), study abroad (3%). **Reserve Officers Training Corps (ROTC):** Army ROTC: Offered at cooperating institution (Marquette University); Navy ROTC: Offered at cooperating institution (Marquette University); Air Force ROTC: Offered at cooperating institution (Marquette University). **Faculty and instruction (2005-2006):** Total instructional faculty: 120 full-time, 93 part-time (74% men; 26% women; 11% minorities). Full-time faculty with Ph.D. or other terminal degree: 65%. Student/faculty ratio: 12/1. Classes of fewer than 20 students: 47%; of 20 to 49 students: 53%; of 50 or more students: 0%. **Advanced Placement and International Baccalaureate credit:** AP tests may be used for: Credit and/or placement. Scores accepted: 4, 5. International Baccalaureate exams may be used for: Credit and/or placement. **Freshmen returning for sophomore year:** 76%. **Graduation rates:** Four-year: 36%; five-year: 53%; six-year: 55%. **Graduate study:** 5% of students pursue further study immediately upon graduation; 17% within one year. Fields in which graduates pursue further study: Master of Business Administration (MBA), 25%; law, 7%; medicine, 3%; engineering, 65%.

COSTS AND FINANCIAL AID

Financial aid office: (414) 277-7511. **Expenses (2006-2007):** Tuition and fees 2006-2007: $26,100; room/board: $6,189. Estimated books and supplies: $1,500; transportation: $2,000; personal expenses: $1,800. **Financial aid:** Priority filing date for institution's financial aid form: March 15. In 2005-2006, 89% of undergraduates applied for financial aid. Of those, 80% were determined to have financial need; 17% had their need fully met. Average financial aid package (proportion receiving): $16,569 (80%). Average amount of gift aid, such as scholarships or grants (proportion receiving): $13,217 (80%). Average amount of self-help aid, such as work study or loans (proportion receiving): $3,792 (71%). Average need-based loan (excluding PLUS or other private loans): $3,390. Among students who received need-based aid, the average percentage of need met: 70%. Among students who received aid based on merit, the average award (and the proportion receiving): $14,263 (16%). The average athletic scholarship (and the proportion receiving): $0 (0%). Average amount of debt of borrowers graduating in 2005: $31,818. Proportion who borrowed: 85%.

CAMPUS LIFE AND EXTRACURRICULAR ACTIVITIES

Campus housing available (% using): coed dorms (99%), special housing for disabled students (1%). Students who live in college-owned, operated, or affiliated housing: 46%. **Student employment:** During the 2005-2006 academic year, 12% of undergraduates worked on campus. Average per-year earnings: $4,000. **Clubs and organizations:** Number of student organizations: 72. Activities include: choral groups, literary magazine, music ensembles, pep band, radio station, student government, student newspaper, symphony orchestra. Number of fraternities: 3; sororities: 2. Proportion of men in fraternities: 3%; of women in sororities: 5%. Average proportion of students who stay on campus on weekends: 52%. **Sports program (2005-2006):** Member of NCAA III. *Men's intercollegiate varsity sports:* baseball, basketball, cross-country, golf, ice hockey, soccer, tennis, track and field (indoor), track and field (outdoor), volleyball, wrestling. *Women's intercollegiate varsity sports:* basketball, cross-country, golf, soccer, softball, tennis, track and field (indoor), track and field (outdoor), volleyball.

SERVICES AND FACILITIES

Basic services: nonremedial tutoring, women's center, placement service, health service, health insurance, other. **Remedial assistance:** reading, math, writing, study skills, other. **Counseling services:** minority student, career, military, personal, veteran student, academic, older student, psychological. **For learning-disabled students:** School does not offer a structured program with separate admission and additional fees. Total undergraduates in learning-disabled program or receiving services: 48. Services include: remedial math, reading machines, tape recorders, diagnostic testing service, untimed tests, note-taking services, oral tests, learning center, readers, extended time for tests, tutors, priority registration, priority seating, proofreading services, texts on tape, typist/scribe, exams on tape or computer, other testing accomodations. **Library:** Number of titles: 48,164; number of current serial subscriptions: 481. **Information technology resources:** Students are required to lease or own a computer. Number of campus computers available to all students: 250. School has a wireless network. Approximate number of users that can be accommodated: 5,500. Proportion of college-owned housing units wired for high-speed internet access: 100%. **Campus safety:** Security services offered: 24-hour foot-and-vehicle patrols, late-night transport/escort service, 24-hour emergency telephones, lighted pathways/sidewalks, controlled dormitory access (key, security card, etc.).

TRANSFER AND INTERNATIONAL STUDENTS
Transfer students: May apply for admission for the following academic terms: Fall, Winter, Spring, Summer. Applicants need a minimum number of credits to apply. For fall 2005: Transfer applications received: 443. Transfer applicants offered admission: 248. Transfer applicants enrolled: 132. **International students:** Number of foreign undergraduates: 40 (2% of student body). Number of countries represented: 19. Minimum TOEFL score required: 550 (paper); 213 (computer). Average TOEFL score: 580 (paper).

Mount Mary College

- **Address:** 2900 N. Menomonee River Parkway, Milwaukee, WI 53222
- **Website:** http://www.mtmary.edu
- **Private; Religious affiliation:** Roman Catholic
- **Enrollment:** 921 full-time; 531 part-time

KEY STATS
- ✔ **U.S News College Ranking:** 70, Universities–Master's (Midwest)
- ✔ **ACT Score (25th/75th percentile):** 16-22
- ✔ **Tuition:** 2006-2007: $18,128

Selectivity: Selective	**Room/board:** $5,990
Acceptance rate: 66%	**Average debt:** $19,040
Student/faculty ratio: 10/1	**Proportion who borrowed:** 75%

UNDERGRADUATE STUDENT BODY STATS
2005-2006 enrollment: 921 full-time; 531 part-time. Men: 3%; women: 97%. **Ethnic makeup:** African American: 18%; American-Indian: 1%; Asian American: 5%; Hispanic: 5%; White: 70%; International: 1%. **Religious preference:** Protestant: 18%; Jewish: 1%; No preference: 35%; Roman Catholic: 34%; Other: 12%.

ADMISSIONS FACTS AND FIGURES
Phone: (800) 321-6265. **Email:** admiss@mtmary.edu. **Website:** http://www.mtmary.edu. **Application deadlines for fall 2007:** Regular decision: Rolling. Early decision: Not offered. Early action: Not offered. Admission can be deferred. **Application fee:** $25. Common application is accepted. **To apply online, go to:** http://www.mtmary.edu/apply.htm. **Admissions requirements/recommendations:** High school units required (recommended): English: 4 (4); Mathematics: 2 (3); Science: 2 (2); Foreign language: 0 (2); Social studies: 2 (2); History: 2 (2); Academic electives: 2 (0); Total units: 16 (16). Tests: The college uses SAT or ACT scores in admissions decisions. Either SAT or ACT required. For admission to the fall 2007 entering class, the school will accept: ACT with writing, ACT without writing. Campus visit: Recommended. Admissions interview: Recommended. Off-campus interview: May be arranged. **Factors that count in admissions decisions:** *Academic:* Secondary school record: Very important. Class rank: Important. Letters of recommendation: Considered. Essay: Considered. *Nonacademic:* Interview: Considered. Extracurricular activities: Considered. Talent/ability: Important. Character/personal qualities: Important. Alumni/ae relationship: Not considered. Geographical residence: Not considered. State residency: Not considered. Religious affiliation/commitment: Not considered. Minority status: Not considered. Volunteer work: Considered. Work experience: Considered. **Other schools with the greatest overlap in applicants:** Alverno College. **Admissions statistics for the fall 2005 entering class:** Total applicants: 438. Total accepted: 288. Freshmen enrolled: 160; 8% were from out of state. Overall acceptance rate: 66%. **Credentials of fall 2005 freshmen:** 24% ranked in the top 10 percent of their high school class; 50% were in the top 25 percent, and 79% were in the top half. (Proportion submitting class standing: 80%.) **Average high school grade point average:** 3.0. **First-year students who submitted SAT scores:** 4%. Scores (25/75 percentile): Verbal: 510-650, Math: 400-600, Combined: 910-1250. **First-year students submitting ACT scores:** 85%. Scores (25/75 percentile): English: 15-22, Math: 16-21, Composite: 16-22.

ACADEMICS
Year founded: 1913. **Academic calendar:** Semester. **Degrees offered:** bachelor's, post-bachelor's certificate, master's. **Most popular majors:** 25% health professions and related clinical sciences, 25% visual and performing arts, 16% business, management, marketing, and related support services, 6% social sciences, 5% English language and literature/letters. **Major fields of study:** biological and biomedical sciences; business, management, marketing, and related support services; communication, journalism, and related programs; computer and information sciences and support services; education; English language and literature/letters; foreign languages, literatures, and linguistics; health professions and related clinical sciences; history; legal professions and studies; mathematics and statistics; multi/interdisciplinary studies; philosophy and religious studies; physical sciences; psychology; public administration and social service professions; security and protective services; social sciences; theology and religious vocations; visual and performing arts. **Areas of required coursework:** arts/fine arts, humanities, mathematics, English (including composition), philosophy, sciences (biological or physical), history, social science, other. **Pre-professional programs:** pre-law, pre-dentistry, pre-medicine, pre-veterinary science, pre-optometry, other. **Special academic programs (% participation):** accelerated program (17%), distance learning, double major (4.5%), dual enrollment, honors program (6%), independent study, internships (36%), liberal arts/career combination, student-designed major (1%), study abroad (15%), teacher certificate program (12%). **Teacher certification offered in:** early childhood, elementary, middle/junior high, secondary. **Faculty and instruction (2005-2006):** Total instructional faculty: 64 full-time, 134 part-time (22% men; 78% women; 5% minorities). Full-time faculty with Ph.D. or other terminal degree: 64%. Student/faculty ratio: 10/1. Classes of fewer than 20 students: 86%; of 20 to 49 students: 13%; of 50 or more students: 1%. **Advanced Placement and International Baccalaureate credit:** AP tests may be used for: Credit and/or placement. Scores accepted: 4, 5. International Baccalaureate exams may be used for: Credit and/or placement. **Freshmen returning for sophomore year:** 63%. **Graduation rates:** Four-year: 41%; five-year: 46%; six-year: 54%. **Graduate study:** 10% of students pursue further study within one year.

COSTS AND FINANCIAL AID
Financial aid office: (414) 256-1258. **Expenses (2006-2007):** Tuition and fees 2006-2007: $18,128; room/board: $5,990. Estimated books and supplies: $1,000; transportation: $1,036; personal expenses: $1,454. **Financial aid:** Priority filing date for institution's financial aid form: March 1. In 2005-2006, 76% of undergraduates applied for financial aid. Of those, 67% were determined to have financial need; 19% had their need fully met. Average financial aid package (proportion receiving): $11,550 (67%). Average amount of gift aid, such as scholarships or grants (proportion receiving): $7,158 (67%). Average amount of self-help aid, such as work study or loans (proportion receiving): $4,842 (61%). Average need-based loan (excluding PLUS or other private loans): $4,410. Among students who received need-based aid, the average percentage of need met: 68%. Among students who received aid based on merit, the average award (and the proportion receiving): $7,287 (19%). The average athletic scholarship (and the proportion receiving): $0 (0%). Average amount of debt of borrowers graduating in 2005: $19,040. Proportion who borrowed: 75%.

CAMPUS LIFE AND EXTRACURRICULAR ACTIVITIES
Campus housing available (% using): women's dorms (100%). Students who live in college-owned, operated, or affiliated housing: 12%. **Clubs and organizations:** Number of student organizations: 42. Activities include: choral groups, dance, drama/theater, literary magazine, music ensembles, student government, student newspaper. Number of fraternities: 0; sororities: 0. Average proportion of students who stay on campus on weekends: 9%. **Sports program (2005-2006):** Member of NCAA III. *Women's intercollegiate varsity sports:* basketball, soccer, softball, tennis, volleyball.

SERVICES AND FACILITIES
Basic services: nonremedial tutoring, placement service, day care, health service, health insurance. **Remedial assistance:** reading, math, writing, study skills. **Counseling services:** minority student, career, personal, academic, older student, psychological, religious. **For learning-disabled students:** School does not offer a structured program with separate admission and additional fees. Total undergraduates in learning-disabled program or receiving services: 26. Services include: remedial math, remedial English, reading machines, remedial reading, tape recorders, other special classes, untimed tests, note-taking services, oral tests, learning center, readers, extended time for tests, tutors, priority registration, priority seating, texts on tape, typist/scribe, other testing accomodations. **Library:** Number of titles:

795,246; number of current serial subscriptions: 210. **Information technology resources:** Students are not required to lease or own a computer. Number of campus computers available to all students: 336. School does not have a wireless network. Proportion of college-owned housing units wired for high-speed internet access: 100%. **Campus safety:** Security services offered: 24-hour foot-and-vehicle patrols, late-night transport/escort service, 24-hour emergency telephones, lighted pathways/sidewalks, controlled dormitory access (key, security card, etc).

TRANSFER AND INTERNATIONAL STUDENTS

Transfer students: May apply for admission for the following academic terms: Fall, Spring, Summer. Applicants do not need a minimum number of credits to apply. For fall 2005: Transfer applications received: 403. Transfer applicants offered admission: 252. Transfer applicants enrolled: 160. **International students:** Number of foreign undergraduates: 17 (1% of student body). Number of countries represented: 8. Minimum TOEFL score required: 500 (paper); 173 (computer). Average TOEFL score: 550 (paper).

Northland College

- **Address:** 1411 Ellis Avenue, Ashland, WI 54806
- **Website:** http://www.northland.edu
- **Private; Religious affiliation:** United Church of Christ
- **Enrollment:** 649 full-time; 90 part-time

KEY STATS

✔ **U.S News College Ranking:** 25, Comp. Coll.–Bachelor's (Midwest)
✔ **ACT Score (25th/75th percentile):** 22-26
✔ **Tuition:** 2006-2007: $20,789
  Selectivity: More selective **Room/board:** $5,970
  Acceptance rate: 75% **Average debt:** $18,893
  Student/faculty ratio: 13/1 **Proportion who borrowed:** 81%

UNDERGRADUATE STUDENT BODY STATS

2005-2006 enrollment: 649 full-time; 90 part-time. Men: 42%; women: 58%. **Ethnic makeup:** African American: 2%; American-Indian: 3%; Asian American: 1%; Hispanic: 2%; White: 91%; International: 1%.

ADMISSIONS FACTS AND FIGURES

Phone: (715) 682-1224. **Email:** admit@northland.edu. **Website:** http://www.northland.edu. **Application deadlines for fall 2007:** Regular decision: August 15. Early decision: Not offered. Early action: Not offered. Admission can be deferred. **Application fee:** $25. Common application is accepted. **Admissions requirements/recommendations:** High school units required (recommended): English: 3 (4); Mathematics: 3 (3); Science: 3 (3); Foreign language: 0 (2); Social studies: 3 (3); History: 3 (3); Academic electives: 3 (4); Total units: 3 (17). Tests: The college uses SAT or ACT scores in admissions decisions. Either SAT or ACT required. For admission to the fall 2007 entering class, the school will accept: ACT with writing, ACT without writing. Campus visit: Recommended. Admissions interview: Recommended. Off-campus interview: May be arranged. **Factors that count in admissions decisions:** *Academic:* Secondary school record: Very important. Class rank: Important. Letters of recommendation: Considered. Standardized test scores: Important. Essay: Considered. *Nonacademic:* Interview: Considered. Extracurricular activities: Considered. Talent/ability: Considered. Character/personal qualities: Considered. Alumni/ae relationship: Considered. Geographical residence: Not considered. State residency: Considered. Religious affiliation/commitment: Considered. Minority status: Considered. Volunteer work: Considered. Work experience: Considered. **Other schools with the greatest overlap in applicants:** College of the Atlantic; Green Mountain College; Lawrence University; University of Minnesota–Twin Cities; University of Wisconsin–Stevens Point. **Admissions statistics for the fall 2005 entering class:** Total applicants: 804. Total accepted: 605. Freshmen enrolled: 180; 67% were from out of state. Overall acceptance rate: 75%. **Credentials of fall 2005 freshmen:** 26% ranked in the top 10 percent of their high school class; 50% were in the top 25 percent, and 78% were in the top half. (Proportion submitting class standing: 90%.) **Average high school grade point average:** 3.5. **First-year students who submitted SAT scores:** 16%. Scores (25/75 percentile): Verbal: 510-590, Math: 510-620, Combined: 1020-1210. **First-year students submitting ACT scores:** 84%. Scores (25/75 percentile): English: 22-26, Math: 22-26, Composite: 22-26.

ACADEMICS

Year founded: 1892. **Academic calendar:** 4-1-4. **Degrees offered:** bachelor's. **Most popular majors:** 25% education, 25% natural resources and conservation, 15% biological and biomedical sciences, 15% business, management, marketing, and related support services, 10% physical sciences. **Major fields of study:** biological and biomedical sciences; business, management, marketing, and related support services; computer and information sciences and support services; education; history; liberal arts and sciences studies, and humanities; mathematics and statistics; natural resources and conservation; philosophy and religious studies; physical sciences; psychology; social sciences; visual and performing arts. **Areas of required coursework:** arts/fine arts, humanities, mathematics, English (including composition), philosophy, sciences (biological or physical), history, social science. **Pre-professional programs:** pre-law, pre-medicine, pre-theology, pre-veterinary science. **Special academic programs (% participation):** accelerated program (1%), double major (10%), exchange student program (domestic) (5%), external degree program (3%), honors program (20%), independent study (60%), internships (50%), student-designed major (10%), study abroad (2%), teacher certificate program (30%). **Teacher certification offered in:** elementary, middle/junior high, secondary. **Cooperative education programs:** engineering, natural science, other. **Faculty and instruction (2005-2006):** Total instructional faculty: 40 full-time, 41 part-time (64% men; 36% women; 7% minorities). Full-time faculty with Ph.D. or other terminal degree: 65%. Student/faculty ratio: 13/1. Classes of fewer than 20 students: 77%; of 20 to 49 students: 23%. **Advanced Placement and International Baccalaureate credit:** AP tests may be used for: Credit and/or placement. International Baccalaureate exams may be used for: Credit only. **Freshmen returning for sophomore year:** 91%. **Graduation rates:** Six-year: 42%. **Graduate study:** Fields in which graduates pursue further study: law, 2%; medicine, 3%; arts and sciences, 10%; veterinary medicine, 10%.

COSTS AND FINANCIAL AID

Financial aid office: (715) 682-1255. **Expenses (2006-2007):** Tuition and fees 2006-2007: $20,789; room/board: $5,970. Estimated books and supplies: $800; transportation: $800; personal expenses: $1,500. **Financial aid:** Priority filing date for institution's financial aid form: April 15. In 2005-2006, 94% of undergraduates applied for financial aid. Of those, 86% were determined to have financial need; 22% had their need fully met. Average financial aid package (proportion receiving): $15,302 (86%). Average amount of gift aid, such as scholarships or grants (proportion receiving): $10,783 (85%). Average amount of self-help aid, such as work study or loans (proportion receiving): $4,923 (85%). Average need-based loan (excluding PLUS or other private loans): $4,397. Among students who received need-based aid, the average percentage of need met: 80%. Among students who received aid based on merit, the average award (and the proportion receiving): $10,137 (14%). The average athletic scholarship (and the proportion receiving): $0 (0%). Average amount of debt of borrowers graduating in 2005: $18,893. Proportion who borrowed: 81%.

CAMPUS LIFE AND EXTRACURRICULAR ACTIVITIES

Campus housing available (% using): coed dorms (85%), women's dorms (14%), apartment for single students (0%), cooperative housing (1%), other housing options. Students who live in college-owned, operated, or affiliated housing: 65%. **Student employment:** During the 2005-2006 academic year, 60% of undergraduates worked on campus. Average per-year earnings: $1,200. **Clubs and organizations:** Number of student organizations: 50. Activities include: choral groups, concert band, dance, drama/theater, jazz band, literary magazine, music ensembles, musical theater, radio station, student government, student newspaper, student film society, symphony orchestra, television station, yearbook. Number of fraternities: 0; sororities: 0. Average proportion of students who stay on campus on weekends: 90%. **Sports program (2005-2006):** Member of NCAA III. *Men's intercollegiate varsity sports:* baseball, basketball, cross-country, ice hockey, soccer. *Women's intercollegiate varsity sports:* basketball, cross-country, soccer, softball, volleyball.

SERVICES AND FACILITIES

Basic services: nonremedial tutoring, women's center, placement service, health service, health insurance. **Remedial assistance:** reading, math, writing, study skills. **Counseling services:** minority student, career, personal, academic, psychological, birth control, religious. **For learning-disabled students:** School does not offer a structured program with separate admission and additional fees. Services include: remedial math, remedial English, remedial reading, tape recorders, videotaped classes, note-taking services, oral tests, readers, extended time for tests, tutors, early syllabus, priority seating, proofreading services, texts on tape, typist/scribe, exams on tape or computer, other testing accomodations. **Library:** Number of titles: 75,000; number of current serial subscriptions: 260. **Information technology resources:** Students are not required to lease or own a computer. Number of campus computers available to all students: 400. School has a wireless network. Proportion of college-owned housing units wired for high-speed internet access: 100%. **Campus safety:** Security services offered: late-night transport/escort service, 24-hour emergency telephones, lighted pathways/sidewalks, student patrols, controlled dormitory access (key, security card, etc).

TRANSFER AND INTERNATIONAL STUDENTS

Transfer students: May apply for admission for the following academic terms: Fall, Winter. Applicants need a minimum number of credits to apply. For fall 2005: Transfer applications received: 159. Transfer applicants offered admission: 92. Transfer applicants enrolled: 52. **International students:** Number of foreign undergraduates: 10 (1% of student body). Minimum TOEFL score required: 525 (paper). Average TOEFL score: 600 (paper).

Ripon College

- ■ **Address:** 300 Seward Street, Ripon, WI 54971-0248
- ■ **Website:** http://www.ripon.edu
- ■ **Private**
- ■ **Enrollment:** 953 full-time; 26 part-time

KEY STATS

✔ **U.S News College Ranking:** third tier, Liberal Arts Colleges
✔ **ACT Score (25th/75th percentile):** 21-27
✔ **Tuition:** 2006-2007: $22,437

Selectivity: More selective	**Room/board:** $6,060
Acceptance rate: 81%	**Average debt:** $16,492
Student/faculty ratio: 14/1	**Proportion who borrowed:** 90%

UNDERGRADUATE STUDENT BODY STATS

2005-2006 enrollment: 953 full-time; 26 part-time. Men: 50%; women: 50%. **Ethnic makeup:** African American: 3%; American-Indian: 1%; Asian American: 2%; Hispanic: 3%; White: 90%; International: 1%.

ADMISSIONS FACTS AND FIGURES

Phone: (920) 748-8337. **Email:** adminfo@ripon.edu. **Website:** http://www.ripon.edu. **Application deadlines for fall 2007:** Regular decision: Rolling. Early decision: Not offered. Early action: Not offered. Admission can be deferred. **Application fee:** $30. Common application is accepted. **Admissions requirements/recommendations:** High school units required (recommended): English: 4; Mathematics: 2 (4); Science: 2 (4); Foreign language: (2); Social studies: 2 (4); Total units: 17. Tests: The college uses SAT or ACT scores in admissions decisions. Either SAT or ACT required. For admission to the fall 2007 entering class, the school will accept: ACT with writing, ACT without writing. Campus visit: Recommended. Admissions interview: Recommended. Off-campus interview: May be arranged. **Factors that count in admissions decisions:** *Academic:* Secondary school record: Very important. Class rank: Important. Letters of recommendation: Important. Standardized test scores: Very important. Essay: Important. *Nonacademic:* Interview: Important. Extracurricular activities: Important. Talent/ability: Important. Character/personal qualities: Very important. Alumni/ae relationship: Considered. Geographical residence: Not considered. State residency: Not considered. Religious affiliation/commitment: Not considered. Minority status: Considered. Volunteer work: Very important. Work experience: Considered. **Other schools with the greatest overlap in applicants:** Carthage College; Marquette University; St. Norbert College; University of Wisconsin–La Crosse; University of Wisconsin–Madison. **Admissions statistics for the fall 2005 entering class:** Total applicants: 976. Total accepted: 791. Freshmen enrolled: 262; 29% were from out of state. Overall acceptance rate: 81%. **Credentials of fall 2005 freshmen:** 23% ranked in the top 10 percent of their high school class; 50% were in the top 25 percent, and 87% were in the top half. (Proportion submitting class standing: 88%.) **Average high school grade point average:** 3.4. **First-year students who submitted SAT scores:** 17%. Scores (25/75 percentile): Verbal: 480-650, Math: 500-620, Combined: 980-1270. **First-year students submitting ACT scores:** 83%. Scores (25/75 percentile): English: N/A, Math: N/A, Composite: 21-27.

ACADEMICS

Year founded: 1851. **Academic calendar:** Semester. **Degrees offered:** bachelor's. **Most popular majors:** 12% English language and literature, 10% biology, 10% business administration and management, 10% history, 10% psychology. **Major fields of study:** area, ethnic, cultural, and gender studies; biological and biomedical sciences; business, management, marketing, and related support services; communication, journalism, and related programs; computer and information sciences and support services; education; English language and literature/letters; foreign languages, literatures, and linguistics; history; mathematics and statistics; natural resources and conservation; parks, recreation, leisure, and fitness studies; philosophy and religious studies; physical sciences; psychology; social sciences; visual and performing arts. **Areas of required coursework:** arts/fine arts, humanities, English (including composition), sciences (biological or physical), social science, other. **Pre-professional programs:** pre-law, pre-dentistry, pre-medicine, pre-theology, pre-veterinary science, pre-optometry, pre-pharmacy. **Special academic programs (% participation):** accelerated program (2%), double major (34%), exchange student program (domestic) (10%), independent study (20%), internships (10%), student-designed major (3%), study abroad (20%), teacher certificate program (17%). **Teacher certification offered in:** early childhood, elementary, middle/junior high, secondary, bilingual/bicultural. **Reserve Officers Training Corps (ROTC):** Army ROTC: Offered on campus. **Faculty and instruction (2005-2006):** Total instructional faculty: 52 full-time, 33 part-time (60% men; 40% women; 4% minorities). Full-time faculty with Ph.D. or other terminal degree: 92%. Student/faculty ratio: 14/1. Classes of fewer than 20 students: 58%; of 20 to 49 students: 40%; of 50 or more students: 2%. **Advanced Placement and International Baccalaureate credit:** AP tests may be used for: Credit and/or placement. Scores accepted: 4, 5. International Baccalaureate exams may be used for: Credit and/or placement. **Freshmen returning for sophomore year:** 85%. **Graduation rates:** Four-year: 60%; five-year: 68%; six-year: 68%. **Graduate study:** 21% of students pursue further study immediately upon graduation; 28% within one year; 50% within five years. Fields in which graduates pursue further study: Master of Business Administration (MBA), 4%; law, 8%; medicine, 7%; theology (or the seminary), 3%; education, 10%; arts and sciences, 63%.

COSTS AND FINANCIAL AID

Financial aid office: (920) 748-8101. **Expenses (2006-2007):** Tuition and fees 2006-2007: $22,437; room/board: $6,060. Estimated books and supplies: $750; transportation: $175; personal expenses: $800. **Financial aid:** Priority filing date for institution's financial aid form: March 1. In 2005-2006, 94% of undergraduates applied for financial aid. Of those, 75% were determined to have financial need; 41% had their need fully met. Average financial aid package (proportion receiving): $18,534 (75%). Average amount of gift aid, such as scholarships or grants (proportion receiving): $14,326 (75%). Average amount of self-help aid, such as work study or loans (proportion receiving): $5,310 (61%). Average need-based loan (excluding PLUS or other private loans): $4,453. Among students who received need-based aid, the average percentage of need met: 93%. Among students who received aid based on merit, the average award (and the proportion receiving): $14,807 (18%). The average athletic scholarship (and the proportion receiving): $0 (0%). Average amount of debt of borrowers graduating in 2005: $16,492. Proportion who borrowed: 90%.

CAMPUS LIFE AND EXTRACURRICULAR ACTIVITIES

Campus housing available (% using): coed dorms (23%), women's dorms (9%), men's dorms (13%), sorority housing (22%), fraternity housing (33%). Students who live in college-owned, operated, or affiliated housing: 82%. **Student employment:** During the 2005-2006 academic year, 21% of undergraduates worked on campus. Average per-year earnings: $794. **Clubs and organizations:** Number of student organizations: 45. Activities include: choral groups, concert band, dance, drama/theater, jazz band, literary magazine, music ensembles, musical theater, pep band, radio station, student government, student newspaper, student film society, symphony orchestra, television station, yearbook. Number of fraternities: 5; sororities: 3. Proportion of men in fraternities: 23%; of women in sororities: 15%. Average proportion of students who stay on campus on weekends: 80%. **Sports program (2005-2006):** Member of NCAA III. *Men's intercollegiate varsity sports:* baseball, basketball, cross-country, football, golf, soccer, swimming and diving, tennis, track and field (indoor), track and field (outdoor). *Women's intercollegiate varsity sports:* basketball, cross-country, golf, soccer, softball, swimming and diving, tennis, track and field (indoor), track and field (outdoor), volleyball.

SERVICES AND FACILITIES

Basic services: nonremedial tutoring, placement service, health service, health insurance. **Remedial assistance:** reading, writing, study skills. **Counseling services:** minority student, career, military, personal, academic, birth control. **For learning-disabled students:** School does not offer a structured program with separate admission and additional fees. Total undergraduates in learning-disabled program or receiving services: 21. Services include: tape recorders, untimed tests, note-taking services, oral tests, readers, extended time for tests, tutors, proofreading services, texts on tape, exams on tape or computer, other. **Library:** Number of titles: 185,000; number of current serial subscriptions: 341. **Information technology resources:** Students are not required to lease or own a computer. Number of campus computers available to all students: 150. School has a wireless network. Approximate number of users that can be accommodated: 1,000. Proportion of college-owned housing units wired for high-speed internet access: 100%. **Campus safety:** Security services offered: late-night transport/escort service, 24-hour emergency telephones, lighted pathways/sidewalks, controlled dormitory access (key, security card, etc).

TRANSFER AND INTERNATIONAL STUDENTS

Transfer students: May apply for admission for the following academic terms: Fall, Spring. Applicants need a minimum number of credits to apply. For fall 2005: Transfer applications received: 58. Transfer applicants offered admission: 40. Transfer applicants enrolled: 27. **International students:** Number of foreign undergraduates: 12 (1% of student body). Number of countries represented: 11. Minimum TOEFL score required: 550 (paper); 213 (computer). Average TOEFL score: 570 (paper).

Silver Lake College

- **Address:** 2406 S. Alverno Road, Manitowoc, WI 54220
- **Website:** http://www.sl.edu
- **Private; Religious affiliation:** Roman Catholic
- **Enrollment:** 214 full-time; 415 part-time

KEY STATS

✔ **U.S News College Ranking:** third tier, Universities–Master's (Midwest)
✔ **ACT Score (25th/75th percentile):** 17-23
✔ **Tuition:** 2006-2007: $17,108

Selectivity: Less selective	**Room/board:** $6,200
Acceptance rate: 83%	**Average debt:** $18,934
Student/faculty ratio: 9/1	**Proportion who borrowed:** 70%

UNDERGRADUATE STUDENT BODY STATS

2005-2006 enrollment: 214 full-time; 415 part-time. Men: 26%; women: 74%. **Ethnic makeup:** American-Indian: 4%; Hispanic: 1%; White: 94%. **Religious preference:** Roman Catholic: 37%; Unknown: 37%; Lutheran: 14%; Other: 12%.

ADMISSIONS FACTS AND FIGURES

Phone: (920) 686-6175. **Email:** admslc@silver.sl.edu. **Website:** http://www.sl.edu. **Application deadlines for fall 2007:** Regular decision: Rolling. Early decision: Not offered. Early action: Not offered. Admission can be deferred. **Application fee:** $35. Common application is accepted. **To apply online, go to:** http://www.wisconsinmentor.org/Applications/Silver_Lake_College/apply.html. **Admissions requirements/recommendations:** High school units required (recommended): English: 3; Mathematics: 2; Science: 1; Foreign language: 0; Social studies: 1; History: 1; Academic electives: 7; Total units: 16. Tests: The college uses SAT or ACT scores in admissions decisions. Neither SAT nor ACT required. For admission to the fall 2007 entering class, the school will accept: ACT with writing, ACT without writing. Campus visit: Recommended. Admissions interview: Recommended. Off-campus interview: May be arranged. **Factors that count in admissions decisions:** *Academic:* Secondary school record: Very important. Class rank: Important. Letters of recommendation: Considered. Standardized test scores: Important. Essay: Not considered. *Nonacademic:* Interview: Considered. Extracurricular activities: Not considered. Talent/ability: Considered. Character/personal qualities: Considered. Alumni/ae relationship: Not considered. Geographical residence: Not considered. State residency: Not considered. Religious affiliation/commitment: Not considered. Minority status: Not considered. Volunteer work: Not considered. Work experience:

Considered. **Other schools with the greatest overlap in applicants:** Lakeland College; Marian College; St. Norbert College; University of Wisconsin–Stevens Point. **Admissions statistics for the fall 2005 entering class:** Total applicants: 102. Total accepted: 85. Freshmen enrolled: 33; 3% were from out of state. Overall acceptance rate: 83%. **Credentials of fall 2005 freshmen:** 3% ranked in the top 10 percent of their high school class; 26% were in the top 25 percent, and 50% were in the top half. (Proportion submitting class standing: 91%.) **Average high school grade point average:** 3.0. **First-year students submitting ACT scores:** 93%. Scores (25/75 percentile): English: 15-22, Math: 16-22, Composite: 17-23.

ACADEMICS

Year founded: 1935. **Academic calendar:** Semester. **Degrees offered:** certificate, associate, bachelor's, master's. **Most popular majors:** 27% business administration and management, 12% psychology, 11% human resources management/personnel administration, 10% accounting, 9% early childhood education and teaching. **Major fields of study:** biological and biomedical sciences; business, management, marketing, and related support services; computer and information sciences and support services; education; English language and literature/letters; history; mathematics and statistics; psychology; public administration and social service professions; theology and religious vocations; visual and performing arts. **Areas of required coursework:** arts/fine arts, humanities, computer literacy, mathematics, English (including composition), philosophy, sciences (biological or physical), history, social science, other. **Pre-professional programs:** pre-dentistry, pre-medicine, pre-theology, pre-veterinary science, other. **Special academic programs (% participation):** accelerated program (25%), double major (7%), internships (7%), student-designed major, teacher certificate program (24%). **Teacher certification offered in:** early childhood, special education, elementary, middle/junior high, secondary. **Faculty and instruction (2005-2006):** Total instructional faculty: 25 full-time, 115 part-time (41% men; 59% women; 3% minorities). Full-time faculty with Ph.D. or other terminal degree: 56%. Student/faculty ratio: 9/1. Classes of fewer than 20 students: 97%; of 20 to 49 students: 3%. **Freshmen returning for sophomore year:** 70%. **Graduation rates:** Four-year: 19%; five-year: 58%; six-year: 56%.

COSTS AND FINANCIAL AID

Financial aid office: (920) 686-6122. **Expenses (2006-2007):** Tuition and fees 2006-2007: $17,108; room/board: $6,200. Estimated books and supplies: $890; transportation: $1,000; personal expenses: $1,200. **Financial aid:** Priority filing date for institution's financial aid form: March 15. In 2005-2006, 87% of undergraduates applied for financial aid. Of those, 79% were determined to have financial need; 20% had their need fully met. Average financial aid package (proportion receiving): $12,752 (79%). Average amount of gift aid, such as scholarships or grants (proportion receiving): $8,555 (79%). Average amount of self-help aid, such as work study or loans (proportion receiving): $4,084 (72%). Average need-based loan (excluding PLUS or other private loans): $3,688. Among students who received need-based aid, the average percentage of need met: 73%. Among students who received aid based on merit, the average award (and the proportion receiving): $3,510 (8%). The average athletic scholarship (and the proportion receiving): $2,000 (1%). Average amount of debt of borrowers graduating in 2005: $18,934. Proportion who borrowed: 70%.

CAMPUS LIFE AND EXTRACURRICULAR ACTIVITIES

Campus housing available (% using): apartment for single students (100%). Students who live in college-owned, operated, or affiliated housing: 10%. **Student employment:** During the 2005-2006 academic year, 30% of undergraduates worked on campus. Average per-year earnings: $1,000. **Clubs and organizations:** Number of student organizations: 17. Activities include: choral groups, concert band, dance, jazz band, literary magazine, music ensembles, opera, student government. Number of fraternities: 0; sororities: 0. Average proportion of students who stay on campus on weekends: 75%. **Sports program (2005-2006):** *Women's intercollegiate varsity sports:* basketball.

SERVICES AND FACILITIES

Remedial assistance: reading, math, writing, study skills. **Counseling services:** career, academic. **For learning-disabled students:** School does not offer a structured program with separate admission and additional fees. Services include: remedial math, remedial English, remedial reading, note-taking services, oral tests, readers, extended time for tests, tutors, take home exams. **Library:** Number of titles: 60,288; number of current serial subscriptions: 277. **Information technology resources:** Students are not required to lease or own a computer. Number of campus computers available to all students: 50. School has a wireless network. Approximate number of users that can be accommodated: 40. Proportion of college-owned housing units wired for high-speed internet access: 0%. **Campus safety:** Security services offered: 24-hour emergency telephones, lighted pathways/sidewalks.

TRANSFER AND INTERNATIONAL STUDENTS
Transfer students: May apply for admission for the following academic terms: Fall, Spring, Summer. Applicants need a minimum number of credits to apply. For fall 2005: Transfer applications received: 96. Transfer applicants offered admission: 76. Transfer applicants enrolled: 51. **International students:** Number of foreign undergraduates: 1.

St. Norbert College

- **Address:** 100 Grant Street, De Pere, WI 54115-2099
- **Website:** http://www.snc.edu
- **Private; Religious affiliation:** Roman Catholic
- **Enrollment:** 1,922 full-time; 65 part-time

KEY STATS
- ✔ **U.S News College Ranking:** 4, Comp. Coll.–Bachelor's (Midwest)
- ✔ **ACT Score (25th/75th percentile):** 21-27
- ✔ **Tuition:** 2006-2007: $23,497

Selectivity: More selective	**Room/board:** $6,319
Acceptance rate: 86%	**Average debt:** $24,808
Student/faculty ratio: 14/1	**Proportion who borrowed:** 65%

UNDERGRADUATE STUDENT BODY STATS
2005-2006 enrollment: 1,922 full-time; 65 part-time. Men: 43%; women: 57%. **Ethnic makeup:** African American: 1%; American-Indian: 1%; Asian American: 1%; Hispanic: 2%; White: 93%; International: 2%. **Religious preference:** Protestant: 13%; Jewish: 1%; Buddhist: 1%; No preference: 1%; Unknown: 32%; Roman Catholic: 51%.

ADMISSIONS FACTS AND FIGURES
Phone: (800) 236-4878. **Email:** admit@snc.edu. **Website:** http://www.snc.edu. **Application deadlines for fall 2007:** Regular decision: Rolling. Early decision: Send application by: December 1; Decision sent by: December 15. Early action: Not offered. Admission can be deferred. **Application fee:** $25. Common application is accepted. **To apply online, go to:** http://www.snc.edu/admit/appform1.htm. **Admissions requirements/recommendations:** High school units required (recommended): English: (4); Mathematics: (3); Science: (3); Foreign language: (2); Social studies: (2); History: (2); Total units: (16). Tests: The college uses SAT or ACT scores in admissions decisions. Either SAT or ACT required. For admission to the fall 2007 entering class, the school will accept: ACT with writing, ACT without writing. Campus visit: Recommended. Admissions interview: Recommended. Off-campus interview: May be arranged. **Factors that count in admissions decisions:** *Academic:* Secondary school record: Very important. Class rank: Considered. Letters of recommendation: Considered. Standardized test scores: Important. Essay: Considered. *Nonacademic:* Interview: Considered. Extracurricular activities: Considered. Talent/ability: Considered. Character/personal qualities: Considered. Alumni/ae relationship: Considered. Geographical residence: Not considered. State residency: Not considered. Religious affiliation/commitment: Not considered. Minority status: Not considered. Volunteer work: Considered. Work experience: Considered. **Other schools with the greatest overlap in applicants:** Marquette University; University of Wisconsin–Eau Claire; University of Wisconsin–Green Bay; University of Wisconsin–Madison; University of Wisconsin–Oshkosh. **Admissions statistics for the fall 2005 entering class:** Total applicants: 1,683. Total accepted: 1,453. Freshmen enrolled: 511; 28% were from out of state. Accepted through early-decision or early-action plans: 4%. Overall acceptance rate: 86%. Early-decision acceptance rate: 96%. Non-early acceptance rate: 86%. **Credentials of fall 2005 freshmen:** 27% ranked in the top 10 percent of their high school class; 56% were in the top 25 percent, and 90% were in the top half. (Proportion submitting class standing: 76%.) **Average high school grade point average:** 3.2. **First-year students submitting ACT scores:** 96%. Scores (25/75 percentile): English: 20-27, Math: 21-27, Composite: 21-27.

ACADEMICS
Year founded: 1898. **Academic calendar:** Semester. **Degrees offered:** bachelor's, master's. **Most popular majors:** 20% business/commerce, 11% com-

munication studies/speech communication and rhetoric, 11% elementary education and teaching, 6% history, 5% English language and literature. **Major fields of study:** biological and biomedical sciences; business, management, marketing, and related support services; communication, journalism, and related programs; computer and information sciences and support services; education; English language and literature/letters; foreign languages, literatures, and linguistics; history; liberal arts and sciences studies, and humanities; mathematics and statistics; multi/interdisciplinary studies; natural resources and conservation; philosophy and religious studies; physical sciences; psychology; social sciences; visual and performing arts. **Areas of required coursework:** arts/fine arts, humanities, mathematics, English (including composition), philosophy, sciences (biological or physical), history, social science, other. **Special academic programs (% participation):** distance learning, double major (13%), English as a Second Language (ESL) (1%), honors program (10%), independent study (3%), internships (18%), student-designed major, study abroad (27%), teacher certificate program (23%), other. **Teacher certification offered in:** early childhood, elementary, middle/junior high, secondary, bilingual/bicultural. **Reserve Officers Training Corps (ROTC):** Army ROTC: Offered on campus. **Faculty and instruction (2005-2006):** Total instructional faculty: 109 full-time, 68 part-time (62% men; 38% women; 5% minorities). Full-time faculty with Ph.D. or other terminal degree: 92%. Student/faculty ratio: 14/1. Classes of fewer than 20 students: 53%; of 20 to 49 students: 46%; of 50 or more students: 0%. **Advanced Placement and International Baccalaureate credit:** AP tests may be used for: Credit and/or placement. Scores accepted: 3. International Baccalaureate exams may be used for: Credit and/or placement. **Freshmen returning for sophomore year:** 84%. **Graduation rates:** Four-year: 64%; five-year: 70%; six-year: 72%. **Graduate study:** 14% of students pursue further study immediately upon graduation.

COSTS AND FINANCIAL AID
Financial aid office: (920) 403-3071. **Expenses (2006-2007):** Tuition and fees 2006-2007: $23,497; room/board: $6,319. Estimated books and supplies: $500; transportation: $350; personal expenses: $750. **Financial aid:** Priority filing date for institution's financial aid form: March 1. In 2005-2006, 78% of undergraduates applied for financial aid. Of those, 66% were determined to have financial need; 39% had their need fully met. Average financial aid package (proportion receiving): $16,958 (65%). Average amount of gift aid, such as scholarships or grants (proportion receiving): $11,522 (64%). Average amount of self-help aid, such as work study or loans (proportion receiving): $4,656 (53%). Average need-based loan (excluding PLUS or other private loans): $4,524. Among students who received need-based aid, the average percentage of need met: 88%. Among students who received aid based on merit, the average award (and the proportion receiving): $7,054 (30%). The average athletic scholarship (and the proportion receiving): $0 (0%). Average amount of debt of borrowers graduating in 2005: $24,808. Proportion who borrowed: 65%.

CAMPUS LIFE AND EXTRACURRICULAR ACTIVITIES
Campus housing available (% using): coed dorms (65%), women's dorms (11%), apartment for single students (7%), special housing for disabled students (1%), other housing options (16%). Students who live in college-owned, operated, or affiliated housing: 77%. **Student employment:** During the 2005-2006 academic year, 36% of undergraduates worked on campus. Average per-year earnings: $1,732. **Clubs and organizations:** Number of student organizations: 68. Activities include: choral groups, concert band, drama/theater, jazz band, literary magazine, music ensembles, musical theater, radio station, student government, student newspaper, student film society, television station. Number of fraternities: 4; sororities: 5. Proportion of men in fraternities: 6%; of women in sororities: 8%. Average proportion of students who stay on campus on weekends: 80%. **Sports program (2005-2006):** Member of NCAA III. *Men's intercollegiate varsity sports:* baseball, basketball, cross-country, football, golf, ice hockey, soccer, tennis, track and field (indoor), track and field (outdoor). *Women's intercollegiate varsity sports:* basketball, cheerleading, cross-country, golf, soccer, softball, swimming and diving, tennis, track and field (indoor), track and field (outdoor), volleyball.

SERVICES AND FACILITIES
Basic services: nonremedial tutoring, women's center, placement service, day care, health service, health insurance. **Remedial assistance:** reading, math, writing, study skills. **Counseling services:** minority student, career, military, personal, veteran student, academic, older student, psychological, birth control, religious. **For learning-disabled students:** School does not offer a structured program with separate admission and additional fees. Total undergraduates in learning-disabled program or receiving services: 37.

Services include: remedial math, remedial English, remedial reading, tape recorders, note-taking services, learning center, readers, extended time for tests, tutors, priority registration, priority seating, substitution of courses, texts on tape, typist/scribe, exams on tape or computer, other testing accomodations. **Library:** Number of titles: 220,030; number of current serial subscriptions: 675. **Information technology resources:** Students are not required to lease or own a computer. Number of campus computers available to all students: 219. School has a wireless network. Approximate number of users that can be accommodated: 175. Proportion of college-owned housing units wired for high-speed internet access: 99%. **Campus safety:** Security services offered: late-night transport/escort service, 24-hour emergency telephones, lighted pathways/sidewalks, student patrols, controlled dormitory access (key, security card, etc).

TRANSFER AND INTERNATIONAL STUDENTS

Transfer students: May apply for admission for the following academic terms: Fall, Spring, Summer. Applicants do not need a minimum number of credits to apply. For fall 2005: Transfer applications received: 103. Transfer applicants offered admission: 79. Transfer applicants enrolled: 46. **International students:** Number of foreign undergraduates: 47 (2% of student body). Number of countries represented: 16. Minimum TOEFL score required: 550 (paper); 213 (computer). Average TOEFL score: 555 (paper).

University of Wisconsin–Eau Claire

- **Address:** 105 Garfield Avenue, Eau Claire, WI 54701
- **Website:** http://www.uwec.edu
- **Public**
- **Enrollment:** 9,374 full-time; 689 part-time

KEY STATS
✔ **U.S News College Ranking:** 26, Universities–Master's (Midwest)
✔ **ACT Score (25th/75th percentile):** 22-26
✔ **Tuition:** 2006-2007: $5,502 in state, $12,977 out of state
  Selectivity: More selective   **Room/board:** $4,936
  Acceptance rate: 70%   **Average debt:** $16,953
  Student/faculty ratio: 20/1   **Proportion who borrowed:** 65%

UNDERGRADUATE STUDENT BODY STATS

2005-2006 enrollment: 9,374 full-time; 689 part-time. Men: 41%; women: 59%. **Ethnic makeup:** American-Indian: 1%; Asian American: 3%; Hispanic: 1%; White: 94%; International: 1%.

ADMISSIONS FACTS AND FIGURES

Phone: (715) 836-5415. **Email:** admissions@uwec.edu. **Website:** http://www.uwec.edu. **Application deadlines for fall 2007:** Regular decision: Rolling. Early decision: Not offered. Early action: Not offered. Admission cannot be deferred. **Application fee:** $35. Common application is not accepted. **To apply online, go to:** http://www.uwec.edu/admissions. **Admissions requirements/recommendations:** High school units required (recommended): English: 4; Mathematics: 3; Science: 3; Foreign language: 2; Social studies: 3; Academic electives: 2; Total units: 17. Tests: The college uses SAT or ACT scores in admissions decisions. Either SAT or ACT required. For admission to the fall 2007 entering class, the school will accept: ACT with writing, ACT without writing. Campus visit: Recommended. Admissions interview: Recommended. Off-campus interview: Not available. **Factors that count in admissions decisions:** *Academic:* Secondary school record: Very important. Class rank: Very important. Letters of recommendation: Considered. Standardized test scores: Important. Essay: Considered. *Nonacademic:* Interview: Considered. Extracurricular activities: Considered. Talent/ability: Considered. Character/personal qualities: Considered. Alumni/ae relationship: Considered. Geographical residence: Not considered. State residency: Not considered. Religious affiliation/commitment: Not considered. Minority status: Considered. Volunteer work: Considered. Work experience: Considered. **Other schools with the greatest overlap in applicants:** University of Minnesota–Twin Cities; University of Wisconsin–La Crosse; University of Wisconsin–Madison; University of Wisconsin–Oshkosh; University of Wisconsin–Stevens Point. **Admissions statistics for the fall 2005 entering class:** Total applicants: 7,134. Total accepted: 5,007. Freshmen enrolled: 2,068; 24% were from out of state. Overall acceptance rate: 70%. **Size of waiting list:** 103 applicants; enrolled from waiting list: 54. **Credentials of fall**

2005 freshmen: 23% ranked in the top 10 percent of their high school class; 60% were in the top 25 percent, and 95% were in the top half. (Proportion submitting class standing: 95%.) **First-year students who submitted SAT scores:** 3%. Scores (25/75 percentile): Verbal: 520-630, Math: 540-640, Combined: 1060-1270. **First-year students submitting ACT scores:** 99%. Scores (25/75 percentile): English: 21-26, Math: 22-26, Composite: 22-26.

ACADEMICS

Year founded: 1916. **Academic calendar:** Semester. **Degrees offered:** associate, transfer-associate, terminal-associate, bachelor's, post-bachelor's certificate, master's, post-master's certificate. **Most popular majors:** 25% business, management, marketing, and related support services, 11% education, 9% health professions and related clinical sciences, 8% communication, journalism, and related programs, 6% visual and performing arts. **Major fields of study:** area, ethnic, cultural, and gender studies; biological and biomedical sciences; business, management, marketing, and related support services; communication, journalism, and related programs; computer and information sciences and support services; education; English language and literature/letters; foreign languages, literatures, and linguistics; health professions and related clinical sciences; history; mathematics and statistics; parks, recreation, leisure, and fitness studies; philosophy and religious studies; physical sciences; psychology; public administration and social service professions; security and protective services; social sciences; visual and performing arts. **Areas of required coursework:** arts/fine arts, humanities, computer literacy, mathematics, English (including composition), philosophy, foreign languages, sciences (biological or physical), history, social science. **Pre-professional programs:** pre-law, pre-dentistry, pre-medicine, pre-theology, pre-veterinary science, pre-optometry, pre-pharmacy, other. **Special academic programs (% participation):** accelerated program (2%), cooperative (work-study plan) program (2%), distance learning (2%), double major (7%), dual enrollment (1%), English as a Second Language (ESL) (1%), exchange student program (domestic) (2%), honors program (5%), independent study (14%), internships (51%), liberal arts/career combination (9%), study abroad (16%), teacher certificate program (14%). **Teacher certification offered in:** early childhood, special education, elementary, middle/junior high, secondary. **Cooperative education programs:** computer science, health professions, humanities, natural science, social/behavioral science. **Faculty and instruction (2005-2006):** Total instructional faculty: 401 full-time, 107 part-time (53% men; 47% women; 7% minorities). Full-time faculty with Ph.D. or other terminal degree: 86%. Student/faculty ratio: 20/1. Classes of fewer than 20 students: 28%; of 20 to 49 students: 59%; of 50 or more students: 13%. **Advanced Placement and International Baccalaureate credit:** AP tests may be used for: Credit only. Scores accepted: 3, 4, 5. International Baccalaureate exams may be used for: Credit only. **Freshmen returning for sophomore year:** 81%. **Graduation rates:** Four-year: 19%; five-year: 51%; six-year: 57%.

COSTS AND FINANCIAL AID

Financial aid office: (715) 836-3373. **Expenses (2006-2007):** Tuition and fees 2006-2007: $5,502 in state, $12,977 out of state; room/board: $4,936. Estimated books and supplies: $450; transportation: $700; personal expenses: $2,114. **Financial aid:** Priority filing date for institution's financial aid form: April 15. In 2005-2006, 67% of undergraduates applied for financial aid. Of those, 41% were determined to have financial need; 73% had their need fully met. Average financial aid package (proportion receiving): $7,206 (41%). Average amount of gift aid, such as scholarships or grants (proportion receiving): $4,389 (23%). Average amount of self-help aid, such as work study or loans (proportion receiving): $5,039 (38%). Average need-based loan (excluding PLUS or other private loans): $4,332. Among students who received need-based aid, the average percentage of met need: 94%. Among students who received aid based on merit, the average award (and the proportion receiving): $1,670 (10%). Average amount of debt of borrowers graduating in 2005: $16,953. Proportion who borrowed: 65%.

CAMPUS LIFE AND EXTRACURRICULAR ACTIVITIES

Campus housing available (% using): coed dorms (77%), women's dorms (9%), men's dorms (5%), apartment for single students (9%). Students who live in college-owned, operated, or affiliated housing: 40%. **Student employment:** During the 2005-2006 academic year, 15% of undergraduates worked on campus. Average per-year earnings: $1,800. **Clubs and organizations:** Number of student organizations: 180. Activities include: choral groups, concert band, dance, drama/theater, jazz band, literary magazine, marching band, music ensembles, musical theater, opera, pep band, radio station, student government, student newspaper, student film society, symphony orchestra, television station. Number of fraternities: 5; sororities: 3. Proportion of men in fraternities: 1%; of women in sororities: 1%. **Sports**

program (2005-2006): Member of NCAA III. **Men's intercollegiate varsity sports:** basketball, cross-country, football, golf, ice hockey, swimming and diving, tennis, track and field (indoor), track and field (outdoor), wrestling. **Women's intercollegiate varsity sports:** basketball, cross-country, golf, gymnastics, ice hockey, soccer, softball, swimming and diving, tennis, track and field (indoor), track and field (outdoor), volleyball.

SERVICES AND FACILITIES

Basic services: nonremedial tutoring, women's center, placement service, day care, health service, health insurance, other. **Remedial assistance:** reading, math, writing, study skills. **Counseling services:** minority student, career, military, personal, veteran student, academic, older student, psychological, birth control. **For learning-disabled students:** School does not offer a structured program with separate admission and additional fees. Total undergraduates in learning-disabled program or receiving services: 45. Services include: remedial math, remedial English, reading machines, remedial reading, tape recorders, note-taking services, oral tests, learning center, readers, extended time for tests, tutors, priority registration, priority seating, substitution of courses, texts on tape, typist/scribe, exams on tape or computer, other testing accomodations, waiver of foreign language degree requirement, waiver of math degree requirement. **Library:** Number of titles: 764,275; number of current serial subscriptions: 2,448. **Information technology resources:** Students are not required to lease or own a computer. Number of campus computers available to all students: 1,150. School has a wireless network. Approximate number of users that can be accommodated: 4,500. Proportion of college-owned housing units wired for high-speed internet access: 100%. **Campus safety:** Security services offered: 24-hour foot-and-vehicle patrols, late-night transport/escort service, 24-hour emergency telephones, lighted pathways/sidewalks, controlled dormitory access (key, security card, etc).

TRANSFER AND INTERNATIONAL STUDENTS

Transfer students: May apply for admission for the following academic terms: Fall, Winter, Spring, Summer. Applicants do not need a minimum number of credits to apply. For fall 2005: Transfer applications received: 1,416. Transfer applicants offered admission: 868. Transfer applicants enrolled: 497. **International students:** Number of foreign undergraduates: 103 (1% of student body). Number of countries represented: 43. Minimum TOEFL score required: 525 (paper).

University of Wisconsin–Green Bay

- **Address:** 2420 Nicolet Drive, Green Bay, WI 54311
- **Website:** http://www.uwgb.edu
- **Public**
- **Enrollment:** 4,519 full-time; 1,103 part-time

KEY STATS

✔ **U.S News College Ranking:** 70, Universities–Master's (Midwest)
✔ **ACT Score (25th/75th percentile):** 21-25
✔ **Tuition:** 2006-2007: $5,716 in state, $13,190 out of state

Selectivity: Selective	**Room/board:** $4,780
Acceptance rate: 66%	**Average debt:** $12,222
Student/faculty ratio: 23/1	**Proportion who borrowed:** 61%

UNDERGRADUATE STUDENT BODY STATS

2005-2006 enrollment: 4,519 full-time; 1,103 part-time. Men: 34%; women: 66%. **Ethnic makeup:** African American: 1%; American-Indian: 1%; Asian American: 3%; Hispanic: 1%; White: 93%; International: 1%.

ADMISSIONS FACTS AND FIGURES

Phone: (920) 465-2111. **Email:** uwgb@uwgb.edu. **Website:** http://www.uwgb.edu. **Application deadlines for fall 2007:** Regular decision: Rolling. Early decision: Not offered. Early action: Not offered. Admission can be deferred. **Application fee:** $35. Common application is not accepted. **To apply online, go to:** http://apply.wisconsin.edu. **Admissions requirements/recommendations:** High school units required (recommended): English: 4 (4); Mathematics: 3 (3); Science: 3 (3); Foreign language: 0 (2); Social studies: 3 (3); History: 0 (0); Academic electives: 2 (2); Total units: 17 (19). Tests: The college uses SAT or ACT scores in admissions decisions. Either SAT or ACT required. For admission to the fall 2007 entering class, the school will accept: ACT with writing, ACT without writing. Campus visit: Recommended. Admissions interview: Neither required nor recommended. Off-campus interview: May be arranged. **Factors that count in admissions decisions:** *Academic:* Secondary school record: Very important. Class rank: Considered. Letters of recommendation: Considered. Standardized test scores: Very important. Essay: Considered. *Nonacademic:* Interview: Considered. Extracurricular activities: Very important. Talent/ability: Important. Character/personal qualities: Considered. Alumni/ae relationship: Not considered. Geographical residence: Not considered. State residency: Considered. Religious affiliation/commitment: Not considered. Minority status: Considered. Volunteer work: Considered. Work experience: Considered. **Other schools with the greatest overlap in applicants:** University of Wisconsin–Eau Claire; University of Wisconsin–Madison; University of Wisconsin–Milwaukee; University of Wisconsin–Oshkosh; University of Wisconsin–Stevens Point. **Admissions statistics for the fall 2005 entering class:** Total applicants: 3,350. Total accepted: 2,222. Freshmen enrolled: 910; 4% were from out of state. Overall acceptance rate: 66%. **Size of waiting list:** 211 applicants; enrolled from waiting list: 25. **Average high school grade point average:** 3.3. **First-year students who submitted SAT scores:** 2%. Scores (25/75 percentile): Verbal: 478-558, Math: 520-610, Combined: 998-1168. **First-year students submitting ACT scores:** 98%. Scores (25/75 percentile): English: 20-25, Math: 20-26, Composite: 21-25.

ACADEMICS

Year founded: 1965. **Academic calendar:** Semester. **Degrees offered:** certificate, associate, bachelor's, post-bachelor's certificate, master's. **Most popular majors:** 20% business administration and management, 19% developmental and child psychology, 9% biomedical sciences, 9% communication, journalism, and related programs, 5% social sciences. **Major fields of study:** biological and biomedical sciences; business, management, marketing, and related support services; communication, journalism, and related programs; computer and information sciences and support services; education; English language and literature/letters; foreign languages, literatures, and linguistics; health professions and related clinical sciences; history; liberal arts and sciences studies, and humanities; mathematics and statistics; multi/interdisciplinary studies; natural resources and conservation; philosophy and religious studies; physical sciences; psychology; social sciences; visual and performing arts. **Areas of required coursework:** arts/fine arts, humanities, mathematics, English (including composition), sciences (biological or physical), social science, other. **Pre-professional programs:** pre-law, pre-dentistry, pre-medicine, pre-veterinary science, pre-optometry, pre-pharmacy. **Special academic programs (% participation):** cross-registration (1%), distance learning (5%), double major (30%), dual enrollment (1%), English as a Second Language (ESL) (1%), exchange student program (domestic) (1%), external degree program (2%), independent study (60%), internships (45%), liberal arts/career combination (5%), student-designed major (1%), study abroad (10%), teacher certificate program (10%). **Teacher certification offered in:** elementary, middle/junior high, secondary, bilingual/bicultural. **Reserve Officers Training Corps (ROTC):** Army ROTC: Offered on campus. **Faculty and instruction (2005-2006):** Total instructional faculty: 179 full-time, 100 part-time (53% men; 47% women; 10% minorities). Full-time faculty with Ph.D. or other terminal degree: 88%. Student/faculty ratio: 23/1. Classes of fewer than 20 students: 27%; of 20 to 49 students: 58%; of 50 or more students: 16%. **Advanced Placement and International Baccalaureate credit:** AP tests may be used for: Credit and/or placement. Scores accepted: 3, 4, 5. International Baccalaureate exams may be used for: Credit and/or placement. **Freshmen returning for sophomore year:** 77%. **Graduation rates:** Four-year: 18%; five-year: 43%; six-year: 44%. **Graduate study:** 10% of students pursue further study immediately upon graduation; 15% within one year; 25% within five years. Fields in which graduates pursue further study: Master of Business Administration (MBA), 20%; law, 5%; medicine, 10%; education, 20%; arts and sciences, 45%.

COSTS AND FINANCIAL AID

Financial aid office: (920) 465-2075. **Expenses (2006-2007):** Tuition and fees 2006-2007: $5,716 in state, $13,190 out of state; room/board: $4,780. Estimated books and supplies: $700; transportation: $720; personal expenses: $1,890. **Financial aid:** Priority filing date for institution's financial aid form: April 15. In 2005-2006, 78% of undergraduates applied for financial aid. Of those, 57% were determined to have financial need; 40% had their need fully met. Average financial aid package (proportion receiving): $7,839 (55%). Average amount of gift aid, such as scholarships or grants (proportion receiving): $4,609 (31%). Average amount of self-help aid, such as work study or loans (proportion receiving): $4,154 (40%). Average need-based loan (excluding PLUS or other private loans): $4,030. Among students who received need-based aid, the average percentage of need met: 79%. Among students who received aid based on merit, the average award (and the proportion receiving): $2,890 (2%). The average athletic scholarship (and the proportion receiving): $6,219 (1%). Average amount of debt of borrowers graduating in 2005: $12,222. Proportion who borrowed: 61%.

CAMPUS LIFE AND EXTRACURRICULAR ACTIVITIES

Campus housing available (% using): coed dorms (40%), apartment for single students (60%). Students who live in college-owned, operated, or affiliated housing: 33%. **Student employment:** During the 2005-2006 academic year, 20% of undergraduates worked on campus. Average per-year earnings: $1,000. **Clubs and organizations:** Number of student organizations: 94. Activities include: choral groups, dance, drama/theater, jazz band, literary magazine, music ensembles, pep band, radio station, student government, student newspaper, television station. Number of fraternities: 1; sororities: 1. Proportion of men in fraternities: 1%; of women in sororities: 1%. Average proportion of students who stay on campus on weekends: 35%. **Sports program (2005-2006):** Member of NCAA I. *Men's intercollegiate varsity sports:* basketball, cross-country, golf, nordic skiing, soccer, swimming and diving, tennis. *Women's intercollegiate varsity sports:* basketball, cross-country, nordic skiing, soccer, softball, swimming and diving, tennis, volleyball.

SERVICES AND FACILITIES

Basic services: nonremedial tutoring, placement service, health service, health insurance. **Remedial assistance:** math, writing. **Counseling services:** minority student, career, personal, veteran student, academic, psychological, birth control, religious. **For learning-disabled students:** School does not offer a structured program with separate admission and additional fees. Services include: remedial math, remedial English, tape recorders, untimed tests, note-taking services, readers, extended time for tests, priority registration, priority seating, texts on tape. **Library:** Number of titles: 339,003; number of current serial subscriptions: 5,299. **Information technology resources:** Students are not required to lease or own a computer. Number of campus computers available to all students: 600. School has a wireless network. Proportion of college-owned housing units wired for high-speed internet access: 96%. **Campus safety:** Security services offered: 24-hour foot-and-vehicle patrols, late-night transport/escort service, 24-hour emergency telephones, lighted pathways/sidewalks, student patrols, controlled dormitory access (key, security card, etc).

TRANSFER AND INTERNATIONAL STUDENTS

Transfer students: May apply for admission for the following academic terms: Fall, Spring, Summer. Applicants need a minimum number of credits to apply. For fall 2005: Transfer applications received: 1,327. Transfer applicants offered admission: 878. Transfer applicants enrolled: 611. **International students:** Number of foreign undergraduates: 37 (1% of student body). Number of countries represented: 26. Minimum TOEFL score required: 500 (paper).

University of Wisconsin–La Crosse

- **Address:** 1725 State Street, La Crosse, WI 54601
- **Website:** http://www.uwlax.edu
- **Public**
- **Enrollment:** 7,720 full-time; 413 part-time

KEY STATS

- ✔ **U.S News College Ranking:** 20, Universities–Master's (Midwest)
- ✔ **ACT Score (25th/75th percentile):** 23-27
- ✔ **Tuition:** 2006-2007: $5,550 in state, $13,000 out of state

Selectivity: More selective	**Room/board:** $5,020
Acceptance rate: 67%	**Average debt:** $16,793
Student/faculty ratio: 22/1	**Proportion who borrowed:** 67%

UNDERGRADUATE STUDENT BODY STATS

2005-2006 enrollment: 7,720 full-time; 413 part-time. Men: 41%; women: 59%. **Ethnic makeup:** African American: 1%; American-Indian: 1%; Asian American: 3%; Hispanic: 1%; White: 94%; International: 1%.

ADMISSIONS FACTS AND FIGURES

Phone: (608) 785-8939. **Email:** admissions@uwlax.edu. **Website:** http://www.uwlax.edu. **Application deadlines for fall 2007:** Regular decision: Rolling. Early decision: Not offered. Early action: Not offered. Admission cannot be deferred. **Application fee:** $35. Common application is not accepted. **To apply online, go to:** http://www.apply.wisconsin.edu. **Admissions requirements/recommendations:** High school units required (recommended): English: 4 (4); Mathematics: 3 (4); Science: 3 (4); Foreign language: 0 (3); Social studies: 3 (4); History: 0 (0); Academic electives: 4 (2); Total units: 17 (21). Tests: The college uses SAT or ACT scores in admissions decisions. Either SAT or ACT required. For admission to the fall 2007 entering class, the school will accept: ACT with writing, ACT without writing. Campus visit: Recommended. Admissions interview: Neither required nor recommended. Off-campus interview: Not available. **Factors that count in admissions decisions:** *Academic:* Secondary school record: Very important. Class rank: Very important. Letters of recommendation: Considered. Standardized test scores: Very important. Essay: Important. *Nonacademic:* Interview: Considered. Extracurricular activities: Considered. Talent/ability: Considered. Character/personal qualities: Considered. Alumni/ae relationship: Not considered. Geographical residence: Considered. State residency: Considered. Religious affiliation/commitment: Not considered. Minority status: Considered. Volunteer work: Considered. Work experience: Considered. **Other schools with the greatest overlap in applicants:** Marquette University; University of Minnesota–Twin Cities; University of Wisconsin–Eau Claire; University of Wisconsin–Madison. **Admissions statistics for the fall 2005 entering class:** Total applicants: 6,347. Total accepted: 4,282. Freshmen enrolled: 1,764; 16% were from out of state. Overall acceptance rate: 67%. **Size of waiting list:** 385 applicants; enrolled from waiting list: 330. **Credentials of fall 2005 freshmen:** 30% ranked in the top 10 percent of their high school class; 80% were in the top 25 percent, and 97% were in the top half. (Proportion submitting class standing: 92%.) **First-year students who submitted SAT scores:** 3%. Scores (25/75 percentile): Verbal: 500-610, Math: 520-660, Combined: 1020-1270. **First-year students submitting ACT scores:** 98%. Scores (25/75 percentile): English: 22-27, Math: 23-27, Composite: 23-27.

ACADEMICS

Year founded: 1909. **Academic calendar:** Semester. **Degrees offered:** associate, bachelor's, master's, doctorate. **Most popular majors:** 9% kinesiology and exercise science, 8% biology/biological sciences, 7% elementary education and teaching, 7% psychology, 6% marketing/marketing management. **Major fields of study:** biological and biomedical sciences; business, management, marketing, and related support services; communication, journalism, and related programs; computer and information sciences and support services; education; English language and literature/letters; foreign languages, literatures, and linguistics; health professions and related clinical sciences; history; mathematics and statistics; parks, recreation, leisure, and fitness studies; philosophy and religious studies; physical sciences; psychology; public administration and social service professions; social sciences; visual and performing arts. **Areas of required coursework:** arts/fine arts, humanities, computer literacy, mathematics, English (including composition), sciences (biological or physical), history, social science, other. **Pre-professional programs:** pre-law, pre-dentistry, pre-medicine, pre-veterinary science, pre-optometry, pre-pharmacy, other. **Special academic programs:** cooperative (work-study plan) program, cross-registration, distance learning, double major, dual enrollment, English as a Second Language (ESL), honors program, independent study, internships, study abroad, teacher certificate program. **Teacher certification offered in:** early childhood, special education, elementary, middle/junior high, secondary. **Reserve Officers Training Corps (ROTC):** Army ROTC: Offered on campus. **Faculty and instruction (2005-2006):** Total instructional faculty: 339 full-time, 109 part-time (58% men; 42% women; 13% minorities). Full-time faculty with Ph.D. or other terminal degree: 79%. Student/faculty ratio: 22/1. Classes of fewer than 20 students: 39%; of 20 to 49 students: 53%; of 50 or more students: 8%. **Advanced Placement and International Baccalaureate credit:** AP tests may be used for: Credit and/or placement. Scores accepted: 3, 4, 5. International Baccalaureate exams may be used for: Credit and/or placement. **Freshmen returning for sophomore year:** 87%. **Graduation rates:** Four-year: 21%; five-year: 55%; six-year: 61%. **Graduate study:** 23% of students pursue further study immediately upon graduation.

COSTS AND FINANCIAL AID

Financial aid office: (608) 785-8604. **Expenses (2006-2007):** Tuition and fees 2006-2007: $5,550 in state, $13,000 out of state; room/board: $5,020. Estimated books and supplies: $300; transportation: $730; personal expenses: $2,000. **Financial aid:** Priority filing date for institution's financial aid form: March 15. In 2005-2006, 87% of undergraduates applied for financial aid. Of those, 66% were determined to have financial need; 79% had their need fully met. Average financial aid package (proportion receiving): $4,885 (66%). Average amount of gift aid, such as scholarships or grants (proportion receiving): N/A (29%). Average amount of self-help aid, such as work study or loans (proportion receiving): N/A (66%). Among students who received need-based aid, the average percentage of need met: 86%. Among students who received aid based on merit, the average award (and the proportion receiving): $3,875 (12%). Average amount of debt of borrowers graduating in 2005: $16,793. Proportion who borrowed: 67%.

CAMPUS LIFE AND EXTRACURRICULAR ACTIVITIES
Campus housing available (% using): coed dorms (61%), apartment for single students (12%), special housing for disabled students (8%), special housing for international students (19%). Students who live in college-owned, operated, or affiliated housing: 36%. **Clubs and organizations:** Number of student organizations: 182. Activities include: choral groups, concert band, dance, drama/theater, jazz band, literary magazine, marching band, music ensembles, musical theater, pep band, radio station, student government, student newspaper, student film society, symphony orchestra, television station. Number of fraternities: 3; sororities: 2. Proportion of men in fraternities: 1%; of women in sororities: 1%. Average proportion of students who stay on campus on weekends: 66%. **Sports program (2005-2006):** Member of NCAA III. *Men's intercollegiate varsity sports:* baseball, basketball, cross-country, football, swimming and diving, tennis, track and field (indoor), track and field (outdoor), wrestling. *Women's intercollegiate varsity sports:* basketball, cross-country, gymnastics, soccer, softball, swimming and diving, tennis, track and field (indoor), track and field (outdoor), volleyball.

SERVICES AND FACILITIES
Basic services: women's center, placement service, day care, health service, health insurance. **Remedial assistance:** reading, math, writing, study skills. **Counseling services:** minority student, career, personal, veteran student, academic, older student, psychological. **For learning-disabled students:** School does not offer a structured program with separate admission and additional fees. Total undergraduates in learning-disabled program or receiving services: 62. Services include: reading machines, tape recorders, note-taking services, oral tests, readers, extended time for tests, priority registration, texts on tape, exams on tape or computer, other testing accomodations. **Library:** Number of titles: 687,207; number of current serial subscriptions: 3,160. **Information technology resources:** Students are not required to lease or own a computer. Number of campus computers available to all students: 600. School has a wireless network. Approximate number of users that can be accommodated: 1,800. Proportion of college-owned housing units wired for high-speed internet access: 100%. **Campus safety:** Security services offered: 24-hour foot-and-vehicle patrols, 24-hour emergency telephones, lighted pathways/sidewalks, controlled dormitory access (key, security card, etc).

TRANSFER AND INTERNATIONAL STUDENTS
Transfer students: May apply for admission for the following academic terms: Fall, Winter, Spring, Summer. Applicants need a minimum number of credits to apply. For fall 2005: Transfer applications received: 1,003. Transfer applicants offered admission: 672. Transfer applicants enrolled: 409. **International students:** Number of foreign undergraduates: 59 (1% of student body). Number of countries represented: 41. Minimum TOEFL score required: 550 (paper); 213 (computer).

University of Wisconsin–Madison

- **Address:** 500 Lincoln Drive, Madison, WI 53706
- **Website:** http://www.wisc.edu
- **Public**
- **Enrollment:** 27,441 full-time; 2,665 part-time

KEY STATS
- ✔ **U.S News College Ranking:** 34, National Universities
- ✔ **ACT Score (25th/75th percentile):** 26-30
- ✔ **Tuition:** 2005-2006: $6,284 in state, $20,284 out of state

Selectivity: More selective	**Room/board:** $6,500
Acceptance rate: 68%	**Average debt:** $18,630
Student/faculty ratio: 13/1	**Proportion who borrowed:** 45%

UNDERGRADUATE STUDENT BODY STATS
2005-2006 enrollment: 27,441 full-time; 2,665 part-time. Men: 46%; women: 54%. **Ethnic makeup:** African American: 3%; American-Indian: 1%; Asian American: 5%; Hispanic: 3%; White: 85%; International: 3%.

ADMISSIONS FACTS AND FIGURES
Phone: (608) 262-3961. **Email:** onwisconsin@admissions.wisc.edu. **Website:** http://www.wisc.edu. **Application deadlines for fall 2007:** Regular decision: February 1. Early decision: Not offered. Early action: Not offered. Admission can be deferred. **Application fee:** $35. Common application is not accepted. To apply online, go to: http://www.apply.wisconsin.edu. **Admissions requirements/recommendations:** High school units required (recommended): English: 4 (4); Mathematics: 3 (4); Science: 3 (4); Foreign language: 2 (4); Social studies: 3 (4); Academic electives: 2 (2); Total units: 17 (20). Tests: The college uses SAT or ACT scores in admissions decisions. Either SAT or ACT required. For admission to the fall 2007 entering class, the school will accept ACT with writing. Campus visit: Recommended. Admissions interview: Neither required nor recommended. **Factors that count in admissions decisions:** *Academic:* Secondary school record: Very important. Class rank: Very important. Letters of recommendation: Important. Standardized test scores: Important. Essay: Considered. *Nonacademic:* Interview: Considered. Extracurricular activities: Considered. Talent/ability: Considered. Character/personal qualities: Considered. Alumni/ae relationship: Considered. Geographical residence: Not considered. State residency: Important. Religious affiliation/commitment: Not considered. Minority status: Considered. Volunteer work: Considered. Work experience: Considered. **Other schools with the greatest overlap in applicants:** Marquette University; University of Illinois–Urbana-Champaign; University of Minnesota–Twin Cities; University of Wisconsin–Eau Claire; University of Wisconsin–La Crosse. **Admissions statistics for the fall 2005 entering class:** Total applicants: 21,682. Total accepted: 14,718. Freshmen enrolled: 6,141; 39% were from out of state. Overall acceptance rate: 68%. **Credentials of fall 2005 freshmen:** 56% ranked in the top 10 percent of their high school class; 91% were in the top 25 percent, and 99% were in the top half. (Proportion submitting class standing: 75%.) **Average high school grade point average:** 3.7. **First-year students who submitted SAT scores:** 31%. Scores (25/75 percentile): Verbal: 560-670, Math: 600-700, Combined: 1160-1370. **First-year students submitting ACT scores:** 83%. Scores (25/75 percentile): English: N/A, Math: N/A, Composite: 26-30.

ACADEMICS
Year founded: 1848. **Academic calendar:** Semester. **Degrees offered:** bachelor's, master's, post-master's certificate, first professional, first professional certificate, doctorate. **Most popular majors:** 6% political science and government, 5% English language and literature, 5% psychology, 4% communication studies/speech communication and rhetoric, 4% economics. **Major fields of study:** agriculture, agriculture operations, and related sciences; architecture and related services; area, ethnic, cultural, and gender studies; biological and biomedical sciences; business, management, marketing, and related support services; communication, journalism, and related programs; computer and information sciences and support services; education; engineering; English language and literature/letters; family and consumer sciences/human sciences; foreign languages, literatures, and linguistics; health professions and related clinical sciences; history; legal professions and studies; mathematics and statistics; multi/interdisciplinary studies; natural resources and conservation; parks, recreation, leisure, and fitness studies; philosophy and religious studies; physical sciences; psychology; public administration and social service professions; social sciences; visual and performing arts. **Areas of required coursework:** humanities, mathematics, English (including composition), foreign languages, sciences (biological or physical), social science, other. **Special academic programs (% participation):** accelerated program (14%), cooperative (work-study plan) program (5%), distance learning (40%), double major (24%), dual enrollment (1%), English as a Second Language (ESL) (3%), honors program (4%), independent study (46%), internships (20%), liberal arts/career combination (1%), student-designed major (1%), study abroad (18%), teacher certificate program (5%). **Teacher certification offered in:** early childhood, special education, elementary, middle/junior high, secondary, bilingual/bicultural. **Cooperative education programs:** agriculture, engineering. **Reserve Officers Training Corps (ROTC):** Army ROTC: Offered on campus; Navy ROTC: Offered on campus; Air Force ROTC: Offered on campus. **Faculty and instruction (2005-2006):** Total instructional faculty: 2,365 full-time, 610 part-time (63% men; 37% women; 14% minorities). Full-time faculty with Ph.D. or other terminal degree: 92%. Student/faculty ratio: 13/1. Classes of fewer than 20 students: 43%; of 20 to 49 students: 39%; of 50 or more students: 18%. **Advanced Placement and International Baccalaureate credit:** AP tests may be used for: Credit only. Scores accepted: 3, 4, 5. International Baccalaureate exams may be used for: Credit only. **Freshmen returning for sophomore year:** 93%. **Graduation rates:** Four-year: 43%; five-year: 74%; six-year: 78%. **Graduate study:** 20% of students pursue further study immediately upon graduation; 30% within one year; 42% within five years.

COSTS AND FINANCIAL AID

Financial aid office: (608) 262-3060. **Expenses (2005-2006):** Tuition and fees 2005-2006: $6,284 in state, $20,284 out of state; room/board; $6,500. Estimated books and supplies: $860; transportation: $430; personal expenses: $1,920. **Financial aid:** In 2005-2006, 74% of undergraduates applied for financial aid. Of those, 41% were determined to have financial need; 43% had their need fully met. Average financial aid package (proportion receiving): $11,288 (39%). Average amount of gift aid, such as scholarships or grants (proportion receiving): $4,928 (17%). Average amount of self-help aid, such as work study or loans (proportion receiving): $4,631 (34%). Average need-based loan (excluding PLUS or other private loans): $3,813. Among students who received aid based on merit, the average award (and the proportion receiving): $2,935 (15%). The average athletic scholarship (and the proportion receiving): $15,202 (2%). Average amount of debt of borrowers graduating in 2005: $18,630. Proportion who borrowed: 45%.

CAMPUS LIFE AND EXTRACURRICULAR ACTIVITIES

Campus housing available: coed dorms, women's dorms, men's dorms, apartments for married students, apartment for single students, other housing options. Students who live in college-owned, operated, or affiliated housing: 26%. Average per-year earnings: $7,000. **Clubs and organizations:** Number of student organizations: 729. Activities include: choral groups, concert band, dance, drama/theater, jazz band, literary magazine, marching band, music ensembles, musical theater, opera, pep band, radio station, student government, student newspaper, student film society, symphony orchestra, television station, yearbook. Number of fraternities: 26; sororities: 11. Proportion of men in fraternities: 9%; of women in sororities: 8%. **Sports program (2005-2006):** Member of NCAA I. *Men's intercollegiate varsity sports:* basketball, crew, cross-country, football, golf, ice hockey, soccer, swimming and diving, tennis, track and field (indoor), track and field (outdoor), wrestling. *Women's intercollegiate varsity sports:* basketball, crew, cross-country, golf, ice hockey, lightweight crew, rowing, soccer, softball, swimming and diving, tennis, track and field (indoor), track and field (outdoor), volleyball.

SERVICES AND FACILITIES

Basic services: nonremedial tutoring, women's center, placement service, day care, health service, health insurance. **Counseling services:** minority student, career, military, personal, veteran student, academic, older student, psychological, birth control. **For learning-disabled students:** School does not offer a structured program with separate admission and additional fees. Services include: untimed tests, note-taking services, oral tests, learning center, readers, extended time for tests, tutors, priority registration, priority seating, texts on tape, other testing accomodations. **Library:** Number of titles: 7,348,117; number of current serial subscriptions: 55,164. **Information technology resources:** Students are not required to lease or own a computer. Number of campus computers available to all students: 3,300. School has a wireless network. Proportion of college-owned housing units wired for high-speed internet access: 100%. **Campus safety:** Security services offered: 24-hour foot-and-vehicle patrols, late-night transport/escort service, 24-hour emergency telephones, lighted pathways/sidewalks, student patrols, controlled dormitory access (key, security card, etc).

TRANSFER AND INTERNATIONAL STUDENTS

Transfer students: May apply for admission for the following academic terms: Fall, Spring, Summer. Applicants need a minimum number of credits to apply. For fall 2005: Transfer applications received: 3,763. Transfer applicants offered admission: 2,048. Transfer applicants enrolled: 1,169. **International students:** Number of foreign undergraduates: 923 (3% of student body). Number of countries represented: 91. Minimum TOEFL score required: 550 (paper); 213 (computer). Average TOEFL score: 577 (paper).

University of Wisconsin–Milwaukee

- **Address:** PO Box 413, Milwaukee, WI 53201
- **Website:** http://www.uwm.edu
- **Public**
- **Enrollment:** 18,856 full-time; 4,060 part-time

KEY STATS

✔ **U.S News College Ranking:** fourth tier, National Universities
✔ **ACT Score (25th/75th percentile):** 20-24
✔ **Tuition:** 2006-2007: $6,860 in state, $16,432 out of state

Selectivity: Selective	**Room/board:** $6,950
Acceptance rate: 81%	**Average debt:** $16,492
Student/faculty ratio: 20/1	**Proportion who borrowed:** 63%

UNDERGRADUATE STUDENT BODY STATS

2005-2006 enrollment: 18,856 full-time; 4,060 part-time. Men: 46%; women: 54%. **Ethnic makeup:** African American: 7%; American-Indian: 1%; Asian American: 4%; Hispanic: 4%; White: 83%; International: 1%.

ADMISSIONS FACTS AND FIGURES

Phone: (414) 229-2222. **Email:** uwmlook@uwm.edu. **Website:** http://www.uwm.edu. **Application deadlines for fall 2007:** Regular decision: August 1. Early decision: Not offered. Early action: Not offered. Admission can be deferred. **Application fee:** $35. Common application is not accepted. **To apply online, go to:** http://www.apply.wisconsin.edu. **Admissions requirements/recommendations:** High school units required (recommended): English: 4 (4); Mathematics: 3 (3); Science: 3 (3); Foreign language: 0 (2); Social studies: 3 (3); Academic electives: 2 (2); Total units: 17 (19). Tests: The college uses SAT or ACT scores in admissions decisions. Either SAT or ACT required. For admission to the fall 2007 entering class, the school will accept: ACT with writing, ACT without writing. Campus visit: Recommended. Admissions interview: Neither required nor recommended. Off-campus interview: Not available. **Factors that count in admissions decisions:** *Academic:* Secondary school record: Important. Class rank: Very important. Letters of recommendation: Considered. Standardized test scores: Very important. Essay: Considered. *Nonacademic:* Interview: Considered. Extracurricular activities: Considered. Talent/ability: Considered. Character/personal qualities: Considered. Alumni/ae relationship: Not considered. Geographical residence: Not considered. State residency: Considered. Religious affiliation/commitment: Not considered. Minority status: Considered. Volunteer work: Considered. Work experience: Considered. **Other schools with the greatest overlap in applicants:** Marquette University; University of Wisconsin–La Crosse; University of Wisconsin–Madison; University of Wisconsin–Oshkosh; University of Wisconsin–Whitewater. **Admissions statistics for the fall 2005 entering class:** Total applicants: 11,238. Total accepted: 9,070. Freshmen enrolled: 4,300; 3% were from out of state. Overall acceptance rate: 81%. **Credentials of fall 2005 freshmen:** 7% ranked in the top 10 percent of their high school class; 26% were in the top 25 percent, and 67% were in the top half. (Proportion submitting class standing: 91%.) **Average high school grade point average:** 3.1. **First-year students who submitted SAT scores:** 3%. Scores (25/75 percentile): Verbal: 470-610, Math: 480-600, Combined: 950-1210. **First-year students submitting ACT scores:** 97%. Scores (25/75 percentile): English: 18-24, Math: 19-25, Composite: 20-24.

ACADEMICS

Year founded: 1956. **Academic calendar:** Semester. **Degrees offered:** certificate, bachelor's, post-bachelor's certificate, master's, post-master's certificate, doctorate. **Most popular majors:** 24% business, management, marketing, and related support services, 9% education, 9% health professions and related clinical sciences, 8% communication, journalism, and related programs, 7% visual and performing arts. **Major fields of study:** architecture and related services; area, ethnic, cultural, and gender studies; biological and biomedical sciences; business, management, marketing, and related support services; communication, journalism, and related programs; computer and information sciences and support services; education; engineering; English language and literature/letters; foreign languages, literatures, and linguistics; health professions and related clinical sciences; history; liberal arts and sciences studies, and humanities; mathematics and statistics; multi/interdisciplinary studies; natural resources and conservation; parks, recreation, leisure, and fitness studies; philosophy and religious studies; physical sciences; psychology; public administration and social service professions; security and protective services; social sciences; visual and performing arts. **Areas of required coursework:** arts/fine arts, humanities, mathematics, English (including composition), foreign languages, sciences (biological or physical), history, social science, other. **Pre-professional programs:** pre-law, pre-dentistry, pre-medicine, pre-pharmacy. **Special academic programs:** accelerated program, cooperative (work-study plan) program, cross-registration, distance learning, double major, dual enrollment, English as a Second Language (ESL), external degree program, honors program, independent study, internships, liberal arts/career combination, student-designed major, study abroad, teacher certificate program. **Teacher certification offered in:** early childhood, special education, elementary, middle/junior high, secondary, bilingual/bicultural. **Cooperative education programs:** computer science, engineering. **Reserve Officers Training Corps (ROTC):** Army ROTC: Offered at cooperating institution (Marquette University); Air Force ROTC: Offered at cooperating institution (Marquette University). **Faculty and instruction (2005-2006):** Total instructional faculty: 1,046 full-time, 353 part-time (54% men; 46% women; 18% minorities). Full-time faculty with Ph.D. or other terminal degree: 81%. Student/faculty ratio: 20/1. Classes of fewer than 20 students: 35%; of 20 to 49 students: 50%; of 50 or more students: 15%. **Advanced Placement and International Baccalaureate credit:** AP tests may be used for: Credit and/or placement. Scores accepted: 3, 4, 5. International Baccalaureate exams may be used for: Credit and/or placement. **Freshmen returning for sophomore year:** 72%. **Graduation rates:** Four-year: 13%; five-year: 34%; six-year: 42%.

COSTS AND FINANCIAL AID
Financial aid office: (414) 229-6300. **Expenses (2006-2007):** Tuition and fees 2006-2007: $6,860 in state, $16,432 out of state; room/board: $6,950. Estimated books and supplies: $950; transportation: $1,848; personal expenses: $1,600. **Financial aid:** Priority filing date for institution's financial aid form: March 1. In 2005-2006, 80% of undergraduates applied for financial aid. Of those, 64% were determined to have financial need; 25% had their need fully met. Average financial aid package (proportion receiving): $5,966 (53%). Average amount of gift aid, such as scholarships or grants (proportion receiving): $4,587 (23%). Average amount of self-help aid, such as work study or loans (proportion receiving): $3,880 (44%). Average need-based loan (excluding PLUS or other private loans): $3,722. Among students who received need-based aid, the average percentage of need met: 57%. Among students who received aid based on merit, the average award (and the proportion receiving): $1,970 (2%). The average athletic scholarship (and the proportion receiving): $666 (0%). Average amount of debt of borrowers graduating in 2005: $16,492. Proportion who borrowed: 63%.

CAMPUS LIFE AND EXTRACURRICULAR ACTIVITIES
Campus housing available (% using): coed dorms (80%), apartment for single students (17%), special housing for disabled students (3%). Students who live in college-owned, operated, or affiliated housing: 12%. **Clubs and organizations:** Number of student organizations: 265. Activities include: choral groups, concert band, dance, drama/theater, jazz band, literary magazine, music ensembles, musical theater, pep band, radio station, student government, student newspaper, student film society, symphony orchestra. Number of fraternities: 12; sororities: 9. Average proportion of students who stay on campus on weekends: 65%. **Sports program (2005-2006):** Member of NCAA I. **Men's intercollegiate varsity sports:** baseball, basketball, cross-country, soccer, swimming and diving, track and field (indoor), track and field (outdoor). **Women's intercollegiate varsity sports:** basketball, cross-country, soccer, swimming and diving, tennis, track and field (indoor), track and field (outdoor), volleyball.

SERVICES AND FACILITIES
Basic services: nonremedial tutoring, women's center, placement service, day care, health service. **Remedial assistance:** reading, math, writing, study skills. **Counseling services:** minority student, career, veteran student, academic, older student, birth control. **For learning-disabled students:** School does not offer a structured program with separate admission and additional fees. Total undergraduates in learning-disabled program or receiving services: 321. Services include: remedial math, remedial English, reading machines, remedial reading, tape recorders, diagnostic testing service, note-taking services, oral tests, learning center, readers, extended time for tests, tutors, exams on tape or computer, other. **Library:** Number of titles: 2,088,025; number of current serial subscriptions: 6,394. **Information technology resources:** Students are not required to lease or own a computer. Number of campus computers available to all students: 1,000. School has a wireless network. Approximate number of users that can be accommodated: 2,400. Proportion of college-owned housing units wired for high-speed internet access: 100%. **Campus safety:** Security services offered: 24-hour foot-and-vehicle patrols, late-night transport/escort service, 24-hour emergency telephones, lighted pathways/sidewalks, controlled dormitory access (key, security card, etc).

TRANSFER AND INTERNATIONAL STUDENTS
Transfer students: May apply for admission for the following academic terms: Fall, Winter, Spring, Summer. Applicants do not need a minimum number of credits to apply. For fall 2005: Transfer applications received: 4,417. Transfer applicants offered admission: 2,602. Transfer applicants enrolled: 1,507. **International students:** Number of foreign undergraduates: 116 (1% of student body). Number of countries represented: 55. Minimum TOEFL score required: 520 (paper); 190 (computer). Average TOEFL score: 530 (paper).

University of Wisconsin—Oshkosh

- **Address:** 800 Algoma Boulevard, Oshkosh, WI 54901
- **Website:** http://www.uwosh.edu
- **Public**
- **Enrollment:** 8,538 full-time; 1,202 part-time

KEY STATS
✔ **U.S News College Ranking:** third tier, Universities–Master's (Midwest)
✔ **ACT Score (25th/75th percentile):** 20-24
✔ **Tuition:** 2005-2006: $4,981 in state, $15,027 out of state

Selectivity: Selective	**Room/board:** $4,884
Acceptance rate: 79%	**Average debt:** $16,000
Student/faculty ratio: 20/1	**Proportion who borrowed:** 70%

UNDERGRADUATE STUDENT BODY STATS
2005-2006 enrollment: 8,538 full-time; 1,202 part-time. Men: 40%; women: 60%. **Ethnic makeup:** African American: 1%; American-Indian: 1%; Asian American: 3%; Hispanic: 1%; White: 93%; International: 1%.

ADMISSIONS FACTS AND FIGURES
Phone: (920) 424-0202. **Email:** oshadmuw@uwosh.edu. **Website:** http://www.uwosh.edu. **Application deadlines for fall 2007:** Regular decision: Rolling. Early decision: Not offered. Early action: Not offered. Admission can be deferred. **Application fee:** $35. Common application is not accepted. **To apply online, go to:** http://apply.wisconsin.edu. **Admissions requirements/recommendations:** High school units required (recommended): English: 4; Mathematics: 3 (4); Science: 3 (4); Social studies: 3; History: 1; Academic electives: 4; Total units: 17. Tests: The college uses SAT or ACT scores in admissions decisions. Either SAT or ACT required. For admission to the fall 2007 entering class, the school will accept: ACT with writing, ACT without writing. Campus visit: Neither required nor recommended. Admissions interview: Neither required nor recommended. Off-campus interview: Not available. **Factors that count in admissions decisions:** *Academic:* Secondary school record: Very important. Class rank: Important. Letters of recommendation: Considered. Standardized test scores: Important. Essay: Considered. *Nonacademic:* Interview: Not considered. Extracurricular activities: Considered. Talent/ability: Considered. Character/personal qualities: Not considered. Alumni/ae relationship: Not considered. Geographical residence: Not considered. State residency: Not considered. Religious affiliation/commitment: Not considered. Minority status: Considered. Volunteer work: Not considered. Work experience: Considered. **Other schools with the greatest overlap in applicants:** University of Wisconsin–Eau Claire; University of Wisconsin–La Crosse; University of Wisconsin–Stevens Point; University of Wisconsin–Whitewater. **Admissions statistics for the fall 2005 entering class:** Total applicants: 4,777. Total accepted: 3,796. Freshmen enrolled: 1,634; 2% were from out of state. Overall acceptance rate: 79%. **Credentials of fall 2005 freshmen:** 11% ranked in the top 10 percent of their high school class; 38% were in the top 25 percent, and 89% were in the top half. (Proportion submitting class standing: 91%.) **Average high school grade point average:** 3.3. **First-year students submitting ACT scores:** 97%. Scores (25/75 percentile): English: 19-24, Math: 18-25, Composite: 20-24.

ACADEMICS
Year founded: 1871. **Academic calendar:** Semester. **Degrees offered:** certificate, bachelor's, master's. **Most popular majors:** 20% business, management, marketing, and related support services, 16% education, 11% health

professions and related clinical sciences, 8% communication, journalism, and related programs, 7% social sciences. **Major fields of study:** biological and biomedical sciences; business, management, marketing, and related support services; communication, journalism, and related programs; computer and information sciences and support services; education; health professions and related clinical sciences; history; mathematics and statistics; philosophy and religious studies; psychology; public administration and social service professions; social sciences. **Areas of required coursework:** arts/fine arts, humanities, mathematics, English (including composition), sciences (biological or physical), social science. **Pre-professional programs:** pre-law, pre-dentistry, pre-medicine, pre-veterinary science, pre-optometry, pre-pharmacy. **Special academic programs:** accelerated program, cooperative (work-study plan) program, distance learning, double major, English as a Second Language (ESL), exchange student program (domestic), honors program, independent study, internships, student-designed major, study abroad, teacher certificate program, weekend college. **Teacher certification offered in:** early childhood, special education, elementary, middle/junior high, secondary, bilingual/bicultural. **Reserve Officers Training Corps (ROTC):** Army ROTC: Offered on campus. **Faculty and instruction (2005-2006):** Total instructional faculty: 381 full-time, 185 part-time (52% men; 48% women; 10% minorities). Full-time faculty with Ph.D. or other terminal degree: 85%. Student/faculty ratio: 20/1. Classes of fewer than 20 students: 27%; of 20 to 49 students: 60%; of 50 or more students: 13%. **Freshmen returning for sophomore year:** 75%. **Graduation rates:** Four-year: 15%; five-year: 40%; six-year: 46%.

COSTS AND FINANCIAL AID

Financial aid office: (920) 424-3377. **Expenses (2005-2006):** Tuition and fees 2005-2006: $4,981 in state, $15,027 out of state; room/board: $4,884. Estimated books and supplies: $750; transportation: $350; personal expenses: $525. **Financial aid:** Priority filing date for institution's financial aid form: March 15. Average amount of debt of borrowers graduating in 2005: $16,000. Proportion who borrowed: 70%.

CAMPUS LIFE AND EXTRACURRICULAR ACTIVITIES

Campus housing available (% using): coed dorms (98%), women's dorms, men's dorms, sorority housing (1%), fraternity housing (1%). Students who live in college-owned, operated, or affiliated housing: 34%. **Student employment:** During the 2005-2006 academic year, 16% of undergraduates worked on campus. Average per-year earnings: $4,350. Activities include: choral groups, dance, drama/theater, jazz band, literary magazine, music ensembles, radio station, student government, student newspaper, student film society, television station. Proportion of men in fraternities: 3%; of women in sororities: 3%. **Sports program (2005-2006):** Member of NCAA III. *Men's intercollegiate varsity sports:* baseball, basketball, cross-country, football, riflery, soccer, swimming and diving, tennis, track and field (indoor), track and field (outdoor), wrestling. *Women's intercollegiate varsity sports:* basketball, cross-country, golf, gymnastics, riflery, soccer, softball, swimming and diving, tennis, track and field (indoor), track and field (outdoor), volleyball.

SERVICES AND FACILITIES

Basic services: nonremedial tutoring, women's center, placement service, day care, health service, health insurance. **Remedial assistance:** reading, math, writing, study skills. **Counseling services:** minority student, career, military, personal, veteran student, academic, older student, psychological, birth control. **For learning-disabled students:** School offers a structured program with separate admission and additional fees. Services include: remedial math, other testing accommodations, remedial English, reading machines, remedial reading, tape recorders, videotaped classes, note-taking services, oral tests, learning center, readers, extended time for tests, tutors, exams on tape or computer, other testing accomodations. **Library:** Number of titles: 606,070; number of current serial subscriptions: 4,297. **Information technology resources:** Students are not required to lease or own a computer. Number of campus computers available to all students: 500. School has a wireless network. Approximate number of users that can be accommodated: 100. Proportion of college-owned housing units wired for high-speed internet access: 100%. **Campus safety:** Security services offered: 24-hour foot-and-vehicle patrols, late-night transport/escort service, 24-hour emergency telephones, lighted pathways/sidewalks, student patrols, controlled dormitory access (key, security card, etc).

TRANSFER AND INTERNATIONAL STUDENTS

Transfer students: May apply for admission for the following academic terms: Fall, Spring, Summer. Applicants do not need a minimum number of credits to apply. For fall 2005: Transfer applications received: 1,555. Transfer applicants offered admission: 1,357. Transfer applicants enrolled:

840. **International students:** Number of foreign undergraduates: 72 (1% of student body). Minimum TOEFL score required: 523 (paper); 193 (computer).

University of Wisconsin–Parkside

- **Address:** 900 Wood Road, Kenosha, WI 53141-2000
- **Website:** http://www.uwp.edu
- **Public**
- **Enrollment:** 3,545 full-time; 1,308 part-time

KEY STATS

✔ **U.S News College Ranking:** fourth tier, Universities–Master's (Midwest)
✔ **ACT Score (25th/75th percentile):** 18-22
✔ **Tuition:** 2005-2006: $4,995 in state, $15,043 out of state

Selectivity: Less selective	**Room/board:** $4,950
Acceptance rate: 92%	**Average debt:** N/A
Student/faculty ratio: 18/1	**Proportion who borrowed:** N/A

UNDERGRADUATE STUDENT BODY STATS

2005-2006 enrollment: 3,545 full-time; 1,308 part-time. Men: 43%; women: 57%. **Ethnic makeup:** African American: 9%; American-Indian: 1%; Asian American: 3%; Hispanic: 6%; White: 79%; International: 1%.

ADMISSIONS FACTS AND FIGURES

Phone: (262) 595-2355. **Email:** admissions@uwp.edu. **Website:** http://www.uwp.edu. **Application deadlines for fall 2007:** Regular decision: August 1. Early decision: Not offered. Early action: Not offered. Admission can be deferred. **Application fee:** $35. Common application is not accepted. **To apply online, go to:** http://www.apply.wisconsin.edu. **Admissions requirements/recommendations:** High school units required (recommended): English: 4 (4); Mathematics: 3 (4); Science: 3 (4); Foreign language: 0 (2); Social studies: 3 (3); History: 0 (1); Academic electives: 4 (4); Total units: 17 (22). Tests: The college uses SAT or ACT scores in admissions decisions. Neither SAT nor ACT required. For admission to the fall 2007 entering class, the school will accept: ACT with writing, ACT without writing. Campus visit: Neither required nor recommended. Admissions interview: Neither required nor recommended. Off-campus interview: Not available. **Factors that count in admissions decisions:** *Academic:* Secondary school record: Very important. Class rank: Very important. Letters of recommendation: Considered. Standardized test scores: Considered. Essay: Considered. *Nonacademic:* Interview: Considered. Extracurricular activities: Considered. Talent/ability: Considered. Character/personal qualities: Considered. Alumni/ae relationship: Considered. Geographical residence: Not considered. State residency: Not considered. Religious affiliation/commitment: Not considered. Minority status: Considered. Volunteer work: Considered. Work experience: Considered. **Other schools with the greatest overlap in applicants:** University of Wisconsin–Milwaukee; University of Wisconsin–Stevens Point. **Admissions statistics for the fall 2005 entering class:** Total applicants: 1,868. Total accepted: 1,726. Freshmen enrolled: 877; 5% were from out of state. Overall acceptance rate: 92%. **Credentials of fall 2005 freshmen:** 5% ranked in the top 10 percent of their high school class; 23% were in the top 25 percent, and 56% were in the top half. (Proportion submitting class standing: 89%.) **First-year students submitting ACT scores:** 90%. Scores (25/75 percentile): English: N/A, Math: N/A, Composite: 18-22.

ACADEMICS

Year founded: 1968. **Academic calendar:** Semester. **Degrees offered:** certificate, bachelor's, master's. **Most popular majors:** 21% business, management, marketing, and related support services, 11% security and protective services, 9% social sciences, 8% communication, journalism, and related programs, 8% psychology. **Major fields of study:** biological and biomedical sciences; business, management, marketing, and related support services; communication, journalism, and related programs; computer and information sciences and support services; English language and literature/letters; foreign languages, literatures, and linguistics; health professions and related clinical sciences; history; liberal arts and sciences studies, and humanities; mathematics and statistics; parks, recreation, leisure, and fitness studies; philosophy and religious studies; physical sciences; psychology; security and protective services; social sciences; visual and performing arts. **Areas of required coursework:** arts/fine arts, mathematics, English (including composition), foreign languages, sciences (biological or physical), social science, other. **Pre-professional programs:** pre-law, pre-dentistry, pre-medicine, pre-veterinary science, pre-optometry, pre-pharmacy, other. **Special academic programs:** accelerated program, distance learning, double major, dual enrollment, exchange student program (domestic), honors program, independent study, internships, liberal arts/career combination, study abroad, teacher certificate program, weekend college, other. **Teacher certification offered in:** early childhood, elementary, middle/junior high, secondary. **Reserve Officers Training Corps (ROTC):** Army ROTC: Offered at cooperating institution (Marquette University). **Faculty and instruction (2005-2006):** Total instructional faculty: 181 full-time, 132 part-time (56% men; 44% women; 19% minorities). Full-time faculty with Ph.D. or other terminal degree: 74%. Student/faculty ratio: 18/1. Classes of fewer than 20 students: 46%; of 20 to 49 students: 45%; of 50 or more students: 9%. **Advanced Placement and International Baccalaureate credit:** AP tests may be used for: Credit and/or placement. Scores accepted: 3, 4, 5. International Baccalaureate exams may be used for: Credit and/or placement. **Freshmen returning for sophomore year:** 64%. **Graduation rates:** Four-year: 9%; five-year: 23%; six-year: 29%.

COSTS AND FINANCIAL AID
Financial aid office: (262) 595-2004. **Expenses (2005-2006):** Tuition and fees 2005-2006: $4,995 in state, $15,043 out of state; room/board: $4,950. Estimated books and supplies: $784; transportation: $1,060; personal expenses: $1,328. **Financial aid:** Priority filing date for institution's financial aid form: March 15.

CAMPUS LIFE AND EXTRACURRICULAR ACTIVITIES
Campus housing available: coed dorms, apartment for single students, special housing for disabled students, special housing for international students. Students who live in college-owned, operated, or affiliated housing: 16%. **Student employment:** During the 2005-2006 academic year, 12% of undergraduates worked on campus. Average per-year earnings: $3,000. **Clubs and organizations:** Number of student organizations: 72. Activities include: choral groups, concert band, dance, drama/theater, jazz band, literary magazine, music ensembles, musical theater, pep band, radio station, student government, student newspaper, symphony orchestra. Number of fraternities: 5; sororities: 7. Proportion of men in fraternities: 1%; of women in sororities: 1%. Average proportion of students who stay on campus on weekends: 25%. **Sports program (2005-2006):** Member of NCAA II. *Men's intercollegiate varsity sports:* baseball, basketball, cross-country, golf, soccer, track and field (indoor), track and field (outdoor), wrestling. *Women's intercollegiate varsity sports:* basketball, cross-country, soccer, softball, track and field (indoor), track and field (outdoor), volleyball.

SERVICES AND FACILITIES
Basic services: nonremedial tutoring, women's center, placement service, day care, health service, health insurance. **Remedial assistance:** reading, math, writing, study skills. **Counseling services:** minority student, military, personal, veteran student, academic, psychological, birth control, other. **For learning-disabled students:** School does not offer a structured program with separate admission and additional fees. Services include: remedial math, remedial English, reading machines, remedial reading, untimed tests, note-taking services, learning center, extended time for tests, tutors. **Information technology resources:** Students are not required to lease or own a computer. Number of campus computers available to all students: 228. School has a wireless network. Proportion of college-owned housing units wired for high-speed internet access: 100%. **Campus safety:** Security services offered: 24-hour foot-and-vehicle patrols, late-night transport/escort service, 24-hour emergency telephones, lighted pathways/sidewalks, student patrols, controlled dormitory access (key, security card, etc).

TRANSFER AND INTERNATIONAL STUDENTS
Transfer students: May apply for admission for the following academic terms: Fall, Spring, Summer. Applicants need a minimum number of credits to apply. For fall 2005: Transfer applications received: 611. Transfer applicants offered admission: 573. Transfer applicants enrolled: 356. **International students:** Number of foreign undergraduates: 53 (1% of student body). Number of countries represented: 24. Minimum TOEFL score required: 525 (paper).

University of Wisconsin–Platteville

- **Address:** 1 University Plaza, Platteville, WI 53818
- **Website:** http://www.uwplatt.edu
- **Public**
- **Enrollment:** 5,180 full-time; 595 part-time

KEY STATS
✔ **U.S News College Ranking:** 55, Universities–Master's (Midwest)
✔ **ACT Score (25th/75th percentile):** 20-25
✔ **Tuition:** N/A

Selectivity: Selective	**Room/board:** N/A
Acceptance rate: 85%	**Average debt:** N/A
Student/faculty ratio: 20/1	**Proportion who borrowed:** N/A

UNDERGRADUATE STUDENT BODY STATS
2005-2006 enrollment: 5,180 full-time; 595 part-time. Men: 62%; women: 38%. **Ethnic makeup:** African American: 1%; Asian American: 1%; Hispanic: 1%; White: 97%.

ADMISSIONS FACTS AND FIGURES
Phone: (800) 362-5515. **Email:** admit@uwplatt.edu. **Website:** http://www.uwplatt.edu. **Application deadlines for fall 2007:** Regular decision: Rolling. Early decision: Not offered. Early action: Not offered. Admission can be deferred. **Application fee:** $35. Common application is not accepted. **To apply online, go to:** http://www.apply.wisconsin.edu/. **Admissions requirements/recommendations:** High school units required (recommended): English: 4; Mathematics: 3 (3); Science: 3; Foreign language: 0; Social studies: 3; History: 0; Academic electives: 4; Total units: 17. Tests: The college uses SAT or ACT scores in admissions decisions. ACT required. For admission to the fall 2007 entering class, the school will accept: ACT with writing, ACT without writing. Campus visit: Recommended. Admissions interview: Neither required nor recommended. Off-campus interview: May be arranged. **Factors that count in admissions decisions:** *Academic:* Secondary school record: Very important. Class rank: Very important. Letters of recommendation: Considered. Standardized test scores: Very important. Essay: Not considered. *Nonacademic:* Interview: Considered. Extracurricular activities: Considered. Talent/ability: Considered. Character/personal qualities: Not considered. Alumni/ae relationship: Not considered. Geographical residence: Important. State residency: Important. Religious affiliation/commitment: Not considered. Minority status: Not considered. Volunteer work: Not considered. Work experience: Not considered. **Admissions statistics for the fall 2005 entering class:** Total applicants: 3,075. Total accepted: 2,620. Freshmen enrolled: 1,218; 15% were from out of state. Overall acceptance rate: 85%. **Credentials of fall 2005 freshmen:** 12% ranked in the top 10 percent of their high school class; 35% were in the top 25 percent, and 77% were in the top half. (Proportion submitting class standing: 94%.) **First-year students submitting ACT scores:** 99%. Scores (25/75 percentile): English: 19-25, Math: 20-27, Composite: 20-25.

ACADEMICS
Year founded: 1866. **Academic calendar:** Semester. **Degrees offered:** certificate, diploma, associate, transfer-associate, bachelor's, master's. **Most popular majors:** 24% engineering, 13% business, management, marketing, and related support services, 12% education, 9% security and protective services, 8% agriculture, agriculture operations, and related sciences. **Major fields of study:** agriculture, agriculture operations, and related sciences; biological and biomedical sciences; business, management, marketing, and related support services; communication, journalism, and related programs; communications technologies/technicians and support services; computer and information sciences and support services; education; engineering; engineering technologies/technicians; English language and literature/letters; foreign languages, literatures, and linguistics; history; mathematics and statistics; multi/interdisciplinary studies; natural resources and conservation; philosophy and religious studies; physical sciences; psychology; security and protective services; social sciences; visual and performing arts. **Areas of required coursework:** arts/fine arts, humanities, mathematics, English (including composition), foreign languages, sciences (biological or physical), history, social science. **Pre-professional programs:** pre-law, pre-dentistry, pre-medicine, pre-veterinary science, pre-optometry, pre-pharmacy. **Special academic programs:** cooperative (work-study plan) program, distance learning, double major, dual enrollment, English as a Second Language (ESL),

exchange student program (domestic), external degree program, honors program, independent study, internships, liberal arts/career combination, student-designed major, study abroad, teacher certificate program. **Teacher certification offered in:** early childhood, special education, elementary, middle/junior high, adult education, secondary. **Cooperative education programs:** agriculture, art, business, computer science, education, engineering, humanities, natural science, social/behavioral science, technologies, vocational arts, other. **Reserve Officers Training Corps (ROTC):** Army ROTC: Offered at cooperating institution (University of Dubuque, Iowa). **Faculty and instruction (2005-2006):** Total instructional faculty: 249 full-time, 99 part-time (67% men; 33% women; 13% minorities). Full-time faculty with Ph.D. or other terminal degree: 83%. Student/faculty ratio: 20/1. Classes of fewer than 20 students: 51%; of 20 to 49 students: 44%; of 50 or more students: 5%. **Advanced Placement and International Baccalaureate credit:** AP tests may be used for: Credit only. Scores accepted: 2, 3, 4, 5. **Freshmen returning for sophomore year:** 78%. **Graduation rates:** Four-year: 13%; five-year: 41%; six-year: 52%. **Graduate study:** 6% of students pursue further study immediately upon graduation. Fields in which graduates pursue further study: law, 6%; medicine, 11%; engineering, 6%; education, 26%; arts and sciences, 51%.

COSTS AND FINANCIAL AID
Financial aid office: (608) 342-1836. **Financial aid:** Priority filing date for institution's financial aid form: March 15.

CAMPUS LIFE AND EXTRACURRICULAR ACTIVITIES
Campus housing available: coed dorms, women's dorms, men's dorms, sorority housing, fraternity housing. Students who live in college-owned, operated, or affiliated housing: 39%. **Student employment:** During the 2005-2006 academic year, 21% of undergraduates worked on campus. Average per-year earnings: $2,448. **Clubs and organizations:** Number of student organizations: 170. Activities include: choral groups, concert band, drama/theater, jazz band, literary magazine, marching band, music ensembles, musical theater, pep band, radio station, student government, student newspaper, symphony orchestra, television station. Number of fraternities: 9; sororities: 5. Proportion of men in fraternities: 3%; of women in sororities: 2%. Average proportion of students who stay on campus on weekends: 40%. **Sports program (2005-2006):** Member of NCAA III. *Men's intercollegiate varsity sports:* baseball, basketball, cross-country, football, soccer, track and field (indoor), track and field (outdoor), wrestling. *Women's intercollegiate varsity sports:* basketball, cross-country, golf, soccer, softball, track and field (indoor), track and field (outdoor), volleyball.

SERVICES AND FACILITIES
Basic services: nonremedial tutoring, women's center, placement service, day care, health service, health insurance. **Remedial assistance:** reading, math, writing, study skills. **Counseling services:** minority student, career, military, personal, veteran student, academic, older student, psychological, birth control, religious. **For learning-disabled students:** School does not offer a structured program with separate admission and additional fees. Total undergraduates in learning-disabled program or receiving services: 68. Services include: remedial math, remedial English, reading machines, tape recorders, note-taking services, oral tests, extended time for tests, tutors, priority registration, priority seating, texts on tape, exams on tape or computer, other testing accomodations, waiver of foreign language degree requirement, waiver of math degree requirement. **Library:** Number of titles: 363,432; number of current serial subscriptions: 1,993. **Information technology resources:** Students are not required to lease or own a computer. Number of campus computers available to all students: 1,000. School has a wireless network. Approximate number of users that can be accommodated: 1,000. Proportion of college-owned housing units wired for high-speed internet access: 100%. **Campus safety:** Security services offered: 24-hour foot-and-vehicle patrols, 24-hour emergency telephones, lighted pathways/sidewalks, controlled dormitory access (key, security card, etc).

TRANSFER AND INTERNATIONAL STUDENTS
Transfer students: May apply for admission for the following academic terms: Fall, Spring, Summer. Applicants do not need a minimum number of credits to apply. For fall 2005: Transfer applications received: 595. Transfer applicants offered admission: 449. Transfer applicants enrolled: 326. **International students:** Number of foreign undergraduates: 22. Number of countries represented: 14. Minimum TOEFL score required: 500 (paper); 173 (computer).

University of Wisconsin–River Falls

- **Address:** 410 S. Third Street, River Falls, WI 54022
- **Website:** http://www.uwrf.edu
- **Public**
- **Enrollment:** 5,289 full-time; 384 part-time

KEY STATS
✔ **U.S News College Ranking:** 59, Universities–Master's (Midwest)
✔ **ACT Score (25th/75th percentile):** 20-23
✔ **Tuition:** 2006-2007: $5,454 in state, $12,978 out of state
   Selectivity: Selective   **Room/board:** $4,450
   Acceptance rate: 79%   **Average debt:** $14,756
   Student/faculty ratio: 20/1   **Proportion who borrowed:** 68%

UNDERGRADUATE STUDENT BODY STATS
2005-2006 enrollment: 5,289 full-time; 384 part-time. Men: 40%; women: 60%. **Ethnic makeup:** African American: 1%; Asian American: 3%; Hispanic: 1%; White: 93%; International: 1%.

ADMISSIONS FACTS AND FIGURES
Phone: (715) 425-3500. **Email:** admit@uwrf.edu. **Website:** http://www.uwrf.edu. **Application deadlines for fall 2007:** Regular decision: Rolling. Early decision: Not offered. Early action: Not offered. Admission can be deferred. **Application fee:** $35. Common application is not accepted. **To apply online, go to:** http://apply.wisconsin.edu. **Admissions requirements/recommendations:** High school units required (recommended): English: 4; Mathematics: 2; Science: 2; Foreign language: (2); Social studies: 3; Academic electives: 4; Total units: 17. Tests: The college uses SAT or ACT scores in admissions decisions. ACT required. For admission to the fall 2007 entering class, the school will accept: ACT with writing, ACT without writing. Campus visit: Neither required nor recommended. Admissions interview: Neither required nor recommended. Off-campus interview: May be arranged. **Factors that count in admissions decisions:** *Academic:* Secondary school record: Very important. Class rank: Very important. Letters of recommendation: Considered. Standardized test scores: Very important. Essay: Considered. *Nonacademic:* Interview: Considered. Extracurricular activities: Considered. Talent/ability: Considered. Character/personal qualities: Considered. Alumni/ae relationship: Considered. Geographical residence: Considered. State residency: Considered. Religious affiliation/commitment: Not considered. Minority status: Not considered. Volunteer work: Considered. Work experience: Considered. **Other schools with the greatest overlap in applicants:** University of Minnesota–Twin Cities; University of Wisconsin–Eau Claire; University of Wisconsin–La Crosse; University of Wisconsin–Madison; University of Wisconsin–Stevens Point. **Admissions statistics for the fall 2005 entering class:** Total applicants: 3,239. Total accepted: 2,567. Freshmen enrolled: 1,209; 43% were from out of state. Overall acceptance rate: 79%. **Size of waiting list:** 256 applicants; enrolled from waiting list: 49. **Credentials of fall 2005 freshmen:** 14% ranked in the top 10 percent of their high school class; 37% were in the top 25 percent, and 78% were in the top half. (Proportion submitting class standing: 98%.) **First-year students submitting ACT scores:** 97%. Scores (25/75 percentile): English: N/A, Math: N/A, Composite: 20-23.

ACADEMICS
Year founded: 1874. **Academic calendar:** Semester. **Degrees offered:** certificate, bachelor's, post-bachelor's certificate, master's, post-master's certificate. **Most popular majors:** 62% business, management, marketing, and related support services, 8% communication, journalism, and related programs, 6% computer and information sciences and support services, 6% social sciences, 4% foreign languages, literatures, and linguistics. **Major fields of study:** agriculture, agriculture operations, and related sciences; biological and biomedical sciences; business, management, marketing, and related support services; communication, journalism, and related programs; computer and information sciences and support services; education; English language and literature/letters; foreign languages, literatures, and linguistics; health professions and related clinical sciences; history; liberal arts and sciences studies, and humanities; mathematics and statistics; multi/interdisciplinary studies; natural resources and conservation; physical sciences; psychology; public administration and social service professions; social sciences; visual and performing arts. **Areas of required coursework:** arts/fine arts, humanities, mathematics, English (including composition), sciences (biological or physical), social science, other. **Pre-professional pro-**

grams: pre-law, pre-dentistry, pre-medicine, pre-veterinary science, pre-pharmacy. Special academic programs: cooperative (work-study plan) program, distance learning, double major, dual enrollment, English as a Second Language (ESL), exchange student program (domestic), external degree program, honors program, independent study, internships, student-designed major, study abroad, teacher certificate program. Teacher certification offered in: elementary, secondary. Cooperative education programs: agriculture, business, education. Faculty and instruction (2005-2006): Total instructional faculty: 215 full-time, 195 part-time (; 5% minorities). Student/faculty ratio: 20/1. Advanced Placement and International Baccalaureate credit: AP tests may be used for: Credit only. Scores accepted: 3, 4, 5. International Baccalaureate exams may be used for: Credit only. Freshmen returning for sophomore year: 78%. Graduation rates: Four-year: 26%; five-year: 55%; six-year: 57%.

COSTS AND FINANCIAL AID

Financial aid office: (715) 425-3141. Expenses (2006-2007): Tuition and fees 2006-2007: $5,454 in state, $12,978 out of state; room/board: $4,450. Estimated books and supplies: $200; transportation: $800; personal expenses: $1,106. Financial aid: Priority filing date for institution's financial aid form: March 15. In 2005-2006, 73% of undergraduates applied for financial aid. Of those, 48% were determined to have financial need; 20% had their need fully met. Average financial aid package (proportion receiving): $6,343 (48%). Average amount of gift aid, such as scholarships or grants (proportion receiving): $2,610 (37%). Average amount of self-help aid, such as work study or loans (proportion receiving): $1,226 (47%). Average need-based loan (excluding PLUS or other private loans): $3,046. Among students who received need-based aid, the average percentage of need met: 82%. Among students who received aid based on merit, the average award (and the proportion receiving): $1,510 (5%). The average athletic scholarship (and the proportion receiving): $0 (0%). Average amount of debt of borrowers graduating in 2005: $14,756. Proportion who borrowed: 68%.

CAMPUS LIFE AND EXTRACURRICULAR ACTIVITIES

Campus housing available (% using): coed dorms (62%), women's dorms (11%), fraternity housing (7%), apartment for single students (10%), special housing for disabled students (10%). Students who live in college-owned, operated, or affiliated housing: 98%. Student employment: During the 2005-2006 academic year, 25% of undergraduates worked on campus. Average per-year earnings: $1,500. Clubs and organizations: Number of student organizations: 150. Activities include: choral groups, concert band, dance, drama/theater, jazz band, literary magazine, music ensembles, musical theater, radio station, student government, student newspaper, student film society, symphony orchestra, television station. Number of fraternities: 4; sororities: 4. Proportion of men in fraternities: 3%; of women in sororities: 2%. Average proportion of students who stay on campus on weekends: 30%. Sports program (2005-2006): Member of NCAA III. Men's intercollegiate varsity sports: basketball, cross-country, football, ice hockey, swimming and diving, track and field (indoor), track and field (outdoor). Women's intercollegiate varsity sports: basketball, cross-country, golf, ice hockey, soccer, softball, swimming and diving, tennis, track and field (indoor), track and field (outdoor), volleyball.

SERVICES AND FACILITIES

Basic services: nonremedial tutoring, placement service, day care, health service, health insurance. Remedial assistance: reading, math, writing, study skills. Counseling services: minority student, career, military, personal, veteran student, academic, psychological, birth control. For learning-disabled students: School does not offer a structured program with separate admission and additional fees. Services include: remedial math, remedial English, reading machines, tape recorders, note-taking services, oral tests, readers, extended time for tests, tutors, substitution of courses, texts on tape, exams on tape or computer, other testing accomodations, other. Library: Number of titles: 314,119; number of current serial subscriptions: 1,143. Information technology resources: Students are not required to lease or own a computer. Number of campus computers available to all students: 750. School does not have a wireless network. Proportion of college-owned housing units wired for high-speed internet access: 100%. Campus safety: Security services offered: 24-hour foot-and-vehicle patrols, late-night transport/escort service, 24-hour emergency telephones, lighted pathways/sidewalks, controlled dormitory access (key, security card, etc.).

TRANSFER AND INTERNATIONAL STUDENTS

Transfer students: May apply for admission for the following academic terms: Fall, Winter, Spring, Summer. Applicants do not need a minimum number of credits to apply. For fall 2005: Transfer applications received: 831. Transfer applicants offered admission: 613. Transfer applicants enrolled: 438. International students: Number of foreign undergraduates: 44 (1% of student body). Number of countries represented: 15. Minimum TOEFL score required: 500 (paper); 180 (computer).

University of Wisconsin–Stevens Point

- Address: 2100 Main Street, Stevens Point, WI 54481
- Website: http://www.uwsp.edu
- Public
- Enrollment: 7,746 full-time; 607 part-time

KEY STATS

✔ U.S News College Ranking: 37, Universities–Master's (Midwest)
✔ ACT Score (25th/75th percentile): 20-25
✔ Tuition: 2006-2007: $5,465 in state, $14,617 out of state
  Selectivity: Selective   Room/board: $4,643
  Acceptance rate: 80%   Average debt: $17,065
  Student/faculty ratio: 21/1   Proportion who borrowed: 69%

UNDERGRADUATE STUDENT BODY STATS

2005-2006 enrollment: 7,746 full-time; 607 part-time. Men: 46%; women: 54%. Ethnic makeup: African American: 1%; American-Indian: 1%; Asian American: 2%; Hispanic: 1%; White: 94%; International: 1%.

ADMISSIONS FACTS AND FIGURES

Phone: (715) 346-2441. Email: admiss@uwsp.edu. Website: http://www.uwsp.edu. Application deadlines for fall 2007: Regular decision: Rolling. Early decision: Not offered. Early action: Not offered. Admission can be deferred. Application fee: $35. Common application is not accepted. To apply online, go to: http://apply.wisconsin.edu. Admissions requirements/recommendations: High school units required (recommended): English: 4; Mathematics: 3; Science: 3; Social studies: 3; Total units: 17. Tests: The college uses SAT or ACT scores in admissions decisions. Either SAT or ACT required. For admission to the fall 2007 entering class, the school will accept: ACT with writing, ACT without writing. Campus visit: Recommended. Admissions interview: Neither required nor recommended. Off-campus interview: Not available. Factors that count in admissions decisions: Academic: Secondary school record: Very important. Class rank: Very important. Letters of recommendation: Important. Standardized test scores: Very important. Essay: Important. Nonacademic: Interview: Not considered. Extracurricular activities: Considered. Talent/ability: Considered. Character/personal qualities: Considered. Alumni/ae relationship: Not considered. Geographical residence: Not considered. State residency: Not considered. Religious affiliation/commitment: Not considered. Minority status: Considered. Volunteer work: Considered. Work experience: Considered. Admissions statistics for the fall 2005 entering class: Total applicants: 4,583. Total accepted: 3,681. Freshmen enrolled: 1,523; 6% were from out of state. Overall acceptance rate: 80%. Credentials of fall 2005 freshmen: 14% ranked in the top 10 percent of their high school class; 42% were in the top 25 percent, and 91% were in the top half. (Proportion submitting class standing: 92%.) Average high school grade point average: 3.4. First-year students who submitted SAT scores: 1%. Scores (25/75 percentile): Verbal: 465-575, Math: 438-605, Combined: 903-1180. First-year students submitting ACT scores: 98%. Scores (25/75 percentile): English: 19-25, Math: 20-25, Composite: 20-25.

ACADEMICS

Year founded: 1894. Academic calendar: Semester. Degrees offered: certificate, associate, bachelor's, master's, doctorate. Most popular majors: 9% biology/biological sciences, 9% business administration and management, 8% communication studies/speech communication and rhetoric, 5% elementary education and teaching, 5% psychology. Major fields of study: area, ethnic, cultural, and gender studies; biological and biomedical sciences; business, management, marketing, and related support services; communication, journalism, and related programs; computer and information sciences and support services; education; English language and literature/letters; foreign languages, literatures, and linguistics; health professions and related clinical sciences; history; liberal arts and sciences studies, and humanities; mathematics and statistics; multi/interdisciplinary studies; natural resources and conservation; parks, recreation, leisure, and fitness studies; philosophy and religious studies; physical sciences; psychology; public administration and social service professions; social sciences; visual and performing arts. **Areas of required coursework:** arts/fine arts, humanities, mathematics, English (including composition), sciences (biological or physical), history, social science, other. **Pre-professional programs:** pre-law, pre-dentistry, pre-medicine, pre-veterinary science, pre-optometry, pre-pharmacy, other. **Special academic programs:** accelerated program, cooperative (work-study plan) program, distance learning, double major, dual enrollment, English as a Second Language (ESL), independent study, internships, student-designed major, study abroad, teacher certificate program. **Teacher certification offered in:** early childhood, special education, elementary, secondary. **Cooperative education programs:** agriculture, art, business, computer science, education, engineering, health professions, home economics, humanities, natural science, social/behavioral science, technologies, vocational arts. **Reserve Officers Training Corps (ROTC):** Army ROTC: Offered on campus. **Faculty and instruction (2005-2006):** Total instructional faculty: 357 full-time, 80 part-time (60% men; 40% women; 7% minorities). Full-time faculty with Ph.D. or other terminal degree: 87%. Student/faculty ratio: 21/1. Classes of fewer than 20 students: 33%; of 20 to 49 students: 54%; of 50 or more students: 14%. **Advanced Placement and International Baccalaureate credit:** AP tests may be used for: Credit and/or placement. Scores accepted: 3, 4, 5. International Baccalaureate exams may be used for: Credit and/or placement. **Freshmen returning for sophomore year:** 78%. **Graduation rates:** Four-year: 19%; five-year: 52%; six-year: 57%. **Graduate study:** 11% of students pursue further study immediately upon graduation. Fields in which graduates pursue further study: Master of Business Administration (MBA), 4%; law, 5%; medicine, 5%; dentistry, 1%; education, 8%; arts and sciences, 38%.

COSTS AND FINANCIAL AID
Financial aid office: (715) 346-4771. **Expenses (2006-2007):** Tuition and fees 2006-2007: $5,465 in state, $14,617 out of state; room/board: $4,643. Estimated books and supplies: $450; transportation: $304; personal expenses: $1,677. **Financial aid:** In 2005-2006, 85% of undergraduates applied for financial aid. Of those, 49% were determined to have financial need; 72% had their need fully met. Average financial aid package (proportion receiving): $6,885 (47%). Average amount of gift aid, such as scholarships or grants (proportion receiving): $4,496 (25%). Average amount of self-help aid, such as work study or loans (proportion receiving): $4,797 (44%). Average need-based loan (excluding PLUS or other private loans): $4,234. Among students who received need-based aid, the average percentage of need met: 95%. Among students who received aid based on merit, the average award (and the proportion receiving): $1,973 (6%). The average athletic scholarship (and the proportion receiving): $0 (0%). Average amount of debt of borrowers graduating in 2005: $17,065. Proportion who borrowed: 69%.

CAMPUS LIFE AND EXTRACURRICULAR ACTIVITIES
Campus housing available (% using): coed dorms (90%), women's dorms (5%), men's dorms (5%), special housing for international students. Students who live in college-owned, operated, or affiliated housing: 37%. **Student employment:** During the 2005-2006 academic year, 26% of undergraduates worked on campus. Average per-year earnings: $1,928. **Clubs and organizations:** Number of student organizations: 180. Activities include: choral groups, concert band, dance, drama/theater, jazz band, literary magazine, music ensembles, musical theater, opera, pep band, radio station, student government, student newspaper, student film society, symphony orchestra, television station. Number of fraternities: 4; sororities: 3. Proportion of men in fraternities: 1%; of women in sororities: 1%. **Sports program (2005-2006):** Member of NCAA III. *Men's intercollegiate varsity sports:* baseball, basketball, cross-country, football, ice hockey, swimming and diving, track and field (indoor), track and field (outdoor), wrestling. *Women's intercollegiate varsity sports:* basketball, cross-country, golf, ice hockey, soccer, softball, swimming and diving, tennis, track and field (indoor), track and field (outdoor), volleyball.

SERVICES AND FACILITIES
Basic services: nonremedial tutoring, women's center, placement service, day care, health service. **Remedial assistance:** reading, math, writing, study skills. **Counseling services:** minority student, career, military, personal, veteran student, academic, older student, psychological, birth control, religious. **For learning-disabled students:** School does not offer a structured program with separate admission and additional fees. Total undergraduates in learning-disabled program or receiving services: 89. Services include: remedial math, remedial English, reading machines, remedial reading, other special classes, note-taking services, oral tests, learning center, read-

ers, extended time for tests, tutors, priority registration, priority seating, texts on tape, other testing accomodations. **Library:** Number of titles: 1,035,370; number of current serial subscriptions: 3,622. **Information technology resources:** Students are not required to lease or own a computer. Number of campus computers available to all students: 1,074. School has a wireless network. Proportion of college-owned housing units wired for high-speed internet access: 100%. **Campus safety:** Security services offered: 24-hour foot-and-vehicle patrols, late-night transport/escort service, 24-hour emergency telephones, lighted pathways/sidewalks, student patrols, controlled dormitory access (key, security card, etc).

TRANSFER AND INTERNATIONAL STUDENTS
Transfer students: May apply for admission for the following academic terms: Fall, Spring, Summer. Applicants need a minimum number of credits to apply. For fall 2005: Transfer applications received: 1,289. Transfer applicants offered admission: 985. Transfer applicants enrolled: 703. **International students:** Number of foreign undergraduates: 117 (1% of student body). Number of countries represented: 28. Minimum TOEFL score required: 525 (paper); 193 (computer).

University of Wisconsin–Stout

- **Address:** 1 Clock Tower Plaza, Menomonie, WI 54751
- **Website:** http://www.uwstout.edu
- **Public**
- **Enrollment:** 6,606 full-time; 735 part-time

KEY STATS
✔ **U.S News College Ranking:** 68, Universities–Master's (Midwest)
✔ **ACT Score (25th/75th percentile):** 19-23
✔ **Tuition:** 2005-2006: $6,592 in state, $16,925 out of state

Selectivity: Selective	**Room/board:** $4,572
Acceptance rate: 81%	**Average debt:** $18,496
Student/faculty ratio: 20/1	**Proportion who borrowed:** 73%

UNDERGRADUATE STUDENT BODY STATS
2005-2006 enrollment: 6,606 full-time; 735 part-time. Men: 51%; women: 49%. **Ethnic makeup:** African American: 1%; American-Indian: 1%; Asian American: 2%; Hispanic: 1%; White: 95%; International: 1%.

ADMISSIONS FACTS AND FIGURES
Phone: (715) 232-1411. **Email:** admissions@uwstout.edu. **Website:** http://www.uwstout.edu. **Application deadlines for fall 2007:** Regular decision: Rolling. Early decision: Not offered. Early action: Not offered. Admission cannot be deferred. **Application fee:** $35. Common application is not accepted. **To apply online, go to:** http://www.apply.wisconsin.edu. **Admissions requirements/recommendations:** High school units required (recommended): English: 4 (4); Mathematics: 3 (3); Science: 3 (3); Foreign language: 0 (2); Social studies: 3 (3); History: 0 (0); Academic electives: 4 (4); Total units: 17 (19). Tests: The college uses SAT or ACT scores in admissions decisions. Either SAT or ACT required. For admission to the fall 2007 entering class, the school will accept: ACT with writing, ACT without writing. Campus visit: Recommended. Admissions interview: Recommended. Off-campus interview: May be arranged. **Factors that count in admissions decisions:** *Academic:* Secondary school record: Considered. Class rank: Very important. Letters of recommendation: Considered. Standardized test scores: Very important. Essay: Considered. *Nonacademic:* Interview: Considered. Extracurricular activities: Considered. Talent/ability: Considered. Character/personal qualities: Considered. Alumni/ae relationship: Considered. Geographical residence: Not considered. State residency: Not considered. Religious affiliation/commitment: Not considered. Minority status: Considered. Volunteer work: Considered. Work experience: Considered. **Other schools with the greatest overlap in applicants:** University of Minnesota–Twin Cities; University of Wisconsin–Eau Claire; University of Wisconsin–River Falls; University of Wisconsin–Stevens Point; Winona State University. **Admissions statistics for the fall 2005 entering class:** Total applicants: 3,953. Total accepted: 3,205. Freshmen enrolled: 1,694; 35% were from out of state. Overall acceptance rate: 81%. **Credentials of fall 2005 freshmen:** 6% ranked in the top 10 percent of their high school class; 28% were in the top 25 percent, and 73% were in the top half. (Proportion submitting class standing: 92%.) **Average high school grade point average:** 3.2.

First-year students submitting ACT scores: 94%. Scores (25/75 percentile): English: 17-23, Math: 17-24, Composite: 19-23.

ACADEMICS

Year founded: 1891. **Academic calendar:** 4-1-4. **Degrees offered:** certificate, bachelor's, master's, post-master's certificate. **Most popular majors:** 17% business administration and management, 9% design and applied arts, 7% early childhood education and teaching, 7% hospitality administration/management, 6% human development and family studies. **Major fields of study:** business, management, marketing, and related support services; communications technologies/technicians and support services; computer and information sciences and support services; education; engineering; engineering technologies/technicians; English language and literature/letters; family and consumer sciences/human sciences; health professions and related clinical sciences; mathematics and statistics; psychology; science technologies/technicians; visual and performing arts. **Areas of required coursework:** arts/fine arts, humanities, mathematics, English (including composition), philosophy, sciences (biological or physical), history, social science. **Pre-professional programs:** pre-law, other. **Special academic programs:** accelerated program, cooperative (work-study plan) program, cross-registration, distance learning, double major, dual enrollment, exchange student program (domestic), external degree program, honors program, independent study, internships, study abroad, teacher certificate program. **Teacher certification offered in:** early childhood, special education, elementary, vo-tech, secondary. **Cooperative education programs:** art, business, computer science, education, engineering, home economics, humanities, natural science, social/behavioral science, technologies, vocational arts. **Reserve Officers Training Corps (ROTC):** Army ROTC: Offered on campus. **Faculty and instruction (2005-2006):** Total instructional faculty: 289 full-time, 105 part-time (58% men; 42% women; 8% minorities). Full-time faculty with Ph.D. or other terminal degree: 78%. Student/faculty ratio: 20/1. Classes of fewer than 20 students: 33%; of 20 to 49 students: 60%; of 50 or more students: 7%. **Advanced Placement and International Baccalaureate credit:** AP tests may be used for: Credit only. Scores accepted: 3, 4, 5. **Freshmen returning for sophomore year:** 73%. **Graduation rates:** Four-year: 14%; five-year: 41%; six-year: 48%. **Graduate study:** 9% of students pursue further study within one year.

COSTS AND FINANCIAL AID

Financial aid office: (715) 232-1363. **Expenses (2005-2006):** Tuition and fees 2005-2006: $6,592 in state, $16,925 out of state; room/board: $4,572. Estimated books and supplies: $314; transportation: $720; personal expenses: $1,666. **Financial aid:** Priority filing date for institution's financial aid form: March 15. In 2005-2006, 74% of undergraduates applied for financial aid. Of those, 50% were determined to have financial need; 50% had their need fully met. Average financial aid package (proportion receiving): $7,467 (50%). Average amount of gift aid, such as scholarships or grants (proportion receiving): $4,177 (25%). Average amount of self-help aid, such as work study or loans (proportion receiving): $4,541 (49%). Average need-based loan (excluding PLUS or other private loans): $3,880. Among students who received need-based aid, the average percentage of need met: 85%. Among students who received aid based on merit, the average award (and the proportion receiving): $2,087 (7%). The average athletic scholarship (and the proportion receiving): $0 (0%). Average amount of debt of borrowers graduating in 2005: $18,496. Proportion who borrowed: 73%.

CAMPUS LIFE AND EXTRACURRICULAR ACTIVITIES

Campus housing available (% using): coed dorms (91%), apartment for single students (9%), special housing for disabled students. Students who live in college-owned, operated, or affiliated housing: 40%. **Student employment:** During the 2005-2006 academic year, 21% of undergraduates worked on campus. Average per-year earnings: $1,494. **Clubs and organizations:** Number of student organizations: 120. Activities include: choral groups, concert band, dance, drama/theater, jazz band, literary magazine, marching band, music ensembles, musical theater, pep band, radio station, student government, student newspaper, student film society. Number of fraternities: 5; sororities: 3. Proportion of men in fraternities: 2%; of women in sororities: 3%. Average proportion of students who stay on campus on weekends: 60%. **Sports program (2005-2006):** Member of NCAA III. *Men's intercollegiate varsity sports:* baseball, basketball, cross-country, football, ice hockey, track and field (indoor), track and field (outdoor). *Women's intercollegiate varsity sports:* basketball, cross-country, gymnastics, soccer, softball, tennis, track and field (indoor), track and field (outdoor), volleyball.

SERVICES AND FACILITIES

Basic services: nonremedial tutoring, women's center, placement service, day care, health service. **Remedial assistance:** reading, math, writing, study skills. **Counseling services:** minority student, career, personal, veteran student, academic, older student, psychological, birth control. **For learning-disabled students:** School does not offer a structured program with separate admission and additional fees. Total undergraduates in learning-disabled program or receiving services: 168. Services include: remedial math, remedial English, reading machines, tape recorders, other special classes, diagnostic testing service, untimed tests, note-taking services, readers, extended time for tests, priority registration, priority seating, texts on tape, other testing accomodations, other. **Library:** Number of titles: 226,424; number of current serial subscriptions: 1,769. **Information technology resources:** Students are not required to lease or own a computer. Number of campus computers available to all students: 875. School has a wireless network. Approximate number of users that can be accommodated: 4,500. Proportion of college-owned housing units wired for high-speed internet access: 100%. **Campus safety:** Security services offered: 24-hour foot-and-vehicle patrols, 24-hour emergency telephones, lighted pathways/sidewalks, controlled dormitory access (key, security card, etc).

TRANSFER AND INTERNATIONAL STUDENTS

Transfer students: May apply for admission for the following academic terms: Fall, Spring, Summer. Applicants do not need a minimum number of credits to apply. For fall 2005: Transfer applications received: 1,146. Transfer applicants offered admission: 881. Transfer applicants enrolled: 581. **International students:** Number of foreign undergraduates: 47 (1% of student body). Number of countries represented: 27. Minimum TOEFL score required: 500 (paper); 173 (computer). Average TOEFL score: 525 (paper).

University of Wisconsin–Superior

- **Address:** Belknap and Catlin, PO Box 2000, Superior, WI 54880-4500
- **Website:** http://www.uwsuper.edu
- **Public**
- **Enrollment:** 2,133 full-time; 450 part-time

KEY STATS

✔ **U.S News College Ranking:** third tier, Universities–Master's (Midwest)
✔ **ACT Score (25th/75th percentile):** 20-24
✔ **Tuition:** 2005-2006: $5,188 in state, $6,302 out of state

Selectivity: Selective	Room/board: $4,422
Acceptance rate: 74%	Average debt: N/A
Student/faculty ratio: 18/1	Proportion who borrowed: N/A

UNDERGRADUATE STUDENT BODY STATS

2005-2006 enrollment: 2,133 full-time; 450 part-time. Men: 40%; women: 60%. **Ethnic makeup:** African American: 1%; American-Indian: 3%; Asian American: 1%; Hispanic: 1%; White: 89%; International: 5%.

ADMISSIONS FACTS AND FIGURES

Phone: (715) 394-8230. **Email:** admissions@uwsuper.edu. **Website:** http://www.uwsuper.edu. **Application deadlines for fall 2007:** Regular decision: Rolling. Early decision: Not offered. Early action: Not offered. Admission can be deferred. **Application fee:** $35. Common application is not accepted. **To apply online, go to:** http://www.apply.wisconsin.edu. **Admissions requirements/recommendations:** High school units required (recommended): English: 4; Mathematics: 3; Science: 3; Foreign language: 0; Social studies: 3; Academic electives: 4; Total units: 17. Tests: The college uses SAT or ACT scores in admissions decisions. Either SAT or ACT required. For admission to the fall 2007 entering class, the school will accept: ACT with writing, ACT without writing. Campus visit: Recommended. Admissions interview: Recommended. Off-campus interview: May be arranged. **Factors that count in admissions decisions:** *Academic:* Secondary school record: Important. Class rank: Important. Letters of recommendation: Considered. Standardized test scores: Important. Essay: Considered. *Nonacademic:* Interview: Considered. Extracurricular activities: Considered. Talent/ability: Considered. Character/personal qualities: Considered. Alumni/ae relationship: Considered. Geographical residence: Considered. State residency: Not considered. Religious affiliation/commitment: Not considered. Minority status:

Considered. Volunteer work: Considered. Work experience: Considered. **Other schools with the greatest overlap in applicants:** University of Minnesota–Duluth; University of Minnesota–Twin Cities; University of Wisconsin–Eau Claire; University of Wisconsin–Madison; University of Wisconsin–River Falls. **Admissions statistics for the fall 2005 entering class:** Total applicants: 918. Total accepted: 679. Freshmen enrolled: 346; 41% were from out of state. Overall acceptance rate: 74%. **Credentials of fall 2005 freshmen:** 14% ranked in the top 10 percent of their high school class; 44% were in the top 25 percent, and 82% were in the top half. (Proportion submitting class standing: 90%.) **First-year students who submitted SAT scores:** 5%. Scores (25/75 percentile): Verbal: 490-605, Math: 500-625, Combined: 990-1230. **First-year students submitting ACT scores:** 91%. Scores (25/75 percentile): English: 19-24, Math: 18-24, Composite: 20-24.

ACADEMICS

Year founded: 1893. **Academic calendar:** Semester. **Degrees offered:** certificate, associate, bachelor's, master's, post-master's certificate. **Most popular majors:** 21% business, management, marketing, and related support services, 19% education, 8% communication, journalism, and related programs, 8% social sciences, 7% public administration and social service professions. **Major fields of study:** biological and biomedical sciences; business, management, marketing, and related support services; communication, journalism, and related programs; computer and information sciences and support services; education; English language and literature/letters; health professions and related clinical sciences; history; legal professions and studies; liberal arts and sciences studies, and humanities; mathematics and statistics; multi/interdisciplinary studies; physical sciences; psychology; public administration and social service professions; security and protective services; social sciences; transportation and materials moving; visual and performing arts. **Areas of required coursework:** arts/fine arts, humanities, computer literacy, mathematics, English (including composition), philosophy, sciences (biological or physical), history, social science, other. **Pre-professional programs:** pre-law, pre-medicine, pre-veterinary science, pre-optometry, pre-pharmacy. **Special academic programs:** cooperative (work-study plan) program, cross-registration, distance learning, double major, dual enrollment, exchange student program (domestic), external degree program, independent study, internships, liberal arts/career combination, student-designed major, study abroad, teacher certificate program. **Teacher certification offered in:** early childhood, special education, elementary, middle/junior high, secondary. **Cooperative education programs:** engineering, natural science. **Reserve Officers Training Corps (ROTC):** Air Force ROTC: Offered at cooperating institution (University of Minnesota-Duluth). **Faculty and instruction (2005-2006):** Total instructional faculty: 118 full-time, 52 part-time (59% men; 41% women; 9% minorities). Full-time faculty with Ph.D. or other terminal degree: 72%. Student/faculty ratio: 18/1. Classes of fewer than 20 students: 48%; of 20 to 49 students: 48%; of 50 or more students: 4%. **Advanced Placement and International Baccalaureate credit:** AP tests may be used for: Credit and/or placement. Scores accepted: 3, 4, 5. International Baccalaureate exams may be used for: Credit only. **Freshmen returning for sophomore year:** 69%. **Graduation rates:** Six-year: 34%. **Graduate study:** 13% of students pursue further study immediately upon graduation. Fields in which graduates pursue further study: law, 1%; education, 4%; arts and sciences, 3%; veterinary medicine, 2%.

COSTS AND FINANCIAL AID

Financial aid office: (715) 394-8200. **Expenses (2005-2006):** Tuition and fees 2005-2006: $5,188 in state, $6,302 out of state; room/board: $4,422. Estimated books and supplies: $860; transportation: $770; personal expenses: $1,760. **Financial aid:** Priority filing date for institution's financial aid form: April 15. In 2005-2006, 76% of undergraduates applied for financial aid. Of those, 60% were determined to have financial need; 33% had their need fully met. Average financial aid package (proportion receiving): $6,242 (59%). Average amount of gift aid, such as scholarships or grants (proportion receiving): $4,592 (34%). Average amount of self-help aid, such as work study or loans (proportion receiving): $4,109 (52%). Average need-based loan (excluding PLUS or other private loans): $3,664. Among students who received aid based on merit, the average award (and the proportion receiving): $2,454 (3%). The average athletic scholarship (and the proportion receiving): $0 (0%).

CAMPUS LIFE AND EXTRACURRICULAR ACTIVITIES

Campus housing available (% using): coed dorms (72%), women's dorms (26%), special housing for disabled students (1%), other housing options (1%). Students who live in college-owned, operated, or affiliated housing: 22%. **Student employment:** During the 2005-2006 academic year, 15% of undergraduates worked on campus. Average per-year earnings: $2,126.

Clubs and organizations: Number of student organizations: 60. Activities include: choral groups, concert band, dance, drama/theater, jazz band, music ensembles, radio station, student government, student newspaper, symphony orchestra, television station. Number of fraternities: 0; sororities: 1. Average proportion of students who stay on campus on weekends: 65%. **Sports program (2005-2006):** Member of NCAA III. ***Men's intercollegiate varsity sports:*** baseball, basketball, cross-country, ice hockey, soccer, track and field (indoor), track and field (outdoor). ***Women's intercollegiate varsity sports:*** basketball, cross-country, golf, ice hockey, soccer, softball, track and field (indoor), track and field (outdoor), volleyball.

SERVICES AND FACILITIES

Basic services: nonremedial tutoring, women's center, placement service, day care, health service, health insurance. **Remedial assistance:** reading, math, writing, study skills. **Counseling services:** minority student, career, military, personal, veteran student, academic, older student, psychological, birth control, religious. **For learning-disabled students:** School does not offer a structured program with separate admission and additional fees. Total undergraduates in learning-disabled program or receiving services: 30. Services include: remedial math, remedial English, tape recorders, learning center, extended time for tests, tutors, texts on tape, other. **Library:** Number of titles: 259,202; number of current serial subscriptions: 806. **Information technology resources:** Students are not required to lease or own a computer. Number of campus computers available to all students: 325. School has a wireless network. Approximate number of users that can be accommodated: 700. Proportion of college-owned housing units wired for high-speed internet access: 100%. **Campus safety:** Security services offered: 24-hour foot-and-vehicle patrols, late-night transport/escort service, 24-hour emergency telephones, lighted pathways/sidewalks, controlled dormitory access (key, security card, etc).

TRANSFER AND INTERNATIONAL STUDENTS

Transfer students: May apply for admission for the following academic terms: Fall, Spring, Summer. Applicants do not need a minimum number of credits to apply. For fall 2005: Transfer applications received: 634. Transfer applicants offered admission: 525. Transfer applicants enrolled: 368. **International students:** Number of foreign undergraduates: 131 (5% of student body). Number of countries represented: 32. Minimum TOEFL score required: 525 (paper); 197 (computer). Average TOEFL score: 540 (paper).

University of Wisconsin–Whitewater

- **Address:** 800 W. Main Street, Whitewater, WI 53190
- **Website:** http://www.uww.edu
- **Public**
- **Enrollment:** 8,572 full-time; 815 part-time

KEY STATS

✔ **U.S News College Ranking:** 51, Universities–Master's (Midwest)
✔ **ACT Score (25th/75th percentile):** 20-24
✔ **Tuition:** 2006-2007: $5,518 in state, $13,701 out of state

Selectivity: Selective	**Room/board:** N/A
Acceptance rate: 73%	**Average debt:** $17,394
Student/faculty ratio: 22/1	**Proportion who borrowed:** 63%

UNDERGRADUATE STUDENT BODY STATS

2005-2006 enrollment: 8,572 full-time; 815 part-time. Men: 49%; women: 51%. **Ethnic makeup:** African American: 4%; American-Indian: 1%; Asian American: 2%; Hispanic: 2%; White: 90%; International: 1%.

ADMISSIONS FACTS AND FIGURES

Phone: (262) 472-1440. **Email:** uwwadmit@mail.uww.edu. **Website:** http://www.uww.edu. **Application deadlines for fall 2007:** Regular decision: Rolling. Early decision: Not offered. Early action: Not offered. Admission can be deferred. **Application fee:** $35. Common application is not accepted. **To apply online, go to:** http://www.apply.wisconsin.edu. **Admissions requirements/recommendations:** High school units required (recommended): English: 4 (4); Mathematics: 3 (4); Science: 3 (4); Foreign language: 2 (2); Social studies: 3 (4); Academic electives: 4; Total units: 19 (20). Tests: The college uses SAT or ACT scores in admissions decisions. Neither SAT nor ACT required. For admission to the fall 2007 entering class, the school will accept: ACT with writing, ACT without writing. Campus visit: Recommended. Admissions interview: Neither required nor recommended. Off-campus interview: Not available. **Factors that count in admissions decisions:** *Academic:* Secondary school record: Very important. Class rank: Very important. Letters of recommendation: Considered. Standardized test scores: Very important. Essay: Important. *Nonacademic:* Interview: Considered. Extracurricular activities: Important. Talent/ability: Important. Character/personal qualities: Important. Alumni/ae relationship: Considered. Geographical residence: Important. State residency: Very important. Religious affiliation/commitment: Considered. Minority status: Very important. Volunteer work: Important. Work experience: Important. **Admissions statistics for the fall 2005 entering class:** Total applicants: 5,423. Total accepted: 3,980. Freshmen enrolled: 1,712; 6% were from out of state. Overall acceptance rate: 73%. **Credentials of fall 2005 freshmen:** 8% ranked in the top 10 percent of their high school class; 32% were in the top 25 percent, and 79% were in the top half. (Proportion submitting class standing: 93%.) **Average high school grade point average:** 3.2. **First-year students who submitted SAT scores:** 3%. Scores (25/75 percentile): Verbal: N/A, Math: N/A, Combined: N/A. **First-year students submitting ACT scores:** 98%. Scores (25/75 percentile): English: 18-24, Math: 19-25, Composite: 20-24.

ACADEMICS

Year founded: 1868. **Academic calendar:** Semester. **Degrees offered:** associate, bachelor's, master's. **Most popular majors:** 32% business, management, marketing, and related support services, 14% education, 9% communication, journalism, and related programs, 9% social sciences, 4% computer and information sciences and support services. **Major fields of study:** area, ethnic, cultural, and gender studies; biological and biomedical sciences; business, management, marketing, and related support services; communication, journalism, and related programs; computer and information sciences and support services; education; engineering technologies/technicians; English language and literature/letters; foreign languages, literatures, and linguistics; health professions and related clinical sciences; history; liberal arts and sciences studies, and humanities; mathematics and statistics; multi/interdisciplinary studies; physical sciences; psychology; public administration and social service professions; social sciences; visual and performing arts. **Areas of required coursework:** arts/fine arts, humanities, mathematics, English (including composition), sciences (biological or physical), history, social science. **Pre-professional programs:** pre-law, pre-dentistry, pre-medicine, pre-veterinary science, pre-optometry, pre-pharmacy, other. **Special academic programs (% participation):** accelerated program (.5%), cooperative (work-study plan) program, cross-registration (.5%), distance learning (3%), double major (5%), dual enrollment (1%), English as a Second Language (ESL) (.5%), exchange student program (domestic), external degree program, honors program (3%), independent study (4%), internships (10%), student-designed major (.5%), study abroad (3%), teacher certificate program (22%), weekend college (18%). **Teacher certification offered in:** early childhood, special education, elementary, middle/junior high, secondary, bilingual/bicultural. **Reserve Officers Training Corps (ROTC):** Army ROTC: Offered on campus; Air Force ROTC: Offered on campus. **Faculty and instruction (2005-2006):** Total instructional faculty: 405 full-time, 102 part-time (54% men; 46% women; 15% minorities). Full-time faculty with Ph.D. or other terminal degree: 83%. Student/faculty ratio: 22/1. Classes of fewer than 20 students: 42%; of 20 to 49 students: 54%; of 50 or more students: 4%. **Advanced Placement and International Baccalaureate credit:** AP tests may be used for: Credit only. Scores accepted: 3, 4, 5. **Freshmen returning for sophomore year:** 77%. **Graduation rates:** Four-year: 19%; five-year: 43%; six-year: 52%. **Graduate study:** 17% of students pursue further study immediately upon graduation; 17% within one year.

COSTS AND FINANCIAL AID

Financial aid office: (262) 472-1130. **Expenses (2006-2007):** Tuition and fees 2006-2007: $5,518 in state, $13,701 out of state; room/board: N/A. **Financial aid:** Priority filing date for institution's financial aid form: March 15. In 2005-2006, 67% of undergraduates applied for financial aid. Of those, 47% were determined to have financial need; 50% had their need fully met. Average financial aid package (proportion receiving): $6,527 (44%). Average amount of gift aid, such as scholarships or grants (proportion receiving): $4,739 (20%). Average amount of self-help aid, such as work study or loans (proportion receiving): $4,022 (40%). Average need-based loan (excluding PLUS or other private loans): $3,822. Among students who received need-based aid, the average percentage of need met: 75%. Among students who received aid based on merit, the average award (and the proportion receiving): $2,091 (7%). The average athletic scholarship (and the proportion

receiving): $0 (0%). Average amount of debt of borrowers graduating in 2005: $17,394. Proportion who borrowed: 63%.

CAMPUS LIFE AND EXTRACURRICULAR ACTIVITIES

Campus housing available (% using): coed dorms (97%), women's dorms (3%), sorority housing, fraternity housing, special housing for disabled students, special housing for international students. Students who live in college-owned, operated, or affiliated housing: 40%. **Student employment:** During the 2005-2006 academic year, 26% of undergraduates worked on campus. Average per-year earnings: $1,530. **Clubs and organizations:** Number of student organizations: 170. Activities include: choral groups, concert band, dance, drama/theater, jazz band, literary magazine, marching band, music ensembles, musical theater, pep band, radio station, student government, student newspaper, symphony orchestra, television station. Number of fraternities: 6; sororities: 8. Proportion of men in fraternities: 4%; of women in sororities: 4%. Average proportion of students who stay on campus on weekends: 35%. **Sports program (2005-2006):** Member of NCAA III. *Men's intercollegiate varsity sports:* baseball, basketball, cross-country, football, soccer, swimming and diving, tennis, track and field (indoor), track and field (outdoor), wrestling. *Women's intercollegiate varsity sports:* basketball, bowling, cross-country, golf, gymnastics, soccer, softball, swimming and diving, tennis, track and field (indoor), track and field (outdoor), volleyball.

SERVICES AND FACILITIES

Basic services: nonremedial tutoring, women's center, placement service, day care, health service, other. **Remedial assistance:** reading, math, writing, study skills, other. **Counseling services:** minority student, career, military, personal, veteran student, academic, older student, psychological, birth control, religious, other. **For learning-disabled students:** School does not offer a structured program with separate admission and additional fees. Total undergraduates in learning-disabled program or receiving services: 195. Services include: remedial math, remedial English, reading machines, remedial reading, tape recorders, other special classes, note-taking services, learning center, readers, extended time for tests, tutors, priority registration, typist/scribe, exams on tape or computer, waiver of foreign language degree requirement, waiver of math degree requirement, other. **Library:** Number of titles: 670,308; number of current serial subscriptions: 4,078. **Information technology resources:** Students are not required to lease or own a computer. Number of campus computers available to all students: 1,300. School has a wireless network. Approximate number of users that can be accommodated: 3,000. Proportion of college-owned housing units wired for high-speed internet access: 100%. **Campus safety:** Security services offered: 24-hour foot-and-vehicle patrols, late-night transport/escort service, 24-hour emergency telephones, lighted pathways/sidewalks, controlled dormitory access (key, security card, etc).

TRANSFER AND INTERNATIONAL STUDENTS

Transfer students: May apply for admission for the following academic terms: Fall, Winter, Spring, Summer. Applicants need a minimum number of credits to apply. For fall 2005: Transfer applications received: 1,339. Transfer applicants offered admission: 739. Transfer applicants enrolled: 595. **International students:** Number of foreign undergraduates: 51 (1% of student body). Number of countries represented: 21. Minimum TOEFL score required: 500 (paper); 175 (computer).

Viterbo University

- **Address:** 900 Viterbo Drive, La Crosse, WI 54601
- **Website:** http://www.viterbo.edu
- **Private; Religious affiliation:** Roman Catholic
- **Enrollment:** 1,429 full-time; 435 part-time

KEY STATS

✔ **U.S News College Ranking:** 68, Universities–Master's (Midwest)
✔ **ACT Score (25th/75th percentile):** 19-24
✔ **Tuition:** 2005-2006: $16,660

Selectivity: Selective	**Room/board:** $5,430
Acceptance rate: 82%	**Average debt:** N/A
Student/faculty ratio: 10/1	**Proportion who borrowed:** N/A

UNDERGRADUATE STUDENT BODY STATS

2005-2006 enrollment: 1,429 full-time; 435 part-time. Men: 28%; women: 72%. **Ethnic makeup:** African American: 1%; Asian American: 2%; Hispanic: 1%; White: 94%; International: 1%. **Religious preference:** Protestant: 43%; No preference: 7%; Unknown: 7%; Roman Catholic: 43%.

ADMISSIONS FACTS AND FIGURES

Phone: (608) 796-3010. **Email:** admission@viterbo.edu. **Website:** http://www.viterbo.edu. **Application deadlines for fall 2007:** Regular decision: Rolling. Early decision: Not offered. Early action: Not offered. Admission can be deferred. **Application fee:** $25. Common application is accepted. **To apply online, go to:** http://www.wisconsinmentor.org/AdmissionApp/. **Admissions requirements/recommendations:** High school units required (recommended): English: 3 (4); Mathematics: 2 (2); Science: 2 (2); Foreign language: (2); Social studies: 2 (2); Academic electives: 5 (5); Total units: 16 (19). Tests: The college uses SAT or ACT scores in admissions decisions. ACT required. For admission to the fall 2007 entering class, the school will accept: ACT with writing, ACT without writing. Campus visit: Recommended. Admissions interview: Recommended. Off-campus interview: May be arranged. **Factors that count in admissions decisions:** *Academic:* Secondary school record: Important. Class rank: Important. Letters of recommendation: Important. Standardized test scores: Very important. Essay: Considered. *Nonacademic:* Interview: Important. Extracurricular activities: Considered. Talent/ability: Important. Character/personal qualities: Very important. Alumni/ae relationship: Considered. Geographical residence: Not considered. State residency: Not considered. Religious affiliation/commitment: Not considered. Minority status: Not considered. Volunteer work: Considered. Work experience: Not considered. **Other schools with the greatest overlap in applicants:** University of Wisconsin–Eau Claire; University of Wisconsin–La Crosse; University of Wisconsin–Madison; University of Wisconsin–Stevens Point; Winona State University. **Admissions statistics for the fall 2005 entering class:** Total applicants: 1,098. Total accepted: 899. Freshmen enrolled: 296; 27% were from out of state. Overall acceptance rate: 82%. **Credentials of fall 2005 freshmen:** 12% ranked in the top 10 percent of their high school class; 35% were in the top 25 percent, and 69% were in the top half. (Proportion submitting class standing: 90%.) **Average high school grade point average:** 3.2. **First-year students submitting ACT scores:** 92%. Scores (25/75 percentile): English: 18-24, Math: 18-23, Composite: 19-24.

ACADEMICS

Year founded: 1890. **Academic calendar:** Semester. **Degrees offered:** associate, transfer-associate, bachelor's, post-bachelor's certificate, master's. **Most popular majors:** 33% health professions and related clinical sciences, 17% business, management, marketing, and related support services, 14% education, 7% multi/interdisciplinary studies, 7% visual and performing arts. **Major fields of study:** biological and biomedical sciences; business, management, marketing, and related support services; computer and information sciences and support services; education; English language and literature/letters; foreign languages, literatures, and linguistics; health professions and related clinical sciences; liberal arts and sciences studies, and humanities; mathematics and statistics; multi/interdisciplinary studies; philosophy and religious studies; physical sciences; psychology; public administration and social service professions; security and protective services; social sciences; theology and religious vocations; visual and performing arts. **Areas of required coursework:** arts/fine arts, humanities, mathematics, English (including composition), philosophy, sciences (biological or physical), history, social science, other. **Pre-professional programs:** pre-law, pre-dentistry, pre-medicine, pre-veterinary science, pre-optometry, pre-pharmacy, other. **Special academic programs (% participation):** cross-registration (0%), distance learning (.9%), double major (.7%), dual enrollment (.5%), independent study (24.7%), internships (12.5%), liberal arts/career combination (.5%), student-designed major (9.2%), study abroad (.7%), teacher certificate program (12.5%), other (0%). **Teacher certification offered in:** early childhood, elementary, vo-tech, middle/junior high, secondary. **Reserve Officers Training Corps (ROTC):** Army ROTC: Offered at cooperating institution (University of Wisconsin–La Crosse). **Faculty and instruction (2005-2006):** Total instructional faculty: 119 full-time, 105 part-time (40% men; 60% women; 3% minorities). Full-time faculty with Ph.D. or other terminal degree: 59%. Student/faculty ratio: 10/1. Classes of fewer than 20 students: 75%; of 20 to 49 students: 24%; of 50 or more students: 1%. **Advanced Placement and International Baccalaureate credit:** AP tests may be used for: Credit only. Scores accepted: 3, 4, 5. International Baccalaureate exams may be used for: Credit only. **Freshmen returning for sophomore year:** 68%. **Graduation rates:** Four-year: 36%; five-year: 48%; six-year: 49%. **Graduate study:** 15% of students pursue further study within one year.

Fields in which graduates pursue further study: Master of Business Administration (MBA), 4%; law, 9%; medicine, 24%; dentistry, 2%; theology (or the seminary), 4%; education, 7%; arts and sciences, 47%; veterinary medicine, 2%.

COSTS AND FINANCIAL AID

Financial aid office: (608) 796-3900. **Expenses (2005-2006):** Tuition and fees 2005-2006: $16,660; room/board: $5,430. Estimated books and supplies: $650; transportation: $700; personal expenses: $1,800. **Financial aid:** Priority filing date for institution's financial aid form: March 15.

CAMPUS LIFE AND EXTRACURRICULAR ACTIVITIES

Campus housing available (% using): coed dorms (63%), apartment for single students (32%), other housing options (5%). Students who live in college-owned, operated, or affiliated housing: 17%. **Student employment:** During the 2005-2006 academic year, 16% of undergraduates worked on campus. Average per-year earnings: $382. **Clubs and organizations:** Number of student organizations: 28. Activities include: choral groups, dance, drama/theater, literary magazine, music ensembles, musical theater, opera, pep band, student government, student newspaper. Number of fraternities: 0; sororities: 0. Average proportion of students who stay on campus on weekends: 50%. **Sports program (2005-2006):** Member of NAIA. *Men's intercollegiate varsity sports:* baseball, basketball, soccer. *Women's intercollegiate varsity sports:* basketball, soccer, softball, volleyball.

SERVICES AND FACILITIES

Basic services: nonremedial tutoring, placement service, health service, health insurance, other. **Remedial assistance:** reading, math, writing, study skills, other. **Counseling services:** career, personal, academic, older student, psychological, religious, other. **For learning-disabled students:** School does not offer a structured program with separate admission and additional fees. Total undergraduates in learning-disabled program or receiving services: 43. Services include: remedial math, remedial English, reading machines, remedial reading, tape recorders, other special classes, untimed tests, note-taking services, oral tests, learning center, readers, extended time for tests, tutors, early syllabus, priority registration, priority seating, proofreading services, substitution of courses, texts on tape, typist/scribe, exams on tape or computer, other testing accomodations, waiver of foreign language degree requirement, waiver of math degree requirement, other. **Library:** Number of titles: 92,036; number of current serial subscriptions: 466. **Information technology resources:** Students are not required to lease or own a computer. Number of campus computers available to all students: 291. School has a wireless network. Approximate number of users that can be accommodated: 150. Proportion of college-owned housing units wired for high-speed internet access: 95%. **Campus safety:** Security services offered: 24-hour foot-and-vehicle patrols, late-night transport/escort service, 24-hour emergency telephones, lighted pathways/sidewalks, controlled dormitory access (key, security card, etc).

TRANSFER AND INTERNATIONAL STUDENTS

Transfer students: May apply for admission for the following academic terms: Fall, Spring, Summer. Applicants do not need a minimum number of credits to apply. For fall 2005: Transfer applications received: 538. Transfer applicants offered admission: 196. Transfer applicants enrolled: 272. **International students:** Number of foreign undergraduates: 23 (1% of student body). Number of countries represented: 15. Minimum TOEFL score required: 550 (paper); 213 (computer).

Wisconsin Lutheran College

- **Address:** 8800 W. Bluemound Road, Milwaukee, WI 53226
- **Website:** http://www.wlc.edu
- **Private; Religious affiliation:** Lutheran
- **Enrollment:** 663 full-time; 28 part-time

KEY STATS

✔ **U.S News College Ranking:** 20, Comp. Coll.–Bachelor's (Midwest)
✔ **ACT Score (25th/75th percentile):** 22-27
✔ **Tuition:** 2006-2007: $18,650

Selectivity: More selective	**Room/board:** $6,140
Acceptance rate: 82%	**Average debt:** $14,638
Student/faculty ratio: 10/1	**Proportion who borrowed:** 71%

UNDERGRADUATE STUDENT BODY STATS

2005-2006 enrollment: 663 full-time; 28 part-time. Men: 38%; women: 62%. **Ethnic makeup:** African American: 1%; Asian American: 1%; Hispanic: 1%; White: 95%; International: 1%. **Religious preference:** Roman Catholic: 4%; Protestant: 7%; No preference: 4%; Lutheran: 71%; other Lutheran (non-WELS/ELS): 9%; Other: 5%.

ADMISSIONS FACTS AND FIGURES

Phone: (414) 443-8811. **Email:** admissions@wlc.edu. **Website:** http://www.wlc.edu. **Application deadlines for fall 2007:** Regular decision: Rolling. Early decision: Not offered. Early action: Not offered. Admission cannot be deferred. **Application fee:** $20. Common application is accepted. **To apply online, go to:** http://www.wlc.edu/admissions/. **Admissions requirements/recommendations:** High school units required (recommended): English: 4 (4); Mathematics: 3 (4); Science: 2 (3); Foreign language: 2 (4); History: 2 (2); Academic electives: 3 (3); Total units: 16 (20). Tests: The college uses SAT or ACT scores in admissions decisions. Either SAT or ACT required. For admission to the fall 2007 entering class, the school will accept: ACT with writing, ACT without writing. Campus visit: Recommended. Admissions interview: Recommended. Off-campus interview: May be arranged. **Factors that count in admissions decisions:** *Academic:* Secondary school record: Very important. Class rank: Important. Letters of recommendation: Important. Standardized test scores: Important. Essay: Considered. *Nonacademic:* Interview: Important. Extracurricular activities: Important. Talent/ability: Considered. Character/personal qualities: Important. Alumni/ae relationship: Considered. Geographical residence: Considered. State residency: Considered. Religious affiliation/commitment: Important. Minority status: Considered. Volunteer work: Considered. Work experience: Not considered. **Admissions statistics for the fall 2005 entering class:** Total applicants: 504. Total accepted: 411. Freshmen enrolled: 180; 19% were from out of state. Overall acceptance rate: 82%. **Credentials of fall 2005 freshmen:** 23% ranked in the top 10 percent of their high school class; 50% were in the top 25 percent, and 84% were in the top half. (Proportion submitting class standing: 91%.) **Average high school grade point average:** 3.5. **First-year students who submitted SAT scores:** 5%. Scores (25/75 percentile): Verbal: N/A; Math: N/A, Combined: N/A. **First-year students submitting ACT scores:** 97%. Scores (25/75 percentile): English: 21-27, Math: 21-27, Composite: 22-27.

ACADEMICS

Year founded: 1973. **Academic calendar:** Semester. **Degrees offered:** bachelor's. **Most popular majors:** 17% communication studies/speech communication and rhetoric, 12% elementary education and teaching, 11% psychology, 7% art/art studies, 7% history. **Major fields of study:** biological and biomedical sciences; business, management, marketing, and related support services; communication, journalism, and related programs; education; English language and literature/letters; foreign languages, literatures, and linguistics; history; mathematics and statistics; multi/interdisciplinary studies; philosophy and religious studies; physical sciences; psychology; social sciences; theology and religious vocations; visual and performing arts. **Areas of required coursework:** arts/fine arts, humanities, mathematics, English (including composition), foreign languages, sciences (biological or physical), history, social science, other. **Pre-professional programs:** pre-law, pre-dentistry, pre-medicine, pre-veterinary science, pre-pharmacy, other. **Special academic programs:** double major, dual enrollment, independent study, internships, student-designed major, study abroad, teacher certificate program. **Teacher certification offered in:** early childhood, elementary, middle/junior high, secondary. **Reserve Officers Training Corps (ROTC):** Army ROTC: Offered at cooperating institution (Marquette University); Navy ROTC: Offered at cooperating institution (Marquette University); Air Force ROTC: Offered at cooperating institution (Marquette University). **Faculty and instruction (2005-2006):** Total instructional faculty: 51 full-time, 45 part-time (64% men; 36% women). Full-time faculty with Ph.D. or other terminal degree: 67%. Student/faculty ratio: 10/1. Classes of fewer than 20 students: 72%; of 20 to 49 students: 28%; of 50 or more students: 0%. **Advanced Placement and International Baccalaureate credit:** AP tests may be used for: Credit and/or placement. Scores accepted: 3, 4, 5. **Freshmen returning for sophomore year:** 77%. **Graduation rates:** Four-year: 49%; five-year: 64%; six-year: 68%.

COSTS AND FINANCIAL AID

Financial aid office: (414) 443-8856. **Expenses (2006-2007):** Tuition and fees 2006-2007: $18,650; room/board: $6,140. Estimated transportation: $300; personal expenses: $1,440. **Financial aid:** Priority filing date for institution's financial aid form: March 1. In 2005-2006, 82% of undergraduates applied for financial aid. Of those, 73% were determined to have financial need; 29% had their need fully met. Average financial aid package (proportion receiving): $14,493 (73%). Average amount of gift aid, such as scholarships or grants (proportion receiving): $10,377 (73%). Average amount of self-help aid, such as work study or loans (proportion receiving): $4,702 (64%). Average need-based loan (excluding PLUS or other private loans): $3,580. Among students who received need-based aid, the average percentage of need met: 86%. Among students who received aid based on merit, the average award (and the proportion receiving): $10,638 (23%). Average amount of debt of borrowers graduating in 2005: $14,638. Proportion who borrowed: 71%.

CAMPUS LIFE AND EXTRACURRICULAR ACTIVITIES

Campus housing available: women's dorms, men's dorms, apartment for single students. Students who live in college-owned, operated, or affiliated housing: 78%. **Student employment:** During the 2005-2006 academic year, 20% of undergraduates worked on campus. Average per-year earnings: $1,700. **Clubs and organizations:** Number of student organizations: 26. Activities include: choral groups, concert band, dance, drama/theater, jazz band, music ensembles, pep band, student government, student newspaper, yearbook. Number of fraternities: 0; sororities: 0. Average proportion of students who stay on campus on weekends: 50%. **Sports program (2005-2006):** Member of NCAA III. *Men's intercollegiate varsity sports:* baseball, basketball, cross-country, football, golf, soccer, track and field (indoor), track and field (outdoor). *Women's intercollegiate varsity sports:* basketball, cross-country, golf, soccer, softball, tennis, track and field (indoor), track and field (outdoor), volleyball.

SERVICES AND FACILITIES

Basic services: nonremedial tutoring, placement service, health service. **Counseling services:** minority student, career, personal, veteran student, academic, older student, psychological, birth control, religious. **For learning-disabled students:** School does not offer a structured program with separate admission and additional fees. Services include: tape recorders, videotaped classes, untimed tests, note-taking services, learning center, extended time for tests, tutors, other. **Library:** Number of titles: 71,716; number of current serial subscriptions: 3,208. **Information technology resources:** Students are not required to lease or own a computer. Number of campus computers available to all students: 250. School has a wireless network. Approximate number of users that can be accommodated: 30. Proportion of college-owned housing units wired for high-speed internet access: 100%. **Campus safety:** Security services offered: 24-hour foot-and-vehicle patrols, late-night transport/escort service, lighted pathways/sidewalks, controlled dormitory access (key, security card, etc).

TRANSFER AND INTERNATIONAL STUDENTS

Transfer students: May apply for admission for the following academic terms: Fall, Spring, Summer. Applicants do not need a minimum number of credits to apply. For fall 2005: Transfer applicants enrolled: 30. **International students:** Number of foreign undergraduates: 9 (1% of student body). Number of countries represented: 7. Minimum TOEFL score required: 550 (paper); 213 (computer).

Wyoming

University of Wyoming

- **Address:** 1000 E. University Avenue, Laramie, WY 82071
- **Website:** http://www.uwyo.edu
- **Public**
- **Enrollment:** 7,699 full-time; 1,811 part-time

KEY STATS

✔ **U.S News College Ranking:** third tier, National Universities
✔ **ACT Score (25th/75th percentile):** 20-26
✔ **Tuition:** 2006-2007: $3,515 in state, $10,055 out of state

Selectivity: Selective	**Room/board:** $6,861
Acceptance rate: 95%	**Average debt:** $16,742
Student/faculty ratio: 15/1	**Proportion who borrowed:** 46%

UNDERGRADUATE STUDENT BODY STATS

2005-2006 enrollment: 7,699 full-time; 1,811 part-time. Men: 47%; women: 53%. **Ethnic makeup:** African American: 1%; American-Indian: 1%; Asian American: 1%; Hispanic: 4%; White: 92%; International: 1%.

ADMISSIONS FACTS AND FIGURES

Phone: (307) 766-5160. **Email:** Why-wyo@uwyo.edu. **Website:** http://www.uwyo.edu. **Application deadlines for fall 2007:** Regular decision: August 10. Early decision: Not offered. Early action: Not offered. Admission can be deferred. **Application fee:** $30. Common application is not accepted. To apply online, go to: http://uwadmnweb.uwyo.edu/admissions/apply_now.asp. **Admissions requirements/recommendations:** High school units required (recommended): English: 4 (4); Mathematics: 3 (3); Science: 3 (3); Foreign language: (2); Total units: 13 (19). Tests: The college uses SAT or ACT scores in admissions decisions. Either SAT or ACT required. For admission to the fall 2007 entering class, the school will accept: ACT with writing, ACT without writing. Campus visit: Recommended. Admissions interview: Neither required nor recommended. Off-campus interview: May be arranged. **Factors that count in admissions decisions:** *Academic:* Secondary school record: Very important. Class rank: Not considered. Letters of recommendation: Considered. Standardized test scores: Very important. Essay: Considered. *Nonacademic:* Interview: Considered. Extracurricular activities: Considered. Talent/ability: Considered. Character/personal qualities: Considered. Alumni/ae relationship: Not considered. Geographical residence: Not considered. State residency: Considered. Religious affiliation/commitment: Not considered. Minority status: Not considered. Volunteer work: Not considered. Work experience: Not considered. **Admissions statistics for the fall 2005 entering class:** Total applicants: 3,155. Total accepted: 3,008. Freshmen enrolled: 1,421; 44% were from out of state. Overall acceptance rate: 95%. **Credentials of fall 2005 freshmen:** 20% ranked in the top 10 percent of their high school class; 48% were in the top 25 percent, and 80% were in the top half. (Proportion submitting class standing: 90%.) **Average high school grade point average:** 3.4. **First-year students who submitted SAT scores:** 23%. Scores (25/75 percentile): Verbal: 480-610, Math: 500-610, Combined: 980-1220. **First-year students submitting ACT scores:** 90%. Scores (25/75 percentile): English: 19-26; Math: 19-26, Composite: 20-26.

ACADEMICS

Year founded: 1886. **Academic calendar:** Semester. **Degrees offered:** certificate, bachelor's, master's, post-master's certificate, first professional, doctorate. **Most popular majors:** 6% elementary education and teaching, 5% business administration and management, 5% nurse/nursing assistant/aide and patient care assistant, 4% psychology, 3% criminal justice/safety studies. **Major fields of study:** agriculture, agriculture operations, and related sciences; area, ethnic, cultural, and gender studies; biological and biomedical sciences; business, management, marketing, and related support services; communication, journalism, and related programs; computer and information sciences and support services; education; engineering; English lan-

guage and literature/letters; family and consumer sciences/human sciences; foreign languages, literatures, and linguistics; health professions and related clinical sciences; history; liberal arts and sciences studies, and humanities; mathematics and statistics; multi/interdisciplinary studies; natural resources and conservation; parks, recreation, leisure, and fitness studies; philosophy and religious studies; physical sciences; psychology; public administration and social service professions; security and protective services; social sciences; visual and performing arts. **Areas of required coursework:** arts/fine arts, humanities, mathematics, English (including composition), sciences (biological or physical), social science, other. **Pre-professional programs:** pre-law, pre-dentistry, pre-medicine, pre-optometry, other. **Special academic programs:** accelerated program, distance learning, double major, dual enrollment, English as a Second Language (ESL), exchange student program (domestic), external degree program, honors program, independent study, internships, student-designed major, study abroad, teacher certificate program. **Teacher certification offered in:** early childhood, special education, elementary, middle/junior high, secondary. **Cooperative education programs:** agriculture, business, education, health professions, home economics, natural science, social/behavioral science, technologies, vocational arts. **Reserve Officers Training Corps (ROTC):** Army ROTC: Offered on campus; Air Force ROTC: Offered on campus. **Faculty and instruction (2005-2006):** Total instructional faculty: 651 full-time, 53 part-time (65% men; 35% women; 8% minorities). Full-time faculty with Ph.D. or other terminal degree: 84%. Student/faculty ratio: 15/1. Classes of fewer than 20 students: 40%; of 20 to 49 students: 50%; of 50 or more students: 9%. **Advanced Placement and International Baccalaureate credit:** AP tests may be used for: Credit and/or placement. Scores accepted: 3, 4, 5. International Baccalaureate exams may be used for: Credit only. **Freshmen returning for sophomore year:** 76%. **Graduation rates:** Four-year: 29%; five-year: 49%; six-year: 58%.

COSTS AND FINANCIAL AID

Financial aid office: (307) 766-2116. **Expenses (2006-2007):** Tuition and fees 2006-2007: $3,515 in state, $10,055 out of state; room/board: $6,861. Estimated books and supplies: $1,200; transportation: $889; personal expenses: $2,200. **Financial aid:** Priority filing date for institution's financial aid form: February 1. In 2005-2006, 59% of undergraduates applied for financial aid. Of those, 44% were determined to have financial need; 23% had their need fully met. Average financial aid package (proportion receiving): $7,017 (43%). Average amount of gift aid, such as scholarships or grants (proportion receiving): $3,272 (28%). Average amount of self-help aid, such as work study or loans (proportion receiving): $3,250 (38%). Average need-based loan (excluding PLUS or other private loans): $4,022. Among students who received need-based aid, the average percentage of need met: 75%. Among students who received aid based on merit, the average award (and the proportion receiving): $1,434 (17%). The average athletic scholarship (and the proportion receiving): $2,973 (31%). Average amount of debt of borrowers graduating in 2005: $16,742. Proportion who borrowed: 46%.

CAMPUS LIFE AND EXTRACURRICULAR ACTIVITIES

Campus housing available: coed dorms, sorority housing, fraternity housing, apartments for married students, apartment for single students, special housing for disabled students, other housing options. Students who live in college-owned, operated, or affiliated housing: 23%. **Student employment:** During the 2005-2006 academic year, 25% of undergraduates worked on campus. Average per-year earnings: $1,021. **Clubs and organizations:** Number of student organizations: 189. Activities include: choral groups, concert band, dance, drama/theater, jazz band, literary magazine, marching band, music ensembles, musical theater, opera, pep band, radio station, student government, student newspaper, symphony orchestra, television station. Number of fraternities: 8; sororities: 4. Proportion of men in fraternities: 5%; of women in sororities: 5%. **Sports program (2005-2006):** Member of NCAA I. *Men's intercollegiate varsity sports:* basketball, cross-country, football, golf, swimming and diving, track and field (indoor), track and field (outdoor), wrestling. *Women's intercollegiate varsity sports:* basketball, cross-country, golf, soccer, swimming and diving, tennis, track and field (indoor), track and field (outdoor), volleyball.

SERVICES AND FACILITIES

Basic services: nonremedial tutoring, women's center, day care, health service, health insurance. **Counseling services:** minority student, career, military, personal, veteran student, academic, older student, psychological, birth control. **For learning-disabled students:** School does not offer a structured program with separate admission and additional fees. Total undergraduates in learning-disabled program or receiving services: 95. Services include: reading machines, tape recorders, other special classes, note-taking services, learning center, readers, extended time for tests, tutors, priority registration, texts on tape, other testing accomodations, other. **Library:** Number of titles: 1,366,006; number of current serial subscriptions: 11,642. **Information technology resources:** Students are not required to lease or own a computer. Number of campus computers available to all students: 1,226. School has a wireless network. Approximate number of users that can be accommodated: 4,375. Proportion of college-owned housing units wired for high-speed internet access: 100%. **Campus safety:** Security services offered: 24-hour foot-and-vehicle patrols, late-night transport/escort service, 24-hour emergency telephones, lighted pathways/sidewalks, controlled dormitory access (key, security card, etc).

TRANSFER AND INTERNATIONAL STUDENTS

Transfer students: May apply for admission for the following academic terms: Fall, Spring, Summer. Applicants need a minimum number of credits to apply. For fall 2005: Transfer applications received: 1,825. Transfer applicants offered admission: 1,716. Transfer applicants enrolled: 1,022. **International students:** Number of foreign undergraduates: 110 (1% of student body). Number of countries represented: 48. Minimum TOEFL score required: 525 (paper); 197 (computer). Average TOEFL score: 590 (paper).

Index of Schools

Marquette University, 1692
Mars Hill College, 1204
Marshall University, 1670
Martin Methodist College, 1498
Martin University, 667
Mary Baldwin College, 1617
Marygrove College, 896
Maryland Institute College of Art, 797
Marylhurst University, 1325
Marymount Manhattan College, 1120
Marymount University, 1618
Maryville College, 1499
Maryville University of St. Louis, 972
Marywood University, 1389
Massachusetts College of Art, 841
Massachusetts College of Liberal Arts, 842
Massachusetts Institute of Technology, 843
Master's College and Seminary, 411
Mayville State University, 1235
McDaniel College, 798
McKendree College, 614
McMurry University, 1532
McNeese State University, 762
McPherson College, 721
Medaille College, 1121
Memphis College of Art, 1500
Menlo College, 412
Mercer University, 558
Mercy College, 1122
Mercyhurst College, 1390
Meredith College, 1205
Merrimack College, 844
Mesa State College, 463
Messiah College, 1391
Methodist College, 1206
Metropolitan State College of Denver, 464
Metropolitan State University, 927
Miami University–Oxford, 1269
Michigan State University, 897
Michigan Technological University, 898
MidAmerica Nazarene University, 722
Mid-Continent University, 744
Middle Tennessee State University, 1501
Middlebury College, 1594
Midland Lutheran College, 1011
Midway College, 745
Midwestern State University, 1533
Miles College, 334
Millersville University of Pennsylvania, 1392
Milligan College, 1502
Millikin University, 615
Mills College, 413
Millsaps College, 948
Milwaukee Institute of Art and Design, 1693
Milwaukee School of Engineering, 1694
Minneapolis College of Art and Design, 927
Minnesota State University–Mankato, 928
Minnesota State University–Moorhead, 929
Minot State University, 1236
Mississippi College, 949
Mississippi State University, 950
Mississippi University for Women, 952
Mississippi Valley State University, 953
Missouri Baptist University, 973
Missouri Southern State University, 973
Missouri State University, 974
Missouri Valley College, 975

Missouri Western State University, 976
Molloy College, 1123
Monmouth College, 617
Monmouth University, 1045
Montana State University–Billings, 995
Montana State University–Bozeman, 996
Montana State University–Northern, 997
Montana Tech of the University of Montana, 997
Montclair State University, 1047
Montreat College, 1207
Montserrat College of Art, 845
Moore College of Art and Design, 1393
Moravian College, 1394
Morehead State University, 746
Morehouse College, 559
Morgan State University, 799
Morningside College, 700
Morris College, 1460
Mount Aloysius College, 1395
Mount Holyoke College, 846
Mount Ida College, 847
Mount Marty College, 1475
Mount Mary College, 1695
Mount Mercy College, 701
Mount Olive College, 1208
Mount St. Mary College, 1124
Mount St. Mary's College, 414
Mount St. Mary's University, 800
Mount Union College, 1270
Mount Vernon Nazarene University, 1271
Mountain State University, 1671
Muhlenberg College, 1396
Murray State University, 747
Muskingum College, 1273
Myers University, 1274

N

National Hispanic University, 414
National University, 415
National-Louis University, 618
Nazareth College of Rochester, 1125
Nebraska Wesleyan University, 1012
Neumann College, 1397
New College of California, 415
New College of Florida, 521
New England College, 1029
New England Conservatory of Music, 848
New Jersey City University, 1048
New Jersey Institute of Technology, 1048
New Mexico Highlands University, 1067
New Mexico Institute of Mining and Technology, 1067
New Mexico State University, 1068
New School University, 1126
New York Institute of Technology, 1127
New York University, 1128
Newberry College, 1461
Newbury College, 848
Newman University, 723
Niagara University, 1129
Nicholls State University, 763
Nichols College, 849
Norfolk State University, 1619
North Carolina A&T State University, 1209
North Carolina Central University, 1210
North Carolina School of the Arts, 1211
North Carolina State University–Raleigh, 1212
North Carolina Wesleyan College, 1213

North Central College, 618
North Dakota State University, 1237
North Georgia College and State University, 560
North Greenville University, 1462
North Park University, 622
Northeastern Illinois University, 620
Northeastern State University, 1302
Northeastern University, 850
Northern Arizona University, 356
Northern Illinois University, 621
Northern Kentucky University, 748
Northern Michigan University, 899
Northern State University, 1476
Northland College, 1696
Northwest Christian College, 1326
Northwest Missouri State University, 976
Northwest Nazarene University, 586
Northwest University, 1649
Northwestern College, 702
Northwestern College, 930
Northwestern Oklahoma State University, 1303
Northwestern State University of Louisiana, 764
Northwestern University, 623
Northwood University, 900
Norwich University, 1595
Notre Dame College of Ohio, 1274
Notre Dame de Namur University, 416
Nova Southeastern University, 522
Nyack College, 1130

O

Oakland City University, 667
Oakland University, 901
Oakwood College, 335
Oberlin College, 1275
Occidental College, 417
Oglethorpe University, 561
Ohio Dominican University, 1276
Ohio Northern University, 1277
Ohio State University–Columbus, 1278
Ohio University, 1280
Ohio Valley University, 1672
Ohio Wesleyan University, 1281
Oklahoma Baptist University, 1304
Oklahoma Christian University, 1305
Oklahoma City University, 1306
Oklahoma Panhandle State University, 1307
Oklahoma State University, 1308
Oklahoma Wesleyan University, 1309
Old Dominion University, 1620
Olivet College, 902
Olivet Nazarene University, 624
Oral Roberts University, 1310
Oregon Institute of Technology, 1327
Oregon State University, 1328
Otis College of Art and Design, 418
Ottawa University, 723
Otterbein College, 1282
Ouachita Baptist University, 366
Our Lady of Holy Cross College, 765
Our Lady of the Lake University, 1534

P

Pace University, 1131
Pacific Lutheran University, 1650
Pacific Northwest College of Art, 1329
Pacific Union College, 418

Pacific University, 1329
Paine College, 562
Palm Beach Atlantic University, 523
Park University, 976
Patten University, 419
Paul Quinn College, 1535
Peace College, 1214
Pennsylvania College of Technology, 1398
Pennsylvania State University–University Park, 1400
Pennsylvania State–Erie, The Behrend College, 1398
Pepperdine University, 420
Peru State College, 1013
Pfeiffer University, 1215
Philadelphia University, 1401
Philander Smith College, 367
Piedmont College, 563
Pikeville College, 749
Pine Manor College, 851
Pittsburg State University, 723
Pitzer College, 421
Plymouth State University, 1030
Point Loma Nazarene University, 423
Point Park University, 1402
Polytechnic University, 1132
Pomona College, 424
Portland State University, 1330
Post University, 478
Prairie View A&M University, 1535
Pratt Institute, 1133
Presbyterian College, 1463
Prescott College, 357
Princeton University, 1049
Principia College, 625
Providence College, 1438
Purdue University–Calumet, 668
Purdue University–North Central, 669
Purdue University–West Lafayette, 670

Q

Queens University of Charlotte, 1216
Quincy University, 626
Quinnipiac University, 479

R

Radford University, 1621
Ramapo College of New Jersey, 1050
Randolph-Macon College, 1622
Randolph-Maçon Woman's College, 1623
Reed College, 1331
Regent University, 1625
Regis College, 852
Regis University, 464
Reinhardt College, 564
Rensselaer Polytechnic Institute, 1134
Rhode Island College, 1439
Rhode Island School of Design, 1440
Rhodes College, 1503
Rice University, 1536
Richard Stockton College of New Jersey, 1051
Rider University, 1053
Ringling School of Art and Design, 524
Ripon College, 1697
Rivier College, 1031
Roanoke College, 1625
Robert Morris College, 627
Robert Morris University, 1403
Roberts Wesleyan College, 1135

University of Detroit Mercy, 906
University of Dubuque, 705
University of Evansville, 677
University of Findlay, 1289
University of Florida, 531
University of Georgia, 571
University of Great Falls, 999
University of Hartford, 487
University of Hawaii–Hilo, 579
University of Hawaii–Manoa, 580
University of Houston, 1561
University of Houston–Downtown, 1562
University of Idaho, 587
University of Illinois–Chicago, 636
University of Illinois–Springfield, 637
University of Illinois–Urbana-Champaign, 638
University of Indianapolis, 678
University of Iowa, 706
University of Judaism, 446
University of Kansas, 727
University of Kentucky, 753
University of La Verne, 446
University of Louisiana–Lafayette, 768
University of Louisiana–Monroe, 769
University of Louisville, 754
University of Maine–Augusta, 779
University of Maine–Farmington, 779
University of Maine–Fort Kent, 780
University of Maine–Machias, 781
University of Maine–Orono, 782
University of Maine–Presque Isle, 783
University of Mary, 1238
University of Mary Hardin-Baylor, 1563
University of Mary Washington, 1629
University of Maryland–Baltimore County, 805
University of Maryland–College Park, 806
University of Maryland–Eastern Shore, 807
University of Maryland–University College, 808
University of Massachusetts–Amherst, 861
University of Massachusetts–Boston, 862
University of Massachusetts–Dartmouth, 863
University of Massachusetts–Lowell, 864
University of Memphis, 1511
University of Miami, 532
University of Michigan–Ann Arbor, 907
University of Michigan–Dearborn, 908
University of Michigan–Flint, 909
University of Minnesota–Crookston, 937
University of Minnesota–Duluth, 938
University of Minnesota–Morris, 939
University of Minnesota–Twin Cities, 940
University of Mississippi, 955
University of Missouri–Columbia, 983
University of Missouri–Kansas City, 984
University of Missouri–Rolla, 985
University of Missouri–St. Louis, 986
University of Mobile, 345
University of Montana, 1000
University of Montana–Western, 1001
University of Montevallo, 346
University of Nebraska–Kearney, 1015
University of Nebraska–Lincoln, 1016
University of Nebraska–Omaha, 1017
University of Nevada–Las Vegas, 1021
University of Nevada–Reno, 1023
University of New England, 784
University of New Hampshire, 1034

University of New Haven, 488
University of New Mexico, 1069
University of New Orleans, 769
University of North Alabama, 347
University of North Carolina–Asheville, 1221
University of North Carolina–Chapel Hill, 1222
University of North Carolina–Charlotte, 1223
University of North Carolina–Greensboro, 1224
University of North Carolina–Pembroke, 1225
University of North Carolina–Wilmington, 1226
University of North Dakota, 1239
University of North Florida, 534
University of North Texas, 1564
University of Northern Colorado, 469
University of Northern Iowa, 707
University of Notre Dame, 679
University of Oklahoma, 1316
University of Oregon, 1332
University of Pennsylvania, 1416
University of Pittsburgh, 1417
University of Pittsburgh–Bradford, 1418
University of Pittsburgh–Greensburg, 1419
University of Pittsburgh–Johnstown, 1420
University of Portland, 1333
University of Puget Sound, 1654
University of Redlands, 447
University of Rhode Island, 1443
University of Richmond, 1630
University of Rio Grande, 1290
University of Rochester, 1174
University of San Diego, 448
University of San Francisco, 450
University of Science and Arts of Oklahoma, 1317
University of Scranton, 1421
University of Sioux Falls, 1479
University of South Alabama, 348
University of South Carolina–Aiken, 1466
University of South Carolina–Columbia, 1467
University of South Carolina–Upstate, 1468
University of South Dakota, 1480
University of South Florida, 535
University of Southern California, 451
University of Southern Indiana, 680
University of Southern Maine, 785
University of Southern Mississippi, 956
University of St. Francis, 639
University of St. Francis, 681
University of St. Mary, 728
University of St. Thomas, 941
University of St. Thomas, 1565
University of Tampa, 536
University of Tennessee, 1512
University of Tennessee–Chattanooga, 1513
University of Tennessee–Martin, 1514
University of Texas of the Permian Basin, 1571
University of Texas–Arlington, 1566
University of Texas–Austin, 1567
University of Texas–Brownsville, 1568
University of Texas–Dallas, 1569
University of Texas–El Paso, 1570
University of Texas–Pan American, 1572
University of Texas–San Antonio, 1573
University of Texas–Tyler, 1574
University of the Arts, 1422
University of the Cumberlands, 755
University of the District of Columbia, 504
University of the Incarnate Word, 1575

About the Authors and Editors

Founded in 1933, Washington, D.C.-based *U.S.News & World Report* delivers a unique brand of journalism to its 11.1 million weekly magazine readers and the 84,000-plus daily visitors to usnews.com. In 1983, *U.S. News* began its exclusive annual rankings of American colleges and universities. The *U.S. News* education franchise is second to none. Its annual college and graduate school rankings are among the most eagerly anticipated magazine issues in the country.

Anne McGrath, the book's editor, is a deputy editor at *U.S.News & World Report*, where she has covered higher education and primary and secondary education, in addition to health and medicine. Previously, she was managing editor of "America's Best Colleges" and "America's Best Graduate Schools," the two *U.S. News* annual publications featuring rankings of the country's liberal arts colleges and universities.

Robert Morse is the director of data research at *U.S.News & World Report*. He is in charge of the research, data collection, methodologies, and survey design for the annual "America's Best Colleges" rankings and "America's Best Graduate Schools" rankings.

Brian Kelly is the executive editor of *U.S.News & World Report*. As the magazine's No. 2 editor, he oversees the weekly magazine, the website, and newsstand books. He is a former editor at the *Washington Post* and the author of three books.

Acknowledgments

The editors would like to thank the many people whose effort and expertise are reflected in this project. In addition to the work of writers at *U.S. News*, we'd like to acknowledge the contributions of freelance writers **Carolyn Kleiner Butler**, **Kristin Davis**, **Jessica Shoemaker**, **Ann Wright** (vice president for the southwest region at the College Board), and **Joyce Slayton Mitchell** (director of college advising at Nightingale-Bamford School). The work involved in producing the directory, the index of majors, and the U.S. News Insider's Index was handled by deputy director of data research **Sam Flanigan**. We'd also like to thank several experts in college admissions who read portions of the manuscript and gave us their feedback: **Arlene Cash**, vice president for enrollment management at Spelman College; **Scott Friedhoff**, vice president for enrollment at Allegheny College; **Nancy Hargrave Meislahn**, dean of admission and financial aid at Wesleyan University; and **Nanci Tessier**, vice president for enrollment management at Saint Anselm College.

Notes

Notes

Notes

Notes

Notes

Notes

Notes

Notes

Notes

Notes

Notes

Notes

Notes

Notes

Notes

Notes

Notes

Notes

Notes

Notes

Notes

Notes

Notes

Notes

Notes

Notes

Notes

Notes

Notes

Notes

Notes

Notes